CASSELL'S

SPANISH–ENGLISH ENGLISH–SPANISH DICTIONARY

DICCIONARIO ESPAÑOL–INGLÉS INGLÉS–ESPAÑOL

Cassell's

Spanish – English
English – Spanish
Dictionary

Diccionario
Español – Inglés
Inglés – Español

Completely revised by

ANTHONY GOOCH, M.A. (Edin.)
Director of Hispanic Studies, London School of Economics and Political Science, University of London

ANGEL GARCÍA de PAREDES
Ldo. en Filosofía y Letras (Madrid)

CASSELL LTD.

London

CASSELL LTD.
1 Vincent Square,
London SW1P 2PN

Completely revised and reset edition 1978
3rd impression 1986

ISBN 0 304 52290 2

Printed and bound in the USA

Contents
Materias

Prólogo

Un diccionario bilingüe es el lazo de unión más útil y preciso entre dos lenguas—que, a su vez, son vehículos de expresión de una cultura. Pese a los fulgurantes avances de la tecnología y de la lingüística de nuestros días, ningún otro medio ha podido desplazarlo en su misión multisecular de intermediario de dos culturas recíprocas. A diferencia de un diccionario monolingüe, que está dirigido exclusivamente a personas con un grado variable de formación intelectual en *una* lengua y que se mueven dentro del ámbito de esa lengua, el diccionario bilingüe consta de dos partes claramente definidas. En el caso de este diccionario, de una parte española y de otra inglesa. En ambas partes, las palabras que encabezan los artículos no se definen ni se explican, sino que se traducen lo más fielmente posible por sus equivalentes en el otro idioma.

Si un hispanohablante, por ejemplo, busca una palabra inglesa que ha oído o leído cuyo significado ha ignorado hasta entonces, acudirá a la parte inglesa y encontrará el equivalente castellano que más o menos exactamente cuadra al vocablo inglés. Si, por el contrario, quiere expresarse en inglés y no dispone de la palabra inglesa adecuada, acudirá a la parte española en donde encontrará el equivalente inglés con sus distintos usos y matices. De este modo, el diccionario persigue la doble finalidad de facilitar la comprensión de una palabra determinada y de ayudar a su expresión correcta.

El buen uso de cualquier diccionario no está exento de dificultades. El lector deberá cerciorarse en primer lugar del contexto en que aparece la palabra que quiere encontrar y, entre las diversas y a veces muy numerosas acepciones de la cabeza de artículo, seleccionar la que mejor se conforme con el contexto. Para ayudar al lector en esta tarea, hemos fragmentado los artículos lo más claramente posible en sus correspondientes acepciones y matices, agregando en casi todos los casos uno o varios ejemplos ilustrativos.

Casi veinte años median entre la primera edición del diccionario Cassell y la presente edición. La revisión que hemos llevado a cabo ha supuesto una labor tal que bien puede decirse que el nuevo diccionario apenas conserva del antiguo sino su título. En estos veinte años, las profundas modificaciones que han tenido lugar en ambos idiomas son tales que nos han obligado a actualizar el diccionario y remodelar su contenido. En la medida de lo posible, hemos intentado incluir las innumerables palabras nuevas que han surgido de las transformaciones sociopolíticas y económicas de los dos decenios últimos.

Hemos prestado especial atención al tratamiento del registro de cada palabra, velando siempre por hallar el equivalente más preciso. Ello ha supuesto un cambio metodológico con respecto al antiguo diccionario que nos ha llevado a reorganizar la mayoría de los artículos y a desglosarlas en sus diversos matices y en sus frecuentes acepciones. Esperamos con esto haber reducido al máximo el margen de error en el peliagudo problema de seleccionar la palabra justa y exacta.

Hemos intentado, también en la medida de lo posible, dar cabida a un buen número de americanismos de uso corriente tanto en la America Sajona como en la América Latina. Muchos de ellos van encontrando aceptación creciente de este lado del Atlántico y su presencia en nuestro diccionario está con creces justificada. Igualmente hemos dado cabida a numerosos coloquialismos, que son parte del lenguaje cotidiano y que deben figurar a justo título en un diccionario moderno.

El presente diccionario está ideado para servir de ayuda a quienes, de una u otra manera, se interesan por inglés o por el español. Hemos tenido particularmente en cuenta a los estudiantes de uno u otro idioma y los problemas con que se enfrentan. Asimismo, hemos tenido presente a las personas que hacen un uso práctico del conocimiento de idiomas, traductores, intérpretes, hombres de negocio y, en definitiva, a todos aquéllos que precisan de un instrumento de trabajo útil, rápido y riguroso.

A. G. de P.

Preface

Traduttore, traditore—a time-honoured adage to daunt not the translator proper alone but hardly less the hapless lexicographer. Notwithstanding, in the present work the challenge has been met with a fair degree of dogged determination that, within the limitations of human frailty and fallibility, *le mot juste*, *la palabra exacta*, the precise term should be run to ground.

It goes without saying that the purpose of a bilingual dictionary is to provide translations, not definitions, and accurate translations, not approximate ones. This we have laboured to do, but beyond this lies the more subtle question of register, to which we have devoted considerable attention. To the maximum degree possible, learned has been paired with learned, standard with standard, colloquial with colloquial, slang with slang, technical with technical, and so on. Thus, a high-register expression such as 'I am not unaware that . . .' will be conveyed by something of the order of *no se me oculta que . . .*, while a low-register 'to go off the deep end' will be rendered in some such form as *subirse por las paredes*.

The question of context, is, of course, of prime linguistic importance, and even this difficult area has been dealt with in the new Cassell by the inclusion of large numbers of illustrative examples.

Another oft-repeated saw calculated to damp the spirits of the lexicographer and his readers has it that 'by the time they appear in print all dictionaries are hopelessly out of date'. Nevertheless, here too we have endeavoured to confound leaden tradition by the eleventh-hour inclusion of a substantial body of new-wave socio-political, economic and colloquial vocabulary—total neologisms and old words with new semantic faces alike—e.g. *amnistiar*, *ideologizar*, *plebiscitar*, *politizar*, *jemsbondesco*, *catastrofismo*, *consumismo*, *dedismo /digitalismo*, *inmovilismo*, *sinsostenismo*, *pornocracia*, *síndrome de abstención*.

As in the case of other languages, Spanish is being inundated with anglicisms, many of which rapidly undergo a greater or lesser degree of morphological and/or semantic change. This phenomenon, too, we have done our best to reflect by the inclusion of such terms as *ranking*, *standing*, *timing*, *credibilidad*, *managerman*, *mass-media*, *off-side/orsay*, *penalty*, *relax*, *sexy*, *show*. Because of change, modification or extension of sense or usage many of these terms fall into the vexed category of *falsos amigos*, an area of far greater complexity and danger than is generally realized. For instance, *mass-media*, in its plural (masculine) form, has the same sense as the English word, but it also has a singular (feminine) form, which means 'bulk of society, general run of people'; while *timing*, although retaining its English sense, has also acquired the meaning 'rate of progress'.

The Spanish of Spain is, in a similar manner, increasingly subject to the impingement of Latin-American usage and, although this is, in fact, in many cases merely Anglo-Saxon influence at second hand, the importance of American Spanish, like that of American English, is of course very great, and the fact is extensively reflected in the volume now before the reader.

The destinies of English and Spanish, both international languages with vast ramifications in the New World, both languages of vast lexical wealth, much of it of common origin, are fast becoming inextricably intertwined; the relationship between them is an increasingly complex and fascinating one; our aim has been and is, within the modest compass of this volume, to throw a sharp semantic light on that relationship, for all those who would delve into it—students, scholars and philologists, interpreters and translators, economists, sociologists and politicians, *aficionados* and businessmen.

The work has been revised, up-dated and enlarged on so comprehensive a scale that little indeed remains of the original compilation. Yet, buried in the pages of the new Cassell there lies still something of Peers, Barragán, Vinyals, Mora, Jones and Sage. To them and to all the many others who have contributed to it, our remembrance and thanks.

What remains to be said in conclusion could scarcely be put better than it was many a long semantic change ago by Dr. Johnson. Let him, then, speak for us once more: 'I have laboured to perform all the parts of a faithful lexicographer: but I have not always executed my own scheme, or satisfied my own expectations. The work, whatever proofs of diligence and attention it may exhibit, is yet capable of many improvements.'

A.G.

Advice to the User

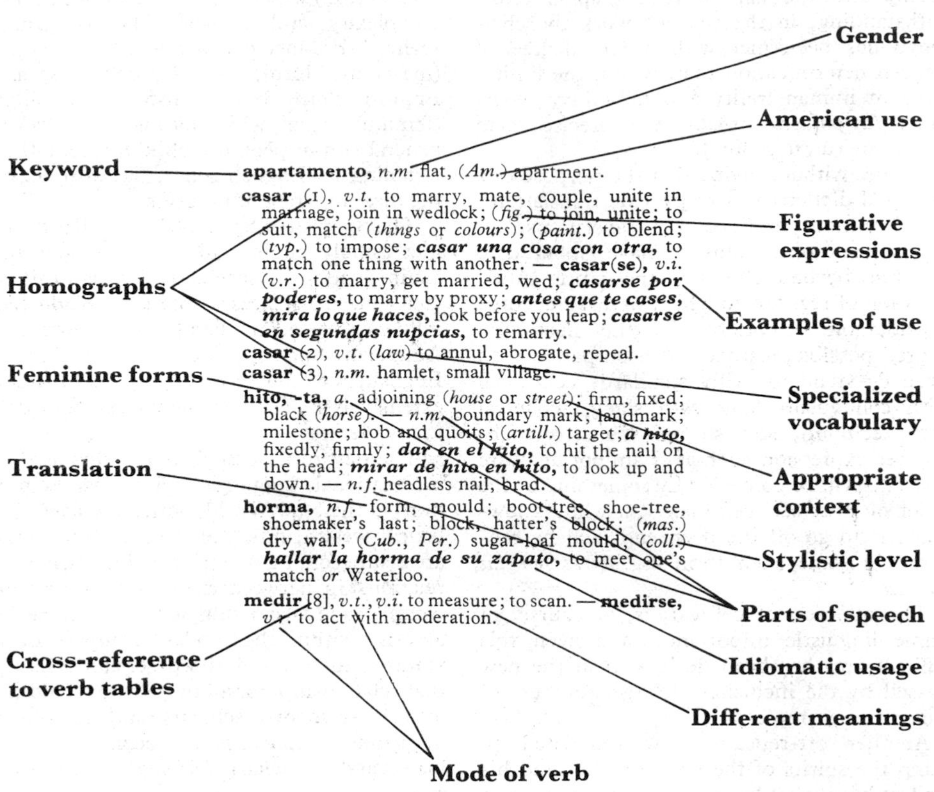

Gender
American use
Keyword
apartamento, n.m. flat, (Am.) apartment.
casar (1), v.t. to marry, mate, couple, unite in marriage, join in wedlock; (fig.) to join, unite; to suit, match (things or colours); (paint.) to blend; (typ.) to impose; casar una cosa con otra, to match one thing with another. — casar(se), v.i. (v.r.) to marry, get married, wed; casarse por poderes, to marry by proxy; antes que te cases, mira lo que haces, look before you leap; casarse en segundas nupcias, to remarry.
casar (2), v.t. (law) to annul, abrogate, repeal.
casar (3), n.m. hamlet, small village.
hito, -ta, a. adjoining (house or street); firm, fixed; black (horse). — n.m. boundary mark; landmark; milestone; hob and quoits; (artill.) target; a hito, fixedly, firmly; dar en el hito, to hit the nail on the head; mirar de hito en hito, to look up and down. — n.f. headless nail, brad.
horma, n.f. form, mould; boot-tree, shoe-tree, shoemaker's last; block, hatter's block; (mas.) dry wall; (Cub., Per.) sugar-loaf mould; (coll.) hallar la horma de su zapato, to meet one's match or Waterloo.
medir [8], v.t., v.i. to measure; to scan. — medirse, v.r. to act with moderation.
Figurative expressions
Homographs
Examples of use
Feminine forms
Specialized vocabulary
Translation
Appropriate context
Stylistic level
Parts of speech
Cross-reference to verb tables
Idiomatic usage
Different meanings
Mode of verb

Key to Spanish Pronunciation

Vowels

i	s*ee*n
e	l*a*te
a	p*a*st (Northern English)
o	s*o*ldier
u	b*oo*t

Diphthongs

ie	*Ya*le
ei	p*ay*ing
eu	p*ea*r, *Ju*ly; *e-u* run together
ai, ay	sk*y*
au	c*ow*
oi, oy	b*oy*
ue	*w*ay

Consonants

b, v (*initial*)	*b*est
b, v (*intervocalic*)	like *b* without lips touching
c (*before a, o, u or consonant*), k, qu	*k*ind
c (*before e or i*), z	*th*ink
ch	*ch*oose
d (*initial*)	*d*ear
d (*intervocalic*)	*th*ere
f	*f*ind
g (*before a, o, u or consonant*)	*g*ain
g (*before e or i*), j	lo*ch* (Scots)
h	*h*onour
l	*l*ong
ll	mi*ll*ion
m	*m*ice
n	ba*nn*er
ñ	o*ni*on
p	co*pp*er
r	la*r*ge (Scots)
rr	*r*ound (Scots)
s	goo*s*e
t	*t*ank
w	like Spanish b, v
x (*intervocalic*)	a*x*e *or* pi*gs*kin *or* e*gg*s
x (*before consonant*)	e*x*treme *or* pa*s*te
y	*y*ellow

American Spanish

The following are the main features which distinguish the pronunciation of American from that of Castilian Spanish; they also occur in Southern Spain

c (*before e or i*), z	goo*s*e
ll (*in many regions of Spain and of Spanish America*)	*y*ellow
ll (*Argentina, Uruguay*)	plea*s*ure
s (*at end of word or before a consonant; in parts of Southern Spain and America*)	*h*ail

Note on Spanish Gender

As a general rule, nouns ending in *-a*, *-ción*, *-gión*, *-sión*, *-tión*, *-xión*, *-dad*, *-tad*, *-tud*, *-ez* and *-umbre* are feminine; all other nouns are masculine. In the body of the text genders are given only where this rule does not apply or in order to clarify its application.

Spanish Verbs

ORTHOGRAPHIC CHANGING VERBS

Group **A.** abarcar: ***c*** changes to ***qu*** before ***e.***

Present Indicative	*Participles*	*Imperative*	*Preterite*
abarco	abarcando		abar***qu***é
abarcas	abarcado	abarca	abarcaste
abarca			abarcó
abarcamos			abarcamos
abarcáis		abarcad	abarcasteis
abarcan			abarcaron

Group **B.** ahogar: ***g*** changes to ***gu*** before ***e.***

Present Indicative	*Participles*	*Imperative*	*Preterite*
ahogo	ahogando		aho***gu***é
ahogas	ahogado	ahoga	ahogaste
ahoga			ahogó
ahogamos			ahogamos
ahogáis		ahogad	ahogasteis
ahogan			ahogaron

Group **C.** cazar: ***z*** changes to ***c*** before ***e.***

Present Indicative	*Participles*	*Imperative*	*Preterite*
cazo	cazando		ca***c***é
cazas	cazado	caza	cazaste
caza			cazó
cazamos			cazamos
cazáis		cazad	cazasteis
cazan			cazaron

Group **D.** vencer and esparcir: ***c*** changes to ***z*** before ***o*** and ***a.***

Present Indicative	*Participles*	*Imperative*	*Preterite*
ven***z***o	venciendo		vencí
vences	vencido	vence	venciste
vence			venció
vencemos			vencimos
vencéis		venced	vencisteis
vencen			vencieron
espar***z***o	esparciendo		esparcí
esparces	esparcido	esparce	esparciste
esparce			esparció
esparcimos			esparcimos
esparcís		esparcid	esparcisteis
esparcen			esparcieron

Group **E.** coger and afligir: ***g*** changes to ***j*** before ***o*** and ***a.***

Present Indicative	*Participles*	*Imperative*	*Preterite*
co***j***o	cogiendo		cogí
coges	cogido	coge	cogiste
coge			cogió
cogemos			cogimos
cogéis		coged	cogisteis
cogen			cogieron
afli***j***o	afligiendo		afligí
afliges	afligido	aflige	afligiste
aflige			afligió
afligimos			afligimos
afligís		afligid	afligisteis
afligen			afligieron

Group **F.** delinquir: ***qu*** changes to ***c*** before ***o*** and ***a.***

Present Indicative	*Participles*	*Imperative*	*Preterite*
delin***c***o	delinquiendo		delinquí
delinques	delinquido	delinque	delinquiste
delinque			delinquió
delinquimos			delinquimos
delinquís		delinquid	delinquisteis
delinquen			delinquieron

Group **G.** distinguir: ***gu*** changes to ***g*** before ***o*** and ***a.***

Present Indicative	*Participles*	*Imperative*	*Preterite*
distin***g***o	distinguiendo		distinguí
distingues	distinguido	distingue	distinguiste
distingue			distinguió
distinguimos			distinguimos
distinguís		distinguid	distinguisteis
distinguen			distinguieron

Present Subjunctive	*Imperfect Subjunctive*		*Future Subjunctive*
abar***qu***e	abarcara	abarcase	abarcare
abar***qu***es	abarcaras	abarcases	abarcares
abar***qu***e	abarcara	abarcase	abarcare
abar***qu***emos	abarcáramos	abarcásemos	abarcáremos
abar***qu***éis	abarcarais	abarcaseis	abarcareis
abar***qu***en	abarcaran	abarcasen	abarcaren
aho***gu***e	ahogara	ahogase	ahogare
aho***gu***es	ahogaras	ahogases	ahogares
aho***gu***e	ahogara	ahogase	ahogare
aho***gu***emos	ahogáramos	ahogásemos	ahogáremos
aho***gu***éis	ahogarais	ahogaseis	ahogareis
aho***gu***en	ahogaran	ahogasen	ahogaren
ca***c***e	cazara	cazase	cazare
ca***c***es	cazaras	cazases	cazares
ca***c***e	cazara	cazase	cazare
ca***c***emos	cazáramos	cazásemos	cazáremos
ca***c***éis	cazarais	cazaseis	cazareis
ca***c***en	cazaran	cazasen	cazaren
ven***z***a	venciera	venciese	venciere
ven***z***as	vencieras	vencieses	vencieres
ven***z***a	venciera	venciese	venciere
ven***z***amos	venciéramos	venciésemos	venciéremos
ven***z***áis	vencierais	vencieseis	venciereis
ven***z***an	vencieran	venciesen	vencieren
espar***z***a	esparciera	esparciese	esparciere
espar***z***as	esparcieras	esparcieses	esparcieres
espar***z***a	esparciera	esparciese	esparciere
espar***z***amos	esparciéramos	esparciésemos	esparciéremos
espar***z***áis	esparcierais	esparcieseis	esparciereis
espar***z***an	esparcieran	esparciesen	esparcieren
co***j***a	cogiera	cogiese	cogiere
co***j***as	cogieras	cogieses	cogieres
co***j***a	cogiera	cogiese	cogiere
co***j***amos	cogiéramos	cogiésemos	cogiéremos
co***j***áis	cogierais	cogieseis	cogiereis
co***j***an	cogieran	cogiesen	cogieren
afli***j***a	afligiera	afligiese	afligiere
afli***j***as	afligieras	afligieses	afligieres
afli***j***a	afligiera	afligiese	afligiere
afli***j***amos	afligiéramos	afligiésemos	afligiéremos
afli***j***áis	afligierais	afligieseis	afligiereis
afli***j***an	afligieran	afligiesen	afiigieren
delin***c***a	delinquiera	delinquiese	delinquiere
delin***c***as	delinquieras	delinquieses	delinquieres
delin***c***a	delinquiera	delinquiese	delinquiere
delin***c***amos	delinquiéramos	delinquiésemos	delinquiéremos
delin***c***áis	delinquierais	delinquieseis	delinquiereis
delin***c***an	delinquieran	delinquiesen	delinquieren
distin***g***a	distinguiera	distinguiese	distinguiere
distin***g***as	distinguieras	distinguieses	distinguieres
distin***g***a	distinguiera	distinguiese	distinguiere
distin***g***amos	distinguiéramos	distinguiésemos	distinguiéremos
distin***g***áis	distinguierais	distinguieseis	distinguiereis
distin***g***an	distinguieran	distinguiesen	distinguieren

Present Indicative	*Participles*	*Imperative*	*Preterite*
Group **H.** fraguar: ***gu*** changes to ***gü*** before ***e.***			
fraguo	fraguando		frag***üé***
fraguas	fraguado	fragua	fraguaste
fragua			fraguó
fraguamos			fraguamos
fraguáis		fraguad	fraguasteis
fraguan			fraguaron
Group **I.** argüir: ***üi*** changes to ***uy*** before a vowel.			
arg***uy***o	arg***uy***endo		argüí
arg***uy***es	argüido	arg***uy***e	argüiste
arg***uy***e			arg***uy***ó
argüimos			argüimos
argüís		argüid	argüisteis
arg***uy***en			arg***uy***eron
Group **J.** bullir: ***i*** is elided before a vowel.			
bullo	bull***e***ndo		bullí
bulles	bullido	bulle	bulliste
bulle			bull***ó***
bullimos			bullimos
bullís		bullid	bullisteis
bullen			bull***e***ron
Group **K.** tañer and ceñir: ***i*** is elided before a vowel; ***e*** in the stem sometimes changes to ***i.***			
taño	tañ***e***ndo		tañí
tañes	tañido	tañe	tañiste
tañe			tañ***ó***
tañemos			tañimos
tañéis		tañed	tañisteis
tañen			tañ***e***ron
c***i***ño	c***i***ñ***e***ndo		ceñí
c***i***ñes	ceñido	c***i***ñe	ceñiste
c***i***ñe			c***i***ñ***ó***
ceñimos			ceñimos
ceñís		ceñid	ceñisteis
c***i***ñen			c***i***ñ***e***ron
Group **L.** variar: ***i*** takes an accent when the stress falls on it.			
var***í***o	variando	var***í***a	varié
var***í***as	variado		variaste
var***í***a			varió
variamos			variamos
variáis		variad	variasteis
var***í***an			variaron
Group **M.** atenuar: ***u*** takes an accent when the stress falls on it.			
aten***ú***o	atenuando	aten***ú***a	atenué
aten***ú***as	atenuado		atenuaste
aten***ú***a			atenuó
atenuamos			atenuamos
atenuáis		atenuad	atenuasteis
aten***ú***an			atenuaron
Group **N.** creer: ***i*** changes to ***y*** before a vowel; before a consonant it takes an accent.			
creo	cre***y***endo		creí
crees	cre***í***do	cree	cre***í***ste
cree			cre***y***ó
creemos			cre***í***mos
creéis		creed	cre***í***steis
creen			cre***y***eron
Group **O.** huir: ***i*** changes to ***y*** before a vowel.			
hu***y***o	hu***y***endo		huí[1]
hu***y***es	huído	hu***y***e	huiste
hu***y***e			hu***y***ó
huimos			huimos
huís[1]		huid	huisteis
hu***y***en			hu***y***eron

[1]The accents on these two forms may be omitted in ***huir*** but not in any other verb.

Present Subjunctive	*Imperfect Subjunctive*		*Future Subjunctive*
fragüe	fraguara	fraguase	fraguare
fragües	fraguaras	fraguases	fraguares
fragüe	fraguara	fraguase	fraguare
fragüemos	fraguáramos	fraguásemos	fraguáremos
fragüéis	fraguarais	fraguaseis	fraguareis
fragüen	fraguaran	fraguasen	fraguaren
arguya	arguyera	arguyese	arguyere
arguyas	arguyeras	arguyeses	arguyeres
arguya	arguyera	arguyese	arguyere
arguyamos	arguyéramos	arguyésemos	arguyéremos
arguyáis	arguyerais	arguyeseis	arguyereis
arguyan	arguyeran	arguyesen	arguyeren
bulla	bullera	bullese	bullere
bullas	bulleras	bulleses	bulleres
bulla	bullera	bullese	bullere
bullamos	bulléramos	bullésemos	bulléremos
bulláis	bullerais	bulleseis	bullereis
bullan	bulleran	bullesen	bulleren
taña	tañera	tañese	tañere
tañas	tañeras	tañeses	tañeres
taña	tañera	tañese	tañere
tañamos	tañéramos	tañésemos	tañéremos
tañáis	tañerais	tañeseis	tañereis
tañan	tañeran	tañesen	tañeren
ciña	ciñera	ciñese	ciñere
ciñas	ciñeras	ciñeses	ciñeres
ciña	ciñera	ciñese	ciñere
ciñamos	cinéramos	ciñésemos	ciñéremos
ciñáis	ciñerais	ciñeseis	ciñereis
ciñan	ciñeran	ciñesen	ciñeren
varíe	variara	variase	variare
varíes	variaras	variases	variares
varíe	variara	variase	variare
variemos	variáramos	variásemos	variáremos
variéis	variarais	variaseis	variareis
varíen	variaran	variasen	variaren
atenúe	atenuara	atenuase	atenuare
atenúes	atenuaras	atenuases	atenuares
atenúe	atenuara	atenuase	atenuare
atenuemos	atenuáramos	atenuásemos	atenuáremos
atenuéis	atenuarais	atenuaseis	atenuareis
atenúen	atenuaran	atenuasen	atenuaren
crea	creyera	creyese	creyere
creas	creyeras	creyeses	creyeres
crea	creyera	creyese	creyere
creamos	creyéramos	creyésemos	creyéremos
creáis	creyerais	creyeseis	creyereis
crean	creyeran	creyesen	creyeren
huya	huyera	huyese	huyere
huyas	huyeras	huyeses	huyeres
huya	huyera	huyese	huyere
huyamos	huyéramos	huyésemos	huyéremos
huyáis	huyerais	huyeseis	huyereis
huyan	huyeran	huyesen	huyeren

Spanish Verbs

Present Indicative	*Participles*	*Imperative*	*Preterite*

Group **P.** aullar (all verbs, of any conjugation, having the diphthongs ***ai, au*** or ***eu*** in the stem): ***i*** or ***u*** takes an accent when the stress falls on it.

Present Indicative	*Participles*	*Imperative*	*Preterite*
a***ú***llo	aullando		aullé
a***ú***llas	aullado	a***ú***lla	aullaste
a***ú***lla			aulló
aullamos			aullamos
aulláis		aullad	aullasteis
a***ú***llan			aullaron

Group **Q.** garantir: defective, occurring only in those forms where the ***i*** is present in the verb ending, *viz.* the entire imperfect, preterite, future, conditional, both imperfect subjunctives, the future subjunctive and the forms of the present indicative and imperative given below.

Present Indicative	*Participles*	*Imperative*	*Preterite*
	garantiendo		garantí
	garantido		garantiste
			garantió
garantimos			garantimos
garantís		garantid	garantisteis
			garantieron

IRREGULAR VERBS

Present Indicative	*Participles*	*Imperative*	*Future Indicative*	*Preterite*

Group **1.** cerrar: ***e*** changes to ***ie*** when the stress falls on it.

Present Indicative	*Participles*	*Imperative*	*Future Indicative*	*Preterite*
c***ie***rro	cerrando		cerraré	cerré
c***ie***rras	cerrado	c***ie***rra	cerrarás	cerraste
c***ie***rra			cerrará	cerró
cerramos			cerraremos	cerramos
cerráis		cerrad	cerraréis	cerrasteis
c***ie***rran			cerrarán	cerraron

Group **2.** perder: ***e*** changes to ***ie*** when the stress falls on it.

Present Indicative	*Participles*	*Imperative*	*Future Indicative*	*Preterite*
p***ie***rdo	perdiendo		perderé	perdí
p***ie***rdes	perdido	p***ie***rde	perderás	perdiste
p***ie***rde			perderá	perdió
perdemos			perderemos	perdimos
perdéis		perded	perderéis	perdisteis
p***ie***rden			perderán	perdieron

Group **3.** cernir: ***e*** changes to ***ie*** when the stress falls on it.

Present Indicative	*Participles*	*Imperative*	*Future Indicative*	*Preterite*
c***ie***rno	cerniendo		cerniré	cerní
c***ie***rnes	cernido	c***ie***rne	cernirás	cerniste
c***ie***rne			cernirá	cernió
cernimos			cerniremos	cernimos
cernís		cernid	cerniréis	cernisteis
c***ie***rnen			cernirán	cernieron

Group **4.** rodar: ***o*** changes to ***ue*** when the stress falls on it.

Present Indicative	*Participles*	*Imperative*	*Future Indicative*	*Preterite*
r***ue***do	rodando		rodaré	rodé
r***ue***das	rodado	r***ue***da	rodarás	rodaste
r***ue***da			rodará	rodó
rodamos			rodaremos	rodamos
rodáis		rodad	rodaréis	rodasteis
r***ue***dan			rodarán	rodaron

Group **5.** mover: ***o*** changes to ***ue*** when the stress falls on it.

Present Indicative	*Participles*	*Imperative*	*Future Indicative*	*Preterite*
m***ue***vo	moviendo		moveré	moví
m***ue***ves	movido	m***ue***ve	moverás	moviste
m***ue***ve			moverá	movió
movemos			moveremos	movimos
movéis		moved	moveréis	movisteis
m***ue***ven			moverán	movieron

Group **6.** advertir: ***e*** (or in some cases ***i***) changes to ***ie*** when the stress falls on it; ***e*** changes to ***i*** in some forms.

Present Indicative	*Participles*	*Imperative*	*Future Indicative*	*Preterite*
adv***ie***rto	adv***i***rtiendo		advertiré	advertí
adv***ie***rtes	advertido	adv***ie***rte	advertirás	advertiste
adv***ie***rte			advertirá	adv***i***rtió
advertimos			advertiremos	advertimos
advertís		advertid	advertiréis	advertisteis
adv***ie***rten			advertirán	adv***i***rtieron

Present Subjunctive	*Imperfect Subjunctive*		*Future Subjunctive*
a***ú***lle	aullara	aullase	aullare
a***ú***lles	aullaras	aullases	aullares
a***ú***lle	aullara	aullase	aullare
aullemos	aulláramos	aullásemos	aulláremos
aulléis	aullarais	aullaseis	aullareis
a***ú***llen	aullaran	aullasen	aullaren
	garantiera	garantiese	garantiere
	garantieras	garantieses	garantieres
	garantiera	garantiese	garantiere
	garantiéramos	garantiésemos	garantiéremos
	garantierais	garantieseis	garantiereis
	garantieran	garantiesen	garantieren
c***ie***rre	cerrara	cerrase	cerrare
c***ie***rres	cerraras	cerrases	cerrares
c***ie***rre	cerrara	cerrase	cerrare
cerremos	cerráramos	cerrásemos	cerráremos
cerréis	cerrarais	cerraseis	cerrareis
c***ie***rren	cerraran	cerrasen	cerraren
p***ie***rda	perdiera	perdiese	perdiere
p***ie***rdas	perdieras	perdieses	perdieres
p***ie***rda	perdiera	perdiese	perdiere
perdamos	perdiéramos	perdiésemos	perdiéremos
perdáis	perdierais	perdieseis	perdiereis
p***ie***rdan	perdieran	perdiesen	perdieren
c***ie***rna	cerniera	cerniese	cerniere
c***ie***rnas	cernieras	cernieses	cernieres
c***ie***rna	cerniera	cerniese	cerniere
cernamos	cerniéramos	cerniésemos	cerniéremos
cernáis	cernierais	cernieseis	cerniereis
c***ie***rnan	cernieran	cerniesen	cernieren
r***ue***de	rodara	rodase	rodare
r***ue***des	rodaras	rodases	rodares
r***ue***de	rodara	rodase	rodare
rodemos	rodáramos	rodásemos	rodáremos
rodéis	rodarais	rodaseis	rodareis
r***ue***den	rodaran	rodasen	rodaren
m***ue***va	moviera	moviese	moviere
m***ue***vas	movieras	movieses	movieres
m***ue***va	moviera	moviese	moviere
movamos	moviéramos	moviésemos	moviéremos
mováis	movierais	movieseis	moviereis
m***ue***van	movieran	moviesen	movieren
adv***ie***rta	adv***i***rtiera	adv***i***rtiese	adv***i***rtiere
adv***ie***rtas	adv***i***rtieras	adv***i***rtieses	adv***i***rtieres
adv***ie***rta	adv***i***rtiera	adv***i***rtiese	adv***i***rtiere
adv***i***rtamos	adv***i***rtiéramos	adv***i***rtiésemos	adv***i***rtiéremos
adv***i***rtáis	adv***i***rtierais	adv***i***rtieseis	adv***i***rtiereis
adv***ie***rtan	adv***i***rtieran	adv***i***rtiesen	adv***i***rtieren

Group **7.** dormir: *o* changes to *ue* when the stress falls on it; *o* changes to *u* in some forms.

Present Indicative	*Participles*	*Imperative*	*Future Indicative*	*Preterite*
d*ue*rmo	d*u*rmiendo		dormiré	dormí
d*ue*rmes	dormido	d*ue*rme	dormirás	dormiste
d*ue*rme			dormirá	d*u*rmió
dormimos			dormiremos	dormimos
dormís		dormid	dormiréis	dormisteis
d*ue*rmen			dormirán	d*u*rmieron

Group **8.** pedir: *e* changes to *i* when the stress falls on it and in some other cases.

Present Indicative	*Participles*	*Imperative*	*Future Indicative*	*Preterite*
p*i*do	p*i*diendo		pediré	pedí
p*i*des	pedido	p*i*de	pedirás	pediste
p*i*de			pedirá	p*i*dió
pedimos			pediremos	pedimos
pedís		pedid	pediréis	pedisteis
p*i*den			pedirán	p*i*dieron

Group **9.** padecer: *c* changes to *zc* before *o* and *a*.

Present Indicative	*Participles*	*Imperative*	*Future Indicative*	*Preterite*
pade*zc*o	padeciendo		padeceré	padecí
padeces	padecido	padece	padecerás	padeciste
padece			padecerá	padeció
padecemos			padeceremos	padecimos
padecéis		padeced	padeceréis	padecisteis
padecen			padecerán	padecieron

Group **10.** agorar: *o* changes to *üe* when the stress falls on it.

Present Indicative	*Participles*	*Imperative*	*Future Indicative*	*Preterite*
ag*üe*ro	agorando		agoraré	agoré
ag*üe*ras	agorado	ag*üe*ra	agorarás	agoraste
ag*üe*ra			agorará	agoró
agoramos			agoraremos	agoramos
agoráis		agorad	agoraréis	agorasteis
ag*üe*ran			agorarán	agoraron

Group **11.** andar:

Present Indicative	*Participles*	*Imperative*	*Future Indicative*	*Preterite*
ando	andando		andaré	and***uve***
andas	andado	anda	andarás	and***uviste***
anda			andará	and***uvo***
andamos			andaremos	and***uvimos***
andáis		andad	andaréis	and***uvisteis***
andan			andarán	and***uvieron***

Group **12.** asir:

Present Indicative	*Participles*	*Imperative*	*Future Indicative*	*Preterite*
asgo	asiendo		asiré	así
ases	asido	ase	asirás	asiste
ase			asirá	asió
asimos			asiremos	asimos
asís		asid	asiréis	asisteis
asen			asirán	asieron

Group **13.** caber:

Present Indicative	*Participles*	*Imperative*	*Future Indicative*	*Preterite*
quepo	cabiendo		***cabré***	***cupe***
cabes	cabido	cabe	***cabrás***	***cupiste***
cabe			***cabrá***	***cupo***
cabemos			***cabremos***	***cupimos***
cabéis		cabed	***cabréis***	***cupisteis***
caben			***cabrán***	***cupieron***

Group **14.** caer:

Present Indicative	*Participles*	*Imperative*	*Future Indicative*	*Preterite*
caigo	ca*y*endo		caeré	caí
caes	ca*í*do	cae	caerás	ca*í*ste
cae			caerá	ca*y*ó
caemos			caeremos	ca*í*mos
caéis		caed	caeréis	ca*í*steis
caen			caerán	ca*y*eron

Group **15.** deducir:

Present Indicative	*Participles*	*Imperative*	*Future Indicative*	*Preterite*
ded*uzc*o	deduciendo		deduciré	***deduje***
deduces	deducido	deduce	deducirás	***dedujiste***
deduce			deducirá	***dedujo***
deducimos			deduciremos	***dedujimos***
deducís		deducid	deduciréis	***dedujisteis***
deducen			deducirán	***dedujeron***

Present Subjunctive	*Imperfect Subjunctive*		*Future Subjunctive*
d*ue*rma	d*u*rmiera	d*u*rmiese	d*u*rmiere
d*ue*rmas	d*u*rmieras	d*u*rmieses	d*u*rmieres
d*ue*rma	d*u*rmiera	d*u*rmiese	d*u*rmiere
d*u*rmamos	d*u*rmiéramos	d*u*rmiésemos	d*u*rmiéremos
d*u*rmáis	d*u*rmierais	d*u*rmieseis	d*u*rmiereis
d*ue*rman	d*u*rmieran	d*u*rmiesen	d*u*rmieren
p*i*da	p*i*diera	p*i*diese	p*i*diere
p*i*das	p*i*dieras	p*i*dieses	p*i*dieres
p*i*da	p*i*diera	p*i*diese	p*i*diere
p*i*damos	p*i*diéramos	p*i*diésemos	p*i*diéremos
p*i*dáis	p*i*dierais	p*i*dieseis	p*i*diereis
p*i*dan	p*i*dieran	p*i*diesen	p*i*dieren
pade*zc*a	padeciera	padaciese	padeciere
pade*zc*as	padecieras	padecieses	padecieres
pade*zc*a	padeciera	padeciese	padeciere
pade*zc*amos	padeciéramos	padeciésemos	padeciéremos
pade*zc*áis	padecierais	padecieseis	padeciereis
pade*zc*an	padecieran	padeciesen	padecieren
ag*üe*re	agorara	agorase	agorare
ag*üe*res	agoraras	agorases	agorares
ag*üe*re	agorara	agorase	agorare
agoremos	agoráramos	agorásemos	agoráremos
agoréis	agorarais	agoraseis	agorareis
ag*üe*ren	agoraran	agorasen	agoraren
ande	and***uviera***	and***uviese***	and***uviere***
andes	and***uvieras***	and***uvieses***	and***uvieres***
ande	and***uviera***	and***uviese***	and***uviere***
andemos	and***uviéramos***	and***uviésemos***	and***uviéremos***
andéis	and***uvierais***	and***uvieseis***	and***uviereis***
anden	and***uvieran***	and***uviesen***	and***uvieren***
as***ga***	asiera	asiese	asiere
as***gas***	asieras	asieses	asieres
as***ga***	asiera	asiese	asiere
as***gamos***	asiéramos	asiésemos	asiéremos
as***gáis***	asierais	asieseis	asiereis
as***gan***	asieran	asiesen	asieren
quepa	***cupiera***	***cupiese***	***cupiere***
quepas	***cupieras***	***cupieses***	***cupieres***
quepa	***cupiera***	***cupiese***	***cupiere***
quepamos	***cupiéramos***	***cupiésemos***	***cupiéremos***
quepáis	***cupierais***	***cupieseis***	***cupiereis***
quepan	***cupieran***	***cupiesen***	***cupieren***
caiga	ca*y*era	ca*y*ese	ca*y*ere
caigas	ca*y*eras	ca*y*eses	ca*y*eres
caiga	ca*y*era	ca*y*ese	ca*y*ere
caigamos	ca*y*éramos	ca*y*ésemos	ca*y*éremos
caigáis	ca*y*erais	ca*y*eseis	ca*y*ereis
caigan	ca*y*eran	ca*y*esen	ca*y*eren
dedu*zc*a	dedu*j*era	dedu*j*ese	dedu*j*ere
dedu*zc*as	dedu*j*eras	dedu*j*eses	dedu*j*eres
dedu*zc*a	dedu*j*era	dedu*j*ese	dedu*j*ere
dedu*zc*amos	dedu*j*éramos	dedu*j*ésemos	dedu*j*éremos
dedu*zc*áis	dedu*j*erais	dedu*j*eseis	dedu*j*ereis
dedu*zc*an	dedu*j*eran	dedu*j*esen	dedu*j*eren

Present Indicative	*Participles*	*Imperative*	*Future Indicative*	*Preterite*
Group **16.** dar:				
doy	dando		daré	***di***[1]
das	dado	da	darás	***diste***
da			dará	***dio***[1]
damos			daremos	***dimos***
dais		dad	daréis	***disteis***
dan			darán	***dieron***
Group **17.** decir:				
digo	***diciendo***		***diré***	***dije***
d*i*ces	***dicho***	***di***	***dirás***	***dijiste***
d*i*ce			***dirá***	***dijo***
decimos			***diremos***	***dijimos***
decís		decid	***diréis***	***dijisteis***
d*i*cen			***dirán***	***dijeron***
Group **18.** estar:				
estoy	estando		estaré	***estuve***
estás	estado	***está***	estarás	***estuviste***
está			estará	***estuvo***
estamos			estaremos	***estuvimos***
estáis		estad	estaréis	***estuvisteis***
están			estarán	***estuvieron***
Group **19.** haber:				
he	habiendo		***habré***	***hube***
has	habido	***hé***	***habrás***	***hubiste***
ha			***habrá***	***hubo***
hemos			***habremos***	***hubimos***
habéis		habed	***habréis***	***hubisteis***
han			***habrán***	***hubieron***
Group **20.** hacer:				
hago	haciendo		***haré***	***hice***
haces	***hecho***	***haz***	***harás***	***hiciste***
hace			***hará***	***hizo***
hacemos			***haremos***	***hicimos***
hacéis		haced	***haréis***	***hicisteis***
hacen			***harán***	***hicieron***
Group **21.** ir[2]:				
voy	***yendo***		iré	***fui***
vas	ido	***vé***	irás	***fuiste***
va			irá	***fue***
vamos			iremos	***fuimos***
vais		id	iréis	***fuisteis***
van			irán	***fueron***
Group **22.** oír:				
oigo	***oyendo***		oiré	oí
o*y*es	***oído***	***oye***	oirás	o*í*ste
o*y*e			oirá	o*y*ó
o*í*mos			oiremos	o*í*mos
oís		***oíd***	oiréis	o*í*steis
o*y*en			oirán	o*y*eron
Group **23.** placer:				
pla***zc***o *or* pla***zg***o	placiendo		placeré	plací
places	placido	place	placerás	placiste
place			placerá	plació *or* ***plugo***
placemos			placeremos	placimos
placéis		placed	placeréis	placisteis
placen			placerán	placieron

[1] In compounds ***-dí, -dió.***
[2] Imperfect: ***iba, -as, -a, íbamos, ibais, iban.***

Present Subjunctive	*Imperfect Subjunctive*		*Future Subjunctive*
dé[1]	***diera***	***diese***	***diere***
des	***dieras***	***dieses***	***dieres***
dé[1]	***diera***	***diese***	***diere***
demos	***diéramos***	***diésemos***	***diéremos***
deis[1]	***dierais***	***dieseis***	***diereis***
den	***dieran***	***diesen***	***dieren***
diga	***dijera***	***dijese***	***dijere***
digas	***dijeras***	***dijeses***	***dijeres***
diga	***dijera***	***dijese***	***dijere***
digamos	***dijéramos***	***dijésemos***	***dijéremos***
digáis	***dijerais***	***dijeseis***	***dijereis***
digan	***dijeran***	***dijesen***	***dijeren***
esté	***estuviera***	***estuviese***	***estuviere***
estés	***estuvieras***	***estuvieses***	***estuvieres***
esté	***estuviera***	***estuviese***	***estuviere***
estemos	***estuviéramos***	***estuviésemos***	***estuviéremos***
estéis	***estuvierais***	***estuvieseis***	***estuviereis***
estén	***estuvieran***	***estuviesen***	***estuvieren***
haya	***hubiera***	***hubiese***	***hubiere***
hayas	***hubieras***	***hubieses***	***hubieres***
haya	***hubiera***	***hubiese***	***hubiere***
hayamos	***hubiéramos***	***hubiésemos***	***hubiéremos***
hayáis	***hubierais***	***hubieseis***	***hubiereis***
hayan	***hubieran***	***hubiesen***	***hubieren***
haga	***hiciera***	***hiciese***	***hiciere***
hagas	***hicieras***	***hicieses***	***hicieres***
haga	***hiciera***	***hiciese***	***hiciere***
hagamos	***hiciéramos***	***hiciésemos***	***hiciéremos***
hagáis	***hicierais***	***hicieseis***	***hiciereis***
hagan	***hicieran***	***hiciesen***	***hicieren***
vaya	***fuera***	***fuese***	***fuere***
vayas	***fueras***	***fueses***	***fueres***
vaya	***fuera***	***fuese***	***fuere***
vayamos[2]	***fuéramos***	***fuésemos***	***fuéremos***
vayáis	***fuerais***	***fueseis***	***fuereis***
vayan	***fueran***	***fuesen***	***fueren***
oiga	***oyera***	***oyese***	***oyere***
oigas	***oyeras***	***oyeses***	***oyeres***
oiga	***oyera***	***oyese***	***oyere***
oigamos	***oyéramos***	***oyésemos***	***oyéremos***
oigáis	***oyerais***	***oyeseis***	***oyereis***
oigan	***oyeran***	***oyesen***	***oyeren***
plazca *or* ***plazga***	placiera	placiese	placiere
plazcas	placieras	placieses	placieres
plazca	placiera *or* ***pluguiera***	placiese *or* ***pluguiese***	placiere *or* ***pluguiere***
plazcamos	placiéramos	placiésemos	placiéremos
plazcáis	placierais	placieseis	placiereis
plazcan	placieran	placiesen	placieren

[1] In compounds ***-de, -déis.***
[2] Jussive ***vamos.***

Present Indicative	*Participles*	*Imperative*	*Future Indicative*	*Preterite*
Group **24.** poder:				
p***ue***do	***pudiendo***		***podré***	***pude***
p***ue***des	podido		***podrás***	***pudiste***
p***ue***de			***podrá***	***pudo***
podemos			***podremos***	***pudimos***
podéis			***podréis***	***pudisteis***
p***ue***den			***podrán***	***pudieron***
Group **25.** poner:				
pongo	poniendo		***pondré***	***puse***
pones	***puesto***	***pon***[1]	***pondrás***	***pusiste***
pone			***pondrá***	***puso***
ponemos			***pondremos***	***pusimos***
ponéis		poned	***pondréis***	***pusisteis***
ponen			***pondrán***	***pusieron***
Group **26.** querer:				
qu***ie***ro	queriendo		***querré***	***quise***
qu***ie***res	querido	***quiere***	***querrás***	***quisiste***
qu***ie***re			***querrá***	***quiso***
queremos			***querremos***	***quisimos***
queréis		quered	***querréis***	***quisisteis***
qu***ie***ren			***querrán***	***quisieron***
Group **27.** raer: Identical with caer (**14**) but has the following alternative forms: ***raigo*** *or* ***rayo***				
Group **28.** reír:				
río	***riendo***		reiré	reí
ríes	re***í***do	***ríe***	reirás	re***í***ste
ríe			reirá	***rio***
reímos			reiremos	re***í***mos
reís		***reíd***	reiréis	re***í***steis
ríen			reirán	***rieron***
Group **29.** roer:				
roo, ***roigo*** *or* ***royo***	ro***y***endo		roeré	roí
roes	ro***í***do	roe	roerás	ro***í***ste
roe			roerá	ro***y***ó
roemos			roeremos	ro***í***mos
roéis		roed	roeréis	ro***í***steis
roen			roerán	ro***y***eron
Group **30.** saber:				
sé	sabiendo		***sabré***	***supe***
sabes	sabido	sabe	***sabrás***	***supiste***
sabe			***sabrá***	***supo***
sabemos			***sabremos***	***supimos***
sabéis		sabed	***sabréis***	***supisteis***
saben			***sabrán***	***supieron***
Group **31.** salir:				
salgo	saliendo		***saldré***	salí
sales	salido	***sal***	***saldrás***	saliste
sale			***saldrá***	salió
salimos			***saldremos***	salimos
salís		salid	***saldréis***	salisteis
salen			***saldrán***	salieron
Group **32.** ser[2]:				
soy	siendo		seré	***fui***
eres	sido	***sé***	serás	***fuiste***
es			será	***fue***
somos			seremos	***fuimos***
sois		sed	seréis	***fuisteis***
son			serán	***fueron***

[1] In compounds ***-pón.***
[2] Imperfect: ***era, -as, -a, éramos, erais, eran.***

Present Subjunctive	*Imperfect Subjunctive*		*Future Subjunctive*
pueda	***pudiera***	***pudiese***	***pudiere***
puedas	***pudieras***	***pudieses***	***pudieres***
pueda	***pudiera***	***pudiese***	***pudiere***
podamos	***pudiéramos***	***pudiésemos***	***pudiéremos***
podáis	***pudierais***	***pudieseis***	***pudiereis***
puedan	***pudieran***	***pudiesen***	***pudieren***
ponga	***pusiera***	***pusiese***	***pusiere***
pongas	***pusieras***	***pusieses***	***pusieres***
ponga	***pusiera***	***pusiese***	***pusiere***
pongamos	***pusiéramos***	***pusiésemos***	***pusiéremos***
pongáis	***pusierais***	***pusieseis***	***pusiereis***
pongan	***pusieran***	***pusiesen***	***pusieren***
quiera	***quisiera***	***quisiese***	***quisiere***
quieras	***quisieras***	***quisieses***	***quisieres***
quiera	***quisiera***	***quisiese***	***quisiere***
queramos	***quisiéramos***	***quisiésemos***	***quisiéremos***
queráis	***quisierais***	***quisieseis***	***quisiereis***
quieran	***quisieran***	***quisiesen***	***quisieren***
raiga *or* ***raya***			
ría	***riera***	***riese***	***riere***
rías	***rieras***	***rieses***	***rieres***
ría	***riera***	***riese***	***riere***
riamos	***riéramos***	***riésemos***	***riéremos***
riáis	***rierais***	***rieseis***	***riereis***
rían	***rieran***	***riesen***	***rieren***
roa, ***roiga*** *or* ***roya***	***royera***	***royese***	***royere***
roas	***royeras***	***royeses***	***royeres***
roa	***royera***	***royese***	***royere***
roamos	***royéramos***	***royésemos***	***royéremos***
roáis	***royerais***	***royeseis***	***royereis***
roan	***royeran***	***royesen***	***royeren***
sepa	***supiera***	***supiese***	***supiere***
sepas	***supieras***	***supieses***	***supieres***
sepa	***supiera***	***supiese***	***supiere***
sepamos	***supiéramos***	***supiésemos***	***supiéremos***
sepáis	***supierais***	***supieseis***	***supiereis***
sepan	***supieran***	***supiesen***	***supieren***
salga	saliera	saliese	saliere
salgas	salieras	salieses	salieres
salga	saliera	saliese	saliere
salgamos	saliéramos	saliésemos	saliéremos
salgáis	salierais	salieseis	saliereis
salgan	salieran	saliesen	salieren
sea	***fuera***	***fuese***	***fuere***
seas	***fueras***	***fueses***	***fueres***
sea	***fuera***	***fuese***	***fuere***
seamos	***fuéramos***	***fuésemos***	***fuéremos***
seáis	***fuerais***	***fueseis***	***fuereis***
sean	***fueran***	***fuesen***	***fueren***

Spanish Verbs

Present Indicative	*Participles*	*Imperative*	*Future Indicative*	*Preterite*
Group **33.** tener:				
tengo	teniendo		***tendré***	***tuve***
t*ie*nes	tenido	***ten***[1]	***tendrás***	***tuviste***
t*ie*ne			***tendrá***	***tuvo***
tenemos			***tendremos***	***tuvimos***
tenéis		tened	***tendréis***	***tuvisteis***
t*ie*nen			***tendrán***	***tuvieron***
Group **34.** traer:				
traigo	tra*y*endo		traeré	***traje***
traes	tra*í*do	trae	traerás	***trajiste***
trae			traerá	***trajo***
traemos			traeremos	***trajimos***
traéis		traed	traeréis	***trajisteis***
traen			traerán	***trajeron***
Group **35.** valer:				
valgo	valiendo		***valdré***	valí
vales	valido	***val*** *or* vale	***valdrás***	valiste
vale			***valdrá***	valió
valemos			***valdremos***	valimos
valéis		valed	***valdréis***	valisteis
valen			***valdrán***	valieron
Group **36.** venir:				
vengo	***viniendo***		***vendré***	***vine***
v*ie*nes	venido	***ven***[2]	***vendrás***	***viniste***
v*ie*ne			***vendrá***	***vino***
venimos			***vendremos***	***vinimos***
venís		venid	***vendréis***	***vinisteis***
v*ie*nen			***vendrán***	***vinieron***
Group **37.** ver[3]:				
veo	viendo		veré	vi
ves	***visto***	ve	verás	viste
ve			verá	vio
vemos			veremos	vimos
veis		ved	veréis	visteis
ven			verán	vieron

[1] In compounds ***-tén.***
[2] In compounds ***-vén.***
[3] Imperfect: ***veía, -as, -a, -amos, -ais, -an.***

Present Subjunctive	*Imperfect Subjunctive*		*Future Subjunctive*
tenga	***tuviera***	***tuviese***	***tuviere***
tengas	***tuvieras***	***tuvieses***	***tuvieres***
tenga	***tuviera***	***tuviese***	***tuviere***
tengamos	***tuviéramos***	***tuviésemos***	***tuviéremos***
tengáis	***tuvierais***	***tuvieseis***	***tuviereis***
tengan	***tuvieran***	***tuviesen***	***tuvieren***
traiga	***trajera***	***trajese***	***trajere***
traigas	***trajeras***	***trajeses***	***trajeres***
traiga	***trajera***	***trajese***	***trajere***
traigamos	***trajéramos***	***trajésemos***	***trajéremos***
traigáis	***trajerais***	***trajeseis***	***trajereis***
traigan	***trajeran***	***trajesen***	***trajeren***
valga	valiera	valiese	valiere
valgas	valieras	valieses	valieres
valga	valiera	valiese	valiere
valgamos	valiéramos	valiésemos	valiéremos
valgáis	valierais	valieseis	valiereis
valgan	valieran	valiesen	valieren
venga	***viniera***	***viniese***	***viniere***
vengas	***vinieras***	***vinieses***	***vinieres***
venga	***viniera***	***viniese***	***viniere***
vengamos	***viniéramos***	***viniésemos***	***viniéremos***
vengáis	***vinierais***	***vinieseis***	***viniereis***
vengan	***vinieran***	***viniesen***	***vinieren***
vea	viera	viese	viere
veas	vieras	vieses	vieres
vea	viera	viese	viere
veamos	viéramos	viésemos	viéremos
veáis	vierais	vieseis	viereis
vean	vieran	viesen	vieren

English Abbreviations used in the Dictionary

a.	adjective
abbr.	abbreviation
abl.	ablative
acc.	accusative
adv.	adverb
aer.	aeronautics
agric.	agriculture
alch.	alchemy
alg.	algebra
Am.	(North) America(n)
anat.	anatomy
anc.	ancient
And.	Andes
Ant.	Antilles
ant.	antiquated
anth.	anthropology
Arab.	Arabic
arch.	architecture
archæol.	archæology
Arg.	Argentina
arith.	arithmetic
arm.	armour
art.	article, artistic
artill.	artillery
astrol.	astrology
astron.	astronomy
augm.	augmentative
aux. v.	auxiliary verb
bact.	bacteriology
Bibl.	Bible, Biblical
bibliog.	bibliography
biol.	biology
Bol.	Bolivia
bookb.	bookbinding
bot.	botany
build.	building
c.	circa (=about)
Carib.	Caribbean
carp.	carpentry
Cat.	Catalonia
Celt.	Celtic
Cent. Am.	Central America
ceram.	ceramics
Ch.	Church
chem.	chemistry
Chi.	Chile
cine.	cinema
civ. eng.	civil engineering
class.	classical
Col.	Colombia
coll.	colloquial
com.	commerce
compar.	comparative
conch.	conchology
conj.	conjunction
contempt.	contemptuously
contr.	contraction
cook.	cooking
coop.	coopering
C.R.	Costa Rica
craniol.	craniology
cryst.	crystallography
Cub.	Cuba
dat.	dative
def.	definite, definitive
defect.	defective verb
demons.	demonstrative
dent.	dentistry
deriv.	derivation
dial.	dialect
dim.	diminutive
diplom.	diplomacy
disj.	disjunctive
Dom.	Dominican Republic
dynam.	dynamics
Ec.	Ecuador
eccles.	ecclesiastical
econ.	economics
educ.	education
e.g.	exempli gratia (=for example)
elec.	electricity
ellip.	elliptical
embryol.	embryology
Eng.	English
engin.	engineering
ent.	entomology
equit.	equitation
E.S.	El Salvador
esp.	especially
ethn.	ethnology
etym.	etymology
exclam.	exclamation
f.	feminine
falc.	falconry
fam.	familiar
fenc.	fencing
fig.	figuratively
for.	foreign
fort.	fortification
found.	foundry
freq.	frequentative
fut.	future
G.	German
Gael.	Gaelic
gen.	genitive
geneal.	genealogy
geog.	geography
geol.	geology
geom.	geometry
ger.	gerund
Goth.	Gothic
Gr.	Greek
gram.	grammar
Guat.	Guatemala
Heb.	Hebrew
her.	heraldry
Hisp. Am.	Hispanic America
hist.	history
Hond.	Honduras
hort.	horticulture
hunt.	hunting
hydrost.	hydrostatics
hyg.	hygiene
ichth.	ichthyology
i.e.	id est (=that is)
imper.	imperative
imperf.	imperfect
impers.	impersonal
indef. art.	indefinite article
indic.	indicative
inf.	infinitive
interj.	interjection
interrog.	interrogative
intr.	intransitive
inv.	invariable
I.O.U.	I owe you
iron.	ironical
irreg.	irregular
jewel.	jewellery
joc.	jocular
L.	Latin
Lit.	literature
lit.	literally
log.	logic

m.	masculine	**pres. p.**	present participle
mach.	machinery	**print.**	printing
mas.	masonry	**pron.**	pronoun
math.	mathematics	**pros.**	prosody
mech.	mechanics	**Prov.**	Provençal
med.	medicine, mediæval	**prov.**	provincial
metal.	metallurgy	**psych.**	psychology
metaph.	metaphysics	**pugil.**	pugilism
meteor.	meteorology	**pyr.**	pyrotechnics
Mex.	Mexico	**r.**	reflexive
mil.	military	**rad.**	radio
mill.	milling	**railw.**	railway
min.	mineralogy	**R.C.**	Roman Catholic
mint.	minting	**reflex.**	reflexive
motor.	motoring	**reg.**	registered
mus.	music	**relig.**	religion
myth.	mythology	**rel. pron.**	relative pronoun
n.	noun	**remonstr.**	remonstrative
nat. hist.	natural history	**rhet.**	rhetoric
naut.	nautical	**Rom.**	Roman
neg.	negative	**s.**	south
neol.	neologism	**sci.**	science
neut.	neuter	**sculp.**	sculpture
newsp.	newspaper	**sew.**	sewing
Nic.	Nicaragua	**shoe.**	shoemaking
nom.	nominative	**sing.**	singular
N.T.	New Testament	**sl.**	slang
numis.	numismatics	**s.o.**	someone
obj.	objective	**Span.**	Spanish
obs.	obsolete	**sth.**	something
obsc.	obscene	**Stock Exch.**	Stock Exchange
onomat.	onomatopœic	**subj.**	subjunctive
O. Prov.	Old Provençal	**subst.**	substantive
opt.	optics	**suf.**	suffix
orig.	origin	**superl.**	superlative
orn.	ornithology	**surg.**	surgery
o.s.	oneself	**surv.**	surveying
O. Sp.	Old Spanish	**syl.**	syllable
p.	past; participle	**t.**	transitive
palæont.	palæontology	**tail.**	tailoring
Pan.	Panama	**tan.**	tanning
Par.	Paraguay	**tauro.**	tauromachy
parl.	parliamentary	**teleg.**	telegraphy
part.	participle	**telev.**	television
pass.	passive	**theat.**	theatre
path.	pathology	**theol.**	theology
pej.	pejorative	**therap.**	therapeutics
Per.	Peru	**therm.**	thermionics
perf.	perfect	**topog.**	topography
pers.	person, personal	**tr.**	transitive
petrol.	petrology	**trig.**	trigonometry
pharm.	pharmacology	**typ.**	typography
phil.	philosophy	**univ.**	university
Philip.	Philippines	**Ur.**	Uruguay
philol.	philology	**U.S.A.**	United States of America
phon.	phonetics	**usu.**	usually
photo.	photography	**v.**	verb
phrenol.	phrenology	**Val.**	Valencia
phys.	physics	**Ven.**	Venezuela
physiol.	physiology	**verb. a.**	verbal adjective
pl.	plural	**vet.**	veterinary
poet.	poetry, poetical	**v.i.**	verb intransitive
polit.	politics	**v.r.**	verb reflexive
poss.	possessive	**v.t.**	verb transitive
p.p.	past participle	**vulg.**	vulgar
P.R.	Puerto Rico	**W. Indies**	West Indies
pref.	prefix	**weav.**	weaving
prep.	preposition	**zool.**	zoology
pres.	present	[. . .]	see, see also

A, a, *n.f.* letter A, a; ***no sabe ni la a,*** he is a perfect ignoramus; ***a por a y be por be,*** point by point, minutely.

a, *prep.* to, at, on, by, in, up to, according to, as, as if, for, against, with, toward, upon, until, of, after, *etc. It governs the dative and accusative cases:* ***(se) lo doy a mi padre,*** I give it to my father; ***se lo he quitado,*** I've taken it from him. *Before proper nouns, personified nouns and occasionally before other nouns, in the accusative case,* ***a*** *is a symbol of that case and is not translated:* ***veo a mi madre,*** I see my mother; ***conozco a Juan,*** I know John. *It indicates direction, purpose, limit, approval, interval, action, location, rate* or *quantity, request, time, distance, command, manner, instrument* or *means,* e.g.: ***voy a París,*** I am going to Paris; ***han subido a verme,*** they have come up to see me; ***un viaje a Marte,*** a trip to Mars; ***ella me enseñó a cantar,*** she taught me (how) to sing; ***aprendió a nadar,*** he learnt to swim; ***empezaron a gritar,*** they began to shout; ***sentado a (en) la mesa,*** sitting at the table; ***espere a (en) la puerta,*** wait at the door; ***a cinco kilómetros de Burgos,*** three miles from Burgos; ***a cuatro grados bajo cero,*** four degrees below zero; ***a lo lejos,*** in the distance; ***al alcance de,*** within reach of; ***al aire libre,*** in the fresh *or* open air; ***al sol, a la luz del sol,*** in the sun; ***a las tres de la tarde,*** at three in the afternoon; ***al mediodía,*** at midday; ***a medianoche,*** at midnight; in the middle of the night; ***de tres a cuatro,*** from three to four; ***a mi gusto,*** to my taste; ***a mi pesar,*** to my regret; ***con el agua a la cintura,*** with water up to the waist; ***a la orilla del río,*** on the bank of the river; ***a mi lado,*** at my side; ***el azúcar se vende a tres pesos el quintal,*** sugar is sold at three pesos per hundredweight; ***hacer el seguro al tres por ciento,*** to effect the insurance at three per cent; ***a instancias de mi hermano,*** at my brother's request; ***a la española, a lo español,*** in *or* after the Spanish fashion, Spanish-style; ***a lo loco,*** wildly, crazily; ***a guisa de,*** in the manner of; ***a modo de,*** by way of; ***morir a hierro,*** to die by the sword; ***oler a vino,*** to smell of wine; ***a su disposición,*** at your disposal; ***a voluntad,*** at will; ***a manos llenas,*** liberally, by handfuls; ***a mano,*** by hand; ***a máquina,*** by machine; ***a fuerza de,*** by dint of; ***a fuerza bruta,*** by brute force; ***a pedazos,*** in pieces, piecemeal; ***cara a cara,*** face to face; ***paso a paso,*** step by step; ***poco a poco,*** little by little; ***a caballo,*** on horseback; ***a pie,*** on foot; ***a bordo,*** on board, aboard; ***a mi fe,*** upon my honour. *It forms many idiomatic and adverbial phrases:* ***a decir verdad,*** to tell the truth; ***a propósito,*** on purpose; incidentally, by the way; ***al fin, al final,*** at last, finally, in the end; ***al azar,*** at random; ***a su servicio,*** in his service; ***una pintura al óleo,*** an oil painting; ***a mi llegada,*** on my arrival; ***a oscuras,*** in the dark; ***a lo que parece,*** as it seems; ***a lo que dice,*** to judge by what he says; ***a sabiendas,*** on purpose, deliberately; ***a trueque,*** in exchange; ***a la verdad,*** truly; ***a lo menos,*** at least; ***a ojos vistas,*** plainly, publicly; ***a veces,*** sometimes; ***a pesar de,*** in spite of; ***al poco rato,*** shortly afterwards; ***a los dos años,*** two years later; ***al día siguiente,*** (on) the following day; ***al año,*** a year later; a year, per year; ***al mes,*** a month later; a month, per month. *When followed by an infinitive, it represents:* if, if . . . not, but for: e.g.: ***a no ser por Vd.,*** but for you. *Idiomatic phrase:* ***¿a que (no) . . .?*** I'll bet you can (not) . . ., e.g.: ***¿a que no lo aciertas?*** I'll bet you can't guess it? *It coalesces with the article* **el,** *forming* **al: *al hombre,*** to the man; ***traducir al inglés,*** to translate into English. *This masculine article is also used before the infinitive of verbs used as nouns;* ***al entrar,*** on entering; ***al saberlo,*** on hearing of it, on learning about it. *It is used before the infinitive of verbs of action governed by other verbs:* ***vamos a pasear, a comer, a beber,*** let us go for a walk, (let us) eat, (let us) drink.

a-, *pref. denotes privation* or *negation as:* ***acromático,*** achromatic; ***amoral,*** amoral; ***apolítico,*** indifferent to politics; ***ateísmo,*** atheism.

Aarón, *n.m.* Aaron.

aarónico, aaronita, *a.* Aaronic, pertaining to Aaron *or* his descendants.

aba, (1), *n.f.* an absolute unit of lineal measure, about 6 feet.

¡aba! (2), *interj.* look out! beware!

abab, *n.m.* Turkish volunteer sailor employed in the galleys.

ababán, *n.m.* (*Arg.*) fruit tree (*Caesalpinia*).

ababillarse, *v.r.* (*Chi.*) to become sick with ***babilla*** (*animals*).

ababol, *n.m.* red poppy [AMAPOLA].

abacá, *n.m.* plant of the banana family; fibre of the plant called Manila hemp; material made of this fibre.

abacería, *n.f.* grocery store.

abacero, -ra, *n.m.f.* grocer.

abacial, *a.* abbatial.

ábaco, *n.m.* abacus; washing-trough.

abacorar, *v.t.* (*Hisp. Am.*) to harass, press hard; to attack boldly; to surprise; to hold improperly (*in dancing*).

abactor, *n.m.* (*Hisp. Am.*) cattle thief.

abad, *n.m.* abbot; ***abad bendito (mitrado),*** crosiered (mitred) abbot; ***si bien canta el abad no le va en zaga el monaguillo,*** the servant does not fall far short of his master.

abada, *n.f.* rhinoceros.

abadanar, *v.t.* to dress *or* finish like sheepskin.

abadejo, *n.m.* (*orn.*) firecrest, goldcrest; (*ent.*) Spanish fly, blistering beetle; (*ichth.*) pollack, codfish; (*ichth.*) ***abadejo largo,*** ling.

abadengo, -ga, *a.* abbatial.

abadernar, *v.t.* (*naut.*) to fasten with short ropes.

abadesa, *n.f.* abbess.

abadí, *a.* applied to the descendants of Mohammed ben Ismail ben Abad, founder of the kingdom of Seville (11th cent.).

abadía, *n.f.* abbey.

abadiado, *n.m.* dignity of an abbot, abbotship.

abajadero, *n.m.* downhill slope.

abajador, *n.m.* stable boy; (*min.*) pit boy; (*surg.*) depressor.

abajamiento, *n.m.* depression; humiliation; discount, reduction.

abajar, *v.t.* to lower.

abajeño, -ña, *a.* (*Hisp. Am.*) pertaining to the lowland. — *n.m.f.* (*Hisp. Am.*) lowlander; (*Col.*) northerner.

abajino, -na, *a., n.m.f.* (*Chi.*) (inhabitant) of the northern territories.

abajo, *adv.* under, underneath, below; down; downstairs; ***escalera abajo,*** down (the) stairs; ***río abajo,*** down river, downstream; ***cuesta abajo,*** downhill; ***venirse abajo,*** to come (tumbling) down, fall to the ground, collapse; ***¡abajo el rey!*** down with the king! ***más abajo de,*** lower than, further down than.

abalanzar [C], *v.t.* to balance, compare; to throw, impel. — **abalanzarse,** *v.r.* to throw oneself, dart, rush impetuously; ***abalanzarse a los peligros,*** to rush into danger; ***abalanzarse sobre,*** to pounce *or* swoop down upon.
abalaustrado, -da, *a.* balustered.
abaldonar, *v.t.* to debase, revile.
abaleador, -ra, *n.m.f.* grain cleaner *or* separator.
abaleaduras, *n.f.pl.* siftings, chaff.
abalear, *v.t.* to clean *or* separate (*grain*) from chaff.
abaleo, *n.m.* (*agric.*) cleaning *or* separating of grain.
abalizamiento, *n.m.* (*naut.*) buoying.
abalizar [C], *v.t.* (*naut.*) to lay down buoys (in). — **abalizarse,** *v.r.* (*naut.*) to take bearings.
abalorio, *n.m.* glass, bead; bead-work; (*fig.*) showy article of little value; ***no valer un abalorio,*** to be worthless.
abalsamado, -da, *a.* like *or* impregnated with balsam; made fragrant.
abalsamar, *v.t.* to give the consistency *or* quality of balsam to (*a liquid*); to make fragrant.
aballestar, *v.t.* to tense.
abanar, *v.t.* to fan.
abanderado, *n.m.* standard-bearer; colour-sergeant.
abanderamiento, *n.m.* registration (*ship*); conscription.
abanderar(se), *v.t.* (*v.r.*) to register (*a ship*), give a certificate of registration (to); to conscript.
abanderizador, -ra, *n.m.f.* ringleader.
abanderizar [C], *v.t.* to organize in bands; to stir up revolution (in *or* among). — **abanderizarse,** *v.r.* to band together.
abandonadamente, *adv.* carelessly, negligently, with abandon.
abandonado, -da, *a.* abandoned, forsaken; helpless; forlorn; lost; profligate; slovenly.
abandonamiento, *n.m.* forlornness; slovenliness; profligacy, debauchery.
abandonar, *v.t.* to forsake, leave, give up. — **abandonarse,** *v.r.* to give oneself up (to); to let oneself go; ***abandonarse a*** or ***en manos de la suerte,*** to give oneself up to chance, trust to luck.
abandonismo, *n.m.* defeatism.
abandono, *n.m.* abandon(ment); neglect.
abanicar [A], *v.t.* to fan. — **abanicarse,** *v.r.* to fan oneself.
abanicazo, *n.m.* blow with a fan.
abanico, *n.m.* fan; range, spread; (*naut.*) derrick; crane; spritsail; (*fort.*) defensive parapet of wood; (*arch.*) fan-light; (*arch.*) winding stairs; semi-circular window; (*min.*) ventilator; ***en abanico,*** fan-shaped; ***abanico de culpas,*** talebearer; ***parecer un abanico de tonta,*** to be very restless.
abanillo, abanino, *n.m.* pleated collar; ruffle, frill.
abaniqueo, *n.m.* fanning; swinging motion; (*fig.*) exaggerated gesturing in speaking.
abaniquería, *n.f.* fan shop *or* factory.
abaniquero, *n.m.* fan-maker; fan-dealer; fan painter *or* decorator.
abano, *n.m.* fan; hanging-fan, punkah, ventilator.
abantar, *v.i.* to brag, boast.
abanto, -ta, *a.* (*fam.*) timid (*bull*); undecided. — *n.m.* (*orn.*) African vulture.
abañar, *v.t.* to grade (*seeds etc.*).
abaratador, -ra, *a.* that cheapens.
abaratamiento, *n.m.* lowering of prices, cheapening.
abaratar, *v.t.* to cheapen, lower the price of. — **abaratar(se),** *v.i.*, (*v.r.*) to fall in price.
abarbar, *v.i.* to raise bees; (*agric.*) to take root.
abarbetar, *v.t.* to grasp firmly; (*naut.*) to fasten with gaskets; (*mil.*) to fortify.
abarca, *n.f.* sandal.
abarcador, -ra, *a.* embracing; monopolistic.
abarcadura, *n.f.*, **abarcamiento,** *n.m.* embrace.
abarcar [A], *v.t.* to embrace, take in; ***quien mucho abarca poco aprieta,*** grasp all lose all; (*Ec.*) to brood, hatch; (*Mex.*) to monopolize.
abarcía, *n.f.* (*med.*) inordinate hunger.
abarcón, *n.m.* iron ring, hoop; pole-ring in carriages; large iron clamp.
abarloar(se), *v.t.* (*v.r.*) (*naut.*) to dock; to bring alongside; to moor at a wharf.
abarquería, *n.f.* sandal shop *or* factory.
abarquero, -ra, *n.m.f.* maker *or* seller of sandals.
abarquillado, -da, *a.* rolled up; curled up.
abarquillamiento, *n.m.* curling up, rolling-up; warping.
abarquillar(se), *v.t.* (*v.r.*) to curl up; to warp, buckle up.
abarracar(se) [A], *v.i.* (*v.r.*) (*mil.*) to encamp in huts *or* barracks.
abarrado, -da, *a.* corded *or* striped (*material*).
abarraganamiento, *n.m.* concubinage.
abarraganarse, *v.r.* to take to concubinage.
abarrajar, *v.t.* to force, impel; to assault; to trip.
abarrancadero, *n.m.* precipice; place full of pitfalls; (*fig.*) difficult situation.
abarrancado, -da, *a.* stranded.
abarrancamiento, *n.m.* fall into a pit; (*naut.*) stranding; embarrassment.
abarrancar [A], *v.t.* to ditch. — *v.i.* (*naut.*) to run aground. — **abarrancarse,** *v.r.* to fall into a pit; to get into difficulties, become embarrassed.
abarrar, *v.t.* to hurl, fling.
abarraz, *n.m.* (*bot.*) louse-wort.
abarredera, *n.f.* broom, carpet-sweeper; anything that sweeps and cleans.
abarrotar, *v.t.* to tie, bind; to bar, strengthen with bars; (*naut.*) to stow (*cargo*); to overfill, cram.
abarrote, *n.m.* (*Hisp. Am.*) ***tienda de abarrotes,*** retail grocery store.
abarrotero, *n.m.* (*Hisp. Am.*) grocer.
abarse, *v.r.* (*defective, used only in the infinitive and the second person* (*sing. and pl.*) *of the imperative:* **ábate, abáos**) to go; to move aside; to get away.
abasí, *a.* (*hist.*) Abbasid.
abastamiento, *n.m.* provisioning; supplying with stores, provisions, *etc.*
abastar, *v.t.* to provision, supply.
abastardar, *v.t.* to degenerate.
abastecedor, -ra, *a.* who supplies. — *n.m.f.* supplier.
abastecer(se) [9], *v.t.* (*v.r.*) to supply, provision, purvey.
abastecimiento, *n.m.* provisioning, supplying; supplies.
abastero, *n.m.* (*Cub., Chi.*) purveyor of livestock, fruit *or* vegetables.
abastionado, -da, *a.* similar to *or* protected by bastions.
abastionar, *v.t.* (*mil.*) to fortify with bastions.
abasto, *n.m.* supply of provisions; (*com.*) supply; ***plaza de abastos,*** public market; ***no dar abasto,*** not to be able to cope *or* manage; ***tenemos tanto trabajo que no damos abasto,*** we have so much work we can't cope with it all; ***no doy abasto a escribir tantas cartas,*** I can't cope with so much letter writing.
abatanar, *v.t.* to beat *or* full (*cloth*).
abatatar, *v.t.* to intimidate, confuse. — **abatatarse,** *v.r.* to become confused.
abate, *n.m.* abbé, French *or* Italian priest.
abatí, *n.m.* (*Arg., Par.*) maize; liquor of maize.
abatida, *n.f.* (*mil.*) abattis.
abatidamente, *adv.* dejectedly.
abatidero, *n.m.* drain trench.
abatido, -da, *a.* downcast; dejected; spiritless; discouraged; crestfallen; faint; dismayed; abject; mean; (*coll.*) knocked down (*in value* or *price*); (*com.*) depreciated *or* fallen in price *or* demand.

abatidura, *n.f.* sudden descent of a bird of prey on its quarry.

abatimiento, *n.m.* depression, low spirits; (*naut.*) ***abatimiento del rumbo,*** leeway; (*aer.*) drift.

abatir, *v.t.* to throw *or* cast down, bring down, knock down; to shoot down; to kill; to humble, debase; to overwhelm; to discourage, dishearten; (*mech.*) to lower, depress; to dismount, take apart. — *v.i.* to descend, stoop. — **abatirse,** *v.r.* to become disheartened, dismayed *or* depressed; to swoop; (*naut.*) to have leeway; (*aer.*) to drift; ***abatirse al suelo,*** to throw oneself to the ground; ***abatirse con dificultad,*** not to be easily disheartened; ***abatirse en*** or ***por los contratiempos,*** to become disheartened by setbacks.

abayado, -da, *a.* (*bot.*) similar to a berry; (*Arg.*) bay-like (*horses*).

abazón, *n.m.* cheek-pouch.

abdicación, *n.f.* abdication; renunciation.

abdicar [A], *v.t., v.i.* to abdicate; to renounce; ***abdicar de,*** to abandon; ***abdicar en,*** to abdicate in favour of.

abdomen, *n.m.* abdomen.

abdominal, *a.* abdominal.

abducción, *n.f.* (*anat.*) abduction; (*log., math., law*) abduction.

abducir [15], *v.t.* (*log., math.*) to abduce.

abductor, *a.* abducent. — *n.m.* (*anat.*) abducent muscle; abductor.

abecé, *n.m.* ABC, the alphabet; rudiments; ***no saber el abecé,*** to be a dunce.

abecedario, *n.m.* alphabet; spelling-book, primer.

abedul, *n.m.* birch-tree.

abeja, *n.f.* (*ent.*) bee; ***abeja albañila,*** mason bee; ***abeja machiega, maesa*** or ***maestra,*** honey bee; ***abeja madre*** or ***reina,*** queen bee; ***abeja neutra*** or ***obrera,*** worker bee.

abejar, *a.* ***uva abejar,*** grape much liked by bees. — *n.m.* bee-hive; apiary.

abejarrón, *n.m.* bumble-bee.

abejaruco, *n.m.* (*orn.*) bee-eater.

abejeo, *n.m.* buzz, hum.

abejera, *m.f.* bee-hive; (*bot.*) bee-wort, balm-mint.

abejero, *n.m.* bee-keeper.

abejilla, -jita, -juela, *n.f.* little bee.

abejón, *n.m.* (*ent.*) drone; hornet; rustic game; (*Hisp. Am.*) ***hacer abejón,*** to heckle; to boo.

abejorreo, *n.m.* buzz, buzzing.

abejorro, *n.m.* (*ent.*) bumble-bee; cockchafer; (*fig.*) tedious individual.

abejuno, -na, *a.* relating to the bee.

abela, *n.f.* black poplar.

abelmosco, *n.m.* (*bot.*) abelmosk (*Hibiscus abelmoschus*); musk-okra, moschatel (*Adoxa moschatellina*).

abellacado, -da, *a.* mean-spirited, degraded.

abellacar [A], *v.t.* to make base. — **abellacarse,** *v.r.* to become base.

abellotado, -da, *a.* in the form of an acorn.

abellotar, *v.t.* to shape like an acorn. — **abellotarse,** *v.r.* to take the shape of an acorn.

abemoladamente, *adv.* softly.

abemolar, *v.t.* to soften (*the voice*); (*mus.*) to flatten, make flat.

abencerraje, *a.* (*coll.*) ill-mannered, coarse. — *n.m.pl.* (**abencerrajes**), Moorish family.

abéndula, *n.f.* blade of water-wheel.

aberenjenado, -da, *a.* aubergine-coloured; lilac.

aberenjenar(se), *v.t.* (*v.r.*) to make (become) the colour of aubergine.

aberración, *n.f.* aberration; deviation; mania.

aberrante, *a.* aberrant.

aberrar, *v.i.* to be mistaken *or* misled; to deviate; to err.

aberrugado, -da, *a.* warty.

aberrugarse, *v.r.* to become covered with warts.

abertal, *a.* (*soil*) easily cleft *or* cracking with drought. — *n.m.* crack; small opening.

abertura, *n.f.* aperture, opening; cleft, crevice, fissure; gap; slit; cove, inlet; (*fig.*) openness (of mind).

abesanar, *v.t.* (*And.*) to divide (*arable land*) into plots.

abesón, *n.m.* (*bot.*) dill.

abestiado, -da, *a.* beast-like.

abestiarse, *v.r.* to become an animal; to descend to the level of an animal.

abetal, *n.m.* place covered with silver firs.

abete, *n.m.* (*bot.*) silver fir-tree; hook for holding cloth while cutting it.

abético, -ca, *a.* relating to the fir-tree.

ab(i)etina, *n.f.* (*chem.*) abietin.

abetinote, abietino, *n.m.* rosin of the silver fir.

abeto, *n.m.* (*bot.*) fir; yew-leaved fir; silver tree; spruce; ***abeto blanco, plateado*** or ***de hojas de tejo,*** silver fir; ***abeto falso, rojo*** or ***del Norte,*** spruce.

abetuna, *n.f.* fir-tree sprout.

abetunado, -da, *a.* resembling bitumen.

abetunar, *v.t.* to cover with pitch.

abey, *n.m.* (*bot.*) abey tree; (*bot.*) ***abey macho,*** jacaranda.

abiar, *n.m.* camomile.

abiertamente, *adv.* openly, frankly, candidly.

abierto, -ta, *a.* open, clear; sincere, candid, frank; (*bot.*) full-blown; ***campo abierto,*** open country; ***carta abierta,*** open letter; (*com.*) ***cuenta abierta,*** open account; (*com.*) ***letra abierta,*** open credit; ***pueblo abierto,*** unfortified town; ***ciudad abierta,*** open city; ***puerto abierto,*** free port; ***a pecho abierto,*** openly, straightforwardly, frankly.

abietineas, *n.f.pl.* (*bot.*) plants forming the genus *Abies*.

abigarradamente, *adv.* in a variegated manner.

abigarrado, -da, *a.* variegated, many-coloured, motley, mottled, speckled; incoherent.

abigarrar, *v.t.* to paint with diverse ill-matched colours; to fleck, variegate.

abigeato, *n.m.* (*law*) theft of cattle.

abigeo, *n.m.* (*law*) cattle-thief.

abigotado, -da, *a.* having *or* wearing a moustache.

abintestato, *n.m.* legal adjudication of an intestate estate.

abiótico, -ca, *a.* not life-producing *or* life-supporting.

abipón, -pona, *n.m.f.* (*Hisp. Am.*) Indian of a tribe on the river Paraná.

abirritar, *v.t.* (*med.*) to lessen irritation.

abisagrar, *v.t.* to hinge, fix hinges to.

abisal, *a.* abysmal; deep-sea (*fauna*).

abiselación, *n.f.* bevelling.

abiselado, -da, *a.* bevelled.

abiseladura, *n.f.* bevelment.

abiselar, *v.t.* to bevel.

Abisinia, *n.f.* Abyssinia.

abisinio, -nia, *a. n.m.f.* Abyssinian.

abismado, -da, *a.* dejected, depressed; absorbed in thought.

abismal, *a.* abysmal. — *n.m.* clasp-nail, shingle-nail.

abismar, *v.t.* to sink. — **abismarse,** *v.r.* to become engrossed (**en,** in); to become lost in thought.

abismático, -ca, *a.* abysmal.

abismo, *n.m.* abyss, gulf; immense depth; hell; (*fig.*) anything profound and unfathomable.

abita, *n.f.* (*naut.*) bitt.

abitadura, *n.f.* (*naut.*) a turn of the cable round the bitts.

abitaque, *n.m.* (*arch.*) rafter; joist.

abitar(se), *v.t.* (*v.r.*) (*naut.*) to bitt.

abitón, *n.m.* (*naut.*) topsail-sheet bitt.

abizcochado, -da, *a.* in the form of a sponge-cake.

abjuración, *n.f.* abjuration, recantation.
abjurar, *v.t.* to abjure, forswear.
ablación, *n.f.* (*surg.*) ablation.
ablactación, *n.f.* weaning.
ablactar, *v.t.* to wean.
ablanar [ABLANEDO].
ablandabrevas, *n.m.f. inv.* (*coll.*) good-for-nothing.
ablandadizo, -za, *a.* soothing; easily persuaded.
ablandador, -ra [ABLANDANTE].
ablandamiento, *n.m.* softening.
ablandante, *a.* soothing, mollifying.
ablandar [9], *v.t., v.i.* to soften, mollify, mellow, mitigate, assuage; to loosen; to run in (*motor vehicle*); to melt, relent; to soothe; to soften up (*by bombardment*); ***ablandar las piedras,*** to melt a heart of stone.
ablandativo, -va, *a.* mollifying.
ablanedo, *n.m.* (*Asturia*) hazel-nut *or* filbert plantation.
ablano, *n.m.*, hazel-tree; filbert-tree [AVELLANO].
ablaquear, *v.t.* to dig around to water *or* air (*plants, trees*).
ablativo, *n.m.* (*gram.*) ablative (case).
ablator, *n.m.* (*vet.*) ablator.
ablegado, *n.m.* ablegate.
ablegar [B], *v.t.* to send away.
ablepsia, *n.f.* (*med.*) ablepsia, loss of sight; (*fig.*) loss of mental powers.
ablución, *n.f.* ablution, washing, cleansing.
abnegación, *n.f.* self-denial; self-sacrifice.
abnegado, -da, *a.* self-sacrificing.
abnegar(se) [1B], *v.t.* (*v.r.*) to renounce; to deny oneself.
abobado, -da, *a.* stupefied.
abobamiento, *n.m.* stupefaction.
abobar, *v.t.* to stupefy. —**abobarse,** *v.r.* to become stupefied.
abocadear, *v.t.* to tear away *or* out by biting.
abocado, -da, *a.* mild, smooth, agreeable (*wines*).
abocamiento, *n.m.* meeting, interview; parley.
abocar [A], *v.t.* to open the mouth of (*bag*); to decant; to bring near; ***estar abocado a,*** to be staring in the face; ***abocar la artillería,*** to bring the guns to bear; (*naut.*) to enter, negotiate (*river, strait, channel*). — *v.i.* (*naut.*) to enter the mouth of a river *etc.* — **abocarse,** *v.r.* to approach; to meet by appointment.
abocardado, -da, *a.* wide-mouthed.
abocardar, *v.t.* to widen *or* expand the mouth of (*tube, hole etc.*); to ream; to countersink.
abocardo, *n.m.* (*min.*) large drill.
abocetado, -da, *a.* unfinished, rough (*pictures*); sketchy.
abocetar, *v.t.* to make a rough sketch of.
abocinado, -da, *a.* vault-shaped; shaped like a trumpet *or* horn; said of speech produced with extra lip rounding.
abocinadura, *n.f.*, **abocinamiento,** *n.m.* (*arch.*) arch.
abocinar, *v.t.* to shape like a trumpet. — *v.i.* to walk with head lowered (*horses*).
abochornado, -da, *a.* flushed, put to shame; abashed; (*bot.*) scorched.
abochornar, *v.t.* to overheat; (*fig.*) to shame, make blush. **abochornarse,** *v.r.* (*fig.*) to blush; (*agric.*) to wilt, dry up from excessive heat; ***abochornarse de algo,*** to be ashamed of something; ***abochornarse por alguien,*** to blush *or* feel ashamed for someone.
abofeteable, *a.* capable *or* deserving of slapping.
abofeteador, -ra, *a.* buffeting, slapping. — *n.m.f.* buffeter, slapper.
abofeteamiento, *n.m.* slapping.
abofetear, *v.t.* to slap.
abogacía, *n.f.* profession of a lawyer *or* advocate; law (*subject or profession*).
abogada, *n.f.* lady lawyer; mediatrix; counsellor's wife.
abogadear, *v.i.* to play the advocate (*used contemptuously*).
abogaderas, *n. f.pl.* (*Hisp. Am.*) captious *or* insidious arguments.
abogadesco, -ca, *a.* [ABOGADIL].
abogadil, *a.* (*fam.*) lawyerish.
abogadillo, *n.m.* petty, minor *or* third-rate lawyer.
abogadismo, *n.m.* legal interference *or* chicanery.
abogado, *n.m.* solicitor, lawyer, advocate, barrister, (*Am.*) attorney; counsellor; mediator; ***abogado de secano,*** quack lawyer, charlatan; ***abogado del diablo,*** Devil's advocate; ***abogado firmón*** or ***trampista,*** shyster (*prepared to sign anything*); ***recibirse de abogado,*** to be called to the bar, (*Am.*) to be admitted to the bar.
abogar [B], *v.i.* to advocate, plead; (*fig.*) to intercede, mediate; ***abogar por alguien,*** to plead for s.o.
abohetado, -da, *a.* inflated, swollen.
abolengo, *n.m.* ancestry, lineage.
abolible, *a.* abolishable.
abolición, *n.f.* abolition, abrogation, extinction.
abolicionismo, *n.m.* abolitionism.
abolicionista, *n.m.f.* abolitionist.
abolir [Q], *v.t. and defective* (*the only moods and persons used are those which end in* ***i***). to abolish, annul, revoke, repeal.
abolitivo, -va, *a.* that abolishes.
abolorio, *n.m.* ancestry.
abolsado, -da, *a.* bag-shaped, purse-shaped; pursed up, puckered.
abolladura, *n.f.* dent, indentation.
abollar, *v.t.* to dent.—**abollarse,** *v.r.* to get dented.
abollón, *n.m.* (*bot.*) bud, first shoot (*vine*); dent.
abollonadura, *n.f.* dent.
abollonamiento, *n.m.* (*bot.*) budding.
abollonar, *v.t.* to dent. — *v.i.* to bind.
abomaso, *n.m.* (*vet.*) abomasum.
abombado, -da, *a.* convex, arched; (*fig.*) deafened, stunned, giddy.
abombar, *v.t.* to give a convex form to; (*fig., fam.*) to deafen, confuse.
abominable, *a.* abominable, detestable, odious, heinous.
abominablemente, *adv.* abominably.
abominación, *n.f.* abomination; detestation; abhorrence.
abominar, *v.t., v.i.* to abominate; to detest, abhor.
abonable, *a.* payable, due for payment; which can be subscribed to.
abonadamente, *adv.* with security *or* guarantee.
abonado, -da, *a.* trustworthy; likely; fit for; ***país abonado para el comunismo,*** country ripe for Communism. — *n.m.f.* subscriber (*telephone, newspaper etc.*); ticket holder (*for a theatre, concert, bullfight etc. season*).
abonador, -ra, *a. n.m.f.* (*com.*) (person) who goes bail, guarantor, surety; (*agric.*) manurer. — *n.m.* barrel-maker's auger.
abonamiento, *n.m.* bail, security.
abonanzar [C], *v.i.* (*naut.*) to grow calm; to clear up.
abonar, *v.t.* to pay for; to guarantee, back up; to manure, put fertilizer on; ***abonar de más, de menos,*** to overpay, underpay. — **abonarse,** *v.r.* to subscribe (*to*); to buy a ticket for the season.
abonaré, *n.m. inv.* promissory note; bill.
abono, *n.m.* security, guarantee; subscription, (*Am.*) dues; allowance, discount; season ticket, (*Am.*) commutation ticket; receipt, voucher; ***abono parcial*** or ***a cuenta,*** payment on account; manure, fertilizer.
aboquillado, -da, *a.* filter-tipped (*cigarette*).
aboquillar, *v.t.* to add a mouthpiece to; (*arch.*) to

enlarge (an opening) on one side and narrow it on the other; (*arch.*) to bevel, chamfer.
abordable, *a.* accessible.
abordador, *n.m.* (*naut.*) boarder.
abordaje, *n.m.* (*naut.*) (act of) boarding (*a ship*); (*naut.*) fouling of two ships; ***abordaje culpable,*** collision due to negligence; ***abordaje fortuito,*** unavoidable collision; ***abordaje recíproco,*** both-to-blame collision.
abordar, *v.t.* (*naut.*) to board (*a ship*), to run foul of (*a ship*); (*fig.*) to approach (*a person*); to undertake (*business*); ***abordar un tema,*** to tackle a subject. — *v.i.* to put into port; ***abordar*** (***una nave***) ***a*** *or* ***con otra,*** to run foul (*one ship*) of another.
abordo, *n.m.* the act of boarding a ship.
aborigen, *a.* aboriginal. — *n.m.pl.* (**aborígenes**), aborigines.
aborlonado, -da, *a.* (*Chi., Col.*) ribbed, striped (*cloth*).
aborrachado, -da, *a.* high-coloured red; inflamed, flushed, purplish.
aborrascado, -da, *a.* stormy.
aborrascarse [A], *v.r.* to become stormy.
aborrecedor, -ra, *n.m.f.* hater, detester.
aborrecer [9], *v.t.* to hate, abhor; to desert (*of birds*); ***aborrecer de muerte,*** to hate like poison; ***lo tengo aborrecido,*** I am heartily sick of it *or* sick to death of it. — **aborrecerse,** *v.r.* to hate each other.
aborrecible, *a.* hateful, detestable.
aborreciblemente, aborrecidamente, *adv.* hatefully, odiously.
aborrecimiento, *n.m.* hate, detestation, abhorrence; tediousness, boredom.
aborregado, -da, *a.* fleecy (*sky*).
aborregarse, *v.r.* to become fleecy (*sky*); (*Am.*) to get dull *or* stupid.
abortamiento, *n.m.* abortion.
abortar, *v.t.* to abort, make miscarry. — *v.i.* to abort, have a miscarriage; (*fig.*) to miscarry, go wrong.
abortivamente, *adv.* abortively; untimely, inopportunely.
abortivo, -va, *a.* abortive; producing abortion. — *n.m.* abortive.
aborto, *n.m.* miscarriage, abortion; monster; hideous creature; (*fig.*) failure.
abortón, *n.m.* miscarriage (*of an animal*); unborn lamb's skin.
aborujar, *v.t.* to make lumpy *or* tufty. — **aborujarse,** *v.r.* to become lumpy *or* tufty; to muffle oneself up.
abotagarse [B], **abotargarse** [B], *v.r.* to become swollen, inflated *or* bloated; (*fig.*) to become stupefied *or* besotted.
abotellarse, *v.r.* to become full of bubbles (*said of glass*).
abotijarse, *v.r.* to become pot-bellied.
abotinado, -da, *a.* shaped like a half-gaiter, spat-shaped; laced-up (*shoes*).
abotonador, *n.m.* button-hook.
abotonar, *v.t.* to button. — *v.i.* to bud. — **abotonarse,** *v.r.* to button up (one's coat).
abovedado, -da, *a.* (*arch.*) arched, vaulted.
abovedar, *v.t.* (*arch.*) to arch, vault, make vault-shaped.
aboyado, -da, *a.* rented with oxen for ploughing (*of a farm*).
aboyar, *v.t.* (*naut.*) to lay down buoys in. — *v.i.* to float.
abozalar, *v.t.* to muzzle.
abra, *n.f.* bay, haven; cove, creek; gorge, fissure; (*Col.*) half section (of a door *or* window).
abracar [A], *v.t.* (*Cub., C.R., Ec., Per.*) to gird, surround, embrace.
abracijo, *n.m.* (*fam.*) embrace, hug.
Abrahán, *m.* Abraham.
abrandecosta, *n.m.* (*Cub.*) a hard-wood tree (*Bunchosia nitida*).
abrasadamente, *adv.* ardently.
abrasado, -da, *a.* red-hot, burning.
abrasador, -ra, *a.* fiercely hot, scorching.
abrasamiento, *n.m.* burning; scorching.
abrasante, *a.* burning.
abrasar, *v.t.* to burn, scorch *or* inflame; to dry up; (*fig.*) to squander. — **abrasarse,** *v.r.* to glow red-hot; to be agitated by any violent passion; ***abrasarse vivo,*** to be consumed with passion; to wither; to be nipped (*by cold*); ***abrasarse de amor,*** to be passionately in love; ***abrasarse en deseos,*** to be dying with longing *or* desire.
abrasilado, -da, *a.* of the colour of brazil-wood.
abrasión, *n.f.* (*geol., med.*) abrasion, graze.
abraxas, *n.m. inv.* abraxas; abraxas stone.
abrazadera, *n.f.* clasp, clamp, cleat, band, gasket; (*print.*) brace, bracket.
abrazado, -da, *a.* (*fam.*) imprisoned.
abrazador, -ra, *a.* embracing. — *n.m.f.* embracer; hook.
abrazamiento, *n.m.* embracing.
abrazante, *a.* embracing.
abrazar [C], *v.t.* to embrace, throw one's arms round, hug, clasp; to clamp, cleat; to contain, comprise; to surround; to accept, follow; ***abrazar la vida religiosa,*** to embrace *or* adopt a religious vocation. — **abrazarse,** *v.r.* (***a, con, de***) to embrace, clasp.
abrazo, *n.m.* embrace, clasp, hug.
abrebocas, *n.m. inv.* mouth prop, gag.
abrebotellas, *n.m. inv.* bottle opener.
abrecartas, *n.m. inv.* paper knife (*for opening letters*).
abrecoches, *n.m. inv.* doorman.
ábrego, *n.m.* south wind.
abrelatas, *n.m. inv.* tin-opener.
¡abrenuncio! *interj.* out! never!
abrepuño, *n.m.* (*bot.*) lesser burdock; milk thistle.
abretonar, *v.t.* (*naut.*) to lash (*the guns*) to the ship's side.
abrevadero, *n.m.* watering-place (*for cattle*); drinking trough.
abrevado, -da, *a.* watered; steeped (*leather*); moistened; (*med.*) damp.
abrevador, *n.m.* one who waters cattle; drinking trough.
abrevar, *v.t.* to water (*cattle*); to irrigate; to moisten (*skins*) with water; to size (*before painting*); to wet down (*a wall*). — *v.i.* to water (*of cattle*). — *v.r.* ***abrevarse en,*** to become bathed in (*blood, tears etc.*).
¡abrevia! *interj.* hurry up!
abreviación, *n.f.* abbreviation, shortening; abridgment; reduction.
abreviadamente, *adv.* briefly, in short.
abreviador, -ra, *a., n.m.f.* (one) who shortens *or* abridges. — *n.m.* (*eccles.*) pontifical officer who issues briefs and bulls.
abreviaduría, *n.f.* office of the pontifical issuer of briefs.
abreviar, *v.t.* to abridge, shorten, cut short, reduce. — *v.i.* to hasten; ***abreviar con,*** to make short work of; ***abreviar en*** + *inf.*, not to take long to + *inf.*
abreviativo, -va, *a.* abbreviatory, abridging.
abreviatura, *n.f.* abbreviation; contraction; ***en abreviatura,*** in abbreviation, in abbreviated form.
abreviaturía, *n.f.* office of the pontifical issuer of briefs.
abribonarse, *v.r.* to become a rascal.
abridero, -ra, *a.* easily opened; free-stone, free-shell (*of peaches*); aperitive. — *n.m.* (*bot.*) free-stone peach.
abridor, -ra, *a.* open, opening. — *n.m.* nectarine, free-stone peach-tree; ear-drop *or* wire (for pierced ears); opener; grafting-knife; ***abridor de***

láminas, engraver; ***abridor en hueco,*** die- *or* punch-sinker; ***abridor de guantes,*** glove-stretcher; ***abridor de latas,*** tin-opener.

abrigadero, *n.m.* (*naut.*) sheltered place, shelter.

abrigado, -da, *a.* warm (*clothes*), sheltered, covered. — *n.m.* shelter.

abrigador, -ra, *a.* (*Mex., Per.*) that which covers *or* protects well; ***gabán muy abrigador,*** very warm overcoat. — *n.m.f.* (*Mex.*) concealer of a crime.

abrigaño, *n.m.* shelter (for cattle); (*agric.*) matting (for protecting plants).

abrigar [B], *v.t.* to shelter, protect, cover, lodge; (*fig.*) to support, nourish; to cherish, warm; ***abrigar una duda,*** to harbour a doubt; ***abrigar una queja,*** to brood over a grievance; ***abrigar esperanzas,*** to cherish hopes; ***abrigar planes,*** to foster plans. — **abrigarse,** *v.r.* to take shelter; to wrap oneself up well; ***abrigarse bajo techado,*** to (take) shelter indoors, get under cover; ***abrigarse con ropa,*** to protect oneself with clothes; ***abrigarse del aguacero,*** to shelter from the heavy rain; ***abrigarse en el portal,*** to take shelter in the doorway.

abrigo, *n.m.* shelter, protection, cover; overcoat, wrap, (*Am.*) topcoat; (*naut.*) harbour, haven; ***al abrigo de,*** sheltered from; under protection of; shielded by; ***prenda de*** (***mucho***) ***abrigo,*** (very) heavy clothing; ***abrigo de entretiempo,*** spring *or* light-weight coat; ***abrigo antiaéreo,*** air-raid shelter.

abril, *n.m.* April; (*fig.*) youth; (*pl.*) (*fig.*) years; ***los dieciséis abriles,*** sweet sixteen; ***estar hecho*** or ***parecer un abril,*** to look youthful; ***abril, aguas mil,*** April showers; ***tiene quince abriles,*** she has seen fifteen summers.

abrileño, -ña, *a.* April, relating to *or* like April.

abrillantado, -da, *a.* brilliant, shining, sparkling; ***fruta abrillantada,*** crystallized fruit. — *n.m.* operation of imparting brilliance.

abrillantador, *n.m.* diamond cutter and polisher.

abrillantar, *v.t.* to cut and polish (*diamonds*), to make (*sth.*) sparkle; to polish, brighten; to impart brilliance to; to gloss (*photographic prints*).

abrimiento, *n.m.* opening.

abrir [*p.p.* **abierto**], *v.t.* to open, unlock, unfasten, uncover, unseal; to begin, inaugurate; to engrave; to expand, separate, distend; to cut open, cleave, rend, dig; ***abrir*** (***una***) ***cuenta,*** to open an account; ***abrir la corona,*** to shave the tonsure; ***abrir el ojo,*** to get on the alert; ***abrir paso,*** to clear the way; ***abrir la mano,*** to let *or* ease up; to become more liberal; (*naut.*) ***abrir registro,*** to begin to take in cargo; ***abrir zanjas,*** to dig trenches; ***abrir la marcha,*** to lead the way; ***abrir la procesión,*** to head the procession; ***abrir brecha en un muro,*** to make a breach in a wall; ***abrir brecha,*** to make advances (*to s.o.*), tempt; ***abrir camino*** or ***calle,*** to clear the way; to force a path; (*fig.*) to advance, facilitate; give the means of success to; to remove obstacles; ***abrir trincheras,*** to dig trenches; ***abrir un canal,*** to cut a canal; ***en un abrir y cerrar de ojos,*** in the twinkling of an eye; very quickly; ***abrir los oídos,*** to open one's ears; ***abrirle los ojos a uno,*** to undeceive s.o., open s.o.'s eyes; ***abrir tanto ojo,*** to stare in amazement; ***abrir el apetito*** or ***las ganas,*** to awaken *or* whet the appetite; ***abrir su pecho a alguien,*** to confide in s.o., unbosom o.s. to s.o.; ***abrir*** (***una lámina***) ***a buril,*** to engrave; ***abrir de arriba abajo,*** to open from top to bottom; ***abrir en canal,*** to slit from top to bottom, rip open. — *v.i.* to open, unfold; to extend; ***abre el tiempo,*** the weather is clearing up. — **abrirse,** *v.r.* to open, expand, crack, gape, yawn; to confide, unbosom o.s., communicate; ***abrir(se) una vía de agua,*** to spring a leak; ***abrirse las cataratas del cielo,*** to begin to rain *or* pour; ***la madera se abre,*** the wood cracks; ***abrirse con alguien,*** to confide in s.o.

abrochador, *n.m.* button-hook.

abrochadura, *n.f.* buttoning, fastening.

abrochar, *v.t.* to button up, do up, buckle, fasten with hooks and eyes; (*Hisp. Am.*) to chastise, punish, reprehend. — **abrocharse,** *v.r.* to do one's buttons up.

abrogación, *n.f.* (*law*) abrogation, repeal.

abrogar [B], *v.t.* (*law*) to abrogate, annul, repeal.

abrogatorio, -ria, *a.* abrogative.

abrojal, *n.m.* thistly ground.

abrojillo, *n.m.* small thistle.

abrojín, *n.m.* (*ichth.*) purple sea-snail.

abrojo, *n.m.* thistle; thorn; prickle; (*mil.*) caltrop; (*bot.*) crowfoot; (*pl.*) (*naut.*) hidden rocks (in the sea); (*fig.*) difficulties.

abromado, -da, *a.* (*naut.*) hazy, foggy; worm-eaten.

abromarse, *v.r.* (*naut.*) to become worm-eaten.

abroncar [A], *v.t.* (*fam.*) to annoy, vex, irritate.

abroquelado, -da, *a.* (*bot.*) in the form of a shield.

abroquelar, *v.t.* (*naut.*) to box-haul. — **abroquelarse,** *v.r.* to shield *or* defend oneself; ***abroquelarse con su inocencia,*** to defend oneself by one's innocence.

abrótano, *n.m.* (*bot.*) southern-wood.

abrotoñar, *v.i.* (*bot.*) to bud, sprout.

abrumado, -da, *a.* weary; overwhelmed, overcome.

abrumador, -ra, *a.* oppressive; overwhelming, crushing.

abrumar, *v.t.* to crush, overwhelm, oppress; to weary. — **abrumarse,** *v.r.* to become filled with anxiety; to turn misty.

abrupto, -ta, *a.* craggy, rugged; steep.

abrutado, -da, *a.* brutish, bestial.

abruzo, -za, *a., n.m.f.* Abruzzian.

absceso, *n.m.* (*med.*) abscess.

abscisa, *n.f.* (*geom.*) abscissa.

abscisión, *n.f.* (*med.*) incision.

absentismo, *n.m.* absenteeism.

ábside, *n.m.* (*arch.*) apse.

absidiola, *n.f.* (*arch.*) apse chapel.

absintina, *n.f.* (*chem.*) absinthin.

absintio, *n.m.* (*bot.*) absinthe.

absintismo, *n.m.* (*med.*) absinthism.

absolución, *n.f.* absolution, pardon, acquittal; (*law*) ***absolución de la demanda,*** finding for the defendant; (*law*) ***absolución de la instancia,*** dismissal of the case; ***absolución libre,*** acquittal.

absoluta, *n.f.* [ABSOLUTO].

absolutamente, *adv.* absolutely.

absolutismo, *n.m.* autocracy; despotism, absolutism.

absolutista, *a., n.m.f.* absolutist.

absoluto, -ta, *a.* absolute, unconditional; imperious, despotic; (*log.*) universal (*proposition*); (*mil.*) ***licencia absoluta,*** discharge; ***lo absoluto,*** the absolute; ***dominio absoluto,*** freehold. — *adv.* ***en absoluto,*** absolutely, absolutely not; *almost always used negatively, as in:* ***no me gusta en absoluto,*** I don't like it at all; ***¿le molesta que pase? en absoluto,*** do you mind if I come in? not at all. — *n.f.* dogma; universal proposition; ipse dixit, dictum; total discharge from military service.

absolutorio, -ria, *a.* (*law.*) absolving, absolutory.

absolvederas, *n.f.pl.* (*fam.*) readiness with which some priests give absolution; ***buenas absolvederas,*** easy absolution.

absolvente, *a.* absolving.

absolver [5], *v.t.* to absolve; to acquit; ***absolver del cargo,*** to absolve from the charge; ***absolver de una obligación,*** to release from an obligation.

absorbencia, *n.f.* absorbability; absorption.

absorbente, *a.* absorbent; engrossing, demanding, absorbing, possessive; ***una mujer absorbente,***

a possessive woman; ***una vida absorbente,*** a demanding life. — *n.m.* absorbent; absorber.

absorber, [*p.p.* **absorbido, absorto**] *v.t.* to absorb; drink in; to engross.

absorbible, *a.* (*physiol.*) absorbable.

absorción, *n.f.* absorption.

absortar, *v.t.* to cause rapture; to strike with amazement.

absorto, -ta, *a.* absorbed in thought; amazed.

abstemio, -mia, *a.* abstemious. — *n.m.f.* teetotaller.

abstención, *n.f.* abstention; self-denial; forbearance.

abstencionismo, *n.m.* non-participation (*in political matters*).

abstencionista, *a.*, *n.m.f.* (*politics*) abstentionist.

abstenerse [33], *v.r.* to abstain, forbear, refrain; ***abstenerse de lo vedado,*** to abstain from what is prohibited; ***abstenerse de hacer algo,*** to refrain from doing something.

abstergente, *a.*, *n.m.* (*med.*) cleansing; detergent; abstergent.

absterger [E], *v.t.* (*med.*) to absterge; to cleanse.

abstersión, *n.f.* (*med.*) abstersion, cleansing, purification.

abstersivo, -va, *a.* (*med.*) cleansing; detergent.

abstinencia, *n.f.* abstinence; forbearance; fasting; ***día de abstinencia,*** day of abstinence.

abstinente, *a.* abstinent.

abstinentemente, *adv.* abstinently.

abstracción, *n.f.* abstraction; preoccupation.

abstractivo, -va, *a.* abstractive.

abstracto, -ta, *a.* abstract; ***en abstracto,*** in the abstract.

abstraer [34, *p.p.* **abstraído, abstracto**], *v.t.* to abstract. — *v.i.* ***abstraer de,*** to leave aside. — **abstraerse,** *v.r.* to become absorbed; to allow one's mind *or* attention to wander.

abstraído, -da, *a.* withdrawn; preoccupied, lost in thought.

abstruso, sa, *a.* difficult, abstruse, obscure.

absuelto, -ta, *a.* acquitted, absolved.

absurdamente, *adv.* absurdly.

absurdidad, *n.f.* absurdity.

absurdo, -da, *a.* absurd, nonsensical. — *n.m.* absurdity, nonsense, piece of nonsense; ***reducción al absurdo,*** reductio ad absurdum.

abubilla, *n.f.* (*orn.*) hoopoe.

abubo, *n.m.* (*prov.*, *bot.*) fruit of ***cermeño***; (*fig.*) simpleton, ninny.

abuchear, *v.t.* (*coll.*) to boo, catcall, shout down.

abucheo, *n.m.* (*coll.*) booing, catcalling.

abuela, *n.f.* grandmother; old woman, crone; ***no necesita*** or ***no tiene*** or ***se le ha muerto la abuela,*** he doesn't need a trumpeter (*i.e.* he is continually praising himself); (*iron.*) ***cuénteselo a su abuela,*** tell that to your grandmother *or* to the marines.

abuelo, *n.m.* grandfather; (*mainly as pl.*) ancestor, forebear; old man.

abuhardillado, -da, *a.* like a garret, garret shaped; attic shaped.

abuinche, *n.m.* (*Col.*) machete used to fell and strip the bark of cinchona trees.

abuje, *n.m.* (*Cub.*, *PR.*) a tick attacking human beings.

abulense, *a.* of, from *or* to do with Avila. — *n.m.f.* native of Avila.

abulia, *n.f.* acute apathy, pathological indolence *or* lack of will.

abúlico, -ca, *a.* acutely apathetic, pathologically weak-willed.

abultadamente, *adv.* in a bulky *or* protruding manner.

abultado, -da, *a.* big, bulky, massive, protruding; (*fig.*) exaggerated; ***abultado de facciones,*** coarse, big-featured; ***abultado de carnes,*** squat, thick-set.

abultar, *v.t.* to make bulky; (*fig.*) to exaggerate. — *v.i.* to be large *or* bulky; to loom large; ***abulta mucho,*** it takes up a lot of room.

abundamiento, *adv. phrase* ***a mayor abundamiento,*** moreover, furthermore, to boot. — *n.m.* abundance, plenty.

abundancia, *n.f.* abundance, plenty; opulence; fertility, fruitfulness; ***cuerno de la abundancia,*** horn of plenty; ***de la abundancia del corazón habla la boca,*** one speaks of what is nearest one's heart.

abundancial, *a.* abundant; (*gram.*) ***adjetivo abundancial,*** adjective of abundance.

abundante, *a.* abundant, plentiful, copious.

abundantemente, *adv.* abundantly.

abundar, *v.i.* to abound (***de*** or ***en,*** with *or* in); ***abundar en riquezas,*** to abound in wealth; ***abundan ahora las frutas,*** fruit is plentiful now; ***abundar en,*** to give further weight to; (*Arg.*) to exaggerate.

abundosamente, *adv.* abundantly, plentifully.

abundoso, -sa, *a.* abundant, plentiful.

abuñolar, abuñuelar [4], *v.t.* to shape like a fritter.

abuñuelado, -da, *a.* fritter-shaped.

¡abur! *interj.* adieu! farewell! goodbye!

aburar, *v.t.* to burn, scorch.

aburelado, -da, *a.* of dark red wool; like fustian.

aburelar, *v.t.* to give a reddish colour to.

aburguesado, -da, *a.* middle-class.

aburguesarse, *v.r.* to become bourgeois *or* middle-class, to sink into an (upper) middle-class rut, adopt (upper) middle-class attitudes.

aburilar, *v.t.* to engrave.

aburrado, -da, *a.* brutish.

aburrarse, *v.r.* to become brutish.

aburrición, *n.f.* (*coll.*) boredom; weariness.

aburrido, -da, *a.* weary, bored; tiresome, boring.

aburrimiento, *n.m.* weariness; tediousness, boredom; annoyance.

aburrir, *v.t.* to tire, bore, weary, annoy, vex; (*fam.*) to venture, hazard; to spend. — **aburrirse,** *v.r.* to be, get bored; ***aburrirse con*** or ***de todo,*** to become bored with everything.

aburujar(se), *v.t.* (*v.r.*) [ABORUJAR].

abusante, *a.* abusing.

abusador, -ra, *a.* which takes unfair advantage of. — *n.m.f.* s.o. who takes unfair advantage of, misuses.

abusar, *v.i.* to take advantage; to misuse, use unfairly; to overdo it; to outstay one's welcome; ***abusar de,*** to make bad use of; to take advantage of; to impose upon; ***abusar de la amistad,*** to abuse friendship.

abusión, *n.f.* abuse; superstition.

abusionero, -ra, *a.* superstitious. — *n.m.* fortuneteller, soothsayer.

abusivamente, *adv.* abusively.

abusivo, -va, *a.* abusive.

abuso, *n.m.* abuse, misuse; ***abuso de autoridad,*** abuse of authority; ***abuso de confianza,*** breach of trust; ***abuso de privilegio,*** abuse of privilege.

abusón, -sona, *a.* (*coll.*) given to taking advantage of, given to abusing (*hospitality, friendship etc.*).

abyección, *n.f.* abjectness; servility.

abyecto, -ta, *a.* abject; servile.

acá, *adv.* here, this way, hither, this side; ***¿de cuando acá?*** since when?; ***ven acá,*** come along, come here; ***acá no se estila,*** this is not the custom here; ***acá y allá, acá y acullá,*** here and there; ***más acá,*** nearer, closer; ***muy acá,*** right here; ***de acá para allá,*** to and fro; ***desde entonces acá,*** since that time; ***acá en la tierra, acá abajo,*** here below; ***por acá,*** here, hereabouts, this way; ***para acá,*** hither, here; ***sin más acá, ni más allá,*** without more ado.

acabable, *a.* that can be finished, practicable; achievable.

acabadamente, *adv.* completely, perfectly.

acabado, -da, *a.* perfect, complete, consummate, well-finished, faultless; (*fam.*) old; worn-out, ruined. — *n.m.* last touch; finish.

acabador, -ra, *a.* finishing. — *n.m.f.* finisher, completer.

acabalar, *v.t.* to complete, finish.

acaballadero, *n.m.* time when and place where sires cover mares.

acaballado, -da, *a.* like a horse; ***de cara acaballada,*** horse-faced; ***narices acaballadas,*** horse-like nostrils.

acaballar, *v.t.* to cover, serve (*mares*).

acaballerado, -da, *a.* gentlemanly; noble.

acaballerar, *v.t.* to knight; to make (a person) behave as a gentleman. — **acaballerarse,** *v.r.* to conduct o.s. as a gentleman.

acaballonar, *v.t.* (*agric.*) to ridge (*land*).

acabamiento, *n.m.* end, completion, death; consummation.

acabar, *v.t., v.i.* to finish (off), end, conclude, complete, make, achieve; to exhaust; to sell out; to destroy; to finish up; (*coll.*) *¡acabáramos!* at last! at long last!; ***acabar con,*** to finish, destroy, extirpate; ***acabar con el negocio,*** to make an end of the affair; ***acabar de hacer una cosa,*** to finish doing something; ***por fin he acabado de escribir la carta,*** I've finished writing the letter at last; ***no acaban de decidirse,*** they can't quite make up their minds *or* they can't make up their minds; ***acabar de*** (+*inf.*), to have just (+*p.p.*); ***acaba de salir, venir,*** he has just gone out, arrived; ***acababa de salir, venir,*** he had just gone out, arrived; ***está acabado de salir . . .,*** it is fresh from . . ., it is just out; ***la espada acaba en punta,*** the sword ends in a point; ***acabar en bien,*** to terminate successfully; ***acabar mal,*** to come to a bad end; ***acabar por*** or +*pres. part.*, to end up by; ***acabó por enfadarse, acabó enfadándose,*** he ended up by losing his temper. — **acabarse,** *v.r.* to die, end, be finished; to grow feeble *or* less; to diminish; to become exhausted; to be *or* run out of; ***se me acaba el agua,*** my water is running out, I am getting short of water; ***se me ha acabado la paciencia,*** my patience is exhausted; ***es cosa de nunca acabarse,*** it is an endless affair; ***es el cuento de nunca acabar,*** it's a never-ending business; ***acabados son cuentos,*** there is an end to it (*conversation, dispute*); ***!se acabó!*** it's finished, over, done; that's it.

acabellado, -da, *a.* light chestnut (*colour*).

acabestrado, -da, *a.* similar to a halter.

acabestrar, *v.t.* to fit with a halter.

acabestrillar, *v.i.* to go fowling with a stalking-horse *or* ox.

acabijo, *n.m.* (*coll.*) end, termination, conclusion.

acabildar, *v.t.* to unite *or* form into a group. — **acabildarse,** *v.r.* to gang up (***contra,*** on).

acabe, *n.m.* completion.

acabóse, *n.m.* (*fam.*) end; ***ser una cosa el acabóse,*** to be the end, the limit *or* the last straw.

acabronado, -da, *a.* resembling a buck; utterly swinish.

acacia, *n.f.* (*bot.*) acacia.

acacharse, *v.r.* (*coll.*) [AGACHARSE]; (*Chi.*) to become stagnant (*market*).

acachetar, *v.t.* to strike (*the bull*) with the poniard.

academia, *n.f.* academy; school; correspondence school; tutorial establishment; learned society; ***academia de idiomas,*** language school; ***La Academia*** (=***La Real Academia de la Lengua***), Spanish Royal Academy of the Language.

académicamente, *adv.* in an academic sense.

academicismo, *n.m.* academic term *or* expression.

académico, -ca, *a.* academic(al). — *n.m.* academician; member of a Royal Society.

acadenillar, *v.t.* to form like a small chain.

acaecedero, -ra, *a.* contingent, conceivable as happening.

acaecer [9], *v.i. def.* to happen, come to pass; ***acaecer en tal tiempo,*** to happen at a certain time; ***acaecer (algo) a alguien,*** to happen (something) to s.o.; ***acaeció que yo estaba allí,*** it so happened that I was there.

acaecimiento, *n.m.* event, incident, occurrence.

acahé, *n.m.* (*Par.*) magpie.

acahual, *n.m.* (*Mex.*) (*bot.*) sunflower.

acahualillo, *n.m.* Mexican variety of tea.

acal, *n.m.* (*Mex.*) canoe; vessel.

acalabazado, -da, *a.* similar to a pumpkin *or* gourd.

acalabazarse [C], *v.r.* to become like a pumpkin *or* gourd; (*fig.*) to become brutish.

acalabrotar, *v.t.* (*naut.*) to make (a cable) by intertwining three ropes each containing three strands.

acalaca, *n.f.* (*Hisp. Am.*) ant.

acalambrarse, *v.r.* to contract (*muscles*) with cramp; to get (a) cramp.

acaldar, *v.t.* (*Per.*) to intimidate, overwhelm, oppress; to accommodate, arrange, set down. — **acaldarse,** *v.r.* to settle down.

acalefo, -fa, *a., n.m.f.* (*zool.*) acalephan. — **acalefos,** *n.m.pl.* (*zool.*) Acalephæ.

acalenturado, -da, *a.* feverish.

acalenturarse, *v.r.* to become feverish.

acalia, *n.f.* (*bot.*) marsh-mallow.

acaloradamente, *adv.* excitedly, heatedly.

acalorado, -da, *a.* excited, heated, fiery, angry, irritated.

acaloramiento, *n.m.* ardour, heat, excitement.

acalorar, *v.t.* to overheat, inflame, urge on; to encourage, promote. — **acalorarse,** *v.r.* to grow heated *or* excited; ***acalorarse por, en*** or ***con la disputa,*** to become heated by, in *or* because of the debate.

acaloro, *n.m.* overheating, suffocation.

acalote, *n.m.* (*Mex.*) (*orn.*) wading bird (*Tantalus mexicanus*).

acallar, *v.t.* to quiet, hush; to mitigate, assuage.

acamaleonado, -da, *a.* chameleon-like.

acamar, *v.t.* to blow down; to lay (plants) flat (*storm*). — **acamarse,** *v.r.* to be blown down.

acamastronarse, *v.r.* (*Per.*) to become sly, crafty *or* cunning.

acambrayado, -da, *a.* cambric-like.

acamellado, -da, *a.* camel-like.

acamellonar, *v.i.* (*Cent. Am., Mex.*) to make ridges with plough *or* spade.

acampado, -da, *a.* encamped.

acampamento, *n.m* (*mil.*) encampment, camp.

acampanado, -da, *a.* bell-shaped.

acampador, -ra, *n.m.f.* camper.

acampanar(se), *v.t., v.i.* (*v.r.*) to shape (*or* be shaped) like a bell.

acampar(se), *v.t., v.i.* (*v.r.*) to encamp.

acampo, *n.m.* (*agric.*) pasture land.

acanalado, -da, *a.* passing through a channel; channelled, striate, fluted, corrugated, grooved, slotted; ***hoja acanalada,*** slotted blade.

acanalador, *n.m.* (*mech.*) grooving-plane.

acanaladura, *n.f.* (*arch.*) groove, stria, striation.

acanalar, *v.t.* to channel; to flute, groove, corrugate.

acanallarse, *v.r.* to become a cad *or* rotter.

acandilado, -da, *a.* lamp-shaped; dazzled.

acandilar, *v.t.* to shape like a lamp.

acanelado, -da, *a.* cinnamon-coloured, cinnamon-flavoured.

acanillado, -da, *a.* making furrows; ribbed, striped (*of cloth*).

acansinarse, *v.r.* to become lazy *or* slow.

acantáceas, *n.f.pl.* (*bot.*) Acanthaceæ.

acantáceo, -cea, *a.* (*bot.*) acanthaceous.

acantalear, *v. impers.* to hail large hailstones.

acantarar, *v.t.* to measure out with milk-pitchers.

acantilado, -da, *a.* steep, sheer; ***costa acantilada,*** precipitous coast. — *n.m.* cliff.

acantilar, *v.i.* (*naut.*) to founder against cliffs.

acanto, *n.m.* (*bot.*) prickly thistle; (*arch.*) acanthus.

acántolis, *n.m. inv.* (*Cub.*) reptile covered with sharp-pointed tubercles.

acantonamiento, *n.m.* cantonment; quartering; billeting.

acantonar, *v.t.* to quarter, billet (*troops*). — **acantonarse,** *v.r.* to be provided with quarters, take up billets.

acañaverear, *v.t.* to wound with sharp-pointed canes.

acañoneamiento, *n.m.* cannonade.

acañonear, *v.t.* to cannonade.

acaparador, -ra, *a.* monopolizing. — *n.m.f.* monopolizer; hoarder.

acaparamiento, *n.m.* monopoly; cornering; hoarding.

acaparar, *v.t.* to monopolize; to corner; to hoard up.

acaparrarse, *v.r.* to come to terms, close a bargain.

acaparrosado, -da, *a.* copperas-hued.

acapillar, *v.t.* to grasp, seize.

acápite, *n.m.* (*Hisp. Am.*) separate paragraph.

acapizarse [C], *v.r.* (*coll., prov.*) to grapple; to clinch.

acaponado, -da, *a.* capon-like; effeminate; ***rostro acaponado,*** hairless face; ***voz acaponada,*** shrill voice.

acaracolado, -da, *a.* spiral-shaped; winding.

acaraira, *n.f.* (*Cub.*) bird of prey.

acarambanado, -da, *a.* covered in icicles; icicle-shaped.

acaramelado, -da, *a.* caramel-like; sickly-sweet; (*fam.*) over-polite, mealy-mouthed, spoony, mawkish.

acaramelar, *v.t.* to make like caramel; (*fig.*) to butter up. — **acaramelarse,** *v.r.* to become spoony *or* smarmy.

acarar, *v.t.* to confront, face, brave.

acardenalado, -da, *a.* covered with weals, livid.

acardenalar, *v.t.* to beat black and blue. — **acardenalarse,** *v.r.* to become covered with weals.

acareamiento, *n.m.* confronting, facing.

acarear, *v.t.* to face, brave; (*fig.*) to bring something into line with something else.

acariciador, -ra, *a.* fondling, caressing. — *n.m.f.* fondler.

acariciar, *v.t.* to stroke, caress, fondle; to cherish; to touch lightly; ***acariciar un proyecto,*** to cherish a plan.

acarminado, -da, *a.* carmine-coloured.

acarnerado, -da, *a.* having the head shaped like sheep (*horses*).

ácaro, *n.m.* (*zool.*) acarus; ***ácaro de queso,*** cheese-mite.

acarralar(se), *v.t.* (*v.r.*) to drop (*a thread*). — *v.r.* to spoil through frost (*grapes*).

acarrarse, *v.r.* to seek shade (*sheep*).

acarrazar(se) [C], *v.t.* (*v.r.*) (*coll., prov.*) to grab, hold hard in a scuffle.

acarreadizo, -za, *a.* portable.

acarreador, -ra, *a.* carrying, transporting. — *n.m.f.* carrier, porter, bearer.

acarreamiento, *n.m.* carrying, cartage; (*pl.*) supplies.

acarrear, *v.t.* to carry, cart, convey, transport; to bring *or* wash down (*floods etc.*); to cause, occasion; ***acarrear a lomo,*** to carry on the back; ***acarrear en ruedas,*** to carry on wheels; ***acarrear por agua,*** to carry by water; ***eso acarreó su desgracia,*** that brought about his misfortune. — **acarrearse,** *v.r.* to bring upon oneself.

acarreo, *n.m.* carrying, cartage; ***cosas de acarreo,*** freight; ***tierras de acarreo,*** alluvium; (*pl.*) supplies.

acarreto (hilo de), *n.m.* packthread.

acarroñar, *v.i.* (*Col.*) to cower, quail; to flag.

acartonado, -da, *a.* pasteboard-like; wizened.

acartonamiento, *n.m.* wizening; hardening like cardboard.

acartonarse, *v.r.* (*fam.*) to become wizened, shrivelled.

acasamatado, -da, *a.* (*mil.*) having *or* resembling a casemate.

acasanate, *n.m.* (*Mex.*) black bird which destroys the maize lands.

acaseramiento, *n.m.* (*Per.*) patronizing of a shop.

acaserarse, *v.r.* (*Chi., Per.*) to become a regular customer; to become fond of; (*Hisp. Am.*) to be a stay-at-home.

acaso, *adv.* maybe, perhaps; perchance; ***por si acaso,*** in case; ***por si acaso no viene,*** in case he doesn't come. — *n.m.* chance.

acastañado, -da, *a.* reddish-brown.

acastillaje, *n.m.* (*naut.*) upper works of a ship; superstructure.

acastillar, *v.t.* to put the upper works on (*a ship*).

acastorado, -da, *a.* similar to beaver fur.

acatable, *a.* worthy of respect *or* reverence.

acatadamente, *adv.* respectfully.

acataléctico, acatalecto, *a.* (*poet.*) acatalectic.

acatalepsia, *n.f.* (*med.*) acatalepsy.

acataléptico, -ca, *a.* acataleptic.

acatamiento, *n.m.* esteem, respect; veneration, reverence, obeisance; acknowledgment; worship; observance.

acatante, *a., n.m.f.* respectful (person).

acatar, *v.t.* to respect, revere, do homage to; to worship; to observe.

acatarrarse, *v.r.* to catch cold.

acatéchili, *n.m.* (*orn.*) (*Mex.*) green finch (*Fringila mexicana*).

acates, *n.m. inv.* Achates, true friend.

acatitado, *a.* similar to ***catite,*** sugar-loaf; ***sombrero acatitado,*** sugar-loaf hat.

acato, *n.m.* reverence; observance.

acaudalado, -da, *a.* wealthy, opulent.

acaudalador, -ra, *a.* that hoards. — *n.m.f.* hoarder.

acaudalar, *v.t.* to hoard up (*riches*); (*fig.*) to acquire, store up (*knowledge, reputation etc.*).

acaudillador, -ra, *a.* commanding, leading. — ***n.m.*** commander (*of troops*); leader.

acaudillamiento, *n.m.* command (*of troops*); leadership (*of a group*).

acaudillar, *v.t.* to command (*troops*); to lead (*party, band*).

acaule, *a.* (*bot.*) wanting a stem; short-stemmed.

accedente, *a.* acceding.

acceder, *v.i.* to accede, agree, consent; ***acceder al dictamen de alguien,*** to accept s.o.'s judgement; ***acceder a la petición,*** to accede to *or* grant the request.

accesibilidad, *n.f.* accessibility.

accesible, *a.* accessible, approachable; attainable; ***accesible a todos,*** accessible to all.

accesión, *n.f.* accession; accessory; (*med.*) access of a fever; paroxysm.

accésit, *n.m.* second prize *or* award.

acceso, *n.m.* access; carnal intercourse; accession to property; (*med.*) access, attack, bout; ***acceso de tos,*** fit of coughing; ***es persona de fácil acceso,*** he is very approachable; ***avenida de acceso,*** approach road, entrance; ***acceso prohibido,*** no entry; ***acceso dirigido desde (la) tierra,*** ground-controlled approach.

accesoriamente, *adv.* accessorily.

accesorio, -ria, *a.* accessory, additional; ***obras accesorias,*** outworks. — *n.f.* outbuilding.

accidentado, -da, *a.* agitated, perturbed; full of incidents, eventful; broken, irregular; ***sesión accidentada,*** rough *or* stormy session; ***viaje accidentado,*** eventful journey; ***terreno accidentado***, broken country. — *n.m.f.* casualty.

accidental, *a.* accidental, fortuitous, chance.

accidentalmente, *adv.* accidentally, by chance.

accidentario, -ria, *a.* accidental.

accidentarse, *v.r.* to be seized with a fit *or* sudden illness; to have an accident, become a casualty.

accidente, *n.m.* accident, chance, mischance; irregularity, unevenness; (*gram.*) accidence; ***accidente de trabajo,*** industrial accident; ***por accidente,*** by chance; ***accidentes del terreno,*** irregularity *or* unevenness in the terrain.

acción, *n.f.* action; act; lawsuit; (*com.*) share, (*Am.*) stock; ***acción directa,*** direct action, violence; ***acción de gracias,*** thanksgiving; ***acción industrial,*** share in a company; ***acción liberada,*** free share.

accionamiento, *n.m.* setting in motion; operation.

accionar, *v.t.* (*mech.*) to operate, move. — *v.i.* to gesticulate.

accionista, *n.m.f.* (*com.*) shareholder, stockholder.

accipitrino, -na, *a.* accipitral; rapacious, predatory; keen-sighted.

acebadamiento, *n.m.* (*vet.*) surfeit.

acebal, *n.m.*, **acebedo, -da,** *n.m.f.* plantation of holly-trees.

acebo, *n.m.* (*bot.*) holly-tree; holly.

acebolladura, *n.f.* damage to a tree from splitting of the woody layers.

acebrado, -da, *a.* striped like a zebra.

acebuchal, *a.* belonging to wild olives. — *n.m.* grove of wild olives.

acebuche, *n.m.* (*bot.*) wild olive-tree.

acebucheno, -na, *a.* belonging to the wild olive.

acebuchina, *n.f.* fruit of the wild olive.

acecinado, -da, *a.* smoked, dried (*meat*); (*fig.*) dried-up, withered, wizened.

acecinar, *v.t.* to salt and dry (*meat*). — **acecinarse,** *v.r.* to grow wizened.

acechadera, *n.f.* vantage point.

acechador, -ra, *a.* prying, intruding; spying; ambushing. — *n.m.f.* look-out, observer; prier.

acechanza, *n.f.* spying, watching, stalking.

acechar, *v.t.* to waylay, lie in wait for; to spy on, watch.

acecho, *n.m.* waylaying, lying in ambush; ***al*** or ***en acecho,*** lying in wait, in ambush.

acechón, -chona, *a.*, *n.m.f.* [ACECHADOR]; ***hacer la acechona,*** to scrutinize, be inquisitive.

acedamente, *adv.* sourly, bitterly.

acedar, *v.t.* to sour, embitter; to displease, vex. — **acedarse,** *v.r.* to become acid, sour, vexed *or* displeased; (*bot.*) to turn yellow (*leaves*).

acedera, *n.f.* (*bot.*) sorrel; (*chem.*) ***sal de acedera,*** oxalate of potash.

acederaque, *n.m.* (*bot.*) bead-tree.

acederilla, *n.f.* (*bot.*) wood-sorrel.

acederón, *n.m.* (*bot.*) variety of sorrel.

acedía, *n.f.* acidity, heart-burn; (*fig.*) melancholia; (*ichth.*) plaice.

acedo, -da, *a.* acid, sour; (*fig.*) harsh, unpleasant.

acefalía, *n.f.*, **acefalismo,** *n.m.* headlessness; (*fig.*) lack of leadership.

acéfalo, -la, *a.* (*zool.*) acephalous, headless; (*fig*) without a leader.

aceguero, *n.m.* wood-gatherer.

aceitada, *n.f.* spilled oil; cake kneaded with oil.

aceitar, *v.t.* to oil; to rub with oil.

aceitazo, *n.m.* thick oil.

aceite, *n.m.* oil, olive oil, vegetable oil; (*paint*) medium; ***aceite alcanforado,*** camphorated oil; ***aceite combustible,*** fuel oil; ***aceite de abeto,*** resin; ***aceite de algodón,*** cottonseed oil; ***aceite de anís,*** sweet aniseed brandy; ***aceite de arder*** or ***quemar,*** lamp *or* fuel oil; ***aceite de ballena,*** whale oil; ***aceite de ben,*** behen oil; ***aceite de cacahuete,*** peanut oil; ***aceite de cada,*** juniper oil; ***aceite de cañamón,*** hemp-oil; ***aceite de carbón,*** coal-oil; ***aceite de coco,*** coconut oil; ***aceite de colza,*** colza, rape oil; ***aceite de comer*** or ***guisar,*** table *or* cooking oil; ***aceite de creosota,*** creosote oil; ***aceite de crotón,*** croton oil; ***aceite de esperma,*** sperm oil; ***aceite de fusel,*** fusel oil; ***aceite de gaulteria,*** oil of wintergreen; ***aceite de hígado de bacalao,*** cod-liver oil; ***aceite de linaza,*** linseed oil; ***aceite de Macasar,*** Macassar oil; (*chem.*) ***aceite de neroli,*** neroli oil; ***aceite de oliva,*** olive oil; ***aceite de palma,*** palm oil; ***aceite de palo,*** copaiba balsam; ***aceite de patas de vaca*** or ***de pie de buey,*** neat's-foot oil; ***aceite de pescado,*** fish-oil; ***aceite de ricino,*** castor oil; ***aceite de vitriolo,*** oil of vitriol; ***aceite de trementina,*** oil of turpentine; ***aceite esencial de rosas,*** attar of roses; (*paint.*) ***aceite graso, litargiriado*** or ***secante,*** drying oil; ***aceite mineral,*** mineral oil; ***aceite pesado,*** diesel oil; ***aceite vegetal,*** vegetable oil; ***aceite virgen,*** virgin olive oil; ***aceite volátil,*** volatile oil; ***cundir como mancha de aceite,*** to spread like an oil-stain; ***caro como aceite de Aparicio,*** excessively dear; ***dejarle a uno freír en su aceite,*** to let someone stew in his own juice; ***echar aceite al fuego,*** to add fuel to the flames; ***quien el aceite mesura las manos se unta,*** touch pitch and you'll get black.

aceitería, *n.f.* oil-shop.

aceitero, -ra, *a.* appertaining to oil. — *n.m.f.* oil-seller; oiler. — *n.m.* (*Carib.*) satin-wood. — *n.f.* woman who sells oil; oil-jar, oil-cruet, oil-horn, oil-can; (*mech.*) oil-cup; (*pl.*) cruets for oil and vinegar.

aceitillo, *n.m.* very light oil; perfumed toilet oil; (*bot.*) snowberry; mountain damson.

aceitón, *n.m.* lubricating olive-oil; olive oil dregs; thick dirty oil; insect secretion that causes plant fungus.

aceitoso, -sa, *a.* oily, greasy.

aceituna, *n.f.* olive; ***aceituna corval,*** olive larger than average; ***aceituna de la reina*** or ***gordal,*** queen olive; ***aceituna zorzaleña*** or ***picudilla,*** crescent olive; ***aceituna manzanilla,*** manzanilla olive; ***aceituna rellena,*** stuffed olive; ***aceitunas zapateras,*** over-ripe and off-colour olives; ***llegar a las aceitunas,*** to arrive late *or* at the end.

aceitunado, -da, *a.* olive-coloured, sallow. — *n.f.* olive season, olive harvest.

aceitunero, -ra, *n.m.f.* person who gathers, carries *or* sells olives. — *n.m.* olive depot.

aceituní, *n.m.* arabesque work.

aceitunil, *a.* olive-coloured, olive-like.

aceitunillo, *n.m.* (*bot.*) satin-wood.

aceituno, *n.m.* (*bot.*) olive-tree; (*Hond.*) Talcochote tree; ***aceituno silvestre,*** satin-wood.

acelajado, -da, *a.* having wisps of cloud.

aceleración, *n.f.* acceleration; speeding.

aceleradamente, *adv.* speedily, swiftly, hastily.

acelerado, -da, *a.* accelerated, speedy. — *n.f.* rev, burst of speed.

acelerador, *n.m.* accelerator.

aceleramiento, *n.m.* acceleration; hastening.

acelerante, *a.* accelerating,

acelerar, *v.t.* to accelerate, hasten, hurry forward, expedite. — **acelerarse,** *v.r.* to make haste; to move quickly.

aceleratriz, *a.* (*mech.*) accelerative; (*mech.*) ***fuerza aceleratriz,*** accelerating motion.

acelerómetro, *n.m.* (*aer.*) accelerometer.
acelerón, *n.m.* rev, burst of speed; ***dar*** or ***pegar acelerones,*** to rev hard, speed.
acelga, *n.f.* (*bot.*) Swiss chard, spinach beet; ***cara de acelga,*** sallow face; miserable face.
acémila, *n.f.* mule; beast of burden; pack animal; (*fig.*) clod, dolt, blockhead, dull plodder.
acemilar, *a.* pertaining to beasts of burden.
acemilería, *n.f.* stable where mules are kept.
acemilero, -ra, *a.* belonging to mules. — *n.m.* muleteer.
acemita, *n.f.* bran bread.
acemite, *n.m.* fine bran, porridge, wheaten flour.
acendrado, -da, *a.* purified; refined; stainless; of the highest order *or* quality; ***fe acendrada,*** unblemished faith, faith of the highest order.
acendramiento, *n.m.* refinement, purification (*metals*).
acendrar, *v.t.* to purify *or* refine (*metals*); (*fig.*) to free from stain; ***acendrarse (el amor) con*** or ***en las contrariedades,*** to become purified *or* be tempered by adversity (*of love*).
acensuar [M], *v.t.* to tax (*property*).
acento, *n.m.* accent; tone, modulation; inflection of the voice; ***acento agudo,*** acute accent; ***acento ortográfico,*** written accent; ***acento prosódico*** or ***tónico,*** tonic accent, emphasis.
acentuación, *n.f.* accentuation; stress.
acentuar [M], *v.t.* to accentuate, stress; to exaggerate.
aceña, *n.f.* water-mill.
aceñero, *n.m.* miller.
acepar, *v.i.* to take root.
acepción, *n.f.* (*gram.*) meaning, sense; ***acepción de personas,*** favouritism.
acepillador, -ra, *n.m.f.* planer. — *n.f.* planing-machine.
acepilladura, *n.f.* planing; wood-shaving.
acepillar, *v.t.* to plane; to brush (*clothes*); (*fam.*) to polish (*manners*).
aceptable, *a.* acceptable; admissible.
aceptablemente, *adv.* acceptably.
aceptación, *n.f.* acceptance; approbation; (*com.*) acceptance of a draft; ***aceptación expresa,*** absolute acceptance; ***aceptación condicional,*** qualified acceptance; ***aceptación mercantil,*** trade acceptance; ***aceptación de personas,*** favouritism; ***tener aceptación,*** to be popular.
aceptador, -ra, *a.*, *n.m.f.* [ACEPTANTE]; ***aceptador de personas,*** one who practises favouritism.
aceptante, *a.* accepting. — *n.m.* acceptant.
aceptar, *v.t.* to accept; (*com.*) ***aceptar una letra,*** to accept responsibility for payment.
acepto, -ta, *a.* acceptable, agreeable; ***acepto a la nobleza y plebe,*** agreeable to the nobility and people. — *n.m.* acceptance.
acequia, *n.f.* irrigation ditch; (*Per.*) rivulet.
acequiador, *n.m.* irrigation channel maker.
acequiar [L], *v.t.* to cover (*a field*) with irrigation channels.
acequiero, *n.m.* irrigation channel keeper.
acera, *n.f.* pavement, (*Am.*) sidewalk; row of houses (on either side of a street); (*arch.*) surface (*wall*); stone slab (*wall*).
aceración, *n.f.* hardening with steel.
acerado, -da, *a.* made of steel; (*fig.*) strong; sharp (*voice*).
acerar, *v.t.* to point *or* edge with steel; to harden with steel; to strengthen; (*fig.*) to fortify, give courage to; to pave; to strengthen (*wall*) with stone slabs. — **acerarse,** *v.r.* to take courage.
acerbamente, *adv.* harshly; cruelly, rigorously; bitterly.
acerbidad, *n.f.* harshness, bitterness; acerbity, asperity; rigour, cruelty.
acerbo, -ba, *a.* harsh, bitter; sharp; (*fig.*) severe, cruel.
acerca de, *adv.* about, concerning, relating to; ***acerca de lo dicho,*** concerning *or* relating to what has been said.
acercamiento, *n.m.* approximation, approaching; rapprochement.
acercar [A], *v.t.* to place near, put closer, bring *or* draw up. — **acercarse,** *v.r.* to come near *or* nearer; ***acercarse a,*** to approach, get near *or* close to.
ácere, *n.m.* (*bot.*) maple-tree.
acerico, acerillo, *n.m.* pin-cushion; small pillow.
acerino, -na, *a.* (*poet.*) of steel, steel-like.
acernadar, *v.t.* (*vet.*) to apply ash poultices to (*horses*).
acero, *n.m.* steel; (*fig.*) sword; small edged *or* pointed weapon; ***acero de aleación,*** alloy steel; ***acero de crisol,*** crucible steel; ***acero de herramientas,*** tool steel; ***acero inoxidable,*** stainless steel; ***acero adamascado, damasquino,*** Damascus, damask steel; ***acero dulce, suave,*** soft steel; ***acero de alta velocidad, de corte rápido,*** high-speed steel; ***acero moldeado, colado, fundido,*** cast steel; ***espada de buenos aceros,*** sword of well-tempered steel; (*pl.*)(*fig.*) courage, spirit; appetite; ***tener buenos, valientes aceros,*** to be courageous.
acerola, *n.f.* fruit *or* berry of the azerole tree.
acerolo, *n.m.* (*bot.*) azerole tree.
acérrimamente, *adv.* strenuously; vigorously.
acérrimo, -ma, *a.* *superl. of* **acre**; very strong (*taste, odour*); very vigorous, harsh *or* tenacious in the extreme; (*fig.*) very staunch *or* stalwart; ***enemigo acérrimo,*** bitter, unremitting foe.
acerrojar, *v.t.* to bolt, lock.
acertadamente, *adv.* opportunely; correctly, properly; successfully.
acertado, -da, *a.* right, correct; successful, sure; well aimed, well planned, well thought out; fit, proper.
acertante, *n.m.f.* winner.
acertar [I], *v.t.* to guess *or* get right, work out correctly. — *v.i.* to hit the mark, succeed; ***acertar a,*** to happen to; to manage to; ***acertó a pasar,*** he happened to pass by; ***no acierto a expresarme,*** I can't manage to express myself properly, I can't find the right words to express my meaning; ***no acertamos a comprenderla,*** we failed to understand her; ***por fin acertamos con la casa,*** we found the right house at last; ***acertaron en el pronóstico,*** they were right in their forecast.
acertijo, *n.m.* riddle, conundrum, guessing game.
aceruelo, *n.m.* small packsaddle.
acervo, *n.m.* heap, store; (*law*) undivided estate.
acescencia, *n.f.* acescence, turning sour; inclination to acidity.
acescente, *a.* (*chem.*) acescent; turning sour, acid.
acetábulo, *n.m.* cruet; Roman measure; (*anat.*) acetabulum.
acetal, *n.m.* (*chem.*) acetal.
acetanilida, *n.f.* (*chem.*) acetanilide.
acetato, *n.m.* acetate.
acetería, *n.f.* pickled vegetables.
acético, -ca, *a.* acetic; vinegary.
acetificación, *n.f.* acidification.
acetificar, *v.t.* to convert into vinegar.
acetileno, *n.m.* ***gas acetileno,*** acetylene gas.
acetílico, -ca, *a.* (*chem.*) acetylic.
acetilo, *n.m.* (*chem.*) acetyl.
acetímetro, *n.m.* acetimeter.
acetín, *n.m.* (*bot.*) satin-wood.
acetona, *n.f.* acetone.
acetosa (1), *n.f.* (*bot.*) sorrel.
acetosidad, *n.f.* acidity.
acetosilla, *n.f.* wood-sorrel.
acetoso, -sa (2), *a.* acetous.

acetre, *n.m.* small bucket; holy-water basin.
acetrinarse, *v.r.* to become sallow.
acezar [C], *v.i.* to pant, be winded, gasp.
acezo, *n.m.* panting, short-windedness, gasping.
acezoso, -sa, *a.* panting, short-winded.
aciago, -ga, *a.* unlucky, ill-fated, ill-starred.
acial, aciar, *n.m.* (*vet.*) barnacle, twitch; (*Cent. Am.*) whip.
aciano, *n.m.* (*bot.*) corn-flower.
acíbar, *n.m.* aloes; aloe-tree; (*fig.*) bitterness; sorrow.
acibarado, -da, *a.* embittered.
acibarador, -ra, *a.* embittering.
acibaramiento, *n.m.* embitterment.
acibarar, *v.t.* to put aloes into; (*fig.*) to make bitter, embitter.
aciberar, *v.t.* to grind very fine.
acicalado, -da, *a.* polished, immaculate; spruce, dapper. — *n.m.* polishing.
acicalador, -ra, *a.* embellishing, polishing, burnishing, furbishing. — *n.m.* burnishing tool.
acicaladura, *n.f.*, **acicalamiento,** *n.m.* burnishing; sprucing up.
acicalar, *v.t.* to polish, burnish; to bedeck; embellish. — **acicalarse,** *v.r.* (*fig.*) to spruce oneself up.
acicate, *n.m.* spur; (*fig.*) goad, incentive.
acicatear, *v.t.* to spur on.
acíclico, -ca, *a.* (*elec.*) acyclic.
acicular, *a.* needle-shaped; (*bot.*) acicular.
aciche, *n.m.* paving-hammer; brick-hammer; tiling-trowel.
ácidamente, *adv.* acidly.
acidaque, *n.m.* Mohammedan marriage settlement.
acidez, *n.f.* acidity, sourness.
acidia, *n.f.* sloth; negligence.
acidificación, *n.f.* (*chem.*) acidification.
acidificante, *a.* acidifying.
acidificar [A], *v.t.* to acidify.
acidimetría, *n.f.* acidimetry.
acidioso, -sa, *a.* slothful; negligent.
ácido, -da, *a.* acid, sour; harsh; tart. — *n.m.* (*chem.*) acid; ***ácido bórico,*** boric acid, boracic acid; ***ácido cítrico,*** citric acid; ***ácido fluorhídrico,*** hydrofluoric acid; ***ácido nucléico,*** nucleic acid; ***ácido pantoténico,*** pantothenic acid; ***ácido prúsico,*** prussic acid; ***ácido salicílico,*** salicylic acid.
acidulado, -da, *a.* acidulated; sour.
acidular, *v.t.* to acidulate; to make sour.
acídulo, -la, *a.* (*chem.*) acidulous; sour; tart.
acierto, *n.m.* hitting the mark, accurate shot; right move, right thing to do *or* say; success.
acigarrado, -da, *a.* (*Chi.*) rough, hoarse, harsh, husky-voiced.
aciguatado, -da, *a.* jaundiced.
aciguatarse, *v.r.* to catch jaundice.
acijado, -da, *a.* copper-coloured *or* copperas-coloured.
acije, *n.m.* copperas; ferrous sulphate.
acijoso, -sa, *a.* copperas-coloured.
acimboga, *n.f.* a variety of citron tree.
ácimo, -ma [ÁZIMO].
acimut, *n.m.* (*astron.*) azimuth.
acimutal, *a.* (*astron.*) azimuthal.
acincelar, *v.t.* to engrave, carve, chisel.
acinesia, *n.f.* (*med.*) akinesia.
ácino, *n.m.* (*bot., anat.*) acinus.
ación, *n.f.* stirrup-leather.
acionera, *n.f.* (*Arg., Chi.*) part of a saddle.
acionero, *n.m.* maker of stirrup-leathers.
acipado, -da, *a.* close-woven.
acirate, *n.m.* landmark; limit; elevated ground, mound.

acitara, *n.f.* partition-wall; rail (of a bridge); cover (of chair *or* saddle).
acitrón, *n.m.* candied citron.
acivilarse, *v.r.* (*Chi.*) to marry before a registrar.
aclamable, *a.* laudable.
aclamación, *n.f.* acclamation, acclaim.
aclamar, *v.t.* to acclaim, applaud.
aclamatoriamente, *adv.* with acclaim.
aclamatorio, -ria, *a.* with acclaim.
aclaración, *n.f.* explanation, clarification; brightening; rinsing.
aclarador, -ra, *a.* explanatory. — *n.m.* a kind of loom comb.
aclarar, *v.t.* to make clear; to explain; to clarify; to brighten; to rinse; to thin down; ***aclarar la voz,*** to clear the throat; ***aclarar los colores,*** to brighten up *or* lighten the colours. — **aclarar(se),** *v.i.* (*v.r.*) to clear up, brighten up; ***el día (se) aclara,*** the day is brightening up; ***nuestro amigo no se aclara,*** our friend does not explain his meaning clearly; our friend does not come out into the open *or* does not put his cards on the table.
aclaratoriamente, *adv.* explanatorily.
aclaratorio, -ria, *a.* explanatory.
aclarecer [9], *v.t.* to lighten, illuminate; to enlighten, elucidate, explain.
aclimatación, *n.f.* acclimatizing, acclimatization.
aclimatar(se), *v.t.* (*v.r.*) to acclimatize, (*Am.*) acclimate.
aclocar [4], *v.i.* to brood, hatch (*eggs*). — **aclocarse,** *v.r.* to become broody; (*fig.*) to sprawl.
acmé, *n.m.* top, highest point, culmination.
acné, *n.m.* (*med.*) acne.
acobardamiento, *n.m.* cringing, climbing down.
acobardar, *v.t.* to daunt, intimidate, cow. — **acobardarse,** *v.r.* to become frightened, to lose courage, back *or* climb down, shrink.
acobijar, *v.t.* (*agric.*) to mulch.
acobijo, *n.m.* (*agric.*) mulch.
acobrado, -da, *a.* copper-hued.
acoceamiento, *n.m.* kicking.
acocear, *v.t.* to kick; (*fig.*) to trample upon, oppress.
acocil, -le, -li, *n.m.* (*Mex.*) crayfish.
acocotar [ACOGOTAR].
acocote, *n.m.* (*Mex.*) long gourd used to extract the juice of maguey.
acocharse, *v.r.* to crouch; to cringe.
acochinadamente, *adv.* filthily.
acochinado, -da, *a.* dirty, filthy.
acochinar, *v.t.* (*coll.*) to corner and murder; to corner (*a pawn in chess*). — **acochinarse,** *v.r.* to get smeared *or* filthy.
acodado, -da, *a.* elbowed; cranked (*axle*); (*naut.*) toggled.
acodadura, *n.f.* bending, leaning on the elbow; nudging, jostling; (*agric.*) layering.
acodalamiento, *n.m.* (*arch.*) propping; staying.
acodalar, *v.t.* (*arch.*) to prop, shore, stay.
acodar, *v.t.* to elbow, bend; to lean the elbow upon; (*agric.*) to layer; (*arch.*) to prop, stay; (*carp.*) to square (*timber*). — **acodarse,** *v.r.* to lean *or* rest on one's elbow(s).
acoderamiento, *n.m.* (*naut.*) bringing the broadside to bear.
acoderar, *v.t.* (*naut.*) to put a spring on a cable; to bring the broadside to bear.
acodiciar, *v.t.* to covet. — **acodiciarse,** *v.r.* to become covetous.
acodillado, -da, *a.* elbowed; bent into an angle.
acodillar, *v.t.* to bend into an elbow *or* angle; to make tricks (*in shadow, at cards*). — *v.i.* to touch the ground with knee (*animals*); (*fig.*) ***acodillar con la carga,*** to sink *or* sag under a burden.
acodo, *n.m.* (*agric.*) layer.
acogedizo, -za, *a.* easy to gather.

acogedor, -ra, *a.* sheltering, protecting; welcoming; cosy.

acoger [E], *v.t.* to welcome, receive; (*fig.*) to accept (*opinions*); to protect, shelter; ***acoger en casa,*** to receive in the house. — **acogerse,** *v.r.* to seek protection; to take shelter; (*fig.*) ***acogerse a,*** to avail oneself of; ***acogerse bajo sagrado,*** to seek refuge *or* asylum.

acogeta, *n.f.* shelter, cover, place of safety; evasion.

acogible, *a.* receivable, acceptable.

acogida, *n.f.* reception; welcome; hospitality; (*com.*) ***dar acogida a una letra,*** to honour a bill *or* draft; ***buena*** or ***mala acogida,*** welcome, good *or* bad reception.

acogimiento, *n.m.* welcome.

acogollar, *v.t.* to cover up (*plants*) for protection. — *v.i.* to bud forth. — **acogollarse,** *v.r.* to grow to a round head.

acogombradura, *n.f.* (*agric.*) banking (*earth*); digging up the ground about plants.

acogombrar, *v.t.* to earth up; to bank.

acogotado, -da, *a.* strangled; (*fig., coll.*) ***estar acogotado,*** to be up to one's neck (in debts).

acogotador, -ra, *n.m.f.* (*prov.*) slaughterer, feller (*of oxen etc.*); (*fam.*) bore.

acogotar, *v.t.* to kill with a rabbit-punch; to strangle.

acojinamiento, *n.m.* (*mech.*) cushioning (*of piston*).

acojinar, *v.t.* to quilt; to cushion.

acolada, *n.f.* accolade.

acolar, *v.t.* (*her.*) to quarter *or* unite (two coats of arms).

acolchar, *v.t.* to quilt; to pad; (*naut.*) to intertwine.

acolchonar, *v.t.* (*Hisp. Am.*) to quilt, cushion.

acólita, *n.f.* (*Chi.*) female acolyte.

acolitado, *n.m.* order of acolytes.

acolitar, *v.i.* to serve as an acolyte.

acólito, *n.m.* acolyte; assistant.

acolladores, *n.m.pl.* lanyards.

acolladura, *n.f.* covering of earth round the base of a trunk.

acollar [4], *v.t.* (*agric.*) to hill up earth round (*the base of a trunk*); to shear the neck of (*sheep*); (*naut.*) to caulk (*a ship*); to haul by the lanyards.

acollarado, -da, *a.* ring-necked (*birds*).

acollarar, *v.t.* to yoke *or* harness (*horses, oxen etc.*); to leash (*hounds*). — **acollararse,** *v.r.* to get married, (*fam.*) to get hitched.

acollonar, *v.t.* (*coll.*) to intimidate. — **acollonarse,** *v.r.* to become frightened, get into a funk.

acombado, -da, *a.* warped.

acombar, *v.t.* to bend, warp. — **acombarse,** *v.r.* to become warped.

acomedido, -da, *a.* (*Hisp. Am.*) obsequious, obliging, compliant.

acomedirse [8], *v.r.* (*Hisp. Am.*) to be obliging, volunteer.

acomejenarse, *v.r.* (*Hisp. Am.*) to become infested with termites.

acometedor, -ra, *a.* aggressive. — *n.m.f.* aggressor, attacker.

acometer, *v.t.* to attack, assault; to charge; (*fig.*) to go for; to undertake; to connect, install (*gas etc.*); ***acometer por la espalda,*** to assault in the back; ***ser acometido de un síncope,*** to be seized by a fainting fit; ***le acometió el sueño,*** sleep overtook him.

acometida, *n.f.*, **acometimiento,** *n.m.* attack, assault; fit of illness; connection (*gas etc.*).

acometividad, *n.f.* combativeness, fighting spirit, aggressiveness.

acomodable, *a.* adaptable.

acomodación, *n.f.* arrangement.

acomodadizo, -za, *a.* accommodating, cooperative, obliging.

acomodado, -da, *a.* suitable, fit; comfortably off, well-to-do; moderate, reasonable.

acomodador, -ra, *a.* conciliating. — *n.m.f.* usher, attendant (*theatre, cinema etc.*).

acomodamiento, *n.m.* fitness; suitability; arrangement.

acomodar, *v.t.* to accommodate, arrange; to settle; to adapt; to compound, compromise. — *v.i.* to fit, suit. — **acomodarse,** *v.r.* to condescend, comply, put up (with); to fit in (with); to accept; ***acomodarse al tiempo,*** to fit in with things as they are; ***acomodarse a*** or ***con otro dictamen,*** to conform to another judgment; ***acomodarse en una casa,*** to make oneself at home.

acomodaticio, -cia, *a.* compliant, accommodating; (*Bibl.*) metaphorical.

acomodativo, -va, *a.* accommodative.

acomodo, *n.m.* employment, place, situation; arrangement, adjustment; (*Chi.*) finery, ornament.

acompañado, -da, *a.* accompanied; (*coll.*) frequented (*thoroughfare*). — *n.m.* (*law*) consultant.

acompañador, -ra, *a.* accompanying. — *n.m.f.* chaperon, companion; attendant; (*mus.*) accompanist.

acompañamiento, *n.m.* attendance, retinue; (*mus.*) accompaniment; supernumeraries at a theatre; (*her.*) ornament round an escutcheon.

acompañante, *a., n.m.f.* companion, chaperon.

acompañar, *v.t.* to go *or* come with, accompany, attend; to lead along; to join, unite; to enclose; (*mus.*) to accompany; (*in letters*) ***le acompaño,*** I send you herewith; ***acompañar a dar un paseo,*** to go for a walk with; ***acompañar con*** or ***de pruebas,*** to accompany with proofs. — **acompañarse,** *v.r.* (*mus.*) to accompany oneself; ***acompañarse al piano,*** to accompany oneself at *or* on the piano.

acompasadamente, *adv.* rhythmically; calmly.

acompasado, -da, *a.* measured by the compass; rhythmic; (*coll.*) quiet and slow in tone; of fixed, regular habits.

acompasar, *v.t.* to measure with dividers and rule; (*mus.*) to divide (*a score*) into equal parts.

acomplexionado, -da, *a.* of good *or* bad constitution.

acomunarse, *v.r.* to band together; to league for a common purpose, combine.

aconchabarse, *v.r.* to gang up; to plot, conspire.

aconchar, *v.t.* to push to a place of safety; (*naut.*) to run aground.

acondicionado, -da, *a.* of good *or* bad disposition (*persons*) *or* condition (*goods*); ***aire acondicionado,*** air conditioning.

acondicionamiento, *n.m.* drying (*silk*) after manufacture; ***acondicionamiento de aire,*** air conditioning.

acondicionar, *v.t.* to dispose, constitute; to prepare, arrange, fix. — **acondicionarse,** *v.r.* to acquire a certain quality *or* condition; to qualify.

acongojadamente, *adv.* in anguish.

acongojado, -da, *a.* anguished, grieved.

acongojador, -ra, *a.* afflicting.

acongojar, *v.t.* to grieve, sadden, oppress, afflict. — **acongojarse,** *v.r.* to become grieved, to be filled with anguish.

aconitina, *n.f.* (*chem.*) aconitine.

acónito, *n.m.* aconite, wolf's-bane.

aconsejable, *a.* advisable.

aconsejado, -da, *a.* ***bien*** (***mal***) ***aconsejado,*** well- (ill-) advised.

aconsejador, -ra, *a.* advising, counselling. — *n.m.f.* adviser, counsellor.

aconsejar, *v.t.* to advise, counsel. — **aconsejarse,** *v.r.* to take counsel, consult (**de,** of, **con,** with); seek *or* get advice (**de,** from); ***aconsejarse mejor,*** to think better of it; ***aconsejarse con la almohada,*** to consult one's pillow, sleep on it;

aconsejarse de sabios, to take advice from the wise, accept sensible advice.

aconsonantar, *v.t.* to make (*a word*) rhyme (*with another*). — *v.i.* to rhyme.

aconstelado, -da, *a.* (*astron.*) constellated.

acontecedero, -ra, *a.* possible, conceivable.

acontecer [9], *v. impers.* (*used only in the inf. and third person sing. and pl.*) to happen, come about, take place, occur; ***lo acontecido,*** that which has *or* had happened; the occurrence.

acontecimiento, *n.m.* event, incident, occurrence, happening.

acopado, -da, *a.* shaped like a wine-glass, rounded.

acopar, *v.t.* (*naut.*) to hollow. — *v.i.* (*bot.*) to form a rounded head.

acopetado, -da, *a.* tufted, crested.

acopetar, *v.t.* to make tufted *or* crested.

acopiador, -ra, *a., n.m.f.* (*com.*) (one) who collects *or* stores up, who corners the market in goods. — *n.m.f.* speculator, monopolist.

acopiamiento, *n.m.* gathering *or* buying up (*goods*); speculation.

acopiar, *v.t.* to gather, store up; to corner (*goods*); to speculate in.

acopio, *n.m.* gathering, storing; store.

acoplado, -da, *a.* attached, fitted, adjusted; coupled. — *n.m.* (*Hisp. Am.*) trailer; tow.

acopladura, *n.f.* coupling, junction.

acoplamiento, *n.m.* coupling, joining, connection, joint; ***acoplamiento de manguito,*** sleeve coupling; ***acoplamiento de rebajo,*** rabbeted joint; ***acoplamiento inductivo,*** (flux) linkage; ***acoplamiento universal,*** universal joint.

acoplar, *v.t.* to couple, join, adjust, fit; to yoke; to mate (*animals*); to settle differences between. — **acoplarse,** *v.r.* to make up matters, be agreed; (*coll.*) to have sexual intercourse, mate.

acoquinamiento, *n.m.* knuckling under.

acoquinar, *v.t.* (*fam.*) to terrify, intimidate, cow. — **acoquinarse,** *v.r.* to be terrified, knuckle under, get into a funk.

acoralado, -da, *a.* coralline.

acorar, *v.t.* to afflict, sadden, grieve. — *v.i.* (*bot.*) to fade. — **acorarse,** *v.r.* to be grieved, waste away with grief.

acorazado, -da, *a.* ironclad, armour-plated. — *n.m.* armoured ship; ironclad, battleship; ***acorazado de bolsillo,*** pocket battleship.

acorazamiento, *n.m.* supplying armour to ships.

acorazar [C], *v.t.* to armour, provide with armour-plating; to shield. — **acorazarse,** *v.r.* to harden *or* shield o.s. (***contra,*** against).

acorazonado, -da, *a.* heart-shaped.

acorchamiento, *n.m.* sponginess; shrivelling; withering.

acorchar, *v.t.* to line with cork. — **acorcharse,** *v.r.* to turn into cork; to shrivel; to become stale (*fruits*); (*fig.*) to become numb (*morally*) *or* sluggish.

acordable, *a.* tunable.

acordada (1), *n.f.* (*law*) order, decree; ***carta acordada,*** granted charter.

acordadamente, *adv.* by common consent; with mature deliberation; harmoniously.

acordado, -da (2), *a.* agreed.

acordar [4], *v.t.* to decide, agree upon; to grant; to reconcile; to resolve; to tune (*musical instruments*); to dispose (*figures in a picture*); to make level *or* flush. — *v.i.* to agree, be in agreement; ***acordar*** + *inf.*, to agree to + *inf.* — **acordarse,** *v.r.* to remember; to be agreed; ***acordarse con alguien,*** to come to an agreement with s.o.; ***acordarse de,*** to remember; ***acordarse remotamente de algo,*** to have a vague recollection of s.th.; ***si mal no me acuerdo,*** if I remember rightly; (*coll.*) ***si te vi no me acuerdo,*** and that was the end of it.

acorde, *a.* agreed; in tune; in agreement; coinciding in opinion; in harmony. — *n.m.* (*mus.*) chord; harmony of sound *or* colours.

acordeladura, *n.f.*, **acordelamiento,** *n.m.* measuring by cord *or* rule.

acordelar, *v.t.* to measure with a cord; to chalk out; to align.

acordemente, *adv.* by common consent, harmoniously.

acordeón, *n.m.* accordion.

acordeonista, *n.m.f.* accordionist.

acordonado, -da, *a.* surrounded; made in the form of a cord; (*Mex.*) lean (*animals*).

acordonar, *v.t.* to make in the form of a cord *or* rope; to lace (*shoes etc.*); to mill (*coin*); to cord, twine; to cordon off.

acornar [4], **acornear,** *v.t.* to butt with the horns, gore.

acorneador, -ra, *a.* butting. — *n.m.f.* animal which butts.

ácoro, *n.m.* (*bot.*) sweet flag.

acorralamiento, *n.m.* corralling; cornering.

acorralar, *v.t.* to corral; to corner.

acorrer, *v.t.* to succour. — *v.i.* to run (***a,*** to). — **acorrerse,** *v.r.* to take shelter.

acorrucarse, [A], *v.r.* [ACURRUCARSE].

acortable, *a.* reducible, shrinkable.

acortamiento, *n.m.* shortening; (*astron.*) curtation.

acortar, *v.t.* to shorten, lessen, reduce; to check, halt, pull up; ***acortarle a uno la palabra,*** to cut s.o. short; ***acortar la marcha,*** to slow down, slacken speed; ***acortar la vela,*** to shorten sail. — *v.i.* to take a short cut. — **acortarse,** *v.r.* to contract, shrink; to become embarrassed; to back down.

acorullar, *v.t.* (*naut.*) to ship (*oars*).

acorvar, *v.t.* to bend, curve.

acosador, -ra, *a.* harassing.

acosar, *v.t.* to pursue *or* press hard, hound, dog, harass; to beset; to corner; to vex, molest; to corral and test mettle of (*bulls*).

acosijar, (*Mex.*) [ACOSAR].

acoso, *n.m.* harassment, relentless pursuit; training, corralling and testing (*bulls*).

acostado, -da, *a.* stretched out, laid down; in bed; closely related; friendly; favoured; (*naut.*) on beam ends. — *n.m.* (*Hisp. Am.*) childbirth; sexual intercourse.

acostamiento, *n.m.* laying down; lying down; support, favour, protection; stipend, emolument.

acostar [4], *v.t.* to lay down; to put to bed; (*naut.*) to bring (*a ship*) alongside the shore. — **acostarse,** *v.r.* to lie down, go to bed; (*coll.*) ***acostarse con las gallinas,*** to go to bed very early; (*naut.*) to have a list; to heave over.

acostumbradamente, *adv.* customarily.

acostumbrado, -da, *a.* accustomed; customary, usual.

acostumbrar, *v.t.* to accustom, make used; ***acostumbrar a una persona a hacer algo,*** to get s.o. used to doing sth. — *v.i.* to be accustomed, used to; ***no acostumbro fumar tanto,*** I am not used to smoking so much. — **acostumbrarse,** *v.r.* to get used (to), become accustomed (to); ***acostumbrarse a los trabajos,*** to accustom o.s. to work.

acotación, *n.f.* bounds, limit; annotation, marginal note; (*theat.*) directions; (*surv.*) elevation (*marked on a map*).

acotamiento, *n.m.* limitation.

acotada, *n.f.* (*bot.*) nursery.

acotar, *v.t.* to limit, set bounds to; to mark out; to mark elevations on; to annotate, make marginal notes on; to accept; to vouch for; to prune (*trees*); (*fam.*) to select.

acotiledóneo, -nea, *a.* (*bot.*) acotyledonous, not provided with seed leaves. — *n.f.pl.* (**acotiledóneas**) (*bot.*) Acotyledons.

acotillo, *n.m.* sledge-hammer.

acoyundar, *v.t.* to yoke.
acoyuntar, *v.t.* to form a partnership (*two one-horse farmers*).
acracia, *n.f.* (*polit.*) opposition to authority.
ácrata, *a.*, *n.m.f.* (*polit.*) (one) opposed to all authority.
acre (1), *a.* acrid, bitter, sour; pungent; mordant; keen; acrimonious; ***acre de condición,*** acrimonious by nature.
acre (2), *n.m.* acre.
acrecencia, *n.f.* (*law*) increase, growth.
acrecentadamente, *adv.* increasingly.
acrecentador, -ra, *a.* increasing. — *n.m.f.* one that increases.
acrecentamiento, *n.m.* increase, growth.
acrecentar(se) [1], *v.t.* (*v.r.*), **acrecer(se)** [9], *v.t.* (*v.r.*) to increase; to promote, advance, foster.
acreditadamente, *adv.* creditably; with guarantees.
acreditado, -da, *a.* accredited; reputable, held in esteem.
acreditar, *v.t.* to assure, affirm; to verify, prove; to give credit to; (*com.*) to credit, recommend; to answer for, guarantee; to accredit, authorize. — **acreditarse,** *v.r.* to gain a reputation; ***acreditarse de loco*** or ***de necio,*** to mark oneself as a madman *or* fool; ***acreditarse con alguien,*** to gain s.o.'s confidence; ***acreditado en*** or ***para su oficio,*** having a good standing in his job.
acreditativo, -va, *a.* creditable.
acreedor, -ra, *a.* deserving, meritorious; ***acreedor a la gratitud de la patria,*** worthy of *or* entitled to the country's gratitude. — *n.m.f.* creditor.
acremente, *adv.* sourly, bitterly; with acrimony.
acribador, -ra, *a.* sifting. — *n.m.f.* sifter.
acribar, *v.t.* to sift.
acribillador, -ra, *a.* sieve-like; tormenting, molesting. — *n.m.f.* one who pierces; tormentor, molester.
acribillar, *v.t.* to pierce like a sieve; to riddle (*with shot*); (*coll.*) to pester, badger; ***acribillar a preguntas,*** to ply (mercilessly) with questions, pepper with questions; ***le acribillan los acreedores,*** his creditors hound him; ***está acribillado de deudas,*** he is up to his eyes in debt.
acrídidos, *n.m.pl.* (*ent.*) locusts.
acridófago, -ga, *a.*, *n.m.f.* living on locusts.
acriminable, *a.* incriminatory.
acriminación, *n.f.* accusation, incrimination.
acriminador, -ra, *a.* accusing. — *n.m.f.* accuser.
acriminar, *v.t.* to accuse, impeach; (*law*) to aggravate.
acrimonia, *n.f.* acrimony, sharpness, sourness; asperity (of expression); sharpness (of temper); vehemence (in talking).
acrimonial, *a.* acrimonious.
acrimoniosamente, *adv.* acrimoniously.
acrimonioso, -sa, *a.* acrimonious.
acriollado, -da, *a.* (*Hisp. Am.*) adapted to local customs.
acriollarse, *v.r.* (*Hisp. Am.*) to adopt national customs.
acrisolación, *n.f.* purification.
acrisoladamente, *adv.* in a pure way.
acrisolado, -da, *a.* pure; tried, tested.
acrisolador, -ra, *a.* refining. — *n.m.f.* refiner, assayer (*metals*).
acrisolar, *v.t.* to refine, purify, assay (*metals*); (*fig.*) to cleanse, make pure, purge of all dross.
acristianar, *v.t.* (*coll.*) to baptize.
acritud, *n.f.* acrimony; sharpness; asperity.
acróbata, *n.m.f.* acrobat.
acrobático, -ca, *a.* acrobatic.
acromático, -ca, *a.* achromatic.
acromatismo, *n.m.* achromatism.
acromatizar [C], *v.t.* to achromatize.
acromial, *a.* (*anat.*) acromial.
acrómico, -ca, *a.* achromic.
acromio, acromión, *n.m.* (*anat.*) acromion.
acrónicamente, *adv.* (*astron.*) acronychally.
acrónico, -ca, *a.* (*astron.*) acronychal.
acróstico, -ca, *a.* acrostic.
acrotera, *n.f.* (*arch.*) acroterium.
acta, *n.f.* act *or* record of proceedings; certificate of election; ***acta de matrimonio,*** marriage certificate; ***acta de nacimiento,*** birth certificate; ***acta de nacionalidad,*** registry certificate; ***acta notarial,*** affidavit; ***levantar acta,*** to draw up and execute a certificate *or* affidavit; to report, book (*of police*); (*pl.*) acts, minutes *or* records of communities, councils *or* conferences; ***libro de actas,*** minute-book; ***actas de los santos,*** lives of the saints.
actínico, -ca, *a.* actinic.
actinio, *n.m.* actinium, metallic element.
actinométrico, -ca, *a.* (*opt.*) actinometric.
actinómetro, *n.m.* (*opt.*) actinometer.
actinota, *n.f.* actinolite.
actitud, *n.f.* attitude, position; ***en actitud de,*** showing an intention to, ready *or* poised to, about to.
activamente, *adv.* actively.
activar, *v.t.* to push, make brisk, hasten, hurry; to expedite, activate, get moving; to poke, stir; (*fam.*) to buck up.
actividad, *n.f.* activity, liveliness; ***poner en actividad,*** to put in operation; ***estar en plena actividad,*** to be in full swing.
activista, *n.m.f.* activist, agitator.
activo, -va, *a.* active, quick, diligent; ***voz activa,*** suffrage. — *n.m.* (*com.*) assets, outstanding claims; ***en activo,*** on *or* in active service; ***por activa o por pasiva,*** from any angle.
acto, *n.m.* act, action; event; ceremony; public function; thesis defended in universities; ***acto continuo, acto seguido,*** immediately afterwards; ***en el acto,*** at once, instantly; ***acto inaugural,*** opening, opening ceremony; ***acto de presencia,*** formal attendance; ***sala de actos,*** assembly hall; ***actos públicos,*** public *or* official occasions; ***Actos de los Apóstoles,*** Acts of the Apostles.
actor, *n.m.* actor, performer, player; (*law*) claimant, plaintiff.
actora, *n.f.* (*law*) plaintiff; ***parte actora,*** prosecution.
actriz, *n.f.* actress; ***primera actriz,*** leading lady.
actuación, *n.f.* action, actions, performance, behaviour; (*pl.*) (*law*) proceedings.
actuado, -da, *a.* skilled, experienced.
actual, *a.* present; present-day; topical.
actualidad, *n.f.* present situation *or* state of affairs; ***en la actualidad,*** at the present time; ***estar de actualidad,*** to be topical *or* in the news; ***ser de mucha actualidad,*** to be highly topical; (*pl.*) current affairs *or* events, topical news.
actualizar [C], *v.t.* to make *or* bring up-to-date, modernize. — **actualizarse,** *v.r.* to get up to date, (*fam.*) get with it.
actualmente, *adv.* at present, at the present time, nowadays.
actuante, *n.m.f.* defender of a thesis (*in universities etc.*); one who performs (*in general*).
actuar [M], *v.t.* to put into action. — *v.i.* to act, perform; to support *or* defend a thesis (*at university*); ***actuar de,*** to act as; ***actuar sobre,*** to act on *or* upon.
actuario, *n.m.* clerk of a court of justice; actuary; ***actuario de seguros,*** insurance expert.
acuadrillar, *v.t.* to form into a band *or* gang; to command, lead, head (*a band*).
acuafortista, *n.m.f.* etcher.

acuantiar [L], *v.t.* to determine the quantity *or* amount of.
acuarela, *n.f.* water-colour.
acuarelista, *n.m.f.* water-colour artist.
Acuario, *n.m.* (*astron.*, *astrol.*) Aquarius.
acuario, *n.m.* aquarium.
acuartelado, -da, *a.* confined to barracks (*troops*).
acuartelamiento, *n.m.* quartering troops; quarters.
acuartelar, *v.t.* to quarter, billet (*troops*); to confine (*troops*) to barracks; (*naut.*) ***acuartelar las velas,*** to bear (*sails*) to windward. — **acuartelarse,** *v.r.* to take up quarters; to withdraw.
acuartillar, *v.i.* to bend in the quarters under a heavy load (*beasts of burden*).
acuate, *n.m.* (*Mex.* **acoatl**) water snake.
acuático, -ca, acuátil, *a.* aquatic.
acuatinta, *n.f.* aquatint.
acuatizaje, *n.m.* (*aer.*) alighting on (the) water.
acuatizar [C], *v.i.* (*aer.*) to alight on (the) water.
acubar, *v.t.* to shape like a pail *or* bucket. — **acubarse,** *v.r.* (*coll.*) to become intoxicated.
acubilar, *v.t.* to shelter (*cattle*).
acucia, *n.f.* zeal, diligence, haste; eagerness, longing.
acuciador, -ra, acuciante, *a.* (desperately) pressing, urgent.
acuciamiento, *n.m.* goading, prodding.
acuciar, *v.t.* to goad, prod; to harass; to hasten.
acuciosamente, *adv.* zealously, actively; diligently; eagerly.
acucioso, -sa, *a.* zealous, eager.
acuclillarse, *v.r.* to crouch, squat.
acucharado, -da, *a.* spoon-shaped.
acucharar, *v.t.* to shape like a spoon.
acuchillado, -da, *a.* cut, slashed, stabbed; (*fig.*) made cautious by bitter experience; slashed (*of garments*).
acuchillador, -ra, *a.* quarrelsome. — *n.m.f.* bully; bravo.
acuchillar, *v.t.* to cut, stab, knife, hack; to slash (*clothes*); to plane down, smooth. — **acuchillarse,** *v.r.* to fight with knives *or* swords.
acudimiento, *n.m.* aid, assistance.
acudir, *v.i.* to run in, come in *or* up, rush; to go *or* come to the rescue; to resort *or* repair (to); ***acudir a,*** to have recourse to.
acueducto, *n.m.* aqueduct.
ácueo, -cuea, *a.* watery, aqueous.
acuerdado, -da, *a.* constructed by line *or* rule.
acuerdo, *n.m.* agreement, accord; meeting; resolution, decision; harmony (of colours); ***de acuerdo,*** all right; (*coll.*) O.K.; ***de acuerdo con,*** complying with, in accordance with; ***libro del acuerdo,*** book of resolutions; ***estar en*** or ***fuera de su acuerdo,*** to be in *or* not to be in one's right mind; ***estar de acuerdo,*** to agree; ***ponerse de acuerdo,*** to come to an agreement, to agree; ***volver sobre*** or ***de su acuerdo,*** to change one's mind; ***volver en su acuerdo,*** to regain one's senses.
acuidad, *n.f.* acuity; subtlety; visual sharpness.
acuitadamente, *adv.* with (great) affliction.
acuitado, -da, *a.* afflicted, grieved, sorrowful.
acuitar, *v.t.* to afflict, grieve. — **acuitarse,** *v.r.* to grieve, be grieved.
acular, *v.t.* to force into a corner; to make (*s.o., sth.*) back up. — **acularse,** *v.r.* to set one's back (*against sth.*); (*naut.*) to back up on a shoal.
aculebrinado, -da, *a.* made in the form of a culverin.
aculeiforme, *a.* in the form of a goad *or* sting.
acúleo, -lea, *a.* (*zool.*) aculeate, armed with *or* having a sting.
acullá, *adv.* there; yonder, on the other side; opposite; ***aquí y acullá,*** here and there.
acumen, *n.m.* acumen, discernment.
acuminado, -da, *a.* (*bot.*) acuminate, ending in a point.
acumíneo, -nea, *a.* ending in a point.
acumuchar, *v.t.* (*Chi.*) to pile up.
acumulación, *n.f.* accumulation, gathering, conglomeration, heap; storing up.
acumuladamente, *adv.* cumulatively.
acumulador, -ra, *a.* accumulating, amassing. — *n.m.f.* accumulator, hoarder; (*elec.*) storage battery, accumulator; ***acumulador de ferro-níquel*** or ***de hierro-níquel,*** ferro-nickel alkaline cell; ***acumulador de plomo-ácido,*** lead acid cell; ***acumulador flotante,*** floating battery.
acumulante, *a.* amassing, accumulating.
acumular, *v.t.* to accumulate, heap together, pile up, treasure up, hoard, lay up.
acumulativamente, *adv.* accumulatively.
acumulativo, -va, *a.* accumlative.
acunar, *v.t.* to rock in a cradle.
acuñación, *n.f.* coining, minting; wedging.
acuñador, -ra, *a.* coining, minting; wedging. — *n.m.f.* minter, coiner. — *n.m.* wedge; (*print.*) shooting-stick.
acuñar, *v.t.* to coin, mint; to wedge, fasten with wedges; to key, lock; (*print.*) to quoin; ***acuñar dinero,*** to mint money; ***acuñar una palabra,*** to coin a word.
acuosidad, *n.f.* wateriness.
acuoso, -sa, *a.* watery, aqueous.
acupuntura, *n.f.* (*surg.*) acupuncture.
acure, *n.m.* (*Col.*, *Ven.*) guinea pig.
acurrarse, *v.r.* (*Cub.*) to imitate Andalusian pronunciation and ways.
acurrucarse [A], *v.r.* to huddle *or* curl up.
acusable, *a.* accusable, indictable.
acusación, *n.f.* accusation, impeachment, indictment, charge.
acusado, -da, *a.* accused; marked; ***acusada mejoría,*** marked improvement. — *n.m.f.* defendant, accused.
acusador, -ra, *a.* accusing, prosecuting. — *n.m.f.* accuser, prosecutor; informer.
acusante, *a.* accusing, prosecuting.
acusar, *v.t.* to accuse, charge, prosecute, indict; to announce (*winning cards*); ***acusar cansancio,*** to show signs of weariness; ***acusar recibo,*** to acknowledge receipt; ***acusar las cuarenta,*** to call out the forty honour points (*at cards*); (*law*) ***acusar la rebeldía,*** to summon a defaulter. — **acusarse,** *v.r.* ***acusarse de algo,*** to confess something.
acusativo, *n.m.* (*gram.*) accusative (case).
acusatorio, -ria, *a.* accusatory.
acuse, *n.m.* accusation; announcement (*of winning cards*); ***acuse de recibo,*** acknowledgment of receipt.
acusetas, *n.m. inv.*, **acusete,** *n.m.* (*Hisp. Am.*) talebearer.
acusón, -sona, *a.* talebearing, tell-tale. — *n.m.f.* talebearer, tell-tale.
acústica, *n.f.* acoustics.
acústico, -ca, *a.* acoustic; ***tubo acústico,*** speaking-tube; ***trompetilla acústica,*** ear-trumpet, auriphone.
acusticón, *n.m.* electric sound-amplifier.
acutángulo, *a.* (*geom.*) acute-angled.
acutí, *n.m.* (*Arg.*) guinea pig.
achacable, *a.* imputable.
achacar [A], *v.t.* to impute, put down (to); ***achacó su fracaso a negligencia,*** he put his failure down to carelessness; to frame an excuse.
achacosamente, *adv.* sickly.
achacoso, -sa, *a.* sickly, weak, ailing.
achachay, *n.m.* (*Col.*) children's game.
achaflanadura, *n.f.* chamfering.
achaflanar, *v.t.* to chamfer.
achagual, *n.m.* (*Hisp. Am.*) South American fish.

achahuistlarse, *v.r.* (*Mex.*) to contract a disease from a plant.
achajuanarse, *v.r.* (*Col.*) to suffer from working in hot weather (*animals*).
achamparse, *v.r.* (*Chi.*) to keep s.o. else's property.
achancharse, *v.r.* (*Per.*) to become lazy.
achantarse, *v.r.* (*coll.*) to climb down, sing small.
achaparrado, -da, *a.* stunted (*tree*); ***hombre achaparrado,*** short thick-set man.
achaparrarse, *v.r.* to grow stunted.
achaque, *n.m.* (habitual) ailment *or* indisposition; (*coll.*) excuse, pretext; (*fam.*) period, menstruation; ***saber poco de achaques de amores,*** to know little of love's afflictions.
achaquiento, -ta, *a.* sickly, unhealthy.
achares, *n.m.pl.* jealousy; ***dar achares a alguien,*** to make s.o. jealous.
acharolado, -da, *a.* resembling patent leather; treated with japan varnish.
acharolador, -ra, *a.* that varnishes; that gives the appearance of patent leather. — *n.m.f.* japan varnisher.
acharoladura, *n.f.* japan varnishing; patent leathering.
acharolar, *v.t.* to varnish like patent leather; to japan.
achatado, -da, *a.* flattened; ***nariz achatada,*** flat nose.
achatamiento, *n.m.* flattening.
achatar, *v.t.* to flatten. — **achatarse,** *v.r.* to become flat.
achicado, -da, *a.* abashed; timid, reserved.
achicador, *n.m.* (*naut.*) scoop (for bailing boats); (*min.*) bailer, scooper.
achicadura, *n.f.*, **achicamiento,** *n.m.* timidity; (*naut.*) bailing.
achicar [A], *v.t.* to reduce, diminish, lessen; (*coll.*) to intimidate, humble, belittle; to bail (*a boat*), drain (*a mine*); (*Hisp. Am.*) to kill; ***achicar un cabo,*** to shorten a rope. — **achicarse,** *v.r.* to humble oneself, make oneself small, climb down; ***X se achica demasiado,*** X makes too little of himself *or* takes too much of a back seat.
achicoria, *n.f.* (*bot.*) chicory.
achicorial, *n.m.* chicory field.
achicharradero, -ra, *n.m.f.* place of scorching heat; ***el teatro es un achicharradero,*** the theatre is like an oven.
achicharrador, -ra, *a.* searing, scorching, fiercely hot.
achicharrar, *v.t.* to scorch, sear, roast; to irritate; ***me achicharra la sangre,*** he gets on my nerves.
achichinque, *n.m.* (*min.*) scooper, bailer.
achiguarse, *v.r.* (*Arg.*, *Chi.*) to warp, bulge, sag.
achilenarse, *v.r.* to adopt Chilean ways.
achimero, *n.m.* (*Hisp. Am.*) pedlar, hawker.
achinado, -da, *a.* like a Chinaman, of a Chinese type; (*Arg.*) dark-red; resembling an Indian (in colour or features).
achinar, *v.t.* (*coll.*) to cut the face of; to scare; to corner.
achinelado, -da, *a.* slipper-shaped.
achinelar, *v.t.* to give (*shoes*) the form of a slipper.
ach(i)ote, *n.m.* (*Mex.*, *bot.*) arnotto-tree.
achique, *n.m.* scooping, bailing, draining.
achispado, -da, *a.* tipsy.
achispar, *v.t.* (*coll.*) to make (*s.o.*) tipsy. — **achisparse,** *v.r.* to get tipsy.
achocadura, *n.f.* hurling against something hard; stoning; wound from a stone.
achocar [A], *v.t.* to hurl against something hard; to wound with a stone, stone; to strike; to hoard.
achocolatado, -da, *a.* chocolate-coloured, chocolate-like.
achocharse, *v.r.* (*coll.*) to become senile.
acholado, -da, *a.* (*Hisp. Am.*) half Indian; half-breed, mestizo.
acholar, *v.t.* (*Hisp. Am.*) to make blush; to shame. — **acholarse,** *v.r.* to become ill from heat.
achorizado, -da, *a.* sausage-like.
achubascarse [A], *v.r.* to get showery, become overcast and threatening.
achucutarse, achucuyarse, *v.r.* (*Cent. Am.*) to become down-hearted; to lose courage; to wither.
achuchador, -ra, *a.* bullying. — *n.m.f.* bully.
achuchamiento, *n.m.* jostling; squeezing.
achuchar, *v.t.* (*coll.*) to incite, stir up; (*coll.*) to push around, jostle; to squeeze, crush, crumple; ***está muy achuchado,*** he is very hard up.
achuchón, *n.m.* (*coll.*) squeeze.
achulado, -da, *a.*, *n.m.f.* truculent, bragging, bullying (type). — *n.m.* man kept by a woman.
achulaparse, achularse, *v.r.* to become truculent; to (allow oneself to) be kept by a woman.
achunchar, *v.t.* (*Hisp. Am.*) to frighten; to shame; to cast the evil eye on.
achupaya, *n.f.* (*Hisp. Am.*) a plant of the Bromeliaceæ family.
achura, *n.f.* (*Per.*, *min.*) richest part of a seam; (*Arg.*) offal.
adafina, *n.f.* Jewish stew.
adagio, *n.m.* proverb; saying; adage; (*mus.*) adagio, slow time.
adala, *n.f.* (*naut.*) pump dale.
adalid, *n.m.* champion; leader, chief; commander.
adamado, -da, *a.* effeminate. — *n.f.* (*fam.*) la-di-da woman.
adamantino, -na, *a.* (*poet.*) adamantine.
adamarse, *v.r.* to become effeminate.
adamascado, -da, *a.* damask-like.
adamascador, -ra, *a.*, *n.m.f.* (s.o.) that manufactures damask.
adamascar [A], *v.t.* to damask.
adámico, -ca, *a.* Adamic.
adamismo, *n.m.* back-to-nature doctrine.
adamita, *n.m.* Adamite.
Adán, *n.m.* Adam; (*coll.*) slovenly individual.
adanismo, *n.m.* [ADAMISMO].
adaptabilidad, *n.f.* adaptability.
adaptable, *a.* adaptable.
adaptación, *n.f.* adaptation; fitting; alteration.
adaptador, -ra, *a.* adapting. — *n.m.f.* adapter.
adaptante, *a.* adapting. — *n.m.f.* adapter.
adaptar, *v.t.* to adapt, fit, apply; to make suitable. — **adaptarse,** *v.r.* to adapt (oneself) (to); get used (to).
adaraja, *n.f.* (*arch.*, *carp.*) toothing.
adarce, *n.m.* dry sea-froth; (*pl.*) carbonate of lime.
adarga, *n.f.* oval *or* heart-shaped leather shield; targe.
adargar [B], *v.t.* to shield, protect, defend.
adarguero, *n.m.* maker of shields.
adarguilla, *n.f.* small shield.
adarme, *n.m.* half a drachm, sixteenth part of an ounce, 179 centigrams; bit; ***no me gusta un adarme,*** I don't like it one little bit; ***por adarmes,*** very sparingly.
adarvar, *v.t.* to paralyse, bewilder, stun. — **adarvarse,** *v.r.* to faint, become unconscious.
adarve, *n.m.* (*mil.*, *arch.*) passage *or* walk behind a parapet; (*fig.*) protection, defence.
adatar, *v.t.* to enter in a ledger; to credit.
adaza, *n.f.* (*bot.*) sorghum.
adazal, *n.m.* esparto thread.
adecenamiento, *n.m.* forming by tens.
adecenar, *v.t.* to form *or* count by tens.
adecentar, *v.t.* to clean up, straighten up, tidy up, do up, set in order.
adecuación, *n.f.* fitting, adaptation.
adecuadamente, *adv.* fitly, properly, suitably.

adecuado, -da, *a.* adequate, fit, suitable, right.

adecuar, *v.t.* to fit, suit, adapt, make suitable.

adefagia, *n.f.* (*zool.*) voracity.

adéfago, -ga, *a.* (*zool.*) voracious; adephagous.

adefesio, *n.m.* (*coll.*) nonsense, absurdity; extravagant *or* outlandish garb *or* figure, ridiculous-looking object; (*coll.*) sight.

adehala, *n.f.* gratuity, perquisite, tip, extra.

adehesamiento, *n.m.* converting (*land*) into pasture; pasturage.

adehesar, *v.t.* to convert (*land*) into pasture.

adelantadamente, *adv.* beforehand; in advance.

adelantado, -da, *a.* anticipated; advanced; developed; precocious; early (*fruit etc.*); fast (*clock, watch*); ***por adelantado,*** in advance. — *n.m.* governor-general.

adelantamiento, *n.m.* progress, improvement; furtherance, advancement, betterment; promotion; governor-generalship; province under governor-general.

adelantar, *v.t.* to advance, promote, forward; to overtake; to pay beforehand. — *v.i.* to advance, make progress *or* headway; to grow; to improve; to be fast, gain (*watch, clock*). — **adelantarse,** *v.r.* ***adelantarse a,*** to take the lead (*over*), get ahead (*of*), cut in ahead (*of*); (*coll.*) steal a march (*on*), beat (*s.o.*) to it.

adelante, *adv.* ahead; forward, onward; higher up; farther off; ***en adelante, de hoy en adelante, de aquí en adelante,*** henceforth, in future, for the future; ***más adelante,*** later on; ***hacia adelante,*** forward(s). — *interj.* come in!; go on! forward!

adelanto, *n.m.* advance, progress; (*com.*) advance payment.

adelfa, *n.f.* (*bot.*) oleander; rose-bay.

adelfal, adelfar, *n.m.* (*bot.*) plantation of rose-bay trees.

adélfico, -ca, *a.* (*poet.*) bitter, cruel.

adelfilla, *n.f.* (*bot.*) rose-bay, willow herb.

adelgazador, -ra, *a.* slimming, thinning.

adelgazamiento, *n.m.* slimming, reducing; slenderness.

adelgazar [C], *v.t.* to make thin *or* slender; to taper. — *v.i.* to slim; to lose weight; to get thin, reduce; to split hairs; ***régimen de adelgazar,*** slimming diet.

adeliñar, *v.i.* to make a bee-line (*for sth.*).

adema, *n.f.,* **ademe,** *n.m.* (*min.*) shore; strut; prop.

ademán, *n.m.* gesture, attitude; ***en ademán de,*** showing intention to; ***hacer ademán de,*** to make a move to.

ademar, *v.t.* (*min.*) to shore, prop.

además, *adv.* moreover, further; furthermore; besides; ***además de,*** besides; ***además de lo referido,*** in addition to *or* besides the matter referred to.

adenografía, *n.f.*(*med.*) treatise on the glands.

adenoideo, -dea, *a.* adenoid; ***tumor adenoideo, vegetación adenoidea,*** adenoids.

adenología, *n.f.* (*med.*) part of anatomy dealing with the glands.

adenoso, -sa, *a.* glandular.

adensar, *v.t.* to condense. — **adensarse,** *v.r.* to become thick(er).

adentelladura, *n.f.* biting; (*arch.*) toothing.

adentellar, *v.t.* to bite, catch with the teeth; (*fig.*) to get one's teeth into; ***adentellar una pared,*** to leave toothing-stones *or* bricks to continue a wall. — **adentellarse,** *v.r.* to become angry.

adentrar(se), *v.i.* (*v.r.*) to go into; to go more deeply into.

adentro, *adv.* within, inwardly, internally, inside; ***de botones adentro,*** in one's heart; ***tierra adentro,*** inland; ***mar adentro,*** out at sea; ***nunca me entró de dientes adentro,*** I never could endure him; ***barrer hacia adentro,*** to have one's eye to the main chance. — *interj.* come in! in you go! — *n.m.pl.* (**adentros**) ***pensé para mis adentros,*** I thought to myself.

adepto, *n.m.* initiate; supporter, follower.

aderezadamente, *adv.* with seasonings, adornments *or* embellishments.

aderezador, -ra, *a.,n.m.f.* (s.o.) that adorns, dresses *or* embellishes. — *n.m.* (*carp.*) jointing-plane.

aderezamiento, *n.m.* adorning, embellishing, dressing.

aderezar [C], *v.t.* to adorn, embellish; to prepare; to season; to dress (*salad*); to clean, repair; to mix (*drinks*); to blend (*wines, tea*); to gum (*silks*); to size (*stuffs*). — **aderezarse,** *v.r.* to adorn, embellish, dress oneself.

aderezo, *n.m.* dressing and adorning; finery; gum, starch *etc.* (*used for stiffening*); set of jewellery; trappings (*of a horse*); furniture; hilt, hook and other appendages (*of a sword*); ***aderezo de mesa,*** seasoning, condiments.

aderra, *n.f.* rush rope; esparto rope.

adestrado, -da, *a.* broken in; (*her.*) on the dexter side of the escutcheon.

adestrador, -ra [ADIESTRADOR].

adestramiento [ADIESTRAMIENTO].

adestrar [I] [ADIESTRAR].

adeudado, -da, *a.* indebted, in debt.

adeudar, *v.t.* to owe; to be subject to (*duty etc.*); (*com.*) to charge, debit. — *v.i.* to fall due; to become related by marriage. — **adeudarse,** *v.r.* to incur debt.

adeudo, *n.m.* indebtedness; custom-house duty; (*com.*) debit, charge.

adherencia, *n.f.* alliance; adherence; adhesion; (*fig.*) relationship; bond, friendship; ***tener adherencias,*** to have connections.

adherente, *a.* adhesive, adherent. — *n.m.* follower, adherent; (*pl.*) equipment, accessories.

adherir [6], *v.i.* to adhere, stick (*to*). — **adherirse,** *v.r.* to hold, stick fast; to adhere (*to*); ***adherir(se) a un dictamen,*** to espouse *or* embrace a judgment *or* decision.

adhesión, *n.f.* adhesion, adherence.

adhesividad, *n.f.* adhesiveness.

adhesivo, -va, *a.* adhesive.

adiafa, *n.f.* tip given to seamen at the end of a voyage.

adiamantado, -da, *a.* adamantine.

adiamantar, *v.t.* to adorn with diamonds.

adición, *n.f.* addition, extension; bill; remark *or* note put to accounts; ***adición de la herencia,*** acceptance of an inheritance.

adicionable, *a.* addible, that can be added.

adicional, *a.* supplementary, additional.

adicionalmente, *adv.* additionally.

adicionar, *v.t.* to make additions, add to; to extend, prolong.

adicto, -ta, *a.* addicted, attached. — *n.m.f.* supporter, follower, devotee.

adiestrable, *a.* trainable.

adiestrador, -ra, *n.m.f.* trainer, instructor.

adiestramiento, *n.m.* training, instruction.

adiestrar, *v.t.* to train, instruct, coach. — **adiestrarse,** *v.r.* ***adiestrarse a*** + *inf.* or ***en*** + *noun,* to practise.

adietar, *v.t.* to put on a diet.

adinamia, *n.f.* (*med.*) debility, adynamia, prostration.

adinámico, -ca, *a.* (*med.*) lacking strength.

adinerado, -da, *a.* rich, wealthy, moneyed.

adinerar, *v.t.* (*prov.*) to convert into currency. — **adinerarse,** *v.r.* (*coll.*) to become rich *or* wealthy.

adintelado, -da, *a.* (*arch.*) straight; flat.

¡adiós! *interj.* good-bye, cheerio; hello, hi (*e.g. on passing s.o. in street*).

adipal, *a.* greasy.

adipocira, *n.f.* adipocere.

adiposidad, *n.f.* fatness, adiposity.
adiposo, -sa, *a.* fat, adipose; ***tejido adiposo,*** adipose tissue.
adir [21], *v.t.* (*law*) to accept, receive (*an inheritance*).
adisonismo, *n.m.* (*med.*) Addison's disease.
aditamento, *n.m.* addition; (*pl.*) attachments, accessories.
aditicio, *n.m.* additive.
aditivo, -va, *a.* additive.
adiva, *n.f.*, **adive,** *n.m.* jackal.
adivas, *n.f.pl.* (*vet.*) vives.
adivinable, *a.* guessable.
adivinación, *n.f.* divination; guessing.
adivinador, -ra, *a.* divining. — *n.m.f.* soothsayer; guesser.
adivinaja, *n.f.* (*coll.*) puzzle, riddle, conundrum.
adivinamiento, *n.m.* divination.
adivinanza, *n.f.* (*coll.*) prophecy; prediction; enigma, riddle; guess; divination.
adivinar, *v.t.* to guess, divine, solve; ***adivinarle a alguien el pensamiento,*** to read s.o.'s mind.
adivinatorio, -ria, *a.* divinatory.
adivino, -na, *n.m.f.* soothsayer; prophet, fortune-teller; wizard; guesser; (*ent.*) praying mantis.
adjetivación, *n.f.* adjectival use; (*gram.*) agreement.
adjetival, *a.* adjectival.
adjetivar, *v.t.* to make agree; (*gram.*) to give adjectival value to. —**adjetivarse,** *v.r.* to be used adjectivally.
adjetivo, -va, *a.* adjectival. — *n.m.* adjective; ***adjetivo calificativo,*** qualifying adjective; ***adjetivo comparativo,*** comparative adjective; ***adjetivo determinativo,*** limiting adjective; ***adjetivo gentilicio,*** proper adjective; ***adjetivo superlativo,*** superlative adjective.
adjudicación, *n.f.* adjudication; award; 'knocking-down' (*at auction*); ***adjudicación de quiebra,*** adjudication in bankruptcy; ***adjudicación procesal,*** judicial award.
adjudicador, -ra, *a.* adjudging, adjudicating. — *n.m.f.* adjudger; adjudicator.
adjudicar [A], *v.t.* to adjudge, adjudicate; to auction; to award; ***adjudicar el contrato,*** to award the contract. — **adjudicarse,** *v.r.* to appropriate.
adjudicatario, -ria, *n.m.f.* grantee; successful bidder.
adjudicativo, -va, *a.* adjudicative; adjudicating.
adjunción, *n.f.* (*law*) adjunction; (*gram.*) zeugma.
adjuntamente, *adv.* jointly; in the same place.
adjuntar, *v.t.* to add, join; to enclose (*in a letter*).
adjunto, -ta, *a.* joined, annexed; enclosed, attached; associate, adjunct; ***profesor adjunto,*** (assistant) lecturer. — *n.m.* addition; adjective. — *n.m.f.* enclosure; partner. — *n.f.* (*com.*) letter enclosed in another.
adjutor, -ra, *a.* helping, adjuvant. — *n.m.f.* helper; assistant.
adminicular, *v.t.* (*law*) to support, corroborate; to substantiate, provide additional proof (of).
adminículo, *n.m.* aid, prop, support; (*pl.*) articles carried for emergency use.
administrable, *a.* administrable.
administración, *n.f.* administration, management; ***en administración,*** in trust; ***administración accesoria,*** ancillary administration; ***administración activa,*** executive office; ***administración contenciosa,*** legal *or* judicial administration; ***administración con testamento anexo,*** administration with will attached; ***administración de impuestos,*** tax collector's office; ***administración de lotería,*** State Lottery office *or* shop; ***por administración,*** by the government, officially.
administrador, -ra, *a.* administrating. — *n.m.f.* administrator; steward, bailiff; trustee; ***administrador de aduanas,*** collector of customs duties; ***administrador de correos,*** postmaster.
administrar(**se**), *v.t.* (*v.r.*) to administer, manage.
administrativamente, *adv.* administratively.
administrativo, -va, *a.* administrative.
administratorio, -ria, *a.* (*law*) belonging to an administration *or* administrator.
admirable, *a.* admirable, praiseworthy.
admirablemente, *adv.* admirably.
admiración, *n.f.* admiration; wonder; (*gram.*) exclamation mark (¡ !).
admirador, -ra, *a.* admiring. — *n.m.f.* admirer.
admirando, -da, *a.* worthy of admiration.
admirar, *v.t.* to admire; to marvel *or* wonder at; to astonish, amaze, astound; ***me admira su osadía,*** his daring astonishes me. — **admirarse,** *v.r.* to wonder, be astonished; to be surprised (at); ***admirarse de un suceso,*** to wonder at an occurrence.
admirativamente, *adv.* in a wondering manner; admiringly.
admirativo, -va, *a.* admiring; wondering.
admisible, *a.* admissible, allowable.
admisión, *n.f.* admission, acceptance.
admitir, *v.t.* to receive, admit; to concede; to accept; to allow, suffer, brook; ***el asunto no admite dilación,*** the affair admits *or* allows of no delay.
admonición, *n.f.* admonition, warning.
admonitor, *n.m.* monitor (*in some religious communities*).
adnato, -ta, *a.* (*bot.*, *physiol.*) adnate. — *n.f.* (*anat.*) conjunctiva.
adobado, *n.m.* pickled meat (*esp. pork*).
adobador, -ra, *a.* pickling, preserving. — *n.m.f.* dresser, preparer.
adobamiento, *n.m.* dressing; preserving; tanning.
adobar, *v.t.* to dress, prepare, pickle (*pork or other meats*); to cook; to tan (*hides*). — *v.r.* to paint oneself up.
adobasillas, *n.m. inv.* chair-mender.
adobe, *n.m.* adobe, dried mud, mud brick.
adobeño, -ña, *a.* of adobe.
adobera, *n.f.* adobe mould; (*Hisp. Am.*) cheese in brick shape; mould (for making cheese).
adobería, *n.f.* adobe works; tannery.
adobino, -na, *a.* of adobe.
adobío, *n.m.* front wall (of a blast-furnace).
adobo, *n.m.* repairing, mending; pickle, sauce; dressing for seasoning; ingredients for dressing leather *or* cloth; pomade, cosmetic.
adocenadamente, *adv.* in a common *or* ordinary manner.
adocenado, -da, *a.* common, ordinary; counted by the dozen, numerous.
adocenamiento, *n.m.* commonplaceness; counting *or* selling by dozens.
adocenar, *v.t.* to count *or* sell by dozens; to make ordinary. — **adocenarse,** *v.r.* to become ordinary.
adoctrinamiento, *n.m.* indoctrination.
adoctrinar, *v.t.* to instruct; to indoctrinate.
adolecer [9], *v.i.* to be afflicted (with); to suffer (from). — **adolecerse,** *v.r.* to sympathize, be sorry.
adolec(**i**)**ente,** *a.* suffering, patient, ailing.
adolescencia, *n.f.* youth, adolescence.
adolescente, *a.* young, adolescent. — *n.m.f.* adolescent, teenager.
adolorido, -da, *a.* afflicted; heart-sick; grieved.
adomiciliarse, *v.r.* to take up one's abode.
adonde, *adv.* where; ***¿adónde?*** *adv.* where? whither? to what place?
adondequiera, *adv.* wherever; anywhere.
adónico, adonio, *n.m.* adonic (verse).
adónide, *n.m.* greenhouse.
Adonis, *n.m.* Adonis.

adonis, *n.m. inv.* (*fig.*) handsome youth; (*bot., ent., ichth.*) adonis.
adonizarse [C], *v.r.* to adorn o.s.
adopción, *n.f.* adoption.
adopcionismo, *n.m.* Adoptionism.
adoptable, *a.* adoptable.
adoptado, -da, *n.m.f.* adopted person.
adoptador, -ra, *a.* adopting. — *n.m.f.* adopter.
adoptante, *a.* adopting. — *n.m.f.* adopter.
adoptar, *v.t.* to adopt, father; to embrace (*an opinion*); ***adoptar un acuerdo,*** to pass a resolution; ***adoptar por hijo,*** to adopt as a son.
adoptivo, -va, *a.* adoptive; adopted.
adoquier, adoquiera, *adv.* anywhere, where you please.
adoquín, *n.m.* paving-stone; cobble-stone; (*coll.*) block-head, clot.
adoquinado, *n.m.* paving.
adoquinar, *v.t.* to pave.
ador, *n.m.* time allotted for irrigation.
adorable, *a.* adorable.
adoración, *n.f.* adoration, worship; ***Adoración de los Reyes Magos,*** Epiphany.
adorador, -ra, *a.* adoring. — *n.m.f.* adorer; worshipper.
adorante, *a.* adoring. — *n.m.f.* adorer; worshipper.
adorar, *v.t.* to adore, worship; ***adorar a Dios,*** to worship God.
adoratorio, *n.m.* (*Hisp. Am.*) Indian temple, teocalli.
adoratriz, *n.f.* cloistered nun.
adormecedor, -ra, *a.* soporiferous, soporific.
adormecer [9], *v.t.* to make sleepy *or* drowsy; (*fig.*) to lull asleep; (*fig.*) to calm, lull. — **adormecerse,** *v.r.* to fall asleep; to grow benumbed *or* torpid; (*fig.*) to grow *or* persist (*in sth.*).
adormecido, -da, *a.* sleepy, half-asleep, drowsy.
adormeciente, *a.* soporific.
adormecimiento, *n.m.* drowsiness, slumber, sleepiness; numbness.
adormidera, *n.f.* (*bot.*) opium poppy.
adormilarse, adormitarse, *v.r.* to doze off, become drowsy.
adornable, *a.* that can be adorned.
adornador, -ra, *a.* adorning, decorating. — *n.m.f.* adorner, decorator.
adornante, *a.* decorating, adorning. — *n.m.f.* adorner, decorator.
adornar, *v.t.* to adorn, ornament, decorate, grace, embellish; to garnish.
adornista, *n.m.* decorator; painter.
adorno, *n.m.* adornment, ornament, decoration; finery; ***de adorno,*** ornamental, decorative; ***adorno de escaparates,*** window-dressing.
adosar, *v.t.* to place back to back; ***adosar algo a*** (***contra***), to place sth. with its back to, lean up against.
adquiridor, -ra, *a.* acquiring. — *n.m.f.* acquirer, purchaser.
adquir(i)ente, *a.* acquiring. — *n.m.f.* acquirer, purchaser.
adquirir [6], *v.t.* to acquire, obtain, get; ***adquirir la certeza*** or ***la certidumbre de que,*** to become certain *or* convinced that.
adquisición, *n.f.* acquisition, purchase.
adquisidor, -ra, *a.* acquiring. — *n.m.f.* acquirer, purchaser.
adquisitivo, -va, *a.* (*law*) acquisitive; ***poder adquisitivo, capacidad adquisitiva,*** purchasing power.
adquisividad, *n.f.* acquisitiveness.
adra, *n.f.* turn, time, successive order; portion of the inhabitants of a town.
adragante, *a.* ***goma adragante,*** gum tragacanth.
adraganto, *n.m.* tragacanth.
adral, *n.m.* hurdle; side-board (*cart*).
adrazo, *n.m.* alembic for distilling sea-water.
adrede, *adv.* on purpose, deliberately.
adrenalina, *n.f.* (*chem.*) adrenaline.
adrián, *n.m.* bunion; (*orn.*) magpie's nest.
adriático, -ca, *a., n.m.f.* Adriatic.
adrizado, -da, *a.* (*naut.*) righted. — *n.m.* (*naut.*) set of halyards.
adrizar [C], *v.t.* (*naut.*) to right. — **adrizarse,** *v.r.* (*naut.*) to right itself.
adrolla, *n.f.* fraud, trick.
adrollar, *v.t.* to cheat, trick.
adrollero, *n.m.* one who buys *or* sells dishonestly.
adscribir [*p.p.* **adscri(p)to**], *v.t.* to assign; to appoint to a place *or* employment. — **adscribirse,** *v.r.* to inscribe o.s.
adscripción, *n.f.* nomination, appointment; adscription.
adsorbente, *a.* adsorptive.
adsorber, *v.t.* to adsorb.
adsorción, *n.m.* adsorption.
adstringente [ASTRINGENTE].
aduana, *n.f.* custom-house; ***aduana seca,*** inland custom-house; ***en la aduana,*** in bond; ***arancel de aduanas,*** tariff; ***corredor de aduana,*** custom-house broker; ***derecho de aduana,*** customs duty; ***pasar por todas las aduanas,*** to undergo a close examination.
aduanar, *v.t.* to enter (*goods*) at the custom-house; to pay customs duty on; to put in bond.
aduanero, -ra, *a.* belonging to the custom-house. — *n.m.* custom-house officer; revenue officer.
aduanilla, *n.f.* (*Hisp. Am.*) general store.
aduar, *n.m.* Arab village; itinerant Arab camp; horde of gipsies; (*Hisp. Am.*) Indian settlement.
adúcar, *n.m.* silk from outer part of cocoon and cloth made from it.
aducción, *n.f.* adducing; ***addución de pruebas,*** production of evidence.
aducir [15], *v.t.* to adduce, cite; to provide, furnish.
aductor, *a.* ***músculo aductor,*** adducent muscle. — *n.m.* (*anat.*) adductor (*muscle*).
aduendado, -da, *a.* fairy-like, gnome- *or* goblin-like.
adueñarse, *v.r.* to take possession, gain control (***de***, of).
adufa, *n.f.* (*Val.*) sluice; lock.
adufe, *n.m.* timbrel, tambourine; (*coll.*) silly talker.
adufero, -ra, *n.m.f.* tambourine-player.
aduja, *n.f.* (*naut.*) coil of rope *or* cable.
adujar, *v.t.* (*naut.*) to coil (*cable, chain*). — **adujarse,** *v.r.* to twist *or* curl oneself up in a small space.
adula, *n.f.* common pasture-ground.
adulación, *n.f.* adulation, flattery, fawning.
adulador, -ra, *a.* flattering, fawning. — *n.m.f.* flatterer, fawner.
adular, *v.t.* to flatter, fawn on.
adularia, *n.f.* (*min.*) variety of feldspar.
adulatorio, -ria, *a.* flattering.
adulear, *v.i.* (*prov.*) to bawl, cry out.
adulero, *n.m.* driver of horses *or* mules.
adulón, -lona, *a.* crawling, toadying. — *n.m.f.* crawler, toady.
adúltera, *n.f.* [ADÚLTERO].
adulterable, *a.* liable to adulteration.
adulteración, *n.f.* adulteration; falsification.
adulterador, -ra, *a.* adulterating, adulterant. — *n.m.f.* adulterator, adulterant; falsifier.
adulterante, *a.* adulterating. — *n.m.f.* adulterant.
adulterar, *v.t.* to adulterate, corrupt, falsify. — ***v.i.*** to commit adultery. — **adulterarse,** *v.r.* to become corrupted *or* adulterated.
adulterino, -na, *a.* adulterine, adulterous, begotten in adultery, bastard; (*fig.*) adulterated, falsified, false, fake, forged.

adulterio, *n.m.* adultery.
adúltero, -ra, *a.* adulterous; (*fig.*) base, corrupted. — *n.m.f.* adulterer, adulteress.
adultez, *n.f.* adulthood.
adulto, -ta, *a., n.m.f.* adult, grown-up.
adulzar [C], *v.t.* to sweeten; to soften; to render (*metals*) more ductile.
adumbración, *n.f.* shade, shadow (*esp. in art*); adumbration.
adumbrar, *v.t.* to shade, shadow.
adunar, *v.t.* to unite, join, unify. — **adunarse,** *v.r.* to become associated.
adunco, -ca, *a.* curved.
adunia, *adv.* abundantly.
adustez, *n.f.* grimness, sternness; gloominess, sullenness.
adusto, -ta, *a.* grim, stern, severe, austere; gloomy, sullen.
advenedizo, -za, *a.* newly come *or* arrived. — *n.m.f.* newcomer, outsider; intruder, upstart, parvenu.
advenidero, -ra, *a.* future, coming, forthcoming.
advenimiento, *n.m.* arrival; advent; ***esperar como al santo advenimiento,*** to wait in high expectation.
advenir [36], *v.i.* to come, arrive; to occur.
adventicio, -cia, *a.* accidental, adventitious, chance; (*law*) coming otherwise than by direct succession.
adventismo, *n.m.* (*relig.*) doctrine of the Adventists.
adventista, *a., n.m.f.* (*relig.*) Adventist.
adverado, -da, *a.* certified.
adverar, *v.t.* to certify, authenticate.
adverbial, *a.* adverbial.
adverbializar [C], *v.t.* (*gram.*) to give adverbial value to.
adverbio, *n.m.* adverb.
adversario, -ria, *n.m.f.* adversary, opponent, antagonist, foe. — *n.m.pl.* (**adversarios**) reference notes.
adversativo, -va, *a.* (*gram.*) adversative.
adversidad, *n.f.* adversity, misfortune, calamity; affliction, hardship.
adverso, -sa, *a.* adverse, calamitous.
advertencia, *n.f.* warning, advice; remark, notice.
advertidamente, *adv.* advisedly, deliberately.
advertido, -da, *a.* forewarned; wide-awake, with one's eyes open; experienced.
advertimiento, *n.m.* warning, advice; remark; notice.
advertir [6], *v.t.* to notice, take notice of, observe; to warn, advise, notify; to be aware of; ***es de advertir,*** it should be noticed; ***he de advertir,*** I must point out; ***te advierto que es muy tarde,*** it's very late, mind you. — **advertirse,** *v.r.* to notice, become aware.
Adviento, *n.m.* Advent.
advocación, *n.f.* dedication (*to saint etc.*).
advocar, *v.t.* to call upon.
adyacencia, *n.f.* adjacency. — *n.f.pl.* (***adyacencias***) surroundings, neighbourhood.
adyacente, *a.* adjacent, contiguous.
adyuntivo, -va, *a.* conjunctive; joining.
aechar [AHECHAR].
aeración, *n.f.* aeration; ventilation.
aerear, *v.t.* to aerate.
aéreo, -rea, *a.* aerial; (pertaining to) air; overhead; (*fig.*) airy, light, fantastic; (*poet.*) tall, lofty; ***ataque aéreo,*** air raid.
aerífero, -ra, *a.* aeriferous, air-conducting.
aerificación, *n.f.* gasification.
aerificar [A], *v.t.* to gasify. — **aerificarse,** *v.r.* to be converted into gas.
aeriforme, *a.* (*chem.*) aeriform, gaseous.
aéro-atómico, -ca, *a.* air-atomic.
aeróbico, -ca, *a.* (*bact.*) aerobic.
aerobio, *n.m.* (*bact.*) aerobic.
aerobús, *n.m.* airbus.
aerodinámico, -ca, *a.* aerodynamic; stream-lined. — *n.f.* aerodynamics.
aeródromo, *n.m.* aerodrome, (*Am.*) airfield.
aeroembolismo, *n.m.* (*path.*) aeroembolism.
aeroescala, *n.f.* [AEROSCALA].
aerofagia, *n.m.* (*med.*) aerophagia.
aerófano, -na, *a.* diaphanous, transparent.
aerofaro, *n.m.* aerial beacon.
aerofluyente, aeroforme, *a.* stream-lined.
aerofobia, *n.f.* aerophobia.
aerófobo, -ba, *a.* suffering from aerophobia.
aerófono, -na, *a.* amplifying (*voice*). — *n.m.* aerophone.
aeróforo, -ra, *a.* air-conducting.
aerofoto, *n.f.* aerophotograph.
aerofotografía, *n.f.* aerophotography (*art, process*); aerophotograph (*picture*).
aerofotografiar, *v.t.* to photograph from the air.
aerofumigación, *n.f.* crop dusting *or* fumigating.
aerógamo, -ma, *a.* (*bot.*) flowering.
aerografía, *n.f.* aerography.
aerógrafo, *n.m.* atomizer; air brush.
aerograma, *n.m.* aerogram; wireless message.
aerolínea, *n.f.* air line.
aerolito, *n.m.* aerolite, meteoric stone.
aerología, *n.f.* aerology.
aerólogo, -ga, *n.m.f.* aerologist.
aeromancia, *n.f.* aeromancy.
aeromántico, -ca, *a.* appertaining *or* relating to aeromancy. — *n.m.f.* student of aeromancy.
aeromapa, *n.m.* air map.
aeromecánico, -ca, *a.* aeromechanical. — *n.f.* aeromechanics.
aeromedicina, *n.f.* aviation medicine.
aerometría, *n.f.* aerometry.
aerómetro, *n.m.* aerometer.
aeromodelismo, *n.m.* model-aeroplane building.
aeromodelista, *n.m.f.* model-aeroplane builder.
aeromodelo, *n.m.* model aeroplane.
aeromotor, *n.m.* aeromotor.
aeromoza, *n.f.* air hostess, stewardess.
aeronato, -ta, *a.* born in a plane during a flight.
aeronauta, *n.m.f.* aeronaut.
aeronáutico, -ca, *a.* aeronautic. — *n.f.* aeronautics.
aeronave, *n.f.* airship, dirigible; airliner; space ship; ***aeronave cohete,*** rocket ship.
aeropista, *n.f.* (*aer.*) air strip.
aeroplano, *n.m.* aeroplane; (*Am.*) airplane.
aeroplano-nodriza, *n.m.* (*aer.*) tanker plane.
aeropostal, *a.* air mail.
aeropropulsor, *n.m.* (*aer.*) aeroplane engine; (*aer.*) ***aeropropulsor por reacción,*** jet engine.
aeroscala, *n.f.* (*aer.*) fuel stop; transit point.
aeroscopia, *n.f.* aeroscopy.
aerostación, *n.f.* aerostation; air navigation.
aeróstata, *n.m.f.* aerostat, balloonist.
aerostático, -ca, *a.* aerostatic. — *n.f.* aerostatics.
aeróstato, *n.m.* aerostat, air balloon.
aerostero, *n.m.* (*mil.*) air soldier.
aerotecnia, *n.f.* air technology.
aeroterapia, *n.t.* aerotherapeutics, aerotherapy.
aerotermo, -ma, *a.* (*phys.*) applied to hot-air furnaces.
aeroterrestre, *a.* air-ground.
aerotransportado, -da, *a.* air-borne.
aerovía, *n.f.* air corridor.
afabilidad, *n.f.* affability, amiability, pleasantness, geniality.
afabilísimo, -ma, *a. superl.* extremely affable, amiable, pleasant *or* genial.

afable, *a.* affable, agreeable, amiable, pleasant.
afabulación, *n.f.* putting into fable form.
afabular, *v.t.* to put into fable form.
áfaca, *n.f.* (*bot.*) yellow vetch.
afamado, -da, *a.* celebrated, noted, famous, renowned.
afamar, *v.t.* to make famous, give fame to. — **afamarse,** *v.r.* to become renowned.
afán, *n.m.* eagerness; urge; ***afán de,*** eagerness *or* urge to +*infin.*, for +*noun*; (*pl.* **afanes**) labours, toils.
afanadamente, *adv.* eagerly.
afanador, -ra, *a.* eager; industrious. — *n.m.f.* one eager (*for riches etc.*).
afanar, *v.i.* to toil, labour, strive (eagerly), be eager; ***afanar, afanar y nunca medrar,*** much toil and little profit. — **afanarse,** *v.r.* to busy o.s.; ***afanarse por nada,*** to waste effort, strive to no purpose; to fuss over nothing.
afaneso, *n.f.* arsenite of copper.
afaníptero, -ra, *a.* wingless; (*zool.*) aphanipterous. — *n.m.pl.* (**afanípteros**) (*ent.*) Aphaniptera, Siphonaptera.
afanita [ANFIBOLITA].
afanosamente, *adv.* eagerly.
afanoso, -sa, *a.* eager.
afantasmado, -da, *a.* phantasmal, ghost-like; (*fam.*) vain, conceited, presumptuous.
afarallonado, -da, *a.* steep, with steep cliffs, craggy.
afarolarse, *v.r.* (*Hisp. Am., coll.*) to become excited; to make a fuss; to lose one's temper.
afasia, *n.f.* (*med.*) aphasia.
afeable, *a.* that can *or* deserves to be made ugly; censurable.
afeamiento, *n.m.* making ugly, defacing; condemnation.
afear, *v.t.* to make (look) ugly, deface, disfigure, spoil; to decry, condemn.
afeblecerse [9], *v.r.* to grow feeble *or* delicate.
afección, *n.f.* affection, inclination, fondness; (*med.*) disease, complaint.
afectable, *a.* impressionable; susceptible.
afectación, *n.f.* affectation.
afectado, -da, *a.* affected.
afectar, *v.t.* to feign; to affect, assume (*a manner*); to affect, influence; (*law*) to charge, impose, put a tax on. — **afectarse,** *v.r.* to be moved, feel emotion, be distressed.
afectísimo, -ma, *a. superl.* very affectionate, most loving; yours sincerely.
afectividad, *n.f.* affectibility; affectionateness; capacity for feeling *or* emotion.
afectivo, -va, *a.* affective; emotional.
afecto, -ta, *a.* fond, inclined; well-affected; (*law*) subject to; attached. — *n.m.* affection, love, fondness; (*paint.*) lively interpretation.
afectuosidad, *n.f.* fondness, affection.
afectuoso, -sa, *a.* loving, fond, affectionate.
afeitadora, *n.f.* (electric) shaver.
afeitadura(s), *n.f.* (*engin.*) shaving(s).
afeitar, *v.t.* to shave; to beautify; to clip (*plants, trees etc.*); to trim the tail and mane of (*a horse*). — **afeitarse,** *v.r.* to shave; to make up.
afeite, *n.m.* paint, rouge, cosmetic; make-up.
afelio, *n.m.* (*astron.*) aphelion.
afelpado, -da, *a.* like plush *or* velvet; (*fig.*) shaggy; (*naut.*) ***palletes afelpados,*** cased mats. — *n.m.* grass mat.
afelpar, *v.t.* to make like plush *or* velvet; to pad.
afeminación, *n.f.* effeminacy.
afeminado, -da, *a.* effeminate.
afeminamiento, *n.m.* effeminacy.
afeminar, *v.t.* to make effeminate. — **afeminarse,** *v.r.* to become effeminate.
aferente, *a.* (*med.*) afferent.
aféresis, *n.f. inv.* (*gram.*) aphæresis.
aferrado, -da, *a.* headstrong, stubborn; obstinate, tenacious.
aferrador, -ra, *a.* grasping. — *n.m.* clamp.
aferramiento, *n.m.* grasping, grappling, seizing; headstrongness, obstinacy; (*naut.*) mooring; ***aferramiento de las velas,*** furling of the sails.
aferrar [1], *v.t., v.i.* to grasp, grapple, seize; (*naut.*) to furl; to moor, anchor; to interlock. — **aferrarse,** *v.r.* (*naut.*) to fasten to each other; ***aferrarse a su opinión,*** to cling doggedly to one's own view.
aferravelas, *n.f.pl.* (*obs., naut.*) rope bands, gaskets; furling-lines.
aferruzado, -da, *a.* angry, irate; glowering.
afestonado, -da, *a.* festoon-like.
Afganistán, *n.m.* Afghanistan.
afgano, -na, *a., n.m.f.* Afghan.
afianzador, -ra, *a.* guaranteeing. — *n.m.f.* guarantor.
afianzamiento, *n.m.* security, guarantee, bail; prop, support; fastening, securing.
afianzar [C], *v.t.* to guarantee; to vouch for, stand bail *or* surety for; to prop, support, buttress, secure, fasten. — **afianzarse,** *v.r.* to secure one's hold; ***afianzarse en su posición,*** to secure *or* consolidate one's position, become consolidated in one's position.
afición, *n.f.* fondness *or* liking (for), keenness (on); fans, supporters (*esp. of bullfight*); ***tener afición a,*** to have a liking for, be keen on; ***esto indignó a la afición,*** this made the fans indignant; ***afición, ciega razón,*** love is blind.
aficionado, -da, *a.* fond (of), keen (on); ***ser aficionado a,*** to be fond of *or* keen on. — *n.m.f.* amateur; fan, supporter, addict.
aficionar, *v.t.* to cause to like, get keen on; ***él me aficionó a los toros,*** he got me keen on bullfighting, I owe my keenness on bullfighting to him. — *v.r.* ***aficionarse a,*** to become fond of, acquire a liking for, get keen on.
afiche, *n.m.* (*Hisp. Am.*) poster.
afidávit, *n.m.* affidavit.
afiebrado, -da, *a.* feverish.
afijación, *n.f.* (*gram.*) affixation.
afijo, -ja, *a.* affixed. — *n.m.* (*gram.*) affix.
afiladera, *n.f.* whetstone.
afilado, -da, *a.* sharp, keen; slender, thin, tapering.
afilador, -ra, *a.* sharpening. — *n.m.* knife-grinder; sharpener; leather razor-strop.
afiladura, *n.f.* sharpening, whetting.
afilalápices, *n.m.inv.* pencil sharpener.
afilamiento, *n.m.* slenderness (*face, nose or fingers*); sharpening, whetting.
afilar, *v.t.* to sharpen, make *or* get sharp, put an edge on, whet, grind; to taper; ***afilar el ingenio,*** to sharpen one's wits. — **afilarse,** *v.r.* to grow thin *or* narrow; to taper (away); ***afilarse las uñas,*** to make ready (*for sth. difficult*), to prepare for the fray.
afiliación, *n.f.* affiliation.
afiliado, -da, *a.* affiliated. — *n.m.* member.
afiliar [L], *v.t.* to affiliate. — *v.r.* ***afiliarse a,*** to become affiliated *or* associated to, join.
afiligranado, -da, *a.* filigree, filigreed; ornamented; ornate, elaborate; delicate, neat.
afiligranar, *v.t.* to filigree; to embellish, ornament.
áfilo, -la, *a.* (*bot.*) leafless.
afilón, *n.m.* whetstone; steel, knife-sharpener, razor-strop.
afilorar, *v.t.* (*Hisp. Am.*) to adorn, bedeck.
afilosofado, -da, *a.* like a philosopher, having pretensions to being a philosopher.
afín *a.* contiguous, adjacent; allied, related, similar; ***x y afines,*** x and the like. — *n.m.f.* relative.
afinación, *n.f.* completion; last touch; refining (*metals*); tuning (*musical instruments*).

afinado, *n.m.* (*mus.*) tuning.

afinador, -ra, *a.* finishing; tuning. — *n.m.f.* finisher; piano-tuner. — *n.m.* tuning-key.

afinamiento, *n.m.* completion; refining; refinement; fineness of manners.

afinar (1), *v.t.* to complete; to polish; to trim (*binding*); to tune (*instruments, voice*); to refine (*metals*). — **afinarse,** *v.r.* to become polished, refined, civilized, astute, keen *or* sagacious.

afinar (2), *v.t.* (*Chi.*) to finish, conclude.

afincamiento, *n.m.* settlement.

afincar [A], *v.i.* to buy real estate. — **afincarse,** *v.r.* to settle down, establish oneself.

afinidad, *n.f.* affinity; attraction; relationship by marriage.

afino, *n.m.* refining (of metals).

afión, *n.m.* opium.

afir, *n.m.* (*vet.*) horse medicine made up of juniper-berries.

afirmación, *n.f.* statement, assertion, affirmation.

afirmado, *n.m.* road-bed.

afirmador, -ra, *a.* affirming. — *n.m.f.* affirmer.

afirmar, *v.t.* to state, affirm, assert; to make fast, secure. — **afirmarse,** *v.r.* to hold fast; to steady o.s., make o.s. firm; ***afirmarse en lo dicho,*** to stick to one's guns.

afirmativo, -va, *a.* affirmative.

afistular, *v.t.* to render fistulous.

aflato, *n.m.* breath, wind; (*fig.*) inspiration.

aflautada, *a.* high-pitched, flute-like (*voice*).

aflechado, -da, *a.* (*bot.*) arrow-shaped.

aflicción, *n.f.* affliction, sorrow, grief, anguish.

aflictivo, -va, *a.* afflicting, distressing, grieving, grievous; (*law*) ***pena aflictiva,*** corporal punishment.

aflicto, -ta, *a.* (*poet.*) grieved.

afligido, -da, *a.* distressed, grieving.

afligimiento [AFLICCIÓN].

afligir [E], *v.t.* to afflict, grieve; to cause sorrow to. — **afligirse,** *v.r.* to grieve; ***afligirse con, de*** or ***por,*** to be grieved at.

aflojadura, *n.f.* relaxation, loosening, slackening.

aflojamiento, *n.m.* slackening; abatement.

aflojar, *v.t.* to loosen, slacken, relax; ***aflojar el ánimo,*** to ease up, take things easier, relax; ***aflojar la cuerda*** or ***las riendas,*** to let up, relax discipline *or* vigilance; (*fam.*) ***aflojar la pasta,*** to pay up, cough up the cash. — *v.i.* to ease up, abate; ***aflojó en el estudio,*** he let up in his studying; ***aflojó la fiebre,*** the fever abated. — **aflojarse,** *v.r.* to lose enthusiasm *or* courage.

aflorado, -da, *a.* choice, exquisite; best, most perfect.

afloramiento, *n.m.* (*min.*) outcrop; springing *or* gushing forth (*water, oil etc.*); sifting (*flour, grain*).

aflorar, *v.t.* to sift; to purify, refine. — *v.i.* (*min.*) to crop out; to spring *or* gush forth (*water, oil etc.*).

afluencia, *n.f.* flow, flowing, inflow, influx; rush; crowd; plenty, abundance; fluency, volubility.

afluente, *a.* inflowing; eloquent. — *n.m.* tributary (*of a river*).

afluir [O], *v.i.* to flow, pour in *or* into; to flock in.

aflujo, *n.m.* (*med.*) afflux, influx; crowd.

afofado, -da, *a.* spongy, soft.

afofar, *v.t.* to make spongy. — **afofarse,** *v.r.* to become soft, spongy.

afogar [B], *v.t.* to suffocate, choke.

afogarar, *v.t.* to scorch, burn up.

afoliado, -da, *a.* (*bot.*) leafless.

afollar [4], *v.t.* to blow with bellows; (*fig.*) to fold in the shape of bellows; (*build.*) to work badly. — *v.i.* to become blistered, puff up, hollow (*walls*).

afondar, *v.t.* to put under water, submerge. — **afondar(se),** *v.i.* (*v.r.*) (*naut.*) to sink, founder.

afonía, *n.f.* (*med.*) aphonia, loss of voice.

afónico, -ca, *a.* voiceless; having lost one's voice; ***estar afónico,*** to have lost one's voice.

afonización, *n.f.* unvoicing.

afonizar [C], *v.t.* to unvoice.

áfono, -na, *a.* aphonous.

aforado, -da, *a.* privileged.

aforador, *n.m.* gauger, appraiser; gauge.

aforamiento, *n.m.* gauging, appraisement.

aforar [4; *irregular when used in sense of 'to give privileges'*], *v.t.* to gauge, measure; to appraise; to give privileges to; to hold, contain, have room for; ***este estadio afora 50,000 personas,*** this stadium has capacity for *or* seats 50,000 people.

aforisma, *n.f.* (*vet.*) tumour (*in animals*).

aforismo, *n.m.* aphorism.

aforístico, -ca, *a.* aphoristic.

aforo, *n.m.* gauging; appraisement; capacity, seating capacity.

aforrar, *v.t.* to line (*clothes, vessels, tubes etc.*); (*naut.*) to sheathe.

aforro, *n.m.* lining; (*naut.*) rounding, sheathing; (*nuat.*) waist (of a ship).

afortunadamente, *adv.* luckily, fortunately.

afortunado, -da, *a.* fortunate, happy, lucky.

afosarse, *v.r.* (*mil.*) to entrench o.s.; to dig in.

afoscarse [A], *v.r.* (*naut.*) to become hazy.

afrailado, -da, *a.* monk-like; (*print.*) having a friar patch.

afrailar, *v.t.* (*agric.*) to prune, trim (*trees*).

afrancesado, -da, *a.* frenchified, French-like. — *n.m.f.* Spanish sympathizer with the French, especially during the Napoleonic invasion (1808-1813).

afrancesamiento, *n.m.* frenchification.

afrancesar, *v.t.* to gallicize, frenchify; to give a French termination *or* turn to (words). — **afrancesarse,** *v.r.* to imitate the French; ape things French.

afranelado, -da, *a.* flannel-like.

afrecho, *n.m.* bran.

afrenillar, *v.t.* (*naut.*) to bridle (*oars*).

afrenta, *n.f.* affront, dishonour, outrage, insult.

afrentar, *v.t.* to affront, insult.

afrentoso, -sa, *a.* ignominious; insulting; outrageous.

afretar, *v.t.* (*naut.*) to scrub and clean (*the bottom of a vessel*); to rub, scour.

África, *n.f.* Africa; ***África del Sudoeste,*** South-West Africa; ***África del Norte,*** North Africa.

africanista, *a.*, *n.m.f.* Africanist.

africano, -na, *a.*, *n.m.f.* African.

áfrico, *n.m.* south-west wind [ÁBREGO].

afrodisia, *n.f.* aphrodisia.

afrodisíaco, -ca, *a.* aphrodisiac, aphrodisian. — *n.m.* aphrodisiac.

afroditario, *n.m.* aphrodisiac.

afrontado, -da, *a.* (*her.*) face to face.

afrontamiento, *n.m.* confrontation.

afrontar, *v.t.* to confront; to meet, face up to. — *v.i.* to face.

afrontilar, *v.t.* (*Mex.*) to tie (*cattle*) by the horns.

afta, *n.f.* (*med.*) aphthæ, thrush.

afuera, *adv.* outside, outwardly, in public. — *interj.* ***¡afuera!*** out! clear out! — *n.f.pl.* (**afueras**) suburbs, outskirts; (*fort.*) open ground around a fortress.

afufa, *n.f.* (*coll.*) flight; ***estar uno sobre las afufas,*** to be arranging to escape; (*coll.*) ***tomar las afufas,*** to do a bunk, scarper.

afufar(se), *v.i.* (*v.r.*) (*coll.*) to do a bunk, scarper.

afusion, *n.f.* (*med.*) affusion, shower-bath.

afusionar, *v.t.* (*med.*) to administer an affusion to.

afuste, *n.m.* gun-carriage; ***afuste de mortero,*** mortar-bed; emplacement.

agá, *n.m.* Turkish officer.
agabachar, *v.t.* to frenchify. — **agabacharse,** *v.r.* to become frenchified.
agacé, *a.* (*Par.*) Indian aboriginal.
agachada, *n.f.* trick, wile; trickiness.
agachadiza, *n.f.* (*orn.*) snipe; (*coll.*) ***hacer la agachadiza,*** to duck (down), duck out of sight.
agachar, *v.t.* to lower, bow down, bend; ***agachar las orejas,*** to climb down, put one's tail between one's legs. — **agacharse,** *v.r.* (*coll.*) to stoop, bend down, duck.
agachona, *n.f.* (*orn.*) Mexican wader.
agafar, *v.t.* (*prov., coll.*) to seize, grasp, pinch.
agafita, *n.f.* oriental turquoise.
agalbanado, -da, *a.* indolent, lazy, shiftless.
agalerar, *v.t.* (*naut.*) to tip (*an awning*).
agalgado, -da, *a.* similar to a greyhound.
agalibar, *v.t.* (*naut.*) to squadron.
agalla, *n.f.* (*bot.*) gall-nut; (*vet.*) wind-galls (*of a horse*); screw-thread (*of boring rod*); the side of the head of birds corresponding to the temple; (*pl.*) tonsils; fish-gills; (*coll.*) courage, guts; ***tener agallas,*** to have guts.
agallado, -da, *a.* (*Cub.*) steeped in an infusion of gall nuts.
agalladura, *n.f.* cicatricule, tread (*of egg*).
agallato, *n.m.* gallate.
agállico, -ca, *a.* gallic, derived from nut-galls.
agallón, *n.m.* large gall-nut; (*arch.*) echinus; (*pl.*) strings of large silver beads hollowed like gall-nuts; wooden beads put to rosaries.
agallonado, -da, *a.* (*arch.*) ornamented with echinus.
agalludo, -da, *a.* (*Hisp. Am.*) cunning, astute, foxy.
agamí, *n.m.* (*orn.*) trumpeter.
agamitar, *v.i.* to bleat like a small deer.
ágamo, -ma, *a.* (*biol.*) agamic, asexual.
agamuzado, -da, *a.* chamois-coloured, buff, like chamois-leather.
agamuzar [C], *v.t.* to dress (*skins*) like chamois-leather.
agangrenarse, *v.r.* to gangrene.
ágape, *n.m.* agape, banquet, love-feast.
agarbado, -da [GARBOSO].
agarbanzado, -da, *a.* like a chick-pea.
agarbanzar [C], *v.i.* (*prov., agric.*) to bud, sprout.
agarbarse, *v.r.* to bend, stoop down, crouch.
agarbillar, *v.t.* (*agric.*) to bind *or* tie in sheaves.
agardamarse, *v.r.* (*prov.*) to become worm-eaten, (*wood*).
agarduñar, *v.t.* to steal.
agareno, -na, *a.* Mohammedan.
agárico, *n.m.* (*bot.*) agaric, fungus.
agarrada (1), *n.f.* (*coll.*) wrangle, squabble, set-to, row.
agarraderas, *n.f.pl.* (*coll.*) protection, patronage; ***tener buenas agarraderas,*** to have influence *or* friends in the right place.
agarradero, *n.m.* hold, haft, handle; thing *or* place to hold on to; (*naut.*) anchorage.
agarrado, -da (2), *a.* (*coll.*) mean, miserable, stingy, tight-fisted.
agarrador, -ra, *a.* grasping, seizing. — *n.m.f.* grasper, seizer; (*coll.*) bailiff. — *n.m.* sad-iron holder; catchpole.
agarrafar, *v.t.* (*coll.*) to grasp; to grapple hard in a struggle with; to grab hold of. — **agarrafarse,** *v.r.* to come to close grips.
agarrante, *a.* grasping.
agarrar, *v.t.* to catch, grab, grasp, lay hold of. — *v.i.* to take, to take root; to catch on; (*Hisp. Am.*) ***agarrar para,*** to head for; to strike out for. — **agarrarse,** *v.r.* to grab hold, hang on; (*coll.*) to take hold of (*disease*); (*coll.*) ***agarrarse de,*** to grasp at; ***agarrarse a un clavo ardiendo,*** to go to incredible lengths; (*coll.*) ***agarrarse de los pelos,*** to despair; to come to blows; ***se le agarró la fiebre,*** the fever took hold of him.
agarre [AGARRADERO].
agarro, *n.m.* grasp, hold.
agarrochador, *n.m.* pricker, goader.
agarrochar, *v.t.* to prick with a spike *or* spear; to goad; (*naut.*) to brace (*the yards*).
agarrón, *n.m.* (*Hisp. Am.*) grasp, clutch, hold; jerk; row, brawl, fight.
agarrotado, -da, *a.* garrotted; (*coll.*) stiff, rigid.
agarrotar, *v.t.* to bind with ropes; to squeeze hard; to garrotte. — **agarrotarse,** *v.r.* to go stiff *or* rigid; to seize up; to become twisted.
agasajado, *n.m.* guest (of honour).
agasajador, -ra, *a., n.m.f.* attentive, considerate (person).
agasajar, *v.t.* to receive and treat well, to regale, entertain; fête, wine and dine.
agasajo, *n.m.* fine reception *or* welcome, lavish treatment *or* entertainment; party (in someone's honour); attention shown; friendly present; afternoon refreshment.
agasón, *n.m.* stable boy, groom.
ágata, *n.f.* agate.
agatoideo, -dea, *a.* that leads to good; that seems good.
agavanza, *n.f.* dog rose (*fruit*).
agavanzo, *n.m.* dog rose (*plant, fruit*).
agave, *n.f.* (*bot.*) agave, century-plant; fibre of the agave.
agavillado, -da, *a.* (*agric.*) sheaved; (*coll.*) ruffian-like.
agavilladora, *n.f.* (*mech.*) binder, binding machine (*sheaves*).
agavillar, *v.t.* (*agric.*) to bind *or* tie in sheaves. — **agavillarse,** *v.r.* (*coll.*) to band together; to gang up.
agazapada, *n.f.* refuge of game.
agazapar, *v.t.* (*coll.*) to nab (*a person*). — **agazaparse,** *v.r.* (*coll.*) to hide, lurk, crouch (down).
agencia, *n.f.* agency; commission; agent's bureau, office; (*Hisp. Am.*) pawnshop; ***agencia de noticias,*** news agency.
agenciador, -ra, *a.* negotiating, promoting. — *n.m.f.* agent, promoter, negotiator.
agenciar [L], *v.t.* to bring about, engineer, to get. — **agenciarse,** *v.r.* to manage, get along; to get, get hold of, come by.
agencioso, -sa, *a.* diligent, active; officious.
agenda, *n.f.* note-book; desk *or* pocket calendar; diary.
agenesia, *n.f.* (*med.*) impotence; sterility.
agente, *a.* acting. — *n.m.* agent; policeman; (*gram.*) agent; ***agente consular,*** consular agent; ***agente de cambio y bolsa,*** stock-broker; ***agente inmobiliario,*** estate agent, (*Am.*) realtor; ***agente de negocios,*** promoter; ***agente de policía,*** police officer; ***agente de prensa,*** agency journalist; ***agente de turismo,*** travel agent; ***agente fiscal,*** assistant attorney; ***agente provocador,*** agent provocateur; (*chem.*) ***agente reductor,*** reducing agent; ***agente secreto,*** secret agent; ***agente viajero,*** sales representative.
agerasia, *n.f.* old age free from indispositions.
agermanarse, *v.r.* to join a gang of thieves; (*Hisp. Am.*) to ape German ways.
agestado, -da, *a.* ***bien*** or ***mal agestado,*** well- *or* ill-featured.
agestión, *n.f.* accumulation, agglomeration.
agibílibus, *n.m. inv.* (*coll.*) smartness, sharpness, quickness on the up-take.
agible, *a.* feasible, practicable.
agigantado, -da, *a.* gigantic, huge, colossal; (*coll.*) exaggerated, extraordinary; out of the ordinary; ***a pasos agigantados,*** by leaps and bounds.
agigantar, *v.t.* to make huge; to exaggerate.
ágil, *a.* nimble, agile, fast, light.

agilar, *v.i.* (*Hisp. Am.*) to hasten; to be brief.
agilidad, *n.f.* agility, nimbleness, lightness.
agilitar, agilizar [C], *v.t.* to render nimble; to make active; to speed up. — **agilitarse, agilizarse,** *v.r.* to become nimble; to limber up.
agio, agiotaje, *n.m.* (*com.*) agio, agiotage; exchange of paper money for coin *or* coin for bills; speculation; usury.
agiotador, agiotista, *n.m.* speculator; usurer.
agiotar, *v.i.* to speculate; to practise usury.
agitable, *a.* easily agitated; that can be shaken.
agitación, *n.f.* agitation, flurry, flutter, fretting; excitement.
agitado, -da, *a.* agitated, hectic, stormy; ***sesión agitada,*** stormy session.
agitador, -ra, *n.m.f.* agitator, trouble-maker.
agitanarse, *v.r.* to become gipsy-like; to behave like a gipsy.
agitar, *v.t.* to agitate, excite; to stir, shake; to wave. — **agitarse,** *v.r.* to flutter, move about; to become agitated, disturbed, excited; to get rough (*sea*).
aglomeración, *n.f.* agglomeration, heaping up; ***horas de mayor aglomeración,*** rush hours.
aglomerado, -da, *a.* agglomerate. — *n.m.* agglomerate; briquette.
aglomerante, *a.* agglomerative; agglomerant, binder.
aglomerar(se), *v.t.* (*v.r.*) to heap *or* pile up, agglomerate.
aglutinación, *n.f.* agglutination.
aglutinado, -da, *a.* agglutinate.
aglutinante, *a.* agglutinating, cementing, binding. — *n.m.* cementing material; linking agent; (*med.*) sticking-plaster.
aglutinar, *v.t.* to glue together, agglutinate, link, bind.
aglutinativo, -va, *a.* agglutinative.
agnación, *n.f.* (*law*) agnation.
agnado, -da, *a., n.m.f.* agnate.
agnaticio, -cia, *a.* agnatic.
agnición, *n.f.* (*poet.*) recognition (*of a person in a poem or drama*).
agnocasto, *n.m.* chaste-tree, agnus castus.
agnomento, *n.m.* agnomen.
agnominación, *n.f.* (*rhet.*) paronomasia.
agnosia, *n.f.* ignorance.
agnosticismo, *n.m.* agnosticism.
agnóstico, -ca, *a., n.m.f.* agnostic.
agnusdéi, *n.m.* Agnus Dei.
agobiado, -da, *a.* bent, oppressed; overwhelmed; hunch-backed.
agobiar, *v.t.* to weigh *or* bow down, (over)burden; to oppress, overwhelm; ***está agobiado de trabajo,*** he is weighed down with work; ***le agobian los quehaceres, los años, las penas,*** he is overwhelmed by his duties, age, worries. — **agobiarse,** *v.r.* ***agobiarse con, de*** or ***por los años,*** to become oppressed by age.
agobio, *n.m.* oppression, weight, burden; dejection, load.
agogía, *n.f.* drain; water outlet (*in mines*).
agolar, *v.t.* (*naut.*) to furl (*sails*).
agolpamiento, *n.m.* crowding, rush; thronging.
agolpar, *v.t.* to heap, pile up. — **agolparse,** *v.r.* to crowd, rush; to throng.
agonal, *a.* agonistic. — *n.f.pl.* (**agonales**) agones.
agonía, *n.f.* death-agony, throes of death; (*fig.*) anguish, extreme sorrow *or* suffering.
agónico, -ca, *a.* in the throes of death, dying.
agonioso, -sa, *a.* persistent; importunate; ***niño agonioso,*** insistent *or* importunate child.
agonística, *n.f.* athletics; science of combat.
agonístico, -ca, *a.* agonistic.
agonizante, *a., n.m.f.* dying (person). — *a., n.m.* (monk) who assists dying person.
agonizar [C], *v.t.* to assist (dying persons). — *v.i.* to be dying; (*fig.*) to be in extreme suffering or anguish; ***estar agonizando,*** to be in the agony of death.
ágono, -na, *a.* agonic, without angles.
agora, *adv.* (*obs.*) now.
ágora, *n.f.* agora.
agorador, -ra [AGORERO].
agorafobia, *n.f.* (*path.*) agoraphobia, dread of open spaces.
agorar [4], *v.t.* to divine, foretell, prognosticate.
agorería, *n.f.* divination.
agorero, -ra, *a.* divinatory; prophetic, ominous; ill-omened. — *n.m.f.* soothsayer, fortune-teller, diviner.
agorgojarse, *v.r.* (*agric.*) to be destroyed by grubs (*seeds etc.*).
agostadero, *n.m.* summer pasture.
agostado, -da, *a.* parched, consumed, extinguished; gathered; ploughed.
agostador, -ra, *a., n.m.f.* that dries up *or* parches; (*coll.*) spendthrift.
agostamiento, *n.m.* parching up.
agostar, *v.t.* to wither, burn up; to kill prematurely; to plough; to get rid of weeds. — *v.i.* to burn up, parch, wither; to graze in August; to spend August. — **agostarse,** *v.r.* to fade away, wither.
agostero, *n.m.* harvest-man; religious mendicant who begs corn in August.
agostizo, -za, *a.* weak, sickly, scrawny; born in August. — *n.m.* colt foaled in August.
agosto, *n.m.* August; harvest-time; harvest; ***hacer su agosto,*** to make hay while the sun shines, make one's pile.
agotable, *a.* exhaustible.
agotado, -da, *a.* exhausted; out of print (*books*); (*com.*) sold out.
agotador, -ra, *a.* exhausting.
agotamiento, *n.m.* exhaustion, utter fatigue.
agotante, *a.* exhausting.
agotar, *v.t.* to exhaust; to wear out; to use up, run through (*money*); to sell out, run out of; to drain off (*liquid*). — **agotarse,** *v.r.* to become exhausted; to go out of print *or* stock, be sold out.
agovía [ALBORGA].
agracejina, *n.f.* (*bot.*) barberry fruit.
agracejo, *n.m.* unripened grape; unripe fallen olive; (*bot.*) barberry.
agraceño, -ña, *a.* sour, tart.
agracero, -ra, *a.* applied to vines with fruit that never ripens. — *n.f.* verjuice cruet.
agraciado, -da, *a.* favoured, good-, nice- *or* pleasant-looking, pretty; lucky, — *n.m.f.* winner.
agraciar [L], *v.t.* to favour; to grace; to reward; to award; to pardon.
agracillo, *n.m.* (*bot.*) barberry.
agradable, *a.* agreeable, pleasing, pleasant, enjoyable.
agradar, *v.i.* to please; ***me agrada,*** it pleases me, I like it.
agradecer [9], *v.t.* to be grateful for, thank for; ***se lo agradezco,*** I'm grateful to you for it; ***no me lo agradezca a mí,*** don't thank *me* for it; ***le agradecería que viniera pronto,*** I should be grateful if you would come early.
agradecido, -da, *a.* grateful, thankful.
agradecimiento, *n.m.* gratitude, gratefulness, thankfulness.
agrado, *n.m.* pleasure, liking; pleasantness; willingness; ***esto no es de su agrado,*** this is not to his liking; ***es hombre de mucho agrado,*** he's a very agreeable person.
agrafia, *n.f.* (*path.*) agraphia.
agraja [ADARAJA].
agramadera, *n.f.* brake for dressing flax *or* hemp; scutcher.

agramado, *n.m.* braking, scutching (*flax, hemp*).
agramador, -ra, *n.m.f.* flax *or* hemp dresser. — *n.m.* brake, scutch.
agramaduras, *n.f.pl.* hemp refuse.
agramar, *v.t.* to brake, scutch (*flax or hemp*).
agramilador, *n.m.* (*build.*) brick-trimmer.
agramilar, *v.t.* to trim (*bricks*); (*arch.*) to paint to resemble bricks; to mark out; to make even.
agramiza, *n.f.* stalk (*of hemp*); hemp refuse.
agrandamiento, *n.m.* enlargement, expansion, aggrandizement.
agrandar, *v.t.* to enlarge, increase, aggrandize. — **agrandarse,** *v.r.* to increase, grow larger.
agranelar, *v.t.* to pebble (*leather*); to grain.
agranitado, -da, *a.* granite-like.
agranujado, -da, *a.* grain-shaped; (*coll.*) behaving like a rogue *or* scoundrel.
agranujar, *v.t.* to grain; to give a granular finish to. — **agranujarse,** *v.r.* (*coll.*) to become a rascal *or* rogue.
agrario, -ria, *a.* agrarian.
agrarismo, *n.m.* agrarianism.
agravación, *n.f.* aggravation; worsening.
agravador, -ra, *a.* aggravating.
agravamiento, *n.m.* worsening.
agravante, *a.* aggravating. — *n.m.* (*law*) aggravating circumstance.
agravar, *v.t.* to weigh down, make heavier; to impose a tax *or* an assessment on; to aggravate, make worse; to exaggerate. — **agravarse,** *v.r.* to become worse; ***la enfermedad se agrava,*** the illness is getting worse.
agravatorio, -ria, *a.* aggravating.
agraviado, -da, *a.* injured, offended; (*law*) ***parte agraviada,*** aggrieved party.
agraviador, -ra, *a.* offending, wrongful, injurious. — *n.m.f.* injurer, wronger, offender.
agraviante, *a.* wronging, offending.
agraviar, *v.t.* to wrong, offend, injure. — **agraviarse,** *v.r.* to be aggrieved, take offence, be piqued.
agravio, *n.m.* wrong, offence, insult; (*law*) tort; injury, damage; ***agravio personal,*** personal tort; ***agravio civil,*** civil injury; ***agravio marítimo,*** maritime tort; ***agravio protervo,*** wanton injury; ***deshacer agravios,*** to right wrongs; (*law*) ***escrito de agravios,*** appeal; writ.
agravión, *a.* (*Chi.*) touchy.
agravioso, -sa, *a.* offensive, insulting.
agraz, *n.m.* verjuice; unripe grape; (*coll.*) displeasure; (*bot.*) barberry; ***en agraz,*** unseasonably; ***este proyecto está todavía en agraz,*** this plan is still in *or* at an embryonic stage; ***echar a uno el agraz en el ojo,*** to say something unpleasant to s.o.
agrazada, *n.f.* verjuice-water with sugar.
agrazar [C], *v.t.* (*coll.*) to embitter, displease, vex. — *v.i.* to taste sour.
agrazón, *n.m.* wild grape, grape which does not ripen; gooseberry-bush; (*coll.*) displeasure, resentment.
agrecillo, *n.m.* unripe grape *or* olive; barberry.
agredido, -da, *a., n.m.f.* assaulted, injured (person *or* party).
agredir [Q], *v.t.* to assault, attack, set about.
agregación, *n.f.* aggregation.
agregado, *n.m.* aggregate; attaché; concrete block; (*Hisp. Am.*) tenant-farmer; ***agregado militar,*** military attaché.
agregar [B], *v.t.* to add; to attach; to join together, collect.
agremán, *n.m.* passementerie, trimming, braid, ribbon.
agremiación, *n.f.* unionization; union.
agremiado, *n.m.* guild-member.
agremiar [M], *v.t.* to form into a guild *or* union.
agresión, *n.f.* aggression, attack, assault.
agresividad, *n.f.* aggressiveness, pugnacious self-assertion.
agresivo, -va, *a.* aggressive.
agresor, -ra, *a.* aggressive, assaulting. — *n.m.f.* aggressor, assaulter.
agreste, *a.* rural; rough (*country*); (*coll.*) uncouth.
agrete, *a.* sourish, tartish.
agria (1), *n.f.* (*med.*) herpes, tetter; (*min.*) very sloping gallery.
agriar [L *and regular*], *v.t.* to make bitter, make sour; to embitter, exasperate. — **agriarse,** *v.r.* to become bitter *or* embittered, turn sour *or* acid; to become embittered *or* exasperated.
agriaz, *n.m.* (*bot.*) bead-tree.
agrícola, *a.* agricultural. — *n.m.f.* agriculturist.
agricultor, *n.m.* husbandman, farmer, agriculturist.
agricultura, *n.f.* agriculture.
agridulce, *a.* bitter-sweet, sweet-and-sour.
agridulzura, *n.f.* bitter-sweetness.
agriera, *n.f.* (*Hisp. Am.*) acidity, heartburn.
agrietamiento, *n.m.* cracking.
agrietar(se), *v.t.* (*v.r.*) to crack, split.
agrifolio, *n.m.* (*bot.*) holly-tree.
agrilla (1), *n.f.* (*bot.*) sorrel.
agrillado, -da, *a.* cricket-like.
agrillarse, *v.r.* (*agric.*) to shoot, sprout [GRILLARSE].
agrillo, -lla (2), *a.* sourish, tartish.
agrimensor, *n.m.* land-surveyor.
agrimensorio, -ria, *a.* appertaining to surveying.
agrimensura, *n.f.* land surveying; survey.
agrimonia, *n.f.* (*bot.*) agrimony, liverwort.
agringarse [B], *v.r.* (*Hisp. Am.*) to ape North-American ways.
agrio, -ria (2), *a.* sour, acid, tart; citrus (*fruit*); rough, uneven; brittle, unmalleable (*metals*); clashing (*colours*); (*coll.*) sharp, unpleasant; ***una respuesta agria,*** a tart reply. — *n.m.* sour juice; (*pl.*) (*bot.*) citrus fruit; citrus fruit trees; citrus fruit juices. — *n.f.* (*coll.*) ***mascar las agrias,*** to hide one's bad temper.
agrión, *n.m.* (*vet.*) callosity (*horses*); (*bot.*) bead-tree.
agripalma, *n.f.* (*bot.*) motherwort.
agrisado, -da, *a.* greyish.
agrisar, *v.t.* to colour grey. — **agrisarse,** *v.r.* to become greyish.
agrisetado, -da, *a.* like flowered silk; grey-coloured.
agro (1), *n.m.* land, countryside.
agro (2), **-ra,** *a.* acid, sour; (*coll.*) tart, sharp. — *n.m.* (*bot.*) citron.
agrología, *n.f.* ecology.
agronometría, *n.f.* agronomics.
agronomía, *n.f.* agronomy, agronomics.
agronómico, -ca, *a.* agronomic, agronomical.
agrónomo, -ma, *a.* agronomic. — *n.m.f.* agronomist.
agropecuario, -ria, *a.* appertaining to land and cattle; ***riqueza agropecuaria,*** land and cattle wealth.
agrostema, *n.f.* (*bot.*) corn-cockle; rose-campion.
agrósteo, -tea, *a.* gramineous. — *n.f.pl.* (**agrósteas**) (*bot.*) Agrostis.
agróstide, *n.f.* (*bot.*) bent-grass.
agrostografía, *n.f.* agrostography.
agrumación, *n.f.* clotting, curdling.
agrumar, *v.t.* to curdle, clot. — **agrumarse,** *v.r.* to curdle, become clotted.
agrupación, *n.f.* cluster, crowd, group; grouping.
agrupamiento, *n.m.* (*com.*) association, group, merger; cartel.
agrupar, *v.t.* to group, cluster. — **agruparse,** *v.r.* to gather in groups, crowd together.

agrura, *n.f.* acidity; acerbity; orchard of citrus trees.

agua, *n.f.* water, liquid, fluid; rain; sea; (*chem.*) liquor distilled from flowers *etc.*; lustre (*diamonds*); (*naut.*) leak; (*arch.*) slope of roof; (*pl.*) mineral waters (*in general*); gloss (*feathers, stone, wood*); clouds (*in silk and other stuffs*); urine; tide;
(*in nature*) ***agua de lluvia,*** rain water; ***agua abajo,*** downstream; ***agua arriba,*** upstream; ***¡agua va!*** look out, water coming down! ***agua muerta,*** still water; ***agua dulce,*** fresh water; ***agua fresca,*** cool *or* cold water; ***agua (de) sal, agua salobre,*** salt(y) water, brine; ***agua de manantial,*** spring water; ***agua de pozo,*** well water; ***agua termal,*** hot-spring water;
(*domestic*) ***agua corriente*** or ***viva,*** running water; ***agua suave (blanda, delgada),*** soft water; ***agua dura (cruda, gorda),*** hard water; ***agua potable*** or ***de beber,*** drinking water; ***agua de pantoque*** or ***de sentina,*** bilge water; ***aguas negras*** or ***de albaña,*** sewage;
(*in special uses*) ***agua bendita,*** holy water; ***agua de Colonia,*** eau-de-Cologne; ***agua de cepas,*** wine; ***agua oxigenada,*** hydrogen peroxide; ***agua fuerte,*** aqua fortis; etching; ***agua de alhucema*** or ***de espliego,*** lavender water; ***agua de azahar*** or ***de nafa,*** orange-flower water; (*coll.*) ***agua de cerrajas,*** nought; ***agua gaseosa,*** aerated water, fizzy lemonade; ***agua de seltz,*** soda water; ***se me hace la boca agua,*** my mouth waters;
(*naut., sing. & pl.*) ***¡hombre al agua!*** man overboard! ***aguas chifles*** or ***muertas,*** neap-tides; ***aguas vivas,*** spring-tides; ***aguas de creciente (de menguante),*** rising (ebb) tide; ***aguas mayores,*** equinoctial tide; ***aguas menores,*** ordinary tide; ***aguas juridiccionales,*** territorial waters; ***aguantar aguas,*** to back water (*with oars*); ***arrollar agua,*** to go at full speed; ***hacer agua,*** to leak;
(*other pl. uses*) (*chem.*) ***aguas madres,*** mother-liquid; (*anat.*) ***hacer aguas,*** to pass water; (*anat.*) ***aguas mayores,*** fæces; (*anat.*) ***aguas menores,*** urine;
(*fig.*) ***sin decir agua va,*** without a word of warning; ***agua arriba,*** against the current; ***ahogarse en poca agua*** or ***en un vaso de agua,*** to be easily daunted *or* flustered, to make a mountain out of a molehill; ***no alcanzar para agua,*** to scrape a bare living, barely make ends meet; ***bailarle a uno el agua,*** to dance attendance on *or* humour s.o., keep s.o. happy; ***cubrir aguas,*** to put on the roof (*of a building*); ***echar el agua a,*** to baptize; ***echarle a uno un jarro de agua fría,*** to throw cold water on; ***echarse al agua,*** to take the plunge, go ahead regardless; ***estar entre dos aguas,*** to be undecided, sit on the fence; ***estar con el agua al cuello,*** to be up to one's eyes; ***guardarse del agua mansa,*** to beware of the (apparently) meek and mild; ***quedarse en agua de cerrajas,*** to flop, fizzle out, come to nothing; ***no hallar agua en el mar,*** not to see sth. under one's very nose, not to see the wood for the trees; ***este dinero me viene como agua de mayo,*** this money comes in very handy *or* just right; ***pasado por agua,*** soft-boiled (*egg*).

aguacatal, *n.m.* avocado plantation.

aguacate, *n.m.* avocado pear; alligator-pear; (*min.*) pear-shaped emerald.

aguacatillo, *n.m.* variety of the avocado pear-tree.

aguacero, *n.m.* heavy shower, downpour.

aguacibera, *n.f.* watering.

aguacha, *n.f.* (*coll.*) foul water.

aguachar, *n.m.* pool, puddle.

aguachar(nar), *v.t.* to flood; (*Chi.*) to tame (*horses*). — **aguacharse,** *v.r.* (*Arg.*) to get fat in idleness (*horses*).

aguachento, -ta, *a.* (*Hisp. Am.*) sodden.

aguachirle, *a.* wishy-washy (*wine, soup etc.*). — *n.m.* watery stuff.

aguada, *n.f.* (*build.*) priming; watering-station; (*min.*) flood (*in a mine*); (*naut.*) fresh water supplies; (*art*) water-colour sketch *or* outline; (*naut.*) ***hacer aguada,*** to take on fresh water; (***pintura***) ***a la aguada,*** water-colour (picture).

aguaderas, *n.f.pl.* wing-coverts; crates for carrying water on horseback.

aguadero, -ra, *a.* waterproof; ***capa aguadera,*** waterproof cape. — *n.m.* drinking-trough.

aguadija, *n.f.* water, humour in pimples *or* sores.

aguado, -da, *a.* watered-down.

aguador, -ra, *n.m.f.* water-carrier; sprocket of a water-wheel; (*mil.*) ***aguador del real,*** sutler.

aguaducho, *n.m.* freshet; stall for selling water.

aguadura, *n.f.* (*vet.*) catarrh (*in horses*); abscess in the hoof (*horses*).

aguafiestas, *n.m.f. inv.* kill-joy, spoil-sport; (*coll.*) wet blanket.

aguafuerte, *n.f.* etching; etched plate.

aguagoma, *n.f.* gum-water.

aguaitamiento, *n.m.* spying, watching.

aguaitar, *v.t.* to lie in wait for; to spy upon.

aguajaque, *n.m.* fennel gum.

aguajas, *n.f.pl.* (*vet.*) ulcers above the hoofs.

aguaje, *n.m.* sea current *or* stream; (*naut.*) watering station; tidal wave; whirlpool, eddy at rudder; wake (*of a ship*).

aguajoso, -sa, *a.* watery.

agualdar, *v.t.* to colour like dyer's weed.

agualí, *n.f.* (*sl.*) office, fees of assessor.

agualó, *n.m.* (*sl.*) assessor, adviser.

agualluvia, *n.f.* rain-water.

aguamala, *n.f.*, **aguamar,** *n.m.* (*ichth.*) medusa, jelly-fish.

aguamanil, *n.m.* water-jug, ewer; wash-basin, wash-stand.

aguamanos, *n.m. inv.* water for washing the hands; wash-basin, wash-stand.

aguamarina, *n.f.* aquamarine.

aguamelar, *v.t.* to mix with honey and water; to sweeten.

aguamiel, *n.f.* honeywater; nectar; mead-must; (*Hisp. Am.*) sugar cane and water; (*Mex.*) unfermented juice of maguey.

aguamotor, *n.m.* water motor.

aguanafa, *n.f.* (*prov.*) orange-flower water.

aguanieve, *n.f.* sleet.

aguanieves, *n.f. inv.* (*orn.*) water wagtail.

aguanosidad, *n.f.* serous humours; wateriness.

aguanoso, -sa, *a.* watery.

aguantable, *a.* tolerable, bearable.

aguantaderas, *n.f.pl.* endurance, patience.

aguantar, *v.t.* to support; to suffer, stand, bear, endure, abide, put up with; ***no le*** or ***lo aguanto,*** I can't stand him. — *v.i.* to hold out, stick it out, last out, stand one's ground; ***hay que aguantar hasta mañana,*** we must stick it out until to-morrow; ***hay que reírse y aguantar,*** you just have to grin and bear it. — **aguantarse,** *v.r.* to restrain o.s.; to lump it, take it; ***si no te gusta, te aguantas,*** if you don't like it, you (must) lump it.

aguante, *n.m.* staying power; endurance; resistance; patience; ***tiene aguante,*** he can stick it; ***navío de aguante,*** ship that carries a stiff sail.

aguañón, *n.m.* constructor of hydraulic machines.

aguapié, *n.m.* third-rate wine, red biddy.

aguar [M], *v.t.* to water down; to mar, spoil, pour cold water on; ***aguar la fiesta,*** to spoil the fun. — **aguarse,** *v.r.* (*vet.*) to become ill from drinking water when perspiring (*horses*).

aguará, *n.m.* (*Arg.*) large fox.

aguardada, *n.f.* wait, waiting.

aguardar, *v.t.* to wait for, await, expect. — *v.i.* to wait. — *v.r.* (*coll.*) ***¡aguárdate!*** hold on! hang on!

aguardentado, -da, *a.* addicted to drinking ***aguardiente***; containing ***aguardiente.***

aguardentería, *n.f.* spirits-shop.
aguardentero, -ra, *n.m.f.* maker *or* retailer of spirits. — *n.f.* spirit-flask.
aguardentoso, -sa, *a.* mixed with *or* similar to spirits; alcoholic; ***voz aguardentosa,*** voice of a person who drinks, rough, beery voice.
aguardiente, *n.m.* Spanish aquavitæ, (unmatured) brandy; ***aguardiente de caña,*** rum; ***aguardiente de cabeza,*** first spirits drawn from the still, first running.
aguardillado, -da, *a.* garret-like.
aguardo, *n.m.* covert, hide.
aguarrás, *n.m.* oil of turpentine.
aguasarse, *v.r.* to become facetious; to become ill-mannered.
aguasol, *n.m.* (*bot.*) blight.
aguate, *n.m.* (*Hisp. Am.*) prickle.
aguatero, *n.m.* (*Hisp. Am.*) water carrier *or* vendor.
aguatinta, *n.f.* aquatint, etching.
aguatocha, *n.f.* pump; fire-engine.
aguatoso, -sa, *a.* (*Hisp. Am.*) spiny, prickly.
aguaturma, *n.f.* (*bot.*) Jerusalem artichoke.
aguaverde, *n.f.* green jellyfish.
aguavientos, *n.m. inv.* (*bot.*) yellow sage-tree.
aguavilla, *n.f.* (*bot.*) red-berried arbutus.
aguaza, *n.f.* lymph, aqueous humour; sap.
aguazal, *n.m.* marshy area, fenland.
aguazar [C], *v.t.* to make marshy *or* watery.
aguazo, *n.m.* gouache.
aguazoso, -sa, *a.* watery.
agudamente, *adv.* sharply, keenly; ingeniously; finely.
agudeza, *n.f.* sharpness (*instruments*); acuteness, subtlety, fineness; witticism, repartee; acumen, smartness.
agudizarse, *v.r.* to become (more) acute *or* pronounced.
agudo, -da, *a.* acute; sharp; keen; (*mus.*) high-pitched; ***palabra aguda,*** oxytone; ***agudo de ingenio,*** quick-witted; (*geom.*) ***ángulo agudo,*** acute angle.
Águeda, *n.f.* Agatha.
agüela, *n.f.* (*sl.*) cloak, mantle.
agüera, *n.f.* irrigation trench.
agüero, *n.m.* omen; ***de mal agüero,*** ill-omened; ***ave de mal agüero,*** bird of ill omen; ***ser de buen agüero,*** to augur well.
aguerrir [Q], *v.t.* (*defective*) to inure to war; to harden; to season (*troops*). — **aguerrirse,** *v.r.* (*defective*) to become inured to war; to become hardened.
aguijada, *n.f.* goad; prod.
aguijador, -ra, *a.* goading, spurring, stimulating. — *n.m.f.* goader, spurrer; instigator, stimulator.
aguijadura, *n.f.* goading.
aguijar, *v.t.* to goad; to incite. — *v.i.* to quicken one's pace.
aguijón, *n.m.* sting (*of bee, wasp etc.*); prick, prickle; spur, goad; thorn (*plants*); stimulus; ***dar coces contra el aguijón,*** to kick against the pricks.
aguijonamiento, *n.m.* pricking.
aguijonazo, *n.m.* thrust with a goad.
aguijoneador, -ra, *a.* pricking. — *n.m.f.* one who pricks or goads.
aguijoneadura, *n.f.* goading, spurring.
aguijoneamiento, *n.m.* goading, spurring.
aguijonear, *v.t.* to prick, goad; to goad on.
águila, *n.f.* eagle; (*Hisp. Am.*) swindler; (*astron.*) Aquila; good cigar; ***ser un águila,*** to be a lynx; ***águila barbuda,*** lammergeyer; ***águila blanca,*** bald eagle; ***águila caudal, cabdal*** or ***real,*** royal *or* golden eagle; ***águila de mar*** or ***marina,*** sea eagle; ***águila gallinera,*** Egyptian vulture; ***águila imperial,*** imperial eagle; ***águila monoeva,*** harpy eagle; ***águila pescadora,*** osprey; ***águila ratonera,*** buzzard. — *n.m.* lynx, smart fellow; (*ichth.*) eagle ray; ***un águila del foro,*** a legal eagle.
aguileña (1), *n.f.* (*bot.*) columbine; aquilegia.
aguileño, -ña (2), *a.* aquiline; hooked, hawk-nosed; hawk-eyed.
aguilera, *n.f.* eyrie.
aguilillo, -lla, *a.* (*Hisp. Am.*) swift (*horses*).
aguilón, *n.m.* boom (*of a crane*), jib; square clay tube; (*arch.*) gable wall; large eagle [ÁGUILA].
aguilucho, *n.m.* eaglet; harrier.
agüilla, *n.f.* moisture; seepage; (*And.*) drizzle.
aguinaldo, *n.m.* Christmas bonus; (*bot.*) bindweed.
agüista, *n.m.f.* one who takes the waters at a spa.
aguja, *n.f.* needle, knitting-needle; bodkin; spire; stylus (*gramophone*); points, switch-rail; (*ichth.*) needle-fish, horn-fish; needle-shell; hand (*of a watch*), style (*of a dial*); pole, prop; under-pinning beam (*bridge*); meat-pie; customs officer's spike; ***aguja colchonera,*** quilting *or* tufting needle; ***aguja de arrear*** or ***de enjalmar, aguja salmera*** or ***saquera,*** saddler's *or* packing needle; ***aguja de fogón,*** gun-pin; ***aguja de gancho,*** crochet-hook; ***aguja de marcar,*** theodolite; ***aguja de mechar, aguja mechera,*** larding-needle, skewer; ***aguja de tejer,*** knitting needle; ***aguja loca,*** compass which does not point to N.; (*naut.*) ***aguja de bitácora, aguja magnética, aguja de marear,*** mariner's compass; ***aguja de hacer punto*** or ***calceta,*** knitting-needle; (*bot.*) ***aguja de pastor, aguja de Venus,*** shepherd's needle; ***buscar una aguja en un pajar,*** to look for a needle in a haystack; ***conocer la aguja de marear,*** to know what's what, know one's job; ***meter aguja y sacar reja,*** to give a sprat to catch a salmon; ***alabar uno sus agujas,*** to blow one's own trumpet; (*pl.*) ribs (*of animal*); distemper (*horse*).
agujadera, *n.f.* needlewoman, knitter.
agujal, *n.m.* hole left by beams *or* props.
agujazo, *n.m.* prick with a needle.
agujerear, *v.t.* to make a hole *or* holes in; to pierce, bore, prick.
agujero, *n.m.* hole; den; needle-maker, needle-seller.
agujeta, *n.f.* lace, string *or* latchet tipped with tags; shoe-strap, shoe-string; (*orn.*) godwit; (*pl.*) aches and pains, fatigue; ***tener agujetas,*** to be all aches and pains, be fagged out.
agujetero, *n.m.* (*Hisp. Am.*) needle-case.
agujón, *n.m.* (*ichth.*) needle-fish.
agujuela, *n.f.* brad.
aguosidad, *n.f.* lymph.
aguoso, -sa, *a.* watery.
¡agur! *interj.* (*coll.*) adieu, farewell.
agusanarse, *v.r.* to become worm-eaten.
agustina (1), *n.f.* (*bot.*) anemone.
agustiniano, -na, *a.* Augustinian.
Agustín, *n.m.* Augustine.
agustino, -na (2), *a., n.m.f.* Augustinian, Austin (monk, nun).
agutí, *n.m.* agouti.
aguzadero, -ra, *a.* sharpening. — *n.m.f.* sharpener. — *n.m.* place where wild boars sharpen their tusks. — *n.f.* whetstone.
aguzador, -ra, *a.* sharpening. — *n.m.f.* sharpener.
aguzadura, *n.f.* sharpening, whetting; steel used to forge new cutting edge *or* point on plough.
aguzamiento, *n.m.* sharpening, whetting.
aguzanieves, *n.f. inv.* (*orn.*) wagtail.
aguzar [C], *v.t.* to whet, sharpen; to incite, goad on; ***aguzar el ingenio,*** to sharpen one's wits; ***aguzar las orejas,*** to prick up one's ears; ***aguzar el diente*** or ***los dientes,*** to whet one's appetite; ***aguzar la vista,*** to sharpen *or* peel one's eyes.
aguzonazo, *n.m.* lunge, thrust.
¡ah! *interj.* oh!

ahebrado, -da, *a.* fibrous, thread-like.
ahechadero, *n.m.* place for winnowing.
ahechador, -ra, *a.* sifting, winnowing. — *n.m.f.* sifter, winnower.
ahechaduras, *n.f.pl.* winnowings.
ahechar, *v.t.* to sift, winnow.
ahecho, *n.m.* winnowing.
ahelear, *v.t.* to gall, embitter. — *v.i.* to taste bitter.
ahelgado, -da, *a.* jag-toothed.
aherrojamiento, *n.m.* fettering, shackling, enchainment.
aherrojar, *v.t.* to put in irons; to chain, fetter, shackle; (*fig.*) to oppress, subjugate.
aherrumbrar, *v.t.* to make rusty; to give the taste *or* colour of iron to. — **aherrumbrarse,** *v.r.* to become rusty.
aherrumbroso, -sa, *a.* rusty, rusted.
ahervorarse, *v.r.* to become heated (*cereals*).
ahí, *adv.* there; here; ***de ahí a poco,*** shortly afterwards; ***de ahí que,*** with the result that, hence; ***por ahí,*** that way (*direction*); about, roughly; ***por ahí se andan,*** there's not much in it, they are about equal; ***irse por ahí,*** to go out (*on a spree*).
ahidalgado, -da, *a.* gentlemanly.
ahijadero, *n.m.* sheep nursery, breeding place for sheep.
ahijado, -da, *n.m.f.* godchild; protégé.
ahijador, *n.m.* shepherd in charge of a sheep nursery.
ahijar, *v.t.* to adopt; to espouse (*cause etc.*); to impute; to attribute. — *v.i.* to bring forth young; (*agric.*) to bud, shoot, sprout.
¡ahijuna! *interj.* (*Hisp. Am.*) Lord! Heavens!
ahilar, *v.t.* to line up, form into single file. — **ahilarse,** *v.r.* to become faint *or* weak; to turn sour; to grow thin; to go in single file.
ahilo, *n.m.* faintness, weakness.
ahincado, -da, *a.* determined, resolute, stubborn; vehement.
ahincar [A], *v.t.* to urge, press, drive. — **ahincarse,** *v.r.* to make haste.
ahínco, *n.m.* determination, resoluteness, tenacity; earnestness, insistence.
ahitar, *v.t.* to stuff, gorge; to surfeit, satiate.
ahitera, *n.f.* (*coll.*) overeating, stuffing, gorging.
ahito, -ta, *a.* gorged, satiated; sick (***de,*** of). — *n.m.* indigestion, surfeit.
ahobachonarse, *v.r.* to become lazy *or* shiftless.
ahocicar [A], *v.i.* (*naut.*) to pitch, plunge; (*Hisp. Am.*) to give in, yield.
ahocinado, *n.m.* gorge, narrow passage.
ahocinarse, *v.r.* to run in deep and narrow ravines (*rivers*).
ahogadero, *n.m.* hangman's rope; stifling, overcrowded place; throat-band; halter.
ahogadizo, -za, *a.* easily drowned *or* stifled; harsh, unpalatable (*fruits*); heavier than water, non-floating (*wood*); ***carne ahogadiza,*** flesh of drowned *or* suffocated animals.
ahogado, -da, *a.* close, unventilated, stuffy; (too) tight, tight fitting, muffled, half-smothered.
ahogador, -ra, *n.m.f.* choker.
ahogamiento, *n.m.* drowning, suffocation; distress, hardship.
ahogar [B], *v.t.* to choke, throttle, stifle; to smother; to drown; to oppress; to quench, extinguish; to swamp (*plants*); ***ahogar las penas,*** to drown one's sorrows. — **ahogarse,** *v.r.* to become suffocated; to drown; (*naut.*) to founder; ***ahogarse de risa,*** to choke with *or* die of laughter; ***ahogarse de calor,*** to be *or* become suffocated by (the) heat; ***ahogarse en un vaso de agua*** or ***en poca agua,*** to get flustered over nothing, make a mountain out of a molehill.
ahogaviejas, *n.f. inv.* (*bot.*) dill.
ahogo, *n.m.* oppression; anguish; tightness (*chest*), suffocation; distress, affliction; embarrassment; ***pasar un ahogo,*** to have a nasty experience; to go through a tight spell *or* squeeze.
ahoguijo, *n.m.* (*vet.*) quinsy, swollen throat.
ahoguío, *n.m.* oppression in the chest.
ahojar, *v.t.* (*prov., agric.*) to browse.
ahombrado, -da, *a.* (*coll.*) manly, mannish.
ahondar, *v.t.* to dig, deepen, sink; to go deep into. — *v.i.* to go deep; to go deeply (***en,*** into). — **ahondarse,** *v.r.* to become deeper.
ahonde, *n.m.* going deep.
ahora, *adv.* now, at present, just now; a moment ago; in a moment; ***por ahora,*** for the present, for the time being; ***hasta ahora,*** hitherto, so far, until now; ***ahora bien,*** well, all the same; ***desde ahora,*** henceforth, from now on; ***ahora mismo,*** at once, this moment, right now, this very instant; ***de ahora,*** of the present day.
ahorcado, -da, *n.m.f.* hanged person; ***mentar la soga en casa del ahorcado,*** to touch on a sore point, raise a painful subject.
ahorcadura, *n.f.* hanging.
ahorcajarse, *v.r.* to sit astride.
ahorcalobo, *n.m.* (*bot.*) herb Paris.
ahorcamiento, *n.m.* hanging.
ahorcaperro, *n.m.* (*naut.*) running knot.
ahorcar [A], *v.t.* to hang; ***ahorcar los hábitos,*** to leave the priesthood. — **ahorcarse,** *v.r.* to hang onself.
ahorita, *adv.* (*coll.*) just now; this minute, right now; ***ahorita mismo,*** this very moment, right away, at once.
ahormar, *v.t.* to fit, shape, adjust; to break in (*shoes etc.*); to block (*hats*); (*fig.*) to bring to reason. — **ahormarse,** *v.r.* to adjust oneself to; to become adapted to.
ahornagamiento, *n.m.* (*agric.*) drying up, parching; dryness.
ahornagarse [B], *v.r.* (*agric.*) to get *or* become parched *or* burned.
ahornar, *v.t.* to put in the oven. — **ahornarse,** *v.r.* to get burned.
ahorquillado, -da, *a.* forked.
ahorquillar, *v.t.* to stay, prop up (*with forks*); to make fork-shaped.
ahorrador, -ra, *a.* economizing. — *n.m.f.* economizer, saver.
ahorramiento, *n.m.* saving.
ahorrar, *v.t.* to save, economize; to spare; to free, emancipate; ***ahórrese Vd. palabras,*** save your breath; ***no ahorrárselas con nadie,*** to be afraid of nobody.
ahorrativa, *n.f.* (*coll.*) [AHORRATIVO].
ahorratividad, *n.f.* thriftiness.
ahorrativo, -va, *a.* thrifty, saving, sparing. — *n.f.* (*coll.*) saving, economy, thrift.
ahorrillos, *n.m.pl.* small savings.
ahorro, *n.m.* saving, economy; (*pl.*) savings; ***caja de ahorros,*** savings-bank.
ahoyadura, *n.f.* digging, hole digging.
ahoyar, *v.t.* to dig holes in.
ahuate, *n.m.* (*Hond., Mex.*) prickly hair (*plants*).
ahuchador, -ra, *a.* hoarding, miserly. — *n.m.f.* hoarder, miser.
ahuchamiento, *n.m.* hoarding, miserliness.
ahuchar, *v.t.* to hoard up.
ahuecadera, *n.f.* pick.
ahuecado, -da, *a.* hollow, pompous, affected.
ahuecamiento, *n.m.* hollowing; softening, fluffing up; pompousness.
ahuecar [A], *v.t.* to make hollow, scoop out; to loosen up, fluff up, soften; to give a pompous tone to. — *v.i.* (*coll.*) to clear off; ***ahueca (el ala),*** clear off, beat it.
ahuehué, ahuehuete, *n.m.* (*bot.*) Mexican conifer.
ahuesado, -da, *a.* bony, bone-like.
ahuevar, *v.t.* to clarify (*wine*) with the white of eggs.

ahulado, *n.m.* (*Hisp. Am.*) waterproof oil-cloth.

ahumado, -da, *a.* smoky; smoked; smoke-cured; ***lentes ahumados,*** dark glasses. — *n.f.* smoke signal. — *n.m.* smoking, curing.

ahumador, -ra, *a.* smoking, curing. — *n.m.f.* smoker, curer.

ahumadura, *n.f.*, **ahumamiento,** *n.m.* smoking, curing.

ahumar, *v.t.* to smoke; to cure in smoke; to fill with smoke. — *v.i.* to smoke, emit smoke. — **ahumarse,** *v.r.* to become smoky *or* smoked up; (*coll.*) to get tight.

¡ahur! *interj.* (*coll.*) adieu! farewell!

ahurrugado, -da, *a.* (*agric.*) badly tilled *or* cultivated.

ahusado, -da, *a.* spindle-shaped, slender, tapering.

ahusar, *v.t.* to make slender as a spindle; to taper. — **ahusarse,** *v.r.* to taper; to become slender.

ahuyentador, -ra, *a.* scaring, frightening.

ahuyentar, *v.t.* to drive away; to frighten away, put to flight; to drive out; to banish (*care*). — **ahuyentarse,** *v.r.* to flee, run away.

aijada, *n.f.* goad.

ailanto, *n.m.* (*bot.*) ailanthus tree.

aimará, *a.* (*Hisp. Am.*) pertaining to an Indian race on Lake Titicaca (*Peru-Bol.*).

aína(s), *adv.* (*obs.*) quickly; almost; easily, well-nigh; ***no tan aínas,*** not so easily.

aindiado, *a.* (*Hisp. Am.*) Indian-looking.

airado, -da, *a.* angry, wrathful, furious; (*fig.*) depraved, perverse; ***vida airada,*** life of vice.

airamiento, *n.m.* wrath, anger.

airar [P], *v.t.* to anger. — **airarse,** *v.r.* to grow angry; ***airarse con*** or ***contra alguien,*** to become angry with s.o.; ***airarse de*** or ***por algo,*** to become angry at sth.

airampo, *n.m.* (*Per.*, *bot.*) a tinctorial cactus.

aire, *n.m.* air; atmosphere, wind; briskness (*horse*); gait, aspect, look; vanity; beauty; vigour; (*coll.*) attack of paralysis; (*mus.*) air, tune; trifle, frivolity; ***aire colado,*** cold draught; ***aires naturales,*** native air; ***aire acondicionado,*** air conditioning; ***aire comprimido,*** compressed air; ***beber los aires*** or ***los vientos por,*** to be desperately keen on; ***azotar el aire,*** to act to no purpose, labour in vain; ***creerse del aire,*** to be credulous; ***hablar al*** or ***en el aire,*** to talk idly; ***tomar (el) aire,*** to take a walk; ***¿qué aires le traen a Vd. por acá?*** what (good wind) brings you here? ***al aire libre,*** in the open air, out of doors; ***en aire,*** in a good humour; ***en el aire,*** in the air, in suspense; ***de buen (mal) aire,*** in a pleasing (peevish) manner; ***estar en el aire,*** to be pending; ***empañar el aire,*** to darken the sky (*of clouds etc.*); (*fig.*) ***fundar en el aire,*** to build on insufficient foundations; ***se da*** or ***tiene un aire con,*** it has the look of, it rather resembles; (*fig.*) ***aire de suficiencia,*** air of conceit; ***aire popular,*** popular song; ***castillos en el aire,*** castles in the air; (*jewel.*) ***guarnición al aire,*** open setting; ***palabras al aire,*** idle talk; ***dar aire a,*** to get rid of quickly; (*coll.*) ***darse aires,*** to put on airs; ***echar al aire,*** to uncover, reveal; ***hacerse aire,*** to fan oneself; (*coll.*) ***guardarle*** or ***llevarle el aire a uno,*** to vanish into thin air; to humour s.o.; ***mudar (de) aires,*** to get a change of scene; ***mudarse a cualquier aire,*** to be fickle *or* easily influenced; ***ofenderse del aire,*** to be very touchy; (*coll.*) ***sustentarse del aire,*** to eat very little; to live on vain hopes; to be taken in by flattery.

airear, *v.t.* to air, ventilate; to aerate, charge with gas. — **airearse,** *v.r.* to take the air; to cool oneself; to get aired; to catch cold.

airecillo, *n.m.* (*dim.*) gentle breeze; ***airecillo protector,*** something of a patronizing air.

airón (1), *n.m.* strong wind.

airón (2), *n.m.* aigrette; panache; crest; (*orn.*) grey heron.

airosidad, *n.f.* gracefulness, elegance.

airoso, -sa, *a.* airy, light; graceful, elegant; successful, triumphant; ***salir airoso,*** to come forth triumphant.

aislable, *a.* separable; that can be isolated *or* insulated.

aislación, *n.f.* insulation; ***aislación de sonido,*** sound-proofing.

aislacionismo, *n.m.* isolationism.

aislacionista, *n.m.f.* isolationist.

aislado, -da, *a.* isolated, separate, single; insulated.

aislador, -ra, *a.* isolating, insulating. — *n.m.f.* isolator. — *n.m.* (*elec.*, *phys.*) insulator.

aislamiento, *n.m.* isolation; detachment; loneliness; insulation.

aislar [P], *v.t.* to isolate, separate, detach; to insulate. — **aislarse,** *v.r.* to isolate, seclude oneself; to become isolated.

¡ajá!, ¡ajajá! *interj.* aha! ha! ha! fine! good!

ajabeba, *n.f.* Moorish flute.

ajacintado, -da, *a.* hyacinth-like.

ajada, *n.f.* garlic sauce.

ajadizo, -za, *a.* easily faded, withered, crumpled.

ajador, -ra, *a.* fading, withering, crumpling.

ajamiento, *n.m.* fading, withering, crumpling.

ajamonarse, *v.r.* (*coll.*) to grow stout, get fat (*women*); (*Hisp. Am.*) to wither, dry up.

ajaquecarse [A], *v.r.* to get a headache.

ajar (1), *n.m.* garlic field. — *v.t.* to spoil, mar, muss, tarnish; to crumple; cause to fade *or* wither. — **ajarse,** *v.r.* to wither, fade; to become spoiled *or* crumpled; to get mussed.

ajar (2), *v.t.* to crack; to chip, splinter.

ajaraca, *n.f.* (*arch.*) arabesque.

ajarafe, *n.m.* table-land, terrace.

ajardinar, *v.t.* to landscape.

aje, *n.m.* (*usu. pl.*) complaint, weakness; (*Cub.*, *bot.*) yam; (*Hond.*) cochineal.

ajea, *n.f.* brushwood for fuel.

ajear, *v.i.* to cry like a hunted partridge; (*Ec.*) to swear.

ajebe, *n.m.* rock alum.

ajedrea, *n.f.* (*bot.*) savory.

ajedrecista, *n.m.f.* chess-player.

ajedrez, *n.m.* chess; chess set; (*naut.*) netting, grating.

ajedrezado, -da, *a.* chequered. — *n.m.* chequerwork.

ajedrezamiento, *n.m.* chequerwork.

ajedrezar [C], *v.t.* to chequer-work.

ajedrista, *a.* related to the game of chess.

ajenabe, ajenabo, *n.m.* (*bot.*) wild mustard.

ajenar, *v.t.* to alienate.

ajengibre, *n.m.* (*bot.*) ginger.

ajenjo, *n.m.* (*bot.*) wormwood; absinthe.

ajeno, -na, *a.* another's; foreign; inappropriate; free; unaware; detached; ***en casa ajena,*** in somebody else's house; ***por causas ajenas a nuestra voluntad,*** for reasons beyond our control; ***ser ajeno a,*** to have no connection with; ***estar ajeno,*** to have one's mind on other things.

ajenuz, *n.m.* (*bot.*) field fennel-flower.

ajeo, *n.m.* cry (*partridge*); ***perro de ajeo,*** setter (*dog*).

ajerezado, -da, *a.* sherry-type (*wine*).

ajero, -ra, *n.m.f.* vendor of garlic. — *n.m.* proprietor of garlic field.

ajesuitado, -da, *a.* (*Hisp. Am.*) Jesuitical, crafty.

ajete, *n.m.* young garlic; leek *or* garlic sauce.

ajetrear, *v.t.* to harass, exhaust. — **ajetrearse,** *v.r.* to bustle about, wear oneself out.

ajetreo, *n.m.* bustle, agitation.

ají, *n.m.* (*pl.* **ajíes**) (*bot.*) chili; chili sauce; green *or* red pepper; (*Hisp. Am.*) ***ponerse como un ají,*** to turn as red as a beetroot.

ajiaceite, *n.m.* garlic and olive-oil sauce.

ajiaco, *n.m.* (*Hisp. Am.*) chili sauce; Spanish stew seasoned with garlic; (*Hisp. Am.*) ***estar como un ajiaco,*** to be in a bad mood.

ajicarar, *v.t.* to shape like a cup.

ajicero, -ra, *a.* (*Chi.*) pertaining to chili. — *n.m.f.* (*Chi.*) seller of chili. — *n.m.* (*Chi.*) vase for keeping chili.

ajicola, *n.f.* (*art.*) glue made of kidskin boiled with garlic.

ajicomino, *n.m.* sauce made of garlic and cumin seed.

ajigotar, *v.t.* (*coll.*) to smash into bits.

ajilimoje, ajilimójili, *n.m.* (*coll.*) pepper-and-garlic sauce; (*pl.* **ajilimojes, ajilimójilis**) (*coll.*) bits and pieces.

ajillo, *n.m.* young garlic; chopped garlic.

ajimez, *n.m.* (*arch.*) mullioned window.

ajipa, *n.f.* (*bot.*) artichoke, Jerusalem artichoke.

ajipuerro, *n.m.* (*bot.*) wild leek.

ajironar, *v.t.* to patch; to tear, rend, slit.

ajizal, *n.m.* chili field.

ajo, *n.m.* (*bot.*) garlic; (*coll.*) paint (*cosmetic*); (*coll.*) oath, swear word; (*bot.*) ***ajo de chalote,*** shallot; (*bot.*) ***ajo moruno,*** chive; (*bot.*) ***ajo silvestre,*** moly; ***diente de ajo,*** clove of garlic; ***harto de ajos,*** ill-bred, uncouth; ***tieso como un ajo,*** stiff and stilted, proud and haughty; ***revolver el ajo,*** to stir up trouble; ***¡bueno anda el ajo!*** a fine *or* nice state things are in! ***andar*** or ***estar en el ajo,*** to be in the picture *or* in the know, to have a hand in it; ***hacer morder el ajo,*** to make (*s.o.*) eat humble pie; ***ajo blanco,*** garlic soup. — *interj.* ***¡ajó! ¡ajó!*** goo, dada (*used to encourage infants to speak*).

-ajo, aja, *suffix dim., pej. e.g.* **colgajo,** rag, tatter; **lagunajo,** puddle; **migaja,** crumb.

ajobar, *v.t.* to carry on the back.

ajobilla, *n.f.* clam.

ajobo, *n.m.* burden, heavy load; (action of) carrying; (*fig.*) fatiguing work.

ajofaina [JOFAINA].

ajolín, *n.m.* bug.

ajolio, *n.m.* (*prov.*) oil and garlic sauce.

ajolote, *n.m.* (*zool.*) axolotl, mud puppy.

ajomate, *n.m.* (*bot.*) conferva.

ajonje, ajonjo, *n.m.* bird-lime.

ajonjear, *v.t.* (*Hisp. Am.*) to fondle, stroke.

ajonjera, *n.f.*, **ajonjero,** *n.m.* (*bot.*) carline thistle.

ajonjolí, *n.m.* (*bot.*) sesame.

ajoqueso, *n.m.* dish of garlic and cheese.

ajorar, *v.t.* to carry away by force.

ajorca, *n.f.* bracelet, anklet, bangle.

ajordar, *v.i.* (*prov.*) to bawl.

ajornalar, *v.t.* to hire by the day.

ajote, *n.m.* (*bot.*) water-germander.

ajuagas, *n.f.pl.* (*vet.*) malanders.

ajuanet(e)ado, -da, *a.* having bunions, bunion-like; ***rostro ajuanetado,*** face with prominent cheekbones.

ajuar, *n.m.* bridal apparel; trousseau; bridal *or* household furniture.

ajudiado, -da, *a.* Jewish, Jew-like.

ajuiciado, -da, *a.* judicious, prudent.

ajuiciamiento, *n.m.* judiciousness, sagacity.

ajuiciar [L], *v.t.* to bring to one's senses, reform. — **ajuiciar(se),** *v.i.* (*v.r.*) to come to one's senses, mend one's ways.

ajumarse, *v.r.* (*And., Hisp. Am.*) to get drunk.

ajustabilidad, *n.f.* adjustability.

ajustado, -da, *a.* right, exact; close-fitting, tight.

ajustador, -ra, *a.* fitting, adjusting. — *n.m.* close-fitting waistcoat *or* jacket; (*print.*) justifier, pager; (*mech.*) adapter, fitter, adjuster, adjusting tool, coupler.

ajustamiento [AJUSTE].

ajustar, *v.t.* to adjust, fit, regulate; to engage, hire; to arrange (for); reconcile, settle; to fasten; to fix (*prices etc.*); to fit tightly; (*print.*) to page; ***se ajustó el reloj,*** he fastened on his watch; ***ajustó la ventana,*** he fastened the window; ***ajustó el precio en 20 ptas.,*** he fixed the price at 20 ptas.; ***me ajusta mucho esta camisa,*** this shirt is very tight; ***ajustar cuentas con,*** to have it out (with). — *v.i.* to fit. — **ajustarse,** *v.r.* to fit; to be engaged, hired; to come to terms, to reach an agreement; ***ajustarse a*** + *inf.*, to comply with, to agree to; ***la llave se ajusta a la cerradura,*** the key fits into the lock; ***ajustarse a la razón,*** to conform to reason.

ajuste, *n.m.* fit (*of clothes*), fitting, adjustment; compromise, settlement, reconciliation; engagement, hiring; (*print.*) paging, making-up.

ajusticiado, -da, *n.m.f.* executed convict.

ajusticiar, *v.t.* to execute, put to death.

al, *contraction of* **a** *and* **el.** to the, at the (*before masc. noun*); *used with inf. of verbs with equivalence of English* on + *pres. part.*; *it also indicates immediate moment of action or co-existence*: ***al salir del sol,*** at sunrise; ***al anochecer,*** at nightfall; ***al nacer,*** at birth; ***al acabar la vida,*** at the moment of dying.

ala, *n.f.* (*naut., bot., aer., arch.*) wing, row, file; (*football*) wing; (*mil.*) flank; brim (*of hat*); (*anat.*) auricle (*of ear, heart*); (*aer.*) blade (*of screw propeller*); fin (*of fish*); (*bot.*) sneeze-weed; (*arch.*) eaves; (*fig.*) presumption; leaf (*of door, table*); (*fort.*) curtain; (*naut.*) ***ala de gavia,*** main-top studding-sails; (*slang*) ***ala de mosca,*** cheating at cards; (*naut.*) ***ala de proa,*** head of the ship; (*naut.*) ***ala de sobremesana,*** mizzen-top studding-sails; (*naut.*) ***ala de velacho,*** fore studding-sails; (*aer.*) ***ala en delta,*** delta wing; (*aer.*) ***ala en flecha,*** backswept wing; (*coll.*) ***ahuecar el ala,*** to take wing, disappear; ***arrastrar el ala,*** to court, make love to; (*pl.*) (*naut.*) upper studding-sails; (*fig.*) boldness, protection; (*poet.*) speed, rapidity; ***caérsele a uno las alas del corazón,*** to be dismayed, lose heart; ***cortar las alas a,*** to clip (s.o.'s) wings; to take (s.o.) down a peg; ***tomar alas,*** to take liberties; ***volar con propias alas,*** to stand on one's own feet; ***dar alas,*** to protect, encourage; ***estar bajo el ala de alguien,*** to be under s.o.'s wing.

Alá, *n.m.* Allah.

¡ala! *interj.* (*naut.*) pull! haul!

alabado, -da, *a.* praised. — *n.m.* hymn in praise of the Sacrament; (*Chi.*) ***al alabado,*** at daybreak.

alabador, -ra, *a.* praising; complimentary. — *n.m.f.* applauder, praiser.

alabamiento, *n.m.* praise.

alabamio, *n.m.* (*chem.*) alabamine.

alabancero, -ra, *a.* (*coll.*) fawning, flattering.

alabancia, *n.f.* praise, laudation.

alabancioso, -sa, *a.* (*coll.*) boastful, ostentatious.

alabandina, *n.f.* manganese sulphide; garnet, almandine.

alabanza, *n.f.* praise, commendation, glory; ***la alabanza propia envilece,*** self-praise debaseth; ***cantar las alabanzas de uno,*** to sing s.o.'s praises; ***amontonar alabanzas*** (***sobre***), to heap praises (on).

alabar, *v.t.* to praise, extol. — **alabarse,** *v.r.* to boast; to show oneself pleased (at); ***alabarse de valiente,*** to boast of one's courage; ***mucho me alabo de su triunfo,*** I am very pleased at his success.

alabarda, *n.f.* halberd.

alabardado, -da, *a.* halberd-shaped.

alabardazo, *n.m.* blow with a halberd.

alabardero, *n.m.* halberdier; (*theat.*) hired applauder, claqueur.

alabastrado, -da, *a.* alabaster-like.

alabastrino, -na, *a.* alabastrine. — *n.f.* thin sheet of alabaster.

alabastro, *n.m.* alabaster.

álabe, *n.m.* drooping branch; blade (*water-wheel*); (*mech.*) cam; mat (*carts*).
alabear, *v.t.* to warp. — **alabearse,** *v.r.* to become warped.
alábega, *n.f.* (*bot.*) sweet-basil.
alabeo, *n.m.* warping.
alabiado, -da, *a.* lipped, irregularly edged (*coins*).
alacena, *n.f.* cupboard, closet; (*naut.*) locker.
alaciar [L], *v.t.* to make limp *or* lifeless.
alacrán, *n.m.* scorpion; ring in bit of bridle; chain *or* link in sleeve-button; swivel; (*ent.*) ***alacrán cebollero,*** mole cricket; (*ichth.*) ***alacrán marino,*** angler.
alacranado, -da, *a.* bitten by a scorpion; infected (*by vice* or *disease*).
alacridad, *n.f.* alacrity, eagerness.
alacha, *n.f.*, **alache,** *n.m.* anchovy.
alachero, -ra, *n.m.f.* seller of anchovies.
alada, *n.f.* [ALADO]
aladares, *n.m.pl.* forelocks over the temples.
aladica, *n.f.* winged ant.
aladierna, *n.f.* (*bot.*) mock-privet; buckthorn.
Aladino, *n.m.* Aladdin.
alado, -da, *a.* winged; (*fig.*) light, swift, fleet. — *n.f.* fluttering of wings.
aladrada, *n.f.* (*prov.*) furrow.
aladrar, *v.t.* (*prov.*) to plough.
aladrería, *n.f.* (*prov.*) agricultural implements.
aladrero, *n.m.* (*carp.*) prop-maker (*mines*); (*prov.*) plough-maker.
aladres, *n.m.pl.* baying (*hounds*).
aladro, *n.m.* (*prov.*) plough, ploughed land.
aladroque, *n.m.* (*prov.*) anchovy.
alafia, *n.f.* (*coll.*) ***pedir alafia,*** to beg pardon *or* forgiveness.
álaga, *n.f.* spelt.
alagadizo, -za, *a.* easily flooded.
alagar [B], *v.t.* to make ponds *or* lakes in. — **alagarse,** *v.r.* to become flooded.
alagartado, -da, *a.* variegated, motley; lizard-like.
alagunado, -da, *a.* lagoon-like.
alajor, *n.m.* ground rent.
alajú, *n.m.* nougat; gingerbread.
alalá, *n.m.* popular song.
alalagmo, *n.m.* war-whoop [LELILÍ].
alalía, *n.f.* (*med.*) aphonia.
alalimón [ALIMÓN].
alalino, -na, *a.* dumb.
alama, *n.f.* (*bot.*) fodder plant.
alamar, *n.m.* frog and braid trimming; gimp.
alambicadamente, *adv.* subtly, with subtlety.
alambicado, -da, *a.* distilled; over-refined; (*fig.*) euphuistic, precious, oversubtle; given sparingly.
alambicamiento, *n.m.* distillation; affectation; subtlety; euphuism.
alambicar [A], *v.t.* to distil; to over-refine. — *v.r.* ***alambicarse los sesos,*** to cudgel one's wits; (*Hisp. Am.*) to sell cheap with a large turnover.
alambique, *n.m.* still, alembic; ***por alambique,*** sparingly.
alambor, *n.m.* (*arch.*) bevelling; (*fort.*) scarp, inside slope.
alamborado, -da, *a.* bevelled, sloped.
alambrado, -da, *a.* wiry; wired. — *n.m.* wire mesh, netting; (*elec.*) wiring. — *n.f.* wire fence, screen; (*mil.*) wire entanglement, barbed wire.
alambrador, -ra, *a.* wiring. — *n.m.* wirer.
alambraje, *n.m.* (*elec.*) wiring.
alambrar (1), *v.t.* to enclose, fence *or* string with wire; (*elec.*) to wire.
alambrar (2), *v.i.* (*prov.*) to clear (*sky*).
alambre, *n.m.* wire; cowbells; (*fig.*) wiry person; high-wire; ***alambre cargado,*** live wire; ***alambre conejo,*** rabbit-wire (*for snares*), ***alambre de latón,*** brass wire; (*rad.*) ***alambre de entrada,*** lead-in wire; ***alambre de espino*** or ***de púas,*** barbed wire; (*rad.*) ***alambre de tierra,*** earth wire; (*telev.*) ***alambre gemelo,*** twin lead; (*elec.*) ***alambre para artefactos,*** fixture wire; ***alambre para timbres eléctricos,*** wire for electric bells; ***alambre sin aislar,*** bare wire.
alambrecarril, *n.m.* aerial railway, cable railway.
alambrera, *n.f.* wire screen; fire guard; wire cover (*for food*).
alambrería, *n.f.* wire shop; agglomeration of wire.
alambrero, *n.m.* wireworker; (*coll.*) telegraph maintenance man.
alámbrico, -ca, *a.* wire-made.
alambrista, *n.m.f.* high-flier, acrobat.
alameda, *n.f.* poplar grove; public walk; avenue.
alamín, *n.m.* clerk appointed to inspect weights and measures; surveyor of buildings; irrigation inspector.
alaminazgo, *n.m.* office of the ***alamín.***
alamirré, *n.m.* (*obs.*) sign in musical notation.
álamo, *n.m.* (*bot.*) poplar; ***álamo blanco,*** white poplar; ***álamo de Italia,*** Lombardy poplar; ***álamo negro,*** black poplar; ***álamo temblón,*** aspen.
alampar, *v.t.* to crave after (*food and drink*). — *v.r.* ***alamparse por,*** to crave for.
alamud, *n.m.* square bolt for a door.
alanceador, -ra, *a.* lancing. — *n.m.f.* lancer.
alanceadura, *n.f.*, **alanceamiento,** *n.m.* lancing, spearing.
alancear, *v.t.* to spear, lance.
alandrearse, *v.r.* to become dry, stiff and white (*of silkworms*).
alandro, *n.m.* (*fig.*) trifle.
alanés, *n.m.* (*Mex.*) large deer.
alangarí, *n.m.* (*slang*) pardon, excuse; pain, cramp.
Alano, *n.m.* Alan, Allen.
alano, *n.m.* mastiff, wolfhound; ***los alanos,*** the Alani.
alantoideo, -dea, *a.* allantoid.
alanzado, -da, *a.* lance-like, spear-like; lanced, speared.
alanzar [C], *v.t.* to throw lances at, spear.
alaqueca, *n.f.*, **alaqueque,** *n.m.* bloodstone.
alar (1), *a.* wing; alar. — *n.m.* (*bot.*) overhanging roof. — *n.m.pl.* (**alares**) horse-hair snare; (*slang*) breeches.
alar (2), *v.t.* (*naut.*) to haul [HALAR].
alárabe, alarbe, *a., n.m.f.* Arabian. — *n.m.* (*fig.*) unmannerly person; ***portarse como un alarbe,*** to behave badly.
alarconiano, -na, *a.* of Alarcón.
alarde, *n.m.* review, parade (*soldiers*); show, display, ostentation; ***hacer alarde de,*** to make a show of, boast of.
alardear, *v.i.* to boast, brag, show off; ***alardear de,*** to boast of.
alardeo, *n.m.* boastfulness.
alardoso, -sa, *a.* ostentatious, boastful.
alargadero, -ra, *a.* that can be lengthened. — *n.f.* (*chem.*) nozzle; lengthening tube; (*naut.*) lengthening bar (*compasses*).
alargado, -da, *a.* extended, elongated. — *n.f.* extension, lengthening; ***dar la alargada,*** to pay out more string *or* rope.
alargador, -ra, *a.* stretching, lengthening. — *n.m.* extension cord.
alargamiento, *n.m.* extension, lengthening; (*eng.*) elongation.
alargar [B], *v.t.* to lengthen, extend, stretch out; to protract, prolong, dwell over; to increase; to reach *or* hand (*sth. to s.o.*); to pay out (*rope, cable etc.*); to spin out (*money etc.*); ***alargar el paso,*** to lengthen one's stride, hurry; ***alargar el dinero*** (***el sueldo***), to spin out one's money (salary), make one's money (salary) go a long way;

alargar las uñas, to show one's claws *or* teeth. — **alargarse,** *v.r.* to get longer, become prolonged; to expatiate, dwell; to go *or* pop around; ***los días se van alargando,*** the days are gradually drawing out; ***se alargó mucho en su conferencia,*** he made his lecture very long; ***me voy a alargar a la casa de al lado,*** I'm just going to drop in next door.

alarguez, *n.m.* (*bot.*) dog-rose.

alaria, *n.f.* potter's finishing iron.

alarida, *n.f.* hue and cry; yelling; baying.

alarido, *n.m.* yell, howl, scream; ***pegar un alarido,*** to let out a yell.

alarifazgo, *n.m.* (*Arab.*) office of builder.

alarife, *n.m.* architect, builder, clerk of works.

alarije, *n.f.* grape.

alarma, *n.m.* alarm, alert, warning; ***falsa alarma,*** false alarm; ***dar la alarma,*** to raise the alarm.

alarmador, -ra, *a.* alarming. — *n.m.f.* alarmist.

alarmante, *a.* alarming.

alarmar, *v.t.* to alarm, alert; to call to arms.

alarmativo, -va, *a.* alarming.

alármega, *n.f.* (*bot.*) wild rue.

alarmista, *a.* alarming. — *n.m.* alarmist, scaremonger.

alaroz, *n.m.* framework (*door*).

alastrar, *v.t.* to throw back (*the ears*); (*naut.*) to ballast. — **alastrarse,** *v.r.* to cower, squat close, lie flat (*of game*).

alátere, *n.m.* (*coll.*) side-kick.

alaterno, *n.m.* (*bot.*) mock-privet, buckthorn.

alatinado, -da, *a.* Latinized; affected.

alatrón, *n.m.* froth of saltpetre; purified saltpetre.

alaureado, -da, *a.* laurel-like.

alavanco, *n.m.* wild duck.

alavense, alavés, -vesa, *a., n.m.f.* (*native*) of Alava.

alazán, -zana, alazano, -na, *a.* sorrel-coloured, chestnut-coloured. — *n.m.f.* sorrel horse. — *n.f.* wine press; oil press.

alazo, *n.m.* blow with a wing.

alazor, *n.m.* (*bot.*) bastard saffron.

alba (I), *n.f.* dawn, first light; alb, white vestment; (*sl.*) sheet; ***al alba,*** at daybreak; ***al quebrar, romper, rayar del alba,*** at the first light of day.

albaca, *n.f.* (*bot.*) sweet-basil.

albacara, *n.f.* (*fort.*) round tower, enclosing bailey.

albacea, *n.m.f.* testamentary executor *or* executrix.

albaceazgo, *n.m.* executorship.

albacora, *n.f.* (*ichth.*) tunny; (*bot.*) early large fig.

albada, *n.f.* morning serenade; (*prov., bot.*) soapwort; (*Mex.*) attack at dawn.

albahaca, *n.f.* (*bot.*) sweet-basil.

albahaquero, *n.m.* flowerpot.

albaicín, *n.m.* hilly quarter (of a town).

albaida, *n.f.* (*bot.*) shrubby gypsophila.

albaire, *n.m.* (*sl.*) hen's egg.

albalá, *n.m.f.* royal letters patent; statement; proof.

albanado, -da, *a.* (*sl.*) sleepy, asleep.

albando, -da, *a.* incandescent, white-hot (*metals*).

albanega, *n.f.* hair-net; net for catching partridges *or* rabbits.

albaneguero, -ra, *n.m.f.* (*sl.*) player at dice.

albanés, -nesa, *a., n.m.f.* Albanian.

Albania, *n.f.* Albania.

albañal, *n.m.* sewer, drain; dung-heap; ***salir uno por el albañal,*** to come out badly in an affair.

albañil, *n.m.* mason, bricklayer.

albañilear, *v.t.* to build, construct.

albañilería, *n.f.* masonry; brickwork, bricklaying.

albaquía, *n.f.* remnant, residue, balance.

albar, *a.* white.

albaracino, -na, *a.* leprous.

albarada, *n.f.* dry-stone wall; temporary whiteness.

albarán, *n.m.* placard announcing apartments to let; (public) document.

albarazado, -da, *a.* affected with white leprosy; marbled; variegated; pale, whitish; (*Mex.*) cross-bred of Chinese and Indian; ***uva albarazada,*** marble-coloured grape.

albarazo, *n.m.* white leprosy.

albarca, *n.f.* sandal.

albarcoque, *n.m.* apricot.

albarcoquero, *n.m.* apricot-tree.

albarda, *n.f.* packsaddle; ***albarda sobre albarda,*** more still, yet more of the same thing.

albardado, -da, *a.* having different-coloured skin at the loins (*cattle*); (*prov.*) meat in butter.

albardar, *v.t.* to put a packsaddle on; to lard (*fowls*).

albardear, *v.t.* (*Hisp. Am.*) to annoy, pester, nettle.

albardela, *n.f.* small saddle.

albardería, *n.f.* packsaddle shop *or* trade.

albardero, -ra, *n.m.f.* packsaddle maker *or* seller.

albardilla, *n.f.* batter; small packsaddle; coping-stone; border (of a garden bed); wool-tuft; sadiron holder; lardon.

albardillar, *v.t.* to hood (*a hawk*); to lard (*fowls*).

albardín, *n.m.* (*bot.*) mat-weed.

albardón, *n.m.* large packsaddle.

albardoncillo, *n.m.* small packsaddle.

albardonería, *n.f.* packsaddle trade *or* shop.

albardonero, *n.m.* packsaddle maker.

albarejo, albarigo, *n.m.* pure, summer *or* white wheat.

albareque, *n.m.* fishing-net.

albarico, *n.m.* white wheat; summer wheat.

albaricoque, *n.m.* apricot.

albaricoquero, *n.m.* apricot-tree.

albarillo, *n.m.* rapid guitar strumming; (*bot.*) white apricot.

albarizo, -za, *a.* whiting (*earth*). — *n.m.* dishcloth. — *n.f.* salt-water lagoon.

albarrada, *n.f.* dry wall; earth wall; trench, ditch; enclosure; earthenware jar.

albarrana, *n.f.* (*bot.*) ***cebolla albarrana,*** squill-onion; ***torre albarrana,*** watch-tower.

albarranilla, *n.f.* squill-onion.

albarraz, *n.m.* (*bot.*) louse-wort; (*med.*) white leprosy.

albarrazar [C], *v.t.* to dye.

albarsa, *n.f.* fisherman's basket.

albatoza, *n.f.* small covered boat; dinghy.

albatros, *n.m. inv.* (*orn.*) albatross.

albayaldar, *v.t.* to cover with white lead, give the colour of white lead to.

albayalde, *n.m.* white-lead, ceruse.

albazano, -na, *a.* dark chestnut.

albear, *n.m.* clay-pit, marl-pit, loam-pit; lime-pit. — *v.i.* to whiten, show white; (*Hisp. Am.*) to rise early.

albedrío, *n.m.* free-will; (*law*) precedent, unwritten law; ***libre albedrío,*** free-will; will; impulsiveness, wilfulness; ***al albredrío de uno,*** according to one's pleasure *or* desire, as one likes; ***hazlo a tu albedrío,*** do as you please.

albéitar, *n.m.* veterinary surgeon.

albeitería, *n.f.* veterinary surgery.

albellanino, *n.m.* (*bot.*) cornel tree.

albellón, *n.m.* sewer.

albenda, *n.f.* hangings of white linen.

albendera, *n.f.* gadabout.

albengala, *n.f.* turban gauze.

albéntola, *n.f.* fine fishing-net.

alberca, *n.f.* pond, pool (*esp. for irrigation*); ***en alberca,*** roofless.

albercoque, *n.m.* apricot.

albérchiga, *n.f.*, **albérchigo,** *n.m.* clingstone peach.

alberchiguero, *n.m.* clingstone peach-tree.

albergar [B], *v.t.* to lodge, accommodate, house; to shelter; to harbour, foster, cherish; ***albergar esperanzas,*** to harbour *or* cherish hopes. — **albergar(se),** *v.i.* (*v.r.*) to lodge; to take shelter.

albergue, *n.m.* lodging, shelter; hostel; refuge, hut; ***albergue de turismo,*** tourist hotel.

alberguería, *n.f.* poor-house; asylum; place of shelter.

albericoque, *n.m.* apricot.

albero, -ra, *a.* white. — *n.m.* whitish earth; dish-cloth.

alberquero, *n.m.* pool tender, one who tends pools.

Alberto, *n.m.* Albert.

albica, *n.f.* white clay.

albicante, *a.* whitening, bleaching.

albicaudo, -da, *a.* (*zool.*) white-tailed.

albicaulo, -la, *a.* (*bot.*) white-stemmed.

albiceps, *a. inv.* (*zool.*) white-headed, white-faced.

albicerato, -ta, *a.* colour of white wax. — *n.m.* fig.

albicie, *n.f.* whiteness.

albícolo, -la, *a.* (*zool.*) white-necked.

albido, -da, *a.* whitish.

albiflor, -ra, *a.* (*bot.*) white-flowered.

albigense, *a.*, *n.m.f.* Albigensian. — *n.m.pl.* (**albigenses**) Albigenses.

albihar, *n.m.* (*bot.*) ox-eye.

albilabro, -ra, *a.* white-lipped.

albilla, *n.f.*, **albillo** (1), *n.m.* early white grape.

albillo (2), *n.m.* wine of white grape.

albín, *n.m.* bloodstone; carmine pigment.

albina (1), *n.f.* salt-water marsh; salt; nitre.

albinismo, *n.m.* albinism.

albino, -na (2), *a.*, *n.m.* albino; (*Mex.*) octoroon. — *n.f.* albiness.

Albión, *n.f.* Albion.

albita, *n.f.* (*min.*) white feldspar, albite.

albitana, *n.f.* fence to enclose plants; (*naut.*) apron; (*naut.*) ***albitana del codaste,*** inner post.

albo, -ba (2), *a.* (*poet.*) snow white.

alboaire, *n.m.* glazed tile-work.

albogalla, *n.f.* gall-nut.

albogue, *n.m.* pastoral flute; cymbal.

alboguear, *v.i.* to play the ***albogue.***

alboguero, -ra, *n.m.f.* maker, seller *or* player of ***albogues.***

alboheza, *n.f.* (*bot.*) marsh-mallow.

albohol, *n.m.* (*bot.*) red poppy; bindweed.

albollón, *n.m.* drain, sewer.

albóndiga, *n.f.* meat ball, fish-cake.

albor, *n.m.* whiteness; dawn; (*pl.* ***albores***) dawn; early days.

alborada, *n.f.* dawn of day; (*mil.*) action fought at dawn; morning serenade.

albórbola, *n.f.* shouting and yelling (*for joy*).

alborear, *v.i.* to dawn.

alborga, *n.f.* mat-weed sandal.

albornía, *n.f.* large glazed jug.

alborno, *n.m.* (*bot.*) alburnum.

albornoz, *n.m.* burnoose; bathrobe.

alboronía, *n.f.* dish of aubergine *or* egg-plant, tomatoes, pumpkins and pimento.

alboroque, *n.m.* treat at the conclusion of a bargain, good-will.

alborotadizo, -za, *a.* easily excited.

alborotado, -da, *a.* tumultuous, in a state of uproar.

alborotador, -ra, *a.* riotous; agitating. — *n.m.f.* agitator, rioter.

alborotapueblos, *n.m. inv.* rabble-rouser; (*coll.*) gay noisy fellow.

alborotar, *v.t.* to stir up, arouse, excite, agitate; to set in a state of uproar; ***alborotar la calle,*** to disturb the neighbourhood. — **alborotar(se),** *v.i.* (*v.r.*) to get excited; to riot; to make a rumpus, create uproar; (*naut.*) to become rough (*sea*).

alboroto, *n.m.* disturbance, riot, tumult, turmoil; outcry, hubbub, din, uproar.

alborozador, -ra, *a.* mirthful, gay, creating joy. — *n.m.f.* promoter of mirth *or* gaiety.

alborozar [C], *v.t.* to make joyful *or* joyous, fill with delight, exhilarate.

alborozo, *n.m.* joy, delight, exhilaration.

albotín, *n.m.* (*bot.*) terebinth.

albrán, *n.m.* young duck.

albricias, *n.f.pl.* reward for good news; present. — *interj.* hurray! jolly good! congratulations!

albuco, *n.m.* (*bot.*) asphodel.

albudeca, *n.f.* inferior watermelon.

albufera, *n.f.* (large salt-water) lagoon.

albugíneo, -nea, *a.* (*zool.*) entirely white.

albugo, *n.m.* (*med.*) leucoma.

albuhera, *n.f.* lake, lagoon; irrigation pool.

álbum, *n.m.* album; ***álbum de recortes,*** scrap-book.

albumen, *n.m.* (*bot.*) albumen.

albúmina, *n.f.* (*chem.*) albumin.

albuminado, -da, *a.* albuminous.

albuminar, *v.t.* (*phot.*) to albumenize.

albuminoideo, -dea, *a.* albuminoid.

albuminoso, -sa, *a.* albuminous.

albur (1), *n.m.* (*ichth.*) dace.

albur (2), *n.m.* risk, chance; first draw (at monte); ***correr un albur,*** to run a risk; (*pl.* **albures**) card game.

albura, *n.f.* perfect whiteness; white of egg; (*bot.*) alburnum.

alburno, *n.m.* (*bot.*) alburnum; (*ichth.*) ablet.

alca, *n.f.* (*orn.*) razorbill.

alcabala, *n.f.* excise, sales tax; ***alcabala del viento,*** duty paid by a visiting merchant.

alcabalatorio, *n.m.* tax-register.

alcabalero, *n.m.* tax-gatherer, revenue officer.

alcabor, *n.m.* (*prov.*) flue (*of chimney*).

alcacel, alcacer, *n.m.* green barley; barley field.

alcací, alcacil, *n.m.* (*bot.*) wild artichoke.

alcachofa, *n.f.* (*bot.*) artichoke.

alcachofado, -da, *a.* like an artichoke. — *n.m.* dish of artichokes.

alcachofal, *n.m.* artichoke bed *or* field.

alcachofero, -ra, *a.* (*bot.*) producing *or* selling artichokes. — *n.m.f.* seller of artichokes. — *n.f.* artichoke plant.

alcahaz, *n.m.* aviary.

alcahazada, *n.f.* cageful of birds.

alcahazar [C], *v.t.* to cage (*birds*).

alcahuete, -ta, *n.m.f.* procurer, bawd, pimp, go-between; blind, cover; (*coll.*) concealer; gossip; (*theat.*) entr'acte curtain.

alcahuetear, *v.i.* to pimp, procure; to act as a go-between; to act as a front man.

alcahuetería, *n.f.* bawdry; procuring.

alcaicería, *n.f.* raw silk exchange.

alcaico, *a.*, *n.m.* alcaic (verse).

alcaide, *n.m.* governor of a castle; gaoler, warden.

alcaidesa, *n.f.* wife of a governor *or* gaoler.

alcaidía, *n.f.* office, dwelling *or* territory of a governor *or* gaoler.

alcaldada, *n.f.* petty tyranny, abuse of authority.

alcalde, *n.m.* mayor; game of cards; ***tener el padre alcalde,*** to have a friend at court; ***alcalde de monterilla,*** small-town mayor.

alcaldear, *v.i.* (*coll.*) to lord it; be bossy.

alcaldesa, *n.f.* mayoress.

alcaldía, *n.f.* office *or* jurisdiction of a mayor; town hall, city hall.

alcalescencia, *n.f.* (*chem.*) alkalization; alkalescence.

alcalescente, *a.* (*chem.*) alkalescent.

alcalescer, *v.t.* (*chem.*) to alkalify.
álcali, *n.m.* (*chem.*) alkali.
alcalífero, -ra, *a.* alkaline.
alcalificable, *a.* (*chem.*) alkalifiable.
alcalígeno, -na, *a.* alkaligenous, producing alkali.
alcalímetro, *n.m.* alkalimeter.
alcalinidad, *n.f.* alkalinity.
alcalino, -na, alcalizado, -da, *a.* (*chem.*) alkaline.
alcalización, *n.f.* (*chem.*) alkalization.
alcalizar [C], *v.t.* (*chem.*) to alkalize.
alcaloide, *n.m.* alkaloid.
alcaloideo, -dea, *a.* alkaloid.
alcaller, *n.m.* potter.
alcallería, *n.f.* pottery.
alcam, *n.m.* (*bot.*) bitter apple.
alcamonías, *n.f.pl.* spices.
alcana, *n.f.* (*bot.*) privet.
alcance, *n.m.* pursuit; arm's length, reach; (*com.*) deficit; scope, extent; range (*firearms*); compass; capacity, ability; supplement; extra collection (*post*); (*mil.*) soldier's net pay after official deductions; (*print.*) copy; stop-press; result; (*vet.*) tumour in the pastern; ***al alcance de,*** within reach *or* range of; ***al alcance de la mano,*** within reach; ***alcance agresivo,*** striking range; ***alcance de la vista*** (***del oído***), sight, eyeshot (earshot); ***de corto*** (***largo***) ***alcance,*** short- (long-) range; ***ir a alguien en los alcances,*** to spy upon; ***dar alcance a,*** to catch up with; ***de cortos alcances,*** of limited intelligence; ***seguirle a uno los alcances,*** to pursue s.o.
alcancía, *n.f.* money-box; earthenware ball filled with ashes *or* flowers for missiles; (*pl.*) (*mil.*) combustible balls; (*sl.*) brothel-keeper.
alcándara, *n.f.* perch (of a falcon); clothes-horse.
alcandía, *n.f.* (*bot.*) sorghum, Indian millet.
alcandial, *n.m.* millet field.
alcandora, *n.f.* beacon, bonfire; white tunic.
alcanfor, *n.m.* camphor.
alcanforada, *n.f.* camphor-scented shrub.
alcanforar, *v.t.* to camphorate. — **alcanforarse,** *v.r.* (*Hisp. Am.*) to vaporize, vanish, disappear.
alcanforero, *n.m.* camphor-tree.
alcántara, *n.f.* wooden receptacle for velvet in the loom.
alcantarilla, *n.f.* small bridge; culvert, drain, sewer.
alcantarillado, *n.m.* sewage system.
alcantarillar, *v.t.* to make sewers in.
alcantarillero, *n.m.* sewer-man.
alcanzable, *a.* within reach; obtainable; easily attained.
alcanzado, -da, *a.* hard up, short of money.
alcanzadura, *n.f.* (*vet.*) tumour in the pastern, attaint.
alcanzar [C], *v.t.* to attain, reach; to overtake, come *or* catch up with; to grasp, perceive, understand; to hit, strike; to be born early enough to know, to live long enough to know; ***alcanzar el blanco,*** to reach *or* strike the target; ***alcancé a mi bisabuelo,*** I knew my great-grandfather. — *v.i.* ***alcanzar a*** or ***hasta,*** to reach as far as, attain to; ***alcanzar a***+*infin.*, to manage to, succeed in; ***alcanzar para,*** to be sufficient for. — **alcanzarse,** *v.r. impers.* ***no se me alcanza cuál pueda ser su propósito,*** I can't understand, imagine *or* conceive what his object can be.
alcaparra, *n.f.* (*bot.*) caper.
alcaparrado, -da, *a.* dressed with capers. — *n.f.* portion of capers.
alcaparral, *n.m.* caper-field.
alcaparro, *n.m.*, **alcaparrera,** *n.f.* caper plant.
alcaparrón, *n.m.* (*bot.*) caper (*bud, berry*).
alcaparrosa, *n.f.* (*min.*) copperas.
alcaraván, *n.m.* (*orn.*) stone curlew.
alcaravea, *n.f.* (*bot.*) caraway (*seed, plant*).
alcarceña, *n.f.* (*bot.*) bitter-vetch; tare.
alcarcil, *n.m.* (*bot.*) wild artichoke.
alcarracería, *n.f.* earthenware factory *or* shop.
alcarracero, -ra, *n.m.f.* potter; shelf for earthenware.
alcarraza, *n.f.* clay jar.
alcarria, *n.f.* barren plateau.
alcartaz, *n.m.* paper cone.
alcatara, *n.f.* still.
alcatifa, *n.f.* fine carpet *or* rug; (*mas.*) layer of earth.
alcatife, *n.m.* (*sl.*) silk.
alcatraz, *n.m.* (*orn.*) gannet, solan; (*bot.*) arum.
alcaucil, *n.m.* wild artichoke.
alcauciar, *v.t.* (*Hisp. Am.*) to shoot dead.
alcaudón, *n.m.* (*orn.*) butcher-bird, shrike.
alcayata, *n.f.* spike; hook.
alcazaba, *n.f.* (*fort.*) citadel.
alcázar, *n.m.* castle; fortress; fortified palace; (*naut.*) quarter-deck.
alcazuz, *n.m.* liquorice.
alce, *n.m.* (*zool.*) moose, elk; cut (*cards*); gathering (*sugar cane*); (*print.*) gathering for binding.
alcedo, *n.m.* maple grove.
alcino, *n.m.* (*bot.*) wild basil.
alción, *n.m.* (*orn.*) halcyon, kingfisher; (*astron.*) principal star of the Pleiades.
alcista, *a.* rising, upward. — *a.*, *n.m.* (*com.*) bull.
alcoba, *n.f.* bedroom; ***alcoba de respeto,*** guest room.
alcocarra, *n.f.* gesture, grimace.
alcohol, *n.m.* alcohol; spirit; (*min.*) galena; ***alcohol absoluto,*** absolute alcohol; ***alcohol amílico,*** amyl alcohol; ***alcohol de arder*** or ***desnaturalizado,*** methylated spirit, (*Am.*) denatured alcohol; ***alcohol de grano,*** grain alcohol; ***alcohol de madera,*** wood alcohol; ***alcohol etílico,*** ethyl alcohol; ***alcohol metílico,*** methyl alcohol; ***alcohol para fricciones,*** surgical spirit, (*Am.*) rubbing alcohol; ***alcohol vinílico,*** vinyl alcohol; ***lamparilla de alcohol,*** spirit lamp, (*Am.*) alcohol lamp.
alcoholado, -da, *a.* of a darker colour round the eyes (*cattle*); alcoholized. — *n.m.* (*med.*) alcoholized compound.
alcoholar, *v.t.* to distil alcohol from; to dye *or* paint with antimony; (*naut.*) to tar after caulking; to pulverize.
alcoholera, *n.f.* vessel for alcohol *or* antimony.
alcohólico, -ca, *a.* alcoholic.
alcoholímetro, alcoholómetro, *n.m.* alcoholometer, breathalyser.
alcoholismo, *n.m.* alcoholism.
alcoholización, *n.f.* (*chem.*) alcoholization.
alcoholizado, -da, *a.* alcoholized. — *n.m.f.* alcoholic.
alcoholizar [C], *v.t.* to alcoholize; to fortify (*wines*). — **alcoholizarse,** *v.r.* to become alcoholic.
alcolla, *n.f.* large glass bulb *or* decanter.
alcor, *n.m.* hill, rise.
Alcorán, *n.m.* Koran.
alcoranista, *n.m.* Koran expounder *or* scholar.
alcorcí, *n.m.* jewel *or* valuable trinket.
alcornocal, *n.m.* plantation of cork-trees.
alcornoque, *n.m.* (*bot.*) cork oak; (*fig.*) blockhead.
alcornoqueño, -ña, *a.* belonging to the cork-tree.
alcorque, *n.m.* cork-wood clog *or* sole; hollow for irrigation water.
alcorza, *n.f.* sugar icing.
alcorzado, -da, *a.* iced (*cake*).
alcorzar [C], *v.t.* to ice (*cake*); to polish, adorn.
alcotán, *n.m.* (*orn.*) hobby hawk.
alcotana, *n.f.* (*build.*) pickaxe, mattock.
alcrebite, *n.m.* sulphur.
alcribís, *n.m.* tuyère, tewel.
alcubilla, *n.f.* reservoir.

alcucero, -ra, *a.* (*coll.*) greedy; sweet-toothed. — *n.m.f.* maker *or* seller of tin oil-bottles *or* cruets.
alcucilla, *n.f.* small oil-can.
alcurnia, *n.f.* ancestry, lineage.
alcuza, *n.f.* oil-bottle; cruet; oil-can, oiler; ***razonar como una alcuza,*** to use absurd arguments.
alcuzada, *n.f.* cruetful of oil.
alcuzazo, *n.m.* blow with an oil-cruet *or* oil-can.
alcuzcuz, *n.m.* couscous.
aldaba, *n.f.* knocker; door-handle, door-latch; cross-bar; hitching ring; ***agarrarse de*** or ***tener buenas aldabas,*** to have pull, influence *or* friends in the right place.
aldabada, *n.f.* knock, rap with knocker; (*fig.*) twinge of conscience.
aldabazo, aldabonazo, *n.m.* loud knock.
aldabear, *v.i.* to rap *or* knock at the door.
aldabeo, *n.m.* knocking.
aldabía, *n.f.* cross-beam.
aldabilla, *n.f.* small knocker, latch, catch.
aldabón, *n.m.* large knocker; trunk-handle *or* haft.
aldea, *n.f.* small village.
aldeaniego, -ga, *a.* belonging to a village; rustic.
aldeano, -na, *a.* village, country, rustic. — *n.m.f.* villager, countryman, countrywoman.
aldehido, *n.m.* aldehyde.
aldehuela, *n.f.* little village, wretched *or* miserable (little) village.
aldeorrio, aldeorro, *n.m.* (*contempt.*) insignificant *or* miserable little village.
alderredor, *adv.* around [ALREDEDOR].
aldino, *a.* Aldine.
aldiza, *n.f.* (*bot.*) cornflower.
aldora, *n.f.* sorghum.
aldrán, *n.m.* country wine peddler.
aleación, *n.f.* alloy.
alear (1), *v.t.* to alloy.
alear (2), *v.i.* to flutter; to move the wings *or* arms quickly; to convalesce.
aleatorio, -ria, *a.* fortuitous, chance; relating to games of chance; (*law*) aleatory.
alebrarse [1], **alebronarse,** *v.r.* to lie flat; to cower.
aleccionador, -ra, *a.* instructive; ***ésta ha sido una experiencia aleccionadora,*** this experience has taught me a lesson *or* opened my eyes.
aleccionamiento, *n.m.* instruction.
aleccionar, *v.t.* to teach, instruct.
alece, aleche, *n.m.* (*ichth.*) anchovy; ragout of fish-liver.
alecrín, *n.m.* (*Hisp. Am.*) verbenaceous tree; (*ichth.*) tiger-shark.
alectórico, -ca, *a.* relative to cocks; cock-like.
alechigar [B], *v.t.* (*obs.*) to soften; to sweeten. — **alechigarse,** *v.r.* to turn milky.
alechugado, -da, *a.* pleated, curled.
alechugar [B], *v.t.* to curl like a lettuce leaf; to plait; to flute.
alechuguinado, -da, *a.* dandy-like, dude-like, foppish.
aleda, *n.f.* ***cera aleda,*** propolis, bee-glue.
aledaño, -ña, *a.* bordering, confining, neighbouring. — *n.m.* boundary, border, limit; (*pl.* **aledaños**) surroundings, outskirts.
alefanginas, *n.f.pl.* purgative pills made of spices.
alefris, *n.m. inv.*, **alefriz,** *n.m.* (*naut.*) mortise, rabbet (*on the keel, stem and sternpost*).
alefrizar [C], *v.t.* (*naut.*) to mortise, rabbet.
alegación, *n.f.* allegation, argument.
alegamar, *v.t.* to fertilize with mud *or* silt.
alegar [B], *v.t.* to allege; to put forward; to adduce. — *v.i.* to plead; ***¿tiene Vd. algo que alegar?*** have you anything to say (in your defence)?
alegato, *n.m.* (*law*) allegation; presentation, summing-up.
alegoría, *n.f.* allegory.
alegórico, -ca, *a.* allegorical.
alegorista, *n.m.f.* allegorist.
alegorizar [C], *v.t.* to turn into allegory, allegorize.
alegra, *n.f.* (*naut.*) reamer, auger.
alegrador, -ra, *a.* cheering. — *n.m.* spill (*for lighting cigars*); (*pl.* **alegradores**) (*tauro.*) banderillas.
alegrar (1), *v.t.* to cheer (up), make glad *or* happy, delight; to stir up (*fire*); to brighten, enliven. — **alegrarse,** *v.r.* to be glad, delighted; (*coll.*) to get tipsy *or* merry; ***alegrarse de, con*** or ***por,*** to be glad of *or* because of; ***alegrarse de*** + *inf.*, to be glad to + *inf.*
alegrar (2), *v.t.* (*naut.*, *mech.*) to widen (a hole).
alegre, *a.* merry, cheerful, happy, gay, sunny; reckless; tipsy; ***un cielo alegre,*** a bright sky; ***alegre de cascos,*** fast.
alegría, *n.f.* gaiety, joy; cheerfulness, happiness.
alegrillo, -lla, *a.* rather merry.
alegro, *n.m.* (*mus.*) allegro.
alegrón, *n.m.* (*coll.*) sudden joy; ***me llevé un alegrón,*** I was really delighted *or* bucked.
alejamiento, *n.m.* withdrawal; distance; estrangement.
Alejandría, *n.f.* Alexandria; Alessandria.
alejandrino, -na, *a.* of *or* from Alexandria; relating to Alexander the Great; (*poet.*) ***verso alejandrino,*** Alexandrine verse.
Alejandro, *n.m.* Alexander.
alejar, *v.t.* to move aside, move away; to keep at a distance; to drive away. — **alejarse,** *v.r.* to go *or* move away, move to a distance, move further off.
alejijas, *n.f.pl.* barley porridge.
Alejo, *n.m.* Alexis.
alejur, *n.m.* paste of nuts and honey.
alelado, -da, *a.* stupefied, bewildered.
alelamiento, *n.m.* stupidity, foolishness; day dreaming.
alelar, *v.t.* to make stupid; to bewilder. — **alelarse,** *v.r.* to become stupefied.
alelí, *n.m.* wallflower.
aleluya, *n.f.* hallelujah; joy, merriment; Easter-time; (*bot.*) wood-sorrel; (*pl.* **aleluyas**) Easter tract; (*coll.*) poor verses, doggerel; very thin person *or* animal.
alema, *n.f.* quantity of water allotted for purposes of irrigation.
alemán, -mana (1), *a.*, *n.m.f.* German. — *n.m.* German (*language*).
alemana (2), **alemanda,** *n.f.* ancient Spanish dance of German *or* Flemish origin.
Alemania, *n.f.* Germany; (**la**) ***Alemania Occidental,*** West Germany; (**la**) ***Alemania Oriental,*** East Germany.
alemánico, -ca, *a.* Germanic.
alemanisco, -ca, *a.* applied to cloth made in Germany; huckaback; damask (*table-linen*).
alenguar, *v.t.* to agree about *or* negotiate concerning (*pasture lands* or *pasturage*).
alentada (1), *n.f.* long *or* deep breath; ***de una alentada,*** in one breath.
alentado, -da (2), *a.* spirited, courageous; haughty; (*Hisp. Am.*) healthy, in good condition.
alentador, -ra, *a.* encouraging, cheering.
alentar [1], *v.t.* to encourage, inspire, cheer; to comfort; ***alentar con la esperanza,*** to encourage with hope; ***alentar a,*** to encourage to. — *v.i.* to breathe.
aleonado, -da, *a.* lion-like; tawny.
aleonar, *v.t.* (*Hisp. Am.*) to stir up, agitate, arouse.
alepantado, -da, *a.* (*Hisp. Am.*) bemused, distracted.
alépido, -da, *a.* devoid of scales *or* shell.
alepín, *n.m.* bombazine.
alerce, *n.m.* (*bot.*) larch-tree; ***alerce africano,*** sandarac.

alergia, *n.f.* allergy.
alérgico, -ca, *a.* allergic.
alero, *n.m.* eaves; gable-end, corona; water-table; hood-moulding; splash-board; (*pl.*) partridge snares.
alerón, *n.m.* (*aer.*) aileron.
alertar, *v.t.* to alert, make watchful; to put on guard.
alerto, -ta, *a.* alert, watchful, vigilant. — **alerta,** *adv.* on the alert; ***estar alerta,*** to be on the alert. — **alerta,** *n.m.* (*mil.*) alert; watchword.
alerzal, *n.m.* larch grove.
alesna, *n.f.* awl.
alesnado, -da, *a.* awl-shaped, pointed.
aleta, *n.f.* small wing; (*fish's*) fin; (*arch.*) aletta; (*mech.*) leaf (*of a hinge*), teeth (*of a pinion*), blade (*of a screw-propeller*); fender, mudguard (*of car*); (*pl.*) (*naut.*) fashion pieces.
aletado, -da, *a.* winged, finned. — *n.f.* stroke *or* flap (*of wings*).
aletargamiento, *n.m.* state of lethargy.
aletargar [B], *v.t.* to make lethargic. — **aletargarse,** *v.r.* to fall into lethargy; to go into hibernation.
aletazo, *n.m.* blow with the wing *or* fin.
aletear, *v.i.* to flutter, flap, beat wings *or* fins.
aleteo, *n.m.* beating, fluttering *or* flapping of wings; (*fig.*) palpitation.
aleto, *n.m.* osprey.
aletría, *n.f.* (*prov.*) vermicelli, noodles.
aleudar, *v.t.* to leaven. — **aleudarse,** *v.r.* to become fermented, rise.
aleutiano, -na, *a., n.m.f.* Aleutian, Aleut.
aleve, *a.* treacherous, perfidious; ***acción aleve,*** act of treachery. — *n.m.f.* traitor.
alevilla, *n.f.* white moth.
alevinador, -ra, *a., n.m.f.* (one) who stocks ponds with fry.
alevinamiento, *n.m.* breeding young fish; stocking (*water*) with young fish.
alevinar, *v.t.* to stock with fry.
alevino, *n.m.* (*ichth.*) fry, young fish.
alevosa (1), *n.f.* ranula, tumour under the tongue.
alevosía, *n.f.* treachery, perfidy, breach of faith; ***con alevosía,*** treacherously; ***con premeditación y alevosía,*** with malice aforethought.
alevoso, -sa (2), *a.* treacherous; malicious. — *n.m.f.* traitor.
alexifármaco, -ca, *a.* (*med.*) alexipharmic, antidotal. — *n.m.* antidote.
aleya, *n.f.* verse of Koran.
alezna, *n.f.* (*prov.*) black mustard seed.
alezo, *n.m.* (*med.*) draw-sheet; large bandage (*maternity*).
alfa, *n.f.* alpha, beginning, commencement.
alfábega, *n.f.* (*bot.*) sweet-basil.
alfabético, -ca, *a.* alphabetical.
alfabetizar, *v.t.* to place in alphabetical order; to teach how to read and write.
alfabeto, *n.m.* alphabet.
alfaguara, *n.f.* copious spring.
alfaida, *n.f.* tidewater (*in a river*).
alfajía, *n.f.* (*carp.*) wood frame for windows and doors; lintel.
alfajor, *n.m.* sweetmeat.
alfalfa, *n.f.*, **alfalfe,** *n.m.* (*bot.*) lucerne, alfalfa.
alfalfal, alfalfar, *n.m.* lucerne-field.
alfana, *n.f.* strong and spirited horse.
alfandoque, *n.m.* (*Hisp. Am.*) paste made with molasses, cheese and ginger.
alfaneque, *n.m.* (*orn.*) lanner; tent, booth.
alfanjado, -da, *a.* shaped like a cutlass.
alfanjazo, *n.m.* wound with a cutlass.
alfanje, *n.m.* cutlass, scimitar; (*ichth.*) sword-fish.
alfanjete, *n.m.* small cutlass.
alfanjón, *n.m.* large, powerful cutlass.
alfanjonazo, *n.m.* cut with a large cutlass.
alfaque, *n.m.* shoal, sand-bar.
alfaquí, *n.m.* Mohammedan doctor of laws.
alfar (1), *n.m.* pottery; clay.
alfar (2), *v.i.* to gallop stiffly.
alfaraz, *n.m.* Moorish horse for light cavalry.
alfarda, *n.f.* (*prov.*) duty paid for the irrigation of lands; (*arch.*) thin beam.
alfardero, *n.m.* (*prov.*) collector of duty for irrigation.
alfardilla, *n.f.* gold *or* silver braid; (*prov.*) small tax for cleaning culverts.
alfardón, *n.m.* duty paid for irrigation; (*mech.*) washer.
alfareme, *n.m.* Arab head-dress.
alfarería, *n.f.* pottery.
alfarero, *n.m.* potter.
alfargo, *n.m.* master beam of an oil-mill.
alfarje, *n.m.* lower stone of an oil-mill; ceiling ornamented with carved work; wainscot.
alfarijía, *n.f.* (*carp.*) wood frame for windows and doors.
alfarma, *n.f.* (*bot.*) wild rue.
alfayate, *n.m.* (*obs.*) tailor.
alféizar, *n.m.* (*arch.*) embrasure; window sill *or* ledge.
alfeñicado, -da, *a.* weakly, delicate; (*coll.*) affected.
alfeñicarse [A], *v.r.* to become thin *or* delicate; (*coll.*) to be fussy.
alfeñique, *n.m.* sugar paste; sugar baby; (*coll.*) delicate person; affectation; make-up.
alferazgo, *n.m.*, **alferecía** (1), *n.f.* ensigncy, dignity of an ensign.
alferecía (2), *n.f.* epilepsy (*in infants*).
alférez, *n.m.* standard-bearer; ensign; second lieutenant; ***alférez de navío,*** lieutenant.
alficoz, *n.m.* cucumber.
alfil, *n.m.* bishop (*chess*).
alfiler, *n.m.* pin; scarf-pin; brooch; ***alfiler de París,*** wire nail; (*pl.*) pin-money; ***con todos sus alfileres, con veinticinco alfileres,*** dressed *or* dolled up, dressed up to the nines; ***no cabe (ni) un alfiler,*** there's not a scrap of room, it's crammed *or* packed; ***tener*** or ***llevar la lección*** or ***la asignatura cogida*** or ***prendida con alfileres,*** to have mugged *or* swotted up the lesson *or* the subject very shakily; ***estar cogido*** or ***prendido con alfileres,*** to be put together with spit and glue, be shaky.
alfilerazo, *n.m.* pinprick, jab; (*fig.*) dig, hint.
alfilerera (1), *n.f.* seed of the geranium and other plants of the same natural order.
alfilerero, -ra (2), *n.m.f.* maker *or* seller of pins.
alfiletero, *n.m.* pin-case, needle-case.
alfitete, *n.m.* paste made of coarse wheat flour *or* semolina.
alfolí, *n.m.* granary; salt warehouse.
alfoliar [L], *v.t.* to store.
alfoliero, alfolinero, *n.m.* keeper of a granary *or* salt depot.
alfombra (1), *n.f.* carpet; rug.
alfombra (2), *n.f.* (*med.*) German measles.
alfombrado, *n.m.* carpeting; set of carpets.
alfombrar, *v.t.* to carpet.
alfombrero, -ra, *n.m.f.* carpet-maker *or* seller.
alfombrilla (1), *n.f.* small carpet, rug.
alfombrilla (2), *n.f.* (*med.*) German measles.
alfombrista, *n.m.* carpet dealer, sewer and layer.
alfóncigo, alfónsigo, *n.m.* pistachio; pistachio-tree.
alfonsí, alfonsino, -na (1), *a.* Alphonsine, of King Alfonso.
alfonsina (2), *n.f.* solemn rite performed in the University of Alcalá.
Alfonso, *n.m.* Alfonso, Alphonse.

alforfón, *n.m.* (*bot.*) buckwheat.
alforja, *n.f.* saddle-bag, knapsack; provision; ***hacer alforjas,*** to make preparations; ***para este viaje no se necesitan alforjas,*** no preparations are needed for this journey.
alforjero, -ra, *n.m.f.* maker *or* seller of saddle-bags; one who carries the bags with provisions. — *n.m.* lay brother who begs alms.
alforza, *n.f.* horizontal pleat, tuck; hem; (*coll.*) clipping; large seam; scar; secret place (*heart*).
alforzar [C], *v.t.* to pleat, tuck.
alfoz, *n.m.* narrow mountain pass; district; dependent area; outskirts, environs.
Alfredo, *n.m.* Alfred.
alga, *n.f.* (*bot.*) alga, seaweed.
algaba, *n.f.* wood, forest.
algaceo, -cea, *a.* (*bot.*) like seaweed.
algadonera, *n.f.* (*bot.*) cudweed.
algaida, *n.f.* ridge of shifting sand; sand-dune; jungle, brush.
algaido, -da, *a.* (*prov.*) thatched.
algalaba, *n.f.* (*bot.*) white bryony, wild hops.
algalia (1), *n.f.* civet, civet-cat.
algalia (2), *n.f.* (*med.*) catheter.
algaliar [L], *v.t.* to perfume with civet.
algaliero, -ra, *a., n.m.f.* (one) who likes perfumes, especially civet.
algara (1), *n.f.* thin film (*covering an egg, onion etc.*).
algara (2), *n.f.* foraging party of cavalry; cavalry raid, foray; scouting expedition.
algarabía, *n.f.* Arabic; (*coll.*) gabble, gibberish; din, clamour, uproar; (*bot.*) centaury.
algaracear, *v.i.* (*Hisp. Am.*) to snow lightly.
algarada, *n.f.* outcry; sudden onslaught; surprise attack; ancient battering-ram; catapult.
algarero, -ra, *a.* prating, chattering, talkative. — *n.m.* raiding cavalryman.
algarrada, *n.f.* driving bulls into the pen; bull-baiting; battering-ram.
algarroba, *n.f.* (*bot.*) carob bean, locust bean.
algarrobal, *n.m.* carob grove.
algarrobilla, *n.f.* (*bot.*) vetch.
algarrobo, *n.m.* (*bot.*) carob-tree.
algazara, *n.f.* Moorish battle cry; uproar, din; riot.
algazul, *n.m.* (*bot.*) ice plant.
álgebra, *n.f.* algebra; (*med.*) art of setting joints.
algebraico, -ca, algébrico, -ca, *a.* algebraic.
algebrista, *n.m.* algebraist; bone-setter.
algente, *a.* (*poet.*) algid, cold.
algidez, *n.f.* (*med.*) icy coldness.
álgido, -da, *a.* (*med.*) algid, icy; culminating; ***punto álgido,*** culminating point, climax.
algo, *adv.* somewhat, rather, a little; ***algo difícil,*** somewhat difficult. — *pron.* something; ***algo por el estilo,*** something of the sort; ***¿algo más?*** anything else? ***más vale algo que nada,*** a little is better than nothing; ***algo es algo,*** it's something.
algodón, *n.m.* cotton; cotton wool; (*bot.*) cotton-plant; ***algodón en rama,*** raw cotton; ***algodón de altura,*** upland cotton; ***algodón hidrófilo,*** cotton wool, (*Am.*) absorbent cotton; ***algodón pólvora,*** guncotton; (*pl.*) silk *or* cotton fibres; ear plugs; ***criado entre algodones,*** molly-coddled; ***llevar, meter*** or ***tener entre algodones,*** to treat with excessive care, molly-coddle.
algodonal, *n.m.* cotton-plantation; cotton-plant.
algodonar, *v.t.* to cover *or* fill with cotton.
algodoncillo, *n.m.* milkweed.
algodonería, *n.f.* cotton-factory; cotton-trade.
algodonero, -ra, *a.* (appertaining to) cotton. — *n.m.f.* cotton dealer. — *n.m.* cotton-plant; cotton-wood poplar.
algodonoso, -sa, *a.* cottony, woolly, covered with thick down; insipid, tasteless (*certain fruits*).
algonquino, -na, *a.* (*philol.*) Algonquian. — *n.m.f.* Algonquin.
algorfa, *n.f.* grain loft.
algorín, *n.m.* olive bin.
algoritmia, *n.f.*, **algoritmo,** *n.m.* algorithm.
algoso, -sa, *a.* weedy, full of seaweed.
alguacil, *n.m.* alguazil; constable, peace-officer; bailiff; (*zool.*) short-legged spider, jumping spider.
alguacilazgo, *n.m.* office.
alguacilillo, *n.m.* horseman who heads the procession of bullfighters into the ring.
alguarín, *n.m.* (*prov.*) store-room; bucket in which flour falls from the mill-stones.
alguaza, *n.f.* (*prov.*) hinge.
alguien, *pron.* somebody, someone.
algún, *a.* some, any (*before masc. sing. nouns and adjs.*). — *adv.* ***algún tanto,*** somewhat, a little, rather.
alguno, -na, *a.* some, any; not any; ***alguno que otro,*** a few, one or two; ***alguna que otra vez,*** on the odd occasion; ***alguna vez,*** a few times, on occasion; ever; ***¿lo ha visto Vd. alguna vez?*** have you ever seen it?; ***no tengo dinero alguno,*** I have no money whatsoever. — *pron.* some one, someone.
alhadida, *n.f.* (*obs.*) copper sulphate.
alhaja, *n.f.* jewel, gem; (*fig.*) gem (*person, object of great value*); (*iron.*) ***una buena alhaja,*** a fine fellow.
alhajar, *v.t.* to bejewel, adorn; to fit up; to furnish.
alhamel, *n.m.* (*prov.*) beast of burden; labourer; muleteer.
alhandal, *n.m.* (*pharm.*) coloquintida, colocynth, bitter apple.
alharaca, *n.f.* clamour, outcry, hullabaloo, tremendous fuss; ***hacer alharacas,*** to make a tremendous hullabaloo *or* fuss.
alharaquiento, -ta, *a.* clamorous, strident.
alhárgama, alharma, *n.f.* (*bot.*) wild rue.
alhelí, *n.m.* (*bot.*) wallflower.
alheña, *n.f.* henna; powdered henna; blight, mildew; ***estar hecho alheña,*** to be worn out, fagged out.
alheñar, *v.t.* to dye with privet (*henna*). — **alheñarse,** *v.r.* to become mildewed (*corn*).
alhoja, *n.f.* skylark.
alholva, *n.f.* (*bot.*) fenugreek.
alhóndiga, *n.f.* public granary; wheat exchange.
alhondiguero, *n.m.* keeper of a public granary.
alhorma, *n.f.* Moorish camp *or* royal tent; Moorish sanctuary *or* place of refuge.
alhorre, *n.m.* (*med.*) meconium; skin eruption (*in the newly born*).
alhoz [ALFOZ].
alhucema, *n.f.* (*bot.*) lavender.
alhumajo, *n.m.* pine-needles.
ali, *n.m.* sequence of two *or* three playing cards.
aliabierto, -ta, *a.* open-winged, with wings spread.
aliacán, *n.m.* jaundice.
aliacanado, -da, *a.* jaundiced.
aliáceo, -cea, *a.* aliaceous, like garlic.
aliado, -da, *a.* allied, confederate. — *n.m.f.* ally.
aliadófilo, -la, *a.* pro-Ally.
aliaga, *n.f.* (*bot.*) furze, gorse.
aliagar, *n.m.* place covered with furze.
alianza, *n.f.* alliance; wedding ring; (*Bibl.*) covenant; ***Santa Alianza,*** Holy Alliance; ***Triple Alianza,*** Triple Alliance; ***Alianza para el Progreso,*** Alliance for Progress.
aliar [L], *v.t.* to ally. — **aliarse,** *v.r.* to become allied; to form an alliance.
aliara, *n.f.* horn goblet.
aliaria, *n.f.* (*bot.*) garlic mustard.
alible, *a.* nutritious, nourishing.
álica, *n.f.* pottage of spelt and pulse.

alicaído, -da, *a.* with drooping wings; (*coll.*) drooping, crestfallen, dejected.
alicántara, *n.f.* viper.
alicante, *n.m.* viper; nougat; Alicante wine.
alicantina (1), *n.f.* (*coll.*) artifice, stratagem, trick.
alicantino, -na (2), *a.*, *n.m.f.* (native) of Alicante.
alicario, -ria, *a.* relating to spelt. — *n.m.* spelt-miller.
alicatado, *n.m.* tiling.
alicatar, *v.t.* (*build.*) to tile.
alicates, *n.m.pl.* pliers.
Alicia, *n.f.* Alice; ***Alicia en el país de las Maravillas,*** Alice in Wonderland.
aliciente, *n.m.* inducement, incentive, attraction.
alicortar, *v.t.* to clip the wings of.
alicuanta, *a.* aliquant; ***parte alicuanta,*** aliquant number.
alícuota, *a.* aliquot, proportional; ***parte alícuota,*** aliquot number *or* part.
alidada, *n.f.* alidade, index of a quadrant; geometrical ruler.
alídeo, -dea, *a.* (*bot.*) similar to garlic.
alídico, -ca, *a.* mixed with garlic.
alienable, *a.* alienable, capable of alienation.
alienación, *n.f.* (*law, med.*) alienation; lunacy.
alienado, -da, *a.* insane. — *n.m.f.* insane person.
alienar, *v.t.* to alienate; to transfer (*property*).
alienista, *n.m.* (*med.*) alienist, mental specialist.
aliento, *n.m.* breath, breathing; spirit, courage; enterprise; scent; ***cobrar aliento,*** to revive, take heart; ***contener el aliento,*** to hold one's breath; ***dar aliento (a),*** to encourage; ***dejar sin aliento,*** to leave breathless; ***tomar aliento,*** to get one's breath; ***de mucho aliento,*** arduous (*work, task etc.*); ***de un aliento,*** in one breath; ***mal aliento,*** bad breath; ***nuevo aliento,*** second wind; ***sin aliento,*** out of breath.
alier, *n.m.* (*naut.*) rower; marine on watch.
alifa, *n.f.* (*prov.*) second-year sugar-cane.
alifafe, *n.m.* callous tumour on horse's hock; (*coll.*) chronic complaint.
alifar, *v.t.* (*prov.*) to polish, burnish.
alifara, *n.f.* (*prov.*) gratuity, tip; collation, lunch.
alifático, -ca, *a.* (*chem.*) aliphatic.
alífero, -ra, *a.* aliferous, winged.
aliforme, *a.* aliform, wing-shaped.
aligación, *n.f.*, **aligamiento,** *n.m.* alligation, mixture, union; tying *or* binding together.
aligar [B], *v.t.* to tie; to unite. — **aligarse,** *v.r.* to become united *or* allied.
aliger, *n.m.* cross guard (of a sword).
aligeramiento, *n.m.* alleviation, lightening; hastening.
aligerar, *v.t.* to lighten, alleviate; to ease; to hasten; to shorten. — **aligerarse,** *v.r.* to become lighter; to hurry.
alígero, -ra, *a.* (*poet.*) winged; fleet, swift.
aligustre, *n.m.* (*bot.*) privet.
aligustrón, *n.m.* (*bot.*) wax privet.
alijado, -da, *a.* (*naut.*) buoyant; eased, lightened, shortened.
alijador, -ra, *n.m.f.* smuggler; (*naut.*) lighterman; one who separates the seed from cotton; (*naut.*) ***lanchón alijador,*** lighter.
alijar (1), *n.m.* uncultivated ground; (*pl.*) common pasture land.
alijar (2), *v.t.* (*naut.*) to unload, lighten (*a ship*); to smuggle; to gin (*cotton*); to sandpaper.
alijarar, *v.t.* to divide (*waste lands*) for cultivation.
alijarero, *n.m.* cultivator of wasteland.
alijariego, -ga, *a.* relating to waste lands.
alijo, *n.m.* lighterage; ginning; smuggled goods, contraband cache.
alilaya, *n.f.* (*Hisp. Am.*) flimsy excuse.
alimaña, *n.f.* destructive animal *or* creature, beast of prey; (*pl.*) (*fig.*) vermin.
alimañero, *n.m.* gamekeeper who destroys ***alimañas.***
alimentación, *n.f.* nourishment, nutrition; feed, feeding; food, meals; ***alimentación general,*** general foodstuffs.
alimentador, -ra, *a.* nourishing, feeding. — *n.m.* feed-tank; feeder.
alimental, *a.* alimental, nutritive.
alimentante, *n.m.f.* (*law*) maintainer.
alimentar, *v.t.* to nourish, feed; to maintain, sustain; to nurture, nurse; to cherish, foster (*hopes etc.*). — *v.i.* to be nourishing; ***esto alimenta mucho,*** this is very nourishing. — **alimentarse,** *v.r.* to feed; ***alimentarse con*** or ***de,*** to feed on, live on.
alimentario, -ria, *a.* alimentary, nutritious.
alimenticio, -cia, *a.* nutritious; to do with food, of food; ***productos alimenticios,*** food products, foodstuffs.
alimentista, *n.m.f.* pensioner.
alimento, *n.m.* nourishment, nutriment, food; incentive, encouragement; (*pl.*) foodstuffs; alimony, allowance; ***alimento combustible, energético, respiratorio*** or ***termógeno,*** carbohydrate; ***alimento plástico*** or ***reparador,*** protein.
alimentoso, -sa, *a.* alimentary, nutritious.
álimo, *n.m.* (*bot.*) orach, mountain spinach.
alimoche, *n.m.* (*orn.*) vulture, Pharaoh's chicken.
alimón, *adv.* (*tauro.*) ***al alimón,*** with the cape held by two bullfighters; ***hacer al alimón,*** to do together *or* alternating one with another (*of two persons*).
alimonado, -da, *a.* lemon-like, lemon-shaped.
alimonarse, *v.r.* to turn yellowish (*leaves*).
alindado, -da, *a.* affectedly elegant, dandified.
alindamiento, *n.m.* act of putting limits (*property*).
alindar (1), *v.t.* to mark off. — *v.i.* to be contiguous; ***alindar con,*** to border on.
alindar (2), *v.t.* to embellish, adorn.
alindongarse, *v.r.* to overdress.
alineación, *n.f.* alignment, lining up.
alineador, -ra, *a.* aligning. — *n.m.f.* aligner.
alinear, *v.t.* to align, line up. — **alinearse,** *v.r.* (*mil.*) to fall into line.
aliñar, *v.t.* to arrange, adorn; to dress, season (*food*).
aliño, *n.m.* dress, ornament, decoration; cleanliness; dressing, seasoning (*for food*), preparation.
aliñoso, -sa, *a.* dressed, decked out, decorated; careful, attentive.
alioli, *n.m.* garlic and olive-oil sauce.
alionar, *v.t.* (*Hisp. Am.*) to stir up, agitate.
alionín, *n.m.* (*orn.*) bottle tit, long-tailed tit.
alipata, *n.m.* (*Philip.*) poison tree.
alípede, *a.* (*poet.*) with winged feet, swift, nimble.
alípedo, -da, *a.* (*zool.*) cheiropterous, alipedous.
aliquebrado, -da, *a.* broken-winged; (*fig.*) crestfallen, dejected.
aliquebrar [1], *v.t.* to break the wings of.
alirrojo, -ja, *a.* red-winged.
alisador, -ra, *a.* polishing, smoothing. — *n.m.f.* polisher, planisher, smoothing-iron; silk-stick; tool to shape wax candles.
alisadura, *n.f.* planing, smoothing, polishing; (*pl.*) shavings, cuttings.
alisar (1) *v.t.* to plane, smooth down; to flatten (*hair*); to polish, burnish; to mangle. — **alisarse,** *v.r.* to become smooth *or* polished.
alisar (2), *n.m.*, **aliseda,** *n.f.* plantation of alder-trees.
alisios, *n.m.pl.* east winds, trade winds.
alisma, *n.f.* (*bot.*) water-plantain.
aliso, *n.m.* (*bot.*) alder-tree.
alistador, *n.m.* one who enrols *or* enlists; one who keeps accounts.
alistamiento, *n.m.* enlistment, enrolment.

alistar, *v.t.* to enlist, enrol, recruit; to make ready. — **alistarse,** *v.r.* to enlist, enrol; to get ready; ***alistarse en un cuerpo,*** to enlist in a corps.

aliteración, *n.f.* alliteration.

alitierno, *n.m.* (*bot.*) mock privet.

aliviadero, *n.m.* overflow pipe; (*fig.*) outlet, safety valve.

aliviador, -ra, *a.* helping, assisting, labour-saving; palliative. — *n.m.f.* (*sl.*) fence, receiver of stolen goods.

aliviar [L], *v.t.* to lighten; to relieve, mitigate, assuage, soothe; to hasten, speed up; (*coll.*) to steal, pinch. — **aliviarse,** *v.r.* to become lighter *or* relieved; to get better.

alivio, *n.m.* alleviation; mitigation; relief; comfort, calm; (*law-slang*) plea; attorney.

alizace, *n.m.* trench *or* excavation for the foundations of a building.

alizar [C], *n.m.* dado *or* wainscoting of tiles.

aljaba, *n.f.* quiver.

aljafana, *n.f.* wash-bowl, basin for washing.

aljafifar, *v.t.* to mop, clean, wash.

aljama, *n.f.* assembly of Moors *or* Jews; mosque; synagogue; ***mezquita aljama,*** main mosque.

aljamía, *n.f.* Spanish of Moors *or* Jews; Spanish written in Arabic alphabet.

aljarafe, *n.m.* tableland; flat roof.

aljarfa, *n.f.*, **aljarfe, aljerife,** *n.m.* tarred fishing-net.

aljévena, *n.f.* (*prov.*) wash-bowl.

aljez, *n.m.* crude gypsum, plaster of Paris.

aljezar, *n.m.* pit of gypsum.

aljezón, *n.m.* gypsum, plaster of Paris.

aljibe, *n.m.* cistern; (*naut.*) tank boat, water tender; oil tanker.

aljibero, *n.m.* cistern-keeper.

aljimierado, -da, *a.* shaved, trimmed.

aljofaina, *n.f.* wash-bowl; basin for washing; basin, earthen jug.

aljófar, *n.m.* imperfect pearl; pearl trimming; (*poet.*) dewdrop.

aljofarar, *v.t.* to adorn with pearls; to cause to imitate pearls.

aljofifa, *n.f.* floor mop.

aljofifar, *v.t.* to mop.

aljonje, *n.m.* bird-lime [AJONJE].

aljonjera, aljonjero, aljonjolí [AJONJERA, AJONJERO, AJONJOLÍ].

aljor, *n.m.* gypsum.

aljorozar [C], *v.t.* (*Hisp. Am.*) to smooth *or* make smooth with plaster.

aljuba, *n.f.* jubbah.

alma (1), *n.f.* soul; heart; mind, spirit; human being; strength, vigour; substance; staff, frame; web (*of beam, nail etc.*); (*mech.*) attic ridge, scaffolding pole; (*arm.*) bore, core (*of rope, casting*); (*naut.*) body (*of a mast*); ghost, phantom, apparition; sound-post (*violin etc.*); mould (*for casting statues*); ***alma mía, mi alma,*** my dear, my love, dear heart; ***me da el alma que...,*** my heart tells me that; ***poner el alma en,*** to put one's heart and soul into; ***llevar en el alma,*** to bear *or* carry in one's heart; ***no tener alma,*** to be heartless *or* pitiless; ***se me parte el alma de verlo,*** my heart breaks *or* it breaks my heart to see it; ***se me cayó el alma a los pies,*** my heart sank; ***con alma y vida,*** with all one's heart, wholeheartedly; ***alma de Caín,*** heartless person; ***alma de Dios,*** simpleton; thoroughly good-natured person; ***alma de cántaro,*** phlegmatic person; ***alma en pena,*** soul in torment; ***alma nacida*** or ***viviente*** (*in neg. phrase*), not a living soul; ***me pesa*** or ***lo siento en el alma,*** I deeply *or* keenly regret it; ***dar, entregar*** or ***rendir el alma,*** to give up the ghost, expire; ***estar con el alma en un hilo,*** to be in suspense; ***echar el alma atrás*** or ***a las espaldas,*** to stifle one's conscience *or* scruples; ***romperse el alma,*** to break one's neck; ***tener el alma bien puesta,*** to have guts.

almacén, *n.m.* warehouse; store, shop; (*esp. in pl.*) department store; (*photo.*) magazine; (*Hisp. Am.*) grocery shop; ***tener en almacén,*** to have in store; ***gastar mucho almacén,*** to dress gaudily.

almacenador, *n.m.* warehouseman.

almacenaje, *n.m.* warehouse rent.

almacenamiento, *n.m.* warehousing, storing.

almacenar, *v.t.* to store (*in warehouse*); to store up; to hoard.

almacenero, -ra, *n.m.f.* warehouse-keeper.

almacenista, *n.m.* warehouse owner; shopkeeper; wholesale merchant; (*Hisp. Am.*) wholesale grocer.

almáciga, *n.f.* (*bot.*) mastic; nursery of trees.

almacigar [B], *v.t.* to perfume with mastic.

almácigo, *n.m.* mastic-tree; plant nursery.

almaciguero, -ra, *a.* relating to a plant nursery.

almádana, almádena, almádina, *n.f.* large stone hammer; spalling hammer.

almadén, *n.m.* mine.

almadía, *n.f.* canoe, raft.

almadiarse [L], *v.r.* to become *or* get sea-sick.

almadiero, *n.m.* raft-pilot.

almadraba, *n.f.* tunny-fishery; net used for fishing tunny.

almadrabero, *n.m.* tunny-fisher.

almadraque, *n.m.* (*obs.*) quilted cushion, mattress.

almadreña, *n.f.* wooden shoe, clog.

almaganeta, *n.f.* large stone hammer.

almagesto, *n.m.* almagest.

almagra, *n.f.*, **almagre,** *n.m.* red earth, red ochre, Indian red; mark, sign.

almagral, *n.m.* place abounding in red ochre.

almagrar, *v.t.* to colour with red ochre; to defame; to mark; (*vulg.*) to injure in a quarrel.

almaizal, almaizar, *n.m.* gauze veil worn by Moors; sash worn by priests.

almajaneque, *n.m.* (*mil.*) battering-ram.

almajara, *n.f.* well-manured ground, forcing-bed.

almajo, *n.m.* seaweed.

almaleque, *n.f.* long robe.

almanaque, *n.m.* almanac; calendar; ***hacer almanaques,*** to muse, to be pensive; to make hasty predictions.

almanaquero, -ra, *n.m.f.* maker *or* vendor of almanacs.

almancebe, *n.m.* fishing-net.

almandino, -na, *a.* of red garnet.

almanguena, *n.f.* red ochre, Indian red.

almanta, *n.f.* space between rows of vines and olive-trees; ridge between two furrows; tree nursery; (*agric.*) ***poner a almanta,*** to plant vines closely and in disorder.

almarada, *n.f.* triangular poniard; sandal needle; sulphur remover.

almarbatar, *v.t.* to join (*two pieces of wood*).

almarcha, *n.f.* town on marshy ground.

almarga, *n.f.* marl-pit.

almario, *n.m.* wardrobe; clothes-press.

almarjal, *n.m.* plantation of glasswort; marshy ground.

almarjo, *n.m.* (*bot.*) glasswort.

almaro, *n.m.* (*bot.*) germander.

almarrá, *n.m.* cotton-gin.

almarraja, almarraza, *n.f.* sprinkling bottle.

almártaga (1), **almártega,** *n.f.* (*chem.*) litharge; massicot.

almártaga (2), **almártiga,** *n.f.* halter.

almartigón, *n.m.* rough halter.

almástiga, *n.f.* mastic.

almastigado, -da, *a.* containing mastic.

almatrero, *n.m.* shad fisherman.

almatriche, *n.m.* irrigation channel.
almatroque, *n.m.* shad net.
almazara, *n.f.* oil-mill.
almazarero, *n.m.* oil-miller.
almazarrón, *n.m.* red ochre; Indian red.
almea (1), *n.f.* poetess and dancer.
almea (2), *n.f.* bark of the storax-tree; (*bot.*) star-headed water-plantain.
almear, *n.m.* haystack; loft.
almecina, *n.f.* (*prov.*) hackberry.
almeja, *n.f.* clam.
almejar, *n.m.* clam-bed.
almejía, *n.f.* small cloak.
almena, *n.f.* merlon; (*pl.*) battlements.
almenaje, *n.m.* series of merlons; battlements.
almenar, *n.m.* cresset. — *v.t.* to crown with merlons.
almenara (1), *n.f.* beacon.
almenara (2), *n.f.* (*prov.*) outlet channel, overflow ditch.
almendra, *n.f.* almond; kernel; almond-shaped diamond; cut-glass drop; fine cocoon; ***almendras garapiñadas,*** sugared almonds; ***almendra mollar,*** soft-shelled almond; ***dama de la media almendra,*** prudish lady.
almendrado, -da, *a.* almond-like. — *n.m.* macaroon. — *n.f.* almond milk.
almendral, *n.m.* almond grove.
almendrero, *n.m.* almond salver.
almendrilla, *n.f.* almond-shaped file (*locksmith's*); gravel (*for road repair*); (*pl.*) almond-shaped diamond ear-rings.
almendro, *n.m.* almond-tree.
almendruco, *n.m.* green almond.
almenilla, *n.f.* merlon-shaped trimming.
almete, *n.m.* helmet; soldier wearing a helmet.
almez, almezo, *n.m.* (*bot.*) hackberry, nettle-tree.
almeza, *n.f.* (*bot.*) hackberry.
almiar, *n.m.* haystack.
almíbar, *n.m.* syrup.
almibarado, -da, *a.* syrupy; honeyed, over-sweet, cloying.
almibarar, *v.t.* to preserve in syrup; to honey, make sweet.
almicantarat, *n.f.* (*astron.*) circle parallel to the horizon.
almidón, *n.m.* starch.
almidonado, -da, *a.* starched; (*coll.*) spruce; dapper; stiff. — *n.m.* starching.
almidonar, *v.t.* to starch.
almidonería, *n.f.* starch factory *or* shop.
almidonero, -ra, *n.m.f.* starcher; maker *or* seller of starch.
almifor, *n.m.* (*sl.*) horse.
almifora, *n.f.* (*sl.*) she-mule.
almiforero, *n.m.* horse-thief.
almijara, *n.f.* oil-depot, oil-tank (*in the Almadén mines*).
almila, *n.f.* kiln.
almilla, *n.f.* close-fitting jacket; short military jacket worn beneath armour; (*carp.*) tenon; breast of pork.
almimbar, *n.m.* pulpit of a mosque.
alminar, *n.m.* minaret.
almiranta, *n.f.* (*naut.*) flagship; admiral's wife.
almirantazgo, *n.m.* (*naut.*) admiralty; admiral's dues; admiral-ship.
almirante, *n.m.* admiral, commander of a fleet; women's headgear; (*prov.*) swimming-master.
almirez, *n.m.* brass mortar; wood-engraver's tool of tempered steel.
almirón, *n.m.* (*prov., bot.*) wild chicory.
almizclar, *v.t.* to perfume with musk.
almizcle, *n.m.* musk.
almizcleño, -ña, *a.* musky. — *n.f.* (*bot.*) musk, grape-hyacinth.
almizclero, -ra, *a.* musky. — *n.m.* musk-deer. — *n.f.* musk-rat.
almo, -ma (2), *a.* (*poet.*) creating, vivifying; holy, venerable, sacred; beneficent.
almocadén, *n.m.* (*obs.*) captain of infantry; n.c.o. commanding a cavalry platoon; (*Morocco*) justice of peace; sergeant of Moorish levies.
almocafrar, *v.t.* to dibble.
almocafre, *n.m.* dibble, weeding hoe.
almocárabes, almocarbes, *n.m.pl.* (*arch.*) bow-knot *or* loop-shaped ornaments.
almocatracía, *n.f.* duty on broadcloths and woollen goods.
almoceda, *n.f.* (*prov.*) impost on water for irrigation; right of irrigation on certain days.
almocela, *n.f.* ancient hood.
almocrate, *n.m.* sal-ammoniac.
almocrí, *n.m.* reader of the Koran in a mosque.
almodí, almudí, almudín, *n.m.* public granary; (*prov.*) measure containing six ***cahices*** *or* bushels.
almodón, *n.m.* baking-flour.
almodrote, *n.m.* sauce for aubergine *or* egg-plant; (*coll.*) hotchpotch.
almófar, *n.m.* mail head-cover under the helmet.
almofía, *n.f.* wash-bowl, basin.
almoflate, *n.m.* saddler's round knife.
almofrej, *n.m.* travelling canvas *or* leather bag for mattress.
almogama, *n.f.* (*naut.*) stern-post of a ship.
almogárabe, almogávar, *n.m.* expert raider, forager; Arab mercenary in the Aragonese army.
almogavarear, *v.i.* (*mil.*) to raid.
almogavaría, almagavería, *n.f.* body of raiding troops.
almohada, *n.f.* pillow, bolster; cushion; pillow-case; (*arch.*) rough wall stone; (*naut.*) piece of timber on which the bowsprit rests; ***aconsejarse*** or ***consultar con la almohada,*** to sleep on it (*an idea*); ***dar almohada a,*** to raise (*a lady*) to the nobility.
almohade, *a., n.m.f.* Almohade.
almohadilla, *n.f.* small pillow *or* bolster; pad; working case; sewing cushion; pad (*of harness*); (*arch.*) rough wall stone; (*vet.*) callous excrescence (*on the backs of mules and horses*).
almohadillado, -da, *a.* (*arch.*) cushioned. — *n.m.* (*arch.*) relief; padding.
almohadillar, *v.t.* to cushion; to pad.
almohadón, *n.m.* large pillow.
almohatre, almojatre, *n.m.* sal-ammoniac.
almohaza, *n.f.* curry-comb.
almohazador, *n.m.* groom.
almohazar [C], *v.t.* to curry, groom with a curry-comb.
almojábana, *n.f.* cheese cake; cruller.
almojarifazgo, *n.m.* (*obs.*) import *or* export duty; custom house.
almojarife, *n.m.* (*obs.*) tax-gatherer; custom-house officer.
almojaya, *n.f.* putlog.
almona, *n.f.* public stores; shad-fishery; (*prov.*) soap-manufactory.
almóndiga [ALBÓNDIGA].
almoneda, *n.f.* public auction; second-hand *or* junk shop.
almonedear, *v.t.* to sell by auction.
almoradux, *n.m.* (*bot.*) sweet marjoram.
almorávide, *a., n.m.f.* Almoravides.
almorejo, *n.m.* (*bot.*) bottle grass.
almorí, almurí, *n.m.* honey cake.
almoronía [ALBORONÍA].
almorranas, *n.f.pl.* (*med.*) piles.
almorraniento, -ta, *a., n.m.f.* (s.o.) suffering from piles.
almorrefa, *n.f.* triangular tile; mosaic floor.
almorta, *n.f.* (*bot.*) blue vetch.

almorzada, *n.f.* double-handful.
almorzar [4C], *v.t.* to eat for lunch; (*obs.*) to have for breakfast; ***almorzar chuletas,*** to have chops for lunch. — *v.i.* to (have) lunch; (*obs.*) to have breakfast.
almotacén, *n.m.* inspector of weights and measures; inspector's office; (*Morocco*) overseer of markets.
almotacenazgo, *n.m.* inspector's office and duty.
almotacenía, *n.f.* fee paid to the market-clerk *or* inspector; inspectorship.
almozala, *n.f.* quiet; blanket.
almozárabe, *a., n.m.f.* (Christian) subject to the Moors in Spain.
almud, *n.m.* measure of grain (*about* 4.625 *litres*); ***almud de tierra,*** measure of land (*about half an acre* or 2000 *sq.m.*).
almudada, *n.f.* ground which takes one ***almud*** of seed.
almudejo, *n.m.* each of the weights kept by the ***almudero.***
almudero, *n.m.* keeper of weights and measures for grain.
almudí, almudín, *n.m.* Castilian measure (*about* 4000 *litres*).
almuecín, almuédano, *n.m.* muezzin.
almuérdago, *n.m.* mistletoe.
almuertas, *n.f.pl.* (*prov.*) duty on cereals sold.
almuerza, *n.f.* double-handful.
almuerzo, *n.m.* lunch, luncheon; (*obs.*) breakfast.
almunia, *n.f.* orchard, vegetable garden.
almutazaf, *n.m.* (*prov.*) inspector of weights and measures.
alnado, -da, *n.m.f.* stepchild.
alo, *n.m.* (*Mex.*) crested parrot.
aloaria, *n.f.* (*arch.*) vault.
alobadado, -da, *a.* bitten by a wolf; (*vet.*) suffering from anthrax.
alobunado, -da, *a.* wolf-coloured (*hair*).
alocado, -da, *a.* wild, reckless. — *n.m.f.* madcap.
alocar [A], *v.t.* to drive mad *or* crazy.
alocución, *n.f.* allocution, address, harangue; speech.
alodial, *a.* (*law*) allodial, free, exempt.
alodio, *n.m.* freehold possession.
áloe, *n.m.* (*bot.*) aloes-tree, aloes; ***palo áloe,*** aloes-wood.
aloético, -ca, *a.* aloetic.
aloína, *n.f.* aloin, active principle of aloes.
aloja, *n.f.* metheglin, mead.
alojado, *n.m.* billeted soldier.
alojamiento, *n.m.* lodging, accommodation; quartering, billeting; (*naut.*) steerage; (*pl.*) (*mil.*) camp, quarters.
alojar, *v.t.* to lodge, let lodgings to; to accommodate, house, put up; to quarter, billet (*troops*). — **alojarse,** *v.r.* to lodge, put up, take lodgings.
alojería, *n.f.* place where mead is made *or* sold.
alojero, -ra, *n.m.f.* one who mixes *or* sells mead; box near the pit in theatres.
alomar, *v.t.* to plough in wide furrows. — **alomarse,** *v.r.* to become strong in back and loins (*of horses*).
alón, *n.m.* plucked wing; wing of chicken (*for eating*).
alondra, *n.f.* (*orn.*) lark.
alongamiento, *n.m.* delay; distance; separation; lengthening, extension.
alongar [4B], *v.t.* to remove, put at a distance, separate; to lengthen, prolong, extend, stretch. — **alongarse,** *v.r.* to move away.
alonso [TRIGO].
alópata, *n.m.* allopath, allopathist.
alopatía, *n.f.* allopathy.
alopático, -ca, *a.* allopathic.
alopecia, *n.f.* (*med.*) alopecia, baldness.
alopecuro, *n.m.* (*bot.*) foxtail grass.
alopiado, -da, *a.* opiate, composed of opium.
aloque, *a.* light red (*of wine*). — *n.m.* mixture of red and white wine.
aloquín, *n.m.* stone enclosure in a wax bleachery.
alosa, *n.f.* (*ichth.*) shad.
alosna, *n.f.* (*bot.*) wormwood.
alotar, *v.t.* (*naut.*) to reef, lash, make fast.
alotropía, *n.f.* (*chem.*) allotropy.
alotrópico, -ca, *a.* (*chem.*) allotropic.
alotropo, *n.m.* allotrope.
alpaca, *n.f.* alpaca; nickel silver.
alpamato, *n.m.* (*Arg., bot.*) tea shrub.
alpañata, *n.f.* piece of chamois-skin.
alpargata, *n.f.* hemp sandal.
alpargatado, -da, *a.* shaped like a hemp sandal.
alpargatar, *v.i.* to make hemp sandals.
alpargatazo, *n.m.* blow with a hemp sandal.
alpargatería, *n.f.* hemp sandal shop *or* factory.
alpargatero, -ra, *n.m.f.* maker *or* seller of hemp sandals.
alpargatilla, *n.m.f.* crafty *or* designing person.
alpechín, *n.m.* olive ooze.
alpechinera, *n.f.* vat *or* large jar to hold ***alpechín.***
alpende, *n.m.* shed.
alpérsico [ALBÉRCHIGO].
Alpes, *n.m.pl.* Alps.
alpes, *n.m.pl.* high mountains.
alpestre, *a.* alpine; Alpine; (*fig.*) mountainous, wild.
alpinismo, *n.m.* mountain-climbing, mountaineering.
alpinista, *n.m.f.* mountain-climber, mountaineer.
alpino, -na, *a.* Alpine.
alpiste, *n.m.* bird-seed, canary-seed; ***quedarse alpiste,*** to be disappointed.
alpistela, alpistera, *n.f.* sesame-seed cake.
alpistero, *n.m.* sieve for canary-seed.
alquequenje, *n.m.* winter-cherry.
alquería, *n.f.* farm-house.
alquermes, *n.m. inv.* kermes, cordial; (*pharm.*) medicinal syrup.
alquerque, *n.m.* shredding place.
alquez, *n.m.* wine measure (193 *litres*).
alquibla, *n.f.* kiblah.
alquicel, alquicer, *n.m.* cloak; cover for benches, tables *etc.*
alquifol, *n.m.* (*min.*) zaffre, zaffer.
alquilador, -ra, *n.m.f.* renter, hirer; proprietor; tenant.
alquilamiento, *n.m.* (act of) hiring *or* letting.
alquilar, *v.t.* to let, hire, rent. — **alquilarse,** *v.r.* to be to let *or* for hire.
alquiler, *n.m.* rent, rental; hire, fee; (act of) letting *or* hiring; ***de alquiler,*** for hire, to let, to rent; ***alquiler de una casa,*** house-rent, rental; ***coche de alquiler,*** coach *or* car for hire, hackney carriage.
alquilona, *n.f.* charwoman, charlady.
alquimia, *n.f.* alchemy.
alquímico, -ca, *a.* alchemistic, alchemical.
alquimila, *n.f.* (*bot.*) lady's mantle.
alquimista, *n.m.* alchemist.
alquinal, *n.m.* veil *or* head-dress (for women).
alquitara, *n.f.* still, alembic; ***por alquitara,*** sparingly.
alquitarar, *v.t.* to distil; (*fig.*) to refine, make subtle (*style etc.*).
alquitira, *n.f.* tragacanth.
alquitrán, *n.m.* tar, pitch; ***alquitrán mineral*** or ***de hulla,*** coal-tar; ***alquitrán vegetal,*** wood tar.
alquitranado, *n.m.* (*naut.*) tarpaulin, tarred cloth; (*naut.*) ***cabos alquitranados,*** black *or* tarred cordage.
alquitranar, *v.t.* to tar.

alrededor, *adv.* around; ***alrededor de,*** about, around. — *n.m.pl.* (**alrededores**) environs, outskirts.

alrota, *n.f.* coarse tow.

Alsacia, *n.f.* Alsace; ***Alsacia-Lorena,*** Alsace-Lorraine.

alsaciano, -na, *a., n.m.f.* Alsatian.

álsine, *n.m.* (*bot.*) chickweed.

alta (1), *n.f.* court dance; dancing exercise; fencing bout; (*mil.*) record of entry into service; discharge (*from hospital*); (*sl.*) window, tower, belfry; ***dar de alta,*** to declare fit for (military) service; to discharge (from hospital); ***darse de alta,*** to return to duty (after illness); to join, become a member.

altabaque, *n.m.* needle-work basket; work-basket.

altabaquillo, *n.m.* (*bot.*) small bindweed, convolvulus.

altamente, *adv.* highly, strongly, extremely, perfectly, entirely; (*fig.*) in a distinguished manner.

altamisa, *n.f.* (*bot.*) mugwort.

altana (1), *n.f.* (*sl.*) temple, church.

altanado, -da, *a.* (*slang*) married.

altanería, *n.f.* falconry; haughtiness, arrogance, loftiness.

altanero, -ra, *a.* soaring (*of birds of prey*); haughty, arrogant, lofty.

altano, -na (2), *a.* (*naut.*) (*wind*) blowing alternately from the sea and the land.

altar, *n.m.* altar; ***altar mayor,*** high altar; ***conducir*** or ***llevar al altar,*** to take to the altar, (marry).

altarero, -ra, *n.m.f.* altar-maker *or* dresser; one who decks *or* adorns altars.

altarreina, *n.f.* (*bot.*) milfoil.

altavoz, *n.m.* loudspeaker.

altea, *n.f.* (*bot.*) marshmallow.

altearse, *v.r.* to rise, stand out.

alterabilidad, *n.f.* changeableness, mutability.

alterable, *a.* changeable, alterable; excitable; easily upset.

alteración, *n.f.* alteration; disturbance, upset; agitation, disorder; fastness *or* unevenness (*pulse*).

alterador, -ra, *a.* altering, disturbing, upsetting.

alterante, *a.* altering, disturbing, upsetting; (*med.*) alterative.

alterar, *v.t.* to alter, change, transform; to disturb, upset; to adulterate, corrupt; to agitate, irritate. — **alterarse,** *v.r.* to become disturbed, agitated *or* annoyed; to be put out *or* upset (***por,*** by).

altercado, *n.m.* altercation, controversy, wrangle, quarrel.

altercador, -ra, *a.* wrangling, arguing, bickering. — *n.m.f.* wrangler, arguer.

altercar [A], *v.i.* to quarrel, bicker, wrangle.

alternación, *n.f.* alternation.

alternadamente, *adv.* alternately, by turns.

alternador, *n.m.* (*elec.*) alternator.

alternancia, *n.f.* alternation.

alternar, *v.t.* to alternate, perform by turns; change (*for sth. else*). — *v.i.* to alternate; to mix, mingle, have social intercourse; ***alternar en sociedad,*** to mix in society.

alternativa, *n.f.* [ALTERNATIVO].

alternativamente, *adv.* alternately, by turns.

alternativo, -va, *a.* alternate; alternating; ***cultivo alternativo,*** rotation of crops. — *n.f.* alternative, option, choice; service by turn; (*pol.*) option; (*tauro.*) ceremony of becoming a full matador; ***tomar la alternativa,*** to become *or* be accepted as a fully-fledged matador.

alterno, -na, *a.* alternate, alternating.

alteza, *n.f.* (*title*) Highness; height, elevation, sublimity.

altibajo, *n.m.* velvet brocade; downward cut *or* thrust (*with sword*); (*pl.*) unevenness (*of ground*); ups and downs, vicissitudes.

altilocuencia, *n.f.* grandiloquence.

altilocuente, altílocuo, -cua, *a.* pompous, bombastic, high-sounding, grandiloquent.

altillo, *n.m.* hillock; attic.

altimetría, *n.f.* (*geom.*) altimetry.

altimétrico, -ca, *a.* (*geom.*) altimetric.

altímetro, -tra, *a.* altimetric. — *n.m.* altimeter.

altiplanicie, *n.f.* high plateau, tableland; uplands.

altiplano, *n.m.* (*Bol., Per.*) [ALTIPLANICIE].

Altísimo, *n.m.* (the) Most High.

altisonante, altísono, -na, *a.* altisonant; high-flown; high-sounding.

altitonante, *a.* (*poet.*) thundering.

altitud, *n.f.* altitude, height.

altivarse, altivecerse [9], *v.r.* to put on airs.

altivez, altiveza, *n.f.* haughtiness, arrogance.

altivo, -va, *a.* haughty, lofty, arrogant, overbearing.

alto, -ta (1), *a.* high, tall; upper; elevated, superior; deep; loud, strong (*voice*); (*naut.*) ***alta mar,*** high seas, open sea; ***altas horas,*** early *or* small hours; ***alto relieve,*** high-relief; ***alto horno,*** blast-furnace; (*naut.*) ***de alto bordo,*** sea-going. — *adv.* loudly, aloud, highly; ***de alto a abajo,*** from top to bottom; ***en alto,*** up high, above. — *n.m.* height, high ground; storey, floor; ***altos y bajos,*** ups and downs; ***casa de tres altos,*** three-storied house; ***lo alto,*** the heavens above; ***de lo alto,*** from above, from on high; ***estar en*** (***todo***) ***lo alto,*** to be (right) at the top; ***por todo lo alto,*** in grand style; (*Hisp. Am.*) mountain, pile; (*pl., Hisp. Am.*) upper stories.

alto (2), *n.m.* (*mil.*) halt; ***hacer alto,*** to stop, halt. — *interj.* stop! halt!; ***¡alto ahí!*** stop there! halt there!

altoparlante, *n.m.* loud speaker.

altor, *n.m.* height.

altozano, *n.m.* height; hill; (*Hisp. Am.*) atrium; paved terrace *or* platform in front of a church.

altramuz, *n.m.* (*bot.*) lupin.

altruísmo, *n.m.* altruism.

altruísta, *a.* altruistic, selfless. — *n.m.f.* altruist.

altura, *n.f.* height; loftiness; elevation; altitude; (*naut.*) latitude; ***las alturas,*** the heavens, Heaven; ***altura meridiana,*** meridian altitude; ***pesca de altura,*** deep-sea fishing; ***estar a la altura de,*** to be up to *or* equal to (*task, situation*); to be abreast of (*times*); (*geog.*) to be opposite, off; ***a estas alturas,*** at this (late) stage.

alubia, *n.f.* (*bot.*) French bean.

aluciar [L], *v.t.* to polish, burnish, brighten.

alucinación, *n.f.*, **alucinamiento,** *n.m.* hallucination.

alucinador, -ra, *n.m.f.* hallucinator.

alucinar, *v.t.* to dazzle, blind; to delude. — **alucinarse,** *v.r.* to deceive oneself; ***alucinarse con promesas,*** to delude oneself with promises.

alucón, *n.m.* (*orn.*) barn-owl.

alud, *n.m.* avalanche, landslide.

aluda, *n.f.* [ALUDO].

aludel, *n.m.* (*chem.*) sublimating pots; aludel.

aludir, *v.i.* to allude, refer.

aludo, -da, *a.* winged, large-winged. — *n.f.* (*ent.*) winged ant *or* emmet.

alumbrado, *n.m.* lighting (system); (*pl.*) Illuminati.

alumbrador, -ra, *a.* illuminating.

alumbramiento, *n.m.* illumination; childbirth.

alumbrante, *a.* illuminating. — *n.m.* (*theat.*) lighting operator.

alumbrar (1), *v.t.* to light, illuminate; to give light to; to enlighten; to find (*underground water*); to remove the earth from around (*vines*). — *v.i.* to give light; to give birth to a child. — **alumbrarse,** *v.r.* (*coll.*) to get tipsy *or* lit up.

alumbrar (2), *v.t.* to treat with alum.

alumbre, *n.m.* alum; ***alumbre de rasuras,*** potassium carbonate; ***alumbre de roca,*** rock alum; ***alumbre sacarino,*** saccharine alum.
alumbrera, *n.f.* (*min.*) alum mine.
alumbrería, *n.f.* alum factory.
alúmbrico, -ca, alumbrífero, -ra, *a.* aluminous.
alumbroso, *a.* aluminous.
alúmina, *n.f.* (*chem.*) alumina.
aluminato, *n.m.* (*chem.*) aluminate.
alumínico, -ca, *a.* containing alumina; aluminous.
aluminífero, -ra, *a.* aluminiferous.
aluminio, *n.m.* (*chem.*) aluminium, (*Am.*) aluminum.
aluminita, *n.f.* aluminite.
aluminoso, -sa, *a.* aluminous.
alumnado, *n.m.* student body.
alumno, -na, *n.m.f.* pupil; student; foster-child.
alunamiento, *n.m.* (*naut.*) billowing (*of sails*).
alunarse, *v.r.* to go mad, become a lunatic; to become tainted (*meat, fish*); to billow out (*sails*).
alunarado, -da, *a.* covered in spots, dots *or* moles.
alunita, *n.f.* (*min.*) alunite, alumstone.
alunizaje, *n.m.* moon-landing.
alunizar [C], *v.i.* to land on the moon.
alusión, *n.f.* allusion, reference, hint.
alusivo, -va, *a.* allusive, hinting.
alustrar, *v.t.* to give lustre to, polish.
alutación, *n.f.* (*min.*) stratum of grains of gold.
alutrado, -da, *a.* otter-coloured.
aluvial, *a.* (*geol.*) alluvial.
aluvión, *n.m.* alluvion; alluvium; (*fig.*) flood.
alveario, *n.m.* (*anat.*) canal; alveary.
álveo, *n.m.* bed (*of a river*).
alveolar, *a.* alveolar.
alvéolo, *n.m.* alveolus, alveole; small cavity.
alverja, alverjana [ARVEJA].
alvino, -na, *a.* (*med.*) alvine.
alza, *n.f.* (*com.*) rise; piece of leather put round a last to make the shoe wider; (*artill.*) hind-sight; (*print.*) overlay, frisket sheet; instrument used in rope-walks; (*com.*) ***jugar al alza,*** to speculate on a rise.
alzacuello, *n.m.* clergyman's collar; (*fig., coll.*) dog-collar; neckstock *or* tie.
alzada, *n.f.* [ALZADO].
alzadamente, *adv.* for a cash settlement, for a lump sum.
alzado, -da, *a.* raised, lifted; fixed, settled. — *n.m.* cash settlement, lump sum; (*arch.*) elevation; (*print.*) gathering; height (*of ship*); fraud; fraudulent bankrupt. — *n.f.* height (*of horses*); appeal; ***juez de alzadas,*** judge in appeal cases.
alzador, -ra, *a.* lifting, raising. — *n.m.* (*print.*) gatherer; gathering-room.
alzafuelles, *n.m.f. inv.* flatterer.
alzamiento, *n.m.* elevation, raising, lifting; rise; outbidding (*auction*); revolt, rising; ***el Alzamiento,*** the 1936 uprising led by General Franco; fraudulent bankruptcy.
alzapaño, *n.m.* curtain-holder *or* loop.
alzapié, *n.m.* snare.
alzaprima, *n.f.* lever, wedge; (*naut.*) heaver; (*mech.*) fulcrum.
alzaprimar, *v.t.* to raise with a lever; (*fig.*) to incite, spur on.
alzapuertas, *n.m. inv.* dumb player; supernumerary.
alzar [C], *v.t.* to raise (*price, load, siege, voice etc.*); to heave, lift up; to erect; to carry off; to hide; to lock up; to cut (*cards*); (*print.*) to collate (*printed sheets*); to elevate (*the host in celebrating mass*); (*naut.*) to heave; to repeal (*a decree of excommunication*); ***alzar el precio,*** to raise the price; ***alzar el codo,*** to drink; ***alzar el dedo,*** to raise the forefinger; ***alzar la casa*** or ***los reales,*** to leave a house, break up house *or* camp; (*naut.*) ***alzar velas,*** to set sail; ***alzar cabeza,*** to get over a disaster *or* difficult period; ***alzar un entredicho,*** to raise an injunction; ***alzar la mesa,*** to clear away the table (*after meals*); ***alzar la tienda,*** to close the shop; ***alzar el grito,*** to cry out; ***alzar la mano,*** to raise one's hand; ***alzar mano (de),*** to abandon; ***alzar por jefe*** or ***rey,*** to proclaim as chief *or* king. — **alzarse,** *v.r.* to rise in revolt; to rise (from one's knees); ***alzarse con el reino,*** to usurp the kingdom; ***alzarse en rebelión,*** to rise in revolt; ***alzarse con el dinero,*** to make off with *or* embezzle the money; ***alzarse con el santo y la limosna,*** to make off with everything.
alzaválvulas, *n.m. inv.* (*mech.*) tappet.
allá, *adv.* there, yonder, over there; thither; way back; ***allá él*** or ***Vd.,*** that's his *or* your look out; ***allá en América,*** over in America; ***allá por los años veinte,*** back in the twenties; ***allá veremos,*** we shall see, that remains to be seen; ***más allá,*** farther, further, beyond; ***muy allá,*** much beyond, far beyond; ***no es muy allá,*** it's not much good; ***el más allá,*** the afterlife; ***más allá de,*** beyond; ***por allá,*** there, thereabouts; ***allá se las haya,*** let him shift for himself; ***¡allá va eso!*** look out! take that! how's that!
allanador, -ra, *a.* levelling. — *n.m.f.* leveller. — *n.m.* gold-beater's paper.
allanamiento, *n.m.* levelling; smoothing; consent; (*law*) ***allanamiento de morada,*** housebreaking.
allanar, *v.t.* to level, make even; to flatten; to iron out (*difficulties*); to pacify, subdue; ***allanar el camino,*** to pave the way; ***allanar la casa,*** to break into the house. — **allanarse,** *v.r.* to acquiesce, conform; to abide (by).
allariz, *n.m.* linen (manufactured at Allariz in Galicia).
allegadizo, -za, *a.* gathered *or* piled up at random.
allegado, -da, *a.* near, close; related. — *n.m.f.* relative, relation; close friend.
allegador, -ra, *a.* gathering, collecting. — *n.m.f.* gatherer, collector. — *n.m.* gathering board.
allegamiento, *n.m.* collection, union; collecting, uniting; reaping, gathering; close friendship, relationship.
allegar [B], *v.t.* to collect, gather, reap; to add, unite; ***allegar fondos,*** to raise funds. — *v.i.* to approach, arrive. — **allegarse,** *v.r.* to approach, arrive; ***allegarse a,*** to become attached to, become a follower *or* adept of.
allende, *adv.* on the other side, beyond; besides; ***allende el mar,*** overseas; (*fam.*) America, Spanish America.
allí, *adv.* there, yonder, in that place; then; ***aquí y allí,*** here and there; ***de allí,*** thence; ***por allí,*** that way, thereabouts; ***allí mismo,*** right there, in that very place *or* spot; ***allí dentro,*** in there; ***de allí que,*** hence.
alloza, *n.f.* green (wild) almond.
allozar, *n.m.* almond grove.
allozo, *n.m.* (*bot.*) (wild) almond-tree.
alludel [ALUDEL].
ama, *n.f.* mistress (*of the house*); landlady; woman owner; ***ama de casa,*** housewife; ***ama de llaves,*** housekeeper; ***ama de cría*** or ***de leche,*** wet-nurse; ***ama seca,*** children's nurse.
amabilidad, *n.f.* kindness; ***tener la amabilidad de,*** to be so kind as to, be kind enough to.
amabilísimo, -ma, *a. superl.* extremely kind, most kind.
amable, *a.* kind.
amacayo, *n.m.* (*Am., bot.*) flower-de-luce.
amaceno, -na, *a.* Damascene. — *n.m.* (*bot.*) damson.
amacigado, -da, *a.* of yellowish *or* mastic colour.
amación, *n.f.* (mystic) love; deep love.
amacollarse, *v.r.* (*agric.*) to throw out shoots.
amacrático, -ca, *a.* amacratic.
amachetear, *v.t.* to strike and cut with a machete, hack.
amachinarse, *v.r.* (*Hisp. Am.*) to live in concubinage.

amadamarse [ADAMARSE].
amado, -da, *n.m.f.* beloved, sweetheart.
amador, -ra, *a.* loving. — *n.m.f.* lover.
amadrigar [B], *v.t.* to welcome, take in, receive with open arms. — **amadrigarse,** *v.r.* to burrow; to live in retirement.
amadrinar, *v.t.* to couple, yoke together; (*naut.*) to join (*one thing to another*); to act as godmother to; to favour, uphold.
amadroñado, -da, *a.* resembling arbutus-berries (***madroños***).
amaestramiento, *n.m.* instruction, training, coaching.
amaestrar, *v.t.* to instruct; to master, dominate; to lead; to train, coach; ***amaestrar un caballo,*** to train a horse.
amagar [B], *v.t., v.i.* to threaten, show signs *or* symptoms (of); to feint; ***amaga la tormenta,*** the storm is gathering. — **amagarse,** *v.r.* (*coll.*) to hide.
amago, *n.m.* threat; threatening movement; symptom (*of disease*); sign; feint.
ámago, *n.m.* beebread; loathing, nausea, disgust.
amainar, *v.t.* (*naut.*) to lower (*the sails*); to relax. — *v.i.* to subside, lessen, moderate; ***ha amainado el viento,*** the wind has dropped. — **amainarse,** *v.r.* to yield; to give way (to).
amaine, *n.m.* (act of) lowering the sails.
amaitinar, *v.t.* to spy (up)on.
amajadar, *v.t.* to fertilize (*a field*) with sheep. — *v.i.* to be in the fold (*sheep, goats etc.*).
amalecita, amalequita, *a., n.m.f.* Amalekite.
amalgama, *n.f.* (*chem.*) amalgam.
amalgamación, *n.f.* amalgamation.
amalgamador, -ra, *a.* amalgamating. — *n.m.f.* amalgamator.
amalgamar, *v.t.* to amalgamate. — **amalgamarse,** *v.r.* to become amalgamated.
amallarse, *v.r.* (*Chi.*) to leave a gambling party when winning money.
amamantamiento, *n.m.* suckling, nursing.
amamantar, *v.t.* to nurse; to feed, give suck to.
Amán, *n.m.* (Muscat and) Oman.
amán, *n.m.* (*Morocco*) peace, amnesty.
amancebamiento, *n.m.* concubinage.
amancebarse, *v.r.* to (begin to) live in concubinage *or* in sin.
amancillar, *v.t.* to stain; to spot, sully; to tarnish.
amandina, *n.f.* (*chem.*) amandine.
amanear, *v.t.* to hobble (*horse*).
amanecer [9], *v.i.* to dawn; to arrive *or* rise at break of day; to begin to appear; ***cuando Dios amanece, para todos aparece,*** the sun shines on good and bad alike; ***no por mucho madrugar, amanece más temprano,*** you can't force time *or* push the clock; ***amanecí en Madrid,*** morning found me in Madrid. — *n.m.* dawn; ***al amanecer,*** at daybreak.
amanecida, *n.f.* daybreak.
amaneciente, *a.* rising, dawning; ***arreboles al oriente, agua amaneciente,*** red sky in the morning, shepherd's warning.
amanerarse, *v.r.* to adopt a mannerism; to become affected.
amanita, *n.f.* (*bot.*) agaric.
amanojamiento, *n.m.* handful.
amanojar, *v.t.* to gather by handfuls.
amansador, -ra, *a.* taming, subduing, appeasing; soothing. — *n.m.f.* tamer, subduer; appeaser; (*Chi., Ec., Mex.*) horse breaker.
amansamiento, *n.m.* taming, subduing; soothing, appeasement; tameness.
amansar, *v.t.* to tame, subdue, pacify; to domesticate; to soothe, appease, placate.
amantar, *v.t.* (*coll.*) to cloak, blanket.
amante, *a.* loving. — *n.m.f.* lover. — *n.m.pl.* (*naut.*) moorings; hawser.
amantillar, *v.t.* (*naut.*) to top (*lifts*); to hoist (*one end of the yard-arm*) higher.
amantillo, *n.m.* (*naut.*) lift.
amanuense, *n.m.* amanuensis.
amanzanar, *v.t.* (*Arg.*) to divide (*an area*) into squares *or* blocks.
amañar, *v.t.* to do cleverly *or* skilfully; to fake. — **amañarse,** *v.r.* to be *or* get handy, acquire skill, become expert; ***amañarse con cualquiera,*** to get on well with anybody.
amaño, *n.m.* cleverness, cunning way (of doing a thing); (*pl.*) tools, instruments; intrigue, machinations.
amapola, *n.f.* (*bot.*) poppy.
amar, *v.t.* to love; ***amar de corazón,*** to love wholeheartedly; ***amar con locura,*** to love madly.
amaracino, *a.* (*pharm.*) containing marjoram. — *n.m.* marjoram ointment.
amáraco, *n.m.* (*bot.*) marjoram.
amaraje, *n.m.* (*aer.*) alighting *or* landing on water.
amarantáceo, -cea, *a.* (*bot.*) amaranthine. — *n.f.pl.* (**amarantáceas**) (*bot.*) Amaranthaceæ.
amarantina, *n.f.* (*bot.*) amaranthine.
amaranto, *n.m.* (*bot.*) amaranth.
amarar, *v.i.* (*aer.*) to alight on water.
amargado, -da, *n.m.f.* embittered person.
amargaleja, *n.f.* (*bot.*) sloe.
amargar [B], *v.t.* to make bitter; to embitter; to spoil (*party, fun etc.*). — **amargarse,** *v.r.* to become *or* get bitter *or* embittered.
amargo, -ga, *a.* bitter; with an acrid taste; painful. — *n.m.* bitterness, bitter taste; sweetmeat of bitter almonds; (*pl.*) bitters.
amargón, *n.m.* (*bot.*) dandelion.
amargor, *n.m.* bitterness.
amargoso, -sa, *a.* bitterish.
amarguera, *n.f.* (*bot.*) wild horse-radish.
amarguillo, -lla, *a.* bitterish. — *n.m.* bitter-almond sweetmeat.
amargura, *n.f.* bitterness.
amaricado, -da, *a.* (*coll.*) effeminate, queer.
amarilídeo, -dea, *a.* (*bot.*) amaryllidaceous. — *n.f.pl.* (**amarilídeas**) (*bot.*) Amaryllidaceæ.
amarilis, *n.f. inv.* (*bot.*) amaryllis.
amarilla, *n.f.* [AMARILLO].
amarillear, *v.t.* to make yellow. — *v.i.* to be *or* show yellow.
amarillecer [9], *v.i.* to turn *or* become yellow.
amarillejo, -ja, amarillento, -ta, *a.* yellowish, inclining to yellow, yellowy.
amarillez, *n.f.* yellowness; pallor.
amarillo, -lla, *a.* yellow. — *n.m.* yellow; disease of silkworms. — *n.f.* gold coin; liver disease (of sheep).
amarilloso, -sa, *a.* yellowish.
amarinar, *v.t.* to salt (*fish*); (*naut.*) to man (*a ship*).
amariposado, -da, *a.* (*bot.*) papilionaceous, butterfly-like.
amaro, *n.m.* (*bot.*) common clary.
amarra, *n.f.* (*naut.*) cable, hawser; martingale; (*naut.*) 'belay', 'lash' *or* 'fasten'; (*fig.*) protection shelter; ***cortar las amarras,*** to cut the cable; (*fig.*) to cut loose.
amarraco, *n.m.* score of five points (*cards*).
amarradero, *n.m.* tying *or* hitching post; (*fig.*) tie (obligation, restriction); (*naut.*) mooring berth.
amarradura, *n.f.* tying, fastening; (*naut.*) moorage.
amarraje, *n.m.* (*naut.*) moorage dues.
amarrar, *v.t.* to tie, fasten, lash; to cheat (*at cards*).
amarrazones, *n.m.pl.* (*naut.*) ground-tackle.
amarre, *n.m.* (*naut.*) tying, fastening, mooring; cheating (*at cards*).
amarrido, -da, *a.* dejected, gloomy, melancholy.
amartelamiento, *n.m.* (*coll.*) spooning, necking, lovemaking.

amartelar, *v.t.* to make lovesick. — **amartelarse,** *v.r.* (*fam.*) to get a crush (***de,*** on); (*fam.*) ***están muy amartelados,*** they are very gone on each other.
amartillar, *v.t.* to hammer; to cock (*gun, pistol*).
amarulencia, *n.f.* resentment, bitterness.
amasada, *n.f.* batch of dough.
amasadera, *n.f.* kneading-trough.
amasadero, *n.m.* kneading-place.
amasador, -ra, *a.* kneading. — *n.m.f.* kneader; mortar-mixer.
amasadura, *n.f.* kneading.
amasamiento, *n.m.* (act of) uniting *or* joining; kneading; (*med.*) massage.
amasar, *v.t.* to knead, mix; (*med.*) to massage; to cook up; ***amasar dinero,*** to amass money.
amasijo, *n.m.* dough; kneading; mixture; medley, hodgepodge; task; plot, intrigue; mess, stew, concoction.
amatar, *v.t.* (*Ec.*) to cause a sore on (*a horse*).
amate, *n.m.* (*Mex.*) fig-tree.
amatista, *n.f.* (*min.*) amethyst.
amatividad, *n.f.* (*phrenol.*) amativeness.
amatorio, -ria, *a.* amatory, of love.
amaurosis, *n.f. inv.* (*med.*) amaurosis.
amaurótico, -ca, *a.* (*med.*) amaurotic.
amauta, *n.m.* (*Hisp. Am.*) Inca sage.
amayorazgar [B], *v.t.* to entail.
amazacotado, -da, *a.* heavy, thick, stodgy, ponderous; clumsy.
amazona, *n.f.* Amazon; mannish woman; lady rider; riding-habit; (*Hisp. Am.*) large parrot.
Amazonas, *n.m.* Amazon (*river*).
amazónico, -ca, amazonio, -nia, *a.* Amazonian.
amba, *n.f.* (*bot.*) mangrove fruit.
ambages, *n.m.pl.* maze; circumlocution; roundabout expression; quibbling; beating about the bush; ***sin rodeos ni ambages,*** without beating about the bush.
ambagioso, -sa, *a.* roundabout, involved, tortuous.
ámbar, *n.m.* amber; ***ámbar gris,*** ambergris; ***ámbar negro,*** jet.
ambarar, *v.t.* to perfume with amber.
ambarilla, *n.f.* (*bot.*) amber-seed.
ambarino, -na, *a.* relating to amber; amber-like. — *n.f.* (*chem.*) ambrine.
Amberes, *n.f.* Antwerp.
amberino, -na, *a., n.m.f.* (native *or* inhabitant) of Antwerp.
ambición, *n.f.* ambition.
ambicionar, *v.t.* to be ambitious for, have ambitions of; to aspire to; to covet.
ambicioso, -sa, *a.* ambitious; over-ambitious; covetous; greedy; (*bot.*) climbing. — *n.m.f.* self-seeking individual.
ambidextro, -ra, *a.* ambidextrous.
ambientación, *n.f.* (creating) atmosphere, setting.
ambiental, *a.* of atmosphere; to do with setting; environmental.
ambientar, *v.t.* to set, set the scene of; to give atmosphere to; to get into the right frame of mind; to put in the picture.
ambiente, *a.* ambient; surrounding. — *n.m.* atmosphere, environment, surroundings; ***este sitio tiene mucho ambiente,*** this place is very lively *or* full of life; ***aquí no hay ambiente,*** there's no life here, there's nothing doing here, it's dead here; ***X aquí no tiene ambiente,*** X hasn't got the right conditions here, conditions are not favourable to X here, things aren't right for X here.
ambigú, *n.m.* buffet-supper; refreshment room.
ambigüedad, *n.f.* ambiguity.
ambiguo, -gua, *a.* ambiguous.
ambir, *n.m.* (*Hisp. Am.*) tobacco juice *or* stain.
ámbito, *n.m.* area; sphere; compass, limited space; scope, limit.
ambivalencia, *n.f.* ambivalence.
ambivalente, *a.* ambivalent.
amblar, *v.i.* to amble, pace.
ambleo, *n.m.* short thick wax-candle; candlestick.
ambligonio, -nia, *a.* obtuse-angled.
ambliopía, *n.f.* (*med.*) amblyopia.
ambo, *n.m.* (*Hisp. Am.*) two-piece (man's) suit.
ambón, *n.m.* ambo.
ambos, -bas, *a.pl.* both; ***ambos a dos, ambas a dos,*** both, both together.
ambrosía, *n.f.* ambrosia.
ambrosiano, -na, *a.* Ambrosian.
Ambrosio, *n.m.* Ambrose.
ambuesta, *n.f.* contents held in the hollow of two hands.
ambulación, *n.f.* ambulation.
ambulancia, *n.f.* ambulance; field-hospital; ***ambulancia de correos,*** mail coach.
ambulanciero, -ra, *n.m.f.* ambulance driver; nurse.
ambulante, *a.* ambulatory, itinerant, roving, of no fixed abode. — *n.m.* ***ambulante de correos,*** mail-coach official.
ambular, *v.i.* to wander about.
ambulativo, -va, *a.* ambulatory, roving, shifting, itinerant.
ambulatorio, -ria, *a.* ambulatory.
ameba, *n.f.* amœba.
amebeo, -bea, *a., n.m.f.* (dialogue) in verse.
amechar, *v.t.* to put wicks in (lamps *or* candles); to lard (*meat*).
amedrentador, -ra, *a.* threatening, terrifying, frightening.
amedrentar, *v.t.* to frighten, terrify; put the fear of God into; to intimidate.
ámel, *n.m.* district chief.
amelar, *v.i.* to make honey (*bees*).
amelcochar, *v.t.* (*Hisp. Am.*) to pulp molasses into.
amelga, *n.f.* ridge (between two furrows).
amelgado, *n.m.* (*prov.*) hillock, boundary; unevenly grown wheat.
amelgar [B], *v.t.* to open furrows in; to mark (*boundaries*) with mounds.
amelía, *n.f.* district governed by an ***ámel.***
amelo, *n.m.* (*bot.*) golden starwort.
amelonado, -da, *a.* melon-shaped; (*coll.*) silly.
amelonarse, *v.r.* to go silly.
amén (1), *adv.* besides; ***amén de,*** besides, in addition to.
amén (2), *n.m.* amen, so be it; ***decir a todo amén,*** to agree to everything; ***en un decir amén,*** in an instant.
amenaza, *n.f.* threat, menace.
amenazador, -ra, *a.* threatening.
amenazante, *a.* threatening, menacing, impending.
amenazar [C], *v.t.* to threaten, menace; ***amenazar de muerte,*** to threaten with death; ***amenazó (con) matarme,*** he threatened to kill me.
amencia, *n.f.* (*obs.*) dementia.
amenguamiento, *n.m.* diminution, lessening.
amenguar [H], *v.t.* to defame, dishonour; to diminish, lessen.
amenidad, *n.f.* agreeableness, pleasantness.
amenizar [C], *v.t.* to make pleasant *or* agreeable.
ameno, -na, *a.* pleasant, delightful; ***una película amena,*** an entertaining film; ***un libro ameno,*** a readable book.
amenorrea, *n.f.* (*med.*) amenorrhœa, suppression of the menses.
amentáceo, -cea, *a.* (*bot.*) amentaceous.
amentar [1], *v.t.* to lace (*shoes etc.*).
amento, *n.m.* shoe-lace; leather string; (*bot.*) ament.
amerar, *v.t.* to soak, mix with water. — **amerarse,** *v.r.* to become sodden.
amerengado, -da, *a.* like meringue, containing meringue; (*coll.*) affected, mincing.

América, *n.f.* America; ***(la) América Central,*** Central America; ***(la) América del Norte,*** North America; ***(la) América del Sur,*** South America; ***(la) América Latina,*** Latin America.

americana (I), *n.f.* coat, jacket.

americanismo, *n.m.* (*gram.*) Americanism (*applied to Hisp. Am. words and phrases*); admiration *or* sympathy for anything American.

americanista, *n.m.f.* scholar devoted to American studies; Americanist.

americanizar [C], *v.t.* to Americanize. — **americanizarse,** *v.r.* to become Americanized, go American.

americano, -na (2), *a.*, *n.m.f.* American; South American, Spanish American.

amerindio, -dia, *a.*, *n.m.f.* Amerindian, American Indian.

ameritar, *v.i.* to have *or* gain worth, show *or* prove one's worth.

amerizar [C], *v.i.* [AMARAR].

amestizado, -da, *a.* like a half-breed.

ametalado, -da, *a.* metallic, metal-like.

ametista, *n.f.*, **ametisto,** *n.m.* (*min.*) amethyst.

ametrallador, *n.m.* machine-gunner.

ametralladora, *n.f.* machine-gun.

ametrallar, *v.t.* to machine-gun; (*fig.*) ***ametrallar con preguntas,*** to fire questions at (mercilessly).

amezquinarse, *v.r.* to complain.

amezquindarse, *v.r.* to become sad.

amia, *n.f.* (*ichth.*) cub shark; bow fin.

amianto, *n.m.* asbestos.

amiba, *n.f.* amœba.

amiboideo, -dea, *a.* amœboid, amœbic.

amicísimo, -ma, *a. superl.* most friendly.

amida, *n.f.* (*chem.*) amide.

amidina, *n.f.* (*chem.*) amidin.

amidol, *n.m.* (*photo.*) amidol.

amiento, *n.m.* leather strap (*to secure helmet*); shoelace; leather string.

amiga (I), *n.f.* (*prov.*) primary *or* elementary school.

amigable, *a.* friendly.

amigar [B], *v.t.* to make (people) friends; to acquaint. — **amigarse,** *v.r.* to become friends; to live in concubinage.

amigdaláceo, -cea, *a.* (*bot.*) amygdalaceous. — *n.f.pl.* (**amigdaláceas**) Amygdalaceæ.

amígdalas, *n.f.pl.* (*med.*) tonsils.

amigdalina, *n.f.* (*chem.*) amygdalin.

amigdalitis, *n.f. inv.* tonsillitis.

amigdalotomía, *n.f.* (*surg.*) tonsillectomy.

amigo, -ga (2), *a.* friendly; fond, keen; ***países (puertos) amigos,*** friendly countries (ports); ***es muy amigo de dar consejos,*** he's very fond of giving advice. — *n.m.f.* friend; lover; ***amigo del alma*** *or* ***del corazón,*** bosom friend; ***es muy amigo mío,*** he's a great friend of mine; ***tener cara de pocos amigos,*** to be stern-faced *or* severe, look forbidding; ***¡(para que) tenga usted amigos!*** that's friends for you!; ***amigo reconciliado, enemigo doblado,*** don't trust a reconciled friend; ***a muertos y a idos, no hay (más) amigos,*** out of sight, out of mind; ***cuanto más amigos, más claros,*** let there be no secrets between friends. — *n.f.* mistress.

amigote, *n.m.* (*coll.*) pal, buddy, crony.

amiláceo, -cea, *a.* amylaceous, starchy.

amilanado, -da, *a.* cowardly; intimidated.

amilanamiento, *n.m.* cowering fear.

amilanar, *v.t.* to frighten, terrify; to intimidate, cow. — **amilanarse,** *v.r.* to become terrified *or* cowed.

Amílcar, *n.m.* Amilcar.

amillaramiento, *n.m.* tax assessment.

amillarar, *v.t.* to assess the tax on.

amillonado, -da, *a.* liable to pay a tax called ***millones***; wealthy, opulent. — *n.m.f.* millionaire, very rich person.

amimar, *v.t.* to wheedle, flatter, fondle, pet.

amín, *n.m.* (*Morocco*) tax collector.

amina, *n.f.* (*chem.*) amine.

amínico, -ca, *a.* (*chem.*) aminic.

aminoácidos, *n.m.pl.* (*chem.*) amino acids.

aminoración, *n.f.* lessening; diminution.

aminorar, *v.t.* to lessen, diminish.

amir, *n.m.* ameer, amir.

amirí, *a.* applied to the descendants of Ibn Abi'Amir Mohammed (called Almanzor in Spain).

amistad, *n.f.* friendship; (friendly) connection, friend; concubinage; ***hacer las amistades,*** to become reconciled, make up; ***romper las amistades,*** to fall out; ***trabar amistad,*** to strike up a friendship.

amistar, *v.t.* to reconcile (*enemies*), make (*people*) friends. — **amistarse,** *v.r.* to become reconciled; to become acquainted *or* friends.

amistoso, -sa, *a.* friendly, amicable, cordial.

amito, *n.m.* (*eccles.*) amice.

amnesia, *n.f.* (*med.*) amnesia.

amnésico, -ca, *a.* amnesic.

amnícola, *a.* growing along rivers.

amnios, *n.m. inv.* (*zool.*) amnion, fœtal envelope.

amniótico, -ca, *a.* amniotic.

amnistía, *n.f.* amnesty.

amnistiar [L], *v.t.* to give amnesty, grant pardon to.

amo, *n.m.* master; master of a house; employer; head of a family; proprietor; overseer; foster-father; lord; (*coll.*) boss; (*pl.*) master and mistress; landlord and his wife; (*Chi., Mex.*) ***nuestro amo,*** the consecrated host; ***amo de casa,*** householder; ***el ojo del amo engorda el ganado,*** the best work is done in the master's presence; ***asentar con amo,*** to contract for service; (*coll.*) ***ser el amo del cotarro,*** to rule the roost.

amoblar [4], *v.t.* to furnish.

amoceto, *n.m.* larva of river lamprey.

amodita, *n.f.* horned serpent.

amodorrado, -da, *a.* heavy with sleep, drowsy.

amodorramiento, *n.m.* drowsiness, sleepiness.

amodorrante, *a.* soporific.

amodorrarse, *v.r.* to get drowsy; to grow numb; to fall asleep.

amodorrido, -da, *a.* drowsy, sleepy.

amogotado, -da, *a.* knoll-shaped, humped; paplike.

amohecerse [9], *v.r.* to grow rusty *or* mouldy.

amohinar, *v.t.* to irritate, worry; to fret. — **amohinarse,** *v.r.* to become annoyed, fretful *or* peevish.

amojamado, -da, *a.* dried up, shrivelled.

amojamar, *v.t.* to dry and smoke (*tunny-fish*). — **amojamarse,** *v.r.* to dry up, shrivel up.

amojelar, *v.t.* (*naut.*) to seize (*a cable*).

amojonador, *n.m.* one who sets landmarks.

amojonamiento, *n.m.* setting of landmarks.

amojonar, *v.t.* to set landmarks to.

amoladera, *n.f.* whetstone, grindstone.

amolador, -ra, *a.* grinding, sharpening; boring. — *n.m.* grinder, sharpener; (*coll.*) bore, tiresome person.

amoladura, *n.f.* whetting, grinding; (*pl.*) grit.

amolar [4], *v.t.* to grind, sharpen, whet; (*coll.*) to give a pain in the neck to, bore.

amoldador, -ra, *a.* moulding.

amoldamiento, *n.m.* moulding, fitting, modelling.

amoldar, *v.t.* to mould; to adapt, fit, model; to brand (*cattle*). — **amoldarse,** *v.r.* to adapt oneself.

amole, *n.m.* soap root *or* bark.

amollar, *v.t.* (*naut.*) to ease off; to pay out. — *v.i.* to play low (*cards*); to yield, give in.

amollentar, *v.t.* to soften.

amolletado, -da, *a.* roll- *or* loaf-shaped.

amomo, *n.m.* (*bot.*) grain of paradise.
amonarse, *v.r.* (*coll.*) to get tight.
amondongado, -da, *a.* (*coll.*) fat, flabby; coarse.
amonedación, *n.f.* coinage; coining.
amonedado, -da, *a.* monied, wealthy.
amonedar, *v.t.* to coin, mint.
amonestación, *n.f.* admonition, warning; (*pl.*) marriage banns; ***correr las amonestaciones,*** to publish banns of marriage.
amonestador, -ra, *a.* admonishing, warning. — *n.m.f.* monitor; admonisher.
amonestamiento, *n.m.* admonishment.
amonestar, *v.t.* to advise, forewarn; to admonish; to publish (*banns of marriage*).
amoniacal, *a.* ammoniacal, ammoniated.
amoníaco, -ca, *a.* ammoniac. — *n.m.* ammonia; gum resin.
amónico, -ca, *a.* ammoniac, ammoniacal; ammoniated.
amonio, *n.m.* (*chem.*) ammonium.
amonita, *n.f.* (*zool.*) ammonite.
amontar, *v.t.* to put to flight, chase off. — **amontarse,** *v.r.* to take cover *or* shelter; to take to the hills *or* mountains.
amontillado, *n.m.* amontillado sherry.
amontonadamente, *adv.* in heaps; chaotically.
amontonamiento, *n.m.* heaping, accumulating, gathering; conglomeration, pile.
amontonar, *v.t.* to heap, pile, stack, accumulate, hoard, congest, crowd. — **amontonarse,** *v.r.* to pile up; to crowd together; to drift, bank up (of snow).
amor, *n.m.* love, affection; (*bot.*) great bur parsley, burdock; (*bot.*) ***amor de hortelano,*** goosegrass; ***amor mío,*** my love *or* dear; ***amor al arte,*** love of art; ***por amor de,*** for the love *or* sake of; ***por amor de Dios,*** for the love of God; ***amor propio,*** self-esteem, pride, amour propre; ***a su amor,*** at one's ease; ***en amor y compañía,*** in friendship, harmoniously; ***al amor del fuego*** or ***de la lumbre,*** by the fireside *or* hearth; ***amor con amor se paga,*** one good turn deserves another; ***donde hay amor, hay dolor,*** there's no rose without a thorn; (*pl.*) gallantry; amours; love affairs; ***con*** or ***de mil amores,*** with the greatest pleasure; (*bot.*) ***amores (mil),*** red valerian.
amoral, *a.* amoral.
amoralidad, *n.f.* amorality.
amoralismo, *n.m.* (*phil.*) amoralism.
amoratado, -da, *a.* black-and-blue.
amoratar, *v.t.* to turn purple; to make black and blue. — **amoratarse,** *v.r.* to turn purple; to go black and blue.
amorcillo, *n.m.* figurine of Cupid; passing fancy, flirtation.
amordazar [C], *v.t.* to gag, muzzle; (*naut.*) to fasten with bitts.
amorecer [9], *v.t.* to mate (*ram with ewe*).
amorfia, *n.f.* amorphism.
amorfo, -fa, *a.* amorphous.
amorgar [B], *v.t.* to drug (*fish*) with olive pulp.
amoricones, *n.m.pl.* (*coll.*) love glances, flirtation.
amorío, *n.m.* love-affair, love-making, amour.
amoriscado, -da, *a.* Moorish, Moorish-looking.
amormado, -da, *a.* suffering from glanders (*horses*).
amormío, *n.m.* (*bot.*) sea-daffodil.
amorosidad, *n.f.* amorousness, love, affection; ***con amorosidad,*** with loving care.
amoroso, -sa, *a.* loving, affectionate, pleasing; gentle, mild, serene.
amorrar, *v.i.* (*coll.*) to hold down the head; to muse; to be sullen; (*naut.*) to pitch. — **amorrarse,** *v.r.* to sulk.
amorreo, -rrea, *a.* concerning *or* pertaining to the biblical Amorites.
amorronar, *v.t.* (*naut.*) to roll and knot (*a flag*); to make (*a waft*) for hoisting as a signal of distress.
amortajar, *v.t.* to shroud (*a corpse*).
amortecer [9], *v.t.* to deaden, muffle. — **amortecerse,** *v.r.* to faint; to die away.
amorteicmiento, *n.m.* swoon, fainting; deadening, muffling.
amortiguación, *n.f.,* **amortiguamiento,** *n.m.* softening, dulling, deadening; cushioning, absorbing.
amortiguador, -ra, *a.* softening, deadening, muffling, absorbing. — *n.m.f.* softener, reducer. — *n.m.* (*mech.*) shock-absorber; bumper; buffer, damper.
amortiguar [H], *v.t.* to deaden, muffle; to cushion, absorb (*blow, shock, effect*); to soften, tone down (*colour*); to damp down (*fire*).
amortizable, *a.* redeemable (*annuities etc.*), inalienable, payable.
amortización, *n.f.* liquidation, paying off (*a debt*), amortization; (*com.*) redemption, paying off; ***caja*** or ***fondo de amortización,*** sinking fund.
amortizar [C], *v.t.* to amortize; to pay off, pay back, repay (*debts*); to recoup, recover (*money sunk in business*); to render (*an estate*) inalienable by transferring (*it*) to a community; to suppress (*offices etc.*); to refund.
amoscar [A], *v.t.* to drive away (*flies*). — **amoscarse,** *v.r.* to get irritable, peeved, annoyed; to get suspicious.
amosquilado, -da, *a.* (*prov.*) tormented with flies (*cattle*).
amostachado, -da, *a.* moustached.
amostazar [C], *v.t.* (*coll.*) to exasperate, provoke. — **amostazarse,** *v.r.* to get irritated *or* peeved.
amotinado, -da, *a.* mutinous, rebellious; riotous. — *n.m.f.* mutineer, insurgent, rebel; rioter.
amotinador, -ra, *a.* mutinous, riotous, rabble-rousing. — *n.m.f.* inciter to mutiny *or* riot, rabble-rouser.
amotinamiento, *n.m.* mutiny, rebellion, insurrection; rioting.
amotinar, *v.t.* to incite to mutiny, rebellion *or* riot. — **amotinarse,** *v.r.* to mutiny, riot.
amover [4], *v.t.* to remove; to dismiss.
amovibilidad, *n.f.* revocableness; removability.
amovible, *a.* removable; revocable.
ampac, *n.m.* (*bot.*) champac.
ampara, *n.f.* (*prov., law*) embargo, confiscation.
amparador, -ra, *a.* protecting, defending, sheltering. — *n.m.f.* protector, defender.
amparar, *v.t.* to shelter; to protect, help, support, assist; (*prov.*) to confiscate; (*Hisp. Am.*) to fulfil the requirements for registering and working (*a mine*); (*law*) ***amparar en la posesión,*** to maintain in possession. — **ampararse,** *v.r.* to enjoy favour *or* protection; to defend oneself; to seek shelter; ***ampararse a,*** to have recourse to, seek the protection of; ***ampararse de,*** to seek the protection of, avail oneself of.
amparo, *n.m.* favour, aid, succour, protection; guardianship; refuge; (*law*) confiscation; (*prov.*) fragment, chip; (*sl.*) prisoner's advocate; asylum, shelter; (*Hisp. Am.*) registration of mine ownership.
ampelideo, -dea, *a.* (*bot.*) ampelideous. — (*n.f.pl.*) **ampelideas,** ampelopsis.
ampelografía, *n.f.* viticulture.
ampelográfico, -ca, *a.* viticultural.
ampelógrafo, -fa, *n.m.f.* viticulturist.
amper, amperio, *n.m.* (*elec.*) ampere; ***amperio hora,*** ampere hour; ***amperio vuelta,*** ampere turn.
amperaje, *n.m.* amperage.
amperímetro, *n.m.* amperemeter.
amplexicaulo, -la, *a.* (*bot.*) amplexicaul.
amplexo, -xa, *a.* (*bot.*) amplexifoliate.

ampliación, *n.f.* enlargement, extension, expansion.
ampliador, -ra, *a.* amplifying, enlarging. — *n.m.f.* amplifier, enlarger.
ampliar [L], *v.t.* to broaden, enlarge, extend.
ampliativo, -va, *a.* enlarging.
amplificación, *n.f.* enlargement; (*rhet.*) amplification.
amplificador, -ra, *a.* amplifying, enlarging. — *n.m.f.* (*photo.*) enlarger. — *n.m.* (*rad.*) amplifier.
amplificar [A], *v.t.* to amplify, enlarge, extend.
amplificativo, -va, *a.* amplifying, enlarging.
amplio, -lia, *a.* ample, extensive; large, full, roomy; broad, wide.
amplitud, *n.f.* extent, greatness, fullness; roominess; (*astron.*) amplitude.
ampo, *n.m.* whiteness; ***blanco como el ampo de la nieve,*** white as snow.
ampolla, *n.f.* blister; vial, cruet; bubble; lamp bulb; ampoule.
ampollar, *a.* resembling a bladder, bubble *or* blister. — *v.t.* to blister; to hollow. — **ampollarse,** *v.r.* to become blistered, hollow *or* bulb-like; to form blisters *or* bubbles.
ampolleta, *n.f.* small vial *or* cruet; hour-glass; bulb; (*naut.*) sand-glass.
ampón, -pona, *a.* frothy, redundant; bulky, large, puffed up.
amprar, *v.i.* (*prov.*) to borrow.
ampulosidad, *n.f.* pomposity, verbosity, bombast.
ampuloso, -sa, *a.* pompous, bombastic, flowery.
amputación, *n.f.* amputation.
amputar, *v.t.* to amputate.
amuchachado, -da, *a.* boyish, childish.
amueblar, *v.t.* to furnish.
amugamiento, *n.m.* (act of) setting landmarks.
amugronamiento, *n.m.* layering.
amugronar, *v.t.* to layer (*the shoot of a vine*).
amujerado, -da, *a.* effeminate.
amujeramiento, *n.m.* effeminacy.
amular, *v.i.* to be sterile (*mares*).
amulatado, -da, *a.* mulatto-like.
amuleto, *n.m.* amulet.
amunicionar, *v.t.* to supply with ammunition.
amuñecado, -da, *a.* puppet-like.
amura, *n.f.* (*naut.*) beam (of a ship); tack (of a sail).
amurada, *n.f.* (*naut.*) interior side of a ship.
amurallar, *v.t.* to surround with walls, wall in.
amurar, *v.t.* (*naut.*) to fasten (*corner of sail*) for tacking; to haul on (*a sail*) by the tack. — *v.i.* to tack.
amurcar [A], *v.t.* to gore.
amurco, *n.m.* goring.
amurillar, *v.t.* (*agric.*) to earth up.
amurriarse, *v.r.* to become melancholic *or* sullen; to become downcast; to be under the weather.
amusco, -ca, *a.* brown.
amusgar [B], *v.t.* to throw back (*ears*); to screw up (*eyes*).
amuso, *n.m.* (*hist.*) marble slab with the signs of the compass; mariner's compass.
Ana, *n.f.* Ann(e), Anna.
ana (1), *n.f.* ell.
ana(2), *n.f.* abbreviation to signify equal parts.
anabaptismo, *n.m.* Anabaptism.
anabaptista, *a.*, *n.m.f.* Anabaptist.
anacarado, -da, *a.* like mother-of-pearl.
anacardino, -na, *a.* mixed with anacardium. — *n.f.* confection made of anacardium *or* cashew-nut.
anacardo, *n.m.* cashew-tree, cashew-nut.
anacatártico, -ca, *a.* (*med.*) emetic.
anaclástica, *n.f.* (*opt.*) anaclastics.
anaco, *n.m.* (*Bol., Per.*) dress of Indian women; (*Ec.*) women's hairdressing.
anaconda, *n.f.* (*Hisp. Am.*) anaconda.
anacoreta, *n.m.f.* anchorite, hermit.
anacorético, -ca, *a.* anchoretical.
anacreóntico, -ca, *a.* Anacreontic.
anacrónico, -ca, *a.* anachronistic, anachronous.
anacronismo, *n.m.* anachronism.
ánade, *n.m.f.* duck.
anadear, *v.i.* to waddle.
anadeja, *n.f.* duckling.
anadeo, *n.m.* waddle.
anadino, -na, *n.m.f.* duckling, young duck.
anadón, *n.m.* young duck; non-floating log.
anadoncillo, *n.m.* grown duckling.
anaerobio, *a.* (*biol.*) anaerobic.
anafalla, anafaya, *n.f.* thick corded silk.
anafe, anafre, *n.m.* portable stove.
anafilaxis, *n.f. inv.* (*med.*) anaphylaxis.
anáfora, *n.f.* (*rhet.*) anaphora.
anafrodisia, *n.f.* (*med.*) anaphrodisia.
anafrodisíaco, -ca, *a.* (*med.*) anaphrodisiac.
anafrodita, *a.*, *n.m.f.* (person) abstaining from sexual pleasures.
anáglifo, *n.m.* (*arch.*) vase, vessel *or* other work adorned with sculpture in bas-relief.
anagnórisis, *n.f. inv.* (*poet.*) anagnorisis, recognition.
anagoge, anagogia, *n.f.* anagoge, anagogy.
anagógicamente, *adv.* anagogically.
anagógico, -ca, *a.* anagogical.
anagrama, *n.m.* anagram.
anagramático, -ca, *a.* anagrammatical.
anagramatizador, -ra, *n.m.f.* anagrammatist.
anagramatizar [C], *v.t.* to anagrammatize.
anaiboa, *n.m.* (*Cuba*) cassava juice.
anal, *a.* anal, relating to the anus.
analectas, *n.m.pl.* analects, literary gleanings.
analéptico, -ca, *a.* (*med.*) analeptic; comforting, restorative.
anales, *n.m.pl.* annals.
analfabetismo, *n.m.* illiteracy.
analfabeto, -ta, *a.*, *n.m.f.* illiterate.
analgesia, *n.f.* (*med.*) analgesia.
analgésico, -ca, *a.* (*med.*) analgesic.
analgesina, *n.f.* (*chem.*) antipyrine.
análisis, *n.m. inv.* analysis; (*gram.*) parsing; (*math.*) analysis; ***análisis cualitativo*** (***cuantitativo***), qualitative (quantitative) analysis; ***análisis gramatical,*** parsing.
analista (1), *n.m.* annalist.
analista (2), *n.m.* analyst.
analítico, -ca, *a.* analytical. — *n.f.* analytics.
analizable, *a.* analysable.
analizador, -ra, *a.* analysing. — *n.m.f.* analyst; analyser.
analizar [C], *v.t.* to analyse; (*gram.*) to parse.
analogía, *n.f.* analogy, resemblance.
analógico, -ca, *a.* analogic, analogical.
analogismo, *n.m.* (*med.*) empiricism.
análogo, -ga, *a.* analogous, similar; (*biol.*) analogue.
anamorfosis, *n.f. inv.* (*phys.*) anamorphosis.
ananá(s), *n.f.* (*bot.*) pineapple.
anapelo, *n.m.* (*bot.*) wolf's-bane.
anapesto, *n.m.* anapæst.
anaquel, *n.m.* shelf.
anaquelería, *n.f.* shelving, case of shelves.
anaranjado, -da, *a.* orange-coloured. — *n.m.* orange (*colour*).
anarquía, *n.f.* anarchy.
anárquico, -ca, *a.* anarchical.
anarquismo, *n.m.* anarchism.
anarquista, *a.* anarchical. — *n.m.f.* anarchist.
anarquizar [C], *v.t.* to spread anarchism *or* anarchy in.
anasarca, *n.f.* (*med.*) general dropsy.

anascote, *n.m.* twilled woollen serge.
anastasia, *n.f.* (*bot.*) mugwort.
anastomosis, *n.f. inv.* (*anat.*) anastomosis.
anástrofe, *n.f.* (*rhet.*) anastrophe.
anata, *n.f.* annates, yearly income; ***media anata,*** the annates of the half-year.
anatema, *n.f.*, **anatematismo,** *n.m.* anathema; excommunication.
anatematizar [C], *v.t.* to anathematize, excommunicate.
anatife, *n.m.* (*ichth.*) goose-barnacle.
anatista, *n.m.* officer for the half-year's annates.
anatolio, -lia, *a.*, *n.m.f.* Anatolian.
anatomía, *n.f.* anatomy.
anatómico, -ca, *a.* anatomical. — *n.m.f.* anatomist.
anatomista, *n.m.f.* anatomist.
anatomizar [C], *v.t.* to anatomize, dissect; (*art.*) to bring out, emphasize (*bones and muscles*).
anavajado, -da, *a.* knife-scarred.
anca, *n.f.* croup (*of a horse*); haunch; (*frog's*) leg; (*coll.*) buttock; ***a ancas, a las ancas,*** behind; (*coll.*) ***llevar*** or ***traer a las ancas a alguien,*** to keep *or* maintain somebody.
ancado, -da, *a.* (*vet.*) stringhalted, stringtied. — *n.m.* stringhalt.
ancianidad, *n.f.* old age.
anciano, -na, *a.* elderly. — *n.m.f.* elderly person.
ancillar, *a.* ancillary.
ancla, *n.f.* anchor; (*slang*) hand; (*naut.*) ***ancla de la esperanza,*** sheet-anchor; ***ancla de servidumbre,*** bower anchor; ***zafar el ancla para dar fondo,*** to clear the anchor for coming to; ***uñas del ancla,*** anchor arms; ***pico del anca,*** bill of the anchor; ***echar anclas,*** to anchor; ***levar anclas,*** to weigh anchor; ***estar sobre el ancla*** or ***las anclas,*** to be anchored, be at anchor.
ancladero, *n.m.* anchorage, anchoring-place.
anclaje, *n.m.* casting anchor; anchoring-ground; ***derecho de anclaje,*** anchorage rights.
anclar, *v.i.* to anchor, cast anchor.
anclote, *n.m.* stream-anchor, grapnel, kedge.
anclotillo, *n.m.* kedge-anchor.
ancolia, *n.f.* (*bot.*) columbine.
ancón, *n.m.*, **anconada,** *n.f.* small cove, inlet, bay; (*Mex.*) corner, angle, nook.
áncora, *n.f.* anchor.
ancoraje, *n.m.* anchorage; anchoring; anchors.
ancorar, *v.i.* to anchor, cast anchor.
ancorca, *n.f.* yellow ochre.
ancorel, *n.m.* stone sinker (for fishing nets).
ancorería, *n.f.* anchor-forge.
ancorero, *n.m.* anchor-smith.
ancudo, -da, *a.* big-rumped.
ancusa, *n.f.* (*bot.*) alkanet.
ancusina, *n.f.* (*chem.*) alkanet.
ancuviña, *n.f.* (*Chi.*) Indian grave.
ancharia, *n.f.* width of cloth (*among merchants and traders*).
ancheta, *n.f.* small quantity (*of goods*); profit.
anchicorto, -ta, *a.* wide and short.
ancho, -cha, *a.* broad, wide; full, ample, loose, loose-fitting; ***a sus anchas,*** at one's ease; ***tener (la) manga ancha,*** to have a generous conscience, be liberal-minded, be easy-going *or* understanding; ***estar más ancho que largo,*** to be as pleased as Punch; ***¡ancha es Castilla!*** there's room for all tastes *or* views. — *n.m.* width, breadth; ***ancho de vía,*** track gauge.
ancho(v)a, *n.f.* anchovy.
anchura, *n.f.* width, breadth; spaciousness, extensiveness; fullness, ampleness.
anchuroso, -sa, *a.* broad, wide, spacious, ample, extensive.
andábata, *n.m.* blindfolded gladiator.
andaboba, *n.f.* card-game.
andada, *n.f.* [ANDADO].
andaderas, *n.f.pl.* go-cart.
andadero, -ra, *a.* passable, fit *or* suitable for walking; wandering. — *n.m.f.* runner, walker.
andado, -da, *a.* beaten, trodden (*path*); worse for wear; elapsed; threadbare; customary. — *n.f.* thin hard-baked cake; track, trail, pathway; (*pl.*) tracks (of game); ***volver a las andadas,*** to get up to one's old tricks.
andador, -ra, *a.* swift, good at walking *or* running; wandering. — *n.m.f.* good walker. — *n.m.* junior minister of justice; messenger (of a court); (*naut.*) fine sailor; alley, garden path; (*pl.* **andadores**) reins (*for child*); ***no necesito*** or ***puedo andar sin andadores,*** I can look after myself.
andadura, *n.f.* gait, pacing; amble.
andahuertas, *n.f. inv.* (*orn.*) garden warbler.
Andalucía, *n.f.* Andalusia.
andaluz, -za, *a.*, *n.m.f.* Andalusian.
andaluzada, *n.f.* typical piece of Andalusian behaviour, talk *or* exaggeration; typical piece of Andalusian stuff *or* rubbish (*e.g. play* or *film*); typical Andalusian yarn *or* tall story.
andamiada, *n.f.*, **andamiaje,** *n.m.* scaffolding.
andamio, *n.m.* scaffold, platform; (*coll.*) footwear; (*naut.*) gang-plank.
andana, *n.f.* row, line; tier; (*coll.*) ***llamarse andana,*** to go back on a promise.
andanada, *n.f.* (*naut.*) broadside; grandstand (*bull-ring*); (*coll.*) reproof, reprimand, tirade; ***soltarle a uno una andanada,*** to give s.o. a real blowing-up *or* dressing-down.
andancia, *n.f.* (*And., Hisp. Am.*) slight epidemic.
andaniño, *n.m.* go-cart, baby-walker.
andante, *a.* walking, errant; ***caballero andante,*** knight errant; ***es la inutilidad andante,*** he is the personification of uselessness. — *n.m.* (*mus.*) andante.
andantesco, -ca, *a.* belonging to knighthood *or* knight-errantry.
andanza(s), *n.f* (*pl.*) wandering(s), travel(s); life, doings, actions; ***buena (mala) andanza,*** good (bad) fortune.
andar, *n.m.* (*pl.* **andares**) gait; pace; walking; ***a largo andar,*** in the long run; ***estar a un andar,*** to be within walking distance; ***el andar del tiempo,*** the passing of time.

andar [11], *v.i.* to walk, go on foot; to go, come; to work, function (*machine*); to run; to be; to get along, be going;

(*to walk, go*) ***andar a cuerpo,*** to go out without a coat; ***andar de la ceca a la meca,*** to go wandering *or* roaming about; ***andar a gatas,*** to go on all fours; ***a todo andar,*** at full speed; ***¡anda a paseo!*** clear out!; ***andar a tientas,*** to feel one's way; ***andar tras,*** to run after; ***andar de acá para allá,*** to wander *or* roam about, wander hither and thither; ***andar de prisa,*** to walk *or* go quickly; ***andar de puntillas,*** to walk on tip-toe; ***andar a caballo (en bicicleta, en coche),*** to ride on horseback (on a bicycle, in a car); ***andar tierras,*** to go places;

(*to function* or *work*) ***andar a derechas,*** to work properly; ***andar al uso,*** to conform; ***anda el mundo al*** or ***del revés,*** the world is upside down; ***andar manga por hombro,*** to be topsy-turvy *or* higgledy-piggledy; ***andar a las malas,*** to be on bad terms; ***todo se andará,*** all in good time;

(*to walk, go: fig.*) ***andar de capa caída,*** to be down on one's luck; ***andar a la caza de algo,*** to be in pursuit of sth.; ***andar con la cara descubierta,*** to act openly; ***andar en carnes*** or ***en cueros,*** to go stark naked; ***andar por los cerros de Ubeda,*** to be off the point; ***andar en coche,*** to be sitting pretty; ***andar en malos pasos,*** to be up to sth.; to have gone off the rails; ***andar en dares y tomares, andar en dimes y diretes, andar la tuya sobre la mía,*** to argue the toss; ***andar con pies de plomo*** to go very cautiously;

andar a puñetazos (puñaladas), to fight with fists (knives); ***andando el tiempo,*** in the course of time; ***dime con quién andas y te diré quién eres,*** a man is known by the company he keeps; ***andar en palmas,*** to be universally applauded, be a great success, be a hit; ***andar a sombra de tejado,*** to be in hiding, be on the run; ***andar con un palmo de lengua,*** to have one's tongue hanging out, be utterly fagged out; ***andar en la danza,*** to be involved in the affair, have a hand in it; ***andar a la que salta,*** to be on the look-out (for every opportunity); ***andar con el tiempo,*** to move with the times; ***andar holgado,*** to be comfortably off; ***andar listo,*** to be active *or* diligent; ***¡anda listo!*** he's got another think coming; ***anda que bebe los vientos por ella,*** he's in a terrible state over her, he's absolutely mad on her; ***quién mal anda, mal acaba,*** he who lives ill, dies ill; ***andar a vueltas con,*** to be busy with;

(to be) ***andar*** *is often used as an auxiliary verb instead of* **estar**: ***los negocios andan bien,*** business is good; ***andar alegre,*** to be merry; ***andar de boca en boca, andar en coplas,*** to be the talk of the town; ***andar en mangas de camisa,*** to be in one's shirt-sleeves; ***anda mal de dinero,*** he is hard up; ***anda por ahí,*** he is somewhere around; ***¡ande yo caliente, y ríase la gente!*** I'm all right, Jack!

— *v.r.* ***andarse con cumplidos,*** to stand upon ceremony; ***andarse por las ramas,*** to beat about the bush; ***andarse con cuidado,*** to go carefully; ***no andarse con rodeos,*** not to beat about the bush; ***no andarse con miramientos,*** to go ahead regardless; to make no bones about things.

andaraje, *n.m.* wheel (*of well*); frame (*of a garden roller*).

andariego, -ga, *a.* wandering, roving. — *n.m.f.* good walker.

andarín, -rina, *a.* walking. — *n.m.f.* (*coll.*) good walker, fast walker. — *n.f.* (*orn.*) swallow. — *n.m.pl.* (**andarines**) young partridges.

andarivel, *n.m.* cable ferry, cable way; (*naut.*) girt-line, safety rope; (*Arg.*) temporary *or* rope bridge; (*Arg.*) swimming lane; (*Col.*) trinkets.

andarríos, *n.m. inv.* wagtail.

andas, *n.f.pl.* bier *or* litter with shafts.

andén, *n.m.* platform; (*Hisp. Am.*) pavement.

andero, *n.m.* litter-bearer.

Andes, *n.m.pl.* Andes.

andinismo, *n.m.* (*Hisp. Am.*) mountaineering, climbing.

andinista, *n.m.f.* (*Hisp. Am.*) mountaineer, climber.

andino, -na, *a.* Andean.

ándito, *n.m.* gallery, corridor (*round a building*); sidewalk.

andolina, andorina, *n.f.* (*orn.*) swallow.

andón, *a.* (*Col., Cub., Ven.*) roving.

andorga, *n.f.* belly; ***llenar la andorga,*** to fill one's belly.

andorina [ANDOLINA].

Andorra, *n.f.* Andorra.

andorra, *n.f.* (*coll.*) gadabout.

andorrano, -na, *a., n.m.f.* Andorran.

andorrear, *v.i.* to gad about; to bustle about.

andorrero, -ra, *a.* gadabout; bustling.

andosco, -ca, *a., n.m.f.* two-year-old (*livestock*).

andrajero, -ra, *n.m.f.* rag-picker.

andrajo, *n.m.* rag, tatter; good-for-nothing.

andrajoso, -sa, *a.* ragged, tattered.

Andrés, *n.m.* Andrew.

andriana, *n.f.* (*obs.*) woman's gown.

andrina, *n.f.* (*bot.*) sloe.

andrino, *n.m.* (*bot.*) sloe-tree, blackthorn.

androfobia, *n.f.* androphobia.

andrógino, -na, *a.* androgynous. — *n.m.f.* (*bot., zool.*) androgyny.

androide, *n.m.* android.

Andrómeda, *n.f.* (*astron.*) Andromeda.

andrómina, *n.f.* (*coll.*) trick, fraud, piece of humbug, artifice.

androsemo, *n.m.* (*bot.*) St. John's wort.

andularios, *n.m.pl.* (*coll.*) long, trailing gown.

andullo, *n.m.* bale of tobacco; plug tobacco; (*naut.*) fender, shield.

andurriales, *n.m.pl.* byways, out-of-the-way place(s), place(s) off the beaten track.

anea, *n.f.* (*bot.*) bulrush, rush; ***silla de anea,*** rush-work chair.

aneaje, *n.m.* alnage, ell measure.

anear, *v.t.* to measure by ells; (*prov.*) to rock (*a cradle*).

aneblar [I], *v.t.* to cloud; to darken. — **aneblarse,** *v.r.* to become overcast.

anécdota, *n.f.* anecdote.

anecdótico, -ca, *a.* anecdotal.

anecdotista, *n.m.f.* anecdotist.

aneciarse, *v.r.* to become stupid.

anegable, *a.* subject to flooding, easily flooded.

anegación, *n.f.* flooding.

anegadizo, -za, *a.* subject to flooding, easily flooded.

anegar [B], *v.t.* to flood, inundate, submerge; to drown; to waterlog.

anegociado, -da, *a.* busy.

anejín, anejir, *n.m.* popular proverb put to music.

anejo, -ja, *a.* annexed, joined; accessory, dependent. — *n.m.* annex; dependency; supplement; benefice *or* church dependent upon another.

aneldo, *n.m.* (*bot.*) common dill.

aneléctrico, -ca, *a.* (*phys.*) anelectrical, non-electric.

anélido, -da, *n.m.f.* (*zool.*) annelid. — *n.m.pl.* (**anélidos**) Annelida.

anemia, *n.f.*(*med.*) anæmia.

anémico, -ca, *a.* anæmic.

anemografía, *n.f.* anemography.

anemográfico, -ca, *a.* anemographic.

anemometría, *n.f.* anemometry.

anemómetro, *n.m.* anemometer.

anémona, anémone, *n.f.* (*bot.*) anemone; wind-flower; ***anémona de mar,*** sea-anemone.

anemoscopio, *n.m.* anemoscope.

anepigráfico, -ca, *a.* without title *or* inscription.

anequín, *adv. phrase* ***a*** or ***de anequín,*** so much a head (*applied to the shearing of sheep*).

aneroide, *a., n.m.* (*phys.*) aneroid (barometer).

anestesia, *n.f.*(*med.*) anæsthesia.

anestesiar, *v.t.* to anæsthetize.

anestésico, -ca, *a., n.m.* anæsthetic.

aneurisma, *n.m.f.* (*med.*) aneurism.

anexar, *v.t.* to annex, join, attach.

anexidades, *n.f.pl.* annexes, belongings, appurtenances.

anexión, *n.f.* annexation.

anexionismo, *n.m.* annexationism.

anexionista, *a., n.m.f.* annexationist.

anexo, -xa, *a.* joined, annexed. — *n.m.* annexe; enclosure.

anfibio, -bia, *a.* amphibious. — *n.m.f.* amphibian. — *n.m.pl.* (**anfibios**) Amphibia.

anfibiografía, *n.f.*(*zool.*) amphibiography.

anfibiográfico, -ca, *a.* (*zool.*) amphibiographic.

anfíbol, *n.m.* (*min.*) amphibole.

anfibólico, -ca, *a.* amphibolous.

anfibolita, *n.f.* (*geol.*) amphibolite.

anfibología, *n.f.* (*rhet.*) amphibology.

anfibológicamente, *adv.* amphibologically.

anfibológico, -ca, *a.* (*rhet.*) amphibological.

anfíbraco, *n.m.* (*poet.*) amphibrach.

anfímacro, *n.m.* (*poet.*) amphimacer.

anfión, *n.m.* opium (*in the East Indies*).

anfioxo, *n.m.* (*zool.*) amphioxus.
anfípodo, -da, *a.* amphipod. — *n.m.pl.* (**anfípodos**) Amphipoda.
anfipróstilo, *n.m.* (*arch.*) amphiprostyle.
anfisbena, anfisibena, *n.f.* amphisbæna.
anfiscios, *n.m.pl.* (*geog.*) amphiscii.
anfiteatro, *n.m.* amphitheatre.
anfitrión, -riona, *n.m.f.* host, hostess.
Anfitrite, *n.f.* (*myth., astron.*) Amphitrite.
ánfora, *n.f.* amphora.
anfractuosidad, *n.f.* (*anat.*) anfractuosity; indentation; irregularity; twisting nature.
anfractuoso, -sa, *a.* anfractuous; irregular; twisting.
angaria, *n.f.* (*law*) angary.
angarillar, *v.t.* to put panniers on (*horses etc.*).
angarillas, *n.f.pl.* hand barrow; panniers; cruet-stand.
angarillón, *n.m.* large basket; large hand-barrow; (*coll.*) large clumsy body.
angaripola, *n.f.* striped calico; (*pl.*) gaudy, ostentatious ornaments on clothes.
ángaro, *n.m.* fire beacon.
angazo, *n.m.* instrument for catching shell-fish.
ángel, *n.m.* angel; (*ichth.*) angel-fish; (*artill.*) cross-bar shot; ***ángel custodio, ángel de la guarda,*** guardian angel; ***ángel malo,*** evil genius, devil; ***tener ángel,*** to have charm.
Ángela, *n.f.* Angela.
angélica (1), *n.f.* (*bot.*) angelica; ***angélica palustre,*** wild angelica; ***angélica carlina,*** carline thistle.
angelical, angélico, -ca (2), *a.* angelic(al).
angelico, angelito, *n.m.* little angel; baby; (*coll.*) ***estar con los angelitos,*** to be in the land of nod.
angelón, *n.m.* great angel; ***angelón de retablo,*** fat child.
angelote, *n.m.* large figure of an angel; chubby child, large *or* fat good-natured child; (*ichth.*) angel-fish.
ángelus, *n.m. inv.* angelus.
angina, *n.f.* (*med.*) angina, quinsy; ***angina de pecho,*** angina pectoris; (*pl.*) sore throat; ***tener anginas,*** to have a sore throat *or* tonsillitis.
anginoso, -sa, *a.* (*med.*) anginal, anginose.
angiografía, *n.f.* angiography.
angiospermo, -ma, *a.* (*bot.*) angiosperm. — *n.f.pl.* (**angiospermas**) Angiospermæ.
angla (1), *n.f.* cape, promontory.
anglesita, *n.f.* (*min.*) anglesite.
anglicanismo, *n.m.* anglicanism.
anglicano, -na, *a., n.m.f.* Anglican; ***la iglesia anglicana,*** the Anglican Church, Church of England.
anglicismo, *n.m.* anglicism.
anglo, -gla (2), *a.* Anglian. — *n.m.f.* Angle.
angloamericano, -na, *a., n.m.f.* Anglo-American.
anglocatólico, -ca, *a., n.m.f.* Anglo-Catholic.
angloespañol, -la, *a., n.m.f.* Anglo-Spanish (*person*).
anglófilo, -la, *a., n.m.f.* Anglophile.
anglófobo, -ba, *a., n.m.f.* Anglophobe.
angloíndio, -dia, *a., n.m.f.* Anglo-Indian.
angloiranio, -nia, *a., n.m.f.* Anglo-Iranian.
anglomanía, *n.f.* Anglomania; enthusiasm for England *or* English things.
anglómano, -na, *a., n.m.f.* Anglomaniac.
anglonormando, -da, *a., n.m.f.* Anglo-Norman.
anglonorteamericano, -na, *a., n.m.f.* Anglo-American.
angloparlante, *a.* English-speaking. — *n.m.f.* English-speaker.
anglosajón, -jona, *a., n.m.f.* Anglo-Saxon.
angolán, *n.m.* (*bot.*) alangium.
angorra, *n.f.* canvas *or* leather apron.
angostar, *v.t., v.i.* to narrow, contract.
angosto, -ta, *a.* narrow.
angostura, *n.f.* narrowness; narrow pass; strait.
angosturina, *n.f.* angostura bitters.
angra, *n.f.* small bay, cove.
angrelado, -da, *a.* (*her.*) engrailed.
anguarina, *n.f.* loose knee-length coat.
anguiforme, *a.* anguiform, serpent-like.
anguila, *n.f.* (*ichth.*) eel; (*pl.*) (*naut.*) launching-ways; ***anguila de cabo,*** rope's end, lash; ***escurrirse como una anguila,*** to be as slippery as an eel.
anguilazo, *n.m.* stroke with a rope's end.
anguilero, -ra, *n.m.f.* eel basket. — *n.f.* eel-buck, eel-pot; eel tank.
anguiliforme, *a.* (*ichth.*) eel-like.
anguililla, *n.f.* small irrigation channel.
anguina, *n.f.* (*vet.*) vein of the groins.
angula, *n.f.* elver, baby eel.
angular, *a.* angular; ***piedra angular,*** corner-stone.
angulema, *n.f.* coarse linen (*manufactured at Angoulême*); (*coll.*) fulsome flatteries.
ángulo, *n.m.* angle, corner, nook; (*astron.*) ***ángulo acimutal,*** azimuth; (*aer.*) ***ángulo de ataque,*** angle of attack; (*aer.*) ***ángulo de balance,*** angle of bank *or* roll; (*railw.*) ***ángulo de contingencia,*** interior intersection angle (*of two tangents*); (*aer.*) ***ángulo de resistencia nula,*** angle of zero lift; ***ángulo entrante,*** re-entrant angle; convex angle; (*geom.*) ***ángulo externo*** (***interno***), exterior (interior) angle; (*astron.*) ***ángulo horario,*** hour angle; ***ángulo recto,*** right angle; (*railw.*) ***ángulo tangencial,*** deflection angle (*from a tangent to a curve*); ***ángulos alternos externos*** (***internos***), alternate exterior (interior) angles; ***ángulos correspondientes,*** corresponding *or* interior-exterior angles; ***ángulos opuestos por el vértice,*** vertical angles.
anguloso, -sa, *a.* angular, sharp; sharp-cornered.
angurria, *n.f.* (*coll.*) strangury.
angustia, *n.f.* anguish, anxiety, agony of mind, (deep) distress; ***angustia existencial, vital,*** anxiety state; (*sl.*) prison; (*pl.*) (*sl.*) galleys.
angustiar, *v.t.* to cause (*s.o.*) anguish *or* anxiety, afflict, worry, distress. — **angustiarse,** *v.r.* to be (deeply) distressed, suffer agonies of mind.
angustioso, -sa, *a.* deeply distressing, agonizing; prone to anxiety.
anhelación, *n.f.* (*med.*) anhelation; panting; yearning; longing.
anhelante [ANHELOSO].
anhelar, *v.t.* to desire eagerly, crave, yearn *or* long for. — *v.i.* to gasp for breath; (+*inf.*) to long to, to yearn to.
anhélito, *n.m.* difficult breathing.
anhelo, *n.m.* anxiousness, eagerness, yearning, longing.
anheloso, -sa, *a.* panting, gasping for breath; eager, yearning.
anhídrico, -ca, *a.* (*chem.*) anhydrous.
anhídrido, *n.m.* (*chem.*) anhydride; ***anhídrido carbónico,*** carbon dioxide, carbonic acid gas; ***anhídrido sulfúrico,*** sulphur trioxide.
anhidrita, *n.f.* anhydrite.
anhidro, -ra, *a.* (*chem.*) anhydrous.
anhidrosis, *n.f. inv.* (*med.*) anhydrosis.
aní, *n.m.* (*Hisp. Am., orn.*) ani.
aniaga, *n.f.* (*prov.*) annual wage.
anidar, *v.t.* to cherish, shelter. — *v.i.* to nest; (*fig.*) to dwell.
anidiar, *v.t.* (*prov.*) to whitewash; to spring-clean.
anidio, *n.m.* (*prov.*) whitewashing; spring-cleaning.
anieblar [ANUBLAR].
aniego, *n.m.* abnegation.
anilina, *n.f.* (*chem.*) aniline.
anilla, *n.f.* curtain ring.

anillado, -da, *a.* ring-shaped, annulated. — *n.m.* (*zool.*) annelid.
anillar, *v.t.* to form into rings *or* circles; to ring.
anillejo, anillete, *n.m.* small ring.
anillo, *n.m.* ring, circuit; ring (*for finger*); ring (*of a turbine*); circular band; (*arch.*) astragal; (*naut.*) hank, grommet; (*slang*) fetters, irons; ***venir como anillo al dedo,*** to come just at the right time, be just right *or* just the thing; ***de anillo,*** honorary (*of posts, dignities etc.*); ***anillo del Pescador,*** (*papal*) fisherman's ring.
ánima, *n.f.* soul; (*artill.*) bore (*of gun*); (*pl.*) ringing of bells at sunset for prayers for souls in purgatory.
animación, *n.f.* animation, bustle, life, liveliness; (*pl.* **animaciones**) entertainment, floor show.
animador, -ra, *a.* animating, enlivening; encouraging, inspiring. — *n.m.f.* animator, enlivener; entertainer, comedian; master of ceremonies, chairman.
animadversión, *n.f.* antagonism, enmity, hostility, ill will.
animal, *a.* animal. — *n.m.* animal, creature, brute; ***animal de bellota,*** hog; (*fig. unfavourable* or *favourable*) ***¡qué animal!*** what a brute *or* beast! what an uncouth blighter! what a clumsy oaf! what a (magnificent) fellow! what a devil!
animalada, *n.f.* (*coll.*) stupid *or* clumsy thing to do *or* say; smashing thing to do *or* say; terrific amount, hell of a lot.
animalazo, animalote, *n.m.* big animal, hulking creature, hefty great brute; uncouth blighter.
animálculo, *n.m.* animalcule.
animalejo, animalillo, *n.m.* little animal *or* creature; miserable *or* wretched little animal *or* creature.
animalia, *n.f.* animals, animal kingdom.
animalidad, *n.f.* animality.
animalismo, *n.m.* animalism.
animalización, *n.f.* (*med.*) animalization.
animalizar [C], *v.t.* to animalize; to make into animal substance. — **animalizarse,** *v.r.* to sink to animal level.
animalucho, *n.m.* wretched *or* ugly little creature.
animar, *v.t.* to animate, enliven, put (some) life into; to entertain; to inspire, incite, excite; to encourage, comfort. — **animarse,** *v.r.* to get lively *or* merry; to cheer up, take heart.
anime, *n.f.* (*bot.*) courbaril.
animero, *n.m.* one who asks charity for souls in purgatory.
anímico, -ca, *a.* of the mind; spiritual; psychic.
animismo, *n.m.* animism.
animita, *n.f.* (*Hisp. Am.*) firefly.
ánimo, *n.m.* soul; spirit; will; courage; mind, thought; intention; encouragement; ***¡ánimo!*** courage! cheer up! buck up!; ***¡ánimo y adelante!*** press on!; ***se me cayó el ánimo,*** my heart sank; ***estado de ánimo,*** state *or* frame of mind; ***presencia de ánimo,*** presence of mind; ***tener ánimo de,*** to have a mind to, intend to; ***dar ánimo(s) a,*** to encourage, cheer up.
animosidad, *n.f.* courage, spirit; animosity.
animoso, -sa, *a.* brave, courageous, spirited.
aniñado, -da, *a.* child-like.
aniñarse, *v.r.* to grow childish.
anión, *n.m.* (*elec.*) anion.
aniquilación, *n.f.* annihilation.
aniquilador, -ra, *a.* annihilating, destroying.
aniquilamiento, *n.m.* annihilation, destruction.
aniquilar, *v.t.* to annihilate, destroy, crush. — **aniquilarse,** *v.r.* (*fig.*) to decline, decay, waste away; to become emaciated; to humble o.s.
anís, *n.m.* (*bot.*) anise; aniseed; anisette; (*pl.* **anises**) sugar-coated aniseeds.
anisado, -da, *a.* mixed with aniseed; anise-like; ***aguardiente anisado,*** aniseed brandy. — *n.m.* action of adding anise.
anisar, *n.m.* aniseed field. — *v.t.* to flavour with anise.
anisete, *n.m.* anisette.
anisillo, *n.m.* appetizer.
anisófilo, -la, *a.* (*bot.*) anisophyllous.
anisómero, -ra, *a.* (*bot.*) anisomerous.
anisométrico, -ca, *a.* (*min.*) anisometric.
anivelar [NIVELAR].
aniversario, -ria, *n.m.* anniversary; yearly requiem.
anjeo, *n.m.* coarse linen; burlap.
ano, *n.m.* (*anat.*) anus.
anoa, *n.f.* anoa, buffalo.
anoche, *adv.* last night.
anochecedor, -ra, *a.* nocturnal.
anochecer [9], *n.m.* dusk, nightfall, twilight; ***al anochecer,*** at dusk. — *v.i.* to grow dark; to be, find o.s. at nightfall; ***anochecí agotado,*** by nightfall I was worn out; ***nos anocheció en Madrid,*** night found us in Madrid.
anochecida, *n.f.* nightfall.
anodinar, *v.t.* to administer anodyne medicines to.
anodinia, *n.f.* (*med.*) anodynia, painlessness.
anodino, -na, *a.* anodyne; (*coll.*) insipid, dull, flat, colourless, uninteresting. — *n.m.* (*med.*) anodyne.
ánodo, *n.m.* (*phys.*) anode.
anofeles, *n.f. inv.* anopheles (mosquito).
anomalía, *n.f.* anomaly.
anomalístico, -ca, *a.* anomalistic.
anómalo, -la, *a.* anomalous.
anón, *n.m.* (*bot.*) custard-apple tree.
anona, *n.f.* (*bot.*) anona, custard-apple; store of provisions.
anonáceo, -cea, *a.* (*bot.*) anonaceous. — *n.f.pl.* (**anonáceas**) Anonaceæ.
anonadación, *n.f.*, **anonadamiento,** *n.m.* annihilation, obliteration, effacement.
anonadar, *v.t.* to annihilate, obliterate, crush; to humiliate.
anónimo, -ma, *a.* anonymous, nameless. — *n.m.* anonym; anonymity; anonymous letter.
anoria [NORIA].
anormal, *a.* abnormal.
anormalidad, *n.f.* abnormality.
anortita, *n.f.* (*min.*) anorthite.
anorza, *n.f.* (*bot.*) white bryony.
anotación, *n.f.* annotation, note.
anotador, -ra, *a.* annotating. — *n.m.f.* commentator, annotator.
anotar, *v.t.* to note, jot down; to annotate.
anquera, *n.f.* (*Mex.*) hind covering (*for horses*).
anqueta, *n.f.* small rump; ***estar de media anqueta,*** to be seated lopsidedly.
anquialmendrado, -da, *a.* having an almond-shaped rump.
anquiboyuno, -na, *a.* (*vet.*) having a rump like an ox.
anquilosar, *v.t.* to ankylose, fossilize, paralyse. — **anquilosarse,** *v.r.* to become fossilized, paralysed *or* stagnant.
anquilosis, *n.f. inv.* (*anat., vet.*) ankylosis, stiff joint.
anquirredondo, -da, *a.* (*vet.*) round-rumped.
anquiseco, -ca, *a.* thin-rumped.
ansa [HANSA].
ánsar, *n.m.* goose, gander.
ansarería, *n.f.* goose farm.
ansarero, -ra, *n.m.f.* gooseherd; goosegirl.
ansarino, -na, *a.* relating to geese. — *n.m.* gosling.
ansarón, *n.m.* large goose.
anseático [HANSEÁTICO].
ansí, *adv.* (*obs.*) so, thus.
ansia, *n.f.* anguish; eagerness; longing, yearning; voracious hunger; (*pl.*) nausea, retching.

ansiar [L and regular], *v.t.* to desire eagerly, long *or* yearn for; ***ansío saberlo,*** I long to know.
ansiedad, *n.f.* anxiety; nervous tension; eagerness; longing, yearning.
ansioso, -sa, *a.* anxious; eager; longing, yearning; voraciously hungry.
anta (1), *n.f.* (*zool.*) elk.
anta (2), *n.f.* obelisk; needle; (*arch.*) antæ.
antagallas, *n.f.pl.* (*naut.*) spritsail reef-bands.
antagónico, -ca, *a.* antagonistic.
antagonismo, *n.m.* antagonism.
antagonista, *n.m.f.* antagonist.
antañazo, *adv.* (*coll.*) way back, in days of yore *or* bygone days.
antaño, *adv.* in days of yore *or* bygone days.
antañón, -ñona, *a.* ancient, very old.
Antares, *n.m.* (*astron.*) Antares.
antártico, -ca, *a.* antarctic. — *n.m.* the Antarctic (*ocean*). — *n.f.* Antarctica (*continent*).
Antártida, *n.f.* Antarctica.
ante-, *pref.* fore, before.
ante (1), *n.m.* (*zool.*) elk; African antelope; dressed buck *or* buffalo skin; buckskin, suede; (*paint.*) buff-colour.
ante (2), *prep.* before, in the presence of, in front of; in face of; to, with regard to; ***valor ante el peligro,*** courage in face of danger; ***postura ante la vida,*** attitude to life; ***embajador ante la Santa Sede,*** ambassador to the Holy See; ***ante todo,*** first of all, to begin with. — *n.m.* first course, starter; (*Per.*) refreshing beverage; (*Mex.*) dessert made of egg, coconut, almond etc.; (*Guat.*) syrup.
anteado, -da, *a.* buff-coloured.
antealtar, *n.m.* chancel.
anteanoche, *adv.* the night before last.
anteanteanoche, *adv.* three nights ago.
anteanteayer, *adv.* three days ago.
anteantier, *adv.* (*coll.*) three days ago.
antear, *v.t.* to cover with *or* make like chamois leather.
anteayer, *adv.* the day before yesterday.
antebrazo, *n.m.* fore-arm; (*vet.*) shoulder, fore-thigh.
antecama, *n.f.* bedside carpet *or* rug.
antecámara, *n.f.* antechamber; lobby, hall.
antecapilla, *n.f.* ante-chapel.
antecedencia, *n.f.* antecedence; lineage, origin.
antecedente, *a.*, *n.m.* antecedent.
anteceder, *v.t.* to precede, go before *or* in front of.
antecesor, -ra, *a.* antecedent. — *n.m.f.* predecessor. — *n.m.* forefather; (*pl.*) ancestors.
anteco, -ca, *a.* (*geog.*) relating to the Antœci. — *n.m.pl.* (**antecos**) Antœci.
antecoger [E], *v.t.* to grasp and carry *or* lead in front of one; (*prov.*) to gather in (*fruit*) before the due time.
antecolumna, *n.f.* (*arch.*) column of a portico.
antecoro, *n.m.* entrance leading to the choir.
Antecristo [ANTICRISTO].
antecuerpo, *n.m.* (*arch.*) projection, balcony.
antedata, *n.f.* antedate.
antedatar, *v.t.* to antedate.
antedecir [17], *v.t.* to predict, foretell.
antedía, *adv.* before the fixed day.
antedicho, -cha, *a.* aforesaid.
antediluviano, -na, *a.* antediluvian.
antefirma, *n.f.* title above signature.
antefoso, *n.m.* (*fort.*) second ditch.
antehistórico, -ca, *a.* prehistoric.
anteiglesia, *n.f.* (*prov.*) parochial church and municipal district (*of some places in Vizcaya*); church-porch.
anteislámico, *a.* pre-Islam(ic).
antejo, *n.m.* (*Cub.*) antejo tree.
antelación, *n.f.* preference; precedence in order of time; ***con antelación,*** in advance, beforehand.
antemano, *adv. phrase*: ***de antemano,*** beforehand.
antemeridiano, -na, *a.* in the forenoon.
antemural, antemuro, *n.m.*, **antemuralla,** *n.f.* fort, rock *or* mountain serving as defence to a fortress; safeguard.
antena, *n.f.* (*naut.*) lateen yard; (*ent.*) antenna; (*rad.*) aerial; (*pl.*) antennæ.
antenacido, -da, *a.* premature (*baby*).
antenatal, *a.* pre-natal.
antenífero, -ra, *a.* (*ent.*) antenniferous.
anteniforme, *a.* (*ent.*) antenniform.
antenoche, *adv.* the night before last; before dusk *or* twilight.
antenombre, *n.m.* title prefixed to a proper name, as ***Don, San*** *etc.*
anténula, *n.f.* antennule; feeler.
antenupcial, *a.* before marriage, antenuptial.
anteojero, -ra, *n.m.f.* spectacle maker *or* seller. — *n.f.* spectacle-case; (*pl.*) blinkers.
anteojo, *n.m.* spy-glass; eye-glass; ***anteojo de larga vista,*** telescope; ***anteojo de puño*** or ***de teatro,*** opera-glass; (*pl.*) spectacles, eye-glasses; opera-glasses; ***anteojos de camino*** or ***de enfermos,*** goggles.
antepagar [B], *v.t.* to pay for in advance.
antepalco, *n.m.* (*theat.*) small antechamber to a box.
antepasado, -da, *a.* elapsed *or* passed; ***la semana antepasada,*** the week before last. — *n.m.pl.* (**antepasados**) ancestors, predecessors, forefathers.
antepecho, *n.m.* breastwork, parapet, bridge-rail, railing; breast harness; breastbeam (*of a loom*); (*min.*) breast.
antepenúltimo, -ma, *a.*, *n.m.f.* antepenultimate, antepenult; third last, last but two.
anteponer [25], *v.t.* to prefer, place before. — **anteponerse,** *v.r.* to place oneself first, push forward.
anteportada, *n.f.* fly-leaf bearing the title only of a book.
anteproyecto, *n.m.* preliminary plan, first draft.
antepuerta, *n.f.* portière, curtain placed before a door; (*fort.*) anteport.
antepuerto, *n.m.* (*naut.*) outer port, anteport.
antequino, *n.m.* (*arch.*) quarter-round moulding.
antera, *n.f.* (*bot.*) anther.
anterior, *a.* earlier, preceding, previous, going before, former; front.
anterioridad, *n.f.* priority, precedence; ***con anterioridad a,*** previous to, earlier than.
antero, *n.m.* worker in suède.
antes, *adv.* before, formerly; earlier, first; rather, better; ***haga esto antes,*** do this first; ***cuanto antes, lo antes posible,*** as soon as possible; ***cuanto antes mejor,*** the sooner the better; ***antes bien,*** rather, on the contrary; ***antes hoy que mañana,*** better to-day than to-morrow. — *conj.* ***antes (de) que*** + *subj.* before; ***antes que,*** rather than. — *prep.* ***antes de,*** before.
antesacristía, *n.f.* room leading to the sacristy.
antesala, *n.f.* anteroom, antechamber; ***hacer antesala,*** to dance attendance (*in an antechamber*), kick one's heels.
antestatura, *n.f.* (*fort.*) small entrenchment of palisades and sandbags.
antetemplo, *n.m.* portico (*of a church*).
antever [37], *v.t.* to foresee.
antevíspera, *n.f.* two days before.
anti-, *pref.* anti-, against; before.
antia, *n.f.* (*ichth.*) lampuga, mutton-fish.
antiácido, *a.* antacid.
antiaéreo, -rea, *a.* anti-aircraft.
antiafrodisíaco, -ca, *a.* anaphrodisiac.
antiálcali, *n.m.* antalkali.
antialcohólico, -ca, *a.* antialcoholic.

antiapoplético, -ca, *a.* (*med.*) antiapoplectic.
antiapóstol, *n.m.f.* anti-apostle.
antiar, *n.m.* (*bot., chem.*) antiar resin; antiar.
antiarina, *n.f.* (*chem.*) antiarin.
antiaris, *n.m.* (*bot.*) upas-tree.
antiartístico, -ca, *a.* inartistic.
antiartrítico, -ca, *a., n.m.* (*med.*) antarthritic.
antiasmático, -ca, *a., n.m.* (*med.*) antasthmatic.
antibaby, *a.* ***píldora antibaby,*** contraceptive pill.
antibactérico, -ca, *a.* antibacterial.
antibilioso, -sa, *a.* antibilious.
antibiosis, *n.f. inv.* (*biol.*) antibiosis.
antibiótico, -ca, *a., n.m.* antibiotic.
anticanónico, -ca, *a.* anticanonical; unorthodox.
anticartel, *a. inv.* anti-monopoly, (*Am.*) antitrust.
anticatarral, *a., n.m.* (*med.*) anticatarrhal.
anticatólico, -ca, *a.* anticatholic.
anticausótico, -ca, *a.* febrifugal. — *n.m.* febrifuge.
anticiclón, *n.m.* anticyclone.
anticientífico, -ca, *a.* unscientific; unscholarly.
anticipación, *n.f.* anticipation, foretaste; ***con anticipación,*** in advance.
anticipado, -da, *a.* premature; (*agric.*) early; (*com.*) advanced, in advance (*payment*); ***venta anticipada,*** ticket booking. — *n.f.* unexpected thrust *or* blow (*in fencing*).
anticipador, -ra, *a.* anticipating. — *n.m.f.* anticipator.
anticipante, *a.* anticipating; (*med.*) anticipant.
anticipar, *v.t.* to anticipate, forestall; to take up beforehand; to advance. — **anticiparse (a),** *v.r.* to be *or* get ahead (of), beat to it, steal a march (on); to jump the gun.
anticipo, *n.m.* advance, advance payment; deposit; foretaste.
anticívico, -ca, *a.* anticivic.
anticlerical, *a.* anticlerical.
anticlericalismo, *n.m.* anticlericalism.
anticlímax, *n.m.f.* anticlimax.
anticlinal, *a.* (*geol.*) anticlinal. — *n.m.* anticline.
anticohesor, *n.m.* (*rad.*) anti-coherer.
anticombustible, *a., n.m.* non-inflammable.
anticomunista, *a., n.m.f.* anticommunist.
anticoncepcional, *a., n.m.* contraceptive.
anticonceptivo, -va, *a.* (of) birth control, contraceptive.
anticongelante, *n.m.* antifreeze.
anticonstitucional, *a.* unconstitutional, anticonstitutional.
anticresis, *n.f. inv.* (*law*) agreement to yield the fruits of a farm till a debt is paid.
anticristiano, -na, *a.* antichristian.
Anticristo, *n.m.* Antichrist.
anticrítica, *n.f.* counter-criticism.
anticrítico, *n.m.* opponent of a critic.
anticuado, -da, *a.* antiquated, out of date, old-fashioned, obsolete.
anticuar, *v.t.* to antiquate, outdate. — **anticuarse,** *v.r.* to become antiquated *or* old-fashioned.
anticuario, -ria, *n.m.f.* antiquarian.
anticuerpo, *n.m.* (*bact.*) antibody.
antidáctilo, *n.m.* (*poet.*) anapæst.
antideportivo, -va, *a.* unsportsmanlike.
antiderrapante, *a.* non-skid.
antideslizante, *a.* non-slip.
antideslumbrante, *an.* antidazzle, antiglare.
antidisentérico, -ca, *a.* antidysenteric.
antidoral, *a.* (*law*) remuneratory, remunerative.
antidotario, *n.m.* pharmacopœia; place in a pharmacy for antidotes; dispensary.
antídoto, *n.m.* antidote.
antieconómico, -ca, *a.* uneconomic, unprofitable.
antiemético, -ca, *a.* (*med.*) antemetic.
antiepiléptico, -ca, *a.* (*med.*) antepileptic.
antier, (*coll.*) [ANTEAYER].
antiesclavista, *a., n.m.f.* antislave; antislaver.
antiescorbútico, -ca, *a.* antiscurvy.
antiescrofuloso, -sa, *a.* antiscrofulous.
antiespasmódico, -ca, *a., n.m.* antispasmodic.
antiestético, -ca, *a.* unæsthetic; unsightly.
antifaz, *n.m.* mask.
antifebril, *a.* (*med.*) antifebrile, febrifugal.
antifernales, *a.pl.* said of possessions given by the husband to the wife as security for her dowry.
antiflogístico, -ca, *a., n.m.* (*med.*) antiphlogistic.
antífona, *n.f.* antiphon, anthem.
antifonal, *a., n.f.,* **antifonario,** *a., n.m.* antiphonal, antiphonary.
antifonero, *n.m.* precentor.
antífrasis, *n.f. inv.* (*rhet.*) antiphrasis.
antifricción, *n.f.* (*mech.*) anti-friction.
antigás, *a. inv.* protecting from poisonous gases; ***careta antigás,*** gas mask.
Antígona, *n.f.* Antigone.
antigramatical, *a.* ungrammatical.
antigripal, *a.* antiflu.
antigualla, *n.f.* antique; ancient custom *or* object; thing of the past, piece of out-moded *or* out-dated junk, rubbish *or* nonsense; old fogey, has-been.
antiguamente, *adv.* formerly, in former times, in olden days.
antiguarse [H], *v.r.* to become antiquated *or* out-of-date.
antigüedad, *n.f.* antiquity; oldness; ancient times; antique; seniority.
antiguo, -gua, *a.* antique, ancient, old; having been long in a position *or* employment, senior; ***a la antigua,*** in the ancient manner, in an old-fashioned way; ***de antiguo,*** of old, from days gone by; ***Antiguo Testamento,*** Old Testament. — *n.m.* aged *or* senior member; old boy, former pupil; ***los antiguos,*** the ancients.
antihelio, *n.m.* anthelion.
antihelmíntico, -ca, *a., n.m.* anthelmintic.
antiherpético, -ca, *a.* (*med.*) antiherpetic.
antiherrumbroso, -sa, *a.* antirust, rust-resisting.
antihigiénico, -ca, *a.* unhygienic.
antihistérico, -ca, *a.* (*med.*) antihysteric.
antihumano, -na, *a.* inhuman.
antiinflacionista, *a.* anti-inflationary.
antilogía, *n.f.* contradiction.
antilógico, -ca, *a.* illogical.
antílope, *n.m.* (*zool.*) antelope.
antillano, -na, *a., n.m.f.* native of *or* relating to the Antilles, West Indian.
Antillas, *n.f.pl.* West Indies, Antilles; ***Antillas Francesas,*** French West Indies; ***Antillas Mayores,*** Greater Antilles; ***Antillas Menores,*** Lesser Antilles.
antimilitarista, *a., n.m.f.* anti-militarist.
antiministerial, *a.* anti-ministerial.
antimonárquico, -ca, *a.* antimonarchical, anti-royalist.
antimonial, *a.* antimonial.
antimoniato, *n.m.* antimoniate.
antimónico, -ca, *a.* antimonic.
antimonio, *n.m.* antimony.
antinacional, *a.* anti-national.
antinatural, *a.* unnatural.
antinefrítico, -ca, *a.* (*med.*) antinephritic.
antinomia, *n.f.* antinomy.
antinómico, -ca, *a.* implying antinomy; contradictory.
antiobrero, -ra, *a.* antilabour.
Antíoco, *n.m.* Antiochus.
antioqueno, -na, *a., n.m.f.* Antiochian.
antioqueño, -ña, *a., n.m.f.* (native) of Antioquia (*Colombia*).
Antioquía, *n.f.* Antioch.

antipalúdico, -ca, *a., n.m. (med.)* anti-malarial.
antipapa, *n.m.* antipope.
antipapado, *n.m.* dignity of antipope.
antipapal, *a.* anti-papal.
antipara, *n.f.* folding screen; gaiter.
antiparalítico, -ca, *a. (med.)* antiparalytic.
antiparras, *n.f.pl. (coll.)* spectacles.
antipartido, *a. inv., n.m.* antiparty.
antipatía, *n.f.* antipathy, aversion, dislike; disagreeableness, unpleasantness; unfriendliness.
antipático, -ca, *a.* antipathetic, disagreeable, uncongenial, unpleasant, unfriendly, nasty; ***me es muy antipático,*** I don't like him one bit *or* at all.
antipatizar [C], *v.i.* to feel *or* arouse antipathy *or* dislike.
antipatriótico, -ca, *a.* unpatriotic.
antiperistáltico, -ca, *a. (med.)* antiperistaltic.
antiperístasis, *n.f. inv.* antiperistasis.
antiperistático, -ca, *a.* belonging to antiperistasis.
antipestilencial, *a. (med.)* anti-plague.
antipirético, -ca, *a., n.m. (med.)* antipyretic.
antipirina, *n.f. (chem.)* antipyrine.
antípoca, *n.f.* agreement to lease.
antipocar [A], *v.t.* to execute *(a lease).*
antípoda, *a. (geog.)* antipodal. — *n.f.pl.* **(antípodas)** antipodes; *(coll.)* persons of opposite dispositions *or* manners.
antipolítico, -ca, *a.* anti-political.
antipolo, *n.m.* antipole.
antiprotón, *n.m. (phys. and chem.)* antiproton.
antipútrido, -da, *a. (med.)* antiseptic.
antiquísimo, -ma, *a. superl.* extremely ancient.
antiquismo, *n.m.* archaism.
antirrábico, -ca, *a. (med.)* anti-rabies.
antirreligioso, -sa, *a., n.m.f.* anti-religious (person).
antirreumático, -ca, *a., n.m. (med.)* anti-rheumatic.
antirrevolucionario, -ria, *a., n.m.f.* anti-revolutionary.
antirrino, *n.m. (bot.)* antirrhinum, snapdragon.
antirrobo, *a. inv.* burglar-proof.
antisabático, -ca, *a., n.m.f.* anti-Sabbatarian.
antiscio, -cia, *a., n.m.f. (geog.)* [ANTECO].
antisemita, *n.m.f.* anti-Semite.
antisemítico, -ca, *a.* anti-Semitic.
antisemitismo, *n.m.* anti-Semitism.
antisepsia, *n.f. (med.)* antisepsis.
antiséptico, -ca, *a. n.m.* antiseptic.
antisifilítico, -ca, *a., n.m. (med.)* antisyphilitic.
antisísmico, -ca, *a.* earthquake-proof.
antisocial, *a.* antisocial; opposed to society and order.
antisocialista, *a., n.m.f.* anti-socialist.
antisonoro, *a.* sound-proof.
antistrofa, *n.f.* antistrophe.
antiteísmo, *n.m.* antitheism.
antitérmico, -ca, *a. (phys.)* non-conducting.
antítesis, *n.f. inv.* antithesis.
antitético, -ca, *a.* antithetic, antithetical.
antitípico, -ca, *a.* antitypal, antitypical.
antitipo, *n.m.* antitype.
antitóxico, -ca, *a. (med.)* antitoxic, preventing poisoning.
antitoxina, *n.f.* antitoxin.
antitrinitario, -ria, *a., n.m.f.* anti-Trinitarian.
antituberculoso, -sa, *a. (med.)* antituberculous.
antivarioloso, -sa, *a. (med.)* anti-smallpox.
antivenenoso, -sa, *a.* antidotal. — *n.m.f.* antidote.
antivenéreo, -rea, *a. (med.)* anti-venereal.
antiverminoso, -sa, *a.* vermifugal.
antizímico, -ca, *a. (chem.)* non-fermenting.
antófago, -ga, *a.* flower-eating.
antófilo, -la, *a.* flower-loving. — *n.m.f.* flower-lover.
antojadizo, -za, *a.* capricious, unpredictable.
antojarse, *v.r.* to seem. — *v. impers.* to fancy, take a (sudden) fancy to; to seem (likely), imagine; ***se me antoja bastante difícil,*** I fancy it is pretty difficult; ***se me antoja que va a llover,*** I've got a feeling it's going to rain; ***antojársele a uno*** + *inf.*, to take it into one's head to + *inf.*, ***se le antojó irse a América,*** he took it into his head to go to America; ***antojársele a alguien los dedos huéspedes,*** to be over-suspicious, be excessively wary.
antojera, *n.f.* spectacle-case; blinker *(for horses).*
antojero, *n.m.* spectacle-maker.
antojo, *n.m.* whim, caprice, fancy; craving, hankering; mole, birth-mark.
antojuelo, *n.m.* petty *or* trifling caprice, fancy *or* whim.
antología, *n.f.* anthology.
Antón, Antonio, *n.m.* Ant(h)ony.
Antonieta, *n.f.* Antoinette.
antónimo, -ma, *a., n.m. (gram.)* antonym.
Antoñito, *n.m.* Tony.
antonomasia, *n.f. (rhet.)* antonomasia; ***por antonomasia,*** *(loosely used for)* par excellence.
antonomástico, -ca, *a.* antonomastic.
antor, -ra, *n.m.f.* one who, in ignorance, sells stolen goods.
antorcha, *n.f.* torch, taper, flambeau; cresset.
antorchero, *n.m.* torch holder *or* socket; cresset.
antracita, *n.f.* anthracite.
antracítico, -ca, *a.* anthracitic.
ántrax, *n.m. (med.)* anthrax.
antro, *n.m.* cavern, den; *(coll.)* low dive; *(med.)* antrum.
antropofagia, *n.f.* anthropophagy, cannibalism.
antropófago, -ga, *a.* cannibalistic, man-eating. — *n.m.f.* cannibal, man-eater.
antropografía, *n.f.* anthropography.
antropoide, *a.* anthropoid.
antropología, *n.f.* anthropology.
antropológico, -ca, *a.* anthropological.
antropólogo, *n.m.* anthropologist.
antropómetra, *n.m.* anthropometrist.
antropometría, *n.f.* anthropometry.
antropomorfismo, *n.m.* anthropomorphism.
antropomorfita, *n.m.f.* anthropomorphist.
antropomorfo, -fa, *a.* anthropomorphous.
antroposofía, *n.f.* anthroposophy.
antruejo, *n.m.* carnival.
antucá, *n.m.* parasol.
antuerpiense, *a.* appertaining to Antwerp. — *n.m.f.* native *or* inhabitant of Antwerp.
antuviada, *n.f. (coll.)* blow *or* stroke.
antuviar, *v.t.* to forestall, anticipate; *(coll.)* to be first in striking *or* attacking.
antuvión, *n.m. (coll.)* sudden, unexpected blow *or* attack; ***de antuvión,*** unexpectedly.
anual, *a.* annual, yearly.
anualidad, *n.f.* annuity, yearly payment, pension *or* rent.
anuario, *n.m.* year-book, trade directory, yearly report.
anúbada, *n.f.* call to war.
anubarrado, -da, *a.* clouded, cloudy; *(paint.)* with cloud effects.
anublado, -da, *a. (sl.)* blind.
anublar, *v.t.* to cloud, darken, dim, overcast, obscure. — **anublarse,** *v.r.* to become cloudy; *(agric.)* to become blasted, withered *or* mildewed; *(fig.)* to fall through.
anublo, *n.m.* mildew.
anudadura, *n.f.,* **anudamiento,** *n.m.* knotting, tying, joining; withering, pining.

anudar, *v.t.* to knot; to join, unite; to resume. — **anudarse,** *v.r.* to become knotted; to wither, fade, pine away; ***se le anudó la garganta,*** he got a lump in his throat, a lump came to his throat.

anuencia, *n.f.* compliance, consent.

anuente, *a.* complying, consenting.

anuir, *v.i.* to assent, agree, consent.

anulación, *n.f.* nullification, abrogation, cancellation.

anulador, -ra, *a.* repealing. — *n.m.f.* repealer.

anular (1), *v.t.* to annul, nullify, cancel, rescind, cancel out. — **anularse,** *v.r.* to take a back seat, efface oneself.

anular (2), *a.* ring-shaped, annular. — *n.m.* ring-finger.

anulativo, -va, *a.* having the power of making void, invalidating.

ánulo, *n.m.* ring, circle.

anuloso, -sa, *a.* annular.

anunciación, *n.f.* Annunciation; Day of the Annunciation, Lady Day (March 25).

anunciador, -ra, *a.* announcing; advertising. — *n.m.f.* announcer; advertiser. — *n.m.* (*elec.*) annunciator.

anunciante, *a., n.m.f.* [ANUNCIADOR].

anunciar, *v.t.* to announce, proclaim; to notify; to advertise; to foretell, harbinger.

anuncio, *n.m.* announcement; advertisement; notice; omen; sign; prediction; harbinger; (*com.*) advice; ***anuncios clasificados*** or ***por palabras,*** classified advertisements; ***anuncio iluminoso,*** illuminated sign.

anuo, *a.* annual.

anúteba, *n.f.* call to war; defence tax.

anverso, *n.m.* obverse.

anvir, *n.m.* (*Carib.*) tobacco beverage.

anzolero, -ra, *n.m.f.* maker of *or* dealer in fish-hooks.

anzuelo, *n.m.* fish-hook; (*coll.*) allurement, inducement; fritter; (*fig.*) ***caer en, picar en*** or ***tragar el anzuelo,*** to swallow the bait.

aña, *n.f.* nanny.

añacal, *n.m.* wheat carrier; baker's board.

añacalero, *n.m.* (*prov.*) carrier of building materials.

añada, *n.f.* good *or* bad season; tract (*of arable land*).

añadido, *n.m.* hair-switch; addition.

añadidura, *n.f.* addition; extra; make-weight; ***por añadidura,*** further, furthermore, in addition, besides, to boot.

añadir, *v.t.* to add; to increase.

añafea, *n.f.* ***papel de añafea,*** coarse paper.

añafil, *n.m.* Moorish trumpet.

añafilero, *n.m.* ***añafil,*** player.

añagaza, *n.f.* lure, decoy (*birds*); allurement, enticement.

añal, *a.* annual; ***cordero añal,*** yearling lamb. — *n.m.* anniversary; offering for some deceased person that is made one year after funeral.

añalejo, *n.m.* ecclesiastical almanac.

añas, *n.f. inv.* (*Per.*) South American fox.

añascar [A], *v.t.* to collect *or* gather little by little; to entangle, muddle. — **añascarse,** *v.r.* to become entangled.

añasco, *n.m.* entanglement, muddle.

añejar, *v.t.* to make old. — **añejarse,** *v.r.* to change, grow old; to age.

añejo, -ja, *a.* old (*wine, bacon*).

añicos, *n.m.pl.* pieces, bits; ***hacer añicos de,*** to smash to smithereens; ***hacerse añicos,*** to wear oneself out.

añil, *n.m.* (*bot.*) indigo (plant); indigo dye-stuff.

añilar, *v.t.* to blue (*clothes*); to dye with indigo.

añilería, *n.f.* indigo plantation, mill *or* works.

añinero, -ra, *n.m.f.* lambskin dresser, dealer in lambskins.

añinos, *n.m.pl.* lambs' wool, unshorn lambskin.

año, *n.m.* year; (*pl.*) birthday; old age; ***entre año,*** during the year; ***por los años setenta,*** about *or* around the seventies; ***al año,*** yearly, a year; ***por año,*** per year; ***todos los años,*** every year; ***tiene 30 años,*** he's 30 (years old); ***año bisiesto,*** leap year; ***año económico,*** financial year; ***año escolar*** or ***lectivo,*** school *or* academic year; ***año secular,*** last year of the century; ***tierra de año y vez,*** land cultivated *or* bearing fruit only once in every two years; ***celebrar los años,*** to celebrate one's birthday; ***estar de buen año,*** to be in the pink of health, be hale and hearty; ***estar entrado en años,*** to be getting on *or* elderly; ***perder año,*** to lose a year (*in one's studies*); ***ser del año de la nana,*** to be donkeys' years old, be as old as the hills; ***¡mal año!*** a plague on it!

añojal, *n.m.* fallow land.

añojo, -ja, *n.m.f.* yearling calf *or* lamb.

añoranza, *n.f.* homesickness; nostalgia; longing, yearning.

añorar, *v.t.* to long *or* yearn for.

añoso, -sa, *a.* aged, heavy with years.

añublar [ANUBLAR].

añublo, *n.m.* mildew, blight.

añudador, -ra, *a.* knotty, tying. — *n.m.f.* one who knots *or* ties.

añudar [ANUDAR].

añusgar [B], *v.i.* to choke; to be displeased *or* vexed.

aojador, -ra, *a., n.m.f.* (one) with the evil eye.

aojadura, *n.f.,* **aojamiento,** *n.m.* witchcraft, evil eye, curse, spell.

aojar, *v.t.* to bewitch, put the evil eye on, curse.

aojo, *n.m.* evil eye.

aojusgar [B], *v.i.* to choke (*while eating*).

aónides, *n.f.pl.* (the) Muses.

aoristo, *n.m.* (*gram.*) aorist, past tense.

aorta, *n.f.* (*anat.*) aorta.

aorteurismo, *n.m.* aneurism of the aorta.

aórtico, -ca, *a.* aortic.

aovado, -da, *a.* ovate, oviform, egg-shaped.

aovar, *v.i.* to lay eggs.

aovillar, *v.t.* to wind (*wool*) into balls. — **aovillarse,** *v.r.* to curl up.

apabellonado, -da, *a.* tent-like.

apabilar, *v.t.* to trim the wick of (*a candle*). — **apabilarse,** *v.r.* to lose courage.

apabullar, *v.t.* (*coll.*) to flatten, crush; to overwhelm; to abash.

apabullo, *n.m.* (*coll.*) flattening, crushing.

apacentadero, *n.m.* pasture-land.

apacentador, -ra, *n.m.f.* one who tends cattle. — *n.m.* herdsman, pasturer.

apacentamiento, *n.m.* tending of grazing cattle; pasturage.

apacentar [1], *v.t.* to tend (*grazing cattle*); to put out to graze. — **apacentarse,** *v.r.* to feed (***con, de,*** on).

apacibilidad, *n.f.* mildness, pleasantness; gentleness; calmness, peacefulness.

apacible, *a.* mild, pleasant, affable; still, quiet, placid, calm, peaceful.

apaciguador, -ra, *a.* pacifying, appeasing. — *n.m.f.* pacifier, appeaser, peace-maker.

apaciguamiento, *n.m.* pacification, appeasement.

apaciguar [H], *v.t.* to pacify, appease, calm, still. — *v.i.* (*naut.*) to abate. — **apaciguarse,** *v.r.* to become calm; to calm down.

apacorral, *n.m.* (*Hond., bot., med.*) apacorral tree.

apache, *a.* Apache; thuggish. — *n.m.* Apache; thug.

apacheta, *n.f.* (*Per.*) hilltop cairn; (*Arg., pol.*) pressure group; (*Arg., com.*) huge profit.

apachurrar, *v.t.* (*Hisp. Am.*) to crush, flatten, squash.

apadrinador, -ra, *a.* protecting; sponsoring. — *n.m.f.* patron, protector; sponsor, backer.

apadrinamiento, *n.m.* sponsorship, support.
apadrinar, *v.t.* to act as second in a duel to; to act as godfather to; to act as best man for; to be a patron to; to sponsor, back, support.
apagable, *a.* extinguishable, quenchable.
apagadizo, za, *a.* tending to go out easily, hard to keep alight.
apagado, -da, *a.* dull, lifeless; muffled, very quiet; extinct; out.
apagador, -ra, *a.* extinguishing. — *n.m.f.* damper, extinguisher.
apagaincendios, *n.m. inv.* fire-extinguisher.
apagamiento, *n.m.* (*fig.*) dullness; loss of interest.
apagapenoles, *n.m.pl.* (*naut.*) leech-ropes, leech-lines.
apagar [B], *v.t.* to quench, put out, extinguish; to switch *or* turn off; (*art*) to soften (*colours*); (*mech.*) to deaden; (*artill.*) to silence (*the enemy's guns*); ***apagar la sed,*** to quench one's thirst; ***apagar la cal,*** to slake lime; ***¡apaga y vámonos!*** let's drop it, we'd better give it up as a bad job.—**apagarse,** *v.r.* to become extinguished, die out, go out.
apagavelas, *n.m. inv.* snuffers.
apagón, *n.m.* black-out, power cut *or* failure.
apainelado, -da, *a.* (*arch.*) elliptical.
apaisado, -da, *a.* oblong, elongated.
apajarado, -da, *a.* (*Hisp. Am.*) scatterbrained, crazy.
apalabrar, *v.t.* to agree to (*sth.*) by word of mouth; to bespeak, engage beforehand, reserve; to appoint (*a meeting*) for consultation.
apalache, *a.* Appalachian.
Apalaches, *n.m.pl.* Appalachians.
apalancar [A], *v.t.* to lever (up). — *v.i.* (*coll.*) to lump it.
apaleamiento, *n.m.* shovelling, heaping; beating, drubbing.
apalear, *v.t.* to shovel, heap; to beat, drub; to winnow.
apaleo, *n.m.* heaping; beating; winnowing.
apanalado, -da, *a.* honey-combed.
apancle, *n.m.* (*Hisp. Am.*) irrigation channel.
apancora, *n.f.* (*ichth.*) sea-urchin.
apandar, *v.t.* (*coll.*) to pinch, swipe.
apandillar(se), *v.t.* (*v.r.*) to form into a band, faction, gang *or* party.
apandorgarse [B], *v.r.* (*coll.*) to get lazy.
apanojado, -da, *a.* (*bot.*) paniculate.
apantallar, *v.t.* to screen, shield; (*Hisp. Am.*) to amaze, dazzle.
apantanar, *v.t.* to flood, make marshy *or* swampy. — **apantanarse,** *v.r.* to get bogged down.
apantuflado, -da, *a.* shaped like a slipper.
apañado, -da, *a.* handy, useful with one's hands, good at doing things.
apañadura, *n.f.* fixing, arranging; mending; wrapping; grasping, pinching, filching; (*pl.*) trimming on counterpanes.
apañamiento, *n.m.* [APAÑADURA].
apañar, *v.t.* to fix (up), arrange; to mend, patch; to dress, wrap; to grasp, seize; to pinch; (*coll.*) ***estar apañado,*** to be in a fix, have had it; ***¡estamos apañados!*** we've had it! we're for it! — **apañárselas,** *v.r.* to get fixed up, fend for oneself; ***que se las apañe*** (***solo***), let him fend for himself.
apaño, *n.m.* fixing, mending; arrangement, understanding, something fixed up (*esp. of immoral* or *illegal nature*); seizing, filching.
apañuscar [A], *v.t.* (*coll.*) to rumple, crush, crumple; to pilfer.
apapagayado, -da, *a.* parrot-like; shaped like a parrot's beak.
aparador, *n.m.* sideboard, dresser; credence-table; workshop; show-window.
aparadura, *n.f.* (*naut.*) garbel, garboard-plank.
aparar, *v.t.* to prepare; (*carp.*) to adze, dub; to close (*shoe-uppers*); (*agric.*) to dress, weed (*plants*); to hold out (*skirt, hands*); to catch sth.; (*naut.*) ***aparar un navío,*** to dub a ship; ***aparar en*** or ***con la mano,*** to catch in *or* with the hand.— **apararse,** *v.r.* to prepare, adorn *or* arrange o.s.
aparasolado, -da, *a.* umbrella-like; (*bot.*) umbelliferous.
aparatarse, *v.r.* (*Col.*) to become overcast; to threaten snow *or* hail (*sky*); to adorn oneself ostentatiously.
aparatero, -ra, *a.* (*prov., Chi.*) boasting, exaggerating.
aparato, *n.m.* apparatus, piece of equipment, device, appliance; machine; mechanism, system; (radio) set; (hearing) aid; pomp, show, ceremony, ostentation; signs, symptoms; ***aparato respiratorio,*** respiratory system; ***aparato vendedor,*** slot machine, (*Am.*) vending machine.
aparatosidad, *n.f.* ostentation.
aparatoso, -sa, *a.* pompous, showy; (*coll.*) ostentatious; (*coll.*) spectacular.
aparcadero, *n.m.* parking place.
aparcamiento, *n.m.* parking; car-park, (*Am.*) parking lot.
aparcar [A], *v.t., v.i.* to park.
aparcería, *n.f.* (*agric.*) land-leasing; ***en aparcería,*** in league.
aparcero, -ra, *n.m.f.* (*agric.*) leaser; sharecropper.
apareamiento, *n.m.* matching, mating; pairing, coupling.
aparear(se), *v.t.* (*v.r.*) to match, mate, couple, pair.
aparecer(se) [9], *v.i.* (*v.r.*) to appear, turn up, show up.
aparecido, *n.m.* ghost.
aparejado, -da, *a.* apt, fit, ready.
aparejador, -ra, *n.m.f.* assistant architect, assistant engineer; overseer (of a building); (*naut.*) rigger.
aparejar, *v.t.* to get ready; to prepare; to harness; (*naut.*) to rig; to furnish; to size; (*paint.*) to prime; to prepare for building.
aparejo, *n.m.* preparation, disposition; harness, gear; (*paint.*) priming; sizing (*of canvas* or *board*); (*mech.*) tackle, set of pulleys; (*build.*) bond; (*naut.*) tackle and rigging; furniture; ***aparejo real,*** main-tackle; (*pl.*) apparatus, tools, instruments *or* materials necessary for a trade.
aparentar, *v.t.* to pretend; to feign, affect; to look (*older, younger*); ***tiene veinte años, pero aparenta más,*** she's twenty, but she looks older.
aparente, *a.* apparent; seeming; fit, suited; evident; (*coll.*) impressive-looking.
aparición, *n.f.* apparition, appearance, vision.
apariencia, *n.f.* appearance, outward appearance, aspect, look; indication, probability; ***las apariencias engañan,*** appearances are deceptive; ***juzgar por las apariencias,*** to judge by appearance(s); ***salvar las apariencias,*** to keep up appearances, save face.
aparrado, -da, *a.* vine-like, shrubby; stocky, thick-set.
aparragarse [B], *v.r.* (*Hisp. Am.*) to bend, crouch, squat.
aparrar, *v.t.* to espalier. — **aparrarse,** *v.r.* to spread; (*Hisp. Am.*) to squat, crouch.
aparroquiar, *v.t.* to get customers *or* clients for.
apartación, *n.f.* distribution, division.
apartadamente, *adv.* privately, apart; separately.
apartadero, *n.m.* siding; lay-by; sorting-room (*for wool*); (*agric.*) free pasture place (*beside a road*); place for bulls (*before bullfight*).
apartadijo, *n.m.* small part, share, portion; alcove, cubicle, recess; ***hacer apartadijos*** (***de***), to divide *or* split up.
apartadizo, -za, *a.* unsociable, stand-offish. — *n.m.* alcove, cubicle, recess.
apartado, -da, *a.* withdrawn; side *or* back (*street*); out of the way, off the beaten track. — *n.m.* side room, cubicle; special delivery mail; **poste**

restante box; smelting-house; smelting, assaying; board of cattle ranchers; penning (*of bulls*); vocabulary entry; section; distribution; ***hacer el apartado (de),*** to separate *or* divide up.

apartador, -ra, *n.m.f.* separator, divider, sorter; smelter.

apartamento, *n.m.* flat, (*Am.*) apartment.

apartamiento, *n.m.* separation; retirement; remoteness; estrangement; apartment.

apartar, *v.t.* to separate, divide; to set *or* put aside; to take *or* turn aside; to push away; to pen; to sort; to shunt; ***le apartaron de esta idea,*** they got him away from this idea. — **apartarse,** *v.r.* to turn aside *or* away, stand aside, get out of the way; to withdraw *or* retire.

aparte, *adv., prep.* apart (from), aside; ***esto aparte, aparte (de) esto,*** this apart, this aside, apart from this. — *n.m.* fresh paragraph; aside; ***punto y aparte,*** full stop, fresh paragraph.

apartidar, *v.t.* to side with.

aparvar, *v.t.* to heap (*grain*) for threshing; to heap, throw together.

apasionadamente, *adv.* passionately; in a prejudiced *or* bigoted way.

apasionado, -da, *a.* passionate, passionately fond, devoted. — *n.m.f.* passionate admirer, fan, devotee.

apasionamiento, *n.m.* passion; intense emotion *or* enthusiasm.

apasionante, *a.* thrilling, enthralling, fascinating.

apasionar, *v.t.* to inspire (a) passion in; to fill with enthusiasm. — *v.r.* ***apasionarse de*** or ***por,*** to be *or* become passionately fond of, be *or* become madly keen on.

apaste, *n.m.* (*Guat., Hond., Mex.*) earthenware tub.

apasturar, *v.t.* (*obs.*) to pasture, forage.

apatanado, -da, *a.* rustic, boorish, uncouth.

apatía, *n.f.* apathy.

apático, -ca, *a.* apathetic, indifferent.

apatuscar [A], *v.t.* to botch.

apatusco, *n.m.*(*coll.*) ornament, adornment.

apayasar, *v.t.* to make clownish.

apea, *n.f.* rope fetter, hobble (*for horses*).

apeadero, *n.m.* alighting-place; wayside station; horse-block; halt; pied-à-terre.

apeador, -ra, *a.* dismounting. — *n.m.* land-surveyor; (*pl.*) (*arch.*) props, supports.

apeamiento, *n.m.* surveying.

apear, *v.t.* to help alight, step down *or* dismount; to survey; to fell (*a tree*); to block, scotch (*a wheel*); to take (*sth.*) down from its place; (*artill.*) to dismount (*a gun*); to dissuade; to ford (*a river*); to remove, surmount (*difficulties*); to hobble (*a horse*); (*arch.*) to prop (*a building*); ***nadie le apea de su burro,*** he cannot be persuaded. — **apearse,** *v.r.* to alight; to get off *or* out.

apechugar [B], *v.i.* (*coll.*) to face, undertake with spirit; ***apechugar con todo,*** to lump it, put up with everything.

apedazar [C], *v.t.* to tear into pieces; to patch, mend, repair.

apedernalado, -da, *a.* flinty, hard, insensitive.

apedreado, -da, *a.* spotted, variegated; pitted with smallpox.

apedreamiento, *n.m.* lapidation, stoning; hailing.

apedrear, *v.t.* to stone; to lapidate. — *v. impers.* to hail.

apedreo [APEDREAMIENTO].

apegarse [B], *v.r.* to attach o.s. (***a,*** to); to grow fond (***a,*** of).

apego, *n.m.* attachment, fondness; inclination; liking.

apegualar, *v.i.* (*Arg., Chi.*) to use a girth for fastening and securing horses, etc.

apelación, *n.f.* (*law*) appeal; (*med., coll.*) consultation; (*law*) ***dar por desierta la apelación,*** to declare null and void; (*law*) ***interponer apelación,*** to state intent to appeal; ***no hay apelación, no tiene apelación,*** it's a hopeless case.

apelado, -da, (1) *a.* (*law*) successful in appeal.

apelado, -da, (2) *a.* of the same coat *or* colour (*horses*).

apelambrar, *v.t.* to remove hair from (*hide*).

apelante, *a.* appellate. — *n.m.f.* appellant.

apelar, *v.i.* to appeal, have recourse (to); to refer (to); ***apelar a,*** to appeal to; ***apelar de,*** to appeal against.

apelativo, -va, *a., n.m.f.* appellative.

apeldar, *v.t.* (*coll.*) ***apeldarlas,*** to take to one's heels.

apelde, *n.m.* (*coll.*) flight, escape; bell rung before daybreak (*in Franciscan convents*).

apelmazado, -da, *a.* heavy, solid, stodgy, thick.

apelmazadura, *n.f.,* **apelmazamiento,** *n.m.* heaviness, solidness, stodginess, thickness.

apelmazar [C], *v.t.* to cram *or* pack together, make solid *or* thick.

apelotonar, *v.t.* to form into balls.

apellar, *v.t.* to dress (*leather*).

apellidar, *v.t.* to call by name; to proclaim; to call to arms.

apellido, *n.m.* surname, (*Am.*) family name; epithet; call to arms; force called to arms; mobilization order; cry; (*coll.*) ***se nos metió en casa con todo el apellido,*** he moved in on us lock, stock and barrel *or* with his whole family.

apenachado, -da, *a.* plumed, crested.

apenar, *v.t.* to grieve.

apenas, *adv.* scarcely, hardly, barely; no sooner (than); as soon (as).

apencar [A], *v.i.* (*coll.*) to lump it; ***apencar con una cosa,*** to put up with sth.

apéndice, *n.m.* appendix; supplement.

apendicitis, *n.f. inv.* (*med.*) appendicitis.

apendicular, *a.* appendicular.

apenino, -na, *a.* Apennine.

apeo, *n.m.* survey, mensuration of lands and buildings; (*arch.*) propping; prop, stay.

apeonar, *v.i.* to walk *or* run swiftly (*birds, esp. partridges*).

apepsia, *n.f.* (*med.*) apepsy, indigestion.

aperador, *n.m.* one in charge of agricultural implements; wheelwright; foreman (*in a mine*).

aperar, *v.i.* to carry on the trade of a wheelwright.

apercibimiento, *n.m.* preparation; foresight; arrangement; advice, warning; (*law*) threat, summons.

apercibir, *v.t.* to provide, get ready, prepare; to warn, advise; (*law*) to summon; ***apercibirse de ropa,*** to equip o.s. with clothes; ***apercibirse de algo,*** to become aware of sth., to realize sth.

apercollar [4], *v.t.* (*coll.*) to collar, seize by the neck; to steal, snatch.

aperdigar [B], *v.t.* to broil (*partridges, meat*) slightly.

apergaminado, -da, *a.* parchment-like, shrivelled.

apergaminarse, *v.r.* (*coll.*) to become dried up.

aperiódico, *a., n.m.* (*phys.*) aperiodic.

aperitivo, -va, *a.* aperitive, appetizing; (*med.*) aperient. — *n.m.* appetizer; apéritif; (*med.*) aperient.

aperlado, -da, *a.* of pearly colour.

apernar [I], *v.t.* to seize by the legs.

apero, *n.m.* sheep-fold; set of implements; outfit of tools; (*Hisp. Am.*) riding accoutrements.

aperreado, -da, *a.* wretched, lousy; ***vida aperreada,*** dog's life, miserable existence.

aperrear, *v.t.* to set the dogs on; to harass, plague, pester.

aperreo, *n.m.* (*coll.*) dog's life, wretched existence.

apersogar [B], *v.t.* (*Mex.*) to tether (*a horse*) by the neck.

apersonado, -da, *a.* ***bien (mal) apersonado,*** of good (bad) appearance *or* presence.

apersonarse, *v.r.* (*law*) [PERSONARSE].

apertura, *n.f.* opening; reading (*of a will*).

aperturismo, *n.m.* (*pol.*) policy of opening up, liberalization.

apesadumbar, apesarar, *v.t.* to afflict, grieve.

apesgar [B], *v.t.* to overburden; to overwhelm.

apestar, *v.t.* to infect with the plague; (*fig.*) to corrupt, turn putrid; to pester, vex, annoy. — *v.i.* to stink; ***aquí apesta,*** there is a foul smell here.

apestoso, -sa, *a.* pestilent, foul-smelling, stinking; sickening, nauseating.

apétalo, -la, *a.* (*bot.*) apetalous.

apetecer [9], *v.t.* (*often impers.*) to fancy, feel like, have a hankering for; ***me apetece una cerveza,*** I feel like a beer; ***le apetecía bañarse,*** he fancied a bath(e); ***no me apetece en absoluto que venga,*** I'm not at all keen on his coming. — *v.i.* to be attractive, have appeal, be welcome.

apetecible, *a.* desirable, appetizing, tempting.

apetencia, *n.f.* appetite, desire, craving, urge.

apetite, *n.m.* sauce, appetizer; inducement.

apetitivo, -va, *a.* appetitive, appetizing.

apetito, *n.m.* appetite, desire; ***abrir el apetito,*** to whet the appetite.

apetitoso, -sa, *a.* appetizing; palatable, tasty.

apezonado, -da, *a.* nipple-shaped.

apezuñar, *v.i.* to sink the hoofs into the ground.

apiadar, *v.t.* to move to pity. — **apiadarse,** *v.r.* — ***de,*** to take *or* have pity on, have mercy on.

apiaradero, *n.m.* owner's reckoning of his livestock.

apiario, -ria, *a.* bee-like. — *n.m.* apiary.

apicararse, *v.r.* to go to the dogs, become depraved, degenerate into a rogue, knave, cad *or* rotter.

ápice, *n.m.* apex; crux; trifle, jot, iota; (*gram.*) graphic accent; ***estar en los ápices de algo,*** to be well up in sth.; ***no falta (ni) un ápice,*** there's not an iota missing.

ápices, *n.m.pl.* (*bot.*) anthers.

apícola, *a.* appertaining to bee-keeping.

apículo, *n.m.* (*bot.*) small, keen point.

apicultor, -ra, *n.m.f.* bee-keeper, apiarist.

apicultura, *n.f.* bee-keeping, apiculture.

apilada, *n.f.* dried chestnut.

apilador, -ra, *a.* piling. — *n.m.f.* piler.

apilar, *v.t.* to pile *or* heap up.

apilonar, *v.t.* (*Hisp. Am.*) to pile (up).

apimpollarse, *v.r.* to put forth bud, germinate.

apiñado, -da, *a.* shaped like a pine-cone.

apiñadura, *n.f.*, **apiñamiento,** *n.m.* congestion, pressing *or* squeezing together, crowd, throng.

apiñar, *v.t.* to bunch, cram, crowd, crush, jam, press *or* squeeze together. — **apiñarse,** *v.r.* to crowd, throng.

apio, *n.m.* (*bot.*) celery; (*bot.*) ***apio caballar*** or ***equino,*** smallage, wild chicory; (*bot.*) ***apio de ranas,*** buttercup, crowfoot.

apiolar, *v.t.* to gyve (*a hawk*); to tie by the legs; (*fig.*) to seize, apprehend; (*coll.*) to kill, murder.

apiparse, *v.r.* (*coll.*) to gorge.

apirético, -ca, *a.* (*med.*) apyretic.

apirexia, *n.f.* (*med.*) apyrexia.

apisonadora, *n.f.* steam roller.

apisonamiento, *n.m.* stamping *or* flattening down.

apisonar, *v.t.* to ram *or* stamp down, flatten.

apitonamiento, *n.m.* (*zool.*) putting forth tenderlings; (*agric.*) sprouting, budding; passion, anger.

apitonar, *v.t.* to pierce, break through. — *v.i.* to put forth horns; (*agric.*) to bud, sprout. — **apitonarse,** *v.r.* (*coll.*) to exchange insults.

apívoro, -ra, *a.* bee-eating.

apizarrado, -da, *a.* slate-coloured.

aplacable, *a.* appeasable.

aplacación, *n.f.* (*obs.*), **aplacamiento,** *n.m.* appeasement; stay of execution.

aplacador, -ra, *a.* appeasing, placating. — *n.m.f.* appeaser.

aplacar [A], *v.t.* to appease, pacify, mitigate, calm down.

aplacerado, -da, *a.* (*naut.*) level and shallow; (*Hisp. Am.*) open, cleared of trees.

aplacible, *a.* pleasant.

aplaciente, *a.* pleasing.

aplacimiento, *n.m.* pleasure.

aplanadera, *n.f.* roller, leveller.

aplanador, -ra, *a.* levelling. — *n.m.* leveller; (*mech.*) battledore, brusher, riveter; cylinder roller; (*typ.*) planer, planishing mallet.

aplanamiento, *n.m.* levelling, flattening; (*fig.*) dejection, depression; prostration.

aplanar, *v.t.* to level, make level *or* even, flatten; (*coll.*) to cast down, make dejected; ***estar aplanado por el calor,*** to be laid out by the heat.

aplanético, -ca, *a.* (*opt.*) aplanatic.

aplantillar, *v.t.* to adjust *or* fit (*stones etc.*) according to pattern.

aplastante, *a.* crushing.

aplastar, *v.t.* flatten, crush.

aplaudidor, -ra, *a.* applauding. — *n.m.f.* one who applauds.

aplaudir, *v.t.* to applaud.

aplauso, *n.m.* applause; approbation.

aplayar, *v.i.* to overflow (*rivers*).

aplazamiento, *n.m.* convocation, citation; summons; deferring, postponement; adjournment.

aplazar [C], *v.t.* (*obs.*) to summon; to postpone, put off; to adjourn.

aplebeyar, *v.t.* to debase, degrade.

aplicable, *a.* applicable.

aplicación, *n.f.* application, diligence; (*sew.*) appliqué.

aplicado, -da, *a.* studious, industrious.

aplicar [A], *v.t.* to apply; to destine; to attribute, impute; (*law*) to adjudge; ***aplicar el oído,*** to listen attentively. — *v.r.* ***aplicarse a los estudios,*** to get down seriously to study.

aplique, *n.m.* fitting, light fitting, fixture.

aplomado, -da, *a.* lead-coloured, leaden, containing lead; confident, self-assured.

aplomar, *v.t.* (*build.*) to plumb; (*arch.*) to put vertically. — *v.i.* (*build.*) to plumb; to be perpendicular.

aplomo, *n.m.* aplomb, self-assurance, self-confidence, self-possession; (*mus.*) exactness; (*art*) due proportion; plumb, plumb-bob, plummet.

apnea, *n.f.*(*med.*) apnœa.

apocado, -da, *a.* spineless, feeble-spirited, irresolute, pusillanimous, timid.

Apocalipsis, *n.m.* Apocalypse, Apocalypsis.

apocalíptico, -ca, *a.* apocalyptic(al).

apocamiento, *n.m.* spinelessness, feeble-spiritedness, lack of resolution, pusillanimity, timidity.

apocar [A], *v.t.* to lessen; to humiliate; to cramp, contract. — **apocarse,** *v.r.* to be(come) cowed; to climb down.

apócema, apócima [PÓCIMA].

apocopar, *v.t.* to apocopate, shorten.

apócope, *n.f.* apocope.

apócrifo, -fa, *a.* apocryphal.

Apócrifos, *n.m.pl.* (*Bibl.*) Apocrypha.

apodar, *v.t.* to nickname; to scoff at, ridicule.

apodencado, -da, *a.* pointer-like, hound-like.

apoderado, *n.m.* one empowered *or* authorized (*by law*); agent, manager (*e.g. of bullfighter*).

apoderar, *v.t.* to empower, authorize. — **apoderarse,** *v.r.* — ***de algo,*** take possession of, take hold of, grab, grasp *or* seize sth.

apodíctico, -ca, *a.* apodictic.

ápodo, -da, *a.* (*zool.*) apodal.

apodo, *n.m.* nickname.
apófige, *n.f.* (*arch.*) apophyge.
apófisis, *n.f. inv.* (*med.*) apophysis.
apogeo, *n.m.* (*astron.*) apogee; height, summit, pinnacle; climax, heyday.
apógrafo, *n.m.* apograph, copy.
apolilladura, *n.f.* moth-hole.
apolillar, *v.t.* to gnaw, eat, infest (*moths*). — **apolillarse,** *v.r.* to get *or* become moth-eaten.
apolinar, apolíneo, -nea, *a.* (*poet.*) of *or* belonging to Apollo.
apologético, -ca, *a.* apologetic, appertaining to apologetics.
apología, *n.f.* apology, apologia.
apológico, -ca, *a.* relating to an apologue.
apologista, *n.m.f.* apologist.
apólogo, -ga, *a.* [APOLÓGICO]. — *n.m.* apologue.
apoltronarse, *v.r.* to get lazy, loaf *or* sprawl about.
apomazar [C], *v.t.* to glaze, burnish with pumice-stone.
aponeurosis, *n.f. inv.* (*med.*) aponeurosis.
apopar, *v.t., v.i.* (*naut.*) to steer into wind, tide *or* current.
apoplejía, *n.f.* (*med.*) apoplexy.
apoplético, -ca, *a.* apoplectic.
aporcadura, *n.f.* (*agric.*) hilling, earthing-up, banking-up.
aporcar [A], *v.t.* (*agric.*) to hill, earth up.
aporcelanado, -da, *a.* resembling porcelain.
aporisma, *n.m.* (*surg.*) ecchymosis.
aporismarse, *v.r.* to become an ecchymosis.
aporracear, (*prov.*) [APORREAR].
aporrar, *v.i.* (*coll.*) to be mute *or* tongue-tied. — **aporrarse,** *v.r.* (*coll.*) to become a nuisance.
aporreado, *n.m.* (*Cub.*) spiced-meat dish.
aporreamiento, *n.m.* beating, pommelling, cudgelling, clubbing.
aporrear, *v.t.* to beat, cudgel, club. — **aporrearse,** *v.r.* to toil, slave, labour.
aporreo, *n.m.* cudgelling, pommelling *or* beating; drudgery, toil.
aporrillarse, *v.r.* to swell in the joints.
aportación, *n.f.* contribution; share.
aportaderas, *n.f.pl.* pannier, box (*carried on horses* or *mules*); grape tub.
aportadero, *n.m.* stopping place (*for ships* or *persons*); landing-place.
aportar, *v.t.* to bring, contribute. — *v.i.* to turn *or* show up.
aportillar, *v.t.* to breach (*a wall* or *rampart*); to break down, break open. — **aportillarse,** *v.r.* to tumble down, collapse.
aposentador, -ra, *n.m.f.* lodging-house keeper, inn-keeper; billeter.
aposentamiento, *n.m.* lodging; settling down.
aposentar, *v.t.* to lodge, give lodging to. — **aposentarse,** *v.r.* to take lodgings.
aposento, *n.m.* room, apartment; lodging; (*obs.*) box (*in theatre*).
aposesionar, *v.t.* to give possession to. — **aposesionarse,** *v.r.* to take possession.
aposición, *n.f.* (*gram.*) apposition.
apositivo, -va, *a.* (*gram.*) appositional.
apósito, *n.m.* (*med.*) dressing.
aposta, *adv.* deliberately.
apostadero, *n.m.* naval station; dock-yard; fuelling station.
apostador, -ra, *n.m.f.* one who bets, better, punter.
apostal, *n.m.* (*prov.*) good fishing-place (*in a river*).
apostáleos, *n.m.pl.* (*naut.*) gun planks.
apostar [4], *v.t.* to bet, wager, stake; ***apuesto a que no viene,*** I bet (that) he won't come. — **apostarse,** *v.r.* to take up a position.
apostasía, *n.f.* apostasy.
apóstasis, *n.f. inv.* (*med.*) abscess.
apóstata, *n.m.f.* apostate; forsaker, abjurer.
apostatar, *v.i.* to apostatize, abjure, forsake, fall away; ***apostatar de la fe,*** to abjure one's faith.
apostema, *n.f.* (*med.*) abscess, tumour.
apostemación, *n.f.* (*obs.*) formation of an abscess.
apostemar, *v.t.* (*med.*) to form *or* cause an abscess in.
apostemero, *n.m.* (*med.*) bistoury, scalpel.
apostemoso, -sa, *a.* apostematous.
apostilla, *n.f.* marginal note, annotation, rider, apostil.
apostillar, *v.t.* to make marginal notes in *or* to, annotate. — **apostillarse,** *v.r.* to break out in pimples.
apóstol, *n.m.* apostle.
apostolado, *n.m.* apostolate; apostleship; (the) twelve apostles.
apostólicamente, *adv.* apostolically; (*coll.*) simply, poorly, unostentatiously.
apostólico, -ca, *a.* apostolic.
apostrofar, *v.t.* to apostrophize; to insult.
apóstrofe, *n.m.f.* (*rhet.*) apostrophe; (*fig.*) taunt, insult.
apóstrofo, *n.m.* (*gram.*) apostrophe.
apostura, *n.f.* poise, fine *or* imposing bearing.
aposturaje, *n.m.* (*naut.*) top-timber, futtock.
apote, *adv.* (*coll.*) abundantly, galore.
apotegma, *n.m.* apophthegm, maxim.
apoteósico, -ca, *a.* deifying; glorifying; (*coll.*) terrific, tremendous, superb; (*coll.*) catastrophic, disastrous.
apoteosis, *n.f. inv.* apotheosis, deification; exaltation.
apoyabrazos, *n.m. inv.* arm-rest.
apoyadero, *n.m.* prop, support.
apoyador, -ra, *a.* supporting. — *n.m.* support, prop.
apoyadura, *n.f.* flow of milk to the udders *or* breasts.
apoyar, *v.t.* to lean, rest, support; to hold up; to back (up); to droop, lower (*the head*).
apoyatura, *n.f.* (*mus.*) appoggiatura.
apoyo, *n.m.* prop, stay; support; backing; ***con apoyo de,*** with the support of, with backing from.
apozarse [C], *v.r.* (*Chi., Col.*) to form a pool.
apreciable, *a.* appreciable, valuable; esteemed, worthy of esteem; considerable, substantial, noticeable, worthy of being taken into account.
apreciación, *n.f.* appreciation, appraisal, appraisement, assessment; ***error de apreciación,*** error of judgement.
apreciador, -ra, *n.m.f.* appraiser.
apreciar, *v.t.* to appreciate, esteem; to appraise, estimate; ***apreciar en mucho,*** to hold in high esteem; ***apreciar a alguien en su verdadero valor,*** to appreciate s.o.'s true value, appreciate s.o. fully.
apreciativo, -va, *a.* appreciative.
aprecio, *n.m.* appreciation, esteem; appraisement, valuation.
aprehender, *v.t.* to apprehend, seize; (*phil.*) to comprehend, grasp.
aprehensión, *n.f.* seizure, capture; (*phil.*) comprehension.
apremiador, -ra, *a.* compelling, pressing.
apremiante, *a.* urgent, pressing.
apremiar, *v.t.* to press, urge.
apremio, *n.m.* pressure, constraint; (*law*) judicial compulsion.
aprendedor, -ra, *a.* learning. — *n.m.f.* learner.
aprender, *v.t., v.i.* to learn; ***aprender a escribir,*** to learn to write; ***aprender de memoria,*** to learn by heart.
aprendiz, -za, *n.m.f.* apprentice; ***aprendiz de todo, oficial de nada,*** Jack of all trades, master of none.

aprendizaje, *n.m.* apprenticeship; ***hacer su aprendizaje,*** to serve one's apprenticeship.
aprensador, -ra, *a.* pressing. — *n.m.f.* presser.
aprensar [PRENSAR].
aprensión, *n.f.* apprehension; scruple, fear; mistrust, suspicion; (*med.*) hypochondria; squeamishness.
aprensivo, -va, *a.* apprehensive; (*med.*) hypochondriac.
apresador, -ra, *a.* seizing, capturing. — *n.m.* privateer; captor, plunderer.
apresamiento, *n.m.* hold; capture; seizure.
apresar, *v.t.* to seize, grasp; to arrest.
aprestar, *v.t.* to prepare, make ready, arrange; to gum, size (*materials*). — **aprestarse,** *v.r.* to get ready (***a,*** to).
apresto, *n.m.* preparation, accoutrement; ***esta tela no tiene apresto,*** this cloth has no body.
apresuración, *n.f.* haste.
apresurado, -da, *a.* hasty.
apresuramiento, *n.m.* hastiness.
apresurar, *v.t.* to hasten, hurry; ***apresurarse por llegar a tiempo,*** to hurry in order to be in time.
apretadamente, *adv.* tightly, closely, fast.
apretadera, *n.f.* strap, rope (*for tying*); (*pl.*) (*coll.*) pressing requests, entreaties.
apretadero, *n.m.* truss.
apretadizo, -za, *a.* easily bound *or* compressed.
apretado, -da, *a.* tight; compact, thick, dense, cramped; difficult, arduous, dangerous.
apretador, -ra, *a.* pressing, tightening. — *n.m.* presser, rammer; quoin-wedge; waistcoat; soft stays (*for children*); broad bandage (*for infants*); hair-net.
apretadura, *n.f.* compression, constriction.
apretamiento, *n.m.* crowd, jam, crush; closeness.
apretar [1], *v.t.* to press; to tighten, squeeze; to jam, pack *or* press down *or* hard; ***apretarle a uno la mano,*** to squeeze *or* shake s.o.'s hand; ***apretar los dientes,*** to clench one's teeth; ***apretarle a uno las clavijas*** or ***los tornillos,*** to put the squeeze *or* put pressure on s.o.; ***apretar el paso,*** to speed up, get a move on; ***apretar los puños,*** to clench one's fists; ***sabe dónde le aprieta el zapato,*** he knows what's good for him *or* which side his bread is buttered on; ***quien mucho abarca poco aprieta,*** grasp all, lose all. — *v.i.* to make itself felt, be *or* become severe (*heat, pain etc.*); ***está apretando mucho el calor,*** the heat is really making itself felt; ***apretar a correr,*** to start off running.
apretón, *n.m.* sharp pressure, firm grip *or* hug; dash, sprint; sharp pain, twinge; ***apretón de manos,*** hand-shake.
apretujar, *v.t.* (*coll.*) to squeeze *or* keep on squeezing, squash *or* keep on squashing.
apretujón, *n.m.* hard squeeze.
apretura, *n.f.* crowd, crush; straits; want, need; (*fig.*) fix; narrow confined place.
apriesa [APRISA].
aprietatuercas, *n.m. inv.* (*engin.*) wrench.
apriete (1), *n.m.* tightening.
aprieto (1), *n.m.* fix, jam, tight spot, difficulty; crush.
aprieto (2), **apriete** (2), *pres. indic.*; *pres. subj.* [APRETAR].
apriorismo, *n.m.* apriorism.
aprisa, *adv.* quickly.
apriscar [A], *v.t.* to gather (*sheep*) in the fold.
aprisco, *n.m.* sheep-fold.
aprisionar, *v.t.* to confine, imprison; to put in chains; (*fig.*) to bind.
aproar, *v.t.* (*naut.*) to turn the prow (of). — *v.i.* to head (for).
aprobable, *a.* approvable.
aprobación, *n.f.* approbation, approval.
aprobado, *n.m.* pass (*in examination*).
aprobador, -ra, *a.* approving. — *n.m.f.* approver.
aprobante, *a.* approving.
aprobar [4], *v.t.* to approve; to pass (*an examination, a candidate*).
aprobativo, -va, *a.* approbatory.
aprobatorio, -ria, *a.* approbatory, approving.
aproches, *n.m.pl.* (*mil.*) approaches.
aprontar, *v.t.* to prepare *or* deliver quickly.
apropiación, *n.f.* appropriation, assumption.
apropiado, -da, *a.* appropriate, fit.
apropiador, -ra, *a.* appropriating. — *n.m.f.* appropriator.
apropiar, *v.t.* to appropriate, assume; to accommodate, fit, apply. — **apropiarse,** *v.r.* to possess o.s. of, to appropriate to o.s.; ***apropiarse (de) algo,*** to appropriate sth.
apropincuación, *n.f.* approach.
apropincuarse, *v.r.* (*coll.*) to approach, draw near.
aprovechable, *a.* serviceable; usable.
aprovechado, -da, *a.* studious, diligent; selfish. — *n.m.f.* opportunist.
aprovechamiento, *n.m.* profit; utilization, exploitation; progress, benefit.
aprovechar, *v.t.* to profit by, make good use of. — *v.i.* to be useful *or* profitable; to progress. — **aprovecharse,** *v.r.* — ***de,*** to avail o.s. of; to take unfair advantage of, abuse, exploit.
aprovisionador, -ra, *n.m.f.* provider, purveyor; caterer, victualler.
aprovisionar, *v.t.* to victual, stock, supply.
aproximación, *n.f.* approximation; nearness; bringing near.
aproximadamente, *adv.* nearly, about, approximately.
aproximado, -da, *a.* approximate; ***cálculo aproximado,*** rough estimate.
aproximar(**se**), *v.t.* (*v.r.*) to approximate; to bring, move near; to approach.
aproximativo, -va, *a.* approaching; approximate.
ápside, *n.m.* (*astron.*) apsis, apogee (*of the moon*); (*arch.*) apse, apsis.
áptero, -ra, *a.* (*ent.*) apterous, wingless.
aptitud, *n.f.* aptitude; fitness; ability; capacity; suitability.
apto, -ta, *a.* apt; fit; suitable; ***apto para todo,*** ready *or* fit for anything.
apuesta (1), *n.f.* bet, wager.
apuesto (1), **-ta** (2), *a.* smart, spruce, neat and tidy.
apuesto (2), **apueste,** *pres. indic.*; *pres. subj.* [APOSTAR].
apulgarar, *v.i.* to press with the thumb, push. — **apulgararse,** *v.r.* to become spotted (*with damp* or *mildew*).
apulso, *n.m.* (*astron.*) appulse.
apunarse, *v.r.* (*Hisp. Am.*) to contract mountain-sickness.
apunchar, *v.t.* to twine, part (*in comb making*).
apuntación, *n.f.* annotation, note, memorandum, memorial; (musical) notation.
apuntado, -da, *a.* pointed at both ends.
apuntador, -ra, *n.m.f.* (*theat.*) prompter.
apuntalamiento, *n.m.* propping, shoring up, supporting.
apuntalar, *v.t.* to prop, shore up, support; (*naut.*) to shore (*a vessel*).
apuntamiento, *n.m.* pointing, aiming; abstract, summary; annotation; judicial report.
apuntar, *v.t.* to point, aim; to point out, indicate; to note, jot down; to sketch; to stitch, tack lightly; to mend; to wager (*in games*); to fasten; to sharpen; (*theat.*) to prompt. — *v.i.* to begin to appear *or* show; to hint; ***apuntar a un blanco,*** to aim at a target; ***apunta el día,*** day is breaking; ***apuntar y no dar,*** to fail to live up to expectation *or* promise. — **apuntarse,** *v.r.* to sign on *or* up; to

begin to turn (*of wine*); to get tight *or* tipsy; ***apuntarse a una sociedad,*** to join a society; ***me apunto,*** I'm on, count me in.

apunte, *n.m.* annotation, memorandum; note; rough sketch; stake (*in games*); (*theat.*) prompt-book, prompting; (*coll.*) rascal, crafty person; aim.

apuntillar, *v.t.* to finish off.

apuñadar, *v.t.* (*prov.*) to strike with the fist.

apuñalado, -da, *a.* shaped like a dagger.

apuñalar, *v.t.* to stab.

apuñar, *v.t.* to seize with the fist, grab. — *v.i.* to tighten *or* clench the fist.

apuñear, *v.t.* (*coll.*) to strike with the fist.

apuracabos, *n.m. inv.* candlestick; save-all.

apuración, *n.f.* refining; investigating; draining (*to the lees*); embarrassment, fluster.

apuradamente, *adv.* barely, barely in time, only just, in great haste, with great difficulty.

apurador, -ra, *a.* refining, purifying; consuming. — *n.m.f.* refiner, purifier; candlestick.

apuramiento, *n.m.* [APURACIÓN].

apuranieves, *n.m. inv.* [AGUZANIEVES].

apurar, *v.t.* to purify; to clear up, verify, investigate minutely; to consume, exhaust, drain; to hurry, push; ***apurar todos los recursos,*** to exhaust every expedient. — **apurarse,** *v.r.* to get embarrassed; to get flustered; (*coll.*) get into a dither *or* tizzy; (*Hisp. Am.*) to hurry.

apurativo, -va, *a.* (*med.*) detersive.

apuro, *n.m.* stringency, strait, want; ***estar en un apuro,*** to be in a tight spot; to be hard up.

aquejar, *v.t.* to afflict.

aquejoso, -sa, *a.* afflicted, grieved.

aquél, *m.*, **aquélla,** *f.*, **aquéllos,** *m.pl.*, **aquéllas,** *f.pl. dem. pron.* the former, the first mentioned. — *n.m.* indescribable quality; charm, air, grace; ***Juana tiene aquél,*** Jane has charm.

aquel, *m.*, **aquella,** *f. dem. a.*, *dem. pron.* that (one), that (one) yonder. — **aquellos,** *m.pl.*, **aquellas,** *f.pl.* those (ones), those (ones) yonder. — **aquello,** *neut. dem. pron.* that; that matter; there; ***aquello me encanta,*** I love it there; ***ya salió aquello,*** I knew you were going to say that.

aquelarre, *n.m.* witches' Sabbath; (*fig.*) rumpus, din, uproar.

aquende, *adv.* on this side, hither, here.

aqueo, -quea, *a.*, *n.m.f.* Achæan.

aquerenciarse, *v.r.* to become deeply attached (*to a place*).

aquese, *m.*, **aquesa,** *f.*, **aqueso,** *neut. dem. pron.* (*obs.*) that. — **aquesos,** *m.pl.*, **aquesas,** *f.pl.* (*obs.*) those.

aqueste, *m.*, **aquesta,** *f.*, **aquesto,** *neut. dem. pron.* (*obs.*) this, that. — **aquestos,** *m.pl.*, **aquestas,** *f.pl.* (*obs.*) these.

áqueta, *n.f.* (*ent.*) cicada, harvest fly.

aquí, *adv.* here, hither; at this point; ***aquí mismo,*** right here; ***aquí dentro,*** inside here, in here; ***aquí fuera,*** out here; ***he aquí,*** behold; ***de aquí para allí,*** to and fro, up and down; ***de aquí,*** from here; hence; ***de aquí a 20 años,*** 20 years from now; ***por aquí,*** this way, through here; here, hereabouts; ***de aquí en adelante,*** from now on, henceforth; ***hasta aquí,*** hitherto, so far.

aquiescencia, *n.f.* acquiescence, consent.

aquietar, *v.t.* to quiet, lull, pacify, hush, allay; to set at rest.

aquifolio, *n.m.* (*bot.*) holly-tree.

aquilatación, *n.f.*, **aquilatamiento,** *n.m.* assay; assaying; examination.

aquilatar, *v.t.* to assay (*gold, silver, gems; graduation of pearls*); to examine closely; to go into fine detail over.

aquilea, *n.f.* (*bot.*) milfoil, yarrow.

aquilino, -na, *a.* (*poet.*) aquiline.

aquilón, *n.m.* north wind; North.

aquilonal, aquilonar, *a.* northerly, northern; wintry.

aquillado, -da, *a.* keel-shaped; (*naut.*) long-keeled.

Aquisgrán, *n.m.* Aachen, Aix-la-Chapelle.

aquistar, *v.t.* to acquire; to conquer.

aquivo, -va, *a.* Achæan.

Ara, *n.f.* (*astron.*) Ara.

ara (1), *n.f.* altar; ***en aras de,*** for the sake of; ***sacrificar en aras de,*** to sacrifice to *or* for.

ara (2), *n.m.* (*orn.*) blue and yellow macaw.

árabe, *a.* Arabian. — *n.m.f.* Arab. — *n.m.* Arabic (*language*).

arabesco, -ca, *a.* Arabian. — *n.m.* arabesque.

Arabia, *n.f.* Arabia; ***la Arabia Saudita,*** Saudi Arabia.

arábico, -ca, arábigo, -ga, *a.* Arabian; ***goma arábiga,*** gum arabic. — *n.m.* Arabic; ***estar una cosa en arábigo,*** to be gibberish.

arabio, -bia, *a.* Arabian, Arabic. — *n.m.f.* Arab.

arabismo, *n.m.* Arabism.

arabista, *n.m.f.* Arabist, Arabic scholar.

arabizar [E], *v.t.* to Arabize, make Arabic *or* Arab-like.

arable, *a.* (*agric.*) arable.

arácnido, -da, *a.* (*zool.*) arachnidan, arachnidean. — *n.m.* arachnid; (*pl.* **arácnidos**) Arachnida.

aracnoides, *n.f. inv.* (*anat.*) arachnoid membrane.

aracnología, *n.f.* (*nat. hist.*) arachnology.

arada, *n.f.* (*agric.*) ploughing; ploughed ground; land ploughed in a day.

arado, *n.m.* plough, (*Am.*) plow.

arador, -ra, *a.* ploughing. — *n.m.* ploughman; (*zool.*) harvest-mite; handworm, ring-worm.

aradro, *n.m.* (*prov.*) plough.

aradura, *n.f.* ploughing; (*prov.*) land ploughed in a day.

aragonés, -nesa, *a.*, *n.m.f.* Aragonese.

aragonito, *n.m.* (*min.*) aragonite.

araguato, *n.m.* (*Hisp. Am.*) American monkey.

araguirá, *n.m.* (*Arg.*) araguirá bird.

aralia, *n.f.* aralia; spikenard.

aramaico, -ca, *a.* Aramaic.

arambel, *n.m.* rag, tatter.

arameo, -mea, *a.*, *n.m.f.* Aramaic, Aramæan. — *n.m.* Aramaic (*language*).

aramio, *n.m.* fallow field, ground *or* land.

arán, *n.m.* (*prov., bot.*) sloe (*tree and fruit*).

arana, *n.f.* trick.

arancel, *n.m.* tariff, scale of dues *or* duties (*esp. customs*).

arancelario, -ria, *a.* to do with tariffs *or* duties (*esp. customs*).

arandanedo, *n.m.* cranberry patch.

arándano, *n.m.* bilberry, blueberry; cranberry.

arandela, *n.f.* socket-pan (*of candlestick*); (*mech.*) ring; (*mech.*) washer; axle-guard; rivet-plate, collar-plate; (*obs.*) guard (*round staff of lance*); nave-box (*of gun-carriage*); glass candelabrum.

arandillo, *n.m.* (*orn.*) marsh warbler; (*prov.*) hip-pad, bustle.

aranero, -ra, *a.* deceitful, tricky. — *n.m.f.* trickster, cheat.

arangorri, *n.m.* (*ichth.*) arangorri fish.

aranoso, -sa [ARANERO].

aranzada, *n.f.* measure of land (447 *deciares; in Córdoba* 367 *deciares; in Sevilla* 475 *deciares*).

araña, *n.f.* (*zool.*) spider; (*ichth.*) sting-bull, common weaver, sea-spider; chandelier, girandole, sconce; (*bot.*) crowfoot; bird net *or* trap; (*coll.*) selfish *or* calculating person; (*prov.*) scuffle, scramble; (*Chi.*) a light two-wheeled carriage.

arañada, *n.f.* collection of spiders; scratch.

arañador, -ra, *a.* scratching, scraping. — *n.m.f.* scratcher, scraper.

arañamiento, *n.m.* scratching; scraping.

arañar, *v.t.* to scratch; (*coll.*) to scrape (*stringed* *instruments*); (*coll.*) to scrape together, scrape up (*money etc.*).

arañazo, *n.m.* scratch.

arañero, -ra, *a.* (*prov.*) wild, untameable (*bird*). — *n.m.* spider-catcher.

araño, *n.m.* scratch, nipping, slight wound.

arañón, *n.m.* (*prov.*) sloe (*tree and fruit*).

arañuela, *n.f.* small spider; (*bot.*) crowfoot.

arañuelo, *n.m.* (*zool.*) red spider; spider grub.

arapenne, *n.m.* (*obs.*) ancient measure of 120 square feet.

aráquida, *n.f.* (*bot.*) peanut.

arar (1), *v.t.* to plough.

arar (2), *n.m.* sandarac tree.

aratada, *n.f.* (*prov.*) bad turn.

araticú, *n.m.* (*Hisp. Am.*) (*bot.*) cherimoya.

aratoso, -sa, *a.* (*prov.*) heavy, annoying.

araucano, -na, Araucanian, Araucarian.

araucaria, *n.f.* (*bot.*) araucaria pine.

arauja, *n.f.* creeping plant (*Asclepiadaceae*).

aravico, *n.m.* (ancient Peruvian) bard.

arazá, *n.m.* (*Arg.*, *Par.*, *Ur.*) guava tree.

arbalestrilla, *n.f.* (*math.*) arbalest, cross-staff.

arbellón, *n.m.* (*prov.*) gutter, draining channel.

arbitrable, *a.* arbitrable.

arbitración, *n.f.* (*law*) arbitration.

arbitrador, -ra, *a.* arbitrating. — *n.m.* arbitrator, umpire, referee, judge.

arbitraje, *n.m.* arbitration; (*com.*) arbitrage.

arbitral, *a.* arbitral.

arbitramento, arbitramiento, *n.m.* arbitration; (*law*) arbitrament.

arbitrante, *a.* arbitrating.

arbitrar, *v.t.* to arbitrate, adjudge. — *v.i.* to contrive ways and means.

arbitrariedad, *n.f.* arbitrariness.

arbitrario, -ria, arbitrativo, -va, *a.* arbitrary; depending on arbitration; (*law*) arbitral.

arbitrio, *n.m.* free will; means, expedient; arbitration; (*law*) discretionary judgment, decision, adjudication; (*pl.*) rates; ***propios y arbitrios,*** ways and means.

arbitrista, *n.m.f.* schemer, projector, contriver; Utopian political thinker.

árbitro, -ra, *n.m.f.* arbitrator, arbiter, referee, umpire.

árbol, *n.m.* (*bot.*) tree; (*naut.*) mast; (*mech.*) arbor, shaft, axle, spindle; body (*of shirt*); (*slang*) body; crown post (*of winding stairs*); ***árbol genealógico,*** genealogical tree; (*bot.*) ***árbol de Judas*** or ***de Judea*** or ***del amor,*** Judas tree; (*Bib.*, *bot.*) ***árbol de la vida,*** tree of life; (*Bib.*) ***árbol de la ciencia del bien y del mal,*** tree of the knowledge of good and evil; (*bot.*) ***árbol del pan,*** breadfruit tree; (*bot.*) ***árbol del paraíso,*** Paradise *or* China tree; (*bot.*) ***árbol del viajero,*** traveller's tree; (*bot.*) ***árbol de pie,*** seedling; (*mech.*) ***árbol de transmisión*** or ***de asiento,*** transmission shaft; (*mech.*) ***árbol de mando, árbol motor,*** drive shaft; (*mech.*) ***árbol de levas,*** camshaft; ***quien a buen árbol se arrima, buena sombra le cobija,*** he who has good friends enjoys good protection; ***del árbol caído todos hacen leña,*** everyone takes advantage of a man who is down; (*pl.* **árboles**) timber, (*Am.*) lumber.

arbolado, -da, *a.* wooded; (*naut.*) masted; high (*of sea*); ***mar arbolado,*** high seas. — *n.m.* woodland.

arboladura, *n.f.* (*naut.*) masts and spars.

arbolar, *v.t.* to hoist, set upright; (*naut.*) to mast (*a ship*), ensign, flag. — **arbolarse,** *v.r.* to rear (*horse*).

arbolario, -ria, *a.*, *n.m.f.* (*coll.*) madcap, scatterbrain(ed). — *n.m.* (*bot.*) nursery.

arboleda, *n.f.* grove.

arboledo, *n.m.* woodland.

arbolejo, *n.m.* (miserable *or* wretched) little tree.

arbolete, *n.m.* branch of a tree on which to fasten lime twigs; (*fig.*) trap.

arbolillo, *n.m.* (miserable *or* wretched) little tree; (*min.*) side (of a blast-furnace).

arbolista, *n.m.f.* arboriculturist.

arbolito, *n.m.* (nice *or* delightful) little tree.

arbollón, *n.m.* drain, sewer; ***salir por el arbollón,*** to come off badly.

arbóreo, -rea, *a.* arboreal, arboraceous.

arborescencia, *n.f.* arborescence.

arborescente, *a.* arborescent.

arboricultura, *n.f.* arboriculture.

arboriforme, *a.* tree-like in shape.

arborista [ARBOLISTA].

arborización, *n.f.* (*min.*, *med.*) arborization.

arborizado, -da, *a.* having the appearance of foliage; arborescent, dendritic.

arborizar [C], *v.t.* to make tree-like. — *v.i.* to cultivate trees.

arbotante, *n.m.* vault (supporting arch); flying buttress.

arbusto, *n.m.* shrub.

arca, *n.f.* chest, coffer, safe; tempering oven; ark; mollusc; lumber room; ***arca de Noé,*** Noah's ark; ***arca de la alianza,*** Ark of the Covenant; ***arca de agua,*** reservoir, water tower; (*anat.*) ***arca del cuerpo,*** human trunk; (*fig.*) ***arca cerrada,*** closed book, dark horse, unknown quantity; ***el buen paño en el arca se vende,*** good quality needs no pushing; (*pl.*) cavities of the body under the ribs; treasury.

arcabucear, *v.t.* to shoot *or* execute with an harquebus.

arcabucería, *n.f.* (*mil.*) troop of harquebusiers; salvo of harquebuses; harquebus factory.

arcabucero, *n.m.* harquebus maker; harquebusier.

arcabucete, *n.m.* small harquebus.

arcabuco, *n.m.* densely wooded mountain.

arcabuz, *n.m.* harquebus.

arcabuzazo, *n.m.* harquebus shot *or* wound.

arcacil [ALCAUCIL].

arcada, *n.f.* retch, retching; (*arch.*) arcade, row of arches.

arcade, *a.*, *n.m.f.*, **arcadio, -dia,** *a.* Arcadian.

arcador, *n.m.* wool-beater.

arcaduz, *n.m.* conduit, pipe; bucket; (*fig.*) channel; ***llevar una cosa por sus arcaduces,*** to conduct an affair through the proper channels.

arcaico, -ca, *a.* archaic.

arcaísmo, *n.m.* archaism.

arcaísta, *n.m.f.* archaist.

arcaizar [C], *v.t.*, *v.i.* to archaize.

arcángel, *n.m.* archangel.

arcangelical, arcangélico, -ca, *a.* archangelic.

arcano, -na, *a.* secret, recondite, cryptic, mysterious. — *n.m.* arcanum.

arcar [A], *v.t.* to arch; to beat (*wool*).

arcaz, *n.m.* large chest.

arcazón, *n.m.* (*prov.*) osier; willow-plot.

arce, *n.m.* (*bot.*) maple-tree.

arcedianato, *n.m.* archdeaconship, archdeaconry.

arcediano, *n.m.* archdeacon.

arcedo, *n.m.* maple grove.

arcén, *n.m.* border, brim, edge; curbstone (*well*); margin, hard shoulder *or* verge (*road*).

arcifinio, -nia, *a.* having natural boundaries (*territory*).

arcilla, *n.f.* clay.

arcillar, *v.t.* to clay.

arcilloso, -sa, *a.* clayey, argillaceous.

arciprestazgo, *n.m.* office of archpriest.

arcipreste, *n.m.* archpriest.

arco, *n.m.* (*geom.*) arc; (*arch.*) arch, bridge; bow; (*mus.*) bow; ***arco iris,*** rainbow.

arcón, *n.m.* large chest.
arcosa, *n.f.* (*min.*) arkose.
archicofradía, *n.f.* privileged brotherhood.
archidiácono, *n.m.* archdeacon.
archidiócesis, *n.f. inv.* archdiocese.
archiducado, *n.m.* archdukedom, archduchy.
archiducal, *a.* archducal.
archiduque, *n.m.* archduke.
archiduquesa, *n.f.* archduchess.
archilaúd, *n.m.* large lute.
archimillonario, -ria, *a., n.m.f.* multi-millionaire.
archipámpano, *n.m.* (*coll.*) ***archipámpano de las Indias,*** Grand Panjandrum.
archipiélago, *n.m.* archipelago.
archivador, *n.m.* filing cabinet.
archivar, *v.t.* to file; to file away; (*coll.*) to hide away.
archivero, -ra, *n.m.f.*, **archivista,** *n.m.f.* archivist, keeper of the records.
archivo, *n.m.* archive(s); file(s); (*coll.*) secret place.
archivolta, *n.f.* (*arch.*) archivolt.
arda, *n.f.* squirrel.
ardalear, *v.i.* to yield thin *or* poor bunches of grapes.
árdea, *n.f.* stone-curlew; heron.
ardentía, *n.f.* heat; phosphorescence (*of sea*); heartburn.
ardentísimo, -ma, *a. superl.* [ARDIENTE], extremely ardent.
ardeola, *n.f.* (*orn.*) squacco heron.
arder, *v.i.* to burn, blaze; (*poet.*) to glitter, glisten, shine; to rot (*manure*); to be inflamed; ***estar ardiendo de cólera,*** to be blazing with rage; (*coll.*) ***está que arde,*** he's fuming; ***arder en deseos de,*** to be consumed with a passion to (*do sth.*). — **arderse,** *v.r.* to burn up, become consumed (*grain in hot weather*).
ardero, -ra, *a.* squirrel-hunter (*dog*).
ardeviejas, *n.f. inv.* (*bot., coll.*) gorse, furze.
ardid, *n.m.* stratagem, artifice, ruse.
ardido, -da, *a.* brave, courageous; daring, bold, fearless.
ardiente, *a.* ardent, burning, hot, fervent; (*fig.*) fiery, feverish; passionate; (*poet.*) glowing red, like fire.
ardilla, *n.f.* squirrel; ***andar como ardilla,*** to be restless, be a fidget; (*fig.*) ***ser una ardilla,*** to be very quick *or* smart.
ardimiento, *n.m.* conflagration; intrepidity, valour, courage.
ardínculo, *n.m.* (*vet.*) abscess (*horses*).
ardiondo, -da, *a.* valiant, courageous.
ardite, *n.m.* farthing; (*coll.*) ***no vale un ardite,*** it's not worth a brass farthing *or* a twopenny cuss; (*coll.*) (***no***) ***me importa un ardite,*** I don't give a damn.
ardor, *n.m.* ardour, heat, hotness, fieriness; vivacity; valour; fervency, eagerness; (*med.*) fever; heartburn.
ardoroso, -sa, *a.* fiery; ardent, passionate.
arduo, -dua, *a.* arduous, difficult; (*poet.*) steep, lofty.
área, *n.f.* area; are.
areca, *n.f.* areca palm *or* nut.
arefacción, *n.f.* drying; arefaction.
areito, *n.m.* popular song and dance (of the Caribbean).
arel, *n.m.* large sieve.
arelar, *v.t.* to sift.
arena, *n.f.* sand; arena; (*pl.*) (*med.*) gravel; ***arena movediza,*** quicksand.
arenáceo, -cea, *a.* arenaceous, gravelly, sandy.
arenal, *n.m.* sandy ground, stretch of sand, strand; quicksand bed.
arenalejo, *n.m.* small sandy place.
arenar, *v.t.* to sand; to rub *or* cover with sand.
arencado, -da, *a.* herring-like; (*fig.*) dried-up, skinny.
arencar [A], *v.t.* to salt and dry (*sardines etc.*).
arencón, *n.m.* (*ichth.*) large herring.
arenería, *n.f.* sand-pit.
arenero, -ra, *n.m.f.* dealer in sand. — *n.m.* sand-box.
arenga, *n.f.* harangue.
arengador, -ra, *a.* haranguing. — *n.m.f.* haranguer.
arengar [B], *v.t., v.i.* to harangue, deliver a speech (to).
arenilla, *n.f.* moulding sand; powder to dry writing; (*med.*) calculus; (*pl.*) granulated saltpetre.
arenisco, -ca, *a.* sandy. — *n.f.* (*min.*) sandstone.
arenoso, -sa, *a.* sandy.
arenque, *n.m.* (*ichth.*) herring; ***arenque ahumado,*** kipper.
arenquero, -ra, *n.m.f.* herring dealer. — *n.f.* (*sl.*) coarse, low woman; *n.f.* herring fishing-net.
aréola, *n.f.* (*anat., biol., med.*) areola; circle (round the nipple).
areómetro, *n.m.* aræometer; hydrometer.
areopagita, *n.m.* Areopagite.
areópago, *n.m.* Areopagus.
areóstilo, *n.m.* (*arch.*) aræostyle.
areotectónica, *n.f.* areotectonics.
arepa, *n.f.* (*Hisp. Am.*) corn griddle cake.
arestil, arestín, *n.m.* (*bot.*) perennial umbelliferous plant with dark blue flowers; (*vet.*) skin eruption, rash.
arestinado, -da, *a.* (*vet.*) afflicted with thrush.
arete, *n.m.* ear-ring.
aretino, -na, *a., n.m.f.* (native) of Arezzo.
arfada, *n.f.* (*naut.*) pitching (*ship*).
arfar, *v.i.* (*naut.*) to pitch.
argadijo, argadillo, *n.m.* reel, bobbin, winder; (*prov.*) large wicker basket; (*coll.*) blustering, noisy *or* interfering person.
argado, *n.m.* trick, artifice; absurdity, nonsense.
argal, *n.m.* argol, crude tartar.
argalia, *n.f.* catheter.
argallera, *n.f.* (*carp.*) saw for (cutting grooves).
argamandel, *n.m.* rag, tatter.
argamandijo, *n.m.* collection of small tools *or* implements.
argamasa, *n.f.* mortar.
argamasado, *n.m.* quantity of mortar.
argamasar, *v.t.* to mix (*mortar*); to plaster, cement. — *v.i.* to make mortar.
argamasón, *n.m.* large dry piece of mortar.
árgana, *n.f.* (*mech.*) crane; (*pl.*) wicker baskets (*carried by horses*).
arganel, *n.m.* ring in an astrolabe.
arganeo, *n.m.* (*naut.*) anchor-ring.
árgano, *n.m.* (*mech.*) crane.
argavieso, *n.m.* whirlwind.
argayar, *v. impers.* to fall down (*landslide*).
argayo (1), *n.m.* landslide; (*prov.*) ***argayo de nieve,*** avalanche.
argayo (2), *n.m.* (monk's) coarse cloak.
Argel, *n.m.* Algiers.
argel, *a.* (said of a horse) having a white right hind foot.
Argelia, *n.f.* Algeria.
argelino, -na, *a., n.m.f.* Algerian.
argema, argemón, *n.m.* (*med.*) argema.
argemone, *n.f.* (*bot.*) prickly *or* horned poppy.
argén, *n.m.* (*her.*) white *or* silver (colour), argent.
argentado, -da, *a.* silvered, silvery; slashed (*shoes*). — *n.f.* ladies' cosmetic.
argentador, -ra, *a.* silvery. — *n.m.* silversmith.
argentar, *v.t.* to silver, plate, adorn with silver; to polish like silver.

argentario, *n.m.* silversmith; governor of the mint.
argénteo, -tea, *a.* silvery; silver-plated; silver-white.
argentería, *n.f.* embroidery in gold *or* silver.
argentero, *n.m.* silversmith.
argentífero, -ra, *a.* silver-bearing.
Argentina, *n.f.* Argentina, the Argentine.
argentina (1), *n.f.* (*bot.*) satin cinquefoil.
argentinismo, *n.m.* Argentinism.
argentino, -na (2), *a.* silvery, argentine; Argentinian, Argentine. — *n.m.f.* Argentinian, Argentine. — *n.m.* argentino (five gold pesos) (*coin*).
argento, *n.m.* (*poet.*) silver; ***argento vivo,*** quicksilver; (*chem.*) ***argento vivo sublimado,*** corrosive sublimate.
argentoso, -sa, *a.* mixed with silver.
argila, argilla [ARCILLA].
argiloso, -sa [ARCILLOSO].
argo, *n.m.* (*chem.*) argon.
argolla, *n.f.* (large) ring, collar, hoop.
argolleta, *n.f.* (small) ring.
argollón, *n.m.* very large ring.
árgoma, *n.f.* (*bot.*) furze, gorse.
argomal, *n.m.* area of furze, heath.
argomón, *n.m.* large, prickly furze.
argonauta, *n.m.* Argonaut; (*zool.*) paper-nautilus; cuttlefish.
Argos, *n.m.* (*myth.*) Argus; Argos; Argo; (*fig.*) lynx-eyed person.
argot, *n.m.* slang.
argucia, *n.f.* subtlety, sophistry; ruse, trick.
argüe, *n.m.* (*naut.*) windlass, capstan.
arguellarse, *v.r.* (*prov.*) to become emaciated.
arguello, *n.m.* (*prov.*) emaciation, loss of weight.
árguenas, árgueñas, *n.f.pl.* handbarrow, panniers; saddlebags; (*Chi.*) wicker baskets (*on horse*).
argüidor, -ra, *a.* argumentative. — *n.m.f.* arguer.
argüir [I], *v.t.* to allege; to imply, infer. — *v.i.* to argue, dispute.
argumentación, *n.f.* argumentation.
argumentador, -ra, *a.* argumentative; reasoning. — *n.m.f.* arguer, reasoner, disputer.
argumentar, *v.t., v.i.* to argue.
argumentista, *n.m.f.* arguer, reasoner.
argumento, *n.m.* argument; plot (*of story* or *play*).
arguyente, *a.* arguing, opposing. — *n.m.f.* arguer.
aria (1), *n.f.* (*mus.*) aria.
ariano, -na [ARIO].
aribar, *v.t.* (*obs.*) to reel (*yarn*) into skeins.
aribo, *n.m.* (*obs.*) reel for making skeins.
aricado, *n.m.* (*agric.*) light ploughing, cross harrowing.
aricar [A], *v.t.* (*agric.*) to plough lightly; [ARREJACAR].
aridecer(se) [9], *v.t., v.i.* (*v.r.*) to make, be *or* become dry *or* arid.
aridez, *n.f.* dryness, aridity, aridness.
árido, -da, *a.* arid, dry; (*fig.*) arid, dry. — *n.m.pl.* (**áridos**) dry goods.
arienzo, *n.m.* old Castilian coin.
arieta, *n.f.* (*mus.*) arietta.
arietar, *v.t.* to ram, batter.
ariete, *n.m.* battering-ram; (*naut.*) ram; ***ariete hidráulico,*** hydraulic ram.
arietino, -na, *a.* resembling a ram's head.
arijo, -ja, *a.* (*agric.*) light, easily tilled.
arillo, *n.m.* ear-ring; neck-stock frame.
arimez, *n.m.* prominence *or* projection (*of building*).
arincarse [A], *v.r.* to be *or* become constipated.
ario, -ria (2), *a., n.m.f.* Aryan.
arisaro, *n.m.* (*bot.*) wake-robin.
arisblanco, -ca, *a.* white-bearded (*wheat*).
ariscarse [A], *v.r.* to become sullen *or* stand-offish.
arisco, -ca, *a.* churlish, surly, sullen; stand-offish, unsociable, unfriendly.
arisnegro, -ra, arisprieto, -ta, *a.* black-bearded (*wheat*).
arista, *n.f.* (*bot.*) arista; beard, awn (*of grains*); hemp-stalk; edge; (*geom.*) intersection; (*pl.*) (*mil.*) salient angles.
aristado, -da, *a.* awned, bearded, aristate.
aristarco, *n.m.* Aristarch, severe critic.
aristino, *n.m.* (*vet.*) thrush; wheals.
aristocracia, *n.f.* aristocracy.
aristócrata, *n.m.f.* aristocrat.
aristocrático, -ca, *a.* aristocratic.
aristoloquia, *n.f.* (*bot.*) birthwort.
aristón, *n.m.* (*arch.*) edge, corner; (*arch.*) groin, groin-rib; (*mus.*) barrel-organ.
aristoso, -sa, *a.* having many beards *or* awns.
aristotélico, -ca, *a.* Aristotelian.
aristotelismo, *n.m.* Aristotelianism.
aritmancia, aritmomancia, *n.f.* arithmancy, arithmomancy.
aritmético, -ca, *a.* arithmetical. — *n.m.f.* arithmetician. — *n.f.* arithmetic.
aritmómetro, *n.m.* calculating machine.
arjorán, *n.m.* ciclamor.
arlar, *v.t.* to hang (*fruit*) in bunches for preserving.
arlequín, *n.m.* harlequin; Neapolitan ice-cream.
arlequinado, -da, *a.* parti-coloured (*clothes*). — *n.f.* harlequin's trick *or* joke.
arlo, *n.m.* (*bot.*) barberry; fruit hung in bunches to be preserved.
arlota, *n.f.* tow of flax *or* hemp.
arma, *n.f.* weapon, arm; force; branch (*of the three services*); (*pl.*) armorial bearings; coat of arms; (*fig.*) means, power; ***arma de infantería,*** infantry; ***las armas,*** the fighting services; ***arma arrojadiza,*** missile weapon; ***arma blanca,*** steel-bladed weapon (*sword, knife*); ***arma corta,*** pistol; ***arma de fuego,*** fire-arm, gun; ***arma negra,*** fencing foil; ***maestro de armas,*** fencing master; ***hecho de armas,*** feat of arms; ***alzarse en armas,*** to rise up in arms; ***pasar por las armas,*** to put to the sword, execute; ***poner en armas,*** to arm; ***ponerse en armas,*** to prepare, get ready; ***rendir las armas,*** to lay down one's arms; ***tocar al arma, tocar arma,*** to sound the call to arms; ***sobre las armas,*** under arms; ***¡a las armas!*** to arms!
armada, *n.f.* navy; fleet, squadron; ***la Armada Invencible,*** the Spanish Armada; (*hunt.*) party of beaters.
armadera, *n.f.* keel, main timber.
armadía, *n.f.* raft, float.
armadijo, *n.m.* trap, snare.
armadillo, *n.m.* (*zool.*) armadillo.
armado, *n.m.* Roman soldier (*in religious processions*).
armador, *n.m.* outfitter, shipowner; privateer, cruiser; (*mech.*) framer, adjuster, fitter; jacket.
armadura, *n.f.* armour; (*mil., elec.*) armature; (*elec.*) yoke (*of a magnet*); framework, shell (*of building*); (*mech.*) fitting, setting; truss; (*anat.*) skeleton.
armajal [MARJAL].
armajo, *n.m.* (*bot.*) glasswort.
armamento, *n.m.* armament; accoutrements; (*naut.*) equipment.
armar, *v.t.* to arm; to man; (*carp.*) to bind, mount, truss, put together; (*mech.*) to set, frame, mount, piece, adjust, make true, rig up; to plate (*with gold* or *silver*); to reinforce (*concrete*); (*naut.*) to equip, fit out, put (*a ship*) in commission; (*naut.*) ***armar los remos,*** to man the oars; ***armar caballero,*** to dub knight; ***armar ruido,*** to make a din *or* racket; (*coll.*) ***armar una bronca,*** to start a row; (*coll.*) ***armarla*** or ***armar la gorda,*** to start a hell of a row, kick up a hell of a fuss;

(*coll.*) ***buena se va a armar,*** there's going to be hell to pay; ***armar un escándalo,*** to kick up a shindy. — **armarse,** *v.r.* — ***(uno) un lío,*** to get into a muddle *or* mess; ***armarse de paciencia,*** to possess one's soul in patience; ***armarse de valor,*** to pluck up courage.

armario, *n.m.* wardrobe, cupboard, (*Am.*) closet; ***armario de luna,*** wardrobe with mirror.

armatoste, *n.m.* unwieldy *or* lumbering great object; (*coll.*) hefty useless person.

armazón, *n.m.* (*anat.*) skeleton. — *n.f.* framework, skeleton; mounting.

armelina, *n.f.* ermine skin.

armella, *n.f.* screw-eye.

arménico, -ca, *a.* Armenian. — *n.m.* Armenian bole; Armenian stone.

armenio, -nia, *a., n.m.f.* Armenian (*person*). — *n.m.* Armenian (*language*).

armería, *n.f.* armoury, arsenal; gunsmith's trade *or* shop; heraldry.

armero, *n.m.* armourer, gunsmith; keeper of arms; (*mil.*) rack *or* stand for fire-arms.

armífero, -ra, armígero, -ra, *a.* warlike; (*poet.*) armed, armour-bearing. — *n.m.* squire, shield-bearer.

armila, *n.f.* (*arch.*) part of base of a column.

armilar, *a.* ***esfera armilar,*** armillary sphere.

armilla, *n.f.* (*arch.*) astragal.

armillado, -da, *a.* armillary; surrounded by rings.

armiñado, -da, *a.* trimmed *or* lined with ermine; ermine-white.

armiño, *n.m.* (*zool.*) ermine.

armipotente, *a.* (*poet.*) mighty in war.

armisonante, *a.* (*poet.*) bearing resounding arms.

armisticio, *n.m.* armistice.

armón, *n.m.* (*mil.*) limber, guncarriage.

armonía, *n.f.* harmony; concord.

armónico, -ca, *a.* harmonic, harmonious; proportionate, musical, rhythmical. — *n.f.* harmonica.

armonio, *n.m.* harmonium, small reed-organ.

armonioso, -sa, *a.* harmonious, pleasant-sounding.

armonista, *n.m.f.* harmonist.

armonización, *n.f.* harmonization.

armonizar [C], *v.t., v.i.* to harmonize; ***armonizar con,*** to be in keeping with.

armosín, *n.m.* thin silk, taffeta.

armuelle, *n.m.* (*bot.*) orach, mountain spinach.

arna, *n.f.* (*prov.*) beehive.

arnacho, *n.m.* (*bot.*) rest-harrow.

Arnaldo, *n.m.* Arnold.

arnaúte, *a., n.m.f.* Albanian.

arnés, *n.m.* harness; armour; (*pl.* **arneses**) harness, trappings.

árnica, *n.f.* (*bot.*) arnica; wolf's-bane.

arnillo, *n.m.* arnillo fish.

aro (1), *n.m.* hoop; serviette ring; rim; ***entrar por el aro,*** to come to heel, knuckle under; to settle down.

aro (2), *n.m.* (*bot.*) wild arum, lords-and-ladies.

¡aro! (3), *interj.* (*Chi.*) word with which a singer, dancer *or* talker is stopped, and presented with a drink.

aroca, *n.f.* linen made in Arouca (Portugal).

aroma, *n.m.* aromatic gum, balsam, wood *or* herb; aroma, perfume, fragrance. — *n.f.* aroma flower.

aromaticidad, *n.f.* aromatic quality, perfume.

aromático, -ca, *a.* aromatic, fragrant.

aromatización, *n.f.* aromatization.

aromatizador, -ra, *a.* perfuming. — *n.m.* aromatizer.

aromatizante, *a.* fragrant, aromatizing.

aromatizar [C], *v.t.* to aromatize, perfume.

aromo, *n.m.* (*bot.*) aroma tree.

aromoso, -sa, *a.* aromatic, fragrant.

arón, *n.m.* (*bot.*) arum.

aroza, *n.m.* foreman (*in iron-works* or *forge*).

arpa, *n.f.* (*mus.*) harp.

arpado, -da, *a.* serrated, toothed; (*poet.*) sweetly singing (*bird*).

arpadura, *n.f.* scratch.

arpar, *v.t.* to rend, scratch, claw, tear to pieces.

arpegio, *n.m.* (*mus.*) arpeggio.

arpella, *n.f.* (*orn.*) buzzard, marsh-harrier.

arpeo, *n.m.* (*naut.*) grappling-iron.

arpía, *n.f.* (*myth., coll.*) harpy; (*coll.*) jade, ugly shrew.

arpillera, *n.f.* sackcloth, burlap.

arpista, *n.m.f.* (*mus.*) harpist; (*Chi.*) common thief.

arpón, *n.m.* harpoon.

arponado, -da, *a.* harpoon-like.

arponar, arponear, *v.t., v.i.* to harpoon.

arponero, *n.m.* harpooner; harpoon-maker.

arqueada, *n.f.* (*mus.*) stroke with the bow; (*pl.*) retching.

arqueador, *n.m.* ship-gauger; wool-beater.

arqueaje, arqueamiento, *n.m.* gauging (*of a ship*); tonnage measurement.

arquear (1), *v.t.* to arch; to beat (*wool*); ***arquear las cejas,*** to raise one's eyebrows. — *v.i.* to retch.

arquear (2), *v.t.* (*naut.*) to gauge (*ships*); to check; to audit.

arqueo (1), *n.m.* arching.

arqueo (2), *n.m.* (*naut.*) gauging; (*naut.*) tonnage, burden; check, checking; audit.

arqueología, *n.f.* archæology.

arqueológico, -ca, *a.* archæologic(al).

arqueólogo, *n.m.* archæologist.

arquería, *n.f.* series of arches; (*Mex.*) aqueduct.

arquero (1), *n.m.* archer; bowmaker; hooper.

arquero (2), *n.m.* treasurer, cashier.

arqueta, *n.f.* small chest.

arquetipo, *n.m.* archetype.

arquetón, *n.m.* large chest.

arquibanco, *n.m.* bench with drawers.

arquidiócesis [ARCHIDIÓCESIS].

arquiepiscopal, *a.* archiepiscopal.

arquilla, arquita, *n.f.* little chest; coach-box.

arquillo, *n.m.* small bore (*locksmith's*).

arquimesa, *n.f.* writing-desk, escritoire.

arquisinagogo, *n.m.* principal in the synagogue.

arquitecto, *n.m.* architect.

arquitectónico, -ca, *a.* architectural; architectonic.

arquitectura, *n.f.* architecture.

arquitrabe, *n.m.* architrave.

arquivolta, *n.f.* archivolt.

arrabal, *n.m.* suburb, outer quarter; lower class district; (*pl.*) environs, outskirts.

arrabalero, -ra, *a., n.m.f.* suburban(ite); (*coll.*) ill-bred (person).

arrabillado, -da, *a.* (*agric.*) blighted (*wheat*).

arrabio, *n.m.* cast-iron.

arracada, *n.f.* ear-ring (with pendant).

arracimarse, *v.r.* to cluster; to form bunches.

arraclán, *n.m.* alder-tree.

arráez, *n.m.* captain *or* master of Arab ship.

arraigadas, *n.f.pl.* (*naut.*) futtock-shrouds.

arraigado, -da, *a.* fixed, deep-rooted, secure; inveterate. — *n.m.* (*naut.*) mooring.

arraigar [B], *v.i.* to take *or* strike root; (*law.*) to pledge land as guarantee. — **arraigarse,** *v.r.* to settle down; to become rooted.

arraigo, *n.m.* settling in a place; landed property; ***hombre*** or ***persona de arraigo,*** landlord, property-owner; ***tener arraigo,*** to own property; ***fianza de arraigo,*** guarantee by mortgage.

arraigue, *n.m.* settling down, taking root.

arralar, *v.i.* to become thin *or* sparse; (*agric.*) to yield thin bunches of grapes.

arramblar, *v.t.* to leave covered with sand and

gravel (*after floods*); (*fig.*) to sweep away. — *v.i.* ***arramblar con todo,*** to go *or* clear off with everything.

arranca, *n.f.* plucking (*fruit*).

arrancaclavos, *n.m. inv.* nail-puller.

arrancada, *n.f.* (*coll.*) sudden departure; violent sally; (*naut.*) sudden increase in speed.

arrancadera, *n.f.* leading bell (*for cattle*).

arrancadero, *n.m.* starting-point; (*prov.*) thickest part (of a gun-barrel).

arrancador, -ra, *a.* extirpating, destroying. — *n.m.f.* extirpator, destruction.

arrancadura, *n.f.*, **arrancamiento,** *n.m.* extirpation, pulling out, destruction.

arrancapinos, *n.m. inv.* (*coll.*) dwarf, small person.

arrancar [A], *v.t.* to extirpate, root out, root up, pull up, force out, wrest, pull out, tear out, draw out; to carry off; to expectorate; ***arrancar de raíz*** or ***de cuajo,*** to pull up *or* tear out by the roots; to eradicate. — *v.i.* to start, start off; to set sail; to originate. — **arrancarse,** *v.r.* to get moving, suddenly start to move, rush forward (*esp. of bulls*).

arrancasiega, *n.f.* (*agric.*) poor grain half mowed and half pulled up; (*prov.*) quarrel, dispute.

arrancasondas, *n.m. inv.* drill extractor, grab.

arranciarse, *v.r.* to become rancid.

arranchar, *v.t.* (*naut.*) to coast; (*naut.*) to brace. — **arrancharse,** *v.r.* to mess together.

arranque, *n.m.* pulling up, wrenching, wrench; outburst; burst, sally; sudden impulse; sudden jerk *or* start; (*mech., motor.*) start, starter, starting (*gear*); (*arch.*) arch springer *or* spring.

arranquera, *n.f.* (*Cub., Mex.*) financial straits.

arrapar, *v.t.* (*vulg.*) to snatch away, carry off.

arrapiezo, *n.m.* tatter, rag; urchin, ragamuffin.

arrapo, *n.m.* rag, tatter.

arras, *n.f.pl.* security, earnest (*of contract*); 13 coins given by a bridegroom to his bride at a wedding; dowry; earnest-money, pledge, handsel.

arrasado, -da, *a.* satiny.

arrasadura, *n.f.* levelling with a strickle.

arrasamiento, *n.m.* levelling, razing to the ground.

arrasar, *v.t.* to level; to raze to the ground, destroy; to level with a strickle; to fill to the brim. — **arrasar(se),** *v.i.* (*v.r.*) to clear up, turn fine (*of the weather*); ***arrasarse de*** or ***en lágrimas,*** to become filled with tears (*eyes*).

arrastrada, *n.f.* [ARRASTRADO].

arrastraderas, *n.f.pl.* (*naut.*) lower studding-sails.

arrastradero, *n.m.* log path, dragging road; place where dead animals are dragged from bull-ring; (*naut.*) careening place.

arrastrado, -da, *a.* base, low, vile, wretched; knavish, rascally. — *n.m.* good-for-nothing, wretch; rascal. — *n.f.* good-for-nothing, degraded creature; whore.

arrastramiento, *n.m.* dragging; crawling.

arrastrante, *a.* dragging; crawling.

arrastrar, *v.t.* to drag, drag along *or* down, carry along *or* down, haul along *or* down; to attract; to prompt, move, urge; ***arrastrar en su caída,*** to drag down in its fall; ***arrastrar los pies,*** to shuffle, drag one's feet; ***arrastrar por tierra,*** to drag along the ground. — *v.i.* to creep, crawl; to hang down to the ground; to follow suit (*at cards*); ***hacer una cosa arrastrando,*** to do a thing reluctantly. — **arrastrarse,** *v.r.* to debase oneself, crawl.

arrastre, *n.m.* dragging, haulage, drayage; leading a trump; slope (*in a mining shaft*); (*Mex.*) mining mill.

arrate, *n.m.* pound (*weight*).

arratonado, -da, *a.* gnawed by mice.

arrayán, *n.m.* (*bot.*) myrtle.

arrayanal, *n.m.* myrtle field.

¡arre! *interj.* gee! get up! gee up!; ***¡arre allá!*** get out of the way!

arreada, *n.f.* (*Arg., Mex.*) cattle theft; (*Arg.*) recruiting.

arreador, *n.m.* (*Hisp. Am.*) muleteer; foreman, overseer.

arreala, *n.f.* pasturage toll.

arrear, *v.t.* to drive (*horses, mules etc.*); to urge on; to harness; (*Arg., Mex.*) to steal (*cattle*). — *v.i.* to hurry up; ***el que venga detrás que arree,*** the devil take the hindmost. — *interj.* (*coll.*) ***¡arrea!*** get moving!; good heavens!

arrebañaderas, *n.f.pl.* grappling-irons (*for dragging a well*).

arrebañador, -ra, *a.* gleaning, gathering. — *n.m.f.* gleaner, gatherer.

arrebañadura, *n.f.* gleaning, picking up; (*pl.*) scraps, remains (*food*).

arrebañar [REBAÑAR].

arrebatadizo, -za, *a.* excitable, inflammable, prone to violence.

arrebatado, -da, *a.* sudden, rapid, violent; reckless, rash, impetuous; flushed.

arrebatador, -ra, *a.* captivating, ravishing, enthralling.

arrebatamiento, *n.m.* rage, fury; ecstasy, rapture.

arrebatar, *v.t.* to carry off, snatch; to captivate, charm; to enrapture, delight. — **arrebatarse,** *v.r.* (*agric.*) to get parched *or* scorched; to get overcooked; ***arrebatarse de ira,*** to be carried away by anger.

arrebatiña, *n.f.* scrimmage, scramble, scuffle.

arrebato, *n.m.* surprise; sudden attack, paroxysm; fit, fury, rage; rapture.

arrebatoso, -sa, *a.* sudden, abrupt, prone to sudden fury.

arrebol, *n.m.* red sky *or* cloud; rouge.

arrebola, *n.f.* group of red clouds.

arrebolada, *n.f.* red clouds.

arrebolar, *v.t.* to paint red. — **arrebolarse,** *v.r.* to rouge.

arrebolera, *n.f.* rouge-box, rouge-seller; (*bot.*) four o'clock, marvel of Peru.

arrebollarse, *v.r.* to fall headlong.

arrebozar [C], *v.t.* (*cook.*) to dip in, cover (*with butter, sugar etc.*); to wrap up.

arrebozo [REBOZO].

arrebujadamente, *adv.* confusedly, in a muddle.

arrebujar, *v.t.* to jumble together; to huddle; to wrap.

arreciar, *v.i.* to grow worse *or* stronger; to increase in force, intensity *or* violence; ***arrecia el frío,*** it's getting colder.

arrecife, *n.m.* road paved with stone; (*naut.*) reef.

arrecirse [Q], *v.r.* to become numb; ***arrecirse de frío,*** to grow stiff with cold.

arrechucho, *n.m.* fit of anger; impulse; (*coll.*) slight attack, touch (*of an ailment*).

arredilar, *v.t.* to fold (*sheep*); to pen (*cattle*).

arredondar, arredondear [REDONDEAR].

arredramiento, *n.m.* moving back; backing out; dismay, fear.

arredrar, *v.t.* to drive back; to daunt; ***no arredrarse ante nada,*** to be daunted by nothing.

arregazar [C], *v.t.* to tuck in, turn up.

arreglado, -da, *a.* neat, tidy; regular; moderate, reasonable; ***a un precio arreglado,*** at a reasonable price.

arreglar, *v.t.* to arrange, fix, settle; to adjust, regulate; to repair; to put in order, tidy up; (*min.*) to level; ***arreglarse con alguien,*** to come to an arrangement *or* understanding with s.o.; ***arreglarse por las buenas,*** to settle matters amicably; ***arreglarse a la razón,*** to see *or* conform to reason; ***arreglarse (solo)*** or ***arreglárselas (solo),*** to fend for oneself, manage by oneself; (*coll., vulg.*) ***te voy a arreglar,*** I'm going to fix you.

arreglo, *n.m.* arrangement; agreement, settlement, understanding, sth. fixed up (*often of illegal* or *amorous nature*); ***con arreglo a,*** in accordance with.

arregostarse, *v.r.* — ***a,*** to become fond of, (*coll.*) take a fancy to; to relish.

arrejacar [A], *v.t.* to harrow, rake, cross-hoe.

arrejaco, *n.m.* (*orn.*) swift, martin.

arrejada, *n.f.* (*agric.*) plough-staff.

arrejaque, *n.m.* fishing-fork (*with three prongs*); fish-spear; (*orn.*) swift, martin.

arrejerar, *v.t.* (*naut.*) to make (a ship) fast by casting two anchors fore and one aft.

arrela, arrelde, *n.m.* weight (*of* 4 *pounds* or 1.8 *kg.*).

arrellanarse, *v.r.* to loll, sprawl, sit back at ease.

arremangar [B], *v.t.* to turn *or* tuck up. — **arremangarse,** *v.r.* to turn one's sleeves up; (*fig.*) to roll one's sleeves up, get ready.

arremango, *n.m.* turning *or* tucking up.

arrematar, (*coll.*) [REMATAR].

arremedar [REMEDAR].

arremetedero, *n.m.* (*mil.*) point of attack; weak point.

arremetedor, -ra, *a.* assaulting, aggressive. — *n.m.f.* assailant, aggressor.

arremeter, *v.t.* to assail, attack, charge; ***arremeter contra,*** to charge against.

arremetida, *n.f.* assault, attack, charge; start (*of horses*).

arremolinarse, *v.r.* to whirl, eddy; to crowd, throng together, mill about.

arrempujar, *v.t.* to push, jostle.

arremueco, arremuesco, *n.m.* (*Col.*) caress, fondling.

arrendable, *a.* rentable, farmable, tenantable.

arrendación, *n.f.* renting, letting; lease; rental.

arrendadero, *n.m.* ring for tethering horses.

arrendador, -ra, *n.m.f.* landlord, lessor; hirer, tenant, lessee, holder; farmer; (*slang*) receiver of stolen goods, fence; horse-trainer.

arrendajo, *n.m.* (*orn.*) mocking bird.

arrendamiento, *n.m.* renting, letting, hiring, lease, rental.

arrendante, *n.m.f.* lessor.

arrendar (1) [I], *v.t.* to rent, let, lease, hire; ***no arriendo la ganancia,*** I don't give much fo his chances.

arrendar (2) [I], *v.t.* to bridle, tie (*a horse*); to train (*a horse*).

arrendar (3) [I], *v.t.* to imitate.

arrendatario, -ria, *a.* renting, hiring. — *n.m.f.* lessee, tenant.

arreo (1), *n.m.* dress, ornament, decoration; (*pl.*) harness, trappings, appurtenances, accessories.

arreo (2), *adv.* successively, uninterruptedly.

arrepápalo, *n.m.* fritter, pancake.

arrepentido, -da, *n.m.f.* penitent. — *n.f.* reformed woman.

arrepentimiento, *n.m.* repentance, contrition; lock of hair; (*paint.*) correction; (*law*) mitigating circumstance.

arrepentirse [6], *v.r.* — ***de,*** to repent of, rue, regret.

arrepistar, *v.t.* to grind (*rags*) into pulp (*paper making*).

arrepisto, *n.m.* grinding *or* pounding rags.

arrepollado, -da, *a.* cabbage-like.

arrepsia, *n.f.* irresolution.

arrepticio, -cia, *a.* possessed by the devil.

arrequesonarse, *v.r.* to curdle.

arrequife, *n.m.* singeing-iron (*cotton gins*).

arrequives, *n.m.pl.* dress trimmings; (*coll.*) ornaments, adornments; (*coll.*) circumstances; requisites.

arrestado, -da, *a.* intrepid, bold, audacious.

arrestar, *v.t.* (*mil.*) to place under arrest; to submit to detention. — **arrestarse,** *v.r.* to rush boldly (***a,*** to).

arresto, *n.m.* (*mil.*) arrest, detention; daring, guts, spirit; ***tener arresto(s),*** to have guts.

arretín, *n.m.* moreen.

arretranca [RETRANCA].

arrevesado, -da [REVESADO].

arrezafe, *n.m.* (*bot.*) spear-plume thistle; place covered in brambles *or* thistles.

arrezagar [B], *v.t.* to raise; to turn up, tuck up.

arria, *n.f.* drove (*of beasts*).

arriada, *n.f.* [RIADA]; (*naut.*) taking in (*sails*).

arrial [ARRIAZ].

arrianismo, *n.m.* Arianism.

arriano, -na, *a., n.m.f.* Arian.

arriar [L], *v.t.* (*naut.*) to lower, strike; (*naut.*) to loosen, slacken; to flood; ***arriar la bandera,*** to strike the colours; ***arriar las velas,*** to take in sail; ***arriar un cabo,*** to pay out a cable *or* line.

arriata, *n.f.,* **arriate,** *n.m.* narrow flower bed *or* border; trellis; causeway, path.

arriaz, *n.m.* hilt-bar (*of sword*).

arriba, *adv.* above, up, high up; on high, on top, upstairs; over; (*naut.*) aloft; ***¡arriba!*** up you get! on your feet! up you go! ***(más) arriba de,*** above, higher than; ***de arriba,*** from above, from on high; ***calle arriba,*** up the street; ***río arriba,*** up the river, upstream; ***de cinco pesetas para arriba,*** from five pesetas (upwards); ***de Madrid para arriba,*** north of Madrid; ***de arriba (a) abajo,*** from head to foot; from top to bottom; from start to finish; ***mirar de arriba abajo,*** to look up and down.

arribada, *n.f.* (*naut.*) arrival; ***arribada forzosa,*** emergency call; ***de arribada,*** in distress.

arribaje, *n.m.* (*naut.*) arrival, landing.

arribar, *v.i.* to arrive; (*naut.*) to put into harbour; to fall off to leeward; (*naut.*) to reach; (*coll.*) to recover (*from an illness* or *financial calamity*); (*coll.*) to accomplish one's desire.

arribazón, *n.f.* great influx of fish, abundance.

arribeño, -ña, *a.* (*Hisp. Am.*) highland, upland. — *n.m.f.* highlander, uplander.

arribo, *n.m.* arrival, landing.

arricés, *n.m.* buckle (*of stirrup-strap*).

arricete, *n.m.* shoal, sand-bank.

arridar, *v.t.* (*naut.*) to haul taut.

arriendo (1), *n.m.* letting, renting, hiring.

arriendo (2), *pres. indic.* [ARRENDAR].

arriería, *n.f.* occupation of muleteer, driving of mules.

arriero, *n.m.* muleteer.

arriesgado, -da, *a.* perilous, dangerous, hazardous, risky; daring.

arriesgar [B], *v.t.* to risk, jeopardize. — **arriesgarse,** *v.r.* to risk oneself, take a risk; ***arriesgarse a*** + *inf.*, to risk + *ger.*; ***arriesgarse en,*** to venture on; ***arriesgarse fuera,*** to venture out; ***quien no se arriesga no pasa la mar,*** nothing venture, nothing win.

arrimadero, *n.m.* scaffolding; stool; stand; support.

arrimadillo, *n.m.* mat; wainscot; dado.

arrimadizo, -za, *a.* made to be placed against *or* joined to a thing; (*fig.*) parasitic, sponging.

arrimadero, *n.m.* scaffolding; stool; stand; support. those in front of it.

arrimadura, *n.f.* approaching.

arrimar, *v.t.* to bring, draw *or* place near; to give (*blow*); (*naut.*) to stow (*the cargo*); to lay aside, put by, reject; ***arrimar una cosa,*** to put something out of the way; ***arrimar el hombro,*** to put one's shoulder to the wheel; ***arrimar el ascua a su sardina,*** to have one's eye to the main chance. — **arrimarse,** *v.r.* — ***a,*** to lean (against); to join; to seek the protection of; ***arrimarse (al toro),*** to work close (to the bull).

arrime, *n.m.* area surrounding jack (*bowls*).

arrimo, *n.m.* placing against, beside *or* near; staff, stick, crutch; protection; help, support; (*arch.*) idle wall, wall bearing no load; (*Cub.*) separating wall, fence *or* hedge.

arrimón, *n.m.* idler, loafer; (*coll.*) ***hacer el arrimón,*** to stagger along a wall; ***estar de arrimón,*** to stand idle, loaf about.

arrinconamiento, *n.m.* retreat, retirement.

arrinconar, *v.t.* to put in a corner; to corner; to put out of the way; to neglect; to withdraw one's favour *or* protection from. — **arrinconarse,** *v.r.* to retire from the world; ***arrinconarse en casa,*** to live in retirement.

arriñonado, -da, *a.* kidney-shaped.

arriostrar, *v.t.* (*naut.*) to brace (*a frame*).

arrisar, *v.t.* to make pleasant *or* agreeable.

arriscado, -da, *a.* craggy; bold, intrepid, rash; ***caballo arriscado,*** high-mettled horse.

arriscador, -ra, *n.m.f.* (*prov.*) gleaner of olives.

arriscamiento, *n.m.* intrepidity, daring.

arriscar [A], *v.t.* to risk. — **arriscarse,** *v.r.* to dare; to be proud *or* arrogant; to plunge over a cliff (*flocks*); to ascend (*cliff*); (*E.S.*, *Per.*) to dress smartly.

arrisco, *n.m.* risk.

arrizafa [RUZAFA].

arrizar [C], *v.t.* (*naut.*) to reef; to stow; to lash, tie; ***arrizar el ancla,*** to stow the anchor.

arroaz, *n.m.* (*zool.*) dolphin.

arroba, *n.f.* arroba (*weight of about* 25 *lbs.* or 11.5 *kgs.*); (*fig.*) ***por arrobas,*** in large quantities, by the ton; (*coll.*) ***tener dinero por arrobas,*** to have masses, bags *or* pots of money.

arrobadizo, -za, *a.* prone to falling into ecstasy and rapture.

arrobador, -ra, *a.* entrancing, ravishing.

arrobamiento, *n.m.* entrancement, ecstasy, rapture.

arrobar, *v.t.* to entrance, fill with ecstasy *or* rapture.

arrobinar, *v.t.* to consume, corrupt.

arrobo, *n.m.* rapture, ecstasy.

arrocabe, *n.m.* (*arch.*) wooden frieze; frieze-like ornament; top cross-beam.

arrocado, -da, *a.* distaff-like.

arrocero, -ra, *a.* (of) rice; ***molino arrocero,*** rice mill. — *n.m.f.* rice grower *or* dealer.

arrocinado, -da, *a.* hack-like; stupid, stubborn.

arrocinar, *v.t.* to reduce to animal level. — **arrocinarse,** *v.r.* to sink to animal level, become dull *or* stupid; to fall blindly in love.

arrodajarse, *v.r.* (*Hisp. Am.*) to squat.

arrodear [RODEAR].

arrodelarse, *v.r.* to protect oneself with a buckler *or* round shield.

arrodillada, *n.f.* kneeling.

arrodilladura, *n.f.*, **arrodillamiento,** *n.m.* kneeling.

arrodillar, *v.t.* to make (*s.o.*) kneel down. — **arrodillarse,** *v.r.* to kneel (down).

arrodrigar [B], **arrodrigonar,** *v.t.* to prop (*vines*).

arrogación, *n.f.* arrogation; adoption.

arrogador, -ra, *n.m.f.* adopter; one who makes a proud claim.

arrogancia, *n.f.* fine bearing *or* style, stately carriage; haughtiness, loftiness; valour, courage.

arrogante, *a.* having a fine bearing *or* style, grand, majestic; haughty; valiant.

arrogar [B], *v.t.* to arrogate; to claim; to adopt.

arrojadizo, -za, *a.* for throwing, to be thrown; ***arma arrojadiza,*** missile weapon.

arrojado, -da, *a.* bold, fearless, intrepid; rash, foolhardy.

arrojador, -ra, *a.* throwing, flinging.

arrojar, *v.t.* to throw, cast, fling, hurl, dash; to throw out, emit; (*Hisp. Am.*) to throw away; to vomit; (*agric.*) to bring *or* shoot forth; ***arrojar luz sobre,*** to cast *or* shed light on; (*com.*) ***arrojar un balance de 20.000,*** to show *or* give a balance of 20,000.

arrojo, *n.m.* boldness, intrepidity, fearlessness; dash.

arrollado, -da, *n.m.* (*Chi.*) rolled joint of meat.

arrollador, -ra, *a.* rolling, winding; overwhelming, sweeping. — *n.m.* roller.

arrollamiento, *n.m.* (*elec.*) winding, rolling, coiling.

arrollar, *v.t.* to roll up, wind; to roll *or* sweep away; (*fig.*) to overwhelm.

arromadizarse [C], *v.r.* to catch (a) cold.

arromanzar [C], *v.t.* to translate into the vernacular.

arromar, *v.t.* to blunt, dull.

arronzar [C], *v.t.* (*naut.*) to raise with levers. — *v.i.* (*naut.*) to incline too much to leeward.

arropamiento, *n.m.* wrapping up.

arropar, *v.t.* to dress, cover, wrap, clothe; ***arropar el vino,*** to mix wine with boiled must; ***arropar las viñas,*** to cover the roots of the vines.

arrope, *n.m.* grape *or* honey syrup.

arropea, *n.f.* iron, fetter, shackle.

arropera, *n.f.* vessel for holding ***arrope.***

arropía, *n.f.* (*prov.*) toffee.

arropiero, -ra, *n.m.f.* (*prov.*) maker *or* seller of toffee.

arrostrar, *v.t.* to defy, face; to face up to; ***arrostrar los peligros (la muerte),*** to brave dangers (death).

arroyada, *n.f.*, **arroyadero,** *n.m.* channel; gully; flood; freshet.

arroyar, *v.t.* to make gullies in. — **arroyarse,** *v.r.* to form *or* run in gullies; (*agric.*) to become blighted (*grain*).

arroyo, *n.m.* rivulet, small river, stream, brook; gutter; (*fig.*) street; ***arroyos de sangre,*** streams of blood.

arroyuela, *n.f.* (*bot.*) loosestrife; [SALICARIA].

arroyuelo, *n.m.* rill, small brook, rivulet.

arroz, *n.m.* rice.

arrozal, *n.m.* rice-field.

arruar [M], *v.i.* to grunt (*hunted wild boar*).

arrufadura, *n.f.* (*naut.*) sheer.

arrufar, *v.t.* (*naut.*) to camber, form sheer of. — **arrufarse,** *v.r.* (*obs.*) to snarl.

arrufianado, -da, *a.* ruffianly, roguish, knavish, scoundrelly; impudent.

arrufo [ARRUFADURA].

arruga, *n.f.* wrinkle, crease.

arrugación, *n.f.*, **arrugamiento,** *n.m.* wrinkling, creasing.

arrugar [B], *v.t.* to wrinkle, rumple, crease; ***arrugar el entrecejo*** or ***la frente,*** to knit one's brow, frown. — **arrugarse,** *v.r.* (*sl.*) to scarper, bunk.

arrugia, *n.f.* (*min.*) gold-mine.

arruinador, -ra, *a.* ruinous, destructive. — *n.m.f.* ruiner, demolisher.

arruinamiento, *n.m.* ruin, destruction.

arruinar, *v.t.* to ruin, destroy. — **arruinarse,** *v.r.* to go to ruin; to become bankrupt; (*coll.*) to go bust.

arrullador, -ra, *a.* lulling, soothing.

arrullar, *v.t.* to lull; to court, woo. — *v.i.* to bill and coo.

arrullo, *n.m.* billing and cooing; lullaby.

arruma, *n.f.* (*naut.*) cargo space (*in the hold*).

arrumaco, *n.m.* caress; (*coll.*) eccentric dress *or* ornament; ***hacer arrumacos a,*** to fuss, fondle.

arrumaje, *n.m.* (*naut.*) stowage.

arrumar, *v.t.* (*naut.*) to stow. — **arrumarse,** *v.r.* (*naut.*) to become overcast (*horizon*).

arrumazón, *n.m.* (*naut.*) stowage; overcast horizon.

arrumbación, *n.f.* ranging wine-casks (*in cellars*).

arrumbadas, *n.f.pl.* (*naut.*) bulwarks (*at bow of rowing-galley*).

arrumbador, -ra, *a.* heaping, piling. — *n.m.f.* heaper, piler. — *n.m.* (*naut.*) steersman; wine-cellar worker.

arrumbamiento, *n.m.* (*naut.*) bearing.

arrumbar, *v.t.* to put, cast *or* sweep aside, put away *or* out of the way; to line up (*wine casks*); (*naut.*) to determine (*direction*). — *v.i.* (*naut.*) to steer the proper course. — **arrumbarse,** *v.r.* (*naut.*) to take bearings.

arrunflarse, *v.r.* to have a flush of cards of the same suit.

arrurruz, *n.m.* arrowroot.

arsáfragra, *n.f.* (*bot.*) water-parsnip.

arsenal, *n.m.* arsenal; dockyard, shipyard, navy-yard.

arseniato, *n.m.* (*chem.*) arsenate.

arsenical, *a.* arsenical.

arsénico, *n.m.* arsenic.

arsenioso, -sa, *a.* arsenious.

arsenito, *n.m.* arsenite.

arsolla, *n.f.* (*bot.*) lesser burdock, milk-thistle.

arsonvalización, *n.f.* (*med.*) high-frequency treatment.

arta, *n.f.* (*bot.*) plantain, ribwort.

artalejo, artalete, *n.m.* tart, pie.

artanica, artanita, *n.f.* cyclamen, sowbread.

arte, *n.m.f.* art; skill, craft, cunning; intrigue; fishing-net; ***usar de arte,*** to be astute, artful *or* cunning; ***no tener arte ni parte en una cosa,*** to have nothing to do with sth.; (*cook.*) ***arte cisoria,*** art of carving; ***arte manual,*** craft; ***arte mayor,*** Spanish verse of ten to twelve syllables; ***arte menor,*** Spanish verse of six to eight syllables; ***arte plumaria,*** art of embroidering featherwork; ***buen arte,*** skilfulness; ***mal arte,*** awkwardness; ***el séptimo arte,*** the cinema. — *n.f.pl.* arts; ***bellas artes,*** fine arts; ***artes gráficas,*** graphic arts; ***artes liberales,*** liberal arts; ***artes y oficios,*** arts and crafts.

artefacto, *n.m.* contrivance; appliance, device.

artejo, *n.m.* finger-joint, knuckle; (*ent.*) leg segment.

artemisa, artemisia, *n.f.* (*bot.*) artemisia, mugwort.

artera (1), *n.f.* (*prov.*) iron instrument for marking bread before it is baked.

artería, *n.f.* cunning, craftiness, artfulness.

arteria, *n.f.* (*anat.*) artery; (*fig.*) main road; (*railw.*) trunk line; (*elec.*) feeder.

arterial, *a.* arterial.

arteriografía, *n.f.* arteriography.

arteriola, *n.f.* small artery.

arteriología, *n.f.* (*anat.*) arteriology.

arteriosclerosis, *n.f. inv.* (*med.*) arteriosclerosis, hardening of the arteries.

arterioso, -sa, *a.* arterial; abounding in arteries.

arteriotomía, *n.f.* (*anat.*) arteriotomy.

artero, -ra (2), *a.* crafty, cunning, artful.

artesa, *n.f.* dug-out; kneading trough.

artesano, *n.m.* artisan, craftsman.

artesiano, -na, *a.* artesian.

artesilla, *n.f.* small trough; game *or* exercise on horseback; trough for a draw-well.

artesón, *n.m.* wash-tub; (*arch.*) carved panel (*on ceilings and vaults*).

artesonado, -da, *a.* (*arch.*) panelled. — *n.m.* ceiling of carved panels; panelling.

artesonar, *v.t.* to make (*troughs*); (*arch.*) to panel (*ceilings* or *vaults*).

artesuela, *n.f.* small kneading trough.

artete, *n.m.* drag-net.

artético, -ca, *a.* afflicted with arthritis; arthritic.

ártico, -ca, *a.* arctic, northern; ***polo ártico,*** north pole.

articulación, *n.f.* articulation; joint; (*bot.*) geniculation.

articulado, -da, *a.* articulate. — *n.m.* (*law*) articles; (*pl.*) (*zool.*) Articulata.

articulador, -ra, *a.* articulating.

articular, *a.* articular. — *v.t.* to articulate; to join; (*law*) to article.

articulista, *n.m.f.* writer of articles, columnist.

artículo, *n.m.* article; item; joint; ***artículo definido*** or ***determinado*** (***indefinido*** or ***indeterminado***), definite (indefinite) article; ***artículo de fondo,*** leader, editorial; ***artículos de consumo*** (***de cuero***), consumer (leather) goods; ***artículos de primera necesidad,*** basic commodities, essentials; ***hacer el artículo,*** to push one's goods *or* wares.

artifara, artife, *n.m.* (*sl.*) bread.

artifero, *n.m.* (*sl.*) baker.

artífice, *n.m.f.* artificer, artist; inventor, contriver; (*fig.*) author.

artificial, *a.* artificial, man-made; ***fibra artificial,*** man-made fibre; ***fuegos artificiales,*** fireworks.

artificializar, *v.t.* to make *or* render artificial; to give an air of *or* lend artificiality to.

artificiero, *n.m.* (*artill.*) artificer.

artificio, *n.m.* workmanship, craft; trick, cunning, artifice; guilefulness, finesse; (*mech.*) contrivance, device, appliance.

artificioso, -sa, *a.* skilful, ingenious; affected, unnatural; false, deceptive.

artiga, *n.f.* breaking up new land; land newly broken up.

artigar [B], *v.t.* to break, burn and level (*land*) before cultivation.

artilugio, *n.m.* worthless contrivance *or* device; ruse, scheme, trick.

artillado, *n.m.* artillery, guns.

artillar, *v.t.* to furnish with artillery. — **artillarse,** *v.r.* (*sl.*) to arm o.s.

artillería, *n.f.* gunnery; artillery, ordnance; ***parque de artillería,*** artillery depot; ***artillería de sitio,*** siege guns; ***artillería antiaérea,*** anti-aircraft guns; ***artillería gruesa,*** heavy artillery; ***artillería de avancarga,*** muzzle-loading artillery; ***artillería de retrocarga,*** breech-loading artillery; ***artillería de montaña,*** mountain artillery; ***artillería de campaña,*** field artillery.

artillero, *n.m.* gunner; artillery-man.

artimaña, *n.f.* trap, snare, gin; stratagem, artifice.

artimón, *n.m.* (*naut.*) mizen-sail.

artina, *n.f.* fruit of the box-tree.

artista, *n.m.f.* artist; craftsman; performer, showman.

artístico, -ca, *a.* artistic.

artizar [C], *v.t.* to perform ingeniously.

arto, *n.m.*, **artos,** *n.m. inv.* (*bot.*) box-tree.

artocárpeo, -pea, *a.* (*bot.*) artocarpous.

artolas, *n.f.pl.* back-to-back seats (*for two persons on the same horse*).

artrítico, -ca, *a.* arthritic.

artritis, *n.f. inv.* (*med.*) arthritis.

artritismo, *n.m.* (*med.*) arthritism.

artrodia, *n.f.* (*anat.*) arthrodia.

artrografía, *n.f.* description of the joints.

artrón, *n.m.* (*anat.*) arthrosis, articulation.

artrópodo, -da, *a.* (*zool.*) arthropodal, arthropodous. — *n.m.f.* (*zool.*) arthropod. — *n.m.pl.* (*zool.*) Arthropoda.

artuña, *n.f.* ewe whose lamb has perished.

Arturo, *n.m.* Arthur; (*astron.*) Arcturus.

arugas, *n.f.pl.* (*bot.*) feverfew.

árula, *n.f.* (*archæol.*) small altar.

arundense, *a., n.m.f.* (native) of Arunda (modern Ronda).
arundíneo, -nea, *a.* (*bot.*) arundinaceous, arundineous, reedy.
aruñar, (*coll.*) [ARAÑAR].
aruñazo, (*coll.*) [ARAÑAZO].
arúspice, *n.m.* haruspex; augurer, soothsayer.
aruspicina, *n.f.* haruspicy.
arveja, *n.f.* (*bot.*) vetch, tare; (*Chi.*) green pea.
arvejal, arvejar, *n.m.* field sown with ***arveja.***
arvejana, arvejera [ARVEJA].
arvejo, *n.m.* (*bot.*) pea.
arvejón, *n.m.* (*bot., prov.*) chickling-vetch, blue vetch.
arvejona, *n.f.,* **arvejote,** *n.m.* (*prov.*) vetch *or* tare.
arvela, *n.f.* (*orn.*) martin-fisher.
arvense, *a.* growing in sown fields.
arza, *n.f.* (*naut.*) hoisting-tackle; (*naut.*) sling, strap (*for blocks*).
arzobispado, *n.m.* archbishopric.
arzobispal, *a.* archiepiscopal.
arzobispo, *n.m.* archbishop.
arzolla, *n.f.* (*bot.*) lesser burdock, milk-thistle.
arzón, *n.m.* fore *or* hind bow (*of a saddle*); saddle-tree.
as, *n.m.* ace.
asá, *adv.* ***ni así ni asá,*** neither one way nor another *or* nor t'other.
asa (1), *n.f.* handle; ear (*of vase*); (*coll.*) ear; ***en asas,*** akimbo.
asa (2), *n.f.* juice (*of certain plants*); (*prov.*) holly-tree; ***asa dulce,*** gum benzoin, gum benjamin; ***asa fétida,*** asafœtida, a gum resin.
asacar [A], *v.t.* to withdraw; to invent; to pretend; to impute.
asación, *n.f.* (*pharm.*) decoction.
asadero, -ra, *a.* fit for roasting.
asado, -da, *a., n.m.* roast; (*Hisp. Am.*) steak; (*build.*) topping-off ceremony.
asador, *n.m.* spit; jack; (*naut.*) ***asador de bomba,*** pump-hook.
asadura, *n.f.* entrails (*of an animal*), chitterlings; liver, lights; (*fig.*) ***echar las asaduras,*** to work one's guts out; ***tener asadura,*** to be stolid; to be extremely lazy.
asaeteador, -ra, *a.* (*fig.*) harassing, annoying. — *n.m.* archer, bowman. — *n.f.* archeress.
asaetear, *v.t.* to riddle with arrows; (*fig.*) to annoy, harass.
asaetinado, -da, *a.* resembling satin.
asainetado, -da, *a.* (*theat.*) farcical.
asalariado, *n.m.* wage-earner; hireling.
asalariar, *v.t.* to pay wages to.
asalmonado, -da, *a.* salmon-like.
asaltador, -ra, *a.* assaulting, assailing. — *n.m.f.* assailant, assaulter.
asaltar, *v.t.* to assault, storm; to surprise, fall upon; (*fig.*) to beset; ***me asaltó la duda,*** I was suddenly beset by doubt.
asalto, *n.m.* assault; ***asalto de armas,*** fencing bout; ***dar asalto,*** to assault; ***por asalto,*** by storm; ***guardia de asalto,*** riot squad.
asamblea, *n.f.* assembly, meeting, congress; (*mil.*) assembly (*bugle-call*).
asambleísta, *n.m.f.* member of an assembly.
asar, *v.t.* to roast; to bake; ***manzanas asadas,*** baked apples; ***asar a la parrilla,*** to grill; (*coll.*) ***asar a alguien,*** to pester s.o. to death. — **asarse,** *v.r.* (*coll.*) ***asarse de calor*** or ***asarse vivo,*** to be stewed *or* scorching hot.
asarabácara, asáraca, *n.f.* (*bot.*) wild ginger *or* nard.
asarcia, *n.f.* emaciation.
asarero, *n.m.* (*bot.*) blackthorn, sloe-tree.
asargado, -da, *a.* serge-like.
asarina, *n.f.* (*bot.*) bastard asarum.
ásaro, *n.m.* (*bot.*) asarum.
asativo, -va, *a.* (*pharm.*) dressed *or* boiled in its own juice.
asaz, *adv.* (*obs.*) sufficiently, abundantly.
asbestino, -na, *a.* appertaining to asbestos.
asbesto, *n.m.* asbestos.
ascalonia, *n.f.* (*bot.*) seed onion; shallot.
áscar, *n.m.* army (*in Morocco*).
áscari, *n.m.* Moroccan infantryman.
ascárides, *n.f.pl.* ascarid worms.
ascendencia, *n.f.* ancestry, origin.
ascendente, *a.* ascendant; ascending, up.
ascender [2], *v.t.* to promote. — *v.i.* to ascend, climb, go up, mount, rise; to get promoted, rise (*in one's profession*); (*com.*) ***ascender a,*** to amount to.
ascendiente, *a.* ascendant, ascending. — *n.m.f.* ancestor, forebear. — *n.m.* ascendency, influence; precedent; ***tener ascendiente sobre,*** to have ascendency over.
ascensión, *n.f.* ascension; ascent; raising; (*eccles.*) Ascension (*of Our Lord*) ; exaltation (*to the papal throne*); rising point (*of the equator*); (*astron.*) ***ascensión recta,*** right ascension.
ascensional, *a.* (*astron.*) ascensional; rising.
ascensionista, *a.* climbing, ascending. — *n.m.f.* balloonist; climber.
ascenso, *n.m.* rise; promotion.
ascensor, *n.m.* lift, (*Am.*) elevator; ***ascensor de municiones,*** ammunition hoist.
asceta, *n.m.* ascetic.
ascético, -ca, *a.* ascetic. — *n.f.* ascetics.
ascetismo, *n.m.* asceticism.
ascidia (1), *a.* ascidian. — *n.f.* (*zool.*) Ascidium, ascidian.
ascidio, -dia (2), *a.* (*bot.*) pitcher-like. — *n.f.* (*bot.*) pitcher-like leaf.
asciro, *n.m.* (*bot.*) St. Peter's wort, St. Andrew's cross.
ascítico, -ca, *a.* (*med.*) dropsical.
ascitis, *n.f. inv.* (*med.*) ascites, dropsy.
asclepiadea, *n.f.* (*bot.*) swallow-wort.
asclepiadeo, *n.m.* (*poet.*) Asclepiad.
asco, *n.m.* disgust, loathing, nausea; ***es un asco,*** it's disgusting, sickening *or* revolting; it's utterly worthless *or* rotten; ***me da asco,*** it makes me (feel) sick; ***le tengo asco,*** I loathe him; ***estar hecho un asco,*** to be in a revolting, atrocious *or* pitiful state; ***estoy hecho un asco,*** I feel shocking; ***hacer ascos a,*** to turn one's nose up at.
ascua, *n.f.* red-hot coal, burning ember; ***estar en*** or ***sobre ascuas,*** to be on tenter-hooks; ***pasar sobre ascuas,*** to glide lightly over (*difficulty, awkward point etc.*); ***estar hecho un ascua,*** to be all spick and span *or* spruced up; ***arrimar el ascua a su sardina,*** to look after number one, keep one's eye to the main chance; ***¡ascuas!*** ouch! that hurts!
aseado, -da, *a.* clean, neat, tidy.
asear, *v.t.* to clean, tidy up.
asechador, -ra, *a.* ensnaring. — *n.m.f.* ensnarer, waylayer.
asechamiento, *n.m.,* **asechanza,** *n.f.* waylaying; artifice, trick, stratagem, snare.
asechar, *v.t.* to waylay, be on the watch for, lie in ambush for.
asedado, -da, *a.* silky.
asedar, *v.t.* to make like silk.
asediador, -ra, *a.* besieging. — *n.m.f.* besieger.
asediar, *v.t.* to besiege, blockade; (*fig.*) to beset.
asedio, *n.m.* siege, blockade.
aseglararse, *v.r.* to leave the priesthood, become a layman.
asegundar, *v.t.* to repeat at once.
asegurable, *a.* insurable.
aseguración, *n.f.* insurance contract.

asegurado, -da, *n.m.f.* insured (person).
asegurador, -ra, *a.* insuring, assuring. — *n.m.f.* insurer, assurer, underwriter.
aseguramiento, *n.m.* securing; insuring; (*law*) security, safety; insurance, assurance.
asegurar, *v.t.* to secure, fasten, fix; to affirm, assure; to preserve; (*com.*) to guarantee; to insure. — **asegurarse,** *v.r.* to make sure (***de,*** of); ***asegurarse de que,*** to make sure that.
aseidad, *n.f.* (*theol.*) aseity.
aselarse, *v.r.* (*prov.*) to roost.
asemejar, *v.t.* to make similar. — **asemejarse,** *v.r.*, — ***a,*** to resemble.
asendereado, -da, *a.* beaten, well-trodden.
asenderear, *v.t.* to chase, pester; to open a track in.
asengladura [SINGLADURA].
asenso, *n.m.* assent, consent, acquiescence, credence, credit; ***no dar asenso,*** not to credit *or* believe; ***no dar su asenso,*** not to agree.
asentada (1) [SENTADA(1)].
asentaderas, *n.f.pl.* (*coll.*) buttocks, seat.
asentadillas, *adv. phrase* ***a asentadillas,*** side-saddle.
asentado, -da (2), *a.* steady, calm; stable.
asentador, *n.m.* bricklayer; plate-layer; setter-up; razor-strop; blacksmith's turning chisel.
asentamiento, *n.m.* (*law*) establishment, settlement; prudence, sanity.
asentar [1], *v.t.* to seat; to place; to affirm, fix, lay down, settle, state; to establish, found, set up; to note down, enter up; to level, smooth; to hone, sharpen; to deal (*blows*); (*law*) to award; to settle (*food*). — *v.i.* to be fitting *or* suitable; to settle. — **asentarse,** *v.r.* to settle (down); to remain undigested.
asentimiento, *n.m.* assent, consent.
asentir [6], *v.i.* to assent, agree.
asentista, *n.m.* contractor; supplier.
aseñorado, -da, *a.* lordly, pompous, snobbish, affecting superiority.
aseo, *n.m.* cleanliness; neatness; toilet; ***cuarto de aseo,*** toilet-room, wash-room.
asépalo, -la, *a.* (*bot.*) without sepals.
asepsia, *n.f.* (*med.*) asepsis.
aséptico, -ca, *a.* (*med.*) aseptic.
asequi, *n.m.* (*prov.*) cattle duty.
asequible, *a.* attainable, obtainable, reasonable, within one's reach; ***de precio asequible,*** reasonably priced.
aserción, *n.f.* assertion, affirmation.
aserenar, *v.t.* [SERENAR].
aserradero, *n.m.* sawmill; saw-horse.
aserradizo, -za, *a.* that can be sawn (easily).
aserrado, -da, *a.* serrate, serrated, dented; saw-like.
aserrador, -ra, *n.m.f.* sawyer.
aserradura, *n.f.* sawing; cut in sawing; (*pl.*) saw-dust.
aserrar [SERRAR].
aserrín [SERRÍN].
aserruchar [SERRUCHAR].
asertivo, -va, *a.* assertive.
aserto, *n.m.* assertion, affirmation.
asertorio, -ria, *a.* affirmatory.
asesar, *v.i.* to become prudent; to acquire discretion.
asesinar, *v.t.* to murder; to assassinate.
asesinato, *n.m.* murder; assassination.
asesino, -na, *a.* murderous; ***mirada asesina,*** murderous look. — *n.m.f.* murderer, murderess; assassin.
asesor, -ra, *a.* advising, consulting. — *n.m.f.* adviser, consultant
asesorar, *v.t.* to advise, counsel. — **asesorarse,** *v.r.* to get *or* take (expert) advice.
asesoría, *n.f.* advising, consulting; adviser's *or* consultant's fee *or* office.
asestadura, *n.f.* aim, aiming; firing, shooting.
asestar, *v.t.* to aim; to deal (*blow*); to fire; (*fig.*) to try to injure.
aseveración, *n.f.* asseveration, affirmation.
aseveradamente, *adv.* affirmatively.
aseverar, *v.t.* to asseverate, affirm.
aseverativo, -va, *a.* affirming, asseverating.
asfaltado, *n.m.* asphalt surface.
asfaltar, *v.t.* to asphalt.
asfáltico, -ca, *a.* asphalt(ic).
asfalto, *n.m.* asphalt.
asfíctico, -ca, asfíxico, -ca, *a.* asphyxial.
asfixia, *n.f.* (*med.*) asphyxia.
asfixiador, -ra, *a.* asphyxiating, suffocating.
asfixiante, *a.* asphyxiating.
asfixiar, *v.t.* (*med.*) to asphyxiate, suffocate.
asfódelo, *n.m.* (*bot.*) asphodel.
así, *adv.* so, thus, in this way, like that; (*followed by a verb in the subjunctive mood*) would that; ***así como,*** as well as; ***así que,*** as soon as; therefore; ***así así,*** so-so; middling; ***así que llegó,*** as soon as he arrived; ***así me estoy,*** it's all the same to me; ***así pues,*** therefore; ***así sea,*** so be it; ***así y todo,*** even so; ***así te aspen,*** the devil take you.
Asia, *n.f.* Asia; (***el***) ***Asia Menor,*** Asia Minor; (***el***) ***Asia Sudoriental,*** Southeast Asia.
asiático, -ca, *a.* Asiatic; (*fig.*) luxurious. — *n.m.f.* Asiatic.
asidera, *n.f.* (*Arg.*) strap with rings (*for fastening the lasso*).
asidero, *n.m.* handle, holder; (*fig.*) opportunity, pretext.
asiduidad, *n.f.* assiduity, diligence.
asiduo, -dua, *a.* assiduous, diligent.
asiento (1), *n.m.* seat; seat (*in tribunal* or *court of justice*); bottom (*of a vessel*); sediment; treaty; spot, site; settling; (*fig.*) solidity; stability, permanence; contract; (*com.*) entry; (*fig.*) judgment; registry, list, roll; bit (*bridle*); ***hombre de asiento,*** prudent man; ***asiento de los esmaltes,*** edging of enamels; ***asiento de puente levadizo,*** bed of a drawbridge; ***asiento de plaza,*** enlistment; ***asiento del estómago,*** indigestion; ***estar de asiento,*** to be established in a sure place; ***tomar asiento,*** to take a seat; ***asiento de colmenas,*** open apiary; ***asiento de molino*** or ***de tahona,*** millstone; ***asiento de negros,*** contract for supplying slaves; ***no calentar el asiento,*** to stay a short time; ***quedarse de asiento,*** to remain in a place; ***hacer*** or ***tomar asiento,*** to establish oneself; (*pl.*) posteriors, seat; bindings; collar and cuff bands; variety of pearls flat on one side.
asiento (2), *pres. indic.* [ASENTAR].
asiento (3), *pres. indic.* [ASENTIR].
asignable, *a.* assignable.
asignación, *n.f.* assignation; grant, subsidy; salary; distribution, partition; destination.
asignado, *n.m.* assignat.
asignar, *v.t.* to assign, mark out; to ascribe, attribute.
asignatura, *n.f.* subject (*academic discipline*).
asilar, *v.t.* to shelter; to place in an asylum.
asilo (1), *n.m.* asylum, sanctuary, place of shelter and refuge; harbourage; protection.
asilo (2), *n.m.* (*ent.*) asilus, hornet-fly.
asilla, *n.f.* small handle; slight pretext; collar-bone.
asimetría, *n.f.* asymmetry.
asimétrico, -ca, *a.* asymmetrical, irregular, uneven.
asimiento, *n.m.* grasp; (*fig.*) attachment, affection.
asimilable, *a.* assimilable.
asimilación, *n.f.* assimilation.
asimilar, *v.t.* to assimilate, absorb, take in; to make similar; to grant (*rights, honours*). — **asimilarse,** *v.r.* — ***a,*** to resemble.

asimilativo, -va, *a.* assimilating, assimilative.
asimismo, *adv.* in the same way, in like manner.
asimplado, -da, *a.* like a simpleton.
asincrónico, -ca, *a.* asynchronous, untimed.
asincronismo, *n.m.* asynchronism.
asíntota, *n.f.* (*geom.*) asymptote.
asir [12], *v.t.* to grasp, grip, seize. — *v.i.* (*agric.*) to strike *or* take root. — **asirse,** *v.r.* — ***a*** or ***de,*** to grasp, take hold of, hang on to.
Asiria, *n.f.* Assyria.
asiriano, -na, asirio, -ria, *a., n.m.f.* Assyrian.
asiriología, *n.f.* Assyriology.
asiriológico, -ca, *a.* Assyriological.
asiriólogo, *n.m.* Assyriologist.
asistencia, *n.f.* attendance, presence; people present; assistance; (*Hisp. Am.*) board, meals; (*Mex.*) intimate drawing room; (*pl.*) allowance; alimony.
asistencial, *a.* (of) social work *or* welfare; ***Estado asistencial,*** welfare state.
asistenta, *n.f.* charwoman, daily help.
asistente, *a.* attendant; attending, present. — *n.m.f.* assistant; one present, person present; (*mil.*) batman.
asistir, *v.t.* to assist; to attend, serve, wait on; ***¡Dios nos asista!*** God help us!; ***asistir a los enfermos,*** to tend the sick; ***le asiste la razón,*** right is on his side. — *v.i.* to attend, be present; ***asistir a una reunión,*** to attend a meeting; ***asistir de oyente,*** to attend as a non-graduating student.
asistolia, *n.f.* (*path.*) asystole.
asma, *n.f.* (*med.*) asthma.
asmático, -ca, *a.* asthmatic.
asna, *n.f.* she-ass; (*pl.*) (*carp.*) rafters.
asnacho, asnallo, *n.m.* (*bot.*) rest-harrow, cammock.
asnada, *n.f.* (*coll.*) asininity, foolish action.
asnado, *n.m.* prop, side-wall timber (*in mines*).
asnal, *a.* asinine; (*coll.*) stupid, obstinate.
asnería, *n.f.* (*coll.*) stud of asses; (*coll.*) foolish action.
asnico, *n.m.* little ass; (*prov.*) fire-irons.
asnilla, *n.f.* stanchion, prop.
asnillo, *n.f.* little ass; (*ent.*) field-cricket.
asnino, -na, *a.* asinine, ass-like.
asno, *n.m.* ass; ***bajarse del asno,*** to admit (an) error; ***caerse del asno,*** to realize.
asobarcar [A], *v.t.* (*coll.*) to carry under the arm; to raise to the armpits (*clothes*).
asobiar, *v.t.* (*prov.*) to whistle.
asobinarse, *v.r.* to fall face downwards (*horses*).
asobío, *n.m.* (*prov.*) whistle.
asocairarse, *v.r.* (*naut.*) to shelter behind a cape *or* point.
asocarronado, -da, *a.* crafty, sly, cunning.
asociación, *n.f.* association; fellowship, copartnership.
asociado, -da, *a.* associate, associated. — *n.m.f.* associate; (*com.*) partner.
asociar, *v.t.* to associate. — **asociarse,** *v.r.* to form a partnership; ***asociarse a,*** to become a partner in.
asolación, asoladura, *n.f.* desolation, devastation.
asolador, -ra, *a.* destroying, desolating, devastating.
asolamiento, *n.m.* devastation, desolation.
asolanar, *v.t.* to parch, dry up.
asolapar, *v.t.* (*tailoring*) to make lapels on; to overlap (*tiles*).
asolar [4], *v.t.* to raze to the ground, lay waste devastate; to burn, parch. — **asolarse,** *v.r.* to settle (*liquids*).
asoldadar, asoldar [4], *v.t.* to hire, employ, sign on.
asolear, *v.t.* to sun, expose to the sun. — **asolearse,** *v.r.* to sun o.s.; to become sunburnt; (*vet.*) to become affected by the sun (*horses*).
asomada, *n.f.* (brief) appearance; point from which something is first seen.
asomar, *v.t.* to show, stick out. — *v.i.* to (begin to) appear, become visible, loom; to show, stick out. — **asomarse,** *v.r.* (*coll.*) to (begin to) get tipsy; ***asomarse a*** or ***por la ventana,*** to look out of the window.
asombradizo, -za, *a.* easily astonished.
asombrador, -ra, *a.* astonishing, amazing.
asombramiento, *n.m.* astonishment, amazement.
asombrar, *v.t.* to shade; to astonish, amaze. — **asombrarse,** *v.r.* to be amazed (***de,*** at).
asombro, *n.m.* astonishment, amazement; ***no salgo de mi asombro,*** I can't get over my astonishment, I can't get over it, I can't credit it.
asombroso, -sa, *a.* wonderful, astonishing, marvellous.
asomo, *n.m.* indication, mark, sign, trace, hint; touch; ***ni por asomo,*** not by a long shot, not a ghost of a chance.
asonada, *n.f.* mob; riot.
asonancia, *n.f.* assonance; consonance.
asonantado, -da, *a.* assonant.
asonantar, *v.t.* make assonant. — *v.i.* to assonate.
asonante, *a., n.m.f.* assonant.
asonar [4], *v.i.* to be assonant; to accord.
asordar, *v.t.* to deafen.
asosegar [1B] [SOSEGAR].
asotanar, *v.t.* to make into a cellar.
aspa, *n.f.* cross, cross-shaped figure, cross-piece; reel; sail, arm (*windmill*); ***aspa de San Andrés,*** Saint Andrew's cross (X); ***en aspa,*** cross-wise, X-wise.
aspadera, *n.f.* (*mech.*) reel.
aspado, -da, *a.* with the arms extended like a cross; (*coll.*) trussed up.
aspador, -ra, *a.* winding, reeling. — *n.m.f.* reeler. — *n.m.* reel.
aspalato, *n.m.* (*bot.*) rosewood.
aspalto, *n.m.* (*paint.*) dark-coloured paint.
aspar, *v.t.* to reel; to crucify; (*coll.*) to vex, get on the nerves of; ***que me aspen si es cierto,*** I'll be hanged if it's true; ***así lo aspen no lo hará,*** wild horses won't make him do it. — **asparse,** *v.r.* to writhe; to slave; ***trabaja que se aspa,*** he works himself to death.
aspaventero, -ra, aspaventoso, -sa, *a.* given to wild shows of emotion, wildly emotional.
aspaviento, *n.m.* violent display of emotion; ***hacer aspavientos,*** to make a wild show of emotion.
aspearse, *v.r.* to become sore (through much walking) (*feet, hoofs*).
aspecto, *n.m.* sight, appearance, look, aspect, countenance; (*arch.*) outlook; (*astron.*) aspect.
asperarteria, *n.f.* windpipe, trachea.
asperear, *v.i.* to be rough and acrid to the taste.
asperete, *n.m.* sour taste.
aspereza, *n.f.* asperity, acerbity, acrimony; roughness, ruggedness, harshness; ***limar asperezas,*** to smooth away the rough edges.
aspergear, aspergiar, *v.t.* to sprinkle.
asperges, *n.m. inv.* (*eccles.*) asperges; aspergillum, sprinkler.
asperidad, *n.f.* asperity; roughness; harshness; rough place.
asperiego, -ga, *a.* sour, cider (*apple*).
asperilla, *n.f.* (*bot.*) woodruff.
asperillo, *a.* tartish, sourish. — *n.m.* [ASPERETE].
asperjar, *v.t.* to sprinkle; to spray.
áspero, -ra, *a.* rough, rugged; harsh; (*fig.*) sour, sharp.
asperón, *n.m.* detergent sandstone.
aspérrimo, -ma, *a. superl.* [ÁSPERO].
aspersión, *n.f.* aspersion, sprinkling, spraying.
aspersorio, *n.m.* water-sprinkler; (*eccles.*) aspersorium.

áspid(e), *n.m.* (*zool.*) asp; ***lengua de áspid,*** venomous tongue; small ancient gun.
aspidistra, *n.f.* (*bot.*) aspidistra.
aspilla, *n.f.*(*prov.*) dip-stick.
aspillera, *n.f.* (*mil.*) loophole.
aspillerar, *v.t.* to make loopholes in.
aspiración, *n.f.* aspiration; inspiration; intake, suction; (*mus.*) short pause.
aspirado, -da, *a.* (*gram.*) aspirate.
aspirante, *a.* aspiring. — *n.m.f.* candidate, applicant.
aspirar, *v.t.* to breathe in; to aspirate. — *v.i.* to aspire (***a,*** to).
aspirina, *n.f.* (*chem.*) aspirin.
aspro, *n.m.* asper, a Turkish coin.
asquear, *v.t.* to revolt, disgust. — *v.i.* to feel nausea.
asquerosidad, *n.f.* disgusting, loathsome, revolting *or* sickening thing; filthy object.
asqueroso, -sa, *a.* disgusting, loathsome, revolting, sickening; filthy.
asta, *n.f.* shaft; staff, flagstaff; handle; horn; antler; (*naut.*) anchor-shank; ***a media asta,*** at half-mast; ***dejar en las astas del toro,*** to leave in the lurch.
ástaco, *n.m.* crawfish, crayfish.
astado, *n.m.* Roman pikeman; bull.
astático, -ca, *a.* astatic.
asteísmo, *n.m.* (*rhet.*) delicate irony.
astenia, *n.f.*(*med.*) asthenia, debility.
asténico, -ca, *a.* (*med.*) asthenic.
asteria, *n.f.* (*min.*) star-stone, cat's-eye; (*zool.*) starfish.
asterisco, *n.m.* asterisk.
asterismo, *n.m.* (*astron., min.*) asterism.
astero, *n.m.* Roman pikeman.
asteroide, *a., n.m.* asteroid.
astigmático, -ca, *a.* astigmatic.
astigmatismo, *n.m.* (*med.*) astigmatism.
astil, *n.m.* handle (*of axe, hatchet etc.*); shaft (*of arrow*); beam (*of balance*); steelyard; quill.
astilla, *n.f.* splinter; ***de tal palo, tal astilla,*** a chip off the old block, like father, like son; ***sacar astilla,*** to benefit, profit (*from sth.*).
astillar, *v.t.* to splinter.
astillazo, *n.m.* crack, noise made by a splinter when torn from the block; blow from flying splinter.
Astillejos, Astilejos, *n.m.pl.* (*astron.*) Castor and Pollux.
astillero, *n.m.* rack (*for lances, spears, pikes etc.*); shipyard.
astillón, *n.m.* large splinter.
astilloso, -sa, *a.* splintery.
astracán, *n.m.* astrakhan (*cloth* or *fur*).
astrágalo, *n.m.* (*arch.*) astragal; (*bot.*) milk-vetch; (*artill.*) mouldings (*on a cannon*); (*anat.*) astragalus; round moulding.
astral, *a.* astral. — *n.m.* (*prov.*) small hatchet *or* axe.
astreñir [K], [ASTRINGIR].
astricción, *n.f.* astriction; (*med.*) costiveness.
astrictivo, -va, *a.* astrictive, astringent, styptic.
astricto, -ta, *a.* contracted, compressed; bound, obliged, constrained.
astrífero, -ra, *a.* (*poet.*) starry.
astringencia, *n.f.* astringency, astriction; (*med.*) costiveness.
astringente, *a., n.m.f.* (*med.*) astringent.
astringir [E], *v.t.* (*med.*) to astringe, contract, compress; (*fig.*) to oblige, bind, constrain.
astro, *n.m.* heavenly body; (*fig.*) star, luminary, leading light.
astrografía, *n.f.* astrography.
astrolabio, *n.m.* astrolabe.
astrolatría, *n.f.* astrolatry.
astrologar [B], *v.t., v.i.* to astrologize.
astrología, *n.f.* astrology.
astrológico, -ca, *a.* astrological, astrologic.
astrólogo, -ga, *a.* astrologic. — *n.m.f.* astrologer.
astronauta, *n.m.* astronaut.
astronáutico, -ca, *a.* astronautic(al). — *n.f.* astronautics.
astronave, *n.f.* spaceship; ***astronave tripulada,*** manned spaceship.
astronavegación, *n.f.* space travel.
astronomía, *n.f.* astronomy.
astronómico, -ca, *a.* astronomic(al); (*coll.*) astronomical, exorbitant.
astrónomo, *n.m.* astronomer.
astroso, -sa, *a.* ill-fated; (*fig.*) shabby, ragged, slovenly.
astucia, *n.f.* cunning, craft, trick, craftiness; astuteness.
astucioso, -sa, *a.* astute, shrewd.
astur, -ra, *a., n.m.f.* (native) of Asturias; (*hist.*) Asturian.
asturiano, -na, *a., n.m.f.* Asturian; native of Asturias.
Asturias, *n.f.pl.* Asturias.
asturión, *n.m.* small horse; (*ichth.*) [ESTURIÓN].
astuto, -ta, *a.* astute, cunning, sly.
asuardado, -da, *a.* stained, spotted (*cloth*).
asubiar, *v.i.* (*prov.*) to shelter against the rain.
asuejón, *n.m.* great ass; very stupid person.
asueto, *n.m.* short holiday, day off; leisure.
asumir, *v.t.* to assume, take upon o.s.; (*law*) [AVOCAR].
asunción, *n.f.* elevation to a higher dignity; feast of the Assumption.
asunto, *n.m.* matter; subject; affair, business; (***pl.***) business; ***en asunto de,*** in the matter of; ***asuntos exteriores,*** foreign affairs.
asuramiento, *n.m.* burning (*food*).
asurar, *v.t.* to burn (*food*); (*agric.*) to parch, scorch; (*fig.*) to pester.
asurcano, -na, *a.* adjacent, neighbouring.
asurcar [A], *v.t.* to furrow; to plough.
asuso, *adv.* (*obs.*) upwards.
asustadizo, -za, *a.* easily frightened *or* scared; scary.
asustar, *v.t.* to frighten, scare.
atabaca, *n.f.* (*prov., bot.*) groundsel.
atabacado, -da, *a.* tobacco-coloured.
atabal, *n.m.* kettle-drum; timbrel; kettle-drummer.
atabalear, *v.i.* to drum; to clatter; to paw, stamp (*horses*).
atabalejo, atabalete, *n.m.* small kettle-drum.
atabalero, *n.m.* kettle-drummer.
atabanado, -da, *a.* (*vet.*) spotted white.
atabardillado, -da, *a.* appertaining to *or* like spotted fever.
atabe, *n.m.* vent, spiracle (*in water-pipes*).
atabillar, *v.t.* to fold (*cloth*) with selvedges out.
atabladera, *n.f.* roller (*to level sown land*).
atablar, *v.t.* to level (*sown land*).
atacable, *a.* attackable.
atacadera, *n.f.* blast rammer.
atacado, -da, *a.* (*fig., coll.*) irresolute, undecided; miserable, mean.
atacador, -ra, *n.m.f.* aggressor. — *n.m.* ramrod, rammer (*for a gun*).
atacadura, *n.f.,* **atacamiento,** *n.m.* attaching, fastening, fitting; plugging.
atacamita, *n.f.* (*min.*) atacamite.
atacante, *a.* attacking; (*coll.*) irritating.
atacar [A], *v.t.* to fit (*clothes*) tight to the body; to button; to ram, force (*charge into fire-arms*); to attack, assault, assail; (*coll.*) to get on the nerves of, irritate; ***me ataca,*** he gets on my nerves.
atacir, *n.m.* (*astrol.*) division of the celestial arch into twelve parts.

ataderas, *n.f.pl.* (*coll.*) garters.

atadero, *n.m.* cord, rope; place where a thing is tied; tying; halter-ring; ***no tener atadero,*** to be crazy, incomprehensible *or* nonsensical; to be uncontrollable.

atadijo, *n.m.* (*coll.*) ill-shaped little bundle.

atado, -da, *a.* pusillanimous, good-for-nothing. — *n.m.* bundle, parcel, something tied together.

atador, -ra, *a.* tying, binding. — *n.m.f.* (*agric.*) binder.

atadura, *n.f.* fastening; cord; tying together; (*fig.*) union, connection; knot, loop; lace; limitation, restriction; ***sin ataduras,*** unfettered, unimpeded, untrammelled.

atafagar [B], *v.t.* to choke, suffocate; to stupefy; to pester.

atafetanado, -da, *a.* resembling taffeta.

atagallar, *v.i.* (*naut.*) to crowd sail.

ataguía, *n.f.* coffer-dam.

ataharre, *n.m.* broad crupper (*of a packsaddle*).

atahona [TAHONA].

atahonero [TAHONERO].

atahorma, *n.f.* osprey.

atahulla, *n.f.* plot of arable land.

ataifor, *n.m.* deep dish; round table.

atairar, *v.t.* to cut mouldings in (*panels*); to mould (*panels and frames*).

ataire, *n.m.* moulding (*in panels and frames of doors and windows*).

atajadero, *n.m.* barrage; sluice-gate.

atajadizo, *n.m.* partition wall.

atajador, -ra, *a.* intercipient. — *n.m.f.* interceptor; (*mil.*) scout; (*Chi.*) boy who tends horses; ***atajador de ganado,*** sheep-stealer.

atajamiento, *n.m.* interception.

atajante, *a.* intercepting.

atajar, *v.t.* to cut; to cut short, interrupt; to cut off, intercept, stop; to partition off. — *v.i.* to take a short cut. — **atajarse,** *v.r.* to get embarrassed *or* flustered; to panic.

atajea, atajía [ATARJEA].

atajo, *n.m.* short-cut (*road* or *path*); division; cut (*in MS., play etc.*); ward *or* guard (*made by a weapon in fencing*); obstruction; interception, stopping; ***echar por el atajo,*** to take a short cut; ***dar atajo a,*** to cut short; ***no hay atajo sin trabajo,*** there is no convenience without some inconvenience.

atalajar, *v.t.* (*artill.*) to harness and hitch (*horses to a carriage*).

atalaje, *n.m.* (*coll.*) tools, implements; (*artill.*) breast-harness; draft.

atalantar, *v.t.* to agree; to please; to bewilder, daze.

atalaya, *n.f.* watch-tower; vantage point. — *n.m.* guard placed in a watch-tower; look-out.

atalayador, -ra, *n.m.f.* look-out; (*fig.*) spy, prier.

atalayar, *v.t.* to observe, watch (over); to scan; (*fig.*) to pry into, spy on.

atalayero, *n.m.* advance scout.

ataludar, *v.t.* to slope; to embank.

atalvina [TALVINA].

atamiento, *n.m.* (*coll.*) pusillanimity, poor-spiritedness.

atanasia (1), *n.f.* (*bot.*) costmary, alecost.

atanasia (2), *n.f.* (*print.*) 14-point type-face.

atanor, *n.m.* tile-drain.

atanquía, *n.f.* depilatory; refuse of silk.

atañer [K], *v.i.* to be concerned, appertain.

atapar [TAPAR].

ataque, *n.m.* attack, onset; (*mil.*) offensive works; (*med.*) fit.

ataquiza, *n.f.* (*agric.*) layering (*vine*).

ataquizar [C], *v.t.* to layer, lay (*vine*).

atar, *v.t.* to tie, bind, fasten; to stop; ***loco de atar,*** raving mad; (*fig.*) ***atar cabos,*** to put two and two together; ***atar corto,*** to keep on a tight rein; ***atar de pies y manos,*** to tie hand and foot. — **atarse,** *v.r.* to become confused.

ataracea [TARACEA].

ataracear [TARACEAR].

atarantado, -da, *a.* (*coll.*) restless, wild.

atarantamiento, *n.m.* stunning, bewilderment.

atarantar, *v.t.* (*coll.*) to stun, bewilder.

ataraxia, *n.f.* ataraxia, ataraxy.

atarazana, *n.f.* arsenal; dockyard; shed (*in rope-works*); (*prov.*) cellar.

atarazar [C], *v.t.* to bite, wound, tear with the teeth.

atardecer [9], *v.i.* to grow late, draw towards evening; to be, find oneself in the evening. — *n.m.* evening; ***al atardecer,*** in the evening.

atareado, -da, *a.* (exceedingly) busy.

atarear, *v.t.* to load with work. — **atarearse,** *v.r.* to busy o.s., toil.

atarjea, *n.f.* drainpipe, sewer; sewer connection; tank, trough.

atarquinar, *v.t.* to bemire.

atarraga, *n.f.* (*bot.*) elecampane.

atarragar [B], *v.t.* to fit (*a shoe to a horse's foot*).

atarrajar, *v.t.* to cut the thread of (*a screw*).

atarraya, *n.f.* casting-net.

atarugamiento, *n.m.* plugging; wedging; (*coll., fig.*) state of fluster.

atarugar [B], *v.t.* to bung, plug; to wedge; to cram, stuff; (*coll., fig.*) to silence. — **atarugarse,** *v.r.* (*coll., fig.*) to get flustered.

atasajar, *v.t.* to jerk (*beef*).

atascadero, atascamiento, *n.m.* mudhole; bog; obstruction; stoppage; traffic jam.

atascar [A], *v.t.* to stop up, plug; to bung up, obstruct, jam. — **atascarse,** *v.r.* to get stuck, get bogged down; to stuff, gorge.

atasco, *n.m.* clogging, jamming; obstruction; traffic jam.

ataúd, *n.m.* coffin, (*Am.*) casket.

ataudado, -da, *a.* coffin-shaped.

ataujía, *n.f.* damascening.

ataurique, *n.m.* ornamented plaster-work.

ataviar [L], *v.t.* to deck out, trim, adorn, embellish, accoutre.

atávico, -ca, *a.* atavistic.

atavío, *n.m.* dress; ornament; finery; gear, accoutrement.

atavismo, *n.m.* atavism.

ataxia, *n.f.* (*med.*) ataxy.

atáxico, -ca, *a.* (*med.*) ataxic.

atea [ATEO].

atediar, *v.t.* to bore, weary.

ateísmo, *n.m.* atheism.

ateísta, *n.m.f.* [ATEO].

ateje, *n.m.* (*Cub., bot.*) ateje tree.

atejo, *n.m.* (*Col.*) parcel, bundle.

atelaje, *n.m.* team; harness.

atelar, *v.t.* to harness.

atemorizar [C], *v.t.* to terrify, strike with terror.

atemperación, *n.f.* tempering.

atemperante, *a.* soothing; tempering.

atemperar, *v.t.* to temper; to soften, mollify, assuage, calm; to modify, accommodate.

atenazar [C], *v.t.* to grip firmly.

atención, *n.f.* attention; attentiveness; civility, kindness; contract of sale (*in wool trade*); (*pl.* **atenciones**) business, affairs; ***en atención a,*** in view of; ***prestar atención,*** to pay attention. — *interj.* (*mil.*) attention!

atendedor, -ra, *n.m.f.* (*print.*) one who checks from original MSS., reader.

atendencia, *n.f.* attention.

atender [2], *v.t.* (*v.i.*) to attend (to), be attentive (to), mind; to heed, hearken; to show civility, attention

or courtesy (to); (*print.*) to check from original MSS.
atendible, *a.* worthy of consideration *or* attention.
atenebrarse, *v.r.* (*poet.*) to become obscured.
ateneísta, *n.m.f.* member of a cultural club.
ateneo, *n.m.* cultural club.
atenerse [33], *v.r.* to abide, rely; ***atenerse a,*** to abide by; to depend *or* rely on; to keep *or* stick to; ***atenerse a lo convenido,*** to keep to what has been agreed; ***no saber a qué atenerse,*** not to know where one stands.
ateniense, *a., n.m.f.* Athenian.
atentación, *n.f.* (*law*) illegal procedure.
atentado, -da, *a.* prudent, moderate; tactful. — *n.m.* (*law*) outrage; attempt on the life (*of s.o.*).
atentar, *v.i.* to attempt to commit a crime; ***atentar contra la vida de,*** to make an attempt on the life of; ***atentar contra la propiedad,*** to attack property. — **atentarse** [1], *v.r.* to restrain oneself.
atentatorio, -ria, *a.* (*law*) illegal, unlawful; prejudicial.
atento, -ta, *a.* attentive; polite, civil, courteous. — *adv.* seeing that, in consideration of; ***atento a la explicación,*** in view of the explanation.
atenuación, *n.f.* attenuation.
atenuante, *a.* attenuant; diluent; lessening. — *n.m.pl.* (**atenuantes**) (*law*) extenuating circumstances.
atenuar [M], *v.t.* to attenuate, diminish; to lessen.
ateo, -tea, *a.* atheistic. — *n.m.f.* atheist.
atepocate, *n.m.* (*Mex.*) frog spawn, tadpole.
atercianado, -da, *a.* afflicted with a tertian fever.
aterciopelado, -da, *a.* velvet-like, velvety.
aterimiento, *n.m.* stiffness from cold, numbness.
aterino, *n.m.* atherine, sand smelt.
aterirse [Q], *v.r.* to grow stiff with cold.
atermancia, *n.f.* (*phys.*) athermancy.
atérmano, -na, *a.* (*phys.*) athermanous.
aterrador, -ra, *a.* terrifying, horrifying.
aterrajar, *v.t.* to work (*with the draw-plate*); to thread (*a screw*); to tap (*with the die*).
aterraje, *n.m.* (*naut.*) landfall; (*aer.*) landing.
aterramiento, *n.m.* ruin, destruction; terror.
aterrar [1], *v.t.* to terrify; to destroy; to pull down, strike down; to cover with earth; (*min.*) to dump (*rubbish*). — *v.i.* to land.
aterrerar, *v.t.* (*min.*) to dump (*rubbish*).
aterrizaje, *n.m.* (*aer.*) landing.
aterrizar [C], *v.i.* (*aer.*) to land.
aterronar, *v.t.* to clod; to make lumpy.
aterrorizar [C], *v.t.* to terrify.
atesador, *n.m.* (*mech.*) stretcher, tightener; brace pin.
atesar [1], *v.t.* (*naut.*) to haul taut; to brace, tighten.
atesorador, -ra, *n.m.f.* hoarder.
atesorar, *v.t.* to treasure, hoard; to possess.
atestación, *n.f.* attestation, deposition, testimony.
atestado (1), **-da,** *a.* stubborn, pig-headed.
atestado (2), *n.m.* certificate, "certified correct" note; (*pl.*) testimonials.
atestadura, *n.f.* cramming, stuffing; extra must (*for filling up casks*).
atestamiento, *n.m.* cramming, stuffing, filling.
atestar (1) [1], *v.t.* to cram, pack, stuff; to crowd; to fill up (*pipes* or *butts of wine*) with must.
atestar (2) [*regular*], *v.t.* (*law*) to attest, witness; to affirm.
atestiguación, *n.f.*, **atestiguamiento,** *n.m.* deposition, testimony, testifying.
atestiguar [H], *v.t.* to testify to, witness.
atetado, -da, *a.* mammillated, mammiform.
atetar, *v.t.* to suckle, give suck to; (*prov.*) to suck.
atetillar, *v.t.* (*agric.*) to dig a trench round (*roots of trees*).
atezamiento, *n.m.* tanning; blackening.
atezar [C], *v.t.* to tan; to blacken. — **atezarse,** *v.r.* to get tanned *or* weathered.
atibar, *v.t.* (*min.*) to fill up.
atiborrar, *v.t.* to cram, stuff.
aticismo, *n.m.* Atticism; concise and elegant expression.
aticista, *a., n.m.f.* Attic, elegant (*writer*).
ático, -ca, *a.* Attic, elegant. — *n.m.* Attic dialect; (*arch.*) ornamental masonry (*set above the cornice*); (*arch.*) top floor.
atierre (1), *n.m.* (*min.*) caving in; landslide, collapse.
atierre (2), *pres. subj.* [ATERRAR].
atiesar, *v.t., v.i.* to stiffen.
atifle, *n.m.* potter's trivet.
atigrado, -da, *a.* marked like a tiger's skin; striped.
atijara, *n.f.* merchandise, freight; recompense.
atijarero, *n.m.* carrier.
atildado, -da, *a.* foppish, affected; affectedly dressed.
atildadura, *n.f.*, **atildamiento,** *n.m.* affectation (*in dress*); nicety.
atildar, *v.t.* to place a tilde on (the letter n); (*fig.*) to dress *or* adorn affectedly.
atinadamente, *adv.* accurately, pertinently.
atinado, -da, *a.* accurate, right; sensible.
atinar, *v.i.* to hit the mark *or* the target; (*fig.*) to hit upon it, to guess right.
atíncar, *n.m.* (*chem.*) tincal, borax.
atinconar, *v.t.* (*min.*) to prop up.
atinente, *a.* appertaining.
atingencia, *n.f.* relation; contiguity.
atiplar, *v.t.* to raise the pitch of (*a musical instrument*).
atirantar, *v.t.* (*arch.*) to make taut, brace.
atiriciarse, *v.r.* to contract jaundice.
atisbadero, *n.m.* peep-hole.
atisbador, -ra, *a.* prying, nosy. — *n.m.f.* prier, snooper, spy.
atisbadura, *n.f.* prying, snooping.
atisbar, *v.t.* to pry into, spy on, watch.
atisbo, *n.m.* suggestion, sign, hint, touch.
atisuado, -da, *a.* like gold *or* silver tissue.
atizadero, *n.m.* fire-poker; (*min.*) furnace door.
atizador, -ra, *a.* inciting. — *n.m.* poker; feeder.
atizar [C], *v.t.* to stir up, poke, prod; to incite.
atizonar, *v.t.* (*build.*) to bond with headers; to embed (*a beam*) in a wall. — **atizonarse,** *v.r.* (*agric.*) to be smutted (*of grain*).
atlante, *n.m.* (*arch.*) telamon; (*pl.*) (*arch.*) atlantes.
Atlántico, *n.m.* Atlantic (Ocean).
atlántico, -ca, *a.* Atlantic.
Atlas, *n.m.* Atlas; ***el Atlas,*** the Atlas Mountains.
atlas, *n.m.inv.* atlas.
atleta, *n.m.* athlete.
atlético, -ca, *a.* athletic.
atletismo, *n.m.* athletics.
atmósfera, *n.f.* atmosphere.
atmosférico, -ca, *a.* atmospherical.
atoaje, *n.m.* (*naut.*) towage, tow, towing.
atoar, *v.t.* (*naut.*) to tow. — *v.i.* (*naut.*) to be towed.
atoba, *n.f.* (*prov.*) adobe.
atocinado, -da, *a.* fat, fleshy.
atocinar, *v.t.* to cut up (*a pig*); to make into bacon; (*coll.*) to butcher, slaughter. — **atocinarse,** *v.r.* (*coll.*) to get infuriated *or* wild; (*coll.*) to fall head over heels in love.
atocha, *n.f.* (*bot.*) esparto.
atochal, *n.m.* esparto field.
atochar, *n.m.* esparto field. — *v.t.* to fill with esparto; to stuff.
atochón, *n.m.* panicle of esparto; esparto cane *or* rush.
atol, atole, *n.m.* (*Hisp. Am.*) cornflour gruel; (*Mex., fig.*) deceit, trick.

atoleadas, *n.f.pl.* (*Hond.*) festivities celebrated between July and December.
atolillo, *n.m.* (*C.R.*, *Hond.*) gruel made of flour, sugar and eggs.
atolón, *n.m.* atoll.
atolondrado, -da, *a.* hare-brained, giddy, thoughtless, heedless, crazy.
atolondramiento, *n.m.* bewilderment; heedlessness, craziness; state of fluster *or* dither.
atolondrar, *v.t.* to bewilder; to fluster; to stun. — **atolondrarse,** *v.r.* to get flustered, get into a dither.
atolladero, *n.m.* mudhole; (*fig.*) difficult *or* burdensome situation; ***estar metido en un atolladero,*** to be bogged down, be in a hole; ***salir del atolladero,*** to get out of a fix.
atollarse, *v.r.* (*lit.*, *fig.*) to get bogged down, get stuck.
atomicidad, *n.f.* atomicity.
atómico, -ca, *a.* atomic.
atomismo, *n.m.* atomism.
atomista, *n.m.f.* atomist.
atomístico, -ca, *a.* atomical.
atomizar [C], *v.t.* to atomize.
átomo, *n.m.* atom.
atona, *n.f.* ewe that rears another's lamb.
atondar, *v.t.* to urge on (*a horse*) with one's legs.
atonía, *n.f.* (*med.*) atony.
atónico, -ca, *a.* (*gram.*, *med.*) atonic.
atónito, -ta, *a.* thunderstruck, flabbergasted, nonplussed.
átono, -na, *a.* (*gram.*) atonic, unaccented.
atontamiento, *n.m.* stupefaction, dazed state.
atontar, *v.t.* to knock silly, daze, stun; to bewilder, confuse.
atopile, *n.m.* (*Mex.*) foreman in charge of irrigation waters.
atora, *n.f.* (*Bibl.*) Mosaic law.
atoramiento, *n.m.* choking, obstruction.
atorar (1), *v.t.* to obstruct; to choke, jam. — **atorarse,** *v.r.* [*regular*] to stick in the mud.
atorar (2) [4], *v.t.* to cut (*firewood*).
atormentador, -ra, *a.* tormenting. — *n.m.f.* tormentor, tormentress.
atormentar, *v.t.* to torment; to torture. — **atormentarse,** *v.r.* to suffer agony *or* agonies of mind.
atornillar, *v.t.* to screw; to screw in, on *or* up.
atorozonarse, *v.r.* (*vet.*) to suffer from colic *or* gripes.
atorra, *n.f.* (*prov.*) linen petticoat.
atorrante, *n.m.* (*Arg.*) loafer; good-for-nothing.
atortolar, *v.t.* (*coll.*) to intimidate; (*coll.*) to rattle.
atortorar, *v.t.* (*naut.*) to frap; (*naut.*) to strengthen by means of a tourniquet.
atortujar, *v.t.* to squeeze, flatten.
atosigador, -ra (1), *a.* poisonous. — *n.m.* poisoner.
atosigador, -ra (2), *a.* pressing, urgent. — *n.m.* urger.
atosigamiento, *n.m.* poisoning; harassing.
atosigante, *a.* pressing, urgent.
atosigar (1) [B], *v.t.* to poison.
atosigar (2) [B], *v.t.* (*fig.*) to harass, press (hard).
atoxicar [A], *v.t.* to poison.
atóxico, -ca, *a.* non-poisonous.
atrabajar, *v.t.* to keep (*s.o.*) very busy; to make (*s.o.*) work hard.
atrabancar [A], *v.t.* to do in a hurry.
atrabanco, *n.m.* hurry, hurrying.
atrabiliario, -ria, *a.* atrabiliary, melancholy; splenetic, bitter-tempered; (*med.*) bilious; (*med.*) ***cápsula atrabiliaria,*** atrabiliary capsule.
atrabilis, *n.f. inv.* (*med.*) atrabiliousness, black bile; (*coll.*) melancholy; bitter temper.
atracable, *a.* (*naut.*) easy to berth.
atracada, *n.f.* (*naut.*) berthing, docking; (*coll.*) overeating, gluttony.
atracadero, *n.m.* (*naut.*) landfall; landing-place, berthing place.
atracador, *n.m.* hold-up man, armed bandit.
atracar (1) [A], *v.t.* to hold up, rob. — **atracarse,** *v.r.* to stuff o.s. with food, to gorge o.s.
atracar (2) [A], *v.t.* to berth, bring alongside (*a quay* or *pier*). — *v.i.* to berth.
atracción, *n.f.* attraction; show; ***parque de atracciones,*** funfair, (*Am.*) carnival.
atraco, *n.m.* hold-up, robbery.
atracón, *n.m.* stuffing, gluttony; ***darse un atracón de pasteles,*** to stuff o.s. with cakes.
atractivo, -va, *a.* attractive, engaging, enchanting. — *n.m.* charm, attraction; inducement.
atractriz, *a.f.* (*phys.*) attracting; ***fuerza atractriz,*** attractive power.
atraer [34], *v.t.* to attract, lead, lure; to charm, captivate.
atrafagar [B], *v.i.* to labour, toil.
atragantarse, *v.r.* to choke, get sth. stuck in one's throat; to get tied up (*in one's speech*); ***atragantarse con una espina,*** to get a fish-bone stuck in one's throat; (*fig.*) ***ese tío se me atraganta*** or ***se me ha atragantado,*** I can't stomach that chap.
atraíble, *a.* attractable.
atraicionar [TRAICIONAR].
atraidorado, -da, *a.* treacherous, faithless, perfidious.
atraillar [P], *v.t.* to leash; to follow (*game*) guided by a dog on leash.
atramento, *n.m.* ink-black.
atramparse, *v.r.* to get trapped *or* snared; to get choked, blocked *or* stopped up; to get jammed *or* stuck.
atramuz [ALTRAMUZ].
atrancar [A], *v.t.* to bar (*a door*); to block up. — *v.i.* (*coll.*) to take long steps; to read hurriedly.
atranco, atranque, *n.m.* blockage, stoppage; obstruction; difficulty.
atrapamoscas, *n.f. inv.* (*bot.*) Venus's flytrap.
atrapar, *v.t.* (*coll.*) to catch; grab; to trap, ensnare; to take in.
atrás, *adv.* back, at the back, behind; past; ***¡atrás!*** back! get back!; ***hacia atrás,*** backwards; ***dejar atrás,*** to leave behind; ***quedarse atrás,*** to get left behind, lag behind; ***hacerse atrás,*** to get *or* move back.
atrasado, -da, *a.* backward; behind (the times); late; slow (*clock*); in arrears; retarded; ***país atrasado,*** backward country; ***número atrasado,*** back number (*of magazine etc.*); ***niño mentalmente atrasado,*** mentally retarded *or* deficient child.
atrasar, *v.t.* to slow (down), retard; to put, set *or* turn back; to postpone, put off. — *v.i.* to be slow, to lose (*of watch*). — **atrasarse,** *v.r.* to be late, arrive late; to take a long time; to get behindhand *or* into arrears.
atraso, *n.m.* backwardness; delay; slowness (*watch*); (*pl.*) arrears; (*coll.*) ***¡esto es un atraso!*** this is hopeless *or* a dead loss!
atravesado, -da, *a.* squint-eyed; half-breed; (*coll.*) awkward, difficult, nasty, bloody-minded.
atravesador, -ra, *a.* traversing, crossing.
atravesaño [TRAVESAÑO].
atravesar [1], *v.t.* to stretch across; to run through; to cross, cross over, pass over, go through; to wager, bet; (*coll.*) to bewitch; to lay (*a trump*) (*cards*); (*naut.*) to lie to; ***atravesar la ciudad,*** to pass through the city; ***atravesar un madero en la calle,*** to lay a beam across the street; ***atravesar el pecho de un balazo,*** to shoot through the breast. — **atravesarse,** *v.r.* to interfere; (*naut.*) to cross the course of another vessel;

to bet, stake, wager; ***atravesarse con alguien,*** to get *or* be on bad terms with s.o.

atrayente, *a.* attractive.

atreguado, -da, *a.* foolish; lunatic; under truce.

atreguar [H], *v.t.* to give a truce to. — **atreguarse,** *v.r.* to agree to a truce.

atrenzo, *n.m.* (*Hisp. Am.*) conflict, difficulty.

atresia, *n.f.* (*med.*) atresia.

atresnalar, *v.t.* (*agric.*) to stack, stook.

atreverse, *v.r.* to dare; to venture; ***atreverse con todo,*** to take anything on; ***no atreverse a hablar,*** not to dare to speak.

atrevido, -da, *a.* bold, audacious, daring, fearless; forward, insolent.

atrevimiento, *n.m.* boldness, audacity, daring; effrontery, impudence.

atribución, *n.f.* conferring; power; prerogative; attribute.

atribuible, *a.* attributable.

atribuir [O], *v.t.* to attribute, ascribe, impute; to put down (to).

atribulación, *n.f.* tribulation, affliction.

atribular, *v.t.* to afflict, grieve.

atributivo, -va, *a.* attributive.

atributo, *n.m.* attribute; (*log.*) predicate.

atrición, *n.f.* (*relig.*) attrition; (*vet., obs.*) contraction of the principal nerve.

atril, *n.m.* lectern, music-stand; easel.

atrilera, *n.f.* ornamental cover for a lectern.

atrincheramiento, *n.m.* entrenchment.

atrio, *n.m.* atrium; porch, portico.

atrípedo, -da, *a.* (*zool.*) black-footed.

atrirrostro, -ra, *a.* (*orn.*) black-beaked.

atrincherar, *v.r.* to entrench, fortify with trenches.

atrito, -ta, *a.* contrite.

atrocidad, *n.f.* atrocity, atrociousness, heinousness, wickedness, cruelty; (*coll.*) shocking *or* utterly stupid thing to do *or* say; ***come una atrocidad,*** he eats a terrific amount.

atrochar, *v.i.* to take a short cut.

atrofia, *n.f.* atrophy; wasted condition; stunted *or* retarded state.

atrofiarse, *v.r.* to fall into a state of atrophy; to waste away; to become stunted *or* retarded.

atrófico, -ca, *a.* atrophic; wasted; stunted, retarded.

atrojar, *v.t.* (*agric.*) to garner. — **atrojarse,** *v.r.* (*Hisp. Am., coll.*) to be stumped.

atrompetado, -da, *a.* trumpet-like.

atronado, -da, *a.* unreflecting, inconsiderate, precipitate, reckless.

atronador, -ra, *a.* thundering.

atronadura, *n.f.* crack *or* split (*in wood*); (*vet.*) tumour (*in the pastern*).

atronamiento, *n.m.* thundering; deafening noise; stunned state; (*vet.*) crepance.

atronar [4], *v.t.* to deafen; to make a din in (*a place*); to stun, knock silly; to stop the ears of (*horses*); to kill (*bulls*) by blow on nape of neck; ***atronar la calle,*** to kick up a racket in the street, make an infernal din in the street. — **atronarse,** *v.r.* to become affected by thunder (*chickens, silkworms etc.*).

atronerar, *v.t.* to make loopholes in.

atropar, *v.t.* to group together, assemble in groups. — **atroparse,** *v.r.* to gang up.

atropelladamente, *adv.* confusedly, helter-skelter, pell-mell.

atropellado, -da, *a.* hasty, precipitate, reckless.

atropellador, -ra, *a.* trampling, violating. — *n.m.f.* trampler, transgressor, violator.

atropellamiento, *n.m.* trampling under foot; confusedness, precipitation.

atropellar, *v.t.* to trample down, tread under foot; to knock down, run over; to ride roughshod over; to do hurriedly; to abuse, misuse, violate. — **atropellarse,** *v.r.* to rush, be precipitate, act hastily *or* recklessly.

atropello, *n.m.* upset; trampling; abuse, outrage.

atropina, *n.f.* (*chem.*) atropine.

atroz, *a.* atrocious, cruel, heinous, inhuman, barbarous; (*coll.*) terrific, tremendous, fiendish; ***hace un frío atroz,*** it's wickedly cold.

atrozar [C], *v.t.* (*naut.*) to truss (*a yard*) to the mast.

atruchado, -da, *a.* trout-coloured (*cast-iron graining*).

atruhanado, -da, *a.* scurrilous, rascally.

atuendo, *n.m.* pomp, show; attire, get-up, rig-out.

atufadamente, *adv.* peevishly, morosely, angrily.

atufamiento [ATUFO].

atufar, *v.t.* to vex, irritate. — *v.i.* to smell bad, stink; ***esta carne atufa,*** this meat smells. — **atufarse,** *v.r.* to get heated (up), worked up *or* steamed up, get into a state; to become affected by fumes; to turn sour (*wine*).

atufo, *n.m.* vexation, irritation, annoyance; (*coll.*) fume, stew.

atumultuar [H], *v.t.* [TUMULTUAR].

atún, *n.m.* tunny, tunny-fish, tuna; (*coll., fig.*) ***pedazo de atún,*** blockhead.

atunara, *n.f.* tunny fishing-ground.

atunera, *n.f.* tunny fish-hook.

atunero, *n.m.* tunny fisherman *or* salesman.

aturar (1), *v.t.* (*coll.*) to close tightly.

aturar (2), *v.i.* to act judiciously.

aturdidor, -ra, *a.* that stuns *or* flusters.

aturdimiento, *n.m.* daze, bewilderment, fluster, confusion.

aturdir, *v.t.* to daze, stun, fluster, bewilder, confuse. — **aturdirse,** *v.r.* to become dazed; to get into a dither.

aturrullar, *v.t.* (*coll.*) to confuse, disconcert, confound, perplex, bewilder.

atusador, -ra, *a.* trimming; smoothing.

atusar, *v.t.* to trim; to smooth down; to trim (*plants*). — **atusarse,** *v.r.* (*fig.*) to dress (o.s.) with affectation.

atutía, *n.f.* (*chem.*) tutty; oxide of zinc ointment.

auca (1), *n.f.* goose.

auca (2), *a., n.m.f.* Araucanian.

audacia, *n.f.* audacity, boldness.

audaz, *a.* bold, audacious, daring.

audible, *a.* audible.

audición, *n.f.* audition, hearing.

audiencia, *n.f.* audience, hearing, reception; audience-chamber; law court; high court; law officers (*appointed to institute some judicial inquiry*); ***dar audiencia,*** to hold a levee; to give audience; (*law*) ***hacer audiencia,*** to sit and determine lawsuits; ***recibir en audiencia,*** to grant an audience to.

audífono, *n.m.* audiphone.

audiofrecuencia, *n.f.* audiofrequency.

audiómetro, *n.m.* audiometer.

auditivo, -va, *a.* auditive, auditory. — *n.m.* telephone ear-piece.

auditor, *n.m.* judge; auditor; ***auditor de la nunciatura,*** papal legal adviser (*in Spain*); ***auditor de guerra*** (***de marina***), military (naval) legal adviser.

auditoría, *n.f.* office of ***auditor.***

auditorio, -ria, *a.* auditory. — *n.m.* auditorium; audience.

auge, *n.m.* (*fig.*) boom; height.

augita, *n.f.* (*min.*) augite.

augur, *n.m.* augur.

auguración, *n.f.* augury.

augural, *a.* augural.

augurar, *v.t.* to augur, foretell, prophesy.

augurio, *n.m.* augury.

augustal, *a.* Augustan.

augusto, -ta, *a.* august, magnificent, majestic.
aula, *n.f.* lecture hall; class room; (*poet.*) palace.
aulaga, *n.f.* (*bot.*) furze, whin, gorse.
aulagar, *n.m.* gorse heath.
áulico, -ca, *a.* aulic, courtly. — *n.m.* courtier.
aulladero, *n.m.* place where wolves meet and howl.
aullador, -ra, *a.* howling.
aullante, *a.* howling.
aullar [P], *v.i.* to howl.
aullido, aúllo, *n.m.* howl.
aumentable, *a.* augmentable.
aumentación, *n.f.* increase; (*rhet.*) climax.
aumentador, -ra, *a.* augmenting.
aumentante, *a.* augmenting, increasing.
aumentar, *v.t.* to increase, enlarge, augment, magnify. — *v.i.* to increase, grow; ***las dificultades van aumentando,*** the difficulties are growing.
aumentativo, -va, *a.* augmentative.
aumento, *n.m.* increase, augmentation, enlargement, growth, rise, (*Am.*) raise; magnifying power (*of a telescope* or *lens*); ***ir en aumento,*** to increase, grow.
aún, *adv.* yet, still; ***aún . . . cuando,*** still . . . when.
aun, *adv.* even; yet, as yet, still; ***aun así,*** even so. — *conj.* ***aun cuando,*** even though, although.
aunar [P], *v.t.* to unite, join, assemble; to incorporate, merge.
auniga, *n.f.* (*Philip.*) auniga bird.
aunque, *conj.* though; even if.
¡aúpa! *interj.* (*coll.*) up you get! up with you!; (*coll.*) ***de aúpa,*** fabulous, fantastic, super; ***coche*** (***chica***) ***de aúpa,*** smashing car (girl); ***comer de aúpa,*** to have a slap-up meal.
aupar [P], *v.t.* (*coll.*) to help up, lift up, raise up; (*coll.*) to praise.
aura (1), *n.f.* (*orn.*) turkey buzzard.
aura (2), *n.f.* (*poet.*) gentle breeze; (*fig.*) favour, applause; (*med.*) aura; ***aura popular,*** popularity.
auranciáceo, -cea, *a.*(*bot.*) orange-like.
áureo, -rea, *a.* golden, gold; (*poet.*) aureate. — *n.m.* (ancient) gold coin; weight of four scruples.
auréola, aureola, *n.f.* aureola, halo.
aureolar, *v.t.* to adorn with an aureole *or* halo.
aurero, *n.m.* (*Cub.*) place where vultures gather.
auricalco, *n.m.* copper, bronze, brass.
aurícula, *n.f.* (*anat.*) auricle; (*bot.*) lobe (*on leaf*).
auricular, *a.* auricular. — *n.m.* telephone ear-piece receiver.
aurífero, -ra, *a.* auriferous, gold-bearing.
Auriga, *n.m.* (*astron.*) Auriga, Wagoner.
auriga, *n.m.* (*poet.*) charioteer.
aurígero, -ra, *a.* auriferous, gold-bearing.
aurista, *n.m.f.* (*med.*) aurist, ear specialist.
aurívoro, -ra, *a.* (*poet.*) greedy for gold.
aurora, *n.f.* dawn, daybreak; flush of dawn; roseate colour; (*fig.*) harbinger; beverage of almond milk and cinnamon; (*naut.*) morning-watch gun; ***aurora boreal,*** aurora borealis, northern lights; ***despuntar*** or ***romper la aurora,*** to dawn, break (*of day*).
aurragado, -da, *a.* badly tilled and cultivated.
auscultación, *n.f.* (*med.*) auscultation.
auscultar, *v.t.* (*med.*) to auscultate, sound.
ausencia, *n.f.* absence; ***guardarle a alguien*** (***la***) ***ausencia,*** to wait faithfully for s.o., be faithful to s.o.
ausentarse, *v.r.* to absent oneself; to go away, leave.
ausente, *a.* absent; (*fig.*) ***está ausente,*** his mind is not on the subject.
ausentismo, *n.m.* absenteeism.
auspicio, *n.m.* auspice.
austeridad, *n.f.* austerity; severity.
austero, -ra, *a.* austere; severe, stern.
austral, *a.* austral, southern.
Australia, *n.f.* Australia.
australiano, -na, *a.*, *n.m.f.* Australian.
Austria, *n.f.* Austria.
austríaco, -ca, *a.*, *n.m.f.* Austrian.
Austria-Hungría, *n.f.* Austria-Hungary.
austrino, -na, *a.* belonging to the house of Austria.
austro, *n.m.* south wind; south.
austrohúngaro, -ra, *a.*, *n.m.f.* Austro-Hungarian.
autarcía, autarquía, *n.f.* autarchy, (*Am.*) autarky.
auténtica, *n.f.* [AUTÉNTICO].
autenticación, *n.f.* authentication.
autenticar [A], *v.t.* to authenticate, attest.
autenticidad, *n.f.* authenticity.
auténtico, -ca, *a.* authentic, genuine, real; (*law*) attested. — *n.f.* original, authentic text; certificate, attestation.
autillo (1), *n.m.* Inquisition act *or* decree.
autillo (2), *n.m.* (*orn.*) barn-owl, screech-owl.
auto (1), *n.m.* act; judicial decree *or* sentence; writ, warrant, edict, ordinance; (*pl.*) pleadings and proceedings (*in a lawsuit*); ***auto de fe,*** auto-da-fé; ***auto interlocutorio,*** interlocutory sentence; ***auto sacramental,*** allegorical religious play; (*fam.*) ***estar en*** (***los***) ***autos,*** to know (*sth.*) profoundly; to be well up (*in sth.*); ***poner en autos,*** to inform.
auto (2), *n.m.* (*coll.*) car, automobile.
autoanálisis, *n.m. inv.* self-analysis.
autobiografía, *n.f.* autobiography.
autobiográfico, -ca, *a.* autobiographical.
autobiógrafo, -fa, *n.m.f.* autobiographer.
autoblasto, *n.m.* (*biol.*) autoblast.
autobomba, *n.f.* motor pump.
autobombo, *n.m.* blowing one's own trumpet, self-glorification.
autobote, *n.m.* motorboat.
autobús, *n.m.* bus.
autocamión, *n.m.* motor-lorry.
autocar, *n.m.* coach.
autocarril, *n.m.* (*railw.*) multi-diesel unit.
autocasa, *n.f.* trailer, caravan.
autoclave, *a.* self-regulating (*cooking vessel*). — *n.m.* steam-pressure sterilizing apparatus.
autoconciencia, *n.f.* self-consciousness.
autocopiar, *v.t.* (*com.*) to duplicate, multiply.
autocopista, *n.m.* (*com.*) autocopyist; duplicator; duplicating machine.
autocracia, *n.f.* autocracy.
autócrata, *n.m.f.* autocrat.
autocrático, -ca, *a.* autocratic.
autocrítica, *n.f.* self-criticism.
autóctono, -na, *a.* autochthonic, aboriginal. — *n.m.f.* autochthon.
autodefensa, *n.f.* self-defence.
autodeterminación, *n.f.* self-determination.
autodidacto, -ta, *a.*, *n.m.f.* self-taught (person).
autodidaxia, *n.f.* facility for self-teaching.
autodirigido, -da, *a.* self-guided.
autodominio, *n.m.* self-control.
autódromo, *n.m.* car racing track.
autoencendido, *n.m.* self-ignition.
auto-escuela, *n.f.* driving school.
autofecundación, *n.f.* (*bot.*) close fertilization.
autógamo, -ma, *a.* (*bot.*) autogamous.
autogénesis, *n.f. inv.* (*physiol.*) autogeny, autogony.
autógeno, -na, *a.* welding by means of oxygen and acetylene.
autogiro, *n.m.* (*aer.*) autogiro.
autogobierno, *n.m.* self-government.
autógrafa [AUTÓGRAFO].
autografía, *n.f.* autography; facsimile reproduction; duplicating office.
autografiar [L], *v.t.* to autograph; to duplicate.

autográfico, -ca, *a.* autographical, facsimile.
autógrafo, -fa, *a.* autograph, autographic. — *n.m.* autograph.
autohipnosis, *n.f. inv.* self-hypnotism.
autoinducción, *n.f.* (*elec.*) self-induction.
autointoxicación, *n.f.* (*path.*) autointoxication, autotoxæmia.
automación, *n.f.* automation.
autómata, *n.m.* automaton; (*coll.*) zombie.
automático, -ca, *a.* automatic.
automatismo, *n.m.* automatism.
automatización, *n.f.* automation.
automatizar [C], *v.t.* to automate; (*coll.*) to turn into an automaton.
automedonte, *n.m.* (*myth.*) Automedon.
automotor, -ra, automotriz, *a.* self-acting, self-moving, self-propelling. — *n.m.* autorail.
automóvil, *a.* self-moving. — *n.m.* (motor-)car, (*Am.*) automobile.
automovilismo, *n.m.* motoring.
automovilista, *n.m.f.* motorist.
autonomía, *n.f.* autonomy, home rule; range.
autonómico, -ca, *a.* autonomous.
autonomista, *a.*, *n.m.f.* autonomist.
autónomo, -ma, *a.* autonomous, free.
autopista, *n.f.* motorway, (*Am.*) turnpike.
autoplastia, *n.f.* (*surg.*) autoplasty.
autopropulsado, -da, *a.* self-propelled.
autopropulsión, *n.f.* self-propulsion.
autoprotección, *n.f.* self-preservation.
autopsia, *n.f.* (*med.*) post-mortem, autopsy.
autópsido, -da, *a.* (*min.*) glittering, having a metallic lustre.
autor, -ra, *n.m.f.* author, authoress; maker; composer; writer; (*obs.*) manager (*of a theatre*); (*law*) plaintiff, claimant; perpetrator (*of crime*).
autorcillo, *n.m.* petty *or* third-rate author *or* writer.
autoría, *n.f.* (*obs.*) direction (*of a theatrical company*).
autoridad, *n.f.* authority; authoritative quotation.
autoritario, -ria, *a.* authoritarian.
autoritarismo, *n.m.* authoritarianism.
autoritativo, -va, *a.* authoritative.
autorizable, *a.* authorizable.
autorización, *n.f.* authorization.
autorizado, -da, *a.* authoritative; official; ***fuente autorizada,*** official source.
autorizador, -ra, *a.* authorizing. — *n.m.f.* one who authorizes.
autorizamiento, *n.m.* authorization.
autorizar [C], *v.t.* to authorize, empower.
autorretrato, *n.m.* self-portrait.
autorzuelo [AUTORCILLO].
autoservicio, *n.m.* self-service (*shop* or *restaurant*).
autostop, *n.m.* hitch-hiking; ***hacer autostop,*** to hitch-hike.
autosugestión, *n.f.* (*med.*) auto-suggestion.
autotécnica, *n.f.* automotive engineering.
autotipia, *n.f.* (*photo.*) autotype.
autumnal, *a.* (*poet.*) autumnal.
Auvernia, *n.f.* Auvergne.
auxiliador, -ra, *a.* helping; rescuing, saving. — *n.m.f.* helper; rescuer, saver.
auxiliante, *a.* aiding, assisting; rescuing.
auxiliar (1), *a.* auxiliary; helping, assistant. — *n.m.* assistant, auxiliary.
auxiliar (2) [L *and regular*], *v.t.* to aid, help, assist; to attend (*a dying person*).
auxiliatorio, -ria, *a.* (*law*) auxiliary.
auxilio, *n.m.* aid, assistance, help; rescuing, saving; ***acudir en auxilio de,*** to come to the aid *or* rescue of; ***primeros auxilios,*** first aid; ***auxilio en carretera,*** highway assistance *or* rescue service; ***auxilio social,*** social work.
avacado, -da, *a.* cow-like.
avadarse, *v.r.* to become fordable.
avahar, *v.t.* to warm with breath *or* vapour. — **avahar(se),** *v.i.* (*v.r.*) to fume; to give off vapour.
aval, *n.m.* guarantee, surety; endorsement, counter-signature; (*pers.*) guarantor; (*polit.*) guarantee of conduct.
avalancha, *n.f.* avalanche; (*fig.*) flood.
avalar, *v.t.* (*com.*) to endorse, countersign; to back.
avalentado, -da, avalentonado, -da, *a.* bragging, boasting, arrogant.
avalo, *n.m.* slight movement; earthquake.
avalorar, *v.t.* to estimate, price, value, evaluate.
avaluación, *n.f.* valuation, appraisement, assessment.
avaluar [M], *v.t.* to value, appraise, estimate, assess.
avalúo, *n.m.* valuation, appraisement.
avallar, *v.t.* to barricade, fence in.
avambrazo, *n.m.* armlet.
avampiés, *n.m. inv.* spatterdash.
avancarga (de), *n.f.* muzzle loader.
avance, *n.m.* (*mil.*) advance; progress; (*com.*) account, statement, balance-sheet; payment in advance; (*cine.*) trailer.
avanecerse [9], *v.r.* to become stale (*fruit*).
avantrén, *n.m.* (*mil.*) limbers (*of a gun-carriage*).
avanzado, -da, *a.* advanced, liberal, progressive. — *n.f.* (*mil.*) van, outpost, reconnoitring troop.
avanzar [C], *v.t.* to advance, increase. — *v.i.* (*mil.*) to advance; to come *or* go on, come *or* go forward.
avanzo, *n.m.* (*com.*) estimate, tender; balance-sheet.
avaricia, *n.f.* avarice, cupidity, greed.
avaricioso, -sa, avariento, -ta, *a.* avaricious, covetous, niggardly, miserly. — *n.m.f.* miser, niggard.
avaro, -ra, *a.* avaricious, miserly; ***avaro de gloria,*** eager for glory. — *n.m.f.* miser, tightwad.
avasallador, -ra, *a.* enslaving; overbearing. — *n.m.f.* enslaver.
avasallamiento, *n.m.* enslavement, servitude; subjection.
avasallar, *v.t.* to subdue, subject, enslave, reduce to vassalage; to overbear; (*coll.*) ***sin avasallar, ¿eh?*** no browbeating, if you don't mind!
avatar, *n.m.* avatar; (*pl.* **avatares**) vicissitudes.
ave, *n.f.* bird, fowl; ***ave del Paraíso,*** bird of paradise; ***ave pasajera*** or ***de paso,*** bird of passage; ***ave de corral,*** barnyard fowl; ***ave de rapiña,*** bird of prey.
avecica, avecilla, avecita, *n.f.* small bird.
avecinar, *v.t.* to bring near; to domicile. — **avecinarse,** *v.r.* to approach; to take up residence.
avecindamiento, *n.m.* (act of) taking up residence *or* settling.
avecindar, *v.t.* to register as a resident. — **avecindarse,** *v.r.* to take up residence.
avechucho, *n.m.* (*orn.*) sparrow-hawk; wretched bird; (*coll.*) ragamuffin.
avejentar, *v.t.* to make look old, age. — **avejentarse,** *v.r.* to get to look old, age.
avejigar [B], *v.t.* to produce blisters in. — **avejigar(se),** *v.i.* (*v.r.*) to blister.
avellana, *n.f.* filbert, hazel-nut.
avellanador, *n.m.* fraise, countersink-bit, rose-bit.
avellanal, avellanar (1), *n.m.* plantation of hazel-nut trees.
avellanar (2), *v.t.* to countersink; to shrivel (up).
avellanero, -ra, *n.m.f.* dealer in nuts and filberts. — *n.f.* hazel-tree, filbert-tree.
avellanica, *n.f.* small filbert.
avellano, *n.m.* hazel-nut tree.
¡Ave María! *interj.* good gracious!
avemaría, *n.f.* Ave Maria; Hail Mary; rosary bead; ***al avemaría,*** at nightfall; ***en un avemaría,*** in an instant.
avena, *n.f.* (*bot.*) oats; (*poet.*) pastoral flute *or* pipe.
avenáceo, -cea, *a.* oat-like.

avenado, -da, *a.* fickle, inconstant, wild; crazy.
avenal, *n.m.* oatfield.
avenamiento, *n.m.* draining, drainage.
avenar, *v.t.* to drain.
avenate (1), *n.m.* water-gruel, oatmeal-gruel.
avenate (2), *n.m.* (*prov.*) fit of madness.
avenenar [ENVENENAR].
avenencia, *n.f.* agreement, arrangement, understanding.
avenible, *a.* adaptable, flexible.
aveníceo, -cea, *a.* oaten.
avenida (1), *n.f.* flood, freshet; avenue; approach, access.
avenido, -da (2), *a.* ***bien*** (***mal***) ***avenidos,*** living on good (bad) terms.
avenidor, -ra, *a.* mediating, pacifying. — *n.m.f.* mediator, pacifier.
avenimiento, *n.m.* convention, accord, reconciliation; agreement, arrangement.
avenir [36], *v.t.* to reconcile. — **avenirse,** *v.r.* to reach a reconciliation; to come to an agreement; to come to a compromise; ***avenirse a,*** to agree (reluctantly) to, come round to, see one's way to; ***por fin se avino,*** he eventually agreed *or* came round.
aventador, -ra, *a.* fanning, winnowing. — *n.m.f.* (*agric.*) fanner, winnower. — *n.m.* (*agric.*) pitchfork; esparto scoop *or* fan; (*min.*) pump-valve.
aventadura, *n.f.* (*vet.*) wind-gall.
aventajado, -da, *a.* advantageous; excellent, superior, outstanding; ***alumno aventajado,*** outstanding pupil; ***estatura aventajada,*** superior stature. — *n.m.* (*mil., obs.*) soldier having additional pay.
aventajar, *v.t.* to give an advantage to; to do better than, outdo, excel, surpass.
aventamiento, *n.m.* fanning, winnowing.
aventar [1], *v.t.* to fan; to winnow; (*coll.*) to expel, drive away; (*Cub.*) to expose (*sugar*) to sun and air. — **aventarse,** *v.r.* to become inflated; (*coll.*) to escape, run away; (*prov.*) to become tainted; (*naut.*) to burst.
aventura, *n.f.* adventure, enterprise.
aventurar, *v.t.* to venture, hazard, risk, endanger, expose. — **aventurarse,** *v.r.* to venture (***a,*** to).
aventurero, -ra, *a.* adventurous, venturesome. — *n.m.* adventurer. — *n.f.* adventuress.
averdugado, -da, *a.* blotchy, pimply.
avergonzar [10c], *v.t.* to shame, abash, put to shame. — **avergonzarse,** *v.r.* to feel ashamed *or* embarrassed.
avería (1), *n.f.* damage; breakdown; (*naut.*) average; ***avería gruesa,*** general average.
avería (2), *n.f.* collection of birds; poultry yard, aviary.
averiar [L], *v.t.* to damage. — **averiarse,** *v.r.* to break down.
averiguación, *n.f.* investigation, inquiry; inquest; ascertainment.
averiguador, -ra, *a.* investigating, inquiring. — *n.m.f.* searcher, inquirer.
averiguar [H], *v.t.* to inquire into, investigate; to ascertain, find out.
averío, *n.m.* flock of birds; (*prov.*) beast of burden.
averno, *n.m.* (*poet.*) hell; (*myth.*) Avernus.
averroísmo, *n.m.* Averroism.
averroísta, *n.m.f.* Averroist.
averrugado, -da, *a.* warty, pimply.
aversión, *n.f.* aversion.
avertín, *n.m.* (*med.*) melancholia; (*vet.*) colic (*cattle*).
avestruz, *n.m.* ostrich; (*coll.*) ignoramus.
avetado, -da, *a.* veined, streaked.
avetarda [AVUTARDA].
avetoro, *n.m.* (*orn.*) bittern.
avezado, -da, *a.* experienced.
avezar [C], *v.t.* to accustom, get used (to).
aviación, *n.f.* aviation; air force; ***bombardeos realizados por la aviación alemana,*** bombing carried out by the German Air Force.
aviador, -ra (1), *n.m.f.* aviator.
aviador, -ra (2), *a.* equipping, providing. — *n.m.* provider; caulking auger; (*Chi.*) mining financier; (*Hisp. Am.*) one who lends money *or* implements to farmers.
aviar (1) [L], *v.t.* to get ready, prepare; to equip, provide; to lend; (*min.*) to enlarge; (*naut.*) to caulk; (*fam.*) ***estar aviado,*** to have had it, be up the creek; ***¡estamos aviados!*** we've had it, we're up the creek, we're done for, we're for it. — **aviárselas,** *v.r.* (*fam.*) to manage, make out, get by.
aviar (2), *a.* appertaining to birds.
aviciar, *v.t.* (*agric.*) to encourage luxuriant growth in; (*prov.*) to manure.
avícola, *a.* appertaining to poultry-farming.
avicultor, -ra, *n.m.f.* aviarist, poultry-farmer.
avicultura, *n.f.* aviculture, poultry-farming.
avidez, *n.f.* greed, covetousness, avidity.
ávido, -da, *a.* greedy, covetous; eager, anxious.
aviejarse, *v.r.* to grow old.
avienta, *n.f.* (*agric.*) winnowing.
aviento (1), *n.m.* pitchfork.
aviento (2), *pres. indic.* [AVENTAR].
avieso, -sa, *a.* irregular, crooked, out of rule; (*fig.*) perverse, vicious, ill-willed.
avigorar, *v.t.* to invigorate, revive.
avilantarse, *v.r.* to become insolent.
avilantez, avilanteza, *n.f.* forwardness, boldness, insolence.
avilés, -lesa, *a., n.m.f.* (native) of Avila.
avillanar, *v.t.* to make boorish, debase.
avinado, -da, *a.* wine-coloured; bibulous.
avinagrado, -da, *a.* vinegary, sour; (*coll.*) harsh-tempered; bitter, crabbed, peevish, morose.
avinagrar, *v.t.* to sour, make acid *or* bitter.
aviñonense, *a., n.m.f.* (native) of Avignon.
avío, *n.m.* preparation, provision; (*prov.*) rations; (*Hisp. Am.*) money advanced; (*pl.*) (*coll.*) equipment, tackle; ***avíos de pescar,*** fishing-tackle; ***hacer su avío,*** to look after one's own interests.
avión, *n.m.* (*orn.*) martin, martlet, swift; (*aer.*) aeroplane, aircraft; ***avión a turbohélice,*** turbo-prop plane; ***avión de caza*** or ***de combate,*** fighter plane; ***avión a*** or ***de chorro, avión de propulsión a chorro, avión a reacción,*** jet aircraft.
avioneta, *n.f.* light aircraft; trainer.
avisado, -da, *a.* cool-headed, level-headed, prudent, wary; ***mal avisado,*** ill-advised, rash.
avisador, -ra, *a.* advising, informing. — *n.m.f.* adviser, admonisher; announcer, informer; messenger.
avisar, *v.t.* to inform, let (*s.o.*) know; to advise; to admonish; ***avíseme con tiempo,*** let me know in good time, give me due warning.
aviso, *n.m.* notice; announcement; advice, warning; prudence, care, attention; (*naut.*) advice-boat, despatch-boat; (*sl.*) pimp, pander; ***andar*** or ***estar sobre aviso,*** to be on one's guard.
avispa, *n.f.* wasp.
avispado, -da, *a.* (*coll.*) smart, quick on the uptake; (*sl.*) suspicious, circumspect.
avispar, *v.t.* to spur; (*coll.*) to stir up, prod; (*Chi., sl.*) to scare, frighten. — **avisparse,** *v.r.* to smarten up one's ideas.
avispedar, *v.t.* (*sl.*) to look at with suspicion *or* carefully.
avispero, *n.m.* wasps' nest; swarm of wasps; (*coll.*) trouble spot; (*med.*) carbuncle.
avispón, *n.m.* hornet; (*sl.*) thief who spies out likely places to rob.
avistar, *v.t.* to catch sight of. — **avistarse,** *v.r.* to have an interview.
avitelado, -da, *a.* parchment-like.

avituallamiento, *n.m.* victualling.
avituallar, *v.t.* (*mil.*) to victual, supply with provisions.
avivado, *n.m.* heightening (*textile colours*); first operation in mirror silvering; pumice rubbing before gilding (*bronze statues*); jewellery's final polish; (*art*) final touch.
avivador, -ra, *a.* enlivening, reviving. — *n.m.f.* enlivener, hastener. — *n.m.* (*carp.*) fluting-plane; rabbet-plane; (*arch.*) ornamental line; (*arch.*) quirk; (*prov.*) perforated paper for raising silkworms.
avivamiento, *n.m.* enlivening, quickness; revival.
avivar, *v.t.* to quicken, enliven, brighten; to hasten; to inflame; to revive, vivify; to heighten (*colours*); (*carp.*) to rabbet; ***avivar el ojo,*** to keep on the alert; ***avivar el paso,*** to hasten one's steps.
avizor, -ra, *a.* watchful; ***estar ojo avizor,*** to keep a sharp look-out, be on the alert. — *n.m.* spy; (*pl.*) (*sl.*) eyes.
avizorador, -ra, *a.* watching, spying. — *n.m.f.* watcher, spy.
avizorar, *v.t.* to watch attentively, spy on.
avocación, *n.f.*, **avocamiento,** *n.m.* (*law*) evocation; (*law*) removing a lawsuit to a higher court.
avocar [A], *v.t.* (*law*) to evoke.
avoceta, *n.f.* (*orn.*) avocet.
avolcanado, -da, *a.* volcanic.
avucasta [AVUTARDA].
avugo, *n.m.* (*bot.*) fruit of ***avuguero,*** very small early pear.
avuguero, *n.m.* (*bot.*) pear tree.
avulsión, *n.f.* (*surg.*) extirpation.
avutarda, *n.f.* (*orn.*) bustard, wild turkey.
avutardado, -da, *a.* bustard-like.
¡ax! *interj.* exclamation of pain; ouch!
axil, *a.* axial; (*zool.*) axillary.
axila, *n.f.* (*bot.*) axilla; (*med.*) armpit.
axilar, *a.* (*bot., zool.*) axillar, axillary.
axinita, *n.f.* (*min.*) axinite.
axioma *n.m.* axiom, maxim.
axiomático, -ca, *a.* axiomatic, axiomatical.
axiómetro, *n.m.* (*naut.*) axiometer.
axis, *n.m. inv.* (*anat.*) axis, second vertebra.
axo, *n.m.* (*Per.*) woollen garment (*worn by Indian women*).
axoideo, -dea, *a.* (*anat.*) axoid, axoidean.
ay, *n.m.* sigh, moan; ***estar en un ay,*** to be in pain. — *interj.* alas! ***¡ay de mí!*** alas, woe is me! ***¡ay de los vencidos!*** woe to the vanquished!
aya, *n.f.* nanny, nurse-maid.
ayacuá, *n.m.* (*Arg.*) small devil (*Indian folklore*).
ayahuasa, *n.f.* (*Ec.*) narcotic plant.
ayate, *n.m.* (*Mex.*) cloth made of maguey fibre.
ayear, *v.i.* to wail, bemoan.
ayecahue, *n.m.* (*Chi.*) nonsense, absurdity.
ayer, *adv.* yesterday; (*fig.*) formerly; lately, not long ago; ***de ayer acá, de ayer a hoy,*** since yesterday, overnight. — *n.m.* the (recent) past, days gone by.
ayermar, *v.t.* to make waste, desert; to demolish, raze.
ayo, *n.m.* manservant.
ayocote, *n.m.* (*Mex.*) kidney bean.
ayocuantoto, *n.m.* (*Mex.*) ayocuantoto bird.
ayote, *n.m.* (*Hisp. Am.*) pumpkin.
ayotera, *n.f.* (*Hisp. Am.*) pumpkin, gourd.
ayúa, *n.f.* (*Hisp. Am.*) ayua tree.
ayuda, *n.f.* help, aid, assistance; comfort; enema; (*naut.*) preventer-rope; ***ayuda de cámara,*** valet; ***ayuda de costa,*** financial help; gratification; ***ayuda de parroquia,*** chapel of ease.
ayudador, -ra, *a.* helping, assisting. — *n.m.f.* assistant, helper; chief shepherd.
ayudanta, *n.f.* female assistant.
ayudante, *a.* helping, assisting. — *n.m.* (*mil.*) adjutant; (*mil.*) aide-de-camp; assistant; assistant lecturer.
ayudantía, *n.f.* adjutancy; office of adjutant.
ayudar, *v.t.* to aid, help, assist; ***ayudar a misa,*** to serve (at) Mass; ***a quien madruga, Dios le ayuda,*** the early bird catches the worm; ***ayúdate, y ayudarte ha,*** God helps those who help themselves.
ayuga, *n.f.* (*bot.*) ground-pine; (*bot.*) summer cypress goose-foot.
ayunador, -ra, ayunante, *a.*, *n.m.f.* (person) who fasts *or* observes fast-days.
ayunar, *v.t.* (*coll.*) ***ayunarle a uno,*** to fear *or* respect someone. — *v.i.* to fast; (*coll.*) ***ayunar después de harto,*** to fast after a good meal; ***harto ayuna quien mal come,*** a bad meal is no better than fasting.
ayuno, -na, *a.* fasting; (*fig.*) ignorant. — *n.m.* fast, abstinence; (*coll.*) ***quedarse en ayunas,*** not to understand, to be none the wiser.
ayunque [YUNQUE].
ayuntador, -ra, *a.* uniting, joining. — *n.m.f.* one who unites.
ayuntamiento, *n.m.* union, joint; corporation *or* body of magistrates (*in cities* or *towns*); town-council; municipal government; (***casa de***) ***ayuntamiento,*** town-hall, guild-hall; ***ayuntamiento sexual,*** sexual intercourse, copulation.
ayuso, *adv.* (*obs.*) below.
ayustar, *v.t.* (*naut.*) to splice.
ayuste, *n.m.* (*naut.*) splice, splicing; scarf, scarfing.
azabachado, -da, *a.* jet-black.
azabache, *n.m.* (*min.*) jet; (*orn.*) titmouse; (*pl.*) trinkets of jet.
azabara, *n.f.* (*bot.*) common aloe.
azacán, -cana, *a.* toiling, labouring. — *n.m.* water-carrier; labourer; (*coll.*) ***andar*** or ***estar hecho un azacán,*** to toil, labour, be worked to death.
azacaya, *n.f.* (*prov.*) conduit, water-pipe.
azache, *a.* silk (*of an inferior quality*).
azada, *n.f.* (*agric.*) spade, hoe.
azadada, *n.f.*, **azadazo,** *n.m.* blow with a spade *or* hoe.
azadilla, *n.f.* gardener's hoe.
azadón, *n.m.* mattock, hoe; ***azadón de peto*** or ***de pico,*** pickaxe.
azadonada, *n.f.* blow with pickaxe *or* hoe; (*coll.*) ***a la primera azadonada,*** lucky first stroke; at first sight; at once.
azadonar, *v.t.* to dig with a spade, hoe *or* pickaxe.
azadonazo, *n.m.* stroke with a mattock.
azadonero, *n.m.* digger.
azafata, *n.f.* lady of the queen's wardrobe; air-hostess.
azafate, *n.m.* low, flat-bottomed basket *or* tray.
azafatero, *n.m.* tray maker *or* seller.
azafrán, *n.m.* saffron; (*bot.*) saffron, crocus; (*paint.*) saffron colour; ***azafrán bastardo, romí*** or ***romín,*** safflower, bastard saffron; (*chem.*) ***azafrán de Marte,*** iron rust; ***azafrán del timón,*** after-piece of the rudder.
azafranado, -da, *a.* saffron-coloured; saffrony.
azafranal, *n.m.* plantation of saffron.
azafranamiento, *n.m.* saffron-dyeing.
azafranar, *v.t.* to tinge, mix *or* dye with saffron.
azafranero, -ra, *n.m.f.* dealer in saffron.
azafranina, *n.f.* (*chem.*) safranin.
azagadero, azagador, *n.m.* path *or* pass for cattle.
azagaya, *n.f.* javelin, spear.
azagayada, *n.f.* cast of a javelin.
azagor, *n.m.* verdigris.
azahar, *n.m.* orange, lemon *or* citron flower; orange blossom; ***agua de azahar,*** orange-flower water.
azainado, -da, *a.* (*prov.*) perfidious, treacherous.

azainador, -ra, *a.* (*prov.*) treacherous. — *n.m.* (*prov.*) traitor. — *n.f.* traitress.
azainamiento, *n.m.* (*prov.*) perfidy, treachery.
azainar, *v.t.* (*prov.*) to make treacherous. — **azainarse,** *v.r.* (*prov.*) to turn traitor.
azalá, *n.m.* Mohammedan prayer.
azalea, *n.f.* (*bot.*) azalea.
azamboa, *n.f.* fruit of citron tree.
azamboero, azamboo, *n.m.* (*bot.*) citron tree.
azanahoriate, azanoriate, *n.m.* preserved carrot; (*coll.*) flattery.
azanca, *n.f.* (*min.*) subterranean spring.
azandar, *n.m.* (*bot., prov.*) sandalwood.
azanoria [ZANAHORIA].
azaque, *n.m.* tax paid by Moslems.
azar, *n.m.* chance, hazard; accident, misfortune; unlucky card *or* throw at dice; destiny; ***al azar,*** at random; on the off-chance.
azarandar [ZARANDAR].
azararse, *v.r.* to get flustered, get into a dither.
azarbe, *n.m.* irrigation trench *or* drain.
azarbeta, *n.f.* small irrigation trench.
azarcón, *n.m.* red oxide of lead; (*paint.*) vermilion; bright orange colour; (*prov.*) earthen pot.
azarja, *n.f.* instrument for winding raw silk.
azarolla, *n.f.* (*bot.*) haw; (*prov.*) fruit of the true service-tree.
azarollo, *n.m.* (*bot., prov.*) true service-tree.
azaroso, -sa, *a.* chequered, eventful, difficult; risky, hazardous, dangerous.
azaúcho, *n.m.* (*bot.*) wild fig.
azaya, *n.f.* (*bot., prov.*) spike, French lavender.
azcón, *n.m.*, **azcona,** *n.f.* dart, javelin.
azemar, *v.t.* to fit; to smooth.
azenoria [ZANAHORIA].
azi, *n.m.* curd of milk and vinegar used for cheese-making.
azímico, -ca, *a.* opposed to fermentation.
ázimo, -ma, *a.* azymous, unleavened.
azimut, *n.m.* (*astron.*) azimuth.
azimutal, *a.* azimuthal.
aznacho, *n.m.* (*bot.*) Scotch fir; rest-harrow.
aznallo [AZNACHO].
azoado, -da, *a.* nitrogenous.
azoar, *v.t.* (*chem.*) to azotize.
azoato, *n.m.* (*chem.*) nitrate.
azocar [A], *v.t.* (*naut.*) to tighten; (*Cub.*) to over-tighten.
ázoe, *n.m.* (*chem.*) nitrogen.
azofaifa, *n.f.* (*bot.*) jujube berry.
azofaifo, *n.m.* (*bot.*) jujube-tree.
azófar, *n.m.* latten, brass.
azofra, *n.f.* personal assistance; (*prov.*) ridgeband (*of harness*).
azofrar, *v.i.* (*prov.*) to assist personally.
azogado, -da, *a.* (*coll.*) quivering, trembling; restless, fidgety.
azogamiento, *n.m.* quicksilvering; (*coll.*) shaking, agitation.
azogar [B], *v.t.* to quicksilver; to slake (*lime*). — **azogarse,** *v.r.* to become salivated; to be affected by mercury vapours; (*coll.*) to become agitated, perturbed.
azogue (1), *n.m.* (*min.*) mercury, quicksilver; ship carrying quicksilver (to Spanish America); ***ser un azogue, tener azogue en las venas,*** to be restless *or* fidgety.
azogue (2), *n.m.* market-place.
azoguejo, *n.m.* small market-place.
azoguería, *n.f.* (*min.*) amalgamating works.
azoguero, *n.m.* (*min.*) amalgamator.
azoico, -ca, *a.* (*geol.*) azoic; (*chem.*) nitric.
azolar [4], *v.t.* (*carp.*) to adze.
azolvar, *v.t.* to obstruct (*water-conduits*). — **azolvarse,** *v.r.* to become obstructed, choked.
azolve, *n.m.* (*Mex.*) sludge obstructing a water-conduit.
azor, *n.m.* (*orn.*) goshawk; (*sl.*) thief.
azoramiento, *n.m.* fluster, dither.
azorar, *v.t.* to fluster, throw into a dither. — **azorarse,** *v.r.* to get flustered, get into a dither.
azorero, *n.m.* (*slang*) accomplice of a thief; receiver of stolen goods, fence.
Azores, *n.f.pl.* ***las —,*** the Azores.
azorrado, -da, *a.* fox-like; (*naut.*) water-logged.
azorramiento, *n.m.* heaviness of the head, drowsiness.
azorrarse, *v.r.* to become drowsy from heaviness; (*naut.*) to pitch through being water-logged.
azotable, *a.* deserving a whipping.
azotacalles, *n.m.f. inv.* (*coll.*) street-lounger, idler.
azotado, -da, *a.* variegated (*flowers*). — *n.m.* publicly whipped criminal; (*obs.*) flagellant, one who lashes himself for mortification. — *n.f.* severe whipping *or* spanking.
azotador, -ra, *a.* whipping. — *n.m.f.* whipper.
azotaina, azotina, *n.f.* (*coll.*) beating, flogging.
azotalengua, *n.f.* (*bot., prov.*) goose-grass.
azotamiento, *n.m.* whipping.
azotaperros, *n.m. inv.* church beadle appointed to enforce silence and throw out dogs.
azotar, *v.t.* to whip, lash, scourge; to flail; to beat down; to afflict, punish; ***azotar las calles,*** to lounge about the streets; ***azotar el aire,*** to act to no purpose.
azotazo, *n.m.* severe lash.
azote, *n.m.* whip, lash; spank; (*fig.*) calamity, affliction; (*fig.*) scourge (person); (*pl.*) (*obs.*) public whipping; ***besar el azote,*** to kiss the rod, resign oneself to punishment; ***no salir de azotes y galeras,*** never to prosper; ***azotes y galeras,*** dull fare.
azotea, *n.f.* flat roof.
azótico, -ca, *a.* (*chem.*) azotic.
azozobrar, *v.t.* to fill with anguish; to worry unduly.
azre, *n.m.* (*bot.*) maple-tree.
azteca, *a., n.m.f.* Aztec. — *n.m.* Aztec language.
azúcar, *n.m.f.* sugar; ***azúcar blanco (-ca), de flor, de florete*** or ***refino (-na),*** white sugar, first quality refined sugar; ***azúcar cande, candi*** or ***piedra,*** rock candy; ***azúcar extrafino,*** castor sugar, (*Am.*) powdered sugar; (*chem.*) ***azúcar de leche,*** milk-sugar; ***azúcar de lustre,*** castor sugar; ***azúcar de pilón,*** loaf-sugar; (*chem.*) ***azúcar de plomo,*** sugar of lead; ***azúcar de redoma,*** crystallized sugar in syrup-jars; (*chem.*) ***azúcar de Saturno,*** sal Saturni; ***azúcar mascabado (-da), quebrado (-da)*** or ***muscovado (-da),*** unclarified sugar; ***azúcar moreno (-na), negro (-ra)*** or ***terciado (-da),*** brown sugar; ***azúcar en terrón,*** lump-sugar; ***azúcar en polvo,*** granulated *or* castor sugar; ***azúcar y canela,*** sorrel-grey (*horse*); ***azúcar rosado (-da),*** rose-coloured candy-floss.
azucarado, -da, *a.* (*coll.*) sugary, honeyed; (*pej.*) smarmy.
azucarar, *v.t.* to sugar, sweeten; to ice *or* coat with sugar; (*fig.*) to sugar over.
azucarero, -ra, *a.* relating to sugar. — *n.m.* foreman in sugar factory; (*orn.*) honey-creeper. — *n.m.f.* sugar-basin, sugar-bowl.
azucarí, *a.* (*prov.*) sugary, sweet (*fruits*).
azucarillo, *n.m.* (hard) candy floss; (*theat.*) cut in orchestral piece; (*mil., sl.*) shoe.
azucena, *n.f.* (*bot.*) white lily.
azucenal, *n.m.* white lily nursery.
azuche, *n.m.* (*engin.*) pile ferrule.
azud, *n.m.* **azuda,** *n.f.* dam (*with a sluice* or *flood-gate*); waterwheel.
azuela, *n.f.* adze; ***azuela de construcción,*** shipwright's adze; ***azuela curva,*** hollow adze.

azufaifa, azufeifa, *n.f.* (*bot.*) jujube berry.
azufaifo, azufeifo, *n.m.* (*bot.*) jujube tree.
azufrado, -da, *a.* sulphureous; sulphuretted; sulphury.
azufrador, *n.m.* sulphurator, machine for drying and bleaching linen; instrument for sulphuring vines.
azufral, *n.m.*, **azufrera,** *n.f.* sulphur mine.
azuframiento, *n.m.* sulphuration; sulphurization.
azufrar, *v.t.* to sulphurate; to sulphurize.
azufre, *n.m.* sulphur.
azufrín, *n.m.* sulphurous wick *or* candle.
azufrón, *n.m.* (*min.*) powder pyrites.
azufroso, -sa, *a.* sulphureous.
azul, *a.* blue. — *n.m.* blue; ***azul celeste,*** sky blue, light blue; ***azul marino,*** navy blue; ***azul oscuro,*** dark blue; ***azul de Prusia,*** Prussian blue; ***azul turquí,*** indigo.
azulado, -da, *a.* blue, bluish.
azulador, -ra, *a.*, *n.m.f.* (one) who *or* (that) which dyes blue.
azulamiento, *n.m.* (act of) dyeing blue.
azulaque, *n.m.* (*hydrost.*) packing stuff; (*naut.*) stuff for caulking bottom of ship.
azular, *v.t.* to dye *or* colour blue.
azulear, *v.i.* to have a bluish shade; to show blue.
azulejado, -da, *a.* tiled.
azulejar, *v.t.* to tile.
azulejería, *n.f.* tile-works; tiling.
azulejero, *n.m.* tiler.
azulejo (1), *n.m.* glazed tile.
azulejo (2), *n.m.* (*bot.*) cornflower; (*orn.*) bee-eater.
azulete, *n.m.* slight tinge of blue given to linen to make it look white, blueing.
azulino, -na, *a.* bluish.
azuloso, -sa, *a.* blue, bluish.
azumar, *v.t.* to dye (*hair*).
azumbar, *n.m.* (*bot.*) star-headed water-plantain; spikenard; storax-tree gum.
azumbrado, -da, *a.* measured by ***azumbres***; (*coll.*) sozzled.
azumbre, *n.f.* liquid measure of four pints.
azuquero, *n.m.* (*prov.*) sugar-basin.
azur, *a.*, *n.m.* (*her.*) azure.
azurita, *n.f.* (*min.*) azurite.
azut, (*prov.*) [AZUD].
azutero, *n.m.* (*prov.*) sluice-master.
azuzador, -ra, *a.* inciting, instigating. — *n.m.f.* instigator.
azuzar [C], *v.t.* to halloo; to set dogs on to; (*fig.*) to incite; to egg *or* urge on, stir up.
azuzón, -zona, *n.m.f.* instigator.

B

B, b, *n.f.* letter B, b; pronounced as a plosive (similarly to English ***b***) after a pause and after a nasal consonant; pronounced as a bi-labial fricative (a sound with no exact correspondence in English; rather softer than the English ***b***, it is produced by joining the lips without pressure) in all other positions; ***saber algo b por b*** or ***b por c*** or ***c por b,*** to know something in all its details.

baba, *n.f.* drivel, spittle; ***se le cae la baba,*** he raves about it; he is rather silly.

bababuí, *n.m.* (*Hisp. Am.*) mocking bird.

babada [BABILLA].

babadero, babador [BABERO].

babaza, *n.f.* slime; slug.

babazorro, -rra, *a.* (*prov.*) uncouth, rustic. — *n.m.* (*coll., prov.*) clown, ill-bred man.

babear, *v.i.* to dribble, slaver.

Babel, *n.m.f.* Babel; (*coll.*) bedlam; confusion, disorder.

babeo, *n.m.* drivelling, slavering.

babera, *n.f.* beaver (*of a helmet*); bib.

babero, *n.m.* bib, chin-cloth.

baberol, *n.m.* beaver (*of a helmet*).

Babia, *n.f.* area of Leon; (*coll.*) ***estar en Babia,*** to be in the clouds; to daydream.

babieca, *a., n.m.f.* ignorant, stupid (person); idiot.

Babilonia, *n.f.* Babylon(ia); (*coll.*) bedlam.

babilónico, -ca, *a.* Babylonian; gigantic, magnificent; (*coll.*) noisy.

babilonio, -nia, *a., n.m.f.* Babylonian.

babilla, *n.f.* thin skin (*about the flanks of cattle*).

babirusa, *n.m.* (*zool.*) babiroussa.

bable, *n.m.* Asturian dialect.

babón, -bona, *a.* [BABOSO].

babor, *n.m.* (*naut.*) port, larboard; ***a babor todo,*** hard a-port; ***de babor a estribor,*** athwart ship.

babosa (1), *n.f.* slug; (*prov.*) young onion; (*sl.*) silk; (*agric.*) vine which produces malmsey wine.

babosear, *v.t., v.i.* to dribble; to slobber *or* drool (over).

baboseo, *n.m.* dribbling, slavering; (*coll.*) cloying sentimentality, schmaltz.

babosillo, -lla, babosuelo, -la, *a.* rather dribbly; (*coll.*) drooling; half daft.

baboso, -sa (2), *a.* drivelling, slavering; (*coll.*) sickeningly sentimental; daft. — *n.m.f.* driveller, slaverer.

babucha, *n.f.* heelless slipper, mule.

babuino, *n.m.* (*zool.*) baboon; (*med.*) pustule on lips; (*fig.*) grotesque figure; dwarf; idiot; coward.

baca (1), *n.f.* luggage rack (*of a vehicle*).

baca (2), *n.f.* (*bot.*) berry; (*orn.*) African falcon *or* eagle.

bacalada, *n.f.* whole dried codfish.

bacaladero, -ra, *a.* cod-fish(ing). — *n.m.* cod-fishery; cod-fishing vessel.

bacalao, bacallao, *n.m.* codfish; dried cod; (*coll.*) skinny object, bag of bones; (*coll.*) ***cortar el bacalao,*** to be boss, rule the roost, run the show.

bacallar, *n.m.* rustic, yokel.

bacanal, *a.* bacchanalian. — *n.f.* (*fig.*) orgy; (*pl.*) bacchanalia.

bacante, *n.f.* bacchante; (*pl.*) Bacchae.

bácara, *n.f.,* **bácaris,** *n.f. inv.* (*bot.*) common clary.

bacará, bacarrat, *n.m.* baccarat.

bacelar, *n.m.* arbour with grape-vines.

bacera, *n.f.* (*vet.*) swelling of the belly.

baceta, *n.f.* (*obs.*) basset; stock (*card-games*).

bacía, *n.f.* metal basin; shaving-dish; barber's basin; wash-pot.

bacífero, -ra, *a.* (*bot.*) bacciferous, berry-bearing.

baciforme, *a.* (*bot.*) bacciform, berry-shaped.

báciga, *n.f.* a game played with three cards.

bacilar, *a.* (*biol.*) bacillary; (*min.*) of coarse fibre.

baciliforme, *a.* bacilliform.

bacilo, *n.m.* bacillus, bacterium.

bacillar, *n.m.* new vineyard.

bacín, *n.m.* chamber-pot; poor-box; (*coll.*) despicable object.

bacina, *n.f.* (*prov.*) poor-box.

bacinada, *n.f.* filth, slops; (*coll.*) despicable action.

bacinero, -ra, *n.m.f.* collector of oblations in church.

bacineta, *n.f.* small bowl; offertory box; pan (*of gun-lock*).

bacinete, *n.m.* basnet, bacinet, basinet; (*anat.*) pelvis.

bacinica, bacinilla, *n.f.* small chamber-pot; small poor-box.

bacívoro, -ra, *a.* (*zool.*) baccivorous, berry-eating.

Baco, *n.m.* (*myth.*) Bacchus; (*fig.*) wine.

baconiano, -na, *a.* Baconian.

bacteria, *n.f.* bacterium.

bacteriología, *n.f.* bacteriology.

bacteriológico, -ca, *a.* bacteriological.

bacteriólogo, -ga, *n.m.f.* bacteriologist.

bactris, *n.m. inv.* (*bot.*) South American palm.

báculo, *n.m.* walking-stick, staff; (*fig.*) support, relief, comfort, aid; ***báculo pastoral,*** bishop's crozier; ***José es el báculo de mi vejez,*** Joseph is the comfort of my old age.

bache, *n.m.* pot-hole; air-pocket; sweating place (*for sheep before shearing*); ***estar en un bache,*** to be low in spirits; to have struck a thin patch.

bachear, *v.t.* to fill holes in (*a road*).

bachiller (1), *n.m.f.* holder of a degree *or* matriculation certificate.

bachiller (2), **-ra,** *a.* garrulous, loquacious.

bachilleramiento, *n.m.* conferring *or* obtaining the degree of bachelor.

bachillerar, *v.t.* to confer the degree of bachelor on. — **bachillerarse,** *v.r.* to graduate as bachelor.

bachillerato, *n.m.* baccalaureate, senior school certificate.

bachillerear, *v.i.* (*coll.*) to prattle, babble.

bachillería, *n.f.* (*coll.*) prattle, babble.

bada, *n.f.* rhinoceros.

badajada, *n.f.* stroke of the clapper (*bell*); (*coll.*) idle talk.

badajear, *v.i.* (*coll.*) to chatter.

badajo, *n.m.* clapper (*of a bell*); (*coll.*) idle talker.

badajocense, *a., n.m.f.* (native) of Badajoz.

badal, *n.m.* (*prov.*) shoulder and ribs of butcher's meat.

badallar, *v.i.* (*prov.*) to yawn.

badán, *n.m.* trunk (*of a body*).

badana, *n.f.* dressed sheep-skin, basil; (*coll.*) ***zurrarle a alguien la badana,*** to tan s.o.'s hide; to give s.o. a dressing-down.

badano, *n.m.* (*carp.*) chisel.

badaza, *n.f.* cord for lacing bonnets to sails.

badea, *n.f.* (*bot.*) bad melon *or* water-melon; insipid yellowish cucumber; (*coll.*) dull, insipid fellow; (*coll.*) insubstantial thing.

badén, *n.m.* channel made by rain-water; catch-drain; (*pl.* **badenes**) bumpy road, uneven surface.

baderna, *n.f.* (*naut.*) thrummed cable.

badián, *n.m.,* **badiana,** *n.f.* (*bot.*) Indian anise; aniseed.

badil, -la, *n.m.f.* fire-shovel; ***dar con la badila en los nudillos,*** to rap over the knuckles.

badilazo, *n.m.* blow with a fire-shovel.

badina, *n.f.* (*prov.*) puddle.

badomía, *n.f.* nonsense, absurdity.

badulaque, *n.m.* (*obs.*) cosmetic; (*obs.*) ragout of stewed livers; (*coll.*) unreliable fellow.

bafea, *n.f.* waste, rubbish, filth.
bafear, *v.i.* (*prov.*) to emit fumes *or* vapour.
bafetas, *n.f.pl.* (*com.*) white cotton cloth, indiana.
baffle, *n.m.* (*rad.*) baffle.
baga, *n.f.* (*prov.*) rope to tie burdens on the backs of beasts; little head of flax; (*Cub.*, *bot.*) baga tree.
bagacera, *n.f.* (*Cub.*) place in sugar-mills where the bagasse is dried in the sun.
bagaje, *n.m.* (*mil.*) baggage; beast of burden; ***bagaje mayor,*** horse, mule; ***bagaje menor,*** donkey; ***bagaje cultural,*** stock of culture.
bagajero, *n.m.* driver of military baggage transport.
bagar [B], *v.i.* to yield the seed (*flax*).
bagarino, *n.m.* volunteer *or* paid oarsman.
bagasa, *n.f.* prostitute, harlot.
bagatela, *n.f.* bagatelle, trifle; (*Chi.*) bagatelle billiard table *or* game.
bagazo, *n.m.* bagasse; oil-cake; husk (*flax*); pressed pulp.
bago, *n.m.* (*prov.*) district, country area.
bagre, *a.* (*Hisp. Am.*) gaudy, showy; coarse, crude. — *n.m.* (*Hisp. Am.*) catfish.
bagual, *a.* (*Hisp. Am.*) wild; brutish.
baguarí, *n.m.* (*Hisp. Am.*) crane.
¡bah! *interj.* bah!
baharí, *n.m.* (*orn.*) sparrow-hawk.
bahía, *n.f.* bay.
bahorrina, *n.f.* (*coll.*) slops; collection of filthy things; (*coll.*) rabble.
bahuno, -na [BAJUNO].
baila, *n.f.* (*ichth.*) hog-fish.
bailable, *a.* for dancing; ***música bailable,*** dance music. — *n.m.* dance number *or* tune; dance turn.
bailadero, *n.m.* public dancing-place.
baila(d)or, -ra, *n.m.f.* Flamenco dancer.
bailar, *v.i.* to dance; to spin; to wobble, be unsteady; (*fig.*) ***bailarle a uno el agua,*** to humour s.o., keep s.o. happy; (*fig.*) ***bailar uno al son que le tocan,*** to do as one is told, toe the line.
bailarín, -rina, *a.* dancing. — *n.m.f.* ballet dancer.
baile (1), *n.m.* dance; dancing; ball; (*sl.*) thief; ***baile de disfraces, máscaras*** or ***trajes,*** fancy-dress ball, masquerade; ***baile de cuenta*** or ***de figuras,*** figure *or* square dance; (*med.*) ***baile de San Vito,*** chorea, St. Vitus's dance; ***baile de etiqueta,*** formal dance; ***siga el baile,*** on with the motley.
baile (2), *n.m.* (*Andorra*, *prov.*) bailiff.
bailía, *n.f.*, **bailiazgo,** *n.m.* bailiwick.
bailiaje, *n.m.* commandery of a Military Order.
bailío, *n.m.* knight commander of a Military Order.
bailotear, *v.i.* (*coll.*) to dance around, jive (around).
bailoteo, *n.m.* dancing about, jigging (about).
baivel, *n.m.* square bevel (*used by stone-masons*).
bajá, *n.m.* (*pl.* **bajaes**) pasha.
baja (1), *n.f.* fall in price; [ALEMANDA]; casualty; vacancy; (*com.*) ***jugar a la baja,*** to speculate on a fall; ***dar de baja,*** to discharge (*from hospital*); to drop, cross off (*from a list, membership etc.*); ***darse de baja,*** to drop out, withdraw, quit; (*mil.*) ***ser baja,*** to cease belonging to a corps; ***estar en baja,*** to be on the decline *or* wane; to droop; to fail, diminish.
bajada, *n.f.* descent, incline, slope; inclination (*of an arch*); ***bajada de agua,*** rain-water pipe.
bajadizo, -za, *a.* descending, sloping gently.
bajalato, *n.m.* office *or* territory of a pasha.
bajamanero, *n.m.* (*sl.*) pickpocket.
bajamano, *adv.* (*sl.*) under the arm. — *n.m.* (*sl.*) shoplifter.
bajamar, *n.f.* low water, low tide; ebb tide.
bajar, *v.t.* to lower, let down; to bring *or* take down; ***bajar el punto,*** to temper; ***bajarle a uno los humos,*** to knock s.o. down a peg or two; ***bajar los ojos,*** to cast one's eyes down; to be ashamed; ***bajar la cabeza,*** to bow one's head; to humble oneself; ***bajar la voz,*** to speak softly; ***bajar las orejas,*** to humble oneself; to yield. — *v.i.* to go *or* come down, fall. — **bajarse,** *v.r.* to stoop; to dismount, get down.
bajaraque, *n.m.* (*Cub.*) wretched hut, hovel *or* cabin; (*Guat.*, *Hond.*) lath-and-mud for walls.
bajel, *n.m.* (*naut.*) vessel.
bajelero, *n.m.* owner *or* master of a vessel.
bajero, -ra, *a.* (*prov.*) lower, under.
bajete, *a.* shortish. — *n.m.* shortish person; (*mus.*) baritone; counterpoint exercise.
bajeza, *n.f.* base act *or* behaviour; (*fig.*) lowliness, lowness.
bajial, *n.m.* (*Per.*) marsh.
bajillo, *n.m.* (*prov.*) stand-cask for wine.
bajío, *n.m.* shoal, sand-bank, flat; (*Hisp. Am.*) lowland; (*fig.*) ***dar en un bajío,*** to run into trouble.
bajista, *n.m.* (*com.*) bear (*stocks*).
bajito, -ta, *a.* shortish, rather low. — *adv.* softly, quietly (*voice*).
bajo, -ja (2), *a.* short, low; ***bajo de ley,*** debased, alloyed; ***bajo de color,*** faint; ***Los Países Bajos,*** the Low Countries; ***con los ojos bajos,*** with downcast eyes; ***sentimientos bajos,*** base feellings; ***hablar bajo*** or ***en voz baja,*** to speak in a low voice; ***por lo bajo,*** secretly; softly. — *adv.* (be)low. — *n.m.* deep place; shoal, sand-bank; (*mus.*) bass; ***bajo de arena,*** sand-bank; ***bajo relieve,*** bas-relief. — *prep.* under, beneath; ***bajo mano,*** secretly; ***bajo condición,*** conditionally; ***bajo pena de muerte,*** on pain of death; ***bajo palabra de caballero,*** on the word of a gentleman; ***bajo techado,*** indoors; ***bajo tutela,*** under the care of a guardian.
bajoca, *n.f.* (*prov.*, *bot.*) French bean; (*prov.*) dead silkworm.
bajocar, *n.m.* (*prov.*) plot of French beans.
bajón, *n.m.* (*mus.*) bassoon; bassoon-player; (*coll.*) decline (*in health, fortune etc.*); ***dar*** or ***pegar un bajón,*** to go downhill, go off.
bajonazo, *n.m.* blow with a bassoon; ghastly din made by bassoon; (*tauro.*) low thrust with the sword.
bajoncillo, *n.m.* fagottino, descant bassoon.
bajonista, *n.m.* bassoon-player.
bajuelo, -la, *a.* lowish, shortish.
bajuno, -na, *a.* base, low, vile.
bajura, *n.f.* lowness, shortness; shallow water; ***pesca de bajura,*** shallow-water *or* inshore fishing.
bala, *n.f.* ball, bullet, shot; sweetmeat; bale; wax ball filled with water *or* perfume used in carnival; printer's inking-roller; paper packet of ten reams; ***bala de cadena*** or ***encadenada,*** chain-shot; ***bala enramada,*** bar-shot; ***bala fría,*** spent bullet; ***bala perdida,*** stray bullet; ***bala roja,*** red-hot incendiary ball; (*adv. phrase*) ***como una bala,*** like a shot; (*coll.*) ***es un(a) bala (perdida),*** he's a chap who has got off the tracks *or* gone off the rails, *or* taken a wrong turn.
balada, *n.f.* ballad, song; (*sl.*) arrangement, agreement.
baladí, *a.* trivial, minor, unimportant.
balador, -ra, *a.* bleating.
baladrar, *v.i.* to scream, screech, whoop.
baladre, *n.m.* (*bot.*) rose-bay.
baladrero, -ra, *a.* screaming, screeching, whooping.
baladro, *n.m.* scream, screech, whoop.
baladrón, -rona, *n.m.f.* boaster, bragger.
baladronada, *n.f.* piece of boasting, brag(ging), bravado.
baladronar, baladronear, *v.i.* to boast, brag.
bálago, *n.m.* grain chaff *or* straw; heap of chaff; soap bubbles *or* suds.
balagre, *n.m.* (*Hond.*, *bot.*) rush.
balaguero, *n.m.* rick of straw.

balaj, balaje, *n.m.* balas, spinel ruby.
balance, *n.m.* oscillation, swinging; (*fencing*) poise, equilibrium; (*naut.*) rolling, rocking; dance step *or* setting; (*fig.*) vacillation, fluctuation; (*com.*) balance, balancing, balance-sheet; (*Hisp. Am.*) rocking-chair; (*fig.*) toll; ***el triste balance fueron diez muertos,*** the tragic toll was ten dead (*e.g. of an accident*).
balancear, *v.t.* to balance; to poise. — **balancear(se),** *v.i.* (*v.r.*) (*naut., aer.*) to roll, rock; to swing; (*fig.*) to waver.
balanceo, *n.m.* balancing; oscillation; rocking, rolling; swinging.
balancero, *n.m.* weigh-master (*in a mint*).
balancín, *n.m.* splinter-bar, futchel, whipple-tree, swingle-tree, whiffle-tree; (*mech.*) cross-beam, balance-beam; minting-mill; (*zool.*) balancer, rope-walker's balancing pole; seesaw; (*pl.* **balancines**) (*naut.*) yard-lifts.
balandra, *n.f.* (*naut.*) sloop.
balandrán, *n.m.* cassock.
balandro, *n.m.* (*naut.*) small sloop; yacht; (*Cub.*) fishing smack.
bálano, balano, *n.m.* (*anat.*) end of penis; (*ichth.*) acorn-barnacle.
balante, *a.* bleating.
Balanza, *n.f.* (*astron., astrol.*) Libra, (the) Balance.
balanza, *n.f.* scales; balance; judgment; ***balanza de comercio,*** balance of trade; ***en balanza, en balanzas,*** doubtful, in danger; (*fig.*) ***poner en balanza,*** to raise doubts about.
balanzario, *n.m.* balancer, weigh-master (*in a mint*).
balanzón, *n.m.* cleaning-pan (*used by jewellers, platers etc.*).
balar, *v.i.* to bleat; (*coll.*) ***balar por,*** to crave.
balastaje, *n.m.* ballasting (*road*).
balastar, *v.t.* to ballast (*road*).
balaste, balasto, *n.m.* (*railw.*) ballast, layer of gravel.
balastera, *n.f.* (*railw.*) quarry of stone *or* gravel used for ballasting.
balate, *n.m.* terrace margin; sloping terrace; border of a trench; (*zool.*) sea-slug.
balausta, balaustra, *n.f.* (*bot.*) variety of pomegranate.
balaustrado, -da, *a.* balustered. — *n.f.* balustrade.
balaustral, *a.* balustered.
balaustre, balaústre, *n.m.* baluster.
balay, *n.m.* (*Hisp. Am.*) wicker basket; (*Cub.*) wooden plate for winnowing rice.
balazo, *n.m.* shot, gunshot; bullet wound; ***acribillado a balazos,*** bullet-riddled.
balboa, *n.m.* (*Panama*) gold coin.
balbucear, *v.i.* to stutter, stammer.
balbuceo, *n.m.* stammer(ing), stutter(ing).
balbuciente, *a.* stammering, stuttering.
balbucir [Q] [BALBUCEAR].
balbusardo, *n.m.* (*orn.*) osprey, sea-eagle.
Balcanes, *n.m.pl.* (the) Balkans.
balcánico, -ca, *a.* Balkan.
balcarrotas, *n.f.pl.* (*Mex.*) plaited hair style adopted by the Indians.
balcón, *n.m.* balcony.
balconaje, *n.m.,* **balconería,** *n.f.* range of balconies, balcony work.
balconcillo, *n.m.* small balcony.
balda (1), *n.f.* shelf; trifle.
baldadura, *n.f., n.m.* crippled state; (*coll.*) state of being worn out.
baldamiento, *n.m.* [BALDADURA].
baldanza, *adv. phrase.* ***de baldanza,*** wandering.
baldaquín, baldaquino, *n.m.* canopy, baldachin.
baldar, *v.t.* to cripple; to trump; (*coll.*) ***estar baldado,*** to be worn out.
balde (1), *adv.* (***de***) ***balde,*** gratis, free of charge; ***en balde,*** in vain; ***estar de balde,*** not to be wanted; to be lazy *or* unoccupied.
balde (2), *n.m.* bucket.
baldear, *v.t.* (*naut.*) to swab (*decks*); to clean; to bail.
baldeo, *n.m.* washing down, swabbing (*decks*).
baldés, *n.m.* soft dressed skin (*for gloves etc.*).
baldío, -día, *a.* untilled, uncultivated; useless, vain; idle, lazy; vagabond. — *n.m.* waste land.
baldo, -da (2), *a.* having to renounce (*cards*). — *n.m.* renounce (*cards*).
baldón, *n.m.* affront; blot, disgrace.
baldonar, baldonear, *v.t.* to affront, insult; to disgrace.
baldosa, *n.f.* floor tile, paving tile.
baldosado, *n.m.* tiled floor, paved flooring, tile paving.
baldosar, *v.t.* to tile, flag.
baldosín, *n.m.* small tile.
baldosón, *n.m.* large tile *or* flagstone.
baldragas, *n.m. inv.* weak-kneed individual.
Balduino, *n.m.* Baldwin.
balduque, *n.m.* narrow red tape.
balear (1), *v.t.* (*prov.*) [ABALEAR]; (*Hisp. Am.*) to fire *or* shoot at, to wound *or* kill with bullets.
balear (2), **baleárico, -ca, baleario, -ria,** *a., n.m.f.* Balearic.
Baleares, *n.f.pl.* ***las*** (***Islas***) —, Balearic Islands.
baleo, *n.m.* rug, mat; (*prov.*) esparto scoop *or* fan.
balería, *n.f.,* **balerío,** *n.m.* (*artill.*) pile of balls *or* shot.
balero, *n.m.* bullet-mould; (*Mex.*) cup-and-ball (*toy*).
baleta, *n.f.* small bale of goods.
balhurria, *n.f.* (*slang*) rabble.
balido, *n.m.* bleat, bleating.
balín, *n.m.* small-bore bullet.
balista, *n.f.* ballista.
balístico, -ca, *a.* ballistic.
balitadera, *n.f.* deer call.
balitar, *v.i.* to bleat frequently.
baliza, *n.f.* (*naut.*) buoy.
balizamiento [ABALIZAMIENTO].
balneario, -ria, *a.* pertaining to baths. — *n.m.* watering-place, spa.
balompié, *n.m.* (*obs.*) football, soccer.
balón, *n.m.* (large) ball; football; (large) bale; balloon; ***balón de oxígeno,*** oxygen balloon.
baloncesto, *n.m.* basket-ball.
balota, *n.f.* ballot; small voting ball.
balotada, *n.f.* leap (*horse*).
balotar, *v.i.* to ballot.
balsa (1), *n.f.* pool, pond; (*prov.*) half a butt of wine; (***tranquilo***) ***como una balsa de aceite,*** as calm as a mill-pond; (*prov.*) ***balsa de sangre,*** pond from which water is drawn with difficulty.
balsa (2), *n.f.* (*naut.*) raft, float; balsa, balsa-wood.
balsadera, *n.f.,* **balsadero,** *n.m.* ferry.
balsamera, *n.f.* flask for balsam.
balsamerita, *n.f.* small flask for balsam.
balsámico, -ca, *a.* balsamic, balmy.
balsamina, *n.f.* balsam-apple, balsamine.
balsamita, *n.f.* (*bot.*) hedge-mustard; ***balsamita mayor,*** watercress.
bálsamo, *n.m.* balsam, balm; (*med.*) purest part of the blood; ***bálsamo de Judea*** or ***de Meca,*** true balsam, balm of Gilead; ***bálsamo del Canadá,*** Canada balsam; ***bálsamo del Perú,*** Peru balsam; (*fig.*) ***ser un bálsamo,*** to be very fragrant, generous *or* perfect (*old wine*).
balsar, *n.m.* marshy and brambly ground.
balsear, *v.t.* to ferry *or* cross (*a river*) on rafts *or* floats.
balsero, *n.m.* ferryman.
balsete, *n.m.* (*prov.*) small puddle, pool.

balso, *n.m.* (*naut.*) rope with loops for raising men *or* goods on board ship; sling.
balsopeto, *n.m.* (*coll.*) large pouch carried near the breast; (*coll.*) bosom.
bálteo, *n.m.* officer's belt.
Báltico, *n.m.* (the) Baltic (Sea).
báltico, -ca, *a.* Baltic.
baltra, *n.f.* (*prov.*) belly, paunch.
baluarte, *n.m.* bastion, bulwark; (*fig.*) defence, support; ***baluarte de la fe,*** bulwark of the faith.
balumba, *n.f.* bulk; heap; pile of stuff.
balumbo, *n.m.* bulky load, mass *or* object.
Ballena, *n.f.* (*astron.*) Whale, Cetus.
ballena, *n.f.* (*zool.*) whale; train-oil; whalebone.
ballenato, *n.m.* whale-calf.
ballenero, -ra, *a.* appertaining to whaling. — *n.m.* whale-boat; whaler.
ballesta, *n.f.* cross-bow, ballista; snare (*for birds*); carriage-spring; (*aut.*) car-spring; (*pl.* (*sl.*) saddle-bags; ***a tiro de ballesta,*** a stone's throw away.
ballestada, *n.f.* shot from a cross-bow.
ballestazo, *n.m.* blow from the arrow of a cross-bow.
ballesteador, *n.m.* cross-bowman, arbalister.
ballestear, *v.t.* to shoot with a cross-bow.
ballestera, *n.f.* loophole for cross-bows.
ballestería, *n.f.* big-game hunting; archery; armoury for cross-bows; number of cross-bows *or* bowmen.
ballestero, *n.m.* archer, arbalister, cross-bowman; cross-bow maker; king's armourer; ***ballestero de maza,*** mace-bearer; ***ballestero de corte,*** king's porter.
ballestilla, *n.f.* small whiffle-tree; (*vet.*) fleam; cross-staff; (*naut.*) forestaff; (*sl.*) cheating trick (*cards*).
ballestón, *n.m.* large cross-bow, arbalest; (*sl.*) cheating trick (*cards*).
ballestrinque, *n.m.* (*naut.*) clovehitch.
ballico, *n.m.* (*bot.*) rye-grass.
ballueca, *n.f.* (*bot.*) wild oats.
bamba, *n.f.* fluke (*billiards*); (*prov.*) swing on cords; (*prov.*) sponge roll.
bambalear(se) [BAMBOLEAR(SE)].
bambalina, *n.f.* (*theat.*) fly.
bambarria, *n.f.* fluke (*billiards*); (*coll.*) fool, idiot.
bambarrión, *n.m.* (*coll.*) great fluke.
bambochada, *n.f.* painting representing a banquet *or* drunken feast, with grotesque figures.
bamboche, *n.m.* (*coll.*) plump red-faced fellow.
bambolear(se), *v.i.* (*v.r.*) to sway.
bamboleo, *n.m.* swaying, rocking, rolling.
bambolla, *n.f.* (*coll.*) show, showiness, ostentation; sham, façade; ***darse bambolla,*** to show off, talk big; to put on a front.
bambollero, -ra, *a.* showy, flashy; sham.
bambú, *n.m.* (*bot.*) bamboo.
bambuco, *n.m.* (*Col.*) folk-dance.
bambusáceo, -cea, *a.* bamboo-like. — *n.f.pl.* (**bambusáceas**) bamboos.
banana, *n.f.* banana.
bananal, *n.m.* banana plantation.
bananero, -ra, *a.* appertaining to bananas. — *n.m.* banana tree.
banano, *n.m.* banana tree.
banas, *n.f.pl.* (*Hisp. Am.*) matrimonial banns.
banasta, *n.f.* large basket.
banastero, -ra, *n.m.f.* basket-maker, basket-dealer. — *n.m.* (*sl.*) prison governor, (*Am.*) prison warden.
banasto, *n.m.* large round basket; (*sl.*) prison.
banca, *n.f.* bench; bank; banking; stand (*market*); Philippine canoe; ***hacer saltar la banca,*** to break the bank.
bancada, *n.f.* bench (*for shearing cloth*); (*mech.*) bed, base; quantity of cloth prepared for shearing; (*arch.*) piece of masonry; (*naut.*) rower's bench; (*min.*) step.
bancal, *n.m.* oblong plot; cultivated terrace; bench-cover.
bancalero, *n.m.* weaver of bench-covers.
bancario, -ria, *a.* banking, financial.
bancarrota, *n.f.* bankruptcy, failure; ***hacer bancarrota,*** to go bankrupt.
bancaza, *n.m.* (*naut.*) bench.
bancazo, *n.m.* (*coll.*) clout *or* wallop delivered with a bench; huge *or* superb bank.
banco, *n.m.* form, bench, pew; (*mech.*) bed, table, frame, horse; (*arch.*) pediment; (*naut.*) course; school, shoal (*of fishes*); (*naut.*) large sand-bank, shoal; (*com.*) bank; (*geol.*) stratum; (*slang*) prison; (*pl.*) cheeks of the bit of a bridle; ***banco de compensación*** or ***de liquidación,*** clearing bank; ***banco de hielo,*** ice-bank, iceberg; ***banco de niebla,*** fog bank; ***banco de pruebas,*** testing bench; ***banco de sangre,*** blood bank.
banda, *n.f.* sash; band, gang, party; (military) band, (brass) band; bank, border, edge; side; cushion (*of billiard-table*); (*eccles.*) humeral veil; (*prov.*) felloe (*wheel*); (*print.*) platen-rail; (*naut.*) ***arriar en banda,*** to loose (*the ropes*); ***cerrarse en banda,*** to be adamant; (*naut.*) ***caer*** or ***estar en banda,*** to be hanging loosely; (*naut.*) ***dar a la banda,*** to heel; ***tomar por banda,*** to get a craze *or* fad for; to take a dislike to; ***banda sonora,*** sound track; ***banda transportadora,*** conveyor belt; ***de banda a banda,*** from side to side.
bandada, *n.f.* covey; flock (*of birds*).
bandarria, *n.f.* (*naut.*) iron maul.
bandazo, *n.m.* (*naut.*) breaking of a wave on the side of a ship; heave, lurch, jolt; ***dar*** or ***pegar bandazos,*** to heave *or* roll from side to side, lurch about.
bandeado, -da, *a.* striped.
bandearse, *v.r.* to fend *or* shift for oneself, manage.
bandeja, *n.f.* tray.
bandera, *n.f.* banner, standard, flag, ensign; (*mil.*) company (*Foreign Legion*); (*naut.*) ***bandera de popa,*** ensign; (*naut.*) ***bandera de proa,*** jack; (*naut.*) ***bandera de inteligencia,*** signalling flag; ***bandera de recluta,*** recruiting party; (*naut.*) ***arriar bandera,*** to strike the colours, surrender; (*fig.*) ***a banderas desplegadas,*** openly; ***con banderas desplegadas,*** with flying colours; ***alzar*** or ***levantar bandera,*** to raise the flag; (*fig.*) ***llevarse la bandera,*** to carry the day; (*fig.*) ***militar bajo la bandera de,*** to fight on the side of; ***rendir la bandera,*** to strike the flag.
bandereta, banderita, *n.f.* bannerette, small flag.
banderetas, *n.f.pl.* (*mil.*) camp colours.
bandería, *n.f.* band, faction.
banderilla, *n.f.* banderilla; ***clavarle, plantarle*** or ***ponerle a alguien banderillas,*** to taunt s.o.
banderillear, *v.t.* to stick banderillas into (*bulls*).
banderillero, *n.m.* one who thrusts banderillas into the bull.
banderín, *n.m.* camp colours; small flag; railway signal; standard; ***banderín de enganche,*** recruiting post.
banderizar(se) [C], *v.t.* (*v.r.*) to divide into bands *or* parties.
banderizo, -za, *a.* factious; (*fig.*) turbulent, seditious.
banderola, *n.f.* banderol, camp colours; signalling flag; streamer, pennon.
bandidaje, *n.m.* banditry, brigandage.
bandido, *n.m.* bandit.
bandín, *n.m.* (*naut.*) seat in a row-galley.
bando (1), *n.m.* proclamation, edict; ***echar bando,*** to publish a law.
bando (2), *n.m.* faction, party; shoal (*of fish*).
bandola (1), *n.f.* bandore, mandolin.
bandola (2), *n.f.* (*naut.*) jury-mast.

bandolera, *n.f.* bandolier; female bandit.
bandolerismo, *n.m.* banditry, brigandage.
bandolero, *n.m.* bandit.
bandolín, *n.m.* small bandore *or* mandolin.
bandolina, *n.f.* bandoline, hair fixative.
bandujo, *n.m.* large sausage; (*prov., coll.*) bowel, intestine; belly.
bandullo, *n.m.* (*vulg.*) belly, bowels, intestines.
bandurria, *n.f.* bandurria, bandore.
bandurrista, *n.m.f.* (*mus.*) bandore player.
bánova, *n.f.* (*prov.*) bed-quilt, bed-cover.
banquera, *n.f.* (*prov.*) bee-house; site *or* frame for beehives.
banquero, *n.m.* banker; (*sl.*) prison governor, (*Am.*) prison warden.
banqueta, *n.f.* bench; stool; (*mil.*) banquette; (*Mex.*) pavement; (*artill.*) ***banqueta de cureña,*** gun-carriage bed; (*naut.*) ***banqueta de calafate,*** caulking-stool.
banquete, *n.m.* banquet, feast.
banquetear(se), *v.t., v.i.* (*v.r.*) to banquet, feast.
banquillo, *n.m.* small bench; (*law*) ***banquillo de los acusados,*** dock; enclosure (*for prisoners*).
banzo, *n.m.* cheek of embroidering-frame; jamb; sloping bank of canal.
bañada, *n.f.* bath; swim.
bañadera, *n.f.* (*naut.*) skeet; (*Hisp. Am.*) bath(tub).
bañadero, *n.m.* water-hole, watering place.
bañado, *n.m.* chamber-pot; (*Hisp. Am.*) swamp, marsh land.
bañador, *n.m.* bathing costume.
bañar, *v.t.* to bathe, wash; to flood, fill; to dip, soak; to coat, cover; ***murallas bañadas por el mar,*** walls washed by the sea; ***habitación bañada de luz (sol),*** room bathed in *or* flooded with light (sunlight). — **bañarse,** *v.r.* to bath, take *or* have a bath; to bathe, take *or* have a bathe *or* swim, go for a bathe *or* swim; ***bañarse en agua de rosas,*** to walk on air, be delighted.
bañero, -ra, *n.m.f.* bath-owner; bath-keeper; bathing-attendant. — *n.f.* bath(tub).
bañil, *n.m.* water-hole, watering place.
bañista, *n.m.f.* taker of waters (*at a spa*).
baño, *n.m.* bath; bath-tub; bath-room; bathing; coat, covering (*paint.*); (*obs.*) Moorish prison; ***baño de asiento,*** hip-bath; ***calentar al baño (de) María,*** to warm by bain-marie; (*fam.*) ***nos dio un auténtico baño de historia,*** he gave us an earful of history; (*pl.*) bathing-place; spa; watering-place.
bañón, *n.m.* (*bot.*) ***palo de bañón,*** mock privet.
bao, *n.m.* (*naut.*) beam, cross-timber.
baobab, *n.m.* (*bot.*) baobab.
baptisterio, *n.m.* baptistry.
baque, *n.m.* thud.
baquear, *v.i.* (*naut.*) to sail with the current.
baqueta, *n.f.* ramrod; switch; ***tratar a la baqueta,*** to treat harshly; ***aprender a la baqueta,*** to learn the hard way; (*pl.*) drumsticks; (*mil.*) ***carrera de baquetas,*** running the gauntlet.
baquetazo, *n.m.* blow, knock, wallop; ***ha sufrido muchos baquetazos,*** he's had lots of knocks, he's been through the mill.
baquetear, *v.t.* to make run the gauntlet; to beat; to harass; ***estar baqueteado,*** to have received many a knock, be inured by experience.
baqueteo, *n.m.* (*mil.*) gauntlet; (*fig.*) annoyance, vexation.
baquetilla, *n.f.* small rod.
baquía, *n.f.* (*Hisp. Am.*) knowledge of local country *or* terrain; experience.
baquiano, -na, *a.* skilful, experienced. — *n.m.* local guide.
báquico, -ca, *a.* bacchanalian; Bacchic.
baquio, *n.m.* (*poet.*) metrical foot.
báquira, *n.f.* (*Hisp. Am.*) wild-hog.
bar, *n.m.* bar.
baraca, *n.f.* (*Morocco*) divine gift ascribed to sherifs and hermits.
barago, *n.m.* wicker tray for drying chestnuts.
barahá, *n.f.* Jewish term for prayer.
barahunda, *n.f.* uproar; chaos.
baraja, *n.f.* pack (*of cards*); (*coll.*) ***jugar con dos barajas,*** to play a double game; ***peinar la baraja,*** to shuffle two packs of cards.
barajador, -ra, *n.m.f.* chicaner, caviller.
barajadura, *n.f.* shuffling (*cards*); scuffle.
barajar, *v.t., v.i.* to shuffle (*cards*); to mix.
barajón, *n.m.* snow-shoe.
baranda, *n.f.* railing, banister.
barandado, barandaje, *n.m.* balustrade.
barandal, *n.m.* handrail; railing.
barandilla, *n.f.* balustrade, small railing.
barangay, *n.m.* (*Philip.*) tribal government.
baraño, *n.m.* (*prov.*) new-mown hay.
barata, *n.f.* [BARATO].
baratador, -ra, *n.m.f.* barterer, trader.
baratar, *v.t.* to barter, traffic.
baratear, *v.t.* to cheapen, undersell.
baratería, *n.f.* (*law*) fraud; (*law*) ***baratería de capitán*** or ***de patrón,*** barratry.
baratero, *n.m.* one who exacts money from winning gamblers.
baratía, *n.f.* (*Col.*) cheapness.
baratijas, *n.f.pl.* trinkets, trifles.
baratillero, -ra, *n.m.f.* seller of second-hand goods *or* articles; keeper of second-hand shop.
baratillo, *n.m.* second-hand shop; bargain counter; heap of trifling articles for sale; (*coll.*) shambles.
baratista, *n.m.f.* barterer, trafficker.
barato, -ta, *a.* cheap; easy. — *adv.* cheaply. — *n.m.* bargain *or* sale; money given by winning gamblers; ***de barato,*** free, gratis; ***dar de barato,*** to allow for the sake of argument; to take for granted; ***echar*** or ***meter a barato,*** to heckle; to jeer at. — *n.f.* barter; cheapness; (*Mex.*) bargain sale.
báratro, *n.m.* (*poet.*) hell; (*Bibl.*) Sheol; abysm.
baratura, *n.f.* cheapness.
baraúnda, *n.f.* uproar; chaos.
baraustador, *n.m.* (*sl.*) dagger.
baraustar [P], *v.t.* to aim, point; to ward off, deflect (*blow*).
barba, *n.f.* chin; beard; whiskers; first swarm of bees; top of a bee-hive; wattle; ***barba cerrada,*** thick, heavy beard; (*coll.*) ***barbas de chivo*** or ***de macho,*** pointed beard; man having such a beard; ***hacerle a uno la barba,*** to shave s.o.; (*fig.*) to annoy *or* irritate s.o.; to flatter s.o.; ***atusarse la barba,*** to smooth *or* stroke one's beard; ***mesarle a uno la barba,*** to pull s.o. by the beard; to affront *or* insult s.o. grievously; ***se nos ha subido a las barbas,*** he's got above himself (with us); ***tentarse la barba,*** to feel one's way, go warily; ***andar, estar con*** or ***traer la barba sobre el hombro,*** to be on the alert, be cautious; ***llevar de la barba,*** to lead by the nose; ***mentir por la barba,*** to tell barefaced lies; (*bot.*) ***barba cabruna,*** yellow goat's beard; (*bot.*) ***barba de Aarón,*** green dragon arum; ***barba a barba,*** face to face; ***por barba,*** per capita, apiece; ***en sus barbas,*** to his face; (*pl.*) (*astron.*) beard (*comet*); slender roots; fibres; rough edges, deckles (*of paper*); vanes (*of a quill*); (*vet.*) ranula. — *n.m.* actor who plays old men's parts.
barbacana, *n.f.* (*mil.*) barbican; churchyard wall; loophole.
barbacoa, *n.f.* (*Hisp. Am.*) barbecue.
Barbada, *n.f.* ***la —,*** Barbados.
barbada (1), *n.f.* lower jaw (*of horse*); bridle-curb; (*ichth.*) dab, small flatfish.
barbado, -da (2), *a.* bearded, barbed, barbated. — *n.m.* big fellow, full-grown chap; transplanted

vine *or* tree; (*bot.*) shoot, sucker; (*sl.*, *zool.*) buck; ***plantar de barbado,*** to transplant.

barbaja, *n.f.* (*bot.*) cut-leaved viper's-grass; (*pl.*) (*agric.*) first roots (*of plants*).

barbaján, *n.m.* (*Hisp. Am.*) bumpkin, yokel; (*Am.*) hick.

barbar, *v.i.* to grow a beard; to rear bees; (*agric.*) to strike root.

barbárico, -ca, *a.* barbarous, barbarian.

barbaridad, *n.f.* barbarity, barbarism, cruelty; (*coll.*) shocking, terrible *or* stupid thing to do *or* say; (*coll.*) hell of a lot; (*coll.*) ***¡qué barbaridad!*** good Lord!

barbarie, *n.f.* (*fig.*) barbarousness, savagery.

barbarismo, *n.m.* barbarism.

barbarizar [C], *v.t.* to make barbarous *or* savage; to fill with barbarisms.

bárbaro, -ra, *a.* barbaric, barbarian; savage; crude, coarse; (*coll.*) terrific, magnificent; ***¡qué bárbaro!*** how super! what a chap!

barbarote, -ta, *a.* (*coll.*) shockingly barbarous; utterly crude, coarse.

barbato, -ta, *a.* having the tail before the nucleus (*comets*).

barbaza, *n.f.* shaggy great beard.

barbear, *v.t.* to reach with the chin; (*Mex.*) to shave; (*Mex.*) to throw down (*a steer*). — *v.i.* to be almost as high (**con,** as); (*naut.*) ***barbeando,*** lying alongside. — **barbearse,** *v.r.* (*fig.*) to be very stiff (*with s.o.*).

barbechada, *n.f.* (*agric.*) fallowing.

barbechar, *v.t.* (*agric.*) to fallow; to plough for seeding.

barbechera, *n.f.* series of ploughings; (act of) ploughing; fallow season.

barbecho, *n.m.* fallow; first ploughing of the ground; ploughed land ready for sowing.

barbería, *n.f.* barber's shop.

barberil, *a.* pertaining to a barber, barber-like.

barberillo, *n.m.* twopenny ha'penny barber.

barbero, -ra, *a.* (*Hisp. Am.*) flattering, fawning. — *n.m.* barber.

barbeta, *n.f.* (*naut.*) gasket; (*artill.*) barbette; (*artill.*, *fort.*) ***a barbeta,*** en barbette.

barbián, -biana, *a.* (*coll.*) bold, insolent, cheeky.

barbiblanco, -ca, *a.* grey- *or* white-bearded.

barbicacho *n.m.* ribbon tied under the chin.

barbicano, -na, *a.* grey-bearded.

barbicastaño, *a.* with a chestnut-coloured beard.

barbiespeso, -sa, *a.* having a thick beard.

barbihecho, -cha, *a.* freshly shaven.

barbijo, *n.m.* (*Arg.*, *prov.*) chin-strap; scar on face.

barbilampiño, -ña, *a.* clean-shaven, beardless.

barbilindo, -da, *a.* foppish, dandyish.

barbilucio, -cia, *a.* smooth-faced.

barbiluengo, -ga, *a.* long-bearded.

barbilla, *n.f.* chin; (*ichth.*) barbel; (*carp.*) rabbet; (*vet.*) ranula.

barbillera, *n.f.* roll of tow (*in wine casks*); bandage put under the chin of a dead person.

barbimoreno, -na, *a.* dark-bearded.

barbinegro, -ra, *a.* black-bearded.

barbiponiente, *a.* (*coll.*) beginning to grow a beard; apprenticed.

barbipungente, *a.* just growing a beard; with a thin beard.

barbiquejo [BARBOQUEJO].

barbirrapado, -da, *a.* having a cropped beard.

barbirrojo, -ja, *a.* red-bearded.

barbirrubio, -bia, *a.* fair-bearded.

barbirrucio, -cia, *a.* grey-bearded, grizzled.

barbitaheño, -ña, *a.* red-bearded.

barbiteñido, -da, *a.* having a dyed beard.

barbo, *n.m.* (*ichth.*) barbel; ***barbo de mar,*** surmullet.

barbón, *n.m.* full-bearded man; Carthusian lay-brother; (*zool.*) buck.

barboquejo, barbuquejo, *n.m.* chin-strap, hat-guard.

barbotar, *v.t.*, *v.i.* to mumble, mutter.

barbote, *n.m.* beaver (*of helmet*).

barbudo, -da, *a.* having a full beard. — *n.m.* vine transplanted with the roots; (*sl.*, *zool.*) buck; (*coll.*, *Hisp. Am.*) guerrilla.

barbulla, *n.f.* babble, hubbub.

barbullar, *v.i.* to babble.

barbullón, -llona, *a.* babbling. — *n.m.f.* (*coll.*, babbler.

barca, *n.f.* boat; bark; ***barca de pesca,*** (small) fishing boat.

barcada, *n.f.* boat trip; boat-load.

barcaje, *n.m.* ferryage; freightage, freight; boat fare.

barcal, *n.m.* (*prov.*) wooden trough, pan *or* tray.

barcarola, *n.f.* barcarole.

barcaza, *n.f.* barge, lighter; lighterage.

barcelonés, -nesa, *a.*, *n.m.f.* (native) of Barcelona.

barceno, -na, *a.* dappled.

barceo, *n.m.* dry bass *or* sedge (*for mats, ropes etc.*).

barcia, *n.f.* chaff, siftings.

barcina (1), *n.f.* (*Hisp. Am.*) esparto net-bag; large truss of straw.

barcinar, *v.t.* (*prov.*) to carry (*sheaves*).

barcino, -na (2), *a.* dappled.

barco, *n.m.* boat, ship; shallow gorge.

barcolongo. barcoluengo, *n.m.* (*hist.*) swift-sailing ship; oblong boat with a large bow.

barcón, barcote, *n.m.* big boat.

barchilón, *n.m.* (*Hisp. Am.*) male nurse (*in hospital*).

barchilla, *n.f.* (*prov.*) measure for grain.

barda (1), *n.f.* (*obs.*) bard, horse-armour.

barda (2), *n.f.* wall top *or* cover; low stone *or* mud wall; (*prov.*) young oak tree; (*naut.*) large, threatening cloud.

bárdago, *n.m.* (*naut.*) pendant.

bardaguera, *n.f.* (*bot.*) willow.

bardaja, bardaje, *n.m.* sodomite.

bardal, *n.m.* thatched wall *or* fence; mud wall covered at the top with straw *or* brushwood; ***saltando bardales,*** overcoming all difficulties.

bardana, *n.f.* (*bot.*) burdock.

bardanza, *n.f.* ***andar de bardanza,*** to wander to and fro, wander about.

bardar, *v.t.* to thatch (*fences*).

bardiota, *a.*, *n.m.* (of) the Byzantine imperial guard.

bardiza, *n.f.* (*prov.*) cane fence.

bardo, *n.m.* bard.

bardoma, *n.f.* (*prov.*) filth, mud.

bardomera, *n.f.* (*prov.*) brush *or* weeds carried off by a stream.

baría, *n.f.* (*Cub.*) baria tree.

bario, *n.m.* (*min.*) barium.

barisfera, *n.f.* (*geol.*) (the) centre of mass of the earth.

barita, *n.f.* (*min.*) baryta, barytes.

baritel, *n.m.* (*min.*) hoisting machine.

barítico, -ca, *a.* baric, relating to barium.

baritina, *n.f.* barium sulphate, heavy spar.

barítono, *n.m.* (*mus.*) baritone.

barjuleta, *n.f.* knapsack, haversack; tool-bag.

barloa, *n.f.* cable (*for mooring a ship to another*).

barloar, *v.t.* to bring alongside a ship *or* wharf. — **barloar(se),** *v.i.* (*v.r.*) to draw alongside a ship *or* wharf.

barloventear, *v.i.* (*naut.*) to ply to windward; (*coll.*) to beat about, tack about, rove about.

barlovento, *n.m.* (*naut.*) windward; ***costa de barlovento,*** weather shore; ***costado de barlovento,*** weather side; (*coll.*) ***ganar el barlovento de,*** to get to windward of.

barnacla, *n.f.* (*zool.*) barnacle; (*orn.*) sea-goose.
barnicillo, *n.m.* thin *or* slight veneer.
barniz, *n.m.* varnish (*finish*); veneer; printer's ink.
barnizado, *n.m.* (*art*) varnishing.
barnizador, -ra, *a.* varnishing. — *n.m.f.* varnisher.
barnizar [C], *v.t.* to varnish.
barógrafo, *n.m.* barograph.
barología, *n.f.* barology.
barometría, *n.f.* barometry.
barométrico, -ca, *a.* barometric, barometrical.
barómetro, *n.m.* barometer.
barón, *n.m.* baron.
baronesa, *n.f.* baroness.
baronía, *n.f.* barony.
baroscopio, *n.m.* baroscope.
baroto, *n.m.* (*Philip.*) small boat.
barquear, *v.t.* to take over by boat. — *v.i.* to go about in a boat.
barqueo, *n.m.* boating.
barquero, *n.m.* waterman, ferryman, boatman; (*ent.*) water-bug.
barqueta, *n.f.*, **barquete,** *n.m.* small boat.
barquía, *n.f.* (*naut.*) fishing-boat; fishing-net.
barquichuelo, *n.m.* wretched little craft.
barquilla, *n.f.* conical mould for wafers; little boat, wherry; airship-car; balloon-basket; (*naut.*) log.
barquillero, -ra, *n.m.f.* maker *or* seller of rolled wafers. — *n.m.* wafer-mould.
barquillo, *n.m.* cock-boat; thin rolled wafer.
barquín, *n.m.*, **barquinera,** *n.f.* large bellows (*for furnaces*).
barquinazo, *n.m.* violent heave *or* jolt; ***dar pegar barquinazos,*** to heave, sway *or* jolt violently *or* heavily (from side to side).
barquinero, *n.m.* bellows-maker.
barquino, *n.m.* wine-skin.
barra, *n.f.* (*mech.*) bar, beam, rod; strip; crow-bar, lever; (*naut.*) sand-bar; ingot; Spanish game played with iron bars; barrier (*of court-room*); gross-spun thread in defective cloth; (*her., naut.*) bar; (*mus.*) bar-line; (*Hisp. Am., coll.*) gang, clique; chase bar; shaft (*of a carriage*); thill; (*naut.*) spar; (*pl.*) saddletrees; (*Hisp. Am.*) mining shares; (*her.*) stripes, bars; clamps of embroidery-frame; ***barra de labios,*** lipstick; ***de barra a barra,*** from side to side and from one end to the other; (*coll.*) ***estirar la barra,*** to do one's utmost to attain something; (*fig.*) ***llevar a la barra,*** to impeach; ***sin pararse en barras,*** regardless of obstacles; ***tirar a la barra,*** to play the game of ***barra***; (*coll.*) ***tirar la barra,*** to get the highest price possible; to do all in one's power to attain anything; ***sin daño de barras,*** without injury or danger; ***estar en barras,*** to be on the point of settling an affair.
barrabás, *n.m.* (*coll.*) evil *or* wicked person.
barrabasada, *n.f.* (*coll.*) evil *or* wicked thing (to do); wild *or* crazy thing (to do).
barraca, *n.f.* cabin, hut; (*prov.*) cottage, rustic dwelling; (*Hisp. Am.*) storage shed, warehouse; (*pl.*) (*Mex.*) shanty town.
barraco, *n.m.* ancient naval gun.
barracón, *n.m.* large hut *or* cabin; shed.
barrado, -da, *a.* corded; ribbed; striped; (*her.*) barred.
barragán, *n.m.* camlet; waterproof woollen stuff; overcoat of such material.
barragana, *n.f.* concubine.
barraganería, *n.f.* concubinage.
barraganete, *n.m.* (*naut.*) top-timber, futtock.
barral, *n.m.* (*prov.*) demijohn.
barranca, *n.f.* gorge, ravine; ***a trancas y a barrancas,*** limpingly, haltingly, laboriously.
barranco, *n.m.* gully, gorge, ravine; (*fig.*) (great) difficulty, obstruction.
barrancoso, -sa, *a.* full of gorges, gullies *or* ravines; broken, uneven; precipitous.
barranquera [BARRANCA].
barraquero, *n.m.* (*prov.*) hut-constructor; (*Hisp. Am.*) owner of a store *or* warehouse.
barrar (1), *v.t.* to daub, smear.
barrar (2), *v.t.* to bar, barricade.
barrate, *n.m.* little joist *or* rafter.
barrear, *v.t.* to bar, barricade; (*prov.*) to cancel, cross off. — *v.i.* to graze a knight's armour with a lance. — **barrearse** (1), *v.r.* (*obs.*) to entrench oneself.
barrearse (2), *v.r.* (*prov.*) to wallow (*pigs and boars*).
barreda, *n.f.* barricade, barrier, fence.
barredero, -ra, *a.* that drags alone; sweeping; ***red barredera,*** drag-net, sweep-net. — *n.m.* baker's long-handled oven mop *or* swab. — *n.f.* road-sweeping machine; (*Hisp. Am.*) broom; (*pl.*) (*naut.*) studding-sail.
barredor, -ra, *a.* sweeping. — *n.m.f.* sweeper.
barreduela, *n.f.* (*prov.*) small enclosed square *or* place.
barredura, *n.f.* sweeping; (*pl.*) sweepings, remains, residue, refuse, chaff.
barrelotodo, *n.m. inv.* one who collects and makes use of everything.
barrena, *n.f.* gimlet, borer, drill; ***barrena grande,*** auger, borer; ***barrena pequeña*** or ***de mano,*** gimlet; (*obs.*) ***barrena de gusano,*** wimble, rock-drill; ***barrena de disminución,*** taper auger; ***barrena de guía,*** centre-bit; (*aer.*) ***entrar en barrena,*** to go into a spin.
barrenador, *n.m.* blaster, driller; (*naut.*) auger, borer.
barrenamiento, *n.m.* boring, drilling.
barrenar, *v.t.* to bore, auger, drill; to blast; (*fig.*) to foil, frustrate; (*fig.*) to violate (*laws, rights*); (*naut.*) ***barrenar un navío,*** to scuttle a ship; ***barrenar una roca*** (***mina***), to blast a rock (mine).
barrendero, -ra, *n.m.f.* sweeper, cleaner.
barrenero, *n.m.* maker *or* seller of augers *or* drills; blaster, driller.
barrenillo, *n.m.* (*ent.*) borer; (*bot.*) disease in trees caused by borer.
barreno, *n.m.* large borer *or* auger; bored hole, blast-hole; blast; (*fig.*) vanity; (*naut.*) ***dar barreno a,*** to scuttle (*a ship*).
barreño, *n.m.* pan, tub.
barrer, *v.t.* to sweep; to sweep away, sweep clean; to mow down; (*mil.*) to enfilade; (*naut.*) to rake; ***barrer hacia dentro,*** to have one's eye to the main chance.
barrera (1), *n.f.* barrier, fence; cupboard (*for crockery*); bar; (*fig.*) obstacle, difficulty; tollgate, turnpike; (*railw.*) half-barrier (*at crossing*); (*bullring*) front seat; ***barrera de golpe,*** automatic *or* self-closing gate; ***ver los toros desde la barrera,*** to sit on the fence, be a mere onlooker.
barrera (2), *n.f.* clay-pit; mound (*of earth*).
barrero, *n.m.* potter; clay-pit; (*prov.*) eminence, ridge of hills; bog, quagmire; (*Hisp. Am.*) salty soil.
barreta, *n.f.* small bar; shoe-lining; (*prov.*) bar of toffee.
barretear, *v.t.* to fasten with bars; to line (*a shoe*).
barretero, *n.m.* (*min.*) one who works with a pick, wedge *or* crow.
barretina, *n.f.* Phrygian cap; Catalonian cap.
barriada, *n.f.* outer district *or* suburb; (*pl., Per.*) shanty town.
barrial, *a.* clayey. — *n.m.* (*obs.*) muddy spot.
barrica, *n.f.* cask.
barricada, *n.f.* barricade.
barrido, *n.m.* sweeping; sweepings, remains.

barriga, *n.f.* belly; bulge (*in a wall*).
barrigón, -gona, barrigudo, -da, *a.* (*coll.*) big-bellied, pot-bellied.
barriguera, *n.f.* belly-band, girth.
barril, *n.m.* barrel, cask.
barrila, *n.f.* (*prov.*) short round jug.
barrilamen, *n.m.*, **barrilería,** *n.f.* stock of casks *or* barrels; barrel factory *or* shop.
barrilejo, *n.m.* runlet, small barrel.
barrilero, *n.m.* cooper, barrel-maker *or* vendor.
barrilete, *n.m.* dice box; (*carp.*) holdfast, dog, clamp; (*zool.*) spider crab; (*prov.*) keg; kite (*toy*); (*mus.*) barrel, part of a clarinet near mouthpiece; (*naut.*) mouse.
barrilla, *n.f.* (*bot.*) saltwort, glasswort; (*pl.*) saltwort ashes.
barrillar, *n.m.* saltwort plantation; saltwort pits.
barrillero, -ra, *a.* (*bot.*) salsolaceous.
barrillo, *n.m.* pimple.
barrio, *n.m.* district, quarter; ***barrio comercial,*** shopping *or* business district; ***barrio residencial,*** residential district; (*coll.*) ***el otro barrio,*** the other *or* next world; (*coll.*) ***irse para el otro barrio,*** to peg out, kick the bucket; ***andar*** or ***estar*** (***vestido***) ***de barrio,*** to wear plain, simple dress.
barriscar [A], *v.t.* (*prov.*) to sell in bulk; (*prov.*) to sweep brusquely.
barrisco, *adv. phrase,* ***a barrisco,*** higgledy-piggledy; pell-mell.
barrita, *n.f.* small bar.
barrizal, *n.m.* muddy place; clay-pit.
barro (1), *n.m.* mud, clay; earthenware; ***barro cocido,*** terra-cotta; (*sl.*) ***dejar en el barro,*** to leave in the lurch.
barro (2), *n.m.* pimple.
barroco, -ca, *a.* baroque.
barrocho, *n.m.* barouche.
barrón, *n.m.* sand *or* beach grass.
barroquismo, *n.m.* baroque style *or* taste; extravagant *or* wildly exaggerated style *or* taste.
barroso, -sa (1), *a.* muddy; terra-cotta colour.
barroso, -sa (2), *a.* pimply.
barrote, *n.m.* (thick) iron bar; iron band; table-clamp; (*carp.*) brace.
barrotín, *n.m.* (*naut.*) wooden lattice-lath.
barrueco, *n.m.* pearl of irregular form; (*geol.*) nodule.
barrumbada, *n.f.* (*coll.*) boastful *or* extravagant thing to do *or* say.
barruntador, -ra, *a.* conjecturing, guessing, sensing. — *n.m.* guesser.
barruntar, *v.t.* to conjecture, guess, surmise; to sense, suspect; to glimpse; to get wind of.
barrunte, *n.m.* indication, presentiment, sign.
barrunto, *n.m.* conjecture, guess; sensing, suspicion; glimpse; adumbration.
bartola, *n.f.* (*coll.*) paunch; ***echarse, tenderse*** or ***tumbarse a la bartola,*** to lie back lazily, to sprawl carelessly.
bartolillo, *n.m.* small three-cornered meat *or* cream pie.
bartolina, *n.f.* (*Hisp. Am.*) small, narrow, dark dungeon.
Bartolomé, *n.m.* Bartholomew.
bartulear, *v.i.* (*Chi.*) to cavil, rack one's brains.
bartuleo, *n.m.* (*Chi.*) racking one's brains.
bártulos, *n.m.pl.* goods and chattels; (*coll.*) ***coger los bártulos,*** to clear out; ***liar los bártulos,*** to pack (ready to go).
baruca, *n.f.* (*coll.*) artifice, cunning, deceit.
barulé, *n.m.* upper part of the stockings rolled over the knee.
barullero, -ra, *n.m.f.* busybody.
barullo, *n.m.* (*coll.*) bustle; uproar; chaos.
barzal, *n.m.* bramble-patch.
barzón, *n.m.* stroll, saunter; (*agric.*) ring of a yoke; (*C.R.*) leather strap for yoking oxen; ***dar*** or ***hacer barzones,*** to loiter, idle about.
barzonear, *v.i.* to saunter; to loiter about.
barzoque, berzoque, *n.m.* (*coll.*) Satan; evil spirit.
basa (1), *n.f.* (*arch.*) pedestal, base; (*fig.*) basis, foundation.
basa (2), *n.f.* (*prov.*) pool, pond.
basácula, *n.f.* locker of the thumb-plate (*in a stocking-frame*).
basada, *n.f.* (*naut.*) cradle, stocks.
basal, *a.* basic, basal.
basáltico, -ca, *a.* basaltic, of basalt.
basalto, *n.m.* (*min.*) basalt.
basamento, *n.m.* (*arch.*) base and pedestal.
basanita, *n.f.* (*min.*) basanite; touchstone; (*zool.*) crustacean.
basar, *v.t.* to base, to support; (*surv.*) to start from a fixed base-line; ***¿en qué se basa usted para decir eso?*** what grounds *or* basis have you for saying this?
basáride, *n.f.* (*zool.*) bassariscus (*a species of racoon*).
basca, *n.f.* qualm; queasiness; feeling of sickness; (*vet.*) distemper; (*coll.*) fit of anger; ***tener bascas,*** to retch.
bascosidad, *n.f.* filth.
báscula, *n.f.* platform-scale; weighing-machine; (*fort.*) bascule-bridge.
bascuñana, *n.f.* (*bot.*) Barbary wheat.
base, *n.f.* base, basis; grounds; foundation; (*surv.*) base-line; ***a base de,*** on the basis of.
basicidad, *n.f.* (*chem.*) basicity.
básico, -ca, *a.* basic.
báside, basideo, *n.m.* (*bot.*) basidium.
basilea, *n.f.* (*sl.*) gallows, gibbet.
basílica, *a.* (*anat.*) ***vena basílica,*** basilic vein. — *n.f.* basilica (*church*).
basilicón, *n.m.* (*med.*) basilicon, ointment.
basilio, -lia, *a.*, *n.m.f.* Basilidian (monk *or* nun).
basilisco, *n.m.* basilisk; (*coll.*) ***estar hecho un basilisco,*** to be in a rage.
basquear, *v.i.* to retch.
basquilla, *n.f.* blood disease (*in sheep*).
basquiña, *n.f.* (outer) skirt.
basta (1), *n.f.* basting, tacking; mattress tufting.
bastaje, *n.m.* porter, carrier.
bastante, *a.* sufficient, enough; competent. — *adv.* enough; quite, rather; (*coll.*) fairly, pretty.
bastantear, *v.i.* (*law*) to acknowledge the validity of a power of attorney.
bastanteo, *n.m.* acknowledgment of a power of attorney.
bastantero, *n.m.* (*law*) officer who examined powers of attorney.
bastar, *v.i.* to suffice, be enough; ***bastan dos*** or ***basta con dos,*** two are enough, two will be sufficient; ***¡basta ya!*** that's (quite) enough, that will do (now); ***basta de tonterías,*** that's enough nonsense; ***bastar a*** or ***para,*** to be sufficient to; ***bastarse a sí mismo,*** to be self-sufficient.
bastarda (1), *n.f.* locksmith's fine file; (*obs.*) piece of ordnance; (*naut.*) lateen mainsail.
bastardeamiento, *n.m.* degeneracy, degeneration; depravation; bastardy.
bastardear, *v.t.* to bastardize; to debase; to adulterate, corrupt. — *v.i.* to degenerate, deteriorate.
bastardelo, *n.m.* notary's draft book; blotter.
bastardía, *n.f.* bastardy; baseness; corruption, depravity.
bastardilla, *n.f.* italics; flute.
bastardo, -da (2), *a.* bastard, illegitimate; spurious; (*print.*) bastard (type). — *n.m.* bastard; (*zool.*) boa (*snake*); saddle; (*naut.*) parrel rope.
baste, *n.m.* (*sew.*) basting, tacking; saddle cushion.
bastear, *v.t.* to baste; to stitch *or* sew loosely.

basterna, *n.m.* member of the Bastarnæ (people). — *n.f.* cart; horse-drawn Roman litter.

bastero, *n.m.* maker *or* retailer of packsaddles.

basteza, *n.f.* coarseness, crudeness.

bastidor, *n.m.* frame; stretcher (*for canvas*); window-sash; wing (*of stage scenery*); holder (*for photographic plates*); stage scenery; ***entre bastidores,*** behind the scenes, off stage, secretly.

bastilla, *n.f.* hem.

bastillado, -da, *a.* (*her.*) with merlons pointing downwards.

bastillar, *v.t.* to hem.

bastimentar, *v.t.* to victual, supply with provisions.

bastimento (1), *n.m.* supply of provisions; (*naut.*) vessel, boat; building, structure.

bastimento (2), *n.m.* mattress tufting.

bastión, *n.m.* bastion, bulwark.

bastionado, -da, *a.* fortified; provided with bulwarks.

basto (1), **-ta** (2), *a.* coarse, crude, rough.

basto (2), *n.m.* pack-saddle (*for beasts of burden*); pad; ace of clubs (*cards*); (*pl.*) clubs (*cards*); ***bastos son triunfos,*** clubs are trumps; ***a basto*** [ABASTO].

bastón, *n.m.* cane, stick, baton; roller (*of a silk-frame*); (*bot., prov.*) young reed *or* shoot; (*arch.*) fluted moulding; (*her.*) vertical bars; ***empuñar el bastón,*** to seize the reins, take command; ***meter el bastón,*** to intervene, make peace.

bastonada, *n.f.*, **bastonazo,** *n.m.* blow with a stick; bastinado.

bastoncillo, *n.m.* small cane *or* stick (*used in velvet-loom*); narrow lace trimming.

bastonear, *v.t.* to cane, beat with a stick; to stir (*must*) with a stick. — *v.i.* (*prov.*) to eat young shoots (*cattle*).

bastonera, *n.f.* umbrella-stand.

bastonería, *n.f.* walking-stick shop.

bastonero, *n.m.* cane maker *or* seller; master of ceremonies; deputy prison governor.

basura, *n.f.* refuse, rubbish, (*Am.*) garbage; trash; ***cubo de la basura,*** dustbin, (*Am.*) garbage can.

basurero, *n.m.* dustman, (*Am.*) garbage man; dustbin, (*Am.*) garbage can; refuse heap, rubbish dump.

bata, *n.f.* dressing-gown, (*Am.*) bathrobe; (*obs.*) frock with train. — *n.m.* (*Philip.*) child; young Indian servant.

batacazo, *n.m.* (*fig.*) heavy fall, cropper; ***darse un batacazo,*** to come a cropper.

batahola, *n.f.* (*coll.*) hurly-burly, bustle, hubbub.

batalla, *n.f.* battle; saddle seat; wheelbase; (*artill.*) battle-piece; ***campo de batalla,*** battlefield; ***batalla campal,*** pitched battle; ***en batalla,*** in battle array; ***presentar batalla,*** to offer battle; ***librar batalla,*** to do *or* join battle.

batallador, -ra, *a.* battling; fencing. — *n.m.f.* battler, warrior; fencer.

batallante, *a.* battling, fighting.

batallar, *v.i.* to battle, fight; to fence; (*fig.*) to contend, strive, struggle.

batallón, *n.m.* battalion.

batallona, *a.* ***cuestión batallona,*** bone of contention, moot point.

batán, *n.m.* fulling-mill.

batanar, *v.t.* to full (*cloth*).

batanear, *v.t.* (*coll.*) to bang, beat, handle roughly.

batanero, *n.m.* fuller; cloth-worker.

batanga, *n.f.* (*Philip.*) bamboo outrigger on boats.

bataola [BATAHOLA].

batata, *n.f.* (*bot.*) sweet-potato.

batatar, *n.m.* sweet-potato field.

batatero, -ra, *n.m.f.* sweet-potato vendor.

bátavo, -va, *a.*, *n.m.f.* Batavian.

batayola, *n.f.* (*naut.*) rail.

batea, *n.f.* tray; (*naut.*) punt; open wagon with low sides; washing trough.

batehuela, *n.f.* small wooden bowl *or* tray.

batel, *n.m.* (*naut.*) small vessel; (*pl.*) (*sl.*) gang of roughs *or* thieves.

batelada, *n.f.* boat-load.

batelejo, *n.m.* small boat.

batelero, *n.m.* boatman.

bateo, *n.m.* (*coll.*) baptism.

batería, *n.f.* battery; battering; (*theat.*) footlights; (*mus.*) percussion instruments (*in an orchestra* or *band*); ***batería de cocina,*** set of kitchen utensils; ***en batería,*** in a row, in line, lined up.

batero, -ra, *n.m.f.* dressmaker.

batey, *n.m.* (*Cub.*) central complex on sugar plantation.

batiboleo, *n.m.* (*Hisp. Am.*) noisy stir, bustle.

batiborrillo, batiburrillo, *n.m.* hodge-podge, mixed medley.

baticola, *n.f.* crupper.

baticulo, *n.m.* (*naut.*) cordage, rigging; lateen mizen-sail.

batida (1), *n.f.* battue, hunting-party (*sport*); reconnaissance; minting (*coins*).

batidera, *n.f.* (*build.*) beater; instrument for cutting honeycombs.

batidero, *n.m.* continuous beating *or* striking; beating-place; collision; uneven ground; (*pl.*) (*naut.*) wash-boards; sail-tablings.

batido, -da (2), *a.* shot, chatoyant (*silk*). — *n.m.* wafer *or* biscuit batter; beaten eggs; beating; milk shake.

batidor, -ra, *a.* beating. — *n.m.* (*mech.*) beater; scout; (*prov., hunt.*) beater; one of the guard of honour who ride before a royal coach; outrider; haircomb; ***batidor de cáñamo,*** hemp-dresser; ***batidor de oro,*** gold-beater. — *n.f.* (food) mixer, beater, whisk.

batiente, *a.* beating; (*mil.*) ***a tambor batiente,*** with drums beating; ***reír(se) a mandíbula batiente,*** to guffaw. — *n.m.* jamb; leaf of door; place where the sea beats against shore *or* dyke; damper (*of a piano*); (*naut.*) vertical frame of gun-port.

batihoja, *n.m.* gold-beater.

batimento, *n.m.* (*paint.*) shade.

batimetría, *n.f.* bathymetry.

batimiento, *n.m.* beating.

batín, *n.m.* (short) dressing-gown, (man's) dressing-gown, (*Am.*) bathrobe.

batintín, *n.m.* Chinese gong.

bationdeo, *n.m.* fluttering (*of a banner* or *curtain*).

batiportar, *v.t.* (*naut.*) to house (*a gun*).

batiporte, *n.m.* (*naut.*) frame (*of gun-port*).

batir, *v.t.* to beat, pound, strike; to whip, whisk; to beat *or* batter down; to clap; to coin, mint; ***batir el campo,*** to reconnoitre the ground *or* terrain; (*naut.*) ***batir banderas,*** to salute with the colours; to strike colours; (*mil.*) ***batir tiendas,*** to strike camp; ***batir las olas,*** to ply the seas; ***batir(se) el cobre,*** to make determined efforts, put up a really good fight *or* show, give a good account of oneself. — **batirse,** *v.r.* to fight; to fight a duel; ***batirse en duelo,*** to fight a duel.

batista, *n.f.* batiste, fine cambric.

bato, *n.m.* simpleton, rustic.

batochar, *v.t.* to mix (*the hairs and fibres in hat-making*).

batojar, *v.t.* to beat down (*the fruit of a tree*).

batología, *n.f.* tautology, needless repetition.

batológico, -ca, *a.* tautological.

batometría, *n.f.* bathymetry.

batómetro, *n.m.* batometre, bathymetre.

batracio, -cia, *a.*, *n.m.f.* (*zool.*) batrachian. — *n.m.pl.* Batrachia.

batraco, *n.m.* tumour on the tongue.

batuda, *n.f.* series of jumps on a trampoline.

Batuecas, *n.f.pl.* (*coll.*) ***estar en las Batuecas,*** to have one's head in the clouds.
batueco, *n.m.* (*prov.*) addled egg.
batuque, *n.m.* rowdy dance; confusion, disorder.
batuquear, *v.t.* (*Hisp. Am.*) to flap, to move in a violent manner.
baturrada, *n.f.* cloddish *or* uncouth thing to do *or* say.
baturrillo, *n.m.* hotchpotch; (*coll.*) medley, potpourri.
baturro, -rra, *a.* uncouth. — *n.m.f.* peasant from Aragon; (*fig.*) clod, yokel.
batuta, *n.f.* (*mus.*) conductor's baton; ***llevar la batuta,*** to have the whip-hand, call the tune.
baúl, *n.m.* chest, trunk; (*coll.*) belly; ***baúl mundo,*** Saratoga trunk.
baulero, *n.m.* trunk maker *or* seller.
bauprés, *n.m.* (*naut.*) bowsprit.
bausán, -sana, *n.m.f.* effigy; mannikin; (*coll.*) fool, idiot.
bautismal, *a.* baptismal.
bautismo, *n.m.* baptism, christening; ***fe de bautismo,*** certificate of baptism; ***bautismo de fuego,*** baptism by fire.
bautista, *n.m.* one who baptizes; Baptist; ***San Juan Bautista*** or ***El Bautista,*** St. John the Baptist.
bautisterio, *n.m.* baptistry.
bautizante, *a.* baptizing, christening.
bautizar [C], *v.t.* to baptize, christen; to name, call; (*coll.*) to nick-name; to throw water over; ***bautizar el vino,*** to water down wine.
bautizo, *n.m.* baptism; christening party.
bauza, *n.f.* rough chunk *or* piece of wood.
bauzado, *n.m.* (*prov.*) roof of a hut.
bávaro, -ra, *a.*, *n.m.f.* Bavarian.
Baviera, *n.f.* Bavaria.
baya (1), *n.f.* (*bot.*) berry.
bayadera, *n.f.* bayadère, Oriental dancer.
bayal, *a.* long-stemmed, fine-fibred (*flax*). — *n.m.* lever used in raising millstones.
bayeta, *n.f.* baize, baize cloth, duster; floor cloth.
bayetón, *n.m.* blanket-cloth, heavy coating, cloth for coats; (*Hisp. Am.*) long baize poncho.
bayetuno, -na, *a.* appertaining to baize.
bayo, -ya (2), *a.* bay. — *n.m.f.* bay (*horse*); ***uno piensa el bayo*** (***y otro el que le ensilla***), he who gives orders has one idea, he who takes them (often has) another. — *n.m.* silkworm moth.
bayoco (1), *n.m.* Italian copper coin.
bayoco (2), *n.m.* (*prov.*) unripe *or* withered fig.
bayón, *n.m.* (*Philip.*) sack made of matting for bailing.
bayona, *n.f.* bow oar; scull used for steering.
bayoneta, *n.f.* bayonet; ***a la bayoneta,*** with fixed bayonets; ***armar*** or ***calar la bayoneta,*** to fix bayonets.
bayonetazo, *n.m.* bayonet thrust *or* wound.
bayosa, *n.f.* (*sl.*) sword.
bayú, *n.m.* (*Cub.*) brothel.
bayuca, *n.f.* (*coll.*) tavern.
baza (1), *n.f.* trick (*at cards*); ***hacer baza,*** to get on, be successful; ***meter baza,*** to get one's spoke in, to butt in; ***no poder*** (***conseguir***) ***meter baza,*** to be unable to get a word in edgeways; ***no deja meter baza a nadie,*** he doesn't let anyone get a word in edgeways.
bazagón, -gona, *a.* chattering, gossiping.
bazar, *n.m.* bazaar, market-place; toy shop; department store.
bazo, -za (2), *a.* brownish-yellow. — *n.m.* (*anat.*) spleen.
bazofia, *n.f.* offal; waste *or* rotten food, mush; rubbish, trash, filth.
bazucar [A], **bazuquear,** *v.t.* to shake (*liquids*); to agitate, shake.
bazuqueo, *n.m.* shaking, stirring (*of liquids*); (*fig.*) jumble.
be (1), *n.m.* baa; bleating.
be (2), *n.f.* letter B; ***Ce por be,*** from A to Z, in detail.
beata, *n.f.* [BEATO].
beatería, *n.f.* sanctimoniousness, exaggerated *or* insufferable piety, goody-goodiness.
beaterio, *n.m.* house inhabited by pious women.
beático, -ca, *a.* hypocritical.
beatificación, *n.f.* beatification.
beatificar [A], *v.t.* to beatify.
beatífico, -ca, *a.* (*theol.*) beatific, beatifical.
beatilla, *n.f.* fine linen.
beatísimo, -ma, *a. superl.* most holy, most blessed; ***beatísimo Padre,*** Most Holy Father (*the Pope*).
beatitud, *n.f.* beatitude, blessedness, holiness; bliss; ***su beatitud,*** his Beatitude.
beato, -ta, *a.* happy, blessed; (*coll.*) sanctimonious, exaggeratedly *or* insufferably pious, goody-goody. — *n.m.f.* (*coll.*) sanctimonious, over-pious *or* insufferably devout person, religious crack-pot.
beatón, -tona, *a.* atrociously sanctimonious. — *n.m.f.* atrociously sanctimonious person.
bebedero, -ra, *a.* drinkable. — *n.m.* drinking-trough (*for birds*); place where birds drink; spout; (*pl.*) strips for facing revers and sleeves.
bebedizo, -za, *a.* drinkable. — *n.m.* medicinal potion; love potion; philtre; poisonous draught.
bebedor, -ra, *a.* tippling. — *n.m.f.* drinker, tippler, boozer.
beber, *n.m.* drinking; drink. — *v.t.* to drink; (*naut.*) ***beber agua,*** to ship a sea; ***beberse las lágrimas,*** to keep back one's tears; ***beber los vientos por,*** to sigh *or* long for; ***sin comerlo ni beberlo,*** without even trying; without any merit, blame *or* responsibility; ***beber algo,*** to have sth. to drink; ***estar bebido,*** to have had a drink or two. — *v.i.* to drink; (*fig.*) to imbibe, drink up; ***beber de*** or ***en,*** to drink out of; (*coll.*) ***beber en buenas fuentas,*** to get information from good sources; ***beber a*** or ***por la salud de alguien,*** to drink s.o.'s health; ***beber como una cuba,*** to drink like a fish. — **beberse,** *v.r.* to drink up *or* down; (*coll.*) to polish off.
beberrón, -rrona, *a.* tippling. — *n.m.f.* tippler.
bebible, *a.* drinkable.
bebida, *n.f.* drink, beverage; (*Am.*) liquor.
bebistrajo, *n.m.* (*coll.*) rotten drink, concoction.
beborrotear, *v.i.* (*coll.*) to tipple.
beca, *n.f.* sash worn over student's gown; fellowship, scholarship, bursary; tippet worn by ecclesiastics.
becabunga, *n.f.* (*bot.*) brooklime.
becada, *n.f.* (*orn.*) woodcock.
becafigo, *n.m.* (*orn.*) fig-pecker.
becardón, *n.m.* (*prov.*, *orn.*) snipe.
becario, *n.m.* holder of a scholarship.
becerra, *n.f.* heifer; (*bot.*) snapdragon; (*prov.*) lump of dough (*in cakes and bread*).
becerrada, *n.f.* bullfight with young bulls.
becerrero, *n.m.* cowherd.
becerril, *a.* concerning cows *or* bulls; bovine; calf.
becerrilla, *n.f.* very young heifer.
becerrillo, *n.m.* tanned and dressed calfskin; small *or* young calf.
becerro, *n.m.* young bull; tanned and dressed calfskin; church register; register of privileges and nobility; (*zool.*) ***becerro marino,*** sea-calf, seal; ***el culto del becerro de oro,*** the worship of the golden calf.
becoquín, *n.m.* cap with ear-flaps; coif.
becoquino, *n.m.* (*bot.*) honeywort.
becuadrado, *n.m.* (*mus.*) natural; first property in plain-song *or* Gregorian mode.
becuadro, *n.m.* (*mus.*) sign (♮) denoting a natural tone.

becuna, *n.f.* (*ichth.*) becuna.
bedano, *n.m.* (*prov.*) large chisel.
bedel, *n.m.* beadle; porter, servitor.
bedelía, *n.f.* beadleship; office of porter.
bedelio, *n.m.* bdellium, an aromatic gum.
bederre, *n.m.* (*sl.*) hangman, executioner.
beduino, -na, *a.*, *n.m.f.* Bedouin. — *n.m.* (*fig.*) barbarian, barbarous person.
beduro, *n.m.* (*mus.*) natural.
befa (1), *n.f.* jeer(ing), mocking, scoffing, taunt(ing).
befabemí, *n.m.* (*mus.*) Hypophrygian mode (*plain chant*).
befadura, *n.f.* scoffing, taunt; moving of lips (*horse*).
befar, *v.t.* to jeer at, mock, scoff at, taunt. — *v.i.* to move the lips and endeavour to catch the chain of the bit (*horses*).
befo, -fa (2), *a.* blubber-lipped; knock-kneed. — *n.m.* lip (*of an animal*); (*zool.*) monkey.
begardo, -da, *n.m.f.* Beghard.
begonia, *n.f.* (*bot.*) begonia.
begoniáceo, -cea, *a.* relating to the begonia.
behetría, *n.f.* town whose inhabitants were free and could elect any lord; (*fig.*) chaos, pandemonium.
béisbol, *n.m.* baseball.
bejín, *n.m.* (*bot.*) puff-ball; (*coll.*) touchy person; peevish child.
bejuco, *n.m.* (*bot.*) bindweed; thin reed; rattan.
bejuquillo, *n.m.* small gold chain made in China; (*bot.*) root of ipecacuanha.
belcho, *n.m.* (*bot.*) horse-tail tree.
beldad, *n.f.* beauty; belle.
beldar, *v.t.* (*agric.*) to winnow.
belemnita, *n.f.* (*geol.*) belemnite.
belemnítico, -ca, *a.* (*geol.*) belemnitic.
Belén, *n.m.* Bethlehem.
belén, *n.m.* crib, Christmas crib, Nativity scene; (*coll.*) bedlam, pandemonium; (*coll.*) difficulty, risk; (*coll.*) gossip, mischief; ***meterse en belenes,*** to get into difficulties, get into a fix.
beleño, *n.m.* (*bot.*) henbane.
belérico, *n.m.* (*bot.*) myrobalan.
belez, *n.f.*, **belezo,** *n.m.* receptacle, vessel; household article; (*prov.*) jar (*for oil* or *wine*).
belfo, -fa, *a.* blubber-lipped. — *n.m.* lip (*animals*).
belga, bélgico, -ca, *a.*, *n.m.f.* Belgian.
Bélgica, *n.f.* Belgium.
belicismo, *n.m.* war spirit, war-mongering.
belicista, *a.* warlike, war-mongering. — *n.m.* war-mongerer.
bélico, -ca, *a.* appertaining to war; ***material bélico,*** war material.
belicosidad, *n.f.* bellicosity, pugnacity, warlike spirit.
belicoso, -sa, *a.* warlike, bellicose, aggressive.
beligerancia, *n.f.* belligerence, belligerency; (*coll.*) influence, say; ***a usted no le han dado beligerancia en este asunto, no tienes beligerancia en este asunto,*** you have no say in this matter.
beligerante, *a.*, *n.m.f.* belligerent.
belígero, -ra, *a.* (*poet.*) warlike.
belísono, -na, *a.* with martial *or* warlike sound.
belitre, *a.* (*coll.*) low, vile, base. — *n.m.* (*coll.*) rascal, rogue.
belitrería, *n.f.* knavishness, rascality.
belitrero, *n.m.* (*sl.*) double-crosser.
belorta, *n.f.* (*agric.*) clasp-ring (*of plough*).
bellacada, *n.f.* nest of rogues; knavish act *or* deed.
bellacamente, *adv.* knavishly, in rascally fashion.
bellaco, -ca, *a.* sly, cunning; base, vile. — *n.m.* rogue, scoundrel, knave.
bellacuelo, -la, *n.m.* petty rogue, miserable knave.
belladona, *n.f.* (*bot.*) belladonna, deadly nightshade.
bellaquear, *v.i.* to behave in a roguish, artful *or* base manner.
bellaquería, *n.f.* knavery, roguery; cunning, cheating; vile act *or* word.
bellerife, *n.m.* (*slang*) judge's servant.
belleza, *n.f.* beauty, fairness, handsomeness.
bellico, *n.m.* (*bot.*) oat.
bello, -lla, *a.* beautiful, handsome, fair, fine; ***el bello sexo,*** the fair sex; ***Bellas Artes,*** fine arts; ***la Bella Durmiente,*** The Sleeping Beauty.
bellorio, -ria, *a.* greyish, mouse-coloured (*horse*).
bellota, *n.f.* acorn; acorn-shaped balsam *or* perfume-box; carnation bud; acorn-shaped fringeless tassel.
bellote, *n.m.* large round-headed nail.
bellotear, *v.i.* to feed on acorns.
bellotera, *n.f.* woman who gathers *or* sells acorns; season for gathering acorns and pig fattening; acorn crop; holm-oak grove.
bellotero, *n.m.* man who gathers acorns; oak tree.
bemol, *a.* (*mus.*) flat. — *n.m.* (*mus.*) flat; flat sign (♭); softness, smoothness; (*coll.*) ***tener bemoles,*** to be a tough proposition.
bemolado, -da, *a.* (*mus.*) flat, lowered a semitone.
ben, *n.m.* (*bot.*) behen.
bencina, *n.f.* (*chem.*) benzine; (*Arg.*) petrol.
bendecidor, -ra, *a.* blessing, blesser.
bendecir [17, *imperative* **bendice,** *future regular, p.p.* **bendito, bendecido**], *v.t.* to bless; to consecrate; to praise, exalt.
bendición, *n.f.* benediction, blessing; grace; ***echar la bendición a,*** to bless; (*coll., fig.*) to say goodbye to; ***trabaja que es una bendición,*** it does one good to see how hard *or* well he works; (*iron.*) ***miente que es una bendición,*** he is a glorious liar; (*pl.*) ***bendiciones nupciales,*** marriage ceremony.
bendito, -ta, *a.* blessed, saintly; happy, fortunate; (*coll.*) blasted, damned, wretched; ***agua bendita,*** holy water. — *n.m.* simpleton, simple-minded soul.
benedícite, *n.m.* travel permission sought by ecclesiastics; grace before meal; Song of the Three Holy Children.
benedicta, *n.f.* (*med.*) benedict, electuary.
benedictino, -na, *a.* Benedictine. — *n.m.* Benedictine (*monk* or *liqueur*).
benedictus, *n.m. inv.* (*mus.*) benedictus.
benefactor, -ra, *n.m.f.* benefactor, benefactress.
beneficencia, *n.f.* beneficence, charity; welfare; ***función de beneficencia,*** charity performance.
beneficentísimo, -ma, *a. superl.* extremely beneficent, highly charitable.
beneficiable, *a.* deserving of charity; eligible.
beneficiación, *n.f.* benefaction.
beneficiado, -da, *n.m.f.* beneficiary.
beneficiador, -ra, *a.* beneficent, doing good. — *n.m.f.* benefactor.
beneficial, *a.* (*eccles.*) relating to benefices.
beneficiar, *v.t.* to benefit, do good to; to improve; (*agric.*) to cultivate; (*min.*) to work, exploit; to process; to serve; (*com.*) to sell at a discount; (*eccles.*) to confer a benefice on. — **beneficiarse,** *v.r.* to do o.s. good, benefit, profit (**de,** from, by); to make a good thing (**de,** out of); to take undue *or* unfair advantage (**de,** of).
beneficiario, *n.m.* beneficiary.
beneficio, *n.m.* benefit, favour; utility, profit; (*agric.*) cultivation; (*min.*) development; (*min.*) process; perquisite of employment; selling at a discount; (*theat.*) benefit (*performance, proceeds*); (*law*) benefit, right by law *or* charter; (*eccles.*) benefice, ecclesiastical living; ***beneficio bruto,*** gross profit; ***beneficio neto,*** net profit; ***tomar a beneficio de inventario,*** to pay no attention (to), ignore, treat with contempt; ***no tener oficio ni beneficio,*** to have neither profession nor means of support.

beneficioso, -sa, *a.* beneficial, advantageous, profitable.
benéfico, -ca, *a.* beneficial; beneficent, charitable; ***con fines benéficos,*** for charity, for charitable purposes.
benemérito, -ta, *a.* meritorious, worthy; ***benemérito de la patria,*** well-deserving of the country. — *n.f.* ***La Benemérita,*** the Civil Guard (*Guardia Civil*).
beneplácito, *n.m.* approval, consent, placet.
benevolencia, *n.f.* benevolence.
benevolente, *a.* benevolent, kind.
benévolo, -la, *a.* benevolent, benign, kind.
bengala, *n.f.* (*bot.*) cane; (*mil.*) baton, sceptre; Bengal stripes; (***luz de***) ***bengala,*** Bengal light; sparkler; flare.
bengalí, *a., n.m.f.* Bengali, Bengalee. — *n.m.* Bengali language; (*orn.*) Bengal finch.
benignidad, *n.f.* benignity, kindness, graciousness, mercifulness; mildness (*of climate, weather etc.*).
benigno, -na, *a.* benign, merciful, kind; (*fig.*) mild, temperate; non-malignant.
Benito, *n.m.* Benedict.
benito, -ta, *a., n.m.f.* Benedictine (friar *or* nun).
Benjamín, *n.m.* Benjamin; youngest son, darling.
benjamita, *a., n.m.f.* (one) descended from the tribe of Benjamin.
benjuí, *n.m.* benzoin.
benzoato, *n.m.* (*chem.*) benzoate.
benzoico, *a.* (*chem.*) benzoic.
benzol, *n.m.* (*chem.*) benzol.
benzolina, *n.f.* (*chem.*) benzoline.
beocio, -cia, *a.* Bœotian; (*fig.*) stupid, dull. — *n.m.f.* dunce.
beodez, *n.f.* drunkenness.
beodo, -da, *a.* drunk, drunken. — *n.m.f.* drunkard, inebriate.
beorí, *n.m.* (*zool.*) American tapir.
beque, *n.m.* (*naut.*) head (*of a ship*); crew's water-closet; (*fig.*) chamber-pot.
béquico, -ca, *a.* efficacious against coughs.
berberecho, *n.m.* (*ichth.*) cockle.
berberí, berberisco, -ca, *a., n.m.f.* native of Barbary, Berber.
Berbería, *n.f.* Barbary.
berberís, *n.m.* (*bot.*) barberry, berberry.
bérbero, bérberos, *n.m.* barberry (*tree and fruit*); confection made of barberry fruit.
berbí, *n.m.* woollen cloth.
berbiquí, *n.m.* (*carp.*) brace and bit.
berceo, *n.m.* (*bot.*) bass, sedge.
bercería, *n.f.* vegetable market.
bercero, -ra, *n.m.f.* greengrocer.
bereber, *a., n.m.f.* native of Barbary, Berber.
berenjena, *n.f.* (*bot.*) egg-plant, aubergine.
berenjenal, *n.m.* egg-plant plantation; (*fig.*) difficulties, troubles; (*fig.*) ***meterse en un berenjenal,*** to get into a fix.
berenjenín, *n.m.* (*bot.*) egg-plant.
bergamota, *n.f.* (*bot.*) bergamot (*fruit, essence* or *snuff*).
bergamote, bergamoto, *n.m.* (*bot.*) bergamot-tree.
bergante, *n.m.* brazen-faced villain, ruffian, rascal.
bergantín, *n.m.* (*naut.*) brig, brigantine.
bergantinejo, *n.m.* (*naut.*) small brig.
bergantón, bergantonazo, *n.m.* great villain.
beriberi, *n.m.* (*med.*) beriberi.
berilo, *n.m.* (*min.*) beryl.
berlanga, *n.f.* card game.
berlina, *n.f.* berlin (*carriage*); front compartment (*of a stage-coach* or *railway carriage*); ***estar, quedar, poner en berlina,*** to be, be left, place in a ridiculous position.
berlinés, -nesa, *a., n.m.f.* (native) of Berlin.
berlinga, *n.f.* pole (*of green wood used for stirring molten metal*); (*prov.*) (clothes-line) post; (*prov.*) tall, gawky person; (*naut.*) round timber.
berlingar [B], *v.t.* to stir (*molten metal*) with a pole.
berma, *n.f.* (*fort.*) berm.
bermejal, *n.m.* (*Cub.*) bright red soil.
bermejear, *v.i.* to be *or* show up (as) vermilion (colour); to tend to vermilion.
bermejecer [9], *v.i.* to turn vermilion; to blush.
bermejizo, -za, *a.* tending to vermilion.
bermejo, -ja, *a.* vermilion.
bermejuela, *n.f.* (*ichth.*) rochet; (*prov., bot.*) heather.
bermejura, *n.f.* vermilion colour.
bermellón, *n.m.* vermilion.
Bermudas, *n.f.pl.,* ***las —,*** Bermuda.
Bernabé, *n.m.* Barnabas.
bernardina, *n.f.* (*coll.*) tall story.
bernardo, -da, *a., n.m.f.* Bernardine (monk *or* nun). — *n.m.* (*zool.*) hermit-crab.
bernegal, *n.m.* bowl, drinking-cup, cup with scalloped edges; (*Ven.*) earthen jar.
bernés, -nesa, *a., n.m.f.* Bernese, (native) of Berne.
bernia, *n.f.* rug; rug cloak.
berquera, *n.f.* confectioner's wire sieve *or* tray.
berra, berraza, *n.f.* tall watercress.
berraña, *n.f.* coarse watercress.
berrazal, berrizal, *n.m.* cress-bed.
berrear, *v.i.* to low, bellow; to bawl, squall, yell. — **berrearse,** *v.r.* (*coll.*) to squeal, spill the beans.
berrenchín, *n.m.* odour (*emitted by furious wild boar*); (*coll.*) tantrum.
berrendearse, *v.r.* (*prov.*) to grow yellow (*wheat*).
berrendo, -da, *a.* two-coloured; spotted. — *n.m.* pronghorn deer.
berreón, -rreona, *a.* (*prov.*) bawling, squalling, yelling.
berrera, *n.f.* (*bot.*) water parsnip.
berrido, *n.m.* bellow, low(ing); bawl, squall, yell.
berrín [BEJÍN (*coll.*)].
berrinche, *n.m.* (*coll.*) fit of temper, tantrum.
berro, *n.m.* (*bot.*) watercress.
berrocal, *n.m.* craggy *or* rocky place.
berroqueño, -ña, *a.* stone-hard, granitic; ***piedra berroqueña,*** granite stone.
berrueco, *n.m.* (*med.*) tumour in the pupil of the eye; rock.
berso, berzo, *n.m.* (*prov.*) cradle.
berta, *n.f.* lace collar *or* pelerine.
berza, *n.f.* (*bot.*) cabbage; (*bot.*) ***berza de pastor,*** white goosefoot; (*bot.*) ***berza de perro*** or ***perruna,*** milkweed; ***estar en berza,*** to be in the blade (*of corn*); (*coll.*) ***mezclar berzas con capachos,*** to get things all mixed up. — *n.m.* (**berza**) country bumpkin, yokel, (*fam.*) clod.
berzal, *n.m.* cabbage patch.
besable, *a.* kissable.
besador, -ra, *a.* kissing.
besalamano, *n.m.* 'with compliments' card *or* note.
besamanos, *n.m. inv.* levée, court-day; salute performed by kissing someone's hand.
besana, *n.f.* (first) furrow, furrowing.
besante, *n.m.* (*numis., her.*) bezant.
besar, *v.t.* to kiss; (*coll.*) to graze, touch lightly; ***llegar y besar el santo,*** to succeed straight away; ***besarle a alguien la mano*** or ***los pies,*** expressions of respect and courtesy, often used in the abbreviated forms Q.B.S.M., Q.B.S.P., *etc.*
besico, *n.m.* (*bot.*) ***besico de monja,*** Indian heart.
besito, *n.m.* (delightful) little kiss.
beso, *n.m.* kiss; (*coll.*) ***comerse a besos,*** to kiss repeatedly and vehemently.
besotear, *v.t.* to slobber over.
besoteo, *n.m.* excessive kissing, slobbery kissing.
besque, *n.m.* (*prov.*) bird-lime.

bestezuela, *n.f.* small beast, small creature.
bestia, *n.f.* beast; ***bestia de silla,*** saddle-mule; ***bestia de carga,*** beast of burden. — *n.m.* (*fig.*) brute; oaf; idiot; ***hacer el bestia,*** to play the oaf; to act the goat.
bestiaje, bestiame, *n.m.* assembly of beasts of burden.
bestial, *a.* bestial, brutal; (*coll.*) smashing, terrific; enormous.
bestialidad, *n.f.* bestiality; (*coll.*) terrific amount.
bestializarse [C], *v.r.* to sink to animal level.
bestiario, *n.m.* bestiary.
bestión, *n.m.* (*arch.*) grotesque animal figure.
béstola, *n.f.* ploughstaff.
besucador, -ra, *a.* (*coll.*) kissing, necking. — *n.m.f.* (*coll.*) kisser, necker.
besucar [A], *v.t.* (*coll.*) to kiss, neck with.
besucón, -cona, *a.* (*coll.*) much given to kissing *or* necking. — *n.m.f.* (*coll.*) exaggerated kisser *or* necker.
besugada, *n.f.* dish, meal *or* feast of bream; (*coll.*) idiotic thing to do *or* say.
besugo, *n.m.* (*ichth.*) (sea) bream; red gilt-head; (*coll.*) nitwit; ***ojos de besugo,*** glazed, staring eyes, vacant eyes.
besuguero, -ra, *n.m.f.* vendor of sea-bream. — *n.m.* sea-bream transporter; (*prov.*) fishing-tackle for sea-bream. — *n.f.* fish-kettle.
besuquear, *v.t.* to kiss slobberingly, slobber over.
besuqueo, *n.m.* slobbery kissing.
beta, *n.f.* thread, tape; (*naut.*) esparto cord; (*naut.*) piece of cordage used as tackle.
betarraga, betarrata, *n.f.* (*bot.*) beetroot.
betel, *n.m.* (*bot.*) betel, betel-pepper.
betería, *n.f.* (*naut.*) cordage (*aboard a ship*).
bético, -ca, *a.*, *n.m.f.* (native) of Baetica, Andalusian.
betlemita, *n.m.f.* native of Bethlehem.
betlemítico, -ca, *a.* appertaining to Bethlehem.
betón, *n.m.* concrete, hydraulic cement; bee-glue; (*med.*) colostrum.
betónica, *n.f.* (*bot.*) betony.
betuláceo, -cea, *a.* belonging to the genus birch, birchen.
betuminoso, -sa, *a.* bituminous.
betún, *n.m.* bitumen, pitch; shoe blacking, shoe polish; (*hydrost.*) packing; ***betún de Judea,*** Jew's pitch.
betunería, *n.f.* bitumen; shoe-polish factory *or* shop.
betunero, *n.m.* maker *or* seller of pitch *or* shoe polish; boot-black, shoe shiner.
bezaar, bezar, bezoar, *n.m.* (*med.*) bezoar.
bezante [BESANTE].
bezo, *n.m.* blubber lip; (*med.*) proud flesh.
bezoar, *n.m.* (*zool.*) bezoar.
bezoárdico, -ca, bezoárico, -ca, *a.* relating to bezoar. — *n.m.* antidote; ***bezoárdico mineral,*** peroxide of antimony.
bezote, *n.m.* (*Hisp. Am.*) ring worn by Indians in lower lip.
bezudo, -da, *a.* blubber-lipped.
biajaiba, *n.f.* biajaiba fish.
biangulado, -da, biangular, *a.* biangular.
biazas, *n.f.pl.* saddlebags.
bíbaro, *n.m.* (*zool.*) beaver.
bibero, *n.m.* linen cloth.
biberón, *n.m.* infant's feeding-bottle.
bibijagua, *n.f.* destructive ant.
Biblia, *n.f.* Bible.
bíblico, -ca, *a.* Biblical.
bibliófilo, *n.m.* bibliophile, book-lover.
bibliografía, *n.f.* bibliography.
bibliográfico, -ca, *a.* bibliographical.
bibliógrafo, *n.m.* bibliographer.
bibliomanía, *n.f.* bibliomania, mania for books.
bibliómano, *n.m.f.* bibliomaniac, book fiend.
biblioteca, *n.f.* library; ***biblioteca de consulta,*** reference library; ***biblioteca circulante,*** lending library.
bibliotecario, -ria, *n.m.f.* librarian.
bica, *n.f.* (*prov.*) unleavened maize-tart, maize-cake.
bical, *n.m.* (*ichth.*) male salmon.
bicameral, *a.* (*pol.*) two-chamber, having an upper and a lower house.
bicapsular, *a.* (*bot.*) bicapsular.
bicarbonato, *n.m.* (*chem.*) bicarbonate.
bíceps, *n.m. inv.* biceps muscle.
bicerra, *n.f.* (*zool.*) wild goat.
bicicleta, *n.f.* bicycle.
biciclo, *n.m.* large bicycle; penny-farthing.
bicipital, *a.* (*anat.*) bicipital.
bicípite, *a.* bicephalous.
bicloruro, *n.m.* (*chem.*) bichloride.
bicoca, *n.f.* trifle; (*coll.*) piece of cake, walk-over.
bicolor, *a.* two-coloured.
bicóncavo, -va, *a.* concavo-concave.
biconvexo, -xa, *a.* convexo-convex.
bicoquete, bicoquín, *n.m.* cap with ear-flaps.
bicorne, *a.* (*poet.*) two-horned.
bicornio, -nia, *a.* two-horned. — *n.m.* two-cornered hat.
bicorpóreo, -rea, *a.* bicorporal, bicorporate.
bicos, *n.m.pl.* gold trimmings on skullcaps.
bicromato, *n.m.* (*chem.*) bichromate.
bicromía, *n.f.* two-colour print.
bicuadrado, -da, *a.* (*math.*) biquadratic; ***ecuación bicuadrada,*** biquadratic equation.
bicuento, *n.m.* billion.
bicuspidado, -da, bicúspide, *a.* bicuspid.
bicha, *n.f.* (*coll.*) used by the superstitious to replace the word ***culebra,*** considered to be of ill omen; ***mentar la bicha,*** to raise an unpleasant subject; (*arch.*) fantastic caryatid; (*Col.*) small grub *or* insect.
bicharraco, *n.m.* (*coll.*) revolting, loathsome creature.
bichear, *v.t.* to spy on.
bichero, *n.m.* (*naut.*) boat-hook.
bichito, *n.m.* (delightful) little creature.
bicho, *n.m.* insect; creature; fighting bull; (*coll.*) ***es un mal bicho,*** he's a nasty bit of work, nasty customer; (*coll.*) ***bicho raro,*** funny chap, peculiar individual; (*coll.*) ***bicho viviente,*** living soul.
bidé, *n.m.* bidet.
bidente, *a.* (*poet.*) bidentate. — *n.m.* (*poet.*) bident, two-pronged fork.
biela, *n.f.* (*mech.*) connecting-rod; tie-rod.
bielda, *n.f.* large pitchfork.
bieldar, *v.t.* to winnow with a pitchfork.
bieldero, -ra, *n.m.f.* maker *or* vendor of pitchforks.
bieldo, bielgo, *n.m.* winnowing fork.
bien, *a.* ***de casa bien,*** of good family. — *adv.* well; right, all right; properly; very, hard; easily; fully; gladly, willingly; about; ***el proyecto salió bien,*** the plan turned out well *or* all right; ***estamos bien,*** we are all right *or* fine; ***hazlo bien,*** do it properly; ***llegó bien tarde,*** he arrived very *or* pretty late; ***trabaja bien poco,*** he does precious little work; ***bien se conoce que tienes dinero,*** it's easy to see you have money; ***bien andaríamos cinco kilómetros antes de ver el pueblo,*** we must have walked a good three miles before we saw the village; ***entérate bien,*** get full details; get your facts right; ***yo bien quisiera ir, pero no puedo,*** I'd gladly go *or* I'd be only too glad to go, but I can't; ***bien avenidos,*** on good terms; ***ahora bien,*** all the same, nevertheless; ***de bien en mejor,*** better and better; ***más bien,*** rather, somewhat; ***más bien lento,*** on the slow side; ***o bien,*** or else; ***¿y bien?*** so what? ***tener a bien***

hacer algo, to consider it fitting to do sth.; to see fit to do sth.; to see one's way to doing sth.; — *conj.* ***bien que, si bien,*** though, although; ***no bien,*** no sooner, hardly, scarcely; ***no bien había llegado . . .,*** scarcely had he arrived . . .; ***bien . . . bien . . .,*** either . . . or. . . . — *n.m.* good; well-being, welfare; dearest, darling; (*pl.*) property, fortune, riches; ***hombre de bien,*** honest man; ***bienes dotales,*** dower; ***bienes gananciales,*** property acquired during married life; ***bienes libres,*** unencumbered estate; ***bienes mostrencos,*** unclaimed property; ***bienes muebles,*** goods and chattels; ***bienes inmuebles*** or ***raíces,*** real estate, (*Am.*) realty; ***bienes semovientes,*** livestock; ***bien con bien se paga,*** one good turn deserves another; ***del bien al mal no hay un canto de real,*** good and bad are (often) not far apart; ***contar*** or ***decir mil bienes de,*** to speak very highly of, praise highly.

bienal, *a.* biennial.

bienamado, -da, *a.* cherished, well-beloved.

bienandante, *a.* happy, successful, prosperous.

bienandanza, *n.f.* felicity, prosperity, success.

bienaventurado, -da, *a.* blessed, happy; fortunate; (*iron.*) simple, simple-minded.

bienaventuranza, *n.f.* beatitude; bliss, felicity, happiness; (*pl.*) (the) beatitudes.

bienestar, *n.m.* well-being, comfort, happiness.

bienfortunado, -da, *a.* fortunate.

biengranada, *n.f.* (*bot.*) curl-leaved goose-foot.

bienhablado, -da, *a.* well-spoken.

bienhadado, -da, *a.* lucky, fortunate.

bienhecho, -cha, *a.* well-made.

bienhechor, -ra, *a.* charitable. — *n.m.f.* benefactor, benefactress.

bienintencionado, -da, *a.* well-intentioned, well-meaning.

bienio, *n.m.* biennium, term *or* period of two years.

bienllegado, -da, *a.*, *n.f.* welcome.

bienmandado, -da, *a.* obedient, submissive.

bienmesabe, *n.m.* meringue.

bienoliente, *a.* fragrant.

bienparecer, *n.m.* (face-saving) compromise.

bienquerencia, *n.f.* goodwill, esteem; affection.

bienquerer, *n.m.* goodwill; affection. — [26], *v.t.* to be well disposed to.

bienqueriente, *n.m.f.* well-wisher.

bienquistar, *v.t.* to conciliate, reconcile.

bienquisto, -ta, *a.* well-loved, highly thought of.

bienteveo, *n.m.* hut built on piles for watching vineyards.

bienvenida, *n.f.* welcome.

bienvivir, *v.i.* to live well *or* uprightly.

bienza, *n.f.* (*prov.*) pellicle (*of egg, onion*); membrane.

bierva, *n.f.* (*prov.*) milch-cow.

bierzo, *n.m.* linen made in El Bierzo.

bies, *n.m. inv.* bias (*of materials*); ***al bies,*** slanting, slantwise.

bifásico, -ca, *a.* (*elec.*) two-phase.

bife, *n.m.* (*Hisp. Am.*) boneless cutlet *or* fillet.

bífero, -ra, *a.* (*bot.*) fructifying twice a year.

bífido, -da, *a.* (*bot.*) bifid.

bifilar, *a.* (*elec.*) two-wired.

biflor, bifloral, bifloro, -ra, *a.* (*bot.*) biflorate, biflorous.

bifoliado, -da, *a.* (*bot.*) bifoliate.

biforme, *a.* (*poet.*) biformed, biform.

bifronte, *a.* (*poet.*) bifront.

biftec, *n.m.* steak; (*pl.* **biftecs**).

biftequera, *n.f.* (*Chi.*) beefsteak broiler.

bifurcación, *n.f.* parting of the ways; (*railway*) branch; (*road*) junction.

bifurcarse [A], *v.r.* to fork, divide; to branch off *or* out.

biga, *n.f.* chariot.

bigamia, *n.f.* bigamy; (*law*) second marriage.

bígamo, -ma, *a.* bigamous. — *n.m.f.* bigamist; twice-married person; person married to widow *or* widower.

bigarada, *n.f.* (*bot.*) sour orange.

bigarda (1), *n.f.* (*prov.*) tip-cat (*children's game*).

bigardear, *v.i.* (*coll.*) to idle *or* loaf about *or* around.

bigardía, *n.f.* jest; fiction, dissimulation.

bigardo, -da (2), *a.* lazy, loutish. — *n.m.* idler, loafer, lazy lout.

bigardón, -dona, *a.* utterly lazy, loutish. — *n.m.* lazy great lout.

bigardonear, (*prov., coll.*) [BIGARDEAR].

bigardonería, *n.f.* (*coll.*) loafing, loutishness.

bígaro, bigarro, *n.m.* (*ichth.*) sea-snail.

bigarra, *n.f.* (*mech.*) horse-power pole (*in horse-mill*).

bigarrado, -da [ABIGARRADO].

bigeno, -na, *a.* producing twice yearly.

bignonia, *n.f.* (*bot.*) bignonia.

bigorella, *n.f.* heavy stone for sinking a fish trap.

bigornia, *n.f.* two-horned anvil; (*sl.*) ***los de bigornia,*** bullies, roughs, toughs.

bigornio, *n.m.* (*sl.*) boaster; bully, rough.

bigorrilla, *n.f.* (*naut.*) round seam (*in material*).

bigotazo, *n.m.* large moustache, handlebar moustache.

bigote, *n.m.* moustache; (*print.*) dash rule; (*min.*) slag tap; (*pl.*) whiskers; ***no tener malos bigotes,*** to be not bad looking; (*fig.*) ***tener bigote(s),*** to be resolute, have guts; to be a tough proposition, a hard nut to crack.

bigotera, *n.f.* leather cover (*for moustaches*); ribbon bow (*formerly worn by women on the breast*); folding seat (*put in the front of a carriage*); small compass; fur edging (*of slippers*); toe-cap; (*min.*) hole in vats for the discharge of scoria; (*prov.*) swindle, trick; (*pl.*) marks left on upper lip after drinking.

bigotudo, -da, *a.* heavily moustached *or* bewhiskered.

bija, *n.f.* (*bot.*) heart-leaved arnotto, bixa; (*com.*) anatta; (*Hisp. Am.*) concoction of seeds of this plant and vermilion used by Indians to daub their bodies.

bijago, *n.m.* (*ichth.*) bijago fish.

bilabiado, -da, *a.* (*bot.*) bilabiate.

bilabial, *a.* (*gram.*) bilabial.

bilao, *n.m.* (*Philip.*) tray made of reed.

bilateral, *a.* bilateral.

bilbaíno, -na, *a.* appertaining to Bilbao. — *n.m.f.* native of Bilbao.

biliar, biliario, -ria, *a.* (*med.*) biliary.

bilingüe, *a.* bilingual.

bilingüismo, *n.m.* bilingualism.

bilioso, -sa, *a.* (*med.*) bilious.

bilis, *n.f. inv.* bile, gall; (*fig.*) spleen; ***descargar la bilis,*** to vent one's spleen.

bilítero, -ra, *a.* biliteral, of two letters.

bilma, *n.f.* (*Hisp. Am.*) poultice.

bilmar, *v.t.* (*Hisp. Am.*) to place poultices on, apply a poultice to.

bilobado, -da, *a.* (*anat.*) bilobate.

bilocación, *n.f.* (*theol.*) bilocation.

bilocarse [A], *v.r.* to be in two places simultaneously.

bilogía, *n.f.* book in two parts.

biltrotear, *v.i.* (*coll.*) to ramble about the streets; to gad about.

biltrotero, -ra, *n.m.f.* gossip; gadabout.

billa, *n.f.* pocketing a ball after it has struck another (*billiards*).

billalda, billarda, *n.f.* tip-cat (*children's game*).

billar, *n.m.* (game of) billiards; billiard-table; billiard-hall; ***billar romano,*** pin-table.

billarde, *n.m.* (*barrel-making*) instrument for curving staves.

billarista, *a., n.m.f.* billiard player.
billete, *n.m.* ticket; banknote, (*Am.*) bill; note; (*arch., her.*) billet; ***billete de abonado,*** season ticket, (*Am.*) commutation ticket; ***billete de ida y vuelta,*** return ticket, (*Am.*) round trip ticket; ***billete kilométrico,*** mileage ticket; ***billete de regalo,*** complimentary ticket.
billetero, *n.m.* wallet, (*Am.*) billfold.
billón, *n.m.* billion (*a million millions*), (*Am.*) trillion.
billonésimo, -ma, *a., n.m.* billionth.
bimaculado, -da, *a.* two-coloured.
bimano, -na, *a.* two-handed.
bimba, *n.f.* (*coll.*) top-hat.
bimbalete, *n.m.* (*Mex.*) prop; buttress, pillar.
bimbral [MIMBRAL].
bimbre [MIMBRE].
bimembre, *a.* having two members.
bimensual, *a.* twice-monthly.
bimestral, *a.* two-monthly.
bimestre, *a.* [BIMESTRAL]. — *n.m.* period of two months; two months' rent, pension *or* salary.
bimetálico, -ca, *a.* bimetallic.
bimetalismo, *m.* bimetallism.
bimetalista, *a.* bimetallic. — *n.m.f.* bimetallist.
bimotor, -ra, *a.* (*aer.*) twin-engined.
bina, *n.f.,* **binazón,** *n.m.* digging *or* ploughing a second time.
binación, *n.f.* (*eccles.*) celebration of the Mass twice on the same day.
binadera, *n.f.* (*agric.*) hoe.
binado, -da, *a.* (*bot.*) geminative.
binador, *n.m.* digger; hoe, weeding-fork.
binar, *v.t.* to plough *or* dig (*ground*) for the second time; to hoe and weed (*vines*) for the second time. — *v.i.* (*eccles.*) to celebrate two Masses on the same day.
binario, -ria, *a.* binary.
binocular, biocular, *a.* (*med.*) binocular.
binóculo, *n.m.* binocle.
binomio, *n.m.* (*alg.*) binomial; ***binomio de Newton,*** binomial theorem.
binubo, -ba, *a., n.m.f.* twice-married (person).
binza, *n.f.* pellicle (*of egg, onion*); any thin membrane; (*prov.*) tomato *or* capsicum seed.
bioblasto, *n.m.* bioblast.
bioculado, -da, *a.* two-eyed.
biodinámica, *n.f.* biodynamics.
biogénesis, *n.f. inv.,* **biogenia,** *n.f.* biogenesis.
biogenético, -ca, biogénico, -ca, *a.* biogenetic.
biografía, *n.f.* biography.
biografiado, -da, *n.m.f.* subject of a biography.
biografiar [L], *v.t.* to write a biography of (*s.o.*).
biográfico, -ca, *a.* biographical.
biógrafo, -fa, *n.m.f.* biographer.
biología, *n.f.* biology.
biològico, -ca, *a.* biological.
biólogo, *n.m.* biologist.
biomagnetismo, *n.m.* biomagnetism.
biombo, *n.m.* (folding) screen.
biometría, *n.f.* biometry.
biomía, *n.f.* (*ent.*) cattle-fly.
bionomía, *n.f.* bionomics.
bioplasma, *n.m.* bioplasm.
bioquímico, -ca, *a.* biochemical. — *n.m.f.* biochemist. — *n.f.* biochemistry.
biótico, -ca, *a.* biotic.
biotita, *n.f.* (*min.*) biotite.
bióxido, *n.m.* (*chem.*) dioxide.
bipartición, *n.f.* bipartition.
bipartidismo, *n.m.* two-party system.
bipartido, -da, *a.* bipartite.
bipedal, *a.* bipedal.
bípedo, -da, *a., n.m.f.* biped.
bipersonal, *a.* for two (people).
bipétalo, -la, *a.* (*bot.*) bipetalous.
biplano, -na, *a., n.m.* (*aer.*) biplane.
biplaza, *n.m.* two-seater (*aeroplane*); two-seater (*car*), (*Am.*) roadster.
bipolar, *a.* bipolar.
bipontino, -na, *a., n.m.f.* native of *or* relating to Zweibrücken (*in the Palatinate*).
biribís, *n.m.* roulette.
biricú, *n.m.* sword-belt.
birimbao, *n.m.* (*mus.*) jew's-harp, jew's-trump.
birla, *n.f.* (*prov.*) ninepin, skittle.
birlador, *n.m.* (*coll.*) filcher, pincher, swiper.
birlar, *v.t.* to bowl a second time (*from the place where the ball stopped the first time*); (*coll.*) to filch, pinch, swipe; to outwit; to kill, knock down at a blow.
birlesca, *n.f.* (*sl.*) (pack of) thieves.
birlesco, *n.m.* (*sl.*) thief.
birlí, *n.m.* (*print.*) blank space at bottom of printed page; printer's earnings.
birlibirloque, *n.m.* (*coll.*) ***por arte de birlibirloque,*** (as if) by magic.
birlo, birloche, *n.m.* (*sl.*) thief.
birlocha, *n.f.* paper-kite.
birlocho, *n.m.* barouche.
birlón, *n.m.* (*prov.*) jack pin, large middle skittle (*in the game of ninepins*).
birlonga, *n.f.* type of ombre; ***a la birlonga,*** carelessly.
Birmania, *n.f.* Burma.
birmano, -na, *a.* appertaining to Burma, Burmese. — *n.m.f.* Burmese. — *n.m.* Burmese (*language*).
birreactor, *a.* twin-jet. — *n.m.* twin-jet (*aircraft*).
birrectángulo, -la, *a.* (*geom.*) having two right angles.
birreme, *a., n.m.* bireme; having two banks of oars.
birreta, *n.f.* biretta, cardinal's cap.
birrete, *n.m.* biretta; cap (*worn by professors, judges etc.*).
birretina, *n.f.* small biretta *or* cap.
birria, *n.f.* (*coll.*) third-rate object; rotten stuff; rubbish, trash, mess.
bis, *adv.* twice; ***¡bis! ¡bis!*** encore!
bisabuelo, *n.m.,* **bisabuela,** *n.f.* great-grandfather *or* -mother.
bisagra, *n.f.* hinge; shoemaker's boxwood polisher.
bisalto, *n.m.* (*prov.*) pea.
bisanual, bisanuo, -nua, *a.* (*bot.*) biennial.
bisar, *v.t.* to repeat (*music*).
bisasado, -da, *a.* twice-roasted.
bisbís, *n.m.* game resembling roulette.
bisbisar, bisbisear, *v.t., v.i.* to mutter, mumble.
bisbiseo, *n.m.* mutter, muttering, mumbling.
biscúter, *n.m.* bubble car.
bisecar [A], *v.t.* to bisect.
bisección, *n.f.* bisection.
bisector, -triz, *a.* (*geom.*) bisecting. — *n.f.* bisector (*of an angle*).
bisecular, *a.* two centuries old.
bisel, *n.m.* bevelled edge (*of a looking-glass*); bevel; chamfer.
biselado, *n.m.* bevelling.
biselamiento, *n.m.* bevelling.
biselar, *v.t.* to bevel.
bisemanal, *a.* twice-weekly.
bisexual, *a.* bisexual.
bisiesto, *a.* bissextile (*year*); ***año bisiesto,*** leap-year.
bisilábico, -ca, bisílabo, -ba, *a.* bisyllabic, two-syllabled.
bismuto, *n.m.* (*min.*) bismuth.
bisnieto, -ta, *n.m.f.* great-grandson, great-granddaughter.

bisojo, -ja, *a.* squinting, squint-eyed. — *n.m.f.* squinter.
bisonte, *n.m.* (*zool.*) bison.
bisoñada, bisoñería, *n.f.* (*coll.*) stupid *or* rash thing done *or* said by a newcomer; practical joke played on a newcomer.
bisoñé, *n.m.* (small) wig, toupee.
bisoño, -ña, *a.* (*mil.*) raw, undisciplined; green. — *n.m.f.* novice, greenhorn.
bispón, *n.m.* roll of oilcloth *or* tarpaulin (used by sword-cutlers).
bistec, *n.m.* (*pl.* **bistecs**) steak.
bístola, *n.f.* (*prov.*) plough-shaft.
bistorta, *n.f.* (*bot.*) bistort, snake-weed.
bistraer [34], *v.t.* (*prov.*) to advance *or* receive in advance (*money*); (*coll.*) to pilfer; to draw out, entice.
bistre, bistro, *n.m.* (*art*) bistre.
bistrecha, *n.f.* (*law*) payment made in advance.
bisturí, *n.m.* (*surg.*) bistoury, scalpel.
bisulco, -ca, *a.* (*zool.*) bisulcate, cloven-footed, cloven-hoofed.
bisulfato, *n.m.* bisulphate.
bisulfito, *n.m.* bisulphite.
bisulfuro, *n.m.* disulphide.
bisunto, -ta, *a.* dirty, greasy.
bisutería, *n.f.* cheap *or* imitation jewellery.
bisutero, *n.m.* maker *or* seller of cheap jewellery.
bita, *n.f.* (*naut.*) bitt.
bitácora, *n.f.* (*naut.*) binnacle.
bitadura, *n.f.* (*naut.*) cable bitt.
bitango, *a.* ***pájaro bitango,*** kite (*toy*).
bitar, *v.t.* (*naut.*) to bitt.
bitola, *n.f.* callipers.
bitones, *n.m.pl.* (*naut.*) pins (*of capstan*).
bitongo, -ga, *a.* (*prov.*) ***niño bitongo,*** overgrown child.
bitoque, *n.m.* bung, plug, stopper.
bitor, *n.m.* (*orn.*) corn-crake.
bitumen, *n.m.* bitumen.
bituminización, *n.f.* bituminization.
bituminizar [C], *v.t.* to bituminize.
bituminoso, -sa, *a.* bituminous.
bivalvo, -va, bivalvulado, -da, bivalvular, *a.* bivalve, bivalvular.
bixineas, *n.f.pl.* (*bot.*) Bixaceæ.
biza, *n.f.* (*ichth.*) bonito.
Bizancio, *n.m.* Byzantium.
bizantinismo, *n.m.* corruption by luxury; excessive ornamentation; useless *or* excessively involved argument *or* discussion.
bizantino, -na, *a.* appertaining to *or* of Byzantium, Byzantian, Byzantine; useless, excessively involved. — *n.m.f.* Byzantine.
bizarrear, *v.i.* to act in a valiant and spirited manner.
bizarría, *n.f.* valour, spirit; generosity.
bizarro, -rra, *a.* valiant, spirited; generous.
bizazas, *n.f.pl.* saddlebags.
bizacha [VIZCACHA].
bizcar [A] [BIZQUEAR].
bizco, -ca, *a.* cross-eyed, squinting, squint-eyed; ***dejar a uno bizco,*** to leave s.o. goggle-eyed, gasping. — *n.m.f.* squinter.
bizcochada, *n.f.* biscuit *or* sponge and milk soup; long split French roll.
bizcochar, *v.t.* to re-heat, warm up (*bread*).
bizcochería, *n.f.* art of biscuit *or* sponge-cake making; sponge-cake shop.
bizcochero, -ra, *n.m.f.* biscuit *or* sponge-cake maker *or* seller.
bizcocho, *n.m.* biscuit, ship's biscuit, hard tack; sponge-cake; bisque; plaster; whiting; ***bizcocho borracho,*** tipsy cake.
bizcorneado, -da, *a.* (*print.*) folded crookedly (*page*); (*Cub.*) cross-eyed, squinting.
bizcorneto, -ta, *a.* cross-eyed, squinting.
bizcotela, *n.f.* iced sponge-cake.
bizma, *n.f.* poultice.
bizmar, *v.t.* to poultice.
bizna, *n.f.* membrane (*separating walnut-kernel*).
biznaga, *n.f.* (*bot.*) bishop's weed; (*Hisp. Am.*) cactus.
biznieto, -ta [BISNIETO].
bizquear, *v.i.* to squint.
blanca (1), *n.f.* old copper coin; (*prov., orn.*) magpie; (*mus.*) minim; ***blanca morfea*** [ALBARAZO]; (*vet.*) white scurf, tetter, ringworm; ***no tener blanca*** or ***estar sin blanca,*** to be broke.
blancal, *a.* white-footed (*partridge*).
blancarte, *n.m.* (*min.*) residue, rubbish.
blanco, -ca (2), *a.* white; blank; ***Blanca Nieves,*** Snow White; ***ropa blanca,*** linen; ***arma blanca,*** steel weapon; (*her.*) ***armas blancas,*** argent. — *n.m.f.* white person; coward. — *n.m.* white colour; white spot *or* hairs (*on animals*); (*theat.*) interval; (*print.*) recto form; (*chem.*) bleach, white dye; blank; blank space; target; ***blanco de huevo,*** eggshell cosmetic; ***blanco de la uña,*** half-moon of the nail; ***dar en el blanco,*** to hit the mark; ***blanco de ballena,*** spermaceti; ***blanco de España,*** Spanish white, whiting; ***blanco de plomo,*** white lead; ***blanco del ojo,*** white of the eye; ***de punta en blanco,*** dressed up to the nines; ***en blanco,*** blank; ***muebles en blanco,*** unpainted furniture; ***una noche en blanco,*** a sleepless night; ***quedarse en blanco,*** to miss the point; ***pasar en blanco,*** to omit.
blancor, *n.m.,* **blancura,** *n.f.* whiteness; (*vet.*) ***blancura del ojo,*** white film on the eye.
blancote, -ta, *a.* excessively *or* unpleasantly white *or* pale.
blancuzco, -ca, *a.* whitish, dirty white.
blanda (1), *n.f* (*sl.*) bed.
blandeador, -ra, *a.* softening.
blandeamiento, *n.m.* softening.
blandear (1), *v.t.* to soften (down).
blandear (2), *v.t.* to brandish, flourish.
blandengue, *a., n.m.f.* soft *or* spineless (person); (*coll.*) softy.
blandicia, *n.f.* softness; flattery.
blandiente, *a.* brandishing, quivering.
blandir [Q], *v.t.* to brandish, flourish.
blando, -da (2), *a.* soft; (too) easy-going; mild; (*mus.*) flatted; ***blando de boca,*** tender-mouthed (*horse*). — *adv.* (**blando**) gently, softly.
blandón, *n.m.* large wax torch with one wick; large church candlestick.
blanducho, -cha, blandujo, -ja, *a.* (*coll.*) oversoft, flabby, pappy, soggy.
blandura, *n.f.* softness; weakness (*character*); (*med.*) lenitive *or* emollient application; white cosmetic; mild temperature; blandishment; ***¡basta de blanduras!*** that's enough *or* we've had enough soft behaviour *or* soft talk!
blandurilla, *n.f.* pomade.
blanduzco, -ca [BLANDUCHO].
blanqueación, *n.f.* whitening, bleaching; white-washing; blanching.
blanqueador, -ra, blanqueante, *a.* whitewashing; whitening, bleaching; blanching. — *n.m.f.* white-washer; whitener, bleacher; blancher.
blanqueadura, blanqueamiento, *n.f.* whitening, bleaching.
blanquear, *v.t.* to make white, whitewash; to whiten, bleach; to blanch; to wax (*honeycombs*). — *v.t.* to be, show up *or* stand out white.
blanquecedor, *n.m.* officer in the mint who burnishes coins.
blanquecer [9], *v.t.* to whiten, bleach; to blanch.

blanquecimiento, *n.m.* blanching; burnishing (*metals*).
blanquecino, -na, *a.* whitish.
blanqueo, *n.m.* whitewash; whitening, bleaching.
blanquería, *n.f.* bleaching-place, bleach-field.
blanqueta, *n.f.* coarse blanket; (*coll.*) ***en blanquetas,*** in (one's) underwear; cleaned out, broke.
blanquete, *n.m.* cosmetic for whitening the skin; whitewash.
blanquición, *n.f.* blanching (*metals*).
blanquillo, -lla, *a.* very white (*flour, bread*). — *n.m.* (*Chi., Per.*) white peach; (*Hisp. Am.*) small fish; (*Mex.*) egg; ***soldado blanquillo,*** foot-soldier dressed in white.
blanquimento, blanquimiento, *n.m.* bleaching liquid.
blanquinoso, -sa, *a.* whitish.
blanquizal, blanquizar, *n.m.* clay-pit.
blanquizco, -ca, blanquizo, -za, *a.* whitish.
blao, *a., n.m.* (*her.*) azure.
Blas, *n.m.* Blaise; (*iron.*) ***díjolo Blas, punto redondo,*** you're always right.
blasfemador, -ra, *a.* blaspheming, swearing. — *n.m.f.* blasphemer, swearer.
blasfemante, *a., n.m.f.* [BLASFEMADOR].
blasfemar, *v.i.* to blaspheme; to curse; ***blasfemar de la virtud,*** to rail against virtue.
blasfematorio, -ria, *a.* blasphemous.
blasfemia, *n.f.* blasphemy, blaspheming; ***decir blasfemias,*** to blaspheme.
blasfemo, -ma, *a.* blasphemous; cursing. — *n.m.f.* blasphemer, curser, swearer.
blasido, *n.m.* yellowing (of linen).
blasón, *n.m.* heraldry, blazonry; arms, coat of arms, armorial bearings; honour, glory; ***hacer blasón de,*** to boast *or* brag about.
blasonador, -ra, *a.* boasting, bragging.
blasonante, *a.* vainglorious, boasting.
blasonar, *v.t.* to blazon (forth); to extol. — *v.i.* (*fig.*) to boast, brag; ***blasonar de valiente,*** to brag of one's courage.
blasonería, *n.f.* boasting, bravado.
blasónico, -ca, *a.* relating to heraldry.
blasonista, *n.m.* heraldry expert.
blastema, *n.m.* (*biol.*) blastema.
blastodermo, *n.m.* (*biol.*) blastoderm.
blaterón, -rona, *a.* chattering, gossipy (*person*).
blavo, -va, *a.* yellowish-grey and reddish colour.
ble, *n.m.* handball game.
bledo, *n.m.* (*bot.*) wild amaranth; (*coll.*) **(*no*) *me importa un bledo,*** I don't give a damn.
bledomora, *n.f.* (*bot., prov.*) spinach.
blefaritis, *n.f. inv.* (*med.*) blepharitis, inflammation of the eyelids.
blefaroplastia, *n.f.* (*surg.*) blepharoplasty.
blefaróstato, *n.m.* (*surg.*) blepharostat.
blenda, *a.* (*min.*) blende.
blenia, *n.m.* (*ichth.*) blenny.
blenorragia, *n.f.* (*med.*) blennorrhœa.
blenorrágico, -ca, *a.* blennorrhagic.
blenorrea, *n.f.* (*med.*) chronic blennorrhœa, gleet.
bletonismo, *n.m.* water-divining power.
blinda, *n.f.* (*fort.*) blindage.
blindado, -da, *a.* iron-plated, armoured, armour-plated.
blindaje, *n.m.* (*mil.*) blindage; armour plate; (*naut.*) ***planchas de blindaje,*** armour-plate.
blindar, *v.t.* (*mil., naut.*) to armour-plate.
blocao, *n.m.* (*mil.*) block-house; pill-box.
blondina, *n.f.* narrow silk lace, narrow blonde lace.
blondo, -da, *a.* flaxen, blond. — *n.f.* silk lace, blonde lace.
bloque, *n.m.* block.
bloqueador, -ra, *a.* blockading. — *n.m.f.* blockader.
bloquear, *v.t.* (*naut.*) to blockade; to lay siege to; (*print.*) to block.
bloqueo, *n.m.* blockade.
blusa, *n.f.* blouse, (*Am.*) shirt-waist.
boa, *n.f.* (*zool.*) boa, boa constrictor.
boalaje, *n.m.* pasture ground; (*prov.*) tax paid by cattle-owner.
boato, *n.m.* pomp, show.
bobada, *n.f.* foolish thing to do *or* say.
bobalías, *n.m.f. inv.* (*coll.*) stupid person, dolt, blockhead.
bobalicón, -cona, bobazo, -za, *n.m.f.* nincompoop, utter fool.
bobarrón, -rrona, *n.m.f.* nincompoop, utter fool.
bobatel, *n.m.* (*coll.*) dolt, fool, simpleton.
bobático, -ca, *a.* silly, stupid, foolish.
bobear, *v.i.* to act *or* talk foolishly, fool about.
bobería, *n.f.* foolery, foolishness, silliness.
bóbilis, *adv.* (*coll.*) ***de bóbilis bóbilis,*** without even having to try *or* make an effort; without paying.
bobillo, *n.m.* big-bellied jug; modesty-piece.
bobina, *n.f.* reel, bobbin; (*elec.*) coil.
bobitonto, -ta, *a.* (*coll.*) hopelessly foolish *or* silly.
bobo, -ba, *a.* foolish, daft, silly; ***pájaro bobo,*** penguin; (*Hisp. Am.*) (baby's) comforter; (*Hisp. Am.*) bobo fish; ***manga boba,*** wide *or* bell sleeve; ***sopa boba,*** free gift; ***a bobas,*** foolishly, in a silly fashion. — *n.m.* kind of ruff worn by women; (stage) buffoon; (*Cub.*) old maid (*card game*); (*sl.*) stolen goods recovered by owner; ***bobo de Capirote*** or ***de Coria,*** utter fool, dunce, simpleton; ***hacerse el bobo,*** to make o.s. out to be a fool, act the fool. — *n.m.f.* fool, dimwit, silly person; (*iron.*) ***entre bobos anda el juego,*** there are no flies on any *or* either of them.
bobote, -ta, *a., n.m.f.* great idiot *or* simpleton.
boca, *n.f.* mouth; entrance, opening, hole; nozzle; muzzle; taste, flavour (*of wine*); distance between compass points; (*naut.*) hatchway; hole (of fish-trap); (*fam.*) mouth to feed; (*pl.*) pincers (*of crabs etc.*); ***boca de espuerta, boca rasgada,*** very large *or* wide mouth, huge mouth; ***boca de gachas,*** mumbling, indistinct *or* sloppy speaker; ***boca de fuego,*** gun; ***boca de riego,*** hydrant; ***boca del estómago,*** pit of the stomach; ***lo tengo sentado en la boca del estómago,*** I can't stand (the sight of) him; ***como boca de lobo,*** as black as pitch; ***a boca, de boca,*** by word of mouth; ***a boca de cañón,*** at close range; ***a boca de costal,*** at a rough estimate; ***pedir algo a boca llena,*** to cry out for sth.; ***andar de boca en boca,*** to be the talk of the town; ***hablar por boca de ganso,*** to parrot the views of others; (*fam.*) ***¡cállate la boca!*** belt up! pipe down!; ***hacer boca,*** to whet one's appetite; ***decir una cosa con la boca chica,*** to offer a thing without really meaning it; ***estar*** or ***quedarse con la boca abierta,*** to gape; ***mentir con toda la boca,*** to lie shamelessly; ***no descoser la boca,*** not to open one's mouth; ***no caérsele a alguien de la boca una cosa,*** to harp continually on sth.; ***me lo has quitado de la boca,*** you've taken the words right out of my mouth; ***repulgar la boca,*** to purse one's lips; (*fam.*) ***no decir esta boca es mía,*** not to say a word; ***taparle a alguien la boca,*** to shut somebody up; ***dice todo lo que se le viene a la boca,*** he says everything that comes into his head; ***en boca cerrada no entran moscas,*** silence is best; ***torcer la boca,*** to pull a face (*of disapproval*), to frown; ***de la mano a la boca desparece la sopa,*** there's many a slip 'twixt cup and lip; ***a boca de invierno,*** about the beginning of winter; ***a boca (de) jarro,*** point-blank; ***a boca de noche,*** at nightfall; ***boca arriba,*** face up; on one's back; ***boca abajo,*** face downwards; ***boca con boca,*** face to face; ***a pedir de boca,*** to one's heart's delight; ***de manos a***

boca, all of a sudden; ***quien tiene boca se equivoca***, anybody can make a mistake, to err is human; ***por la boca muere el pez***, it is easy to give o.s. away by talking too much.
bocabarra, *n.f.pl.* (*naut.*) bar-hole (*in the capstan* or *windlass*).
bocacalle, *n.f.* entry, end *or* opening (*of a street*), street turning *or* junction.
bocacaz, *n.m.* opening left in the weir *or* dam (*of a river*).
bocací, bocacín, *n.m.* fine glazed buckram.
bocacha, *n.f.* hideous great mouth; blunderbuss with trumpet-like mouth.
bocadear, *v.t.* to break down *or* up.
bocadillo, *n.m.* sandwich, savoury roll, snack; thin kind of linen; narrow ribbon *or* tape; (*Ven., Col.*) guava jelly wrapped in banana leaves; (*Hond., Mex.*) coconut preserve; (*Cub.*) sweet potato jelly; ***tomar un bocadillo***, to have a snack.
bocado, *n.m.* mouthful, morsel (*of food*); gobbet; modicum, small portion; bite; bit (*of a bridle*); (*pl.*) dried fruit preserve; ***en un bocado***, at one gulp; at one go; ***comer(se) algo a bocados***, to eat sth. by biting chunks out of it, chew sth.; ***sacar un buen bocado***, to get a good *or* substantial share; ***salir con el bocado en la boca***, to go out *or* leave immediately after eating; ***no tener para un bocado***, not to have a brass farthing.
bocal (1), *n.m.* wide-mouthed wine pitcher.
bocal (2), *n.m.* mouthpiece; sluice.
bocallave, *n.f.* keyhole.
bocamanga, *n.f.* cuff, wristband; opening (*of sleeve*).
bocamina, *n.f.* entrance (*to a mine*); shaft.
bocanada, *n.f.* mouthful (*of liquid*); puff (*of smoke*); blast (*of air, heat*); rush, onrush, crush (*of people*); (*pl.*) (*fam.*) boasting, bragging; ***una bocanada de aire caliente***, a blast *or* wave of hot air.
bocarón, *n.m.* wind-chest (*of an organ*), wind-trunk.
bocarte, *n.m.* ore-crusher, stamp-mill; (*prov.*) baby *or* young sardine.
bocartear, *v.t.* to crush (*ore*).
bocateja, *n.f.* front tile (*on each line of roof-tiling*).
bocatijera, *n.f.* socket (*for pole of a four-wheeled coach*).
bocaza, *n.f.* (*fam.*) (ugly) great mouth.
bocazas, *n.m. inv.* braggart, loud-mouthed individual.
bocazo, *n.m.* (*min.*) fizzled-out explosion.
bocear, bocezar [C], *v.i.* (*vet.*) to move the lips from one side to the other (*horses etc.*).
bocel, *n.m.* (*arch.*) fluted moulding; fluting-plane.
bocelar, *v.t.* to make fluted mouldings in.
bocera, *n.f.* crumbs sticking to the lip after eating.
boceras, *n.m. inv.* (*coll.*) big mouth.
boceto, *n.m.* sketch, outline, draft.
bocezar [BOCEAR].
bocín, *n.m.* hub-cap; feedpipe.
Bocina, *n.f.* (*astron.*) Little Bear.
bocina, *n.f.* trumpet; horn, hooter; shell used as horn; (*mech.*) bushing.
bocinar, *v.i.* to blow a horn; to hoot.
bocinero, *n.m.* trumpeter, horn-blower.
bocio, *n.m.* (*med.*) goitre.
bocón, -cona, *a.*, *n.m.f.* wide-mouthed *or* loud-mouthed (person), braggart.
bocoy, *n.m.* hogshead, large barrel *or* cask.
bocudo, -da, *a.* big-mouthed.
bocha, *n.f.* wooden bowl; (*pl.*) game of bowls.
bochado, *n.m.* (*sl.*) executed prisoner.
bochar, *v.t.* (*bowls*) to hit and move.
bochazo, *n.m.* blow of one bowl against another.
boche, *n.m.* donkey, chuck-farthing game; (*slang*) executioner.
bochinche, *n.m.* (*coll.*) uproar, din, racket.
bochinchero, -ra, *a.* riotous.
bochorno, *n.m.* heavy, sultry weather; shame; embarrassment.
bochornoso, -sa, *a.* heavy, sultry (*weather*); shameful; embarrassing.
boda, *n.f.* wedding; wedding party; ***Bodas de Camacho***, lavish feast; ***bodas de diamante, de oro, de plata***, diamond, golden, silver wedding; ***no va a bodas***, he doesn't go in for amusement.
bodega, *n.f.* wine cellar *or* vault; vintage; store cellar; hold (*of ship*); (*Hisp. Am.*) grocery shop.
bodegaje, *n.m.* (*Hisp. Am.*) warehouse dues.
bodegón, *n.m.* cheap eating house; (*paint.*) still life.
bodegonear, *v.i.* to go on a pub crawl.
bodegoneo, *n.m.* pub crawling.
bodegonero, -ra, *n.m.f.* keeper of a low eating-house *or* tavern.
bodeguero, -ra, *a.* appertaining to vine growing *or* wine cellars. — *n.m.f.* owner of vineyards *or* wine cellars; (*Hisp. Am.*) retail grocer.
bodigo, *n.m.* manchet brought as church offering.
bodijo, *n.m.* (*coll.*) third-rate wedding.
bodollo, *n.m.* (*prov.*) pruning hook *or* knife.
bodón, *n.m.* magnificent *or* slap-up wedding; pool that dries up in summer.
bodoque, *n.m.* clay pellet; lump; hole embroidery; (*fam.*) clot, dolt.
bodoquera, *n.f.* mould in which pellets are formed; cradle of (cross-bow); pea shooter, blowgun, blow-pipe.
bodorrio, *n.m.* (*coll.*) third-rate wedding.
bodrio, *n.m.* poor *or* thin soup *or* broth, poor man's soup *or* stew; hodge podge; mess; mixture of hog's blood and onions for sausages.
bóer, *a.*, *n.m.f.* Boer.
boezuelo, *n.m.* stalking ox (*used in partridge shooting*).
bofada, *n.f.* stew; large quantity of lungs and lights.
bofe, *n.m.* lung; (*pl.*) lights; ***echar el bofe*** or ***los bofes***, to gasp, pant; to sweat, toil.
bofeña, *n.f.* (*prov.*) sausage of pork lights and lungs.
bofeta, *n.f.* thin stiff cotton material.
bofetada, *n.f.* slap, buffet, box; ***darle a alguien una bofetada***, to slap s.o.; to rebuff s.o.
bofetón, *n.m.* hard slap; (*theat.*) revolving door trick.
bofia, *n.f.* (*sl.*) police; ***la bofia***, the cops, fuzz.
bofo, -fa [FOFO].
boga (1), *n.f.* (*naut.*) rowing; vogue, fashion; ***estar en boga***, to be fashionable, all the rage. — *n.m.f.* (*naut.*) rower.
boga (2), *n.f.* (*ichth.*) cackerel.
boga (3), *n.f.* (*prov.*) small two-edged knife.
bogada (1), *n.f.* stroke (*rowing*).
bogado (2), *n.f.* (*prov.*) bucking (clothes) with lye.
bogador, -ra, *n.m.f.* rower.
bogadura, *n.f.* rowing.
bogante, *a.* rowing.
bogar [B], *v.i.* to row.
bogavante (1), *n.m.* (*naut.*) strokesman (*of a row-galley*).
bogavante (2), *n.m.* (*zool.*) large lobster.
bogotano, -na, *a.*, *n.m.f.* (person) appertaining to *or* (native) of Bogota.
boguear, *v.i.* to fish cackerel.
boguera, *n.f.* net for catching cackerel.
bohardilla [BUHARDA].
bohemiano, -na, *a.*, *n.m.f.* Bohemian.
bohémico, -ca, *a.* appertaining to Bohemia.
bohemio, -mia, *a.*, *n.m.f.* Bohemian; bohemian; gipsy. — *n.m.* short cloak (*formerly worn by the royal archers*). — *n.f.* bohemianism.
bohemo, -ma, *a.*, *n.m.f.* (*geog.*) Bohemian.

bohena, boheña, *n.f.* (*prov.*) sausage of pork lights and lungs.

bohío, *n.m.* (*Hisp. Am.*) hut.

bohordo, *n.m.* (*bot.*) blade of flag; (*bot.*) scape; short spear *or* dart (*used in tournaments*); stalk (*of a cabbage run to seed*).

boicot, *n.m.* boycott.

boicotear, *v.t.* to boycott.

boicoteo, *n.m.* boycotting.

boíl, *n.m.* ox stall.

boina, *n.f.* beret.

boira, *n.f.* (*prov.*) fog.

boj, *n.m.* (*bot.*) box, box tree, box wood; shoemaker's box wood tool; (*naut.*) [BOJEO].

boja, *n.f.* (*bot.*) southern wood.

bojar, *v.t.* to scrape (*leather*) clean.

boje, *n.m.* (*prov.*) dolt, clod; (*prov.*) box tree.

bojear, *v.t.* (*naut.*) to measure the perimeter of (*an island* or *cape*). — *v.i.* to measure.

bojedal, *n.m.* plantation of box trees.

bojeo, bojo, *n.m.* (*naut.*) act of sailing round an island and measuring it; perimeter (*of an island* or *cape*).

bojiganga, *n.f.* company of strolling players.

bojote, *n.m.* (*Hisp. Am.*) bundle, parcel.

bojotero, *n.m.* (*Col.*) worker in a sugar mill.

bol (1), *n.m.* Armenian bole, red earth.

bol (2), *n.m.* punch bowl.

bol (3), *n.m.* fishing smack.

bola, *n.f.* ball; globe; marble; blacking (*for shoes*); grand slam (*at cards*); (*coll.*) lie, trick, deceit, twist; (*naut.*) truck; signalling ball; (*sl.*) fair, market; (*Ven.*) tamale; ***a bola vista,*** frankly, openly; (*bot.*) ***bola de nieve,*** viburnum; ***escurrir la bola,*** to flee; ***dale bola,*** what, again!

bolada, *n.f.* throw *or* cast of a ball *or* bowl; stroke (*in billiards*); (*artill.*) chase.

bolaga, *n.f.* (*prov., bot.*) flax-leaved daphne.

bolandistas, *n.m.pl.* Bollandists.

bolantín, *n.m.* fine packthread.

bolaño, *n.m.* stone missile.

bolar, *a.* ***tierra bolar,*** bole earth, bole armeniac.

bolazo, *n.m.* violent blow (*with a bowl*); ***de bolazo,*** hurriedly, carelessly.

bolchaca, *n.f.*, **bolchaco,** *n.m.* (*prov.*) purse; pocket.

bolchevique, bolchevista, *a.*, *n.m.f.* Bolshevik, Bolshevist.

bolchevismo, *n.m.* Bolshevism.

boldina, *n.f.* (*chem.*) alkaloid from jalap.

boldo, *n.m.* (*bot.*) jalap (*from Chile*).

bolea, *n.f.* (*artill.*) whipple tree (*of a carriage*).

boleador, *n.m.* (*vulg.*) wrestler; (*sl.*) thief (at fairs and markets).

boleadoras, *n.f.pl.* (*Arg.*) lariat with balls at one end to catch animals by the legs.

bolear, *v.t.* to cast, launch; (*Arg.*) to throw the bolas at (an animal); (*Arg., fig.*) to confuse, entangle; to cheat, deceive. — *v.i.* to play at billiards (*for amusement only*); to throw wooden *or* iron balls (*for a wager*); (*prov.*) to boast, lie.

boleo, *n.m.* bowling; bowling green *or* pitch; place where balls are thrown.

bolera, *n.f.* bowling alley.

bolero, *n.m.* bolero; bolero dancer.

boleta, *n.f.* ticket; warrant; billet slip; small package of tobacco; ***darle a alguien la boleta,*** to give s.o. the sack.

boletería, *n.f.* (*Hisp. Am.*) ticket office.

boletero, *n.m.* (*mil.*) billeting officer; (*Hisp. Am.*) ticket agent, ticket seller; ticket collector.

boletín, *n.m.* bulletin; pay warrant; lodging billet; journal; (*com.*) price list.

boleto, *n.m.* voting paper; raffle ticket; (*bot.*) mushroom; (*Hisp. Am.*) ticket.

bolichada, *n.f.* game of bowls; throw of drag-net; fish caught in a drag-net; (*fig.*) lucky stroke; ***de una bolichada,*** at one throw, all at once.

boliche (1), *n.m.* jack, small ball (*in bowls*); skittles (*game, ground*); furnace for lead-smelting *or* charcoal burning; inferior tobacco (*from Puerto Rico*).

boliche (2), *n.m.* small drag-net (and all the small fish caught in it); (*pl.*) (*naut.*) foretop bowlines and topgallant bowlines.

bolichero (1), **-ra,** *n.m.f.* one who keeps a pigeon-hole *or* troll-madam table.

bolichero (2), *n.m.* (*prov.*) fisherman who uses a drag-net; seller of small fish caught in drag-nets.

bolicho, *n.m.* (*prov.*) shrimp-net.

bólido, *n.m.* fiery meteor, shooting star; (*aut.*) racing car; (*coll.*) hot-rod.

bolígrafo, *n.m.* ball-point pen.

bolillo, *n.m.* lace-bobbin; iron pin (*in pool billiards*); (*vet.*) bone in which hoof is joined; mould for starching lace cuffs; starched lace cuff; (*pl.*) bars of sweet paste; ***encaje de bolillo*** or ***de bolillos,*** bobbin lace.

bolín, *n.m.* jack, small ball (*in bowls*); (*coll.*) ***de bolín, de bolán,*** recklessly.

bolina, *n.f.* (*naut.*) bowline; sounding-line; (*naut.*) flogging; (*coll.*) row, rumpus, shindy; (*naut.*) ***ir*** or ***navegar de bolina,*** to sail close to the wind; ***echar de bolina,*** to make idle boasts.

bolineador, -ra, bolinero, -ra, *a.* (*naut.*) good at bowline sailing.

bolinear, *v.i.* (*naut.*) to haul up the bowline; to sail close to the wind.

bolinga, *n.f.* (*naut.*) main-topsail.

bolisa, *n.f.* (*prov.*) embers, hot cinders.

bolívar, *n.m.* (*Ven.*) silver coin (*monetary unit of Venezuela*).

bolivariano, -na, *a.* relating to Simón Bolívar.

Bolivia, *n.f.* Bolivia.

boliviano, -na, *a.* appertaining to *or* (native) of Bolivia. — *n.m.* monetary unit of Bolivia.

bolo (1), *n.m.* skittle; grand slam (*in the game of* ***tresillo***); misère (*in the game of* ***cargadas***); large piece of timber; (*med.*) bolus; (*prov.*) round *or* lace cushion; axis of a winding staircase; (*coll.*) dolt, idiot; actor engaged for one performance; (*pl.*) game of nine-pins; (*coll.*) ***echar a rodar los bolos,*** to start trouble; ***tener bien puestos los bolos,*** to have guts.

bolo (2), *n.m.* (*Philip.*) large knife (*like a machete*) used by the Indians.

bolómetro, *n.m.* (*phys.*) bolometer.

bolón, *n.m.* (*artill.*) square bolt *or* mortar-bed pintle; (*Chi.*) large stone for foundations.

bolonio, -nia, *a.*, *n.m.f.* (student) of the Spanish College at Bologna; (*coll.*) ignorant *or* rattle-brained (person).

boloñés, -ñesa, *a.* Bolognese. — *n.m.f.* person from Bologna.

bolsa, *n.f.* purse, money-bag; bag; (*com.*) stock-exchange; pouch; foot-muff; pocket; paper bag; (*min.*) vein containing the purest gold *or* any other mineral; (*med.*) sac; (*anat.*) scrotum; ***alargar la bolsa,*** to spin the money out; (*bot.*) ***bolsa de pastor,*** shepherd's purse; (*mil.*) ***bolsa de resistencia,*** pocket of resistance; ***bolsa de agua caliente,*** hot-water bottle; ***bolsa de hielo,*** ice-bag; ***bolsa de trabajo,*** labour exchange; ***bolsa de viaje,*** travel bursary; (*com.*) ***jugar a la bolsa,*** to speculate on the stock-exchange; ***¡la bolsa o la vida!*** your money or your life!

bolsada, *n.f.* (*min.*) pocket.

bolsear, *v.t.* (*Hisp. Am.*) to pick the pocket of. — *v.i.* to pucker, pouch (*clothes, materials etc.*).

bolsería, *n.f.* place where purses *or* bags are made *or* sold; bag-making trade; collection of bags *or* purses.

bolsero, -ra, *n.m.f.* maker *or* seller of purses *or* bags.

bolsilla, *n.f.* (*sl.*) false pocket used by card-sharpers.

bolsillo, *n.m.* pocket; purse; ***de bolsillo,*** pocket-size; ***con esto no me meto nada en el bolsillo,*** I'm not getting anything out of this; ***meterse a alguien en el bolsillo,*** to win s.o. over, talk s.o. into sth.; ***tener a alguien en el bolsillo,*** to have won s.o. over, have s.o. just where one wants him; ***rascarse el bolsillo,*** to pay up reluctantly, (*coll.*) fork out.

bolsín, *n.m.* gathering of brokers out of exchange hours; little stock-exchange.

bolsista, *n.m.* stock-broker.

bolso, *n.m.* hand-bag; (*naut.*) bulge (*in sail*).

bolsón, *n.m.* large purse; (*geol.*) large depression; (*min.*) pocket, deposit; (*build.*) large iron ring to hold braces of arches; board lining of the oil-reservoir (*in oil-mills*).

bolla (1), *n.f.* duty on woollens and silks (formerly levied in Catalonia); tax on the manufacture of playing-cards.

bolla (2), *n.f.* (*prov.*) milk-roll; (*Hisp. Am.*) great richness of gold *or* silver ore.

bolladura [ABOLLADURA].

bollar, *v.t.* to put a leaden seal on (*cloths*) (to indicate their manufactory); to emboss.

bollería, *n.f.* bun *or* roll shop; buns; rolls.

bollero, -ra, *n.m.f.* maker *or* seller of buns *or* rolls.

bollo, *n.m.* bun, scone, (*Am.*) biscuit; roll; boss; bump; mound; puff (*in dress*); tuft (*in upholstery*); (*Per.*) silver ingot; (*Col.*) tamale; (*Hond.*) blow; (*coll.*) ***armarse un bollo,*** to get into a muddle, mess *or* fix, get all mixed up; ***no está el horno para bollos,*** this is no time *or* not the right moment for joking *or* for that sort of thing, he is not (we are not etc.) in the mood for joking *or* for that sort of thing.

bollón, *n.m.* boss; brass-headed nail; button, bud; vine bud; button earring, pendant.

bollonado, -da, *a.* bossed, bossy, studded with bosses.

bomba (1), *n.f.* pump; fire engine; bomb(-shell); lamp-globe; earthen jar for skimming oil from water; doggerel; drunkenness; (*mus.*) sliding tube; ***bomba alimenticia*** or ***de alimentación,*** feed-pump; ***bomba de achique,*** baling pump; ***caer como una bomba,*** to fall like a bomb-shell; ***estar echando bombas,*** to be flaming hot; to be going great guns; ***estar a tres bombas,*** to be flaming mad; ***bomba aspirante,*** suction-pump; ***bomba centrífuga*** or ***rotatoria,*** centrifugal-pump; ***bomba impelente,*** force-pump; ***bomba de fuego*** or ***de vaho,*** steam-engine; ***bomba marina,*** water-spout; ***bomba neumática,*** pneumatic pump; ***bomba de vacío,*** vacuum pump; (*naut.*) ***bomba de guimbalete,*** common pump; ***bomba de carena,*** bilge-pump; ***bomba atómica,*** atomic bomb; ***bomba de hidrógeno,*** hydrogen bomb; ***bomba fétida,*** stink bomb; ***bomba volante,*** flying bomb; ***bomba de mano,*** hand grenade; ***a prueba de bombas,*** bomb-proof.

bombáceo, -cea, *a.* (*bot.*) bombacaceous. — *n.f.pl.* (**bombáceas**) Bombacaceæ.

bombacino, *n.m.* bombasine, bombazine.

bombacho, *a.* loose-fitting. — *n.m.pl.* (***pantalones***) ***bombachos,*** plus-fours.

bombar [BOMBEAR].

bombarda, *n.f.* (*mil., mus.*) bombard; (*naut.*) bomb-ketch, bomb-vessel; bombardone, bass reed-stop of a pipe-organ.

bombardear, *v.t.* to bombard; to shell; to bomb.

bombardeo, *n.m.* bombardment; shelling; bombing.

bombardero, -ra, *a.* bombarding. — *n.m.* bombardier; bombing plane, bomber; (*ent.*) bombadier-beetle.

bombardino, bombardón, *n.m.* (*mus.*) bombardone.

bombasí, *n.m.* bombazine, dimity.

bombástico, -ca, *a.* bombastic, high-sounding.

bombax, *n.m.* (*bot.*) bombax.

bombazo, *n.m.* great big bomb; bomb explosion *or* damage.

bombé, *n.m.* light two-wheeled carriage open in front.

bombear, *v.t.* to bomb; to pump; (*fig.*) to praise excessively; to camber.

bombeo, *n.m.* bulge, convexity.

bombero, *n.m.* fireman; pumper; howitzer.

bómbice, *n.m.* (*ent.*) bombyx.

bombicidos, *n.m.pl.* (*ent.*) Bombycidæ.

bombicino, -na, *a.* (*bot.*) silk-like. — *n.m.pl.* (**bombicinos**) (*ent.*) Bombycinæ.

bombilla, *n.f.* (*elec.*) bulb; (*naut.*) hand lantern; (*Hisp. Am.*) tube for sipping ***mate.***

bombillo, *n.m.* water closet trap; sample *or* thief tube; hand-pump, fire-extinguisher.

bombista, *n.m.* manufacturer of pumps *or* glass bulbs.

bombo, -ba (2), *a.* astounded, stunned; (*Hisp. Am.*) lukewarm. — *n.m.* bass-drum; player on bass-drum; (*naut.*) barge, lighter; leather container for numbered balls (*in billiards, lottery etc.*); revolving lottery box; (*fig.*) excessive praise, puff; ***anunciar a bombo y platillo,*** to announce with great fuss; ***darle bombo a alguien*** or ***a algo,*** to praise s.o. *or* sth. to the skies.

bombomido, -da, *a.* (*ent.*) buzzing.

bombón (1), *n.m.* chocolate; ***una caja de bombones,*** a box of chocolates; (*coll.*) ***esta chica es un bombón,*** this girl is a bit of all right.

bombón (2), *n.m.* (*Philip.*) vessel made of cane.

bombona, *n.f.* carboy.

bombonaje, *n.m.* (*bot.*) screw-pine.

bombonera, *n.f.* chocolate box.

Bona, *n.f.* Bonn.

bonachón, -chona, *a., n.m.f.* thoroughly good-natured *or* easy-going (person).

bonaerense, *a., n.m.f.* appertaining to *or* (native) of Buenos Aires.

bonancible, *a.* moderate, calm, fair, serene (*weather, sea*).

bonanza, *n.f.* fair weather; (*fig.*) prosperity, success; (*min.*) bonanza; ***ir en bonanza,*** to sail with fair wind and weather; (*fig.*) to be prosperous.

bonanzoso, -sa, *a.* prosperous.

bonapartismo, *n.m.* Bonapartism.

bonapartista, *a., n.m.f.* Bonapartist.

bondad, *n.f.* goodness, kindness; ***tenga la bondad (de),*** be so kind *or* good (as to).

bondadoso, -sa, *a.* kind, kindly, good-natured.

boneta, *n.f.* (*naut.*) bonnet.

bonetada, *n.f.* (*fam.*) raising one's hat (*in greeting*).

bonete, *n.m.* biretta, hat; cap; (*fig.*) clergyman; bonnet (*of a fortress*); preserve jar; (*anat.*) reticulum (*of ruminants*); ***a tente bonete,*** with perseverance; (*iron.*) ***bravo bonete,*** idiot; ***gran bonete,*** big-wig; ***tirarse los bonetes,*** to quarrel.

bonetería, *n.f.* cap factory *or* shop, millinery.

bonetero, -ra, *n.m.f.* one who makes *or* sells caps; (*bot.*) common spindle-tree, dog-wood.

bonetillo, *n.m.* small cap *or* hat; ornament for the hair.

bonetón, *n.m.* (*Chi.*) game of forfeits.

bonga, *n.f.* (*Philip.*) palm tree.

bongo, *n.m.* (*Cent. Am.*) Indian canoe; (*Cub.*) boat, barge.

boniatillo, *n.m.* (*Cub.*) sweet made of sweet-potato and sugar.

boniato, *n.m.* (*bot.*) sweet-potato.

bonico, -ca, *a.* pretty; cute, dainty; charming, delightful; (*prov.*) ***a bonico,*** quietly, softly.

Bonifacio, *n.m.* Boniface.

bonificación, *n.f.* improvement; increment; extra *or* additional payment, allowance, bonus; discount.

bonificable, *a.* that entitles one to extra *or* additional payment.

bonificar [A], *v.t.* to improve; to increment; to give extra *or* additional payment to; to credit.

bonijo, *n.m.* (*prov.*) ground olive stone.

bonina, *n.f.* (*bot.*) ox-eye camomile.

bonísimo, -ma, *a. superl.* very *or* extremely good.

bonitera, *n.f.* bonito fishing season.

bonito (1), **-ta,** *a.* pretty; cute, dainty; neat, nice; (*iron.*) ***¡en bonito lío se ha metido!*** a fine (old) mess *or* muddle he's got himself into!

bonito (2), *n.m.* (*ichth.*) bonito, striped tunny; (*sl.*) short capeless cloak.

bonitolera, *n.f.* (*prov.*) imitation fish-bait (used in tunny fishing).

bonizal, *n.m.* (*bot.*) panicle-field.

bonizo, *n.m.* (*bot.*) panicle.

bono, *n.m.* voucher; relief ticket (*charity*); (*com.*) bond, certificate.

bonote, *n.m.* coconut fibre; (*naut.*) coir.

bonzo, *n.m.* bonze.

boñiga, *n.f.* dung.

boñigar, *n.m.* kind of round white fig.

boñigo, *n.m.* (piece of) dung, cow-pat.

boom, *n.m.* (*fig.*) boom, explosion; boost.

boque, *n.m.* (*prov., zool.*) buck.

boqué, boquí, *n.m.* (*sl.*) hunger.

boqueada, *n.f.* gasp, gasping; ***dar la última boqueada,*** to breathe one's last; ***dar*** or ***estar dando las boqueadas,*** to be on one's last legs.

boquear, *v.t.* to pronounce, utter. — *v.i.* to gape, gasp; to breathe one's last; (*coll.*) to be in its last stages.

boquera, *n.f.* sluice (*in irrigation canal*); door (*of hayloft*); (*prov.*) opening (*in enclosures for cattle*); (*prov.*) cesspool; (*med.*) lip sore, mouth sore *or* ulcer.

boquerón, *n.m.* wide opening, large hole; [BOQUERA]; (*ichth.*) (fresh) anchovy.

boquete, *n.m.* gap, small opening.

boquiabierto, -ta, *a.* open-mouthed; (*fig.*) gaping, astonished.

boquiancho, -cha, *a.* wide-mouthed.

boquiangosto, -ta, *a.* narrow-mouthed.

boquiblando, -da, *a.* tender-mouthed (*horse*); (*fig.*) indiscreet (*speaker*).

boquiconejuno, -na, *a.* rabbit-mouthed; hare-lipped (*horse*).

boquiduro, -ra, *a.* hard-mouthed (*horse*).

boquifresco, -ca, *a.* fresh-mouthed (*horse*); (*coll.*) cheeky.

boquifruncido, -da, *a.* pucker-mouthed.

boquihendido, -da, *a.* slit-mouthed (*horse*).

boquihundido, -da, *a.* sunken-mouthed (*horse*).

boquilindo, -da, *a.* foppish.

boquilla, *n.f.* lower opening (*of breeches*); opening (*in irrigation canal*); chisel-cut, mortise; cigar- *or* cigarette-holder; mouthpiece (*of a wind-instrument*); bomb-hole; burner (*of lamp*); mouth (*of a scabbard*); lighting tip (*of cigar*); filter tip; (*build.*) verge, course; (*mech.*) nozzle; ***habla de boquilla,*** he doesn't mean what he says, he's not to be taken at his word, he's not reliable.

boquimuelle, *a.* tender-mouthed; (*fig.*) soft.

boquín (1), *n.m.* coarse baize.

boquín (2), *n.m.* executioner, hangman.

boquina, *n.f.* (*prov.*) buckskin.

boquinegro, -gra, *a.* black-mouthed (*animals*). — *n.m.f.* snail.

boquipando, -da, *a., n.m.f.* prudent, discreet, slow (speaker). — *n.m.f.* (*iron.*) gossip, chatterbox.

boquirrasgado, -da, *a.* slit-mouthed.

boquirroto, -ta, *a.* (*coll.*) talkative.

boquirrubio, -bia, *a.* simple, artless. — ***n.m.*** pretty boy.

boquiseco, -ca, *a.* dry-mouthed; (*fig.*) showy, insubstantial.

boquisumido, -da, *a.* sunken-mouthed.

boquita, *n.f.* (delightful *or* charming) little mouth.

boquitorcido, -da, boquituerto, -ta, *a.* wry-mouthed, having a crooked mouth.

boquiverde, *a., n.m.f.* foul-mouthed (speaker).

boracita, *n.f.* (*min.*) boracite.

borásico, -ca, *a.* (*chem.*) boracic.

boratado, -da, *a.* mixed with boric acid.

boratero, -ra, *a.* (*Chi.*) of borate. — *n.m.* (*Chi.*) worker in a borate mine. — *n.f.* (*Chi.*) borate mine.

borato, *n.m.* (*chem.*) borate.

bórax, *n.m.* (*chem.*) borax.

borbolla, *n.f.* bubble.

borbollar, borbollear, borbollonear, *v.i.* to bubble out, gush out.

borbolleamiento, *n.m.* bubbling.

borbollón, borbotón, *n.m.* bubbling, gushing; ***salir a borbollones*** or ***a borbotones,*** to bubble *or* gush forth, out *or* over, spill forth, out *or* over.

Borbón, *n.m.* Bourbon.

borbónico, -ca, *a.* Bourbon.

borbonismo, *n.m.* Bourbonism.

borbonista, *a., n.m.f.* Bourbonist.

borbor, *n.m.* bubbling.

borborigmo, *n.m.* (*med.*) rumbling (*in the bowels*).

borboritar, *v.i.* to bubble up, gush forth *or* out.

borborito (*prov.*) [BORBOLLÓN].

borbotar, *v.i.* to gush out, boil over.

borbotón [BORBOLLÓN].

borceguí, *n.m.* buskin, half-boot; laced shoe.

borceguinería, *n.f.* shop where buskins are made *or* sold.

borceguinero, -ra, *n.m.f.* maker *or* retailer of buskins.

borcelana, *n.f.* (*prov.*) wash-bowl.

borcellar, *n.m.* brim (*of vessel*).

borda (1), *n.f.* (*naut.*) main-sail (*of galley*); gunwale; ***tirar, arrojar, echar por la borda,*** to throw overboard; (*fig.*) to throw away, jettison, ditch.

borda (2), *n.f.* hut, cottage.

bordada, *n.f.* (*naut.*) board, tack; (*coll.*) promenade, stroll; (*naut.*) ***dar bordadas,*** to tack; (*coll.*) to go back and forth.

bordadillo, *n.m.* (*obs.*) double-flowered taffeta.

bordado, *n.m.* embroidery, embroidering; ***bordado de cadeneta,*** chain-stitch embroidery; ***bordado de canutillo,*** gold *or* silver twist embroidery; ***bordado de recamado*** or ***de realce,*** raised embroidery.

bordador, -ra, *n.m.f.* embroiderer.

bordadura, *n.f.* embroidery; embroidering; (*her.*) bordure.

bordaje, *n.m.* (*naut.*) side-planks.

bordar, *v.t.* to embroider; ***bordar de realce,*** to do raised embroidery; ***bordar con*** or ***de oro,*** to embroider with gold; ***bordar en cañamazo,*** to embroider on canvas; (*coll.*) ***hacer algo bordado,*** to do sth. really well; ***lo hizo bordado,*** he made a really good *or* beautiful job of it.

borde (1), *a.* wild, savage, uncultivated; bastard (*child*).

borde (2), *n.m.* border, brim, brink, edge, ledge, margin, fringe, verge; (*Am.*) shoulder (*of road*); hem; ***al borde de la guerra,*** on the brink *or* verge of war.

bordear, *v.t.* to border, edge; to skirt, go round. — *v.i.* to walk on the edge *or* border; (*naut.*) to ply to windward.

bordelés, -lesa, *a., n.m.f.* appertaining to *or* (native) of Bordeaux.

bordeo, *n.m.* (*naut.*) boarding, tacking.

bordillo, *n.m.* kerb.

bordo, *n.m.* (*naut.*) side (*of a ship*); tack; ***a bordo,*** on board (*ship*); ***al bordo*** or ***bordo con bordo,*** alongside; (*naut.*) ***de alto bordo,*** ocean-going; (*fig.*) important, high-up; (*naut.*) ***dar bordos,*** to tack.

bordón, *n.m.* (pilgrim's) staff; refrain *or* burden (*of a song*); toll, knell; pet phrase, catch phrase; bass-string; snare (*of side drum*); (*surg.*) gut; (*print.*) omission in setting-up.

bordonado, -da, *a.* (*her.*) pommée, pommetty.

bordoncillo, *n.m.* catchword, refrain.

bordonear, *v.t.* to beat. — *v.i.* to try the ground with a staff *or* stick; to beat, cudgel, club; (*fig.*) to rove *or* wander about begging.

bordonería, *n.f.* wandering idly about on pretence of devotion.

bordonero, -ra, *n.m.f.* vagrant, vagabond, tramp.

bordura, *n.f.* (*her.*) bordure.

boreal, *a.* boreal, northern.

bóreas, *n.m.* Boreas, (the) north wind.

Borgoña, *n.f.* Burgundy.

borgoña, *n.m.* Burgundy wine.

borgoñón, -ñona, *a., n.m.f.* appertaining to *or* (native) of Burgundy; ***a la borgoñona,*** in the Burgundy fashion.

borgoñota, *n.f.* ancient helmet.

borguil, *n.m.* (*prov.*) haystack.

bórico, -ca, *a.* (*chem.*) boric.

borla, *n.f.* tassel; (*pl.*) (*bot.*) amaranth; ***borla para polvos de tocador,*** toilet powder-puff; ***tomar la borla,*** to graduate as a doctor *or* master.

borlica, borlita, *n.f.* small tassel.

borlilla, *n.f.* (*bot.*) anther.

borlón, *n.m.* large tassel, [BORLA]; napped, tufted stuff made of thread and cotton yarn; (*pl.* **borlones**) (*bot.*) amaranth.

borne (1), *a.* brittle, splintery (*wood*).

borne (2), *n.m.* end of a lance; (*bot.*) kind of oak; (*elec.*) binding post, binding screw; terminal; (*sl.*) gallows, gibbet.

borneadero, *n.m.* (*naut.*) berth (of a ship at anchor); swinging berth.

borneadizo, -za, *a.* pliant, flexible, easily warped *or* bent.

bornear, *v.t.* to bend, turn, twist; (*arch.*) to model and cut (*pillars*) all round; (*arch.*) to hoist, move and set down (*building blocks etc.*); (*arch.*) to mark out; to make sure (*sth.*) is level *or* straight. — *v.i.* (*prov.*) to edge, sidle, pirouette; (*naut.*) to swing around the anchor.—**bornearse,** *v.r.* to warp, turn.

borneo, *n.m.* turning *or* winding action; swinging motion (in dancing); warping; (*naut.*) swinging around the anchor.

bornero, -ra, *a.* blackish (*mill-stone*); ground (*by such a stone*).

borní, *n.m.* (*orn.*) falcon.

bornido, *n.m.* (*sl.*) hanged man.

bornizo, *a.* said of cork obtained from the first stripping. — *n.m.* (*prov., agric.*) stem, sucker.

boro, *n.m.* (*chem.*) boron.

borona, *n.f.* (*bot.*) millet, maize; (*prov.*) bread made from millet *or* maize flour; (*Hisp. Am.*) crumb *or* bit of bread.

borra (1), *n.f.* yearling ewe; coarse *or* flock wool; goat's hair; nap (*of cloth*); floss, fluff; cotton; tax *or* duty on sheep; lees, sediment, waste; silk waste; (*coll.*) idle talk, trash; ***meter borra,*** to put in padding (*in writing etc.*).

borra (2), *n.f.* borax.

borrable, *a.* effaceable, erasable, eradicable.

borracha, *n.f.* (*coll.*) [BORRACHO].

borrachada [BORRACHERA].

borrachear, *v.i.* to get drunk often, booze.

borrachera, borrachería, *n.f.* drunkenness, hard-drinking; drunken spree, binge; (*coll., fig.*) craziness.

borrachero, *n.m.* (*bot.*) stramonium.

borrachez [BORRACHERA].

borrachín, *n.m.* inveterate *or* hopeless drunkard.

borracho, -cha, *a.* drunk; violet *or* flush coloured; (*coll., fig.*) blind, crazed (*with passion etc.*); ***bizcocho borracho,*** tipsy cake. — *n.f.* (*coll.*) borachio, leather wine-bag.

borrachón, *n.m.* great drunkard.

borrachuela, *n.f.* (*bot.*) bearded darnel, ray-grass.

borrador, *n.m.* rough copy *or* draft; blotter; rough-book; (*prov.*) satchel.

borradura, *n.f.* erasure, scratching out, effacement.

borragíneo, -nea, *a.* (*bot.*) appertaining to plants of the Boraginaceæ family.

borraj, *n.m.* borax; tincal.

borraja, *n.f.* (*bot.*) borage; (*coll., fig.*) ***quedarse en agua de borrajas,*** to come to nothing.

borrajear, *v.t.* to scribble, scrawl.

borrajo, *n.m.* embers, hot ashes, cinders; dead pine leaves.

borrar, *v.t.* to cross out, strike out; to efface, erase, rub out; to blot; (*fig.*) to expunge, obliterate.

borrasca, *n.f.* (*lit., fig.*) storm; tempest, squall; (*Mex.*) exhaustion of a mine.

borrascoso, -sa, *a.* stormy, squally; (*fig.*) boisterous, tempestuous.

borrasquero, -ra, *a.* (*coll.*) revelling.

borregada, *n.f.* large flock of sheep *or* lambs.

borrego, -ga, *n.m.f.* lamb (*not yet two years old*); (*coll.*) easily influenced person. — *n.m.pl.* (*coll.*) fleecy clouds; ***no hay tales borregos,*** there is no sign *or* trace of them *or* it.

borregoso, -sa, *a.* fleecy.

borreguero, -ra, *a.* suitable for lambs (*pasture land*); (*coll.*) easily influenced. — *n.m.f.* shepherd, shepherdess (*who tends lambs*).

borreguil, *a.* appertaining to lambs; (*coll.*) easily influenced.

borreguito, *n.m.* (delightful) little lamb. — *n.m.pl.* (*fig.*) white horses.

borrén, *n.m.* panel (*of saddle*).

borrica, *n.f.* she-ass.

borricada, *n.f.* drove of asses; (*coll.*) silly *or* foolish thing to do *or* say.

borrico, *n.m.* ass; (*carp.*) trestle; ***puesto en el borrico,*** hell bent *or* set on sth.

borricote, *n.m.* (*coll.*) utter ass; plodder.

borrilla, *n.f.* lamb's first coat; downy matter (covering fruits).

borriqueño, -ña, *a* asinine

borriquería [BORRICADA].

borriquero, *n.m.* ass-driver *or* keeper.

borriquete, *n.m.* (*carp.*) trestle; (*naut.*) fore-topsail.

borriquillo, -lla, borriquito, -ta, *n.m.f.* little ass [BORRICO].

borro, *n.m.* lamb not two years old; duty on sheep.

borrón (1), *n.m.* blot, smudge, blur; (*fig.*) blemish; stigma; (*pl.* **borrones**) (*print.*) excess of paste on overlay.

borrón (2), *n.m.* (*prov.*) pile of weeds burnt for manure.

borronear, *v.t., v.i.* to scribble (on).

borronista, *n.m.f.* scribbler.

borroso, -sa, *a.* turbid, muddy; blurred; illegible; ***letra borrosa,*** indistinct hand writing.

borrufalla, *n.f.* (*prov., coll.*) empty sounds *or* words, bombast.

borrumbada, *n.f.* (*fam.*) extravagant expense; boastful saying.

boruca, *n.f.* (*fam.*) noise, hubbub, uproar.

boruga, *n.f.* (*Cub.*) curd mixed with sugar.

borujo, burujo, *n.m.* small lump; mass of ground and pressed olive stones; oilcake.

borujón, *n.m.* bump on the head (caused by a blow); lump; (*fam.*) untidy heap; disorderly crowd; [BORUJO].
boruquiento, -ta, *a.* (*Mex.*) boisterous, noisy, lively.
borusca, *n.f.* withered leaf.
boscaje, *n.m.* cluster of trees, grove; wooded country; (*paint.*) woodland scene.
Bósforo, *n.m.* Bosphorus.
bosníaco, -ca, bosnio, -nia, *a.*, *n.m.f.* Bosnian.
bosque, *n.m.* wood; forest; ***bosque maderable,*** timber-yielding forest.
bosquecillo, *n.m.* small wood, coppice, grove.
bosquejar, *v.t.* to make a rough sketch of; to outline.
bosquejo, *n.m.* (*paint.*) sketch; outline.
bosquete, *n.m.* bosket, small wood.
bosquimán, bosquimano, *n.m.* bushman (*S. Africa*).
bosta, *n.f.* dung, manure.
bostear, *v.i.* (*Arg., Chi.*) to excrete (*animals*).
bostezador, -ra, *a.* yawning, gaping. — *n.m.f.* yawner, gaper.
bostezante, *a.* yawning, gaping.
bostezar [C], *v.i.* to yawn, gape.
bostezo, *n.m.* yawn, yawning.
bota (1), *n.f.* boot; ***botas de montar,*** riding-boots; ***estar con las botas puestas,*** to be (all) ready *or* prepared; ***morir con las botas puestas,*** to die with one's boots on, die in harness; (*coll.*, *fig.*) ***ponerse las botas,*** to go to town, to do justice to sth. (*e.g. a meal*).
bota (2), *n.f.* wine skin; cask.
botabala, *n.f.* ramrod.
botacuchar, *v.i.* to meddle, interfere.
botada, *n.f.* quantity of staves; (*naut.*) launch, launching.
botador, -ra, *a.* throwing, pitching. — *n.m.f.* thrower, pitcher. — *n.m.* punch, instrument for forcing out nails; (dentist's) crow-bill; (*naut.*) starting-pole, boat-hook; (*print.*) quoin-adjusting tool.
botadura, *n.f.* (*naut.*) launch, launching.
botafuego, *n.m.* (*artill.*) linstock, match-staff; (*coll.*) irritable, quick-tempered person.
botafumeiro, *n.m.* large incensory.
botagueña, *n.f.* sausage (made of pigs' haslets).
botalón, *n.m.* (*naut.*) jib boom.
botamen, *n.m.* (*naut.*) collection of water-casks; all the pots and jars in a chemist's shop.
botana, *n.f.* patch *or* plug (to stop up a hole in a leather wine-bag *or* cask); (*coll.*) plaster (on a wound); (*coll.*) scar.
botanero, *n.m.* instrument for applying patches to casks and leather wine-bags.
botánico, -ca, *a.* botanic, botanical. — *n.m.f.* botanist. — *n.f.* botany.
botanista, *n.m.f.* botanist.
botanizar [C], *v.i.* to botanize.
botanomancia, *n.f.* superstitious divination by herbs.
botante de caza, *n.m.* (*naut.*) cradle (used for launching ships).
botar, *v.t.* to cast, pitch, throw, launch, fling; (*Hisp. Am.*) to throw away; to sack, fire; (*naut.*) to shift (*the helm*); ***botar al agua,*** to launch. — *v.i.* to bounce, (re)bound. — **botarse,** *v.r.* (*equit.*) to buck.
botaratada, *n.f.* rash, wild *or* madcap thing to do *or* say.
botarate, *a.*, *n.m.* (*coll.*) madcap, scatterbrain.
botarel, *n.m.* (*arch.*) buttress, abutment, spur, counterfort.
botarete, *a.* (*arch.*) vault-supporting (*arch*).
botarga, *n.f.* (*obs.*) loose breeches, galligaskins; motley dress; harlequin, buffoon; (kind of) large sausage; (*prov.*) tumbler (*toy*) (used at bull-fights).
botasilla, *n.f.* bugle signal for the cavalry to saddle
botavante, *n.m.* (*naut.*) boarding-pike.
botavara, *n.f.* (*naut.*) boom *or* pole, gaff, sprit; boat-hook; ***botavara de cangreja,*** gaff-sail boom.
bote (1), *n.m.* thrust with a pike, lance, *or* spear; bound, jump.
bote (2), *n.m.* pot, jar; tin, (*Am.*) can; kitty; ***estar de bote en bote,*** to be packed *or* crammed; ***chupar del bote,*** to be a drone *or* parasite.
bote (3), *n.m.* (*naut.*) (rowing) boat; ***bote salvavidas,*** life-boat; ***bote de lastre,*** ballast-lighter.
botecario, *n.m.* war tribute.
botella, *n.f.* bottle, flask; (*phys.*) ***botella de Leiden,*** Leyden jar.
botellazo, *n.m.* blow with a bottle.
botellería, *n.f.* bottle factory.
botellero, *n.m.* bottle manufacturer *or* dealer; wire basket for bottles; bin, bottle-rack (in wine-cellars).
botellón, *n.m.* large bottle, demijohn.
botequín, *n.m.* (*naut.*) cock-boat, small boat.
botería, *n.f.* (*naut.*) collection of casks of wine; shop for the sale of leather wine-bags and casks.
botero (1), *n.m.* maker *or* vendor of leather bags and bottles (for wine, oil etc.).
botero (2), *n.m.* boatman, wherry-man; ***Pero Botero,*** the Devil.
botete, *n.m.* mosquito.
boteza, *n.f.* (*obs.*) rudeness, boorishness.
botica, *n.f.* apothecary's shop; medicine (in general); shop; (*slang*) drapery shop; ***hay de todo como en botica,*** there is everything under the sun.
boticaria, *n.f.* (female) apothecary.
boticario, *n.m.* apothecary; (*sl.*) draper; ***venir como pedrada en ojo de boticario,*** to be just right.
botifuera, *n.f.* (*prov.*) discount, bonus to purchaser; (*prov.*) wine-measurer's perquisite; (*prov.*) tip, gratuity.
botiga, *n.f.* (*prov.*) shop.
botiguero, *n.m.* (*prov.*) shopkeeper.
botija, *n.f.* earthen jug; ***estar hecho una botija,*** to have got stout *or* fat.
botijero, -ra, *n.m.f.* maker *or* seller of jugs.
botijo, *n.m.* round earthen jar with spout and handle; (*fam.*) ***tren botijo,*** excursion train.
botiller, *n.m.* person in charge of wines.
botillero, *n.m.* maker *or* seller of cold drinks and refreshments.
botillería, *n.f.* soda-fountain and light refreshment saloon; war tribute; pantry, larder.
botillo, *n.m.* small leather wine-bag.
botín (1), *n.m.* half-boot; spat.
botín (2), *n.m.* booty.
botina, *n.f.* half-boot.
botinería, *n.f.* boot shop *or* factory.
botinero, -ra, *a.* black-footed (*cattle*). — *n.m.* boot-maker; soldier who guards *or* sells booty.
botiquín, *n.m.* medicine chest, medicine *or* first-aid kit; first-aid station.
botivoleo, *n.m.* recovering a ball at the rebound.
boto (1), **-ta** (3), *a.* blunt; dim-witted, dull.
boto (2), *n.m.* small skin (*for wine, oil etc.*); (*prov.*) large gut filled with lard.
botón, *n.m.* (*bot.*) sprout, bud; button; tip (*of a foil in fencing*); knob (*of doors, windows, furniture*); annulet (*of balusters, keys*); (*prov.*) piece of wood which fastens a fowling-net; crank-pin; dowel; handle; (*bot.*) ***botón de oro,*** creeping double-flowered crowfoot; ***de botones adentro,*** inwardly; ***de botones afuera,*** outwardly.
botonadura, *n.f.* set of buttons.
botonar, *v.i.* to germinate, bud.

botonazo, *n.m.* thrust with fencing-foil.
botonería, *n.f.* button shop.
botonero, -ra, *n.m.f.* button-maker; button-seller. — *n.f.* (*carp.*) socket for stanchion, dowel.
botones, *n.m. inv.* page-boy, buttons.
botor, *n.m.* tumour.
bototo, *n.m.* (*Hisp. Am.*) gourd *or* calabash for water.
botulina, *n.f.* (*med.*) botuline.
botulismo, *n.m.* botulism.
botuto, *n.m.* (*Hisp. Am.*) stem (*of papaw fruit*); war trumpet (*of the Orinoco Indians*).
bou, *n.m.* joint casting of a net by two boats; boat.
bourel, *n.m.* cork buoy with flag signal.
bovage, bovático, *n.m.* ancient duty on horned cattle (*levied in Catalonia*).
bóveda, *n.f.* (*arch.*) vault; ***bóveda celeste,*** vault of heaven, firmament; ***bóveda craneal,*** cranial cavity; (*anat.*) ***bóveda palatina,*** palatine vault, palate; ***bóveda de jardín,*** bower.
bovedilla, *n.f.* (*arch.*) small vault; (*naut.*) counter.
bóvido, -da, bovino, -na, *a.* bovine.
box, *n.m.* shoemaker's box-wood tool.
boxeador, *n.m.* boxer.
boxear, *v.i.* to box.
boxeo, *n.m.* boxing.
bóxer, *n.m.* boxer (dog).
boxibalón, *n.m.* punch-bag.
boya, *n.f.* (*naut.*) buoy; net-float; ***boya de campana,*** bell buoy; ***boya pantalón,*** breeches buoy; ***boya salvavidas,*** life-buoy.
boyada, *n.f.* drove of oxen.
boyal, *a.* (*relating to*) cattle.
boyante, *a.* buoyant, floating; (*naut.*) drawing light, sailing well; (*fig.*) prosperous, successful.
boyar, *v.i.* (*naut.*) to float, be afloat.
boyarín, *n.m.* small buoy *or* net-float [BOYA].
boyazo, *n.m.* large ox [BUEY].
boyera, boyeriza, *n.f.* ox-stall, cow-shed.
boyerizo, *n.m.* ox-herd, ox-driver.
boyero, *n.m.* ox-herd, ox-driver, cowherd.
boyezuelo, *n.m.* young *or* small ox [BUEY].
boyo, *n.m.* serpent.
boyuda, *n.f.* (*sl.*) pack of cards.
boyuno, -na, *a.* bovine.
boza, *n.f.* (*naut.*) rope with one end fast in a ring-bolt; (*naut.*) stopper.
bozal, *a.* (*slave*) newly arrived (*from Africa*); (*coll.*) inexperienced; stupid, foolish; wild, not broken in, untamed (*horse*). — *n.m.f.* (*coll.*) novice, greenhorn. — *n.m.* muzzle; bells (on a harness); (*Hisp. Am.*) temporary headstall.
bozalejo, *n.m.* small muzzle [BOZAL].
bozo, *n.m.* down (*preceding growth of beard*); exterior of mouth; headstall.
braba, *n.f.* large net.
brabante, *n.m.* Brabant *or* Flemish linen.
brabanzón, -zona, *a., n.m.f.* (native) of Brabant.
brabera, *n.f.* (*arch.*) vent *or* air-hole of cave etc.
brabio, *n.m.* prize, reward.
bracarense, *a., n.m.f.* (native) of Braga (Portugal).
braceada, *n.f.* violent extension of the arms.
braceado, *n.m.* action of stirring molten metal; brewing, mashing.
braceador, -ra, *a.* (*riding*) drawing up the front legs too much. — *n.m.* coiner, minter.
braceaje, *n.m.* coinage; beating the metal for coinage (in the mint); (*naut.*) depth of water, sounding; soundings.
bracear, *v.t.* (*naut.*) to brace. — *v.i.* to move *or* swing the arms; to do the crawl (*swimming*); (*fig.*) to strive, struggle; (*prov., equit.*) to draw up the fore-feet; to stir molten metal.
braceo, *n.m.* threshing of arms.
braceral, *n.m.* brace (*armour*).
bracero, -ra, *a.* thrown by hand (*weapon, dart etc.*). — *n.m.* (hired) hand; day-labourer. — *n.f.* tenon-saw.
bracete, *n.m.* small arm; ***de bracete,*** arm-in-arm.
bracillo, *n.m.* branch (of the bridle-bit).
bracitendido, -da, *a.* indolent, lazy.
bracito, *n.m.* little arm [BRAZO].
bracmán, *n.m.* Brahmin.
braco, -ca, *a.* (*coll.*) snub-nosed; ***perro braco,*** pointer dog.
bráctea, *n.f.* (*bot.*) bract.
bracteal, *a.* (*bot.*) bracteal.
bractéola, *n.f.* (*bot.*) bracteole.
bradipepsia, *n.f.* (*med.*) bradypepsia.
brafonera, *n.f.* brace (*armour*).
braga, *n.f.* hoisting-rope; (*pl.*) knickers; pants, panties; ***calzarse las bragas,*** to wear the trousers *or* breeches.
bragada (1), *n.f.* (*vet.*) flat *or* inside part of the thigh.
bragado, -da, (2), *a.* (*vet.*) having the crotch of a different colour from the rest of the body; (*fig.*) ill-disposed, of depraved sentiments; (*coll.*) energetic, firm; ***un tío bragado,*** a fellow with guts.
bragadura, *n.f.* (*anat.*) crotch; crutch (*of trousers*).
bragar [B], *v.t.* (*artill.*) to suspend in the prolonge.
bragazas, *n.m. inv.* hen-pecked man.
braguerista, *n.m.* surgical truss maker *or* vendor.
braguero, *n.m.* (*med.*) surgical truss, brace, bandage (*for a rupture*); (*artill., naut.*) breeching; (*Per.*) martingale.
bragueta, *n.f.* fly (*of trousers*); cod-piece.
braguetazo, *n.m.* marriage for money; (*fam.*) ***dar*** or ***pegar el braguetazo,*** to marry (for) money (*said of a man*).
braguetero, -ra, *a.* (*fam.*) lecherous, lascivious. — *n.m.* lecher.
braguillas, *n.m. inv.* (*fig.*) newly breeched child; (*fig.*) ugly, undersized child.
brahmán, brahmín, *n.m.* Brahmin,
brahmánico, -ca, brahmínico, -ca, *a.* Brahminic(al).
brahmanismo, *n.m.* Brahminism.
brahón, *n.m.*, **brahonera,** *n.f.* (*obs.*) fold surrounding the upper part of the sleeve.
brama, *n.f.* rut, mating season (*of deer and other wild animals*).
bramadera, *n.f.* rattle (*toy*); call *or* horn (*used by shepherds and keepers of plantations*); (*Col., Cub.*) vent, chimney (*of furnaces*).
bramadero, *n.m.* rutting-place (*of deer and other wild animals*); (*Hisp. Am.*) post in corral (*for tying animals*).
bramador, -ra, *a.* roaring, bellowing. — *n.m.f.* roarer, bellower. — *n.m.* (*sl.*) town-crier.
bramante (1), *a.* roaring, bellowing.
bramante (2), *n.m.* pack-thread, hemp-cord, twine; Brabant linen.
bramar, *v.i.* to roar, bellow.
bramido, *n.m.* roar, bellow.
bramil, *n.m.* [GRAMIL]; (*carp.*) marking-gauge.
bramo, *n.m.* (*sl.*) bawl, cry; alarm.
bramón, *n.m.* (*sl.*) sneak.
bramona, *n.f.* (*vulg.*) ***soltar la bramona,*** to curse and swear.
bran de Inglaterra, *n.m.* old Spanish dance.
branca, *n.f.* point (*of a horn*); (*bot.*) ***branca ursina,*** brankursine, bear's breech.
brancada, *n.f.* drag-net, sweep-net.
branchas, *n.f.pl.* gills (*of fish*).
brandales, *n.m.pl.* (*naut.*) ladder-ropes.
brandar, *v.i.* (*naut.*) to rock.
brandís, *n.m.* (*obs.*) great-coat.
branque, *n.m.* (*naut.*) stem.
branquia, *n.f.* gill (*of fish*).

branquiado, -da, *a.* branchiate.
branquial, *a.* branchial.
branquífero, -ra, *a.* branchiferous.
branza, *n.f.* fastening ring (*of galley-slave's chain*).
braña, *n.f.* (*prov.*) summer pasture; (*prov.*) brushwood.
braquiado, -da, *a.* (*bot.*) brachiate.
braquial, *a.* brachial.
braquicéfalo, -la, *a.* brachycephalic.
braquigrafía, *n.f.* shorthand.
braquígrafo, *n.m.* shorthand-writer.
braquiópodo, -da, braquípodo, -da, *a.* brachiopodous. — *n.m.f.* brachiopod.
braquiotomía, *n.f.* (*surg.*) arm amputation.
brasa, *n.f.* live coal, red-hot coal *or* wood, burning ember; (*slang*) thief; ***estar hecho unas brasas,*** to be flushed, red-faced; ***estar en brasas,*** to be on edge; ***salir de llamas y caer en brasas,*** to go from the frying pan into the fire; ***pasar como sobre brasas,*** to skate over, touch upon superficially.
brasca, *n.f.* (*chem., min.*) coating of coal-powder and clay (in furnaces).
brascar [A], *v.t.* (*chem.*) to cover the interior of (crucibles) with ***brasca.***
braserillo, *n.m.* small fire-pan; small cigar-lighter.
braserito, *n.m.* small pan to hold coals.
brasero, *n.m.* brazier, pan to hold coals; fire-pan; funeral-pile; (*sl.*) theft; (*Mex.*) hearth, fireplace.
Brasil, *n.m.* Brazil.
brasil, *n.m.* (*obs.*) rouge; ***palo brasil,*** Brazil wood.
brasilado, -da, *a.* of a red *or* Brazil-wood colour; ruddy.
brasileño, -ña, *a., n.m.f.* Brazilian.
brasilete, *n.m.* inferior Brazil wood, Jamaica wood.
brasilina, *n.f.* (*chem.*) brazilin.
brasmología, *n.f.* science which studies the tides.
bravata, *n.f.* bravado.
bravatero, *n.m.* (*slang*) bully, hector.
braveador, -ra, *a.* bullying, hectoring. — *n.m.f.* bully, hector.
bravear, *v.i.* to bully, hector.
bravera, *n.f.* vent *or* chimney (*of ovens*).
braveza, *n.f.* bravery, valour; fighting spirit.
bravío, -vía, *a.* wild, fierce, rough. — *n.m.* fierceness, savageness. — *n.f.* shrew.
bravo, -va, *a.* brave, valiant, manful, fearless; (*fam.*) savage, wild, fierce; (*coll.*) severe, intractable; rude, unpolished, uncivilized; (*coll.*) luxurious, sumptuous, expensive; excellent, fine; ***mar brava,*** rough sea. — *n.m.* (*sl.*) judge. — *interj.* ***¡bravo!*** bravo!
bravone, *n.m.* bravo, hector, braggart.
bravosidad, *n.f.* elegance; arrogance, bravado.
bravote, *n.m.* (*sl.*) bravo, bully.
bravucón, -cona, *a.* (*fam.*) boastful, braggart. — *n.m.f.* boaster, braggart.
bravura, *n.f.* ferocity, fierceness; courage, manliness.
braza, *n.f.* (*anat., naut.*) fathom; (arm-)stroke; (*naut.*) brace.
brazada, *n.f.* arm movement; arm-stroke; armful.
brazado, *n.m.* armful, truss (*of hay*).
brazaje, *n.m.* [BRACEAJE]; (*naut.*) depth of water.
brazal, *n.m.* brace (*armour*); clasp (of shield); brassard; bracelet; arm-band; (*naut.*) headrail.
brazalete, *n.m.* armlet, bracelet; brace (*armour*).
brazalote, *n.m.* (*naut.*) brace pendant.
brazo, *n.m.* arm (*of body, sea, balance-beam, lever, chair*); upper part of arm; branch (*of chandelier, tree*); fore-leg, fore-foot (*of quadrupeds*); (*fig.*) valour, strength, power; (*pl.*) protectors, defenders; hands, labourers; ***brazo de candelero,*** branch of a chandelier; ***brazo de cruz,*** cross-bar; ***brazo del mar,*** arm of the sea; ***estar hecho un brazo de mar,*** to be all poshed up, to be dressed up to the nines; ***brazos del reino,*** estates of the realm; ***brazo real, secular*** or ***seglar,*** secular arm, temporal authority; ***con los brazos abiertos,*** with open arms; ***con los brazos cruzados,*** with folded arms, standing idly by; ***cruzarse de brazos,*** to stand idly by; ***huelga de brazos caídos,*** go-slow (strike); ***brazo a brazo,*** hand to hand; ***a brazo partido,*** with all one's might; ***asidos*** or ***cogidos del brazo,*** arm-in-arm; ***darle a alguien los brazos,*** to embrace s.o.; ***no dar su brazo a torcer,*** to stick to one's guns; ***ser el brazo derecho de alguien,*** to be s.o.'s right-hand man; ***tener brazo,*** to be strong *or* tough; ***vivir por su brazo,*** to live by one's labours.
brazolas, *n.f.pl.* (*naut.*) coamings (*of the hatchways*).
brazuelo, *n.m.* small arm; shoulder *or* fore-thigh (*of beasts*); branch (*of bridle-bit*).
brea, *n.f.* pitch, tar.
brear, *v.t.* to pitch, tar; (*coll.*) to treat roughly, give a rough time of it to; to beat (up); ***le brearon a golpes,*** they gave him a beating.
brebaje, *n.m.* concoction; (*naut.*) grog.
brebajo, *n.m.* (*prov., vet.*) drench.
breca, *n.f.* (*ichth.*) bleak.
brecol, *n.m.*, **brecolera,** *n.f.* (*bot.*) broccoli.
brecha, *n.f.* breach, opening; ***abrir brecha, batir en brecha,*** to breach, open *or* make a breach; ***montar la brecha,*** to start an assault *or* attack; ***estar siempre en la brecha,*** to be always on the job *or* at the ready.
brechar, *v.i.* (*sl.*) to play with loaded dice.
brechero, *n.m.* (*sl.*) player with loaded dice.
brecho, *n.m.* (*ichth.*) mutton-fish.
brega, *n.f.* strife, affray, fight, scuffle, scrap; (*fig.*) practical joke, jest, trick; ***dar brega,*** to play a trick; ***andar a la brega,*** to toil, labour.
bregar (1) [B], *v.t.* to work (*dough*) with a rolling-pin.
bregar (2) [B], *v.i.* to fight, struggle; to toil, labour.
bregón, *n.m.* baker's rolling-pin.
brema, *n.m.* (*prov., ichth.*) sheepshead.
bren, *n.m.* bran.
brenca, *n.f.* sluice-post; (*bot.*) maidenhair.
brenga, *n.f.* (*prov.*) bundle of fibres and filaments twisted round a trunk.
breña, *n.f.*, **breñal, breñar,** *n.m.* rough brambly ground, heath.
breñoso, -sa, *a.* rough and brambly.
breque, *n.m.* (*ichth.*) bleak; ***ojo de breque,*** bleary eye.
bresca, *n.f.* honeycomb.
brescar [A], *v.t.* to extract (*honeycombs*) from a beehive.
breslinga, *n.f.* (*bot.*) strawberry.
bretador, *n.m.* cry *or* whistle to call birds.
Bretaña, *n.f.* Brittany; ***Gran Bretaña,*** Great Britain.
bretaña, *n.f.* fine linen made in Brittany; (*bot.*) hyacinth.
brete (1), *n.m.* shackle, fetter; (*fig.*) perplexity, difficulty; (*Arg.*) place in the corral where beasts are branded; ***poner a alguien en un brete,*** to put someone in a tight spot; ***estar en un brete,*** to be in a tight spot.
brete (2), *n.m.* (*Philip.*) leaves of betel.
bretesado, -da, *a.* scalloped, serrated (*sash, band etc.*).
bretón (1), **-tona,** *a., n.m.f.* Breton. — *n.m.* Breton language.
bretón (2), *n.m.* (*bot.*) borecole, kale.
breva, *n.f.* early fig; early large acorn; choice cigar; (*coll.*) bargain; good thing; piece of luck; ***no caerá esa breva,*** we shan't have any such luck.
breval, *n.m.* (*bot.*) early fig-tree.
breve, *a.* brief, short; ***en breve,*** shortly, before long. — *n.m.* apostolic brief. — *n.f.* (*mus.*) breve.

brevedad, *n.f.* brevity, briefness, shortness.
brevera, *n.f.* (*prov.*) [BREVAL].
brevete, *n.m.* memorandum.
brevetín [EVANGELIO].
breviario, *n.m.* breviary; abridgment, epitome; (*print.*) brevier, small size of type; (*slang*) quick worker.
brevipenne, *a.* (*zool.*) brevipennate.
brevípodo, -da, *a.* (*zool.*) breviped.
brevirrostro, -ra, *a.* (*orn.*) brevirostrate.
brezal, *n.m.* heath.
brezo, *n.m.* (*bot.*) heather.
briaga, *n.f.* thick bass-weed rope; hoisting rope.
brial, *n.m.* rich silken skirt *or* petticoat.
briba, *n.f.* loafing; ***andar a la briba,*** to loaf about; ***hombre de la briba,*** good-for-nothing fellow.
bribar, *v.i.* to loaf about.
bribia, *n.f.* (*sl.*) beggar's tale of woe; ***echar la bribia,*** to go a-begging.
bribión, *n.m.* (*sl.*) master in the art of begging.
bribón, -bona, *a., n.m.f.* vagrant; knave, scoundrel, rascal.
bribonada, *n.f.* piece of knavery.
bribonazo, -za, *n.m.f.* utter rascal, scamp *or* good-for-nothing.
bribonear, *v.i.* to loaf about; to behave in a rascally fashion.
bribonería, *n.f.* vagabondage; roguery.
bribonesco, -ca, *a.* knavish, rascally.
bribonzuelo, -la, *n.m.f.* petty rascal *or* good-for-nothing.
bricbarca, *n.f.* barque.
bricho, *n.m.* spangle, tinsel.
brida, *n.f.* bridle; bridle-rein; horsemanship; clamp; (*pl., surg.*) fibrous membranes in wounds; ***a la brida,*** riding with low saddle and long stirrup; ***a toda brida,*** hell for leather.
bridecú, *n.m.* sword-belt.
bridón, *n.m.* horseman riding with low saddle and long stirrup; horse accoutred with low saddle and long stirrup; small bridle; snaffle-bit; (*poet.*) fine horse.
brigada, *n.f.* (*mil.*) brigade; gang, party, squad; — *n.m.* (***sargento***) ***brigada,*** sergeant-major.
brigadero, *n.m.* civilian who tends beasts of burden in the army.
brigadier, *n.m.* (*mil.*) brigadier (general); (*naut.*) officer commanding a division of a fleet.
brigadiera, *n.f.* (*fam.*) brigadier's wife.
brigantina (1), *n.f.* brigandine (*coat of mail*).
brigantino, -na (2), *a.* appertaining to *or* of Brigantium (*mod.* La Coruña).
Brígida, *n.f.* Bridget.
brigola, *n.f.* (*mil.*) battering-ram.
Briján, *n.m.* ***saber más que Briján,*** to be very wise and cautious.
brillador, -ra, *a.* [BRILLANTE].
brillante, *a.* brilliant; bright, shining, sparkling, radiant, glossy, glittering. — *n.m.* brilliant, diamond.
brillantez, *n.f.* brilliance; brilliancy; (*fig.*) splendour.
brillantina, *n.f.* brilliantine; percaline; mineral powder (for polishing metal).
brillar, *v.i.* to shine, sparkle, glisten, glitter, gleam; ***brillar por su ausencia,*** to be conspicuous by one's absence.
brillo, *n.m.* brilliancy, brilliance, brightness, luminousness, lustre, splendour, glitter.
brin, *n.m.* (*prov.*) fragment *or* pistil of saffron; fine canvas, sail-cloth.
brincador, -ra, *a.* leaping, jumping.
brincar [A], *v.t.* to bounce (*a child on one's knee etc.*). — *v.i.* to leap, jump, frisk, skip, gambol, hop; (*coll.*) to be *or* get hopping mad, go off the deep end.
brincia [BRIZNA].
brinco, *n.m.* leap, jump, frisk, hop, skip, gambol, bounce, bound; small jewel for head-dress; ***en un brinco,*** in a jiffy.
brincho, *n.m.* flush (*in card-game **quínolas***).
brindador, -ra, *n.m.f.* inviter; toaster.
brindar, *v.t.* to offer; (*tauro.*) to dedicate (*a bull*). — *v.i.* to drink s.o.'s health, toast. — **brindarse,** *v.r.* to offer (***a,*** to); ***se brindó a pagar,*** he offered to pay.
brindis, *n.m. inv.* offer; dedication; toast.
brinete, *n.m.* sail-cloth.
bringulata, *n.f.* (*naut.*) pump handle *or* brake.
brinquiño, *n.m.* gewgaw, small trinket; sweetmeat (from Portugal); ***estar*** or ***ir hecho un brinquiño,*** to be very spruce.
brinzal, *n.m.* (*bot.*) blade, slip, sprig, shoot.
briñolas, *n.f.pl.* prunes.
briñolero, *n.m.* (*bot.*) olive-tree.
briñón, *n.m.* (*bot.*) nectarine.
brío, *n.m.* vigour, spirit, mettle; gusto; ***bajarle a alguien los bríos,*** to calm *or* cool s.o. down; to put the brake on s.o.; to bring s.o. down a peg or two.
briol, *n.m.* (*naut.*) brail.
briolín, *n.m.* (*naut.*) bunt-line.
briología, *n.f.* bryology.
brión, *n.m.* (*naut.*) fore-foot.
brionia, *n.f.* (*bot.*) briony.
brios, *interj.* ***¡voto a brios!*** by Jove!
brioso, -sa, *a.* vigorous, spirited.
briqueta, *n.f.* briquette, briquet.
brisa (1), *n.f.* breeze.
brisa (2), *n.f.* bagasse of pressed grapes.
brisada, brisura, *n.f.* (*her.*) label.
brisca, *n.f.* card game.
briscar [A], *v.t.* to embroider *or* weave with gold *or* silver twist.
brisera, *n.f.* glass screen (*for a candle*).
británico, -ca, *a.* British, Britannic. — *n.f.* (*bot.*) great water dock.
britano, -na, *a., n.m.f.* (ancient) Briton.
briza, *n.f.* fog, haze.
brizar [C], *v.t.* to (rock in the) cradle.
brizna, *n.f.* (*bot.*) filament, string (*of beans etc.*); blade (*of grass*); fragment, splinter, chip; morsel, minute piece.
brizo, *n.m.* rocking cradle.
broa (1), *n.f.* (*naut.*) shallow dangerous creek *or* cove.
broa (2), *n.f.* biscuit *or* cracker.
broca, *n.f.* (weaving) reel, bobbin; (*engin.*) drill, bit; (*shoe*) tack.
brocadillo, *n.m.* brocade of inferior quality.
brocado, -da, *a.* brocaded. — *n.m.* brocade.
brocadura, *n.f.* bear's bite.
brocal, *n.m.* curb-stone (*of a well*); metal ring (*of sword scabbard*); steel ornament (*on shield*); (*min.*) mouth (*of a shaft*); (*mil.*) bush (*reinforcement of cannon's mouth*); ***brocal de bota,*** mouthpiece of leather wine bottle.
brocamantón, *n.m.* brooch set with gems.
brocatel, *n.m.* brocade, damask of hemp and silk; ***mármol brocatel,*** Spanish marble with white veins; ***brocatel de seda,*** silk brocade.
brocato, *n.m.* (*prov.*) [BROCADO].
brocino, *n.m.* bump (*on the head*).
brócula, *n.f.* drill (*for piercing metals*).
bróculi, *n.m.* (*bot.*) broccoli.
brocha (1), *n.f.* brush (*for painting, shaving etc.*); loaded dice; ***pintor de brocha gorda,*** house painter; crude *or* heavy-handed painter, dauber.
brocha (2), *n.f.* stroke (*of brush*).
brochado, -da, *a.* brocaded.
brochadura, *n.f.* set of hooks and eyes.
brochal, *n.m.* (*arch.*) joist.

brochar, *v.i.* to daub.
brochazo, *n.m.* stroke, brush-stroke.
broche, *n.m.* brooch; clasp, clip; hasp; hook and eye; ***broche de oro,*** crowning glory, finishing touch.
brocheta, *n.f.* skewer, spit.
brochón, *n.m.* large brush, whitewash brush, plasterer's brush.
brodio [BODRIO].
brollador, -ra, *a.* gushing out, boiling over; spitting. — *n.m.* fountain, jet.
brollar *v.t.* to spit. — *v.i.* to gush out, boil over.
broma (1), *n.f.* joke, jest; fun; ship-worm; ***broma pesada,*** practical joke, unpleasant *or* nasty joke; ***darle, gastarle*** or ***hacerle una broma a alguien,*** to play a joke on s.o.; ***de*** or ***en broma,*** in fun.
broma (2), *n.f.* oatmeal gruel; (*build.*) riprap.
bromar, *v.t.* to gnaw (*of ship-worm*).
bromato, *n.m.* (*chem.*) bromate.
bromatografía, *n.f.* description of alimentary substances.
bromatología, *n.f.* treatise on foods.
bromatometría, *n.f.* calculation of food quantity necessary to maintain the human body in good condition.
bromazo, *n.m.* practical joke, unpleasant *or* nasty joke.
bromear(**se**), *v.i.* (*v.r.*) to joke, make fun, jest.
bromelia, *n.f.* (*bot.*) pineapple.
bromhidrato, *n.m.* (*chem.*) hydrobromate, hydrobromide.
bromhídrico, -ca, *a.* (*chem.*) hydrobromic.
bromhidrosis, bromidrosis, *n.f. inv.* (*med.*) fetid sweating.
brómico, -ca, *a.* (*chem.*) bromic.
bromífero, -ra, *a.* containing bromine.
bromismo, *n.m.* (*med.*) bromism.
bromista, *a.* joking. — *n.m.f.* joker.
bromo (1), *n.m.* (*chem.*) bromine.
bromo (2), *n.m.* (*bot.*) brome grass.
bromurado, -da, *a.* (*chem., med.*) bromic, bromine.
bromuro, *n.m.* (*chem.*) bromide.
bronca (1), *n.f.* (*coll.*) wrangle; row, ticking off; ***echarle a alguien una bronca,*** to tick s.o. off; to give s.o. a dressing-down *or* rocket.
bronce, *n.m.* bronze; (*poet.*) trumpet, bell, cannon; (*numis.*) copper coin; ***edad de bronce,*** Bronze Age; (*coll.*) ***gente del bronce,*** gay, determined people; ***escribir en bronce una cosa,*** to make sth. unforgettable; ***ser de bronce*** or ***un bronce,*** to be hard-hearted; to be robust and indefatigable.
bronceado, *n.m.* bronzing; (sun-)tan.
bronceadura, *n.f.* bronzing.
broncear, *v.t.* to bronze; to (sun-)tan.
broncería, *n.f.* collection of brass *or* bronze articles.
broncia, *n.f.* (*min.*) pyrites.
broncina, *n.f.* bronze-powder.
broncíneo, -nea, *a.* bronze.
broncista, *n.m.* worker in bronze.
bronco, -ca (2), *a.* rough, coarse, unpolished; brittle (*metals*); (*fig.*) rude, hard, abrupt (*character*); harsh, hoarse (*voice, instrument*); ***bronco de genio,*** of crusty *or* gruff temperament.
broncocele, *n.m.* (*surg.*) bronchocele.
bronconeumonía, *n.f.* (*med.*) broncho-pneumonia.
broncotomía, *n.f.* (*surg.*) bronchotomy.
broncha (1), *n.f.* short poniard; jewel.
broncha (2), *n.f.* white-washing brush.
bronquedad, *n.f.* harshness, roughness; abruptness; rudeness; brittleness.
bronquial, *a.* (*anat.*) bronchial.
bronquina, *n.f.* (*fam.*) dispute, contention, quarrel.
bronquio, *n.m.* (*anat.*) bronchus, bronchial tube.
bronquitis, *n.f. inv.* (*med.*) bronchitis.
broquel, *n.m.* shield, buckler; (*fig.*) support, protection; (*naut.*) position of sails when taken aback.
broquelarse [ABROQUELARES].
broquelazo, *n.m.* stroke with shield *or* buckler.
broquelero, *n.m.* maker *or* wearer of shields *or* bucklers; (*fig.*) wrangler, disputer.
broquelete, *n.m.* small buckler.
broquelillo, *n.m.* small ear-ring.
broquer, *n.m.* small door of fyke.
broqueta, *n.f.* skewer, spit.
bróquil, *n.m.* (*prov.*) [BRECOL].
brosquil, *n.m.* (*prov.*) sheep-fold, sheep-cote.
brota, *n.f.* bud, shoot.
brotación, brotadura, *n.f.* budding.
brotador, -ra, *a.* budding.
brótano, *n.m.* (*bot.*) southern-wood; bud, shoot.
brotar, *v.t.* to grow, bring forth. — *v.i.* to bud, germinate, put forth shoots; to spring (forth *or* up), come out, gush, flow *or* rush out; (*fig.*) to issue, break out, appear.
brote, broto, *n.m.* shoot, sprout(ing), bud(ding); outburst, outbreak; (breaking out in a) rash; (*prov.*) bit, crumb, fragment.
brotón, *n.m.* (*obs.*) large clasp; bud, shoot, tender twig; thicket, brushwood; (*fig.*) useless stuff.
broza, *n.f.* brush, brushwood, undergrowth; rubbish; (*fig.*) padding; (*print.*) brush; ***quitar la broza,*** to clear the ground *or* way; ***meter broza,*** to pad, put *or* stick in padding; ***gente de toda broza,*** people of every description.
brozador [BRUZADOR].
brozar [E], *v.t.* (*print.*) [BRUZAR].
brozno, -na, *a.* rough, coarse, uncouth.
brozoso, -sa, *a.* covered in brushwood.
brucero, *n.m.* brush and broom maker *or* seller.
bruces, *adv. phrase* ***de bruces,*** face downwards; ***caer*** (***dar***) ***de bruces,*** to fall (flat) on one's face.
brucita, *n.f.* (*min.*) hydrate of magnesia, brucite.
bruco, *n.m.* plant-louse.
brugo, *n.m.* moth larva; plant-louse.
bruja, *a.* very fine (*sand*). — *n.f.* (*orn.*) owl; witch, sorceress; (*coll.*) hag, shrew.
Brujas, *f.* Bruges.
brujear, *v.i.* to practise *or* go in for witchcraft.
brujería, *n.f.* witchcraft, sorcery.
brujesco, -ca, *a.* appertaining to witchcraft.
brujido, *n.m.* diamond dust.
brujidor, *n.m.* glazier's nippers.
brujir, *v.t.* to trim (*glass*) with nippers.
brujo, *n.m.* sorcerer, wizard.
brújula, *n.f.* magnetic needle; (*naut.*) compass; (gun) sight; peep-hole; ***perder la brújula,*** to lose control; to lose one's grip.
brujulear, *v.t.* slowly to uncover (*one's cards*); (*coll.*) to guess (at). — *v.i.* to know *or* find one's way around.
brujuleo, *n.m.* act of gradually uncovering one's cards; (*coll.*) guessing; knowing *or* finding one's way around.
brulote, *n.m.* (*naut.*) fire-ship.
bruma, *n.f.* (*sea*) mist, haze.
brumador, -ra [ABRUMADOR].
brumal, *a.* misty, hazy; brumal.
brumar [ABRUMAR].
brumazón, *n.m.* heavy *or* thick (sea) mist *or* haze.
brumo, *n.m.* refined wax.
brumoso, -sa, *a.* misty, hazy.
brunella, *n.f.* (*bot.*) self-heal.
bruno, -na, *a.* dark brown, darkish. — *n.m.* black plum *or* damson; plum *or* damson tree.
bruñidera, *n.f.* board for polishing wax.
bruñido, *n.m.* polish(ing), burnish(ing).
bruñidor, -ra, *a.* burnishing, polishing. — *n.m.f.*

burnisher, polisher (*person*). — *n.m.* burnisher (*tool*).
bruñidura, *n.f.* burnishing, polishing.
bruñimiento, *n.m.* polishing, burnishing; polish.
bruñir [K], *v.t.* to burnish, polish; (*coll.*) to put rouge on.
bruño, *n.m.* (*bot.*) damson (*fruit and tree*).
brusca (1), *n.f.* (*Cub.*) brushwood.
bruscate, *n.m.* hash of lambs' and goats' chitterlings.
brusco, -ca (2), *a.* rough; brusque, abrupt, short. — *n.m.* (*bot.*) knee-holly, butcher's broom; waste (*in harvesting*). — *n.f.* (*naut.*) bevel, sweep *or* rounding of masts.
brusela, *n.f.* lesser periwinkle; (*pl.*) jeweller's tongs *or* tweezers.
Bruselas, *n.f.* Brussels.
bruselense, *a.*, *n.m.f.* appertaining to *or* (native) of Brussels.
brusquedad, *n.f.* brusqueness, abruptness.
brusquería, *n.f.* (*fam.*) brusqueness.
brutal, *a.* brutal; savage, bestial; (*coll.*) ***una cantidad brutal,*** a terrific amount.
brutalidad, *n.f.* brutality, savageness, brutishness.
brutalizarse [C], *v.r.* to become brutal.
bruteza, *n.f.* roughness, want of polish.
bruto, -ta, *a.* coarse; beastly, brutish; gross; unpolished, rough; thick-headed; ***peso bruto,*** gross weight; ***beneficio bruto,*** gross profit; ***en bruto,*** in the rough; ***madera en bruto,*** rough timber; ***diamante en bruto,*** uncut diamond. — *n.m.* brute, beast; (*poet.*) ***noble bruto,*** horse; (*coll.*) ***pedazo de bruto,*** thick-headed lout, thundering ass.
bruza, *n.f.* horse-brush; stove-brush; scrubbing-brush; printer's brush.
bruzador, *n.m.* (*print.*) inclined table for cleaning type.
bruzar [C], *v.t.* to brush.
bu, *n.m.* (*coll.*) bogy, bugbear; (*coll.*) scarecrow; ***hacerle a alguien el bu,*** to scare *or* terrify s.o.; ***que viene el bu,*** here is *or* comes the bogyman.
búa, buba, *n.f.* (*med.*) pustule, small tumour; (*pl.*) buboes.
búbalo, -la, *n.m.f.* African antelope.
bubático, -ca, *a.* bubonic, having buboes *or* glandular tumours.
bubón, *n.m.* morbid tumour.
bubónico, -ca, *a.* bubonic; ***peste bubónica,*** bubonic plague, Black Death.
buboso, -sa, *a.* afflicted with pustules.
bucal, *a.* relating to the mouth; ***por vía bucal,*** by mouth, through the mouth.
bucanero, *n.m.* buccaneer.
bucara, *n.f.* (*bot.*) grape.
bucarán, *n.m.* (*prov.*) buckram.
bucardo, *n.m.* (*prov.*) wild buck.
bucare, *n.m.* (*Ven.*) shade tree.
búcaro, *n.m.* fragrant clay; (drinking) vessel, jug; vase.
buccelación, bucelación, *n.f.* action of stopping hæmorrhage; (*med.*) ligature of open vein *or* artery.
buccino, *n.m.* buccinum, whelk.
buceamiento [BUCEO].
bucear, *v.i.* to dive; to swim underwater; to search underwater.
bucéfalo, *n.m.* (*coll.*) stupid, dull man.
bucentauro, *n.m.* (*myth.*) Bucentaur.
buceo, *n.m.* diving; underwater swimming; underwater searching.
bucero, -ra, *a.* black-nosed (*dog*).
bucinador, *n.m.* (*anat.*) buccinator.
bucle, *n.m.* ringlet, curl, lock of hair; (*fig.*) loop.
buco (1), *n.m.* opening, aperture, gap.
buco (2), *n.m.* (*zool.*) buck (*goat*).
bucólico, -ca, *a.* bucolic, pastoral. — *n.m.* bucolic poet. — *n.f.* bucolic, pastoral poem; (*coll.*) food.
bucosidad, *n.f.* (*naut.*) tonnage.
bucranio, *n.m.* (*arch.*) bucranium.
buchada, *n.f.* mouthful.
buche, *n.m.* (*orn.*) craw, crop; maw, stomach (*of quadrupeds*); mouthful (*of fluid*); young sucking ass, foal; bags *or* pucker (*in clothes*); (*coll.*) bosom, breast; (*coll.*) belly, stomach; tunny-fish net; ***hacer buche,*** to bag, be baggy; (*coll.*) ***sacarle a alguien el buche,*** to make s.o. cough up *or* spit out what he knows.
buchete, *n.m.* puffed out *or* inflated cheek.
buchillo, *n.m.* (*prov.*) large knife *or* dagger.
buchón, -chona, *a.* baggy, pouched; ***paloma buchona,*** pouter pigeon.
budare, *n.m.* (*Ven.*) large baking pan.
búdico, -ca, *a.* Buddhic, Buddhistic.
budín, *n.m.* pie; ***budín de verduras,*** vegetable pie.
budinera, *n.f.* pie-dish.
budión, *n.m.* (*ichth.*) peacock-fish.
budismo, *n.m.* Buddhism.
budista, *n.m.f.* Buddhist.
buega, *n.f.* (*prov.*) landmark, boundary.
buen, *a.* (*apocope of* BUENO, *used before a singular masculine noun and before an infinitive verb used as a substantive*) good; ***buen dinero,*** good money; ***el buen decir,*** correct *or* proper speech; ***El Buen Pastor,*** The Good Shepherd; (*iron.*) ***¡buen pájaro es ése!*** a fine fellow he is!
buenaboya, *n.m.* volunteer seaman (in a galley).
buenamente, *adv.* freely, spontaneously; conveniently, easily; ***ven, si buenamente puedes,*** come if it's convenient, come if it doesn't put you out; ***hágalo como buenamente pueda,*** do it as best you can.
buenandanza, *n.f.* prosperity, felicity, success.
buenaventura, *n.f.* fortune, good luck; ***decirle a alguien la buenaventura,*** to tell s.o.'s fortune.
bueno, -na, *a.* good; kind; simple; fine; right; sound; (*coll.*) funny, amusing; surprising, amazing; ***buenos días,*** good day, good morning; ***buenas palabras,*** conciliatory, polite *or* pleasant language; ***buenas tardes,*** good afternoon, good evening; ***buenas noches,*** good evening, good night; ***a la buena de Dios,*** at random, on chance, taking a chance; ***de buena gana,*** willingly; ***de buenas a buenas,*** freely, willingly, gratefully; ***a*** (or ***por las***) ***buenas,*** with good grace; of one's own accord; ***¡buena es ésa!*** that's *or* she's a fine one!; ***¡estaría bueno!*** that would be a fine thing!; ***bueno está,*** that's all right; enough, no more; ***estar de buenas,*** to be in a good mood; ***estoy bueno,*** I am well; ***lo bueno es que quiere enseñar a su maestro,*** the extraordinary thing is that he now presumes to teach his master. — *adv.* very well, all right; enough, no more; ***¿adónde bueno?*** where are you going?; ***¿de dónde bueno?*** where are you coming from?; (*iron.*) ***¡bueno anda el ajo!*** here's a pretty state of things! — *n.m.* good (mark).
buenparecer, *n.m.* good looks *or* appearance.
bueña, *n.f.* (*prov.*) sausage.
buera, *n.f.* (*prov.*) pustule *or* pimple (*in the mouth*).
buey, *n.m.* ox, bullock; (*pl.* **bueyes**) (*sl.*) cards; ***buey marino,*** sea-calf; ***buey de cabestrillo*** or ***de caza,*** stalking-ox; ***a paso de buey,*** at a snail's pace; ***habló el buey y dijo mu,*** he only opens his mouth to put his foot in it; ***el buey suelto bien se lame,*** a man with no ties has the best of things.
bueyerizo [BOYERIZO].
bueyuno, -na, [BOYUNO].
bufa, *n.f.* [BUFO].
bufador, -ra, *a.* puffing, blowing. — *n.m.* volcanic eruption.
bufalino, -na, *a.* of buffalo.

búfalo, -la, *n.m.f.* buffalo. — *n.m.* buff-stick, buff-wheel.
bufanda, *n.f.* muffler, scarf.
bufante, *a.* puffing, blowing.
bufar, *v.i.* to puff and blow (with anger), snort; to spit (*cats*).
bufarda, *n.f.* garret window; (*prov.*) lower opening of a charcoal-burner's furnace.
bufete, *n.m.* bureau; desk *or* writing-table; (*fig.*) lawyer's office *or* clientele; ***abrir bufete,*** to start practice as a lawyer.
buffet, *n.m.* sideboard; buffet, refreshment-bar; (*Per.*) dining-car.
bufí, *n.m.* watered camlet.
bufia, *n.f.* (*sl.*) bag *or* butt of wine.
bufido, *n.m.* bellow, roar, snort.
bufo, -fa, *a.* comic, farcical; ***ópera bufa,*** comic opera. — *n.m.f.* comic singer, harlequin, buffoon. — *n.f.* joke, jest(ing), buffoonery.
bufón, -fona, *a.* funny comical. — *n.m.f.* buffoon, merry-andrew, clown, jester.
bufonada, *n.f.* buffoonery, jest.
bufonear(se), *v.i.* (*v.r.*) to play the fool; to jest, make fun.
bufonería [BUFONADA].
bufonesco, -ca, *a.* buffoonish, farcical.
bufonizar [C], *v.i.* [BUFONEAR].
bugada, *n.f.* buck, lye, clothes-bleach.
bugalla, *n.f.* (*bot.*) gall-nut, gall-apple.
buganvilla, *n.f.* (*bot.*) bougainvillæa.
bugir [E], *v.t.* (*naut.*) to caulk.
bugle, *n.f.* (*mus.*) bugle.
buglosa, *n.f.* (*bot.*) alkanet, bugloss.
búgula, *n.f.* (*bot.*) bugle.
buharda, buhardilla, *n.f.* dormer-window; attic, garret; skylight.
buhardo, buharro, *n.m.* eagle-owl.
buhedera, *n.f.* embrasure, loop-hole.
buhedo, *n.m.* marly earth; pondlet.
buhero, *n.m.* owl-keeper.
búho, *n.m.* owl; (*coll.*) unsocial person; (*slang*) sneak, nark.
buhonería, *n.f.* hawking, peddling; pedlar's box.
buhonero, *n.m.* hawker, pedlar.
buir [O], *v.t.* to polish, burnish; to sharpen.
buitre, *n.m.* vulture.
buitrero, -ra, *a.* vulturine, vulturish, vulturous. — *n.m.* vulture-fowler. — *n.f.* place to catch vultures.
buitrón, *n.m.* osier basket (*to catch fish*); partridge net; snare (*for game*); (*Hisp. Am.*) furnace where silver is smelted.
bujarasol, *n.m.* (*prov., bot.*) fig with reddish pulp.
bujarrón, *a., n.m.* (*vulg.*) sodomite.
buje, *n.m.* axle-box, bush-box; iron ring; pillow (*of a shaft*).
bujeda, *n.f.*, **bujedal, bujedo,** *n.m.* plantation of box-trees.
bujería, *n.f.* gewgaw, bauble, knick-knack.
bujeta, *n.f.* wooden box; perfume box; case for a perfume-bottle.
bujía, *n.f.* (wax *or* stearine) candle; candle-stick; candle-power; (*med.*) bougie, catheter; (*motor*) sparking-plug.
bujier, *n.m.* chief *or* head of the ***bujiería.***
bujiería, *n.f.* office at court where wax candles were kept.
bula, *n.f.* bulla, (papal) bull; ***bula de carne,*** dispensation from fasting; ***no poder con la bula,*** to be worn out, extremely weak; ***tener bula para todo,*** to be allowed to act as one pleases, have a completely free hand.
bular, *v.t.* (*obs.*) to brand (*prisoners, slaves*).
bulario, *n.m.* collection of papal bulls.
bulbar, *a.* (*med.*) bulbaceous, bulbous, bulbose.
bulbífero, -ra, *a.* (*bot.*) bulbiferous.
bulbillo, *n.m.* (*bot.*) bulbil.
bulbo, *n.m.* (*bot., anat.*) bulb.
bulboso, -sa, *a.* bulbous.
bulero, *n.m.* distributor of papal bulls.
buleto, *n.m.* brief granted by the Pope *or* his legate; apostolic letter.
bulevar, *n.m.* boulevard.
Bulgaria, *n.f.* Bulgaria.
búlgaro, -ra, *a., n.m.f.* Bulgarian. — *n.m.* Bulgarian language.
bulí, *n.m.* (*Philip.*) palm-tree.
bulimia, *n.f.* (*med.*) bulimia, voracious appetite.
bulista, *a.* in charge of the register of papal bulls.
bulo, *n.m.* false rumour, hoax.
bulto, *n.m.* bulk; lump; parcel; (*art*) bust; pillow-case; bundle, package; ***figura*** or ***imagen de bulto,*** figure (image) in sculpture; ***bulto redondo,*** round sculpture; ***a bulto,*** roughly, at a guess; ***buscar a uno el bulto,*** to harass s.o.; ***coger*** or ***pescar a alguien el bulto,*** to lay hold of *or* seize s.o.; ***escurrir, guardar*** or ***huir el bulto,*** to dodge the column; to pass the buck; ***poner de bulto,*** to emphasize, stress; ***ser de bulto,*** to be clear *or* evident.
bululú, *n.m.* strolling (protean) player; (*Ven.*) tumult, riot, commotion.
bulla, *n.f.* noise, hubbub; bustle; (*prov.*) haste, hurry; ***meter bulla,*** to kick up a racket; ***meter a bulla,*** to confuse, obstruct.
bullaje, *n.m.* noisy crowd.
bullanga, *n.f.* din, hubbub.
bullar, *v.t.* (*prov.*) to mark (*goods*) with lead seal to show origin; (*hunt.*) to kill (*the boar*) while the dogs hold it down.
bullarengue, *n.m.* (*fam.*) bustle (*dress*); (*Cub.*) feigned, artificial thing; (*vulg.*) behind.
bullebulle, *n.m.f.* (*fam.*) busybody, bustler, hustler.
bullente, *a.* bubbling, boiling.
bullicio, *n.m.* bustle; hubbub, uproar.
bullicioso, -sa, *a.* lively, restless, bustling; noisy, clamorous; busy; seditious, turbulent; boisterous. — *n.m.f.* rioter, sedition-monger.
bullidor, -ra, *a.* bustling, lively, restless.
bullir [J], *v.t.* to move, stir. — *v.i.* to boil, bubble up; to swarm, teem; to abound; to move about, stir; to bustle; (*coll.*) to itch, be restless. — **bullirse,** *v.r.* to stir, show signs of life.
bullón, *n.m.* dye bubbling up in a boiler; metallic ornament for large books; (*sew.*) puff.
bumerán, *n.m.* boomerang.
buneto, *n.m.* hedge sparrow.
bunga, *n.f.* (*Cub.*) small orchestra; deceit, lie.
bungo, *n.m.* (*Nic.*) flat-boat.
buniato [BONIATO].
bunio, *n.m.* (*bot.*) turnip grown for seed.
búnker, búnquer, *n.m.* (*pol.*) entrenched extreme right wing, diehard right-wing elements.
bunkeriano, bunqueriano, *a.* (*pol.*) (of the) entrenched extreme right wing.
buñolería, *n.f.* fritter shop.
buñolero, -ra, *n.m.f.* maker *or* seller of fritters.
buñuelo, *n.m.* fritter; (*coll.*) bungle, mess.
buque, *n.m.* (*naut.*) bulk, capacity, burden (*o a ship*); hull (*of a ship*); vessel, ship; ***buque escuela,*** training-ship; ***buque insignia,*** flag-ship; ***buque de guerra,*** warship, man-of-war; ***buque carguero,*** cargo ship *or* vessel; ***buque cisterna,*** tanker; ***buque correo,*** mail-boat; ***buque faro,*** light-ship; ***buque gemelo,*** sister-ship; ***buque mercante,*** merchant vessel; ***buque mixto,*** vessel equipped to sail under canvas *or* steam.
buqué, *n.m.* bouquet (*of wine*).
buquetino, *n.m.* (*zool.*) bouquetin, ibex.
buratina, *n.f.* silk *or* wool cloth; Persian silk.
burato, *n.m.* crape, crape cloth; transparent veil.

burba, *n.f.* African coin of small value.
burbuja, *n.f.* bubble.
burbujear, *v.i.* to bubble.
burbujeo, *n.m.* bubbling.
burbujita, *n.f.* small *or* tiny bubble.
burchaca, *n.f.* pilgrim's leather bag.
burche, *n.m.* tower (fort).
burcho, *n.m.* (*naut.*) large sloop *or* barge.
burda (1), *n.f.* (*naut.*) back-stay.
burdégano, *n.m.* hinny.
burdel, *a.* libidinous. — brothel; (*coll.*) mad-house, chaos.
Burdeos, *n.f.* Bordeaux.
burdeos, *n.m.inv.* claret.
burdinalla, *n.f.* (*obs.*) sprit-topsail-stay.
burdo, -da (2), *a.* coarse, crude, rough and ready.
burel, *n.m.* (*her.*) bar (*ninth part of a shield*); (*naut.*) fid, marline-spike; (*naut.*) wooden mould of scupper-plug.
burelado, *a.* (*her.*) with five metal and five coloured bars.
burelete, *n.m.* (*her.*) cord tying plumes and lambrequins.
burengue, *n.m.* (*prov.*) mulatto slave.
bureo, *n.m.* court of justice (*for members of royal household*); entertainment, amusement, spree; ***irse de bureo,*** to go on a spree.
bureta, *n.f.* (*chem.*) burette, dropping-tube.
burga, *n.f.* hot spring.
burgado, *n.m.* edible snail.
burgalés, -lesa, *a.*, *n.m.f.* appertaining to *or* (native) of Burgos. — *n.m.* ancient coin made in Burgos.
burgo, *n.m.* borough.
burgomaestre, *n.m.* burgomaster.
burgués, -guesa, *a.* (of the) middle class; bourgeois. — *n.m.f.* middle-class citizen; burgess.
burguesía, *n.f.* burgess-ship; bourgeoisie; middle class(es).
burguesismo, *n.m.* bourgeois qualities, middle-class attitudes.
burí, *n.m.* (*Philip.*) buri, talipot palm.
buriel, *a.* reddish, dark red. — *n.m.* kersey, dark red coarse cloth.
buril, *n.m.* burin, engraver's tool, graver; ***buril de punta,*** sharp-pointed burin; ***buril chaple redondo,*** gouge-pointed burin; ***buril chaple en forma de escoplo,*** chisel-pointed burin.
burilada, *n.f.* line *or* stroke of a burin; silver taken by an assayer for testing.
buriladura, *n.f.* engraving with a burin.
burilar, *v.t.* to engrave with a burin *or* graver.
burjaca, *n.f.* pilgrim's leather bag.
burla, *n.f.* scoff(ing), mockery, sneer; hoax; gibe, jeer; cheat; deceit; ***burla pesada,*** no joke, nasty trick; ***burla burlando,*** in an easy way, without effort; ***de burla,*** in jest; ***decir una cosa entre burlas y veras,*** to say sth. half jokingly; ***hablar de burlas,*** to speak with one's tongue in one's cheek; ***hacer burla de,*** to mock, make fun of; ***no aguantar burlas,*** to have no sense of humour; to stand no nonsense; ***no hay peor burla que la verdadera,*** there is no more cutting gibe than an apposite one.
burladero, -ra, *a.* joking, scoffing. — *n.m.* refuge *or* covert in a bullring; (*railw.*) vaulted niche in tunnels.
burlador, -ra, *a.* joking, mocking. — *n.m.f.* wag, jester, scoffer, mocker, practical joker. — *n.m.* libertine, seducer; conjurers' cup; concealed squirt.
burlar, *v.t.* to mock, laugh at; to deceive, dodge, trick; to hoax; ***burlar la ley,*** to trick *or* evade the law. — **burlarse,** *v.r.* to make fun (***de,*** of), laugh *or* scoff (***de,*** at).
burlería, *n.f.* fun, drollery; pun; artifice; yarn, romantic story; deceit, illusion; derision, reproach; chaff, banter, ridicule.
burlesco, -ca, *a.* burlesque, comical, funny.
burleta, *n.f.* (*fam.*) little trick, fun, joke.
burlete, *n.m.* weather-strip, draught excluder.
burlón, -lona, *a.* bantering, mocking, facetious. — *n.m.f.* banterer, jester, mocker, scoffer. — *n.m.* mocking-bird.
burlote, *n.m.* small bank (*gambling*).
buro, *n.m.* (*prov.*) chalk, marl.
buró, *n.m.* bureau, writing-desk.
burocracia, *n.f.* bureaucracy; officialdom.
burócrata, *n.m.f.* bureaucrat.
burocrático, -ca, *a.* bureaucratic.
burra, *n.f.* [BURRO].
burrada, *n.f.* drove of asses; (*coll.*) asinine *or* crazy thing to do *or* say; (*coll.*) colossal *or* terrific amount.
burrajear [BORRAJEAR].
burrajo, *n.m.* dry stable-dung (*for fuel*).
burral, *a.* (*fam.*) brutal.
burreño, *n.m.* hinny.
burrero, *n.m.* ass-keeper *or* -driver who sells asses' milk.
burriciego, -ga, *a.* short-sighted; (*coll.*) slow-witted.
burrillo, *n.m.* (*coll.*) ecclesiastical almanac.
burrito, *n.m.* (attractive *or* nice) little donkey.
burro, -rra, *a.* dim-witted; pig-headed; blundering, ham-fisted. — *n.m.* ass, donkey; saw-horse; wheel (*of a reel*); windlass; burro (*card game*); ***burro de carga,*** pack-ass; (*fig.*) hard worker; ***burro cargado de letras,*** learned jackass; ***puesto en el burro,*** obstinately determined; ***no apearse del burro,*** to stick to one's guns.— *n.f.* she-ass; (*fig.*) dim-witted *or* thick-headed woman *or* creature; (*fig.*) patient hard-working woman; ***panza de burra,*** parchment inscribed with university degree, (*coll.*) sheepskin; ***descargar la burra,*** to shift (the) work on to s.o. else.
burrumbada, *n.f.* (*fam.*) boastful saying.
bursario, -ria, *a.* baggy, purse-like.
bursátil, *a.* relating to the stock exchange *or* stock market.
burujo, *n.m.* pack, lump (*of wool, dough*); parcel, package; bagasse (*from olives, grapes etc.*).
burujón [BORUJÓN].
busaca, *n.f.* (*Hisp. Am.*) bag.
busardas, *n.f.pl.* (*naut.*) breast-hooks, compass-timbers.
busardo, *n.m.* buzzard.
busca, buscada, *n.f.* search, hunt, pursuit; hunting party; ***en busca de,*** in search of.
buscador, -ra, *a.* searching; (*mil.*) ***buscador del blanco,*** homing (*e.g. missile*). — *n.m.f.* searcher; ***buscador de oro,*** gold prospector. — *n.m.* (view-) finder (*optical appliances*).
buscaniguas, *n.m. inv.* (*Hisp. Am.*) squib, fire-cracker.
buscapié, *n.m.* hint; (*fig.*) key.
buscapiés, *n.m. inv.* squib-cracker; serpent fire-cracker.
buscapleitos, *n.m.f. inv.* (*Hisp. Am.*) trouble-maker.
buscar [A], *v.t.* to seek, search *or* look for; (*slang*) to pinch, pilfer; ***buscar a tientas,*** to grope for; ***buscarle tres pies al gato,*** to ask *or* look for trouble; to see difficulties where there are none; ***buscarse la vida*** (or ***buscársela***), to earn one's living, to make one's way in the world; ***buscar a alguien, buscarle a alguien la lengua,*** to provoke s.o.; ***buscar pan de trastrigo,*** to look for the impossible; ***buscar por donde salir,*** to look for a way out; ***cada uno busca a los suyos,*** like seeks like.
buscarruidos, *n.m.f. inv.* (*coll.*) mischief-maker, quarrelsome person; (*naut.*) scout ship.
buscavidas, *n.m.f. inv.* (*coll.*) busybody; person good at getting on *or* making his way in the world.

busco (1), *n.m.* threshold (*of a sluice-gate*).
busco (2), *n.m.* track (*of an animal*).
buscón, -cona, *a.* searching. — *n.m.f.* swindler. — *n.f.* harlot.
busilis, *n.m. inv.* (*coll.*) crux, heart (*of question, matter*); ***dar en el busilis,*** to hit the mark.
busingote, *n.m.* hat.
búsqueda, *n.f.* search (*de*, for).
busquillo, *n.m.* (*bot.*) myosotis; (*zool.*) tiny dog; (*Chi.*, *Per.*) diligent *or* active person.
busquizal, *n.m.* (*prov.*) very brambly place.
busto, *n.m.* (*art*) bust.
bustrófedon, *n.m.* a method of writing from left to right and right to left alternately.
butaca, *n.f.* arm-chair, easy-chair; (*theat.*) stall, (*Am.*) orchestra seat.
butano, *n.m.* (*chem.*) butane.
buten, *adv. phrase* (*sl.*) ***de buten,*** terrific, smashing.
butifarra, *n.f.* pork sausage (*made in Catalonia, Valencia, and Balearic Is.*); (*coll.*) baggy loose sock *or* stocking; (*Per.*) ham sandwich.
butifarrería, *n.f.* pork sausage making *or* shop.
butifarrero, -ra, *n.m.f.* pork sausage maker *or* seller.
butilo, *n.m.* (*chem.*) butyl.
butiondo, -da, *a.* lustful, lewd, obscene.
butiráceo, -cea, *a.* butyraceous.
butirato, *n.m.* (*chem.*) butyrate.
butírico, -ca, *a.* butyric.
butirina, *n.f.* (*chem.*) butyrine.
butiro, *n.m.* butter.
butiroso, -sa, *a.* buttery.
botomeo, -mea, *a.* (*bot.*) butomaceous.
butomo, *n.m.* (*bot.*) butomus.
butrino, butrón, *n.m.* osier basket (*to catch fish*)
buya, *n.m.* (*zool.*) beaver.
buyador, *n.m.* (*prov.*) brazier, worker in brass.
buyes, *n.m.pl.* (*slang*) cards.
buyo, *n.m.* (*Philip.*) leaf of the betel-vine.
buz, *n.m.* kiss of respect and reverent regard; lip; ***hacer el buz,*** to do homage; (*pej.*) to bow and scrape.
buzamiento, *n.m.* (*geol.*) dip.
búzano, *n.m.* diver; culverin.
buzar [C], *v.i.* (*geol.*) to dip.
buzardas, *n.f.pl.* (*naut.*) breast-hooks, fore-hooks.
buzcorona, *n.f.* blow on the head given in fun while the hand is being kissed.
buzo, *n.m.* diver; (*orn.*) buzzard; ancient vessel.
buzón, *n.m.* conduit, canal; letter-box, pillar-box; bung, lid *or* cover; hook (*to remove the lids of melting-pots*); sluice (*of mill*).
buzonera, *n.f.* (*prov.*) drain *or* gutter (*in court-yard*).

C

C, c, *n.f.* letter C, c.
ca (1), *conj.* (*obs.*) because, for.
¡ca! (2) *interj.* oh no! come, now! come off it!
cabal, *a.* exact; perfect, complete, full, accomplished; faultless, consummate; ***no estar en sus cabales,*** not to be in one's right mind. — *adv.* exactly, just so; ***¿dijo eso? — ¡cabal!*** did he say that? — his very words!
cábala, *n.f.* cabbala; (*fig.*) superstitious divination; (*coll.*) cabal, intrigue, plot.
cabalar, *v.t.* to complete.
cabalgada, *n.f.* foray, raid; cavalcade, troops of horsemen *or* riders.
cabalgador, -ra, *n.m.f.* rider, horseman, horsewoman; (*obs.*) horse-block.
cabalgadura, *n.f.* mount; beast of burden.
cabalgante, *a.* on horseback.
cabalgar [B], *v.t.* to ride (*a horse*); to mount (*a gun*); to cover (*a mare*). — *v.i.* to ride, go riding; to mount on horseback; to parade on horseback.
cabalgata, *n.f.* cavalcade.
cabalhuste, *n.m.* saddle (with high semicircular pommel and cantle).
cabalino, -na, *a.* (*poet., myth.*) applied to Pegasus, Mount Helicon, and the Hippocrene spring.
cabalismo, *n.m.* cabbalism.
cabalista, *n.m.* cabbalist.
cabalístico, -ca, *a.* cabbalistic.
cabalito (*fam.*) [CABALMENTE].
cabalmente, *adv.* exactly, just so; completely, perfectly, fully.
caballa, *n.f.* (*ichth.*) mackerel.
caballada, *n.f.* group of horses.
caballaje, *n.m.* serving of mares and she-asses; money paid for that service.
caballar, *a.* (pertaining to the) horse; equine; ***ganado caballar,*** horses.
caballear, *v.i.* (*fam.*) to go riding (often).
caballejo, *n.m.* (wretched) little horse, nag; rack (*for torture*).
caballerato, *n.m.* pontifical benefice granted to laymen; privilege of gentleman *or* esquire in Catalonia.
caballerear, *v.i.* to set up as a gentleman; to act the knight *or* gentleman.
caballeresco, -ca, *a.* of knights, chivalrous; courtly (*literature*).
caballerete, *n.m.* young knight *or* gentleman; (*iron.*) fine young gentleman; (*coll.*) spruce presumptuous young gentleman.
caballería, *n.f.* (riding) mount; horse riding; cavalry; knighthood; share of spoils given to a knight; (*prov.*) pension given by grandees to knights fighting for them; agrarian measure of 60 ***fanegas*** (96 acres), *or* (*Cub.*) of 33 acres, *or* (*P.R.*) of 190 acres; ***caballería mayor,*** saddle-horse, mule; ***caballería menor,*** ass, jackass; ***libros de caballería,*** books of knight-errantry; ***caballería andante,*** knight-errantry; ***caballería ligera,*** light cavalry; ***orden de caballería,*** order of chivalry.
caballerito, *n.m.* young gentleman; (*iron.*) fine young gentleman.
caballeriza, *n.f.* stable; stud.
caballerizo, *n.m.* head groom (*of a stable*); stable hand; ***caballerizo de campo*** or ***del rey,*** equerry to the king; ***caballerizo mayor del rey,*** master of the King's horse.
caballero, -ra, *a.* riding; (*fig.*) obstinate, determined. — *n.m.* knight, nobleman, cavalier; rider, horseman; gentleman; sir; (*orn.*) redshank; Spanish dance; (*fort.*) cavalier; surplus mound of earth in a clearing; (*bot.*) ***espuela de caballero,*** larkspur; ***caballero andante,*** knight-errant; ***caballero cubierto,*** grandee (who keeps his head covered in the king's presence); ***caballero de industria,*** swindler; ***caballero de hábito,*** knight of the military orders; ***caballero novel,*** novice knight; ***iba caballero sobre un asno,*** he was riding on an ass; ***ser todo un caballero,*** to be every inch a gentleman; ***armar caballero a,*** to knight; ***de caballero a caballero,*** as between gentlemen; ***poderoso caballero es don dinero,*** money is power.
caballerosidad, *n.f.* chivalry; gentlemanliness.
caballeroso, -sa, *a.* chivalrous; gentlemanly.
caballerote, *n.m.* (*coll.*) clumsy *or* loutish knight.
caballeta, *n.f.* (*ent.*) grasshopper.
caballete, *n.m.* little horse; (*arch.*) ridge (*of gable-roof*); (*carpenter's*) horse; stand (*for saddles*); bench, trestle; horse (*for torture*); (*chimney*) cap *or* cowl; ridge (*between furrows*); bridge (*of the nose*); brake (*for dressing hemp and flax*); (*painter's*) easel; (*potter's*) trivet; (*orn.*) breast-bone; (*print.*) gallows (*of printing-press*).
caballino, -na, *a.* equine, appertaining to horses. — *n.m.* (*bot.*) aloes.
caballista, *n.m.* horseman; (*prov.*) mounted highwayman, brigand; (*prov.*) horse-trainer.
caballito, *n.m.* small horse, pony; (nice) little horse; (*naut.*) trestle; (*pl.*) roundabout, merry-go-round; (*Per.*) Indian coracle; ***caballito del diablo,*** dragon fly; ***caballito de mar,*** sea horse; ***caballito de Bamba,*** worthless person *or* thing.
caballo, *n.m.* horse; queen (*Spanish cards*); knight (*chess*); (*carp.*) trestle; cross-thread (*in reel* or *skein*); (*med.*) bubo; (*prov.*) strong vine-shoot; (*Hisp. Am.*) ***caballo aguililla,*** very swift horse; ***caballo alazán,*** sorrel horse; ***caballo de batalla,*** battle-horse, charger; (*fig.*) forte, speciality; main point, crux (*of discussion*); big test, hurdle; ***caballo de buena boca,*** person easily satisfied, especially as regards food; ***caballo de carga,*** pack-horse; ***caballo castrado*** or ***capado,*** gelding; ***caballo de caza,*** hunter; ***caballo corredor*** or ***de carrera,*** race-horse; ***caballo del diablo,*** dragonfly; ***caballo desbocado,*** runaway horse; ***caballo de escuela,*** horse well broken-in at the manège; ***caballo frisón,*** draught-horse; (*mil.*) ***caballo de Fris(i)a,*** cheval-de-frise; ***caballo de mano,*** horse on the right-hand side of the pole; led horse; ***caballo medroso*** or ***espantadizo,*** skittish horse; ***caballo matado,*** galled horse; ***caballo marino, de agua*** or ***de mar,*** river-horse, hippopotamus; (*ichth.*) sea-horse; ***caballo de montar,*** saddle-horse; ***caballo moro,*** piebald horse; ***caballo overo,*** red and white spotted horse; ***caballo picazo,*** pied horse; (*coll.*) ***caballo de palo,*** vessel; rack (*for torture*); ***caballo de posta,*** post-horse; ***caballo rabón,*** docked horse; ***caballo de regalo*** or ***de albada,*** state horse; ***caballo retinto,*** shining black horse; ***caballo rubicán,*** speckled white horse; ***caballo rucio rodado,*** dapple-grey horse; ***caballo de silla,*** horse on the left-hand side of the pole; ***caballo de tiro,*** draught-horse; ***caballo tordo,*** dapple bay horse; ***caballo de vapor,*** horse-power; ***caballo de vara,*** shaft-horse; ***a caballo,*** on horseback; ***a caballo regalado no le mires el diente,*** don't look a gift horse in the mouth; ***a mata caballo,*** at break-neck speed; ***ir en el caballo de San Francisco,*** to go on foot *or* on Shanks's pony; ***a uña de caballo,*** at top speed, full-tilt; ***poner a alguien a caballo,*** to get someone started.
caballón, *n.m.* border, bank of earth; ridge (*between two furrows*).
caballona, *n.f.* queen (*chess*).
caballote, *n.m.* horse, torture rack.
caballuno, -na, *a.* equine, horse-like.
cabana, *n.f.* (*naut.*) customs-officer's office; strong boat.
cabaña, *n.f.* hut, cottage, cabin; large flock of ewes *or* breeding sheep; drove of mules for carrying

grain; baulk-line (*in billiards*); (*paint.*) landscape with cottage and domestic animals.

cabañal, *a.* used by sheep *or* cattle (*road*). — *n.m.* village of huts; (*prov.*) cattle-shelter.

cabañería, *n.f.* weekly rations allowed to shepherds.

cabañero, -ra, *a.* of *or* belonging to a drove *or* flock. — *n.m.* drover, shepherd. — *n.f.* (*prov.*) cattle road, drove; ***perro cabañero,*** sheep-dog.

cabañil, *a.* belonging to a shepherd's hut. — *n.m.* muleteer.

cabañuela, *n.f.* small hut *or* cottage; weather forecast made in August for the following year; (*pl.*) ***fiesta de las Cabañuelas,*** Jewish feast of the tabernacles.

cabás, *n.m.* small pannier, shopping-bag.

cabe (1), *n.m.* stroke by which two balls are hit in the game of ***argolla***; ***cabe de pala,*** lucky chance; ***dar un cabe al bolsillo de,*** to damage (*s.o.'s*) business interests, fortune, etc.

cabe (2), *prep.* (*poet.*) near, hard by, nigh.

cabeceado, *n.m.* thickening of line in a letter.

cabeceador, -ra, *a.* nodding; (*naut.*) pitching.

cabecear, *v.t.* to make (*letters*) with thick strokes; to put (*the head-piece*) to a book; to bind (*clothes or rugs*); to foot (*stockings*); (*agric.*) to plough (*headland*); to head (*wine*) (*by adding old wine to give it strength*). — *v.i.* to nod (*in sleep, assent*); to shake the head in disapproval; to raise *or* lower the head (*of horses*); to lurch (*of carriages*); to incline to one side, hang over, tilt (*of load*); (*naut.*) to pitch.

cabeceo, *n.m.* nodding; nod of the head; (*naut.*) pitching.

cabecequia, *n.m.* inspector of sluices and drains.

cabecera, *n.f.* head (*of bed, table*); upper end; head-waters; head-board (*bed*); seat of honour; capital (*of province, region* or *district*); bridge-head; head-line; head-piece (*book*); head-piece *or* vignette; bolster; (*gambling*) fixed bank; (*arch.*) sanctuary; (*min.*) foreman (*of drillers*); (*pl.*) (*print.*) quoins, wedges; ***médico de cabecera,*** family doctor; ***nunca dejó la cabecera de su padre,*** he never left his father's bedside.

cabecería, *n.f.* obstinacy, stubbornness; (*fig.*) primacy, primateship.

cabecero, *n.m.* (*carp.*) hood-mould, hood-moulding.

cabeciancho, -cha, *a.* broad- *or* flat-headed (*nails* or *studs*).

cabecil, *n.m.* padded ring (*for carrying objects on the head*).

cabecilla, *n.m.* gang leader, rebel leader; ringleader.

cabellar(se), *v.i.* (*v.r.*) to grow hair; to put on false hair.

cabellera, *n.f.* (head of) hair; long hair; tail (*of comet*).

cabello, *n.m.* hair (*of head*); (*pl.*) large sinews (*in mutton*); fibres (*of maize*); ***cabello de ángel,*** preserve of fruit cut into small threads; ***cabello rizado,*** curly hair; ***asirse de un cabello,*** to clutch at a straw; ***cortar, hender*** or ***partir un cabello en el aire,*** to be very sharp-witted; ***en cabellos,*** bare-headed; ***estar pendiente de un cabello,*** to be hanging by a hair *or* thread; ***llevar de un cabello,*** to lead by the nose; ***tropezar en un cabello,*** to make a mountain out of a molehill; ***no falta un cabello,*** no detail is missing; ***traído por los cabellos,*** quite out of place, nothing to do with the subject, far-fetched.

cabelludo, -da, *a.* hairy; (*bot.*) fibrous; ***cuero cabelludo,*** scalp.

caber [13], *v.i.* to be capable of being contained; to have room *or* entry; to fit; to be possible; to fall to one's lot; to befall (*good* or *bad luck*); ***todo cabe,*** there is room for everything; everything is possible; ***cabe hacerlo mejor,*** it can be done better, there is room for improvement; ***cabe intentar alguna otra cosa,*** there's no reason why sth. else should not be attempted; ***cabe otra posibilidad,*** there is *or* exists another possibility; ***no cabe duda,*** there is *or* can be no doubt; ***no me cabe en la cabeza,*** it's beyond my comprehension; ***me cabe la honra de presentarlo,*** it is my honour to introduce him; ***no cabe en sí,*** he is beside himself with delight, he can't contain himself; he is very conceited; ***en él cabe todo,*** one can expect anything from him; ***no cabe más,*** there is room for no more; there is no more to be desired; ***me cupo en suerte ir,*** it fell to my lot to go.

cabero, -ra, *a.* (*Mex.*) last, final. — *n.m.* (*prov.*) handle maker (*for tools and implements*).

cabestraje, *n.m.* halter; fee paid to a drover.

cabestrar, *v.t.* to halter. — *v.i.* to fowl with a stalking-ox.

cabestrear, *v.i.* to follow docilely when led by a halter (*beasts*).

cabestrería, *n.f.* shop where halters and collars are made and sold.

cabestrero, -ra, *a.* (*prov.*) that can be led by a halter. — *n.m.* halter and collar maker *or* seller; fishing-net. — *n.f.* fishing-net cord.

cabestrillo, *n.m.* sling; gold *or* silver chain; (*carp.*) (kind of) hoop; (*naut.*) small cord; ***buey de cabestrillo,*** stalking-ox; ***llevar el brazo en cabestrillo,*** to have one's arm in a sling.

cabestro, *n.m.* halter; bell-ox; gold *or* silver chain; (*coll.*) blockhead; ***llevar*** or ***traer del cabestro,*** to lead by the nose.

cabeza, *n.f.* (*lit., fig.*) head; capital (*of province, region* or *district*); (*anat.*) rounded part of certain bones; (*pl.*) (*naut.*) bow and stern; ***cabeza de ajo(s),*** head of garlic; ***cabeza de chorlito,*** scatterbrain; (*prov., bot.*) ***cabeza de gigante,*** sunflower bud; ***cabeza mayor,*** head (*of cattle*); ***cabeza menor,*** head (*of sheep, goat etc.*); (*bot.*) ***cabeza de dragón,*** snapdragon; ***cabeza de olla,*** scum, skimmings; ***cabeza de partido,*** capital (*of district*); (*bot.*) ***cabeza de perro,*** common celandine; (*mil.*) ***cabeza de puente,*** bridge-head; ***cabeza de turco,*** scapegoat; ***cabeza moruna,*** light-coloured horse with black head; ***cabeza redonda,*** blockhead; Roundhead (*English Parliamentarian, 17th cent.*); ***cabeza torcida,*** hypocrite; ***mala cabeza,*** hare-brained irresponsible person; ***abrirle a alguien la cabeza,*** to cut s.o.'s head open; ***a la cabeza,*** in front, at the head; ***se me va la cabeza,*** I'm feeling giddy; ***bajar*** or ***doblar la cabeza,*** to bow down one's head; ***calentarle a uno la cabeza,*** to bother *or* worry s.o.; ***ando de cabeza,*** I'm harassed, I don't know whether I'm coming or going; ***el país va de cabeza,*** the country is going to the dogs; ***calentarse la cabeza,*** to bother one's head; ***caer(se) de cabeza,*** to fall head first *or* headlong; ***se dio de cabeza en el suelo,*** he fell head first on to the floor; ***lo hizo para darle en la cabeza a su suegro,*** he did it to give his father-in-law one in the eye; ***escarmentar en cabeza ajena,*** to learn from another's mistakes; ***más vale (ser) cabeza de ratón que cola de león,*** it is better to be a big fish in a small pond than a small fish in a big pond; ***levantar cabeza,*** to get one's head above water, get on one's feet; ***no levantar cabeza,*** to have one's nose to the grindstone; ***se le ha metido en la cabeza ir hoy,*** he has got it into his head to go today; ***meter la cabeza en,*** to get in on; ***meterse de cabeza,*** to plunge *or* throw oneself in headlong *or* wholeheartedly; ***por cabeza,*** per head, per capita; ***nunca (se) me ha pasado por la cabeza semejante idea,*** such an idea has never crossed *or* entered my mind; ***perder la cabeza,*** to lose one's head; ***quebrarse*** or ***romperse la cabeza,*** to rack one's brains; ***sentar la cabeza,*** to settle down, become sensible; ***se le subió a la cabeza,*** it went to his head; ***no tener dónde volver la cabeza,*** to have no one to turn to; ***tener mala cabeza,*** to be scatterbrained; ***tocado de la cabeza,*** wrong in the head. — *n.m.* head (*of family, army etc.*); ***cabeza de familia,*** head of

the family; head of the household; ***cabeza mayor,*** head of the family.
cabezada, *n.f.* shake of the head; blow *or* butt given with *or* received on the head; nod; halter, nose-band; (*naut.*) pitch(ing); headstall; cord (*for stitching headband of a book*); instep, upper (*of a boot*); highest part (*of piece of ground*); ***dar cabezadas,*** to nod (*in sleep*); ***echar una cabezada,*** to have a snooze.
cabezal, *n.m.* small pillow; (*surg.*) compress; bolster; forepart (*of carriage*); post (*of a door*); narrow mattress.
cabezalejo, *n.m.* little pillow *or* bolster; small compress.
cabezalero, -ra, *n.m.* executor, executrix (*of a will*).
cabezazo, *n.m.* butt, header.
cabezo, *n.m.* summit (*of a mountain*); hillock; (*naut.*) reef; shirt collar.
cabezón, -zona, *a.* large-headed; (*coll.*) pig-headed, stubborn. — *n.m.f.* large head; tax list *or* register; shirt collar; opening of a garment for the head; ***cabezón de cuadra,*** halter, nose-band; ***cabezón de serreta,*** serrated nose-ring; ***llevar*** or ***traer de cabezones,*** to lead by the nose.
cabezonada, *n.f.* (*fam.*) obstinacy, pig-headedness.
cabezorro, *n.m.* (*fam.*) disproportionately large head.
cabezota, *a., n.m.f.* large-headed (person); pig-headed, stubborn (person).
cabezudo, -da, *a.* large-headed; (*coll.*) pig-headed, obstinate, stubborn; (*coll.*) heady (*liquor*); (*agric.*) headed (*runner, stem*). — *n.m.* (*ichth.*) mullet; large-headed dwarf (*in procession*); pig-headed individual.
cabezuela, *n.f.* small head; coarse flour; wine sediment; rosebud from which rose water is distilled; (*bot.*) eryngo, ragwort-leaved centaury. — *n.m.f.* dolt, blockhead, simpleton, hare-brained fellow.
cabezuelo, *n.m.* little head *or* top.
cabida, *n.f.* capacity; ***aquí no tienen cabida,*** there's no room for them here; ***dar cabida a,*** to make room for.
cabido, *n.m.* landmark; knight of the Order of Malta.
cabila, *n.f.* tribe (*of Berbers*).
cabildada, *n.f.* (*fam.*) hasty *or* unwise decision of a council.
cabildante, *n.m.* (*Hisp. Am.*) councillor.
cabildear, *v.i.* to lobby; to scheme, plot.
cabildeo, *n.m.* lobbying; intrigue, scheming.
cabildero, *n.m.* lobbyist; intriguer.
cabildo, *n.m.* chapter (*of a cathedral* or *collegiate church*); meeting of a chapter; municipal council.
cabileño, -ña, *a.* appertaining to a Berber tribe. — *n.m.f.* member of a Berber tribe.
cabilla, *n.f.* dowel; (*naut.*) treenail; belaying-pin.
cabillador, *n.m.* maker of belaying-pins.
cabillero, *n.m.* (*naut.*) rack for holding belaying-pins.
cabillo, *n.m.* (*bot.*) flower-stalk, leaf-stalk; fruit-stem.
cabimiento, *n.m.* capacity, content, space; right of claiming a commandery in the Order of Malta.
cabina, *n,f.* cabin; (*cine.*) projection room; ***cabina telefónica,*** call-box, telephone kiosk, (*Am.*) phone-booth.
cabio, *n.m.* lintel; flooring joist; breastsummer (*of a chimney*); top *or* bottom piece (*of a window-* or *door-frame*); rafter.
cabizbajo, -ja, *a.* crestfallen, downcast.
cabizcaído, -da [CABIZBAJO].
cable, *n.m.* cable, rope, hawser; cable's length; cable(gram); ***cable de cadena,*** chain cable; ***cable eléctrico,*** electric cable; ***cable submarino,*** submarine cable.
cablegrafiar [L], *v.t., v.i.* to cable.
cablegráfico, -ca, *a.* cable.
cablegrama, *n.m.* cable(gram).
cablero, -ra, *a.* cable-laying. — *n.m.* cable ship.
Cabo, *n.m.* (the) Cape; ***Cabo de Buena Esperanza,*** Cape of Good Hope; ***Cabo de Hornos,*** Cape Horn.
cabo, *n.m.* end; extremity, stub, stump; cape, headland; handle; string, rope; lowest card (*in the game* ***revesino***); (*mil.*) corporal; (*prov.*) paragraph, article; parcel *or* package; (*naut.*) cord; (*pl.*) tail and mane (of horses); loose pieces, bits and pieces, odds and ends; divisions (*of a discourse*); (*mil.*) ***cabo de ala*** or ***de fila,*** guide, fugleman; (*prov.*) ***cabo de armería,*** manorial residence; ***cabo de barra,*** last payment *or* balance of account; (*naut.*) ***cabo de columna,*** guide; ***cabo suelto,*** loose end; ***atar cabos,*** to put two and two together; ***al cabo de un año,*** after a year; in a year's time; ***estar al cabo (de la calle),*** to know all about it; (*fig.*) to know it all; (*fig.*) ***estar al cabo de la calle de todo,*** to be blasé; ***estar (muy) al cabo,*** to be (very) near one's end; ***llevar a cabo,*** to carry through *or* out; ***volver a coger el cabo,*** to pick up the thread again (*e.g. in a speech*); ***cabo de maestranza,*** foreman; (*naut.*) ***cabo de presa,*** prize-master; ***(al fin y) al cabo,*** after all; finally, in the end; ***dar cabo a una cosa,*** to finish *or* perfect a thing; ***dar cabo de una cosa,*** to finish sth. off; ***de cabo a cabo*** or ***a rabo,*** from head to tail, from top to bottom, from end to end.
cabotaje, *n.m.* (*naut.*) coasting-trade, coastal shipping *or* traffic.
Cabra, *n.f.* (*astron.*) Capella.
cabra, *n.f.* goat; (*mil.*) catapult; (*Col., Cub.*) loaded dice; (*Chi.*) light two-wheeled carriage; (*bot.*) ***barba de cabra,*** goat's-beard; ***pata de cabra,*** shoemaker's burnishing tool; ***pie de cabra,*** two-pronged lever; ***estar como una cabra,*** to be as crazy as a coot; ***la cabra siempre tira al monte,*** what is bred in the bone will out in the flesh; ***meterle a uno las cabras en el corral,*** to intimidate someone; ***cabra montés,*** wild goat; ***piel de cabra,*** goatskin; (*pl.*) red marks on legs caused by fire.
cabrahigal, cabrahigar (1), *n.m.* grove *or* plantation of wild fig-trees.
cabrahigar (2),[B], *v.t.* to caprificate.
cabrahigo, *n.m.* wild fig-tree; wild fig.
cabrearse, *v.r.* to get into a filthy temper, to get hopping made; to get ratty.
cabreo (1), *n.m.* (*prov.*) church register.
cabreo (2), *n.m.* (*coll.*) vile temper, ratty state.
cabrería, *n.f.* goat's shelter; goat's milk dairy.
cabrerizo, -za, *a.* goatish. — *n.m.f.* goatherd. — *n.f.* hut for goatherds.
cabrero, -ra, *n.m.f.* goatherd.
cabrestante, *n.m.* capstan.
cabrevación, *n.f.* (*prov.*) survey of royal property.
cabrevar, *v.t.* (*prov.*) to survey (*royal property*).
cabreve, *n.m.* (*prov.*) survey of royal property.
cabria, *n.f.* wheel and axle; winch, windlass; hoist; axle-tree; (*naut.*) sheers.
cabrieta, *n.f.* (*mach.*) jack.
cabrihigación, cabrahigadura, *n.f.* caprification.
cabrilla, *n.f.* (*ichth.*) serran; (*carp.*) trestle, bench; (*pl.*) (*astron.*) Pleiades; marks on the legs made by continual proximity to the fire; (*naut.*) white-caps; ducks and drakes (*game*).
cabrillear, *v.i.* (*naut.*) to form whitecaps.
cabrilleo, *n.m.* waves forming whitecaps.
cabrio, *n.m.* (*carp.*) bridging-joist; rafter, beam.
cabrío, *a.* goatish. — *n.m.* flock of goats; ***macho cabrío,*** buck, he-goat.
cabriola, *n.f.* caper; nimble leap; gambol; hop, skip, jump.
cabriolar, cabriolear, *v.i.* to caper, cut capers; to jump, frisk.

cabriolé, *n.m.* sleeveless cloak; cabriolet.
cabriolista, *n.m.f.* caperer.
cabrión, *n.m.* (*naut.*) piece of wood at the back of a gun-carriage.
cabrionar, *v.t.* (*naut.*) to fix ***cabriones*** to (gun-carriages).
cabrita, *n.f.* ancient catapult.
cabritero, -ra, *n.m.f.* dealer in kid-skins.
cabritilla, *n.f.* kid(-skin).
cabritillo, *n.m.* corset.
cabrito, *n.m.* kid, young goat.
cabrituno, -na, *a.* appertaining to the kid.
cabrón, *n.m.* buck, he-goat; (*coll.*) cuckold; (*fig., obsc.*) bugger, bastard; (*Hisp. Am.*) pimp, pander.
cabronada, *n.f.* (*obsc.*) rotten, filthy *or* vile trick.
cabroncete, cabronzuelo, *n.m.* small he-goat; (*coll.*) despicable (little) cuckold; (*fig., obsc.*) miserable (little) bugger.
cabruno, -na, *a.* goatish, goat-like.
cabruñar, *v.t.* (*prov.*) to sharpen (*a scythe*) by hammering the edge.
cabruño, *n.m.* (*prov.*) sharpening of a scythe.
cabú, *n.m.* (*prov.*) barren ground.
cabujón, *n.m.* (*jewel.*) cabochon.
caburé, *n.m.* (*Arg., Par.*) small hawk.
cabuya, *n.f.* (*bot.*) common American agave; sisal-grass, sisal-hemp; (*prov., Hisp. Am.*) cord *or* rope made of aloes; (*Hisp. Am.*) ***dar cabuya a,*** (*fig.*) to tie, fasten; (*Hisp. Am.*) ***ponerse en la cabuya,*** to begin to understand, to see daylight.
cabuyera, *n.f.* cords supporting a hammock.
cabuyería, *n.f.* (*naut.*) small cordage.
caca, *n.f.* (*vulg.*) shit; (*fam.*) number two; (*fig., fam.*) filth, dirt; mess, botch; ***¡caca!*** dirty! don't touch! leave it alone!
cacahual, *n.m.* plantation of cacao-trees.
cacahuete, cacahuey, *n.m.* (*bot.*) peanut.
cacahuetero, -ra, *n.m.f.* peanut seller *or* vendor.
cacalote, *n.m.* (*Mex.*) raven; (*Hisp. Am., metal.*) rosette copper.
cacao (1), *n.m.* (*bot.*) cacao-tree; cacao-nut, -bean; cacao; ***manteca de cacao,*** cacao-butter.
cacao (2), *n.m.* (*fam.*) ***armar un cacao,*** to kick up a din *or* shindy; (*Hisp. Am.*) ***pedir cacao,*** to beg for mercy.
cacaotal, *n.m.* cacao plantation.
cacaraña, *n.f.* pit (*caused by small-pox*).
cacareador, -ra, *a.* cackling (*hen*); crowing (*cock*); (*coll.*) boastful, bragging.
cacarear, *v.i.* to crow, cackle. — *v.t.* to trumpet, vaunt; ***el tan cacareado plan de desarrollo,*** the much-vaunted development plan.
cacareo, *n.m.* crowing, cackling; (*coll.*) boasting, trumpeting, vaunting.
cacarizo, -za, *a.* (*Mex.*) pock-marked.
cacarro, *n.m.* (*prov.*) oak-gall.
cacatúa, *n.f.* (*orn.*) cockatoo.
cacaxtle, *n.m.* (*Mex.*) crate (*to carry goods*).
cacear, *v.t.* to stir with a dipper *or* ladle.
caceo, *n.m.* stirring with a ladle.
cacera, *n.f.* irrigating channel, ditch.
cacería, *n.f.* hunt; hunting party; hunting bag (*game bagged*); (*paint.*) hunting scene.
cacerina, *n.f.* cartridge-box *or* pouch.
cacerola, *n.f.* stew-pan, saucepan.
caceta, *n.f.* small colander (used by apothecaries).
cacica, *n.f.* wife of an Indian chief; (*pol.*) wife of a party boss.
cacical [CACIQUIL].
cacicato [CACICAZGO].
cacicazgo, *n.m.* dignity *or* territory of a chief *or* ***cacique***; political fief; (*pol.*) area controlled by party boss; power of party boss.
cacimba, *n.f.* hole dug on the sea-shore (in the search for fresh water); bucket; fishing-net; (*coll.*) top-hat.
cacique, *n.m.* cacique, Indian chief; political leader, wire-puller *or* boss.
caciquería, *n.f.* political bossing, wire-pulling, jobbery.
caciquil, *a.* appertaining to a cacique *or* (*pol.*) party boss.
caciquismo, *n.m.* control by political bossing, jobbery.
caciquista, *a.* appertaining to *or* partisan of a ***cacique*** or ***caciquismo.***
cacle, *n.m.* (*Mex.*) leather sandal.
caco, *n.m.* pickpocket; (*coll.*) coward.
cacodilato, *n.m.* (*chem.*) cacodylate.
cacodílico, -ca, *a.* (*chem.*) cacodylic.
cacodilo, *n.m.* (*chem.*) cacodyl.
cacofonía, *n.f.* cacophony, horrible din, hideous row.
cacofónico, -ca, *a.* cacophonous, hideous.
cacogástrico, -ca, *a.* (*med.*) cacogastric.
cacografía, *n.f.* cacography.
cacomite, *n.m.* tiger flower.
cacomiztle, *n.m.* (*Mex.*) (*zool.*) cacomistle.
cacomorfia, *n.f.* (*med.*) cacomorphia.
cacoquimia (1), *n.f.* (*med.*) cacochymy.
cacoquímico, -ca, *a.* (*med.*) cacochymic.
cacoquimio, -mia (2), *n.m.f.* one suffering from melancholy.
cácteo, -tea, *a.* (*bot.*) cactaceous, cactal, cactoid. — *n.f.pl.* (**cácteas**) cacti.
cacto, *n.m.* (*bot.*) cactus.
cacumen, *n.m.* top, height; (*coll.*) acumen, nous.
cacha (1), *n.f.* each of the two leaves of a razor *or* knife handle; buttock, cheek; (*prov.*) buttock, seat; ***hasta las cachas,*** up to the hilt.
cachaco, *n.m.* (*Col., Ec., Ven.*) dandy.
cachada, *n.f.* stroke of one top against another (*game of tops*); (*Col., Hond.*) thrust with the horns (*from animals*).
cachado, *n.m.* (*carp.*) wood sawn in the middle.
cachalote, *n.m.* sperm whale.
cachamarín, *n.m.* (*naut.*) coasting lugger.
cachano, *n.m.* (*fam.*) the devil; ***llamar a cachano,*** to ask *or* call in vain.
cachapa, *n.f.* (*Ven.*) corn bread with sugar.
cachapucha, *n.f.* (*coll.*) hotchpotch.
cachar, *v.t.* to break in pieces; to divide (*a plank*) in two lengthwise with a saw *or* axe.
cacharpari, *n.m.* (*Per.*) farewell supper and dance.
cacharrería, *n.f.* crockery-store; collection of pots and pans.
cacharrero, -ra, *n.m.f.* maker *or* seller of crockery.
cacharro, *n.m.* pot *or* pan; crock, old crock; ***este coche es un cacharro,*** this car is a wreck *or* a piece of junk.
cachava, *n.f.* (shepherd's) crook, staff; shinny.
cachavazo, *n.m.* (*coll.*) swipe, wallop.
cachavona, *n.f.* (*prov.*) cudgel *or* club.
cachaza, *n.f.* slowness, sluggishness, phlegmatic nature; (*Hisp. Am.*) rum; first froth on cane-juice when boiled to make sugar.
cachazudo, -da, *a., n.m.f.* slow, phlegmatic, sluggish (person). — *n.m.* (*Hisp. Am.*) tobacco worm.
cache, *a.* (*Arg.*) coarse, unpolished (*person*).
cachear, *v.t.* to search *or* frisk (*for weapons*).
cachemarín, *n.m.* coasting lugger.
cachemir, *n.m.*, **cachemira,** *n.f.* cashmere.
cacheo, *n.m.* search, frisking.
cachera, *n.f.* coarse shaggy cloth *or* baize.
cacheta, *n.f.* tooth *or* ward in lock *or* latch.
cachete, *n.m.* slap; fat cheek; poniard (*for killing cattle*).
cachetear, *v.t.* to slap, smack.

cachetero, *n.m.* short poniard; bull-fighter who delivers the coup de grâce.
cachetina, *n.f.* hand-to-hand fight.
cachetudo, -da, *a.* plump-cheeked, chubby-faced.
cachicamo, *n.m.* (*Hisp. Am.*) armadillo.
cachicán, *n.m.* overseer, foreman; (*coll.*) smart *or* cunning man.
cachicuerno, -na, *a.* having a horn handle.
cachidiablo, *n.m.* (*fam.*) hobgoblin; one disguised in a devil's mask.
cachifo, -fa, *n.m.f.* (*Col.*, *Ven.*, *coll.*) boy, girl.
cachifollar, *v.t.* (*fig.*) to flatten, squash.
cachigordo, -da, *a.* (*fam.*) short and plump.
cachillada, *n.f.* litter of young animals.
cachimán, *n.m.* (*fam.*) hiding-place.
cachimba, *n.f.* (*Hisp. Am.*) spring, well; (tobacco) pipe; revolver; empty cartridge; ***chupar cachimba,*** to smoke a pipe; to suck one's thumb.
cachimbo, *n.m.* (*Hisp. Am.*) (tobacco) pipe; sugar mill.
cachipolla, *n.f.* (*ent.*) day-fly; May-fly.
cachiporra, *n.f.*, **cachiporro,** *n.m.* (*prov.*) club, cudgel.
cachiporrazo, *n.m.* blow with a club.
cachirulo, *n.m.* earthen, glass *or* tin pot (*for liquors*); head ornament (*formerly worn by women*); (*vulg.*) paramour; (*prov.*) small cup; small three-masted vessel; (*Mex.*) lining of chamois for riding trousers.
cachivache, *n.m.* (*fig.*) lying, worthless fellow; (*pl.*) pots and pans; old crocks; goods and chattels; tools of the trade.
cachizo, -za, *a.* that can be hewn.
cacho (1), *n.m.* slice, piece, chunk; card game; (*fam.*) ***es un cacho de bestia,*** he is a great lout.
cacho (2), *n.m.* (*ichth.*) surmullet.
cacho (3), *n.m.* (*Hisp. Am.*) horn, drinking horn.
cacho (4), **-cha** (2), *a.* bent, crooked.
cacholas, *n.f.pl.* (*naut.*) cheeks (*of masts*); (*naut.*) bee-blocks (*of bowsprit*).
cachón, *n.m.* breaker (*wave*); small waterfall.
cachondearse, *v.r.* (*vulg.*) to be *or* get sexy; to take the micky.
cachondeo, *n.m.* sexiness; micky-taking; crazy *or* mad business, farce.
cachondez, *n.f.* rut; randiness, sexiness.
cachondo, -da, *a.* in heat, in rut; sexy, randy.
cachopo, *n.m.* (*prov.*) dry trunk, stump (*of a tree*).
cachorra (1), *n.f.* (*prov.*) soft hat.
cachorreña, *n.f.* (*prov.*, *fam.*) tardiness, slowness; (*pl.*) (*prov.*) soup made of garlic, oil, chillies, vinegar and salt.
cachorrillo, *n.m.* small puppy; pocket pistol.
cachorro, -ra (2) *n.m.f.* puppy; cub, whelp; pocket pistol.
cachú, *n.m.* catechu, cutch.
cachúa, *n.f.* (*Bol.*, *Ec.*, *Per.*) Indian dance.
cachucha, *n.f.* row-boat; man's cloth *or* fur cap; Andalusian dance and song in triple measure.
cachuchear, *v.t.* (*prov.*, *fam.*) to coax.
cachuchero, *n.m.* maker *or* seller of caps *or* of pin and needle-cases; (*sl.*) gold thief.
cachucho (1), *n.m.* oil-measure (*containing* 2.8 *fl. oz.*); pin- *or* needle-case; row-boat; (*prov.*) earthen pot; (*sl.*) gold; gold currency.
cachucho (2), *n.m.* (*ichth.*) red snapper.
cachuela, *n.f.* fricassee of rabbits' livers and lights; stew; gizzard.
cachuelo, *n.m.* (*ichth.*) dace.
cachulera, *n.f.* (*prov.*) cavern, hiding-place.
cachumba, *n.f.* (*Philip.*) cachumba plant; saffron substitute.
cachumbo, *n.m.* (*Hisp. Am.*) hard shell (*of coconut* or *other fruit*).
cachunde, *n.f.* cachou, aromatic chewing paste of amber, musk and catechu; catechu.
cachupanda [CUCHIPANDA].
cachupín, -pina, *n.m.f.* (*Mex.*) Spanish settler.
cada (1), *a. inv.* every, each, ***cada uno, cada cual,*** everyone, each one; ***cada quisque,*** every son of a gun; ***cada loco con su tema,*** everyone has his hobby-horse; ***cada vez más,*** more and more; ***cada vez que,*** every time that; whenever; ***cada (y) cuando que,*** whenever; provided that; ***cada tres días,*** every three days.
cada (2), *n.m.* (*bot.*) juniper-tree.
cadahalso, *n.m.* shed, cabin.
cadalecho, *n.m.* (*prov.*) bed made of the branches of trees.
cadalso, *n.m.* platform, stage, stand; scaffold, gallows.
cadañal, *a.* annual, yearly.
cadañego, -ga, *a.* annual, yearly; (*bot.*) bearing abundant fruit yearly.
cadañero, -ra, *a.* lasting a year; annual, yearly; giving birth every year.
cadarzo, *n.m.* coarse, entangled silk which cannot be spun; cover of the cocoon; (*prov.*) narrow silk ribbon.
cádava, *n.f.* (*prov.*) burnt stump of furze.
cadáver, *n.m.* corpse, dead body.
cadavérico, -ca, *a.* cadaveric; (*fig.*) cadaverous; corpse-like.
cadejo, *n.m.* entangled hair; small skein; threads put together to make tassels.
cadena, *n.f.* (*lit.*, *fig.*) chain; chain-gang; (*arch.*) buttress; frame; wooden hearth-fender; figure (*in dancing*); ***balas de cadena,*** chain-shot; ***cadena de montañas,*** mountain range; ***cadena perpetua,*** life imprisonment; ***cadena de puerto,*** harbour boom; ***estar en cadena,*** to be in prison.
cadencia, *n.f.* cadence, measure, rhythm; fall (*of the voice*); flow (*of verses* or *periods*); rate, velocity (*of fire*); (*mus.*) cadenza.
cadenciado, -da, cadencioso, -sa, *a.* rhythmical, harmonious.
cadeneta, *n.f.* lace *or* needle-work wrought in the form of a chain, chain-stitch; headband (*of a book*).
cadenilla, *n.f.* small ornamental chain.
cadenita, *n.f.* small chain.
cadente, *a.* decaying, declining; going to ruin; well-modulated, rhythmical.
cadera, *n.f.* hip; coxa.
caderillas, *n.f.pl.* bustle; dress-hoops.
caderudo, -da, *a.* large-hipped.
cadetada, *n.f.* (*fam.*) wild action; schoolboy prank.
cadete, *n.m.* (*mil.*) cadet; ***hacer el cadete,*** to play the fool.
cadi, *n.m.* (*Ec.*) ivory-nut palm.
cadí, *n.m.* cadi.
cadillar, *n.m.* place where bur-parsley grows.
cadillo, *n.m.* (*bot.*) (great) bur-parsley; prickly burweed; common burdock; wart (*on skin*); (*prov.*) puppy; (*pl.*) first warp threads.
cadmía, *n.f.* sublimated oxide of zinc, tutty.
cadmio, *n.m.* (*min.*) cadmium; calamine; ***amarillo de cadmio***, cadmium yellow.
cado, *n.m.* (*prov.*) ferret-hole.
cadoce, cadoz, *n.m.* (*ichth.*, *prov.*) gudgeon.
cadozo, *n.m.* whirlpool.
caducante, *a.* doting, in decline.
caducar [A], **caduquear,** *v.i.* to dote; to fall into disuse; to become out-dated *or* superannuated; (*com.*, *law*) to expire, lapse.
caduceador, *n.m.* king at arms, who proclaimed peace and carried the caduceus.
caduceo, *n.m.* caduceus.
caducidad, *n.f.* (*law*) expiry; decrepitude.
caducífloro, -ra, *a.* (*bot.*) caducous.

caduco, -ca, *a.* senile; decrepit; in decline; (*bot.*) deciduous; ***mal caduco,*** epilepsy; (*anat.*) ***membrana caduca,*** decidua.

caduquear [CADUCAR].

caduquez, *n.f.* decrepitude, senility.

caedizo, -za, *a.* ready to fall; (*bot.*) deciduous.

caedura, *n.f.* loose threads falling from the loom.

caer(se) [14], *v.i.* (*v.r.*) to fall, drop *or* tumble down, off *or* over; to fall *or* come (under); to hang down, droop; to fit, suit, become; to be (situated); to decrease, decline; to deviate (from one's path); to fall due; to fall to one's lot; to see, realize, understand; to fade (*colours*); ***caer de pie,*** to fall on one's feet; ***caer(se) redondo,*** to fall flat, go out like a light; ***caer a plomo, caer de plano,*** to fall, drop *or* descend sheer *or* vertically; ***el sol cae de plano,*** the sun is beating straight down; ***cae cerca,*** it is *or* lies near *or* nearby; ***esta chaqueta le cae bien,*** this jacket fits him *or* suits him; ***el pescado me ha caído mal,*** the fish has disagreed with me *or* upset me; ***le cayó mal la noticia,*** the news upset him; ***cayó bien allí,*** he went down well there, he was well received there; ***las ventanas caen al río,*** the windows look onto the river; ***caer en culpa,*** to become guilty of an offence; (*fig.*) ***con las orejas caídas,*** with one's tail between one's legs; ***le cayó en suerte un destino bueno,*** as luck would have it he got a good post(ing) *or* job; ***no caigo,*** I don't get it; I can't recall it; ***por fin cayó,*** it eventually dawned on him; ***le ha caído la lotería,*** he has won a lottery prize; (*fig.*) he's had a stroke of luck; ***estar*** (***una cosa***) ***al caer,*** to be ripe; to be about to arrive, happen etc.; ***caer sobre el enemigo,*** to fall upon the enemy; ***dejar caer,*** to drop; ***ya caigo en ello*** or ***en la cuenta,*** now I see, now I get it; now I remember; ***caer en cama, enfermo*** or ***malo,*** to fall ill, be taken ill; ***caer en la cuenta,*** to realize; ***el día cae,*** day draws to a close; ***al caer*** (***de***) ***la tarde,*** at nightfall, at dusk; ***caer en falta,*** to fall into error, commit a misdeed; ***caer en flor,*** to be cut off in one's youth, die prematurely; ***caer en saco roto,*** to fall on deaf ears; ***caer en desgracia,*** to fall into disgrace; ***caer en gracia,*** to please, be agreeable, find favour; ***caer el plazo,*** to fall due; ***caerse de suyo,*** to be obvious *or* self-evident; ***caerse*** (***una cosa***) ***de su peso,*** to be evident; ***me caigo de sueño,*** I'm dropping with sleep; ***se me cayó de la memoria,*** I forgot it; ***caérsele a uno la cara de vergüenza,*** to blush deeply with shame; ***caerse a pedazos,*** to fall to pieces; ***caerse de ánimo,*** to become dejected; ***caérsele a uno las alas del corazón,*** to become discouraged.

cafar, *v.i.* (*sl.*) to escape.

café, *n.m.* coffee; coffee-tree; coffee-berry; coffee-house, café.

caféico, -ca, *a.* (*chem.*) caffeic.

cafeína, *n.f.* caffeine.

cafería, *n.f.* village.

cafetal, *n.m.* coffee plantation.

cafetalista, *n.m.f.* (*Cub.*) owner of coffee plantation.

cafetería, *n.f.* coffee bar, refreshment *or* snack bar.

cafetero, -ra, *a.* appertaining to coffee. — *n.m.f.* one who gathers coffee-berries; coffee grower; coffee-maker *or* seller; owner of coffee-house *or* café. — *n.f.* coffee-pot; kettle.

cafetín, *n.m.* small café, miserable little place.

cafeto, *n.m.* (*bot.*) coffee-tree.

cafetucho, *n.m.* wretched little café, dump.

caficultor, *n.m.* (*Cent. Am.*) coffee grower.

caficultura, *n.f.* (*Cent. Am.*) coffee growing.

cáfila, *n.m.* (*fam.*) series, string (*of people, things* or *animals*); caravan.

cafiroleta, *n.f.* (*Cub.*) sweetmeat made of sweet-potatoes, grated coconut and sugar.

caftán, *n.m.* caftan.

caga(a)ceite, *n.m.* missel thrush.

cagachín, *n.m.* small reddish mosquito; tiny bird.

cagada (1), *n.f.* dung; (*vulg.*) shit; (*com.*) blunder, mistake.

cagadero, *n.m.* lavatory; (*vulg.*) bog.

cagado, -da (2), *a.* (*vulg.*) cowardly, poor-spirited. — *n.m.* (*vulg.*) coward, funker, miserable object, pitiful specimen.

cagafierro, *n.m.* scoria, dross (*of iron*).

cagajón, *n.m.* dung (*of horses, mules and asses*).

cagalaolla, *n.m.* masquerader; clown.

cagalar, *n.m.* (*anat.*) cæcum.

cagalera, *n.f.* diarrhœa.

cagaluta [CAGARRUTA].

cagancia, *n.f.* (*vulg.*) shit.

caganidos, *n.m. inv.* (*prov.*) one who frequently changes his residence.

cagaoficios, *n.m.f. inv.* (*fam.*) rolling stone.

cagar [B], *v.t., v.i.* (*vulg.*) to shit; (*fig.*) to mess *or* muck up; to soil, stain, defile. — **cagarse,** *v.t.* to dirty one's pants.

cagarrache, *n.m.* one who washes the olive-pits in an oil-mill; (*orn.*) missel thrush.

cagarria, *n.f.* morel (*edible mushroom*).

cagarropa, *n.m.* small reddish mosquito.

cagarruta, *n.f.* dung (*sheep, goats, hares and mice*).

cagatinta(s), *n.m.* pen-pusher.

cagatorio [CAGADERO].

cagón, -gona, *a., n.m.f.* (person) troubled with diarrhœa; (*coll.*) cowardly, funky (person).

caguama, *n.f.* turtle (of the Caribbean).

cagueta, *n.m.f.* (*fam.*) funker, coward.

cahiz, *n.m.* measure of twelve ***fanegas,*** *or* 188 bushels.

cahizada, *n.f.* land sufficient to contain one ***cahiz*** of seed.

cáico, *n.m.* (*Cub.*) large reef *or* shoal.

caíd, *n.m.* (*hist.*) cadi.

caída, *n.f.* fall; downfall; falling off, drop, lapse; hang (*clothes, curtains etc.*); (*geol.*) dip; fallen woman; (*Philip.*) interior gallery overlooking the courtyard; ***tener buena caída,*** to hang well; ***a la caída de la tarde,*** at nightfall, at dusk; ***a la caída del sol,*** at sunset; (*pl.*) coarse wool cut off the skirts of a fleece.

caído, *n.m.* (*pl.*) ***los caídos,*** the Fallen; ***día de los caídos,*** Remembrance Day. — *p.p.* [CAER].

caigua, *n.f.* (*Per.*) pumpkin.

caiguá, *a., n.m.f.* (*Hisp. Am.*) Indian inhabiting mountains of Uruguay, Paraná and Paraguay.

caimacán, *n.m.* vizier.

caimán, *n.m.* alligator; (*coll., fig.*) shark.

caimiento, *n.m.* fall, drop; droop; (*fig.*) dejection, languidness, lowness of spirits.

caimito, *n.m.* (*Hisp. Am.*) star apple.

Caín, *n.m.* Cain; ***pasar las de Caín,*** to go through Hell.

caique, *n.m.* (*naut.*) caique, small boat, ketch.

cairel, *n.m.* false hair *or* wig; fringe trimming; furbelow, flounce.

cairelar, *v.t.* to fringe.

Cairo, *n.m.* Cairo.

cairota, *a., n.m.f.* of *or* native of Cairo.

caja, *n.f.* box, case; coffin; chest; crate; body (*of carriage*); safe, cash-box; gun-stock; socket; cavity, hole; (*mil.*) drum, drum case *or* frame; frame; (*com.*) cash, funds; cashier's office; cash-desk; printer's case; well (*of staircase*); (*bot.*) seed-case; (*naut.*) block, pulley; ***caja de ahorros,*** savings-bank; ***caja de amortización,*** Department of Public Debts; Sinking Fund Department; (*com.*) ***caja de caudales,*** safe; ***caja de coche,*** body of a coach; (*law*) ***caja de consulta,*** brief; ***caja del cuerpo,*** torso; ***caja de engranajes, de velocidades*** or ***de cambios,*** gear-box, (*Am.*) transmission; ***caja de***

música, musical-box; (*mil.*) ***caja de recluta-miento,*** recruiting-office; (*com.*) ***caja registra-dora,*** cash register; (*anat.*) ***caja del tambor,*** drum, middle ear cavity; ***libro de caja,*** cash-book; ***despedir*** or ***echar (a alguien) con cajas destempladas,*** to send (s.o.) packing; ***en caja,*** in hand (*cash*); ***meter a alguien en caja,*** to bring s.o. to heel; ***no estar en caja,*** to feel out of sorts; (*print.*) ***caja alta,*** upper case; ***caja baja,*** lower case.

cajel, *a.* ***naranja cajel,*** blood-orange.

cajera, *n.f.* woman cashier; (*naut.*) sheave-hole.

cajería, *n.f.* box shop.

cajero, *n.m.* box-maker; cashier; treasurer; (*Am.*) teller; reservoir (*in irrigation canals*).

cajeta, *n.f.* little box; (*prov.*) poor box; (*naut.*) plaited cord; (*Cub.*) tobacco pouch; (*C.R., Mex.*) box of jelly.

cajete, *n.m.* (*Guat., Mex.*) flat earthen bowl.

cajetilla, *n.f.* packet (*of cigarettes*).

cajetín, *n.m.* very small box; (*print.*) fount-case, letter-case; stamp (*mark and instrument*).

cají, *n.m.* caji fish.

cajiga, *n.f.* (*bot.*) muricated oak, gall oak.

cajigal, *n.m.* plantation of muricated oaks.

cajilla, *n.f.* (*bot.*) capsule.

cajista, *n.m.f.* (*print.*) compositor.

cajita, *n.f.* small box.

cajo, *n.m.* (bookbinder's) groove.

cajón, *n.m.* large box, case, chest; drawer, till; locker; space between shelves (of a book-case); (*arch.*) space between buttress and wall; mould for casting; wooden stand *or* shed for selling provisions; (*Mex.*) dry-goods store; (*Chi.*) ravine; (*naut.*) ***cajón de dique*** or ***de grada,*** dam, caisson; dock-gate; ***ser de cajón,*** to be obvious *or* elementary; ***cajón de sastre,*** hotch-potch, medley; muddle-head.

cajonada, *n.f.* (*naut.*) locker.

cajoncito, *n.m.* small box; little drawer.

cajonera, *n.f.* chest of drawers (in a vestry); set of lockers.

cajonería, *n.f.* set of drawers; tall-boy, chiffonier.

cajonero, *n.m.* (*min.*) operative in charge of water-extracting implements.

cajonga, *n.f.* (*Hond.*) omelet of maize.

cajuela, *n.f.* small box.

cal, *n.f.* lime; ***cal ahogada, apagada*** or ***muerta,*** slaked lime; ***cal viva,*** quick *or* unslaked lime; ***cal hidráulica,*** hydraulic lime; ***cerrado a cal y canto,*** tight shut; ***negar a cal y canto,*** to deny flatly; ***dar una de cal y otra de arena,*** not to overdo either one thing or the other, strike a (happy) balance *or* medium.

cala, *n.f.* cove, creek; sample cut *or* slice (*of melon*); probe, test, boring; dipstick, (*Am.*) bayonet; (*med.*) suppository; (*naut.*) hold; (*bot.*) calla-lily; (*slang*) hole; ***hacer cala y cata,*** to test for quantity *or* quality.

calaba, *n.m.* (*bot.*) [CALAMBUCO].

calabacear, *v.t.* (*coll.*) to fail, plough; to reject, send away with a flea in the ear.

calabacera, *n.f.* (*bot.*) pumpkin, gourd-plant; woman vendor of this fruit.

calabacero, *n.m.* retailer of pumpkins; (*slang*) picklock, burglar.

calabacil, *a.* ***pera calabacil,*** calabash pear.

calabacilla, *n.f.* bitter gherkin; core of gourd-shaped tassel; pear-shaped ear-ring.

calabacín, *n.m.* (*bot.*) marrow, (*Am.*) squash; courgette; (*coll.*) dolt.

calabacino, *n.m.* dry gourd, calabash, bottle.

calabacita, *n.f.* small pumpkin.

calabaza, *n.f.* (*bot.*) pumpkin, gourd; (*fig.*) bumpkin, clod; (*sl.*) picklock, skeleton-key; ***dar calabazas a,*** to fail, plough; to jilt, send away with a flea in the ear; ***llevar calabazas,*** to be jilted, go away with a flea in the ear.

calabazada, *n.f.* blow (*with* or *on the head*); ***darse de calabazadas,*** to make strenuous efforts.

calabazar, *n.m.* pumpkin patch.

calabazate, *n.m.* candied pumpkin.

calabazazo, *n.m.* blow (*from a pumpkin*).

calabazo, *n.m.* gourd, calabash; pumpkin; (*naut.*) old tub; (*Cub.*) musical instrument.

calabazón, *n.m.* large gourd *or* pumpkin.

calabazona, *n.f.* (*prov.*) large winter pumpkin.

calabazuela, *n.f.* plant grown in the Sierra de Sevilla and used against viper bites.

calabobos, *n.m. inv.* (*fam.*) drizzle.

calabocero, *n.m.* jailer, warden.

calabozaje, *n.m.* fee paid by prisoners to the jailer.

calabozo (1), *n.m.* dungeon.

calabozo (2), *n.m.* pruning-hook *or* knife; (*Cub.*) small sickle.

calabrés, -resa, *a., n.m.f.* Calabrian.

calabriada, *n.f.* mixture; concoction; mixture of red and white wine; balderdash.

calabriar, *v.t.* to confuse, embroil, mix.

calabrotar [ACALABROTAR].

calabrote, *n.m.* (*naut.*) laid rope.

calacuerda, *n.f.* beating of drums as summons to attack.

calada, *n.f.* soaking, wetting-through; rapid flight of birds of prey; ***dar una calada a,*** to give a dressing-down.

caladera, *n.f.* (*prov.*) net for fishing mullet.

caladero, *n.m.* suitable place for casting fishing-nets.

caladio, *n.m.* (*bot.*) caladium.

caladizo, -za, *a.* (*fig.*) smart, sharp.

calado, *n.m.* open-work (*in metal, stone, wood* or *linen*); fretwork; (*naut.*) draught (*of a vessel*); (*pl.*) lace cape *or* deep collar.

calador, *n.m.* perforator, borer; one who does open-work; (*naut.*) caulking iron; (*surg.*) bougie, probe.

caladora, *n.f.* (*Ven.*) large canoe.

caladre, *n.f.* (*orn.*) lark.

caladura, *n.f.* cutting and tasting (of fruits).

calafate, calafateador, *n.m.* (*naut.*) caulker; shipwright.

calafateado, *n.m.* caulking.

calafateadura, *n.f.* caulking.

calafatear, *v.t.* (*naut.*) to caulk.

calafateo, *n.m.* caulking.

calafatería, *n.f.* caulking.

calafatín, *n.m.* caulker's boy *or* mate.

calafraga, *n.f.* (*bot.*) saxifrage.

calagozo, *n.m.* bill-hook, hedging-hook.

calagraña, *n.f.* table grape (not suitable for wine).

calaguala, *n.f.* (*Per.*) medicinal fern.

calaguasca, *n.f.* (*Col.*) anisette.

calahorra, *n.f.* public office where bread was distributed in times of scarcity.

calaíta, *n.f.* (*min.*) turquoise.

calaje, *n.m.* (*prov.*) chest, trunk, coffer.

calajería [CAJONERÍA].

calalú, *n.m.* (*Cub.*) potage of vegetables.

calaluz, *n.m.* (*Philip.*) (*naut.*) small vessel.

calamaco, *n.m.* calamanco.

calamar, *n.m.* squid, ink-fish.

calambac, *n.m.* (*bot.*) aloes-wood, kalamba, eaglewood.

calambre, *n.m.* spasm, twinge; cramp; electric shock.

calambuco, -ca, *a.* (*Hisp. Am.*) sanctimonious. — *n.m.* (*Hisp. Am.*) calaba tree; jug; pail; milk-churn.

calamento, *n.m.* soaking of fishing-nets.
calamidad, *n.f.* calamity; (*fam.*) ***ser una calamidad,*** to be a dead loss, be hopeless.
calamillera, *n.f.* pot-hook (*of a crane*).
calamina, piedra calaminar, *n.f.* calamine.
calaminta, *n.f.* (*bot.*) calamint.
calamita, *n.f.* loadstone; magnetic needle.
calamitación, *n.f.* (*phys.*) magnetization.
calamite, *n.m.* little green tree-frog.
calamiteas, *n.f. inv.* (*bot.*) calamite.
calamitoso, -sa, *a,* calamitous, disastrous.
cálamo, *n.m.* calamus; (*poet.*) pen; ancient flute; (*bot.*) ***cálamo aromático,*** sweet-flag.
calamocano, -na, *a.* fuddled, tipsy, unsteady; doting.
calamoco, *n.m.* icicle.
calamocha, *n.f.* dull yellow ochre.
calamochazo [CALAMORRAZO].
calamón (1), *n.m.* (*orn.*) purple water-hen, gallinule; round-headed nail.
calamón (2), *n.m.* stay (*to support beam of oil-mill*).
calamorra, *a.* woolly-faced (*sheep*). — *n.f.* (*coll.*) head.
calamorrada, *n.f.* blow with *or* on the head; nod (*in sleep*).
calamorrar, *v.t.* to butt.
calamorrazo, *n.m.* (*fam.*) blow on the head.
calamorro, *n.m.* (*Chi.*) coarse shoe.
calandraca, *n.f.* (*naut.*) mess of hard-tack.
calandrajo, *n.m.* (*fam.*) tatter; (old) rag; (*coll.*) ragamuffin; (*prov.*) invention, supposition.
calandria (1), *n.f.* (*orn.*) lark; calender.
calandria (2), *n.f.* (*sl.*) town-crier; winch, windlass. — *n.m.f.* malingerer (*in hospital*).
cálanis, *n.m. inv.* (*bot.*) sweet-flag.
calaña, *n.f.* pattern; sample; model, form; (*fig.*) kind, sort; breed, ilk; cheap cane-ribbed fan.
calañés, *a.* ***sombrero calañés,*** Andalusian hat.
calapatillo, *n.m.* weevil, grub.
calapé, *n.m.* (*Hisp. Am.*) turtle roasted in its shell.
calar (1), *v.t.* to penetrate, soak through, permeate, drench; to go through, pierce, perforate; (*coll.*) to see through; to slice and sample; to make open-work in (*metal, wood, linen* or *paper*); (*mech.*) to wedge; (*slang*) to pick (*pockets*); (*naut.*) to raise *or* lower by means of a pole; (*naut.*) to soak, submerge (*fishing-tackle*); (*Col.*) to crush, vex, humble; (*Mex.*) to take out a sample from (*a bale*; ***calar la bayoneta,*** to fix bayonets; ***calar el can de una escopeta,*** to cock a gun; ***calar una cuba,*** to gauge a barrel *or* cask; ***calar un mélon,*** to take a sample slice out of a melon; (*naut.*) ***calar el palo,*** to step the mast; ***le tengo calado,*** I've got him sized up, I can see through him; (*naut.*) ***calar el timón,*** to hang the rudder. — *v.i.* (*naut.*) to draw. — **calarse,** *v.r.* to get drenched *or* soaked; ***calarse el sombrero,*** to pull down one's hat; ***calarse hasta los huesos,*** to get soaked to the skin.
calar (2), *a.* calcareous. — *n.m.* lime-quarry.
calasancio, -cia, *a.* [ESCOLAPIO].
calato, -ta, *a.* (*Per.*) naked.
Calatrava, *n.f.* Calatrava, order of knighthood.
calatravo, -va, *a., n.m.f.* appertaining to *or* member of the Order of Calatrava.
calavera, *n.f.* skull. — *n.m.* tyke, rake.
calaverada, *n.f.* wild escapade, mad thing to do.
calaverear, *v.i.* to act wildly *or* like a rake; to lead the life of a rake.
calavernario, *n.m.* charnel-house, ossuary.
calaverón, *n.m.* utter rake.
calboche, *n.m.* (*prov.*) perforated earthenware pan (*for roasting chestnuts*).
calbote, *n.m.* (*prov.*) bread made of acorns *or* chestnuts; roasted chestnut.
calca, *n.f.* (*sl.*) road, highway; (*pl.*) footsteps, footprints.
calcable, *a.* fordable, navigable; traceable.
calcado, *n.m.* tracing.
calcador, -ra, *n.m.f.* tracer. — *n.m.* style (*instrument*).
calcáneo, *n.m.* (*anat.*) calcaneum.
calcañal, calcañar, *n.m.* heel, heel-bone.
calcañuelo, *n.m.* bee disease.
calcar [A], *v.t.* to trace; to trample upon; (*fig.*) to copy, imitate, model (on).
calcáreo, -ra, *a.* calcareous.
calcatrife, *n.m.* (*slang*) drudge; common labourer.
calce, *n.m.* (steel) tyre; (iron *or* steel) shoe (*plough*); wedge; wheel shoe, brake-lining; (*Guat., Mex.*) bottom, foot, end.
calcedonia, *n.f.* chalcedony.
calceolaria, *n.f.* (*bot.*) calceolaria, slipperwort.
calcés, *n.m.* (*naut.*) mast-head.
calceta, *n.f.* stocking; (*fig.*) fetter; (*prov.*) sausage; ***hacer calceta,*** to knit.
calcetería, *n.f.* hosier's shop; hosier's trade; hosiery.
calcetero, -ra, *n.m.f.* one who makes, mends *or* sells stockings, hosier. — *n.m.* (*sl.*) one who puts the fetters on.
calcetín, *n.m.* sock.
calceto, *a., n.m.* (*Col., C.R.*) (chicken) with feathers covering its legs.
calcetón, *n.m.* thick stocking (*worn under boots*).
calcicloro, *n.m.* chloride of lime.
cálcico, -ca, *a.* (*chem.*) calcic.
calciferrita, calcioferrita, calcoferrita, *n.f.* (*min.*) calcio-ferrite.
calcificación, *n.f.* (*med.*) calcification.
calcificar [A], *v.t.* to calcify.
calcil, *n.m.* light tawny colour.
calcilla, *n.f.* (*prov.*) footless stocking; gaiter; (*pl.*) short, narrow breeches; (*fam.*) ***es un calcillas,*** he is a short man; he is a timid man; ***poner calcilla a,*** to praise unduly.
calcímetro, *n.m.* calcimetre.
calcina, *n.f.* mortar.
calcinación, *n.f.*, **calcinamiento,** *n.m.* (*chem.*) calcination.
calcinador, -ra, *a.* calcining. — *n.m.f.* calciner.
calcinar, *v.t.* to calcine; to burn, blacken.
calcinatorio, -ria, *a.* calcinatory.
calcinero, *n.m.* lime-burner.
calcio, *n.m.* calcium.
calcita, *n.f.* (*min.*) calcite.
calco, *n.m.* tracing; copy, imitation; (*sl.*) shoe.
calcografía, *n.f.* chalcography; place where engravings are made.
calcografiar, *v.t.* to engrave on copper.
calcógrafo, *n.m.* chalcographer, engraver; engraving machine.
calcomanía, *n.f.* transfer.
calcopirita, *n.f.* (*min.*) chalcopyrite.
calcorrear, *v.i.* (*sl.*) to run.
calcorreo, *n.m.* (*sl.*) running.
calcorro, *n.m.* (*sl.*) shoe.
calculable, *a.* calculable.
calculación, *n.f.* calculation.
calculadamente, *adv.* in a calculating manner.
calculador, -ra, *a.* calculating; (***máquina***) ***calculadora,*** calculating machine, computer.
calcular, *v.t.* to calculate, reckon, compute, estimate; to work out.
calculativo, -va, *a.* calculative.
calculatorio, -ria, *a.* calculating.
calculiforme, *a.* pebble-shaped.
calculista, *a.* calculating. — *n.m.* schemer.
cálculo, *n.m.* calculation, computation; estimate;

count; (*math.*) calculus; (*med.*) calculus, gallstone; (*pl.*) (*med.*) lithiasis.
calculoso, -sa, *a.*, *n.m.f.* (*med.*) calculous (sufferer).
calcha, *n.f.* (*Chi.*) fetlock (*of horse*); (*Arg., Chi.*) workman's clothing and bedding.
calchacura, *n.f.* (*Chi.*) lichen (*used in medicine*).
calchona, *n.f.* (*Chi.*) bogeyman; witch.
calda, *n.f.* (act of) warming *or* heating; stoking (*furnaces etc.*); (*pl.*) hot springs; ***dar una calda,*** to reheat (*in the forge*).
caldaico, -ca, *a.*, *n.m.f.* Chaldean, Chaldee; Chaldaic. — *n.m.* Chaldean language.
caldaria, *n.f.* ***ley caldaria,*** trial by water.
caldario, *n.m.* caldarium.
caldeamiento, *n.m.* heating.
caldear, *v.t.* to warm, heat; to weld (*iron*).
caldeo, -dea, *a.*, *n.m.f.* Chaldaic.
caldera, *n.f.* boiler; sugar-kettle; shell (*of kettle-drum*); (*min.*) sump (*of well*); (*Arg.*) coffee-pot; kettle; (*Chi.*) tea-pot; (*coll.*) ***calderas de Pero Botero,*** Hell; ***caldera de vapor,*** steam-boiler; ***caldera tubular,*** tubular boiler.
calderada, *n.f.* cauldronful.
calderería, *n.f.* boiler-maker's shop *or* trade.
calderero, *n.m.* coppersmith; boilermaker; tinker.
caldereta, *n.f.* small cauldron, kettle, pot; kettleful; stoup, holy-water basin; stew; (*Mex.*) chocolate-pot; (*Hisp. Am.*) thunderstorm.
calderil, (*prov.*) *n.m.* notched pole (for supporting cooking pots).
calderilla, *n.f.* coppers, small change; (*bot.*) grossulaceous plant.
caldero, *n.m.* cauldron; copper; cauldronful.
calderón, *n.m.* large copper cauldron *or* kettle [CALDERA]; (*prov.*) tip-cat; (*arith.*) mark of a thousand (.ↀ); (*gram., print.*) orthographic sign denoting paragraph (¶); (*mus.*) sign indicating pause (𝄐); (*mus.*) pause and flourish executed during same.
calderoniano, -na, *a.* appertaining to *or* characteristic of Pedro Calderón de la Barca.
calderuela, *n.f.* small kettle; dark lantern (used to drive partridges into the net).
caldibache, caldivache [CALDUCHO].
caldillo, *n.m.* gravy; (*Mex.*) sauce with ragout *or* fricassee.
caldo, *n.m.* broth; clear soup; (*Mex.*) juice of sugar cane; (*Mex.*) marigold; salad dressing; juice; ***caldo de carne,*** consommé, beef-tea; (*fig.*) ***amargarle el caldo a alguien,*** to spoil things for s.o.; (*pl.*) (*com.*) wine oil and all juices extracted from fruits; wines.
caldoso, -sa, *a.* thin, having much stock (*soup*).
calducho, *n.m.* thin, tasteless broth *or* stock.
calduda, *n.f.* (*Chi.*) moist pie made with eggs, sultanas, olives etc.
cale, *n.m.* light blow *or* tap.
calé, *a.* gipsy. — *n.m.* gipsy; gipsy language.
calecer [9], *v.i.* to become heated.
calecico, *n.m.* small chalice.
caledonio, -nia, *a.*, *n.m.f.* Caledonian.
calefacción, *n.f.* heating; ***calefacción central,*** central heating.
calefactorio, *n.m.* calefactory.
calembé, *n.m.* (*Cub.*) bathing trunks.
calenda, *n.f.* part of the martyrology which treats of the acts of the saints of the day; (*pl.*) kalends; ***las calendas griegas,*** the Greek Kalends, never.
calendario, *n.m.* calendar; ***hacer calendarios,*** to muse; to forecast hastily.
calendarista, *n.m.f.* calendarer.
caléndula, *n.f.* marigold.
calentador, *a.* heating, warming. — *n.m.* heater; warmer, warming-pan; (*coll.*) large, clumsy watch.
calentamiento, *n.m.* warming, heating; overheating; inflammation.
calentano, -na, *a.* (*Hisp. Am.*) lowlands. — *n.m.f.* (*Hisp. Am.*) lowlander.
calentar [1], *v.t.* to warm, heat, make hot; (*coll.*) to beat; ***le calentó las orejas,*** he boxed his ears. — **calentarse,** *v.r.* to become heated, worked up (*in an argument*); to heat up, warm up; to be on heat (*animals*); ***calentarse la cabeza,*** to worry one's head.
calentito, -ta, *a.* nice and warm; piping hot; (*coll.*) nice and sexy.
calentón, -tona, *a.* unpleasantly warm *or* hot; tepid; very sexy *or* randy. — *n.m.* warming *or* heating up quickly; over-heating; ***darse un calentón,*** to warm oneself up, have a warm.
calentorro, -rra, *a.* revoltingly warm *or* hot; tepid; very sexy *or* randy.
calentucho, -cha, *a.* revoltingly warm *or* hot; tepid.
calentura, *n.f.* fever, temperature; mouth rash.
calenturiento, -ta, *a.* feverish; (*fig.*) wild; (*Chi.*) consumptive.
calenturilla, *n.f.* slight fever.
calenturón, *n.m.* violent fever.
calenturoso, -sa, *a.* feverish.
caleño, -ña, *a.* producing lime. — *n.f.* (*prov.*) limestone.
calepino, *n.m.* (*coll.*) Latin dictionary.
calería, *n.f.* place where lime is burnt *or* sold.
calero, -ra, *a.* calcareous. — *n.m.* lime-burner, lime-maker, lime-seller. — *n.f.* lime-kiln; lime-quarry; fishing smack.
calés, *n.m.*, **calesa** (1), *n.f.* two-wheeled calash, chaise.
calesa (2), *n.f.* (*prov.*) maggot.
calesera, *n.f.* Andalusian bolero-jacket; waistcoat.
calesero, *n.m.* driver of a calash, coachman.
calesín, *n.m.* light chaise.
calesinero, *n.m.* coachman.
caleta, *n.f.* (*naut.*) small cove, creek, inlet; (*Hisp. Am.*) ship plying small cabotage; (*Ven.*) guild of carriers. — *n.m.* (*sl.*) thief who steals through a hole.
caletero, *n.m.* (*Ven.*) docker, (*Am.*) longshoreman; (*sl.*) thief's accomplice.
caletre, *n.m.* (*fam.*) brain-box; sense.
cali, *n.m.* (*chem.*) alkali.
calibeo, -bea, *a.* (*med.*) chalybeate.
cálibes, *n.m.pl.* Chalybes.
calibración, *n.f.* calculation; gauging.
calibrador, *n.m.* calibre-gauge; callipers.
calibrar, *v.t.* to calibrate (*a ball* or *firearm*); to gauge, measure, reckon.
calibre, *n.m.* calibre; ***compás de calibres,*** callipers; ***de mucho calibre,*** substantial; high quality.
calicanto, *n.m.* (*bot.*) allspice; stone masonry.
calicata, *n.f.* (*min.*) trial pit; sounding (*of ground*).
caliciflora, *a.* (*bot.*) calyciflorate.
caliciforme, *a.* (*bot.*) calyciform.
calicillo, *n.m.* (*bot.*) calycle.
calicinal, caliciniano, -na, *a.* (*bot.*) calycine.
calicó, *n.m.* calico.
caliculado, -da, *a.* (*bot.*) calycled.
calicular, *a.* (*bot.*) calyculate.
calículo, *n.m.* calycle.
calicut, *n.m.* calicut silk.
caliche, *n.m.* pebble burnt in a brick; crust of lime flaking from a wall; (*prov.*) crack (*in vessel*); (*prov.*) game of quoits; (*Chi.*) saltpetre; (*Per.*) mound of earth left in extracting saltpetre.
calidad, *n.f.* quality; (*med.*) fever, heat; stipulation; (*pl.* **calidades**) conditions, rules (*in card games*); personal gifts; ***a calidad de que,*** on condition that; ***en calidad de,*** as *or* in the capacity of.
calidez, *n.f.* (*med.*) heat, fever.

cálido, -da, *a.* warm, hot.
calidoscópico, -ca, *a.* kaleidoscopic.
calidoscopio, *n.m.* kaleidoscope.
calientacamas, *n.m. inv.* warming-pan, bed-warmer.
calientapiés, *n.m. inv.* foot-warmer.
calientaplatos, *n.m. inv.* plate-warmer.
caliente, *a.* warm, hot; (*fig.*) heated; hot; on heat; ***caliente de cascos,*** hot-headed; ***hacer algo en caliente,*** to do sth. in the heat of the moment; ***ande yo caliente, y ríase la gente,*** people may laugh, but I am all right; let them think what they like, I'm fine.
califa, *n.m.* caliph.
califato, *n.m.* caliphate.
calífero, -ra, *a.* calciferous.
calificable, *a.* qualifiable.
calificación, *n.f.* qualification; judgment; label; grade, mark (*in examination*).
calificador, *n.m.* qualifier; censor; moderator (*in examinations*); ***calificador del Santo Oficio,*** ecclesiastical censor of books.
calificar [A], *v.t.* to qualify; to assess, grade; to authorize; ***calificar de irresponsable,*** to call irresponsible, stamp as irresponsible. — **calificarse,** *v.r.* to prove one's noble birth and descent according to law.
calificativo, -va, *a.* (*gram.*) qualifying. — *n.m.* name, description.
californiano, -na, californio, -nia, *a., n.m.f.* Californian.
califórnico, -ca, *a.* relating to California.
cáliga, *n.f.* sandal (*worn by Roman soldiers*); (*pl.*) (bishop's) gaiters.
calígine, *n.f.* (heat) haze, mist.
caliginoso, -sa, *a.* hazy, misty.
caligrafía, *n.f.* calligraphy, penmanship.
caligrafiar [L], *v.t.* to calligraph.
caligráfico, -ca, *a.* calligraphic.
calígrafo, *n.m.* calligrapher, good penman.
calilla, *n.f.* suppository; (*Hisp. Am.*) bother; pest; hardship.
calima, *n.f.* (*naut.*) buoy of strung corkfloats.
calimaco, *n.m.* calamanco.
calimba, *n.f.* (*Cub.*) branding-iron.
calimbar, *v.t.* (*Cub.*) to brand.
calimbo, *n.m.* (*min.*) kernel of eagle-stone.
calimoso, -sa [CALINOSO].
calimote, *n.m.* centre cork-float of seine.
calina (1), *n.f.* (heat) haze, mist.
calinda, *n.f.* (*Cub.*) calinda dance.
calino, -na (2), *a.* containing lime.
calinoso, -sa, *a.* vapoury, misty, hazy.
Calíope, *n.f.* Calliope.
calípedes, *n.m. inv.* (*zool.*) sloth.
caliptriforme, *a.* (*bot.*) calyptriform.
caliptro, *n.m.* (*bot.*) calyptra.
calisaya, *n.f.* cinchona.
calistenia, *n.f.* callisthenics.
cáliz, *n.m.* chalice; (*bot.*) calyx; (*poet.*) cup, goblet; ***apurar el cáliz de la amargura,*** to drain the cup of bitterness.
calizo, -za, *a.* calcareous, limy. — *n.f.* calcite.
calma, *n.f.* [CALMO].
calmante, *a.* sedative, soothing. — *n.m.* (*med.*) sedative, tranquillizer.
calmar, *v.t.* to calm (down), quieten, pacify, soothe; to relieve. — *v.i.* to be calm; to be becalmed; to abate. — **calmarse,** *v.r.* to calm down; to abate.
calmazo, *n.m.* great calm; phlegm; (*naut.*) dead calm.
calmear, *v.i.* to become calm; to calm gradually.
calmil, *n.m.* (*Mex.*) tilled and sown field adjoining a farmhouse.
calmita, *n.f.* calmness; phlegm.
calmo, -ma, *a.* uncultivated, untilled; treeless, barren; fallow; ***mar calma,*** calm sea. — *n.f.* (*naut.*) calm; calmness, tranquillity, composure, quiet, stillness, phlegm, slowness, tardiness; lull; doldrums; (*naut.*) ***calma chicha,*** dead calm; (*naut.*) ***en calma,*** motionless, becalmed (*sea*).
calmoso, -sa, *a.* calm, tranquil, quiet; (*coll.*) slow, sluggish.
calmuco, *a., n.m.f.* Kalmuck.
caló, *n.m.* gipsy slang; cant.
calobiótica, *n.f.* good *or* orderly living.
calocéfalo, -la, *a.* having a beautiful head.
calofilo, -la, *a.* (*bot.*) having beautiful leaves.
calofriarse [L], **calosfriarse,** *v.r.* to shiver with cold; to feel chilly.
calofrío, calosfrío, *n.m.* chill, shiver.
calología, *n.f.* æsthetics.
calomel, *n.m.,* **calomelanos,** *n.m.pl.* (*med.*) calomel.
calón, *n.m.* pole for keeping fishing-nets extended; fathom (pole); (*min.*) sand-covered iron vein (*in Vizcaya*).
caloña, *n.f.* fine *or* damages for slander.
calóptero, -ra, *a.* handsome-winged.
calor, *n.m.* (*phys.*) heat, hotness; warmth; fieriness, fervour; fever; ***calor canicular,*** sweltering heat; ***asarse*** or ***freírse de calor,*** to be stewing *or* sweltering with heat; ***tiene calor,*** he's hot; ***coger*** (***entrar en***) ***calor,*** to get warm; ***dar calor,*** to give out warmth *or* heat; to make feel hot; ***hace calor,*** it is hot (*weather*); ***tomarse algo con calor,*** to undertake sth. enthusiastically; ***no me da ni frío ni calor,*** I don't care either way, it's immaterial to me.
calorescencia, *n.f.* calorescence.
caloría, *n.f.* calory.
caloriamperímetro, *n.m.* (*elec.*) ammeter.
caloricidad, *n.f.* caloricity.
calórico, *n.m.* caloric; heat; ***calórico radiante,*** radiant heat.
calorífero, -ra, *a.* heat-giving. — *n.m.* stove, heater; furnace; foot-warmer; ***calorífero de aire,*** hot-air radiator; ***calorífero de vapor,*** steam-radiator.
calorificación, *n.f.* caloricity.
calorífico, -ca, *a.* calorific.
calorífugo, -ga, *a.* heat-resisting.
calorimetría, *n.f.* (*phys.*) calorimetry.
calorimétrico, -ca, *a.* (*phys.*) calorimetric.
calorímetro, *n.m.* (*phys.*) calorimeter.
calorimotor, *n.m.* (*phys.*) calorimotor.
calorina (*prov.*) [CALINA].
caloso, -sa, *a.* porous (*paper*).
calostro, *n.m.* colostrum.
calota, *n.f.* medicated ringworm cap.
calote, *n.m.* (*prov.*) fraud, hoax.
calotipia, *n.f.* calotype.
caloyo, *n.m.* unborn *or* new-born lamb *or* kid; (*mil., prov.*) raw recruit.
calpamulo, -la, *a.* (*Mex.*) half-breed.
calpixque, *n.m.* (*Mex.*) collector of taxes (*from Indians*).
calpul, *n.m.* (*Hisp. Am.*) meeting, assembly; Indian mound.
calquín, *n.m.* (*Arg.*) Andean eagle.
calseco, -ca, *a.* cured with lime.
calta, *n.f.* (*bot.*) caltha, marsh marigold.
calucha, *n.f.* (*Bol.*) inner rind (*of coconut, almond etc.*).
caluma, *n.f.* (*Per.*) gorge (*Andes*); (*Per.*) Indian village.
calumbarse, *v.r.* (*prov.*) to plunge, dive.
calumbo, *n.m.* (*prov.*) plunge, dive, diving.
calumnia, *n.f.* calumny, slander.

calumniador, -ra, *a.* calumniating, slanderous. — *n.m.f.* calumniator, slanderer.

calumniar, *v.t.* to calumniate, slander.

calumnioso, -sa, *a.* calumnious, slanderous.

calungo, *n.m.* (*Col.*) curly-haired dog.

caluro, *n.m.* (*Hisp. Am.*) climbing bird.

caluroso, -sa, *a.* warm; hot.

caluyo, *n.m.* (*Bol.*) Indian dog-dance.

calva, *n.f.* [CALVO].

calvar, *v.t.* to hit the top of (post *or* horn in the game of ***calva***); to cheat, deceive.

calvario, *n.m.* Calvary; (*coll.*) cross, ordeal; debts.

calvatorio, -ria, *a.* appertaining to baldness.

calvatrueno, *n.m.* (*fam.*) baldness of the whole head; (*coll.*) wild person.

calvaza, *n.f.* big bald pate.

calverizo, -za, *a.* having many bare *or* barren spots (*ground*).

calvero, *n.m.* clearing; clay-pit.

calvez, calvicie, *n.f.* baldness.

calvijar[CALVERO].

calvinismo, *n.m.* Calvinism.

calvinista, *a. n.m.f.* Calvinist.

calvitar [CALVERO].

calvo, -va, *a.* bald, hairless, bald-headed, bald-pated; bare, treeless; napless, threadbare. — *n.f.* bald head *or* patch; treeless *or* bare patch, clearing; threadbare *or* napless patch; (a) game; ***calva de almete,*** crest of a helmet.

calza, *n.f.* breeches; (*fam.*) hose; ribbon (*tied on certain animals*); wedge, scotch (*of a wheel etc.*); (*pl.*) (*slang*) fetters; ***en calzas prietas,*** in a tight fix.

calzacalzón, *n.m.* galligaskins.

calzada, *n.f.* causeway; roadway (*as opposed to pavement*); highway.

calzadera, *n.f.* hempen cord; lace; shoe, drag (*wheel*).

calzado, *n.m.* footwear; (*sl.*) person in fetters.

calzador, *n.m.* shoe-horn; (*Arg.*) pen-holder; ***entra con calzador,*** it takes some doing.

calzadura, *n.f.* act of putting on the shoes; tip for this service; felloe (*of a cart-wheel*).

calzar(se) [C], *v.t.* (*v.r.*) to put on (*shoes, gloves, spurs etc.*); to prop up; to wedge, chock; (*print.*) to overlay, raise, underlay; (*naut.*) ***calzar el ancla,*** to shoe the anchor; ***calzo el 40,*** I take size 7 (*shoes etc.*).

calzo, *n.m.* (*print.*) frisket-sheet, overlay; (*mech.*) wedge, quoin; shoe (*of a felloe*); (*naut.*) skid, chock, bed, shoe; (*rail.*) block, brake-shoe.

calzón, *n.m.* long trouser [CALZA]; safety rope (*used by masons and painters*); ombre; (*Mex.*) disease of the sugar cane; (*pl.* **calzones**) breeches, trousers, (*naut.*) ***en calzones,*** sails arranged as goose-wings; ***calzon(es) blanco(s),*** pants, trunks (*underwear*); ***calzon(es) corto(s),*** knicker-bockers; ***calzarse los calzones,*** to wear the trousers; ***tener bien puestos los calzones,*** to be very manly.

calzonazos, *n.m. inv.* (*coll.*) henpecked husband.

calzoncillos, *n.m.pl.* pants, (*Am.*) underpants.

calzoneras, *n.f.pl.* (*Mex.*) trousers buttoned all the way down both sides.

calla, *n.f.* (*Hisp. Am., agric.*) dibble.

callada (1), *n.f.* meal consisting principally of tripe.

callada (2) [CALLADO].

calladito, *n.m.* (*Chi.*) popular dance.

callado, -da (2), *a.* silent, taciturn; reserved. — *n.f.* silence (*in certain phrases*); (*naut.*) lull; ***a las calladas*** or ***de callada,*** privately, on the quiet; ***dar la callada por respuesta,*** to answer by silence.

callana, *n.f.* (*Hisp. Am.*) flat earthen bowl (*for toasting maize* or *corn*); metallic scoria; crucible (*for assaying metals*); (*Chi.*) big pocket-watch; (*Per.*) flowerpot.

callandico, callandito, *adv.* (*fam.*) in a very low voice, quietly, softly, silently; very secretly, slyly.

callandriz, *n.m.* sly, secretive person.

callao, *n.m.* river pebble; flat ground covered with boulders (*in Canary Islands*).

callapo, *n.m.* (*Chi., min.*) prop, stay; step (*of a ladder* or *stairs in mines*); (*Per.*) stretcher (*in mines*).

callar, *v.t.* to keep quiet, hush up, not to mention; ***callar la verdad,*** to keep the truth quiet; ***callar la boca*** or ***el pico,*** to hold one's tongue, shut up. — **callar(se),** *v.i.* (*v.r.*) to be, become *or* fall silent; be, become *or* keep quiet; to make no reply; to stop talking, playing etc.; ***¡cállate! ¡cállese!*** shut up!; ***¡calla! ¡calle!*** (*fig.*) you don't say! you can't mean it! nonsense!; ***las mata callando,*** he's a quiet, crafty, sly one; ***quien calla otorga,*** silence gives consent; ***al buen callar llaman Sancho,*** silence is golden.

calle, *n.f.* street; lane; (*sl.*) freedom; (*print.*) vertical *or* oblique space; ***calle arriba*** or ***abajo,*** up *or* down the street; ***calle mayor,*** main street, high street; ***abrir*** or ***hacer calle,*** to clear a passage; to make way; ***alborotar la calle,*** to disturb the neighbourhood; ***azotar calles,*** to lounge about the streets; ***dejar en la calle,*** to leave penniless, destitute; ***echar a la calle, poner*** (***plantar***) ***en la calle,*** to throw *or* chuck out, sack; ***echar por la calle de en medio,*** to go ahead regardless; ***echarse a la calle,*** to go out into the street(s); to mutiny, rebel, riot; ***llevarse de calle,*** to carry away, overwhelm; ***rondarle la calle a,*** to court, woo; ***llevarse a la gente de calle,*** to be irresistible, carry all before one; ***quedarse en la calle,*** to be left with nothing.

callear, *v.t.* to clear the walks in (*a vineyard*).

callecalle, *n.m.f.* (*Chi.*) medicinal plant of the Iridaceæ family.

calleja, *n.f.* small street, alley; (*sl.*) escape.

callejear, *v.i.* to walk *or* hang about the streets; to ramble, to wander about.

callejeo, *n.m.* strolling, wandering, loafing.

callejero, -ra, *a.* fond of gadding about. — *n.m.f.* gadabout, gadder, loiterer. — *n.m.* street directory and guide; publisher's list of subscribers.

callejo, *n.m.* (*prov.*) pit *or* trap (*for game*).

callejón, *n.m.* alley, narrow lane; narrow mountain pass; ***callejón sin salida,*** blind alley, dead end, cul-de-sac; (*fig.*) deadlock.

callejoncillo, *n.m.* narrow passage; small lane.

callejuela, *n.f.* alley, lane, narrow passage.

callialto, -ta, *a., n.m.f.* horse-shoe having swelling welts *or* borders.

callicida, *n.f.* corn-remover.

callista, *n.m.f.* chiropodist.

callo, *n.m.* corn, callous (*on feet, hands etc.*); (*surg.*) callus; (*fig., fam.*) ugly creature; (*pl.*) tripe.

callón, -llona, *a.* silent, reserved. — *n.m.* whet-stone, rubber (*for awl*).

callosidad, *n.f.* callosity; (*pl.* **callosidades**) wens.

calloso, -sa, *a.* callous, corny, corneous, horny.

cama, *n.f.* bed; bedstead; place (*in hospitals, schools*); lair *or* couch (*of wild animals*); litter, straw, bedding (*for animals and plants*); (*mech.*) cam; cog; catch; tooth; bed plate; base; (*geol.*) layer, stratum; felloe (*of a wheel*); sheath (*of a plough*); cheek (*of a bridle*); ***cama camera*** or ***sencilla,*** single bed; ***cama de matrimonio,*** double bed; ***caer uno en cama,*** to fall ill; (*fig.*) ***échate en tu cama y piensa en lo de tu casa,*** go to bed and sleep on it; ***estar en, guardar, hacer cama,*** to be confined to bed; ***hacer cama redonda,*** to sleep (all) in the same bed; (*fig.*) ***levantarse por los pies de la cama,*** to get out of bed on the wrong side.

camachuelo, *n.m.* linnet.

camada, *n.f.* litter, brood (*of young animals*); layer; (*min.*) floor of struts; (*coll.*) band (*of thieves*);

ser de la misma camada, to be of the same brood, breed, ilk.
camafeo, *n.m.* cameo.
camagua, *a.* (*Hisp. Am.*) said of maize beginning to ripen.
camahuas, *n.m.pl.* (*Peru*) Camahua people.
camahueto, *n.m.* (*Chi.*) dragon, monster.
camal, *n.m.* hempen halter; pole (*for suspending dead pig*); chain (*for slaves*); (*prov.*) thick branch; (*Per.*) principal slaughterhouse.
camáldula, *n.f.* religious order of Benedictines.
camaldulense, *a.*, *n.m.f.* of *or* belonging to the order of ***Camáldula.***
camaleón, *n.m.* (*zool.*) chameleon; (*coll.*) turn-coat; (*Bol.*) iguana; (*Cub.*) green tree-climbing lizard; ***camaleón mineral,*** permanganate of potash.
camaleonesco, -ca, *a.* chameleonic.
Camaleopardo, *n.m.* (*astron.*) Camelopardalis.
camalero, *n.m.* (*Per.*) slaughterman; butcher.
camalote, *n.m.* (*Hisp. Am.*) river plant forming a floating island.
camama, *n.f.* (*coll.*) sham, humbug.
camambú, *n.m.* (*Hisp. Am.*) camambu plant.
camamila, *n.f.* (*bot.*) common camomile.
camanance, *n.m.* (*C.R.*) dimple.
camanchaca, *n.f.* (*Chi.*, *Per.*) thick fog.
camándula, *n.f.* chaplet *or* rosary of one *or* three decades; (*coll.*) hypocrisy, astuteness; ***tener muchas camándulas,*** to be very tricky.
camandular, camandulear, *v.i.* to feign religious devotion, be a hypocrite.
camandulense, *a.*, *n.m.f.* belonging to the religious order of ***Camáldula*** *or* reformed Benedictines.
camandulería, *n.f.* hypocrisy, insincerity, dissimulation; prudery.
camandulero, -ra, *a.* tricky, hypocritical. — *n.m.f.* hypocrite, trickster, rogue.
camanonca, *n.f.* material formerly used for lining.
camao, *n.m.* (*Cub.*) small wild pigeon.
cámara, *n.f.* chamber; granary, barn; (*naut.*) cabin; (*motor.*) inner tube; (*photo.*) camera; (*pl.*) diarrhœa; ***cámara apostólica,*** pontifical exchequer; ***cámara del rey,*** royal exchequer; ***Cámara de los Comunes,*** House of Commons; ***Cámara de los Lores,*** House of Lords; ***Cámara alta,*** Upper House; ***Cámara baja,*** Lower House; ***cámara mortuoria,*** funeral parlour, chapel of rest; ***cámara obscura,*** camera obscura; ***cámara de comercio,*** chamber of commerce; ***ayuda de cámara,*** valet; ***moza de cámara,*** chambermaid; ***pintor de cámara,*** court painter; ***irse uno de cámaras,*** to suffer from diarrhœa.
camarada, *n.m.* comrade, mate, chum.
camaradería, *n.f.* comradeship.
camaraje, *n.m.* rent for a granary.
camaranchón, *n.m.* garret, attic.
camarera, *n.f.* waitress; chambermaid; lady-in-waiting.
camarería, *n.f.* place *or* employment of a chambermaid; ancient perquisite of the lord chamberlain.
camarero, *n.m.* waiter; chamberlain; steward; keeper of stores.
camareta, *n.f.* small bed-chamber; (*naut.*) small cabin; deck-cabin; midshipman's cabin; (*Arg.*, *Chi.*, *Per.*) maroon (*firework*).
camareto, *n.m.* (*Cub.*) sweet potato.
camarico, *n.m.* (*Hisp. Am.*) offering of the Indians to their priests and afterwards to the Spaniards; (*Chi.*) favourite place; (*Chi.*) love affair.
camariento, -ta, *a.* having diarrhœa.
camarilla, *n.f.* (palace) clique.
camarín, *n.m.* small room; place behind an altar where images are dressed and ornaments destined for that purpose are kept; (*theat.*) dressing-room; closet; private office.
camarista, *n.m.* member of the supreme council. — *n.f.* maid of honour to the queen and the ***infantas*** of Spain.
camarlengato, *n.m.* office of a ***camarlengo.***
camarlengo, *n.m.* lord of the bed-chamber of the kings of Aragon; chamberlain to the Pope.
camarón, *n.m.* large shrimp, small prawn; (*C.R.*) tip, gratuity.
camaronero, -ra, *n.m.f.* prawn *or* shrimp seller; shrimper. — *n.f.* shrimp-net. — *n.m.* (*Per.*, *orn.*) kingfisher.
camarote, *n.m.* (*naut.*) state-room, berth, cabin.
camarotero, *n.m.* (*Hisp. Am.*) cabin steward.
camarroya, *n.f.* (*bot.*) wild chicory.
camasquince, *n.m.f.* meddlesome person.
camastra, *n.f.* (*Chi.*) cunning, trickery.
camastrear, *v.t.* (*Chi.*) to dissemble.
camastro, *n.m.* rickety old bed.
camastrón, -rona, *a.*, *n.m.f.* (*coll.*) artful, cunning, sly (*person*).
camastronería, *n.f.* artfulness, cunning, slyness.
camatón, *n.m.* (*prov.*) small bundle of firewood.
camauro, *n.m.* Pope's red cap.
camba, *n.f.* cheek (*of a bridle*); (*prov.*) felloe; (*pl.*) gores, V-shaped pieces in garments.
cambado, -da, *a.* bowlegged.
cambalache, *n.m.* (*coll.*) barter; bartering, swap, swapping; (*Arg.*) second-hand shop.
cambalachear, *v.t.* to barter, swap.
cambalachero, -ra, *a.* bartering. — *n.m.f.* barterer.
cambalada, *n.f.* (*prov.*) stagger, swaying; ***ir dando cambaladas,*** to stagger along.
cambaleo, *n.m.* strolling troupe of players.
cambar, *v.t.* to bend; to curve.
cámbaro, *n.m.* crab.
cambera, *n.f.* net (*for crab and shrimp fishing*).
cambeto, -ta, *a.* (*Ven.*) bowlegged.
cambiable, *a.* fit to be bartered; exchangeable.
cambiada, *n.f.* (*equit.*) change of gait; (*naut.*) change (*of course etc.*).
cambiadizo, -za, *a.* changeable, changing.
cambiador, -ra, *a.* changing. — *n.m.* barterer, money-changer; (*sl.*) brothel proprietor; (*Chi.*, *Mex.*, *railw.*) switchman.
cambiamiento, *n.m.* change, alteration, mutation.
cambiante, *a.* changing; bartering, exchanging. — *n.m.* banker, money-changer; (*pl.*) iridescence; shot, chatoyant fabrics.
cambiar, *v.t.*, *v.i.* to change, alter; to exchange; to veer (*wind*); ***cambiar la peseta,*** to be sick; ***cambiar de propósito,*** to change one's plans; ***cambiar de idea,*** to change one's mind; ***cambiar de manos,*** to change hands; ***cambiar (alguna cosa) con, por otra,*** to exchange (*one thing*) for another; ***cambiar plata en calderilla,*** to change silver into small copper coins. — **cambiarse,** *v.r.* to change, turn (***en,*** into); to veer (*wind*); ***se cambió su alegría en tristeza,*** their joy turned to sorrow.
cambiavía, *n.m.* (*Cub.*, *Mex.*, *railw.*) switch; switchman.
cambiazo, *n.m.* (sudden) change-over, switch-over; ***dar (pegar) el cambiazo,*** to do a (quick) switch.
cambija, *n.f.* reservoir, basin of water.
cambín, *n.m.* round rush fishing-basket *or* net.
cambio, *n.m.* change, alteration; small change; (*com.*) premium paid *or* received (*for negotiating bills, changing money etc.*); (*com.*) quotation price (*of stocks and shares*); (*com.*) rate of exchange (*of money*); (*railw.*) switch, point; (*law*) barter, exchange; ***letra de cambio,*** bill of exchange; ***libre cambio,*** free trade; ***cambio minuto,*** rate of money exchange; ***a las primeras de cambio,*** at the first opportunity; all of a sudden; ***a cambio (de),*** in exchange (for); ***en cambio,*** on the other hand, instead.
cambista, *n.m.* money-changer, money-broker; ***libre cambista,*** free-trader.

Camboya, *n.f.* Cambodia.
camboyano, -na, *a.*, *n.m.f.* Cambodian. — *n.m.* Cambodian (*language*).
cambray, *n.m.* cambric, fine linen.
cambrayón, *n.m.* coarse cambric.
cambriano, -na, cámbrico, -ca, *a.* (*geol.*) Cambrian. — *a.*, *n.m.f.* Cambrian, Welsh.
cambrillón, *n.m.* inner sole of shoe.
cambrón, *n.m.* (*bot.*) buckthorn; hawthorn; (*pl.* **cambrones**) brambles.
cambronal, *n.m.* thicket of briars, brambles etc.
cambronera, *n.f.* (*bot.*) box-thorn.
cambrún, *n.m.* (*Col.*) home-made wool cloth.
cambucho, *n.m.* (*Chi.*) paper cone; cornucopia; waste-basket; hut, hovel; straw envelope for bottles; small kite (*toy*).
cambuí, *n.m.* American myrtle-tree.
cambuj, *n.m.* child's cap; veil; mask.
cambujo, -ja, *a.* reddish-black (*donkey*); (*Mex.*) mestizo; half-breed.
cambullón, *n.m.* (*Per.*) imposition, swindle; (*Col., Mex.*) second-hand shop; barter.
cambur, *n.m.* banana.
camedafne, *n.f.* (*bot.*) dwarf-bay; daphne.
camedrio, *n.m.*, **camedris,** *n.m. inv.* (*bot.*) wall-germander, germander speedwell.
camedrita, *n.f.* germander wine.
camelador, -ra, *a.* cajoling; deceiving. — *n.m.f.* cajoler; deceiver.
camelar, *v.t.* (*fam.*) to win over (*a person, woman*); to butter up, cajole; to deceive, take in.
camelete, *n.f.* large cannon.
camelia, *n.f.* (*bot.*) camellia; (*Cub.*) poppy.
camélidos, *n.m.pl.* mammalians belonging to the camel and dromedary group.
camelo, *n.m.* (*fam.*) fake, blarney; put-up job, gimmick.
camelote, *n.m.* camlet.
camelotero, -ra, *n.m.f.* camlet maker *or* vendor.
camelotina, *n.f.* cameline, fine camlet.
camelotón, *n.m.* coarse camlet.
camella, *n.f.* she-camel; ridge (*in ploughed land*); wooden trough *or* milk-pail; bow (*of animal's yoke*).
camellar, *a.* camel-like, camelish.
camellería, *n.f.* employment of a camel-driver.
camellero, *n.m.* keeper *or* driver of camels.
camello, *n.m.* (*zool.*) camel; ancient cannon; (*naut.*) camel; ***camello pardal,*** giraffe.
camellón, *n.m.* ridge (*turned up by plough* or *spade*); drinking-trough (*for cattle*); camlet.
camena, *n.f.* (*poet.*) Muse.
camera (1), *n.f.* (*Col.*) wild rabbit.
camero, -ra (2), *a.* belonging to a single bed. — *n.m.f.* upholsterer; one who lets beds on hire.
Camerón, *n.m.* Cameroons.
camia, *n.f.* (*Philip.*) camia tree.
camibar, *n.m.* (*C.R., Nic.*) copaiba tree; balsam of copaiba.
cámica, *n.f.* (*Chi.*) slope (*of roof*).
camilucho, -cha, *n.m.f.* (*Hisp. Am.*) Indian farm labourer.
camilla, *n.f.* stretcher; couch; (***mesa***) ***camilla,*** table with heater underneath.
camillero, *n.m.* stretcher-bearer.
caminada, *n.f.* day's journey.
caminador, -ra, *n.m.f.* good walker.
caminante, *n.m.f.* wayfarer; passer-by. — *n.m.* running footman; (*Chi.*) small lark.
caminar, *v.i.* to walk; to go; to travel; to trek; to move along.
caminata, *n.f.* (*fam.*) long walk, trek.
caminero, -ra, *a.* relating to the road; ***peón caminero,*** road-man.
camini, *n.m.* (*Arg.*) best quality maté.
camino, *n.m.* road, lane, path; way, route; ***camino trillado,*** beaten track; (*mil.*) ***camino cubierto,*** covert-way; ***camino de herradura,*** bridle-path; ***camino de hierro,*** iron road, railway; ***camino de Santiago,*** Milky Way; ***camino de sirga,*** tow path; ***camino real,*** highroad, highway; (*fig.*) royal road; ***camino vecinal,*** country, local road; ***abrir camino,*** to clear, lead the way; ***abrirse camino,*** to make one's way, get on; ***coger el camino,*** to go off, clear out; ***echarse al camino,*** to take to the road(s) (*as a robber, highwayman*); ***estar de camino,*** to be on the way; to be travelling; to be in travelling attire, dressed for the road; (*fig.*) ***ir fuera de camino,*** to be off the rails, up the creek; ***ir por buen camino,*** to be on the right track, have the right idea; ***interceptar el camino,*** to bar, block the way; ***llevar camino de,*** to show signs of, look likely to; ***salirle a alguien al camino,*** to go to meet s.o., meet s.o. on the way; to hold s.o. up (*of highwayman etc.*); ***traer a*** (***al***) ***buen camino,*** to put right, put on the right road; ***ponerse en camino,*** to set off, start out; ***quedarse a medio camino,*** to stop half-way; ***romper un camino,*** to open up a new road.
camión, *n.m.* lorry, (*Am.*) truck.
camionaje, *n.m.* truck transport, truckage.
camioneta, *n.f.* motor-van.
camisa, *n.f.* shirt; shift, chemise; (snake's) slough; thin skin (*of almonds* or *other fruit*); (*mil.*) chemise; jacket, case, casing; lining (*of a furnace*); incandescent gas-mantle; paper wrapper of documents; (*print.*) linen case for roller; (*Chi.*) paper-lining; jacket, cover (*of book*); (*naut.*) ***camisa embreada,*** fire-chemise; ***camisa de fuerza,*** strait-jacket; (*naut.*) ***camisa de una vela,*** body of a sail; ***dejar a uno sin camisa,*** to take the shirt off s.o.'s back: ***jugar*** (***empeñar, vender***) ***hasta la camisa,*** to stake (pawn, sell) the very shirt off one's back; ***meterse en camisa de once varas,*** to get out of one's depth, to bite off more than one can chew; to meddle with other people's business; ***no llegarle a uno la camisa al cuerpo,*** to be on tenter-hooks; ***en mangas de camisa,*** in shirt sleeves.
camisería, *n.f.* shirt-shop; men's outfitters.
camisero, -ra, *n.m.f.* shirt-maker.
camiseta, *n.f.* vest; (sport) shirt.
camisola, *n.f.* (labourer's) shirt; blouse.
camisolín, *n.m.* shirt-front; tucker; camisole; dicky; chemisette, modesty vest.
camisón, *n.m.* night-shirt; night-dress; (*Hisp. Am.*) chemise.
camisote, *n.m.* hauberk.
camistrajo, *n.m.* (*fam.*) pallet, poor bed.
camita, *a.*, *n.m.f.* Hamite.
camítico, -ca, *a.* Hamitic.
camoatí, *n.m.* (*River Plate*) wasp.
camocán, *n.m.* brocade.
camodar, *v.t.* (*sl.*) to disarrange, muddle.
camomila, *n.f.* (*bot.*) camomile.
camón, *n.m.* large bed; portable throne; conservatory, glass-enclosed balcony; curved piece of a water-wheel frame; (*arch.*) lath frame; ***camón de vidrios,*** glass partition; (*pl.* **camones**) oak tyres of cart-wheels.
camoncillo, *n.m.* stool.
camorra, *n.f.* (*fam.*) quarrel, wrangle; ***armar camorra,*** to make trouble, pick a quarrel; ***buscar camorra,*** to (be) look(ing) for a fight.
camorrear, *v.i.* (*Aragon, fam.*) to make trouble.
camorrista, *a.*, *n.m.f.* quarrelsome, pugnacious (*person*).
camote, *n.m.* (*Hisp. Am.*) sweet potato; (*Hisp. Am.*) infatuation; (*Hisp. Am.*) lover, mistress; (*Hisp. Am.*) lie, fib; (*Mex.*) knave, scoundrel; (*E.S.*) wale, welt; (*Ec., Mex.*) silly, stupid.
camotear, *v.i.* (*Mex.*) to roam, loiter.

camotero, -ra, *n.m.f.* (*Mex.*) seller of sweet potatoes.
camotillo, *n.m.* (*Per.*) sweet potato jam; (*Mex.*) violet-coloured wood with black streaks; (*E.S., Guat., Hond.*) curcuma; (*C.R.*) sago.
camp, *a.* (typical) of the forties, forties' style; outmoded; (*fam.*) old hat.
campa, *a.* ***tierra campa,*** plain; treeless (*ground*).
campal, *a.* belonging to the field, camp, open country; ***batalla campal,*** pitched battle.
campamento, *n.m.* camp, encampment.
campana, *n.f.* bell; bell glass, bell jar; canopy (*of electrical fixture*); bottom (*of a well*); (*fig.*) parish church, parish; curfew; ***campana de chimenea,*** hood of a chimney; ***campana de buzo,*** diving-bell; ***campana de rebato,*** alarm-bell; ***campana de cristal,*** bell-glass; ***a toque de campana,*** at the sound of a bell; (*fig.*) at the double; ***doblar las campanas,*** to toll the knell; ***echar las campanas a vuelo,*** to rejoice loudly, cry out from the housetops; ***oír campanas y no saber dónde,*** to have a vague notion *or* recollection; (*naut.*) ***picar la campana,*** to sound the bell.
campanada, *n.f.* stroke, ring, sound of a bell; (*fig.*) scandal, sensational report; ***dar una (la) campanada,*** to create a stir, cause a scandal.
campanario, *n.m.* belfry; ***de campanario,*** local, mean, narrow-minded, short-sighted; ***política de campanario,*** local, petty politics; narrow-minded, short-sighted policy.
campanear, *v.t., v.i.* to ring (*bells*); to spread abroad. — **campanearse,** *v.r.* to strut, swagger.
campanela, *n.f.* fancy step (*in dancing*); (*mus.*) natural stroke (*guitar*).
campaneo, *n.m.* bell-ringing, chime; (*coll.*) strut(ting), swagger(ing).
campanero, *n.m.* bell-founder; bell-ringer; (*Ven.*) (*orn.*) bellbird.
campanil, *a.* ***metal campanil,*** bell-metal. — *n.m.* belfry, bell tower.
campanilla, *n.f.* small bell, door-bell, hand-bell; electric chime; (*naut.*) cabin-bell; (*bot.*) bell-flower; small bubble; (*anat.*) epiglottis, uvula; little tassel, bell-shaped dress fringe; (*print.*) loose, ill-adjusted type; ***persona de (muchas) campanillas,*** distinguished person, V.I.P.
campanillazo, *n.m.* violent ringing of a bell; signal given with a bell.
campanillear, *v.i.* to ring often, reverberate.
campanilleo, *n.m.* ringing, jingle, tinkle.
campanillero, *n.m.* bellman, town crier.
campano, *n.m.* cattle-bell.
campanología, *n.f.* campanology.
campanólogo, -ga, *n.m.f.* (*mus.*) campanologist.
campante, *a.* (*fam.*) self-satisfied, cheerful; ***tan campante,*** as pleased as Punch.
campanudo, -da, *a.* bell-shaped; puffed up (*clothes*); (*fig.*) resonant, ringing; pompous, high-sounding; (*bot.*) campanulate, campanular.
campánula, *n.f.* (*bot.*) bell-flower, campanula.
campanuláceo, -cea, *a.* (*bot.*) campanulaceous. — *n.f.pl.* Campanulaceæ.
campaña, *n.f.* level country; (*Hisp. Am.*) country; (*mil.*) campaign; (*mil.*) each year of active service; (*naut.*) ***campaña naval,*** cruise; ***batir*** or ***correr la campaña,*** to reconnoitre; (*mil.*) ***salir a campaña,*** take the field.
campañista, *n.m.* (*Chi.*) highland shepherd.
campañol, *n.m.* (*zool.*) field-mouse.
campar, *v.i.* to excel, stand out; (*mil.*) to encamp, be encamped; ***campar con su estrella,*** to be fortunate; ***campar por su respeto,*** to be a lone wolf, to go one's own way.
campeador, *a.* surpassingly valiant. — *n.m.* combatant, warrior.
campear, *v.i.* to be in the field; to pasture; to frisk about; to grow, crop out; to excel, be eminent; (*mil.*) to campaign; reconnoitre.
campechana (1), *n.f.* (*Cub. Mex.*), refreshing drink; (*Ven.*) hammock; (*Ven.*) harlot.
campechanía, *n.f.* (*prov.*) frankness, heartiness.
campechano, -na (2), *a.* frank, hearty, open, hail-fellow-well-met; (*Mex.*) native of *or* belonging to Campeche. — *n.f.* (*naut.*) grating, lattice-work.
campeche, *n.m.* Campeche wood, log-wood.
campeón, -peona, *n.m.f.* champion.
campeonato, *n.m.* championship.
campero, -ra, *a.* exposed to the weather in the open field; unsheltered, unhoused, sleeping out (*cattle*); (*Mex.*) having a gait like gentle trotting horses; ***fiesta campera,*** country festivity. — *n.m.* friar who superintends a farm; field-guard.
campesino, -na, *a.* rural, rustic, country. — *n.m.f.* countryman, peasant.
campestre, *a.* rural, country-like.
campilán, *n.m.* (*Philip.*) straight, long sabre broadening at the point.
campillo, *n.m.* small field; common, public land.
camping, *n.m.* camping; camping site; picnic; ***hacer camping,*** to go camping.
campiña, *n.f.* flat tract of arable land, field; country; landscape.
campirano, -na, *a.* (*Hisp. Am.*) churlish, unmannerly. — *n.m.f.* countryman, countrywoman; expert in farming; tamer; horse-breaker.
campista, *n.m.* (*Hisp. Am.*) owner *or* partner of a mine; foreman inspecting cattle on the savanna.
campo, *n.m.* field; country; countryside; district; (*fig.*) scope, range, sphere; (*mil.*) camp; (*her.*) field; ground of patterned materials, papers etc.; (*paint.*) background, groundwork; ***campo de Agramante,*** babel, bedlam; ***campo de batalla,*** battlefield; ***campo de concentración,*** concentration camp; prisoner-of-war camp; ***campo de honor,*** duelling-ground; field of honour; ***campo magnético,*** magnetic field; ***campo raso,*** flat country; plain; ***campo de trabajo,*** work camp; ***campo visual,*** field of vision; ***campos Elíseos,*** Elysian fields; ***hombre de campo,*** country lover; ***hombre del campo,*** countryman; ***a campo raso,*** in the open field, out of doors; ***a campo traviesa*** or ***travieso,*** cross-country; ***batir, descubrir*** or ***reconocer el campo,*** to reconnoitre; ***dejar el campo abierto (expedito, libre),*** to leave the field *or* way clear; ***dar campo a,*** to give free range to; ***echarse al campo,*** to take to the country; to rise in revolt; ***juntar campo,*** to raise an army; ***levantar el campo,*** to raise camp; to pack up; ***partir el campo,*** to mark out a duelling ground; ***quedar el campo por uno, quedar señor del campo,*** to carry the day, come out best.
camposanto, *n.m.* churchyard, graveyard.
camuatí, *n.f.* (*Arg.*) hut, cabin.
camucha, *n.f.* (*fam.*) wretched little bed.
camuesa, *n.f.* (*bot.*) pippin, apple.
camueso, *n.m.* (*bot.*) pippin-tree; (*coll.*) dunce, fool.
camuflaje, *n.m.* camouflage.
camuflar, *v.t.* to camouflage.
camuliano, -na, *a.* (*Hond.*) beginning to ripen.
camuñas, *n.f.pl.* all seeds except barley, wheat and rye; (*coll.*) ***el tío Camuñas,*** the bogeyman.
camuza [GAMUZA].
can (1), *n.m.* dog; (*arch.*) bracket, shoulder, corbel; modillion; trigger (*of gun*); ancient piece of ordnance; ***can de busca,*** terrier; ***Can Mayor,*** Canis Major; ***Can Menor,*** Canis Minor.
can (2), *n.m.* khan, prince *or* chief (*N. Asia*), governor (*Persia*).
cana (1), *n.f.* (*Cub.*) wild palm-tree.
cana (2), [CANO].
canabíneo, -nea, *a.* pertaining to the hemp family. — *n.f.pl.* (**canabíneas**), hemp family.
canáceo, -cea, *a.* (*bot.*) cannaceous. — *n.f.pl.* (**canáceas**) Cannaceæ.
canaco, -ca, *a., n.m.f.* (*Hisp. Am., pej.*) appertaining to the yellow races; brothel keeper.

canacuate, *n.m.* (*Mex.*) large aquatic serpent.
Canadá, *n.m.* Canada.
canadiense, *a., n.m.f.* Canadian.
canadillo, *n.m.* horse-tail tree.
canadio, *n.m.* metal of the platinum group.
canal, *n.m.* channel; canal; waterway; (*anat.*) duct; pharynx. — *n.m.f.* long, narrow dell; gas- *or* water-pipe, conduit; gutter, duct, pantile; drinking-trough; (*arch.*) stria, groove; crease, slot in metal *or* wood-work; animal carcase cleaned and gutted; weaver's comb; hemp once hackled; front edge of a book; ***Canal de la Mancha,*** English Channel; ***canal maestra,*** principal gutter (*of roof*); ***abrir en canal,*** to cut from top to bottom, slit open.
canalado, -da, *a.* fluted, corrugated. — *n.m.* (*prov.*) aqueduct cavity.
canaladura, *n.f.* (*arch.*) vertical groove.
canaleja, *n.f.* small canal; small drinking-trough; mill-hopper spout.
canalera, *n.f.* (*prov.*) roof-gutter; (*prov.*) rain falling from this gutter.
canaleta, *n.f.* (*Chi.*) mill-hopper spout.
canalete, *n.m.* single- or double-bladed paddle for canoeing; small oar; (*naut.*) winding-frame for spun yarn.
canalí, *n.m.* (*Cub.*) paddle for canoeing made of palm.
canalizable, *a.* that can be canalized.
canalización, *n.f.* canalization; (*elec.*) wiring.
canalizar [C], *v.t.* to open a channel, make a canal in; to channel.
canalizo, *n.m.* narrow channel between two islands *or* sand-banks.
canalón, *n.m.* gutter; priest's hat.
canalla, *n.f.* rabble, scum. — *n.m.* (*coll.*) bounder, cad, rotter.
canallada, *n.f.* caddish thing to do.
canallesco, -ca, *a.* caddish, base.
canameño, *n.m.* (*Hisp. Am.*) hammock.
canana, *n.f.* cartridge-belt.
cananeo, -nea, *a.* appertaining to Canaan. — *n.m.f.* Canaanite.
cananga, *n.f.* fragrant plant used in perfumery.
canapé, *n.m.* sofa, couch, settee; savoury.
Canarias, *n.f.pl.* Canary Islands.
canariera, *n.f.* large cage for canaries.
canario, -ria, *a.* appertaining to the Canary Islands. — *n.m.* canary; Canary Islands dance; (*naut.*) barge; (*Chi.*) generous tipper; water-filled toy-whistle (*imitating song of canary*).
canasta, *n.f.* basket, crate, hamper.
canastada, *n.f.* basketful, crateful.
canastero, -ra, *n.m.f.* basket-maker *or* seller; (*Chi.*) fruit and vegetable pedlar; (*Chi.*) assistant baker; (*Chi.*) blackbird.
canastilla, *n.f.* small basket; gift (*to ladies of the court*); layette.
canastillo, *n.m.* small wicker tray; small basket.
canasto, *n.m.* basket. — *interj.* ***¡canastos!*** crikey!
cancagua, *n.f.* (*Chi.*) fine sand (*used for brick-making and building*).
cáncamo, *n.m.* gum, resin; hook; surge, swell (*sea*).
cancamurria, *n.f.* (*coll.*) sadness, melancholy.
cancamusa, *n.f.* (*coll.*) trick.
cancán, *n.m.* cancan; ample petticoat.
cáncana (1), *n.f.* punishment-stool.
cáncana (2), *n.f.* spider.
cancanear, *v.i.* (*fam.*) to rove, wander about; (*Hisp. Am.*) to stammer.
cáncano, *n.m.* (*fam.*) louse.
cancel, *n.m.* iron-work door *or* screen (*in churches etc.*).
cancela, *n.f.* front-door grating *or* screen.
cancelación, *n.f.* cancellation.
cancelar, *v.t.* to cancel, annul.
cancelaría, cancelería, *n.f.* papal chancery.
cancelariato, *n.m.* chancellorship.
cancelario, *n.m.* chancellor (*of a university*).
Cáncer, *n.m.* (*astron., astrol.*) Cancer.
cáncer, *n.m.* (*med.*) cancer.
cancerar, *v.t.* to render cancerous; (*fig.*) to consume, destroy; (*fig.*) to mortify, punish, reprove. — **cancerarse,** *v.r.* to get cancer; to turn cancerous.
Cancerbero, *n.m.* (*myth.*) Cerberus; (*fig.*) watch-dog, guard.
cancerif ɔrme, *a.* cancriform.
canceroso, -sa, *a.* cancerous.
cancilla, *n.f.* lattice *or* wicker door *or* gate.
canciller, *n.m.* chancellor.
cancillerato, *n.m.* chancellorship.
cancilleresco, -ca, *a.* belonging to a chancellery.
cancillería, *n.f.* chancellery.
cancín, *n.m.* puppy; one-year-old sheep.
canción, *n.f.* song; tune; rhyme; lay; ***canción de cuna,*** cradle-song, lullaby; ***mudar de canción,*** to change one's tune; ***volver a la misma canción,*** to harp back to the same old tune.
cancioncita, *n.f.* (delightful) little song, tune *or* ditty.
cancionero, *n.m.* song-book, collection of lyrics; (*mus.*) book of airs.
cancioneta, *n.f.* little song, canzonet.
cancionista, *n.m.f.* folk-singer, ballad-singer.
canco, *n.m.* earthenware stewpot; flower-pot; (*Bol.*) buttock, rump; wide hips.
cancón, *n.m.* (*fam.*) bogeyman.
cancrinita, *n.f.* (*min.*) variety of nepheline with carbonate of lime.
cancro, *n.m.* canker.
cancrófago, -ga, *a.* crab-eating.
cancroide, *n.m.* (*med.*) cancroid.
cancroideo, -dea, *a.* cancroid, cancriform.
cancha, *n.f.* pit (*cockfighting*); (*Hisp. Am.*) roasted corn *or* broad beans; (*Hisp. Am.*) (pelota) court; ***cancha de tenis,*** tennis court; (*Hisp. Am.*) sports field *or* ground; race course. — *interj.* (*Arg.*) ***¡cancha!*** give way! out of the way!
canchal, *n.m.* rocky ground, stony place.
canchalagua, canchelagua, *n.f.* (*Per.*) medicinal plant.
cancho, *n.m.* big boulder *or* rock.
candado, *n.m.* padlock; (*prov.*) tendril (*of vine*); (*Col.*) goatee.
candaliza, *n.f.* (*naut.*) brail.
candamo, *n.m.* ancient rustic dance.
candar, *v.t.* to padlock.
cándara, *n.f.* (*prov.*) sifting-screen, sieve.
cande, candi, *a.* candied; ***azúcar cande,*** sugar-candy.
candeal, candial, *a.* white and of first quality (*flour*); ***pan candeal,*** bread made of white wheat; ***trigo candeal,*** white wheat, summer wheat.
candela, *n.f.* candlestick; candle; flower *or* blossom of chestnut-tree; inclination of the balance-needle to the object weighed; light, fire; ***se acabó la candela,*** it's sold out, it's finished; ***arrimar candela,*** to give a drubbing; ***arrimarse a la candela,*** to seek protection; ***como unas candelas,*** bright, gay; (*naut.*) ***en candela,*** in a vertical position (*masts*); ***estar con la candela en la mano,*** to be dying.
candelabro, *n.m.* candelabrum, candelabra.
candelada, *n.f.* bonfire, blaze.
candelaria, *n.f.* Candlemas; (*bot.*) mullein.
candelecho, *n.m.* hut built on piles for watching a vineyard.
candeleja, *n.f.* (*Chi., Per.*) socket pan of a candle-stick.
candelejón, -jona, *a.* (*Chi., Col., Per.*) naïve, silly.

candelerazo, *n.m.* blow given with a candlestick.

candelero, *n.m.* candlestick; student's lamp; fishing-torch; candle-maker *or* seller; (*naut.*) stanchion; (*naut.*) ***candelero ciego,*** stanchion without top ring; (*naut.*) ***candelero de ojo,*** eye-stanchion; ***estar en candelero,*** to be in the news, be topical.

candelilla, *n.f.* (*surg.*) bougie, catheter; (*bot.*) blossom (*of holm-oak and cork-trees*); (*bot.*) catkin, ament; children's game; (*Cub.*) hem; (*Hisp. Am.*) glow-worm, firefly; (*Hisp. Am.*) jack-o'-lantern; will-o'-the-wisp, ignis fatuus; (*coll.*) ***se le hacen candelillas los ojos,*** his eyes light up (*with interest, desire etc.*).

candelizo, *n.m.* icicle, shoot of ice.

candencia, *n.f.* candescence, incandescence, white heat.

candente, *a.* candescent, incandescent, white-hot; red-hot; ***cuestión candente,*** burning question.

candi [CANDE].

candial [CANDEAL].

candidación, *n.f.* crystallization (*of sugar*).

candidato, *n.m.* candidate, runner.

candidatura, *n.f.* candidature, candidateship; list of candidates.

candidez, *n.f.* whiteness; ingenuousness, simplicity.

cándido, -da, *a.* white, snowy; guileless, simple.

candiel, *n.m.* sweetmeat (*made of white wine, eggs, sugar etc.*).

candil, *n.m.* oil-lamp; (*coll.*) point (*of cocked hat*); (*coll.*) long irregular fold (*in petticoats*); top (*of stag's horn*); (*Mex.*) chandelier; (*Cub.*) pink fish; (*pl.* **candiles**) (*bot.*) wake-robin; ***baile de candil,*** rustic ball; ***a moco de candil,*** closely; ***ni buscado con un candil,*** just the thing, the very man for the job; ***candil sin mecha,*** white elephant, useless object; ***candil en la calle y oscuridad en la casa,*** a bright spark outside but a dull dog at home.

candilada, *n.f.* (*coll.*) oil spilt from a lamp.

candileja, *n.f.* oil receptacle (*for a lamp*); (*bot.*) lucerne; (*pl.*) footlights; limelight.

candilejo, *n.m.* small kitchen-lamp; (*bot.*) lucerne.

candilera, *n.f.* (*bot.*) lampwick.

candilero, *n.m.* (*prov.*) drilled slat (*for hanging lamps*).

candiletear, *v.i.* (*prov.*) to idle, roam about.

candiletero, -ra, *n.m.f.* (*prov.*) idler, gossip.

candilillos, *n.m.pl.* (*bot.*) wake-robin.

candilón, *n.m.* large oil lamp.

candiota, *a., n.m.f.* Candiot, Cretan. — *n.f.* barrel *or* keg (*wine*); large earthen jar (*wine*).

candiotera, *n.f.* wine-cellar; collection of casks.

candiotero, *n.m.* cooper; maker *or* seller of casks.

candita, *n.f.* (*min.*) black aluminate of magnesia.

candombe, *n.m.* (*Hisp. Am.*) low, coarse Negro dance.

candongo, -ga, *a., n.m.f.* (*coll.*) toadying, toady; shirker. — *n.f.* (*coll.*) cajolery; (*coll.*) merry, playful trick, practical joke; (*fam.*) draught-mule; (*Hond., med.*) binder; (*naut.*) storm-sail; (*pl.*) (*Col.*) earrings.

candonguear, *v.t.* (*coll.*) to sneer at; jeer at; to tease; to play practical jokes on. — *v.i.* to shirk work.

candonguero, -ra, *a.* joking, teasing. — *n.m.f.* (*coll.*) practical joker; toady.

candor, *n.m.* sparkling whiteness; purity; ingenuousness, candour, simplicity.

candoroso, -sa, *a.* ingenuous, simple-minded.

candujo, *n.m.* (*slang*) padlock.

cané, *n.m.* card game.

caneca (1), *n.f.* stone bottle.

canecillo, *n.m.* (*arch.*) corbel, truss, modillion, cantilever; console.

caneco, -ca (2), *a.* (*Bol.*) intoxicated, drunk.

canéfora, *n.f.* jar, vase.

canela, *n.f.* [CANELO].

canelado, -da, *a.* cinnamon-coloured.

canelar, *n.m.* cinnamon-tree plantation.

canelero, *n.m.* cinnamon-tree.

canelo, -la, *a.* cinnamon-coloured. — *n.m.* (*bot.*) cinnamon-tree; ***hacer el canelo,*** to play the fool; ***hacerse el canelo,*** to drag one's feet. — *n.f.* (*bot.*) cinnamon; ***canela fina,*** first-rate stuff.

canelón, *n.m.* gargoyle; gutter; icicle; tubular fringe; bullion (*on epaulets*); cinnamon candy; (*pl.* **canelones**) ends of a cat-o'-nine-tails; cannelloni.

canequí, *n.m.* fine muslin.

canero, *n.m.* (*prov.*) coarse bran.

canesú, *n.m.* corset-cover; yoke (*of shirt* or *blouse*).

caney, *n.m.* (*Cub.*) bend (*of river*); (*Cub., Ven.*) log cabin.

canfeno, *n.m.* (*chem.*) carbohydrate (*made by treating artificial camphor with lime*).

canfín, *n.m.* (*C.R.*) petroleum.

canforado, -da, *a.* camphorated.

canforato, *n.m.* (*chem.*) camphorate.

canforero, *n.m.* (*bot.*) camphor-tree.

canfórico, -ca, *a.* (*chem.*) camphoric.

canforífero, -ra, *a.* (*bot.*) producing camphor.

canga, *n.f.* (*prov.*) coupling, yoking; cang; (*Hisp. Am.*) iron ore mixed with clay.

cangagua, *n.f.* (*Ec.*) earth for making adobe.

cangalla, *n.f.* (*prov.*) rag, tatter; (*slang*) cart; (*Col.*) emaciated person *or* animal; (*Arg., Per.*) coward; (*Arg., Chi.*) slag; (*Bol.*) harness with pack-saddle.

cangallar, *v.t.* to steal; (*sl.*) to fence, sell (*stolen goods*).

cangallero, *n.m.* (*sl.*) carter, wagoner.

cangallo, *n.m.* (*prov.*) nickname given to a lanky person; (*prov.*) heel-bone; (*prov.*) damaged object; (*sl.*) car, cart.

cangilón, *n.m.* water-wheel bucket.

cangre, *n.m.* (*Cub.*) stem of yucca.

cangreja, *a.* ***vela cangreja,*** boom-sail, gaff-sail.

cangrejal, *n.m.* crab ground; crayfish ground.

cangrejero, -ra, *n.m.f.* one who catches *or* sells crabs *or* crayfish. — *n.m.* (*orn.*) crab-catcher. — *n.f.* (*Chi.*) nest of crabs.

cangrejo, *n.m.* crab; crayfish; (*naut.*) boom, gaff; ***cangrejo de mar,*** crab; ***cangrejo de río,*** fresh-water crayfish.

cangrena [GANGRENA].

cangrenarse [GANGRENARSE].

cangrenoso, -sa [GANGRENOSO].

cangro, *n.m.* (*Hisp. Am., med.*) cancer.

canguelo, *n.m.* (*sl.*) funk; ***tener canguelo,*** to be in a funk.

cangüeso, *n.m.* cangueso fish.

canguil, *n.m.* (*Ec.*) maize.

canguro, *n.m.* kangaroo.

cania, *n.f.* small nettle.

caníbal, *a., n.m.* cannibal, man-eater; (*fig.*) savage.

canibalismo, *n.m.* cannibalism; (*fig.*) savagery.

canica, *n.f.* marble; (*pl.*) (game of) marbles.

canicie, *n.f.* whiteness (*of hair*).

Canícula, *n.f.* Dogstar.

canícula, *n.f.* dog-days.

canicular, *a.* canicular, belonging to the Dogstar. — *n.m.pl.* (**caniculares**) dog-days.

caniculario, *n.m.* beadle (*who ejects dogs from church*).

caniculoso, -sa, *a.* [CANICULAR].

cánidos, *n.m.pl.* (*zool.*) Canidæ.

canijo, -ja, *a., n.m.f.* (*coll.*) feeble, weak, sickly (individual).

canil, *n.m.* coarse bread, dog's bread; (*prov.*) canine tooth.

canilla, *n.f.* shinbone; end bone; tap, faucet, spigot;

reel, bobbin, spool; unevenness of the woof (*in thickness* or *colour*); (*fam.*) slender legs; (*Per.*) game of dice; (*Col.*) calf (*of the leg*); (*Mex.*) (*fig.*) strength, fortitude, courage; ***irse de canilla,*** to suffer from diarrhœa; (*fam.*) to have verbal diarrhœa.

canillado, -da, *a.* ribbed *or* striped.

canillera (1), *n.f.* (*Col.*) awe, dread, anxiety.

canillero, -ra (2), *n.m.f.* maker of weaver's quills. — *n.m.* faucet, spigot-hole (*in casks*). — *n.f.* greave, jamb (*armour*).

canime, *n.m.* (*Col.*) canime tree.

caninez, *n.f.* ravenous hunger.

canino, -na, *a.* canine; ***hambre canina,*** wolfish *or* ravenous hunger; ***dientes caninos,*** eye-teeth, canine teeth. — *n.f.* excrement of dogs.

caniquí, *n.m.* fine muslin.

canísimo, -ma, *a. superl.* very grey *or* white (*hair*).

canje, *n.m.* (*mil., dipl., com.*) exchange, barter, swop; ***canje de prisioneros,*** exchange of prisoners.

canjeable, *a.* exchangeable.

canjear, *v.t.* to exchange, barter, swop.

cano, -na (2), *a.* hoary, grey-haired; (*poet.*) white. — *n.f.* grey hair: ***echar una cana al aire,*** to go on a spree; ***peinar*** or ***tener canas,*** to be grey-haired *or* old.

canoa, *n.f.* canoe; motor-boat; ***sombrero de canoa,*** shovel-hat.

canoero, -ra, *n.m.f.* canoeist.

canoi, *n.m.* (*Hisp. Am.*) fishing basket.

canon, *n.m.* canon, rule; catalogue, list; standard, norm; governmental *or* municipal loan; (*law*) land tax; (*min.*) royalty; (*pl.* **cánones**) canons, canon law.

canonesa, *n.f.* canoness.

canónica (1), *n.f.* conventual life.

canonical, *a.* canonical, relating to canon, prebendary; (*coll.*) comfortable, easy (*life*).

canonicato, *n.m.* canonry; (*coll.*) sinecure.

canonicidad, *n.f.* canonicity.

canónico, -ca (2), *a.* canonical, canonic.

canóniga, *n.f.* (*coll.*) siesta; nap before a meal.

canónigo, *n.m.* canon, prebendary; ***vida de canónigo,*** comfortable life.

canonista, *n.m.* canonist.

canonizable, *a.* worthy of canonization.

canonización, *n.f.* canonization.

canonizar [C], *v.t.* to canonize; (*fig.*) to applaud, praise.

canonjía, *n.f.* canonry; (*coll.*) sinecure.

canope, *n.m.* (*archæol.*) canopic vase.

canoro, -ra, *a.* melodious.

canoso, -sa, *a.* hoary, grey-haired.

canotié, *n.m.* straw-hat.

canquén, *n.m.* (*Chi.*) wild goose.

cansable, *a.* easily tired.

cansado, -da, *a.* weary, tired; tiring; tedious, tiresome; ***vista cansada,*** weak eyesight.

cansancio, *n.m.* weariness, fatigue, tiredness.

cansar, *v.t.* to weary, tire, fatigue.

cansera, *n.f.* (*coll.*) fatigue, weariness; importunity.

cansí, *n.m.* (*Cub.*) Indian hut.

cansino, -na, *a.* weary; tedious.

canso, -sa (*prov.*) [CANSADO].

cantable, *a.* singable; (*mus.*) that is sung slowly. — *n.m.* lyrics, musical part of a ***zarzuela***; (*mus.*) cantabile; majestic, simple melody.

cantábrico, -ca, cántabro, -ra, *a., n.m.f.* Cantabrian, of Cantabria; ***el mar cantábrico,*** the Bay of Biscay.

cantada, *n.f.*(*mus.*) cantata.

canta(d)or, -ra, *n.m.f.* Flamenco singer.

cantal, *n.m.* block of stone; stony ground.

cantalear, *v.i.* to coo, warble (*doves*).

cantaleta, *n.f.* charivari; tin-pan serenade; (*fig.*) pun, jest, joke, humbug; ***dar cantaleta a,*** to make fun of.

cantaletear, *v.t.* (*Hisp. Am.*) to harp on; (*Mex.*) to deride, laugh at; to lecture.

cantalinoso, -sa, *a.* stony, pebbly.

cantante, *a.* singing. — *n.m.f.* singer.

cantar, *n.m.* song, canticle; tune; poem; ***Cantar de los Cantares,*** Song of Songs; ***cantar de gesta,*** epic poem; ***ése es otro cantar,*** that is another matter, that is another kettle of fish. — *v.t., v.i.* to sing; to chant; to praise. — *v.i.* (*fig.*) to announce the trump (*at cards*); (*naut.*) to sound the whistle; to sing shanties; (*coll.*) to squeal, spill the beans; ***cantar de plano,*** to make a full confession, make a clean breast of it; ***cantar misa,*** to say mass; ***cantarlas claras,*** to speak out, do some plain speaking; ***el gallo canta,*** the cock crows; (***los dineros del sacristán,***) ***cantando se vienen y cantando se van,*** easy come, easy go; ***quien mal canta, bien le suena,*** we are all blind to our own defects; ***quien canta, sus males espanta,*** he who sings frightens away his woes; ***en menos que canta un gallo,*** in a twinkling.

cántara, *n.f.* large, narrow-mouthed pitcher; milk-churn.

cantarela, *n.f.* treble (*of violin* or *guitar*).

cantarera [CANTERERO].

cantarería, *n.f.* shop where pitchers and jars are sold.

cantarero, -ra, *n.m.f.* potter; dealer in pitchers, jars etc. — *n.f.* shelf (*for pitchers, jars etc.*).

cantárida, *n.f.* cantharis, Spanish-fly; cantharides, blistering-plaster; blister (*raised by this plaster*).

cantaridina, *n.f.* (*chem.*) cantharidine.

cantarín, -rina, *a.* (*coll.*) sing-song; keen on singing.

cántaro, *n.m.* large pitcher; measure for liquids (*varying from* $2\frac{1}{2}$ *to* 4 *gals.*); vessel into which votes are put; (*Mex.*) bassoon; ***a cántaros,*** galore, by the bucketful; ***llover a cántaros,*** to bucket down, pour (*with rain*).

cantata, *n.f.* (*mus.*) cantata.

cantatriz, *n.f.* (*obs.*) female singer.

cantazo, *n.m.* blow from *or* with a stone.

cantear, *v.t.* to work the edge of (*stone*); to put *or* set on its *or* their narrow edge.

canteles, *n.m.pl.* (*naut.*) ends of old ropes put under casks to keep them steady.

cantera, *n.f.* quarry; (*fig.*) source, place of supply.

cantería, *n.f.* art of hewing stone; building made of hewn stone; portion of hewn stone.

canterios, *n.m.pl.* transverse roof-beams.

cantero, *n.m.* stone-cutter; end, edge; (*prov.*) ***cantero de heredad,*** piece of ground; ***cantero de pan,*** crust of bread.

canticio, *n.m.* (*coll.*) tiresome singing.

cántico, *n.m.* canticle; hymn.

cantidad, *n.f.* quantity, amount; number; (*gram.*) duration of a syllable; ***¡me ha costado una cantidad*** (***de dinero***)***!*** it has cost me a terrific amount!; ***en cantidad,*** in large amounts, generously, lavishly; ***tiene cantidad de dinero,*** he has bags of money; (*phys.*) ***cantidad de movimiento,*** momentum.

cantiga, *n.f.* troubadour poem.

cantil, *n.m.* steep rock; cliff; shelf (*coastal, sea*).

cantilena, cantinela, *n.f.* ballad; (*coll.*) same old song *or* thing.

cantillo, *n.m.* small pebble used in a children's game; corner, angle.

cantimpla, *a.* simple-minded.

cantimplora, *n.f.* siphon; water-cooler; water bottle; (*Am.*) canteen; (*Guat.*) goiter; (*Col.*) powder flask.

cantina, *n.f.* wine-cellar; canteen; station buffet.

cantinela [CANTILENA].

cantinera, *n.f.* vivandière.

cantinero, *n.m.* butler; sutler, canteen-keeper.

cantiña, *n.f.* (*coll.*) popular song.

cantizal, *n.m.* stony ground, place covered in stones.

canto (1), *n.m.* singing; epic; canto; chant, song, canticle; ***canto gregoriano*** or ***llano,*** Gregorian chant, plainsong; ***al canto,*** right away; for sure, bank on it; (*coll.*) ***al canto del gallo,*** at cock-crow; ***en canto llano,*** in a straightforward manner, simply; ***ser canto llano,*** to be straightforward.

canto (2), *n.m.* end; edge; side; end piece (*of a loaf*); back (*of a knife*); front edge (*of a book*); stone, pebble; game of throwing the stone (*duck on a rock*); quarry-stone, block, ***a canto,*** very near; ***de canto,*** on edge, on its *or* their side; ***ya puedes darte con un canto en los dientes,*** you can count yourself lucky; ***canto pelado*** or ***rodado,*** boulder.

cantollanista, *n.m.f.* expert in plain-song.

cantomanía, *n.f.* singing mania.

cantón (1), *n.m.* corner; canton; cantonment; (*her.*) canton; (*Hond.*) isolated plateau; (*carp.*) ***cantón redondo,*** coarse file.

cantón (2), *n.m.* (*Mex.*) imitation cashmere.

cantonada, *n.f.* (*prov.*) corner; ***dar cantonada a,*** to dodge, evade.

cantonal, *a.* cantonal. — *n.m.f.* cantonalist rebel, secessionist.

cantonalismo, *n.m.* cantonal spirit; policy of decentralization into cantons; secessionism.

cantonalista, *a.*, *n.m.f.* cantonalist.

cantonar [ACANTONAR].

cantonear, *v.i.* to hang about street corners.

cantoneo (*fam.*) [CONTONEO].

cantonero, -ra, *a.* loafing, idling. — *n.m.* loafer; bookbinder's gilding instrument. — *n.f.* corner-plate, clip; angle-iron, corner-bracket; photo corner fixer; street-walker.

cantor, -ra, *a.* singing, that sings. — *n.m.f.* singer; song-bird; (*slang*) squealer, one who spills the beans; ***los maestros cantores,*** the Master Singers.

cantoral, *n.m.* chorus-book.

cantorral [CANTIZAL].

cantoso, -sa, *a.* stony, pebbly.

cantú, *n.m.* (*Per.*) cantu plant.

cantúa, *n.f.* (*Cub.*) sweetmeat (*of sweet potato, coconut, sesame and sugar*).

cantuariense, *a.* of *or* belonging to Canterbury.

cantueso, *n.m.* (*bot.*) French lavender, spike.

canturía, *n.f.* singing exercise, vocal music, musical composition; monotonous singing; method of singing musical compositions.

canturrear, canturriar, *v.i.* (*fam.*) to hum, chant.

canturria, *n.f.* humming, chanting.

cantuta, *n.f.* (*Per.*) carnation plant.

cánula, *n.f.* cannula.

canular, *a.* cannular.

canutero, *n.m.* pincase.

canutillo, *n.m.* small tube; glass bead; gold *or* silver twist.

canuto, *n.m.* (reed) internode; tube, small tube; ***meterle a alguien la peste en un canuto,*** to make s.o. worried for no cause, fill s.o. with anxiety for no good reason, make a mountain out of a molehill.

caña, *n.f.* (*bot.*) cane, reed; walking-stick, cane; stem, stalk; bone (*of arm* or *leg*); (*min.*) gallery; (*arch.*) shaft (*of column* or *pillar*); (*anat.*) marrow; (*naut.*) helm, tiller; (small) glass of beer; long, narrow tumbler (*for* ***manzanilla*** *wine*); Andalusian song; flaw (*in a sword's blade*); leg (*of boot, stocking*); (*glass-blower's*) pipe; groove (*for the barrel of a firearm*); (*carp.*) shank; reed (*of wind-instruments*); (*naut.*) ***¡caña a babor!*** port the helm! ***caña de un cañón,*** chase of a gun; ***caña dulce, de azúcar*** or ***melar,*** sugar-cane; ***caña de pescar,*** fishing-rod; (*naut.*) ***caña del ancla,*** anchor shank; (*naut.*) ***caña del timón,*** tiller; (*anat.*) ***caña del pulmón,*** windpipe; ***caña del trigo,*** stem of corn; ***caña de vaca,*** shin-bone of beef and its marrow; (*pl.*) jousts; ***correr cañas,*** to joust with reed spears; ***las cañas se tornan lanzas,*** what began in jest may end in earnest.

cañacoro, *n.m.* (*bot.*) Indian shot, Indian reed.

cañada, *n.f.* glen, dale; dell, glade; cattle-path; shin-bone marrow; (*prov.*) measure of wine.

cañadilla, *n.f.* purple murex.

cañaduz, *n.m.* (*Col., prov.*) sugar-cane.

cañafístola, cañafístula, *n.f.* (*bot.*) cassia-tree and its fruit.

cañaheja, cañaherla, cañajelga, *n.f.* (*bot.*) common fennel-plant; (*bot.*) ***cañaheja hedionda,*** madder, Thapsia.

cañahua, *n.f.* (*Per.*) Indian millet from which ***chicha*** is made.

cañahuate, *n.m.* (*Col.*) lignum vitæ.

cañal, *n.m.* cane *or* reed plantation; cane weir (*for fishing*); small sluice *or* channel (*for catching fish*).

cañaliega *n.f.* cane *or* reed weir (*for fishing*).

cáñama, *n.f.* assessment of taxes.

cañamacero, -ra, *n.m.f.* canvas-maker *or* seller.

cañamal, cañamar, *n.m.* hemp-field.

cañamazo, *n.m.* coarse canvas, canvas for embroidery; embroidered canvas; burlap; (*Cub.*) wild plant used as fodder.

cañamelar, *n.m.* sugar-cane plantation.

cañameño, -ña, *a.* hempen, made of hemp.

cañamiel, *n.f.* sugar-cane.

cañamiza, *n.f.* bagasse of hemp.

cáñamo, *n.m.* hemp; cloth made of hemp; hemp-cord; ***cáñamo de Manila,*** manila hemp; ***cáñamo en rama,*** undressed hemp.

cañamón, *n.m.* hempseed.

cañamoncillo, *n.m.* very fine sand.

cañamonero, -ra, *n.m.f.* vendor of hempseed.

cañar, *n.m.* cane *or* reed plantation; weir for catching fish.

cañareja, *n.f.* common fennel plant.

cañariego, -ga, *a.* accompanying a drove; ***pellejos cañariegos,*** skins of sheep that die on the road.

cañarroya, *n.f.* pellitory, wall-pellitory.

cañavera, *n.f.* common reed-grass.

cañaveral, *n.m.* cane *or* reed-bed.

cañaverear, *v.t.* to wound with sharp-pointed canes.

cañaverería, *n.f.* place where reeds are sold.

cañaverero, -ra, *n.m.f.* retailer of canes *or* reeds.

cañazo, *n.m.* swipe with a cane; (*fig.*) ***dar cañazo,*** to cast down, make dejected.

cañedo, *n.m.* plantation of canes *or* reeds.

cañería, *n.f.* pipe; ***cañería maestra,*** main.

cañero, *n.m.* conduit-maker, director of water- *or* gas-works; (*Mex.*) peon in a sugar mill; (*Cub.*) seller of sugar-cane; (*Hond.*) owner of a sugar plantation; (*Mex.*) sugar-cane warehouse; (*prov.*) angler.

cañeta, *n.f.* reed-grass.

cañete, *n.m.* small tube; (*bot.*) ***ajo cañete,*** red-bulbed garlic.

cañí, *n.m.* gipsy.

cañihueco, cañivano, *a.* applied to a variety of wheat which gives good flour.

cañilavado, -da, *a.* thin, lank-limbed.

cañilla, cañita, *n.f.* small cane *or* reed.

cañillera, *n.f.* jambe.

cañiza, *a.* having the vein on one side (*wood*). — *n.f.* coarse linen; (*prov.*) sheepfold-fence, hurdle.

cañizal, cañizar, *n.m.* bed of canes *or* reeds.

cañizo, *n.m.* hurdle; frame (*for rearing silkworms*); frame (*of car-tilt*); lath frame (*of plaster ceiling etc.*); (*prov.*) wicker door *or* gate; (*naut.*) flake.

caño, *n.m.* tube, pipe; gutter; conduit, spout, spring, jet (*of water*); cellar; organ-pipe; (*min.*) gallery; (*prov.*) warren, burrow; (*naut.*) channel at entrance to seaports.
cañocal, *a.* (*naut.*) easily split (*wood*).
cañón, *n.m.* cannon; gun; gun-barrel; tube *or* pipe; fold, quilling (*of garment*); quill (*pen*); down (*feathers, hair*); (*Col.*) tree-trunk; canyon, gorge; (*Per.*) road, highway; (*min.*) gallery; (*mech.*) socket; bit (*of bridle*); well (*of staircase*); (*slang*) tramp, homeless rogue; ***cañón de chimenea,*** chimney (flue); ***cañón de órgano,*** organ-pipe; ***cañón obús,*** howitzer.
cañonazo, *n.m.* cannon-shot; report and damage caused by a cannon-shot; fire, firing; ***atraer los cañonazos del enemigo,*** to draw the enemy's fire.
cañonear, *v.t.* to bombard, shell, fire on.
cañoneo, *n.m.* bombarding, shelling, firing.
cañonería, *n.f.* collection of guns, cannon; collection of organ-pipes.
cañonero, -ra, *n.m.* gunner; gun-boat. — *n.f.* embrasure for cannon; (*mil.*) large tent; (*naut.*) gunport; (*Mex.*) holster; ***lancha cañonera,*** armed sloop.
cañota, *n.f.* panicled sorghum.
cañucela, *n.f.* slender cane *or* reed.
cañuela, *n.f.* small reed; fescue-grass.
cañutazo, *n.m.* (*coll.*) hint, suggestion, whisper, tale, gossip.
cañutería, *n.f.* collection of organ-pipes; gold *or* silver embroidery.
cañutero [CANUTERO].
cañutillo [CANUTILLO].
cañuto [CANUTO].
caoba, caobana, *n.f.*, **caobo,** *n.m.* (*bot.*) mahogany-tree, mahogany-wood.
caolín, *n.m.* kaolin, china clay.
caos, *n.m.* chaos; (*fig.*) confusion, shambles.
caótico, -ca, *a.* chaotic, in disorder and confusion.
capa, *n.f.* cape, cloak, mantle; cover; layer, stratum; hider, harbourer; coat, coating, covering; third mould (*in casting bells*); (*build.*) bed, course; (*com.*) primage; cigar's outer leaf; ***capa aguadera*** or ***gascona,*** waterproof cape *or* cloak; (*naut.*) tarred canvas covering for mast; ***capa del cielo,*** canopy of heaven; (*naut.*) ***capa de fogonaduras,*** mast-coat; ***capa consistorial*** or ***magna,*** cope worn by officiating bishops; (*bot.*) ***capa de rey,*** three-coloured amaranth; ***capa de coro*** or ***pluvial,*** pluvial *or* choir-cope; ***capa rota,*** secret emissary; ***capa torera,*** bull-fighter's cape; (*naut.*) ***capa del timón,*** rudder-coat; ***de capa y gorra,*** unceremoniously, informally; ***comedia de capa y espada,*** cloak and dagger play; ***gente de capa negra,*** middle-class townspeople; ***gente de capa parda,*** rustics, countrypeople; ***hombre de buena capa,*** man of genteel bearing; ***andar*** or ***ir de capa caída,*** to be down at heel, be in a bad way; ***defender a capa y espada,*** to defend with all one's might; ***defender su capa,*** to look after oneself; (*fig.*) ***echar la capa al toro,*** to stake everything; (*naut.*) ***esperar, estar, estarse*** or ***ponerse a la capa,*** to lie to; to watch for an opportunity; ***hacer de su capa un sayo,*** to do as one pleases; ***quitar a uno la capa,*** to rob; to skin; ***una buena capa todo lo tapa,*** a good appearance is very useful.
capá, *n.m.* capa-tree.
capacete, *n.m.* helmet, casque.
capacidad, *n.f.* capacity; (*fig.*) means; (*fig.*) ability, capability; (*law*) legal qualification.
capacitar, *v.t.* to capacitate, equip, qualify; (*Chi.*) to commission, empower, delegate.
capacha, *n.f.* frail, hamper.
capacho, *n.m.* hamper, frail, large basket; hempen pressing-bag in oil-mills; (*orn.*) common owl, barn owl.
capada, *n.f.* capeful, cloakful.
capador, *n.m.* gelder; whistle used by gelders.
capadura, *n.f.* castration; castration scar; inferior quality tobacco leaf.
capar, *v.t.* to geld, castrate; (*coll.*) to curtail, diminish.
caparazón, *n.m.* caparison; saddle-cover, carriage-cover, piano-cover; hempen nose-bag; carcass (*of a fowl*); shell (*of insects and crustaceans*).
caparra, *n.f.* sheep-louse; deposit; (*prov.*) caper-tree.
caparrilla, *n.f.* small tick which molests bees.
caparro, *n.m.* (*Per.*, *Ven.*) small white monkey.
caparrós, *n.m.* (*prov.*), **caparrosa,** *n.f.* copperas; ***caparrosa azul,*** copper sulphate; ***caparrosa blanca,*** sulphate of zinc; ***caparrosa verde,*** iron sulphate.
capasurí, *n.m.* (*C.R.*) deer.
capataz, *n.m.* overseer, foreman.
capaz, *a.* capacious, ample, roomy, spacious; (*fig.*) capable, fit, competent; (*coll.*) ***es capaz de no contestarte,*** he's quite capable of not answering you.
capaza, *n.f.* (*prov.*) hempen pressing-bag.
capazo, *n.m.* hempen basket, large frail; esparto mat; swipe given with a cloak.
capciosidad, *n.f.* artfulness, cunning.
capcioso, -sa, *a.* artful, cunning; ***pregunta capciosa,*** leading question.
capea, *n.f.* cloak stealing; amateur bullfight with calf (*in which the animal is not killed*).
capeador, *n.m.* amateur bull-fighter.
capear, *v.t.* to strip *or* rob of a cloak; to fight (*a bull*) with the cape; (*coll.*) to dodge; ***capear el temporal,*** to weather the storm. — *v.i.* (*naut.*) to lie to.
capelán, caplán, *n.m.* (*ichth.*) capelin.
capelanero, caplanero, *n.m.* capelin fisher and vendor.
capelina, *n.f.* head bandage.
capelo, *n.m.* dues formerly received by bishops from their clergy; cardinal's hat; cardinalate; (*Hisp. Am.*) glass bell.
capellada, *n.f.* toe-piece (*of a shoe*); repair (*to the vamp of shoe*).
capellán, *n.m.* chaplain, padre; ***capellán castrense,*** army chaplain; ***capellán de honor,*** king's private chaplain; ***capellán mayor de los ejércitos,*** vicar-general of the army; ***capellán de navío,*** naval chaplain.
capellanía, *n.f.* chaplaincy.
capellar, *n.m.* Moorish cloak.
capellina, *n.f.* head-piece of a helmet *or* casque; hood worn by country-people; trooper armed with a helmet.
capeo, *n.m.* challenging and teasing a bull with a cloak; (*pl.*) amateur bullfight with calf.
capeón, *n.m.* young bull challenged with a cloak.
capero, *n.m.* priest wearing cope in church; cloak-rack.
caperol, *n.m.* (*naut.*) top of stem.
caperucear, *v.t.* to remove (*headgear*) as salute.
caperucita, *n.f.* ***Caperucita roja,*** Little Red Riding Hood.
caperuza, *n.f.* pointed hood *or* cap; (*coll.*) ***dar en caperuza a uno,*** to frustrate s.o.'s aims and designs; ***caperuza de chimenea,*** chimney-cowl.
caperuzón, *n.m.* large hood.
capeta, *n.f.* short collarless cape *or* cloak [CAPA].
capetonada, *n.f.* violent vomiting (*affecting Europeans*) when in torrid zone.
capi, *n.m.* (*Chi.*) pod, capsule; (*Hisp. Am.*) maize.
capia, *n.f.* (*Arg.*) sweetmeat made of maize and sugar; (*Col.*) tender maize.
capialzado, -da, *a.*, *n.m.f.* (*arch.*) arched cap-piece; rear-arch, rear-vault.
capialzar [C], *v.t.* (*arch.*) to give a splay to.

capialzo, *n.m.* (*arch.*) slope of intrados.
capibara, *n.m.* (*zool.*) capybara.
capicatí, *n.m.* (*Par.*) Cyperaceæ herb *or* drink.
capicúa, *n.m.* symmetrical number; palindrome.
capichola, *n.f.* ribbed silk material.
capidengue, *n.m.* small cloak worn by ladies.
capigorrista, capigorrón, *n.m.* (*coll.*) vagabond; sloven, sly fellow; student who never takes a high degree; one who has taken minor orders.
capilar, *a.* capillary.
capilaridad, *n.f.* capillarity; (*phys.*) capillary attraction.
capilla, *n.f.* hood; cowl of monk *or* friar; chapel; priests and others taking part in chapel services; Capella; chapter *or* assembly of collegians; (*bot.*) pod, seed-vessel; (*print.*) proof-sheet; ***capilla ardiente,*** lighted room where a dead body lies in state; (*naut.*) ***caja de capilla,*** chest for chapel ornaments; ***estar en capilla,*** to be awaiting execution; (*coll.*) to be anxiously waiting (*to take an examination etc.*).
capillada, *n.f.* hoodful.
capillejo, *n.m.* small christening-cap; skein of sewing-silk.
capiller, capillero, *n.m.* clerk *or* sexton of a chapel; churchwarden.
capillita, *n.f.* small chapel; niche; collection-box. — *n.m.* (*coll.*) church worker, parish helper.
capillo, *n.m.* child's cap; baptismal cap; christening fee; hood (*of hawk*); cloth covering a church-offering; rosebud; toepiece lining; cap (*of a distaff*); silk cocoon; net (*for catching rabbits*); colander (*for wax*); (*anat.*) prepuce; first wrapper (*of cigar-fillings*); (*naut.*) tin *or* wooden binnacle-cover; (*naut.*) canvas covering (*of shroud ends*); ***capillo de hierro,*** helmet, casque.
capilludo, -da, *a.* hood-like, cowl-like.
capín, *n.m.* (*Hisp. Am.*) fodder plant.
capingo, *n.m.* (*Chi.*) short and narrow cape.
capipardo, *n.m.* artisan, working-man.
capirotada, *n.f.* batter (*of herbs, eggs etc.*); (*Mex.*) pauper's grave.
capirotazo, *n.m.* fillip, blow, swipe.
capirote, *a.* having head of a different colour from that of the body (*cattle*). — *n.m.* hood (*academic, hawk, carriage etc.*); (penitent's) cap; flick, fillip; ***tonto de capirote,*** dunce, numskull; ***hacer mangas y capirotes de un asunto,*** to deal arbitrarily *or* in an off-hand fashion with a matter.
capirucho, *n.m.* (*coll.*) [CAPIROTE].
capisayo, *n.m.* cloak, mantle, mantelet; vestment (*worn by bishops*); (*Col.*) vest.
capiscol, *n.m.* precentor; (*slang*) cock, rooster.
capiscolía, *n.f.* precentorship.
capita, *n.f.* small cloak.
capitá, *n.m.* (*Hisp. Am.*) capita bird.
capitación, *n.f.* capitation; poll-tax, head-money.
capital, *a.* capital, principal, relating to the head; leading, great; excellent, unsurpassed; essential, vital; ***enemigo capital,*** chief enemy; ***error capital,*** capital error; ***pecado capital,*** deadly sin; ***pena capital,*** capital punishment, death penalty. — *n.f.* capital (*city*); provincial capital, main town; (*fort.*) capital. — *n.m.* capital (*wealth*); husband's fortune at marriage; (*com.*) capital stock; (*com.*) ***capital desembolsado,*** paid-up capital; ***capital líquido,*** net balance of assets; ***capital social,*** nominal capital, authorized capital.
capitalidad, *n.f.* status of capital city.
capitalismo, *n.m.* capitalism.
capitalista, *a., n.m.f.* capitalistic; capitalist.
capitalizable, *a.* that can be capitalized.
capitalización, *n.f.* capitalization.
capitalizador, -ra, *a., n.m.f.* that capitalizes.
capitalizar [C], *v.t.* to capitalize, realize; to compound.
capitán, *n.m.* captain; leader; commander (*of a ship*); ***capitán de bandera,*** flag captain; ***capitán de corbeta,*** lieutenant commander; ***capitán de fragata,*** commander; ***capitán general de ejército,*** field-marshal; ***capitán general,*** commander-in-chief of a military district; ***capitán de navío,*** captain; (*naut.*) ***capitán del puerto,*** port-captain, harbour-master.
capitana, *n.f.* admiral's ship, flagship; (*fam.*) captain's wife; (*fam.*) woman leader of troops.
capitanear, *v.t.* to captain, command, lead.
capitanía, *n.f.* captainship, captaincy; port dues; ***capitanía de puerto,*** harbour-master's office; ***capitanía general,*** rank of a captain-general; residence and office of a captain-general.
capitel, *n.m.* (*arch.*) capital; spire.
capitelado, -da, *a.* (*arch.*) adorned with capitals; (*bot.*) capitate, capitated.
capitolino, -na, *a.* Capitolian, Capitoline.
capitolio, *n.m.* capitol; any lofty *or* majestic public building; acropolis; (*Hisp. Am.*) senate house.
capitón, *n.m.* striped mullet.
capitoné, *n.m.* removal van.
capítula, *n.f.* chapter (*passage of Scripture*).
capitulación, *n.f.* capitulation; (*pl.* **capitulaciones**) stipulation, agreement; marriage articles *or* contract; document embodying these articles.
capitulado, *n.m.* capitulation, contract.
capitulador, -ra, *a.* that capitulates. — *n.m.f.* capitulator.
capitulante, *a.* capitulating.
capitular, *a.* (*eccles.*) capitular. — *n.m.* (*eccles.*) capitular. — *n.f.pl.* (**capitulares**) capitulary. — *v.t.* (*law*) to impeach. — *v.i.* to conclude an agreement; to draw up the articles of a contract; to compound; to dispose, resolve; to sing prayers at the divine office; (*mil.*) to capitulate.
capitulario, *n.m.* prayer book.
capitulear, *v.t.* to lobby.
capituleo, *n.m.* lobbying.
capituliforme, *a.* (*bot.*) capitate.
capítulo, *n.m.* (*eccles.*) chapter, council; chapter-house; commission; chapter (*of a book*); heading, entry; subject, matter; ***capítulo de culpas,*** impeachment; ***capítulos matrimoniales,*** marriage articles; ***llamar*** or ***traer a capítulo,*** to take to task.
caplán [CAPELÁN].
caplanero [CAPELANERO].
capnomancia, capnomancía, *n.f.* capnomancy.
capó, *n.m.* (*motor.*) bonnet.
capoc, *n.m.,* **capoca,** *n.f.* kapok.
capolado, *n.m.* (*prov.*) hash, mince.
capolar, *v.t.* to cut into pieces; (*prov.*) to mince *or* chop up (*meat*); (*prov.*) to decapitate, behead.
capón (1), *a.* castrated, gelded. — *n.m.* gelding; capon; faggot, bundle of brushwood; (*naut.*) anchor-stopper at the cathead; ***capón de galera,*** kind of cold soup; ***capón de leche,*** capon fattened in a coop.
capón (2), *n.m.* (*coll.*) blow on the head with knuckle of middle finger; (*coll.*) ***capón de ceniza,*** blow on the forehead with rag filled with ashes.
capona, *n.f.* epaulette without fringe; shoulder-knot; sleeveless surplice; ***llave capona,*** key worn by a lord of the bed-chamber.
caponar, *v.t.* to tie up (*the runners of vines*); (*naut.*) to fasten (*the anchor*) to the cathead.
caponera, *n.f.* leading mare; coop (*to fatten poultry*); (*coll.*) jail; (*fort.*) caponiere; (*coll.*) place where one lives well at other people's expense.
capoquero, *n.m.* kapok-tree.
caporal, *n.m.* chief, ringleader; (*Hisp. Am.*) head-man, chief cowherd; (*sl.*) cock, rooster; (*mil.*) corporal.
capota, *n.f.* head (*of teasel* or *fuller's thistle*); bonnet; hood (*of vehicles*); collarless cape.
capotazo, *n.m.* (*tauro.*) flick *or* flourish of cape.

capote, *n.m.* cloak; (*tauro.*) cape; poncho; (*mil.*) greatcoat; (*coll.*) thick mist *or* cloud; ***dar capote a,*** to flabbergast; to leave without anything to eat; to prevent from taking any tricks (*cards*); (*Hisp. Am.*) to hoodwink; ***decir para su capote,*** to say to o.s.; ***echar un capote,*** to cover up, help out *or* lend a hand (*by covering up*), draw attention away from (*in conversation*).
capotear, *v.t.* to fight (*a bull*) with the cape; to trick; to handle, get round; to dodge, evade; ***capoteárselas,*** to manage, make out, get by.
capoteo, *n.m.* (*tauro.*) cape-work.
capotera, *n.f.* (*Hisp. Am.*) hat *or* clothes rack; (*Ven.*) travelling-bag (*made of canvas*).
capotero, *n.m.* maker of cloaks *or* capes.
capotillo, *n.m.* cape, mantlet; ***capotillo de dos faldas,*** short, loose jacket open at the sides.
capotudo, -da, *a.* frowning.
caprario, -ria, *a.* capric, caprine.
caprico, -ca, *a.* (*chem.*) capric.
Capricornio, *n.m.* (*astron.*, *astrol.*) Capricorn.
capricho, *n.m.* caprice, fancy, whim; (*mus.*, *art*) caprice, capriccio.
caprichoso, -sa, *a.* capricious, flighty; wilful.
caprichudo, -da, *a.* capricious; stubborn, wilful.
caprificación, *n.f.* caprification.
caprino, -na, *a.* (*poet.*) caprine, goatish.
caprípede, caprípedo, -da, *a.* (*poet.*) goat-footed.
caproico, -ca, *a.* (*chem.*) caproic.
capsicina, *n.f.* (*chem.*) capsicine.
cápsico, *n.m.* (*bot.*) capsicum.
capsueldo, *n.m.* (*prov.*) discount for payment in advance.
cápsula, *n.f.* metal cap, capsule; cartridge shell.
capsular, *a.* capsular. — *v.t.* to cap (*bottle*).
captación, *n.f.* captation; grasping; attraction; capture; harnessing (*of water*); (*rad.*) tuning, picking up.
captador, -ra, *a.* captivating, fascinating. — *n.m.f.* inveigler.
captar, *v.t.* to attract; to catch; to grasp; to win over; to impound (*water*); to pick up (*radio signals*); ***captarse simpatías,*** to win favour.
captatorio, -ria, *a.* (*law*) underhand, undue.
captura, *n.f.* (*law*) capture, seizure; catch, catching.
capturar, *v.t.* (*law*) to apprehend, arrest; to catch, capture.
capuana, *n.f.* (*coll.*) spanking.
capuceta, *n.f.*, **capucete,** *n.m.* (*prov.*) act of ducking (*a person*).
capucha, *n.f.* hood, cowl; (*print.*) circumflex accent.
capuchino, -na, *a.*, *n.m.f.* Capuchin (*monk, nun*). — *n.f.* (*bot.*) nasturtium; portable lamp with extinguisher; confection of yolk of egg; (*pl.*) (*print.*) two or more frames joined together at the top.
capucho, *n.m.* cowl, hood.
capuchón, *n.m.* lady's evening cloak with hood; short domino [CAPUCHO].
capuleto, *n.m.* capulet.
capulí, *n.m.* (*Hisp. Am.*, *bot.*) capulin; calabur tree.
capúlidos, *n.m.pl.* (*zool.*) family of the limpets (*Mollusca*).
capulina, *n.f.* (*Hisp. Am.*) fruit of the capulin; calabur tree; (*Mex.*) poisonous black spider; (*Mex.*) harlot.
capultamal, *n.m.* (*Mex.*) tamale of capulí.
capullo, *n.m.* cocoon; bud; acorn-cup; chestnut bur; coarse stuff of floss-silk; (*anat.*) prepuce; ***en capullo,*** in embryo; ***seda de capullos,*** or ***de todo capullo,*** floss-silk; ***capullo ocal,*** cocoon made by two or more silkworms together.
capuz, *n.m.* cowl; hooded cloak; dive, duck; ducking.
capuzar [C], *v.t.* to duck; (*naut.*) to overload at the bows.
caquéctico, -ca, *a.* cachectic. — *n.m.f.* (*med.*) person suffering from cachexia.
caquexia, *n.f.* (*med.*) cachexia; (*bot.*) chlorosis, etiolation.
caqui, *n.m.* date plum; khaki.
caquino, *n.m.* (*Mex.*) guffaw, loud laughter.
car, *n.m.* (*naut.*) lower and thicker end of a lateen-yard.
cara (I), *adv.* facing; ***de cara,*** facing; ***cara adelante,*** forward; ***cara al sol,*** facing the sun. — *n.f.* face; look, appearance; surface; obverse; (*geom.*) face, plane, surface; ***cara de juez*** or ***de guardia,*** stern face; ***cara de ajo*** or ***de perro,*** surly face; ***cara de pocos amigos*** or ***de vinagre,*** sour face; ***cara de acelga,*** pale, sallow face; ***cara a cara,*** face to face; ***cara de cartón,*** wrinkled face; ***cara de hereje,*** ugly mug; ***cara de aleluya, de Pascua*** or ***de risa,*** smiling, cheerful face; ***cara de Viernes Santo,*** sad, lean face; ***cara o cruz,*** heads or tails; ***a primera cara,*** at first sight; ***a cara descubierta,*** openly; ***caérsele a uno la cara de vergüenza,*** to blush with shame; ***cruzarle a alguien la cara,*** to strike s.o. across the face; ***dar la cara,*** to show one's face; to face the music; ***dar*** (***sacar***) ***la cara por,*** to stand up for, defend; to take responsibility for (on behalf of); ***echarle a alguien algo en cara,*** to throw sth. in s.o.'s face, upbraid s.o. for sth., tax s.o. with sth.; ***en la cara se le conoce,*** his face gives him away; you can tell what he's like from his face; ***hacer cara a,*** to face (up to); ***lavarle a una cosa la cara,*** to give sth. a quick clean up, fix sth. up quickly; ***no saber dónde se tiene la cara,*** not to have a clue, not to know the first thing about it; ***le sale a la cara,*** you can see it in his face; ***no tener a quien volver la cara,*** to have no one to turn to; ***no tener cara para,*** not to have the face (nerve) to; ***tener cara de,*** to look like; ***tener buena cara,*** to look well (in good health); to look good (attractive, appetizing); ***tener mala cara,*** to look ill, not to look well; ***tener el sol de cara,*** to have the sun in one's eyes; ***poner buena*** (***mala***) ***cara a,*** to receive favourably (badly); (*iron.*) ***por su bella*** (***linda***) ***cara,*** just (solely) for his pretty face; ***ya nos veremos las caras,*** we'll have this out sooner or later.
caraba, *n.f.* (*coll.*) end, limit; ***esto es la caraba,*** this is the end.
cáraba, *n.f.* boat used in the Levant.
carabao, *n.m.* (*Philip.*) caraboo, buffalo.
cárabe, *n.m.* amber.
carabela, *n.f.* (*naut.*) caravel; (*prov.*) large basket, tray.
carabelón, *n.m.* (*naut.*) small caravel.
carábico, -ca, *a.* (*ent.*) similar *or* relating to the beetle.
carabina, *n.f.* carbine, rifle; (*coll.*) chaperon; ***ser la carabina de Ambrosio,*** to be hopeless *or* a dead loss.
carabinazo, *n.m.* carbine shot *or* report; carbine wound *or* damage.
carabinero, *n.m.* carabineer; frontier *or* coast guard; customs guard.
carablanca, *n.m.* (*Col.*, *C.R.*) Cebus monkey.
cárabo, *n.m.* small Moorish boat; (*ent.*) beetle; (*orn.*) large horned owl; setter dog.
carabú, *n.m.* carabu tree.
caraca, *n.f.* (*Cub.*) maize cake.
caracal, *n.m.* (*Hisp. Am.*) lynx.
caracará, *a.* (*Par.*) appertaining to an Indian tribe living on the banks of the river Paraná; (*Arg.*) caracara bird.
caracas, *n.m. inv.* (*Ven.*) cacao (*from the coast of Caracas*); (*Mex.*, *coll.*) chocolate; (*pl.*) tribe of the Guaraní.
caracatcy, *n.m.* (*Cub.*) Cuban nightjar.
caracoa, *n.f.* (*Philip.*) small rowing-barge.
caracol, *n.m.* (*zool.*) snail; spiral shell; (*mech.*) snail-wheel; (*arch.*, *equit.*) caracole; (*anat.*) cochlea; twisted coil of hair worn on the temples; (*Mex.*) nightdress; (*Mex.*) embroidered blouse; ***hacer***

caracoles, to stagger; ***escalera de caracol,*** winding *or* spiral staircase. — *interj.* (*coll.*) ***¡caracoles!*** Lord!

caracola, *n.f.* (*prov., zool.*) triton; shell, conch; trumpet, horn.

caracolada, *n.f.* dish of snails.

caracolear, *v.i.* (*equit.*) to caracole.

caracoleo, *n.m.* caracoling.

caracolero, -ra, *n.m.f.* snail-gatherer, snail-seller.

caracolillo, *n.m.* snail-flowered kidney-bean; veined mahogany; ***café caracolillo,*** pea-bean coffee; (*pl.*) shell-like fringes, trimmings on clothes.

caracolito, *n.m.* small snail.

carácter, *n.m.* (*pl.* **caracteres**) character, temperament, disposition, nature; firmness, energy; letter; mark, brand (*on animals*); ***en su carácter de,*** in his capacity as; ***una mujer de buen*** or ***mal carácter,*** a good- *or* bad-tempered woman; ***caracteres de imprenta,*** printing types.

caracterismo, *n.m.* characteristics.

característico, -ca, *a.* characteristic, typical. — *n.m.* character actor. — *n.f.* character actress; characteristic, feature; trait, quality, attribute; (*math.*) characteristic.

caracterizable, *a.* that may be characterized.

caracterizar [C], *v.t.* to characterize; to confer a distinction on; to play a part properly. — **caracterizarse,** *v.r.* to dress and make up for a part.

caracú, *n.m.* (*Arg.*) race of cattle bred specially for meat.

caracha, *n.f.*, **carache,** *n.m.* (*Chi., Per.*) itch, scab; (*Per.*) mange (*of llamas*).

carado, -da, *a.* ***biencarado, -da,*** pleasant-faced, agreeable-looking; ***malcarado, -da,*** evil-faced, evil-looking.

caradura, *n.f.* (*coll.*) face, cheek, nerve. — *n.m.* (*coll.*) cheeky blighter, thick-skinned fellow, rascal; ***tener la caradura de,*** to have the cheek to.

caraguatá, *n.f.* (*Par.*) sisal.

caraguay, *n.m.* (*Bol.*) large lizard.

caraira, *n.f.* (*Cub.*) sparrow-hawk.

caraja, *n.f.* square sail.

carajillo, *n.m.* black coffee with brandy.

caramanchel, *n.m.* (*naut.*) hatchway cover; (*Arg.*) eating house; (*Chi.*) canteen; (*Col.*) den, low place; (*Ec.*) hawker's *or* pedlar's basket.

caramanchelero, *n.m.* (*Hisp. Am.*) hawker, pedlar.

caramanchón, *n.m.* garret.

caramayola, *n.f.* (*Chi., mil.*) water-bottle.

caramba (I), *n.f.* ancient headgear for women.

¡caramba! (2), *interj.* (*coll.*) good Lord!, Heavens!, I say!

carambanado, -da, *a.* frozen, forming icicles.

carámbano, *n.m.* icicle.

carambillo, *n.m.* (*bot.*) salt-wort.

carambola (I), *n.f.* cannon (*in billiards*); (*bot.*) fruit of the ***carambolo*** tree; (*coll.*) coincidence, fluke; (*coll.*) trick; (*coll.*) ***por carambola,*** by chance, by a fluke.

¡carambola! (2), *interj.* I say!

carambolaje, *n.m.* cannon score (*billiards*).

carambolear, *v.t.* to cannon (*at billiards*).

carambolero, *n.m.* [CARAMBOLISTA].

carambolista, *n.m.f.* one good at making cannons (*billiards*).

carambolo, *n.m.* carambolo tree.

caramel (I), *n.m.* caramel.

caramel (2), *n.m.* (*ichth.*) atherine.

caramelizar [C], *v.t.* to convert into caramel.

caramelo, *n.m.* caramel; sweet; (*pl.*) sweets.

caramiello, *n.m.* (*León and Ast.*) woman's hat.

caramillar, *n.m.* salt-wort plantation.

caramilleras, *n.f.pl.*(*prov.*) pot-hooks.

caramillo, *n.m.* flageolet, small flute; (*bot.*) salt-wort; deceit, trick; gossip, tale-telling; confused heap of things; ***armar*** or ***levantar un caramillo,*** to make mischief.

caramilloso, -sa, *a.* (*fam.*) peevish, touchy.

caramuzal, *n.m.* Turkish boat.

carancho, *n.m.* (*Arg., Bol.*) carancho bird; (*Per.*) owl.

carandaí, *n.m.* (*Arg.*) tall palm-tree.

caranegra, *n.m.f.* (*Arg.*) black-faced sheep; (*Col., C.R., Ven.*) black-faced monkey.

caranga, *n.f.* louse.

carángano, *n.m.* louse; (*Col.*) Indian musical instrument.

carantamaula, *n.f.* (*coll.*) hideous mask; (*coll.*) ugly, hard-featured person.

carantoña, *n.f.* ugly (false) face; painted old hag; (*pl.*) (*coll.*) fawning, wheedling.

carantoñero, -ra, *n.m.f.* (*fam.*) flatterer, wheedler, cajoler.

caráota, *n.f.* (*Ven.*) french bean.

carapacho, *n.m.* carapace; shell (*of crustaceans*); (*Cub.*) shell-fish cooked in the shell; (*Per.*) Carapacho Indian.

carapato, *n.m.* castor oil.

¡carape! *interj.* Lord!

carapulca, *n.f.* (*Per.*) dish made of meat, dry potato and chilli.

caraqueño, -ña, *a., n.m.f.* (native) of Caracas.

carasol, *n.m.* sunny place, sun-gallery.

carátula, *n.f.* mask; hideous face; (*fig.*) histrionic art; bee-net.

caratulero, *n.m.* maker *or* seller of masks.

carava, *n.f.* peasant holiday gathering.

caravana, *n.f.* caravan, (*Am.*) trailer; group, crowd, stream, queue.

caravanera, *n.f.* caravanserai.

caravanero, *n.m.* caravaneer.

caravanista, *n.m.f.* caravanist.

caravanseray, caravanserrallo, *n.m.* caravanserai.

caray (I), *n.m.* tortoise-shell.

¡caray! (2), *interj.* Lord! blimey!

carayá, *n.m.* (*Arg., Col.*) howling monkey.

caraza, *n.f.* great big face; (*fam.*) big mug.

cárbaso, *n.m.* fine flax; ancient tunic; (*poet.*) sail of a ship.

carbinol, *n.m.* methylic alcohol.

carbol, *n.m.* phenol, carbolic acid.

carbólico, -ca, *a.* carbolic.

carbón, *n.m.* coal; charcoal; carbon-pencil; carbon (*arc lamp*); coal-brand; (*agric.*) smut; ***carbón animal,*** bone-black; ***carbón de bujía,*** cannel (coal); ***carbón de leña*** or ***vegetal,*** charcoal; ***carbón graso,*** soft coal; ***carbón mineral*** or ***de piedra,*** coal.

carbonado, -da, *a.* carbonaceous. — *n.m.* black diamond. — *n.f.* broiled chop *or* steak.

carbonalla, *n.f.* refractory mortar.

carbonar, *v.t.* to carbonize.

carbonatar, *v.t.* to carbonate.

carbonato, *n.m.* carbonate.

carboncillo, *n.m.* fine coal; charcoal (*pencil*); black sand; wheat smut.

carbonear, *v.t.* to char, make into charcoal.

carboneo, *n.m.* carbonization; charcoal-making, charring.

carbonería, *n.f.* coal-yard, coal-shop.

carbonero, -ra, *a.* relating to coal *or* charcoal. — *n.m.* (*orn.*) colemouse, coal-titmouse; charcoal-burner *or* -seller; collier, coal-man, coal-miner; coal-merchant. — *n.f.* wood prepared for burning into charcoal; charcoal kiln; coal-bin, -bunker, -shed *or* -cellar; woman who sells charcoal; (*Col.*) coal mine; (*Chi.*) tender (*of a locomotive*); (*naut.*) main staysail.

carbónico, -ca, *a.* carbonic.
carbónidos, *n.m.pl.* carbon and its compounds.
carbonífero, -ra, *a.* carboniferous, coal-bearing.
carbonilla, *n.f.* fine coal, coal dust; coal smuts; smutty black smoke (*from trains*).
carbonización, *n.f.* carbonization.
carbonizar [C], *v.t.* to carbonize, char.
carbono, *n.m.* carbon.
carbonoso, -sa, *a.* carbonaceous, coaly.
carborundo, *n.m.* (*chem.*) carborundum.
carbuncal, *a.* carbuncular.
carbunclo, carbunco, *n.m.* carbuncle (*precious stone*); carbuncle, anthrax.
carbuncoso, -sa, *a.* carbuncular.
carbúnculo, *n.m.* carbuncle (*precious stone*).
carburación, *n.f.* carburization.
carburador, *n.m.* carburettor.
carburante, *a.* containing hydrocarbon. — *n.m.* fuel.
carburar, *v.t.* to carburet, carburize; ***el coche no carbura bien,*** the car isn't running smoothly.
carburo, *n.m.* (*chem.*) carbide; carburet.
carca, *a., n.m.* hopelessly reactionary; wretched Carlist *or* Tory.
carcaj, *n.m.* quiver; case in which the cross may be borne in a procession; Moorish anklet, (*Hisp. Am.*) rifle-case.
carcajada, *n.f.* guffaw.
carcamal, *n.m.* (*coll.*) old fogey, old dodderer.
carcamán, *n.m.* (*naut.*) old tub; (*Cub.*) foreigner of low status; (*Per.*) presumptuous, conceited, but unworthy person; (*Arg.*) Italian (*especially Genoese*).
cárcamo, *n.m.* hollow in which a water-wheel turns.
carcañal, calcañar, *n.m.* heel-bone, calcaneum.
cárcava, carcavina, *n.f.* gully made by torrents of water; hedge; ditch; grave; mound; (*mil.*) enclosure.
cárcavo, *n.m.* (*obs.*) pit *or* cavity of the abdomen.
carcavuezo, *n.m.* deep pit.
cárcel, *n.f.* prison, gaol; coulisse (*of a sluice-gate*); (*carp.*) clamp, cramp, clasp; cheek (*of printing-press*).
carcelaje, carceraje, *n.m.* gaoler's fees, prison fees.
carcelario, -ria, *a.* relating to a prison.
carcelería, *n.f.* imprisonment; bail offered for a prisoner; ***guardar carcelería,*** to be confined within bounds (*a prisoner*).
carcelero, -ra, *a.* ***fiador carcelero,*** one who stands bail *or* surety for a prisoner; ***fianza carcelera,*** bail, surety. — *n.m.* gaoler, keeper, warder. — *n.f.* gaoleress, wardress; popular Andalusian song dealing with prisoner's tribulations.
carceraje [CARCELAJE].
carcinoma, *n.f.* carcinoma.
carcinomatoso, -sa, *a.* carcinomatous.
carcinosis, *n.f. inv.* carcinosis.
cárcola, *n.f.* treadle (*of loom*).
carcoma, *n.f.* death-watch beetle, wood-worm, wood-fretter; dust made by wood-worm; (*fig.*) gnawing anxiety; (*slang*) road, highway, footpath.
carcomer, *v.t.* to gnaw, eat away (*of wood-worm*); to undermine slowly.
carcomido, -da, *a.* worm-eaten.
carda, *n.f.* carding; card (*instrument*); (*bot.*) card-thistle, teasel; (*coll.*) severe reproof, censure; (*naut.*) small vessel like a galley; ***gente de*** (***la***) ***carda,*** bullies, ruffians, toughs; ***dar una carda,*** to reprimand severely; ***todos somos de la carda,*** we are all of the same ilk.
cardada, *n.f.* portion of wool carded at one operation.
cardadería, cardería, *n.f.* carding factory; card factory.
cardador, -ra, *n.m.f.* carder, comber. — *n.m.* (*zool.* myriapod.
cardadura, *n.f.* carding, combing (*wool*).
cardamina, *n.f.* cardamine, lady's smock, cuckoo-flower.
cardamomo, *n.m.* cardamom.
cardar, *v.t.* to card *or* comb; to teasel; ***cardarle a uno la lana,*** to reprimand someone bitterly and severely; to skin someone (*gambling*).
cardelina, *n.f.* goldfinch.
cardenal (1), *n.m.* (*eccles.*) cardinal; (*orn.*) Virginian nightingale; cardinal-bird.
cardenal (2), *n.m.* weal.
cardenalato *n.m.* cardinalate, cardinalship.
cardenalicio, -cia, *a.* belonging to a cardinal.
cardencha, *n.f.* (*bot.*) teasel; comb, card (*instrument*).
cardenchal, *n.m.* place where teasels grow.
cardenchoso, -sa, *a.* teasel-like.
cardenillo, *n.m.* verdigris; paris green.
cárdeno, -na, *a.* livid, bluish-purple, mauve; piebald (*bull*); opaline (*water*); (*bot.*) ***lirio cárdeno,*** purple iris.
cardero, *n.m.* [CARDADOR].
cardíaca (1), *n.f.* motherwort.
cardiáceo, -cea, *a.* heart-shaped.
cardíaco, -ca (2) *a.* cardiac, cardiacal; suffering from heart-disease. — *n.m.f.* person suffering from heart-disease.
cardialgia, *n.f.* cardialgy, heart-burn.
cardiálgico, -ca, *a.* cardialgic.
cardias, *n.m. inv.* cardiac orifice (*of the stomach*).
cardillo, *n.m.* golden thistle.
cardinal, *a.* cardinal; essential, paramount, utmost.
cardiografía, *n.f.* cardiography.
cardiógrafo, *n.m.* cardiograph.
cardiología, *n.f.* cardiology.
cardítico, -ca, *a.* cardiac.
cardizal, *n.m.* land covered with thistles and weeds.
cardo, *n.m.* thistle; (*Par.*) sisal; ***cardo ajonjero*** or ***aljonjero,*** carline thistle; ***cardo bendito*** or ***santo,*** blessed thistle, centaury; ***cardo corredor, estelado*** or ***setero,*** creeping thistle, erigeron; ***cardo huso,*** bastard saffron; ***cardo lechero*** or ***mariano,*** milk-thistle; ***cardo borriqueño, borriquero*** or ***silvestre,*** spear-plume *or* Scotch thistle; ***más áspero que un cardo,*** harsher than a thistle; ***ser un cardo borriquero,*** to be a country bumpkin.
cardón, *n.m.* (*bot.*) teasel; carding, teaseling.
Cardona, *n.m.* (*only in*) ***más listo que Cardona,*** smart as the Devil.
cardonal, *n.m.* (*Hisp. Am.*) place abounding in thistles.
cardoncillo, *n.m.* milk-thistle.
carducha, *n.f.* large iron comb *or* card (*for wool*).
cardume, cardumen, *n.m.* shoal (*of fishes*).
carduzador, -ra, *n.m.f.* carder; (*slang*) fence, receiver of stolen goods.
carduzal [CARDIZAL].
carduzar [C], *v.t.* to card *or* comb (*wool*).
carear, *v.t.* to bring face to face, confront; (*fig.*) to compare; to tend (*sheep* or *cattle*); to clean (*base of sugar-loaf*). — **carearse,** *v.r.* to meet *or* come face to face; ***carearse con,*** to face, confront.
carecer [9], *v.i.* to lack, be lacking in, be without; ***carecer de medios,*** to lack means; ***carece de sentido,*** there is no sense to it, it doesn't make sense.
careciente [CARENTE].
carecimiento, *n.m.* [CARENCIA].
carena, *n.f.* (*naut.*) careenage, careening; (*coll.*) banter; (*coll.*) ***dar carena a,*** to tease, reprove in jest.
carenadura, *n.f.* careenage.

carenar, *v.t.* (*naut.*) to careen; ***carenar de firme,*** to overhaul completely.
carencia, *n.f.* need, want, lack.
carenero, *n.m.* (*naut.*) careenage, careening-place.
carente, *a.* lacking; ***carente de interés,*** lacking in interest, uninteresting.
careo, *n.m.* confrontation (*of criminals* or *witnesses*); act of bringing face to face; interrogation; (*prov.*) corn-plot for hog-feeding; (*prov.*) fodder; (*prov.*) gossip, chat.
carero, -ra, *a.* (*coll.*) who charges high prices; dear, expensive.
carestía, *n.f.* scarcity; famine; high cost of living; high prices; dearness.
careto, -ta, *a.* marked with a white spot *or* stripe (*horses*). — *n.f.* mask; fencing mask; bee-keeper's mask; ***careta antigás,*** gas-mask; ***quitarle a uno la careta,*** to unmask, expose.
carey, *n.m.* tortoise-shell turtle; tortoise-shell.
carga, *n.f.* load, burden; freight, cargo, lading; charge (*of fire-arms, mines, furnaces etc.*); (*fig.*) duty, toll, tax; (*fig.*) burden; weight, load, pressure; (*mil.*) charge; (*vet.*) poultice; ***a cargas,*** abundantly, in plenty; ***bestia de carga,*** beast of burden; ***carga abierta,*** bayonet *or* sword charge in open formation; ***carga cerrada,*** bayonet *or* sword charge in close formation; ***a carga cerrada,*** in bulk; ***carga de caballería,*** cavalry charge; (*eng.*) ***carga fija,*** dead load; ***carga de fractura*** or ***de rotura,*** breaking load; (*hydrost.*) ***carga hidrostática,*** head; ***carga mayor,*** burden suitable for horse *or* mule; ***carga menor,*** load suitable for an ass; (*eng.*) ***carga móvil,*** live load; ***carga personal,*** obligatory personal service; ***carga real,*** king's tax, land tax; ***carga útil,*** payload; ***acodillar con la carga,*** to sink down under a burden; to be unable to fulfil one's duties; ***echar la carga a otro,*** to put the main load on to another; ***echar las cargas a otro,*** to throw the blame upon another; ***echarse uno con la carga,*** to give up in despair; ***sentarse*** (***una carga***), to settle (*a load*); ***ser de ciento en carga,*** to be run-of-the-mill, commonplace; ***soltar la carga,*** to throw off a duty *or* responsibility; ***terciar la carga,*** to divide the load; ***volver a la carga,*** to harp on a subject.
cargadal, *n.m.* (*prov.*) silt (*in rivers and drains*).
cargadera, *n.f.* (*naut.*) down-haul, brail; (*Col.*) suspenders.
cargadero, *n.m.* loading *or* unloading bay *or* platform; (*arch.*) lintel.
cargadilla, *n.f.* (*coll.*) increase of a debt through accumulation of interest.
cargado, -da, *a.* loaded, full; sultry (*weather*); pregnant (*sheep*); strong (*tea, coffee etc.*); ***cargado de espaldas,*** round-shouldered, stooping. — *n.m.* Spanish step in dancing. — *n.f.pl.* (**cargadas**) card game.
cargador, *n.m.* shipper, freighter; loader, stevedore; carrier, porter; charger; (*arch.*) post put in a door *or* window; pitchfork (*for straw*); rammer, ramrod.
cargamento, *n.m.* (*naut.*) cargo, shipment.
cargante, *a., n.m.f.* unbearable, insufferable, annoying (*person*).
cargar [B], *v.t.* to load; to overload, burden, make heavy, weigh down; to impose, lay; to charge; (*fig.*) to get on the nerves of, annoy; (*com.*) to debit, book, charge to account; (*naut.*) to furl *or* unfurl; (*mil.*) to charge; (*vet.*) to poultice; ***cargar los dados,*** to load the dice; (*com.*) ***cargar a flete,*** to ship on freight; (*naut.*) ***cargar arriba una vela,*** to clew up a sail; ***cargar la concienca,*** to burden one's conscience; ***cargar la mano (en),*** to overdo it, go to far, use too much (of); — *v.i.* to lean, rest; to load up; to fall (*of stress*); (*bot.*) to bear fruit in abundance; ***cargar a (en) hombros,*** to hoist on one's shoulders, bear on the shoulders; ***cargó con todo,*** he took everything away; he (under)took responsibility for everything, dealt with everything. — **cargarse,** *v.r.* to lean (*the body*) towards; to incline towards; (*com.*) to agree with the sum debited to one's account; to become cloudy *or* heavier (*weather*); (*with **de***) to become full, overburdened; (*fig.*) to get browned off, fed up; ***cargarse de hijos,*** to load o.s. down with children; ***cargarse de razón,*** to see that one has right fully on one's side.
cargareme, *n.m.* receipt, voucher.
cargazón, *n.f.* cargo; heaviness (*in any part of the body*); cloudiness; (*Arg.*) botch; (*Chi.*) abundance of fruit (*on trees, plants etc.*); heavy, overcast sky.
cargo, *n.m.* load, loading; burden; load (*of stones of one-third cubic metre*); load (*of pressed grapes for repressing*); (*com.*) total receipts; charge, accusation; (*law*) count; post, position; office; (*Chi.*) (*law*) certificate (*issued by the court and appended to legal documents indicating date and hour of receipt*); care, charge, keeping; duty *or* obligation; ministry; command; management; fault *or* deficiency of duty; ***cargo concejil,*** compulsory municipal office; ***cargo de conciencia,*** remorse, sense of guilt; (*com.*) ***cargo y data,*** creditor and debtor; ***hacer cargo a uno de una cosa,*** to entrust s.o. with sth.; ***hacerse cargo de algo,*** to take sth. upon o.s.; ***esto está a cargo de fulano,*** so-and-so is in charge of *or* responsible for this.
cargoso, -sa, *a.* heavy, grave, annoying, vexatious.
carguero, -ra, *a.* burden-bearing, freight-carrying. — *n.m.* cargo-boat; (*Arg.*) beast of burden.
carguío, *n.m.* cargo, freight; load.
cari, *a.* (*Arg., Chi.*) light brown colour; *n.m.* (*Hisp Am.*) blackberry; (*Arg.*) poncho; (*Chi.*) Indian pepper.
caria, *n.f.* (*arch.*) shaft (*of column*).
cariacedo, -da, *a.* disagreeable, ill-tempered.
cariaco, *n.m.* (*Cub.*) popular dance; (*Ec.*) beverage made from sugar-cane.
cariacontecido, -da, *a.* down-in-the-mouth.
cariacos, *n.m.pl.* (*ethn.*) Caribs.
cariacuchillado, -da, *a.* scarred (*face*).
cariado, -da, *a.* carious, decayed.
cariadura, *n.f.* (*med.*) caries.
cariaguileño, -ña, *a.* aquiline (*face*).
carialegre, *a.* smiling, cheerful.
carialzado, -da, *a.* with uplifted face.
cariampollado, -da, cariampollar, *a.* round-faced, plump-cheeked.
cariancho, -cha, *a.* broad-faced.
cariarse [L], *v.r.* (*med.*) to become carious, decayed.
cariátide, *n.f.* (*arch.*) caryatid.
caríbal, *n.m.* cannibal, man-eater.
caribe, *a., n.m.f.* Carib, Indian (from West Indies). — *n.m.* Carib language; (*fig.*) savage.
caribello, *a.* having white spots on the forehead (*bull*).
caribito, *n.m.* fresh-water bream.
cariblanco, *n.m.* (*C.R.*) small wild boar.
caribobo, -ba, *a.* stupid-looking.
caribú, *n.m.* caribou, cariboo.
carica, *n.f.* (*prov.*) spotted kidney bean.
caricato, *n.m.* opera buffoon; comedian.
caricatura, *n.f.* caricature; cartoon.
caricatural, *a.* caricatural.
caricaturar, caricaturizar [C], *v.t.* to caricature.
caricaturesco, -ca, *a.* caricatural.
caricaturista, *n.m.f.* caricaturist; cartoonist.
caricia, *n.f.* caress, stroke.
caricioso, -sa, *a.* fondling, caressing.
caricompuesto, -ta, *a.* with composed, circumspect face.
caricorto, -ta, *a.* small-featured *or* fine (*face*).
caricoso, -sa, *a.* fig-shaped.
caricuerdo, -da, *a.* with a grave, reserved expression.

carichato, -ta, *a.* flat-faced.
caridad, *n.f.* charity; alms; ***la caridad bien entendida empieza por uno mismo,*** charity begins at home.
caridelantero, -ra, *a.* (*coll.*) brazen-faced, impudent.
caridoliente, *a.* pained-looking.
cariedón, *n.m.* nut-weevil.
carientismo, *n.m.* (*rhet.*) dissimulated irony.
carie(s), *n.f.* (*med.*) caries, decay; (*agric.*) blight; (*coll.*) ***tener una carie,*** to have a decayed *or* carious tooth.
cariexento, -ta, *a.* (*fam.*) shameless, brazen-faced.
carifruncido, -da, *a.* (*coll.*) cross-looking, frowning.
carigordo, -da, *a.* fat-faced.
cariharto, -ta, *a.* round-faced.
carihermoso, -sa, *a.* fair of face.
carijusto -ta, *a.* hypocritical.
carilampiño, *a.* smooth-faced, beardless.
carilargo, -ga, *a.* long-faced.
carilavado, -da, *a.* clean-faced; beaming.
carilucio, -cia, *a.* shiny-faced.
carilla (1), *n.f.* (bee-keeper's) mask; page (*of book*); (*Aragonese*) silver coin.
carilleno, -na, *a.* plump-faced, full-faced.
carillo, -lla (2), *a.* rather dear, on the expensive side. — *n.m.f.* beloved, betrothed, lover.
carillón, *n.m.* (*mus.*) carillon.
carimba, *n.f.* (*Per.*) branding mark; (*Cub.*) branding-iron.
carimbo, *n.m.* (*Bol.*) branding-iron.
carimohino, -na, *a.* glum-faced, gloomy-looking.
carinegro, -ra, *a.* dark, swarthy-complexioned.
carininfo, -fa, *a.* with girlish face, effeminate.
cariñana, *n.f.* ancient head-dress resembling a nun's wimple.
cariñar, *v.i.* (*prov.*) to be homesick.
cariñena, *n.f.* Cariñena wine.
cariño, *n.m.* love, affection, tenderness, fondness; dear, darling; (*pl.*) tender *or* endearing expressions; ***con cariño,*** lovingly.
cariñoso, -sa, *a.* affectionate, loving, fond, kind.
caripálido, -da, *a.* pale-faced.
caripando, -da, *a.* foolish-looking.
cariparejo, -ja, *a.* (*coll.*) impassive.
carirraído, -da, *a.* (*coll.*) brazen-faced, impudent.
carirrechoncho, -cha, *a.* (*fam.*) chubby-faced.
carirredondo, -da, *a.* round-faced.
carirromo, -ma, *a.* flat-featured.
cariseto, *n.m.* coarse woollen cloth.
carisma, *n.m.* charisma.
carita, *n.f.* (dainty *or* sweet) little face.
caritán, *n.m.* (*Philip.*) gatherer of tuba.
caritativo, -va, *a.* charitable.
carite, *n.m.* (*Cub.*) sawfish.
caritieso, -sa, *a.* stiff-faced.
cariz, *n.m.* appearance, aspect, look; ***este asunto va tomando mal cariz,*** this business is beginning to look nasty.
carla, *n.f.* coloured cloth.
carlán, *n.m.* person with certain rights and jurisdiction of a district in Aragon.
carlanca, *n.f.* spiked iron collar; (*sl.*) shirt-collar; (*Col., C.R.*) shackle, fetter; (*Chi., Hond.*) burdensome, onerous person; (*pl.*) roguery, trickery; ***tener muchas carlancas,*** to be very cunning and crafty.
carlancón, -cona, *a., n.m.f.* cunning and crafty (individual).
carlanga, *n.f.* (*Mex.*) rag, tatter.
carlanía, *n.f.* dignity and district of a ***carlán.***
carlear, *v.i.* to pant.
carleta, *n.f.* file (*for smoothing iron*); (*min.*) Anjou slate.
carlín, *n.m.* ancient silver coin.
carlina, *n.f.* carline thistle.
carlinga, *n.f.* (*naut.*) step (*of a mast*); (*aer.*) cockpit.
carlismo, *n.m.* Carlism.
carlista, *a., n.m.f.* Carlist.
carlita, *n.f.* reading-glasses.
Carlitos, *n.m.* Charlie.
Carlos, *n.m.* Charles.
carlota, *n.f.* Charlotte pudding.
carlovingio, -gia, *a., n.m.f.* Carolingian.
carmañola, *n.f.* jacket with narrow collar; carmagnole (*song*).
carmel, *n.m.* plantain.
carmelina, *n.f.* second quality vicuña wool.
carmelita, *a.* Carmelite; (*Hisp. Am.*) brown. — *n.m.f.* Carmelite. — *n.f.* nasturtium flower.
carmelitano, -na, *a.* belonging to the order of the Carmelites.
Carmelo, *n.m.* order of Mount Carmel.
carmen (1), *n.m.* (*prov.*) country-house and garden; villa.
carmen (2), *n.m.* Carmelite order.
carmen (3), *n.m.* verse, poem.
carmenador, *n.m.* teaser, comber (*workman* or *machine*); carding-engine *or* machine.
carmenadura, *n.f.* teasing (*wool, silk etc.*).
carmenar, *v.t.* to tease, card, unravel (*wool* or *silk*); to comb, disentangle (*hair*); (*coll.*) to pull (*the hair*); (*coll.*) to rob, cheat (*of valuables*).
carmes, *n.m. inv.* (*ent.*) kermes.
carmesí, *a.* carmine, scarlet, crimson. — *n.m.* cochineal powder; crimson, scarlet, red silk material.
carmín, *n.m.* carmine, colouring matter of cochineal; carmine (*colour*); (*bot.*) wild red rose; ***carmín bajo,*** pale rose-colour.
carminativo, -va, *a., n.m.f.* (*med.*) carminative.
carminoso, -sa, *a.* reddish.
carnación, *n.f.* carmine; (*her., paint.*) carnation; flesh colour.
carnada, *n.f.* bait; (*coll.*) artifice, trap.
carnadura, *n.f.* muscularity, robustness; (*surg.*) incarnation.
carnaje, *n.m.* salt beef; carnage.
carnal, *a.* carnal, sensual; (*fig.*) earthly, worldly; german(e); ***primo carnal,*** first cousin.
carnalidad, *n.f.* carnality, sensuality.
carnaval, *n.m.* carnival.
carnavalada, *n.f.* carnival stunt.
carnavalesco, -ca, *a.* carnival-like.
carnaza, *n.f.* fleshy side (*of hide* or *skin*); bait; (*coll.*) fleshiness.
carne, *n.f.* meat; pulp (*of fruit*); (*lit., fig.*) flesh; ***carne ahogadiza,*** meat of a drowned animal; ***carne cediza,*** tainted meat; ***carne de cañón,*** cannon-fodder; ***carne de horca,*** gallows-bird(s); ***carne fiambre,*** cold meat; (*fig.*) ***carne de gallina,*** goose-flesh; ***carne magra, mollar*** or ***momia,*** lean meat; ***carne de membrillo,*** quince jelly; ***carne de pelo,*** flesh of small quadrupeds (*rabbits etc.*); ***carne de pluma,*** flesh of fowls; ***carne de sábado,*** head, pluck, feet of slaughtered animals; giblets of fowls; ***carne de perro,*** really tough individual; really hard-wearing stuff; ***carne de vaca*** (***de cerdo, de cordero***), beef (pork, lamb *or* mutton); ***carne nueva,*** first meat sold after Lent; ***carne salvajina,*** venison; (*fig.*) ***carne sin hueso,*** sinecure; ***carne trifa,*** meat cut by a Hebrew butcher; ***carne viva,*** quick flesh (*in a wound*); ***carne viciosa,*** proud flesh; ***carnes blancas,*** white meats; ***criar*** (***echar***) ***carnes,*** to put on weight; ***estar metido en carnes,*** to have got fat (hefty); ***estar en carne viva,*** to be raw; ***estar en carnes vivas,*** to be stark naked; ***hacer carne,*** to butcher, slaughter; ***hacerse carne,*** to flay oneself; ***poner toda la carne en el*** (***al***) ***asador,***

to stake everything, to give it everything one's got; ***ser carne y sangre,*** to be kith and kin; ***ser de carne y hueso,*** to be flesh and blood; (*fig.*) ***ser uña y carne,*** to be very close; ***no ser ni carne ni pescado,*** to be neither one thing nor the other; ***le temblaban las carnes (de miedo),*** he was shivering in his shoes.

carnear, *v.t.* (*Hisp. Am.*) to slaughter; (*Chi.*) to swindle, cheat; (*Mex.*) to kill, stab.

carnecería [CARNICERÍA].

carnecilla, *n.f.* caruncle, lump.

carnerada, *n.f.* flock of sheep.

carneraje, *n.m.* tax *or* duty on sheep.

carnerario, *n.m.* (*prov.*) charnel-house.

carnereamiento, *n.m.* penalty for the trespass of sheep.

carnerear, *v.t.* to kill (*sheep*) for trespassing.

carnerero, *n.m.* shepherd.

carneril, *a.* to do with sheep. — *n.m.* sheep-walk, sheep-run.

carnero, *n.m.* sheep, mutton; (*prov.*) sheep-skin; family vault, charnel-house, burying place; (*Arg., Bol., Per.*) llama; (*Arg., Chi., coll.*) weak-minded person; scab; ***carnero marino,*** seal; ***carnero de simiente,*** ram kept for breeding; (*coll.*) ***no hay tales carneros,*** there is no truth in it; there is no such thing.

carneruno, -na, *a.* belonging to sheep; sheep-like, sheepish.

carnestolendas, *n.f.pl.* Shrovetide.

carnet, *n.m.* memorandum book; season-ticket; ***carnet de conducir,*** driving licence.

carnicería, *n.f.* butcher's shop; (*fig.*) carnage, massacre slaughter; (*Ec.*) slaughterhouse.

carnicero, -ra, *a.* carnivorous (*animals*); (*fig.*) blood-thirsty; applied to pastures for cattle about to be slaughtered; (*coll.*) fond of meat. — *n.m.f.* butcher. — *n.m.pl.* (*zool.*) Carnivora.

carnicol, *n.m.* hoof (*cloven*); (*pl.* **carnicoles**) knuckle-bones (*game*).

carnificación, *n.f.* (*med.*) carnification.

carnificarse [A], *v.r.* (*med.*) to carnify.

carniforme, *a.* flesh-like.

carniseco, -ca, *a.* lean, scraggy.

carnívoro, -ra, *a.* carnivorous (*animal*). — *n.m.* carnivore; (*pl.*) Carnivora.

carniza, *n.f.* (*coll.*) left-over meat; cats' meat, dogs' meat; decayed flesh.

carnosidad, *n.f.* proud flesh; carnosity; fleshiness.

carnoso, -sa, carnudo, -da, *a.* fleshy; full of marrow; pulpy (*fruit*).

carnuz, *n.m.* (*prov.*) tainted meat.

carnuza, *n.f.* coarse sheep meat.

caro (1) **-ra** (2), *a.* dear, expensive; beloved; ***cara mitad,*** better half. — *adv.* dear, dearly.

caro (2), *n.m.* (*Cub.*) dish made of crab roes and cassava.

caroba, *n.f.* carob.

caroca, *n.f.* decoration in public festivities; farce; (*coll.*) cajolery.

carocha, carrocha, *n.f.* eggs (*of bees and other insects*).

carochar, carrochar, *v.i.* to lay eggs (*bees and other insects*).

carola, *n.f.* carol, song and dance.

carolingio, -gia, *a., n.m.f.* Carolingian.

carolino, -na, *a., n.m.f.* of *or* from Caroline Islands (*Pacific*); Caroline.

carolus, *n.m. inv.* Flemish coin (*16th century*).

caromomia, *n.f.* dry flesh of a mummy.

carona, *n.f.* saddle padding *or* lining; part of the animal's back which bears the saddle; (*sl.*) shirt; ***a carona,*** bare-backed; ***esquilar*** or ***hacer la carona,*** to shear the back of a mount; ***blando de carona,*** having the back tender where the saddle goes; (*coll.*) said of a person who is lazy, feeble *or* addicted to falling in love; ***corto*** or ***largo de carona,*** short- *or* long-backed (*mount*).

caroñoso, -sa, *a.* old and galled (*animals*).

caroquero, -ra, *a.* caressing; honey-worded. — *n.m.f.* wheedler, flatterer.

carosiero, *n.m.* palm-tree.

carosis, *n.f. inv.* profound stupor.

carótico, -ca, *a.* (*med.*) relating to stupor. *n.m.*— cure for stupor.

carótido, -da, *a.* carotid. — *n.f.* the carotid artery.

carozo, *n.m.* (*prov.*) core (*of apple, pear etc.*); cob (*of maize*).

carpa, *n.f.* (*ichth.*) carp; part torn off from a bunch of grapes; (*Hisp. Am.*) canvas tent.

carpanel, *n.m.* (*arch.*) elliptic arch.

carpanta, *n.f.* (*coll.*) ravenous hunger; (*prov.*) laziness; (*Mex.*) crowd of noisy people; loose-living set.

Cárpatos, *n.m.pl.* Carpathians.

carpe, *n.m.* hornbeam.

carpedal, *n.m.* plantation of hornbeam-trees.

carpelo, *n.m.* carpel.

carpeta, *n.f.* table-cover; folder, file, letter-file, portfolio; writing-case; docket (*of stock-exchange quotations*); small curtain *or* screen (*before the door of a tavern*); (*prov.*) envelope.

carpetazo, *n.m.* swipe with a folder; ***dar carpetazo a,*** to shelve; to put away and forget.

carpetovetónico, -ca, *a.* (*fig.*) utterly *or* hopelessly Spanish.

carpiano, -na, *a.* (*zool.*) carpal.

carpidor, *n.m.* (*Hisp. Am.*) hoe.

carpincho, *n.m.* (*Hisp. Am.*) capybara.

carpintear, *v.i.* to carpenter.

carpintería, *n.f.* carpentry, woodwork; carpenter's shop.

carpintero, *n.m.* carpenter, joiner, woodworker; ***carpintero de blanco,*** joiner; ***carpintero de armar*** or ***de obras de afuera,*** carpenter who timbers *or* roofs houses; ***carpintero de prieto*** or ***de carretas,*** cartwright, wheelwright; ***carpintero de ribera*** or ***de navío,*** ship-carpenter, shipwright; ***maestro carpintero de remos,*** master oar-maker; (*orn.*) ***pájaro carpintero,*** carpenter-bird, woodpecker.

carpir(se), *v.i.* (*v.r.*) to wrangle, quarrel; to scrape, scratch, tear; to stun; (*Hisp. Am.*) to clear (*the ground*) with a hoe.

carpo, *n.m.* carpus, wrist.

carpobálsamo, *n.m.* (*bot.*) fruit of balsam-fir.

carpófago, -ga, *a.* carpophagous.

carpología, *n.f.* carpology.

carqueroles, *n.m.pl.* parts of velvet loom.

carquesa, *n.f.* glass-furnace.

carquexia, *n.f.* medicinal broom.

carraca (1), *n.f.* carrack; navy-yard.

carraca (2), *n.f.* rattle; ratchet.

carraco, -ca (3), *a.* old, withered, decrepit.

carrada, *n.f.* cart-load, cartful.

carragaheen, *n.m.* carrageen.

carral (1), *n.m.* barrel, butt, vat.

carral (2), *n.m.* (*prov.*) decrepit old man.

carraleja, *n.f.* oil beetle.

carralero, *n.m.* cooper.

carranca, carrancha, *n.f.* spiked iron collar.

carranza, *n.f.* spike (*of iron collar*).

carrao, *n.m.* (*Ven.*) (*orn.*) crane; (*Col., Cub.*) heavy, coarse shoes.

carraón, *n.m.* short-stemmed wheat.

carrasca, *n.f.* holly-oak, holm-oak.

carrascal, carrascalejo, *n.m.* holm-oak grove.

carrasco, *n.m.* holm-oak, Corsican pine.

carraspada, *n.f.* negus (*beverage*).

carraspante, *a.* harsh, rough.

carraspear, *v.i.* to clear one's throat; to suffer from hoarseness.

carraspeño, -ña, *a.* gruff, hoarse.
carraspeo, *n.m.* hoarseness; clearing of throat.
carraspera, *n.f.* (*coll.*) hoarseness; sore throat, frog-in-the-throat.
carraspique, *n.m.* candytuft.
carrasposo, -sa, *a.* suffering from chronic hoarseness *or* sore throat; (*Col.*, *Ven.*) rough to the touch.
carrasqueño, -ña, *a.* belonging to the holm-oak; (*prov.*) harsh, sharp.
carrejo, *n.m.* corridor, passage.
carrera, *n.f.* run, race; race-track; road; (*astron.*) course; avenue; line, parting of the hair; (*arch.*) beam, girder; ladder, run (*in stocking*); career, profession; course (*of a pageant* or *procession*); (*naut.*) steamer route *or* run; coach *or* stage line; Spanish step in dancing; (*pl.*) races, horse-racing; (*mil.*) ***carrera de baquetas,*** gauntlet (*punishment*); (*fig.*) series of troubles; ***de carrera,*** swiftly, rashly; ***carrera del émbolo,*** stroke of the piston; ***carrera de Indias,*** trade between Spain and Spanish America; ***carrera del sol,*** the sun's course; ***a la carrera,*** at full speed; ***dar carrera a uno,*** to pay for s.o.'s education; ***estar en carrera,*** to begin to earn one's living; ***hacer carrera,*** to succeed, get on; ***hacer la carrera,*** to walk the streets; ***no poder hacer carrera con*** or ***de alguno,*** to be unable to bring s.o. to reason; ***poner a uno en carrera,*** to provide s.o. with a job.
carrerilla, *n.f.* rapid movement in a Spanish dance; (*mus.*) run, flourish, roulade of an octave; ***decir de carrerilla,*** to say off pat.
carrerista, *n.m.f.* turfite; punter, better; racing cyclist. — *n.m.* outrider of the royal carriage.
carrero, *n.m.* carman, carrier, carter, ox-cart driver, vanman.
carreta, *n.f.* waggon.
carretada, *n.f.* cartful, cart-load; (*coll.*) ***a carretadas,*** by the cart-load.
carretaje, *n.m.* cartage, carting fee.
carretal, *n.m.* rough, ragged ashlar.
carrete, *n.m.* spool, bobbin, reel; fishing-reel; (*elec.*, *wire.*) bobbin, wireless induction coil; ***dar carrete,*** to pay out (*line*); ***dar carrete a uno,*** to keep s.o. dangling.
carreteador, *n.m.* carter, waggon-driver.
carretear, *v.t.* to cart, convey in a cart; to drive (*a cart*). — *v.i.* (*Cub.*) loud chatter of parrots *or* parrakeets (*especially when young*). — **carretearse,** *v.r.* to draw unevenly (*of oxen and mules*).
carretel, *n.m.* (*prov.*) fishing-reel, line-reel; (*naut.*) log-reel.
carretela, *n.f.* calash; (*Chi.*) omnibus, stage-coach.
carreteo, *n.m.* cart transport, carting.
carretera, *n.f.* road, high-road, highway; ***carretera de circunvalación,*** by-pass, (*Am.*) cut-off.
carretería, *n.f.* number of carts; carter's trade; cartwright's yard; wheelwright's shop.
carreteril, *a.* appertaining to carters.
carretero, *a.* ***camino carretero,*** cart (waggon) road. — *n.m.* cartwright; carter, driver; (*sl.*) card-sharper; ***jurar como un carretero,*** to swear like a trooper.
carretil, *a.* belonging to a cart; ***camino carretil,*** cart-road.
carretilla, *n.f.* small cart; push-cart, wheelbarrow, hand-cart; railway truck; baby-walker, child's go-cart; squib, cracker; instrument for decorating bread and cakes; (*Arg.*, *Ur.*) heavy goods vehicle drawn by three mules; (*Chi.*) long narrow cart, waggon; (*Arg.*, *Chi.*) jaw, jawbone; ***de carretilla,*** automatically, off pat, by heart; ***carretilla de equipaje,*** baggage-truck; (*coll.*) ***saber de carretilla,*** to know off pat.
carretillada, *n.f.* wheelbarrow-load.
carretillero, *n.m.* one who guides *or* pushes a wheelbarrow.
carretón, *n.m.* cart, go-cart; truck; dray; child's chair; knife-grinder's cart; ***carretón de lámpara,*** pulley used for raising and lowering lamps (*in churches*).
carretonada, *n.f.* truck-load, waggon-load.
carretoncillo, *n.m.* small go-cart; sled, sledge, sleigh.
carretonero, *n.m.* drayman, truck-man.
carricoche, *n.m.* waggonette; rickshaw; (*coll.*) old-fashioned cart *or* coach; (*prov.*) muck-cart, dung-cart.
carricuba, *n.f.* water-cart.
carriego, *n.m.* osier fishing-trap; rough basket (*for bleaching flax-yarn*).
carriel, *n.m.* (*Col.*, *Ec.*, *Ven.*) muleteer's girdle; (*C.R.*) travelling valise; (*C.R.*) reticule.
carril, *n.m.* rut, cart-rut; narrow road, cartway; lane; furrow; (*railw.*) rail; ***salirse de sus carriles,*** to go off the track *or* rails.
carrilada, carrilera, *n.f.* rut, cart-rut; (*Cub.*) railway siding; (*Col.*) grate, grillage.
carrilano, *n.m.* (*Chi.*) railway worker; (*Chi.*) thief, bandit.
carrillada, *n.f.* oily *or* medullar substance of a hog's cheek.
carrillar, *n.m.* tackle used to hoist light goods from the hold of a ship. — *v.t.* (*naut.*) to hoist with a tackle.
carrillera, *n.f.* jaw; chin-strap, chin-stay.
carrillo, *n.m.* cheek; hoisting tackle, pulley; ***carrillos de monja boba, de trompetero,*** full, plump cheeks; ***comer*** or ***masticar a dos carrillos,*** to eat voraciously; to have two strings to one's bow.
carrilludo, -da, *a.* plump- *or* round-cheeked.
carriola, *n.f.* truckle-bed, trundle-bed; carriole, small chariot, curricle.
carriquí, *n.m.* (*Col.*) carriqui bird.
carrizada, *n.f.* line of barrels towed on the water.
carrizal, *n.m.* land covered in reed-grass.
carrizo, *n.m.* (*bot.*) common reed-grass.
carro, *n.m.* cart; carriage; cart-load, carriageful; (*Hisp. Am.*) car; carriage-frame; (*sl.*) gambling; (*print.*) bed, carriage (*of press*); carriage (*of typewriter*); (*railw.*) truck, (*Am.*) freight car; ***carro de oro,*** fine shot camlet; ***carro de basura,*** dust-cart; ***carro de riego,*** water-cart; ***carro de volteo,*** tip-car, tilt-car; ***carro fuerte,*** lorry, truck; (*astron.*) ***Carro Mayor,*** Great Bear; (*astron.*) ***Carro Menor,*** Little Bear; ***carro triunfal,*** triumphal chariot; (*fig.*) ***cogerle a uno el carro,*** to be unlucky; ***tirar del carro,*** to bear the brunt; (*fig.*) ***untar el carro,*** to bribe, wheedle; ***¡alto el carro!*** hold your horses!
carrocería, *n.f.* shop where carriages are made, repaired *or* sold; (*motor.*) body, bodywork.
carrocero, *n.m.* carriage- *or* coach-builder.
carrocilla, *n.f.* small coach.
carrocín, *n.m.* gig.
carrocha, *n.f.* seminal substance *or* eggs of insects.
carrochar [CAROCHAR].
carromatero, *n.m.* carter, carman.
carromato, *n.m.* covered waggon.
carrón, *n.m.* hodful of bricks.
carronada, *n.f.* carronade.
carroñar, *v.t.* to infect (*sheep*) with the scab.
carroño, -ña, *a.* putrefied, putrid, rotten. — *n.f.* carrion.
carroñoso, -sa, *a.* foul-smelling.
carroza, *n.f.* coach, carriage; ***carroza alegórica,*** float; (*naut.*) awning.
carrozal, *a.* appertaining to coach-building.
carruaje, *n.m.* carriage; vehicle.
carruajero, *n.m.* waggoner, driver.
carruata, *n.f.* agave from Guyana.
carruco, *n.m.* small cart, hodful of tiles.
carrucha, *n.f.* pulley.

carrucho, *n.m.* wretched (little) cart.

carrujado, -da, *a.* corrugated, wrinkled. — *n.m.* (*sew.*) fluting, gathering, shirring.

carrujo, *n.m.* tree-top.

carta, *n.f.* letter; playing card; chart; royal ordinance; charter; menu; ***carta abierta,*** open letter; (*com.*) letter of credit for unlimited amount; ***carta blanca,*** carte blanche; ***carta certificada,*** registered letter; ***carta(s) credencial(es)*** or ***carta de creencia,*** credential(s); ***carta de ahorro,*** letters of enfranchisement; ***carta de crédito,*** letter of credit; ***carta de dote,*** document detailing a wife's dowry; (*law*) ***carta de espera*** or ***moratoria,*** moratorium; ***carta de examen,*** diploma; (*com.*) ***carta de fletamento,*** charter-party; ***carta de gracia*** or ***forera,*** royal grant of privileges; (*law*) reversion contract; judicial writ; ***carta de guía,*** passport; (*eccles.*) ***carta de hermandad,*** introduction; ***carta de hidalguía*** or ***ejecutoria*** (***de hidalguía***), letters patent of nobility; (*law*) ***carta de libre,*** guardian's discharge; ***carta de marca,*** letters of marque; ***carta de marear,*** sea chart; ***Carta Magna,*** Magna Carta; ***carta de naturaleza,*** letters of naturalization: ***carta de pago,*** acquittance, receipt, discharge (*of a debt etc.*); ***carta de presentación,*** letter of introduction; ***carta de sanidad,*** bill of health; ***carta de seguridad,*** safeguard, protection; ***carta de Urías,*** trap, snare, treacherous letter; ***carta de vecindad,*** burghership certificate; ***carta de venta,*** bill of sale; ***carta de vuelta,*** dead letter; ***carta en lista,*** letter 'to be called for', letter in *poste restante*; ***carta orden,*** mandatory letter; ***carta pastoral,*** pastoral; ***carta pécora,*** document written on parchment; ***carta plomada,*** document with lead seal; ***carta puebla,*** certificate of rights over land; ***carta receptoria,*** warrant, voucher; ***carta requisitoria,*** letters requisitorial; ***carta viva,*** messenger who delivers a message verbally; ***cartas*** or ***letras expectativas,*** royal *or* papal announcement of forthcoming appointment; ***a carta cabal,*** irreproachably; completely; ***a la carta,*** à la carte, (*Am.*) European plan; ***carta canta,*** there is documentary evidence, it can be proved; (*fig.*) ***echar las cartas,*** to tell a person's fortune by cards; ***enseñar las cartas,*** to show one's hand; ***jugar a cartas vistas, poner las cartas boca arriba,*** to play a straight game, act openly, put *or* lay one's cards on the table; ***no estar en cartas,*** to be without precedent, unheard-of; ***perder con buenas cartas,*** to lose despite having a strong hand; (*fig.*) ***traer*** (or ***venir con***) ***malas cartas,*** to have a poor *or* weak hand; to have the odds against one; ***no ver carta(s),*** to have a bad run of cards; ***no saber a qué carta quedarse,*** not to know where one stands; ***tomar cartas*** (***en***), to take a hand (in); take sides (in); ***hablen cartas y callen barbas,*** actions speak louder than words; ***por carta de más o de menos se pierden los juegos,*** a miss is as good as a mile.

cartabón, *n.m.* (drawing) triangle; (*shoemaker's*) slide-rule; (topographic) octagonal prism; ***echar el cartabón,*** to adopt measures to attain one's end.

cartafolio, *n.m.* sheet of paper, folio.

cartagenero, -ra, *a.*, *n.m.f.* (native) of Cartagena. — *n.f.* flamenco dance.

cartaginense, cartaginés, -nesa, *a.*, *n.m.f.* Carthaginian, (native) of Carthage.

Cartago, *n.f.* Carthage.

cártama, *n.f.*, **cártamo,** *n.m.* bastard saffron.

cartapacio, *n.m.* memorandum-book; writing-case; (*fig.*, *fam.*) lengthy screed.

cartazo, *n.m.* long letter; (*coll.*) letter *or* paper containing a severe reproof.

cartear, *v.i.* to play out low cards to see how the game stands. — **cartearse,** *v.r.* to correspond regularly.

cartel, *n.m.* poster; mural reading-card (*for teaching children*); (*Am.*) bill-board; cartel; agreement; sardine fishing-net; lampoon; ***tener cartel,*** to have a good name, be popular.

cartela, *n.f.* slip of paper *or* other form of memorandum; (*arch.*) modillion, console, bracket; iron stay (*supporting a balcony*).

cartelera, *n.f.* bill-board, hoarding; amusement-guide.

cartelero, *n.m.* bill-poster, bill-sticker.

carteo, *n.m.* correspondence, exchange of letters.

cárter, *n.m.* (*mech.*) housing; ***sumidor del cárter,*** sump, (*Am.*) oil-pan.

cartera, *n.f.* pocket-book, wallet, (*Am.*) billfold; document case, brief-case; pocket-flap; (*fig.*) portfolio (*office of cabinet minister*); (*com.*) assets; ***cartera de pedidos,*** order book.

cartería, *n.f.* employment of letter-carrier; sorting-room (*in post-office etc.*).

carterista, *n.m.* pickpocket.

cartero, *n.m.* postman.

cartesianismo, *n.m.* Cartesianism.

cartesiano, -na, *a.*, *n.m.f.* Cartesian.

carteta, *n.f.* lansquenet.

cartílago, *n.m.* cartilage.

cartilla, *n.f.* clergyman's certificate of ordination; children's primer, spelling book; ***cartilla de ahorros,*** savings book; ***cartilla de racionamiento,*** ration book; ***no saber la cartilla,*** to have not a clue; ***cantarle*** or ***leerle a uno la cartilla,*** to read s.o. the riot act, to lecture *or* warn s.o.; ***no estar en la cartilla,*** to be uncommon, out of the ordinary.

cartismo, *n.m.* Chartism.

cartista, *a.*, *n.m.f.* Chartist.

cartita, *n.f.* short letter, brief note.

cartivana, *n.f.* linen *or* paper strip (*for binding single sheets*).

cartografía, *n.f.* cartography.

cartográfico, -ca, *a.* cartographic.

cartógrafo, *n.m.* cartographer, map-maker.

cartología, *n.f.* cartology.

cartomancia, *n.f.* cartomancy, fortune-telling by cards.

cartomántico, -ca, *a.* relating to cartomancy. — *n.m.f.* fortune-teller by cards.

cartómetro, *n.m.* curvimeter.

cartón, *n.m.* pasteboard, cardboard; carton; cartoon (*for fresco, tapestry etc.*); iron ornament representing the leaves of plants; (*art*) ***cartón piedra,*** papier-mâché.

cartonaje, *n.m.* cardboard packaging.

cartonería, *n.f.* cardboard *or* millboard factory *or* shop.

cartonero, -ra, *a.* relating to cardboard. — *n.m.f.* maker *or* vendor of pasteboard, cardboard articles. — *n.f.pl.* paper-making wasps.

cartuchera, *n.f.* cartridge-box; cartridge-belt.

cartuchería, *n.f.* cartridge-factory; stock of cartridges.

cartucho, *n.m.* cartridge; roll of coins; paper cornet; (*lit.*, *fig.*) ***quemar el último cartucho,*** to fire one's last round, use up one's last resource.

cartuja, *n.f.* Carthusian order; Charterhouse.

cartujano, -na, *a.* Carthusian.

cartujo, *a.* Carthusian. — *n.m.* Carthusian monk; (*coll.*) taciturn man; hermit, recluse.

cartulario, *n.m.* cartulary, archives, registry; archivist.

cartulina, *n.f.* cartridge paper; thin cardboard.

cartusana, *n.f.* fancy braid.

caruata, *n.f.* (*Ven.*) agave.

carúncula, *n.f.* caruncle; wattle; ***carúncula lagrimal,*** lachrymal gland.

carunculado, -da, *a.* carunculate, carunculated.

caruncular, *a.* caruncular.

caruto, *n.m.* genipap.

carvajal, carvallar, carvalledo, *n.m.* oak grove.
carvajo, carvallo, *n.m.* (*prov.*) oak.
carvi, *n.m.* caraway-seed.
cas, *n.f.* (*prov.*) apocope of casa; (*C.R.*) cas tree.
casa, *n.f.* house; home, household; business house, firm; checker, square (*on chessboard etc.*); ***casa abierta,*** residence and office *or* studio combined; ***casa central*** or ***matriz,*** head office, headquarters; ***casa cuartel,*** barracks and residential quarters combined; ***casa de banca,*** banking house; ***casa de baños,*** public baths; ***casa de beneficencia,*** poor house; ***casa de comidas,*** eating house; ***casa de comercio,*** trading *or* business house; ***casa(s) consistorial(es), casa de la villa,*** town hall, city hall; ***casa cuna*** or ***de expósitos,*** foundling home; ***casa de camas, de citas, de trato(s), pública*** or ***de mancebía,*** brothel; ***casa de campo*** or ***de placer y recreo,*** country-house; ***casa de corrección,*** reformatory, approved school; ***casa de correos,*** post-office; ***casa de empeños*** or ***de préstamos,*** pawnshop; ***casa de fieras,*** menagerie, zoo; (*prov.*) ***casa de ganado,*** barn with stable beneath; ***casa de huéspedes,*** guest-house, boarding-house; ***casa de juego,*** gambling-house; ***casa de labor*** or ***de labranza,*** farm, farmhouse; ***casa de locos*** or ***de orates,*** lunatic asylum, madhouse; (*fig.*) noisy, riotous house; ***casa de maternidad,*** maternity hospital; ***casa de modas,*** fashion house; ***casa de moneda,*** mint; ***casa de postas,*** post-house; ***casa de socorro,*** first-aid station, emergency hospital; (*fam.*) ***casa de tía,*** prison, clink, nick; ***casa de tócame Roque*** or ***de trueno,*** crazy, chaotic house(hold); ***casa de vacas,*** dairy; ***casa de vecindad,*** tenement; ***casa fuerte,*** stronghold; rich and powerful family; ***casa llana,*** unfortified country-seat; ***casa mortuoria,*** house of deceased person; ***casa paterna,*** house of one's father, home; ***casa profesa,*** convent, monastery; ***casa real,*** royal household; ***casa robada,*** poorly furnished house; ***casa solariega,*** ancestral home; ***levantar la casa,*** to move (*house*); ***asentar casa,*** to set up house; ***cada uno en su casa y Dios en la de todos,*** let every man live in his own home and harmony will prevail; ***caérsele a uno la casa a cuestas,*** to have the house fall about one's ears; ***casa con dos puertas mala es de guardar,*** a house with many doors is difficult to guard; ***convida la casa,*** it's on the house; ***empezar la casa por el tejado,*** to put the cart before the horse; ***de fuera vendrá quien de casa nos echará*** it is often an outsider who ousts the established; ***se deshizo la casa,*** the family came down in the world; the family broke up; ***echar la casa por la ventana,*** to spend lavishly; ***entrar como Pedro por su casa,*** to behave as if one owns the place; ***estar de casa,*** to be casually *or* comfortably dressed; ***guardar la casa,*** to be confined to the house; ***hacer casa,*** to get rich; ***se le llueve la casa,*** he is beginning to go downhill; ***mientras en mi casa estoy, rey me soy,*** a man's house is his castle; ***no caber en toda la casa,*** to be in a vile temper; ***no parar en casa,*** never to be at home; ***no tener casa ni hogar,*** to be homeless; ***poner casa,*** to set up house *or* home; ***ser muy de (su) casa,*** to be very fond of home life; (*prov.*) ***tener casa y tinelo,*** to keep open house; ***mucho hablar y la casa por barrer,*** plenty of talk but no work done, talking won't get the work done; ***ya sabe usted dónde tiene su casa,*** treat my house as your own, my house is at your disposal; make yourself at home (*expression of courtesy*).
casabe, *n.m.* manioc cake; cassava bread.
casaca, *n.f.* coat, dress-coat; (*coll.*) marriage, wedding; ***volver la casaca,*** to turn one's coat, change sides.
casación, *n.f.* cassation, abrogation, repeal.
casacón, *n.m.* cassock; greatcoat.
casadero, -ra, *a.* marriageable, eligible.
casado, -da, *n.m.f.* married man, woman. — *n.m.* (*print.*) imposition; ***el casado casa quiere,*** newly-weds need a house of their own.
casal, *n.m.* manor, country-house; farmhouse (*Hisp. Am.*) couple, pair.
casalicio, *n.m.* house, building.
casamata, *n.f.* casemate.
casamentero, -ra, *a.* match-making. — *n.m.f.* match-maker, marriage-maker.
casamiento, *n.m.* marriage, wedding; matrimony.
casampulga, *n.f.* (*E.S., Hond.*) poisonous spider.
casamuro, *n.m.* (*fort.*) single wall without a terreplein.
casapuerta, *n.f.* porch, entrance.
casaquilla, *n.f.,* **casaquín,** *n.m.* short jacket.
casar (1), *v.t.* to marry, mate, couple, unite in marriage, join in wedlock; (*fig.*) to join, unite; to suit, match (*things* or *colours*); (*paint.*) to blend; (*typ.*) to impose; ***casar una cosa con otra,*** to match one thing with another. — **casar(se),** *v.i.* (*v.r.*) to marry, get married, wed; ***casarse por poderes,*** to marry by proxy; ***antes que te cases, mira lo que haces,*** look before you leap; ***casarse en segundas nupcias,*** to remarry.
casar (2), *v.t.* (*law*) to annul, abrogate, repeal.
casar (3), *n.m.* hamlet, small village.
casarón, *n.m.* big house; large ramshackle house.
casatienda, *n.f.* tradesman's shop and house combined.
casca, *n.f.* skin of pressed grapes; oak-bark; (*prov.*) bad liquor; ring-shaped fruit-cake.
cascabel, *n.m.* small bell; hawk-bell; sleigh-bell; cascabel (*of a cannon*); ***serpiente de cascabel,*** rattlesnake; ***echar*** or ***soltar el cascabel a otro,*** to shift the burden on to s.o. else; ***poner el cascabel al gato,*** to bell the cat; ***ser un cascabel,*** to be a scatterbrained fellow; ***tener un cascabel,*** to be worried, anxious.
cascabela, *n.f.* (*C.R.*) rattlesnake.
cascabelada, *n.f.* rattle, jingling of small bells; (*coll.*) crazy thing to do *or* say.
cascabelear, *v.t.* (*coll.*) to feed with vain hopes; to bamboozle. — *v.i.* to act without foresight or prudence.
cascabelero, -ra, *a., n.m.f.* scatterbrained (person). — *n.m.* baby's rattle (*toy*).
cascabelillo, *n.m.* small black plum.
cascabillo, *n.m.* tiny bell; hawkbell; (*bot.*) glume; cup of an acorn.
cascaciruelas, *n.m.f. inv.* (*coll.*) mean, despicable person.
cascada, *n.f.* cascade, waterfall.
cascadura, *n.f.* cracking, breaking up.
cascajal, cascajar, *n.m.* place covered in gravel and pebbles; place in which the husks of grapes are thrown.
cascajera, *n.f.* gravelly, pebbly place.
cascajo, *n.m.* gravel; broken stone, rubble; (*coll.*) useless object, piece of junk; small copper coin; ***estar hecho un cascajo,*** to be a wreck.
cascajoso, -sa, *a.* gravelly, covered in stones.
cascamajar, *v.t.* to crack slightly.
cascamiento, *n.m.* cracking.
cascante, *a.* cracking; (*fig.*) tedious.
cascanueces, *n.m. inv.* nut-cracker.
cascapiedras, *n.m. inv.* stone-breaker.
cascapiñones, *n.m. inv.* pine-nut cracker (*instrument and operative*).
cascar [A], *v.t.* to crack, break into pieces; to crunch; (*coll.*) to beat, hit, strike; (*sl.*) ***cascarla,*** to kick the bucket; (*coll.*) ***le cascaron bien,*** they gave him a good hiding; (*coll.*) ***le cascaron un multazo,*** they stung him for a large fine; (*coll.*) ***estar cascado,*** to be a physical wreck; ***tiene la voz cascada,*** his voice is cracked, husky. — *v.i.* (*coll.*) to keep on tediously, be a pain-in-the-neck.
cáscara, *n.f.* rind, shell, peel, husk; (*prov.*) silk-cocoon; (*prov.*) dried red pepper; (*bot.*) bark; (*pl.*)

(*sl.*) knee socks; ***ser de la cáscara amarga,*** to be full of mischief; to hold advanced views; to be (a) homosexual, (*fam.*) a pansy, gay, (a) queer.

cascarada, *n.f.* (*sl.*) brawl; uproar.

¡cáscaras! *interj.* Lord! good grief!

cascarela, *n.f.* lansquenet (*card game*).

cascarilla, *n.f.* Peruvian bark, Jesuit's bark, quinine; cosmetic made of powdered eggshell; thin metal covering.

cascarillero, *n.m.* gatherer of Peruvian bark.

cascarillina, *n.f.* bitter principle of quinine.

cascarillo, *n.m.* (*Hisp. Am.*) shrub from which the cinchona bark is obtained.

cascarón, *n.m.* thick rind; shell, eggshell (especially when broken); (*arch.*) calotte, vault, arch; trick in ***cascarela***; (*Mex.*) eggshell filled with confetti; (*Ur.*) cork tree; (*naut.*) ***cascarón de nuez,*** cockleshell; ***salir del cascarón,*** to come out of one's shell, begin to live.

cascarrabias, *n.m.f. inv.* (*coll.*) irritable person, spitfire.

cascarria, *n.f.* dried mud (*on clothes*).

cascarrojas, *n.m.pl.* insects *or* worms (*in ships*).

cascarrón, -rrona, *a.* (*coll.*) rough, harsh, rude. — *n.m.* (*naut.*) stiff wind.

cascarudo, -da, *a.* having a thick rind *or* shell.

cascaruleta, *n.f.* wheat; (*coll.*) noise made by the teeth when one is chucked under the chin.

casco, *n.m.* skull, cranium; broken fragment; (*prov.*) quarter (*of orange, lemon etc.*); skin (*of onion*); crown (*of hat*); casque, helmet, headpiece; cask; (empty) bottle; saddle-tree; hoof; hull (*of a ship*); (*pl.*) heads of livestock without the tongues or brains; (*fam.*) head; (*med.*) ringworm cap; (*vet.*) ***casco atronado,*** injured hoof; ***casco de casa,*** framework of house; ***casco de mantilla,*** foundation material of mantilla; ***casco de población, casco urbano,*** city centre; ***alegre*** or ***ligera de cascos,*** fast, impulsive; ***barrenado de cascos,*** scatter-brained; ***calentarle a alguien los cascos,*** to worry s.o., fill s.o.'s head with wild ideas; ***romperse los cascos,*** to rack one's brains.

cascol, *n.m.* (*Ec.*) resin.

cascote, *n.m.* piece of rubbish *or* rubble.

cascotería, *n.f.* rubble-work.

cascudo, -da, *a.* large-hoofed.

casea, *n.f.* casein.

caseación, *n.f.* curdling of milk (*for cheese-making*).

caseasa, *n.f.* casease.

caseato, *n.m.* salt formed by combining lactic acid with a base.

caseico, -ca, *a.* caseic; caseous; lactic.

caseificación, *n.f.* caseation.

caseificar [A], *v.t.* to transform into casein; to separate *or* precipitate the casein from (*the milk*).

caseína, *n.f.* casein.

cáseo, -sea, *a.* caseous. — *n.m.* curd.

caseoso, -sa, *a.* caseous; cheesy.

casería, *n.f.* manor with out-buildings for farm-hands; housewifery.

caserillo, *n.m.* homespun linen.

caserío, *n.m.* cluster of houses (*in the country*); small village, hamlet.

caserna, *n.f.* barrack.

casero, -ra, *a.* domestic, homely, home-bred; home-made. — *n.m.f.* landlord, landlady; house-agent; caretaker, (*Am.*) janitor; tenant, lessee; familiar; ***baile casero,*** family dance; ***lienzo casero,*** home-spun linen; ***mujer casera,*** home-loving woman; ***pan casero,*** home-made bread.

caserón, *n.m.* large, rambling house.

caseta, *n.f.* cabin; shed; bathing-hut.

casetón, *n.m.* (*arch.*) rosette.

casi, *adv.* almost, nearly; scarcely; ***casi casi,*** very nearly; (*coll.*) ***casi nada,*** hardly anything; ***casi sí,*** I rather think I will; ***casi no,*** scarcely, hardly; I don't think I will, actually.

casia, *n.f.* bastard cinnamon; cassia, leguminous plant.

casicontrato, *n.m.* quasi-contract.

casilla, *n.f.* keeper's lodge; railway guard's hut; booth; locker; (*Cub.*) trap, snare (*to catch birds*); (*Ec.*) water-closet; (*pl.*) pigeon-holes; ruled columns in accounts; squares (*of chess-board*); points (*of backgammon-table*); (*coll.*) ***sacar a alguien de sus casillas,*** to drive s.o. up the wall, make s.o. hopping mad.

casiller, *n.m.* palace servant who emptied slops etc.

casillero, *n.m.* set of pigeon-holes *or* lockers; store-keeper in naval dockyards.

casillo, *n.m.* (*iron.*) trifling matter, slight case.

casimba, *n.f.* (*Cub., Per.*) water reservoir.

casimir, *n.m.*, **casimira** (1), *n.f.* [CACHEMIR].

casimiro, -ra (2), *a.* (*Hisp. Am.*) short-sighted; squint-eyed; one-eyed.

casinete, *n.m.* (*Arg., Chi., Hond.*) low quality cashmere; (*Ec., Ven.*) cheap woollen cloth.

casinita, *n.f.* feldspar of barytes.

casino, *n.m.* men's club; ***casino de juego,*** casino.

casiopea, *n.f.* Cassiopeia.

casis, *n.m.* black currant.

casita, *n.f.* (dear) little house; cottage; ***casita de campo,*** nice little house in the country, country cottage.

casiterita, *n.f.* cassiterite.

caso, *n.m.* case; occurrence; contingency; ***caso de conciencia,*** matter of *or* for conscience; ***caso de honra*** matter *or* question of honour; ***caso fortuito,*** act of God, unforeseen occurrence; (*eccles.*) ***caso reservado,*** case to be decided by higher authority; ***a caso hecho,*** on purpose, deliberately; ***caer en mal caso,*** to get into a spot, unpleasant position; ***dado caso (que),*** supposing (that); ***se da el caso,*** you find *or* get cases (*instances*); ***(en) caso (de) que,*** in the event of, should; ***caso de que venga,*** should he come; ***en todo caso,*** at all events; if at all; ***estar en el caso,*** to be in the picture; ***no hacer (venir) al caso, no ser del caso,*** to be beside the point, to be irrelevant; ***hablar al caso,*** to speak to the point; ***vamos al caso,*** let's get to the point; ***(no) hacer caso de (a),*** to take (no) notice of, pay (no) attention to; ***hacer caso omiso de,*** to ignore, omit, leave out; ***poner por caso,*** to give (take) as an example; ***verse en el caso de,*** to be forced to; ***el caso es que,*** the fact is *or* remains that; what matters is that; ***en el mejor de los casos,*** at (the) best; ***en el peor de los casos,*** at (the) worst, if the worst comes to the worst; ***dado el caso, en caso de necesidad,*** should the occasion *or* need arise, if it comes to it; (*coll.*) ***es un caso,*** he's (a) hopeless (case).

casoar, *n.m.* cassowary.

casolero, -ra, *a.* (*prov.*) home-loving.

casón, *n.m.* large, rambling house.

casorio, *n.m.* (*coll.*) poor, second-rate marriage *or* wedding.

caspa, *n.f.* dandruff, scurf.

caspera, *n.f.* scurf-comb.

caspia (1), *n.f.* (*prov.*) core (*apple*).

caspicias, *n.f.pl.* (*fam.*) remains, left-overs.

caspio, -pia (2), *a., n.m.f.* Caspian.

caspiroleta, *n.f.* (*Am.*) egg-nog.

¡cáspita! *interj.* Heavens!; by Jove!; gracious me!

casposo, -sa, *a.* covered in dandruff.

casquería, *n.f.* offal-shop; offal.

casquero, *n.m.* offal-seller.

casquetazo, *n.m.* blow given with the head, header.

casquete, *n.m.* helmet, casque; skull-cap, cap; wig, periwig; (*mech.*) cap; (*conch.*) helmet-shell; cataplasm (*to remove scurf*).

casquiacopado, -da, *a.* cup-hoofed.

casquiblando, -da, *a.* soft-hoofed.

casquiderramado, -da, *a.* wide-hoofed.
casquijo, *n.m.* gravel; ballast-material.
casquilucio, -cia, *a.* feather-brained.
casquilla, *n.f.* cell of the queen-bee.
casquillo, *n.m.* tip, cap; ferrule, socket; iron arrow-head; cartridge-cap; spent cartridge; (*Hisp. Am.*) horseshoe; (*Hond.*) sweat-band (*in hats*).
casquimuleño, -ña, *a.* narrow-hoofed like mules.
casquite, *a.* (*Ven.*) sour.
casquivano, -na, *a.* feather-brained; empty-headed.
casta, *n.f.* [CASTO].
Castálidas, *n.f.pl.* Muses.
castalio, -lia, *a.* castalian.
castaña, *n.f.* [CASTAÑO].
castañal, castañar, *n.m.* chestnut-grove.
castañazo, *n.m.* great wallop; crashing bore.
castañeda, *n.f.*, **castañedo,** *n.m.* chestnut-grove.
castañero, -ra, *n.m.f.* dealer in chestnuts. — *n.m.* palmiped dove. — *n.f.* (*prov.*) district rich in chestnut-trees.
castañeta, *n.f.* snapping of the fingers; castanet.
castañetada, *n.f.*, **castañetazo,** *n.m.* blow with a castanet; sound made by a chestnut bursting in the fire; cracking of the joints.
castañete, *a.* brownish.
castañeteado, *n.m.* sound of castanets.
castañetear, *v.t.* to rattle (*the castanets*). — *v.i.* to chatter (*teeth*); to crackle.
castañeteo, *n.m.* clicking (*fingers* or *castanets*); chattering (*teeth*).
castaño, -ña, *a.* chestnut, chestnut-coloured; reddish-brown. — *n.m.* chestnut-tree; chestnut-wood; ***castaño de Indias,*** horse-chestnut-tree; (*coll.*) ***pasa de castaño oscuro,*** it's too much, it's a bit thick. — *n.f.* chestnut; chestnut-shaped jar, demijohn; chignon; (*Mex.*) small barrel; (*coll.*) bore, pain-in-the-neck; wallop; drunkenness; ***castaña de Indias,*** wild *or* horse-chestnut; ***castaña de Pará*** or ***del Brasil,*** Brazil nut; ***coger una castaña,*** to get sozzled; ***dar la castaña,*** to bore to death; ***sacarle a alguien las castañas del fuego,*** to help s.o. out of a jam; to do s.o.'s dirty work.
castañuelo, -la, *a.* of a light chestnut colour (*horses*). — *n.f.* castanet; round tuberous-rooted cyperus; (*coll.*) ***estar como unas castañuelas,*** to be as happy as a sand-boy.
castellana (1), *n.f.* chatelaine mistress (*of a castle*); stanza (*in old Spanish poetry*).
castellanía, *n.f.* castellany.
castellanismo, *n.m.* expression peculiar to Castile.
castellanización, *n.f.* Castilianization (*of a foreign word*).
castellanizar [C], *v.t.* to Castilianize; to turn (*a foreign word*) into a Spanish one.
castellano, -na (2), *a.*, *n.m.f.* Castilian. — *a.* said of a mule got by a jackass and a mare. — *n.m.* Castilian *or* Spanish language; castellan *or* warden (*of a castle*); ancient Spanish coin; ***a la castellana,*** in the Castilian *or* Spanish fashion; (*fig.*) ***en castellano***, in plain language.
castellar, *n.m.* St. John's wort, tutsan.
casticidad, *n.f.* correctness, purity (*of language, customs etc.*).
casticismo, *n.m.* purism; true nature, authentic *or* genuine spirit.
casticista, *n.m.f.* purist.
castidad, *n.f.* chastity, purity.
castigable, *a.* punishable.
castigación, *n.f.* castigation, punishment; revision and correction (*of a written work*).
castigadera, *n.f.* strap *or* rope (*for tying the clapper of a wether's bell*).
castigador, -ra, *a.* castigating, chastising. — *n.m.f.* punisher, chastiser, castigator.
castigar [B], *v.t.* to punish, castigate, chastise. chasten; to strain, overwork; to correct (*proofs etc.*); to break in (*animals*); (*tauro.*) to wear down. — *v.t.*, *v.i.* (*coll.*) to be tough, hard on; to play hard to get (*of women*); ***castigar el cuerpo,*** to drive o.s. hard (*physically*); ***castigar el estómago,*** to restrict o.s. to frugal fare; ***castigar la vista,*** to strain one's sight.
castigo, *n.m.* punishment, chastisement; correction; hard use; (*coll.*) curse, pest, insufferable nuisance; ***ser de castigo,*** to be terribly hard, burdensome, insufferable.
castila, *a.* (*Philip.*) nickname applied to Spaniards. — *n.m.* Spanish language.
Castilla, *n.f.* Castile; ***ancha es Castilla,*** it takes all sorts to make a world.
castillado, -da, *a.* (*her.*) castellated.
castillaje, *n.m.* castle-toll.
castillejo, *n.m.* small castle, scaffolding; go-cart.
castillería, *n.f.* toll for transit through castle property.
castillete, *n.m.* small castle.
castillo, *n.m.* castle; cell of queen-bee; mounting (*of a velvet-loom*); (*mil.*) wooden tower (*on the back of an elephant*); total capacity (*of cart*); ***castillo de fuego,*** fireworks; ***castillo de naipes,*** house of cards, flimsy structure; (*naut.*) ***castillo de proa,*** forecastle; ***castillo roquero,*** castle built on a rock; (*fig.*) ***hacer castillos en el aire,*** to build castles in the air *or* in Spain; ***Juan es un castillo,*** John is a towering fellow.
castina, *n.f.* (*chem., metal.*) flux.
castizar, *v.t.* (*fig.*) to purify, refine.
castizo, -za, *a.* of noble descent; of good stock; pure-blooded; pure (*language*); idiomatic (*language*); authentic, real; genuinely popular *or* typical; truly Spanish; prolific. — *n.m.f.* (*Mex.*) quadroon.
casto, -ta, *a.* pure, chaste. — *n.f.* caste, clan, breed; race; (*fig.*) kind, quality; ***cruzar castas,*** to cross breeds; ***hacer casta,*** to get a particular breed (*of some animal*).
castor, *n.m.* beaver; beaver-skin, -cloth *or* -felt; (*Mex.*) fine red baize.
Cástor, *n.m.* (*astron.*) Castor; ***Cástor y Pólux,*** St. Elmo's fire.
castora, *n.f.* (*prov., fam.*) top-hat.
castorcillo, *n.m.* rough, hairy serge.
castoreño, -ña, *a.* made of beaver; ***sombrero castoreño,*** beaver hat.
castóreo, *n.m.* (*pharm.*) castoreum.
castorina, *n.f.* oil extracted from castoreum; beaverteen.
castra, *n.f.* pruning; pruning season.
castración, *n.f.* castration, gelding, spaying.
castradera, *n.f.* honey extractor.
castrado, *n.m.* eunuch.
castrador, *n.m.* gelder, castrator.
castradura, *n.f.* castration; castration scar.
castrametación, *n.f.* castrametation, encamping.
castrapuercas, *n.f. inv.*, **castrapuercos,** *n.m. inv.* gelder's whistle.
castrar, *v.t.* to geld, castrate, spay; to dry up (*sores, wounds*); to prune (*trees* or *plants*); to cut (*honeycombs*) from beehives.
castrazón, *n.f.* cutting of honeycombs out of hives; season when this is done.
castrense, *a.* appertaining to the army, military; ***cura castrense,*** padre.
castro (1), *n.m.* castration.
castro (2), *n.m.* hopscotch; (*prov.*) headland; (*prov.*) hill-top castle.
castrón, *n.m.* castrated goat; (*Cub.*) hog.
casual, *a.* chance, coincidental; (*coll.*) ***por un casual,*** by any chance.
casualidad, *n.f.* chance, coincidence; ***por casualidad,*** by chance.

casualismo, *n.m.* casualism.
casualista, *n.m.f.* casualist.
casuáridos, *n.m.pl.* family of the cassowaries.
casuario, *n.m.* cassowary.
casuca, casucha, *n.f.* (*coll.*) miserable house *or* hovel.
casuísta, *a.* casuistic, casuistical. — *n.m.f.* casuist.
casuística, *n.f.* casuistry.
casuístico, -ca, *a.* casuistical.
casulla, *n.f.* chasuble; (*Hond.*) grain of rice with its husk.
casullero, *n.m.* maker of chasubles and other vestments.
cata, *n.f.* trying, tasting; trial, sample; plummet (*for measuring heights*); (*Col., Mex.*) trial excavation (*of a mine*); (*Col.*) hidden thing; ***dar cata,*** to examine, observe; ***dar a cata,*** to put on trial.
catabre, catabro, *n.m.* (*Col.*) shell of calabash.
catacaldos, *n.m.f. inv.* wine-taster; (*fig.*) inconstant fickle person.
catacáustico, -ca, *a., n.f.* catacoustic(s).
cataclismo, *n.m.* cataclysm; catastrophe; upheaval.
cataclismología, *n.f.* history of floods and terrestrial catastrophes.
cataclismológico, -ca, *a.* cataclysmal, cataclysmic.
cataclismólogo, *n.m.* cataclysmist.
catacresis, *n.f. inv.* (*rhet.*) catachresis.
catacumbas, *n.f.pl.* catacombs.
catador, *n.m.* taster, sampler; ***catador de vinos,*** wine-taster.
catadura, *n.f.* tasting; (*coll.*) face, expression, look; ***tiene mala catadura,*** he (it) has an ugly (evil) look, I don't like the look of him (it).
catafalco, *n.m.* catafalque.
catafractarios, *n.m.pl.* mounted knights in armour.
catafractos, *n.m.pl.* cataphracted fish.
catalán, -lana, *a., n.m.f.* Catalan, Catalonian. — *n.m.* Catalan (*language*).
catalanismo, *n.m.* Catalanism; Catalonian autonomy movement; doctrine of Catalan autonomy.
catalanista, *n.m.f.* Catalanist.
cataléctico, -ca, catalecto, -ta, *a., n.m.f.* (*poet.*) catalectic (verse); ***catalectos,*** anthology.
catalejo, *n.m.* telescope.
catalepsia, *n.f.* catalepsy.
cataléptico, -ca, *a., n.m.f.* (*med.*) cataleptic.
catalicón, *n.m.* catholicon, panacea.
catalicores, *n.m. inv.* pipette.
Catalina, *n.f.* Catherine; ***rueda catalina,*** Catherine wheel.
catalineta, *n.f.* (*ichth.*) catalufa fish.
cátalisis, *n.f. inv.* catalysis.
catalítico, -ca, *a.* catalytic.
catalizador, *n.m.* catalyzer, catalyst.
catalogable, *a.* that can be catalogued.
catalogación, *n.f.* cataloguing.
catalogador, -ra, catalógrafo, -fa, *n.m.f.* cataloguer.
catalogar [B], *v.t.* to catalogue, list.
catálogo, *n.m.* catalogue, list.
catalufa, *n.f.* carpet material; double taffeta; (*ichth.*) catalufa fish.
Cataluña, *n.f.* Catalonia.
catán, *n.m.*, **catana,** *n.f.* Indian cutlass.
catanga, *n.f.* (*Arg.*) black beetle; (*Chi.*) green scarab; (*Col.*) fish trap; (*Bol.*) one-horse cart.
catante, *a.* tasting; looking.
cataplasma, *n.f.* cataplasm, poultice. — *n.m.f.* (*coll.*) bore, pain-in-the-neck.
catapléctico, -ca, *a.* relating to cataplexy.
cataplexia, *n.f.* cataplexy.
¡cataplum! *interj.* bang!, crash!, wallop!
catapulta, *n.f.* catapult.
catapún, *a.* ***del año catapún,*** donkey's years old.
catar, *v.t.* to taste, try, sample; to look (at), examine, investigate, inspect; to respect, esteem; to cut (*combs*) out of beehives.
cataraña, *n.f.* (*orn.*) sheldrake.
catarata, *n.f.* cataract, waterfall; (*med.*) cataract; ***abrirse las cataratas del cielo,*** to begin to pour; (*surg.*) ***batir la catarata,*** to couch a cataract.
catarinita, *n.f.* (*Mex.*) parakeet.
cátaros, *n.m.pl.* catharists.
catarral, *a.* catarrhal.
catarribera, *n.m.* falconer; (*iron.*) lawyer in search of briefs.
catarriento, -ta, *a.* catarrhous.
catarro, *n.m.* catarrh; cold.
catarroso, -sa, *a., n.m.f.* catarrhal; (person) subject to colds; having a cold.
catarsis, *n.f.* catharsis.
catártico, -ca, *a.* cathartic, purging.
catartina, *n.f.* cathartin.
catasalsas, *n.m.f. inv.* (*coll.*) sauce-taster.
catastro, *n.m.* cadastre; fiscal property register.
catástrofe, *n.f.* catastrophe.
catastrofismo, *n.m.* attitude of gloom and doom, gloom- *or* doom-mongering.
catata, *n.f.* (*Cub.*) maté.
catatán, *n.m.* (*Chi.*) (*coll.*) punishment, penalty.
cataviento, *n.m.* (*naut.*) dog-vane; weather-cock.
catavino, *n.m.* small jug *or* cup for tasting wine; small hole in wine-vessel for tasting the wine.
catavinos, *n.m. inv.* wine-taster, sampler; (*coll.*) tippler.
cate, *n.m.* (*prov.*) blow, slap; (*coll.*) fail (*mark*); (*Philip.*) half a pound.
cateador, *n.m.* (*Hisp. Am.*) prospector; geologist's hammer.
catear, *v.t.* to procure, solicit; (*coll.*) to fail (*in an examination*); (*Arg., Chi., Per.*) to prospect.
catecismo, *n.m.* catechism.
catecú, *n.m.* catechu.
catecuménico, -ca, *a.* catechumenical.
catecúmeno, -na, *n.m.f.* catechumen.
cátedra, *n.f.* cathedra; chair (*of a professor*); professorship; (*eccles.*) see; ***cátedra del Espíritu Santo,*** pulpit; ***cátedra de San Pedro,*** the Holy See; ***pasear la cátedra,*** to lecture to an empty class-room; ***poner*** or ***sentar cátedra (de),*** to hold forth (on); to lay down the law (about).
catedral, *a., n.f.* cathedral.
catedralicio, -cia, *a.* appertaining to a cathedral.
catedralidad, *n.f.* status of a cathedral church.
catedrático, *n.m.* professor; contribution paid to bishops and prelates.
categorema, *n.f.* (*log.*) categorem.
categoría, *n.f.* category; class, rank, status; ***hombre de categoría,*** man of rank *or* (high) standing.
categórico, -ca, *a.* categorical, categoric; flat.
catenaria, *a., n.f.* catenary, chain; ***reacción catenaria*** or ***en cadena,*** chain reaction.
catenular, *a.* catenarian.
catequesis, *n.f. inv.* catechizing.
catequismo, *n.m.* catechism; religious instruction.
catequista, *n.m.f.* catechist.
catequístico, -ca, *a.* catechetic, catechetical, catechistical.
catequización, *n.f.* catechizing, catechism.
catequizador, -ra, *n.m.f.* persuasive arguer.
catequizante, *a.* catechizing. — *n.m.f.* catechizer, catechist.
catequizar [C], *v.t.* to catechize, instruct in religious doctrine; (*fig.*) to induce, persuade.
caterético, -ca, *a.* (*med.*) erosive.
caterva, *n.f.* multitude, throng, crowd, swarm, mob.
catete, *n.m.* (*Chi.*) Old Nick, the Devil.

catéter, *n.m.* (*surg.*) catheter.
cateterismo, *n.m.* sounding with a catheter *or* probe.
cateterizar [C], *v.t.* to sound with a catheter.
cateto, *n.m.* (*geom.*) leg (*of a right-angled triangle*); (*fig.*) country bumpkin, yokel.
catey, *n.m.* (*Cub.*) small cockatoo; palm-tree.
catilinaria, *a.* catilinarian. — *n.f.* denunciatory tirade.
catimbao, *n.m.* (*Chi., Per.*) figures of paste-board appearing in Corpus Christi procession; (*Chi., fig.*) ridiculously dressed person; (*Chi.*) clown; (*Per.*) squat, dumpy person.
catín, *n.m.* copper-refining crucible.
catinga, *n.f.* (*Hisp. Am.*) bad smell (*as of sweat*); (*Chi., contempt.*) nickname given by sailors to soldiers.
catión, *n.f.* (*elec.*) cation.
catire, *a., n.m.f.* (*Hisp. Am.*) blond, light-haired (*offspring of mulatto and white*).
catite, *n.m.* loaf of the finest refined sugar; light slap; ***dar catite a,*** to beat.
cato, *n.m.* japan earth *or* catechu.
catoche, *n.m.* (*Mex.*) bad temper.
catódico, -ca, *a.* cathodic.
cátodo, *n.m.* cathode.
catolicidad, *n.f.* catholicity.
catolicísimo, -ma, *a. superl.* extremely devout Catholic.
catolicismo, *n.m.* Catholicism.
católico, -ca, *a.* catholic; universal; (*coll.*) ***no estar muy católico,*** to feel out of sorts; to be not too good. — *n.m.f.* Catholic.
catolicón, *n.m.* (*pharm.*) electuary.
catón, *n.m.* primer, reading-book (*for children*); (*fig.*) severe censor.
catonizar [C], *v.t.* to censure severely.
catopter, *n.m.* (*opt.*) speculum.
catóptrico, -ca, *a.* catoptric. — *n.f.* catoptrics.
catoptromancia, *n.f.* catoptromancy.
catorce, *a., n.m.* fourteen; fourteenth.
catorceno, -na, *a.* fourteenth; aged fourteen. — *n.f.* collection, set of fourteen units.
catorzavo, -va, *a., n.m.* one-fourteenth (*part*).
catre, *n.m.* cot, small bedstead; ***catre de mar,*** hammock, cot; ***catre de tijera,*** camp-bed, field-bed.
catricofre, *n.m.* folding-bed, bed-lounge, press-bed which shuts up.
catrintre, *n.m.* (*Chi.*) cheese made with skim-milk; (*Chi.*) beggar.
caturra, *n.f.* (*Chi.*) small parrot *or* parakeet.
catzo, *n.m.* (*Ec.*) bumblebee.
cauba, *n.f.* (*Arg.*) cauba tree.
cauca, *n.m.* (*Col., Ec.*) herb cultivated as fodder.
caucalis, *n.m.* (*bot.*) bur-parsley, bur-weed.
caucáseo, -sea, caucasiano, -na, *a.* Caucasian.
caucásico, -ca, *a.* Caucasian.
Caúcaso, *n.m.* Caucasus.
cauce, *n.m.* river-bed; channel.
caución, *n.f.* caution, precaution; security *or* pledge; bond, bail; (*law*) ***caución de indemnidad,*** bail-bond; surety, guarantee, gage; ***caución juratoria,*** parole.
caucionar, *v.t.* to take precautions against (*loss* or *harm*); to bail.
caucha, *n.f.* (*Chi.*) thistle.
cauchal, *n.m.* rubber plantation *or* patch.
cauchera, *n.f.* rubber-yielding plant.
cauchero, *n.m.* collector of rubber.
cauchil, *n.m.* (*prov.*) small well *or* reservoir.
caucho, *n.m.* rubber.
cauchotina, *n.f.* rubber solution.
cauda, *n.f.* train (*of bishop's robe*).
caudal, *a.* having much water; (*zool.*) caudal; ***águila caudal,*** red-tailed eagle. — *n.m.* property, fortune, means, wealth; capital principal sum, stock; volume (*of water*); (*fig.*) plenty, abundance, wealth.
caudaloso, -sa, *a.* having much water; copious, abundant; rich, wealthy.
caudatario, *n.m.* (*eccles.*) train-bearer; (*coll.*) adulator.
caudato, -ta, *a.* having a tail (*comet*); having a refrain (*sonnet*).
caudatrémula, *n.f.* wagtail.
caudillaje, *n.m.* leadership; tyranny.
caudillismo, *n.m.* bossism, dictatorship.
caudillo, *n.m.* chief, leader, head; (*mil.*) commander.
caudimano, *a.* (*zool.*) having a prehensile tail.
caudón, *n.m.* shrike.
caula, *n.f.* (*Chi., Hond.*) trick, deceit, cunning.
caulescente, *a.* (*bot.*) caulescent.
caulícolo, caulículo, *n.m.* (*arch.*) caulis.
caulífero, -ra, *a.* (*bot.*) cauliferous.
caulifloro, -ra, *a.* (*bot.*) with flowers growing on the top of the stem.
cauliforme, *a.* (*bot.*) cauliform.
caulinario, -ria, *a.* (*bot.*) cauline.
cauque, *n.m.* (*Chi.*) large mackerel; (*Chi., fig.*) quick, clever person; (*Chi., iron.*) dull, stupid person.
cauro, *n.m.* north-west wind.
causa, *n.f.* cause; (*law*) case, trial; (*Chi.*) light meal; (*Per.*) potato salad; ***a causa de,*** owing to, on account of; (*law*) ***acriminar una causa,*** to aggravate an action; (*law*) ***conocer de una causa,*** to judge an action; (*law*) ***dar la causa por conclusa,*** to wind up the action; (*law*) ***hacer causa,*** to bring an action; ***hacer uno la causa de otro,*** to take up s.o.'s case.
causador, -ra, *a.* causing, causative. — *n.m.f.* occasioner.
causahabiente, *n.m.* person holding a right from others.
causal, *a.* (*gram.*) causative, causal. — *n.f.* ground on which sth. is done.
causalidad, *n.f.* cause, origin; causality, causation.
causante, *a.* causative, causing, occasioning; (*coll.*) guilty, responsible. — *n.m.* causer, occasioner; (*law*) person from whom a right is derived.
causar, *v.t.* to cause; (*prov.*) to sue.
causativo, -va, *a.* causative.
causear, *v.t.* (*Chi.*) to defeat, overcome. — *v.i.* to have a meal *or* snack.
causeo, *n.m.* (*Chi.*) light meal *or* snack.
causídico, -ca, *a.* (*law*) causidical, forensic. — *n.m.* advocate, counsellor.
causón, *n.m.* burning fever of short duration.
causticación, *n.f.* conversion into causticity; cauterization.
causticar [A], *v.t.* to make caustic.
causticidad, *n.f.* causticity; pungent satire.
cáustico, -ca, *a.* caustic, burning; (*fig.*) caustic, biting. — *n.m.* (*med.*) caustic. — *n.f.* (*math.*) caustic curve.
causticóforo, -ra, *a.* cauterizing. — *n.m.* cauter, cautery (*instrument*).
cautela, *n.f.* caution, care; artfulness, craft, cunning; (*eccles.*) ***absolver a cautela,*** to give the benefit of the doubt.
cautelar, *v.t.* to prevent. — **cautelarse,** *v.r.* — ***de,*** to guard against.
cauteloso, -sa, *a.* cautious, wary.
cauterio, *n.m.* cauterization; cautery; (*fig.*) eradication, rooting out.
cauterización, *n.f.* cauterization, cauterizing.
cauterizador, -ra, *a.* cauterizing. — *n.m.f.* one who *or* that which cauterizes.
cauterizante, *a.* cauterizing.

cauterizar [C], *v.t.* to cauterize; to eradicate (*an evil*); to correct harshly; to brand.
cautín, *n.m.* soldering-iron.
cautivador, -ra, *a.* captivating.
cautivante, *a.* captivating.
cautivar, *v.t.* to capture; (*fig.*) to captivate, charm; to win over.
cautiverio, *n.m.,* **cautividad,** *n.f.* captivity.
cautivo, -va, *a., n.m.f.* captive; (*poet.*) captivated.
cauto, -ta, *a.* cautious, wary.
cava, *n.f.* digging and earthing (*vines*); wine-cellar.
cavacote, *n.m.* mound, small hillock of earth.
cavadiza, *a.* dug out of a pit (*sand*).
cavador, *n.m.* digger.
cavadura, *n.f.* digging.
cavalillo, *n.m.* ditch, trench.
cavar, *v.t.* to dig (out). — *v.i.* — ***en,*** to go deeply (into), penetrate.
cavatina, *n.f.* cavatina.
cavazón, *n.f.* digging.
caverna, *n.f.* cave, cavern; (*med.*) ulcer *or* wound cavity.
cavernidad, cavernosidad, *n.f.* cavernousness.
cavernilla, *n.f.* small cavern.
cavernoso, -sa, *a.* cavernous, caverned.
caveto, *n.m.* (*arch.*) concave moulding forming quadrant of a circle.
cavia, *n.f.* circular excavation made at the foot of a tree to collect water.
caviar, *n.m.* caviare.
cavicornios, *n.m.pl.* family of hollow-horned ruminants.
cavidad, *n.f.* cavity, hollow.
cavilación, *n.f.* pondering, deep thought.
cavilar, *v.t.* to ponder (over). — *v.i.* to ponder.
cavilosidad, *n.f.* pondering; brooding.
caviloso, -sa, *a.* deep in thought; brooding.
cay, *n.m.* (*Arg.*) capuchin monkey.
cayada, *n.f.,* **cayado,** *n.m.* shepherd's crook; bishop's crozier; walking-stick.
cayán, *n.m.* (*Philip.*) boat awning.
cayana, *n.f.* (*Arg., Col.*) large baking pan.
cayanco, *n.m.* (*Hond.*) poultice of hot herbs.
cayapear, *v.i.* (*Ven.*) to combine for assault and battery.
cayente, *a.* falling.
cayeputi, *n.m.* cajuput-tree; cajuput oil.
cayo, *n.m.* islet, cay, key.
cayuco, *n.m.* (*Hisp. Am.*) a fishing boat.
caz, *n.m.* millrace.
caza, *n.m.* pursuit plane, fighter; ***caza de escolta,*** escort fighter. — *n.f.* chase, pursuit; hunt, hunting; fowling; shooting; game (*wild animals* or *birds*); ***caza mayor,*** big game (hunting); ***caza menor,*** shooting, fowling; small game; (*obs.*) fine linen cloth; ***partida de caza,*** hunting-party; ***trompa de caza,*** hunting-horn; ***alborotar*** or ***levantar la caza,*** to start the game; (*fig.*) to start the ball rolling; (*fig.*) ***andar*** or ***ir a caza de,*** to go in pursuit of; ***andar a caza de gangas,*** to go bargain-hunting; ***dar caza a,*** to pursue; (*fig.*) to go after *or* in pursuit of (*employment, secret etc.*); (*naut.*) to give chase to; (*lit., fig.*) ***espantar la caza,*** to frighten the game away; ***ir de caza,*** to go hunting; ***llevar de caza,*** to take hunting; (*lit., fig.*) ***seguir la caza,*** to pursue the quarry, follow the scent *or* trail.
cazabe, *n.m.* cassava; cassava flour; cassava bread.
cazaclavos, *n.m. inv.* nail-puller.
cazada, *n.f.* capacity of a ***cazo,*** ladleful.
cazadero, *n.m.* hunting-ground.
cazador, -ra, *a.* hunting, chasing. — *n.m.* hunter, huntsman, sportsman, chaser; ***cazador de dotes,*** fortune hunter; ***cazador furtivo,*** poacher; (*pl.* **cazadores**) light infantry. — *n.f.* huntress; (hunting) jacket.
cazar [C], *v.t., v.i.* to chase, pursue; to hunt; to shoot; to catch; (*coll.*) to get, get hold of, land; (*naut.*) to haul (*sheets*) taut; ***cazó la idea en seguida,*** he caught on to the idea at once; ***las caza al vuelo,*** he's very quick on the up-take.
cazasubmarinos, *n.m. inv.* submarine chaser.
cazatorpedero, *n.m.* (*naut.*) destroyer.
cazcalear, *v.i.* (*coll.*) to fuss about.
cazcarria, *n.f.* splashings of mud (*on clothes*).
cazcarriento, -ta, *a.* (*coll.*) splashed, bemired.
cazcorvo, -va, *a.* bow-legged.
cazo, *n.m.* ladle; scoop; pot, pan, saucepan; (*coll.*) fright, ugly woman.
cazolada, *n.f.* panful.
cazoleja, *n.f.* small saucepan; pan (*of firelock*).
cazolero, cazoletero, *a., n.m.* (*coll.*) cotquean, man who does women's work in the kitchen.
cazoleta, *n.f.* small saucepan; pan (*of firelock*); boss *or* defence (*of shield*); hand-guard (*of sword*); perfume; censer; pipe-bowl.
cazolilla, cazolita, *n.f.* small saucepan.
cazolón, *n.m.* large earthen pot *or* stew-pan.
cazón, *n.m.* dogfish, small shark; brown sugar.
cazonal, *n.m.* shark fishing-tackle; (*coll.*) difficulty, muddle.
cazonete, *n.m.* (*naut.*) toggle.
cazudo, -da, *a.* having a thick back (*knives*).
cazuela, *n.f.* earthen stewing-pan, casserole; stew, casserole; (*theat., coll.*) the gods; place reserved for women; (*print.*) wide composing stick holding several lines.
cazumbrar, *v.t.* to join (*staves*) with hempen cords.
cazumbre, *n.m.* hempen cord to join staves.
cazumbrón, *n.m.* cooper.
cazurro, -rra, *a., n.m.f.* (*coll.*) dour and crafty (person).
cazuz, *n.m.* ivy.
ce (1), *n.f.* letter C; ***ce por be,*** A to Z, in full detail; ***por ce o por be,*** for one reason or another.
¡ce! (2), *interj.* hark! here! come here!
cea, *n.f.* thigh-bone.
ceanoto, *n.m.* New Jersey tea, redroot.
cearina, *n.f.* cearin.
ceática, (1), *n.f.* [CIÁTICO].
ceático, -ca, (2), *a.* [CIÁTICO].
ceba, *n.f.* fattening (*of domestic animals*); (*fig.*) stoking (*of furnaces*).
cebada (1), *n.f.* barley; ***cebada perlada,*** pearl-barley.
cebadal, *n.m.* barley-field.
cebadar, *v.t.* to feed (*animals*).
cebadazo, -za, *a.* appertaining to barley; ***paja cebadaza,*** barley-straw.
cebadera, *n.f.* nose-bag; barley-bin; (*naut.*) sprit-sail; (*min.*) furnace-charger.
cebadería, *n.f.* barley-market.
cebadero, *n.m.* feeding-place (*fowls, game etc.*); breeder and feeder of hawks; ostler; mule carrying the feed; bell-mule; (*min.*) mouth for feeding a furnace; dealer in barley; (*art*) scene of domestic birds feeding.
cebadilla, *n.f.* wild barley; (*bot.*) sneeze-wort; powdered hellebore-root used as snuff.
cebado, -da (2), *a.* (*her.*) ravening.
cebador, *n.m.* priming-horn, powder-horn.
cebadura, *n.f.* feeding, fattening (*of domestic animals*).
cebar, *v.t.* to fatten (*animals*); to cram, stuff; to prime (*firearm*); to feed (*fire, furnace* or *lamp*); to bait (*fish-hook*); to light (*rocket* or *other kind of fireworks*); to remagnetize (*needle*); to cherish a passion *or* desire. — *v.t., v.i.* to penetrate; to take hold (of); to stick fast (to); — **cebarse,** *v.r.* — ***en,*** to vent one's fury *or* rage on; to gloat over; ***cebarse en su víctima,*** to gloat over one's victim.

cebellina, *n.f.* sable; sable-fur.
cebetera, *n.f.* bag for priming materials.
cebiche, *n.m.* (*Per.*) dish made of fish and chilli.
cebil, *n.m.* (*River Plate*) sumac tree.
cebo, *n.m.* feed, fodder; fattening (*of animals*); bait; priming (*of guns*); (*min.*) charge (*of furnaces*); incentive.
cebolla, *n.f.* onion; onion-bulb; bulbous root; oil-receptacle (*of lamp*); rose-nozzle *or* -strainer; (*bot.*) ***cebolla albarrana,*** squill; (*bot.*) ***cebolla escalonia,*** shallot.
cebollada, *n.f.* onion ragout.
cebollana, *n.f.* chive.
cebollar, *n.m.* patch of onions
cebollero, -ra, *n.m.f.* onion-seller.
cebolleta, *n.f.* spring onion, (*Am.*) scallion.
cebollino, *n.m.* onion seedling; onion seed; chive; ***escardar cebollinos,*** to do nothing useful; ***mandar a alguien a escardar cebollinos,*** to tell s.o. to go to hell.
cebollón, *n.m.* large onion.
cebolludo, -da, *a.* bulbous, having a bulb; onion-shaped; (*coll.*) portly.
cebón, -bona, *a., n.m.f.* fattened (animal); (*coll.*) fatty, fat stuff.
ceboncillo, *n.m.* fatling.
cebra, *n.f.* zebra.
cebrado, -da, *a.* striped like the zebra.
cebruno, -na, *a.* deer-coloured; deer-like.
cebú, *n.m.* zebu; (*Arg.*) howling-monkey.
ceburro [CANDEAL].
ceca, *n.f.* mint (*for coining money*); (*Spanish Morocco*) money; ***de la Ceca a la Meca.*** to and fro, hither and thither.
cecal, *a.* caecal.
ceceamiento [CECEO].
cecear, *v.t.* to call by making the sound ***ce-ce.*** — *v.i.* to lisp; to pronounce ***s*** as [θ].
ceceo, *n.m.* lisping, lisp; pronunciation of ***s*** as if it were [θ].
ceceoso, -sa, *a., n.m.f.* lisper, lisping.
cecesmil, *n.m.* (*Hond.*) plantation of early maize.
cecial, *n.m.* dried and cured hake, haddock etc.
Cecilio, *n.m.* Cecil.
cecina, *n.f.* salt dried meat; jerked meat.
cecinar, *v.t.* to salt and dry (*meat*).
cecografía, *n.f.* braille.
cecográfico, -ca, *a.* appertaining to braille.
cecógrafo, *n.m.* braille writer.
ceda (1) [ZETA].
ceda (2), *n.f.* horse-hair.
cedacear, *v.i.* to fail, decrease (*sight*).
cedacería, *n.f.* sieve shop.
cedacero, *n.m.* maker *or* seller of sieves.
cedacillo (1), **cedacito,** *n.m.* small sieve.
cedacillo (2), *n.m.* quaking-grass.
cedazo, *n.m.* sieve; bolt, bolter; large fishing-net.
cedazuelo, *n.m.* small sieve.
cedente, *a.* ceding, granting. — *n.m.* conveyer, assigner, transferrer.
ceder, *v.t.* to yield, give up, make over, convey, deliver up, transfer, cede; ***¡ceda el paso!*** out of the way! give way!; ***ceder su asiento,*** to give up one's seat. — *v.i.* to yield, give way, give in; (*mech.*) to sag, slacken; to drop, abate; ***ceder a la razón,*** to give in to reason; ***ceder de su derecho,*** to give up (surrender) a part of one's rights, a part of one's entitlement.
cedilla, *n.f.* cedilla.
cedizo, -za, *a.* putrid, rotten; ***carne cediza,*** tainted meat.
cedoaria, *n.f.* zedoary.
cedras, *n.f.pl.* saddle-bags of skin.
cedreleón, *n.m.* oil of cedar.
cedreno, *n.m.* base of cedar oil.
cedria, cedrilla, *n.f.* resin from the cedar.
cédride, *n.f.* fruit of the cedar-tree.
cedrino, -na, *a.* cedarn, of cedar, cedar.
cedrito, *n.m.* beverage of sweet wine and cedar-resin.
cedro, *n.m.* cedar; ***cedro de España,*** savin, Spanish cedar; ***cedro de la India,*** deodar; ***cedro del Líbano,*** cedar of Lebanon.
cedróleo, *n.m.* essential oil of cedar.
cédula, *n.f.* scrip; slip of paper *or* parchment; bill, decree; order; warrant; share; Government security, stock; ***cédula de abono,*** order remitting a tax; ***cédula ante diem,*** secretary's summons to members of a society; ***cédula de cambio,*** bill of exchange; ***cédula personal*** or ***de vecindad,*** identity document; ***cédula real,*** royal letters patent; ***echar cédulas,*** to draw *or* cast lots.
cedulaje, *n.m.* fees *or* dues paid for royal letters patent.
cedulario, *n.m.* collection of royal letters patent.
cedulón, *n.m.* proclamation, public notice; edict; (*fig.*) lampoon.
cefalalgia, *n.f.* headache.
cefalea, *n.f.* violent headache, migraine.
cefáleo, -lea, *a.* cephalous.
cefálico, -ca, *a.* cephalic.
céfalo, *n.m.* (*ichth.*) mullet.
cefaloídeo, -dea, *a.* cephaloid.
Cefeo, *n.m.* (*astron.*) Cepheus.
céfiro, *n.m.* zephyr; zephyr (*material*).
cefo, *n.m.* large African monkey.
cegador, -ra, *a.* blinding.
cegajo, *n.m.* two-year-old billy-goat.
cegajoso, -sa, *a.* blear-eyed, watery-eyed.
cegar [IB], *v.t.* to blind, make blind; to block, close, wall up, cover over *or* in; ***cegar un pozo,*** to stop up a well. — *v.i.* to go blind; ***cegarse de cólera,*** to get *or* become blinded by anger.
cegarra, *a., n.m.f.* [CEGATO].
cegato, -ta, *a., n.m.f.* short-sighted, myopic (person).
cegatoso, -sa, *a.* blear-eyed.
ceguecillo, -lla, ceguezuelo, -la, *a., n.m.f.* poor little blind (child, old man etc.).
ceguedad, *n.f.* (*fig.*) blindness.
ceguera, *n.f.* (*lit., fig.*) blindness.
ceiba, *n.f.* silk-cotton tree; sea-moss, alga.
Ceilán, *n.m.* Ceylon.
ceilanés, -nesa, *a., n.m.f.* Ceylonese.
ceja, *n.f.* eyebrow; edging (*clothes, books etc.*); summit (*mountain*); brow (*of a hill*); ridge of clouds (*round a hill*), cloud-cap; bridge (*stringed instruments*); rim; (*arch.*) weather-moulding; (*carp.*) rabbet; (*Hisp. Am.*) narrow path (*in a forest*); ***arquear las cejas,*** to raise one's eyebrows; ***estar hasta las cejas de trabajo,*** to be up to one's eyes in work; ***fruncir las cejas,*** to knit one's brows, frown; ***se le ha metido entre ceja y ceja ir,*** he has got it into his head to go, he is set on going; ***tener entre ceja y ceja,*** to be set on (*sth.*); to have a dislike for (*s.o.*); ***quemarse las cejas,*** to burn the midnight oil.
cejadero, *n.m.* hold-back strap (*of a harness*); harness trace.
cejar, *v.i.* to back (away, out); (*fig.*) to give way; to let up, relax; to slacken (off).
cejijunto, -ta, *a.* beetle-browed; (*fig.*) frowning.
cejilla, *n.f.* (*mus.*) bridge.
cejinegro, -ra, *a.* having black eyebrows.
cejo, *n.m.* river mist *or* fog; esparto cord.
cejudo, -da, *a.* beetle-browed.
cejuela, *n.f.* small eyebrow.
celada, *n.f.* sallet, helm, helmet (*without visor*); snare, ambush; artful dodge *or* trick; horse-soldier with helmet; part of the key of the cross-bow; ***caer en la celada,*** to fall into the trap; ***celada borgoñota,*** helmet without a visor; ***en celada,*** secretly.

celador, -ra, *a.* vigilant, watchful. — *n.m.f.* watcher; caretaker; curator; warden; inspector.
celaje, *n.m.* skylight; (*fig.*) omen, harbinger; (*pl.*) cloud effects, coloured clouds; (*naut.*) scud (*clouds*).
celajería, *n.f.* (*naut.*) scud (*clouds*).
celandés, -desa, *a.*, *n.m.f.* (person) from *or* belonging to Zealand (*Netherlands*).
celar, *v.t.* to see to, attend to; to watch, spy on (*through fear, jealousy*); to supervise, control; to cover, conceal; to carve, engrave.
celda, *n.f.* cell.
celdilla, *n.f.* cell; cellule; niche.
celebérrimo, -ma, *a. superl.* extremely famous.
celebración, *n.f.* celebration, solemn performance; praise, acclamation, applause.
celebradamente, *adv.* with celebration.
celebrador, -ra, *a.* praising, applauding, celebrating.
celebrante, *a.* celebrating. — *n.m.* celebrant.
celebrar, *v.t.*, to celebrate; to praise; to hold (*a meeting etc.*); ***lo celebro mucho,*** I am delighted (to hear it). — **celebrarse,** *v.r.* to take place; to be held.
célebre, *a.* celebrated, renowned, famous; (*coll.*) ***Juan es célebre,*** John is a (real) character.
celebridad, *n.f.* celebrity; renown, fame; public celebration.
celebro, [CEREBRO].
celemín, *n.m.* measure (*equivalent to half a peck*); quantity contained in such a measure.
celeminada, *n.f.* quantity of grain contained in a ***celemín.***
celeminero, *n.m.* ostler.
celeque, *a.* (*E.S.*, *Hond.*) tender (*fruits*).
célere, *a.* swift, fleet. — *n.m.* one of the select three hundred knights of ancient Roman nobility. — *n.f.pl.* (*myth.*) (the) Hours.
celeridad, *n.f.* celerity, velocity, swiftness.
celeste, *a.* celestial, heavenly; (***azul***) ***celeste,*** sky-blue, azure.
celestial, *a.* celestial, heavenly; (*coll.*) ***música celestial,*** nonsense, moonshine.
celestialidad, *n.f.* glory; beatitude.
celestino, -na, *a.*, *n.m.f.* Celestine, Celestinian (*monk* or *nun*); (*coll.*) bawd, pander, procurer, procuress. — *n.f.* (*min.*) celestine, celestite.
celfo [CEFO].
celia, *n.f.* brew.
celíaco, -ca, *a.* cœliac. — *n.f.* cœliac artery; chylific diarrhœa.
celibato, *n.m.* celibacy; (*coll.*) bachelor.
célibe, *n.m.f.* bachelor, spinster, unmarried person, celibate.
célico, -ca, *a.* (*poet.*) celestial, heavenly.
celidonia, *n.f.* common celandine.
celinda, *n.f.* syringa.
celindrate, *n.m.* ragout made with coriander-seed.
celo, *n.m.* zeal, ardour; heat, rut; (*pl.*) jealousy; ***dar celos a,*** to make jealous; ***tener celos,*** to be jealous.
celosía, *n.f.* lattice (*window*); venetian blind; jealousy.
celoso, -sa, *a.* zealous; jealous; (*naut.*) unsteady; highly sensitive.
celotipia, *n.f.* jealousy.
celsitud, *n.f.* elevation, grandeur; highness (*a title, now expressed by* ***alteza***).
celta, *a.*, *n.m.f.* Celt, Celtic. — *n.m.* Celtic (*language*).
celtibérico, -ca, celtiberio, -ria, celtíbero, -ra, *a.*, *n.m.f.* Celtiberian.
celticismo, *n.m.* Celticism.
céltico, -ca, *a.* Celtic.
celtismo, *n.m.* Celticism; love for the study of things Celtic.
celtista, *n.m.f.* Celtologist.
celtohispánico, -ca, celtohispano, -na, *a.* Celto-Spanish.
celtómano, -na, *a.*, *n.m.f.* Celtomaniac.
célula, *n.f.* cell, cellule.
celulado, -da, *a.* cellulate, cellulated.
celular, celulario, -ria, *a.* cellular (*system of isolation in prisons*); ***coche celular,*** black Maria.
celuliforme, *a.* cellulated.
celulilla, *n.f.* very small cell; small cellule *or* cavity.
celuloide, *n.m.* celluloid.
celulosidad, *n.f.* cellulosity.
celuloso, -sa, *a.* cellulose, cellulous. — *n.f.* cellulose; wood pulp.
celladura, *n.f.* repairing of broken cask-hoops.
cellar, *a.* forged (*iron*).
cellenco, -ca, *a.* (*coll.*) decrepit.
cellisca, *n.f.* sleet (storm).
cellisquear, *v.i.* to sleet.
cello, *n.m.* hoop (*used in cooperage*).
cementación, *n.f.* cementation.
cementar, *v.t.* to cement; (*min.*) to precipitate.
cementatorio, -ria, *a.* relating to cementation.
cementerial, *a.* relating to a cemetery.
cementerio, *n.m.* cemetery, churchyard, graveyard.
cemento, *n.m.* cement; ***cemento de Portland,*** Portland cement.
cementoso, -sa, *a.* like cement.
cena, *n.f.* supper, dinner; ***la Ultima Cena,*** the Last Supper.
cenaaoscuras, *n.m.f. inv.* (*coll.*) recluse; miser.
cenáculo, *n.m.* cenacle, literary group; Cenacle (*place of Last Supper*).
cenacho, *n.m.* basket *or* hamper (*for fruit, vegetables etc.*).
cenadero, *n.m.* summer-house; supper-room.
cenador, *n.m.* summer-house; arbour, bower; open gallery round a court-yard (*in a Spanish house*).
cenaduría, *n.f.* (*Mex.*) eating-house (*where food is served only at night*).
cenagal, *n.m.* bog, quagmire, slough; (*fig.*) mess, predicament, bad business.
cenagoso, -sa, *a.* muddy, miry, marshy.
cenal, *n.m.* topgallant sail (*of felucca*).
cenancle, *n.m.* (*Mex.*) cob (*maize*).
cenar, *v.t.* to have, eat for supper, dinner; ***¿qué cenaste?*** what did you have for supper?; ***cené pescado,*** I had fish for supper. — *v.i.* to have supper, dinner; ***ya han cenado, ya están cenados,*** they have (already) had supper; ***vengo cenado,*** I have (already) had supper (elsewhere).
cenata, *n.f.* (*Col.*, *Cub.*) convivial supper amongst friends.
cencapa, *n.f.* (*Per.*) (llama's) halter.
cenceño, -ña, *a.* lean, thin, slight, slender; ***pan cenceño,*** unleavened bread.
cencerra, *n.f.* [CENCERRO].
cencerrada, *n.f.* charivari (*at the door of a widower on the night of his re-marriage*).
cencerrear, *v.i.* to jingle continually (*cow-bells etc.*); (*coll.*) to make a din, kick up a racket *or* row.
cencerreo, *n.m.* jingling, rattling; din, racket.
cencerro, *n.m.* bell (*worn by cattle*); ***a cencerros tapados,*** by stealth; ***cencerro zumbón,*** bell worn by leading beast of a drove.
cencerrón, *n.m.* small bunch of grapes remaining ungathered.
cencido, -da, *a.* untilled, uncultivated; untrodden.
cencuate, *n.m.* (*Mex.*) poisonous snake.
cendal, *n.m.* gauze; scarf used by the priest for the consecration at Mass; barbs of a feather; Moorish vessel with xebec rigging, and usually armed; (*pl.* **cendales**) cotton for an inkstand.
cendea, *n.f.* (*prov.*) in Navarre, municipal borough composed of several villages.

cendra, cendrada, *n.f.* bone-dust paste used for cupels; (*fig.*) ***ser (vivo como) una cendra,*** to be as lively as a cricket.
cenefa, *n.f.* border; edge; band, hem, stripe (*on a piece of cloth etc.*); centre part of a chasuble; hangings, flounce, valance, trimming; (*naut.*) top rim, paddle-box rim; (*naut.*) awning.
cení, *n.m.* fine brass *or* bronze.
cenia, *n.f.* irrigation water-wheel; plot watered in this way.
cenicero, *n.m.* ash-bin, ash-pit, ash-pan; ash-tray.
Cenicienta, *n.f.* Cinderella.
ceniciento, -ta, *a.* ash-coloured, ashen.
cenicilla, *n.f.* (*bot.*) oidium.
cenismo, *n.m.* mixture of dialects.
cenit, cénit, *n.m.* zenith.
cenital, *a.* zenith, zenithal; (*fig.*) peak.
cenizal [CENICERO].
cenizo, -za, *a.* ash-coloured. — *n.m.* goose-foot; (*coll.*) ***ser un cenizo,*** to be a jinx. — *n.f.* ash, ashes, cinders; (*paint.*) size (*on canvas*); (*bot.*) oidium; ***miércoles de ceniza,*** Ash Wednesday; ***huir de la ceniza y caer en las brasas,*** to fall from the frying-pan into the fire; ***tomar uno la ceniza,*** to receive the ashes on Ash Wednesday; (*pl.*) ashes; ***cenizas azules,*** lapis lazuli; ***cenizas de estaño,*** putty; ***cenizas graveladas,*** weed-ashes; ***cenizas de vegetales,*** potash; ***convertir en cenizas,*** to reduce to ashes.
cenizoso, -sa, *a.* ashen; ashy.
cenobio, *n.m.* monastery.
cenobita, *n.m.f.* cœnobite monk, nun.
cenobítico, -ca, *a.* cœnobitical.
cenobitismo, *n.m.* cœnobitism.
cenojil, *n.m.* garter.
cenopegias, *n.f.pl.* Jewish feast of Tabernacles.
cenotafio, *n.m.* cenotaph.
cenote, *n.m.* (*Mex.*) water reservoir in caves.
censal, *a.* (*prov.*) [CENSUAL]. — *n.m.* (*prov.*) annual ground-rent.
censalista (*prov.*) [CENSUALISTA].
censatario, *n.m.* vassal; one who pays an annuity out of his estate; lessee; farmer.
censo, *n.m.* agreement for settling an annuity; annual ground-rent, rental, lease; income; census; poll-tax; (*fig.*) burden, charge; ***censo de agua,*** water-tax; ***censo de por vida,*** life annuity; ***censo redimible,*** redeemable annuity.
censontli, censontle, *n.m.* (*Mex.*) mocking-bird.
censor, *n.m.* censor; censorious critic *or* person.
censoría, *n.f.* censorship; censor's office.
censorino, -na, censorio, -ria, *a.* censorial; censorious.
censual, *a.* belonging to a lease, annuity *or* rent; rental.
censualista, *n.m.f.* lessor, annuitant; copy-holder.
censura, *n.f.* censoring; censorship.
censurable, *a.* censurable; reprehensible; objectionable.
censurador, -ra, *a.* censorious. — *n.m.* censor; fault-finder.
censurante, *a.* censorious, censoring.
censurar, *v.t.* to censor; to censure, criticize, condemn.
censuratorio, -ria, *a.* censorial.
censurista, *a.* critical, carping. — *n.m.f.* critic, fault-finder.
centaura, *n.f.* (*bot.*) centaury; ***centaura mayor,*** greater centaury; ***centaura menor,*** lesser centaury.
centaureo, -rea, *a.* gentianic. — *n.f.* [CENTAURA]; gentian; (*pl.*) Gentiana.
centauro, *n.m.* (*myth.*) centaur; (*astron.*) Centaur.
centavo, -va, *a.* centesimal. — *n.m.* cent.
centella, *n.f.* lightning; flash; spark; (*sl.*) sword; (*Chi.*) crowfoot, buttercup; ***como una centella,*** like a flash.
centellador, -ra, *a.* brilliant, flashing.
centellante, centelleante, *a.* gleaming, glittering, sparkling, flashing.
centellar, centellear, *v.i.* to gleam, glitter, sparkle, flash, twinkle.
centelleo, *n.m.* gleam(ing), glitter(ing), sparkle, sparkling; scintillation.
centén, *n.m.* Spanish gold coin worth twenty-five pesetas (*i.e. one hundred reales*).
centena, *n.f.* [CENTENO].
centenada, *n.f.* hundred; ***a centenadas,*** by the hundred, in hundreds.
centenal, *n.m.* centenary; rye-field.
centenar, *n.m.* hundred; rye-field; ***a centenares,*** by the hundred, in hundreds.
centenario, -ria, *a.* centenary, centennial. — *a., n.m.f.* centenarian. — *n.m.* centenary, centennial.
centenaza, *a.* appertaining to rye; ***paja centenaza,*** rye-straw.
centenero, -ra, *a.* good for rye (*soil*).
centeno (1), *n.m.* rye.
centeno (2), **-na,** *a.* hundred. — *n.f.* hundred; century.
centenoso, -sa, *a.* mixed with rye.
centesimal, *a.* centesimal, hundredth.
centésimo, -ma, *a., n.m.f.* centesimal, hundredth.
centiárea, *n.f.* centiare, square metre, hundredth part of an are.
centígrado, -da, *a.* centigrade.
centigramo, *n.m.* centigram.
centilitro, *n.m.* centilitre.
centiloquio, *n.m.* work divided into a hundred parts *or* chapters.
centillero, *n.m.* (*Chi.*) seven-light candelabra.
centimano, -na, *a.* (*poet.*) hundred-handed.
centímetro, *n.m.* centimetre.
céntimo, -ma, *a.* hundredth. — *n.m.* copper coin, centime; hundredth part of any monetary unit.
centinela, *n.m.f.* sentry, sentinel; ***centinela perdida,*** forlorn hope; ***centinela de vista,*** prisoner's guard; (*mil.*) ***hacer*** or ***estar de centinela,*** to stand sentry, to be on guard.
centinodia, *n.f.* knot-grass, persicaria.
centípedo, -da, *a.* centipedal. — *n.m.* (*zool.*) centipede.
centiplicado, -da [CENTUPLICADO].
centollo, *n.m.*, **centolla,** *n.f.* spider-crab.
centón, *n.m.* patch-work quilt; (*fig., lit.*) cento; (*mil.*) coarse covering (*for military equipment*).
centonar, *v.t.* to pile, heap up untidily; (*fig.*) to compile (*centos*).
centrado, -da, *a.* (*her.*) having sth. on centre of globe *or* sphere.
central, *a.* central. — *n.f.* central, head office; headquarters; ***central (telefónica),*** (telephone) exchange; ***central eléctrica,*** power station.
centralidad, *n.f.* central situation.
centralilla, centralita, *n.f.* local telephone exchange; sub-exchange.
centralismo, *n.m.* centralism.
centralista, *a., n.m.f.* centralist.
centralización, *n.f.* centralization.
centralizador, -ra, *a.* centralizing; relating to centralization.
centralizar [C], *v.t.* to centralize.
centrar, *v.t.* to centre.
céntrico, -ca, *a.* central, focal; ***punto céntrico,*** focal point; ***vive en un sitio céntrico,*** he lives very near the centre of town.
centrifugador, -ra, *a.* centrifugal.
centrifugar [B], *v.t.* to centrifuge.
centrífugo, -ga, *a.* centrifugal; ***bomba centrífuga,*** centrifugal pump; ***fuerza centrífuga,*** centrifugal force.

centrina, *n.f.* crab.
centripetencia, *n.f.* attraction to the centre.
centrípeto, -ta, *a.* centripetal.
centrisco, *n.m.* trumpet-fish.
centro, *n.m.* centre; middle; (*Ec.*) short flannel dress; (*Cub.*) transparent skirt; (*Cub.*) suit; (*Hond., Mex.*) waistcoat; ***centro docente,*** educational centre; (*phys.*) ***centro de gravedad,*** centre of gravity; ***centro de mesa,*** centre-piece (*for a table*); ***centros nerviosos,*** nerve centres; (*fig.*) ***estar en su centro,*** to be in one's element.
centroamericano, -na, *a., n.m.f.* (native) of Central America.
centrobárico, -ca, *a.* centrobaric.
centroide, *n.m.* (*math.*) centrode.
centunviral, *a.* centumviral.
centunvirato, *n.m.* centumvirate.
centunviro, *n.m.* centumvir.
centuplicación, *n.f.* centuplication.
centuplicado, -da, *a.* centuplicated, multiplied a hundredfold; ***por centuplicado,*** a hundredfold, greatly increased.
centuplicador, -ra, *a., n.m.f.* centuplicating, multiplying a hundredfold.
centuplicar [A], *v.t.* to centuplicate, multiply a hundredfold; greatly to increase.
céntuplo, -la, *a., n.m.f.* centuple, hundredfold.
centuria, *n.f.* century; (Roman) century.
centurión, *n.m.* centurion.
centurionazgo, *n.m.* office of a centurion.
cenzalino, -na, *a.* relating to the mosquito.
cénzalo, *n.m.* mosquito.
ceñido, -da, *a.* tight; close-fitting; close; narrow-waisted; tight for money, hard-up; ***curva ceñida,*** sharp bend.
ceñidor, *n.m.* belt, girdle, sash.
ceñidura, *n.f.* girding; contraction, reduction, restriction.
ceñiglo, *n.m.* white goose-foot.
ceñir [8K], *v.t.* to gird, girdle, circle, surround; to hem in; (*fig.*) to reduce, contract, abbreviate; ***ceñir espada,*** to gird *or* wear a sword; ***ceñir la plaza,*** to besiege the town; (*naut.*) ***ceñir el viento,*** to haul the wind; ***ceñir con*** or ***de flores,*** to girdle with flowers. — **ceñirse,** *v.r.* to confine, limit *or* restrict oneself; to cut down; ***ceñirse a lo justo,*** to restrict oneself to essentials; ***ceñirse a las circunstancias,*** to adapt oneself to circumstances.
ceño, *n.m.* frown; lowering *or* threatening appearance; band, hoop, ring; (*vet.*) circle round top of horse's hoof; ***arrugar (fruncir) el ceño,*** to knit one's brow, frown.
ceñoso, -sa [CEÑUDO].
ceñudo, -da, *a.* frowning; forbidding, grim, stern.
ceo, *n.m.* dory.
cepa, *n.f.* vine-stock; underground stub (*of tree-stem*); stump, stub; (*fig.*) origin, stock (*of a family*); root (*of horns* or *tails of animals*); (*arch.*) pier (*of an arch*); ***de buena cepa,*** of good family, origin *or* stock; of good quality.
cepeda, cepera, *n.f.* land overgrown with heath.
cepejón, *n.m.* butt-end of a branch torn from the trunk.
cepellón, *n.m.* earth left round the roots of a plant for transplanting.
cepilladura, *n.f.* planing; (*pl.*) shavings.
cepillamiento, *n.m.* planing.
cepillar, *v.t.* to brush; to plane.
cepillo, *n.m.* almsbox, collection box, poor-box, charity-box; (*carp.*) plane; brush; ***cepillo de dientes,*** tooth-brush.
cepo, *n.m.* bough *or* branch (*of a tree*); stock (*of an anvil*); (*naut.*) bilboes; stocks (*for punishment*); (shoemaker's) horse; trap, snare; reel (*for winding silk*); poor-box; stocks (*of gun-carriage*); (*zool.*) [CEFO]; (*mech.*) block, socket, clasp, clamp, joining-press; ***cepo del ancla,*** anchor-stock; (*pl.*) notched cleats; (*interj., coll.*) ***¡cepos quedos!*** hands off! stop! no more of that!
cepón, *n.m.* large stub of tree *or* vine-stock.
ceporro, *n.m.* old vine pulled up (*for fuel*); (*fig.*) clod, thick-headed person; chubby child; ***estar hecho un ceporro,*** to be sleeping like a log.
cequí, *n.m.* sequin (*Venetian gold coin*).
cequia [ACEQUIA].
cera, *n.f.* wax; wax tapers, wax candles; ***cera aleda,*** bee-glue, propolis; ***cera de dorar,*** gold size; ***cera de los oídos,*** ear-wax; ***cera toral,*** unbleached wax; ***cera vieja,*** ends of wax candles; ***cera virgen,*** virgin wax; ***no hay más cera que la que arde,*** that's all there is, that's it; ***ser una cera*** or ***como una cera,*** to be malleable; ***melar las ceras,*** to fill the combs with honey.
ceracate, *n.f.* yellow agate.
ceráceo, -cea, *a.* cereous, waxy.
ceración, *n.f.* fusing of metal.
cerafolio, *n.m.* common chervil.
cerámico, -ca, *a.* ceramic. — *n.f.* ceramic art; ceramics, pottery.
ceramista, *n.m.f.* ceramist, potter.
ceramita, *n.f.* precious stone; brick stronger than granite.
cerapez, *n.f.* (cobbler's) wax.
cerasina, *n.f.* cerasin.
cerasiote, *n.m.* purge containing cherry-juice.
cerasta, cerastas, *n.f.*, **ceraste, cerastes,** *n.m.* cerastes, horned serpent.
ceratias, *n.m.* double-tailed comet.
cerato, *n.m.* oil and wax ointment.
ceratoideo, -dea, *a.* ceratoid.
ceratótomo, *n.m.* ceratotome.
ceraunia, *n.f.* thunderbolt (*stone*).
ceraunómetro, *n.m.* apparatus for measuring intensity of lightning.
ceraunoscopión, *n.m.* ceraunoscope.
cerbatana, *n.f.* pop-gun; pea-shooter; blow-pipe; acoustic trumpet (*for the deaf*); ancient culverin; ***hablar por cerbatana,*** to speak through an intermediary.
cerbero, *n.m.* Cerberus; shrub with poisonous sap.
cerca (de), *adv., prep.* near(ly) close (to); ***cerca de tu casa,*** near your house; ***son cerca de las ocho,*** it is nearly eight o'clock; ***embajador cerca de Su Majestad Británica,*** ambassador to His (Her) Britannic Majesty; ***aquí cerca*** or ***cerca de aquí,*** close by, near here; ***de cerca,*** at close quarters; ***tocar de cerca,*** to affect closely, to concern directly. — *n.f.* wall, fence; ***cerca viva,*** hedge. — *n.m.* ***tener buen*** or ***mal cerca,*** to admit *or* not to admit of close examination; (*pl., paint.*) objects in the foreground.
cercado, *n.m.* enclosure, fenced-in *or* walled-in garden *or* field; (*Per.*) territorial division.
cercador, -ra, *a.* enclosing. — *n.m.f.* hedger, encloser. — *n.m.* blunt chisel used in repoussé-work.
cercadura, *n.f.* enclosure, fence, wall.
cercamiento, *n.m.* enclosing; surrounding.
cercanía, *n.f.* nearness, proximity; (*pl.*) vicinity, neighbourhood; surroundings; ***tren de cercanías,*** suburban train.
cercano, -na, *a.* near, close by; ***cercano a su fin,*** nearing its end.
cercar [A], *v.t.* to enclose, fence, hem in, encircle; to surround, crowd about; to pale; (*mil.*) to besiege, invest.
cercén, *adv.* ***a cercén,*** close (*to the root*), all around; completely.
cercenadera, *n.f.* clipping-knife (*used by wax-chandlers*).
cercenador, -ra, *a.* clipping. — *n.m.f.* clipper.
cercenadura, *n.f.* clipping, retrenchment; (*pl.*) cuttings.

cercenar, *v.t.* to pare, clip, lop off (*ends* or *extremities*); to abridge, curtail, lessen, reduce.

cercera, *n.f.* (*prov.*) strong northerly wind.

cerceta, *n.f.* widgeon; (*pl.*) first growth of a deer's antlers.

cercillo, *n.m.* ear-ring; ***cercillo de vid,*** vine tendril.

cerciorar, *v.t.* to assure. — **cerciorarse,** *v.r.* to make certain *or* sure, check (up).

cerco, *n.m.* hoop; ring; rim, border, edge; halo; (*mil.*) siege; circle; frame (*of door, picture* or *window*); ***en cerco,*** round about; ***la luna tiene cerco,*** the moon has a ring round it; ***alzar*** or ***levantar el cerco,*** to raise the siege; ***poner cerco a,*** to lay siege to.

cercopiteco, *n.m.* long-tailed monkey.

cercote, *n.m.* fishing-net.

cercha, *n.f.* wooden rule (*for measuring convex* or *concave objects*); skeleton pattern *or* frame (*for building vaults* or *arches*); segment (*of a rim*); rim (*of a rudder*).

cerchar, *v.t.* to plant (vine-cuttings).

cerchearse, *v.r.* (*prov.*) to sag.

cerchón, *n.m.* (*arch.*) [CIMBRA].

cerda, *n.f.* hair (*of horse's tail* or *mane*); bristle; new-mown but unthrashed cereals; bundle (*of unhackled flax*); (*zool.*) sow; ***cerda de puerco,*** hog's bristle; ***ganado de cerda,*** swine; (*pl.*) snares.

cerdada, *n.f.* herd of swine; (*coll.*) filthy *or* rotten trick.

cerdamen, *n.m.* (set of) bristles.

cerdear, *v.i.* to be weak in the fore-quarter (*animals*); to grate, rasp (*musical instrument*); (*coll.*) to make excuses; to cut up rusty.

Cerdeña, *n.f.* Sardinia.

cerdito, *n.m.* piglet; (dear) little pig, piggy.

cerdo, *n.m.* (*lit., fig.*) hog, pig; (*meat*) pork; ***cerdo de matanza (engorde),*** pig (to be) specially fattened up; ***cerdo marino,*** porpoise.

cerdoso, -sa, *a.* bristly.

cerdudo, -da [CERDOSO].

cereal, *a., n.m.f.* cereal.

cerealina, *n.f.* cerealin.

cerebelitis, *n.f.* inflammation of the cerebellum.

cerebelo, *n.m.* cerebellum.

cerebral, *a.* cerebral; (*fig.*) cold, calculating.

cerebralidad, *n.f.* cerebralism; intellectual vigour.

cerébrico, -ca, *a.* cerebric.

cerebrino, -na, *a.* cerebral. — *n.f.* cerebrin.

cerebritis, *n.f.* encephalitis.

cerebro, *n.m.* cerebrum; (*lit., fig.*) brain(s).

cerebroespinal, *a.* cerebro-spinal.

cerebroideo, -dea, *a.* encephaloid.

cerebropatía, *n.f.* encephalopathy.

cereceda, *n.f.* cherry-orchard; (*sl.*) (galley-slaves') chain.

cerecilla, *n.f.* pod (*of red pepper*).

cerecita, *n.f.* small cherry.

cereiforme, *a.* cherry-shaped.

cereleón [CERATO].

ceremonia, *n.f.* ceremony; pomp, formality; ***de ceremonia,*** formal, with ceremony *or* pomp; ***sin ceremonias,*** without formality, unceremoniously; ***lo hace de pura ceremonia,*** he does it as a pure formality.

ceremonial *a., n.m.* ceremonial.

ceremoniático, -ca, *a.* ceremonious.

ceremoniero, -ra, *a.* addicted to formality.

ceremonioso, -sa, *a.* ceremonious; formal.

cereño, -ña, *a.* wax-coloured (*dog*).

céreo, -rea, *a.* cereous, waxy.

cereolita, *n.f.* soft waxy-looking lava.

cerería, *n.f.* chandlery.

cerero, *n.m.* wax-chandler; ***cerero mayor,*** royal chandler.

ceresina, *n.f.* cerasin.

cerevisina, *n.f.* brewer's yeast.

cereza, *n.f.* cherry; cerise; ***cereza garrafal,*** large white-heart cherry; ***cereza mollar,*** soft cherry; ***cereza póntica,*** small black cherry.

cerezal, *n.m.* cherry orchard.

cerezo, *n.m.* cherry tree; cherry wood; ***cerezo silvestre,*** dog-cherry tree.

ceribón, *n.m.* (*obs.*) surrender by an insolvent debtor of his estate to his creditors; (*obs.*) ***hacer ceribones,*** to make affectedly submissive compliments.

cérico, -ca, *a.* relating to an acid resulting from oxidation of cerium.

cerífero, -ra, *a.* producing *or* yielding wax.

cerífica, *a.* cerographical; ***pintura cerífica,*** wax painting.

cerificación, *n.f.* purifying of wax.

cerificador, *n.m.* wax-purifying apparatus.

cerificar [A], *v.t.* to purify (*wax*).

ceriflor, *n.m.* honey-wort, honey-flower.

cerilla, *n.f.* wax taper (*in rolls*); wax match; ear wax; cold cream.

cerillero, -ra, *n.m.f.* match seller; matchbox.

cerillo, *n.m.* (*prov.*) wax match.

cerina, *n.f.* cerin.

cerio, *n.m.* cerium.

cerita, *n.f.* (*min.*) cerite.

cermeña, *n.f.* pear.

cermeño, *n.m.* pear tree; (*fig.*) boor, clod.

cernada, *n.f.* leached ashes; ash sizing; ash poultice.

cernadero, cernaguero, *n.m.* coarse linen strainer (*for leach-tub*); material of linen *or* linen and silk (*for collars*).

cernedero, *n.m.* apron (*worn in sifting flour*); bolting-place.

cernedor, -ra, *n.m.f.* bolting-machine, bolter, sifter.

cerneja, *n.f.* fetlock.

cernejudo, -da, *a.* having shaggy fetlocks.

cerner [2], *v.t.* to sift, bolt; (*fig.*) to scrutinize, examine minutely; (*fig.*) to refine, purify. — ***v.i.*** to bud and blossom; (*fig.*) to drizzle. — **cernerse,** *v.r.* to sway, waddle; to hover; to hang threateningly (***sobre,*** over).

cernícalo, *n.m.* kestrel, sparrow hawk; (*fig.*) clod, thick-headed fellow; (*slang*) woman's cloak; ***coger*** or ***pillar un cernícalo,*** to get sozzled.

cernidillo, *n.m.* drizzle; swagger.

cernido, *n.m.* sifting; sifted flour.

cernidura, *n.f.* sifting.

cernir [3], *v.t.* [CERNER].

cero, *n.m.* cipher, zero, naught; ***ser un cero,*** or ***un cero a la izquierda,*** to be a mere cipher.

ceroferario, *n.m.* (*eccles.*) candelabrum bearer.

cerografía, *n.f.* cerography.

cerográfico, -ca, *a.* cerographical.

cerógrafo, *n.m.* cerographist; (*archæol.*) wax seal.

ceroideo, -dea, *a.* cereous; (*min.*) scaly.

ceroleína, *n.f.* constituent of bees-wax.

cerollo, -lla, *a.* green and soft (*grain*).

ceroma, *n.f.* ointment.

ceromancia, *n.f.* ceromancy.

ceromático, -ca, *a.* containing oil and wax.

ceromiel, *n.m.* ointment of wax and honey.

cerón, *n.m.* dregs of pressed wax.

ceróneo, *n.m.* embrocation.

ceroplasta, *n.m.* modeller in wax.

ceroplástica, *n.f.* ceroplastics.

cerote, *n.m.* (shoemaker's) wax; (*coll.*) panic, funk.

cerotear, *v.t.* to wax (*thread*).

cerotero, *n.m.* piece of felt used to wax twine (*in making rockets*).

ceroto [CERATO].

cerquillo, *n.m.* small circle, hoop; seam *or* welt (*of shoe*); ring (*of hair* or *tonsure*).
cerquita, *adv.* quite *or* very near, nice and near *or* handy.
cerrada (1), *n.f.* spinal hide *or* skin.
cerradero, -ra, *a.* locked; locking (*device*). — *n.m.f.* lock; locker. — *n.m.* staple *or* hole which receives the bolt of a lock; purse-strings; ***echar la cerradera,*** to turn a deaf ear.
cerradizo, -za, *a.* that may be locked *or* fastened.
cerrado, -da (2), *a.* close, reserved, secretive; uncomprehending, obtuse; heavy *or* broad (*accent*); overcast, cloudy; thick (*beard*); ***a puño cerrado,*** staunch; staunchly; ***barba cerrada,*** heavy, thick beard; ***noche cerrada,*** pitch-dark (*night*); ***a ojos cerrados,*** blindly, unquestioningly, without hesitation; ***a puerta cerrada,*** behind closed doors, privately, secretly; in camera. — *n.m.* enclosure; closed shop; ***cerrado de cascos*** or ***de mollera,*** obtuse, thick.
cerrador, -ra, *a.* locking, shutting. — *n.m.* fastener; locker, shutter; porter, door-keeper; tie, fastening.
cerradura, *n.f.* locking *or* shutting up; lock; (*obs.*) enclosure; ***cerradura embutida,*** mortise lock; ***cerradura de golpe*** or ***de muelle,*** spring-lock; ***cerradura de loba,*** lock with wards shaped like a wolf's teeth; ***cerradura de molinillo,*** lock with revolving tube for keyshaft.
cerraja, *n.f.* lock; (*bot.*) common sow-thistle; ***todo quedó en agua de cerrajas,*** all came to naught.
cerrajear, *v.i.* to work as a locksmith.
cerrajería, *n.f.* locksmith's trade, shop, *or* forge.
cerrajero, *n.m.* locksmith.
cerrajón, *n.m.* steep, craggy cliff.
cerramiento, *n.m.* closure, shutting *or* locking up.
cerrar [1], *v.t., v.i.* to close, shut; to lock, fasten; to stop up; to plug; to clench; to turn off; to close, fence in; to finish, terminate, put an end to; to engage (*the enemy*); ***cerrar la carta,*** to seal the letter, ***cerrar la cuenta,*** to close the account; ***cerrar un contrato,*** to conclude a contract; ***cerrar los estudios,*** to wind up one's studies; ***cerrar el paso,*** to bar *or* block the way; ***cerrar la boca, el pico*** or ***los labios,*** to shut up; ***cerrar en falso,*** to shut faultily, insecurely; ***cerrar la marcha,*** to bring up the rear; ***cerrar los oídos,*** to turn a deaf ear; (*lit., fig.*) ***cerrar el ojo*** (***los ojos***), to shut one's eye(s); ***la puerta cierra mal,*** the door doesn't shut properly; ***cerrar con*** (***contra***) ***el enemigo,*** to close with *or* engage the enemy; ***cerrar la noche,*** to get dark; ***al cerrar del día,*** at night-fall; ***¡Santiago y cierra España!*** up, Spaniards, and at 'em! — **cerrarse,** *v.r.* to heal up; to become set, obdurate; to get cloudy, overcast.
cerrazón, *n.f.* gathering storm clouds; thick-headedness, obdurateness; (*Hisp. Am.*) ridge, spur (*of mountain range*).
cerrejón, *n.m.* hillock.
cerrería, *n.f.* laxity, licence.
cerrero, -ra, *a.* untamed, running wild; lofty, haughty; (*Hisp. Am.*) rude, rough; (*Ven.*) bitter; ***caballo cerrero,*** unbroken horse.
cerreta, *n.f.* (*naut.*) bulwarks.
cerril, *a.* uneven, rough; wild, unbroken, untamed; (*coll.*) boorish, uncouth; ***puente cerril,*** very narrow bridge.
cerrilla, *n.f.* die (*for milling coins*).
cerrillar, *v.t.* to mill (*coins*).
cerrillo, *n.m.* (*bot.*) grama; (*pl.*) dies (*for milling coined metal*).
cerrión, *n.m.* icicle.
cerro, *n.m.* neck (*of animal*); backbone, ridge (*formed by backbone*); hill; cleaned flax *or* hemp; ***en cerro,*** bareback; unadorned; ***echar por esos cerros, echar, irse*** or ***andarse por los cerros de Ubeda,*** to go, get *or* wander off the track *or* subject, ramble on.
cerrojazo, *n.m.* slamming (*of bolt*).
cerrojillo, *n.m.* (*orn.*) wagtail, warbler.
cerrojo, *n.m.* bolt, latch; ***tentar cerrojos,*** to try all ways and means.
cerrón, *n.m.* coarse fabric.
cerruma, ceruma, *n.f.* pastern.
cerrumado, -da, *a.* having weak *or* defective pasterns.
certamen, *n.m.* (*obs.*) duel, battle; competition, contest.
certeneja, *n.f.* (*Mex.*) small and deep reservoir; (*Chi.*) pit dug in a river bed.
certería, *n.f.* accuracy; good aim.
certero, -ra, *a.* sure, certain; accurate; well-aimed, on the mark.
certeza, *n.f.* certainty, certitude; ***tengo la certeza de que vendrá,*** I am certain that he will come.
certidumbre, *n.f.* certainty; (*obs.*) security, obligation to fulfil an engagement.
certificable, *a.* certifiable; registrable.
certificación, *n.f.* certificate; certification; attestation (*of the truth of a fact* or *event*); registration.
certificado, *n.m.* certificate.
certificador, -ra, *a.* certifying; registering. — *n.m.f.* certifier.
certificar [A], *v.t.* to certify, guarantee; to register (*a letter* or *postal packet*); (*law*) to prove by a public instrument.
certificativo, -va, certificatorio, -ria, *a.* certifying.
certísimo, -ma, *a. superl.* absolutely true *or* sure.
certitud, *n.f.* certitude, certainty.
ceruleína, cerulina, *n.f.* (*chem.*) cerulein, cerulin.
cerúleo, -lea, *a.* cerulean, sky-blue.
cerumen, *n.m.* ear-wax.
ceruminoso, -sa, *a.* ceruminous.
cerusa, *n.f.* ceruse.
cerusita, *n.f.* cerusite.
cerval, cervario, -ria, *a.* appertaining to deer; ***tener un miedo cerval,*** to be scared to death.
cervantesco, -ca, cervantino, -na, *a.* like, in the style of, relating *or* peculiar to, Cervantes.
cervantismo, *n.m.* study, influence *or* expression of Cervantes.
cervantista, *a., n.m.f.* student of Cervantes.
cervantófilo, -la, *a., n.m.f.* admirer *or* lover of Cervantes.
cervatica, *n.f.* locust.
cervatillo, *n.m.* musk-deer; young fawn.
cervato, *n.m.* fawn.
cerveceo, *n.m.* fermentation of beer.
cervecería, *n.f.* brewery; ale-house; beer-saloon.
cervecero, -ra, *a.* appertaining to beer. — *n.m.f.* brewer, beer-seller. — *n.m.* set of beer-jugs and -glasses.
cerveza, *n.f.* beer, ale.
cervicabra, *n.f.* gazelle.
cervical, cérvico, -ca, cervicular, *a.* cervical.
cérvidos, *n.m.pl.* cervidæ, deer.
cervigudo, -da, *a.* high-necked, thick-necked; (*fig.*) obstinate, stubborn.
cerviguillo, *n.m.* thick nape (*of neck*).
cervillera, *n.f.* helmet, casque.
cervino, -na, *a.* cervine, appertaining to deer; ***el monte Cervino,*** the Matterhorn.
cerviolas, *n.f.pl.* (*naut.*) cat-heads.
cerviz, *n.f.* cervix, nape (*of neck*); ***doblar*** or ***bajar la cerviz,*** to humble o.s.; ***levantar la cerviz,*** to grow proud; ***ser de dura cerviz,*** to be headstrong, unruly.
cervuno, -na, *a.* cervine, appertaining to deer; of the colour of deer.
cesación, *n.f.,* **cesamiento,** *n.m.* cessation, ceasing, pause; ***cesación a divinis,*** canonical suspension of divine service (*in a desecrated church*).

cesante, *a.* out of office, suspended from office, unemployed. — *n.m.* out of office *or* suspended civil servant.
cesantía, *n.f.* suspension from civil service, (state of) being out of office *or* unemployed; pension.
César, *n.m.* Cæsar, emperor; ***o César o nada,*** all or nothing.
cesar, *v.i.* to cease, stop; to leave *or* go out of office; to be dismissed *or* suspended (*from a post*); ***cesó de llover,*** it stopped raining; ***sin cesar,*** ceaselessly, continually.
cesáreo, -rea, *a.* Cæsarian, imperial; (***operación***) ***cesárea,*** Cæsarian (operation).
cesariano, -na, cesarino, -na, *a.* Cæsarian.
cesarismo, *n.m.* Cæsarism, despotism.
cese, *n.m.* ceasing, cessation; dismissal, suspension; stoppage (*of salary*); end; ***cese de alarma,*** all clear; ***cese de*** or ***el fuego,*** cease fire.
cesible, *a.* (*law*) that may be ceded; transferable.
cesión, *n.f.* cession *or* transfer; assignment, conveyance; resignation; concession; ***cesión de bienes,*** surrender of property.
cesionario, -ria, cesonario, -ria, *n.m.f.* (*law*) cessionary.
cesionista, *n.m.f.* transferrer, assignor, grantor.
césped, *n.m.* sod, grass plot, turf, sward, lawn; bark (*growing over cut made by pruning*); ***césped inglés,*** lawn.
cespedera, *n.f.* field where grass sods are cut.
cespitar, *v.i.* to hesitate, vacillate.
cespitoso, -sa, *a.* cespitose.
cesta, *n.f.* basket, pannier, hamper; scoop *or* racket (*pelota*); ***llevar la cesta,*** to (have to) play gooseberry.
cestada, *n.f.* basketful.
cestería, *n.f.* basket-shop *or* factory; basket-making.
cestero, -ra, *n.m.f.* basket-maker, basket-seller.
cestico, -ca; cestillo, -lla; cestito, -ta, *n.m.f.* small basket.
cesto, *n.m.* basket; cestus; ***cesto de los papeles,*** waste-paper basket; (*Am.*) waste basket; ***coger agua en cesto,*** to labour in vain; ***estar hecho un cesto,*** to be overcome (*by sleep, drink etc.*); ***estar metido en el cesto,*** to be spoiled (*children*); (*coll.*) ***ser un cesto,*** to be a boor, clod.
cestodos, *n.m.pl.* Cestoidea.
cestoide, cestoideo, -dea, *a.* cestoid.
cestón, *n.m.* large pannier, large basket; (*mil.*) gabion.
cestonada, *n.f.* (*mil.*) gabionade.
cesura, *n.f.* cæsura.
ceta [ZETA].
cetáceo, -cea, *a.* cetaceous. — *n.m.f.* cetacean; *n.m.pl.* cetacea.
cetaria, *n.f.* hatchery.
cetarina, *n.f.* extract of Iceland lichen.
cetario, *n.m.* breeding place of whales.
cetina, *n.f.* spermaceti.
cetís, *n.m.* old Galician and Portuguese coin.
cetra, *n.f.* leather shield (*formerly used by Spaniards*).
cetrarina, *n.f.* bitter element found in certain lichens.
cetre, *n.m.* (*obs.*) holy-water basin; (*prov.*) assistant acolyte.
cetrería, *n.f.* falconry, hawking.
cetrero, *n.m.* verger; falconer, hawker.
cetrífero, *n.m.* (*poet.*) one who bears a sceptre.
cetrino, -na, *a.* citrine; citrinous; sallow.
cetro, *n.m.* sceptre; (*eccles.*) rod, verge; wand, staff; perch, roost; ***cetro de locura,*** jester's bauble with cap and bells; ***empuñar el cetro,*** to ascend to the throne.
ceugma, *n.f.* (*rhet.*) zeugma.
ceutí, *a., n.m.f.* appertaining to *or* (native) of Ceuta. — *n.m.* coin of Ceuta.
cía, *n.f.* hip-bone, huckle-bone.
ciaboga, *n.f.* (*naut.*) putting about, turn.
ciaescurre, *n.m.* (*naut.*) putting about.
cianato, *n.m.* cyanate.
cianea [LAZULITA].
cianhidrato, *n.m.* hydrocyanate.
cianhídrico, -ca, *a.* hydrocyanic.
ciánico, -ca, *a.* cyanic.
ciánido, *n.m.* cyanide.
cianina, *n.f.* cyanine.
cianita, *n.f.* cyanite.
cianoférrico, -ca, *a.* ferrocyanic.
cianoferro, *n.m.* ferrocyanide.
cianógeno, *n.m.* cyanogen.
cianómetro, *n.m.* cyanometer.
cianopatía, *n.f.*, **cianosis,** *n.m.* cyanosis.
cianosado, -da, *a.* suffering from cyanosis.
cianótico, -ca, *a.* relating to cyanosis. — *a., n.m.f.* [CIANOSADO].
cianotipia, *n.f.* cyanotype.
cianuro, *n.m.* cyanide.
ciar [L], *v.i.* to back water; (*fig.*) to soft-pedal.
ciático, -ca, *a.* sciatic. — *n.f.* sciatica; (*Per.*) poisonous tree-frern.
ciatófero, -ra, *a.* cyathiform.
cibal, *a.* appertaining to food.
Cibeles, *n.f.* (*myth.*) Cybele; (*astron.*) earth.
cibera, *n.f.* quantity of wheat put at once in the hopper; seeds *or* grains fit for animal food; coarse remains of crushed grain *or* fruit; (*prov.*) hopper in a corn-mill.
cibica, *n.f.* clout, hurter (*of axle-tree*); (*naut.*) staple, clamp.
cibicón, *n.m.* large clout.
cíbolo, -la, *n.m.f.* bison, American buffalo.
ciborio, *n.m.* ciborium.
cibui, *n.m.* (*Per.*) cedar.
cicada, *n.f.* cicada.
cicatear, *v.i.* (*coll.*) to act in a mean *or* stingy way; to show reluctance to pay.
cicatería, *n.f.* niggardliness, stinginess.
cicaterillo, -lla, *a., n.m.f.* rather stingy (person).
cicatero, -ra, *a., n.m.f.* niggardly *or* stingy (person). — *n.m.* (*sl.*) pickpocket.
cicateruelo, -la, *a., n.m.f.* (person) on the mean *or* stingy side, rather mean *or* stingy (little) (beggar).
cicatricera, *n.f.* volunteer military nurse.
cicatriz, *n.f.* cicatrix, scar.
cicatrizante, *a.* cicatrizing, healing.
cicatrizar(se) [C], *v.t., v.i.* (*v.r.*) to cicatrize, heal (up), skin (over).
cicatrizativo, -va, *a.* cicatrizing, healing.
cícera, cicércula, cicercha, *n.f.* small chick-pea.
cícero, *n.m.* (*print.*) pica; measure unit equivalent to 12 points.
cicerone, *n.m.* cicerone, guide.
ciceroniano, -na, *a., n.m.f.* Ciceronian.
ción, *n.m.* (*prov.*) tertian.
ciclada, *n.f.* (woman's) tunic.
ciclamen, ciclamino, *n.m.* cyclamen.
ciclamor, *n.m.* sycamore, Judas tree.
ciclán, *a., n.m.* one-testicled (*animal*).
ciclar, *v.t.* to polish, burnish (*precious stones*).
ciclatón, *n.m.* (woman's) tunic.
cíclico, -ca, *a.* cyclic, cyclical.
ciclismo, *n.m.* cycling.
ciclista, *n.m.f.* cyclist.
ciclo, *n.m.* cycle.
ciclógrafo, *n.m.* cyclograph.
cicloidal, cicloideo, -dea, *a.* cycloidal.
cicloide, *n.f.* cycloid.
ciclometría, *n.f.* cyclometry.
ciclométrico, -ca, *a.* relating to cyclometry.
ciclómetro, *n.m.* cyclometer.

ciclón, *n.m.* cyclone.
ciclonal, *a.* cyclonic.
cíclope, *n.m.* (*myth., zool.*) cyclops.
ciclópeo, -pea, ciclópico, -ca, *a.* cyclopean; gigantic.
ciclorama, *n.m.* cyclorama.
ciclosis, *n.f.* cyclosis.
ciclostilo, *n.m.* cyclostyle.
cicuración, *n.f.* taming of wild animals.
cicurar, *v.t.* to tame (*wild animals*).
cicuta, *n.f.* hemlock; ***beber la cicuta,*** to drink *or* take hemlock.
cicutado, -da, *a.* impregnated with hemlock juice.
cicutina, *n.f.* hemlock poison.
cid, *n.m.* chief, leader; ***el Cid Campeador,*** national hero of Spain.
cidra, *n.f.* citron.
cidrada, *n.f.* candied peel.
cidral, *n.m.* citron grove.
cidrayote, chilacayote, *n.m.* American gourd.
cidro, *n.m.* citron-tree.
cidronela, *n.f.* common balm.
ciegayernos, *n.m. inv.* (*coll.*) fraud, sham, humbug.
ciego, -ga, *a.* (*lit., fig.*) blind; ***obediencia ciega,*** blind obedience. — *n.m.* (*anat.*) cæcum; large black-pudding. — *n.m.f.* blind man *or* woman; ***a ciegas,*** blindly, in the dark, heedlessly; ***ciego de ira,*** blind with rage; (*fig.*) ***dar palos de ciego,*** to try to do sth. in the dark, to grope for a solution.
cieguecico, -ca, cieguecito, -ta, cieguillo, -lla, cieguito, -ta, cieguezuelo, -la, *a., n.m.f.* (poor) little blind (boy, man, girl, woman, creature).
cielito, *n.m.* (*Arg.*) tune and dance; (little) darling.
cielo, *n.m.* sky; heaven; climate; ceiling; (*fig.*) darling; ***bajado, llovido*** or ***venido del cielo,*** heaven-sent; ***un cielo benigno,*** a mild climate; ***cielo borreguero,*** fleecy sky; ***cielo de la boca,*** roof of the mouth; ***cielo de la cama,*** bed-canopy; ***¡santo(s) cielo(s)!, ¡cielos!,*** good heavens!; (*naut.*) ***cielo viejo,*** glimpse of blue sky; ***cielo raso,*** ceiling; ***dormir a cielo raso,*** to sleep in the open (air); ***a cielo abierto,*** in the open (air); ***a cielo descubierto,*** in the open; ***escupir al cielo,*** to have sth. boomerang; ***comprar*** or ***ganar el cielo,*** to buy *or* win one's way to Heaven; ***está hecho un cielo,*** he's being a darling; ***mudar (de) cielo,*** to go somewhere else, have a change of air; ***mover cielo y tierra,*** to move heaven and earth; ***poner el grito en el cielo,*** to raise Cain; ***poner en el cielo*** or ***los cielos,*** to praise to the skies; ***ver el cielo abierto,*** to see a way out; ***ver el cielo por un embudo,*** to see the world through blinkers; ***venirse el cielo abajo,*** to pour, bucket down.
ciempiés, *n.m. inv.* centipede; (*coll.*) third-rate rigmarole.
cien, *a.* (one) hundred (*used before nouns for* **ciento**).
ciénaga, *n.f.* marsh, bog, quagmire.
ciencia, *n.f.* knowledge, learning; science; ***ciencias exactas,*** (exact) science(s); ***ciencia infusa,*** God-given knowledge; ***gaya ciencia,*** art of verse-making *or* poetry; ***a ciencia cierta,*** for certain; ***no lo sé a ciencia cierta,*** I don't know for certain; ***a ciencia y paciencia (de),*** on sufferance (from).
cienmilésimo, -ma, *a.* hundred-thousandth.
cienmilímetro, *n.m.* hundredth part of a millimetre.
cienmilmillonésimo, -ma, *a.* hundred-thousand-millionth.
cieno, *n.m.* mud, mire, slime; (*fig.*) filth.
ciente, *a.* learned, knowledgeable.
científico, -ca, *a.* appertaining to learning; scientific. — *n.m.f.* man *or* woman of learning, scholar; scientist.
ciento, *a., n.m.* hundred(th), a hundred, one hundred; ***por ciento,*** per cent; ***por cientos,*** by the hundred; ***ciento por ciento,*** (a) hundred per cent; ***el diez por ciento,*** ten per cent.
cientopiés, *n.m. inv.* centipede.
cierna, *n.f.* anther of blossom (*vines, corn*).
cierne, *n.m.* blossoming, flowering; ***estar en cierne(s),*** to be in bloom; (*fig.*) to be in its infancy, early stages.
cierrapuertas, *n.m. inv.* automatic door-closing apparatus.
cierre, *n.m.* closing, closure; fastening, locking, shutting; bolt; latch; lock; clasp, fastener, snap; ***cierre de cañón,*** breechblock; ***cierre metálico,*** flexible metal roller-shutter (*for shops etc.*); ***cierre hidráulico,*** hydraulic *or* water seal.
cierro, *n.m.* closure; (*prov.*) ***cierro de cristales,*** glass-covered balcony *or* veranda.
ciertamente, *adv.* certainly, indeed.
cierto, ta, *a.* certain; sure; true. — *adv.* certainly, indeed; ***cierto profesor,*** a certain teacher; ***saber de cierto,*** to know for certain; ***es cierto que,*** it's true that; ***lo cierto es que,*** the truth of the matter is that; what is certain is that; ***ciertos son los toros,*** the story *or* report is true, it's a fact; ***me dan por cierto que,*** I am assured that; ***no, por cierto,*** no, by no means; ***sí, por cierto,*** certainly, indeed; ***por cierto (que),*** by the way, incidentally; ***estar en lo cierto,*** to be (quite) right. — *n.f.* (*sl.*) death.
cierva, *n.f.* deer, hind.
ciervo, *n.m.* deer, stag, hart; ***ciervo volante,*** stag-beetle.
cierzas, *n.f.pl.* shoots, suckers (*of vine*).
cierzo, *n.m.* cold north wind; ***tener ventana al cierzo,*** to be haughty.
cifac, cifaque, *n.m.* peritoneum.
cifosis, *n.f. inv.* (*med.*) kyphosis.
cifra, *n.f.* cipher; code; figure; abbreviation; ***en cifras y en palabras,*** in figures and words; ***una cifra asombrosa,*** an astounding figure; ***en cifra,*** in code; cryptically; in brief.
cifrador, -ra, *a., n.m.f.* (one) writing in cipher.
cifrar, *v.t.* to cipher, write in cipher; (*fig.*) to abridge, summarize; to enclose; ***cifrar las esperanzas (en),*** to set *or* place one's hopes on *or* in.
cigala, *n.f.* crayfish.
cigarra, *n.f.* grasshopper, cicada, harvest-fly; (*sl.*) bag, purse.
cigarral, *n.m.* (*in Toledo*) country-house *or* mansion and grounds.
cigarrera, *n.f.* cigar seller *or* maker; cigar-case, cigar-cabinet.
cigarrería, *n.f.* (*Hisp. Am.*) tobacconist's shop.
cigarrero, *n.m.* cigar maker *or* dealer.
cigarrillo, *n.m.* cigarette.
cigarrista, *n.m.* heavy smoker.
cigarro, *n.m.* cigar; cigarette; ***cigarro puro,*** cigar.
cigarrón, *n.m.* grasshopper; (*sl.*) large purse [CIGARRA].
cigofileo, -lea, *a.* (*bot.*) zygophyllaceous. — *n.f.pl.* (**cigofileas**) zygophyllum.
cigoma, *n.m.* (*anat.*) zygoma.
cigomático, -ca, *a.* zygomatic.
cigoñal, *n.m.* swape-well; (*fort.*) beam for raising drawbridge.
cigoñino, *n.m.* young stork.
cigoñuela, *n.f.* (*orn.*) stilt.
cigua, *n.f.* cigua tree.
ciguatera, *n.f.* (*Hisp. Am.*) food-poisoning.
cigüeña, *n.f.* (*orn.*) stork; crank (*of bell*); (*mech.*) crane; winch.
cigüeñal, *n.m.* crankshaft.
cigüeñear, *v.i.* to make a noise with the beak (*stork*).
cigüeño, *n.m.* (*obs.*) male stork; (*prov.*) tall, silly-looking person.

cigüeñuela, *n.f.* (*mech.*) small crank; (*naut.*) ***cigüeñuela de la caña del timón,*** gooseneck of the tiller.
cigüete, *n.f.* white grape.
cija, *n.f.* granary; sheep shelter; (*prov.*) dungeon.
cilampa, *n.f.* (*C.R., E.S.*) drizzle.
cilanco, *n.m.* pool (*left by a river*).
cilantro, *n.m.* (*bot.*) coriander.
ciliado, -da, cilífero, -ra, *a.* ciliate.
ciliar, *a.* ciliary, belonging to the eye-brows.
cilicio, *n.m.* hair-cloth; cilice, hair-shirt; (*mil.*) coarse cover for armaments.
cilindrada, *n.f.* cylinder capacity.
cilindrado, *n.m.* calendering, rolling.
cilindrar, *v.t.* to roll, calender.
cilíndrico, -ca, *a.* cylindrical; cylindriform.
cilindro, *n.m.* cylinder, drum; roller; cylinder-press; (*mech.*) chamber; ***cilindro de escarchar,*** silversmith's roll; ***cilindro estriado,*** fluted cylinder.
cilindroide, *n.m.* cylindroid.
cilindroideo, -dea, *a.* cylindrical.
cilla, *n.f.* granary; tithe; tithe-barn.
cillazgo, *n.m.* store-house fees (*paid by persons concerned on tithes kept in a granary*).
cillerero, *n.m.* cellarist *or* butler (*in some religious houses*).
cilleriza, *n.f.* nun (*who directs the domestic affairs of a convent*).
cillero, *n.m.* keeper (*of a granary* or *tithe-barn*); granary; cellar, store-house.
cima, *n.f.* summit, top; (*bot.*) cyme; ***por cima,*** at the top; lightly, cursorily, superficially; ***mirar por cima una cosa,*** to look at sth. cursorily; ***dar cima a,*** to carry through, finish off.
cimacio, *n.m.* (*arch.*) cyma, cymatium, ogee.
cimar, *v.t.* to clip the tops of (*hedges, plants etc.*).
cimarrón, -rrona, *a.* (*Hisp. Am.*) wild, unruly. — *a., n.m.* (*naut.*) lazy (sailor). — *n.m.f.* runaway slave, maroon; (*Arg.*) black mate.
cimbalaria, *n.f.* ivy-wort.
cimbalero, cimbalista, *n.m.* cymbalist.
cimbalillo, cimbanillo, *n.m.* small church-bell.
címbalo, *n.m.* cymbal.
címbara, *n.f.* short, broad scythe.
cimbel, *n.m.* decoy-pigeon; cord (*with which such pigeons are made fast*).
cimboga [ACIMBOGA].
cimborio, cimborrio, *n.m.* dome.
cimbornales, *n.m.pl.* (*naut.*) scupper-holes.
cimbra, *n.f.* (*arch.*) wooden frame (*for constructing an arch*); cradling; (*naut.*) curvature; (*naut.*) ***cimbra de una tabla,*** bending of a board.
cimbrado, *n.m.* quick, bending movement (*in Spanish dance*); (*arch.*) fixing of arch frame.
cimbrar(se) [CIMBREAR].
cimbrear, *v.t.* to make vibrate; to bend; to sway; to beat, cane; to place a cradling in (*an arch*). — **cimbrearse,** *v.r.* to vibrate; to bend; to sway.
cimbre, *n.m.* underground gallery *or* passage.
cimbreante, *a.* bending; swaying; flexible, pliant; lithe, supple, willowy.
cimbreño, -ña [CIMBREANTE].
cimbreo, *n.m.* vibrating; bending; swaying; vibrating, bending *or* swaying movement.
cimbronazo, *n.m.* stroke (*with foil* or *flat of sword*); (*Col., C.R.*) violent nervous jerk.
cimbroso, -sa [CIMBREANTE].
cimentación, *n.f.* (laying of) foundation.
cimentado, *n.m.* refining (*of gold*).
cimentador, -ra, *a.* founding; (*min.*) refining. — *n.m.f.* founder; (*min.*) refiner.
cimentar [I], *v.t.* to lay the foundation(s) of *or* for; to found, ground, establish; to refine (*gold*).
cimenterio [CEMENTERIO].
cimento, *n.m.* (*geol.*) cement.
cimero, -ra, *a.* topmost, at the top. — *n.f.* crest (*of helmet* or *coat of arms*).
cimiento, *n.m.* foundation; (*fig.*) basis, base, groundwork; ***abrir los cimientos,*** to break ground.
cimillo, *n.m.* flexible twig to which decoy-bird is attached.
cimitarra, *n.f.* scimitar, falchion.
cimofana, *n.f.* cymofane, cat's-eye.
cimorra, *n.f.* (*vet.*) glanders.
cimótico, -ca, *a.* (*med.*) zymotic.
cinabrino, -na, *a.* resembling cinnabar.
cinabrio, *n.m.* cinnabar; vermilion.
cinámico, -ca, *a.* (*chem.*) cinnamonic.
cinamida, *n.f.* (*chem.*) cinnamate.
cinamomo, *n.m.* (*bot.*) bead-tree; cinnamon; (*Philip.*) privet.
cinc, *n.m.* zinc.
cinca, *n.f.* infraction (*of ninepins rules*); ***hacer cinca en el juego de bolos,*** to lose five points at ninepins.
cincel, *n.m.* chisel.
cincelado, *n.m.* chiselling, engraving.
cincelador, *n.m.* engraver, sculptor, stone-cutter.
cinceladura, *n.f.* chasing, carving.
cincelar, *v.t.* to chisel, engrave, carve, chase.
cincelería, *n.f.* shop *or* factory where chiselling *or* engraving is done.
cincelito, *n.m.* small chisel.
cíncico, -ca, *a.* zinciferous, zincoid, zinky.
cinco, *a., n.m.* five, fifth; five-spotted (*card*); (*Ven.*) five-string guitar; (*Chi., C.R.*) silver coin (5 *centavos*); ***decirle a alguien cuántas son cinco,*** to tell s.o. what's what; ***no sabe cuántas son cinco,*** he hasn't a notion; ***¡vengan esos cinco!*** shake! let's have your hand on that.
cincoañal, *a.* five-year-old (*animal*).
cincoenrama, *n.f.* common cinquefoil.
cincograbado, *n.m.* zincograph.
cincografía, *n.f.* zincography.
cincomesino, -na, *a.* five-month-old.
cincona, *n.f.* (*bot.*) cinchona; quinine.
cinconáceo, -cea, *a.* cinchonaceous.
cinconina, *n.f.* (*chem.*) cinchonine.
cincuenta, *a.* fifty, fiftieth. — *n.m.* fifty.
cincuentañal, *a.* fifty-year-old.
cincuentavo, -va, *a., n.m.* fiftieth.
cincuenteno, -na, *a.* fiftieth.
cincuentón, -tona, *a., n.m.f.* quinquagenarian.
cincuesma, *n.f.* Pentecost.
cincha, *n.f.* girth, cinch; ***a revientacinchas,*** at breakneck speed; ***ir rompiendo cinchas,*** to go hell for leather.
cinchadura, *n.f.* girthing.
cinchar, *v.t.* to girth, cinch up; to fasten with iron hoops.
cinchera, *n.f.* girth-place (*on mule, horse etc.*); (*vet.*) girth sore.
cincho, *n.m.* belly-band; belt; girdle, sash; tyre; iron hoop; (*arch.*) projecting rib (*of arch*); (*Mex.*) cinch; plated esparto band (*of vessel for moulding cheese*); (*vet.*) hoof ring.
cinchón, *n.m.* (*River Plate*) strip of rawhide (*used as cinch*); (*Ec.*) hoop (*of iron*); (*Col.*) overload.
cinchuela, *n.f.* small girth; narrow ribbon.
cine, *n.m.* cinema; films; cine camera; ***cine hablado*** or ***sonoro,*** talking films; ***cine mudo,*** silent films; ***cine en relieve,*** three-dimensional films; ***ir al cine,*** to go to the cinema, pictures, movies.
cineasta, *n.m.f.* film producer; film actor *or* actress.
cinefacción, *n.f.* cineration, reduction to ashes.
cinefacto, -ta, *a.* reduced to ashes.
cineficar, *v.t.* to reduce to ashes.

cinegético, -ca, *a.* appertaining to hunting (*with dogs*). — *n.f.* hunting (*with dogs*).
cinelandia, *n.f.* filmland.
cinemateca, *n.f.* film library.
cinemático, -ca, *a.* kinematic. — *n.f.* kinematics.
cinematografía, *n.f.* cinematography.
cinematografiar [L], *v.t.*, *v.i.* to film.
cinematográfico, -ca, *a.* cinematographic, film.
cinematógrafo, *n.m.* cinematograph; films; cinema.
cinematurgo, *n.m.* author of dramas for the cinema.
cinemómetro, *n.m.* apparatus for measuring the velocity of movement.
cineración, *n.f.* cineration.
cinerario, -ria, *a.* cinerary; ***urna cineraria,*** cinerary urn. — *n.f.* (*bot.*) cineraria.
cinéreo, -rea, *a.* cinerious.
cinericio, -cia, *a.* ashy.
cineriforme, *a.* ash-like.
cingalés, -lesa, *a.*, *n.m.f.* Cingalese.
cíngaro, -ra, *a.*, *n.m.f.* gipsy.
cinglado, *n.m.* blooming (*of metals*).
cinglador, *n.m.* large hammer (*for blooming metals*).
cingladora, *n.f.* bloomery.
cinglar, *v.t.*, *v.i.* (*naut.*) to scull; to bloom (*metals*).
cingleta, *n.f.* (*naut.*) rope with cork (*to buoy up a net*).
cíngulo, *n.m.* girdle (*of priest's alb*); ancient military badge.
cínico, -ca, *a.*, *n.m.f.* cynical (person), cynic; barefaced *or* brazen (person); unprincipled.
cínife, *n.m.* mosquito.
cinismo, *n.m.* cynicism; barefacedness, brazenness; lack of principle.
cinocéfalo, *n.m.* (*zool.*) cynocephalus, dogfaced baboon.
cinoglosa, *n.f.* (*bot.*) hound's tongue.
Cinosura, *n.f.* (*astron.*) Cynosure; Pole star, Lesser Bear.
cinquén, *n.m.* ancient Spanish coin.
cinqueño, cinquillo, *n.m.* (game of) ombre (*played by five persons*).
cinquero, *n.m.* zinc-worker.
cinta, *n.f.* [CINTO].
cintadero, *n.m.* part of a cross-bow to which the string is fastened.
cintagorda, *n.f.* coarse hempen net (*for the tunny fishery*).
cintajos, cintarajos, *n.m.pl.* rotten *or* tawdry (old) ribbons.
cintar, *v.t.* (*arch.*) to adorn with fillets *or* scrolls.
cintarazo, *n.m.* swipe (*with flat of sword*).
cintarear, *v.t.* (*coll.*) to swipe with a sword.
cinteado, -da, *a.* adorned with ribbons.
cintería, *n.f.* ribbons; ribbon-shop *or* -trade.
cintero, -ra, *n.m.f.* seller *or* weaver of ribbons. — *n.m.* belt, girdle; (*prov.*) bandage, truss; halter, cable, rope.
cintilla, *n.f.* small ribbon; narrow tape.
cintillo, *n.m.* hat-band; ring set with precious stones.
cinto, -ta, *p.p.* [CEÑIR], *a.* encircled, girdled, girt. — *n.m.* belt; waist; (*obs.*) ***cinto de onzas*** or ***de oro,*** inner belt for carrying money. — *n.f.* ribbon; tape; band, strip; (*obs.*) girdle; strong hempen net (*used in tunny-fishing*); lowest part of pastern (*of a horse*); first course (*of floor-tiles*); kerb-stone; (*arch.*, *her.*) fillet; (*arch.*) scroll; tape-measure; film; (*naut.*) wale; ***cinta aislante,*** insulating tape; ***cinta de embrague,*** clutch band; ***cinta de freno,*** brake lining; ***cinta magnetofónica,*** recording tape; ***cinta métrica,*** (decimal) tape-measure; ***cinta de sombrero,*** hat-band; ***cinta de teleimpresor, de teletipo,*** ticker tape; ***cinta de transporte,*** conveyor belt; ***en cinta,*** under subjection; liable to restraint.
cintón, *n.m.* (*naut.*) strake.
cintra, *n.f.* (*arch.*) curve (*of arch* or *vault*).
cintrado, -da, *a.* (*arch.*) curved.
cintrel, *n.m.* (*arch.*) rule *or* line (*placed in centre of dome for arching*).
cintura, *n.f.* waist; girdle, belt; throat (*of chimney*); (*naut.*) rope knot; (*fig.*) ***meter en cintura,*** to bring to heel.
cinturilla, *n.f.* small girdle *or* belt; waist ornament.
cinturón, *n.m.* belt; sword-belt; sash; (*fig.*) belt, circle; ***cinturón de castidad,*** chastity belt; ***cinturón de seguridad,*** safety belt; ***cinturón salvavidas,*** life belt.
cinzolín, *n.m.* reddish-mauve colour.
cipariso, *n.m.* (*poet.*) cypress.
cipayo, *n.m.* sepoy.
cipión, *n.m.* walking-stick.
cipo, *n.m.* (*arch.*) cippus; milestone.
cipolino, -na, *a.*, *n.m.* cipolin.
cipote, *a.* (*Col.*) dull, stupid; (*Guat.*) chubby, fat (*E.S.*, *Hond.*, *coll.*) urchin, little rogue.
ciprés, *n.m.* cypress.
cipresal, *n.m.* cypress grove.
cipresino, -na, *a.* appertaining to *or* resembling the cypress.
ciprino (1), **-na, ciprio, -ria, cipriota,** *a.*, *n.m.f.* Cyprian, Cypriot.
ciprino (2), *n.m.* (*ichth.*) cyprine.
cipripedio, *n.m.* (*bot.*) cypripedium.
ciquiribaile, *n.m.* (*sl.*) thief.
ciquiricata, *n.f.* (*coll.*) caress; flattery.
ciquitroque, *n.m.* fried tomatoes, pimentoes etc.
circaeto, *n.m.* moor-buzzard.
circe, *n.f.* Circe; artful, deceitful woman.
circinado, -da, *a.* (*bot.*) circinate.
circo, *n.m.* circus; amphitheatre.
circón, *n.m.* zircon.
circona, *n.f.* zirconate.
circonio, *n.m.* zirconium.
circuición, *n.f.*, **circuimiento,** *n.m.* surrounding, encircling.
circuir [O], *v.t.* to surround, compass, encircle.
circuito, *n.m.* circuit; ***corto circuito,*** short circuit.
circulación, *n.f.* circulation; traffic; movement.
circulador, -ra, *a.* circulating, circulative. — *n.m.f.* circulator.
circulante, *a.* circulatory, circulating, circulative, circling; ***biblioteca circulante,*** lending library.
circular, *a.* circular. — *n.f.* circular (*letter*). — *v.t.* to circularize; to circulate. — *v.i.* to circulate, move, travel round; to go from hand to hand, point to point; ***¡circulen! ¡circulen!*** move along there, come along now!
circulatorio, -ria, *a.* circulatory.
círculo, *n.m.* (*lit.*, *fig.*) circle; ring; club; (*geom.*) ***círculo máximo,*** great circle; (*geom.*) ***círculo menor,*** lesser *or* small circle; ***círculo vicioso,*** vicious circle.
circumcirca, *adv.* (*coll.*) about, thereabout.
circumpolar, *a.* circumpolar.
circuncenital, *a.* (*astron.*) surrounding the zenith.
circuncidante, *a.* circumcising.
circuncidar, *v.t.* to circumcise; to diminish, clip, curtail.
circuncisión, *n.f.* circumcision; festival of the Circumcision (*New Year's Day*).
circunciso, -sa, *a.* circumcised; (*fig.*) Jewish, Moorish.
circundante, *a.* surrounding, encircling.
circundar, *v.t.* to surround, encircle, compass.
circunferencia, *n.f.* circumference.
circunferencial, *a.* circumferential, circular, surrounding.
circunferente, *a.* circumscribing.

circunflejo, -ja, *a.* (*anat.*, *gram.*) circumflex; ***acento circunflejo,*** circumflex accent.
circunfuso, -sa, *a.* circumfluent.
circunlocución, *n.f.*, **circunloquio,** *n.m.* circumlocution.
circunnavegable, *a.* circumnavigable.
circunnavegación, *n.f.* circumnavigation.
circunnavegante, *n.m.* circumnavigator.
circunnavegar [B], *v.t.* to circumnavigate.
circunscribir [*p.p.* **circunscrito**], *v.t.* to circumscribe, enclose, encircle. — **circunscribirse,** *v.r.* to limit, restrict o.s. (***a,*** to).
circunscripción, *n.f.* circumscription.
circunsolar, *a.* circumsolar.
circunspección, *n.f.* circumspection.
circunspecto, -ta, *a.* circumspect.
circunstancia, *n.f.* circumstance; detail; ***circunstancia agravante,*** aggravating circumstance; ***circunstancia atenuante,*** extenuating circumstance; ***circunstancia eximente,*** exculpatory circumstance; ***en las circunstancias,*** in the circumstances; ***refirió el caso con todas sus circunstancias,*** he gave a detailed account of the matter.
circunstanciado, -da, *a.* circumstantial, detailed, minute.
circunstancial, *a.* circumstantial.
circunstante, *a.* surrounding; present. — *n.m.pl.* (**circunstantes**) bystanders.
circunvalación, *n.f.* surrounding; (*fort.*) circumvallation; ***carretera de circunvalación,*** ring *or* circular road.
circunvalar, *v.t.* to surround, encircle; (*fort.*) to circumvallate.
circunvecino, -na, *a.* neighbouring, contiguous, adjacent.
circunvención, *n.f.* circumvention.
circunvenir [36], *v.r.* to circumvent; to over-reach.
circunvolar [4], *v.t.* to fly round.
circunvolución, *n.f.* circumvolution; ***circunvolución cerebral,*** cerebral convolution.
circunyacente, *a.* surrounding, adjacent.
cirial, *n.m.* processional candlestick.
cirigallo, -lla, *n.m.f.* idler, wastrel.
cirigaña, *n.f.* (*prov.*) flattery; (*prov.*) practical joke; trifle.
cirineo, *n.m.* (*coll.*) mate, assistant.
cirio, *n.m.* wax taper *or* candle; ***cirio pascual,*** paschal candle.
cirolar, *n.m.* plum tree orchard.
cirolero, *n.m.* plum tree.
ciroso, -sa, *a.* cereous.
cirro, *n.m.* (*surg.*) scirrhus; (*bot.*, *meteor.*, *zool.*) cirrus.
ciruela, *n.f.* plum; ***ciruela pasa,*** prune; ***ciruela amacena*** or ***damascena,*** damson plum; ***ciruela claudia,*** greengage; ***ciruela de yema,*** yellow plum.
ciruelar, *n.m.* plum-tree orchard.
ciruelica, ciruelilla, ciruelita, *n.f.* small plum.
ciruelo, *n.m.* plum-tree; (*coll.*) fool, idiot.
cirugía, *n.f.* surgery; ***cirugía estética,*** face lifting; ***cirugía mayor*** (***menor***), major (minor) surgery; ***cirugía nerviosa,*** neurosurgery; ***cirugía plástica,*** plastic surgery.
cirujano, *n.m.* surgeon.
cisalpino, -na, *a.* cisalpine.
cisca, *n.f.* reed-grass.
ciscar, *v.t.* (*obsc.*) to shit. — **ciscarse,** *v.r.* (*obsc.*) to shit one's pants.
cisco, *n.m.* fine *or* small coal; (*coll.*) uproar, shindy, wrangle; ***armar un cisco,*** to kick up a shindy; ***esto es un cisco,*** this is chaos; ***hacer cisco,*** to smash to smithereens.
ciscón, *n.m.* cinders.
cisión, *n.f.* incision.
cisípedo, *a.* toe-footed.
cisma, *n.m.f.* schism; discord.
cismático, -ca, *a.*, *n.m.f.* schismatic.
cismontano, -na, *a.* situated on this side of the mountains.
cisne, *n.m.* (*orn.*) swan; (*astron.*) Cygnus; (*sl.*) prostitute.
cisneo, -nea, *a.* swan-like.
cisoria, *a.* ***arte cisoria,*** art of carving (*meat*).
cisquera, *n.f.* receptacle for small coal.
cisquero, *n.m.* seller of small coal.
cista, *n.f.* (*archæol.*) cist.
ciste, *n.m.* (*surg.*) cyst.
cistel, cister, *n.m.* Cistercian order.
cisterciense, *a.*, *n.m.f.* Cistercian.
cisterna, *n.f.* cistern; water-tank.
cisticerco, *n.m.* cystic worm.
cístico, -ca, *a.* (*surg.*) cystic.
cistina, *n.f.* (*chem.*) cystine.
cisura, *n.f.* incisure, incision.
cita, *n.f.* assignation, appointment, rendezvous, date; citation; quotation.
citable, *a.* citable, quotable.
citación, *n.f.* citation, quotation; (*law*) summons, judicial notice.
citador, -ra, *a.* citing; quoting; summoning. — *n.m.f.* citer; quoter; summoner.
citar, *v.t.* to make an appointment with; to quote, cite; (*law*) to summon; (*law*) to give judicial notice to; to incite, provoke (*the bull*).
cítara, *n.f.* zither, cithern.
citara, *n.f.* partition-wall; (*mil.*) troops covering the flanks.
citarista, *n.m.f.* zither-player.
citarón, *n.m.* socle with wooden framework.
citatorio, -ria, *a.* (*law*) summoning. — *n.f.* (*law*) summons.
citereo, -rea, *a.* (*poet.*) cytherean.
citerior, *a.* hither, nearer, towards this part; (*hist.*) ***España citerior,*** the north-eastern part of Spain.
cítiso, *n.m.* shrub-trefoil, cytisus.
¡cito! *interj.* here, boy! (*to call dogs*).
cítola, *n.f.* clack, clapper (*in corn-mills*).
citote, *n.m.* (*coll.*) summons, judicial citation.
citra, *adv.* on this side.
citramontano, -na, *a.* cismontane.
citrato, *n.m.* (*chem.*) citrate.
cítrico, -ca, *a.* (*chem.*) citric.
citrino, -na, *a.* citrine, citrinous, lemon-coloured. — *n.f.* (*min.*) citrine; (*chem.*) essential oil of lemon.
citrón, *n.m.* lemon; (*P.R.*) lime.
ciudad, *n.f.* town; city; ***ciudad jardín,*** garden city.
ciudadanía, *n.f.* citizenhood, citizenship.
ciudadano, -na, *a.* appertaining to towns, cities *or* citizens. — *n.m.f.* citizen; town-dweller, city-dweller.
ciudadela, *n.f.* citadel.
civeta, *n.f.* civet cat.
civeto, *n.m.* civet perfume.
cívico, -ca, *a.* civic; public-spirited; ***espíritu cívico,*** public spirit.
civil, *a.* civil. — *n.m.f.* civilian; (***los***) ***civiles,*** Civil Guards.
civilidad, *n.f.* public-spiritedness; sociability; (*obs.*) meanness, vileness.
civilismo [CIVISMO].
civilista, *n.m.* student of *or* authority on civil law; (*Hisp. Am.*) antimilitarist.
civilizable, *a.* civilizable.
civilización, *n.f.* civilization.
civilizador, -ra, *a.* civilizing. — *n.m.f.* civilizer.
civilizar [C], *v.t.* to civilize. — **civilizarse,** *v.r.* to become civilized.

civismo, *n.m.* public-spirit(edness).
cizalla, *n.f.* shears; sheet-metal shears; shearing machine; paper cutters; (*surg.*) bone forceps; chips, shavings; (*pl.*) shears.
cizallar, *v.t.* to shear.
cizaña, *n.f.* (*bot.*) darnel; tare; (*fig.*) discord; ***sembrar cizaña,*** to sow discord.
cizañador, -ra, *a., n.m.f.* (one) who sows discord.
cizañar, *v.t.* to sow discord among. — *v.i.* to sow discord.
cizañero, -ra, *a., n.m.f.* troublemaking, troublemaker.
clac, *n.m.* opera-hat; cocked hat.
claco, *n.m.* (*Mex.*) ancient copper coin of small value.
clacopacle, *n.m.* (*Mex., bot.*) birthwort.
clacota, *n.f.* (*Mex.*) small tumour *or* boil.
clachique, *n.m.* (*Mex.*) unfermented pulque.
clamador, -ra, *a.* clamorous, crying out. — *n.m.f.* clamourer.
clamar, *v.t.* to clamour for, cry out for. — *v.i.* to clamour, cry out; ***clamar al cielo,*** to cry out to Heaven.
clamor, *n.m.* clamour, outcry; plaint; knell.
clamoreada, *n.f.* outcry, clamour.
clamorear, *v.t.* to clamour; to implore insistently. — *v.i.* to toll.
clamoreo, *n.m.* clamouring; knell.
clamoroso, -sa, *a.* clamorous, loud, noisy.
clamosidad, *n.f.* clamorousness.
clan, *n.m.* clan; clique, faction; mob, crowd.
clandestinidad, *n.f.* secrecy; secret nature; (*pol.*) underground.
clandestino, -na, *a.* clandestine, secret, undercover.
clanga [PLANGA].
clangor, *n.m.* (*poet.*) clarion, blare.
clara, *n.f.* [CLARO].
claraboya, *n.f.* skylight; transom.
clarea, *n.f.* mulled wine.
clarear, *v.t.* to light, give light to; to make light *or* clear; to rinse. — *v.i.* to grow *or* get light, dawn; to clear (up) (*weather*). — **clarearse,** *v.r.* to show through; to show *or* reveal one's intentions, give oneself away.
clarecer [9], *v.i.* to dawn, grow light.
clarete, *n.m.* claret (*wine*).
claridad, *n.f.* clarity, brightness, light; clearness, distinctness; glory (*of the blessed*); ***claridad de la vista*** or ***de los ojos,*** clearness of sight; ***con claridad,*** clearly, distinctly; frankly; (*pl.*) plain language, plain truths; ***entre amistades, claridades,*** there should be frankness between friends; ***le dije dos claridades,*** I gave him a piece of my mind.
clarificable, *a.* that can be clarified.
clarificación, *n.f.* brightening; clarifying, purifying.
clarificador, -ra, *a.* clarifying. — *n.m.f.* clarifier; (*Cub.*) clarifying pan (*sugar*).
clarificar [A], *v.t.* to brighten, make lighter; to clarify, purify.
clarificativo, -va, *a.* clarifying, purifying.
clarífico, -ca, *a.* resplendent.
clarilla, *n.f.* (*prov.*) lye (*of ashes* or *any alkaline salt*).
clarimente, *n.m.* beautifying lotion; (*paint.*) cleanser and colour-reviver.
clarimentos, *n.m.pl.* (*paint.*) lights.
clarín, *n.m.* bugle, clarion; bugler; organ-stop; fine cambric; (*Chi.*) sweet pea; (*orn.*) tropical thrush.
clarinado, -da, *a.* (*her.*) applied to animals with bells in their harness. — *n.f.* clarion call; (*fig.*) blast, broadside.
clarinero, *n.m.* bugler.
clarinete, *n.m.* clarinet; clarinet-player.
clarinetista, *n.m.* clarinet-player.
clarión, *n.m.* crayon, chalk.
clarioncillo, *n.m.* white crayon, pastel.
clarisa, *n.f.* nun of the order of St. Clare.
clarísimo, -ma, *a. superl.* absolutely clear; most illustrious.
clarividencia, *n.f.* clear-sightedness.
clarividente, *a., n.m.f.* clear-sighted (person).
claro, -ra, *a.* clear; bright; light; thin; sparse; weak; open, frank; (*obs.*) illustrious; ***colores claros,*** light colours; ***vamos claros,*** let's get things clear *or* straight; ***a las claras,*** clearly, plainly. — *adv.* ***¡claro (está)!*** of course, obviously; ***de claro en claro,*** from beginning to end; ***pasar la noche de claro en claro,*** to have a sleepless night; ***por lo claro,*** obviously, clearly; ***poner en claro,*** to make clear, to clarify; ***sacar en claro,*** to get clear *or* straight; ***no he sacado nada en claro,*** I haven't been able to draw any conclusion. — *n.m.* skylight; break, gap, interval, space; (*paint.*) light; (*naut.*) break (*in the clouds*); clearing, glade; ***claro de luna,*** moonlight; (*pl.*) (*lit., fig.*) loopholes; (*arch.*) openings, windows. — *n.f.* white (*of egg*); thin part (*of badly woven cloth*); (*coll.*) short interval (*of fine weather on a wet day*); bald spot.
claror, *n.m.* resplendence; brightness.
claroscuro, *n.m.* chiaroscuro, light and shade; monochrome; combination of light and heavy strokes in penmanship.
clarucho, -cha, *a.* thinnish, poor, watery (*soup*).
clascal, *n.m.* (*Mex.*) maize omelet.
clase, *n.f.* class; rank; kind, sort; species, family; form, class; classroom; lesson; ***de cualquier clase,*** of any kind *or* description; (*naut.*) ***clases de navío,*** rates of ships; ***clases de tropa,*** non-commissioned officers; ***clase media,*** middle-class; ***clases pasivas,*** pensioners; ***clase(s) alta(s),*** upper classes; (*coll.*) ***tiene mucha clase,*** he is very classy.
clasicidad, *n.f.* classicality.
clasicismo, *n.m.* classicism.
clasicista, *n.m.f.* classicist.
clásico, -ca, *a.* classic, classical; (*coll.*) typical. — *n.m.* classic; ***los clásicos,*** the classics; ***es lo clásico,*** it's what you always find, it's the usual thing, it's the same old story.
clasificación, *n.f.* classification.
clasificador, -ra, *a.* classifying, classificatory. — *n.m.f.* classifier. — *n.m.* filing-cabinet.
clasificar [A], *v.t.* to classify, class.
claudicación, *n.f.* limp, halting; (*fig.*) faltering, wavering.
claudicante, *a.* halting, limping; (*fig.*) faltering, wavering.
claudicar [A], *v.i.* to limp, go haltingly; (*fig.*) to waver, falter; to betray one's creed.
claustrado, -da, *a.* cloistered.
claustrero, -ra [CLAUSTRADO].
claustrillo, *n.m.* small cloister, small hall.
claustro, *n.m.* cloister; university council; (*fig.* monastic state; ***claustro de profesores,*** academic staff; ***claustro materno,*** womb.
claustrofobia, *n.f.* claustrophobia.
cláusula, *n.f.* clause.
clausular, *v.t.* to close; to terminate.
clausura, *n.f.* inner recess (*of convent*); claustration, confinement, monastic life; closure, cloture.
clausurar, *v.t.* to close, terminate.
clava, *n.f.* cudgel, club; (*naut.*) scupper.
clavadizo, -za, *a.* nail-studded.
clavado, -da, *a.* nail-studded; exactly right, dead on; exactly like *or* alike, identical; ***es clavado a su padre,*** he's the spitting image of his father.
clavadura, *n.f.* pricking (*in horse-shoeing*).
clavar, *v.t.* to nail; to nail, force *or* stick in, drive home; to fix; to prick; (*coll.*) to overcharge, skin;

(*artill.*) to spike, nail up (*guns*); to set in gold *or* silver; (*mil.*) to ground (*arms*); ***clavar los ojos (la mirada, la vista) en,*** to fix one's eyes on, gaze *or* stare at; ***clavarle el diente a,*** to sink *or* get one's teeth into; ***clavar un clavo con la cabeza,*** to beat one's head against a brick wall; ***que me lo claven en la frente,*** tell that to the marines.

clavario, -ria, *n.m.f.* keeper of the keys.

clavazón, *n.m.* (set of) nails.

clave, *n.m.* clavichord. — *n.f.* (*arch.*) keystone; key; code; (*mus.*) clef; ***la clave de todo está en,*** the key to the whole thing lies in, the answer to the whole business is in; ***en clave,*** in code; ***echar la clave,*** to close, conclude, wind up.

clavel, *n.m.* carnation; ***clavel coronado,*** grass pink; ***clavel reventón,*** large *or* double-flowered carnation.

clavelito, *n.f.* small pink.

clavellina, *n.f.* pink; (*artill.*) vent stopple.

clavelón, *n.m.* marigold.

claveque, *n.m.* rock crystal (*cut like a diamond*).

clavera (1), *n.f.* nail mould; nail hole; (*prov.*) boundary landmark.

clavería, *n.f.* office and dignity of key-bearer; (*Mex.*) treasury (*of cathedral*).

clavero, -ra (2), *n.m.f.* keeper of the keys; treasurer, cashier. — *n.m.* clove-tree; key-bearer (*of some military orders*).

clavete, *n.m.* tack; (*mus.*) plectrum.

clavetear, *v.t.* to nail, stud; to point *or* tag (*a lace*); (*fig.*) to settle, wind up.

clavicordio, *n.m.* clavichord.

clavicornio, -nia, *a., n.m.f.* (*ent.*) clavicorn.

clavícula, *n.f.* clavicle, collar-bone.

clavicular, *a.* clavicular.

clavija, *n.f.* pin; peg; treenail; pintle; lever, switch (*instrument board*); ***clavija maestra,*** fore axle-tree pintle; ***apretar las clavijas,*** to put on the pressure.

clavijera, *n.f.* (*prov.*) opening (*in mud walls to let in the water*).

clavijero, *n.m.* bridge (*of clavichord*); (*hat and coat*) rack.

clavillo, clavito, *n.m.* small nail, brad, tack rivet (*of buckle*); (*bot.*) clove.

clavímano, -na, *a.* having club-shaped hands.

claviórgano, *n.m.* instrument with strings like a clavichord and pipes like an organ.

clavo, *n.m.* nail, spike; corn (*on foot*); snag; spot (*in eye*); (*surg.*) tent, lint; (*bot.*) clove; (*naut.*) rudder; (*vet.*) pastern tumour; (*surg.*) scab; (*min.*) rich vein; ***clavo de rosca,*** screw nail; (*vet.*) ***arrimar el clavo,*** to prick (*in shoeing*); ***clavo de herradura,*** hobnail; ***clavo romano,*** picture-hanging hook; ***agarrarse a un clavo ardiendo,*** to clutch at anything; ***no dejar clavo ni estaca en pared,*** to leave nothing at all in a place; ***de clavo pasado,*** hopeless; well-known: easy; (*fig.*) ***dar en el clavo,*** to hit the nail on the head; ***dar una en el clavo y ciento en la herradura,*** hardly ever to be right; ***hacer clavo,*** to set (*mortar*); ***no importa un clavo,*** it does not matter a damn; ***remachar el clavo,*** to overdo it; to go on unnecessarily; ***como un clavo,*** dead on, on the dot.

clazol, *n.m.* (*Mex.*) bagasse of sugar cane.

clemátide, *n.f.* (*bot.*) traveller's joy, clematis, virgin's bower.

clemencia, *n.f.* clemency, mercy, forbearance.

clemente, *a.* merciful.

clepsidra, *n.f.* water-clock; hour-glass.

cleptomanía, *n.f.* kleptomania.

cleptomaníaco, -ca, cleptómano, -na, *a., n.m.f.* kleptomaniac.

clerecía, *n.f.* clergy; priesthood.

clerical, *a.* clerical.

clericalismo, *n.m.* clericalism.

clericato, *n.m.* clergy, priesthood.

clericatura, *n.f.* [CLERICATO].

clerigalla, *n.f.* (*coll.*) wretched *or* rotten priests.

clérigo, *n.m.* clergyman, cleric; clerk; ***clérigo de corona,*** tonsured cleric; ***clérigo de misa,*** priest; ***clérigo de misa y olla,*** ignorant priest.

cleriguicia [CLERIGALLA].

cleriguillo, *n.m.* petty clergyman.

clerizón, *n.m.* (*prov.*) chorister.

clerizonte, *n.m.* fake priest; (*coll.*) ill-bred *or* shabby priest; wretched priest.

clero, *n.m.* clergy; ***clero regular,*** regular clergy.

clerofobia, *n.f.* hatred of clergy, anti-clericalism.

clerófobo, -ba, *a.* anti-clerical.

cliente, *n.m.f.* customer, patron, client; (*obs.*) protégé; (*med.*) patient.

clientela, *n.f.* clientele, customers, patrons; protection, patronage; (*med.*) practice.

clima, *n.m.* climate; clime.

climatérico, -ca, *a.* climacteric; critical; (*coll.*) ***estar climatérico,*** to be ill-humoured.

climático, -ca, *a.* climatic; (*fig.*) changeable, fickle.

climatología, *n.f.* climatology.

climatológico, -ca, *a.* climatological.

clímax, *n.m.* (*rhet.*) climax.

clin [CRIN].

clínico, -ca, *a.* clinic, clinical. — *n.m.f.* (*eccles.*) clinic. — *n.f.* (*med.*) clinic; private hospital; clinical medicine; ***hospital clínico,*** teaching hospital; ***clínica de reposo,*** nursing home.

clinométrico, -ca, *a.* clinometrical.

clinómetro, *n.m.* (*naut.*) clinometer.

clinopodio *n.m.* (*bot.*) wild basil, calamint.

clip, *n.m.* (paper-)clip.

clíper, *n.m.* (*naut.*) clipper.

clisado, *n.m.* stereotyping; stereotypography.

clisador, *n.m.* (*print.*) stereotyper.

clisar, *v.t.* (*print.*) to stereotype.

clisé, *n.m.* (*print.*) stereotype, cliché.

clistel, clister, *n.m.* (*med.*) clyster.

clistelera, *n.f.* woman who administers clysters.

clisterizar [C], *v.t.* to administer clysters to.

clitómetro, *n.m.* (*surveying*) clinometer.

clivoso, -sa, *a.* (*poet.*) gradually descending, declivous, sloping.

clo, *n.m.* cluck (*hen*).

cloaca, *n.f.* cloaca; sewer; drain; (*zool.*) large intestine (*of fowls etc.*).

clocar [A], *v.i.* [CLOQUEAR].

clon, *n.m.* clown.

cloque, *n.m.* boat-hook; gaff (*used for tunny-fishing*).

cloquear, *v.t.* to gaff (*tunny-fish*). — *v.i.* to cluck (*hens*).

cloqueo, *n.m.* cluck(ing).

cloquera, *n.f.* broodiness (*in fowls*).

cloquero, *n.m.* gaff handler.

cloral, *n.m.* (*chem.*) chloral.

clorato, *n.m.* (*chem.*) chlorate.

clorhidrato, *n.m.* (*chem.*) chloral-hydrate.

clorhídrico, -ca, *a.* (*chem.*) hydrochloric.

clórico, -ca, *a.* chloric; ***ácido clórico,*** chloric acid.

clorita, *n.f.* (*min.*) chlorite.

clorítico, -ca, *a* (*min.*) chloritic.

cloro, *n.m.* (*chem.*) chlorine.

clorofílico, ca, *a.* appertaining to chlorophyll.

clorofilo, -la, *a.* (*bot.*) having green *or* yellow leaves. — *n.f.* chlorophyll.

clorofórmico, -ca, *a.* relating to chloroform.

cloroformización, *n.f.* chloroforming.

cloroformizador, -ra, *n.m.f.* chloroformer.

cloroformizar [C], *v.t.* to chloroform.

cloroformo, *n.m.* chloroform.

cloromicetina, *n.f.* chloromycetin.

clorosis, *n.f.* (*med.*) chlorosis, green-sickness.
cloroso, -sa, *a.* (*chem.*) chlorous.
clorótico, -ca, *a.* chlorotic; suffering from chlorosis.
clorurado, -da, *a.* containing chloride.
clorurar, *v.t.* to chloridize.
cloruro. *n.m.* chloride; ***cloruro de cal,*** chloride of lime; ***cloruro de sodio*** or ***cloruro sódico,*** sodium chloride.
club, *n.m.* club; ***club náutico,*** yacht(ing) club.
clubista, *n.m.* club-man, member of a club.
clueco, -ca, *a.* broody; (*coll.*) decrepit. — *n.f.* broody hen.
coa, *n.f.* (*Hisp. Am.*) hoe; (*Chi.*) gaol slang.
coacción, *n.f.* compulsion, coercion.
coacervación, *n.f.* piling, heaping together.
coacervar, *v.t.* to heap together.
coacreedor, -ra, *n.m.f.* joint creditor.
coactivo, -va, *a.* coercive, compelling.
coacusado, -da, *a.* (*law.*) accused jointly. — *n.m.f.* (*law*) co-respondent; fellow-prisoner.
coacusar, *v.t.* (*law*) to accuse jointly.
coadjutor, *n.m.* coadjutor, assistant, associate.
coadjutora, *n.f.* coadjutrix.
coadjutoría *n.f.* coadjutorship, office of a coadjutor; right of survivorship of a coadjutor.
coadministrador, *n.m.* co-trustee (*of a diocese*), co-administrator.
coadquirente, coadquiriente, *a.* purchasing jointly.
coadquiridor, -ra, coadquisidor, -ra, *n.m.f.* joint-purchaser.
coadquirir [6], *v.t.* to purchase jointly.
coadquisición, *n.f.* joint purchase.
coadunación, *n.f.*, **coadunamiento,** *n.m.* coadunation, close union.
coadunar, *v.t.* to join closely together.
coadyutor, *n.m.* coadjutor.
coadyutorio, -ria, *a.* co-operative.
coadyuvador, -ra, *n.m.f.* fellow-helper, assistant.
coadyuvante, *a.* helping, assisting.
coadyuvar, *v.t.* to help, assist.
coagente, *n.m.* coagent, associate.
coagulable, *a.* easily coagulating.
coagulación, *n.f.* coagulation, curdling.
coagulador, -ra, coagulante, *a.* coagulating, curdling.
coagular(se), *v.t.* (*v.r.*) to coagulate, congeal; to curdle.
coágulo, *n.m.* clot; coagulum.
coaguloso, -sa, *a.* coagulating, coagulated.
coairón, *n.m.* (*prov.*) piece of timber.
coaita, *n.f.* (*Cent. Am.*) monkey.
coalescencia, *n.f.* coalescence.
coalición, *n.f.* coalition.
coalicionarse, *v.r.* to form a coalition.
coalicionista, *n.m.f.* coalitionist.
coaltar, *n.m.* coal-tar.
coalla, *n.f.* woodcock.
coapóstol, *n.m.* fellow-apostle.
coarrendador, *n.m.* joint-lessor.
coarrendamiento, *n.m.* joint-tenancy.
coarrendar, *v.t.* to rent jointly.
coarrendatario, *n.m.* joint-tenant.
coartación, *n.f.* limitation, restriction; (*eccles.*) obligation to be ordained within a given time.
coartada, *n.f.* alibi; ***probar la coartada,*** to prove one's alibi.
coartador, -ra, *a.* restraining. — *n.m.f.* restrainer.
coartar, *v.t.* to limit, restrict, curtail.
coartatorio, -ria, *a.* limiting, restrictive.
coasignatorio, -ria, *n.m.f.* joint-assignee.
coasociación, *n.f.* co-partnership.
coasociado, -da, *n.m.f.* co-partner.
coasociarse, *v.r.* to go into partnership.
coate, -ta, *a.* (*Mex.*) twin.
coautor, -ra, *n.m.f.* co-author, joint-author.
coba, *n.f.* (*Morocco*) sultan's tent; (*Morocco*) dome, cupola; shrine *or* tomb (*of dervish*); (*coll.*) amusing lie; chat; buttering up, soft soap; ***dar coba a,*** to butter up *or* soft soap.
cobáltico, -ca, *a.* (*chem.*) cobaltic.
cobaltina, *n.f.* cobaltite.
cobalto, *n.m.* cobalt.
cobaltocre, *n.m.* cobalt-bloom.
cobanillo, *n.m.* small basket (*used during vintage*).
cobarcho, *n.m.* barrier net (*tunny fishing*).
cobarde, *a.* cowardly; (*fig.*) poor (*sight*). — *n.m.f.* coward.
cobardear, *v.i.* to be cowardly, act in a cowardly way.
cobardía, *n.f.* cowardliness, cowardice.
cobayo, -ya, *n.m.f.* guinea-pig.
cobea, *n.f.* (*Cent. Am.*) cobea plant.
cobertera, *n.f.* lid, cover; procuress; (*prov.*) white water-lily; (*pl.*) two middle feathers (*of hawk's tail*).
cobertizo, *n.m.* pent-roof, penthouse; shed.
cobertor, *n.m.* coverlet, quilt, counterpane, bedspread.
cobertura, *n.f.* cover, covering; act of grandee of Spain in covering himself in presence of king.
cobija, *n.f.* ridge-tile; (*prov.*) short mantilla; cover; fine feather; (*Mex.*) shawl; (*pl.*) (*Col., Mex.*) bedclothes.
cobijador, -ra, *a.* covering, protective.
cobijadura, *n.f.* (*act of*) covering.
cobijamiento [COBIJO].
cobijar, *v.t.* to cover, protect; to shelter, lodge.
cobijo, *n.m.* cover(ing), protection; shelter(ing).
cobijón, *n.m.* (*Col.*) leather *or* hide covering (*for a pack-horse*).
cobil, *n.m.* corner, angle.
cobla, *n.f.* (*mus.*) Sardana band.
cobo, *n.m.* (*Cub.*) giant snail; (*C.R.*) blanket.
cobra, *n.f.* number of mares (*for treading out the corn*); rope (*for yoking oxen*); (*zool.*) cobra; (*hunt.*) (*act of*) retrieving.
cobrable, cobradero, -ra, *a.* collectable, recoverable.
cobrador, -ra, *n.m.f.* collector, receiver (*of money*); conductor (*of bus, tram etc.*); ***perro cobrador,*** retriever (*dog*).
cobramiento, *n.m.* [COBRANZA].
cobranza, *n.f.* collection, receiving, recovery; (*hunt.*) retrieving (*game*).
cobrar, *v.t.* to collect, receive, be paid; to retrieve (*game*); to gain, acquire; to charge; to pull in, draw in (*rope etc.*); ***le ha cobrado afición al estudio,*** he's become keen on study; ***le ha cobrado cariño a Juan,*** he's become fond of John; ***cobrar ánimo,*** to take heart, courage; ***cobrar carnes,*** to put on weight; ***cobrar fuerzas,*** to gather strength; ***cobrar un cheque,*** to cash *or* draw a cheque; ***cobra buena fama y échate a dormir,*** once you get a good name, you need worry no more. — *v.i.* to get paid; (*coll.*) ***¡vas a cobrar!*** you're going to cop it! you're in for it! — **cobrarse,** *v.r.* to make up for sth. and more, to get more than one's money back.
cobratorio, -ria, *a.* appertaining to collecting *or* receiving; collectable.
cobre, *n.m.* copper; brass kitchen utensils; ***cobre de cecial,*** pair of dried fish; ***cobre quemado,*** sulphate of copper; ***cobre verde,*** malachite; (*coll.*) ***batir el cobre,*** to labour stoutly. ***batirse el cobre,*** to fight tooth and nail; (*pl.*) brass (*instruments of orchestra*).
cobreño, -ña, *a.* copper.
cobrizo, -za, *a.* coppery, cupreous; copper-coloured; (*min.*) cupric.

cobro, *n.m.* collecting, receiving (*money, tax etc.*); ***poner cobro,*** to be careful, take care; ***poner cobro en algo,*** to take steps to get sth.; ***poner en cobro,*** to keep in a safe place; ***ponerse en cobro,*** to find a safe refuge.
coca, *n.f.* (*bot.*) coca; (*prov.*) [TARASCA]; (*naut.*) small vessel; (*woman's*) side-hair; (*coll.*) head; (*coll.*) rap on the head; (*prov.*) cake; kink; (*naut.*) knot (*in cable*); ***coca de Levante,*** Indian berry.
cocacho, *n.m.* (*Arg., Ec., Per.*) rap on the head.
cocada, *n.f.* (*Bol., Col.*) coconut candy.
cocador, -ra, *a.* wheedling, coaxing, flattering. — *n.m.f.* coaxer, flatterer, wheedler.
cocaína, *n.f.* cocaine.
cocal, *n.m.* (*Per.*) grove of Indian berries; (*Ven.*) coconut plantation.
cocán, *n.m.* (*Per.*) breast (*of fowl*).
cocar [A], *v.t.* to make faces at; (*coll.*) to coax, flatter.
cocarar, *v.t.* to supply with coca-leaves.
cocaví, *n.m.* (*Hisp. Am.*) coca and provisions for a journey.
coccicultura, *n.f.* cochineal-insect cultivation.
coccíneo, -nea, *a.* purple, purplish.
cocción, *n.f.* boiling, cooking.
coceador, -ra, *a.* kicking. — *n.m.f.* kicker.
coceadura, *n.f.*, **coceamiento,** *n.m.* kicking.
cocear, *v.i.* to kick; ***cocear contra el aguijón,*** to kick against the pricks.
cocedero, -ra, *a.* easily boiled *or* cooked. — *n.m.* kitchen; place where wine is boiled.
cocedizo, -za, *a.* easily boiled *or* cooked.
cocedor, *n.m.* one whose business is to boil must; baking-oven.
cocedura, *n.f.* boiling; cooking.
cocer [5D], *v.t.* to boil; to bake (*bread, bricks, tiles* or *earthenware*); (*Hisp. Am.*) to cook; (*surg.*) to maturate. — *v.i.* to boil, ferment, cook, seethe; to ret.
cocido, *n.m.* Spanish stew.
cociembre, *n.f.* (*prov.*) fermentation (*of wine*).
cociente, *n.m.* quotient.
cocimiento, *n.m.* boiling, cooking, decoction; bath *or* mordant (*for dyeing*).
cocina, *n.f.* cookery, cooking, cuisine; kitchen; kitchen-stove; (*naut.*) galley; ***libro de cocina,*** cookery book; ***cocina francesa,*** French cooking *or* cuisine; ***cocina económica,*** cooking range, kitchen range.
cocinar, *v.t.* to cook. — *v.i.* (*coll.*) to meddle.
cocinera, *n.f.* cook.
cocinero, *n.m.* cook, chef; ***haber sido cocinero antes que fraile,*** to know the ropes.
cocinilla, cocinita, *n.f.* small kitchen; camping-stove; chafing-dish; fireplace. — *n.m.* interfering *or* nosy person, meddler.
cocle [CLOQUE].
cóclea, *n.f.* cochlea.
coclear, *a.* (*bot.*) cochlean, cochlear. — *n.m.* half a drachm.
coclearia, *n.f.* cochlearia, scurvy-grass.
coclero, -ra, *n.m.f.* harpooner.
coclillo, *n.m.* vine pest.
coco, *n.m.* (*bot.*) coco-palm; coconut; (*ent.*) coccus; (*prov.*) muslin; berry (*used for rosary beads*); (*coll.*) bogy, bogeyman; (*coll.*) head, nut; (*coll.*) grimace, (ugly) face; (*Cub.*) white ibis; ***agua*** or ***leche de coco,*** coconut milk; ***más feo que un coco,*** as ugly as sin; ***meterse algo en el coco,*** to get sth. into one's head *or* nut; ***hacer cocos (a),*** to wheedle; to make eyes (at), flirt (with).
cocó, *n.m.* (*Cub.*) whitish earth (*used in masonry and for making concrete*).
cocobacilo, *n.m.* bubonic plague bacillus.
cocobacteria, *n.f.* primitive form of bacteria.
cocobálsamo, *n.m.* fruit of the balm of Gilead.
cocobolo, cocolobo, *n.m.* cocobolo tree.
cocodrilo, *n.m.* (*zool.*) crocodile; (*railw.*) alarm-signal; ***lágrimas de cocodrilo,*** crocodile tears.
cocol, *n.m.* (*Mex.*) bread roll.
cocolero, *n.m.* (*Mex.*) baker of bread rolls.
cocolía, *n.f.* (*Mex.*) spite, ill-will, dislike.
cocoliche, *n.m.* (*Arg., Ur.*) pidgin Spanish (*used by foreigners, especially Italian immigrants*); (*contempt.*) Italian immigrant.
cocoliste, *n.m.* (*Mex.*) epidemic fever.
cocolita, *n.f.* (*min.*) coccolith.
cócora, *a., n.m.f.* boring, tedious (person).
cocoso, -sa, *a.* worm-eaten, gnawed by grubs.
cocotal, *n.m.* coco-palm grove.
cocote [COGOTE].
cocotero, *n.m.* coco-palm.
cocui, *n.m.* (*Ven.*) agave.
cocuiza, *n.f.* (*Mex., Ven.*) strong rope (*made of agave fibre*).
cocula, *n.f.* (*bot.*) cocculus.
cocuma, *n.f.* (*Per.*) roasted ear of corn.
cocuyo, cucuyo, *n.m.* fire-beetle.
cocha, *n.f.* [COCHO].
cochama, *n.m.* (*Col.*) cochama fish.
cochambre, *n.f.* filth, filthiness; foul *or* filthy object.
cochambrería, *n.f.* (*coll.*) heap of filth; foul object *or* place.
cochambrero, -ra, cochambroso, -sa, *a.* foul, filthy.
cocharro, *n.m.* wooden *or* stone dish, cup, platter.
cochastro, *n.m.* young sucking-boar.
cochayuyo, *n.m.* (*Hisp. Am.*) edible sea-weed.
coche, *n.m.* coach, carriage; (motor) car, (*Am.*) automobile; ***coche de alquiler,*** hired car, car for hire; ***coche de plaza,*** cab, hansom carriage; ***coche de punto,*** hackney cab; ***coche de collleras,*** coach drawn by pairs of mules; (*railw.*) ***coche cama,*** sleeping-car; ***coche celular,*** black Maria, police van, (*Am.*) patrol wagon; (*railw.*) ***coche comedor,*** dining-car; (*fig.*) ***coche parado,*** balcony *or* window overlooking busy thoroughfare; ***ir en el coche de San Fernando,*** to go by Shanks's pony; ***coche de línea,*** long distance bus *or* coach; ***coche fúnebre,*** hearse.
cochecito, cochecillo, *n.m.* pram; wheel-chair; ***cochecito de niño,*** pram, perambulator, (*Am.*) baby carriage.
cochear, *v.i.* to drive; to go by car.
cocheril, *a.* (*contempt.*) relating to coachmen.
cochero, -ra, *a.* easily cooked. — *n.m.* coachman; (*astron.*) Auriga; ***puerta cochera,*** carriage-entrance. — *n.f.* carriage *or* coach house; depot *or* garage (*buses, trams etc.*).
cocherón, *n.m.* large coach-house; engine-house.
cochevira, *n.f.* lard.
cochevís [COGUJADA].
cochifrito, *n.m.* fricassee of kid *or* lamb.
cochigato, *n.m.* (*Mex., orn.*) wader.
cochinada, *n.f.* (*coll.*) mean, dirty trick.
cochinata, *n.f.* (*naut.*) rider.
cochinear, *v.i.* (*fam.*) to behave in a filthy manner.
cochinería, *n.f.* (*coll.*) filthy *or* foul thing to do *or* say.
cochinero, -ra, *a.* suitable for pigs; (*coll.*) short, quick (*gait*). — *n.f.* pig-sty.
cochinilla, *n.f.* cochineal-insect; wood louse; cochineal; ***cochinilla de humedad,*** damp louse.
cochinillo, *n.m.* sucking-pig.
cochino, -na, *a.* (*coll.*) filthy; rotten; vile. — *n.m.f.* pig, sow. — *n.f.* sow.
cochiquera, *n.f.* (*lit., fig.*) pig-sty.
cochistrón, -rona, *n.m.f.* (*coll.*) filthy *or* revolting person.
cochite hervite, *a., adv., n.m.* (*coll.*) helter-skelter.
cochitril, *n.m.* pig-sty; (*coll.*) filthy hovel.

cocho, -cha, *p.p. irreg.* [COCER] baked, boiled. — *n.m.f.* (*prov.*) pig; (*prov.*) filthy person. — *n.f.* sow; (*min.*) small reservoir of water; (*Per.*) large clear space; (*Chi., Ec.*) lagoon, pool.
cochura, *n.f.* baking, boiling; dough for a batch of bread; (*min.*) calcination.
cochurero, *n.m.* furnace-man, stoker.
cochurra, *n.f.* (*Cub.*) sweetmeat of guava with seeds.
coda, *n.f.* (*prov.*) tail; (*mus.*) coda; (*carp.*) wedge.
codadura, *n.f.* (*agric.*) layer (*of vine*).
codal, *a., n.m.* elbow-shaped; measuring a cubit. — *n.m.* one cubit (*in length*); elbow-piece (*of armour*); cubit-long wax candle; (*vine*) shoot; (*arch.*) buttress; (*carp.*) frame (*of hand-saw*); (*carp.*) square; (*min.*) prop, shore.
codaste, *n.m.* (*naut.*) stern (*post*).
codazo, *n.m.* nudge; dig of the elbow; ***darle (pegarle) un codazo a alguien,*** to nudge s.o., dig s.o. with one's elbow.
codeador, *n.m.* (*naut.*) timber-measurer.
codear, *v.t.* (*naut.*) to measure (*timber*) into cubits. — *v.i.* to elbow, jostle. — **codearse,** *v.r.* to rub shoulders, hobnob, mix (**con,** with).
codeína, *n.f.* (*chem.*) codeine.
codelincuencia, *n.f.* complicity.
codelincuente, *a., n.m.f.* accomplice, partner in crime.
codemandante, *a., n.m.f.* co-plaintiff, joint-plaintiff.
codemandar, *v.t.* (*law*) to prosecute *or* sue jointly.
codeo, *n.m.* elbowing; nudging; hobnobbing.
codera, *n.f.* elbow itch; elbow patch; baggy elbow; (*naut.*) stern-fast.
codesera, *n.f.* cytisus plantation.
codeso, *n.m.* (*bot.*) hairy cytisus, bean-trefoil.
codetenido, -da, *n.m.f.* fellow-prisoner.
codetentar [2], *v.t.* to detain jointly (*another's property*).
codeudor, -ra, *n.m.f.* joint-debtor.
códice, *n.m.* codex.
codicia, *n.f.* greed, covetousness, cupidity; ***la codicia rompe el saco,*** grasp all, lose all.
codiciable, *a.* covetable.
codiciador, -ra, *a., n.m.f.* covetous (person).
codiciante, *a.* coveting.
codiciar, *v.t.* to covet.
codicilar, *a.* codicillary.
codicilo, *n.m.* codicil.
codicioso, -sa, *a.* greedy, covetous; grasping; desirous; industrious; ***es muy codicioso de su tiempo,*** he is very sparing of his time.
codificación, *n.f.* codification.
codificador, -ra, *a.* codifying. — *n.m.f.* codifier.
codificar [A], *v.t.* to codify.
código, *n.m.* code (*of laws*); ***código civil,*** civil code; (*naut.*) ***código de señales,*** signal code.
codillera, *n.f.* elbow *or* knee tumour.
codillo, *n.m.* bend, elbow, angle; codille; shoulder (*of quadrupeds*); stirrup (*of saddle*); branch stump; ham-bone; ***jugársela de codillo a,*** to trick out of sth.; to outwit; ***tirar al codillo a,*** to do everything possible to harm.
codirector, -ra, *n.m.f.* joint-director, joint-directress.
codo, *n.m.* elbow; cubit; (*mech.*) angle, elbow, knee; shoulder (*of quadrupeds*); ***dar de codo a,*** to nudge; ***alzar, empinar*** or ***levantar el codo,*** to drink, tipple; ***comerse los codos de hambre,*** to be starving; ***hablar por los codos,*** to talk one's head off; ***hasta los codos,*** up to one's eyes.
codón, *n.m.* leather cover for a horse's tail.
codonante, *a.* giving jointly. — *n.m.f.* joint-donor.
codoñate, *n.m.* preserved quinces.
codorniz, *n.f.* quail.
coeducación, *n.f.* coeducation.
coeducar [A], *v.t.* to coeducate.
coeficiencia, *n.f.* coefficiency.
coeficiente, *a.* co-operating. — *n.m.* (*alg.*) coefficient; ***coeficiente de seguridad,*** safety factor; ***coeficiente de trabajo,*** working stress.
coelector, -ra, *n.m.f.* joint-elector.
coemperador, *n.m.* associate emperor.
coendú, *n.m.* (*Hisp. Am.*) porcupine.
coepíscopo, *n.m.* fellow bishop.
coercer [D], *v.t.* to coerce.
coercibilidad, *n.f.* (*phys.*) compressibility.
coercible, *a.* coercible; (*phys.*) compressible.
coerción, *n.f.* (*law*) coercion.
coercitivo, -va, *a.* coercive, that forces *or* compels.
coesencial, *a.* coessential.
coetáneo, -nea, *a.* contemporary; contemporaneous; ***coetáneo de Cervantes,*** contemporary with Cervantes.
coeternidad, *n.f.* coeternity.
coeterno, -na, *a.* coeternal.
coevo, -va, *a.* coeval, contemporary.
coexistencia, *n.f.* coexistence.
coexistente, *a.* coexistent.
coexistir, *v.i.* to coexist; to live together.
coextenderse [2], *v.r.* to become coextensive.
coextenso, -sa, *a.* coextensive.
cofa, *n.f.* (*naut.*) mast top; crow's nest.
cofia, *n.f.* head-dress, head-gear; coif.
cofiador, -ra, *n.m.f.* (*law*) joint guarantor.
cofín, *n.m.* small basket; fruit-box.
cofosis, *n.f. inv.* cophosis, deafness.
cofrade, *n.m.f.* confrère; member (*of a confraternity, sisterhood* or *brotherhood*); (*sl.*) ***cofrade de pala,*** burglar's accomplice.
cofradía, *n.m.* confraternity, brotherhood, sisterhood; association, guild.
cofre, *n.m.* chest, coffer, trunk; (car) boot; (*print.*) coffin.
cofrecillo, *n.m.* small chest.
cofrero, *n.m.* chest-maker *or* seller.
cofto, -ta, *a.* [COPTO].
cofundador, -ra, *a.* co-founding. — *n.m.f.* co-founder.
cogedero, -ra, *a.* ready to be picked. — *n.m.* handle. — *n.f.* rod (*for gathering esparto-grass*); box (*for catching swarming bees*); pole (*for gathering fruit*).
cogedizo, -za, *a.* which can easily be collected *or* gathered.
cogedor, -ra, *a.* collecting, gathering. — *n.m.f.* collector, gatherer. — *n.m.* dustpan; coal *or* ash shovel; tax-gatherer.
cogedura, *n.f.* gathering *or* collecting.
coger [E], *v.t.* to catch, take, grab, grasp, seize; to get; to gather, pick; to take up, occupy; to hold; to gore; ***coger de (por) la mano,*** to take, grasp *or* seize by the hand; ***coger casa,*** to take a house; ***coger a puñados,*** to gather *or* grab by the handful; ***coger descuidado*** or ***desprevenido,*** to catch *or* take off guard, unawares, unprepared; ***coger in fraganti,*** to catch in the act, red-handed; ***coger en casa,*** to catch, find at home; ***coger a solas,*** to catch, find, get alone; ***le cogió un coche,*** a car got him, he was struck by a car; ***coger la ocasión por los pelos,*** to seize the opportunity; ***a lo mejor te cojo la palabra,*** I may take you up on that, hold you to that; ***coger el rábano por las hojas,*** to get hold of the wrong end of the stick; ***le cogieron miedo,*** they became *or* got frightened of him; ***le cogimos odio,*** we came to hate him, got to hate him; ***coger la calle*** or ***la puerta,*** to clear out; ***coger las calles,*** to seize (control of) the streets; ***coge toda la calle,*** it takes up, occupies the whole street; (*fig.*) he acts as if he owns the place; ***coger los trastos,*** to pack up; ***coger las de Villadiego,*** to take to one's heels; ***cogerlas al vuelo,*** to be quick on the up-take; (*coll.*) ***¡te cogí!*** I've got you there! I've got you now! — *v.i.* (*coll.*) to fit in, go in;

have room; (*coll.*) ***cogió y se largó,*** he went and cleared out *or* off. — **cogerse,** *v.r.* to catch; (*fig.*) ***cogerse los dedos,*** to burn one's fingers.
cogetrapos, *n.m. inv.* ragman.
cogida, *n.f.* gathering, harvesting; catching, hook(ing), gore, goring (*bull-fighting*).
cogido, *n.m.* fold, gather, pleat (*in clothes, curtains etc.*).
cogimiento, *n.m.* gathering, collecting, catching.
cogitabilidad, *n.f.* cogitativeness.
cogitable, *a.* cogitable.
cogitabundo, -da, *a.* pensive, musing, cogitative.
cogitación, *n.f.* reflection, cogitation, meditation.
cogitar, *v.t.* to reflect, meditate, muse, cogitate.
cogitativo, -va, *a.* cogitative.
cognación, *n.f.* cognation, relationship.
cognado, -da, *n.m.f.* cognate, blood relation.
cognaticio, -cia, *a.* cognate.
cognático, -ca, *a.* (*law*) cognate.
cognición, *n.f.* cognition.
cognomento, *n.m.* agnomen.
cognominar, *v.t.* to name, to make known (as); to cognominate.
cognoscible, *a.* cognoscible.
cognoscitivo, -va, *a.* cognitive, having the power of knowing.
cogollero, *n.m.* (*Cub.*) tobacco worm.
cogollo, *n.m.* heart (*of cabbage, lettuce etc.*); shoot (*of plant*); tree-top, summit (*of pine*); (*fig.*) heart, essence; pick.
cogón, *n.m.* (*Philip.*) bamboo (*used for thatching*).
cogotazo, *n.m.* blow on the back of the neck.
cogote, *n.m.* nape, back of the neck; crest (*at the back of the helmet*); (*fig.*) ***ser tieso de cogote,*** to be stiff-necked.
cogotera, *n.f.* nape-protector; sun-bonnet (*for beasts of burden*); hair combed down on the neck.
cogotudo, -da, *a.* thick-necked; (*coll.*) haughty.
cogucho, *n.m.* coarse sugar.
cogujada, *n.f.* crested lark.
cogujón, *n.m.* corner (*of mattress* or *bolster*).
cogujonero, -ra, *a.* pointed (*like the corners of mattresses and bolsters*).
cogulla, *n.f.* (monk's) cowl.
cogullada, *n.f.* (pig's) dewlap.
cohabitación, *n.f.* cohabitation.
cohabitador, -ra, *a., n.m.f.* (person) cohabiting, living with another.
cohabitar, *v.i.* to cohabit, live together.
cohecha, *n.f.* last tillage (*before sowing the crop*).
cohechador, -ra, *a.* bribing. — *n.m.f.* briber, suborner.
cohechar, *v.t.* to bribe, suborn; (*obs.*) to force, oblige; (*agric.*) to plough just before sowing.
cohecho, *n.m.* bribery; graft; (*agric.*) season for ploughing.
cohén, *n.m.f.* soothsayer; procurer, pimp.
coheredar, *v.t.* to inherit jointly.
coheredera, *n.f.* coheiress, joint heiress.
coheredero, *n.m.* co-heir, joint heir.
coherencia, *n.f.* coherence; joint inheritance; (*phys.*) cohesion.
coherente, *a.* coherent.
cohesión, *n.f.* cohesion.
cohesivo, -va, *a.* cohesive.
cohesor, *n.m.* (*rad.*) coherer.
cohete, *n.m.* rocket, sky-rocket; ***cohete de salvamento,*** life rocket, flare; ***cohete de señales,*** signal rocket; ***salió como un cohete,*** he shot out like a streak of lightning.
cohetería, *n.f.* rocketry.
cohetero, *n.m.* rocket maker *or* seller.
cohibente, *a.* (*phys.*) bad conductor (*of electricity*).
cohibición, *n.f.* inhibition, embarrassment, state of being *or* feeling ill at ease.
cohibidor, -ra, *a.* inhibiting, constraining.
cohibir, *v.t.* to inhibit, embarrass, make (*s.o.*) feel awkward *or* ill at ease.
cohobación, *n.f.* (*chem.*) repeated distillation.
cohobar, *v.t.* to distil repeatedly.
cohobo, *n.m.* deer-skin; (*Ec., Per.*) deer.
cohollo [COGOLLO].
cohombral, *n.m.* cucumber-bed.
cohombrar, *v.t.* (*agric.*) (*prov.*) to earth up (*plants*).
cohombrillo, *n.m.* gherkin.
cohombro, *n.m.* cucumber; fritter; ***cohombro de mar*** sea-cucumber.
cohonder, *v.t.* to corrupt; to vilify.
cohondimiento, *n.m.* corruption, reproach, infamy.
cohonestar, *v.t.* to give an honest *or* decent appearance to.
cohorte, *n.m.* cohort; (*fig.*) crowd, legion.
coigual, *a.* coequal.
coigualdad, *n.f.* coequality.
coila, *n.f.* (*Chi.*) fraud, lie.
coima, *n.f.* perquisite (*received by keeper of gaming-table*); mistress, concubine.
coime, coimero, *n.m.* keeper of a gaming-table; scorer (*at billiards*).
coincidencia, *n.f.* coincidence; concurrence.
coincidente, *a.* coincident, coincidental; coinciding.
coincidir, *v.i.* to coincide; to concur; ***coincidimos en el ascensor,*** (by chance) we went up in the same lift.
coinquilino, -na, *n.m.f.* joint-tenant.
coinquinación, *n.f.* staining, stain.
coinquinar, *v.t.* to stain, sully.
cointeresado, -da, *a.* jointly interested. — *n.m.f.* sharer, partner.
coipo, *n.m.* (*Arg., Chi.*) coypu.
coirón, *n.m.* (*Bol., Chi., Per.*) thatching grass.
coito, *n.m.* coition, coitus.
coja (I), *n.f.* (*coll.*) lewd woman.
cojal, *n.m.* knee-cap (*worn by carders*).
cojear, *v.i.* to limp, hobble; (*fig.*) to falter, waver, lapse, slip; ***cojean del mismo pie,*** they're tarred with the same brush, they're birds of a feather; ***ya sabemos de qué pie cojea,*** we are well aware of his weak spot, his leanings, his traits.
cojera, *n.f.* lameness, limp, hobble.
cojijo, *n.m.* slight complaint *or* injury; grub, insect.
cojijoso, -sa, *a.* peevish, irritable.
cojín, *n.m.* cushion; saddle-pad; (*naut.*) pillow.
cojinete, *n.m.* cushionet, small pillow [COJÍN]; pad; (*railw.*) chair; (*mech.*) bearing; (*print.*) roller-clamp; ***cojinete de bolas,*** ball-bearing.
cojitranco, -ca, *a., n.m.f.* (*contempt.*) mean and lame (person).
cojo, -ja (2) *a.* lame; limping, halt(ing); unsteady, lop-sided (*chair, table*). — *n.m.f.* lame person, cripple; ***una frase coja,*** an incomplete sentence; ***cojo de nacimiento,*** lame from birth.
cojobo, *n.m.* (*Cub.*) cojobo tree.
cojón, *n.m.* (*obsc.*) testicle, ball.
cojubo, *a.* entire, not gelt *or* castrated (*animal*).
cojuelo, -la, *a., n.m.f.* lame and mischievous.
cok [COQUE].
col, *n.f.* cabbage; ***entre col y col,*** every now and again.
cola, *n.f.* tail; train (*of dress*); end (*of a piece of cloth*); tail-end, hind part; queue; glue; (*arch.*) inside joint; (*fort.*) gorge; gum; (*mus.*) sustained note on final syllable; (*bot.*) cola, kola; ***cola de caballo,*** pony-tail; (*bot.*) horse-tail; (*fort.*) ***cola de golondrina,*** horn-work; (*carp.*) ***cola de milano*** or ***de pato,*** dove-tail; swallow-tail, fan-tail; (*arch.*) ***a cola de milano,*** dovetail moulding; ***cola de pescado,*** fish glue, isinglass; ***cola de retal*** or ***de retazos,*** painters' size; ***cola fuerte,*** adhesive gum; ***a la cola,*** at the end, right at the

back; ***ser arrimado a la cola,*** to be dim-witted; ***hacer cola,*** to queue (up); (*coll.*) ***tener*** or ***traer cola,*** to have consequences.

colaboración, *n.f.* collaboration.

colaborador, -ra, *n.m.f.* collaborator.

colaborar, *v.i.* to collaborate.

colación, *n.f.* collation; critical comparison; conferring (*of degrees*); conference (*on spiritual matters*); sweetmeats (*given to servants on Christmas Eve*); precinct *or* district of a parish; ***sacar*** or ***traer a colación,*** to bring in *or* up, introduce.

colacionar, *v.t.* to collate; to compare.

colactáneo, -nea, *n.m.f.* foster-brother, foster-sister.

colachón, *n.m.* guitar with a long handle.

colada (1), *n.f.* wash, washing; soaking of clothes *or* linen in lye; lye; linen soaked in lye; common, open ground; road for cattle; tap (*of furnace*); col (*of mountain*); (*coll.*) good sword; ***todo saldrá en la colada,*** it will all come out in the wash, truth will out; (*coll.*) you'll catch it sooner or later.

coladera, *n.f.* strainer, colander, wax-chandler's sieve; (*Mex.*) sewer, drain.

coladero, *n.m.* colander, drainer, strainer; filtering bag; narrow passage; (*min.*) hole (*for dumping ore*).

coladizo, -za, *a.* penetrating, filtering through easily, runny; (*coll.*) subtle, artful.

colado, -da (2), *a.* ***aire colado,*** (cold) draught; ***hierro colado,*** cast iron.

colador, *n.m.* colander; (*eccles.*) collator; (*print.*) leach-tub.

coladora, *n.f.* laundress, washerwoman; washing machine.

coladura, *n.f.* straining; (*coll.*) blunder, faux pas, slip.

colágeno, -na, *a.* gummy, gummiferous.

colaina [ACEBOLLADURA].

colaire, *n.m.* (*prov.*) draughty place.

colambre [CORAMBRE].

colana, *n.f.* beverage, draught.

colanilla, *n.f.* small sliding bolt (*doors, windows*).

colaña, *n.f.* railing *or* low partition (*on stairs* or *in granaries*); (*prov.*) joist.

colapez, *n.f.*, **colapiscis,** *n.f. inv.* isinglass.

colapso, *n.m.* (*med.*) collapse.

colar (1), *v.t.* (*eccles., regular in this sense*) to collate, confer.

colar (2) [4], *v.t.* to strain; to sieve; to bleach in lye; (*coll.*) to pass off (*false money*); (*coll.*) ***está colado,*** he's gone on her. — *v.i.* to slip *or* get through; ***eso no cuela,*** that won't wash, no one is going to swallow that. — **colarse,** *v.r.* to slip in; to slip up, blunder; ***se coló de rondón en la fiesta,*** he slipped unasked (*or* uninvited) into the party.

colateral, *a.* collateral; side, placed at either side.

colativo, -va, *a.* straining, filtering; (*eccles.*) relating to collation.

colcótar, *n.m.* colcothar, jewellers' rouge.

colcha, *n.f.* bedspread, coverlet, quilt, counterpane.

colchadura, *n.f.* quilting.

colchar, *v.t.* to quilt; (*naut.*) ***colchar cabos,*** to lay *or* twist ropes.

colchero, -ra, *n.m.f.* quilt-maker.

cólchico [CÓLQUICO].

colchón, *n.m.* mattress; ***colchón de pluma,*** feather-bed; ***colchón de muelles,*** spring mattress; ***colchón de tela metálica,*** woven wire mattress; ***colchón de viento,*** air-cushion, air-bed.

colchoncillo, *n.m.* small mattress.

colchonería, *n.f.* mattress-shop; bedding.

colchonero, -ra, *n.m.f.* mattress-maker *or* vendor.

colchoneta, *n.f.* long thin cushion; long thin mattress.

coleada, *n.f.* swish, wag (*of tail*); (*Hisp. Am.*) act of felling a steer by the tail.

coleador, *n.m.* (*Hisp. Am.*) man who throws a bull by its tail.

coleadura, *n.f.* swishing, wagging (*of tail*); wriggling.

colear, *v.t.* (*Hisp. Am.*) to hold *or* throw by the tail. — *v.i.* to shake, swish *or* wag (the tail); to wriggle; ***todavía colea,*** it's still dragging on, there's life in it yet, we haven't heard the last of it; ***vivito y coleando,*** (very much) alive and kicking.

colección, *n.f.* collection, (*path.*) abscess, gathering.

coleccionador, -ra, *n.m.f.* collector.

coleccionar, *v.t.* to collect.

coleccionista, *n.m.f.* collector.

colecta, *n.f.* (church) collection; collect.

colectación, *n.f.* levy; collecting (*of rates, taxes* or *dues*).

colectar, *v.t.* to collect (*taxes etc.*).

colecticio, -cia, *a.* raw, undisciplined (*troops*); collectaneous (*book*).

colectividad, *n.f.* collectivity, community.

colectivismo, *n.m.* collectivism.

colectivista, *a., n.m.f.* collectivist.

colectivo, -va, *a.* collective; ***nombre colectivo,*** collective noun. — *n.m.* (*Arg.*) bus.

colector, *n.m.* collector, gatherer; water-conduit; (*elec.*) commutator.

colecturía, *n.f.* collectorship; tax office.

colédoco, *n.m.* common bile duct.

colega, *n.m.* colleague.

colegatario, -ria, *n.m.f.* co-legatee, co-heir.

colegiación, *n.f.* formation of collegiate group.

colegiado, -da, *a.* collegiate; belonging to a professional body.

colegial, *a.* collegiate. — *n.m.* collegian, schoolboy; (*coll.*) greenhorn, novice.

colegiala, *n.f.* schoolgirl, collegian.

colegiarse, *v.r.* to form *or* join a professional association.

colegiata, *n.f.* collegiate church.

colegiatura, *n.f.* fellowship, scholarship.

colegio, *n.m.* (private secondary) school, academy; college; student body; professional body.

colegir [8E], *v.t.* to gather, collect; to gather, infer, deduce.

colegislador, -ra, *a.* co-legislative.

coleo, *n.m.* [COLEADURA].

coleóptero, -ra, *a.* (*ent.*) coleopterous.

colera, *n.f.* ornament (*for horse's tail*).

cólera, *n.f.* choler, bile; (*fig.*) anger, fury, rage, passion. — *n.m.* (*med.*) cholera; gummed cotton cloth; ***montar en cólera,*** to fly into a rage; ***descargar la cólera en uno,*** to vent one's rage on s.o.

colérico, -ca, *a.* choleric, raging, furious.

colero, *n.m.* (*Hisp. Am., min.*) supervisor-assistant.

coleta, *n.f.* pigtail; postscript, rider; ***cortarse la coleta,*** to give up one's profession *or* trade (*esp. bullfighting*), retire, pack in *or* up; ***tener*** or ***traer coleta,*** to have consequences.

coletazo, *n.m.* swish *or* swipe of *or* from a tail.

coletear, *v.i.* to flap, flop, swish.

coleteo, *n.m.* flap(ping), flop(ping), swish(ing).

coletero, *n.m.* maker of doublets.

coletilla, *n.f.* short pigtail; postscript, rider, footnote, tail-piece; refrain, tag.

coletillo, *n.m.* sleeveless doublet.

coleto, *n.m.* buff jacket; (*coll.*) body, one's body; (*coll.*) inner self; ***dije para mi coleto,*** I said to myself; ***echarse al coleto,*** to eat up, drink down, finish *or* polish off.

coletón, *n.m.* (*Ven.*) burlap; sackcloth.

colgadero, -ra, *a.* fit to be hung up. — *n.m.* hanger, hook, peg, rack.

colgazido, -da, *a.* hanging. — *n.m.* pent-house, pent-roof.

colgado, -da, *a.* hanging.
colgadura, *n.f.* hanging(s), drapery; ***colgadura(s) de cama,*** bed hangings; ***colgaduras de papel pintado,*** paper hangings.
colgajo, *n.m.* (hanging *or* flapping) rag *or* tatter; ***colgajo de uvas,*** bunch of grapes hung up to be preserved; (*surg.*) portion of healthy skin left to cover a wound.
colgamiento, *n.m.* hanging.
colgandero, -ra, *a.* hanging.
colgante, *a.* hanging. — *n.m.* (*arch.*) festoon; earring, pendant; (*mech.*) hanger; ***puente colgante,*** suspension-bridge.
colgar [4B], *v.t.* to hang, suspend; to string up; to adorn; ***colgar algo de un clavo,*** to hang sth. on a nail; ***lo colgaron,*** they hanged him, strung him up; ***colgar los hábitos,*** to doff the cassock, leave the Church; (*coll.*) ***dejar colgado,*** to leave high and dry, at a loose end; ***quedarse colgado,*** to be left high and dry, at a loose end; (*coll.*) ***colgar a uno,*** to give s.o. a birthday present. — *v.i.* to hang, dangle; to depend.
colibacilo, *n.m.* coli bacillus.
coliblanco, -ca, *a.* white-tailed.
colibrí, *n.m.* colibri, humming-bird.
colicano, -na, *a.* having grey hair in the tail.
colicitante, *a., n.m.f.* joint-bidder.
cólico, -ca, *a.* (*med.*) belonging to the colon. — *n.m.* colic, gripes, stomach upset. — *n.f.* colic.
colicoli, *n.m.* (*Chi.*) gadfly.
colicuable, *a.* easily dissolved.
colicuación, *n.f.* melting *or* dissolving; (*med.*) colliquation.
colicuante, *a.* dissolving.
colicuar, *v.t.* to melt, dissolve.
colicuativo, -va, *a.* (*med.*) causing colliquation.
colicuecer [9], *v.t.* to fuse, melt.
coliche, *n.m.* (*fam.*) informal party.
colidir, *v.i.* to dash *or* knock (against).
colífero, -ra, *a.* cauliferous.
coliflor, *n.f.* cauliflower.
coligación, *n.f.* colligation, binding together; union, alliance.
coligado, -da, *n.m.f.* leaguer, covenanter, associate.
coligadura, *n.f.*, **coligamiento,** *n.m.* colligation.
coligar(se) [B], *v.t.* (*v.r.*) to confederate, colligate; to join, ally.
coligrueso, -sa, *a.* thick-tailed.
colilla, *n.f.* train (*of gown*); cigarette end, stub.
colillero, -ra, *n.m.f.* one who gathers cigarette ends.
colín, *a.* short-tailed (*horse*). — *n.m.* (*Mex.*) bird, quail; bread stick, toast stick *or* finger.
colina, *n.f.* hill; (*chem.*) cholestrin, cholesterine.
colinabo, *n.m.* swede.
colindante, *a.* adjacent, contiguous.
colindar, *v.i.* to be adjacent, contiguous.
colineta, *n.f.* (*prov.*) table centrepiece.
colino, *n.m.* cabbage-seed; cabbage-nursery.
colipava, *a.* broad-tailed (*pigeon*).
coliquidador, *n.m.* joint-liquidator.
colirio, *n.m.* (*med.*) collyrium, eye-drops.
colirrábano, *n.m.* kohlrabi.
colisa, *n.f.* swivel-gun.
coliseo, *n.m.* coliseum.
colisión, *n.f.* (*lit., fig.*) collision, crash, clash; chafe, soreness caused by friction.
colitigante, *n.m.f.* joint-litigant.
colitis, *n.f. inv.* (*med.*) colitis.
coliza, (*naut.*) [COLISA].
colmado, -da, *a.* abundant, plentiful, overflowing. — *n.m.* grocer's shop; eating house.
colmar, *v.t.* to heap up; to fill to the brim; to stock, store (*granary*); (*fig.*) to heap on; ***colmar de mercedes,*** to heap favours on.
colmena, *n.f.* beehive; ***tener la casa como una colmena,*** to have one's house well stocked with provisions.
colmenar, *n.m.* apiary.
colmenero, -ra, *n.m.f.* bee-keeper; ***oso colmenero,*** bear who eats the honey from beehives.
colmenilla, *n.f.* morel, edible mushroom.
colmillada, *n.f.* fang *or* tusk wound.
colmillar, *a.* belonging to the canine teeth.
colmillazo, *n.m.* large eye-tooth *or* fang; gash with a fang *or* eye-tooth.
colmillo, *n.m.* eye-tooth, canine tooth; fang; tusk; ***mostrar los colmillos,*** to show one's teeth; ***tener los colmillos retorcidos,*** to be foxy, sharp, smart, be an old hand; ***escupir por un colmillo,*** to brag, talk big; to be condescending *or* superior.
colmilludo, -da, *a.* having prominent canine teeth, large fangs *or* tusks; (*fig.*) foxy, sharp, smart.
colmo, -ma, *a.* heaped up, full to the brim, overflowing. — *n.m.* (*lit., fig.*) top, limit; (*prov.*) thatched roof; ***llegar a colmo,*** to reach perfection; ***llenar con colmo,*** to fill to the brim *or* to overflowing; ***para colmo,*** to crown (it) all; ***es el colmo,*** it's the limit *or* end.
colobo, *n.m.* (*Hisp. Am.*) catarrhine monkey.
colocación, *n.f.* placing, setting; arrangement, layout, position; employment, place, situation.
colocar [A], *v.t.* to place, position, set, lay; to arrange; to give employment to, get a situation for; ***colocar por orden,*** to place in order; ***está colocado de conductor,*** he has a job as a driver. — **colocarse,** *v.r.* to take up a position; to find a position, get a job; ***se colocaron al lado de la puerta,*** they took up a position beside the door.
colocolo, *n.m.* (*Chi.*) wild cat.
colocutor, -ra, *n.m.f.* collocutor.
colodión, *n.m.* collodion.
colodra, *n.f.* milk pail; wine bucket; drinking horn; (*prov.*) wooden case for mower's whetstone; (*coll.*) ***ser una colodra,*** to be a toper *or* tippler.
colodrazgo, *n.m.* tax *or* duty on wine sold in small quantities.
colodrillo, *n.m.* occiput, back part of the head.
colodro, *n.m.* wooden shoe; (*prov.*) wine measure.
colofón, *n.m.* colophon; afterword, postscript; (*coll.*) finishing touch.
colofonia, *n.f.* colophony.
colofónico, -ca, *a.* colophonic.
colofonita, *n.f.* light-green *or* red garnet.
colofonona, *n.f.* (*chem.*) colophonate.
colografía, *n.f.* photoprinting.
colÓgrafo, *n.m.* collograph.
coloidal, *a.* colloidal.
coloide, *a., n.m.* colloid.
coloidico, -ca, coloideo, -dea, *a.* colloid.
Colombia, *n.f.* Colombia; ***la Colombia Británica,*** British Columbia.
colombiano, -na, *a., n.m.f.* Colombian.
colombino, -na, *a.* Columbian, appertaining to Columbus.
colombofilia, *n.f.* fancy for pigeon-breeding.
colombófilo, -la, *a., n.m.f.* pigeon-fancier.
colombroño, *n.m.* namesake.
colon, *n.m.* colon; clause.
colonato, *n.m.* system of colonial land settlement.
colonche, *n.m.* (*Mex.*) strong drink made from cactus sap and sugar.
colonés, -nesa, *a., n.m.f.* (person) of *or* from Cologne.
colonia, *n.f.* colony; settlement; silk ribbon (*two fingers wide*); (***agua de***) ***colonia,*** eau-de-Cologne.
colonial, *a* colonial; oversea. — *n.m.pl.* (**coloniales**) grocery products; ***tienda de coloniales,*** grocer's shop.

colónico, -ca, *a.* biliary.
colonizable, *a.* colonizable.
colonización, *n.f.* colonization.
colonizador, -ra, *a.* colonizing. — *n.m.f.* colonizer.
colonizar [C], *v.t.* to colonize.
colono, *n.m.* colonist, settler; tenant farmer.
coloño, *n.m.* (*prov.*) load of wood (*carried on head* or *back*).
coloquíntida, *n.f.* coloquintida, colocynth, bitter apple.
coloquintina, *n.f.* (*chem.*) colocynthin.
coloquio, *n.m.* colloquy; dialogue, discussion; discussion (group); talk.
color, *n.m.* colour, hue; colouring; complexion; flush, blush; (*fig.*) pretext; ***color muerto*** or ***quebrado,*** pale *or* faded colour; ***color vivo,*** bright colour; ***de*** (***en***) ***color***(***es***), coloured; ***colores nacionales,*** national colours; (*fig.*) ***mudar de color,*** to change colour; (*fig.*) ***pintar con negros colores,*** to paint a black picture of; ***ponerse de mil colores,*** to gò livid; ***robar el color,*** to cause to fade; ***sacarle a uno los colores*** (***a la cara*** or ***al rostro***), to make someone blush; ***salirle a uno los colores*** (***a la cara*** or ***al rostro***), to flush, blush; ***so color de,*** on pretence of, under pretext of; ***tomar color,*** to begin to show results; ***tomar el color,*** to take the dye well; ***un color se le iba y otro se le venía,*** his colour came and went; ***ver de color de rosa,*** to see through rose-coloured spectacles.
coloración, *n.f.* colouring, coloration.
colorado, -da, *a.* coloured; red; ruddy, florid; ***ponerse colorado,*** to go red, blush, flush.
colorador, -ra, *a.* colouring, tinting. — *n.m.f.* colourist.
colorante, *a., n.m.* colouring.
colorar, *v.t.* to dye, colour, stain.
colorativo, -va, *a.* colouring.
colorear, *v.t.* to colour, palliate, excuse, make plausible. — *v.i.* to redden, go red.
colorete, *n.m.* rouge.
colorido, *n.m.* (*art*) colouring, colour.
coloridor, -ra, *n.m.f.* (*art*) colourist.
colorímetro, *n.m.* colorimeter.
colorín, *n.m.* (*orn.*) linnet; (*pl.* **colorines**) flashy, garish colours; ***colorín colorado este cuento se ha acabado,*** and so our tale ends.
colorir [Q], *v.t.* to colour. — *v.i.* to become coloured.
colorista, *n.m.f.* (*art*) colourist.
colosal, *a.* colossal, huge.
coloso, *n.m.* Colossus, giant; (*fig.*) ***el coloso americano,*** the American giant.
colostro, *n.m.* colostrum.
colotipia, *n.f.* (*print.*) collotype.
colpa, *n.f.* (*min.*) colcothar (*used as a flux*).
cólquico, *n.m.* colchicum, meadow saffron.
colúbridos, colubrinos, *n.m.pl.* coluber.
coludir, *v.i.* (*law*) to conspire, act in collusion.
columbial, *a.* (*orn.*) columbine.
columbino, -na, *a.* columbine; dove-like, innocent.
columbio, *n.m.* (*min.*) columbium, niobium.
columbrador, -ra, *a., n.m.f.* descrying, glimpsing; one who descries *or* glimpses.
columbrar, *v.t.* to descry, glimpse, see afar off, spy at a distance; (*fig.*) to guess at, suspect.
columbrete, *n.m.* (*naut.*) low islet (*suitable for anchoring*).
columelar, *a.* canine (*tooth*).
columna, *n.f.* column; pillar; support; (*naut.*) line (*of warships*); (*fig.*) ***quinta columna,*** fifth column; ***columnas de Hércules,*** pillars of Hercules; ***columna mingitoria,*** public urinal; ***columna salomónica*** (***entorchada***), wreathed (twisted) column; ***columna vertebral,*** vertebral *or* spinal column; (*mil.*) ***columna volante,*** flying column.
columnación, *n.f.* (*arch.*) columnication.
columnar, *n.m.* colonnade.
columnario, -ria, *a.* relating to money minted in Spanish America.
columnata, *n.f.* colonnade.
columnilla, *n.f.* (*bot.*) columella.
columnita, *n.f.* short, slender column.
columpiar(se), *v.t.* (*v.r.*) to swing. — *v.r.* (*coll.*) to blunder.
columpio, *n.m.* swing.
colurión, *n.m.* lesser butcher-bird, flusher.
colusión, *n.f.* collusion.
colusor, *n.m.* partner in collusion.
colusorio, -ria, *a.* collusive.
colutorio, *n.m.* gargle.
coluvie, *n.f.* gang of ruffians; (*fig.*) den of iniquity.
colza, *n.f.* (*bot.*) colza, rape.
colla, *n.f.* gorget; row of fish traps; (*naut.*) last oakum (*placed in a seam*); channel (*of an auger*); (*Philip.*) storm preceding the monsoons; (*Bol.*) Indian from the Andean plains; (*Arg.*) Indian mestizo.
collación [COLACIÓN].
collada, *n.f.* col; steady wind.
colladía, *n.f.* series of hillocks.
collado, *n.m.* hill; fell.
collar, *n.m.* necklace; chain; collar; (*mech.*) collet.
collarada, *n.f.* shirt-collar; wild pigeon.
collarcito, *n.m.* small necklace; dainty little necklace.
collarejo, *n.m.* small collar *or* necklace; miserable little collar *or* necklace.
collarín, *n.m.* small collar, necklet; priest's collar *or* stock; coat-collar; ring (*of bomb-fuse*).
collarino, *n.m.* half-circle (*at top of column*).
collazo, *n.m.* labourer; bondsman, serf.
colleja, *n.f.* lamb's lettuce, corn-salad; (*pl.*) thin nerves (*in sheep's neck*).
collera, *n.f.* collar, horse-collar, breast-harness (*for draught animals*); gang of convicts chained together; ***collera de yeguas,*** pair of mares; ***collera de palomos,*** brace of pigeons.
collerón, *n.m.* large harness collar; light fancy collar (*for carriage horse*).
colleta, *n.f.* (*prov.*) small cabbage.
collón, -llona, *a.* cowardly. — *n.m.f.* (*coll.*) coward, poltroon.
collonada, collonería, *n.f.* cowardliness, cowardice.
coma, *n.f.* comma; (*mus.*) fifth part of a tone; support (*in choir-stalls*); mane; ***punto y coma,*** semicolon; ***sin faltar una coma,*** in minutest detail. — *n.m.* (*med.*) coma, stupor.
comadrazgo, *n.m.* spiritual relationship between a child's mother and godmother.
comadre, *n.f.* midwife; name given reciprocally by the mother and godmother of a child; (*coll.*) procuress; (*coll.*) woman friend; gossip; ***las alegres comadres de Windsor,*** the Merry Wives of Windsor.
comadrear, *v.i.* to gossip.
comadreja, *n.f.* weasel.
comadreo, *n.m.* gossiping.
comadrería, *n.f.* gossip, tittle-tattle.
comadrero, -ra, *a.* lazy and gossiping. — *n.m.f.* lazy gossiper.
comadrón, *n.m.* male midwife, accoucheur.
comadrona, *n.f.* midwife.
comal, *n.m.* (*Mex.*) flat earthenware pan (*for cooking maize cake*).
comalia, comalición, *n.f.* (*vet.*) dropsy.
comandamiento [MANDAMIENTO].
comandancia, *n.f.* command; commander's office.
comandanta, *n.f.* commander's *or* major's wife; flagship.

comandante, *n.m.* commander, commandant; major; ***comandante en jefe,*** commander-in-chief; ***comandante mayor,*** paymaster.

comandar, *v.t.* to command jointly; to compel.

comandita, *n.f.* (*com.*) silent partnership; ***compañía*** or ***sociedad en comandita,*** limited *or* joint-stock company.

comanditar, *v.i.* (*com.*) to promote, act as promoter.

comanditario, -ria, *a.* (*com.*) relating to the ***comandita.*** — *n.m.f.* (*com.*) sleeping-partner, (*Am.*) silent partner; shareholder. — *n.m.* (*law*) joint-mandatory.

comando, *n.m.* (*mil.*) commando; duffle-coat.

comarca, *n.f.* locality, area, district, region.

comarcano, -na, *a.* neighbouring; local; bordering (upon).

comarcar [A], *v.t.* to plant (*trees*) in lines. — *v.i.* to border (upon), be on the borders.

comatoso, -sa, *a.* comatose.

comba, *n.f.* [COMBO].

combadura, *n.f.* curvature, camber, warping, bending, bulging.

combar(se), *v.t.* (*v.r.*) to bend, curve, warp.

combate, *n.m.* combat, fight, engagement; bout; (*fig.*) struggle; ***poner fuera de combate,*** to put out of action.

combatible, *a.* combatable, conquerable.

combatidor, *n.m.* hard fighter.

combatiente, *a.* combating, fighting. — *n.m.* combatant, fighter, soldier.

combatir, *v.t.*, *v.i.* to combat, fight; to beat, buffet; (*naut.*) ***combatir a la retreta,*** to keep up a running fight.

combatividad, *n.f.* combativeness, fighting spirit.

combeneficiado, *n.m.* joint-curate *or* prebendary.

combés, *n.m.* (*naut.*) waist (*of ship*); open space.

combinable, *a.* combinable.

combinación, *n.f.* combination; permutation; (*railw.*) connection; slip, petticoat.

combinador, -ra, *a.* combining. — *n.m.f.* one that combines. — *n.m.* (*elec.*) controller.

combinar, *v.t.* to combine, join, unite, connect; (*chem.*) to compound; ***combinar una cosa con otra,*** to combine one thing with another.

combinatorio, -ria, *a.* combinative, combining, uniting, compounding.

combleza, *n.f.* mistress (*kept by a married man*).

comblezo, *n.m.* one who lives in concubinage with a married woman.

combo, -ba, *a.* bent, warped. — *n.m.* stand *or* frame (*for casks*); (*Chi.*) fisticuff; (*Arg.*) stone-breaking hammer. — *n.f.* curve, bend, warp, bulge; skipping-rope; skipping; ***saltar a la comba,*** to skip.

comboso, -sa, *a.* curved, warped.

comburente, *a.* (*phys.*) inducing combustion.

combustibilidad, *n.f.* (*phys.*) combustibility.

combustible, *a.* combustible. — *n.m.* fuel.

combustión, *n.f.* combustion, burning; ***combustión espontánea,*** spontaneous combustion.

combusto, -ta, *a.* burnt, consumed.

comedero, -ra, *a.* eatable, edible. — *n.m.* feeding-place, eating-trough; ***limpiarle a uno el comedero,*** to deprive s.o. of his livelihood.

comedia, *n.f.* play; drama; comedy; theatre; ***es una comedia,*** it's a farce; ***comedia de capa y espada,*** cloak and dagger play; ***comedia de costumbres,*** comedy of manners, social play; ***comedia de enredo,*** comedy of intrigue; ***hacer la comedia,*** to pretend, put on an act.

comedianta, *n.f.* actress; (*fig.*) play-actress.

comediante, *n.m.* player, actor; (*fig.*) play-actor.

comediar, *v.t.* to divide into equal shares; to average.

comedido, -da, *a.* polite, courteous; sparing; moderate, prudent, discreet.

comedimiento, *n.m.* politeness, courteousness; prudence; discretion, moderation.

comedio, *n.m.* middle; intermediate period.

comediógrafo, *n.m.* playwright.

comedión, *n.m.* (*contempt.*) long, tedious comedy *or* play.

comedirse [8], *v.r.* to restrain o.s.; to exercise prudence.

comedón, *n.m.* blackhead, pimple.

comedor, -ra, *a.*, *n.m.f.* big eater. — *n.m.* dining-room.

comején, *n.m.* wood-fretter moth; (*Hisp. Am.*, *Philip.*) white ant.

comejenera, *n.f.* breeding-place for moths *or* ants; (*Ven.*) thieves' den.

comelón, -lona, *a.* [COMILÓN].

comendador, *n.m.* commander (*of an order of knighthood*); prefect (*of religious houses*).

comendadora, *n.f.* mother superior; Mercederian nun.

comendaticio, -cia, *a.* (*eccles.*) commendatory (*letter*).

comendatorio, -ria, *a.* recommendatory. — *n.m.* (*eccles.*) commendator.

comendero, *n.m.* commendator, beneficiary of the crown.

comensal, *n.m.f.* retainer; table companion; (fellow-)diner.

comensalía, *n.f.* house *or* table companionship.

comentador, -ra, *n.m.f.* commentator, annotator, glosser; ***comentador de textos,*** glosser of texts.

comentar, *v.t.*, *v.i.* to comment (on); to gloss; (*coll.*) to discuss; to gossip (about).

comentario, *n.m.* commentary; remark, comment; (*pl.*) talk; ***hacer un comentario,*** to pass a remark.

comentarista, *n.m.f.* commentator; ***comentarista deportivo,*** sports commentator.

comento, *n.m.* comment, commenting, explanation.

comenzante, *a.* beginning. — *n.m.f.* beginner.

comenzar [IC], *v.t.*, *v.i.* to commence, begin; ***comenzar a hablar,*** to begin to speak; ***comenzar por reñir*** or ***comenzar riñendo,*** to start by quarrelling.

comer, *n.m.* food, sustenance. — *v.t.* to eat; (*fig.*) to consume, eat away; to cause to fade; ***come que te come,*** eating away; ***come lo que sea,*** he'll eat anything; ***le come la envidia,*** he is consumed with envy; ***sin comerlo ni beberlo,*** innocently; effortlessly. — *v.i.* to eat, feed; to dine; to have lunch; ***comer a dos manos,*** to wolf *or* bolt one's food; ***comer con gana,*** to eat heartily; ***comer como una lima*** or ***como un sabañón,*** to have the appetite of a wolf; ***ser de buen comer,*** to have a good appetite; ***comer por cuatro,*** to eat (enough) for four; ***come que da gusto,*** it's a pleasure to see how he enjoys his food; ***come de todo,*** he is easy to please (*as regards food*); ***comer de gorra,*** to eat at the expense of others; ***comer de viernes*** or ***de vigilia,*** to abstain from meat; ***ganar de comer,*** to earn a living; ***no tener qué comer,*** to have nothing to eat; to be down and out; ***dar de comer a,*** to feed; ***quedarse sin comer,*** to go without one's lunch, food; ***el comer y el rascar, todo es empezar,*** getting started is always the most difficult part. — **comerse,** *v.r.* to eat up, consume; to skip; ***se lo comió todo,*** he ate it all up; ***se come las palabras,*** he mumbles his words; ***se la comía con los ojos,*** he was positively devouring her with his eyes; ***se comió una fortuna,*** he ran through a fortune; ***te has comido un letra,*** you've left a letter out; ***comerse una ficha,*** to take a piece (*chess etc.*); ***tú te lo guisas, tú te lo comes,*** you make your bed and you must lie on it; ***con su pan se lo coma,*** let him get on with it *or* lump it; ***se come de envidia,*** he is consumed with envy; ***comerse unos a otros,*** to be at daggers drawn.

comerciable, *a.* marketable; (*fig.*) sociable, affable, easy to get on with.

comercial, *a.* commercial trading, business; ***esto no es comercial,*** this is not a business *or* paying proposition.

comerciante, *a.* trading. — *n.m.f.* trader, merchant, dealer.

comerciar, *v.i.* to trade, deal; to have intercourse *or* communication; ***comerciar en granos,*** to deal in grain; ***comerciar al por mayor,*** to deal wholesale; ***comerciar al por menor,*** to trade retail.

comercio, *n.m.* trade, commerce, traffic; mart, shop, business, commercial establishment; shops, shopping facilities; intercourse; communication; card game; ***comercio de cabotage,*** coasting trade; ***comercio exterior,*** foreign trade; ***comercio interior,*** home trade; ***comercio sexual (social),*** sexual (social) intercourse.

comestible, *a.* eatable, edible, comestible. — *n.m.pl.* (**comestibles**) provisions, food.

cometa, *n.m.* comet. — *n.f.* kite; card game.

cometario, -ria, *a.* (*astron.*) cometic, cometary.

cometedor, -ra, *a.* offending, perpetrating. — *n.m.f.* offender, criminal, perpetrator.

cometer, *v.t.* to commit; to charge, entrust; to undertake; (*com.*) to order; (*gram.*) to employ (*figures of speech*); ***cometer una falta,*** to make a mistake; ***cometer al brazo secular,*** to commit, surrender to the secular arm.

cometido, *n.m.* commission, charge, trust; duty, task; ***esto no es de su cometido,*** this is not his province *or* concern.

cometografía, *n.f.* cometography.

cometología, *n.f.* (*astron.*) cometology.

comezón, *n.f.* itch, itching; (*fig.*) restlessness, eagerness.

comible, *a.* eatable.

comicalla, *a.* reserved, taciturn. — *n.m.f.* sulky, taciturn person.

comicial, *a.* (*connected with*) election.

comicidad, *n.f.* comicalness, humour.

comicios, *n.m.pl.* assembly; electoral meeting; elections.

cómico, -ca, *a.* comic, ludicrous, comical; relating to the stage, dramatic. — *n.m.f.* actor, actress, player; comedian; ***cómico de la legua,*** strolling player.

comida, *n.f.* food; meal, lunch, dinner; (*fig.*) ***cambiar la comida,*** to throw up; ***comida hecha, compañía deshecha,*** interest served, friendship fades; ***reposar la comida,*** to rest after meals.

comidilla, *n.f.* (*coll.*) talk; gossip, topic of conversation; ***comidilla de la ciudad,*** talk of the town.

comienzo, *n.m.* beginning, start, commencement, inception.

comihuelga, *a.* working little but eating heartily; lazy, good-for-nothing.

comilitón, *n.m.* fellow-soldier.

comilitona, *n.f.* (*coll.*) [COMILÓN].

comilón, -lona, *a.* heavy eating. — *n.m.f.* heavy eater. — *n.f.* (*coll.*) slap-up meal, grand blow-out, spread.

comilla, *n.f.* small comma; (*pl.*) inverted commas.

cominear, *v.i.* (*coll.*) to meddle, fuss around.

cominero, -ra, *a.* meddlesome, interfering. — *n.m.f.* busybody, meddler.

cominillo, *n.m.* darnel grass.

comino, *n.m.* cumin plant and seed; (*coll.*) ***no se me da un comino,*** I don't care (give) a damn.

comiquear, *v.i.* (*fam.*) to put on amateur performances.

comiquería, *n.f.* troop of amateur players.

comisar, *v.t.* to confiscate, seize.

comisaría, *n.f.* police station.

comisariato, *n.m.* commissariat.

comisario, *n.m.* commissary, deputy; ***alto comisario,*** high commissioner; ***comisario de cuartel*** or ***de barrio,*** justice of the peace (*of a ward*); ***comisario de policía,*** commissioner of police; ***comisario de entradas,*** receptionist (*in hospitals*); ***comisario de guerra,*** head of the commissariat; ***comisario general,*** commissary-general of the army; ***comisario ordenador,*** assistant quarter-master.

comiscar [A] [COMISQUEAR].

comisión, *n.f.* commission; trust; committee; (*com.*) ***comisión mercantil,*** commission, percentage.

comisionado, -da, *a.* commissional. — *n.m.f.* commissioner; (*com.*) agent, proxy; ***comisionado de apremios,*** bailiff, sheriff's officer.

comisionar, *v.t.* to commission, depute, empower, appoint.

comisionista, *n.m.f.* (*com.*) commission-merchant, commission-agent.

comiso, *n.m.* (*law*) confiscation (*of prohibited goods*); confiscated goods; (*com.*) seizure; (*law*) foreclosure of an emphyteusis.

comisorio, -ria, *a.* (*law*) binding.

comisquear, *v.t.* to peck *or* nibble at.

comistión, *n.f.* commixture, mixture.

comistrajo, *n.m.* (*coll.*) hodge-podge, concoction, messy food.

comisura, *n.f.* (*anat.*) commissure; corner (*of lips etc.*).

comisural, *a.* (*anat.*) commissural.

comital, *a.* relating to the dignity of a count *or* countship.

comité, *n.m.* committee.

comitente, *a.* commissioning. — *n.m.f.* client.

comitiva, *n.f.* suite, retinue; procession.

cómitre, *n.m.* galley slave driver, overseer; sea-captain.

comiza, *n.f.* (*ichth.*) barbel.

como, *adv.*, *conj.* as; such as; inasmuch as; like; if; that; about; ***blanco como la nieve,*** white as snow; ***se portó como un cobarde,*** he behaved like a coward; ***la manera como lo dijo,*** the way (in which) he said it; ***como lo vuelvas a decir,*** if you dare to say it again; ***como no vengas pronto,*** unless you come soon; ***tanto como,*** as much as; ***así como, tan luego como,*** as soon as; ***como que, como quiera que*** or ***como sea que,*** since; ***está como a cinco kilómetros,*** it is about five kilometres away; ***está como atontado,*** he is sort of stunned.

cómo, *exclam.*, *interrog.* how!, why!; how?, what?, why?, how is it that?; ***¿cómo?*** what?; ***¿cómo te encuentras?*** how do you feel?; ***dime cómo fue,*** tell me how it happened; ***¡cómo grita!*** how he shouts!; ***¿cómo no me lo has dicho?*** how is it you didn't tell me? why didn't you tell me?; ***¿cómo no?*** what do you expect?, of course; ***¡cómo!*** you can't mean it! it's not possible!

comodable, *a.* (*law*) which can be lent *or* borrowed.

comodante, *n.m.f.* (*law*) lender by commodation.

comodatario, *n.m.* (*law*) borrower by commodation.

comodato, *n.m.* (*law*) commodate, commodation.

comodidad, *n.f.* comfort; convenience; (*pl.* **comodidades**) creature comforts.

comodín, *n.m.* joker (*cards*); (*coll.*) general substitute.

comodista, *a.*, *n.m.f.* selfish (person); comfort-loving (person).

cómodo, -da, *a.* comfortable; convenient. — *n.m.* utility, profit, convenience. — *n.f.* chest of drawers, (*Am.*) dresser.

comodón, -dona, *a.* (*fam.*) comfort-loving; reluctant to put oneself out.

comodoro, *n.m.* commodore.

comóforo, -ra, *a.* comose, hairy.

comorar, *v.i.* to dwell *or* live together.

comótico, -ca, *a.* beautifying, embellishing.
compacidad, *n.f.* [COMPACTIBILIDAD].
compactar, *v.t.* (*Col., Chi.*) to consolidate.
compactibilidad, *n.f.* compactness.
compacto, -ta, *a.* compact, close, dense.
compadecer [9], *v.t.* to feel sorry for, sympathize with, pity. — **compadecerse,** *v.r.* — ***de,*** to pity, feel sorry for, take pity on; to have mercy on; — ***con,*** to go (well) with.
compadraje, *n.m.* clique, ring.
compadrar, *v.i.* to become a godfather *or* godmother; to become a friend *or* sponsor; to concur *or* tally (with).
compadrazgo, *n.m.* spiritual relationship between a child's parents and the godfather; clique.
compadre, *n.m.* father *or* godfather (*with respect to each other*); mate, chum, pal.
compadrería, *n.f.* friendship, companionship.
compaginación, *n.f.* combining; (*print.*) paging; arrangement.
compaginador, *n.m.* coupler; combiner; collator.
compaginar, *v.t.* (*fig.*) to arrange, combine; (*print.*) to page up; to collate. — **compaginarse,** *v.r.* to fit, agree; ***lo uno se compagina con lo otro,*** the one thing fits with the other.
companage, compango, *n.m.* snack.
compañerismo, *n.m.* good fellowship, comradeship.
compañero, -ra, *n.m.f.* companion, comrade, chum, fellow, mate; (*fig.*) counterpart, match; ***compañero de cuarto,*** room-mate; ***compañero de colegio,*** school-mate; ***compañero de armas,*** comrade in arms; ***compañero de juego,*** playmate; partner; ***compañero de viaje,*** fellow traveller.
compañía, *n.f.* companionship; company; fellowship, partnership; gathering; (*theat.*) troop; ***compañía de la legua,*** strolling company of players; ***Compañía de Jesús,*** Society of Jesus; ***compañía anónima,*** stock company; ***compañía de seguros,*** insurance company; ***compañía matriz,*** parent company; ***hacer compañía a,*** to keep company; ***ir en compañía,*** to go together (*with others*); ***trabajar en compañía,*** to work together *or* in partnership.
compañón, *n.m.* testicle.
comparabilidad, *n.f.* comparability.
comparable, *a.* comparable.
comparación, *n.f.* comparison, comparing; ***en comparación con,*** in *or* by comparison with, compared with; ***las comparaciones son odiosas,*** comparison is odious.
comparado, -da, *a.* comparative (*grammar*); ***filología comparada,*** comparative philology.
comparador, *n.m.* (*phys.*) comparator.
comparanza, *n.f.* comparison.
comparar, *v.t.* to compare; ***comparar una cosa con otra,*** to compare one thing with another.
comparativo, -va, *a.* comparative.
comparecencia, *n.f.* (*law*) appearance (*in court*).
comparecer [9], *v.i.* to appear (*in court*).
compareciente, *n.m.f.* (*law*) person appearing (*in court*).
comparendo, *n.m.* (*law*) summons, citation.
comparición, *n.f.* (*law*) appearance; (*law*) summons.
compariente, *a.* akin, kin, kindred.
comparsa, *n.f.* masquerade (*in carnival*). — *n.m.f.* (*theat.*) extra; (*fig.*) figure-head, puppet; ***gobierno comparsa,*** puppet government.
comparte, *n.m.* (*law*) joint-party.
compartimiento, *n.m.* division (*into parts*); compartment; (*aer.*) curtain (*of airship*); ***compartimiento estanco,*** water-tight compartment.
compartir, *v.t.* to divide (*into equal parts*); to share; ***compartir las penas con otro,*** to share one's sorrows with s.o. else.
compás, *n.m.* compass; pair of compasses; callipers; (*mus.*) beat, rhythm, time; pace; territory assigned to a monastery; (*mus.*) ***a compás,*** in (right) time; ***al compás de,*** in time with; ***fuera de compás,*** out of time, off beat; ***compás de dos por cuatro,*** two-four time; ***compás de espera,*** pause for the duration of a bar; short break *or* interruption; temporary expedient; ***con un compás de espera,*** in the meantime; ***llevar el compás,*** to keep *or* beat time; ***ir con el compás,*** to keep in time; ***ir con el compás en la mano,*** to proceed accurately *or* methodically; ***estar en compás,*** to be within proper bounds; ***salirse de compás,*** to go off the rails, get out of line.
compasado, -da, *a.* measured, judicious, sensible.
compasamiento, *n.m.* measuring with compasses.
compasar, *v.t.* to measure (*with a rule and compass*); (*fig.*) to regulate; (*mus.*) to divide into bars; (*naut.*) ***compasar una carta de marear,*** to prick a chart.
compasible, *a.* compassionate, deserving pity.
compasillo, *n.m.* (*mus.*) quadruple measure.
compasión, *n.f.* compassion, pity, sympathy, mercifulness.
compasivo, -va, *a.* compassionate, merciful, sympathetic.
compaternidad, *n.f.* spiritual relationship between a child's parents and its godfather.
compatibilidad, *n.f.* compatibility.
compatible, *a.* compatible; ***compatible con la justicia,*** consistent with justice.
compatricio, -cia, compatriota, *n.m.f.* fellow countryman *or* woman, compatriot.
compatrón, -rona [COMPATRONO].
compatronato, *n.m.* rights and duties of joint-patronage.
compatrono, -na, *n.m.f.* fellow-patron *or* patroness.
compelación, *n.f.* (*law*) interrogatory; (*rhet.*) apostrophe.
compelativo, -va, *a.* interrogative, interrogatory.
compeler, *v.t.* to compel (***a,*** to).
compendiador, -ra, *a.* summarizing. — *n.m.f.* summarizer.
compendiar, *v.t.* to summarize, abridge.
compendio, *n.m.* compendium, abridgment, summary; ***en compendio,*** briefly.
compendiosamente, *adv.* briefly.
compendioso, -sa, *a.* brief, compendious.
compendista, *n.m.* author of a compendium.
compendizar [C] [COMPENDIAR].
compenetración, *n.f.* mutual understanding, interpenetration.
compenetrarse, *v.r.* — ***de,*** to make o.s. thoroughly familiar (with); to steep o.s. (in); to enter fully into the spirit (of); ***compenetrarse con alguien,*** to get in tune with s.o.
compensable, *a.* that can be compensated.
compensación, *n.f.* compensation; equivalent; ***banco de compensación,*** clearing bank.
compensador, -ra, *a.* compensating. — *n.m.* compensator, balance *or* pendulum.
compensar, *v.t.* to compensate; to clear (*a cheque*); to make up for; ***compensar una cosa con otra,*** to counterbalance one thing with another; (*coll.*) ***no compensa,*** it's not worth it.
compensativo, -va, compensatorio, -ria, *a.* compensatory.
competencia, *n.f.* competition; competence; concern, province; ***no es de su competencia,*** it's not his concern *or* province; ***a competencia,*** competitively.
competente, *a.* competent; able, capable.
competer, *v.i.* to belong, appertain, concern.
competición, *n.f.* competition, contest.
competidor, -ra, *a.* competing, contesting. — *n.m.f.* competitor, contender.

competir [8], *v.i.* to contest, contend; to compete.
compilación, *n.f.* compilation.
compilador, -ra, *a.* compiling. — *n.m.f.* compiler, collector.
compilar, *v.t.* to compile.
compinche, *n.m.f.* (*coll.*) pal, chum, crony.
complacedero, -ra [COMPLACIENTE].
complacedor, -ra [COMPLACIENTE].
complacencia, *n.f.* pleasure, gratification; satisfaction.
complacer [23], *v.t.* to please, oblige, give satisfaction to, humour; ***le voy a complacer,*** I'm going to satisfy your wishes; ***me complace poderle decir que,*** I'm pleased to be able to tell you that. — **complacerse,** *v.r.* to take pleasure *or* delight (***en,*** in).
complaciente, *a.* accommodating, obliging, helpful.
complacimiento, *n.m.* [COMPLACENCIA].
complectivo, -va, complectorio, -ria, *a.* (*bot.*) complected, joined together.
complejidad, *n.f.* complexity.
complejo, -ja, *a.* complex, complicated. — *n.m.* complex.
complementar, *v.t.* to complement, complete.
complementario, -ria, *a.* complementary, completing.
complemento, *n.m.* complement; (*gram.*) predicate; accomplishment; completion.
completar, *v.t.* to complete.
completas, *n.f.pl.* (*eccles.*) compline.
completivo, -va, *a.* completive, absolute.
completo, -ta, *a.* complete; full; full up; full house; ***por completo,*** completely, fully.
complexidad, *n.f.* complexity.
complexión, *n.f.* (*physiol.*) constitution; build; ***de complexión recia,*** having a tough constitution; strongly built.
complexional, *a.* constitutional.
complexionar, *v.t.* to reform the constitution *or* build of.
complexo, -xa, *a.* [COMPLEJO].
complicación, *n.f.* complication, complicatedness.
complicado, -da, *a.* complicated.
complicador, -ra, *a.* complicating.
complicar [A], *v.t.* to complicate; to make difficult; to implicate, involve; ***están complicados los dos,*** they are both involved. — **complicarse,** *v.r.* to become complicated; to become involved; ***se complica la vida,*** he makes things difficult for himself, goes looking for trouble.
cómplice, *n.m.f.* accomplice, abettor; ***cómplice en el delito,*** accessory to the crime.
complicidad, *n.f.* complicity.
complot, *n.m.* plot, conspiracy.
componedor, -ra, *n.m.f.* repairer; composer, compositor. — *n.m.* (*print.*) composing-stick; (*law*) ***amigable componedor,*** arbitrator.
componenda, *n.f.* compromise.
componente, *a., n.m.* component.
componer [25], *v.t.* to compose, put together; to arrange, compound; to draw up; to repair, mend; to adorn, trim, decorate; to settle (*differences*); ***componer el semblante,*** to compose one's countenance. — **componerse,** *v.r.* to deck o.s. out; ***allá se las componga,*** let him get on with it; ***componérselas,*** to shift for o.s.
componible, *a.* mendable, compoundable.
comporta, *n.f.* (*prov.*) large basket (*for grape harvesting*); (*Per.*) mould (*used in the solidification of refined sulphur*).
comportable, *a.* supportable, tolerable.
comportación, *n.f.* joint-carrying; deportment, behaviour.
comportamiento, *n.m.* behaviour, conduct.
comportar, *v.t.* to carry jointly; to involve; (*fig.*) to tolerate, suffer. — **comportarse,** *v.r.* to behave.
comporte, *n.m.* behaviour, conduct; deportment.
composición, *n.f.* composition; essay; making up; repair, mending; ***hacer composición de lugar,*** to size up the situation.
compositivo, -va, *a.* (*gram.*) compositive, synthetic.
compositor, -ra, *a.* composing. — *n.m.f.* (*mus.*) composer. — *n.m.* (*print.*) compositor.
compostura, *n.f.* composition, accommodation, agreement, adjustment; repairing, mending; neatness, cleanliness; adulterating mixture; composure; circumspection, modesty, sedateness.
compota, *n.f.* stewed fruit.
compotera, *n.f.* dish for stewed fruit.
compra, *n.f.* purchase, buy; buying; ***compra a plazos,*** hire purchase, (*Am.*) instalment plan; ***hacer la compra,*** to do the shopping; ***ir de compras,*** to go shopping.
comprable, compradero, -ra, compradizo, -za, *a.* purchasable.
comprachilla, *n.f.* (*Guat.*) blackbird.
comprado, *n.m.* card game.
comprador, -ra, *a.* buying, purchasing. — *n.m.f.* buyer, purchaser, shopper.
comprante, *a.* buying, purchasing.
comprar, *v.t., v.i.* to buy, purchase; to shop; ***comprar al contado,*** to buy cash down; ***comprar a plazos,*** to buy on hire purchase, (*Am.*) the instalment plan; ***comprar por kilos,*** to buy by the kilo; ***comprar de comer,*** to buy food; ***le hemos comprado dos,*** we have bought two for him *or* from him.
compraventa, *n.f.* buying and selling.
comprehensivo, -va [COMPRENSIVO].
comprendedor, -ra, *a.* comprehending, understanding; comprehensive.
comprender, *v.t.* to comprehend, understand; to comprise, contain.
comprensibilidad, *n.f.* comprehensibility; comprehensiveness.
comprensible, *a.* comprehensible, understandable; ***comprensible para todos,*** understandable to all.
comprensión, *n.f.* comprehension, understanding.
comprensividad, *n.f.* (*capacity for*) understanding.
comprensivo, -va, *a.* understanding; comprising, containing.
comprensor, -ra, *a., n.m.f.* (one) that understands, embraces; (*theol.*) blessed.
compresa, *n.f.* (*surg.*) compress; sanitary towel.
compresbítero, *n.m.* fellow-priest.
compresibilidad, *n.f.* compressibility.
compresible, *a.* compressible.
compresión, *n.f.* compression, pressure; (*gram.*) synæresis.
compresivo, -va, *a.* compressive, compressing, condensing.
compresor, -ra, *a.* compressing. — *n.m.* compressor; ***compresor de aire,*** air-compressor.
comprimario, -ria, *n.m.f.* singer of secondary parts.
comprimente, *a.* compressing, oppressing, constraining.
comprimible, *a.* compressible.
comprimido, *n.m.* (*pharm.*) tablet.
comprimidor, -ra, *a.* compressive.
comprimir, *v.t.* to compress, condense; to constrain, repress, restrain. — **comprimirse,** *v.r.* to restrain oneself.
comprobación, *n.f.* check, checking; verification.
comprobador, -ra, *a.* checking; verifying. — *n.m.f.* verifier, tester.
comprobante, *a.* proving, attesting, substantiating. — *n.m.* check, proof; voucher, certificate, receipt.
comprobar [4], *v.t.* to verify, check, test.
comprofesor, -ra, *n.m.f.* colleague.

comprometedor, -ra, *a.* compromising; jeopardizing. — *n.m.f.* compromiser; jeopardizer.
comprometer, *v.t.* to compromise; to expose, jeopardize, endanger; to make liable, put under an obligation, bind. — **comprometerse,** *v.r.* to commit o.s.; to compromise o.s.; ***comprometerse a,*** to undertake to.
comprometido, -da, *a.* awkward, risky; embarrassing; (*pol.*) committed.
comprometimiento, *n.m.* undertaking; agreement; predicament, embarrassment, jeopardy.
compromisario, *n.m.* arbitrator, umpire, referee; elector of political delegate.
compromisorio, -ria, *a.* (*law*) pronounced by arbiters (*decisions etc.*); stipulating arbitration (*clauses etc.*). — *n.m.* obligation, agreement, embarrassment, predicament; engagement.
comprovincial, *a.* suffragan (*bishop*).
comprovinciano, -na, *a.*, *n.m.f.* from the same province.
compuerta, *n.f.* hatch, half-door; lock, sluice, flood-gate; door-curtain (*of coach*); ***compuerta de marea,*** tide-gate.
compuesto, -ta, *a.* composed; dressed up, neat and tidy; composite. — *n.m.* compound.
compulsa, *n.f.* (*law*) certified copy; collation, comparison.
compulsador, -ra, *n.m.f.* one who collates *or* compares.
compulsar, *v.t.* (*law*) to make an authentic copy *or* transcript of; to compare, collate.
compulsión, *n.f.* compulsion, forcing.
compulsivo, -va, *a.* compulsive.
compulsor, -ra, *a.* compulsory. — *n.m.f.* compelling, forceful person.
compulsorio, -ria, *a.* (*law*) relating to a judicial decree to obtain a certified copy. — *n.m.f.* (*law*) order for a certified copy.
compunción, *n.f.* compunction, contrition, repentance.
compungido, -da, *a.* contrite, remorseful.
compungir [E], *v.t.* to move to compunction. — **compungirse,** *v.r.* to feel compunction, contrition, remorse.
compungivo, -va, *a.* pricking, stinging.
compurgación, *n.f.* (*law*) compurgation, vindication.
compurgador, *n.m.* (*law*) compurgator.
compurgar [B], *v.t.* (*law*) to prove the innocence of by compurgation.
computación, *n.f.* computation, calculation.
computadamente, *adv.* by computation.
computador, -ra, *a.* computing, calculating. — *n.f.* computer.
computar, *v.t.* to compute, calculate.
computista, *n.m.f.* computer.
cómputo, *n.m.* computation, calculation.
comulación, *n.f.* accumulation.
comulgante, *a.* (*eccles.*) of an age to communicate. — *n.m.f.* (*eccles.*) communicant.
comulgar [B], *v.t.* to communicate, administer communion to. — *v.i.* to communicate, receive communion; (*coll.*) ***comulgar con ruedas de molino,*** to be very credulous, swallow anything.
comulgatorio, *n.m.* communion rail.
común, *a.* common; ordinary. — *n.m.* community, public; water-closet, lavatory; ***en común,*** in common; ***tener en común*** or ***de común,*** to have in common; ***por lo común,*** in general, generally; ***el común de las gentes,*** the general run of people.
comuna, *n.f.* commune; main irrigation channel *or* water-pipe.
comunal, *a.* common, communal. — *n.m.* commonalty.
comunero, -ra, *a.* popular, common, pleasing to the people; appertaining to the communities of Castile. — *n.m.* commoner; joint-holder of a tenure of lands; (*pl.* **comuneros**) villages with commonage.
comunes, *n.m.pl.* the (House of) Commons.
comunial, *a.* communal.
comunicabilidad, *n.f.* communicability, communicableness.
comunicable, *a.* communicable.
comunicación, *n.f.* communication; connection; (*pl.* **comunicaciones**) post, telephone, telegraph; ***Palacio de Comunicaciones,*** (the) Post Office.
comunicado, *n.m.* communiqué.
comunicador, -ra, *a.* communicating. — *n.m.f.* communicator.
comunicante, *a.* communicating. — *n.m.f.* communicant.
comunicar [A], *v.t.*, *v.i.* to communicate, impart; ***comunicar con el exterior,*** to communicate with the outside world. — **comunicarse,** *v.r.* ***comunicarse (dos lagos) entre sí,*** to be joined together (*two lakes*); ***comunicarse por señas,*** to communicate by signs.
comunicativo, -va, *a.* communicative, open, forthcoming.
comunicatorio, -ria, *a.* ***letras comunicatorias,*** testimonial letters.
comunidad, *n.f.* community; ***de comunidad,*** in common, jointly, collectively; (*pl.* **comunidades**) popular risings in Castile (16*th cent.*).
comunión, *n.f.* communion; fellowship; (Holy) Communion; ***comunión carlista,*** carlism.
comunísimo, -ma, *a.* *superl.* extremely common, very general.
comunismo, *n.m.* communism.
comunista, *a.*, *n.m.f.* communist.
comunistizante, *a.* with leanings to communism. — *n.m.f.* fellow traveller.
comunistizar [C], *v.t.* to communize. — **comunistizarse,** *v.r.* to become communist.
comuña, *n.f.* maslin, mixed corn and rye; (*prov.*) partnership.
comunitario, -ria, *a.* communal; (of the) community; (of the) European Economic Community.
con, *prep.* with; (*preceding Spanish infinitive*), by (*followed by English gerund*); (*followed by Spanish infinitive*), although; in; toward; ***con pagar, se eximió del servicio,*** by paying he was exempted from military service; ***con ser tan difícil, lo hizo,*** notwithstanding its being so difficult he did it; ***con que Vd. me hubiera escrito,*** if you had only written to me; ***con que así es,*** so that's that; ***afable con los niños,*** kind to children; ***llevarse bien con otro,*** to get on well with another person; ***con lluvia,*** in the rain; ***con sol,*** in the sun.
conacho, *n.m.* (*Per.*) mortar (*for pounding gold-ore*).
conato, *n.m.* attempt; endeavour; tendency.
concadenamiento, *n.m.* concatenation.
concadenar, *v.t.* to concatenate, link together.
concambio, *n.m.* exchange.
concanónigo, *n.m.* fellow-canon.
concatedralidad, *n.f.* union of two cathedral churches.
concatenación, *n.f.* concatenation.
concausa, *n.f.* joint cause.
concavidad, *n.f.* [CÓNCAVO].
concavar, *v.t.* to dig jointly.
cóncavo, -va, *a.* concave, hollow. — *n.m.f.* concavity, hollow.
concebible, *a.* conceivable.
concebir [8], *v.t.*, *v.i.* (*lit.*, *fig.*) to conceive; (*coll.*) ***no lo concibo,*** it's beyond my comprehension; ***¿usted concibe que se haga esto?*** can you credit this being done?
concedente, *a.* conceding.

conceder, *v.t.* to concede; to bestow, grant.
concejal, -la, *n.m.f.* councillor.
concejalía, *n.f.* councillorship.
concejil, *a.* common; public; relating to the municipal council.
concejo, *n.m.* municipal council; council board; session; ***casa del concejo,*** town hall.
concelebramiento, *n.m.* (*eccles.*) concelebrating.
concelebrar, *v.t.* (*eccles.*) to concelebrate.
conceller, *n.m.* councillor (*in Catalonia*).
concento, *n.m.* concert, concord of voices, harmony.
concentrabilidad, *n.f.* quality of being concentrated.
concentrable, *a.* that which can be concentrated.
concentración, *n.f.* concentration.
concentrado, *n.m.* concentrate.
concentrador, -ra, *a.* concentrating. — *n.m.f.* concentrator.
concentrar(se), *v.t.* (*v.r.*) to concentrate; to concentre; ***concentrar el interés en,*** to focus (one's) interest on; ***concentrarse con los cinco sentidos,*** to apply one's full attention.
concentratividad, *n.f.* concentrativeness.
concentricidad, *n.f.* concentricity.
concéntrico, -ca, *a.* (*geom.*) concentric.
concentuoso, -sa, *a.* harmonious.
concepción, *n.f.* (*lit., fig.*) conception; notion; (*festival of*) the Immaculate Conception.
concepcional, *a.* (*phil.*) conceptional.
concepcionario, -ria, *n.m.f.* defender of the dogma of the Immaculate Conception.
conceptáculo, *n.m.* (*bot.*) conceptacle.
conceptear, *v.i.* to give smart repartees.
conceptibilidad, *n.f.* imaginativeness.
conceptible, *a.* conceivable, imaginable.
conceptismo, *n.m.* ingenious style; euphuism; conceit.
conceptista, *n.m.* ingenious stylist; euphuist; wit; punster.
conceptividad, *n.f.* conceivableness, conceivability.
conceptivo, -va, *a.* conceptive.
concepto, *n.m.* concept, idea; flash of wit, epigram, pun; opinion, judgment; ***formar un concepto,*** to form an opinion; ***tener en buen (mal) concepto,*** to have a good (poor) opinion of; ***en concepto de,*** by way of, under the heading of.
conceptor, -ra, *a.* conceiving, imagining. — *n.m.f.* conceptionist, imaginer.
conceptuar [M], *v.t.* to conceive, judge, deem, form an opinion of; ***ser conceptuado de inteligente,*** to be deemed intelligent.
conceptuosidad, *n.f.* witticism, pithiness; ingenuity, ingeniousness.
conceptuoso, -sa, *a.* ingenious, witty.
concernencia, *n.f.* relation.
concerniente, *a.* concerning, touching, relating; ***en lo concerniente a,*** as for, with regard to; ***lo concerniente al negocio,*** what concerns the business.
concernir [3Q], *v. impers.* to regard, concern; to appertain, belong (to).
concertación, *n.f.* contest, fight, dispute.
concertadamente, *adv.* by agreement; in conjunction.
concertador, -ra, *a.* concerting, arranging. — *n.m.f.* arranger; ***maestro concertador,*** choirmaster.
concertamiento, *n.m.* [CONCERTACIÓN].
concertante, *a.* concerting, arranging, planning; (*mus.*) concerted, arranged for two or more voices.
concertar [1], *v.t.* to concert; to arrange; to make agree; (*com.*) to close (*a deal*); to tune (*musicil instruments*); to compare; (*hunt.*) to beat, start *or* rouse (the game); ***concertar las paces entre dos contrarios,*** to arrange peace between two parties. — *v.i.* to agree; to harmonize. — **concertarse,** *v.r.* to be arranged; to go hand in hand; to agree; to conspire.
concertina, *n.f.* (*mus.*) concertina.
concertino, *n.m.* orchestra leader.
concertista, *n.m.f.* (*mus.*) performer; concert artist.
concesible, *a.* admissible, grantable.
concesión, *n.f.* concession; grant; acknowledgment.
concesionario, *n.m.* (*law*) grantee, concessionary.
concesivo, -va, *a.* that may be granted.
concia, *n.f.* prohibited part of a forest.
conciencia, *n.f.* conscience; consciousness; awareness; conscientiousness; ***cargar la conciencia,*** to burden one's conscience; ***descargar la conciencia,*** to unburden one's conscience, get a load off one's conscience *or* mind; ***adquirir*** or ***tomar conciencia de,*** to become conscious *or* aware of; ***en conciencia,*** in conscience, in all honesty; ***a conciencia,*** conscientiously, thoroughly.
concienciación, concientización, *n.f.* creation of a state of (social *or* political) awareness.
concienciar, concientizar, *v.t.* to create *or* foster a state of (social *or* political) awareness in.
concienzudo, -da, *a.* conscientious, scrupulous, thorough.
concierto, *n.m.* concert; contract, agreement, accommodation; good order, arrangement; (*mus.*) concert; concerto; (*hunt.*) beating; ***de concierto,*** in concert *or* agreement.
conciliable, *a.* reconcilable, capable of conciliation.
conciliábulo, *n.m.* (*coll.*) secret meeting.
conciliación, *n.f.* conciliation, reconcilement; affinity; favour, good will.
conciliador, -ra, *a.* conciliating. — *n.m.f.* conciliator.
conciliar, *a.* conciliar. — *n.m.* councillor, member of a council. — *v.t.* to reconcile; to conciliate; to harmonize; to win, gain; ***conciliar el sueño,*** to woo *or* induce sleep. — **conciliarse,** *v.r.* to win, gain; ***conciliarse el respeto de todos,*** to win everyone's respect.
conciliatorio, -ria, *a.* conciliatory; ***palabras conciliatorias,*** conciliatory words.
concilio, *n.m.* council; decrees of a council.
concino, -na, *a.* concinnous, harmonious (*language*).
concisión, *n.f.* conciseness, brevity.
conciso, -sa, *a.* concise, brief.
concitación, *n.f.* instigation, stirring up.
concitador, -ra, *a.* inciting, provoking. — *n.m.f.* instigator, inciter.
concitamiento, *n.m.* [CONCITACIÓN].
concitar, *v.t.* to excite, stir up.
concitativo, -va, *a.* inciting, stirring up.
conciudadanía, *n.f.* fellow-citizenship.
conciudadano, -na, *n.m.f.* fellow-citizen, fellow-countryman.
conclave, cónclave, *n.m.* conclave.
conclavista, *n.m.* domestic attending on cardinals in a conclave.
concluidor, -ra, *a.* concluding.
concluir [O], *v.t.* to conclude, terminate, close; to infer, deduce; (*fenc.*) to disarm. — *v.i.* to conclude, end; ***concluir con algo,*** to finish with sth. — **concluirse,** *v.r.* to finish, come to an end.
conclusión, *n.f.* conclusion; (*law*) winding-up; ***en conclusión,*** finally, in conclusion; ***llegó a la conclusión de que,*** he came to the conclusion that; ***sacar una conclusión,*** to draw a conclusion.
conclusivo, -va, *a.* conclusive, final, concluding.
concluso, -sa, *a.* concluded, closed, terminated; (*law*) ***dar por concluso,*** consider (as) closed.
concluyente, *a.* conclusive.
concofrade, *n.m.* confrère, fellow of the same brotherhood.

concoidal, *a.* (*geom.*) conchoidal.

concoide, *a.* (*geom.*) conchoid. — *n.f.* (*math.*) conchoid.

concoideo, -dea, *a.* conchoidal, shell-like.

concolega, *n.m.* fellow-collegian.

concología, *n.f.* conchology.

concomerse, *v.r.* (*coll.*) to smart, be vexed.

concomezón, concomimiento, concomio, *n.m.* (*coll.*) smart(ing), vexation.

concomitancia, *n.f.* concomitance.

concomitante, *a.* concomitant.

concomitar, *v.t.* to accompany.

concón, *n.m.* (*Chi.*) barn-owl; (*Chi.*) wind from land.

concordable, *a.* concordant, conformable, agreeable.

concordación, *n.f.* co-ordination, combination.

concordador, -ra, *a.* conciliating, pacifying. — *n.m.f.* conciliator, moderator, peace-maker.

concordancia, *n.f.* concord, agreement; (*pl.*) concordance, index.

concordante, *a.* concordant, agreeing.

concordar [4], *v.t., v.i.* to accord, agree, conform, make agree; ***la copia concuerda con el original,*** the copy conforms to the original; ***el adjetivo concuerda en género y número con el substantivo,*** the adjective agrees with the noun in gender and number.

concordato, -ta, *n.m.f.* concordat.

concordativo, -va, concorde, *a.* concordant, agreeing, tallying.

concordatorio, -ria, *a.* relating to a concordat.

concordia, *n.f.* concord, conformity; (*law*) agreement, settlement; linked finger-rings; ***de concordia,*** in agreement, by common consent.

concorpóreo, -rea, *a.* (*theol.*) concorporate, of the same body.

concreado, -da, *a.* created jointly.

concreción, *n.f.* concretion; specific nature.

concrecionar(se), *v.t.* (*v.r.*) to concrete, form concretions.

concrecionario, -ria, *a.* concretionary.

concrescencia, *n.f.* (*bot.*) concrescence.

concrescible, *a.* capable of concreting.

concretación, *n.f.,* **concretamiento,** *n.m.* concreteness, concretion.

concretador, -ra, *a.* concreting.

concretamente, *adv.* concretely, specifically; to give a case in point; to be exact; ***fuimos tarde, concretamente a las diez,*** we went late, at ten to be precise.

concretar, *v.t.* to make concrete, definite *or* specific; to pinpoint. — **concretarse,** *v.r.* to confine o.s. (***a,*** to).

concreto, -ta, *a.* concrete, definite, specific; ***en concreto*** [CONCRETAMENTE]. — *n.m.* concretion.

concubina, *n.f.* concubine.

concubinariamente, *adv.* in concubinage.

concubinario, *n.m.* concubinary.

concubinato, concubinismo, *n.m.* concubinage.

concúbito, *n.m.* coition.

concuerda, *adv.* ***por concuerda,*** certified accurate as per original (*said of a copy*).

conculcación, *n.f.* trampling; infringement, violation.

conculcador, -ra, *a.* infringing, trampling. — *n.m.f.* infringer, trampler.

conculcar [A], *v.t.* to trample under foot; to infringe, violate.

concuna, *n.f.* (*Col.*) wild pigeon.

concuñado, -da, *n.m.f.* brother-in-law, sister-in-law (*confined to persons married to two brothers* or *sisters*).

concupiscencia, *n.f.* concupiscence, lust.

concupiscente, *a.* concupiscent.

concupiscible, *a.* that awakens desire.

concurrencia, *n.f.* concurrence, coinciding; coming together; attendance, gathering; help, aid.

concurrente, *a.* concurrent, coinciding; coming together; attending, present. — *n.m.f.* one present; habitué.

concurrido, -da, *a.* crowded; well-attended; frequented, busy.

concurrir, *v.i.* to concur; to coincide, converge; to gather, come together; to go (to), attend; to help; to compete.

concursante, *n.m.f.* participant, competitor; applicant; one who puts in a tender.

concursar, *v.t.* (*law*) to declare insolvent. — *v.i.* to take part *or* compete (***en,*** in); to put in a tender.

concurso, *n.m.* confluence; attendance; assistance; contest, competition; call for tenders; ***concurso hípico,*** riding contest *or* display; ***fuera de concurso,*** hors concours; ***con el concurso de,*** with the assistance of; ***concurso de acreedores,*** meeting of creditors.

concusión, *n.f.* concussion; (*law*) extortion.

concusionario, *n.m.* extortioner.

concha (1), *n.f.* shell, sea-shell, carapace; tortoise-shell; oyster; (*arch.*) volute; shell-guard (*of dagger* or *cutlass*); shell-shaped covering (*of spike of Indian corn*); prompter's box; nether millstone; ancient copper coin; horse-shoe bay; very good cigar; ***Concha,*** popular contraction of ***Concepción*** (*girl's name*); (*anat.*) ***concha auditiva,*** concha; ***meterse en su concha,*** to go into one's shell; ***tener muchas conchas,*** to be very reserved and wary.

conchabanza, *n.f.* manner of making o.s. comfortable; (*coll.*) plotting, conspiracy.

conchabar, *v.t.* to unite, join; to mix (*wool*). — **conchabarse,** *v.r.* to gang up, plot together, conspire; to make o.s. snug.

conchabo, *n.m.* (*Hisp. Am.*) domestic servant's contract.

concháceo, -cea, *a.* having a bivalve shell. — *n.m.f.* lamellibranch molluscs.

conchado, -da, *a.* crustaceous, shelly, scaly.

conchal, *a.* high-class (*silk*).

conchífero, -ra, *a.* conchiferous, shell-bearing.

conchil, *n.m.* (*zool.*) murex.

concho, -cha (2), *a.* (*Ec.*) of the same colour as the lees of beer and chicha. — *n.m.* (*Hisp. Am.*) lees, dregs.

conchoidal, *a.* (*zool.*) conchoid.

conchoso, -sa, *a.* (*zool.*) scaly, shelly.

conchudo, -da, *a.* scaly, shelly; (*coll.*) knowing, wary, close, reserved.

conchuela, *n.f.* small shell; sea-bed covered with broken shells.

condado, *n.m.* earldom, dignity of an earl; county.

condal, *a.* of an earl *or* count; relating to an earldom; ***Ciudad Condal,*** Barcelona.

conde, *n.m.* earl, count; gipsy leader; (*prov.*) overseer.

condecente, *a.* fit, proper.

condecoración, *n.f.* decoration.

condecorar, *v.t.* to decorate.

condena, *n.f.* sentence (*of a condemned criminal*), term of imprisonment; penalty.

condenable, *a.* worthy of condemnation.

condenación, *n.f.* condemnation; damnation; (*coll.*) ***es una condenación,*** it is unbearable; he is a pest.

condenado, -da, *a.* damned; (*fam.*) blasted, cursed. — *n.m.f.* reprobate.

condenador, -ra, *a.* condemning, damning. — *n.m.f.* condemner, blamer, censurer.

condenar, *v.t.* to condemn; to damn, censure, blame; to stop, shut *or* nail up (*a door, window, passage etc.*); ***condenar a trabajos forzados,*** to sentence to penal servitude *or* hard labour. — **condenarse,** *v.r.* to be damned.

condenatorio, -ria, *a.* (*law*) condemnatory; damnatory.
condensabilidad, *n.f.* condensability.
condensable, *a.* condensable.
condensación, *n.f.* condensation.
condensador, -ra, *a.* condensing. — *n.m.* condenser; ***condensador de fuerzas,*** accumulator; ***condensador eléctrico,*** storage-battery; ***condensador de chorro,*** jet condenser; ***condensador de mezcla,*** mixing condenser; ***condensador de superficie,*** surface condenser.
condensamiento, *n.m.* [CONDENSACIÓN].
condensante, *a.* condensing.
condensar, *v.t.* to condense.
condensativo, -va, *a.* condensing.
condesa, *n.f.* countess.
condescendencia, *n.f.* acquiescence, willingness to comply, compliance.
condescender [2], *v.i.* to condescend, acquiesce, comply, yield; ***condescender a los ruegos,*** to yield to the supplications; ***condescender con la instancia,*** to comply with the request; ***condescender en reiterarse,*** to agree to repeat o.s.
condescendiente, *a.* compliant, acquiescent, willing to comply.
condesil (*iron.*) [CONDAL].
condesito, -ta, *n.m.f.* (dapper) young count *or* earl, (sweet) little countess.
condestable, *n.m.* high constable, commander-in-chief of the army; master gunner.
condestablía, *n.f.* constableship, dignity of high constable.
condición, *n.f.* condition, state; disposition; rank; circumstance; ***a condición de que*** or ***bajo la condición de que,*** on condition that; ***las condiciones son inmejorables,*** the conditions *or* terms are unbeatable; ***estar en buenas condiciones,*** to be in good condition; ***carne en malas condiciones,*** bad meat, meat that is not fresh; ***estar en condiciones de,*** to be in a position to; ***hombre de condición,*** man of rank; ***persona de humilde condición,*** person of humble birth; ***tener condición,*** to be of a sharp disposition.
condicional, *a.* conditional; (*law*) ***libertad condicional,*** parole.
condicionar, *v.t.* to condition. — *v.i.* to agree, fit.
condignidad, *n.f.* suitability.
condigno, -na, *a.* condign, suitable, appropriate.
condileo, -lea, condiloideo, -dea, *a.* (*anat.*) condylar, condyloid.
cóndilo, *n.m.* (*anat.*) condyle.
condimentador, -ra, *a.* seasoning. — *n.m.f.* seasoner.
condimentar, *v.t.* to season.
condimenticio, -cia, *a.* seasoning.
condimento, *n.m.* condiment, seasoning.
condiscípulo, -la, *n.m.f.* fellow-scholar, fellow-student, schoolfellow.
condolecerse [CONDOLERSE].
condolencia, *n.f.* condolence.
condolerse [5], *v.r.* to condole; ***condolerse de,*** to sympathize with, be sorry for.
condominio, *n.m.* condominium, joint-ownership.
condómino, *n.m.f.* condominus, joint-owner.
condonación, *n.f.* condonation, pardoning.
condonante, *a.* condoning, forgiving, remitting.
condonar, *v.t.* to pardon, forgive, condone.
condonatorio, -ria, *a.* (*law*) condoning, remitting (*sentence*). — joint-donatory.
cóndor, *n.m.* (*orn.*) condor; (*Chi., Ec.*) gold coin.
condotiero, *n.m.* condottiere.
cóndrico, -ca, *a.* relating to cartilage.
condrila, *n.f.* common gum-succory.
condrín, *n.m.* (*Philip.*) weight for precious metals (0·3768 *grammes*).

conducción, *n.f.* conveyance, transportation, cartage; piping; leading, guiding, bringing; contract at a stipulated rate; conduction (*of liquids*); driving (*of vehicles*).
conducencia [CONDUCCIÓN].
conducente, *a.* conducive, leading.
conducir [15], *v.t., v.i.* to conduct, guide; to convey; to drive (*a vehicle*); to contract at a fixed rate *or* salary; ***conducir en carreta,*** to transport in a cart; ***conducir por mar,*** to convey by sea. — **conducirse,** *v.r.* to behave.
conducta, *n.f.* conduct, behaviour; transport (*of currency* or *bullion*); currency *or* bullion transported; handling; contract with a doctor to attend the sick of a given district; doctor's remuneration for this work; new recruits conducted to the regiments; stipulation, agreement; ***mejorar de conducta,*** to change *or* mend one's ways.
conductero, *n.m.* convoy leader.
conductibilidad, *n.f.* conductibility.
conductible, *a.* conveyable, conductible.
conductividad, *n.f.* conveying power, conductivity.
conductivo, -va, *a.* leading, conductive, conveying *or* transporting.
conducto, *n.m.* conduit; duct; channel; canal; ***por conducto de,*** through; ***por (los) conductos oficiales,*** through (the) official channels.
conductor, -ra, *a.* conducting, guiding. — *n.m.f.* leader, guide; driver (*of vehicle*); (*phys.*) conductor, conveyer.
condueño, *n.m.f.* joint-owner.
conduerma, *n.f.* (*Ven.*) drowsiness, heaviness.
condumio, *n.m.* (*coll.*) food, grub.
conduplicación, *n.f.* reduplication.
conduplicado, -da, conduplicativo, -va, *a.* conduplicate.
condutal, *n.m.* spout (*of roof-gutter*).
conectador, *n.m.* connecter (*contact-plug*).
conectar, *v.t.* (*mech.*) to connect, couple. — *v.i.* (*radio*) to go over; ***conectamos con Barcelona,*** we are going over to Barcelona.
coneja, *n.f.* [CONEJO].
conejal, conejar, *n.m.* rabbit warren.
conejear, *v.t.* to dodge. — *v.i.* to crouch, hide; to cower.
conejero, -ra, *a.* rabbit-hunting (*dog*). — *n.m.f.* breeder and vendor of rabbits. — *n.f.* rabbit hole, burrow; warren; (*coll.*) den, dive.
conejillo, *n.m.* little rabbit; ***conejillo de Indias,*** guinea-pig.
conejito, -ta, *n.m.f.* young, small *or* baby rabbit.
conejo, -ja, *n.m.f.* rabbit; ***conejo albar,*** white rabbit. — *n.f.* female rabbit, doe; ***es una coneja,*** she breeds like a rabbit, she's always having children.
conejuno, -na, *a.* relating, similar to the rabbit. — *n.f.* rabbit down *or* fur.
cóneo, -nea, *a.* conic.
conexidades, *n.f.pl.* adjuncts, appurtenances.
conexión, *n.f.* connection.
conexionar, *v.t.* to connect; to put in touch.
conexivo, -va, *a.* connective.
conexo, -xa, *a.* connected; (*law*) united, linked.
confabulación, *n.f.* confabulation; conspiracy, plot, scheming.
confabulador, -ra, *n.m.f.* schemer, plotter; story teller.
confabular(se), *v.i.* (*v.r.*) to confabulate, plot, scheme.
confarreación, *n.f.* confarreation.
confección, *n.f.* confection, making (up), tailoring; (*pharm.*) preparation; ***traje de confección,*** ready-made suit.
confeccionador, -ra, *a.* confectioning. — *n.m.f.* manufacturer (*of wearing apparel* or *handiwork*).

confeccionar, *v.t.* to make, put together; to prepare, make up (*clothes, prescriptions etc.*).
confederación, *n.f.* confederation, confederacy.
confederado, -da, *a.* confederate, confederated. — *n.m.f.* confederate.
confederar, *v.t.* to confederate. — **confederarse,** *v.r.* to combine *or* join in confederation (**con,** with).
confederativo, -va, *a.* confederative.
conferencia, *n.f.* conference; lecture; (trunk) call.
conferenciar, *v.i.* to confer; to lecture.
conferenciante, *n.m.f.* lecturer.
conferimiento, *n.m.* conferment.
conferir [6], *v.t.* to confer, bestow; to compare. — *v.i.* to confer.
confesa, *n.f.* [CONFESO].
confesable, *a.* avowable.
confesado, -da, *n.m.f.* (*coll.*) confessant, penitent.
confesante, *a.* confessing; (*law*) declaratory. — *n.m.* (*obs.*) penitent, confessant.
confesar(se) [I], *v.t., v.i.* (*v.r.*) to confess; to hear *or* make confession.
confesión, *n.f.* confession.
confesional, *a.* denominational; confessional.
confes(i)onario, *n.m.* confessional; treatise with rules for confession.
confesionista, *n.m.f.* confessionist, Lutheran.
confeso, -sa, *a.* (*law*) confessed; converted (*Jew*). — *n.m.* lay brother. — *n.f.* widow become a nun.
confesor, *n.m.* confessor.
confesorio, -ria, *a.* (*law*) appertaining to avowry.
confeti, *n.m.* confetti.
confiable, *a.* trustworthy, reliable.
confiado, -da, *a.* confident; unwary, trusting, unsuspicious.
confiador, *n.m.* (*law*) joint surety.
confianza, *n.f.* confidence, trust, reliance; reliability; familiarity, informality, liberty; ***persona de confianza,*** reliable *or* trustworthy person; ***en confianza,*** in confidence, confidentially; ***tiene mucha confianza en sí mismo,*** he is very self-confident, self-assured; ***se toma muchas confianzas,*** he takes too many liberties; ***hay confianza,*** there's no need for formality, we're all friends here.
confianzudo, -da, *a.* over-familiar, given to taking (too many) liberties.
confiar [L], *v.t.* to confide, entrust. — *v.i.* to trust, rely; ***confío en que llegue pronto,*** I trust he will arrive soon; I am relying on his arriving soon. — **confiarse,** *v.r.* to be trusting; to confide; ***no te confíes,*** don't bank on it, don't be too sure; ***se confió a su tío,*** he confided in his uncle.
confidencia, *n.f.* confidence; secret.
confidencial, *a.* confidential.
confidente, *a.* faithful, sure, trusty. — *n.m.f.* confidant, confidante; secret agent, spy. — *n.m.* sofa for two, tête-à-tête.
configuración, *n.f.* configuration.
configurar, *v.t.* to configure, form.
confín, *a.* [CONFINANTE]. — *n.m.* limit, boundary, confine, border.
confinación, *n.f.,* **confinamiento,** *n.m.* confining, confinement; banishing, exiling.
confinante, *a.* bordering.
confinar, *v.t.* to banish, exile; to confine. — *v.i.* to border (**con,** on).
confingir [E], *v.t.* (*pharm.*) to mix into one mass.
confirmación, *n.f.* confirmation.
confirmado, -da, *n.m.f.* confirmee.
confirmador, -ra, *a.* confirming. — *n.m.f.* confirmer.
confirmando, -da, *n.m.f.* confirmee.
confirmante, *a.* confirming. — *n.m.f.* confirmer.
confirmar, *v.t.* to confirm. — **confirmarse,** *v.r.* to be confirmed; ***confirmarse en su dictamen,*** to be confirmed, strengthened in one's opinion *or* judgment.
confirmativo, -va, confirmatorio, -ria, *a.* confirmatory.
confiscación, *n.f.* confiscation, forfeiture.
confiscar [A], *v.t.* to confiscate.
confitado, -da, *a.* hopeful, full of expectation.
confitar, *v.t.* to candy; to sweeten.
confite, *n.m.* sweetmeat; confectionery; ***morder en un confite,*** to be hand in glove, intimate.
confitente, *a.* confessed; penitent.
confitera, *n.f.* [CONFITERO].
confitería, *n.f.* confectioner's shop, sweet-shop, confectionery.
confitero, -ra, *n.m.f.* confectioner. — *n.m.* tray for sweetmeats. — *n.f.* jar *or* box for sweetmeats.
confitico, confitillo, confitito, *n.m.* ornamented coverlet.
confitura, *n.f.* candied fruit, preserve.
confiturería, *n.f.* fruit preserving.
confiturero, -ra, *n.m.f.* fruit preserver.
conflagración, *n.f.* conflagration.
conflagrar, *v.t.* to set on fire.
conflátil, *a.* fusible.
conflictividad, *n.f.* (essential) element of conflict *or* strife, controversial nature.
conflictivo, -va, *a.* of conflict *or* strife, controversial.
conflicto, *n.m.* conflict.
confluencia, *n.f.* confluence, conflux.
confluente, *a.* confluent. — *n.m.* confluence (*of rivers*).
confluir [O], *v.i.* to join, meet, come together.
conformación, *n.f.* conformation.
conformador, *n.m.* shaper, hat-block.
conformar, *v.t.* to make conform. — *v.i.* to conform, fit. — **conformarse,** *v.r.* to resign o.s.; ***conformarse con la situación,*** to resign o.s. to the situation.
conforme, *a.* agreeing, in agreement; ***estamos conformes,*** we are agreed. — *adv.* as; ***conforme a,*** according to; ***conforme con,*** complying with.
conformidad, *n.f.* conformity, conformance, agreement; compliance; resignation; shape; ***de*** or ***en conformidad con,*** in accordance with.
conformismo, *n.m.* docile conformity.
conformista, *n.m.f.* conformist.
confortable, *a.* comfortable.
confortación, *n.f.* comfort, consolation.
confortador, -ra, *a.* comforting. — *n.m.f.* comforter, consoler, strengthener.
confortamiento, *n.m.* comfort, consolation.
confortante, *a., n.m.f.* [CONFORTADOR]. — *n.m.* mitten.
confortar, *v.t.* to comfort, console, cheer.
confortativo, -va, *a.* comforting, strengthening, cheering. — *n.m.* cordial; solace.
conforte, *n.m.* comfort, solace.
confracción, *n.f.* breaking.
confraguación, *n.f.* alloying, fusing (*metals*).
confraguar [H], *v.t.* [FRAGUAR].
confraternidad, *n.f.* confraternity, brotherhood.
confraternizar [C], *v.i.* to fraternize.
confricación, *n.f.* friction.
confricar, *v.t.* to rub.
confrontación, *n.f.* confrontation; comparison, comparing; natural affinity.
confrontante, *a.* confronting.
confrontar, *v.t.* to confront, collate, compare; ***confrontar un texto con otro,*** to compare one text with another. — *v.i.* to border (upon). — **confrontar(se),** *v.i.* (*v.r.*) to be opposite, stand facing one another; (*fig.*) to agree in sentiments and opinion.
confucianismo, *n.m.* Confucianism.

confuciano, -na, confucionista, *a.*, *n.m.f.* Confucian.
confulgencia, *n.f.* refulgence.
confundible, *a.* that can be confused, indistinguishable.
confundimiento, *n.m.* confusion; perplexity.
confundir, *v.t.* to confuse, mistake, mix up; to confound, throw into confusion, bewilder, perplex; to defeat, confute; to humiliate, embarrass; ***confundir una cosa con otra,*** to mistake one thing for another. — **confundirse,** *v.r.* to make a mistake, go wrong; ***me he confundido por completo,*** I've made a complete mistake.
confusión, *n.f.* confusion, tumult; confusedness, muddle; bewilderment; embarrassment.
confusionismo, *n.m.* (deliberate) creation of confusion, (deliberate) clouding of issues.
confuso, -sa, *a.* confused; muddled, vague; bewildered; embarrassed; ***en confuso,*** confusedly.
confutación, *n.f.* confutation, disproof, refutation.
confutador, -ra, *a.* confuting, refutatory. — *n.m.f.* refuter.
confutar, *v.t.* to confute, disprove.
confutatorio, -ria, *a.* [CONFUTADOR].
conga, *n.f.* conga (*music, dance*).
congelación, *n.f.* freezing; congealing; ***congelación de salarios,*** wage freeze.
congelador, *a.*, *n.m.* freezing; freezer.
congelamiento, *n.m.* freezing; congealing.
congelante, *a.* freezing; congealing.
congelar(se), *v.t.* (*v.r.*) to freeze; to congeal.
congénere, *a.* congeneric, kindred. — *n.m.f.* kindred person *or* thing.
congenial, *a.* akin, like.
congenialidad, *n.f.* affinity.
congeniar, *v.i.* to get on well (**con,** with).
congénito, -ta, *a.* congenital, connate.
congerie, *n.f.* congeries, heap, mass.
congestibilidad, *n.f.* tendency to become congested.
congestible, congestionable, *a.* liable to congestion.
congestión, *n.f.* congestion.
congestional, *a.* (*med.*) congestive.
congestionar, *v.t.* (*med.*) to congest. — **congestionarse,** *v.r.* to get congested *or* flushed.
congestivo, -va, *a.* (*med.*) congestive.
conglobación, *n.f.* conglobation; (*fig.*) mixture, union; (*rhet.*) accumulation of proofs.
conglobar, *v.t.* to conglobate, heap together.
conglomeración, *n.f.* conglomeration, accumulation.
conglomerado, *n.m.* conglomerate.
conglomerar, *v.t.* to conglomerate.
conglutinación, *n.f.* conglutination.
conglutinante, *a.*, *n.m.* conglutinant.
conglutinar, *v.t.* to conglutinate, cement, adhere.
conglutinativo, -va, *a.*, *n.m.* conglutinative.
conglutinoso, -sa, *a.* glutinous.
Congo, *n.m.* Congo.
congo, *n.m.* (*Mex., Cub.*) hog's hind leg; (*Hond.*) congo fish; (*C.R., E.S.*) howling monkey.
congoja, *n.f.* agony, affliction, grief; anguish, anxiety of mind.
congojar [ACONGOJAR].
congojoso, -sa, *a.* anguished.
congoleño, -ña, congolés, -lesa, *a.*, *n.m.f.* Congolese.
congolona, *n.f.* (*C.R.*) wild chicken.
congorocho, *n.m.* (*Ven.*) centipede.
congosto, *n.m.* canyon, gorge.
congraciador, -ra, *a.* ingratiating.
congraciamiento, *n.m.* ingratiation.
congraciarse, *v.r.* to ingratiate o.s.; ***congraciarse con alguien,*** to get into s.o.'s good books.
congratulación, *n.f.* congratulation, satisfaction, delight.
congratulador, -ra, *a.* congratulating, satisfying, delighting.
congratular, *v.t.* to congratulate, compliment. — **congratularse,** *v.r.* to be delighted, rejoice; ***me congratulo del (buen) éxito de la empresa,*** I am delighted at the success of the undertaking.
congratulatorio, -ria, *a.* congratulatory.
congregación, *n.f.* congregation; assembly; ***congregación de los fieles,*** Catholic *or* universal church.
congregacionalismo, *n.m.* Congregationalism.
congregacionalista, *a.*, *n.m.f.* Congregationalist.
congregante, -ta, *n.m.f.* congregant; member of a religious body.
congregar(se), [B], *v.t.* (*v.r.*) to assemble, meet, congregate, gather.
congresista, *n.m.f.* member of a congress *or* conference.
congreso, *n.m.* congress; conference; assembly; intercourse.
congrio, *n.m.* conger eel.
congruencia, *n.f.* congruence, congruity; (*coll.*) circumstance.
congruente, *a.* congruent, congruous; fitting, suitable.
congruísmo, *n.m.* (*theol.*) congruism.
congruísta, *n.m.f.* (*theol.*) congruist.
congruo, -rua, *a.* congruous; apt, fit, suitable. — *n.f.* income requisite for a priest; corresponding share.
conicidad, *n.f.* (*geom.*) conicalness.
conicina, conina, *n.f.* (*chem.*) conine.
cónico, -ca, *a.* conical, conic, cone-shaped.
conífero, -ra, *a.* coniferous. — *n.f.* conifer.
coniforme, *a.* coniform, conical, cone-shaped.
conio, *n.m.* (*bot.*) conium.
conirrostro, -ra, *a.* (*orn.*) having a conical beak.
conivalvo, -va, *a.* (*zool.*) having a conical shell.
coniza, *n.f.* great flea-bane.
conjetura, *n.f.* conjecture, surmise, guess.
conjeturable, *a.* conjecturable.
conjeturador, -ra, *a.* conjecturing, guessing.
conjetural, *a.* conjectural.
conjeturar, *v.t.*, *v.i.* to conjecture, surmise, guess.
conjuez, *n.m.* co-judge.
conjugable, *a.* that may be conjugated.
conjugación, *n.f.* conjugation.
conjugador, -ra, *a.* conjugating. — *n.m.f.* conjugate.
conjugar [B], *v.t.* to conjugate.
conjunción, *n.f.* conjunction; union.
conjuntivitis, *n.f.* conjunctivitis.
conjuntivo, -va, *a.* conjunctive, connective.
conjunto, -ta, *a.* conjunct, joint. — *n.m.* whole; ensemble; twin-set; chorus; side, team; ***en (su) conjunto,*** as a whole, all together.
conjura, conjuración, *n.f.* conspiracy, plot.
conjurado, -da, *n.m.f.* conspirator.
conjurador, *n.m.* conjuror; exorcist; conspirator.
conjuramentar, *v.t.* to conjure, bind by oath, swear in.
conjurante, *a.* conjuring; conspiring. — *n.m.f.* conjuror; conspirator.
conjurar, *v.t.*, *v.i.* to bind by oath. — *v.t.* to entreat, implore; (*fig.*) to avert, ward off. — *v.i.* to conspire, plot. — **conjurarse,** *v.r.* to plot, conspire together.
conjuro, *n.m.* conjuration; exorcism; incantation; entreaty.
conllevador, -ra, *a.* bearing, enduring; helping to bear *or* endure.
conllevar, *v.t.* to bear, suffer, endure.
conmemorable, *a.* commemorable.

conmemoración, *n.f.* remembrance, commemoration.
conmemorador, -ra, conmemorante, *a.* commemorating. — *n.m.f.* commemorator.
conmemorar, *v.t.* to commemorate.
conmemorativo, -va, *a.* commemorative.
conmemoratorio, -ria, *a.* commemorative.
conmensal [COMENSAL].
conmensalía [COMENSALÍA].
conmensurabilidad, *n.f.* commensurability.
conmensurable *a.* commensurable.
conmensuración, *n.f.* commensuration.
conmensurar, *v.t.* to measure equally, in proportion.
conmensurativo, -va, *a.* commensurating.
conmigo, *pron.* with me, with myself.
conmilitón, *n.m.* comrade; fellow-soldier.
conminación, *n.f.* commination, threat.
conminador, -ra, *a.* threatening.
conminar, *v.t.* to threaten (**con,** with); (*law*) to order.
conminativo, -va, *a.* threatening; compulsory.
conminatorio, -ria, *a.* comminatory, threatening. — *n.f.* threatening order.
conmiseración, *n.f.* commiseration, pity, compassion, sympathy.
conmistión, conmistura, conmixtión, *n.f.* commixion, commixture.
conmisto, -ta, conmixto, -ta, *a.* mixed, mingled.
conmoción, *n.f.* commotion, stir; ***conmoción cerebral,*** concussion.
conmonitorio, *n.m.* written narration of an event; (*law*) reminder to subordinate judge.
conmovedor, -ra, *a.* moving, touching.
conmover [5], *v.t.* to disturb; to move, touch. — **conmoverse,** *v.r.* to be moved; ***se conmovió mucho por*** or ***ante la desgracia de su amigo,*** he was deeply moved by his friend's misfortune.
conmunitario, -ria, *a.* [COMUNITARIO].
conmutabilidad, *n.f.* commutability.
conmutable, *a.* commutable.
conmutación, *n.f.* commutation, exchange.
conmutador, -ra, *a.* commutating. — *n.m.* (*elec.*) commutator; switch.
conmutar, *v.t.* to commute, exchange; ***conmutar una cosa con*** or ***por otra,*** to exchange one thing for another; ***conmutar una pena en otra,*** to commute one penalty for another.
conmutatriz, *n.f.* (*elec.*) current converter.
connato, -ta, *a.* (*bot.*) connate.
connatural, *a.* connatural, inborn.
connaturalidad, *n.f.* inherency.
connaturalización, *n.f.* naturalization.
connaturalizarse [C], *v.r.* to accustom o.s., become inured *or* acclimatized.
connivencia, *n.f.* connivance.
connivente, *a.* conniving.
connotación, *n.f.* connotation; distant relationship.
connotado, *n.m.* distant relationship.
connotante, *a.* connoting.
connotar, *v.t.* to connote; to imply.
connotativo, -va, *a.* (*gram.*) connotative.
connovicio, -cia, *n.m.f.* (*eccles.*) fellow-novice.
connubial, *a.* connubial, matrimonial.
connubio, *n.m.* matrimony, marriage, wedlock.
connumerar, *v.t.* to enumerate, include in a number.
cono, *n.m.* cone; hopper.
conocedor, -ra, *a.*, *n.m.f.* (one) well-acquainted *or* knowledgeable (**de,** with *or* about); connoisseur, expert, judge. — *n.m.* (*prov.*) chief herdsman.
conocencia, *n.f.* (*law*) confession.
conocer [9], *v.t.* to know, get to know, be *or* become acquainted with, make the acquaintance of, meet; to recognize; to experience; to perceive, realize; ***conocer de vista,*** to know by sight; ***le conocí en Madrid,*** I met him, made his acquaintance in Madrid; ***dar a conocer,*** to make known; ***darse a conocer,*** to make o.s. known; ***quien no te conozca, que te compre,*** once bitten, twice shy, you won't catch me again. — *v.i.* to try (*a case in law*); to be versed (*in a subject*); ***conocer de una causa, de un asunto,*** to try a case, be versed in a matter.
conocible, *a.* cognoscible, cognizable, knowable.
conocido, -da, *a.* well-known. — *n.m.f.* acquaintance.
conocimiento, *n.m.* knowledge; comprehension, understanding, cognition, notice, experience; consciousness; acquaintance; (*com.*) note of hand; (*law*) cognizance; (*com.*) ***conocimiento de embarque,*** bill of lading; receipt, acknowledgment; ***obrar con conocimiento de causa,*** to act with (full) knowledge of the facts; ***lo ha puesto en conocimiento del alcalde,*** he has notified the mayor of it; ***ha venido en conocimiento del decano,*** it has come to the dean's notice; ***perder el conocimiento,*** to lose consciousness; (*pl.* **conocimientos**) knowledge, learning.
conopeo, *n.m.* canopy.
conopial, *a.* (*arch.*) relating to a canopy; ***arco conopial,*** ogee arch.
conque, *conj.* so. — *n.m.* (*coll.*) condition; ***conqué,*** means; (*coll.*) ***no tener el conqué,*** not to have the wherewithal.
conquibus, *n.m.* (*coll.*) cash, wherewithal.
conquiforme, *a.* conchiform, shell-shaped.
conquilífero, -ra, *a.* [CONCHÍFERO].
conquiliología, *n.f.* conchology.
conquiliológico, -ca, *a.* conchological.
conquiliólogo, -ga, *n.m.f.* conchologist.
conquista, *n.f.* conquest; gain; achievement.
conquistable, *a.* conquerable; attainable.
conquistador, -ra, *a.* conquering. — *n.m.f.* conqueror, conquistador; (*coll.*) lady-killer.
conquistar, *v.t.* to conquer, win (over).
conrear, *v.t.* to grease (*wool*); to hoe; to treat, apply a particular process to (*land, cloth etc.*).
conregnante, *a.* jointly reigning.
conreinar, *v.i.* to reign jointly.
conreo, *n.m.* application of particular process (*to land etc.*).
consabido, -da, *a.* well-known, time-honoured; hackneyed, much abused.
consabidor, -ra, *n.m.f.* one possessing knowledge jointly with others.
consagrable, *a.* consecratable.
consagración, *n.f.* consecration, dedication.
consagrado, -da, *a.* consecrate(d); sacred; time-honoured; ***una frase consagrada,*** a stock phrase.
consagrante, *a.* consecrating, consecrative. — *n.m.* consecrator, officiant.
consagrar, *v.t.* to consecrate, hallow, make sacred; to devote; to dedicate; (*fig.*) to make (*word, phrase*) accepted; ***consagrarse al estudio,*** to devote *or* dedicate o.s. to study.
consanguíneo, -nea, *a.* consanguineous, cognate, kindred. — *n.m.f.* kin, blood relation; half-brother *or* half-sister by the same father.
consanguinidad, *n.f.* consanguinity.
consciente, *a.* conscious, aware.
conscripción, *n.f.* (*mil.*) conscription.
consectario, *a.* next; belonging to the same sect. — *n.m.f.* co-religionist. — *n.m.* corollary.
consecución, *n.f.* attainment, obtaining, achievement.
consecuencia, *n.f.* consequence; consistency; inference; ***en consecuencia,*** consequently, therefore; ***guardar consecuencia,*** to be consistent; ***sacar en consecuencia,*** to draw as a

conclusion; ***tener*** or ***traer consecuencias,*** to entail consequences; (*coll.*) ***traer a consecuencia,*** to bring in *or* up; ***traer en consecuencia,*** to adduce.

consecuencial, *a.* consequential, resulting.

consecuente, *a.* consequent; consistent. — *n.m.* consequence, (*math.*) consequent.

consecutivo, -va, *a.* consecutive.

conseguimiento, *n.m.* attainment, obtaining.

conseguir [8G], *v.t.* to get, obtain, attain; to achieve; ***conseguir hacer algo,*** to succeed in doing sth.; ***por fin consiguió que lo hiciera,*** he finally managed to get him to do it.

conseja, *n.f.* fable, fairy-tale; (old wives') tale; illegal assembly; ***el lobo está en la conseja,*** there's a spy in the camp.

consejero, -ra, *a.* advisory. — *n.m.* counsellor, adviser; member of board of directors, executive. — *n.f.* female adviser.

consejo, *n.m.* counsel, advice; council; advisory board, consulting body; ***un consejo,*** a piece of advice; (*law*) ***consejo de familia,*** family council; ***consejo de guerra,*** court-martial; council of war; ***consejo de ministros,*** cabinet council; ***entrar en consejo,*** to begin consultation; ***presidente del consejo de ministros,*** Prime Minister; ***tomar consejo de,*** to consult; (*pl.*) advice.

consenso, *n.m.* consensus, consent, assent.

consentido, -da, *a.* spoiled (*child*); acquiescent (*cuckold*). — *n.m.* cuckold.

consentidor, -ra, *a.* consenting, acquiescing, acquiescent. — *n.m.f.* one who consents *or* acquiesces.

consentimiento, *n.m.* consent, acquiescence; pampering, coddling.

consentir [6], *v.t.* to allow, permit, tolerate; to allow of, admit, suffer; to coddle, pamper, spoil; ***le consienten todos los caprichos,*** they give in to all his whims, let him have every whim; ***esto no se puede consentir,*** this cannot be tolerated *or* endured; ***está muy consentido,*** he's terribly spoiled. — *v.i.* to consent, agree, acquiesce; to begin to give (way), come loose, weaken; ***por fin consintió en hacerlo,*** he finally agreed to do it.

conserje, *n.m.* keeper, warden; concierge, caretaker, janitor; (hotel) porter.

conserjería, *n.f.* janitorship, wardenship; warden's dwelling, janitor's office; caretaker's lodge *or* quarters; porter's lodge.

conserva, *n.f.* preserve; preserved food; tinned food; convoy; ***conservas alimenticias,*** tinned foods; ***navegar en conserva,*** to sail in convoy.

conservable, *a.* preservable.

conservación, *n.f.* preservation.

conservador, *a.* preserving. — *n.m.f.* preserver; (*polit.*) conservative. — *n.m.* conservator; (*eccles.*) ***juez conservador,*** person appointed to defend the rights of a community; ***conservador de museo,*** curator of a museum.

conservaduría, *n.f.* conservatorship, curatorship.

conservadurismo, *n.m.* conservatism.

conservante, *a.* preserving.

conservar, *v.t.* to conserve, preserve, maintain; to keep, hold on to; ***consérvalo,*** keep it, hold on to it; ***don José se conserva (muy) bien,*** Don José wears well; ***está (muy) bien conservado,*** he looks young for his age.

conservativo, -va, *a.* conserving, preservative.

conservatoría, *n.f.* place *or* office of a ***juez conservador***; privilege *or* exemption issued by him.

conservatorio, -ria, *a.* conserving, preservative. — *n.m.* conservatoire.

conservería, *n.f.* art of making *or* canning preserve; cannery, place where canned goods are made *or* sold.

conservero, -ra, *a.* preparer of conserves.

considerable, *a.* considerable; substantial; large.

consideración, *n.f.* consideration; regard; importance; ***en consideración a,*** in consideration of, considering; ***tomar en consideración,*** to take into consideration *or* account; ***guardar (tener) consideraciones,*** to show considerateness; ***ser de consideración,*** to be considerable *or* of importance.

considerado, -da, *a.* considerate, thoughtful; esteemed, respected.

considerando, *n.m.* (*law*) whereas; ***considerando que,*** whereas.

considerante, *a.* considering.

considerar, *v.t.* to consider, think over; to judge; to regard, deem; to treat with consideration *or* respect; ***se considera innecesario,*** it is deemed unnecessary.

consiervo, *n.m.* fellow-slave.

consigna, *n.f.* password, watchword; motto; rules, regulations; left-luggage office, (*Am.*) check room.

consignación, *n.f.* consignation, consignment, shipment.

consignador, *n.m.* (*com.*) consignor.

consignar, *v.t.* to assign; to consign; to record, put on record; (*law*) to deposit in trust.

consignatario, *n.m.* (*law*) trustee, mortgagee; (*com.*) consignee.

consigo, *pers. pron.* with oneself, with himself, herself, themselves, yourself, yourselves; ***hablar consigo (mismo),*** to talk to oneself.

consiguiente, *a.* consequent, resulting. — *n.m.* (*log.*) consequent; ***por consiguiente,*** therefore, consequently.

consiliario, -ria, *n.m.f.* adviser; counsellor.

consintiente, *a.* consenting, agreeing.

consistencia, *n.f.* soundness, solidity, firmness, solidness.

consistente, *a.* firm, solid, sound.

consistir, *v.i.* to consist (*en,* in *or* of); ***la obra consiste en tres volúmenes,*** the work is made up of three volumes; ***el secreto consiste en hablar poco,*** the secret lies in not talking too much; ***todo consiste en firmar un papel,*** it's purely a matter of signing a piece of paper.

consistorial, *a.* consistorial; ***casa(s) consistorial(es),*** town hall, guild hall.

consistorialmente, *adv.* in *or* by consistory.

consistorio, *n.m.* (*eccles.*) consistory; town-hall; municipal council; ***consistorio divino,*** tribunal of God.

consocio, -cia, *n.m.f.* partner, associate.

consola, *n.f.* console-table, pier-table, console.

consolable, *a.* consolable, relievable.

consolación, *n.f.* consolation, comfort; forfeit (*cards*); ***premio de consolación,*** consolation prize.

consolador, -ra, *a.* consolatory, comforting. — *n.m.f.* consoler, comforter.

consolante, *a.* comforting, consoling, soothing.

consolar [4], *v.t.* to console, comfort; ***consolar a alguien en su dolor,*** to console s.o. in their sorrow; ***consolarse en Dios,*** to find consolation in God.

consolativo, -va, consolatorio, -ria, *a.* consolatory, comforting.

consólida, *n.f.* (*bot.*) comfrey; (*bot.*) ***consólida real,*** larkspur.

consolidable, *a.* that can be consolidated.

consolidación, *n.f.* consolidation.

consolidado, *n.m.* consolidated fund.

consolidar, *v.t.* to consolidate; to fund (*debts*).

consolidativo, -va, *a.* consolidating, consolidatory.

consonancia, *n.f.* consonance, harmony; rhyme; conformity, congruency; ***estar (ir) en consonancia con,*** to be in accord, accordance *or* keeping with.

consonante, *a.* consonant, concordant, consistent; rhyming. — *n.m.* rime, rhyme; (*mus.*) consonous *or* corresponding sound. — *n.f.* (*gram.*) consonant.

consonar [4], *v.i.* to harmonize; to rhyme; to agree, conform, fit.
cónsone, *a.* concordant; consonous. — *n.m.* chord.
cónsono, -na, *a.* consonous; consonant, harmonious.
consorcio, *n.m.* partnership; marital union; consortium.
consorte, *n.m.f.* consort; partner; (*pl.*) (*law*) accomplices, confederates; associates, joint-parties (*to a lawsuit*).
conspicuo, -cua, *a.* conspicuous, obvious; eminent, famous, distinguished.
conspiración, *n.f.* conspiracy, plot.
conspirador, -ra, *n.m.f.* conspirator, plotter.
conspirar, *v.i.* to conspire, plot; (*fig.*) to concur.
constancia, *n.f.* constancy, perseverance, steadiness; certainty; proof, written evidence, record; ***dejar constancia de una cosa,*** to leave sth. on record.
constante, *a.* constant, steady; known for certain; consisting (of); ***constante en la amistad,*** steadfast in friendship. — *n.f.* constant, constant value, constant feature.
constantinopolitano, -na, *a., n.m.f.* native of *or* pertaining to Constantinople.
constar, *v.i.* to be certain; to be on record; to be made up *or* composed (of); to scan (*verse*); ***me consta que lo hizo,*** I know for certain that he did it; ***y*** (***que***) ***conste que,*** let it be known that, I want it known that, for the record, mind you; ***consta en las actas,*** it is recorded in the minutes; ***hacer constar,*** to make known, put on record; ***la obra consta de cuatro tomos,*** the work is made up of *or* comprises four volumes.
constelación, *n.f.* constellation; climate.
consternación, *n.f.* consternation, panic, dismay.
consternar, *v.t.* to consternate, dismay. — **consternarse,** *v.i.* to be dismayed; ***se consternó ante esta noticia,*** he was dismayed by this news.
constipación, *n.f.* cold, chill.
constipado, *n.m.* cold, chill.
constipar, *v.t.* to give a cold to. — **constiparse,** *v.r.* to catch a cold.
constipativo, -va, *a.* constrictive.
constitución, *n.f.* constitution.
constitucional, *a.* constitutional. — *n.m.* constitutionalist.
constitucionalidad, *n.f.* constitutionality.
constitucionalismo, *n.m.* constitutionalism.
constituidor, -ra, *a.* constituting, establishing. — *n.m.f.* constitutor.
constituir [O], *v.t.* to constitute; to set up, establish; to make up; to represent; ***esto constituye el único peligro,*** this represents *or* is the only danger; ***constituirse en juez,*** to set o.s. up as a judge.
constitutivo, -va, *a.* constitutive. — *n.m.* constitutor.
constituyente, *a.* constituting, constituent. — *n.f.pl.* (**constituyentes**) ***Cortes constituyentes,*** Spanish Parliament.
constreñimiento, *n.m.* constraint, compulsion.
constreñir [8K], *v.t.* to constrain, compel, force; (*med.*) to constipate.
constricción, *n.f.* constriction.
constrictivo, -va, *a.* (*med.*) binding, astringent; constrictive, constringent.
constrictor, -ra, *a.* constrictive. — *n.m.* (*med.*) constrictor.
constringente, *a.* constringent.
construcción, *n.f.* construction, building; edifice, structure; ***construcción naval,*** shipbuilding.
constructor, -ra, *a.* constructing. — *n.m.f.* builder, constructor; ***constructor de buques,*** shipbuilder.
construir, *v.t.* to construct; to build; (*gram.*) to construe.
constuprador, *n.m.* corrupter, raper.
constuprar, *v.t.* to rape, corrupt.
consubstancial, *a.* consubstantial.
consuegrar, *v.i.* to become reciprocal fathers- *or* mothers-in-law.
consuegro, -ra, *n.m.f.* joint father-in-law, joint mother-in-law.
consuelda, *n.f.* (*bot.*) comfrey.
consuelo, *n.m.* consolation, comfort; joy; ***sin consuelo,*** disconsolately, inconsolably.
consueta, *n.m.* (*theat.*) prompter. — *n.f.* (*eccles., prov.*) almanac; (*pl.*) short prayers.
consuetudinal, consuetudinario, -ria, *a.* consuetudinary, customary, generally practised; (*eccles.*) habitually sinning; ***derecho consuetudinario,*** law of custom, common law.
cónsul, *n.m.* consul; ***cónsul general,*** consul-general.
consulado, *n.m.* consulate; consulship.
consular, *a.* consular.
consulta, *n.f.* consultation, consulting; (*med.*) practice; (*med.*) surgery; (professional) opinion; ***tengo que hacerte una consulta,*** I have to, must consult you (ask you) about sth.; (*med.*) ***horas de consulta,*** consulting hours.
consultación, *n.f.* consultation.
consultante, *a., n.m.* consulting, consultant; consulter.
consultar, *v.t., v.i.* to consult, consult about; to deliberate; ***le he consultado,*** I've consulted him; ***lo he consultado con él*** or ***se lo he consultado,*** I've consulted him (asked him) about it; ***consultar con la almohada,*** to sleep on it; ***consultar con el bolsillo,*** to consult one's pocket, see how one's funds are.
consultivo, -va, *a.* consultative, advisory.
consultor, -ra, *a.* advising, consulting. — *n.m.f.* consultant, consulter, consultee; consultor; adviser, counsel, counsellor.
consultorio, *n.m.* information bureau; consulting-room, surgery; readers' queries (*section in press*).
consumación, *n.f.* consummation, fulfilment; ***hasta la consumación de los siglos,*** to the end of time.
consumado, -da, *a.* consummate, perfect, accomplished; ***hecho consumado,*** fait accompli; ***ladrón consumado,*** consummate thief, past master at thievery.
consumador, -ra, *a.* consummating, consummative. — *n.m.f.* consummator.
consumar, *v.t.* to consummate, perfect, complete.
consumero, *n.m.* excise-officer, exciseman.
consumición, *n.f.* [CONSUMO]; item consumed; ***80 pts. por consumición,*** 80 pesetas per item *or* 80 pesetas minimum charge.
consumido, -da, *a.* thin, emaciated; worn out.
consumidor, -ra, *a.* consuming. — *n.m.f.* consumer.
consumir, *v.t.* to consume, use up; (*coll.*) to afflict, grieve; ***consumir el caudal,*** to run through one's fortune. — *v.t., v.i.* (*eccles.*) to communicate. — **consumirse,** *v.r.* to waste away; to wear out; to fret, pine, be grieved; ***consumirse a fuego lento,*** to burn away slowly; ***consumirse con la fiebre,*** to waste away through fever.
consumismo, *n.m.* consumerism, ethos of the consumer society, consumer society mentality.
consumista, *a.* (of the) consumer society.
consumo, *n.m.* consumption; (*pl.*) municipal excise-duty.
consunción, *n.f.* consumption, wasting away.
consuno, *adv.* ***de consuno,*** jointly, in accord.
consuntivo, -va, *a.* consuming, consumptive.
consunto, -ta, *a.* (*obs.*) used up, wasted away.
consustancial, *a.* consubstantial.
consustancialidad, *n.f.* consubstantiality.

contabilidad, *n.f.* book-keeping, accountancy.
contabilizar [C], *v.t.* to calculate, reckon, count up, tot up.
contable, *n.m.* accountant, book-keeper.
contactar, *v.t.* to contact, get in touch with.
contacto, *n.m.* contact, touch; ***póngase en contacto con él,*** get in touch with him.
contadero, -ra, *a.* countable, numerable. — *n.m.* turnstile.
contado, -da, *a.* scarce, rare; ***contadas personas,*** very few people; ***contadas veces,*** rarely; ***tiene los días contados,*** his days are numbered; ***al contado,*** cash down; ***de contado,*** immediately; ***por de contado,*** certainly, of course.
contador, -ra, *a.* counting. — *n.m.f.* book-keeper, accountant, auditor, cashier. — *n.m.* official receiver; counter, desk; comptometer; meter (*for gas etc.*); automatic counter; cash register.
contaduría, *n.f.* accountantship, accountancy; counting-house; auditorship; cashier's office; (*theat.*) box-office.
contagiar, *v.t.* to infect; to corrupt. — **contagiarse,** *v.r.* to become infected; ***se contagió de sus amigos,*** he was infected by his friends.
contagio, *n.m.* contagion, infectiousness, infection; corruption, perversion.
contagiosidad, *n.f.* contagiousness.
contagioso, -sa, *a.* contagious, catching; perverting.
contal, *n.m.* string of beads for counting.
contaminable, *a.* contaminable.
contaminación, *n.f.* contamination, pollution.
contaminador, -ra, *a.* contaminating, polluting.
contaminar, *v.t.* to contaminate, pollute, infect; to corrupt.
contante, *a.* ***dinero contante y sonante,*** ready money, cash.
contar [4], *v.t.* to count, reckon, number; to relate, tell; to charge, enter; ***contar con,*** to rely *or* count on; ***cuenta conmigo,*** count on me; ***cuenta con las simpatías de todo el mundo,*** he is liked by everyone; ***cuenta con su favor,*** he enjoys their favour; ***cuénteselo a su tía,*** tell that to the Marines.
contemperante, *a.* temperate, tempering, moderating.
contemperar, *v.t.* to temper, moderate.
contemplación, *n.f.* contemplation; (*coll.*) ***no andarse con contemplaciones,*** to make no bones about it, make no concessions, stand no nonsense, come straight to the point.
contemplador, -ra, *a.* contemplating, contemplative. — *n.m.f.* contemplator.
contemplar, *v.t.*, *v.i.* to contemplate; to pamper, humour, keep happy.
contemplativo, -va, *a.* contemplative, meditative; lenient.
contemporaneidad, *n.f.* contemporaneousness, contemporaneity.
contemporáneo, -nea, *a.* contemporaneous, contemporary. — *n.m.f.* contemporary.
contemporización, *n.f.*, **contemporizamiento,** *n.m.* temporization, compromising.
contemporizador, -ra, *a.* temporizing, compromising. — *n.m.f.* temporizer, compromiser.
contemporizar [C], *v.i.* to temporize, compromise.
contención, *n.f.* containing, holding; checking, restraining; contention, contest, (law) suit; ***muro de contención,*** containing wall.
contencioso, -sa, *a.* contentious; litigious; disputatious.
contendedor, *n.m.* contender, antagonist.
contender [2], *v.i.* to contend, fight, strive; to contest, conflict, debate, litigate; to discuss, argue, expostulate.
contendiente, *a.*, *n.m.f.* contending (party); disputant, litigant.
contendor, *n.m.* contender, antagonist.
contenedor, -ra, *a.* containing, holding. — *n.m.f.* holder, container, receptacle.
contenencia, *n.f.* suspension (*in flight of birds*); movement (*in Spanish dance*); (*obs. law*) ***contenencia a la demanda,*** demurer.
contener [33], *v.t.* to contain, comprise, hold, embrace; to restrain, curb, check, hold back; ***iba a contestar, pero se contuvo,*** he was going to answer, but he refrained *or* forebore.
contenido, -da, *a.* moderate, temperate. — *n.m.* contents.
conteniente, *a.* containing, comprising.
contenta, *n.f.* [CONTENTO].
contentadizo, -za, *a.* easy to please, easily pleased.
contentamiento, *n.m.* contentment, joy, satisfaction.
contentar, *v.t.* to content, please; (*com.*) to endorse; ***no se contenta con nada,*** he is pleased *or* satisfied with nothing; ***contentarse con su suerte,*** to be contented with one's lot.
contentible, *a.* contemptible.
contentivo, -va, *a.* containing, comprising; (*surg.*) covering, binding (*bandages*).
contento, -ta, *a.* content, contented; happy, glad. — *n.m.* contentment, joy, pleasure, satisfaction; (*law*) discharge, release (*of debt*); ***a contento,*** to one's satisfaction; ***no caber de contento,*** to be overjoyed. — *n.f.* welcome gift, present; certificate of good conduct; (*com.*) endorsement.
contera, *n.f.* chape (*of scabbard*); button *or* tip (*of the cascabel of a gun*); ferrule (*of an umbrella* or *walking-stick*); refrain (*of song*); end, completion; ***echar la contera,*** to finish, end, terminate; ***por contera,*** ultimately, finally.
contérmino, -na, *a.* contiguous, bordering.
conterráneo, -nea, *a.*, *n.m.f.* compatriot.
contertuliano, -na, contertulio, -lia, *n.m.f.* member of a group habitually gathered for conversation.
contestable, *a.* disputable, questionable.
contestación, *n.f.* answer, reply; contestation, dispute; (socio-political) protest, argument; (*law*) ***contestación a la demanda,*** plea; answer to the complaint; ***no tiene contestación,*** it's unanswerable *or* indisputable.
contestar, *v.t.*, *v.i.* to answer, reply; to confirm; to prove, attest; to plead to an action; to accord, agree; ***contestar (a) la pregunta,*** to answer the question.
contestatario, -ria, *a.* (of) (socio-political) protest; (*fam.*) bolshie.
conteste, *a.* (*law*) confirming the evidence of another witness. — *n.m.f.* confirmation witness.
contexto, *n.m.* contexture; context.
contextuar [M], *v.t.* to prove textually.
contextura, *n.f.* contexture; frame and structure (of the human body).
conticinio, *n.m.* dead of night.
contienda, *n.f.* contest, dispute, conflict, contention, strife, struggle, fight.
contignación, *n.f.* floor-boards; lath-work (*of ceiling*).
contigo, *pron.* with you; ***contigo pan y cebolla,*** anything will do as long as I am with you.
contigüidad, *n.f.* contiguity, proximity.
contiguo, -gua, *a.* contiguous, next, adjacent; ***contiguo al jardín,*** next to the garden.
continencia, *n.f.* continence; graceful bow in a dance; capacity, containing.
continental, *a.* continental.
continente, *a.* containing; continent. — *n.m.* container; continent, mainland; countenance, mien.
contingenica, *n.f.* contingency; possibility; hazard.
contingente, *a.* contingent, fortuitous, accidental. — *n.m.* contingent, quota, share; contingency.
contingible, *a.* that may happen, possible.

continuación, *n.f.* continuation, continuity, continuance; protraction, lengthening; ***a continuación (de),*** immediately afterwards (after); ***dijo a continuación que,*** he then went on to say that.

continuado, -da, *a.* continuous, sustained, steady.

continuador, -ra, *a.* continuing. — *n.m.f.* continuer, continuator.

continuar [M], *v.t., v.i.* to continue, go on, keep on; to remain, stay; ***continúe usted,*** go on; ***continuó hablando,*** he went on talking, continued to talk; ***continuó en su puesto,*** he remained at his post; ***continúa en Amberes,*** he is still in Antwerp; ***se continuará,*** to be continued.

continuidad, *n.f.* continuity; ***con solución de continuidad,*** discontinuously, with breaks *or* interruptions; ***sin solución de continuidad,*** continuously, without any break *or* interruption.

continuismo, *n.m.* (dogged) preservation of the status quo, commitment to the status quo.

continuo, -nua, *a.* continuous, continual; constant. — *n.m.* whole, composition of united parts; yeoman of the guard; ***a la continua, de continuo,*** continually, continuously.

contonearse, *v.r.* to strut, swagger.

contoneo, *n.m.* strutting, swaggering.

contorcerse [5D], *v.r.* to contort, writhe, twist.

contorción, *n.f.* contortion; twisting, writhing.

contornado, -da, *a.* (*her.*) distorted, turned towards the sinister side of the shield.

contornar, contornear, *v.t.* to contour, outline; to go *or* wind round (*a place*).

contorneado, -da, *a.* (*bot.*) convoluted.

contorneo, *n.m.* turning, winding; contouring, outlining.

contorno, *n.m.* contour, outline; (*pl.*) environs, neighbourhood; ***en contorno,*** round about.

contorsión, *n.f.* contortion, twist; grimace, wry motion, queer gesture.

contorsionista, *n.m.f.* contortionist.

contra, *n.m.* opposite, opposite sense; (*mus.*) organ-pedal; (*pl.*) organ-pipes forming lowest bass. — *n.f.* (*coll.*) snag; counter (*fencing*). — *prep.* against, contrary to, counter; ***contra viento y marea,*** in the teeth of all opposition; ***en contra de,*** against, in opposition to; ***ir en contra de,*** to run counter to; ***hacer*** or ***llevar la contra a,*** to go against, oppose, contradict; ***el pro y el contra,*** the pros and cons.

contraabertura, *n.f.* (*surg.*) counter-opening.

contraabrir [*p.p.* **contraabierto**], *v.t.* (*surg.*) to make a counter-opening in.

contraaletas, *n.f.pl.* (*naut.*) counter-fashion pieces.

contr(a)almirante, *n.m.* rear-admiral.

contraalmohadón, *n.m.* (*arch.*) voussoir on coussinet.

contraamantillos, *n.m.pl.* (*naut.*) preventer-lifts, counter-braces.

contraamura, *n.f.* (*naut.*) preventer-tack.

contraaproches, *n.m.pl.* (*fort.*) counter-approaches.

contraarmiños, *n.m.pl.* (*her.*) black field with white spots.

contraataguía, *n.f.* second *or* reinforcing coffer-dam.

contraataque, *n.m.* counter-attack; (*pl.*) counter-approaches.

contraaviso, *n.m.* counter-advice.

contrabajo, *n.m.* double-bass; bass (*voice and singer*).

contrabalancear, *v.t.* to counterbalance, counterpoise; (*fig.*) to compensate; ***las dos cosas se contrabalancean,*** the two things cancel each other out.

contrabalanceo, *n.m.* counterbalancing.

contrabalanza, *n.f.* counterbalance, counterpoise.

contrabanda, *n.f.* (*her.*) band sinister.

contrabandear, *v.i.* to smuggle.

contrabandista, *a.* smuggling. — *n.m.f.* smuggler, contrabandist.

contrabando, *n.m.* contraband, smuggling; smuggled goods; ***meter*** or ***pasar algo de contrabando,*** to smuggle sth. in; ***contrabando de guerra,*** contraband of war.

contrabarrado, -da, *a.* (*her.*) counter-barred shield.

contrabarrera, *n.f.* second row of seats in the inner barrier in a bull-ring.

contrabasa, *n.f.* pedestal.

contrabatería, *n.f.* (*mil.*) counter-battery.

contrabatir, *v.t.* to fire upon the enemy's batteries; to return the fire of.

contrabolina, *n.f.* (*naut.*) preventer-bowline.

contrabracear, *v.t.* (*naut.*) to counter-brace.

contrabranque, *n.m.* (*naut.*) stemson.

contrabraza, *n.f.* (*naut.*) preventer-brace.

contrabrazola, *n.f.* (*naut.*) coaming (*of a scuttle*).

contracaja, *n.f.* (*print.*) right-hand upper.

contracalcar [A], *v.t.* to trace the reversed impression of.

contracambiada, *n.f.* changing of the fore-foot by a horse.

contracambio, *n.m.* (*com.*) re-exchange; ***en contracambio,*** in exchange.

contracanal, *n.m.* counter-channel; branch canal.

contracandela, *n.f.* (*Cub.*) back-fire made to prevent the spread of a forest fire.

contracarrera, *n.f.* reinforcement to joist *or* girder.

contracarril, *n.m.* check-rail, guard-rail, safety-rail.

contracarta [CONTRAESCRITURA].

contracción, *n.f.* contraction; (*econ.*) recession; (*gram.*) synæresis.

contracebadera, *n.f.* (*naut*). sprit-topsail.

contracédula, *n.f.* counter-decree.

contracifra, *n.f.* cipher-key.

contraclave, *n.f.* (*arch.*) voussoir next to key-stone.

contracodaste, *n.m.* (*naut.*) inner stern-post.

contracorriente, *n.f.* countercurrent, reverse current; cross-current; (*fig.*) backwash; ***a contracorriente,*** against the current.

contracosta, *n.f.* coast opposite another.

contracostado, *n.m.* (*naut.*) sheathing.

contracruz, *n.f.* (*naut.*) spilling-line.

contractable, *a.* contractible.

contráctil, *a.* contractile, contractible.

contractilidad, *n.f.* contractility, contractibility.

contractivo, -va, *a.* contractive.

contracto, -ta, *a.* contracted; ***forma contracta,*** contracted form.

contractual, *a.* contractual.

contractura, *n.f.* contracture; contraction.

contracuartel, *n.m.* (*her.*) counter-quarter.

contracuartelado, -da, *a.* (*her.*) counter-quartered.

contracuerdas, *n.f.pl.* (*naut.*) outward deck-planks.

contracultural, *a.* anti-Establishment, alternative, underground.

contracurva, *n.f.* (*railw.*) reversed curved rail; ***curva y contracurva,*** double bend.

contrachapado, *n.m.* plywood.

contradancista, *n.m.f.* dancer of country-dance.

contradanza, *n.f.* quadrille, cotillon, cotillion.

contradecir [17], *v.t.* to contradict, gainsay.

contradenuncia, *n.f.* (*law*) counter-accusation.

contradicción, *n.f.* contradiction, gainsaying; ***espíritu de contradiccion,*** contrariness.

contradictor, -ra, *a.* contradictive, contradicting, conflicting. — *n.m.f.* contradictor.

contradictorio, -ria, *a.* contradictory, conflicting. — *n.f.* (*log.*) contradictory.

contradique, *n.m.* counterdike.

contradriza, *n.f.* (*naut.*) second halliard.

contradurmente, contradurmiente, *n.m.* (*naut.*) clamp.
contraedicto, *n.m.* counter-edict.
contraeje, *n.m.* countershaft.
contraemboscada, *n.f.* counter-ambush.
contraembozo, *n.m.* cloak-strap.
contraemergente, *a.* counter-salient.
contraendosar, *v.t.* to repass (*a bill of exchange*) to the first endorser.
contraendoso, *n.m.* repassing of a bill of exchange to the first endorser.
contraer(se), [34], *v.t.*, *v.i.* (*v.r.*) to contract; to limit, confine; ***contraer amistad con,*** to strike up a friendship with; ***contraer deudas,*** to incur debt; ***contraer una enfermedad,*** to contract *or* get a disease or illness; ***contraer matrimonio,*** to contract marriage.
contraescarpa, *n.f.* counterscarp.
contraescota, *n.f.* (*naut.*) preventer-sheet.
contraescotín, *n.m.* (*naut.*) preventer topsail-sheet.
contraescritura, *n.f.* (*law*) deed revoking a former one.
contraestay, *n.m.* (*naut.*) preventer-stay.
contrafacción, *n.f.* imitation, counterfeit.
contrafactor, *n.m.* counterfeiter.
contrafajado, -da, *a.* (*her.*) having the fillets opposed in colour *or* metal.
contrafallar, *v.t.* to trump another trump (*cards*).
contrafallo, *n.m.* act of trumping another trump.
contrafianza, *n.f.* indemnity-bond.
contrafigura, *n.f.* (*theat.*) double.
contrafilo, *n.m.* sharp back edge of sword near point.
contraflorado, -da, *a.* (*her.*) having flowers opposed in metal *or* colour.
contrafoque, *n.m.* fore-top staysail.
contraforjar, *v.t.* to beat (*iron*) on the flat and side alternately.
contrafoso, *n.m.* (*theat.*) second cellar under stage; (*fort.*) outer ditch *or* moat.
contrafuero, *n.m.* infringement of a charter *or* privilege.
contrafuerte, *n.m.* girth-strap; stiffener (*shoe*); (*arch.*) counterfort, abutment, buttress; spur (*of mountain*); (*fort.*) fort opposite another.
contrafuerzas, *n.f.pl.* opposing forces.
contrafuga, (*mus.*) counterfugue.
contragolpe, *n.m.* counter-stroke, back-stroke; (*path.*) contrecoup.
contraguardia, *n.f.* (*fort.*) counter-guard.
contraguía, *n.f.* near *or* left-hand mule (*of a team*).
contrahacedor, -ra, *a.* counterfeiting, imitating. — *n.m.f.* imitator, counterfeiter.
contrahacer [20], *v.t.* to counterfeit, forge; to imitate, copy; to pirate (*an author's works*). — **contrahacerse,** *v.r.* to feign, dissemble.
contrahaz, *n.f.* wrong side (*of a piece of cloth*).
contrahecho, -cha, *a.* hump-backed, deformed.
contrahechura, *n.f.* copy, imitation.
contrahierba, *n.f.* medicinal plant.
contrahilera, *n.f.* (*arch.*) second *or* parallel row.
contrahilo, *a.* cross-grain; ***a contrahilo,*** across the grain; against the grain; (*sew.*) on the cross.
contrahoradar, *v.t.* to bore on the opposite side.
contrahuella, *n.f.* (*arch.*) rise (*of step* or *stair*).
contraindicación, *n.f.* (*med.*) contraindication.
contraindicante, *n.m.* (*med.*) contraindicant.
contraindicar [A], *v.t.* (*med.*) to contraindicate.
contralecho, *adv.* (*arch.*) ***a contralecho,*** cross-bond, laid vertically.
contralibrar, *v.t.* to draw (*a bill*) to cover o.s.
contraliga, *n.f.* counter-league.
contralínea, *n.f.* defence ditch and parapet.
contralizo, *n.m.* (*weav.*) back leash.
contralor, *n.m.* (*mil.*) controller, inspector.
contraloría, *n.f.* controllership; controller's office.
contralto, *n.m.f.* contralto, counter-tenor.
contraluz, *n.f.* cross-light; ***mirar una cosa a contraluz,*** to look at sth. against the light, hold sth. up to the light.
contramaestra, *n.f.* mainsail.
contramaestre, *n.m.* petty officer; boatswain; overseer, foreman.
contramalla, contramalladura, *n.f.* double-meshed net (*for catching fish*).
contramallar, *v.t.* to make double-meshed nets.
contramandar, *v.t.* to countermand.
contramangas, *n.f.pl.* oversleeves.
contramaniobra, *n.f.* counter-manœuvre *or* movement.
contramano, *adv.* ***a contramano,*** the wrong way, in the wrong direction.
contramarca, *n.f.* countermark; duty on goods.
contramarcar [A], *v.t.* to countermark.
contramarco, *n.m.* interior frame (*of french window etc.*).
contramarcha, *n.f.* countermarch, reverse.
contramarchar, *v.i.* to countermarch.
contramarea, *n.f.* counter-tide.
contramesana, *n.f.* mizzen-mast.
contramina, *n.f.* countermine; (*min.*) driftway, heading.
contraminar, *v.t.* (*mil.*) to countermine; (*fig.*) to counterwork.
contramolde, *n.m.* counter *or* second mould.
contramotivo, *n.m.* counter melody; phrase in double counterpoint.
contramuelle, *n.m.* counter-mole; duplicate spring.
contramuñones, *n.m.pl.* (*artill.*) metallic reinforcements of the trunnions.
contramuralla, *n.f.*, **contramuro,** *n.m.* (*fort.*) countermure.
contranatural, *a.* unnatural.
contraofensiva, *n.f.* counteroffensive.
contraoferta, *n.f.* counteroffer.
contraorden, *n.f.* countermand, counter order.
contrapalanquín, *n.m.* (*naut.*) preventer clew-garnet.
contrapalmejar, *n.m.* (*naut.*) kelson.
contrapar, *n.m.* (*arch.*) rafter.
contraparte, *n.f.* opposite side; flat side (*of embossed work*); (*mus.*) counterpoint.
contrapartida, *n.f.* (*com.*) cross-entry, correction (*in double entry book-keeping*).
contrapás, *n.m.* walking step.
contrapasar, *v.i.* to go over to the other side *or* party.
contrapaso, *n.m.* back step; second part.
contrapear, *v.t.* to make into two-ply (*wood*).
contrapechar, *v.t.* to make (*a horse*) strike its breast against that of another horse.
contrapelo, *adv.* ***a contrapelo,*** against the grain; ***a contrapelo de,*** against the opposition of.
contrapesar, *v.t.* to counterpoise, counter-balance; to compensate, offset.
contrapeso, *n.m.* counterpoise, counter-balance, counterweight; makeweight; rope dancer's pole; plummet.
contrapeste, *n.m.* remedy against plague.
contrapié, *n.m.* (*hunt.*) failure of scent, losing of trail; (*fig.*) trap, snare.
contrapilastra, *n.f.* counter-pilaster; wooden draught-excluder on doors and windows.
contraplancha, *n.f.* second plate (*in engraving*).
contrapolicía, *n.f.* secret police watching ordinary police.
contrapóliza, *n.f.* (*com.*) policy which annuls another.
contraponedor, -ra, *a.* comparing, contrasting; opposing. — *n.m.f.* comparer; opposer.

contraponer [25], *v.t.* to set against; to oppose; to compare, contrast.
contraposición, *n.f.* contraposition, counterview, contrast; ***en contraposición de,*** as compared with.
contrapozo, *n.m.* counter-blast.
contrapresión, *n.f.* back-pressure.
contraprincipio, *n.m.* counter-principle.
contraproducente, *a.* self-defeating, producing the opposite of the desired effect; (*coll.*) pointless, useless.
contrapromesa, *n.f.* counter-promise.
contraproposición, *n.f.* counter-proposition.
contrapropósito, *n.m.* counter-aim.
contraprotesto, *n.m.* counter-protest; (*com.*) second protest (*to a bill*).
contraproyectar, *v.t.* to counterplan; to prepare (*a counterplan*).
contraproyecto, *n.m.* counter-project; counter-plan, counter-scheme.
contraprueba, *n.f.* counter-proof; (*print.*) second proof.
contrapuerta, *n.f.* screen-door, double door; (*fort.*) counter-port.
contrapugnar, *v.t.* to fight back against.
contrapuntante, *n.m.* singer in counterpoint.
contrapuntarse, contrapuntearse, *v.r.* to exchange sarcasms.
contrapuntear, *v.t.* to sing in counterpoint; to taunt; *v.i.* to be sarcastic.
contrapuntista, *n.m.* contrapuntist.
contrapuntístico, -ca, *a.* contrapuntal.
contrapunto, *n.m.* counterpoint.
contrapunzar [C], *v.t.* to rivet with a punch.
contrapunzón, *n.m.* punch; gunsmith's countermark.
contraquerella, *n.f.* (*law*) cross-action.
contraquilla, *n.f.* (*naut.*) false keel.
contrariamente, *adv.* contrarily, contrariwise; on the other hand.
contrariar [L], *v.t.* to cross, thwart; to annoy, vex.
contrariedad, *n.f.* opposition; annoyance, vexation. irritation, bother; setback, disappointment.
contrario, -ria, *a.* contrary, contradictory, opposite, opposed, adverse; ***ser contrario a,*** to be against *or* opposed to; ***tiempo contrario,*** adverse weather. — *n.m.f.* opponent, adversary. — *n.m.* contrary, opposite; ***al contrario, por el contrario, por lo contrario,*** on the contrary, quite the opposite; ***al contrario de Juan,*** unlike John; ***de lo contrario, en caso contrario,*** otherwise, if not; ***no ha dicho nada en contrario,*** he has said nothing to the contrary. — *n.f.* contrariness, opposition; ***llevar la contraria a,*** to go against, go counter to, oppose, contradict.
contrarraya, *n.f.* cross-hatching line (*in engraving*).
contrarrayar, *v.t.* to cross-hatch.
contrarreforma, *n.f.* counter-reformation.
contrarregistro, *n.m.* control, second checking.
contrarreguera, *n.f.* lateral ditch *or* drain (*in irrigated ground*).
contrarreparo, *n.m.* (*fort.*) countermure, counterscarp.
contrarréplica, *n.f.* rejoinder, counter-reply, retort.
contrarrestar, *v.t.* to check, counteract; to return (*a ball*).
contrarresto, *n.m.* checking, counteraction; player receiving (*service*).
contrarretablo, *n.m.* back of altar-piece.
contrarrevolución, *n.f.* counter-revolution.
contrarrevolucionario, -ria, *a., n.m.f.* counter-revolutionary.
contrarroda, *n.f.* (*naut.*) stemson.
contrarronda, *n.f.* (*mil.*) second round (*night patrol*).
contrarrotura, *n.f.* (*vet.*) plaster, poultice.
contrasalida, *n.f.* (*mil.*) counter-sally.
contrasalva, *n.f.* (*mil.*) counter-salute.
contrasazón, *n.f.* unseasonableness, inopportuneness.
contraseguro, *n.m.* repayment insurance contract.
contrasellar, *v.t.* to counter-seal.
contrasello, *n.m.* counter-seal.
contrasentido, *n.m.* contradiction in terms.
contraseña, *n.f.* countersign; countermark; (*mil.*) watchword; password; (*theat.*) ***contraseña de salida,*** re-admission ticket.
contrasignar [CONTRASELLAR].
contrasignatorio, *n.m.* one who countersigns.
contrasol, *n.m.* (*hort.*) bell-glass, sunshade.
contrastable, *a.* contrastable.
contrastador, -ra, *a.* contrasting.
contrastante, *a.* contrasting.
contrastar, *v.t.* to resist, oppose; to hall-mark; to assay; to check; to constrast. — *v.i.* to contrast.
contraste, *n.m.* contrast; opposition; assay; assayer (*of weights and measures* or *metals*); assayer's office; assayer's seal *or* mark; sudden change of the wind; public weighing of raw silk.
contrata, *n.f.* contract, deed; ***contrata de arriendo,*** lease; ***contrata de fletamento,*** charter-party.
contratablacho, *n.m.* double lock.
contratación, *n.f.* trade, commerce, traffic, transaction.
contratajamar, *n.m.* buttress of bridge-piles.
contratante, *a.* contracting. — *n.m.* contractor, party to a contract.
contratapa, *n.f.* double lid *or* cover.
contratar, *v.t.* to contract; to hire, engage, take on.
contratecho, *n.m.* double roof.
contratela, *n.f.* (*hunt.*) second enclosure of canvas to trap game.
contratiempo, *n.m.* mishap, contretemps; ***a contratiempo,*** in syncopated time; (*pl.*) (*equit.*) unruly movements.
contratista, *n.m.f.* contractor.
contrato, *n.m.* contract, covenant; deed, indenture; ***hacer un contrato,*** to draw up a contract; ***contrato a la gruesa*** or ***a riesgo marítimo,*** respondentia; ***contrato de arrendamiento,*** lease; ***contrato de compra y venta,*** contract of bargain and sale; ***contrato de retrovendendo,*** contract of sale and return; (*fig.*) ***contrato leonino,*** one-sided pact.
contratorpedero, *n.m.* torpedo-boat destroyer.
contratreta, *n.f.* counterplot.
contratrinchera, *n.f.* (*fort.*) counter-approaches.
contravalación, *n.f.* (*fort.*) contravallation.
contravalar, *v.t.* to form a line of contravallation round.
contravalor, *n.m.* equivalent (*value*).
contravapor, *n.m.* back-pressure steam; ***dar contravapor,*** to (put into) reverse.
contravención, *n.f.* contravention, transgression, violation, offence.
contraveneno, *n.m.* counter-poison, antidote.
contravenir [36], *v.i.* — ***a,*** to contravene, transgress, violate.
contraventana, *n.f.* window-shutter; storm-shutter.
contraventor, -ra, *a.* contravening, infringing. — *n.m.f.* transgressor.
contravertiente, *n.m.* unevenness opposing the free flow of waters.
contravidriera, *n.f.* double window; storm-window; double-glazing.
contravirar, *v.t.* (*naut.*) to turn in an opposite direction.
contravisita, *n.f.* second visit (*as check on previous visit*).
contravoluta, *n.f.* (*arch.*) inner volute.

contray, *n.m.* Courtrai cloth.
contrayente, *a.*, *n.m.f.* betrothed; contracting (*marriage*) party.
contrecho, -cha [CONTRAHECHO].
contribución, *n.f.* contribution; tax; rates; ***contribución de sangre,*** military service; ***contribución industrial,*** excise tax.
contribuidor, -ra, *a.* contributing. — *n.m.f.* contributor.
contribuir [o], *v.t.*, *v.i.* to contribute; to pay as tax; to pay tax; ***contribuir (con) 1.000 pts.,*** to contribute 1,000 pesetas; ***contribuir a,*** to contribute to; ***este artículo contribuye,*** this article attracts tax, tax is payable on this article.
contribulado, -da, *a.* grief-stricken, afflicted.
contributario, -ria, *n.m.f.* fellow tax-payer, co-tax-payer.
contributivo, -va, *a.* appertaining to tax-paying.
contribuyente, *a.* contributing, contributory. — *n.m.f.* tax-payer.
contrición, *n.f.* contrition, compunction.
contrín, *n.m.* weight used in the Philippines (*about* 6 *grains*).
contrincante, *n.m.* competitor, rival, opponent; fellow contestant, candidate.
contristar, *v.t.* to afflict, sadden.
contrito, -ta, *a.* contrite.
control, *n.m.* control; check; ***puesto de control,*** check point.
controlar, *v.t.* to control; to check.
controversia, *n.f.* controversy, dispute.
controversista, *n.m.* controversialist, disputant.
controvertible, *a.* controvertible, disputable.
controvertir [6], *v.t.*, *v.i.* to controvert, dispute.
contubernio, *n.m.* cohabitation, concubinage; (*fig.*) infamous alliance; (international) conspiracy.
contumacia, *n.f.* obstinacy, obduracy, stubbornness; (*law*) contumacy, default.
contumaz, *a.* obstinate, obdurate, stubborn; contumacious; (*med.*) germ-carrying (*substances*).
contumelia, *n.f.* contumely, abuse.
contumelioso, -sa, *a.* contumelious, abusive.
contundente, *a.* blunt, bruising, producing a contusion; (*fig.*) forceful, forcible, crushing, irresistible; ***argumento contundente,*** crushing, decisive argument.
contundir, *v.t.* to contuse, bruise, pound.
conturbación, *n.f.* perturbation, distress.
conturbado, -da, *a.* turbulent.
conturbador, -ra, *a.* perturbing. — *n.m.f.* perturber.
conturbar, *v.t.* to perturb.
conturbativo, -va, *a.* perturbing.
contusión, *n.f.* contusion, bruise.
contuso, -sa, *a.* having *or* suffering from contusion. — *p.p. irreg.* [CONTUNDIR].
contutor, *n.m.* joint guardian, co-guardian.
conuco, *n.m.* (*Col.*, *Cub.*, *Ven.*) small plot of land.
convalaria, *n.f.* (*bot.*) convallaria, lily of the valley.
convalecencia, *n.f.* convalescence; ***casa de convalecencia,*** convalescent home.
convalecer [9], *v.i.* to convalesce, be convalescent; (*fig.*) to recover; ***convalecer de una enfermedad,*** to recover from sickness.
convaleciente, *a.*, *n.m.f.* convalescent.
convalidación, *n.f.* (*law*) confirmation, ratification, recognition.
convalidar, *v.t.* (*law*) to ratify, confirm, recognise.
convecino, -na, *a.* neighbouring. — *n.m.f.* fellow-neighbour.
convelerse, *v.r.* (*med.*) to have convulsions.
convencedor, -ra, *a.* convincing. — *n.m.f.* convincer.
convencer [D], *v.t.* to convince, persuade; ***le convencieron de (para) que se fuera,*** they persuaded him to leave; ***por fin se convenció de que era imposible,*** he finally came to the conclusion that it was hopeless.
convencimiento, *n.m.* conviction, certainty; ***en el convencimiento de que,*** in the belief *or* believing that; ***tengo el convencimiento de que,*** I am certain that.
convención, *n.f.* convention.
convencional, *a.* conventional, conventionary. — *n.m.* conventionalist.
convencionalismo, *n.m.* conventionalism, conventionality.
convenible, *a.* able to be agreed on, reasonable, negotiable.
conveniencia, *n.f.* congruity; profit, advantage; suitability, desirability; agreement; service, employ; norm of respectability; (*pl.*) (*obs.*) emoluments, perquisites; income, property.
conveniente, *a.* advantageous, desirable, suitable, expedient; fit; opportune, proper, respectable; ***será conveniente que lo hagas pronto,*** it will be a good idea if you do it soon.
convenio, *n.m.* convention, agreement.
convenir [36], *v.i.* to agree; to fit, correspond; to be a good idea, be advisable, be desirable; ***convenir con,*** to agree with; ***convenir en,*** to agree to, on *or* about; ***no me conviene que vengas mañana,*** it doesn't suit me for you to come tomorrow; ***conviene advertírselo,*** it will be a good idea *or* advisable to warn him.
conventícula, *n.f.*, **conventículo,** *n.m.* conventicle.
convento, *n.m.* convent, nunnery; monastery.
conventual, *a.* conventual, monastic. — *n.m.* conventual, monk; member of landed Franciscan order.
conventualidad, *n.f.* conventual life; assignment of monk to a monastery.
convergencia, *n.f.* convergence, coming together.
convergente, *a.* converging, convergent, coming together.
converger [E], **convergir** [E], *v.i.* to converge, come together, merge; (*fig.*) to agree.
conversable, *a.* conversable, sociable.
conversación, *n.f.* conversation; subject *or* topic of conversation; talk, discussion; ***la conversación vino a recaer sobre el matrimonio,*** the conversation came round to marriage; ***¿quién sacó esta conversación?*** who brought up this topic of conversation?; ***trabar conversación,*** to start up a conversation; ***conversaciones de alto nivel,*** high-level talks *or* discussions.
conversador, -ra, *n.m.f.* good talker.
conversar, *v.i.* to converse, talk; (*mil.*) to change front, wheel; ***conversar con,*** to talk to, with; ***conversar sobre,*** to talk on, about.
conversión, *n.f.* conversion; transformation; (*rhet.*) apostrophe; (*mil.*) wheel, wheeling.
conversivo, -va, *a.* having the power of converting.
converso, -sa, *n.m.f.* convert. — *n.m.* lay brother.
convertible, *a.* convertible.
convertibilidad, *n.f.* convertibility.
convertidor, -ra, *a.* converting. — *n.m.* (*metal.*, *elec.*) converter.
convertir [6], *v.t.* to convert, change, transform; ***este problema se ha convertido en una pesadilla,*** this problem has become a nightmare; ***el agua se convirtió en hielo,*** the water turned to ice; ***se ha convertido al catolicismo,*** he has become converted to Catholicism.
convexidad, *n.f.* convexity.
convexo, -xa, *a.* convex.
convexocóncavo, -va, *a.* convexo-concave.
convicción, *n.f.* conviction.
conviccional, *a.* of conviction.
convicto, -ta, *a.* (*law*) convicted, guilty.
convictor, *n.m.* (*prov.*) boarder, pensioner in a college.

convictorio, *n.m.* students' quarters (*in Jesuit colleges*).
convidado, -da, *n.m.f.* guest, person invited; ***convidado de piedra,*** silent guest. — *n.f.* (*coll.*) invitation to drink, treat.
convidador, -ra, *a.* inviting. — *n.m.f.* host; one who stands drinks.
convidar, *v.t.* to invite, stand, treat; (*fig.*) to incite, induce; ***convidar a comer,*** to invite to lunch; ***el frío convida a andar,*** the cold tempts one to walk.
convincente, *a.* convincing.
convite, *n.m.* feast, treat; banquet.
convival, *a.* convivial.
convivencia, *n.f.* living together; coexistence.
conviviente, *a.* living together. — *n.m.f.* one who lives with others, cohabitant.
convivir, *v.i.* to live together; to coexist.
convocación, *n.f.* convocation.
convocador, -ra *a.* convening, summoning. — *n.m.f.* convener, summoner.
convocar [A], *v.t.* to convene, convoke, summon, call together; to acclaim; ***convocar a junta,*** to summon a meeting.
convocatorio, -ria, *a.* summoning, convoking. — *n.f.* letter of convocation, notice of meeting, summons; session of examinations (*university*).
convolución, *n.f.* convolution.
convóluto, -ta, *a.* (*bot., zool.*) convolute, convoluted.
convolvuláceo, -cea, *a., n.f.* (*bot.*) convolvulus.
convólvulo, *n.m.* (*bot.*) convolvulus; (*ent.*) vine-borer, vine-fretter.
convoy, *n.m.* convoy; train; (*fig.*) cruet-stand; (*coll.*) suite, retinue.
convoyar, *v.t.* to convoy, escort, guard.
convulsible, *a.* liable to convulsions.
convulsión, *n.f.* upheaval; (*med.*) convulsion.
convulsionar, *v.t.* to cause upheaval in; (*med.*) to produce convulsions in.
convulsionario, -ria, *a.* (*med.*) convulsionary; causing upheaval. — *n.m.pl.* (**convulsionarios**) (*hist.*) convulsionists.
convulsivo, -va, *a.* convulsive.
convulso, -sa, *a.* convulsed.
conyúdice [CONJUEZ].
conyugable, *a.* marriageable.
conyugal, *a.* conjugal, connubial; ***vida conyugal,*** married life.
cónyuge, *n.m.* married partner.
conyugicida, *n.m.f.* (*law*) murderer of husband *or* wife.
conyugicidio, *n.m.* (*law*) murder of husband *or* wife.
coña, *n.f.* (*vulg.*) joking, facetiousness; ***estar de coña,*** to be in a joking mood.
coñac, *n.m.* cognac, brandy.
cooperación, *n.f.* co-operation.
cooperador, -ra, *a.* co-operative. — *n.m.f.* co-operator.
cooperante, *a.* co-operating, co-operant, coactive.
cooperar, *v.i.* to co-operate; ***cooperar a una empresa,*** to co-operate in an undertaking.
cooperario, *n.m.* co-operator.
cooperativo, -va, *a.* co-operative. — *n.f.* co-operative society.
coopositor, -ra, *n.m.f.* fellow candidate, competitor.
cooptación, *n.f.* co-optation.
coordenada, *n.f.* (*geom.*) co-ordinate; (*pl.*) parameters, set limits, (given) framework, terms of reference.
coordinación, *n.f.* co-ordination.
coordinado, -da, *a.* (*geom.*) co-ordinate.
coordinador, -ra, *a.* co-ordinating.
coordinamiento, *n.m.* [COORDINACIÓN].
coordinar, *v.t.* to co-ordinate.
copa, *n.f.* cup; goblet, wine-glass; tree-top; crown (*of hat*); roof (*of oven*); glassful; brazier, fire-pan; (*pl.*) hearts (*at cards*); bosses (*of bridle*); ***tomar una copa,*** to have a drink.
copado, -da, *a.* tufted (*tree*). — *n.f.* crested lark.
copador, *n.m.* wooden hammer for copper *or* brass beating.
copaiba, *n.f.* copaiba tree.
copal, *n.m.* copal.
copaljocol, *n.m.* (*Mex.*) copaljocol tree.
copanete, cópano, *n.m.* skiff.
copar, *v.t.* (*mil.*) to get (*cut off and capture*); (*elec.*) to take, sweep (*all votes*); (*cards etc.*) to win *or* take (all), sweep the board of *or* walk off with (everything); ***los hemos copado,*** we've got them; ***estamos copados,*** it's all up with us, we've had it, we're copped.
coparticipación, *n.f.* joint-participation.
copartícipe, *n.m.f.* (*law*) joint-sharer *or* participator.
copazo, *n.m.* large wine-glass *or* glass of wine; large snowflake.
cope, *n.m.* thickest part of fishing-net.
copear, *v.i.* to sell drinks by the glass; to go drinking.
copela, *n.f.* (*metal.*) cupel.
copelación, *n.f.* cupellation.
copelar, *v.t.* to cupel.
Copenhague, *n.m.* Copenhagen.
copeo, *n.m.* sale of drinks by the glass; drinking.
copera, *n.f.* cupboard for glasses, cabinet.
copernicano, -na, *a.* Copernican.
Copérnico, *n.m.* Copernicus.
copero, *n.m.* (*obs.*) cup-bearer; sideboard.
copete, *n.m.* small portion of flax etc. ready on distaff for spinning; toupee; crest, tuft; (*fig.*) top, summit; upper (*of a shoe*); forelock (*of a horse*); crownwork (*of furniture*); projecting top (*of ice-cream*); (*fig.*) conceitedness, uppishness; ***de alto copete,*** upper crust, of noble rank, of high standing; ***asir la ocasión por el copete,*** to seize opportunity by the forelock; ***estar hasta el copete,*** to be fed up to the teeth; ***tener copete,*** to be conceited *or* uppish.
copetón, *n.m.* (*Col.*) crested sparrow.
copetudo, -da, *a.* tufted; (*coll.*) conceited, uppish. — *n.f.* lark; (*Cub.*) marigold.
copey, *n.m.* (*Hisp. Am.*) copey tree.
copia, *n.f.* copiousness, plenty, abundance; copy, duplicate; counterpart; image, likeness.
copiador, -ra, *a.* copying. — *n.m.f.* copyist, copier, transcriber. — *n.m.* (*com.*) letter-book; (*fig.*) imitator; duplicating *or* copying machine.
copiante, *a., n.m.f.* [COPIADOR].
copiar, *v.t.* to copy, duplicate; (*poet.*) to describe, depict; to ape, mimic; ***copiar al pie de la letra,*** to copy word for word; ***copiar del natural,*** to draw from life.
copilador, -ra, *a.* compiling. — *n.m.f.* compiler.
copilar, *v.t.* to compile.
copilla, *n.f.* cigar-lighter; chafing-dish.
copín, *n.m.* Asturian grain-measure (*of half a peck*).
copina, *n.f.* (*Mex.*) whole skin.
copinar, *v.t.* (*Mex.*) to remove the whole skin from.
copioso, -sa, *a.* copious, abundant, plentiful.
copismo, *n.m.* servile imitation.
copista, *n.m.f.* copyist, transcriber.
copita, *n.f.* small cup *or* glass; nice drink.
copito, *n.m.* small snowflake.
copla, *n.f.* couplet, stanza; ballad, popular song, satirical verse; pair, couple; ***andar en coplas,*** to be notorious; ***coplas de ciego,*** folk ballads; ***echar coplas a uno,*** to speak ill of s.o.; (*pl.*) (*fam.*) verses.
coplear, *v.i.* to compose couplets *or* ballads.
copleja, *n.f.* wretched little ballad.
coplero, -ra, *n.m.f.* ballad-seller; folk singer.

coplista, *n.m.f.* poetaster.
coplones, *n.m.pl.* third-rate verses.
copo, *n.m.* small bundle (*of cotton, hemp, silk etc. on distaff ready for spinning*); snowflake; bottom (*of purse-seine*); fishing with purse-seine; cornering, grabbing; ***poco a poco, hila la vieja el copo,*** little strokes fell great oaks.
copón, *n.m.* large cup; (*eccles.*) ciborium.
coposo, -sa, *a.* [COPADO].
copra, *n.f.* copra.
copròfago, -ga, *a.* coprophagous.
coprolito, *n.m.* coprolite; (*med.*) intestinal calculus.
copropiedad, *n.f.* joint-property.
copropietario, -ria, *a.* owning jointly. — *n.m.f.* joint-owner.
cóptico, -ca, *a.* Coptic.
copto, -ta, *a.* Coptic. — *n.m.f.* Copt (*person*). — *n.m.* Coptic (*language*).
copudo, -da, *a.* tufted, bushy, thick-topped (*of trees*).
cópula, *n.f.* joining, coupling; copulation; (*log.*) copula; (*arch.*) cupola.
copulación, *n.f.* copulation.
copulador, -ra, *a.* copulatory.
copular, *v.t.* to pair, couple. — *v.i.* to copulate.
copulativo, -va, *a.* joining; (*gram.*) copulative.
coque, *n.m.* coke.
coquera, *n.f.* head of top (*toy*); concavity (*in a stone*); coal-scuttle.
coquetear, *v.i.* to flirt; to behave coquettishly.
coqueteo, *n.m.* coquetry, flirting.
coquetería, *n.f.* coquetry, coquettishness, flirtatiousness.
coqueto, -ta, *a.* flirtatious, coquettish. — *n.m.f.* flirt. — *n.f.* coquette; dressing-table.
coquetón, -tona, *a.* delightful, sweet, cute; terribly flirtatious; ***sombrero coquetón,*** cute hat. — *n.m.* terrible one for the girls. — *n.f.* terrible flirt.
coquí *n.m.* (*Cub.*) insect of marshy lands.
coquimbo, *n.m.* (*Hisp. Am.*) burrowing owl.
coquina, *n.f.* wedge shell.
coquito, *n.m.* gesture, grimace, face (*to amuse children*); (*Mex.*) turtledove; (*Chi., Ec.*) fruit of palm tree.
coráceo, -cea [CORIÁCEO].
coracero, *n.m.* cuirassier; (*coll.*) poor cigar.
coracina, *n.f.* small breastplate.
coracora, *n.f.* (*Philip.*) coasting vessel.
coracha, *n.f.* (*Hisp. Am.*) leather bag.
corada, *n.f.* (*prov.*) offal.
coraje, *n.m.* mettle, spirit; fierceness; irritation, vexation; (*coll.*) ***me da coraje,*** it makes me wild.
corajina, *n.f.* (*fam.*) fit of anger.
corajudo, -da, *a.* ill-tempered.
coral (1), *n.m.* coral; (*pl.* **corales**) strings of coral; (turkeys') wattles. — *n.f.* coral snake.
coral (2), *a.* choral, of a choir. — *n.f.* choir.
coralero, -ra, *n.m.f.* worker *or* dealer in corals.
coralífero, -ra, *a.* coralliferous.
coraliforme, *a.* coralliform.
coralíneo, -nea, *a.* coralline.
coralino, -na, *a.* coralline. — *n.f.* coralline (*seaweed and polyzoa*).
corambre, *n.f.* hides, skins, pelts; skin bag (*for oil* or *wine*).
corambrero, *n.m.* dealer in hides and skins.
Corán, *n.m.* Koran.
coránico, -ca, *a.* Koranic.
coranvobis, *n.m.* (*coll.*) appearance of a corpulent solemn person.
coraza, *n.f.* cuirass; shield; (*naut.*) armour-plating; turtle-shell.
coraznada, *n.f.* fricassee of animals' hearts.
corazón, *n.m.* heart; spirit; (loom) cam; ***blando de corazón,*** soft-hearted; ***ábrele tu corazón,*** open your heart to him; ***se me arranca el corazón, se me rompe el corazón,*** my heart bleeds; ***se me dilató el corazón, se me ensanchó el corazón,*** I was *or* felt heartened, the cockles of my heart were warmed; ***se le encogió el corazón, se le heló el corazón,*** his heart was chilled; ***hacer de tripas corazón,*** to pluck up courage; ***llevar el corazón en la mano,*** to wear one's heart on one's sleeve; ***no tener corazón para,*** not to have the heart to; ***tener el corazón bien puesto,*** to have (plenty of) guts; ***me dio un vuelco el corazón,*** my heart turned over; ***me da el corazón que,*** my heart tells me that, I can feel in my bones that; ***Dios le tocó en el corazón,*** God softened his heart; ***de*** (***todo***) ***corazón,*** wholeheartedly, with all one's heart; ***no le cabe el corazón en el cuerpo,*** he is big-hearted; ***no tener corazón,*** to have no heart; ***no tener uno corazón para hacer, decir etc.,*** not to have the heart to do, say etc.; ***se me parte el corazón de verlo,*** it breaks my heart to see it; ***le sale del corazón,*** he speaks from the heart; ***meterle a alguien el corazón en un puño,*** to put s.o. on edge; ***tener uno un corazón de bronce,*** to be hard-hearted.
corazonada, *n.f.* hunch, intuition, presentiment, foreboding; (*coll.*) entrails, chitterlings.
corazoncico, corazoncito, *n.m.* dear little heart.
corazoncillo *n.m.* St. John's wort.
corbachada, *n.f.* lash.
corbacho, *n.m.* (*obs.*) pizzle, cowhide whip.
corbata, *n.f.* neck-tie, cravat; streamer (*of flag-*[*staff*]); ribbon, insignia.
corbatería, *n.f.* necktie-shop.
corbatero, -ra, *n.m.f.* maker *or* vendor of neck-ties.
corbatín, *n.m.* small neck-tie, bow-tie; stock, closely fitting neck-cloth; ***irse*** or ***salirse por el corbatín,*** to be long-necked (*person*).
corbatinero, -ra, *a.* relating to neck-ties. — *n.m.f.* [CORBATERO].
corbato, *n.m.* cooler, worm (*of a still*).
corbatón, *n.m.* (*naut.*) small knee, bracket.
corbe, *n.m.* ancient dry measure.
corbeta, *n.f.* corvette; ***corbeta de guerra,*** sloop.
Córcega, *n.f.* Corsica.
corcel, *n.m.* steed, charger.
corcesca, *n.f.* ancient barbed spear.
corcino, *n.m.* young deer.
corconera, *n.f.* grey-black duck.
corcova, *n.f.* hump, hunch-back; protuberance.
corcovado, -da, *a.* hump-backed, hunch-backed. — *n.m.f.* hunchback.
corcovar, *v.t.* to bend, curve; to make crooked.
corcovear, *v.i.* to curvet, cut capers.
corcoveo, *n.m.* curvet, curvetting.
corcoveta, *n.f.* small hump *or* hunch. — *n.m.f.* (*coll.*) crook-back, hunch-back.
corcovo, *n.m.* curvet; (*coll.*) crookedness, unfair proceeding.
corcusido, *n.m.* rough *or* bad darn(ing).
corcusir, *v.t.* (*coll.*) to darn *or* patch clumsily.
corcha, *n.f.* cork; wine-cooler; beehive; (*naut.*) laying of a rope.
corchador, *n.m.* rope-laying sailor.
corchar, *v.t.* to lay (*a rope*).
corche, *n.m.* cork-soled sandal *or* shoe.
corchea, *n.f.* quaver.
corchera, *n.f.* wine-bucket.
corcheta, *n.f.* eye (*of hook* or *clasp*).
corchete, *n.m.* clasp, hook and eye; locket, small lock; crotch, hook; brace, bracket; catchpole.
corcho, *n.m.* cork; beehive; cork box (*for eatables*); cork mat; cork-soled clog *or* sandal; float (*of fishing-line*); ***flotar*** or ***sobrenadar como corcho en el agua,*** to come up smiling, rise

above adversity; ***tener cara de corcho,*** to be thick-skinned.
corchoso, -sa, *a.* corky.
corchotaponero, -ra, *a.* appertaining to the manufacture of cork stoppers.
corda, *n.f.* (*naut.*) ***estar a la corda,*** to be close-hauled, lying-to.
cordado, -da, *a.* (*her.*) corded.
cordaje, *n.m.* cordage; (*naut.*) rigging.
cordal (1), *a.*, *n.f.* (***muela***) ***cordal,*** wisdom tooth.
cordal (2), *n.m.* tailpiece (*of stringed instrument*); mountain range.
cordato, -ta, *a.* wise, prudent, judicious, discreet.
cordel, *n.m.* cord, thin rope, line; distance of five steps; ***mozo de cordel,*** porter, carrier; ***a cordel,*** in a straight line; ***trazar a cordel,*** to plan in a straight line, draw up in straight *or* parallel lines; (*coll.*) ***no le des cordel,*** don't encourage him.
cordelado, -da, *a.* corded (*ribbons* or *garters*).
cordelazo, *n.m.* lash with a cord.
cordelejo, *n.m.* (miserable) little cord; (*fig.*) fun, jest, joke; ***dar cordelejo,*** to chaff, banter.
cordelería, *n.f.* rope trade; cord-making; cord-making factory *or* shop; cordage; rope-walk; (*naut.*) rigging.
cordelero, -ra, *a.* to do with cord *or* rope-making. — *n.m.f.* rope-maker *or* seller. — *n.m.pl.* (**cordeleros**) cordeliers.
cordelito, *n.m.* fine, thin cord.
cordellate, *n.m.* grogram.
cordera, *n.f.* (*lit.*, *fig.*) lamb.
cordería, *n.f.* cordage.
corderilla, *n.f.* little ewe-lamb.
corderillo, *n.m.* young lamb; lambskin dressed with the fleece.
corderino, -na, corderuno, -na, *a.* appertaining to lambs. — *n.f.* lambskin.
cordero, *n.m.* (*lit.*, *fig.*) lamb; dressed lambskin; ***cordero añal,*** yearling lamb; ***cordero pascual,*** paschal lamb; ***cordero lechal, recental,*** sucking lamb; ***ésa es la madre del cordero,*** that's where the trouble lies, where the answer is.
corderuela, *n.f.* little ewe-lamb.
cordeta, *n.f.* (*prov.*) bast rope.
cordezuela, *n.f.* fine small rope.
cordíaco, -ca, *a.* [CARDÍACO].
cordial, *a.* cordial, hearty, affectionate; invigorating, reviving (*of medicine*); ***dedo cordial,*** middle finger. — *n.m.* cordial, tonic.
cordialidad, *n.f.* cordiality, heartiness.
cordialmente, *adv.* cordially, heartily, affectionately; (*at end of letter*) sincerely.
cordifoliado, -da, *a.* with heart-shaped leaves.
cordiforme, *a.* cordiform, heart-shaped.
cordila, *n.f.* spawn (*of tunny-fish*).
cordilo, *n.m.* African lizard.
cordilla, *n.f.* sheep's guts (*used as cat's meat*).
cordillera, *n.f.* cordillera, chain, range (*of mountains*).
cordillerano, -na, *a.* appertaining to a cordillera. — *n.m.f.* inhabitant *or* native of a cordillera.
cordita, *n.f.* cordite.
corditis, *n.f.* inflammation of the vocal cords.
córdoba, *n.m.* (*Nic.*) monetary unit, peso.
cordobán, *n.m.* cordovan leather; (*fig.*) ***dejar a alguien en cordobán,*** to skin s.o.
cordobana, (*coll.*) ***andar a la cordobana,*** to go naked.
cordobanero, -ra, *n.m.f.* cordovan tanner.
cordobés, -besa, *a.*, *n.m.f.* (person) of *or* belonging to Córdoba.
cordón, *n.m.* rope, cord, string; girdle; cordon; shoe-lace, (*Am.*) shoestring; ***cordón umbilical,*** umbilical cord; ***cordón sanitario,*** sanitary cordon; (*pl.* **cordones**) rope strands; ***cordones de zapato(s),*** shoe-laces.
cordonazo, *n.m.* swipe with rope *or* cord; ***cordonazo de San Francisco,*** autumn equinoctial storm(s).
cordoncillo, *n.m.* milling (*coins*).
cordonería, *n.f.* cord- *or* lace-making; lace *or* cord trade; lace- *or* cord-factory *or* shop.
cordonero, -ra, *n.m.f.* cord- *or* lace-maker *or* seller.
cordura, *n.f.* sanity, common-sense.
Corea, *n.f.* Korea; ***la Corea del Norte,*** North Korea; ***la Corea del Sur,*** South Korea.
corea, *n.f.* dance accompanied by a chorus; (*med.*) chorea, St. Vitus' Dance.
coreado, -da, *a.* sung *or* played in chorus; choral; choric; ***música coreada,*** chorus, choral music.
coreano, -na, *a.*, *n.m.f.* Korean. — *n.m.* Korean (*language*).
corear, *v.t.* to add choral accompaniment to; to play *or* sing in chorus; (*fig.*) ***no hace más que corear a su jefe,*** he merely repeats his boss's tune.
coreo, *n.m.* choree, trochee; connected harmony of choruses.
coreografía, *n.f.* choreography.
coreográfico, -ca, *a.* choreographic.
coreógrafo, *n.m.* choreographer.
corete, *n.m.* leather washer (*under nails, nuts etc.*).
corezuelo, *n.m.* small pelt *or* hide; sucking-pig; crackling (*of roasted sucking-pig*).
cori, *n.m.* St. John's wort.
coriáceo, -cea, *a.* appertaining to leather.
coriámbico, -ca, *a.*, *n.m.* choriambic.
coriambo, *n.m.* choriambus.
coriandro, *n.m.* coriander.
coribante, *n.m.* corybant, priest of Cybele.
coribántico, -ca, *a.* corybantian, corybantic.
corifeo, *n.m.* coryphæus; (*fig.*) leader; (*coll.*) follower.
corimbifloro, -ra, *a.* (*bot.*) corymbiate.
corimbiforme, *a.* corymbiform.
corimbo, *n.m.* corymb.
corindón, *n.m.* corundum.
corínti(c)o, -ti(c)a, *a.*, *n.m.f.* Corinthian.
corista, *n.m.* chorister. — *n.m.f.* chorus singer. — chorus girl.
corito, *a.* naked; (*fig.*) timid, pusillanimous.
coriza (1), *n.f.* (*med.*) coryza.
coriza (2), *n.f.* (*prov.*) sandal; clog.
corladura, *n.f.* vermeil (*varnish*), silver-gilt.
corlar, corlear, *v.t.* to put vermeil varnish on.
corma, *n.f.* stocks; (*fig.*) clog, hobble; (*fig.*) hindrance.
cormorán, *n.m.* cormorant.
cornac(a), *n.m.* elephant keeper, driver, mahout; elephant tamer.
cornada, *n.f.* thrust with a bull's horn, gore; thrust with a foil.
cornadillo, *n.m.* ***emplear*** or ***poner su cornadillo,*** to do one's bit.
cornado, *n.m.* old copper coin; (*coll.*) ***no vale un cornado,*** it is not worth a farthing.
cornadura, *n.f.* horns (*of an animal*).
cornal, cornil, *n.m.* strap (*for yoking oxen by the horns*).
cornalina, *n.f.* cornelian.
cornalón, *a.* big-horned (*bull*).
cornamenta, *n.f.* horns (*of an animal*).
cornamusa, *n.f.* brass horn *or* trumpet; bagpipe; (*naut.*) belaying cleat.
cornatillo, *n.m.* horn olive.
córnea, *n.f.* [CÓRNEO].
corneador, -ra, *a.* butting, horning, goring.
cornear, *v.t.* to butt, horn, gore.
corneja, *n.f.* crow.
cornejal, *n.m.* place abounding in cornel *or* dogwood.

cornejalejo, *n.m.* pod.
cornejo, *n.m.* dogwood, cornel.
cornelina, *n.f.* cornelian.
córneo, -nea, *a.* horny, corneous. — *n.f.* cornea.
cornerina, *n.f.* cornelian.
cornero, *n.m.* ***cornero de pan,*** crust of bread.
corneta, *n.f.* bugle, cornet; swine-herd's horn; (*obs.*) cornet, banderol; (*naut.*) broad pennant; (*obs., mil.*) cornet, troop of cavalry; head-dress of sisters of charity; ***corneta acústica,*** ear-trumpet; ***corneta de posta,*** postilion's *or* post horn. — *n.m.* cornet-player, bugler; (*obs., mil.*) cornet.
cornete, *n.m.* (*anat.*) cartilage of nose.
cornetilla, *n.f.* ***pimiento de cornetilla,*** chilli.
cornetín, *n.m.* small bugle; cornet-à-piston; player of such instrument.
cornezuelo, *n.m.* small horn; (*bot.*) horn olive; (*vet.*) instrument for bleeding horses; (*bot.*) ergot of rye.
corniabierto, -ta, *a.* having widespread horns.
cornial, *a.* horn-shaped.
corniapretado, -da, *a.* with close-set horns.
cornicabra, *n.f.* turpentine-tree; horn olive; wild fig-tree.
cornidelantero, -ra, *a.* with horns pointing forward.
cornífero, -ra, *a.* (*geol.*) corniferous.
corniforme, *a.* corniform, horn-shaped.
cornigacho, -cha, *a.* with horns pointing downwards.
cornígero -ra, *a.* (*poet.*) horned, cornigerous.
cornija, *n.f.* (*arch.*) cornice.
cornijal, *n.m.* angle *or* corner (*of building*); (*eccles.*) purificator (*at Mass*).
cornijamento, cornijamiento, cornijón, *n.m.* entablature; corner (*of street*).
cornil [CORNAL].
corniola, *n.f.* cornelian.
cornipríeto, -ta, *a.* having close-set horns.
cornisa, *n.f.* cornice; corniche, coastal promenade.
cornisamento, cornisamiento, cornisón, *n.m.* entablature.
corniveleto, -ta, *a.* having horns turned upward.
cornizo, corno, *n.m.* cornelian cherry tree.
cornizola, *n.f.* wild cherry.
Cornualles, *n.f.* Cornwall.
cornucopia, *n.f.* cornucopia; mirror with sconces.
cornudilla, *n.f.* hammer-fish.
cornudo, *a.* horned. — *n.m.* (*coll.*) cuckold.
cornúpeta, *a., n.m.f.* butting (animal); bull.
coro, *n.m.* choir; choir-loft; chorus; ***a coro,*** in chorus; ***de coro,*** by heart, by rote; ***hablar (rezar) a coros,*** to speak (pray) alternately; ***hacerle coro a alguien,*** to chorus *or* second s.o.
corocha, *n.f.* vine-fretter, vine-grub.
corografía, *n.f.* chorography.
corográfico, -ca, *a.* chorographical.
corógrafo, -fa, *n.m.f.* chorographer.
coroideo, -dea, *a.*, **coroides,** *n.f.* (*anat.*) choroid.
corojal, *n.m.* plantation of ***corojos.***
corojo, *n.m.* palm bearing an oily nut.
corolario, *n.m.* corollary.
corolífero, -ra, *a.* corollate.
corología, *n.f.* chorology.
corona, *n.f.* crown; coronet; tonsure; wreath; chaplet (*beads*); rosary of seven decades; halo; (*arch., astron., bot.*) corona; (*eccles.*) corona, chandelier; (*fort.*) crown-work; (*naut.*) pendant (rope); (*vet.*) ***corona del casco,*** cornet; (*bot.*) ***corona de rey*** or ***real,*** three-toothed globularia; ***abrir la corona,*** to tonsure; ***ceñir(se) la corona,*** to assume the crown.
coronación, *n.f.* coronation; crowning; (*arch.*) coping (*of walls*).
coronado, *n.m.* tonsured priest.
coronador, -ra, *a.* crowning, finishing. — *n.m.f.* crowner, finisher.
coronal, *a.* belonging to the frontal bone. — *n.m.* frontal bone.
coronamiento, *n.m.* (*arch.*) coping; crowning; (*naut.*) taffrail.
coronar, *v.t.* to crown, top, cap; to finish, complete; ***para coronar la fiesta,*** as a final touch. — **coronarse,** *v.r.* to be crowned.
coronario, -ria, *a.* coronary, extremely refined (*gold*); (*bot.*) coronate; (*anat.*) coronary (*arteries, veins*). — *n.f.* crown-wheel of watch.
corondel, *n.m.* (*print.*) reglet, column-rule; (*pl.* **corondeles**) watermark lines.
coronel, *n.m.* colonel; (*arch.*) cyma, top-moulding; (*her.*) crown.
coronela, *a.* of a colonel's flag, company etc. — *n.f.* colonel's wife.
coronelía, *n.f.* colonelship.
corónide, *n.f.* end, crowning, consummation.
coroniforme, *a.* coronate.
coronilla, *n.f.* crown (*of the head*); (*bot.*) coronilla; ***ando de coronilla,*** I'm harassed, I don't know whether I'm on my head or my heels; ***esto me trae de coronilla,*** this is driving me up the wall; ***estoy hasta la coronilla,*** I'm fed up to the teeth, I'm thoroughly browned off.
coronio, *n.m.* (*astron.*) coronium.
coroza, *n.f.* cap worn as mark of infamy; ***ponerle a alguien la coroza (de),*** to mark *or* stigmatize s.o. (as).
corpachón, corpanchón, corpazo, *n.m.* (*fam.*) hulking body *or* carcass.
corpecico, corpecillo, corpecito, *n.m.* small body.
corpezuelo, *n.m.* small body *or* carcass.
corpiñera, *n.f.* bodice-maker.
corpiño, *n.m.* bodice.
corporación, *n.f.* corporation, body, guild; ***la docta corporación,*** the Spanish Academy of the Language; ***en corporación,*** in a body.
corporal, *a.* corporal; ***castigo corporal,*** corporal punishment; ***daño corporal,*** bodily harm. — *n.m.* (*eccles.*) corporal (*cloth*).
corporalidad, *n.f.* corporality.
corporativamente, *adv.* as a body.
corporativo, -va, *a.* corporative.
corporeidad, *n.f.* corporeity; ***tomar corporeidad,*** to take shape.
corporificación, *n.f.* materialization.
corporificar [A], *v.t.* to materialize; (*chem.*) to solidify (*liquid*).
corpóreo, -rea, *a.* corporeal, corporal; ***tomar forma corpórea,*** to take shape.
corps, *n.m.* body, corps; ***guardia de corps,*** royal *or* palace guard; ***sumiller de corps,*** Lord Chamberlain.
corpudo, -da, *a.* having a big *or* hefty body.
corpulencia, *n.f.* corpulence, hefty build.
corpulento, -ta, *a.* big-framed, heavily *or* heftily built.
corpus, *n.m.* Corpus Christi (*day and procession*).
corpuscular, *a.* corpuscular.
corpusculista, *n.m.* corpuscularian.
corpúsculo, *n.m.* corpuscle.
corral, *n.m.* enclosure; yard, barn-yard, farm-yard, poultry-yard, stock-yard; tenement; fish-pond; (*obs.*) open-air theatre; (*fig.*) blank left by students when taking down lectures; ***hacer corrales,*** to play truant.
corralero, -ra, *a.* of the slums *or* gutters; ill-bred, vulgar. — *n.f.* (*prov.*) Andalusian song and dance.
corralillo, *n.m.* small yard.
corraliza, *n.f.* yard.
corralón, *n.m.* large yard; (bull) pen.
correa, *n.f.* leather strap *or* thong, leash; lead; belt; (*arch.*) joist, purlin; ***correa de perro,*** dog's lead; ***correa de transmisión, correa transmisora,***

driving belt; ***correa transportadora,*** conveyor belt; ***correa del ventilador,*** fan belt; ***besar la correa,*** to knuckle under; ***no tener correa,*** not to be able to take it; (*pl.*) duster made of thongs.

correaje, *n.m.* (leather) straps; belting.

correal, *n.m.* dressed reddish deerskin; ***coser*** or ***labrar de correal,*** to stitch with thongs.

correar, *v.t.* to draw out (*wool*).

correazo, *n.m.* swipe *or* lash (*with a leather strap*).

correcalles, *n.m.f. inv.* gadabout, street loafer.

corrección, *n.f.* correction; correctness; good manners.

correccional, *a.* correctional, corrective. — *n.m.* reformatory, approved school.

correccionalismo, *n.m.* reformatory system.

correccionalmente, *adv.* as a corrective, by way of correction.

correccionario, -ria, *n.m.f.* inmate of reformatory.

correctivo, -va, *a., n.m.f.* (*med.*) corrective, antidote.

correcto, -ta, *a.* correct, right; well-mannered. — *p.p. irreg.* [CORREGIR].

corrector, -ra, *a.* correcting, amending. — *n.m.f.* corrector, amender; proof-reader; superior in a convent of St. Francis of Paula.

corredentor, -ra, *n.m.f.* joint-redeemer.

corredero, -ra, *a,* sliding; ***puerta corredera,*** sliding door. — *n.f.* (*obs.*) race-ground; sliding panel; upper grinding-stone; wood-louse; cockroach; lane, street; (*naut.*) log, log-line; (*coll.*) procuress; (*print.*) track, slide, rail; (*mech.*) slide-valve; (*mech.*) tongue, rail, guide, groove, runner; (*mint.*) milling machine; (*naut.*) ***echar la corredera,*** to heave the log.

corredizo, -za, *a.* running, sliding, slip; ***nudo corredizo,*** running knot; ***lazada corrediza,*** slip knot.

corredor, -ra, *a.* running; fast running; (*orn.*) cursorial. — *n.m.* runner; corridor, (*Am.*) aisle; racing driver, cyclist; (*fort.*) covered-way; (*mil.*) scout; (*mil.*) forager; (*com.*) broker; (*sl.*) thief; (*sl.*) catchpole; ***corredor de cambios,*** stock-broker, money-broker; (*com.*) ***corredor de comercio, de lonja*** or ***de mercaderías,*** agent *or* broker; ***corredor de fincas,*** estate *or* land agent, (*Am.*) realtor; ***corredor(a) de oreja,*** stock-broker; (*coll.*) tale-bearer; (*sl.*) pimp, procurer, procuress. — *n.f.pl.* (**corredoras**) (*orn.*) cursores.

corredura, *n.f.* overflow.

correduría, *n.f.* brokerage; broker's office.

correería, *n.f.* strap-maker's trade, shop *or* factory.

correero, -ra, *n.m.f.* strap-maker *or* vendor.

corregencia, *n.f.* co-regency.

corregente, *n.m.f.* co-regent.

corregibilidad, *n.f.* corrigibility.

corregible, *a.* corrigible.

corregidor, -ra, *a.* correcting. — *n.m.f.* corrector. — *n.m.* (*obs.*) royal representative. — *n.f.* (*obs.*) representative's wife.

corregimiento, *n.m.* office *or* district of a corregidor.

corregir [8E], *v.t.* to correct, put right, amend; to adjust; to mitigate, temper; ***corregirse de un defecto,*** to cure o.s. of a defect.

corregüela, correhuela, *n.f.* small strap; child's game; (*bot.*) bindweed; (*bot.*) knotgrass.

correinado, *n.m.* joint reign.

correinante, *a.* reigning jointly.

correjel, *n.m.* sole-leather.

correlación, *n.f.* correlation.

correlacionar, *v.t.* to correlate.

correlativo, -va, correlato, -ta, *a.* correlative.

correligionario, -ria, *a., n.m.f.* (*lit., fig.*) coreligionist.

correndilla, *n.f.* (*coll.*) short run.

correntío, -tía, *a.* current, running; (*coll.*) light, unembarrassed, free. — *n.f.* diarrhœa.

correntón, -tona, *a.* gay, jolly, light-hearted. — *n.m.f.* gadabout.

correntoso, -sa, *a.* (*Hisp. Am.*) swift, of strong current (*rivers*).

correo, *n.m.* courier; messenger; post, mail; ***correos,*** post office; ***correo aéreo,*** air mail; ***correo urgente,*** special delivery; ***tren correo,*** mail train; ***lista de correos,*** poste restante; ***echar una carta al correo,*** to post *or* mail a letter.

correón, *n.m.* large leather strap.

correosidad, *n.f.* leatheriness, toughness.

correoso, -sa, *a.* leathery, tough.

correr (1), *v.t.* to overrun, sweep over, scour; to harass, pursue; to race, gallop (*an animal*); to run (*a risk*); to push home (*a bolt*); to draw (*curtains*); to act as agent for (*a commodity*); to slip, undo (*a knot*); to tip over (*a scale*); to auction; ***correr la comparación,*** to establish the comparison; ***correr monte,*** to hunt (big) game; ***correr peligro,*** to be in danger; ***correr lanzas,*** to joust; ***lo ha corrido todo,*** he's seen life; ***correrla,*** to go on a spree; ***correr fortuna,*** to seek one's fortune; ***correr baquetas,*** to run the gauntlet; ***correr las amonestaciones,*** to publish the banns (*of a marriage*); ***correr los negocios,*** to transact business; ***corre la plaza,*** he acts as commercial agent; (*theat.*) ***correr el telón,*** to drop the curtain; ***correr los mares,*** to see the world, rove over the seas.

correr (2), *v.i.* to run, speed, hasten, race; to flow, stream; to run on, pass, slip away (*time*); to blow (*winds*); to count (from) (*salary etc.*); to become due; to go on, continue; (*com.*) to pass (through) (*the proper channel*); to be current, accepted; to be worth, cost; (*naut.*) to sail with reduced canvas because of strong wind; to be said, be common talk, rumoured; (*Mex.*) to run about carousing at night; ***a todo correr,*** at full speed, flat out, hell for leather; ***corría el año 1906,*** it was the year 1906; ***corre la voz, el rumor,*** it is said, rumoured; (*com.*) ***corre el plazo,*** time is running out, passing; ***correr con uno,*** to be on good terms with s.o.; ***corre a mi cargo,*** I am responsible for it; ***correr con los gastos,*** to bear the expenses; ***correr un velo sobre lo pasado,*** to draw a veil over the past; ***corre que corre,*** he keeps on running; ***correr la voz,*** to pass the word; ***corre pareja(s) con,*** it is akin to; ***me corre prisa,*** I want it urgently; ***corre que se las pela,*** he's running as fast as his legs will carry him; it goes at a hell of a lick; ***correr a rienda suelta,*** to go hell for leather.

correrse, *v.r.* to move *or* shift over; to slide *or* slip out; to flow over, gutter (*candle*); to blush, be abashed; to run (*colours*); ***se corrieron para hacerle sitio,*** they moved over to make room for him; ***se corrió hasta Madrid,*** he got as far as Madrid.

correría, *n.f.* (*mil.*) foray, raid; (*pl.*) wanderings, travels.

correspondencia, *n.f.* correspondence; return, reciprocation; connection (*underground*); ***en justa correspondencia,*** in fair return.

corresponder, *v.i.* to correspond; to reciprocate; to fall (to); ***le correspondió a mi padre darles las gracias,*** it fell to my father to thank them; ***me corresponde el honor de presentarle,*** the honour of introducing him falls to me *or* I am entitled to the honour of introducing him; ***nos corresponden tres,*** we are entitled to three; ***a Francia le corresponde la mitad de esta producción,*** France accounts for half this output.

correspondiente, *a.* corresponding; respective. — *n.m.f.* correspondent; ***el dialecto y la zona del país correspondiente,*** the dialect and the respective area of the country.

corresponsal, *n.m.* correspondent.

corresponsalía, *n.f.* post of newspaper correspondent; ***tiene la corresponsalía del Times***

en Bruselas, he is The Times correspondent in Brussels.

corretaje, *n.m.* broking; brokerage; agent's commission.

corretear, *v.i.* to run, rove *or* wander about; to gad around.

correteo, *n.m.* dashing about.

corretero, -ra *a., n.m.f.* gadabout.

correvedile, correveidile, *n.m.f.* (*coll.*) talebearer, gossip-monger; (*fig., coll.*) go-between.

correverás, *n.m.* spring *or* mechanical toy.

corrido, -da, *a.* running, cursive; continuous, unbroken; generous, over; (*coll.*) (*one*) who has seen life, worldly-wise; ***letra corrida,*** flowing hand; ***juerga corrida,*** constant spree; ***tres kilos corridos,*** a good *or* generous three kilos; ***tres meses corridos,*** a good *or* full three months; ***de corrido,*** by heart; ***saberse de corrido,*** to know off pat, be able to reel off. — *n.m.* wall shed. — *n.f.* sprint, run; (*aer.*) taxiing; ***corrida de toros,*** bullfight; ***de corrida,*** fast, quickly.

corriente, *a.* running; instant, present (*week, month, year*); current; usual, ordinary; easy, easy-flowing; loose; approachable; common; ***corriente y moliente,*** run of the mill. — *n.f.* current; trend; ***corriente de aire,*** draught; ***corriente eléctrica,*** electric current; ***corriente alterna,*** alternating current; ***corriente continua,*** continuous *or* direct current; ***dejarse llevar de la corriente,*** to go with the stream; ***ir contra la corriente,*** to go against the stream; ***estar al corriente (de),*** to be up-to-date *or* informed (about); ***poner al corriente,*** to bring up-to-date, put in the picture.

corrigendo, -da, *n.m.f.* reformatory inmate.

corrillero, -ra, *a.* gossiping.

corrillo, *n.m.* group.

corrimiento, *n.m.* running; guttering; (*med.*) fluxion; (*fig.*) shyness, bashfulness; (*agric.*) blight (*of vine blossoms*); ***corrimiento de tierras,*** landslide, landslip.

corrinche, *n.m.* meeting of low people, rabble.

corrivación, *n.f.* impoundage (*of water*).

corro, *n.m.* circle *or* ring (*of spectators etc.*); round enclosure; children's round dance; ring-a-ring-of-roses; ***hacer corro,*** to form a ring; to make room; ***hacer corro aparte,*** to start a separate party *or* group.

corroborable, *a.* corroborable, confirmable.

corroboración, *n.f.* corroboration.

corroboradamente, *adv.* in corroboration, confirmatively.

corroborador, -ra, *a.* corroboratory, corroborating. — *n.m.f.* corroborator.

corroborante, *a.* corroborating. — *n.m.* (*med.*) corroborative, corroborant.

corroborar *v.t.* to corroborate, confirm; to fortify, strengthen.

corroborativo, -va, *a.* corroborative.

corrobra [ROBRA].

corroer, [29], *v.t.* to corrode; (*fig.*) to eat, gnaw away.

corrompedor, -ra, *a.* corrupting. — *n.m.f.* corrupter.

corromper, *v.t.* to corrupt; to spoil, mar; to bribe. — **corromperse,** *v.r.* to become corrupt *or* corrupted; to spoil; to be spoilt; ***se ha corrompido el cadáver,*** the corpse has gone rotten.

corroncho, *n.m.* (*Col.*) corroncho fish.

corrosal, *n.m.* custard-apple (*tree and fruit*).

corrosible, *a.* easily corroded.

corrosión, *n.f.* corrosion.

corrosivo, -va, *a.* corrosive; ***sublimado corrosivo,*** corrosive sublimate; ***es Vd. corrosivo,*** you undermine everything.

corroyente, *a.* corroding.

corrugación, *n.f.* corrugation.

corrugador, *a., n.m.* (*anat.*) corrugator.

corrulla [CORULLA].

corrumpente, *a.* corrupting.

corrupción, *n.f.* corruption; corruptness; depravity, depravation.

corruptela, *n.f.* corruption; depravation; (*law*) abuse.

corruptibilidad, *n.f.* corruptibility.

corruptible, *a.* corruptible.

corruptivo, -va, *a.* corruptive.

corrupto, -ta, *a.* corrupted, corrupt.

corruptor, -ra, *a.* corrupting. — *n.m.f.* corrupter, perverter.

corrusco, *n.m.* (*coll.*) crust (*of bread*).

corsario, *a., n.m.* corsair, privateer (*man and ship*); pirate.

corsé, *n.m.* corset, stays.

corsear, *v.i.* to cruise as a privateer.

corsetería, *n.f.* corset factory *or* shop.

corsetero, -ra, *n.m.f.* corset maker *or* seller.

corso (1), *n.m.* privateering cruise; ***armar en corso,*** to fit (*a vessel*) as a privateer; ***ir*** or ***salir a corso,*** to cruise as privateer; ***patente de corso,*** letters of marque.

corso (2), **-sa,** *a., n.m.f.* Corsican.

corta (1), *n.f.* felling (trees); cutting (sugar-cane).

cortaalambres, *n.m. inv.* wire-cutter.

cortabolsas, *n.m.f. inv.* pickpocket.

cortacallos, *n.m. inv.* corn-cutter.

cortacigarros, *n.m. inv.* cigar-cutter.

cortacircuitos, *n.m. inv.* (*elec.*) cut-out, circuit breaker.

cortacorriente, *n.m. inv.* (*elec.*) contact-breaker.

cortadera, *n.f.* chisel (*for cutting hot iron*); (*bee-keeper's*) knife; (*Arg., Chi.*) fibre plant.

cortadillo, -lla, *a.* clipped (*coin*). — *n.m.* small tumbler; gill (*liquid measure*); ***azúcar de cortadillo,*** lump sugar; (*fig.*) ***echar cortadillos,*** to speak affectedly; (*fig.*) to drink glasses of wine.

cortado, -da, *a.* short, abrupt; (*her.*) parted in the middle. — *n.m.* caper, leap; ***un (café) cortado,*** coffee with a dash of milk.

cortador, -ra, *a.* cutting. — *n.m.* cutter. — *n.f.* cutting *or* slicing machine; cutting board.

cortadura, *n.f.* cut, cutting; (*fort.*) parapet with embrasures and merlons.

cortafrío, *n.m.* cold chisel, cutting-iron.

cortafuego, *n.m.* (*agric.*) clearing (*left to prevent fire spreading*), firebreak; (*arch.*) fireproof wall (*between buildings*).

cortalápices, *n.m. inv.* pencil-sharpener.

cortamalla, *n.f.* pruning (*of vine-branch*).

cortamiento, *n.m.* cutting.

cortante, *a.* cutting, sharp, biting; short, abrupt. — *n.m.* butcher.

cortapapel, *n.m.* paper-cutter, paper-knife, letter opener.

cortapicos, *n.m. inv.* earwig; (*coll.*) ***cortapicos y callares,*** children should be seen and not heard.

cortapiés, *n.m.* (*fencing*) thrust (*at the legs*).

cortapisa, *n.f.* condition, proviso; obstacle, impediment, hindrance; elegance (*in speaking*).

cortaplumas, *n.m. inv.* penknife.

cortapruebas, *n.m. inv.* (*photo.*) print-cutter.

cortapuros, *n.m. inv.* cigar-cutter.

cortar, *v.t.* to cut; to shear; to trim; to cut away, pare off; to cut short, cut in on, break in on; to switch off; to stop; to curdle; ***cortar el agua,*** to cut *or* turn the water off; ***me ha cortado el hilo del pensamiento,*** he has interrupted *or* upset my train of thought; ***cortar el paso,*** to bar the way; ***cortarle a alguien las alas*** or ***los vuelos,*** to clip s.o.'s wings; ***cortar por lo sano,*** to take drastic measures, cut one's losses; ***cortar las libranzas,*** to stop payment; ***cortar de raíz,*** to eradicate, root out; ***cortar por el camino más corto,*** to take a short cut. — **cortarse,** *v.r.* to be abashed, become confused, get embarrassed *or* tongue-tied; to get chapped, cracked, split; to curdle; ***se ha cortado la leche,*** the milk has turned sour; ***se me han cortado los labios,*** my lips are chapped.

cortarraíces, *n.m. inv.* root-cutter.

cortauñas, *n.m. inv.* nail-clippers.

cortavapor, *n.m.* cut-off (*of an engine*).

cortavidrios, *n.m. inv.* (glazier's) diamond; glass-cutter.

cortaviento, *n.m.* windscreen (*of vehicles*); (*aer.*) wind-shield.

corte (1), *n.m.* cut; cutting; trimming; length (*of material needed for garment*); slit, slash; (*mil.*) tailor's shop; cross-section; felling of trees; arbitration; (*vulg.*) ***corte de manga(s),*** V-sign.

corte (2), *n.f.* (royal) court; levee; suite, retinue; ***la Corte,*** Madrid; ***la corte celestial,*** Heaven; ***hacer la corte a,*** to court, woo; (*pl.*) ***Cortes,*** legislative assembly of Spain

cortedad, *n.f.* smallness; (*fig.*) shyness, diffidence, bashfulness; ***cortedad de medios,*** lack of means.

cortejador, -ra, *a.* courting, wooing. — *n.m.f.* wooer.

cortejante, *a.* courting, wooing. — *n.m.* gallant, beau.

cortejar, *v.t.* to woo; to court; to escort.

cortejo, *n.m.* courting, wooing; gallant, beau; lover, sweetheart; paramour; cortège, procession, train.

corteña, *n.f.* (*print.*) blank page.

cortés, *a.* courteous, polite, civil, mannerly.

cortesanazo, -za, *a.* affectedly polite, fulsome.

cortesanía, *n.f.* courtesy, civility, politeness, good manners.

cortesano, -na, *a.* courtly, court-like; — *n.m.* courtier. — *n.f.* courtesan.

cortesía, *n.f.* courtesy, civility, good manners, politeness; courteousness; compliment; (*print.*) blank left between two chapters; (*obs.*) days of grace for payment of a bill of exchange; expression of respect (*at end of letter*); ***hacer una cortesía,*** to curtsey.

corteza, *n.f.* bark, peel, skin, rind, crust; (*fig.*) rusticity, boorishness; (*orn.*) widgeon.

cortezón, *n.m.* thick bark, rind, crust.

cortezudo, -da, *a.* very barky *or* crusty; (*fig.*) rustic, boorish, unmannerly, unpolished.

cortezuela, *n.f.* thin bark, crust *or* rind.

cortical, *a.* cortical.

cortijada, *n.f.* farm estate; group of buildings round a farmhouse.

cortijero, -ra, *a.* to do with farm estates. — *n.m.f.* owner *or* foreman of a farm estate.

cortijo, *n.m.* farm-estate; ***alborotar el cortijo,*** to stir up trouble, set the cat among the pigeons.

cortil, *n.m.* yard.

cortina, *n.f.* curtain; screen; covering; lees, dregs; ***cortina de agua,*** sheet of water; ***cortina de fuego,*** artillery barrage; ***cortina de humo,*** smoke-screen; ***cortina de muelle,*** sustaining wall, dike; ***correr la cortina,*** to draw the curtain; (*fig.*) to draw a veil (over); (*fig.*) to uncover, disclose; ***descorrer la cortina,*** to draw the curtain back, open the curtain; (*fig.*) to disclose; ***dormir a cortinas verdes,*** to sleep in the open air; ***a cortina corrida,*** in secret, behind closed doors.

cortinaje, *n.m.* (set of) curtains.

cortinal, *n.m.* allotment, plot.

cortinilla, *n.f.* small curtain; curtain (*carriage, car etc.*).

cortinón, *n.m.* large curtain.

cortiña, *n.f.* (*prov.*) allotment, garden plot.

corto, -ta (2), *a.* short, brief; shy, diffident; ***corto de genio,*** diffident; ***corto de luces,*** dull-witted; ***corto de oído,*** hard of hearing; ***corto de vista,*** short-sighted; ***corto circuito,*** short circuit; ***a la corta o a la larga,*** sooner or later; ***atar corto,*** to keep a tight hold on, keep on a short rein; ***no es corto en dar,*** he's a ready *or* lavish giver; ***se quedó corto,*** he didn't go far enough, he didn't do *or* say enough.

cortón, *n.m.* mole-cricket.

corúa, *n.f.* Cuban cormorant.

corulla, *n.f.* place for stowing cordage (*in galleys*).

corundo, *n.m.* corundum.

coruña, *n.f.* coarse canvas.

coruñés, -ñesa, *a., n.m.f.* of *or* belonging to Corunna, native of Corunna.

coruscación, *n.f.* (*phys.*) coruscation, flashing; brilliancy.

coruscante, corusco, -ca, *a.* (*poet.*) coruscant, shining.

coruscar [A], *v.i.* (*poet.*) to shine, coruscate.

corva, *n.f.* [CORVO].

corvadura, *n.f.* curvature; (*arch.*) bend (*of arch or vault*).

corval, *a.* long (*olive*).

corvato, *n.m.* young crow *or* rook.

corvaza, *n.f.* (*vet.*) curb.

corvecito, *n.m.* small crow *or* rook.

corvejón, *n.m.* gambrel, hock, hough; spur (*of a cock*); (*orn.*) cormorant.

corvejos, *n.m.pl.* hock.

corveta, *n.f.* curvet, leap, bound.

corvetear, *v.i.* to curvet, bound, leap.

corvídeo, -dea, *a.* (*orn.*) corvine.

córvidos, *n.m.pl.* corvus genus of birds.

corvillo, *n.m.* bill-hook, pruning-knife; knife; ***miércoles corvillo,*** Ash Wednesday.

corvinera, *n.f.* fishing-net for sea-bass.

corvino, -na, *a.* corvine, raven-like. — *n.f.* corvina fish, drum fish, bass.

corvo, -va, *a.* bent, crooked, arched. — *n.m.* grappling-iron; (*ichth.*) kind of conger. — *n.f.* back of the knee; (*vet.*) curb; ***hasta la(s) corva(s),*** knee-deep.

corzo, -za, *n.m.f.* roe-deer, fallow-deer.

corzuelo, *n.m.* wheat left by threshers.

cosa, *n.f.* thing; something; matter, affair; ***me he dejado una cosa en el coche,*** I've left sth. in the car; ***a otra cosa,*** let's go on to sth. else; ***no es (ninguna) cosa del otro jueves,*** it's nothing very wonderful; ***cosa de oír*** or ***de ver,*** thing worth hearing *or* seeing; ***cosa nunca vista,*** sth. unheard of; ***cosa perdida,*** dead loss; ***¡cosa rara!*** how strange! how extraordinary!; ***cosa de risa,*** laughing-stock; ***como quien no quiere la cosa,*** with an air of indifference, casually; ***como si tal cosa,*** as if nothing had happened; effortlessly; ***es muy poquita cosa,*** he (she) is a poor (miserable) object *or* specimen; ***cosas de viento,*** trifles; ***a cosa hecha,*** with certainty of success; ***es cosa de media hora,*** it's about half an hour; ***son cosas de Juan,*** that's John all over, that's typical of John, that's John's doing; ***dejarlo como cosa perdida,*** to give up as hopeless; ***disponer sus cosas,*** to put one's affairs in order (*before dying*); ***es cosa de nunca acabar,*** it's a never-ending business; ***las cosas de palacio van despacio,*** officialdom moves slowly; ***muchas cosas a su madre,*** kind regards to your mother; ***ni cosa que lo valga,*** nor anything like it; ***no hay tal cosa,*** it is not true; ***no hacer cosa a derechas,*** not to do anything right; ***no sea cosa que,*** lest; ***no es cosa de apurarse,*** it's nothing to get worried about; ***eso es cosa mía,*** that's my business; ***eso no es cosa suya,*** that's no business of yours.

cosaco, -ca, *a., n.m.f.* Cossack; ***beber como un cosaco,*** to drink like a fish. — *n.f.* Cossack dance.

cosaquería, *n.f.* brutal raid, incursion.

cosario, *n.m.* professional errand-doer, one who carries out commissions; professional huntsman.

coscarana, *n.f.* (*prov.*) cracknel.

coscarse [A], *v.r.* (*coll.*) to shrug the shoulders; to be

put out; to flinch; ***ni se coscó,*** he didn't turn a hair *or* bat an eye-lid.
coscoja, *n.f.* kermes oak; dried oak-leaf; ring on bridle-bit.
coscojo, *n.m.* kermes oak-gall; (*pl.*) chains of bridle-bit.
coscolina, *n.f.* (*Mex.*) harlot.
coscomate, *n.m.* (*Mex.*) corn barn.
coscón, -cona, *a., n.m.f.* crafty, sly (*person*); tedious, wearisome (*person*).
coscoroba, *n.f.* (*Arg., Chi.*) small swan.
coscorrón, *n.m.* bump, lump (*on the head*).
coscorronera [CHICHONERA].
cosecante, *n.m.* (*trig.*) cosecant.
cosecha, *n.f.* harvest; harvest-time; crop; ***cosecha de vino,*** vintage; ***de su cosecha,*** of one's own invention.
cosechadora, *n.f.* combine harvester, (*Am.*) harvester, reaping machine.
cosechar, *v.t., v.i.* to reap, harvest.
cosechero, -ra, *n.m.f.* (crop) grower.
cosedizo, -za, *a.* which can be stitched *or* sewed.
coselete, *n.m.* corslet; pikeman; thorax (*of insects*).
coseno, *n.m.* (*trig.*) cosine; ***coseno verso,*** versed cosine.
coser, *v.t.* to sew, stitch; ***coserse la boca*** or ***los labios,*** to remain silent; (*coll.*) ***coser a puñaladas,*** to stab repeatedly; ***coser a preguntas,*** to bombard with questions; ***coserse a (con) alquien,*** to stick close to s.o.; ***es coser y cantar,*** it's child's play, it's a walk-over; ***estar cosido a la(s) falda(s) de su madre,*** to be tied to one's mother's apron strings.
cosera, *n.f.* (*prov.*) piece of land (*that can be irrigated all at once*).
cosetada, *n.f.* quick run, sprint.
cosible, *a.* which can be sewed.
cosicosa [QUISICOSA].
cosido, *n.m.* sewing; ***cosido de la cama,*** quilt and blankets stitched together.
cosidura, *n.f.* (*naut.*) lashing.
cosificar [A], *v.t.* to reduce to the level of an inanimate object *or* chattel.
cosilla, *n.f.* (miserable) little thing.
cosita, *n.f.* (dear) little thing.
cosmética, *n.f.* cosmetics.
cosmético, *n.m.* cosmetic.
cósmico, -ca, *a.* cosmic.
cosmogonía, *n.f.* cosmogony.
cosmogónico, -ca, *a.* cosmogonic(al).
cosmografía, *n.f.* cosmography.
cosmográfico, -ca, *a.* cosmographical.
cosmógrafo, -fa, *n.m.f.* cosmographer.
cosmología, *n.f.* cosmology.
cosmológico, -ca, *a.* cosmological.
cosmólogo, -ga, *n.m.f.* cosmologist.
cosmopolita, *a., n.m.f.* cosmopolitan.
cosmopolitismo, *n.m.* cosmopolitanism.
cosmos, *n.m.* cosmos.
coso, *n.m.* public place (*for bullfights, sports etc.*); main street; wood-worm; ***coso de flores,*** battle of flowers.
cospe, *n.m.* hacking stroke (*in timber-cutting*).
cospel, *n.m.* planchet, coin-blank (*in the mint*).
cospillo, *n.m.* (*prov.*) olive lees, bagasse.
cosque (*fam.*) [COSCORRÓN].
cosquilladizo, -za, *a.* touchy, peevish.
cosquillar, cosquillear, *v.t.* to tickle.
cosquillas, *n.f.pl.* tickling, ticklishness; ***buscarle a alguien las cosquillas,*** to tease, try to annoy s.o.; (*lit., fig.*) ***hacerle a alguien cosquillas,*** to tickle s.o.; (*coll.*) ***tener malas cosquillas,*** to be touchy.
cosquillejas, *n.f.pl.* light tickling.
cosquilleo, *n.m.* tickling.
cosquilloso, -sa, *a.* ticklish; (*fig.*) touchy.
costa, *n.f.* cost; coast, shore; shoemaker's boxwood polisher; ***a costa de,*** at the expense of; ***a mi costa,*** at my expense; ***a poca costa,*** with little effort; ***a toda costa,*** at all costs; (*naut.*) ***dar a la costa,*** to be blown towards the coast; (*pl.*) (*law*) costs; (*law*) ***condenar en costas,*** to sentence to pay costs.
costado, *n.m.* side; flank; ***inglés por los cuatro costados,*** English to the backbone; ***dolor de costado,*** stitch in the side; (*pl.*) race, lineage.
costal, *a.* (*anat.*) costal. — *n.m.* sack; brace (*of frame for making adobe walls*); ***ésa es harina de otro costal,*** that's another kettle of fish; ***estar hecho un costal de huesos,*** to be a bag of bones; (*fam.*) ***el costal de los pecados,*** the human body; ***vaciar el costal,*** to unburden o.s.
costalada, *n.f.* [COSTALAZO].
costalazo, *n.m.* cropper; ***dar(se) un costalazo,*** to come a cropper; to flop down.
costalejo, *n.m.* small sack.
costalero, *n.m.* (*prov.*) porter, carrier.
costalgia, *n.f.* pain in the side.
costana, *n.f.* steep road *or* street; (*naut.*) frame.
costanero, -ra, *a.* coastal, coasting; sloping; ***buque costanero,*** coaster. — *n.f.* slope; (*pl.*) rafters.
costanilla, *n.f.* steep street; gentle slope.
costar [4], *v.i.* to cost; ***me ha costado caro,*** I've had to pay through the nose for it; ***cuesta trabajo creerlo,*** it is hard to believe; ***cueste lo que cueste,*** at all costs.
costarricense, costarriqueño, -ña, *a., n.m.f.* Costa Rican.
coste, *n.m.* cost, price; ***a coste y costas,*** at cost price; ***coste de la vida,*** cost of living.
costear, *v.t.* to pay the cost of; to bear the expense of; (*naut.*) to coast; ***no me lo puedo costear,*** I can't afford it; ***vender una cosa para costear(se) otra,*** to sell one thing in order to pay for another.
costeño, -ña, *a.* [COSTANERO].
costero, -ra, *a.* coastal, coasting. — *n.m.* wood nearest to the bark; (*min.*) side (*of a furnace*); (*min.*) side face (*of a seam*). — *n.f.* side (*of a bale of goods*); outside quire (*of a ream of hand-made paper*); slope, incline; coast; (*naut.*) salmon-fishing season.
costezuela, *n.f.* slight slope.
costil, *a.* (*anat.*) costal.
costilla, *n.f.* rib; (*carp.*) furring; part of an organ bellows; (*coll.*) support; chop, cutlet; (*coll.*) wife; rung (*of chair*); stave (*of barrel*); (*mech.*) cramp-irons, chimney-ties; ***costilla falsa,*** false rib; ***costilla flotante,*** floating rib; (*pl.*) shoulders, back; ***medirle a uno las costillas,*** to cudgel s.o.
costillaje, costillar, *n.m.* ribs; ribbing.
costilludo, -da, *a.* (*coll.*) broad-shouldered.
costino, -na, *a.* [COSTANERO].
costo, *n.m.* cost, price, expense, charges; (*bot.*) alecost, costmary; ***a costo y costas,*** at cost price.
costosamente, *adv.* in a costly way, expensively, extravagantly.
costoso, -sa, *a.* dear, expensive, costly; (*fig.*) hard to obtain.
costra, *n.f.* crust; scab; (wick) snuff; (*coll.*) filthiness, tattiness, messiness; ***costra de azúcar,*** sugar crust (*left in boilers*); (*med.*) ***costra láctea,*** scald head, infantile eczema.
costrada, *n.f.* candied seed-cake.
costroso, -sa, *a.* crusty; scabby; (*coll.*) filthy, tatty, messy.
costumbre, *n.f.* custom, habit; ***novela de costumbres,*** novel of manners; ***usos y costumbres,*** usage and custom; ***las tonterías de costumbre,*** the usual nonsense; ***de costumbre,*** usually, habitually; ***según costumbre,*** according to custom; ***depravar las costumbres,*** to

corrupt morals; ***la costumbre es segunda naturaleza,*** habit is second nature; ***la costumbre hace ley,*** custom creates law; ***es costumbre,*** it is customary; ***tener por costumbre hacer algo,*** to be in the habit of doing sth.

costumbrismo, *n.m.* writing of novels of manners.

costumbrista, *n.m.f.* writer of novels of manners.

costura, *n.f.* seam; needlework, sewing; stitching; riveting; (*naut.*) splicing (*of a rope*); (*mech., carp.*) joint; ***sin costura,*** seamless; ***sentar las costuras,*** to press seams (*in tailoring*); ***sentar a uno las costuras*** to take s.o. to task.

costurera, *n.f.* seamstress.

costurería, *n.f.* work-room (*for sewing*).

costurero, *n.m.* (lady's) work-box *or* table; (*prov.*) sewing-room.

costurón, *n.m.* thick seam; large scar; coarse stitch.

cota, *n.f.* coat of mail (also ***cota de malla***), tabard-coat, coat of arms; callous skin (*on boar's back*); height, height figure.

cotana, *n.f.* mortise, mortise chisel.

cotangente, *n.f.* (*trig.*) cotangent.

cotanza, *n.f.* coutances (*linen*).

cotarrera, *n.f.* (*sl.*) tramp; (*coll.*) gossip, gadabout.

cotarro, *n.m.* charity doss-house; side of a ravine; disorderly meeting *or* group; (*fig.*) ***alboratar el cotarro,*** to set the cat among the pigeons; ***ser el amo del cotarro,*** to rule the roost, boss the show.

cotejar, *v.t.* to compare, confront, collate.

cotejo, *n.m.* comparison, collation.

cotense, *n.m.* (*Mex.*) rough brown linen wrapper.

coterráneo, -nea, *a.* [CONTERRÁNEO].

cotí, *n.m.* tick, ticking (*material*).

cotidianamente, *adv.* daily.

cotidiano, -na, *a.* daily, every day.

cotiledón, *n.m.* (*bot.*) cotyledon.

cotiliforme, *a.* (*bot.*) cotyliform.

cotiloide, cotiloideo, -dea, *a.* (*anat.*) cotyloid.

cotilla, *n.f.* stays, corsets; (*coll.*) gossip.

cotillero, -ra, *n.m.f.* stay-maker, stay-seller; gossip.

cotillo, *n.m.* head, striking side of hammer.

cotillón, *n.m.* cotillion (*dance*).

cotín, *n.m.* back stroke (*given to a ball*).

cotiza, *n.f.* (*her.*) band (*of a shield*); (*Ven.*) Indian sandal.

cotizable, *a.* quotable.

cotización, *n.f.* (*com.*) quotation, price.

cotizado, -da, *a.* (*her.*) banded.

cotizador, -ra, *n.m.f.* quoter, pricer, valuer.

cotizar [C], *v.t.* (*com.*) to quote; to value at a price; (*coll.*) ***estar muy cotizado,*** to be much sought after, be in demand.

coto, *n.m.* reserved ground, preserve; boundary (*mark*); limit; restriction; (*ichth.*) chub; billiard contest; (*Hisp. Am.*) goitre; ***coto redondo,*** estate, large estate; ***coto de caza,*** game preserve; ***poner coto a,*** to put a stop to; to put a limit on, check.

cotobelo, *n.m.* opening in branch of bridle.

cotomono, *n.m.* (*Per., zool.*) ursine howler.

cotón, *n.m.* printed cotton.

cotona, *n.f.* (*Hisp. Am.*) coarse undervest; (*Mex.*) chamois jacket.

cotonada, *n.f.* cotton goods, calico prints.

cotoncillo, *n.m.* button of a maulstick.

cotonía, *n.f.* dimity.

cotorra, *n.f.* small parrot, parakeet; magpie; (*coll.*) talkative woman, chatter-box.

cotorrear, *v.i.* to chatter, gabble.

cotorreo, *n.m.* (*coll.*) chattering, gossiping.

cotorrera, *n.f.* hen-parrot; (*coll.*) talkative woman, chatter-box.

cotorrería, *n.f.* chattering (*of women*).

cotorrón, -rrona, *a.* trying to be young (*old people*).

cototo, *n.m.* (*Arg., Chi.*) bump, lump.

cotral, *a., n.m.f.* worn-out ox *or* cow.

cotudo, -da, *a.* cottony, hairy, fluffy; (*Hisp. Am.*) suffering with goitre.

cotufa, *n.f.* Jerusalem artichoke; titbits, dainties.

cotundo, *n.m.* (*Cub.*) cotundo bird.

coturno, *n.m.* cothurnus, buskin; ***calzar el coturno,*** to use lofty, sublime language; ***de alto coturno,*** of high degree *or* station.

cotutela, *n.f.* joint custody, joint wardship.

cotutor, -ra, *n.m.f.* joint guardian.

cotuza, *n.f.* (*E.S., Guat.*) agouti, agouty.

covacha, *n.f.* wretched cave *or* den.

covachuela, *n.f.* wretched little cave *or* den; poky little (government) office.

covachuelista, *n.m.* wretched clerk *or* white-collared worker; miserable civil servant.

covadera, *n.f.* (*Chi., Per.*) guano bed; (*Col.*) dell.

covalonga, *n.f.* (*Ven.*) quinine plant.

covendedor, -ra, *n.m.f.* joint-vendor.

coxalgia, *n.f.* (*med.*) coxalgia.

coxálgico, -ca, *a.* (*med.*) coxalgic.

coxcojilla, coxcojita, *n.f.* hopscotch; ***a coxcojita,*** hippety-hoppety, jumping on one foot.

coy, *n.m.* (*naut.*) hammock, cot.

coya, *n.f.* (*Per.*) Inca queen *or* princess.

coyunda, *n.f.* shoe-lace, (*Am.*) shoestring; strap (*for yoking oxen*); (*fig.*) wedlock; dominion, subjection.

coyuntura, *n.f.* joint, articulation; (political *or* economic) juncture, situation.

coyuntural, *a.* of the (political *or* economic) situation.

coyuyo, *n.m.* (*Arg.*) large cicada.

coz, *n.f.* kick; recoil (*of a gun*); flowing back (*of water*); butt (*of a pistol*); butt-end (*of log*); heel (*of mast*); ***a coces*** (by) kicking, with kicks; ***dar*** (***tirar***) ***coces,*** to kick (out); (*fig.*) ***dar*** (***tirar***) ***coces contra el aguijón,*** to kick against the pricks; (*fig.*) ***soltar*** (***tirar***) ***una coz,*** to retort brusquely *or* harshly; ***mandar a coces,*** to command *or* rule harshly; ***meterse de hoz y de coz*** (***en***), to plunge headlong *or* wholeheartedly (into).

cozcojilla, cozcojita [COXCOJILLA].

cozolmeca, *n.f.* (*Mex.*) sarsaparilla plant.

crabrón, *n.m.* hornet.

crac, crash, *n.m.* (*com.*) crash, failure, bankruptcy, slump; ***hacer crac,*** to go bankrupt.

cran, *n.m.* (*print.*) nick (*of type*).

craneal, craneano, -na, *a.* cranial.

cráneo, *n.m.* skull, cranium; (*coll.*) ***el cráneo,*** the brain; ***se le ha secado el cráneo, tiene seco el cráneo,*** he has lost his wits.

craneología, *n.f.* craniology.

craneológico, -ca, *a.* craniological.

craneólogo, *n.m.* craniologist.

craneometría, *n.f.* craniometry.

craneómetro, *n.m.* craniometer.

craneoscopia, *n.m.* cranioscopy.

craneotomía, *n.f.* craniotomy.

craniano, -na, *a.* cranial.

crápula, *n.f.* debauchery.

crapulosidad, *n.f.* debauchery.

crapuloso, -sa, *a.* crapulous, debauched.

crascitar, *v.i.* to caw, croak.

crash [CRAC].

crasicaudo, -da, *a.* (*zool.*) thick-tailed.

crasicaulo, -la, *a.* (*bot.*) thick-stemmed.

crasiento, -ta [GRASIENTO].

crasitud, *n.f.* fat; greasiness; (*coll.*) ignorance, stupidity.

craso, -sa, *a.* fat, greasy, oily, unctuous; (*fig.*) crass, gross.

cráter, *n.m.* crater.

craticula, *n.f.* wicket (*in convent through which nuns* *receive the sacrament*); confessional; (*phys.*) diffraction grating.

craza, *n.f.* crucible (*for melting precious metal*).

crea, *n.f.* semi-fine cotton *or* linen stuff.

creable, *a.* creatable.

creación, *n.f.* creation.

creador, -ra, *a.* creative. — *n.m.f.* creator. — *n.m.* Creator.

crear, *v.t.* to create; ***crearse dificultades,*** to make difficulties for o.s.

crébol, *n.m.* (*prov.*) holly tree.

crecedero, -ra, *a.* able to grow; that can be lengthened (*children's clothes*).

crecer [9], *v.i.* to grow, increase, swell, become larger, rise. — **crecerse,** *v.r.* to show guts (*in the face of danger*); to become too big for one's boots.

creces, *n.f.pl.* increase, rise, increment; ***con creces,*** abundantly, lavishly; ***le compensó con creces,*** he more than compensated him.

crecida (1), *n.f.* swelling, freshet, rise, flood.

crecidamente, *adv.* plentifully, abundantly, copiously.

crecidito, -ta, *a.* quite big, pretty tall.

crecido, -da (2), *a.* large, great, big; ***un número crecido,*** a large number.

creciente, *a.* growing, increasing; crescent. — *n.m.* (*her.*) half-moon with points upward. — *n.f.* freshet, swell (*of waters*); leaven; ***creciente de la luna,*** crescent moon; (*naut.*) ***creciente del mar,*** flow, flood-tide.

crecimiento, *n.m.* growth.

credencia, *n.f.* credence-table.

credencial, *a.* credential. — *n.f.pl.* (**credenciales**) credentials.

credibilidad, *n.f.* (*pol.*) credibility.

crédito, *n.m.* credit; credence; reputation; note, bill, order for payment; ***créditos activos,*** assets; ***créditos pasivos,*** liabilities; ***dar a crédito,*** to loan, give on credit; ***dar crédito a,*** to give credit *or* credence to.

credo, *n.m.* creed, credo; ***cada credo,*** every moment; ***en un credo,*** in a trice; ***con el credo en la boca,*** in great risk *or* danger.

credulidad, *n.f.* credulity.

crédulo, -la, *a.* credulous.

creederas, *n.f.pl.* (*coll.*) credulity; ***tener buenas creederas,*** to be very credulous.

creedero, -ra, *a.* credible.

creedor, -ra, *a.* credulous.

creencia, *n.f.* belief.

creer(se) [N], *v.t.,* (*v.r.*) to believe, think; ***creer a ojos cerrados, a macha martillo, a puño cerrado,*** to believe blindly, implicitly, firmly; ***créamelo,*** believe me, take my word for it, mark my words; ***ya lo creo,*** definitely, most certainly, I should think so; ***creo que no vendrá,*** I don't think he'll come; ***se cree que somos tontos,*** he imagines we're fools; ***se lo cree todo,*** he'll swallow anything; ***no me lo creo,*** I'm not having, swallowing *or* taking that; ***Juan se cree en el deber de ir,*** John considers that he is under an obligation to go; ***ver y creer,*** seeing is believing.

crehuela, *n.f.* crash (linen).

creíble, *a.* credible, believable.

crema (1), *n.f.* cream; liqueur; ***crema de (los) zapatos,*** shoe-cream *or* polish.

crema (2), *n.f.* diæresis.

cremación, *n.f.* cremation.

cremallera, *n.f.* (*mech.*) toothed bar, rack, ratch; zip, zip-fastener.

crematístico, -ca, *a.* chrematistic, economic. — *n.f.* chrematistics, political economy.

crematólogo, -ga, *n.m.f.* chrematist, political economist.

crematología, *n.f.* political economy.

crematológico, -ca, *a.* relating to political economy.

crematorio, -ria, *a.* crematory. — *n.m.* cremator (*furnace*); crematorium.

cremento [INCREMENTO].

cremómetro, *n.m.* creamometer.

crémor tártaro, *n.m.* cream of tartar.

cremoso, -sa, *a.* creamy.

crencha, *n.f.* parting (*of hair*); hair on each side of parting.

creosota, *n.f.* creosote.

creosotar, *v.t.* to creosote.

crepitación, *n.f.* crepitation, crackling.

crepitante, *a.* crepitant, crepitating, crackling.

crepitar, *v.i.* to crepitate, crackle.

crepuscular, *a.* crepuscular, of twilight *or* dusk. — *n.m.pl.* (**crepusculares**) crepuscular Lepidoptera.

crepusculino, -na, *a.* crepuscular.

crepúsculo, *n.m.* twilight, dusk.

cresa, *n.f.* fly-blow, fly's egg; larva; egg of queen bee.

creso, *n.m.* Croesus, very wealthy man.

crespilla, *n.f.* agaric.

crespina, *n.f.* hair-net.

crespo, -pa, *a.* crisp; curly, frizzy; unruly, unmanageable; (*bot.*) crisp-leaved; obscure, bombastic (*style*); (*fig.*) angry, displeased, vexed; (*fig.*) elegant; haughty, conceited. — *n.m.* curl.

crespón, *n.m.* crape; crêpe.

cresta, *n.f.* comb, cock's comb; crest; aigrette, tuft; ***alzar*** or ***levantar la cresta,*** to become arrogant, get uppish; ***dar en la cresta,*** to bring (*s.o.*) down a peg.

crestado, -da, *a.* crested, cristate.

crestería, *n.f.* (*arch.*) cresting; (*fort.*) battlements.

crestomatía, *n.f.* chrestomathy.

crestón, *n.m.* large comb *or* crest; (*min.*) outcrop; crest (*of helmet*).

crestudo, -da, *a.* large-crested; (*fig.*) arrogant, conceited, presumptuous.

Creta, *n.f.* Crete.

creta, *n.f.* chalk.

cretáceo, -cea, *a.* cretaceous, chalky.

cretense, *a., n.m.f.* Cretan.

crético, -ca, *a.* Cretan. — *n.m.* cretic.

cretinismo, *n.m.* cretinism, idiocy.

cretino, -na, *a.* cretinous. — *n.m.f.* (*lit., fig.*) cretin, idiot; fool.

cretona, *n.f.* cretonne.

creyente, *a.* believing. — *n.m.f.* believer.

crezneja [CRIZNEJA].

cría, *n.f.* brood (*of animals*); rearing, breeding; child reared by a nurse; ***ama de cría,*** wet nurse; ***cría de abejas,*** bee keeping.

criada, *a., n.f.* [CRIADO].

criadero, -ra, *a.* fruitful, prolific. — *n.m.* nursery (*plants*); breeding-place; fish-hatchery; (*min.*) seam; ***criadero de ostras,*** oyster breeding ground.

criadilla, *n.f.* testicle; lamb-fry; truffle, small loaf; potato.

criado, -da, *a.* brought up; ***bien (mal) criado,*** well- (ill-) bred. — *n.m.* servant. — *n.f.* female servant, maid(servant); ***me ha salido la criada respondona,*** I wasn't banking on that, I wasn't expecting that; that's a new side of him (her).

criador, -ra, *a.* feeding, nourishing; fruitful, fertile, fecund. — *n.m.f.* creator; breeder, raiser. — *n.f.* wet-nurse.

criamiento, *n.m.* renovation, preservation.

criandera, *n.f.* (*Hisp. Am.*) wet-nurse.

crianza, *n.f.* nursing; lactation; breeding, manners, upbringing; ***dar crianza,*** to rear, bring up.

criar [L], *v.t.* to create; to breed, nurse, rear, foster, nourish; to bring up; to grow (*wine*); ***criar***

carnes, to grow fat; ***criar molleja,*** to grow lazy; ***Dios los cría y ellos se juntan,*** birds of a feather flock together.
criatura, *n.f.* creature; infant, child; ***eso es criatura de Juan,*** that's John's doing.
criba, *n.f.* sieve, sifter; screen.
cribado, *n.m.* sieving, sifting.
cribador, -ra, *a.* sieving, sifting. — *n.m.f.* sifter.
cribadura, *n.f.* sifting.
cribar, *v.t.* to sieve, sift; to screen; to sort out.
cribero, -ra, *n.m.f.* maker *or* vendor of sieves.
cribo, *n.m.* sieve.
criboso, -sa, *a.* (*anat.*) cribriform, cribrate, cribrose.
cric, *n.m.* screw-jack, lifting-jack.
crica, *n.f.* trench, fissure; (*anat.*) female pudenda.
cricoides, *a.*, *n.m.* (*anat.*) cricoid.
críquet, *n.m.* cricket.
crimen, *n.m.* crime; murder.
criminación, *n.f.* crimination.
criminal, *a.* criminal; murderous; (*coll., fig.*) murderous, appalling, ghastly; (*coll.*) ***un viaje criminal,*** a murderous *or* ghastly journey; (*coll.*) ***esto es criminal,*** it's (sheer) murder. — *n.m.* criminal; murderer.
criminalidad, *n.f.* criminality; crime-rate.
criminalista, *n.m.* criminalist.
criminalizar [C], *v.t.* to transfer (*a case*) from civil to criminal court.
criminalmente, *adv.* criminally, guiltily; in accordance with criminal law.
criminar, *v.t.* to criminate.
criminología, *n.f.* criminology.
criminosidad, *n.f.* criminality.
criminoso, -sa, *a.* criminal.
crimno, *n.m.* coarse flour of spelt and wheat.
crin, *n.f.* mane, horse-hair; ***tenerse a las crines,*** to hold on with might and main.
crinado, -da, crinito, -ta, *a.* crinite, maned; (*poet.*) long-haired.
crinífero, -ra, *a.* (*zool.*) mane-bearing.
criniforme, *a.* mane-like.
crinoideo, -dea, *a.* (*bot.*) crinoid, lily-shaped. — *n.m.pl.* (**crinoideos**) Crinoidea.
crinolina, *n.f.* crinoline.
crío, *n.m.* (*fam.*) baby, child, infant; kid.
criolita, *n.f.* (*min.*) cryolite.
criollo, -lla, *a.*, *n.m.f.* Creole.
cripta, *n.f.* crypt.
criptogámico, -ca, *a.* (*bot.*) cryptogamic.
criptógamo, -ma, *a.* (*bot.*) cryptogamous. — *n.m.f.* cryptogam.
criptografía, *n.f.* cryptography.
criptográfico, -ca, *a.* cryptographic.
criptógrafo, -fa, *n.m.f.* cryptographer.
criptograma, *n.f.* cryptogram.
criptotelegrafía, *n.f.* code telegraphy.
criptología, *n.f.* cryptology.
cris, *n.m.* creese, kris.
crisálida, *n.f.* pupa, chrysalis.
crisantemo, *n.m.* chrysanthemum.
criselefantino, -na, *a.* chryselephantine.
crisis, *n.f. inv.* crisis.
crisma, *n.m.* chrism. — *n.f.* (*coll.*) nut; ***romperse la crisma,*** to crack one's nut, break one's neck.
crismera, *n.f.* chrismatory.
crisneja [CRIZNEJA].
crisoberilo, *n.m.* chrysoberyl.
crisol, *n.m.* crucible; hearth (*of furnace*).
crisolada, *n.f.* quantity of molten metal in a crucible.
crisolar [ACRISOLAR].
crisolito, *n.m.* chrysolite; ***crisolito oriental,*** yellow topaz.
crisopeya, *n.f.* alchemy.
crisoprasa, *n.f.* chrysoprase.
crispación, *n.f.*, **crispamiento,** *n.m.* (convulsive) contraction *or* contracting, twitch, twitching.
crispante, *a.* twitching, convulsive.
crispar, *v.t.* to convulse, cause contraction *or* twitching in; ***Juan me crispa (los nervios),*** John gets on my nerves.
crispativo, -va, *a.* convulsive.
crispatura, *n.f.* [CRISPACIÓN].
crispir, *v.t.* to marble.
crista, *n.f.* crest (*of helmet*).
cristal, *n.m.* crystal; glass; window-pane, pane of glass; ***doble cristal,*** double glazing; ***cristal de aumento,*** magnifying glass; ***cristal de roca,*** rock crystal; ***cristal hilado,*** spun glass; ***cristal tártaro,*** crystallized cream of tartar.
cristalería, *n.f.* glass-works; glass-ware; glass store.
cristalero, -ra, *n.m.f.* glass-maker *or* -dealer; glazer. — *n.f.* glass-making machine; glass door *or* partition.
cristalino, -na, *a.* crystalline. — *n.m.* (*anat.*) crystalline humour *or* lens.
cristalita, *n.f.* (*geol.*) crystallite.
cristalizable, *a.* crystallizable.
cristalización, *n.f.* crystallization.
cristalizador, -ra, *a.* crystallizing. — *n.m.* crystallizing pan.
cristalizante, *a.* crystallizing.
cristalizar(se), *v.t.*, *v.i.* (*v.r.*) to crystallize.
cristalografía, *n.f.* crystallography.
cristalográfico, -ca, *a.* crystallographic.
cristalógrafo, *n.m.* crystallographer.
cristel, *n.m.* clyster.
cristianar, *v.t.* (*coll.*) to baptize, christen.
cristiandad, *n.f.* Christendom; (*obs.*) Christianity.
cristianesco, -ca, *a.* aping Christian style; that is a travesty of Christian values.
cristianillo, -lla, *n.m.f.* (*contempt.*) nickname given to Spaniards by the Moors.
cristianísimo, -ma, *a. superl.* most Christian.
cristianismo, *n.m.* Christianity.
cristianizar [C], *v.t.* to christianize.
cristiano, -na, *a.*, *n.m.f.* Christian; (*coll.*) ***esto lo entiende todo cristiano,*** everybody will (can) understand that; ***hablar en cristiano,*** to use plain language.
cristífero, -ra, *a.* wearing the sign of the cross.
Cristina, *n.f.* Christina.
cristino, -na, *a.*, *n.m.f.* supporter of Isabel II.
Cristo, cristo, *n.m.* Christ; crucifix; ***¡voto a Cristo!*** zounds!; ***ni por un cristo,*** not on your life; ***le sienta como a un Cristo un par de pistolas,*** it's quite out of place on him; ***vive donde Cristo dio las tres voces,*** he lives in the back of beyond; ***poner a uno como un cristo,*** to reduce s.o. to a ghastly state.
Cristóbal, *n.m.* Christopher.
cristofué, *n.m.* (*Ven.*) bird.
cristus, *n.m. inv.* Christ-cross; Christ-cross row; the alphabet; ***no saber el cristus,*** to be very ignorant; ***estar en el cristus,*** to be at the rudiments.
crisuela, *n.f.* dripping-pan (*of lamp*).
criterio, *n.m.* criterion.
criticable, *a.* open to criticism, criticizable.
criticador, -ra, *a.* critical, criticizing. — *n.m.* critic, censurer, criticizer.
criticar [A], *v.t.* to criticize.
criticastro, *n.m.* criticaster.
criticismo, *n.m.* (*phil.*) criticism.
crítico, -ca, *a.* critical. — *n.m.* critic. — *n.f.* criticism; critique; (the) critics.
criticón, -cona, *a.*, *n.m.f.* terrible (one) for criticizing *or* fault finding, always finding fault; fault-finder.
critiquizar [C], *v.t.* (*coll.*) to over-criticize.
crizneja, *n.f.* rope, plait (*esparto etc.*); braid of hair.
croar, *v.i.* to croak.

croata, *a., n.m.f.* Croat, Croatian. — *n.m.* Croatian (*language*).
crocante, *n.m.* almond cake.
crocino, -na, *a.* croceate, croceous. — *n.m.* (*pharm.*) ointment.
croché, *n.m.* crochet.
cromático, -ca, *a.* chromatic. — *n.f.* chromatics.
cromatismo, *n.m.* (*opt.*) chromatism.
cromato, *n.m.* (*chem.*) chromate.
cromatología, *n.f.* chromatics.
crómico, -ca, *a.* chromic.
cromita, *n.f.* (*min.*) chromite.
cromo, *n.m.* chrome, chromium; chromolithograph; (*coll.*) coloured picture; gaudy picture; (*coll.*) ***estar hecho un cromo,*** to be all dolled up, (flashily) decked out.
cromógeno, -na, *a., n.m.f.* (*biol.*) chromogen.
cromografía, *n.f.* vignette in colours.
cromógrafo, *n.m.* chromograph.
cromolitografía, *n.f.* chromo, chromolithograph; chromolithography.
cromolitografiar [L], *v.t.* to make chromolithographs of.
cromolitográfico, -ca, *a.* chromolithographic.
cromolitógrafo, *n.m.* chromolithographer.
cromosfera, *n.f.* chromatosphere, chromosphere.
cromoso, -sa, *a.* chromic, chromous.
cromotipia, *n.f.* colour printing.
cromotipografía, *n.f.* chromotypography.
crónica (1), *n.f.* chronicle; news-letter, report.
cronicidad, *n.f.,* **cronicismo,** *n.m.* (*med.*) chronic condition.
crónico, -ca (2), *a.* (*med.*) chronic.
cronicón, *n.m.* short chronicle.
cronista, *n.m.f.* chronicler; news-letter writer, correspondent.
cronografía, *n.f.* chronography.
cronográfico, -ca, *a.* chronographic.
cronógrafo, *n.m.* chronograph; chronographer.
cronograma, *n.f.* chronogram.
cronología, *n.f.* chronology; sequence.
cronológico, -ca, *a.* chronological.
cronologista, *n.m.f.,* **cronólogo,** *n.m.* chronologist, chronologer.
cronometrador, -ra, *n.m.f.* time-keeper.
cronometraje, *n.m.* clocking, timing.
cronometrar, *v.t.* to clock, time.
cronometría, *n.f.* chronometry.
cronométrico, -ca, *a.* chronometrical.
cronómetro, *n.m.* chronometer, stop-watch.
cronoscopia, *n.m.* chronoscope.
croqueta, *n.f.* croquette.
croquis, *n.m. inv.* sketch, rough draft.
croscitar, *v.i.* to crow.
crótalo, *n.m.* crotalum (*castanet*); rattle-snake.
crotón, *n.m.* (*bot.*) croton, castor-oil plant.
crotorar, *v.i.* to rattle its bill (*crane, stork*).
cruce, *n.m.* crossing, cross-roads; ***cruce de línea,*** crossed-line; ***cruce giratorio,*** roundabout, (*Am.*) traffic circle.
crucera, *n.f.* withers.
crucería, *n.f.* (*arch.*) boss.
crucero, *n.m.* crucifer, cross-bearer; crossing; (*arch.*) transept; cross-vault; (*print.*) cross-bar (*of a chase*); (*print.*) fold (*in sheet of paper*); (*carp.*) beam; (*naut.*) cruiser; cruise; (*min.*) line *or* plane of cleavage.
cruceta, *n.f.* cross-piece; cross-stitch; (*naut.*) cross-trees.
crucial, *a.* crucial, cross-shaped.
cruciata, *n.f.* gentian.
cruciferario, *n.m.* cross-bearer, crucifer.
crucífero, -ra, *a.* cruciferous; (*bot.*) cruciate. — *n.m.* cross-bearer; crutched friar. — *n.f.pl.* (**crucíferas**) (*bot.*) Cruciferae.
crucificado, -da, *a.* crucified; ***El Crucificado,*** Jesus Christ.
crucificador, *n.m.* crucifier; (*coll.*) tormentor.
crucificar [A], *v.t.* crucify; (*coll.*) to torment.
crucifijo, *n.m.* crucifix.
crucifixión, *n.f.* crucifixion.
cruciforme, *a.* cruciform.
crucígero, -ra, *a.* (*poet.*) cruciferous.
crucillo, *n.m.* push-pin.
crudelísimo, -ma, *a. superl.* extremely cruel.
crudeza, *n.f.* rawness; hardness (*of water*); harshness; (*coll.*) vain boasting; (*pl.*) undigested food.
crudo, -da, *a.* raw, underdone; unripe; harsh; rough; (*coll.*) boastful; unbleached (*linen*); hard to digest; (*med.*) not mature; ***agua cruda,*** hard water; ***tiempo crudo,*** harsh weather; ***seda cruda,*** raw silk; ***cuero crudo,*** untanned leather.
cruel, *a.* cruel; intense; ***cruel con, para*** or ***para con,*** cruel to.
crueldad, *n.f.* cruelty, act of cruelty.
cruelísimo, -ma [CRUDELÍSIMO].
cruento, -ta, *a.* bloody.
crujía, *n.f.* (midship) gangway; passage (*between sanctuary rails in a cathedral*); large open corridor, hall *or* passage; aisle (*of a ward*); ***crujía de piezas,*** suite of rooms in succession; ***pasar crujía*** or ***sufrir una crujía,*** to run the gauntlet; to go through the mill, have a tough time.
crujidero, -ra, *a.* creaky, creaking, crackling, rustling.
crujido, *n.m.* creak, creaking; crackle, crackling; rustle, rustling; gnash, gnashing; flaw (*blade*); ***dar*** (***pegar***) ***un crujido,*** to go crack *or* bang.
crujidor, *n.m.* glass-cutter (*tool*).
crujiente, *a.* crackling, creaking, rustling.
crujir, *v.i.* to rustle, crackle, creak; to gnash; ***allí será el llanto y el crujir de dientes,*** there will be weeping and wailing and gnashing of teeth.
crúor, *n.m.* (*physiol.*) cruor; blood.
cruórico, -ca, *a.* appertaining to cruor.
crup, *n.m.* croup.
crupal, *a.* appertaining to croup.
crural, *a.* (*anat.*) crural, belonging to the thigh.
crustáceo, -cea, *a.* crustaceous. — *n.m.* (*zool.* crustacean.
crústula, *n.f.* thin bark, skin *or* rind.
cruz, *n.f.* cross; reverse (*of coin*); (*vet.*) withers; (*print.*) dagger, obelisk; top (*of tree-trunk where branches begin*); (*astron.*) Southern Cross; (*naut.*) cross-tree; ***en cruz,*** crosswise, with extended arms; ***cruz gamada,*** swastika; ***de la cruz a la fecha,*** from start to finish; ***cruz y raya,*** no more of this, that's an end to it; ***hacerle la cruz a alguien,*** to have done with s.o., want no more to do with s.o.; ***firmar con una cruz,*** to make one's mark; ***quedarse en cruz y en cuadro,*** to be left with nothing; ***hacerse cruces*** (***de***), to be shocked (at *or* by).
cruzado, -da, *a.* cross-bred; crossed; double-breasted; crosswise, transverse, twilled; ***traje cruzado,*** double-breasted suit; ***estarse con los brazos cruzados,*** to be idle. — *n.m.* crusader; knight; manner of playing the guitar; (*obs.*) various coins; figure in dancing. — *n.f.* crusade; cross-roads.
cruzamiento, *n.m.* cross-breeding; crossing, cross-roads; bestowal of knighthood.
cruzar [C], *v.t.* to cross; to lay, place *or* pass across; to go across; (*naut.*) to cruise; to cross-breed; to twill; to (dub) knight; ***cruzar la cara a,*** to slap on the face; ***cruzar los brazos,*** to fold one's arms. — **cruzarse,** *v.r.* to pass each other; ***cruzarse de caballero,*** to be knighted; ***cruzarse de brazos,*** to stand idle; ***cruzarse de palabras,*** to quarrel; ***cruzarse con alguien,*** to bump into s.o.

cu (1), *n.m.* (*Mex.*) ancient temple.
cu (2), *n.f.* the letter Q.
cuaderna, *n.f.* (*naut.*) frame; double fours in backgammon.
cuadernal, *n.m.* (*naut.*) block, tackle.
cuadernillo, *n.m.* quinternion; clerical directory.
cuaderno, *n.m.* writing-book, exercise-book; (*print.*) four sheets of paper placed within each other; (*coll.*) pack of cards; ***cuaderno de bitácora,*** log-book.
cuadra, *n.f.* [CUADRO].
cuadradillo, *n.m.* gusset (*of shirt*); blank (*of key etc.*); cube of sugar; square ruler.
cuadrado, -da, *a.* square; (*fig.*) inflexible. — *n.m.* square, quadrate; clock (*of stocking*); square ruler; gusset (*of sleeve*); (*arith.*) square number; die (*for coining*); (*print.*) quadrat, quad; ***de cuadrado,*** full-faced (*view*). — *n.f.* (*mus.*) breve.
cuadragenario, -ria, *a.*, *n.m.f.* (person who is) forty years old, quadragenarian.
cuadragesimal, *a.* Quadragesimal, Lenten.
cuadragésimo, -ma, *a.* fortieth. — *n.f.* Lent, Quadragesima.
cuadral, *n.m.* angle-brace.
cuadrangular, *a.* quadrangular.
cuadrángulo, -la, *a.* quadrangular. — *n.m.* quadrangle.
cuadrantal, *a.* (*math.*) quadrantal.
cuadrante, *a.* squaring. — *n.m.* quadrant; fourth part of an inheritance; sun-dial; clock face, watch face; (*carp.*) cross-tie, angle-brace; ancient Roman copper coin.
cuadranura, *n.f.* radial crack.
cuadrar, *v.t.* to square, form into a square; (*paint.*) to divide into squares. — *v.i.* to fit, suit, tally, correspond; to adjust. — **cuadrarse,** *v.r.* to stand at *or* to attention; (*fig.*) to put one's foot down, take a firm line; (*equit.*) to stop short.
cuadratín, *n.m.* (*print.*) quadrat.
cuadratura, *n.f.* (*astron.*, *math.*) quadrature; squaring, square; ***la cuadratura del círculo,*** the squaring of the circle.
cuadricenal, *a.* every forty years.
cuadrícula, *n.f.* checker-work, quadrille ruling.
cuadriculado, -da, *a.* cross-section, squared (*paper*).
cuadricular, *a.* checkered; ruled in squares. — *v.t.* to rule in squares.
cuadrienal, *a.* quadrennial.
cuadrienio, *n.m.* quadrennium.
cuadrífloro, -ra, *a.* (*bot.*) having four flowers.
cuadrifoliado, -da, *a.* (*bot.*) quadriphyllous.
cuadriforme, *a.* square-shaped.
cuadrifronte, *a.* four-faced.
cuadriga, *n.f.* quadriga.
cuadril, *n.m.* haunch bone; (*vet.*) croup; hip, thigh.
cuadrilátero, -ra, *a.*, *n.m.* quadrilateral.
cuadriliteral, cuadrilítero, -ra, *a.* quadriliteral.
cuadrilongo, -ga, *a.* rectangular, oblong. — *n.m.* parallelogram, oblong; rectangle; square of infantry.
cuadriloquio, *n.m.* conversation between four persons.
cuadrilla, *n.f.* team; gang; crew; troop; squad; armed band; armed patrol; quadrille.
cuadrillazo, *n.m.* (*Chi.*) ganging up, attack.
cuadrillero, *n.m.* team-, gang- *or* squad-leader; member of a patrol.
cuadrillo, *n.m.* quarrel (*arrow*).
cuadrimestre, *a.* [CUATRIMESTRE].
cuadrinieto, -ta, *n.m.f.* great-great-great-grandson *or* -daughter.
cuadrinomio, *n.m.* (*alg.*) quadrinomial.
cuadripartición, *n.f.* quadripartition.
cuadripartido, -da, *a.* quadripartite, divided into four.
cuadriple [CUÁDRUPLE].
cuadriplicar [CUADRUPLICAR].
cuadrivio, *n.m.* quadrivium; cross-roads.
cuadríyugo, *n.m.* cart with four horses; quadriga.
cuadro, -ra, *a.* square. — *n.m.* square; scene, tableau (*of a play*); picture, painting; square flower-bed; (*print.*) platen; (*mil.*) square (*of troops*); (*mil.*) staff (*of regiment*); (*elec.*) switchboard; touching *or* imposing sight; (*elec.*) ***cuadro de alimentación, distribución*** or ***de interruptores,*** feeder-switchboard, distribution-board; ***cuadro de costumbres,*** sketch of manners; ***cuadros vivos,*** tableaux vivants; ***en cuadro,*** squared; ***estar*** or ***quedarse en cuadro,*** to be friendless and penniless; (*mil.*) to be left with officers only (*said of a body of troops having lost its men*). — *n.f.* stable; hall, drawing-room, saloon; croup (*of horse*); square; ward (*in hospital, barracks etc.*); (*naut.*) quarter of a ship; quarter of a mile; (*Hisp. Am.*) block (*of houses*).
cuadrúmano, -na, *a.* quadrumanous. — *n.m.* quadrumane.
cuadrupedal, *a.* quadrupedal, four-footed.
cuadrupedante, *a.* (*poet.*) quadrupedal.
cuadrúpede, cuadrúpedo, *a.*, *n.m.* quadruped.
cuádruple, *a.* quadruple, fourfold.
cuadruplicación, *n.f.* quadruplication.
cuadruplicar [A], *v.t.* to quadruplicate, quadruple.
cuadruplo, -la, *a.*, *n.m.* quadruple.
cuaga, *n.m.* (*zool.*) quagga.
cuaima, *n.f.* (*Ven.*) poisonous snake; (*fig.*) clever, dangerous, cruel person.
cuajadillo, *n.m.* heavily embroidered silk.
cuajado, -da, *a.* dumbfounded. — *n.m.* mincemeat. — *n.f.* curd.
cuajadura, *n.f.* coagulation, curdling.
cuajaleche, *n.m.* (*bot.*) lady's bed-straw; cheese rennet.
cuajamiento, *n.m.* [CUAJADURA].
cuajar, *n.m.* abomasus, rennet bag. — **cuajar(se),** *v.t.* (*v.r.*) to curd, curdle, coagulate; to cake; (*coll.*) to overdeck. — *v.i.* to take shape; to cover in; to come off.
cuajarejo, *n.m.* abomasus, rennet bag.
cuajarón, *n.m.* clot.
cuajicote, *n.m.* (*Mex.*) carpenter bee.
cuajilote, *n.m.* (*Mex.*) cuajilote tree.
cuajo, *n.m.* rennet; maw; curdling, coagulation; ***arrancar de cuajo,*** to tear up by the roots, eradicate; ***tener buen*** or ***mucho cuajo,*** to be stolid; ***hierba de cuajo,*** cheese rennet.
cuakerismo, cuaquerismo, *n.m.* Quakerism.
cuákero, -ra, cuáquero, -ra, *n.m.f.* Quaker.
cual, *a.*, *rel. pron.* as, such as; ***el cual,*** which, who; ***por lo cual,*** for which reason; ***cual . . . tal,*** just as . . . so; like . . . like; ***cual padre, tal hijo,*** like father, like son. — *adv.* as; ***cual si,*** as if. — *prep.* like. — (**cuál**), *a.*, *interrog. pron.* which?, what?, which one?; ***cuál . . . cuál,*** some . . . some. — *interj.* how!
cualidad, *n.f.* quality.
cualitativo, -va, *a.* qualitative.
cualquier, *indef. a.* (*pl.* **cualesquier**) *contraction of* ***cualquiera*** *used before a noun.*
cualquiera, *indef. a.* (*pl.* **cualesquiera**), any. — *rel. a.* whichever. — *indef. pron.* anyone. — *rel. pron.* whichever, whoever. — *n.m.* anybody, nobody; ***cualquier hombre,*** any man; ***un*** (***hombre***) ***cualquiera,*** a nobody.
cuan (*interrog.*, *interj.* **cuán**), *adv. contraction of* ***cuanto*** (***cuánto***), *not used before a verb,* how; as.
cuando (*interrog.*, *interj.* **cuándo**), *adv.* when; if. — *conj.* though, although, even; sometimes, now and then; since, inasmuch as; ***¿de cuándo acá?*** since when?; ***de cuando en cuando,*** from time to time, now and then; ***¿hasta cuándo?*** until when?; ***cuando más*** or ***cuando mucho,***

at most, at best; ***cuando menos,*** at least; ***cuando quiera,*** when you please; whenever; ***cuando no,*** otherwise; ***el cómo y el cuándo,*** (the) how and when; ***cuando tú lo dices,*** if you say so. — *prep.* at the time of; ***cuando la guerra,*** at the time of the war.

cuantía, *n.f.* amount, quantity; importance; degree; ***de mayor cuantía,*** serious, grave; first-rate; ***de menor cuantía,*** of minor importance, secondary.

cuantiar [L], *v.t.* to value, estimate, appraise.

cuantidad [CANTIDAD].

cuantimás, *adv.* (*coll.*) all the more.

cuantioso, -sa, *a.* copious, numerous, large, substantial.

cuantitativo, -va, *a.* quantitative.

cuanto, -ta (*interrog., interj.* **cuánto, -ta**), *a.* as much as, as many as, all the, whatever. — *adv.* how much; how long; how far; as, the more; respecting; whilst; ***te daré cuanto tengo,*** I'll give you all that I have, as much as I have; ***cuantos quieras,*** as many as you like; (***tanto***) ***. . . cuanto . . .,*** as much as, as long as; ***cuanto más consigues, más pretendes,*** the more you get, the more you want; ***cuanto más que . . .,*** all the more so because; ***cuanto antes,*** as soon as possible; (***en***) ***cuanto . . .,*** as soon as; (***en***) ***cuanto a,*** as regards; ***por cuanto,*** inasmuch as; ***¿cuánto?*** how much?; ***¿cuántos?*** how many?; ***¿cuánto suma?*** how much does it come to?; ***¿cuánto va?*** how much do you bet?; ***¡cuánto tiempo sin verle!*** it's been a long time!; ***cuánto me alegro de verle!*** I'm really delighted to see you; ***¿a cuántos estamos?*** what is the date (*today*)?

cuaquerismo, cuáquero, *n.m.* [CUAKERISMO, CUÁKERO].

cuarango, *n.m.* Peruvian bark-tree.

cuarcífero, -ra, *a.* quartziferous.

cuarcita, *n.f.* quartzite.

cuarenta, *a., n.m.* forty; ***cantarle a alguien las cuarenta,*** to give s.o. a piece of one's mind.

cuarentavo, -va, *a., n.m.f.* fortieth (part).

cuarentena, *n.f.* space of forty days, months *or* years; fortieth part; Lent; forty; quarantine; (*met.*) suspension of assent; ***estar, poner en cuarentena,*** to be, place in quarantine.

cuarentenal, *a.* relating to the number forty.

cuarentón, -tona, *a., n.m.f.* (person) forty years old *or* in his *or* her forties.

cuaresma, *n.f.* Lent; collection of Lenten sermons.

cuaresmal, *a.* Lenten, used in Lent.

cuaresmario, *n.m.* collection of Lenten sermons.

cuarta, *n.f.* [CUARTO].

cuartago, *n.m.* nag.

cuartal, *n.m.* loaf; quarter (*dry measure*).

cuartán, *n.m.* grain measure (*of about* 1 *bushel*); oil measure (*of about* 7 *pints*).

cuartana, *n.f.* (*med.*) quartan.

cuartanal, *a.* (*med.*) quartan intermittent.

cuartanario, -ria, *a.* quartan. — *a., n.m.f.* (person) suffering from a quartan fever.

cuartar, *v.t.* to plough (*ground*) the fourth time.

cuartazo, *n.m.* (*Mex.*) stroke with a whip; (*pl.*) untidy, lazy and corpulent man.

cuartear, *v.t., v.i.* to quarter, divide into four parts; to bid a fourth more (*at sales*); to make a fourth person (*at a game*); to zig-zag up steep and bad roads; (*Mex.*) to whip. — **cuartearse,** *v.r.* to split, rift, crack.

cuartel, *n.m.* quarter, fourth part; district, ward; flower-bed; dwelling; home, tenement, habitation, lodging; barracks; (*her.*) quarter; (*mil.*) quarter, clemency; (*naut.*) hatch; (*poet.*) quatrain; ***dar cuartel,*** to give quarter; (*mil.*) ***cuartel general,*** headquarters; ***cuartel maestre*** (***general***), quartermaster-general; (*mil.*) ***estar de cuartel,*** to be on half-pay.

cuartelada, *n.f.* mutiny, military coup.

cuartelado, *n.m.* (*her.*) quartering.

cuartelar, *v.t.* (*her.*) to quarter.

cuartelero, -ra, *a.* relating to barracks *or* quarters; ***lenguaje cuartelero,*** barrack-room language. — *n.m.* soldier appointed to keep rooms clean.

cuartelesco, -ca, *a.* [CUARTELERO].

cuartelillo, *n.m.* police post.

cuarteo, *n.m.* dodging, swerving, sidestep; cracking; rift, fissure.

cuartero, -ra, *n.m.f.* (*prov.*) collector of the fourth of the crop of grain. — *n.f.* (*in Catalonia*) dry measure (*about* 2 *bushels*); surface measure (*about* 4,306 *square yards*); square timber (15 *feet* × 8 *inches* × 8 *inches*).

cuarterola, *n.f.* quarter-cask; (*Chi.*) short cavalry carbine.

cuarterón, *n.m.* quartern, quarter of a pound; upper part of windows; panel of a door; quadroon.

cuarteta, *n.f.* (*poet.*) quatrain.

cuarteto, *n.m.* (*poet.*) quatrain; (*mus.*) quartet.

cuartilla, *n.f.* quarter; sheet of writing paper; (*print.*) sheet of copy; pastern.

cuartillo, *n.m.* pint; fourth part of a peck; fourth part of a real; (*naut.*) dog watch.

cuartilludo, -da, *a.* with long pasterns.

cuartito, *n.m.* small room.

cuarto, -ta, *a.* fourth. — *n.m.* room; copper coin; crack (*in horse's hoof*); service in the royal palace; joint (*of meat*), (*Am.*) roast; ***cuarto de baño,*** bathroom; ***cuarto de costura,*** sewing-room; ***de tres al cuarto,*** third-rate; ***estar sin*** or ***no tener un cuarto,*** to be penniless; ***echar su cuarto a espadas,*** to butt in (*conversation*); (*pl.*) (*coll.*) money; animal's limbs; ***tener cuartos,*** to have money; ***no hay que dar tres cuartos al pregonero,*** there is no need to tell everyone our business. — *n.f.* quart, sequence of four cards in piquet; quadrant; span (*of the hand*); (*naut.*) point (*of compass*); quart measure; (*prov.*) guide mule; (*mus.*) fourth; (*mil.*) quarter-company of soldiers; (*Mex.*) riding whip. — *n.m.f.* quarter, fourth, fourth part; (*fenc., mil.*) ***cuarto de conversión,*** quarter-wheeling; ***cuarto creciente,*** first quarter of the moon; (*print.*) ***en cuarto,*** quarto.

cuartogénito, -ta, *a., n.m.f.* fourth-born (child).

cuartón, *n.m.* quarter, large joist *or* girder; (*prov.*) measure of wine; oblong patch of farming land.

cuartuco, cuartucho, *n.m.* miserable little room.

cuarzo, *n.m.* quartz.

cuarzoso, -sa, *a.* quartzose.

cuasi, *adv.* almost.

cuasia, *n.f.* (*bot.*) quassia.

cuasicontrato, *n.m.* (*law*) quasi-contract.

cuasidelito, *n.m.* (*law*) quasi-offence.

cuasimodo, *n.m.* first Sunday after Easter, Low Sunday.

cuate, -ta, *a., n.m.f.* (*Mex.*) twin; (*Mex.*) ***eso no tiene cuate,*** that has no equal.

cuatequil, *n.m.* (*Mex.*) maize.

cuaterna, *n.f.* [CUATERNO].

cuaternario, -ria, *a.* quaternary.

cuaternidad, *n.f.* quaternary, quaternity.

cuaterno, -na, *a.* quaternary. — *n.f.* four points (*in lotto*).

cuatezón, -zona, *a.* (*Mex.*) hornless (*ox* or *sheep*).

cuati, *n.m.* (*Arg., Col.*) monkey.

cuatralbo, -ba, *a.* with four white feet (*horse*). — *n.m.* (*obs.*) commander of four galleys.

cuatratuo, -tua, *a., n.m.f.* quadroon.

cuatreño, -ña, *a.* four years old (*cattle*).

cuatrero, *n.m.* horse *or* cattle thief, rustler.

cuatriduano, -na, *a.* lasting four days.

cuatrienio, *n.m.* quadrennium.

cuatrilingüe, *a.* quadrilingual.

cuatrillo, *n.m.* game of cards.

cuatrillón, *n.m.* (*British*) quadrillion.
cuatrimestre, *a.* lasting four months. — *n.m.* period of four months.
cuatrimotor, *a., n.m.* four-engined (aircraft).
cuatrín, *n.m.* (*obs.*) small coin; (*coll.*) cash.
cuatrinca, *n.f.* union of four persons *or* things; four cards of a kind (*in bezique*).
cuatrisílabo, -ba, *a.* quadrisyllabic. — *n.m.* quadrisyllable.
cuatro, *a., n.m.* four, fourth; ***las cuatro,*** four o'clock; ***más de cuatro,*** many; (*coll.*) quite a few people.
cuatrocentista, *n.m.f.* quattrocentist.
cuatrocientos, -tas, *a., n.m. inv.* four hundred.
cuatrodoblar, *v.t.* to quadruple.
cuatropea, *n.f.* horse tax, duty on horse sales.
cuatropeado, *n.m.* step in dancing.
cuatrotanto, *n.m.* quadruple.
Cuba, *n.f.* Cuba.
cuba, *n.f.* cask, tub, vat; tubful, vatful; big-bellied individual; stack (*blast furnace*); ***beber como una cuba,*** to drink like a fish; ***estar hecho una cuba,*** to be sozzled, drunk as a lord.
cubación, *n.f.* (*math.*) cubing.
cubalibre, *n.m.* rum and coke (*drink*).
cubano, -na, *a., n.m.f.* Cuban.
cubeba, *n.f.* (*bot.*) cubeb.
cubebina, *n.f.* (*chem.*) cubebin.
cubería, *n.f.* cooperage, cask-shop.
cubero, *n.m.* cooper; maker *or* vendor of casks; ***a ojo de buen cubero,*** at a rough estimate *or* guess.
cubertura, *n.f.* right of Spanish grandees to remain hatted in king's presence.
cubeta, *n.f.* small barrel, cask, keg, tub, pail, bucket, basin, tray; reservoir of mercury in barometer; base of harp; test-tube.
cubeto, *n.m.* small barrel, pail, tub, vessel.
cúbica (1), *n.f.* woollen material.
cubicación, *n.f.* cubage, cubature.
cubicar [A], *v.t.* to calculate the cubic contents of; to cube.
cúbico, -ca (2), *a.* cubic.
cubículo, *n.m.* cubicle.
cubichete, *n.m.* (*naut.*) weather-boards; (*artill.*) gun apron.
cubierta, *n.f.* cover, covering; envelope; book cover; (*fig.*) pretence, pretext; casing, coat; (*arch.*) facing, roofing; hood (*of carriage*); deck (*of ship*); ***entre cubiertas,*** between decks; ***cubierta alta,*** upper deck; ***cubierta de aterrizaje,*** flight deck; ***cubierta del motor,*** bonnet (*of car*).
cubierto, *n.m.* cover, table service, place (*at table*); fixed-price meal, table d'hôte; shelter, shed; roof; cover, covert; ***ponerse a cubierto,*** to take cover.
cubil, *n.m.* lair (*of wild beasts*); bed (*of river*).
cubilar, *n.m.* lair, sheep-fold. — *v.i.* to take shelter (*sheep*).
cubilete, *n.m.* copper pudding-basin *or* mould; food prepared therein; tumbler, mug, drinking cup; juggler's goblet; dice box; tub (*of ice cream*); (*Col.*) top hat.
cubiletero, *n.m.* pudding basin *or* mould; juggler.
cubilote, *n.m.* cupola furnace.
cubilla, *n.f.* Spanish fly, blistering beetle.
cubillo, *n.m.* (*theat.*) small box near the stage; water cooler.
cubismo, *n.m.* cubism.
cubista, *a., n.m.f.* cubist.
cubital, *a.* cubital.
cúbito, *n.m.* (*anat.*) ulna.
cubo, *n.m.* pail, bucket; mill-pond; barrel (*of watch* or *clock*); socket; (*math., geom.*) cube; (*fort.*) small tower; hub (*of wheel*); (*arch.*) dado, die.
cuboides, *a., n.m. inv.* (*anat.*) cuboid.
cubrecadena, *n.m.* chain-cover.
cubrecama, *n.f.* bed-cover, coverlet, counterpane.
cubrecorsé, *n.m.* camisole, corset cover.
cubremantel, *n.m.* fancy tablecloth.
cubrepiano, *n.m.* cloth cover for piano keyboard.
cubrepiés, *n.m. inv.* foot coverlet; counterpane.
cubreplatos, *n.m. inv.* dish-cover; wire-net cover.
cubrición, *n.f.* covering, copulation (*animals*).
cubriente, *a.* covering; copulating (*animals*).
cubrimiento, *n.m.* covering; roofing.
cubrir [*p.p.* **cubierto**], *v.t.* to cover, overlay, spread over; to face, coat; to shroud, cover up, hood; (*arch.*) to roof; to cover (*animals*); ***cubrir los gastos,*** to cover *or* meet (the) expenses. — **cubrirse,** *v.r.* to put on one's hat; to cloud over.
cuca, *n.f.* [CUCO].
cucador, -ra, *a.* winking.
cucadura, *n.f.*, **cucamiento,** *n.m.* wink; winking.
cucamonas, *n.f.pl.* (*fam.*) caresses, endearments.
cucaña, *n.f.* greased pole; (*coll.*) bargain, piece of cake, walk-over, windfall.
cucañero, -ra, *a., n.m.f.* parasite, hanger-on.
cucar [A], *v.t.* to wink.
cucaracha, *n.f.* cockroach; woodlouse; hazel-coloured snuff.
cucarachera, *n.f.* nest of cockroaches; cockroach trap; (*coll.*) good luck, lucky chance.
cucarda, *n.f.* cockade, badge.
cucarrón, *n.m.* (*Col.*) beetle.
cuclillas, *adv.* ***en cuclillas,*** squatting; ***sentarse en cuclillas,*** to squat (down).
cuclillo, *n.m.* cuckoo; (*fig.*) cuckold.
cuco, -ca, *a.* (*coll.*) cute, ducky; crafty, sharp, smart. — *n.m.f.* caterpillar; cuckoo; card game; gambler. — *n.m.pl.* knickers, pants. — *n.f.* earth-nut; root tubercle (*of sedge*); caterpillar; (*coll.*) gambling woman; (*coll.*) tart; (*Chi.*) heron; ***cuca y matacán,*** card game; (*coll.*) ***mala cuca,*** wicked person; (*pl.*) nuts; (*coll.*) pesetas.
cucú, *n.m.* call of the cuckoo.
cucubá, *n.m.* (*Cub.*) barking owl.
cuculí, *n.m.* (*Chi., Per.*) wild pigeon.
cuculla, *n.f.* cowl; old-fashioned hood.
cucuma, *n.f.* (*Col.*) bread.
cucúrbita, *n.f.* retort (*for distilling*).
cucurbitáceo, -cea, *a.* (*bot.*) cucurbitaceous.
cucurucho, *n.m.* roll *or* cone (*paper*); cornet.
cucha, (*Per.*) [LAGUNA].
cuchar, *n.f.* spoon; ancient corn measure; tax *or* duty on grain.
cuchara, *n.f.* spoon; ladle, scoop; trowel; ***media cuchara,*** mediocre individual; ***meterle a alguien algo con cuchara (de palo),*** to spoon-feed s.o. with sth.; ***meter su cuchara,*** to stick one's oar in.
cucharada, *n.f.* spoonful, ladleful; ***meter su cucharada,*** to stick one's oar in.
cucharadita, *n.f.* teaspoonful.
cucharal, *n.m.* (shepherd's) leather spoon bag.
cucharazo, *n.m.* stroke *or* blow with a spoon.
cucharero, -ra, *n.m.f.* maker *or* seller of spoons. — *n.m.* spoon rack.
cuchareta, *n.f.* small spoon; (*prov.*) wheat; inflammation of liver (*in sheep*); (*Hisp. Am.*) flamingo.
cucharetear, *v.i.* (*coll.*) to stir with a spoon; ***cucharetear en todo,*** to meddle in everything.
cucharetero, -ra, *n.m.f.* maker *or* seller of wooden spoons. — *n.m.* spoon-rack; petticoat fringe.
cucharica, cucharita, *n.f.* small spoon, tea- *or* coffee-spoon.
cucharilla, *n.f.* small spoon; tea- *or* coffee-spoon; (*min.*) scraper; liver disease (*in swine*).
cucharón, *n.m.* ladle, scoop; ***despacharse uno con el cucharón,*** to help o.s. to the best *or* largest part; ***tener el cucharón por el mango,*** to rule the roost, boss the show.
cucharro, *n.m.* (*naut.*) harping.

cuchí, *n.m.* (*Per.*) hog.
cuchichear, *v.i.* to whisper.
cuchicheo, *n.m.* whisper, whispering.
cuchichero, -ra, *a.* whispering. — *n.m.f.* whisperer.
cuchichiar, *v.i.* to call (*partridge*).
cuchilla, *n.f.* blade; razor-blade; kitchen knife; cutter; (*Ur.*) mountain ridge.
cuchillada, *n.f.* slash; gash; (*pl.*) wrangles, quarrels; ***dar cuchillada,*** to play to the gallery; ***estar*** or ***andar a cuchilladas con alguien,*** to be at daggers-drawn with s.o.
cuchillar, *a.* appertaining to knives.
cuchillazo, *n.m.* large knife; knife slash *or* wound.
cuchilleja, *n.f.*, **cuchillejo,** *n.m.* small knife, paring knife.
cuchillera, *n.f.* knife case, scabbard.
cuchillería, *n.f.* cutler's shop; cutlery.
cuchillero, *n.m.* cutler.
cuchillo, *n.m.* knife; gore (*garment, land*); (*arch.*) gable frame; (*pl.*) chief feathers of a hawk's wing; (*naut.*) ***vela de cuchillo,*** triangular sail; ***cuchillo de monte,*** hunter's knife; ***cuchillo mangonero,*** coarse, badly forged knife; ***matar a uno con cuchillo de palo,*** to mortify slowly and relentlessly; ***pasar a cuchillo,*** to put to the sword; ***ser uno cuchillo de otro,*** to be a thorn in s.o.'s side; ***señor de horca y cuchillo,*** utter despot.
cuchipanda, *n.f.* (*coll.*) slap-up do, bean feast.
cuchitril, *n.m.* poky hole, place *or* dump.
cucho, *n.m.* (*Chi.*) conical hat used by countrymen; puss, cat; pooch; dog; hog.
cuchuco, *n.m.* (*Col.*) barley and pork soup.
cuchuchear [CUCHICHEAR].
cuchufleta, *n.f.* joke, quip.
cuchufletero, -ra, *a.* joking. — *n.m.f.* joker.
cuchugo, *n.m.* (*Hisp. Am.*) saddle bag.
cuchuña, *n.f.* (*Chi.*) small sweet water-melon.
cudria, *n.f.* bass rope.
cudú, *n.m.* (*zool.*) koodoo.
cuébano [CUÉVANO].
cuelga, *n.f.* bunch, cluster (*fruit*); string (*vegetables*); (*coll.*) birthday present.
cuelgacapas, *n.m. inv.* cloak hanger, rack.
cuelgaplatos, *n.m. inv.* (wire) plate-holder (*for wall decoration*).
cuelmo, *n.m.* torch, firebrand.
cuelliangosto, -ta, *a.* thin-necked.
cuellicorto, -ta, *a.* short-necked.
cuelligrueso, -sa, *a.* thick-necked.
cuellierguido, -da, *a.* stiff-necked; conceited.
cuellilargo, -ga, *a.* long-necked.
cuello, *n.m.* neck; throat; collar; collar-band; neck-stock; (*fig.*) ***levantar cuello,*** to get on one's feet again; (*fig.*) ***estar a medio cuello,*** to be half way there *or* nearly there.
cuenca, *n.f.* wooden bowl; socket (*of eye*); (river) basin.
cuenco, *n.m.* earthen bowl; cavity, hollow.
cuenda, *n.f.* end of a skein (*of silk* or *thread*); ***madeja sin cuenda,*** tangled business; ***por la cuenda se devana la madeja,*** the right way is the easiest way; ***hasta la cuenda,*** to the end.
cuenta, *n.f.* account; count; bill, (*Am.*) check; bead; ***cuenta corriente,*** current account; ***cuenta de banco,*** bank account, (*Am.*) checking account; ***cuenta pendiente,*** outstanding account; ***cuenta de venta,*** sales account; ***las cuentas del Gran Capitán,*** exorbitant expenses *or* sums; ***la cuenta de la vieja,*** counting on one's fingers; ***a cuenta,*** on account; ***a(l) fin de cuentas,*** when all is said and done; ***en resumidas cuentas,*** in short, to sum up; in other words; ***a esa cuenta,*** at that rate; ***de cuenta,*** of importance; ***por (de) cuenta y riesgo de,*** on the responsibility of; ***por su cuenta,*** off one's own bat, on one's own initiative; as far as one is concerned; (*lit., fig.*) ***ajustar cuentas,*** to settle accounts; ***caer en la cuenta de,*** to (come to) realize; ***eso corre de mi cuenta,*** I'll attend to, see to, look after that; ***eso es cuenta mía,*** that's my affair *or* concern; ***cobrar más de la cuenta,*** to over-charge; ***hablar más de la cuenta,*** to talk too much; ***pasar de la cuenta,*** to be too much; ***dar cuenta de,*** to account for, give (an) account of; to report; to finish *or* polish off; ***echar la cuenta,*** to work out how much it is; ***echar (las, sus) cuentas,*** to work it out, see if it suits; ***echar la cuenta sin la huéspeda,*** to count the gain without reckoning on the cost; ***esto también entra en cuenta,*** this is another point to be taken into account; (*com.*) ***girar la cuenta,*** to make out and send the bill; ***hacer(se) (la) cuenta,*** to imagine, suppose; ***llevar la cuenta,*** to keep a record; ***no quiero cuentas contigo,*** I'll have nothing to do with you; ***por la cuenta que le trae,*** for his own good, in his own interest; ***esto no me tiene*** or ***trae cuenta,*** it's not worth my while, it's not to my advantage; ***pedir cuenta,*** to ask for an explanation; ***perder la cuenta,*** to lose count; ***tener en cuenta,*** to bear in mind; to take into account; ***tribunal de cuentas,*** ministerial finance tribunal, court of inquiry; ***vamos a cuentas,*** let's get down to brass tacks; ***vivir a cuenta de otro,*** to live at another's expense.
cuentacorrentista, *n.m.f.* current account holder.
cuentadante, *a.*, *n.m.f.* (one) having to render account of money held in trust.
cuentagotas, *n.m. inv.* (*med.*) dropper.
cuentahilos, *n.m. inv.* thread-counter; linen-prover.
cuentapasos, *n.m. inv.* pedometer.
cuentecillo, *n.m.* little story.
cuentista, *n.m.f.* yarn-spinner, liar; story-teller; short-story writer.
cuento (1), *n.m.* story, tale, short-story; yarn, lie; million, huge number; butt *or* tip (*of a weapon*); prop, support; ***cuento de cuentos,*** billion, a million millions; ***cuento de viejas,*** old wives' tale; ***cuento de nunca acabar,*** never-ending affair; ***acabados son cuentos,*** the matter is at an end; ***no viene a cuento,*** that's not to the point; ***dejarse de cuentos,*** to come to the point; ***estar en el cuento,*** to be in the picture; ***sin cuento,*** countless; ***traer a cuento,*** to bring in (up); ***va de cuento,*** so the story goes; ***no me vengas con cuentos,*** don't give me that stuff.
cuento (2), **cuente,** *pres. indic.*; *pres. subj.* [CONTAR].
cuentón, -tona [CUENTISTA].
cuera, *n.f.* leather jacket.
cuerda (1), *n.f.* string; rope; halter; c(h)ord; tendon; cat-gut; fuse; mountain chain; (*mus.*) compass; ***cuerda falsa,*** out of tune string; ***cuerda floja,*** tight rope; ***cuerdas vocales,*** vocal cords; (*fig.*) ***andar, bailar en la cuerda floja,*** to vacillate, waver; ***dar cuerda a,*** to wind up (*spring, watch etc.*); (*fig.*) ***no le des cuerda,*** don't encourage him; ***dar una cuerda falsa,*** to strike a (the) wrong note; ***aflojar la cuerda,*** to relax, let up; ***apretar la cuerda,*** to tighten up, make things stiffer; ***eso no es de mi cuerda,*** that's not my line *or* cup of tea; ***(por) bajo cuerda,*** in an underhand manner, on the quiet; ***cuerda de presos,*** chain gang.
cuerdero, *n.m.* (*mus.*) string-maker *or* -seller.
cuerdo, -da (2), *a.* sane; wise, prudent.
cuerna, *n.f.* (set of) horns *or* antlers; horn vessel; hunting-horn.
cuérnago, *n.m.* bed (*of river*).
cuernecico, cuernecillo, cuernecito, *n.m.* small horn.
cuernezuelo, *n.m.* small horn.
cuerno, *n.m.* horn; feeler, antenna; (*mus.*) hunting-horn; side; wing (*of an army* or *fleet*); button (*of manuscript roll*); (*naut.*) outrigger; ***cuerno de la abundancia,*** horn of plenty; ***cuerno de caza,*** hunting horn; ***en los cuernos***

del toro, in jeopardy; ***poner en (sobre) los cuernos de la luna,*** to praise to the skies; ***ponerle a uno los cuernos,*** to cuckold s.o.; ***estar de cuerno con,*** to be on bad terms with; ***¡vete al cuerno!*** go to blazes!; ***¡cuerno!*** gad!; ***no vale un cuerno,*** it's worthless; ***me ha sabido a cuerno quemado,*** it was damned unpleasant, nasty; (*fam.*) ***sobre cuernos, penitencia,*** to add insult to injury; (*pl.*) tips.

cuero, *n.m.* (raw)hide; leather; pelt; wine skin; ***cuero cabelludo,*** scalp; ***cuero exterior (interior),*** outer (inner) skin; ***de cuero,*** leathern; ***en cueros vivos,*** (stark-) naked; ***entre cuero y carne,*** between skin and flesh; (*fig.*) intimately; ***estar hecho un cuero,*** to be drunk; (*pl.*) leather-hangings.

cuerpecito, *n.m.* dainty (nice) little body.

cuerpezuelo, corpezuelo, *n.m.* small body *or* carcass.

cuerpo, *n.m.* body; (*mil.*) corps; (*print.*) size (*of letter*); ***cuerpo de bomba,*** pump barrel; ***cuerpo de bomberos,*** fire-brigade; ***cuerpo de cabrestante,*** capstan-barrel; ***cuerpo de correos,*** post office staff; ***cuerpo de redacción,*** editorial staff; ***cuerpo extraño,*** foreign body; ***¡cuerpo de Cristo*** or ***de Dios! ¡cuerpo de tal! ¡cuerpo de mí!*** by God! Christ!; (*law*) ***cuerpo del delito,*** corpus delicti; (*mil.*) ***cuerpo de ejército,*** army corps; ***cuerpo de guardia,*** (body of men on) guard; ***retrato de medio cuerpo (cuerpo entero),*** half-length (full-length) portrait; (*mil.*) ***cuerpo de reserva,*** reserve corps; ***cuerpo facultativo,*** medical team; (*theol.*) ***cuerpo glorioso,*** body of the blessed after the resurrection; ***no eres cuerpo glorioso,*** you are human like everybody else; (*naut.*) ***cuerpo muerto,*** mooring-buoy; ***cuerpo sin alma,*** dull, lifeless person; (*anat.*) ***cuerpo tiroides,*** thyroid gland; (*mil.*) ***cuerpo volante,*** flying column; ***salir a cuerpo (gentil),*** to go out with no overcoat on; ***a cuerpo descubierto,*** manifestly; without cover; ***cuerpo a cuerpo,*** hand to hand; ***dar con el cuerpo en tierra,*** to fall down; ***dar cuerpo,*** to give body, consistence; ***de cuerpo presente,*** prepared for burial, in state; ***descubrir uno el cuerpo,*** to get off one's guard, lay o.s. open; ***no me lo pide el cuerpo,*** I don't feel like it, the will doesn't move me; ***echar el cuerpo fuera, falsear, huir*** or ***hurtar el cuerpo,*** to dodge (*a blow, duties, obligations etc.*); ***en cuerpo de camisa,*** in one's underwear; ***en cuerpo y alma,*** heart and soul; ***hacer del cuerpo,*** to open bowels; ***no quedarse con nada en el cuerpo,*** to leave nothing unsaid, let it all out; ***tomar cuerpo,*** to take shape; ***tratar a cuerpo de rey*** or ***tratar a qué quieres, cuerpo,*** to feast like a king, entertain lavishly.

cuerria, *n.f.* (*prov.*) fenced circular space for ripening chestnuts.

cuerva, *n.f.* female crow.

cuervo, *n.m.* crow, raven; (*astron.*) Corvus; ***cuervo marino,*** cormorant; ***cuervo merendero,*** rook; ***cría cuervos y te sacarán los ojos,*** nurse a viper, and you'll get what you deserve.

cuesco, *n.m.* stone (*fruit*); dross, scoria; (*obsc*). noisy fart; (*coll.*) ***darse un cuesco,*** to come a cropper.

cuesta, *n.f.* slope, incline, hill, ***cuesto abajo,*** downhill; ***cuesta arriba,*** uphill; ***a cuestas,*** on one's back *or* shoulders; ***llevar a cuestas,*** to carry on one's back, bear the burden of; ***tomar a cuestas,*** to take on, take upon o.s., undertake; ***se me hace muy cuesta arriba,*** it's a great effort for me (to), I find it very hard (to); ***la cuesta de enero,*** after-Christmas slump.

cuestación, *n.f.* charitable appeal, collection for charity, flag day.

cuestecilla, cuestecita, *n.f.* easy slope, slight incline.

cuestión, *n.f.* question, issue, matter, subject; argument, dispute; ***cuestión batallona,*** main issue, crux; ***cuestión candente,*** burning question; ***cuestión de gabinete,*** serious (political *or* public) issue.

cuestionable, *a.* questionable, doubtful.

cuestionador, -ra, *a.* questionary. — *n.m.f.* questioner; examiner.

cuestionar, *v.t., v.i.* to question, dispute, argue (over).

cuestionario, *n.m.* questionary, questionnaire.

cuestor, *n.m.* quæstor; mendicant.

cuestuario, -ria, cuestuoso, -sa, *a.* lucrative.

cuestura, *n.f.* quæstorship.

cuétano, *n.m.* (*E.S.*) caterpillar.

cueto, *n.m.* fortified lofty place; craggy hill.

cueva, *n.f.* cave; den; cellar.

cuévano, *n.m.* basket, hamper, pannier.

cuevecita, *n.f.* small cave.

cuevero, *n.m.* cave-maker, grotto-maker.

cueza (I), *n.f.* grain tax.

cuezo (I), *n.m.* mortar trough; ***meter el cuezo,*** to interfere, intrude, meddle.

cuezo (2), **cueza** (2), *pres. indic.*; *pres. subj.* [COCER].

cugujada, *n.f.* crested lark.

cugulla [COGULLA].

cuicacoche, *n.f.* (*Mex.*) song bird.

cuida, *n.f.* older girl at school who looks after a child.

cuidado, *n.m.* care; carefulness; concern; ***¡cuidado!*** mind! be careful! look out! beware!; ***con cuidado,*** carefully; ***cuidado de, a/c de,*** care of; ***de cuidado,*** dangerous; ***estar de cuidado,*** to be dangerously ill; ***un tío de cuidado,*** a chap who needs watching, a dangerous bloke; ***pierda Vd. cuidado,*** don't worry; ***no hay cuidado,*** there's no fear of that.

cuidadoso, -sa, *a.* careful, painstaking.

cuidante, *a.* careful, heedful, mindful, vigilant.

cuidar, *v.t., v.i.* to take care of, care for, look after, mind; ***cuídalo, (cuida de él),*** look after it (him); ***cuida de que lo haga,*** take care that he does it, see that he does it. — **cuidarse,** *v.r.* to take care of o.s.

cuido, *n.m.* (*prov.*) care, minding.

cuija, *n.f.* (*Mex.*) small, thin lizard; (*fig.*) lean and ugly woman.

cuita, *n.f.* care, grief, affliction, sorrow.

cuitado, -da, *a.* miserable, wretched; sorrowful; pusillanimous.

cuitamiento, *n.m.* bashfulness, timidity, lack of spirit.

cuja, *n.f.* bucket, holder (*on saddle*); bedstead; thigh.

cuje, *n.m.* (*Cub.*) stick (*for hanging tobacco*).

cují, *n.m.* (*Ven.*) huisache tree.

cula, *n.f.* (*coll.*) hoop (*in croquet*).

culada, *n.f.* (*coll.*) bumps-a-daisy; (*pl.*) heaving (*of ship*).

culantrillo, *n.m.* maidenhair fern.

culantro, *n.m.* coriander.

culata, *n.f.* butt(-end); breech (*of gun*); breech-block; back part; cylinder head; buttock, haunch (*of animals*); ***salir el tiro por la culata,*** to misfire, backfire.

culatazo, *n.m.* blow with the butt-end of a fire-arm; recoil, kick (*of gun*).

culazo, *n.m.* big behind.

culcusido [CORCUSIDO].

culebra, *n.f.* snake; worm (*of still*); (*coll.*) trick, practical joke, prank; (*fig.*) viper; ***culebra de cascabel,*** rattlesnake; ***sabe más que las culebras,*** he is very crafty; ***hacer culebra,*** to wriggle; ***liársele a uno la culebra,*** to find o.s. suddenly in grave difficulties.

culebrazo, *n.m.* lash(ing), whipping; practical joke (*played on new arrivals*).

culebrear, *v.i.* to wriggle; to twist and turn, wind, zigzag.

culebreo, *n.m.* wriggling; twisting, winding, zigzagging.
culebrilla, *n.f.* tetter, herpes; fissure (*in gun-barrel*); (*bot.*) dragon-tree.
culebrino, -na, *a.* appertaining to snakes; snake-like. — *n.f.* (*mil.*) culverin; twisting meteor.
culebrón, *n.m.* large snake; (*coll.*) crafty fellow, double-dealer.
culero, -ra, *a.* lazy, tardy. — *n.m.* nappy, (*Am.*) diaper; pip (*disease in birds*). — *n.f.* stain of urine (*in swaddling-clothes*); patch (*on seat of trousers*); (shiny) seat (*trousers*).
culi, *n.m.* coolie.
culinario, -ria, *a.* culinary.
culinegro, -ra, *a.* black-bottomed. — *n.f.* ***dijo la sartén a la caldera ¡quítate allá, culinegra!*** the pot called the kettle black.
culirroto, *a.* having torn seat (*trousers*).
culito, *n.m.* (*fam.*) (cute *or* sweet) little behind.
culminación, *n.f.* (*astron.*) culmination.
culminancia, *n.f.* (*poet.*) height, elevation, summit.
culminante, *a.* culminating.
culminar, *v.i.* to culminate; (*naut.*) to be at high tide.
culo, *n.m.* bottom, behind, backside, posterior, seat; (*obsc.*) arse; (*obsc.*) ***culo de mal asiento,*** fidget arse; ***culo de plomo,*** heavy sitter, lump of lead; ***culo de pollo,*** rough piece of darning; ***culo de vaso,*** imitation (precious) stone.
culombio, *n.m.* (*elec.*) coulomb.
culón, -lona, *a.* big-bottomed.
culote, *n.m.* metal end (*shell, missile*).
culpa, *n.f.* guilt, blame, fault; ***echar la culpa a,*** to put *or* lay the blame on; ***tener la culpa*** (***de***), to be to blame (for); ***yo no tengo la culpa, la culpa no es mía,*** I'm not to blame, it's not my fault, I'm not responsible (*for it*); ***estoy aquí por tu culpa,*** it's your fault that I am here.
culpabilidad, *n.f.* culpability, guilt.
culpable, *a.* culpable, guilty, blameworthy. — *n.m.f.* (*law*) culprit, guilty person.
culpación, *n.f.* crimination, blame.
culpado, -da, *a.* guilty. — *n.m.f.* culprit.
culpar, *v.t.* to blame.
culpeo, *n.m.* (*Chi.*) large fox.
cultalatiniparla, *n.f.* (*coll.*) euphuistic language.
cultedad, *n.f.* (*coll.*) affected style; (*fig.*) fustian.
culteranismo, *n.m.* high-flown style, fustian, euphuism.
culterano, -na, *a.* fustian, euphuistic. — *n.m.f.* euphuist.
cultero, -ra, *a.* [CULTERANO].
cultiparlar, *v.i.* to speak euphuistically.
cultiparlista, *n.m.f.* euphuist.
cultipicaño, -ña, *a.* (*iron.*) knavish and affecting culture.
cultivable, *a.* cultivatable, arable.
cultivador, -ra, *a.* cultivating. — *n.m.f.* cultivator.
cultivadora, *n.f.* cultivating machine.
cultivar, *v.t.* to cultivate; to grow.
cultivo, *n.m.* cultivation; crop; (*bact.*) culture.
culto, -ta, *a.* cultured; educated, cultivated; ***estilo culto,*** academic (learned) style. — *n.m.* cult; worship.
cultor, -ra, *a.* worshipping. — *n.m.f.* worshipper.
cultura, *n.f.* culture; civilization.
cultural, *a.* cultural.
cuma, *n.f.* (*Hisp. Am.*) godmother.
cumarú, *n.m.* (*Cent. Am.*) tonquin bean.
cumbarí, *a., n.m.* (*Arg.*) red chilli.
cumbé, *n.m.* negro dance and tune.
cumbo, *n.m.* (*E.S., Hond.*) calabash.
cumbre, *n.f.* top, summit, peak; climax; height, highlight; ***figura cumbre,*** top figure.
cumbrera, *n.f.* (*arch.*) ridge-pole, tie-beam, roof-tree.
cúmel, *n.m.* kummel.
cumiche, *n.m.* (*Cent. Am.*) youngest, baby (*of a family*).
cumíneo, -nea, *a.* (*bot.*) cumin-like.
cuminol, *n.m.* (*chem.*) cumin-oil.
cúmplase, *n.m.* approval, sanction; (*Hisp. Am.*) presidential assent to Bills passed by parliament.
cumpleaños, *n.m. inv.* birthday.
cumplefaltas, *n.m. inv.* deputy, substitute.
cumplidero, -ra, *a.* expiring (*by a given date*); important, necessary.
cumplido, -da, *a.* full, thorough, complete; ample; courteous, polite, formal. — *n.m.* compliment, expression of courtesy; formality; ***no se ande usted con cumplidos,*** don't stand on ceremony.
cumplidor, -ra, *a.* dependable, reliable, trustworthy. — *n.m.f.* executor (*of a will*).
cumplimentador, -ra, *a.* complimenting.
cumplimentar, *v.t.* to pay a compliment *or* compliments to; to extend appropriate courtesies to; to implement.
cumplimentero, -ra, *a., n.m.f.* (*coll.*) excessively courteous *or* formal, ceremonious (person).
cumplimiento, *n.m.* fulfilling, carrying out; observance; completion; lapse, expiry; courtesy; ***al cumplimiento del plazo,*** on the expiry of the stipulated period; ***por cumplimiento,*** purely as a matter of form.
cumplir, *v.t.* to fulfil, carry out; ***hoy cumple 80 años,*** he is 80 today; ***cumplir años,*** to have a birthday; ***cumplir una condena,*** to serve a sentence; ***cumplir una promesa,*** to keep a promise; ***cumplir el servicio,*** to complete *or* finish one's military service; ***cumplir*** (***uno***) ***su deber,*** to do one's duty. — *v.i.* to fall due, expire; to complete (*one's military service*); to keep one's promise, fulfil one's obligation(s); ***cumplir con su deber,*** to do one's duty; ***cumplir con Dios,*** to do one's duty to God; ***hemos cumplido con él,*** we have fulfilled our obligation(s) to him; ***por cumplir,*** as a matter of form, as a formality. — *impers.* to fall (to); ***me cumple a mí hablar,*** it falls to me to speak. — **cumplirse,** *v.r.* to come about; to fall due.
cumquibus, *n.m. inv.* (*coll.*) wherewithal, cash.
cumulador, -ra, *a.* [ACUMULADOR].
cumular [ACUMULAR].
cumulativo, -va, *a.* cumulative.
cúmulo, *n.m.* heap, pile; terrific number *or* amount; cumulus.
cuna, *n.f.* (*lit., fig.*) cradle; crib, cot; birth-place; birth; space between the horns of cattle; rope-bridge; (*naut.*) stocks; ***de humilde cuna,*** of humble birth; ***de ilustre cuna,*** of illustrious birth; ***casa cuna,*** foundling home.
cunaguaro, *n.m.* (*Ven.*) wild beast.
cunar [ACUNAR].
cuncuna, *n.f.* (*Col.*) wild pigeon; (*Chi.*) caterpillar.
cundido, *n.m.* provision of oil, salt and vinegar given to shepherds; anything spread on bread.
cundidor, -ra, *a.* expanding, growing, spreading.
cundir, *v.i.* to spread; to grow; to go a long way; ***cunde el pánico,*** panic is spreading; ***no me cunde el tiempo*** (***trabajo***), I'm getting very little done, I'm making very little headway; ***le cunde mucho el dinero,*** he makes his money go a long way.
cunear, *v.t.* to rock. — **cunearse,** *v.r.* to rock, sway.
cuneiforme, *a.* cuneiform, wedge-shaped.
cuneo, *n.m.* rocking, swinging.
cunero, -ra, *a., n.m.f.* (*prov.*) foundling; maker *or* vendor of cradles; (*coll.*) ***diputado cunero,*** deputy elected by the influence of the Government. — *n.f.* royal nurse.
cuneta, *n.f.* ditch.
cuña, *n.f.* wedge; quoin; (*fig.*) ***meterse de cuña,*** to force *or* elbow one's way in.
cuñado, -da, *n.m.f.* brother-in-law; sister-in-law.

cuñar, *v.t.* to wedge.
cuñete, *n.m.* keg, firkin.
cuño, *n.m.* die (*for coining money etc.*); die stamp; triangular formation of troops; ***de nuevo cuño,*** newly coined, freshly minted.
cuociente [COCIENTE].
cuodlibeto, *n.m.* quodlibet, thesis; paradox, argument, pungent saying, subtlety.
cuota, *n.f.* quota; subscription, membership fee.
cuotidiano, -na, *a.* quotidian.
cupé, *n.m.* landau, coupé.
cupido, *n.m.* cupid.
cuplé, *n.m.* cabaret song, ballad.
cupletista, *n.f.* music-hall singer.
cupo, *n.m.* quota; contingent.
cupón, *n.m.* coupon; dividend.
cupresino, -na, *a.* (*poet.*) belonging to the cypress-tree.
cúprico, -ca, *a.* cupric; of copper.
cuprífero, -ra, *a.* cupriferous.
cuprita, *n.f.* (*min.*) cuprite.
cuproso, -sa, *a.* cuprous, copper-like.
cúpula, *n.f.* dome, cupola; (*bot.*) cupule.
cupulado, -da, cupular, *a.* (*bot.*) cupular, cupulate.
cupulífero, -ra, *a.* (*bot.*) cupuliferous.
cupuliforme, *a.* cupulate.
cupulino, *n.m.* (*arch.*) lantern, over dome.
cuquillo, *n.m.* cuckoo.
cura, *n.m.* priest; ***cura párroco,*** parish priest; (*eccles.*) ***cura ecónomo,*** locum tenens; ***cura de misa y olla,*** ignorant priest; (*slang*) ***este cura se larga,*** I'm shoving off. — *n.f.* cure, healing; curing, preserving, pickling; ***alargar la cura,*** to prolong a matter unduly; ***cura de almas,*** cure of souls; ***cura de aguas,*** water cure; ***no tiene cura,*** it (he) is hopeless; ***primera cura,*** first aid; ***tener cura,*** to be curable.
curabilidad, *n.f.* curability.
curable, *a.* curable, healable.
curaca, *n.m.* (*Hisp. Am.*) governor, boss.
curación, *n.f.* cure, healing.
curadero, *n.m.* bleachery; curing place.
curadillo, *n.m.* codfish, ling.
curador, -ra, *a.* curing; healing; curatorial. — *n.m.f.* overseer, caretaker; (*law*) guardian; curator, administrator; bleacher; curer; healer.
curaduría, *n.f.* guardianship.
curalotodo, *n.m.* cure-all.
curalle, *n.m.* purging physic.
curandero, -ra, *n.m.f.* quack; witch-doctor.
curanto, *n.m.* (*Chi.*) dish made of meat, shellfish, and vegetables.
curar, (*v.t.*) to cure, heal; to treat; to dress; to cure, preserve, season; ***curar al humo,*** to smoke; ***estar curado de espanto,*** to have seen it all, be blasé. — **curar(se),** *v.i.* (*v.r.*) to recover; to take care (of); to pay attention (to); ***se curó en seguida,*** he recovered, got well at once; ***curarse en salud,*** to take steps beforehand, take evasive action early, forestall events.
curare, *n.m.* (*bot.*) curare.
curarina, *n.f.* (*chem.*) curarine.
curasao, *n.m.* curaçao.
curatela, *n.f.* (*law*) guardianship.
curativo, -va, *a.* curative. — *n.f.* cure, healing.
curato, *n.m.* office of parish priest; parish; care of souls.
curbaril, *n.m.* courbaril; locust tree.
curculio, *n.m.* corn-weevil.
cúrcuma, *n.f.* (*bot.*) turmeric, curcuma.
curcumáceo, -cea, *a.* turmeric.
curcumina, *n.f.* (*chem.*) curcumine, turmeric yellow.
curcusilla, *n.f.* coccyx.
curdo, -da, *a., n.m.f.* Kurdish, Kurd; (*coll.*) ***estar curda,*** to be sozzled; ***coger una curda,*** to get plastered *or* sozzled.
cureña, *n.f.* gun-carriage; gun-stock (*in the rough*); stay (*of cross-bow*); (*fort.*) ***a cureña rasa,*** without a parapet; (*coll.*) without shelter or defence.
cureñaje, *n.m.* (collection of) gun-carriages.
curesca, *n.f.* shear-wool, nap.
curia, *n.f.* ecclesiastical court; bar, legal profession; care; ***curia romana,*** Roman curia.
curial, *a.* curial. — *n.m.* member of the Roman curia; clerk, officer (*of a court*); attorney.
curialesco, -ca, *a.* legalistic.
curiana, *n.f.* cockroach.
curiara, *n.f.* (*Hisp. Am.*) sailing canoe.
curibay, *n.m.* (*River Plate*) pine.
curiel, *n.m.* (*Cub.*) guinea-pig.
curiosear, *v.t., v.i.* to pry (into), snoop, be nosy.
curiosidad, *n.f.* curiosity; inquisitiveness; object o curiosity; (*coll.*) neatness, cleanliness; curio.
curioso, -sa, *a.* curious; inquisitive, prying; (*coll.*) neat, tidy, clean; strange, funny, odd. — *n.m.f.* inquisitive person.
curiquingue, *n.m.* (*Ec., Per.*) vulture.
curricán, *n.m.* spinning tackle.
curro, -rra, *a.* cute, nice; showy.
curruca, *n.f.* linnet, warbler.
currutaco, -ca, *a.* foppish; stocky. — *n.m.* dandy, fop, dude. — *n.f.* belle.
cursado, -da, *a.* experienced, exercised.
cursante, *a.* frequenting, assiduous, studious. — *n.m.f.* scholar, student.
cursar, *v.t.* to frequent; to take (*courses of lectures*), study; to transmit, expedite.
cursería [CURSILERÍA].
cursi, *a.* pretentious, ostentatious, shabby-genteel. — *n.m.f.* pretentious, shabby-genteel person.
cursilería, *n.f.* pretentiousness, ostentation.
cursilón, -lona, *a., n.m.f.* insufferably pretentious *or* ostentatious (person).
cursillo, *n.m.* short course.
cursivo, -va, *a.* cursive. — *n.m.f.* cursive writing; (*print.*) italic; ***letra cursiva,*** flowing hand.
curso, *n.m.* course; turn; route; school session; academic year; ***es de curso legal,*** it is legal tender; ***dar curso a,*** to put through the official channels; ***en curso,*** current; (*pl.*) diarrhœa.
cursómetro, *n.m.* train speed measuring device.
cursor, *n.m.* (*mech.*) slider, slide.
curtación, *n.f.* (*astron.*) curtation.
curtidero, *n.m.* ground bark for tanning.
curtido, *n.m.* tanning; (*pl.*) tanned leather.
curtidor, *n.m.* tanner, leather-dresser.
curtiduría, *n.f.* tan-yard, tannery.
curtiente, *a., n.m.* tanning (material).
curtimbre, *n.f.* tanning; (collection of) tanned hides.
curtimiento, *n.m.* tanning.
curtir, *v.t.* to tan (*hides*); to tan, sunburn; to harden, inure, make experienced. — **curtirse,** *v.r.* to become tanned, sunburnt; to become experienced.
curto, -ta, *a.* (*prov.*) short; dock-tailed.
curú, *n.m.* (*Per.*) larva of the cloth moth.
curubo, *n.m.* (*Col.*) climbing plant.
curuca, curuja, *n.f.* eagle-owl.
curucú, *n.m.* (*Cent. Am.*) climbing bird.
curucurú, *n.m.* (*Hisp. Am.*) disease caused by snake-bite.
curuguá, *n.m.* (*Hisp. Am.*) cassabanana plant.
curupay, *n.m.* (*River Plate*) mimosa tree.
cururo, *n.m.* (*Chi.*) field rat.
cururú, *n.m.* Surinam toad.
curva, *n.f.* [CURVO].
curvatón, *n.m.* (*naut.*) small knee, bracket.
curvatura, curvidad, *n.f.* curvature.
curvicaudo, -da, *a.* curvicaudate.

curvifoliado, -da, *a.* curvifoliate.
curvilíneo, -nea, *a.* curvilinear.
curvímetro, *n.m.* curvometer.
curvo, -va, *a.* curved, crooked, bent. — *n.m.* (*prov.*) enclosed pasture-ground. — *n.f.* curve, bend; (*geom.*) curve-line; (*naut.*) knee; (*naut.*) ***curva de bao,*** spur; (*surv.*) ***curva de nivel,*** contour-line; ***tomar una curva,*** to take a bend.
cusca (cusqui), *n.f.* (*coll.*) ***hacerle a alguien la cusca (cusqui),*** to jigger s.o. up, mess s.o. up.
cuscungo, *n.m.* (*Ec.*) small owl.
cuscurrear, *v.i.* to eat *or* pick crumbs.
cuscurro, *n.m.* crust (*of bread*).
cuscuta, *n.f.* common dodder.
cuscús [ALCUZCUZ].
cusir, *v.t.* (*coll.*) to sew *or* stitch badly, clumsily.
cusma, *n.f.* (*Per.*) coarse shirt.
cuspidado, -da, *a.* (*bot.*) cuspidate.
cúspide, *n.f.* cusp; apex, tip, top, summit, peak; (*geom.*) vertex.
cuspídeo, -dea, *a.* (*bot.*) cuspidate.
custodia, *n.f.* custody, safe-keeping; guardianship; monstrance; tabernacle; guard, keeper, guardian, custodian.
custodiar, *v.t.* to keep, guard, take care of.
custodio, *n.m.* guard, keeper, watchman, custodian.
cusubé, *n.m.* (*Cub.*) sweetmeat made of yucca starch, water, sugar and eggs.
cusumbe, *n.m.* (*Ec.*), **cusumbo,** *n.m.* (*Col.*) coati.
cususa, *n.f.* (*Cent. Am.*) anisette.
cutache, *n.f.* (*Hond.*) long knife.
cutama, *n.f.* (*Chi.*) dull and tedious person.
cutáneo, -nea, *a.* cutaneous.
cúter, *n.m.* (*naut.*) cutter.
cutí, *n.m.* bed-ticking, crash.
cutícula, *n.f.* cuticle.
cuticular, *a.* cuticular.
cutio, *n.m.* labour, work.
cutir, *v.t.* to knock, pound, strike, beat, hammer, dash.
cutis, *n.m.* skin.
cuto, -ta, *a.* (*E.S.*) maimed, without the use of a limb.
cutral, *a.*, *n.m.f.* worn out (*ox* or *cow*).
cutre, *n.m.* (*coll.*) stingy person.
cutusa, *n.f.* (*Col.*) turtle-dove.
cuy, *n.m.* (*Cent. Am.*) guinea-pig.
cuyabra, *n.f.* (*Col.*) wooden bowl.
cuyo, -ya, *poss. and rel. pron.* whose, of whom, of which. — *n.m.* (*coll.*) lover.
cuzcuz [ALCUZCUZ].
¡cuz, cuz! *interj.* call to dogs.
cuzco, *n.m.* dog, mongrel.
cuzma [CUSMA].
cuzqueño, -ña, *a.*, *n.m.f.* (native) of Cuzco.
czar, czarina [ZAR, ZARINA].
czariano, -na [ZARIANO, -NA].

CH

Ch, ch, *n.f.* letter Ch, ch (is always sounded as *ch* in *church*).
cha, *n.f.* (*Hisp. Am.*) tea.
chabacanería, *n.f.* vulgarity, commonness.
chabacano, -na, *a.* vulgar, common. — *n.m.* (*Mex.*) apricot (*tree*).
chabela, *n.f.* (*Bol.*) drink made of wine and chicha.
chabola, *n.f.* shanty (-hut), shack.
chabolismo, *n.m.* shanty living, living in shacks; (tendency to) proliferation of shanty-dwellings.
chabolista, *n.m.f.* shanty-dweller.
chabrana, *n.f.* jamb (*of door* or *window*).
chacal, *n.m.* jackal.
chacalín, *n.m.* (*Hond.*) shrimp.
chacana, *n.f.* (*Ec.*) stretcher.
chacanear, *v.t.* (*Chi.*) to spur hard.
chacarero, *n.m.* (*Hisp. Am.*) farmer; farm hand.
chacarrachaca, *n.f.* (*fam.*) noisy racket *or* row.
chacina, *n.f.* minced pork sausage filling.
chacó, *n.m.* shako.
chacolí, *n.m.* sour red wine (*Basque country*).
chacolotear, *v.i.* to clatter (*loose horseshoe*).
chacoloteo, *n.m.* clatter (*of loose horseshoe*).
chacona, *n.f.* chaconne.
chaconada, *n.f.* jaconet.
chaconero, -ra, *n.m.f.* composer *or* dancer of chaconnes.
chacota, *n.f.* noisy joking, mocking; ***echar*** or ***tomar a chacota,*** to treat as a joke; ***hacer chacota de,*** to make fun of.
chacotear, *v.i.* to joke noisily.
chacoteo, *n.m.* mockery, joking.
chacotero, -ra, *a.* joking, mocking. — *n.m.f.* mocker, joker.
chacra, *n.f.* (*Hisp. Am.*) farm, ranch.
chacuaco, *n.m.* (*Mex.*) silver smelting furnace.
chacha, *n.f.* maid (*servant*).
chachal, *n.m.* (*Per.*) lead pencil.
chachalaca, *n.f.* (*Mex.*) chachalaca, Texas grouse; (*fig.*) chatterbox.
cháchara, *n.f.* (*coll.*) chit-chat, idle talk, prattle.
chacharear, *v.i.* (*coll.*) to chatter, prattle.
chacharero, -ra, chacharón, -rona, *a.* chattering, prattling. — *n.m.f.* chatterer, prattler.
chacho, *n.m.* lad.
chafador, -ra, *a.* crushing, crumpling; (*fig.*) spoiling.
chafadura, *n.f.* flattening; crushing, crumpling; (*fig.*) spoiling.
chafaldete, *n.m.* (*naut.*) clew-line.
chafaldita, *n.f.* (*coll.*) chaff, raillery, jest, banter.
chafalditero, -ra, *a.* (*fam.*) teasing, joking. — *n.m.f.* teaser, banterer.
chafalmejas, *n.m.f. inv.* (*fam.*) dauber, bad painter.
chafalonía, *n.f.* old plate, broken articles of silver.
chafallar, *v.t.* (*coll.*) to botch.
chafallo, *n.m.* coarse patch, botch.
chafallón, -llona, *a.* botching. — *n.m.f.* botcher.
chafandín, *n.m.* vain feather-brained person.
chafar, *v.t.* to flatten; to rumple, crumple; (*fig.*) to spoil; to leave speechless; ***me dejó chafado,*** he left me speechless; ***me ha chafado el plan,*** he has spoiled my chances.
chafardear, *v.i.* to meddle.
chafardero, -ra, *a.*, *n.m.f.* busybody.
chafarotazo, *n.m.* cutlass slash *or* wound.
chafarote, *n.m.* cutlass; sabre.
chafarrinar, *v.t.* to blot, splodge, stain.
chafarrinón, *n.m.* blot, splodge, stain; ***echarle a alguien un chafarrinón,*** to cast aspersions on s.o.
chaflán, *n.m.* bevel, chamfer.
chaflanar, *v.t.* to bevel, chamfer.
chagolla, *n.f.* (*Mex.*) counterfeit coin.
chagorra, *n.f.* (*Mex.*) woman of low class.
chagra, *n.m.* (*Ec.*) countryman.
chagrín, *n.m.* shagreen.
chagual, *n.m.* (*Hisp. Am.*) pineapple plant.
chaguala, *n.f.* (*Hisp. Am.*) nose-ring; (*Col.*) old shoe; long scar; (*Mex.*) slipper.
chagualón, *n.m.* (*Col.*) incense tree.
cháguar, *n.m.* (*Hisp. Am.*) sisal.
chaguarama, *n.m.* (*Cent. Am.*) giant palm tree.
chagüí, *n.m.* (*Ec.*) sparrow.
chahuar, *a.* bay and white (*horse*).
chaima, *a.* (*Ven.*) of the Chaima tribe.
chaira, *n.f.* (shoemaker's) knife; steel (*to sharpen knives*).
chajá, *n.m.* (*Arg.*) screamer bird.
chajal, *n.m.* (*Hisp. Am.*) Indian servant.
chajuán, *n.m.* (*Col.*) sultry weather.
chal, *n.m.* shawl.
chala, *n.f.* (*Per.*) husk (*of maize*).
chalado, -da, *a.* (*coll.*) barmy, crazy, nuts. — *n.m.f.* (*coll.*) crazy person, nut-case.
chalán, -lana (1), *n.m.f.* horse-dealer; (*coll.*) crafty dealer. — *n.m.* (*Hisp. Am.*) horse-breaker.
chalana (2), *n.f.* lighter, scow, wherry.
chalanear, *v.t.*, *v.i.* to deal, trade (*in horses*); (*coll.*) to deal craftily; (*coll.*) to haggle; (*Hisp. Am.*) to break in (*horses*).
chalaneo, *n.m.* horse-dealing; (*coll.*) crafty dealing.
chalanería, *n.f.* (*coll.*) crafty dealing.
chalanero, -ra, chalanesco, -ca, *a.* crafty (*in dealing*).
chalar, *v.t.* to drive crazy. — **chalarse,** *v.r.* to go crazy, lose one's head.
chalate, *n.m.* (*Mex.*) nag.
chalchal, *n.m.* (*River Plate*) conifer.
chalchihuite, *n.m.* (*Mex.*) low-grade emerald; (*E.S.*, *Guat.*) trifle trash.
chaleco, *n.m.* waistcoat; ***chaleco salvavidas,*** life-jacket.
chalequera, *n.f.* female waistcoat-maker.
chalet, *n.m.* chalet, villa.
chalí, *n.m.* mohair.
chalina, *n.f.* cravat, scarf.
chalón, *n.m.* (*Ur.*) shawl.
chalona, *n.f.* dried and salted mutton.
chalote, *n.m.* shallot.
chalupa, *n.f.* sloop, launch, long-boat; (*Mex.*) small canoe; (*Mex.*) corn pancake.
chalupero, *n.m.* boatman, canoe-man.
challulla, *n.f.* (*Per.*) river catfish.
chama, *n.f.* (*vulg.*) barter, exchange.
chamaco, *n.m.* (*Mex.*) boy, lad.
chamada, *n.f.* brushwood-fire; brushwood.
chamagoso, -sa, *a.* (*Mex.*) dirty, filthy; low, vulgar.
chamagua, *n.f.* (*Mex.*) ripening maize field.
chamal, *n.m.* (*Arg.*, *Chi.*) blanket garment.
chamanto, *n.m.* (*Chi.*) striped wrap.
chamar, *v.t.* (*vulg.*) to barter, exchange.
chámara, chamarasca, *n.f.* brushwood-fire; brushwood.
chamarilero, -ra, *n.m.f.* second-hand dealer; junk-dealer.
chamarilería, *n.f.* junk shop.
chamarillero, *n.m.* gambler, card sharper.
chamarillón, -llona, *a.* gambling, card sharping.
chamariz, *n.m.* greenfinch.
chamarón, *n.m.* bottle tit.
chamarra, *n.f.* sheepskin jacket.

chamarro, *n.m.* (*Hond., Mex.*) coarse garment.
chamba, *n.f.* (*coll.*) fluke.
chambado, *n.m.* (*Arg., Chi.*) drinking-horn.
chambelán, *n.m.* chamberlain.
chambelanía, *n.f.* chamberlainship.
chambergo, -ga, *a.* appertaining to the royal guard of Carlos II. — *n.m.* soldier of the royal guard; slouched broad-brimmed hat. — *n.f.* long, wide cassock; broad girdle; a Spanish dance; (*prov.*) very narrow ribbon.
chamberguilla, *n.f.* (*prov.*) very narrow ribbon.
chambilla, *n.f.* stone wall with an iron railing.
chambo, *n.m.* (*Mex.*) barter of grain and seeds.
chambón, -bona, *a.* awkward, unhandy. — *n.m.f.* blunderer, duffer.
chambonada, *n.m.f.* blunder; (*fig.*) fluke.
chambonear, *v.i.* to blunder.
chamborote, *a.* (*Ec.*) applied to white pepper; (*Ec.*) (*fig.*) long-nosed person.
chambra, *n.f.* dressing-jacket.
chamelote, *n.m.* camlet.
chamelotón, *n.m.* coarse camlet.
chamerluco, *n.m.* close jacket with collar.
chamicado, -da, *a.* (*Chi., Per.*) reserved and silent; suffering from after-effects of drunkenness.
chamicera, *n.f.* scorched area (*of forest*).
chamiza, *n.f.* wild cane (*used for thatching*); (*prov.*) brushwood.
chamizo, *n.m.* half-burnt tree *or* log; thatched hut; (*coll.*) gambling den.
chamorro, -rra, *a.* shorn; ***trigo chamorro,*** beardless wheat. — *n.f.* shorn head.
champán, *n.m.* (*naut.*) sampan; champagne.
Champaña, *n.f.* Champagne.
champaña, *n.m.* champagne.
champar, *v.t.* (*coll.*) to give (s.o.) a piece of one's mind.
champear, *v.t.* (*Chi., Ec.*) to close (*a gap* or *flume*) with green sods *or* turf.
champola, *n.f.* (*Cub.*) refreshment made from custard-apple, sugar and ice.
champú, *n.m.* shampoo.
champurrado, *n.m.* (*Mex.*) chocolate made with cornflour.
champurrar, *v.t.* to mix (*drinks*).
chamucera, *n.f.* rowlock, (*Am.*) oarlock.
chamuchina, *n.f.* trifle, trash; (*Hisp. Am.*) populace, rabble.
chamuscar [A], *v.t.* to singe, scorch; to mark.
chamusco, *n.m.* [CHAMUSQUINA].
chamuscón, *n.m.* large scorch *or* singe.
chamusquina, *n.f.* scorching, singeing; (*fig.*) quarrelling, wrangling; ***huele a chamusquina,*** things are getting hot, there's going to be trouble; it smacks of heresy.
chan, *n.m.* (*E.S., Guat.*) lime-leaved sage.
chanada, *n.f.* (*coll.*) trick, deceit.
chanate, *n.m.* (*Mex.*) blackbird.
chanca [CHANCLA].
chancaca, *n.f.* (*Cub., Mex.*) sugar of the second crop; (*Ec.*) paste made of toasted maize ground with honey.
chancadora, *n.f.* (*Chi.*) crusher, grinder.
chancaquita, *n.f.* (*Hisp. Am.*) ***chancaca*** cake.
chancar [A], *v.t.* (*Chi.*) to crush.
chancear(se), *v.i.* (*v.r.*) to joke, jest.
chancero, -ra, *a.* joking, jesting.
chanciller [CANCILLER].
chancillería [CANCILLERÍA].
chancla, *n.f.* heelless slipper; old down-at-heel shoe.
chancleta, *n.f.* heelless slipper; ***en chancleta,*** with shoes worn slipper-like, slipshod. — *n.m.f.* bungler.
chancletear, *v.i.* to go about slipshod.
chancleteo, *n.m.* clatter of slippers.
chanclo, *n.m.* galosh, overshoe, (*Am.*) rubber.
chancro, *n.m.* chancre.
chancuco, *n.m.* (*Col.*) contraband tobacco.
chánccharras máncharras, *n.f.pl.* (*coll.*) ***andar en chánccharras máncharras,*** to beat about the bush.
chanchería, *n.f.* (*Hisp. Am.*) pork-butcher's shop.
chancho, -cha, *a.* (*Hisp. Am.*) dirty, unclean. — *n.m.* hog.
chanchullero, -ra, *a.* tricky, sharp, underhand. — *n.m.f.* trickster, sharper.
chanchullo, *n.m.* (*coll.*) trickery, sharp practice, underhand dealing.
chanfaina, *n.f.* ragout made of offal.
chanflón, -lona, *a.* clumsy. — *n.m.* (*obs.*) old copper coin.
changa, *n.f.* (*Hisp. Am.*) portering, carrying.
changador, *n.m.* (*Hisp. Am.*) porter, carrier.
changle, *n.m.* (*Chi.*) fungus.
changote, *n.m.* oblong iron bar; (*min.*) bloom.
changüí, *n.m.* (*coll.*) hoax, trick; (*Cub.*) low-class dance.
chantado, *n.m.* (*prov.*) wall *or* fence of upright flagstones.
chantaje, *n.m.* blackmail; ***hacer chantaje a,*** to blackmail.
chantajista, *n.m.f.* blackmailer.
chantar, *v.t.* to dress, put on; (*coll.*) to scold, rate; to pave *or* fence with flagstones.
chanto, *n.m.* (*prov.*) flagstone.
chantre, *n.m.* precentor, choir-master.
chantría, *n.f.* precentorship.
chanza, *n.f.* joke, jest, fun; ***hablar de chanza,*** to speak jestingly.
chanzoneta, *n.f.* (*coll.*) joke, jest; ballad, chansonette, merry little song.
chanzonetero, *n.m.* writer of ballads, petty poet.
chapa, *n.f.* metal plate, sheet metal; wood veneer; metal cap; metal badge; metal token; rosy spot on the cheek; (*coll.*) judgment, sense; (*pl.*) game of tossing up coins.
chapado, -da, *a.* ***chapado a la antigua,*** old-fashioned, die-hard.
chapalear, *v.i.* to splash (about), paddle.
chapaleo, *n.m.* splashing, paddling.
chapaleta, *n.f.* valve (*of hydraulic pump*).
chapaleteo, *n.m.* lapping; pattering.
chapapote, *n.m.* tar.
chapar, *v.t.* to plate, coat, veneer; (*fig.*) to settle; to let out.
chaparra, *n.f.* kermes oak; (*obs.*) low-roofed coach; bramble bush.
chaparral, *n.m.* kermes oak grove.
chaparrazo, *n.m.* (*Hond.*) violent shower of rain.
chaparrear, *v.i.* to shower, pour (*rain*).
chaparro, *n.m.* evergreen oak, dwarf oak.
chaparrón, *n.m.* heavy shower (*rain*).
chapatal, *n.m.* quagmire.
chape, *n.m.* (*Chi., Col.*) tress.
chapeador, -ra, *n.m.f.* plater; veneerer.
chapear, *v.t.* to plate; to veneer. — *v.i.* to clatter (*loose horseshoe*).
chapecar [A], *v.t.* (*Chi.*) to braid, plait; (*Chi.*) to string (*onions, garlic etc.*).
chapeo, *n.m.* (*coll.*) titfer, hat.
chapera, *n.f.* inclined plank.
chapería, *n.f.* sheet metal work.
chaperón, *n.m.* (*obs.*) hood, cowl; (*arch.*) wooden support of gutter.
chapeta, *n.f.* red spot on the cheek.
chapetón, -tona, *a., n.m.f.* (*Hisp. Am.*) Spanish immigrant. — *n.m.* (*Mex.*) silver plate on riding harness.

chapetonada, *n.f.* (*Hisp. Am.*) illness affecting newly arrived Europeans.
chapín, *n.m.* chopine; slipper; trunk fish.
chapinazo, *n.m.* blow with a chopine.
chapinería, *n.f.* chopine shop.
chapinero, *n.m.* chopine-maker *or* seller.
chápiro, *n.m.* ***¡voto al chápiro! ¡por vida del chápiro (verde)!*** zounds! by thunder!
chapisca, *n.f.* (*C.R.*) maize harvest.
chapitel, *n.m.* chapiter, capital; spire; jewel bearing (*of a magnetic needle*).
chaple, *n.m.* graver, engraving-tool.
chapó, *n.m.* four- *or* six-handed billiard game.
chapodar, *v.t.* to lop, prune, trim (*trees*); (*fig.*) to curtail, cut down, cut out.
chapodo, *n.m.* pruned *or* trimmed branch.
chapola, *n.f.* (*Col.*) butterfly.
chapón, *n.m.* large ink-stain *or* blot.
chapona, *n.f.* (woman's) morning dress; (*Ur.*) coat, jacket.
chapote, *n.m.* (*Mex.*) black chewing-wax.
chapotear, *v.t.* to wet, damp with a sponge *or* cloth. — *v.i.* to paddle, splash about.
chapoteo, *n.m.* paddling, splashing about.
chapucear, *v.t.* to botch, bungle.
chapucería, *n.f.* botch, bungle, mess; fib, lie.
chapucero, -ra, *a.* bungling, clumsy, messy. — *n.m.f.* botcher, bungler. — *n.m.* blacksmith; dealer in old iron.
chapul, *n.m.* (*Col.*) dragonfly.
chapulín, *n.m.* (*Hisp. Am.*) locust; large cicada.
chapurr(e)ar, *v.t.* to jabber, speak brokenly, mangle; to mix; ***chapurrear el inglés,*** to speak pidgin English.
chapuz, *n.m.* ducking; botch-work; ***dar chapuz a,*** to duck, give a ducking; (*pl.* **chapuces**) mast spars.
chapuza, *n.f.* botch-work.
chapuzar(se) [C], *v.t., v.i.* (*v.r.*) to duck.
chapuzón, *n.m.* (*coll.*) duck, ducking, diving; ***darse (pegarse) un chapuzón,*** to go for a dip (swim).
chaqué, *n.m.* morning coat.
chaqueta, *n.f.* jacket, coat.
chaquete, *n.m.* backgammon.
chaquetear, *v.i.* (*coll.*) to turn coat.
chaquetera, *n.f.* jacket *or* coat maker.
chaquetero, *n.m.* (*coll.*) turncoat.
chaquetilla, *n.f.* short jacket.
chaquetón, *n.m.* short overcoat.
chaquira, *n.f.* glass bead.
charabán, *n.m.* charabanc.
charada, *n.f.* charade.
charadrio, *n.m.* bittern.
charal, *n.m.* (*Mex.*) charal fish.
charamusca, *n.f.* (*Mex.*) twisted candy; (*Per.*) brushwood.
charamusquero, *n.m.* (*Mex.*) seller of candy.
charanga, *n.f.* brass band; din, racket.
charango, *n.m.* (*Per.*) bandore, small guitar.
charanguero, -ra, *a.* clumsy, bungling, botching. — *n.m.f.* botcher, bungler. — *n.m.* (*prov.*) pedlar, hawker; (*prov.*) coaster.
charapa, *n.f.* (*Per.*) small tortoise.
charape, *n.m.* (*Mex.*) intoxicating drink (*made with pulque, ear of maize, honey, clove and cinnamon*).
charata, *n.f.* (Arg.) wood grouse.
charca, *n.f.* (large, natural) pool *or* pond.
charcas, *n.m.pl.* Indians of the Inca empire.
charco, *n.m.* paddle; small pond; (*coll.*) ***pasar el charco,*** to cross the pond (*Atlantic*).
charla, *n.f.* chat, chatting, talk; (*orn.*) chatterer, waxwing.
charlador, -ra, *a.* chattering, talkative. — *n.m.f.* gabbler, prater, chatterbox.
charladuría, *n.f.* prattle; gossip.
charlar, *v.i.* to chat, talk, prattle; to gossip.
charlatán, -tana, *a.* talkative. — *n.m.f.* prater, babbler; charlatan, quack, mountebank.
charlatanear, *v.i.* to prattle, chatter.
charlatanería, *n.f.* prattling; gossip; charlatanry, quackery.
charlatanesco, -ca, *a.* charlatanish.
charlatanismo, *n.m.* charlatanry, quackery, charlatanism.
charlear, *v.i.* to croak.
charlotear, *v.i.* to prattle.
charneca, *n.f.* mastic tree, pistachio tree.
charnecal, *n.m.* plantation of mastic trees.
charnela, charneta, *n.f.* hinge.
charol, *n.m.* varnish, japan, japan-work, lacquer; patent leather; ***darse charol,*** to brag, put on airs.
charolar, *v.t.* to varnish, japan, polish.
charolista, *n.m.* varnisher, japanner.
charpa, *n.f.* baldric; sling.
charque, *n.m.* (*Arg., Mex.*) jerked beef.
charquear, *v.t.* (*Hisp. Am.*) to jerk (*beef*).
charquecillo, *n.m.* (*Per.*) salted and dried conger eel.
charqui, *n.m.* (*Hisp. Am.*) charqui, jerked beef.
charquicán, *n.m.* (*Hisp. Am.*) dish made of charqui, chili, potatoes, beans etc.
charquillo, *n.m.* small pool, puddle.
charra (1), *n.f.* (*Hond.*) wide-brimmed hat with a low crown.
charrada, *n.f.* clownish speech *or* action; country dance; (*coll.*) tawdriness, gaudiness.
charrán, *a.* rascally, knavish. — *n.m.* rogue, rascal.
charranada, *n.f.* knavish *or* roguish thing to do.
charranear, *v.i.* to play the knave, be a rogue.
charranería, *n.f.* rascality, knavery, roguery.
charrasca, *n.f.*, **charrasco,** *n.m.* (*coll.*) trailing sword; clasp-knife.
charrería, *n.f.* tawdriness.
charrete, *n.f.* two-wheeled carriage.
charretera, *n.f.* knee-strap, knee-buckle; epaulet; (*coll.*) shoulder-pad (*for carrying loads*).
charro, -rra (2), *a.* relating to a peasant from Salamanca; (*fam.*) churlish, ill-bred, rustic; (*coll.*) tawdry, showy, gaudy. — *n.m.f.* peasant from Salamanca; churl, boor.
charrúa, *n.m.* River Plate Indians; small craft used as a tugboat.
chasca, *n.f.* brushwood, lops.
chascar [A], *v.t., v.i.* to crack; to click; to crunch; to swallow.
chascarrillo, *n.m.* joke, funny story, quip.
chascás, *n.m.* lancer's helmet.
chasco, *n.m.* joke; deceit, trick; disappointment; ***dar chasco a,*** to disappoint; ***llevarse un chasco,*** to be disappointed.
chascón, -cona, *a.* (*Chi.*) entangled, dishevelled.
chasconear, *v.t.* (*Chi.*) to entangle; to involve in difficulties; (*Chi.*) to pull by the hair.
chasis, *n.m. inv.* frame, chassis.
chasponazo, *n.m.* bullet graze, scrape *or* scratch.
chasqueador, -ra, *a.* joking, fooling; whipping. — *n.m.f.* joker, hoaxer; whipper.
chasquear, *v.t.* to trick; to disappoint; to crack (*whip*). — *v.i.* to crack, snap. — **chasquearse,** *v.r.* to be disappointed *or* frustrated.
chasqui, *n.m.* (*Per.*) Indian runner *or* courier.
chasquido, *n.m.* crack; click; snap.
chatarra, *n.f.* scrap iron, old iron; iron slag.
chatarrero, *n.m.* scrap-iron dealer.
chatedad, *n.f.* flatness; shallowness.
chato, -ta, *a.* flat; flat-nosed. — *n.m.* small glass. — *n.f.* flat bed-pan; short shot-gun; flat-bottomed

boat; (*coll.*) death. — *n.m.f.* flat-nosed person; (*coll.*) dear, duckie.
chatón, *n.m.* large stone (*set in ring* or *brooch*).
chatre, *a.* (*Ec.*) richly attired.
chaucha, *n.f.* (*Arg.*) small coin (*of silver* or *nickel*); (*Arg.*) green bean; (*Chi.*) silver coin (*of low standard*); (*Chi.*) new season potato (*left for seed*).
chauche, *n.m.* red lead paint.
chaucera, *n.f.* (*Chi.*) purse.
chaúl, *n.m.* blue Chinese silk shawl.
chauvinismo, *n.m.* chauvinism, jingoism.
chauvinista, *a.*, *n.m.f.* chauvinist, chauvinistic, jingo.
chaval, -la, *n.m.f.* (*coll.*) boy, lad, kid; girl, lass, kid, bird.
chavarí, *n.m.* linen.
chavasca, *n.f.* brushwood.
chavea, *n.m.* boy, lad, kid.
chaveta, *n.f.* forelock; pin, cotter-pin; ***perder la chaveta,*** to lose one's head; ***estar chaveta,*** to be nuts.
chaya, *n.f.* (*Chi.*) fun; confetti; (*Cub.*) resin shrub.
chayo, *n.m.* (*Chi.*) large sieve.
chayote, *n.m.* (*Mex.*) chayote fruit.
chayotera, *n.f.* (*Cub.*) chayote plant.
chaza, *n.f.* space between two portholes; place and mark where the ball stops (*in pelota*); ***chazas corrientes,*** handicap penalty in pelota; (*equit.*) ***hacer chazas,*** to hop on the hind feet.
chazador, *n.m.* player who stops the ball (*in pelota*); scorer, marker.
chazar [C], *v.t.* to stop (*the ball*) before it reaches the winning-point, mark (*the spot*) where the ball stops (*in pelota*).
che (1), *n.f.* name of the letter Ch.
¡che! (2), *interj.* I say!
checar [A], **chequear,** *v.t.* to check.
checo, -ca (1), *a.*, *n.m.f.* Czech. — *n.m.* Czech language.
checa (2), *n.f.* secret police prison.
checoslovaco, -ca, *a.* Czechoslovak.
Checoslovaquia, *n.f.* Czechoslovakia.
cheira, *n.f.* shoemaker's knife; table steel.
cheje, *n.m.* (*E.S.*, *Hond.*) link (*of a chain*).
chelín, *n.m.* shilling.
chencha, *a.* (*Mex.*) lazy, lay-about.
chepa, *n.f.* (*coll.*) hump, hunch.
chepica, *n.f.* (*Chi.*) gramma-grass.
cheque, *n.m.* cheque, (*Am.*) check.
chequén, *n.m.* (*Chi.*) myrtle.
chercán, *n.m.* (*Chi.*) nightingale.
chercha, *n.f.* (*Hond*). noisy mirth; (*Ven.*) mockery, joke, jest.
cherchar, *v.i.* (*Cent. Am.*) to make fun, joke, jest.
chericles, *n.m.* (*Ec.*) climbing parrot.
cherinol, *n.m.* (*sl.*) leader of a band of robbers.
cherinola, *n.f.* (*sl.*) meeting of robbers *or* ruffians.
cherna, *n.f.* Mediterranean sea-bass.
cherva, *n.f.* castor-oil plant.
chéster, *n.m.* English Cheshire cheese.
cheurón, *n.m.* (*her.*) chevron.
cheuronado, -da, *a.* (*her.*) chevroned.
cheuto, -ta, *a.* (*Chi.*) hare-lipped.
chía, *n.f.* (*obs.*) short black mourning mantle; (*obs.*) cowl; (*bot.*) lime-leaved sage; white medicinal earth.
chibalete, *n.m.* (*print.*) composing-frame.
chibcha, *a.* (*Col.*) Chibcha. — *n.m.* Chibcha language.
chibera, *n.f.* (*Mex.*) coachman's whip.
chibolo, -la, *n.m.f.* (*Ec.*) small round body; bump, bruise.
chiborra, *n.f.* fool's bauble.
chibuquí, *n.m.* chibouk, Turkish pipe.
chica, *n.f.* [CHICO].
chicada [CHIQUILLADA].
chicalé, *n.m.* (*Cent. Am.*) chicalé bird.
chicalote, *n.m.* argemone, prickly Mexican poppy.
chicarrón, *n.m.* strapping, hefty lad.
chicazo, *n.m.* strapping lad; tom-boy; ***María es un chicazo,*** Mary is a tom-boy.
chicle, *n.m.* (*Mex.*) chicle; chewing-gum.
chiclear, *v.i.* to chew gum.
chico, -ca, *a.* small, tiny; young; ***chico con grande,*** mixed; all in all, more or less; ***chico de cuerpo,*** small-built. — *n.m.* child, boy, lad; chap, fellow; ***es (un) buen chico,*** he is a good lad, chap. — *n.f.* girl; maid, servant girl; (*Hisp. Am.*) negro dance; small bottle; (*Mex.*) small silver coin worth three centavos.
chicolear, *v.i.* to flirt; to whisper sweet nothings; to fool about.
chicoleo, *n.m.* (*coll.*) flirting; fooling about.
chicoria, *n.f.* chicory.
chicoriáceo, -cea, *a.* appertaining to chicory.
chicorro [CHICAZO].
chicote, *n.m.* [CHICAZO]; (*coll.*) cigar; (*naut.*) cable end; (*Hisp. Am.*) whip.
chicozapote, *n.m.* (*Mex.*) sapodilla.
chicuelo, -la, *n.m.f.* young boy, lad; young girl, lass.
chicha, *a.* ***calma chicha,*** dead calm, doldrums. — *n.f.* meat (*children's language*); strong drink (*made from fermented maize*); ***tener pocas chichas,*** to be thin *or* weak; ***tener chicha,*** to have guts; (*coll.*) ***no ser ni chicha ni limoná,*** to be neither one thing nor the other.
chícharo, *n.m.* pea.
chicharra, *n.f.* cicada; chatterbox, prattler; rattling toy; ***cantaba la chicharra,*** it was high summer, blazing hot.
chicharrar [ACHICHARRAR].
chicharrero, *n.m.* blazing hot place *or* spot.
chicharro, *n.m.* crackling.
chicharrón, *n.m.* crackling, over-roasted meat; (*coll.*) sun-burnt person.
chichear, *v.t.*, *v.i.* to hiss.
chicheo, *n.m.* hissing.
chichería, *n.f.* (*Mex.*) tavern *or* shop where chicha is sold.
chichicuilote, *n.m.* (*Mex.*) curlew.
chichigua, *n.f.* (*Mex.*, *vulg.*) wet nurse; (*Col.*) worthless trifle.
chichilasa, *n.f.* (*Mex.*) red ant.
chichilo, *n.m.* (*Bol.*) yellow monkey.
chichimeco, -ca, *a.*, *n.m.f.* (*Mex.*) Chichimeca Indian.
chichisbeo, *n.m.* court paid to a lady; wooer.
chicholo, *n.m.* (*River Plate*) sweet wrapped in corn husk.
chichón, *n.m.* bump, lump (*on head*).
chichonera, *n.f.* padded cap.
chichota, *n.f.* jot, tittle.
chifla, *n.f.* whistle; hiss, hissing; paring-knife.
chifladera, *n.f.* whistle.
chiflado, -da, *n.m.f.* crack-brain, crank, crazy person.
chifladura, *n.f.* hissing; whistling; (*coll.*) craze, fad, whim; hobby-horse.
chiflar (1), *v.t.*, *v.i.* to hiss (at), whistle (at): to gulp down. — **chiflarse,** *v.r.* to go potty, go round the bend; to get crazy (***por,*** on *or* about); ***estar chiflado,*** to be cracked *or* up the creek; to be crazy *or* gone (***por,*** on).
chiflar (2), *v.t.* to pare (leather).
chiflato, *n.m.* whistle.
chifle, *n.m.* whistle, call; bird-whistle, decoy; (*obs.*) priming-horn, powder-flask.
chiflete, chiflo, *n.m.* whistle.
chiflido, *n.m.* whistling.

chiflón, *n.m.* (*Hisp. Am.*) draught; (*Mex.*) water spout; (*Mex.*) caving in (*roof, wall etc.*).
chigre, *n.m.* (*Ast.*) cider house.
chigua, *n.f.* (*Chi.*) basket.
chigüil, *n.m.* (*Ec.*) dough made with maize, sugar, butter, eggs, cheese wrapped in green corn husk.
chigüiro, *n.m.* (*Ven.*) capybara.
chihuahua, *n.m.* (*Ec.*) firework.
chilaba, *n.f.* djellabah.
chilacayote, *n.m.* American *or* bottle gourd.
chilacoa, *n.f.* (*Col.*) woodcock.
chilanco, *n.m.* (*Cent. Am.*) river pool.
chilaquil, *n.m.* (*Mex.*) maize omelet with chilli sauce.
chilaquila, *n.f.* (*Guat.*) maize omelet stuffed with cheese, herbs and chilli.
chilar, *n.m.* (*Hisp. Am.*) chilli field.
chilate, *n.m.* (*Cent. Am.*) drink made of chilli, roasted maize and cacao.
chilatole, *n.m.* (*Mex.*) ear of corn cooked with chilli and pork meat.
chilco, *n.m.* (*Chi.*) wild fuchsia.
chilchote, *n.m.* (*Mex.*) very hot chilli.
Chile, *n.m.* Chile.
chile, *n.m.* chilli.
chilenismo, *n.m.* phrase, idiom, colloquialism peculiar to Chileans.
chileno, -na, *a.*, *n.m.f.* Chilean.
chilero, *n.m.* (*Mex.*) (*contempt.*) grocer.
chilindrina, *n.f.* (*coll.*) trifle; jest, joke, fun; chaff, banter.
chilindrinero, -ra, *a.* (*fam.*) jesting, bantering. — *n.m.f.* jester, joker; chatterbox.
chilindrón, *n.m.* card game.
chilmote, *n.m.* (*Mex.*) sauce of chilli and tomato.
chilote, *n.m.* (*Mex.*) drink made with pulque and chilli.
chilpe, *n.m.* (*Ec.*) strip of agave leaf; (*Ec.*) dry leaf of maize; (*Chi.*) rag, tatter.
chiltipiquín, *n.m.* (*Mex.*) small hot chilli.
chiltuca, *n.f.* (*E.S.*) poisonous spider.
chilla, *n.f.* call (*decoy-instrument for foxes, hares etc.*); thin board; (*Chi.*) small fox.
chillado, *n.m.* roof of shingles *or* thin boards; clap-boards.
chillador, -ra, *a.* screaming, shrieking. — *n.m.f.* screamer, shrieker.
chillar, *v.i.* to scream, shriek; to screech; to squeak; (*hunt.*) to imitate birds' notes; (*fig.*) to be loud, garish; to clash, shriek (*of colours*); ***me chillan los oídos,*** my ears are ringing; ***chillarle a alguien,*** to tick (tell) s.o. off.
chilleras, *n.f.pl.* (*naut.*) shot-lockers.
chillería, *n.f.* row, uproar, screeching, screaming.
chillido, *n.m.* squeak, shriek, shrill sound; ***dar un chillido,*** to utter a scream.
chillo, *n.m.* call, whistle (*instrument*).
chillón (1), **-llona,** *a.* (*coll.*) bawling, shrieking, screaming; shrill; (*fig.*) loud, garish (*colours*).
chillón (2), *n.m.* lath nail; ***chillón real,*** spike.
chimachima, chimango, *n.m.* (*Arg.*) beetle-eater.
chimbador, *n.m.* (*Per.*) expert in river crossing.
chimenea, *n.f.* chimney, smoke stack, flue; funnel; fire-place; shaft; (*mil.*) nipple (*of a percussion firearm*); ***caerle a uno algo por la chimenea,*** to have a windfall.
chimó, *n.m.* (*Ven.*) concoction of tobacco and hydrous carbonate of soda, chewed by the Indians.
chimpancé, *n.m.* chimpanzee.
China, *n.f.* China.
china, *n.f.* [CHINO].
chinaca, *n.f.* (*Mex.*) beggars, poor people.
chinama, *n.f.* (*Guat.*) hut, hovel.
chinampa, *n.f.* (*Mex.*) small plot of land (*between the lagoons near Mexico City*).
chinapo, *n.m.* (*Mex.*) obsidian.
chinar, *v.t.* (*build.*) to pebble-dash.
chinarro, *n.m.* large pebble.
chinateado, *n.m.* stratum *or* layer of pebbles.
chinazo, *n.m.* large pebble; blow with a pebble.
chincol, *n.m.* (*Hisp. Am.*) sparrow.
chincual, *n.m.* (*Mex.*) measles.
chinchar, *v.t.* (*coll.*) to needle, nag, pester; (*coll.*) ***te tienes que chinchar,*** you must (just) lump it. — **chincharse,** *v.r.* (*coll.*) to get narked; ***¡a chincharse!*** lump it!
chincharrazo, *n.m.* (*coll.*) blow with the flat of a sword.
chincharrero, *n.m.* place swarming with bugs; (*Col., Ec., Per.*) fishing smack.
chinche, *a.*, *n.m.f.* fussy, finicky (person); nagger, pest. — *n.f.* bed-bug; drawing-pin, (*Am.*) thumb-tack; ***morir como chinches,*** to die like flies.
chinchero, *n.m.* bug-trap.
chincheta, *n.f.* drawing-pin.
chinchilla, *n.f.* chinchilla.
chinchimén, *n.m.* (*Chi.*) sea-otter.
chinchín, *n.m.* tinny noise (*esp. of brass band*); (*Chi.*) evergreen shrub; (*Cub.*) drizzling rain; (*Col.*) your health! (*toast*).
chinchintor, *n.m.* (*Hond.*) viper.
chinchona, *n.f.* (*Hisp. Am.*) quinine.
chinchorrería, *n.f.* fussiness; nagging; pestering.
chinchorrero, -ra, *a.* fussing; nagging; pestering.
chinchorro, *n.m.* small rowing-boat, dinghy; fishing net; (*Ven.*) Indian hammock.
chinchoso, -sa, *a.* fussing; nagging, pestering.
chiné, *a.* chiné (*fabric*).
chinear, *v.t.* (*Cent. Am.*) to carry in the arms *or* on the back.
chinela, *n.f.* slipper.
chinelazo, *n.m.* blow with a slipper.
chinería, *n.f.* Chinese object.
chinero, *n.m.* china-closet.
chinesco, -ca, *a.* Chinese-like; ***a la chinesca,*** in the Chinese manner; ***sombras chinescas,*** shadow pantomime. — *n.m.pl.* (**chinescos**) (*mus.*) bell tree, instrument with small bells.
chinga, *n.f.* (*Hisp. Am.*) skunk; (*C.R.*) sale by auction; (*C.R.*) stub (*of cigar* or *cigarette*); (*Hond.*) jest, banter; (*Ven.*) drunkenness.
chingana, *n.f.* (*Hisp. Am.*) low music-hall.
chingar [B], *v.t.* (*coll.*) to drink; to pester, annoy; to dock the tail of. — **chingarse,** *v.r.* to get tipsy; to get ratty; (*Chi.*) to fail; (*Hisp. Am.*) (*obsc.*) to shit.
chinguirito, *n.m.* (*Mex.*) rum from the lees of sugar.
chino, -na, *a.*, *n.m.f.* Chinese. — *n.m.* Chinese (language); hairless dog; (*Hisp. Am.*) offspring of Indian and mestizo; (*Cub.*) offspring of negro and mulatto; (*Col.*) servant; newsboy; (*Hisp. Am.*) dear, darling; (*Chi.*) Indian; ***engañar a uno como a un chino,*** to deceive s.o. easily. — *n.f.* pebble, small stone; porcelain, china; china-ware; china-root; china-silk *or* linen cloth; game of shutting hands and guessing which contains a pebble; (*Hisp. Am.*) servant girl (*of Indian* or *mestizo blood*); ***poner chinas a,*** to put stumbling blocks in the way of; ***no tener ni una china,*** not to have a brass farthing; ***te ha tocado la china,*** it has fallen to you, it's your baby *or* funeral, you've had it; ***tropezar en una china,*** to make a mountain out of a mole-hill, falter over a trifle.
chipa, *n.m.* (*River Plate*) basket.
chipá, *n.m.* (*River Plate*) cake *or* loaf of maize *or* cassava.
chipaco, *n.m.* (*Arg.*) cake of bran.
chipé, *n.f.* (*sl.*) truth; ***de chipé,*** first rate, smashing.

chipén, *n.f.* (*sl.*) bustle; ***de chipén,*** smashing.
chipichape [ZIPIZAPE].
chipichipi, *n.m.* (*Mex.*) drizzle.
chipile, *n.m.* (*Mex.*) cabbage.
chipilo, *n.m.* (*Bol.*) banana fritter.
chipirón, *n.m.* small squid.
chipojo, *n.m.* (*Cub.*) green lizard.
chipolo, *n.m.* (*Col.*, *Ec.*, *Per.*) ombre.
chipote, *n.m.* (*Cent. Am.*) cuff, slap, box.
Chipre, *n.m.* Cyprus.
chipriota, *a.*, *n.m.f.* Cypriot.
chiqueadores, *n.m.pl.* disks of tortoise shells.
chiquear, *v.t.* (*Cub.*, *Mex.*) to fondle, pamper.
chiqueo, *n.m.* (*Cub.*, *Mex.*) fondling, pampering, caress.
chiquero, *n.m.* pigsty; (*prov.*) hut for goats; bull-pen.
chiquichaque, *n.m.* (*obs.*) sawer, sawyer; chewing noise.
chiquiguite, *n.m.* (*Guat.*, *Mex.*) wicker basket *or* hamper.
chiquilicuatro, *n.m.* (*coll.*) whippersnapper.
chiquillada, *n.f.* childish thing to do *or* say.
chiquillería, *n.f.* (*fam.*) mob of kids.
chiquillo, -lla, *n.m.f.* child, kid, brat, nipper.
chiquirín, *n.m.* (*Guat.*) cicada-like insect.
chiquirritico, -ca, *a.* tiny, wee.
chiquirritín, -tina, chiquitín, -tina, *a.* teeny-weeny.
chiquito, -ta, *a.* nice and small. — *n.m.f.* little boy *or* girl; ***andarse con chiquitas,*** to beat about the bush.
chira, *n.f.* (*C.R.*) banana skin; (*Col.*) shred; (*E.S.*) ulcer, sore.
chirapa, *n.f.* (*Bol.*) rag, tatter; (*Per.*) sun shower.
chirca, *n.f.* (*Cent. Am.*) chirca tree.
chircate, *n.m.* (*Col.*) rough skirt.
chiribico, *n.m.* (*Cub.*) chiribico fish.
chiribitas, *n.f.pl.* (*coll.*) sparks; ***estar echando chiribitas,*** to be flaming *or* blazing mad *or* angry; to be flaming hot; ***ver chiribitas,*** to see spots before the eyes.
chiribital, *n.m.* (*Col.*) untilled land.
chiribitil [CUCHITRIL].
chiricatana, *n.f.* (*Ec.*) rough poncho.
chiricaya, *n.f.* (*Hond.*) sweet made with milk and eggs.
chirigaita, *n.f.* (*prov.*) gourd, calabash.
chirigota, *n.f.* joke, fun; ***tomar a chirigota,*** to treat as a joke.
chirigotero, -ra, *a.* joking, jesting, fun-loving.
chiriguare, *n.m.* (*Ven.*) bird of prey.
chirigüe, *n.m.* (*Chi.*) chirigüe bird.
chirimbolos, *n.m.pl.* (*coll.*) pots and pans.
chirimía, *n.f.* flageolet. — *n.m.* flageolet-player.
chirimoya, *n.f.* cherimoya, custard apple.
chirimoyo, *n.m.* (*Cent. Am.*) cherimoya tree.
chiringo, *n.m.* (*Mex.*) fragment, piece, bit.
chirinola, *n.f.* game resembling ninepins; (*fig.*) trifle; ***estar de chirinola,*** to be in good spirits.
chiripa, *n.f.* (*lit.*, *fig.*) fluke; ***por*** or ***de chiripa,*** by a fluke.
chiripá, *n.m.* (*Arg.*) leg-cover.
chiripear, *v.t.* to fluke (*at billiards*).
chiripero, *n.m.* poor billiard-player who wins by flukes; lucky person.
chirivía, *n.f.* (*bot.*) parsnip; (*orn.*) wagtail.
chirivisco, *n.m.* (*Guat.*) dry brambly place.
chirla, *n.f.* small clam.
chirlador, -ra, *a.* prattling.
chirlar, *v.i.* to prattle.
chirlata, *n.f.* low-class gaming-den; (*naut.*) wedge.
chirle, *a.* (*coll.*) dull, flat, tasteless. — *n.m.* sheep *or* goat dung.
chirlear, *v.i.* (*Ec.*) to chirp.
chirlería, *n.f.* prattle, chat.
chirlo, *n.m.* (knife) slash, scar.
chirlomirlo, *n.m.* tit-bit; thrush.
chirmol, *n.m.* (*Ec.*) dish made with chilli, onions, tomatoes etc.
chirola, *n.f.* (*Hisp. Am.*) silver coin worth 20 centavos.
chirona, *n.f.* (*sl.*) clink, nick (*prison*).
chirote, *n.m.* (*Ec.*, *Per.*) linnet.
chirraca, *n.f.* (*C.R.*) chirraco resin.
chirraco, *n.m.* (*C.R.*) chirraco tree.
chirriador, -ra, *a.* sizzling; creaking; chirping, squeaking.
chirriar, *v.i.* to squeak, creak; to screech; to chatter.
chirrido, *n.m.* squeak(ing), crack(ing); screech(ing); chatter(ing).
chirrión, *n.m.* creaking tumbrel.
chirula, *n.f.* (*prov.*) pan-pipe.
chirulí, *n.m.* (*Ven.*) chiruli bird.
chirulio, *n.m.* (*Hond.*) dish made with beaten eggs, maize, chilli, fruit of the anatta tree and salt.
chirumbela, *n.f.* flageolet; (*Hisp. Am.*) small cup *or* gourd (*for maté*).
chirumen, *n.m.* (*coll.*) brains, grey matter.
¡chis! *interj.* hush! silence!
chiscón, *n.m.* hut, hovel.
chischás, *n.m.* clash, clashing.
chisgarabís, *n.m.* (*coll.*) dabbler; whippersnapper, petty upstart; meddlesome person.
chisguete, *n.m.* (*coll.*) swig; squirt; ***echar un chisguete,*** to take a swig.
chisme, *n.m.* gadget; knick-knack; what-do-you-call-it, thingummy; (*pl.*) gossip, tittle-tattle.
chismear, *v.t.*, *v.i.* to gossip.
chismería, *n.f.* tittle-tattle, gossiping.
chismero, -ra, *a.* [CHISMOSO].
chismografía, *n.f.* (*coll.*) gossip, tattle.
chismorrear, *v.i.* [CHISMEAR].
chismorrero, -ra, *a.* [CHISMOSO].
chismoso, -sa, *a.*, *n.m.f.* gossiping; gossip.
chispa, *n.f.* [CHISPO].
chispazo, *n.m.* (*fig.*) spark, flash; ***el chispazo que originó la guerra,*** the spark that started off the war.
chispeante, *a.* sparkling.
chispear, *v.i.* to sparkle; to spark; to spit (*rain*).
chispero, -ra, *a.* sparking. — *n.m.* blacksmith; spark-catcher; (*coll.*) ***chispero*** (*Madrid equivalent of Cockney*).
chispo, -pa, *a.* (*fam.*) tipsy. — *n.m.* swig. — *n.f.* spark; (*fig.*) tiny bit; wit; ***estar chispa,*** to be tipsy; ***está echando chispas,*** he is blazing mad, in a flaming rage; ***tiene mucha chispa,*** he is very witty; ***no me gusta ni chispa,*** I don't like it one little bit.
chispoleto, -ta, *a.* vivacious, lively.
chisporrotear, *v.i.* to sizzle; to sputter, splutter, gutter, crackle.
chisporroteo, *n.m.* sizzling, crackling, spluttering.
chisposo, -sa, *a.* sputtering, sparkling, sparking.
chisquero, *n.m.* leather bag *or* pouch; pocket lighter.
chistar, *v.i.* to utter (a) sound; ***sin chistar (ni mistar),*** without uttering a word.
chiste, *n.m.* joke, funny story; ***contar chistes,*** to tell *or* crack jokes; ***caer en el chiste,*** to see the joke; to get the point; ***dar en el chiste,*** to get the point; ***la cosa no tiene chiste,*** it's no joke; ***ahí está el chiste,*** that's the point, that's the thing.
chistera, *n.f.* fish-basket; (*coll.*) top-hat.
chistoso, -sa, *a.* funny; witty; facetious.
chita, *n.f.* ankle-bone; knuckle-bone; (*game of*) jacks; ***a la chita callando,*** quietly; on the quiet;

dar en la chita, to hit the nail on the head; ***tirar a dos chitas,*** to have two strings to one's bow; (***no***) ***me importa dos chitas,*** I don't care a damn.
chite, *n.m.* (*Col.*) chite shrub.
chiticalla, *n.m.f.* (*coll.*) secretive person; secret.
chiticallando, *adv.* ***a la chiticallando,*** quietly; on the quiet.
chito, *n.m.* bone on which money is placed in the game of ***chito***; (*coll.*) ***irse a chitos,*** to go on the razzle.
¡chito!, ¡chitón! *interj.* hush!; mum's the word!
chiva (1), *n.f.* (*Cent. Am.*) blanket, coverlet; (*Ven.*) net bag; (*Hisp. Am.*) goatee, imperial.
chivar, *v.t.* to needle, pester; to cheat, take in. — **chivarse,** *v.r.* to inform, squeal, spill the beans.
chivarras, *n.m.pl.* (*Mex.*) shaggy kid breeches.
chivarro, -rra, *n.m.f.* young goat.
chivata, *n.f.* (*prov.*) shepherd's staff.
chivatazo, *n.m.* informing, squealing; ***dar*** or ***pegar el chivatazo,*** to squeal, spill the beans, let the cat out of the bag.
chivato, *n.m.* kid; (*coll.*) informer, squealer, tale-bearer.
chivetero, chivital, *n.m.* kid fold.
chivicoyo, *n.m.* (*Mex.*) chivicoyo bird.
chivillo, *n.m.* (*Per.*) starling.
chivo, -va (2), *n.m.f.* kid. — *n.m.* ***está como un chivo,*** he's as mad as a hatter.
¡cho! *interj.* whoa!
chocante, *a.* jarring; annoying; surprising, astonishing.
chocar [A], *v.t.* to surprise, astonish; to shake (*hands*); ***me choca que no haya venido,*** I'm surprised that he hasn't come; ***¡chócala!*** shake!, your hand on it! — *v.i.* to crash, collide; to clash.
chocarrear, *v.i.* to joke *or* jest coarsely.
chocarrería, *n.f.* buffoonery, low jesting, vulgarity.
chocarrero, -ra, *a.* vulgar, coarse, ribald.
choclar, *v.i.* to drive the ball through the rings (*in* ***argolla***).
choclo, *n.m.* overshoe, galosh; (*Hisp. Am.*) green ear of maize; (*Per.*) cake of maize and sugar.
choclón, *n.m.* driving a ball through the rings (*in* ***argolla***).
choco, *n.m.* small cuttle-fish.
chocolate, *n.m.* chocolate.
chocolatería, *n.f.* chocolate shop.
chocolatero, -ra, *a.* fond of chocolate. — *n.m.f.* maker *or* seller of chocolate. — *n.f.* chocolate-pot.
chocolatina, *n.f.* small chocolate bar.
chocoleo, *n.m.* gallantry, flattery.
chócolo, *n.m.* (*Col.*) clog.
chocoyo, *n.m.* (*Cent. Am.*) parrot.
chocha (1), **chochaperdiz,** *n.f.* woodcock.
chochear, *v.i.* to dote; to be in one's dotage.
chochera, chochez, *n.f.* dotage.
chocho (1), **-cha** (2), *a.* doting; doddering; ***estar chocho por,*** to dote on.
chocho (2), *n.m.* cinnamon candy; (*bot.*) lupin.
chófer, *n.m.* chauffeur; driver.
chofes, *n.m.pl.* lungs; liver and lights.
chofeta, *n.f.* chafing-dish, fire-pan.
chofista, *n.m.* (*obs.*) poor student (*who lived upon offal*).
cholgua, *n.f.* (*Chi.*) mussel.
cholo, -la, *a., n.m.f.* (*Hisp. Am.*) half-breed, mestizo; civilized Indian.
choloque, *n.m.* (*Hisp. Am.*) choloque tree.
cholla, *n.f.* (*coll.*) head, nut, noddle.
choncar, *n.m.* jackdaw.
chongo, *n.m.* (*Mex.*) chignon, bun; (*Guat.*) curl, ringlet; (*Mex.*) joke, jest.
chonguearse (*Mex.*) [CHUNGUEARSE].
chonta, *n.f.* (*Cent. Am., Per.*) hardwood palm tree.
chontaduro, *n.m.* (*Ec.*) palm tree.
chontal, *a., n.m.f.* (*Hisp. Am.*) appertaining to the Chontal tribe; Chontal Indian. — *n.m.* Chontal language.
chopa, *n.f.* (*ichth.*) sea-bream; (*naut.*) poop-house; top-gallant poop.
chopal, *n.m.*, **chopalera, chopera,** *n.f.* grove of black poplar trees.
chope, *n.m.* (*Chi.*) rooting implement; (*Chi.*) oyster tongs.
chopí, *n.m.* (*Arg.*) thrush.
chopo, *n.m.* black poplar tree; (*coll.*) musket.
choque, *n.m.* clash; crash; collision; (*mech.*) impact.
choquezuela, *n.f.* (*anat.*) knee-pan.
chorcha, *n.f.* woodcock.
chordón, *n.m.* raspberry.
choricería, *n.f.* pork-butcher's shop.
choricero, -ra, *n.m.f.* sausage-maker *or* -seller. — *n.f.* sausage-machine.
chorizo, *n.m.* garlic sausage; (acrobat's) counter-poise.
chorla, *n.f.* (*coll.*) head, nut.
chorlito, *n.m.* plover; ***cabeza de chorlito,*** hare-brained person.
chorlo, *n.m.* basalt, schorl, tourmaline.
choro, *n.m.* (*Chi.*) mussel.
chorote, *n.m.* (*Col.*) unglazed chocolate-pot; (*Cub.*) thick drink; (*Ven.*) poor quality chocolate.
choroy, *n.m.* (*Chi.*) small parrot.
chorrada, *n.f.* extra amount (*of liquid*); (*coll.*) drivel, rot.
chorreado, -da, *a.* (*obs.*) of a kind of satin; having striped skin (*cattle*).
chorreadura, *n.f.* dripping; gushing, spouting; drip stain.
chorrear, *v.i.* to drip; to gush, spout, pour.
chorreo, *n.m.* dripping; gushing, spouting; ***este coche es un chorreo de dinero,*** this car is a never-ending expense, positively eats money.
chorrera, *n.f.* drip, spout; drip stain; rapid (*in river*); ornament (*once appended to crosses of military orders*); frill (*of shirt*).
chorretada, *n.f.* (*coll.*) squirt, jet; ***hablar a chorretadas,*** to spurt out one's speech *or* words.
chorrillo, *n.m.* gentle *or* slight flow *or* trickle; ***irse por el chorrillo,*** to go with the current; ***sembrar a chorrillo,*** to sow in a trickle.
chorro, *n.m.* jet, gush, flow, spout, spurt, stream; ***avión de*** (***a***) ***chorro,*** jet aircraft; ***a chorros,*** copiously, lavishly, galore; ***como los chorros del oro,*** spotlessly clean; ***soltar el chorro,*** to burst into a guffaw.
chorroborro, *n.m.* flood; deluge.
chorrón, *n.m.* dressed hemp.
chortal, *n.m.* small pond (*fed by a spring at the bottom*).
chotacabras, *n.f. inv.* goatsucker; churn-owl.
chote, *n.m.* (*Cub.*) chote fruit.
chotearse, *v.r.* to make *or* poke fun, mock.
choteo, *n.m.* (*Cub., coll.*) making *or* poking fun, mocking.
chotis, *n.m. inv.* schottische.
choto, -ta, *n.m.f.* sucking kid; calf; ***estar como un choto,*** to be as crazy as a coot.
chotuno, -na, *a.* sucking (*kid*); poor, starved (*goat* or *lamb*); ***oler a chotuno,*** to smell like a goat.
chova, *n.f.* (*orn.*) chough; jackdaw.
choz, *n.m.* surprise.
choza, *n.f.* hut, hovel.
chozno, -na, *n.m.f.* great-great-great-grandson *or* -daughter.
chozo, *n.m.* small hut, hovel.
chozpar, *v.i.* to gambol, caper.
chozpo, *n.m.* gambol, caper.
chozpón, -pona, *a.* frisky, capering.

chozuela, *n.f.* miserable little hovel.
chubasco, *n.m.* shower; squall; ***aguantar el chubasco,*** to weather the storm, stick it out.
chubascoso, -sa, *a.* showery; squally.
chuca, *n.f.* concave part of a knucklebone.
chucán, -cana, *a.* (*Guat.*) scurrilous, vulgar.
chucanear, *v.i.* (*Guat.*) to jest, joke, make fun.
chucao, *n.m.* (*Chi.*) thrush.
chúcaro, -ra, *a.* (*Hisp. Am.*) wild (*animals*).
chucero, *n.m.* (*mil.*) pikeman; (*slang*) thief, robber.
chucua, *n.f.* (*Col.*) quagmire, bog.
chucuru, *n.m.* (*Ec.*) weasel.
chucuto, -ta, *a.* (*Ven.*) docked, bobtailed.
chucha, *n.f.* pooch, hound; mongrel bitch; (*Hisp. Am.*) opossum. — *interj.* quiet! lie down! (*to dogs*).
chuchazo, *n.m.* (*Cub.*, *Ven.*) whiplash.
chuchear, *v.i.* to fowl with calls, gins and nets; to whisper.
chuchería, *n.f.* manner of fowling with calls, gins and nets; bauble, gewgaw; titbit; knicknack; ***compramos unas chucherías,*** we bought a few bits and pieces, odds and ends.
chucho, *n.m.* (*coll.*) pooch, hound, mongrel; (*Arg.*) shiver; intermittent fever; (*Cub.*, *Ven.*) cowhide whip; (*Chi.*) owl; (*Hisp. Am.*) herring; (*Cub.*) goad; whip; skewer; (*Cub.*) ray-fish.
chuchoca, *n.f.* (*Hisp. Am.*) dry potage of maize.
chuchumeco, *n.m.* contemptible little fellow; (*Mex.*) Chichimec.
chueco, -ca, *a.* (*Hisp. Am.*) bow-legged. — *n.f.* tree stump; small ball (*hockey*); game of hockey; soap-makers' paddle; (*coll.*) fun, trick; (*anat.*) condyle.
chuela, *n.f.* (*Chi.*) small axe, hatchet.
chueta, *n.m.f.* (*Balearic Is.*) descendant of converted Jews
chufa, *n.f.* earthnut; (*obs.*) bravado; joke.
chufar, *v.i.* to mock, scoff.
chufería, *n.f.* ***horchata*** shop.
chufero, -ra, *n.m.f.* earthnut seller.
chufeta, *n.f.* jest, joke; chafing-dish, fire-pan.
chufla, chufleta, *n.f.* taunt, jeer, scoff, gibe.
chufletear, *v.i.* to sneer, taunt, poke fun.
chufletero, -ra, *a.* taunting, sneering. — *n.m.f.* taunter, sneerer.
chula, *n.f.* [CHULO].
chulada, *n.f.* loutishness; rough, pert wit, joke *or* speech.
chulear, *v.t.* to live off (*a woman*). — *v.i.* to act rough, play the tough guy; to throw one's weight about.
chulería, *n.f.* pimping; bravado.
chulesco, -ca, *a.* [CHULO].
chuleta, *n.f.* chop, cutlet; (*carp.*) chips for filling joints; filling; (*coll.*) slap, smack; (*educ.*) crib; (*pl.*) side whiskers.
chulo, -la, *a.* pimpish; aggressive, truculent. — *n.m.* pimp; bellicose person; lout; flashy type; butcher's boy; bull-fighter's assistant. — *n.f.* flashy low-class woman, hussy, wench.
chullo, -lla, *a.* (*Ec.*) odd, left of a pair; ***un guante chullo,*** an odd glove. — *n.f.* (*prov.*) slice of meat.
chumacera, *n.f.* (*naut.*) thole-pin, rowlock; (*mech.*) journal bearing.
chumbe, *n.m.* (*Col.*, *Per.*) band, cord, belt.
chumbera, *n.f.* prickly pear, cactus.
chumbo, *n.m.* prickly pear.
chumpipe, *n.m.* (*Guat.*) turkey.
chuncho, *n.m.* (*Per.*) wild Indian tribesman; (*Per.*) marigold.
chunga, *n.f.* joke, jest, banter, fun; ***estar de chunga,*** to be in a joking mood.
chungón, -gona, *a.*, *n.m.f.* jesting, joking, facetious.
chunguearse, *v.r.* (*coll.*) to chaff, gibe, jest.
chunguero, -ra, *a.* joking, jesting. — *n.m.f.* joker, jester.
chuño, *n.m.* (*Hisp. Am.*) starch (*of potato*).
chupa, *n.f.* short jacket; (*coll.*) ***poner como chupa de dómine,*** to criticize savagely, tear to pieces.
chupable, *a.* suckable.
chupadero, -ra, *a.* sucking, absorbent. — *n.m.* (baby's) teething-ring.
chupado, -da, *a.* (*coll.*) lean, emaciated; (*print.*) tall, thin (*letters*). — *n.f.* suck, sucking; pull, draw, drag (*at pipe etc.*).
chupador, -ra, *a.* sucking, absorbing. — *n.m.f.* sucker, suckling. — *n.m.* (baby's) teething-ring; (*bot.*, *zool.*) sucker.
chupadura, *n.f.* suck, sucking.
chupaflor, chupamirto, *n.m.* (*Mex.*, *Ven.*) humming-bird.
chupalandero, *n.m.* (*prov.*) snail.
chupalla, *n.f.* straw hat; chupalla plant.
chupar, *v.t.*, *v.i.* to suck, draw, milk, sap; to absorb; (*coll.*) to sponge; ***le chupa la sangre a la gente,*** he's a blood sucker; (*coll.*) ***chupar del bote,*** to sponge, be a sponger *or* parasite. — **chuparse,** *v.r.* to suck; to smoke; to endure; ***está de chuparse los dedos,*** it makes one smack one's lips; ***me chupé la conferencia entera,*** I stuck the lecture out to the bitter end; (*coll.*) ***¡chúpate ésa!*** put that in your pipe and smoke it!
chupatintas, *n.m. inv.* (*contempt.*) pen-pusher.
chupativo, -va, *a.* sucking.
chupe, *n.m.* (*Chi.*, *Per.*) hotchpotch dish.
chupeta, *n.f.* short jacket; (*naut.*) round-house.
chupetada, *n.f.* suck.
chupete, *n.m.* (baby's) dummy.
chupetear, chuperretear, *v.t.* to suck away at.
chupeteo, *n.m.* (continuous) sucking.
chupetilla, *n.f.* (*naut.*) glass cover (*for hatch-way*).
chupetín, *n.m.* jerkin, doublet.
chupetón, *n.m.* hard suck.
chupinazo, *n.m.* great clout *or* wallop.
chupón, -pona, *a.* (*coll.*) sucking; sponging. — *n.m.f.* sponger, blood-sucker, parasite. — *n.m.* (*bot.*) sucker; piston (*of suction-pump*); suction action; ***a la barca la cogió un chupón,*** the boat was sucked under.
chuquiragua, *n.f.* (*Hisp. Am.*) chuquiragua plant.
chuquisa, *n.f.* (*Chi.*, *Per.*) good-time girl.
churana, *n.f.* (*Hisp. Am.*) Indian quiver.
churco, *n.m.* (*Chi.*) churco plant.
churcha, *n.f.* (*Hisp. Am.*) opossum.
churdón, *n.m.* raspberry bush
churla, *n.f.*, **churlo,** *n.m.* canvas bag *or* sack.
churo, *n.m.* (*Ec.*) curl, ringlet; snail.
churra, *n.f.* [CHURRO].
churrasco, *n.m.* (*Hisp. Am.*) barbecued meat.
churre, *n.m.* (*coll.*) thick, dirty grease; filth.
churrería, *n.f.* fritter shop.
churrero, -ra, *n.m.f.* maker *or* seller of fritters.
churretada, *n.f.* filthy *or* greasy mess *or* stain (*on hands* or *face*).
churrete, *n.m.* filthy *or* greasy spot *or* stain (*on hands* or *face*).
churriana, *n.f.* (*vulg.*) strumpet.
churriburri, *n.m.* cur; rabble.
churriento, -ta, *a.* greasy, filthy.
churrigueresco, -ca, *a.* (*arch.*) churrigueresque, Spanish baroque; (*fig.*) over-loaded, tawdry, loud.
churriguerismo, *n.m.* (*arch.*) churrigueresque *or* Spanish baroque style.
churriguerista, *n.m.* churrigueresque *or* Spanish baroque architect.
churro, -rra, *a.* coarse, coarse-wooled. — *n.m.f.* coarse-wooled sheep. — *n.m.* fritter; (*coll.*) botch. — *n.f.* grouse.
churrullero, *a.* prattling, gossipy. — *n.m.f.* prattler, tattler, gossip.

churrupear, *v.i.* to sip at.
churruscar [A], *v.t.* to burn, scorch.
churrusco, *n.m.* burnt toast.
churumbel, *n.m.* (*slang*) kid, brat.
churumbela, *n.f.* flageolet; (*Hisp. Am.*) maté cup.
churumen [CHIRUMEN].
churumo, *n.m.* juice, substance.
¡chus!, *interj.* here, boy! (*to dogs*); ***no decir chus ni mus,*** to say not a word.
chuscada, *n.f.* pleasantry, drollery, joke.
chusco, -ca, *a.* droll, funny.
chusma, *n.f.* galley-slaves; rabble, mob, scum.
chuspa, *n.f.* (*Hisp. Am.*) pouch, bag, game-bag.
chusque, *n.m.* (*Col.*) bamboo.
chut, *n.m.* shot (*football*).
chutar, *v.i.* to shoot (*football*); (*coll.*) to go, work, function.
chutazo, *n.m.* superb shot (*football*).
chute, *n.m.* (*Cent. Am.*) prick, goad, spur.
chuva, *n.f.* (*Hisp. Am.*) spider monkey.
chuza, *n.f.* (*Mex.*) strike (*in bowling*).
chuzar [C], *v.t.* (*Col.*) to prick, goad.
chuzazo, *n.m.* pike thrust *or* wound.
chuzo, *n.m.* pike, short pike; (*Hisp. Am.*) whip; (*coll.*) ***echar chuzos,*** to boast, brag; ***a chuzos,*** heavily, galore; (*coll.*) ***llover, nevar*** or ***caer chuzos,*** to rain, snow *or* hail heavily; (*coll.*) ***caen chuzos de punta,*** it is pouring *or* bucketing down, raining cats and dogs.
chuzón, -zona, *a.*, *n.m.f.* sly, crafty (person); witty, clever, adroit (person) (*in conversation*). — *n.m.* large pike.
chuzonería, *n.f.* mockery, mimicry; craftiness.

D

D, d, *n.f.* letter D, d.
dable, *a.* feasible, possible, practicable.
daca (*contraction of* ***da acá***), give here; ***toma y daca,*** give and take, tit for tat.
dación, *n.f.* (*law*) handing over, yielding.
dactilado, -da, *a.* finger-shaped.
dactílico, -ca, *a.* dactylic.
dactiliforme, *a.* (*arch.*) palm-shaped.
dáctilo, *n.m.* dactyl.
dactilografía, *n.f.* dactylography, typewriting.
dactilografiar [L], *v.t.* to typewrite.
dactilográfico, -ca, *a.* relating to typewriting.
dactilógrafo, -fa, *n.m.f.* typist.
dactiloscopia, *n.f.* identification through the study of finger-prints.
dactiloscópico, -ca, *a.* relating to the study of finger-prints.
dádiva, *n.f.* gift, present, offering; ***dádivas quebrantan peñas,*** a golden key unlocks all doors.
dadivosidad, *n.f.* liberality, generosity, munificence.
dadivoso, -sa, *a., n.m.f.* liberal, generous, munificent (person).
dado, -da, *a.* given; ***dado que,*** given *or* assuming that. — *n.m.* die (*pl.* dice); block; pivot-collar; (*naut.*) crossbar; (*arch.*) dado; ***cargar los dados,*** to load the dice; ***corre el dado,*** we're in luck; ***está como un dado,*** it fits perfectly; ***como venga el dado,*** as things turn out, as it comes.
dador, -ra, *a.* giving. — *n.m.f.* donor, giver. — *n.m.* bearer (*of letter*); (*com.*) drawer (*of a bill of exchange*).
daga, *n.f.* dagger; line of bricks (*in a kiln*); ***llegar a las dagas,*** to come to blows.
dagón, *n.m.* large dagger.
daguerrotipado, *n.m.* daguerreotype.
daguerrotipar, *v.t.* to daguerreotype.
daguerrotipia, *n.f.* daguerreotyping.
daguerrotipo, *n.m.* daguerreotype.
daguilla, *n.f.* (*prov.*) hollow knitting-needle; (*Cub.*) lace-bark tree.
daifa, *n.f.* mistress, concubine.
dala, *n.f.* pump-dale.
¡dale! *interj.* ***¡dale que dale!*** not again!, here we go again!
dalia, *n.f.* dahlia.
dalmática, *n.f.* dalmatic.
daltoniano, -na, *a., n.m.f.* colour-blind (person).
daltonismo, *n.m.* Daltonism, colour-blindness.
dallador, *n.m.* (*prov.*) mower, scytheman.
dallar, *v.t.* to mow.
dalle, *n.m.* scythe, sickle.
dama, *n.f.* lady; mistress, concubine; king (*at draughts*); queen (*at chess*); leading-lady; fallow deer; (*metal.*) crucible-door; ***dama cortesana,*** courtesan; ***dama de honor,*** bridesmaid; lady-in-waiting; patron lady; ***dama de noche,*** night jasmine; (*theat.*) ***dama joven,*** young lead; (*theat.*) ***primera dama,*** leading lady; ***soplar la dama,*** to huff the king (*at draughts*); (*coll.*) tu cut out a rival; to beat to it; ***ser (una mujer) muy dama,*** to be very ladylike, refined; (*pl.*) (game of) draughts, (*Am.*) checkers.
damaceno, -na, damasceno, -na, *a., n.m.f.* Damascene. — *n.f.* damson plum.
damajuana, *n.f.* demijohn.
damascado, -da, *a.* damask, damascene.
Damasco, *n.m.* Damascus.
damasco, *n.m.* damask; damson (*tree and plum*).
damasina, *n.f.* light damask.
damasquillo, *n.m.* [DAMASINA]; (*prov.*) apricot.
damasquinado, *n.m.* damascene work.
damasquinador, -ra, *a., n.m.f.* (one) who *or* (that) which damascenes.
damasquinar, *v.t.* to inlay, damascene (*steel*).
damasquino, -na, *a.* damascened; ***a la damasquina,*** Damascus fashion.
damería, *n.f.* prudery; nicety.
damero, *n.m.* checker-board, draught-board.
damisela, *n.f.* young lady, damsel; (*coll.*) courtesan.
damnación, *n.f.* damnation.
damnificador, -ra, *a.* damaging, injuring. — *n.m.f.* damager, injurer.
damnificar [A], *v.t.* to damage, hurt, injure.
danchado, -da, *a.* (*her.*) dentate, indented.
dandismo, *n.m.* dandyism.
danés, -nesa, dánico, -ca, *a.* Danish. — *n.m.f.* Dane. — *n.m.* Danish language.
dango, *n.m.* gannet.
danta, *n.f.* tapir.
dante, *a.* giving.
dantellado, -da, *a.* (*her.*) dentated, serrated.
dantesco, -ca, *a.* Dantesque; (*fam.*) nightmarish.
danubiano, -na, *a.* Danubian.
Danubio, *n.m.* Danube.
danza, *n.f.* dance; dancing; ***danza de cintas,*** maypole dance; ***danza de espadas,*** sword-dance; (*coll.*) quarrel, fight; ***meterle a uno en la danza,*** to involve s.o. in the dispute; ***meterse en danza de espadas,*** to mix in quarrels; ***¿por dónde va la danza?*** which way does the wind blow?
danzado, *n.m.* dance.
danzador, -ra, *a.* dancing. — *n.m.f.* dancer.
danzante, -ta, *n.m.f.* dancer; (*iron.*) fine fellow.
danzar [C], *v.t., v.i.* to dance; (*coll.*) to butt in.
danzarín, -rina, *a.* dancing; much given to dancing. — *n.m.f.* fine dancer; (*coll.*) meddler.
danzón, *n.m.* (*Cub.*) slow dance.
dañable, *a.* prejudicial; condemnable.
dañador, -ra, *a., n.m.f.* damaging, harmful, injurious (person).
dañar, *v.t.* to hurt, harm, damage.
dañino, -na, *a.* hurtful, harmful, destructive, injurious (*animals*).
daño, *n.m.* damage, hurt, harm, injury; (*com.*) ***daños y perjuicios,*** damages; ***en daño de,*** to the detriment *or* injury of; ***hacer daño a,*** to damage, hurt, harm, injure; ***hacerse daño,*** to hurt o.s.
dañoso, -sa, *a.* damaging, hurtful, harmful.
dar [16], *v.t.* to give, give out; to deal, deal out (*cards*); to show (*results*); to show, put on (*films etc.*); to hit, strike; to strike (*the hour*); ***dar de alta,*** to discharge (*from hospital, army etc.*); to enter, inscribe (*in army register*); ***dar de baja,*** to discharge; to record as absent; to remove from list of members; ***dar de barato,*** to admit *or* allow for the sake of argument; ***dar de balde,*** to give gratis *or* for nothing; ***dar los buenos días,*** to bid *or* wish good day; ***no da ni los buenos días,*** he is as mean as sin; ***dar una carcajada,*** to let out a guffaw; ***dar la cara por alguien,*** to stand up for s.o.; ***dar de comer,*** to feed; ***dar a conocer,*** to make known; ***dar diente con diente,*** to shiver with cold; ***dar (en) qué pensar,*** to make one think *or* give one food for thought; ***no dar golpe,*** not to do a stroke of work; ***dar en entender,*** to insinuate, hint; ***dar ejemplo,*** to set an example; ***dar la enhorabuena,*** to congratulate; ***dar a la estampa,*** to send to press; ***dar fiado,*** to give credit; ***dar fe,*** to certify; (*naut.*) ***dar fondo,*** to cast anchor; ***dar fruto,*** to yield, bear fruit; ***me dan ganas de llorar,*** I feel like crying; ***dar gracias,*** to thank; ***dar un grito,*** to utter a scream; ***dar guerra,*** to give trouble, be a nuisance; ***da gusto,*** it warms one's heart; ***da pena,*** it breaks one's heart; ***dar que hablar,*** to give cause for scandal; ***dar que hacer,***

to give trouble, make work; ***dar a luz,*** to give birth; ***dar a la luz,*** to publish; ***dar de mano,*** to pack up *or* in; ***dar la mano a,*** to shake hands with; ***me dio el día,*** he ruined my day for me; ***nos dio la noche,*** he gave us a terrible night; ***dar el pésame,*** to express condolence; ***no da pie con bola,*** he can't put a foot right; ***lo da por bien empleado,*** he considers it worth while, he doesn't regret it; ***lo da por concluido, hecho,*** he considers it finished, settled; ***dar prestado,*** to lend; ***dar razón de,*** to give an account of, account for, give information about; ***no supieron darme razón,*** they were unable to give me any information *or* explanation; ***dar la razón a X,*** to acknowledge *or* say that X is right; ***dar rienda suelta a,*** to give free rein to; ***dar saltos,*** to jump about; ***dar el sí,*** to say yes, accept, agree; ***donde las dan las toman,*** it works both ways; ***dar tregua,*** to grant a respite *or* breathing space; ***dar voces,*** to cry *or* shout out, yell out; ***dar una vuelta,*** to take a turn *or* stroll, go for a ride *or* spin; ***ahí me las den todas,*** if I don't get anything worse than that I shan't complain; ***dar de palos,*** to beat, give a drubbing; ***dar la bienvenida,*** to welcome; ***lo mismo me da, igual me da, tanto me da,*** it's all the same to me; ***dar de lado,*** to slight, cold-shoulder, ignore, pass over; ***dar la lata,*** to nag, pester, bother; ***dar la casualidad de que,*** it so happens that; ***me da rabia,*** it infuriates me; ***me da el corazón que,*** I have a feeling that. — *v.i.* to look out (***a,*** onto), overlook (*of windows etc.*); to fall down; to strike (*the hour*); ***dar al traste con,*** to demolish, destroy, ruin; ***dar con,*** to find, come upon (*after searching*); ***dar en,*** to commit (*an error*); ***dar en blando,*** to get easily; to meet with no resistance; ***dar en duro,*** to encounter difficulties; ***dar en vacío,*** to fall on stony ground *or* on deaf ears; ***dar en ello,*** to hit upon it, realize it; ***dar contra,*** to hit against; ***dar en, dar a alguien por,*** to take it into one's head to; ***dio en beber, le dio por beber,*** he took to drink; ***dio en coleccionar sellos,*** he took it into his head to start collecting stamps; ***dio en una manía,*** he got a craze *or* fad; ***dar en el blanco,*** to hit the mark; ***dar en la llaga,*** to hit where it hurts, get on the raw; ***dar de sí,*** to give (way), stretch; (*fig.*) ***no da más de sí,*** he can't manage any more; that's as far as he goes. — **darse,** *v.r.* to give in, surrender; to happen, occur; to produce, yield (*fruit etc.*); to devote o.s. (***a,*** to); — ***por,*** to think, consider o.s.; ***darse a conocer,*** to make o.s. known; ***darse de baja,*** to resign, quit, leave; (*fig.*) ***darse la mano,*** to be birds of a feather; ***darse maña para,*** to have ability for, be good at, manage well at; ***darse a merced,*** to surrender unconditionally; (*coll.*) ***darse un atracón,*** to have a blow-out (*meal*); ***darse prisa,*** to make haste; ***darse por aludido,*** to take the hint; ***darse a la vela,*** to set sail; ***darse por vencido,*** to give up *or* in; ***a mí no me la das,*** you're not taking me in; ***dárselas de,*** to make o.s. out to be; ***se me da el naipe,*** I'm in luck (*at cards*).

dardabasí, *n.m.* hawk, kite.

dardada, *n.f.* blow with a dart.

dardo, *n.m.* dart; dart-fish, dace; (*fig.*) sarcasm; ***dardo de pescador,*** harpoon, fizgig.

dares y tomares, *n.m.pl.* (*coll.*) give and take; (*coll.*) disputes, arguments.

dársena, *n.f.* inner harbour, basin.

dartros, *n.m.pl.* (*med.*) dartre.

darviniano, -na, *a.* Darwinian.

darvinismo, *n.m.* Darwinism.

darvinista, *n.m.f.* Darwinian, Darwinist.

dasímetro, *n.m.* baroscope.

dasocracia, *n.f.* forestry.

dasocrático, -ca, *a.* appertaining to forestry.

dasonomía, *n.f.* forestry.

dasonómico, -ca, *a.* appertaining to forestry.

data, *n.f.* date; item (*of statement* or *account*); outlet (*of a reservoir*); plum; ***estar de mala data,*** to be in a bad temper; ***de larga data,*** of long standing.

datar, *v.t.* to date; (*com.*) to credit on account. — *v.i.* ***datar de,*** to date from.

datario, *n.m.* datary.

dátil, *n.m.* (*bot.*) date; (*zool.*) date-shell; (*sl.*) finger.

datilado, -da, *a.* date-like.

datilera, *n.f.* date-palm.

datismo, *n.m.* (*rhet.*) redundant use of synonymous terms.

dativo, -va, *a.*, *n.m.* dative.

dato, *n.m.* datum, fact; clue; detail; (*pl.*) data.

datura, *n.f.* thorn-apple.

daturina, *n.f.* (*chem.*) daturine.

dauco, *n.m.* wild carrot.

davalar, *v.i.* (*naut.*) to drift.

davídico, -ca, *a.* Davidic(al).

daza, *n.f.* (*bot.*) sorghum.

de (1), *prep.* of; out of; from; by; with; as; for; about; on; in; to; ***de balde,*** free gratis; ***de día (noche),*** by day (night); ***de forma*** or ***manera que,*** so that, in such a way that; ***de fuerza,*** forcibly; ***de golpe,*** all at once, suddenly; ***de intento,*** on purpose; ***¡desdichado de mí!*** woe is me!; ***el libro de Juan,*** John's book; ***de prisa,*** quickly, hurriedly; ***le dieron de palos,*** they gave him a beating, drubbing; ***es de Sevilla,*** he is *or* comes from Seville; ***salió del despacho,*** he came out of *or* left the office; ***mesa de madera,*** wooden table; ***sombrero de fieltro,*** felt hat; ***curso de español,*** Spanish course; ***¿de qué habla Vd.?*** what are you talking about?; ***es un hombre de bien,*** he is an upright man; ***es un muchacho de talento,*** he is a talented boy; ***es hora de trabajar,*** it's time to work; ***el bueno de Carlos,*** good old Charles; ***ese pícaro de muchacho,*** that rascal of a boy; ***de una vez,*** once and for all; ***de un trago,*** at one gulp; ***recado de escribir,*** writing-set; ***cuarto de baño,*** bathroom; ***máquina de coser,*** sewing-machine; ***máquina de escribir,*** typewriter; ***cantaba de alegría,*** she was singing for joy; ***la señora del sombrero rojo,*** the lady with the red hat; ***el hombre del traje gris,*** the man in the grey suit; ***esto es fácil de hacer,*** this is easy to do; ***trabaja de ingeniero,*** he works as an engineer; ***de haberlo sabido, habría ido,*** had I heard about it, I should have gone; ***el precio es de cien pesetas,*** the price is one hundred pesetas; ***doña Inés Ruiz de González,*** Mrs. Inez Gonzalez (*née Ruiz*).

de (2), *n.f.* letter D.

dea, *n.f.* (*poet.*) goddess.

deambular, *v.i.* to stroll (about), wander (about).

deambulatorio, *n.m.* (*arch.*) nave round main chapel.

deán, *n.m.* dean.

deanato, deanazgo, *n.m.* deanship.

debajo, *adv.* under, underneath, below; ***debajo de,*** beneath, under; ***quedar debajo,*** to get the worst of it.

debate, *n.m.* debate.

debatible, *a.* debatable.

debatir, *v.t.*, *v.i.* to debate. — **debatirse,** *v.r.* to struggle; ***se debatía entre la vida y la muerte,*** he was struggling between life and death.

debe, *n.m.* (*com.*) debit.

debelación, *n.f.* conquest, conquering.

debelador, -ra, *n.m.f.* conqueror, victor.

debelar, *v.t.* to conquer, subdue, vanquish.

deber, *n.m.* duty; debt; (school) exercise; ***cumplir con el deber,*** to do one's duty; ***hacer sus deberes,*** to do one's exercises *or* home-work. — *v.t.*, *v.i.* to owe; to be obliged, have to; must, ought; ***debes hacerlo,*** you ought to do it; ***debía, debería*** or ***debiera ir,*** I ought to go; ***he debido*** or ***debí ir,*** I ought to have gone; ***deben (de) ser las ocho,*** it must be eight o'clock.

debidamente, *adv.* duly, properly.
debido, -da, *a.* due, proper; ***como es debido,*** as it should be, as is right and proper.
debiente, *a.* owing. — *n.m.f.* debtor.
débil, *a.* feeble, weak; faint, slight.
debilidad, *n.f.* debility, weakness, feebleness.
debilitación, *n.f.* debilitation, weakening.
debilitar, *v.t.* to debilitate, weaken, enervate.
débito, *n.m.* debt; ***débito conyugal,*** conjugal duty.
debó, *n.m.* skin-scraper.
debutante, *a.* beginning. — *n.m.f.* beginner; débutante.
debutar, *v.i.* to begin; to make one's first appearance *or* début; to come out (*in society*).
decacordo, *n.m.* (*mus.*) decachord.
década, *n.f.* decade.
decadario, -ria, *a.* decadal.
decadencia, *n.f.* decline, decadence; ***ir en decadencia,*** to be on the decline.
decadente, *a.* declining, decadent. — *n.m.f.* decadent.
decadentismo, *n.m.* (*Lit.*) decadence.
decadentista, *a.*, *n.m.f.* decadent (person).
decaedro, *n.m.* decahedron.
decaer [14], *v.i.* to decay, decline; (*naut.*) to fall to leeward; to subside.
decagonal, *a.* decagonal.
decágono, *n.m.* decagon.
decagramo, *n.m.* decagram.
decaído, -da, *a.* low (*in spirits*).
decaimiento, *n.m.* decay, decline, depression.
decalco, *n.m.* transfer (*of drawing*); counter-tracing.
decalitro, *n.m.* decalitre.
decálogo, *n.m.* decalogue.
decalvación, *n.f.* shaving of the head.
decalvante, *a.* shaving (*the head*); (*med.*) producing baldness.
decalvar, *v.t.* to crop, shave the head of (*as punishment*).
decámetro, *n.m.* decametre.
decampar, *v.i.* (*mil.*) to decamp.
decanato, *n.m.* deanery, deanship.
decania, *n.f.* farm *or* parish church belonging to a monastery.
decano, *n.m.* senior member; dean, doyen; (*fig.*) grand old man.
decantación, *n.f.* decantation, pouring off.
decantador, *n.m.* decanter.
decantar, *v.t.* to decant; to puff up, praise up.
decapitación, *n.f.* decapitation, beheading.
decapitar, *v.t.* to decapitate, behead.
decápodo, -da, *a.* decapodal. — *n.m.pl.* (**decápodos**) Decapoda.
decárea, *n.f.* decare (1000 *sq. metres*).
decasílabo, -ba, *a.* decasyllabic.
decemnovenal, decemnovenario, *a.* lunar *or* Metonic (*cycle*).
decena, *n.f.* [DECENO].
decenal, *a.* decennial.
decenar, *n.m.* ten, group, gang *or* team of ten.
decenario, -ria, *a.* decennary, decennial. — *n.m.* decennary; rosary of ten beads.
decencia, *n.f.* decency, respectability, propriety.
decenio, *n.m.* decade.
deceno, -na, *a.* tenth. — *n.f.* denary; ten, about ten; (*mus.*) tenth.
decentar [1], *v.t.* to begin to use, cut the first slice of; to begin to impair; to gall. — **decentarse,** *v.r.* to get bed sores.
decente, *a.* decent, respectable; modest, reasonable.
decenvir [DECENVIRO].
decenviral, *a.* decemviral.
decenvirato, *n.m.* decemvirate.
decenviro, *n.m.* decemvir.
decepción, *n.f.* disillusion(ment), disappointment.
decepcionar, *v.t.* to disillusion, disappoint.
deciárea, *n.f.* deciare.
decible, *a.* expressible.
decidero, -ra, *a.* that can be said *or* told.
decidido, -da, *a.* determined, resolute.
decidir, *v.t.* to decide, determine, resolve. — **decidir(se),** *v.i.* (*v.r*) to make up one's mind; ***decidieron ir, se decidieron a ir,*** they decided to go, they made up their minds to go.
decidor, -ra, *a.* witty. — *n.m.f.* wit, witty talker, raconteur.
decigramo, *n.m.* decigram.
decilitro, *n.m.* decilitre.
decimal, *a.* decimal; belonging to tithes.
décimanovena, *n.f.* register (*of pipe-organ*).
decímetro, *n.m.* decimetre.
décimo, -ma, *a.* tenth. — *n.m.f.* tenth. — *n.m.* tenth part of lottery ticket. — *n.f.* ten-line stanza.
décimoctavo, -va, *a.* eighteenth.
décimocuarto, -ta, *a.* fourteenth.
decimonónico, -ca, *a.* nineteenth century; (*fig.*) old-fashioned, Victorian.
décimonono, -na, décimonoveno, -na, *a.* nineteenth.
décimoquinto, -ta, *a.* fifteenth.
décimoséptimo, -ma, *a.* seventeenth.
décimosexto, -ta, *a.* sixteenth.
décimotercero, -ra, décimotercio, -cia, *a.* thirteenth.
deciocheno, -na, *a.* eighteenth.
decir, *n.m.* speech; way of speaking; saying; ***es un decir,*** it's a (mere) figure of speech, it's just a manner of speaking; ***el decir de las gentes,*** public opinion. — [17], *v.t.*, *v.i.* to say; to tell; to call, name; ***como dijo el otro,*** as they say; ***como quien no dice nada*** or ***la cosa,*** as if it didn't matter in the least, casually nonchalantly; ***como si dijéramos, por decirlo así,*** as it were, so to speak; ***decir a uno cuántas son cinco,*** to tell *or* tick s.o. off; ***decir entre*** or ***para sí, decir para su capote,*** to say to o.s.; ***decir nones,*** to say nay, refuse; ***decir una cosa por otra,*** to say one thing instead of another; ***decir su parecer,*** to give one's opinion; ***es decir,*** that is to say; ***por mejor decir,*** more properly speaking; ***mejor dicho,*** more properly speaking, rather; ***no digamos,*** not to mention, to say nothing of; ***no es tímida, que digamos,*** she is not shy, to say the least of it; ***¡no digo nada!*** you should just have seen it; ***ni que decir tiene que, huelga decir que,*** needless to say . . . ; ***le importa un bledo el qué dirán,*** he doesn't care two hoots about what people may think (*or* say); ***¿qué quiere decir eso?*** what does that mean?; ***mañana, digo pasado mañana,*** tomorrow, I mean the day after tomorrow; ***¡diga!*** hello! (*telephone*); ***decir y hacer, dicho y hecho,*** no sooner said than done; ***dime con quién andas y te diré quién eres,*** a man is known by the company he keeps. — *v.i.* to harmonize; ***decir bien (mal) con una cosa,*** to go well (badly) with sth. — **decirse,** *v.r.* to be called; to be said; ***se dice,*** it is said, they say; ***decírselo a uno deletreado,*** to spell it out.
decisión, *n.f.* decision; determination, resolution.
decisivo, -va, *a.* decisive.
decisorio, -ria, *a.* (*law*) decisive.
declamación, *n.f.* declamation; delivery (*manner of reciting*).
declamador, -ra, *a.* declaiming, reciting. — *n.m.f.* declaimer, reader, reciter.
declamar, *v.i.* to declaim, recite.
declamatorio, -ria, *a.* declamatory.
declarable, *a.* declarable.
declaración, *n.f.* declaration, statement; proposal (*of marriage*); (*law*) deposition.

declarado, -da, *a.* self-confessed, unabashed.
declarador, -ra, *a.* declaring, stating. — *n.m.f.* declarer.
declarante, *a.* declaring, stating. — *n.m.f.* (*law*) declarant; witness.
declarar, *v.t.* to declare, state; (*law*) to find; ***declarar culpable,*** to find guilty. — *v.i.* to make a statement. — **declararse,** *v.r.* to come out (***contra,*** against; ***por,*** for), declare (***por,*** for); to propose (*marriage*).
declarativo, -va, *a.* declarative.
declaratorio, -ria, *a.* declaratory.
declinabilidad, *n.f.* declinability.
declinable, *a.* (*gram.*) declinable.
declinación, *n.f.* (*gram.*) declension; decline, decay; deviation; (*astron.*) declination.
declinado, -da, *a.* (*bot.*) declinate.
declinador, *n.m.* declinator.
declinante, *a.* declining, bending down.
declinar, *v.t.* to decline. — *v.i.* to decline; to lean over, deviate, have deviation *or* declination; to decay, diminish, fall off *or* away, sink; ***va declinando el día,*** the day is drawing to a close.
declinatoria, *n.f.* declinatory (*plea*).
declinatorio, *n.m.* declinator (*instrument*).
declinómetro, *n.m.* declinometer.
declive, declivio, *n.m.* declivity, downward inclination, downhill, descent, slope, fall; ***en declive,*** slanting, sloping.
declividad, *n.f.* declivity.
decocción, *n.f.* decoction; (*surg.*) amputation.
decoctivo, -va, *a.* (*med.*) digestive.
decoloración, *n.f.* decoloration; discoloration.
decomisar, *v.t.* to confiscate, seize, forfeit.
decomiso, *n.m.* confiscation, forfeiture, seizure.
decoración, *n.f.* decoration, ornament; theatrical scenery; memorizing.
decorado, *n.m.* decoration, ornamentation; scenery, setting, décor; thing committed to memory.
decorador, *n.m.* decorator; scene-setter.
decorar, *v.t.* to decorate, adorn; to learn by heart; to recite, repeat.
decorativo, -va, *a.* decorative.
decoro, *n.m.* honour; respect; decorum, propriety.
decoroso, -sa, *a.* decorous, decent.
decorticación, *n.f.* decortication.
decrecer [9], *v.i.* to decrease.
decreciente, *a.* decreasing, diminishing.
decrecimiento, *n.m.* decrease.
decremento, *n.m.* decrement, decrease, diminution.
decrepitación, *n.f.* (*chem.*) decrepitation.
decrepitante, *a.* crackling.
decrepitar, *v.t., v.i.* to decrepitate; to crackle.
decrépito, -ta, *a.* decrepit, fallen into decay.
decrepitud, *n.f.* decrepitude.
decretal, *a.* decretal. — *n.f.pl.* (**decretales**) decretals.
decretalista, *n.m.* decretist.
decretar, *v.t.* to decree; (*law*) to give a decree (*in a suit*).
decretero, *n.m.* (*obs.*) list of criminals and verdicts; collection of decrees.
decretista, *n.m.* decretist.
decreto, *n.m.* decree.
decretorio, -ria, *a.* (*med.*) decretory, critical, determining.
decúbito, *n.m.* recumbent *or* lying position.
decumbente, *a.* recumbent, reclining.
decuplar, decuplicar [A], *v.t.* to decuple, multiply by ten.
décuplo, -la, *a.* tenfold.
decuria, *n.f.* decury; group of ten (*students, soldiers etc.*).
decuriato, *n.m.* student of a decuria.
decurión, *n.m.* decurion; monitor over ten pupils; commander set over a decuria.
decurionato, *n.m.* decurionate.
decurrencia, *n.f.* (*bot.*) decurrence.
decurrente, *a.* (*bot.*) decurrent.
decursas, *n.f.pl.* (*law*) arrears of rent.
decurso, *n.m.* course, lapse, passage *or* passing of time.
decusación, *n.f.* decussation, intersection.
decusado, -da, *a.* (*bot.*) decussated.
dechado, *n.m.* sample, pattern, standard design, example, model; sampler; ***dechado de virtudes,*** model of virtue, paragon.
dedada, *n.f.* small portion; (*coll.*) ***dedada de miel,*** taste of honey.
dedal, *n.m.* thimble; leathern finger-stall; thimble-full.
dedalera, *n.f.* foxglove.
dédalo, *n.m.* labyrinth, maze.
dedeo, *n.m.* (*mus.*) fingers; fingering.
dedicación, *n.f.* dedication; consecration; inscription.
dedicante, *a.* dedicating.
dedicar(**se**) [A], *v.t.* (*v.r.*) to dedicate (o.s.), devote (o.s.), consecrate (o.s.); ***dedicarse a,*** to devote o.s. to.
dedicativo, -va, *a.* dedicative, dedicatory.
dedicatorio, -ria, *a.* dedicatory. — *n.f.* dedication; inscription.
dedignar, *v.t.* to disdain, scorn, despise.
dedil, *n.m.* finger-stall; (*sl.*) ring.
dedillo, *n.m.*, ***saberse al dedillo,*** to have at one's finger-tips.
dedismo, *n.m.* (*fam.*) jobs for the boys, system of arbitrary appointment.
dedo, *n.m.* finger, toe; finger's breadth; ***dedo anular,*** ring- *or* third finger; ***dedo cordial*** or ***corazón,*** middle finger; ***dedo índice,*** index-finger, forefinger; ***dedo pulgar*** or ***gordo,*** thumb; ***dedo auricular*** or ***meñique,*** little finger; ***estar a dos dedos de,*** to be on the verge of; ***antojársele a uno los dedos huéspedes,*** to be exceedingly suspicious; (*fig.*) ***cogerse*** or ***pillarse los dedos,*** to burn one's fingers; (*fig.*) ***chuparse los dedos,*** to smack one's lips; ***dar un dedo de la mano por,*** to give one's right arm for *or* to; ***derribar con un dedo,*** to knock down with a feather; ***ir al dedo malo,*** to go for the weak spot; ***poner el dedo en la llaga,*** to put one's finger on the sore spot; ***no se mama el dedo,*** he's no fool, he's all there; ***métele un dedo en la boca,*** he's not such a fool as he looks; ***no tiene dos dedos de frente,*** he's not very bright; ***métele los dedos,*** sound him out, pump him; (*fig.*) ***morderse los dedos,*** to bite *or* chew one's nails; ***poner los cinco dedos en la cara a,*** to slap in the face; ***ponerse el dedo en la boca,*** to keep quiet; ***señalar con el dedo,*** to point at, single out.
dedocracia, *n.f.* [DEDISMO].
dedolar [4], *v.t.* (*surg.*) to make an oblique incision in.
deducción, *n.f.* deduction; inference, conclusion; (*mus.*) diatonic scale.
deducible, *a.* deducible, inferable.
deduciente, *a.* deducing, inferring.
deducir [15], *v.t.* to deduce, infer; (*law*) to allege (*in pleading*); (*com.*) to deduct, discount; (*math.*) to derive; ***deducir de*** or ***por lo dicho,*** to infer from what has been said.
deductivo, -va, *a.* deductive.
defalcar [DESPALCAR].
defecación, *n.f.* defecation; purification.
defecador, -ra, *a.* defecating, purifying. — *n.f.* defecator, purifier (*in sugar refining*).
defecar [A], *v.t.* to defecate; to clarify, purify. — *v.i.* to defecate.

defección, *n.f.* defection, desertion.
defectible, *a.* faulty, defective, lacking.
defectivo, -va, *a.* defective, faulty.
defecto, *n.m.* defect, fault, failing, flaw; (*law*) ***a defecto,*** by default; (*pl.*) (*print.*) sheets lacking *or* left over (*from an edition* or *issue*).
defectuoso, -sa, *a.* defective, deficient, faulty.
defendedero, -ra, *a.* defensible.
defendedor, -ra, *a.* defending. — *n.m.* defender.
defender [2], *v.t.* to defend, shield. — **defenderse,** *v.r.* to hold one's own; to manage, get by.
defendible, *a.* defendable, defensible.
defenecer [9], *v.t.* (*prov.*) to close (*an account*).
defenecimiento, *n.m.* (*prov., com.*) settlement.
defenestración, *n.f.* throwing (*people*) from windows, defenestration.
defenestrar, *v.t.* to throw (*people*) from windows.
defensa, *n.f.* defence; backs (*football*); (*pl.*) horns, tusks, antlers (*animals*); (*naut.*) skids, fenders.
defensión, *n.f.* safeguard, defence; [DEFENSA].
defensivo, -va, *a.* defensive. — *n.m.* protection. — *n.f.* defensive; ***estar*** or ***ponerse a la defensiva,*** to be *or* go on the defensive.
defensor, -ra, *a.* defending, protecting. — *n.m.f.* defender, protector; counsel for the defence.
defensoría, *n.f.* duty and office of a defender.
defensorio, *n.m.* plea, defence.
deferencia, *n.f.* deference.
deferente, *a.* deferring, deferential.
deferir [6], *v.t.* to transfer (*jurisdiction* or *power*). — *v.i.* to defer, yield.
deficiencia, *n.f.* deficiency.
deficiente, *a.* defective, faulty, deficient.
déficit, *n.m.* deficit.
definible, *a.* definable.
definición, *n.f.* definition; (*pl.* **definiciones**) statutes of military orders.
definido, -da, *a.* definite. — *n.m.* thing defined.
definidor, -ra, *a.* defining. — *n.m.* definer; definitor (*of religious order*).
definir, *v.t.* to define; (*paint.*) to put the finishing touches to.
definitivo, -va, *a.* final; ***en definitiva,*** in conclusion, to sum up.
definitorio, *n.m.* (*eccles.*) governing chapter; assembly of a religious order and place where chapter is held.
deflagración, *n.f.* deflagration.
deflagrador, -ra, *a.* deflagrating. — *n.m.* (*phys., min.*) deflagrator, igniter.
deflagrar, *v.i.* to deflagrate.
deflector, *n.m.* deflector.
deflegmación, *n.f.* (*med.*) expectoration; (*chem.*) rectification.
deflegmar, *v.t.* to dephlegmate.
deflexión, *n.f.* deflection, deflexure.
deflujo, *n.m.* recession (*of the moon from a planet*); abundant fluxion.
defoliación, *n.f.* defoliation.
deformación, *n.f.* deformation; defacing.
deformador, -ra, *a.* deforming. — *n.m.f.* deformer, disfigurer.
deformar, *v.t.* to deform; to disfigure; to warp, put out of shape; (*rad.*) to distort; (*mech.*) to strain. — **deformarse,** *v.r.* to become deformed; to get distorted; to get out of *or* lose shape; to warp.
deformatorio, -ria, *a.* deforming, disfiguring.
deforme, *a.* deformed, disfigured, misshapen; hideous.
deformidad, *n.f.* deformity; hideousness; (*fig.*) gross error; perversion.
defraudación, *n.f.* defrauding, fraud; tax-evasion.
defraudador, -ra, *a.* defrauding; disappointing. — *n.m.f.* defrauder, defaulter.
defraudar, *v.t.* to defraud, rob, cheat; to disappoint; to frustrate; to intercept (*light*); ***me has defraudado,*** you've disappointed me.
defuera, *adv.* externally, on the outside; ***por defuera,*** on the outside.
defunción, *n.f.* death, decease, demise; (*obs.*) obsequies.
degeneración, *n.f.* degeneration, degeneracy.
degenerado, -da, *a., n.m.f.* degenerate (person).
degenerante, *a.* degenerating.
degenerar, *v.i.* to degenerate (***en,*** into).
deglución, *n.f.* deglutition; swallowing.
deglutidor, -ra, *a.* swallowing.
deglutir, *v.t., v.i.* to swallow.
degollación, *n.f.* throat-cutting.
degolladero, *n.m.* throttle, windpipe; slaughtering place; scaffold; (*obs.*) barrier (*in pit of theatre*); ***llevar al degolladero,*** to lead to the slaughter.
degollado, *n.m.* low neck (*cut in a garment*); sheath (*of plough*); (*build.*) joint.
degollador, -ra, *a.* throat-cutting. — *n.m.* throat-cutter, executioner.
degolladura, *n.f.* cutting of the throat; slender part (*of balustrade*); low neck (*cut in a garment*).
degollante, *a.* throat-cutting; (*coll.*) unbearable, insufferable. — *n.m.f.* pain in the neck; crashing bore.
degollar [10], *v.t.* to behead, cut the throat of; to cut low (*dresses*); to make a mess of, murder, ruin; to cut in on (*a story etc.*); ***Juan me degüella,*** I can't bear *or* stand John.
degollina, *n.f.* (*coll.*) slaughter, butchery; massacre.
degradación, *n.f.* degradation, degrading; deprivation of status; debasement; (*paint.*) degradation, diminution; blending.
degradante, *a.* degrading.
degradar, *v.t.* to degrade, debase, deprive (*of place, dignity* or *honours*); (*paint.*) to shade down.
degüello (1), *n.m.* beheading; decollation; throat cutting; neck *or* narrow part (*of dart etc.*); massacre; ***tira a degüello,*** he means business; (*mil.*) ***entrar a degüello en,*** to put a town to the sword.
degüello (2), *pres. indic.* [DEGOLLAR].
degustación, *n.f.* degustation, tasting, sampling.
dehesa, *n.f.* pasture-ground; cattle-range.
dehesar, *v.t.* to turn into pasture-ground.
dehesero, *n.m.* keeper of pasture-ground.
dehiscencia, *n.f.* (*bot.*) dehiscence.
dehiscente, *a.* (*bot.*) dehiscent.
deicida, *a., n.m.f.* deicidal, deicide.
deicidio, *n.m.* deicide.
deidad, *n.f.* deity.
deificación, *n.f.* deification.
deificar [A], *v.t.* to deify.
deífico, -ca, *a.* deific.
deiforme, *a.* deiform, godlike.
deípara, *a.* deiparous (*the Virgin Mary*).
deísmo, *n.m.* deism.
deísta, *a.* deistic. — *n.m.f.* deist.
deja, *n.f.* prominence (*between two fissures*).
dejación, *n.f.* abandonment, relinquishment, giving up; (*law*) assignment; ***dejación de bienes,*** assignment of one's property to one's creditors.
dejadez, *n.f.* neglect, carelessness; lassitude.
dejado, -da, *a.* indolent; negligent, careless, lax; ***dejado de la mano de Dios,*** God-forsaken. — *n.f.* relinquishment.
dejamiento, *n.m.* lassitude, indolence; carelessness.
dejar, *v.t.* to leave; to let; to yield, give; ***dejar aparte, a un lado,*** to leave aside, on one side; ***dejar atrás,*** to leave behind; (*fig.*) ***¡déjame bien!*** give me a good write up!, don't let me down!; (*fig.*) ***me dejó muy mal,*** he gave me a very poor write-up, he conveyed a very poor impression of me, he let me down; ***dejar bien sentado,*** to make clear *or*

plain; ***dejar caer,*** to let go of, let slip, drop; ***dejar con la palabra en la boca,*** to leave (*s.o.*) in mid-sentence; ***dejar con un palmo de narices,*** to disappoint, let down, dash (*s.o.'s*) hopes; ***dejar con la boca abierta,*** to flabbergast; ***dejar dicho,*** to leave word *or* orders; ***dejar el campo libre,*** to leave the field *or* way clear; ***dejar en blanco,*** to leave blank; ***me dejó en ayunas,*** I was none the wiser afterwards; ***dejar en cueros,*** to skin, leave with nothing; ***dejar frío*** or ***helado,*** to leave speechless; ***el viaje me dejó molido,*** I was worn out after the journey; ***dejar olvidado,*** to forget, leave behind; ***dejar para mañana, para más tarde,*** to leave until tomorrow, until later; ***dejar paso a,*** to let through, make way for; ***dejar plantado,*** to leave in the lurch; ***dejar por imposible,*** to give up as hopeless; ***dejar mucho por decir,*** to leave a great deal unsaid; ***no dejar títere con cabeza,*** to pull completely to pieces; to spare no one; ***dejó caer en la conversación que,*** he casually hinted that; ***déjalo correr,*** let it go *or* rip, let it take its course; ***no me dejes de la mano,*** don't let me go; ***déjame en Serrano,*** drop me *or* put me down in Serrano St.; ***te dejaré en tu casa,*** I'll drop you at your home, I'll take *or* see you home; ***¡déjame en paz!*** leave me alone! ***déjalo de mi cuenta,*** leave it to me. — *v.i.* to leave off, stop, give up; to fail; ***¡deja!, que lo hago yo,*** leave it!, I'll do it; ***deja de hacer ruido,*** stop making a noise; ***dejó de fumar,*** he stopped *or* gave up smoking; ***no dejes de venir,*** don't fail to come, be sure to come; ***no deja de tener razón,*** he's right all the same, he's still right. — **dejarse,** *v.r.* to neglect o.s., let o.s. go downhill; ***me dejaré caer por tu casa,*** I'll drop in at your place; ***déjate de tonterías (cuentos),*** stop talking rot *or* rubbish; ***déjate de rodeos,*** stop beating about the bush; ***se dejó decir que,*** he let it out that, let it slip (out) that; ***dejarse llevar de,*** to allow o.s. to be carried away by; ***se deja querer,*** he (passively) accepts adoration.

dejativo, -va, *a.* lazy, indolent, languid.

deje, *n.m.* after-taste; accent.

dejillo, *n.m.* slight after-taste; slight accent.

dejo, *n.m.* [DEJACIÓN]; after-taste; accent.

del, *contraction of the preposition* **de** *and the article* **el.**

delación, *n.f.* delation, giving away, denunciation.

delantal, *n.m.* apron; pinafore.

delante, *adv.* before, in front, ahead; ***delante de,*** before, in front of; ***ir delante,*** to go ahead, in front; ***pasó por delante de la tienda,*** he passed the shop.

delantero, -ra, *a.* fore, foremost, front. — *n.m.* fore, front; front postilion; forward (*in games*). — *n.f.* front, fore end, fore part; front seats; front edge (*of book*); lead, advantage; (*football*) forward line; boundary line; ***coger (tomar) la delantera,*** to get ahead, be in the lead; (*pl.* **delanteras**) leather breeches.

delatable, *a.* that can be denounced.

delatante, *a.* informing, denouncing.

delatar, *v.t.* to inform against, denounce, give away.

delator, -ra, *a.* denouncing. — *n.m.f.* informer, denouncer.

delco, *n.m.* (*engin.*) distributor (*head*).

deleble, *a.* deletable, erasable.

delectación, *n.f.* delectation, pleasure, delight.

delegación, *n.f.* delegation; delegating; power conferred; proxy; local branch.

delegado, -da, *n.m.f.* delegate, commissioner, deputy, proxy; ***consejero delegado,*** deputy chairman; ***ministro delegado,*** deputy minister.

delegante, *a.* delegating.

delegar [B], *v.t.* to delegate.

delegatorio, -ria, *a.* containing a delegation, delegatory.

deleitable, *a.* delectable, delightful.

deleitabilísimo, -ma, *a. superl.* most delectable.

deleitación, *n.f.* delectation.

deleitamiento, *n.m.* delight, pleasure.

deleitante, *a.* delighting.

deleitar, *v.t.* to please, delight. — **deleitarse,** *v.r.* to delight, take pleasure (***en*** or ***con,*** in).

deleite, *n.m.* delight, pleasure.

deleitoso, -sa, *a.* delightful, pleasing.

deletéreo, -rea, *a.* deleterious, poisonous.

deletreador, -ra, *a.* spelling. — *n.m.f.* speller.

deletrear, *v.t., v.i.* to spell (out); to decipher, interpret.

deletreo, *n.m.* spelling (out).

deleznable, *a.* fragile, frail, unsubstantial, unstable; brittle, crumbly; perishable; slippery.

délfico, -ca, *a.* Delphic, Delphian, of Delphi.

delfín (1), *n.m.* dolphin.

delfín (2), *n.m.* dauphin.

delfina (1), *n.f.* (*chem.*) delphinine.

delfina (2), *n.f.* dauphiness.

delfínidos, *n.m.pl.* (*ichth.*) dolphin family.

delfino, *n.m.* (*bot.*) delphinium.

Delfos, *n.f.* Delphi.

delgadez, *n.f.* thinness, leanness; acuteness, ingenuity.

delgado, -da, *a.* thin, lean; lank, gaunt; acute, ingenious; poor (*soil*). — *adv.* ***hilar delgado,*** to make fine distinctions, go into fine detail; ***hilar demasiado delgado,*** to split hairs. — *n.m.* (*naut.*) dead-rising; (*pl.*) flanks (*of animals*).

delgaducho, -cha, *a.* over-thin, skinny.

deliberación, *n.f.* deliberation.

deliberadamente, *adv.* deliberately.

deliberado, -da, *a.* deliberate.

deliberante, *a.* deliberating, deliberative.

deliberar, *v.t., v.i.* to deliberate, consider.

deliberativo, -va, *a.* deliberative.

delicadez, delicadeza, *n.f.* delicacy; delicateness; finesse; touchiness; squeamishness; scrupulousness; tenderness.

delicado, -da, *a.* delicate; considerate, tender; dainty; ticklish, tricky; touchy; particular, fastidious; scrupulous; subtle, ingenious.

delicia, *n.f.* delight; ***hacer las delicias de,*** to be the delight of.

delicioso, -sa, *a.* delicious, delightful.

delictivo, -va, delictuoso, -sa, *a.* unlawful, felonious.

delicuescencia, *n.f.* deliquescence.

delicuescente, *a.* deliquescent.

deligación, *n.f.* deligation; bandaging.

deligatorio, -ria, *a.* (*surg.*) relating to bandaging.

delimitación, *n.f.* delimitation.

delimitar, *v.t.* to delimit, set the limits of, mark off.

delincuencia, *n.f.* delinquency.

delincuente, *a.* delinquent, offending. — *n.m.f.* delinquent, criminal, offender.

delineación, *n.f.* delineation, draft.

delineador, -ra, *a.* delineating, delineatory. — *n.m.f.* delineator.

delineamiento, *n.m.* delineation.

delineante, *a.* delineating. — *n.m.f.* draughtsman.

delinear, *v.t.* to delineate, outline, draft.

delinquimiento, *n.m.* delinquency, fault, transgression.

delinquir [F], *v.i.* to commit an offence, transgress.

deliquio, *n.m.* swoon, fainting-fit; ecstasy, rapture.

delirante, *a.* delirious, raving.

delirar, *v.i.* to rave, be delirious; to rant.

delirio, *n.m.* delirium; ranting; raving; frenzy, rapture; ***tiene delirios de grandeza,*** he has delusions of grandeur.

delito, *n.m.* crime, offence.
delta, *n.f.* delta.
deltoideo, -dea, *a.* deltoid, triangular.
deltoides, *a.* deltaic, deltoid. — *n.m.* deltoid muscle.
deludir, *v.t.* to delude, deceive.
delusivo, -va, *a.* delusive, fallacious.
delusorio, -ria, *a.* delusive, delusory; fallacious, deceptive.
demacración, *n.f.* emaciation.
demacrar(se), *v.t.,* (*v.r.*) to emaciate, waste away.
demagogia, *n.f.* demagogy.
demagógico, -ca, *a.* demagogic.
demagogo, -ga, *a.* demagogic. — *n.m.f.* demagogue.
demanda, *n.f.* demand, petition, request; alms-begging; search, quest; enterprise; attempt; (*com.*) demand; (*law*) claim; ***la oferta y la demanda,*** supply and demand; ***morir en la demanda,*** to die in the attempt; ***poner demanda,*** to issue a writ; ***que Dios me lo demande,*** may God call me to account for it.
demandadero, -ra [MANDADERO].
demandado, -da, *n.m.f.* defendant, accused.
demandador, -ra, *a.* demanding. — *n.m.f.* (*law*) claimant, plaintiff.
demandante, *a.* [DEMANDADOR].
demandar, *v.t.* to demand, claim, request; to covet, wish for, desire; (*law*) to enter into an action against, sue.
demarcación, *n.f.* demarcation.
demarcador, -ra, *a.* demarcating, dividing. — *n.m.* boundary-surveyor.
demarcar [A], *v.t.* to survey, mark out bounds and limits of; (*naut.*) to determine the bearings of.
demás, *a.* remaining, other; ***y demás,*** and so on, and all the rest of it; ***por demás,*** uselessly, in vain; excessively; ***por lo demás,*** for the rest, apart from this.
demasía, *n.f.* excess; audacity, insolence; outrage; (*min.*) space between two claims; ***en demasía,*** excessively.
demasiadamente, *adv.* [DEMASIADO].
demasiado, -da, *a., pron.* too much; (*pl.*) too many; ***demasiadas veces,*** too often; ***tengo demasiados,*** I have too many. — *adv. inv.* too, too much; ***demasiado pronto,*** too soon; ***hablas demasiado,*** you talk too much.
demasiarse, *v.r.* to go too far.
demediar, *v.t.* to halve; to use up half of; to reach the middle of.
demencia, *n.f.* dementia, insanity.
dementar, *v.t.* to drive insane. — **dementarse,** *v.r.* to become demented, go insane.
demente, *a.* demented, insane. — *n.m.f.* lunatic.
demérito, *n.m.* demerit, defect, fault.
demeritorio, -ria, *a.* unworthy, undeserving; demeritorious.
demisión, *n.f.* submission, humility.
democracia, *n.f.* democracy.
demócrata, *a.* democratic. — *n.m.f.* democrat.
democrático, -ca, *a.* democratic.
democratizar [C], *v.t.* to democratize, make democratic.
demografía, *n.f.* demography.
demográfico, -ca, *a.* demographic; ***problema demográfico,*** population problem.
demógrafo, *n.m.* demographer.
demoledor, -ra, *a.* demolishing. — *n.m.f.* demolisher.
demoler [5], *v.t.* to demolish, pull *or* tear down.
demolición, *n.f.* demolition.
demonche, *n.m.* (*coll.*) devil — *interj.* ***¡demonches!*** the devil! the deuce!
demoníaco, -ca, *a.* demoniacal, devilish, fiendish.
demonio, *n.m.* demon, devil, fiend; ***¡demonio!*** the deuce; ***se da a (todos) los demonios, se le llevan (todos) los demonios,*** he gets all worked up, he gets into a real stew; ***tener el demonio dentro del cuerpo,*** to be terribly restless *or* mischievous; ***hace un frío de mil pares de demonios,*** it's fiendishly *or* perishing cold.
demonolatría, *n.f.* demonolatry.
demonología, *n.f.* demonology.
demonomanía, *n.f.* demonomania.
demonomaníaco, -ca, *a.* suffering from demonomania.
demontre [DEMONCHE].
demora, *n.f.* delay, procrastination; (*Hisp. Am.*) period of eight months (*that Indians were obliged to work in mines*); (*com.*) demurrage; (*naut.*) bearing; ***sin demora,*** without delay.
demorar, *v.t.* to delay, retard. — *v.i.* to tarry, linger, delay; to stop over, halt (*on the way*); (*naut.*) to bear. — **demorarse,** *v.r.* to delay.
demóstenes, *n.m.* (*fig.*) eloquent speaker, orator.
demostino, -na, *a.* Demosthenean.
demostrable, *a.* that can be proved.
demostración, *n.f.* demonstration; proof, proving.
demostrador, -ra, *a.* demonstrating. — *n.m.f.* demonstrator.
demostrar [4], *v.t.* to demonstrate, prove, show.
demostrativo, -va, *a.* demonstrative; ***esto es demostrativo de,*** this is proof of.
demudación, *n.f.* change of countenance.
demudar, *v.t.* to change, upset, disturb. — **demudarse,** *v.r.* to turn *or* go pale *or* white.
demulcente, *a., n.m.* (*med.*) demulcent, emollient.
denario, -ria, *a.* denary. — *n.m.* denarius.
dendriforme, *a.* dendriform.
dendrita, *n.f.* (*min.*) dendrite; fossil tree.
dendrítico, -ca, *a.* dendritic.
dendrografía, *n.f.* dendrology.
dendrográfico, -ca, *a.* relating to dendrology.
dendroide, dendroideo, -dea, *a.* dendroid.
denegación, *n.f.* denial, refusal.
denegar [1B], *v.t.* to refuse, reject, turn down.
denegatorio, -ria, *a.* rejecting.
denegrecer [9], *v.t.* to blacken, darken. — **denegrecerse,** *v.r.* to become blackened, dark.
denegrido, -da, *a.* black, dark; blackened, darkened.
denegrir, *v.t.* [DENEGRECER].
dengoso, -sa, *a.* mincing, finicky, fussy.
dengue, *n.m.* mincing affectation; finickiness; woman's cape with long points; (*med.*) dengue.
denguero, -ra [DENGOSO].
denigración, *n.f.* denigration, insult.
denigrante, *a.* denigrating, insulting. — *n.m.f.* denigrator.
denigrar, *v.t.* to denigrate, insult.
denigrativo, -va, *a.* denigrating, insulting, disparaging.
denodado, -da, *a.* valiant, resolute, intrepid.
denominación, *n.f.* denomination, name, designation.
denominadamente, *adv.* distinctly, markedly.
denominador, -ra, *a.* denominating. — *n.m.f.* denominator.
denominar, *v.t.* to denominate, call, give a name to.
denominativo, -va, *a.* denominative.
denostadamente, *adv.* ignominiously, insultingly.
denostador, -ra, *a.* insulting, vilifying. — *n.m.* vilifier, railer, reviler.
denostar [4], *v.t.* to revile, abuse, insult.
denotación, *n.f.* denotation.
denotar, *v.t.* to denote.
denotativo, -va, *a.* denoting.
densidad, *n.f.* density; denseness; thickness; closeness; solidness.
densímetro, *n.m.* (*phys.*) densimeter.
denso, -sa, *a.* dense; thick; close; solid.

dentado, -da, *a.* dentate, dentated, serrated, toothed; crenated; cogged; pronged.
dentadura, *n.f.* (set of) teeth; ***dentadura postiza,*** false teeth, denture.
dental, *a.* dental. — *n.m.* ploughshare-bed; tooth (*of harrow*). — *n.f.* (*phon.*) dental.
dentar [I], *v.t.* to tooth, cut teeth in, furnish with teeth, cogs *or* prongs. — *v.i.* to teethe, cut teeth.
dentario, -ria, *a.* dental. — *n.f.* (*bot.*) tooth-wort.
dentejón, *n.m.* yoke (*for oxen*).
dentelaria, *n.f.* (*bot.*) plumbago.
dentelete, *n.m.* (*arch.*) dentil.
dentellado, -da, *a.* tooth-edged, serrated, toothed. — *n.f.* bite, toothmark; ***a dentelladas,*** with the teeth.
dentellar, *v.i.* to have one's teeth chattering.
dentellear, *v.t.* to nibble.
dentellón, *n.m.* (*arch.*) moulding (*of cornice*); tooth, cam (*of lock*); dentil.
dentera, *n.f.* tooth-edge, tingling pain in the teeth; ***me da dentera,*** it sets my teeth on edge.
denticina, *n.f.* teething-powder.
dentición, *n.f.* dentition, teething.
denticulado, -da, denticular, *a.* denticular, denticulated.
dentículo, *n.m.* (*arch.*) denticle, dentil.
dentiforme, *a.* dentiform.
dentífrico, -ca, *a.* tooth. — *n.m.* dentifrice.
dentina, *n.f.* dentine.
dentista, *n.m.f.* dentist.
dentivano, -na, *a.* having long and big teeth with gaps.
dentolingual, *a.* dentilingual.
dentón, -tona, *a.* large-toothed. — *n.m.* dentex fish.
dentro, *adv.* within, inside; ***hacia dentro,*** inwards; ***por*** (***de***) ***dentro,*** inside; ***dentro de casa,*** indoors; ***dentro de poco,*** shortly, before long; ***dentro del año,*** in the course of the (present) year; ***dentro de un año,*** in a year's time; ***dentro de lo que cabe,*** as far as circumstances allow, as far as is practicable; ***barrer para dentro,*** to have one's eye to the main chance.
dentudo, -da, *a.* [DENTÓN].
denudación, *n.f.* denudation.
denudar, *v.t.* to strip, bare, denude.
denuedo, *n.m.* valour, intrepidity, resoluteness.
denuesto (1), *n.m.* affront, insult, abuse.
denuesto (2), *pres. indic.* [DENOSTAR].
denuncia, *n.f.* denunciation, accusation; report (*to the police*).
denunciable, *a.* fit to be denounced.
denunciación [DENUNCIA].
denunciador, -ra, *a.* denunciating, denouncing. — *n.m.f.* denunciator, denouncer, accuser.
denunciante, *a.*, *n.m.f.* [DENUNCIADOR].
denunciar, *v.t.* to denounce, denunciate, report; to make known, give notice of; to indicate, show; to apply for the registration of (*a claim*).
denunciatorio, -ria, *a.* denunciatory.
denuncio, *n.m.* (*min.*) registration of a claim.
denutrición, *n.f.* denutrition.
deñarse [DIGNARSE].
deontología, *n.f.* deontology.
deparar, *v.t.* to afford, furnish, present.
departamental, *a.* departmental.
departamento, *n.m.* department; (*naval*) district; (*railway*) compartment; administrative division.
departidor, -ra, *a.* conversing, talking. — *n.m.f.* talker, converser.
departir, *v.i.* to converse, talk.
depauperación, *n.f.* (*med.*) debility, exhaustion.
depauperar, *v.t.* to impoverish; (*med.*) to debilitate, weaken, exhaust.
dependencia, *n.f.* dependence, dependency; branch office; relation; business, affair; staff, employees; (*pl.*) accessories; (*arch.*) outbuildings.
depender, *v.i.* — ***de,*** to depend on; to be dependent on; to be the responsibility of.
dependienta, *n.f.* shop assistant, salesgirl.
dependiente, *a.* dependent, depending, subordinate. — *n.m.* shop assistant, salesman.
depilación, *n.f.* depilation.
depilar, *v.t.* (*med.*) to depilate.
depilatorio, -ria, *a.*, *n.m.* depilatory.
depleción, *n.f.* (*med.*) depletion.
depletivo, -va, *a.* (*med.*) depletive, depletory.
deplorable, *a.* deplorable, lamentable, regrettable.
deplorar, *v.t.* to deplore, bewail, lament.
deponente, *a.* deposing, deponent. — *n.m.f.* deponent, deposer; (*law*) witness.
deponer [25], *v.t.* to lay aside; to declare; to remove from office, depose; to lay down (*arms*). — *v.i.* to make a statement; to defecate.
depopulador, -ra, *a.* depopulating, devastating. — *n.m.f.* depopulator, devastator.
deportación, *n.f.* deportation; banishment.
deportado, -da, *n.m.f.* deported person, deportee.
deportar, *v.t.* to deport; to banish.
deporte, *n.m.* sport; pastime.
deportismo, *n.m.* sport, addiction to sport.
deportista, *a.* sporting. — *n.m.f.* sportsman, sportswoman.
deportividad, *n.f.* sportsmanship, sporting spirit.
deportivo, -va, *a.* sport, sporting, sportive; (*coll.*) casual, airy, gay, cheery.
deposición, *n.f.* deposition; statement; removal (*from office*); evacuation (*of bowels*).
depositador, -ra, *a.* depositing, entrusting. — *n.m.f.* depositor, one who leaves in trust.
depositante, *a.* depositing, entrusting.
depositar, *v.t.* to deposit; to lay *or* set down; to entrust, confide; to put (*a person*) judicially in a position where he is free to manifest his will; to enclose, contain. — **depositarse,** *v.r.* to settle (*dregs, sediment*).
depositaría, *n.f.* depository, repository; subtreasury; trusteeship.
depositario, -ria, *a.* relating to a depositor, depositary. — *n.m.f.* depositary, trustee, receiver.
depósito, *n.m.* deposit; trust; depositary; (*com.*) store, depot, warehouse; (*mech.*) chamber; (*med.*) abscess, tumour; (*min.*) alluvium; (*mil.*) depot; (*chem.*) precipitate, sediment, deposit; ***depósito de agua,*** water tank; reservoir; ***depósito de*** (***la***) ***gasolina,*** petrol tank; ***depósito de cadáveres,*** mortuary; ***en depósito,*** in trust.
depravación, *n.f.* depravation, depravity.
depravado, -da, *a.* depraved.
depravador, -ra, *a.* depraving, corrupting. — *n.m.f.* depraver, corrupter.
depravar, *v.t.* to deprave, corrupt. — **depravarse,** *v.r.* to become depraved.
deprecación, *n.f.* entreaty.
deprecante, *a.* entreating, beseeching.
deprecar [A], *v.t.* to entreat, beseech.
deprecativo, -va, deprecatorio, -ria, *a.* entreating, beseeching.
depreciación, *n.f.* depreciation; devaluation.
depreciar, *v.t.* to depreciate; to devalue.
depredación, *n.f.* depredation, plundering, looting, pillaging; extortion.
depredador, *n.m.* depredator.
depredar, *v.t.* to depredate, pillage, loot.
depresión, *n.f.* depression; (*naut.*) ***depresión de horizonte,*** dip of the horizon.
depresivo, -va, *a.* depressive, depressing.
depresor, -ra, *a.* depressing. — *n.m.f.* oppressor. — *n.m.* (*anat., surg.*) depressor.
deprimente, *a.* depressing.

deprimir, *v.t.* to depress; to press down; (*fig.*) to humiliate. — **deprimirse,** *v.r.* to get depressed.

depurable, *a.* cleansable, purifiable.

depuración, *n.f.* purification; purge.

depurador, -ra, *a.* purifying. — *n.m.f.* purifier.

depurar, *v.t.* to cleanse, purify.

depurativo, -va, *a.*, *n.m.* (*med.*) depurative, depurant.

depuratorio, -ria, *a.* depuratory, purifying.

deputar [DIPUTAR].

deque, *conj.* (*coll.*) as soon as.

derecera [DERECHERA].

derecha, *n.f.* [DERECHO].

derechamente, *adv.* in a proper *or* upright manner.

derechera, *n.f.* direct road, short cut.

derechero, *a.* straight, honest, upright. — *n.m.* clerk appointed to collect fees and taxes.

derechista, *a.*, *n.m.f.* (*polit.*) right-wing.

derecho, -cha, *a.* right; straight; right-hand; standing upright; ***hecho y derecho,*** fully-fledged. — *adv.* straight, straight on; ***todo derecho,*** straight ahead. — *n.m.* right; right side; law; ***al derecho,*** the right way round; ***conforme a derecho, según derecho,*** according to law and justice; ***de derecho,*** by right; ***derecho de gentes,*** ius gentium; international law; ***derecho de visita,*** right of search; ***estudiante de derecho,*** law student; ***no hay derecho,*** it is not right, it's not fair; ***usar uno de su derecho,*** to exercise one's rights; ***derecho consuetudinario,*** common law; ***derecho criminal*** or ***penal,*** criminal law, ***derecho natural,*** natural right; (*pl.*) fees, duties, dues; ***derechos de aduana,*** customs duties; ***derechos consulares,*** consular fees; ***derechos de almacenaje*** or ***depósito,*** warehouse dues, storage; ***derechos de anclaje,*** anchorage dues; ***derechos de entrada,*** import duties; ***derechos de herencia,*** death duties, (*Am.*) inheritance tax; ***derechos de muelle,*** wharfage, pierage; ***derechos de puerto,*** harbour *or* port dues; ***derechos reales,*** inheritance tax; ***derechos de remolque,*** towage. — *n.f.* right hand, right side; (*polit.*) right; (*mil.*) ***¡derecha!*** right-about! ***hacer algo a derechas,*** to do sth. properly; ***a tuertas o a derechas,*** by hook or by crook.

derechura, *n.f.* rectitude, right way; ***en derechura,*** by the most direct road; without delay.

derelicción, *n.f.* dereliction.

deriva, *n.f.* (*naut.*, *aer.*) drift, drifting; ***ir a la deriva,*** to drift, be adrift; ***empezar a ir a la deriva,*** to go adrift.

derivable, *a.* derivable, deducible.

derivación, *n.f.* derivation; descent; deduction, inference; drawing off (*water etc.*); (*elec.*) loss of current (*through damp etc.*); (*elec.*) branch; (*elec.*) shunt connection.

derivado, -da, *a.*, *n.m.f.* (*math.*, *gram.*) derivative. — by-product.

derivador, -ra, *a.* deriving. — *n.m.* (*phys.*) graduator.

derivar, *v.t.* to derive; to draw off, turn aside. — *v.i.* to derive, be derived, come (from); to go off course. — **derivarse,** *v.r.* to derive, be derived; to go off course; ***esta palabra (se) deriva del árabe,*** this word derives (comes) from Arabic.

derivativo, -va, *a.*, *n.m.* derivative.

derivo, *n.m.* derivation.

derivómetro, *n.m.* drift meter.

dermatitis, *n.f. inv.* dermatitis.

dérmatoesqueleto, *n.m.* dermatoskeleton.

dermatoideo, -dea, *a.* dermatoid.

dermatología, *n.f.* dermatology.

dermatológico, -ca, *a.* appertaining to dermatology.

dermatólogo, *n.m.* dermatologist.

dermesto, *n.m.* larder beetle.

derogable, *a.* repealable.

derogación, *n.f.* revocation, repeal, annulment, abolition; curtailment, diminution.

derogador, -ra, *a.* repealing, abolishing.

derogar [B], *v.t.* to revoke, repeal, annul, abolish; to curtail, diminish; to amend.

derogatorio, -ria, *a.* (*law*) repealing, annulling.

derrabar, *v.t.* to dock the tail of.

derrama, *n.f.* apportionment (*of tax*).

derramadamente, *adv.* profusely, lavishly; extravagantly; in a disorderly manner.

derramadero, *n.m.* dumping-place; weir; spillway.

derramado, -da, *a.* prodigal, wasteful.

derramador, -ra, *a.* prodigal, wasteful. — *n.m.f.* prodigal, waster, spendthrift.

derramamiento, *n.m.* spilling, shedding, overflow; scattering, spreading; ***derramamiento de sangre,*** bloodshed, spilling of blood.

derramaplaceres, derramasolaces, *n.m.f. inv.* killjoy, wet blanket.

derramar, *v.t.* to spill, shed; to scatter; to spread; to apportion (*taxes*); ***derramar la hacienda,*** to squander one's inheritance. — **derramarse,** *v.r.* to spill over, overflow.

derrame, *n.m.* spilling; loss, leakage, overflow; (*arch.*) bevel, splay (*window etc.*), declivity; outlet (*of ravine*); (*med.*) effusion, discharge; (*naut.*) draught (*from sail*); slop; ***derrame de sangre,*** hæmorrhage; ***derrame cerebral,*** cerebral hæmorrhage.

derramo, *n.m.* chamfer, splay, flare, bevel (*of door* or *window*).

derrapar, *v.i.* to skid.

derrape, *n.m.* (*naut.*, *aer.*) yawing; (*motor.*) skid.

derraspado, -da, *a.* beardless (*wheat*).

derredor, *n.m.* contour; ***al*** or ***en derredor,*** round about, round, around.

derrelicto, *n.m.* (*naut.*) derelict. — *p.p.* [DERRELINQUIR].

derrelinquir [F], *v.t.* to abandon, forsake.

derrenegar [IB], *v.i.* — ***de,*** to hate, detest, loathe.

derrengada, *n.f.* (*prov.*) step in dancing.

derrengadura, derrengamiento, *n.f.* hip dislocation; lameness; (*coll.*) state of being fagged out, aching all over.

derrengar [IB, *modern* B], *v.t.* to cripple, sprain the hip of, strain the spine of, break the back of; to bend, make crooked. — **derrengarse,** *v.r.* (*coll.*) to knock o.s. up, fag o.s. out; (*coll.*) ***estar derrengado,*** to be fagged out, be a mass of aches and pains.

derretido, -da, *a.* (*fig.*) soppy, sloppy. — *n.m.* concrete.

derretimiento, *n.m.* melting; (*fig.*) soppiness, sloppiness.

derretir [8], *v.t.* to melt; (*coll.*) to squander. — **derretirse,** *v.r.* to melt; (*coll.*) to go weak at the knees, sloppy *or* soppy.

derribado, -da, *a.* having low buttocks (*horses*).

derribador, -ra, *a.* demolishing, pushing over *or* down, knocking over *or* down. — *n.m.* cowpuncher.

derribar, *v.t.* to demolish, overthrow, to push *or* knock over *or* down; to shoot *or* bring down (*aircraft*); ***derribar por tierra,*** to knock to the ground.

derribo, *n.m.* demolition, pulling down; knocking down (*fighting bulls*); (*pl.*) debris.

derrocadero, *n.m.* precipice.

derrocamiento, *n.m.* throwing *or* falling, throwing *or* pulling down; overthrow.

derrocar [4A, *modern* A], *v.t.* to cast *or* throw down; to overthrow.

derrochador, -ra, *a.* wasteful, squandering. — *n.m.f.* prodigal, spendthrift, squanderer.

derrochar, *v.t.* to squander; ***derrochar salud,*** to be brimming over with health.

derroche, *n.m.* squandering, extravagance, waste; profusion, abundant *or* lavish display.
derrochón, -chona, *a., n.m.f.* squandering; squander-bug, spendthrift.
derrostrarse, *v.r.* to injure one's face.
derrota, *n.f.* defeat; course, route; path; post-harvest pasture rights.
derrotar, *v.t.* to defeat, beat; to wear out, bring low. — **derrotarse,** *v.r.* (*naut., aer.*) to deviate from course; (*coll.*) to get worn out, get knocked up.
derrote, *n.m.* butt, thrust (*of a bull's horn*).
derrotero, *n.m.* course; track; (collection of) sea-charts; (*fig.*) course, way (*of life* or *conduct*).
derrotismo, *n.m.* defeatism.
derrotista, *a., n.m.f.* defeatist.
derrubiar, *v.t.* to wash away, erode.
derrubio, *n.m.* washing away, erosion, alluvion, alluvium.
derruir [O], *v.t.* to demolish, pull *or* tear down; ***casa derruida,*** house in ruins.
derrumbadero, *n.m.* precipice; (*fig.*) danger, risk, hazard.
derrumbamiento, *n.m.* collapse.
derrumbar, *v.t.* to pull, throw *or* fling down. — **derrumbarse,** *v.r.* to collapse, cave in.
derrumbe, *n.m.* precipice; (*min.*) landslide, collapse, caving in.
derviche, *n.m.* dervish.
desabarrancamiento, *n.m.* dragging out, extricating.
desabarrancar [A], *v.t.* to drag *or* pull out, disentangle, extricate.
desabastecer [I], *v.t.* to cut off from supplies; to leave unprovided.
desabastecido, -da, *a.* without supplies *or* provisions.
desabastecimiento, *n.m.* stopping of supplies.
desabejar, *v.t.* to take (*bees*) from a hive.
desabocar [A], *v.i.* to sail out.
desabollador, -ra, *a.* planishing, removing dents. — *n.m.* planisher (*tool*).
desabolladura, *n.f.* removal of dents.
desabollar, *v.t.* to remove dents from.
desabonarse, *v.r.* to discontinue one's subscription, season ticket etc.
desabono, *n.m.* cancellation, discontinuation (*of subscription etc.*); ***hablar en desabono de,*** to speak to the prejudice of.
desabor, *n.m.* insipidity, tastelessness, lack of enthusiasm; ***coger con desabor,*** to receive without enthusiasm.
desabordarse, *v.r.* to get clear of a ship (*which has run foul of one's own*).
desaborido, -da, *a.* tasteless, insipid; dull, flat.
desabotonar, *v.t.* to unbutton. — *v.i.* (*fig.*) to bloom, blossom. — **desabotonarse,** *v.r.* to become unbuttoned; to undo one's buttons.
desabrido, -da, *a.* tasteless, insipid; kicking (*cross-bow* or *gun*); surly, disagreeable; unsettled, unpleasant (*weather*).
desabrigado, -da, *a.* lightly clothed; uncovered; unprotected, defenceless; (*naut.*) unsheltered, exposed (*roadstead*).
desabrigar [B], *v.t.* to uncover; to take off (s.o.'s) clothes; to deprive of shelter. — **desabrigarse,** *v.r.* to take off one's outer clothes; ***no te desabrigues,*** keep your warm clothes on, don't take your coat (*pullover etc.*) off.
desabrigo, *n.m.* lack of covering, clothing, sheltering *or* protection; (*fig.*) want of protection.
desabrimiento, *n.m.* insipidity (*in food*); (*fig.*) surliness, unpleasantness; recoil (*of firearms* or *crossbow*).
desabrir, *v.t.* to give a bad taste to; to annoy. — **desabrirse,** *v.r.* — ***de,*** to become annoyed, vexed, surly.
desabrochamiento, *n.m.* unbuttoning, unfastening.
desabrochar, *v.t.* to unbutton, unfasten, unclasp.
desacaloramiento, *n.m.* cooling off.
desacalorarse, *v.r.* to cool off.
desacatado, -da, *a.* disrespectful.
desacatador, -ra, *a., n.m.f.* disrespectul (person).
desacatamiento [DESACATO].
desacatar, *v.t.* to treat disrespectfully; to show irreverence to; to disobey; to show contempt for.
desacatarrarse, *v.r.* to get rid of a cold.
desacato, *n.m.* disrespect, irreverence; disobedience; (*law*) contempt (*of court*).
desacedar, *v.t.* to remove acidity from.
desaceitar, *v.t.* to remove oil and grease from.
desaceración, *n.f.* removing *or* wearing out of steel (*in a tool*).
desacerar, *v.t.* to wear out the steel in (*a tool*). — **desacerarse,** *v.r.* to lose its steel (*tool*).
desacerbar, *v.t.* to sweeten, soothe, temper.
desacertado, -da, *a.* mistaken, wrong; unsuccessful, ill-advised.
desacertar [I], *v.t.* to get wrong. — *v.i.* to be wrong, make a mistake.
desacidificación, *n.f.* (*chem.*) deacidification.
desacidificar [A], *v.t.* (*chem.*) to remove acid from, deacidify.
desacidular, *v.t.* to remove acid from.
desacierto, *n.m.* error, mistake, blunder.
desacobardar, *v.t.* to free from fear; to give courage to.
desacollar, *v.t.* to dig a hollow round (*vines*).
desacomodado, -da, *a.* badly off, in straitened circumstances; awkward, bothersome, uncomfortable.
desacomodamiento [DESACOMODO].
desacomodar, *v.t.* to make things awkward for; to dismiss, discharge.
desacomodo, *n.m.* awkward circumstances; loss of job.
desacompañamiento, *n.m.* lack of company *or* society, solitude, loneliness.
desacompañar, *v.t.* to cease to accompany, abandon.
desaconsejable, *a.* inadvisable.
desaconsejado, -da, *a.* ill-advised, unwise.
desaconsejar, *v.t.* to dissuade.
desacoplar, *v.t.* to unfasten, disconnect, uncouple.
desacordado, -da [DESACORDE].
desacordante, *a.* discordant.
desacordar [4], *v.t.* to make discordant, put out of tune; to cause disagreement in. — **desacordarse,** *v.r.* to get out of tune, to fall into disagreement; to become forgetful.
desacorde, *a.* discordant, out of tune; in disagreement.
desacordonar, *v.t.* to undo, loosen.
desacorralar, *v.t.* to bring (*a bull*) into the arena *or* open field; to let cattle out of the yard.
desacostumbrado, -da, *a.* unusual, unaccustomed.
desacostumbrar, *v.t.* to disaccustom; to break of a habit. — **desacostumbrarse,** *v.r.* to get out of practice, get out of the habit.
desacotar, *v.t.* to open up; to raise the ban on; to withdraw (from); to refuse, reject.
desacoto, *n.m.* opening up; removal of ban.
desacreditador, -ra, *a.* discrediting.
desacreditar, *v.t.* to discredit, bring discredit on, injure the reputation of. — **desacreditarse,** *v.r.* to become discredited, lose one's reputation, fall into disrepute.
desacuartelar, *v.t.* (*mil.*) to remove from barracks.
desacuerdo (1), *n.m.* disaccord, disagreement; error, mistake; forgetfulness; mental derangement.
desacuerdo (2), *pres. indic.* [DESACORDAR].

desacuñar, *v.t.* (*print.*) to unwedge, remove the quoins from; (*mint.*) to remove the die of *or* from.
desaderezar [C], *v.t.* to ruffle, disarrange. — **desaderezarse,** *v.r.* to become disarranged, untidy.
desadeudar, *v.t.* to clear, extricate from debt. — **desadeudarse,** *v.r.* to pay one's debts.
desadoquinar, *v.t.* to remove paving-stones from.
desadorar, *v.t.* to cease to worship.
desadormecer [9], *v.t.* to wake, rouse from sleep; to free from numbness.
desadornar, *v.t.* to denude, lay bare, divest of ornaments.
desadorno, *n.m.* lack of ornaments.
desadujar, *v.t.* to undo the ropes from (*a sail*).
desadvertidamente, *adv.* inadvertently, inconsiderately.
desadvertido, -da, *a.* inadvertent, heedless.
desadvertimiento, *n.m.* inadvertence, heedlessness.
desadvertir [6], *v.t.* to give no heed to, take no notice of.
desafear, *v.t.* to improve the appearance of.
desafección, *n.f.* disaffection.
desafecto, -ta, *a.* disaffected; opposed. — *n.m.* ill-will, dislike.
desaferramiento, *n.m.* weighing anchor.
desaferrar [I], *v.t.* to loosen, unfasten; to unfurl (*sails*); to unmoor; to weigh (*anchor*); to talk (*s.o.*) out of his views.
desafiadero, *n.m.* duelling-ground.
desafiador, -ra, *a.* challenging; defying; competing. — *n.m.f.* challenger; duellist; competitor, rival.
desafiante, *a.* defiant, defying.
desafiar [L], *v.t.* to defy, challenge; to dare; to rival, compete with.
desafición, *n.f.* disaffection.
desaficionar, *v.t.* to cause to lose liking *or* taste (***de,*** for). — **desaficionarse,** *v.r.* to lose liking *or* taste (***de,*** for).
desafijar [DESAHIJAR].
desafilar, *v.t.* to blunt, dull (*edge, point*). — **desafilarse,** *v.r.* to become blunt, dull.
desafinación, *n.f.* discordance, dissonance.
desafinado, -da, *a.* dissonant, out of tune, discordant.
desafinar, *v.i.* to be out of tune; to sing out of tune; to speak off the point. — **desafinarse,** *v.r.* to get out of tune.
desafío, *n.m.* challenge; duel.
desaforado, -da, *a.* lawless; outrageous; (*fig.*) huge, excessive, exorbitant.
desaforar [4], *v.t.* to encroach upon the rights *or* privileges of. — **desaforarse,** *v.r.* to act outrageously, insolently.
desaforrar, *v.t.* to take the lining from.
desafortunado, -da, *a.* unlucky, unfortunate.
desafrancesar, *v.t.* to divest of frenchified ways and manners.
desafuero, *n.m.* excess, violence, outrage, injustice, infraction (*of the law*).
desagarrar, *v.t.* (*coll.*) to loose, release, let go of.
desagitadera, *n.f.* instrument for removing honeycomb from the hive.
desagitar, *v.t.* to remove (*honeycombs*) from the hive.
desagraciar, *v.t.* to spoil, detract from.
desagradable, *a.* disagreeable, unpleasant.
desagradar, *v.t.* to displease; ***me desagrada su conducta,*** I dislike his behaviour.
desagradecer [9], *v.t.* to be ungrateful for.
desagradecido, -da, *a.* ungrateful; ***desagradecido al beneficio,*** ungrateful for the favour; ***desagradecido con*** or ***para con su bienhechor,*** ungrateful to his benefactor. — *n.m.f.* ungrateful person.
desagradecimiento, *n.m.* ingratitude.
desagrado, *n.m.* displeasure; reluctance; ***con desagrado,*** reluctantly.
desagraviador, -ra, *a.* indemnifying. — *n.m.f.* indemnifier.
desagraviar, *v.t.* to make amends to; to right wrong done to; to give satisfaction to; to indemnify.
desagravio, *n.m.* amends; righting (*of wrong*); satisfaction (*for injury*); compensation.
desagregación, *n.f.* separation, segregation.
desagregar [B], *v.t.* to separate, segregate.
desagriar, *v.t.* to take the acidity *or* sharpness from; (*fig.*) to mollify; to appease.
desaguadero, *n.m.* drain, outlet, waste-pipe; (*fig.*) drain (*of money*).
desaguador, -ra, *a.* draining. — *n.m.* waste-pipe, drain.
desaguamiento, *n.m.* drainage; outlet, waste-pipe, drain.
desaguar [H], *v.t.* to drain; (*fig.*) to squander, waste. — *v.i.* to empty, flow (*into*). — **desaguarse,** *v.r.* to discharge (the body) waste by vomit *or* stool.
desaguazar [C], *v.t.* to drain.
desagüe, *n.m.* outlet, drain, drainage; waste.
desaguisado, -da, *a.* lawless, illegal, unjust. — *n.m.* injury, outrage, wrong; (*coll.*) hash, bungle, mess, muck-up.
desaherrojar, *v.t.* to unchain; unshackle.
desahijar, *v.t.* to wean, separate (*young*) from dams. — **desahijarse,** *v.r.* to swarm (*bees*).
desahitarse, *v.r.* to relieve indigestion.
desahogado, -da, *a.* impudent, brazen-faced; free, clear, unencumbered; in comfortable circumstances, comfortably off; (*naut.*) having sea-room.
desahogar [B], *v.t.* to ease, relieve, alleviate; to give vent to. — **desahogarse,** *v.r.* to find relief, let off steam, give vent to one's feelings.
desahogo, *n.m.* relief, alleviation; giving vent; ample room; unbosoming of feelings; impudence; ***vivir con desahogo,*** to be comfortably off.
desahuciar, *v.t.* to give up (all) hope for; to declare past recovery; to give up as a lost cause; to evict.
desahucio, *n.m.* eviction (*of a tenant*).
desahumado, -da, *a.* smokeless, smoke-free; mild, faded, vapid; flat (*liquors*).
desahumar, *v.t.* to free from smoke.
desainadura, *n.f.* (excessive) loss of fat from overwork (*horses*).
desainar [P], *v.t.* to cause (excessive) loss of fat in (*horses*).
desairadamente, *adv.* gracelessly, slightingly.
desairado, -da, *a.* graceless; ***hacer un papel desairado,*** to cut a poor figure.
desairar, *v.t.* to slight, snub, ignore; to rebuff.
desaire, *n.m.* slight, rebuff, disdain, snub; awkwardness; ***tragarse un desaire,*** to swallow an affront.
desaislarse [P], *v.r.* to cease to be isolated, leave one's seclusion.
desajustar, *v.t.* to mismatch, unfit, disarrange, disadjust. — **desajustarse,** *v.r.* to withdraw from an agreement; to get out of order.
desajuste, *n.m.* disagreement; breaking (*of a contract*); dislocation, being out of place *or* loose; discrepancy, error.
desalabanza, *n.f.* disparagement.
desalabar, *v.t.* to disparage; to criticize.
desalabear, *v.t.* (*carp.*) to straighten; take the warp out of; to true up.
desalabeo, *n.m.* (*carp.*) straightening, unwarping.
desalado, -da, *a.* anxious, eager; in a rush; unsalted.
desalar, *v.t.* to cut the wings of; to desalt, unsalt. — **desalarse,** *v.r.* to rush, dash; ***desalarse por,*** to yearn for, crave for.

desalazón, *n.f.* (*chem.*) desalting.
desalbardar, *v.t.* to unsaddle (*packhorse etc.*).
desalcoholizar [C], *v.t.* to remove the alcohol from.
desalentadamente, *adv.* dispiritedly.
desalentador, -ra, *a.* dispiriting, discouraging.
desalentar [I], *v.t.* to wind, put out of breath; (*fig.*) to discourage, dispirit. — **desalentarse,** *v.r.* to become dispirited, discouraged.
desalfombrar, *v.t.* to remove carpeting from, uncarpet.
desalforjar, *v.t.* to remove from a saddlebag; to take the saddlebags off. — **desalforjarse,** *v.r.* (*coll.*) to loosen one's garments, make o.s. easy.
desalhajar, *v.t.* to dismantle, strip (*a room*).
desaliento (1), *n.m.* discouragement, dispiritedness, faintheartedness.
desaliento (2), *pres. indic.* [DESALENTAR].
desalineación, *n.f.* disalignment.
desalinear, *v.t.* to disalign, put out of alignment.
desaliñado, -da, *a.* slovenly, unkempt, untidy.
desaliñar, *v.t.* to disarrange, disorder, ruffle, untidy.
desaliño, *n.m.* slovenliness, untidiness, carelessness; (*pl.*) (*obs.*) long diamond ear-rings.
desalisamiento, *n.m.* ruffling (*of smooth hair*); sorting (*of paper, rags etc.*).
desalisar, *v.t.* to ruffle (*hair*); to sort (*rags etc. in paper-mill*).
desalivar, *v.i.* to salivate.
desalmacenar, *v.t.* to remove *or* collect from warehouse *or* depot.
desalmado, -da, *a.* soulless; inhuman, merciless, ruthless, pitiless, heartless.
desalmamiento, *n.m.* soullessness; ruthlessness, pitilessness.
desalmar, *v.t.* to weaken; to disturb. — **desalmarse,** *v.r.* to long, yearn.
desalmenar, *v.t.* to strip of battlements.
desalmidonar, *v.t.* to take the starch out of.
desalojamiento, *n.m.* dislodging; evacuation.
desalojar, *v.t.* to dislodge, evict; to evacuate, leave; to clear. — *v.i.* to clear out, leave.
desalquilado, -da, *a.* untenanted, unrented, vacant.
desalquilar, *v.t.* to leave, vacate, give up; to evict, make leave *or* vacate. — **desalquilarse,** *v.r.* to become vacant *or* untenanted.
desalterar, *v.t.* to calm down, quieten.
desalucinación, *n.f.* dishallucination.
desalumbrado, -da [DESLUMBRADO].
desalumbramiento, *n.m.* [DESLUMBRAMIENTO].
desamable, *a.* unlovable; unworthy of love.
desamador, -ra, *a., n.m.f.* (one) who does not love.
desamanerarse, *v.r.* to lose one's mannerisms *or* affectations.
desamar, *v.t.* to cease loving; to detest, hate.
desamarrar, *v.t.* (*naut.*) to unmoor, cast off; to untie, unbind, unlash.
desamarre, *n.m.* unmooring, untying.
desamasado, -da, *a.* dissolved, disunited.
desambientado, -da, *a.* out of place, out of one's element, lost.
desamazacotar, *v.t.* to make lighter *or* less tedious.
desambientar, *v.t.* to put out of place; ***estar desambientado,*** to be out of place, not to have settled down.
desamigado, -da, *a.* estranged.
desamistarse, *v.r.* to fall out, quarrel.
desamoblar [4], *v.t.* [DESAMUEBLAR].
desamodorrar, *v.t.* to rouse from drowsiness, lethargy.
desamoldar, *v.t.* to unmould; (*fig.*) to change the shape of, deform.
desamontonar, *v.t.* to unpile, unheap.
desamor, *n.m.* lack of affection, coldness, indifference; dislike, aversion.
desamorado, -da, *a.* cold-hearted; unloving.
desamorar, *v.t.* to kill love in.
desamoroso, -sa, *a.* unloving.
desamorrar, *v.t.* (*coll.*) to cheer up.
desamortizable, *a.* redeemable; that can be disentailed.
desamortización, *n.f.* disentail.
desamortizador, -ra, *a., n.m.f.* disentailing (*person* or *thing*).
desamortizar [C], *v.t.* to free from mortmain; to disentail.
desamotinarse, *v.r.* to cease from mutiny.
desamparador, -ra, *a.* abandoning, deserting. — *n.m.f.* forsaker.
desamparar, *v.t.* to forsake, abandon; to leave unprotected *or* helpless; (*law*) to relinquish; (*naut.*) to dismantle, dismast.
desamparo, *n.m.* abandonment, desertion; forlornness, helplessness; dereliction.
desamueblado, -da, *a.* unfurnished.
desamueblar, *v.t.* to strip of furniture.
desamurar, *v.t.* to raise *or* free the tack of (*a sail*).
desanclar, desancorar, *v.t.* to unanchor.
desandadura, *n.f.* turning back, retracing of one's steps.
desandar [11], *v.t.* to retrace, go back over; ***desandar lo andado,*** to retrace one's steps; (*fig.*) to go back to the beginning.
desandrajado, -da, *a.* ragged, tattered.
desangramiento, *n.m.* bleeding to excess *or* to death.
desangrar, *v.t.* to bleed to excess *or* to death; to empty (*a pond etc.*); (*fig.*) to bleed. — **desangrarse,** *v.r.* to lose a lot of blood; to bleed to death; to lose *or* pour out one's lifeblood.
desanidar, *v.i.* to forsake the nest (*birds*). — **desanidarse,** *v.r.* to dislodge.
desanimado, -da, *a.* (*com.*) dull, flat.
desanimar, *v.t.* to dishearten, dispirit, discourage. — **desanimarse,** *v.r.* to get discouraged, lose heart; ***no hay que desanimarse,*** we must keep our spirits up.
desánimo, *n.m.* discouragement, downheartedness, despondency.
desanublar, *v.t.* to clear up.
desanudadura, *n.f.* unknotting, untying; disentangling.
desanudar, desañudar, *v.t.* to unknot, untie, loosen; (*fig.*) to disentangle, clarify.
desaojadera, *n.f.* woman supposed to break the spell of the evil eye.
desaojar, *v.t.* to break the spell of *or* counteract the evil eye in.
desapacibilidad, *n.f.* disagreeableness, unpleasantness; brusqueness; inclemency.
desapacible, *a.* disagreeable, unpleasant; brusque; inclement.
desapadrinar, *v.t.* to disapprove (of); to disavow.
desaparear, *v.t.* to unmatch, disjoin, separate (*a pair*).
desaparecer [9], *v.i.* to disappear (*from sight*), vanish.
desaparecimiento, *n.m.* disappearing.
desaparejar, *v.t.* to unhitch, unharness; to unrig (*a ship*).
desaparición, *n.f.* disappearance.
desaparroquiar, *v.t.* to remove from a parish; to drive customers away from. — **desaparroquiarse,** *v.r.* to lose one's parish; to lose customers; to cease to be a customer.
desapasionado, -da, *a.* dispassionate, cool, impartial, unbiased.
desapasionarse, *v.r.* to lose enthusiasm, cool (off).
desapegar [B], *v.t.* to detach, pull away, separate. —

desapegarse, *v.r.* to cease to feel attached, lose fondness, cool.
desapego [DESPEGO].
desapercibido, -da, *a.* unprovided; unprepared; unguarded, unaware; unnoticed; ***pasar desapercibido,*** to go unnoticed.
desapercibimiento, *n.m.* unpreparedness.
desapestar, *v.t.* to disinfect.
desapiadado, -da [DESPIADADO].
desaplicación, *n.f.* want of application, lack of studiousness, laziness.
desaplicado, -da, *a.* unstudious, lazy.
desaplomar, *v.t.* to put out of plumb.
desapoderado, -da, *a.* impetuous, wild, unbridled, ungovernable.
desapoderamiento, *n.m.* dispossession; withdrawing of powers; boundless liberty *or* licence.
desapoderar, *v.t.* to dispossess, take powers away from.
desapolillar, *v.t.* to clear of moths. — **desapolillarse,** *v.r.* (*fig.*) to get rid of the cobwebs, get some (fresh) air.
desaporcar [A], *v.t.* to remove the earth from around (*plants*).
desaposentar, *v.t.* to turn out, drive out.
desaposesionar, *v.t.* to dispossess.
desapoyar, *v.t.* to remove support from.
desapreciar, *v.t.* not to value; to underestimate.
desaprecio, *n.m.* lack of appreciation, disregard.
desaprender, *v.t.* to unlearn.
desaprensar, *v.t.* to take the gloss off (*fabrics*); to ease, free from pressure.
desapretar [I], *v.t.* to slacken, loosen, loose; (*fig.*) to set at ease, free from anxiety.
desaprisionar, *v.t.* to release, set at liberty.
desaprobación, *n.f.* disapproval.
desaprobar [4], *v.t.* to disapprove (of).
desapropiación, desaprobamiento, *n.m.* renunciation, divesting (*of property*).
desapropio, *n.m.* alienation, transfer *or* divesting (*of property*).
desaprovechado, -da, *a.* lazy (*student*).
desaprovechamiento, *n.m.* backwardness; waste; negligence; ill-use, poor-use; lack of progress (*in studying*).
desaprovechar, *v.t.* to waste, misspend; to fail to make use of, fail to profit by, fail to take advantage of; ***desaprovechar una ocasión,*** to miss an opportunity. — *v.i.* to be backward, make small *or* no progress.
desapuntalar, *v.t.* to take away props *or* supports from.
desapuntar, *v.t.* to unstitch; to throw *or* put (*a gun*) out of aim.
desaquellarse, *v.r.* (*coll.*) to become disheartened.
desarbolar, *v.t.* to unmast, dismast.
desarbolo, *n.m.* unmasting.
desarenar, *v.t.* to clear of sand.
desareno, *n.m.* clearing of sand.
desarmador, *n.m.* trigger (*of gun*).
desarmadura, *n.f.*, **desarmamiento,** *n.m.* disarming, disarmament.
desarmar, *v.t.* to disarm; to dismantle; to dismount, take apart (*machines etc.*); (*naut.*) to lay up; to make (*a bull*) butt in the air. — *v.i.* to disarm.
desarme, *n.m.* disarming, disarmament.
desarraigar [B], *v.t.* to uproot; to eradicate, root out, extirpate; to expel.
desarraigo, *n.m.* eradication, uprooting.
desarrancarse [A], *v.r.* to desert, separate from a body *or* association.
desarrapado, -da, *a.* ragged.
desarrebozadamente, *adv.* frankly, openly.
desarrebozar [C], *v.t.* to unmuffle; to uncover, reveal.
desarrebujar, *v.t.* to disentangle, unbundle; uncover; to clear up.
desarreglado, -da, *a.* disarranged; disorderly, out of order; dishevelled, slovenly; irregular, unpredictable.
desarreglar, *v.t.* to upset, disorder, disarranage — **desarreglarse,** *v.r.* to lose one's regular habits.
desarreglo, *n.m.* disorder, disarrangement; irregularity; slovenliness.
desarrendar [I], *v.t.* to break, give up the lease of; to unbridle (*a horse*).
desarrimar, *v.t.* to remove, separate; to dissuade.
desarrimo, *n.m.* want of support.
desarrollar, *v.t.* to unroll, unfurl, unfold; (*fig.*) to develop; to expand; (*fig.*) to work out. — **desarrollarse,** *v.r.* to develop, grow, expand; to take place; ***la acción de la novela se desarrolla en Galicia,*** the action of the novel takes place (is set) in Galicia.
desarrollismo, *n.m.* growth *or* expansion ethos *or* policy.
desarrollo, *n.m.* development, growth, expansion.
desarropar, *v.t.* to uncover, unwrap.
desarrugar [B], *v.t.* to unwrinkle, take creases out of, smooth out; ***desarrugar el entrecejo,*** to unknit the brow.
desarrumar, *v.t.* to unstow, shift (*cargo*).
desarticulación, *n.f.* (*surg.*) disarticulation.
desarticular, *v.t.* to disarticulate; to disconnect (*machine etc.*).
desartillar, *v.t.* to take (*the guns*) out of (*a ship* or *fortress*).
desarzonar, *v.t.* to unhorse.
desasado, -da, *a.* without handles.
desaseado, -da, *a.* dirty, slovenly, untidy.
desasear, *v.t.* to (make) dirty.
desasegurar, *v.t.* to make unsteady; to cancel the insurance on.
desasentar [I], *v.t.* to displace, move, remove. — *v.i.* (*fig.*) to displease. — **desasentarse,** *v.r.* to stand up.
desaseo, *n.m.* uncleanliness, dirtiness; untidiness, slovenliness.
desasimiento, *n.m.* loosening, letting loose; (*fig.*) disinterest, disaffection; estrangement.
desasimilación, *n.f.* (*physiol.*) disassimilation.
desasir [12], *v.t.* to release, let go of. — **desasirse,** *v.r.* — ***de,*** to break *or* get loose *or* free from; to give up, relinquish.
desasnar, *v.t.* (*coll.*) to knock the rough edges off, give a little polish to, educate a little.
desasociable, *a.* unsociable.
desasociar, *v.t.* to disassociate, separate.
desasosegado, -da, *a.* uneasy, anxious.
desasosegar [IB], *v.t.* to make uneasy, anxious.
desasosiego, *n.m.* restlessness, uneasiness.
desastrado, -da, *a.*, *n.m.f.* wretched, unfortunate, miserable (person); ragged, battered, shabby (person).
desastre, *n.m.* disaster.
desastroso, -sa, *a.* disastrous.
desatacar [A], *v.t.* to loosen, untie, undo, unbutton, unclasp; to remove the wad from (*a firearm*); ***desatacar la escopeta,*** to draw the charge from a gun. — **desatacarse,** *v.r.* to unfasten one's trousers.
desatado, -da, *a.* frantic, crazy, in a mad rush.
desatador, -ra, *n.m.f.* one who loosens, unfastens *or* unties; absolver.
desatadura, *n.f.*, **desatamiento,** *n.m.* untying, loosening.
desatancar [A], *v.t.* to clear, unblock.
desatar, *v.t.* to loose, loosen, untie, unravel, unleash, unbind, unfasten, unhitch, undo (*a knot*); to solve; to dissolve, liquefy. — **desatarse,** *v.r.* to lose all restraint; ***desatarse en denuestos.***

to burst forth in abuse; ***se desató la tormenta,*** the storm burst.
desatascar [A], *v.t.* to free, clear, unblock, extricate.
desataviar [L], *v.t.* to strip of ornaments and decorations.
desatavío, *n.m.* untidiness, disarray.
desate, *n.m.* loosing, loosening; disorderly conduct; unrestrained talk; ***desate de vientre,*** looseness of the bowels.
desatención, *n.f.* lack of attention, inattention; disregard, disrespect.
desatender [2], *v.t.* to neglect; to disregard, ignore, take no notice of.
desatentado, -da, *a.* ill-advised, unwise; heedless wild.
desatentar [1], *v.t.* to perturb the mind of.
desatento, -ta, *a.* inattentive, careless; rude, unmannerly; heedless, thoughtless.
desaterrar [1], *v.t.* (*Hisp. Am.*) to free (*a mine*) from debris.
desatesorar, *v.t.* to remove *or* spend the treasure of.
desatiento, *n.m.* lack of sense of touch; restlessness, uneasiness.
desatierre, *n.m.* (*Hisp. Am., min.*) dumping ground.
desatinado, -da, *a.* crazy, preposterous, wild. — *n.m.* crazy *or* wild individual.
desatinar, *v.t.* to drive crazy. — *v.i.* to do *or* say crazy things; to go off the rails, go up the creek.
desatino, *n.m.* crazy *or* wild thing to do *or* say, utter nonsense, folly.
desatolondrarse, *v.r.* to pull o.s. together.
desatollar, *v.t.* to pull out of the mud *or* mire; to extricate.
desatontarse, *v.r.* to come down to earth, face facts.
desatorar, *v.t.* (*naut.*) to shift (*cargo*); (*min.*) to clear (*a gallery*).
desatornillar [DESTORNILLAR].
desatracar [A], *v.t., v.i.* (*naut.*) to cast off, move away.
desatraer [34], *v.t.* to separate, disjoin.
desatraillar [P], *v.t.* to unleash.
desatrampar, *v.t.* to clear.
desatrancar [A], *v.t.* to unbar, to clear.
desatufarse, *v.r.* to get some fresh air; to calm down, cool off.
desaturdirse, *v.r.* to pull o.s. together.
desautoridad, *n.f.* want of authority.
desautorización, *n.f.* withdrawal of authorization; disavowal.
desautorizadamente, *adv.* without authorization; in an unauthorized fashion.
desautorizar [C], *v.t.* to withdraw authority *or* authorization from; to deny, disavow; to ban, prohibit.
desavahar, *v.t.* to air, ventilate; to (allow to) cool. — **desavaharse,** *v.r* to relax, enjoy o.s.
desavecindado, -da, *a.* deserted, unoccupied.
desavecindarse, *v.r.* to move (*to another area*).
desavenencia, *n.f.* discord, disagreement, quarrel.
desavenir [36], *v.t.* to cause to fall out *or* quarrel. — **desavenirse,** *v.r.* to fall out, quarrel.
desaventajado, -da, *a.* disadvantageous; unfavourable; inferior; backward, slow.
desaviar [L], *v.t.* to mislead, lead astray; to strip of necessaries.
desavío, *n.m.* going astray; want of necessary means; inconvenience; ***me hace mucho desavío,*** it upsets my arrangements; it's a great nuisance.
desavisado, -da, *a.* unwary, innocent, naïve.
desavisar, *v.t.* to cancel, countermand, disavow.
desayudar, *v.t.* to refrain from assisting; to prevent from being aided.
desayunar, *v.i.* to (have) breakfast; ***estoy (vengo) desayunado,*** I've (already) had breakfast. — **desayunarse,** *v.r.* — ***de,*** (*coll.*) to hear (about), get news (of); ***ahora me desayuno de ello,*** this is the first I've heard of it, it's news to me, (it seems that) I'm the last one to hear about it.
desayuno, *n.m.* breakfast.
desazogar [B], *v.t.* to take the quicksilver backing from (*a mirror*).
desazón, *n.m.* insipidity, want of taste *or* flavour; anxiety, uneasiness, discomfort, restlessness; strained atmosphere; unfitness *or* unsuitability of soil.
desazonar, *v.t.* to render tasteless; to annoy; to cause discomfort *or* uneasiness in. — **desazonarse,** *v.r.* to become uneasy *or* off-colour.
desbabar(se), *v.i.,* (*v.r.*) to drivel, slaver.
desbagar [B], *v.t.* to extract (*flax-seed*) from the capsule.
desbancar [A], *v.t.* to win all the money from; to clear of benches; to oust, unseat; ***desbancar al casino,*** to break the bank.
desbandada, *n.f.* (*mil.*) disbandment; rout; ***a la desbandada,*** in disorder, in rout, helter-skelter.
desbandarse, *v.r.* to disband, flee in disorder, break up, scatter.
desbarajustar, *v.t.* to throw into disorder *or* confusion.
desbarajuste, *n.m.* disorder, chaos, shambles, muddle, mess.
desbaratadamente, *adv.* in disorder.
desbaratado, -da, *a.* (*coll.*) debauched; in disorder.
desbaratador, -ra, *n.m.f.* destroyer; debaucher.
desbaratamiento, *n.m.* disorder, chaos.
desbaratar, *v.t.* to ruin, spoil, wreck; to thwart; to rout, throw into confusion; to take to pieces; to squander. — *v.i.* to talk nonsense. — **desbaratarse,** *v.r.* to go to pieces.
desbarate, desbarato, *n.m.* rout(ing), smash(ing); disorder; waste, squandering; ***desbarate de vientre,*** loose bowels.
desbarbado, -da, *a.* beardless.
desbarbar, *v.t.* (*coll.*) to shave; to trim; to cut off filaments from.
desbarbillar, *v.t.* to prune the roots of (*young vines*).
desbardar, *v.t.* to unthatch.
desbarrar, *v.i.* to throw, hurl, fling an iron bar (*sport*); (*fig.*) to ramble, get off the point; to talk nonsense, act foolishly.
desbarretar, *v.t.* to unbolt, unbar.
desbarrigado, -da, *a.* little-bellied.
desbarrigar [B], *v.t.* (*coll.*) to rip open the belly of, disembowel.
desbarro, *n.m.* nonsense, craziness, stupidity.
desbastador, *n.m.* chisel, hewer, paring-tool.
desbastadura, *n.f.* planing, trimming, polishing, hewing.
desbastar, *v.t.* to plane down, smooth down, roughdress, trim, remove the rough parts from; to wear down, use up; (*fig.*) to take the rough edges off; (*fig.*) give a little education, refinement *or* polish to.
desbaste, *n.m.* roughdressing, smoothing down; refining.
desbastecido, -da [DESABASTECIDO].
desbautizarse [C], *v.r.* (*coll.*) to get annoyed *or* impatient.
desbazadero, *n.m.* wet, slippery place.
desbeber, *v.i.* (*coll.*) to discharge urine.
desbecerrar, *v.t.* to wean (*calves*).
desblanquecido, -da, desblanquiñado, -da, *a.* blanched, bleached, off-white.
desbloquear, *v.t.* (*com.*) to unfreeze.
desbocado, -da, *a.* wide-mouthed (*cannon*); broken-faced (*tool*); broken-lipped *or* edged (*jar*);

wild, frantic, amuck; runaway (*horse*); (*fig.*) foul-mouthed.

desbocamiento, *n.m.* running away (*horses*); foul-mouthedness.

desbocar [A], *v.t.* to break the brim of (*a jug, mug* or *other vessel*); ***este abrigo tiene desbocado el cuello,*** this overcoat sags open at the neck. — *v.i.* to disembogue. — **desbocarse,** *v.r.* to take the bit between the teeth, run away, run riot, bolt; to start using foul language, let o.s. go.

desbonetarse, *v.r.* (*coll.*) to take off one's cap.

desboquillar, *v.t.* to break the mouth of (*a vessel*); to break *or* remove the stem of (*a pipe etc.*); to break the nozzle of.

desbordamiento, *n.m.* overflowing.

desbordante, *a.* overflowing.

desbordar, *v.i.* to overflow, run over. — **desbordarse,** *v.r.* to overflow; (*fig.*) to run riot, break all bounds.

desbornizar [C], *v.t.* to take the cork from (*trees*).

desborrar, *v.t.* to burl (*cloth*); to cut *or* lop off.

desbotonar, *v.t.* (*Cub.*) to cut the buds of (*tobacco plants*).

desbozar [C], *v.t.* to clear.

desbragado, -da, *a.* (*contempt.*) unbreeched. — *n.m.f.* one of the dispossessed, wretch.

desbraguetado, -da, *a.* having the fore part of the breeches unbuttoned and open.

desbravador, *n.m.* horse-breaker.

desbravar, desbravecer [9], *v.t.* to tame, break in (*horses*). — *v.i.* to moderate, diminish in strength, abate. — **desbravarse, desbravecerse,** *v.r.* to moderate.

desbrazarse [C], *v.r.* to extend one's arms violently.

desbrevarse, *v.r.* to lose body and strength (*wine*).

desbridar, *v.t.* (*surg.*) to debride.

desbriznar, *v.t.* to shred; to cut up small; to string (*beans*); to pluck the stamens of.

desbroce, *n.m.* clearing (away).

desbrozar [C], *v.t.* to clear.

desbrozo, *n.m.* clearing (away); rubbish cleared.

desbruar, *v.t.* to clean of grease.

desbrujar, *v.t.* to crumble, break up small.

desbuchar [DESEMBUCHAR].

desbulla, *n.f.* part of an oyster remaining on the shell.

desbullador, *n.m.* oyster-fork.

desbullar, *v.t.* to extract (*an oyster*) from its shell.

desca, *n.f.* (*naut.*) tar-pot.

descabal, *a.* imperfect, incomplete.

descabalar, *v.t.* to make incomplete; to take away a part of; to spoil a set of (*e.g. china*).

descabalgadura, *n.f.* dismounting (*from a horse*).

descabalgar [B], *v.t.* to dismount (*gun*). — *v.i.* to dismount (*from a horse*).

descabellado, -da, *a.* wild, crazy, hare-brained, preposterous.

descabellamiento, *n.m.* absurdity.

descabellar(se), *v.t.* (*v.r.*) to dishevel, tousle, rumple (*hair*); to kill (*a bull*) by stabbing in the back of the neck.

descabello, *n.m.* killing (*a bull*) by stabbing in the back of the neck.

descabestrar, *v.t.* to unhalter.

descabezamiento, *n.m.* beheading; lopping off; racking of brain.

descabezar [C], *v.t.* to behead; to lop the top off; to begin to overcome; ***descabezar un sueño,*** to have a snooze *or* nap. — **descabezarse,** *v.r.* (*coll.*) to cudgel *or* rack one's brains; to shed the grain (*cereals*).

descabritar, *v.t.* to wean (*kids*).

descabullirse [J] [ESCABULLIRSE].

descacilar, descafilar, *v.t.* to trim (*bricks*).

descachar, *v.t.* (*Hisp. Am.*) to cut off the horns of (*an animal*).

descachazar [C], *v.t.* (*Hisp. Am.*) to remove the froth from (*boiling cane juice*).

descaderar, *v.t.* to injure the hip of.

descadillar, *v.t.* to cut off the loose ends of (*the warp*).

descaecer [9], *v.i.* to decline, languish; (*naut.*) to edge away.

descaecido, -da, *a.* weak, feeble, languishing.

descaecimiento, descaimiento, *n.m.* weakness, debility, decay, languor.

descalabazarse [C], *v.r.* (*coll.*) to rack one's brains.

descalabradura, *n.f.* wound in the head.

descalabrar, *v.t.* to wound in the head; to hurt, injure; to cause loss to. — **descalabrarse,** *v.r.* to hurt *or* cut one's head.

descalabro, *n.m.* disaster, great loss, calamity.

descalandrajar, *v.t.* to rip *or* tear to shreds.

descalar, *v.t.* to unship (*the helm*).

descalcador, *n.m.* (*naut.*) rave-hook; (*carp.*) claw.

descalcar [A], *v.t.* to remove (the) old oakum from (*seams*).

descalce, *n.m.* (*agric.*) baring (*root of a tree*); undermining.

descalcez, *n.f.* barefootedness.

descalcificación, *n.f.* decalcification.

descalificación, *n.f.* disqualification; discrediting.

descalificar [A], *v.t.* to disqualify; to discredit.

descalostrado, -da, *a.* having passed the days of the first milk.

descalzado, -da, *a.* having receded gums (*teeth*).

descalzador, *n.m.* bootjack; crowbar.

descalzamiento, *n.m.* taking off (*shoes etc.*); (*agric.*) baring.

descalzar [C], *v.t.* to take off the shoes and/or stockings of; (*agric.*) to bare; to unwedge; to undermine. — **descalzarse,** *v.r.* to take off one's shoes and/or stockings; to lose a shoe (*horses*).

descalzo, -za, *a.* barefooted; discalced (*friars and nuns*).

descamación, *n.f.* (*med.*) desquamation.

descambiar, *v.t.* to return (*sth. already exchanged*), swap back again.

descaminar, *v.t.* to lead astray, mislead; to seize; ***no anda descaminado del todo,*** he is not altogether on the wrong lines. — **descaminarse,** *v.r.* to go astray, lose the way; to go off the track.

descamino, *n.m.* leading *or* going astray; aberration; seizure; goods seized.

descamisado, -da, *a.* shirtless; destitute. — ***n.m.f.*** one of the dispossessed *or* underprivileged, underdog.

descampado, -da, *a.* bare, clear, open. — ***n.m.*** wasteland, waste *or* bare ground; ***en descampado,*** in (the) open country.

descansadamente, *adv.* in a leisurely manner.

descansadero, *n.m.* resting-place.

descansado, -da, *a.* quiet, tranquil, leisurely; ***vida descansada,*** quiet, easy life.

descansar, *v.t.* to rest, lean. — *v.i.* to rest; to pause.

descansillo, *n.m.* landing (*of a staircase*).

descanso, *n.m.* rest; pause, break, interval; (*theat.*) interval, (*Am.*) intermission; aid; landing; (*mech.*) resting-place, support; (*mil.*) ***en su lugar, descanso,*** parade rest, stand at ease.

descantar, *v.t.* to clear of stones.

descantear, *v.t.* to smooth corners *or* angles of; to splay, chamfer, edge.

descanterar, *v.t.* to cut the crusts off (*bread*).

descantillar, descantonar, *v.t.* to break the end *or* edge of, chip; to take away a part of.

descantillón [ESCANTILLÓN].

descañar, *v.t.* to break the stem of.

descañonar, *v.t.* to pluck out the feathers of; to shave close; (*fig.*) to fleece, skin.

descaperuzar [C], *v.t.* to take off the cowl *or* hood of.
descaperuzo, *n.m.* taking off the cowl, hood *or* hunting-cap.
descapillar, *v.t.* to take off the hood of.
descarado, -da, *a.* brazen, barefaced, cheeky, saucy.
descararse, *v.r.* to start being cheeky *or* impudent; to make o.s. unpleasantly clear.
descarbonatar, descarburar, *v.t.* to decarbonize.
descarga, *n.f.* discharge; unburdening, unloading; round, volley, firing; exoneration; ***descarga de aduana,*** customs clearance; ***descarga cerrada,*** volley.
descargadero, *n.m.* wharf, unloading-place.
descargador, *n.m.* discharger, unloader, stevedore, lighterman; (*artill.*) wad-hook.
descargadura, *n.f.* bones which a butcher removes from meat.
descargar [B], *v.t.* to discharge; to unload, disburden, lighten, ease; to empty; to remove the flap and bones of (*meat*); (*naut.*) to brace (*alee*); to clear (*the sails* or *yards*); to lay on, inflict (*blows*); ***descargar la conciencia,*** to unburden *or* ease one's conscience; ***descargar la ira en alguien,*** to vent one's anger upon s.o. — *v.i.* to flow, empty (into); to burst (*a storm*). — **descargarse,** *v.r.* to clear o.s. (*of a charge*); to resign; ***descargarse de algo en alguien,*** to unload sth. on s.o.
descargo, *n.m.* unloading, unburdening; acquittal, discharge; (*law*) plea, answer to an impeachment; (*com.*) acquittance, receipt, release, discharge; ***en descargo de mi conciencia,*** for the satisfaction of my conscience; ***testigo de descargo,*** witness for the defence; ***en su descargo,*** in his favour, in justification of him.
descargue, *n.m.* unloading.
descariñarse, *v.r.* to lose affection (for), cool (towards).
descariño, *n.m.* coolness, loss of affection.
descarnado, -da, *a.* thin, lean; bare; blunt, outspoken. — *n.f.* (*personification of*) death.
descarnador, *n.m.* scraper.
descarnadura, *n.f.* divesting of flesh.
descarnar, *v.t.* to remove *or* scrape the flesh from; to lay bare; (*fig.*) to remove from earthly things. — **descarnarse,** *v.r.* to lose flesh, get thin.
descaro, *n.m.* impudence, effrontery, barefacedness, sauciness, cheekiness.
descarriamiento [DESCARRÍO].
descarriar, *v.t.* to lead astray, mislead, misguide; to cut out (*cattle*). — **descarriarse,** *v.r.* to go astray, go off the track; (*fig.*) to go wrong.
descarrilamiento, *n.m.* derailment.
descarrilar, *v.t.* to derail, send off the rails. — *v.i.* to run off the rails, jump the track. — **descarrilarse,** *v.r.* (*coll.*, *fig.*) to get off the track, go off the rails.
descarrío, *n.m.* going astray, losing one's way.
descartar, *v.t.* to discard, dismiss, brush aside; ***esto queda descartado,*** this is out. — **descartarse,** *v.r.* to discard (*at cards*); to excuse o.s.; to shirk.
descarte, *n.m.* cards discarded (*from a hand*); evasion, shirking; rejection, casting aside.
descasamiento, *n.m.* separation.
descasar, *v.t.* to separate, disunite; (*print.*) to upset the position of. — **descasarse,** *v.r.* to separate.
descascar [A], *v.t.* [DESCASCARAR]. — **descascarse,** *v.r.* to break to pieces; (*coll.*) to brag.
descascarador, -ra, *n.m.f.* huller, husker.
descascarar, *v.t.* to peel, shell, shuck.
descascarillar, *v.t.* to peel, remove shell of. — **descascarillarse,** *v.r.* to peel *or* flake off.
descaspar, *v.t.* to remove dandruff from.
descasque, *n.m.* decortication (*particularly of the cork-tree*).
descastado, -da, *a.* cold, lacking in affection.
descastar, *v.t.* to exterminate, wipe out. — **descastarse,** *v.r.* to cut off family ties.
descatolizar [C], *v.t.* to cause to abandon Catholicism.
descaudalado, -da, *a.* penniless.
descebar, *v.t.* to unprime (*firearms*).
descendencia, *n.f.* descent; descendants, issue.
descendente, *a.* descending, (coming) down.
descender [2], *v.i.* to descend, to come, go *or* flow down; (*fig.*) to stoop (to); to drop, fall (*temperature*).
descendiente, *a.* descending. — *n.m.* descendant, offspring.
descendimiento, *n.m.* descent, taking down, lowering.
descensión, *n.f.* descent, coming down.
descenso, *n.m.* descent; lowering; fall, drop; decline.
descentrado, -da, *a.* off-centre, off-beam; all-at-sea; unadapted.
descentralización, *n.f.* decentralization.
descentralizador, -ra, *a.* decentralizing. — *n.m.f.* decentralizer.
descentralizar [C], *v.t.* to decentralize.
descentrar, *v.t.* to uncentre, knock off centre; (*coll.*) to put off one's stroke, leave all at sea.
desceñidura, *n.f.* ungirding, loosening.
desceñir [8K], *v.t.* to ungird, take off (*girdle, belt, crown*).
descepar, *v.t.* to pull up by the roots; to eradicate, extirpate; (*naut.*) to remove the stocks from (*an anchor*).
descerar, *v.t.* to take the empty combs from (*a beehive*).
descercado, -da, *a.* open, unfenced.
descercador, *n.m.* one who forces the enemy to raise a siege.
descercar [A], *v.t.* to tear *or* pull down the wall *or* fence of; to raise the siege of; to force the enemy to raise the siege of.
descerezar [C], *v.t.* (*Hisp. Am.*) to pulp (*coffee berry*).
descerrajado, -da, *a.* (*coll.*) wicked, evil.
descerrajadura, *n.f.* forcing, wrenching off locks *or* bolts.
descerrajar, *v.t.* to burst *or* force open; (*coll.*) ***le descerrajaron un tiro,*** they let him have it, shot him.
descerrumarse, *v.r.* (*vet.*) to wrench the pastern joint (*horses*).
descervigar [B], *v.t.* to twist the neck of.
descifrable, *a.* decipherable.
descifrador, -ra, *n.m.f.* decipherer.
descifrar, *v.t.* to decipher; to decode; (*fig.*) to unravel.
descimbramiento, *n.m.* (*arch.*) removing the centering.
descimbrar, *v.t.* (*arch.*) to remove the centering of.
descimentar, *v.t.* to demolish the foundations of.
descinchar, *v.t.* to ungirth.
desclavador, *n.m.* nail-puller; claw-wrench.
desclavar, *v.t.* to remove the nails from; to remove (*gems*) from a setting.
descoagulación, *n.f.* decoagulation.
descoagulante, *a.* decoagulating.
descoagular(se), *v.t.* (*v.r.*) to decoagulate.
descobajar, *v.t.* to separate (*grapes*) from the stem.
descobijar, *v.t.* to uncover, deprive of shelter.
descocado, -da, *a.* (*coll.*) brazen, barefaced, shameless.
descocar [A], *v.t.* to clean, clear insects from (trees). — **descocarse,** *v.r.* (*coll.*) to become *or* get brazen.
descocedura, *n.f.* digestion.
descocer [5D], *v.t.* to digest.

descoco, *n.m.* cheek, barefacedness, boldness, brazenness.
descodar, *v.t.* (*prov.*) to unstitch, rip.
descoger [E], *v.t.* to spread, extend, unfold.
descogollar, *v.t.* to take out the heart from; to strip (*a tree*) of shoots.
descogotado, -da, *a.* with the neck exposed, low-necked.
descogotar, *v.t.* to knock *or* cut the horns off (*a stag*).
descolar, *v.t.* to dock, cut off tail of; (*carp.*) to unglue.
descolchar, *v.t.* (*naut.*) to untwist (*a cable*).
descolgar [4B], *v.t.* to unhang, take down, let down. — **descolgarse,** *v.r.* to let o.s. down, come down, slip down; to come out (with); to appear suddenly *or* unexpectedly, show up, turn up.
descoligado, -da, *adj.* not belonging to a league; non-union.
descolmar, *v.t.* to level off; (*fig.*) to diminish.
descolmillar, *v.t.* to pull out *or* break the eye-teeth, fangs *or* tusks of.
descolocar, *v.t.* to put out of place; to lay off (*from work*).
descoloramiento, *n.m.* fading; discolouration.
descolorar, *v.t.* to bleach, fade; to discolour.
descolorido, -da, *a.* bleached, faded; discoloured.
descolorimiento, *n.m.* fading; discoloration.
descolorir, *v.t.* to bleach, fade; to discolour.
descolladamente, *adv.* loftily, haughtily.
descollado, -da, *a.* lofty, haughty; outstanding.
descollamiento [DESCUELLO (I)].
descollante, *a.* outstanding.
descollar [4], *v.i.* to stand out, be outstanding, tower (above).
descombrar, *v.t.* to clear, clear of debris.
descombro, *n.m.* clearing.
descomedido, -da, *a.* excessive, disproportionate; beyond all bounds; rude, insolent.
descomedimiento, *n.m.* rudeness, incivility.
descomedirse [8], *v.r.* to be rude *or* disrespectful; to forget o.s.
descomer, *v.i.* (*coll.*) to defecate.
descomodidad, *n.f.* discomfort; inconvenience.
descompadrar, *v.t.* to cause to fall out. — *v.i.* to fall out.
descompás, *n.m.* excess; want of measure *or* proportion.
descompasado, -da, *a.* excessive, disproportionate; out of time *or* tune; beyond rule *or* measure.
descompasarse, *v.r.* to go beyond bounds, go too far, be excessive.
descompletar, *v.t.* to render incomplete.
descomponer [25], *v.t.* to decompose; to put out of order; to disturb, unsettle, upset; to set at odds; to break up *or* down. — **descomponerse,** *v.r.* to decompose, rot; to get out of order, become upset; to show (deep) emotion (*in the face*); to lose one's temper, lose control; (*coll.*) to go to the dogs; to change for the worse (*weather*).
descomposición, *n.f.* decomposition, rotting; separation, analysis; breaking up *or* down; (*fig.*) discomposure; ***descomposición de vientre,*** looseness of bowels.
descompostura, *n.f.* slovenliness, untidiness; lack of restraint; want of modesty; disrespectful conduct; illness.
descompuesto, -ta, *a.* impudent, insolent.
descomulgado, -da, *a.* wicked, perverse.
descomulgador, *n.m.* excommunicator.
descomulgar [B], *v.t.* to excommunicate.
descomunal, *a.* monstrous, enormous, huge, colossal.
descomunión, *n.f.* excommunication.
desconcertado, -da, *a.* disorderly.
desconcertador, -ra, *n.m.f.* disturber, disconcerter.
desconcertadura, *n.f.* discomposure, disturbance, confusion.
desconcertante, *a.* disconcerting, baffling, bewildering, perplexing.
desconcertar [I], *v.t.* to disorder, upset; to disconcert, baffle, bewilder, perplex; (*anat.*) to dislocate. — **desconcertarse,** *v.r.* to be disconcerted; ***se desconcertó al verme,*** he was put out *or* taken aback at seeing me.
desconcierto, *n.m.* disorder, chaos, confusion, muddle; perplexity, bewilderment.
desconcordia, *n.f.* discord, disagreement.
desconchado, *n.m.* part of wall from which plaster has fallen, flaked *or* peeled off; ***la pared tiene muchos desconchados,*** the plaster is falling off the wall everywhere.
desconchadura, *n.f.* falling off, peeling (*plaster, glaze*).
desconchar, *v.t.* to strip of plaster *or* glaze.
desconchón [DESCONCHADO].
desconectar, *v.t.* to disconnect, cut off. — **desconectarse,** *v.r.* (*fig., fam.*) to switch off, put the shutters up.
desconfiado, -da, *a.* distrustful, suspicious.
desconfianza, *n.f.* distrust, mistrust; suspicion.
desconfiar [L], *v.i.* — ***de,*** to distrust, mistrust, be suspicious of; to have little hope; ***desconfío de que salga bien,*** I doubt whether *or* I have little hope that it will turn out all right.
desconformar, *v.i.* to dissent, disagree, differ in opinion. — **desconformarse,** *v.r.* to fall out.
desconforme [DISCONFORME].
descongelar, *v.t.* to defrost, unfreeze.
descongestión, *n.f.* decongestion.
decongestionar, *v.t.* to decongest, clear; to ease pressure on.
desconocer [9], *v.t.* not to know; to be unaware of; not to recognize; to pretend not to know; to disavow; ***Madrid está desconocido,*** Madrid has changed out of all recognition, you wouldn't know *or* recognize Madrid now; ***me desconoció,*** he ignored me.
desconocido, -da, *a.* unknown, unfamiliar, strange. — *n.m.f.* stranger.
desconocimiento, *n.m.* ignorance; unawareness; ungratefulness.
desconsiderado, -da, *a.* inconsiderate, thoughtless; rash.
desconsiderar, *v.t.* to be inconsiderate to, have no regard for.
desconsolación, *n.f.* [DESCONSUELO (I)].
desconsolado, -da, *a.* disconsolate, grief-stricken.
desconsolar [4], *v.t.* to distress, grieve.
desconsuelo (I), *n.m.* affliction, grief, sorrow; empty feeling (*in stomach*); ***es un desconsuelo verlo,*** it's heart-breaking to see it.
desconsuelo (2), **desconsuele,** *pres. indic.*; *pres. subj.* [DESCONSOLAR].
descontagiar, *v.t.* to disinfect.
descontar [4], *v.t.* to discount, deduct; ***dar por descontado,*** to take for granted; ***por descontado que,*** needless to say.
descontendadizo, -za, *a.* hard to please, fussy.
descontentamiento, *n.m.* [DESCONTENTO].
descontentar, *v.t.* to discontent, displease, dissatisfy.
descontento, -ta, *a.* discontented, dissatisfied, displeased. — *n.m.* discontent, dissatisfaction, displeasure.
descontinuación [DISCONTINUIDAD].
descontinuar [M] [DISCONTINUAR].
descontinuo, -nua [DISCONTINUO].
desconvenible, *a.* disagreeing.
desconvenir [36], *v.i.* to disagree; not to match, not to suit.

desconversable, *a.* unsociable, retiring.
desconvidar, *v.t.* to cancel an invitation to.
descopar, *v.t.* to lop the top off.
descorazonado, -da, *a.* disheartened, dejected, dispirited.
descorazonamiento, *n.m.* low spirits, down-heartedness, despondency.
descorazonar, *v.t.* to tear out the heart of; to dishearten, discourage.
descorchador, *n.m.* decorticator; uncorker; cork-screw.
descorchar, *v.t.* to decorticate; to uncork; to break open.
descordar [4], *v.t.* [DESENCORDAR]; to kill (*bull*) by stabbing it in the cervix.
descorderar, *v.t.* to deprive (*ewes*) of their lambs.
descornar [4], *v.t.* to dishorn. — **descornarse,** *v.r.* (*coll.*) to rack one's brains.
descoronar, *v.t.* to take the top *or* crown from; uncrown.
descorrear, *v.i.* to shed the velvet of the antlers.
descorregido, -da, *a.* incorrect; disarranged.
descorrer, *v.t.* to draw back, open; to run back over. — *v.i.* to drip, trickle.
descorrimiento, *n.m.* dripping, trickling.
descortés, *a.* impolite, uncivil, unmannerly, rude.
descortesía, *n.f.* discourtesy, impoliteness, incivility, rudeness.
descortezador, *n.m.* decorticator.
descortezadura, *n.f.*, **descortezamiento,** *n.m.* decortication, excortication; bark taken off.
descortezar [C], *v.t.* to bark, strip of bark; to peel; to remove the crust of; (*fig.*) to give a little polish *or* education to.
descortinar, *v.t.* to destroy the ramparts of.
descosedura, *n.f.* ripping, unseaming.
descoser, *v.t.* to rip, unstitch, unseam; to disjoin, separate; (*naut.*) to unlash; ***no descoser los labios,*** not to say a word. — **descoserse,** *v.r.* to let one's tongue run on; (*coll.*) to break wind.
descosido, *n.m.* babbler, prater; rip, torn seam; ***como un descosido,*** eagerly, avidly, wildly.
descostarse, *v.r.* to draw away (from).
descostillar, *v.t.* to unrib; to break the ribs of; to beat on the ribs. — **descostillarse,** *v.r.* to fall violently on one's back.
descostrar, *v.t.* to remove the crust *or* scab from.
descotar, *v.t.* [ESCOTAR (1)].
descote [ESCOTE].
descoyuntamiento, *n.m.* dislocation; (*coll.*) being knocked up.
descoyuntar, *v.t.* dislocate, disjoint; to put out of gear; (*fig.*) to get on the nerves of. — **descoyuntarse,** *v.r.* to get out of joint; ***descoyuntarse de risa,*** to split one's sides with laughter.
descrecencia, *n.f.* [DECREMENTO].
descrecer [9], *v.t., v.i.* [DECRECER].
descrecimiento [DECREMENTO].
descrédito, *n.m.* discredit, loss of reputation.
descreer [N], *v.t.* to disbelieve.
descreído, -da, *a.* unbelieving. — *n.m.f.* unbeliever.
descreimiento, *n.m.* unbelief.
descremar, *v.t.* to skim (*milk*).
descrestar, *v.t.* to remove the crest *or* comb from; (*Hisp. Am., coll.*) to cheat, take in.
descriarse [L], *v.r.* to weaken, pine, waste away.
describir [*p.p.* **descrito**], *v.t.* to describe.
descripción, *n.f.* description, word-picture; (*law*) inventory, schedule.
descriptivo, -va, *a.* descriptive.
descriptor, -ra, *a., n.m.f.* (person) describing.
decrismar, *v.t.* (*eccles.*) to remove the chrism from; (*coll.*) to clout on the head. — **descrismarse,** *v.r.* (*coll.*) to crack one's skull; (*coll.*) to get ratty; to rack one's brains.
descristianar, *v.t.* to dechristianize.
descruzar [C], *v.t.* to uncross.
descuadernar, *v.t.* to unbind (*books*); to dismember, pull apart.
descuadrillado, *n.m.* (*vet.*) sprain (*in the haunch*).
descuadrillarse, *v.r.* to sprain the haunches (*horses*); to get cut off from the main party *or* body.
descuajar, *v.t.* to decoagulate, unclot; to uproot, root out; to dishearten.
descuajaringarse [B], *v.r.* (*coll.*) to come apart at the joints, fall to pieces; (*coll.*) to get knocked up; ***descuajaringarse de risa,*** to split one's sides laughing.
descuaje, descuajo, *n.m.* (*agric.*) uprooting, rooting out.
descuartelar, *v.t.* (*mil.*) to remove (*troops*) from barracks; (*naut.*) to unfurl (*sails*).
descuartizamiento, *n.m.* quartering; breaking *or* cutting in pieces; carving up.
descuartizar [C], *v.t.* to carve (up).
descubierto, -ta, *a.* patent, manifest; bareheaded, exposed. — *n.m.* exposition of the Sacrament; overdraft; ***al descubierto,*** in the open; defenceless; (*com.*) ***en descubierto,*** overdrawn; ***girar en descubierto,*** to utter a false cheque; ***dejar al descubierto,*** to lay bare; ***quedarse al descubierto,*** to be left in an exposed position. — *n.f.* crustless pie; (*mil.*) reconnaissance, reconnoitring; (*naut.*) scanning of the horizon; ***a la descubierta,*** openly, in the open.
descubridero, *n.m.* eminence (*commanding an extensive view*); lookout post.
descubridor, -ra, *n.m.f.* discoverer, finder; (*mil.*) scout.
descubrimiento, *n.m.* discovery; disclosure.
descubrir [*p.p.* **descubierto**], *v.t.* to discover, find out; to uncover, disclose, reveal; to disclose, make known; to descry, make out. — **descubrirse,** *v.r.* to uncover one's head, take one's hat off.
descuello (1), *n.m.* loftiness, haughtiness; overtopping; pre-eminence, superiority.
descuello (2), *pres. indic.* [DESCOLLAR].
descuento, *n.m.* discount; deduction.
descuernacabras, *n.m. inv.* cold north wind.
descuidado, -da, *a.* careless, negligent; unprepared, off one's guard.
descuidar, *v.t.* to neglect, forget, overlook; to relieve from care; to divert the attention of. — *v.i.* to be careless; ***descuida, lo haré yo,*** don't worry, I'll do it; ***descuide usted,*** have no fear. — **descuidarse,** *v.r.* to be careless; ***como te descuides, perderás el tren,*** if you are not careful *or* if you don't watch out, you'll miss the train.
descuidero, *n.m.* pickpocket.
descuido, *n.m.* carelessness, neglect, negligence, forgetfulness, want of attention; oversight, slip; ***al descuido,*** casually, nonchalantly.
descuitado, -da, *a.* carefree.
descular, *v.t.* to break the bottom *or* end of.
deschavetarse, *v.r.* (*Hisp. Am., coll.*) to go screwy *or* nuts.
deschuponar, *v.t.* (*agric.*) to strip (*a tree*) of its shoots *or* suckers.
desdar, *v.t.* to turn in the opposite direction; to turn in an anticlockwise direction; to unwind.
desde, *conj.* ***desde que,*** since. — *prep.* from; since, after; ***desde . . . hasta,*** from . . . to, as far as; ***desde ahora,*** from now on; ***desde entonces,*** from then on, ever since; ***desde luego,*** of course; at once, from the start; ***desde niño,*** from one's childhood; ***desde hace un año,*** for a year past.
desdecir [17], *v.t.* to belie, contradict, gainsay. — *v.i.* to be unworthy (***de,*** of); ***este tomo no desdice en absoluto de los anteriores,*** this volume is in no way inferior to the preceding ones.

— **desdecirse,** *v.r.* to take one's words back; to go back on what one has said.
desdén, *n.m.* disdain, contempt, scorn; slight; ***con desdén,*** contemptuously, slightingly; ***al desdén,*** with studied neglect, casually.
desdentado, -da, *a.* toothless — *n.m.pl.* (**desdentados**) (*zool.*) edentates.
desdentar [I], *v.t.* to draw the teeth of.
desdeñable, *a.* contemptible, despicable; negligible; ***una cantidad no desdeñable,*** a sum not to be scorned, a not inconsiderable sum.
desdeñadamente, *adv.* disdainfully, scornfully.
desdeñador, -ra, *n.m.f.* scorner, disdainer.
desdeñar, *v.t.* to disdain, scorn, ignore. — **desdeñarse,** *v.r.* to disdain, scorn (to); not to deign (to).
desdeñoso, -sa, *a.* disdainful, contemptuous.
desdevanar, *v.t.* to unwind.
desdibujarse, *v.r.* to get blurred, faded, shadowy, vague, indeterminate.
desdicha (I), *n.f.* misfortune, adversity; misery.
desdichado, -da, *a.* unfortunate, luckless, hapless, sorry, wretched. — *n.m.f.* sorry creature, wretch; (*coll.*) ***es un desdichado,*** he is a pitiful creature.
desdicho, -cha (2), *p.p.* [DESDECIR].
desdinerar, *v.t.* to impoverish, drain of money.
desdoblamiento, *n.m.* unfolding; splitting; ***desdoblamiento de (la) personalidad,*** split personality.
desdoblar, *v.t.* to unfold, split.
desdonado, -da, *a.* graceless, insipid, dull.
desdonar, *v.t.* to take back a gift from.
desdoncellar, *v.t.* to deflower.
desdorar, *v.t.* to take the gilt off; (*fig.*) to tarnish, sully.
desdoro, *n.m.* dishonour, blemish, blot, stigma.
deseable, *a.* desirable.
deseado, -da, *a.* desired, wish for.
deseador, -ra, *n.m.f.* desirer, wisher.
desear, *v.t.* to desire, wish for; ***estoy deseando que llegue,*** I'm looking forward to his arrival, longing for him to get here.
desecación, *n.f.* exsiccation, desiccation.
desecamiento, *n.m.* desiccation, exsiccation; drying, draining.
desecante, *a.* drying. — *n.m.f.* (*chem.*) dryer, desiccator.
desecar [A], *v.t.* to desiccate, dry (up); to drain.
desecativo, -va, *a.* desiccative, exsiccant. — *n.m.* healing plaster.
desecha, *n.f.* coda.
desechadamente, *adv.* vilely, despicably.
desechar, *v.t.* to reject, throw out; to cast aside, cast out; to refuse, exclude; to unlock, unfasten (*keys*); ***lo que uno desecha, otro lo ruega,*** one man's meat is another man's poison.
desecho, *n.m.* rejected item *or* article; (*pl.*) scraps, dregs, debris; rubbish.
desedificación, *n.f.* scandal, evil example.
desedificar [A], *v.t.* to set a bad example to, scandalize.
deseguida, *adv.* (*coll.*) at once, straight away.
desejecutar, *v.t.* (*law*) to exonerate (*a debtor*).
deselectrizar [C], *v.t.* (*elec.*) to discharge; to de-electrify; disconnect.
deselladura, *n.f.* unsealing.
desellar, *v.t.* to unseal.
desembalaje, *n.m.* unpacking.
desembalar, *v.t.* to unpack.
desembaldosar, *v.t.* to unpave, untile.
desembanastar, *v.t.* to unpack, uncrate; (*coll.*) to draw (*a sword*). — *v.i.* (*coll.*) to prate. — **desembanastarse,** *v.r.* to break out, break loose; (*coll.*) to alight (*from a carriage*).
desembarazado, -da, *a.* free, unencumbered, easy, free and easy; nonchalant; clear, open, unrestrained; ***modales desembarazados,*** easy manners.
desembarazar [C], *v.t.* to free; to remove an impediment from, clear, extricate, disencumber; to vacate, clear out from. — **desembarazarse,** *v.r.* to get rid (***de,*** of); (*Hisp. Am.*) to give birth.
desembarazo, *n.m.* disembarrassment, disencumbrance, ease; nonchalance; extrication.
desembarcadero, *n.m.* landing-place; quay, wharf.
desembarcar [A], *v.t.* to unship, unload; to disembark. — *v.i.* to disembark, land, go ashore; to end (at a landing) (*staircase*).
desembarco, *n.m.* disembarkation, landing; unshipment, unloading; landing (*of stairs*).
desembargar [B], *v.t.* to remove impediments from, free; (*law*) to raise an embargo on *or* the seizure of.
desembargo, *n.m.* (*law*) raising an embargo *or* seizure.
desembarque, *n.m.* landing, disembarkation, unloading.
desembarrancar [A], *v.t.* to refloat (*a stranded vessel*).
desembarrar, *v.t.* to clear of mud.
desembaular [P], *v.t.* to remove from a trunk; (*fig.*) to cough up, let out.
desembebecerse [9], *v.r.* to come down to earth, come back to reality, snap out of it.
desembelesarse, *v.r.* [DESEMBEBECERSE].
desemblantarse, *v.r.* [DEMUDARSE].
desembocadero, *n.m.* [DESEMBOCADURA].
desembocadura, *n.f.* mouth (*of river*); exit, outlet (*of street etc.*).
desembocar [A], *v.i.* to disembogue, flow out (into); to end (at), lead (to).
desembojar, *v.t.* to remove (*cocoons of the silkworm*) from the southern-wood.
desembolsar, *v.t.* to disburse, pay out, lay out, fork out.
desembolso, *n.m.* disbursement, expenditure, outgoings.
desemborrachar, *v.t.* to sober up.
desemboscarse [A], *v.r.* to get out of the woods; to get clear of an ambush.
desembotar, *v.t.* to sharpen, sharpen up. — **desembotarse,** *v.r.* to get one's head clear, get one's wits about one; (*coll.*) to shake it off, snap out of it.
desembozar [C], *v.t.* to unmuffle, uncover; to free, unblock. — **desembozarse,** *v.r.* (*fig.*) to show one's true colours.
desembozo, *n.m.* uncovering (*the face*).
desembragar [B], *v.t.* to declutch, ungear, disconnect.
desembrague, *n.m.* declutching.
desembravecer [9], *v.t.* to domesticate, tame.
desembravecimiento, *n.m.* taming, reclaiming from wildness.
desembrazar [C], *v.t.* to hurl *or* fling violently.
desembriagar [B], *v.t.* [DESEMBORRACHAR].
desembridar, *v.t.* to unbridle.
desembrollar, *v.t.* to unravel, clear, disentangle, disembroil.
desembuchar, *v.t.* to disgorge; (*fig.*) to cough up.
desemejante, *a.* dissimilar, unlike.
desemejanza, *n.f.* dissimilitude, unlikeness, dissimilarity.
desemejar, *v.t.* to change the look of. — *v.i.* to differ, be dissimilar.
desempacar [A], *v.t.* to unpack. — **desempacarse,** *v.r.* to grow calm, be appeased.
desempachar, *v.t.* to relieve indigestion in. — **desempacharse,** *v.r.* to stop being diffident, cease to have qualms.
desempacho, *n.m.* ease, forwardness.
desempalagar [B], *v.t.* to uncloy; to clear.

desempañar, *v.t.* to clean, clear, demist; to change nappy of.
desempapelar, *v.t.* to unwrap; to strip of paper.
desempaquetar, *v.t.* to unpack, take out of a packet.
desemparejar, *v.t.* to unmatch, make unequal *or* uneven.
desemparentado, -da, *a.* without relatives *or* kin.
desemparvar, *v.t.* to gather (*threshed corn*) in heaps.
desempatar, *v.t.* to settle (*a tied election*); to play off a tie between *or* in.
desempedrar [I], *v.t.* to unpave; (*fig.*) ***desempedrar la calle,*** to pound the pavement, roam the streets.
desempegar [B], *v.t.* to remove (the) pitch from.
desempeñar, *v.t.* to redeem, take out of pawn; to free from debt *or* obligation; to discharge (*a duty*); to fill (*an office*); to act *or* play (*a part*). — **desempeñarse,** *v.r.* to get clear.
desempeño, *n.m.* redeeming, redemption; performance, fulfilment, discharge.
desemperezar(se) [C], *v.i.* (*v.r.*) to get moving, shake off sloth.
desempobrecerse [9], to extricate o.s. from poverty.
desempolvar, desempolvorar, *v.t.* to dust.
desempolvadura, *n.f.* dusting.
desemponzoñar, *v.t.* to cure from the effects of poison; to free from poison.
desempotrar, *v.t.* to take *or* pull out (*sth. embedded*).
desempulgadura, *n.f.* unbending of a bow.
desempulgar [B], *v.t.* to unbend (*a bow*).
desenalbardar, *v.t.* to take the packsaddle(s) off.
desenamorar, *v.t.* to destroy love *or* affection in. — **desenamorarse,** *v.r.* to lose love *or* affection; cool.
desenastar, *v.t.* to take the handle from.
desencabalgar [B], *v.t.* to dismount (*cannon*).
desencabestrar, *v.t.* to disentangle (*a beast*) from the halter.
desencadenar, *v.t.* to unchain; to unleash, let loose, trigger off. — **desencadenarse,** *v.r.* to break, break out (*storm, conflict etc.*).
desencajado, -da, *a.* haggard, drawn.
desencajadura, *n.f.* unjointing, disconnection.
desencajamiento, desencaje, *n.m.* disjointing, dislocation; haggard expression.
desencajar, *v.t.* to disjoint, unjoin, disconnect, put out of place *or* gear; to disarticulate. — **desencajarse,** *v.r.* to become disjointed; to become drawn *or* haggard.
desencajonar, *v.t.* to take out of a box, crate *or* pen.
desencalabrinar, *v.t.* to clear, free, unbefuddle.
desencallar, *v.t., v.i.* to refloat (*a stranded ship*).
desencaminar, *v.t.* to mislead, lead astray.
desencantamiento, *n.m.* disenchantment.
desencantar, *v.t.* to disenchant; to disillusion.
desencantarar, *v.t.* to draw (*names*) (*for an election*); to exclude (*from an election*).
desencanto, *n.m.* disenchantment; disillusion.
desencapillar, *v.t.* (*naut.*) to unrig.
desencapotadura, *n.f.* stripping off (*a cloak*).
desencapotar, *v.t.* to strip (*s.o.*) of a coat; (*coll.*) to uncover, reveal; to raise and keep up the head of (*a horse*). — **desencapotarse,** *v.r.* to clear, clear up, begin to look brighter.
desencaprichar, *v.t.* to get *or* talk out of, make snap out of. — **desencapricharse,** *v.r.* to get over it, snap out of it.
desencarcelar, *v.t.* to release, set at liberty.
desencarecer [9], *v.t.* to lower the price of. — *v.i.* to come down in price.
desencargar [B], *v.t.* to cancel an order for.
desencarnar, *v.t.* to prevent (*dogs*) from eating game; (*fig.*) to lose one's liking for.
desencastillar, *v.t.* to drive out, dislodge; to uncover, reveal.
desencerrar [I], *v.t.* to free from confinement; to open; to disclose.
desencintar, *v.t.* to remove the ribbons from; to remove the kerb from.
desenclavar, *v.t.* to unnail; (*fig.*) to dislodge.
desenclavijar, *v.t.* to take the pins *or* pegs out of.
desencoger [E], *v.t.* to unshrink; to unfold. — **desencogerse,** *v.r.* to lose inhibition.
desencogimiento, *n.m.* naturalness, ease.
desencoladura, *n.f.* ungluing.
desencolar, *v.t.* to unglue.
desencolerizarse [C], *v.r.* to calm down.
desenconar, *v.t.* to calm, soothe, assuage.
desencono, *n.m.* calming, soothing, mitigating.
desencordar [I], *v.t.* (*mus.*) to unstring.
desencordelar, *v.t.* to untie, undo the strings of.
desencorvar, *v.t.* to straighten, unbend.
desencrespar, *v.t.* to uncurl.
desencuadernar, *v.t.* to unbind, remove binding from.
desenchufar, *v.t.* to unplug, disconnect.
desendemoniar, desendiablar, *v.t.* to exorcise, drive out an evil spirit from.
desendiosar, *v.t.* to humble.
desenfadaderas, *n.f.pl.* ***tener buenas desenfadaderas,*** to be resourceful.
desenfadado, -da, *a.* easy, nonchalant; uninhibited; wide, spacious.
desenfadar, *v.t.* to appease, mollify. — **desenfadarse,** *v.r.* to calm down.
desenfado, *n.m.* ease, nonchalance, uninhibited manner.
desenfaldar, *v.t.* to untack the skirt of.
desenfangar [B], *v.t.* to clean, free of mud *or* filth.
desenfardar, desenfardelar, *v.t.* to unpack.
desenfilar, *v.t.* to defilade.
desenfocar [A], *v.t.* to put *or* get out of focus, not to get in focus.
desenfrailar, *v.i.* to leave the monastic life; (*coll.*) to come out from subjection; (*coll.*) to rest for a time (*from business etc.*).
desenfrenado, -da, *a.* unbridled, unrestrained, wild, frantic; wanton.
desenfrenamiento [DESENFRENO].
desenfrenar, *v.t.* to unbridle. — **desenfrenarse,** *v.r.* to give rein to one's passions and desires; to become unleashed; to run wild; to throw all caution to the wind.
desenfreno, *n.m.* unruliness, wantonness; lack of all restraint *or* inhibition; debauchery; wild *or* frantic behaviour.
desenfundar, *v.t.* to unsheathe, draw *or* take out.
desenfurecerse [9], *v.r.* to calm down.
desengalanar, *v.t.* to strip of ornaments.
desenganchar, *v.t.* to unhook; to take down from a hook; to unharness; to uncouple; to disengage; to unhitch.
desenganche, *n.m.* unharnessing.
desengañar, *v.t.* to undeceive, disabuse; to disillusion. — **desengañarse,** *v.r.* to become disillusioned *or* disabused, lose (all) one's illusions; ***desengáñese usted,*** don't kid *or* fool yourself (about it), have no illusions, make no mistake (about it).
desengaño, *n.m.* undeceiving, disabusal; disappointment, disillusion; bitter lesson (*of experience*).
desengarrafar, *v.t.* to release, let go of.
desengarzar [C], *v.t.* (*jewel.*) to take out of a setting; to unstring (*pearls etc.*).
desengastar, *v.t.* to take (*a jewel*) from its setting.
desengomar, *v.t.* to ungum, unsize.
desengoznar, *v.t.* to unhinge.
desengranar, *v.t.* to disengage, unmesh.
desengrane, *n.m.* disengaging, unmeshing.

desengrasar, *v.t.* to remove (the) grease from. — *v.i.* to lose weight.
desengrase, *n.m.* removal of grease.
desengrilletar, *v.t.* (*naut.*) to knock off a coupling link from.
desengrosar [I], *v.t.* to make thinner *or* leaner, reduce. — *v.i.* to get thinner *or* leaner.
desengrudamiento, *n.m.* removal of sticky paste.
desengrudar, *v.t.* to unglue, unpaste.
desenguantarse, *v.r.* to remove one's gloves.
desenhebrar, *v.t.* to unthread.
desenhornar, *v.t.* to take out of the oven.
desenjaezar [C], *v.t.* to remove (the) trappings from (*horse*).
desenjalmar, *v.t.* to remove the packsaddle from.
desenjaular, *v.t.* to uncage; to let out of the cage; (*coll.*) to let out of clink *or* jail.
desenlabonar [DESLABONAR].
desenlace, *n.m.* dénouement; conclusion, end, unravelling; outcome.
desenladrillar, *v.t.* to take up the bricks *or* tiles from (*a floor*).
desenlazar [C], *v.t.* to unlace, untie, loose; to bring to a dénouement *or* issue; to unravel.
desenlodar, *v.t.* to remove (the) mud from.
desenlosar, *v.t.* to unpave, take up the flagstones from.
desenlutar, *v.t.* to take out of mourning. — **desenlutarse,** *v.r.* to leave off mourning.
desenmallar, *v.t.* to take (*fish*) out of the net.
desenmarañar, *v.t.* to disentangle, unravel.
desenmascaramiento, *n.m.* unmasking; exposure.
desenmascarar, *v.t.* to unmask; (*fig.*) to expose.
desenmohecer [9], *v.t.* to remove the mould, mildew *or* rust from.
desenmudecerse [9], *v.r.* to recover one's speech; to break one's silence.
desenojar, *v.t.* to appease, mollify.
desenojo, *n.m.* appeasement, moderation of anger.
desenredar, *v.t.* to disentangle, unravel.
desenredo, *n.m.* disentangling, unravelling; dénouement.
desenrollar, *v.t.* to unroll, unwind.
desenronquecer [9], *v.t.* to free from hoarseness.
desenroscar [9], *v.t.* to uncoil; to unscrew; to untwist.
desensabanar, *v.t.* (*coll.*) to take the sheets off.
desensamblar, *v.t.* (*carp.*) to disjoint, separate.
desensañar, *v.t.* to pacify, appease.
desensartar, *v.t.* to unthread, unstring.
desensebar, *v.t.* to strip of fat. — *v.i.* to leave off work for a time; to change for a better job; to take away the taste of fat.
desenseñar, *v.t.* to correct wrong teaching in.
desensillar, *v.t.* to unsaddle.
desensoberbecerse [9], *v.r.* to moderate one's pride, be humbled.
desensortijado, -da, *a.* uncurled; dislocated, displaced.
desentablar, *v.t.* to rip up planks *or* boards from; (*fig.*) to disturb, disarrange; to break off.
desentalingar [B], *v.t.* to untangle the chain-cable (*of an anchor*).
desentarimar, *v.t.* to remove a platform *or* stand from.
desentarquinar, *v.t.* to clear.
desentenderse [2], *v.r.* to wash one's hands (***de,*** of); ***me desentiendo de este asunto,*** I want nothing more to do with this business.
desentendido, -da, *a.* ***no te hagas el desentendido,*** don't pretend you don't know; ***se hizo el desentendido,*** he didn't take the hint.
desenterramiento, *n.m.* disinterment, exhumation; (*fig.*) unearthing.
desenterrar [I], *v.t.* to disinter, dig up, unearth; (*fig.*) to dig *or* rake up; ***desenterrar los muertos,*** to slander the dead.
desentierramuertos, *n.m. inv.* calumniator of the dead.
desentoldar, *v.t.* to take away the awning from; (*fig.*) to strip of ornaments.
desentonación, *n.f.* dissonance, false tune.
desentonado, -da, *a.* out of tune, discordant.
desentonamiento, *n.m.* [DESENTONACIÓN].
desentonar, *v.t.* to humble; to wound the pride of. — *v.i.* (*mus.*) to be out of tune; to clash; to be out of place. — **desentonarse,** *v.r.* to raise one's voice rudely.
desentono, *n.m.* discord; harsh tone; false note; (*fig.*) rude tone.
desentornillar, *v.t.* to unscrew.
desentorpecer [9], *v.t.* to free from numbness *or* torpor, restore life *or* movement to. — **desentorpecerse,** *v.r.* to liven *or* smarten up, snap out of it.
desentrampar, *v.t.* to free from debt, get out of debt.
desentrañar, *v.t.* to eviscerate, disembowel; (*fig.*) to decipher, unravel. — **desentrañarse,** *v.r.* to give one's all.
desentrenamiento, *n.m.* want of training *or* practice.
desentrenarse, *v.r.* to get out of training *or* practice.
desentronizar [C], *v.t.* to dethrone.
desentumecer [9], **desentumir,** *v.t.* to free from numbness, restore life *or* movement to.
desenvainar, *v.t.* to unsheathe; to bare, uncover; (*coll.*) ***desenvainar el sable,*** to make ready to touch s.o. for money *or* a loan.
desenvelejar, *v.t.* to strip (*a vessel*) of sails.
desenvendar, [DESVENDAR].
desenvenenar, *v.t.* to free from prison.
desenvergar [B], *v.t.* to unbend (*a sail*).
desenviolar, *v.t.* to purify (*a desecrated place*), reconsecrate.
desenvoltura, *n.f.* ease (of manner), easy manner, self-assurance, nonchalance, freedom from inhibition; forwardness.
desenvolvedor, -ra, *n.m.f.* unfolder, investigator.
desenvolver [5, ***p.p.*** **desenvuelto**], *v.t.* to unfold, unwrap; (*fig.*) to decipher, unravel; to develop; to enlarge upon. — **desenvolverse,** *v.r.* (*coll.*) to make out, get along; ***se desenvuelve muy bien,*** he is making out fine, getting along very well.
desenvolvimiento, *n.m.* unfolding, development.
desenvuelto, -ta, *a.* easy in manner, self-assured, nonchalant, uninhibited; forward.
desenzarzar [C], *v.t.* to disentangle; to separate.
deseo, *n.m.* desire; wish; longing; ***arde en deseos de,*** he is longing *or* yearning to; ***a (la) medida de su deseo,*** in accordance with your wishes; ***tengo deseos de volver,*** I feel like going back; ***le vino en deseo matarlo,*** he was seized with a desire to kill him.
deseoso, -sa, *a.* desirous, longing, eager.
desequido, -da, *a.* parched.
desequilibrado, -da, *a.*, *n.m.f.* unbalanced (person).
desequilibrar, *v.t.* to unbalance, throw out of balance.
desequilibrio, *n.m.* disequilibrium, unbalance.
deserción, *n.f.* desertion; (*law*) abandonment of a suit (*by the appellant*).
deserrado, -da, *a.* free from error.
desertar, *v.t.* to desert, abandon, drop. — *v.i.* to desert.
desertor, -ra, *n.m.f.* deserter.
deservicio, *n.m.* disservice; failure in duty to s.o.
deservidor, *n.m.* he who fails in serving another.
deservir [8], *v.t.* to disserve, serve badly; to fail in one's duty to.

desescamar, *v.t.* to scale.
desescombrar, *v.t.* to clear of rubble.
deseslabonar, *v.t.* to cut the links of a chain; [DESLABONAR].
desespaldar, *v.t.* to break *or* dislocate the back *or* shoulder of.
desespaldillar [DESPALDILLAR].
desesperación, *n.f.* despair, desperation; *(coll.)* ***es una desesperación,*** it's intolerable, infuriating.
desesperado, -da, *a.* desperate, despairing, at one's wits end. — *n.m.f.* person with nothing to lose, who will stop at nothing; desperado.
desesperante, *a.* exasperating, infuriating.
desesperanza, *n.f.* despair.
desesperanzar [C], *v.t.* to deprive of hope.
desesperar, *v.t.* to cause to despair; to exasperate. — *v.i.* to despair, lose hope (of); ***desesperó de conseguirlo,*** he despaired of achieving it. — **desesperarse,** *v.r.* ***Juan se desespera fácilmente,*** John gets exasperated easily.
desespigar [B], *v.t.* thresh *(grain).*
desestancar [A], *v.t.* to free from a monopoly.
desestañar, *v.t.* to remove tin from; to unsolder.
desesterar, *v.t.* to take up mats from.
desestero, *n.m.* taking up mats.
desestibar, *v.t.* to unstow.
desestima, *n.f.* disesteem, lack of esteem; rejection.
desestimación, *n.f.* lack of esteem.
desestimador, -ra, *a.* contemning, despising. — *n.m.f.* contemner, despiser.
desestimar, *v.t.* to disesteem, have no esteem for; to reject.
desfacedor, *n.m.* *(obs.)* ***desfacedor de entuertos,*** righter of wrongs, undoer of injuries.
desfacer *(obs.)* [DESHACER].
desfachatado, -da, *a.* *(coll.)* shameless, brazen, barefaced.
desfachatez, *n.f.* *(coll.)* impudence, effrontery, cheek.
desfajar, *v.t.* to ungird.
desfalcador, -ra, *a.* embezzling. — *n.m.f.* embezzler.
desfalcar [A], *v.t.* to lop, cut off; to peculate, embezzle; to unseat, dislodge.
desfalco, *n.m.* diminution, diminishing, detracting; embezzlement, peculation.
desfallecer [9], *v.i.* to faint, faint away; to weaken.
desfalleciente, *a.* fainting, weak.
desfallecimiento, *n.m.* languor; fainting; weakness.
desfasar, *v.t.* to put out of phase, out of step, out of time, out of tune; ***estar desfasado,*** to be out of phase, out of time, etc.; not to be on the same wavelength; to overlap.
desfavor *(obs.)* [DISFAVOR].
desfavorable, *a.* unfavourable.
desfavorecedor, -ra, *n.m.f.* disfavourer, contemner.
desfavorecer [9], *v.t.* to disfavour, not to favour; to cease to favour; not to be to the good *or* advantage of.
desfiguración, *n.f.*, **desfiguramiento,** *n.m.* disfigurement; deforming.
desfigurar, *v.t.* to disfigure; to deform; to disguise; to blur, obscure; to distort, misrepresent.
desfijar, *v.t.* to unfix, detach.
desfiladero, *n.m.* defile, gorge, canyon.
desfilar, *v.i.* to file by, march past; to pass (through).
desfile, *n.m.* filing past, march past, parade, procession.
desflecar [A], *v.t.* to remove the fringe *or* border from.
desflemar, *v.t.* to dephlegmate. — *v.i.* to expectorate.
desfloración, *n.f.* defloration.
desfloramiento, *n.m.* deflowering.
desflorar, *v.t.* to deflower; to sully; to skate *or* skim over *(a subject).*
desflorecer [9], *v.i.* to lose (the) flower.
desflorecimiento, *n.m.* falling of flowers.
desfogar [B], *v.t.* to vent, give vent to; to slake *(lime).* — *v.i.* to break, burst *(a storm).* — **desfogarse,** *v.r.* to let off steam.
desfogonar, *v.t.* to burst the vent of *(a cannon).*
desfogue, *n.m.* vent, venting.
desfollonar, *v.t.* to trim, prune.
desfondar, *v.t.* to remove *or* stave in the bottom of; *(agric.)* to dig deeply. — **desfondarse,** *v.r.* to have the bottom fall out of one's life *or* existence; *(coll.)* to go (all) to pieces; *(coll.)* ***el pobre chico se ha desfondado,*** the bottom has gone out of the poor chap's life.
desfonde, *n.m.* staving in; deep digging.
desformar, *v.t.* to disfigure, deform.
desfortalecer [9], *v.t.* to dismantle, demolish; to take the garrison from.
desforzarse [C], *v.r.* to take revenge.
desfosforar, *v.t.* to dephosphorize.
desfrenar, *v.t.* [DESENFRENAR].
desfrutar, *v.t.* to take the fruit from *(a tree)* before it is ripe.
desgaire, *n.m.* carelessness; casualness; ***al desgaire,*** casually, unconcernedly, nonchalantly.
desgajadura, *n.f.* tearing off.
desgajar, *v.t.* to tear off, tear away, wrench off, rend. — **desgajarse,** *v.r.* to break away; ***se desgajó un trozo,*** a piece broke off, fell away.
desgaje, *n.m.* breaking away, tearing off.
desgalgadero, *n.m.* precipice.
desgalgar [B], *v.t.* to precipitate, throw down headlong.
desgalichado, -da, *a.* *(coll.)* ungainly, gawky.
desgana, *n.f.* want of appetite; reluctance; ***con desgana,*** reluctantly.
desganarse, *v.r.* to lose one's appetite, go off one's food; ***está muy desganado,*** he's completely off his food.
desganchar, *v.t.* to lop off the branches of.
desgañitarse, *v.r.* *(coll.)* to shout o.s. hoarse.
desgarbado, -da, *a.* ungraceful, gawky, ungainly.
desgarbo, *n.m.* gracelessness, gawkiness.
desgargantarse, *v.r.* *(coll.)* to scream o.s. hoarse.
desgargolar, *v.t.* to ripple *(flax, hemp)*; to take *(a board* or *stave)* from a groove.
desgaritar(se), *v.i.* *(v.r.)* *(naut.)* to lose the course; to lose the way, go astray; to give up an undertaking.
desgarrado, -da, *a.* licentious, dissolute; shameless, brazen.
desgarrador, -ra, *a.* tearing; heart-breaking, heart-rending.
desgarradura, *n.f.* rent, rip.
desgarrar, *v.t.* to rend, tear, rip; to cough up.
desgarro, *n.m.* rent, rip, tear; effrontery, impudence; swagger, swaggering.
desgarrón, *n.m.* large rent *or* tear; tatter.
desgastar, *v.t.* to wear away *or* down; to use up.
desgaste, *n.m.* wear, wearing down, wear and tear; attrition; ***guerra de desgaste,*** war of attrition.
desgaznatarse [DESGAÑITARSE].
desglosar, *v.t.* to blot out a note *or* comment in; to separate *(sheets)* from a book *or* document; to break down, analyse.
desglose, *n.m.* break-down, analysis.
desgobernado, -da, *a.* disorderly; ungovernable.
desgobernar [I], *v.t.* to upset the government of; to misgovern, misrule; to steer *(a ship)* carelessly; *(med.)* to dislocate, disjoint *(bones)*; to mismanage, handle badly. — **desgobernarse,** *v.r.* to get out of control.

desgobierno, *n.m.* mismanagement; misgovernment, misrule; maladministration; (*med.*) dislocation (*of bones*).
desgolletar, *v.t.* to break the neck of (*a bottle*); to loosen the neck *or* collar of.
desgomar, *v.t.* to ungum, unsize.
desgonzar [C], *v.t.* to upset, disrupt.
desgorrarse, *v.r.* to pull off one's hat *or* cap.
desgoznar, *v.t.* to unhinge; to disjoint, put out of joint.
desgracia, *n.f.* misfortune; mishap; bad luck; bereavement, sorrow; disgrace; gracelessness; ***desgracias personales,*** casualties; ***caer en desgracia,*** to fall into disgrace; ***por desgracia,*** unfortunately, unhappily.
desgraciadamente, *adv.* unfortunately, unhappily.
desgraciado, -da, *a.* unhappy, luckless, unfortunate, unlucky, hapless; graceless; disagreeable. — *n.m.f.* poor devil, wretched creature, miserable *or* pitiful object.
desgraciar, *v.t.* to spoil, mar, ruin; to maim, cripple; to displease. — **desgraciarse,** *v.r.* to get spoiled, broken etc.; to lose favour; to fall out.
desgramar, *v.t.* to clear of panic grass.
desgranador, -ra, *n.m.f.* sheller, thresher; flail.
desgranamiento, *n.m.* (*artill.*) grooves (*formed in the gun-barrel and venthole by the expanding force of powder*).
desgranar, *v.t.* to shake out grain from (*ears of corn etc.*); to thresh, flail; to shell, shuck; to clear of grapes; to wear away (*vents, bores*). — **desgranarse,** *v.r.* to come loose, scatter; to wear away; to pass away; ***se desgranan las horas,*** the hours pass away.
desgrane, *n.m.* shelling (*of grain*); picking off (*of grapes*).
desgranzar [C], *v.t.* to separate chaff from (*grain*); (*art*) to give the first grinding to (*colours*).
desgrasar, *v.t.* to remove grease from.
desgrase, *n.m.* removal of grease.
desgravar, *v.t.* to reduce duty *or* tax on.
desgreñar, *v.t.* to dishevel, disarrange the hair of.
desguace, *n.m.* breaking up, scrapping (*ships*).
desguarnecer [9], *v.t.* to strip of trimmings; to dismantle; to unharness; to disarm; to withdraw the garrison from.
desguarnir, *v.t.* (*naut.*) to remove rope, chain etc. from (*a capstan* or *set of pulleys*).
desguazar [C], *v.t.* to roughdress; to break up, scrap (*ships*).
desguince, *n.m.* rag knife; [ESGUINCE].
desguindar, *v.t.* (*naut.*) to lower, bring down. — **desguindarse,** *v.r.* to slide down a rope.
desguinzar [C], *v.t.* to cut (*cloth* or *rags in paper-mills*).
deshabitado, -da, *a.* uninhabited, deserted, untenanted.
deshabitar, *v.t.* to leave, move out of (*a house*); to depopulate, unpeople.
deshabituación, *n.f.* disaccustoming; freeing from a habit.
deshabituar [M], *v.t.* to disaccustom, to free from a habit. — **deshabituarse,** *v.r.* to get out of a habit *or* out of practice.
deshacedor, *n.m.* undoer; ***deshacedor de agravios*** or ***entuertos,*** righter of wrongs.
deshacer [20], *v.t.* to undo; to smash (up), cut up; to take apart; to cancel; to melt; to run through; to upset; ***deshacer agravios,*** to redress wrongs; ***estar deshecho,*** to be done up *or* fagged out; ***está deshecho por la muerte de su hijo,*** the death of his son has been a terrible blow to him. — **deshacerse,** *v.r.* to break up; ***deshacerse como el humo,*** to vanish like smoke; ***deshacerse de,*** to get rid of; ***deshacerse trabajando,*** to wear o.s. out with work; ***deshacerse en lágrimas,*** to dissolve *or* melt into tears.
deshambrido, -da, *a.* famished, starving.
desharrapado, -da, *a.* ragged, in tatters.
desharrapamiento, *n.m.* living in rags, destitution.
deshebillar, *v.t.* to unbuckle.
deshebrar, *v.t.* to unthread; to separate into threads *or* filaments.
deshecha, *n.f.* [DESHECHO].
deshechizar [C], *v.t.* to free from a spell *or* enchantment.
deshechizo, *n.m.* breaking of a magic spell.
deshecho, -cha, *a.* violent; ***borrasca deshecha,*** violent, full-force squall *or* storm; ***fuga deshecha,*** precipitate flight; rout. — *n.f.* pretence; polite farewell; burden, refrain; step in a Spanish dance; ***hacer la deshecha,*** to dissemble, feign, pretend. — *p.p.* [DESHACER].
deshelar [1], *v.t.* to thaw (out), defrost.
desherbar [1], *v.t.* to weed.
desheredar, *v.t.* to disinherit. — **desheredarse,** *v.r.* (*fig.*) to degenerate.
deshermanar, *v.t.* to break up, split, unmatch, unpair.
desherradura, *n.f.* (*vet.*) footsoreness; injury done to a horse's foot by being unshod.
desherrar [1], *v.t.* to unchain; to unshoe. — **desherrarse,** *v.r.* to lose a shoe.
desherrumbrar, *v.t.* to clear of rust.
deshidratar, *v.t.* to dehydrate, remove the water from. — **deshidratarse,** *v.r.* to become dehydrated *or* dried up; to lose all the liquid from one's body.
deshielo (1), *n.m.* thaw.
deshielo (2), **deshiele,** *pres. indic.; pres. subj.* [DESHELAR].
deshijar, *v.t.* (*Cub.*) to remove suckers from (*plants*).
deshilachar, *v.t.* to make ragged, fray; ***tiene los bordes deshilachados,*** the edges are frayed.
deshiladiz, *n.m.* (*prov.*) silk refuse.
deshilado, -da, *a.* ***a la deshilada,*** in single file; stealthily. — *n.m.* open work, drawn work, embroidery (*on linen*).
deshiladura, *n.f.* ravelling out.
deshilar, *v.t.* to ravel; to fray; to shred, shred up (*meat*); (*sew.*) to draw threads.
deshilvanado, -da, *a.* disjointed, disconnected, incoherent.
deshilvanar, *v.t.* (*sew.*) to unbaste, untack; to separate.
deshincar [A], *v.t.* to pull *or* draw out.
deshinchadura, *n.f.* going down of a swelling.
deshinchar, *v.t.* to deflate; to reduce the swelling *or* puffiness of; to appease, allay. — **deshincharse,** *v.r.* to go down (*swelling*); ***ante esta crítica se deshinchó,*** he was deflated by this criticism, the wind was taken out of his sails by this criticism.
deshipotecar [A], *v.t.* to cancel a mortgage on; pay off the mortgage on.
deshojador, *n.m.* stripper of leaves.
deshojar, *v.t.* to strip of leaves *or* petals.
deshoje, *n.m.* fall of leaves, defoliation.
deshollejar, *v.t.* to pare, peel, strip, husk; to shell (*beans etc.*); to skin (*grapes*).
deshollinador, *n.m.* chimney-sweep; turk's-head; (*coll.*) prying individual.
deshollinar, *v.t.* to sweep (*chimneys*); to clean; (*coll.*) to pry into.
deshonestarse, *v.r.* to throw propriety to the winds.
deshonestidad, *n.f.* immodesty, lewdness, indecency.
deshonesto, -ta, *a.* immodest, lewd, indecent.
deshonor, *n.m.* dishonour; disgrace.
deshonorar, *v.t.* to dishonour, disgrace; to deprive of office *or* dignity.
deshonra, *n.f.* dishonour, disgrace; shame; seduction, rape; ***tener a deshonra,*** to consider *or* hold as dishonourable.

deshonrabuenos, *n.m.f. inv.* calumniator, libeller, slanderer; degenerate.
deshonrador, -ra, *a.* dishonouring. — *n.m.f.* dishonourer, disgracer, defamer; seducer.
deshonrar, *v.t.* to dishonour, disgrace; to defame, insult; to seduce.
deshonrible, *a.* (*coll.*) shameless, contemptible.
deshonroso, -sa, *a.* dishonourable; disgraceful, ignominious.
deshora, *n.f.* ***a deshora,*** very late; inopportunely.
deshorado, -da, *a.* untimely.
deshornar, *v.t.* to take out of the oven.
deshuesar, *v.t.* to bone; to stone.
deshumanizar [C], *v.t.* to dehumanize.
deshumano, -na, *a.* inhuman.
deshumedecer [9], *v.t.* to deprive of moisture, dry up.
desiderable, *a.* desirable.
desiderata, *n.f.* request list.
desiderativo, -va, *a.* desirous; of desire.
desiderátum, *n.m.* peak of perfection, desideratum.
desidia, *n.f.* indolence, apathy.
desidioso, -sa, *a.* indolent, apathetic.
desierto, -ta, *a.* deserted, waste, lonely; ***declarar desierto,*** to declare null and void. — *n.m.* desert, wilderness, waste; ***voz que clama en el desierto,*** voice crying in the wilderness.
designación, *n.f.* designation.
designar, *v.t.* to designate, name, appoint; to plan.
designativo, -va, *a.* designative.
designio, *n.m.* design, purpose, intention.
desigual, *a.* unequal; changeable, variable; uneven, irregular; broken; arduous; (*obs.*) excessive, extreme; ***pareja desigual,*** ill-assorted pair.
desigualar, *v.t.* to make unequal *or* uneven. — **desigualarse,** *v.r.* to surpass, excel.
desigualdad, *n.f.* inequality; difference, variableness; unevenness, roughness; (*math.*) sign of inequality (<, >).
desilusión, *n.f.* disillusionment; disappointment.
desilusionar, *v.t.* to disullusion, disenchant; to disappoint.
desimaginar, *v.t.* to blot out, obliterate from the mind.
desimanar [DESIMANTAR].
desimantación, *n.f.* demagnetization.
desimantar(se), *v.t.* (*v.r.*) to demagnetize.
desimponer [25], *v.t.* (*print.*) to break up the imposition of (*a forme*).
desimpresionar, *v.t.* to undeceive.
desinclinar, *v.t.* to disincline.
desincorporación, *n.f.* disincorporation.
desincorporar, *v.t.* to separate; to dissolve, wind up.
desinencia, *n.f.* (*gram.*) desinence, ending.
desinfección, *n.f.* disinfection; disinfecting.
desinfectador, *n.m.* disinfecting apparatus; disinfector.
desinfectante, *a.* disinfecting. — *n.m.* disinfectant.
desinfectar, *v.t.* to disinfect.
desinficionamiento, *n.m.* disinfection.
desinficionar, *v.t.* to disinfect, free from infection.
desinflamar, *v.t.* to cure *or* remove inflammation from.
desinflar, *v.t.* to deflate. — **desinflarse,** *v.r.* to be deflated; ***se desinfló,*** all the wind went out of his sails; he lost all his drive *or* enthusiasm.
desinsaculación, *n.f.* act of drawing names from an urn *or* ballot-box.
desinsacular, *v.t.* to draw from an urn *or* ballot-box.
desinsectar, *v.t.* to clear of insects.
desintegrar, *v.t.* to disintegrate.
desinterés, *n.m.* disinterestedness; impartiality; unselfishness.
desinteresadamente, *adv.* disinterestedly, generously, selflessly; impartially.
desinteresado, -da, *a.* disinterested; impartial, unbiased.
desinteresarse, *v.r.* to lose interest.
desinvernar [I], *v.i.* (*mil.*) to leave winter quarters.
desistencia, *n.f.,* **desistimiento,** *n.m.* desistance; waiving.
desistir, *v.i.* to desist; to waive (*a right*); ***desistir de,*** to desist *or* cease from, give up.
desjarretadera, *n.f.* knife for hamstringing cattle.
desjarretar, *v.t.* to hamstring, hock.
desjarrete, *n.m.* hamstringing.
desjugar [B], *v.t.* to take the juice from.
desjuntamiento, *n.m.* disjunction, separation.
desjuntar, *v.t.* to separate, sever, disjoin.
desjurar, *v.t.* to forswear, retract (*an oath*).
deslabonar, *v.t.* to unlink, disjoin; (*fig.*) to sever.
desladrillar [DESENLADRILLAR].
deslamar, *v.t.* to clear of mud.
deslastrar, *v.t.* to unballast.
deslatar, *v.t.* to remove the laths from.
deslavado, -da, *a.* impudent, barefaced.
deslavadura, *n.f.* superficial washing *or* rinsing.
deslavar, *v.t.* to wash, wet superficially; to rinse superficially; to take away the colour, force, vigour from.
deslavazado, -da, *a.* floppy, limp; drooping; flat; disjointed.
deslazar [C], *v.t.* to unlace; to untie.
desleal, *a.* disloyal.
deslealtad, *n.f.* disloyalty.
deslechar, *v.t.* (*prov.*) to remove dirt from.
deslechugar [B], **deslechuguillar,** *v.t.* to prune; to clear.
desleidura, *n.f.,* **desleimiento,** *n.m.* mixing (in) (*with liquid*).
desleír [28], *v.t.* to mix (in) (*with liquid*). — **desleírse,** *v.r.* to dissolve; ***deslíase en leche,*** mix with milk.
deslendrar [I], *v.t.* to clear of nits.
deslenguado, -da, *a.* shameless, brazen, foul-mouthed.
deslenguamiento, *n.m.* foul-mouthedness.
deslenguar [H], *v.t.* to cut out the tongue of. — **deslenguarse,** *v.r.* (*coll.*) to use foul language.
desliar (1) [L], *v.t.* to loose, untie, undo.
desliar (2) [L], *v.t.* to separate the lees from.
desligadura, *n.f.,* **desligamiento,** *n.m.* untying; disjoining.
desligar [B], *v.t.* to loosen, untie, unbind; (*fig.*) to unravel; to absolve (*from ecclesiastical censure*); to excuse (*from an obligation*); (*mus.*) to play *or* sing staccato. — **desligarse,** *v.r.* to break away (*from*), cut one's ties (*with*), cut o.s. off (*from*).
deslindable, *a.* limitable, capable of demarcation.
deslindador, *n.m.* one who marks boundaries; land-surveyor.
deslindamiento, *n.m.* demarcation; survey of boundaries.
deslindar, *v.t.* to mark the boundaries, define the limits of, draw the line between; to make plain.
deslinde, *n.m.* demarcation.
desliñar, *v.t.* to clean (*fulled cloth*) before it goes to press.
deslío, *n.m.* separating from lees.
desliz, *n.m.* slipping; sliding; false step; slip (up), blunder.
deslizable, *a.* that which can slip *or* slide.
deslizadero, -ra, deslizadizo, -za, *a.* slippery, slippy. — **deslizadero,** *n.m.* slippery place.
deslizador, *n.m.* (*aer.*) glider.
deslizamiento, *n.m.* slip, slipping; sliding; skidding.
deslizar [C], *v.i.* to slip, slide, glide (along). —

deslizarse, *v.r.* to slip, slide, glide (along); (*fig.*) to slip up; to sneak (in *or* out).
deslomadura, *n.f.* breaking the back of.
deslomar, *v.t.* to break the back of. — **deslomarse,** *v.r.* to fag o.s. out.
deslucido, -da, *a.* tarnished, spoilt; dull, flat.
deslucimiento, *n.m.* tarnishing; dullness, flatness.
deslucir [9], *v.t.* to tarnish, mar, spoil; ***la fiesta resultó deslucida,*** the party was a flop.
deslumbrador, -ra, *a.* dazzling, glaring.
deslumbrado, -da, *a.* dazzled; dazed; unsure.
deslumbramiento, *n.m.* dazzle, glare; (*fig.*) bewilderment.
deslumbrante, *a.* dazzling, glaring.
deslumbrar, *v.t.* to dazzle; (*fig.*) to daze, bewilder.
deslustración, *n.f.* tarnishing, sullying.
deslustrador, -ra, *a.* tarnishing, dulling. — *n.m.f.* tarnisher.
deslustrar, *v.t.* to dull, tarnish, take the lustre from; to frost (*glass*); to dim, blot (*reputation etc.*).
deslustre, *n.m.* dulling, tarnishing; removal of lustre; blot, stain (*on reputation etc.*).
deslustroso, -sa, *a.* unbecoming, ugly.
desmadejamiento, *n.m.* shakiness, totteriness, weakness.
desmadejar, *v.t.* to make shaky, tottery *or* weak. — **desmadejarse,** *v.r.* (*fig.*) to go floppy, begin to loll.
desmadrado, -da, *a.* motherless (*animal*).
desmadrar, *v.t.* to separate (*animal*) from its mother.
desmajolar [4], *v.t.* to root up (*vines*); to untie (*shoe-laces*).
desmalazado, -da, *a.* drooping, weak; dejected.
desmalladura, *n.f.* cutting of meshes, unmeshing.
desmallar, *v.t.* to cut the meshes of, unmesh.
desmamar, *v.t.* to wean.
desmamonar, *v.t.* to cut off the young shoots of (*vines* or *trees*).
desmán (1), *n.m.* excess; outrage.
desmán (2), *n.m.* (*zool.*) musk-rat.
desmanarse, *v.r.* to stray from a flock *or* herd.
desmandamiento, *n.m.* excess; outrage; insubordination.
desmandar, *v.t.* to countermand; to revoke; to repeal. — **desmandarse,** *v.r.* to get out of hand, get out of control, rebel against authority; to run amuck; to throw off all restraint.
desmanear, *v.t.* to unhobble, unshackle.
desmangar [B], *v.t.* to remove the handle from.
desmanotado, -da, *a.* awkward, clumsy, bungling.
desmantecar [A], *v.t.* to remove the lard from.
desmantelado, -da, *a.* ruinous, dilapidated.
desmantelar, *v.t.* to dismantle; (*naut.*) to unmast, unrig.
desmaña, *n.f.* clumsiness, awkwardness.
desmañado, -da, *a.* clumsy, awkward.
desmarañar, *v.t.* to disentangle.
desmarcar, *v.t.* to remove marks from.
desmarrido, -da, *a.* dejected; exhausted.
desmatar, *v.t.* to clear of undergrowth.
desmayado, -da, *a.* faint, fainting; pale, wan.
desmayar, *v.t.* to dismay, discourage. — *v.i.* to lose courage, lose heart. — **desmayarse,** *v.r.* to faint, swoon.
desmayo, *n.m.* swoon, fainting-fit; languor, weakness; dismay, discouragement; (*bot.*) weeping-willow; ***sin desmayo,*** unfalteringly.
desmazalado, -da, *a.* weak, shaky; drooping, dejected.
desmedido, -da, *a.* disproportionate, excessive, out of all proportion, boundless.
desmedirse [8], *v.r.* to forget o.s.; to go too far; to lose self-control.
desmedrar(se), *v.t., v.i.* (*v.r.*) to deteriorate.
desmedro, *n.m.* deterioration.
desmejorar, *v.t.* to deteriorate, impair.
desmelancolizar [C], *v.t.* to cheer up, enliven.
desmelar [1], *v.t.* to take honey from (*a hive*).
desmelenamiento, *n.m.* (*fam.*) breaking loose, bursting free, letting rip.
desmelenar, *v.t.* to dishevel, disarrange the hair of.
desmelene [DESMELENAMIENTO].
desmembración, *n.f.* dismemberment; breaking up.
desmembrador, -ra, *n.m.f.* divider; one who dismembers.
desmembrar [1], *v.t.* to dismember; to break up; to divide.
desmemoria, *n.f.* forgetfulness; loss of memory.
desmemoriado, -da, *a.* forgetful. — *n.m.f.* person suffering from loss of memory.
desmemoriarse, *v.r.* to become forgetful; to lose one's memory.
desmenguar [H], *v.t.* to lessen, diminish.
desmentida, *n.f.* act of giving the lie, denial.
desmentir [6], *v.t.* to give the lie to; to contradict, deny; to belie; to do things unworthy of. — *v.i.* to be unworthy (***de,*** of). — **desmentirse,** *v.r.* to take back what one has said; to go back on one's word, belie one's words.
desmenuzable, *a.* brittle, easily crumbled.
desmenuzador, -ra, *a.* crumbling. — *n.m.f.* crumbler; minute scrutinizer.
desmenuzar [C], *v.t.* to break up small, crumble; (*fig.*) to sift, examine in minute detail.
desmeollar, *v.t.* to remove the marrow from.
desmerecedor, -ra, *a.* unworthy, undeserving.
desmerecer [9], *v.t.* to be *or* become unworthy *or* undeserving of. — *v.i.* to go off *or* down; to compare unfavourably (with).
desmerecimiento, *n.m.* demerit, unworthiness.
desmesura, *n.f.* excess, want of moderation.
desmesurado, -da, *a.* disproportionate, excessive; beyond the bounds of reasonableness.
desmesurar, *v.t.* to disorder, disarrange. — **desmesurarse,** *v.r.* to go too far, forget oneself, become unreasonable.
desmigajar, *v.t.* to break up small, crumble (up).
desmigar [B], *v.t.* to take the pap from (*bread*).
desmilitarizar [C], *v.t.* to demilitarize.
desmineralización, *n.f.* (*med.*) demineralization.
desmirriado, -da (*coll.*) [ESMIRRIADO].
desmitificación, *n.f.* debunking.
desmitificar [A], *v.t.* to debunk.
desmocha, desmochadura, *n.f.* [DESMOCHE].
desmochar, *v.t.* to lop *or* cut the top off, clip, trim; to cut; (*fig.*) to touch lightly on, skate over.
desmoche, *n.m.* lopping *or* cutting off; (*fig.*) thinning *or* weeding out, cutting (down).
desmocho, *n.m.* things lopped *or* cut off.
desmogar [B], *v.i.* to cast the horns (*deer*).
desmogue, *n.m.* casting of the horns.
desmolado, -da, *a.* having lost the molar teeth.
desmoldar, *v.t.* to remove from a mould.
desmonetización, *n.f.* demonetization.
desmonetizar [C], *v.t.* to demonetize.
desmontador, -ra, *n.m.f.* dismounter.
desmontadura, *n.f.* felling, clearing; dismounting.
desmontaje, *n.m.* uncocking (*firearms*); taking down, dismounting.
desmontar, *v.t.* to fell (*trees*); to clear; to level; to uncock (*firearms*); to take down, dismount; to take to pieces, dismantle. — *v.i.* to dismount (*from horse*).
desmonte, *n.m.* felling, clearing; levelling; cut; cleared *or* levelled ground; (*fig.*) waste ground.
desmoñar, *v.t.* (*coll.*) to loosen the hairknot of.
desmoralización, *n.f.* demoralization.
desmoralizar [C], *v.t.* to demoralize; to corrupt.

desmoronadizo, -za, *a.* easily crumbled, crumbly.
desmoronar, *v.t.* to cause to crumble (away). — **desmoronarse,** *v.r.* to crumble away; ***se desmoronó la pared,*** the wall crumbled, collapsed.
desmostarse, *v.r.* to lose (its) must.
desmotadera, *n.f.* burler; burling-iron.
desmotador, -ra, *a.* burling. — *n.m.f.* burler.
desmotar, *v.t.* to burl; to gin.
desmovilización, *n.f.* demobilization.
desmugrar, *v.t.* to remove the grease *or* filth from.
desmullir, *v.t.* to squash flat, make hard.
desmurador, *n.m.* (*prov.*) mouser (*cat*).
desmurar, *v.t.* (*prov.*) to knock down the walls of; to clear of mice *or* rats.
desnarigado, -da, *a.* noseless.
desnarigar [B], *v.t.* to cut off the nose of. — **desnarigarse,** *v.r.* to bang *or* bump one's nose.
desnatar, *v.t.* to skim; (*fig.*) to cream, cream off the best from; to remove the scum from; to remove the slag *or* dross from.
desnaturalización, *n.f.* denaturalization; (*chem.*) denaturation.
desnaturalizado, -da, *a.* unnatural; ***alcohol desnaturalizado,*** methylated spirits, (*Am.*) denatured alcohol.
desnaturalizar [C], *v.t.* to denaturalize, banish; to denature; to make unnatural, pervert; to alter *or* spoil the (essential) nature of; to twist the sense of.
desnegamiento, *n.m.* denial; retraction.
desnegarse [1B], *v.r.* to recant, go back on what one has said.
desnervar, desnerviar [ENERVAR].
desnevar [1], *v.i.* to thaw.
desnieve, *n.m.* thaw.
desnivel, *n.m.* unevenness; difference in standards; gradient, drop, slope; ***playa en desnivel,*** sloping beach.
desnivelación, *n.f.* unevenness; difference in levels; making uneven.
desnivelar, *v.t.* to make uneven; (*fig.*) to upset.
desnucar [A], *v.t.* to break *or* dislocate the back of the neck of, give a rabbit punch to.
desnudador, -ra, *a.* denuding. — *n.m.f.* one who denudes.
desnudamiento, *n.m.* undressing.
desnudar, *v.t.* to strip, undress; to denude; to uncover, lay bare; (*coll., fig.*) to fleece; (*naut.*) to unrig; ***desnudar la espada,*** to draw one's sword; ***desnudar un santo para vestir a otro,*** to rob Peter to pay Paul.
desnudez, *n.f.* nudity, nakedness, bareness.
desnudo, -da, *a.* naked, nude, bare; (*fig.*) empty-handed; ***desnudo nací, desnudo me hallo,*** naked I was born, and naked I am; (*fig.*) ***estoy desnuda,*** I haven't a thing to wear. — *n.m.* (*art*) nude.
desnutrición, *n.f.* (*med.*) malnutrition, undernourishment.
desnutrirse, *v.r.* to become undernourished.
desobedecer [9], *v.t.* to disobey; to fail to respond to.
desobediencia, *n.f.* disobedience.
desobediente, *a.* disobedient.
desobligar [B], *v.t.* to release from an obligation; to disoblige, offend; to alienate the good will of.
desobstrucción, *n.f.* removal of obstructions *or* obstacles, clearing.
desobstruente, *a., n.m.* (*med.*) deobstruent.
desobstruir [O], *v.t.* to clear.
desocupación, *n.f.* leisure; unemployment.
desocupado, -da, *a.* idle; unemployed; free, empty, vacant. — *n.m.f.* idler; unemployed person.
desocupar, *v.t.* to vacate, leave, empty; to evacuate. — **desocuparse,** *v.r.* to leave work.
desodorante, *a., n.m.* deodorant.
desoír [22], *v.t.* to pay no heed to, ignore.
desojar, *v.t.* to break the eye of (*a needle*). — **desojarse,** *v.r.* to look hard; to strain one's eyes.
desolación, *n.f.* desolation; (*fig.*) affliction, grief.
desolado, -da, *a.* desolate; disconsolate.
desolar [4], *v.t.* to desolate, lay waste; to afflict, grieve.
desoldar [4], *v.t.* to unsolder, unweld.
desolladero, *n.m.* slaughter-house (*where animals are flayed*).
desollado, -da, *a.* (*coll.*) forward, impudent, brazen.
desollador, -ra, *n.m.f.* flayer; extortioner. — *n.m.* (*orn.*) shrike.
desolladura, *n.f.* flaying, skinning; excoriation, barking; (*fig.*) fleecing.
desollar [4], *v.t.* to flay, skin; to excoriate, bark; (*fig.*) to fleece; (*fig.*) to pull *or* tear to pieces (*by criticism*).
desollón, *n.m.* barking, scraping.
desonzar [C], *v.t.* to discount *or* deduct a number of ounces from; (*fig.*) to slander.
desopilar, *v.t.* to clear.
desopilativo, -va, *a.* (*med.*) deobstruent.
desopinar, *v.t.* to defame, discredit.
desoprimir, *v.t.* to free from oppression.
desorbitado, -da, *a.* excessive, disproportionate, extortionate; bulging, popping out (*eyes*).
desorbitar, *v.t.* to make excessive, exaggerate, blow up.
desorden, *n.m.* disorder; untidiness.
desordenadamente, *adv.* in a disorderly way.
desordenado, -da, *a.* disorderly; untidy, slovenly.
desordenamiento, *n.m.* disorder.
desordenar, *v.t.* to disorder, throw into confusion, disarrange, make untidy, upset.
desorejador, -ra, *n.m.f.* one who cuts off ears.
desorejamiento, *n.m.* cutting off of ears.
desorejar, *v.t.* to cut off the ears of.
desorganización, *n.f.* disorganization.
desorganizadamente, *adv.* in a disorganized way.
desorganizador, -ra, *a.* disorganizing. — *n.m.f.* disorganizer.
desorganizar [C], *v.t.* to disorganize; to throw into confusion.
desorientar, *v.t.* to throw (*s.o.*) off his bearings; to mislead, lead astray; (*fig.*) to put out, baffle. — **desorientarse,** *v.r.* to lose one's bearings.
desorillar, *v.t.* to cut off the edge *or* border from.
desortijado, -da, *a.* (*vet.*) sprained.
desortijar, *v.t.* (*agric.*) to hoe *or* weed for the first time.
desosada, *n.f.* (*sl.*) tongue.
desosar [4, ***h*** *precedes* ***ue***], *v.t.* to bone, unbone; to stone (*fruit*).
desovar, *v.i.* to spawn.
desove, *n.m.* spawning; spawning season.
desovillar, *v.t.* to unwind; (*fig.*) to unravel, disentangle.
desoxidación, *n.f.* derusting.
desoxidante, *a.* derusting, rust removing. — *n.m.* rust remover.
desoxidar, *v.t.* to derust.
desoxigenación, *n.f.* deoxygenation.
desoxigenar, *v.t.* to deoxygenate, deoxidize.
despabiladeras, *n.f.pl.* snuffers.
despabilado, -da, *a.* wide awake; smart, quick-witted, all-there.
despabilador, -ra, *a.* snuffing (*candles*). — *n.m.* candle-snuffer.
despabiladura, *n.f.* snuff (*of candle*); (*fig.*) ***de pronto tuvo una despabiladura,*** he suddenly woke up.
despabilar, *v.t.* to snuff, trim the wick of; to smarten *or* liven up; to finish *or* polish off; (*coll.*) to

pinch, rob; (*fig.*) to bump off, do in. — **despabilarse,** *v.r.* to wake up; to brighten up; ***¡despabílate!*** wake up! pull your socks up!
despacio, *adv.* slowly, carefully, with attention. — *interj.* take it easy!, go easy!
despacioso, -sa, *a.* slow, sluggish.
despacito, *adv.* (*coll.*) very slowly, nice and gently, gingerly; with great care *or* attention. — *interj.* take it very easy!; ***despacito y buena letra,*** tread very carefully; just take it nice and easy.
despachaderas, *n.f.pl.* (*coll.*) ***tener buenas despachaderas,*** to be quick to answer; to be blunt *or* outspoken, not to beat about the bush.
despachador, -ra, *n.m.f.* expeditor; (*Hisp. Am.*) (*min.*) filler of trucks in an adit.
despachar, *v.t.* to dispatch; to get done promptly; to attend to; to dismiss, discharge; to sell, issue; to clear (*at customs*). — *v.i.* to do business; to give birth (*a woman*). — **despacharse,** *v.r.* to get finished; ***se despachó a gusto con él,*** he gave him a good piece of his mind; ***despacharse a gusto,*** thoroughly to enjoy o.s.
despacho, *n.m.* dispatch; dispatching; attending (to); clearance (*at customs*); dismissal, discharge; office, room; study; ***despacho de billetes,*** ticket-office; ***despacho de localidades,*** box-office; ***secretario de despacho,*** personal secretary.
despachurrar, *v.t.* to squash, flatten; (*fig.*) to make a mess of.
despajadura, *n.f.* winnowing; (*min.*) sifting.
despajar, *v.t.* to winnow; (*min.*) to sieve.
despajo, *n.m.* winnowing.
despaldar, *v.t.* to break *or* dislocate the shoulder *or* back of.
despaldillar, *v.t.* to break *or* dislocate the shoulder of.
despalillar, *v.t.* to remove the stems from, stem (*grapes etc.*); to strip (*tobacco*).
despalmador, *n.m.* careening-place; hoof-paring knife.
despalmar, *v.t.* to careen; to pare; to clear of grass.
despampanador, *n.m.* pruner of vines.
despampanadura, *n.f.* pruning (*vines*).
despampanante, *a.* (*coll.*) stunning, smashing, terrific.
despampanar, *v.t.* to prune (*vines*); (*coll.*) to stun. — **despampanarse,** *v.r.* (*coll.*) to let off steam; (*coll.*) to come a cropper.
despamplonar, *v.t.* to separate the shoots of (*plants*). — **despamplonarse,** *v.r.* (*fig.*) to sprain one's hand.
despanar, *v.t.* to clear of wheat.
despancar [A], *v.t.* (*Hisp. Am.*) to husk (*maize*).
despancijar, despanzurrar, *v.t.* (*coll.*) to rip *or* smash open; to squash.
despapar, *v.i.* to carry the head too high (*horse*).
despapucho, *n.m.* (*Per.*) absurdity, nonsense.
desparecer [9] [DESAPARECER].
desparejar, *v.t.* to break, break up, split (*a pair*); to mismatch; ***llevas los guantes desparejados,*** you are wearing odd gloves.
desparpajado, -da, *a.* nonchalant, free and easy, self-assured.
desparpajar, *v.t.* to undo in a disorderly way. — *v.i.* (*coll.*) to prattle.
desparpajo, *n.m.* nonchalance, easy manner, self-assurance; (*Hisp. Am.*) disorder, disturbance, turmoil.
desparramador, -ra, *n.m.f.* scatterer; squanderer.
desparramar, *v.t.* to spread, scatter, spill; to squander; to dissipate.
desparramo, *n.m.* (*Hisp. Am.*) spreading, scattering; squandering; (*Chi.*) disorder, disturbance.
despartidor, *n.m.* separator; conciliator.
despartir, *v.t.* to separate; to conciliate.
desparvar, *v.t.* to pile up for winnowing.
despasar, *v.t.* to unreeve (*rope etc.*); to remove (*cable etc.*) from a windlass.
despatarrada, *n.f.* the splits (*in certain Spanish dances*); (*coll.*) splits (*of the legs*).
despatarrar, *v.t.* to cause to open the legs wide; (*coll.*) to flabbergast. — **despatarrarse,** *v.r.* to do the splits.
despatillar, *v.t.* to cut off the sideboards of; to break off the arm of (*an anchor*); (*carp.*) to tenon.
despavesadura, *n.f.* snuffing (*candle etc.*).
despavesar, *v.t.* to blow the ashes off.
despavorido, -da, *a.* terrified, in panic.
despavorir(se) [Q], *v.i.* (*v.r.*) (*defective, having only the tenses and persons containing the letter **i***) to be *or* become terrified.
despeadura, *n.f.* (*vet.*) surbating, foundering, lameness (*horses*).
despeamiento, *n.m.* (*vet.*) foundering.
despear, *v.t.* to founder (*horses*).
despectivo, -va, *a.* contemptuous, derogatory; supercilious; pejorative.
despechar, *v.t.* to slight, make indignant; to drive to despair; (*coll.*) to wean.
despecho, *n.m.* spite; exasperation; ***a despecho,*** reluctantly, unwillingly; ***a despecho de,*** in spite of, despite; ***con despecho,*** angrily, spitefully; ***por despecho,*** in a fit of exasperation *or* pique.
despechugadura, *n.f.* cutting off the breast of a fowl; uncovering the breast.
despechugar [B], *v.t.* to cut off the breast of (*a fowl*). — **despechugarse,** *v.r.* (*coll.*) to uncover one's breast.
despedazamiento, *n.m.* tearing, smashing; cutting to pieces.
despedazar [C], *v.t.* to cut, tear *or* smash to pieces. — **despedazarse,** *v.r.* to fall to pieces; ***despedazarse de risa,*** to split one's sides laughing; ***se me despedaza el corazón,*** my heart is breaking, it breaks my heart.
despedida, *n.f.* leave-taking, farewell, parting; send-off; dismissal, discharge; last stanza in popular songs.
despedimiento, *n.m.* [DESPEDIDA].
despedir [8], *v.t.* to throw off *or* out, give off *or* out; to dismiss, fire, sack; to see off, see to the door, say good-bye to; ***despide mucho calor,*** it gives off a lot of heat. — **despedirse,** *v.r.* to take one's leave, say good-bye; to give (one's) notice; ***despídete de ese dinero,*** (you can) say good-bye to that money; ***despedirse a la francesa,*** to leave without saying good-bye, take French leave.
despedregar [B], *v.t.* to clear of stones.
despegable, *a.* that may be unglued, detachable.
despegado, -da, *a.* detached, indifferent, cool, cold, lacking in affection.
despegadura, *n.f.* detaching, ungluing.
despegamiento [DESPEGO].
despegar [B], *v.t.* to unglue, unstick, detach; ***no despega los labios,*** he doesn't say a word. — *v.i.* to take off (*aircraft*). — **despegarse,** *v.r.* to become detached; to grow cool *or* indifferent.
despego, *n.m.* indifference, coldness, lack of affection.
despegue, *n.m.* take off (*aircraft*).
despeinar, *v.t.* to disarrange, ruffle the hair of.
despejado, -da, *a.* bright, clear-headed; clear, cloudless; clear, wide (*forehead*).
despejar, *v.t.* to clear, free; to clear up; to find the value of; ***despejen(se),*** clear the way (there).— **despejarse,** *v.r.* to clear (up), brighten (up); to drop (*fever*).
despeje, despejo, *n.m.* clearing, freeing; clearing up; brightness, clear-headedness.
despeluchar, *v.t.* to ruffle the hair of; to wear away the hair, fluff *or* surface from (*velvet etc.*).
despeluzamiento, *n.m.* dishevelling (*hair*); making hair stand on end.

despeluzar, *v.t.* to tousle, dishevel, rumple (*hair*); (*Cub.*) to ruin (financially), leave penniless, (*coll.*) skin. — **despeluzarse,** *v.r.* to stand on end (*hair*).
despeluznar [ESPELUZNAR].
despeluznante [ESPELUZNANTE].
despellejadura [DESOLLADURA].
despellejar, *v.t.* to skin, flay; (*fig.*) to tear to bits.
despenar, *v.t.* to console; to put out of misery, kill; (*Chi.*) to drive to despair.
despendedor, -ra, *a.* spendthrift. — *n.m.f.* spendthrift.
despender, *v.t.* to spend, expend; (*fig.*) to squander.
despensa, *n.f.* pantry, larder; store of provisions; stewardship; marketing; year's supply of fodder; (*naut.*) steward's room.
despensería, *n.f.* office of steward.
despensero, -ra, *n.m.f.* caterer; steward; dispenser.
despeñadero, -ra, *a.* steep, precipitous. — *n.m.* precipice, cliff; (*fig.*) risk, danger.
despeñadizo, -za, *a.* steep, precipitous.
despeñar, *v.t.* to precipitate, fling *or* hurl down.
despeño, despeñamiento, *n.m.* flinging *or* hurling down; fall, drop; diarrhœa.
despepitar, *v.t.* to remove the seeds from; to gin. — **despepitarse,** *v.r.* to scream one's head off; to be crazy (about), rave (about).
despercudir, *v.t.* to cleanse, clean.
desperdiciador, -ra, *a.*, *n.m.f.* squanderer, waster, wastrel.
desperdiciar, *v.t.* to squander, waste.
desperdicio, *n.m.* waste; (*usually pl.*) garbage, refuse, remains, offal; ***no tiene desperdicio,*** it can all be used, it's worth every penny; (*iron.*) ***este niño no tiene desperdicio,*** this child is a little marvel.
desperdigar [B], *v.t.* to scatter.
desperecerse [9], *v.r.* to crave, long, desire eagerly.
desperezarse [C], *v.r.* to stretch one's limbs; to rouse up; to shake off one's sloth.
desperezo, *n.m.* stretching one's limbs; rousing up.
desperfecto, *n.m.* deterioration, wear and tear; slight damage; blemish, flaw; defect.
desperfilar, *v.t.* (*art*) to soften the lines of (*a painting*); (*mil.*) to camouflage; to mask the outlines of. — **desperfilarse,** *v.r.* to become shadowy.
despernada, *n.f.* step (*in dancing*).
despernar [1], *v.t.* to cut *or* injure the legs of; to tire, make footsore.
despertador, -ra, *a.* awakening, arousing. — *n.m.f.* awakener; (*sl.*) knocker-up. — *n.m.* alarm-clock.
despertamiento, *n.m.* awakening.
despertar [1], *v.t.* to awaken, wake, wake up, rouse; to whet. — **despertar(se),** *v.i.* (*v.r.*) to wake up.
despestañar, *v.t.* to pluck out the eyelashes of. — **despestañarse,** *v.r.* to look hard, strain one's eyes; (*Arg.*) to swot.
despezar, [C], *v.t.* (*plumbing*) to taper; (*arch.*) to divide into constituent parts.
despezo, *n.m.* (*plumbing*) taper [DESPIEZO].
despezonar, *v.t.* to remove the nipple *or* stem from; to separate.
despezuñarse, *v.r.* to injure a hoof; (*Hisp. Am.*) to rush; (*Hisp. Am.*) to take pains.
despiadado, -da, *a.* pitiless, ruthless, merciless, unmerciful.
despicar [A], *v.t.* to mollify. — **despicarse,** *v.r.* to become mollified; to get one's own back.
despichar, *v.t.* to give out; (*Hisp. Am.*) to crush, squash. — *v.i.* (*coll.*) to kick the bucket, pop off.
despidiente, *n.m.* (*build.*) board placed between a hanging scaffold and the wall; (*arch.*) ***despidiente de agua,*** flashing.
despido (1), *n.m.* dispatch; discharge; dismissal.
despido (2), *pres. indic.* [DESPEDIR].
despiece, *n.m.* break-down, break-up (*analysis*).
despierto, -ta, *a.* awake; (*fig.*) alive, quick, quick-witted, smart, all there. — *p.p.* [DESPERTAR].
despiezo, *n.m.* (*arch.*) juncture, bonding (*of one stone with another*).
despilarar, *v.t.* (*Hisp. Am.*, *min.*) to knock down the props from.
despilfarrado, -da, *a.* ragged, tattered; prodigal, wasteful.
despilfarrador, -ra, *n.m.f.* squanderer, waster, extravagant person.
despilfarrar, *v.t.* to squander, waste.
despilfarro, *n.m.* waste, squandering, extravagance; shabbiness.
despimpollar, *v.t.* to prune (*vines*).
despinces, *n.m.pl.* tweezers.
despintar, *v.t.* to remove the paint from; (*fig.*) to distort, disfigure. — **despintarse,** *v.r.* to lose paint *or* colour; (*fig.*) to fade, become forgotten; ***no se me despinta ese tipo,*** I'll never forget the fellow, I can see the fellow clearly (in my mind's eye).
despinte, *n.m.* (*Chi.*) inferior ore.
despinzadera, *n.f.* burler.
despinzar [C], *v.t.* to burl.
despinzas, *n.f.pl.* burling-tweezers.
despiojador, *n.m.* delouser.
despiojar, *v.t.* to clean of lice, delouse; to free from poverty.
despiporren, *n.m.* (*coll.*) limit, end; ***es el despiporren,*** it's the limit.
despique, *n.m.* getting one's own back.
despistado, -da, *a.*, *n.m.f.* absent-minded, woolly-headed (person).
despistar, *v.t.* to throw off the scent *or* track, throw off, give the slip; to mislead, fox. — **despistarse,** *v.r.* to lose the way, get lost; to get muddled, make a mistake, get the wrong idea, get hold of the wrong end of the stick, get on the wrong track *or* tack.
despiste, *n.m.* absent-mindedness, woolly-headedness.
despitorrado, *a.* (*tauro.*) with a broken horn.
despizcar [A], *v.t.* to break up small. — **despizcarse,** *v.r.* to make great efforts.
desplacer, *n.m.* displeasure, chagrin. — [9] *v.t.* to displease.
desplantación, *n.f.* uprooting.
desplantar, *v.t.* (*obs.*) to uproot; to throw out of plumb. — **desplantarse,** *v.r.* to lose one's erect posture (*in fencing* or *dancing*).
desplante, *n.m.* oblique posture (*in fencing* or *dancing*); piece of arrogance *or* insolence; piece of defiance.
desplatar, *v.t.* to separate silver from.
desplate, *n.m.* separating (*silver from other metals*).
desplayar, *v.i.* to go out, ebb.
desplazamiento, *n.m.* (*naut.*) displacement.
desplazar [C], *v.t.* to displace; to move, shift; to dislodge, oust.
desplegadura, *n.f.* unfolding, spreading out.
desplegar [1B], *v.t.* to unfold, display; to spread, lay out; (*mil.*) to deploy; to unfurl. — **desplegarse,** *v.r.* to spread (itself) out; ***desplegarse en abanico,*** to fan out.
despleguetear, *v.t.* to remove folds from.
despliegue, *n.m.* unfurling, unfolding; display(ing); (*mil.*) deploying, deployment.
desplomar, *v.t.* to put out of plumb. — **desplomarse,** *v.r.* to collapse; to tumble *or* topple down; to break (*waves*).
desplome, *n.m.* tumbling down, collapse; leaning *or* toppling over; (*arch.*) overhang(ing); (*aer.*) pancaking.
desplomo, *n.m.* tilt, being out of plumb (*wall*).
desplumadura, *n.f.* deplumation.
desplumar, *v.t.* to pluck; (*fig.*) to fleece, skin.

despoblación, *n.f.* depopulation.
despoblado, *n.m.* deserted spot, wilderness; open country; ***robo en despoblado,*** highway robbery.
despoblador, -ra, *a.* depopulating.
despoblar [4], *v.t.* to depopulate; to strip *or* empty (*a place*); (*min.*) to leave undermanned. — **despoblarse,** *v.r.* to become deserted; to become depopulated, lose its population, be bled of its population.
despojador, -ra, *a.* despoiling. — *n.m.f.* despoiler.
despojar, *v.t.* to strip, despoil; (*coll.*) to fleece. — **despojarse,** *v.t.* to divest o.s. (***de,*** of).
despojo, *n.m.* spoliation; spoils; plunder; slough; (*pl.*) offal, remains, leavings; secondhand building materials; mortal remains.
despolarización, *n.f.* depolarization.
despolarizar [C], *v.t.* to depolarize.
despolvar, *v.t.* to dust.
despolvorear, *v.t.* to dust; to sprinkle.
despopularizar [C], *v.t.* to render unpopular.
desportillar, *v.t.* to chip the edge of, chip; to notch.
desposado, -da, *a.* newly wed.
desposando, -da, *n.m.f.* person about to be married, betrothed.
desposar, *v.t.* to join in matrimony, wed. — **desposarse,** *v.r.* to get betrothed *or* married.
desposeer [N], *v.t.* to dispossess.
desposeído, -da, *n.m.f.* underprivileged individual, underdog.
desposeimiento, *n.m.* dispossession.
desposorio, *n.m.* (*esp. pl.*) betrothal; wedding, nuptials.
despostar, *v.t.* (*Hisp. Am.*) to cut up (*a carcass*).
despostillar (*Mex.*) [DESPORTILLAR].
déspota, *n.m.* despot.
despótico, -ca, *a.* despotic.
despotismo, *n.m.* despotism.
despotizar [C], *v.t.* (*Arg., Chi., Per.*) to tyrannize.
despotricar [A], *v.i.* (*coll.*) to rant, rant on, kick up a fuss, complain.
despreciable, *a.* contemptible, despicable; ***una cantidad nada despreciable,*** a sum not to be scorned, a not inconsiderable amount.
despreciador, -ra, *a.* despising, scorning. — *n.m.f.* despiser, scorner.
despreciar, *v.t.* to scorn, despise; to slight, rebuff; to reject; to ignore.
despreciativo, -va, *a.* scornful, derogatory.
desprecio, *n.m.* scorn, contempt; slight, rebuff; disregard.
desprender, *v.t.* to detach, break away, break off; to give off, give out. — **desprenderse,** *v.r.* to break off, come loose, fall away; to give up, part with (***de***); to be inferred; ***le cuesta desprenderse de esta sortija,*** it is an effort for her to part with this ring; ***de esto se desprenden muchas cosas,*** a great deal may be inferred from this.
desprendido, -da, *a.* disinterested, selfless; generous.
desprendimiento, *n.m.* detaching; coming loose, working loose; coming out, issue; selflessness; indifference; (*art*) descent from the Cross; ***desprendimiento de tierras,*** landslip, landslide.
despreocupación, *n.f.* unconcern, carefreeness, casualness, nonchalance.
despreocupado, -da, *a.* unconcerned, carefree, easy-going.
despreocuparse, *v.r.* to cease to concern *or* worry o.s., stop bothering.
desprestigiar, *v.t.* to impair the prestige of, discredit.
desprestigio, *n.m.* loss of prestige, discredit.
desprevención, *n.f.* improvidence, want of caution.
desprevenido, -da, *a.* unprovided; unprepared; ***coger desprevenido a alguien,*** to catch *or* take s.o. unawares.
desproporción, *n.f.* disproportion.
desproporcionado, -da, *a.* disproportionate; out of proportion.
desproporcionar, *v.t.* to disproportion.
despropositado, -da, *a.* absurd, ridiculous, preposterous.
despropósito, *n.m.* absurdity, preposterous *or* irrelevant nonsense.
desproveer [N, *p.p.* **desproveído, desprovisto**], *v.t.* to deprive of provisions *or* necessaries.
desprovisto, -ta, *a.* — ***de,*** unprovided, devoid (of).
despueble (1), *n.m.* depopulation.
despueblo, despueble (2), *pres. indic.; pres. subj.* [DESPOBLAR]
después, *adv.* after; afterwards, next, then, later; ***después de,*** after; next to; ***después*** (***de***) ***que,*** after; ***después de todo,*** after all, when all is said and done.
despulir, *v.t.* to tarnish; to frost.
despulpado, *n.m.* pulp extraction.
despulpar, *v.t.* to extract the pulp from.
despulsar, *v.t.* to leave lifeless. — **despulsarse,** *v.r.* to faint; to get worked up; ***despulsarse por,*** to yearn, long for.
despumación, *n.f.* skimming.
despumar, *v.t.* to skim.
despuntador, *n.m.* (*Mex.*) mineral separator; (*Mex.*) geological hammer.
despuntadura, *n.f.* blunting.
despuntar, *v.t.* to blunt; to crop, cut off, wear out (*a point*); to cut away the dry combs of (*a beehive*); (*naut.*) to round (*a cape*). — *v.i.* to bud, sprout; to begin to show *or* appear; to stand out, excel, be outstanding; to dawn, break (*day*); ***al despuntar del día,*** at break of day.
desquejar, *v.t.* to slip (*a plant*).
desqueje, *n.m.* slipping (*a plant*).
desquerer [26], *v.t.* to lose affection *or* liking for, cease to love *or* like.
desquiciado, -da, *a.* off balance; (*coll.*) off one's rocker.
desquiciar, *v.t.* to unhinge, disjoint; to unsettle, upset. — **desquiciarse,** *v.r.* to lose control, go off the rails.
desquijaramiento, *n.m.* breaking jaws.
desquijarar, *v.t.* to break the jaws of; (*naut.*) to break the cheek of (*a block*).
desquijerar, *v.t.* (*carp.*) to tenon.
desquilatar, *v.t.* to lower the value of (*gold*); (*fig.*) to debase.
desquitar, *v.t.* to compensate for loss etc. — **desquitarse,** *v.r.* to make up for sth.; to get one's own back; to get even *or* square, turn the tables.
desquite, *n.m.* compensation, making up for sth.; getting one's own back.
desrabotar, *v.t.* to cut off the tail of.
desramar, *v.t.* to strip of branches.
desrancharse, *v.r.* to withdraw from a mess (*regimental etc.*).
desraspar, *v.t.* to remove the stalk from (*grapes*); to remove the bones from (*fish*).
desrastrojar, *v.t.* (*agric.*) to remove stubble from.
desratizar [C], *v.t.* to clear of rats.
desrazonable, *a.* unreasonable.
desreglarse [DESARREGLARSE].
desreputación, *n.f.* (*coll.*) dishonour, disrepute.
desriñonarse, *v.r.* (*coll.*) to wear o.s. out, get fagged out.
desrizar [C], *v.t.* to uncurl; (*naut.*) to unfurl.
desroblar, *v.t.* to unrivet.
destacado, -da, *a.* outstanding, conspicuous, notable, distinguished.
destacamento, *n.m.* detachment.
destacar [A], *v.t.* (*mil.*) to detach, detail; to make

stand out, highlight, emphasize. — **destacarse,** *v.r.* to stand out, be conspicuous.
destaconar, *v.t.* to wear out the heels of.
destajador, *n.m.* smith's hammer.
destajar, *v.t.* to settle the terms for (*a job*); to cut (*cards*).
destajero, destajista, *n.m.* pieceworker.
destajo, *n.m.* job, piecework, task-work; ***a destajo,*** by the job, on a piecework basis; ***hablar a destajo,*** to chatter one's head off; ***trabajar a destajo,*** to work hurriedly, feverishly.
destalonar, *v.t.* to wear out the heels of; to detach, tear out; (*vet.*) to level the hoofs of.
destallar, *v.t.* to prune.
destapada, *n.f.* pie without upper crust.
destapar, *v.t.* to uncover, uncork, unplug, take the cover, lid *or* cap off, open. — **destaparse,** *v.r.* to get uncovered; to lose one's bedclothes; (*fig.*) to come out into the open, show one's true feelings *or* colours; (*fig.*) to lose control, fly off the handle.
destape, *n.m.* (*fam.*) nudity, stripping; (*fig.*) stripping *or* laying bare, taking the lid *or* wraps off things.
destapiar, *v.t.* to unwall.
destaponar, *v.t.* to uncork, unstopper.
destartalado, -da, *a.* ramshackle, rambling.
destazar [C], *v.t.* to cut up (*carcasses*).
destechadura, *n.f.* unroofing.
destechar, *v.t.* to unroof.
destejar, *v.t.* to untile; (*fig.*) to leave defenceless.
destejer, *v.t.* to unweave, unknit.
destellar, *v.t.*, *v.i.* to sparkle, twinkle, flash.
destello, *n.m.* sparkle, twinkle, flash; ***a veces tiene destellos de inteligencia,*** he has occasional flashes of intelligence.
destemplado, -da, *a.* out of tune; inharmonious; intemperate, disagreeable, harsh; ***echar con cajas destempladas,*** to throw out unceremoniously, fling out.
destemplanza, *n.f.* inclemency (*of weather*); (*med.*) being out of sorts, seediness, feverishness; intemperance, lack of moderation.
destemplar, *v.t.* to disturb *or* upset the harmony of; to put out of tune; to infuse; to untemper. — **destemplarse,** *v.r.* to get out of sorts; to lose one's equanimity *or* moderation; (*Hisp. Am.*) to have the teeth on edge.
destemple, *n.m.* lack *or* loss of temper (*in metals*); being out of tune; [DESTEMPLANZA].
destentar [I], *v.t.* to lead out of temptation; to remove temptation from.
desteñir [8K], *v.t.* to undye; to fade. — *v.i.* to fade; ***esta tela no destiñe,*** this is a fast-colour fabric.
desternillarse, *v.r.* to break one's cartilages; to break a tendon; ***desternillarse de risa,*** to split one's sides with laughter.
desterradero, *n.m.* wilderness, wilds, waste.
desterrado, -da, *n.m.f.* exile, banished person.
desterrar [I], *v.t.* to banish; to exile; to remove earth from; ***desterrar la tristeza,*** to put sorrow aside.
desterronar, *v.t.* to break the clods of; to harrow.
destetamiento, *n.m.* weaning.
destetar, *v.t.* to wean; (*fig.*) to force s.o. to fend for himself; ***destetarse uno con una cosa,*** to have known a thing from one's cradle.
destete, *n.m.* weaning.
desteto, *n.m.* weaned livestock; place where newly weaned mules are kept.
destiempo, *adv.* ***a destiempo,*** at the wrong time (*too early, too late*).
destiento, *n.m.* surprise, shock.
destierre (1), *n.m.* cleaning (*ore*).
destierro (1), *n.m.* exile, banishment; place of exile; (*fig.*) wilderness, wilds.
destierro (2), **destierre** (2), *pres. indic.; pres. subj.* [DESTERRAR].
destilable, *a.* distillable.
destilación, *n.f.* distillation; flow of humours; filtration.
destiladera, *n.f.* still, distiller; (*Hisp. Am.*) filter.
destilador, -ra, *a.* distilling. — *n.m.f.* distiller. — *n.m.* still; filtering-stone.
destilar, *v.t.* to distil; to filter; ***la llaga destilaba sangre,*** blood was oozing from the wound. — *v.i.* to distil, drop, fall in drops; to filter.
destilatorio, -ria, *a.* distillatory, distilling. — *n.m.* distillery; still.
destinar, *v.t.* to destine; to post, station, send; to assign.
destino, *n.m.* destiny; destination; appointment, post, position, job; (*mil.*) posting, stationing; purpose; use; ***con destino a,*** bound for, going to.
destiño (1), *n.m.* piece of blackish *or* greenish dry honeycomb.
destiño (2), (***él***) **destiño** (3), *pres. indic.; 3rd pers. sing. pret.* [DESTEÑIR].
destitución, *n.f.* dismissal, removal from office; depriving, deprivation.
destituir [O], *v.t.* to dismiss, remove from office; to deprive.
destocar [A], *v.t.* to uncoif; to pull off the cap *or* head-dress from.
destorcer [5D], *v.t.* to untwist; (*fig.*) to straighten out. — **destorcerse,** *v.r.* (*naut.*) to deviate from course; to drift.
destornillado, -da, *a.* (*fig., fam.*) with a screw loose.
destornillador, *n.m.* unscrewer; screwdriver.
destornillamiento, *n.m.* unscrewing; (*fig.*) craziness, wildness.
destornillar, *v.t.* to unscrew. — **destornillarse,** *v.r.* (*fig.*) to go screwy, go crazy.
destoserse, *v.r.* to feign a cough, clear the throat.
destostarse [4], *v.r.* to lose sunburn.
destrabar, *v.t.* to unfetter, untie, unhobble; to separate.
destraillar, *v.t.* to unleash (*dogs*).
destral, *n.m.* small hatchet *or* axe.
destramar, *v.t.* to unweave, undo the warp of; (*obs.*) to unravel *or* defeat (*a plot*).
destrejar, *v.i.* to act skilfully.
destrenzar [C], *v.t.* to unbraid, unplait, untwine.
destreza, *n.f.* dexterity, skill.
destrincar [A], *v.t.* (*naut.*) to loose, unlash.
destripacuentos, *n.m.f. inv.* (*coll.*) interrupter, butter-in, heckler.
destripador, *n.m.* ripper.
destripar, *v.t.* to disembowel, gut; to rip open, smash open; to take the inside out of; (*coll.*) to interrupt and spoil (*a story*).
destripaterrones, *n.m. inv.* (*coll.*) country bumpkin, clod, yokel.
destrísimo, -ma, *a. superl.* highly dexterous.
destriunfar, *v.t.* to draw out all the trumps from.
destrizar [C], *v.t.* to smash into pieces *or* to smithereens; to tear to shreds. — **destrizarse,** *v.r.* (*fig.*) to go to pieces; (*fig.*) to fly off the handle.
destrocar [A], *v.t.* to return (*a thing bartered*).
destrón, *n.m.* a blind man's guide.
destronamiento, *n.m.* dethronement.
destronar, *v.t.* to dethrone; to oust.
destroncamiento, *n.m.* detruncation, lopping down of trees; ruination.
destroncar [A], *v.t.* to detruncate, lop (*a tree*) down; to maim, mutilate; to ruin, destroy; to interrupt, cut short; ***destroncar un discurso,*** to interrupt a speech; (*Chi., Mex.*) to uproot, extirpate.
destrozador, -ra, *n.m.f.* destroyer, mangler.
destrozar [C], *v.t.* to smash to pieces, shatter; to mangle.

destrozo, *n.m.* smashing to pieces, shattering; (*pl.*) damage, havoc.
destrozón, -zona, *a.* destructive; hard on (*clothes*).
destrucción, *n.f.* destruction.
destructibilidad, *n.f.* destructibility.
destructible, *a.* destructible.
destructivo, -va, *a.* destructive.
destructor, -ra, *a.* destructive, destroying. — *n.m.f.* destroyer, harasser; (*naut.*) destroyer.
destructorio, -ria, *a.* destroying.
destrueco (1), **destrueque** (1), *n.m.* return of an exchange, re-exchange.
destrueco (2), **destrueque** (2), *pres. indic.; pres. subj.* [DESTROCAR].
destruible, *adj.* destructible.
destruidor, -ra, *a.* destroying. — *n.m.f.* destroyer.
destruir [O], *v.t.* to destroy. — **destruirse,** *v.r.* (*alg.*) to cancel out.
destruyente, *a.* destroying.
destusar, *v.t.* (*Hisp. Am.*) to husk (*maize*).
desucación, *n.f.* juice extraction.
desudar, *v.t.* to wipe off sweat from.
desuellacaras, *n.m. inv.* (*coll.*) face-scraper; (*fig.*) shameless person.
desuello (1), *n.m.* flaying, skinning; fleecing; (*fig.*) shamelessness; ***esto es un desuello,*** it's sheer robbery.
desuello (2), **desuelle,** *pres. indic.; pres. subj.* [DESOLLAR].
desuncir [D], *v.t.* to unyoke.
desunión, *n.f.* disunion; discord.
desunir, *v.t.* to disunite, separate, part; (*fig.*) to occasion discord between.
desuñar, *v.t.* to tear off the nails of; to pull out the dead roots of (*plants*). — **desuñarse,** *v.r.* (*coll., fig.*) to work one's fingers to the bone; to plunge into vice etc.
desuñir, *v.t.* (*Arg., prov.*) to unyoke.
desurcar [A], *v.t.* to remove *or* undo furrows in.
desurdir, *v.t.* to unravel, unweave; to upset, stop, frustrate (*a plot etc.*).
desusado, -da, *a.* out of use, obsolete; unusual.
desusar, *v.t.* to disuse, discontinue the use of. — **desusarse,** *v.r.* to become obsolete, fall into disuse.
desuso, *n.m.* disuse; obsoleteness; ***caer en desuso,*** to fall into disuse; ***dejar en desuso,*** to abandon the use of, give up using.
desustanciar, *v.t.* to deprive of substance, weaken.
desvahar, *v.t.* to trim off the dead parts of (*a plant*).
desvaído, -da, *a.* faded, pale, colourless; lank.
desvainadura, *n.f.* shelling (*beans etc.*).
desvainar, *v.t.* to shell.
desvalido, -da, *a.* unprotected, helpless; destitute.
desvalijador, *n.m.* rifler, robber.
desvalijamiento, *n.m.* rifling.
desvalijar, *v.t.* to rifle.
desvalimiento, *n.m.* want of protection, helplessness; destitution.
desvalor, *n.m.* (*obs.*) cowardice; lack of merit.
desvalorizar [C], *v.t.* to diminish the value of, devalue.
desván, *n.m.* garret, loft, attic.
desvanecer [9], *v.t.* to cause to vanish; to dispel, dissipate; to efface. — **desvanecerse,** *v.r.* to vanish; to faint, swoon.
desvanecidamente, *adv.* haughtily.
desvanecimiento, *n.m.* vanishing; dispelling; fading; faint(ing), swoon(ing); haughtiness.
desvarar, *v.t.* to set afloat, re-float. — **desvararse,** *v.r.* to slip, glide.
desvariado, -da, *a.* delirious, raving; nonsensical; long and rank (*branches etc.*).
desvariar [L], *v.i.* to be delirious, rave, rant.
desvarío, *n.m.* delirium, raving; wild *or* crazy nonsense; eccentricity, whim.
desvedar, *v.t.* to lift the ban on.
desvelamiento, *n.m.* watchfulness; [DESVELO].
desvelar, *v.t.* to keep awake, make sleepless; to wake up. — **desvelarse,** *v.r.* to be unable to sleep, stay awake; ***desvelarse por,*** to do everything possible to; to be anxious about.
desvelo, *n.m.* sleeplessness; anxiety, concern.
desvenar, *v.t.* to remove the veins from; to extract (*ore*) from veins; to strip (*tobacco leaves*); to raise (*the bit*) of a bridle.
desvencijado, -da, *a.* rickety, tumble-down, falling apart.
desvencijar, *v.t.* to make rickety, disjoint.
desvendar, *v.t.* to unbandage, take off a bandage from.
desveno, *n.m.* arch (*of a bit*).
desventaja, *n.f.* disadvantage, drawback.
desventajoso, -sa, *a.* disadvantageous, unfavourable, unprofitable, detrimental.
desventar [1], *v.t.* to vent, let out the air from.
desventura, *n.f.* misfortune.
desventurado, -da, *a.* unfortunate; wretched; spiritless; pusillanimous. — *n.m.f.* spiritless person, wretch.
desvergonzado, -da, *a.* impudent; shameless; immodest.
desvergonzarse [C], *v.r.* to throw modesty *or* pretence to the winds; to show one's true colours.
desvergüenza, *n.f.* impudence; effrontery, shamelessness; impudent *or* shameless thing to do *or* say.
desvestir(se) [8], *v.t.* (*v.r.*) to undress, strip unclothe.
desvezar [C], *v.t.* (*prov.*) to cut the young shoots of (*vines*).
desviación, *n.f.* deviation; diversion, diverting, turning aside, deflection; (*med.*) extravasation.
desviacionismo, *n.m.* deviationism.
desviadero, *n.m.* (*railw.*) siding.
desviar [L], *v.t.* to divert, deflect, turn aside; to dissuade; (*fenc.*) to ward off; (*railw.*) to switch. — **desviarse,** *v.r.* to deviate, turn away, turn off, wander; to swerve.
desvío, *n.m.* deviation; deflection; turning aside *or* away; estrangement, coolness; (*build.*) wall support (*scaffolding*); (*Hisp. Am.*) railway siding.
desvirar, *v.t.* to pare off the rough edges of; to trim the edges of; (*naut.*) to reverse (*capstan*).
desvirgar [B], *v.t.* to deflower.
desvirtuar [M], *v.t.* to weaken; to detract from, spoil.
desvitrificar [A], *v.t.* to devitrify.
desvivirse, *v.r.* to go out of one's way, go to any trouble, lean over backwards; ***se desvive por el dinero,*** he'll do anything for money, to get money.
desvolvedor, *n.m.* nut-wrench.
desvolver [5, *p.p.* **desvuelto**], *v.t.* to alter the shape of; to turn up (*soil*); to unscrew.
desyemar, *v.t.* to remove buds from.
desyerbador, -ra, *a.* weeding.
desyerbar, *v.t.* to weed.
deszocar [A], *v.t.* to hurt, wound *or* disable (*foot*).
deszumar, *v.t.* to extract the juice from.
detalladamente, *adv.* in detail.
detallar, *v.t.* to detail, particularize; to tell in detail; to retail.
detalle, *n.m.* detail, particular; detailed list *or* account; retail; piece of thoughtfulness *or* consideration, courtesy; ***al detalle,*** retail; ***vender al detalle,*** to sell retail; ***tiene muchos detalles,*** he is very thoughtful *or* considerate.
detallista, *a., n.m.f.* thoughtful, considerate (person); painstaking, meticulous (individual). — *n.m.f.* retailer.
detasa, *n.f.* (*railw.*) rebate.

detectar, *v.t.* to detect, spot.
detective, *n.m.* detective.
detector, *n.m.* detector.
detención, *n.f.* detention; arrest; stop, stopping; thoroughness.
detenedor, -ra, *n.m.f.* detainer, stopper, arrester.
detener [33], *v.t.* to stop; to detain, keep back, hold back; to check; to arrest. — **detenerse,** *v.r.* to stop, come to a halt; to pause; to linger, tarry.
detenido, -da, *a.* thorough, careful, painstaking; hesitant; mean.
detenimiento, *n.m.* thoroughness, great care.
detentación, *n.f.* (*law*) withholding (*of an estate etc.*) from its rightful owner.
detentador, *n.m.* (*law*) deforcer.
detentar, *v.t.* to hold; (*law*) to keep unlawfully; ***detentar un cargo,*** to hold an office *or* position; ***detenta la marca (el récord),*** he holds the record.
detergente, *a., n.m.* detergent.
deterger [E], *v.t.* (*med.*) to cleanse, deterge.
deterioración, *n.f.* [DETERIORO].
deteriorado, -da, *a.* shop-soiled, (*Am.*) shop-worn.
deteriorar, *v.t.* to make bad; to damage, spoil, wear out, impair. — **deteriorarse,** *v.r.* to deteriorate; (*fig.*) to go down-hill; to become dilapidated, sink into a state of dilapidation, go to wrack and ruin.
deterioro, *n.m.* deterioration, dilapidation, damage, wear and tear.
determinable, *a.* determinable, ascertainable.
determinación, *n.f.* decision; determining, determination; ***tomar una determinación,*** to take *or* make a decision.
determinado, -da, *a.* determinate; definite; given, specified; ***a una hora determinada,*** at a given time; ***en determinados casos,*** in certain cases.
determinante, *a.* determining, determinative. — *n.m.* (*gram.*) determining verb.
determinar, *v.t.* to determine, decide; to specify; to bring about. — **determinarse,** *v.r.* — ***a,*** to make up one's mind to, resolve to.
determinativo, -va, *a.* determinative.
determinismo, *n.m.* (*phil.*) determinism.
determinista, *a., n.m.* (*phil.*) determinist.
detersión, *n.f.* (*med.*) cleansing, detersion.
detersivo, -va, *a.* detersive.
detersorio, -ria, *a., n.m.f.* detergent.
detestable, *a.* detestable, atrocious, deplorable, abominable.
detestación, *n.f.* detestation, abomination.
detestar, *v.t.* to detest, hate, loathe.
detienebuey, *n.m.* (*bot.*) rest-harrow.
detonación, *n.f.* detonation, report.
detonar, *v.i.* to detonate, explode.
detorsión, *n.f.* (*med.*) distortion.
detracción, *n.f.* detraction; defamation; slander; withdrawal.
detractar, *v.t.* to defame, slander.
detractor, -ra, *a.* detracting, slandering. — *n.m.* detractor, slanderer.
detraer [34], *v.t.* to detract, remove, take away; to defame, slander, libel.
detrás, *adv.* behind, after, at the back, in the rear; ***detrás de,*** behind, at the back of; ***por detrás,*** behind, at the back; ***ir detrás de,*** to go after.
detrimento, *n.m.* detriment, damage, harm; ***con (sin) detrimento de,*** with (without) detriment to.
detrítico, -ca, *a.* detrital, detritic.
detritus, *n.m.* detritus.
deuda (1), *n.f.* debt; ***duedas activas,*** assets; ***deuda consolidada,*** funded debt; ***deudas pasivas,*** liabilities; ***sin deudas,*** clear; ***perdónanos nuestras deudas,*** forgive us our trespasses; ***la deuda,*** public debt; ***estar en deuda con,*** to be indebted to.
deudo, -da (2), *n.m.f.* relative, kinsman; (*pl.*) kith and kin.
deudor, -ra, *a.* indebted. — *n.m.f.* debtor.
Deuteronomio, *n.m.* Deuteronomy.
deutóxido, *n.m.* (*chem.*) dioxide.
devalar, *v.i.* (*naut.*) to drift, deviate from course.
devaluar [M], *v.t., v.i.* to devalue, devaluate.
devanadera, *n.f.* reel, spool, bobbin; winding-frame; (*pl.*) (*theat.*) revolving wings.
devanador, -ra, *a.* reeling, winding. — *n.m.* winder; ***devanador de lanzadera,*** shuttle-winder.
devanar, *v.t.* to reel, spool, wind (*yarn etc.*). — **devanarse,** *v.r.* ***devanarse los sesos,*** to rack one's brains.
devanear, *v.i.* to rave, be delirious, talk nonsense.
devaneo, *n.m.* delirium, craziness; crazy whim, wild pursuit; flirtation, fooling about.
devantal [DELANTAL].
devastación, *n.f.* devastation.
devastador, -ra, *a.* devastating. — *n.m.f.* devastator.
devastar, *v.t.* to devastate, lay waste.
devengar [B], *v.t.* to collect; to yield; ***derechos a devengar,*** duties due for settlement.
devenir [36], *v.i.* to happen; to become; ***el devenir,*** the shape of things to come.
devoción, *n.f.* devotion, devotedness; devoutness, piety; ***no es santo de mi devoción,*** I'm not keen on him, it etc.; he, it etc. is not my cup of tea.
devocionario, *n.m.* prayer-book.
devolución, *n.f.* return, restitution; devolution.
devolutivo, -va, *a.* (*law*) restorable.
devolver [5, *p.p.* **devuelto**], *v.t.* to return, give, send *or* pay back; (*coll.*) to throw up, vomit.
devoniano, -na, *a* (*geol.*) Devonian.
devorador, -ra, *a.* devouring, ravenous. — *n.m.f.* devourer.
devorar, *v.t.* to devour, swallow up, wolf (down).
devotería, *n.f.* sanctimoniousness.
devoto, -ta, *a.* devout, godly, pious. — *n.m.f.* devotee.
dexiocardia, *n.f.* dextrocardia.
dextrina, *n.f.* dextrine.
dextrógiro, -ra, *a.* dextrogyrous.
dextrorso, -sa, *a.* dextrorse.
dextrosa, *n.f.* dextrose.
deyección, *n.f.* (*geol.*) debris; (*med.*) defecation.
deyector, -ra, *a.* ejector, ejecting.
dezmable, *a.* tithable.
dezmar [DIEZMAR].
dezmatorio, *n.m.* tithing; place in which tithes are collected.
dezmeño, -ña, dezmero, -ra, *a.* belonging to tithes. — *n.m.* payer *or* collector of tithes.
dezmería, *n.f.* tithe-land.
día, *n.m.* day; daylight; ***a días,*** at times; ***buenos días,*** good day, good morning; ***al día,*** a day, per day; up to date; ***de día,*** by day; ***al otro día,*** on the next day; ***progresa de día en día,*** he gets better every day; ***lo fue dejando de un día para otro,*** he kept putting it off from one day to the next; ***en su día,*** in due course; ***dar los días a,*** to wish a happy birthday to; ***tiene días,*** he has his days, he has good days *or* off days; ***todo el santo día,*** the whole blessed day; ***de hoy en ocho días,*** a week today; ***hombre de días*** or ***entrado en días,*** elderly man; ***los días de uno,*** one's birthday; ***no se van los días en balde,*** time tells; ***más días hay que longanizas,*** there is no hurry *or* urgency; ***es del día,*** it's to-day's, it's fresh; ***un día sí y otro no,*** every other day; ***días caniculares,*** dog days; ***día de cutio, día laborable,*** work-day, working day; ***día de descanso*** or ***de asueto,*** holiday, day off; ***día de fiesta, día festivo, día feriado,*** holiday; ***día de***

guardar, día de precepto, holy day of obligation; ***día de Reyes,*** Epiphany; ***día del juicio,*** doomsday; ***día de los difuntos,*** All Souls' Day; ***día de recibo,*** at-home day; ***día entre semana,*** week-day; ***día señalado,*** red-letter day; ***día diado,*** appointed day; ***uno que otro día,*** some day or another; ***el día menos pensado,*** when least expected; ***hoy en día,*** nowadays; ***el mejor día,*** some fine day; ***mañana será otro día,*** tomorrow is another day; ***abrir, despuntar*** or ***romper el día,*** to break (*day*); ***vivir al día,*** to live from hand to mouth.

diabasa, *n.f.* (*geol.*) diabase.

diabetes, *n.f.* diabetes.

diabético, -ca, *a.* diabetic.

diabeto, *n.m.* automatic flushing cistern.

diabla, *n.f.* (*coll.*) she-devil; carding-machine; two-wheeled carriage; ***a la diabla,*** carelessly, anyhow.

diablear, *v.i.* (*coll.*) to get up to mischief, play pranks.

diablejo, *n.m.* (engaging) little devil, scamp.

diablesa, *n.f.* (*coll.*) she-devil.

diablillo [DIABLEJO].

diablo, *n.m.* devil, demon, fiend; (*coll.*) ***aquí hay mucho diablo,*** there's more to it than meets the eye; ***anda*** or ***está el diablo en Cantillana,*** there's a rumpus going on; ***el diablo anda suelto,*** the devil's on the loose; ***dar a todos los diablos,*** to give up as a bad job; ***darse a todos los diablos,*** to go off the deep end; ***el diablo harto de carne se metió fraile,*** young sinner, old saint; (*fig.*) ***el diablo las carga,*** it may back-fire on you; ***¡el diablo que lo entienda!*** it's beyond me!; ***diablo cojuelo,*** artful devil; ***como un diablo,*** like hell; ***correr como un diablo,*** to go hell for leather; ***ser (de) la piel del diablo,*** to be of the devil's brood; ***sus buenas intenciones se las llevó el diablo,*** his good intentions (all) went down the drain; ***tener uno el diablo en el cuerpo,*** to be the very devil, get up to all manner of tricks.

diablotín, diabolín, *n.m.* sweet *or* chocolate (*wrapped in paper with a joke, saying etc. written on it*).

diablura, *n.f.* piece of devilry *or* mischief, prank, lark.

diabólico, -ca, *a.* diabolical, devilish.

diábolo, *n.m.* diabolo (*game*).

diacitrón, *n.m.* candied lemon-peel.

diacodión, *n.m.* syrup of poppy.

diaconado, diaconato, *n.m.* deaconship.

diaconal, *a.* diaconal.

diaconía, *n.f.* deaconry.

diaconisa, *n.f.* deaconess.

diácono, *n.m.* deacon.

diacrítico, -ca, *a.* diacritic, diacritical.

diacústico, -ca, *a.* diacoustic. — *n.f.* diacoustics.

diadema, *n.f.* diadem; tiara; halo.

diademado, -da, *a.* diademed.

diado, *a.* ***día diado,*** appointed day.

diafanidad, *n.f.* transparency, diaphanousness, sparkling clarity.

diáfano, -na, *a.* transparent, diaphanous, sparklingly clear.

diaforesis, *n.f. inv.* (*med.*) diaphoresis.

diafragma, *n.m.* (*anat.*) diaphragm.

diafragmático, -ca, *a.* diaphragmatic.

diagnosis, *n.f.* (*med.*) diagnosis.

diagnosticar [A], *v.t.* (*med.*) to diagnose.

diagnóstico, -ca, *a.* (*med.*) diagnostic. — *n.m.* diagnosis.

diagonal, *a.* diagonal. — *n.f.* (*geom.*) diagonal.

diágrafo, *n.m.* diagraph.

diagrama, *n.m.* diagram.

diálaga, *n.f.* (*min.*) diallage.

dialéctico, -ca, *a.* dialectic, dialectical. — *n.m.* dialectician. — *n.f.* dialectics; (*pol.*) debate.

dialecto, *n.m.* dialect.

dialogal, *a.* dialogical.

dialogar [B], *v.i.* to dialogue, talk, communicate, discuss *or* exchange views.

dialogístico, -ca, *a.* dialogistic.

dialogizar [C] [DIALOGAR].

diálogo, *n.m.* dialogue; debate; talk, communication; ***todo diálogo es imposible,*** any attempt at communication *or* mutual comprehension is out of the question.

dialoguista, *n.m.* dialogist.

dialtea, *n.f.* marsh-mallow ointment.

diamantado, -da, *a.* diamond-like.

diamante, *n.m.* (*min.*) diamond; miner's lamp; glass-cutter; (*lit., fig.*) ***diamante en bruto,*** rough diamond.

diamantino, -na, *a.* adamantine.

diamantista, *n.m.* diamond-cutter; jeweller.

diametral, *a.* diametrical.

diámetro, *n.m.* diameter.

diana, *n.f.* (*mil.*) reveille; bull's-eye (*target*); (*poet.*) moon; ***hacer diana,*** to hit the bull's-eye, score a bull's-eye.

dianche, diantre, *n.m.* (*coll.*) deuce, devil.

diapasón, *n.m.* diapason; fingerboard; tuning-fork; pitch; pitch pipe.

diaplejía, *n.f.* (*med.*) general paralysis.

diapositiva, *n.f.* slide, transparency.

diaprea, *n.f.* plum.

diaquilón, *n.m.* (*pharm.*) diachylon.

diariamente, *adv.* daily, every day.

diario, -ria, *a.* daily. — *n.m.* diary; daily newspaper; daily household expenses; (*com.*) ***libro diario,*** day-book, journal; (*naut.*) ***diario de navegación,*** log-book.

diarista, *n.m.f.* diarist; journalist.

diarrea, *n.f.* diarrhœa.

diarreico, -ca, diárrico, -ca, *a.* (*med.*) diarrhœic.

diáspero, diaspro, *n.m.* jasper.

diáspora, *n.f.* diaspora; ***se produjo una diáspora,*** they all ran for it, they all cleared off, they all scattered.

diástilo, *n.m.* (*arch.*) diastyle.

diatérmano, -na, diatérmico, -ca, *a.* diathermanous.

diatesarón, *n.m.* (*mus.*) diatessaron.

diatómico, -ca, *a.* (*chem.*) diatomic.

diatónico, -ca, *a.* (*mus.*) diatonic.

diatriba, *n.f.* diatribe.

dibujante, *n.m.f.* designer, draughtsman, draughtswoman; illustrator; cartoonist.

dibujar, *v.t., v.i.* to draw; to design; to depict; to sketch. — **dibujarse,** *v.r.* to take form, stand out; to be outlined.

dibujo, *n.m.* design, drawing; pattern; picture; sketch; ***dibujo del natural,*** drawing from life *or* nature; ***dibujo lineal,*** instrument drawing; ***dibujos animados,*** animated cartoons; ***no te metas en dibujos,*** don't do anything too elaborate.

dicacidad, *n.f.* pertness, banter, sauciness.

dicaz, *a.* keen, biting (*word*).

dicción, *n.f.* diction.

diccionario, *n.m.* dictionary.

diccionarista, *n.m.f.* dictionary compiler, lexicographer.

diciembre, *n.m.* December.

dicotomía, *n.f.* dichotomy.

dicotómico, -ca, dicótomo, -ma, *a.* dichotomous.

dictado, *n.m.* dictation; title, style; (*pl.*) dictates, promptings (*of conscience etc.*); ***escribir al dictado,*** to take (down) dictation.

dictador, *n.m.* dictator.

dictadura, *n.f.* dictatorship.

dictáfono, *n.m.* dictaphone.

dictamen, *n.m.* judgment, decision; opinion, findings, report; ***tomar dictamen de,*** to take counsel of.
dictaminar, *v.i.* to express an opinion; to report.
díctamo, *n.m.* (*bot.*) dittany; ***díctamo blanco*** or ***real,*** white fraxinella.
dictar, *v.t.*, *v.i.* to dictate; (*fig.*) to prompt.
dictatorial, dictatorio, -ria, *a.* dictatorial.
dicterio, *n.m.* vituperation.
dicha, *n.f.* happiness, bliss, joy, delight; good fortune, good luck; ***por dicha,*** fortunately; ***nunca es tarde si la dicha es buena,*** all's well that ends well.
dicharachero, -ra, *a.* (*coll.*) amusing, witty and lively (*in conversation*). — *n.m.f.* jokester, wag.
dicharacho, *n.m.* (*coll.*) crude *or* vulgar expression; piece of waggishness.
dichero, -ra (*prov.*, *coll.*) [DICHARACHERO].
dicho, *n.m.* saying; saw; ***del dicho al hecho, hay gran trecho,*** talk and action are two very different things; (*pl.*) marriage pledge. — ***p.p.*** [DECIR]; ***mejor dicho,*** rather, I mean; ***propiamente dicho,*** proper, strictly speaking; ***diez, mejor dicho once,*** ten, I mean eleven; ***Castilla propiamente dicha,*** Castille proper; ***lo dicho,*** that's settled then, it's agreed; I'll hold you to that.
dichoso, -sa, *a.* happy, blissful; delighted; (*fig.*, *fam.*) blessed, blasted, damned.
didáctico, -ca, *a.* didactic. — *n.f.* didactics.
didascálico, -ca, *a.* didactic.
diecinueve, *a.*, *n.m.* nineteen(th).
diecinueveavo, -va, *a.* nineteenth.
dieciochavo, -va, dieciocheno, -na, *a.* eighteenth. — *n.m.* cloth; old coin (*Valencia*).
dieciocho, *a.*, *n.m.* eighteen(th).
dieciséis, *a.*, *n.m.* sixteen(th).
dieciseisavo, -va, dieciseseno, -na, *a.* sixteenth.
diecisiete, *a.*, *n.m.* seventeen(th).
diecisieteavo, -va, *a.* seventeenth.
diedro, -ra, *a.* (*geom.*) dihedral.
Diego, *n.m.* James.
dieléctrico, -ca, *a.* dielectric.
diente (1), *n.m.* tooth; fang; (*mech.*) cog; prong (*of fork*); clove (*of garlic*); ***diente de león,*** dandelion; ***diente de lobo,*** spike; burnisher; ***diente de perro,*** chisel; (*bot.*) dog-tooth violet; (*sew.*) sampler; ***apretar los dientes,*** to clench *or* grit one's teeth; ***está dando diente con diente,*** his teeth are chattering; ***crujir de dientes,*** gnashing of teeth; ***hacer rechinar los dientes,*** to grind one's teeth; ***hincar el diente en,*** to sink one's teeth into; (*fig.*) to get one's teeth into; ***tener buen diente,*** to be a good eater; ***echar los dientes,*** to cut (one's) teeth, teethe; ***enseñar los dientes,*** to show one's teeth; ***hablar entre dientes,*** to mumble, mutter; ***se me ponen los dientes largos,*** I am *or* feel green with envy; ***ése no me entra de los dientes adentro,*** I can't stomach that chap; ***de dientes afuera,*** insincerely, outwardly.
diente (2), *pres. subj.* [DENTAR].
dientecico, dientecillo, dientecito, *n.m.* little tooth.
diéresis, *n.f.* diæresis.
diestro, -ra, *a.* right; skilful, dexterous; right-handed; able; ***a diestro y a siniestro,*** recklessly; right, left and centre. — *n.m.* skilful fencer; matador, bullfighter; halter, bridle; ***llevar del diestro,*** to lead by the halter. — *n.f.* right hand; ***juntar diestra con diestra,*** to join forces.
dieta, *n.f.* diet; ***está a dieta,*** he is on a diet, he mustn't eat; (*pl.*) expenses (per day).
dietario, *n.m.* account *or* record book.
dietético, -ca, *a.* dietetic. — *n.f.* dietetics.
diez, *a.*, *n.m.* ten, tenth; ***diez de bolos,*** pin placed alone in front of ninepins; ***a las diez,*** at ten o'clock; (*coll.*) ***hacer las diez de últimas,*** to queer one's own pitch.
diezmal, *a.* decimal, tenth.
diezmar, *v.t.* to decimate; to tithe.
diezmero, *n.m.* one who pays *or* collects a tithe.
diezmesino, -na, *a.* ten-month.
diezmilésimo, -ma, *a.* ten-thousandth.
diezmilmillonésimo, -ma, *a.* ten-thousand-millionth.
diezmillonésimo, -ma, *a.* ten-millionth.
diezmo, *n.m.* tithe.
difamación, *n.f.* defamation, slander, libelling.
difamador, -ra, *a.* defamatory. — *n.m.f.* defamer, libeller.
difamar, *v.t.* to defame, libel.
difamatorio, -ria, *a.* defamatory, libellous.
diferencia, *n.f.* difference; ***a diferencia de,*** in contrast to, unlike; ***hacer diferencias,*** to discriminate; ***partir la diferencia,*** to split the difference.
diferenciación, *n.f.* differentiation.
diferencial, *a.*, *n.f.* differential.
diferenciar, *v.t.* to differentiate; to distinguish. — **diferenciarse,** *v.r.* to be different, differ (***de,*** from).
diferente, *a.* different.
diferir [6], *v.t.* to defer, postpone, adjourn, put off. — *v.i.* to differ, be different.
difícil, *a.* difficult, hard; unlikely; ***es difícil que venga ya,*** he's not likely to come now.
difícilmente, *adv.* hardly, scarcely; with difficulty.
dificultad, *n.f.* difficulty, hardness; objection; obstacle; ***tiene dificultad para andar,*** he has difficulty in walking; ***tiene dificultad para las matemáticas,*** he has difficulty *or* trouble with maths; ***hemos tenido muchas dificultades,*** we have had a great deal of trouble; ***me puso bastantes dificultades,*** he put quite a few difficulties in my way, he raised quite a few objections.
dificultador, -ra, *a.* hindering, causing difficulty. — *n.m.f.* hinderer, one who raises difficulties.
dificultar, *v.t.* to hinder, interfere with, make difficult; to consider unlikely.
dificultoso, -sa, *a.* difficult, hard, laborious, awkward.
difidación, *n.f.* declaration of war; manifesto justifying such a declaration.
difidencia, *n.f.* distrust.
difidente, *a.* distrustful.
difilo, -la, *a.* (*bot.*) two-leafed.
difluir [O], *v.i.* to be diffused, spread out, flow away.
difracción, *n.f.* (*opt.*) diffraction.
difteria, *n.f.* (*med.*) diphtheria.
diftérico, -ca, *a.* diphtheritic.
difteritis, *n.f.* (*med.*) diphtheritis.
difuminar, *v.t.* to blur, make vague.
difumino, *n.m.* blur, vagueness; [ESFUMINO].
difundir, *v.t.* to diffuse, spread; to divulge, publish abroad; (*rad.*) to broadcast; ***está muy difundido,*** it is very wide-spread.
difunto, -ta, *a.* defunct, dead, deceased, late. — *n.m.* dead person; ***día de los difuntos,*** All Souls' Day.
difusamente, *adv.* diffusely, diffusedly, vaguely.
difusible, *a.* diffusible.
difusión, *n.f.* diffusion; diffuseness, vagueness; spreading; (*rad.*) broadcasting.
difusivo, -va, *a.* diffusive.
difuso, -sa, *a.* diffuse, vague; wordy. — ***p.p.*** [DIFUNDIR].
difusor, -ra, *a.* diffusive; (*rad.*) broadcasting. — *n.m.* diffuser (*sugar manufacture*).
digástrico, -ca, *a.* digastric.
digerible, *a.* digestible.
digerir [6], *v.t.* to digest; to take in.
digestible, *a.* digestible.

digestión, *n.f.* digestion; ***hacer la digestión,*** to digest one's food.
digestivo, -va, *a., n.m.* digestive.
digesto, *n.m.* (*law*) digest.
digestor, *n.m.* digester (*apparatus*).
digitación, *n.f.* fingering.
digitado, -da, *a.* (*bot., zool.*) digitate.
digital, *a.* (*anat.*) digital. — *n.f.* (*bot.*) digitalis, foxglove; ***impresión digital,*** fingerprint.
digitalina, *n.f.* (*chem.*) digitalin.
digitalismo, *n.m.* [DEDISMO].
dígito, -ta, *a.* digital. — *n.m.* (*math., astron.*) digit.
dignación, *n.f.* condescension; deigning.
dignarse, *v.r.* to condescend, deign; ***se dignó recibirlos,*** he condescended to receive them; ***dígnese pasar por (la) secretaría,*** please be so kind as to call in at the office.
dignatario, *n.m.* dignitary.
dignidad, *n.f.* dignity; dignitary.
dignificante, *a.* (*theol.*) dignifying.
dignificar [A], *v.t.* to dignify.
digno, -na, *a.* worthy; fitting; decent; honest.
digresión, *n.f.* digression.
digresivo, -va, *a.* digressive.
dihueñe, dihueñi, *n.m.* (*Chi.*) tree fungus.
dije (1), *n.m.* charm, trinket; (*coll., fig.*) gem; (*pl.*) bravado, bragging.
dije (2), *pret.* [DECIR].
dilaceración, *n.f.* rending, ripping apart *or* to pieces.
dilacerar, *v.t.* to lacerate, tear *or* rip apart *or* to pieces.
dilación, *n.f.* delay, procrastination; dilation; protraction.
dilapidación, *n.f.* squandering.
dilapidador, -ra, *a.* squandering. — *n.m.f.* squanderer.
dilapidar, *v.t.* to squander.
dilatabilidad, *n.f.* (*phys.*) quality of dilatation.
dilatable, *a.* dilatable.
dilatación, *n.f.* dilation, expansion; prolixity; serenity in grief; ***dilatación lineal,*** linear expansion.
dilatado, -da, *a.* broad, spreading, vast; long-drawn-out.
dilatador, -ra, *a.* dilating, expanding; retarding, causing delay. — *n.m.f.* one who dilates *or* expands. — *n.m.* (*surg.*) dilator.
dilatar, *v.t.* to dilate, widen, broaden, expand; to prolong, protract; to postpone; to disseminate, spread abroad. — **dilatarse,** *v.r.* to tarry, linger; (*fig.*) — ***en,*** to dwell (on), go into lengthy detail (about).
dilatorio, -ria, *a.* (*law*) dilatory, delaying. — *n.f.* delay, procrastination; (*law*) time granted by a court to a debtor, grace; ***andarse con dilatorias,*** to keep putting things off.
dilección, *n.f.* predilection; strong affection.
dilecto, -ta, *a.* dearly beloved.
dilema, *n.m.* dilemma.
diligencia, *n.f.* diligence; dispatch; speed; stage-coach; (*pl.*) business, formality.
diligenciar, *v.t.* to dispatch, deal with, attend to.
diligenciero, *n.m.* agent.
diligente, *a.* diligent; prompt, quick.
dilogía, *n.f.* ambiguity.
dilucidación, *n.f.* elucidation.
dilucidador, -ra, *a.* elucidating. — *n.m.f.* elucidator.
dilucidar, *v.t.* to elucidate.
dilucidario, *n.m.* explanatory writing.
dilución, *n.f.* dilution.
diluente, *a.* diluent.
diluir [O], *v.t.* to dilute.
dilusivo, -va, *a.* delusive.
diluvial, *a.* (*geol.*) diluvial.
diluviano, -na, *a.* diluvian.
diluviar, *v. impers.* to pour with rain.
diluvio, *n.m.* deluge, flood; downpour.
dille, *n.m.* (*Chi.*) cicada.
dimanación, *n.f.* springing, issuing; origin.
dimanante, *a.* springing, originating.
dimanar, *v.i.* — ***de,*** to spring, issue, arise (from), originate (in).
dimensión, *n.f.* dimension; extent; ***de grandes dimensiones,*** of large proportions.
dimensional, *a.* dimensional.
dimes, *n.m.pl.* ***andar en dimes y diretes,*** to bicker, squabble.
diminución [DISMINUCIÓN].
diminuir [O], *v.t.* [DISMINUIR].
diminutamente, *adv.* sparingly; minutely.
diminutivo, -va, *a., n.m.* diminutive.
diminuto, -ta, *a.* minute, diminutive, tiny.
dimisión, *n.f.* resignation (*of office etc.*); ***presentar la dimisión,*** to tender *or* hand in one's resignation.
dimisorias, *n.f.pl.* (*eccles.*) letters dimissory; dismissal.
dimitir, *v.t., v.i.* to resign.
dimorfismo, *n.m.* dimorphism.
dimorfo, -fa, *a.* dimorphous.
din, *n.m.* (*coll.*) cash, lolly.
dina, *n.f.* (*phys.*) dyne.
Dinamarca, *n.f.* Denmark.
dinamarqués, -quesa, *a.* Danish. — *n.m.f.* Dane. *n.m.* Danish (*language*).
dinamia, *n.f.* dynam.
dinámico, -ca, *a.* dynamic. — *n.f.* dynamics.
dinamismo, *n.m.* dynamism.
dinamista, *a.* dynamistic. — *n.m.f.* dynamist; terrorist.
dinamita, *n.f.* dynamite.
dinamitero, -ra, *n.m.f.* dynamiter.
dínamo, *n.f.* dynamo.
dinamoeléctrico, -ca, *a.* dynamo-electric.
dinamométrico, -ca, *a.* dynamometric.
dinamómetro, *n.m.* dynamometer.
dinasta, *n.m.* dynast.
dinastía, *n.f.* dynasty.
dinástico, -ca, *a.* dynastic.
dinastismo, *n.m.* loyalty to a dynasty.
dinerada, *n.f.* [DINERAL].
dineral, *n.m.* fortune, packet, enormous amount of money.
dinerillo, *n.m.* modest bit of money; (*iron.*) pretty penny; ***su dinerillo le habrá costado,*** it must have cost him a pretty penny.
dinero, *n.m.* money; denarius; ***alzarse con el dinero,*** to go off with the takings; ***dinero contante (y sonante), dinero en efectivo,*** ready money, spot cash; ***dinero en mano,*** ready money; ***dinero llama dinero,*** money makes money; ***dinero menudo, dinero suelto,*** loose change, petty cash; ***estar*** or ***andar mal de dinero,*** to be short of cash; ***los dineros del sacristán, cantando se vienen y cantando se van,*** easy come, easy go; ***¡adiós mi dinero!*** I've had it, he's had it; that's torn it *or* done it; ***poderoso caballero es don dinero,*** money talks.
dineroso, -sa, *a.* moneyed, rich.
dingo, *n.m.* (*zool.*) dingo.
dingolondango(s), *n.m.* (*coll.*) soft-soaping; (*coll., fig.*) rot, gibberish.
dinosauro, *n.m.* dinosaur.
dintel, *n.m.* lintel.
dintelar, *v.t.* to fit with lintels.
dintorno, *n.m.* (*arch., art*) outline (*within the contour*).
diñar, *v.t.* (*coll.*) ***diñarla,*** to kick the bucket.

diocesano, -na, *a.* diocesan. — *n.m.* diocesan.
diócesis, *n.f. inv.* diocese.
dionisia, *n.f.* blood-stone.
dionisíaco, -ca, *a.* Dionysiac.
dioptría, *n.f.* (*opt.*) diopter.
dióptrico, -ca, *a.* dioptric, dioptrical. — *n.f.* dioptrics.
diorama, *n.m.* diorama.
diorita, *n.f.* (*min.*) diorite.
Dios, *n.m.* God; ***¡con Dios!*** farewell, cheerio; ***¡santo Dios!*** heavens!; ***no (lo) quiera Dios,*** God forbid; ***sea como Dios quiera,*** God's will be done; ***Dios le guarde,*** God be with you; ***se armó la de Dios es Cristo,*** there was a great to-do, shindy; ***a Dios rogando y con el mazo dando,*** praise the Lord and pass the ammunition; ***¡alabado sea Dios!*** God be praised!; ***¡bendito sea Dios!*** good Lord! good heavens!; ***¡por Dios!*** good God! good heavens! for God's sake!; ***¡válgame Dios!*** bless my soul!; ***¡válgate Dios!*** God preserve you!; ***¡Dios nos asista, nos coja confesados, nos la depare buena*** or ***nos tenga de su mano!*** God help us!; ***a la buena de Dios,*** any old how; ***lo hizo como Dios le dio a entender,*** he did it according to his lights, as best he could; ***amanecerá Dios y medraremos,*** tomorrow will be another day, sooner or later our luck will change; ***cuando Dios amanece, para todos amanece,*** God sends his rain on just and unjust alike; ***Dios aprieta, pero no ahoga,*** God does not try us beyond our strength; ***bien sabe Dios que . . .,*** honestly, truly; ***¡sabe Dios!*** heaven knows!; ***como hay Dios,*** as sure as two and two make four; ***como Dios manda,*** properly, decently; ***me costó Dios y ayuda convencerlo,*** it was a terrific effort persuading him, it required a terrific effort to persuade him; ***Dios los cría, y ellos se juntan,*** birds of a feather flock together; ***Dios dará,*** the Lord will provide; ***Dios dirá,*** we shall see; God will decide; ***este niño de Dios,*** this blessed child; ***estaba de Dios,*** it was fated (to happen); ***¡que de Dios goce! ¡que Dios haya!*** God rest his soul!; (*iron.*) ***¡Dios te la depare buena!*** and the best of luck!; ***Dios mediante,*** God willing, Deo volente; ***quien madruga, Dios le ayuda,*** the early bird catches the worm; ***plega*** or ***plegue a Dios,*** please God; ***poner a Dios por testigo,*** to call God to witness; ***yo no sirvo ni a Dios ni al diablo,*** I'm not taking sides, I don't care either way; ***como Dios sea servido,*** as God wills; ***Dios sobre todo,*** it rests with God; ***que venga Dios y lo vea (y lo oiga),*** it's incredible; ***estaba de Dios que pasara esto,*** this was bound to happen, it was fated *or* written; ***el hombre propone y Dios dispone,*** man proposes, God disposes; ***no le ha llamado Dios por el camino de la paciencia,*** he is not notable for his patience; ***no me importa maldita de Dios la cosa,*** I don't care two hoots (about it); ***tentar a Dios,*** to tempt Providence; ***¡vive Dios! ¡voto a Dios!*** that's bad luck, that's a bad business; by God!; ***le ha venido Dios a ver,*** that's a real stroke of good luck for him.
dios, *n.m.* god, idol.
diosa, *n.f.* goddess.
diostedé, *n.m.* (*Hisp. Am.*) toucan.
dipétalo, -la, *a.* (*bot.*) dipetalous.
diploma, *n.m.* diploma.
diplomacia, *n.f.* diplomacy; tact.
diplomático, -ca, *a.* diplomatic; tactful. — *n.m.* diplomatist, diplomat. — *n.f.* diplomatics; diplomacy.
dipsomanía, *n.f.* dipsomania.
dipsómano, -na, *n.m.f.* dipsomaniac.
díptero, -ra, *a.* dipteran; dipterous. — *n.m.pl.* **(dípteros)** (*ent.*) diptera.
díptico, *n.m.*, **díptica,** *n.f.* diptych.
diptongar [B], *v.t.*, *v.i.* to diphthongize.
diptongo, *n.m.* diphthong.
diputación, *n.f.* functions of an M.P.; deputation; local government *or* body.
diputada, *n.f.* lady representative *or* M.P.
diputado, *n.m.* representative; ***diputado a Cortes,*** member of Spanish parliament, congressman.
diputador, -ra, *a.* constituent. — *n.m.f.* constituent.
diputar, *v.t.* to appoint as a representative; to depute, delegate, commission; to consider, deem.
dique, *n.m.* dyke, dam; (*fig.*) barrier; (*min.*) outcrop; ***dique seco,*** dry dock; ***dique flotante,*** floating dock.
dirección, *n.f.* direction; directing; managing; editorship; management; steering; (postal) address; ***dirección general,*** ministerial department; ***dirección única,*** one-way street; (*engin.*) ***dirección asistida,*** power steering.
directivo, -va, *a.* directive, directing, managing; ***junta directiva,*** board of directors *or* governors. *n.m.* director. — *n.f.* directive, instruction; board of directors *or* governors.
directo, -ta, *a.* direct; straight; ***tren directo,*** through train; ***(velocidad) directa,*** top (*gear*); (*rad., telev.*) ***en directo,*** live.
director, -ra, *a.* directing, guiding. — *n.m.f.* director; manager; chief; editor; (prison) governor, (*Am.*) warden; ***director de escena,*** stage manager; ***director de orquestra,*** conductor; ***director de pompas fúnebres,*** undertaker, (*Am.*) mortician; ***director espiritual,*** confessor, religious director; ***director general,*** head of a ministerial department.
directoral, *a.* directoral.
directorial, *a.* pertaining to a directory.
directorio, -ria, *a.* directive, directorial. — *n.m.* directory; directorate.
directriz, *a.f.*, *n.f.* (*geom.*) directrix; (*pl.*) ***(líneas) directrices,*** guide lines, norms.
dirigente, *a.* directing, leading; ruling. — *n.m.f.* leader.
dirigible, *a.* dirigible; directable. — *n.m.* dirigible airship.
dirigir [E], *v.t.* to direct; to manage, govern, control, supervise; to lead, head; to guide; to address (*letter*); to conduct (*orchestra*); to point (*gun*); to steer (*ship*). — **dirigirse,** *v.r.* — **a,** to address; to apply (to); to go *or* turn (to, towards); ***dirigir la palabra a,*** to speak to, address.
dirigismo, *n.m.* state control.
dirimente, *a.* annulling.
dirimible, *a.* annullable.
dirimir, *v.t.* to annul, dissolve; to settle, solve.
disanto, *n.m.* holy-day.
discantar, *v.t.*, *v.i.* to descant.
discante, *n.m.* descant.
disceptación, *n.f.* discourse.
disceptar, *v.i.* to discourse.
discernidor, -ra, *a.* discerning. — *n.m.f.* discerner.
discernimiento, *n.m.* discernment, judgment, insight, discrimination; (*law*) appointment of a guardian.
discernir [E], *v.t.* to discern, distinguish, discriminate, judge; (*law*) to appoint (*a guardian*).
disciplina, *n.f.* discipline; scourge, whip.
disciplinable, *a.* disciplinable.
disciplinadamente, *adv.* with discipline; in strict order.
disciplinado, -da, *a.* marbled, variegated (*flowers*).
disciplinal, *a.* disciplinary.
disciplinante, *a.* disciplinary. — *n.m.* disciplinant, flagellant.
disciplinar, *v.t.* to discipline; to instruct, drill; to scourge, whip.
disciplinario, -ria, *a.* disciplinary; ***batallón disciplinario,*** punishment squad.
disciplinazo, *n.m.* lash.

discipulado, *n.m.* discipleship; teaching, instruction; disciples; pupils.
discipular, *a.* discipular.
discípulo, -la, *n.m.f.* disciple; pupil.
disco, *n.m.* disk; (gramophone) record; quoit; discus; traffic light(s).
discóbolo, *n.m.* discobolus.
discoidal, discoide, discoideo, -dea, *a.* disk-like, discoidal.
díscolo, -la, *a.* ungovernable; intractable.
discoloro, -ra, *a.* (*bot.*) having leaves of differently coloured sides.
disconforme, *a.* disagreeing, in disagreement.
disconformidad, *n.f.* disconformity; disagreement.
discontinuación, *n.f.* discontinuation.
discontinuar [M], *v.t.* to discontinue, suspend.
discontinuidad, *n.f.* lack of continuity.
discontinuo, -nua, *a.* discontinuous, broken.
disconveniencia [INCONVENIENCIA].
disconveniente, *a.* [INCONVENIENTE].
disconvenir [36] [DESCONVENIR].
discordancia, *n.f.* discordance, disagreement.
discordante, *a.* discordant, dissonant.
discordar [4], *v.i.* to be discordant, out of tune; to disagree.
discorde, *a.* discordant; (*mus.*) dissonant.
discordia, *n.f.* discord, disagreement.
discoteca, *n.f.* record library; discotheque.
discrasia, *n.f.* (*med.*) cacochymia.
discreción, *n.f.* discretion; circumspection; wit; ***a discreción,*** at one's own discretion; ***rendirse a discreción,*** to surrender unconditionally.
discrecional, *a.* discretional, optional; ***parada discrecional,*** request stop.
discrepancia, *n.f.* discrepancy.
discrepante, *a.* discrepant, differing.
discrepar, *v.i.* to differ, disagree.
discretear, *v.i.* to try to be clever, show off (*verbally*).
discreteo, *n.m.* (verbal) showing off.
discreto, -ta, *a.* discreet; unobtrusive; sensible; witty; (*coll.*) fair, not bad, reasonable. — *n.m.f.* (*eccles.*) counsellor to the Superior.
discrimen, *n.m.* hazard, risk, peril; difference, diversity.
discriminar, *v.t., v.i.* to discriminate (against).
disculpa, *n.f.* excuse, apology.
disculpabilidad, *n.f.* excusability, pardonableness.
disculpable, *a.* excusable, pardonable.
disculpar, *v.t.* to excuse, forgive. — **disculparse,** *v.r.* to apologize (***de,*** for).
discurrir, *v.t.* to think up, invent, devise; to infer, conjecture. — *v.i.* to go *or* roam about; to flow (*river*); to pass (*time*); to think, reason; ***no discurro bien,*** I can't think clearly.
discursante, *n.m.f.* speech-maker.
discursar, *v.i.* to discourse (***sobre*** or ***acerca de,*** on).
discursear, *v.i.* (*coll., iron.*) to make speeches, harangue.
discursista, *n.m.f.* one given to speech-making.
discursivo, -va, *a.* discursive; reflective, meditative.
discurso, *n.m.* discourse; reasoning; speech; oration; course (*of time*); (*gram.*) ***partes del discurso,*** parts of speech.
discusión, *n.f.* discussion; argument.
discutible, *a.* disputable; debatable, questionable.
discutidor, -ra, *a.* arguing. — *n.m.f.* arguer.
discutir, *v.t., v.i.* to discuss; to dispute; to debate, argue (about); to haggle (over), (*Am.*) dicker (about).
disecación, *n.f.* stuffing, taxidermy.
disección, *n.f.* dissection, anatomy.
disecador, -ra, *n.m.f.* stuffer, taxidermist.
disecar [A], *v.t.* to stuff (*animals etc.*); to dissect.
disecea, *n.f.* (*med.*) high-tone deafness.
disector, -ra, *n.m.f.* dissector, anatomist.
diseminación, *n.f.* dissemination; scattering.
diseminador, -ra, *a.* disseminating. — *n.m.f.* disseminator.
diseminar, *v.t.* to disseminate, scatter.
disensión, *n.f.* dissension; strife.
disenso, *n.m.* dissent, disagreement.
disentería, *n.f.* dysentery.
disintérico, -ca, *a.* dysenteric, dysenterical.
disentimiento, *n.m.* dissent, disagreement.
disentir [6], *v.i.* to dissent, disagree; ***disiento de usted,*** I disagree with you.
diseñador, -ra, *n.m.f.* designer.
diseñar, *v.t.* to design, draw; to sketch, outline.
diseño, *n.m.* design, drawing; sketch, outline; plan, pattern.
disertación, *n.f.* dissertation, disquisition.
disertador, -ra, *a.* given to discoursing. — *n.m.f.* discourser, expounder.
disertante, *n.m.f.* speaker.
disertar, *v.i.* to discourse (***sobre*** or ***acerca de,*** on).
diserto, -ta, *a.* eloquent, able.
disfavor, *n.m.* disfavour; bad turn.
disformar [DEFORMAR].
disforme [DEFORME].
disformidad [DEFORMIDAD].
disfraz, *n.m.* disguise; fancy dress; ***baile de disfraces,*** fancy-dress ball; (*fig.*) ***es un disfraz,*** it looks a sight.
disfrazar [C], *v.t.* to disguise; (*fig.*) to cloak, cover; (*coll.*) to make (s.o.) look a sight; ***iba disfrazada,*** she was in disguise; (*coll.*) she looked a sight. — **disfrazarse,** *v.r.* to disguise, masquerade (***de,*** as).
disfrutar, *v.t., v.i.* to enjoy; to enjoy o.s.; ***disfruta de buena salud,*** he enjoys good health; ***disfruta con el coche,*** he enjoys himself in the car; ***disfruta haciéndole sufrir,*** he gets pleasure from making him suffer.
disfrute, *n.m.* enjoyment, benefit, use.
disgregación, *n.f.* disintegration; scattering.
disgregar [B], *v.t.* to disintegrate; to scatter.
disgregativo, -va, *a.* disintegrating; scattering.
disgustar, *v.t.* to displease; to upset; ***me disgusta,*** I dislike it; ***no disgustes a tu padre,*** don't upset your father. — **disgustarse,** *v.r.* to be displeased *or* upset; ***se disgustó mucho con la noticia,*** he was very upset by the news.
disgustillo, *n.m.* minor *or* petty upset.
disgusto, *n.m.* displeasure; upset; nasty shock, unpleasantness; row, set-to; ***cualquier día tendrán un disgusto con ese niño,*** sooner or later they are going to get a nasty shock with that child; ***hacer algo a disgusto,*** to do sth. reluctantly; ***estar*** (***sentirse***) ***a disgusto,*** not to feel at home, to feel uncomfortable.
disidencia, *n.f.* dissidence, dissent.
disidente, *a.* dissident. — *n.m.f.* dissenter.
disidir, *v.i.* to dissent, disagree.
disílabo, -ba, *a.* disyllabic.
disimetría, *n.f.* dissymmetry.
disimétrico, -ca, *a.* unsymmetrical.
disímil, *a.* dissimilar, unlike.
disimilar, *a.* dissimilar.
disimilaridad, *n.f.* dissimilarity.
disimilitud, *n.f.* unlikeness.
disimulable, *a.* concealable.
disimulación, *n.f.* dissimulation, covering-up.
disimulado, -da, *a.* dissembling, underhand, undercover; ***hacerse el disimulado,*** to pretend not to hear, understand etc.
disimulador, -ra, *a.* dissembling. — *n.m.f.* dissembler.
disimular, *v.t., v.i.* to dissemble; to cover up, feign, pretend; to hide, conceal.

disimulo, *n.m.* dissimulation; pretence, covering-up; ***hacer algo con disimulo,*** to do sth. in an underhand way.
disipación, *n.f.* dissipation.
disipado, -da, *a.* dissipated.
disipador, -ra, *a.* squandering, spendthrift. — *n.m.f.* spendthrift, prodigal.
disipar, *v.t.* to dissipate, dispel; to scatter; to misspend, squander. — **disiparse,** *v.r.* to clear (away); ***se disipó la niebla,*** the fog cleared.
dislalia, *n.f.* (*path.*) dysphonia.
dislate, *n.m.* nonsense, absurdity.
dislocación, dislocadura, *n.f.* dislocation.
dislocar [A], *v.t.* to dislocate, displace, disjoint.
dismembración [DESMEMBRACIÓN].
disminución, *n.f.* diminution; ***ir en disminución,*** to dwindle, narrow, shrink, taper.
disminuir [O], *v.t.* to diminish, cut down, lessen, lower, decrease; to belittle; ***sentirse disminuido,*** to feel small. — **disminuir(se),** *v.i.* (*v.r.*) to diminish, drop, dwindle, fall, lessen.
disociación, *n.f.* dissociation.
disociar, *v.t.* to dissociate.
disolubilidad, *n.f.* dissolubility.
disoluble, *a.* dissoluble.
disolución, *n.f.* dissolution; break(ing) up; (*chem.*) solution; dissoluteness; (*com.*) ***disolución de sociedad,*** dissolution of partnership.
disolutivo, -va, *a.* dissolvent.
disoluto, -ta, *a.* dissolute.
disolvente, *a.* dissolvent. — *n.m.f.* dissolver.
disolver [5, *p.p.* **disuelto**], *v.t.* to dissolve; to break up.
disón, *n.m.* (*mus.*) discord.
disonancia, *n.f.* dissonance; discord.
disonante, *a.* dissonant; discordant.
disonar [4], *v.i.* to be dissonant *or* discordant; to disagree.
dísono, -na, *a.* dissonant.
dispar, *a.* dissimilar, different, disparate.
disparada, *n.f.* (*Hisp. Am.*) hasty start, sudden run *or* flight; ***a la disparada,*** at full speed, like a shot.
disparadero, *n.m.* trigger; ***esto me puso en el disparadero de pegarle,*** this drove me to hit him, this was the last straw and I hit him.
disparador, *n.m.* shooter; trigger; release (*mechanism*); ratchet-wheel (*in clockwork*); (*naut.*) anchor-tripper; notch (*of crossbow*).
disparar, *v.t.* to shoot, fire, discharge, release, let off, trigger off; to hurl, fling. — **dispararse,** *v.r.* to go off (*gun*); to dash off, bolt (*horse*); to start to race *or* career round (*machine etc.*); (*coll.*) to lose control, fly off the handle; ***salió disparado,*** he shot out, rushed out; ***va disparado,*** he's going hell for leather, belting along; ***está disparado,*** he's running wild, out of control.
disparatado, -da, *a.* crazy, wild, preposterous.
disparatador, -ra, *a.* talking nonsense. — *n.m.f.* talker of nonsense.
disparatar, *v.i.* to behave *or* talk crazily *or* wildly.
disparate, *n.m.* crazy *or* wild thing to do *or* say; rubbish, bunk; (*coll.*) terrific amount, hell of a lot; (*coll.*) crude *or* foul expression.
disparatorio, *n.m.* lot of nonsense *or* rubbish.
disparatoso, -sa, *a.* given to talking nonsense, given to malapropisms.
disparejo, -ja, *a.* uneven.
disparidad, *n.f.* disparity.
disparo, *n.m.* shot; shooting, firing; discharge, report; release, letting loose.
dispendio, *n.m.* waste, squandering, excessive outlay.
dispendioso, -sa, *a.* costly, expensive; squandering.
dispensa, *n.f.* dispensation.
dispensable, *a.* dispensable; excusable.
dispensación, *n.f.* dispensation.
dispensador, -ra, *a.* dispensing. — *n.m.f.* dispenser.
dispensar, *v.t.* to dispense; to excuse, forgive; ***dispense, dispénseme,*** I beg your pardon, I apologize.
dispensario, *n.m.* surgery; clinic.
dispepsia, *n.f.* dyspepsia.
dispéptico, -ca, *a.* dyspeptic.
dispersar, *v.t.* to disperse; to scatter.
dispersión, *n.f.* dispersion, dispersal.
dispersivo, -va, *a.* dispersing.
disperso, -sa, *a.* dispersed, scattered.
displicencia, *n.f.* superciliousness, contemptuous indifference.
displicente, *a.* supercilious, contemptuous, indifferent.
disponedor, -ra, *a.* disposing; arranging. — *n.m.f.* disposer, arranger.
disponente, *a.* disposing, arranging.
disponer [25], *v.t.* to dispose; to arrange, lay out. — *v.i.* — ***de,*** to have at one's disposal; to dispose of. — **disponerse,** *v.r.* — ***a,*** to make *or* get ready to.
disponibilidad, *n.f.* availability; (*pl.* **disponibilidades**) resources.
disponible, *a.* available.
disposición, *n.f.* disposition, arrangement; layout; disposal; aptitude, inclination; willingness (*to work, co-operate etc.*); state of readiness, determination; provision, stipulation; resolution; ***a la disposición de usted,*** at your disposal; ***estar en disposición de,*** to be ready to; ***última disposición,*** last will and testament; ***tomar disposiciones,*** to take steps *or* measures.
dispositivo, -va, *a.* dispositive. — *n.m.* device, contrivance.
dispuesto, -ta, *a.* prepared, ready; willing — *p.p.* [DISPONER]; ***estar dispuesto a,*** to be prepared, ready *or* willing to; ***bien dispuesto,*** well-disposed; ***mal dispuesto,*** ill-disposed.
disputa, *n.f.* dispute; disputation; ***sin disputa,*** beyond dispute.
disputable, *a.* disputable, debatable.
disputador, *a.* disputing. — *n.m.* disputant, disputer.
disputar, *v.t.*, *v.i.* to dispute, argue (over), debate; to haggle (over), (*Am.*) dicker (about).
disquisición, *n.f.* disquisition.
distancia, *n.f.* distance; ***a distancia,*** far off, at a distance; ***control*** or ***mando a distancia,*** remote control; ***guardar la(s) distancia(s),*** to keep one's distance.
distanciamiento, *n.m.* estrangement.
distanciar, *v.t.* to place at a distance; to put farther apart; to estrange. — **distanciarse,** *v.r.* — ***de,*** to get *or* move away (from), put distance between o.s. (and); to become estranged; ***están distanciados,*** they are estranged.
distante, *a.* distant, remote; off.
distar, *v.i.* to be distant, remote, far; ***distar de,*** to be far from; to be (*a specified distance*) from; ***dista tres kilómetros de aquí,*** it is three kilometres away; ***dista (mucho) de ser perfecto,*** he is far from perfect.
distender, *v.t.* to distend; to relax; to sprain.
distensión, *n.f.* distension; relaxation; détente.
dístico, *a.* (*bot.*) distichous. — *n.m.* distich.
distinción, *n.f.* distinction; distinctness; ***a distinción de,*** as distinct from, unlike.
distingo, *n.m.* subtle distinction; reservation.
distinguible, *a.* distinguishable.
distinguido, -da, *a.* distinguished; ***con mis más distinguidos saludos,*** your most obedient servant.
distinguir [G], *v.t.* to distinguish; to make distinctions between, discriminate between, tell; to

single out; to make out, see vaguely; ***no distingue lo bueno de lo malo,*** he can't tell good from bad. — **distinguirse,** *v.r.* to stand out; to be distinguished *or* different *(from)*; ***se distingue por su esplendidez,*** he is notable for his generosity.
distintivo, -va, *a.* distinctive. — *n.m.* distinctive mark *or* feature; badge.
distinto, -ta, *a.* distinct; different.
distorsión, *n.f.* distortion; twisting; spraining.
distorsionar, *v.t.* to distort, twist.
distracción, *n.f.* distraction; diversion, amusement, hobby; carelessness, oversight; absent-mindedness; ***por distracción,*** for amusement; through an oversight.
distraer [34], *v.t.* to distract, distract the attention of; to amuse, entertain, relax; to pilfer. — **distraerse,** *v.r.* to amuse o.s., relax, get one's mind off things; to allow one's attention to wander.
distraídamente, *adv.* absent-mindedly.
distraído, -da, *a.* absent-minded; entertaining; ***hacerse el distraído,*** to pretend not to notice.
distraimiento, *n.m.* [DISTRACCIÓN].
distribución, *n.f.* distribution, apportionment, division; ***cuadro*** or ***tablero de distribución,*** switchboard.
distribuidor, -ra, *a.* distributing. — *n.m.* *(mech.)* distributor; ***distribuidor automático,*** slot-machine.
distribuir [O], *v.t.* to distribute, deliver; to allot, apportion.
distributivo, -va, *a.* distributive.
distributor, -ra, *a.* distributing. — *n.m.f.* distributor.
distribuyente, *a.* distributing. — *n.m.f.* distributor.
distrito, *n.m.* district; area; constituency.
disturbar, *v.t.* to disrupt.
disturbio, *n.m.* distubance, riot.
disuadir, *v.t.* to dissuade, deter.
disuasión, *n.f.* dissuasion.
disuasivo, -va, *a.* dissuasive, deterrent; ***fuerza disuasiva nuclear,*** nuclear deterrent.
disyunción, *n.f.* disjunction.
disyuntivo, -va, *a.* disjunctive. — *n.f.* dilemma, alternative.
disyuntor, *n.m.* *(elec.)* circuit-breaker.
dita, *n.f.* security, bond; surety, bondsman; *(Chi., Guat.)* debt, liability.
diteísmo, *n.m.* ditheism.
diteísta, *a.* ditheistic. — *n.m.f.* ditheist.
ditirámbico, -ca, *a.* dithyrambic.
ditirambo, *n.m.* dithyramb.
dítono, *n.m.* *(mus.)* ditone.
diuca, *n.f.* *(Arg., Chi., orn.)* warbler; *(Arg., Chi., coll.)* teacher's pet.
diurno, -na, *a.* diurnal. — *n.m.* diurnal, prayer-book. — *n.m.f.* *(pl.)* diurnal animals *or* plants.
diuturnidad, *n.f.* diuturnity, long duration.
diuturno, -na, *a.* diuturnal, lasting.
diva, *n.f.* [DIVO].
divagación, *n.f.* rambling, wandering, digression.
divagador, -ra, *a.* roaming; digressing. — *n.m.f.* rambler; digresser.
divagar [B], *v.i.* to ramble, roam; to digress.
diván, *n.m.* divan.
divergencia, *n.f.* divergence.
divergente, *a.* divergent.
divergir [B], *v.i.* to diverge; to dissent.
diversidad, *n.f.* diversity; variety.
diversificación, *n.f.* diversification.
diversificar [A], *v.t.* to diversify, vary.
diversiforme, *a.* diversiform.
diversión, *n.f.* diversion, amusement, entertainment.
diversivo, -va, *a.* *(med.)* divertive.
diverso, -sa, *a.* diverse, different; *(pl.)* various.
divertido, -da, *a.* amusing, funny; gay, jolly, merry.
divertimiento, *n.m.* diversion; amusement; divertimento, divertissement.
divertir [6], *v.t.* to divert; to amuse, entertain; *(coll.)* ***estamos divertidos,*** we've had it, that's torn it. — **divertirse,** *v.r.* to amuse o.s., have a good time.
dividendo, *n.m.* dividend.
divididero, -ra, *a.* divisible, to be divided.
dividir, *v.t.* to divide, split. — **dividirse,** *v.r.* to divide, separate, split, part, branch; *(coll.)* ***no me puedo dividir,*** I can't do two jobs at the same time, I can't be in two places at the same time.
dividuo, -dua, *a.* *(law)* divisible.
divieso, *n.m.* *(med.)* furuncle, boil.
divinal, *a.* *(poet.)* divine.
divinamente, *adv.* divinely; admirably, beautifully.
divinatorio, -ria, *a.* divinatory.
divinidad, *n.f.* divinity, deity; *(fig.)* delight, exquisite thing.
divinización, *n.f.* divinization.
divinizar [C], *v.t.* to deify, to sanctify; to extol.
divino, -na, *a.* divine; *(fig.)* exquisite.
divisa, *n.f.* [DIVISO].
divisar, *v.t.* to descry, make out, catch sight of, sight; *(her.)* to vary.
divisibilidad, *n.f.* divisibility.
divisible, *a.* divisible.
división, *n.f.* division.
divisional, *a.* divisional.
divisionario, -ria, *a.* divisional; fractional.
divisivo, -va, *a.* divisible, divisive.
divismo, *n.m.* *(fig.)* deification; hero-worship.
diviso, -sa, *a.* divided. — *n.f.* emblem; motto, slogan; foreign currency; *(her.)* device; *(tauro.)* beed insignia; *(law)* second-line inheritance. — *p.p.* [DIVIDIR].
divisor, -ra, *a.* dividing. — *n.m.* *(math.)* divisor. — *n.m.f.* divider, separator.
divisorio, -ria, *a.* dividing, divisionary. — *n.m.* *(print.)* copy-holder. — *n.f.* *(geog.)* divide; ***(línea) divisoria,*** divide; ***divisoria de aguas,*** watershed.
divo, -va, *a.* *(poet.)* godlike, divine. — *n.m.* top opera singer, star; *(fig.)* god. — *n.f.* *(poet.)* goddess; diva, prima donna.
divorciar, *v.t.* to divorce, give a divorce to; to separate. — **divorciarse,** *v.r.* to divorce, get a divorce; to separate, split up.
divorcio, *n.m.* divorce; separation; breach.
divulgación, *n.f.* divulgation; spreading; popularization.
divulgador, -ra, *a.* divulging; spreading; popularizing. — *n.m.f.* divulger; popularizer.
divulgar [B], *v.t.* to divulge, publish, spread abroad; to popularize.
diz *(contraction of* ***dícese****)*, it is said, people say.
dizque *(contraction of* ***dícese que*** or ***dice que****)*, *n.m.* *(usually in pl.)* rumour.
do (1), *adv.* *(obs.)* where.
do (2), *n.m.* *(mus.)* C, do, ut; ***do de pecho,*** highest tenor note; ***dar el do de pecho,*** to make it.
dobla, *n.f.* doubloon; *(coll.)* doubling a stake; *(Chi.)* right of one day's free mining granted by a mine owner; ***jugar a la dobla,*** to keep on doubling one's stake *(in gambling)*.
dobladillo, *n.m.* hem; strong yarn for knitting.
doblado, -da, *a.* thick-set; stocky; broken, uneven; deceitful, double-dealing. — *n.m.* measure of the fold in cloth; *(And.)* loft.
dobladura, *n.f.* fold, crease.
doblaje, *n.m.* *(cin.)* dubbing.
doblamiento, *n.m.* doubling, folding, bending.

doblar, *v.t.* to double; to fold; to bend; (*cine.*) to dub; (*coll.*) to cripple; to (go) round (*cape, corner etc.*); to overtake, (*Am.*) pass. — *v.i.* to toll the passing-bell; ***doblar a muerto,*** to toll the death-knell. — **doblarse,** *v.r.* to bend, bow, stoop; to yield, give way.
doble, *a.* double, twofold, twin; thick, heavy (*cloth*); thick-set; two-faced, deceitful; (*chem.*) binary. — *n.m.* double; fold, crease; double-dealing; toll of the passing-bell; (*cine., theat.*) double; (*com.*) carrying over (*stock exchange*); ***al doble,*** doubly.
doblegable, *a.* pliant, pliable, flexible; easily folded.
doblegadizo, -za, *a.* easily bent or folded.
doblegar [B], *v.t.* to bend, curve; to force to yield. — **doblegarse,** *v.r.* to bend; to yield, give way.
doblemente, *adv.* doubly; twice.
doblescudo, *n.m.* (*bot.*) shield-fern; shepherd's purse.
doblete, *a.* of medium thickness. — *n.m.* doublet; stroke (*at billiards*).
doblez, *n.m.* crease, ply, fold; fold mark. — *n.m.f.* duplicity, doubleness, double-dealing; ***sin dobleces,*** straight, honest, frank.
doblón, *n.m.* doubloon (*coll.*); ***escupir doblones,*** to show off one's wealth.
doblonada, *n.f.* (*coll.*) mint of money, piles of money.
doce, *a., n.m.* twelve, twelfth; ***las doce,*** twelve o'clock.
doceañista, *a., n.m.* to do with *or* supporter of the Spanish Constitution of 1812.
doceavo, -va, *a., n.m.* twelfth.
docena, *n.f.* [DOCENO].
docenal, *a.* sold by dozens.
docenario, -ria, *a.* containing a dozen.
docencia, *n.f.* teaching; teaching experience.
doceno, -na, *a.* twelfth. — *n.m.* cloth with twelve hundred threads in the warp. — *n.f.* dozen; ***docena de fraile,*** baker's dozen; ***a docenas,*** by the dozen; ***de éstos no entran dos en docena,*** you don't find many of these.
docente, *a.* educational; teaching; ***personal docente,*** teaching staff.
dócil, *a.* docile, tractable.
docilidad, *n.f.* docility, tractableness.
docimástico, -ca, *a.* docimastic.
dock, *n.m.* dock.
docto, -ta, *a.* learned.
doctor, -ra, *n.m.* doctor (*of law, medicine etc.*) — *n.f.* (*coll.*) doctor's wife; blue-stocking.
doctorado, *n.m.* doctorate, doctorship; (*fig.*) ***tener el doctorado en,*** to know all about, be an expert on.
doctoral, *a.* doctoral; ***juicio doctoral,*** authoritative opinion. — *n.m.* canon. — *n.f.* canonry.
doctoramiento, *n.m.* conferring *or* taking of doctorate.
doctorando, *n.m.* candidate for doctorate.
doctorar, *v.t.* to confer a doctorate on. — **doctorarse,** *v.r.* to take *or* get one's doctorate.
doctorcillo, *n.m.* (*coll.*) third-rate (little) doctor.
doctrina, *n.f.* doctrine; learning; Sunday school; catechism; (*Hisp. Am.*) curacy.
doctrinador, -ra, *a.* instructing, teaching. — *n.m.f.* instructor, teacher.
doctrinal, *a.* doctrinal, relating to doctrine. — *n.m.* manual of precepts.
doctrinante, *a.* instructing.
doctrinar [ADOCTRINAR].
doctrinario, -ria, *a.* doctrinarian. — *n.m.f.* doctrinaire.
doctrinero, *n.m.* teacher of Christian doctrine; (*Hisp. Am.*) curate, parish priest.
doctrino, *n.m.* charity child; ***parecer un doctrino,*** to be diffident and shy.
documentación, *n.f.* documentation; documents; (identity) papers.
documental, *a.* documental, documentary. — *n.m.* documentary (*film*); ***pruebas documentales,*** documentary evidence.
documentalmente, *adv.* with proper documents.
documentar, *v.t.* to document; to substantiate; to inform, put in the picture. — **documentarse,** *v.r.* to get the required information *or* facts; (*fig.*) to do one's homework, get o.s. in the picture.
documento, *n.m.* document.
dodecaedro, *n.m.* (*geom.*) dodecahedron.
dodecágono, *n.m.* (*geom.*) dodecagon.
dodecasílabo, -ba, *a.* twelve-syllable, dodecasyllabic.
dogal, *n.m.* halter; noose, slip-knot; ***estar con el dogal al cuello,*** to be up to one's neck, in a terrible predicament.
dogaresa, *n.f.* wife of the doge.
dogma, *n.m.* dogma.
dogmático, -ca, *a.* dogmatic. — *n.m.f.* dogmatist.
dogmatismo, *n.m.* dogmatism.
dogmatista, *n.m.* propounder of heretical doctrines.
dogmatizador, dogmatizante, *n.m.* dogmatizer, dogmatist.
dogmatizar [C], *v.t.* to dogmatize; to teach doctrines opposed to the Roman Catholic religion.
dogo, *n.m.* bulldog; doge.
dogre, *n.m.* (*naut.*) dogger.
doladera, *n.f.* cooper's adze.
dolador, *n.m.* stone-cutter; timber-cutter.
doladura, *n.f.* shavings; chips.
dolaje, *n.m.* wine absorbed by cask.
dolama, *n.f.* chronic ailment *or* indisposition.
dolame, *n.m.* long-standing hidden disease (*in horses*).
dolar [4], *v.t.* to rough-hew, dress.
dólar, *n.m.* dollar.
dolencia, *n.f.* ailment, complaint.
doler [5], *v.i.* to ache, hurt, give pain; to grieve; ***me duele la cabeza,*** my head aches; ***me duele el tener que decir que no,*** it grieves me to have to refuse; ***ahí le duele,*** there's the rub; ***no le duele el dinero,*** he doesn't mind spending money. — **dolerse,** *v.r.* — ***de,*** to grieve at, feel sorrow for.
doliente, *a.* aching, ailing, suffering; sick; sorrowful; sorrowing. — *n.m.* mourner; sufferer.
dolo, *n.m.* fraud, deceit, trick.
dolobre, *n.m.* stone-hammer.
dolomía, dolomita, *n.f.* (*min.*) dolomite.
dolomítico, -ca, *a.* dolomitic.
dolor, *n.m.* pain, aching, ache; grief, sorrow, regret, repentance; ***dolor de cabeza,*** headache; ***dolor de muelas,*** toothache; ***dolor de tripas,*** griping; ***dolor sordo,*** dull ache; ***dolores de parto,*** birth-pangs, labour pains; ***¡qué dolor!*** how sad!
dolora, *n.f.* short, sentimental philosophic poem.
dolorcillo, dolorcito, *n.m.* slight pain, twinge.
dolorido, -da, *a.* doleful, afflicted; aching, painful; sore, tender.
doloroso, -sa, *a.* painful, distressing. — *n.f.* Mater Dolorosa, Our Lady of Sorrows.
doloso, -sa, *a.* deceitful; fraudulent.
dóllimo, *n.m.* (*Chi.*) freshwater mollusc.
dom, *n.m.* (*eccles.*) title of Carthusian and Benedictine monks.
doma, *n.f.* breaking in, taming; subduing; ***la doma de la bravía,*** the taming of the shrew.
domable, *a.* tamable.
domador, -ra, *n.m.f.* horse-breaker; tamer.
domadura [DOMA].
domar, *v.t.* to break in, tame; to curb, subdue.
domeñar, *v.t.* to master, subdue, curb, harness.

domesticable, *a.* tamable.
domesticar [A], *v.t.* to tame, domesticate. — **domesticarse,** *v.r.* to become civilized.
domesticidad, *n.f.* domesticity; domestication.
doméstico, -ca, *a.* domestic; domesticated. — *n.m.f.* domestic, servant.
domestiquez, *n.m.* tameness.
domiciliar, *v.t.* to domicile, give domicile to, house; ***estar domiciliado en,*** to have one's home *or* address at. — **domiciliarse,** *v.r.* to take up residence.
domiciliario, *a.* domiciliary. — *n.m.* inhabitant, citizen; ***arresto domiciliario,*** house arrest.
domicilio, *n.m.* residence, domicile, home; home address.
dominación, *n.f.* domination; dominance; (*mil.*) high ground, commanding position; (*pl.* **dominaciones**) dominations (*order of angels*).
dominador, -ra, *a.* dominating. — *n.m.f.* dominator.
dominante, *a.* domineering; dominant, commanding; prevailing; ***viento dominante,*** prevailing wind.
dominar, *v.t.* to dominate, master, command; to overlook, command a view of; ***domina tres idiomas,*** he has a command of three languages. — **dominarse,** *v.r.* to control o.s.; ***no sabe dominarse,*** he can't control *or* restrain himself.
dominativo, -va, *a.* dominative.
dómine, *n.m.* teacher of Latin; pedant.
domingada, *n.f.* Sunday festival.
domingo, *n.m.* Sunday; ***domingo de Pasión,*** Passion Sunday; ***domingo de Ramos,*** Palm Sunday; ***domingo de Resurrección,*** Easter Sunday; ***domingo de Cuasimodo,*** Low Sunday; ***domingo de Carnaval*** or ***de piñata,*** Shrove Sunday; ***traje de domingo,*** Sunday best.
dominguejo, *n.m.* (*Hisp. Am.*) nonentity.
dominguero, -ra, *a.* (of) Sunday; (*fig.*) week-end.
dominguillo, *n.m.* tumbler (*toy*); (bull-ring) dummy; ***traer a alguien como un dominguillo,*** to order *or* boss s.o. about.
domínica, *n.f.* (*eccles.*) Sunday.
dominical, *a.* (of) Sunday; dominical; feudal.
dominicano, -na, *a., n.m.f.* (native) of the Dominican Republic; Dominican.
dominicatura, *n.f.* (*prov.*) duty of vassalage.
dominico, -ca, *a., n.m.f.* Dominican (friar *or* nun). — *n.m.* dominico-bird. — *n.f.* (*Hisp. Am.*) small banana.
dominio, *n.m.* dominion; control, mastery, command; domination, rule; domain; (*law*) fee; ***es del dominio público,*** it's common knowledge; ***perder el dominio de sí mismo,*** to lose control of o.s.
dominó, *n.m.* domino (*hooded robe*); dominoes (*game*).
domo, *n.m.* (*arch.*) dome, cupola.
dompedro, *n.m.* (*bot.*) morning-glory; commode.
don, *n.m.* Spanish title for a gentleman, used only before the Christian name; gift; ***don de gentes,*** charm, winning ways; ***don de palabra,*** facility of speech; ***don de lenguas,*** gift for languages; ***don de mando,*** aptitude for command.
dona, *n.f.* (*obs.*) woman, lady; (*Chi.*) bequest; (*pl.*) wedding presents given by bridegroom to bride.
donación, *n.f.* donation, act of donating; bequest.
donadío, *n.m.* (*prov.*) property derived from royal grants.
donado, -da, *n.m.f.* lay-brother, lay-sister.
donador, -ra, *a.* donating. — *n.m.f.* donor.
donaire, *n.m.* charm, gracefulness; wittiness; witticism.
donairoso, -sa, *a.* charming, graceful; witty.
donante, *a.* giving. — *n.m.f.* donor, giver; ***donante de sangre,*** blood donor.
donar, *v.t.* to donate, give.
donatario, -ria, *n.m.f.* donee.
donativo, *n.m.* donation, gift.
doncel, *a.* mellow, mild; ***pino doncel,*** timber of young pines without knots; ***vino doncel,*** mild-flavoured wine. — *n.m.* king's page; chaste youth.
doncella, *n.f.* maid, maiden, damsel; lady's maid; chambermaid; (*ichth.*) peacock fish.
doncellez, *n.f.* virginity, maidenhood.
donde (*interrog., interj.* **dónde**), *adv.* where; ***donde quiera,*** anywhere; ***donde las dan, las toman,*** tit for tat, give and take; ***donde no,*** otherwise; ***¿hacia dónde?*** whither; ***¿por dónde?*** whereabouts? which way?; ***¡mira por dónde!*** there you are! and you know what?
dondequiera, *adv.* anywhere; wherever; ***por dondequiera,*** everywhere.
dondiego, *n.m.* fop, dandy; (*bot.*) jalap; (*bot.*) ***dondiego de noche,*** marvel of Peru; (*bot.*) ***dondiego de día,*** morning-glory.
donguindo, *n.m.* pear.
donillero, *n.m.* sharper, trickster, decoy, roper-in.
donjuán [DONDIEGO].
donosidad [DONOSURA].
donoso, -sa, *a.* charming and witty; (*iron.*) ***¡donosa contestación!*** a fine answer!
donostiarra, *a., n.m.f.* (native) of San Sebastián.
donosura, *n.f.* charming wit.
doña, *n.f.* title used before Christian name of married ladies *or* widows.
doñear, *v.i.* (*coll.*) to womanize.
doquier, doquiera [DONDEQUIERA].
dorada, *n.f.* [DORADO].
doradilla, *n.f.* (*ichth.*) [DORADA]; (*bot.*) scale fern.
doradillo, *a.* (*Arg., C.R.*) honey-coloured (*horses*). — *n.m.* fine brass wire; satin-wood; (*orn.*) wagtail.
dorado, -da, *a.* golden, gilt. — *n.m.* golding, gilt. — *n.f.* (*ichth.*) gilt-head; (*astron.*) dorado; (*Cub.*) poisonous fly.
dorador, *n.m.* gilder.
doradura, *n.f.* gilding.
doral, *n.m.* (*orn.*) fly-catcher.
dorar, *v.t.* to gild; (*cook.*) to brown; (*fig.*) to sugar-coat; ***dorar la píldora,*** to sugar the pill.
dórico, -ca, *a.* (*arch.*) Doric.
dorio, -ria, *a., n.m.f.* Dorian.
dormán, *n.m.* dolman.
dormida, *n.f.* night's sleep; sleeping period; night's resting place.
dormidero, -ra, *a.* sleepy, soporiferous, narcotic. — *n.m.* resting-place for cattle. — *n.f.* garden poppy; (*Cub.*) sensitive mimosa; (*pl.*) sleepiness; ***tiene buenas dormideras,*** he sleeps well.
dormilón, -lona, *a.* sleepy-headed. — *n.m.* sleepy-head. — *n.f.* armchair; pearl earring; (*Hisp. Am.*) mimosa.
dormir [7], *v.t.* to put to sleep; to sleep off; ***dormir la mona,*** to sleep it off; ***dormir la siesta,*** to take a nap after dinner. — *v.i.* to sleep; to spend the night; to rest; ***dormir a pierna suelta,*** to sleep soundly; ***dormir como un leño, como un tronco, como un lirón,*** to sleep like a log; ***dormir sobre,*** to sleep on (*problem etc.*); ***dormir al sereno,*** to sleep in the open. — **dormirse,** *v.r.* to go *or* get to sleep, fall asleep; to oversleep; (*naut.*) to sink down heavily at the prow.
dormirlas, *n.m. inv.* hide-and-seek (*game*).
dormitar, *v.i.* to doze, snooze, have forty winks.
dormitivo, *n.m.* dormitive.
dormitorio, *n.m.* bedroom; dormitory.
dornajo, *n.m.* trough.
Dorotea, *n.f.* Dorothy.
dorsal, *a.* dorsal.
dorso, *n.m.* back; dorsum.
dos, *a.* two; (***coche***) ***de dos plazas,*** two-seater (motor-car), (*Am.*) roadster. — *n.m.* two; second; deuce; ***dos de mayo,*** the second of May; ***de dos en dos,*** two by two, by couples; two abreast; ***en***

un dos por tres, in a twinkling; ***viene cada dos por tres,*** he keeps popping in; (*pl.*) ***los dos,*** both (of them), the two (of them); ***aquí entre los dos,*** between you and me. — *n.f.pl.* ***las dos,*** two o'clock; both (of them), the two (of them).
dosalbo, -ba, *a.* having two white stockings (*horses*).
dosañal, *a.* biennial.
doscientos, -tas, *a., n.m.f.pl.* two hundred.
dosel, *n.m.* canopy.
doselera, *n.f.* valance, drapery of a canopy.
dosificar [A], *v.t.* to dose; to proportion.
dosis, *n.f. inv.* dose.
dotación, *n.f.* endowment; settlement, dowry; crew, complement (*of ship*); staff, personnel.
dotador, -ra, *n.m.f.* endower, donor.
dotal, *a.* dotal.
dotar, *v.t.* to endow; to provide, fit; to staff (*an office*); to man (*a ship*); ***estar dotado de,*** to be endowed with.
dote, *n.m.* stock of counters (*in cards*). — *n.f.* dowry; (*pl.*) endowments, gifts.
dovela, *n.f.* voussoir (*of an arch*).
dovelaje, *n.m.* voussoirs.
dovelar, *v.t.* to hew (*a stone*) in curves for an arch.
dozavado, -da, *a.* twelve-sided; in twelve parts.
dozavo, -va, *a., n.m.f.* twelfth part.
draba, *n.f.* whitlow-grass.
dracma, *n.f.* drachm; drachma.
draconiano, -na, *a.* Draconian.
dracúnculo, *n.m.* guinea-worm.
draga, *n.f.* dredge; (*naut.*) dredger.
dragado, *n.m.* dredging.
dragaminas, *n.m. inv.* minesweeper.
dragante, *n.m.* (*bot.*) goat's thorn; (*naut.*) pillow (*of the bowsprit*).
dragar [B], *v.t.* to dredge.
drago, *n.m.* dragon-tree.
dragomán, *n.m.* dragoman.
dragón, *n.m.* dragon; flying lizard; (*mil.*) dragoon; (*vet.*) white spot (*on the eyes*); furnace feed-hole; (*astron.*) Draco; (*bot.*) dragon-tree; (*ichth.*) ***dragón marino,*** greater weever; (*prov.*) toy kite.
dragona, *n.f.* female dragon; (*mil.*) shoulder-knot; (*Mex.*) cape, cloak; (*Chi., Mex.*) wrist-strap (*of a sword*).
dragoncillo, *n.m.* little dragon; little dragoon; (*obs.*) dragon (*musket*).
dragonear, *v.i.* (*Hisp. Am.*) — ***de,*** to boast, brag (about), make o.s. out to be (sth.), play the (sth.).
dragontea, dragontía, *n.f.* (*bot.*) green dragon.
dragontino, -na, *a.* dragonish, of dragons, dragon.
drama, *n.m.* drama; play.
dramático, -ca, *a.* dramatic. — *n.m.f.* dramatist; dramatic actor *or* actress. — *n.f.* dramatic art, dramatics.
dramatismo, *n.m.* drama, dramatic effect.
dramatización, *n.f.* dramatization.
dramatizar [C], *v.t.* to dramatize.
dramaturgia, *n.f.* dramaturgy, dramatic art.
dramaturgo, -ga, *n.m.f.* dramatist.
dramón, *n.m.* melodrama, blood-and-thunder stuff.
drástico, -ca, *a.* drastic.
drecera, *n.f.* straight row (*of houses, trees etc.*)
drenaje, *n.m.* drainage.
drenar, *v.t.* to drain.
dríada, dríade, *n.f.* dryad.
driblar, *v.t., v.i.* to dribble.
dril, *n.m.* drill; denim.
drino, *n.m.* tree-snake.
driza, *n.f.* halyard.
drizar, *v.t.* (*naut.*) dope; (*obs.*) to hoist (*the yards*).
droga, *n.f.* drug, dope; (*fig.*) fib; deceit; nuisance; (*Hisp. Am.*) debt; deceit, trick.
droguería, *n.f.* hardware store and druggist's, drysaltery.
droguero, -ra, *n.m.f.* drysalter; cheat.
droguete, *n.m.* drugget.
droguista, *n.m.f.* [DROGUERO].
dromedario, *n.m.* dromedary.
dropacismo, *n.m.* (*med.*) depilatory.
druida, *n.m.* druid.
druídico, -ca, *a.* druidic, druidical.
druidismo, *n.m.* druidism.
drupa, *n.f.* (*bot.*) drupe.
druso, -sa, *a.* Drusian. — *n.m.* Druse. — *n.f.* (*min.*) druse.
dúa, *n.f.* (*min.*) gang of workmen.
dual, *a., n.m.* dual.
dualidad, *n.f.* duality.
dualismo, *n.m.* dualism.
dualista, *a.* dualistic. — *n.m.* dualist..
dubio, *n.m.* (*law*) doubtful point *or* issue.
dubitable, *a.* open to doubt *or* question.
dubitación, *n.f.* dubitation.
dubitativo, -va, *a.* dubitative, conjectural; ***oración (cláusula) dubitativa,*** 'if' clause.
ducado, *n.m.* duchy, dukedom; ducat.
ducal, *a.* ducal.
ducentésimo, -ma, *a.* two-hundredth.
dúctil, *a.* ductile.
ductilidad, *n.f.* ductility; malleability.
ductivo, -va, *a.* conducive.
ductor, *n.m.* guide, leader; (*surg.*) probe.
ducha (1), *n.f.* shower; stripe (*in cloth*); ***ducha de agua fría,*** cold shower.
duchar, *v.t.* to give a shower. — **ducharse,** *v.r.* to have *or* take a shower.
ducho, -cha (2), *a.* experienced, skilled.
duda, *n.f.* doubt, misgiving; ***sin duda,*** doubtless; ***sin duda alguna,*** without any shadow of doubt; ***la duda ofende,*** that should go without saying; it goes without saying; ***poner en duda,*** to call in question.
dudable, *a.* doubtful, doubtable.
dudar, *v.t., v.i.* to doubt; to hesitate; ***lo dudo,*** I doubt it; ***dudo de su honradez,*** I doubt his honesty; ***dudó en aceptarlo,*** he hesitated to accept; ***dudo (de) que venga hoy,*** I doubt whether he'll come today.
dudilla, *n.f.* sneaking doubt.
dudoso, -sa, *a.* doubtful, dubious; hesitating.
duela (1), *n.f.* (*cooper's*) stave; fluke.
duelaje [DOLAJE].
duelista, *n.m.* duellist.
duelo (1), *n.m.* sorrow, grief; mourning, bereavement; (assemblage of) mourners; condolence; duel; (*pl.*) troubles; hardship; ***duelos y quebrantos,*** dish of eggs and haslet.
duelo (2), **duela** (2), *pres. indic.; pres. subj.* [DOLER].
duende, *n.m.* (hob)goblin, pixie, gremlin, sprite, leprechaun; ***andar como (parecer un) duende,*** to get up to unexpected tricks; to turn up unexpectedly; ***tener duende,*** to have it, have sth., have what it takes.
duendecillo, *n.m.* elf, little pixie.
duendo, -da, *a.* tame, gentle.
dueña, *n.f.* (*obs.*) mistress, dame; chaperone, duenna; owner, proprietress; ***poner a uno como no digan dueñas,*** to give s.o. a dressing-down; to tear s.o. to pieces.
dueñesco, -ca, *a.* (*coll.*) duenna-like, matronly.
dueño, *n.m.* owner, proprietor, landlord; master; ***dueño de sí mismo,*** self-controlled; ***ser dueño de sí mismo,*** to be one's own master; ***eres muy dueño de hacerlo,*** you are perfectly entitled to do it; ***es usted muy dueño,*** you are welcome, help yourself; ***hacerse dueño de,*** to make o.s. master of.
duermevela, *n.m.* (*coll.*) doze, snooze; fitful sleep.
duerna, *n.f.* trough.

duerno, *n.m.* trough; (*print.*) double sheet of paper.
dueto, *n.m.* duo, duet.
dugo, *n.m.* (*Hisp. Am.*) help, aid.
dugongo, *n.m.* (*zool.*) dugong.
dula, *n.f.* common pasture-ground; irrigated land from common ditch.
dulcamara, *n.f.* (*bot.*) bitter-sweet.
dulce, *a.* sweet; gentle, soft; fresh (*water*); ductile. — *n.m.* sweetmeat; ***dulce de membrillo,*** quince jelly; ***a nadie le amarga un dulce,*** I wouldn't say no to that; (*pl.*) sweet(s), (*Am.*) candy.
dulcecillo, -lla, dulcecito, -ta, *a.* sweetish, rather sweet.
dulcedumbre, *n.f.* sweetness.
dulcémele, *n.m.* (*mus.*) dulcimer.
dulcería, *n.f.* confectioner's (shop).
dulcero, -ra, *a.* fond of sweets, sweet-toothed. — *n.m.f.* confectioner. — *n.f.* sweet-jar, sweet-tray.
dulcificación, *n.f.* dulcification.
dulcificante, *a.* dulcifying, sweetening.
dulcificar [A], *v.t.* to dulcify, sweeten.
dulcinea, *n.f.* (*coll.*) sweetheart; (*fig.*) ideal.
dulcísono, -na, *a.* sweet-toned.
dulero, *n.m.* herdsman.
dulzainero, *n.m.* flageolet-player.
dulzaino, -na, *a.* (*coll.*) too sweet, cloying. — *n.f.* (*mus.*) flageolet; (*coll.*) pile of sweet stuff.
dulzamara [DULCAMARA].
dulzarrón, -rrona, dulzón, -zona, *a.* over-sweet, sickly, cloying.
dulzor, *n.m.* sweetness, sweet taste.
dulzura, *n.f.* sweetness; gentleness; mildness.
dulzurar, *v.t.* (*chem.*) to edulcorate.
duma, *n.f.* douma.
duna, *n.f.* dune.
dundo, -da, *a.* (*Hisp. Am.*) silly, stupid.
Dunquerque, *n.m.* Dunkirk.
dúo, *n.m.* (*mus.*) duo, duet.
duodécimo, -ma, *a.* twelfth.
duodenal, *a.* duodenal.
duodenario, -ria, *a.* lasting twelve days.
duodeno, -na, *a.* twelfth. — *n.m.* (*anat.*) duodenum.
duomesino, -na, *a.* of two months.
dupla, *n.f.* extra dish given in colleges on special days.
duplex, dúplex, *a.* (*teleg.*) duplex.
dúplica, *n.f.* (*law*) rejoinder.
duplicación, *n.f.* duplication, doubling.
duplicado, -da, *a.* duplicate. — *n.m.* duplicate; ***por duplicado,*** in duplicate.
duplicador, -ra, *a.* duplicating. — *n.m.* duplicator (*machine*).
duplicar [A], *v.t.* to duplicate, double; (*law*) to answer (*replication*).
dúplice, *a.* double.
duplicidad, *n.f.* duplicity; doubleness.
duplo, *a., n.m.* double, twice as much.
duque, *n.m.* duke; (*coll.*) fold (*in mantillas*); ***gran duque,*** grand duke; eagle owl.
duquecito, duquesito, *n.m.* young duke; duke's heir.
duquesa, *n.f.* duchess.
dura (1) [DURACIÓN].
durable [DURADERO].
durabilidad, *n.f.* durability, (long) life.
duración, *n.f.* duration; ***ser de mucha duración,*** to be long-lasting *or* hard-wearing.
duradero, -ra, *a.* lasting, durable.
duraluminio, *n.m.* duraluminium.
duramadre, duramáter, *n.f.* (*anat.*) dura mater.
duramente, *adv.* hard; harshly.
durante, *adv.* during, for, in; ***durante mucho tiempo,*** for a long time.
durar, *v.i.* to last, go on (for); to wear well; ***todavía me dura,*** I still have some left.
duraznero, *n.m.* peach tree.
duraznillo, *n.m.* persicary.
durazno, *n.m.* peach; peach tree.
dureza, *n.f.* hardness, firmness; toughness; harshness; (*med.*) callosity; ***dureza de corazón,*** hard-heartedness.
durillo, -lla, *a.* rather hard, hardish, toughish, stiffish. — *n.m.* (*bot.*) dogwood; (*vet.*) callosity.
durmiente, *a.* sleeping, dormant. — *n.m.* (*arch.*) dormant, dormer; (*naut.*) clamp, shelf; (*railw.*) cross-tie, sleeper.
duro, -ra (2), *a.* hard, firm; tough; stiff; harsh; ***a duras penas,*** with difficulty, scarcely, just; ***tomar las duras con las maduras*** or ***estar a las duras y a las maduras,*** to take the rough with the smooth; ***duro de corazón,*** hard-hearted; ***duro de mollera,*** thick, stupid; ***duro de oído,*** hard of hearing; ***ser duro de pelar,*** to be a hard nut to crack; ***ser duro con,*** to be hard on. — *adv.* hard, forcibly, violently; (*coll.*) ***duro y parejo,*** with firmness and steadiness; ***¡duro con ello!*** stick at it!; ***¡duro con él!*** stick (lay) into him, let him have it. — *n.m.* five-peseta coin, five pesetas; ***faltó el canto de un duro,*** it was a near thing, a close shave.
duunviro, *n.m.* duumvir.
duunviral, *a.* duumviral.
duunvirato, *n.m.* duumvirate.
dux, *n.m.* doge.

E

E, e, *n.f.* letter E, e; used instead of *y* when the following word begins with *i* or *hi*; e.g. ***Juan e Ignacio; padre e hijo.*** This rule does not apply at the beginning of interrogation or exclamation, or when the following word begins with the syllable *hie*; e.g. ***¿y Ignacio?***; ***¡y Isidro también!***; ***tigre y hiena.***

¡ea! *interj.* come on!; that's that, that's final.

easonense, *a.*, *n.m.f.* (native) of San Sebastián.

ebanista, *n.m.* cabinet-maker.

ebanistería, *n.f.* cabinet-work; cabinet-making; cabinet-maker's shop.

ébano, *n.m.* ebony, ebony-wood.

ebenáceo, -cea, *a.* (*bot.*) ebenaceous.

ebonita, *n.f.* ebonite.

ebriedad, *n.f.* inebriation.

ebrio, -ria, *a.* inebriated, intoxicated.

ebulición, ebullición, *n.f.* ebullition, boiling; ***en ebullición,*** in ferment.

ebúrneo, -nea, *a.* (*poet.*) eburnian.

eccehomo, *n.m.* Ecce Homo; (*coll.*) pitiable wretch.

eclampsia, *n.f.* (*med.*) eclampsia.

eclecticismo, *n.m.* eclecticism.

ecléctico, *a.*, *n.m.f.* eclectic.

Eclesiástico, *n.m.* Ecclesiasticus.

eclesiástico, -ca, *a.* ecclesiastic, ecclesiastical. — *n.m.* clergyman.

eclesiastizar [C], *v.t.* to transfer to ecclesiastical use *or* ownership.

eclímetro, *n.m.* (*surv.*) clinometer.

eclipsable, *a.* that may be eclipsed.

eclipsar, *v.t.* to eclipse; to outshine. — **eclipsarse,** *v.r.* to be *or* become eclipsed; (*fig.*) to drop into the background, fall into a secondary position; to disappear, fade out.

eclipse, *n.m.* eclipse.

eclíptica, *n.f.* ecliptic.

eclisa, *n.f.* (*railw.*) fish-plate.

eclosión, *n.f.* opening out, blossoming forth, birth.

eco, *n.m.* echo; (distant) sound; ***ecos de sociedad,*** society news and gossip, marriages and events; ***ecos del frente,*** rumblings from the (war-) front; ***hacer eco a, hacerse eco de,*** to echo, repeat slavishly, give wider currency to; ***tener eco,*** to attract attention, be widely commented on.

ecoico, -ca, *a.* (*poet.*) relating to echoes.

ecología, *n.f.* ecology.

ecólogo, *n.m.* ecologist.

economato, *n.m.* guardianship, trusteeship; company store; armed forces' store *or* shop.

economía, *n.f.* economy; sparingness, thrift; saving; ***hacer economías,*** to make savings *or* cuts, economize.

económicamente, *adv.* economically; from the point of view of economics.

económico, -ca, *a.* economical; economic; thrifty; inexpensive.

economista, *n.m.f.* economist.

economizar [C], *v.t.* to economize; to save; ***no economizar esfuerzos,*** to spare no effort.

ecónomo, *n.m.* trustee; guardian; ecclesiastical administrator; acting parish priest.

ectoplasma, *n.m.* ectoplasm.

ecuable, *a.* equitable; (*mech.*) uniform (*motion*).

ecuación, *n.f.* (*alg.*) equation.

Ecuador, *n.m.* ***el —,*** Ecuador.

ecuador, *n.m.* equator.

ecuánime, *a.* equable.

ecuanimidad, *n.f.* equanimity, equableness.

ecuatorial, *a.* equatorial. — *n.m.* equatorial telescope.

ecuatoriano, -na, *a.*, *n.m.f.* Ecuadorian.

ecuestre, *a.* equestrian.

ecuménico, -ca, *a.* ecumenic(al).

ecuo, -cua, *a.* (*obs.*) just, right.

ecuóreo, -rea, *a.* (*poet.*) (belonging to the) sea.

eczema, *n.m.* (*med.*) eczema.

echacantos, *n.m. inv.* (*coll.*) despicable fellow.

echacorvear, *v.i.* (*coll.*) to procure, pimp.

echacorvería, *n.f.* (*coll.*) procuring, pimping.

echacuervos, *n.m. inv.* (*coll.*) procurer, pimp; cheat, impostor.

echada, *n.f.* [ECHADO].

echadero, *n.m.* place of rest, place to stretch out.

echadillo, *n.m.* (*coll.*) foundling.

echadizo, -za, *a.* spying; subtly disseminated; rejected, discarded. — *n.m.f.* spy; (*coll.*) foundling.

echado, -da, *a.* (*C.R.*) indolent, lazy. — *n.m.f.* (*obs.*) foundling. — *n.m.* (*min.*) dip (*of a vein*). — *n.f.* cast, throw; (*sport*) man's length (*on the ground*); (*Arg.*, *Mex.*) boast, bluff; lie, fib.

echador, -ra, *a.* throwing. — *n.m.f.* thrower; coffee waiter.

echadura, *n.m.f.* brooding, hatching; winnowing; ***echadura de pollos,*** brood of chickens.

echamiento, *n.m.* cast, throw; throwing, expulsion, casting out; rejection; ejection.

echapellas, *n.m. inv.* wool-soaker.

echaperros, *n.m. inv.* beadle who drives dogs out of church.

echar, *v.t.*, *v.i.* to cast, throw; to fling, chuck, pitch; to toss; to cast away; to throw out; to put in *or* into; to put on; to deal out; to throw into (*a bag*); to play (*a game*); to give; to give out, give off; to post; to couple (*animals*) sexually; to lay (*blame*); to pour out; ***echar abajo, por tierra,*** or ***por el suelo,*** to throw, pull *or* tear down; ***echar a pique,*** to sink, send to the bottom; ***echar en cara,*** to reproach; ***echar al mundo,*** to give birth to; ***echar a la calle,*** to throw out; ***echar a la lotería*** or ***a una rifa,*** to buy lottery *or* raffle tickets; ***echar las cartas,*** to tell a person's fortune; ***echar una carta,*** to post a letter; ***echar a cara o cruz,*** to toss a coin; ***echar a patadas,*** to kick out; ***echar a perder,*** to spoil, ruin; ***echar con cajas destempladas,*** to throw out unceremoniously; ***echar bravatas,*** to brag, boast; ***echar aceite*** or ***leña al fuego,*** to add fuel to the flames; ***echar el agua a un niño,*** to baptize a child; ***echar a galeras*** or ***a presidio,*** to sentence to the galleys *or* gaol; ***echar las bendiciones a,*** to bless on marriage; ***echar carnes,*** to put on flesh; ***echar chispas, rayos, centellas,*** or ***fuego,*** to be hopping mad, fuming; ***echar de menos,*** to miss (*a person* or *thing*); ***echar de ver,*** to notice; ***echar cálculos*** or ***cuentas,*** to reckon up, work it out (*bill, sum etc.*); ***¿qué edad le echas?*** how old do you make him?; ***echar un bando,*** to publish a proclamation *or* an edict; ***echar una película,*** to put on a film; (*fig.*) ***echar a alguien un discurso*** or ***un sermón,*** to give s.o. a lecture; ***echar ternos*** or ***tacos,*** to swear; ***echar de comer,*** to give sth. to eat; ***echar el bofe*** or ***los bofes,*** to puff and blow; to wear o.s. out; (*naut.*) ***echar el ancla,*** to cast anchor; ***echar el cuerpo fuera,*** to back out; ***echar a broma,*** to take as a joke; ***echar la culpa a alguien,*** to put (throw) the blame on s.o.; ***echar el guante,*** to throw down the gauntlet; ***echar el guante a,*** to grab, catch, seize; (*coll.*) ***echar los hígados por,*** to slave for; (*naut.*); ***echar toda la vela,*** to crowd sail; ***echar maldiciones,*** to curse; ***echar hojas*** or ***flores,*** to put forth leaves *or* flowers; ***echar raíces,*** to take root; ***echar los dientes,*** to cut one's teeth; ***echar pelillos a la mar,*** to bury the hatchet; ***echar suertes,*** to cast *or* draw lots; ***echar tierra a,*** to hush up, keep quiet; ***echar pie a tierra,*** to alight, dismount; ***echar un remiendo a,*** to patch up; ***echar la llave (a),***

to lock; ***echar una partida (de cartas)***, to play a hand (*cards*); ***echar una mano***, to lend a hand; ***echar mano de***, to have recourse to, resort to; ***echar mano a***, to catch, grab, collar; ***echar un pitillo***, to have a fag, smoke; ***echar un trago***, to take a swig, have a drink; ***echar en saco roto***, to pay no heed to, forget all about; ***echarlo todo a rodar***, to ruin the whole thing. — *v.i.* to begin, start (***a***, to); ***echar a correr***, to start to run, break into a run; ***echar a llover***, to begin to rain; ***echaron por otro camino***, they took another road *or* track; ***echaron calle arriba***, they set off up the street; ***echar por la calle de en medio***, to go *or* bash ahead regardless. — **echarse**, *v.r.* to lie down, throw o.s. down, stretch out; to throw o.s. (into); ***se echó el viento***, the wind dropped, died down; ***echarse a perder***, to spoil, go off, go bad; (*fig.*) ***echarse atrás***, to draw back; to back down; ***echarse a un lado***, to draw to one side; ***echarse a***, to begin *or* start to; ***echárselas de***, to make o.s. out to be, brag of being.

echarpe, *n.m.* stole; shawl; scarf.

echazón, *n.f.* throwing; (*naut.*) jettison.

echona, *n.f.* (*Arg.*, *Chi.*) sickle.

eda, *n.f.* lodger, (*Am.*) roomer.

edad, *n.f.* age; ***de edad***, elderly; ***de cierta edad, de edad madura***, of mature years; ***mayor de edad***, of age; ***mayor edad***, majority; ***menor de edad***, under age; ***menor edad***, minority; ***edad de piedra, bronce, hierro***, Stone, Bronze, Iron Age; ***edad media***, Middle Ages; ***alta edad media***, early Middle Ages; ***baja edad media***, late Middle Ages; ***edad del pavo***, awkward age (*in children*).

edecán, *n.f.* (*mil.*) aide-de-camp.

edema, *n.m.* (*med.*) œdema.

edén, *n.m.* Garden of Eden, paradise.

edición, *n.f.* edition; publication; ***edición príncipe***, first edition.

edicto, *n.m.* edict.

edículo, *n.m.* small building; shrine; niche.

edificación, *n.f.* construction, building; edification.

edificador, -ra, *a.* constructing, building; edifying. — *n.m.f.* constructor, builder; edifier.

edificante, *a.* edifying.

edificar [A], *v.t.* to construct, build; to edify.

edificativo, -va, *a.* edifying.

edificatorio, -ria, *a.* edificatory.

edificio, *n.m.* edifice, building.

edil, *n.m.* ædile; councillor.

edilidad, *n.f.* ædileship.

Edimburgo, *n.m.* Edinburgh.

editar, *v.t.* to publish.

editor, -ra, *a.* publishing; ***(casa) editora***, publishing house. — *n.m.* publisher.

editorial, *a.* editorial, publishing. — *n.m.* editorial, leader. — *n.f.* publishing house.

Edipo, *n.m.* Oedipus.

edredón, *n.m.* eiderdown, (*Am.*) comforter.

educable, *a.* educable.

educación, *n.f.* education; upbringing; breeding; ***educación física***, physical training; ***buena (mala) educación***, good (bad) manners; ***eso es una falta de educación***, that is bad form.

educador, -ra, *a.* educating. — *n.m.f.* education(al)ist.

educando, -da, *n.m.f.* pupil, student.

educar [A], *v.t.* to educate; to bring up; to train.

educativo, -va, *a.* educational.

educción, *n.f.* eduction.

educir [15], *v.t.* to educe, bring out.

edulcoración, *n.f.* sweetening.

edulcorante, *n.m.* sweetener.

edulcorar, *v.t.* to sweeten.

efe, *n.f.* letter F.

efebo, *n.m.* adolescent, ephebe.

efectismo, *n.m.* (*art*) (straining after) effect.

efectista, *a.* (*art*) sensational, theatrical, striving after effect.

efectivamente, *adv.* (yes) indeed, sure enough; you're quite right, that's it, just as I, you, he etc. said.

efectividad, *n.f.* effectiveness; ***con efectividad desde***, with effect from, as from.

efectivo, -va, *a.* real, actual; effective; permanent; ***hacer efectivo***, to put into effect, implement; to make valid. — *n.m.* (*com.*) cash; ***en efectivo***, in hard cash; ***efectivo en caja***, cash in hand; ***efectivos militares***, forces, available strength.

efecto, *n.m.* effect, result; end, purpose; ***a efectos de***, for the purpose of; ***a ese*** or ***tal efecto***, to that end; ***al efecto***, for the purpose; ***en efecto***, indeed, so indeed (it is), sure enough; ***por efecto de***, as a result of; (*mech.*) ***de simple efecto, doble efecto***, single acting, double acting; ***llevar a***, or ***poner en efecto***, to carry out, put into effect; ***hacer*** or ***surtir efecto***, to have the desired result, work; ***tener efecto***, to take effect, take place; ***tener por efecto***, to have as a result, to result in; (*pl.*) assets, goods; (*com.*) bills, drafts; ***efectos públicos***, public securities; ***efectos a pagar***, bills payable; ***efectos a recibir***, bills receivable; ***efectos en cartera***, securities in hand.

efectuación, *n.f.* accomplishment.

efectuar [M], *v.t.* to effect, effectuate, accomplish, carry out. — **efectuarse**, *v.r.* to take place.

efémera, *n.f.* (*med.*) ephemeral (*fever*).

efeméride, *n.f.* anniversary; event, date; (*pl.*) daily record; ***efemérides astronómicas***, ephemeris.

efémero, *n.m.* (*bot.*) stinking iris.

efendi, *n.m.* effendi.

efervescencia, *n.f.* effervescence.

efervescente, *a.* effervescent.

efesino, -na, efesio, -sia, *a.*, *n.m.f.* Ephesian.

efetá, *adv.* ephetha (*in baptism*).

eficacia, *n.f.* efficacy; efficiency.

eficaz, *a.* efficacious, effective; efficient.

eficiencia, *n.f.* efficiency; effectiveness.

eficiente, *a.* efficient; effective.

efigie, *n.f.* effigy, image.

efímero, -ra, *a.* ephemeral, fleeting. — *n.f.* (*med.*) ephemeral (*fever*); (*ent.*) mayfly.

eflorecerse [9], *v.r.* (*chem.*) to effloresce.

eflorescencia, *n.f.* (*bot.*, *chem.*) efflorescence; (*med.*) eruption (*on face*).

eflorescente, *a.* (*chem.*) efflorescent.

efluente, *adj.* effluent.

efluvio, *n.m.* effluvium; exhalation, emanation.

efod, *n.m.* ephod.

efugio, *n.m.* subterfuge, shift, evasion.

efundir, *v.t.* to effuse, pour out, spill.

efusión, *n.f.* effusion, pouring out, shedding; effusiveness.

efuso, -sa, *a.* effused. — *p.p. irreg.* [EFUNDIR].

égida, *n.f.* ægis.

egilope, *n.f.* (*bot.*) wild bastard oat.

egipcíaco, -ca, egipciano, -na, egipcio, -cia, *a.*, *n.m.f.* Egyptian.

Egipto, *n.m.* Egypt.

egiptología, *n.f.* Egyptology.

egiptólogo, *n.m.* Egyptologist.

égira, *n.f.* hegira.

égloga, *n.f.* eclogue.

egoísmo, *n.m.* selfishness, egoism.

egoísta, *a.* selfish, egoistic. — *n.m.f.* egoist.

ególatra, *a.* self-worshipping.

egolatría, *n.f.* self-worship.

egotismo, *n.m.* egotism.

egregio, -gia, *a.* egregious, illustrious.

egrena, *n.f.* iron clamp.

egresar, *v.i.* (*Arg., Chi.*) to leave; to pass out, graduate.
egresión, *n.f.* egression.
egreso, *n.m.* departure; debit; (*pl.*) outgoings.
egrisador, *n.m.* box for diamond-dust.
egrisar, *v.t.* to cut (*diamonds*).
¡eh! *interj.* eh! hey there! I say! — *interrog.* **¿eh?** eh? (*i.e. isn't it? aren't you? etc.*).
eider, *n.m.* eider (*duck*).
eirá, *n.m.* (*Arg., Par.*) large fox.
eje, *n.m.* axis; axle-tree, axle; shaft, spindle, arbor; (*mech.*) ***eje auxiliar,*** countershaft; (*geom.*) ***eje conjugado,*** minor axis (*of an ellipse*); (*geom.*) ***eje de abscisas,*** axis of abscissæ; (*geom.*) ***eje de coordenadas,*** co-ordinate axis; ***eje delantero,*** front axle; (*geom.*) ***eje de ordenadas,*** axis of ordinates; ***eje trasero,*** rear axle; (*astron.*) ***eje terrestre,*** axis of the earth; ***partir por el eje,*** to upset completely, throw right out of gear.
ejecución, *n.f.* execution; carrying out; performance; (*law*) judicial writ; distraint.
ejecutable, *a.* executable, performable.
ejecutante, *a.* executing. — *n.m.* performer; (*law*) distrainor.
ejecutar, *v.t.* to execute; to carry out; to perform; (*law*) to distrain.
ejecutivo, -va, *a.* executive; prompt, quick, expeditious. — *n.m.* executive.
ejecutor, -ra, *a.* executing. — *n.m.f.* executor; executer; distrainor.
ejecutoría, *n.f.* office of an executive officer.
ejecutoriar, *v.t.* to confirm (*a judicial sentence*); (*fig.*) to establish the truth of.
ejecutorio, -ria, *a.* (*law*) executory, firm. — *n.f.* (*law*) writ *or* decree of execution; judgment; letters patent of nobility; authority.
ejemplar, *a.* exemplary. — *n.m.* specimen; copy.
ejemplificación, *n.f.* exemplification.
ejemplificar [A], *v.t.* to exemplify.
ejemplo, *n.m.* example, instance; ***dar ejemplo,*** to set an example; ***por ejemplo,*** for instance; ***poner de ejemplo,*** to give as an example.
ejercer [D], *v.t., v.i.* to exercise; to practise, perform; to exert; ***ejercer influencia en*** or ***sobre,*** to exert influence on.
ejercicio, *n.m.* exercise, practice; drill; financial year; paper (*in an examination*); ***en ejercicio,*** practising; in office; ***el ejercicio hace maestro,*** practice makes perfect.
ejercitación, *n.f.* exercise, practice.
ejercitante, *a.* exercising, training. — *n.m.f.* one in a spiritual retreat.
ejercitar, *v.t.* to exercise; to practise; to train, drill.
ejército, *n.m.* army; ***ejércitos de tierra, mar y aire,*** armed forces; ***cuerpo de ejército,*** army-corps.
ejido, *n.m.* common public land.
ejión, *n.m.* (*arch.*) corbel; purlin; bracket.
ejote, *n.m.* (*Hisp. Am.*) string bean.
el, *defin. art. m. sing.* the; (*pl.* **los**).
él, *pron. pers. m.* 3rd *pers. sing.* he; him; it; (*pl.* **ellos**) they; them.
elaboración, *n.f.* elaboration; manufacture; working out.
elaborado, -da, *a.* elaborate.
elaborador, -ra, *a.* elaborating; manufacturing. — *n.m.f.* manufacturer.
elaborar, *v.t.* to manufacture, produce; to work; to work out.
elación, *n.f.* haughtiness; magnanimity; pompous style.
elamí, *n.m.* (*mus.*) Phrygian mode as used in plain-song.
elasticidad, *n.f.* (*phys.*) elasticity, springiness.
elástico, -ca, *a.* elastic. — *n.m.* elastic, elastic band, material etc. — *n.f.* vest; (sports) vest shirt.
elaterio, *n.m.* (*bot.*) squirting cucumber.
elche, *n.m.* apostate, renegade (*from Christianity*).
ele, *n.f.* letter L.
eléboro, elébor, *n.m.* hellebore.
elección, *n.f.* election; choice.
electivo, -va, *a.* elective.
electo, -ta, *a.* elect. — *p.p.* [ELEGIR].
elector, -ra, *a.* electing. — *n.m.* elector.
electorado, *n.m.* electorate.
electoral, *a.* electoral; ***colegio electoral,*** polling station; electoral college.
electoralismo, *n.m.* electioneering.
electorero, *n.m.* (*polit.*) agent, canvasser.
electricidad, *n.f.* electricity.
electricista, *n.m.* electrician.
eléctrico, -ca, *a.* electric, electrical.
electrificación, *n.f.* electrification.
electrificar [A], *v.t.* to electrify.
electrizable, *a.* electrifiable.
electrizador, -ra, electrizante, *a.* electrifying. — *n.m.f.* electrifier.
electrizar [C], *v.t.* to electrify.
electro, *n.m.* amber, electrum.
electrocución, *n.f.* electrocution.
electrocutar, *v.t.* to electrocute.
electrodinámico, -ca, *a.* electrodynamic. — *n.f.* electrodynamics.
electrodo, *n.m.* electrode.
electroencefalografía, *n.f.* electro-encephalography.
electroimán, *n.m.* electro-magnet.
electrólisis, *n.f. inv.* electrolysis.
electrolítico, -ca, *a.* electrolytic.
electrólito, *n.m.* electrolyte.
electrolización, *n.f.* electrolization.
electrolizar [C], *v.t.* to electrolyze.
electromagnético, -ca, *a.* electro-magnetic.
electromagnetismo, *n.m.* electro-magnetism.
electrometría, *n.f.* electrometry.
electrométrico, -ca, *a.* electrometric.
electrómetro, *n.m.* electrometer.
electromotor, -ra, *a.* electromotive. — *n.m.* electromotor.
electromotriz, *a.* electromotive; ***fuerza electromotriz,*** electromotive force.
electrón, *n.m.* electron.
electronegativo, -va, *a.* electronegative.
electropositivo, -va, *a.* electropositive.
electroquímico, -ca, *a.* electrochemical. — *n.f.* electrochemistry.
electroscopio, *n.m.* electroscope.
electrotecnia, *n.f.* electrotechnics.
electroterapia, *n.f.* electrotherapy, electrotherapeutics.
electrotipia, *n.f.* electrotyping.
electrotípico, -ca, *a.* electrotypic.
elefante, -ta, *n.m.f.* elephant.
elefantíasis, *n.f.* elephantiasis.
elefantino, -na, *a.* elephantine; (of) ivory.
elegancia, *n.f.* elegance, stylishness, smartness; finesse.
elegante, *a.* elegant, stylish, smart; ***no es elegante*** + *inf.*, it's not nice, not good form (to).
elegía, *n.f.* elegy.
elegíaco, -ca, *a.* elegiac.
elegible, *a.* eligible.
elegido, -da, *a.* elect, chosen. — *n.m.pl.* (**elegidos**) (the) elect, (the) chosen.
elegir [8E], *v.t.* to elect; to choose.
élego, -ga, *a.* elegiac.
elemental, *a.* elemental; elementary.
elemento, *n.m.* element; (*coll.*) fellow, bloke;

estar en su elemento, to be in one's element; (*pl.*) elements; means, resources.
elemí, *n.m.* elemi, gum resin.
Elena, *n.f.* Helen.
elenco, *n.m.* index, catalogue; (*theat.*) company, cast.
elevación, *n.f.* elevation; rise; height; raising; ecstasy; haughtiness; (*artill.*) ***tirar por elevación,*** to fire with an elevation.
elevado, -da, *a.* elevated; tall, high; sublime, exalted.
elevador, *a.* elevating, hoisting, lifting. — *n.m.* hoist.
elevamiento, *n.m.* elevation; ecstasy, rapture.
elevar, *v.t.* to elevate; to raise, lift, hoist; (*fig.*) to exalt. — **elevarse,** *v.r.* to rise, soar.
elfo, *n.m.* elf.
elidir, *v.t.* to debilitate; (*gram.*) to elide.
elijación, *n.f.* (*pharm.*) seething.
elijar, *v.t.* to seethe.
eliminación, *n.f.* elimination.
eliminador, -ra, *a.* eliminating. — *n.m.f.* eliminator.
eliminar, *v.t.* to eliminate; to get rid of.
elipse, *n.f.* (*geom.*) ellipse.
elipsis, *n.f.* (*gram.*) ellipsis.
elipsoidal, *a.* ellipsoidal.
elipsoide, *n.m.* ellipsoid.
elipticidad, *n.f.* ellipticity.
elíptico, -ca, *a.* elliptic, elliptical.
elíseo, -sea, elisio, -sia, *a.* Elysian.
elisión, *n.f.* (*gram.*) elision.
elitario, -ria, *a.* (of the) élite.
elíxir, elixir, *n.m.* elixir.
elocución, *n.f.* elocution.
elocuencia, *n.f.* eloquence.
elocuente, *a.* eloquent.
elogiador, -ra, *a.* praising, eulogistic. — *n.m.f.* eulogist.
elogiar, *v.t.* to praise, laud, eulogize.
elogio, *n.m.* eulogy, praise.
elongación, *n.f.* elongation.
elote, *n.m.* (*Mex.*) ear of green corn; (*C.R.*, *Hond.*, *coll.*) ***pagar uno los elotes,*** to get the blame, be made the scapegoat.
elucidación, *n.f.* elucidation.
elucidar, *v.t.* to elucidate.
eludible, *a.* avoidable, preventable.
eludir, *v.t.* to elude, avoid.
ella, *pron. pers. f.* 3rd *pers. sing.* she; her; it; (*pl.*) they; them; ***ahora es ella,*** this is it; ***después será ella,*** the rub will come later.
elle, *n.f.* letter LL.
ello, *pron. neut.* it; ***ello es que,*** the fact is that.
emaciación, *n.f.* emaciation.
emanación, *n.f.* emanation.
emanar, *v.i.* to emanate, issue.
emancipación, *n.f.* emancipation.
emancipador, -ra, *a.* emancipating. — *n.m.f.* emancipator.
emancipar, *v.t.* to emancipate. — **emanciparse,** *v.r.* to become emancipated.
emasculación, *n.f.* emasculation.
embabiamiento, *n.m.* (*coll.*) woolgathering, having one's head in the clouds.
embachar, *v.t.* to pen (*sheep*) to be shorn.
embadurnador, -ra, *a.* daubing. — *n.m.f.* dauber.
embadurnar, *v.t.* to (be)smear, (be)daub.
embaidor, -ra, *a.* swindling. — *n.m.f.* swindler, cheat, crook.
embaimiento, *n.m.* swindling, cheating, crookedness.
embair [Q], *v.t.* to swindle, cheat, take in.
embajada, *n.f.* embassy; mission; (*coll.*) bothersome business, bore.
embajador, *n.m.* ambassador; ***embajador cerca de,*** ambassador to.
embajadora, *n.f.* ambassadress; ambassador's wife.
embalador, *n.m.* packer.
embalaje, *n.m.* packing, baling.
embalar, *v.t.* to pack, bale; ***papel de embalar,*** brown paper, (*Am.*) kraft. — **embalar(se),** *v.i.* (*v.r.*) (*sport*) to sprint; (*coll.*) to start to rush off, go tearing off, go off at a tangent; ***no te embales,*** don't start off, hold on, steady; ***estar*** or ***ir embalado,*** to be going flat out; to be hard at it.
embaldosado, *n.m.* tile-floor; tiling.
embaldosar, *v.t.* to tile.
embalsadero, *n.m.* pool of (stagnant) rain-water; swamp.
embalsamador, -ra, *n.m.f.* embalmer.
embalsamamiento, *n.m.* embalming.
embalsamar, *v.t.* to embalm; to perfume.
embalsar, *v.t.* to dam (up); (*naut.*) to sling, hoist.
embalse, *n.m.* damming (up); dam, reservoir; (*naut.*) slinging.
embalumar, *v.t.* to load up, overload, burden.
emballenador, -ra, *n.m.f.* corset-maker.
emballenar, *v.t.* to stiffen with whalebone.
emballestado, -da, *a* (*vet.*) contracted (*hoof*). — *n.m.* contraction of the nerves in animals' feet.
emballestarse, *v.r.* to get ready to discharge a crossbow.
embanastar, *v.t.* to put into a basket; to crate; to pack in.
embancar, *v.i.* (*naut.*) to run aground. — **embancarse,** *v.r.* (*Mex.*) to stick to the walls of the furnace.
embarazada, *n.f.* pregnant woman.
embarazador, -ra, *a.* embarrassing; hindering.
embarazar [C], *v.t.* to embarrass; to hinder, impede; to make pregnant.
embarazo, *n.m.* embarrassment; hindrance; pregnancy.
embarazoso, -sa, *a.* embarrassing; awkward.
embarbascarse [A], *v.r.* to get entangled; to get muddled.
embarbecer [9], *v.i.* to have a beard appearing.
embarbillar, *v.t.* to join planks *or* beams together; to rabbet.
embarcación, *n.f.* craft, vessel; embarkation; ***embarcación menor,*** small craft.
embarcadero, *n.m.* wharf, quay; pier; jetty.
embarcador, -ra, *n.m.f.* shipper, loader.
embarcar [A], *v.t.* to embark, ship. — **embarcar(se),** *v.i.* (*v.r.*) to embark, go aboard; ***embarcarse en,*** to embark on.
embarco, *n.m.* embarkation.
embardar, *v.t.* to thatch.
embargador, -ra, *n.m.f.* (*law*) sequestrator, attacher.
embargante, *a.* impeding, restraining; ***no embargante,*** notwithstanding.
embargar [B], *v.t.* to impede, restrain; to overcome (*emotion*); (*law*) to seize, attach; to lay an embargo on.
embargo, *n.m.* indigestion; (*law*) embargo, sequestration; seizure, attachment; ***sin embargo,*** nevertheless, however, yet.
embarnizador, *n.m.* varnisher.
embarnizadura, *n.f.* varnishing.
embarnizar [C], *v.t.* to varnish.
embarque, *n.m.* embarkation; shipment.
embarradilla, *n.f.* (*Mex.*) small sweet pie.
embarrador, *n.m.* plasterer, dauber; (*fig.*) trouble-maker, mischief-maker.
embarradura, *n.f.* smearing with mud; smear *or* stain of mud.

embarrancar [A], *v.i.* (*naut.*) to run aground. — **embarrancarse,** *v.r.* to get bogged down, stuck in mud *or* mire.
embarrar (1), *v.t.* to dedaub; to besmear with mud; (*prov.*) to rough-cast with plaster.
embarrar (2), *v.t.* to prise up *or* lift with a bar.
embarrilador, *n.m.* barrel packer.
embarrilar, *v.t.* to barrel, put in a barrel.
embarrotar, *v.t.* to bar; to strengthen with bars.
embarullador, -ra, *a.* muddling. — *n.m.f.* muddler.
embarullar, *v.t.* (*coll.*) to muddle, make a mess of.
embasamiento, *n.m.* (*arch.*) foundation.
embastar, *v.t.* to baste, to tack.
embaste, *n.m.* basting.
embastecer [9], *v.i.* to become corpulent *or* fleshy. — **embastecerse,** *v.r.* to become gross *or* coarse.
embate, *n.m.* onslaught; buffet(ing), dash(ing); ***embates de la fortuna,*** buffeting of fortune.
embaucador, -ra, *a.* deceiving; deceptive. — *n.m.* cheat, one who takes another in.
embaucamiento, *n.m.* deception, taking in of another.
embaucar [A], *v.t.* to cheat, take in.
embaular, *v.t.* to pack in a trunk; (*coll.*) to cram *or* pack in, tuck in, tuck away.
embausamiento, *n.m.* amazement, astonishment, bewilderment.
embazador, *n.m.* person who dyes things brown; object which can be dyed brown.
embazadura, *n.f.* brown dye; (*fig.*) amazement, astonishment.
embazar [C], *v.t.* to dye brown; to dumbfound; to hinder. — **embazarse,** *v.r.* to become sick *or* tired (of).
embebecer [9], *v.t.* to enrapture. — **embebecerse,** *v.r.* to become enraptured.
embebecimiento, *n.m.* rapture.
embebedor, -ra, *a.* imbibing. — *n.m.f.* imbiber.
embeber, *v.t.* to imbibe, drink in; to soak; to embed, fit in; to include; (*sew.*) to take in. — *v.i.* to shrink. — **embeberse,** *v.r.* to become lost in thought.
embecadura, *n.f.* (*arch.*) spandrel.
embelecador, -ra, *n.m.f.* cheat.
embelecar [A], *v.t.* to cheat, take in.
embeleco, *n.m.* cheat, fraud; (*coll.*) pest.
embeleñar, *v.t.* to stupefy, drug with henbane; to charm, fascinate.
embelesamiento, *n.m.* rapture, ecstasy.
embelesar, *v.t.* to charm, enrapture, entrance, captivate.
embeleso, *n.m.* rapture, ecstasy, delight.
embellaquecerse, *v.r.* to become a knave.
embellecer [9], *v.t.* to embellish, beautify.
embellecimiento, *n.m.* embellishing, beautifying.
embermejar, embermejecer [9], *v.t.* to dye red; to make blush. — *v.i.* to blush.
emberrenchinarse, emberrincharse, *v.r.* (*coll.*) to fly into a tantrum.
embestida, *n.f.* onslaught, onset, charge.
embestidor, -ra, *a.* onrushing, charging. — *n.m.f.* cadger.
embestidura, *n.f.* onslaught, onset, charge.
embestir [8], *v.t.* to rush at, charge against; (*coll.*) to touch for money.
embetunar, *v.t.* to cover with pitch; to put polish on (*shoes*).
embicar [A], *v.t.* (*naut.*) to top; ***embicar las vergas,*** to top the yards. — *v.i.* (*Arg., Chi.*) to steer straight for the coast.
embijar, *v.t.* to paint with red-lead; (*Hond., Mex.*) to soil, smear, tarnish.
emblandecer [9], *v.t.* to soften; (*fig.*) to mollify.
emblanquecer [9], *v.t.* to whiten, bleach.
emblanquecimiento, *n.m.* bleaching, whitening.
emblema, *n.m.* emblem, badge.
emblemático, -ca, *a.* emblematic.
embobamiento, *n.m.* open-mouthed amazement, gaping wonder.
embobar, *v.t.* to amaze; to make gape with astonishment. — **embobarse,** *v.r.* to be struck with amazement; to begin to gape with amazement; to become stupefied.
embobecer [9], *v.t.* [EMBOBAR].
embobecimiento [EMBOBAMIENTO].
embocadero, embocador, *n.m.* mouth, outlet.
embocado, -da, *a.* dry-sweet (*wine*).
embocador [EMBOCADERO].
embocadura, *n.f.* mouth, entrance; mouthpiece; taste (*of wine*); (*arch.*) proscenium arch; ***tener buena embocadura,*** to have a good mouth (*horse*); (*coll.*) ***tomar la embocadura,*** to jump the first hurdles.
embocar [A], *v.t.* to enter *or* put through; to make swallow; to gobble up, gulp down; to spring on.
embochinchar, *v.i.* (*Hisp. Am.*) to make a row.
embodegar [B], *v.t.* to store in a cellar (*wine, olives*).
embojar, *v.t.* to arrange branches for (*silk-worms*).
embojo, *n.m.* branches placed for silk-worms.
embolada, *n.f.* piston-stroke.
embolado, *n.m.* (*theat.*) minor role; (*tauro.*) bull with tipped horns; (*coll.*) fib, trick.
embolar, *v.t.* to tip the horns of (*bulls*); to apply gilding size to; to shine, polish (*shoes*).
embolia, *n.f.* embolism.
embolismador, -ra, *a.* detracting. — *n.m.f.* detractor.
embolismal, *a.* intercalary.
embolismar, *v.t.* (*coll.*) to gossip about.
embolismo, *n.m.* embolism; (*fig.*) muddle, confusion; (*coll.*) gossip, fib, falsehood.
émbolo, *n.m.* (*mech.*) piston, plunger; embolus; ***émbolo buzo,*** plunger, sucker (*of a pump*).
embolsar, *v.t.* to put in a purse; to pocket.
embolso, *n.m.* pocketing (*money*).
embonar, *v.t.* to improve; (*naut.*) to sheathe; (*Cub., Mex.*) to fit, suit; to be becoming to (*s.o.*).
embono, *n.m.* (*naut.*) sheathing.
emboñigar [B], *v.t.* to plaster with cow-dung.
emboque, *n.m.* passage (*through any narrow space*); (*coll.*) cheat, fraud.
emboquillar, *v.t.* to tip (*a cigarette*); (*min.*) to make the entrance of (*a shaft*); to make a drill-hole in.
embornal, *n.m.* (*naut.*) scupper-hole.
emborrachador, -ra, *a.* intoxicating.
emborrachamiento, *n.m.* (*coll.*) drunkenness.
emborrachar, *v.t.* to make drunk. — **emborracharse,** *v.r.* to get drunk.
emborrar, *v.t.* to pad, wad, stuff with hair, wool etc.; to card (*wool*) a second time; (*fig., fam.*) to make s.o. swallow (*a lie*).
emborrascar [A], *v.t.* to provoke, enrage. — **emborrascarse,** *v.r.* to become stormy; (*fig.*) to be spoiled, ruined (*business*); (*Arg., Hond., Mex., min.*) to become exhausted (*seam*).
emborrazamiento, *n.m.* larding (*a fowl*).
emborrazar [C], *v.t.* to lard (*a fowl*).
emborricarse [A], *v.r.* (*coll.*) to become stupefied; to become infatuated.
emborrizar [A], *v.t.* to give the first combing to (*wool*).
emborronador, -ra, *a.* blotting.
emborronar, *v.t.* to blot; (*fig.*) to scribble.
emborrullarse, *v.r.* (*coll.*) to wrangle.
emboscada, *n.f.* ambush; ***tender una emboscada a,*** to ambush.
emboscadura, *n.f.* ambush(ing).
emboscar [A], *v.t.* (*mil.*) to place in ambush. — **emboscarse,** *v.r.* to take to *or* hide in the forest

or woods; to lie in ambush; (*mil. slang*) to be a shirker.
embosquecer [9], *v.i.* to become wooded.
embotador, -ra, *a.* blunting, dulling.
embotadura, *n.f.* bluntness, dullness.
embotamiento, *n.m.* blunting; bluntness, dullness; stupefaction.
embotar, *v.t.* to (make) blunt *or* dull; to put in a jar. — **embotarse,** *v.r.* to get blunt *or* dull.
embotellado, *n.m.* bottling.
embotellador, -ra, *a.* bottling. — *n.m.f.* bottler.
embotellamiento, *n.m.* congestion, (traffic) jam.
embotellar, *v.t.* to bottle; to block, jam. — **embotellarse,** *v.r.* to get jammed; (*coll.*) to mug, bone *or* swot up (*a subject*).
embotijar, *v.t.* to put in jars *or* jugs; to insulate (*floors*). — **embotijarse,** *v.r.* to swell up, get puffy; to go weepy; to get irritable *or* angry.
embovedar, *v.t.* to arch, vault; to put *or* hide in a vault.
embozado, -da, *a.*, *n.m.f.* (person) muffled, wrapped up to the eyes.
embozar [C], *v.t.* to muffle *or* wrap up to the eyes; to mask, disguise; to muzzle.
embozo, *n.m.* muffler; fold back (*in top part of sheet*); (*fig.*) dissimulation; ***quitarse el embozo,*** to drop one's mask.
embrace, *n.m.* curtain-clasp.
embracilado, -da, *a.* (*coll.*) carried about in the arms (*children*).
embragar [B], *v.t.* to connect, engage by means of a clutch; (*naut.*) to sling.
embrague, *n.m.* (*naut.*) slinging; clutch; coupling.
embravecer [9], *v.t.* to irritate, enrage. — *v.i.* to become strong (*plants*). — **embravecerse,** *v.r.* to get angry; to get rough (*sea*); to become more violent.
embravecimiento, *n.m.* fury, rage.
embrazadura, *n.f.* embracing; handle (*of a shield etc.*).
embrazar [C], *v.t.* to clasp (*a shield*). — *v.i.* (*mech.*) to engage (*gears*).
embreado, *n.m.*, **embreadura,** *n.f.* (*naut.*) tarring, pitching.
embrear, *v.t.* (*naut.*) to tar, pitch.
embregarse [B], *v.r.* to quarrel, wrangle.
embreñarse, *v.r.* to hide in a thicket *or* among brambles.
embriagar [B], *v.t.* to intoxicate, inebriate; (*fig.*) to transport, enrapture. — **embriagarse,** *v.r.* to become inebriated.
embriaguez, *n.f.* intoxication, inebriation; (*fig.*) rapture.
embridar, *v.t.* to bridle.
embriología, *n.f.* embryology.
embriológico, -ca, *a.* embryological.
embriólogo, -ga, *n.m.f.* embryologist.
embrión, *n.m.* embryo; ***en embrión,*** in embryo.
embrionario, -ria, *a.* embryonic.
embroca, embrocación, *n.f.* (*pharm.*) embrocation.
embrocar [A], *v.t.* to empty (*a vessel*) into another; to wind (*thread*) upon a bobbin; (*med.*) to apply embrocation; (*shoemaking*) to fasten with tacks to the last; (*tauro.*) to toss between the horns; (*Hond.*, *Mex.*) to place upside down (*vessel, plate etc.*).
embrochado, -da, *a.* embroidered.
embrochalar, *v.t.* to support (*a beam*) by a cross-piece *or* stay.
embrolla, *n.f.* [EMBROLLO].
embrolladamente, *adv.* in a tangled way.
embrollador, -ra, *a.* embroiling, confusing. — *n.m.f.* embroiler, trouble-maker.
embrollar, *v.t.* to entangle, confuse, muddle up; to embroil.
embrollo, *n.m.* tangle, confusion, muddle, mess; embroiling; (*fig.*) lie, cheat.
embrollón, -llona, *n.m.f.* [EMBROLLADOR].
embrolloso, -sa, *a.* tangled, confused, tricky.
embromado, -da, *a.* (*naut.*) misty, hazy.
embromador, -ra, *a.* joking. — *n.m.f.* joker, jokester.
embromar, *v.t.* to play a joke on; to make fun of; to tease.
embroquelarse, *v.r.* to shield o.s.
embroquetar, *v.t.* to skewer the legs of (*fowls*).
embrosquilar, *v.t.* (*prov.*) to put (*cattle*) into a fold.
embrujar, *v.t.* to bewitch.
embrujo, *n.m.* bewitchment, spell, charm.
embrutecer [9], *v.t.* to make brutish, sottish, dull and stupid. — **embrutecerse,** *v.r.* to become besotted, dull and stupid.
embrutecimiento, *n.m.* brutishness, sottishness, dullness.
embuchado, *n.m.* sausage; fraud; (*theat.*) lines added by actor.
embuchar, *v.t.* to stuff.
embudador, -ra, *n.m.f.* person using funnel (*for filling*).
embudar, *v.t.* to put a funnel into; to funnel in; to trick, deceive.
embudista, *n.m.* deceiver, trickster.
embudo, *n.m.* funnel; (bomb-) hole; deceit, trick; (*coll.*) ***ley del embudo***, discriminatory law; one-sided contract.
embullar, *v.i.* (*Hisp. Am.*) to stir; to make a noise.
embullarse, *v.r.* (*Cub.*) to make merry.
embullo, *n.m.* (*Hisp. Am.*) gaiety, revelry.
emburujar, *v.t.* (*coll.*) to jumble, muddle. — **emburujarse,** *v.r.* (*Hisp. Am.*) to wrap o.s. up.
embuste, *n.m.* fib, falsehood; (*pl.*) gewgaws, baubles, trinkets.
embustear, *v.i.* to fib, tell falsehoods.
embustería, *n.f.* (*coll.*) deceit, fibbing.
embustero, -ra, *n.m.f.* fibber.
embusteruelo, -la, *n.m.f.* little fibber.
embutidera, *n.f.* instrument for riveting tin-work.
embutido, *n.m.* inlaying, inlaid work; sausage; (*Hisp. Am.*) lace, insertion.
embutir, *v.t.* to inlay; to insert; to stuff, pack tightly; to force *or* cram in; (*naut.*) to worm; (*coll.*) ***se embutió un montón de comida,*** he shovelled down, crammed in a great pile of food.
eme, *n.f.* letter M.
emendable, *a.* amendable.
emendación, *n.f.* emendation; amends.
emendador, *n.m.* emendator.
emendar [ENMENDAR].
emergencia, *n.f.* emerging; emergency; (*opt.*) emergence; ***en caso de emergencia,*** in an emergency.
emergente, *a.* emergent, issuing, resulting.
emerger [E], *v.i.* to emerge (*from water*).
emérito, -ta, *a.* emeritus.
emersión, *n.f.* (*astron.*) emersion.
emético, -ca, *a.*, *n.m.f.* emetic. — *n.m.* tartar emetic.
emigración, *n.f.* emigration.
emigrado, -da, *a.*, *n.m.f.* emigré.
emigrante, *a.*, *n.m.f.* emigrant.
emigrar, *v.i.* to emigrate.
eminencia, *n.f.* eminence.
eminencial, *a.* eminent.
eminente, *a.* eminent.
eminentísimo, -ma, *a. superl.* most eminent.
emir, *n.m.* emir, ameer.
emisario, *n.m.* emissary; (*physiol.*) emunctory.
emisión, *n.f.* emission; (*rad.*) broadcast; issue; (*com.*) ***nueva emisión,*** new issue.
emisor, -ra, *a.* emitting; (*rad.*) broadcasting. —

n.m. (*rad.*) transmitter, broadcasting apparatus. — *n.f.* transmitting station.
emitir, *v.t.* to emit, send forth; to issue; to utter; (*rad.*) to broadcast.
emoción, *n.f.* emotion; excitement.
emocional, *a.* emotional.
emocionante, *a.* moving; thrilling, exciting.
emocionar, *v.t.* to arouse emotion in; to excite, thrill. — **emocionarse,** *v.r.* to be moved, touched; to be thrilled.
emoliente, *a., n.m.* emollient.
emolumento, *n.m.* emolument.
emotivo, -va, *a.* emotive, emotional.
empacar, *v.t.* to pack up, put in bales. — **empacarse** [A], *v.r.* to become obstinate, stubborn; to become peeved and sulky; (*Hisp. Am.*) to balk (*horse*).
empacón, -cona, *a.* (*Arg., Per.*) obstinate, subborn; balky (*horse*).
empachado, -da, *a.* awkward, timid, bashful; (*naut.*) overloaded.
empachar, *v.t.* to hinder, impede, embarrass; to surfeit, give indigestion; to disguise. — **empacharse,** *v.r.* to get ashamed, embarrassed; to stuff o.s. (*with food*), get indigestion.
empacho, *n.m.* embarrassment; bashfulness; surfeit, indigestion; hindrance; ***sin empacho,*** without any qualms; ***no tener empacho en,*** not to have any qualms about.
empachoso, -sa, *a.* embarrassing; bashful; rich, cloying.
empadronador, *n.m.* census-taker.
empadronamiento, *n.m.* census; list of persons liable to pay taxes.
empadronar, *v.t.* to take a census of; to register in a census.
empajar, *v.t.* to cover *or* stuff with straw; (*Col., Chi.*) to thatch; (*Arg., Cub., P.R.*) to cram, surfeit, overload with insubstantial food.
empalagamiento, *n.m.* cloying, surfeit.
empalagar [B], *v.t.* to cloy, nauseate, surfeit; (*fig.*) to sicken, weary, bore.
empalago, *n.m.* cloyingness, sickly sweetness.
empalagoso, -sa, *a.* cloying, over-sweet, sickly sweet, sickening, palling; (*fig.*) smarmy.
empalamiento, *n.m.* impalement, impaling.
empalar, *v.t.* to impale.
empaliada, *n.f.* (*prov.*) hangings of bunting.
empaliar, *v.t.* (*prov.*) to adorn with hangings.
empalizada, *n.f.* palisade, pale-fence, stockade.
empalizar [C], *v.t.* to pale, palisade.
empalmadura, *n.f.* dovetailing; joint; coupling; splicing.
empalmar, *v.t.* to scarf, dovetail; to couple, join; to splice; (*coll.*) ***empalmar un constipado con otro,*** to catch *or* get one cold after another; ***empalmar un pitillo con otro,*** to chain-smoke; ***empalmarla,*** to start *or* get talking. — *v.i.* to connect, link (up).
empalme, *n.m.* (*carp.*) scarf; join; connection; jointing; splicing; (*railw.*) junction.
empalomado, *n.m.* loose-stone damming wall.
empalomar, *v.t.* to sew (*a bolt-rope*) to a sail.
empalletado, *n.m.* bulwark formed of sailors' hammocks.
empamparse, *v.r.* (*Hisp. Am.*) to get lost in the pampa.
empanadilla, *n.f.* small pie; moveable footstep in carriages.
empanado, -da, *a.* having no windows *or* openings. —*n.f.* pie, (*Am.*) deep pie; ***hacer una empanada,*** to fix it, cover it up, fiddle it.
empanar, *v.t.* to bake in a pie; to breadcrumb, cover in breadcrumbs; to sow with wheat. — *v.i.* to yield heavily. — **empanarse,** *v.r.* (*agric.*) to be choked with too much seed.
empandar, *v.t.* to bend; to warp.
empandillar, *v.t.* (*coll.*) to fix (*cards*) in order to cheat; to bamboozle.
empantanar, *v.t.* to swamp; (*fig.*) to hold up; ***la cosa está empantanada,*** it's bogged down, it's hanging fire; ***lo tienen todo empantanado,*** they are letting it all stagnate; ***me dejó empantanado,*** he left me in the lurch, he left me in it.
empañadura, *n.f.* swaddling clothes.
empañar, *v.t.* to swaddle; to mist up *or* over, steam up *or* over; to blur, dull; to sully, tarnish.
empañetar, *v.t.* (*Col., C.R., Ec., Ven.*) to plaster (*walls, ceilings etc.*).
empañicar [A], *v.t.* (*naut.*) to furl.
empapar, *v.t.* to soak, drench; to soak up. — **empaparse,** *v.r.* to get soaked; to steep o.s. (***de,*** in); (*coll.*) ***para que te empapes,*** put that in your pipe and smoke it.
empapelado, *n.m.* papering, paper-hanging; wallpaper; paper lining.
empapelador, *n.m.* paper-hanger.
empapelar, *v.t.* to wrap in paper; to paper (*a wall*); (*coll.*) to tie up in legalities and red tape; to put on a charge, book, give a ticket to; ***le voy a empapelar,*** I'm going to drop him in it, get him into trouble.
empapirotar, *v.t.* (*coll.*) to doll up, deck out.
empapujar, *v.t.* (*coll.*) to make (*s.o.*) eat too much, stuff.
empaque, *n.m.* baling; (*fig.*) imposing *or* lordly bearing, fine presence, grand style; (*Chi., Per., P.R.*) impudence, sauciness.
empaquetador, -ra, *n.m.f.* packer.
empaquetadura, *n.f.* packing; gasket.
empaquetar, *v.t.* to pack, bale; (*fig.*) to stuff, pack in; (*coll.*) to get into trouble.
emparamarse, *v.r.* (*Hisp. Am.*) to freeze to death.
emparamentar, *v.t.* to adorn.
emparamento, emparamiento, *n.m.* (*law, prov.*) sequestration.
emparchar, *v.t.* to cover with plasters.
empardar, *v.t.* (*prov., Arg.*) to draw, tie.
emparedado, *n.m.* sandwich.
emparedamiento, *n.m.* confinement, shutting up; immuring; reclusion.
emparedar, *v.t.* to confine, shut up; to immure, wall up *or* in.
emparejador, -ra, *n.m.f.* matcher, fitter.
emparejadura, *n.f.* matching.
emparejamiento, *n.m.* matching, making equal.
emparejar, *v.t.* to pair, match; to level, flush; to set ajar. — *v.i.* to come level with; to equal. — **emparejarse,** *v.r.* to pair (off).
emparentado, -da, *a.* related (*by marriage*).
emparentar [I], *v.t.* to relate *or* join (*by marriage*). — *v.i.* to become related (*by marriage*).
emparrado, *n.m.* vine arbour.
emparrar, *v.t.* to embower, form bowers of vine branches in *or* on.
emparrillado, *n.m.* (*engin.*) grillage.
emparrillar, *v.t.* to grill.
emparvar, *v.t.* to heap up (*grain*) for threshing.
empastador, *n.m.* paste-brush; (*Hisp. Am.*) bookbinder.
empastar, *v.t.* to fill (*a tooth*); to paste; (*paint.*) to impaste; to bind (*a book*) in a stiff cover; (*Arg., Chi., Guat., Mex.*) to turn into a meadow. — **empastarse,** *v.r.* (*Arg., Chi.*) to swell (*animal's belly*); (*Chi.*) to become weed-grown (*land*).
empaste, *n.m.* filling (*of tooth*); binding (*of book*); (*art.*) impasto.
empastelar, *v.t.* (*coll.*) to arrange, fix, fiddle; (*print.*) to pie.
empatadera, *n.f.* (*coll.*) checking, impeding.
empatar, *v.t.* to hinder, obstruct; (*Hisp. Am.*) to join, splice; to couple, connect. — *v.i.* to tie, draw.
empate, *n.m.* tie, draw.

empavesada, *n.f.* bulwark formed of shields; (*naut.*) fringed cloth used to cover boat-seats etc.
empavesado, *n.m.* soldier covered by a shield; (*naut.*) dressing (*of ship*).
empavesar, *v.t.* to spread waistcloths on; to dress (*a ship*); to veil (*a monument*); (*coll.*) to doll up, deck out.
empavonar, *v.t.* to blue (*iron* or *steel*); (*Col., P.R.*) to smear, grease.
empecatado, -da, *a.* incorrigible; cursed, confounded.
empecer [9], *v.t.* (*obs.*) to injure. — *v.i.* to be an obstacle; ***esto no empece para,*** this is no obstacle to.
empecimiento, *n.m.* damage; obstacle.
empecinado, *a.* obstinate, stubborn. — *n.m.* dealer in pitch.
empecinar, *v.t.* to cover in pitch.
empecinarse, *v.r.* to get stubborn.
empedernido, -da, *a.* hard-hearted; inveterate.
empedernir [Q], *v.t.* to indurate, harden. — **empedernirse,** *v.r.* to become hardened; to become hard-hearted.
empedrado, -da, *a.* flecked with clouds; dappled (*horses*); pitted from smallpox. — *n.m.* stone pavement; paving.
empedrador, *n.m.* paver.
empedrar [I], *v.t.* to pave with stones; (*fig.*) to strew, bespatter (***de,*** with).
empega, *n.f.* pitch; mark of pitch.
empegado, *n.m.* tarpaulin.
empegadura, *n.f.* coat of pitch.
empegar [B], *v.t.* to pitch, cover with pitch, mark with pitch.
empeguntar, *v.t.* to mark (*animals*) with pitch.
empeine (1), *n.m.* instep; vamp; pubes; (*obs.*) hoof.
empeine (2), *n.m.* tetter, ringworm.
empeine (3), *n.m.* (*prov.*) cotton flower.
empeinoso, -sa, *a.* affected by ringworm.
empelar, *v.i.* to grow hair.
empelazgarse [B], *v.r.* (*coll.*) to get into a quarrel.
empelechar, *v.t.* to cover *or* face with marble; to join (*marble blocks*).
empelotarse, *v.r.* to get into a wrangle; (*Chi., Col., Cub., Mex.*) to strip; to crowd together.
empeltre, *n.m.* slip (*for grafting*).
empella, *n.f.* vamp (*of a shoe*).
empellar, *v.t.* to push, jostle, shove.
empellejar, *v.t.* to cover *or* line with skins.
empellón, *n.m.* push, shove; ***abrirse paso a empellones,*** to push *or* shove one's way through.
empenachar, *v.t.* to adorn with plumes.
empenta, *n.f.* prop, stay, shore.
empeñadamente, *adv.* strenuously, hard, persistently.
empeñar, *v.t.* to pawn; to pledge; to force; to join (*battle*); to engage on, start. — **empeñarse,** *v.r.* to get into debt; to be set, insist (***en,*** on); ***está empeñado en ir,*** he is set on going.
empeñero, -ra, *n.m.f.* (*Mex.*) pawnbroker.
empeño, *n.m.* pawn(ing); pledge, pledging; dogged determination, firm purpose; undertaking.
empeoramiento, *n.m.* deterioration; worsening.
empeorar(se), *v.t., v.i.* (*v.r.*) to worsen; ***para empeorar las cosas,*** to make matters worse.
empequeñecer [9], *v.t.* to diminish, make smaller; (*fig.*) to belittle.
emperador, *n.m.* emperor; sword-fish.
emperadora, *n.f.* (*fig.*) top figure, star.
emperatriz, *n.f.* empress.
emperchado, *n.m.* fence of green stakes.
emperchar, *v.t.* to suspend on a perch.
emperejilarse, *v.r.* (*coll.*) to dress up, doll o.s. up, deck o.s. out.
emperezar [C], *v.t.* to delay, put off. — **emperezar(se),** *v.i.* (*v.r.*) to get lazy.
empergaminar, *v.t.* to bind with parchment.
emperifollarse [EMPEREJILARSE].
empernar, *v.t.* to bolt.
empero, *conj.* yet, however; notwithstanding.
emperrarse, *v.r.* — ***en,*** to get set on, get (stubbornly) into one's head.
empesador, *n.m.* broom of rushes (*for smoothing warp on a loom*).
empetatar, *v.t.* (*Guat., Mex., Per.*) to cover with a sleeping mat.
empetro, *n.m.* samphire.
empezar [C], *v.t.* to begin, start.
empicarse [A], *v.r.* to get taken with, get keen on.
empicotadura, *n.f.* pillorying.
empicotar, *v.t.* to pillory.
empilonar, *v.t.* (*Cub.*) to stack (*tobacco leaves*).
empinado, -da, *a.* steep; (*fig.*) stiff, stuck-up.
empinador, -ra, *n.m.f.* (*coll.*) toper.
empinadura, *n.f.*, **empinamiento,** *n.m.* elevation, raising, rising.
empinar, *v.t.* to raise, lift up; ***empinar el codo,*** to drink. — *v.i.* to drink. — **empinarse,** *v.r.* to stand on tiptoe; to rear (*horses*); to tower, rise high; (*aer.*) to zoom up.
empingorotado, -da, *a.* stuck-up, posh.
empingorotar, *v.t.* (*coll.*) to put on top. — **empingorotarse,** *v.r.* to climb, get up.
empino, *n.m.* (*arch.*) summit of a curve.
empiolar, *v.t.* to hobble; to sling by the feet; [APIOLAR].
empíreo, *a.* empyreal; celestial, divine. — *n.m.* empyrean.
empírico, -ca, *a.* empiric, empirical. — *n.m.* empiricist.
empirismo, *n.m.* empiricism.
empitonar, *v.t.* to catch with the horns.
empizarrado, *n.m.* slate roof.
empizarrar, *v.t.* to slate.
emplastadura, *n.f.*, **emplastamiento,** *n.m.* plastering, affixing plasters; applying paint and cosmetics to the face.
emplastar, *v.t.* to apply plasters to; to paint (*the face*); (*coll.*) to stop, check. — **emplastarse,** *v.r.* to get smeared.
emplastecer [9], *v.t.* to level the surface of, smooth.
emplástico, -ca, *a.* gluey, sticky.
emplasto, *n.m.* plaster; poultice; (*coll.*) sight; pain in the neck.
emplástrico, -ca, *a.* glutinous, sticky; (*med.*) suppurative.
emplazador, -ra, *n.m.f.* (*law*) summoner.
emplazamiento (1), *n.m.* (*law*) summons, citation.
emplazamiento (2), *n.m.* placing, siting; position, situation, site.
emplazar (1) [C], *v.t.* to summon; to cite.
emplazar (2) [C], *v.t.* to place, position, site.
empleado, -da, *n.m.f.* employee; clerk; attendant, assistant.
emplear, *v.t.* to employ; to use; ***lo da por bien empleado,*** he considers it to be *or* to have been worth while; ***le está bien empleado,*** it serves him right. — **emplearse,** *v.r.* to be employed, take employment; to occupy o.s.; ***emplearse (a fondo) (en),*** to give (terrifically) full treatment (to), (really) go to town (on).
empleita, *n.f.* plaited strand of bass.
empleitero, -ra, *n.m.f.* one who plaits and sells bass matting.
emplenta, *n.f.* section of mud-wall prefabricated in one piece.
empleo, *n.m.* employ, employment; job; use.
empleomanía, *n.f.* (*coll.*) craze *or* mania for public office.
emplomado, *n.m.* leading; lead roof.
emplomador, *n.m.* leadworker; leadfitter.

emplomar, *v.t.* to lead, fit *or* line with lead; to put lead seals on.
emplumar, *v.t.* to feather; to adorn with plumes; to tar and feather; (*Ec., Ven.*) to send to jail *or* exile; ***emplumarlas,*** to run off, clear out.
emplumecer [9], *v.i.* to fledge, grow feathers.
empobrecer(se) [9], *v.i.* (*v.r.*) to become impoverished.
empobrecimiento, *n.m.* impoverishment.
empodrecer(se) [9], *v.i.* (*v.r.*) [PUDRIR].
empolvar, empolvorar, empolvorizar [C], *v.t.* to dust, powder; to cover with dust *or* powder.
empolvoramiento, *n.m.* covering with dust; powdering.
empollador, -ra, *a.* hatching, brooding. — *n.m.* incubator. — *n.m.f.* hatcher.
empolladura, *n.f.* pupa (*of bees*); (*coll.*) swotting.
empollar, *v.t.* to hatch. — **empollar(se),** *v.i.* (*v.r.*) to breed (*bees*); (*coll.*) ***empollar(se) una asignatura, una materia,*** to swot, swot up, bone up *or* mug up a subject; ***no le cuesta empollar,*** it's no effort for him to swot.
empollón, -llona, *a., n.m.f.* swotting; swot.
emponchado, -da, *a.* (*Arg., Chi., Per.*) wearing a poncho; (*Arg., Per., fig.*) suspicious.
emponzoñador, -ra, *a.* poisonous. — *n.m.f.* poisoner.
emponzoñamiento, *n.m.* poisoning.
emponzoñar, *v.t.* to poison.
empopar, *v.t.* (*naut.*) to poop.
emporcar [A], *v.t.* to soil, dirty, foul.
emporio, *n.m.* emporium, mart.
empotramiento, *n.m.* (*arch.*) embedding.
empotrar, *v.t.* (*arch.*) to embed; to build *or* set in; to mortise; to scarf; to put (*beehives*) in a pit; (*naut.*) to fasten (*cannon*).
empotrerar, *v.t.* (*Hisp. Am.*) to pasture (*cattle etc.*).
empozar [C], *v.t.* to throw into a well; to soak (*flax*). — *v.i.* (*Hisp. Am.*) to stop flowing (*water*). — **empozarse,** *v.r.* (*coll.*) to be pigeonholed.
empradizar [C], *v.t.* to turn into a meadow; (*Col.*) to weed.
emprendedor, -ra, *a.* enterprising.
emprender, *v.t.* to undertake; to venture *or* embark upon; ***emprender la marcha,*** to set out; ***emprenderla con alguien,*** to pick on, set on *or* go for s.o.
empreñar [PREÑAR].
empresa, *n.f.* enterprise, undertaking; commercial *or* industrial concern, firm; (*her.*) device.
empresarial, *a.* managerial, (of) management.
empresario, *n.m.* contractor; manager; agent; impresario; showman; ***empresario de pompas fúnebres,*** funeral director, undertaker, (*Am.*) mortician.
empréstito, *n.m.* loan.
emprimado, *n.m.* last combing of wool.
emprimar, *v.t.* to give the last combing to (*wool*); (*paint.*) to prime; (*coll.*) to deceive.
empuchar, *v.t.* to put (*skeins of yarn*) into buck *or* lye.
empujar, *v.t.* to push, shove; to force, press.
empuje, *n.m.* push, drive, thrust.
empujón, *n.m.* push, shove; ***a empujones,*** pushing, shoving; by fits and starts.
empulgadura, *n.f.* stretching the cord of a crossbow.
empulgar [B], *v.t.* to stretch (*the cord of*) a crossbow.
empulgueras, *n.f.pl.* wings of a crossbow; thumbscrews; ***apretar las empulgueras a uno,*** to put the screw on s.o.
empuntar, *v.t.* (*Col., prov.*) to guide, put on the right road; (*Col.*) ***empuntarlas,*** to run away, show a clean pair of heels. — *v.i.* (*Col.*) to go, leave.
empuñador, -ra, *a.* grasping. — *n.m.f.* grasper, clutcher.
empuñadura, *n.f.* hilt; beginning (*of a story*); (*coll., fig.*) ***hasta la empuñadura,*** to the hilt.
empuñar, *v.t.* to clutch, grasp, grip.
empuñidura, *n.f.* (*naut.*) earing.
empurrarse, *v.r.* (*C.R., Guat., Hond.*) to become angry, fly into a violent passion.
emulación, *n.f.* emulation.
emulador, -ra, *a.* emulating. — *n.m.f.* emulator.
emular, *v.t.* to emulate.
emulgente, *a.* (*anat.*) emulgent.
émulo, -la, *n.m.f.* emulator.
emulsión, *n.f.* emulsion.
emulsivo, -va, *a.* emulsive, emulsifying.
emunción, *n.f.* (*med.*) excretion.
emundación, *n.f.* (*obs.*) cleansing.
emuntorio, *n.m.* (*anat.*) emunctory.
en, *prep.* in, into; at; on, upon; for; ***en dos años,*** in two years; ***en la mesa,*** on the table; ***en casa,*** at home; ***en adelante,*** in future; ***convertir en,*** to change *or* turn into; ***en diciendo esto,*** on *or* immediately after saying this; ***en domingo,*** on Sunday; ***le conocí en el andar,*** I knew him by his walk; ***se vendió en £10,000,*** it was sold at *or* for £10,000; ***en alto,*** on high.
enaceitar, *v.t.* to oil, make oily.
enagua, *n.f.* (*usually pl.*) underskirt, petticoat.
enaguachar, *v.t.* to over-fill with water, swamp.
enaguazar [C], *v.t.* to flood, swamp.
enagüillas, *n.f.pl.* short skirt *or* petticoat; kilt.
enajenable, *a.* alienable.
enajenación, *n.f.*, **enajenamiento,** *n.m.* alienation of property; absentmindedness; estrangement; rapture; ***enajenación mental,*** mental derangement.
enajenar, *v.t.* to alienate, transfer *or* give away (*property*); to transport, enrapture. — **enajenarse,** *v.r.* to become estranged; to alienate; ***se ha enajenado de X,*** he has become estranged from X; ***se ha enajenado la amistad de X,*** he has alienated X's friendship.
enálage, *n.f.* (*gram.*) enallage.
enalbar, *v.t.* to bring (*iron* or *steel*) to white heat.
enalbardar, *v.t.* to put a packsaddle on; (*cook.*) to cover with batter; to lard.
enalmagrado, -da, *a.* (*fig.*) vile, despicable.
enalmagrar, *v.t.* to colour with ochre; to dishonour.
enaltecer [9], *v.t.* to exalt, extol.
enamarillecer, *v.i.* to turn yellow.
enamoradizo, -za, *a.* easily infatuated, susceptible.
enamorado, -da, *n.m.f.* lover.
enamorador, -ra, *a.* wooing; love-making. — *n.m.f.* wooer; love-maker.
enamoramiento, *n.m.* infatuation; enamouring.
enamorar, *v.t.* to enamour, cause to fall in love; to captivate; ***estar enamorado de,*** to be in love with. — **enamorarse,** *v.r.* to fall in love (***de,*** with).
enamoricarse [C], *v.r.* (*coll.*) to get infatuated.
enancarse [A], *v.r.* (*Arg., Mex., Per.*) to ride on the croup (*horse*).
enanchar, *v.t.* (*coll.*) to widen.
enangostar, *v.t.* to narrow.
enanito, -ta, *n.m.f.* (delightful) little dwarf.
enano, -na, *a.* dwarfish. — *n.m.f.* dwarf.
enante, *n.m.* water-dropwart.
enarbolar, *v.t.* to hoist; to brandish; ***enarbolar la bandera,*** to hoist the colours. — **enarbolarse,** *v.r.* to rise on the hind legs.
enarcar [A], *v.t.* to hoop (*barrels*); to arch. — **enarcarse,** *v.r.* (*Mex.*) to rise on the hind feet (*horses*).
enardecer [9], *v.t.* to fire with passion, inflame,

kindle. — **enardecerse,** *v.r.* to get inflamed *or* heated.

enardecimiento, *n.m.* inflaming; excitement; passion.

enarenación, *n.f.* plastering (*a wall*).

enarenar, *v.t.* to cover with sand; to gravel. — **enarenarse,** *v.r.* (*naut.*) to run aground.

enarmonar, *v.t.* to raise, rear. — **enarmonarse,** *v.r.* to rise on the hind feet.

enarmónico, -ca, *a.* enharmonic.

enastado, -da, *a.* horned.

enastar, *v.t.* to fix a handle to.

encabalgamiento, *n.m.* gun-carriage; trestlework.

encabalgar [B], *v.t.* to provide horses for; to rest (sth.) (on). — *v.i.* to rest, lean (on).

encaballadura, *n.f.* (*build.*) imbrication.

encaballar, *v.t.* (*build.*) to overlap, imbricate.

encabellecerse [9], *v.r.* to grow hair.

encabestrar, *v.t.* to put a halter on; (*fig.*) to force to obey. — **encabestrarse,** *v.r.* to get entangled in the halter.

encabezadura, *n.f.* scarfing.

encabezamiento, *n.m.* heading; tax-list; census-taking; enrolment of taxable citizens; tax, tribute.

encabezar [C], *v.t.* to head, lead; to put a heading to; to make the tax-roll of; to take a census of; to fortify (*wine*) with alcohol; (*carp.*) to scarf, join. — **encabezarse,** *v.r.* to compromise, settle.

encabillar, *v.t.* (*naut.*) to fasten, secure with spikes, pins *or* bolts.

encabriar, *v.t.* (*arch.*) to put in the rafters for.

encabritarse, *v.r.* to rear up, buck (*horses*); to shoot up, pitch up (*aeroplanes and ships*).

encabullar, *v.t.* (*Cub., P.R., Ven.*) to tie with sisal.

encachado, *n.m.* concrete lining of bridge *or* sewer.

encachar, *v.t.* to line with concrete.

encadenación, encadenadura, *n.f.*, **encadenamiento,** *n.m.* concatenation; chaining, linking, connection.

encadenar, *v.t.* to chain, enchain, fetter, shackle; to link together.

encajador, *n.m.* one who encases, engraves *or* inserts; chasing *or* engraving tool.

encajadura, *n.f.* encasing, inserting, joining; socket groove.

encajar, *v.t.* to encase, drive in, fit in, enclose, insert; (*mech.*) to gear; (*carp.*) to rabbet, join; ***encajar la puerta,*** to push the door to; ***me han encajado esta pesadez,*** they have forced this bore on me; ***le encajó un discurso,*** he forced a long rigmarole on him; ***me han encajado un billete falso,*** they have palmed off a dud note on me; ***le encajé una bofetada,*** I landed him a swipe on the face; (*fig.*) ***encajó bien el golpe,*** he took it on the chin. — *v.i.* to fit; to be relevant, to the point; ***encajar bien,*** to fit well *or* closely. — **encajarse,** *v.r.* to push, squeeze (*o.s. into*); (*fig.*) to intrude, butt in; to put on (*hat, garment etc.*).

encaje, *n.m.* fitting, adjusting; socket, cavity, groove; enchasing; joining together; lace; inlaid work.

encajerado, -da, *a.* (*naut.*) fouled (*rope*).

encajero, -ra, *n.m.* lace-maker; lace-dealer.

encajetillar, *v.t.* to pack (*cigarettes, tobacco*).

encajonado, -da, *a.* flanked by steep banks (*rivers*). — *n.m.* (*arch.*) packed work; coffer-dam.

encajonamiento, *n.m.* packing up in boxes *or* crates; narrowing (*of a river*) in a gorge.

encajonar, *v.t.* to pack up, box, crate; to box in, confine narrowly, squeeze in.

encalabozar [C], *v.t.* (*coll.*) to put into a dungeon *or* prison.

encalabrinado, -da, *a.* headstrong, obstinate, stubborn.

encalabrinar, *v.t.* to affect the head of, make dizzy; to excite, irritate. — **encalabrinarse,** *v.r.* (*coll.*) to become headstrong, obstinate.

encalada, *n.f.* metal piece of harness.

encalador, *n.m.* lime-pit *or* vat (*for hides*).

encaladura, *n.f.* whitewashing.

encalambrarse, *v.r.* (*Chi., Col., Mex., P.R.*) to become numb.

encalamocar [A], *v.t.* (*Col., Ven.*) to make stupid *or* besotted.

encalar, *v.t.* to whitewash; to lime; to stow.

encalmadura, *n.f.* overheating.

encalmarse, *v.r.* (*vet.*) to get overheated; (*naut.*) to become becalmed.

encalostrarse, *v.r.* to become sick by sucking the first milk (*child*).

encalvecer [9], *v.i.* to grow bald.

encalladero, *n.m.* (*naut.*) shoal, sand-bank.

encalladura, *n.f.* (*naut.*) grounding, stranding.

encallar, *v.i.* (*naut.*) to run aground; to get stuck.

encallecer [9], *v.i.* to get corns. — **encallecerse,** *v.r.* to become hardened *or* callous.

encallejonar, *v.t.* to force into a narrow place.

encamación, *n.f.* (*min.*) struts and scaffolding.

encamar, *v.t.* to put to bed, lay down; (*min.*) to prop up. — **encamarse,** *v.r.* to take to bed; to lie *or* crouch down (*animals*); to get beaten flat (*crops*).

encamarar, *v.t.* to store (*grain*).

encambijar, *v.t.* to store (*water*).

encambrar, *v.t.* to store.

encambronar, *v.t.* to enclose with hedges; to strengthen with iron.

encaminadura, *n.f.*, **encaminamiento,** *n.m.* directing; putting on the right road.

encaminar, *v.t.* to guide, put on the right road, show the way; to direct; ***estar bien (mal) encaminado,*** to be on the right (wrong) tracks *or* lines. — **encaminarse,** *v.r.* to take the road (to), set out (to), direct one's steps (to); to be directed (towards), be intended (for).

encamisada, *n.f.* (*mil.*) camisade; (*obs.*) masquerade by night.

encamisar, *v.t.* to put a shirt on. — **encamisarse,** *v.r.* to put a shirt over one's clothes for a camisade.

encamotarse, *v.r.* (*Arg., Chi., C.R., Ec.*) to fall in love (with).

encampanado, -da, *a.* bell-shaped; (*Mex., P.R.*) ***dejar encampanado,*** to leave in the lurch.

encanalar, encanalizar, *v.t.* to channel.

encanallarse, *v.r.* (*fig.*) to sink low, become a rotter.

encanarse, *v.r.* to stiffen with anger.

encanastar, *v.t.* to pack in baskets *or* hampers.

encancerarse, *v.r.* to become affected with cancer.

encandecer, *v.t.* to heat to a white heat.

encandelar, *v.i.* to bud (*trees*).

encandiladera, encandiladora, *n.f.* (*coll.*) procuress, bawd.

encandilado, -da, *a.* high-cocked (*hats*).

encandilar, *v.t.* to dazzle, daze; to excite; (*coll.*) to stir (*the fire*). — **encandilarse,** *v.r.* to shine *or* flash (*eyes*).

encanecer [9], *v.i.* to grow grey-haired *or* white-haired; to grow old.

encanijamiento, *n.m.* weakness, sickliness, feebleness.

encanijar, *v.t.* to make (*an infant*) thin and sickly. — **encanijarse,** *v.r.* to become weak, feeble *or* sickly.

encanillar, *v.t.* to wind on spools *or* bobbins.

encantación, *n.f.* enchantment; incantation, spell, charm.

encantado, -da, *a.* haunted.

encantador, -ra, *a.* delightful, charming, enchanting. — *n.m.f.* enchanter, charmer, sorcerer; enchantress, sorceress.

encantamiento, *n.m.* enchantment; incantation.

encantar, *v.t.* to bewitch; to enchant; to charm;

to delight; ***me encanta nadar,*** I love swimming; ***encantado (de conocerle),*** delighted (to meet you).
encantarar, *v.t.* to put into a jar *or* ballot-box.
encante, *n.m.* auction; flea-market.
encanto, *n.m.* enchantment, charm, spell; delight.
encantorio, *n.m.* (*coll.*) enchantment.
encantusar, *v.t.* (*coll.*) [ENGATUSAR].
encanutar, *v.t.* to flute, roll; to put into a tube *or* pipe.
encañada, *n.f.* gorge.
encañado, *n.m.* water-conduit; trellis of canes *or* reeds.
encañador, -ra, *n.m.f.* spool-winder.
encañadura, *n.f.* strong rye-straw (*for stuffing straw-beds, packsaddle etc.*).
encañar, *v.t.* to stake (*plants*); to channel (*water*); to drain; to wind (*silk*). — *v.i.* to form *or* grow into stalk (*corn*).
encañizada, *n.f.* fish weir; reed trellis.
encañonar, *v.t.* to put into tubes *or* pipes; to plait, fold; to wind (*silk*) on cane quills. — *v.i.* to grow feathers, fledge (*birds*); to point a gun (at).
encapacetado, -da, *a.* covered with a helmet.
encapachadura, *n.f.* number of baskets of olives ready for pressing.
encapachar, *v.t.* to put into a basket; to protect (*the shoots of grapes*) from the sun.
encapado, -da, *a.* cloaked, wearing a cloak.
encapazar [C], *v.t.* to put into a basket.
encaperuzar [C], *v.t.* to hood.
encapillado, *n.m.* ***lo encapillado,*** what one has on.
encapilladura, *n.f.* (*naut.*) rigging.
encapillar, *v.t.* to hood *or* cowl; (*naut.*) to rig; (*min.*) to start a new gallery in. — **encapillarse,** *v.r.* to put on (*clothes*) over the head.
encapirotado, -da, *a.* wearing a hood.
encapotadura, *n.f.*, **encapotamiento,** *n.m.* scowl, frown; lowering sky.
encapotar, *v.t.* to cloak; to veil, muffle. — **encapotarse,** *v.r.* (*fig.*) to scowl, frown; to become cloudy; to carry the head too low (*horses*); ***el cielo está encapotado,*** the sky is over-cast.
encapricharse, *v.r.* to get a whim, fancy *or* mania into one's head; to take a fancy (***con,*** to); to get a crush (***con,*** on).
encapuchar, *v.t.* to cover with a hood.
encapuzar [C], *v.t.* to cover with a cowl.
encarado, -da, *a.* faced; ***bien*** or ***mal encarado,*** well- *or* ill-favoured.
encaramar, *v.t.* to raise, elevate; to praise up, extol. — **encaramarse,** *v.r.* to climb (up); to get high up, reach a high position.
encaramiento, *n.m.* pointing, aiming (*gun*).
encarar, *v.t.* to aim, point, level. — **encarar**(**se**), *v.i.* (*v.r.*) — ***con,*** to face, bring o.s. face to face with.
encaratularse, *v.r.* to mask o.s.
encarcavinar, *v.t.* to put in a grave, bury; to put in a ditch; to choke with a foul odour.
encarcelación, *n.f.* incarceration.
encarcelar, *v.t.* to imprison; (*arch.*) to embed in mortar; (*carp.*) to clamp; (*naut.*) to woold.
encarecedor, -ra, *a.* praising. — *n.m.f.* praiser, extoller.
encarecer [9], *v.t.* to raise the price of; to stress; to praise; to recommend strongly. — **encarecer**(**se**), *v.i.* (*v.r.*) to get dearer, go up (*in price*).
encarecidamente, *adv.* earnestly.
encarecimiento, *n.m.* increase in price *or* cost; stressing; earnestness; ***con encarecimiento,*** earnestly.
encargado, -da, *a.* in charge. — *n.m.f.* person in charge; manager; ***encargado de negocios,*** chargé d'affaires.
encargar [B], *v.t.* to entrust (to), put under the care (of), put in charge (of) (*sth.*); to charge, urge; to order, place an order for; ***le han encargado (de) la administración,*** they have entrusted the administration to him *or* they have entrusted him with the administration; ***de eso me encargo yo,*** I'll see to that. — **encargarse,** *v.r.* — ***de,*** to take charge of, look after, see to, and deal with.
encargo, *n.m.* charge, command, commission, request; (*com.*) order; ***hecho de encargo,*** made to order, tailor-made.
encariñar, *v.t.* to inspire love *or* affection in. — **encariñarse,** *v.r.* to become fond (***con,*** of).
encarna, *n.f.* fleshing.
encarnación, *n.f.* incarnation, embodiment; (*art*) carnation, flesh-colour.
encarnadino, -na, *a.* incarnadine.
encarnado, -da, *a.* incarnate; flesh-coloured, incarnadine; red. — *n.m.* flesh-colour, incarnadine, red.
encarnadura, *n.f.* natural state of flesh in a wound in regard to healing power; ***buena (mala) encarnadura,*** quick- (slow-) healing flesh.
encarnamiento, *n.m.* (*surg.*) incarnation, healing over.
encarnar, *v.t.* to incarnate, embody, personify; to bait (*a hook*); to flesh (*hounds*); to colour (*a sculpture*). — *v.i.* to become incarnate; to take on bodily *or* human form; (*surg.*) to heal over, incarn; to enter the flesh (*a weapon*). — **encarnarse,** *v.r.* to eat from the game (*hounds*); to mix, unite (*with another body*).
encarnativo, -va, *a.* (*surg.*) incarnative.
encarne, *n.m.* game flesh (*given to hounds*).
encarnecer [9], *v.i.* to grow fat and fleshy.
encarnizado, -da, *a.* bloodshot; bloody, fierce.
encarnizamiento, *n.m.* fleshing (*of hounds*); cruelty, savagery.
encarnizar [C], *v.t.* to flesh (*hounds*); to make cruel, savage *or* frenzied. — **encarnizarse,** *v.r.* to be *or* become greedy for flesh; to become frenzied; ***encarnizarse con,*** to treat with savage cruelty.
encaro, *n.m.* stare; (*prov.*) blunderbuss; aiming *or* levelling (*a gun*).
encarpetar, *v.t.* (*Arg., Chi., Ec., Per.*) to shelve, to pigeonhole.
encarrilar, encarrillar, *v.t.* to direct, guide, put on the rails, put on the right track. — **encarrilarse,** *v.r.* (*naut.*) to be fouled in the sheave of a block.
encarroñar, *v.t.* to infect, corrupt.
encarrujado, -da, *a.* (*Mex.*) rugged, rough (*ground*); curled, kinky.
encarrujar, *v.t.* to curl, coil, twist.
encartación, *n.f.* enrolment under a charter; recognition of vassalage; lands held under charter (*particularly in Biscay*).
encartamiento, *n.m.* outlawry, proscription; sentence against absent criminals; [ENCARTACIÓN].
encartar, *v.t.* to outlaw, ban, proscribe; to include, enrol, enter in a register; (*law*) to summon; to deal (*in card games*). — **encartarse,** *v.r.* to be unable to discard (*in card games*).
encarte, *n.m.* having to follow suit (*in card games*).
encartonador, -ra, *n.m.f.* one who applies boards (*bookbinding*).
encartonar, *v.t.* to bind (*books*) in boards.
encartuchar, *v.t.* (*Ec., Chi., Col., P.R.*) to roll, wrap, coil.
encasar, *v.t.* to set (*a bone*).
encascabelado, -da, *a.* adorned with bells.
encascotar, *v.t.* (*build.*) to cover with a layer of rubble.
encasillado, *n.m.* set of pigeonholes; patterns of squares; list of government candidates.
encasillar, *v.t.* to pigeonhole, classify; to assign to a voting district.
encasquetar, *v.t.* to pull on *or* down (*hat*); to hammer, drive *or* force in (*idea etc.*); to force

(*speech etc.*) (on s.o.) — **encasquetarse,** *v.t.* to be set on.
encasquillar, *v.t.* (*Hisp. Am.*) to shoe (*horses*). — **encasquillarse,** *v.r.* to jam (*firearms*).
encastar, *v.t.* to improve (*a breed*) by cross-breeding. — *v.i.* to breed.
encastillado, -da, *a.* (*fig.*) haughty, lofty.
encastillador, -ra, *n.m.f.* scaffolder, spiderman; (*fig.*) headstrong person.
encastillamiento, *n.m.* fortification with castles; piling up; firm stand; (*fig.*) sticking to one's guns.
encastillar, *v.t.* to fortify with castles. — *v.i.* to make the cell of the queen bee. — **encastillarse,** *v.r.* to shut o.s. up in a castle; (*fig.*) to stick to one's guns.
encastrar, *v.t.* (*mech.*) to engage, mesh.
encastre, *n.m.* cogged connection; socket.
encauchado, -da, *n.m.* (*Hisp. Am.*) rubber poncho.
encauchar, *v.t.* to cover with rubber.
encausar, *v.t.* to prosecute, sue.
encauste, *n.m.* encaustic, painting.
encáustico, -ca, *a.* encaustic.
encausto, *n.m.* enamelling, encaustic painting.
encauzamiento, *n.m.* channelling.
encauzar [C], *v.t.* to channel.
encavarse, *v.r.* to run to ground (*animals*), hide.
encebadamiento, *n.m.* (*vet.*) surfeit, repletion.
encebadar, *v.t.* (*vet.*) to surfeit with barley.
encebollado, *n.m.* stew of beef and onions.
encefálico, -ca, *a.* encephalic.
encefalitis, *n.f.* encephalitis.
encéfalo, *n.m.* encephalon.
encelamiento, *n.m.* jealousy; rut.
encelar, *v.t.* to excite jealousy in, make jealous; to put in rut. — **encelarse,** *v.r.* to become jealous; to get in rut.
encella, *n.f.* cheese-mould.
encellar, *v.t.* to mould (*cheese* or *curds*).
encenagado, -da, *a.* mixed *or* filled with mud.
encenagamiento, *n.m.* wallowing in mire; (*fig.*) wallowing in vice.
encenagarse [B], *v.r.* to get covered in mire *or* filth; (*fig.*) to sink into (the) mire *or* filth.
encencerrado, -da, *a.* carrying a cow-bell.
encendedor, *n.m.* lighter; ***encendedor de bolsillo,*** pocket lighter.
encender [2], *v.t.* to kindle, light, set fire to; (*fig.*) to inflame, stir, arouse. — **encenderse,** *v.r.* to take fire, be kindled; to blush; ***encenderse en ira,*** to become aflame with rage.
encendidamente, *adv.* ardently.
encendido, -da, *a.* inflamed; ardent; bright (*colours*). — *n.m.* (motor) ignition.
encendimiento, *n.m.* kindling, lighting; glow; ardour, eagerness.
encenizar [C], *v.t.* cover with ashes.
encentadura, *n.f.*, **encentamiento,** *n.m.* broaching; taking up, starting.
encentar, *v.t.* to broach; to take up, start. — **encentarse,** *v.r.* to develop bed-sores.
encepador, *n.m.* gun-stocker.
encepadura, *n.f.* (*carp.*) tie-joint.
encepar, *v.t.* to put in the stocks; to stock (*gun* or *anchor*); (*carp.*) to join with ties. — *v.i.* to take root. — **enceparse,** *v.r.* to become fouled on the anchor (*cable*).
encepe, *n.m.* (*agric.*) taking firm root, rooting.
encerado, -da, *a.* wax-coloured, like wax; thick. — *n.m.* oil-cloth, oilskin; window-blind; (*naut.*) tarpaulin; sticking-plaster; blackboard.
enceramiento, *n.m.* waxing.
encerar, *v.t.* to wax; to stain with wax; (*build.*) to thicken (*lime*). — *v.i.* to turn yellow (*grain*).
encerotar, *v.t.* to wax (*thread*).
encerradero, *n.m.* sheepfold, pen.
encerrador, -ra, *a.* shutting *or* locking up. — *n.m.f.* shutter, locker. — *n.m.* penner of cattle (*in slaughterhouse*).
encerradura, *n.f.*, **encerramiento,** *n.m.* locking up, shutting in; confinement.
encerrar [I], *v.t.* to lock up, shut in; (*fig.*) to confine; to include, embrace.
encerrona, *n.f.* (*coll.*) voluntary retreat *or* retirement; trap; whole day examination; ***preparar*** or ***tender una encerrona (a),*** to set a trap (for).
encespedar, *v.t.* to turf.
encestar, *v.t.* to put into a basket.
encía, *n.f.* gum (*of mouth*).
encíclico, -ca, *a.* encyclic. — *n.f.* encyclical.
enciclopedia, *n.f.* encyclopædia.
enciclopédico, -ca, *a.* encyclopædian.
enciclopedista, *a.*, *n.m.f.* encyclopædist.
encierra, *n.f.* (*Chi.*) locking up a drove in the abattoir; (*Chi.*) winter pasture.
encierro (1), *n.m.* enclosing *or* locking up; confinement; enclosure; religious retreat; seclusion; (*coll.*) lock-up; penning.
encierro (2), *pres. indic.* [ENCERRAR].
encima, *adv.* above, over; on top; over and above; ***encima de,*** above, over, on top of; ***por encima,*** overhead; superficially; ***poner la mano encima a,*** to get hold of; to lay hands on; ***no le he puesto la mano encima en dos años,*** I haven't touched it for two years; ***está siempre encima de mí,*** he is always keeping an eye on me; (*fig.*) ***mirar por encima del hombro,*** to look down on; ***pasó por encima de nosotros,*** it passed over us; ***eso está por encima de mi inteligencia,*** that is beyond my intelligence; ***lo hará por encima de la voluntad de su padre,*** he'll do it against (in spite of) his father's will.
encimar, *v.t.* to place on top; to raise high; (*Col.*, *Per.*) to give extra. — **encimarse,** *v.r.* to rise above.
encime, *n.m.* (*Col.*) extra gift, bonus.
encina, *n.f.* evergreen oak, holm-oak, ilex.
encinal, encinar, *n.m.* evergreen oak grove.
encinta, *a.* pregnant.
encintado, *n.m.* kerb (*of pavement*).
encintar, *v.t.* to adorn with ribbons; to make pregnant; to put kerbs on.
encismar, *v.t.* (*coll.*) to sow discord in *or* among.
encisto, *n.m.* encysted tumour.
encizañar, *v.t.* to sow discord among.
enclaustrar, *v.t.* to shut up in a convent *or* monastery, cloister.
enclavadura, *n.f.* (*carp.*) groove; embedding.
enclavar, *v.t.* to nail; to prick (*horses*) in shoeing; to pierce through; to fit in; (*coll.*) to hoodwink.
enclave, *n.m.* enclave.
enclavijar, *v.t.* to unite *or* join; to put pegs in, peg.
enclenque, *a.*, *n.m.f.* weak, feeble (person); sickly, ailing (person). — *n.m.f.* weakling.
enclítico, -ca, *a.* (*gram.*) enclitic.
enclocar(**se**) [A], **encloquecer**(**se**) [9], **encoclar**(**se**), *v.i.* (*v.r.*) to go broody.
encobar(**se**), *v.i.* (*v.r.*) to sit on eggs (*to hatch them*).
encobijar, *v.t.* to cover, protect, shelter.
encobrado, -da, *a.* containing copper; copper-coloured.
encocorar, *v.t.* (*coll.*) to annoy.
encofrado, *n.m.* (*min.*) plank lining, timbering.
encofrar, *v.t.* (*min.*) to plank, timber.
encoger [E], *v.t.*, *v.i.* to shrink, contract, shorten. — **encogerse,** *v.r.* to shrink; to become shy, diffident *or* inhibited; to begin to feel small; to get scared; ***se me encoge el corazón,*** my heart breaks, it numbs my heart; ***se me encogió el ombligo,*** I felt scared stiff; ***encogerse de hombros,*** to shrug one's shoulders.
encogidamente, *adv.* bashfully; awkwardly.

encogido, -da, *a.* diffident, inhibited, bashful.
encogimiento, *n.m.* contraction, contracting, shrinkage; diffidence, inhibition, bashfulness.
encohetar, *v.t.* to scourge, harass (*a bull*) with squibs. — **encohetarse,** *v.r.* (*C.R.*) to become furious *or* enraged.
encojar, *v.t.* to cripple, lame. — **encojarse,** *v.r.* to become lame; (*coll.*) to feign sickness.
encolado, *n.m.* clarification (*of wine*); dressing (*in weaving*).
encoladura, *n.f.*, **encolamiento,** *n.m.* gluing; priming, sizing; clarification (*of wine*); dressing (*in weaving*).
encolar, *v.t.* to glue; to clarify (*wine*); to size; to dress (*in weaving*).
encolerizar [C], *v.t.* to anger, infuriate. — **encolerizarse,** *v.r.* to become angry, get in a rage.
encomendable, *a.* commendable.
encomendado, *n.m.* subordinate of a knight commander.
encomendamiento, *n.m.* commission, charge.
encomendar [1], *v.t.* to recommend, commend; to entrust; to bestow the rank of knight commander on. — *v.i.* to hold a knight-commandery. — **encomendarse,** *v.r.* to commit o.s. (*to another's protection*); to put o.s. (*in another's hands*); to send compliments (*to s.o.*); ***sin encomendarse (ni) a Dios ni al Diablo,*** without so much as a by your leave.
encomendero, *n.m.* agent; commissioner (*of Indian territory*).
encomiador, -ra, *a.* praising. — *n.m.f.* praiser.
encomiar, *v.t.* to eulogize, praise, extol.
encomiasta, *n.m.* encomiast, panegyrist.
encomiástico, -ca, *a.* encomiastic.
encomienda, *n.f.* commission, charge; complimentary message; Indian territory entrusted to a Spanish colonist; commandery (*in a military order*); lands *or* rents belonging to a commandery; badge of a knight commander; patronage, protection, support; (*Arg., Chi., Col., Per.*) parcel post; (*pl.*) compliments, respects.
encomio, *n.m.* (*obs.*) praise, encomium, eulogy.
encompadrar, *v.i.* (*coll.*) to contract relationship as godfather; to become good friends.
enconamiento, *n.m.* inflammation, festering; (*fig.*) anger.
enconar, *v.t.* to inflame; (*fig.*) to embitter *or* poison; to arouse rancour in. — **enconarse,** *v.r.* to become embittered; to fester, rankle.
enconcharse, *v.r.* to retire into one's shell.
encono, *n.m.* festering, soreness; (*fig.*) rancour, bitterness; resentment.
enconoso, -sa, *a.* inflaming; rancorous.
enconrear, *v.t.* to oil (*wool*) that is to be carded.
encontradamente, *adv.* in a conflicting way.
encontradizo, -za, *a.* which may be met on the way; ***hacerse el encontradizo,*** to bump into someone (*apparently by accident but really on purpose*).
encontrado, -da, *a.* conflicting, contrary.
encontrar [4], *v.t.* to meet, encounter; to find. — **encontrarse,** *v.r.* to meet, meet each other; to collide, crash; to clash; to find o.s.; to be; ***encontrarse con alguien,*** to meet, run into, bump into, come across s.o.; ***me encontraba en Londres,*** I was in London; ***me encontré una cartera,*** I found a wallet; ***se encontró con una sorpresa,*** he met with a surprise; ***no me encontraba bien,*** I wasn't feeling well; ***están encontrados,*** they are at loggerheads.
encontrón, *n.m.*, **encontronazo,** *n.m.* collision, clash, crash.
encopetado, -da, *a.* grand, upper-class, superior, (*coll.*) posh. — *n.m.* (*arch.*) cathetus.
encopetar, *v.t.* to dress (*the hair*) high; (*fig.*) to raise high up. — **encopetarse,** *v.r.* to become very grand *or* high-class, get above o.s.
encorachar, *v.t.* to put in a leather bag.
encorajar, *v.t.* to encourage; to inflame. — **encorajarse,** *v.r.* to get furious.
encorajinar, *v.t.* to infuriate, enrage.
encorar [4], *v.t.* to cover with leather; to cause (*wounds*) to granulate. — **encorar(se),** *v.i.* (*v.r.*) to heal, granulate (*wounds*).
encorazado, -da, *a.* covered with a cuirass; covered with leather.
encorchadora, *n.f.* corking machine.
encorchar, *v.t.* to hive (*bees*); to cork (*bottles*).
encorchetar, *v.t.* to put hooks *or* clasps on; to hook *or* clasp.
encordar [4], *v.t.* to string (*musical instruments*); to bind, lash with ropes.
encordelar, *v.t.* to string; to bind with cords *or* strings.
encordonar, *v.t.* to cord; to tie with string.
encorecer [9], *v.t.* to cause the formation of skin over (*a wound*). — **encorecer(se),** *v.i.* (*v.r.*) [ENCORAR].
encoriación, *n.f.* skinning, healing.
encornado, -da, *a.* horned.
encornadura, *n.f.* shape, position of horns; set of horns.
encornudar, *v.t.* to cuckold. — *v.i.* to begin to get horns.
encorozar [C], *v.t.* to cover (*a criminal's head*) with a ***coroza*** *or* cone-shaped cap.
encorralar, *v.t.* to enclose, keep in a yard; to corral (*cattle*).
encorrear, *v.t.* to tie up with straps.
encorsetar, *v.t.* to corset.
encortinar, *v.t.* to fit with curtains, hang curtains in.
encorvada, *n.f.* bending, doubling; ungraceful way of dancing; (*coll.*) ***hacer la encorvada,*** to malinger.
encorvadura, *n.f.*, **encorvamiento,** *n.m.* bending; crookedness, curvature.
encorvar, *v.t.* to bend, curve, crook.—**encorvarse,** *v.r.* to bend, go crooked; to warp; to have a leaning (*towards*); to buck.
encostillado, *n.m.* (*min.*) timbering.
encostradura, *n.f.* incrustation, crust.
encostrar, *v.t.* to crust, incrust; to roughcast. — **encostrarse,** *v.r.* to become crusty; to develop a crust *or* scab.
encovadura, *n.f.* depositing in a cellar.
encovar [4], *v.t.* to put in a cellar; to guard, conceal, enclose, lock up, shut up. — **encovarse,** *v.r.* to hide.
encrasar, *v.t.* to fatten, thicken (*liquids*); to manure (*land*). — **encrasarse,** *v.r.* (*agric.*) to become more fertile.
encrespador, *n.m.* curling-iron, curling-tongs.
encrespadura, *n.f.* curling.
encrespamiento, *n.m.* curling; standing on end (*hair*); roughness (*sea*).
encrespar, *v.t.* to curl; to make (*hair*) stand on end; to ruffle (*feathers etc*). — **encresparse,** *v.r.* to become rough (*sea*); to bristle with rage, get furious.
encrestado, -da, *a.* having a crest *or* comb; (*fig.*) haughty, lofty.
encrestarse, *v.r.* to stiffen the crest; to get proud, haughty.
encrucijada, *n.f.* cross-way, cross-roads; ambush, snare.
encrudecer [9], *v.t.* to make raw; to exasperate, irritate.
encruelecer [9], *v.t.* to make cruel. — **encruelecerse,** *v.r.* to become cruel.
encuadernación, *n.f.* binding (*books*).
encuadernador, -ra, *n.m.f.* binder; book-binder.
encuadernar, *v.t.* to bind (*books*); to combine; ***sin encuadernar,*** unbound.

encuadrar, *v.t.* to frame; to fit, adjust.
encuarte, *n.m.* extra horse (*to help a coach uphill*).
encubar, *v.t.* to put into casks etc.; to timber.
encubertar, *v.t.* to overspread with cloth *or* silk, caparison, trap, adorn. — **encubertarse,** *v.r.* to cover o.s. with armour.
encubierta (1), *n.f.* fraud, deceit.
encubiertamente, *adv.* secretly; deceitfully.
encubierto (1), **-ta** (2), *p.p.* [ENCUBRIR].
encubierto (2), *pres. indic.* [ENCUBERTAR].
encubridor, -ra, *a.* hiding, concealing. — *n.m.f.* concealer; procurer, bawd.
encubrimiento, *n.m.* concealment, hiding; (*law*) sheltering (*a criminal*).
encubrir [*p.p.* **encubierto**], *v.t.* to hide, conceal, cover up, hush up.
encuentro (1), *n.m.* encounter; meeting; clash, collision; find, finding; (*arch.*) angle, nook, corner; joint of the wings next to the breast; point of shoulder-blades (*in quadrupeds*); (*sport*) match, bout; ***ir al encuentro de,*** to go to meet; ***salirle a uno al encuentro,*** to go out to meet, to meet half way; (*pl.*) temples (*loom*).
encuentro (2), *pres. indic.* [ENCONTRAR].
encuerar, *v.t.* (*Cub., Mex.*) to undress, strip.
encuesta, *n.f.* survey; inquiry; inquest; (opinion) poll; interview.
encuitarse, *v.r.* to grieve.
enculatar, *v.t.* to cover (*hive*).
encumbrado, -da, *a.* high, elevated; lofty, stately.
encumbramiento, *n.m.* raising, elevation, elevating; height, eminence.
encumbrar, *v.t.* to climb to the top of; to raise, raise high, exalt, elevate. — **encumbrarse,** *v.r.* to raise o.s. high; to become proud.
encunar, *v.t.* to put (*child*) in the cradle; (*tauro.*) to catch between the horns.
encureñado, -da, *a.* mounted on the carriage (*cannon*).
encurtidos, *n.m.pl.* pickles.
encurtir, *v.t.* to pickle.
enchancletar(se), *v.i.* (*v.r.*) to go slipshod.
enchapar, *v.t.* to veneer; to cover with metal plates.
encharcada, *n.f.* pool, puddle.
encharcar [A], *v.t.* to flood, swamp. — **encharcarse,** *v.r.* to become flooded, swamped, covered in puddles.
enchavetar, *v.t.* (*naut.*) to fasten with cotter pins.
enchilada, *n.f.* (*Guat., Mex.*) pancake of maize with chilli.
enchilado, *n.m.* (*Cub.*) shellfish and chilli dish.
enchilar, *v.t.* (*C.R., Hond., Mex.*) to season with chilli; (*Mex.*) to vex, pique; (*C.R.*) to play practical jokes on.
enchinar, *v.t.* (*Mex.*) to curl (*hair*).
enchipar, *v.t.* (*Chi., Per.*) to cover (*sugar-loaves*) with straw.
enchiquerar, *v.t.* (*tauro*) to pen in; (*coll.*) to pen.
enchironar, *v.t.* (*coll.*) to put in clink.
enchivarse, *v.r.* (*Col., Ec., coll.*) to get ratty.
enchuecar [A], *v.t.* (*Chi., Mex.*) to bend, curve.
enchufado, -da, *a., n.m.f.*(person) holding a job through influence.
enchufar, *v.t.* to plug *or* fit in, connect; (*coll.*) to get a job for. — **enchufarse,** *v.r.* to get o.s. a job (*by influence*), get o.s. in.
enchufe, *n.m.* socket; plug; fitting in; (*coll.*) sinecure, cushy job; (*fig.*) connections, strings.
enchufismo, *n.m.* jobs-for-the-boys system, old-boy network.
enchufista, *n.m.f.* one good at getting jobs for himself *or* herself.
ende, *adv.* (*obs.*) there; ***por ende,*** therefore.
endeble, *a.* feeble, weak, frail; flimsy.
endeblez, *n.f.* feebleness; flimsiness.
endeblucho, -cha, *a.* weakish; flimsyish.
endécada, *n.f.* eleven years.
endecágono, *n.m.* hendecagon.
endecasílabo, -ba, *a.* hendecasyllabic. — *n.m.* hendecasyllable.
endecha, *n.f.* dirge, doleful song.
endechadera, *n.f.* paid female mourner (*at funerals*).
endechar, *v.t.* to sing funeral songs to. — **endecharse,** *v.r.* to grieve; to mourn.
endechoso, -sa, *a.* (*obs.*) mournful, doleful.
endehesar, *v.t.* to put out to pasture.
endémico, -ca, *a.* endemic.
endemoniado, -da, *a.* devilish; fiendish; (*fig.*) blasted, cursed, damned.
endemoniar, *v.t.* to possess with a devil *or* the Devil; (*fig.*) to infuriate.
endentado, -da, *a.* (*her.*) serrated.
endentar [1], *v.t.* to fit with teeth; to engage, mesh.
endentecer [9], *v.i.* to cut teeth, teethe.
endeñado, -da, *a.* (*prov.*) damaged, hurt.
enderezadamente, *adv.* rightly, directly, justly.
enderezado, -da, *a.* fit, appropriate.
enderezador, *n.m.* righter; straightener; ***enderezador de entuertos*** or ***agravios,*** righter, redresser of wrongs.
enderezadura, *n.f.* straight road.
enderezamiento, *n.m.* straightening; guiding, directing, setting right.
enderezar [C], *v.t.* to straighten, unbend; to rectify, right, set right; to set upright; to direct; to address; to dedicate. — **enderezarse,** *v.r.* to straighten up; to right o.s. *or* itself; to be directed (towards).
endérmico, -ca, *a.* endermic.
endeudarse, *v.r.* to contract debts, get into debt.
endevotado, -da, *a.* pious; devoted, fond.
endiabladamente, *adv.* devilishly; horribly, abominably.
endiablado, -da, *a.* devilish, diabolical; (*fig.*) blasted, damned. — *n.f.* boisterous masquerade.
endiablar, *v.t.* to possess with a devil *or* the Devil; (*fig.*) to infuriate.
endíadis, *n.f. inv.* (*rhet.*) hendiadys.
endibia, *n.f.* (*bot.*) endive.
endilgar [B], *v.t.* (*coll.*) to polish *or* knock off quickly; to deal (*a blow*); to spring (*sth. unpleasant*) (on), unload (*a bore*) (onto); to stick (*a name, label etc.*) (on); ***me han endilgado esta lata,*** they've unloaded this bore on me, fobbed this bore off on me.
endiosamiento, *n.m.* conceit; abstraction, ecstasy; deification.
endiosar, *v.t.* to deify, set up as a god. — **endiosarse,** *v.r.* to become conceited; to become lost in ecstasy.
enditarse, *v.r.* to contract debts.
endoblado, -da, *a.* applied to a lamb which sucks its own mother and another ewe.
endomingarse [B], *v.r.* (*coll.*) to put on one's Sunday best.
endorsar, *v.t.* (*com.*) to endorse.
endorso, *n.m.* (*com.*) endorsement.
endosador, endosante, *n.m.* endorser.
endosar, *v.t.* (*com.*) to endorse *or* indorse (*draft etc.*); (*coll.*) to fob off, land (*sth.*) (on); (*coll.*) to saddle with, lumber with.
endosatario, -ria, *n.m.f.* (*com.*) endorsee.
endoselar, *v.t.* to canopy.
endoso, *n.m.* [ENDORSO]; (*coll.*) fobbing, landing, lumbering with sth.
endriago, *n.m.* fabulous monster.
endrino, -na, *a.* of sloe colour. — *n.m.* blackthorn, sloe-tree. — *n.f.* sloe.
endrogarse [B], *v.r.* (*Chi., Mex., Per.*) to contract debts.

endulzadura, *n.f.*, **endulzamiento,** *n.m.* sweetening.
endulzar [C], *v.t.* to sweeten; to soothe, soften; (*art*) to tone down.
endurador, -ra, *a.* parsimonious, miserly, niggardly. — *n.m.f.* miser.
endurar, *v.t.* to endure, suffer, bear; to put off, delay; to harden. — *v.i.* to be thrifty.
endurecer [9], *v.t.* to harden, toughen, stiffen; to inure, accustom to hardship.
endurecimiento, *n.m.* hardness; hardening; obdurateness; hardheartedness.
ene, *n.f.* letter N; (*coll.*) ***ene de palo,*** gallows; (*coll.*) ***ser de ene,*** to be a necessary consequence, inevitable; ***eso costará ene pesetas,*** that will cost *x* pesetas.
enea, *n.f.* (*bot.*) reed-mace, rush, cat-tail.
Eneas, *n.m.* Aeneas.
eneasílabo, -ba, *a.* of nine syllables.
enebral, *n.m.* juniper-tree grove.
enebrina, *n.f.* juniper berry.
enebro, *n.m.* juniper.
Eneida, *n.f.* Aeneid.
enejar, *v.t.* to put an axle on; to fasten to an axle.
eneldo, *n.m.* dill.
enema, *n.f.* enema, clyster.
enemigo, -ga, *a.* — ***de,*** inimical, unfriendly; adverse, hostile, contrary (to). — *n.m.f.* enemy, foe; devil; ***ser enemigo de,*** to be against; (***a***) ***enemigo que huye, puente de plata,*** good riddance, let an enemy who flees depart in peace. — *n.f.* hatred, enmity, ill-will.
enemistad, *n.f.* hatred, enmity.
enemistar, *v.t.* to make an enemy of. — **enemistarse,** *v.r.* — ***con,*** to become an enemy of; to fall out with.
éneo, -nea, *a.* (*poet.*) brazen, of brass.
energía, *n.f.* energy; power.
enérgico, -ca, *a.* energetic, vigorous.
energúmeno, -na, *n.m.f.* energumen, person possessed by an evil spirit; (*fig.*) madman, raving lunatic.
enero, *n.m.* January; ***la cuesta de enero,*** after-Christmas drag *or* slump.
enervación, *n.f.* enervation; irritation.
enervador, -ra, *a.* enervating; irritating.
enervamiento, *n.m.* enervation; irritation.
enervar, *v.t.* to enervate; to irritate, exasperate; ***X me enerva,*** X gets on my nerves.
enfadadizo, -za, *a.* easily annoyed, peevish, irritable.
enfadar, *v.t.* to anger, annoy, vex. — **enfadarse,** *v.r.* to get angry *or* annoyed.
enfado, *n.m.* anger, vexation, annoyance.
enfadoso, -sa, *a.* vexatious, annoying, troublesome, bothersome.
enfaldar, *v.t.* to lop off the lower branches of (*trees*); to tuck up (*the skirt*).
enfaldo, *n.m.* tucking up.
enfangar [B], *v.t.* to soil with mud. — **enfangarse,** *v.r.* to get stuck in the mud; (*fig.*) to sink into (the) mire *or* filth.
enfardador, *n.m.* packer, one who packs bales etc.
enfardar, *v.t.* to pack, bale.
enfardelador, *n.m.* packer.
enfardeladura, *n.f.* packing, baling.
enfardelar, *v.t.* to pack, bale.
énfasis, *n.m.f. inv.* emphasis; bombast.
enfático, -ca, *a.* emphatic; bombastic.
enfebrecido, -da, *a.* feverish.
enfermar, *v.t.* to make sick; (*coll.*) to get on the nerves of. — *v.i.* to fall ill.
enfermedad, *n.f.* sickness, illness, malady; disease.
enfermería, *n.f.* infirmary; sick-quarters, sick-bay.
enfermero, -ra, *n.m.f.* nurse.
enfermizo, -za, *a.* sickly; unhealthy.
enfermo, -ma, *a.* diseased, sick, infirm, ill. — *n.m.f.* invalid; patient.
enfermucho, -cha, *a.* a bit off colour, rather groggy.
enfervorizar [C], *v.t.* to inflame, fill with fervour.
enfeudación, *n.f.* infeudation, enfeoffment.
enfeudar, *v.t.* to feoff, enfeoff, invest with a right *or* an estate.
enfielar, *v.t.* to counterpoise, balance.
enfiestarse, *v.r.* (*Hisp. Am.*) to amuse o.s.; to enjoy o.s.
enfilar, *v.t.* to line up, place in a row; to aim, sight; to string; to enfilade; ***enfilar la calle,*** to go straight up *or* down the street. — *v.i.* to make *or* head for.
enfisema, *n.m.* emphysema.
enfistolarse, *v.r.* to become a fistula.
enfiteusis, *n.f.* (*law*) emphyteusis, lease.
enflaquecer [9], *v.t.* to make thin *or* lean. — **enflaquecer(se),** *v.i.* (*v.r.*) to get thin *or* feeble; to flag.
enflaquecimiento, *n.m.* thinness, emaciation.
enflautado, -da, *a.* (*coll.*) inflated, turgid. — *n.f.* (*Hond., Per.*) blunder, absurdity.
enflautador, -ra, *n.m.f.* (*coll.*) deceiver; procurer.
enflautar, *v.t.* to blow, swell; (*coll.*) to procure; (*coll.*) to deceive, trick; to incite to do evil; (*Col., Mex.*) to put in; to annoy, bother with an oft-repeated story.
enflechado, -da, *a.* ready to discharge (*of a bent bow and arrow*).
enfocar [A], *v.t.* (*photo.*) to focus; (*fig.*) to slant; to approach, tackle.
enfoque, *n.m.* (*opt.*) focusing; approach.
enfoscado, *n.m.* (*build.*) mortar covering holes.
enfoscar [A], *v.t.* (*build.*) to fill with mortar. — **enfoscarse,** *v.r.* to get sullen; to get overcast; to become absorbed.
enfrailar, *v.t.* to make a monk *or* friar. — **enfrailarse,** *v.r.* to become a friar.
enfranquecer [9], *v.t.* to frank; to free, make free.
enfrascamiento, *n.m.* absorption.
enfrascar [A], *v.t.* to put in a flask *or* bottle. — **enfrascarse,** *v.r.* to get deeply engaged *or* engrossed in.
enfrenador, -ra, *a.* bridling, restraining. — *n.m.f.* bridler; restrainer; one who puts on a bridle.
enfrenamiento, *n.m.* bridling.
enfrenar, *v.t.* to curb, restrain, bridle; to put the brake on.
enfrentamiento, *n.m.* confrontation.
enfrentar, *v.t.* to confront, put face to face; to face. — **enfrentarse,** *v.r.* — ***con,*** to face; to oppose.
enfrente, *adv.* opposite, facing; ***enfrente de,*** opposite.
enfriadera, *n.f.* refrigerator; cooler.
enfriadero, enfriador, *n.m.* cooling-place; cold storage; refrigerator.
enfriamiento, *n.m.* cooling; refrigeration; cold, chill.
enfriar [L], *v.t.* to refrigerate; to cool. — **enfriarse,** *v.r.* to cool down, cool off; to grow cold; to catch cold.
enfrontar, *v.t.* to confront. — *v.i.* to face, oppose.
enfullar, *v.i.* (*coll.*) to cheat.
enfundadura, *n.f.* casing; putting into cases *or* sheaths.
enfundar, *v.t.* to case, put into a case; to sheathe.
enfurecer [9], *v.t.* to enrage, madden, make furious. — **enfurecerse,** *v.r.* (*fig.*) to rage; to grow boisterous *or* furious.
enfurecimiento, *n.m.* fury.
enfurruñarse, *v.r.* (*coll.*) to get sulky *or* pettish.
enfurruscarse [A] (*Chi., coll.*) [ENFURRUÑARSE].
enfurtir, *v.t.* to full (*cloth*); to felt.
engabanado, -da, *a.* wearing an overcoat.

engafar, *v.t.* to hook; to bend (*a crossbow*); to slip the safety-catch of (*a gun*).
engaitador, -ra, *n.m.f.* (*coll.*) wheedler, coaxer; deceiver, swindler.
engaitar, *v.t.* (*coll.*) to coax, wheedle; to deceive, swindle.
engalanar, *v.t.* to deck, adorn; (*naut.*) to dress (*a ship*).
engalgar [B], *v.t.* to pursue closely, not to lose sight of; to scotch (*a wheel*); (*naut.*) to back (*an anchor*).
engallado, -da, *a.* upright, erect; haughty.
engallador, *n.m.* martingale.
engalladura, *n.f.* red spot (*in the yolk of an egg*).
engallarse, *v.r.* to draw o.s. up arrogantly; to get cocky; to keep the head up (*horses*).
enganchador, *n.m.* hooker; (*mil.*) crimp, one who decoys others into military service.
enganchamiento [ENGANCHE].
enganchar, *v.t.* to clasp, hook, hitch; to connect, link, couple; to recruit, sign up; (*fig.*) to hook, land, catch, get. — **engancharse,** *v.r.* to get caught *or* tangled; to enlist, sign on *or* up.
enganche, *n.m.* hooking, hitching, coupling; hooking device; enlisting, signing on *or* up; ***banderín de enganche,*** recruiting centre.
engandujo, *n.m.* twisted thread (*of a fringe*).
enganchón, *n.m.* gash, rent, tear.
engañabobos, *n.m. inv.* (*coll.*) trickster; fooltrap.
engañadizo, -za, *a.* easily deceived.
engañador, -ra, *a.* deceiving. — *n.m.f.* deceiver, cheat.
engañapastores, *n.m. inv.* (*orn.*) nightjar.
engañar, *v.t.* to deceive, mislead, delude, cheat, fool, hoax, trick, swindle; to while away (*time*); to ward off (*hunger*); to make (*food*) appetizing; ***esto engaña (a) la vista,*** this is deceptive. — **engañarse,** *v.r.* to deceive o.s., delude o.s.; to be wrong *or* mistaken; ***no hay que engañarse,*** we must not delude ourselves; ***se engañan,*** they deceive themselves, are deceived, are mistaken.
engañifa, *n.f.* (*coll.*) trick, deceit, deception, fraud.
engañifla, *n.f.* (*Chi., prov.*) [ENGAÑIFA].
engaño, *n.m.* deceit, deception; fraud; hoax; lure; ***no te llames a engaño,*** don't say you didn't know, don't say you were deceived.
engañoso, -sa, *a.* deceptive, misleading.
engarabatar, *v.t.* (*coll.*) to hook. — **engarabatarse,** *v.r.* to get crooked.
engarabitar(se), *v.i.* (*v.r.*) to ascend, climb.
engaratusar (*Guat., Hond., Mex.*) [ENGATUSAR].
engarbarse, *v.r.* to perch on the highest branches of a tree (*birds*).
engarbullar, *v.t.* (*coll.*) to make a mess of; to involve, entangle.
engarce, *n.m.* hooking; setting, stringing.
engargantar, *v.t.* to put into the throat. — *v.i.* to thrust the foot into the stirrup; to interlock; to put into gear.
engargolar, *v.t.* to join (*pipes*).
engaritar, *v.t.* to provide with sentry boxes, fortify; (*coll.*) to fool, deceive, trick.
engarrafador, *n.m.* grappler.
engarrafar, *v.t.* (*coll.*) to grab, seize.
engarrotar, *v.t.* to garrotte; to squeeze hard. — **engarrotarse,** *v.r.* (*Arg.*) to become numb with cold.
engarzador, -ra, *n.m.f.* one who links *or* enchains; stringer of beads.
engarzar [C], *v.t.* to link, string, wire; to set, enchase, mount; to curl.
engastador, -ra, *a.* setting, encasing (*gems*). — *n.m.f.* setter.
engastar, *v.t.* to set (*gems*); to encase.
engaste, *n.m.* encasing, setting (*gems*); pearl flat on one side.
engatado, -da, *a.* thievish (*cat etc.*). — *n.m.f.* petty robber, pilferer; sharper.
engatar, *v.t.* (*coll.*) to cheat, deceive; wheedle.
engatillado, -da, *a.* thick, high-necked (*horses and bulls*).
engatillar, *v.t.* (*arch.*) to bind with a cramping-iron.
engatusador, -ra, *a.* (*coll.*) coaxing, wheedling. — *n.m.f.* coaxer, wheedler.
engatusamiento, *n.m.* (*coll.*) coaxing, wheedling.
engatusar, *v.t.* (*coll.*) to inveigle, coax, cajole, wheedle.
engazador, -ra [ENGARZADOR].
engazar [C], *v.t.* to dye (*cloth*); to link; (*naut.*) to strap (*blocks*).
engendrable, *a.* that may be engendered.
engendrador, -ra, *a.* generating. — *n.m.f.* engenderer; begetter.
engendramiento, *n.m.* begetting, generating.
engendrar, *v.t.* to beget, breed; to engender, generate.
engendro, *n.m.* fœtus; shapeless embryo, monster, abortion; (*fig.*) abortive scheme; (*coll.*) mess.
engibar, *v.t.* to make humped; (*fig.*) to irritate; (*sl.*) to receive (*stolen goods*).
engina, *n.f.* (*obs.*) quinsy.
englandado, -da, englantado, -da, *a.* (*her.*) acorned.
englobar, *v.t.* to include, comprise; to lump together.
engolado, -da, *a.* (*coll.*) pompous, bombastic, stilted; (*her.*) engouled.
engolamiento, *n.m.* pompousness, bombast, affected tone.
engolfar(se), *v.i.* (*v.r.*) to go far out to sea; (*coll.*) to get lazy, become a layabout.
engolillado, -da, *a.* wearing a ruff; old-fashioned.
engolondrinarse, *v.r.* (*coll.*) to get conceited; to get infatuated.
engolosinar, *v.t.* to allure, entice. — **engolosinarse,** *v.r.* to get keen (**con,** on).
engollar, *v.t.* to make (*a horse*) carry his head high.
engolletado, -da, *a.* (*coll.*) haughty, conceited.
engolletarse, *v.r.* (*coll.*) to get conceited *or* haughty.
engomadura, *n.f.* gumming; coat which bees lay over their hives before making wax.
engomar, *v.t.* to glue, gum, size.
engorar [4], *v.t.* to addle.
engorda, *n.f.* (*Chi., Mex.*) number of animals fattened at one time.
engordadero, *n.m.* sty to fatten hogs; time and food for fattening hogs.
engordador, -ra, *a.* fattening. — *n.m.f.* one who fattens.
engordar, *v.t.* to fatten, make fat. — **engordar(se),** *v.i.* (*v.r.*) to fatten, get fat.
engorde, *n.m.* fattening.
engorro, *n.m.* awkward, tricky *or* bothersome business, bore, pain-in-the-neck.
engorroso, -sa, *a.* awkward, tricky, finicky, bothersome, tedious.
engoznar, *v.t.* to put hinges on; to hinge.
Engracia, *n.f.* Grace.
engranaje, *n.m.* (*mech.*) gear(ing), mesh(ing).
engranar, *v.i.* to gear, (inter)mesh, interlock, tooth, connect.
engrandar, *v.t.* to increase, make larger.
engrandecer [9], *v.t.* to enlarge, aggrandize, augment; to extol, exalt; to magnify.
engrandecimiento, *n.m.* increase, enlargement; aggrandizement; extolling.
engranerar, *v.t.* to store in a granary.
engranujarse, *v.r.* to become covered with pimples; to become a rogue *or* rascal.
engrapar, *v.t.* (*build., carp.*) to cramp, unite with cramp-irons; to staple.
engrasación, *n.f.* oiling, greasing, lubrication.
engrasador, *n.m.* oiler, lubricator.

engrasar, *v.t.* to oil, grease, lubricate; to dress (*cloth*); (*prov.*) to manure; to stain with grease; to pickle. — **engrasarse,** *v.r.* (*Mex.*) to contract lead-poisoning.
engrase, *n.m.* greasing, lubrication; grease.
engredar, *v.t.* to clay; to chalk; to cover with marl *or* fuller's earth.
engreído, -da, *a.* conceited.
engreimiento, *n.m.* conceitedness, conceit.
engreír [28], *v.t.* to make conceited. — **engreírse,** *v.r.* to get conceited; (*Hisp. Am.*) to get keen (on).
engrescar [A], *v.t.* to incite to quarrel, set at odds.
engrifar, *v.t.* to crisp, curl, crimp; to make bristle. — **engrifarse,** *v.r.* to bristle; to rear up (*horses*).
engrillar, *v.t.* to fetter; to shackle; (*P.R.*, *Ven.*) to lower (*the head*) too much (*horses*).
engrillarse, *v.i.* to sprout (*plants*).
engrilletar, *v.t.* (*naut.*) to join with shackles.
engringarse [B], *v.r.* (*coll.*) to go *or* get foreign.
engrosar [4], *v.t.* to enlarge; to swell; to thicken; to make fat; to manure; ***engrosar las filas,*** to swell the ranks.
engrudador, *n.m.* paster.
engrudamiento, *n.m.* pasting, glueing.
engrudar, *v.t.* to paste, glue.
engrudo, *n.m.* paste, glue.
engruesar, *v.i.* [ENGROSAR].
engrumecerse [9], *v.r.* to clot; to curdle; to go lumpy.
engualdrapar, *v.t.* to caparison with rich trappings.
enguantado, -da, *a.* wearing gloves.
enguantar(se), *v.t.* (*v.r.*) to put gloves on.
enguedejado, -da, *a.* having long locks *or* tresses.
enguijarrar, *v.t.* to pave with pebbles.
enguillar, *v.t.* (*naut.*) to wind a thin rope around (*a thicker one*).
enguirnaldar, *v.t.* to garland, adorn with garlands.
enguizgar [B], *v.t.* to incite, arouse, spur on.
engullidor, -ra, *n.m.f.* gobbler, wolfer.
engullir [J], *v.t.* to gobble, wolf (down).
engurrio, *n.m.* sadness, blues.
engurruñarse, *v.r.* (*coll.*) to get the blues.
enharinar, *v.t.* to cover with flour.
enhastiar [L] [HASTIAR].
enhastillar, *v.t.* to put (*arrows*) in a quiver.
enhatijar, *v.t.* to cover (*the mouths of hives*) with matting for transportation.
enhebrar, *v.t.* to string, thread.
enhenar, *v.t.* to cover with hay, wrap up in hay.
enherbolar, *v.t.* to poison with herbs (*heads of arrows etc.*).
enhestador, -ra, *n.m.f.* one who erects.
enhestadura, *n.f.*, **enhestamiento,** *n.m.* erection.
enhestar [1], *v.t.* to set upright; to raise; to erect. — **enhestarse,** *v.r.* to rise upright.
enhetradura, *n.f.* (*obs.*) entangling, entanglement.
enhielar, *v.t.* to mix with gall *or* bile.
enhiesto, -ta, *a.* erect, upright. — *p.p.* [ENHESTAR].
enhilado, -da, *a.* well-arranged, well-disposed, in good order, in line.
enhilar, *v.t.* to thread; (*fig.*) to arrange, place in order; to direct. — *v.i.* to set out (*for*).
enhorabuena, *adv.* (*obs.*) all right; well and good. — *n.f.* congratulations. — *interj.* ***¡enhorabuena!*** congratulations, good for you, good show.
enhoramala, *adv.* (*obs.*) in an evil hour; (*coll.*) ***¡vete enhoramala!*** away with you, go to blazes!
enhornar, *v.t.* to put into an oven.
enhorquetar(se), *v.t.* (*v.r.*) (*Arg.*, *Cub.*, *P.R.*) to ride astride.
enhuecar [A] [AHUECAR].
enhuerar, *v.t.* to addle.
enigma, *n.m.* enigma.
enigmático, -ca, *a.* enigmatic, inscrutable, cryptic.
enigmatista, *n.m.* enigmatist.
enjabonadura, *n.f.* soaping, lathering.
enjabonar, *v.t.* to soap, lather; (*fig.*) to soft-soap, butter up; (*coll.*) to give a dressing down to.
enjaezar [C], *v.t.* to caparison, put trappings on (*horse*).
enjagüe, *n.m.* adjudication required by the creditors of a ship.
enjalbegador, -ra, *n.m.f.* whitewasher.
enjalbegadura, *n.f.* whitewashing.
enjalbegar [B], *v.t.* to whitewash.
enjalma, *n.f.* light packsaddle.
enjalmar, *v.t.* to put a packsaddle on.
enjalmero, *n.m.* packsaddle-maker.
enjambradera, *n.f.* queen bee.
enjambradero, *n.m.* swarming place.
enjambrar, *v.t.* to hive. — *v.i.* to breed a new hive, swarm; to produce heavily.
enjambrazón, *n.f.* swarming (*bees*).
enjambre, *n.m.* swarm.
enjambrillo, *n.m.* small *or* secondary swarm.
enjarciadura, *n.f.* rigging (*ship*).
enjarciar, *v.t.* to rig (*ship*).
enjardinar, *v.t.* to trim (*trees*) as in a garden.
enjaretado, *n.m.* grating, lattice-work.
enjaretar, *v.t.* to run a string through the hem of; (*fig.*) to rattle off, rush through; (*coll.*) to spring, fob off, palm off; (*coll.*) to stick in.
enjaular, *v.t.* to cage.
enjebar, *v.t.* to steep in lye; to buck.
enjebe, *n.m.* lye; steeping in lye; bucking.
enjergar [B], *v.t.* (*coll.*) to start and direct (*a business*); to set about (*a matter*).
enjertar, *v.t.* to graft.
enjerto, *n.m.* grafting. — *p.p.* [ENJERTAR].
enjorguinarse, *v.r.* to become a wizard *or* sorcerer.
enjoyar, *v.t.* to adorn with jewels, bejewel; to adorn, embellish; to set with precious stones.
enjoyelado, -da, *a.* bejewelled; wrought into jewels.
enjoyelador, *n.m.* jeweller, jewel-setter.
enjuagadientes, *n.m. inv.* mouthwash.
enjuagadura, *n.f.* rinsing.
enjuagar [B], *v.t.* to rinse.
enjuagatorio, *n.m.* mouthwash.
enjuague, *n.m.* rinse, rinsing; mouthwash; (*fig.*) sth. fixed up, cooked-up business, put-up job.
enjugador, -ra, *n.m.f.* drier. — *n.m.* drum for drying *or* airing linen.
enjugar [B], *v.t.* to dry; to wipe off *or* away; to cancel, wipe out, pay off (*debts*). — **enjugarse,** *v.r.* to grow lean.
enjuiciamiento, *n.m.* judging, appraisal; (*law*) institution of legal proceedings.
enjuiciar, *v.t.* to judge, appraise; (*law*) to prosecute; to indict; to bring a suit *or* action against.
enjulio, enjullo, *n.m.* warp-rod; cloth-beam (*of a loom*).
enjuncar [A], *v.t.* to fasten with stops of grass rope; to ballast.
enjundia, *n.f.* grease, fat; (*fig.*) substance, solid content.
enjundioso, -sa, *a.* fat, fatty; substantial, solid.
enjunque, *n.m.* heavy ballast *or* cargo; kentledge.
enjuramiento, *n.m.* (*obs.*) legal oath.
enjurar, *v.t.* (*obs.*) to yield *or* transfer (*a right*).
enjunta, *n.f.* [ENJUNTO].
enjutar, *v.t.* (*build.*) to dry.
enjutez, *n.f.* dryness; leanness.
enjuto, -ta, *a.* dry; lean; sparing, frugal; ***a pie enjuto,*** without getting one's feet wet; without toil. — *n.m.pl.* (**enjutos**) brushwood; tit-bits to excite thirst. — *n.f.* (*arch.*) spandrel.
enlabiador, -ra, *a.* wheedling. — *n.m.f.* wheedler, cajoler.

enlabiar, *v.t.* to cajole, wheedle, entice by soft words.
enlabio, *n.m.* enticement, alluring, charming by soft words.
enlace (1), *n.m.* connection; liaison; link; interlocking, interlacing; wedding, union *or* linking by marriage.
enlace (2), *pres. subj.* [ENLAZAR].
enlaciar(se), *v.t.* (*v.r.*) to make *or* become languid, lax *or* lank.
enladrillado, *n.m.* brick paving; brickwork.
enladrillador, *n.m.* bricklayer.
enladrilladura, *n.f.* brickwork.
enladrillar, *v.t.* to pave with bricks.
enlagunar, *v.t.* to flood, turn into a swamp.
enlamar, *v.t.* to cover with slime.
enlardar, *v.t.* to rub with grease, baste.
enlargues, *n.m.pl.* rope-ends.
enlatar, *v.t.* to tin, can; to roof with battens.
enlazable, *a.* that can be joined *or* linked.
enlazador, -ra, *n.m.f.* binder, uniter.
enlazadura, *n.f.* **enlazamiento,** *n.m.* binding; uniting, coupling, linking; lacing; connection.
enlazar [C], *v.t.* to tie, bind; to link; to lasso. — **enlazarse,** *v.r.* to be joined in wedlock.
enlechuguillado, -da, *a.* wearing a ruff round the neck.
enlegajar, *v.t.* to tie up into a docket.
enlejiar [L], *v.t.* to buck; (*chem.*) to make into lye.
enlenzar [IC], *v.t.* to strengthen with adhesive strips of cloth.
enligar [B], *v.t.* to snare with bird-lime; to smear with bird-lime. — **enligarse,** *v.r.* to get caught in bird-lime.
enlistonado, *n.m.* lath-work.
enlistonar, *v.t.* to lath.
enlizar [C], *v.t.* to provide with leashes.
enlodadura, *n.f.* soiling, daubing *or* filling with mud.
enlodar, *v.t.* to soil with mud, bemire; to throw mud at; (*min.*) to stop up with clay; (*fig.*) to (be)smirch.
enloquecedor, -ra, *a.* maddening.
enloquecer [9], *v.t.* to drive mad *or* insane; ***le enloquece el fútbol,*** he's crazy on football. — **enloquecer(se),** *v.i.* (*v.r.*) to go mad *or* insane.
enloquecimiento, *n.m.* going mad; madness, insanity.
enlosado, *n.m.* flagging; flagged paving.
enlosar, *v.t.* to lay with flags *or* tiles.
enlozanarse, *v.r.* [LOZANEAR].
enlucido, *n.m.* coat of plaster; plastering.
enlucidor, *n.m.* plasterer.
enlucimiento, *n.m.* plastering; polishing.
enlucir [10], *v.t.* to plaster; to polish.
enlustrecer [9], *v.t.* to brighten, polish.
enlutar, *v.t.* to put into mourning; to put crêpe *or* mourning on; (*fig.*) to darken, cloud.
enllantar, *v.t.* to shoe, rim (*a wheel*).
enllentecer [9], *v.t.* to soften.
enmadejar, *v.t.* (*Chi.*) to reel.
enmaderación, *n.f.*, **enmaderamiento,** *n.m.* woodwork; wainscoting; covering of wood.
enmaderar, *v.t.* to timber; to board *or* plank; to floor with boards.
enmadrarse, *v.r.* to get over-attached to one's mother; ***está muy enmadrado,*** he's completely tied to his mother's apron-strings.
enmagrecer(se), *v.i.* (*v.r.*) to grow lean, lose fat.
enmalecerse [9], *v.r.* to get overgrown with scrub.
enmallarse, *v.r.* to get caught in the meshes of a net.
enmalletado, -da, *a.* fouled (*ropes*).
enmangar [B], *v.t.* to put a handle on.
enmaniguarse [H], *v.r.* (*Cub.*) to revert to jungle; (*Cub., fig.*) to settle in the country.
enmantar, *v.t.* to cover with a blanket. — **enmantarse,** *v.r.* to become melancholy.
enmarañamiento, *n.m.* entanglement; tangle, muddle.
enmarañar, *v.t.* to (en)tangle, muddle (up).
enmararse, *v.r.* to take sea-room.
enmarcar, *v.t.* to frame.
enmaridar(se), *v.i.* (*v.r.*) to take a husband, marry.
enmarillecerse [9], *v.r.* to become pale *or* yellow.
enmaromar, *v.t.* to tie with rope.
enmascarar, *v.t.* to mask.
enmasillar, *v.t.* (*carp.*) to putty.
enmatarse, *v.r.* to hide in the undergrowth.
enmelar [1], *v.t.* to honey, sweeten; to smear with honey. — *v.i.* to produce honey.
enmendación, *n.f.* emendation.
enmendador, -ra, *n.m.f.* emendator, amender.
enmendadura, *n.f.*, **enmendamiento,** *n.m.* [ENMIENDA].
enmendar [1], *v.t.* to amend, emend; to remedy; to correct; to compensate; (*law*) to revise (*a sentence*). — **enmendarse,** *v.r.* to mend one's ways, turn over a new leaf.
enmienda, *n.f.* correction, emendation, amendment; ***poner enmienda a,*** to put right; ***esto no tiene enmienda,*** there's no cure for it; (*pl.*) fertilizer.
enmocecer [9], *v.i.* (*obs.*) to recover the vigour of youth.
enmohecer(se) [9], *v.t.* (*v.r.*) to mildew, make mouldy; to rust; to become mouldy, rusty.
enmohecido, -da, *a.* mildewed, mouldy, musty; rusty.
enmohecimiento, *n.m.* mustiness, mouldiness; rustiness.
enmollecer [9], *v.t.* to soften, mollify, make tender.
enmonarse, *v.r.* (*Chi., Per.*) to get drunk.
enmondar, *v.t.* to remove knots from (*cloth*).
enmontadura, *n.f.* (*obs.*) elevation, erection.
enmontarse, *v.r.* (*Hisp. Am.*) to get covered in undergrowth.
enmordazar [C], *v.t.* to gag, muzzle.
enmudecer [9], *v.t.* to silence, hush. — *v.i.* to fall silent; to become dumb.
enmugrar, *v.t.* (*Chi., Col.*) to soil.
ennegrecer [9], *v.t.* to blacken, darken.
ennegrecimiento, *n.m.* blackening, darkening.
ennoblecedor, -ra, *a.* ennobling.
ennoblecer [9], *v.t.* to ennoble; to enhance.
ennoblecimiento, *n.m.* ennoblement.
ennoviado, -da, *a.* delighted with *or* mad on one's fiancé(e).
ennudecer [9], *v.i.* [ANUDAR].
enodio, *n.m.* fawn, young deer.
enojada, *n.f.* (*coll.*) fit of anger; upset.
enojadizo, -za, *a.* easily angered, irritable, peevish.
enojante, *a.* vexing, annoying.
enojar, *v.t.* to anger; to vex, irritate, annoy, displease, offend. — **enojarse,** *v.r.* to get angry, cross; (*fig.*) to become boisterous, violent (*wind etc.*).
enojo, *n.m.* anger, annoyance, irritation.
enojoso, -sa, *a.* annoying, irritating, vexatious, troublesome.
enología, *n.f.* œnology.
enológico, -ca, *a.* œnological.
enómetro, *n.m.* œnometer.
enorgullecer [9], *v.t.* to make proud. — **enorgullecerse,** *v.r.* to become proud, swell with pride; to take pride (***de,*** in); to feel proud (***de,*** of); to feel pride (***de,*** at).
enorgullecimiento, *n.m.* pride, haughtiness, arrogance.
enorme, *a.* huge, enormous; (*fig.*) terrific.

enormemente, *adv.* enormously; terrifically, to a terrific extent.
enormidad, *n.f.* enormousness; enormity, dreadful thing; terrific amount; terrific effort; awful nonsense, utter rubbish.
enotecnia, *n.f.* technical knowledge of œnology.
enotécnico, -ca, *a.* relating to wine-making.
enquiciar, *v.t.* to hinge, put on hinges; (*fig.*) to put in order; to make firm *or* stable.
enquillotrar, *v.t.* to make conceited. — **enquillotrarse,** *v.r.* (*coll.*) to fall in love.
enquiridión, *n.m.* enchiridion.
enquistado, -da, *a.* (*surg.*) cysted, encysted.
enrabiar, *v.t.* to enrage, anger.
enraizar [C], *v.i.* to take root.
enramada, *n.f.* bower, arbour.
enramar, *v.t.* to embower. — *v.i.* to branch (*trees*).
enramblar, *v.t.* to tenter (*cloth*).
enrame, *n.m.* embowering.
enranciarse, *v.r.* to grow rancid, stale.
enrarecer [9], *v.t.* to thin, rarefy. — **enrarecer(se),** *v.i.* (*v.r.*) to rarefy; to get scarce.
enrarecimiento, *n.m.* rarefaction.
enrasar, *v.t.* (*build.*) to make even *or* level; to flush; to smooth.
enrase, *n.m.* (*build.*) levelling.
enrastrar, *v.t.* (*prov.*) to string (*silk cocoons*).
enrayar, *v.t.* to fix spokes in (*a wheel*); to brake, wedge.
enredadera, *a.* twining, trailing. — *n.f.* climbing plant; bindweed.
enredador, -ra, *a.* entangling. — *n.m.f.* busybody, meddler, mischief-maker.
enredamiento (*obs.*) [ENREDO].
enredar, *v.t.* to (en)tangle, mat, snarl up, muddle up; to net, catch, snare; to embroil, set at odds; to involve; to hold up. — *v.i.* to get up to mischief, mess about, fool around; to meddle. — **enredarse,** *v.r.* to get entangled; to get caught; to get involved; to foul up.
enredo, *n.m.* tangle, entanglement; embroilment, mix-up; mischief; involved plot (*of play*); love affair; (*pl.*) odds and ends, goods and chattels.
enredoso, -sa, *a.* entangled, involved, awkward, bothersome, tedious.
enrehojar, *v.t.* to turn over, stir (*wax*) into sheets (*in order to bleach it*).
enrejado, *n.m.* trellis, lattice; open-work, grillework; grating, railing.
enrejalar, *v.t.* to range (*bricks*) in criss-cross tiers.
enrejar, *v.t.* to surround with railing, grating *or* lattice-work; to fix a grating to; to fence with railing *or* grating; to fix the share to (*a plough*); to wound (*ox's* or *horse's feet*) with a ploughshare; (*Mex.*) to darn.
enrevesado, -da, *a.* intricate, complicated, involved.
enriado, *n.m.* retting of flax *or* hemp.
enriador, -na, *n.m.f.* one who rets flax *or* hemp.
enriar [L], *v.t.* to ret (*flax and hemp*).
enrielar, *v.t.* to make into ingots; (*Chi., Mex.*) to set on rails; (*fig.*) to put on the right track.
enripiar, *v.t.* (*build.*) to fill with rubble.
Enrique, *n.m.* Henry.
enriquecedor, -ra, *a.* enriching. — *n.m.f.* one who enriches.
enriquecer [9], *v.t.* to enrich. — **enriquecer(se),** *v.i.* (*v.r.*) to become rich.
Enriqueta, *n.f.* Henrietta, Harriet.
enriscado, -da, *a.* craggy.
enriscamiento, *n.m.* raising; taking refuge amongst rocks.
enriscar [A], *v.t.* to raise, lift. — **enriscarse,** *v.r.* to take refuge amongst rocks.
enristrar, *v.t.* to couch (*lance*); (*fig.*) to head *or* make straight for; to straighten out (*a problem*); to string (*onions etc.*).
enristre, *n.m.* couching (*a lance*).
enrizamiento, *n.m.* curling.
enrizar [C], *v.t.* (*obs.*) to curl, turn into ringlets.
enrobrescido, -da, *a.* (*obs.*) hard *or* strong like an oak.
enrobustecer [9], *v.t.* to strengthen.
enrocar, *v.t., v.i.* to castle (*in chess*); to place (*flax* or *hemp*) on the distaff.
enrodar, *v.t.* to break on the torture-wheel.
enrodelado, -da, *a.* armed with a shield.
enrodrigonar, *v.t.* to prop (*vines*) with stakes.
enrojar, enrojecer [9], *v.t.* to redden; to make red-hot; to make blush. — **enrojecer(se),** *v.i.* (*v.r.*) to blush; to turn red.
enrojecido, -da, *a.* red; red-hot.
enrolar(se), *v.t.* (*v.r.*) to enrol.
enrollar, *v.t.* to wind, coil, roll up.
enromar, *v.t.* to blunt, dull.
enrona, *n.f.* (*prov.*) refuse, rubbish, debris.
enronar, *v.t.* (*prov.*) to dump (*rubbish*).
enronquecer [9], *v.t.* to make hoarse. — **enronquecer(se),** *v.i.* (*v.r.*) to become hoarse.
enronquecimiento, *n.m.* hoarseness.
enroñar, *v.t.* to cover in scabs *or* scurf. — **enroñarse,** *v.r.* to rust, get rusty.
enroscadura, *n.f.* convolution, coiling, twisting, screwing on *or* in.
enroscar [A], *v.t.* to twist, coil, screw in *or* on; to wind round. — **enroscarse,** *v.r.* to curl.
enrostrar, *v.t.* (*Hisp. Am.*) to reproach with.
enrubiador, -ra, *a.* that turns the hair blond.
enrubiar, *v.t.* to dye blond, bleach.
enrubio, *n.m.* dyeing blond; blond dye, bleach.
enrudecer [9], *v.t.* to make coarse, crude *or* rough. — *v.i.* to get coarse, crude *or* rough.
enruinecer [9], *v.i.* to become base, sink low.
ensabanar, *v.t.* to wrap up in sheets; to cover with plaster of Paris.
ensacador, -ra, *n.m.f.* sacker, bagger.
ensacar [A], *v.t.* to sack, bag, put in a sack *or* bag.
ensaimada, *n.f.* bun.
ensalada, *n.f.* salad; medley, hodge-podge.
ensaladera, *n.f.* salad dish *or* bowl.
ensaladilla, *n.f.* Russian salad; jewel made up of different precious stones; assortment of sweetmeats.
ensalmador, -ra, *n.m.f.* bone-setter; charlatan, quack, witch-doctor.
ensalmar, *v.t.* to set (*bones*); to cure by spells.
ensalmista, *n.m.* charlatan.
ensalmo, *n.m.* spell, enchantment, charm; ***como por ensalmo***, as if by magic.
ensalobrarse, *v.r.* to become salty.
ensalzador, -ra, *a.* praising, extolling. — *n.m.f.* praiser, extoller.
ensalzamiento, *n.m.* praise, extolling.
ensalzar [C], *v.t.* to exalt, extol, praise. — **ensalzarse,** *v.r.* to boast.
ensamblador, *n.m.* joiner.
ensambladura, *n.f.* joinery, joiner's trade; joining; joint.
ensamblaje, *n.m.* joining, coupling; scarfing.
ensamblar, *v.t.* to connect, join, couple; to scarf, dovetail, mortise.
ensamble, *n.m.* [ENSAMBLADURA].
ensancha, *n.f.* enlargement, widening; ***dar ensanchas***, to give too much licence *or* liberty.
ensanchador, -ra, *a.* enlarging, widening; stretching, expanding. — *n.m.* glove-stretcher; widener, stretcher, expander; reamer.
ensanchamiento, *n.m.* enlarging, widening, broadening; stretching, expansion.

ensanchar, *v.t.* to enlarge, widen, broaden; to stretch, expand. — **ensancharse,** *v.r.* to widen, expand; (*fig.*) to get puffed up; ***se me ensancha el corazón,*** my heart warms, it warms my heart.
ensanche, *n.m.* enlargement, widening, broadening; expansion, extension; suburban development, new built-up area.
ensandecer [9], *v.i.* to grow stupid.
ensangrentamiento, *n.m.* blood-staining; blood-shedding.
ensangrentar, *v.t.* to stain with blood, cover in blood, make bloody. — **ensangrentarse,** *v.r.* to get covered in blood; to get into a murderous mood.
ensañamiento, *n.m.* savage *or* ferocious cruelty, savagery; (*law*) aggravating circumstance.
ensañar, *v.t.* to enrage, make savage. — **ensañarse,** *v.r.* — ***con,*** to treat with savage cruelty, vent one's savagery upon.
ensarnecerse [9], *v.r.* to get the itch *or* mange.
ensartar, *v.t.* to string (*beads*); to thread (*a needle*); to skewer, spit; (*coll.*) to rattle off, string off, string together.
ensay, *n.m.* (*mint*) trial, assay, proof.
ensayador, -ra, *n.m.f.* assayer; officer of a mint; rehearser.
ensayar, *v.t.* to assay (*precious metals*); to try out, test; to practise, rehearse. — *v.i.* to rehearse. — **ensayarse,** *v.r.* to practise, train.
ensaye, *n.m.* assay, trial, proof, test (*metals*).
ensayista, *n.m.f.* essayist, essay-writer.
ensayo, *n.m.* test, trial; assay; essay; rehearsal; ***ensayo general,*** dress rehearsal.
ensebar, *v.t.* to grease, tallow.
enselvado, -da, *a.* wooded.
enselvar, *v.t.* to place in ambush. — **enselvarse,** *v.r.* to retire to a forest; to become wooded.
ensenado, -da, *a.* having the form of a cove *or* inlet. — *n.f.* inlet, cove, creek.
ensenar, *v.t.* to put into one's bosom; (*naut.*) to embay.
enseña, *n.f.* ensign, colours, standard.
enseñable, *a.* teachable.
enseñador, -ra, *a.* teaching. — *n.m.f.* instructor, teacher.
enseñanza, *n.f.* tuition, teaching; instruction, education.
enseñar, *v.t.* to teach, train, instruct; to show. — **enseñarse,** *v.r.* to become accustomed, inured, trained.
enseño, *n.m.* (*coll.*) education.
enseñoreador, -ra, *n.m.f.* (*obs.*) person who domineers.
enseñorear, *v.t.* to domineer, lord over. — **enseñorearse,** *v.r.* to take possession *or* control (***de,*** of).
enserar, *v.t.* to cover with matting.
enseres, *n.m.pl.* goods and chattels; implements.
enseriarse, *v.r.* (*Hisp. Am.*) to become serious.
ensiforme, *a.* ensiform, sword-shaped.
ensilaje, *n.m.* ensilage.
ensilar, *v.t.* to ensilage.
ensilvecerse [9], *v.r.* to become a forest *or* wooded.
ensillado, -da, *a.* saddle-backed (*horses*).
ensilladura, *n.f.* saddling; part of horse *or* mule on which saddle is placed.
ensillar, *v.t.* to saddle; (*obs.*) to raise, exalt.
ensimismamiento, *n.m.* being sunk *or* deep in thought.
ensimismarse, *v.r.* to become lost in thought, sunk in a reverie; (*Chi., Col.*) to be in love with o.s.; to become vain.
ensoberbecer [9], *v.t.* to make proud. — **ensoberbecerse,** *v.r.* to become proud and haughty, arrogant; (*naut.*) to become rough (*sea*).
ensoberbecimiento, *n.m.* arrogance, haughtiness.
ensogar [B], *v.t.* to fasten with a rope; to line with rope (*demijohn etc.*).
ensolerar, *v.t.* to fix stands *or* bases to (*beehives*).
ensolver [5, *p.p.* **ensuelto**], *v.t.* to include, enclose; to abridge, contract; (*med.*) to resolve, dissipate.
ensombrecer [9], *v.t.* to darken; to make cloudy.
ensoñar, *v.i.* to day-dream, give o.s. up to reverie.
ensopar, *v.t.* to dip in liquid; to soak.
ensordecedor, -ra, *a.* deafening.
ensordecer [9], *v.t.* to deafen; (*phon.*) to unvoice. — *v.i.* to grow deaf.
ensordecimiento, *n.m.* deafness.
ensortijamiento, *n.m.* crimping, curling, crisping; curls, ringlets; ringing (*of animals*).
ensortijar, *v.t.* to curl, crisp; to ring.
ensotarse, *v.r.* to hide o.s. in a thicket.
ensuciador, -ra, *a.* staining, soiling. — *n.m.f.* defiler, stainer.
ensuciamiento, *n.m.* staining, soiling, defilement, polluting.
ensuciar, *v.t.* to dirty, soil, stain, sully, defile, pollute. — **ensuciarse,** *v.r.* to get dirty, soil o.s.
ensueño, *n.m.* dream, day-dream.
entablación, *n.f.* flooring, boarding; register (*in churches*).
entablado, *n.m.* boarded *or* parquet floor; stage, dais.
entabladura, *n.f.* flooring, boarding, planking.
entablamento, *n.m.* entablature.
entablar, *v.t.* to floor, cover with boards; to board up; to plank; to start, initiate; to bring (*a suit* or *action*); to place (*the men*) on a chessboard; (*surg.*) to splint; (*Arg.*) to train (*cattle, horses etc.*). — **entablarse,** *v.r.* to settle (*wind*).
entable, *n.m.* position (*of chessmen*).
entablillar, *v.t.* (*surg.*) to splint.
entalamado, -da, *a.* (*obs.*) hung with tapestry.
entalamadura, *n.f.* awning (*of a cart etc.*).
entalamar, *v.t.* (*obs.*) to cover with an awning.
entalegar [B], *v.t.* (*com.*) to put in a bag *or* sack; to save, hoard.
entalingar [B], *v.t.* (*naut.*) to clinch (*cable*), fasten (*cable*) to the anchor.
entallable, *a.* capable of being carved.
entallador, *n.m.* sculptor, cutter in wood *or* stone; engraver; carver.
entalladura, *n.f.*, **entallamiento,** *n.m.* sculpture, carving; (*carp.*) groove, mortise, notch.
entallar, *v.t.* to notch, make a cut in; to carve, sculpture, engrave; to make fit closely. — ***v.i.*** **to** fit to the body.
entallecer, *v.i.* (*agric.*) to shoot, sprout.
entapizar [C], *v.t.* to hang *or* adorn with tapestry.
entarascar [A], *v.t.* (*coll.*) to overdress, cover with too many ornaments.
entarimado, *n.m.* boarded *or* parqueted floor.
entarimar, *v.t.* to floor with boards.
entarquinamiento, *n.m.* fertilizing with slime.
entarquinar, *v.t.* to fertilize with slime; to cover with mud, bemire; to reclaim (*swamplands*).
entarugar [B], *v.t.* to pave with wooden blocks.
ente, *n.m.* being; (*coll.*) fellow, chap.
enteco, -ca, *a.* weakly, sickly, feeble.
entejar, *v.t.* (*Hisp. Am.*) to tile (*roofs*).
entelequia, *n.f.* (*phil.*) entelechy; figment of the imagination; something unreal.
entelerido, -da, *a.* numb with cold; shivering from fright; (*C.R., Hond., Ven.*) infirm, weak; lean.
entena, *n.f.* lateen yard.
entenada, *n.f.* stepdaughter.
entenado, *n.m.* stepson.
entenallas, *n.f.pl.* pincers; hand-vice.
entendederas, *n.f.pl.* (*coll.*) understanding; ***tener buenas entendederas,*** to be quick on the uptake.

entendedor, -ra, *n.m.f.* understander, one who understands; ***al buen entendedor, pocas palabras,*** a word to the wise.

entender [1], *n.m.* understanding, opinion; ***a*** or ***según mi entender,*** in my opinion. — [2], *v.t.* to understand; ***dar a entender,*** to hint, give to understand. — *v.i.* — ***de*** or ***en,*** to be expert in, to know all about; to have authority in connection with; ***ya entiendo,*** I've got it now. — **entenderse,** *v.r.* to be clear, understandable; to be understood; to understand each other; to carry on a love affair; ***no se entiende eso conmigo,*** this does not include me; ***entenderse con una cosa,*** to be skilled in sth.; ***cada uno se entiende,*** each puts his own meaning into what he says; ***¿cómo se entiende?*** or ***¿qué se entiende?*** what's the meaning of this, pray?

entendido, -da, *a.* able; knowledgeable; knowing; ***darse por entendido,*** to take a hint; to take notice; ***no darse por entendido,*** not to take the hint; to ignore it.

entendimiento, *n.m.* understanding.

entenebrecer [9], *v.t.* to darken, obscure.

enterado, -da, *a.* informed, well up (in).

enterar, *v.t.* to inform, acquaint; (*Arg., Chi.*) to adjust (*an account*); (*C.R., Cub., Hond., Mex.*) to pay, hand over (*money*). — ***enterarse,*** *v.r.* to find out, learn (***de,*** about); ***estar enterado de,*** to be aware of.

enterciar, *v.t.* (*Cub., Mex.*) to pack (*tobacco etc.*) in bundles of 46 kilogram(me)s.

entereza, *n.f.* entirety; integrity, uprightness; fortitude, firmness, presence of mind.

entérico, -ca, *a.* enteric.

enterizo, -za, *a.* of one piece; whole.

enternecedor, -ra, *a.* touching, moving.

enternecer [9], *v.t.* to soften, make tender; to move (*to compassion*), touch the heart of. — **enternecerse,** *v.r.* to be moved *or* touched.

enternecidamente, *adv.* compassionately.

enternecimiento, *n.m.* pity, compassion.

entero, -ra, *a.* entire, complete, whole; sound, perfect; upright, honest; robust, strong, vigorous; uncorrupted, pure; constant, firm; uncastrated; full-bodied (*cloth*); (*arith.*) integral; ***caballo entero,*** stallion; ***números enteros,*** whole numbers; ***por entero,*** entirely, fully, in full, wholly. — *n.m.* (*arith.*) integer; (*com.*) point; (*Chi., Col., C.R., Mex.*) payment (*especially to public funds*).

enterocolitis, *n.f.* enterocolitis.

enterotomía, *n.f.* enterotomy.

enterrador, *n.m.* grave-digger, sexton; (*ent.*) burying beetle.

enterramiento, *n.m.* burial, interment.

enterrar [1], *v.t.* to inter, bury; (*fig.*) to outlive; (*Chi., Hond., P.R.*) to drive in, force in (*nails etc.*); ***ha enterrado a toda la familia,*** he has outlived the whole family; (*coll.*) ***me va a enterrar,*** he'll be the death of me, he'll be the end of me.— **enterrarse,** *v.r.* to hide away; ***enterrarse en vida,*** to bury o.s., shun society.

enterronar, *v.t.* to cover with clods.

entesamiento, *n.m.* stretching, making taut.

entesar [1], *v.t.* to tense, tauten, make taut.

entestado, -da, *a.* stubborn, obstinate.

entibación, *n.f.* (*min.*) propping; timbering.

entibador, *n.m.* (*min.*) one who shores up mines.

entibar, *v.t.* (*min.*) to prop; to shore up (*mines*).

entibiadero, *n.m.* cooling place.

entibiar, *v.t.* to make lukewarm; to cool; to temper; to moderate. — **entibiarse,** *v.r.* to cool (down).

entibo, *n.m.* (*min.*) prop, stay, shore.

entidad, *n.f.* entity; being; association, body; concern, firm; consequence, moment; ***entidad comercial,*** business concern.

entierro (1), *n.m.* funeral, burial, interment; grave, tomb, sepulchre; funeral procession; hoard.

entierro (2), *pres. indic.* [ENTERRAR].

entigrecerse [9], *v.r.* to become furious *or* enraged.

entinar, *v.t.* to put in a dyeing-vat.

entintar, *v.t.* to stain with ink; to ink, ink in (*a drawing etc.*); to tinge, dye.

entiznar [TIZNAR].

entoldado, *n.m.* tent; group of tents; covering with an awning.

entoldamiento, *n.m.* covering with awnings; overcast state (*of sky*).

entoldar, *v.t.* to adorn with hangings; to cover with an awning. — **entoldarse,** *v.r.* to swell with pride; to dress up; to grow cloudy *or* overcast; ***cielo entoldado,*** overcast sky.

entomizar [C], *v.t.* to tie bass cords around (*boards* or *laths so that the plaster may stick to them*).

entomología, *n.f.* entomology.

entomológico, -ca, *a.* entomological.

entomólogo, *n.m.* entomologist.

entonación, *n.f.* intonation; blowing the bellows (*of an organ*); (*fig.*) haughtiness.

entonadera, *n.f.* blow-lever (*of an organ*).

entonado, -da, *a.* haughty, puffed with pride. — *n.m.* (*photo.*) process of toning.

entonador, -ra, *a.* singing in tune; (*photo.*) toning. — *n.m.f.* one who sings in tune; (*photo.*) one who *or* that which tones. — *n.m.* organ-blower.

entonamiento, *n.m.* intonation; haughtiness.

entonar, *v.t.* to tune; to intone; to intonate; to tone (*prints*); to tone up, back up; to blow the bellows of (*an organ*); to harmonize (*colours*). — *v.i.* to sing in tune. — **entonarse,** *v.r.* to tone o.s. up (*coll.*) to get stuck-up.

entonatorio, *n.m.* book of sacred music.

entonces, *adv.* then; at that time; ***en aquel entonces,*** in those days; ***desde entonces,*** ever since (then); ***por*** (***aquel***) ***entonces,*** about *or* around that time; ***¿entonces?*** so? what then?

entonelar, *v.t.* to barrel, put in casks *or* barrels.

entono, *n.m.* intoning; singing in tune; haughtiness.

entontecer [9], *v.t.* to make foolish; to befuddle. — **entontecer(se),** *v.i.* (*v.r.*) to grow foolish, get stupid *or* besotted.

entontecimiento, *n.m.* becoming foolish *or* stupid; foolishness, besottedness, dullness.

entorchado, *n.m.* twisted silk, gold *or* silver cord (*in embroideries*); gold embroidery (*on uniforms*); bullion fringe; (*pl.*) bass-strings.

entorchar, *v.t.* to make a torch by twisting (*candles*); to make bullion fringe of; (*mus.*) to cover (*a cord*) with wire.

entorilar, *v.t.* to stall, pen (*bulls*).

entornar, *v.t.* to set (*a door* or *window*) ajar; to half-close (*eyes*); to tilt, incline.

entornillar, *v.t.* to form into a screw *or* spiral; to screw.

entorno, *n.m.* environment.

entorpecer, *v.t.* to benumb, to make dull *or* sluggish; to impede, obstruct.

entorpecimiento, *n.m.* numbness, dullness, sluggishness; obstruction.

entortadura, *n.f.* crookedness.

entortar [4], *v.t.* to make crooked; to bend; to make one-eyed.

entosigar [B], *v.t.* to poison.

entozoario, *n.m.* (*zool.*) entozoon.

entrabar, *v.t.* (*prov., Col.*) to hinder, obstruct.

entrada, *n.f.* entrance, entry; doorway, gate; access; admission; admission ticket; avenue, drive; (*theat.*) house (*audience*); intimacy, familiar access; beginning (*of a book, speech etc.*); good hand (*at cards*); commencement (*of a season etc.*); entrée (*course at dinner*); (*naut.*) leak; (*min.*) shift; (*com.*) entry (*in a book*); cash receipts; takings; incomings; income; down payment; ***derechos de entrada,*** import duty; (*coll.*) ***entrada de pavana,*** silly *or* tactless remark; ***entradas de la***

frente, receding forehead *or* hair; ***dar entrada a,*** to allow *or* let in, give admittance to, grant admittance to; ***de entrada,*** for a start, to begin with; from the outset.

entradero, *n.m.* (*prov.*) narrow entrance.

entrador, -ra, *a.* (*C.R., Mex., Ven.*) fearless in business etc.; (*Chi.*) intrusive, interfering. — *n.m.* supplier.

entramado, *n.m.* (*carp.*) framework.

entramar, *v.t.* to make a framework for.

entrambos, -bas, *a.pl.* both.

entrampar, *v.t.* to ensnare, entrap; to deceive, trick; (*coll.*) to entangle; to load with debts. — **entramparse,** *v.r.* to get into debt, get in the red.

entrante, *a.* entering; coming; incoming; ***el mes entrante,*** next month; (*fort.*) ***ángulo entrante,*** re-entering angle.

entraña, *n.f.* [ENTRAÑO].

entrañable, *a.* deep, profound; intimate, close; ***amigo entrañable,*** bosom friend.

entrañar, *v.t.* to bury deep; to entail, involve, imply. — **entrañarse,** *v.r.* to penetrate to the core; to get deeply attached.

entrañizar [C], *v.t.* (*obs.*) to love, be passionately fond of.

entraño, -ña, *a.* (*obs.*) internal, interior. — *n.f* entrail, bowel; (*fig.*) heart; (*fig.*) core; ***de buenas (malas) entrañas,*** good- (evil-) hearted; ***de mis entrañas,*** my dearly beloved; ***no tener entrañas,*** to be heartless; ***dar (hasta) las entrañas,*** to give one's very life-blood, one's all; ***me llega a las entrañas,*** it goes to my heart; ***echar las entrañas,*** to throw up violently; ***sacar las entrañas a,*** to strip bare, strip of everything.

entrapada, *n.f.* coarse crimson cloth.

entrapajar, *v.t.* to bandage with rags.

entrapar, *v.t.* (*obs.*) to powder (*the hair*) for a dry shampoo; to manure with rags. — **entraparse,** *v.r.* to become filthy, clogged *or* matted; to get covered with dust.

entrar, *v.t.* to get in, bring in, take in; to approach, tackle, get at; to enter by force; (*naut.*) to overtake; ***entrar la comida,*** to bring dinner in; ***no pude entrarle en razón,*** I couldn't make him see reason. — *v.i.* — ***a, en, por,*** to go *or* come in *or* into, enter; to flow into; to begin, start; to enter in, into, on *or* upon; to have (free) entry *or* access to; ***entrar bien,*** to fit properly; ***entrar a servir a,*** to enter the service of; ***entró como Pedro por su casa,*** he walked in as if he owned the place; ***ahora entro yo,*** now it's my turn; ***entrar en juego,*** to come into play; ***de éstos entran pocos en docena,*** you don't get many like this; ***en eso ni entro ni salgo,*** that is no concern of mine; ***me entró el deseo de hacerlo,*** I was seized by the desire to do it; ***me entran ganas de matarlo,*** I feel like killing him; ***ése a mí no me entra,*** I can't stand him; ***eso no le entra,*** he won't have it; he can't get it into his head; ***entrado en edad*** or ***en años,*** well on in years; ***hasta bien entrada la tarde,*** well into the evening. — **entrarse,** *v.r.* to get in, force, push *or* barge one's way in.

entrazado, -da, *a.* (*Arg., Chi.*) ***bien*** or ***mal entrazado,*** of good *or* bad disposition *or* figure.

entre, *prep.* between; among, amongst, amidst; ***entre semana,*** on weekdays; ***entre tanto,*** meanwhile; ***entre dos luces,*** at dusk; ***nadar entre dos aguas,*** to sit on the fence; ***entre que llega tarde y no trabaja ...,*** what with his being late and not working ...; ***tener un asunto entre manos,*** to be tied up with a matter; ***traerse algo entre manos,*** to be up to sth.; ***entre bastidores,*** behind the scenes.

entreabrir [*p.p.* **entreabierto**], *v.t.* to half-open, set ajar.

entreacto, *n.m.* interval, intermission, entr'acte; small cigar.

entreancho, -cha, *a.* neither wide nor narrow.

entrecalle, *n.m.* (*arch.*) space *or* groove between two mouldings.

entrecanal, *n.f.* (*arch.*) fillet between flutes.

entrecano, -na, *a.* greyish (*hair*).

entrecasco, *n.m.* [ENTRECORTEZA].

entrecava, *n.f.* shallow digging.

entrecavar, *v.t.* to dig shallow.

entrecejo, *n.m.* space between the eyebrows; (*fig.*) frown, frowning; ***fruncir el entrecejo,*** to knit one's brows.

entrecerca, *n.f.* space between enclosures.

entrecerrar, *v.t.* (*C.R., E.S., Mex.*) to set ajar (*door, window etc.*).

entreclaro, -ra, *a.* lightish.

entrecogedura, *n.f.* catching.

entrecoger [E], *v.t.* to catch, seize, corner; to compel (*by argument* or *threat*).

entrecoro, *n.m.* chancel.

entrecortado, -da, *a.* intermittent, faltering, broken (*voice* or *sound*).

entrecortadura, *n.f.* cut that does not sever, partial cut.

entrecortar, *v.t.* to cut without severing, half-cut.

entrecorteza, *n.f.* imperfection (*in timbers*).

entrecriarse, *v.r.* to grow among others (*plants*).

entrecruzar(se) [C], *v.t.* (*v.r.*) to intercross; to interweave.

entrecubierta, *n.f.* (*naut.*) between decks.

entrecuesto, *n.m.* backbone.

entrechocar(se) [A], *v.i.* (*v.r.*) to collide; to clash.

entredecir [17, *p.p.* **entredicho**], *v.t.* (*obs.*) to interdict, prohibit.

entredicho, *n.m.* interdiction; interdict; ***estar en entredicho,*** to be under a cloud, be suspect; ***poner en entredicho,*** to cast doubt *or* suspicion upon. — *p.p.* [ENTREDECIR].

entredoble, *a.* of medium thickness.

entredós, *n.m.* (*sew.*) insertion; small wardrobe; (*print.*) long primer.

entrefino, -na, *a.* of fair *or* medium quality.

entrega, *n.f.* delivery; handing over; giving up; episode, instalment; selflessness.

entregadero, -ra, *a.* (*com.*) deliverable.

entregador, -ra, *a.* delivering. — *n.m.f.* deliver.

entregamiento, *n.m.* delivery.

entregar [B], *v.t.* to give up, deliver, hand over; (*com.*) to pay, transfer; (*arch.*) to introduce, insert, embed; (*coll.*) ***entregarla,*** to give up the ghost, kick the bucket; ***a entregar,*** to be delivered; to be called for. — **entregarse,** *v.r.* to give o.s. up *or* over (***a,*** to); to surrender; (*mil.*) ***entregarse a discreción,*** to surrender unconditionally; ***entregarse de,*** to receive, to take charge *or* possession of.

entrejuntar, *v.t.* to join the panels of (*door etc.*) to the frame.

entrelazar [C], *v.t.* to interlace, interweave, braid, entwine.

entrelinear, *v.t.* to interline, write between the lines of.

entreliño, *n.m.* space between rows of trees, vines etc.

entrelistado, -da, *a.* striped, variegated.

entrelucir [10], *v.i.* to show through.

entremedias, *adv.* in between; ***entremedias de,*** between, among.

entremés, *n.m.* (*theat.*) interlude; short farce *or* one-act play; (*usu. pl.* **entremeses**) hors-d'œuvres.

entremesear, *v.t.* to enliven with jokes. — *v.i.* to act in an ***entremés.***

entremesista, *n.m.f.* writer of *or* player in an ***entremés.***

entremeter, *v.t.* to insert, place between; [ENTROMETERSE].

entremetido, -da [ENTROMETIDO].

entremetimiento, *n.m.* [ENTROMETIMIENTO].
entremezcladura, *n.f.* intermixture.
entremezclar, *v.t.* to intermingle, intermix, interweave.
entremiche, *n.m.* (*naut.*) chock.
entremiso, *n.m.* long bench (*for cheese-making*).
entremorir [7, *p.p.* **entremuerto**], *v.i.* to flicker; to die away *or* out slowly.
entrenador, -ra, *a.* training. — *n.m.* trainer, coach.
entrenar, *v.t.* to train, coach. — **entrenarse,** *v.r.* to train.
entrencar [A], *v.t.* to put sections in (*a beehive*).
entrenzar [C], *v.t.* to plait.
entreoír [22], *v.t.* to hear indistinctly.
entreordinario, -ria, *a.* middling, so so.
entrepalmadura, *n.f.* (*vet.*) hoof-sore.
entrepanes, *n.m.pl.* pieces of unsown ground between sown patches.
entrepañado, -da, *a.* composed of panels (*of doors*), panelled.
entrepaño, *n.m.* space between pilasters, bay; pier; panel, shelf.
entreparecerse [9], *v.r.* to show through.
entrepaso, *n.m.* rack pace (*horses*).
entrepechuga, *n.f.* flesh within the wishbone of birds.
entrepeines, *n.m.pl.* comb-wool.
entrepelado, -da, *a.* (*vet.*) pied; (*Arg., vet.*) variegated.
entrepelar, *v.i.* to be piebald (*horses*).
entrepernar [1], *v.i.* to put one's legs between those of another.
entrepierna, *n.f.* inner surface of the thigh; (*pl.*) strengthening pieces added to the crotch of breeches; (*Chi.*) (bathing) trunks.
entrepiso, *n.m.* (*min.*) space between galleries.
entreponer [25], *v.t.* to interpose, place between.
entrepretado, -da, *a.* with an injured breast *or* shoulder (*horses*).
entrepuente, *n.m.pl.* (*naut.*) between decks.
entrepunzadura, *n.f.* pricking pain.
entrepunzar [C], *v.t.* to prick slightly.
entrerrenglón, *n.m.* interlineation.
entrerrenglonadura, *n.f.* interlineation, anything written between lines; interlineal note.
entrerrenglonar, *v.t.* to interline.
entresaca, entresacadura, *n.f.* thinning out.
entresacar [A], *v.t.* to pick out, select; to cull, sift; (*agric.*) to thin out.
entresijo, *n.m.* (*anat., zool.*) mesentery; (*fig.*) hidden feature; ***tener muchos entresijos,*** to be very involved *or* tricky.
entresuelo, *n.m.* entresol, mezzanine.
entresurco, *n.m.* space between furrows.
entretalla, entretalladura, *n.f.* bas-relief.
entretallar, *v.t.* to carve in bas-relief; to cut, engrave; to make open-work. — **entretallarse,** *v.r.* to interlock, join.
entretanto, *adv., n.m.* meanwhile; ***en el entretanto,*** in the meantime.
entretecho, *n.m.* (*Chi.*) attic, loft, garret.
entretejedor, -ra, *a.* interweaving.
entretejedura, *n.f.* intertexture.
entretejer, *v.t.* to intertwine, intermix, interweave; to variegate; to mix, mingle, insert.
entretejimiento, *n.m.* intertexture; interweaving; variegation.
entretela, *n.f.* (*sew.*) interlining; buckram; (*pl.*) (*fig.*) heart.
entretelar, *v.t.* (*sew.*) to insert an interlining in.
entretención, *n.f.* (*Hisp. Am.*) amusement, sport, pastime.
entretenedor, -ra, *a.* entertaining. — *n.m.f.* entertainer.
entretener [33], *v.t.* to amuse, entertain; to keep in hope *or* expectation; to hold up; to maintain, keep up; to stave off (*hunger etc.*). — **entretenerse,** *v.r.* to keep o.s. amused; to tarry, dally, linger.
entretenido, -da, *a.* entertaining, amusing; time-consuming; ***dar (con) la entretenida,*** to put off with evasions *or* vain promises. — *n.f.* kept woman.
entretenimiento, *n.m.* amusement, pastime, entertainment; maintenance, upkeep.
entretiempo, *n.m.* spring *or* autumn.
entreuntar, *v.t.* to anoint slightly, smear lightly.
entrevenarse, *v.r.* to diffuse through the veins.
entreventana, *n.f.* window-pier, wall space between windows.
entrever [37], *v.t.* to see indistinctly, catch a glimpse of; to foresee, begin to see, visualize.
entreverado, -da, *a.* intermingled, intermixed; interlarded; streaky.
entreverar, *v.t.* to intermix, intermingle. — **entreverarse,** *v.r.* (*Arg.*) to mix, get to close quarters.
entrevía, *n.f.* rail gauge.
entrevista, *n.f.* meeting; interview.
entrevistar, *v.t.* to interview. — **entrevistarse,** *v.r.* to hold an interview *or* meeting.
entripado, -da, *a.* intestinal; contained in the intestines; ungutted. — *n.m.* (*coll.*) dissembled anger *or* displeasure.
entristecer [9], *v.t.* to grieve, sadden, make (deeply) unhappy. — **entristecerse,** *v.r.* to become (deeply) unhappy.
entristecimiento, *n.m.* sadness; mournfulness.
entrojar, *v.t.* to garner (*grain*).
entrometerse, *v.r.* to meddle, stick one's nose (in), butt (in).
entrometida, *a., n.f.* [ENTROMETIDO].
entrometido, *a.* interfering, meddlesome. — *n.m.* busybody, meddler; intruder.
entrometimiento, *n.m.* meddling; meddlesomeness.
entronar, *v.t.* to enthrone.
entroncar(se) [A], *v.i.* (*v.r.*) to be *or* become related *or* connected (**con,** to *or* with); to connect, link up, join.
entronerar, *v.t.* to pocket (*a ball*) in billiards.
entronización, *n.f.* enthronement.
entronizar [C], *v.t.* to enthrone, place on the throne; to exalt. — **entronizarse,** *v.r.* to get puffed up with pride.
entronque, *n.m.* blood-relationship; connection, link.
entropía, *n.f.* entropy.
entruchada, *n.f.*, **entruchado,** *n.m.* (*coll.*) plot, intrigue, underhand business.
entruchar, *v.t.* (*coll.*) to decoy, lure, entice.
entruchón, -chona, *n.m.f.* decoyer, plotter, schemer.
entrujar, *v.t.* to store (up); to hoard (up).
entuerto, *n.m.* injustice, wrong, injury; (*pl.*) after-pains.
entullecer [9], *v.t.* to check, stop, paralyse. — **entullecer(se),** *v.i.* (*v.r.*) to get crippled.
entumecer [9], *v.t.* to benumb. — **entumecerse,** *v.r.* to get numb; to swell, surge (*sea, rivers etc.*).
entumecimiento, *n.m.* numbness, deadness; swelling.
entumirse, *v.r.* to become numb.
entunicar [A], *v.t.* to clothe with a tunic; to plaster (*a wall*) for fresco painting.
entupir, *v.t.* to tighten, compress, press; to block up, obstruct.
enturbiar, *v.t.* to make muddy, cloudy *or* turbid; (*fig.*) to cloud, obscure, muddle. — **enturbiarse,** *v.r.* to become muddy, troubled (*water*).
entusiasmado, -da, *a.* enthusiastic.

entusiasmar, *v.t.* to fill with enthusiasm; to delight. — **entusiasmarse,** *v.r.* to get filled with enthusiasm; to be delighted.
entusiasmo, *n.m.* enthusiasm.
entusiasta, *a.* enthusiastic. — *n.m.f.* enthusiast.
entusiástico, -ca, *a.* enthusiastic.
énula campana, *n.f.* (*bot.*) elecampane.
enumerable, *a.* numerable, enumerable.
enumeración, *n.f.* enumeration; listing.
enumerar, *v.t.* to enumerate; to list.
enunciación, *n.f.* enunciation.
enunciado, *n.m.* enunciation; terms of reference.
enunciar, *v.t.* to enunciate, state.
enunciativo, -va, *a.* enunciative.
envainador, -ra, *a.* sheathing.
envainar, *v.t.* to sheathe.
envalentonamiento, *n.m.* arrogance; boldness.
envalentonar, *v.t.* to embolden, make bold. — **envalentonarse,** *v.r.* to grow bold *or* daring; to get arrogant.
envalijar, *v.t.* to pack in a portmanteau.
envanecer [34], *v.t.* to make proud *or* vain. — **envanecerse,** *v.r.* to become conceited, proud, haughty *or* vain.
envanecimiento, *n.m.* conceit.
envaramiento, *n.m.* deadness, stiffness, numbness.
envarar, *v.t.* to benumb, stiffen, deaden.
envaronar, *v.i.* to grow up strong *or* robust.
envasador, *n.m.* filler, packer; funnel.
envasar, *v.t.* to pack, sack, bottle, can, put into a container; (*fig.*) to sink (*a sword*) in. — *v.i.* (*fig.*) to drink to excess.
envase, *n.m.* packing, bottling, filling, canning; container.
envedijarse, *v.r.* to get entangled; (*coll.*) to quarrel, get into a scrimmage.
envegarse [B], *v.r.* (*Chi.*) to become a swamp.
envejecer [9], *v.t.* to age; to make (*s.o.*) look old. — **envejecer(se),** *v.i.* (*v.r.*) to age, grow old; to become old-fashioned *or* out of date.
envejecido, -da, *a.* grown old; aged.
envejecimiento, *n.m.* ageing; growing *or* looking old.
envenenador, -ra, *a.* poisonous. — *n.m.f.* poisoner.
envenenamiento, *n.m.* poisoning.
envenenar, *v.t.* to poison, envenom.
enverar, *v.i.* to begin to look ripe.
enverdecer [9], *v.i.* to become green.
envergadura, *n.f.* wing-spread, wing-span; spread, span; breadth (*of sail*); scope.
envergar [B], *v.t.* to bend (*sails*).
envergues, *n.m.pl.* rope-bands.
envero, *n.m.* colour of ripening grapes.
envés, *n.m.* back; wrong side; underside.
envesado, *n.m.* fleshy side (*of hides*).
envestidura, *n.f.* investiture.
envestir [8], *v.t.* to invest.
enviada *n.f.* sending consignment, shipment.
enviadizo, -za, *a.* (regularly) sent.
enviado, *n.m.* messenger; envoy; ***enviado extraordinario,*** envoy extraordinary.
enviador, -ra, *a.* sending. — *n.m.f.* sender.
enviajado, -da, *a.* (*arch.*) oblique, sloped.
enviar [L], *v.t.* to send, remit, dispatch; to ship; ***enviar a paseo,*** to send packing, send away with a flea in the ear.
enviciar, *v.t.* to corrupt, vitiate, spoil. — *v.i.* (*bot.*) to run to leaf. — **enviciarse,** *v.r.* to get addicted (***con,*** to).
envidador, *n.m.* challenger (*at cards*).
envidar, *v.t.*, *v.i.* to bid *or* bet (against).
envidia, *n.f.* envy.
envidiable, *a.* enviable.
envidiar, *v.t.* to envy.
envidioso, -sa, *a.* envious.
envigar [B], *v.t.* to put (the) beams in.
envilecedor, -ra, *a.* debasing, degrading.
envilecer [9], *v.t.* to debase, degrade.
envilecimiento, *n.m.* debasement, degradation.
envinado, -da, *a.* tasting of wine; wine-coloured.
envinagrar, *v.t.* to put vinegar into.
envinar, *v.t.* to mix wine with.
envío, *n.m.* (*com.*) sending, remittance; consignment, shipment.
envión, *n.m.* push, shove.
envirotado, -da, *a.* full of airs, stuck-up.
enviscamiento, *n.m.* daubing with bird-lime.
enviscar [A], *v.t.* to daub with bird-lime; to incite, urge on; to irritate, anger. — **enviscarse,** *v.r.* to become stuck with bird-lime.
envite, *n.m.* stake, bid, bet; invitation, offer; push, shove; ***al primer envite,*** at the start, right off.
enviudar, *v.i.* to become a widower *or* widow.
envoltorio, *n.m.* bundle; parcel.
envoltura, *n.f.* covering, wrapper; envelope; (*pl.*) swaddling-clothes.
envolvedero, envolvedor, *n.m.* wrapper, envelope, cover, wrapping.
envolvente, *a.* enveloping; (*mil.*) outflanking, surrounding.
envolver [5, *p.p.* **envuelto**], *v.t.* to cover, envelop, wrap, wrap up *or* round, bundle (up); to make up into a parcel, bundle *or* packet; to swaddle, muffle; to wind (*thread*); to hem in; to involve; to contain, imply; (*mil.*) to outflank, surround. — **envolverse,** *v.r.* to become involved; to wrap o.s. up.
envolvimiento, *n.m.* envelopment; wrapping; winding; (*mil.*) envelopment.
envuelto, *n.m.* (*Mex.*) maize omelette. — *p.p.* [ENVOLVER].
enyerbarse, *v.r.* (*Hisp. Am.*) to become overgrown with grass; (*Mex.*) to get poisoned.
enyesado, *n.m.* plaster-work.
enyesadura, *n.f.* plastering (*of wine*); plaster-work; (*med.*) putting a plaster cast on.
enyesar, *v.t.* to plaster; to add gypsum to; to put a plaster cast on.
enyugar, *v.t.* to yoke.
enzainarse, *v.r.* to start looking sideways; (*coll.*) to turn treacherous.
enzamarrado, -da, *a.* wearing a sheepskin.
enzarzada, *n.f.* (*obs.*, *mil.*) strong entrenchment camouflaged with thorn-bushes.
enzarzar [C], *v.t.* to cover with brambles; to sow discord among, set at odds. — **enzarzarse,** *v.r.* to get entangled in brambles; to engage (*in thorny business*); to get involved (*in a dispute*); to squabble, wrangle.
enzima, *n.f.* (*biochem.*) enzyme.
enzootia, *n.f.* enzootic.
enzunchar, *v.t.* to bind with iron bands.
enzurdecer(se) [9], *v.i.* (*v.r.*) (*fam.*) to become left-handed.
enzurronar, *v.t.* to bag; (*coll.*) to enclose.
eñe, *n.f.* letter Ñ.
eoceno, -na, *a.*, *n.m.f.* eocene.
eón, *n.m.* aeon.
¡epa! *interj.* (*Hond.*, *Mex.*, *Ven.*) hello!; (*naut.*) ahoy! (*Chi.*) hoy!
epactilla, *n.f.* ecclesiastical (devotional) calendar.
eperlano, *n.m.* (*ichth.*) smelt.
épica, *n.f.* [ÉPICO].
epicarpio, *n.m.* (*bot.*) epicarp.
epicedio, *n.m.* epicedium, elegy.
epiceno, -na, *a.* epicene.
epicentro, *n.m.* epicentre.
epicíclico, -ca, *a.* (*astron.*) epicyclic.

epiciclo, *n.m.* (*astron.*) epicycle.
epicicloide, *n.f.* (*geom.*) epicycloid.
épico, -ca, *a.* epic, heroic. — *n.f.* epic (poetry).
epicráneo, *n.m.* epicranium.
epicureísmo, *n.m.* epicureanism.
epicúreo, -rea, *a.* epicurean.
epidemia, *n.f.* epidemic.
epidemial, epidémico, -ca, *a.* epidemical, epidemic.
epidérmico, -ca, *a.* epidermic.
epidermis, *n.f.* epidermis, scarf-skin, cuticle; ***tener la epidermis fina*** or ***sensible,*** to be very touchy, thin-skinned.
epidota, *n.f.* (*min.*) epidote.
epifanía, *n.f.* Epiphany; Twelfth Night.
epífisis, *n.f.* (*anat.*) epiphysis.
epifito, -ta, *a.* (*bot.*) epiphytic. — *n.f.* epiphyte.
epigástrico, -ca, *a.* epigastric.
epigastrio, *n.m.* epigastrium.
epiglotis, *n.f. inv.* epiglottis.
epígrafe, *n.m.* epigraph; title, heading; inscription; motto.
epigrafía, *n.f.* epigraphy.
epigráfico, -ca, *a.* epigraphic.
epigrafista, *n.m.f.* epigrapher.
epigrama, *n.m.* epigram.
epigramatario, -ria, *a.* epigrammatic. — *n.m.f.* epigrammatist.
epigramático, -ca, *a.* epigrammatic.
epigramatista, epigramista, *n.m.* epigrammatist.
epilepsia, *n.f.* epilepsy.
epiléptico, -ca, *a.* epileptic. — *n.m.f.* epileptic.
epilogación, *n.f.* [EPÍLOGO].
epilogal, *a.* epilogic, compendious.
epilogar [B], *v.t.* to recapitulate, sum up.
epilogismo, *n.m.* (*astron.*) epilogism, cumputation.
epílogo, *n.m.* epilogue, summing up; recapitulation.
epinicio, *n.m.* epinicion.
epiplon, *n.m.* (*anat.*) omentum.
epiqueya, *n.f.* equitable interpretation of the law.
episcopado, *n.m.* bishopric, episcopate; episcopacy.
episcopal, *a.* episcopal.
episcopalismo, *n.m.* episcopalism; episcopalianism.
episcopologio, *n.m.* chronological list of bishops.
episódico, -ca, *a.* episodic.
episodio, *n.m.* episode.
epispástico, -ca, *a.* epispastic.
epistaxis, *n.f.* (*med.*) epistaxis.
epístola, *n.f.* Epistle; epistle.
epistolar, *a.* epistolary.
epistolario, *n.m.* epistolary; collection of letters.
epistolero, *n.m.* epistler.
epístrofe, *n.f.* epistrophe.
epitafio, *n.m.* epitaph.
epitalámico, -ca, *a.* epithalamic.
epitalamio, *n.m.* epithalamium.
epítema, *n.f.* (*med.*) epithem.
epíteto, *n.m.* (*gram.*) epithet.
epitimar, *v.t.* (*med.*) to apply an epithem to.
epítimo, *n.m.* (*bot.*) lesser dodder.
epitomadamente, *adv.* concisely.
epitomador, -ra, *a.* epitomizing. — *n.m.f.* epitomizer.
epitomar, *v.t.* to epitomize, summarize.
epítome, *n.m.* epitome, summary.
epizoario, -ria, *a.* (*zool.*) epizoic, epizoan.
epizootia, *n.f.* (*vet.*) epidemic influenza.
epizoótico, -ca, *a.* epizootic.
época, *n.f.* epoch, age, era; time; ***hacer época,*** to be epoch-making.
epodo, -da, *n.m.f.* epode.
epónimo, -ma, *a.* eponymous. — *n.m.* eponym.
epopeya, *n.f.* epic.
epsomita, *n.f.* Epsom salts.
epulón, *n.m.* great eater.
equiángulo, -la, *a.* equiangular.
equidad, *n.f.* equity, equitableness; reasonableness.
equidiferencia, *n.f.* equidifference; arithmetical progression.
equidistancia, *n.f.* equidistance.
equidistante, *a.* equidistant.
equidistar, *v.i.* to be equidistant.
equidna, *n.m.* echidna.
équido, *n.m.* (*zool.*) equid.
equilátero, -ra, *a.* equilateral.
equilibrar, *v.t.* to balance, equilibrate; to counterpoise, counterbalance.
equilibre, *a.* balanced.
equilibrio, *n.m.* balance, equilibrium, equipoise; counterbalance, counterpoise.
equilibrista, *n.m.* tight-rope walker.
equimosis, *n.m.* (*med.*) ecchymosis.
equino, -na, *a.* (*poet.*) equine. — *n.m.* (*zool., arch.*) echinus.
equinoccial, *a.* equinoctial.
equinoccio, *n.m.* equinox.
equinodermo, -ma, *a., n.m.f.* (*zool.*) echinoderm.
equipaje, *n.m.* luggage, baggage; equipment; (*naut.*) crew; (*mil.*) baggage-train.
equipal, *n.f.* (*Mex.*) wicker chair.
equipar, *v.t.* to equip, fit out.
equiparable, *a.* comparable, collatable.
equiparación, *n.f.* comparison, collation.
equiparar, *v.t.* to compare, collate.
equipo, *n.m.* equipment, fitting out; outfit; crew, gang; team; ***equipo de novia,*** trousseau.
equipolencia, *n.f.* (*log.*) equipollence.
equipolente, *a.* equivalent, equipollent.
equiponderante, *a.* equiponderant.
equiponderar, *v.i.* to equiponderate (*statics*).
equis, *a.* certain (*amount*). — *n.f.* letter X; (*Col., Per.*) small viper; (*coll.*) ***estar hecho una equis,*** to be too drunk to walk straight.
equitación, *n.f.* horsemanship, riding.
equitativamente, *adv.* equitably.
equitativo, -va, *a.* equitable, fair.
equivalencia, *n.f.* equivalence; compensation.
equivalente, *a.* equivalent; compensatory, compensative.
equivaler [35], *v.i.* to be equivalent; to be equal, tantamount.
equivocación, *n.f.* mistake, error.
equivocado, -da, *a.* mistaken, wrong.
equivocar [A], *v.t.* to mistake, get wrong. — **equivocarse,** *v.r.* to be mistaken *or* wrong, go wrong, get it wrong; ***se equivocó de camino,*** he went the wrong way; ***te has equivocado,*** you've made a mistake.
equívoco, -ca, *a.* equivocal; ambiguous; dubious, doubtful; suggestive. — *n.m.* equivocation; ambiguity, double meaning; quid pro quo; misunderstanding.
equivoquista, *n.m.f.* equivocator, quibbler.
era (1), *n.f.* era, age; threshing-floor; vegetable patch, garden-plot; ***era común, cristiana, vulgar*** or ***de Cristo,*** Christian era; ***era española,*** Cæsarian era beginning 38 B.C.
era (2), *imperf. indic.* [SER].
eraje, *n.m.* (*prov.*) virgin honey.
eral, *n.m.* young bull (*under two years old*).
erar, *v.t.* to lay out (*a vegetable garden*).
erario, *n.m.* exchequer, public treasury.
erasmiano, -na, *a., n.m.f.* Erasmian.
erbio, *n.m.* (*chem.*) erbium.
ere, *n.f.* letter R.
erección, *n.f.* erectness, elevation; erection, raising; foundation, establishment.

eréctil, *a.* erectile.
erecto, -ta, *a.* erect, upright.
erector, -ra, *a.* erecting. — *n.m.f.* erector; founder.
eremita, *n.m.* hermit; recluse.
eremítico, -ca, *a.* solitary.
eremitorio, *n.m.* place with one *or* more hermitages.
erg, ergio, *n.m.* erg.
ergástula, *n.f.*, **ergástulo,** *n.m.* slave prison.
ergo, *adv.* therefore, so.
ergotina, *n.f.* (*med.*) ergotine.
ergotismo, *n.m.* (*med.*) ergotism; (*phil.*) sophistry.
ergotista, *a.* debating, arguing. — *n.m.f.* sophist.
ergotizar [C], *v.i.* to argue; to make excessive use of syllogistic argument.
erguido, -da, *a.* straight, upright.
erguimiento, *n.m.* straightening up; erectness.
erguir [8 *or* 3, *in which case the initial* **i** *becomes* **y**], *v.t.* to raise up straight, erect, lift up. — **erguirse,** *v.r.* to draw o.s. up, straighten up, stand *or* sit up straight; to stand, rise; to become arrogant.
erial, eriazo, -za, *a.* unploughed, untilled. — *n.m.* uncultivated land; barren *or* waste land; desert.
erica, *n.f.* heather.
erigir [E], *v.t.* to erect, raise, build; to found, establish; to raise in status; ***erigirse en,*** to set o.s. up as.
erina, *n.f.* (*surg.*) clip (*for holding wound open*).
eringe, *n.f.* field eringo, sea-holly.
erinita, *n.f.* (*min.*) erinite.
erío, -ría, *a.* unploughed. — *n.m.* untilled land.
erisipela, *n.f.* (*path.*) erysipelas.
erístico, -ca, *a.* eristic.
Eritrea, *n.f.* Eritrea.
eritreo, -rea, *a.*, *n.m.f.* Eritrean; ***el*** (***mar***) ***Eritreo,*** the Red Sea.
erizado, -da, *a.* covered with bristles; ***erizado de,*** bristling with.
erizamiento, *n.m.* setting on end; bristling up.
erizar [C], *v.t.* to set on end, bristle. — **erizarse,** *v.r.* to bristle, stand on end.
erizo, *n.m.* (*zool.*) hedgehog; (*bot.*) sea-thistle; prickly husk (*of a chestnut etc.*); (*mech.*) urchin, carding roller; sprocket-wheel, rag-wheel, spur-toothed wheel; (*fort.*) iron spikes set on top of a parapet; (*fig.*) prickly, brusque person; ***erizo de mar*** or ***marino,*** sea-urchin.
erizón, *n.m.* thistle.
ermita, *n.f.* hermitage.
ermitaño, -ña, *n.m.f.* hermit; recluse.
ermitorio [EREMITORIO].
ermunio, *n.m.* (*obs.*) one exempt from tribute and services.
erogación, *n.f.* distribution, division.
erogar [B], *v.t.* to divide, distribute, apportion.
erogatorio, *n.m.* pipe for drawing out liquor.
erosión, *n.f.* erosion, wearing away.
erosionar, *v.t.* to erode, wear away.
erotema, *n.f.* (*rhet.*) interrogation.
erotico, -ca, *a.* erotic. — *n.f.* erotic poetry; eroticism; ***erótica del poder,*** erotic aspect(s) of power, erotic element in (the struggle for) power, power-lust.
erotismo, *n.m.* eroticism.
erotizar [C], *v.t.* to put an erotic element into, give an erotic tinge *or* twist to, make erotic.
erotomanía, *n.f.* erotomania.
erotomaníaco, -ca, *a.*, *n.m.f.* erotomaniac.
errabundo, -da, *a.* wandering; (*fig.*) aimless.
errada, *n.f.* [ERRADO].
erradicación, *n.f.* eradication, extirpation.
erradicar [C], *v.t.* to eradicate, root out.
erradizo, -za, *a.* wandering.
errado, -da, *a.* erring, mistaken; erroneous. — *n.f.* miscue (*in billiards*).
erraj, *n.m.* fuel made from the stones of olives.
errante, *a.* errant; roving, rambling, wandering.
errar [I, *initial* **i** *becomes* **y**], *v.t.* to miss (*target etc.*); to get wrong, mistake; ***errar el camino,*** to take the wrong road, miss one's way. — *v.i.* to wander, roam; to err; ***errar y porfiar,*** to persist in error.
errata, *n.f.* misprint, erratum; ***erratas*** or ***fe de erratas,*** (list *or* table of) errata.
errático, -ca, *a.* wandering; erratic.
errátil, *a.* wavering, erratic.
erre, *n.f.* letter RR; ***erre que erre,*** obstinately, stubbornly.
erróneo, -nea, *a.* erroneous, wrong.
erronía, *n.f.* opposition, dislike, grudge, hatred.
error, *n.m.* error, mistake; ***error craso,*** gross error; ***error de bulto,*** major error.
erso, -sa, *a.* Erse.
erubescencia, *n.f.* erubescence, blush.
eructar, *v.i.* to belch, eructate.
eructo, *n.m.* belch(ing), eructation.
erudición, *n.f.* erudition, learning, scholarship.
erudito, -ta, *a.* erudite, learned, scholarly. — *n.m.f.* scholar; ***erudito a la violeta,*** one having only superficial learning.
eruginoso, -sa, *a.* rusty.
erupción, *n.f.* eruption.
eruptivo, -va, *a.* eruptive.
ervato [SERVATO].
ervilla [ARVEJA].
esa, *a.f.* that; **ésa,** *dem. pron. f.* [ÉSE] that one; ***ésa es buena,*** that's a good one; ***no me vengas con ésa,*** don't give me that stuff; ***ni por ésas,*** not even then, not even like that; ***¡con que ésas tenemos!*** so that's the little game!
esaborío, -ría [DESABORIDO].
esbatimentar, *v.t.* (*art.*) to shade; to shadow.
esbatimento, *n.m.* (*art*) shadow.
esbeltez, esbelteza, *n.f.* slenderness, slimness.
esbelto, -ta, *a.* slender, slim, svelte.
esbirro, *n.m.* bailiff, constable; minion; myrmidon.
esbozar [C], *v.t.* to sketch; to outline, map out.
esbozo, *n.m.* sketch; outline; rough draft.
escabechar, *v.t.* to pickle, souse; (*fig.*) to dye (*hair*); (*coll.*) to do in, bump off; (*coll.*) to plough (*in an examination*).
escabeche, *n.m.* souse, pickle; pickled fish; pickled tunny; ***en escabeche,*** pickled.
escabechina, *n.f.* ravage, havoc; massacre, slaughter; (*coll.*) ploughing (*in an examination*).
escabel, *n.m.* foot-stool; low seat; (*fig.*) stepping-stone.
escabiosa (1), *n.f.* field scabious.
escabioso, -sa (2), *a.* (*med.*) scabious.
escabro, *n.m.* mange; scaly bark.
escabrosidad, *n.f.* unevenness, roughness, broken nature; asperity; scabrousness; bawdiness.
escabroso, -sa, *a.* uneven, rough, rugged, broken; tricky, awkward; scabrous; risqué, bawdy.
escabullimiento, *n.m.* slipping *or* sneaking away *or* out.
escabullirse [J], *v.r.* to slip *or* sneak away *or* out.
escacado, -da, *a.* (*her.*) checkered.
escacharrar, escachiflar, escachifollar, *v.t.* to smash up, wreck, ruin.
escafandra, *n.f.* diving helmet *or* suit; space helmet *or* suit.
escafandro, *n.m.* [ESCAFANDRA].
escafilar, *v.t.* to trim (*a brick* or *tile*).
escafoides, *a.*, *n.m.* scaphoid (*bone*).
escala, *n.f.* step-ladder, ladder; scale; army list; port of call; ***escala de cuerda*** or ***de viento,*** rope-ladder; ***en gran escala,*** on a large scale; ***escala franca,*** free port; ***hacer escala en,*** to call at, put in at, touch at.

escalada, *n.f.* (*mil.*) escalade, scaling, climbing; (*pol.*) escalation.
escalador, -ra, *a.* scaling, climbing. — *n.m.f.* scaler, climber; (*sl.*) cat burglar.
escalafon, *n.m.* (army) list, list; wage scale.
escalamera, *n.m.* rowlock, (*Am.*) oarlock.
escalamiento, *n.m.* scaling, climbing.
escálamo, *n.m.* thole, thole-pin; rowlock, (*Am.*) oarlock.
escalar, *v.t.* to climb, scale; to break into; to open (*the sluice of a ditch*). — *v.i.* (*fig.*) to climb the social ladder.
Escalda, *n.f.* Scheldt.
escaldado, -da, *a.* suspicious, cautious, wary. — *n.f.* (*coll.*) loose woman.
escaldadura, *n.f.* scald.
escaldar, *v.t.* to scald; to make red-hot; to chafe; ***gato escaldado del agua fría huye,*** once bitten, twice shy.
escaleno, *a.* (*geom.*) scalene.
escalentamiento, *n.m.* (*vet.*) inflammation (*of the feet*).
escalentar [I], *v.t.* (*obs.*) to heat, warm; to inflame.
escalera, *n.f.* staircase; stair; ladder; (*cards*) sequence, straight; ***escalera de caracol,*** winding stair; ***escalera de mano,*** ladder; (*naut.*) ***escalera de costado*** or ***escalera real,*** quarter-deck ladder; (*cards*) ***escalera de color*** or ***real,*** flush, straight; ***escalera falsa,*** back stairs; ***escalera mecánica,*** escalator; ***escalera de tijera*** or ***escalera doble,*** step-ladder; (*fig.*) ***de escalera abajo,*** below-stairs.
escalerilla, *n.f.* short ladder; (*mech.*) pinion rack; gangway; ***en escalerilla,*** in degrees.
escaleta, *n.f.* jack (*vehicles*).
escalfador, *n.m.* barber's water-heater; chafing-dish; paint remover (*tool*).
escalfar, *v.t.* to poach (*eggs*).
escalfarote, *n.m.* wide boot lined with wool.
escalfeta, *n.f.* small pan (*for live coals*); chafing-dish; dish-heater.
escalinata, *n.f.* (*arch.*) perron, flight of steps.
escalio, *n.m.* waste land being put in cultivation.
escalmo, *n.m.* rowlock, (*Am.*) oarlock.
escalo, *n.m.* breaking a way in *or* out; breaking and entry.
escalofriante, *a.* chilling; (*fig.*) spine-chilling, blood-curdling.
escalofriar [L], *v.t.* to cause to shake, shiver, shudder.
escalofrío, *n.m.* shiver(ing), shudder(ing); chill.
escalón, *n.m.* step (*of stair*); stepping-stone; rung (*of ladder*); degree, level, grade; (*mil.*) echelon; ***en escalones,*** unevenly made *or* cut.
escalonadamente, *adv.* in staggered progression.
escalonar, *v.t.* to place at intervals, space out; (*mil.*) to echelon; to terrace.
escaloña, *n.f.* shallot, scallion.
escalope, *n.m.* escalope.
escalpar, *v.t.* to scalp.
escalpelo, *n.m.* scalpel.
escalplo, *n.m.* tanner's knife.
escama, *n.f.* scale; fish-scale; flake; (*coll.*) distrust, suspicion.
escamado, -da, *a.* scaled, scaly; (*coll.*) wary. — *n.m.* work wrought with the figure of scales. — *n.f.* embroidery in shape of scales.
escamadura, *n.f.* scaling (*a fish*); (*coll.*) arousing suspicion; embroidery in shape of scales.
escamar, *v.t.* to scale (*fish*); (*coll.*) to arouse distrust *or* suspicion in; to adorn with scales; ***está muy escamado,*** he has become very wary. — **escamarse,** *v.r.* (*coll.*) to begin to smell a rat.
escamochear, *v.i.* (*prov.*) to breed (*bees*).
escamocho, *n.m.* remnants of a meal, left-overs; after-swarm of bees.
escamón, -mona, *a* (*coll.*) very distrustful *or* suspicious.
escamonda, *n.f.* pruning.
escamondadura, *n.f.* pruned branches.
escamondar, *v.t.* to prune (*trees*); to trim.
escamondo, *n.m.* pruning.
escamonea, *n.f.* (*bot.*) scammony.
escamoneado, -da, *a.* relating to scammony.
escamonearse, *v.r.* (*coll.*) to become mistrustful, suspicious.
escamoso, -sa, *a.* scaly, squamous.
escamoteador, -ra, *n.m.f.* sleight-of-hand artist; (*fig.*) sleight-of-hand merchant; diddler.
escamotear, *v.t.* to make disappear by sleight of hand; to whisk *or* spirit away *or* out of sight; to diddle out of.
escamoteo, *n.m.* sleight of hand; diddling.
escampado, -da, *a.* open, clear. — *n.f.* (*coll.*) bright interval, clear spell.
escampar, *v.t.* to clear out (*a place*). — *v.i.* to stop raining; to clear up; to leave off working; (*coll., iron.*) ***¡ya escampa!*** there's a storm brewing!
escampavía, *n.f.* (*naut.*) scout boat; coast-guard cutter.
escampo, *n.m.* clearing out; clearing up.
escamudo, -da, *a.* scaly.
escamujar, *v.t.* to prune.
escamujo, *n.m.* lopped-off olive branch; time of pruning olive trees.
escancia, *n.f.* pouring *or* serving (*wine*).
escanciador, -ra, *a.* pouring, serving (*wine*). — *n.m.f.* cup-bearer.
escanciar, *v.t.* to pour out, serve (*wine*). — *v.i.* to drink wine.
escanda, *n.f.* spelt-wheat.
escandalar, *n.m.* (*naut.*) compass-room (*in a galley*).
escandalera, *n.f.* (*coll.*) racket, uproar; (*fig.*) stink, row, rumpus, hell of a to-do.
escandalizador, -ra, *a.* scandalizing. — *n.m.f.* scandalizer; one who makes a racket.
escandalizar [C], *v.t.* to scandalize, shock. — *v.i.* to kick up a racket *or* din. — **escandalizarse,** *v.r.* to be shocked.
escándalo, *n.m.* scandal, disgrace; din, racket, row; ***dar escándalo,*** to give cause for scandal; ***dar un*** or ***el escándalo,*** to kick up a rumpus, make a scene; ***armar (un) escándalo,*** to kick up a rumpus, make a din; ***armar un escándalo a,*** to give a good ticking-off to.
escandaloso, -sa, *a.* scandalous, disgraceful; noisy, boisterous. — *n.f.* gaff-sail; (*coll.*) ***echar la escandalosa,*** to swear away.
escandallar, *v.t.* (*naut.*) to sound; to sample.
escandallo, *n.m.* (*naut.*) deep-sea lead; sampling; cost accounting; price tag.
escandecer, *v.t.* to irritate, provoke.
escandelar, escandelarete, *n.m.* (*naut.*) compass-room (*in a galley*).
escandia, *n.f.* Cienfuegos wheat.
Escandinavia, *n.f.* Scandinavia.
escandinavo, -va, *a., n.m.f.* Scandinavian.
escandio, *n.m.* (*chem.*) scandium.
escandir, *v.t.* to scan (*verses*).
escanilla, *n.f.* (*prov.*) cradle.
escansión, *n.f.* scansion.
escantillar, *v.t.* (*arch.*) to measure from a point; to gauge; to cut out by templets; to trace lines on.
escantillón, *n.m.* gauge, templet, pattern, rule.
escaña, *n.f.* spelt-wheat.
escañero, *n.m.* seat-keeper.
escaño, *n.m.* bench with a back; seat (*in Parliament*).
escañuelo, *n.m.* foot-stool.
escapada, *n.f.* escape, flight; ***en una escapada,*** in a jiffy; ***hacer una escapada,*** to take a quick trip, pay a rapid visit.

escapar, *v.t.* to drive hard; to free. — **escapar(se),** *v.i.* (*v.r.*) to escape, get away, run away; to leak out; ***escapó a la muerte,*** he escaped death; ***escapar con vida,*** to get away alive; ***se le escapó una palabrota,*** he let slip a coarse expression; ***no se le escapa nada,*** he doesn't miss anything; ***salimos de allí escapados,*** we rushed out *or* off.
escaparate, *n.m.* glass-case; shop-window.
escaparatista, *n.m.f.* window-dresser.
escapatoria, *n.f.* escape, flight, fleeing; (*coll., fig.*) way out.
escape, *n.m.* escape, get away; leak, leakage; way out; subterfuge; escapement (*of a watch*); (*mech., engin.*) exhaust; ***a (todo) escape,*** at full speed, hell for leather.
escapo, *n.m.* (*arch.*) shaft (*of a column*); (*bot.*) stem.
escápula, *n.f.* (*anat.*) scapula, shoulder-blade.
escapular, *a.* (*anat.*) appertaining to the shoulder-blade. — *v.t.* (*naut.*) to round (*a cape*), to clear (*a sand-bank*).
escapulario, *n.m.* scapulary.
escaque, *n.m.* square (*of chessboard*); (*her.*) quartering (*of a coat of arms*); (*pl.*) game of chess.
escaqueado, -da, *a.* checkered, of alternate colours.
escara, *n.f.* (*surg.*) scab, scar, scurf, slough.
escarabajear, *v.t.* (*coll.*) to gnaw, worry. — *v.i.* to crawl around; to scribble, scrawl.
escarabajo, *n.m.* beetle; scarab; (*fig.*) flaw (*in a cast*); (*pl.*) scrawl, scribble.
escarabajuelo, *n.m.* vine-beetle.
escarabídeo, -dea, *a., n.m.f.* scarabæid.
escaramucear, *v.i.* to skirmish.
escaramujo, *n.m.* dog-rose; hip; goose-barnacle.
escaramuza, *n.f.* skirmish; (*fig.*) brush.
escaramuzador, -ra, *n.m.f.* skirmisher.
escaramuzar [C], *v.i.* to skirmish.
escarapela, *n.f.* cockade; rosette; wrangle.
escarapelar(se), *v.i.* (*v.r.*) to wrangle, dispute, quarrel (*women*); (*Col., C.R., Ven.*) to peel, shell, husk; (*Col.*) to rumple; (*Mex., Per.*) to get goose-flesh.
escarbadero, *n.m.* scraping *or* scratching place (*animals*).
escarbadientes, *n.m. inv.* tooth-pick.
escarbador, -ra, *a.* scraping, scratching. — *n.m.* scraper, scratcher.
escarbadura, *n.f.* scraping, scratching.
escarbaorejas, *n.m. inv.* ear-pick.
escarbar, *v.t.* to scrape (at), scratch (at); to pick (at), clean out; to poke, pry (into).
escarbo, *n.m.* scraping, scratching.
escarcela, *n.f.* game-bag; large pouch; cuisse; head-dress (*for women*).
escarceo, *n.m.* choppiness (*sea*); (*pl.*) prancing, cavorting; playing *or* fooling around.
escarcina, *n.f.* cutlass.
escarcha, *n.f.* hoar-frost, white frost, rime.
escarchado, -da, *a.* frosted, chilled. — *n.m.* gold *or* silver embroidery; (cake) icing; ***frutas escarchadas,*** glacé *or* crystallized fruit. — *n.f.* ice-plant.
escarchador, *n.m.* instrument for icing cake.
escarchar, *v.t.* to ice (*cakes*); to crystallize; to dilute (*potter's clay*). — *v.i.* to freeze; to frost.
escarcho, *n.m.* red gurnard.
escarchosa, *n.f.* [ESCARCHADO].
escarda, *n.f.* weed-hook, grubbing-hoe; weeding.
escardadera, *n.f.* woman weeder; hoe.
escardador, -ra, *a.* weeding. — *n.m.f.* weeder. — *n.m.* weeding-hook.
escardadura, *n.f.*, **escardamiento,** *n.m.* weeding.
escardar, escardillar, *v.t.* to weed; (*fig.*) to weed out.
escardillo, *n.m.* (*prov.*) small weed-hook; hoe; thistle-down; flickering light.
escariador, *n.m.* reamer; punch (*used by coppersmiths*).
escariar, *v.t.* to ream.
escarificación, *n.f.* (*surg.*) scarification.
escarificador, *n.m.* (*agric.*) scarifier, harrow, cultivator; (*surg.*) scarificator.
escarificar [A], *v.t.* (*surg., agric.*) to scarify.
escarioso, -sa, *a.* (*bot.*) scarious.
escarizar [C], *v.t.* to clean (*a sore*) by taking away the scurf *or* scab.
escarlador, *n.m.* tool for polishing combs.
escarlata, *n.f.* scarlet; cloth of scarlet colour; (*med.*) scarlet fever.
escarlatina, *n.f.* (*com.*) crimson woollen fabric; (*med.*) scarlet fever.
escarmenador, *n.m.* comb (*for wool etc.*).
escarmenar, *v.t.* to comb (*wool, silk etc.*); to disentangle; to swindle.
escarmentar [I], *v.t.* to teach a lesson to. — *v.i.* to learn a *or* one's lesson; ***escarmentar en cabeza ajena,*** to learn from the experience of another *or* others.
escarmiento, *n.m.* lesson; warning; punishment; ***que esto te sirva de escarmiento,*** let this be a lesson to you.
escarnecedor, -ra, *a,* scoffing, mocking. — *n.m.f.* scoffer, jeerer, mocker, giber.
escarnecer [9], *v.t.* to mock, jeer, scoff, gibe (at).
escarnecimiento, *n.m.* scoffing, derision, mocking, jeering.
escarnio, *n.m.* gibe(ing), mock(ing), jeer(ing).
escaro (1), *n.m.* scarus fish.
escaro (2), **-ra,** *a.* having crooked feet. — *n.m.f.* person with crooked feet.
escarola, *n.f.* ruff, frill; curly-leafed lettuce, cos lettuce.
escarolar, *v.t.* to frill, ruffle.
escarótico, -ca, *a.* (*surg.*) caustic.
escarpa, *n.f.* scarp; steep slope; (*fort.*) escarp.
escarpado, -da, *a.* steep, precipitous.
escarpadura, *n.f.* escarpment; cliff; steep slope.
escarpar, *v.t.* to scarp, escarp; to rasp; to scarf.
escarpe, *n.m.* [ESCARPADURA]; solleret (*armour*).
escarpelo, *n.m.* rasp; scalpel.
escarpia, *n.f.* tenter-hook, meat-hook; spike, *clamp*; (*pl.*) (*sl.*) ears.
escarpiador, *n.m.* clamp, fastener.
escarpiar, *v.t.* (*obs.*) to fasten with clamps.
escarpidor, *n.m.* large-toothed comb.
escarpín, *n.m.* woollen slipper; dancing pump; thin-soled shoe; sock.
escarpión, *adv.* ***en escarpión,*** in the form of a tenter-hook.
escarramanchones, *adv.* (*coll., prov.*) ***a escarramanchones,*** astride.
escarrancharse, *v.r.* (*Cub., Ven., prov.*) to spread the legs wide apart.
escarza, *n.f.* hoof sore (*horses*).
escarzano, -na, *a.* (*arch.*) ***arco escarzano,*** arch less than a semicircle.
escarzar [C], *v.t.* to remove poor *or* dirty honey-combs from (*a hive*).
escarzo (1), *n.m.* operation and time of removing honey from a hive; black comb without honey; floss silk; (*prov.*) fungus growing on trees.
escarzo (2), **-za,** *a.* (*prov.*) lame.
escasear, *v.t.* to spare; to give sparingly. — *v.i.* to to be *or* become scarce, be few and far between.
escasero, -ra, *a.* (*coll.*) sparing, stingy.
escasez, *n.f.* scarcity, shortness; want, need; stinginess.
escaso, -sa, *a.* scanty, small, limited; scarce; bare; short; (*coll.*) stingy; ***dos kilómetros escasos,*** a bare two kilometres; ***andar escaso de,*** to be short of.

escatimar, *v.t.* to stint, curtail, give sparingly.
escatimoso, -sa, *a.* sly, cunning; mean, (*coll.*) stingy.
escatófago, -ga, *a.* scatophagous.
escatología (1), *n.f.* scatology.
escatología (2), *n.f.* eschatology.
escatológico, -ca (1), *a.* scatological.
escatológico, -ca (2), *a.* eschatological.
escaupil, *n.m.* (*Mex.*) padded garment (*used against arrows*); (*C.R.*) game bag.
escavanar, *v.t.* to loosen and weed (*the ground*) with a hoe.
escayola, *n.f.* stucco; scagliola; plaster; ***en escayola,*** in plaster, plastered.
escayolar, *v.t.* to plaster, set in plaster.
escayolista, *n.m.f.* plasterer, plaster setter.
escena, *n.f.* stage; scene; ***estar en escena,*** to be on the stage; ***poner en escena,*** to stage, put on.
escenario, *n.m.* stage; scene, setting.
escénico, -ca, *a.* scenic, stage.
escenificación, *n.f.* staging, production.
escenificar [A], *v.t.* to stage, produce.
escenografía, *n.f.* scenography.
escenográfico, -ca, *a.* scenographic.
escenógrafo, *n.m.* scenographer.
escepticismo, *n.m.* scepticism.
escéptico, -ca, *a., n.m.f.* sceptic, sceptical.
esciagrafía, *n.f.* skiagraphy.
esciagráfico, -ca, *a.* skiagraphic.
esciágrafo, *n.m.* skiagraph.
escila, *n.f.* (*bot.*) squill; ***entre Escila y Caribdis,*** between Scylla and Charybdis.
escinco, *n.m.* (*zool.*) skink.
esciolo, *n.m.* sciolist.
escirro, *n.m.* scirrhus.
escirroso, -sa, *a.* scirrhous.
escisión, *n.f.* scission; schism; split; fission.
escita, *a., n.m.f.,* **escítico, -ca,** *a.* Scythian.
esclarea, *n.f.* common clary.
esclarecedor, -ra, *a.* enlightening. — *n.m.f.* enlightener.
esclarecer [9], *v.t.* to light up, brighten; to clear up, clarify; to make illustrious, ennoble. — *v.i.* to dawn.
esclarecido, -da, *a.* illustrious, distinguished.
esclarecimiento, *n.m.* enlightening; clearing up, clarifying; clarification; illustriousness.
esclava, *n.f.* [ESCLAVO].
esclavina, *n.f.* cape; pilgrim's cloak; tippet; pelerine.
esclavista, *a.* pro-slavery. — *n.m.f.* supporter of slavery.
esclavitud, *n.f.* slavery, bondage, servitude; brotherhood.
esclavizar [C], *v.t.* to enslave.
esclavo, -va, *n.m.f.* slave; member of a brotherhood; ***ser esclavo del deber,*** to be a slave to duty. — *n.f.* slave-bracket.
esclavón, -vona, esclavonio, -nia, *a., n.m.f.* Slav, Slavonic. — *n.m.* Slavonic language. — *n.f.* (*Chi.*) member of a brotherhood.
esclerosis, *n.f. inv.* sclerosis.
esclerótica, *n.f.* sclerotic.
esclusa, *n.f.* sluice, lock, flood-gate.
escoa, *n.f.* bend (*of a ship's rib*).
escoba, *n.f.* broom; ***escoba nueva barre bien,*** new brooms sweep clean; (*bot.*) broom.
escobada, *n.f.* sweep, sweeping; ***dar una escobada,*** to give a quick sweep.
escobadera, *n.f.* woman sweeper.
escobajo, *n.m.* old broom; stalk (*of a bunch of grapes*).
escobar, *n.m.* place where broom grows. — *v.t.* to sweep with a broom.
escobazar [C], *v.t.* to sprinkle with a wet broom.
escobazo, *n.m.* stroke, swipe *or* clout with a broom; (*coll.*) ***echar a escobazos,*** to kick, chuck *or* sling out.
escobén, *n.m.* (*naut.*) hawse-hole.
escobero, -ra, *n.m.f.* maker *or* seller of brooms. — *n.f.* (*bot.*) Spanish broom.
escobilla, *n.f.* brush; whisk, small broom; (*bot.*) bur (*of the teasel*); (*bot.*) tamaric-leaved salt-wort; gold *or* silver sweepings.
escobillón, *n.m.* (*artill.*) swab, push-broom; cannon-sponge.
escobina, *n.f.* chips *or* dust made in boring.
escobo, *n.m.* dense brushwood, briers, brambles.
escobón, *n.m.* large broom; Turk's head; scrubbing-brush; swab.
escocedura, *n.f.* burning pain.
escocer [5D], *v.t., v.i.* to make smart *or* sting; to smart, sting; (*fig.*) to hurt; ***ahí te escuece,*** there's the rub.
escocés, -cesa, *a., n.m.f.* Scots, Scottish, Scotch.
Escocia, *n.f.* Scotland.
escocia, *n.f.* (*arch.*) scotia; codfish.
escocimiento, *n.m.* smarting, stinging.
escoda, *n.f.* stone-cutter's hammer.
escodadero, *n.m.* place where deer rub their horns.
escodar, *v.t.* to hew, cut (*stones*).
escofia, escofieta [COFIA].
escofina, *n.f.* rasp, file; wood-rasp; wire brush.
escofinar, *v.t.* to rasp.
escofión, *n.m.* head-dress made of net-work.
escogedor, -ra, *a.* choosing. — *n.m.f.* selector, chooser.
escoger [E], *v.t.* to choose, pick (out).
escogido, -da, *a.* chosen, choice, select; ***lo más escogido,*** the pick (of the bunch). — *n.f.* (*Cub.*) grading tobacco; (*Cub.*) place where grading takes place.
escogimiento, *n.m.* choosing.
escolanía, *n.f.* boys' choir (*in a monastery*).
escolano, *n.m.* pupil receiving free education in a monastery.
escolapio, -pia, *a.* pertaining to the Scuole Pie. — *n.m.* Piarist.
escolar, *a.* scholastic, school. — *n.m.* student, scholar.
escolaridad, *n.f.* schooling; attendance at school.
escolasticismo, *n.m.* scholasticism.
escolástico, -ca, *a.* scholastic. — *n.m.* schoolman.
escoliador, -ra, escoliasta, *n.m.f.* scholiast.
escoliar, *v.t.* to gloss.
escolimado, -da, *a.* (*coll.*) weak, delicate.
escolimoso, -sa, *a.* (*coll.*) difficult, fastidious, fussy, hard to please.
escolio, *n.m.* scholium; gloss.
escoliosis, *n.f.* (*med.*) scoliosis.
escolopendra, *n.f.* (*zool.*) scolopendra, centipede; marine worm; (*bot.*) spleenwort, common hart's-tongue.
escolta, *n.f.* escort.
escoltar, *v.t.* to escort; to convoy.
escollar, *v.i.* (*Arg., naut.*) to go aground; (*Arg., Chi.*) to fail, fall through.
escollera, *n.f.* breakwater; jetty.
escollo, *n.m.* reef, shelf of rock; snag, pitfall.
escombra, *n.f.* clearing.
escombrar, *v.t.* to clear; to clean.
escombrera, *n.f.* dump, dumping ground.
escombro, *n.m.* rubbish, waste material, debris; small raisin; (*ichth.*) mackerel; ***reducir a escombros,*** to reduce to rubble.
escomerse, *v.r.* to become worn out.
esconce, *n.m.* corner, angle.
escondecucas, *n.m. inv.* (*prov.*) hide-and-seek.
escondedero, *n.m.* hiding-place *or* lurking-place.
esconder, *v.t.* to hide, conceal; (*fig.*) to harbour. —

esconderse, *v.r.* to hide, get out of sight; ***estar*** or ***andar escondido,*** to be hidden, be lurking, be skulking.
escondidamente, *adv.* secretly, stealthily.
escondidas (a), escondidillas (a), *adv.* on the sly, stealthily.
escondidas, *n.f.pl.* (*Arg., Chi., Col., Ec.*) hide-and-seek.
escondidos, *n.m.pl.* (*Per.*) hide-and-seek.
escondimiento, *n.m.* concealment.
escondite, *n.m.* hiding-place, lurking-place; ***jugar al escondite,*** to play hide-and-seek.
escondrijo, *n.m.* hiding-place *or* lurking-place, hide-out.
escontrete, *n.m.* (*naut.*) prop, stay, shore.
esconzado, -da, *a.* angular, oblique.
escoperada, (*obs.*) **escoperadura,** *n.f.* gunwale.
escopero, *n.m.* (*naut.*) pitch-brush; swab.
escopeta, *n.f.* shotgun; ***escopeta de dos cañones,*** double-barrelled gun; ***escopetà negra,*** professional hunter; (*fig.*) ***buena escopeta,*** good shot; ***a tiro de escopeta,*** within gunshot; ***aquí te quiero (ver), escopeta,*** I'd like to see you in my shoes.
escopetar, *v.t.* to clear (*mines*); (*coll.*) to spring suddenly (on).
escopetazo, *n.m.* gunshot; gunshot wound.
escopetear, *v.t.* to shoot *or* keep shooting at. — **escopetearse,** *v.r.* to exchange compliments *or* insults.
escopeteo, *n.m.* gunfire, shooting.
escopetería, *n.f.* crowd armed with guns; repeated gunshots, shooting.
escopetero, *n.m.* musketeer, gunner; gunsmith, armourer.
escopetón, *n.m.* large fowling-piece; ***de escopetón,*** all of a sudden.
escopladura, escopleadura, *n.f.* mortise-hole.
escoplear, *v.t.* to mortise, notch.
escoplo, *n.m.* (*carp.*) chisel.
escopo, *n.m.* (*obs.*) scope, aim.
escora, *n.f.* (*naut.*) level-line; shore; list, heel; ***ángulo de escora,*** heeling angle.
escorar, *v.t.* to shore up, prop. — *v.i.* to list, heel. — **escorarse,** *v.r.* (*Cub., Hond.*) to seek shelter *or* protection from the weather.
escorbútico, -ca, *a.* scorbutic, affected by scurvy.
escorbuto, *n.m.* scurvy.
escorchapín, *n.m.* ancient type of passage-boat, ferry.
escorchar, *v.t.* to flay, skin.
escorche, *n.m.* (*obs., art*) foreshortening.
escordio, *n.m.* water germander.
escoria, *n.f.* dross, slag; (*fig.*) scum, dregs; (*pl.*) volcanic ashes.
escoriáceo, -cea, *a.* scoriaceous.
escoriación, *n.f.* crust, scurf (*on a sore*).
escorial, *n.m.* dumping-place for dross; mine-dump; slag-heap.
escoriar [EXCORIAR].
escorificación, *n.f.* (*chem.*) scorification.
escorificar [A], *v.t.* (*chem.*) to scorify; to reduce to slag.
escorodonia, *n.f.* wood sage.
escorpean, escorpina, *n.f.* (*ichth.*) grouper.
escorpioide, *n.f.* scorpion-grass.
escorpión, *n.m.* scorpion; (*ichth.*) sea-scorpion, scorpion-fish; (*astron.*) Scorpio.
escorpiónideo, -dea, *a.* scorpion-like. — **escorpiónideos,** *n.m.pl.* Scorpionidea.
escorpiuro, *n.m.* caterpillar-plant.
escorrozo, *n.m.* (*coll.*) delight.
escorzado, *n.m.* (*art*) foreshortening.
escorzar [C], *v.t.* (*art*) to foreshorten.
escorzo, *n.m.* (*art*) foreshortening; (*coll.*) forced *or* twisted figure.
escorzón, *n.m.* toad.
escorzonera, *n.f.* viper's-grass.
escota, *n.f.* stone-cutter's hammer; (*naut.*) sheet; (*arch.*) scotia; ***escotas mayores,*** main sheets; ***escotas de gavias,*** topsail sheets; ***escotas de las velas de estay,*** staysail sheets; ***escotas volantes,*** flowing-sheets; ***escotas de barlovento,*** weather-sheets.
escotado, *n.m.*, **escotadura,** *n.f.* low neck; décolletage; arm-hole (*in armour*); large trap-door (*of a stage*).
escotar (1), *v.t.* to cut to fit close; to cut low (*in the neck*).
escotar (2), *v.t.* to draw water from (*a river*) by trenching; (*obs.*) to bail water from (*ship*). — *v.i.* to pay one's share, share the cost.
escote, *n.m.* low neck, décolleté, share, scot, quota; modesty-vest, tucker; ***pagar a escote,*** to go Dutch.
escotero, -ra, *a.* free, disengaged. — *n.f.* sheet-hole.
escotilla, *n.f.* hatchway; ***escotilla mayor,*** main hatchway; ***escotilla de proa,*** fore-hatch; ***escotilla de popa,*** aft hatchway.
escotillón, *n.m.* scuttle, trap-door; stage-trap.
escotín, *n.m.* topsail sheet.
escotismo, *n.m.* Scotism.
escotista, *n.m.* Scotist.
escoznete, *n.m.* (*prov.*) nut-pick.
escozor, *n.m.* smart(ing), sting(ing), burning, soreness.
escriba, *n.m.* scribe.
escribanía, *n.f.* court clerkship; writing-desk; writing-set; portable writing-case; (ornamental) inkstand.
escribano, *n.m.* court clerk; (*obs.*) scrivener; (*obs.*) notary; (*naut.*) purser; ***escribano de cámara,*** clerk of a high court of justice; (*ent.*) ***escribano del agua,*** water-strider, whirligig beetle; ***el mejor escribano echa un borrón,*** even Homer sometimes nods.
escribido, *p.p. reg.* [ESCRIBIR], *used only in the idiom* ***leído y escribido,*** affecting learning, full of academic airs.
escribiente, *n.m.* (office) clerk.
escribir [*p.p.* **escrito**], *v.t., v.i.* to write; to spell; ***escribir a máquina,*** to type (out); ***escribir largo y tendido,*** to write at length; ***estaba escrito,*** it was written *or* fated; ***sobre eso no hay nada escrito,*** there's no rule *or* law about it; ***poner por escrito,*** to put in writing; ***voy a escribir un poco,*** I'm going to do a bit of writing. — **escribirse,** *v.r.* to have *or* hold correspondence (**con,** with), write regularly (**con,** to); ***¿cómo se escribe?*** how do you spell it?
escriño, *n.m.* straw hamper; jewel-box, casket.
escrita, *n.f.* (*ichth.*) spotted skate.
escritillas, *n.f.pl.* lamb's testicles.
escrito, *n.m.* (piece of) writing; (*law*) ***escrito (de agravios),*** writ. — *p.p.* [ESCRIBIR].
escritor, -ra, *n.m.f.* writer.
escritorcillo, -lla, *n.m.f.* petty writer, third-rate writer.
escritorio, *n.m.* writing-desk; cabinet; study; office; counting-house; ***objetos de escritorio,*** stationery.
escritorzuelo, -la, *n.m.f.* miserable writer, hack.
escritura, *n.f.* writing; Scripture; (*law.*) deed, instrument, indenture.
escriturar, *v.t.* (*law*) to bind by deed; to indenture; to engage (*as an artist*); ***estar escriturado,*** to be in articles. — **escriturarse,** *v.r.* to sign articles.
escriturario, -ria, *a.* (*law*) scriptory, scriptorian, scriptural. — *n.m.f.* scripturist.
escrófula, *n.f.* scrofula, king's evil.
escrofularia, *n.f.* figwort.
escrofuloso, -sa, *a.* scrofulous.
escrotal, *a.* scrotal.
escroto, *n.m.* scrotum.

escrupulillo, *n.m.* sneaking scruple *or* qualm; jinglet.

escrupulizar [C], *v.i.* to have scruples *or* qualms.

escrúpulo, *n.m.* scruple, qualm, doubt; (*pharm.*) scruple (20 *grains*); (*astron.*) minute (*on a graduated sphere*); ***escrúpulo de monja,*** childish scruple; ***tener escrúpulos de monja,*** to fuss about trifles.

escrupulosidad, *n.f.* scrupulosity, scrupulousness, conscientiousness; preciseness, nicety.

escrupuloso, -sa, *a.* scrupulous, conscientious; squeamish; nice, precise.

escrutador, -ra, *a.* scrutinizing, searching. — *n.m.f.* scrutinizer, searcher.

escrutar, *v.t.* to scrutinize; to count (*votes*).

escrutinio, *n.m.* scrutiny; counting (*votes*).

escrutiñador, *n.m.* [ESCUDRIÑADOR].

escuadra, *n.f.* (carpenter's) square; triangle (*for geometrical drawing*); knee, angle-iron, angle-tie; (*mil.*) squad; gang; (*naut.*) squadron, fleet; ***a escuadra,*** square; ***falsa escuadra,*** bevel; ***escuadra de agrimensor,*** surveyor's cross; ***fuera de escuadra,*** off the square, oblique; (*Cat.*) ***mozo de escuadra,*** rural policeman.

escuadración, *n.f.* squaring.

escuadrador, *n.m.* squaring-tool.

escuadrar, *v.t.* (*carp.*) to square.

escuadreo, *n.m.* squaring, quadrature (*of an area*).

escuadría, *n.f.* scantling (*of timber*); (*obs.*) square, right-angled rule *or* measure.

escuadrilla, *n.f.* flying squadron; flotilla.

escuadro, *n.m.* (*ichth.*) spotted skate.

escuadrón, *n.m.* squadron; ***escuadrón volante,*** flying column.

escuadronar, *v.t.* to form in squadrons, draw up in rank and file.

escuadronista, *n.m.* cavalry tactician.

escualidez, *n.f.* emaciation, extreme thinness.

escuálido, -da, *a.* extremely thin, emaciated.

escualo, *n.m.* spotted dogfish; shark.

escualor, *n.m.* squalor, filthiness.

escuatina, *n.f.* sea-angel.

escucha, *n.f.* scout; vedette; advanced sentinel, sentry; (*in convents*) chaperon; servant sleeping near her mistress; listening; listening-place; ***a la escucha,*** listening; on the alert; ***en escucha,*** listening out.

escuchador, -ra, *a,* hearing, listening. — *n.m.f.* listener.

escuchante, *a.* listening; hearkening.

escuchar, *v.t., v.i.* to listen (to); to hearken (to); to hear. — **escucharse,** *v.r.* to like the sound of one's own voice; to pay too much attention to o.s.

escudar, *v.t.* to shield; ***se escuda en su enfermedad,*** he makes his illness an excuse.

escuderaje, *n.m.* service of a squire, page *or* footman.

escuderear, *v.t.* to serve as a page *or* squire.

escudería, *n.f.* service of a page, squire *or* footman.

escuderil, *a.* belonging to a page, squire *or* shield-bearer.

escudero, *n.m.* page, squire, shield-bearer; shield-maker; nobleman, one of the gentry.

escuderón, *n.m.* conceited *or* pretentious person.

escudete, *n.m.* scutcheon; gusset; rain stain (*on olives*); (*bot.*) white water-lily.

escudilla, *n.f.* bowl.

escudillar, *v.t.* to pour into bowls; (*fig.*) to domineer.

escudo, *n.m.* shield; escutcheon; coat of arms; gold coin; escudo; back (*of a wild boar*); bandage (*used in bleeding*); backboard (*of a boat*); (*her.*) ***escudo vergeteado,*** arms containing ten or more quarterings.

escudriñador, -ra, *a.* prying; scrutinizing, searching. — *n.m.f.* prier; scrutinizer, searcher.

escudriñamiento, *n.m.* prying, scrutiny.

escudriñar, *v.t.* to scrutinize; to search, sweep with one's gaze; to pry into.

escuela, *n.f.* school; primary *or* elementary school; ***escuela de párvulos,*** infant school; ***escuela especial*** or ***superior,*** school (*of engineering, architecture etc.*); ***escuela normal,*** teacher training college.

escuerzo, *n.m.* (*zool.*) toad; (*coll.*) skinny individual.

escuetamente, *adv.,* baldly, in few words, in a nutshell, without frills.

escueto, -ta, *a.* bare, bald, unadorned, plain, strict.

escueznar, *v.t.* (*prov.*) to extract the kernel from (*nuts*).

escuezno, *n.m.* soft kernel (*of nut*).

escular [A], *v.t.* to spy, to watch; (*Col., C.R., Mex., P.R.*) to search, inspect.

esculpidor, -ra, *n.m.f.* engraver, carver.

esculpir [*p.p.* **esculto**], *v.t., v.i.* to carve, sculpture.

escultor, -ra, *n.m.f.* sculptor, sculptress, carver.

escultórico, -ca, *a.* sculptural, (of) sculpture.

escultura, *n.f.* sculpture.

escultural, *a.* sculptural, statuesque.

escullador, *n.m.* dipper (*for oil*).

escullirse, *v.r.* to slip out, slip away, sneak off.

escuna, *n.f.* schooner.

escupidera, *n.f.* spittoon, cuspidor; (*Arg., Chi., Ec.*) chamber-pot.

escupidero, *n.m.* spitting-place; (*fig.*) situation in which one is exposed to being insulted *or* despised.

escupido, -da, *a.* very spit of; ***Juana es escupida la madre,*** Joan is the spit of her mother. — *n.m.* spittle.

escupidor, -ra, *n.m.f.* great spitter; (*Ec., P.R.*) spittoon, cuspidor; (*Col.*) round plait *or* mat.

escupidura, *n.f.* spitting; spittle; fever sore, efflorescence.

escupir, *v.t., v.i.* to spit, spit at, spit out, spit forth; to throw out, throw off; to break out in the skin (*a rash*); ***escupir en la cara (a),*** to spit in the face (of); ***escupir doblones,*** to be rolling in money; ***escupir al cielo,*** to rail against Heaven; ***no escupir una cosa,*** not to despise sth.

escupitajo, *n.m.,* **escupitina,** *n.f.,* **escupitinajo,** *n.m.* (*coll.*) spit, spittle.

escurana, *n.f.* (*Chi., Col.*) obscurity, darkness.

escurar, *v.t.* to scour (*cloth*).

escurialense, *a.* belonging to *or* similar to the monastery of the Escorial.

escurreplatos, *n.m. inv.* dish-draining rack.

escurribanda, *n.f.* (*coll.*) flight, escape; diarrhœa; whipping, spanking.

escurridero, *n.m.* drain-pipe; drain-hole; drain-board.

escurridizo, -za, *a.* slippery; tricky.

escurrido, -da, *a.* wearing tight-fitting skirts; having narrow hips; (*Mex., P.R.*) abashed, ashamed.

escurriduras, escurrimbres, *n.f.pl.* lees, dregs; (*coll., fig.*) ***llegar a las escurriduras,*** to scrape the barrel.

escurrimiento, *n.m.* dripping; running, draining; wringing; trickling, slipping away.

escurrir, *v.t.* to wring (out); to drain. — **escurrir(se),** *v.i.* (*v.r.*) to drip, trickle; to slip (away); to sneak away; ***escurrir el bulto,*** to dodge the issue.

escusalí, *n.m.* small apron.

escutas, escutillas, *n.f.pl.* (*naut.*) scuttles.

escuteliforme, escutiforme, *a.* (*bot.*) scutiform.

escutolaria, *n.f.* (*bot.*) scutellaria.

escuyer, *n.m.* purveyor of meat to the royal palace.

esdrújulo, -la, *a.* accented on the antepenultimate syllable; ***verso esdrújulo,*** line of verse ending with such a word. — *n.m.* word accented on the antepenultimate syllable.

ese (I), *n.f.* letter S; link of a chain of the form of

this letter; ***andar haciendo eses,*** to reel *or* stagger along; to meander, zig-zag; ***ese o ese,*** S.O.S.
ese (2), **esa,** *a.* that (just over there); (*pl.* **esos, esas**) those (just over there).
ése, ésa, *dem. pron.* that one; the former; (*pl.* **ésos, ésas**) those ones; the former; [ESA].
esencia, *n.f.* essence; scent; ***quinta esencia,*** quintessence; ***en esencia,*** in essence; ***por esencia,*** essentially.
esencial, *a.* essential.
esenciarse, *v.r.* (*obs.*) to become intimately united, become essential.
esenciero, *n.m.* scent bottle.
esenio, -nia, *n.m.f.* Essene.
esfacelo, *n.m.* gangrene.
esfenoides, *n.m.* sphenoid bone.
esfera, *n.f.* sphere; orb; dial *or* face (*clocks*); (*poet.*) heaven; ***esfera armilar,*** armillary sphere; ***esfera celeste,*** celestial sphere; ***esfera terrestre,*** globe; ***esfera de actividad,*** sphere of activity; ***fuera de mi esfera,*** out of my sphere *or* province.
esferal, esférico, -ca, *a.* spherical.
esfericidad, *n.f.* sphericity.
esferista, *n.m.* (*obs.*) astronomer.
esferoidal, *a.* spheroidal.
esferoide, *n.f.* spheroid.
esferómetro, *n.m.* spherometer.
esfinge, *n.f.* sphinx. — *n.m.* hawk-moth.
esfíngido, -da, *a.* of the sphinx- *or* hawk-moth.
esfínter, *n.m.* sphincter.
esflorecer [9], *v.i.* (*chem.*) to effloresce.
esforrocinar, *v.t.* to remove the sprigs *or* shoots from (*a vine*).
esforrocino, *n.m.* sprig shooting from the trunk of a vine.
esforzado, -da, *a.* vigorous, strenuous; courageous, bold.
esforzar [4C], *v.t.* to give strength *or* courage to. — **esforzarse,** *v.r.* to strive, try hard, make vigorous efforts, exert o.s. (***por*** or ***en,*** to).
esfuerzo (1), *n.m.* effort, vigorous exertion; courage; (*engin.*) stress.
esfuerzo (2), *pres. indic.* [ESFORZAR].
esfumado, -da, *a.* (*art*) esfumato.
esfumar, *v.t.* (*art*) to stump; to tone down, blur. — **esfumarse,** *v.r.* to grow blurred; to fade away, vanish (into a haze).
esfuminar [ESFUMAR].
esfumino, *n.m.* (*art*) stump.
esgarrar, *v.t., v.i.* to clear (one's throat).
esgrafiado, *n.m.* (*art*) graffito.
esgrafiar, *v.t.* (*art*) to decorate with graffito.
esgrima, *n.f.* fencing; ***maestro de esgrima,*** fencing-master.
esgrimidor, *n.m.* fencer, fencing-master.
esgrimidura, *n.f.* fencing.
esgrimir, *v.t.* to brandish, wield. — *v.i.* to fence.
esgrimista, *n.m.f.* (*Arg., Chi., Per.*) fencer; fencing-master.
esguazable, *a.* fordable.
esguazar [C], *v.t.* to ford (*river*).
esguazo, *n.m.* fording.
esgucio, *n.m.* (*arch.*) quarter-round moulding.
esguin, *n.m.* young salmon.
esguince, *n.m.* twist, twisting; sprain, spraining; dodge, dodging; frown.
esguízaro, -ra, *a., n.m.f.* (*obs.*) Swiss; ***pobre esguízaro,*** wretch.
eslabón, *n.m.* link (*of chain*); table-steel; steel (*for striking fire with a flint*); black scorpion; hard tumour (*on horses' legs*); (*naut.*) ***eslabones de guimbalete,*** swivels.
eslabonador, *n.m.* chain-maker.
eslabonamiento, *n.m.* linking.
eslabonar, *v.t.* to link, link together.
eslavo, -va, *a., n.m.f.* Slav.
eslinga, *n.f.* (*naut.*) sling, span.
eslingar [B], *v.t.* (*naut.*) to sling up, hoist.
eslora, *n.f.* length (*of a ship*); (*pl.*) beams running from stem to stern.
eslovaco, -ca, *a., n.m.f.* Slovak, Slovakian. — *n.m.* Slovak (*language*).
esloveno, -na, *a., n.m.f.* Slovene, Slovenian. — *n.m.* Slovenian (*language*).
esmaltador, -ra, *n.m.f.* enameller.
esmaltadura, *n.f.* enamelling, enamel-work.
esmaltar, *v.t.* to enamel; (*fig.*) to sprinkle, dot; to adorn, embellish.
esmalte, *n.m.* enamel; enamel-work; smalt.
esmaltín, *n.m.* smalt.
esmerado, -da, *a.* careful, painstaking, conscientious.
esmeralda, *n.f.* emerald.
esmeraldino, -na, *a.* emerald-like.
esmerar, *v.t.* to brighten, polish. — **esmerarse,** *v.r.* — ***por, en,*** to take great pains *or* care to, do one's very best to, strive to.
esmerejón, *n.m.* (*orn.*) merlin, goshawk; (*obs.*) small cannon.
esmeril, *n.m.* emery; (*obs.*) small cannon.
esmerilar, *v.t.* to burnish, polish with emery; to make opaque.
esmero, *n.m.* painstaking care, conscientiousness, neatness.
esmirriado, -da, *a.* thin-looking, emaciated; miserable; straggly.
esmoladera, *n.f.* whetstone.
esmoquin, *n.m.* dinner jacket, (*Am.*) tuxedo.
esmuciarse, *v.r.* (*prov.*) to slip from the hands.
esnob, *a., n.m.f. inv.* snob; novelty-mad.
esnobismo, *n.m.* snobbery; novelty-madness.
esnón, *n.m.* (*naut.*) spencer-mast, try-sail mast.
eso, *dem. pron. neut.* that; ***eso es,*** that's it; ***¿no es eso?*** isn't that it? ***a eso de las cinco,*** about five o'clock; ***eso mismo,*** just so, precisely.
esófago, *n.m.* œsophagus, gullet.
esotérico, -ca, *a.* esoteric.
esotro, esotra, *a., dem. pron.* (*obs.*) this *or* that other; (*pl.* **esotros, esotras**) those others.
espabiladeras, *n.f.pl.* snuffers.
espabilar, *v.t.* to snuff (*candle*). — **espabilarse,** *v.r.* (*coll.*) to pull one's socks up, look sharp.
espaciador, *n.m.* space-bar (*typewriter*).
espaciar, *v.t.* to space, space out; (*print.*) to space, lead. — **espaciarse,** *v.r.* to spread (out); to expatiate, spread o.s.; to enjoy o.s.
espacio, *n.m.* space, room; delay, slowness; (*print.*) lead; (*obs.*) diversion, recreation, pastime; ***espacio de tiempo,*** space *or* length of time.
espaciosidad, *n.f.* spaciousness.
espacioso, -sa, *a.* spacious, roomy; deliberate, slow.
espada, *n.m.* matador; ***primer espada,*** star matador. — *n.f.* sword; swordsman; (*cards*) spade; ***espada blanca,*** sword; ***espada negra*** or ***de esgrima,*** foil; ***entrar con espada en mano,*** to go in sword in hand; to be ready for anything; to be looking for trouble; ***hombre de capa y espada,*** man of no profession; ***verse entre la espada y la pared,*** to find o.s. between the devil and the deep blue sea; ***sacar la espada por,*** to stand up for; ***es una buena espada,*** he is a good swordsman; ***media espada,*** one who is mediocre; ***asentar la espada,*** to put the point of the sword on the ground; ***ceñir espada,*** to be a soldier by profession; ***con la espada desnuda,*** ready for anything; ***quedarse a espadas,*** to be left with nothing; to be disappointed; ***salir con su media espada,*** to interrupt impertinently, butt in; ***tirar de*** (***la***) ***espada,*** to draw one's sword; ***comedia de capa y espada,*** cloak-and-dagger play; ***pez espada,*** swordfish.
espadachín, *n.m.* swashbuckling swordsman; bully.

espadadero, *n.m.* bench for braking flax *or* hemp.
espadado, -da, *a.* (*obs.*) armed with a sword.
espadador, -ra, *n.m.f.* hemp-beater.
espadaña, *n.f.* (*bot.*) reed-mace; belfry.
espadañada, *n.f.* regurgitation; vomiting.
espadañal, *n.m.* place where reed-mace grows.
espadañar, *v.t.* to spread out (*tail feathers*).
espadar, *v.t.* to brake, scutch, swingle (*hemp etc.*).
espadarte, *n.m.* swordfish.
espadería, *n.f.* sword-cutler's shop.
espadero, *n.m.* sword-cutler, blade-smith.
espádice, *n.m.* (*bot.*) spadix.
espadilla, *n.f.* red insignia of the order of Santiago; large oar (*used as helm*); ace of spades; swingle, hemp-brake; hair bodkin; (*bot.*) corn-flag, gladiolus.
espadillar, *v.t.* to brake, scutch, swingle.
espadillazo, *n.m.* adverse fortune (*at cards*) (*when loser holds the ace*).
espadín, *n.m.* small dress sword; rapier.
espadita, *n.f.* small sword.
espadón, *n.m.* large sword, broadsword; military big shot *or* big gun, military strong man; blimp; eunuch.
espadrapo [ESPARADRAPO].
espagírica, *n.f.* metallurgy.
espagírico, -ca, *a.* metallurgic.
espahí, *n.m.* spahi.
espaguetis, *n.m.pl.* spaghetti.
espalda, *n.f.* (*anat.*) back; (*fort.*) shoulder (of a bastion); (*pl.*) back, shoulders; (*mil.*) rearguard; ***a espaldas de alguien,*** behind s.o.'s back; ***echarse a las espaldas,*** to forget all about, not to bother about; ***echarse sobre las espaldas,*** to undertake, take on; ***echar una cosa sobre las espaldas de,*** to saddle with the responsibility of sth.; ***espaldas de molinero,*** broad, strong shoulders; ***cargado de espaldas,*** round-shouldered; ***dar de espaldas,*** to fall on one's back; ***dar las espaldas,*** to turn one's back; ***hablar por las espaldas de,*** to say *or* talk behind the back of; (*Chi., C.R., Hond., P.R.*) ***espaldas vueltas, memorias muertas,*** out of sight of, out of mind; ***hacer espaldas,*** to suffer, bear, be prepared; ***hacer espaldas a,*** to protect, guard; ***tener buenas espaldas,*** to have broad shoulders; ***tener guardadas las espaldas,*** to have good *or* adequate protection; ***tener seguras las espaldas,*** to have one's rear covered; ***tirar*** or ***tumbar de espaldas,*** to flabbergast; ***tornar*** or ***volver las espaldas,*** to turn one's back (*on s.o.*); to turn tail.
espaldar, *n.m.* backplate (*of cuirass*); back (*of seat*); espalier (*in garden*); (*pl.* **espaldares**) tapestry, hangings (*against which chairs lean*).
espaldarazo, *n.m.* accolade, recognition; ***dar el espaldarazo a,*** to give recognition to.
espaldarcete, *n.m.* palette (*ancient armour*).
espaldarón, *n.m.* backplate (*armour*).
espaldear, *v.t.* (*naut.*) to dash against the poop (*waves*).
espalder, *n.m.* stroke, stern rower (*galley*).
espaldera, *n.f.* wall to shelter trees; espalier.
espaldilla, *n.f.* shoulder-blade, scapula; back (*of waistcoat* or *jacket*).
espalditendido, -da, *a.* (*coll.*) stretched on one's back.
espaldón, *n.m.* (*carp.*) tenon; (*fort.*) entrenchment, barrier; (*naut.*) hawse-piece.
espaldonarse, *v.r.* to take cover from the enemy's fire.
espaldudo, -da, *a.* broad-shouldered.
espalera, *n.f.* espalier, trellis-work.
espalmadura, *n.f.* parings (*of hoofs*).
espalmar, *v.t.* to clean (*a ship's bottom*).
espalto, *n.m.* dark-coloured paint; spalt; (*mil., obs.*) glacis.
espantable, *a.* frightful, fearful, ghastly, awful.
espantada, *n.f.* stampede, bolting; ***dar*** or ***pegar la espantada,*** to get cold feet; to make a bolt for it.
espantadizo, -za, *a.* scary, easily frightened.
espantador, -ra, *a.* frightening, terrifying.
espantajo, *n.m.* scarecrow.
espantalobos, *n.m. inv.* bladder *or* bastard senna.
espantamoscas, *n.m. inv.* fly-trap.
espantanublados, *n.m. inv.* (*coll.*) charlatan.
espantapájaros, *n.m. inv.* scarecrow.
espantar, *v.t.* to frighten, scare; to drive *or* chase away, scare off; to dumbfound. — **espantarse,** *v.r.* to get scared, take fright; to shy away.
espantavillanos, *n.m. inv.* (*coll.*) gaudy stuff *or* trinket.
espanto, *n.m.* fright, dread, terror; consternation, wonder; threat; (*Hisp. Am.*) ghost, apparition; ***estar curado de espanto,*** to be blasé; ***ser de espanto,*** to be fearful *or* frightful.
espantoso, -sa, *a.* fearful, dreadful, frightful, horrible.
España, *n.f.* Spain.
español, -la, *a.* Spanish; ***a la española,*** in the Spanish manner. — *n.m.* Spanish (*language.*) — *n.m.f.* Spaniard.
españolada, *n.f.* (*pej.*) typically Spanish thing to do *or* say; typically Spanish stuff.
españoleta, *n.f.* ancient Spanish dance.
españolismo, *n.m.* love of *or* devotion to Spain; Spanishness; Hispanicism.
españolista, *a., n.m.f.* (one) addicted to things Spanish.
españolizar [C], *v.t.* to make Spanish *or* Spanish-like. — **españolizarse,** *v.r.* to go Spanish.
esparadrapo, *n.m.* court-plaster, sticking plaster.
esparagón, *n.m.* grogram.
esparaván, *n.m.* (*vet.*) spavin; (*orn.*) sparrow-hawk; ***esparaván huesoso,*** bone-spavin.
esparavel, *n.m.* casting-net.
esparceta, *n.f.* sainfoin.
esparciata, *a., n.m.f.* Spartan.
esparcidamente, *adv.* distinctly, separately; gaily.
esparcido, -da, *a.* merry, festive, gay.
esparcidor, -ra, *a.* scattering, spreading. — *n.m.f.* scatterer, spreader.
esparcimiento, *n.m.* dissemination, scattering; amusement, recreation, relaxation.
esparcir [D], *v.t.* to scatter, spread (around); to entertain, relax. — **esparcirse,** *v.r.* to take recreation, relax.
esparragado, *n.m.* dish of asparagus.
esparragador, -ra, *n.m.f.* asparagus-grower.
esparragamiento, *n.m.* cultivation of asparagus.
esparragar [B], *v.i.* to grow *or* gather asparagus.
espárrago, *n.m.* (*bot.*) asparagus; pole (*of an awning*); (*min.*) peg-ladder; stud-bolt; ***anda*** or ***vete a freír espárragos,*** go to blazes.
esparraguero, -ra, *n.m.f.* asparagus-seller. — *n.f.* asparagus plant; asparagus-bed; asparagus-plate.
esparraguina, *n.f.* (*min.*) asparagine.
esparrancarse [A], *v.r.* (*coll.*) to spread the legs wide apart.
esparsión, *n.f.* dissemination, dispersion, scattering.
Esparta, *n.f.* Sparta.
espartal, *n.m.* place where esparto grass grows.
espartano, -na, *a., n.m.f.* Spartan.
esparteína, *n.f.* genista alkaloid.
esparteña, *n.f.* rope-sole sandal.
espartería, *n.f.* shop where esparto-work is made *or* sold.
espartero, -ra, *n.m.f.* maker *or* seller of esparto-work.
espartilla, *n.f.* mop of esparto grass.
espartizal [ESPARTAL].
esparto, *n.m.* esparto grass.

espasmo, *n.m.* spasm.
espasmódicamente, *adv.* spasmodically, by fits and starts.
espasmódico, -ca, *a.* spasmodic, jerky.
espata, *n.f.* spathe.
espatarrada, *n.f.* (*coll.*) splits.
espatarrarse, *v.r.* to slip and fall with legs wide open; (*fig.*) to be flabbergasted.
espático, -ca, *a.* spathic.
espato, *n.m.* spar.
espátula, *n.f.* spatula; (*art*) palette-knife; (*zool.*) spoonbill.
espaviento [ASPAVIENTO].
espavorido, -da [DESPAVORIDO].
espay [ESPAHÍ].
especería, *n.f.* grocer's shop, grocery, spicery.
especia, *n.f.* spice.
especial, *a.* special, particular; ***en especial,*** specially.
especialidad, *n.f.* speciality.
especialista, *a., n.m.f.,* specialist.
especialización, *n.f.* specialization; specializing.
especializar(se) [C], *v.t.* (*v.r.*) to specialize; ***especializarse en,*** to specialize in.
especialmente, *adv.* especially.
especiar, *v.t.* to spice.
especie, *n.f.* species; kind, class, sort; matter; event; notion; piece of news; pretext, show; (*fenc.*) feint; ***en especie,*** in kind; ***la especie humana,*** mankind; (*coll.*) ***escapársele a uno una especie,*** to drop a brick; (*coll.*) ***soltar uno una especie,*** to fly a kite.
especiería, *n.f.* grocery, grocer's shop.
especiero, *n.m.* grocer.
especificación, *n.f.* specification.
especificar [A], *v.t.* to name, specify, itemize.
especificativo, -va, *a.* specifical, specifying.
específico, -ca, *a.* specific. — *n.m.* (*med.*) patent medicine.
espécimen, *n.m.* specimen, sample; (*pl.* **especímenes**).
especioso, -sa, *a.* beautiful, well-finished, neat; (*fig.*) specious, deceiving.
especiota, *n.f.* (*coll.*) hoax, faked news, cock-and-bull story.
espectable, *a.* (*obs.*) conspicuous, eminent.
espectacular, *a.* spectacular.
espectáculo, *n.m.* spectacle, show, pageant; ***dar un espectáculo,*** to make a scene.
espectador, -ra, *a.* observing, looking-on. — *n.m.f.* spectator, looker-on; (*pl.* **espectadores**) audience.
espectral, *a.* spectral, ghostly.
espectro, *n.m.* spectre, phantom, ghost; spectrum.
espectrografía, *n.f.* spectrography.
espectrógrafo, *n.m.* spectrograph.
espectroscopia, *n.f.* spectroscopy.
espectroscópico, -ca, *a.* spectroscopic.
espectroscopio, *n.m.* spectroscope.
especulación, *n.f.* speculation.
especulador, -ra, *a.* speculating. — *n.m.f.* speculator.
especular, *v.t.* to speculate on *or* about. — *v.i.* to speculate.
especulativo, -va, *a.* speculative. — *n.f.* speculative faculty.
espéculo, *n.m.* (*surg.*) speculum; (*law*) legal code (*compiled by Alfonso the Wise*).
espejado, -da, *a.* mirror-like.
espejarse, *v.r.* to be reflected.
espejear, *v.i.* to shine, glitter.
espejeo, *n.m.* mirage; illusion.
espejería, *n.f.* mirror factory *or* shop.
espejero, -ra, *n.m.f.* maker *or* seller of mirrors.
espejillo, espejito, *n.m.* little mirror.
espejismo, *n.m.* mirage; illusion.
espejo, *n.m.* looking-glass, mirror; ***espejo de cuerpo entero,*** full-length mirror; ***espejo ustorio,*** burning-glass; (*naut.*) ***espejo de popa,*** stern-frame; ***espejo de los Incas,*** obsidian; ***limpio como un espejo,*** as clean as a new pin; ***mírate en ese espejo,*** learn from that example; ***un espejo de maridos,*** a model for husbands.
espejuela, *n.f.* curve (*of bit*); ***espejuela abierta,*** snaffle.
espejuelo, *n.m.* small looking-glass; specular stone, selenite; leaf (*of mica*); candied citron; lark mirror; (*vet.*) wart (*on pastern*); (*pl.*) spectacles; lenses.
espeleología, *n.f.* speleology, pot-holing.
espeleólogo, *n.m.* speleologist, pot-holer.
espelta, *n.f.* spelt.
espélteo, -tea, *a.* belonging to spelt.
espelunca, *n.f.* cave, cavern.
espeluznante, *a.* hair-raising.
espeluznar, *v.t.* to dishevel the hair of; to make (*s.o.'s*) hair stand on end.
espeque, *n.m.* handspike; pump-brake; lever; (*naut.*) ***espeque de la bomba,*** pump-brake.
espera, *n.f.* wait(ing); expectation; delay; restraint; (*law*) stay, respite; (*mus.*) rest, pause; (*carp.*) rabbet, notch; ***en espera de,*** awaiting, waiting for, in expectation of; ***sala de espera,*** waiting room; ***no tiene espera,*** it admits of no delay, it won't wait.
esperable, *a.* that which may be expected *or* hoped for.
esperador, -ra, *a.* expectant, hoping.
esperantista, *a., n.m.f.* Esperantist.
esperanto, *n.m.* Esperanto.
esperanza, *n.f.* hope; ***dar esperanza(s),*** to give encouragement; to be promising; (*naut.*) ***áncora de la esperanza,*** sheet-anchor; ***llenar la esperanza,*** to fulfil one's hopes; ***alimentarse de esperanzas,*** to feed on (false) hopes; ***tener puesta su esperanza en,*** to pin one's hope(s) on.
esperanzar [C], *v.t.* to give hope to.
esperar, *v.t.* to hope, hope for; to expect; to look forward to. — *v.t., v.i.* to await, wait for; ***esperar a que,*** to wait until; ***esperar sentado,*** to hope against hope. — *v.i.* to hope; to trust; ***quien espera desespera,*** long awaiting ends in despair.
esperezarse [C] [DESPEREZARSE].
esperezo [DESPEREZO].
esperiego, *n.m.* sour-apple tree.
esperma, *n.f.* sperm; ***esperma de ballena,*** spermaceti.
espermático, -ca, *a.* spermatic, seminal.
espermatorrea, *n.f.* spermatorrhœa.
espermatozoario, espermatozoide, *n.m.* spermatozoon.
espernada, *n.f.* end link (*of a chain*).
espernancarse [A], *v.r.* (*Hisp. Am., prov.*) to stretch the legs wide.
esperón, *n.m.* beak, ram (*of warship*); (*coll.*) long wait.
esperpento, *n.m.* fright, sight; absurdity, nonsense; piece of grotesqueness; grotesque tale.
esperriaca, *n.f.* (*prov.*) last pressing (*of grapes*).
espesamiento, *n.m.* coagulation.
espesar, *v.t., v.i.* to thicken; to condense; to coagulate, curdle; to mass, assemble; to make closer, weave tighter (*knitting, material*).
espesativo, -va, *a.* thickening.
espeso, -sa, *a.* thick, dense; close; heavy, thickset; curdy; (*fig.*) dirty, untidy; (*Ven.*) dull, heavy.
espesor, *n.m.* thickness.
espesura, *n.f.* thickness, density; thickset, dense wood; shock of hair; (*fig.*) dirt, dirtiness, untidiness.
espetaperro (a), *adv.* at breakneck speed.
espetar, *v.t.* to skewer, spit; to run through, pierce;

(*coll.*) to spring (sth.) (on); ***le espetó la sorpresa,*** he sprang the surprise on him. — **espetarse,** *v.r.* to stiffen, get stuck up, assume a solemn air.

espetera, *n.f.* kitchen-rack; dresser, kitchen utensils *or* furniture.

espetón, *n.m.* poker; spit; rake; iron prong; large pin; blow given with a spit; (*zool.*) sea-pike, spit-fish.

espía (1), *n.m.f.* spy.

espía (2), *n.f.* (*naut.*) warp; warping.

espiar (1) [L] *v.t.*, *v.i.* to spy, spy on.

espiar (2), *v.i.* (*naut.*) to warp.

espibia, *n.f.*, **espibio, espibión,** *n.m.* (*vet.*) sprain in the neck (*horse*).

espicacéltica, *n.f.* yellow valerian.

espicanardi, espicanardo, *n.f.* spikenard.

espicifloro, -ra, espiciforme, *a.* spicate.

espícula, *n.f.* spicule.

espicúleo, -lea, *a.* spiculate.

espichar, *v.t.* to prick. — *v.i.* (*coll.*) to peg out.

espiche, *n.m.* sharp-pointed weapon; meat-spit; spile, spigot.

espichón, *n.m.* prick, stab (*wound*).

espiga, *n.f.* spike *or* ear (*of grain*); tenon, dowel, peg; pin, tongue, treenail, shank stem; brad; tang (*of a sword, knife, chisel etc.*); fuse (*of a bomb* or *shell*); clapper (*of bell*); mast-head; ***espiga céltica,*** valerian; ***espiga de agua,*** pond-weed; ***espiga de pez,*** herringbone pattern; (*coll.*) ***quedarse a la espiga,*** to remain to the last; to gather up others' fragments.

espigadera, espigadora, *n.f.* gleaner.

espigado, -da, *a.* spike-like; tall, slender, slim.

espigar [B], *v.t.* to glean; to pick out, gather here and there; to tenon. — *v.i.* to ear (*wheat*). — **espigarse,** *v.r.* to go *or* run to seed; to shoot up quickly *or* suddenly.

espigón, *n.m.* sting (*bees*); bearded spike; point (*of a sharp tool* or *dart*); peak; ear (*of corn*); breakwater, pier, jetty; bare, craggy hill.

espiguilla, *n.f.* herring bone (*tweed*); small edging (*of lace, tape etc.*)

espilocho, *n.m.* (*obs.*) poor, destitute person.

espín, *n.m.* ***puerco espín,*** porcupine.

espina, *n.f.* thorn; spine, back-bone; fish-bone; splinter; suspicion; ***espina dorsal,*** spine, back-bone; ***espina de pez,*** herringbone pattern; ***quedarse en la espina,*** to get terribly thin; ***sacarse la espina,*** to get even, get one's own back; ***me da mala espina,*** I smell sth. fishy.

espinaca, *n.f.* (leaf of) spinach.

espinadura, *n.f.* pricking (*with a thorn*).

espinal, *a.* spinal.

espinar, *n.m.* place covered in thorn-bushes, brambles *or* briers; (*fig.*) thorny business. — *v.t.* to prick with thorns; to wound, goad, nettle; to surround (*trees*) with thorn-bushes, brambles *or* briers. — **espinarse,** *v.r.* to get pricked (*by a thorn*), prick o.s. (*on a thorn*).

espinazo, *n.m.* spine, back-bone; (*arch.*) keystone; (*coll.*) ***doblar el espinazo,*** to knuckle under; to get down to it.

espinel, *n.m.* fishing-line with many hooks.

espinela, *n.f.* (*poet.*) [DÉCIMO], octosyllabic ten-line stanza; spinel-ruby.

espineo, -nea, *a.* thorny.

espinera, *n.f.* hawthorn.

espineta, *n.f.* spinet.

espingarda, *n.f.* long Moorish musket; lanky person.

espinilla, *n.f.* shin-bone; blackhead.

espinillera, *n.f.* greave, jambe (*armour*); shin-guard.

espino, *n.m.* hawthorn; buckthorn; ***espino blanco*** or ***majuelo,*** hawthorn; ***espino negro,*** buckthorn; ***espino cerval,*** purging buckthorn; ***espino (artificial),*** barbed wire.

espinosismo, *n.m.* Spinozism.

espinosista, *a.*, *n.m.f.* Spinozist.

espinoso, -sa, *a.* spiny, thorny.

espinzar [C], *v.t.* (*prov.*) to burl.

espiocha, *n.f.* pickaxe.

espión, *n.m.* spy.

espionaje, *n.m.* espionage, spying.

espira, *n.f.* helix, spiral line; turn, whorl (*of a shell*); surbase (*of a column*).

espiración, *n.f.* expiration, breathing out.

espirador, -ra, *a.* breathing out.

espiral, *a.* spiral, helical, winding. — *n.f.* spiral line; coil; hair spring (*of a watch*).

espirante, *a.* breathing out.

espirar, *v.t.* to infuse (*a divine spirit*) (in), inspire. — *v.i.* to breathe out, exhale.

espirativo, -va, *a.* (*theol.*) that which inspires divine spirit; ghost-like; (*coll.*) extremely thin.

espirea, *n.f.* spiræa.

espiritado, -da, *a.* (*coll.*) extremely thin.

espiritar, *v.t.* to demonize, possess with a devil; (*coll.*) to irritate.

espiritismo, *n.m.* spiritualism.

espiritista, *a.*, *n.m.f.* spiritualist.

espiritoso, -sa, *a.* lively, spirited; spirituous.

espíritu, *n.m.* spirit; mind; spiritus; ***dar, despedir*** or ***exhalar el espíritu,*** to give up the ghost; ***levantar el espíritu,*** to give *or* take courage; ***el Espíritu Santo,*** the Holy Ghost; (*coll.*) ***espíritu de la golosina,*** very thin person; ***espíritu de contradicción,*** spirit of contradiction.

espiritual, *a.* spiritual; of the mind.

espiritualidad, *n.f.* spirituality.

espiritualismo, *n.m.* spiritualism.

espiritualista, *a.*, *n.m.f.*, spiritualist.

espiritualización, *n.f.* spiritualization.

espiritualizar [C], *v.t.* to spiritualize. — **espiritualizarse,** *v.r.* to grow thin.

espirituoso, -sa, *a.* spirituous; lively.

espíritusanto, *n.m.* (*C.R.*, *Nic.*) large, white flower of a cactus.

espirómetro, *n.m.* spirometer.

espiroqueta, *n.f.* Spirochæta.

espita, *n.f.* measure of length (8 *in.* or 21 *cms.*); tap, spout, stop-cock, faucet, spigot; (*coll.*) tippler, drunkard.

espitar, *v.t.* to put a faucet in; to tap.

espito, *n.m.* (*print.*) peel, hanger.

esplendente, *a.* (*poet.*) shining, resplendent.

esplender, *v.i.* (*poet.*) to shine.

esplendidez, *n.f.* splendour, magnificence; lavishness, generosity.

espléndido, -da, *a.* splendid, magnificent; glorious; lavish, generous; (*poet.*) resplendent.

esplendor, *n.m.* splendour, glory, magnificence; radiance.

esplendoroso, -sa, *a.* splendid, radiant, glorious.

esplenético, -ca, esplénico, -ca, *a.* splenic.

espliego, *n.m.* lavender.

esplín, *n.m.* spleen.

esplique, *n.m.* bird-snare.

espolada, *n.f.* prick (*with a spur*); (*coll.*) ***espolada de vino,*** draught of wine.

espolazo, *n.m.* (violent) prick (*with a spur*).

espoleadura, *n.f.* spur gall.

espolear, *v.t.* to spur; to spur on.

espoleta, *n.f.* fuse (*bombs etc.*); wish-bone.

espolín, *n.m.* small spur; shuttle (*for brocading* or *flowering*); silk brocade.

espolinar, *v.t.* to brocade, to flower.

espolio, *n.m.* spolium.

espolique, *n.m.* running footman, groom.

espolón, *n.m.* cock's spur; ridge, crag (*of a mountain*); (*engin.*) mole, breakwater, jetty, groyne;

(*arch.*) spur, buttress; (*naut.*) ram (*of a man-of-war*); beak (*of a galley*); (*naut.*) fender-beam; chilblain (*on the heel*); public walk; ***tiene más espolones que un gallo,*** he is an old dog.
espolonada, *n.f.* sudden onset (*of horsemen*).
espolvorear, espolvorizar [C], *v.t.* to powder, sprinkle.
espondaico, -ca, *a.* spondaic.
espondeo, *n.m.* spondee.
espóndil, *n.m.* vertebra.
espóndilo, *n.m.* spondyl, vertebra.
esponja, *n.f.* sponge; ***pasar la esponja,*** to wipe the slate clean; ***tirar la esponja,*** to throw *or* chuck in the sponge, pack it in.
esponjado, -da, *a.* spongy; (*coll.*) stuck-up.
esponjadura, *n.f.* sponging; flaw (*in cast metal*); (*Arg.*) arrogance.
esponjar, *v.t.* to make spongy *or* fluffy, puff up. — **esponjarse,** *v.r.* to puff up; (*fig.*) to get puffed up, conceited; to become glowing with health.
esponjera, *n.f.* sponge-holder.
esponjosidad, *n.f.* sponginess.
esponjoso, -sa, *a.* spongy.
esponsales, *n.m.pl.* betrothal.
esponsalicio, -cia, *a.* nuptial, spousal.
espontáneamente, *adv.* spontaneously, of one's own accord, off one's own bat.
espontanearse, *v.r.* to speak freely *or* openly, open one's heart (***con,*** to).
espontaneidad, *n.f.* spontaneity, spontaneousness.
espontáneo, -nea, *a.* spontaneous. — *n.m.* spectator who jumps into the ring to fight the bull.
espontón, *n.m.* spontoon, half-pike.
espontonada, *n.f.* salute *or* blow with a spontoon.
espora, *n.f.*, **esporo,** *n.m.* (*bot.*) spore.
esporádicamente, *adv.* sporadically, intermittently, off and on, by fits and starts.
esporádico, -ca, *a.* sporadic, off and on, stop-go; ***huelga esporádica,*** stop-go strike.
esportada, *n.f.* frailful, basketful.
esportear, *v.t.* to carry in a frail, pannier *or* basket.
esportilla, *n.f.* small frail.
esportillero, *n.m.* porter, carrier.
esportillo, *n.m.* pannier, frail, basket.
esportón, *n.m.* large pannier *or* frail.
esportonada, *n.f.* basketful.
espórtula, *n.f.* (*prov.*) court fees.
esposa, *n.f.* wife, spouse; (*pl.*) manacles, handcuffs.
esposo, *n.m.* husband, spouse; (*Hisp. Am.*) episcopal ring.
espuela, *n.f.* spur; ***espuela de caballero,*** larkspur; ***calzarse la espuela,*** to be dubbed a knight; ***calzar espuela,*** to be a knight; ***dar espuela,*** to spur; ***estar con las espuelas calzadas,*** to be (all) ready; ***poner espuelas a,*** to spur on.
espuenda, *n.f.* (*prov.*) bank (*of canal*); fringe (*of field*).
espuerta, *n.f.* two-handled basket; ***a espuertas,*** galore.
espulgadero, *n.m.* place where beggars clean themselves from lice *or* fleas.
espulgador, -ra, *n.m.f.* one who cleans off lice *or* fleas.
espulgar [B], *v.t.* to delouse; (*fig.*) to examine closely.
espulgo, *n.m.* delousing.
espuma, *n.f.* foam, lather, froth; scum; ***espuma de nitro,*** saltpetre; ***espuma de mar,*** meerschaum; ***espuma de la sal,*** sea-froth; ***crecer como (la) espuma,*** to shoot up, grow (up).
espumadera, *n.f.* skimmer.
espumador, -ra, *a.* skimming. — *n.m.f.* skimmer.
espumajear, *v.i.* to froth, foam (at the mouth).
espumajo, *n.m.* froth, spume, foam.
espumajoso, -sa, *a.* foamy, frothy, spumous.
espumante, *a.* lathering, foaming, frothing; sparkling (*wine*).
espumar, *v.t.* to skim (off). — *v.i.* to froth, foam; (*fig.*) to grow (up).
espumarajo, *n.m.* ugly foam *or* froth; ***echar espumarajos por la boca,*** to foam at the mouth.
espumear, *v.t.* to raise foam on.
espumero, *n.m.* salt pit.
espumescente, *a.* spumescent.
espumilla, *n.f.* voile; (*Ec., Hond.*) meringue.
espumillón, *n.m.* heavy grogram.
espumosidad, *n.f.* frothiness, foaminess.
espumoso, -sa, *a.* spumy, spumous, frothy, foamy; sparkling (*wine*).
espumuy, *n.f.* (*Guat.*) rock dove.
espundia, *n.f.* (*vet.*) cancerous ulcer, tumour.
espúreo, -rea, espurio, -ria, *a.* spurious.
espurrear, espurriar, *v.t.* to sprinkle, moisten with water held in the mouth.
espurrir, *v.t.* (*prov.*) to stretch out.
esputar, *v.t.* to expectorate.
esputo, *n.m.* spittle, saliva; sputum.
esquebrajar, *v.t.* [RESQUEBRAJAR].
esqueje, *n.m.* (*agric.*) cutting, slip.
esquela, *n.f.* note, short letter; printed card; ***esquela (mortuoria*** or ***fúnebre),*** obituary notice.
esquelético, -ca, *a.* skeletal, skeleton-like.
esqueleto, *n.m.* skeleton; framework; (*Hisp. Am.*) form, application; ***en esqueleto,*** in draft form.
esquema, *n.m.* schema; diagram; outline.
esquemáticamente, *adv.* schematically, in outline, in diagrammatic form.
esquemático, -ca, *a.* schematic, diagrammatic.
esquematismo, *n.m.* schematism.
esquematizar [C], *v.t.* to give in outline *or* in diagrammatic form; to put in a nutshell.
esquena, *n.f.* spine, back-bone.
esquero, *n.m.* leather bag *or* pouch.
esquí, *n.m.* ski.
esquiador, -ra, *n.m.f.* skier.
esquiar [L], *v.i.* to ski.
esquiciar, *v.t.* to sketch, outline.
esquicio, *n.m.* sketch, outline.
esquifada, *n.f.* boat-load; vault (*of a cistern*).
esquifar, *v.t.* to fit out (*a ship*); to provide (*a boat*) with oars.
esquifazón, *n.f.* complement of oars and oarsmen (*on a galley etc.*).
esquife, *n.m.* skiff; cylindrical vault.
esquila, *n.f.* small bell; cattle-bell; sheep-shearing; (*ichth.*) prawn; (*ent.*) water-spider; (*bot.*) squill.
esquilador, -ra, *n.m.f.* sheep-shearer, clipper.
esquilar, *v.t.* to shear, crop, clip; (*fig.*) to fleece, skin; ***sin esquilar,*** unshorn.
esquileo, *n.m.* shearing; shearing season; shearing place.
esquilimoso, -sa, *a.* (*coll.*) fastidious, over-nice.
esquilmar, *v.t.* to harvest; to impoverish.
esquilmeño, -ña, *a.* (*prov.*) fruitful, productive.
esquilmo, *n.m.* harvest; produce (*of vines, cattle etc.*); (*Chi.*) stalk (*of grapes*); (*Mex.*) profits of farming by-products.
esquilo, *n.m.* (*obs.*) shearing; (*prov.*) squirrel.
esquilón, *n.m.* large cattle-bell.
esquimal, *a., n.m.f.* Eskimo.
esquina, *n.f.* corner; outer angle; ***a la vuelta de la esquina,*** round the corner; ***hacer esquina,*** to be on a *or* the corner; ***la casa hace esquina con Diego de León,*** the house is on the corner of Diego de León St.; ***las cuatro esquinas,*** (game of) puss-in-the-corner.
esquinado, -da, *a.* having a chip on one's shoulder.

esquinal, *n.m.* (*prov.*) corner-plate; angle-iron; iron knee.
esquinancia, esquinencia, *n.f.* quinsy.
esquinante, esquinanto, *n.m.* aromatic rush.
esquinar, *v.t.* to form a corner with; to square (*timber*); to set at odds. — *v.i.* to be on the corner. — **esquinarse,** *v.r.* to fall out, quarrel; to get a chip on one's shoulder; ***estar esquinado,*** to have a chip on one's shoulder.
esquinazo, *n.m.* (*coll.*) corner; (*Chi.*) serenade; (*coll.*) ***dar esquinazo a,*** to dodge; to give the slip to.
esquinco, *n.m.* skink, lizard.
esquinela, *n.f.* greave, leg-armour.
esquinzador, *n.m.* rag-room (*in paper-mills*); rag-engine.
esquinzar [C], *v.t.* to cut (*rags*).
esquirla, *n.f.* splinter.
esquirol, *n.m.* (*prov.*) squirrel; (*coll.*) blackleg, scab, strike-breaker.
esquisto, *n.m.* schist; slate.
esquistoso, -sa, *a.* laminated; slaty.
esquite, *n.m.* (*C.R., Hond., Mex.*) pop-corn.
esquivar, *v.t.* to dodge, sidestep. — **esquivarse,** *v.r.* to dodge away, shy away.
esquivez, *n.f.* shyness, aloofness, stand-offishness.
esquivo, -va, *a.* shy, elusive; reserved, aloof, stand-offish.
esquizado, -da, *a.* mottled (*marble*).
esquizofrenia, *n.f.* schizophrenia.
estabilidad, *n.f.* stability, steadiness.
estabilizador, -ra, *a.* giving stability. — *n.m.f.* stabilizer.
estabilizar [C], *v.t.* to stabilize.
estable, *a.* stable, steady; permanent.
establear, *v.t.* to accustom to the cowshed.
establecedor, -ra, *a.* establishing. — *n.m.f.* founder, establisher.
establecer [9], *v.t.* to establish, set up, found; to decree. — **establecerse,** *v.r.* to settle, take up residence, set up in business.
estableciente, *a.* establishing.
establecimiento, *n.m.* establishing, setting up; establishment, settlement; shop, store; statute, ordinance.
establero, *n.m.* cowshed-keeper.
establo, *n.m.* cowshed, (*Am.*) barn.
estabulación, *n.f.* housing in a cowshed.
estaca, *n.f.* stake, pale; stick, bludgeon; grafting-twig; (*agric.*) cutting; (*carp.*) clamp-nail; (*Chi.*) stake *or* claim (*in a mine*).
estacada, *n.f.* palisade, stockade; paling; lists; duelling ground; (*prov.*) new plantation of olives; ***dejar en la estacada,*** to leave in the lurch; ***quedar(se) en la estacada,*** to get left in the lurch; to get beaten; to lose; to fail.
estacar [A], *v.t.* to stake; to enclose, fence with stakes; to tie to a stake; (*Chi., Col., Hond., Ven.*) to sun-dry (*skins*). — **estacarse,** *v.r.* to go stiff as a pole.
estacazo, *n.m.* blow with a stake.
estación, *n.f.* station; season; stop; state, position; ***estación balnearia,*** bathing resort, spa; ***estación de las lluvias,*** rainy season; ***estaciones del Vía Crucis,*** Stations of the Cross; ***estación de ferrocarril,*** railway station, (*Am.*) railroad depot.
estacional, *a.* seasonal; (*astron.*) stationary; ***calenturas estacionales,*** seasonal fevers.
estacionamiento, *n.m.* stationing; parking.
estacionario, -ria, *a.* stationary.
estacionar, *v.t.* to station; to park. — **estacionarse,** *v.r.* to come to a halt; to park; to loiter.
estacionero, -ra, *a., n.m.f.* (devotee) praying frequently at the stations in church.
estacte, *n.m.* oil of myrrh.
estacha, *n.f.* tow-line, hawser; harpoon-rope.
estada, *n.f.* stay, sojourn.
estadal, *n.m.* lineal measure (*about* 11 *ft.* or 3 *m.*); ornament *or* blessed ribbon (*worn round the neck*); (*prov.*) length of wax taper.
estadero, *n.m.* (*obs.*) royal land-surveyor.
estadía, *n.f.* stay; (*com., naut.*) demurrage; (*art*) sitting, session (*model*).
estadio, *n.m.* stadium, sports ground; stage, phase.
estadista, *n.m.* statesman.
estadístico, -ca, *a.* statistical, statistic. — *n.m.* statistician. — *n.f.* statistics.
estadizo, -za, *a.* stagnant; stationary.
estado, *n.m.* state; commonwealth; condition; estate (*class*); (*account*) statement; measure of length (2·17 *yds.* or 2 *m.*); (*pl.*) estates (*representative assembly*); ***Estados Unidos,*** United States; ***estado de guerra,*** state of war; martial law; ***estado de excepción,*** state of emergency; ***estado de ánimo,*** state of mind; ***estado de cosas,*** state of affairs; ***estado general*** or ***llano,*** commoners, common people; (*mil.*) ***estado mayor,*** staff; ***estado mayor general,*** general staff; ***hombre de estado,*** statesman; ***papel del estado,*** government bonds; ***en estado (interesante),*** expecting a baby; (*coll.*) ***en estado de merecer,*** marriageable (*of a girl*).
estadojo, estandorio, estadoño, *n.m.* (*prov.*) stake for supporting side-board of a cart.
Estados Unidos de América, *n.m.pl.* United States of America.
estafa, *n.f.* cheat, swindle; stirrup.
estafador, -ra, *n.m.f.* cheat, swindler.
estafar, *v.t.* to cheat, swindle.
estafermo, *n.m.* quintain, movable figure used in tilting; (*fig.*) dummy, figure of fun.
estafeta, *n.f.* courier; post; sub-post office; diplomatic post-bag.
estafetero, *n.m.* postmaster.
estafetil, *a.* belonging to a courier *or* post.
estafilococo, *n.m.* staphylococcus.
estafisagria, *n.f.* stavesacre, larkspur.
estagnación [ESTANCACIÓN].
estala, *n.f.* port of call; cowshed.
estalación, *n.f.* class, rank, order (*in cathedral churches etc.*).
estalactita, *n.f.* stalactite.
estalagmita, *n.f.* stalagmite.
estalingar [B], *v.t.* to bend (*a cable*).
estallante, *a.* bursting, exploding.
estallar, *v.i.* to explode, burst; (*fig.*) to break out.
estallido, *n.m.* crack, crash; explosion, outburst; ***dar*** or ***pegar un estallido,*** to crash, explode, go bang.
estambor, *n.m.* sternpost.
estambrado, *n.m.* (*prov.*) worsted cloth.
estambrar, *v.t.* to spin into worsted.
estambre, *n.m.* worsted, woollen yarn; (*bot.*) stamen; (*poet.*) ***estambre de la vida,*** thread of life.
Estambul, *n.m.* Istanbul.
estamenara, *n.f.* futtock.
estamento, *n.m.* estate (*class*).
estameña, *n.f.* serge.
estameñete, *n.m.* light serge.
estamíneo, -nea, *a.* made of worsted.
estaminífero, -ra, *a.* staminate.
estampa, *n.f.* print; stamp, mark; picture; ***dar a la estampa,*** to send to press; ***ser la estampa de,*** to be the very image of.
estampación, *n.f.* printing; stamping.
estampado, *n.m.* print, cotton print; cloth-printing; stamping, impression.
estampador, *n.m.* stamper; stamp, punch; one who makes *or* sells prints.

estampar, *v.t.* to stamp, print; to imprint; ***esto se le estampó en la memoria,*** this became fixed *or* engraved in his mind.
estampería, *n.f.* shop for printing *or* selling prints.
estampero, -ra, *n.m.f.* maker *or* seller of prints *or* pictures.
estampía, *n.f.* ***de estampía,*** suddenly, in a rush.
estampida, *n.f.* [ESTAMPIDO]; (*Col., Guat., Mex., Ven.*) stampede; ***dar estampida,*** to crash, go bang.
estampido, *n.m.* explosion, crash, bang, boom; ***dar un estampido,*** to crash, go bang.
estampilla, *n.f.* rubber stamp; ***alférez de estampilla,*** war-time *or* emergency officer; (*Hisp. Am.*) postage stamp.
estampillado, *n.m.* stamping.
estampillar, *v.t.* to stamp; ***alférez estampillado,*** war-time *or* emergency officer.
estancación, *n.f.*, **estancamiento,** *n.m.* stagnation, stagnancy.
estancar [A], *v.t.* to stanch, stop, check, stem; (*com.*) to corner, monopolize; to put an embargo on (*goods*). — **estancarse,** *v.r.* to be(come) stagnant, get bogged down *or* stuck.
estancia, *n.f.* stay; room; habitation; day in hospital *or* fee for it; stanza; (*Hisp. Am.*) ranch, farm.
estanciero, *n.m.* (*Hisp. Am.*) rancher, farmer.
estanco, -ca, *a.* watertight; ***compartimiento estanco,*** watertight compartment. — *n.m.* place where state-monopolized goods are sold; state tobacco shop.
estandarte, *n.m.* standard, banner.
estangurria, *n.f.* strangury; catheter.
estanque, *n.m.* pond; basin, reservoir.
estanquero, -ra, *n.m.f.* keeper of reservoirs; retailer of monopoly goods, state tobacconist.
estanquillero, -ra [ESTANQUERO].
estanquillo, *n.m.* (*Mex.*) small, poor shop; (*Ec.*) tavern.
estantal, *n.m.* buttress.
estante, *a.* being, being in place, fixed, permanent. — *n.m.* shelf; (*prov.*) image-carrier in processions; (*print.*) cabinet; (*Hisp. Am.*) wood-pile; (*pl.*) props (*of crossbeams*).
estantería, *n.f.* shelving; bookcase.
estantigua, *n.f.* procession of phantoms; (*coll.*) scarecrow, fright.
estantío, -tía, *a.* stagnant, stationary; dull, slow, lifeless, spiritless.
estañador, *n.m.* tinner, tinman, pewterer.
estañadura, *n.f.* tinning.
estañar, *v.t.* to tin, cover with tin; to solder.
estañero, *n.m.* tinner; seller of tin-ware.
estaño, *n.m.* tin.
estaquero, *n.m.* year-old buck *or* doe.
estaquilla, estaquita, *n.f.* (*shoe.*) peg; tack, tin-tack; spike, brad.
estaquillador, *n.m.* (*shoe.*) pegging-awl.
estaquillar, *v.t.* to peg, fasten with tacks.
estar [18], *v.i.* to be (*temporarily* or *in a place, state,* or *condition*); to stand; to be ready; ***está escribiendo,*** he is writing; ***¿está Juan (en casa)?*** is Juan in?; ***no, no está,*** no, he is out; ***está fuera,*** he is away; ***no están,*** they are not here *or* there; ***estamos a lunes,*** it is Monday today; ***estamos a cinco,*** today is the fifth; ***¿a cómo estamos?*** or ***¿a cuántos estamos?*** what day of the month is it?; ***las patatas están a tres pesetas,*** potatoes are (selling at) three pesetas; ***está con gripe,*** he's got flu; ***estoy con usted,*** I'm with you; I agree with you; ***está de camarero en un hotel,*** he works as a waiter in an hotel; ***estoy de mudanza,*** I am moving; ***estar de buen*** or ***mal humor,*** to be in a good *or* bad temper; ***estar de pie*** or ***en pie,*** to be standing; ***estar levantado,*** to be up; ***estar de viaje,*** to be away (*travelling*); ***no está en lo que estamos diciendo,*** he's not paying attention to what we are saying; ***estar bien,*** to be all right; to feel all right; ***estar mal,*** to be (all) wrong; not to feel too good; ***el traje no me está bien,*** the suit doesn't fit me; ***¿estamos?*** are we agreed? right?; ***¡ya está bien!*** that's enough! that will do! ***estoy para salir,*** I'm about to leave; ***estar para una cosa,*** to be ready for *or* disposed to do a thing; ***no está para bromas,*** he is not in a joking mood; ***estoy por él,*** I'm all for him; ***estoy por hacerlo,*** I feel inclined to do it; ***esto está por hacer,*** this still has to be done; ***estar sobre sí,*** to be cautious; to be conceited; ***estar a todo,*** to be ready for anything; ***estar a matar,*** to be at daggers drawn; ***estar de más*** or ***de sobra,*** to be superfluous; ***¡están verdes!*** sour grapes!; ***está que bufa,*** he's hopping mad; ***la cosa está que arde,*** the matter is in a very touchy *or* inflammable state, things are hotting up; ***estar a la que salta,*** to be on the lookout for anything that's going; ***están al caer,*** they are just about due, they will be here any time now; ***no puedo estar en todo,*** I can't have my mind *or* attention on everything; ***te está bien empleado,*** it serves you right; ***están mal con él,*** they are on bad terms with him; ***está por ver,*** it remains to be seen; ***hay que estar sobre él,*** you have to keep a close eye on him; ***está visto que,*** it is clear *or* obvious that; ***lo estoy viendo,*** I can see it now (as a recollection); ***lo estoy viendo venir,*** I can see it coming; ***¡estate quieto!*** keep still! stop fidgeting!; ***me estuve tres horas,*** I stayed there three hours.
estarcido, *n.m.* stencilled drawing; outline.
estarcir, *v.t.* to stencil, trace the outlines of.
estarna, *n.f.* small partridge.
estatal, *a.* (of the) state.
estatera, *n.f.* (*obs.*) balance; (*numis.*) stater.
estátice, *n.m.* sea-lavender; ***estátice común,*** sea-gillyflower.
estático, -ca, *a.* static. — *n.f.* statics.
estatismo, *n.m.* state control; static state.
estator, *n.m.* stator.
estatua, *n.f.* statue; ***quedarse hecho una estatua,*** to become paralyzed (*with fright etc.*); to turn to stone.
estatuar, *v.t.* to adorn with statues.
estatuario, -ria, *a.* belonging to statuary. — *n.m.* statuary; sculptor. — *n.f.* statuary, sculpture.
estatúder, *n.m.* (*hist.*) stadholder.
estatuilla, *n.f.* statuette, figurine.
estatuir [IO], *v.t.* to establish, ordain, enact.
estatura, *n.f.* stature, height.
estatutario, -ria, *a.* statutory.
estatuto, *n.m.* statute, statutes.
estay, *n.m.* (*naut.*) stay.
este (1), *n.m.* east.
este (2), **esta,** *a.* this; (*pl.* **estos, estas**) these.
éste, *m.*, **ésta,** *f.*, *dem. pron.* this (one), the latter; (*pl.* **éstos,** *m.*, **éstas,** *f.*) these, the latter.
esté, *pres. subj.* [ESTAR].
esteárico, -ca, *a.* stearic; ***bujías esteáricas,*** stearin candles.
estearina, *n.f.* stearin.
esteatita, *n.f.* steatite, soap-stone.
esteatoma, *n.f.* fatty tumour.
esteba, *n.f.* stevedore's pole; (*bot.*) meadow spear grass.
Esteban, *n.m.* Stephen.
estebar, *v.t.* to put (*cloth*) into the dye-kettle.
estegomia, *n.f.* mosquito.
estela, *n.f.* (*naut.*) wake, trail; (*arch.*) stela.
estelar, *a.* sidereal, stellar; (*fig.*) ***momentos estelares,*** high-water marks.
estelaria, *n.f.* (*bot.*) silvery lady's mantle.
estelífero, -ra, *a.* (*poet.*) starry.
estelión, *n.m.* stellion; toad-stone.
estelionato, *n.m.* fraudulent conveyance.

estelón, *n.m.* toad-stone.
estemple, *n.m.* (*min.*) stemple.
estenocardia, *n.f.* (*med.*) angina pectoris.
estenografía, *n.f.* stenography, shorthand.
estenografiar, *v.t.* to write (in) shorthand.
estenográfico, -ca, *a.* stenographic.
estenógrafo, -fa, *n.m.f.* stenographer.
estenordeste, *n.m.* east-north-east.
estentóreo, -rea, *a.* stentorian, thundering.
estepa, *n.f.* steppe; (*bot.*) rock-rose.
estepar, *n.m.* place covered in rock-roses.
estepilla, *n.f.* white-leaved rock-rose.
estera, *n.f.* mat.
esteral, *n.m.* (*Arg.*) inlet, estuary.
esterar, *v.t.* to cover with mats or matting. — *v.i.* (*coll.*) to put on winter clothes before the proper time.
estercoladura, *n.f.*, **estercolamiento,** *n.m.* manuring.
estercolar [4], *v.t.* to manure.
estercolero, *n.m.* muck-collector; dunghill, muck-heap.
estercolizo, -za, estercoráceo, -cea, *a.* stercoraceous.
estercóreo, -rea, *a.* stercoral.
estercuelo, *n.m.* manuring.
estéreo, *n.m.* stere.
estereofonía, *n.f.* stereophony.
estereofónico, -ca, *a.* stereophonic.
estereografía, *n.f.* stereography.
estereográfico, -ca, *a.* stereographic.
estereógrafo, *n.m.* stereographer.
estereometría, *n.f.* stereometry.
estereométrico, -ca, *a.* stereometric.
estereómetro, *n.m.* stereometer.
estereoscopio, *n.m.* stereoscope.
estereotipado, -da, *a.* stereotype(d); ready-made, set, standard.
estereotipador, *n.m.* stereotyper.
estereotipar, *v.t.* to stereotype; to print from stereotypes.
esteriotipia, *n.f.* stereotypography; stereotyping machine.
estereotípico, -ca, *a.* stereotypic.
estereotomía, *n.f.* stereotomy.
estereria, *n.f.* shop where mat-work is made and sold.
esterero, -ra, *n.m.f.* mat-maker, mat-seller.
estéril, *a.* barren, sterile; pointless; fruitless.
esterilidad, *n.f.* sterility, unfruitfulness, barrenness; (*fig.*) uselessness, futility.
esterilizador, -ra, *a.* sterilizing. — *n.m.f.* sterilizer.
esterilizar [C], *v.t.* to sterilize.
esterilla, *n.f.* small mat; straw plait; narrow gold *or* silver braid; (*Chi.*, *C.R.*, *Ec.*) embroidery canvas; (*Arg.*) cane (*for backs and seats of chairs*).
esterlín, *n.m.* fine glazed buckram.
esterlina, *a.* sterling; ***libra esterlina,*** pound sterling.
esternón, *n.m.* sternum, breastbone.
estero, *n.m.* tideland, estuary; matting, covering with matting; fish nursery *or* pond; (*Hisp. Am.*) swamp; (*Hisp. Am.*) stream.
esterquilinio, *n.m.* dunghill, heap of dung.
estertor, *n.m.* death-rattle; noisy breathing, stertor; ***los estertores del invierno,*** the last throes of winter.
estertoroso, -sa, *a.* stertorous.
esteta, *n.m.f.* æsthete.
estético, -ca, *a.* æsthetic. — *n.f.* æsthetics.
estetoscopia, *n.f.* stethoscopy.
estetoscopio, *n.m.* stethoscope.
esteva, *n.f.* plough-handle; perch (*of a carriage*).
estevado, -da, *a.* bow-legged.
estevón, *n.m.* [ESTEVA].
estezado, *n.m.* dressed deer-skin.
estiaje, *n.m.* low water; low-water season.
estiba, *n.f.* rammer; (*naut.*) stowage.
estibador, *n.m.* stevedore, docker, (*Am.*) longshoreman.
estibar, *v.t.* to compress (*wool*); to stow (*cargo*).
estibia, *n.f.* sprain (*in horse's neck*).
estibina, *n.f.* (*min.*) stibine.
estibio, *n.m.* antimony, stibium.
estiércol, *n.m.* dung, manure.
estigio, -gia, *a.* Stygian.
estigma, *n.m.* stigma; brand; stigmata.
estigmatizador, -ra, *a.* stigmatizing. — *n.m.f.* stigmatizer.
estigmatizar [C], *v.t.* to stigmatize; to brand.
estilar, *v.t.* to draw up in due form. — *v.i.* to be in the habit of. — **estilarse,** *v.r.* to be in fashion *or* vogue; to be the custom; ***ya sabes cómo se las estila,*** you know his ways.
estilete, *n.m.* stiletto; stylet; style; (*surg.*) probe.
estilicidio, *n.m.* dripping, distillation.
estilista, *n.m.f.* stylist.
estilita, *a.* stylitic. — *n.m.* stylite.
estilo, *n.m.* stylus; style; fashion; ***al estilo español,*** after the Spanish manner, Spanish style; ***algo por el estilo,*** sth. of the kind, of the sort *or* like that.
estilóbato, *n.m.* stylobate.
estilográfico, -ca, *a.* stylographic. — *n.f.* fountain pen.
estima, *n.f.* esteem; (*naut.*) dead reckoning.
estimabilidad, *n.f.* estimableness; worthiness.
estimable, *a.* estimable, worthy; computable.
estimación, *n.f.* esteem, estimation, regard; valuation, estimate, appraisement; ***estimación propia,*** self-esteem.
estimador, -ra, *a.* esteeming; estimating. — *n.m.f.* esteemer; estimator.
estimar, *v.t.* to esteem, have regard for; to estimate, appraise, reckon; to consider, deem.
estimativo, -va, *a.* judging, appraising. — *n.f.* faculty of judging, judgment.
estimulante, *a.* stimulating. — *n.m.* stimulant, stimulative.
estimular, *v.t.* to stimulate; to encourage, spur on.
estímulo, *n.m.* stimulus; stimulation; encouragement.
estinco, *n.m.* skink.
estío, *n.m.* summer.
estiomenar, *v.t.* (*med.*) to corrode.
estiómeno, *n.m.* gangrene.
estipendiar, *v.t.* to give a stipend to.
estipendiario, *n.m.* stipendiary.
estipendio, *n.m.* stipend, fee.
estípite, *n.m.* pilaster in form of a reversed pyramid.
estipticar, *v.t.* (*med.*) to apply a styptic to.
estipticidad, *n.f.* (*med.*) stypticity; costiveness.
estíptico, -ca, *a.* (*med.*) styptic, astringent; costive; (*fig.*) miserly, stingy.
estiptiquez, *n.f.* (*Arg.*, *Col.*) costiveness; niggardliness.
estípula, *n.f.* stipule.
estipulación, *n.f.* stipulation.
estipulante, *a.* stipulating. — *n.m.f.* stipulator, convening party.
estipular, *v.t.* to stipulate.
estique, *n.m.* sculptor's tool.
estira, *n.f.* currier's knife.
estirado, -da, *a.* (*fig.*) stiff, excessively formal; (*coll.*) sparing (*with money*). — *n.m.* stretching; drawing.
estirador, -ra, *n.m.* stretcher; drawing-frame.
estirajar, estirazar (*coll.*) [ESTIRAR].
estirajón (*coll.*) [ESTIRÓN].

estiramiento, *n.m.* stretching, pulling; drawing (*metals*).
estirar, *v.t.* to stretch, stretch out, pull taut; to draw (*metals*); ***estirar en frío,*** to cold-draw; (*coll.*) ***estirar la pata,*** to kick the bucket, peg out; ***estirar las piernas,*** to stretch one's legs, go for a stroll; ***estirar el dinero,*** to spin out (the) money, make (the) money go a long way. — **estirarse,** *v.r.* to stretch (*one's limbs*); to put on airs.
estirón, *n.m.* jerk, tug, yank, sharp pull; (*coll.*) ***dar*** or ***pegar un estirón,*** to shoot up quickly *or* suddenly (*in growth*).
estirpe, *n.f.* race, stock; pedigree; strain.
estítico, -ca [ESTÍPTICO].
estivada, *n.f.* land cleared of brushwood (*ready for cultivation*).
estival, estivo, -va, *a.* (of) summer.
esto, *pron. dem. neut.* this; ***en esto,*** at this *or* that point *or* moment; ***por esto,*** so; therefore; for this reason; ***esto es,*** that is, i.e.; that's it.
estocada, *n.f.* thrust, lunge *or* wound (*sword, rapier*).
estocafís, *n.m.* stock-fish.
estofa, *n.f.* quilted silk stuff; (*fig.*) kind, ilk; ***de baja estofa,*** of low ilk, of evil breed.
estofado, *n.m.* stew.
estofador, -ra, *n.m.f.* quilter.
estofar, *v.t.* to quilt; to paint on burnished gold; to size (*carvings*) (*before gilding*); to stew.
estofo, *n.m.* quilting; painting on gilt; sizing.
estoicidad, *n.f.* stoic attitude.
estoicismo, *n.m.* stoicism.
estoico, -ca, *a.* stoic, stoical. — *n.m.* stoic.
estola, *n.f.* stole.
estolidez, *n.f.* stupidity, denseness.
estólido, -da, *a.* stupid, dense.
estolón, *n.m.* large stole; (*bot.*) stolon.
estoma, *n.m.* (*bot.*) stoma.
estomacal, *a.* stomachic, of the stomach.
estomagante, *a.* irritating, insufferable.
estomagar [B], *v.t.* to upset; to irritate, get on the nerves of.
estómago, *n.m.* stomach; ***revolver el estómago a,*** to turn the stomach of; ***tener mucho estómago,*** to have a strong stomach, not to be squeamish; to have a thick skin, be thick-skinned.
estomaguero, *n.m.* stomacher.
estomático, -ca, *a.* (of the) stomach.
estomaticón, *n.m.* stomach-plaster.
Estonia, *n.f.* Estonia.
estonio, -nia, *a., n.m.f.* Estonian. — *n.m.* Estonian (*language*).
estopa, *n.f.* tow; burlap; oakum.
estopada, *n.f.* quantity of tow (*for spinning*).
estopear, *v.t.* to calk with oakum.
estopeño, -ña, *a.* (of) tow.
estopero, *n.m.* sucker (*of a pump*).
estoperol, *n.m.* scupper-nail; tow wick; (*Hisp. Am.*) upholstery nail.
estopilla, *n.f.* finest part of hemp *or* flax; yarn made from this; lawn; fine cloth; cotton cloth, cambric.
estopín, *n.m.* (*artill.*) priming-tube; quick-match.
estopón, *n.m.* coarse tow; cloth made from coarse tow yarns.
estopor, *n.m.* anchor-stopper.
estoposo, -sa, *a.* tow-like, filaceous.
estoque, *n.m.* rapier; (narrow) sword; sword lily.
estoqueador, *n.m.* thruster; matador.
estoquear, *v.t.* to thrust at, stab.
estoqueo, *n.m.* thrusting, stabbing.
estoraque, *n.m.* officinal storax; gum of the storax-tree; sweet gum tree; ***estoraque líquido,*** liquidambar.
estorbador, -ra, *a.* hindering, obstructing. — *n.m.f.* hinderer, obstructor.
estorbar, *v.t.* to hinder, obstruct, impede, hamper; to be *or* get in the way of; (*coll.*) ***le estorba lo negro,*** reading isn't his cup of tea.
estorbo, *n.m.* impediment, hindrance, obstruction, obstacle; nuisance.
estorboso, -sa, *a.* hindering, in the way.
estorcer [5D], *v.t.* (*obs.*) to liberate, evade.
estornija, *n.f.* linchpin-washer.
estornino, *n.m.* starling.
estornudar, *v.i.* to sneeze.
estornudo, *n.m.* sneeze.
estornutatorio, *a., n.m.* sternutatory, sternutative.
estotro, -ra, (*compound pronoun of* ***este, esto, esta*** and ***otro, otra***) this other.
estovar, *v.t.* to cook over a slow fire.
estrabismo, *n.m.* (*med.*) strabismus, squint.
estracilla, *n.f.* small rag; fine rag-paper.
estrada, *n.f.* road, way; (*mil.*) ***estrada encubierta,*** covert-way; ***batir la estrada,*** to reconnoitre.
estradiota, *n.f.* lance; ***a la estradiota,*** riding with long stirrups and stiff legs.
estradiote, *n.m.* Albanian mercenary.
estrado, *n.m.* drawing-room; drawing-room suite; dais, platform; (baker's) board; (*pl.*) courtrooms, halls of justice; (*law.*) ***hacer estrados,*** to hold a court.
estrafalario, -ria, *a.* (*coll.*) eccentric, outlandish; crazy, wild.
estragador, -ra, *a.* corrupting; ruining.
estragamiento, *n.m.* corruption, depravation; ravage, waste, ruin.
estragar [B], *v.t.* to vitiate, deprave, corrupt, spoil; to ravage; ***estragar la cortesía,*** to make a mess of one's etiquette, get it all wrong; ***tiene estragado el paladar,*** his palate is spoiled *or* blunted.
estrago, *n.m.* ravage, ruin, waste, havoc; corruption of morals, depravity; ***hacer estragos,*** to play havoc.
estragón, *n.m.* tarragon wormwood.
estrambosidad, *n.f.* squinting.
estrambote, *n.m.* burden of a song.
estrambótico, -ca, *a.* eccentric; crazy, wild; freakish.
estramonio, *n.m.* common thorn-apple.
estrangol, *n.m.* inflammation (*horse's tongue*).
estrangul, *n.m.* (*mus.*) mouthpiece.
estrangulación, *n.f.* strangling, strangulation; (*hydrost.*) stoppage; (*engin.*) throttling, choke.
estrangulador, -ra, *a.* strangling. — *n.m.f.* strangler; (*engin.*) choke, strangler.
estrangular, *v.t.* to strangle; (*med.*) to strangulate; (*engin.*) to throttle, choke.
estraperlo, *n.m.* black market.
estratagema, *n.f.* stratagem; ruse, trick.
estratega, estratego, *n.m.* strategist.
estrategia, *n.f.* strategy.
estratégico, -ca, *a.* strategic.
estratificación, *n.f.* stratification.
estratificar [A], *v.t.* to stratify.
estratiforme, *a.* stratiform.
estratigrafía, *n.f.* stratigraphy.
estratigráfico, -ca, *a.* stratigraphical.
estrato, *n.m.* stratum, layer; stratus (*cloud*).
estratosfera, *n.f.* stratosphere.
estrave, *n.m.* (*naut.*) stem-knee.
estraza, *n.f.* rag, fragment of cloth; ***papel de estraza,*** coarse wrapping paper, brown paper.
estrazar [C], *v.t.* (*obs.*) to tear, rend into fragments.
estrechamiento, *n.m.* tightening, tightness; narrowing.
estrechar, *v.t.* to tighten; to narrow; to make *or* bring close *or* closer; to press, press on; to clasp,

embrace; ***estrechar la mano de, a,*** to shake the hand of. — **estrecharse,** *v.r.* to narrow, draw in; to get *or* become close *or* closer; to move closer together, move up; to tighten one's belt, pull *or* draw in one's horns, cut down expenses.

estrechez, *n.f.* tightness; narrowness; closeness; pressure; strictness; ***vivir con estrecheces,*** to live in straitened circumstances, on a tight budget.

estrecho, -cha, *a.* tight; narrow; close; short of money; ***de manga estrecha,*** strict; narrow-minded. — *n.m.* party game played at the Feast of the Epiphany; strait; channel; tight spot, fix.

estrechón, *n.m.* flapping (*of sails*); pitching (*in a head sea*).

estrechura, *n.f.* narrowness; closeness; tight spot; narrow passage; straits.

estregadera, *n.f.* scrubbing-brush, mop.

estregadero, *n.m.* rubbing-post; washing place.

estregadura, *n.f.* rubbing, scrubbing.

estregamiento, *n.m.* rubbing, scrubbing.

estregar [IB], *v.t.* to rub, scrub, scour; to scrape, scratch.

estregón, *n.m.* hard *or* rough rub(bing).

estrella, *n.f.* star; star-wheel; linen cloth; (*fig.*) stars, fate; ***estrella de mar,*** starfish; ***estrella de rabo,*** comet; ***estrellas errantes*** or ***erráticas,*** wandering stars; ***estrella fugaz,*** shooting star; ***estrella polar,*** pole star; ***tener estrella*** or ***nacer con estrella,*** to be lucky; ***levantarse con las estrellas,*** to rise early; ***poner por*** or ***sobre las estrellas,*** to praise up, praise to the skies; ***unos nacen con estrella y otros nacen estrellados,*** some are born lucky and some unlucky; (*coll.*) ***ver las estrellas,*** to see stars; ***barras y estrellas,*** the Stars and Stripes.

estrellada (1), *n.f.* (*bot.*) lady's mantle, great stitchwort.

estrelladera, *n.f.* (*cook.*) egg-slice, turnover.

estrelladero, *n.m.* confectioner's pan (*for cooking eggs*, or *for making candied yolks*).

estrellado, -da (2), *a.* starry; ***caballo estrellado,*** horse with a star on its forehead; ***huevos estrellados,*** fried eggs.

estrellamar, *n.f.* (*bot.*) buckthorn plantain; (*ichth.*) starfish.

estrellar, *a.* stellated, starry. — *v.t.* (*coll.*) to dash to pieces, shatter; to fry (*eggs.*) — **estrellarse,** *v.r.* to crash, smash; to fail.

estrellera (1), *n.f.* (*naut.*) burton.

estrellero, -ra (2), *a.* that throws up its head (*horse*).

estrellita, *n.f.* little star.

estrellón, *n.m.* large star; star-shaped piece (*in fireworks*); (*Arg., Chi., Hond.*) collision, crash.

estremecedor, -ra, *a.* frightful, terrifying; shattering.

estremecer [9], *v.t.* to shake; to cause to shake, quiver, shudder *or* tremble.

estremecimiento, *n.m.* trembling, quaking; shaking, shuddering.

estrena, *n.f.* present, gift.

estrenar, *v.t.* to use *or* wear for the first time; to perform for the first time, give the first performance of. — **estrenarse,** *v.r.* to start; to make one's debut; (*coll.*) ***no se estrena,*** he doesn't do a hand's turn.

estreno, *n.m.* first performance; debut; première; commencement.

estrenque, *n.m.* stout bass rope.

estrenuidad, *n.f.* vigour, courage.

estrenuo, -nua, *a.* strongly; courageous.

estreñido, -da, *a.* niggardly.

estreñimiento, *n.m.* costiveness, constipation.

estreñir [8K], *v.t.* to constipate. — **estreñirse,** *v.r.* to get constipated.

estrepada, *n.f.* (*naut.*) long, strong pull (*on a rope etc.*).

estrépito, *n.m.* din, crash, crashing, racket.

estrepitoso, -sa, *a.* crashing, deafening; clamorous; uproarious.

estreptococia, *n.f.* (*path.*) streptococcic infection.

estría, *n.f.* (*arch.*) fluting, stria, groove.

estriadura, *n.f.* (*arch.*) fluting, grooving.

estriar [L], *v.t.* (*arch.*) to flute, striate. — **estriarse,** *v.r.* to become grooved, striated.

estribación, *n.f.* (*arch.*) counter-fort; spur (*of a mountain range*); foothill.

estribadero, *n.m.* prop, stay.

estribar, *v.i.* — ***en,*** to rest on, be based on; to lie in.

estribera, *n.f.* stirrup; (*Arg.*) stirrup strap.

estribería, *n.f.* stirrup store.

estriberón, *n.m.* stepping-stone; (*mil.*) temporary road.

estribillo, *n.m.* refrain; pet word *or* phrase, tag.

estribo, *n.m.* stirrup; brace, stay; prop; stirrup-bolt; buttress, abutment; step, running-board, footboard (*of a coach*); clasp (*of the felloes*); bone (*of the ear*); spur (*of a range*); ***andar*** or ***estar sobre los estribos,*** to be on the alert; ***perder los estribos,*** to lose control, fly off the handle; ***estar con el*** or ***un pie en el estribo,*** to be about to go *or* leave; to have one foot in the grave.

estribor, *n.m.* starboard.

estricnina, *n.f.* strychnine.

estricote, *adv.* ***al estricote,*** all over the place; ***tener al estricote,*** to lead a dance.

estricto, -ta, *a.* strict.

estridente, *a.* strident; shrill.

estridor, *n.m.* strident noise, screech.

estrige, *n.f.* screech-owl.

estrígil, *n.m.* strigil.

estrillar, *v.t.* (*obs.*) to groom, currycomb.

estro, *n.m.* (*poet.*) afflatus, inspiration.

estrobilífero, -ra, *a.* cone-bearing.

estróbilo, *n.m.* cone.

estrobo, *n.m.* (*naut.*) loop (*of stout rope* or *cable*); grummet.

estrofa, *n.f.* strophe, stanza, verse.

estronciana, *n.f.* strontia.

estroncianita, *n.f.* strontianite.

estroncio, *n.m.* strontium.

estropajear, *v.t.* to rub, scour.

estropajeo, *n.m.* rubbing, scrubbing.

estropajo, *n.m.* (dish) scourer; piece of rubbish.

estropajoso, -sa, *a.* ropy; thick, indistinct; stringy; (*coll.*) ragged, slovenly.

estropear, *v.t.* to spoil, ruin, wreck; to cripple, maim.

estropeo, *n.m.* spoiling, ruining, wrecking.

estropicio, *n.m.* (*coll.*) breakage, crash (*of crockery etc.*); racket; mess, wreck.

estrovo, *n.m.* (*naut.*) strap (*for a block*).

estructura, *n.f.* structure.

estructuración, *n.f.* structuration, giving a structure *or* framework (to).

estructural, *a.* structural.

estructurar, *v.t.* to structure, give a structure *or* framework to.

estruendo, *n.m.* clamour, clangour, uproar, racket, din.

estruendoso, -sa, *a.* clamorous.

estrujadura, *n.f.*, **estrujamiento,** *n.m.* squeezing, crushing.

estrujar, *v.t.* to squeeze, crush.

estrujón, *n.m.* big hug; (*lit.*) tight squeeze.

estuación, *n.f.* flow of the tide.

estuante, *a.* hot, boiling, glowing.

estuario, *n.m.* estuary.

estucador, *n.m.* stucco-plasterer.

estucar [A], *v.t.* to stucco.

estuco, *n.m.* stucco; plaster, scagliola; ***ser*** or ***parecer un estuco*** or ***de estuco,*** to be stolid.

estucurú, *n.m.* (*C.R.*) large owl.
estuche, *n.m.* box, casket; case; sheath (*for scissors etc.*); kit; ***ser un estuche,*** to be handy, useful.
estudiante, *n.m.* student.
estudiantil, *a.* student, of students.
estudiantillo, *n.m.* young student, miserable *or* two-penny ha'penny student.
estudiantino, -na, *a.* student; (*coll.*) ***a la estudiantina,*** in the manner of students. — *n.f.* strolling band of students.
estudiantón, *n.m.* plodder, dull *or* slow student.
estudiar, *v.t.*, *v.i.* to study; to draw from nature.
estudio, *n.m.* study; learning; studio; ***con estudio,*** with studied care; ***tener estudios,*** to have studied, be well-educated; ***dar estudios a,*** to pay for the education of.
estudiosidad, *n.f.* studiousness.
estudioso, -sa, *a.* studious. — *n.m.* student, scholar, specialist.
estufa, *n.f.* stove; hot-house; gas *or* electric fire; sweating room; dry bath; drying chamber; small brazier; (*fig.*) ***criar en estufa,*** to mollycoddle.
estufador, *n.m.* stew-pan.
estufero, estufista, *n.m.* maker *or* seller of stoves.
estufilla, *n.f.* small fur-muff; foot-warmer; chafing-dish.
estulticia, *n.f.* stupidity.
estulto, -ta, *a.* stupid.
estuosidad, *n.f.* excessive heat.
estuoso, -sa, *a.* hot, ardent, glowing.
estupefacción, *n.f.* stupefaction, astonishment.
estupefaciente, *a.* stupefacient. — *n.m.* drug, narcotic.
estupefactivo, -va, *a.* stupefying.
estupefacto, -ta, *a.* dumbfounded, nonplussed.
estupendamente, *adv.* extremely well, perfectly well, perfectly; fine, great, super; ***estoy estupendamente,*** I'm fine.
estupendo, -da, *a.* fine, great, super, first-rate, top-hole.
estupidez, *n.f.* stupidity, stupidness.
estúpido, -da, *a.* stupid. — *n.m.f.* silly ass, silly fool.
estupor, *n.m.* stupor; amazement, astonishment.
estuprador, *n.m.* rapist.
estuprar, *v.t.* to rape.
estupro, *n.m.* rape.
estuque, *n.m.* stucco.
estuquería, *n.f.* stuccoing; stucco-work.
estuquista, *n.m.* plasterer, stucco-worker.
esturar, *v.t.* to burn (*food*); to scorch, toast.
esturgar, *v.t.* to polish (*pottery*).
esturión, *n.m.* (*ichth.*) sturgeon.
ésula, *n.f.* a leafy-branched spurge.
esviaje, *n.m.* (*arch.*) obliquity.
etalaje, *n.m.* bosh (*of a blast-furnace*).
etapa, *n.f.* stage; halt; campaign *or* marching ration; ***por etapas,*** by stages, step by step; ***hacer etapa en,*** to make a halt at, break one's journey at; ***quemar etapas,*** to cut out intermediate stages, do a through journey.
éter, *n.m.* ether.
etéreo, -rea, *a.* ethereal.
eterización, *n.f.* etherization.
eterizar, [C], *v.t.* to etherize.
eternal, *a.* eternal.
eternidad, *n.f.* eternity.
eternizar [C], *v.t.* to make eternal *or* never-ending. — **eternizarse,** *v.r.* to spend an endless time, ages, all day *or* all night (***en,*** over); to linger, dwell *or* ponder endlessly (***en,*** upon); ***no me puedo eternizar aquí,*** I haven't got all day *or* all night (to waste here).
eterno, -na, *a.* eternal, everlasting.
eteromancia [HETEROMANCÍA].
eteromanía, *n.f.* etheromania.
eterómano, -na, *a.*, *n.m.f.* etheromaniac.
etesio, *a.* etesian.
ético, -ca, *a.* ethical; [HÉTICO]. — *n.m.f.* ethicist, moralist. — *n.f.* ethics.
etileno, *n.m.* ethylene.
etílico, -ca, *a.* ethylic.
etilo, *n.m.* ethyl.
etimóloga, *n.f.* [ETIMÓLOGO].
etimología, *n.f.* etymology.
etimológico, -ca, *a.* etymological.
etimologista, *n.m.* etymologist.
etimologizar [C], *v.t.* to etymologize.
etimólogo, -ga, *n.m.f.* etymologist.
etiología, *n.f.* etiology.
etíope, *a.*, *n.m.f.* Ethiopian (person).
Etiopía, *n.f.* Ethiopia.
etiópico, -ca, *a.* Ethiopic, Ethiopian. — *n.m.* Ethiopic (*language*).
etiópide, *n.f.* clary, Ethiopian mullein.
etiqueta, *n.f.* etiquette, formality; (*com.*) label, tag, (*Am.*) sticker; ***de etiqueta,*** formal; ***traje*** or ***vestido de etiqueta,*** formal dress.
etiquetero, -ra, *a.* formal, (being) a stickler for etiquette; punctilious.
etites, *n.f. inv.* eagle-stone.
etmoides, *n.m. inv.* ethmoid bone.
étnico, -ca, *a.* ethnic, ethnical.
etnógrafa, *n.f.* [ETNÓGRAFO].
etnografía, *n.f.* ethnography.
etnográfico, -ca, *a.* ethnographic.
etnógrafo, -fa, *n.m.f.* ethnographer.
etnología, *n.f.* ethnology.
etnológico, -ca, *a.* ethnologic(al).
etnólogo, -ga, *n.m.f.* ethnologist.
eubolia, *n.f.* propriety *or* discretion in speech.
eucalipto, *n.m.* eucalyptus.
eucaristía, *n.f.* eucharist.
eucarístico, -ca, *a.* eucharistic(al).
eucologio, *n.m.* (*eccles.*) euchologion, euchology.
eucrasia, *n.f.* eucrasy.
eudiometría, *n.m.* eudiometry.
eudiómetro, *n.m.* eudiometer.
eufemismo, *n.m.* euphemism.
eufonía, *n.f.* euphony.
eufónico, -ca, *a.* euphonic, euphonious.
euforia, *n.f.* resistance to pain and disease; euphoria, elation, exhilaration, exultation.
eufórico, -ca, *a.* elated, exhilarated.
eufrasia, *n.f.* (*bot.*) eyebright.
eugenesia, *n.f.* eugenics.
eunuco, *n.m.* eunuch.
eupepsia, *n.f.* eupepsy.
eupéptico, -ca, *a.* eupeptic, digestive.
euritmia, *n.f.* eurhythmy.
eurítmico, -ca, *a.* eurhythmic.
euro, *n.m.* (*poet.*) Eurus, east wind; ***euro austro*** or ***noto,*** south-east wind.
eurocomunismo, *n.m.* Eurocommunism.
Europa, *n.f.* Europe.
europeizar [C], *v.t.* to europeanize.
europeo, -pea, *a.*, *n.m.f.* European.
euscalduna, *a.*, *n.m.* Basque (*language*).
éuscaro, -ra, eusquero, -ra, *a.*, *n.m.f.* Basque. — *n.m.* Basque language.
eutanasia, *n.f.* euthanasia.
eutrapelia, eutropelia, *n.f.* moderation in pleasures; harmless *or* innocent pastime *or* sport.
eutrapélico, -ca, eutropélico, -ca, *a.* moderate, temperate.
evacuación, *n.f.* evacuation.
evacuante, *a.* evacuant, evacuating.
evacuar, *v.t.* to empty, evacuate; to discharge; to transact, deal with.

evacuativo, -va, evacuatorio, -ria, *a.* evacuative, that which evacuates. — *n.m.* public convenience.
evadir, *v.t.* to escape, shirk, elude, evade. — **evadirse,** *v.r.* to escape, sneak away.
evagación, *n.f.* evagation, wandering.
evaluación, *n.f.* evaluation.
evaluador, -ra, *a.* evaluating.
evaluar [M], *v.t.* to evaluate.
evalúo, *n.m.* (*com.*) valuation, appraisement.
evanescente, *a.* evanescent.
evangeliario, *n.m.* evangelistary.
evangélico, -ca, *a.* evangelic, evangelical.
evangelio, *n.m.* gospel; ***es el Evangelio,*** it's (the) gospel truth.
evangelismo, *n.m.* evangelism.
evangelista, *n.m.* evangelist; gospel-chanter, gospeller.
evangelistero, *n.m.* gospeller; (*obs.*) lectern.
evangelización, *n.f.* evangelization.
evangelizador, -ra, *a.* evangelizing. — *n.m.f.* evangelist.
evangelizar [C], *v.t.* to evangelize.
evaporable, *a.* evaporable.
evaporación, *n.f.* evaporation.
evaporador, -ra, *a.* evaporating.
evaporar, *v.t.* to evaporate. — **evaporarse,** *v.r.* to evaporate.
evaporatorio, -ria, *a.* (*med.*) evaporative.
evaporizar [C], *v.t., v.i.* to vaporize.
evasión, *n.f.* escape, breaking-out, get-away.
evasivo, -va, *a.* evasive. — *n.f.* evasive answer, evasion; ***contestar con evasivas,*** not to give a straight answer, be non-committal, dodge the issue.
evección, *n.f.* (*astron.*) evection.
evento, *n.m.* unforeseen event, contingency; ***a todo evento,*** for any eventuality.
eventual, *a.* chance, possible; temporary.
eventualidad, *n.f.* contingency.
eversión, *n.f.* eversion, destruction, ruin.
evicción, *n.f.* (*law*) eviction.
evidencia, *n.f.* obviousness, clear indication, certainty.
evidenciar, *v.t.* to make evident, obvious, clear *or* plain; to bring into evidence.
evidente, *a.* obvious, evident.
evisceración, *n.f.* evisceration.
evitable, *a.* avoidable.
evitación, *n.f.* avoidance.
evitar, *v.t.* to avoid, shun; to avert; to spare, save.
eviterno, -na, *a.* (*theol.*) imperishable, lasting.
evo, *n.m.* eternity; aeon.
evocación, *n.f.* evocation, evoking.
evocar [A], *v.t.* to evoke, call *or* conjure up; to bring back.
evolución, *n.f.* evolution, development; (*mil., naut.*) evolution, manœuvre.
evolucionar, *v.i.* to evolve; to develop; to alter, change; (*mil., naut.*) to perform evolutions *or* manœuvres.
evolucionismo, *n.m.* evolutionism.
evolucionista, *a., n.m.f.* evolutionist.
evolutivo, -va, *a.* evolutionary, evolving.
exabrupto, *n.m.* sudden outburst, harsh remark.
exacción, *n.f.* exaction; extortion.
exacerbación, *n.f.* exacerbation; exasperation.
exacerbar, *v.t.* to exacerbate; to exasperate.
exactamente, *adv.* exactly, precisely, just so.
exactitud, *n.f.* exactness, accuracy.
exacto, -ta, *a.* exact, accurate.
exactor, *n.m.* tax-gatherer.
exaedro, *n.m.* hexahedron.
exageración, *n.f.* exaggeration.
exagerado, -da, *a.* excessive; hysterical.
exagerador, -ra, *a.* exaggerating. — *n.m.f.* exaggerator.
exagerar, *v.t.* to exaggerate, over-state, get out of all proportion. — *v.i.* to exaggerate, make an awful fuss (*about*).
exagerativo, -va, *a.* exaggerating.
exágono, -na, *a.* hexagonal. — *n.m.* hexagon.
exaltación, *n.f.* exaltation, raising; (*chem.*) sublimation; hot-headedness.
exaltado, -da, *a.* ultra-radical in politics; hot-headed. — *n.m.f.* hot-head.
exaltamiento, *n.m.* exaltation; ultra-radicalism.
exaltar, *v.t.* to exalt; to raise. — **exaltarse,** *v.r.* to get all worked-up, get carried away.
examen, *n.m.* examination; inquiry; search; investigation; inspection, survey.
exámetro, *n.m.* hexameter.
examinador, -ra, *a.* examining. — *n.m.f.* examiner.
examinando, *n.m.* examinee, candidate.
examinante, *a.* examining.
examinar, *v.t.* to examine; to inspect, go over; to inquire into, investigate; to review; to look into; to search, scan; to give an examination to. — **examinarse,** *v.r.* to take *or* sit an examination.
exangüe, *a.* bloodless; (*fig.*) weak, without strength; (*fig.*) lifeless.
exanimación, *n.f.* exanimation.
exánime, *a.* lifeless.
exápodo, -da, *a.* hexapod, six-footed. — *n.m.pl.* (**exápodos**) (*ent.*) Hexapoda.
exarca, exarco, *n.m.* exarch.
exarcado, *n.m.* exarchate.
exasperación, *n.f.* exasperation.
exasperador, -ra, exasperante, *a.* exasperating.
exasperar, *v.t.* to exasperate.
excandecencia, *n.f.* anger.
excandecer [9], *v.t.* to enrage.
excarcelación, *n.f.* setting free, release.
excarcelar, *v.t.* to set free, release.
excavación, *n.f.* excavation, digging up.
excavar, *v.t.* to excavate, dig (up). — *v.i.* to excavate, dig.
excedencia, *n.f.* leave of absence.
excedente, *a.* excessive, exceeding; surplus; on leave of absence *or* paid leave. — *n.m.* surplus.
exceder, *v.t.* to surpass, outdo. — *v.i.* ***—de,*** to exceed, go beyond. — **excederse,** *v.r.* to overstep due bounds, go too far, overreach o.s.; to go beyond *or* exceed one's brief.
Excelencia, *n.m.f.* Excellency (*title*).
excelencia, *n.f.* excellence; ***por excelencia,*** par excellence.
excelente, *a.* excellent, first-rate.
excelentísimo, -ma, *a. superl.* most excellent.
excelsitud, *n.f.* loftiness.
excelso, -sa, *a.* lofty, sublime; ***el Excelso,*** the Most High.
excentricidad, *n.f.* eccentricity.
excéntrico, -ca, *a.* eccentric, eccentrical. — *n.f.* eccentric wheel.
excepción, *n.f.* exception; (*law*) demurrer; ***estado de excepción,*** state of emergency.
excepcional, *a.* exceptional.
excepcionar, *v.t.* (*law*) to enter a demurrer against.
exceptivo, -va, *a.* exceptive.
excepto, *adv.* except, excepting.
exceptuación, *n.f.* exception, exclusion.
exceptuar [M], *v.t.* to except, exclude.
excerpta, *n.f.* compendium.
excesivo, -va, *a.* excessive.
exceso, *n.m.* excess; (*com.*) surplus; ***en exceso,*** excessively; in excess; ***exceso de equipaje, de peso,*** excess luggage, weight.
excisión, *n.f.* (*surg.*) excision.
excitabilidad, *n.f.* excitability.

excitable, *a.* excitable.
excitación, *n.f.* excitation, exciting; excitement, agitation, worked-up state.
excitador, *n.m.* (*elec.*) discharging rod.
excitante, *a.* exciting. — *n.m.* (*elec.*) exciter.
excitar, *v.t.* to excite, stir up, get worked up. — **excitarse,** *v.r.* to get excited, get het-up, get worked-up.
excitativo, -va, *a.* exciting, stimulative.
exclamación, *n.f.* exclamation.
exclamar, *v.t.* to exclaim, cry out.
exclamativo, -va, exclamatorio, -ria, *a.* exclamatory.
exclaustración, *n.f.* (*eccles.*) secularization of monks *or* nuns.
exclaustrado, -da, *n.m.f.* (*eccles.*) secularized monk *or* nun.
exclaustrar, *v.t.* (*eccles.*) to secularize (*monks* or *nuns*).
excluir [O], *v.t.* to exclude, shut out; to debar.
exclusión, *n.f.* exclusion, debarring, shutting out.
exclusivismo, *n.m.* blind adherence to an idea etc., exclusivism.
exclusivista, *a.* exclusive. — *n.m.f.* exclusivist.
exclusivo, -va, *a.* exclusive. — *n.f.* exclusive *or* sole right.
excogitable, *a.* imaginable, conceivable.
excogitar, *v.t.* to excogitate, meditate; to devise.
excomulgación, *n.f.* excommunication.
excomulgado, -da, *a.* (*coll.*) accursed, wicked, perverse.
excomulgador, *n.m.* excommunicator.
excomulgar [B], *v.t.* to excommunicate.
excomunión, *n.f.* excommunication.
excoriación, *n.f.* excoriation, flaying.
excoriar, *v.t.* to excoriate, flay. — **excoriarse,** *v.r.* to graze o.s.
excrecencia, *n.f.* excrescence.
excreción, *n.f.* excretion.
excremental, excrementicio, -cia, excrementoso, -sa, *a.* excremental, excrementitious.
excrementar, *v.i.* to void excrement.
excremento, *n.m.* excrement; (*pl.*) excreta; droppings.
excretar, *v.i.* to excrete; to eject excrement.
excreto, -ta, *a.* excreted, ejected.
excretorio, -ria, *a.* excretory, excretive.
exculpación, *n.f.* exculpation, exoneration.
exculpar, *v.t.* to exculpate, exonerate.
excursión, *n.f.* excursion, outing; trip.
excursionista, *n.m.f.* tripper.
excusa (I), *n.f.* excuse; (*law*) demurrer; (*obs.*) ***a excusas,*** dissemblingly.
excusabaraja, *n.f.* basket with a wickerwork cover.
excusable, *a.* excusable, pardonable.
excusación, *n.f.* excuse.
excusadamente, *adv.* unnecessarily.
excusado, -da, *a.* set apart; reserved; useless, superfluous, unnecessary; ***puerta excusada,*** side *or* private door; ***es pensar en lo excusado,*** it's a waste of time to think of it. — *n.m.* water-closet, toilet-room.
excusador, -ra, *a.* excusing. — *n.m.f.* excuser. — *n.m.* substitute, deputy vicar.
excusalí, *n.m.* small apron.
excusaña, *n.m.* (*obs., mil.*) scout, spy, lookout; (*obs.*) ***a excusañas,*** hiddenly, secretly.
excusar, *v.t.* to excuse; to avoid; to save from the trouble of; to exempt (from); (*with infinitive*) to be excused from, not to have to; ***como vas a venir, excuso escribirte,*** as you are coming, I don't need to write *or* I shan't bother to write; ***excuso decirte*** or ***excusado decirte,*** I don't have *or* need to tell you, needless to say; ***con esto me excusas el tener que salir,*** in this way you save my having to go out; ***así excusamos disgustos,*** like this we avoid upsets *or* unpleasantness.
excuso, -sa (2), (*obs.*) [EXCUSADO].
exea, *n.m.* (*mil.*) scout.
execrable, *a.* execrable, abominable.
execración, *n.f.* execration; (*eccles.*) desecration.
execrador, -ra, *a.* execrating.
execrando, -da, *a.* execrable.
execrar, *v.t.* to execrate, abhor.
execratorio, -ria, *a.* execratory.
exégesis, *n.f.* exegesis.
exégeta, *n.m.* exegete.
exegético, -ca, *a.* exegetic, exegetical.
exención, *n.f.* exemption.
exentar [EXIMIR].
exento, -ta, *a.* exempt; free; detached; isolated; privileged. — *n.m.* (*obs.*) officer of royal guard. — *p.p.* [EXIMIR].
exequátur, *n.m.* exequatur.
exequias, *n.f.pl.* exequies, obsequies.
exequible, *a.* attainable.
exfoliación, *n.f.* exfoliation, defoliation.
exfoliador, *n.m.* (*Chi.*) writing-pad.
exfoliar, *v.t.* to exfoliate.
exhalación, *n.f.* exhalation; shooting star; bolt of lightning; effluvium, fume, vapour.
exhalador, -ra, *a.* exhaling. — *n.m.f.* exhaler.
exhalar, *v.t.* to exhale, breathe out, emit; ***exhalar el espíritu,*** to give up the ghost. — **exhalarse,** *v.r.* to breathe hard; to rush; to have a craze.
exhausto, -ta, *a.* exhausted.
exheredación, *n.f.* disinheritance.
exheredar, *v.t.* to disinherit.
exhibición, *n.f.* exhibition; show; showing off.
exhibir, *v.t.* to exhibit, display, show; to show off; to produce (*documents*).
exhortación, *n.f.* exhortation.
exhortador, -ra, *a.* exhorting. — *n.m.f.* exhorter.
exhortar, *v.t.* to exhort.
exhortatorio, -ria, *a.* exhortatory.
exhorto, *n.m.* (*law*) letters rogatory.
exhumación, *n.f.* exhumation.
exhumar, *v.t.* to exhume, dig up.
exigencia, *n.f.* exigency, requirement, demand.
exigente, *a.* exigent, exacting, demanding.
exigible, exigidero, -ra, *a.* exigible.
exigir [E], *v.t.* to demand, require, exact.
exigüidad, *n.f.* exiguity, exiguousness, scantiness.
exiguo, -gua, *a.* exiguous, scanty.
exiliar, *v.t.* to (send into) exile.
exilio, *n.m.* exile, banishment; place of exile.
eximente, *a.* exempting; ***circunstancia eximente,*** exonerating circumstance.
eximio, -mia, *a.* eminent, distinguished.
eximir [*p.p.* **eximido, exento**], *v.t.* to exempt, free (from); to excuse.
exinanido, -da, *a.* debilitated, very weak, very feeble.
existencia, *n.f.* existence, life; (*pl.*) (*com.*) stocks; (*com.*) ***en existencia,*** in stock.
existente, *a.* existent, extant, existing; (*com.*) in stock.
existimación, *n.f.* estimation, opinion.
existimar, *v.t.* to form an opinion of, judge.
existir, *v.i.* to exist, live, have being.
exitazo, *n.m.* terrific success, smash hit.
éxito, *n.m.* issue, outcome; success; ***tener mucho éxito,*** to be very successful.
Éxodo, *n.m.* Exodus.
exoneración, *n.f.* exoneration.
exonerar, *v.t.* to exonerate.
exorable, *a.* exorable.
exorar, *v.t.* to beg, entreat.

exorbitancia, *n.f.* exorbitance, excessiveness.
exorbitante, *a.* exorbitant, excessive, terrific.
exorcismo, *n.m.* exorcism.
exorcista, *n.m.* exorcizer, exorcist.
exorcizante, *a.* exorcizing. — *n.m.* exorcizer.
exorcizar [C], *v.t.* to exorcize.
exordio, *n.m.* exordium.
exornación, *n.f.* (*rhet.*) embellishment.
exornar, *v.t.* to embellish, adorn.
exortación, *n.f.* exhortation.
exotérico, -ca, *a.* exoteric.
exótico, -ca, *a.* exotic; foreign; unusual.
expandir, *v.t.* to expand; to spread.
expansibilidad, *n.f.* (*phys.*) expansibility.
expansible, *a.* (*phys.*) expansible.
expansión, *n.f.* expansion; recreation.
expansionar, *v.t.* to expand. — **expansionarse,** *v.r.* to let off steam; to relax; to have (some) fun; (*fig.*) let one's hair down.
expansivo, -va, *a.* expansive; extrovert.
expatriación, *n.f.* expatriation.
expatriar, *v.t.* to expatriate. — **expatriarse,** *v.r.* to leave one's country.
expectación, *n.f.* expectance, expectation, expectancy; anticipation.
expectante, *a.* expectant.
expectativa, *n.f.* expectation; expectancy; ***estar a la expectativa,*** to be on the lookout.
expectoración, *n.f.* expectoration.
expectorante, *a.* expectorating. — *n.m.* (*med.*) expectorant.
expectorar, *v.t.* to expectorate.
expedición, *n.f.* expedition; shipment, dispatch; expeditiousness.
expedicionario, -ria, *a.* expeditionary; ***cuerpo expedicionario,*** expeditionary force.
expedicionero, *n.m.* despatcher of pontifical bulls.
expedido, -da [EXPEDITO].
expedidor, -ra, *n.m.f.* (*com.*) despatcher, sender, shipper.
expediente, *n.m.* (*law*) proceedings, action; file; dossier, record; despatch; provision, supply; means, resource, expedient measure; motive, reason; ***cubrir el expediente,*** to keep up appearances; to do the bare minimum; ***dar expediente a,*** to put through; ***formar expediente a,*** to take proceedings against; ***instruir un expediente,*** to prepare a matter for decision *or* for action to be taken; ***incoar expediente,*** to start proceedings.
expedienteo, *n.m.* (*coll.*) red tape.
expedir [8], *v.t.* to facilitate, expedite; to issue; to draw up; to despatch, send, remit, forward, ship.
expeditivo, -va, *a.* expeditious, prompt.
expedito, -ta, *a.* expeditious, prompt.
expelente, *a.* expellant.
expeler [*p.p.* **expelido, expulso**], *v.t.* to expel, eject.
expendedor, -ra, *a.* selling, retailing, retail. — *n.m.f.* dealer, seller; retailer; (*law*) ***expendedor de moneda falsa,*** utterer, passer of counterfeit money.
expendeduría, *n.f.* retail shop where tobacco and other state goods are sold.
expender, *v.t.* to spend, lay out, expend; to sell, retail; (*law*) to pass (*counterfeit money*); (*com.*) to sell on commission.
expendición, *n.f.* expending; selling (*by retail* or *on commission*).
expendio, *n.m.* expense, outlay; (*Arg., Mex., Per.*) selling, retailing; (*Mex.*) tobacconist.
expensar, *v.t.* (*Chi., Mex., law*) to pay costs (of).
expensas, *n.f.pl.* expenses, charges, costs; ***a expensas de,*** at the expense of.
experiencia, *n.f.* experience; experiment.
experimentado, -da, *a.* experienced.
experimentador, -ra, *n.m.f.* experimenter.
experimental, *a.* experimental.
experimentar, *v.t.* to experience, feel, undergo; to test, try out. — *v.i.* to experiment.
experimento, *n.m.* experiment, test.
experto, -ta, *a.* expert. — *n.m.f.* expert.
expiación, *n.f.* expiation, atonement, reparation; purification.
expiar, *v.t.* to expiate, atone for; to cleanse, purify.
expiativo, -va, *a.* expiational.
expiatorio, -ria, *a.* expiatory.
expillo, *n.m.* (*bot.*) feverfew.
expiración, *n.f.* expiration.
expirante, *a.* expiring.
expirar, *v.i.* to expire.
explanación, *n.f.* elaboration, elucidation; levelling.
explanada, *n.f.* esplanade; (*artill.*) platform; (*fort.*) glacis.
explanar, *v.t.* to elaborate on, enlarge on, elucidate; to level, grade.
explayamiento, *n.m.* dwelling, elaborating (on).
explayar, *v.t.* to extend, spread, enlarge. — **explayarse,** *v.r.* to dwell, enlarge *or* elaborate (***en,*** on); to let off steam, relieve one's mind; to relax.
expletivo, -va, *a.* expletive.
explicable, *a.* explicable, explainable.
explicación, *n.f.* explanation.
explicaderas, *n.f.pl.* (*coll.*) ***tener buenas explicaderas,*** to be good at explaining things.
explicador, -ra, *n.m.f.* explainer; demonstrator; glosser.
explicar [A], *v.t.* to explain; ***no me lo explico,*** I can't understand it, I can't credit it, I can't account for it.
explicativo, -va, *a.* explicative, explicatory, explanatory.
explícito, -ta, *n.f.* explicit.
exploración, *n.f.* exploration; scanning.
explorador, -ra, *a.* exploring. — *n.m.f.* explorer; boy *or* girl scout.
explorar, *v.t.* to explore, search, scan; (*mil.*) to scout.
exploratorio, -ria, *a.* exploratory, exploring. — *n.m.* (*med.*) probe; catheter.
explosión, *n.f.* explosion, blast; outburst.
explosivo, -va, *a., n.m.* explosive.
explotable, *a.* exploitable; (*min.*) workable, minable.
explotación, *n.f.* exploitation; development; working; cultivation.
explotar, *v.t.* to exploit; to develop; to work; to cultivate. — *v.i.* to explode.
expoliación, *n.f.* spoliation.
expoliador, -ra, *a.* spoliating. — *n.m.f.* spoliator.
expoliar, *v.t.* to spoliate, plunder, despoil.
exponencial, *a.* (*math.*) exponential.
exponente, *a., n.m.f.* exponent; (*com.*) exhibitor. — *n.m.* (*alg., arith.*) exponent.
exponer [25], *v.t.* to expose, show, exhibit, lay open; to expound; to abandon (*a child*).
exportación, *n.f.* exportation, export; ***derechos de exportación,*** export duties.
exportador, -ra, *a.* exporting. — *n.m.f.* exporter.
exportar, *v.t.* to export.
exposición, *n.f.* exposition; exposé; exhibition, show, display; risk, peril, jeopardy; claim, petition; (*photo.*) exposure.
expositivo, -va, *a.* expositive.
expósito, -ta, *a.* exposed; foundling. — *n.m.f.* foundling.
expositor, -ra, *a.* expounding; exhibiting. — *n.m.f.* expounder; exhibitor.
expremijo, *n.m.* cheese-vat.
expresado, -da, *a.* aforesaid.

expresamente, *adv.* expressly.
expresar [*p.p.* **expresado, expreso**], *v.t.* to express, convey.
expresión, *n.f.* expression; expressiveness; utterance, phrase; squeezing; ***reducir a la mínima expresión,*** to cut to a minimum, cut to the bare minimum; ***muchas expresiones para,*** kindest regards to.
expresionismo, *n.m.* expressionism.
expresivo, -va, *a.* expressive; telling; affectionate.
expreso, -sa, *a.* expressed; express; ***tren expreso,*** express train. — *adv.* expressly, on purpose. — *n.m.* express train; express messenger. — *p.p.* [EXPRESAR].
exprimidera, *n.f.*, **exprimidero,** *n.m.* squeezer.
exprimir, *v.t.* to squeeze (out), press (out).
expropiación, *n.f.* expropriation.
expropiar, *v.t.* to expropriate.
expuesto, -ta, *a.* risky, dangerous. — *p.p.* [EXPONER].
expugnable, *a.* stormable.
expugnación, *n.f.* (*mil.*) storming.
expugnador, *n.m.* (*mil.*) stormer.
expugnar, *v.t.* (*mil.*) to storm, take by storm.
expulsar [*p.p.* **expulsado, expulso**], *v.t.* to expel, throw out; to send down; to cashier.
expulsión, *n.f.* expulsion, expelling.
expulsivo, -va, *a.* expulsive, expelling.
expulso, -sa, *a.* expelled. — *p.p* [EXPELER *and* EXPULSAR].
expulsor, -ra, *a.* expelling, ejecting. — *n.m.f.* expeller, ejector.
expurgación, *n.f.* expurgation, purification.
expurgar [B], *v.t.* to expurgate.
expurgativo, -va, *a.* expurgatory.
expurgatorio, -ria, *a.* expurgatory. — *n.m.* index of the books prohibited by the Inquisition.
expurgo, *n.m.* expurgation.
exquisito, -ta, *a.* exquisite, delicious.
éxtasi, éxtasis, *n.m.* ecstasy; rapture.
extasiarse, *v.r.* to go into raptures.
extático, -ca, *a.* ecstatic.
extemporal, extemporáneo, -nea, *a.* untimely; unpremeditated, extemporaneous.
extender(se) [2, *p.p.* **extendido, extenso**], *v.t.* (*v.r.*) to extend, enlarge, spread (out), expand, stretch (out); to draw up (*a document*); to unfurl, unfold; ***extender un cheque,*** to write out a cheque. — **extenderse,** *v.r.* to extend, spread out, stretch out *or* away; to enlarge upon.
extendido, *a.* widespread.
extendimiento, *n.m.* (*obs.*) extension, dilatation.
extensibilidad, *n.f.* extensibility.
extensión, *n.f.* extension; extent; area, expanse; extensiveness.
extensivo, -va, *a.* extendable; ***disposiciones extensivas a otros grupos,*** provisions which can be extended to cover other groups.
extenso, -sa, *a.* extensive, vast; ***por extenso,*** at length, in detail. — *p.p.* [EXTENDER].
extensor, -ra, *a.* extending. — *n.m.* (*anat.*) extensor (*muscle*).
extenuación, *n.f.* extenuation.
extenuar [M], *v.t.* to extenuate, wear out utterly.
extenuativo, -va, *a.* utterly exhausting.
exterior, *a.* exterior; outward, outer; foreign. — *n.m.* outside, exterior; outward appearance; outdoors; abroad, foreign countries.
exterioridad, *n.f.* outward appearance; outside; outside things.
exteriorizar [C], *v.t.* to show. — **exteriorizarse,** *v.r.* to show, take outward form.
exterminador, -ra, *a.* exterminatory, exterminating. — *n.m.f.* exterminator.
exterminar, *v.t.* to exterminate.
exterminio, *n.m.* extermination.
externado, *n.m.* day-school.
externo, -na, *a.* external; outward; exterior, outside. — *n.m.f.* day-pupil.
extinción, *n.f.* extinction; quenching, extinguishing.
extinguible, *a.* extinguishable.
extinguir [G], *v.t.* to extinguish, quench.
extintivo, -va, *a.* extinctive.
extinto, -ta, *a.* extinct; late, deceased. — *p.p.* [EXTINGUIR].
extintor, *n.m.* fire-extinguisher.
extirpación, *n.f.* extirpation, rooting-out.
extirpador, -ra, *a.* extirpating. — *n.m.f.* extirpator. — *n.m.* (*agric.*) weed-extirpator, cultivator.
extirpar, *v.t.* to extirpate, root out.
extorno, *n.m.* (*insurance*) rebate.
extorsión, *n.f.* extortion; trouble, inconvenience; ***siempre que no te cause ninguna extorsión,*** (always) provided it doesn't cause you any bother, doesn't put you out.
extra, *a.* extra, extra-special, top-quality. — *n.m.f.* extra; ***extra de,*** besides, in addition to.
extracción, *n.f.* extraction; drawing out; (lottery) draw.
extractador, -ra, *a.* abstracting. — *n.m.f.* abstractor.
extractar, *v.t.* to abstract, summarize, give in précis form.
extracto, *n.m.* (*chem.*) extract; précis, summary, abstract; ***extracto de Saturno,*** white lead.
extractor, -ra, *a.* extracting. — *n.m.f.* extractor.
extradición, *n.f.* extradition.
extraente, *a.* extracting. — *n.m.f.* extractor.
extraer [34], *v.t.* to extract, draw out.
extrafino, -na, *a.* superfine; ***azúcar extrafino,*** castor sugar, (*Am.*) powdered sugar.
extrajudicial, *a.* extrajudicial.
extralimitarse, *v.r.* to overstep the mark, go too far, overreach o.s.; to go beyond *or* exceed one's brief.
extramuros, *adv.* outside the walls of a town, outside.
extranjería, *n.f.* alienship; ***de extranjería,*** foreign.
extranjerismo, *n.m.* fondness for foreign things; foreignness; foreign term.
extranjerizar [C], *v.t.* to make foreign. — **extranjerizarse,** *v.r.* to get *or* go foreign.
extranjero, -ra, *a.* foreign, alien. — *n.m.f.* foreigner, alien. — *n.m.* foreign countries; ***está en el extranjero,*** he is abroad.
entranjía (*coll.*) [EXTRANJERÍA].
extranjis, *adv.* (*coll.*) ***de extranjis,*** secretly, undercover, in an underhand way.
extrañación, *n.f.*, **extrañamiento,** *n.m.* banishment, exile.
extrañar, *v.t.* to banish; to alienate; to cut, ignore (*a person*); to surprise; to find strange; not to feel at home in; (*Hisp. Am.*) to miss (*a person*); ***no es de extrañar,*** it's no wonder; ***extraño la cama,*** I can't get used to this bed. — **extrañarse,** *v.r.* — ***de,*** to be surprised at, wonder at, find surprising.
extrañeza, *n.f.* strangeness; wonder, surprise, astonishment.
extraño, -ña, *a.* queer, strange, odd; peculiar; foreign; out of the ordinary; ***cuerpo extraño,*** foreign body.
extraoficial, *a.* non-official, unofficial.
extraordinario, -ria, *a.* extraordinary; special. — *n.m.* extra dish, treat, sth. special; special courier; (*newsp.*) special, extra.
extrarradio, *n.m.* suburbs.
extratémpora, *n.f.* dispensation to take holy orders.
extraterritorial, *a.* extraterritorial.
extraterritorialidad, *n.f.* extraterritoriality.
extravagancia, *n.f.* oddness, wildness, craziness. eccentricity, extravagant thing to do *or* say.

extravagante, *a.* eccentric, freakish, wild, outlandish, crazy. — *n.f.pl.* (**extravagantes**) (*eccles.*) extravagants.
extravasarse, *v.r.* (*med.*) to extravasate, exude.
extravenado, -da, *a.* extravenate.
extravenarse, *v.r.* to exude through the veins.
extraviar [L], *v.t.* to mislead, lead astray; to mislay, lose. — **extraviarse,** *v.r.* to go astray; to lose one's way, get lost.
extravío, *n.m.* deviation; going astray, losing one's way; misplacement; disorder.
extremado, -da, *a.* extreme.
extremar, *v.t.* to carry to extremes, to excessive lengths *or* to the limit. — **extremarse,** *v.r.* to do one's very best, take special pains, go out of one's way.
extremaunción, *n.f.* extreme unction.
extremeño, -ña, *a.*, *n.m.f.* of Estremadura.
extremidad, *n.f.* extreme *or* remote part; end, extremity.
extremista, *a.*, *n.m.f.* extremist.
extremo, -ma, *a.* extreme; utmost. — *n.m.* extreme, furthest point, end; point, matter, detail; ***con extremo, en extremo,*** or ***por extremo,*** extremely, in the utmost degree; ***de extremo a extremo,*** from end to end; ***hacer extremos,*** to overdo it; to be over-demonstrative; ***pasarse al otro extremo,*** to go to the other extreme; ***en último extremo,*** in the last resort.
extremoso, -sa, *a.* extreme, excessive; going *or* running to extremes, inclined to overdo it.
extrínseco, -ca, *a.* extrinsic.
extroversión, *n.f.* extroversion.
extrovertido, -da, *a.*, *n.m.f.* extrovert.
exuberancia, *n.f.* exuberance; luxuriance.
exuberante, *a.* exuberant; luxuriant.
exuberar, *v.i.* (*obs.*) to be exuberant.
exudación, *n.f.* exudation.
exudar, *v.i.* to exude, ooze out.
exulceración, *n.f.* (*med.*) exulceration.
exulcerar, *v.t.* (*med.*) to exulcerate.
exultación, *n.f.* exultation.
exutorio, *n.m.* (*med.*) artificial ulcer.
exvoto, *n.m.* votive offering.
eyaculación, *n.f.* (*med.*) ejaculation.
eyacular, *v.t.* to ejaculate.
eyectar, *v.t.* to eject.
eyector, *n.m.* ejector.

F

F, f, *n.f.* letter F, f.
fa, *n.m.* (*mus.*) fa.
fabada, *n.f.* Asturian stew of pork and beans.
fabla, *n.f.* (*obs.*) talk, speech.
fablilla, *n.f.* tale.
fábrica, *n.f.* fabric, structure; masonry, brickwork; factory, works, plant; manufacture; fabrication; church building fund; ***fábrica de tejidos,*** textile mill; ***fábrica de cerveza,*** brewery; ***valor en fábrica,*** ex-works price.
fabricación, *n.f.* manufacturing; manufacture, make; ***fabricación en serie,*** mass-production.
fabricador, -ra, *a.* fabricating; scheming, devising. — *n.m.f.* fabricator; schemer, inventor, contriver, deviser; (*naut.*) constructor.
fabricante, *a.* manufacturing. — *n.m.* manufacturer, maker.
fabricar [A], *v.t.* to manufacture, make; to build; to fabricate, devise, contrive; ***fabricar en serie,*** to mass-produce.
fabril, *a.* manufacturing, industrial.
fabriquero, *n.m.* manufacturer; churchwarden.
fabuco, *n.m.* (*bot.*) beech-mast.
fábula, *n.f.* fable, legend; story; talk; ***la fábula del pueblo,*** the talk of the village *or* town.
fabulador, *n.m.* fabulist.
fabular, *v.i.* (*obs.*) to invent fables; to gossip.
fabulista, *n.m.* fabulist, writer of fables.
fabuloso, -sa, *a.* fabulous; legendary; terrific.
faca, *n.f.* jack-knife.
facción, *n.f.* faction; (*mil.*) action, combat; (*mil.*) duty; (*pl.* **facciones**) features (*facial*).
faccionario, -ria, *a.* factionary.
faccioso, -sa, *a.* factious, mutinous. — *n.m.f.* insurgent, rebel.
facería, *n.f.* (*prov.*) common pastureland.
faceto, -ta, *a.* (*Hisp. Am.*) merry, lively, witty, gay. — *n.f.* facet; feature.
facial, *a.* facial; intuitive.
facie, *n.f.* face (*of a crystal*).
fácil, *a.* easy; facile; likely; ***es fácil que venga hoy,*** it's quite likely he'll come today; ***es fácil de hacer,*** it is easy to do.
facilidad, *n.f.* ease, easiness, facility; ***facilidades de pago,*** easy terms; ***dar facilidades,*** to make things easy.
facilillo, -lla, facilito, -ta, *a.* pretty easy, nice and easy.
facilitación, *n.f.* facilitation.
facilitar, *v.t.* to facilitate, make easy; to furnish, supply.
facilón, -lona, *a.* ridiculously easy, a walk-over, easy as pie.
facineroso, -sa, *n.m.f.* villain, rogue, criminal.
facistol, *n.m.* lectern.
facón, *n.m.* large jack-knife.
facoquero, -ra, *n.m.f.* wart-hog.
facsímile, *n.m.* facsimile.
factible, *a.* feasible, practicable.
facticio, -cia, *a.* artificial, factitious.
factor, *n.m.* factor; (*railw.*) luggage clerk.
factoraje, *n.m.* factorage, agency.
factoría, *n.f.* factorage, agency; factory; colonial factory.
factorial, *a.* (*math.*) factorial.
factótum, *n.m.* factotum; busybody.
factura, *n.f.* (*com.*) bill, invoice; (*art*) execution; ***factura simulada,*** pro forma invoice.
facturar, *v.t.* (*com.*) to invoice; (*railw.*) to register (*luggage*).
fácula, *n.f.* (*astron.*) facula.
facultad, *n.f.* faculty; school; power, authority.
facultador, -ra, *n.m.f.* one who commissions *or* empowers.
facultar, *v.t.* to empower, commission, authorize.
facultativo, -va, *a.* belonging to a faculty; facultative; optional. — *n.m.* physician.
facundia, *n.f.* eloquence; loquacity.
facundo, -da, *a.* eloquent; loquacious.
facha, *n.f.* (*coll.*) appearance, look; (*fig.*) sight, mess; ***ponerse en facha,*** to get ready; (*naut.*) to lie to; ***estar hecho una facha,*** to be *or* look a sight.
fachado, -da, *a.* (*coll.*) ***bien fachado,*** good-looking; ***mal fachado,*** bad-looking. — *n.f.* façade, front, frontage; frontispiece; ***hacer fachada con,*** to face, front on; ***tiene mucha fachada,*** he's *or* it's all façade.
fachear, *v.i.* (*naut.*) to lie to.
fachenda, *n.f.* (*coll.*) vanity, conceit. — *n.m.* (*coll.*) vain, conceited fellow.
fachendear, *v.i.* (*coll.*) to brag, boast.
fachendista, fachendón, -dona, fachendoso, -sa, *a., n.m.f.* conceited, vain, ostentatious (person).
fachinal, *n.m.* (*Arg.*) marshy land.
fachoso, -sa, *a.* (*coll.*) ugly-faced; looking a sight; (*Chi., Mex.*) conceited, vain.
fada, *n.f.* enchantress, fairy; (*bot.*) small pippin apple.
fading, *n.m.* fading (out).
faena, *n.f.* piece of work, job, task, chore; (*coll.*) dirty *or* rotten trick; (*Cub., Guat., Mex.*) overtime (*in a hacienda*); ***faenas domésticas,*** housework.
faenero, *n.m.* (*Chi.*) farm labourer.
faenista, *n.m.f.* one who plays dirty *or* rotten tricks.
faetón, *n.m.* phaeton.
fagina [FAJINA].
fagocito, *n.m.* (*biol.*) phagocyte.
fagot, *n.m.* bassoon; bassoon-player.
fagotista, *n.m.* bassoon-player.
faisán, *n.m.* pheasant.
faisana, *n.f.* hen pheasant.
faisanería, *n.f.* pheasantry.
faisanero, *n.m.* pheasant rearer.
faja, *n.f.* sash; girdle; fillet; band; swathing-band; strip (*of land*); (*her.*) fess(e); (*arch.*) fascia; (*naut.*) reef-band.
fajadura, *n.f.* swathing, swaddling; (*naut.*) band.
fajamiento, *n.m.* rolling, swathing.
fajar, *v.t.* to swathe, swaddle; to belt, band, girdle; (*coll.*) to give a belting *or* beating to; (*coll.*) ***fajar con,*** to fall on; to attack violently. — **fajarse,** *v.r.* (*Hisp. Am.*) to fight.
fajardo, *n.m.* meat pie, patty; vol-au-vent.
fajeado, -da, *a.* banded, fasciated.
fajero, *n.m.* swaddling-band.
fajín, *n.m.* small band *or* sash; general's sash.
fajina, *n.f.* faggot; toil, labour; bundle, stack, stook; (*mil.*) taps, retreat; (*fort.*) fascine.
fajinada, *n.f.* collection of faggots *or* stooks; fascine-work.
fajo, *n.m.* bundle, sheaf, wad; ***fajo de billetes,*** wad of notes; (*pl.*) swaddling-clothes.
fajón, *n.m.* (*arch.*) large band, roller; large sash; plaster border.
falacia, *n.f.* fallacy, fallaciousness; deceit.
falange, *n.f.* (*mil.*) phalanx; (*anat.*) phalange; (*polit.*) Falange.
falangia, *n.f.*, **falangio,** *n.m.* daddy-long-legs.
falangista, *a., n.m.f.* Falangist.
falárica, *n.f.* javelin.
falaris, *n.f.* (*orn.*) coot.
falaz, *a.* fallacious; deceitful, treacherous.
falbalá, *n.m.* flounce, furbelow; flap (*on the skirt of a coat*).
falca, *n.f.* (*prov.*) small wedge; (*naut.*) wash-board.

falcado, -da, *a.* hooked. — *n.m.* shaped like a scythe; ***carro falcado,*** scythed chariot.
falcar [A], *v.t.* (*obs.*) to reap, to cut with hook *or* sickle; (*prov.*) to wedge.
falce, *n.f.* sickle, reaping-hook; falchion.
falcinelo, *n.m.* glossy ibis.
falcón, *n.m.* (*obs.*) falcon.
falconete, *n.m.* falconet.
falda, *n.f.* skirt; lower slope (*of a hill*); lap; brim (*of a hat*); ***aficionado a las faldas,*** fond of the ladies; ***perrillo de falda,*** lap-dog.
faldamenta, faldamento, *n.m.* (long *or* trailing) skirt.
faldar, *n.m.* tasset, tuille.
faldear, *v.t.* to skirt (*a hill*).
faldellín, *n.m.* short skirt; kilt.
faldero, -ra, *a.* of skirts *or* the lap; ***hombre faldero,*** ladies' man; ***perrillo faldero,*** lap-dog.
faldeta, *n.f.* small skirt; (*theat.*) stage screen.
faldicorto, -ta, *a.* having short skirts.
faldillas, *n.f.pl.* skirts; coat-tails.
faldistorio, *n.m.* bishop's seat.
faldón, *n.m.* hanging drapery; long flowing skirt; coat-tail; flap; shirt-tail; upper millstone; (*arch.*) gable; tympanum; side walls and lintel (*of a chimney*); ***asido a los faldones de,*** under the wing of.
faldriquera, *n.f.* pocket, pouch.
falena, *n.f.* moth.
falencia, *n.f.* misstatement, mistake. — *n.m.f.* (*Arg., Chi., Hond.*) bankruptcy.
falible, *a.* fallible.
fálico, -ca, *a.* phallic.
falimiento, *n.m.* untruth, falsehood; deception, deceit.
falismo, *n.m.* phallic cult, phallic symbolism.
falo, *n.m.* phallus.
falsaamarra, falsamarra, *n.f.* (*naut.*) preventer-rope.
falsabraga, *n.f.* low rampart.
falsada, *n.f.* rapid flight of bird of prey soaring *or* swooping.
falsario, -ria, *a.* falsifying, counterfeiting, forging. — *n.m.f.* forger, counterfeiter, falsifier; crook; liar.
falsarregla, *n.f.* bevel-square, bevel-rule; (*prov., Per., Ven.*) guidelines (*for writing*).
falseable, *a.* falsifiable.
falseador, -ra, *a.* forging, counterfeiting, falsifying. — *n.m.f.* forger, counterfeiter, falsifier.
falseamiento, *n.m.* falsification; misrepresentation.
falsear, *v.t.* to falsify, forge, counterfeit; to misrepresent; to bevel; to penetrate, pierce; ***falsear el cuerpo,*** to dodge *or* duck out of the way. — *v.i.* to slacken, give way; to get out of tune.
falsedad, *n.f.* falsehood; falsity; shakiness.
falseo, *n.m.* bevelling.
falsete, *n.m.* spigot; small door; falsetto voice.
falsía [FALSEDAD].
falsificación, *n.f.* falsification, forgery, counterfeiting.
falsificador, -ra, *a.* forging, counterfeiting. — *n.m.f.* falsifier, counterfeiter, forger.
falsificar [A], *v.t.* to falsify, counterfeit, forge; to fake.
falsilla, *n.f.* guidelines (*for writing*).
falso, -sa, *a.* untrue, false; counterfeit, bogus; sham; vicious (*horses* or *mules*); (*mech.*) temporary; unsubstantial; ***falso flete,*** dead freight; ***falso testimonio,*** false witness; ***puerta falsa,*** back *or* side door; ***en falso,*** falsely; without proper support; ***golpe en falso,*** ill-calculated blow; ***hablar en falso,*** to speak without basis; ***envidar en falso,*** to bluff; ***no levantarás falso testimonio,*** thou shalt not bear false witness; ***cerrar en falso la puerta,*** to leave the door slightly open. — *n.m.* (*sew.*) facing; padding.
falta, *n.f.* [FALTO].
faltante, *a.* wanting, lacking.
faltar, *v.i.* to be lacking, wanting *or* missing; to fail; not to attend, be absent; to be false *or* untrue; to offend (against); to break, not to fulfil; ***faltar a la verdad,*** to offend against the truth; ***faltar al respeto a,*** to be disrespectful to; ***faltar a su palabra,*** to break one's word; ***me faltan palabras,*** words fail me; ***me faltan tres peniques,*** I need *or* am short of threepence; ***falta poco para que venga,*** it won't be long before he's here; ***¡lo que me faltaba!*** the last straw!; ***esto falta por hacer,*** this still has to be done; ***¡no faltaba más!*** of course, naturally, most certainly, by all means.
falto, -ta, *a.* wanting, lacking; deficient, short; ***falto de,*** lacking in, short of. — *n.f.* shortage, lack, absence, want; mistake; fault; flaw, blemish; failure; misdoing, offence; faultiness; shortcoming, failing; (*law*) default; deficiency in weight; stoppage of the period (*in pregnant women*); ***a falta de,*** for want of; ***sin falta,*** without fail; without fault; ***hacer falta,*** to be necessary; ***falta garrafal,*** howler, (*Am.*) boner; ***hacen falta tres más,*** three more are required, we need three more; ***falta de pago,*** non-payment; ***tiene cuatro faltas,*** she is in the fifth month of her pregnancy; ***caer en falta,*** to fail in one's duty; ***poner*** or ***sacar faltas,*** to find fault; ***es una falta de educación,*** it's rude, it's not done, it's not a polite thing to say; ***a falta de pan, buenas son tortas,*** half a loaf is better than no bread.
faltón, -tona, *a.* unreliable; abusive.
faltorra, *n.f.* whopping blunder.
faltrero, -ra, *n.m.f.* pickpocket; petty thief.
faltriquera, *n.f.* pocket, pouch; ***rascar(se) la faltriquera,*** to fork out money reluctantly.
falúa, *n.f.* gig, small boat, tender.
falucho, *n.m.* felucca; (*Arg.*) cocked hat.
falla, *n.f.* [FALLO].
fallada, *n.f.* trumping (*cards*).
fallanca, *n.f.* (*arch.*) flashing, run-off plate.
fallar, *v.t.* to ruff (*cards*); (*law*) to judge, sentence. — *v.i.* to fail, miss, be deficient *or* wanting; to break, give way; (*coll.*) to fall through, not to come off; to ruff (*cards*); (*law*) to judge, pass sentence; ***falló la cosecha,*** the harvest failed; ***no falla,*** it's always the same.
falleba, *n.f.* shutter-bolt.
fallecedero, -ra, fallecedor, -ra, *a.* that may fai *or* be deficient, perishable, exhaustible.
fallecer [9], *v.i.* to decease, die; to run out, fail.
fallecimiento, *n.m.* death, decease, demise.
fallido, -da, *a.* unsuccessful, ineffectual; irrecoverable, uncollectable; bankrupt; ***acto fallido,*** Freudian slip. — *n.m.* bankrupt.
fallo, -lla, *a.* lacking a card of the suit played. — *n.m.* (*law*) judgment, sentence, finding, ruling; (*coll.*) flop, failure, wash out; gap, omission, weak spot; ***echar el fallo,*** to give a ruling, pass sentence; ***no tiene fallo,*** it can't go wrong, it's dead safe. — *n.f.* head-covering; failure, fault; flaw; (*geol.*) fault, break; (*Mex.*) baby's bonnet; (*Val.*) bonfire.
fama, *n.f.* fame, renown; reputation; ***cobra buena fama y échate a dormir,*** get a reputation and you are a made man; ***unos tienen la fama, y otros cardan la lana,*** some do the work and others reap the reward; ***es fama que . . . ,*** rumour has it that. . . .
famélico, -ca, *a.* ravenous, famished.
familia, *n.f.* family; household; kin, clan; relatives; ***cargarse de familia,*** to load o.s. down with children.
familiar, *a.* family, of the family; familiar; conversant; informal; colloquial. — *n.m.* domestic, servant; familiar; relative; familiar spirit.
familiaridad, *n.f.* familiarity.

familiarizar [C], *v.t.* to familiarize, make familiar *or* conversant. — **familiarizarse,** *v.r.* to familiarize o.s., get familiar *or* conversant (**con,** with).
familiatura, *n.f.* position as familiar of the Inquisition; position of famulus.
familión, *n.m.* enormous family.
famoso, -sa, *a.* famous; (*coll.*) great, capital; (*iron.*) priceless; ***tristemente famoso,*** notorious.
fámula, *n.f.* (*coll.*) maidservant.
famular, *a.* (*coll.*) domestic, of servants.
famulato, famulicio, *n.m.* (domestic) service.
fámulo, *n.m.* famulus; (*coll.*) servant.
fanal, *n.m.* lighthouse; large lantern; bell-glass; candle-screen; (*obs., naut.*) poop-lantern.
fanático, -ca, *a.* fanatic, fanatical, bigoted. — *n.m.f.* fanatic, bigot.
fanatismo, *n.m.* fanaticism, bigotry.
fanatizador, -ra, *a.* fanaticizing. — *n.m.f.* one who spreads fanaticism.
fanatizar [C], *v.t.* to fanaticize; to make fanatical.
fandango, *n.m.* fandango; (*fig.*) shindy.
fandanguear, *v.i.* (*coll.*) to kick up a shindy.
fandanguero, -ra, *a., n.m.f.* gay (type).
fané, *a.* faded, withered; (*coll.*) low class, of low social tone.
faneca, *n.f.* (*ichth.*) whiting pout.
fanega, *n.f.* grain measure (*about* 1·5 *bushels*); ***fanega de puño*** or ***de sembradura,*** ground necessary to sow a ***fanega*** of seed; ***fanega de tierra,*** land measure (*about* 1·6 *acres*).
fanegada, *n.f.* [FANEGA DE TIERRA]; ***a fanegadas,*** galore.
fanerógamo, -ma, *a.* phanerogamic. — *n.f.pl.* (**fanerógamas**) phanerograms.
fanferrear, *v.i.* to bully, brag, swagger, show off.
fanfarria, *n.f.* (*coll.*) swagger, arrogance, bluster.
fanfarrón, -rrona, *a.* (*coll.*) swaggering, boasting, showing off. — *n.m.* swaggering boaster, show-off.
fanfarronada, *n.f.* fanfaronade, rodomontade, piece of showing off.
fanfarronear, *v.i.* to brag, show off.
fanfarronería, *n.f.* fanfaronade, bragging.
fanfarronesca, *n.f.* swagger, fanfaronading.
fanfurriña, *n.f.* (*coll.*) fit of the sulks, pettishness, huff.
fangal, fangar, *n.m.* quagmire.
fango, *n.m.* mud, mire.
fangoso, -sa, *a.* muddy, miry.
fano, *n.m.* (*obs.*) fane, temple.
fantaseador, -ra, *a.* fanciful, imaginative.
fantasear, *v.i.* to indulge in fantasy *or* daydream; ***fantasear de,*** to boast of.
fantasía, *n.f.* fantasy, fancy; conceit, vanity; (*mus.*) fantasia; ***de fantasía,*** fancy; (*pl.*) string of pearls.
fantasioso, -sa, *a.* (*coll.*) vain, conceited.
fantasma, *n.m.* ghost, phantom; vain, conceited person. — *n.f.* (*fig.*) scarecrow.
fantasmagoría, *n.f.* phantasmagoria.
fantasmagórico, -ca, *a.* phantasmagoric.
fantasmal, *a.* ghostly.
fantasmón, -mona, *a., n.m.f.* braggart, play-actor, showman.
fantástico, -ca, *a.* fantastic; fanciful; vain, conceited; superb, terrific, wonderful.
fantochada, *n.f.* piece of (conceited) foolery.
fantoche, *n.m.* puppet; foolish figure.
fañado, -da, *a.* one-year-old (*beasts*).
faquín, *n.m.* porter, carrier.
faquir, *n.m.* fakir.
fara, *n.f.* African snake.
farachar, *v.t.* (*prov.*) to beat, clean (*hemp*).
farad, faradio, *n.m.* (*elec.*) farad.
faradización, *n.f.* faradization.
faradizar [C], *v.t.* to faradize.
faralá, *n.m.* flounce, ruffle, frill.
farallón, *n.m.* headland, cliff; outcrop.
faramalla, *a.* (*coll.*) cajoling, deceiving. — *n.f.* (*coll.*) cajolery. — *n.m.f.* (*coll.*) cajoler; deceitful person.
faramallero, -ra, faramallón, -llona, *a.* (*coll.*) cajoling, deceiving; tattling, babbling. — *n.m.f.* deceiver; busybody.
farándula, *n.f.* acting profession; strolling players; (*coll.*) cajolement, eyewash.
farandulear, *v.i.* to brag, show off.
farandulero, -ra, *a.* cajoling, deceiving; tattling. — *n.m.f.* strolling player; (*coll.*) cajoler; tattler.
farandúlico, -ca, *a.* relating to strolling players.
faraón, *n.m.* pharaoh; faro (*card game*); (*fig.*) ace.
faraónico, *a.* pharaonic.
faraute, *n.m.* player who recites the prologue; pursuivant; messenger; (*coll.*) meddling fellow, busybody.
farda, *n.f.* ancient tax; bundle of clothing.
fardaje, *n.m.* bundles, packages, load, luggage.
fardar, *v.i.* (*coll.*) to swank.
farde, *n.m.* (*coll.*) swank(ing).
fardel, *n.m.* bag, knapsack; parcel, bundle.
fardería, *n.f.* [FARDAJE].
fardo, *n.m.* bale, bundle, package; burden, load.
farellón, *n.m.* rocky headland, cliff.
farfalá, *n.f.* flounce, furbelow.
farfallear, *v.i.* to stutter, stammer; to mumble.
farfallón, -llona, *a., n.m.f.* jabbering, stuttering (person); botching, bungling (person).
farfalloso, -sa, *a.* (*prov.*) stuttering, stammering. — *n.m.f.* stutterer, stammerer.
farfán, *n.m.* Christian of Spanish descent in Morocco.
farfante, farfantón, *n.m.* (*coll.*) boaster, braggart, blusterer.
farfantonada, farfantonería, *n.f.* piece of bragging *or* showing off.
fárfara, *n.f.* (*bot.*) coltsfoot; shell membrane (*egg*); ***en fárfara,*** immature; (*fig.*) unfinished, half-done.
farfolla, *n.f.* husk (*maize, millet*).
farfulla, *n.f.* (*coll.*) gabble, gibberish, jabber. — *n.m.f.* (*coll.*) jabberer, gabbler.
farfulladamente, *adv.* hastily and carelessly.
farfullador, -ra, *a.* (*coll.*) stammering. — *n.m.f.* stammerer, mumbler, jabberer.
farfullar, *v.t., v.i.* (*coll.*) to gabble, jabber; to blunder *or* stumble through.
farfullero, -ra, *a.* jabbering, chattering; blundering, bungling.
fargallón, -llona, *a.* (*coll.*) careless, slovenly, untidy. — *n.m.f.* bungler, botcher.
farillón, *n.m.* steep cliff, rock; headland.
farináceo, -cea, *a.* farinaceous.
farinetas, *n.f.pl.* (*prov.*) porridge; pap.
faringe, *n.f.* pharynx.
faríngeo, -gea, *a.* pharyngeal.
faringitis, *n.f.* pharyngitis.
fariña, *n.f.* (*Arg.*) coarse flour of manioc.
farisaico, -ca, *a.* pharisaical, pharisaic.
farisaísmo, fariseísmo, *n.m.* pharisaism; hypocrisy; smugness.
fariseo, *n.m.* pharisee; (*coll.*) tall, lean, ugly person.
farmacéutico, -ca, *a.* pharmaceutical. — *n.m.* pharmacist, chemist, apothecary.
farmacia, *n.f.* pharmacy; chemist's shop, (*Am.*) drug store.
farmacología, *n.f.* pharmacology.
farmacológico, -ca, *a.* pharmacological.
farmacólogo, *n.m.* pharmacologist.
farmacopea, *n.f.* pharmacopœia.
farmacopola, *n.m.* (*coll.*) apothecary, pharmaceutist, chemist.

farmacopólico, -ca, *a.* (*coll.*) pharmaceutical, pharmaceutic.
faro, *n.m.* lighthouse; (*fig.*) beacon; headlight.
farol, *a.* [FAROLERO]. — *n.m.* lantern; lamp; lamp-post; (*tauro.*) feat; (*coll.*) bluff; (*coll.*) bluffer; ***faroles de situación,*** position lights; ***adelante con los faroles,*** press on regardless; ***echarse, marcarse, tirarse un farol*** or ***faroles,*** to bluff.
farola, *n.f.* street lamp.
farolazo, *n.m.* blow given with a lantern; (*Cent. Am., Mex.*) swig.
farolear, *v.i.* (*coll.*) to show off; to bluff; to bluster.
faroleo, *n.m.* showing off; bluffing; blustering.
farolería, *n.f.* place where lanterns are made *or* sold; vulgar display; [FAROLEO].
farolero, -ra, *a.* bluffing; blustering. — *n.m.f.* lantern-maker; lamplighter; show-off; blusterer.
farolillo, *n.m.* Chinese lantern.
farolón, -lona, *a.* showing off; bluffing; blustering. — *n.m.* large lantern; show-off; bluffer; blusterer.
farota, *n.f.* (*coll.*) brazen-faced woman.
farotón, -tona, *a., n.m.f.* (*coll.*) brazen-faced, cheeky, saucy (person).
farpa, *n.f.* pointed scallop (*on the edge of draperies*).
farpado, -da, *a.* scalloped, notched.
farra, *n.f.* (*ichth.*) Swiss salmon; (*Hisp. Am.*) spree, revelry, carousal; ***irse de farra,*** to go on a spree.
fárrago, *n.m.* farrago, medley, hotch-potch.
farraguista, *n.m.f.* muddle-headed individual.
farrear, *v.i.* (*Arg., Chi.*) to go on a spree.
farro, *n.m.* peeled barley; spelt wheat.
farsa, *n.f.* farce; company of strolling players; sham, humbug.
farsanta, *n.f.* actress who plays in farces.
farsante, *n.m.f.* actor in farces; humbug.
farseto, *n.m.* quilted jacket.
farsista, *n.m.f.* writer of farces.
fas, *adv.* (*coll.*) ***por fas o por nefas,*** rightly or wrongly, for one reason or another.
fascicular, *a.* fascicular.
fascículo, *n.m.* fascicle.
fascinación, *n.f.* fascination.
fascinador, -ra, *a.* fascinating. — *n.m.f.* charmer.
fascinante, *a.* fascinating, charming.
fascinar, *v.t.* to fascinate, enchant; to bewitch.
fascismo, *n.m.* fascism.
fascista, *a., n.m.f.* fascist.
fascistizante, *a., n.m.f.* (one) with fascist leanings.
fascistoide, *a., n.m.f.* (one) tainted *or* tinged with fascism; would-be fascist.
fase, *n.f.* phase.
faséolo, *n.m.* kidney bean.
fásoles, *n.m.pl.* French beans.
fastial, *n.m.* cope-stone.
fastidiar, *v.t.* to annoy, irritate; to upset the arrangements of, throw out; ***¡que se fastidie!*** let him lump it; ***¡no fastidies!*** dont be daft, don't talk rot, don't be a pest.
fastidio, *n.m.* annoyance, irritation, bother, nuisance.
fastidioso, -sa, *a.* bothersome, annoying, vexing, tedious, irritating.
fastigio, *n.m.* apex; summit; pediment.
fasto, -ta, *a.* happy, propitious (*day*). — *n.m.* grandeur, splendour, pomp, pageantry, show; (*pl.*) fasti; annals.
fastuoso, -sa, *a.* grand, magnificent, full of pomp and splendour.
fatal, *a.* fatal; fated, inevitable; (*coll.*) ghastly, rotten, lousy; (*law*) fixed, settled, unalterable.
fatalidad, *n.f.* fatality; inevitability; destiny; bad luck; mischance, ill-fortune, mishap, disaster.
fatalismo, *n.m.* fatalism.
fatalista, *a., n.m.f.* fatalist.
fatídico, -ca, *a.* fatidical, ill-fated, fateful.
fatiga, *n.f.* weariness, fatigue; hardship, labour; hard breathing; (*coll.*) ***da fatiga,*** it's embarrassing.
fatigadamente, *adv.* with difficulty, laboriously.
fatigador, -ra, *a.* annoying; tiring.
fatigar [B], *v.t.* to tire, weary, fatigue; to annoy, vex, molest; ***fatigar la caza,*** to pursue game relentlessly.
fatigoso, -sa, *a.* wearisome, tiring; laboured; ***respiración fatigosa,*** laboured breathing.
fatuidad, *n.f.* conceit; foolishness.
fatuo, -tua, *a.* conceited; foolish. — *n.m.* ***fuego fatuo,*** will-o'-the-wisp, ignis fatuus.
fauces, *n.f.pl.* fauces, gullet; jaws.
fauna, *n.f.* fauna.
fauno, *n.m.* faun.
fausto, -ta, *a.* happy, fortunate, successful. — *n.m.* splendour, pageantry, pomp, grandeur.
faustoso, -sa [FASTUOSO].
fautor, -ra, *n.m.f.* helper, abetter, countenancer.
fautoría, *n.f.* aid, help.
favila, *n.f.* (*poet.*) ashes, embers.
favo, *n.m.* (*obs.*) honeycomb; (*med.*) ringworm.
favonio, *n.m.* (*poet.*) westerly wind, zephyr.
favor, *n.m.* favour; good turn; protection, help, service; love-token; ***a favor de,*** in favour of, for, pro; with, with the help of, under cover of; ***por favor,*** please; ***haga el favor de callarse,*** please be silent, kindly be silent, be so good as to be quiet; ***un tanto a favor,*** one up; ***¡favor a la justicia!*** help, in the name of the law!
favorable, *a.* favourable.
favorcillo, *n.m.* small favour *or* service, petty *or* fiddling favour *or* service.
favorecedor, -ra, *a.* favouring, helping. — *n.m.f.* favourer, helper; client, customer; countenancer, friend, well-wisher.
favorecer [9], *v.t.* to favour, befriend; to help, help out; to suit, flatter. — **favorecerse,** *v.r.* to avail o.s. (***de,*** of).
favoreciente, *a.* favouring.
favoritismo, *n.m.* favouritism.
favorito, -ta, *a.* favourite, darling, pet. — *n.m.f.* favourite.
fayado, *n.m.* (*prov.*) garret, lumber-room, attic.
fayanca, *n.f.* unsteady position; ***de fayanca,*** carelessly; negligently.
fayanco, *n.m.* wicker basket.
faz, *n.f.* face; (*arch.*) front; obverse.
fe, *n.f.* faith; trust; faithfulness; promise given; testimonial, certificate; ***dar fe de,*** to testify to; ***fe de bautismo,*** certificate of baptism; (*print.*) ***fe de erratas,*** errata; ***a fe,*** in truth; ***dar fe,*** to attest, cerify; ***dar fe de vida,*** to give signs of life; ***a fe mí*** or ***por mi fe,*** upon my honour; ***a buena fe,*** certainly, without a doubt; ***a la buena fe,*** without deceit; ***de buena fe,*** bona fide; ***de mala fe,*** in bad faith; craftily, deceitfully; ***en fe de lo cual,*** in witness whereof; ***a fe de bueno, de cristiano*** or ***de caballero,*** upon my honour; ***hacer fe,*** to carry conviction; ***prestar fe,*** to assent (to).
fea [FEO].
fealdad, *n.f.* ugliness; hideousness; plainness, homeliness; foulness.
febeo, -bea, *a.* (*poet.*) relating to Phœbus.
feblaje, *n.m.* light weight (*coin*).
feble, *a.* feeble, faint, weak; (*jewel.*) deficient in weight *or* quality. — *n.m.* light coin.
Febo, *n.m.* (*poet.*) Phœbus.
febrera, *n.f.* irrigation ditch.
febrero, *n.m.* February.
febricitante, *a.* feverish.
febrido, -da, *a.* (*obs.*) shining, refulgent.
febrífugo, -ga, *a., n.m.* febrifuge.
febril, *a.* febrile, feverish; (*fig.*) restless, anxious.
fecal, *a.* (*med.*) fæcal.

fecí, *a.* relating to Fez. — *n.m.f.* native of Fez.
fécula, *n.f.* starch, fecula.
feculencia, *n.f.* dregs, lees.
feculento, -ta, *a.* dreggy, foul; starchy.
fecundable, *a.* capable of fecundation, fertilizable.
fecundación, *n.f.* fecundation, fertilization.
fecundante, *a.* fecundating, fertilizing.
fecundar, *v.t.* to fecundate, fertilize.
fecundativo, -va, *a.* fecundating, fertilizing.
fecundidad, *n.f.* fecundity, fertility, fruitfulness.
fecundizar [C], *v.t.* to fertilize, fecundate.
fecundo, -da, *a.* fecund, fertile, fruitful.
fecha (1), *n.f.* date; ***a estas fechas ya habrá llegado,*** he will certainly have arrived by now; ***con fecha de,*** under date of; ***de larga fecha,*** of long standing; ***hasta la fecha,*** to date; ***esta carta ha tardado tres fechas,*** this letter has taken three days to get here.
fechador, *n.m.* dater; (*Chi.*, *Mex.*) postmark.
fechar, *v.t.* to date.
fecho (1), **-cha** (2), *a.* (*obs.*) done, issued, executed (*official documents*).
fecho (2), *n.m.* (*obs.*) [HECHO].
fechoría, *n.f.* villainy, misdeed, mischief.
federación, *n.f.* federation.
federal, *a.* federal. — *n.m.* federalist.
federalismo, *n.m.* federalism.
federar, *v.t.*, *v.i.* to federate.
federativo, -va, *a.* federative.
Federico, *n.m.* Frederick.
féferes, *n.m.pl.* (*Hisp. Am.*) household goods, implements, tools, trinkets.
fehaciente, *a.* (*law*) authentic, reliable.
feísmo, *n.m.* cult of the ugly *or* hideous.
felandrio, *n.m.* water-hemlock.
feldespato, *n.m.* feldspar.
feldmariscal, *n.m.* field-marshal.
felicidad, *n.f.* happiness; success.
felicitación, *n.f.* congratulation; greeting.
felicitar, *v.t.* to congratulate.
félidos, *n.m.pl.* (*zool.*) Felidæ.
feligrés, -resa, *n.m.f.* parishioner.
feligresía, *n.f.* parish; parishioners, congregation.
felino, -na, *a.* feline. — *n.m.f.* felid.
Felipe, *n.m.* Philip.
feliz, *a.* happy; lucky; successful.
felón, -lona, *a.*, *n.m.f.* felon, criminal.
felonía, *n.f.* treachery, disloyalty; felony.
felpa, *n.f.* plush; (*coll.*) reprimand; drubbing; ***toalla de felpa,*** thick towel, nap towel.
felpado, -da, *a.* plushy; velvety; nap.
felpar, *v.t.* to cover with plush.
felpilla, *n.f.* chenille.
felpudo, -da, *a.* plushy; downy. — *n.m.* door-mat.
femenil, *a.* feminine, womanish.
femenino, -na, *a.* feminine; female; ***género femenino,*** feminine gender.
fementido, -da, *a.* false, unfaithful.
femineidad, *n.f.* femininity.
femíneo, -nea, *a.* feminine; effeminate.
feminismo, *n.m.* feminism.
feminista, *a.*, *n.m.f.* feminist.
femoral, *a.* femoral.
fémur, *n.m.* femur.
fenacitina, *n.f.* phenacetin.
fenda, *n.f.* crack, fissure.
fendiente, *n.m.* gash.
fenecer [9], *v.i.* to expire, die, come to an end.
fenecimiento, *n.m.* expiry; death, decease.
fenestrado, -da, *a.* fenestrate.
fenicar, *v.t.* to add carbolic acid to.
fenicio, -cia, *a.*, *n.m.f.* Phœnician.
fénico, *a.* carbolic.
fénix, *n.m.f.* phœnix; (*fig.*) paragon; (*bot.*) palm.
fenogreco, *n.m.* fenugreek.
fenol, *n.m.* phenol.
fenomenal, *a.* phenomenal; (*coll.*) great, smashing, top-hole; terrific; tremendous.
fenomenalismo, *n.m.* phenomenalism.
fenómeno, *n.m.* phenomenon; (*coll.*) (*as adj.*, *adv.*) first-rate, ripping, superb.
feo, fea, *a.* ugly; very plain; nasty; nasty-looking; nasty-sounding; ***la cosa se está poniendo fea,*** it's beginning to look nasty; ***eso está feo,*** it looks bad, it's not done. — *n.m.* slight, snub; ***nos hicieron un feo,*** they slighted *or* snubbed us.
feote, -ta, *a.* quite ugly; big and ugly.
feracidad, *n.f.* fecundity, fertility, fruitfulness.
feral, *a.* ***niño feral,*** child nurtured by a wild creature.
feraz, *a.* fertile.
féretro, *n.m.* bier, coffin.
feria, *n.f.* fair, show; livestock fair *or* show; (*eccles.*) feria; holiday, rest; (*Mex.*) small change; (*pl.*) fairing, present bought at a fair; ***ferias mayores,*** Holy Week celebrations; ***feria segunda, tercera,*** *etc.*, Monday, Tuesday etc.; ***cada uno cuenta de la feria según le va en ella,*** everyone gives his own account of an event.
feriado, -da, *a.* (*law*) ***dia feriado,*** day on which the courts do not sit.
ferial, *a.* ferial. — *n.m.* fair, fairground.
feriante, *a.* attending a fair. — *n.m.f.* dealer *or* trader (*at fairs*).
feriar, *v.t.* to sell, buy, trade, barter; to give fairings to; to purchase at a fair. — *v.i.* to suspend work; to take a holiday.
ferino, -na, *a.* wild, savage, ferocious; ***tos ferina,*** whooping-cough.
fermentable, *a.* fermentable.
fermentación, *n.f.* fermentation.
fermentante, *a.* fermenting.
fermentar, *v.t.* to produce fermentation in; (*fig.*) to rouse, excite, agitate. — **fermentar(se),** *v.i.* (*v.r.*) to ferment; to become agitated.
fermentativo, -va, *a.* fermentative.
fermento, *n.m.* ferment.
fernambuco, *n.m.* Pernambuco wood.
fernandina, *n.f.* linen.
Fernando, *n.m.* Ferdinand.
ferocidad, *n.f.* ferocity, wildness, ferociousness, fierceness, savageness, fury.
feróstico, -ca, *a.* (*coll.*) irritable, wayward; (*coll.*) extremely ugly.
feroz, *a.* ferocious, savage, fierce.
ferra, *n.f.* salmon.
ferrado, -da, *a.* bound, shod, plated with iron. — *n.m.* (*prov.*) corn measure (*about ¼ bushel*); land measure (*from 4 to 6 acres*). — *n.f.* iron-knobbed club.
ferrar [1], *v.t.* to garnish with iron, strengthen with iron plates.
férreo, -rrea, *a.* ferreous; iron, made of iron; stern; ***vía férrea,*** railway.
ferrería, *n.f.* ironworks, foundry; forge.
ferreruelo, *n.m.* short cloak.
ferrete, *n.m.* sulphate of copper; marking-iron.
ferretear [FERRAR].
ferretería, *n.f.* ironworks; hardware; hardware shop.
ferretero, *n.m.* ironmonger, (*Am.*) hardware dealer.
ferricianógeno, *n.m.* ferricyanogen.
ferricianuro, *n.m.* ferricyanide.
férrico, -ca, *a.* ferric.
ferrífero, -ra, *a.* ferriferous, iron-bearing.
ferrificarse [A], *v.r.* to become iron.
ferrizo, -za, *a.* ferreous, iron, of iron.
ferrocarril, *n.m.* railway, (*Am.*) railroad; ***ferrocarril de sangre,*** horse-tramway; ***ferrocarril***

de cable, cable-railway; ***ferrocarril de cremallera,*** rack-railway, mountain railway; ***ferrocarril funicular,*** funicular railway; ***ferrocarril aéreo,*** aerial railway; ***ferrocarril subterráneo,*** underground railway.
ferrocarrilero, -ra, *a. n.m.f.* (*Arg., Col., Ec.*) [FERROVIARIO].
ferrolano, -na, *a. n.m.f.* (native) of Ferrol.
ferrón, *n.m.* iron-worker.
ferroso, -sa, *a.* ferrous.
ferrovía, *n.m.f.* railway, railroad.
ferroviario, -ria, *a.* pertaining to railways. — *n.m.f.* railway worker.
ferrugíneo, -nea, ferruginoso, -sa, *a.* ferruginous.
fértil, *a.* fertile.
fertilidad, *n.f.* fertility.
fertilizante, *a.* fertilizing. — *n.m.* fertilizer.
fertilizador, -ra, *a.* fertilizing.
fertilizar [C], *v.t.* to fertilize.
férula, *n.f.* ferule, cane; (*fig.*) rule, yoke; (*bot.*) ferula; (*surg.*) splint.
ferruláceo, -cea, *a.* ferulaceous.
ferventísimo, -ma, *a. superl.* extremely fervent.
férvido, -da, *a.* fervid, fervent.
ferviente, *a.* fervent.
fervor, *n.m.* fervour, fervidness, fervency.
fervorín, *n.m.* short prayer; short sermon.
fervorizar [C] [ENFERVORIZAR].
fervoroso, -sa, *a.* fervent; pious.
festejador, -ra [FESTEJANTE].
festejante, *a.* entertaining; wooing.
festejar, *v.t.* to entertain, feast, fête; to celebrate; to make love to, woo, court; (*Mex.*) to whip, strike. — **festejarse,** *v.r.* to amuse o.s.
festejo, *n.m.* entertainment, feast, fête; celebration; courtship; (*pl.*) festivities.
festín, *n.m.* feast, banquet.
festinación, *n.f.* speed, haste, hurry.
festinar, *v.t.* (*Hisp. Am.*) to hasten, rush, hurry.
festival, *n.m.* festival (*music, arts*).
festividad, *n.f.* festivity; celebration; rejoicing, merrymaking; holiday; holy day; humour.
festivo, -va, *a.* festive; joyful, light-hearted; festal, festival, pertaining to feasts; humorous; ***día festivo,*** holiday, holy day, feast day, bank holiday.
festón, *n.m.* festoon; scalloped edging.
festonar, festonear, *v.t.* to festoon; to border.
fetal, *a.* fœtal.
feticida, *n.m.f.* abortionist.
feticidio, *n.m.* (*law*) fœticide.
fetiche, *n.m.* fetish.
fetichismo, *n.m.* fetishism.
fetichista, *a.* fetishistic. — *n.m.f.* fetishist.
fetidez, *n.f.* fetidity, fetidness.
fétido, -da, *a.* fetid, foul.
feto, *n.m.* fœtus.
feúcho, -cha, *a.* (*coll.*) rather ugly, plain.
feudal, *a.* feudal.
feudalidad, *n.f.*, **feudalismo,** *n.m.* feudalism.
feudatario, -ria, *a. n.m.f.* feudatory, feudary.
feudista, *n.m.f.* feudist.
feudo, *n.m.* fief, fee, feu, feud, feoff; feudal due; feudal privilege.
fez, *n.m.* fez.
fiable, *a.* trustworthy.
fiado, *n.m.* credit; ***al fiado,*** on credit; ***dar fiado,*** to give credit; ***en fiado,*** on bail.
fiador, -ra, *n.m.f.* bondsman, guarantor, bail. — *n.m.* cloak-fastener; (*mech.*) catch, stop, catch-bolt; locknut, pawl, grip, trigger; safety-catch; tumbler (*of a lock*), detent; (*falc.*) creance; (*coll.*) backside, rump; (*Chi., Ec.*) chin-strap; ***salir fiador,*** to stand surety, bail.
fiambre, *a.* cold (*meat*). — *n.m.* cold meat; (*fig.*) old stuff, old one; (*coll.*) corpse.
fiambrera, *n.f.* lunch-basket *or* container; nest of pots (*for keeping food hot*); (*Arg.*) meat-safe.
fianza, *n.f.* surety, bond, bail, guarantee, security; security (*for loan*), (*Am.*) collateral; pledge; suretyship; ***fianza bancaria,*** bank guarantee; ***fianza de aduana,*** custom-house bond; ***dar fianza,*** to give bail *or* pledge; ***bajo fianza,*** on bail.
fiar [L], *v.t.* to guarantee, warrant, answer for; to sell upon trust; to give credit to; to stand surety, bail for; to confide, commit, entrust. — *v.i.* to give credit; to trust. — **fiarse,** *v.r.* — ***de,*** to trust, rely on; ***ser de fiar,*** to be reliable, trustworthy; ***tan largo me lo fiáis,*** it's a long way off.
fiasco, *n.m.* failure, fiasco.
fíat, *n.m.* consent; (*law*) fiat.
fibra, *n.f.* fibre; (*fig.*) toughness, stamina; (*min.*) vein of ore.
fibrazón, *n.m.* ore-veins (*mine*).
fibrilla, *n.f.* fibril.
fibrina, *n.f.* fibrin.
fibroideo, -dea, *a.* fibroid.
fibroma, *n.m.* (*med.*) fibroma.
fibroso, -sa, *a.* fibrous, stringy.
ficción, *n.f.* fiction, story.
fice, *n.m.* whiting.
ficticio, -cia, *a.* fictitious; fake.
ficto, -ta, *a.* (*obs.*) feigned, artificial, counterfeited.
ficha, *n.f.* chip, counter; piece (*in chess, dominoes etc.*); index *or* filing card; token, disk; record card (*police etc.*); (*fig.*) contract.
fichar, *v.t.* to file particulars of; to put in one's bad books; to sign up *or* on (*football player*).
fichero, *n.m.* card index, file (case).
fidedigno, -na, *a.* trustworthy, reliable.
fideero, -ra, *n.m.f.* maker of vermicelli etc.
fideicomisario, *n.m.* trustee, fiduciary; fidei-commissary.
fideicomiso, *n.m.* trust; feoffment, fidei-commissum.
fideicomitente, *n.m.f.* fidei-commissor.
fidelidad, *n.f.* fidelity; faithfulness, loyalty.
fidelísimo, -ma, *a. superl.* extremely faithful.
fideo, *n.m.* (*coll.*) skinny individual; (*pl.*) vermicelli.
fiduciario, -ria, *a.* fiduciary. — *n.m.f.* trustee, fiduciary.
fiebre, *n.f.* fever; temperature; ***fiebre aftosa,*** foot and mouth disease; ***fiebre amarilla,*** yellow fever; ***fiebre palúdica,*** malaria; ***fiebre tifoidea,*** typhoid fever; ***fiebre del heno,*** hay fever; ***fiebre del oro,*** gold-rush *or* -fever; ***limpio de fiebre,*** free of fever, having no temperature.
fiebrecilla, *n.f.* slight fever *or* temperature.
fiel, *a.* faithful; loyal; true; exact; ***en fiel,*** of equal weight; in even balance. — *n.m.* pointer *or* needle (*of scales*); public inspector (*of weights and measures*); pivot (*of a steelyard*); pin (*of scissors*); arbiter; ***fiel contraste,*** official who weighs and stamps metal; ***fiel de romana,*** inspector of weights; ***fiel medidor,*** inspector of measures; ***los fieles,*** the faithful.
fielato, fielazgo, *n.m.* inspector's office.
fieldad, *n.f.* public inspectorship; surety, guarantee, security.
fieltro, *n.m.* felt; felt rug; felt hat.
fiemo, *n.m.* (*prov.*) dung, manure.
fiera, *n.f.* [FIERO].
fierabrás, *n.m.* (*fig.*) terror.
fiereza, *n.f.* ferocity; fierceness.
fiero, -ra, *a.* fierce; rude, rough; deformed, ugly; terrible, furious; great, huge; wild. — *n.m.pl.* (**fieros**) menaces, threats; ***echar*** or ***hacer fieros,*** to bluster, rant. — *n.f.* wild beast *or* creature; bull; (*fig.*) fiend, devil; ***casa de fieras,*** menagerie; ***está hecho una fiera,*** he's blazing mad,

furious; ***trabaja como una fiera,*** he works like fury *or* like the Devil.

fierro, *n.m.* (*Hisp. Am.*) iron; (*obs.*) fetter (*usually pl.*).

fiesta, *n.f.* feast, entertainment, fête; party; festival; festivity; holiday; holy day; ***hacer fiestas a,*** to fuss, fuss over, make a fuss of; ***hacer fiesta,*** to take a holiday, take a day off; ***aguar la fiesta,*** to spoil the fun, put a dampener on things; ***fiesta de guardar*** or ***de precepto,*** day of obligation to hear mass; ***fiesta de las Cabañuelas*** or ***de los Tabernáculos,*** Feast of Tabernacles; ***fiesta fija*** or ***inmoble,*** fixed feast; ***fiesta movible,*** movable feast; ***fiesta brava*** or ***nacional,*** bull-fighting; ***sala de fiestas,*** night club; ***estar de fiesta,*** to be in good humour; ***no estar para fiestas,*** to be in no mood for fun; ***guardar*** or ***santificar las fiestas,*** to keep feast-days; ***¡se acabó la fiesta!*** that's enough of that! cut it out!; ***tengamos la fiesta en paz,*** let us have no trouble.

fifiriche, *a.* (*C.R., Mex.*) thin, frail, weak. — *n.m.* fop, coxcomb.

figle, *n.m.* (*mus.*) ophicleide.

figón, *n.m.* (low) eating-house.

figonero, -ra, *n.m.f.* keeper of an eating-house.

figueral, *n.m.* fig-tree grove.

figulino, -na, *a.* figuline.

figura, *n.f.* figure; shape, form; countenance; (*mus.*) note; court-card; ***figura de bulto,*** high-relief figure; ***figura de retórica,*** figure of speech; ***alzar figura,*** to draw a horoscope; ***hacer figuras,*** to pull faces; ***figura de delito,*** statutory definition of offence; ***buena (mala) figura,*** good (poor) figure; ***genio y figura hasta la sepultura,*** what's bred in the bone will come out in the flesh.

figurable, *a.* imaginable.

figuración, *n.f.* imagination.

figuradamente, *adv.* figuratively.

figurado, -da, *a.* figurative.

figuranta, *n.f.* figurante.

figurante, *n.m.* figurant.

figurar, *v.t.* to shape, fashion; to adorn (with); to figure, represent; to feign, pretend. — *v.i.* to figure. — **figurarse,** *v.r.* to fancy, imagine.

figurativo, -va, *a.* figurative, representative.

figurería, *n.f.* grimace, affected gesture.

figurero, -ra, *a.* making figures. — *n.m.f.* (*coll.*) person who makes grimaces *or* affected gestures; maker of statuettes.

figurilla, figurita, *n.f.* (*coll.*) insignificant little person; (*art*) figurine, statuette.

figurín, *n.m.* fashion-plate; lay-figure; fashion magazine; (*fig.*) dandy, dude.

figurón, *n.m.* huge grotesque figure; figurehead; (*coll.*) pretentious nobody.

fija, *n.f.* [FIJO].

fijación, *n.f.* fixing; fastening; firmness; stability; billposting.

fijador, -ra, *a.* fixing, fastening; (*photo.*) fixing, fixative. — *n.m.f.* fixer; fastener. — *n.m.* (*build.*) pointer; (*carp.*) setter of doors and windows; (*photo., art*) fixative.

fijamente, *adv.* firmly; fixedly, steadfastly; attentively, intensely; ***mirar fijamente,*** to stare (at).

fijar [*p.p.* **fijado, fijo**], *v.t.* to fix; to make fast, firm *or* stable; to post (*bills*); (*build.*) to point; (*carp.*) to set (*doors and windows*); to affix (*stamps*). — **fijarse,** *v.r.* — ***en,*** to notice; ***fíjate bien,*** mark my words; ***¡fíjate!*** just look! just think of it! well, I never!

fijeza, *n.f.* firmness, stability; steadfastness; ***mirar con fijeza,*** to stare (at).

fijo, -ja, *a.* fixed, firm, secure; permanent, settled; (*mech.*) stationary; ***(de) fijo,*** for certain, dead sure; ***idea fija,*** obsession, idée fixe; ***mirada fija,*** stare, set look. — *n.f.* (*obs.*) door-hinge; (*build.*) pointing-trowel.

fil, *n.m.* (*obs.*) needle (*of scales*); ***fil derecho,*** leap-frog; (*naut.*) ***fil de roda,*** right ahead; ***estar en un fil,*** to be in line; to be equal.

fila, *n.f.* row, line, tier; rank; ***en fila,*** in a row; ***en fila india,*** in single file; ***jefe de fila,*** leader; (*fig.*) ***estar en primera fila,*** to be in the fore-front; ***llamar a filas,*** to summon to the ranks, call up; ***incorporarse a filas,*** to join one's unit; to join up; ***¡rompan filas!*** fall out! dismiss!; (*coll.*) ***tener fila a,*** to have sth. against, have it in for, have a grudge against.

filadiz, *n.m.* floss silk, ferret.

filamento, *n.m.* filament.

filamentoso, -sa, *a.* filamentous.

filandria, *n.f.* filander.

filantropía, *n.f.* philanthropy.

filantrópico, -ca, *a.* philanthropical, philanthropic,

filántropo, -pa, *n.m.f.* philanthropist.

filar, *v.t.* to pay out (*rope*).

filarete, *n.m.* (*obs., naut.*) waist-netting.

filarmonía, *n.f.* love of music.

filarmónico, -ca, *a.* philharmonic. — *n.m.f.* music-lover.

filástica, *n.f.* rope-yarn.

filatelia, *n.f.* philately, stamp-collecting.

filatélico, -ca, *a.* philatelic. — *n.m.f.* philatelist.

filatelista, *n.m.f.* philatelist.

filatería, *n.f.* verbosity.

filatero, -ra, *a.* verbose. — *n.m.f.* incessant talker,

filatura, *n.f.* spinning.

filbán, *n.m.* rough edge (*of a tool*).

filderretor, *n.m.* superfine camlet.

filelí, *n.m.* fine cloth of silk and wool.

fileno, -na, *a.* (*coll.*) delicate, small; effeminate.

filera, *n.f.* fishing-net; spinneret of spiders.

filete, *n.m.* (fillet) steak, (*Am.*) tenderloin; (*sew.*) narrow hem; (*arch.*) listel, fillet; welt (*of a shoe*); small spit (*for roasting*); (*print.*) ornamental line; (*mech.*) edge, border, rim; snaffle-bit; thread (*of a screw*).

filetear, *v.t.* to fillet; to tool.

filetón, *n.m.* (*arch.*) large fillet *or* listel; heavy bullion (*for embroidering*).

filfa, *n.f.* (*coll.*) fib, hoax; fake.

filiación, *n.f.* filiation; relationship, connection; regimental register; personal description, particulars; ***tomar la filiación a,*** to take down (the) particulars of.

filial, *a.* filial. — *n.f.* branch (*of a firm etc.*).

filiar, *v.t.* to take down (the) particulars of; to enlist, sign on *or* up.

filibote, *n.m.* (*obs.*) fly-boat, light vessel.

filibusterismo, *n.m.* filibusterism.

filibustero, *n.m.* filibuster, freebooter; partisan fighting against Spanish colonialism.

filicida, *n.m.f.* (*law*) filicide.

filicidio, *n.m.* (*law*) filicide.

filiforme, *a.* filiform, thread-like.

filigrana, *n.f.* filigree, filigrane; spun work; water-mark (*paper*); delicate *or* elaborate object.

filili, *n.m.* (*coll.*) fineness, delicacy, neatness.

filipéndula, *n.f.* dropwort spiræa.

filipense, *a., n.m.f.* Philippian.

filípica, *n.f.* Philippic.

filipichín, *n.m.* moreen.

Filipinas, *n.f.pl.* Philippines.

filipino, -na, *a., n.m.f.* Filipino, (native) of *or* relating to the Philippine Islands; (*coll.*) ***punto filipino,*** wily character, sharp customer.

filis, *n.f.* knack; trinket, charm.

filisteo, -tea, *a., n.m.f.* Philistine. — *n.m.* (*coll.*) hulking individual.

filmación, *n.f.* filming.

filmar, *v.t.* to film, shoot.
filmina, *n.f.* filmstrip.
filmoteca, *n.f.* film library.
filo, *n.m.* (cutting) edge; arris; ridge; dividing line; (*naut.*) ***filo del viento,*** direction of the wind; ***filo rabioso,*** rough, unpolished edge; ***pasar al filo de la espada,*** to put to the sword; ***por filo,*** exactly, precisely; ***sacar filo a,*** to sharpen; ***arma de dos filos,*** two-edged weapon; ***al filo de,*** dead on, on the dot of.
filocartista, *n.m.f.* collector of postcards.
filófago, -ga, *a.* (*ent.*) phyllophagous.
filología, *n.f.* philology.
filológico, -ca, *a.* philological.
filólogo, -ga, *n.m.f.* philologist.
filomanía, *n.f.* (*bot.*) phyllomania.
filomela, filomena, *n.f.* nightingale.
filón, *n.m.* (*geol.*) vein, seam, mineral layer; (*fig.*) gold-mine.
filonio, *n.m.* (*pharm.*) electuary compounded with honey, opium etc.
filopos, *n.m.pl.* fences of linen erected to direct game towards a particular place.
filoseda, *n.f.* silk and wool *or* silk and cotton cloth.
filoso, -sa, *a.* (*Arg., C.R., Hond.*) sharp, keen edged.
filosofador, -ra, *a.* philosophizing. — *n.m.f.* philosophizer.
filosofal, *a.* ***piedra filosofal,*** philosopher's stone.
filosofar, *v.i.* to philosophize; (*coll.*) to muse.
filosofastro, *n.m.* philosophaster.
filosofía, *n.f.* philosophy; ***filosofía natural,*** natural philosophy; ***filosofía moral,*** moral philosophy.
filosófico, -ca, *a.* philosophical, philosophic.
filosofismo, *n.m.* philosophism.
filosofista, *n.m.f.* philosophist.
filósofo, -fa, *a.* philosophic, philosophical. — *n.m.f.* philosopher.
filoxera, *n.f.* (*ent.*) phylloxera; (*coll.*) drunkenness.
filtración, *n.f.* filtration, filtering.
filtrador, *a.* filtering. — *n.m.f.* filterer. — *n.m.* filter.
filtrar, *v.t.* to filter. — *v.i.* to percolate; to filter (through), seep (through). — **filtrarse,** *v.r.* to filter *or* seep through.
filtro, *n.m.* filter; philtre, love-potion; ***filtro de vacío,*** vacuum filter; ***filtro prensa,*** filter-press.
filván, *n.m.* wire-edge, burr.
filloa, *n.f.* pancake.
fimbria, *n.f.* edge *or* border (*of a skirt*).
fimo, *n.m.* dung, manure.
fimosis, *n.f.* phimosis.
fin, *n.m.* end, ending; aim; limit, boundary; ***al fin, por fin,*** at last, finally; ***en fin,*** in short, to sum up; (*coll.*) well; ***dar fin,*** to come to an end; ***dar*** or ***poner fin a,*** to put an end to; ***dar fin de,*** to destroy; ***a fin de,*** in order to; ***a fin de que,*** in order that; ***a fines de*** or ***del mes,*** towards *or* at the end of the month; ***al fin y al cabo, al fin y a la postre, en fin de cuentas,*** after all, when all is said and done; ***sin fin,*** innumerable, endless; ***correa sin fin,*** endless belt.
finado, -da, *a.* dead, deceased, late. — *n.m.f.* deceased (*person*).
final, *a.* final; ***punto final,*** full stop and end, end; ***Juicio Final,*** Last Judgment. — *n.m.* end; ***al final,*** at *or* in the end.
finalidad, *n.f.* finality; end, purpose.
finalizar [C], *v.t., v.i.* to finalize, terminate.
finamiento, *n.m.* decease, death.
financiero, -ra, *a.* financial. — *n.m.* financier.
finanzas, *n.f.pl.* finances.
finar, *v.i.* to die. — **finarse,** *v.r.* to long, yearn.
finca, *n.f.* estate; real estate, property; ***corredor de fincas,*** estate *or* land agent, (*Am.*) realtor.
fincabilidad, *n.f.* real estate.
fincar [A], *v.i.* to buy real estate.
finchado, -da, *a.* (*coll.*) pompous, vain, conceited.
fincharse, *v.r.* to get pompous, conceited.
finés, -nesa, *a.* Finnic, Finnish. — *n.m.f.* Finn. — *n.m.* Finnish language.
fineta, *n.f.* compact and fine cotton cloth diagonally woven.
fineza, *n.f.* fineness; delicacy; civility, courtesy.
fingido, -da, *a.* feigned, pretended, false; deceitful, two-faced.
fingidor, -ra, *a.* dissembler, simulator, feigner.
fingimiento, *n.m.* simulation, pretence.
fingir [*p.p.* **fingido, ficto**], *v.t.* to feign, pretend.
finible, *a.* capable of being finished.
finiquitar, *v.t.* to conclude, settle. — *v.i.* to conclude, end.
finiquito, *n.m.* settlement; release, quittance; ***dar finiquito a,*** to finish.
finir, *v.i.* (*Chi., Col., Ven.*) to end, finish.
finítimo, -ma, *a.* bordering, contiguous.
finito, -ta, *a.* finite, limited, bounded.
Finlandia, *n.f.* Finland.
finlandés, -desa, *a.* Finnish. — *n.m.f.* Finn. — *n.m.* Finnish (language).
fino, -na, *a.* thin; nice, delicate; sharp (*point*); shrewd, acute, smart; refined, civil; (*naut.*) sharp.
finolis, *a.* lah-di-dah, up-stage.
finquero, *n.m.* land-owner and planter.
finta, *n.f.* ancient tax; feint in fencing.
finura, *n.f.* delicacy; fineness; refinement.
finústico, -ca, (*coll.*) [FINOLIS].
fiñana, *n.m.* black-bearded wheat.
fiord(o), *n.m.* fiord.
fique, *n.m.* (*Col., Mex., Ven.*) fibre of the agave.
firma, *n.f.* signature; signing; (*com.*) firm; ***buena firma,*** house of standing; ***llevar la firma,*** to be empowered to sign the firm's name; ***media firma,*** surname; ***firma en blanco,*** signature put to a blank document; (*fig.*) carte blanche; (*coll.*) ***echar una firma,*** to sign one's name.
firmal, *n.m.* jewelled clasp.
firmamento, *n.m.* firmament.
firmán, *n.m.* firman.
firmante, *n.m.f.* signer, signatory.
firmar, *v.t., v.i.* to sign.
firme, *a.* firm; steady; staunch; ***tierra firme,*** mainland; ***estar en lo firme,*** to be right. — *adv.* hard, firmly; ***de firme,*** hard, staunchly, with a will; ***en firme,*** firm; ***oferta en firme,*** firm offer. — *n.m.* firm, solid ground; road bed; road surface. — *interj.* (*mil.*) ***¡firmes!*** (stand to) attention!
firmeza, *n.f.* firmness, steadiness, steadfastness.
firmón, *n.m.* one who signs another's work.
firuletes, *n.m.pl.* (*Arg., Per.*) dress trimmings; ornaments; adornments.
fiscal, *a.* fiscal. — *n.m.* attorney-general; public prosecutor, (*Am.*) district attorney; ***fiscal de tasas,*** price controller; (*coll.*) intermeddler, prier.
fiscalía, *n.f.* office of public prosecutor *or* price controller.
fiscalización, *n.f.* discharge of a prosecutor's duties.
fiscalizador, -ra, *a.* acting as a prosecutor. — *n.m.f.* prier, censurer, fault-finder.
fiscalizar [C], *v.t.* to control, inspect, scrutinize; to pry into; to criticize, censure.
fisco, *n.m.* national treasury, exchequer; (*Ven.*) copper coin.
fisga, *n.f.* harpoon; (*prov.*) bread of spelt-wheat; spelt-wheat; chaff, banter, raillery; ***hacer fisga de,*** to make fun of.
fisgador, -ra, *n.m.f.* harpooner; banterer.
fisgar [B], *v.t.* to harpoon; to pry into. — **fisgarse,** *v.r.* to make fun (***de,*** of).
fisgón, -gona, *n.m.f.* prier, peeper; mocker.
fisgonear, *v.t.* to pry *or* keep prying into.
fisgoneo, *n.m.* prying.

físico, -ca, *a.* physical; (*Cub., Mex.*) pedantic, prudish. — *n.m.* physicist; physician; physique. — *n.f.* physics.
fisiocracia, *n.f.* physiocracy.
fisiócrata, *n.m.f.* physiocrat.
fisiología, *n.f.* physiology.
fisiológico, -ca, *a.* physiological.
fisiólogo, *n.m.* physiologist.
fisionomía [FISONOMÍA].
fisioquímica, *n.f.* physio-chemistry.
fisioterapia, *n.f.* physiotherapy.
fisípedo, -da, *a.* fissiped, cloven-hoofed.
fisonomía, *n.f.* physiognomy, facial expression.
fisonómico, -ca, *a.* physiognomical.
fisonomista, *n.m.* physiognomist; one with a good memory for faces.
fistol, *n.m.* crafty individual; (*Mex.*) scarf pin.
fístula, *n.f.* water-pipe *or* conduit; (*mus.*) reed, pipe; (*surg.*) fistula.
fistular, *a.* fistular, fistulous.
fistuloso, -sa, *a.* fistulous.
fisura, *n.f.* fissure; cleft.
fitófago, -ga, *a.* phytophagous.
fitografía, *n.f.* phytography.
fitográfico, -ca, *a.* phytographic.
fitógrafo, *n.m.* phytographer.
fitología, *n.f.* phytology.
fitotomía, *n.f.* phytotomy.
flabelación, *n.f.* flabellation.
flabelado, -da, *a.* flabellate.
flabelicornio, *a.* having flabellate antennæ.
flabilífero, -ra, *a.* flabellum-carrying.
flabeliforme, *a.* flabelliform.
flaccidez, flacidez, *n.f.* flaccidity, flabbiness.
fláccido, -da, flácido, -da, *a.* flaccid, flabby.
flaco, -ca, *a.* lean, thin; weak, feeble, frail. — *n.m.* weak point, weakness, foible; ***hacer un flaco servicio,*** to do an ill turn; ***flaco de memoria,*** short of memory; ***vacas flacas,*** lean kine; ***punto flaco,*** weak point.
flacucho, -cha, *a.* scraggy, scrawny, terribly skinny.
flacura, *n.f.* leanness; weakness.
flagelación, *n.f.* flagellation, scourging.
flagelador, -ra, *n.m.f.* flagellator.
flagelante, *n.m.* flagellant.
flagelar, *v.t.* to scourge, flagellate.
flagelo, *n.m.* scourge, flagellum.
flagicio, *n.m.* (*obs.*) heinous crime.
flagrancia, *n.f.* flagrancy, flagrantness.
flagrante, *a.* flagrant, resplendent; ***en flagrante,*** in the very act, red-handed.
flagrar, *v.i.* (*poet.*) to flame, blaze.
flama, *n.f.* flame; reverberation.
flamante, *a.* flaming, bright, resplendent; fresh, brand-new, spick and span.
flamear, *v.t.* to sterilize by flame. — *v.i.* to flame, blaze; (*naut.*) to flutter (*sails*), wave.
flamenco (1), *n.m.* (*orn.*) flamingo.
flamenco (2), **-ca,** *a.* Flemish; (of) Andalusian gipsy; flashy, ostentatious; buxom. — *n.m.f.* Fleming; Andalusian gipsy; (*coll.*) cocky individual. — *n.m.* Flemish (*language*).
flamenquilla, *n.f.* small dish *or* plate; (*bot.*) marigold.
flámeo, *n.m.* ancient bridal veil; flapping, fluttering.
flamero, *n.m.* torch-holder.
flámula, *n.f.* (*naut.*) streamer, pennon; (*bot.*) virgin's bower (*Clematis flammula*).
flan, *n.m.* caramel *or* baked custard.
flanco, *n.m.* side; (*mil., fort.*) flank, flanker; side of a ship.
Flandes, *n.m.pl.* Flanders; ***poner una pica en Flandes,*** to set the Thames on fire.
flanqueante, *a.* flanking.
flanquear, *v.t.* to flank.
flanqueo, *n.m.* flank attack, flanking.
flaquear, *v.i.* to slacken; to flag, weaken, grow feeble, lose vigour.
flaqueza, *n.f.* feebleness; thinness, leanness; foible, frailty, weakness.
flato, *n.m.* flatus, wind; (*Col., Mex., Ven.*) melancholy, sadness, gloom.
flatoso, flatuoso, -sa, *a.* flatuous, windy.
flatulencia, *n.f.* flatulency, wind.
flatulento, -ta, *a.* flatulent, windy.
flauta, *n.f.* flute; ***sonó la flauta,*** it was a fluke; ***cuando pitos flautas, cuando flautas pitos,*** always the opposite of what is wanted.
flautado, -da, *a.* fluted, like a flute. — *n.m.* flute stop (*organ*).
flauteado, *a.* flute-like (*voice*).
flautero, *n.m.* maker of flutes.
flautillo, *n.m.* flageolet, small flute.
flautín, *n.m.* octave flute, piccolo.
flautista, *n.m.f.* flute-player.
flavo, -va, *a.* flavid, golden yellow.
flébil, *a.* mournful, tearful; lamentable.
flebitis, *n.f.* phlebitis.
flebotomía, *n.f.* phlebotomy.
flebotomiano, *n.m.* phlebotomist.
flebotomizar [C], *v.t.* to bleed.
fleco, *n.m.* fringe; ragged edge.
flecha, *n.f.* arrow; (*fort.*) flèche; (*naut.*) front piece (*of cut-water*); sagitta, deflection; sweepback; ***la flecha del parto,*** Parthian shot; ***subir en flecha,*** to shoot up.
flechador, *n.m.* archer.
flechaduras, *n.f.pl.* ratlines.
flechar, *v.t.* to fit an arrow to; to wound *or* kill with an arrow *or* arrows; (*coll.*) to fire with sudden love. — *v.i.* to have a bow drawn (*ready to shoot*).
flechaste, *n.m.* ratline.
flechazo, *n.m.* arrow shot *or* wound; (*coll.*) sudden love, love at first sight.
flechera, *n.f.* (*Ven.*) long canoe.
flechería, *n.f.* shower of arrows.
flechero, *n.m.* archer, bowman; arrow-maker, fletcher.
flegmasía, *n.f.* phlegmasia.
fleje, *n.m.* iron hoop *or* strap.
flema, *n.f.* phlegm; apathy, sluggishness; ***gastar flema,*** to be a phlegmatic *or* stolid individual.
flemático, -ca, *a.* phlegmatic, stolid.
fleme, *n.f.* fleam.
flemón, *n.m.* phlegmon; gumboil.
flemonoso, -sa, *a.* phlegmonous.
flemoso, -sa, *a.* mucous, phlegmy.
flemudo, -da, *a.* (*prov.*) slow, dull, sluggish.
flequillo, *n.m.* fringe; bang (*hair*).
Flesinga, *n.f.* Flushing.
fletador, *n.m.* freighter, charterer.
fletamento, fletamiento, *n.m.* charter, charterage, charter-party.
fletante, *a.*, **fletán,** *n.m.* (*Arg., Chi., Ec., Mex.*) (person) who hires out a ship *or* animal of burden.
fletar, *v.t.* to freight; to charter; to hire; (*Chi., Per.*) to let fly. — **fletarse,** *v.r.* (*Cub., Mex.*) to quit, clear out; (*Arg.*) to butt in.
flete, *n.m.* freight; freightage.
flexibilidad, *n.f.* flexibility, flexibleness; suppleness.
flexibilizar, *v.t.* to make flexible *or* supple; to give *or* lend flexibility, elasticity, *or* suppleness to.
flexible, *a.* flexible; pliant, supple, soft. — *n.m.* flex, (*Am.*) extension cord.
flexión, *n.f.* flexion, flexure.
flexor, -ra, *a.* flexing, bending.
flexuoso, -sa, *a.* (*bot.*) flexuose.
flexura, *n.f.* bend, ply.

flictena, *n.f.* phlyctena.
flirtear, *v.i.* to flirt.
flirteo, *n.m.* flirtation.
flocadura, *n.f.* (*sew.*) fringe trimming.
flogístico, -ca, *a.* phlogistic.
flogisto, *n.m.* phlogiston.
flogosis, *n.f.* phlegmasia.
flojear, *v.i.* to slacken, grow weak.
flojedad, *n.f.* weakness, feebleness; slackness.
flojel, *n.m.* wool shorn from cloth; down, soft feathers.
flojera, *n.f.* (*coll.*) weakness, feebleness; laziness.
flojo, -ja, *a.* loose, slack; floppy, flabby; lazy; weak; feeble; (*Col.*) timid; ***vino flojo,*** thin, poor wine; ***seda floja,*** soft, untwisted silk.
flojucho, -cha, *a.* rather loose *or* slack, weakish, a bit feeble, on the floppy *or* flabby side.
floqueado, -da, *a.* fringed.
flor, *n.f.* flower, blossom; bloom, prime; down (*of fresh fruits*); (*chem.*) floss; maidenhood, virginity; grain (*of tanned leather*); surface (*of the earth*); compliment (*to a lady*); (*gambling*) cheating trick; ***en flor,*** in blossom; ***flor de harina,*** superfine flour; ***flor de la edad,*** prime *or* bloom of youth; ***a flor de agua,*** at water level; ***a flor de tierra,*** at ground level; ***flor de lis,*** fleur-de-lis; ***flor de la canela,*** cassia buds; (*fig.*) the best you can get; (*naut.*) ***flor del viento,*** first puffs of wind after a calm; ***flor y nata,*** cream, flower; ***segar en flor,*** to cut down in the prime of life; (*pl.* **flores**) flowers *or* figures of rhetoric; ***decir*** or ***echar flores,*** pay compliments.
floración, *n.f.* flowering, florescence.
florada, *n.f.* season of flowers best for bee-keepers.
floral, *a.* floral.
florar, *v.i.* to flower, blossom, bloom.
flordelisado, -da, *a.* (*her.*) fleurette; adorned with fleur-de-lis.
flordelisar, *v.t.* (*her.*) to flourish with irises.
floreado, -da, *a.* flowered; ***pan floreado,*** bread made of the finest flour.
florear, *v.t.* to flower, adorn with flowers; to sift the best of (flour). — *v.t.*, *v.i.* to pay compliments (to). — *v.i.* to brandish, flourish; (*mus.*) to flourish on the guitar.
florecer [9], *v.i.* to flower, blossom, bloom; to thrive, flourish, prosper. — **florecerse,** *v.r.* to go mouldy.
florecica, -cilla, -cita, *n.f.* little flower.
floreciente, *a.* flourishing, thriving.
Florencia, *n.f.* Florence.
florentino, -na, *a.*, *n.m.f.* Florentine.
florentísimo, -ma, *a. superl.* extremely flourishing.
floreo, *n.m.* (*fenc.*) flourish (*of foils*); (*mus.*) flourish (*on the guitar*); cross-caper (*in dancing*); (*fig.*) witty, idle talk; (*fig.*) idle pastime.
florera, *n.f.* flower-seller.
florero, -ra, *a.* flattering, complimentary, given to flattery and compliments. — *n.m.* flower vase, pot, stand *or* box; (*art*) flower piece. — *n.f.* flower-seller.
florescencia, *n.f.* (*bot.*) florescence, flowering, efflorescence.
floresta, *n.f.* forest, wood; anthology; collection.
floreta, *n.f.* leather border (*on the edge of a girth*); pile, heap (*in paper mills*).
florete, *n.m.* (fencing) foil; cotton fabric.
floretear, *v.t.* to decorate with flowers. — *v.i.* to fence; to use flourishes.
floretista, *n.m.f.* fencer.
floricultor, -ra, *n.m.f.* floriculturist, flower-grower.
floricultura, *n.f.* floriculture, flower-growing.
floridez, *n.f.* abundance of flowers; floweriness.
florido, -da, *a.* flowery; full of flowers; best, choice, select; ***Pascua florida,*** Easter.
florífero, -ra, florígero, -ra, *a.* floriferous, flower-bearing.
florilegio, *n.m.* florilegium, anthology.
florín, *n.m.* florin.
floripondio, *n.m.* floripondio; (*fig.*) frippery.
florista, *n.m.f.* florist; flower-seller.
floristería, *n.f.* florist's.
florón, *n.m.* large flower; fleuron; rosette; great feat.
flósculo, *n.m.* (*bot.*) floscule, floret.
flota, *n.f.* fleet; ***flota pesquera,*** fishing fleet.
flotable, *a.* floatable; navigable for rafts and logs.
flotación, *n.f.* flotation, floating, flotage; (*naut.*) ***línea de flotación,*** water-line.
flotador, -ra, *a.* floating. — *n.m.* float; floater.
flotadura, *n.f.*, **flotamiento,** *n.m.* flotation, floating.
flotante, *a.* floating; flowing; ***dique flotante,*** floating dock; ***deuda flotante,*** floating debt; ***témpanos flotantes,*** pack-ice, (*Am.*) ice pack.
flotar, *v.i.* to float.
flote, *n.m.* floating; ***a flote,*** afloat; (*fig.*) ***salir a flote,*** to keep one's head above water, survive, come through.
flotilla, *n.f.* flotilla, small fleet.
fluctuación, *n.f.* fluctuation; wavering.
fluctuante, *a.* fluctuating, fluctuant.
fluctuar [M], *v.i.* to fluctuate; to waver; to wave; to totter, be in danger.
fluctuoso, -sa, *a.* fluctuant, wavering.
fluente, *a.* fluent, flowing.
fluidez, *n.f.* fluidness, fluidity; fluency; ***con fluidez,*** fluently, smoothly; ***fluidez de estilo,*** smoothness of style.
fluido, -da, *a.* fluid, flowing. — *n.m.* fluid; ***fluido eléctrico,*** electric current.
fluir [O], *v.i.* to flow; to run.
flujo, *n.m.* flow, flowing; (*med.*) flux, discharge; rising tide; (*path.*) ***flujo blanco,*** whites; ***flujo de risa,*** fit of laughter; ***flujo de palabras,*** flow of words, verbiage; ***flujo de sangre,*** hæmorrhage; ***flujo de vientre,*** loose bowels.
flúor, *n.m.* fluorine; fluor-spar; (*chem.*) flux.
fluorescencia, *n.f.* fluorescence.
fluorescente, *a.* fluorescent.
fluorhídrico, -ca, *a.* fluorhydric, hydrofluoric.
fluórico, -ca, *a.* (*chem.*) fluoric.
fluorina, fluorita, *n.f.* fluor(-spar), fluorite.
fluvial, *a.* fluvial, river.
flux, *n.m.* flush (*at cards*); (*Col.*) set of men's clothes; (*coll.*) ***hacer flux,*** to go broke.
fluxión, *n.f.* cold, catarrh.
fobia, *n.f.* phobia.
foca, *n.f.* seal.
focal, *a.* focal.
foceifiza, *n.f.* mosaic.
focino, *n.m.* goad (*for elephants*).
foco, *n.m.* focus; centre; source; spotlight.
fóculo, *n.m.* small fireplace.
focha, *n.f.* (*orn.*) coot.
fodolí, *a.* (*obs.*) meddlesome, intrusive.
fofadal, *n.m.* (*Arg.*) quagmire.
fofo, -fa, *a.* spongy, soft, flabby.
fogaje, *n.m.* hearth-money; (*Arg.*, *Mex.*) skin eruption, rash; (*Arg.*, *Col.*, *P.R.*, *Ven.*) sultry weather, scorching heat; (*Ec.*) bonfire, flash; (*P.R.*) blush.
fogarada, *n.f.* blaze.
fogarear, *v.t.* (*prov.*) to burn with flame. — **fogarearse,** *v.r.* (*E.S.*) to wilt, get scorched (*vines*).
fogaril, *n.m.* cresset.
fogarín, *n.m.* common hearth (*for field hands*); (*prov.*) intense heat.
fogarizar [C], *v.t.* to set ablaze.
fogata, *n.f.* bonfire, blaze; fougasse.

fogón, *n.m.* kitchen range; touch-hole (*of a cannon*); fire-box; (*naut.*) galley.
fogonadura, *n.f.* (*naut.*) mast-hole.
fogonazo, *n.m.* powder flash; flash in the pan.
fogonero, *n.m.* fireman, stoker.
fogosidad, *n.f.* fire; fiery spirit, fieriness.
fogoso, -sa, *a.* fiery; spirited (*horse etc.*).
fogueación, *n.f.* enumeration of hearths *or* fires.
foguear, *v.t.* to make used *or* get used to gun-fire; to harden, season; to scale (*guns*); to cauterize; ***tropas fogueadas,*** battle-seasoned troops. — **foguearse,** *v.r.* to get used to gun-fire; to get battle-seasoned *or* battle-hardened; to get experienced *or* experience; (*fig.*) ***hay que foguearse,*** one must get experience.
foja, *n.f.* (*law*) leaf (*of manuscript*), folio; (*orn.*) coot.
fole, *n.m.* leather bag (*especially of the bagpipe*).
folgo, *n.m.* foot-warmer, foot-muff.
folía, *n.f.* dance; popular music.
foliáceo, *a.* foliaceous.
foliación, *n.f.* foliation.
foliar, *a.* foliar. — *v.t.* to page, folio.
foliatura, *n.f.* foliation.
folicularío, *n.m.* pamphleteer.
folículo, *n.m.* follicle.
folio, *n.m.* folio; (*print.*) running head; ***folio atlántico,*** atlas folio; ***folio vuelto,*** verso; ***libro en folio,*** folio book; (*bot.*) ***folio índico,*** Indian leaf; ***al primer folio,*** at first sight; (*coll.*) ***de a folio,*** whopping big, whacking great.
folklore, *n.m.* folklore; (*coll.*) rumpus, shindy; (*coll.*) merry-making.
folklórico, -ca, *a.* folkloristic.
folklorismo, *n.m.* typical *or* quaint local stuff; typical trashy local stuff; (*Spain*) cheap toreador and flamenco stuff *or* showmanship.
folklorista, *n.m.* folklorist.
folla, *n.f.* medley; hodgepodge.
follada, *n.f.* puff-pastry pie.
follaje, *n.m.* foliage; gaudy ornament; floweriness; fustian.
follar [4], *v.t.* to blow with bellows; to form in leaves. — **follarse,** *v.r.* (*vulg.*) to discharge wind without noise.
follero, folletero, *n.m.* maker *or* seller of bellows.
folletín, *n.m.* feuilleton; (*coll.*) melodrama, blood-and-thunder stuff.
folletinesco, -ca, *a.* (*coll.*) melodramatic.
folletinista, *n.m.f.* writer of melodramatic blood-and-thunder stuff.
folletista, *n.m.f.* pamphleteer.
folleto, *n.m.* pamphlet, brochure.
follisca, *n.f.* (*Col.*, *Ven.*) dispute, quarrel, wrangle.
follón, -llona, *a.* lazy; knavish, cowardly. — *n.m.* lazy fellow; knave, coward; (*coll.*) mess, muddle; (*coll.*) racket, shindy; (*coll.*) hell of a business; noiseless rocket.
fomentación, *n.f.* fomentation.
fomentador, -ra, *a.* fomenting, encouraging, promoting.
fomentar, *v.t.* to foment; to foster, encourage, promote.
fomento, *n.m.* fomentation; fostering, encouraging, promoting; ***Ministerio de Fomento,*** Ministry of (Public) Works.
fonación, *n.f.* phonation.
fonda, *n.f.* inn, eating-house.
fondable, *a.* fit for anchoring.
fondado, -da, *a.* (*coop.*) reinforced in the heads.
fondeadero, *n.m.* anchoring-place; anchorage; haven.
fondear, *v.t.* (*naut.*) to sound; to search (*a ship*); to examine. — *v.i.* to cast anchor.
fondeo, *n.m.* searching (*a ship*); casting anchor.
fondillón, *n.m.* dregs and lees (*of a cask of liquor*); old Alicante wine.
fondillos, *n.m.pl.* seat (*of trousers*).
fondista, *n.m.f.* innkeeper.
fondo, *n.m.* bottom; bed; back; background; depth; thickness (*diamond*); store; (*Cub.*) boiler (*in sugar mills*); (*Mex.*) white underskirt; capital, fund; (*mech.*) bed; (*mil.*) space occupied by files of soldiers; (*coop.*) head; (*naut.*) ***mar de fondo,*** swell; ***fondo de amortización,*** sinking fund; ***dar fondo,*** to cast anchor; ***de diez en fondo,*** ten abreast; (*naut.*) ***irse a fondo,*** to founder; (*fenc.*) ***tirarse a fondo,*** to thrust home; ***artículo de fondo,*** leading article, editorial; ***a fondo,*** thoroughly; ***al fondo,*** in the background; ***en el fondo,*** at bottom, at heart; ***estar en fondos,*** to be in funds; ***fondos vitalicios,*** life-annuities; ***limpiar fondos,*** to clean a ship's bottom; (*fig.*) to clear up; ***el fondo de la cuestion,*** the heart of the matter; ***tiene buen fondo,*** he is good-hearted; ***a fondo perdido,*** without expectation of return; ***los bajos fondos,*** the underworld.
fondón, -dona, *a.* (*coll.*) fat, hefty; low-bottomed, big-bottomed. — *n.m.* ground of silk *or* velvet; brocade; (*min.*) fondon.
fonema, *n.m.* (*philol.*) phoneme.
fonendoscopio, *n.m.* phonendoscope.
fonético, -ca, *a.* phonetic. — *n.f.* phonetics.
fonetismo, *n.m.* phoneticism.
fonetista, *n.m.f.* phonetician.
fónico, -ca, *a.* phonic.
fonil, *n.m.* funnel.
fonje, *a.* soft, spongy, flabby.
fonografía, *n.f.* phonography.
fonográfico, -ca, *a.* phonographic.
fonógrafo, *n.m.* phonograph.
fonograma, *n.m.* phonogram.
fonolita, *n.f.* (*min.*) phonolite.
fonología, *n.f.* phonology.
fonsadera, *n.f.* personal service during war; ancient war-tax.
fonsado, *n.m.* (*fort.*) foss, ditch.
fonsario, *n.m.* (*obs.*) foss *or* ditch surrounding a fort.
fontal, *a.* fontal.
fontana, *n.f.* fountain, spring.
fontanal, *a.* fontal. — *n.m.* spring; place abounding in springs.
fontanar, *n.m.* spring.
fontanela, *n.f.* (*anat.*) fontanel; (*surg.*) seton-needle.
fontanería, *n.f.* plumbing; pipelaying; water supply system.
fontanero, *n.m.* plumber.
fontezuela, *n.f.* small fountain.
fontículo, *n.m.* (*surg.*) fonticulus, issue.
foque, *n.m.* (*naut.*) jib.
forajido, *n.m.* outlaw, bandit.
foral, *a.* statutory; appertaining to the rights and privileges of a region.
foramen, *n.m.* hole in the nether stone of a mill.
foráneo, -nea, *a.* foreign; from outside.
forastero, -ra, *a.* alien; from outside. — *n.m.f.* stranger, outsider, visitor.
forcejear, *v.i.* to struggle, strive, tussle, contend.
forcejeo, *n.m.* struggle, struggling, tussle, tussling.
forcejón, *n.m.* violent effort.
forcejudo, -da, *a.* strong, hefty.
fórceps, *n.m. inv.* forceps.
forcina, *n.f.* swelling (*tree*); (*obs.*) trident.
forchina, *n.f.* fork-like weapon; (*obs.*) fork.
forense (1), *a.* (*law*) forensic. — *n.m.* coroner.
forense (2), *a.*, *n.m.f.* [FORASTERO].
forero, -ra, *a.* conformable to statute law. — *n.m.* owner of leasehold estate; lessee.
forestal, *a.* forestal; ***repoblación forestal,*** reafforestation.
forillo, *n.m.* backcloth (*in theatrical scenery*).

forja, *n.f.* forge; forging; iron-works, foundry; mortar.
forjador, *n.m.* forger; iron-master, smith; gold-beater.
forjadura, *n.f.* forging.
forjar, *v.t.* to forge; to fashion, shape; to invent.— **forjarse,** *v.r.* to take shape; ***se forjó una leyenda,*** a legend grew up.
forlón, *n.m.* chaise with four seats.
forma, *n.f.* form; shape; mould; cast; last; shaping block; manner, way; convention; (*eccles.*) small host; ***dar forma a,*** to give shape to, shape; ***tomar forma,*** to take shape; ***estar en forma,*** to be in form *or* shape; ***cubrir*** or ***guardar las formas,*** to keep up appearances; to pay lip-service to convention; ***tener buenas formas,*** to be polite, courteous; ***de forma que,*** so that, so; ***de todas formas,*** anyway, anyhow, in any case; ***no hay forma,*** it's hopeless.
formable, *a.* that which may be formed.
formación, *n.f.* formation, forming; setting up; form, shape; education, schooling, training.
formador, -ra, *a.* forming, shaping. — *n.m.f.* former.
formaje, *n.m.* cheese-mould.
formal, *a.* formal; to do with form *or* shape; reliable, punctual; serious.
formalidad, *n.f.* formality; reliability; seriousness.
formalismo, *n.m.* formalism; formality, red-tape.
formalista, *a.* formalistic. — *n.m.f.* formalist, stickler for rules and regulations.
formalizar [C], *v.t.* to formalize; to put into due form *or* shape. — **formalizarse,** *v.r.* to take on proper *or* due form; to get onto a proper *or* official footing; to settle down, become reliable *or* serious; to set in (in earnest) (*rain etc.*).
formar, *v.t.* to form, shape, fashion; to make up; to educate, train. — *v.t., v.i.* (*mil.*) to form *or* line up. — **formarse,** *v.r.* to develop; ***formarse una idea de,*** to get an idea of.
formativo, -va, *a.* formative.
formato, *n.m.* format, size.
formatriz, *a.* forming.
formejar, *v.t.* to clear (*ship*); to trim (*hold*).
formero, *n.m.* (*arch.*) side arch (*of a vault*).
formiato, *n.m.* formic.
formicante, *a.* (*med.*) formicant.
formicarios, formícidos, *n.m.pl.* hymenoptera which carry a sting.
fórmico, *n.m.* (*chem.*) formic; hard tumour.
formidable, *a.* formidable; terrific.
formidoloso, -sa, *a.* timid, timorous, fearful; dreadful, horrible, frightful.
formillón, *n.m.* hat-block, hat-form.
formón, *n.m.* chisel.
fórmula, *n.f.* formula; (*med.*) recipe, prescription.
formular, *v.t.* to formulate; to prescribe; ***formular una protesta,*** to lodge a complaint.
formulario, -ria, *a.* of form, as a matter of form. — *n.m.* formulary, form.
formulismo, *n.m.* formulism; red-tape.
formulista, *a.* formulist, formulistic.
fornáceo, -cea, *a.* to do with ovens.
fornecer [9], *v.t.* (*obs.*) to furnish, provide.
fornecino, -na, *a.* (*obs.*) bastard, illegitimate.
fornicación, *n.f.* fornication.
fornicador, -ra, *a., n.m.f.* fornicator.
fornicar [A], *v.i.* to fornicate.
fornicario, -ria, *a.* relating to fornication.
fornicio, *n.m.* fornication.
fornido, -da, *a.* robust, lusty, sturdy, husky.
fornitura, *n.f.* (*print.*) types cast to complete sorts; (*pl.*) (*mil.*) leather straps (*worn by soldiers*).
foro, *n.m.* forum; bar, legal profession; leasehold; rental; back (*in stage scenery*); (*fig.*) ***desaparecer por el foro,*** to clear out.
forraje, *n.m.* fodder, forage; foraging; (*coll.*) hodgepodge.
forrajeador, *n.m.* forager; fodderer.
forrajear, *v.i.* to forage, collect forage *or* fodder.
forrajera (1), *n.f.* shako guard.
forrajero, -ra (2), *a.* appertaining to forage *or* fodder.
forrar, *v.t.* to line; to cover; (*naut.*) to sheathe, fur, plank. — **forrarse,** *v.r.* to line one's pockets, feather one's nest.
forro, *n.m.* lining; cover; (*naut.*) sheathing, furring, planking; (*naut.*) ***forro de cabos,*** service, serving ropes; (*coll.*) ***ni por el forro,*** not the least bit.
fortachón, -chona, *a.* (*coll.*) burly, hefty.
fortalecedor, -ra, *a.* fortifying.
fortalecer [9], *v.t.* to fortify, strengthen.
fortalecimiento, *n.m.* fortifying, strengthening.
fortaleza, *n.f.* fortitude; vigour, strength; fortress; stronghold; (*pl.*) flaw in a sword blade.
forte, *a.* (*mus.*) loud. — *interj.* (*naut.*) avast!
fortificable, *a.* fortifiable.
fortificación, *n.f.* fortification; ***fortificación de campaña,*** field-fortification.
fortificador, -ra, *a.* fortifying.
fortificante, *a.* fortifying; invigorating.
fortificar [A], *v.t.* to fortify, strengthen, invigorate.
fortín, *n.m.* small fort.
fortitud, *n.f.* (*poet.*) fortitude.
fortuito, -ta, *a.* fortuitous.
fortuna, *n.f.* fortune; chance; fate; good luck; tempest, storm; ***por fortuna,*** luckily; ***probar fortuna,*** to try one's luck; ***al hombre osado la fortuna le da la mano,*** fortune favours the brave.
fortunón, *n.m.* (*coll.*) whacking great fortune, real pile *or* packet, regular mint of money.
forúnculo, *n.m.* (*med.*) boil.
forzado, -da, *a.* forced; ***trabajos forzados,*** hard labour; ***a marchas forzadas,*** by forced marches. — *n.m.* prisoner condemned to the galleys.
forzador, *n.m.* ravisher; forcer.
forzal, *n.m.* back (*of comb*).
forzamento, forzamiento, *n.m.* forcing; raping.
forzar [4C], *v.t.* to force; to break in; to storm; to ravish, rape; ***forzar la vista,*** to strain one's eyes.
forzosamente, *adv.* necessarily; of necessity.
forzoso, -sa, *a.* necessary, unavoidable; ***aterrizaje forzoso,*** forced landing.
forzudo, -da, *a.* strong, vigorous, lusty.
fosa, *n.f.* grave; (*anat.*) fossa.
fosar, *v.t.* to make a pit, dig a trench, ditch *or* foss round.
fosco, -ca, *a.* frowning; dark; sullen, lowering. — *n.f.* haze; (*prov.*) thicket, jungle, thick grove.
fosfático, -ca, *a.* phosphatic.
fosfato, *n.m.* phosphate.
fosfito, *n.m.* phosphite.
fosforado, -da, *a.* phosphated.
fosforero, -ra, *n.m.f.* seller of matches. — *n.f.* match-box.
fosforescencia, *n.f.* phosphorescence.
fosforescente, *a.* phosphorescent.
fosforescer, fosforecer [9], *v.i.* to phosphoresce, shed a phosphorescent light.
fosfórico, -ca, *a.* phosphoric.
fosforita, *n.f.* phosphorite.
fósforo, *n.m.* phosphorus; friction match; morning star.
fosforoscopio, *n.m.* phosphoroscope.
fosforoso, -sa, *a.* phosphorous.
fosfuro, *n.m.* phosphide.
fósil, *a., n.m.* fossil.
fosilífero, -ra, *a.* fossiliferous.
fosilización, *n.f.* fossilization.

fosilizarse [C], *v.r.* to fossilize, become fossilized.
foso, *n.m.* pit; (*theat.*) pit under stage; (*fort.*) moat, ditch, foss.
fotocopia, *n.f.* photocopy.
fotogénico, -ca, *a.* photogenic.
fotograbado, *n.m.* photogravure.
fotografía, *n.f.* photography; photograph.
fotografiar [L], *v.t.* to photograph.
fotográfico, -ca, *a.* photographic.
fotógrafo, *n.m.* photographer.
fotolitografía, *n.f.* photolithography; photolithograph.
fotometría, *n.f.* photometry.
fotómetro, *n.m.* photometer.
fotomontaje, *n.m.* photomontage.
fotón, *n.m.* photon.
fotoquímica, *n.f.* photochemistry.
fotosfera, *n.f.* photosphere.
fototerapia, *n.f.* phototherapeutics, phototherapy.
fototipia, *n.f.* phototypy.
fototipografía, *n.f.* phototypography.
fótula, *n.f.* (*prov.*) flying cockroach.
fotuto, *n.m.* (*Col., Cub.*) whistle; trumpet, horn.
fovila, *n.f.* (*bot.*) fovilla.
frac, *n.m.* dress-coat; tail-coat.
fracasado, -da, *a.* unsuccessful. — *n.m.f.* failure.
fracasar, *v.i.* to fail, be unsuccessful, fall through; (*naut.*) to break up, break to pieces.
fracaso, *n.m.* failure; collapse, crash.
fracción, *n.f.* fraction, part; breaking into parts; faction.
fraccionamiento, *n.m.* division into fractions.
fraccionar, *v.t.* to divide into fractions, break up.
fraccionario, -ria, *a.* fractional; fractionary.
fractura, *n.f.* fracture; breaking; ***fractura complicada,*** compound fracture; ***fractura conminuta,*** comminuted fracture, comminution.
fracturar, *v.t.* to fracture, break.
fraga, *n.f.* raspberry; thicket of brambles.
fragancia, *n.f.* fragrance; good name.
fragante, *a.* fragrant; ***en fragante*** [FLAGRANTE, EN].
fragaria, *n.f.* strawberry.
fragata, *n.f.* frigate; frigate bird; ***fragata ligera,*** corvette.
frágil, *a.* fragile; frail.
fragilidad, *n.f.* fragility; frailty.
fragmentar, *v.t.* to reduce to fragments, break up.
fragmentarismo, *n.m.* fragmentation, tendency to split up, splitting up *or* splintering into small groups.
fragmento, *n.m.* fragment.
fragor, *n.m.* clash, crash, din.
fragoroso, -sa, *a.* noisy, thundering.
fragosidad, *n.f.* unevenness, roughness; denseness, impenetrableness; rugged spot.
fragoso, -sa, *a.* uneven, rough; dense, impenetrable; rugged; noisy, thundering.
fragua, *n.f.* forge.
fraguador, -ra, *a.* scheming. — *n.m.f.* schemer.
fraguar [H], *v.t.* to forge; (*fig.*) to cook up, brew, hatch. — *v.i.* (*mas.*) to set (hard). — **fraguarse,** *v.r.* (*fig.*) to blow up, be in the offing; ***se está fraguando una tormenta,*** there's a storm brewing *or* in the offing.
fragura [FRAGOSIDAD].
frailada, *n.f.* (*coll.*) monkish trick, crude thing to do *or* say.
fraile, *n.m.* friar, monk; (*arch.*) hood (*over a hearth*); fold (*at bottom of a skirt*); (*print.*) friar; fold (*in a leaf*); (*Cub.*) bagasse (*of a sugar-cane*); upright post (*of a floodgate*); ***fraile de misa y olla,*** friar who assists only at the altar and in the choir.
frailear, *v.t.* to prune (*a tree*) close to the trunk.
frailecico, -cillo, *n.m.* little friar; wedge securing the spindle of a silk-reel; (*orn.*) lapwing.
frailecito, *n.m.* husk of the broad bean fashioned by children, as a game, like a monk's cowl.
frailengo, -ga, fraileño, -ña, *a.* monkish.
frailería, *n.f.* (*coll.*) assembly of friars.
frailero, -ra, *a.* friarlike; (*coll.*) very fond of friars.
frailesco, -ca, *a.* (*coll.*) monkish.
frailía, *n.f.* monkishness, monastic life; regular clergy.
frailote, *n.m.* big and coarse friar.
frailuco, *n.m.* despicable friar.
frailuno, -na, *a.* (*coll., pej.*) friarlike, monkish.
frambuesa, *n.f.* raspberry.
frambueso, *n.m.* raspberry-bush.
frámea, *n.f.* javelin, dart.
francachela, *n.f.* (*coll.*) merry meal, banquet, spread; (*Hisp. Am.*) excessive familiarity.
francalete, *n.m.* leather strap with a buckle.
francés, -cesa, *a.* French; ***mal francés,*** venereal disease; ***a la francesa,*** in the French fashion; (*coll.*) ***despedirse a la francesa,*** to take French leave. — *n.m.* Frenchman; French (*language*). — *n.f.* Frenchwoman.
francesada, *n.f.* Frenchism; French business; typical French behaviour; French invasion of Spain in 1808.
francesilla, *n.f.* (*bot.*) turban buttercup; French roll.
Francia, *n.f.* France.
Francisca, *n.f.* Frances.
franciscano, -na, *a., n.m.f.* Franciscan.
Francisco, *n.m.* Francis.
francisco, -ca, *a.* Franciscan.
francmasón, *n.m.* freemason, mason.
francmasonería, *n.f.* freemasonry.
franco, -ca, *a.* frank, open, candid, outspoken; generous, liberal; clear, unobstructed; free, exempt; ***franco de servicio,*** off duty; ***franco de porte,*** carriage free; ***puerto franco,*** free port; ***franco a bordo,*** free on board, f.o.b.; ***lengua franca,*** lingua franca; ***franco-americano,*** Franco-American. — *n.m.* franc (*coin*); (*pl.*) Franks.
francófilo, -la, *a., n.m.f.* Francophile.
francófobo, -ba, *a., n.m.f.* Francophobe.
francolín, *n.m.* francolin.
francote, -ta, *a.* (*coll.*) frank, plain-spoken.
franchipán, *n.m.* frangipane.
franchute, -ta, *n.m.f.* (*contempt.*) Frenchy, Froggy.
franela, *n.f.* flannel.
frange, *n.m.* (*her.*) division of the field of a shield.
frangente, *a.* frangent, fracturing. — *n.m.* accident, disaster, mishap.
frangible, *a.* brittle, frangible, breakable.
frangir [E], *v.t.* to smash to pieces.
frangollar, *v.t.* (*coll.*) to botch, bungle, do (sth.) hurriedly and carelessly; (*obs.*) to grind (*corn*) coarsely.
frangollo, *n.m.* pottage; (*Hisp. Am.*) stew; (*coll.*) mess, botch.
frangollón, -llona, *a.* botching, bungling.
frángula, *n.f.* alder, buckthorn.
franja, *n.f.* fringe; band; strip.
franjar, franjear, *v.t.* to trim, border, put a fringe on.
franjón, *n.m.* wide band *or* strip.
franjuela, *n.f.* narrow little band *or* strip.
franqueamiento [FRANQUEO].
franquear, *v.t.* to free; to exempt, grant immunity to; to grant freely; to clear, open; to frank, stamp; to cross, get over. — **franquearse,** *v.r.* to yield; to open one's heart.
franqueo, *n.m.* franking; postage; liberating, freeing.

franqueza, *n.f.* frankness; generosity; freedom; ***con franqueza,*** candidly, to be quite honest.
franquía, *n.f.* sea-room; (*naut., coll.*) ***ponerse en franquía,*** to get in the open, get clear.
franquicia, *n.f.* exemption from taxes; franchise.
franquismo, *n.m.* Francoism, political system of General Franco.
frasca, *n.f.* dry leaves and small branches.
frasco, *n.m.* flask; bottle; jar.
frase, *n.f.* phrase; sentence; ***frase hecha,*** set phrase; ***frase sacramental,*** set, standard *or* ritual form; ***gastar frases,*** to go in for a lot of verbiage, be wordy.
frasear, *v.t.* to phrase; to adorn with phrases. — *v.i.* to go in for verbiage.
fraseología, *n.f.* phraseology; verbosity.
frasquera, *n.f.* flask-case; bottle-case; (*naut.*) ***frasquera de fuego,*** fire-case *or* fire-chest.
frasqueta, *n.f.* frisket (*of a printing press*).
fratás, *n.m.* plastering trowel.
fratasar, *v.t.* to trowel, smooth with the trowel.
fraterna (1), *n.f.* severe reprimand.
fraternal, *a.* fraternal, brotherly.
fraternidad, *n.f.* fraternity, brotherhood.
fraternizar [C], *v.i.* to fraternize.
fraterno, -na (2), *a.* fraternal, brotherly.
fratricida, *a.* fratricidal. — *n.m.f.* fratricide.
fratricidio, *n.m.* fratricide.
fraude, *n.m.* fraud.
fraudulencia, *n.f.* fraudulence.
fraudulento, -ta, *a.* fraudulent.
fraustina, *n.f.* wooden head (*for fashioning adies' head-dresses*).
fraxinela, *n.f.* white dittany.
fray, *n.m. abbr. of* ***fraile*** *used as an appellation before the names of knights and clergymen of a military order;* ***fray modesto nunca fue prior,*** the timid and faint-hearted never get to the top.
frazada, *n.f.* blanket.
frazadero, *n.m.* maker of blankets.
frazadilla, *n.f.* small *or* light blanket.
frecuencia, *n.f.* frequency; ***con frecuencia,*** often.
frecuentación, *n.f.* frequentation, frequenting; frequent practice.
frecuentador, -ra, *n.m.f.* frequenter.
frecuentar, *v.t.* to frequent, haunt, visit often.
frecuentativo, -va, *a.* frequentative.
frecuente, *a.* frequent; common.
frecuentemente, *adv.* frequently, often.
fregadero, *n.m.* scullery; kitchen sink.
fregado, -da, *a.* (*Arg., Chi.*) annoying, boring (*person*); (*Col.*) stubborn; (*Mex.*) knavish, artful. — *n.m.* scrubbing, scouring; (*coll.*) doubtful affair; racket, shindy, set-to.
fregador, -ra, *a.* scrubbing. — *n.m.f.* scrubbing brush.
fregadura, *n.f.* rubbing, scrubbing, scouring.
fregajo, *n.m.* mop, swab.
fregamiento, *n.m.* friction, rubbing.
fregar [B], *v.t.* to scrub, scour; to rub, swab; to mop (*floor*); to wash (*dishes*); (*Hisp. Am.*) to annoy, bother.
fregatina, *n.f.* (*Chi.*) bother.
fregatriz, fregona, *n.f.* kitchen-maid, scrubbing girl.
fregonil, *a.* (*coll.*) wench-like.
fregotear, *v.t.* to scrub *or* wash up in a slap-dash fashion.
freidura, *n.f.* frying.
freiduría, *n.f.* fried-fish shop.
freile, *n.m.* knight *or* priest of a military order.
freír [28, *p.p.* **frito**], *v.t.* to fry; (*coll.*) to bother, pester; ***al freír será el reír,*** he laughs best who laughs last; ***al freír de los huevos lo verás,*** the proof of the pudding is in the eating; (*coll.*) ***me tienen frito,*** they're driving me up the wall; (*coll.*) ***estoy frito,*** I'm stewed; I'm exasperated. — **freírse,** *v.r.* ***freírse de calor,*** to stew, sizzle with (the) heat; (*coll.*) ***freírsela a alguien,*** to have s.o. on.
fréjol, *n.m.* kidney bean.
frelo, -la, *a.* (*prov.*) delicate, weakly, sickly.
frémito, *n.m.* roar.
frenar, *v.t.* to bridle, to govern by the bridle; to apply the brake to, to brake.
frenazo, *n.m.* sudden *or* sharp braking, jamming on of brakes.
frenería, *n.f.* bridle-making; harness-shop.
frenero, *n.m.* maker *or* seller of bridles; (*railw.*) brakeman.
frenesí, *n.m.* frenzy, fury, madness; distraction, folly.
frenético, -ca, *a.* frantic, frenzied, mad.
frenillar, *v.t.* to bridle (*oars*).
frenillo, *n.m.* (*anat.*) frenum; muzzle; (*naut.*) bridle, fox, ratline; (*Cent. Am., Cub.*) string *or* stay (*of a kite*); ***no tener frenillo en la lengua,*** to be outspoken, not to mince one's words; (*fig.*) ***tener frenillo,*** to speak indistinctly *or* lispingly.
freno, *n.m.* bridle; bit (*of bridle*); brake; catch, check, stop; (*fig.*) curb; ***freno de pedal,*** foot-brake; ***freno neumático,*** air-brake; ***freno de tambor,*** disc-brake; ***beber el freno,*** to bite at the bit; ***morder el freno,*** to chafe at the bit, champ (on) the bit; ***tascar el freno,*** to champ (on) the bit; (*fig.*) to toe the line; ***poner freno a,*** to put the brake on, brake, check.
frenología, *n.f.* phrenology.
frenológico, -ca, *a.* phrenological.
frenólogo, *n.m.* phrenologist.
frenópata, *n.m.* phrenopathist, alienist.
frenopatía, *n.f.* phrenopathy, alienism.
frental, *a.* frontal, of the forehead.
frente, *n.m.* front; face (*of a bastion*); blank space (*at the beginning of a document*); obverse (*of coins*); ***frente a frente,*** face to face; ***al frente de,*** at the head of; ***dar un paso al frente,*** to take a step forward; ***de frente,*** facing; head-on; ***en frente de,*** opposite; ***frente por frente de,*** right opposite; ***sin novedad en el frente,*** all quiet at the (battle-) front. — *n.f.* forehead; brow; (*coll.*) brain, sense; ***arrugar, fruncir la frente,*** to knit one's brow; ***no tener dos dedos de frente,*** to have no sense.
frentero, *n.m.* pad (*to protect a child's forehead*).
freo, *n.m.* channel, strait.
fresa, *n.f.* strawberry; wild strawberry; (*mech.*) milling-tool.
fresada, *n.f.* dish of flour, milk and butter.
fresadora, *n.f.* milling machine.
fresal, *n.m.* strawberry patch.
fresar, *v.t.* to mill; to drill; to machine.
fresca, *n.f.* [FRESCO].
frescachón, -chona, *a.* robust, ruddy; blooming, buxom; brisk (*wind*).
frescal, *a.* lightly salted.
frescales, *n.m. inv.* (*coll.*) cheeky devil *or* hound, fellow with the nerve of the devil.
fresco, -ca, *a.* fresh; cool; (*coll.*) cheeky; (*iron.*) ***¡noticia fresca!*** that's news!; ***largarse con viento fresco,*** to clear out, push off. — *n.m.* cool air; fresco; (*coll.*) cheeky rascal; (*Hisp. Am.*) cool drink; ***quedarse fresco,*** to be disappointed; ***quedarse tan fresco,*** to be unperturbed, quite nonchalant; (*coll.*) ***¡estás tú fresco!*** you've a hope!; you've had it!; ***al fresco,*** in the cool evening air; in the open; ***tomar el fresco,*** to take *or* enjoy the (cool) air; (*coll.*) ***¡es un fresco!*** the fellow has the nerve of the Devil! — *n.f.* cool; cool air; cool evening *or* morning air; (*coll.*) piece of one's mind, biting remark; ***con la fresca,*** in

the cool of evening; ***decir cuatro frescas a,*** to tick off sharply.
frescor, *n.m.* freshness; coolness.
frescote, -ta, *a.* (*coll.*) very healthy, ruddy; thoroughly cheeky.
frescura, *n.f.* coolness; freshness; cheek, nerve.
fresero, -ra, *n.m.f.* strawberry vendor. — *n.f.* strawberry plant.
fresnal, *a.* belonging to the ash-tree.
fresneda, *n.f.* ash-tree grove.
fresnillo, *n.m.* fraxinella.
fresno, *n.m.* ash-tree; ash wood; ***fresno húngaro,*** Hungarian ash; ***fresno americano,*** white ash; ***fresno florido,*** flowering ash.
fresón, *n.m.* strawberry; large strawberry.
fresquillo, -lla, *a.* coolish; rather chilly.
fresquería, *n.f.* (*Hisp. Am.*) ice-cream parlour.
fresquero, -ra, *n.m.f.* vendor of fresh fish. — *n.f.* meat-safe.
fresquete, *n.m.* pretty chilly weather.
fresquilla, *n.f.* peach.
fresquista, *n.m.f.* fresco painter.
fresquito, -ta, *a.* nice and cool; rather chilly; recent, fresh, freshly made. — *n.m.* cool, cool breeze.
freudiano, -na, *a.* Freudian.
freudismo, *n.m.* Freudianism.
frey, *n.m. abbr. of* ***freile*** *used as an appellation before the names of knights and clergymen belonging to a military order.*
frez, *n.f.* dung, droppings.
freza, *n.f.* dung, droppings; spawning, spawning season, spawn; feeding season (*silk-worms*); ground dug up *or* hollow (*left by the rooting* or *scratching of an animal*).
frezada [FRAZADA].
frezar [C], *v.t.* to clean (*hives*). — *v.i.* to eject dung; to spawn; to feed (*silk-worms*); to scratch, root (*game*).
friabilidad, *n.f.* friability.
friable, *a.* friable.
frialdad, *n.f.* coldness; coolness; (*med.*) frigidity.
friático, -ca, *a.* chilly; foolish, graceless, silly.
fricación, *n.f.* friction, rubbing.
fricandó, *n.m.* fricandeau, Scotch collop.
fricar [A], *v.t.* to rub, scour.
fricasé, *n.m.* fricassee.
fricativo, -va, *a.* fricative.
fricción, *n.f.* friction; rubbing.
friccionar, *v.t.* to rub.
friega, *n.f.* friction, rubbing; (*Col., C.R.*) bother, annoyance, nuisance; (*Chi.*) sound beating, flogging.
friera, *n.f.* chilblain.
frigidez, *n.f.* frigidity.
frígido, -da, *a.* frigid.
frigio, -gia, *a., n.m.f.* Phrygian.
frigorífico, -ca, *a.* refrigerating. — *n.m.* refrigerator, fridge, (*Am.*) icebox; refrigerating plant; ***cámara frigorífica,*** cold-storage room *or* chamber.
friísimo, -ma, *a. superl.* extremely cold.
fríjol, *n.m.* kidney-bean.
fringa, *n.f.* (*Hond.*) travelling rug; cloak with sleeves.
fringilago, *n.m.* titmouse.
frío, fría, *a.* cold; cool. — *n.m.* cold, coldness; coolness; (*fig.*) ***ave fría,*** cold fish; ***dejar frío,*** to leave cold, unmoved, unimpressed; ***quedarse frío,*** to go cold, get cold; (*fig.*) to be nonplussed, totally thrown out; ***a sangre fría,*** in cold blood; ***hace frío,*** it's cold (*weather*); ***está frío,*** it's cold; ***es frío,*** he is cold (by nature); ***tiene frío,*** he is cold, feels cold; ***coger frío,*** to catch cold; ***no me da ni frío ni calor,*** I'm indifferent about it.

friolento, -ta, friolero, -ra (1), *a.* chilly; sensitive to cold; ***es muy friolero,*** he feels the cold keenly.
friolera (2), *n.f.* trifle; (*iron.*) ***la friolera de mil libras,*** a trifling thousand pounds.
frisa, *n.f.* frieze; palisade; (*naut.*) lining, packing; (*León*) shawl; (*Arg., Chi.*) nap.
frisado, *n.m.* silk plush, shag.
frisador, -ra, *n.m.f.* frizzler.
frisadura, *n.f.* frizzling, shagging.
frisar, *v.t.* to frizzle, frizz (*cloth*); to rub; (*naut.*) to line, pack. — *v.i.* to get on well; (*fig.*) to be near, approach; ***frisaba en los cuarenta,*** he was getting on for forty.
friso, *n.m.* frieze; wainscot, dado, mop-board.
frísol, *n.m.* kidney-bean.
frisón, -sona, *a., n.m.f.* Frisian. — *n.m.* large draught horse.
frisuelo, *n.m.* kidney-bean; fritter.
frita (1), *n.f.* frit; slag.
fritada, *n.f.* fry, fry-up.
fritilaria, *n.f.* fritillary.
fritillas, *n.f.pl.* fritters.
frito, -ta (2), *a.* fried. — *n.m.* fry, fried food; *p.p.* [FREÍR].
fritura, *n.f.* fry; fritter.
friura, *n.f.* (*prov.*) cold.
frivolidad, *n.f.* frivolity, frivolousness.
frivolité, *n.f.* tatting.
frívolo, -la, *a.* frivolous; trifling.
friz, *n.f.* flower of the beech tree.
froga, *n.f.* (*obs.*) brickwork.
fronda, *n.f.* leaf; frond; foliage; (*surg.*) sling-shaped bandage.
fronde, *n.m.* (*bot.*) frond.
frondescencia, *n.f.* frondescence.
frondífero, -ra, *a.* frondiferous, leaf-bearing.
frondio, -dia, *a.* (*Col.*) peevish, disagreeable; (*Mex.*) dirty, untidy.
frondosidad, *n.f.* frondage, leafiness.
frondoso, -sa, *a.* leafy.
frontal, *a.* frontal; relating to the forehead. — *n.m.* frontal; (*Col., Ec., Mex.*) headstall (*of a bridle*); ***choque frontal,*** head-on collision.
frontalera, *n.f.* brow-band (*of a bridle*); brow-pad (*under a yoke*); (*eccles.*) trimmings (*of an altar frontal*); place where frontals are kept.
frontera, *n.f.* [FRONTERO].
fronterizo, -za, *a.* frontier, border; fronting, opposite.
frontero, -ra, *a.* placed in front, opposite. — **frontero,** *adv.* in front. — *n.m.* governor *or* commander of frontier forces; frontlet *or* brow-pad. — *n.f.* frontier, border; (*arch.*) façade; binder (*of a frail-basket*); side (*of a soft-brick mould*).
frontil, *n.m.* yoke-pad.
frontino, -na, *a.* marked in the face.
frontis, *n.m.* (*arch.*) frontispiece, façade.
frontispicio, *n.m.* front; frontispiece; façade; (*coll.*) face, visage.
frontón, *n.m.* (*arch.*) fronton, pediment; hand-ball court; (*min.*) working face.
frontudo, -da, *a.* broad-browed.
frontura, *n.f.* front (*of a stocking-frame*).
frotación, frotadura, *n.f.* friction, rubbing.
frotador, -ra, *n.m.f.* rubber.
frotamiento, *n.m.* rubbing, friction.
frotante, *a.* rubbing.
frotar, *v.t.* to rub.
frote, *n.m.* friction, rubbing.
fructífero, -ra, *a.* fructiferous, fruit-bearing, fruitful.
fructificación, *n.f.* fructification.
fructificar [A], *v.i.* to fructify, bear *or* yield fruit.
fructuario, -ria, *a.* usufructuary.
fructuoso, -sa, *a.* fruitful.

fruente, *a.* enjoying.
frugal, *a.* frugal, sparing.
frugalidad, *n.f.* frugality.
frugífero, -ra, *a.* (*poet.*) fruit-bearing.
frugívoro, -ra, *a.* frugivorous, feeding on fruit.
fruición, *n.f.* enjoyment, fruition.
fruir [O], *v.i.* to enjoy o.s., have pleasure.
fruitivo, -va, *a.* fruitive, enjoyable.
frumentario, -ria, frumenticio, -cia, *a.* frumentaceous.
frunce, *n.m.* (*sew.*) shirr, shirring, gather; pleat.
fruncidor, *n.m.* (*sew.*) gatherer, pleater, folder.
fruncimiento, *n.m.* shirring, gathering; knitting (*brow*); puckering (*mouth*); (*coll.*) deceit.
fruncir [D], *v.t.* (*sew.*) to gather, shirr; to knit (*brow*); to pucker (*mouth*); ***fruncir el entrecejo,*** to frown. — **fruncirse,** *v.r.* to affect modesty.
fruslería, *n.f.* trifle.
fruslero, -ra, *a.* trifling. — *n.m.* rolling-pin. — *n.f.* brass turnings, clippings.
frustración, *n.f.* frustration.
frustráneo, -nea, *a.* useless, nugatory.
frustrar, *v.t.* to frustrate, baulk, thwart, foil. — **frustrarse,** *v.r.* to fail, miscarry, fall through.
frustratorio, -ria, *a.* frustrative, defeating.
fruta, *n.f.* fruit; ***fruta ajena,*** things coveted; ***fruta nueva,*** novelty, sth. new; ***fruta de sartén,*** fritter; ***fruta del tiempo,*** fruit in season; (*fig.*) anything seasonal *or* recurrent.
frutaje, *n.m.* (*art*) painting of fruits and flowers.
frutal, *a.* fruit (-bearing). — *n.m.* fruit-tree.
frutar, *v.i.* to bear *or* yield fruit.
frutecer [9], *v.i.* to start to bear *or* yield fruit.
frutería, *n.f.* fruit shop, fruiterer's.
frutero, -ra, *a.* fruit. — *n.m.f.* fruit seller *or* grower. — *n.m.* fruit bowl *or* dish; fruit napkin; table centre-piece (*of fruit*); (*paint.*) fruit piece.
frutice, *n.m.* frutex.
fruticoso, -sa, *a.* (*bot.*) fruticose, frutescent; shrubby.
fruticultura, *n.f.* fruit-growing.
frutilla, *n.f.* small fruit; (*Hisp. Am.*) strawberry; bead (*of a rosary*).
frutillar, *n.m.* (*Hisp. Am.*) strawberry-bed.
fruto, *n.m.* fruit; ***dar fruto,*** to yield fruit; ***sacar fruto,*** to derive benefit; ***fruto de bendición,*** legitimate child; ***sin fruto,*** fruitlessly.
¡fu! *interj.* ugh!; ***hacer fu a,*** to turn up one's nose at; (*coll.*) ***ni fu ni fa,*** neither good nor bad, indifferent.
fúcar, *n.m.* opulent man, nabob.
fucilar, *v.i.* to flash, glisten.
fucilazo, *n.m.* fulguration, heat lightning.
fuco, *n.m.* fucus, bladder-wrack, olive sea-weeds.
fucsia, *n.f.* fuchsia.
fucsina, *n.f.* fuchsine.
fuego, *n.m.* fire; light (*for cigarette etc.*); beacon-fire; hearth, fire-place; eruption (*in the skin*); heat (*of an action*); (*vet.*) cautery; ***fuego de San Antón,*** erysipelas; ***fuego de San Telmo,*** St. Elmo's fire; ***fuego fatuo,*** jack-o'-lantern, will-o'-the-wisp, ignis fatuus; ***fuego griego,*** Greek *or* wild fire; ***atizar el fuego,*** to poke *or* stir the fire; (*mil.*) ***hacer fuego,*** to fire; ***echar leña al fuego,*** to add fuel to the flames; ***pegar fuego a,*** to set on fire; ***poner la mano en el fuego,*** to swear on one's oath; ***fuegos artificiales,*** fireworks; (*mil.*) ***fuego graneado,*** drumfire; ***a fuego lento,*** on *or* over a slow fire; ***a sangre y fuego,*** with fire and sword; ***huir del fuego y dar (caer) en las brasas,*** to jump from the frying-pan into the fire; ***romper el fuego,*** to open fire.
fuellar, *n.m.* bright talcum ornament (*on wax tapers*).
fuelle, *n.m.* bellows; blower; (*motor.*) hood, top; clouds (*over mountains*); (*coll.*) tale-bearer; (*sew.*) pucker (*in clothes*); (*prov.*) goat-skin bag.
fuente, *n.f.* fountain; spring, source; service dish, (*Am.*) platter; (*surg.*) seton, small ulcer, issue; ***de fuente fidedigna,*** from a reliable source.
fuentecica, -cilla, -cita, -zuela, *n.f.* small fountain.
fuer, *adv.* ***a fuer de,*** as a, in the manner of; ***a fuer de caballero,*** as a gentleman. — *n.m., contr.* [FUERO].
fuera, *adv.* out, outside; away; off; ***de fuera,*** outside; from (the) outside; ***por fuera,*** on the outside; ***fuera de sí,*** beside o.s.; ***fuera de,*** out of, besides, in addition to; ***fuera de esto,*** apart from this; ***hacia fuera,*** outward; ***fuera de que,*** besides; ***estar fuera,*** to be away; ***fuera de lugar,*** out of place; ***fuera de quicio,*** unhinged; ***fuera de serie,*** unusual, uncommon. — *interj.* out!
¡fuerarropa! *interj.* strip! (*command used in the galleys for the oarsmen to undress*).
fuerista, *n.m.f.* expert in statute law.
fuero, *n.m.* exception, privilege; statute-law and rights (*of a town, region etc.*); jurisdiction; code of local laws and privileges; ***en su fuero interno (interior),*** in his heart of hearts; ***de fuero,*** of right, by right of law.
fuerte, *a.* strong; hard; fast, secure; heavy; thick; intense, severe; loud; ***caja fuerte,*** strong box, safe; ***agua fuerte,*** aqua fortis; ***hacerse fuerte,*** to entrench o.s. — *adv.* hard, strongly, heavily, firmly; ***cenar fuerte,*** to have a heavy supper; ***pisar fuerte,*** to tread firmly.— *n.m.* fort; strong point; forte.
fuerza, *n.f.* strength, force, might, power; ***fuerza animal*** or ***de sangre,*** animal power; ***fuerza mayor,*** superior force, force majeure; ***fuerza pública,*** police; ***fuerza de voluntad,*** will power; ***fuerzas de tierra y de mar,*** land and naval forces; ***fuerzas vivas,*** power *or* pressure groups; ***la fuerza de la costumbre,*** force of habit; ***camisa de fuerza,*** strait-jacket; ***a viva fuerza,*** by main force, by sheer force; ***a fuerza de,*** by dint of; ***a la fuerza, por fuerza,*** necessarily, of necessity, willy-nilly; ***a la fuerza ahorcan,*** needs must (when the Devil drives); ***de grado o por fuerza,*** willingly or unwillingly, willy-nilly; ***hacer fuerza,*** to apply force *or* pressure, strain, pull hard; ***sacar fuerzas de flaqueza,*** to pluck up courage; ***es fuerza que,*** it is necessary *or* unavoidable that.
fuetazo, *n.m.* (*Hisp. Am.*) lash, whip-lash.
fuete, *n.m.* (*Hisp. Am.*) whip.
fufar, *v.i.* to make a spitting noise (*angry cat*).
fufu, *n.m.* (*Col., Cub., P.R.*) pounded mass of yam, plantain etc.
fuga, *n.f.* escape; flight; elopement; leak, leakage; (*mus.*) fugue; ***darse a la fuga,*** to flee, take flight, run away, escape; ***poner en fuga,*** to put to flight.
fugacidad, *n.f.* fugacity, fleetingness.
fugado, -da, *a.* fugato, written in the style of a fugue.
fugarse [B], *v.r.* to flee, run away, escape; to elope.
fugaz, (*poet.*) **fúgido, -da,** *a.* fugacious; fleeting; ***estrella fugaz,*** shooting star.
fugitivo, -va, *a.* fugitive, runaway; fleeting. — *n.m.* fugitive.
fuguillas, *n.m. inv.* (*coll.*) quick-tempered person; jittery individual; hustler, impatient person.
fuina, *n.f.* marten.
ful, *a.* bogus, sham.
fulano, -na, *n.m.f.* so-and-so; ***Fulano de tal,*** So-and-So; ***Fulano, Zutano, Mengano y Perengano,*** (every) Tom, Dick and Harry. — *n.f.* prostitute.
fular, *n.m.* foulard.
fulcro, *n.m.* fulcrum.
fulero, -ra, *a.* bungling; blustering, bluffing; flamboyant.
fulgecer [9], *v.i.* (*poet.*) to shine, be resplendent.

fulgente, *a.* refulgent, brilliant.
fúlgido, -da, *a.* bright, resplendent.
fulgor, *n.m.* resplendence, brilliancy.
fulguración, *n.f.* flash, flashing; (*med.*) lightning stroke.
fulgurante, *a.* resplendent, shining.
fulgurar, *v.i.* to fulgurate, flash, shine with brilliancy; to blaze, flare.
fulguroso, -sa, *a.* fulgorous.
fúlica, *n.f.* (*orn.*) fulica, coot.
fuliginoso, -sa, *a.* fuliginous, dark, sooty, murky.
fulminación, *n.f.* fulmination, thundering.
fulminador, -ra, thundering, fulminating.
fulminante, *a.* fulminating, fulminant, lightning; exploding; (*med.*) violent, deadly. — *n.m.* explosive, fulminant; fulminating powder (*in a percussion cap*).
fulminar, *v.t.* to fulminate; to strike with lightning. — *v.i.* to thunder, fulminate.
fulminato, *n.m.* (*chem.*) fulminate.
fulminatriz, *a.* fulminating.
fulmíneo, -nea, *a.* (*poet.*) fulmineous.
fulmínico, *a.* fulminic (*acid*).
fulminoso, -sa, *a.* fulminatory, thundering.
fulleresco, -ca, *a.* of sharpers and cheats.
fullería, *n.f.* cheating, trickery.
fullero, -ra, *n.m.f.* sharper, cheat, trickster; (*Col.*) tale-bearer, informer.
fullona, *n.f.* (*coll.*) dispute, quarrel, wrangle.
fumable, *a.* smokeable, good to smoke.
fumada, *n.f.* puff, whiff of smoke.
fumadero, *n.m.* smoking-room.
fumador, -ra, *n.m.f.* smoker.
fumante, *a.* smoking; fuming.
fumar, *v.i.* to smoke. — **fumarse,** *v.r.* (*coll.*) to polish off, run through; ***fumarse una clase,*** to skip a class.
fumarada, *n.f.* puff, whiff *or* blast of smoke; pipeful of tobacco.
fumaria, *n.f.* fumitory.
fumarola, *n.f.* fumarole.
fumífero, -ra, *a.* (*poet.*) smoking, emitting smoke.
fumífugo, -ga, *a.* smoke-dispersing.
fumigación, *n.f.* fumigation.
fumigador, *n.m.* fumigator.
fumigar [B], *v.t.* to fumigate.
fumigatorio, -ria, *a.* fumigatory. — *n.m.* perfuming pan.
fumista, *n.m.* stove-maker; seller of stoves; chimney sweep.
fumistería, *n.f.* shop *or* works where stoves are sold *or* repaired.
fumívoro, -ra, *a.* smoke-consuming.
fumorola [FUMAROLA].
fumosidad, *n.f.* smokiness.
fumoso, -sa, *a.* fumy, smoky.
funámbulo, -la, *n.m.f.* funambulist, tight-rope walker, rope-dancer.
función, *n.f.* function; job; show, performance.
funcional, *a.* functional.
funcionamiento, *n.m.* functioning, working, running, operation.
funcionar, *v.i.* to function, work, run.
funcionario, *n.m.* functionary; civil servant, official.
funche, *n.m.* (*Cub., Mex., P.R.*) porridge of maize flour.
funda, *n.f.* case; sheath; covering, cover; wrapper; slip; holster; ***funda de almohada,*** pillow-case.
fundación, *n.f.* foundation; founding; inception.
fundadamente, *adv.* with good foundation.
fundador, -ra, *a.* founding. — *n.m.f.* founder.
fundamental, *a.* fundamental, basic; (*anat.*) ***hueso fundamental,*** sacrum; sphenoid bone; ***piedra fundamental,*** foundation stone.
fundamentar, *v.t.* to lay the foundations of; to ground, set firm, base; to substantiate.
fundamento, *n.m.* foundation; ground-work, ground(s); root, origin; weft, woof; ***sin fundamento,*** groundless.
fundar, *v.t.* to found, set up; to base, ground. — **fundarse,** *v.r.* (***en***), to be based (on); to take as a basis; ***¿en qué se funda usted?*** what is your basis? what grounds do you have?
fundente, *a.* fusing; melting; smelting. — *n.m.* (*chem.*) flux; (*med.*) dissolvent.
fundería, *n.f.* foundry.
fundible, *a.* fusible.
fundíbulo, *n.m.* ballista, catapult.
fundición, *n.f.* fusion; melting; smelting, casting; foundry, smeltery; cast-iron; (*print.*) fount.
fundidor, *n.m.* founder; melter; smelter.
fundir, *v.t.* to fuse; to melt; to smelt; to cast; to merge; (*coll.*) to polish off, get through quickly; (*coll.*) to flog, sell off. — **fundirse,** *v.r.* to fuse, blend, combine, unite; (*elec.*) to fuse, blow; (*Hisp. Am.*) to come to ruin.
fundo, *n.m.* rural property.
fúnebre, *a.* funeral, funereal, mournful, mourning; gloomy, lugubrious; ***director de pompas fúnebres,*** undertaker, (*Am.*) mortician.
funeral, *a.* funeral, funereal. — *n.m.* funeral service.
funerala, *adv.* (*mil.*) ***a la funerala,*** with inverted arms.
funerario, -ria, *a.* funeral, funereal. — *n.f.* undertaker's.
funéreo, -rea, *a.* (*poet.*) mournful, funereal.
funestar, *v.t.* to blot, stain, tarnish, profane.
funesto, -ta, *a.* disastrous, fateful, baneful.
fungible, *a.* consumable; fungible.
fungiforme, *a.* fungiform.
fungir [E], *v.i.* (*Hisp. Am.*) to affect importance; (*Mex.*) to be employed.
fungita, *n.f.* fungite.
fungívero, -ra, *a.* fungiverous.
fungo, *n.m.* (*surg.*) fungus.
fungosidad, *n.f.* fungosity.
fungoso, -sa, *a.* fungous, spongy.
funicular, *a.* funicular; ***ferrocarril funicular,*** funicular railway.
funículo, *n.m.* funicle, funiculus.
fuñicar, *v.i.* to bungle.
fuñique, *a.* awkward; clumsy.
furcia, *n.f.* harlot.
furente, *a.* (*poet.*) furious, frantic, raging.
furgón, *n.m.* transport waggon; baggage-car, freight-car, box-car; van.
furia, *n.f.* fury; rage; (*fig.*) shrew.
furibundo, -da, *a.* furious, raging.
furioso, -sa, *a.* furious, raging.
furo (1), **-ra,** *a.* shy, reserved, unsociable; (*prov.*) ferocious, fierce, wild, untamed.
furo (2), *n.m.* orifice (*of sugar mould*).
furor, *n.m.* furor; fury, rage; ***furor uterino,*** nymphomania; ***hacer furor,*** to be all the rage.
furriel, furrier, *n.m.* quartermaster; clerk of the king's mews.
furriela, furriera, *n.f.* keeper of the keys of the king's palace.
furris, *a.* (*Mex., Ven.*) bad, contemptible; badly made.
furruco, *n.m.* (*Ven.*) drum.
furrusca, *n.f.* (*Col.*) quarrel, brawl.
furtivo, -va, *a.* furtive, clandestine; stealthy; ***cazador furtivo,*** poacher.
furuminga, *n.f.* (*Chi.*) tangle, jumble.
furúnculo [FORÚNCULO].
furunculoso, -sa, *a.* furunculose.
fusa, *n.f.* demi-semiquaver.

fusado, -da, fuselado, -da, *a.* (*her.*) charged with fusils *or* spindles.
fuscar [A], *v.t.* (*obs.*) to obscure.
fusco, -ca, *a.* fuscous, brown, dark. — *n.f.* dark-coloured duck.
fuselaje, *n.m.* (*aer.*) fuselage.
fusibilidad, *n.f.* fusibility.
fusible, fúsil, *a.* fusible.
fusiforme, *a.* fusiform, spindle-shaped.
fusil, *n.m.* rifle, gun; ***fusil de chispa,*** flint-lock, musket; ***fusil rayado,*** rifle; ***fusil de retrocarga,*** breech-loader.
fusilamiento, *n.m.* shooting, execution (*by firing squad*).
fusilar, *v.t.* to shoot, execute (*by firing squad*); (*coll.*) to plagiarize.
fusilazo, *n.m.* musket-shot; rifle-shot; blow with a gun.
fusilería, *n.f.* musketry; body of fusiliers *or* musketeers.
fusilero, *n.m.* fusilier, rifleman.
fusión, *n.f.* fusion; melting; merging; amalgamation; (*com.*) ***fusión de empresas,*** merger.
fusionar, *v.t.* to fuse, amalgamate.
fusionista, *a.* fusionist.
fusique, *n.m.* bottle-shaped snuff-box.
fuslina, *n.f.* smelting-works.
fusor, *n.m.* smelting ladle *or* vessel.
fusta, *n.f.* brushwood; woollen stuff; whip; lateen-rigged lighter.
fustán, *n.m.* fustian; (*Hisp. Am.*) petticoat.
fustanero, *n.m.* fustian manufacturer.
fuste, *n.m.* wood, timber; tree and bows (*of a saddle*); (*poet.*) saddle; shaft (*of a lance*); (*arch.*) fust, shaft (*of a column*); substance, solidness, importance; ***hombre de fuste,*** man of weight and importance.
fustero, *n.m.* (*obs.*) turner, carpenter.
fustete, *n.m.* Venetian sumach; fustic, yellow-wood.
fustigador, -ra, *a.* lashing, thrashing; (*fig.*) savage.
fustigar [B], *v.t.* to whip, thrash; (*fig.*) to lay into.
fustina, *n.f.* smelting place.
fútbol, *n.m.* football.
futbolista, *n.m.* footballer.
futbolístico, -ca, *a.* (of) football.
futesa, *n.f.* trifle, bagatelle.
fútil, *a.* trifling, trivial, of little *or* no account.
futilidad, *n.f.* trifle, triviality, matter of no moment.
futre, *n.m.* (*Hisp. Am.*) fop, dandy.
futurible, *a.*, *n.m.f.* (*pol.*) up and coming (personality), (figure) of *or* for the future.
futuro, -ra, *a.* future. — *n.m.* future; (*coll.*) betrothed, fiancé. — *n.f.* acquired right to an office *or* employment before its vacancy; (*coll.*) betrothed, fiancée.

G

G, g, letter G, g.
gabacho, -cha, *a., n.m.f.* Pyrenean; (*coll.*) Frenchy, Froggy. — *n.m.* (*coll.*) Frenchified language.
gabán, *n.m.* great-coat, overcoat, (*Am.*) topcoat.
gabarda, *n.f.* wild rose.
gabardina, *n.f.* gabardine; raincoat, mackintosh.
gabarra, *n.f.* (*naut.*) lighter, barge.
gabarrero, *n.m.* lighterman, bargee.
gabarro, *n.m.* flaw, defect; mistake, error; burden, annoyance; (*fowl*) pip; (*pastern*) tumour; (*geol.*) nodule.
gabarrón, *n.m.* large barge.
gabasa [BAGASA].
gábata, *n.f.* bowl, small basin for mess on galleys.
gabazo [BAGAZO].
gabela, *n.f.* tax, duty, gabelle; (*fig.*) burden.
gabinete, *n.m.* lady's boudoir, dressing-room; study, library; (*pol.*) cabinet; ***gabinete de lectura,*** reading room; ***gabinete de historia natural,*** natural history collection; ***de gabinete,*** theoretical; parlour.
gablete, *n.m.* gablet.
gabón, *n.m.* powder magazine.
gabote, *n.m.* (*prov.*) shuttlecock.
gabrieles, *n.m.pl.* (*coll.*) cooked chickpeas.
gacel, -la, *n.m.f.* gazelle.
gaceta, *n.f.* gazette, political *or* literary newspaper; government journal; ***mentir más que la gaceta,*** to be an inveterate liar.
gacetera, *n.f.* woman who sells newspapers.
gacetero, *n.m.* gazetteer; news-writer; seller of newspapers.
gacetilla, *n.f.* personal news column; town talk, gossip; scandalmonger.
gacetillero, *n.m.* short-news writer.
gacetista, *n.m.f.* person fond of reading newspapers; newsmonger.
gacha (1), *n.f.* watery mass; (*pl.*) porridge; pap, mush; (*coll.*) soppiness, mush; ***hacerse unas gachas,*** to get mushy *or* soppy.
gacheta, *n.f.* spring catch (*lock*).
gachí, *n.f.* (*sl.*) woman, lass.
gachó, *n.m.* (*sl.*) fellow, guy.
gacho, -cha (2), *a.* turned *or* bent downward; down-curved (*horn*); slouch (*hat*); ***a gachas,*** on all fours; ***con las orejas gachas,*** with one's tail between one's legs.
gachón, -chona, *a., n.m.f.* (*coll.*) sweet and attractive (*person*); sexy (*person*); pampered (*child*).
gachonada, *n.f.* (*coll.*) grace, charm; graceful *or* charming thing to do *or* say.
gachonería, *n.f.* attractiveness; sexiness.
gachumbo, *n.m.* (*Hisp. Am.*) shell of some fruits (*used to make cups and vessels*).
gachupín, -pina, *n.m.f.* (*Mex.*) name given to native of Spain.
gaditano, -na, *a., n.m.f.* (native) of Cadiz.
gaélico, -ca, *a.* Gaelic. — *n.m.* Gaelic (*language*).
gafa, *n.f.* [GAFO].
gafar, *v.t.* to hook, claw; to clench, fasten; to join with clampers; (*coll.*) to put a jinx on.
gafe, *n.m.* jinx.
gafedad, *n.f.* (*med.*) claw hand.
gafete, *n.m.* clasp, hook and eye.
gafo, -fa, *a.* suffering from claw-hand; (*Per.*) paralytic, tremulous. — *n.f.* gaffle, hook (*for bending a crossbow*); cramp (*for holding together*); (*naut.*) grapple fork; (*pl.*) (*naut.*) can hooks; spectacles; spectacle-bows.
gago, -ga, *n.m.f.* (*Per., P.R., Ven.*) stammerer, stutterer.
gaguear, *v.i.* (*Hisp. Am.*) to stutter, stammer.
gaita, *n.f.* flageolet; hurdy-gurdy; bagpipe; hornpipe; (*coll.*) neck; (*coll.*) pest, bore, pain in the neck; ***estar de gaita,*** to be in joking mood; ***templar gaitas,*** to keep people happy, be tactful; ***tener a media gaita,*** to have almost in the bag, within one's grasp.
gaitería, *n.f.* gay and gaudy dress.
gaitero, -ra, *a.* (*coll.*) overgay and facetious; (*coll.*) gaudy, showy, flamboyant. — *n.m.* piper, bagpiper.
gaje, *n.m.* gage; pledge; (*pl.*) perquisites; (*fig.*) ***gajes del oficio,*** occupational hazards.
gajo, *n.m.* broken-off branch; (fruit) cluster; (fruit) segment; (leaf) lobe; spur (*of a mountain, ridge*); prong (*of pitchforks, etc.*).
gajoso, -sa, *a.* branched, pronged.
gala (1), *n.f.* gala; full *or* court dress; elegance; choice, best; show, pomp; (*pl.*) regalia, finery; gifts; beauties; ***de gala,*** gala; full-dress; ***ser (la) gala de,*** to be the pride of; ***hacer gala de,*** to make a show of, show off; ***tener a gala,*** to pride o.s. on, glory in; ***llevarse la gala,*** to take the palm.
galabardera, *n.f.* (*bot.*) wild rose.
galactita, galactite, *n.f.* fuller's earth, alumina.
galactómetro, *n.m.* galactometer, lactometer.
galafate, *n.m.* artful thief, cunning rogue; labourer; constable.
galaico, -ca, *a.* Galician.
galamero, -ra, *a.* sweet-toothed.
galán, *n.m.* handsome fellow; gallant; wooer, lover; ladies' man; (*theat.*) ***primer galán,*** leading man; ***segundo galán,*** second lead; ***galán joven,*** juvenile lead; ***galán de noche,*** night jasmine.
galancete, *n.m.* foppish young fellow; (*theat.*) juvenile.
galanga, *n.f.* galingale.
galano, -na, *a.* spruce, smart; fine; witty; ***cuentas galanas,*** castles in the air.
galante, *a.* gallant; civil, courteous; ***mujer galante,*** demi-mondaine.
galanteador, -ra, *a.* flattering; wooing. — *n.m.f.* flatterer; wooer, flirt.
galantear, *v.t.* to flatter; to woo, flirt with.
galanteo, *n.m.* gallantry, wooing, flirting.
galantería, *n.f.* gallantry, courtesy; flattery; wooing, flirting; elegance, grace; generosity, liberality.
galanura, *n.f.* prettiness; gracefulness, elegance.
galapagar, *n.m.* place where tortoises abound.
galápago, *n.m.* tortoise; (*agric.*) bed (*of a ploughshare*); (*arm.*) frame (*for boring guns*); mould (*for convex tiles*); (*found.*) pig (*of lead* or *tin*); (*mas.*) small centering-frame; (*surg.*) funda; English saddle; (*mil.*) testudo; mantelet, catcastle, sow; (*vet.*) scratch; (*Hond., Ven.*) side-saddle.
galapaguera, *n.f.* tortoise pond.
galapo, *n.m.* (*rope-making*) laying-top.
galardón, *n.m.* guerdon, reward, recompense, prize.
galardonador, -ra, *n.m.f.* remunerator, rewarder.
galardonar, *v.t.* to reward, recompense.
galato, *n.m.* gallate.
galatites, *n.f. inv.* fuller's earth.
galaxia, *n.f.* galactite; galaxy.
galayo, *n.m.* (*prov.*) cliff.
galbana, *n.f.* (*coll.*) laziness.
galbanado, -da, *a.* of the colour of galbanum.
galbanero, -ra, *a.* (*coll.*) lazy.
gálbano, *n.m.* galbanum.
galbanoso, -sa, *a.* lazy.
gálbula, *n.m.* galbulus.
galdrope, *n.m.* wheel-rope.
galdrufa, *n.f.* (*prov.*) top.
gálea, *n.f.* galea.

galeato, -ta, *a.* defensive (*preface*).
galeaza, *n.f.* galleass.
galega, *n.f.* goat's-rue.
galénico, -ca, *a.* Galenic.
galeno, -na, *a.* moderate, soft (*wind*). — *n.m.* (*coll.*) physician; medico. — *n.f.* (*min.*) galena.
gáleo, *n.m.* dogfish.
galeón, *n.m.* galleon.
galeota, *n.f.* galliot.
galeote, *n.m.* galley-slave.
galera, *n.f.* galley; wagon; women's prison; hospital ward; smoothing plane; (*zool.*) mantis crab; line (*cutting off the quotient in division*); furnace (*for distilling sulphur*); subterranean gallery; (*Hond., Mex.*) shed, hut; (*Arg., Chi., Ur.*) silk hat, slouch-hat; ***azotes y galeras,*** humdrum stuff; ***condenar a galeras,*** to send to the galleys.
galerada, *n.f.* waggon-load; (*print.*) galley-proof; type set in a galley.
galerero, *n.m.* waggoner.
galería, *n.f.* gallery; ***hablar para la galería,*** to play to the gallery.
galerín, *n.m.* (*print.*) small galley.
galerita, *n.f.* crested lark.
galerno, *n.m.* **galerna,** *n.f.* gale; north-west gale.
galerón, *n.m.* (*Col., Ven.*) popular air and dance.
Gales, *n.f.* ***el país de Gales,*** Wales.
galés, -lesa, *a., n.m.f.* Welsh; Welshman, Welshwoman. — *n.m.* Welsh (*language*).
galfarro, *n.m.* (*obs.*) magistrate; (*obs.*) loafer; (*prov.*) sparrow-hawk.
galga (1), *n.f.* boulder; greyhound bitch; stone wheel (*that grinds olives*); itch; drag, brake scotch, hub-brake; bier (*for poor people*); (*naut.*) back (*of an anchor*); (*pl.*) long ribbons (*for tying women's shoes*).
galgo (1), *n.m.* greyhound; (*iron.*) ***¡échale un galgo!*** just try to catch it *or* him! just try to find it *or* him!
galgo (2), **-ga** (2), *a.* (*Hisp. Am.*) sweet-toothed.
galgueño, -ña, *a.* of *or* to do with greyhounds.
gálgulo, *n.m.* (*orn.*) blue magpie.
Galia, *n.f.* Gaul.
galibar, *v.t.* (*naut.*) to trace with templates.
gálibo, *n.m.* (*naut.*) pattern, template; (*railw.*) gabarit, gauge; calibre; elegance; (*fig.*) ***de muchos (pocos) gálibos,*** high (low) grade.
galicado, -da, *a.* somewhat Frenchified.
galicanismo, *n.m.* Gallicanism.
galicano, -na, *a.* Gallican.
galiciano, -na, *a.* Galician.
galicismo, *n.m.* Gallicism.
galicista, *n.m.f.* Gallicizer.
gálico, -ca, *a.* Gallic; gallic. — *n.m.* syphilis.
galicoso, -sa, *a.* infected with syphilis.
galileo, -lea, *a., n.m.f.* Galilean. — *n.f.* galilee (*porch*).
galillo, *n.m.* uvula; (*coll.*) windpipe, throat.
galimatías, *n.m.* (*coll.*) gibberish; rigmarole.
galio, *n.m.* cheese-rennet; (*chem.*) gallium.
galiopsis, *n.m. inv.* hedge-nettle.
galiparla, *n.f.* Frenchified Spanish.
galiparlista, *n.m.f.* Gallicizer.
galizabra, *n.f.* lateen-rigged vessel.
galo, -la (2), *a.* Gallic. — *n.m.f.* Gaul. — *n.m.* Gaulish.
galocha, *n.f.* clog; (*pl.*) galoshes, (*Am.*) overshoes, rubbers.
galón (1), *n.m.* braid; stripe.
galón (2), *n.m.* gallon.
galoneador, -ra, *n.m.f.* trimmer.
galoneadura, *n.f.* trimming.
galonear, *v.t.* to bind, trim with braid.
galonero, *n.m.* braid maker.
galonista, *n.m.* (*coll.*) military college prefect.
galop, *n.m.* galop.
galopada, *n.f.* race at the gallop.
galopante, *a.* galloping.
galopar, *v.i.* to gallop.
galope, *n.m.* gallop; ***a galope tendido,*** full tilt, at full speed.
galopeado, -da, *a.* (*coll.*) botched. — *n.m.* beating.
galopear, *v.i.* to gallop.
galopillo, *n.m.* scullion, kitchen-boy.
galopín, *n.m.* ragamuffin; rogue, rascal; clever knave; cabin-boy; scullion.
galopinada, *n.f.* piece of roguery.
galopo, *n.m.* rascal, rogue.
galpito, *n.m.* weak *or* sickly chicken.
galpón, *n.m.* (*Hisp. Am.*) large shed; slaves' quarters; garage; (*Col.*) pottery, tileworks.
galucha, *n.f.* (*Hisp. Am.*) gallop; haste, speed.
galuchar, *v.i.* (*Hisp. Am.*) to gallop.
Galván, *n.m.* (*coll.*) ***no lo entenderá Galván*** Heaven knows.
galvánico, -ca, *a.* galvanic.
galvanismo, *n.m.* galvanism.
galvanización, *n.f.* galvanization.
galvanizar [C], *v.t.* (*lit., fig.*) to galvanize; to electroplate.
galvanómetro, *n.m.* galvanometer.
galvanoplastia, galvanoplástica, *n.f.* galvanoplasty, electrotypy.
galladura, *n.f.* cicatricle, tread (*of an egg.*)
gallarda, *n.f.* [GALLARDO].
gallardear, *v.i.* to act with grace and elegance.
gallardete, *n.m.* pennant, streamer.
gallardetón, *n.m.* broad pennant.
gallardía, *n.f.* graceful air and deportment; gallantry.
gallardo, -da, *a.* fine, of fine bearing; gallant, brave. — *n.f.* galliard (*music and dance*); (*print.*) type of a size between minion and brevier.
gallareta, *n.f.* (*orn.*) coot.
gallarín, *n.m.* ***salir al gallarín,*** to backfire, not to come off.
gallarón, *n.m.* little bustard.
gallaruza, *n.f.* hooded garment, coarse country garment.
gallear, *v.t.* to tread (*cock*). — *v.i.* to throw one's weight about; (*found.*) to have flaws.
gallegada, *n.f.* gathering of Galicians; Galician dance and tune; typical piece of Galician stuff; piece of boasting.
gallego, -ga, *a., n.m.f.* Galician; (*Hisp. Am.*) Spanish immigrant. — *n.m.* Galician (*language*); porter; north-west wind (*in Castile*).
galleo, *n.m.* flaw (*in a casting*).
gallera, *n.f.* cock-pit.
gallería, *n.f.* (*Cub.*) cock-pit.
galleta, *n.f.* biscuit, (*Am.*) cracker; ship-biscuit, hard-tack; (*coll.*) slap; briquet (*of anthracite*); (*Arg., Chi.*) coarse brown bread; (*Arg.*) small gourd (*for maté*).
gallillo, *n.m.* uvula.
gallina, *n.f.* hen; ***gallina ciega,*** blindman's-buff; ***gallina clueca,*** broody hen; ***gallina de Guinea,*** guinea-hen; (*coll.*) ***acostarse con las gallinas,*** to go to bed very early; ***gallina en corral ajeno,*** fish out of water; ***carne de gallina,*** goose flesh. — *n.m.f.* coward, chicken-hearted person.
gallináceo, -cea, *a.* gallinaceous. — *n.f.* gallinacean.
gallinazo, -za, *n.m.f.* (*Hisp. Am.*) turkey buzzard. — *n.f.* hen dung.
gallinería, *n.f.* poulterer's shop; hen-house; hens; poultry; (*coll.*) chicken-heartedness; (*coll.*) bedlam.
gallinero, -ra, *a.* (*falc.*) preying *or* feeding upon fowls. — *n.m.f.* poulterer, poultry-dealer. — *n.m.*

poultry-yard; hen-coop, hen-roost, hen-house; basket (*for carrying poultry*); (*theat.*) gods.

gallineta, *n.f.* European coot; woodcock; (*Hisp. Am.*) guinea-hen.

gallipato, *n.m.* salamander.

gallipava, *n.f.* large hen.

gallipavo, *n.m.* turkey; (*coll.*) false note (*singing*).

gallipollo, *n.m.* cockerel.

gallístico, -ca, *a.* to do with cockfighting.

gallito, *n.m.* small cock; coxcomb, cock-of-the-walk; ***gallito del rey,*** peacock fish.

gallo, *n.m.* cock, rooster; dory; float (*fishing*); wall-board (*of the roof*); false note (*singing*); (*coll.*) cock-of-the-walk, bully; ***gallo de pelea,*** fighting-cock; ***pata de gallo,*** wrinkle; out of place remark, tactless remark; ***peso gallo,*** bantam weight; ***alzar*** or ***levantar el gallo,*** to speak out cockily, pipe up arrogantly; ***bajar el gallo,*** to climb *or* pipe down; (*obs.*) ***al primer gallo,*** in the middle of the night, at the first cock-crow; ***en menos que canta un gallo,*** before you can say Jack Robinson; ***tener mucho gallo,*** to be very cocky; ***otro gallo me cantara*** or ***cantaría,*** there would be a very different story to tell, things would be very different; ***cada gallo canta en su gallinero,*** everyone is master in his own house; (*Mex.*) ***haber comido gallo,*** to be in a fighting mood; ***yo he sido gallo para eso,*** I was a fine *or* great one at that; (*Hisp. Am.*) ***hay gallo tapado,*** I smell a rat; ***tocar un gallo,*** to play a wrong note.

gallobosque, *n.m.* wood-grouse.

gallocresta, *n.f.* wild clary *or* sage.

gallofa (1), *n.f.* food given to pilgrims; alms; vegetables for salad *or* soup; roll, bun; rigmarole; gossip; liturgical calendar.

gallofear, *v.i.* to loaf around begging.

gallofero, -ra, gallofo, -fa (2), *a.* loafing. — *n.m.f.* tramp.

gallón, *n.m.* green sod, turf; (*arch.*) echinus.

gallonada, *n.f.* wall made of sods.

gallote, -ta, *a.* (*C.R., Mex.*) cocky.

galludo, *n.m.* dogfish.

gama (1), *n.f.* (*zool.*) doe, deer.

gama (2), *n.f.* (*mus.*) gamut; (*fig.*) range.

gamarra, *n.f.* martingale.

gamarza, *n.f.* wild rue.

gámbalo, *n.m.* linen cloth.

gambalúa, *n.f.* (*coll.*) gangling lazy fellow.

gámbaro, *n.m.* small prawn.

gamberrada, *n.f.* piece of hooliganism.

gamberrismo, *n.m.* hooliganism.

gamberro, -rra, *n.m.* hooligan. — *n.f.* (*fam.*) coarse creature; tart.

gambesón, *n.m.,* **gambesina,** *n.f.* short quilted jacket.

gambeta, *n.f.* caper, cross-caper; prance; (*Arg., Bol.*) dodge, twist; dodging.

gambetear, *v.i.* to caper; to prance; (*football*) to dribble.

gambeto, *n.m.* long loose garment; quilted great-coat; cap for a new-born baby.

gambito, *n.m.* gambit.

gamboa, *n.f.* quince.

gambota, *n.f.* (*naut.*) counter-timber, arched timber.

gamella, *n.f.* bow (*yoke*); large wooden trough *or* tub; wash-tub; mound made as a boundary line; camlet; (*obs.*) she-camel.

gamellón, *n.m.* large yoke; large tub; trough (*in which grapes are trodden*).

gamezno, *n.m.* young fallow-deer.

gamo, *n.m.* buck; fallow-deer.

gamón, *n.m.* asphodel.

gamonal, *n.m.* place where asphodels flourish; (*Hisp. Am.*) political boss.

gamonoso, -sa, *a.* abounding in asphodels.

gamuno, -na, *a.* of fallow-deer.

gamuza, *n.f.* chamois, shammy(-leather); leather cloth.

gamuzado, -da, *a.* chamois-colour.

gana, *n.f.* wish, desire; ***de buena gana,*** willingly, gladly; ***de mala gana,*** unwillingly, reluctantly; ***tengo ganas de comer,*** I feel like eating; ***no me da la gana,*** I won't; ***no me da la real gana,*** I don't damn well want to; ***hace lo que le da la gana,*** he does just as he pleases; ***me entraron ganas de pegarle,*** I felt like hitting him; ***tenerle ganas a alguien,*** to have it in for s.o.

ganable, *a.* gainable.

ganadería, *n.f.* cattle-raising; cattle-ranch; stock farm; livestock; strain, breed.

ganadero, -ra, *a.* belonging to cattle. — *n.m.f.* grazier, cattle-owner; stock-farmer; cattle-dealer; drover.

ganado, *n.m.* livestock; cattle; stock of bees; (*coll.*) girls; ***ganado mayor,*** large livestock (*cattle etc.*); ***ganado menor,*** small livestock (*sheep, goats*); ***ganado caballar,*** horses; ***ganado de cerda,*** pigs; ***ganado lanar,*** sheep; ***ganado vacuno,*** cattle.

ganador, -ra, *n.m.f.* winner.

ganancia, *n.f.* gain, profit; ***no le arriendo la ganancia,*** I don't give much for his chances.

ganancial, *a.* of *or* to do with earnings and profits; ***bienes gananciales,*** property acquired during marriage.

ganancioso, -sa, *a.* gainful, profitable; winning; ***salir ganancioso,*** to be the winner.

ganapán, *n.m.* labourer, hand; (*fig.*) uncouth individual.

ganapierde, *n.m.* (game of) giveaway.

ganar, *v.t.* to gain, win; to earn; to beat, get the better of; to reach, get to. — *v.i.* to gain, improve; ***ganar por la mano,*** to get ahead of. — **ganarse,** *v.r.* to go off; to escape; ***ganarse a alguien,*** to win s.o. over; ***ganarse la vida,*** to earn one's living, make a living; (*coll.*) ***¡te la vas a ganar!*** you're going to get *or* cop it! you'll be in for it! you'll be for it!

ganchero, *n.m.* (*prov.*) river lumberjack.

ganchillo, ganchito, *n.m.* little hook *or* crotch; crochet needle; crochet.

gancho, *n.m.* hook; crook; coaxer, enticer, decoy, roper-in; pimp; snag, jagged-edged object; pot-hook; (*Hisp. Am.*) hairpin; (*Hisp. Am.*) side-saddle; ***echar el gancho a,*** to hook, land; ***tener gancho,*** to have a way with men.

ganchoso, -sa, ganchudo, -da, *a.* hooked, curved.

gándara, *n.f.* low, rough ground; low wasteland.

gandaya, *n.f.* laziness, idleness; ***ir por la gandaya, andar buscar*** or ***correr la gandaya,*** to loaf, lounge.

gandido, -da, *a.* (*Hisp. Am.*) hungry; gluttonous.

gandinga, *n.f.* (*min.*) washed fine ore; (*Cub., P.R.*) liver stew.

gandir, *v.t.* (*obs.*) to eat.

gandujado, *n.m.* accordion pleating.

gandujar, *v.t.* (*sew.*) to pleat, shirr.

gandul, -la, *a.* idling, loafing. — *n.m.f.* idler, loafer.

gandulear, *v.i.* to idle, loaf.

gandulería, *n.f.* idling, loafing.

ganeta, *n.f.* genet.

ganforro, -rra, *n.m.f.* (*coll.*) rogue, rascal.

ganga, *n.f.* pin-tailed grouse; sand curlew; (*min.*) gangue; (*coll.*) bargain; ***andar a caza de gangas,*** to go bargain-hunting; (*iron.*) ***¡buena ganga!*** a prize specimen! a fine one!

gangarilla, *n.f.* company of strolling players.

ganglio, *n.m.* ganglion.

gangocho, *n.m.* (*Cent. Am., Chi., Mex.*) burlap.

gangoso, -sa, *a.* nasal, twangy.

gangrena, *n.f.* gangrene.

gangrenarse, *v.r.* to become gangrenous.
gangrenoso, -sa, *a.* gangrenous.
ganguear, *v.i.* to speak with a twang, speak through one's nose.
ganguero, -ra, ganguista, *n.m.f.* bargain-hunter.
gánguil, *n.m.* fishing-boat; dump-scow.
ganguista, *a., n.m.f.* bargain-hunting; bargain-hunter.
ganoso, -sa, *a.* desirous, wishing, longing.
gansada, *n.f.* (*coll.*) stupidity.
gansarón, *n.m.* gander; gosling; (*fig.*) lanky, gawky fellow.
ganso, -sa, *n.m.f.* gander, goose; (*fig.*) slow-witted *or* lazy person; ***ganso bravo,*** wild goose; ***hablar por boca de ganso,*** to ape others; ***hacer el ganso,*** to act *or* play the fool.
Gante, *n.m.* Ghent.
gantés, *a., n.m.f.* (native) of Ghent.
ganzúa, *n.f.* picklock; burglar; (*coll.*) pumper, wheedler.
gañán, *n.m.* farm hand; clod.
gañanía, *n.f.* gang of labourers.
gañido, *n.m.* yelp.
gañiles, *n.m.pl.* throat (*of animals*); gills (*of tunny*).
gañir [K], *v.i.* to yelp, howl; to croak, cackle, crow.
gañón, gañote, *n.m.* (*coll.*) gullet; (*prov.*) fritters.
garabatada, *n.f.* hooking.
garabatear, *v.t., v.i.* to hook, catch with a hook; to scribble, scrawl. — *v.i.* (*coll.*) to beat about the bush.
garabateo, *n.m.* hooking; scribbling, scrawling.
garabato, *n.m.* pot-hook; grapple, grapnel, creeper; meat-hook; muzzle; scribble, scrawl; winning ways (*in a woman*); ***mozo de garabato,*** thief.
garabatoso, -sa, *a.* covered in scrawl; attractive.
garabito, *n.m.* market-stall; hook.
garaje, *n.m.* garage.
garambaina, *n.f.* (*coll.*) nonsense, rubbish, drivel, tripe; (*coll.*) illegible scrawl.
garambullo, *n.m.* (*Mex.*) cactus.
garandumba, *n.f.* (*Hisp. Am.*) river barge.
garante, *a.* responsible. — *n.m.f.* warranter, guarantor, surety; bondsman, bail.
garantía, *n.f.* guaranty, guarantee; warranty, security, collateral.
garantir [Q], *v.t.* to guarantee.
garantizar [C], *v.t.* to guarantee, warrant; to endorse, answer for, vouch for.
garañón, *n.m.* stallion jackass; male breeding-camel; (*Chi., Mex.*) stallion horse.
garapacho, *n.m.* shell; (*Cub.*) meat cooked in the shell of crustaceans.
garapiña, *n.f.* sugar coating; scalloped galloon *or* lace; (*Mex., Cub.*) pineapple juice.
garapiñar, *v.t.* to candy, sugar-coat; to ice, frost; ***almendras garapiñadas,*** sugar almonds.
garapiñera, *n.f.* ice-cream freezer; wine-cooler.
garapita, *n.f.* net (*for small fishes*).
garapito, *n.m.* water-skipper, water bug.
garapullo, *n.m.* paper dart; shuttlecock.
garatura, *n.f.* (*tan.*) scraper.
garatusa, *n.f.* piece of coaxing *or* wheedling.
garba, *n.f.* (*prov.*) bastard vetch; (*prov.*) sheaf (*of wheat*).
garbancero, -ra, *a.* to do with chick-peas; (*fig.*) commonplace, dull. — *n.m.* chick-pea dealer.
garbanzal, *n.m.* chick-pea patch *or* field.
garbanzo, *n.m.* chick-pea.
garbanzuelo, *n.m.* small chick-pea; (*vet.*) spavin.
garbar, *v.t.* (*prov.*) to sheaf, sheave.
garbear, *v.t.* to sheaf; to rob, plunder. — *v.i.* to put on airs, put it on. — **garbear(se),** *v.i.* (*v.r.*) to manage, make out.
garbeo, *n.m.* showiness; affected elegance; ***darse un garbeo,*** to take a stroll.
garbera, *n.f.* shock (*of sheaves*).
garbías, *n.m.pl.* omelet (*of herbs, cheese and flour.*)
garbillador, -ra, *a.* sifting, riddling. — *n.m.f.* sifter, riddler.
garbillar, *v.t.* to sift, screen, riddle.
garbillo, *n.m.* sieve, screen, riddle; riddled ore.
garbino, *n.m.* south-west wind.
garbo, *n.m.* gracefulness, grace and ease; graceful and easy carriage *or* bearing; jaunty air; fine style, liberal manner.
garbón, *n.m.* male partridge.
garboso, -sa, *a.* graceful, graceful and easy; jaunty; having fine style; liberal, open-handed.
garbullo, *n.m.* uproar, chaos.
garcero, -ra, *a.* ***halcón garcero,*** heron hawk.
garceta, *n.f.* lesser egret; side locks (*of hair*); (*pl.*) tenderlings, first horns (*of a deer*).
gardenia, *n.f.* gardenia.
garduña (1), *n.f.* marten.
garduño, -ña (2), *n.m.f.* (*coll.*) filcher, petty thief.
garete, *n.m.* (*naut.*) ***al garete,*** adrift.
garfa, *n.f.* claw; ***echar la garfa a,*** to grab, seize, snatch.
garfada, garfiada, *n.f.* clawing; seizing, snatching.
garfear, *v.i.* to hook.
garfio, *n.m.* hook; drag-hook; gaff.
gargajear, *v.i.* to expectorate, spit out phlegm.
gargajeo, *n.m.,* **gargajeada,** *n.f.* spitting out of phlegm.
gargajiento, -ta, gargajoso, -sa, *a.* spitting frequently.
gargajo, *n.m.* phlegm, spit.
garganchón, *n.m.* windpipe, gullet.
garganta, *n.f.* throat, gullet; singing-voice; instep; gorge, canyon, ravine; shaft (*of a column* or *balustrade*); sheath (*of a plough*); (*mech.*) collar, neck, throat, groove (*of a sheave*); ***tener buena garganta,*** to be a good singer; ***tener el agua a la garganta,*** to be in imminent danger; ***lo tengo atravesado en la garganta,*** he sticks in my gizzard.
gargantada, *n.f.* liquid *or* blood (*ejected violently from the throat*).
gargantear, *v.i.* to quaver, warble; (*naut.*) to strap a dead-eye.
garganteo, *n.m.* quavering, warbling, trilling.
gargantil, *n.m.* cutout (*in barber's basin*).
gargantilla, *n.f.* necklace; bead (*of a necklace*).
gárgara, *n.f.* gargling; ***hacer gárgaras,*** to gargle; (*coll.*) ***mandar a alguien a hacer gárgaras,*** to send s.o. packing *or* to blazes.
gargarismo, *n.m.* gargle; gargling.
gargarizar [C], *v.i.* to gargle.
gárgaro, *n.m.* (*Cub., Ven.*) hide-and-seek.
gargavero, *n.m.* [GARGÜERO]; pan-pipe.
gárgol, *a.* empty, addled (*eggs*). — *n.m.* groove, furrow, channel, mortise.
gárgola, *n.f.* gargoyle; linseed.
gargüero, garguero, *n.m.* gullet; windpipe.
garibaldina, *n.f.* garibaldi, loose blouse (*for women* or *children*).
garifalte, *n.m.* gerfalcon.
gariofilea, *n.f.* (*bot.*) common avens, herb-bennet.
garita, *n.f.* sentry-box; porter's lodge; railway-crossing box; water-closet.
gariteear, *v.i.* (*coll.*) to gamble.
garitero, *n.m.* keeper of a gambling den; gambler.
garito, *n.m.* gambling den; profits of gambling.
garla, *n.f.* (*coll.*) talk, chatter.
garlador, -ra, *a.* (*coll.*) chatty, chattering. — *n.m.f.* (*coll.*) babbler, chatterer.
garlante, *a.* (*coll.*) babbling, prattling.
garlar, *v.i.* (*coll.*) to babble, prattle, chatter.

garlito, *n.m.* fish-trap; snare, trap, gin; (*coll.*) ***caer en el garlito,*** to fall into a trap; ***coger en el garlito,*** to catch in the act.
garlocha, *n.f.* goad-stick, ox-goad.
garlopa, *n.f.* jack plane, trying plane.
garma, *n.f.* (*prov.*) steep slope.
garnacha, *n.f.* judge's gown, robe; sweet black grape; company of strolling players.
garniel, *n.m.* muleteer's girdle; (*Ec., Mex.*) handbag.
garoso, -sa, *a.* (*Col., Ven.*) greedy, gluttonous.
garra, *n.f.* claw, paw (*of wild beasts*); talon (*of bird of prey*); (*mech.*) catch, hook, clutch; (*fig.*) hand; (*Arg., Mex.*) corner (*of a hide*); (*Hisp. Am.*) wrinkled piece of rawhide; (*Col.*) leather bag; ***caer en las garras de,*** to fall into the clutches of; (*coll.*) ***echar la garra a,*** to lay one's hands on; to arrest; ***sacar de las garras de,*** to free from; (*pl.*) (*Hisp. Am.*) rags, tatters.
garrafa, *n.f.* carafe, decanter.
garrafal, *a.* large and sweet (*said of cherries*); (*fig.*) great, big, whopping (*lie, blunder etc.*); ***falta garrafal,*** howler, (*Am.*) boner.
garrafiñar, *v.t.* (*coll.*) to snatch away.
garrafón, *n.m.* large carafe; demijohn, carboy.
garrama, *n.f.* (*coll.*) filching, pinching.
garramar, *v.t.* (*coll.*) to filch, pinch.
garrancha, *n.f.* (*bot.*) spathe; (*coll.*) sword; (*Col*). hook.
garrancho, *n.m.* broken branch.
garrapata, *n.f.* sheep-tick; (*mil.*) disabled horse.
garrapatear, *v.i.* to scribble, scrawl.
garrapatero, *n.m.* (*Col., Ec., Ven.*) tick-bird, cow-bird.
garrapato, *n.m.* pot-hook, scrawl.
garrar, garrear, *v.i.* to drag the anchor.
garrido, -da, *a.* handsome, graceful, fine.
garroba, *n.f.* carob bean.
garrobal, *n.m.* grove of carob trees.
garrobilla, *n.f.* chips of carob trees (*for tanning hides*).
garrocha, *n.f.* goad-stick, goad; pole, staff.
garrochada, *n.f.*, **garrochazo,** *n.m.* prick *or* blow with a goad-stick.
garrocheador, *n.m.* goader, pricker.
garrochear, *v.t.* to goad, prick.
garrochón, *n.m.* spear, goad-stick.
garrofa, *n.f.* carob bean.
garrofal, *n.m.* grove of carob trees.
garrón, *n.m.* spur (*of birds*); talon (*of a bird of prey*); paw (*of a rabbit etc.*); (*coll.*) ***tener garrones,*** to be experienced.
garrotal, *n.m.* plantation of olive trees (*made with cuttings*).
garrotazo, *n.m.* blow with cudgel.
garrote, *n.m.* club, cudgel; garrotte; olive cutting; (*prov.*) hazel basket *or* pannier; ***dar garrote a,*** to garrotte.
garrotear, *v.t.* (*Hisp. Am.*) to beat, cudgel.
garrotillo, *n.m.* croup.
garrotín, *n.m.* gipsy dance.
garrubia, *n.f.* carob bean.
garrucha, *n.f.* pulley; sheave.
garrucho, *n.m.* (*naut.*) cringle.
garrudo, -da, *a.* big-clawed; strong, brawny, sinewy.
garrulador, -ra, *a.* garrulous.
garrular, *v.i.* to babble, chatter.
garrulería, *n.f.* prattle, chatter.
garrulidad, *n.f.* garrulity, garrulousness.
gárrulo, -la, *a.* garrulous; chattering, babbling.
garúa, *n.f.* (*Hisp. Am., naut.*) drizzle.
garuar [M], *v.i.* (*Hisp. Am.*) to drizzle.
garujo, *n.m.* concrete.
garulla, *n.f.* loose grapes; (*coll.*) rabble, mob.
garullada, *n.f.* (*coll.*) mob, rabble.
garvín, *n.m.* (*obs.*) net-headdress for women.
garza (1), *n.f.* (*orn.*) heron, purple heron; ***garza real,*** European heron, grey heron.
garzo (1), *n.m.* (*bot.*) agaric.
garzo (2), **-za** (2), *a.* blue (*eye*); blue-eyed.
garzón, *n.m.* boy, lad, youth; (*obs.*) wooer, lover.
garzonear, *v.t.* (*obs.*) to woo, court.
garzonía, *n.f.* (*obs.*) wooing; sowing wild oats.
garzota, *n.f.* night-heron; plumage, aigrette; crest (*of a helmet*).
garzul, *n.m.* (*prov.*) wheat.
gas, *n.m.* gas; gaslight; ***gas pobre,*** producer gas; ***gas hilarante,*** laughing gas; (*mil.*) ***gases asfixiantes,*** poison gas; ***gases lacrimógenos,*** tear gas.
gasa, *n.f.* gauze, muslin; crêpe.
gascón, -cona, gasconés, -nesa, *a., n.m.f.* Gascon.
gasconada, *n.f.* gasconade, boast, bravado.
gasear, *v.t.* to gas.
gaseiforme, *a.* gasiform.
gaseoso, -sa, *a.* gaseous. — *n.f.* soda water.
gasífero, -ra, *a.* gas-conducting.
gasificable, *a.* convertible into gas.
gasificación, *n.f.* gasification.
gasificar [A], *v.t.* to gasify, convert into gas.
gasista, *n.m.* gas fitter.
gasógeno, *n.m.* gazogene; mixture of benzene and alcohol.
gasoleno, *n.m.*, **gasolina,** *n.f.* petrol, (*Am.*) gasoline.
gasolinera, *n.f.* motor boat; petrol station.
gasometría, *n.f.* gasometry.
gasómetro, *n.m.* gasometer; gas-meter.
gasón, *n.m.* large clod of earth; sod.
gastable, *a.* expendable; that can be worn out.
gastadero, *n.m.* (*coll.*) waste; ***gastadero de tiempo,*** waste of time.
gastado, -da, *a.* used-up, worn-out; trite, hackneyed, stale.
gastador, -ra, *a.* wasteful, lavish, extravagant. — *n.m.f.* spender, waster, spendthrift; prodigal. — *n.m.* (*mil.*) pioneer; sapper.
gastamiento, *n.m.* consumption, wearing out.
gastar, *v.t.* to expend, spend (*money, time etc.*); to waste, consume, use up, wear out; to have *or* wear habitually; ***gastar coche,*** to run a car; ***gastar bigote,*** to wear a moustache; ***gastar cumplidos,*** to stand upon ceremony; ***gastar bromas,*** to play jokes. — **gastarse,** *v.r.* to get spent, get used up; ***gastárselas,*** to act, behave.
gasterópodo, -da, *a., n.m.* gast(e)ropod.
gasto, *n.m.* expenditure, expense; (*phys.*) (rate of) flow; use, waste, wear and tear; (*pl.*) charges; (*coll.*) ***hacer el gasto,*** to do all the talking; ***gastos de conservación*** or ***mantenimiento,*** upkeep, maintenance costs; ***gastos de escritorio*** or ***oficina,*** office *or* stationery expenses; ***gastos de explotación,*** working expenses; ***gastos de residencia,*** accommodation costs; ***gastos de representación,*** incidental expenses; ***gastos generales,*** overhead expenses; ***gastos menores*** or ***diarios,*** petty expenses; ***gastos de viaje,*** travelling expenses; ***cubrir gastos,*** to cover expenses; ***pagar los gastos,*** to foot the bill.
gastoso, -sa, *a.* wasteful; lavish; extravagant.
gastricismo, *n.m.* gastricism.
gástrico, -ca, *a.* gastric.
gastritis, *n.f. inv.* gastritis.
gastroenteritis, *n.f. inv.* gastroenteritis.
gastronomía, *n.f.* gastronomy.
gastronómico, -ca, *a.* gastronomic.
gastrónomo, -ma, *n.m.f.* gastronomer, gastronome, gourmet.
gata, *n.f.* she-cat; (*coll.*) woman native of Madrid; (*bot.*) rest-harrow, cammock; (*mil.*) cat-castle;

(*naut.*) cat-head; (*naut.*) ***gata del ancla,*** cat-tackle; ***a gatas,*** on all fours.
gatada, *n.f.* cat-trick, catlike act; cats, litter of cats; turn (*of a hare when closely pursued*); (*coll.*) artful dodge, scurvy trick.
gatallón, *n.m.* (*coll.*) rogue, cheat, scamp.
gatatumba, *n.f.* (*coll.*) fake-up, pretence.
gatazo, *n.m.* large cat; (*coll.*) artful trick, cheat, swindle.
gateado, -da, *a.* feline, catlike; striped, veined. — *n.m.* American striped wood.
gateamiento, *n.m.* scratching; clambering; going on all fours.
gatear, *v.t.* (*coll.*) to scratch, claw; (*coll.*) to steal, pinch. — *v.i.* to climb up, clamber; to go upon all fours.
gatería, *n.f.* (number of) cats; (*coll.*) rabble, gang; cringing servility.
gatero, -ra, *a.* frequented by cats. — *n.m.f.* cat dealer; cat lover. — *n.f.* cat's hole; (*naut.*) cathole.
gatesco, -ca, *a.* (*coll.*) feline, catlike.
gatillazo, *n.m.* click of trigger; (*fig.*) flop.
gatillo, *n.m.* pelican, dentist's forceps; trigger (*of a gun*); nape (*of a bull* or *ox*); (*arch.*) cramp-iron; (*coll.*) boy pickpocket; (*Chi.*) horse's mane.
gatito, -ta, *n.m.f.* kitten.
gato, *n.m.* cat, tom-cat; money-bag, money kept in a bag; (*coll.*) pickpocket, petty thief; shrewd fellow; (*artill.*) gun-searcher; (*mech.*) jack, lifting-jack, cramp-iron; (*coop.*) hopping tongs; (*coll.*) native of Madrid; (*Arg.*) popular dance and its music; (*Per.*) open market; ***gato de algalia,*** civet-cat; ***gato montés,*** wild cat; (*fig.*) ***gato viejo,*** old dog, old hand; ***cuatro gatos,*** a few (odd) people *or* (*sl.*) bods; ***dar gato por liebre,*** to cheat, hoodwink, diddle; ***hay gato encerrado,*** there's sth. fishy about it, there's more to it than meets the eye; ***gato escaldado, del agua fría huye,*** once bitten, twice shy; ***buscar tres pies al gato,*** to look for difficulties where there are none; ***de noche todos los gatos son pardos,*** by night all cats are grey; ***gato con guantes no caza ratones,*** a gloved cat is no mouser; ***correr como gato por ascuas,*** to go like a cat on hot bricks; ***hasta los gatos quieren zapatos,*** everybody wants more than is possible, wants to live beyond their means; ***llevar el gato al agua,*** to accomplish a difficult task.
gatuna (I), **gatuña,** *n.f.* rest-harrow, cammock.
gatuno, -na (2), *a.* catlike, feline.
gatuperio, *n.m.* hotch-potch; (*coll.*) jiggery-pokery.
gauchada, *n.f.* (*Hisp. Am.*) act of a gaucho; cunning thing to do; (*Arg.*) good turn.
gauchaje, *n.m.* (*Arg., Chi.*) assembly of gauchos.
gaucho, -cha, *a., n.m.f.* gaucho. — *a.* (*Arg., Chi.*) rude, boorish; crafty. — *n.m.* (*Arg., Chi., Ur.*) good horseman.
gaudeamus, *n.m. inv.* (*coll.*) feast, entertainment, merrymaking.
gavanza, *n.f.* dog-rose (*flower*).
gavanzo, *n.m.* dog-rose.
gavera, *n.f.* (*Col., Mex., Ven.*) tile *or* brick mould; (*Per.*) form *or* mould (*for mud walls*); (*Col.*) wood mould (*for sugar*).
gaveta, *n.f.* drawer (*of writing desk*).
gavetilla, *n.f.* small desk drawer.
gavia, *n.f.* (*naut.*) topsail, main topsail; top (*in galleys*); ditch; (*orn.*) gull, sea-gull; (*min.*) gang of basket passers; madman's cage.
gaviero, *n.m.* top-man, mast-man.
gavieta, *n.f.* scuttle; bowsprit bee.
gaviete, *n.m.* davit.
gavilán, *n.m.* sparrow-hawk; nib (*of a quill pen*); (*naut.*) iron hook; (*arm.*) quillon (*of a sword*); brad *or* pin (*of a goad-stick*); (*Hisp. Am.*) ingrowing nail, especially on the big toe; (*bot.*) thistle flower.
gavilancillo, *n.m.* young hawk; point of artichoke leaf.
gavilla, *n.f.* sheaf; bundle; (*fig.*) gang (*of low people*); ***gente de gavilla,*** low people.
gavillero, *n.m.* place where sheaves are collected; row of sheaves.
gavina, *n.f.* sea-gull.
gavión, *n.m.* (*mil.*) gabion; (*coll.*) large hat.
gaviota, *n.f.* gull, sea-gull.
gavitel, *n.m.* small buoy.
gavota, *n.f.* gavotte (*dance and tune*).
gaya, *n.f.* [GAYO].
gayado, -da, *a.* motley, striped (*cloth, garment etc.*).
gayadura, *n.f.* striped trimming.
gayar, *v.t.* to trim *or* adorn with coloured stripes.
gayata, *n.f.* (*prov.*) crook, sheep-hook.
gayo, -ya, *a.* gay, bright, showy; ***gaya ciencia,*** art of poesy, minstrelsy. — *n.m.* (*orn.*) jay. — *n.f.* stripe (*on fabrics etc.*); badge (*given to victors in Olympic games*); (*orn.*) magpie; (*sl.*) harlot.
gayola, *n.f.* (*naut.*) cage; (*coll.*) jail; (*prov.*) raised lookout (*in vineyards*).
gayomba, *n.f.* (*bot.*) Spanish broom.
gayuba, *n.f.* (*bot.*) bearberry.
gayubal, *n.m.* bearberry patch.
gaza, *n.f.* loop of a bow; (*naut.*) strap, strop, eye.
gazafatón, gazapatón, *n.m.* blunder, slip (*in talking*).
gazapa, *n.f.* (*coll.*) lie, fib.
gazapela, *n.f.* clamorous wrangling.
gazapera, *n.f.* rabbit-warren; (*coll.*) wrangle, quarrel; (*coll.*) unlawful hiding-place *or* den.
gazapito, *n.m.* small rabbit, bunny.
gazapina, *n.f.* (*coll.*) gang of ruffians; wrangling, quarrelling.
gazapo, *n.m.* young rabbit; (*coll.*) sly fellow; lie; howler, blunder.
gazapón, *n.m.* gaming-house, gambling-den.
gazmiar, *v.i.* to eat tit-bits. — **gazmiarse,** *v.r.* (*coll.*) to complain.
gazmoñada, gazmoñería, *n.f.* prudishness sanctimoniousness.
gazmoñero, -ra, gazmoño, -ña, *a.* prudish; sanctimonious.
gaznápiro, -ra, *n.m.f.* simpleton, booby, daft individual.
gaznar, *v.i.* to croak, caw, cackle.
gaznatada, *n.f.* violent blow on the windpipe; (*Hond., Mex., P.R., Ven.*) cuff.
gaznate, *n.m.* gullet, windpipe; fritter.
gaznatón, *n.m.* blow on the throat; fritter.
gazofia [BAZOFIA].
gazpacho, *n.m.* Andalusian cold soup.
gazuza, *n.f.* (*coll.*) keen appetite, violent hunger; ***tener gazuza,*** to be ravenous, starving.
ge, *n.f.* letter G.
gea, *n.f.* mineral geography (*of an area*).
geato, *n.m.* (*chem.*) geate.
gecónidos, *n.m.pl.* geckonids.
Gedeón, *n.m.* Gideon.
gedeonada, *n.f.* platitude.
gehena, *n.m.* Gehenna, hell.
geico, -ca, *a.* (*chem.*) geic.
géiser, *n.m.* geyser.
gelatina, *n.f.* gelatine, jelly.
gelatinoso, -sa, *a.* gelatinous.
gelatinudo, -da, *a.* (*Hisp. Am.*) gelatinous; phlegmatic, lazy, indolent.
gélido, -da, *a.* (*poet.*) gelid, frigid, icy.
gema, *n.f.* gem; (*bot.*) bud; (*carp.*) slab, flitch.
gemación, *n.f.* (*bot., zool.*) gemmation.
gemebundo, -da, *a.* groaning, moaning.
gemela (I), *n.f.* Arabian jasmine.

gemelo, -la, (2), *n.m.f.* twin. — *n.m.* (*anat.*) gemellus; (*pl.*) binoculars; cuff links; ***gemelos de campaña,*** field glasses; ***gemelos de teatro,*** opera glasses.
Gemelos, *n.m.pl.* (*astron.*, *astrol.*) Gemini.
gemido, *n.m.* groan, moan; wail, whine.
geminación, *n.f.* gemination.
geminar, *v.t.* to geminate.
Géminis, *n.m. inv.* (*astron.*, *astrol.*) Gemini.
géminis, *n.m. inv.* (*pharm.*) plaster.
gemíparo, -ra, *a.* gemmiparous.
gemiquear, *v.i.* (*prov.*, *Chi.*) to whine.
gemir [8], *v.i.* to groan, moan; to wail, whine.
gen, *n.m.* gene.
genciana, *n.f.* gentian.
gendarme, *n.m.* gendarme.
gendarmería, *n.f.* gendarmerie.
genealogía, *n.f.* genealogy, lineage.
genealógico, -ca, *a.* genealogical; ***árbol genealógico,*** family tree.
genealogista, *n.m.* genealogist.
genearca, *n.m.* (*obs.*) head of a family *or* race.
geneático, -ca, *a.* genethliacal.
geneo, *n.m.* (*Per.*) banana.
generable, *a.* generable, that may be begotten *or* produced.
generación, *n.f.* generation; succession, lineage.
generacional, *a.* (of a *or* the) generation; ***conflicto, enfrentamiento, escisión*** or ***incomprensión generacional,*** generation gap.
generador, -ra, *a.* generator; generating. — *n.m.* (*mech.*, *elec.*) generator. — *n.f.* (*math.*) generatrix.
general, *a.* general; common, usual; ***en general, por lo general,*** in general, generally; ***en términos generales,*** in general terms. — *n.m.* general; ***general de brigada,*** brigadier general; ***general de división,*** major general; (*pl.*) ***generales de la ley,*** questions put to a witness as to his personal data.
generala, *n.f.* general's wife; general (*call to arms*).
generalato, *n.m.* generalship.
generalidad, *n.f.* generality, great majority; ***La Generalidad,*** autonomous government of Catalonia.
generalísimo, *n.m.* generalissimo.
generalización, *n.f.* generalization.
generalizar [C], *v.t.* to make general. — *v.i.* to generalize. — **generalizarse,** *v.r.* to become general.
generante, *a.* (*obs.*) generating, engendering.
generar, *v.t.* to generate, produce.
generativo, -va, *a.* generative.
generatriz, *a.* (*geom.*) generating. — *n.f.* (*geom.*) generatrix.
genérico, -ca, *a.* generic.
género, *n.m.* kind; sort; manner, way; (*gram.*) gender; (*lit.*) genre; (*biol.*) genus; ***género humano,*** mankind; ***pintor de género,*** genre painter; ***género chico,*** lesser *or* minor genre; (*pl.*) goods; ***géneros de punto,*** knitted goods.
generosidad, *n.f.* generosity; nobility; valour.
generoso, -sa, *a.* generous; noble; valiant; ***vino generoso,*** rich and full-bodied wine.
Génesis, *n.m. inv.* Genesis.
génesis, *n.f. inv.* genesis.
genetlíaco, -ca, *a.* genethliacal. — *n.f.* genethliacs, astrology.
gengibre, *n.m.* ginger.
genial, *a.* of genius, brilliant; (*coll.*) super, smashing.
genialidad, *n.f.* stroke of genius; originality; eccentricity.
geniazo, *n.m.* violent temper.
genicidio [GENOCIDIO].
geniculado, -da, *a.* geniculate.
geniecillo, *n.m.* sharpish temper; little genie.
genio, *n.m.* genius; temper; bad temper; temperament, disposition; spirit; genie; ***mal genio,*** bad *or* ill temper; ***genio del mal,*** evil spirit; ***genio pronto*** or ***vivo,*** quick temper; ***corto de genio,*** diffident, spiritless; ***echar mal genio,*** to develop a bad temper; ***llevar el genio a,*** to keep happy *or* sweet-tempered; ***genio y figura, hasta la sepultura,*** what's bred in the bone will come out in the flesh.
genioso, -sa, geniudo, -da, *a.* ill-tempered.
genipa, *n.f.* wormwood.
genista, *n.f.* genista; Spanish broom.
genital, *a.* genital. — *n.m.pl.* (**genitales**) genitals.
genitivo, -va, *a.* generative. — *a.*, *n.m.* (*gram.*) genitive.
genitura, *n.f.* (*obs.*) generation, procreation; horoscope; (*obs.*) seed, generating matter.
genízaro, -ra, *a.* [JENÍZARO].
genocida, *a.* genocidal. — *n.m.* genocide.
genocidio, *n.m.* genocide.
genol, *n.m.* (*naut.*) futtock.
Génova, *n.f.* Genoa.
genovés, -vesa, *a.*, *n.m.f.* Genoese.
gente, *n.f.* people; folk, folks; troops, men; clan, nation; ***gente de bien,*** good, honest people, decent folk; ***gente bien,*** superior people, upper *or* smart set; ***gente de alpargata, de capa parda, de pardillo,*** simple, country folk; ***gente del bronce,*** tough, devil-may-care people; ***gente de (la) carda, de gavilla, de (la) vida airada, de mal vivir,*** crooks, scoundrels, people of the underworld; ***gente de coleta,*** bullfighters; ***gente de color,*** coloured people; ***gente de mar,*** seafaring people; ***gente de medio pelo,*** low-class people; ***gente menuda,*** children, youngsters; small fry, people of little account; ***gente de paz,*** friend, friends; ***gente de trato,*** trades-people; ***trato de gentes,*** dealing(s) with people; ***don de gentes,*** gift for getting on well with people; ***hacer gente(s),*** to recruit; to draw a crowd; ***¡a mí, gente!*** help!
gentecilla, *n.f.* petty riff-raff, rabble.
gentil, *a.* genteel, graceful, exquisite; civil, courteous; noble; ***¡gentil necedad!*** a fine piece of nonsense! — *n.m.* gentile, pagan, heathen.
gentileza, *n.f.* gentility, genteelness, grace, gracefulness, exquisiteness, elegance, refinement; civility, courteousness; nobleness.
gentilhombre, *n.m.* (*pl.* **gentileshombres**) gentleman; gentleman-in-waiting; nobleman; kind sir, good man.
gentilicio, -cia, *a.* family; peculiar to a nation, national; tribal; hereditary; (*gram.*) ***nombre gentilicio,*** clan *or* family name.
gentílico, -ca, *a.* heathen, gentile, pagan, heathenish, Hellenic.
gentilidad, *n.f.* gentilism, heathenism, paganism; body of heathens *or* gentiles.
gentilismo, *n.m.* gentilism, heathenism, paganism.
gentilizar [C], *v.t.* to make gentile, paganize. — *v.i.* to gentilize, observe the rites of gentiles *or* heathens.
gentío, *n.m.* crowd, throng.
gentualla [GENTUZA].
gentuza, *n.f.* riff-raff, rabble, scum.
genuflexión, *n.f.* genuflexion, kneeling.
genuino, -na, *a.* genuine, real, true.
geocéntrico, *a.* geocentric.
geoda, *n.f.* geode.
geodesia, *n.f.* geodesy.
geodésico, -ca, *a.* geodesic, geodetic.
geodesta, *n.m.* geodesist; professor of geodesy.
geófago, -ga, *a.*, *n.m.f.* geophagous.
geofísica, *n.f.* geophysics.
geogenia, *n.f.* geogeny.
geogénico, -ca, *a.* geogenic.

geognosia, *n.f.* geognosy.
geognosta, *n.m.* geognost, geologist.
geognóstico, -ca, *a.* geognostic.
geogonía, *n.f.* geogeny.
geogónico, -ca, *a.* geogenic.
geografía, *n.f.* geography; landscape, setting; area, region, part(s).
geográfico, -ca, *a.* geographical.
geógrafo, *n.m.f.* geographer.
geoide, *n.m.* geoid.
geología, *n.f.* geology.
geológico, -ca, *a.* geological.
geólogo, *n.m.* geologist.
geomancia, *n.f.* geomancy.
geomántico, -ca, *a.* geomantic.
geómetra, *n.m.* geometer, geometrician.
geometral, *a.* geometrical, geometric.
geometría, *n.f.* geometry; ***geometría del espacio,*** solid geometry.
geométrico, -ca, *a.* geometrical, geometric.
geomorfía, *n.f.* geomorphy.
geonomía, *n.f.* geonomy.
geonómico, -ca, *a.* geonomic.
geoponía, *n.f.* agriculture; gardening.
geopónico, -ca, *a.* geoponic, agricultural. — *n.f.* geoponics.
geórgica, *n.f.* georgic.
geranio, *n.m.* (*bot.*) geranium; ***geranio de malva,*** nutmeg geranium.
gerencia, *n.f.* (*com.*) managership, management.
gerente, *n.m.* (*com.*) manager.
geriatra, *n.m.f.* geriatrician, geriatrist.
geriatría, *n.f.* geriatrics.
gericaya, *n.f.* (*Mex.*) custard.
gerifalte, *n.m.* gerfalcon; (*fig.*) leader, top man.
germán, *a.* *apocope of* GERMANO.
germanesco, -ca, *a.* belonging to the jargon *or* cant of thieves.
germanía, *n.f.* jargon *or* cant (*of thieves etc.*); slang; concubinage; (*hist.*) Valencian guild league.
germánico, -ca, *a.* Germanic. — *n.m.* Germanic (*group of languages*).
germanio, *n.m.* (*chem.*) germanium.
germanismo, *n.m.* germanism.
germanizar, *v.t.* to germanize.
germano, -na, *a.*, *n.m.f.* Germanic, German.
germanófilo, -la, *a.*, *n.m.f.* Germanophile.
germanófobo, -ba, *a.*, *n.m.f.* Germanophobe.
germen, *n.m.* germ; (*bot.*) germen.
germinación, *n.f.* germination.
germinal, *a.* germinal.
germinar, *v.i.* to germinate, bud.
germinativo, -va, *a.* germinative.
gerundense, *a.*, *n.m.f.* (native) of Gerona.
gerundiada, *n.f.* (*coll.*) bombastic expression.
gerundiano, -na, *a.* (*coll.*) bombastic.
gerundio, *n.m.* (*gram.*) gerund; (*coll.*) pompous and bombastic preacher *or* lecturer, gerund-grinder.
gesta, *n.f.* gest(e), feat, great exploit.
gestación, *n.f.* gestation.
gestatorio, -ria, *a.* gestatory; gestatorial.
gestear, *v.i.* to gesticulate; to make grimaces.
gestero, -ra, *a.* gesticulating; grimacing.
gesticulación, *n.f.* gesticulation; grimacing.
gesticular, *a.* gesticulatory. — *v.i.* to gesticulate; to make faces.
gestión, *n.f.* arrangement; step, measure; conduct, management; ***trámites y gestiones,*** formalities and arrangements.
gestionar, *v.t.* to arrange, fix, fix up; to make arrangements for; to get, get hold of.
gesto, *n.m.* face; wry face, grimace; look; gesture; ***hacer gestos,*** to make faces; ***torcer el gesto,*** to pull a face; ***poner gesto,*** to show annoyance; ***estar de buen*** or ***mal gesto,*** to be in a good *or* bad humour; ***no hacer ni el gesto,*** to make not the slightest move, show not a sign, make no attempt; ***gesto de manos,*** gesture.
gestor, *n.m.* (*com.*) agent.
gestoría, *n.f.* agency, business agency.
gestudo, -da, *a.* (*coll.*) ill-humoured, cross-looking.
giba, *n.f.* hump, hunch, gibbosity; (*coll.*) nuisance, pain-in-the-neck.
gibar, *v.t.* to hump, hunch; (*coll.*) to jigger up, mess up.
gibelino, -na, *a.*, *n.m.f.* Ghibelline.
gibón, *n.m.* gibbon.
gibosidad, *n.f.* gibbosity.
giboso, -sa, *a.* gibbous, crook-backed, hump-backed.
gibraltareño, -ña, *a.*, *n.m.f.* Gibraltarian.
gícama, *n.f.* (*Mex.*) an edible root.
giga, *n.f.* jig (*dance and tune*).
giganta, *n.f.* giantess; (*bot.*) sunflower, acanthus.
gigantazo, -za, *n.m.f.* huge giant.
gigante, *a.* gigantic, giant, huge, mammoth. — *n.m.* giant.
giganteo, -tea, *a.* gigantic, huge, colossal. — *n.f.* (*bot.*) sunflower.
gigantesco, -ca, *a.* gigantic, huge, colossal.
gigantez, *n.f.* gigantism.
gigantilla, *n.f.* large-headed figure.
gigantismo, *n.m.* (*med.*) gigantism.
gigantón, -tona, *n.m.f.* enormous giant. — *n.m.pl.* (**gigantones**) gigantic figures of pasteboard; ***echar los gigantones a alguien,*** to give s.o. a piece of one's mind.
gigote, *n.m.* minced-meat stew; (*coll.*) ***hacer gigote de,*** to make minced meat of.
gijonense, gijonés, -nesa, *a.*, *n.m.f.* (native) of Gijón.
Gil, *n.m.* Giles.
gilvo, -va, *a.* honey-coloured, pinky.
gimelga, *n.f.* (*naut.*) fish, paunch.
gimnasio, *n.m.* gymnasium; school, academy.
gimnasta, *n.m.f.* gymnast, athlete.
gimnástico, -ca, *a.* gymnastic, gymnastical. — *n.f.* gymnastics.
gímnico, -ca, *a.* [GIMNÁSTICO].
gimnosofista, *n.m.* gymnosophist; Indian philosopher.
gimnoto, *n.m.* (*zool.*) gymnotus.
gimotear, *v.i.* to whine, whimper.
gimoteo, *n.m.* whining, whimpering.
ginandra, *a.* (*bot.*) gynandrian, gynandrous.
Ginebra, *n.f.* Geneva.
ginebra (1), *n.f.* gin (*liquor*).
ginebra (2), *n.f.* bedlam, din; card game; rattle.
ginebrada, *n.f.* puff-pastry tart.
ginebrés, -resa, ginebrino, -na, *a.*, *n.m.f.* (native) of Geneva.
gineceo, *n.m.* gynæceum.
ginecocracia, *n.f.* gynæcocracy; gynarchy.
ginecología, *n.f.* gynæcology.
ginesta, *n.f.* genista.
gineta, *n.f.* genet.
gingidio, *n.m.* wild spinach.
gingival, *a.* gingival.
gingivitis, *n.f. inv.* (*med.*) gingivitis.
gira (1), *n.f.* picnic; trip, outing; tour.
girada, *n.f.* gyration, pirouette.
girado, *n.m.* (*com.*) drawee.
girador, girante, *n.m.* (*com.*) drawer.
giralda, *n.f.* vane *or* weather-cock (*in the form of a statue*); ***La Giralda,*** vane on the spire of Seville cathedral tower; name of this tower.

giraldete, *n.m.* rochet, surplice without sleeves.
giraldilla, *n.f.* small vane *or* weather-cock; popular dance (*Asturias*).
girándula, *n.f.* girandole.
girante, *n.m.* (*com.*) drawer.
girar, *v.t.* (*com.*) to send; ***girar dinero,*** to send *or* remit money; ***girar una visita a,*** to pay a visit to. — *v.i.* to revolve, rotate, gyrate, wheel round, spin round, turn, swivel, pivot; (*com.*) to draw (***contra*** or ***a cargo de,*** on).
girasol, *n.m.* sunflower.
giratorio, -ria, *a.* revolving, rotatory, gyrating, turning; ***cruce giratorio,*** roundabout, (*Am.*) traffic circle; ***puerta giratoria,*** revolving door; ***silla giratoria,*** swivel chair.
girifalte, *n.m.* gerfalcon.
girino, *n.m.* whirligig beetle.
giro (1), *n.m.* turn; gyration, revolution, rotation; course, trend; turn of phrase, expression, idiom; (*com.*) draft, money order; (*com.*) trade, circulation, business; ***giro postal,*** postal order.
giro (2), **-ra** (2), *a.* spruce; (*Hisp. Am.*) black and white; (*Hisp. Am.*) yellow; (*Hisp. Am.*) cocky.
girola, *n.f.* apse aisle.
girómetro, *n.m.* revolution counter.
girondino, -na, *a., n.m.f.* Girondist, Girondin.
giroscopio, *n.m.* gyroscope.
giróstato, *n.m.* gyrostat.
giróvago, -ga, *a.* vagabond, wandering.
gis, *n.m.* chalk.
gitanada, *n.f.* gipsylike trick *or* behaviour; cajolerie.
gitanear, *v.i.* to live *or* behave like a gipsy; to cheat; to haggle; to cajole and flatter.
gitanería, *n.f.* gipsies; gipsydom; gipsyism; wheedling, flattery, cajolery.
gitanesco, -ca, *a.* gipsy-like, gipsy; chaotic, messy.
gitanismo, *n.m.* gipsyism; gipsy life.
gitano, -na, *a.* gipsy; artful, sly; mealy-mouthed. — *n.m.f.* gipsy.
glabro, -ra, *a.* glabrous.
glacial, *a.* glacial; (*fig.*) icy, frigid.
glaciar, *n.m.* glacier.
glacis, *n.m. inv.* (*fort.*) glacis.
gladiador, *n.m.* gladiator.
gladiatorio, -ria, *a.* gladiatorial.
gladio, gladíolo, *n.m.* gladiolus.
glande, *n.m.* (glans) penis.
glandífero, -ra, glandígero, -ra, *a.* (*poet., bot.*) glandiferous.
glándula, *n.f.* (*anat., bot.*) gland; ***glándula pineal,*** pineal gland; ***glándula pituitaria,*** pituitary gland.
glandular, *a.* glandular.
glanduloso, -sa, *a.* glandulous.
glasé, *n.m.* glacé; glacé silk.
glaseado, -da, *a.* glacé; glossy, shiny.
glasear, *v.t.* to glacé; to glaze; to calender, satin.
glasto, *n.m.* woad.
glauberita, *n.f.* glauberite.
glaucio, *n.m.* horn poppy.
glauco, -ca, *a.* glaucous; light green. — *n.m.* (*zool.*) glaucus.
glaucoma, *n.m.* glaucoma.
gleba, *n.f.* lump *or* clod (*turned up by the plough*); soil; land; glebe.
gleboso, -sa, *a.* (*prov.*) glebous, turfy.
glera, *n.f.* gravel pit.
glicerina, *n.f.* glycerine.
gliconio, *n.m.* Glyconic (*verse*).
glíptica, *n.f.* glyptics, stone engraving.
gliptografía, *n.f.* glyptography.
global, *a.* global; over-all, all-over.
globiforme, *a.* globe-shaped, spherical.
globo, *n.m.* globe, ball, sphere; globular lamp-shade; balloon; ***globo aerostático,*** aerostat balloon; ***globo cautivo,*** captive balloon; ***globo de barrera,*** barrage balloon; ***globo dirigible,*** dirigible balloon, airship; ***globo sonda,*** sounding balloon; (*fig.*) feeler; ***globo terrestre*** or ***terráqueo,*** terrestrial ball *or* globe; ***globo del ojo,*** eyeball; ***en globo,*** in bulk; as a whole, in toto.
globoso, -sa, *a.* globose, spherical.
globular, *a.* globular, global, globate, spherical.
globulariáceo, -cea, *a.* globularia.
glóbulo, *n.m.* globule; corpuscle.
globuloso, -sa, *a.* globular.
glomerula, *n.f.* glomerule, flower-cluster.
gloria, *n.f.* glory; heaven, bliss; gossamer, transparent gauze; cream tart *or* pie; (*art*) opening in the sky representing angels etc.; boast, pride; (*prov.*) stove; ***estar en la gloria,*** to be as pleased as Punch; ***sin pena ni gloria,*** in commonplace *or* humdrum fashion; ***sabe a gloria,*** it tastes heavenly; ***da gloria verlo,*** it's a treat to see him; ***hacer gloria de,*** to boast of; ***estar en sus glorias,*** to be in one's element. — *n.m.* (*eccles.*) gloria, doxology; (*theat.*) curtain calls.
gloriarse [L], *v.r.* — ***de,*** to glory in, boast *or* be proud of.
glorieta, *n.f.* summer-house, bower, arbour; circus, traffic roundabout, (*Am.*) traffic circle.
glorificación, *n.f.* glorification.
glorificador, -ra, *a.* glorifier. — *n.m.* God.
glorificante, *a., n.m.f.* glorifying; glorifier.
glorificar [A], *v.t.* to glorify. — **glorificarse,** *v.r.* — ***de,*** to glory (in), boast *or* be proud (of).
glorioso, -sa, *a.* glorious, illustrious; holy, blessed; proud; ***La Gloriosa,*** the Holy Virgin; 1868 Revolution in Spain.
glosa, *n.f.* gloss, comment, explanation; gloss *or* rondel; marginal note, footnote; (*mus.*) variation on a theme.
glosador, -ra, *n.m.f.* glosser, commentator.
glosar, *v.t.* to gloss, annotate, comment; to compose a gloss to; (*com.*) to audit (*accounts*); (*mus.*) to vary (*a theme*); (*fig.*) to misconstrue.
glosario, *n.m.* glossary.
glose, *n.m.* glossing, commentating.
glosilla, *n.f.* short gloss, comment; (*print.*) minion type.
glositis, *n.f. inv.* (*med.*) glossitis.
glosopeda, *n.f.* foot-and-mouth disease.
glótico, -ca, *a.* (*zool.*) glottic, glottal.
glotis, *n.f. inv.* (*anat.*) glottis.
glotón, -tona, *a.* gluttonous. — *n.m.f.* glutton.
glotonazo, -za, *n.m.f.* great glutton.
glotonear, *v.i.* to act the glutton, eat gluttonously.
glotonería, *n.f.* gluttony.
gloxínea, *n.f.* (*Col.*) gloxinia.
glucina, *n.f.* (*chem.*) glucina.
glucinio, *n.m.* (*chem.*) glucinum.
glucómetro, *n.m.* (*chem.*) glucometer.
glucosa, *n.f.* glucose.
glucósido, *n.m.* (*chem.*) glucoside.
glucosuria, *n.f.* glycosuria.
gluma, *n.f.* (*bot.*) glume.
gluten, *n.m.* gluten; glue.
glúteo, -tea, *a.* gluteal. — *n.m.* (*fam.*) behind, posterior.
glutinosidad, *n.f.* glutinosity.
glutinoso, -sa, *a.* glutinous.
gnetáceo, -cea, *a.* (*bot.*) gnetaceous.
gnómico, -ca, *a.* gnomic.
gnomo, *n.m.* gnome.
gnomon, *n.m.* gnomon; ***gnomon movible,*** bevel square.
gnomónico, -ca, *a.* gnomonic, gnomonical. — ***n.f.*** gnomonics.

gnosticismo, *n.m.* gnosticism.
gnóstico, *a., n.m.* gnostic.
goa, *n.f.* pig-iron bloom.
gobernación, *n.f.* government; ***Ministerio de la Gobernación,*** Home Office.
gobernador, -ra, *a.* governing. — *n.m.* governor. — *n.f.* governor's wife; female ruler.
gobernalle, *n.m.* rudder, helm.
gobernante, *a.* governing, ruling. — *n.m.f.* ruler.
gobernar [1], *v.t.* to conduct, manage, run; to steer. — *v.t., v.i.* to govern, rule. — **gobernarse,** *v.r.* to manage one's affairs; ***no te gobiernes por eso,*** don't go by that.
gobernativo, -va [GUBERNATIVO].
gobernoso, -sa, *a.* (*coll.*) methodical, systematic, orderly.
gobierna, *n.f.* weather-vane.
gobierno, *n.m.* government, governing, ruling; control; management; steering; rudder, helm; (*Am.*) administration; governorship; governor's office; governor's residence; ***para su gobierno,*** for your guidance *or* information; ***ama de gobierno,*** housekeeper; ***sirva de gobierno,*** let it serve as guidance.
gobio, *n.m.* (*ichth.*) gudgeon.
goce, *n.m.* enjoyment, fruition; possession.
gocete, *n.m.* armpit guards in ancient armour.
gociano, -na, *a., n.m.f.* (native) of Gotland.
gocha, *n.f.* (*coll.*) sow.
gocho, *n.m.* (*coll.*) pig, hog.
godesco, -ca, godible, *a.* joyful, cheerful.
godo, -da, *a., n.m.f.* Goth; Gothic; ***ser godo,*** to be of ancient descent; (*Arg., Can. Isles, Chi., contempt.*) Spaniard; (*Col.*) conservative.
gofio, *n.m.* (*Can. Isles, Hisp. Am.*) roasted flour *or* maize meal; (*Ven.*) sweet made of yucca, pineapple and ginger.
gofo, -fa, *a.* stupid, ignorant, coarse; (*art*) dwarf figure.
gofrar, *v.t.* to goffer.
gol, *n.m.* (*sport*) goal.
gola, *n.f.* gullet, throat; (*mil.*) gorget; ruff, ruche (*collar*); (*fort.*) gorge; (*arch.*) cyma, cymatium.
goldre, *n.m.* quiver.
goleada, *n.f.* great number of goals.
goleador, *n.m.* goal scorer.
golear, *v.i.* to score goals.
goleta, *n.f.* schooner.
golf, *n.m.* golf.
golfán, *n.m.* water-lily.
golfante, *n.m.f.* loafer, scoundrel.
golfear, *v.i.* to loaf, hang around the streets.
golfería, *n.f.* loafing, hanging around the streets; loafers, ragamuffins, scoundrels.
golfillo, *n.m.* urchin, ragamuffin, guttersnipe.
golfín, *n.m.* dolphin; member of a band of thieves.
golfista, *n.m.f.* golf-player, golfer.
golfo, *n.m.* gulf, large bay; main, sea; card game; loafer, tramp; guttersnipe.
goliardesco, -ca, *a.* goliardic.
goliardo, *n.m.* roving clergyman *or* student.
golilla, *n.m.* (*obs.*) magistrate, court clerk; (*Bol.*) gaucho's necktie; (*Chi.*) hub washer.—*n.f.* ruff, collar; (*build.*) joint-pipe; (*mech.*) rim (*of a pipe*); ***ajustar la golilla a,*** to bring to reason.
golillero, -ra, *n.m.f.* collar-maker.
golondrina, *n.f.* swallow; swallowfish; excursion boat; (*Chi.*) pantechnicon; ***golondrina de mar,*** tern; ***una golondrina no hace verano,*** one swallow does not make a summer.
golondrinera, *n.f.* swallow-wort, celandine.
golondrino, *n.m.* male swallow; (*mil.*) deserter; tubfish; large tumour (*in the armpit*).
golondro, *n.m.* (*coll.*) desire, whim; (*coll.*) ***andar en golondros,*** to feed on vain hopes; (*coll.*) ***campar de golondro,*** to live at another's expense.
golosear, *v.i.* to go in for sweet things.
golosina, *n.f.* sweet titbit, sweet morsel; fondness for sweet things; trifle; ***amargar la golosina,*** to spoil things.
golosinar, golosinear, *v.i.* to look for and eat titbits, dainties *or* sweet-meats; to taste and relish nice things; to have a sweet tooth.
goloso, -sa, *a.* having a sweet tooth. — *n.m.f.* one having a sweet tooth; one keen (*on sth.*).
golpazo, *n.m.* violent blow, swipe, wallop; thud *or* thump.
golpe, *n.m.* blow, knock, bump, stroke, swipe; coup; big rush, large throng; big amount; beat (*heart*); spring bolt (*of a lock*); (*sew.*) passementerie trimming; pocket-flap (*of a coat*); witty sally *or* remark; (*fenc.*) movement of attack; hole (*for planting*); number of cuts planted in one hole; (*naut.*) sweep; ***golpe de efecto,*** gag, witty touch; ***golpe de estado,*** coup d'état; ***golpe de fortuna,*** stroke of luck; ***golpe de gracia,*** coup de grâce; finishing stroke; ***golpe de mano,*** surprise attack; hold-up; ***golpe de mar,*** surge, heavy sea; ***golpe de remo,*** oar-stroke; ***golpe de tos,*** fit of coughing; ***golpe de vista,*** glance; intuition; ***a golpes,*** with blows; by fits and starts; ***de golpe,*** all of a sudden; ***de un golpe,*** all at once; ***de golpe y porrazo,*** all of a sudden; ***acusar el golpe,*** to show the effect, feel the pinch; ***dar el golpe,*** to be a sensation, cause a sensation; ***no dar golpe,*** not to do a hand's turn; ***dar un golpe en falso, errar, fallar*** or ***marrar el golpe,*** to miss, fail; ***hacer algo a golpe seguro,*** to do sth. with certainty of success; ***parar el golpe,*** to parry, ward off the blow.
golpeadero, *n.m.* beating *or* striking place; repeated beating *or* striking.
golpeador, -ra, *a.* beating, striking.
golpeadura, *n.f.* beating, hammering, striking.
golpear, *v.t.* to beat, strike, hit, knock, hammer, pound, pummel.
golpeo, *n.m.* repeated beating, striking.
golpete, *n.m.* door-catch, window-catch.
golpetear, *v.t., v.i.* to beat, knock, hammer *or* strike repeatedly.
golpeteo, *n.m.* continued striking; constant hammering *or* battering.
gollería, *n.f.* dainty, delicious morsel; superfluity; trifle.
golletazo, *n.m.* crack on the neck (*of a bottle*); stab in the neck (*of a bull*); quick finish.
gollete, *n.m.* throttle, upper part of the throat; neck (*of a bottle*); neck-band (*of some religious habits*); (*coll.*) ***estar hasta el gollete,*** to be full; to be up to the eyes; to be fed-up.
gollizo, gollizno, *n.m.* gorge, ravine, narrow pass.
goma, *n.f.* gum; rubber; elastic band; rubber-tyre; (*med.*) sheath, condom; ***goma de borrar,*** rubber, eraser; ***goma arábiga,*** gum-arabic; ***goma elástica,*** india-rubber; ***goma laca,*** lac; (*pl.*) (*Hisp. Am.*) galoshes.
gomecillo, *n.m.* (*coll.*) blind person's guide.
gomero, -ra, *a.* pertaining *or* related to rubber. — *n.m.* (*Arg.*) rubber merchant.
gomia, *n.f.* dragon figure; bugbear; glutton; waster.
gomífero, -ra, *a.* gummiferous, gum-bearing.
gomista, *n.m.f.* dealer in rubber goods.
gomorresina, *n.f.* gum-resin.
gomosidad, *n.f.* gumminess, stickiness.
gomoso (1), **-sa,** *a.* gummy, productive of gum; full of viscous humours.
gomoso (2), *n.m.* dandy; (*coll.*) fop, coxcomb.
gonagra, *n.f.* gout which attacks the knees.
gonce, *n.m.* hinge.

góndola, *n.f.* gondola; omnibus, stage; car (*of airship* or *balloon*).
gondolero, *n.m.* gondolier.
gonela, *n.f.* tunic *or* outer garment of silk *or* leather, sleeveless, and reaching to the calf of the leg, worn over the armour; skirt formerly worn by ladies in Aragon.
gonete, *n.m.* dress formerly worn by women.
gonfalón, *n.m.* banner, gonfalon, pennant.
gonfalonier, gonfaloniero, *n.m.* standard-bearer.
gong, gongo, *n.m.* gong.
gongorino, -na, *a.* (*poet.*) gongoresque. — *n.m.f.* Gongoristic.
gongorismo, *n.m.* (*poet.*) Gongorism.
gongorista, *n.f.* (*poet.*) Gongorist.
gongorizar [C], *v.i.* to affect a Gongoristic style.
goniometría, *n.f.* goniometry.
goniométrico, -ca, *a.* goniometric.
goniómetro, *n.m.* goniometer.
gonococo, *n.m.* gonococcus.
gonorrea, *n.f.* gonorrhœa, urethritis.
gonorréico, -ca, *a.* gonorrhœal.
gorbión, gurbión, *n.m.* coarse twisted silk; heavy yarn silk cloth; spurge gum resin.
gordal, *a.* fat, big, fleshy.
gordana, *n.f.* animal fat.
gordito, -ta, *a.* nice and plump.
gordiflón, -lona, gordinflón, -lona, *n.m.f.* (*coll.*) chubby.
gordo, -da, *a.* fat, corpulent, stout; thick; big; ***mentira gorda,*** tall story, whacking great lie; (*coll.*) ***pájaro gordo,*** big noise; (***premio***) ***gordo,*** big prize; ***agua gorda,*** hard water; ***perro gordo,*** ten-cent piece; ***dedo gordo,*** thumb *or* big toe; ***hacer la vista gorda,*** to turn a blind eye; ***se armó la gorda,*** there was a hell of a row; ***pintor de brocha gorda,*** dauber; (*fig.*) ***sudar la gota gorda,*** to sweat blood. — *n.m.* fat, suet, lard. — *n.f.* (*Mex.*) thick maize omelet.
gordolobo, *n.m.* (*bot.*) great mullein.
gordón, -dona, gordote, -ta, *a.* (*coll.*) pretty fat *or* hefty.
gordura, *n.f.* fatness.
gorfe, *n.m.* deep whirlpool.
gorga, *n.f.* hawks' food; (*prov.*) whirlpool.
gorgojarse, *v.r.* to be destroyed by insects (*corn*).
gorgojo, *n.m.* grub, mite, weevil; (*coll.*) little runt.
gorgojoso, -sa, *a.* full of grubs *or* weevils.
gorgón, *n.m.* (*Hisp. Am.*) concrete; parr.
Gorgona, *n.f.* (*myth.*) Gorgon.
gorgorán, *n.m.* grogram.
gorgorear, *v.i.* (*prov.*, *Chi.*) to cry like a turkey-cock.
gorgorita, *n.f.* small bubble; (*pl.*) trilling, quavers.
gorgoritear, *v.i.* (*coll.*) to trill, quaver, warble.
gorgoritos, *n.m.pl.* (*coll.*) trilling, quavering, warbling.
górgoro, *n.m.* (*Mex.*) bubble.
gorgorotada, *n.f.* gulp, swallow (*of liquid*).
gorgotear, *v.i.* to gurgle.
gorgoteo, *n.m.* gurgling.
gorgotero, *n.m.* pedlar, hawker.
gorguera, *n.f.* gorgeret, ruff; (*arm.*) gorget, neck-armour; (*bot.*) involucre.
gorguerán, *n.f.* (*obs.*) grogram.
gorguz, *n.m.* javelin, shaft; (*Mex.*) goad stick.
gorigori, *n.m.* (*coll.*) dirge.
gorila, *n.m.* gorilla.
gorja, *n.f.* throat, throttle; (*coll.*) ***de gorja,*** rejoicing, merrymaking.
gorjal, *n.m.* collar (*of a doublet*); (*arm.*) gorget.
gorjeador, -ra, *a.* trilling, warbling.
gorjear, *v.i.* to chirp, twitter; to trill, warble; to babble, gurgle; (*Hisp. Am.*) to mock.
gorjeo, *n.m.* chirping, twittering; trilling, warbling, babbling, gurgling.
gormar, *v.t.* to vomit.
gorra, *n.f.* cap; (*coll.*) sponging; ***comer de gorra, vivir de gorra, pegar la gorra,*** to sponge (*on people*).
gorrada, gorretada, *n.f.* wave of a cap.
gorrería, *n.f.* cap shop *or* workshop.
gorrero, -ra, *n.m.f.* cap maker *or* seller; sponger.
gorrete, *n.m.* small cap.
gorrín, gorrino, *n.m.* (small) pig, hog; (*fig.*) filthy pig.
gorrinada, gorrinería, *n.f.* (*coll.*) filthy thing to do *or* say.
gorrinera, *n.f.* pigsty.
gorrión, *n.m.* sparrow.
gorrionera, *n.f.* (*coll.*) den.
gorrista, *n.m.f.* sponger.
gorro, *n.m.* cap; bonnet; ***gorro de dormir,*** nightcap; ***gorro frigio,*** Phrygian cap.
gorrón (1), **-rrona,** *a.* sponging. — *n.m.f.* sponger. — *n.f.* trollop.
gorrón (2), *n.m.* round smooth pebble; (*mech.*) spindle, pivot; pillow, swing-block; unhealthy silk-worm.
gorronal, *n.m.* place covered in pebbles.
gorronería, *n.f.* sponging.
gorullo, *n.m.* lump, ball.
gorupo, *n.m.* (*naut.*) granny's bend.
gosipino, -na, *a.* of a cottony surface.
gota, *n.f.* drop; (*med.*) gout; (*arch.*) gutta; (*med.*) ***gota serena,*** amaurosis; (*med.*) ***gota coral*** or ***caduca,*** epilepsy, falling-sickness; ***gotas amargas,*** bitters; ***gota a gota,*** drop by drop; ***no veo ni gota,*** I can't see a thing, (*fam.*) I can't see a sausage; ***no quedar gota de sangre en el cuerpo*** or ***en las venas,*** to be panic-stricken; (*fig.*) ***sudar la gota gorda,*** to sweat blood.
goteado, -da, *a.* spotted, speckled.
gotear, *v.i.* to drop, drip, dribble, leak; to trickle; to spit (*of rain*); to dole things out (*in driblets*); to gutter (*candles*).
gotera, *n.f.* leak, leakage, drip, dripping; drip *or* damp stain; (*arch.*) gutter, valley; valance (*of a canopy* or *tester*); (*agric.*) disease in trees caused by infiltration; chronic ailment; ***la gotera cava la piedra,*** many drops wear away the hardest stone; (*pl.*) (*Hisp. Am.*) environs, outskirts.
gotero, *n.m.* (*Mex.*, *P.R.*) dropper (*for counting* or *measuring drops*).
goterón, *n.m.* large raindrop; (*arch.*) throating.
gótico, -ca, *a.* Gothic; (*fig.*) noble, illustrious; ***letra gótica,*** Gothic characters. — *n.m.* Gothic language.
gotón, -tona, *a.*, *n.m.f.* Goth.
gotoso, -sa, *a.* gouty.
goyesco, -ca, *a.* of Goya, Goyesque.
gozante, *a.* enjoying; joyous.
gozar [C], *v.t.* to enjoy; to enjoy possession of. — *v.i.* to enjoy; to enjoy o.s., have pleasure; ***goza de buena salud,*** he enjoys good health. — **gozarse,** *v.r.* to have enjoyment *or* pleasure, rejoice; ***gozarse en,*** to take pleasure in.
gozne, *n.m.* hinge.
gozo, *n.m.* joy; delight; sudden blaze of dry chips of wood; ***no caber en sí de gozo,*** to be bursting with joy; ***¡mi gozo en un pozo!*** that's torn it! so much for that!; (*pl.*) couplets with a refrain, in praise of the Blessed Virgin or the saints.
gozoso, -sa, *a.* joyful, joyous, gleeful.
gozque, *n.m.* small dog.
grabado, *n.m.* engraving; print, picture, illustration; ***grabado en madera,*** wood-cut; ***grabado al agua fuerte,*** etching; ***grabado al agua tinta,*** aquatint; ***grabado al barniz blando,*** soft-ground etching; ***grabado a puntos,*** stipple

engraving; ***grabado en fondo*** or ***en hueco,*** punch *or* die sinking.
grabador, -ra, *n.m.f.* engraver, cutter, sinker; (*print.*) ***grabador en matrices,*** form-cutter.
grabadura, *n.f.* engraving.
grabar, *v.t.* to engrave, cut, sink.
grabazón, *n.f.* overlay with engraved ornament.
gracejada, *n.f.* (*Hisp. Am.*) clownish joke, buffoonery, jest (*in bad taste*).
gracejar, *v.i.* to jest, joke.
gracejo, *n.m.* wit, wittiness.
gracia, *n.f.* grace; gracefulness; favour; mercy, pardon; wittiness, funniness, amusing quality; witty, funny *or* amusing thing to do *or* say; name; ***estar en gracia de Dios,*** to be in a state of grace; ***hacer gracia de,*** to spare; ***caer en gracia,*** to make a good impression, find favour, please; ***no le hace gracia,*** he doesn't find it funny, he is not amused; ***tiene gracia,*** he *or* it is amusing *or* funny; (*iron.*) ***¡tiene gracia (la cosa)!*** that's a fine thing! the very idea! what a cheek!; ***¡vaya una gracia!*** well, I like that!; ***dar en la gracia de,*** to take to, take into one's head to; ***el niño tiene muchas gracias,*** the child does *or* says lots of cute *or* amusing things; ***¿cuál es su gracia?*** what's your name?; ***de gracia,*** free; ***en gracia a,*** in view of; for the sake of; ***¡que entre la gracia de Dios!*** let the sunlight and air in!; ***Ministerio de Gracia y Justicia,*** Ministry of Justice; (*pl.*) thanks; ***dar gracias,*** to give thanks; to say grace; ***dar las gracias,*** to say thank you.
graciable, *a.* good-natured, affable; easily granted *or* obtained.
grácil, *a.* graceful.
graciola, *n.f.* hedge hyssop.
graciosidad, *n.f.* grace; gracefulness; wit.
gracioso, -sa, *a.* gracious; graceful; amusing, funny, witty; free. — *n.m.* wit, amusing fellow.
grada, *n.f.* step; tier of seats, row of seats; gradins; (altar) predella; (shipyard) slip-way; locutory; harrow.
gradación, *n.f.* gradation; range, variation.
gradado, -da, *a.* having gradins *or* steps.
gradar, *v.t.* to harrow.
gradería, *n.f.* series of steps; series of seats, tiers.
gradiente, *n.m.* (*meteor.*) gradient. — *n.f.* (*Arg., Chi., Ec.*) slope, gradient.
gradilla, *n.f.* small step *or* seat; tile *or* brick mould; small step-ladder.
gradinar, *v.t.* to chisel with a gradine.
gradino, *n.m.* gradine, sculptor's chisel.
gradilo, *n.m.* gladiolus.
grado (1), *n.m.* step (*of a staircase*); degree; rank; grade; (*law*) stage (*of proceedings*); ***grado de longitud*** or ***latitud,*** degree of longitude *or* latitude; ***de grado en grado,*** gradually, by degrees, step by step; ***en grado sumo (superlativo),*** in the highest degree; (*pl.*) minor orders.
grado (2), *n.m.* (*fig.*) will, willingness; ***de grado,*** willingly, gladly; ***mal de mi, tu, su*** etc. ***grado,*** unwillingly; ***de grado o por fuerza,*** willy-nilly; ***de mal grado,*** unwillingly, reluctantly.
gradoso, -sa, *a.* (*obs.*) pleasing, pleasant.
graduable, *a.* adjustable.
graduación, *n.f.* graduation; (*mil.*) rank; (*math.*) scale of degrees; proof (*alcohol*).
graduado, -da, *n.m.f.* graduate.
graduador, *n.m.* graduator, gauger.
gradual, *a.* gradual. — *n.m.* (*eccles.*) response sung at mass between the epistle and the gospel.
graduando, -da, *n.m.f.* undergraduate, candidate for a degree.
graduar [M], *v.t.* to graduate; to grade; to adjust, regulate; to gauge; (*mil.*) to brevet.
gráfico, -ca, *a.* graphic, graphical; vivid. — *n.m.f.* graph.
grafila, *n.f.* milled edge of coin.
grafio, *n.m.* graver for graffito *or* scratch-work.
grafioles, *n.m.pl.* biscuits in the form of an S.
grafito, *n.m.* graphite.
grafolita, *n.f.* grapholite.
grafología, *n.f.* graphology.
grafólogo, *n.m.* graphologist.
grafomanía, *n.f.* graphomania.
grafómetro, *n.m.f.* (*surv.*) graphometer, circumferentor.
gragea, *n.f.* pill.
graja, *n.f.* female rook, crow.
grajal, *a.* belonging to crows, ravens *or* magpies.
grajear, *v.i.* to caw; to chatter.
grajero, -ra, *a.* appertaining to rookeries.
grajo, *n.m.* raven, rook; (*Hisp. Am.*) stench from sweat.
gralario, -ria, *a.* grallatory, wading (*birds*).
grama, *n.f.* (*bot.*) couch-grass, grama-grass.
gramal, *n.m.* place where couch-grass grows.
gramalote, *n.m.* (*Col., Ec., Per.*) fodder crop.
gramalla, *n.f.* long scarlet gown (*worn in ancient times by the magistrates of Catalonia and Aragon*); coat of mail.
gramallera, *n.f.* (*prov.*) pot-hanger.
gramar, *v.t.* (*prov.*) to knead.
gramatical, *a.* grammatical.
gramático, -ca, *a.* grammatical. — *n.m.* grammarian. — *n.f.* grammar; study of the Latin language; (*coll.*) ***gramática parda,*** practical knowledge, horse sense, shrewdness.
gramatiquear, *v.i.* to go into grammatical niceties.
gramatiquería, *n.f.* (tedious) grammatical stuff.
gramil, *n.m.* marking-gauge.
gramilla, *n.f.* scutching board; (*Arg.*) joint grass.
gramíneo, -nea, *a.* (*bot.*) graminaceous.
graminívoro, -ra, *a.* graminivorous, grass-eating.
gramo, *n.m.* gramme, gram.
gramófono, *n.m.* gramophone.
gramola, *n.f.* phonograph; gramophone.
gramómetro, *n.m.* (*print.*) type-gauge.
gramoso, -sa, *a.* pertaining to couch-grass; covered in couch-grass.
grampa, *n.f.* clamp.
gran, *a.* (*contr. of* ***grande*** *used only in sing. before m.* or *f. nouns*), large, big; grand, great; ***gran filósofo,*** great philosopher.
grana, *n.f.* seeding; seeding time; small seed; cochineal; kermes dye; kermesberry; scarlet colour; fine scarlet cloth; ***grana del paraíso,*** grain of paradise, cardamom; (*coll.*) ***ponerse como una grana,*** to go *or* blush as red as a beetroot.
granada, *n.f.* [GRANADO].
granadera, *n.f.* grenadier's pouch.
granadero, *n.m.* grenadier; (*coll.*) very tall person.
granadilla, *n.f.* passion-flower; passion fruit.
granadillo, *n.m.* red ebony.
granadino, -na, *a., n.m.f.* (native) of Granada (*Spain*) *or* New Granada (*Colombia*). — *n.m.* flower of the pomegranate tree. — *n.f.* grenadine.
granado, -da, *a.* select, choice; distinguished, notable; mature, expert; tall, full-grown; gone to seed. — *n.m.* pomegranate tree. — *n.f.* pomegranate; shell; ***granada de mano,*** hand grenade.
granalla, *n.f.* granulation, granulated metal.
granar, *v.i.* to seed.
granate, *n.m.* garnet.
granático, -ca, *a.* deep red, garnet.
granazón, *n.f.* seeding.
Gran Bretaña, *n.f.* Great Britain.
grancolombiano, -na, *a.* pertaining to Greater Colombia.
grande, *a.* large, big; grand, great. — *n.m.* grandee.
grandecito, -cita, *a.* quite *or* pretty big, large *or* tall.

grandemente, *adv.* greatly.
grandevo, -va, *a.* (*poet.*) of advanced age.
grandeza, *n.f.* greatness, bigness; grandeur, grandness; grandeeship; body *or* assembly of grandees.
grandilocuencia, *n.f.* grandiloquence.
grandilocuente, grandílocuo, -cua, *a.* grandiloquent.
grandillón, -llona [GRANDULLÓN].
grandiosidad, *n.f.* greatness, grandeur.
grandioso, -sa, *a.* grandiose; grand.
grandor, *n.m.* size, bigness; greatness.
grandote, -ta, *a.* (*coll.*) hulking great.
grandullón, -llona, *a.* hulking great, gawky.
graneado, -da, *a.* grained, spotted, granulous; (*Per.*) select, choice.
graneador, *n.m.* granulating sieve (*for gunpowder*); place where gunpowder is sifted; tool for stipple-graver.
granear, *v.t.* to sow, seed (*a plot*); to grain (*powder, a lithographic stone*); to stipple (*in engraving*).
granel, *adv.* ***a granel,*** loose; in bulk; lavishly, in abundance.
granelar, *v.t.* to grain (*leather*).
graneo, *n.m.* shedding *or* sowing seed; stippling.
granero, *n.m.* granary; barn; corn-loft.
granete, *n.m.* marking awl, countersink, punch.
granévano, *n.m.* goat's-thorn.
granguardia, *n.f.* grand-guard.
granífero, -ra, *a.* grain-bearing.
granilla, *n.f.* rough nap on cloth.
granillo, *n.m.* small grain; pimple.
granilloso, -sa, *a.* granulous, granular.
granítico, -ca, *a.* granitic, formed of granite.
granito (1), *n.m.* small grain; small pimple; (*pharm.*) granule; small egg (*of a silkworm*).
granito (2), *n.m.* granite.
granívoro, -ra, *a.* granivorous, grain-eating.
granizada, *n.f.* hailstorm; (*fig.*) shower; iced drink.
granizado, *n.m.* iced drink; ***granizado de café,*** iced coffee.
granizar [C], *v.t., v.i.* to hail (down).
granizo, *n.m.* hail.
granja, *n.f.* grange, farm, farmhouse; dairy and poultry farm; ***granja modelo,*** model farm.
granjear, *v.t.* to gain, earn; to win. — *v.i.* (*naut.*) to gain. — **granjearse,** *v.r.* to win, win over; to earn, get.
granjeo, *n.m.* getting; gain, profit; winning, winning over.
granjería, *n.f.* gain, profit; speculation.
granjero, -ra, *n.m.f.* farmer; dairy and poultry farmer; trader.
grano, *n.m.* grain; corn; seed; berry, grape, bean; pimple; (*bot.*) ***granos del paraíso*** or ***amomo,*** grain of paradise; (*coll.*) ***ir al grano,*** to come *or* get to the point; (*iron.*) ***¡ahí es un grano de anís!*** that's no small matter! ***separar el grano de la paja,*** to sort the wheat from the chaff; ***aportar su grano de arena,*** to make one's (modest) contribution.
granoso, -sa, *a.* grained, grainy, granular, granulated.
granuja, *n.f.* loose grapes; grape-seed. — *n.m.* rascal, rogue; urchin.
granujado, -da, *a.* pimply. — *n.f.* dirty trick.
granujería, *n.f.* gang *or* mob of rascals *or* urchins.
granujiento, -ta, *a.* pimply.
granujilla, *n.m.* little rascal.
granujo, *n.m.* (*coll.*) pimple.
granujoso, -sa, *a.* pimply.
gránula, *n.f.* spore (*of cryptogamous plants*).
granulación, *n.f.* granulation.
granular, *a.* granular; pimply. — *v.t.* to granulate.
gránulo, *n.m.* granule.
granuloso, -sa, *a.* granular; granulose.

granza, *n.f.* (*bot.*) madder; (*pl.*) siftings, chaff; dross.
granzón, *n.m.* lump of ore difficult to screen; (*pl.* **granzones**) lumps of straw difficult to sieve and left uneaten by cattle.
grañón, *n.m.* boiled grain of wheat.
grao, *n.m.* landing place; shore, beach.
grapa, *n.f.* clamp, cramp, cramp-iron; staple.
grapadora, *n.f.* stapler, stapling machine.
grapón, *n.m.* large cramp *or* staple.
grasa, *n.f.* [GRASO].
grasera, *n.f.* vessel for fat *or* grease; oil-sump; slush-tub; dripping-pan.
grasería, *n.f.* tallow-chandler's shop.
grasero, *n.m.* (*min.*) slag-dumper.
graseza, *n.f.* fattiness.
grasiento, -ta, *a.* greasy, oily.
grasilla, *n.f.* pounce; (*bot.*) juniper-resin; fine *or* light grease.
graso, -sa, *a.* fat, oily. — *n.f.* grease; fat, ***grasa de ballena,*** whale-oil, blubber; pounce; (*naut.*) slush; (*min.*) slag (*of metals*); gum (*of juniper tree*).
grasones, *n.m.pl.* dish made of flour, milk of almonds, sugar and cinnamon.
grasoso, -sa, *a.* greasy, oily.
grasura, *n.f.* fat, grease.
grata (1), *n.f.* burnisher, smoothing chisel, wire brush.
gratamente, *adv.* pleasantly.
gratar, *v.t.* to brush *or* burnish (*plate*).
gratificación, *n.f.* reward; gratuity; allowance.
gratificador, -ra, *a.* rewarding; tipping.
gratificar [A], *v.t.* to reward; to tip.
grátil, *n.m.* head *or* edge (*of a sail*); luff, leech.
gratis, *adv.* gratis, free, for nothing.
gratisdato, -ta, *a.* gratuitous, given away.
gratitud, *n.f.* gratitude, gratefulness.
grato, -ta (2), *a.* pleasing, pleasant, agreeable; (*com.*) ***su grata,*** your favour.
gratonada, *n.f.* chicken ragout.
gratuito, -ta, *a.* gratuitous; gratis.
gratulación, *n.f.* congratulation; (*obs.*) eagerness to oblige.
gratular, *v.t.* to congratulate. — **gratularse,** *v.r.* to rejoice.
gratulatorio, -ria, *a.* congratulatory.
grava, *n.f.* gravel.
gravamen, *n.m.* burden, obligation; tax, duty; mortgage, encumbrance.
gravar, *v.t.* to weigh on; to burden; to tax; to encumber.
gravativo, -va, *a.* burdensome.
grave, *a.* grave; weighty, heavy; of weight; serious; burdensome; (*mus.*) deep, bass; ***ponerse grave,*** to assume an air of importance; to become critically ill.
gravear, *v.i.* to weigh.
gravedad, *n.f.* gravity; weight, heaviness; graveness, seriousness.
gravedoso, -sa, *a.* self-important, pompous, grave.
gravidez, *n.f.* pregnancy.
grávido, -da, *a.* pregnant; laden, heavy.
gravímetro, *n.m.* gravimeter.
gravitación, *n.f.* gravitation.
gravitar, *v.i.* to gravitate, weigh down (upon).
gravoso, -sa, *a.* burdensome, onerous.
graznador, -ra, *a.* croaking, cawing, cackling.
graznar, *v.i.* to croak, caw, cackle.
graznido, *n.m.* croak, caw, cackle.
greba, *n.f.* (*arm.*) grave.
greca, *n.f.* [GRECO].
Grecia, *n.f.* Greece.
greciano, -na, *a.* Grecian.
grecismo, *n.m.* Græcism.

grecizante, *a.* grecianizing, hellenizing.
grecizar [C], *v.t., v.i.* to græcize, hellenize.
greco, -ca, *a.* Grecian, Greek; ***a la greca,*** in Grecian style. — *n.m.f.* Greek. — *n.f.* Grecian fret, edging, trimming.
grecolatino, -na, *a.* Græco-Latin.
grecorromano, -na, *a.* Græco-Roman.
greda, *n.f.* clay, marl, fuller's earth.
gredal, *a.* clayey. — *n.m.* clay-pit.
gredoso, -sa, *a.* clayey, marly.
grefier, *n.m.* keeper of the rolls (*in the royal house*); official assistant in the ceremony *or* imposition of the Golden Fleece.
gregal (1), *a.* gregarious, going in flocks.
gregal (2), *n.m.* Mediterranean north-east wind.
gregario, -ria, *a.* easily led, sheep-like.
gregoriano, -na, *a.* Gregorian.
gregorillo, *n.m.* neckcloth.
gregorito, *n.m.* (*Mex.*) disappointment; practical joke.
greguería, *n.f.* outcry, confused clamour, hubbub; impressionistic imagery in epigram style.
gregüescos, *n.m.pl.* wide breeches.
greguisco, -ca, *a.* Grecian, Greek.
greguizar [C], *v.t.* to græcize, grecianize.
gremial, *a.* belonging to a guild; professional. — *n.m.* member of a guild; (*eccles.*) gremial.
gremio, *n.m.* guild; fraternity; association; corporation.
grenchudo, -da, *a.* having a long mane.
greña, *n.f.* tangled *or* matted hair; dishevelled hair, shock of hair; entanglement; (*prov., Mex.*) heap of grain laid to be threshed; (*prov.*) first leaves of a vine-shoot; ***andar a la greña,*** to pull one another by the hair; to scrap; to squabble *or* wrangle.
greñudo, -da, *a.* entangled, dishevelled. — *n.m.* shy horse.
gres, *n.m.* sandstone; siliceous clay.
gresca, *n.f.* uproar, shindy; scrap, set-to, wrangle.
grey, *n.f.* (*lit., fig.*) flock.
grial, *n.m.* grail.
griego, -ga, *a.* Greek, Grecian. — *n.m.* Greek language; (*coll.*) gibberish; nonsense; (*coll.*) cheat, gambler; ***hablar en griego,*** to talk gibberish.
griesco, griesgo, *n.m.* (*obs.*) encounter, battle, conflict.
grieta, *n.f.* crevice, crack, cleft; chink, fissure; split; ***grieta(s) en las manos,*** chapping of the hands.
grietarse [AGRIETARSE].
grietecilla, *n.f.* small fissure, crack.
grietoso, -sa, *a.* covered in cracks.
grifa, *n.f.* pot, marijuana.
grifado, -da, *a.* italicized.
grifalto, *n.m.* small culverin.
grifo (1), **-fa** (1), *a., n.m.* (*print.*) italic.
grifo (2), *n.m.* griffin.
grifo (3), **-fa** (2), *a.* frizzy, tangled (*hair*). — *n.m.* (*mech.*) tap, faucet, stop-cock.
grifón, *n.m.* faucet *or* spigot (*of fountains etc.*).
grigallo, *n.m.* (*orn.*) francolin.
gril, *n.m.* grilse.
griliforme, *a.* (*zool.*) shaped like a cricket.
grilla, *n.f.* female cricket; (*coll.*) ***ésa es grilla,*** that's a cock-and-bull story.
grillar, *v.i.* (*obs.*) to chirp (*crickets*). — **grillarse,** *v.r.* to shoot, sprout.
grillera, *n.f.* cricket-cage; (*coll.*) bedlam.
grillero, *n.m.* shackler.
grillete, *n.m.* shackle, fetter.
grillo, *n.m.* (*ent.*) cricket; (*bot.*) shoot, sprout; (*pl.*) fetters, irons, gyves, shackles; (*coll.*) ***olla de grillos,*** bedlam; ***andar a grillos,*** to fritter away one's time.
grima, *n.f.* creeps, horrors; ***da grima,*** it gives me the creeps.
grimoso, -sa, *a.* that gives the creeps *or* horrors.
grímpola, *n.f.* (*naut.*) vane, weather-cock; pennant, streamer.
gringo, *n.m.f.* (*Hisp. Am., contempt.*) blasted foreigner; Yank; ***hablar en gringo,*** to talk gibberish *or* double-Dutch.
griñón (1), *n.m.* wimple.
griñón (2), *n.m.* nectarine.
gripal, *a.* relating to influenza.
gripar, *v.t., v.i.* (*mech.*) to jam.
gripe, *n.f.* influenza.
gripo, *n.m.* (*obs.*) merchant ship.
gris, *a.* grey; (*fig.*) dull. — *n.m.* miniver; (*coll.*) cold, sharp wind; (*coll.*) state policeman.
grisalla, *n.f.* (*art*) grisaille.
grisáceo, -cea, gríseo, -sea, *a.* greyish.
grisar, *v.t.* to polish (*diamonds*).
griseta, *n.f.* flowered silk stuff; disease of trees; French grisette.
grisma, *n.f.* (*Chi., Guat., Hond.*) fragment, mite, crumb.
grisón, -sona, *a., n.m.f.* (native) of the Grisons.
grisú, *n.m.* (*min.*) fire-damp.
grita, *n.f.* clamour, outcry, hubbub, uproar, shouting; (*law*) ***grita foral,*** summons; citation (*Aragon*).
gritador, -ra, *a.* shouting, yelling. — *n.m.f.* shouter, yeller.
gritar, *v.t., v.i.* to shout, cry out, scream, yell; to hoot, boo.
gritería, *n.f.* [GRITERÍO].
griterío, *n.m.* shouting, outcry, hubbub, uproar.
grito, *n.m.* shout, cry, scream, yell, whoop, hoot; ***alzar*** or ***levantar el grito,*** to pipe up insolently; to talk loudly; ***estar en un grito,*** to be in excruciating pain; ***pedir a gritos,*** to cry out for; ***poner el grito en el cielo,*** to raise Cain, kick up a terrific fuss *or* rumpus; ***a grito herido, limpio, pelado*** or ***tendido, a voz en grito,*** at the top of one's voice; ***el último grito,*** the latest fashion *or* rage, dernier cri.
gritón, -tona, *a.* (*coll.*) vociferous, clamorous, bawling.
gro, *n.m.* grogram.
groenlandés, -desa, *a., n.m.f.* (native) of Greenland; Greenlander.
Groenlandia, *n.f.* Greenland.
groera, *n.f.* (*naut.*) ropehole.
gromo, *n.m.* bud, young shoot.
gropos, *n.m.pl.* cotton (*put in inkstands*).
gros, *n.m.* ancient coin of small value.
grosella, *n.f.* redcurrant; gooseberry; ***grosella colorada,*** redcurrant; ***grosella blanca,*** gooseberry; ***grosella negra,*** blackcurrant.
grosellero, *n.m.* redcurrant bush; gooseberry bush.
grosería, *n.f.* grossness; rudeness; coarseness; coarse expression.
grosero, -ra, *a.* gross; rude; coarse.
grosezuelo, -la, *a.* plump(ish).
grosísimo, -ma, *a. superl.* exceedingly stout, exceedingly thick.
grosor, *n.m.* thickness; bulk, size, depth, closeness, compactness.
grosularia, *n.f.* (*min.*) grossular.
grosulariáceo, -cea, *a.* grossularious.
grosularina, grosulina, *n.f.* (*chem.*) grossulin.
grosura, *n.f.* fat, suet, tallow; meat diet; feet and entrails (*animals*); crudeness, coarseness; ***día de grosura,*** Saturday (*formerly so called in Castile*).
grotesco, -ca, *a.* grotesque.
grúa, *n.f.* crane, derrick; ***grúa corredera,*** travelling crane; ***grúa flotante,*** floating crane; ***grúa fija,*** stationary crane; ***grúa de caballete,*** gantry crane.

gruero, -ra, *a.* trained to pursue cranes (*birds of prey*).
grueso, -sa, *a.* thick; corpulent, bulky, stout; (*anat.*) large; (*coll.*) dull, slow. — *n.m.f.* gross, twelve dozen. — *n.m.* bulk, thickness; main body; downstroke (*in penmanship*); ***en grueso,*** in bulk, wholesale; ***por grueso,*** roughly. — *n.f.* (*eccles.*) chief part of prebend.
gruir, *v.i.* to cry (*crane*).
grujidor, *n.m.* small bar used by glaziers (*for trimming glass*).
grujir, *v.t.* to trim *or* pare.
grulla, *n.f.* (*orn.*) crane.
grullada, *n.f.* (*coll.*) flock of cranes; (*coll.*) gang of loafers; (*coll.*) platitude.
grullero, -ra, *a.* crane-hunting (*falcon*).
grullo, *a.* (*Mex.*) ash-coloured (*horse*). — *n.m.* (*Arg., Cub., Mex., Ven.*) 1-dollar coin; (*Arg.*) stallion; country bumpkin, yokel.
grumete, *n.m.* cabinboy, ship's boy; (*sl.*) cat burglar.
grumo, *n.m.* grume, clot; ***grumo de leche,*** curd; lump; cluster, bunch; bud (*of trees*); tip (*of a fowl's wing*).
grumoso, -sa, *a.* grumous, clotty; lumpy.
gruñido, *n.m.* grunt (*of hog*); growl (*of dog*); grumble.
gruñidor, -ra, *a.* grunting, growling, grumbling.
gruñimiento, *n.m.* grunting, growling, grumbling.
gruñir [K], *v.t.* to grunt, growl, grumble; to creak.
gruñón, -ñona, *a., n.m.f.* (*coll.*) grunting, growling, grumbling (person).
grupa, *n.f.* croup, rump (*of horse*); ***volver grupas,*** to turn tail.
grupada, *n.f.* squall, burst of wind and rain; leap of a horse.
grupera, *n.f.* pillion (*horse, motor-cycle*); crupper.
grupo, *n.m.* group; clump, cluster.
grupúsculo, *n.m.* minor *or* splinter group.
gruta, *n.f.* grotto, grot.
grutesco, -ca, *a.* (*art*) grotesque.
¡gua! *interj.* (*Bol., Col., Per., Ven.*) gracious! now, now!
guaba (1), *n.m.* (*West Ind.*) small hairy spider.
guaba (2), *n.f.* (*Hisp. Am.*) fruit of the guamo tree.
guabairo, *n.m.* (*Cub.*) nocturnal insectivorous bird.
guabina, *n.f.* (*Col., Ven.*) guabina fish; (*Col.*) popular peasant melody.
guabirá, *n.m.* (*Arg.*) guabirá tree.
guabo (*C.R., Ec.*) [GUAMO].
guabul, *n.m.* (*Hond.*) banana drink.
guaca, *n.f.* (*Hisp. Am.*) Indian grave; buried *or* hidden treasure; pit (*where green fruit is kept to ripen*).
guacal, *n.m.* (*Hisp. Am.*) calabash tree; calabash; crate.
guacamayo, *n.m.* macaw.
guacamole, *n.m.* (*Cub.*) salad of avocado pear.
guacamote, *n.m.* (*Mex.*) manioc, cassava.
guacia, *n.f.* acacia; acacia gum.
guaco, *n.m.* (*bot.*) guaco; (*orn.*) curassow.
guachapear, *v.t.* (*coll.*) to splash; (*coll.*) to botch. — *v.i.* to clap, clatter.
guachapelí, *n.m.* (*Hisp. Am.*) guachapelí tree.
guáchara (1), *n.f.* (*Cub., P.R.*) fib, lie.
guacharaca, *n.f.* (*Col., Ven., orn.*) chachalaca bird.
guácharo, -ra (2), *a.* sickly, dropsical. — *n.m.* birdling; (*orn.*) oil-bird.
guachinango, -ga, *a.* (*Hisp. Am.*) cunning, sly. — *n.m.f.* (*pej.*) Mexican. — *n.m.* (*ichth.*) braize.
guacho, -cha, *a.* (*Hisp. Am.*) orphan, foundling; homeless, motherless; odd, unmatched. — *n.m.* nestling.
guadafiones, *n.m.pl.* fetter-lock.
guadalajareño, -ña, *a., n.m.f.* (native) of Guadalajara.
guadamací, guadamacil, *n.m.* embossed leather.
guadamacilería, *n.f.* manufacture of embossed leather; embossed leather shop *or* works.
guadamacilero, *n.m.* maker *or* seller of embossed leather.
guadamecí, guadamecil, *n.m.* embossed leather; ***guadamecí brocado,*** gilt *or* silvered embossed leather.
guadameco, *n.m.* ornament (*worn by women*).
guadaña, *n.f.* scythe.
guadañador [GUADAÑERO].
guadañar, *v.t.* to scythe.
guadañero, *n.m.* scythe-man.
guadañil [GUADAÑERO].
guadaño, *n.m.* (*Cádiz, Cub., Mex.*) harbour boat.
guadapero (1), *n.m.* wild pear.
guadapero (2), *n.m.* boy who carries food to harvestmen.
guadarnés, *n.m.* harness-room; harness-keeper; officer of the king's mews.
guadijeño, *a.* belonging to Guadix. — *n.m.* poniard, stiletto.
guadramaña, *n.f.* (*obs.*) trick, fraud; imposition.
guádua, *n.f.* (*Col., Ec., Ven.*) bamboo-cane.
guadual, *n.m.* (*Col., Ec., Ven.*) plantation of bamboo-canes.
guagua (1), *n.f.* trifle; (*Cub., Mex.*) orange scale (*insect*); (*Can. Isles, Cub.*) bus; ***de guagua,*** free, for nothing.
guagua (2), *n.f.* (*Hisp. Am.*) baby.
guaguasí, *n.m.* (*Cub.*) wild tree yielding an aromatic resin.
guagüero, -ra, *n.m.f.* (*Cub.*) bus driver; (*Hisp. Am.*) sponger.
guaicán, *n.m.* (*ichth.*) remora.
guaicurú, *n.m.* (*Arg., Chi.*) medicinal shrub.
guaina, *n.m.* (*Arg., Bol., Chi.*) boy, youth.
guainambí, *n.m.* (*Mex.*) humming-bird.
guaira, *n.f.* (*Hisp. Am.*) smelting furnace; (*naut.*) leg-of-mutton, sail; (*Hisp. Am.*) Indian flute.
guairabo, *n.m.* (*orn.*) night heron.
guairo, *n.m.* (*Hisp. Am.*) small two-masted coaster.
guaita, *n.f.* (*obs.*) night watch, sentinel.
guajacón, *n.m.* (*Cub.*) small fresh-water fish.
guajalote, guajolote, *n.m.* (*Mex.*) turkey; (*coll.*) simpleton.
guajamón, -mona, *a.* (*Cub.*) orange-coloured.
guájar, *n.m.f.*, **guájaras,** *n.f.pl.* fastnesses, roughest part of a mountain.
guaje, *n.m.* (*Mex., Hond.*) calabash, gourd; (*Mex.*) acacia; (*Hond., Mex.*) fool, ninny.
guajear, *v.i.* (*Hisp. Am.*) to play stupid.
guájete por guájete, *adv.* tit for tat.
guajira (1), *n.f.* (*Cub.*) popular song.
guajiro, -ra (2), *a.* (*Cub.*) rustic, rural; boorish; (*Hisp. Am.*) Indian flute. — *n.m.f.* (*Cub.*) white peasant.
¡gualá! *interj.* certainly! (*lit.* by Allah!)
gualatina, *n.f.* dish made of boiled apples, milk of almonds, spice etc.
gualda, *n.f.* [GUALDO].
gualdado, -da, *a.* weld-coloured, yellowish.
gualdera, *n.f.* (*artill.*) trail, bracket; (*carp.*) string-board; (*naut.*) whelp, check.
gualdo, -da, *a.* weld, yellow *or* gold colour. — *n.f.* (*bot.*) weld, dyer's woad, reseda; ***cara de gualda,*** pale face.
gualdón, *n.m.* (*bot.*) base-rocket.
gualdrapa, *n.f.* horse-trappings, sumpter-cloth, housing, foot-cloth; (*coll.*) tatter, rag hanging from clothes.
gualdrapazo, *n.m.* (*naut.*) flap of a sail; jerk.
gualdrapear, *v.t.* to place things head to tail. — *v.i.* (*naut.*) to flap (*sails*).
gualdrapeo, *n.m.* flapping (*sails*).
gualdrapero, *n.m.* ragamuffin, ragged fellow.

gualdrín, *n.m.* weather-strip.
guamá, *n.m.* West Indian tree much used for shade.
guama, *n.f.* (*Col., Ven.*) fruit of the guamo; (*Col.*) guamo-tree.
guamo, *n.m.* tall tree of the Leguminosæ family planted to shade the coffee plant.
guampa, *n.f.* (*Arg.*) drinking horn; (*Arg., Ur.*) horn.
guanabá, *n.m.* (*Cub.*) wading bird.
guanábana, *n.f.* (*bot.*) custard-apple.
guanábano, *n.m.* custard-apple tree.
guanaco, *n.m.* (*Chi.*) guanaco; (*Hisp. Am.*) gawk, gump.
guanajo, *n.m.* (*Cub.*) turkey; (*coll.*) simpleton.
guanche, *n.m.f.* original inhabitant of the Canaries.
guando, *n.m.* (*Hisp. Am.*) litter, stretcher.
guanero, -ra, *a.* of *or* to do with guano. — *n.f.* guano deposit *or* area.
guangoche, *n.m.* (*Hisp. Am.*) burlap.
guangocho, -cha, *a.* (*Mex.*) loose, free-fitting.
guanín, *n.m.* (*Col., W. Ind.*) base gold.
guanina, *n.f.* (*bot.*) stinking weed; (*chem.*) guanine.
guano (1), *n.m.* guano.
guano (2), *n.m.* palm tree.
guantada, *n.f.*, **guantazo,** *n.m.* slap (*with the open hand*).
guante, *n.m.* glove; key-money; ***guantes de cabritilla,*** kid gloves; ***guantes de ante,*** suede gloves; ***arrojar el guante,*** to throw down the gauntlet; ***recoger el guante,*** to take up the gauntlet; ***echar el guante a,*** to get *or* lay hold of, grab; ***echar un guante,*** to have a whip-round; ***salvo el guante,*** excuse my glove; ***como un guante,*** meek and mild, as amenable as you please; (*pl.*) extra amount, tip; ***adobar los guantes a,*** to bribe, tip.
guantelete, *n.m.* gauntlet.
guantería, *n.f.* glover's shop *or* trade.
guantero, *n.m.* glover, glove maker.
guañir [K], *v.i.* (*prov.*) to grunt.
guao, *n.m.* (*bot.*) guao.
guapamente, *adv.* (*coll.*) nonchalantly, with complete ease, without difficulty.
guapear, *v.i.* (*coll.*) to swagger about; throw one's weight about, show off.
guapetón, -tona, *a.* tall and good-looking; well set-up; well-dressed and looking great; flashy and sporty; tough and bullying.
guapeza, *n.f.* (*coll.*) daring, guts; swagger; showiness.
guapo, -pa, *a.* (*coll.*) handsome, good-looking; having guts; showy. — *n.m.f.* (*fam.*) dear, darling, love. — *n.m.* bully, tough; gallant, ladies' man.
guapote, -ta, *a.* (*coll.*) really good- and strong-looking.
guapura, *n.f.* good looks.
guara, *n.f.* (*Cub.*) chestnut tree; (*Hond.*) macaw; (*Chi.*) ridiculous affectation; tawdry ornaments.
guará, *n.m.* (*Hisp. Am.*) wolf of the pampas.
guaraca, *n.f.* (*Chi., Col., Ec., Per.*) sling; whip.
guaracha, *n.f.* (*Cub., P.R.*) Spanish clog-dance and music.
guarache, *n.m.* (*Mex.*) sandal.
guaraguao, *n.m.* (*Cub., P.R.*) predatory bird.
guaraná, *n.f.* (*Hisp. Am., bot.*) guarana, paullinia; paste and stimulating drink made from its seeds.
guarango, *a.* (*Arg., Chi., Ur.*) unmannerly, impudent. — *n.m.* (*Ec., Per., bot.*) wild huisache; (*Ven., bot.*) divi-divi.
guaraní, *a., n.m.* Guarani.
guarapo, *n.m.* (*Hisp. Am.*) juice of the sugar-cane, fermented cane-liquor.
guarapón, *n.m.* (*Arg., Chi., Per.*) wide-brimmed hat.
guarda, *n.m.f.* guard, keeper, custodian. — *n.m.* (*Hisp. Am.*) conductor, ticket-collector. — *n.f.* ward, guard, care, trust, custody; safe-keeping; guardianship; (*law*) observance; guard (*of sword*); ward (*of lock* or *key*); (*bookb.*) flyleaf; outside rib (of fan); (*mech.*) guard, plate; nun who accompanies men through the convent; ***guarda de aduana,*** customs-house officer; ***guarda de coto,*** gamekeeper; ***guarda forestal,*** forest-keeper, forest-ranger. — *interj.* take care! beware! look out!
guardabanderas, *n.m. inv.* (*naut.*) yeoman of signals.
guardabarrera, *n.m.f.* (*railw.*) gate-keeper.
guardabarros, *n.m. inv.* mudguard, fender.
guardabosque, *n.m.* forest-keeper, game-keeper.
guardabrazo, *n.m.* (*arm.*) brassard.
guardabrisa, *n.m.* glass shade for candles; (*motor.*) windscreen.
guardacabras, *n.m. inv.* goatherd.
guardacadenas, *n.m. inv.* (*naut.*) laths (*of chain-wheel*); mudguard.
guardacalada, *n.f.* window *or* opening in a roof.
guardacantón, *n.m.* spur-stone, paving-stone, check-stone.
guardacartuchos, *n.m. inv.* (*naut.*) cartridge-case.
guardacoches, *n.m. inv.* car-park attendant.
guardacostas, *n.m. inv.* revenue cutter; coast-guard ship.
guardacuños, *n.m. inv.* keeper of the dies in the mint.
guardadamas, *n.m. inv.* officer who escorts court ladies.
guardado, -da, *a.* guarded, reserved.
guardador, -ra, *a.* thrifty; observant, law-abiding; stingy. — *n.m.f.* thrifty person; observer; niggard; guardian.
guardafrenos, *n.m. inv.* (*railw.*) guard, (*Am.*) brakeman.
guardafuego, *n.m.* (*naut.*) breaming board; fire-guard.
guardaguas, *n.m. inv.* (*naut.*) spurn-water; (*carp.*) flashing-board; (*motor.*) mudguard, splash leather.
guardagujas, *n.m.* pointsman, switchman.
guardahumo, *n.m.* fire-screen; (*naut.*) smoke-sail.
guardainfante, *n.m.* farthingale, lady's hoop; (*naut.*) capstan whelp.
guardajoyas, *n.m. inv.* keeper of the crown jewels; jewel case.
guardalado, *n.m.* rail, railing (*of bridge*).
guardalmacén, *n.m.* store-keeper, warehouseman.
guardalobo, *n.m.* (*bot.*) poet's cassia.
guardamalleta, *n.f.* pelmet; valance.
guardamancebo, *n.m.* (*naut.*) man-rope.
guardamangel, *n.m.* larder.
guardamangier, *n.m.* officer in charge of victuals and staff payroll.
guardamano, *n.f.* guard (*of sword*).
guardamecha, *n.f.* (*naut.*) match-tub.
guardameta, *n.m.* goalkeeper.
guardamigo, *n.m.* prop (*placed under the chin of criminals while they are flogged*).
guardamonte, *n.m.* guard (*of a gunlock*); forester, keeper (*of a forest*).
guardamuebles, *n.m. inv.* warehouse, store(-room). for furniture; keeper (*of palace furniture*).
guardamujer, *n.f.* maid of honour.
guardapapo, *n.m.* (*arm.*) gorget.
guardapelo, *n.m.* locket.
guardapesca, *n.m.* fishery protection vessel.
guardapiés, *n.m. inv.* skirt.
guardapolvo, *n.m.* dust-guard; dust wrapper, cover; overall, dust-coat; duster, case, cap, lid; inner lid (*of watch*); tongue (*of shoe*); projection (*over a window* or *door*).
guardapuerta, *n.f.* storm-door; door-screen, door-curtain.

guardar, *v.t.* to keep, guard, protect, watch over, defend, take care of; to put away, lay by *or* up, store, store away *or* up, save; to observe, respect; ***guardar cama,*** to keep to one's bed, stay in bed; ***guardar miramientos,*** to show regard *or* deference; ***guardar rencor,*** to harbour a grievance, bear a grudge; ***guardar silencio,*** to keep silent; ***guardar la cara,*** to keep in the background; ***guardar la línea,*** to keep one's figure; ***guardar las apariencias,*** to keep up appearances; ***guardar las distancias,*** to keep one's distance; ***guardar las formas,*** to comply with convention; (*coll.*) ***se la tiene guardada,*** he has got it in for him. — **guardarse,** *v.r.* to be on one's guard (against), look out (for); ***guardarse de,*** to avoid; ***guárdate muy mucho de mentir,*** take jolly good care that you do not lie.

guardarraya, *n.f.* boundary.

guardarrío, *n.m.* (*orn.*) kingfisher.

guardarropa, *n.m.f.* cloakroom attendant; (*theat.*) property-man *or* woman. — *n.m.* cloak-room, coat-room; wardrobe, clothes-press; (*bot.*) lavender-cotton.

guardarropía, *n.f.* (*theat.*) wardrobe; ***de guardarropía,*** make-believe, pretend.

guardarruedas, *n.m. inv.* fender (*to protect the lintel of a house against the wheels of carriages*).

guardasilla, *n.f.* chair rail.

guardasol, *n.m.* sunshade, parasol.

guardatimón, *n.m.* (*naut.*) stern-chaser.

guardavajilla, *n.f.* room for keeping the royal plate *or* table-service.

guardavela, *n.m.* (*naut.*) small purchase rope (*to secure sails*).

guardavía, *n.m.* (*railw.*) signalman, line-keeper.

guardería, *n.f.* keepership; day-nursery.

guardesa, *n.f.* female-keeper; keeper's wife.

guardia, *n.m.* policeman; guardsman; ***guardia municipal,*** policeman; ***guardia de tráfico,*** traffic policeman. — *n.f.* guard; guard duty, turn; (*naut.*) watch; defence, protection; ***guardia de estribor,*** starboard watch; ***guardia de babor,*** larboard watch; (*mil.*) ***estar de guardia,*** to be on duty; ***estar en guardia,*** to be on guard; ***salir de guardia,*** to come off guard; ***guardia municipal,*** town police; ***guardia civil,*** Civil Guard; ***guardia de corps,*** Life Guards; ***guardia de asalto,*** shock police; ***guardia de tráfico,*** traffic police.

guardiamarina, *n.m.* midshipman.

guardián, -diana, *n.m.f.* guard, keeper; warden, watchman. — *n.m.* guardian (*Franciscan order*); (*naut.*) boatswain's mate; quarterman; gunner's yeoman; (*naut.*) hawser.

guardianía, *n.f.* guardianship (*of a convent*).

guardilla, *n.f.* garret, attic; (*sew.*) guard, welt; each of the two extreme thick teeth of a comb.

guardillón, *n.m.* large loft.

guardín, *n.m.* tiller-rope, tiller-chain; port-lanyard.

guardoso, -sa, *a.* frugal, thrifty, parsimonious; niggardly, stingy.

guarecer [9], *v.t.* to shelter, shield. — **guarecerse,** *v.r.* to take refuge *or* shelter.

guarén, *n.m.* (*Chi.*) water-rat.

guarentigio, -gia, *a.* applied to a contract containing a warranty clause.

guaria, *n.f.* (*C.R.*) orchid.

guariao, *n.m.* (*Cub.*) (*orn.*) limpkin.

guaricha, *n.f.* (*Col., Ec., Ven.*) female, woman; (*Ec.*) soldier's moll.

guarida, *n.f.* den, lair; lurking-place, haunt.

guarimán, *n.m.* (*Hisp. Am.*) guariman-tree.

guarín, *n.m.* sucking pig.

guarisapo, *n.m.* (*Chi.*) tadpole.

guarismo, *n.m.* (*arith.*) figure, digit.

guarne, *n.m.* turn of a cable *or* tackle.

guarnecedor, -ra, *a.* garnishing, trimming. — *n.m.f.* garnisher, furnisher, trimmer.

guarnecer [9], *v.t.* to garnish, adorn, decorate, dress, deck, array; (*sew.*) to trim, bind, edge, face, border, line, welt; to provide, furnish; to accoutre, equip; (*build.*) to plaster; (*jewel.*) to set; (*arm.*) to put a guard on (*a sword*); to harness (*horses* or *mules*); (*mil.*) to garrison.

guarnecido, *n.m.* (*build.*) plastering; stucco-work.

guarnés, *n.m.* harness-room.

guarnición, *n.f.* (*sew.*) trimming, binding, edging, valance, welt, flounce, furbelow, garniture, garnish; (*mech.*) packing; (*jewel.*) setting; (*mil.*) garrison; (*arm.*) guard (*of a sword*); (*pl.* **guarniciones**) gears *or* traces (*of mules and horses*); harness; steel armour.

guarnicionar, *v.t.* to garrison.

guarnicionería, *n.f.* shop of a harness-maker; harness making.

guarnicionero, *n.m.* harness-maker.

guarniel, *n.m.* leather pouch; (*Mex.*) powder-flask.

guarnigón, *n.m.* young quail.

guarnimiento, *n.m.* lines *or* ropes for reeving.

guarnir [Q], *v.t.* to trim; (*naut.*) to reeve; to rig.

guaro (1), *n.m.* small parrot.

guaro (2), *n.m.* (*Hisp. Am.*) sugar-cane fire-water.

guarrada, *n.f.* filthy trick.

guarrería, *n.f.* filthiness; filthy thing to do *or* say.

guarro, -rra, *a.* filthy. — *n.m.f.* pig, sow; (*fig.*) filthy pig, filthy person.

¡guarte! *interj.* [*contr.* of ***guárdate***]; take care! beware! look out!

guaruba, *n.f.* (*Hisp. Am.*) red-necked parrot; howling monkey.

guarura, *n.f.* (*Ven.*) large snail.

guasa, *n.f.* [GUASO].

guasanga, *n.f.* (*Hisp. Am.*) shindy.

guasanguero, -ra, *a.* (*Hisp. Am.*) jolly, merry, noisy.

guasasa, *n.f.* (*Cub.*) swarm of mosquitoes.

guasca, *n.f.* (*Hisp. Am.*) cord, thong, whip; ***dar guasca,*** to whip, scourge.

guasearse, *v.r.* to joke, make fun.

guasería, *n.f.* (*Arg., Chi.*) dullness; coarseness.

guaso, -sa, *a.* (*Hisp. Am.*) rustic, rural; coarse, uncouth, churlish. — *n.f.* (*coll.*) joking, fooling, facetiousness; (*And.*) trickiness; (*And.*) tediousness; (*Cub.*) jew-fish; ***estar de guasa,*** to be in a facetious mood.

guasón, -sona, *a.* (*coll.*) joking, mocking. — *n.m.f.* joker, mocker, funny-man.

guasquear, *v.t.* (*Hisp. Am.*) to whip, scourge.

guata, *n.f.* wadding, padded cotton wool; (*Hisp. Am.*) belly, paunch; (*Hisp. Am.*) warping, bulging; ***echar guata,*** to get fat.

guataca, *n.f.* (*Cub.*) spade; (*coll.*) large ear.

guataquear, *v.t.* (*Cub.*) to spade, clear ground with the spade.

guatemalteco, -ca, *a.*, *n.m.f.* Guatemalan.

guateque, *n.m.* party, do; ***flor de guateque,*** party-goer.

guau, *n.m.* (*dog's bark*) bow-wow.

¡guay! *interj.* alas! alack! woe!

guaya, *n.f.* lament.

guayaba, *n.f.* guava, guava apple; (*coll.*) girl, bird, chick; (*Hisp. Am.*) lie.

guayabal, *n.m.* plantation of guava trees.

guayabera, *n.f.* (*Cub.*) short loose jacket.

guayabo, *n.m.* guava tree.

guayaca, *n.f.* (*Arg., Bol., Chi.*) bag, sack.

guayacán, guayaco, *n.m.* lignum-vitæ tree, guaiacum.

guayacana, *n.f.* date-plum.

guayacol, *n.m.* (*chem.*) guaiacol.

guayadero, *n.m.* (*obs.*) wailing room.

guayapil, guayapín, *n.m.* (*Hisp. Am.*) loose Indian dress.

guayaquil, *a.* of Guayaquil. — *n.m.* cacao of Guayaquil.
guayaquileño, -ña, *a., n.m.f.* (native) of Guayaquil.
guayar, *v.i.* (*obs.*) to wail, moan.
guayo, *n.m.* (*Chi.*) guayo tree.
guayuco, *n.m.* (*Col., Ven.*) loin-cloth.
guayusa, *n.f.* (*Ec.*) maté plant.
guazapa, *n.f.* (*Guat., Hond.*) teetotum.
guazubirá, *n.m.* (*Arg.*) wild deer.
gubernamental, *a.* governmental, government.
gubernativo, -va, *a.* administrative, governmental, government.
gubia, *n.f.* (*carp.*) gouge, (*artill.*) vent-searcher.
gubilete, *n.m.* (*obs.*) vase.
guedeja, *n.f.* long lock of hair; (*pl.*) locks.
güeldo, *n.m.* bait.
güelfo, -fa, *a., n.m.f.* Guelph.
guelte, gueltre, *n.m.* money, wealth.
güepil, güipil, *n.m.* (*Mex.*) sack of rich cloth.
güérmeces, *n.m. pl.* morbid swelling (*in the throat of birds of prey*).
guerra, *n.f.* war, warfare; billiards; ***guerra a muerte,*** war to the death, mortal combat; ***guerra sin cuartel,*** war without quarter; ***tener la guerra declarada a,*** to have it in for; ***dar guerra,*** to give trouble *or* bother; ***declarar la guerra a,*** to declare war on; ***armar en guerra,*** to fit *or* equip (*a ship*) for war; ***hacer la guerra,*** to wage war; ***guerra relámpago,*** blitzkrieg; ***guerra fría,*** cold war; ***guerra mundial,*** world war.
guerreador, -ra, *a.* warlike; warring.
guerreante, *a., n.m.f.* warring; warrior.
guerrear, *v.i.* to war, wage war, fight.
guerrero, -ra, *a.* warlike; warring. — *n.m.f.* warrior, fighter. — *n.f.* (*mil.*) tunic.
guerrilla, *n.f.* guerrilla band; card game; ***guerra de guerrillas,*** guerrilla warfare.
guerrillear, *v.i.* to wage guerrilla warfare.
guerrillero, *n.m.* guerrilla fighter; guerrilla leader.
guía, *n.m.f.* guide; leader. — *n.f.* guide, guidance; guide-book; directory; (*com.*) custom-house docket; permit to convey goods; young shoot (*left on a vine* or *tree for training others*); young shoot or sucker (*of a vine*); (*mech.*) guide, rule, guide-bar, guide-pin, guide-screw, guide-tube; (*naut.*) guy, leader, span, hauling-line, preventer-rope; (*pyr.*) fuse; (*min.*) leader; handle-bar (*of a bicycle*); guard (*of a fan*); leader, foremost horse; (jeweller's) guide tool; reins (*for controlling the leader horses*); moustache ends; ***a guías,*** driving four-in-hand; (*pl.*) guidelines.
guiadera, *n.f.* guide *or* conductor (*in mills*); (*pl.*) upright guides (*in oil-mills, mine-lifts etc.*).
guiado, -da, *a.* having a permit.
guiador, -ra, *a.* guiding, directing. — *n.m.f.* guide, director, leader.
guiar [L], *v.t.* to guide, lead, conduct, show the way; to drive; to pilot; to steer; to train (*plants*). — **guiarse,** *v.r.* to be led (by), go (by), follow; ***no te guíes por él,*** don't go by him.
guija, *n.f.* pebble; (*bot.*) blue vetch; (*pl.*) shingle.
guijarral, *n.m.* heap of pebbles, area of shingle.
guijarrazo, *n.m.* blow with a pebble.
guijarreño, -ña, *a.* pebbly; (*coll.*) hardy, strong.
guijarro, *n.m.* (large) pebble.
guijarroso, -sa, *a.* pebbly, shingly.
guijeño, -ña, *a.* pebbly; (*coll.*) hard, relentless.
guijo, *n.m.* gravel; (*mach.*) gudgeon.
guijón, *n.m.* caries.
guijoso, -sa, *a.* gravelly; pebbly.
guilla, *n.f.* plentiful harvest.
guillado, -da, *a.* (*coll.*) cracked, crazy, potty.
guilladura, *n.f.* (*coll.*) crack-pot thing to do *or* say.
guillame, *n.m.* joiner's rabbet-plane.
guillarse, *v.r.* (*coll.*) to get cracked, go crazy *or* potty; (*coll.*) ***guillárselas,*** to clear off, light out, scram.
guilledín, *n.m.* gelding.
Guillelmo, Guillén, Guillermo, *n.m.* William.
guillote, *a.* lazy; simple-minded. — *n.m.* harvester; iron pin.
guillotina, *n.f.* guillotine; ***ventana de guillotina,*** sash window.
guillotinar, *v.t.* to guillotine.
guimbalete, *n.m.* pump handle.
guimbarda, *n.f.* (*carp.*) grooving plane.
guinchar, *v.t.* to prick, goad.
guincho, *n.m.* goad; (*Cub.*) sea-hawk.
guinda, *n.f.* (mazard) cherry; cocktail cherry; glacé cherry; (*naut.*) height of masts.
guindado, -da, *a.* prepared with cherries.
guindajos, *n.m.pl.* (*Cub.*) hangings, fringes, tassels.
guindal, *n.m.* mazard tree, cherry tree.
guindalera, *n.f.* plantation of mazard trees, cherry orchard.
guindaleta, *n.f.* hemp *or* leather rope; fulcrum (*of scales*).
guindaleza, *n.f.* hawser.
guindamaina, *n.f.* (*naut.*) dipping the flag.
guindar, *v.t.* to hoist, lift, winch; (*coll.*) to hang; (*coll.*) to pinch.
guindaste, *n.m.* (*mech.*) horse, frame; (*naut.*) timber-head tackle.
guindilla, *n.f.* cayenne pepper. — *n.m.* (*coll.*) bobby, copper.
guindillo de Indias, *n.m.* red pepper shrub.
guindo, *n.m.* cherry tree; mazard tree; (*coll.*) ***caer(se) de un guindo,*** not to be with it, find o.s. all at sea.
guindola, *n.f.* (*naut.*) triangular hanging stage; lifebuoy; (*naut.*) float of the log.
Guinea, *n.f.* Guinea.
guineo, -nea, *a.* Guinea, Guinean; ***gallina guinea,*** guinea-hen. — *n.m.f.* Guinean, native of Guinea. — *n.m.* negro dance and tune; (*Cub.*) banana. — *n.f.* guinea.
guinga, *n.f.* gingham.
guinja, *n.f.*, **guinjo,** *n.m.* jujube.
guiñada, guiñadura, *n.f.* wink; (*naut.*) yaw, lurch.
guiñador, -ra, *a.* winking. — *n.m.f.* winker.
guiñapiento, -ta, guiñaposo, -sa, *a.* ragged, tattered.
guiñapo, *n.m.* tatter, rag; wretched object; (*Chi.*) ground maize used for brewing chicha.
guiñar, *v.t., v.i.* to wink; to wink at; (*naut.*) to yaw, lurch.
guiño, *n.m.* wink.
guión, *n.m.* hyphen; script; cross, standard; gonfalon; master; leader (*of a dance*); (*mil.*) guidon; (*naut.*) loom (*of an oar*); (*mus.*) repeat.
guionaje, *n.m.* office of guide *or* conductor.
guionista, *n.m.f.* script-writer.
guipar, *v.t.* (*sl.*) to see, see through; ***te he guipado,*** I've caught on to you, I've got your number.
guipuzcoano, -na, *a., n.m.f.* (native) of Guipuzcoa.
güira, *n.f.* (*Hisp. Am.*) calabash tree.
guirigay, *n.m.* (*coll.*) gibberish; jargon; hubbub, uproar.
guirindola, *n.f.* breast, frill (*of shirt*).
guirlache, *n.m.* roast almond caramel.
guirnalda, (*obs.*) **guirlanda,** *n.f.* garland, wreath; (*naut.*) puddening; (*mil.*) light ball; (*bot.*) globe amaranth.
guirnaldeta, *n.f.* small garland.
güiro, *n.m.* (*Hisp. Am.*) green Indian corn stalk; bottle-gourd; (*Cub.*) musical instrument.
guiropa, *n.f.* meat dish.
guirre, *n.m.* (*Can. Isles*) vulture.
guisa, *n.f.* wise, way, manner; ***a guisa de,*** in the manner of; by way of.
guisado, *n.m.* stew; ragout, fricassee.

guisador, -ra, guisandero, -ra, *n.m.f.* cook.
guisantal, *n.m.* pea plot.
guisante, *n.m.* pea; ***guisante de olor,*** sweet-pea.
guisar, *v.t.* to cook; to stew; (*fig.*) to cook up.
guiso, *n.m.* cooked dish; stew.
guisopillo, *n.m.* small water-sprinkler.
guisote, *n.m.* crude *or* coarse dish.
guita (I), *n.f.* string, twine; (*coll.*) cash, dough.
guitar, *v.t.* to sew with string *or* twine.
guitarra, *n.f.* guitar; (*mas.*) muller (*for pulverizing gypsum*).
guitarrazo, *n.m.* blow with a guitar.
guitarrear, *v.i.* to strum (*the guitar*).
guitarrero, -ra, *n.m.f.* guitar-maker; guitar-seller.
guitarresco, -ca, *a.* (*coll.*) of *or* to do with guitars *or* the guitar.
guitarrillo, *n.m.* guitar with four strings.
guitarrista, *n.m.f.* guitarist, guitar-player.
guitarro, *n.m.* four-string guitar.
guitarrón, *n.m.* large guitar; (*coll.*) sharp operator.
guitero, -ra, *n.m.f.* twine-maker.
guito, -ta (2), *a.* (*Arg.*) treacherous, vicious.
guitón, -tona, *n.m.f.* vagrant, vagabond, tramp.
guitonear, *v.i.* to idle about, lead a vagabond life.
guitonería, *n.f.* idleness; vagabond life.
guizazo, *n.m.* (*Cub.*) weed.
guizgar [B], *v.t.* to excite, urge on, egg on.
guizque, *n.m.* boat-hook; (*prov.*) sting (*of a wasp*).
guja, *n.f.* halbert, voulge.
gula, *n.f.* gluttony.
gules, *n.m.pl.* (*her.*) gules.
guloso, -sa, *a.* gluttonous, greedy.
gulusmear, *v.i.* (*coll.*) to eat tit-bits.
gullería [GOLLERÍA].
gulloría, *n.f.* lark.
gúmena, *n.f.* anchor-cable.
gumeneta, *n.f.* small cable.
gumía, *n.f.* Moorish dagger *or* poniard.
gumífero, -ra, *a.* gummiferous, gum-producing.
gurbia (*Hisp. Am.*) [GUBIA].
gurbión, *n.m.* coarse twisted silk; silk material; gum-resin from spurge.
gurdo, -da, *a.* silly, nonsensical.
guripa, *n.m.* (*sl.*) soldier.
gurrar, *v.i.* (*naut.*) to get clear (of another ship).
gurriato, *n.m.* nestling sparrow.
gurrufero, *n.m.* (*coll.*) ugly, vicious nag.
gurrullada, *n.f.* (*coll.*) gang, crowd of people.
gurrumina, *n.f.* (*coll.*) uxoriousness; (*Hisp. Am.*) trifle; (*Hond.*) sly person.
gurrumino, *a.* weak, run-down. — *n.m.* (*coll.*) henpecked husband; (*Bol., Per.*) coward, faint-hearted person; (*Mex., prov.*) small child.
gurullo, *n.m.* (*prov.*) lump, knot.
gurullón, *n.m.* knot (*of wool in cloths*).
gurumete [GRUMETE].
gurupa [GRUPA].
gurupera [GRUPERA].
gurupetín, *n.m.* small crupper.
gurvio, -via, *a.* curved.
gusanear, *v.i.* to itch; to swarm, seethe, teem.
gusanera, *n.f.* place full of worms; (*coll.*) ruling passion.
gusaniento, -ta, *a.* wormy, maggoty.
gusanillo, *n.m.* small worm *or* grub; gold, silver *or* silk twist; twist-stitch embroidery; (*mech.*) bit (of a gimlet *or* auger); (*coll.*) **matar el gusanillo,** to calm *or* allay one's hunger; to calm *or* allay a want *or* feeling of relentlessness.
gusano, *n.m.* worm, maggot, grub; (*fig.*) worm; ***gusano de seda,*** silk-worm; ***gusano de luz,*** glow-worm; ***gusano de la conciencia,*** nagging conscience; ***gusano de San Antón,*** wood-louse; ***gusano revoltón,*** vine inch-worm.
gusarapiento, -ta, *a.* wormy, rotten.
gusarapo, *n.m.* water-worm.
gusil, *n.m.* Russian harp.
gustable, *a.* tastable.
gustadura, *n.f.* tasting, sampling.
gustar, *v.t.* to taste, sample. — *v.i.* to be pleasing (***a,*** to); ***gustar de,*** to take a pleasure in; ***no me gustan las manzanas,*** I don't like apples; ***nos gusta viajar,*** we like travelling; ***como usted guste,*** as you like *or* please.
gustativo, -va, *a.* of taste.
gustazo, *n.m.* (*coll.*) great pleasure; ***darse el gustazo de,*** to enjoy the immense pleasure of, have the tremendous satisfaction of.
gustillo, *n.m.* slight *or* subtle taste *or* flavour.
gusto, *n.m.* taste; flavour, savour; relish; fancy, whim; pleasure; liking; ***de buen gusto,*** in good taste; ***el gusto del día,*** the current taste; ***con mucho gusto,*** with great pleasure; ***dar gusto a,*** to gratify the wishes of; ***gusto dañado (estragado),*** spoiled taste, ruined palate; ***sobre gustos no hay nada escrito,*** there's no accounting for taste; ***darse el gusto de,*** to give o.s. the satisfaction of; ***a mi gusto,*** to my satisfaction; ***estar a gusto,*** to feel at home, comfortable; ***tengo mucho gusto en conocerle,*** I'm very glad to meet you; ***ser del gusto de,*** to be to the liking of; ***coger (tomar) (el) gusto a,*** to get a liking for.
gustosamente, *adv.* gladly, with pleasure.
gustoso, -sa, *a.* tasty, savoury, palatable; agreeable, pleasant, pleasing; glad, willing, ready.
gutagamba, *n.f.* gamboge tree; gamboge gum.
gutapercha, *n.f.* gutta-percha.
gutiámbar, *n.f.* gamboge.
gutífero, -ra, *a.* guttiferous, gum-yielding.
gutiforme, *a.* guttiform.
gutural, *a.* guttural.
guturoso, -sa, *a.* (*bot.*) throated; throaty.
guzla, *n.f.* one-string rebec, gusla.
guzmán, *n.m.* nobleman who formerly served as midshipman *or* cadet.

H

H, h, *n.f.* letter H, h.
ha, *3rd pers. sing. pres. indic.* [HABER].
haba, *n.f.* bean; kernel; voting ball; (*vet.*) tumour; ***haba verde,*** broad bean; ***haba panosa,*** horse bean; ***haba de las Indias,*** sweet-pea; ***son habas contadas,*** it's cut and dried, clear cut; that's all there is to it; it's a sure thing; ***en todas partes cuecen habas,*** you get the same thing everywhere; ***ésas son otras habas,*** that's another kettle of fish.
habado, -da, *a.* (*vet.*) having a tumour; dappled (*as a horse*).
Habana, *n.f.* ***La* —,** Havana.
habanero, -ra, *a., n.m.f.* (native) of Havana. — *n.f.* habanera (*dance and tune*).
habano, -na, *a.* Havana. — *n.m.* Havana cigar.
habar, *n.m.* bean-field.
háber, *n.m.* doctor of the law (*among the Jews*).
haber, *n.m.* property, income, assets (*usu. pl.* **haberes**); (*book-keeping*) credit (*abbr.* Cr.). — *v.t.* [19] (*obs.*) to have; to get, catch. — *aux. v.* [19] to have; ***hemos ido,*** we have gone *or* been; ***habíamos ido,*** we had gone *or* been; ***hemos ido ayer,*** we went yesterday; ***haber de,*** to have to, be to, be bound to, be due to; ***he de ir mañana,*** I have to go to-morrow, I'll be going to-morrow; ***han de llegar pronto,*** they are bound to get here soon. — *v. impers.* (*3rd pers. pres. ind.*, ***hay***) there is, there are; ***hay un hombre aquí,*** there is a man here; ***hay varias personas,*** there are several people; ***ha habido un accidente,*** there has been an accident; ***habrá una guerra,*** there will be a war; ***¿cuánto hay de aquí a . . .?*** how far is it from here to . . . ?; ***lo que hay es,*** the fact is; ***no hay más que ver cómo,*** you only have to see how; ***no hay remedio,*** it can't be helped; ***¿qué hay?*** how are things? what's to do?; ***no hay de qué,*** don't mention it, not at all; ***hay que hacerlo,*** it has to be done; ***¡hay que ver!*** fancy! well!; ***algo habrá,*** there must be a reason; ***¡habrá desvergüenza!*** can you credit such a disgraceful thing?; (*obs.*) ***ha*** (*3rd pers. pres. ind.*), ago; ***tres años ha,*** three years ago; ***poco tiempo ha,*** not long ago. — **haberse,** *v.r.* to behave, conduct o.s.; ***habérselas con,*** to have it out with; to have to deal with.
haberío, *n.m.* beast of burden; livestock.
habichuela, *n.f.* French-bean, kidney-bean.
habiente, *a.* (*law*) having, possessing.
hábil, *a.* clever, skilful, smart; (*law*) fit, able, qualified; ***día hábil,*** working day.
habilidad, *n.f.* cleverness, talent, skill, adroitness; (*pl.* **habilidades**) accomplishments.
habilidoso, -sa, *a.* skilful, clever, adroit.
habilitación, *n.f.* habilitation, qualification; equipment, outfit; office of a paymaster; ***habilitación de bandera,*** concession to a foreign vessel to engage in the coasting trade.
habilitado, *n.m.* paymaster; accountant; (*law*) deputy of a judicial secretary.
habilitador, -ra, *a.* habilitating, qualifying. — *n.m.* qualifier, outfitter.
habilitar, *v.t.* to habilitate, qualify; to prepare, make ready *or* available; to fit out.
habiloso (*Chi.*) [HABILIDOSO].
habitable, *a.* habitable.
habitación, *n.f.* dwelling, habitation; room, bedroom.
habitáculo, *n.m.* dwelling.
habitador, -ra, *n.m.f.* inhabitant, resident, dweller.
habitante, *a.* inhabiting. — *n.m.* inhabitant, dweller, resident.
habitar, *v.t., v.i.* to inhabit, live, dwell, reside (in).
hábito, *n.m.* habit; ***caballero del hábito de Santiago,*** knight of the military order of Saint James; ***el hábito no hace al monje,*** it's not the cowl that makes the monk; ***tener por hábito,*** to be in the habit (of); (*eccles.*) ***tomar el hábito,*** to profess, take vows; (*pl.*) dress of ecclesiastics; (*coll.*) ***ahorcar*** or ***colgar los hábitos,*** to doff the cassock; to abandon a calling *or* profession.
habituación, *n.f.* habituation, accustoming.
habitual, *a.* habitual, usual, customary, regular.
habituar [M], *v.t.* to accustom, habituate, inure. — **habituarse,** *v.r.* to get used (***a,*** to).
habitud, *n.f.* habitude; respect, relation.
habiz, *n.m.* donation, in trust, of immovable property to a Mohammedan religious institution.
habla, *n.f.* speech; language, idiom, dialect; discourse, address; ***de habla española,*** Spanish-speaking; ***me dejó sin habla, me quitó el habla,*** it left me speechless, he left me speechless; ***perdió el habla,*** he lost his speech; ***negar el habla a,*** to cut, not to speak to; ***ponerse al habla con,*** to get in touch *or* contact with; to speak to; ***¡al habla!*** speaking!; ***al habla,*** in contact; (*naut.*) within hailing distance.
hablado, -da, *a.* ***bien hablado,*** well-spoken; ***mal hablado,*** ill-spoken, foul-mouthed.
hablador, -ra, *a.* talkative.
habladuría, *n.f.* impertinent speech; gossip, empty talk.
hablanchín, -china, hablantín, -tina, *a.* (*coll.*) talkative.
hablante, *a.* speaking, talking. — *n.m.f.* speaker.
hablar, *v.t., v.i.* to speak; to talk; to court, woo; (*naut.*) to hail; ***hablar de,*** to talk about; to discuss; to mention; ***hablar con,*** to talk to, speak with; ***hablar a,*** to talk at *or* down to; ***hablar por vicio, hablar por hablar,*** to talk for the sake of it; ***hablar por,*** to speak for; to stand up for; ***hablar al caso,*** to speak to the point; ***hablar alto,*** to talk loudly; ***hablar en cristiano,*** to talk plain Spanish *or* straight Castilian; ***hablar en plata,*** to speak bluntly *or* plainly; ***hablando en plata,*** not to put too fine a point on it; ***hablar entre dientes,*** to mutter, mumble; ***hablar en serio*** or ***de veras,*** to talk in earnest, mean it, mean what one says; ***hablar por demás, hablar de la mar,*** to talk to no purpose, waste one's breath; ***hablar por los codos,*** to talk one's head off; ***hablar por boca de ganso,*** to parrot others, echo what others say; ***hablar a tontas y a locas,*** to talk wildly; ***hablar el último,*** to have the last say *or* word; ***¡ni hablar!*** no fear! not likely! not on your life!; ***dar que hablar,*** to give cause for talk; ***habla tú,*** you do the talking; ***hablen cartas y callen barbas,*** actions speak louder than words; ***no se hablan,*** they do not speak (to one another), they are not on speaking terms; ***no se habla con él,*** he is not on speaking terms with him; ***se habla inglés,*** English spoken.
hablillas, *n.f.pl.* gossip, chitchat; babbling, foolish talk.
hablista, *n.m.f.* professional speaker.
hablistán, *a., n.m.f.* (*coll.*) talkative (person).
habón, *n.m.* wheal.
haca [JACA].
hacán, *n.m.* learned man *or* doctor (*among the Jews*).
hacanea, *n.f.* nag, small horse.
hacecico, hacecillo, hacecito, *n.m.* small sheaf; fascicle; ***hacecillo de rayos luminosos,*** shaft of light.
hacedero, -ra, *a.* feasible, practicable.
Hacedor, *n.m.* Maker.
hacedor, *n.m.* steward, manager of a farm.
hacendado, -da, *a.* landed, owning real estate. — *n.m.* landholder; gentleman farmer; (*Arg.*) rancher.
hacendar [1], *v.t.* to transfer *or* make over (*the property of an estate*). — **hacendarse,** *v.r.* to purchase real estate and settle.
hacendera, *n.f.* [HACENDERO].

hacendero, -ra, *a.* industrious and thrifty. — *n.m.* Almadén miner. — *n.f.* compulsory work.
hacendista, *n.m.f.* economist; financial expert.
hacendoso, -sa, *a.* assiduous, diligent.
hacer [20], *v.t.* to make; to do; to pack (*a case*); to give (*an order*); to cause; to accustom; to play (*a part*); to imagine (*s.o.*) to be; to hold, contain; to have (done); to ask (*a question*); ***hacía a Juan en París,*** I imagined John to be in Paris; ***le hacíamos muy rico,*** we imagined him to be very wealthy; ***hacer acto de presencia,*** to put in an appearance; ***hacer su agosto,*** to make one's pile, make hay while the sun shines; ***hacer aguas,*** to pass water; ***hacer antesala,*** to dance attendance; ***hacer añicos,*** to smash to smithereens; ***hacer la cuenta sin la huéspeda,*** to fail to count the cost, overlook the drawbacks; ***hacer daño,*** to hurt; (*naut.*) ***hacer derrota,*** to set course; ***hacer fiesta,*** to take a holiday *or* day off; ***hacer fiestas a,*** to make a fuss of; ***hacer frente a,*** to face up to, stand up to; ***hacer fuego,*** to fire; (*naut.*) ***hacer fuerza de vela,*** to crowd (on) sail; ***hacer gente,*** to raise soldiers; ***hacer por hacer,*** to do things for the sake of it; (*fig.*) ***no hemos hecho nada,*** we are back where we started, back to square one; ***¿qué se le va a hacer?*** what help is there for it? what can be done about it?; ***hacer juego,*** to place (one's) bets; to match; (*coll.*) ***hacerla buena,*** to make a fine old mess; ***hacer milagros,*** to work miracles; to do wonders; ***hacer oídos de mercader a,*** to turn a deaf ear to; ***hacer mal de ojo a,*** to put the evil eye on; ***hacer pedazos,*** to smash to pieces; ***hacer perder los estribos,*** to push too far; ***hacer presente,*** to recall, bring to (*s.o.'s*) mind; ***hacer saber,*** to make known; ***hacer señas,*** to motion, signal, wave; ***hacer buen tercio,*** to do a good turn; ***hacer la vista gorda,*** to turn a blind eye; (*naut.*) ***hacer agua,*** to leak; ***hacer bancarrota,*** to go bankrupt, go broke; ***hacer caso,*** to pay attention, heed; ***hacer de(l) cuerpo,*** to evacuate the bowels; ***dar que hacer,*** to make work *or* give trouble; ***hacer memoria,*** to try to remember, make an effort to remember; ***hacer de las suyas,*** to get up to one's (usual) tricks; ***hacer de tripas corazón,*** to pluck up courage; ***hacer ver que,*** to pretend that, make out that; ***ha venido a hacer bueno al otro,*** by comparison he makes the other one look good. — *v.i.* to act; to matter; to fit; ***eso no hace al caso,*** that has nothing to do with it; ***hacer por*** or ***para,*** to endeavour, make an effort to; ***hacer (como) que,*** to pretend that; ***hacer de,*** to act as; ***hacer de(l) cuerpo,*** to evacuate the bowels. — **hacerse,** *v.r.* to become, get to be; to grow; to move, shift; ***hacerse con,*** to get, get hold of; ***hacerse a,*** to get used to; ***se hace tarde,*** it's getting late; ***se me hace la boca agua,*** my mouth waters, it makes my mouth water; ***hacerse chiquito,*** to be over-modest, take a back seat; ***no se hizo (de) rogar,*** he didn't have to be asked twice; ***hacerse de nuevas,*** to feign ignorance, pretend that one didn't know. — *v. impers.* to be (*of the weather* or *time*); ***hace aire,*** it's windy; ***hace calor,*** it's warm; ***ayer hizo un año,*** it was a year ago yesterday; ***estar a medio hacer,*** to be half-done; ***estar por hacer,*** to remain still to be done.
hacia, *prep.* toward, towards; about; ***hacia adelante,*** forward; ***hacia atrás,*** backward; ***hacia acá,*** hither; ***hacia allá,*** thither; ***hacia casa, hacia su país,*** homeward; ***hacia popa,*** abaft; ***hacia proa,*** forward; ***hacia el mar,*** seaward; ***hacia las siete,*** about seven o'clock.
hacienda, *n.f.* landed property; farm, ranch; estate, fortune, wealth; finance; ***Ministro de Hacienda,*** Chancellor of the Exchequer; ***Hacienda Pública,*** Exchequer; (*Mex., min.*) ***hacienda de beneficio,*** processing plant *or* works; (*pl.*) domestic work, household duties.
hacina, *n.f.* stack, rick; pile, heap.
hacinador, -ra, *a.* heaping, piling; packing, crowding. — *n.m.f.* heaper, piler.
hacinamiento, *n.m.* heaping, piling; heap, pile; packing, crowding.
hacinar, *v.t.* to heap, pile, stack; to pack, crowd.
hacha (1), *n.f.* axe, hatchet; tomahawk; old Spanish dance; ***hacha de armas,*** battle-axe.
hacha (2), *n.f.* large taper with four wicks; ***hacha de viento,*** flambeau, torch.
hachazo, *n.m.* blow *or* stroke with an axe; (*tauro.*) side blow, grazing blow; (*Col.*) sudden bound (*of a horse*); ***matar a hachazos,*** to hack to death with an axe *or* axes.
hache, *n.f.* letter H; ***llámele usted hache,*** it is the same thing, it doesn't matter what you call it, it doesn't make any difference what you call it; ***por hache o por be,*** for one reason or another.
hachear, *v.t.* to cut with an axe; to hack; to hew. — *v.i.* to wield an axe, hack.
hachero (1), *n.m.* wood-cutter; axeman; (*mil.*) sapper.
hachero (2), *n.m.* torch stand; torch-bearer.
hacheta, *n.f.* small axe, hatchet.
hachich, hachís, *n.m.* hashish.
hacho, *n.m.* firebrand, torch; beacon hill.
hachón, *n.m.* large torch *or* firebrand; cresset.
hachote, *n.m.* large axe.
hachuela, *n.f.* small axe, hatchet.
hada, *n.f.* fairy; ***hada madrina,*** fairy godmother.
hadado, -da, *a.* fateful; magic; ***bien hadado,*** lucky; ***mal hadado,*** ill-fated.
hadar, *v.t.* to divine, foretell; to fate; to cast a spell on.
hado, *n.m.* fate, destiny.
haedo [HAYAL].
hafiz, *n.m.* keeper; overseer, supervisor.
hagiografía, *n.f.* hagiography.
hagiógrafo, *n.m.* hagiographer.
haiga, *n.m.* flashy car, flash bus.
haitiano, -na, *a., n.m.f.* Haitian.
¡hala! *interj.* (*naut.*) pull! haul!; come on! get cracking!; phew! crikey!
halacabuyas, halacuerdas, *n.m. inv.* apprentice sailor; (*coll.*) fresh-water sailor.
halagador, -ra, *a.* flattering.
halagar [B], *v.t.* to flatter; to please, gratify.
halago, *n.m.* flattery.
halagüeño, -ña, *a.* flattering; (*fig.*) bright, rosy, promising.
halar, *v.t., v.i.* (*naut.*) to haul, pull, heave, tug.
halcón, *n.m.* falcon, hawk.
halconado, -da, *a.* falcon-like, hawk-like.
halconcico, halconcillo, halconcito, *n.m.* small *or* young falcon *or* hawk.
halconear, *v.i.* to act brazenly.
halconera, *n.f.* place where falcons are kept.
halconería, *n.f.* falconry.
halconero, *n.m.* falconer, hawk trainer.
halda, *n.f.* skirt; (*prov.*) lapful; packing-bag; (*coll.*) ***poner haldas en cinta,*** to make ready; (*coll.*) ***de haldas o de mangas,*** by hook or by crook.
haldada, *n.f.* skirtful.
haldear, *v.i.* to run along with the skirts flying loose.
haldudo, -da, *a.* full-skirted, with flying skirts.
haleche, *n.m.* anchovy.
halieto, *n.m.* (*orn.*) osprey, fish hawk, sea-eagle.
haliéutica, *n.f.* angling, art of fishing.
halinatrón, *n.m.* native soda.
hálito, *n.m.* breath; vapour, effluvium; (*poet.*) gentle breeze.
halo, halón, *n.m.* (*astron.*) halo.
halófilo, -la, *a.* (*bot.*) halophilous.
halógeno, -na, *a.* (*chem.*) halogen.
halografía, *n.f.* (*chem.*) halography.
haloideo, -dea, *a.* (*chem.*) haloid.
haloque, *n.m.* ancient boat.

halotecnia, *n.f.* science of extracting industrial salts.
haloza, *n.f.* wooden shoe, clog.
halterio, *n.m.* dumb-bell; halter (*of the diptera*).
hallado, -da, *a.* found; ***bien hallado,*** easy, contented; ***mal hallado,*** uneasy, constrained; ***¡bien hallado!*** welcome, glad to see you again.
hallador, -ra, *n.m.f.* finder.
hallar, *v.t.* to find, come across, hit upon; to find out; ***hallar el camino de,*** to find one's way to. — **hallarse,** *v.r.* to be, be present, be found; to feel (*o.s.*); ***hallarse bien con,*** to be pleased with; ***hallarse con,*** to find o.s. with; ***hallarse en todo,*** to butt in everywhere; ***hallárselo todo hecho,*** not to have to do a thing; ***no hallarse,*** not to feel at home, not to have one's bearings.
hallazgo, *n.m.* find, finding, discovery; reward; ***cinco pesos de hallazgo,*** five pesos reward.
hallulla, *n.f.*, **hallullo,** *n.m.* bread baked on embers *or* hot stones; (*Chi.*) fine bread.
hamaca, *n.f.* hammock; deck-chair.
hamacar [A], *v.t.* (*Hisp. Am.*) to rock, swing.
hámago, *n.m.* beebread; (*coll.*) nausea, loathing.
hamaquear, *v.t.* (*Hisp. Am.*) to rock, shake, swing.
hamaquero, *n.m.* hammock-maker; hammock-bearer; hammock-hook.
hambre, *n.f.* hunger; starvation, famine; ***hambre canina,*** ravenous hunger; ***muerto de hambre,*** starving, ravenous; ***a buen hambre no hay pan duro,*** hunger is the best sauce; ***entretener el hambre,*** to stave off hunger (till mealtime); ***matar de hambre,*** to starve to death; ***matar el hambre,*** to satisfy one's hunger; ***morir*(*se*) *de hambre,*** to starve; ***pasar hambre,*** to go hungry; ***tener hambre,*** to be hungry; ***tener hambre de,*** to hunger for *or* after.
hambrear, *v.t.* to starve, famish. — *v.i.* to starve, hunger, go hungry.
hambriento, -ta, *a.* hungry, ravenous; (*Col.*) mean, stingy; ***hambriento de,*** hungry for.
hambrón, -rona, *a.* (*coll.*) hungry, greedy. — *n.m.f.* glutton, heavy eater.
hambruna, *n.f.* (*Hisp. Am.*) mad hunger.
hamburgués, -guesa, *a.*, *n.m.f.* (native) of Hamburg. — *n.f.* hamburger.
hamo, *n.m.* fish-hook.
hampa (1), *n.f.* underworld.
hampesco, -ca, *a.* (of the) underworld.
hampo, -pa (2) [HAMPESCO].
hampón, *n.m.* member of the underworld, tough.
hanega [FANEGA].
hanegada [FANEGADA].
hangar, *n.m.* hangar.
hansa, *n.f.* hanse.
hanseático, -ca, *a.* Hanseatic.
haplología, *n.f.* haplology.
haragán, -gana, *a.* lazy, idling. — *n.m.f.* idler, loafer.
haraganear, *v.i.* to lounge, idle, loaf.
haraganería, *n.f.* idleness, laziness, loafing about.
harakiri, *n.m.* hara-kiri; ***hacerse el harakiri,*** to commit hara-kiri.
harapiento, -ta, haraposo, -sa, *a.* ragged, tattered.
harapo, *n.m.* tatter, rag; ***andar*** or ***estar hecho un harapo,*** to go about in rags.
harca, *n.f.* (*Morocco*) military expedition of conscripted troops; band of rebels.
harem, harén, *n.m.* harem.
harija, *n.f.* mill-dust.
harina, *n.f.* flour; meal; powder; ***harina de maíz,*** cornflour, (*Am.*) cornstarch; ***cerner y sacar poca harina,*** to slave for small return; ***donde no hay harina, todo es mohina,*** poverty brings discord; ***estar metido*(*s*) *en harina,*** to be on the job, be hard at it; to be fat, fleshy; ***ser harina de otro costal,*** to be another kettle of fish.
harinado, *n.m.* flour dissolved in water.
harinero, -ra, *a.* (of) flour. — *n.m.* flour dealer; flour bin.
harinoso, -sa, *a.* floury, mealy, farinaceous.
harma, *n.f.* wild rue.
harmonía [ARMONÍA].
harnero, *n.m.* sieve, sifter; ***estar hecho un harnero,*** to be riddled.
harón, -rona, *a.* slow, sluggish; balky.
haronear, *v.i.* to dawdle, move sluggishly; to be slow; to balk.
haronía, *n.f.* sluggishness, laziness, idleness.
harpa [ARPA].
harpía [ARPÍA].
harpillera, *n.f.* burlap, sackcloth.
hartada, *n.f.* bellyful.
hartar, *v.t.* to glut, stuff, gorge; to sate, satiate; to sicken, weary; ***hartar de palos,*** to beat soundly. — **hartarse,** *v.v.* — ***de,*** to have *or* get one's fill of; to get sick (and tired) of.
hartazgo, hartazón, *n.m.* fill, bellyful; ***darse un hartazgo* (*de*),** to have *or* get one's fill of.
harto, -ta, *a.* satiated, full up; fed up, sick and tired; more than sufficient. — *adv.* enough, well enough, only too well; ***harto sé que,*** I know only too well that.
hartura, *n.f.* satiety, fill; superabundance; full gratification.
hasta, *conj.* even; ***hasta los niños lo hacen,*** even children (can) do it. — *prep.* till, until; to, as far as; as much as; up to, down to; ***hasta ahora,*** till now, up to now; ***hasta aquí,*** so far, hitherto; ***hasta después, hasta luego,*** I'll see you later; ***hasta la vista,*** so long, see you again; ***hasta más no poder,*** to the utmost; ***hasta que,*** until; ***hasta tanto que,*** until, till; ***hasta la médula,*** to the core; ***puede valer hasta cien pesetas,*** it may cost as much as a hundred pesetas.
hastial, *n.m.* (*arch.*) gable-wall; (*min.*) side face of a gallery; big, coarse man.
hastiar [L], *v.t.* to surfeit, sicken; to weary, bore. — **hastiarse,** *v.r.* to weary (***de,*** of).
hastío, *n.m.* surfeit; ennui, feeling of tedium, weariness, boredom.
hataca, *n.f.* large wooden ladle; rolling-pin.
hatajar, *v.t.* to divide (*cattle*) into flocks *or* herds; to separate from the herd *or* flock.
hatajo, *n.m.* small herd *or* flock; (*coll.*) lot, collection; ***hatajo de disparates,*** lot of nonsense.
hatear, *v.i.* to supply shepherds with provisions; (*coll.*) to pack up.
hatería, *n.f.* provisions, supplies *or* equipment for several days (*given to shepherds, miners and farm hands*).
hatero, -ra, *a.* pack (*animal*). — *n.m.f.* (*Hisp. Am.*) rancher; *n.m.* pack carrier.
hatijo, *n.m.* covering of straw *or* feather-grass over beehives.
hatillo, *n.m.* small bundle; a few clothes; (*coll.*) ***echar el hatillo al mar,*** to lose one's temper; (*coll.*) ***coger*** or ***tomar su*** or ***el hatillo,*** to pack off, go away.
hato, *n.m.* herd (*of cattle*); flock (*of sheep*); shepherd's hut; provisions for shepherds; (*Cub., Ven.*) cattle-ranch; pack, bundle (*of clothes*); lot, bunch; gang (*of thugs*); ***andar con el hato a cuestas,*** to be always on the move; ***liar el hato,*** to pack, pack up; (*coll.*) ***menear el hato a,*** to beat up, thrash; ***revolver el hato,*** to stir up trouble.
Haváy, *n.f.* Hawaii.
haxix, *n.m.* hashish.
Haya, *n.f.*, ***La* —,** The Hague.
haya (1), *n.f.* beech tree.
haya (2), *3rd pers. pres. subj.* [HABER].

hayal, hayedo, *n.m.* beech forest.
hayo, *n.m.* (*Col.*) coca; coca leaves prepared for chewing.
hayuco *n.m.* beech mast, fruit of the beech.
haz (1), *n.m.* bunch, bundle; faggot; sheaf; (*mil.*) rank, file; beam, shaft (*rays*); (*bot.*) fascicle. — *n.f.* face, surface; right side (*clothes*); (*arch.*) facing, façade; ***a sobre haz,*** on the surface; ***sobre la haz de la tierra,*** upon the face of the earth; ***ser de dos haces,*** to be two-faced; ***hacer haz,*** to be in line, be flush; ***en haz y en paz,*** by common consent; (*pl.* **haces**) fasces.
haz (2), *2nd pers. imperative* [HACER].
haza, *n.f.* tillable field.
hazaleja, *n.f.* towel.
hazaña, *n.f.* deed, feat, exploit.
hazañería, *n.f.* affected show of fear *or* surprise.
hazañero, -ra, *a.* prudish, affectedly grave, fearful *or* alarmed.
hazañoso, -sa, *a.* valiant, courageous, heroic.
hazcona, *n.f.* dart.
hazmerreír, *n.m.* laughing-stock, figure of fun, butt.
he, *adv.* lo, lo and behold; ***he aquí,*** here is, here are; ***heme aquí,*** here I am; ***helos allí,*** there they are.
hebdómada, *n.f.* hebdomad, week, seven days; seven years.
hebdomadario, -ria, *a.* hebdomadal, hebdomadary, weekly. — *n.m.f.* (*eccles.*) hebdomadary.
Hebe, *n.f.* Hebe.
hebén, *a.* of white grapes; insignificant, of no account.
hebilla, *n.f.* buckle, clasp; ***no faltar hebilla,*** to be perfect.
hebillaje, *n.m.* set of buckles.
hebillero, -ra, *n.m.f.* buckle maker *or* seller.
hebilleta, hebilluela, *n.f.* small buckle.
hebillón, *n.m.* large buckle.
hebra, *n.f.* fibre; thread; staple; grain (*of wood*); needleful of thread; pistil (*of saffron*); (*min.*) vein; ***tabaco de hebra,*** plug tobacco; ***pegar la hebra,*** to strike up a conversation; (*pl.*) (*poet.*) hair.
hebraico, -ca, *a.* Hebraic, Hebrew.
hebraísmo, *n.m.* Hebraism.
hebraísta, *n.m.* Hebraist, Hebrew scholar.
hebraizante, *a.* using Hebraisms. — *n.m.* Hebraist.
hebreo, -rea, *a.*, *n.m.f.* Hebrew. — *n.m.* Hebrew (*language*).
hebrero, *n.m.* œsophagus (*of ruminants*).
Hébridas, *n.f.pl.* Hebrides.
hebroso, -sa, *a.* fibrous, stringy.
hecatombe, *n.f.* hecatomb.
hectárea, *n.f.* hectare.
héctico, -ca, *a.* consumptive.
hectiquez, *n.f.* phthisis.
hectógrafo, *n.m.* hectograph.
hectogramo, *n.m.* hectogram.
hectolitro, *n.m.* hectolitre.
hectómetro, *n.m.* hectometre.
hectóreo, -rea, *a.* like Hector.
hecha (1), *n.f.* (*obs.*) date; (*obs.*) action, act, feat; irrigation tax; ***de esta hecha,*** from this time.
hechiceresco, -ca, *a.* relating to witchcraft, magical.
hechicería, *n.f.* witchcraft, witchery, sorcery, enchantment; fascination, charm.
hechicero, -ra, *a.* bewitching, charming, fascinating. — *n.m.f.* bewitcher, enchanter, enchantress, sorcerer, sorceress, wizard, witch.
hechizar [C], *v.t.* to bewitch, cast a spell on; to enchant, entrance, charm.
hechizo (1), *n.m.* charm, spell; bewitchment, enchantment, fascination; glamour.
hechizo (2), **-za,** *a.* artificial, feigned; made to order; portable, detachable, removable; (*Hisp. Am.*) local, home-produced.
hecho, -cha (2), *a.* made, done; ready-made, finished; fully matured, ripe *or* developed; accustomed, inured, used; ***hecho un león,*** like a lion, furiously angry; ***hecho un Adán,*** in a shocking state; ***estar hecho una sopa,*** to be soaking wet; ***estar hecho un costal de huesos,*** to be nothing but skin and bone; ***hombre hecho y derecho,*** full-grown man; ***trato hecho,*** it's a deal; ***la habitación estaba hecha una pocilga,*** the room looked like *or* had become a pigsty; ***a lo hecho pecho,*** what can't be cured must be endured; (*law*) ***de hecho y de derecho,*** de facto and de jure. — *n.m.* (*law*) point litigated; fact; act, deed; occurrence; ***de hecho,*** in fact, actually, in actual fact; ***el hecho es que,*** the fact of the matter is that; ***Hechos de los Apóstoles,*** Acts of the Apostles. — *p.p.* [HACER]; ***hecho a machete,*** roughly made; ***hecho de encargo,*** made to order; ***bien hecho,*** well done, good show; ***mal hecho,*** bad show, that's not done.
hechura, *n.f.* making, make; confection, making up; form, cut, shape; figure; effigy, statue; build (*of a person*); workmanship; (*fig.*) henchman, creature, puppet; ***esto no tiene hechura,*** this is hopeless.
hedentina, *n.f.* stench, stink, fetidness.
heder [2], *v.i.* to stink, to emit an offensive smell; to vex, annoy, bore, fatigue, be intolerable.
hediondez, *n.f.* strong stench *or* stink; fetidness.
hediondo, -da, *a.* fetid, mephitical, stinking; annoying, wearisome, intolerable; dirty, repulsive; lewd, obscene. — *n.m.* wild Syrian rue.
hedor, *n.m.* stench, stink.
hegemonía, *n.f.* (*pol.*) hegemony, supremacy.
hegemónico, -ca, *a.* (of the) leadership.
héjira, *n.f.* Hegira.
hejots, *n.m.* (*Hisp. Am.*) string bean.
helada, *n.f.* frost; ***helada blanca,*** hoar-frost.
heladera, *n.f.* (*Hisp. Am.*) freezer, refrigerator.
heladería, *n.f.* (*Chi., Col.*) ice cream shop.
heladero, *n.m.* (*Chi.*) ice cream seller *or* maker.
heladizo, -za, *a.* easily congealed.
helado, *n.m.* ice cream; (*prov.*) pink sugar.
helamiento, *n.m.* freezing, frostiness.
helar [1], *v.t.* to freeze, turn to ice; to chill; (*fig.*) to leave aghast, shatter. — *v.i.* to freeze; ***se me heló la sangre,*** my blood ran cold.
!hele or **hétele aquí!** *interj.* behold! here he is!
helechal, *n.m.* fern field.
helecho, *n.m.* fern.
helena (1), *n.f.* (*naut.*) St. Elmo's fire; Castor and Pollux.
helénico, -ca, *a.* Hellenic.
helenio, *n.m.* (*bot.*) elecampane.
helenismo, *n.m.* Hellenism.
helenista, *n.m.f.* Hellenist.
helenístico, -ca, *a.* Hellenistic.
helenizar [C], *v.t.* to hellenize.
heleno, -na (2), *a.* Hellenic. — *n.m.f.* Hellene.
helera, *n.f.* pip (*disease in fowls*).
helero, *n.m.* glacier.
helgado, -da, *a.* jag-toothed, jagged-toothed.
helgadura, *n.f.* space between *or* irregularity of the teeth.
helíaco, -ca, *a.* (*astron.*) heliacal.
heliantemo, *n.m.* (*bot.*) helianthemum.
heliantina, *n.f.* heliantin.
helianto, *n.m.* (*bot.*) helianthus.
hélice, *n.f.* helix; spiral, coil; propeller, screw; (*astron.*) Great Bear.
helicoidal, *a.* helicoidal, spiral.
helicoide, *n.m.* (*geom.*) helicoid.
helicónides, *n.f.pl.* Muses.
heliconio, -nia, *a.* Heliconian.

helicóptero, *n.m.* helicopter.
helio, *n.m.* helium.
heliocéntrico, -ca, *a.* heliocentric.
heliograbado, *n.m.* heliogravure.
heliógrafo, *n.m.* heliograph.
heliograma, *n.m.* heliogram.
heliómetro, *n.m.* heliometer.
helioplastia, *n.f.* helioengraving.
helioscopio, *n.m.* helioscope.
heliosis, *n.f.* heliosis, sunstroke.
helióstata, helióstato, *n.m.* heliostat.
helioterapia, *n.f.* heliotherapy.
heliotipia, *n.f.* heliotype.
heliotropio, heliotropo, *n.m.* heliotrope.
helipuerto, *n.m.* heliport.
helmintiasis, *n.f.* helminthiasis.
helmíntico, -ca, *a.* helminthic.
helminto, *n.m.* helminth.
helvecio, -cia, *a.* Helvetian, Swiss.
helvético, -ca, *a.* Helvetic, Swiss.
hemacrimo, -ma, *a.* (*zool.*) cold-blooded.
hematemesis, *n.f.* (*med.*) hæmatemesis.
hematíe, *n.m.* red cell.
hematina, *n.f.* hæmatin.
hematites, *n.f.* hæmatite.
hematómetro, *n.m.* (*med.*) hæmatometer.
hematosis, *n.f.* hæmatosis.
hematuria, *n.f.* hæmaturia.
hembra, *n.f.* female; eye (*of hook and eye*); nut (*of bolt* or *screw*); holed part *or* section, socket; (*naut.*) ***hembra del timón,*** gudgeon of the rudder.
hembraje, *n.m.* (*Hisp. Am.*) female cattle (*of a herd*); (*joc.*) womenfolk.
hembrear, *v.i.* to womanize; to beget *or* produce females only *or* chiefly.
hembrilla, *n.f.* small female; small nut; small socket; eyebolt.
hemerálope, *a.* hemeralope, hemeralopic.
hemeroteca, *n.f.* newspaper, magazine and periodical library.
hemiciclo, *n.m.* hemicycle; floor (*of Cortes*).
hemicránea, *n.f.* hemicrania, megrim.
hemina, *n.f.* hemina; hemin.
hemiplejía, *n.f.* (*med.*) hemiplegia.
hemíptero, -ra, *a.* hemipteral, hemipteran, hemipterous. — *n.m.* hemipteran; (*pl.*) hemiptera.
hemisférico, -ca, *a.* hemispheric, hemispherical.
hemisferio, *n.m.* hemisphere.
hemisferoidal, *a.* hemispheroidal.
hemistiquio, *n.m.* hemistich.
hemofilia, *n.f.* hæmophilia.
hemofílico, -ca, *a.* hæmophilic. — *n.m.f.* hæmophiliac.
hemoglobina, *n.f.* hæmoglobin.
hemopatía, *n.f.* illness of the blood.
hemoptisis, *n.f.* hæmoptysis.
hemorragia, *n.f.* hæmorrhage, flux of blood.
hemorrágico, -ca, *a.* hæmorrhagic.
hemorroida, hemorroide, *n.f.* (*med.*) piles, hæmorrhoids.
hemorroidal, *a.* hæmorrhoidal.
hemorroisa, *n.f.* woman suffering from an abnormal discharge of blood.
hemorroo, *n.m.* (*zool.*) cerastes.
hemostático, -ca, *a.* hæmostatic.
henal, *n.m.* hayloft.
henar, *n.m.* hayfield.
henchidor, -ra, *n.m.f.* filler.
henchidura, *n.f.* filling, stuffing.
henchimiento, *n.m.* [HENCHIDURA]; (*pl.*) (*naut.*) filling timber.
henchir [8], *v.t.* to fill up, cram, stuff.
hendedor, -ra, *a.* cleaving, splitting.
hendedura [HENDIDURA].
hender [2], *v.t.* to cleave, split, slit, crack; to force one's way through.
hendible, *a.* fissile, cleavable.
hendidura, *n.f.* fissure, crack, cranny, cleft, fissure, crevice.
hendiente, *n.m.* down-stroke of a sword.
hendija (*Hisp. Am.*) [RENDIJA].
hendimiento, *n.m.* cleaving, splitting, cracking.
henequén, *n.m.* henequen.
hénide, *n.f.* (*poet.*) nymph of the meadows.
henificación, *n.f.* tedding, haying.
henificar, *v.t.* to ted, hay.
henil, *n.m.* hayloft, barn.
heno, *n.m.* hay; (*bot.*) crimson clover; ***heno blanco,*** velvet grass.
henojil, *n.m.* garter.
heñir [8K], *v.t.* to knead; (*coll.*) ***hay mucho que heñir,*** there is much to do.
hepático, -ca, *a.* (*med.*) hepatic , liver. — *n.f* liverwort; liverleaf.
heptacordo, *n.m.* heptachord.
heptagonal, heptágono, -na, *a.* heptagonal, seven-sided.
heptarquía, *n.f.* heptarchy.
heptasílabo, -ba, *a.* containing seven syllables.
heptateuco, *n.m.* heptateuch.
heráldico, -ca, *a.* heraldic. — *n.f.* heraldry.
heraldo, *n.m.* herald; harbinger.
herbáceo, -cea, *a.* herby, herbaceous.
herbajar, herbajear, *v.t.* to put (*flocks*) to graze, pasture. — *v.i.* to pasture, graze, browse.
herbaje, *n.m.* herbage, grass, pasture, feeding; pasturage fee; coarse woollen cloth.
herbajero, *n.m.* renter of pasture.
herbar [1], *v.t.* to dress (*skins*) with herbs.
herbario, -ria, *a.* herbal. — *n.m.* herbalist; herbarium; (*zool.*) rumen (*of ruminants*).
herbaza, *n.f.* large weed.
herbazal, *n.m.* grassland; weedy place.
herbecer [9], *v.i.* to begin to grow (*herbs* or *grass*).
herbero, *n.m.* œsophagus (*of a ruminant*).
herbívoro, -ra, *a.* herbivorous.
herbolado, -da, *a.* poisoned (*with juice of plants*).
herbolario, *n.m.f.* herbalist; (*fig.*) scatterbrained person. — *n.m.* herb shop.
herborización, *n.f.* herborization, botanizing.
herborizador, herborizante, *n.m.* herbalist, herborist, herborizer.
herborizar [C], *v.i.* to herborize, botanize, go searching for herbs and plants.
herboso, -sa, *a.* herbous, herby, grassy.
herciano, -na, *a.* (*phys.*) Hertzian.
hercúleo, -lea, *a.* Herculean; herculean.
Hércules, *n.m.* Hercules.
heredad, *n.f.* country place, farm, property, estate.
heredado, -da, *a.* landed, owning real estate. — *n.m.f.* property owner.
heredamiento, *n.m.* landed property, lands.
heredar, *v.t.* to inherit; to leave property to; to institute as heir. — *v.i.* to inherit.
heredero, -ra, *n.m.f.* heir, heiress, inheritor; ***heredero forzoso,*** heir-apparent; ***heredero presunto,*** heir-presumptive.
heredípeta, *n.m.f.* legacy-seeker.
hereditario, -ria, *a.* hereditary.
hereje, *n.m.f.* heretic; (*fig.*) brute.
herejía, *n.f.* heresy; outrage; (*coll.*) ***la estampa de la herejía,*** (one) as ugly as sin.
herejote, -ta, *n.m.f.* (*coll.*) out and out heretic.
herén, *n.m.* vetch.
herencia, *n.f.* inheritance; heritage; heredity; ***derechos de herencia,*** death duties, (*Am.*) inheritance tax.

heresiarca, *n.m.* heresiarch.
herético, -ca, *a.* heretical.
herido, -da, *n.m.f.* wounded *or* injured person. — *n.f.* wound; injury; ***renovar la herida,*** to open the wound *or* an old sore; ***respirar por la herida,*** to show one's resentment; ***restañar las heridas,*** to staunch the wounds; heal the wounds; ***tocar en la herida,*** to get on the quick, touch on a sore spot.
heridor, -ra, *a.* wounding, striking.
herimiento, *n.m.* (*obs.*) wounding; (*gram., obs.*) synalepha, elision.
herir [6], *v.t.* to wound, injure, hurt; to stab; to strike, hit; to pluck, finger; to offend; to move deeply; ***estar, ir*** or ***venir mal herido,*** to be gravely wounded *or* injured.
hermafrodita, hermafrodito, *a., n.m.* hermaphrodite.
hermafroditismo, *n.m.* hermaphroditism.
hermana, *n.f.* [HERMANO].
hermanable, *a.* fraternal, brotherly; compatible.
hermanal, *a.* brotherly, fraternal.
hermanamiento, *n.m.* mating, matching, joining.
hermanar, *v.t., v.i.* to mate, match, join; to pair, couple; to harmonize, make compatible.
hermanastro, -ra, *n.m.f.* step-brother, step-sister.
hermandad, *n.f.* fraternity, brotherhood, sisterhood; confraternity; harmony; ***la Santa Hermandad,*** Spanish rural and judicial police instituted in the 15th century.
hermandarse, *v.r.* to form a religious brotherhood.
hermandino, *n.m.* (*hist.*) fellow of a rebellious movement in Galicia.
hermanear, *v.t.* to treat as a brother.
hermanecer [9], *v.i.* to have a little brother *or* sister born to one.
hermanita, *n.f.* little sister.
hermanito, *n.m.* little brother.
hermano, -na, *a.* sister, twin; ***lenguas hermanas,*** sister languages. — *n.m.* brother; ***hermano carnal,*** brother by the same father and mother; ***hermano de padre,*** brother by the same father, but not the same mother; ***hermano uterino,*** brother by the same mother, but not the same father; ***hermano de leche,*** foster-brother; ***medio hermano,*** half-brother, step-brother; ***hermano político,*** brother-in-law; (*pl.*) brothers and sisters; brethren. — *n.f.* sister.
hermanuco, *n.m.* (*contempt*) lay-brother.
hermenéutico, -ca, *a.* hermeneutic. — *n.f.* (*eccles.*) hermeneutics.
hermético, -ca, hermetical, air-proof, air-tight; (*fig.*) secretive, close.
hermetismo, *n.m.* secretiveness, secrecy, closeness.
hermetizar, *v.t.* to make hermetic *or* air-tight; to shut off from the outside world *or* from outside influence; to give a closed-in quality to.
hermodátil, *n.m.* colchicum.
hermoseador, -ra, *a.* beautifying, embellishing. — *n.m.f.* beautifier, embellisher.
hermoseamiento, *n.m.* beautification, embellishment.
hermosear, *v.t.* to beautify, embellish.
hermoso, -sa, *a.* beautiful, handsome; gorgeous.
hermosura, *n.f.* beauty, handsomeness, fineness; glorious abundance, gorgeous sight; magnificent *or* superb specimen.
hernia, *n.f.* hernia.
herniario, -ria, *a.* hernial.
hernioso, -sa, *a.* herniated.
hernista, *n.m.* hernia surgeon.
Herodes, *n.m.* Herod; ***ir de Herodes a Pilatos,*** to go from pillar to post.
héroe, *n.m.* hero.
heroicidad, *n.f.* heroism, heroic deed.
heroico, -ca, *a.* heroic, heroical; ***a la heroica,*** in the manner of heroic times.
heroína (1), *n.f.* heroine, heroin.
heroína (2), *n.f.* heroin.
heroísmo, *n.m.* heroism.
herpe, *n.m.f.* herpes.
herpético, -ca, *a.* herpetic.
herpil, *n.m.* bag (*of esparto netting*).
herrada, *a.* applied to water in which red-hot iron has been cooled. — *n.f.* wooden pail, bucket.
herradero, *n.m.* branding; place where cattle are branded; season for branding.
herrador, *n.m.* farrier, horse-shoer, smith.
herradora, *n.f.* (*coll.*) farrier's wife.
herradura, *n.f.* horse-shoe; ***arco de herradura,*** horse-shoe arch; ***camino de herradura,*** bridle path; ***mostrar las herraduras,*** to show a clean pair of heels.
herraje, *n.m.* iron-work; pieces of iron.
herramental, *a.* of *or* for tools. — *n.m.* tool-bag; tool-chest.
herramienta, *n.f.* tool, implement; set of tools; (*coll.*) horns; (*coll.*) teeth, grinders.
herrar [1], *v.t.* to shoe (*horses*); to brand (*cattle*); to adorn *or* bind with iron.
herrén, *n.m.* maslin, mixed grain.
herrenal, herreñal, *n.m.* piece of ground in which maslin is sown.
herrera, *n.f.* (*coll.*) blacksmith's wife.
herrería, *n.f.* iron-works; smith's shop, smithy; forge; smith's trade, smithery; clamour, confused noise.
herrerillo, *n.m.* (*orn.*) blue *or* great titmouse.
herrero, *n.m.* blacksmith; iron-worker.
herrerón, *n.m.* bad, clumsy smith.
herreruelo, *n.m.* (*orn.*) coal titmouse.
herrete, *n.m.* tag, tip.
herretear, *v.t.* to tag, tip.
herrezuelo, *n.m.* light piece of iron.
herrial, *a.* applied to certain large black grapes.
herrín, *n.m.* rust.
herrón, *n.m.* quoit; washer; iron prop (*for young trees*); (*Col.*) point (*of a spinning top*).
herronada, *n.f.* violent blow with iron bar; sharp peck.
herrugiento, -ta, *a.* rusty.
herrumbre, *n.f.* rust; irony taste.
herrumbroso, -sa, *a.* rusty.
hertziano, -na, *a.* (*phys.*) Hertzian.
hervencia, *n.f.* boiling.
herventar [1], *v.t.* to boil.
hervidero, *n.m.* boiling; boiling *or* bubbling spring; rattle (*in chest*); swarm, seething mass.
hervidor, *n.m.* kettle; boiler.
herviente, *a.* boiling, seething.
hervir [6], *v.i.* to boil, bubble, seethe; to swarm, teem; ***hacer hervir,*** to boil; ***me hierve la sangre,*** my blood boils.
hervor, *n.m.* boiling; fervour, heat, vigour; ***hervor de la sangre,*** rash; ***alzar*** or ***levantar el hervor,*** to begin to boil; ***dar un hervor,*** to give a short quick boil.
hervoroso, -sa, *a.* fiery, ardent, impetuous.
hesitación, *n.f.* hesitation.
hesitar, *v.i.* to hesitate.
hespéride, hespérido, -da, *a.* relating to the Pleiades; (*poet.*) western. — *n.f.pl.* (**Hespérides**) Hesperides.
hesperidio, -dia, *a.* hesperidium.
Héspero, *n.m.* (*astron.*) the planet Venus; evening star.
¡hete! *interj.* ***¡hete aquí*** or ***ahí!*** here you are! there you are!; lo and behold!
heteo, -tea, *a., n.m.f.* Hittite.
hetera, *n.f.* hetæra.
heteróclito, -ta, *a.* (*gram.*) heteroclite; irregular, abnormal.

heterodoxia, *n.f.* heterodoxy.
heterodoxo, -xa, *a.* heterodox, unorthodox.
heterogeneidad, *n.f.* heterogeneousness, heterogeneity.
heterogéneo, -nea, *a.* heterogeneous.
heteromancia, *n.f.* divination by the flight of birds.
heterónomo, -ma, *a.* heteronomous.
heterópsido, -da, *a.* in a state of alkaline earth, lustreless (*metals*).
hético, -ca, *a.* consumptive.
hetiquez, *n.f.* consumption.
hexacordo, *n.m.* hexachord.
hexaedro, *n.m.* hexahedron, cube.
hexagonal, *a.* hexagonal.
hexágono, -na, *a.* hexagonal. — *n.m.* hexagon.
hexámetro, *n.m.* hexameter.
hexápeda, *n.f.* toise.
hexasílabo, -ba, *a.* containing six syllables.
hez, *n.f.* scum, lees, dregs; dross (*of metals*); grains (*of malt*); ***la hez de la tierra,*** the scum of the earth; (*pl.* **heces**) fæces, excrement.
hi, *n.m.f.* son, daughter; *used only in the compound words* ***hidalgo, hidalguía,*** or *in vulgar phrases like* ***hi de puta,*** son of a whore, ***hi de perra,*** son of a bitch.
híadas, híades, *n.f.pl.* (*astron.*) Hyades, Hyads.
hialino, -na, *a.* hyaline, transparent.
hialitis, *n.f.* (*med.*) hyalitis.
hialóideo, -dea, *a.* vitreous, glass-like.
hialoides, *n.f. inv.* hyaloid membrane.
hialurgia, *n.f.* glass-making.
hiante, *a.* of a verse with a hiatus.
hiato, *n.m.* hiatus; pause; gap.
hibernación, *n.f.* hibernation.
hibernal, hibernizo, -za, *a.* hibernal, wintry.
hibernés, -nesa, *a.* Hibernian, Irish.
hibierno, *n.m.* (*obs.*) winter.
hibridación, *n.f.* hybridization, hybridism.
hibridizar, *v.t.* to make *or* turn hybrid, give *or* lend a hybrid *or* mixed nature *or* character to, bring about a cross in.
híbrido, -da, *a.* hybridous, hybrid. — *n.m.* hybrid.
hicaco, *n.m.* (*W. Ind.*) tree of the rosaceous family.
hicoteca, *n.f.* hiccatee.
hidalgarse [B], *v.r.* to give o.s. the airs of a hidalgo.
hidalgo, -ga, *a.* noble, of noble birth. — *n.m.f.* hidalgo, minor nobleman *or* woman, yeoman, country squire.
hidalgón, -gona, hidalgote, -ta, *n.m.f.* old, ceremonious (minor) nobleman.
hidalguejo, -ja, hidalguelo, -la, hidalguete, -ta, hidalguillo, -lla, *n.m.f.* petty nobleman.
hidalguez, hidalguía, *n.f.* status of minor nobleman *or* yeoman; nobility, nobleness, generosity.
hidatídico, -ca, *a.* (*med.*) hydatid.
hidra, *n.f.* poisonous serpent; hydra; Hydra.
hidrácido, *n.m.* hydracid.
hidragogo, *n.m.* (*med.*) hydragogue.
hidrargírido, -da, *a.* resembling mercury.
hidrargirio, hidrargiro, *n.m.* hydrargyrum, mercury.
hidratable, *a.* able to be hydrated.
hidratación, *n.f.* hydration, hydrating.
hidratado, -da, *a.* hydrate(d).
hidratar, *v.t.* to hydrate.
hidrato, *n.m.* hydrate.
hidráulico, -ca, *a.* hydraulic. — *n.m.* expert in hydraulics. — *n.f.* hydraulics.
hidria, *n.f.* ancient jar *or* pitcher.
hidroavión, *n.m.* hydroplane; seaplane, flying-boat.
hidrobiología, *n.f.* hydrobiology.
hidrocarburo, *n.m.* hydrocarbon.
hidrocéfalo, -la, *a.* hydrocephalous.
hidroclorato, *n.m.* hydrochlorate.
hidroclórico, -ca, *a.* hydrochloric.
hidrodinámico, -ca, *a.* hydrodynamic. — *n.f.* hydrodynamics.
hidroeléctrico, -ca, *a.* hydro-electric.
hidroesfera, *n.f.* hydrosphere.
hidrófana, *n.f.* (*min.*) hydrophane.
hidrofilacio, *n.m.* great cavern full of water.
hidrófilo, -la, *a.* water-loving; absorbent; ***algodón hidrófilo,*** cotton wool, (*Am.*) absorbent cotton.
hidrofobia, *n.f.* hydrophobia; rabies.
hidrófobo, -ba, *a.* suffering from hydrophobia.
hidrófono, *n.m.* hydrophone.
hidrófugo, -ga, *a.* moisture-proof.
hidrogala, *n.m.* mixture of milk and water.
hidrogenar, *v.t.* to hydrogenate.
hidrógeno, *n.m.* hydrogen.
hidrogogía, *n.f.* science of canal making.
hidrografía, *n.f.* hydrography.
hidrográfico, -ca, *a.* hydrographical.
hidrógrafo, *n.m.* hydrographer.
hidrolizar, *v.t.* to hydrolize.
hidrología, *n.f.* hydrology.
hidrológico, -ca, *a.* hydrologic.
hidromancia, *n.f.* hydromancy.
hidromántico, -ca, *a.* hydromantic.
hidromel, hidromiel, *n.m.* hydromel.
hidrometeoro, *n.m.* hydrometeor.
hidrómetra, *n.m.f.* expert in hydrometry.
hidrometría, *n.f.* hydrometry.
hidrómetro, *n.m.* hydrometer.
hidrópata, *n.m.f.* hydropath.
hidropatía, *n.f.* hydropathy.
hidropático, -ca, *a.* hydropathic.
hidropesía, *n.f.* dropsy.
hidrópico, -ca, *a.* hydropic, hydropical, dropsical.
hidroplano, *n.m.* hydroplane.
hidroscopia, *n.f.* hydroscopy.
hidroscopio, *n.m.* hydroscope.
hidrostático, -ca, *a.* hydrostatical. — *n.f.* hydrostatics.
hidrosulfúrico, -ca, *a.* hydrosulphuric, sulphydric.
hidrotecnia, *n.f.* hydraulic engineering; science of constructing hydraulic machines.
hidroterapia, *n.f.* hydrotherapy.
hidroterápico, -ca, *a.* hydrotherapeutic.
hiedra, *n.f.* ivy; ***hiedra terrestre,*** ground ivy.
hiel, *n.f.* gall; bile; (*coll.*) ***echar la hiel,*** to toil, labour; (*coll.*) ***no tener hiel,*** to be meek and mild; (*bot.*) ***hiel de la tierra,*** lesser centaury; (*pl.* **hieles**) hardships, worries.
hielo, *n.m.* ice; iciness; ***punto de hielo,*** freezing point; ***quedarse de hielo,*** to be (left) aghast.
hiemal, *a.* wintry, hibernal.
hiena, *n.f.* hyena.
hienda, *pres. subj.* [HENDER].
hieracio, *n.m.* (*bot.*) hawkweed.
hierático, -ca, *a.* hieratic(al), stiff, upright, grand, majestic.
hierba, *n.f.* grass; herb; herbage; (*pl.*) weeds; herbs; (*among the members of a religious order*) greens, garden-stuff; ***mala hierba,*** weed; ***hierba luisa,*** lemon verbena; (*joc.*) ***y otras hierbas,*** and so forth; ***haber pisado buena*** (***mala***) ***hierba,*** to have had great (little) success; ***ver crecer la hierba,*** to be as sharp as a hawk.
hierbabuena, *n.f.* mint.
hierbatero, *n.m.* (*Chi.*) retailer of fodder, grass etc.
hierofanta, -te, *n.m.* hierophant.
hieroglífico, -ca [JEROGLÍFICO].
hieroscopia, *n.f.* haruspicy.
hierosolimitano, -na [JEROSOLIMITANO].
hierrezuelo [HERREZUELO].
hierro (I), *n.m.* iron; brand; iron head (*of shaft, arrow* or *dart*); pointed weapon; (*naut.* bilboes;

hierro albo, red-hot iron; *hierro colado* or *fundido*, cast-iron; *hierro forjado* or *de fragua*, wrought iron; *hierro cuadrillado*, square iron; *hierro laminado* or *en planchas*, sheet-iron; *hierro varilla*, round iron; *es de hierro*, he is as hard as iron *or* as hard as steel, tireless; *machacar en hierro frío*, to labour in vain; *llevar hierro a Vizcaya*, to carry coals to Newcastle; *quién a hierro mata, a hierro muere*, he who lives by the sword will die by the sword; *quitar hierro a*, to play down, minimize; to take the sting out of; (*pl.*) fetters, shackles.

hierro (2), *pres. indic.* [HERRAR].

higa, *n.f.* fist-shaped charm *or* amulet; derisive gesture of fist and thumb; derision, contempt; *dar higa*, to misfire (*of weapons*); *me importa una higa*, I don't care a rap.

higadilla, *n.f.*, **higadillo,** *n.m.* liver (*of birds, mall animals etc.*); (*pl.*) giblets.

hígado, *n.m.* liver; (*pl.*) (*coll.*) guts; *echar los hígados*, to slave; to puff and blow, sweat and strain; (*coll.*) *malos hígados*, ill-will, hatred; *hasta los hígados*, deeply; *querer comer los hígados a*, to hate the guts of.

higate, *n.m.* fig and pork stew.

higiene, *n.f.* hygiene.

higiénico, -ca, *a.* hygienic.

higienista, *n.m.f.* hygienist.

higienizar [C], *v.t.* to make hygienic.

higo, *n.m.* (*bot.*) fig; *higo chumbo*, prickly pear; *pan de higos*, fig-cake; *de higos a brevas*, once in a blue moon; *no se le da un higo*, he doesn't care a fig.

higrometría, *n.f.* hygrometry.

higrométrico, -ca, *a.* hygrometric.

higrómetro, *n.m.* hygrometer.

higroscopia, *n.f.* hygroscopy.

higroscopio, *n.m.* hygroscope.

higuera, *n.f.* fig-tree; *higuera infernal*, castor-oil plant; *higuera chumba*, prickly pear tree; *sal de higuera*, Epsom salts; *estar en la higuera*, to have one's head in the clouds.

higueral, *n.m.* plantation of fig trees.

higuerón, *n.m.* higuerón tree.

higuito, *n.m.* small fig.

hija, *n.f.* daughter; (*coll.*) dear; *hija política*, daughter-in-law.

hijadalgo, *n.f.* well-born girl *or* woman.

hijastro, -ra, *n.m.f.* step-child; step-son; step-daughter.

hijito, -ta, *n.m.f.* little child.

hijo, *n.m.* son; child; offshoot, offspring; junior (*after a person's name*); *Alejandro Dumas Hijo*, Alexandre Dumas the Younger; *hijo adoptivo*, adopted child; (*fig.*) honorary citizen; (*coll.*) *hijo bastardo, hijo natural, hijo de ganancia* or *hijo de su madre*, bastard; *hijo de bendición*, legitimate child; *hijo de familia*, minor; *hijo del agua*, good sailor; good swimmer; *hijo de leche*, foster-child; *cada hijo de vecino*, every mother's son; *hijo no tener, y nombre le poner*, to count one's chickens before they're hatched.

hijodalgo, *n.m.* [HIDALGO].

hijuela, *n.f.* offshoot; (*eccles.*) pall, chalice cover; (*sew.*) gore; supplementary mattress; estate of a deceased person; rural postal service; (*law*) share of an inheritance; byway; bundle of kindling wood; palm seed.

hijuelo, *n.m.* (*bot.*) shoot.

hila, *n.f.* row, line; thin gut; spinning; *a la hila*, in single file; (*pl.*) (*surg.*) lint; *hilas raspadas*, scraped lint.

hilacha, *n.f.*, **hilacho,** *n.m.* loose *or* ragged thread.

hilachoso, -sa, *a.* ragged, frayed.

hilada, *n.f.* row, line; (*arch.*) course; layer.

hiladillo, *n.m.* ferret silk; narrow ribbon *or* tape.

hilado, *n.m.* spinning; yarn, thread.

hilador, -ra, *a.* spinning. — *n.m.f.* spinner.

hilandería, *n.f.* spinnery, spinning-mill; spinstry.

hilandero, -ra, *n.m.f.* spinner. — *n.m.* spinning-room, spinnery.

hilar, *v.t.* to spin; *hilar delgado* or *fino*, to go into close detail; *hilar demasiado delgado* or *fino*, to split hairs.

hilaracha, *n.f.* loose thread.

hilarante, *a.* laughing; hilarious; *gas hilarante*, laughing gas.

hilaridad, *n.f.* hilarity, mirth.

hilatura, *n.f.* spinning; spun goods.

hilaza, *n.f.* yarn; fibre; uneven thread.

hilera, *n.f.* row, line, file; (*metal.*) wire-drawer; fine thread *or* yarn; (*arch.*) ridge-pole; slit *or* catch (*of a spindle*).

hilero, *n.m.* ripples; thread of a river; current.

hilo, *n.m.* thread, yarn; linen; fibre, filament; wire; flex, (*Am.*) extension cord; line; trickle; edge (*of a sword* or *razor*); (*min.*) seam; *hilo bramante*, pack-thread, twine; *hilo de velas*, sail-maker's yarn; (*naut.*) *hilo de una corriente*, thread of a current; *hilo de perlas*, string of pearls; *a hilo*, following, parallel; without interruption; *al hilo*, along *or* with the thread *or* grain; *al hilo del viento*, with the wind; *ir al hilo del mundo, de la gente*, to go with the crowd, follow the mass; *al hilo de las doce*, at twelve sharp, on the stroke of twelve; *contra hilo*, crosswise, against the grain *or* stream; *hilo a hilo*, steadily; *del hilo al pabilo*, fully; *coger el hilo*, to catch on; *cortar el hilo*, to interrupt the thread; *reanudar el hilo*, to take up the thread; *estar colgado* or *pendiente de un hilo*, to be dangling by a thread; *estar con el alma en un hilo*, to be on tenterhooks; *por el hilo se saca el ovillo*, one thing leads (on) to another.

hilván, *n.m.* (*sew.*) tacking, basting; (*coll.*) *hablar de hilván*, to talk nineteen to the dozen.

hilvanar, *v.t.* (*sew.*) to tack, baste; (*fig.*) to string together, co-ordinate; to put together hurriedly.

himen, *n.m.* (*anat.*) hymen.

himeneo, *n.m.* marriage, nuptials; epithalamium.

himenófilo, *n.m.* filmy fern, lace fern.

himenóptero, -ra, *a.* hymenopterous. — *n.m.* hymenopteran; (*pl.*) hymenoptera.

himnario, *n.m.* hymnary, hymnal.

himno, *n.m.* hymn; anthem.

himnología, *n.f.* hymnology.

himplar, *v.i.* to roar, bellow (*panther, ounce*).

hin, *n.m.* whinny, neigh.

hincadura, *n.f.* driving, sticking, thrusting in.

hincapié, *n.m.* stress, emphasis; *hacer hincapié en*, to stress, emphasize.

hincar [A], *v.t.* to drive, stick, thrust *or* sink in; *hincar el diente* or *los dientes en*, to sink *or* get one's teeth into; *hincar el pico*, to bite the dust; *hincar la rodilla*, to go down on one's knees, knuckle under; *hincarse de rodillas*, to kneel (down).

hincón, *n.m.* ferry-boat; hitching-post.

hincha, *n.f.* (*coll.*) ill-will. — *n.m.f.* (*coll.*) fan.

hinchado, -da, *a.* puffed-up; pompous, bombastic. — *n.f.* (*coll.*) fans, supporters.

hinchar, *v.t.* to puff up, blow up, inflate, swell; *hincharle a alguien el ojo*, to give s.o. a black eye; *se le hincharon las narices*, he got mad, ratty.

hinchazón, *n.m.* swelling; tumefaction; pride, vanity; inflation, bombast.

hiniesta, *n.f.* genista, Spanish broom.

hinnible, *a.* capable of neighing.

hinojal, *n.m.* fennel bed.

hinojo, *n.m.* knee; (*bot.*) fennel; (*bot.*) *hinojo marino*, samphire; *de hinojos*, kneeling.

hintero, *n.m.* baker's kneading table.

hioides, *a.* (*anat.*) hyoid.

hipar, *v.i.* to hiccup; to whimper; to pant; to be fagged out; to long (for).
hipérbola, *n.f.* hyperbola.
hipérbole, *n.f.* hyperbole.
hiperbólico, -ca, *a.* hyperbolic.
hiperbolizar [C], *v.i.* to hyperbolize.
hiperboloide, *n.f.* hyperboloid.
hiperbóreo, -rea, *a.* hyperborean.
hiperclorhidria, *n.f.* hyperchlorhydria.
hipercrisis, *n.f.* extreme crisis.
hipercrítico, -ca, *a.* hypercritical, censorious.
hiperdulía, *n.f.* (*eccles.*) hyperdulia.
hiperemia, hiperhemia, *n.f.* hyperæmia.
hiperémico, -ca, *a.* hyperæmic.
hipericineos, -neas, *n.m.f.pl.* Hypericaceæ.
hipérico, *n.m.* (*bot.*) hypericum.
hipersensible, *a.* hypersensitive.
hipertensión, *n.f.* hypertension.
hipertrofia, *n.f.* hypertrophy.
hipertrofiarse, *v.r.* to hypertrophy.
hipertrófico, -ca, *a.* hypertrophic.
hípico, -ca, *a.* equine, horse.
hipido [*aspirated* ***h***], *n.m.* action and effect of hiccuping; whining.
hipil, *n.m.* (*Hisp. Am.*) loose garment worn by Indians.
hipismo, *n.m.* show jumping.
hipnal, *n.m.* (*obs.*) hypnale.
hipnosis, *n.f.* hypnosis.
hipnótico, -ca, *a., n.m.* hypnotic.
hipnotismo, *n.m.* hypnotism, mesmerism.
hipnotización, *n.f.* hypnotizing, hypnotization.
hipnotizador, -ra, *a.* hypnotizing. — *n.m.f.* hypnotizer, hypnotist.
hipnotizar [C], *v.t.* to hypnotize.
hipo, *n.m.* hiccup; (*fig.*) longing; grudge; ***tener hipo contra,*** to have a grudge against; ***tener hipo por,*** to crave.
hipocampo, *n.m.* sea-horse.
hipocausto, *n.m.* hypocaust.
hipocicloide, *n.f.* hypocycloid.
hipocondria, *n.f.* hypochondria, melancholy.
hipocondríaco, -ca, *a.* hypochondriac, melancholy.
hipocóndrico, -ca, *a.* hypochondriac, hypochondriacal, melancholy, fanciful.
hipocondrio, *n.m.* (*naut.*) hypochondrium.
hipocrás, *n.m.* hippocras, medicated wine.
hipocrático, -ca, *a.* Hippocratic.
hipocrénides, *n.f.pl.* (*poet.*) the Muses.
hipocresía, *n.f.* hypocrisy.
hipócrita, *a.* hypocritical. — *n.m.f.* hypocrite.
hipocritón, -tona, *n.m.f.* (*coll.*) great *or* out and out hypocrite.
hipodérmico, -ca, *a.* hypodermic.
hipódromo, *n.m.* hippodrome, race-course.
hipófisis, *n.f. inv.* (*path.*) hypophysis.
hipofosfito, *n.m.* hypophosphite.
hipogástrico, -ca, *a.* hypogastric.
hipogastrio, *n.m.* hypogastrium.
hipogénico, -ca, *a.* (*geol.*) hypogene.
hipogloso, -sa, *a.* (*zool.*) hypoglossal.
hipogrifo, *n.m.* hippogriff.
hipómanes, *n.m.* hippomanes.
hipomoclio, hipomoclion, *n.m.* fulcrum (*of a lever*).
hiponitrato, *n.m.* subnitrate.
hiponítrico, -ca, *a.* hyponitrous.
hipopótamo, *n.m.* hippopotamus.
hiposo, -sa, *a.* having hiccups.
hipóstasis, *n.f. inv.* (*theol.*) hypostasis.
hipostático, -ca, *a.* hypostatical.
hiposulfato, *n.m.* (*chem.*) hyposulphate.
hiposulfito, *n.m.* (*chem.*) hyposulphite.
hiposulfuroso, *a.* (*chem.*) hyposulphurous.
hipoteca, *n.f.* mortgage; (*law*) hypothec, hypothecation.
hipotecable, *a.* mortgageable.
hipotecar [A], *v.t.* to mortgage.
hipotecario, -ria, *a.* belonging to a mortgage; hypothecary.
hipotenusa, *n.f.* hypotenuse.
hipótesis, *n.f.* hypothesis; theory.
hipotético, -ca, *a.* hypothetic, hypothetical; theoretical.
hipsometría, *n.f.* hypsometry.
hipsométrico, *a.* hypsometric.
hipsómetro, *n.m.* hypsometer.
hircano, -na, *a.* Hyrcanian.
hirco, *n.m.* wild goat.
hircocervo, *n.m.* hircocervus; (*fig.*) fantasy.
hiriente, *a.* wounding, cutting, scathing.
hirma, *n.f.* selvedge, edge (*of cloth*).
hirmar, *v.t.* to make firm, secure.
hirsuto, -ta, *a.* hirsute, hairy, bristly.
hirundinaria, *n.f.* celandine, swallow-wort.
hirviente, *a.* boiling, seething.
hisca, *n.f.* bird-lime.
hiscal, *n.m.* esparto rope of three strands.
hisopada, *n.f.* sprinkling with holy water.
hisopear, *v.t.* to sprinkle holy water on.
hisopillo, *n.m.* mouth swab; (*bot.*) winter-savory.
hisopo, *n.m.* hyssop; (*eccles.*) aspergill, sprinkler; ***hisopo húmedo,*** wool grease.
hispalense, *a., n.m.f.* (native) of Seville.
hispánico, -ca, *a.* Hispanic.
hispanismo, *n.m.* hispanicism.
hispanista, *n.m.f.* Hispanist.
hispanizar, *v.t.* to hispanize.
hispano, -na, *a.* Spanish, Hispanic, Hispano.
Hispanoamérica, *n.f.* Spanish America.
hispanoamericanismo, *n.m.* Hispano-Americanism.
hispanoamericano, -na, *a.* Spanish-American.
hispanoárabe, *a.* Hispano-Arabic.
hispanófilo, -la, *a.* Hispanophile.
híspido, -da, *a.* hispid, bristly.
hispir, *v.t., v.i.* to puff up, make *or* get fluffy.
histeria, *n.f.* hysteria.
histérico, -ca, *a.* hysterical.
histerismo, *n.m.* hysteria.
histerología, *n.f.* hysterology.
histerotomía, *n.m.* hysterotomy.
histología, *n.f.* histology.
histológico, -ca, *a.* histological.
histólogo, *n.m.* histologist.
historia, *n.f.* history; story; (*coll.*) tale, tattle; (*art*) history-piece; ***historia sagrada,*** Sacred History, Scripture; ***una mujer de historia,*** a woman with a past; ***pasar a la historia,*** to become history, become a thing of the past; ***picar en historia,*** to turn out to be more serious than expected; ***no te metas en muchas historias,*** don't go to a lot of trouble *or* bother; ***¡déjate de historias!*** don't give me that stuff *or* nonsense! don't beat about the bush.
historiado, -da, *a.* historiated; storied; (*coll.*) loaded down with ornamentation.
historiador, -ra, *n.m.f.* historian.
historial, *a.* historical. — *n.m.* record, dossier.
historiar [L *and regular*], *v.t.* to write *or* tell the history of; to relate, chronicle, give an account of; (*art*) to depict (*historical events*); (*Hisp. Am.*) to confuse.
histórico, -ca, *a.* historical; historic.
historieta, *n.f.* short story *or* tale; ***historieta cómica,*** comic strip; cartoon; ***historieta muda,*** story without words.
historiógrafo, *n.m.* historiographer.

historión, *n.m.* tedious, long-winded story.
histrión, *n.m.* histrion; theatrical individual.
histriónico, -ca, *a.* histrionic, histrionical.
histrionisa, *n.f.* actress, danseuse.
histrionismo, *n.m.* histrionism; playing to the gallery.
hito, -ta, *a.* adjoining (*house* or *street*); firm, fixed; black (*horse*). — *n.m.* boundary mark; landmark; milestone; hob and quoits; (*artill.*) target; ***a hito,*** fixedly, firmly; ***dar en el hito,*** to hit the nail on the head; ***mirar de hito en hito,*** to look up and down. — *n.f.* headless nail, brad.
hitón, *n.m.* large brad.
hobachón, -chona, *a.* sluggish, fat and lazy. — *n.m.f.* (*Col.*) shy horse.
hocicar [A], *v.t.* to root (up), root among. — to root about; to fall flat; (*coll., fig.*) to come up against (*an obstacle*); (*naut.*) to pitch.
hocico, *n.m.* snout; muzzle; pouting; ***meter el hocico en todo,*** to stick one's nose into everything; (*coll.*) ***poner hocico,*** to pout; (*coll.*) ***caer*** or ***darse de hocicos,*** to fall flat on the face, bang the face (against); ***torcer el hocico,*** to look sullen *or* sulky.
hocicudo, -da, hocicón, -cona, *a.* long-snouted; blubber-lipped.
hocino, *n.m.* (*agric.*) bill, bill-hook; glen, dell; narrow gorge *or* canyon; (*pl.*) fertile spots in glens and dells.
hociquillo, hociquito, *n.m.* little snout.
hogañazo, hogaño, *adv.* nowadays, in the present day and age.
hogar, *n.m.* hearth; furnace; home.
hogaza, *n.f.* large loaf.
hoguera, *n.f.* bonfire.
hoja, *n.f.* leaf; petal; sheet; slip; blade; scale, layer, flake; (*agric.*) strip of land; ***hoja de afeitar,*** razor blade; ***hoja de servicios,*** service record; ***hoja de lata,*** tin-plate; ***hoja de tocino,*** flitch of bacon; ***hoja suelta*** or ***volante,*** handbill, leaflet; (*fig.*) ***hoja de parra,*** fig leaf; ***hoja toledana,*** Toledo blade; ***doblar*** or ***volver la hoja,*** to turn the page; to change *or* drop the subject; ***poner como hoja de perejil,*** to give a dressing down to, tick off properly; to criticize savagely; ***no tiene vuelta de hoja,*** there are no two ways about it, there's no argument about it; (*pl.*) (*arch.*) leaf ornaments, foliation; years of age (*wine*); (*naut.*) ***hojas de las puertas,*** portlids.
hojalata, *n.f.* tin-plate.
hojalatería, *n.f.* tin-plate, tinware; tinshop.
hojalatero, *n.m.* tinman, tinsmith, tinker.
hojaldrado, *a.* flaky.
hojaldrar, *v.t.* to make into puff-pastry.
hojaldre, *n.m.f.* puff-pastry, flaky pastry.
hojaldrista, *n.m.f.* puff-pastry baker.
hojarasca, *n.f.* withered leaves; excessive foliage; empty words, verbiage.
hojear, *v.t.* to turn the leaves of, browse through, peruse. — *v.i.* to flutter, quiver.
hojoso, -sa, hojudo, -da, *a.* leafy.
hojuela, *n.f.* small leaf; pancake; gold *or* silver flat thread; skins of pressed olives.
¡hola! *interj.* hello!; ho! ho!; (*naut.*) hoy! ahoy!
holán, holán batista, *n.m.* cambric; batiste.
Holanda, *n.f.* Holland.
holanda, *n.f.* fine Dutch linen, cambric.
holandés, -desa, *a.* Dutch. — *n.m.f.* Dutchman, Dutchwoman. — *n.m.* Dutch (*language*).
holandeta, holandilla, *n.f.* brown holland.
holgachón, -chona, *a.* (*coll.*) fond of ease and little work.
holgadamente, *adv.* widely, amply, fully, loosely, easily, comfortably.
holgado, -da, *a.* easy; wide, roomy; having plenty, well-to-do; comfortable; at leisure.
holganza, *n.f.* rest, leisure, ease; idleness; recreation, amusement.
holgar [4B], *v.i.* to rest; to be idle; to have free time *or* time off; to be needless; ***huelga decir que,*** needless to say. — **holgarse,** *v.r.* to enjoy o.s., take one's pleasure; to be delighted.
holgazán, -zana, *a.* idle, lazy, slothful. — *n.m.f.* idler, loafer.
holgazanear, *v.i.* to idle, lounge; to be lazy.
holgazanería, *n.f.* idleness, laziness, slothfulness.
holgorio [JOLGORIO].
holgueta, *n.f.* (*coll.*) merrymaking.
holgura, *n.f.* roominess, ample space; ease, comfort; merrymaking.
holocausto, *n.m.* holocaust; burnt sacrifice.
hológrafo, -fa, *a.* holographic, holograph.
holómetro, *n.m.* holometer.
holostérico, *a.* ***barómetro holostérico,*** aneroid barometer.
holladura, *n.f.* trampling; duty paid for the run of cattle.
hollar [4], *v.t.* to tread, tread on *or* down, trample, trample down *or* upon.
hollejo, *n.m.* grapeskin; bean pod, peel, husk.
hollín, *n.m.* soot.
holliniento, -ta, *a.* sooty.
homarrache, *n.m.* clown, buffoon, merry-Andrew.
hombracho, *n.m.* hefty great fellow.
hombrachón, *n.m.* big hefty fellow.
hombrada, *n.f.* manly action.
hombradía, *n.f.* manliness.
hombrazo [HOMBRACHÓN].
hombre, *n.m.* man; ombre; (*law*) ***hombre bueno,*** arbiter, arbitrator, referee; ***hombre de buena capa,*** well-dressed man; ***hombre de bien,*** honest man; ***hombre de pro*** or ***de provecho,*** worthy, useful man; ***hombre de asiento,*** prudent man; ***hombre de corazón,*** courageous man; ***hombre de mundo,*** man of the world; ***hombre de dinero,*** moneyed man; ***hombre de copete,*** man of position; ***hombre de negocios,*** businessman; ***ser muy hombre,*** to be very much a man; ***hombre de edad,*** elderly man; ***hombre de estado,*** statesman; ***hombre de su palabra,*** man of his word; ***hombre de cabeza,*** talented man; ***hombre hecho y derecho,*** grown man; ***hombre de pelo en pecho,*** real he-man; ***¡hombre!*** good heavens, man! good Lord, man!; well, well!; for Goodness' sake!; ***¡hombre al agua!*** man overboard!; ***hombre de armas tomar,*** a man to be reckoned with; ***como un solo hombre,*** as one, unanimously; ***es hombre al agua,*** he's a lost man; ***el hombre propone y Dios dispone,*** man proposes and God disposes; ***hombre prevenido vale por dos,*** forewarned is forearmed.
hombrear, *v.i.* to try to act grown-up; to push with the shoulders. — **hombrearse,** *v.r.* — ***con,*** to strive to equal.
hombrecillo, *n.m.* little man *or* fellow; miserable little man *or* fellow; (*bot.*) hop(s).
hombrera, *n.f.* (*arm.*) pauldron; shoulder pad.
hombretón, *n.m.* hefty fellow.
hombría, *n.f.* manliness; ***hombría de bien,*** uprightness, probity.
hombrillo, *n.m.* (*sew.*) gusset; yoke (*of a shirt*).
hombro, *n.m.* shoulder; ***hombro con hombro,*** shoulder to shoulder; ***encogerse de hombros,*** to shrug one's shoulders; ***llevar a hombro*** or ***sobre los hombros,*** to carry on one's shoulder(s); ***llevar en hombros,*** to carry *or* bear shoulder high; ***arrimar el hombro,*** to put one's shoulder to the wheel; ***echarse al hombro,*** to shoulder, take on; (*fig.*) ***mirar por encima del hombro,*** to look down on.
hombrón, *n.m.* big, lusty man; (*fig.*) great fellow, he-man.
hombronazo, *n.m.* hefty great man *or* fellow.

hombruno, -na, *a.* mannish.
homenaje, *n.m.* homage; tribute; ***en homenaje a,*** in honour of; ***rendir homenaje a,*** to do *or* pay homage to.
homenajear, *v.t.* to pay homage *or* tribute to.
homeópata, *n.m.f.* homœopath(ist).
homeopatía, *n.f.* (*med.*) homœopathy.
homeopático, -ca, *a.* homœopathic.
homérico, -ca, *a.* Homeric.
homicida, *a.* homicidal. — *n.m.f.* homicide, murderer, murderess.
homicidio, *n.m.* homicide, murder.
homiliario, *n.m.* collection of homilies.
homilía, *n.f.* homily.
homilista, *n.m.f.* author *or* writer of homilies.
hominal, *a.* (*nat. hist.*) relating to man.
hominicaco, *n.m.* (*coll.*) paltry fellow; whipper-snapper.
homocéntrico, -ca, *a.* homocentric.
homofonía, *n.f.* homophony.
homófono, -na, *a.* homophonous.
homogeneidad, *n.f.* homogeneity, homogeneousness.
homogéneo, -nea, *a.* homogeneous.
homógrafo, -fa, *a.* homographic. — *n.m.* homograph.
homologación, *n.f.* (*law*) homologation.
homologar [B], *v.t.* (*law*) to homologate; to validate.
homólogo, -ga, *a.* (*geom.*) homologous; (*log.*) synonymous.
homonimia, *n.f.* homonymy.
homónimo, -ma, *a.* homonymous. — *n.m.f.* namesake. — *n.m.* homonym.
homóptero, -ra, *a.* homopteran, homopterous. — *n.m.* homopteran.
homosexual, *a.*, *n.m.f.* homosexual.
homúnculo, *n.m.* homunculus.
honda (1), *n.f.* sling; (*naut.*) ***honda y precinta,*** parbuckle.
hondable, *a.* (*naut.*) soundable.
hondarras, *n.f.pl.* dregs, lees.
hondazo, *n.m.* cast *or* throw with a sling.
hondear, *v.t.* (*naut.*) to sound; to unload (*a vessel*).
hondero, *n.m.* slinger.
hondijo, *n.m.* sling.
hondillos, *n.m.pl.* pieces (*forming seat of trousers*).
hondo, -da (2), *a.* deep, profound; low. — *n.m.* bottom; ***en todo lo hondo,*** right at the bottom.
hondón, *n.m.* bottom; hollow, dell, glen; foot-piece (*of a stirrup*); eye (*of a needle*).
hondonada, *n.f.* hollow, depression, dale.
hondura, *n.f.* depth, profundity; (*fig.*) ***meterse en honduras,*** to get out of depth, get into deep water.
Honduras, *n.f.pl.* Honduras.
hondureño, -ña, *a.*, *n.m.f.* Honduran (person).
honestar, *v.t.* to honour.
honestidad, *n.f.* modesty, decency; purity, chastity; honesty.
honesto, -ta, *a.* modest, decent; pure, chaste; honest; ***estado honesto,*** spinsterhood.
hongo, *n.m.* mushroom; fungus; (***sombrero***) ***hongo,*** bowler (*hat*).
hongoso, -sa, *a.* (*prov.*) fungous, spongy.
honor, *n.m.* honour.
honorable, *a.* honourable.
honorario, -ria, *a.* honorary. — *n.m.* fee, honorarium.
honorífico, -ca, *a.* honorific.
honra, *n.f.* honour, respect; ***tener a mucha honra,*** to be very proud of; ***¡español y a mucha honra!*** Spanish and proud of it!; ***honras fúnebres,*** funeral obsequies.
honradez, *n.f.* honesty; uprightness.
honrado, -da, *a.* honest; upright, fair.
honrador, -ra, *a.* honourer.
honramiento, *n.m.* honouring.
honrar, *v.t.* to honour; to do honour to, be a credit to. — **honrarse,** *v.r.* to deem it an honour.
honrilla, *n.f.* amour propre, self-esteem, pride; modest sense of honour; ***por la negra honrilla,*** because of what people may say.
honroso, -sa, *a.* honourable, creditable.
hontanal, hontanar, *n.m.* place abounding in springs.
hopa, *n.f.* long cassock; sack worn by a condemned man.
hopalanda, *n.f.* student gown.
hopear, *v.t.* to wag the tail (*fox*).
hopo, *n.m.* brush, tail (*fox*); ***seguir el hopo a,*** to dog, pursue closely; ***sudar el hopo,*** to slave, sweat; ***volver el hopo,*** to turn tail.
hora, *adv.* now, at present. — *n.f.* hour; time; ***hora de comer,*** mealtime, lunchtime; ***hora de la verdad,*** moment of truth; ***hora suprema,*** last hour, hour of death; ***horas de trabajo,*** working hours; ***horas extraordinarias,*** overtime; ***horas punta,*** rush hours; ***dar la hora,*** to strike (*clock*); ***pedir hora,*** to make an appointment; ***no ver la hora de,*** to be all impatience to, be unable to wait to; ***no ve la hora de irse,*** he can't wait to go; ***tiene las horas contadas,*** his hours are numbered; ***¿qué hora es?*** what time is it?; ***a la hora,*** on time; ***¡a buena hora! ¡a buenas horas!*** a fine time!; ***llegar a buena hora,*** to arrive early, in good time; ***a estas horas,*** by now, by this time; ***a última hora,*** at the last minute; ***en buena hora,*** happily, luckily; ***en mala hora,*** in an evil hour, unluckily; ***entre horas,*** between meals; ***por horas,*** by the hour, hourly; ***por hora,*** an hour, per hour; (*pl.*) (*eccles.*) hours.
horaciano, -na, *a.* Horatian.
horadable, *a.* capable of being pierced.
horadación, *n.f.* perforation; boring, piercing, tunnelling.
horadado, *n.m.* silk-worm's cocoon bored through.
horadador, -ra, *a.* perforating, boring. — *n.m.f.* perforator, borer.
horadar, *v.t.* to perforate, bore, pierce.
horado, *n.m.* hole bored through; cavern, grotto; cavity.
horambre, *n.m.* hole (*in millstone*).
horario, -ria, *a.* horary, horal, hour. — *n.m.* hour-hand (*of clock* or *watch*); timetable; hours.
horca, *n.f.* gallows, gibbet; (*agric.*) hay-fork, pitch-fork; forked prop; yoke (*for dogs* or *hogs*); rope *or* string (*of onions* or *garlic*); ***señor de horca y cuchillo,*** lord of the manor (*having power of life and death*); ***pasar por las horcas caudinas,*** to be forced to knuckle under; ***mostrar la horca antes que el lugar,*** to meet trouble half-way.
horcado, -da, *a.* forked.
horcadura, *n.f.* fork (*of a tree*).
horcajadas, horcajadillas, *adv.* ***a —,*** astride, astraddle.
horcajadura, *n.f.* crutch (*of legs*).
horcajo, *n.m.* yoke *or* collar (*for mules*); Y-shaped division of the beam (*in oil-mills*); fork *or* confluence (*of two streams*); point of union (*of two mountains* or *hills*).
horcate, *n.m.* hame, collar (*of a horse*).
horco, *n.m.* rope *or* string (*of onions* or *garlic*).
horcón, *n.m.* forked pole.
horchata, *n.f.* orgeat; ***horchata de chufas,*** drink made of earth nuts.
horchatería, *n.f.* place where orgeat is made and sold.
horchatero, -ra, *n.m.f.* maker *or* seller of orgeat.
horda, *n.f.* horde; mob.
hordiate, *n.m.* pearl-barley; barley-water.

hordeína, *n.f.* hordein; finest barley-bran.
horizontal, *a., n.m.f.* horizontal; (*Hisp. Am.*) ***buscar*** or ***tomar la horizontal,*** to lie down.
horizontalidad, *n.f.* horizontality.
horizonte, *n.m.* horizon.
horma, *n.f.* form, mould; boot-tree, shoe-tree, shoemaker's last; block, hatter's block; (*mas.*) dry wall; (*Cub., Per.*) sugar-loaf mould; (*coll.*) ***hallar la horma de su zapato,*** to meet one's match *or* Waterloo.
hormaza, *n.f.* (*mas.*) dry wall.
hormazo, *n.m.* blow with a last *or* block; heap of stones.
hormero, *n.m.* last-maker.
hormiga, *n.f.* (*ent.*) ant; (*med.*) itch; ***ser una hormiga,*** to be very thrifty *or* a busy bee; ***hormiga león,*** ant lion; ***hormiga roja*** or ***silvestre,*** red ant.
hormigo, *n.m.* sifted ash used in smelting quicksilver; (*pl.*) sweetmeat of mashed nuts, honey etc.; coarse parts of ground wheat.
hormigón, *n.m.* concrete; (*vet.*) disease of cattle; (*bot.*) disease of some plants; ***hormigón hidráulico,*** beton, hydraulic mortar; ***hormigón armado,*** reinforced concrete.
hormigonera, *n.f.* concrete mixer.
hormigoso, -sa, *a.* (pertaining to the) ant; full of ants; ant-eaten; itchy.
hormigueamiento [HORMIGUEO].
hormiguear, *v.i.* to swarm; to crawl, creep (*with a sensation of insects*); to teem.
hormigueo, *n.m.* swarming; crawling sensation; (*coll.*) unrest, worry.
hormiguero, -ra, *a.* pertaining to ants, feeding on ants. — *n.m.* anthill; swarm (*of people*); (*orn.*) wryneck; pile of burned compost; (*sl.*) petty thief.
hormiguilla, *n.f.* small ant; tickling *or* creeping sensation; itching.
hormiguillo, *n.m.* tingling, crawling sensation; people ranged in a line who pass materials *or* loads from hand to hand, human chain; (*Mex.*) spicy syrup; almond sweetmeat; (*min.*) amalgamating mixture.
hormiguita, *n.f.* tiny little ant; (*coll.*) very thrifty person, a busy little bee.
hormilla, *n.f.* small last; button-mould.
hormón, *n.m.,* **hormona,** *n.f.* hormone.
hormonal, *a.* hormonal.
hornabeque, *n.m.* (*fort.*) hornwork.
hornablenda, *n.f.* hornblende.
hornacero, *n.m.* (*jewel.*) crucible man.
hornacina, *n.f.* vaulted niche.
hornacho, *n.m.* shaft (*of a mine*); excavation (*formed in a hill, as a sand-pit etc.*); furnace (*for casting statues*).
hornachuela, *n.f.* cave; hut; hole in a wall.
hornada, *n.f.* batch, baking (*of bread, bricks etc.*); melt (*of blast furnace*).
hornaguear, *v.t.* to dig for coal.
hornaguero, -ra, *a.* loose, too large; spacious, roomy; coal-bearing. — *n.f.* pit-coal, hard coal.
hornaje, *n.m.* (*prov.*) fee for baking bread.
hornaza, *n.f.* jeweller's furnace; yellow glazing.
hornazo, *n.m.* Easter cake ornamented with eggs; present given to Lenten preacher.
hornear, *v.i.* to carry on the trade of a baker.
hornería, *n.f.* trade of a baker.
hornero, -ra, *n.m.f.* baker. — *n.m.* (*Arg., Bol.*) oven-bird.
hornija, *n.f.* brushwood (*for heating an oven*).
hornijero, *n.m.* person who supplies an oven with fuel.
hornilla, *n.f.* kitchen stove; grated chamber (*in a masonry kitchen-range*); pigeon-hole (*for nesting*).
hornillo, *n.m.* portable furnace, range *or* stove; (gas *or* electric) ring; (*min.*) blast-hole; (*mil.*) fougade; ***hornillo de atanor,*** athanor (*self-feeding digesting furnace*).
hornito, *n.m.* (*Mex.*) mud-volcano.
horno, *n.m.* oven; kiln; furnace; cavity in which bees lodge; ***horno de ladrillo,*** brick-kiln; ***horno de reverbero,*** reverberatory furnace; ***alto horno,*** blast furnace; ***horno de manga,*** cupola furnace; ***horno de copela,*** cupelling *or* cupellation furnace; ***horno de calcinación,*** calcining furnace; ***no está el horno para bollos,*** it is not the right time, not a suitable moment; it's no time for frivolity.
horometría, *n.f.* horometry.
horón, *n.m.* large round hamper *or* frail.
horópter, horóptero, *n.m.* horopter.
horóscopo, *n.m.* horoscope.
horqueta, *n.f.* forked pole; (*naut.*) outrigger.
horquilla, *n.f.* forked pole, pitchfork; hairpin; (bicycle) fork; (telephone) cradle; (*mech.*) gab, jaw; yoke; rowlock; disease which causes hair to split.
horrendo, -da, *a.* hideous, horrible, fearful, awful, grim, ghastly.
hórreo, *n.m.* granary.
horrero, *n.m.* keeper of a granary.
horribilidad, *n.f.* horribleness, dreadfulness.
horribilísimo, *a.* most horrible.
horrible, *a.* horrible, awful, hideous, dreadful, heinous, ghastly.
horridez, *n.f.* horridness, dreadfulness.
hórrido, -da, *a.* horrid, horrible, hideous.
horrífico, -ca, *a.* horrific, horrifying.
horripilación, *n.f.* horripilation; bristling of the hair.
horripilante, *a.* horrifying, hair-raising.
horripilar, *v.t.* to make (*s.o.'s*) hair stand on end, horrify.
horrisonante, horrísono, -na, *a.* horrisonant.
horro, -rra, *a.* enfranchized; free, disengaged; sterile, barren.
horror, *n.m.* horror; loathsome thing; ***¡qué horror!*** how awful!; ***tener horror a, tener en horror,*** to have a horror of, loathe, detest.
horrorizar [C], *v.t.* to horrify.
horroroso, -sa, *a.* horrible, horrid, hideous, ghastly.
horrura, *n.f.* filth, dirt, dross.
hortaliza, *n.f.* vegetable.
hortatorio, -ria, *a.* hortatory.
hortelano, -na, *a.* (pertaining to) garden *or* orchard. — *n.m.* (*orn.*) ortolan; gardener, horticulturist. — *n.f.* gardener's wife.
hortense, *a.* (pertaining to) kitchen garden *or* orchard; ***plantas hortenses,*** vegetables.
hortensia, *n.f.* hydrangea.
hortera, *n.m.* shop assistant; ***de hortera,*** common, low-class. — *n.f.* wooden bowl.
hortícola, *a.* horticultural.
horticultor, -ra, *n.m.f.* horticulturist.
horticultura, *n.f.* horticulture, gardening.
hosco, -ca, *a.* dark-coloured; sullen, surly; gloomy; proud, arrogant.
hoscoso, -sa, *a.* rough, bristly.
hospedador, -ra, *n.m.f.* host, one who provides lodging.
hospedaje, *n.m.* lodging, board; cost of lodging *or* board.
hospedamiento, *n.m.* lodging, board.
hospedar, *v.t.* to lodge, give lodging, put up. — **hospedar(se),** *v.i.* (*v.r.*) to lodge, have lodgings (in); to stop *or* put up (at); to live (in).
hospedería, *n.f.* hostelry, inn; hospice, place for guests (*in convents*); hostel.
hospedero, -ra, *n.m.f.* host; innkeeper; hospitaller; hosteller.
hospiciano, -na, *n.m.f.* inmate of a poorhouse.

hospicio, *n.m.* hospice; poorhouse; orphan asylum.
hospital, *n.m.* hospital; ***hospital de campaña*** or ***de sangre,*** field hospital; (*coll.*) ***estar hecho un hospital,*** to be a mass of aches and pains.
hospitalario, -ria, *a.* hospitable. — *n.m.f.* hospitaller.
hospitalero, -ra, *n.m.f.* manager of a hospital; hospitaller.
hospitalidad, *n.f.* hospitality; hospitableness; time spent in a hospital.
hospitalito, *n.m.* small hospital.
hospitalización, *n.f.* hospitalization.
hospitalizar [C], *v.t.* to hospitalize.
hosquedad, *n.f.* sullenness, surliness.
hostal, *n.m.* hostelry, inn.
hostelero, -ra, *n.m.f.* innkeeper, tavernkeeper.
hostería, *n.f.* inn, tavern, hostelry.
hostia, *n.f.* host; victim; (*eccles.*) Host, wafer.
hostiario, *n.m.* (*eccles.*) wafer-box.
hostiero, *n.m.* wafer maker. — *n.m.* (*eccles.*) wafer box.
hostigador, -ra, *a.* harassing. — *n.m.f.* harasser.
hostigamiento, *n.m.* harassing, plaguing; lashing, whipping, flogging.
hostigar [B], *v.t.* to harass, plague; to lash, whip, flog; (*Hisp. Am.*) to cloy.
hostigo, *n.m.* lash; weather-beaten wall; beating of rain and winds (*against a wall*).
hostigoso, -sa, *a.* (*Hisp. Am.*) cloying, sickening.
hostil, *a.* hostile.
hostilidad, *n.f.* hostility.
hostilizar [C], *v.t.* to harry, harass.
hotel, *n.m.* hotel; villa, mansion.
hotelería, *n.f.* hotel-keeping.
hotelero, -ra, *a.* of hotels, hotel. — *n.m.f.* hotel-keeper.
hotentote, -ta, *a., n.m.f.* Hottentot.
hoy, *adv.* today; now, nowadays; ***hoy día*** or ***hoy en día,*** nowadays; ***hoy por hoy,*** as things stand at present, the way things are now; ***de hoy en adelante,*** from today on, in future; ***de hoy a mañana,*** before tomorrow; ***antes hoy que mañana,*** the sooner the better; ***hoy por ti y mañana por mí,*** thou today and I tomorrow.
hoya, *n.f.* hole, hollow, pit; grave; dale, valley.
hoyada, *n.f.* dip, depression, hollow.
hoyanca, *n.f.* (*coll.*) potter's field; common grave.
hoyito, *n.m.* small hole; dimple.
hoyo, *n.m.* hole, hollow, pit; indentation, dent; pock-mark; grave.
hoyoso, -sa, *a.* pitted, full of holes.
hoyuela, *n.f.* hollow (*in the neck*).
hoyuelo, *n.m.* little hole; dimple; boy's game.
hoz, *n.f.* sickle, reaping-hook; defile, ravine, narrow pass; (*coll.*) ***de hoz y*** (***de***) ***coz,*** up to the hilt, fully, unreservedly.
hozadero, *n.m.* place where hogs root.
hozadura, *n.f.* hole made by rooting.
hozar [C], *v.t.* to root (*hogs*).
huaca, *n.f.* (*Bol., Per.*) Indian tomb.
huacal, *n.m.* crate; (*Col., Mex., Ven.*) hurdle-basket.
huacatay, *n.f.* (*Hisp. Am.*) mint.
huaco, *n.m.* idol.
huachache, *n.m.* (*Per.*) mosquito.
huaico, *n.m.* (*Per.*) avalanche.
huairuro, *n.m.* (*Per.*) kidney bean (*used as an ornament*).
huango, *n.m.* (*Ec.*) pigtail.
huaquero, *n.m.* (*Per.*) pitcher.
huasca, *n.f.* (*Per.*) whip, lash.
huayno, *n.m.* (*Per.*) Indian dance.
hucha, *n.f.* large chest; money box; toy bank; savings.
huchear, *v.t., v.i.* to hoot (at); to urge on.
¡huchohó! *interj.* word used to call birds.
huebra, *n.f.* ground ploughed in one day by a yoke of oxen; pair of mules with a ploughman hired *or* let out for a day's work.
huebrero, *n.m.* day-labourer who ploughs with a pair of mules; one who lets out mules by the day.
hueco, -ca, *a.* hollow; empty; vain, conceited; resonant, sonorous; pompous; puffed up, inflated; soft, spongy. — *n.m.* hollow, cavity; (stair) well; (lift) shaft; gap, break; free moment; opening; vacancy; (bone) socket. — *n.f.* notch (*of spindle*).
huecograbado, *n.m.* photogravure (*for rotary presses*).
huecú, *n.m.* (*Chi.*) deep slough covered with grass.
huélfago, *n.m.* (*vet.*) heaves.
huelga, *n.f.* strike (*of workmen*); leisure, recreation; (*agric.*) fallow; ***ir a la huelga*** or ***ponerse*** or ***declararse en huelga,*** to go on strike; ***huelga de brazos caídos,*** go-slow; ***huelga de hambre,*** hunger strike; ***huelga patronal,*** lock-out; ***huelga sentada,*** sit-down strike.
huelgo (1), *n.m.* breath, respiration; (*mech.*) wind-age; room, space; ***tomar huelgo,*** to take breath.
huelgo (2), *pres. indic.* [HOLGAR].
huelguista, *n.m.* striker.
huelguístico, -ca, *a.* strike.
huella, *n.f.* tread, treading; impression, mark; trace; trail, track, rut; footprint, footstep; stair-tread; ***huella dactilar*** or ***digital,*** fingerprint; ***seguir las huellas de,*** to follow in the footsteps of; (*cine.*) ***huella de sonido,*** sound track.
huello (1), *n.m.* step (*of an animal*); tread, trodden path, lower part of an animal's hoof.
huello (2), *pres. indic.* [HOLLAR].
huemul, *n.m.* (*Arg., Chi.*) Andes deer.
huequecito, *n.m.* small cavity *or* space.
huerco, *n.m.* (*obs., poet.*) hell; Hades, underworld; (*fig.*) weeper, whiner, unhappy fellow.
huérfago [HUÉLFAGO].
huerfanito, -ta, *n.m.f.* little orphan.
huérfano, -na, *a., n.m.f.* orphan.
huero, -ra, *a.* empty, void; addle, addled; (*Mex.*) fair, blonde; (*coll.*) ***salir huero,*** to turn out bad, flop.
huerta, *n.f.* large vegetable *or* kitchen garden; orchard; irrigated *or* irrigable land.
huertano, -na, *n.m.f.* inhabitant of an irrigated region.
huertero, -ra, *n.m.f.* (*Arg., Per.*) gardener.
huertezuelo, *n.m.* small orchard.
huerto, *n.m.* orchard; garden, kitchen garden.
huesa, *n.f.* grave; ***tener un pie en la huesa,*** to have one foot in the grave.
huesarrón, *n.m.* large bone.
huesecico, huesecito, *n.m.* little bone.
huesera, *n.f.* (*Chi.*) [OSAR (1)].
huesillo, *n.m.* (*Hisp. Am.*) peach dried in the sun.
hueso, *n.m.* bone; stone, pip; (*coll.*) drudgery; (*Hisp. Am.*) good-for-nothing; (*coll.*) hard task-master, tough nut, stickler; (*coll.*) hand; (*coll.*) ***la sin hueso,*** the tongue; ***soltar la sin hueso,*** to talk too much; ***estar en los huesos,*** to be exceedingly thin; to be all skin and grief; ***mondar los huesos,*** to eat up every scrap; ***no dejar hueso sano,*** not to leave a leg to stand upon; ***no estar con sus huesos,*** to care little about one's health; ***tener los huesos molidos, no poder con sus huesos,*** to be worn out, exhausted; ***roerle a uno los huesos,*** to grumble at s.o.; ***dar un hueso que roer,*** to set a difficult and unprofitable task; ***a otro perro con ese hueso,*** tell that to the marines; (*pl.*) bones (*mortal remains*).
huesoso, -sa, *a.* bony, osseous.
huésped, -da, *n.m.f.* guest; lodger, boarder, (*Am.*) roomer; (*obs.*) host, hostess; (*bot.*) host; ***casa de huéspedes,*** boarding house; (*coll.*) ***echar la***

cuenta sin la huéspeda, no contar con la huéspeda, to reckon without all one's commitments, fail to take everything into account.
hueste, *n.f.* host, army; (*pl.*) followers, supporters.
huesudo, -da, *a.* bony, big-boned.
hueva, *n.f.* roe.
huevar, *v.i.* to begin to lay eggs (*birds*).
huevero, -ra, *n.m.f.* egg dealer; egg-cup. — *n.f.* ovarium (*birds*).
huevo, *n.m.* egg; ***huevo de Colón*** or ***de Juanelo,*** sth. which appears difficult to do, but when tried is found to be easy; ***huevos pasados por agua,*** soft-boiled eggs; ***huevos estrellados*** or ***fritos,*** fried eggs; ***huevos escalfados,*** poached eggs; ***huevos moles,*** yolks of eggs, made up with pounded almonds and sugar; ***huevo hilado,*** thread-like sweetmeat made of eggs and sugar; ***huevos revueltos,*** scrambled eggs; (*coll.*) ***sórbete*** or ***chúpate ese huevo,*** put that in your pipe and smoke it; (*coll.*) ***¡límpiate, que estás de huevo!*** you've got a hope!; ***cacarear, y no poner huevo,*** much ado about nothing; ***parecerse como un huevo a una castaña,*** to be totally unlike; ***andar pisando huevos,*** to go gingerly.
hugonote, -ta, *a.*, *n.m.f.* Huguenot.
huida, *n.f.* flight, escape; leak; shying *or* bolting (*horse*).
huidero, -ra, *a.* fleeting. — *n.m.* cover, shelter.
huidizo, -za, *a.* fugitive; evasive, shifty.
huila, *a.* (*Mex.*) crippled, invalid.
huiliento, *a.* (*Chi.*) ragged.
huillín, *n.m.* (*Chi.*) otter.
huincha, *n.f.* (*Chi.*) hair-ribbon.
huir, *v.t.* to flee, fly, avoid, shun. — *v.i.* to flee, fly, run away; to slip away *or* by; ***huir del fuego y dar en las brasas,*** out of the frying pan into the fire.
hule, *n.m.* rubber; oilcloth, oilskin; (*tauro.*) blood, goring.
hulero, *n.m.* rubber-gatherer.
hulla, *n.f.* (soft) coal; ***hulla grasa,*** soft coal; ***hulla magra*** or ***seca,*** hard coal; ***hulla negra,*** short-flame coal; ***hulla azul,*** tide power; ***hulla blanca,*** water power.
hullero, -ra, *a.* (containing *or* pertaining to) (soft) coal. — *n.f.* colliery.
humada, *n.f.* smoke-signal.
humanal, *a.* human.
humanar, *v.t.* to humanize, soften. — **humanarse,** *v.r.* to become human, soften; to become man (*Christ*).
humanidad, *n.f.* humanity; humankind, mankind; human weakness; (*coll.*) corpulence, fleshiness; (*pl.* **humanidades**) humanities.
humanismo, *n.m.* humanism.
humanista, *n.m.f.* humanist.
humanístico, -ca, *a.* humanistic.
humanitario, -ria, *a.* humanitarian.
humanitarismo, *n.m.* humanitarianism, humaneness.
humanizar [C], *v.t.* to humanize, soften.
humano, -na, *a.* human; humane. — *n.m.f.* human (being).
humarazo, *n.m.* dense smoke.
humareda, *n.f.* great deal of smoke; perplexity, confusion.
humazga, *n.f.* hearth-money, fumage.
humazo, *n.m.* dense smoke; (*fig.*) ***humazo de narices,*** displeasure, vexation.
humeante, *a.* smoky, fuming; steaming.
humear, *v.t.* (*Hisp. Am.*) to fumigate. — *v.i.* to smoke, emit smoke, fumes *or* vapours.
humectación, *n.f.* humidification.
humectante, *a.* (*med.*) humidifying.
humectar, *v.t.* (*med.*) to humidify.
humedad, *n.f.* humidity; dampness; moisture, moistness.
humedal, *n.m.* humid ground, marsh.
humedecer [9], *v.t.* to humidify, moisten, dampen.
húmedo, -da, *a.* humid, damp, moist, wet.
humera [*aspirated* ***h***], *n.f.* (*coll.*) drunkenness.
humeral, *a.* (*anat.*) humeral. — *n.m.* (*eccles.*) humeral veil.
húmero, *n.m.* (*anat.*) humerus.
humero, *n.m.* smoke-pipe, chimney-flue; meat-smoking room.
húmido, -da, *a.* (*poet.*) humid.
humildad, *n.f.* humility; humbleness, lowliness.
humilde, *a.* humble, lowly; meek, submissive.
humillación, *n.f.* humiliation; humbling.
humilladero, *n.m.* roadside cross.
humillador, -ra, *a.* humiliating, humbling. — *n.m.f.* humiliator.
humillante, *a.* humiliating, humbling.
humillar, *v.t.* to humiliate; to humble, abase; to bow, bend.
humillo, *n.m.* thin smoke *or* vapour; vanity, petty pride; disease of sucking pigs.
humita, *n.f.* (*Arg.*, *Chi.*, *Per.*) cake of maize and sugar.
humo, *n.m.* smoke; steam, fume; ***irse todo en humo,*** to go up in smoke; ***a humo de pajas,*** lightly, without reflection; ***subirse el humo a las narices,*** to become irritated, get angry; (*pl.*) (*fig.*) conceit, pride, vanity; homes (*in a town* or *village*); ***vender humos,*** to pretend to have influence; ***bajarle a uno los humos,*** to take s.o. down a peg or two.
humor, *n.m.* (*physiol.*) humour; temper, mood, disposition; ***buen*** (***mal***) ***humor,*** good (bad) temper; ***estar de buen humor,*** to be in a good temper; ***seguir el humor a alguien,*** to humour s.o.; ***no estar de humor para,*** not to be in the mood for.
humorado, -da, *a.* ***bien*** (***mal***) ***humorado,*** in a good (bad) humour *or* temper. — *n.f.* whimsical, witty *or* merry thing to do *or* say.
humoral, *a.* humoral.
humorista, *n.m.f.* humorist; (*med.*) humoralist.
humorístico, -ca, *a.* humorous.
humoroso, -sa, *a.* watery, containing fluid.
humoso, -sa, *a.* smoky, fumy.
humus, *n.m.* humus.
hundible, *a.* sinkable.
hundimiento, *n.m.* sinking; foundering; cave-in, subsidence; collapse, downfall.
hundir, *v.t.* to sink, plunge under; to drive in, stave in; to beat *or* pull down; to shatter, crush. — **hundirse,** *v.r.* to sink, go under; to cave in; to collapse.
húngaro, -ra, *a.*, *n.m.f.* Hungarian. — *n.m.* Hungarian (*language*).
Hungría, *n.f.* Hungary.
huno, -na, *a.* Hunnish. — *n.m.f.* Hun.
hupe, *n.f.* punk, touchwood.
hura, *n.f.* carbuncle on the head.
huracán, *n.m.* hurricane.
huracanado, -da, *a.* of hurricane force.
hurañía, *n.f.* unsociableness, standoffishness.
huraño, -ña, *a.* unsociable, standoffish.
hurera, *n.f.* hole; ferret-hole.
hurgar [B], *v.t.* to stir, poke; to stir up; ***peor es hurgallo,*** it is better left alone; ***hurgarse*** (***en***) ***la nariz,*** to pick one's nose.
hurgón, *n.m.* poker, fire-rake; (*coll.*) thrust (*in fencing*).
hurgonada, *n.f.* poking, poke; (*coll.*) thrust (*with a sword*).
hurgonazo, *n.m.* blow with a poker; (*coll.*) thrust (*with a sword*).
hurgonear, *v.t.* to poke; (*coll.*) to thrust.

hurgonero, *n.m.* poker.
hurí, *n.f.* houri.
hurón, -rona, *a.* unsociable, sullen. — *n.m.f.* ferret; (*fig.*) ferreter, prier; sullen individual.
huronear, *v.i.* to (hunt with a) ferret; (*coll.*) to pry, ferret.
huronera, *n.f.* ferret-hole; (*coll.*) lair, den.
huronero, *n.m.* ferret-keeper.
¡hurra! *interj.* hurrah!
hurtable, *a.* that may be stolen.
hurtadillas, *adv.* ***a* —**, by stealth, slyly.
hurtadineros, *n.m. inv.* (*prov.*) money-box, toy bank.
hurtador, -ra, *a.* stealing, thieving. — *n.m.f.* thief.
hurtagua, *n.f.* watering-pot.
hurtar, *v.t.* to steal; to eat away; to cheat; to plagiarize; to remove; ***hurtar el cuerpo,*** to dodge, duck; ***hurtar el hombro,*** to shirk. — **hurtarse,** *v.r.* to withdraw, hide away.
hurto, *n.m.* theft, stealing; thing stolen; (*min.*) driftway, heading; ***a hurto,*** by stealth.
husada, *n.f.* spindleful (*of yarn*).
husaño, *n.m.* large spindle.
húsar, *n.m.* hussar.
husero, *n.m.* beam (*of antler*).
husillo, *n.m.* small spindle; (*mill.*) wheel-spindle *or* shaft; screw-pin; (*pl.*) drains, small channels for draining fens.
husita, *n.m.* Hussite.
husma, *n.f.* [HUSMEO]; (*coll.*) ***andar a la husma,*** to go prying; to be on the look-out *or* watch (for).
husmeador, -ra, *a.* scenting; nosing around. — *n.m.f.* scenter, prier, smeller.
husmear, *v.t.* to scent, get wind of. — *v.i.* (*coll.*) to pry, peep, nose about; to smell high (*meat*).
husmeo, *n.m.* scenting, smelling; prying.
husmo, *n.m.* high smell (*meat*); [HUSMEO]; (*coll.*) ***estar*** or ***andar al husmo,*** to be on the pry.
huso, *n.m.* spindle; (*min.*) drum (*of a windlass*); (*aer.*) fuselage.
huta, *n.f.* hut, huntsman's blind.
hutía, *n.f.* (*zool.*) hutia.
¡huy! *interj.* phew!
huyuyo, -ya (*Cub.*) [HURAÑO].

I

I, i, *n.f.* letter I, i.
ib, *n.m.* (*Mex.*) small kidney-shaped bean.
ibayaú, *n.m.* night bird of the pampas.
ibérico, -ca, iberio, -ria, *a.* Iberian.
ibero, -ra, *a., n.m.f.* Iberian.
iberoamericano, -na, *a., n.m.f.* Ibero-American; Latin-American.
íbice, *n.m.* ibex.
ibis, *n.f.* ibis.
Ibiza, *n.f.* Ibiza.
ibón, *n.m.* lake *or* basin on the slopes of the Pyrenees.
icaco, *n.m.* West Indian cocoa-plum.
icástico, -ca, *a.* natural, without disguise *or* ornament.
icipo, *n.m.* (*Arg.*) creeping plant used for thatching and rope-making.
icnografía, *n.f.* (*arch.*) ichnography, ground-plan; ground-plot.
icnográfico, -ca, *a.* (*arch.*) ichnographical.
iconoclasta, *a.* iconoclastic. — *n.m.f.* iconoclast.
iconografía, *n.f.* iconography.
iconográfico, -ca, *a.* iconographical.
iconólatra, *n.m.* iconolater.
iconología, *n.f.* (*art*) iconology.
iconómaco, *a.* iconoclastic.
iconostasio, *n.m.* (*eccles.*) iconostasis.
icor, *n.m.* (*surg.*) gleet, ichor, watery humour.
icoroso, -sa, *a.* ichorous, serous.
icosaedro, *n.m.* icosahedron.
ictericia, *n.f.* jaundice.
ictericiado, -da, ictérico, -ca, *a.* icterical, jaundiced. — *n.m.f.* jaundiced person.
ictíneo, *n.m.* submarine vessel.
ictiófago, -ga, *a.* fish-eating. — *n.m.f.* ichthyophagist.
ictiología, *n.f.* ichthyology.
ictiológico, -ca, *a.* ichthyologist.
ictiosauro, *n.m.* ichthyosaurus.
ictiosis, *n.f.* ichthyosis.
ichal, *n.m.* (*Per.*) grassland.
icho, ichú, *n.m.* (*Per.*) ichu grass.
ida (1), *n.f.* departure, outgoing; trail (*of game*); (*fenc.*) sally; ***viaje de ida,*** outward trip; ***idas,*** (frequent) visits; ***idas y venidas,*** coming and going; ***en dos idas y venidas,*** in a jiffy; ***ida y vuelta,*** out and home; ***viaje de ida y vuelta,*** return trip, round trip; ***billete de ida y vuelta,*** return ticket.
idea, *n.f.* idea, notion; intention; ***para que te des una idea,*** to give you an idea, so that you can get an idea; ***tener*** or ***llevar (la) idea de,*** to have it in mind to, intend to; ***cambiar de idea,*** to change one's mind; ***tener mala idea,*** to be nasty, spiteful, vicious; ***hacer algo a mala idea,*** to do sth. out of spite.
ideal, *a.* ideal; of ideas; (*coll.*) heavenly, delightful. — *n.m.* ideal.
idealidad, *n.f.* ideality; (*coll.*) heavenly *or* delightful thing.
idealismo, *n.m.* idealism.
idealista, *a.* idealist, idealistic. — *n.m.f.* idealist.
idealizar [C], *v.t.* to idealize.
idear, *v.t.* to think up, devise.
ideático, -ca, *a.* (*Hisp. Am.*) whimsical, capricious.
idéntico, -ca, *a.* identical.
identidad, *n.f.* identity; identicalness.
identificación, *n.f.* identification.
identificar [A], *v.t.* to identify.
ideografía, *n.f.* ideography.
ideología, *n.f.* ideology.
ideológico, -ca, *a.* ideological.
ideologizar [C], *v.t.* to give an ideological content to, give a stiffening of ideology to.
ideólogo, *n.m.* ideologist.
idílico, -ca, *a.* idyllic.
idilio, *n.m.* (*poet.*) idyll; romance.
idioma, *n.m.* language.
idiomático, -ca, *a.* (of) language, linguistic; idiomatic.
idiosincrasia, *n.f.* idiosyncrasy.
idiosincrásico, -ca, *a.* idiosyncratic.
idiota, *a.* idiotic. — *n.m.f.* idiot.
idiotez, *n.f.* idiocy; piece of stupidity.
idiótico, -ca, *a.* idiotic.
idiotismo, *n.m.* ignorance; idiocy; idiom.
ido, -da (2), *a.* having one's head in the clouds; gone, crazy.
idólatra, *a.* idolatrous. — *n.m.f.* idolater, idolatress
dolatradamente, *adv.* idolatrously; madly.
idolatrar, *v.t., v.i.* to idolatrize; to idolize.
idolatría, *n.f.* idolatry.
idolátrico, -ca, *a.* idolatrous.
ídolo, *n.m.* idol.
idoneidad, *n.f.* fitness, suitability.
idóneo, -nea, *a.* fit, suitable.
idos, idus, *n.m.pl.* ides.
iglesia, *n.f.* church; ***La Iglesia,*** the (R.C.) Church; ***iglesia o mar o casa real,*** the church, the sea, or the royal service (*possible career options in the 16th and 17th centuries*); ***llevar a la iglesia,*** to lead to the altar; ***¡iglesia me llamo!*** asylum!; ***con la iglesia hemos topado,*** we are really up against it, it's a hopeless proposition.
ignaro, -ra, *a.* ignorant, unlearned.
ignavia, *n.f.* idleness, laziness; carelessness.
ígneo, -nea, *a.* igneous, of fire.
ignición, *n.f.* ignition, setting on fire.
ignícola, *a.* fire-worshipping. — *n.m.f.* fire-worshipper.
ignífero, -ra, *a.* igniferous.
igniscencia, *n.f.* incandescence.
ignito, -ta, *a.* ignited, inflamed.
ignívomo, -ma, *a.* (*poet.*) vomiting fire.
ignoble, *a.* ignoble.
ignografía, *n.f.* (*arch.*) ichnography.
ignominia, *n.f.* ignominy.
ignominioso, -sa, *a.* ignominious.
ignorancia, *n.f.* ignorance.
ignorante, *a.* ignorant; unaware. — *n.m.* ignoramus.
ignorantón, -tona, *a., n.m.f.* utterly *or* hopelessly ignorant (individual).
ignorar, *v.t.* to be ignorant of, not to know; (*neol.*) to be unwilling *or* refuse to know.
ignoto, -ta, *a.* unknown.
igorrote, *n.m.* (*Philip.*) Igorot, Igorrote.
igual, *a.* equal; same; even. — *n.m.* equal; equals sign. — *adv.* probably; ***nunca vi cosa igual,*** I never saw anything like it; ***(al) igual que,*** in the same way as, just as; ***por igual,*** evenly, without discrimination; ***da*** or ***es igual,*** it makes no difference; ***me es igual,*** it is all the same to me; ***sin igual,*** matchless; ***de igual a igual,*** as equals, on an equal footing; ***igual viene luego,*** very likely *or* probably he'll come later.
iguala, *n.f.* equalization; agreement; annual fee; level.
igualación, *n.f.* equalization; agreement; (*obs.*) equation.
igualado, -da, *a.* with even plumage.
igualador, -ra, *a.* equalizing; levelling. — *n.m.f.* equalizer; leveller.
igualamiento, *n.m.* equalizing, equalization, levelling.

igualar, *v.t.* to equalize; to smooth, level, even; to match; to deem equal; to adjust, fit; to equate. — *v.i.* to be equal (***a,*** to). — **igualarse,** *v.r.* — ***a*** or ***con,*** to equal, be equal to.
igualdad, *n.f.* equality; evenness; equability; ***en igualdad de circunstancias,*** other *or* all things being equal.
igualmente, *adv.* equally; likewise; and the same to you.
iguana, *n.f.* iguana.
iguanodonte, *n.m.* iguanodon.
igüedo, *n.m.* buck.
ijada, *n.f.* flank (*of animal*); loin; stitch (*pain*); (*fig.*) ***tener su ijada,*** to have a weak side *or* point.
ijadear, *v.i.* to pant.
ijar, *n.m.* flank; ***caballo de pocos ijares,*** light-flanked horse.
ilación, *n.f.* illation; connection.
ilapso, *n.m.* trance.
ilativo, -va, *a.* illative.
ilécebra, *n.f.* cajolery, flattery.
ilegal, *a.* illegal, unlawful.
ilegalidad, *n.f.* illegality, unlawfulness.
ilegible, *a.* illegible, unreadable.
ilegitimidad, *n.f.* illegitimacy.
ilegítimo, -ma, *a.* illegitimate.
íleo, *n.m.* (*med.*) ileus.
íleon, *n.m.* (*anat.*) ileum.
ileso, -sa, *a.* unhurt, unharmed, unscathed.
iletrado, -da, *a.* unlettered; illiterate.
ilíaco, -ca (1), *a.* iliac (*relating to the ilium*).
ilíaco, -ca (2), *a.* belonging *or* relating to Ilium *or* Troy.
iliberal, *a.* illiberal.
ilicíneo, -nea, *a.* (*bot.*) ilicaceous.
ilicitano, -na, *a., n.m.f.* (native) of Elche.
ilícito, -ta, *a.* illicit, unlawful.
ilicitud, *n.f.* illicitness, unlawfulness.
ilimitado, -da, *a.* unlimited, boundless, limitless.
ilion, *n.m.* (*anat.*) ilium.
ilíquido, -da, *a.* unliquidated.
iliterato, *a.* unlearned.
ilógico, -ca, *a.* illogical.
ilota, *n.m.f.* helot.
ilotismo, *n.m.* helotism.
iludir, *v.t.* to mock.
iluminación, *n.f.* illumination, lighting; painting in tempera.
iluminado, -da, *a.* illuminate. — *n.m.pl.* (**iluminados**) illuminati.
iluminador, -ra, *a.* illuminating. — *n.m.f.* (*art*) illuminator.
iluminar, *v.t.* to illuminate.
iluminativo, -va, *a.* illuminative.
ilusión, *n.f.* illusion; delusion; expectation; ***no hay que hacerse ilusiones,*** we must be under no delusion, it is useless to harbour false hopes; (*coll.*) ***me hace muchísima ilusión,*** I am looking forward to it no end; I am thrilled to bits by the idea, I am tickled pink at the prospect.
ilusionar, *v.t.* to fill with hope and expectation, thrill. — **ilusionarse,** *v.r.* to build up hopes; to become filled with hope and expectation, feel thrilled.
ilusivo, -va, *a.* illusive, delusive.
iluso, -sa, *a.* deluded, deceived, beguiled. — *n.m.f.* dreamer.
ilusorio, -ria, *a.* illusory, delusive, deceptive; imaginary.
ilustración, *n.f.* illustration; enlightenment; education.
ilustrado, -da, *a.* enlightened; educated.
ilustrador, *a.* illustrating; enlightening. — *n.m.f.* illustrator; enlightener.
ilustrar, *v.t.* to illustrate; to enlighten; to ennoble, impart lustre to. — **ilustrarse,** *v.r.* to acquire learning *or* enlightenment.
ilustrativo, -va, *a.* illustrative.
ilustre, *a.* illustrious.
ilustrísimo, -ma, *a.* most illustrious.
imadas, *n.f.pl.* (*naut.*) ways, sliding planks.
imagen, *n.f.* image, picture; ***a su imagen,*** in his own image; ***imagen de bulto,*** image in high relief.
imaginable, *a.* imaginable.
imaginación, *n.f.* imagination.
imaginar, *v.t., v.i.* to imagine. — **imaginarse,** *v.r.* to imagine, think, fancy.
imaginaria (1), *n.f.* reserve guard; (*mil.*) night guard.
imaginario, -ria (2), *a.* imaginary. — *n.f.* (*math.*) imaginary.
imaginativo, -va, *a.* imaginative. — *n.f.* (capacity for) imagination; ***no tiene imaginativa,*** he has no imagination.
imaginería, *n.f.* imagery; fancy embroidery in colours; (*art*) statuary.
imaginero, *n.m.* sculptor of religious images.
imán (1), *n.m.* magnet; loadstone.
imán (2), *n.m.* imam.
imanación, *n.f.* magnetization.
imanar, *v.t.* to magnetize.
imantación, *n.f.* magnetization.
imantar, *v.t.* to magnetize.
imbécil, *a., n.m.f.* imbecile, half-witted (individual); ***eres un soberano imbécil,*** you're an idiot.
imbecilidad, *n.f.* imbecility; (*coll.*) utterly stupid thing to do *or* say.
imbele, *a.* (*poet.*) unfit for war.
imberbe, *a.* beardless.
imbibición, *n.f.* imbibition.
imbornal, *n.m.* (*naut.*) scupper-hole; drain-hole.
imborrable, *a.* ineffaceable; unforgettable.
imbricación, *n.f.* imbrication.
imbricar [A], *v.t.* to imbricate.
imbuir [O], *v.t.* to imbue.
imbunche, *n.m.* (*Chi.*) Araucanian witch who kidnapped children six months old to change them into monsters; (*Chi.*) ugly and fat child; imbroglio.
imitable, *a.* imitable.
imitación, *n.f.* imitation; ***a imitación de,*** in imitation of; ***perlas (de) imitación,*** imitation pearls.
imitador, -ra, *a.* imitating, aping. — *n.m.f.* imitator, mimic.
imitante, *a.* imitating.
imitar, *v.t.* to imitate; to ape, mimic.
imitativo, -va, *a.* imitative.
imoscapo, *n.m.* (*arch.*) apophyge.
impacción, *n.f.* impact; impaction.
impaciencia, *n.f.* impatience; eagerness.
impacientar, *v.t.* to make impatient, cause to lose patience. — **impacientarse,** *v.r.* to get impatient.
impaciente, *a.* impatient; eager.
impacto, *n.m.* impact.
impagable, *a.* that cannot be paid back; beyond price.
impalpabilidad, *n.f.* impalpability.
impalpable, *a.* impalpable.
impar, *a.* odd, uneven. — *n.m.f.* odd number, thing, person etc.
imparcial, *a.* impartial, unbiased.
imparcialidad, *n.f.* impartiality, freedom from bias.
imparidad, *n.f.* inequality, imparity.
imparipinado, -da, *a.* imparipinnate.
imparisílabo, -ba, *a.* imparisyllabic.
impartible, *a.* indivisible, impossible to share (out).
impartir, *v.t.* to give, give out.

impasable, *a.* impassable.
impasibilidad, *n.f.* impassiveness.
impasible, *a.* impassive.
impavidez, *n.f.* dauntlessness.
impávido, -da, *a.* dauntless, undaunted, unflinching.
impecabilidad, *n.f.* impeccability.
impecable, *a.* impeccable, spotless, faultless.
impedido, -da, *a.* invalid, disabled, crippled.
impedidor, -ra, *a.* impeding, obstructing, hindering.
impediente, *a.* hindering, obstructing.
impedimenta, *n.f.* impedimenta.
impedimento, *n.m.* impediment, obstacle, hindrance, obstruction.
impedir [8], *v.t.* to impede, hinder, obstruct; to prevent.
impeditivo, -va, *a.* impeditive, impeding, hindering.
impelente, *a.* forcing, impelling, propelling.
impeler, *v.t.* to impel, drive *or* move forward; to propel.
impender, *v.t.* to spend, invest.
impenetrabilidad, *n.f.* impenetrability.
impenetrable, *a.* impenetrable, impervious.
impenitencia, *n.f.* impenitence.
impenitente, *a.* impenitent, obdurate.
impensa, *n.f.* (*law*) expense, upkeep expense.
impensado, -da, *a.* unexpected, unforeseen.
imperante, *a.* ruling, commanding; prevailing; (*astrol.*) dominant.
imperar, *v.i.* to rule, reign, hold sway; to prevail, be prevailing.
imperativo, -va, *a.* imperative, commanding. — *n.m.* imperative; ***imperativo categórico,*** categorical imperative. — *n.f.* tone *or* manner of command; ***tomar la imperativa,*** to assume authority *or* an authoritative tone.
imperatoria (I), *n.f.* (*bot.*) masterwort.
imperatorio, -ria (2), *a.* imperatorial.
imperceptible, *a.* imperceptible.
imperdible, *a.* unlosable. — *n.m.* safety pin.
imperdonable, *a.* unpardonable, unforgivable.
imperecedero, -ra, *a.* imperishable, undying.
imperfección, *n.f.* imperfection, fault, flaw, blemish.
imperfecto, -ta, *a.* imperfect, defective, faulty. — *n.m.* (*gram.*) imperfect tense.
imperforación, *n.f.* (*med.*) imperforation.
imperial, *a.* imperial. — *n.f.* imperial, upper deck (*of a stage coach, bus etc.*); (*naut.*) poop-royal.
imperialismo, *n.m.* imperialism.
imperialista, *a.* imperialistic. — *n.m.f.* imperialist.
impericia, *n.f.* lack of skill, inexpertness.
imperio, *n.m.* empire; dominion, command, sway; ***valer un imperio,*** to be of great worth, priceless.
imperiosidad, *n.f.* imperiousness.
imperioso, -sa, *a.* imperious, imperative, overbearing.
imperito, -ta, *a.* unskilled, inexpert.
impermeabilidad, *n.f.* impermeability.
impermeabilización, *n.f.* waterproofing, making waterproof.
impermeabilizante, *a.* waterproofing.
impermeable, *a.* impermeable, water-tight, waterproof, impervious. — *n.m.* raincoat.
impermutable, *a.* unexchangeable.
imperscrutable, *a.* inscrutable.
impersonal, *a.* impersonal; ***verbo impersonal,*** impersonal verb; ***en*** or ***por impersonal,*** impersonally.
impersonalizar [C], *v.t.* to use (*verbs*) impersonally.
impersuasible, *a.* unpersuadable.
impertérrito, -ta, *a.* unperturbed, unshaken.
impertinencia, *n.f.* impertinence.
impertinente, *a.* impertinent. — *n.m.pl.* (**impertinentes**) lorgnette.
imperturbabilidad, *n.f.* imperturbability.
imperturbable, *a.* imperturbable.
impetra, *n.f.* licence, permission; bull granting dubious benefices.
impetrable, *a.* (*law*) impetrable.
impetración, *n.f.* impetration.
impetrador, -ra, *n.m.f.* impetrator.
impetrante, *a.* impetrating. — *n.m.* impetrator.
impetrar, *v.t.* to impetrate, obtain by entreaty; to beg for, beseech.
ímpetu, *n.m.* impetus; impetuosity, thrust, drive.
impetuosidad, *n.f.* impetuosity.
impetuoso, -sa, *a.* impetuous.
impiedad, *n.f.* impiety; impiousness.
impiedoso, -sa, *a.* impious; pitiless.
impío, -pía, *a.* impious, irreligious, godless; pitiless.
impla, *n.f.* wimple; material for wimples.
implacabilidad, *n.f.* implacability.
implacable, *a.* implacable.
implantación, *n.f.* implantation.
implantar, *v.t.* to implant, bring in.
implantón, *n.m.* (*prov.*) piece of timber.
implicación, *n.f.* implication; complicity; contradiction.
implicante, *a.* implicating.
implicar [A], *v.t.* to implicate; to involve, entail; to imply. — *v.i.* to imply contradiction, be an obstacle.
implicatorio, -ria, *a.* implicative; contradictory.
implícito, -ta, *a.* implicit.
imploración, *n.f.* imploration, entreaty.
implorar, *v.t.* to implore, entreat.
implume, *a.* unfeathered, featherless.
impolítico, -ca, *a.* impolitic, indiscreet, imprudent, unwise; impolite. — *n.f.* incivility, discourtesy.
impoluto, -ta, *a.* unpolluted, spotless.
imponderabilidad, *n.f.* imponderability.
imponderable, *a.* imponderable; incalculable.
imponedor, *a.*, *n.m.f.* [IMPONENTE]. — *n.m.* (*print.*) imposer.
imponente, *a.* imposing; depositing; (*coll.*) smashing. — *n.m.f.* depositor.
imponer [25], *v.t.* to impose; to acquaint; to impute falsely; to deposit (*money in a bank*). — *v.i.* to be terrifying; ***estar impuesto en,*** to know all about, be well up in. — **imponerse,** *v.r.* to assert o.s.; to be imperative; ***imponerse a,*** to command respect from; ***imponerse de,*** to learn about, to find out about, acquaint o.s. with.
imponible, *a.* taxable, dutiable.
impopular, *a.* unpopular.
impopularidad, *n.f.* unpopularity.
importable, *a.* (*com.*) importable.
importación, *n.f.* (*com.*) importation, import.
importador, *n.m.* importer.
importancia, *n.f.* importance, import; moment, concern.
importante, *a.* important; considerable.
importar, *v.t.* to amount to; to import; to carry, involve, imply. — *v.i.* to be important be of moment; to matter, be of concern; ***no importa,*** never mind; ***¿qué importa?*** what does it matter?; ***me importa saberlo,*** it is important for me to know about it; ***eso a usted no le importa,*** that's no concern of yours; ***no me importa,*** I don't care.
importe, *n.m.* (*com.*) amount, cost; ***importe medio,*** average amount.
importunación, *n.f.* importunity.
importunador, -ra, *a.* importuning, pestering. — *n.m.f.* importuner, pesterer.
importunar, *v.t.* to importune, pester.

importunidad, *n.f.* importunity, importunacy.
importuno, -na, *a.* importunate.
imposibilidad, *n.f.* impossibility, impracticability, impracticableness.
imposibilitado, -da, *a.* disabled.
imposibilitar, *v.t.* to make impossible.
imposible, *a.* impossible, impracticable, out of the question; ***hacer lo imposible,*** to do one's utmost; ***imposible de toda imposibilidad,*** absolutely out of the question.
imposición, *n.f.* imposition; laying, putting *or* setting upon; tax, charge, duty.
imposta, *n.f.* (*arch.*) impost; springer; fascia.
impostor, -ra, *n.m.f.* impostor.
impostura, *n.f.* imposture, false imputation.
impotable, *a.* undrinkable.
impotencia, *n.f.* impotence; powerlessness.
impotente, *a.* impotent; powerless, unable.
impracticable, *a.* impracticable, unfeasible; impassable.
imprecación, *n.f.* imprecation.
imprecar [A], *v.t.* to imprecate.
imprecatorio, -ria, *a.* imprecatory.
imprecisión, *n.f.* imprecision, vagueness.
impreciso, -sa, *a.* imprecise, vague.
impregnable, *a.* absorbent, porous; saturable.
impregnación, *n.f.* impregnation.
impregnar, *v.t.* to impregnate, saturate.
impremeditación, *n.f.* unpremeditation.
impremeditado, -da, *a.* unpremeditated.
imprenta, *n.f.* printing; printing-office; print; press.
imprescindible, *a.* indispensable.
imprescriptible, *a.* imprescriptible.
impresentable, *a.* unpresentable.
impresión, *n.f.* impression; impress, stamping, stamp; print; printing, press-work; edition, issue.
impresionable, *a.* impressionable.
impresionar, *v.t.* to impress; to shock, affect deeply; (*photo.*) to expose (*a plate*); to record on. — **impresionarse,** *v.r.* to be shocked, deeply moved.
impresionismo, *n.m.* (*art*) impressionism.
impreso, -sa, *a.* printed, stamped. — *n.m.* form; printed matter, print. — *p.p.* [IMPRIMIR].
impresor, *n.m.* printer.
impresora, *n.f.* wife of a printer; female printer.
imprestable, *a.* that cannot be lent.
imprevisible, *a.* unforeseeable.
imprevisión, *n.f.* improvidence, lack of foresight.
imprevisor, -ra, *a.* improvident.
imprevisto, -ta, *a.* unforeseen, unexpected. — *n.m.pl.* (**imprevistos**) unforeseen expenses, events.
imprimación, *n.f.* (*art*) priming; stuff for priming.
imprimadera, *n.f.* (*art*) priming tool.
imprimador, *n.m.* (*art*) primer.
imprimar, *v.t.* (*art*) to prime.
imprimir [*p.p.* **impreso**], *v.t.* to print; to imprint, impress, stamp; to impart.
improbabilidad, *n.f.* improbability, unlikelihood.
improbable, *a.* improbable, unlikely.
improbar [4], *v.t.* to disapprove.
improbidad, *n.f.* improbity, dishonesty.
ímprobo, -ba, *a.* dishonest, wicked; laborious, arduous.
improcedencia, *n.f.* inappropriateness.
improcedente, *a.* inappropriate, out of place, uncalled-for.
improductivo, -va, *a.* unproductive.
impronta, *n.f.* (*art*) cast; stereotype plate.
impronunciable, *a.* unpronounceable.
improperar, *v.t.* to abuse.
improperio, *n.m.* (piece of) abuse, insult.
impropiedad, *n.f.* impropriety, unfitness, inappropriateness.
impropio, -pia, *a.* inappropriate, unsuited, improper, unfit; unbecoming.
improporción, *n.f.* disproportion.
improporcionado, -da, *a.* disproportionate.
improrrogable, *a.* inextensible.
impróspero, -ra, *a.* unprosperous.
improvidencia, *n.f.* improvidence.
impróvido, -da, *a.* improvident, thoughtless.
improvisación, *n.f.* improvisation, extemporization.
improvisado, -da, *a.* improvised; unexpected, sudden.
improvisador, -ra, *a.* improvising. — *n.m.f.* improviser.
improvisar, *v.t., v.i.* to improvise, extemporize.
improviso, -sa, *a.* unexpected, unforeseen; ***de improviso,*** unexpectedly, all of a sudden.
improvisto, -ta, *a.* unexpected, unforeseen; ***a la improvista,*** unexpected, suddenly.
imprudencia, *n.f.* imprudence, indiscretion, recklessness; ***imprudencia temeraria,*** criminal negligence.
imprudente, *a.* imprudent, indiscreet, unwise.
impúber, impúbero, -ra, *a.* impuberate.
impudencia, *n.f.* impudence, shamelessness, immodesty.
impudente, *a.* impudent, shameless.
impudicia, *n.f.* immodesty, indecency, lewdness, impudicity.
impúdico, -ca, *a.* immodest; shameless.
impudor, *n.m.* immodesty, shamelessness.
impuesto, -ta, *a.* imposed; informed; ***estar*** or ***quedar impuesto de una cosa,*** to be well informed about sth. — *n.m.* tax, duty, impost. — *p.p.* [IMPONER].
impugnable, *a.* impugnable.
impugnación, *n.f.* opposition, impugnation, refutation.
impugnador, -ra, *n.m.f.* impugner, objector.
impugnar, *v.t.* to oppose, impugn, contest.
impugnativo, -va, *a.* impugning.
impulsar, *v.t.* to impel, urge on; (*mech.*) to drive, force, move.
impulsión, *n.f.* impulsion, impulse; drive.
impulsivo, -va, *a.* impulsive.
impulso, *n.m.* impulse; prompting; impetus, momentum; ***los impulsos de su corazón,*** the promptings of his heart.
impulsor, -ra, *a.* impelling. — *n.m.f.* impeller.
impune, *a.* unpunished.
impunidad, *n.f.* impunity.
impureza, *n.f.* impurity; unchastity, unchasteness; lewdness.
impurificación, *n.f.* defilement.
impurificar, *v.t.* to defile, render impure; to adulterate.
impuro, -ra, *a.* impure, defiled; adulterated; unchaste, lewd.
imputabilidad, *n.f.* imputability.
imputable, *a.* imputable.
imputación, *n.f.* imputation.
imputador, -ra, *a.* imputing. — *n.m.f.* imputer.
imputar, *v.t.* to impute, ascribe; (*com.*) to credit on account.
inabarcable, *a.* unembraceable, that cannot be taken in *or* encompassed.
inacabable, *a.* interminable, unending, endless.
inaccesibilidad, *n.f.* inaccessibility.
inaccesible, *a.* inaccessible, unapproachable.
inacción, *n.f.* inaction.
inacentuado, -da, *a.* unaccented, unstressed.
inaceptable, *a.* unacceptable.

inactividad, *n.f.* inactivity.
inactivo, -va, *a.* inactive.
inadaptable, *a.* unadaptable.
inadaptado, -da, *a.* unadapted; maladjusted.
inadecuado, -da, *a.* inadequate, unsuitable.
inadmisible, *a.* inadmissible.
inadoptable, *a.* unadoptable.
inadvertencia, *n.f.* inadvertence, oversight.
inadvertido, -da, *a.* inadvertent; careless; unnoticed; ***pasar inadvertido,*** to go unnoticed.
inafectado, -da, *a.* unaffected.
inagotable, *a.* inexhaustible.
inaguantable, *a.* intolerable, insufferable.
inajenable, inalienable, *a.* inalienable.
inalámbrico, -ca, *a.* wireless (*communication*).
inalcanzable, *a.* unattainable.
inalterabilidad, *n.f.* inalterability; impassiveness, imperturbability.
inalterable, *a.* inalterable; impassive, imperturbable.
inalterado, -da, *a.* unchanged; impassive, unperturbed.
inameno, -na, *a.* not agreeable, dull.
inamisible, *a.* inamissible.
inamovible, *a.* immovable.
inamovibilidad, *n.f.* immovability.
inanalizable, *a.* unanalyzable.
inane, *a.* vain, useless.
inanición, *n.f.* (*med.*) inanition, undernourishment.
inanidad, *n.f.* uselessness.
inanimado, -da, *a.* inanimate, lifeless.
inánime, *a.* lifeless; inanimate.
inapagable, *a.* inextinguishable, unquenchable.
inapeable, *a.* incomprehensible, inconceivable; obstinate, stubborn.
inapelable, *a.* without appeal, that cannot be appealed against; inexorable.
inapetencia, *n.f.* want of appetite.
inapetente, *a.* having no appetite.
inaplacable, *a.* unappeasable.
inaplazable, *a.* undeferable.
inaplicable, *a.* inapplicable.
inaplicación, *n.f.* indolence, lack of studiousness.
inaplicado, -da, *a.* indolent, non-studious.
inapreciable, *a.* inestimable, invaluable.
inaprensivo, -va, *a.* without fear of illness etc.
inaprovechado, -da, *a.* wasted.
inarmónico, -ca, *a.* inharmonious.
inarticulado, -da, *a.* inarticulate.
inartístico, -ca, *a.* inartistic.
inasequible, *a.* unattainable.
inasimilable, *a.* unassimilable.
inastillable, *a.* unsplinterable.
inatacable, *a.* (*coll.*) unattackable.
inaudible, *a.* inaudible.
inaudito, -ta, *a.* unheard of.
inauguración, *n.f.* inauguration; unveiling.
inaugural, *a.* inaugural.
inaugurar, *v.t.* to inaugurate; to unveil; to divine by the flight of birds.
inaveriguable, *a.* that cannot be ascertained.
inca, *n.m.* Inca; Peruvian gold coin.
incaico, -ca, *a.* Inca.
incalculable, *a.* incalculable.
incalificable, *a.* unqualifiable; ***es incalificable,*** there is no name for it, it is unspeakable.
incalmable, *a.* unappeasable.
incandescencia, *n.f.* incandescence.
incandescente, *a.* incandescent.
incansable, *a.* indefatigable, unwearied.
incantable, *a.* unsingable.
incapacidad, *n.f.* incapacity; incompetence, disability; incapability.
incapacitar, *v.t.* to incapacitate; to disqualify, disable.
incapaz, *a.* incapable, unable, unfit, incompetent; (*coll.*) utterly hopeless, dead loss.
incasable, *a.* unmarriageable.
incautación, *n.f.* (*law*) seizure (*of property, money etc.*).
incautarse, *v.r.* (*law*) — ***de,*** to seize (*money* or *property*).
incauto, -ta, *a.* incautious, unwary.
incendiar, *v.t.* to set on fire, set fire to. — **incendiarse,** *v.r.* to catch fire.
incendiario, -ria, *a.* incendiary. — *n.m.f.* incendiary, arsonist, fire-raiser.
incendio, *n.f.* fire, blaze; ***incendio provocado,*** arson.
incensación, *n.f.* (*eccles.*) incensation.
incensar [I], *v.t.* to incense (*perfume with incense, burn incense to*); (*fig.*) to flatter, overpraise.
incensario, *n.m.* incensory, thurible.
incensurable, *a.* unblamable.
incentivar, *v.t.* to be *or* give an incentive *or* inducement to.
incentivo, *n.m.* incentive.
incertidumbre, *n.f.* uncertainty, doubt.
incertísimo, -ma, *a.* extremely doubtful.
incesable, *a.* incessant, unceasing.
incesante, *a.* incessant, unceasing.
incesto, *n.m.* incest.
incestuoso, -sa, *a.* incestuous.
incidencia, *n.m.* incident; (*geom.*) incidence.
incidental, *a.* incidental, dependent.
incidente, *a.* incidental; cutting in on. — *n.m.* incident.
incidir, *v.t.* to cut into; to incise. — *v.i.* to fall; ***incidir en,*** to fall into; to fall on; to influence; to have an influence *or* effect (on), impinge (on).
incienso, *n.m.* incense; flattery.
incierto, -ta, *a.* untrue; uncertain, doubtful.
incinerable, *a.* to be incinerated.
incineración, *n.f.* incineration, cremation.
incinerar, *v.t.* to incinerate, cremate.
incipiente, *a.* beginning, incipient.
incircunciso, -sa, *a.* uncircumcised.
incisión, *n.f.* incision, cut.
incisivo, -va, *a.* incisory, cutting; incisive, biting. — *n.m.* incisor.
inciso, -sa, *a.* incised, cut. — *n.m.* (*gram.*) intercalated phrase *or* sentence; clause; comma.
incisorio, -ria, *a.* (*surg.*) incisory.
incitación, *n.f.* incitation, incitement.
incitador, -ra, *a.* inciting. — *n.m.f.* inciter.
incitamento, incitamiento, *n.m.* incitement.
incitante, *a.* inciting.
incitar, *v.t.* to incite.
incitativo, -va, *a.* inciting. — *n.m.* incitement.
incivil, *a.* uncivil, coarse.
incivilidad, *n.f.* incivility, coarseness.
inclasificable, *a.* unclassifiable.
inclemencia, *n.f.* inclemency, harshness; ***a la inclemencia,*** without shelter.
inclemente, *a.* inclement, harsh.
inclinación, *n.f.* inclination; dip, tilt; leaning, bent; bow, nod.
inclinado, -da, *a.* inclined; slanting, sloping.
inclinador, -ra, *a.* inclining.
inclinante, *a.* inclining.
inclinar, *v.t.* to incline; to dip, tilt; to make to lean *or* slant; to bend, bend over *or* down; to bow, bow down. — *v.i.* to take (after). — **inclinarse,** *v.r.* to be *or* become inclined.
ínclito, -ta, *a.* illustrious.
incluir [O, *p.p.* **incluído, incluso**], *v.t.* to include; to enclose; ***todo incluído,*** inclusive terms (*at hotel*), (*Am.*) American plan.

inclusa, *n.f.* [INCLUSO].
inclusero, -ra, *a.*, *n.m.f.* foundling.
inclusión, *n.f.* inclusion.
inclusive, *adv.* inclusively, inclusive (*of days*). — *prep.* including, (*Am.*) through.
inclusivo, -va, *a.* inclusive.
incluso, -sa, *a.* enclosed. — *adv.* even. — *n.m.f.* foundling. — *n.f.* foundling asylum.
incluyente, *a.* including; enclosing.
incoación, *n.f.* (*law*) initiation, opening.
incoagulable, *a.* incoagulable, uncoagulable.
incoar, *v.t.* (*only the infin. and p.p. are used*); (*law*) to inchoate, initiate.
incoativo, -va, *a.* inchoative, inceptive.
incobrable, *a.* irrecoverable, irretrievable; (*com.*) uncollectable.
incoercible, *a.* incoercible.
incógnito, -ta, *a.* unknown; ***de incógnito,*** incognito. — *n.f.* (*lit. fig.*) unknown quantity.
incognoscible, *a.* incognizable, unknowable.
incoherencia, *n.f.* incoherence.
incoherente, *a.* incoherent.
íncola, *n.m.* inhabitant, resident.
incoloro, -ra, *a.* colourless.
incólume, *a.* sound, safe, unharmed, unscathed.
incolumidad, *n.f.* security, safety.
incombinable, *a.* uncombinable.
incombustibilidad, *n.f.* incombustibility.
incombustible, *a.* incombustible, fireproof.
incomerciable, *a.* unsaleable, unmarketable; not negotiable.
incomible, *a.* uneatable, inedible.
incomodar, *v.t.* to incommode, disturb, inconvenience, trouble.
incomodidad, *n.f.* inconvenience; discomfort, uncomfortableness; nuisance, annoyance.
incómodo, -da, *a.* inconvenient; uncomfortable. — *n.m.* inconvenience, discomfort.
incomparable, *a.* incomparable, matchless.
incomparado, -da, *a.* incomparable, matchless.
incompartible, *a.* indivisible, unshareable.
incompasible, incompasivo, -va, *a.* uncompassionate, pitiless.
incompatibilidad, *n.f.* incompatibility; uncongeniality.
incompatible, *a.* incompatible, uncongenial.
incompetencia, *n.f.* incompetency, unfitness, inability.
incompetente, *a.* incompetent, incapable, unfit; (*law*) unqualified.
incomplejo, -ja, *a.* uncomplicated, simple.
incompletamente, *adv.* incompletely.
incompleto, -ta, *a.* incomplete.
incomplexo, -xa, *a.* disconnected, incoherent.
incomponible, *a.* unrepairable, unmendable.
incomportable, *a.* intolerable, unbearable.
incomposición, *n.f.* want of proportion.
incomprehensibilidad, incomprensibilidad, *n.f.* incomprehensibility.
incomprehensible, incomprensible, *a.* incomprehensible.
incomprensión, *n.f.* failure to appreciate *or* understand.
incomprimible, *a.* incompressible.
incomunicabilidad, *n.f.* incommunicability.
incomunicable, *a.* incommunicable.
incomunicado, -da, *a.* incommunicado.
incomunicar [A], *v.t.* to deprive of communication; to isolate; to put in solitary confinement.
inconcebible, *a.* inconceivable.
inconciliable, *a.* irreconcilable.
inconcino, -na, *a.* disordered, disarranged.
inconcluso, -sa, *a.* unfinished.
inconcuso, -sa, *a.* incontrovertible, incontestable.
incondicional, *a.* unconditional; ***amigo incondicional,*** friend through thick and thin.
inconducente, *a.* unconducive.
inconexión, *n.f.* lack of connection.
inconexo, -xa, *a.* unconnected.
inconfesable, *a.* unmentionable, shameful.
inconfeso, -sa, *a.* unconfessed.
inconfidencia, *n.f.* distrust, mistrust.
inconformismo, *n.m.* nonconformism.
inconfundible, *a.* unmistakable.
incongruencia, *n.f.* incongruousness, incongruity.
incongruente, *a.* incongruous, incongruent.
incongruo, -rua, *a.* incongruous.
inconjugable, *a.* inconjugable.
inconmensurabilidad, *n.f.* incommensurability.
inconmensurable, *a.* incommensurable, immeasurable.
inconmovible, *a.* unshakable.
inconmutabilidad, *n.f.* immutability, unchangeableness.
inconmutable, *a.* immutable; incommutable.
inconquistable, *a.* unconquerable, invincible.
inconsciente, *a.* unconscious; unthinking; unaware.
inconsecuencia, *n.f.* inconsistency.
inconsecuente, *a.* inconsistent.
inconservable, *a.* unpreservable.
inconsideración, *n.f.* inconsiderateness, lack of consideration; ill-considered *or* ill-advised attitude *or* nature.
inconsiderado, -da, *a.* ill-considered.
inconsiguiente, *a.* inconsequent.
inconsistencia, *n.f.* unsubstantiality, flimsiness.
inconsistente, *a.* unsubstantial, flimsy.
inconsolable, *a.* inconsolable.
inconstancia, *n.f.* inconstancy, fickleness.
inconstante, *a.* inconstant, changeable, fickle.
inconstitucional, *a.* unconstitutional.
inconsútil, *a.* seamless.
incontable, *a.* innumerable, countless.
incontaminado, -da, *a.* undefiled, uncontaminated.
incontestable, *a.* incontestable, indisputable, unquestionable.
incontinencia, *n.f.* incontinence.
incontinente, *a.* incontinent.
incontinenti, *adv.* at once, instantly.
incontrastable, *a.* indisputable, insuperable; unanswerable.
incontratable, *a.* untractable, unruly.
incontrovertible, *a.* incontrovertible.
inconvencible, *a.* inconvincible.
inconvenible, *a.* uncompromising.
inconveniencia, *n.f.* unsuitability, undesirability; impropriety; absurd thing to do *or* say.
inconveniente, *a.* unsuitable, undesirable; improper. — *n.m.* drawback, disadvantage; objection; ***no tengo inconveniente,*** I have no objection.
inconversable, *a.* unsociable, surly.
inconvertible, *a.* inconvertible.
incordiar, *v.t.* to bother.
incordio, *n.m.* (*med.*) bubo; (*coll.*) nuisance, pest.
incorporación, *n.f.* incorporation.
incorporal, *a.* incorporeal.
incorporar, *v.t.* to incorporate, embody. — **incorporarse,** *v.r.* to sit up (*from reclining position*); to associate, participate; ***incorporarse a,*** to join (*a body, regiment etc.*).
incorporeidad, *n.f.* incorporeity.
incorpóreo, -rea, *a.* incorporeal, bodiless.
incorporo, *n.m.* incorporation.
incorrección, *n.f.* incorrectness, inaccuracy; improper thing to do *or* say.
incorrecto, -ta, *a.* incorrect, inaccurate; improper.

incorregibilidad, *n.f.* incorrigibleness, incorrigibility.
incorregible, *a.* incorrigible.
incorrupción, *n.f.* incorruption.
incorruptibilidad, *n.f.* incorruptibility.
incorruptible, *a.* incorruptible.
incorrupto, -ta, *a.* incorrupt, uncorrupt, uncorrupted; chaste, pure.
incrasar, *v.t.* to incrassate.
increado, -da, *a.* uncreated, increate.
incredibilidad, *n.f.* incredibility, incredibleness.
incredulidad, *n.f.* incredulity, incredulousness.
incrédulo, -la, *a.* incredulous, unbelieving. — *n.m.f.* unbeliever.
increíble, *a.* incredible, unbelievable.
incremento, *n.m.* increment, increase.
increpación, *n.f.* upbraiding, rebuking.
increpador, -ra, *a.* upbraiding, rebuking. — *n.m.f.* rebuker.
increpante, *a.* upbraiding, rebuking.
increpar, *v.t.* to upbraid, rebuke.
incriminación, *n.f.* incrimination.
incriminar, *v.t.* to incriminate; to exaggerate.
incristalizable, *a.* uncrystallizable.
incruento, -ta, *a.* bloodless.
incrustación, *n.f.* incrustation; scale (*in boilers*); (*geol.*) sinter; (*art*) inlaying, inlay work.
incrustar, *v.t.* to incrust, incrustate; to inlay, inset.
incuartación, *n.f.* (*chem.*) quartation.
incubación, *n.f.* incubation; hatching.
incubadora, *n.f.* incubator.
incubar, *v.t.* to incubate; (*fig.*) to hatch (up), brew (up).
íncubo, *n.m.* incubus.
incuestionable, *a.* unquestionable.
inculcación, *n.f.* inculcation; (*print.*) locking.
inculcar [A], *v.t.* to inculcate; (*print.*) to lock up (*type*). — **inculcarse,** *v.r.* to be obstinate.
inculpabilidad, *n.f.* inculpableness, blamelessness.
inculpable, *a.* inculpable, blameless.
inculpación, *n.f.* inculpation.
inculpadamente, *adv.* blamelessly.
inculpar, *v.t.* to inculpate, blame.
incultivable, *a.* uncultivable.
inculto, -ta, *a.* uncultivated; uneducated.
incultura, *n.f.* lack of cultivation; lack of education.
incumbencia, *n.f.* incumbency; responsibility, concern, province, domain; ***no es de mi incumbencia,*** it's not my concern *or* province.
incumbir, *v.i.* to be the concern *or* responsibility (of), be incumbent (upon).
incumplido, -da, *a.* unfulfilled.
incumplimiento, *n.m.* failure to carry out *or* satisfy.
incumplir, *v.t.* to fail to fulfil, carry out *or* satisfy.
incunable, *a.* incunabular. — *n.m.* incunabulum.
incurable, *a.* incurable, hopeless.
incuria, *n.f.* negligence, carelessness.
incurioso, -sa, *a.* negligent, careless.
incurrimiento, *n.m.* incurring.
incurrir [*p.p.* **incurrido, incurso**], *v.i.* — ***en,*** to become liable to, incur, bring on o.s.; to commit (*fault, error*), fall into (*error*).
incursión, *n.f.* (*mil.*) incursion.
incurso, -sa, *p.p.* [INCURRIR].
incusar, *v.t.* to accuse, impute.
incuso, -sa, *a.* incuse.
inda, *n.f.* [INDO].
indagación, *n.f.* investigation, search, inquiry.
indagador, -ra, *a.* investigating, searching. — *n.m.f.* investigator, inquirer.
indagar [B], *v.t.* to investigate, inquire into, conduct an inquiry into.
indagatorio, -ria, *a.* (*law*) investigatory. — *n.f.* (*law*) investigatory.
indebido, -da, *a.* undue, illegal, improper.
indecencia, *n.f.* indecency; indecent *or* low thing to do *or* say.
indecente, *a.* indecent; obscene; low; wretched.
indecible, *a.* inexpressible, unutterable, unspeakable.
indecisión, *n.f.* irresolution, indecision, hesitation, hesitancy.
indeciso, -sa, *a.* irresolute, undecided, hesitant.
indeclinable, *a.* undeclinable; indeclinable.
indecoro, *n.m.* indecorum, indecorousness, lack of propriety.
indecoroso, -sa, *a.* indecorous, improper.
indefectibilidad, *n.f.* indefectibility.
indefectible, *a.* indefectible, unfailing.
indefendible, indefensable, indefensible, *a.* indefensible.
indefenso, -sa, *a.* defenceless.
indeficiente, *a.* indefectible, unfailing.
indefinible, *a.* indefinable, undefinable.
indefinido, -da, *a.* indefinite, indeterminate, undefined.
indehiscente, *a.* (*bot.*) indehiscent.
indeleble, *a.* indelible, ineffaceable.
indeliberación, *n.f.* indeliberation; irreflection.
indeliberado, -da, *a.* indeliberate, indeliberated, unpremeditated.
indelicadeza, *n.f.* indelicacy.
indelicado, -da, *a.* indelicate.
indemne, *a.* undamaged, unhurt, unscathed.
indemnidad, *n.f.* (bond of) indemnity.
indemnizable, *a.* indemnifiable.
indemnización, *n.f.* indemnification, compensation.
indemnizar [C], *v.t.* to indemnify, compensate.
indemostrable, *a.* indemonstrable.
independencia, *n.f.* independence; privacy.
independiente, *a.* independent; private; apart (from).
independientemente, *adv.* independently; irrespectively; apart (from).
indescifrable, *a.* undecipherable.
indescribible, indescriptible, *a.* indescribable.
indeseable, *a.* undesirable.
indesignable, *a.* that cannot be designated.
indestructibilidad, *n.f.* indestructibility.
indestructible, *a.* indestructible.
indeterminable, *a.* indeterminable.
indeterminación, *n.f.* indetermination.
indeterminado, -da, *a.* indeterminate; indefinite.
indevoción, *n.f.* want of devotion.
indevoto, -ta, *a.* not devout, irreligious.
India, *n.f.* ***la* —,** India.
india (I), *n.f.* wealth.
indiada, *n.f.* Indians.
indianista, *n.m.f.* Indianist.
indiano, -na, *a.*, *n.m.f.* Spanish American; West *or* East Indian; (one) back from the Indies *or* America. — *n.f.* printed calico.
Indias, *n.f.pl.* Indies.
indicación, *n.f.* indication; mark, sign; remark; hint.
indicador, -ra, *a.* indicating, indicatory, indicative. — *n.m.* indicator, pointer, gauge, index.
indicante, *a.* indicating. — *n.m.* (*med.*) indicant.
indicar [A], *v.t.* to indicate, point out, show; to hint, suggest.
indicativo, -va, *a.* indicative. — *n.m.* (*gram.*) indicative.
indicción, *n.f.* convening (*of a synod, council etc.*); indiction.
índice, *n.m.* index; hand (*of watch* or *clock*); pointer (*on a sundial*); forefinger; ***índice de crecimiento,***

growth rate; ***índice de materias,*** table of contents.
indiciado, -da, *a.* suspected of a crime *or* vice.
indiciador, -ra, *n.m.f.* one who suspects another.
indiciar, *v.t.* to indicate; to suspect.
indicio, *n.m.* indication, mark, sign; trace; (*law*) ***indicios vehementes,*** circumstantial evidence.
índico, -ca, *a.* (East) Indian.
indiferencia, *n.f.* indifference, unconcern, lukewarmness.
indiferente, *a.* indifferent, unconcerned, lukewarm, cool; (*coll.*) ***eso es indiferente,*** that is immaterial, that makes no difference.
indiferentemente, *adv.* indifferently; with no difference *or* distinction.
indiferentismo, *n.m.* apathy.
indígena, *a., n.m.f.* indigenous, native (person).
indigencia, *n.f.* indigence, destitution.
indigente, *a.* indigent, destitute.
indigerible, indigestible, *a.* indigestible.
indigestar, *v.t.* to cause indigestion in, upset. — **indigestarse,** *v.r.* to get indigestion; ***se le indigestó la comida,*** he got indigestion; (*coll.*) ***se me indigesta X,*** I can't stomach X.
indigestión, *n.f.* indigestion; ill-nature, ill-temper.
indigesto, -ta, *a.* indigestible; undigested; disagreeable.
indignación, *n.f.* indignation.
indignado, -da, *a.* indignant.
indignante, *a.* infuriating; exasperating.
indignar, *v.t.* to make indignant, infuriate. — **indignarse,** *v.r.* to be *or* become indignant, feel indignation *or* a sense of outrage.
indignidad, *n.f.* indignity; unworthiness.
indigno, -na, *a.* unworthy, undeserving; unbecoming; low, contemptible.
índigo, *n.m.* indigo.
indiligencia, *n.f.* negligence, laziness.
indino, -na, *a.* saucy, mischievous.
indio, -dia (2), *a.* Indian; blue, azure. — *n.m.f.* Indian. — *n.m.* (*chem.*) indium.
indirecta, *a.* indirect. — *n.f.* hint, innuendo; ***indirecta del padre Cobos,*** broad hint.
indiscernible, *a.* indiscernible.
indisciplina, *n.f.* indiscipline.
indisciplinable, *a.* indisciplinable.
indisciplinado, -da, *a.* undisciplined, unruly.
indisciplinar, *v.t.* to disturb the discipline of, make rebellious. — **indisciplinarse,** *v.r.* to become undisciplined, get out of hand *or* control.
indiscreción, *n.f.* indiscretion.
indiscreto, -ta, *a.* indiscreet.
indisculpable, *a.* inexcusable.
indiscutible, *a.* unquestionable, indisputable.
indisoluble, *a.* indissoluble, indissolvable.
indispensable, *a.* inexcusable; indispensable.
indisponer [25], *v.t.* to indispose, render unfit; to upset; ***indisponer a alguien con,*** to set s.o. against. — **indisponerse,** *v.r.* to become indisposed; ***indisponerse con,*** to fall out with.
indisponible, *a.* (*law*) that cannot be bequeathed.
indisposición, *n.f.* unpreparedness; indisposition, ailment.
indispuesto, -ta, *a.* indisposed; at variance. — *p.p.* [INDISPONER].
indisputable, *a.* indisputable, incontrovertible.
indistinción, *n.f.* indistinction, indiscrimination.
indistinguible, *a.* undistinguishable, indistinguishable.
indistintamente, *adv.* indistinctly; with no difference *or* distinction, equally.
indistinto, -ta, *a.* indistinct; having *or* making no difference, immaterial.
individuación, *n.f.* individuation.
individual, *a.* individual, personal.
individualidad, *n.f.* individuality.
individualismo, *n.m.* individualism.
individualista, *a.* individualistic. — *n.m.f.* individualist.
individualizar [C], *v.t.* to individualize.
individuar, *v.t.* to individuate, individualize, particularize, specify individually.
individuo, -dua, *a.* individual; indivisible. — *n.m.f.* individual; member, associate, fellow.
indivisamente, *adv.* indivisibly.
indivisibilidad, *n.f.* indivisibility.
indivisible, *a.* indivisible.
indivisión, *n.f.* entirety, completeness.
indiviso, -sa, *a.* undivided; ***pro indiviso,*** joint, jointly.
indo, -da, *a., n.m.f.* Indian.
indócil, *a.* indocile, unruly.
indocilidad, *n.f.* indocility, unruliness.
indocto, -ta, *a.* ignorant, unlearned, uneducated.
indocumentado, -da, *a.* lacking the documents for identification; having no proper knowledge *or* training. — *n.m.f.* one with no proper knowledge *or* training; (*coll.*) ignoramus.
Indochina, *n.f.* ***la —,*** Indo-China.
indochino, -na, *a., n.m.f.* Indo-Chinese.
indoeuropeo, -pea, *a.* Indo-European.
índole, *n.f.* nature.
indolencia, *n.f.* indolence; carelessness; painlessness.
indolente, *a.* indolent; careless; painless.
indoloro, -ra, *a.* painless.
indomable, *a.* untamable, indomitable, unmanageable.
indomado, -da, *a.* untamed.
indomesticable, *a.* untamable.
indoméstico, -ca, *a.* untamed, intractable.
indómito, -ta, *a.* untamed; untamable; indomitable.
Indonesia, *n.f.* Indonesia.
indonesio, -sia, *a., n.m.f.* Indonesian (person).
indostaní, *n.m.* Hindustani (*language*).
indostánico, -ca, *a.* Hindustani.
indotación, *n.f.* (*law*) lack of dowry.
indotado, -da, *a.* unendowed; portionless.
indubitable, *a.* indubitable.
inducción, *n.f.* inducement, persuasion; induction; ***por inducción,*** inductively.
inducimiento, *n.m.* inducement, inducing.
inducir [15], *v.t.* to induce; to lead.
indúctil, *a.* not ductile.
inductivo, -va, *a.* inductive.
inductor, -ra, *a.* (*engin.*) inductive. — *n.m.* (*engin.*) inductor.
indudable, *a.* doubtless, certain.
indulgencia, *n.f.* indulgence; leniency, forbearance.
indulgente, *a.* indulgent, lenient, forbearing.
indultar, *v.t.* to pardon; to exempt.
indultario, *n.m.* one who by virtue of a pontifical privilege can dispense ecclesiastical benefices.
indulto, *n.m.* pardon; exemption.
indumento, *n.m.* apparel.
induración, *n.f.* (*med.*) induration.
industria, *n.f.* industry; business; ingenuity; ***de industria,*** on purpose; ***caballero de industria,*** one who lives by his wits.
industrial, *a.* industrial, manufacturing. — *n.m.* industrialist; owner of a business.
industrialismo, *n.m.* industrialism.
industriar, *v.t.* to instruct, train. — **industriarse,** *v.r.* to manage, find the way, find a way.
industrioso, -sa, *a.* industrious, hard-working.
inedia, *n.f.* undernourishment.
inédito, -ta, *a.* unpublished; new, original; untapped.

inefabilidad, *n.f.* ineffability.
inefable, *a.* ineffable.
inefectivo, -va, *a.* ineffective.
ineficacia, *n.f.* inefficiency; ineffectualness, inefficacy.
ineficaz, *a.* inefficient; ineffectual; inefficacious.
ineficiente, *a.* inefficacious.
inelegancia, *n.f.* inelegance.
inelegante, *a.* inelegant.
ineluctable, *a.* ineluctable.
ineludible, *a.* unavoidable.
inenarrable, *a.* inexpressible, beyond words.
ineptitud, *n.f.* ineptitude, incompetency.
inepto, -ta, *a.* inept, incompetent.
inequívoco, -ca, *a.* unequivocal, unmistakable.
inercia, *n.f.* inertia; force of habit.
inerme, *a.* unarmed.
inerrable, *a.* infallable.
inerrante, *a.* fixed (*of stars*).
inerte, *a.* inert.
inerudito, -ta, *a.* unscholarly.
inervación, *n.f.* innervation.
inescrutable, *a.* inscrutable.
inescudriñable, *a.* unsearchable.
inesperado, -da, *a.* unexpected; unpredictable, unforeseen.
inestabilidad, *n.f.* instability, shakiness.
inestable, *a.* unstable, shaky.
inestimabilidad, *n.f.* inestimableness.
inestimable, *a.* inestimable, invaluable.
inestimado, -da, *a.* (*law*) unestimated, not rated, unappraised, unvalued.
inevitable, *a.* inevitable, unavoidable.
inexactitud, *n.f.* inexactness, inaccuracy.
inexacto, -ta, *a.* inexact, inaccurate.
inexcusable, *a.* inexcusable; essential, that cannot be omitted.
inexhausto, -ta, *a.* unexhausted, unspent.
inexistente, *a.* non-existent.
inexorable, *a.* inexorable, relentless.
inexperiencia, *n.f.* inexperience.
inexperto, -ta, *a.* inexperienced, inexpert.
inexpiable, *a.* inexpiable, unatonable.
inexplicable, *a.* inexplicable, unexplainable.
inexplorado, -da, *a.* unexplored; (*fig.*) virgin.
inexpresivo, -va, *a.* unexpressive.
inexpugnable, *a.* impregnable; impossible to storm.
inextinguible, *a.* inextinguishable, unquenchable.
inextirpable, *a.* ineradicable.
inextricable, *a.* inextricable.
infacundo, -da, *a.* ineloquent.
infalibilidad, *n.f.* infallibility.
infalible, *a.* infallible.
infamación, *n.f.* defamation.
infamador, -ra, *n.m.f.* defamer.
infamante, *a.* infamous, outrageous, shameful.
infamar, *v.t.* to defame, dishonour.
infamativo, -va, *a.* defaming.
infamatorio, -ria, *a.* defamatory, libellous.
infame, *a.* infamous, vile, foul, atrocious.
infamia, *n.f.* infamy; foul *or* atrocious thing.
infancia, *n.f.* infancy; childhood; children.
infando, -da, *a.* unmentionable, unspeakable.
infanta, *n.f.* infanta, princess; female child.
infantado, *n.m.* territory assigned to a prince of the royal blood of Spain.
infante, *n.m.* infante, prince; male child; infantryman; choirboy.
infantería, *n.f.* infantry.
infanticida, *n.m.f.* infanticide, child murderer.
infanticidio, *n.m.* infanticide, child-murder.
infantil, *a.* infantile, childish, childlike.
infantilismo, *n.m.* infantility; infantilism.
infanzón, *n.m.* nobleman.
infanzonado, -da, *a.* pertaining to an ***infanzón.***
infanzonazgo, *n.m.* territory of an ***infanzón.***
infanzonía, *n.f.* nobility.
infartación, *n.f.* (*med.*) infarction.
infarto, *n.m.* (*med.*) infarct; heart attack.
infatigable, *a.* indefatigable, untiring.
infatuación, *n.f.* vanity, conceit.
infatuar [M], *v.t.* to make conceited.
infausto, -ta, *a.* ill-starred; ill-famed.
infebril, *a.* fever-free.
infección, *n.f.* infection.
infeccioso, -sa, *a.* infectious.
infectar, *v.t.* to infect, make septic.
infectivo, -va, *a.* infective, infectious.
infecto, -ta, *a.* infected, tainted; (*coll.*) vile, foul.
infecundidad, *n.f.* infecundity, sterility, infertility.
infecundo, -da, *a.* infecund, infertile, sterile.
infelice, *a.* (*poet.*) [INFELIZ].
infelicidad, *n.f.* unhappiness; misfortune.
infeliz, *a.* unhappy; luckless. — *n.m.f.* luckless, hapless individual; (*coll.*) harmless, miserable object.
inferencia, *n.f.* inference.
inferior, *a.* inferior; lower. — *n.m.f.* subordinate, inferior.
inferioridad, *n.f.* inferiority, lower position.
inferir [6], *v.t.* to infer; to inflict. — **inferirse,** ***v.r.*** to follow, be inferred.
infernáculo, *n.m.* hop-scotch.
infernal, *a.* infernal, hellish.
infernar [I], *v.t.* to damn; to irritate, vex, provoke.
inferno, -na, *a.* (*poet.*) infernal.
ínfero, -ra, *a.* (*poet.*) inferior.
infestación, *n.f.* infestation.
infestar, *v.t.* to infest; to overrun; to fill, flood, swamp.
infesto, -ta, *a.* (*poet.*) harmful.
infeudación, *n.f.* enfeoffment.
infeudar, *v.t.* to enfeoff.
inficionar, *v.t.* to infect, taint.
infidelidad, *n.f.* infidelity, unfaithfulness, faithlessness; unbelief; (whole body of) infidels.
infidelísimo, -ma, *a. superl.* most unfaithful.
infidencia, *n.f.* unfaithfulness, faithlessness; treason; (*law*) misfeasance.
infidente, *a.* unfaithful.
infiel, *a.* infidel; faithless, unfaithful. — ***n.m.f.*** infidel.
infierno, *n.m.* hell; inferno; ***vivir en el quinto infierno,*** to live in the back of beyond.
infigurable, *a.* that which cannot be represented by any figure.
infiltración, *n.f.* infiltration, seeping (through).
infiltrar(se), *v.t.* (*v.r.*) to infiltrate, seep (through).
ínfimo, -ma, *a. superl.* lowest, lowermost, undermost, least; vilest, most abject; most inferior.
infinidad, *n.f.* infinity; infiniteness; endless number.
infinitesimal, *a.* infinitesimal.
infinitésimo, -ma, *a.* infinitely small.
infinitivo, *n.m.* (*gram.*) infinitive.
infinito, -ta, *a.* infinite; ***hasta lo infinito,*** ad infinitum. — *adv.* infinitely, immensely. — ***n.m.*** infinite; infinity.
infinitud, *n.f.* infinitude.
infirmar, *v.t.* (*law*) to invalidate, make null and void.
inflación, *n.f.* inflation; conceit, vanity.
inflacionista, *a.* inflationary.
inflamable, *a.* inflammable.
inflamación, *n.f.* inflammation; igniting.
inflamar, *v.t.* to inflame, set afire, set ablaze.
inflamatorio, -ria, *a.* inflammatory.

inflar, *v.t.* to inflate, blow up.
inflativo, -va, *a.* inflating.
inflexibilidad, *n.f.* inflexibility, inflexibleness.
inflexible, *a.* inflexible, unbending.
inflexión, *n.f.* inflection; bending.
infligir [E], *v.t.* to inflict.
inflorescencia, *n.f.* (*bot.*) inflorescence.
influencia, *n.f.* influence.
influenciar, *v.t.* to influence.
influente, *a.* influencing, influential.
influir [O], *v.t., v.i.* to influence; ***influye mucho en él,*** he influences him a great deal; ***lejos de sufrir influjo, influye ella,*** far from being influenced, it is she who exercises the influence *or* does the influencing.
influjo, *n.m.* influence; rising tide.
influyente, *a.* influential.
infolio, *n.m.* book in folio form.
inforciado, *n.m.* second part of the digest *or* pandects of Justinian.
información, *n.f.* information; report; intelligence; judicial inquiry; (*law*) brief.
informador, -ra, *a.* informing, reporting. — *n.m.f.* informant.
informal, *a.* unreliable, not dependable; badly behaved; informal.
informalidad, *n.f.* lack of reliability; failure to carry out a promise *or* undertaking; informality.
informante, *a.* informing, instructing. — *n.m.* informant.
informar, *v.t.* to inform; to give form *or* shape to. — *v.i.* to inform; to make a report; (*law*) to plead. — **informarse,** *v.r.* to find out (**de,** about); to get *or* obtain information.
informativo, -va, *a.* informative.
informe, *a.* shapeless, formless. — *n.m.* (piece of) information; report; reference, testimonial; (*law*) plea, pleading; (*pl.*) information.
informidad, *n.f.* shapelessness.
infortificable, *a.* that cannot be fortified.
infortuna, *n.f.* adverse influence of the stars.
infortunado, -da, *a.* luckless, hapless.
infortunio, *n.m.* misfortune; mischance.
infosura, *n.f.* (*vet.*) founder.
infracción, *n.f.* infraction, breach, infringement.
infracto, -ta, *a.* steady, not easily moved.
infractor, -ra, *n.m.f.* infractor, breaker, violator, transgressor.
infrangible, *a.* infrangible; inviolable.
infranqueable, *a.* impassable.
infrascripto, -ta, infrascrito, -ta, *a.* undersigned; hereafter mentioned.
infrecuente, *a.* infrequent.
infringir [E], *v.t.* to infringe, violate, break.
infructífero, -ra, infrugífero, -ra, *a.* unfruitful, unprofitable.
infructuosidad, *n.f.* unfruitfulness.
infructuoso, -sa, *a.* fruitless; unsuccessful.
ínfulas, *n.f.pl.* (*eccles.*) infula; ribbon of a bishop's mitre; (*fig.*) airs, conceit; ***tiene ínfulas de noble,*** he has pretensions to nobility.
infumable, *a.* unsmokable (*tobacco*).
infundado, -da, *a.* groundless, baseless.
infundible, *a.* infusible.
infundibuliforme, *a.* (*bot.*) funnel-shaped.
infundir [*p.p.* **infundido, infuso**], *v.t.* to infuse, instil.
infurtir, *v.t.* to full, mill (*clothes*).
infusibilidad, *n.f.* infusibility.
infusible, *a.* infusible.
infusión, *n.f.* infusion; inspiration; (*eccles.*) baptism by sprinkling; ***estar en infusión para,*** to be all set for.
infuso, -sa, *a.* inspired, God-given; ***ciencia infusa,*** inspired knowledge.
infusorio, -ria, *a.* infusorian. — *n.m.pl.* (**infusorios**) infusoria.
ingenerable, *a.* ingenerable.
ingeniar, *v.t.* to conceive, contrive, devise, work out. — **ingeniarse,** *v.r.* to manage, find the *or* a way.
ingeniatura, *n.f.* (*coll.*) ingenuity, subtlety, acuteness, skilful management; (*Hisp. Am.*) engineering.
ingeniería, *n.f.* engineering.
ingeniero, *n.m.* engineer; ***ingeniero agrónomo,*** agricultural engineer; ***ingeniero de caminos, canales y puertos,*** government civil engineer; ***ingeniero electricista,*** electrical engineer; ***ingeniero hidráulico,*** hydraulic engineer; ***ingeniero mecánico,*** mechanical engineer; ***ingeniero de minas,*** mining engineer; ***ingeniero de montes,*** forestry engineer; ***ingeniero naval, de la armarda*** or ***de marina,*** naval engineer; ***ingeniero químico,*** chemical engineer.
ingenio, *n.m.* talent; creative *or* inventive faculty; wit, cleverness, ingenuity; talented individual; engine, device; paper-cutter; (*Hisp. Am.*) sugar mill, sugar plant.
ingeniosidad, *n.f.* ingenuity, ingeniousness, resourcefulness.
ingenioso, -sa, *a.* ingenious, resourceful.
ingénito, -ta, *a.* unbegotten; innate, inborn.
ingente, *a.* huge, colossal.
ingenuidad, *n.f.* ingenuousness.
ingenuo, -nua, *a.* ingenuous, naïve, guileless.
ingerencia, *n.f.* interference, meddling.
ingeridor, *n.m.* grafting-knife.
ingeridura, *n.f.* grafting.
ingerir [6], *v.t.* to ingest; to graft; to insert. — **ingerirse,** *v.r.* to interfere, meddle.
ingerto, -ta, *a.* grafted, ingrafted. — *p.p.* [INGERIR].
ingestión, *n.f.* ingestion, ingesting.
ingina, *n.f.* jaw-bone.
Inglaterra, *n.f.* England.
ingle, *n.f.* groin.
inglés, -lesa, *a.* English; ***a la inglesa,*** in the English fashion. — *n.m.f.* Englishman, Englishwoman. — *n.m.* English (language).
inglesar, *v.t.* to anglicize.
inglesismo, *n.m.* anglicism.
inglete, *n.m.* diagonal; angle of 45°.
inglosable, *a.* admitting no gloss *or* comment.
ingobernable, *a.* ungovernable, unmanageable, unruly.
ingratitud, *n.f.* ingratitude, ungratefulness, unthankfulness.
ingrato, -ta, *a.* ungrateful, unthankful; thankless; harsh, disagreeable. — *n.m.f.* ingrate.
ingrediente, *n.m.* ingredient.
ingresar, *v.t.* to pay in, deposit. — *v.i.* to enter, get in; to join; to come in.
ingreso, *n.m.* entrance, ingress; admission; (*com.*) money paid in; ***derecho de ingreso,*** entrance fee; ***examen de ingreso,*** entrance examination; (*pl.*) income, incomings.
íngrimo, -ma, *a.* (*Hisp. Am.*) entirely alone.
inguinal, inguinario, -ria, *a.* inguinal.
ingurgitación, *n.f.* ingurgitation.
ingurgitar, *v.t.* to ingurgitate, swallow.
ingustable, *a.* unsavoury, unpalatable.
inhábil, *a.* unskilful; unfit, unqualified; inept; incompetent; tactless.
inhabilidad, *n.f.* inability; unskilfulness, lack of skill; incompetence.
inhabilitación, *n.f.* disqualifying; disqualification.
inhabilitar, *v.t.* to disable; to disqualify, incapacitate; to render unfit.
inhabitable, *a.* uninhabitable.
inhabitado, -da, *a.* uninhabited.

inhabituado, -da, *a.* unhabituated, unaccustomed.
inhalación, *n.f.* inhalation.
inhalador, -ra, *a.* inhaling. — *n.m.f.* inhaler.
inhalar, *v.t.* to inhale.
inhartable, *a.* insatiable.
inherencia, *n.f.* inherence, inherency.
inherente, *a.* inherent (*a,* in).
inhestar [I], *v.t.* to erect, set upright.
inhibición, *n.f.* inhibition.
inhibir, *v.t.* to inhibit. — **inhibirse,** *v.r.* to become inhibited; to refrain (from).
inhibitorio, -ria, *a.* inhibitory, inhibiting.
inhiesto, -ta, *a.* erect, upright.
inhonestidad, *n.f.* immodesty, indecency.
inhonesto, -ta, *a.* immodest, indecent.
inhospedable, inhospitable, inhospital, inhospitalario, -ria, *a.* inhospitable.
inhospitalidad, *n.f.* inhospitableness.
inhumanidad, *n.f.* inhumanity.
inhumano, -na, *a.* inhuman.
inhumar, *v.t.* to inhume, inter.
iniciación, *n.f.* initiation.
iniciador, -ra, *a.* initiating, starting. — *n.m.f.* initiator, starter.
inicial, *a.* initial. — *n.f.pl.* (**iniciales**) initials.
iniciar, *v.t.* to initiate; to commence. — **iniciarse,** *v.r.* to be initiated; (*eccles.*) to receive first orders.
iniciativo, -va, *a.* initiating, initiatory. — *n.f.* initiative.
inicuo, -cua, *a.* iniquitous.
inimaginable, *a.* unimaginable.
inimicísimo, -ma, *a. superl.* extremely inimical.
inimitable, *a.* inimitable.
ininteligible, *a.* unintelligible.
iniquidad, *n.f.* iniquity.
iniquísimo, -ma, *a. superl.* most iniquitous.
injerencia [INGERENCIA].
injeridura, *n.f.* graft.
injerir [6], *v.t.* to graft; to insert; to ingest. — **injerirse** [INGERIRSE].
injertar [*p.p.* **injertado, injerto**], *v.t.* to graft, engraft.
injertera, *n.f.* orchard of grafted trees.
injerto, *n.m.* graft, grafting. — *p.p.* [INJERTAR].
injuria, *n.f.* offence, insult, abuse; harm, damage.
injuriador, -ra, *a.* offensive, insulting, abusive. — *n.m.f.* abuser.
injuriante, *a.* offensive, insulting, abusive.
injuriar, *v.t.* to offend, insult, abuse; to harm, damage.
injurioso, -sa, *a.* offensive, insulting, abusive.
injusticia, *n.f.* injustice.
injustificable, *a.* unjustifiable.
injustificadamente, *adv.* unjustifiably.
injustificado, -da, *a.* unjustified.
injusto, -ta, *a.* unjust, unfair.
inlegible, *a.* illegible.
inllevable, *a.* insupportable, unbearable.
inmaculado, -da, *a.* immaculate, spotless, stainless.
inmadurez, *n.f.* immaturity.
inmaduro, -ra, *a.* immature.
inmaleable, *a.* unmalleable.
inmanejable, *a.* unmanageable.
inmanente, *a.* immanent, inherent.
inmarcesible, *a.* unfading, unwithering.
inmarchitable, *a.* unfading.
inmaterial, *a.* immaterial, incorporeal.
inmaterialidad, *n.f.* immateriality.
inmediación, *n.f.* immediacy, immediateness; proximity; (*pl.* **inmediaciones**) environs, neighbourhood, outskirts.
inmediato, -ta, *a.* immediate; adjoining, next; close by, hard by; ***de inmediato,*** immediately. — *n.f.* (*coll.*) immediate action *or* reaction.
inmedicable, *a.* incurable, irremediable.
inmejorable, *a.* unbeatable, that cannot be bettered.
inmemorable, *a.* immemorable, immemorial.
inmemorial, *a.* immemorial.
inmensidad, *n.f.* immensity, immenseness, hugeness, vastness; great multitude *or* number.
inmenso, -sa, *a.* immense, huge, vast.
inmensurable, *a.* immeasurable, measureless.
inmerecido, -da, *a.* unmerited, undeserved.
inmergir [E], *v.t.* (*neol.*) to immerse. — *v.i.* (*astron.*) to disappear in the shadow of *or* behind another heavenly body; [SUMERGIR].
inmérito, -ta, *a.* undeserved, unmerited.
inmeritorio, -ria, *a.* immeritorious, undeserving.
inmersión, *n.f.* immersion.
inmigración, *n.f.* immigration.
inmigrante, *a.* immigrating, immigrant. — *n.m.f.* immigrant.
inmigrar, *v.i.* to immigrate.
inminencia, *n.f.* imminence, nearness.
inminente, *a.* imminent, impending, near, at hand.
inmiscuir [O *and regular*], *v.t.* to mix. — **inmiscuirse,** *v.r.* to interfere, meddle.
inmobiliario, -ria, *a.* real estate, pertaining to real estate. — *n.f.* estate agent's office.
inmoble, *a.* unmovable, immovable, fixed, unaffected; motionless; constant, unchanging.
inmoderación, *n.f.* immoderation, immoderateness; excess.
inmoderado, -da, *a.* immoderate, excessive.
inmodestia, *n.f.* immodesty; indecency, indelicacy.
inmodesto, -ta, *a.* immodest, indelicate.
inmolación, *n.f.* immolation.
inmolador, -ra, *a.* immolating. — *n.m.f.* immolator.
inmolar, *v.t.* to immolate.
inmoral, *a.* immoral.
inmoralidad, *n.f.* immorality.
inmorigerado, -da, *a.* inordinate.
inmortal, *a.* immortal.
inmortalidad, *n.f.* immortality.
inmortalizar [C], *v.t.* to immortalize, perpetuate.
inmortificación, *n.f.* immortification, licentiousness.
inmortificado, -da, *a.* unmortified.
inmotivado, -da, *a.* without reason or cause, unmotivated.
inmoto, -ta, *a.* motionless.
inmovible, *a.* immovable.
inmóvil, *a.* motionless; still, stationary.
inmovilidad, *n.f.* immobility.
inmovilismo, *n.m.* stone-wall resistance to change, dogged preservation of the status quo.
inmudable, *a.* immutable.
inmueble, *a.* (*law*) immovable (*property*). — *n.m.* building (*as a property*); (*pl.*) fixed property.
inmundicia, *n.f.* dirt, filth, filthiness; uncleanliness, impurity, lewdness.
inmundo, -da, *a.* dirty, filthy; unclean, impure.
inmune, *a.* free, exempt; immune.
inmunidad, *n.f.* immunity; exemption.
inmunización, *n.f.* immunization.
inmunizar [C], *v.t.* to immunize.
inmutabilidad, *n.f.* immutability.
inmutable, *a.* immutable, unchanging.
inmutación, *n.f.* change, alteration.
inmutar, *v.t.* to change, alter. — **inmutarse,** *v.r.* to be put out of countenance; ***no se inmutó,*** he didn't bat an eyelid, he didn't turn a hair.
inmutativo, -va, *a.* that which changes *or* causes alterations.
innato, -ta, *a.* innate, inborn.
innavegable, *a.* unnavigable; unseaworthy.

innecesario, -ria, *a.* unnecessary.
innegable, *a.* undeniable.
innoble, *a.* ignoble.
innocuo, -cua, *a.* innocuous, harmless.
innominado, -da, *a.* nameless; ***hueso innominado,*** innominate bone.
innovación, *n.f.* innovation.
innovador, -ra, *a.* innovating. — *n.m.f.* innovator.
innovamiento, *n.m.* innovation.
innovar, *v.t.* to innovate.
innumerabilidad, *n.f.* innumerability, innumerableness.
innumerable, *a.* innumerable, numberless, countless.
innúmero, -ra, *a.* innumerable, numberless, countless.
innutrición, *n.f.* want of nourishment.
inobediencia, *n.f.* want of obedience.
inobediente, *a.* wanting in obedience.
inobservable, *a.* unobservable, inobservable.
inobservancia, *n.f.* inobservance, non-observance
inobservante, *a.* inobservant.
inocencia, *n.f.* innocence; guilelessness.
inocentada, *n.f.* (*coll.*) foolish thing to do *or* say; guileless blunder; practical joke, April-fool joke.
inocente, *a.* innocent; guileless.
inocentón, -tona, *a., n.m.f.* hopelessly simple and guileless (individual).
inoculación, *n.f.* inoculation.
inoculador, -ra, *a.* inoculating. — *n.m.f.* inoculator.
inocular, *v.t.* to inoculate; to contaminate, pervert. — **inocularse,** *v.r.* to get inoculated.
inocuo, -cua, *a.* innocuous.
inodoro, -ra, *a.* inodorous, odourless. — *n.m.* lavatory.
inofensivo, -va, *a.* inoffensive, harmless.
inoficioso, -sa, *a.* inofficious.
inojeta, *n.f.* top (*of a boot*).
inolvidable, *a.* unforgettable, not to be forgotten.
inoperable, *a.* inoperable.
inoperante, *a.* inoperative; useless.
inopia, *n.f.* indigence, poverty, penury; (*coll.*) ***estar en la inopia,*** to have one's head in the clouds, be out of touch; (*coll.*) not with it.
inopinable, *a.* indisputable.
inopinado, -da, *a.* unexpected, unforeseen.
inoportunidad, *n.f.* inopportuneness.
inoportuno, -na, *a.* inopportune; ill-timed; tactless.
inordenado, -da, inordinado, -da, *a.* lacking in order.
inorgánico, -ca, *a.* inorganic.
inoxidable, *a.* inoxidizable, rustless; stainless.
inquebrantable, *a.* unbreakable; unyielding; irrevocable.
inquietador, -ra, *a.* disquieting, disturbing.
inquietante, *a.* disquieting, disturbing.
inquietar, *v.t.* to disquiet, disturb, make uneasy *or* restless, trouble.
inquieto, -ta, *a.* restless; uneasy.
inquietud, *n.f.* restlessness, uneasiness; anxiety.
inquilinato, *n.m.* lease, leasehold; ***impuesto de inquilinato,*** municipal rates.
inquilinaje, *n.m.* (*Chi.*) leasehold.
inquilino, -na, *n.m.f.* tenant; (*law*) lessee.
inquina, *n.f.* (*coll.*) ***tener inquina a,*** to have it in for, bear a grudge against.
inquinamento, *n.m.* infection.
inquinar, *v.t.* to contaminate, pollute.
inquiridor, -ra, *a.* inquiring. — *n.m.f.* inquirer.
inquirir [3, *as if* **inquerir**], *v.t.* to inquire into, look into, investigate.
inquisición, *n.f.* inquisition.
inquisidor, -ra, *a.* inquiring, inquisitive. — *n.m.f* inquirer, examiner. — *n.m.* Inquisitor.
inquisitivo, -va, *a.* inquisitive, inquiring.
inquisitorial, *a.* inquisitorial.
inri, *n.m.* (*fig.*) brand, stigma; insult.
insabible, *a.* unknowable.
insaciabilidad, *n.f.* insatiableness.
insaciable, *a.* insatiable.
insaculación, *n.f.* (*law*) balloting for names.
insaculador, *n.m.* (*law*) balloter.
insacular, *v.t.* to ballot, vote by ballot.
insalivación, *n.f.* insalivation.
insalivar, *v.t.* to insalivate.
insalubre, *a.* insalubrious, unhealthy.
insalubridad, *n.f.* insalubrity, unhealthiness.
insanable, *a.* incurable.
insania, *n.f.* insanity.
insano, -na, *a.* not healthy, unhealthy; insane.
inscribir [*p.p.* **inscrito**], *v.t.* to inscribe; to sign on; to register.
inscripción, *n.f.* inscription; signing on; registration.
insculpir, *v.t.* to engrave, sculpture.
insecable (1), *a.* (*coll.*) that cannot be dried.
insecable (2), *a.* that cannot be divided *or* cut.
insección, *n.f.* incision.
insecticida, *a.* insecticidal. — *n.m.* insecticide.
insectil, *a.* insectile.
insectívoro, -ra, *a.* insectivorous.
insecto, *n.m.* insect, (*Am.*) bug.
insectólogo, -ga, *n.m.f.* entomologist.
inseguridad, *n.f.* insecurity, uncertainty.
inseguro, -ra, *a.* insecure, unsafe; uncertain, dubious; unsteady, not firm.
insembrado, -da, *a.* unsowed, unsown.
inseminación, *n.f.* insemination.
inseminar, *v.t.* to inseminate.
insenescencia, *n.f.* quality of not becoming old, agelessness.
insensatez, *n.f.* stupidity, folly.
insensato, -ta, *a.* insensate, nonsensical, senseless; crazy, wild.
insensibilidad, *n.f.* insensibility; insensitiveness; unfeelingness.
insensibilizar, *v.t.* to make *or* render insensitive, unfeeling, *or* callous.
insensible, *a.* insensitive; unfeeling; gradual, imperceptible.
inseparabilidad, *n.f.* inseparableness, inseparability.
inseparable, *a.* inseparable.
insepulto, -ta, *a.* unburied, uninterred.
inserción, *n.f.* insertion; engrafting.
inserir [6], *v.t.* to insert; to graft.
insertar [*p.p.* **insertado, inserto**], *v.t.* to insert, introduce.
inserto, -ta, *a.* inserted. — *n.m.* insertion.
inservible, *a.* unserviceable, useless.
insidia, *n.f.* ambush, snare: insidious act.
insidiador, -ra, *n.m.f.* plotter, waylayer.
insidiar, *v.t.* to plot against; to waylay, ambush.
insidioso, -sa, *a.* insidious.
insigne, *a.* illustrious.
insignia, *n.f.* decoration, device, badge; standard; (*naut.*) pennant; (*pl.*) insignia.
insignificancia, *n.f.* insignificance.
insignificante, *a.* insignificant.
insinceridad, *n.f.* insincerity.
insinuación, *n.f.* insinuation; innuendo; hint; suggestiveness.
insinuante, *a.* insinuating; hinting; suggestive.
insinuar [M], *v.t.* to insinuate, hint, suggest. — **insinuarse,** *v.r.* to insinuate o.s., work one's way (in), slip *or* creep (in); to begin to come into the

open, start to show one's hand; to act *or* speak suggestively, make (suggestive) advances, drop suggestive hints.
insipidez, *n.f.* insipidity, insipidness.
insípido, -da, *a.* insipid, tasteless, vapid, flat.
insipiencia, *n.f.* ignorance; lack of judgment.
insipiente, *a.* ignorant; lacking in judgment.
insistencia, *n.f.* insistence, persistence, keeping on.
insistente, *a.* insistent, keeping on.
insistir, *v.i.* to insist, persist, keep on.
ínsito, -ta, *a.* inborn.
insociabilidad, *n.f.* unsociability, unsociableness.
insociable, insocial, *a.* unsociable.
insolación, *n.f.* sunstroke, heat-stroke; insolation.
insolar, *v.t.* to insolate, expose to the sun. — **insolarse,** *v.r.* to get sunstroke.
insoldable, *a.* that cannot be soldered.
insolencia, *n.f.* insolence, impudence, effrontery.
insolentar, *v.t.* to make insolent. — **insolentarse,** *v.r.* to get insolent, behave with effrontery.
insolente, *a.* insolent, impudent.
insólito, -ta, unusual, unaccustomed.
insolubilidad, *n.f.* insolubility.
insoluble, *a.* insoluble; unsolvable.
insoluto, -ta, *a.* unpaid.
insolvencia, *n.f.* insolvency.
insolvente, *a.* insolvent.
insomne, *a.* insomnious, sleepless.
insomnio, *n.m.* insomnia, sleeplessness.
insondable, *a.* unfathomable, fathomless; inscrutable.
insonorizar [C], *v.t.* to soundproof.
insonoro, -ra, *a.* soundproof; soundless.
insoportable, *a.* insupportable, intolerable, untenable.
insostenible, *a.* indefensible; untenable.
inspección, *n.f.* inspection; survey; superintendence; control; inspector's office.
inspeccionar, *v.t.* to inspect, examine, oversee.
inspector, -ra, *a.* inspecting. — *n.m.f.* inspector, examiner, overseer, surveyor, controller, superintendent.
inspiración, *n.f.* inspiration; (*med.*) inhalation.
inspirador, -ra, *a.* inspiring. — *n.m.f.* inspirer.
inspirante, *a.* inspiring.
inspirar, *v.t., v.i.* to inspire; to breathe in, inhale. — **inspirarse,** *v.r.* to get, draw *or* derive (one's) inspiration (***en,*** from).
inspirativo, -va, *a.* inspiratory.
instabilidad, *n.f.* [INESTABILIDAD].
instable, *a.* [INESTABLE].
instalación, *n.f.* installation; installing, laying, setting up; plant, factory; fittings; (*gas, electric* or *heating*) system; induction (*of a soldier*); ***instalaciones portuarias,*** port facilities.
instalador, -ra, *a.* installing. — *n.m.f.* installer.
instalar, *v.t.* to install; to set, lay, put in place. — **instalarse,** *v.r.* to settle, settle in, take up one's abode.
instancia, *n.f.* instance; request; petition; application; ***a instancia de,*** at the request of; ***en primera instancia,*** in the first place.
instantáneo, -nea, *a.* instantaneous, momentary. — *n.f.* snapshot.
instante, *a.* instant, urgent, pressing. — *n.m.* instant, moment; ***al instante,*** immediately; ***por instantes,*** incessantly, continually, at every moment; ***a cada instante,*** at every moment; continuously; ***en un instante,*** in a jiffy.
instar, *v.t.* to press, urge. — *v.i.* to be urgent, urge promptness.
instauración, *n.f.* setting-up; restoration.
instaurar, *v.t.* to set up; to renew; restore.
instaurativo, -va, *a.* restorative.
instigación, *n.f.* instigation.
instigador, -ra, *n.m.f.* instigator, abetter.
instigar [B], *v.t.* to instigate, incite, urge.
instilación, *n.f.* instillation.
instilar, *v.t.* to instil.
instintivo, -va, *a.* instinctive.
instinto, *n.m.* instinct; ***por instinto,*** instinctively.
institución, *n.f.* institution; establishment; setting-up; (*obs.*) education, instruction; collation *or* bestowal of a benefice.
institucionalizarse, *v.r.* to become institutionalized, take on the rigidity of an established institution.
instituente, *a.* instituting.
instituidor, -ra, *a.* instituting. — *n.m.f.* institutor, founder.
instituir [O], *v.t.* to institute, establish, found, set up; to appoint, nominate.
instituta, *n.f.* (*law*) institutes (*of Justinian*).
instituto, *n.m.* institute; state secondary school; constitution, rule; ***instituto de segunda enseñanza*** or ***de enseñanza media,*** state secondary school.
institutor, -ra, *a.* instituting, founding. — *n.m.f.* institutor; teacher.
institutriz, *n.f.* governess.
instituyente, *a.* instituting.
instrucción, *n.f.* instruction; teaching; education; knowledge, learning; (*mil.*) drill; (*law*) institution *or* carrying out of proceedings; ***instrucción primaria,*** elementary education; ***instrucción pública,*** public education; (*pl.* **instrucciones**) instructions, directions.
instructivo, -va, *a.* instructive.
instructor, -ra, *a.* instructing. — *n.m.f.* instructor, instructress.
instruir [O], *v.t.* to instruct, teach, train, educate; (*mil.*) to drill; to inform, advise; (*law*) to institute, carry out *or* take (proceedings).
instrumentación, *n.f.* instrumentation, orchestration.
instrumental, *a.* instrumental; (*law*) belonging to legal instruments. — *n.m.* (set of) instruments, kit.
instrumentar, *v.t.* to orchestrate.
instrumentista, *n.m.f.* instrumentalist; instrument maker.
instrumento, *n.m.* instrument; tool; implement; ***instrumento de cuerda,*** stringed instrument; ***instrumento de viento,*** wind instrument; ***instrumento de percusión,*** percussion instrument.
insuave, *a.* rough; unpleasant, disagreeable.
insubordinación, *n.f.* insubordination.
insubordinado, -da, *a.* insubordinate, rebellious.
insubordinar, *v.t.* to incite to insubordination. — **insubordinarse,** *v.r.* to get insubordinate, rebel.
insubsanable, *a.* irreparable.
insubsistencia, *n.f.* instability; groundlessness.
insubsistente, *a.* unstable; groundless.
insubstancial, *a.* unsubstantial.
insubstancialidad, *n.f.* insubstantiality.
insudar, *v.i.* to toil, drudge, slave.
insuficiencia, *n.f.* insufficiency, inadequacy.
insuficiente, *a.* insufficient, inadequate.
insufrible, *a.* intolerable, insufferable, unbearable.
ínsula, *n.f.* (*obs.*) isle, island; (*fig.*) small village, unimportant place.
insulano, -na, *a.* (*obs.*) insular. — *n.m.f.* (*obs.*) islander.
insular, *a.* insular. — *n.m.f.* islander.
insulina, *n.f.* (*med.*) insulin.
insulsez, *n.f.* insipidity, flatness, tastelessness.
insulso, -sa, *a.* insipid, tasteless; (*fig.*) dull, flat, heavy.
insultada, *n.f.* (*Hisp. Am.*) insult.
insultador, -ra, *a.* insulting. — *n.m.f.* insulter.
insultante, *a.* insulting.

insultar, *v.t.* to insult. — **insultarse,** *v.r.* (*coll.*) to have a sudden fit.
insulto, *n.m.* insult; sudden attack; fainting spell.
insumable, *a.* incalculable, innumerable.
insume, *a.* costly, expensive.
insumergible, *a.* unsinkable.
insumir, *v.t.* (*Hisp. Am.*) to consume, use up (*money*). — *v.i.* to ooze.
insumisión, *n.f.* rebelliousness.
insumiso, -sa, *a.* disobedient, rebellious.
insuperable, *a.* insuperable, insurmountable; unsurpassable.
insurgente, *a., n.m.f.* insurgent.
insurrección, *n.f.* insurrection, rebellion.
insurreccional, *a.* (of) insurrection *or* rebellion.
insurreccionar, *v.t.* to raise in insurrection. — **insurreccionarse,** *v.r.* to rise up, rise in revolt.
insurrecto, -ta, *a., n.m.f.* insurgent.
insustancial, *a.* unsubstantial.
intáctil, *a.* intangible, intactible.
intacto, -ta, *a.* untouched, intact, whole, entire.
intachable, *a.* irreproachable, blameless.
intangible, *a.* intangible; not to be touched.
integérrimo, -ma, *a. superl.* most honest *or* upright, irreproachable.
integración, *n.f.* integration.
integral, *a.* integral, whole.
integrante, *a.* integral, integrant.
integrar, *v.t.* to integrate; to make up, form; to reimburse; ***integrado por,*** consisting of, formed by.
integridad, *n.f.* integrality, wholeness, completeness; integrity, honesty, uprightness; virginity, maidenhood.
integrismo, *n.m.* traditionalism.
íntegro, -ra, *a.* integral, entire, complete; upright, honest.
integumento, *n.m.* integument; (*fig.*) disguise, fiction, fable.
intelección, *n.f.* intellection.
intelectivo, -va, *a.* intellective. — *n.f.* intellective.
intelecto, *n.m.* intellect, understanding.
intelectual, *a., n.m.f.* intellectual.
inteligencia, *n.f.* intelligence, understanding; ***estar en inteligencia con,*** to be in collusion with; ***en la inteligencia de que,*** on the understanding that.
inteligenciado, -da, *a.* instructed, informed.
inteligente, *a.* intelligent, clever.
inteligibilidad, *n.f.* intelligibility.
inteligible, *a.* intelligible.
intemperancia, *n.f.* intemperance.
intemperante, *a.* intemperate.
intemperie, *n.f.* outdoor *or* open weather conditions; ***a la intemperie,*** in the open, outdoors.
intempesta, *a.* (*poet.*) ***noche intempesta,*** dead of night.
intempestivo, -va, *a.* untimely, inopportune.
intemporal, *a.* timeless; (*fig., iron*) never-changing, ineffably constant.
intención, *n.f.* intention; intent; viciousness; ***segunda intención,*** hidden *or* double meaning, hidden *or* double purpose; ***de*** or ***con intención,*** deliberately; ***con la mejor intención,*** with the best of intentions; ***de primera intención,*** on (the) first impulse, first, to start with; provisionally; ***tiene su intención,*** there's a purpose behind it, there's a reason for it; ***tener intención de,*** to intend to, have it in mind to; ***tener mala intención,*** to be bloody-minded, be damned nasty.
intencionadamente, *adv.* intentionally, deliberately.
intencionado, -da, *a.* intentioned, inclined, disposed; intentional, deliberate; ***frase intencionada,*** loaded phrase *or* remark.
intencional, *a.* intentional.
intendencia, *n.f.* intendance; intendancy; administrative corps.
intendente, *n.m.* intendant; quartermaster general.
intensidad, *n.f.* intensity.
intensión, *n.f.* intenseness.
intensivo, -va, intenso, -sa, *a.* intensive, intense; ***curso intensivo,*** crash course.
intentar, *v.t.* to try, attempt, endeavour; (*law*) to enter (*an action*), commence (*a lawsuit*).
intento, *n.m.* attempt, try; intent, purpose; ***de intento,*** on purpose, deliberately.
intentona, *n.f.* (*coll.*) rash attempt.
interandino, -na, *a.* inter-Andean.
intercadencia, *n.f.* unevenness, inconstancy; (*med.*) intercadence.
intercadente, *a.* changeable, variable; intercadent.
intercalación, *n.f.* intercalation, insertion.
intercalar, *a.* intercalary. — *v.t.* to intercalate.
intercambiable, *a.* interchangeable.
intercambio, *n.m.* interchange, exchange; trade.
interceder, *v.i.* to intercede.
interceptación, *n.f.* interception.
interceptar, *v.t.* to intercept; to cut, block.
intercesión, *n.f.* intercession.
intercesor, -ra, *a.* interceding. — *n.m.f.* intercessor.
intercesorio, -ria, *a.* intercessory.
interciso, -sa, *a.* cut by half, in the middle; ***día interciso,*** half-holiday.
interclusión, *n.f.* interclusion.
intercolumnio, *n.m.* intercolumniation.
intercomunicación, *n.f.* intercommunication.
intercomunicador, *n.m.* intercom.
intercomunicar [A], *v.t., v.i.* to intercommunicate.
interconectar, *v.t., v.i.* to interconnect.
interconexion, *n.f.* interconnection.
interconfesional, *a.* interdenominational.
intercontinental, *a.* intercontinental.
intercostal, *a.* (*anat.*) intercostal.
intercurrencia, *n.f.* (*path.*) intercurrence.
intercurrente, *a.* intercurrent, intervening.
intercutáneo, -nea, *a.* intercutaneous.
interdecir [17], *v.t.* to interdict, prohibit.
interdental, *a.* interdental.
interdicción, *n.f.* interdiction, prohibition; ***interdicción civil,*** deprivation of civil rights.
interdicto, *n.m.* interdict, prohibition; censure summary possessory proceedings.
interdigital, *a.* interdigital.
interés, *n.m.* interest; ***poner a interés,*** to put out at interest; ***llevar interés,*** to bear interest; ***interés compuesto,*** compound interest; ***intereses creados,*** vested interests; ***tener interés en,*** to be anxious *or* eager to.
interesable, *a.* avaricious, mercenary.
interesado, -da, *a.* self-interested, selfish. — *n.m.f.* interested *or* concerned party *or* person.
interesante, *a.* interesting; reasonable, attractive (*price, scheme, etc.*). (*coll.*) ***estado interesante,*** pregnancy.
interesar, *v.t.* to interest, concern. — *v.i.* to be interesting; to be profitable. — **interesarse,** *v.r.* — ***en*** or ***por,*** to take an interest (in), be interested (in).
interesencia, *n.f.* presence, attendance.
interesente, *a.* present; concurring.
interesillo, *n.m.* slight interest.
interestatal, *a.* interstate.
interestelar, *a.* interstellar, intersidereal.
interfecto, -ta, *n.m.f.* (*law*) victim (*of murder*).
interferencia, *n.f.* (*phys.*) interference.
interfoliar, *v.t.* to interleave (*a book*).
intergubernamental, *a.* intergovernmental.

ínterin, *adv.* meanwhile, interim. — *conj.* while, until, as long as. — *n.m.* interim, temporary; ***en el ínterin,*** in the meantime.
interinar, *v.t.* to fill (*a post*) temporarily; to fill in.
interinato, *n.m.* (*Arg., Chi.*) [INTERINIDAD].
interinidad, *n.f.* interim; temporary post.
interino, -na, *a.* provisional, temporary; pro tempore; acting. — *n.m.f.* holder of a temporary job *or* office.
interior, *a.* interior, internal, inward, inside, inner; home, domestic; ***comercio interior,*** home trade; ***lo interior,*** home affairs; ***Ministerio del Interior,*** Home Office. — *n.m.* interior, inside, inner part; inland; mind, soul; (*pl.* **interiores**) entrails, insides.
interioridad, *n.f.* inside, inward part; act of concealment; (*pl.* **interioridades**) private matters.
interjección, *n.f.* (*gram.*) interjection.
interlínea, *n.f.* (*print.*) lead, space, line.
interlineación, *n.f.* interlineation; (*print.*) leading.
interlineal, *a.* interlineal.
interlinear, *v.t.* to write between lines; (*print.*) to lead, space.
interlocución, *n.f.* interlocution, dialogue, interchange of speech.
interlocutor, -ra, *n.m.f.* interlocutor.
interlocutorio, -ria, *a.* (*law*) interlocutory.
intérlope, *a.* interloping.
interludio, *n.m.* (*mus.*) interlude.
interlunio, *n.m.* interlunar period.
intermaxilar, *a.* intermaxillary.
intermediar, *v.i.* to mediate; to be in the middle *or* in between.
intermediario, -ria, *a.* intermediary. — *n.m.f.* intermediary; mediator; middleman.
intermedio, -dia, *a.* intermediate, intervening; medial. — *n.m.* interval, interim; interlude, intermission; intermezzo.
interminable, *a.* interminable, endless.
intermisión, *n.f.* intermission.
intermitencia, *n.f.* intermittence; (*med.*) intermission.
intermitente, *a.* intermittent.
intermitir, *v.t.* to intermit, discontinue.
internación, *n.f.* internment; moving in *or* inland.
internacional, *a.* international. — *n.f.* International(e).
internacionalismo, *n.m.* internationalism.
internacionalista, *a., n.m.f.* internationalist.
internacionalizar [C], *v.t.* to internationalize.
internado, *n.m.* boarding-school system; state of being a boarder; (body of) boarders.
internar, *v.t.* to lead *or* send inland; to intern; to commit (to an institution). — *v.i.* to go *or* move inland. — **internarse,** *v.r.* to penetrate, go off, strike off *or* plunge (deep) (***en,*** into).
interno, -na, *a.* internal, interior, inside; boarding. — *n.m.f.* boarder.
internodio, *n.m.* internode.
internuncio, *n.m.* interlocutor; (*eccles.*) internuncio.
interpelación, *n.f.* appeal; interpellation.
interpelar, *v.t.* to appeal to, implore the aid of; to interpellate.
interplanetario, -ria, *a.* interplanetary.
interpolación, *n.f.* interpolation.
interpolar, *v.t.* to interpolate; to interrupt.
interponer [25], *v.t.* to interpose, place between; to appoint as a mediator. — **interponerse,** *v.r.* to interpose, intervene, get between.
interposición, *n.f.* interposition, intervention.
interprender, *v.t.* (*mil.*) to take by surprise.
interpresa, *n.f.* (*mil.*) taking by surprise.
interpretable, *a.* interpretable.
interpretación, *n.f.* interpretation; construction; ***interpretacion de lenguas,*** translation bureau.
interpretador, -ra, interpretante, *a.* interpreting. — *n.m.f.* interpreter.
interpretar, *v.t.* to interpret; to translate; to construe; (*theat.*) to act a part; to give a rendering *or* performance of.
interpretativo, -va, *a.* interpretative.
intérprete, *n.m.f.* interpreter; sign.
interpuesto, -ta, *a.* interposed, intervening. — *p.p.* [INTERPONER].
interregno, *n.m.* interreign, interregnum.
interrogación, *n.f.* interrogation; question, inquiry; (*print.*) question mark.
interrogador, -ra, *a.* interrogating, questioning. — *n.m.f.* interrogator, questioner.
interrogante, *a.* interrogative; questioning; interrogating. — *n.m.* question mark.
interrogar [B], *v.t.* to question, interrogate.
interrogativo, -va, *a.* interrogative.
interrogatorio, *n.m.* interrogation; cross-examination.
interrumpido, -da, *a.* interrupted, broken, discontinued.
interrumpir, *v.t.* to interrupt; to suspend, discontinue; to cut in on, cut short; to obstruct, hinder.
interrupción, *n.f.* interruption; discontinuance; stoppage; break, gap.
interruptor, *a.* interrupting. — *n.m.* interrupter; (*elec.*) switch, circuit-breaker; ***interruptor bipolar,*** two-pole switch; ***interruptor de aceite,*** oil-break switch; ***interruptor de dos (tres) direcciones,*** two- (three-) way switch.
intersecarse, [A], *v.r.* (*geom.*) to intersect.
intersección, *n.f.* (*geom.*) intersection.
intersideral, *a.* interstellar.
intersticio, *n.m.* interstice; crevice; chink.
intertropical, *a.* intertropical.
interurbano, -na, *a.* interurban; ***conferencia interurbana,*** trunk call.
interusurio, *n.m.* interest allowed to a woman for the delay in repaying her marriage dowry.
intervalo, *n.m.* interval; stretch, interlapse; break, gap; ***claro*** or ***lúcido intervalo,*** remission of madness, lucid interval.
intervención, *n.f.* intervention; supervision, superintendence; mediation, interposition; auditing accounts.
intervencionismo, *n.m.* (systematic) intervention *or* interference.
intervenir [36], *v.t.* to audit; to take up; to inspect, supervise; to tap (*a telephone line*); to operate on. — *v.i.* to intervene, take part; to intercede, mediate; to happen, occur.
interventor, -ra, *n.m.f.* comptroller, supervisor, inspector, superintendent, auditor.
interviú, *n.f.* (*neol.*) interview.
interviuar, *v.t.* to interview.
intervocálico, -ca, *a.* intervocalic.
interyacente, *a.* interjacent, intervening.
intestado, -da, *a., n.m.* intestate.
intestinal, *a.* intestinal.
intestino, -na, *a.* intestine, internal, domestic. — *n.m.* intestine.
intimación, *n.f.* intimation; hint.
intimar, *v.t.* to intimate, convey, hint. — *v.i.* to become close friends.
intimatorio, -ria, *a.* (*law*) intimating.
intimidación, *n.f.* intimidation.
intimidad, *n.f.* intimacy; close friendship; ***en la intimidad,*** privately, in private.
intimidar, *v.t.* to intimidate.
íntimo, -ma, *a.* intimate; innermost; close; private. — *n.m.f.* close friend, bosom friend.

intitular, *v.t.* to entitle, title.
intocable, *a.* untouchable.
intolerabilidad, *n.f.* intolerableness.
intolerable, *a.* intolerable.
intolerancia, *n.f.* intolerance.
intolerante, *a.* intolerant.
intonso, -sa, *a.* (*poet.*) unshorn; ignorant, unpolished; uncut (*book*).
intorsión, *n.f.* (*bot.*) intortion.
intoxicación, *n.f.* poisoning; food poisoning.
intoxicar [A], *v.t.* (*med.*) to poison; to give food poisoning to.
intradós, *n.m.* (*arch.*) intrados.
intraducible, *a.* untranslatable.
intramuros, *adv.* within the city, within the walls.
intranquilidad, *n.f.* uneasiness, restlessness.
intranquilizar [C], *v.t.* to make uneasy *or* restless, disturb, disquiet.
intranquilo, -la, *a.* uneasy, restless.
intransferible, *a.* untransferable.
intransigencia, *n.f.* intransigence, uncompromisingness.
intransigente, *a.* intransigent, uncompromising.
intransitable, *a.* impassable.
intransitivo, -va, *a.* (*gram.*) intransitive.
intransmisible, *a.* untransmissible.
intransmutabilidad, *n.f.* intransmutability.
intransmutable, *a.* intransmutable.
intratable, *a.* intractable; extremely difficult *or* impossible to deal with; unsociable; impassable.
intravenoso, -sa, *a.* intravenous.
intrepidez, *n.f.* intrepidity, dauntlessness, fearlessness.
intrépido, -da, *a.* intrepid, dauntless, fearless.
intriga, *n.f.* intrigue; embroilment; plot.
intrigante, *a.* intriguing; fascinating.
intrigar [B], *v.t.* to intrigue. — *v.i.* to intrigue, plot, scheme.
intrincación, *n.f.* intricacy.
intrincado, -da, *a.* intricate, involved, elaborate; entangled.
intrincamiento, *n.m.* intricacy.
intrincar [A], *v.t.* to make intricate, involved *or* elaborate; to entangle.
intríngulis, *n.m. inv.* (*coll.*) crafty intention, hidden motive; mystery, enigma; ***tiene su intríngulis,*** there's more to it than meets the eye, there's quite a bit to it.
intrínseco, -ca, *a.* intrinsic, intrinsical.
introducción, *n.f.* introduction; insertion.
introducir [15], *v.t.* to introduce; to bring in; to insert, put in. — **introducirse,** *v.r.* to gain access (to); to interfere, meddle.
introductivo, -va, *a.* introductory, introductive.
introductor, -ra, *a.* introductory. — *n.m.f.* introducer.
introductorio, -ria, *a.* (*law*) introductory.
introito, *n.m.* beginning (*of an oration*); (*eccles.*) introit; (*theat.*) prologue.
intromisión, *n.f.* intromission; insertion; interference, meddling.
introspección, *n.f.* introspection.
introspectivo, -va, *a.* introspective.
introversión, *n.f.* introversion.
introverso, -sa, *a.* introverted.
introvertido, -da, *a.* introvert.
intrusar, *v.t.* to seize unlawfully. — **intrusarse,** *v.r.* to intrude, force one's way in.
intrusión, *n.f.* intrusion; interloping; encroachment; (*law*) trespass.
intrusismo, *n.m.* interloping; gate-crashing.
intruso, -sa, *a.* intrusive. — *n.m.f.* intruder; interloper; gate-crasher.
intubación, *n.f.* (*med.*) intubation, tracheotomy.
intuición, *n.f.* intuition.
intuicionismo, *n.m.* intuitionism.
intuir [O], *v.t.* to feel; to sense, guess at; to have *or* get an intuition *or* inkling of.
intuitivismo, *n.m.* intuitivism.
intuitivo, -va, *a.* intuitive.
intuito, *n.m.* view, look, glance; ***por intuito (de),*** in view (of), in consideration (of).
intumescencia, *n.f.* intumescence, swelling.
intumescente, *a.* intumescent, swollen.
intususcepción, *n.f.* (*med.*) intussusception.
inulto, -ta, *a.* (*poet.*) unavenged, unpunished.
inundación, *n.f.* inundation, flood.
inundante, *a.* inundating, flooding.
inundar, *v.t.* to inundate, flood.
inurbanidad, *n.f.* incivility, inurbanity.
inurbano, -na, *a.* uncivil. inurbane.
inusitado, -da, *a.* unusual, unwonted.
inusual, *a.* unusual.
inútil, *a.* useless.
inutilidad, *n.f.* uselessness; unprofitableness; useless person, dead loss.
inutilizar [C], *v.t.* to render useless; to disable.
invadeable, *a.* unfordable.
invadir, *v.t.* to invade; to encroach upon.
invaginación, *n.f.* (*med.*) invagination.
invaginar, *v.t.* to invaginate.
invalidación, *n.f.* invalidation, invalidity.
invalidar, *v.t.* to invalidate, nullify; to weaken, make helpless.
inválido, -da, *a.* invalid, void, null; disabled. — *n.m.f.* invalid.
invariabilidad, *n.f.* invariability.
invariable, *a.* invariable, constant.
invariación, *n.f.* invariableness.
invariado, -da, *a.* unvaried, constant.
invariante, *a.*, *n.m.f.* invariant, constant.
invasión, *n.f.* invasion.
invasor, -ra, *a.* invading. — *n.m.f.* invader.
invectiva, *n.f.* invective.
invectivar, *v.t.* to heap invective *or* violent abuse upon.
invencibilidad, *n.f.* invincibility.
invencible, *a.* invincible, unconquerable.
invención, *n.f.* invention; fabrication; finding; ***Invención de la Santa Cruz,*** Invention of the Cross.
invencionero, -ra, *a.* inventing, fabricating. — *n.m.f.* inventor, fabricator.
invendible, *a.* unsaleable, unmarketable.
inventar, *v.t.* to invent; to fabricate.
inventariar [L *and regular*], *v.t.* to inventory, list.
inventario, *n.m.* inventory.
inventivo, -va, *a.* inventive. — *n.f.* inventiveness.
invento, *n.m.* invention.
inventor, -ra, *n.m.f.* inventor; fabricator.
inverecundo, -da, *a.* shameless.
inverisímil, *a.* improbable.
inverisimilitud, *n.f.* improbability.
invernáculo, *n.m.* green-house, hot-house, conservatory.
invernada, *n.f.* winter season.
invernadero, *n.m.* winter-quarters; winter pasture; hot-house, conservatory.
invernal, *a.* (of) winter.
invernar [I], *v.i.* to winter.
invernizo, -za, *a.* (of) winter; wintry.
inverosímil, *a.* unlikely; incredible, unbelievable.
inverosimilitud, *n.f.* unlikelihood; incredibleness.
inversión, *n.f.* inversion; investment.

inverso, -sa, *a.* inverse, inverted. — *p.p.* [INVERTIR]; ***a*** or ***por la inversa,*** the other way round, contrariwise, vice versa.
invertebrado, -da, *a.* invertebrate, spineless. — *n.m.pl.* (**invertebrados**), invertebrata.
invertir [6], *v.t.* to invert; to reverse; to invest; to spend, take (*time*).
investidura, *n.f.* investiture.
investigable, *a.* investigable.
investigación, *n.f.* investigation; enquiry; research.
investigador, -ra, *a.* investigating. — *n.m.f.* investigator, research worker.
investigar [B], *v.t.* to investigate, look into, enquire into; to do research on.
investir [8], *v.t.* to invest.
inveterado, -da, *a.* inveterate.
inveterarse, *v.r.* to become inveterate.
invicto, -ta, *a.* invincible, unconquered, unvanquished.
invierno, *n.m.* winter; (*Hisp. Am.*) rainy season.
invigilar, *v.i.* to watch carefully.
inviolabilidad, *n.f.* inviolability, inviolableness.
inviolable, *a.* inviolable; inviolate.
inviolado, -da, *a.* inviolate.
invisibilidad, *n.f.* invisibility.
invisible, *a.* invisible, unseen; (*coll.*) hiding. — *n.m.* (*Hisp. Am.*) hairnet; (*Hisp. Am.*) invisible hairpin; ***en un invisible,*** in less than no time.
invitación, *n.f.* invitation.
invitado, -da, *n.m.f.* person invited, guest.
invitador, -ra, *n.m.f.* inviter, one who invites.
invitar, *v.t.* to invite; to treat. — *v.i.* to stand drinks etc.
invitatorio, *n.m.* (*eccles.*) invitatory.
invocación, *n.f.* invocation.
invocador, -ra, *a.* invoking. — *n.m.f.* invoker.
invocar [A], *v.t.* to invoke.
invocatorio, -ria, *a.* invocatory.
involución, *n.f.* involution.
involucrar, *v.t.* to jumble; to introduce irrelevantly.
involucro, *n.m.* (*bot.*) involucre.
involuntariedad, *n.f.* involuntariness.
involuntario, -ria, *a.* involuntary.
involuto, -ta, *a.* (*bot.*) involute. — *n.f.* (*arch.*) volute; (*geom.*) involute.
invulnerabilidad, *n.f.* invulnerability.
invulnerable, *a.* invulnerable.
inyección, *n.f.* injection; ***inyección hipodérmica*** or ***subcutánea,*** hypodermic injection.
inyectable, *a.* injectable.
inyectado, -da, *a.* congested, inflamed; ***ojos inyectados (de sangre),*** bloodshot eyes.
inyectar, *v.t.* to inject.
inyector, *n.m.* (*mech.*) injector.
ion, *n.m.* (*chem.*) ion.
ionio, *n.m.* (*chem.*) ionium.
ionización, *n.f.* ionization.
ionizar [C], *v.t.* to ionize.
iota, *n.f.* iota.
ipecacuana, *n.f.* ipecacuanha; ***ipecacuana de las Antillas,*** wild ipecac.
ipil, *n.m.* (*bot.*) ipil tree.
ir [21], *v.i.* to go; to come; to suit; ***lo voy entendiendo,*** I'm gradually *or* slowly getting to understand, I'm beginning gradually to grasp it; ***va herido,*** he is wounded; ***va huido,*** he's on the run; ***tenemos que ir a decírselo,*** we must go and tell them; ***no vaya a ser que se caiga,*** we can't have him falling down, we mustn't let him fall down; ***¡ya voy!*** just coming!; ***ir con tiento,*** to go carefully; ***ir a pie,*** to walk, go on foot; ***ir a caballo,*** to ride, go on horseback; ***ir a medias,*** to go halves, go fifty-fifty; ***ir en coche,*** to drive, go by car; ***ir adelante,*** to go ahead; ***van cinco duros a que llego antes,*** I wager 25 pesetas that I'll get there first; ***nada me va en ello,*** I don't stand to gain *or* lose anything by it; ***ir en pos de,*** to go after; ***ir (por) delante,*** to go ahead, lead the way; ***ir a una,*** to act with one accord; ***ir de capa caída,*** to be down-at-heel, down on one's luck, have seen better days; ***ir de campo,*** to go out into the country; to be dressed for the country; ***a gran ir,*** at high speed; ***a todo ir,*** at top speed; ***ir sobre seguro,*** to be sure of one's ground; to play safe; ***¡vaya a paseo!*** go to blazes!; ***¡vaya!*** well, well!; ***¡vaya! con que sí ¿eh?*** well, well, you don't say!; ***esto no me va,*** this doesn't suit me!; ***eso a mí ni me va ni me viene,*** that's of no concern to me; ***entre X y Z va muchísima diferencia,*** there's a world of difference between X and Z; ***ir a parar a,*** to end up in; ***la cosa va de veras*** or ***en serio,*** he, they etc. really mean(s) it, mean(s) business; ***siempre va a lo suyo,*** it is always 'self first' with him; ***vamos por partes,*** let us take one thing at a time; ***si vamos a eso,*** if it comes to that; ***sin ir más lejos,*** to take this alone; ***¡vaya usted a saber!*** it's anybody's guess; ***¡vaya calor!*** talk about heat!; ***¡qué va!*** of course not! nonsense!; ***va vendido,*** he has no protection, he's had it; ***con eso vas que chutas,*** that's all you are going to get, and count yourself lucky; ***a donde fueres, haz lo que vieres,*** when in Rome do as the Romans. — **irse,** *v.r.* to go, go away, go off; to seep out, leak out, run over; to fall apart; to break wind; to lose control (of bodily functions); ***se me va la cabeza,*** I feel dizzy; ***se le fue el pie,*** his foot slipped; ***con la música se le van los pies,*** he can't keep his feet still when he hears music; ***se le van los ojos tras X,*** he can't keep his eyes off X; ***se le fue de la memoria,*** it went out of his head; ***se le fue la mano,*** his hand slipped; he overdid it.
ira, *n.f.* ire, anger, wrath.
iracundia, *n.f.* irascibility,ire, wrath.
iracundo, -da, *a.* ireful, wrathful.
Irak, *n.m.* Iraq.
Irán, *n.m.* Iran.
iraní, iranio, -nia, *a., n.m.f.* Iranian.
iraqués, -quesa, iraquí, *a., n.m.f.* Iraki.
irascible, *a.* irascible.
iridáceo, -cea, *a.* iridaceous.
íride, *n.f.* (*bot.*) stinking iris.
irídeo, -dea, *a.* irideous.
iridio, *n.m.* iridium.
iridiscente, *a.* iridescent.
iris, *n.m.* iris; rainbow; ***iris de paz,*** mediator, peace-maker; (*min.*) opal.
irisado, -da, *a.* rainbow-hued.
irisar, *v.i.* to iridesce.
Irlanda, *n.f.* Ireland.
irlanda, *n.f.* cotton and woollen cloth; Irish linen.
irlandés, -desa, *a.* Irish. — *n.m.* Irishman; Irish (language). — *n.f.* Irishwoman.
ironía *n.f.* (*rhet.*) irony.
irónico, -ca, *a.* ironic(al).
iroqués, -quesa, *a., n.m.f.* Iroquois.
irracional, *a.* irrational; (*math.*) irrational. — *n.m.* brute, animal.
irracionalidad, *n.f.* irrationality.
irradiación, *n.f.* irradiation, radiation.
irradiar, *v.t.* to irradiate, radiate.
irrazonable, *a.* unreasonable.
irreal, *a.* unreal.
irrealidad, *n.f.* unreality.
irrealizable, *a.* unrealizable, unattainable.
irrebatible, *a.* irrefutable.
irreconciliable, *a.* irreconcilable.
irreconocible, *a.* unrecognizable, beyond recognition.
irrecuperable, *a.* irrecoverable, irretrievable.

irrecusable, *a.* unimpeachable.
irredento, -ta, *a.* irredent.
irredentista, *n.m.f.* irredentist.
irredimible, *a.* irredeemable.
irreducible, *a.* irreducible.
irreductible, *a.* irreducible, unyielding.
irreemplazable, *a.* irreplaceable.
irreflexión, *n.f.* rashness, thoughtlessness.
irreflexivo, -va, *a.* inconsiderate, unreflecting, thoughtless.
irreformable, *a.* unreformable.
irrefragable, *a.* irrefragable, irrefutable.
irrefrenable, *a.* irrepressible.
irregular, *a.* irregular.
irregularidad, *n.f.* irregularity.
irreligión, *n.f.* irreligion.
irreligiosidad, *n.f.* irreligiousness.
irreligioso, -sa, *a.* irreligious.
irremediable, *a.* irremediable, incurable; hopeless.
irremisible, *a.* irremissible, unpardonable.
irremunerado, -da, *a.* unremunerated.
irrenunciable, *a.* unrenounceable.
irreparable, *a.* irreparable, irretrievable.
irreprensible, *a.* irreprehensible, irreproachable, blameless.
irrescindible, *a.* unrescindable.
irresistible, *a.* irresistible; unbearable.
irresoluble, *a.* unsolvable, unworkable.
irresolución, *n.f.* irresolution, hesitation, indecision.
irresoluto, -ta, irresuelto, -ta, *a.* irresolute, hesitating, wavering.
irrespetuoso, -sa, *a.* disrespectful.
irrespirable, *a.* unbreathable, suffocating.
irresponsabilidad, *n.f.* irresponsibility.
irresponsable, *a.* irresponsible.
irrestañable, *a.* unstaunchable.
irresuelto, -ta, *a.* irresolute, wavering.
irreverencia, *n.f.* irreverence, disrespect.
irreverenciar, *v.t.* to treat irreverently.
irreverente, *a.* irreverent.
irreversible, *a.* irreversible.
irrevocabilidad, *n.f.* irrevocability.
irrevocable *a.* irrevocable, irreversible.
irrigación, *n.f.* (*med.*) irrigation, enema.
irrigador, *n.m.* (*med.*) irrigator.
irrigar [B], *v.t.* (*med.*) to irrigate.
irrisible, *a.* laughable, ludicrous.
irrisión, *n.f.* derision, ridicule; mockery.
irrisorio, -ria, *a.* derisory, ludicrous, laughable.
irritabilidad, *n.f.* irritability, tendency to ill temper *or* anger.
irritable, *a.* irritable, easily provoked to ill temper *or* anger.
irritación, *n.f.* irritation, exasperation, anger.
irritador, -ra, *a.* irritating, exasperating, angering.
irritamente, *adv.* (*law*) invalidly.
irritamiento, *n.m.* irritation, anger.
irritante, *a.* irritant; irritating; infuriating. — *n.m.* irritant.
irritar, *v.t.* to irritate; to exasperate, infuriate, anger; (*law*) to render null and void.
írrito, -ta, *a.* (*law*) null, void.
irrogar [B], *v.t.* to cause, occasion.
irrompible, *a.* unbreakable.
irruir [O], *v.t.* to storm.
irrumpir, *v.i.* to burst *or* rush (into).
irrupción, *n.f.* irruption; bursting *or* rushing in.
irubú, *n.m.* (*orn.*) turkey buzzard.
Isabel, *n.f.* Elizabeth.
isabelino, -na, *a.* Isabelline; Elizabethan; light bay (*horse*).
isagoge, *n.f.* introduction, exordium.
Isaías, *n.m.* (*Bibl.*) Isaiah.
isatis, *n.m.* Arctic fox.
Isidro, *n.m.* Isidoro, Isidore.
isidro, *n.m.* (*coll.*) bumpkin, yokel.
isla, *n.f.* isle, island; ***en isla,*** isolated(ly); ***Isla de Pascua,*** Easter Island; ***Islas Baleares,*** Balearic Islands; ***Islas de Barlovento,*** Windward Islands; ***Islas Malvinas,*** Falkland Islands; ***Islas de Sotavento,*** Leeward Islands.
islam, *n.m.* Islam.
islámico, -ca, *a.* Islamic.
islamismo, *n.m.* Islamism, Mohammedanism.
islamita, *a.* Islamic. — *n.m.f.* Islamite.
islamizar [C], *v.t.*, *v.i.* to Islamize.
islandés, -desa, *a.* Icelandic. — *n.m.f.* Icelander (*person*). — *n.m.* Icelandic (*language*).
Islandia, *n.f.* Iceland.
islándico, -ca, *a.* Icelandic.
isleño, -ña, *a.* island. — *n.m.f.* islander.
isleo, *n.m.* (small) island.
isleta, *n.f.* small isle, islet.
islilla, *n.f.* (*anat.*) collar-bone.
islote, *n.m.* small barren island; (*fig.*) island; jutting rock (*in sea*).
ismaelita, *a.*, *n.m.f.* Ishmaelite.
isobárico, -ca, *a.* isobaric.
isocronismo, *n.m.* isochronism.
isócrono, *a.* isochronal.
isógono, -na, *a.* (*phys.*) isogonic.
isomería, *n.f.* (*chem.*) isomerism.
isómero, -ra, isomérico, -ca, *a.* isomeric.
isomorfismo, *n.m.* (*min.*) isomorphism.
isomorfo, -fa, *a.* isomorphous, isomorphic.
isoperímetro, -ra, *a.* isoperimetrical.
isoquímeno, -na, *a.* (*meteor.*) isocheimal.
isósceles, *a.* isosceles.
isotermo, -ma, *a.* (*phys.*) isothermal.
isótero, -ra, *a.* (*meteor.*) isotheral.
isótopo, *n.m.* isotope.
isquión, *n.m.* (*anat.*) ischium.
Israel, *n.m.* Israel.
israelí, *a.*, *n.m.f.* Israeli.
israelita, *a.*, *n.m.f.* Israelite.
israelítico, -ca, *a.* Israelitish.
istacayota, *n.f.* (*Mex.*) pumpkin.
istmeño, -ña, *a.*, *n.m.f.* (native) of an isthmus.
ístmico, -ca, *a.* isthmian, isthmic.
istmo, *n.m.* isthmus.
istriar, *v.t.* (*arch.*) to flute.
isuate, *n.m.* (*Mex.*) palm (*the bark of which is used to make mattresses*).
Italia, *n.f.* Italy.
italianizar [C], *v.t.* to Italianize.
italiano, -na, *a.*, *n.m.f.* Italian (person). — *n.m.* Italian (*language*).
itálico, -ca, *a.* Italic; (*print.*) ***letra itálica,*** italics.
italo, -la, *a.* (*poet.*) Italian.
itamo, *n.m.* (*Cub.*) wild plant (*Euphorbia tithimaloides*).
ítem, *adv.* ***ítem*** or ***ítem más,*** also, likewise, furthermore. — *n.m.* item, section, article; addition.
iteración, *n.f.* iteration, repetition.
iterar, *v.t.* to iterate, repeat.
iterativo, -va, *a.* iterative, repeating.
iterbia, *n.f.* (*chem.*) ytterbia.
itérbico, -ca, *a.* ytterbic.
iterbio, *n.m.* (*chem.*) ytterbium.
itinerario, -ria, *a.* itinerary. — *n.m.* itinerary, route; time-table.
itria, *n.f.* (*min.*) yttria.

itrio, *n.m.* yttrium.
iva, *n.f.* (*bot.*) musky bugle.
iza, *n.f.* (*naut.*) hoisting, lifting up.
izaga, *n.f.* place abounding in rushes and reeds.
izaje, *n.m.* (*Hisp. Am.*) hoisting.
izar [C], *v.t.* (*naut.*) to hoist, haul up.
izote, *n.m.* (*bot.*) Spanish dagger.
izquierdear, *v.i.* (*coll.*) to err, go awry, wild *or* astray.
izquierdista, *a.*, *n.m.f.* (*polit.*) Left-winger.
izquierdizante, *a.*, *n.m.f.* (one) having leftish leanings.
izquierdo, -da, *a.* left, left-hand, left-handed; crooked; ***a la izquierda,*** on *or* to the left; (*polit.*) ***de izquierdas,*** Left-wing. — *n.m.f.* left-handed person. — *n.f.* left-hand; (*polit.*) Left, Left-wing.
izquierdoide, *a.*, *n.m.f.* (one) tainted *or* tinged with leftish views; would-be left-winger.
izquierdoso, -sa, *a.* tending to the left, leftish.

J

J, j, *n.f.* letter J, j.
jaba, *n.f.* (*Cub.*) basket; (*Hisp. Am.*) crate.
jabalcón, jabalón, *n.m.* (*arch.*) strut, brace.
jabalconar, *v.t.* to build *or* support with struts.
jabalí, *n.m.* (*zool.*) wild boar.
jabalina, *n.f.* wild sow; javelin, boarspear.
jabardear, *v.t.* to swarm (*bees*).
jabardillo, *n.m.* noisy swarm (*insects* or *birds*); (*coll.*) noisy crowd.
jabardo, *n.m.* small swarm of bees; (*coll.*) noisy crowd.
jabato, *n.m.* young wild boar; (*fig.*) young lion.
jábeca, jábega, *n.f.* sweep-net; fishing smack; dragnet; old-fashioned oven (*for the distillation of mercury in Almadén*).
jabegote, *n.m.* man who draws the sweep-net.
jabeguero, -ra, *a.* pertaining to sweep-net fishing. — *n.m.* sweep-net fisherman.
jabeque, *n.m.* (*naut.*) xebec; (*coll.*) knife slash in the face; (*coll.*) ***pintar un jabeque a,*** to cut *or* mark the face of.
jabera, *n.f.* Andalusian popular song in $\frac{3}{8}$ time.
jabí, *n.m.* (*bot.*) breakax, quebracho; small wild apple; small grape.
jabillo, *n.m.* (*bot.*) sandbox tree.
jabín (*Mex.*) [JABÍ].
jabladera, *n.f.* crozer.
jable, *n.m.* (*coop.*) croze.
jabón, *n.m.* soap; ***jabón de sastre,*** soapstone, French chalk; ***jabón en polvo,*** soap powder; ***agua y jabón,*** soap and water; ***dar un jabón a,*** to give a ticking off to; ***dar jabón a,*** to softsoap, butter up.
jabonado, *n.m.* soaping; wash.
jabonadura, *n.f.* soaping; (*fig.*) ticking off; (*pl.*) soapsuds.
jabonar, *v.t.* to soap; (*coll.*) to tick off.
jaboncillo, *n.m.* soapstone; toilet soap; (*bot.*) soap-tree.
jabonería, *n.f.* soap factory, soap shop.
jabonero, -ra, *a.* soap. — *n.m.f.* soap maker *or* seller. — *n.f.* soap-dish; (*bot.*) soapwort.
jabonete de olor, *n.m.* toilet soap.
jabonoso, -sa, *a.* soapy.
jaborandi, *n.m.* (*bot.*) jaborandi.
jabuco, *n.m.* (*Cub.*) large straw basket.
jaca, *n.f.* pony, cob.
jacal, *n.m.* (*Mex.*) hut.
jacamar, *n.m.* (*orn.*) jacamar.
jacana, *n.f.* (*orn.*) jacana.
jácara, *n.f.* [JÁCARO].
jacaranda, *n.f.* (*bot.*) jacaranda.
jacarandina, jacarandana, *n.f.* slang, vulgar language; assembly of ruffians and thieves.
jacarandoso, -sa, *a.* (*coll.*) jolly, merry, lively.
jacarear, *v.i.* to sing ***jácaras***; (*coll.*) to sing in the streets at night-time; to make *or* pass offensive remarks; to be vexatious, troublesome.
jacarero, *n.m.* ballad singer; wag *or* merry droll, facetious person.
jácaro, -ra, *a.* swaggering. — *n.m.* swaggerer, blusterer. — *n.f.* merry ballad; popular song and dance; roisterers singing and shouting in the streets; (*coll.*) annoyance; story, tale, idle talk, prattle; lie, fable, make-up.
jácena, *n.f.* (*arch.*) girder.
jacerina, *n.f.* coat of mail.
jacilla, *n.f.* mark which a thing leaves upon the ground.
jacinto, *n.m.* (*bot., min.*) hyacinth; ***jacinto de Ceilán,*** zircon; ***jacinto de Compostela,*** red crystallized quartz; ***jacinto occidental,*** topaz; ***jacinto oriental,*** ruby.
jacio, *n.m.* (*naut.*) dead calm.
jaco, *n.m.* nag, jade; coat of mail; short jacket.
jacobinismo, *n.m.* Jacobinism.
jacobino, -na, *a., n.m.* Jacobin.
Jacobo, *n.m.* James.
jactancia, *n.f.* boasting, bragging.
jactancioso, -sa, *a.* boastful, bragging. — *n.m.f.* boaster, bragger.
jactarse, *v.r.* to boast, brag.
jaculatorio, -ria, *a.* ejaculatory. — *n.f.* ejaculation.
jachalí, *n.m.* (*bot.*) custard-apple.
jada, *n.f.* (*prov., agric.*) hoe; spade.
jade, *n.m.* (*min.*) jade.
jadeante, *a.* panting, out of breath.
jadear, *v.i.* to pant.
jadeo, *n.m.* panting.
jadiar, *v.t.* (*prov.*) to dig up; to hoe.
jaecero, -ra, *n.m.f.* harness-maker.
jaén, *n.m.* large white grape.
jaez, *n.m.* harness; kind, type, ilk; (*pl.* **jaeces**), trappings.
jafético, -ca, *a.* Japhetic.
jagua, *n.f.* (*bot.*) genipap.
jaguar, jaguarete, *n.m.* (*zool.*) jaguar.
jaguarzo, *n.m.* (*bot.*) rock-rose.
jaguay, *n.m.* (*Cub.*) tree of yellow wood.
jagüey, *n.m.* (*Hisp. Am.*) basin, pool; (*Hisp. Am.*) tiny mosquito; (*Cub.*) Indian fig.
jaharrar, *v.t.* to plaster.
jaharro, *n.m.* (*mas.*) plaster, plastering.
jahuey (*Arg., Bol., Chi.*) [JAGÜEY].
jai alai, *n.m.* pelota game.
jaiba, *n.f.* (*Cub., zool.*) freshwater crawfish; (*Chi.*) crab.
jaibería, *n.f.* (*Hisp. Am.*) slyness, trickiness.
Jaime, *n.m.* James.
jaique, *n.m.* (Moorish) hooded cloak.
jaira, *n.f.* bevel (*of a plane-bit*).
jairar, *v.t.* to bevel leather.
jaire, *n.m.* bevel cut.
¡ja, ja, ja! *interj.* ha! ha!
jalapa, *n.f.* (*bot.*) jalapa; jalap.
jalar, *v.t.* to pull, haul, tug; (*Hisp. Am.*) to flirt with, court. — **jalarse,** *v.r.* (*Hisp. Am.*) to get drunk; (*Hisp. Am.*) to beat it, clear out.
jalbegar, *v.t.* [ENJALBEGAR]. — *v.t., v.r.* to paint, make up (*the face, one's face*).
jalbegue, *n.m.* whitewash, whitewashing; (*fig.*) paint, make-up.
jaldado, -da, jaldo, -da, jalde, *a.* bright yellow, crocus-coloured.
jaldre, *n.m.* yellow (*peculiar to birds*).
jalea, *n.f.* jelly; (*fig.*) ***hacerse una jalea,*** to go all soft and sloppy; ***jalea del agro,*** conserve of citron; ***jalea de guayaba,*** guava jelly.
jaleador, -ra, *a.* cheering. — *n.m.f.* cheerer (*of hounds, dancers* or *singers*).
jalear, *v.t.* to encourage (*hounds*) with shouts; to cheer (*dancers, singers*) by clapping hands; to urge on; (*Hisp. Am.*) to bother, tease.
jaleco, *n.m.* Turkish jacket.
jaleo, *n.m.* clapping hands, cheering (*to encourage dancers* or *singers*); merry noise, noisy time; (*coll.*) uproar, row; fuss, bother.
jaletina, *n.f.* calf's foot jelly; gelatine.
jalifa, *n.m.* supreme authority in Spanish Morocco (*delegate of the sultan*).
jalma, *n.f.* light packsaddle.
jalmería, *n.f.* packsaddler's trade, packsaddle work.
jalmero, *n.m.* packsaddle maker *or* dealer.
jalón, *n.m.* (*surv.*) flag pole, range pole, stake; (*Hisp. Am.*) jerk, pull, tug; (*Hisp. Am.*) swig, drink; (*fig.*) stage, landmark.

jalonamiento, *n.m.* staking, marking, laying out.
jalonar, *v.t.* (*surv.*) to mark, stake out.
jalonear, *v.t.* (*Hisp. Am.*) to jerk, pull, tug.
jalonero, *n.m.* (*surv.*) rodman.
jaloque, *n.m.* south-east wind.
jallullo, *n.m.* (*prov.*) [HALLULLO].
Jamaica, *n.f.* Jamaica.
jamaica, *n.f.* rum.
jamaicano, -na, jamaiquino, -na, *a., n.m.f.* Jamaican.
jamar, *v.i.* (*sl.*) to have a good nosh.
jamás, *adv.* never; ever; ***nunca jamás,*** never more; ***jamás de los jamases,*** never ever; ***para siempre jamás,*** for ever and ever.
jamba, *n.f.* (*arch.*) jamb.
jambaje, *n.m.* door-frame, window-frame.
jámbico, -ca, *a.* iambic.
jamelgo, *n.m.* (*coll.*) jade, nag.
jamerdana, *n.f.* sewer (*of a slaughterhouse*).
jamerdar, *v.t.* to clean (*the guts of animals*); (*coll.*) to wash hastily.
jamete, *n.m.* rich silk-stuff.
jamón, *n.m.* ham; bacon.
jamona, *a., n.f.* (*coll.*) buxom middle-aged (woman).
jámparo, *n.m.* (*Col.*) small boat *or* canoe.
jamuga, jamugas, *n.f.* mule-chair.
jándalo, -la, *a., n.m.f.* (*coll.*) Andalusian.
jangada, *n.f.* (*coll.*) silly remark *or* idea; (*naut.*) raft, float.
jangua, *n.f.* small armed vessel.
jansenismo, *n.m.* Jansenism.
jansenista, *a., n.m.f.* Jansenist.
Japón, *n.m.* Japan.
japon, -pona, *a., n.m.f.* Japanese.
japonés, -nesa, *a., n.m.f.* Japanese (*person*). — *n.m.* Japanese (*language*).
japuta, *n.f.* (*ichth.*) pomfret.
jaque, *n.m.* check (*in chess*); braggart, bully, tough; saddlebag; smooth combing of the hair; ***jaque mate,*** checkmate; ***¡jaque de aquí!*** out of it! away from here!; ***dar jaque a,*** to check; ***tener en jaque,*** to hold a threat over, keep on edge.
jaquear, *v.t.* to check.
jaqueca, *n.f.* migraine.
jaquel, *n.m.* (*her.*) square; chessboard.
jaquelado, -da, *a.* checkered.
jaquero, *n.m.* fine-toothed comb.
jaqueta, *n.f.* jacket.
jaquetilla, *n.f.* short jacket.
jaquetón, *n.m.* swaggerer, bully, tough.
jáquima, *n.f.* headstall (*of a halter*).
jaquimazo, *n.m.* stroke with the headstall of a halter; (*coll.*) displeasure; disappointment; bad, spiteful turn.
jara, *n.f.* [JARO].
jarabe, *n.m.* syrup; cough-mixture; ***jarabe de pico,*** empty talk, idle promise, lip service.
jarabear, *v.t.* to prescribe syrups for. — **jarabearse,** *v.r.* to make syrups frequently.
jaracolito, *n.m.* (*Per.*) Indian dance.
jaraíz, *n.m.* wine press.
jaramago, *n.m.* (*bot.*) hedge-mustard.
jarameño, -ña, *a.* of the Jarama.
jaramugo, *n.m.* young fish.
jarana, *n.f.* (*coll.*) carousal, revelry; uproar, row; ***irse de jarana,*** to go on a spree.
jaranear, *v.i.* (*coll.*) to carouse.
jaranero, -ra, *a.* merry-making, roistering.
jarano, *n.m.* sombrero.
jarapote, *n.m.* (*prov.*) drug habit.
jarapotear, *v.t.* (*prov.*) to stuff *or* fill with drugs.
jarazo, *n.m.* blow *or* wound with a dart.
jarcia, *n.f.* accoutrements; heaps of things; (*naut.*) tackle; rigging, cordage, shrouds.
jardín, *n.m.* (flower) garden; (*naut.*) privy; (emerald) blemish; ***jardín de infancia,*** kindergarten.
jardincito, *n.m.* small garden.
jardinería, *n.f.* gardening.
jardinero, -ra, *a.* garden, gardening. — *n.m.f.* gardener. — *n.f.* flowerstand, jardinière; basket carriage; open tramcar.
jarearse, *v.r.* (*Hisp. Am.*) to flee, run away; (*Hisp. Am.*) to swing, sway; (*Hisp. Am.*) to die of hunger, starve.
jareta, *n.f.* (*sew.*) casing; (*naut.*) netting, harping.
jaretera [JARRETERA].
jarife [JERIFE].
jarifo, -fa, *a.* showy.
jaro, -ra, *a.* carroty; red (*hog* or *boar*). — *n.m.* thicket; (*bot.*) arum. — *n.f.* (*bot.*) rock-rose; dart, arrow.
jarocho, -cha, *a.* uncouth. — *n.m.f.* uncouth person; (*Mex.*) peasant of Veracruz.
jaropar, jaropear, *v.t.* (*coll.*) to stuff with syrups *or* drugs.
jarope, *n.m.* syrup; (*coll.*) nasty stuff.
jaropeo, *n.m.* (*coll.*) drug overdose.
jaroso, -sa, *a.* covered in brambles.
jarra, *n.f.* earthen jar; pitcher; ***en jarras,*** akimbo.
jarrear, *v.t.* to plaster. — *v.i.* (*coll.*) to draw (*wine* or *water*) with a jug *or* pitcher; (*coll.*) to bucket down, pour with rain.
jarrero, *n.m.* vendor *or* maker of jars.
jarrete, *n.m.* hock; gambrel; ham.
jarretera, *n.f.* garter; Garter (*knighthood order*).
jarrito, *n.m.* small jug *or* pitcher.
jarro, *n.m.* pitcher, jug, pot, ewer; (*prov.*) chatterer; ***echar un jarro de agua (fría) a,*** to pour cold water on.
jarrón, *n.m.* vase, flower-vase; (*arch.*) urn.
jarros, *adv.* **a —,** hard, with great force.
Jartum, *n.m.* Khartoum.
jaspe, *n.m.* (*min.*) jasper.
jaspeadura, *n.f.* marbling.
jaspear, *v.t.* to marble, mottle, vein.
jastial (*arch.*) [HASTIAL].
jateo, -tea, *a.* fox-hunting (*dog*).
jato, -ta, *n.m.f.* calf.
¡jau! *interj.* call to incite animals (*especially bulls*).
Jauja, *n.f.* El Dorado; Cockaigne; (*coll.*) ***vivir en Jauja,*** to live in the lap of luxury.
jaula, *n.f.* cage; crate; (*Hisp. Am.*) open freight car; (*fig.*) ***jaula de locos,*** bedlam, madhouse.
jauría, *n.f.* pack (*of hounds*).
javanés, -nesa, *a. n.m.f.* Javan, Javanese. — *n.m.* Javanese (*language*).
Javier, *n.m.* Xavier.
jayán, *n.m.* hefty fellow.
jazmín, *n.m.* (*bot.*) jessamine, jasmine.
jazmíneo, -nea, *a.* (*bot.*) jasminaceous.
jazminorro, *n.m.* (*bot.*) yellow jasmine.
jazz, *n.m.* (*mus.*) jazz.
¡je, je, je! *interj.* ha, ha!
jebe, *n.m.* rock-alum; (*Hisp. Am.*) india-rubber.
jedive, *n.m.* khedive.
jefatura, *n.f.* headship, leadership; headquarters.
jefe, -fa, *n.m.f.* chief, head, leader; boss; (*mil.*) high-ranking officer, field officer; ***jefe de cocina,*** head cook, chef; ***jefe de estación,*** stationmaster; ***en jefe,*** in chief; ***jefe de día,*** day officer; ***inspector jefe,*** chief inspector; ***redactor jefe,*** chief editor; ***jefe de tren,*** guard, (*Am.*) brakeman.
Jehová, *n.m.* Jehovah.
jeja, *n.f.* (*prov.*) white wheat.
jeito, *n.m.* fishing-net.
jején, *n.m.* (*Cub.*) gnat, gall-midge.
jema, *n.f.* badly squared part (*of a beam*).

eme, *n.m.* distance from the end of the thumb to the end of the forefinger when both are extended; (*coll.*) (woman's) face.
emsbondesco, *a.* (of) James Bond; glamorous.
enabe, jenable, *n.m.* mustard.
engibre, *n.m.* ginger.
eniquén, *n.m.* henequen, sisal hemp.
enízaro, -ra, *a.* mixed, hybrid. — *n.m.* janizary.
eque, *n.m.* sheikh.
era, *n.f.* ground which can be ploughed in a day with a pair of oxen; present, gift.
erapellina, *n.f.* ragged garment.
erarca, *n.m.* (*eccles.*) hierarch; leader.
erarquía, *n.f.* hierarchy; leadership.
erárquico, -ca, *a.* hierarchical.
erarquizar, *v.t.* to give a hierarchical structure to.
erbo, *n.m.* jerboa.
eremiada, *n.f.* jeremiad.
eremías, *n.m.f.* Jeremiah; whiner.
eremiqueo, *n.m.* (*Chi., Cub., P.R.*) persistent supplication; whining.
erez, *n.m.* sherry.
erezano, -na, *a., n.m.f.* (native) of Jerez.
erga, *n.f.* jargon; gibberish; coarse cloth.
ergón, *n.m.* straw mattress; misfit clothes; clumsy oaf; zircon.
erguilla, *n.f.* silk *or* worsted serge.
ericó, *n.f.* Jericho.
ericoplear, *v.t.* (*Guat., Hond.*) to disturb, annoy.
erife, *n.m.* sherif.
erifiano, -na, *a.* sherifian.
erigonza, *n.f.* (*coll.*) jargon; gibberish; piece of stupidity; ***déjate de jerigonzas,*** stop talking rot; stop making a fool of yourself.
eringa, *n.f.* syringe; enema; sausage stuffer; (*coll.*) pest, bore.
eringación, *n.f.* syringing; (*coll.*) plaguing, plague, pest.
eringador, -ra, *a.* syringing; (*coll.*) plaguing, needling.
eringar [B], *v.t.* to syringe; to inject; to give an enema to; (*coll.*) to needle, plague; (*coll.*) to jigger up, muck up. — **jeringarse,** *v.r.* (*coll.*) to lump it.
eringazo, *n.m.* syringing; injecting; (*coll.*) squirt; jab.
eringuilla, *n.f.* hypodermic syringe; (*bot.*) syringa, mock orange.
eroglífico, -ca, *a.* hieroglyphic, hieroglyphical. — *n.m.* hieroglyph, hieroglyphic.
erosolimitano, -na, *a., n.m.f.* (native) of Jerusalem.
erpa, *n.f.* sterile shoot (*of a vine*).
ersey, *n.m.* jersey, jumper, pull-over, sweater.
erricote, *n.m.* pottage of almonds, sugar, sage and ginger.
erusalén, *n.m.* Jerusalem.
esnato, -ta, *a.* child dedicated to Jesus when born.
esucristo, *n.m.* Jesus Christ.
esuita, *a., n.m.f.* Jesuit; cunning, devious *or* sly (person).
esuítico, -ca, *a.* Jesuitical.
esuitismo, *n.m.* Jesuitism.
esús, *n.m.* Jesus; ***en un decir Jesús,*** in a jiffy; ***¡Jesús mil veces!*** good God!; ***no saber ni el Jesús,*** not to know even the alphabet; ***decir los Jesuses,*** to attend dying people; ***morir sin decir Jesús,*** to die very suddenly.
esusear, *v.i.* to repeat often the name of Jesus.
eta, *n.f.* thick and heavy lips; blubber-lip; hog's snout; (*coll.*) mug, phiz; (*mech.*) faucet, cock; (*coll.*) ***estar con mucha jeta,*** to have a long face; (*coll.*) ***poner jeta,*** to pout, pull a face.
etudo, -da, *a.* snouted; grim, gruff.
ji, ji, ji! *interj.* he! he!
íbaro, -ra, *a., n.m.f.* (*Hisp. Am.*) peasant, rustic; (*Mex.*) cross-breed.

jibia, *n.f.* (*zool.*) cuttlefish.
jibión, *n.m.* cuttlefish bone.
jibraltareño, -ña, *a.* [GIBRALTAREÑO].
jícara, *n.f.* chocolate cup; (*Hisp. Am.*) calabash cup.
jicarazo, *n.m.* blow with a chocolate cup; (*coll.*) poisoning; (*coll.*) ***dar un jicarazo,*** to give a poison.
jicarón, *n.m.* large chocolate cup.
jicotea, *n.f.* (*Hisp. Am.*) tortoise; mud-turtle.
jifa, *n.f.* offal (*of slaughtered animals*).
jiferada, *n.f.* stroke with a butcher's knife.
jifería, *n.f.* slaughtering.
jifero, -ra, *a.* belonging to the slaughterhouse; (*coll.*) dirty, filthy, vile. — *n.m.* slaughtering knife; butcher.
jifia, *n.f.* (*ichth.*) xiphias, swordfish.
jiga, *n.f.* jig (*dance and tune*).
jigote [GIGOTE].
jiguilete, *n.m.* indigo-plant.
jijallar, *n.m.* thicket of saltwort.
jijallo, *n.m.* (*bot.*) saltwort.
jijene, *n.m.* (*Hisp. Am.*) sand-fly.
jijona, *n.f.* flinty wheat.
jilguero, *n.m.* (*orn.*) linnet, goldfinch.
jilmaestre, *n.m.* artillery officer (*in charge of horses, mules etc.*).
jilocopo, *n.m.* carpenter bee (*Xylocopa*).
jilote, *n.m.* (*Mex.*) ear (*of green corn*).
jimagua, *n.m.f.* (*Cub.*) twin.
jimelga, *n.f.* (*naut.*) fish (*of a mast*).
jimenzar [C], *v.t.* to ripple (*flax* or *hemp*).
jindama, *n.f.* (*coll.*) fear, funk.
jinestada, *n.f.* sauce made of milk, dates etc.
jineta, *n.f.* (*zool.*) genet; horsemanship; short spear; sergeant's shoulder knot; ***cabalgar*** or ***montar a la jineta,*** to ride with stirrups high and legs bent; ***tener los cascos a la jineta,*** to be hare-brained.
jinete, *n.m.* horseman, rider; cavalryman; pure-bred horse. — *n.f.* horsewoman.
jinetear, *v.t.* (*Hisp. Am.*) to break in (*a horse*). — *v.i.* to ride about on horseback, show off one's horsemanship. — **jinetearse,** *v.r.* (*Hisp. Am.*) to be puffed up.
jinglar, *v.i.* to swing.
jingo, *n.m.* jingo.
jingoísmo, *n.m.* jingoism.
jingoista, *a.* jingo, jingoist, jingoistic. — *n.m.f.* jingo, jingoist.
jinjol, *n.m.* jujube.
jipa, *n.m.* (*Col.*) [JIPIJAPA].
jipato, -ta, *a.* (*Hisp. Am.*) pale, wan; (*Hisp. Am.*) insipid.
jipe, *n.m.* (*Mex.*) [JIPIJAPA].
jipijapa, *n.f.* very fine woven straw. — *n.m.* Panama hat.
jiquilete, *n.m.* (*bot.*) indigo tree.
jira, *n.f.* strip, slip (*of cloth*); picnic, outing: trip, tour.
jirafa, *n.f.* (*zool.*) giraffe.
jirasal, *n.f.* (*bot.*) fruit of the lac tree.
jirel, *n.m.* rich trappings, caparison.
jíride, *n.f.* fetid iris, gladdon.
jiroflé, *n.m.* clove tree.
jirón, *n.m.* shred, tatter; (*sew.*) facing of a shirt; pennant, pointed banner; (*her.*) gyron.
jironado, -da, *a.* shredded, tattered.
jirpear, *v.t.* to dig about (*vines*).
jisca, *n.f.* cylindrical sugar-cane.
jiste, *n.m.* yeast, barm, leaven; froth, head (*beer*).
¡jo! *interj.* whoa!
Joaquín, *n.m.* Joachim.
jobo, *n.m.* (*bot.*) hog plum.
jocó, *n.m.* jocko, ape.
jocoserio, -ria, *a.* jocoserious.

jocosidad, *n.f.* jocularity, jocoseness, jocosity.
jocoso, -sa, *a.* jocose, jocular, humorous, comical.
jocoyote, *n.m.* (*Hisp. Am.*) youngest child, pet.
jocundidad, *n.f.* joviality.
jocundo, -da, *a.* jovial, jolly.
jofaina, *n.f.* wash-basin, wash-bowl.
jojoto, *n.m.* (*Ven.*) maize cooked in milk.
jolgorio, *n.m.* merrymaking, jollification, shindig; shindy, uproar.
jolito, *n.m.* rest, leisure; (*naut.*) calm.
joloano, -na, *a.*, *n.m.f.* (of) Sulu, Suluan.
jollín [JOLGORIO].
Jonás, *n.m.* Jonah.
jónico, -ca, *a.* Ionian, Ionic; (*arch.*) Ionic. — *n.m.f.* Ionian.
jonja, *n.f.* (*Chi.*) mockery.
jonjabar, *v.t.* (*coll.*) to inveigle, wheedle.
¡jopo! *interj.* (*coll.*) out of here! be off!
jorcar [A], *v.t.* (*prov.*) to winnow (*grain*).
Jordán, *n.m.* Jordan (*river*); (*fig.*) fount of youth; regeneration; ***ir al Jordán,*** to be rejuvenated.
Jordania, *n.f.* Jordan (*country*).
jordano, -na, *a.*, *n.m.f.* Jordanian.
jorfe, *n.m.* dry stone wall; steep rock; tor.
Jorge, *n.m.* George.
jorguín, *n.m.* wizard, sorcerer.
jorguina, jorjina, *n.f.* witch, sorceress.
jorguinería, *n.f.* witchcraft.
jornada, *n.f.* day's journey *or* march; working day; stage, journey, trip, travel; king's stay in a royal country residence; summer residence; session; battle; (*mil.*) expedition; occasion, event, circumstance; passage through life; passage from life to eternity; span of life; act (*of a play*); (*print.*) number of sheets printed off in a day; ***jornada intensiva,*** summer time-table, work only in the morning; ***las jornadas de Semana Santa,*** the events *or* ceremonies of Holy Week; ***a grandes*** or ***a largas jornadas,*** by forced marches; ***al fin de la jornada,*** at the end of the day; ***caminar por sus jornadas,*** to go carefully.
jornal, *n.m.* day-work, day's work; day's wages; wage; ***a jornal,*** by the day.
jornalero, *n.m.* day-labourer, journeyman.
joroba, *n.f.* hump; (*coll.*) nuisance, pest.
jorobado, -da, *a.* hump- *or* hunch-backed.
jorobar, *v.t.* (*coll.*) to annoy, bother, jigger up.
jorrar, *v.t.* to haul a sweep-seine.
jorro, *a.* (*Hisp. Am.*) poor (*tobacco*). — *n.m.* (***red de***) ***jorro,*** seine, dragnet.
josa, *n.f.* unfenced orchard.
José, *n.m.* Joseph.
jostrado, -da, *a.* round-headed (*shaft* or *dart*).
Josué, *n.m.* Joshua.
jota (1), *n.f.* letter J; jot, iota; ***no saber*** or ***entender una*** or ***ni jota,*** not to know *or* understand a thing (*about it*); ***sin faltar una jota,*** without anything at all missing, absolutely fully.
jota (2), *n.f.* Spanish dance and tune; vegetable soup; (*Chi.*, *Per.*) Indian sandal.
jote, *n.m.* Chilean vulture.
joule, *n.m.* (*phys.*) joule.
jovada, *n.f.* (*prov.*) ground tilled by a pair of mules in one day.
joven, *a.* young, youthful. — *n.m.f.* youth; young man, young woman.
jovenado, *n.m.* (*eccles.*) juniorate.
jovencísimo, -ma, *a.* extremely young.
jovenzuelo, -la, *n.m.f.* youngster, young shaver.
jovial, *a.* Jovian; jovial, gay, merry, cheerful.
jovialidad, *n.f.* joviality, cheerfulness, good humour.
joya, *n.f.* jewel, piece of jewellery; (*lit.*, *fig.*) gem; present, gift; (*arch.*, *art.*) astragal; ***joya de familia,*** heirloom; ***joyas de fantasía,*** costume jewellery; (*pl.*) trousseau.
joyante, *a.* glossy (*silk*).
joyel, *n.m.* small jewel.
joyelero, *n.m.* jewel-case, jewel-box.
joyería, *n.f.* jeweller's shop; jeweller's trade.
joyero, -ra, *n.m.f.* jeweller. — *n.m.* jewel case, casket; (*Arg.*, *Chi.*, *P.R.*) goldsmith.
joyita, *n.f.* small jewel.
joyo, *n.m.* (*bot.*) bearded darnel, darnel-grass.
joyón, *n.m.* big, ugly jewel.
juaguarzo, *n.m.* (*bot.*) Montpellier rock-rose.
Juan, *n.m.* John; ***Juan Lanas,*** simpleton, good-for-nothing; ***Juan Palomo,*** poor devil.
Juana, *n.f.* Jane, Joan, Jean; ***Juana de Arco,*** Joan of Arc.
juanas, *n.f.pl.* glove stretcher.
juanete, *n.m.* bunion; prominent cheek-bone; (*naut.*) top-gallant sail; ***juanete mayor,*** main-top-gallant sail; ***juanete de sobremesana,*** mizzen-top-gallant sail.
juanetero, *n.m.* sailor in care of the top-gallant sail.
juanetudo, -da, *a.* having bunions.
juanillo, *n.m.* (*Chi.*, *Per.*) gratuity, tip.
juarda, *n.f.* stain in cloth (*due to faulty scouring*).
juardoso, -sa, *a.* stained, spotted (*cloth*).
juay, *n.m.* (*Mex.*) knife.
jubete, *n.m.* doublet covered with mail.
jubetería, *n.f.* shop where ***jubetes*** are sold.
jubetero, *n.m.* maker *or* seller of ***jubetes.***
jubilación, *n.f.* retirement; retirement pension; jubilation.
jubilado, -da, *n.m.f.* retired person, pensioner.
jubilar, *v.t.* to retire, pension off. — *v.i.* to retire; to rejoice. — **jubilarse,** *v.r.* to retire; to rejoice; (*Hisp. Am.*) to decline; (*Hisp. Am.*) to become expert; (*Hisp. Am.*) to play truant.
jubileo, *n.m.* jubilee; great coming and going; (*eccles.*) concession of plenary indulgence; ***por jubileo,*** rarely, happening seldom.
júbilo, *n.m.* jubilation, joy, rejoicing.
jubiloso, -sa, *a.* jubilant, joyful.
jubo, *n.m.* (*Cub.*) small snake.
jubón, *n.m.* doublet, jerkin; waist (*in female dress*).
jubonero, *n.m.* maker of doublets *or* jerkins.
júcaro, *n.m.* hardwood tree.
Judá, *n.m.* Judah.
judaico, -ca, *a.* Judaic, Jewish.
judaísmo, *n.m.* Judaism.
judaizante, *a.* Judaizing. — *n.m.f.* Judaizer, Judaist.
judaizar [PC], *v.t.*, *v.i.* to Judaize.
Judas, *n.m.* Judas; traitor; ***alma de Judas,*** evil individual; ***Judas Iscariote,*** Judas Iscariot; ***estar hecho un Judas,*** to look like a rag-bag.
Judea, *n.f.* Judea.
judería, *n.f.* Jewry, Jewish quarter *or* ghetto; tax on Jews.
judía (1), *n.f.* French bean, kidney-bean; ***judía de careta,*** small spotted French bean.
judicatura, *n.f.* judicature; dignity of a judge.
judicial, *a.* judicial; judiciary.
judiciario, -ria, *a.* astrological. — *n.m.* astrologer.
judiega, *n.f.* inferior olive.
judihuela (1), *n.f.* small French bean.
judihuelo, -la (2), *n.m.f.* young Jew *or* Jewess.
judío, -dia (2), *a.* Jewish. — *n.m.f.* Jew, Jewess; ***judío de señal,*** converted Jew, wearing a distinguishing badge.
judión, *n.m.* large French bean.
Judit, *n.f.* Judith.
juego, *n.m.* play, playing; game; gambling, gaming; hand (*of cards*); set, suit, suite; running gear (*of a vehicle*); free movement, clearance; ***a juego,*** to match, matching; ***descubrir*** (***uno***) ***su juego,*** to show one's hand; ***echar*** or ***tomar a juego,*** to treat as a joke; ***en juego,*** at stake; ***entrar en juego,*** to come into play; ***hacer el***

juego a, to play into the hands of; ***hacer juego***, to place bets; to match, make a set, go together; ***juego de azar*** or ***de suerte***, game of chance; ***juego de bolos***, ninepins; ***juego de cajones***, nest of drawers; ***juego de cartas*** or ***de naipes***, card game; ***juego de manos***, juggling feat; legerdemain; ***juego de niños***, child's game; child's play; ***juego de palabras***, play on words; ***juego de pelota***, handball game; ***juego de prendas***, forfeits; ***juego de té, de café***, tea-set, coffee-set; ***juego limpio***, fair play; ***juego sucio***, foul play; ***no es cosa de juego***, it's no joke; ***poner en juego***, to bring into play; ***por juego***, in play, in fun, as a game; ***seguir el juego a***, to fall in with; ***te conozco el juego***, I (can) see your (little) game. — *pres. indic.* [JUGAR].

jueguecito, *n.m.* little game.

juera, *n.f.* sieve made of esparto.

juerga, *n.f.* (*coll.*) spree, carousal, binge, revelry.

juerguista, *n.m.f.* (*coll.*) reveller.

jueves, *n.m. inv.* Thursday; ***no es nada*** or ***cosa del otro jueves***, it's nothing out of this world, nothing extraordinary; ***jueves de comadres***, Thursday before Lent; ***jueves de compadres***, second Thursday before Lent; ***jueves Santo***, Maundy Thursday.

juez, *n.m.* judge, justice; ***juez de hecho***, lay judge; juror; ***juez de instrucción***, examining magistrate; (*sport*) ***juez de línea***, linesman; (*sport*) ***juez de llegada***, goal judge; ***juez de paz***, justice of the peace; ***juez de primera instancia***, judge of the primary court of claims; (*sport*) ***juez de salida***, starter.

jugada, *n.f.* play; stroke, throw, move; bad turn, dirty trick.

jugadera, *n.f.* shuttle (*for network*).

jugador, -ra, *n.m.f.* player; gamester, gambler; ***jugador de manos***, prestidigitator.

jugar [4B, *as if* **jogar**], *v.t.*, *v.i.* to play; to toy; to gamble; (*com.*) ***jugar a la baja***, to bear the market; (*com.*) ***jugar a la bolsa***, to dabble on the stock exchange; ***jugar al alza***, to bull the market; ***jugar al desquite***, to double the stock; ***jugar al fútbol***, to play football; ***jugar en***, to have a hand in; ***jugar grueso***, to play for big stakes. — **jugarse,** *v.r.* to gamble (away), risk; ***jugarse el pellejo***, to risk one's neck; ***jugarse el todo por el todo***, to stake all, shoot the works; ***jugarse hasta la camisa***, to stake one's last penny; ***jugársela***, to stick one's neck out; ***jugársela a alguien***, to play a dirty trick on s.o.; ***jugarse la vida***, to risk one's life.

jugarreta, *n.f.* (*coll.*) bad turn; dirty trick.

juglándeo, -dea, *a.* (*bot.*) juglandaceous, walnut.

juglar, *n.m.* minstrel, jongleur; mountebank.

juglara, juglaresa, *n.f.* female minstrel *or* jongleur.

juglaresco, -ca, *a.* pertaining to minstrels *or* jongleurs.

juglaría, juglería, *n.f.* minstrels' *or* jongleurs' feasts *or* manners; ***mester de juglaría***, minstrels' poetry.

jugo, *n.m.* sap, juice; substance; ***sacar todo el jugo a***, to get the most out of.

jugosidad, *n.f.* juiciness; substance.

jugoso, -sa, *a.* juicy; substantial.

juguete, *n.m.* toy; plaything; jest, joke; (*theat.*) comedietta; ***por juguete***, jestingly.

juguetear, *v.i.* to play *or* toy about; to frolic, sport.

jugueteo, *n.m.* frolicking, gamboling.

juguetería, *n.f.* toy-shop; toy-trade.

juguetón, -tona, *a.* playful, frolicsome, playsome.

juicio, *n.m.* judgement; sense; opinion: (*law*) trial; ***a juicio de***, in the opinion of; ***asentar el juicio***, to become sensible; ***juicio temerario***, rash *or* hasty judgement; ***no estar en su juicio***, to be out of one's senses; ***no tener juicio***, to be wild; to be a harum-scarum fellow; ***pedir en juicio***, to sue at law; ***perder el juicio***, to go out of one's mind; ***quitar el juicio a***, to drive s.o. out of his mind.

juicioso, -sa, *a.* judicious, sensible, level-headed.

julepe, *n.m.* (*pharm.*) julep; game of cards; (*coll.*) reprimand, punishment; (*Hisp. Am.*) scare, fright, shock.

julepear, *v.t.* (*Arg.*) to alarm, scare; (*Mex.*) to torment, annoy.

juliano, -na, *a.* Julian.

Julio, *n.m.* Julius.

julio (1), *n.m.* July.

julio (2), *n.m.* (*elec.*) joule.

julo, *n.m.* bell-mule, bell-cow.

júmel, *n.m.* Egyptian cotton.

jumenta, *n.f.* she-ass.

jumental, jumentil, *a.* (of the) ass, of asses.

jumento, *n.m.* ass.

jumera, *n.f.* (*coll.*) drunken *or* sozzled state.

juncáceas, *n.f. pl.* (*bot.*) Juncaceæ.

juncada, *n.f.* fritter.

juncago, *n.m.* (*bot.*) bastard rush.

juncal, *a.* of rushes; rush-like; willowy, slender. — *n.m.* rush bed.

juncar, *n.m.* rush bed.

júnceo, -cea, *a.* rush-like. — *n.f.pl.* (**júnceas**) (*bot.*) rush family.

juncia, *n.f.* (*bot.*) cyperus, sedge; ***juncia olorosa***, galangal; ***vender juncia***, to boast, brag.

junciana, *n.f.* (*coll.*) vain boasting.

junciera, *n.f.* earthenware vessel.

juncino, -na, *a.* rushy; made of rushes.

junco (1), *n.m.* (*bot.*) rush, bulrush; ***junco de Indias***, rattan; ***junco florido***, flowering rush; ***junco oloroso***, camel grass.

junco (2), *n.m.* (*naut.*) junk.

juncoso, -sa, *a.* rushy.

jungla, *n.f.* jungle.

junio, *n.m.* June.

júnior, *n.m.* (*eccles.*) junior.

junípero, *n.m.* (*bot.*) juniper.

junquera, *n.f.* (*bot.*) rush.

junqueral, *n.m.* ground covered in rushes.

junquillo, *n.m.* (*bot.*) jonquil; reed, rattan; (*arch.*) round moulding.

junta, *n.f.* [JUNTO].

juntamente, *adv.* jointly, together.

juntar, [*p.p.* **juntado, junto**], *v.t.* to join (together); to bring, get *or* put together; to gather together; to half close, push *or* pull to. — **juntarse,** *v.r.* to join, link up, come *or* get together, gather, meet.

juntera, *n.f.* (*carp.*) jointing-plane.

junto, -ta, *a.* together; close together; ***ya me las pagarás todas juntas***, I'll get even with you. — *p.p.* [JUNTAR]. — *adv. m.* near, close, hard by; at the same time; ***en junto***, together, in all; ***junto a***, next to, by; ***por junto*** or ***de por junto***, in bulk, wholesale; ***todo junto***, altogether. — *n.f.* junta; board; meeting; congress, conference, council, convention, tribunal, assembly; sitting; union, conjunction, junction; (*carp.*) joint, joining, seam; (*mech.*) gasket; (*mech.*) coupling; (*build.*) coursing joint; ***junta de accionistas***, stockholders' meeting; (*com.*) ***junta de acreedores***, meeting of creditors; ***junta de comercio***, board of trade; ***junta de facultad***, academic board; ***junta de gobierno***, governing body; (*med.*) ***junta de médicos***, consultation; ***junta de sanidad***, board of health; ***junta directiva***, board of directors, executive board.

juntura, *n.f.* join, joining, joint; seam; (*naut.*) scarf; (*bot.*) knuckle.

jupa, *n.f.* (*C.R.*) pumpkin.

Júpiter, *n.m.* (*astron.*) Jupiter; (*alch.*) tin.

jura, *n.f.* oath; swearing in; pledge of allegiance.

jurado, *n.m.* jury; juror, juryman.

jurador, -ra, *a.* swearing. — *n.m.f.* swearer.

juraduría, *n.f.* office of a juror.
juramentar, *v.t.* to swear in, put to an oath. — **juramentarse,** *v.r.* to bind o.s. by an oath, be sworn in.
juramento, *n.m.* oath; swearing in; swear word, curse; ***prestar juramento,*** to take an oath, be sworn in; ***proferir juramentos,*** to swear; ***juramento asertorio,*** declaratory oath; ***juramento falso,*** perjury.
jurar, *v.t.* to swear, swear allegiance to; to swear in. — *v.i.* to swear; ***jurar un cargo,*** to take the oath (*before taking up office*); ***me la tiene jurada,*** he has sworn to get even with me.
jurásico, -ca, *a.* Jurassic.
juratoria, *n.f.* Gospel tablet (*for administering the oath*).
juratorio, *a.* juratory; ***caución juratoria, fianza juratoria,*** juratory security, release on oath. — *n.m.* instrument setting forth the oaths taken by Aragonese magistrates.
jurdía, *n.f.* fishing net.
jurel, *n.m.* (*ichth.*) saurel.
jurero, *n.m.* (*Hisp. Am.*) false witness.
jurguina, jurgina, *n.f.* witch, sorceress.
jurídico, -ca, *a.* legal, juridical.
jurisconsulto, *n.m.* jurisconsult; jurist, lawyer.
jurisdicción, *n.f.* jurisdiction.
jurisdiccional, *a.* jurisdictional; ***aguas jurisdiccionales*** or ***mar jurisdiccional,*** territorial waters.
jurisperito, *n.m.* legal expert.
jurisprudencia, *n.f.* jurisprudence.
jurisprudente, *n.m.* jurisprudent, jurist.
jurista, *n.m.* jurist.
juro, *n.m.* right of perpetual property; annuity, pension; ***de juro,*** certainly.
jusbarba, *n.f.* (*bot.*) field myrtle.
jusello, *n.m.* pottage of broth, cheese and eggs.
justa (I), *n.f.* joust, tilt; competition, contest.
justador, *n.m.* tilter, jouster.
justamente, *adv.* precisely; as a matter of fact, as it happens; just so.
justar, *v.i.* to joust, tilt.
justicia, *n.f.* justice. — *n.m.* judge, justice, magistrate; ***de justicia,*** right, fair; ***ir por justicia, pedir justicia,*** to go to law; ***la justicia,*** the authorities; ***sol de justicia,*** pitiless sun; ***tomarse la justicia por su mano,*** to take justice into one's own hands.
justiciable *a.* actionable, justiciable.
justiciero -ra, *a.* justice making, giving *or* doing. — *n.m.f.* stickler for justice.
justificable, *a.* justifiable.
justificación, *n.f.* justification.
justificadamente, *adv.* with justification.
justificador, -ra, *a.* justifying.
justificante, *a.* justifying. — *n.m.* certificate, receipt, written proof.
justificar [A], *v.t.* to justify; to furnish (written) evidence of.
justificativo, -va, *a.* justificative, justifying, justificatory.
justillo, *n.m.* jerkin; corset-cover.
justipreciador, *n.m.* appraiser.
justipreciar, *v.t.* to appraise, set a value to.
justiprecio, *n.m.* appraisement, valuation.
justo, -ta (2), *a.* just; fair; right; rightful, righteous; exact; tight, close-fitting. — *adv.* just; exactly; tight(ly). — *n.m.f.* just *or* righteous individual.
juta, *n.f.* (*Hisp. Am.*) goose.
jutía, *n.f.* (*Cub.*) rat.
juvenil, *a.* juvenile, youthful.
juventud, *n.f.* youthfulness, youth; young people; younger generation.
juvia, *n.f.* (*bot.*) Brazil-nut tree.
juzgado, *n.m.* court (*of justice*); judicature.
juzgamundos, *n.m.f. inv.* (*coll.*) fault-finder.
juzgante, *a.* judging.
juzgar [B], *v.t., v.i.* to judge; ***a juzgar por,*** to judge by, judging from.

K

K, k, *n.f.* letter K, k.
ka, *n.f.* letter K.
kadí, *n.m.* Turkish judge.
kalenda, *n.f.* kalends.
kan, *n.m.* khan.
kantiano, -na, *a.* Kantian.
kantismo, *n.m.* Kantism.
kepis, *inv.* [QUEPIS].
keralila, *n.f.* (*Mex.*) horny flint.
kermes, *n.m. inv.* kermes.
kiliárea, *n.f.* kiliare.
kilo, *n.m.* (*com.*) kilo.
kilográmetro, *n.m.* kilogrammetre.
kilogramo, *n.m.* kilogram(me).
kilolitro, *n.m.* kilolitre.
kilometraje, *n.m.* distance in kilometres.
kilométrico, -ca, *a.* kilometric; (*coll.*) very long, interminable; ***billete kilométrico,*** railway mileage book.
kilómetro, *n.m.* kilometre.
kilovatio, *n.m.* kilowatt.
kimono (*Cub.*) [QUIMONO].
kindergarten, *n.m.* nursery school.
kiosco [QUIOSCO].
kirie, *n.m.* (*eccles.*) kyrie (eleison).
kirieleisón, *n.m.* kyrie eleison; (*coll.*) funeral chant.
knut, *n.m.* knut.
k.o., *n.m.* (*boxing, fig.*) k.o., knock-out; (*boxing*) ***dejar (por) k.o.,*** to k.o., knock-out (*opponent*); (*fig.*) ***me has dejado k.o.,*** you've floored me completely, you astound me.
krausismo, *n.m.* Krausism.
krausista, *n.m.f.* Krausist.
kurdo, -da [CURDO].
Kuwait, Estado del, *n.m.* Kuwait.

L

L, l, *n.f.* letter L, l.
la (1), *def. art., f. sing.* the.
la (2), *pron. pers. acc., f. sing.* her, it.
la (3), *n.m.* (*mus.*) la.
lábaro, *n.m.* labarum.
labe, *n.f.* stain, spot.
laberíntico, -ca, *a.* labyrinthine.
laberinto, *n.m.* labyrinth, maze.
labia, *n.f.* (*coll.*) gift of the gab.
labiado, -da, *a.* (*bot.*) labiate.
labial, *a.* labial.
labiérnago, *n.m.* (*bot.*) mock privet.
labihendido, -da, *a.* hare-lipped.
lábil, *a.* (*chem., phys. etc.*) labile; slippery; fragile, weak, frail.
labio, *n.m.* lip; labium; ***labio hendido*** or ***leporino,*** harelip; ***chuparse los labios,*** to smack one's lips; ***lamerse los labios,*** to lick one's lips; ***morderse los labios,*** to bite one's lip; ***no descoser*** or ***despegar los labios,*** not to open one's mouth; ***sellar los labios (a),*** to impose silence (on); ***no morderse los labios,*** to speak out, be outspoken; ***estar pendiente*** or ***colgado de los labios de alguien,*** to hang on s.o.'s words.
labor, *n.f.* labour, task, toil, work; (*sew.*) needlework; thousand tiles *or* bricks; husbandry, tillage; egg (*of a silkworm*); ***campo de labor,*** cultivated field; ***casa de labor,*** farmhouse; ***finca de labor,*** farming estate; ***labor de equipo,*** teamwork; (*agric.*) ***meter en labor,*** to prepare for sowing; ***profesión, sus labores,*** occupation, housewife.
laborable, *a.* tillable, workable; ***día laborable,*** working day.
laborador, *n.m.* tiller, farmer; worker.
laborante, *a.* tilling, working. — *n.m.* (*Cub.*) conspirator.
laborantismo, *n.m.* (*Cub., polit.*) movement for independence from Spain.
laborar, *v.t.* to till; to work; to scheme.
laboratorio, *n.m.* laboratory.
laborear, *v.t.* to work; to till; to mine; (*naut.*) to reeve, run.
laboreo, *n.m.* working; tilling; mining; (*naut.*) reeving, running.
laborera, *a.* clever, skilful (*of a workwoman*).
laborero, *n.m.* (*Chi.*) foreman *or* overseer (*in mines*).
laboriosidad, *n.f.* industriousness.
laborioso, -sa, *a.* industrious, hard-working.
laborismo, *n.m.* Labour (party).
laborista, *a., n.m.f.* Labour, (member) of the Labour party.
labra, *n.f.* cutting, carving, working.
labrada, *n.f.* [LABRADO].
labradero, -ra, *a.* workable, arable.
labradío, -día, *a.* tillable.
labrado, -da, *a.* wrought, worked, figured. — *n.m.* cutting, carving, working. — *n.m.pl.* (**labrados**) cultivated lands. — *n.f.* land ploughed and fallowed.
labrador, -ra, *n.m.f.* tiller, ploughman; farmer, husbandman, husbandwoman; peasant.
labradoresco, -ca, *a.* farming, peasant.
labradorita, *n.f.* (*min.*) labradorite.
labrandera, *n.f.* seamstress, embroiderer.
labrantín, *n.m.* petty farmer, small farmer, smallholder.
labrantío, -tía, *a.* arable, tillable.
labranza, *n.f.* cultivation, farming; tillage, ploughing; husbandry; farm-land.
labrar, *v.t.* to work, fashion, carve, cut, dress; to plough, till, cultivate; to sew, embroider; to figure, make designs in; to build; to bring about. — *v.i.* to make a lasting impression. — **labrarse,** *v.r.* ***labrarse un porvenir,*** to carve out a future for o.s.
labriego, *n.m.* farm-hand, peasant.
labro, *n.m.* upper lip.
labrusca, *n.f.* wild grape-vine.
laburno, *n.m.* (*bot.*) laburnum.
laca, *n.f.* lac, gum-lac; red colour, lake; lacquer; japan; ***laca en grano,*** seed-lac; ***laca en palillos,*** stick-lac; ***laca en tablillas,*** shellac.
lacayo, *n.m.* lackey; groom; footman; knot of ribbons.
lacayuelo, *n.m.* foot-boy, groom.
lacayuno, -na, *a.* lackey, lackey-like, servile.
lacear, *v.t.* to lace, trim, tie with bows; to beat for game.
lacedemón, lacedemonio, -nia, *a., n.m.f.* Lacedemonian.
laceración, *n.f.* laceration, tearing.
lacerado, -da, *a.* unfortunate, unhappy; leprous.
lacerar, *v.t.* to lacerate; to hurt, damage. — *v.i.* to suffer hardship.
laceria, *n.f.* poverty; hardship.
lacería, *n.f.* set of bows and ribbons.
lacerioso, -sa, *a.* poverty-stricken; wretched.
lacero, *n.m.* lassoer; dogcatcher; poacher.
lacertoso, *a.* muscular, athletic.
lacinia, *n.f.* (*bot.*) lacinia, slender lobe.
laciniado, -da, *a.* (*bot.*) laciniate, slashed.
lacio, -cia, *a.* withered; limp; lank.
lacónico, -ca, *a.* laconic.
laconismo, *n.m.* laconism.
lacra, *n.f.* mark *or* trace (left by illness); defect fault; blot, blemish.
lacrar, *v.t.* to injure the health of; to infect with a disease; to hurt, damage; to seal (*with sealing wax*).
lacre, *n.m.* sealing wax.
lacrimal, *a.* lachrymal.
lacrimatorio, -ria, *a., n.m.f.* lachrymatory.
lacrimógeno, -na, *a.* lachrymogenic, tear, tear-producing; ***gas lacrimógeno,*** tear gas.
lacrimoso, -sa, *a.* weeping, tearful, lachrymose.
lactación, *n.f.* lactation, sucking (*of mother's milk*).
lactancia, *n.f.* lactation, period of suckling.
lactante, *a.* sucking (*child*); suckling, nursing. — *n.m.f.* suckling, sucking child. — *n.m.f.* mother *or* nurse giving suck.
lactar, *v.t., v.i.* to lactate, suckle; to suck (*mother's milk*).
lactario, -ria, *a.* lactary, lacteous, lactescent.
lactato, *n.m.* (*chem.*) lactate.
lácteo, -tea, *a.* lacteous, milky, lacteal, lactean; (of) milk; (*astron.*) ***vía láctea,*** Milky Way; ***productos lácteos,*** dairy produce.
lactescente, *a.* lactescent.
lacticíneo, -nea, *a.* lacteous, milky.
lacticinio, *n.m.* milk *or* milk food.
láctico, -ca, *a.* (*chem.*) lactic.
lactífero, -ra, lactífico, -ca, *a.* lactiferous.
lactina, lactosa, *n.f.* (*chem.*) lactose, lactin, milk sugar.
lactómetro, *n.m.* lactometer.
lactucario, *n.m.* (*pharm.*) lactucarium.
lactumen, *n.m.* (*med.*) lactumen.
lacunario, *n.m.* (*arch.*) lacunar.
lacustre, *a.* lacustrine, of lakes; marshy.
lacha, *n.f.* (*ichth.*) anchovy; (*coll.*) shame; (*coll.*) ***ser de poca lacha,*** not to amount to much.
lada, *n.f.* (*bot.*) rockrose.
ládano, *n.m.* ladanum, labdanum.
ladear, *v.t., v.i.* to tilt, tip, turn on one side, sway. — *v.i.* to skirt; to be even with; to deviate. — **ladearse,** *v.r.* (*Hisp. Am.*) to fall in love; ***ladearse con,*** to fall out with.

ladeo, *n.m.* tipping, tilting; bending; leaning; bent, inclination.
ladera, *n.f.* [LADERO].
ladería, *n.f.* small dale (*on the slope of a mountain*).
ladero, -ra, *a.* lateral, side. — *n.f.* slope, hillside; (*pl.* **laderas**) rails *or* staves (*of a truck*); cheeks (*of a gun-carriage*).
ladierno, *n.m.* (*bot.*) buckthorn.
ladilla (1), *n.f.* crab-louse; (*coll.*) ***pegarse como (una) ladilla,*** to stick like a leech.
ladilla (2), *n.f.* (*bot.*) common barley.
ladillo, *n.m.* shifting panel (*placed in the sides of coaches*).
ladino, -na, *a.* (*obs.*) versed in languages; sagacious, cunning, crafty; linguistic; (*Hisp. Am.*) ***esclavo ladino,*** slave who has served one year. — *n.m.* Ladin (*Romansh*); Ladino (*mixed Spanish and Hebrew*).
lado, *n.m.* side; hand, way; room, space; course, direction; favour, protection; ***al lado,*** close, near by; ***al lado de,*** by the side of, next to; ***dar de lado a,*** to ignore, cut, avoid; ***dejar a un lado,*** to leave aside, leave on one side, leave out; ***de lado,*** sideways, tilted; ***de un lado, de otro lado,*** on one hand, on the other; ***echar a un lado,*** to cast aside; ***echar por otro lado,*** to give another twist *or* interpretation to; ***hacer (un) lado a,*** to make room for; ***hacerse a un lado,*** to step, stand *or* move aside; ***mirar de (medio) lado,*** to look askance at; to look at surreptitiously; ***ponerse al lado de,*** to take sides with, side with; ***por el lado de,*** in the direction of; ***por ningún lado,*** nowhere; ***por todos lados,*** on all sides; ***yo fui por mi lado, él por el suyo,*** I went my way, he went his; (*pl.*) backers, advisers.
ladón, *n.m.* (*bot.*) cistus.
ladra, *n.f.* barking, baying.
ladrador, -ra, *a.* barking.
ladrante, *a.* barking.
ladrar, *v.t., v.i.* to bark, bay; ***me ladra el estómago,*** I'm ravenous.
ladrear, *v.i.* to bark frequently.
ladrería, *n.f.* lazaretto.
ladrido, *n.m.* bark, barking; backbiting.
ladrillado, *n.m.* brick floor.
ladrillador, *n.m.* bricklayer.
ladrillal, *n.m.* brick-yard.
ladrillar, *n.m.* brick-yard. — *v.t.* to brick.
ladrillazo, *n.m.* blow with a brick; (*coll.*) heavy, stodgy food.
ladrillero, *n.m.* maker *or* seller of bricks; brick-mould.
ladrillo, *n.m.* brick; tile.
ladrilloso, -sa, *a.* bricky, made of brick.
ladrón, -rona, *a.* thieving, thievish. — *n.m.f.* thief, robber, burglar; ***ladrón de corazones,*** lady-killer; ***piensa el ladrón que todos son de su condición,*** (you should) speak (only) for yourself. — *n.m.* sluice gate; run of wax. — *n.f.* side *or* branch switch.
ladroncillo, *n.m.* petty thief.
ladronera, *n.f.* den of robbers; filching; money-box; sluice-gate.
ladronería, *n.f.* stealing, robbery, theft.
ladronesco, -ca, *a.* (*coll.*) belonging to thieves, thievish. — *n.f.* mob of thieves.
ladronicio [LATROCINIO].
ladronzuelo, -la, *n.m.f.* petty thief, young filcher, pickpocket.
lagaña, *n.f.* bleariness.
lagañoso, -sa, *a.* blear-eyed.
lagar, *n.m.* wine-press; grape-treading vat; cider-press *or* olive-press, vat.
lagarada, *n.f.* pressful.
lagarero, *n.m.* wine-presser; olive-presser; cider-presser.
lagareta, *n.f.* small wine-press; puddle, pool.
lagarta, *n.f.* female lizard; (*coll.*) sly, cunning woman.
lagartero, -ra, *a.* lizard-hunting. — *n.f.* lizard-hole.
lagartija, *n.f.* small lizard, green *or* wall lizard.
lagartijero, -ra, *a.* lizard-hunting.
lagarto, *n.m.* lizard; (*anat.*) long muscle of the arm; (*coll.*) sly, artful person.
lago, *n.m.* lake; pond; ***lago de leones,*** den of lions; ***lago de Tiberíades,*** Sea of Galilee.
lagotear, *v.i.* (*coll.*) to flatter, wheedle, cajole.
lagotería, *n.f.* (*coll.*) flattery, cajolery.
lagotero, -ra, *a.* (*coll.*) flattering, cajoling, honey-mouthed. — *n.m.f.* flatterer, cajoler.
lágrima, *n.f.* tear; drop; (*bot.*) gromwell; (*bot.*) ***lágrima de David*** or ***de Job,*** Job's tear; ***lágrimas de cocodrilo,*** crocodile tears; ***lágrimas de San Pedro*** or ***de Moisés,*** stones thrown at a person; ***lágrimas de Batavia*** or ***de Holanda,*** Prince Rupert's drops; ***derramar*** or ***verter lágrimas,*** to shed tears; ***deshacerse en lágrimas,*** to burst *or* melt into tears; ***llorar a lágrima viva,*** to shed bitter tears; ***se le saltaban las lágrimas,*** tears were welling to his eyes; ***lo que no va en lágrimas va en suspiros,*** one thing compensates for another.
lagrimable, *a.* lachrymable, lamentable.
lagrimal, *a.* lachrymal. — *n.m.* lachrymal caruncle (*near corner of the eye*).
lagrimar, lagrimear, *v.i.* to weep, shed tears.
lagrimeo, *n.m.* shedding tears.
lagrimón, *n.m.* large tear.
lagrimoso, -sa, *a.* tearful, lachrymose; watery (eyes); (*bot.*) exuding.
laguer, *n.m.* (*Cub.*) lager beer.
laguna, *n.f.* small lake, lagoon; gap (*in a book* or *writing*).
lagunajo, *n.m.* puddle, pool, plashet.
lagunar, *n.m.* (*arch.*) lacunar.
lagunero, -ra, *a.* belonging to a lagoon.
lagunoso, -sa, *a.* marshy, fenny, swampy.
laical, *a.* laical, laic.
laicalizar [C], (*Chi.*) [SECULARIZAR].
laicismo, *n.m.* secularism, laicism.
laico, -ca, *a.* laic, laicist; lay; ***enseñanza laica,*** non-religious education. — *n.m.f.* layman.
laja, *n.f.* flag-stone, slab; (*naut.*) stone flat; (*Col.*) cord made of sisal.
lama (1), *n.f.* slime, silt, ooze; (*bot.*) seaweed; gold *or* silver tissue; dust of ores (*in mines*); fine sand (*used for mortar*).
lama (2), *n.m.* lama (*Tibetan monk*).
lamaísmo, *n.m.* Lamaism.
lamaísta, *n.m.f.* Lamaist.
lambel, *n.m.* (*her.*) lambel, label.
lambrequines, *n.m.pl.* (*her.*) mantelets.
lambrija, *n.f.* tape-worm; (*coll.*) skinny person.
lameculos, *n.m.f. inv.* (*coll.*) bootlicker.
lamedal, *n.m.* marshy and miry place.
lamedero, *n.m.* salt-lick.
lamedor, -ra, *a.* licking. — *n.m.f.* licker. — *n.m.* syrup; (*fig.*) ***dar lamedor,*** to feign a losing game (*in order to mislead one's opponent*).
lamedura, *n.f.* licking.
lamelar, *v.t.* to roll (copper) into sheets.
lameliforme, *a.* lamelliform, in thin layers.
lamentable, *a.* lamentable, deplorable, regrettable.
lamentablemente, *adv.* lamentably.
lamentación, *n.f.* lamentation, lament, wail; ***Muro de las lamentaciones,*** Wailing Wall.
lamentador, -ra, *a.* lamenting, complaining. — *n.m.f.* lamenter, complainer.
lamentar(se), *v.t.* to lament, regret, mourn, bewail, moan. — *v.i.* (*v.r.*) to lament, grieve, wail; to complain.
lamento, *n.m.* lamentation, lament, moan, wail, mourning.

lamentoso, *a.* lamentable; mournful, plaintive.
lameplatos, *n.m. inv.* (*coll.*) glutton, gorger; (*coll.*) one who feeds on leavings.
lamer, *v.t.* to lick; to lap (against).
lamerón, -rona, *a.* (*coll.*) sweet-toothed.
lametón, *n.m.* hard lick, strong lick.
lamia, *n.f.* lamia; shark.
lamido, -da, *a.* emaciated, thin; pale, wan; worn down, very smooth; sleek; prim and proper, over-nice; affected.
lamiente, *a.* licking.
lámina, *n.f.* plate; sheet; lamina; copper-plate; print, engraving, picture, illustration.
laminado, -da, *a.* laminate; laminated, rolled. — *n.m.* lamination, rolling.
laminador, *n.m.* rolling press, rolling mill; metal roller.
laminar, *a.* laminar. — *v.t.* to laminate; to roll.
laminera (1), *n.f.* (*prov.*) bee leading its companions.
laminero, -ra (2), *a.* fond of sweets. — *n.m.f.* manufacturer of metal plates; one who plates shrines for relics.
laminoso, -sa, *a.* laminose.
lamiscar [A], *v.t.* (*coll.*) to lick greedily.
lamoso, -sa, *a.* oozy, slimy, muddy.
lampa, *n.f.* (*Chi.*, *Per.*, *agric.*) shovel; spade.
lampacear, *v.t.* (*naut.*) to swab.
lampar, *v.i.* to be eager (for), hunt about desperately (for), leave no stone unturned (to get).
lámpara, *n.f.* lamp; light; luminous body; grease spot *or* stain; bough placed at the door on festivals *or* rejoicings; (*rad.*) tube, valve, (*Am.*) tube; ***lámpara de soldar,*** blow-lamp, blow-torch; (*coll.*) ***atizar la lámpara,*** to refill the glasses.
lamparería, *n.f.* lamp-factory; lamp-store.
lamparero, -ra, *n.m.f.* maker *or* seller of lamps; lamp-lighter.
lamparilla, *n.f.* small lamp; night-light; camlet; (*bot.*) aspen, trembling poplar; ***lamparilla de alcohol,*** spirit lamp, (*Am.*) alcohol lamp; ***lamparilla de bolsillo,*** torch, (*Am.*) flashlight.
lamparín, *n.m.* lamp-holder, lamp-case.
lamparista, *n.m.f.* maker *or* seller of lamps; lamp-lighter.
lamparón, *n.m.* (large) grease-spot; scrofula; (*vet.*) horse disease.
lamparonoso, -sa, *a.* scrofulous.
lampatán, *n.m.* (*bot.*) chinaroot.
lampazo, *n.m.* (*bot.*) burdock; (*naut.*) swab, mop.
lampiño, -ña, *a.* beardless.
lampión, *n.m.* large lantern.
lampo, *n.m.* (*poet.*) light, splendour.
lamprea, *n.f.* (*ichth.*) lamprey.
lamprear, *v.t.* to dress *or* season with wine and sour gravy.
lamprehuela, lampreílla, *n.f.* (*ichth.*) small lamprey; river lamprey.
lámpsana, *n.f.* (*bot.*) common nipplewort.
lampuga, *n.f.* (*ichth.*) yellow mackerel.
lampuso, -sa, *a.* (*Cub.*, *P.R.*) impudent, bare-faced.
lana, *n.f.* wool; fleece; hair (of some animals); ***lana de vidrio,*** fibre-glass; ***lana en rama,*** uncombed wool; ***perro de lanas,*** poodle; ***ir por lana y salir trasquilado,*** to get sth. one didn't bargain on, get more than one bargained for; ***ser un Juan Lanas,*** to be a nobody.
lanado, -da, *a.* (*bot.*) lanate, wool-like. — *n.f.* (*artill.*) sponge.
lanar, *a.* wool; wool-bearing; ***ganado lanar,*** sheep.
lanaria, *n.f.* (*bot.*) soapwort.
lancán, *n.m.* (*Philip.*) barge.
lance, *n.m.* cast, throw; catch (*in a net*); incident, episode; event; move (*in a game*); pass, stroke; missile (*shot from a bow*); ***lance de fortuna,*** chance, accident; ***lance de honor,*** duel; ***a pocos lances,*** shortly afterwards; ***de lance,*** second hand, at bargain price; ***esto tiene pocos lances,*** there isn't much to it; ***echar buen lance,*** to strike it lucky.
lanceado, -da, *a.* (*bot.*) lanceolate.
lancear [ALANCEAR].
lancéola, *n.f.* (*bot.*) rib-grass plantain.
lanceolado, -da, *a.* (*bot.*) lanceolate.
lancera, *n.f.* lance-rack.
lancero, *n.m.* pikeman, lancer; maker of pikes; (*pl.*) lancers (*music and dance*).
lanceta, *n.f.* (*surg.*) lancet.
lancetada, *n.f.*, **lancetazo,** *n.m.* lancet cut, incision.
lancetero, *n.m.* lancet case.
lancinante, *a.* shooting *or* stabbing (*pains*).
lancita, *n.f.* small lance.
lancurdia, *n.f.* small trout.
lancha, *n.f.* flagstone, slab; (*naut.*) ship's boat; barge; lighter; launch; snare (*for partridges*); ***lancha cañonera,*** gunboat; ***lancha de desembarco,*** landing craft; ***lancha de socorro,*** rescue boat; ***lancha motora,*** motor boat; ***lancha salvavidas,*** lifeboat; ***lancha torpedera,*** torpedo boat.
lanchada, *n.f.* lighter-load.
lanchaje, *n.m.* (*com.*) ferriage; lighterage.
lanchar, *n.m.* flagstone quarry.
lanchazo, *n.m.* blow with a flagstone.
lanchero, *n.m.* bargeman, boatman, oarsman.
lanchón, *n.m.* (*naut.*) lighter, barge.
lanchonero, *n.m.* lighterman, bargeman.
landgrave, *n.m.* landgrave.
landgraviato, *n.m.* landgraviate.
landó, *n.m.* landau.
landre, *n.f.* small tumour; hidden pocket.
landrecilla, *n.f.* round lump (*among the glands*).
landrero, -ra, *n.m.f.* beggar.
landrilla, *n.f.* (*vet.*) tongue-worm.
lanería, *n.f.* wool shop.
lanero, -ra, *a.* (*of*) wool. — *n.m.* wool dealer; wool warehouse; (*orn.*) lanner.
langa, *n.f.* small dry codfish.
langaruto, -ta, *a.* (*coll.*) tall, lank, gangling.
langor, *n.m.* languor.
langosta, *n.f.* (*ent.*) locust; (*ichth.*) lobster.
langostera, *n.f.* lobster-pot.
langostino, *n.m.* (*ichth.*) giant *or* king prawn; Dublin Bay prawn; Chinese prawn.
langostón, *n.m.* (*ent.*) green grasshopper.
languidecer [9], *v.i.* to languish.
languidez, *n.f.* languor.
lánguido, -da, *a.* languid, languorous, torpid, sluggish.
lanífero, -ra, *a.* laniferous, woolbearing.
lanificación, *n.f.*, **lanificio,** *n.m.* woollen manufacturing; woollen goods.
lanilla, *n.f.* nap (*of cloth*); down; swanskin, fine flannel.
lanío, -nía, *a.* woolly.
lanosidad, *n.f.* (*bot.*) down (*of leaves, fruit etc.*).
lanoso, -sa, *a.* woolly.
lansquenete, *n.m.* lansquenet.
lantano, *n.m.* (*chem.*) lanthanum.
lanteja, *n.f.* lentil; ***lantejas son éstas,*** that's all there is.
lanudo, -da, *a.* woolly, fleecy, shaggy.
lanuginoso, -sa, *a.* (*bot.*) lanuginous, downy.
lanza, *n.f.* lance; spear; pike; nozzle; pikeman; pole (*of a coach* or *waggon*); mercenary; ***correr lanzas,*** to joust; ***romper lanzas con,*** to cross swords with; ***romper*** or ***quebrar una lanza*** or ***lanzas por,*** to stand up for, break a lance for; (*Hisp. Am.*) ***ser una lanza,*** to be clever, expert;

lanza en ristre, ready for action; (*pl.*) duty formerly paid by the nobility in lieu of military service.
lanzabombas, *n.m. inv.* bomb-release; trench-mortar.
lanzacohetes, *n.m. inv.* rocket launcher.
lanzadera, *n.f.* shuttle.
lanzado, -da, *a.* at full tilt, hell for leather, rushing madly; out of hand, running wild; (*naut.*) sloping. — *n.f.* blow *or* stroke with a lance; ***a moro muerto gran lanzada,*** it is easy to hit a man when he is down.
lanzador, -ra, *n.m.f.* thrower, ejecter.
lanzafuego, *n.m.* (*artill.*) linstock, match-staff.
lanzallamas, *n.m. inv.* flame-thrower.
lanzamiento, *n.m.* launching; casting, throwing; (*law*) dispossessing, eviction; (*naut.*) flaring (*of bows and knuckle timbers*); rake (*of the stem and stern-post*); ***plataforma*** or ***pista de lanzamiento,*** launching pad; (*pl.*) length of a ship from stem to stern-post.
lanzaminas, *n.m. inv.* minelayer.
lanzar [C], *v.t.* to launch; to hurl, throw, fling, cast; to vomit forth; to put forth; to toss out; to drop, release (*bombs etc.*); (*law*) to dispossess. — **lanzarse,** *v.r.* to hurl *or* fling o.s., rush, dash; to sprint.
Lanzarote, *n.m.* Lancelot.
lanzatorpedos, *n.m. inv.* torpedo tube.
lanzazo, *n.m.* blow *or* stroke with a lance.
lanzón, *n.m.* short and thick goad; dagger.
lanzuela, *n.f.* small lance *or* spear.
laña, *n.f.* brace, clamp, cramp, cramp-iron; green coconut.
lañar, *v.t.* to cramp, clamp; (*prov.*) to prepare (fish) for salting.
laocio, -cia, *a., n.m.f.* Laotian.
Laos, *n.m.* Laos.
lapa, *n.f.* vegetable film (*on the surface of a liquid*); (*ichth.*) limpet; (*bot.*) burdock.
lapachar, *n.m.* swamp, marsh, morass.
lápade, *n.f.* limpet.
lapicero, *n.m.* pencil-case; pencil-holder; propelling pencil.
lápida, *n.f.* tablet, memorial stone; ***lápida mortuoria,*** grave-stone.
lapidación, *n.f.* lapidation, stoning to death.
lapidar, *v.t.* to lapidate, stone to death.
lapidario, -ria, *a.* lapidary; ***frase lapidaria,*** memorable phrase. — *n.m.* lapidary. — *n.f.* lapidary's craft.
lapídeo, -dea, *a.* lapidose.
lapidificación, *n.f.* petrification, lapidification.
lapidificar [A], *v.t.* (*chem.*) lapidify.
lapidoso, -sa, *a.* lapidose.
lapilla, *n.f.* (*bot.*) hound's-tongue.
lapislázuli, *n.m.* lapis-lazuli.
lápiz, *n.m.* black-lead; pencil; ***lápiz de color,*** crayon; ***lápiz de labios,*** lipstick; ***lápiz rojo*** (or ***encarnado***), red ochre; (*coll.*) censor's blue pencil.
lapizar, *n.m.* black-lead mine. — [C], *v.t.* to pencil.
lapo, *n.m.* swipe; slap; swig; spittle.
lapón, -pona, *a.* Lapp, Lappish. — *n.m.f.* Lapp, Laplander. — *n.m.* Lappish (*language*).
Laponia, *n.f.* Lapland.
lapso, *n.m.* lapse, period.
lar, *n.m.* hearth; furnace; (*fig.*) home; (*pl.* **lares**) Lares, household goods.
lardar, lardear, *v.t.* to baste.
lardero, *a.* greasy; ***jueves lardero,*** Thursday before Lent.
lardo, *n.m.* bacon fat, animal fat.
lardón, *n.m.* (*print.*) marginal addition; (*print.*) bite.
lardoso, -sa, *a.* greasy, fatty.
larga, *n.f.* [LARGO].
largamente, *adv.* at (great) length; lavishly.
largar [B], *v.t.* (*naut.*) to pay out (*rope*); (*naut.*) to unfurl (*sail*); (*coll.*) to let have, deliver; to fob off; (*coll.*) to send packing, send off, chuck out; ***largar las velas,*** to set sail. — **largarse,** *v.r.* to clear off, clear out, sheer off; ***¡lárgate!*** scram! beat it!
largo, -ga, *a.* long; lavish; (*coll.*) sharp, smart; ***ése es cuento largo,*** that is a long story; ***eso va para largo,*** that won't be over, ready etc., for quite some time; ***eso viene de largo,*** it has a long history; ***largo de lengua,*** over-free with the tongue; ***largo de uñas,*** light-fingered; ***largo metraje,*** long-running (*film*); (*pl.*) many, quite a number; ***largos años,*** many years; ***3 kilómetros largos,*** a good 3 kilometres. — *adv.* at (great) length; ***a lo largo,*** lengthwise; ***a lo largo de su vida,*** throughout his life; ***a la larga,*** in the long run; ***a la larga o a la corta,*** sooner or later; ***de largo a largo,*** from one end to the other; ***escribir largo y tendido,*** to write at (great) length; (*naut.*) ***navegar a lo largo de la costa,*** to navigate along the coast; ***pasar de largo,*** to pass by, go by, on the other side; ***ponerse de largo,*** to come out (*in society*); (*coll.*) ***ponerse de tiros largos,*** to dress up to the nines. — *n.m.* length; (*mus.*) largo; ***cuan largo,*** to his full length. — *n.f.* (*shoe.*) lengthening piece; longest billiard-cue; ***dar largas a,*** to put off, play for time. — *interj.* ***¡largo!*** or ***¡largo de aquí!*** clear off! buzz off!
largomira, *n.m.* telescope.
largor, *n.m.* length.
largueado, -da, *a.* striped.
larguero, *n.m.* (*carp.*) jamb-post; bolster; (*aer.*) longeron; (*aer.*) spar.
largueza, *n.f.* length; liberality, generosity, munificence.
larguirucho, -cha, *a.* (*coll.*) lanky, gangling.
larguito, -ta, *a.* longish; (*coll.*) nice and long.
largura, *n.f.* length.
lárice, *n.m.* (*bot.*) larch-tree.
laricino, -na, *a.* belonging to the larch-tree.
laringe, *n.f.* (*anat.*) larynx.
laríngeo, -gea, *a.* laryngeal.
laringitis, *n.f.* (*med.*) laryngitis.
laringología, *n.f.* laryngology.
laringoscopia, *n.f.* laryngoscopy.
laringoscopio, *n.m.* laryngoscope.
laringotomía, *n.f.* (*surg.*) laryngotomy.
larva, *n.f.* larva.
larvado, -da, *a.* (*med.*) larvate; embryonic.
larval, *a.* larval; embryonic.
las, *def. art. f.pl.* the; *pers. pron. acc. f.pl.* (*accusative*) them.
lasaña, *n.f.* fritter.
lasca, *n.f.* chip (*from a stone*).
lascar (1) [A], *v.t.* (*naut.*) to ease away, slacken, pay out; (*Mex.*) to hurt, bruise, mangle.
lascar (2), *n.m.* lascar.
lascivia, *n.f.* lasciviousness.
lascivo, -va, *a.* lascivious; wanton, sportive.
láser, *n.m.* benzoin.
laser, *n.m.* laser.
laserpicio, *n.m.* (*bot.*) laserwort.
lasitud, *n.f.* lassitude.
laso, -sa, *a.* languid, drooping, feeble; untwisted (*silk etc.*).
lastar, *v.t.* to pay, answer *or* suffer for another.
lástima, *n.f.* pity; pitiful object; ***me das lástima,*** I feel sorry for you; ***está hecho una lástima,*** he looks a sorry sight, he's in a pitiful state; ***¡qué lástima!*** what a pity! what a shame!
lastimadura, *n.f.* hurt, injury.
lastimar, *v.t.* to hurt, injure, damage, wound; to pity. — **lastimarse,** *v.r.* to hurt o.s.; to feel pity *or* sorrow.

lastimero, -ra, *a.* whining, plaintive; hurtful.
lastimoso, -sa, *a.* pitiful, pathetic.
lasto, *n.m.* receipt given to one who has paid on behalf of another.
lastra, *n.f.* flagstone, slab; boat, lighter.
lastrar, *v.t.* to ballast.
lastre, *n.m.* ballast; stone slat; (*fig.*) burden, dragging weight, handicap; assurance, confidence, aplomb.
lastrón, *n.m.* large stone slat.
lasún, *n.m.* (*ichth.*) loach.
lata (1), *n.f.* tin, (*Am.*) can, tin-can; tin-plate; log; batten, lath; (*coll.*) bore, pest pain in the neck; ***dar la lata (a),*** to bore, pester, give a pain in the neck (to); to nag; ***la lata es que,*** the trouble is that.
latamente, *adv.* at (great) length; in a broad sense.
latania, *n.f.* (*bot.*) latania palm.
latastro, *n.m.* (*arch.*) plinth (*of a pillar*).
lataz, *n.f.* (*zool.*) sea-otter.
latebra, *n.f.* cave, den, hiding-place.
latebroso, -sa, *a.* hiding, furtive.
latente, *a.* latent, dormant.
lateral, *a.* lateral, side.
lateranense, *a.* Lateran.
látex, *n.m.* (*bot.*) latex.
laticaude, *a.* (*zool.*) long-tailed.
latido, *n.m.* beat, throb, pulsation (*of the heart, arteries etc.*); yelp (*of a dog*).
latiente, *a.* beating, throbbing.
latifundio, *n.m.* large landed estate, latifundium.
latifundista, *n.m.f.* owner of a large landed estate; absentee landlord.
latigadera, *n.f.* strap *or* thong (*for lashing the yoke*).
latigazo, *n.m.* lash, whiplash; crack of a whip; (*fig.*) harsh reproof; strong nightcap.
látigo, *n.m.* whip, lash; cinch strap; lashing cord (*for weighing objects with a steelyard*); long plume (*around a hat*).
latiguear, *v.i.* to crack a whip; *v.t.* (*Hisp. Am.*) to lash, whip.
latiguera, *n.f.* cinch-strap.
latiguero, *n.m.* maker *or* seller of whips.
latiguillo, *n.m.* small whip; (*bot.*) stolon; (*theat.*) clap-trap; refrain; stock phrase.
latín, *n.m.* Latin; Latin tongue; ***saber mucho latín,*** to be very cunning.
latinajo, *n.m.* (*coll.*) dog Latin.
latinar, latinear, *v.i.* to speak *or* write Latin; to use Latin phrases often.
latinidad, *n.f.* Latinity, the Latin tongue.
latiniparla, *n.f.* language interspersed with Latin words.
latinismo, *n.m.* Latinism.
latinizar [C], *v.t.* to Latinize. — *v.i.* to use words borrowed from the Latin.
latino, -na, *a.* Latin; ***lengua latina,*** Latin language; ***vela latina,*** lateen sail. — *n.m.f.* Latinist; native of Latium.
latir, *v.i.* to palpitate, pulsate, throb, beat; to yelp, howl.
latitud, *n.f.* breadth, width, extent; (*geog., astron.*) latitude.
latitudinal, *a.* latitudinal.
latitudinario, -ria, *a.* (*theol.*) latitudinarian, liberal.
latitudinarismo, *n.m.* (*theol.*) latitudinarianism.
lato, -ta (2), *a.* broad, wide; large, diffuse.
latón, *n.m.* brass; ***latón en hojas*** (or ***planchas***), latten brass, sheet brass.
latonería, *n.f.* brass trade; brass works; brass shop; brassware.
latonero, *n.m.* brazier, brassworker.
latoso, -sa, *a.* annoying; tedious, tiresome, boring.
latría, *n.f.* latria.
latrina [LETRINA].
latrocinio, *n.m.* theft, thievery, robbery, larceny, burglary.
Latvia, *n.f.* Latvia.
latvio, -via, *a., n.m.f.* Latvian.
laucha, *n.f.* (*Hisp. Am.*) mouse.
laúd, *n.m.* (*mus.*) lute; (*naut.*) craft, catboat; (*zool.*) leather-back turtle.
lauda, *n.f.* tombstone.
laudable, *a.* laudable, praiseworthy.
láudano, *n.m.* (*pharm.*) laudanum.
laudar, *v.t.* (*law*) to give judgment on.
laudatorio, -ria, *a.* laudatory. — *n.f.* panegyric.
laude, *n.f.* inscribed tombstone; (*pl.*) (*eccles.*) lauds; ***a laudes,*** frequently, continually; ***tocar a laudes,*** to blow one's own trumpet.
laudemio, *n.m.* (*law*) dues paid to the lord of the manor on transfers of his landed property.
laudo, *n.m.* (*law*) finding *or* award (*of an arbitrator* or *umpire*).
launa, *n.f.* lamina, thin plate of metal; slate clay.
láurea, *n.f.* laurel wreath.
laureado, -da, *a., n.m.f.* laureate.
laureando, *n.m.* one about to graduate.
laurear, *v.t.* to crown with laurel; to honour, reward; to confer a degree on.
lauredal, *n.m.* plantation of laurel-trees.
laurel, *n.m.* (*bot.*) laurel; laurel wreath; crown o laurel; (*bot.*) ***laurel cerezo,*** cherry-laurel.
laurente, *n.m.* workman (*in paper-mill*).
lauréola, *n.f.* laurel wreath; diadem; (*bot.*) ***lauréola hembra,*** mezereon daphne; ***lauréola macho,*** spurge laurel.
lauríneo, -nea, *a.* (*bot.*) laurineous.
laurino, -na, *a.* belonging to laurel.
lauro, *n.m.* (*bot.*) laurus; glory, honour, fame, triumph.
lauroceraso, laurorreal, *n.m.* cherry-laurel.
lauto, -ta, *a.* rich, opulent.
lava, *n.f.* lava; (*min.*) washing (*of metals*).
lavable, *a.* washable.
lavabo, *n.m.* wash-stand, wash-basin; wash-room; lavatory.
lavacaras, *n.m. inv.* (*coll.*) flatterer.
lavación, *n.f.* (*pharm.*) lotion, wash.
lavadero, *n.m.* washing-place; (*tan.*) vat *or* pit (*for washing hides*); (*min.*) buddling tank; (*Hisp. Am.*) placer (*place where gold deposits are washed*).
lavado, *n.m.* wash, washing; laundry-work; (*art*) aquarelle in a single tint; ***lavado de cerebro,*** brain-washing; interrogation, third degree; picking of brains.
lavador, -ra, *a.* washing. — *n.m.* washer. — *n.f.* washing machine.
lavadura, *n.f.* wash, washing; composition for dressing glove-leather; slops.
lavaje, *n.m.* washing (*of wools*).
lavajo, *n.m.* water-hole.
lavamanos, *n.m. inv.* wash-stand.
lavamiento, *n.m.* washing.
lavanco, *n.m.* wild duck.
lavandera, *n.f.* laundress, washerwoman.
lavandería, *n.f.* laundry.
lavandero, *n.m.* launderer, one who washes.
lavaplatos, *n.m.f. inv.* dish-washer.
lavar, *v.t.* to wash, wash down; ***lavarse los dientes,*** to clean one's teeth.
lavativa, *n.f.* enema; (*fig.*) bore, pain in the neck.
lavatorio, *n.m.* lavation, washing; lavatory, wash-stand; (*pharm.*) lotion; (*eccles.*) maundy; (*eccles.*) lavabo.
lavazas, *n.f.pl.* foul water, slops.
lave, *n.m.* (*min.*) washing.
lavotear(se), *v.t.* (*v.r.*) (*coll.*) to wash hurriedly.
lavoteo, *n.m.* hurried washing.

laxación, *n.f.* loosening, laxation, slackening.
laxamiento, *n.m.* laxation, laxity, laxness, loosening.
laxante, *a.* loosening, softening. — *n.m.* (*med.*) laxative.
laxar, *v.t.* to loosen, soften.
laxativo, -va, *a.*, *n.m.f.* laxative, lenitive.
laxidad, laxitud, *n.f.* laxity, laxness.
laxo, -xa, *a.* lax, slack.
laya, *n.f.* (*agric.*) spade; kind, class, nature.
layador, *n.m.* spadesman.
layar, *v.t.* (*agric.*) to spade, spud.
lazada, *n.f.* bow-knot; (*sew.*) bow; true-lover's knot.
lazador, *n.m.* lassoer.
lazar [C], *v.t.* to lasso.
lazareto, *n.m.* lazaretto, lazaret; pest-house.
lazarillo, *n.m.* blind person's guide.
lazarino, -na, *a.* leprous, lazar-like, lazarly. — *n.m.f.* lazar, leper.
Lázaro, *n.m.* Lazarus.
lázaro, *n.m.* lazar.
lazo, *n.m.* (*sew.*) bow, loop, true-lover's knot; bond, chain, tie, lasso, knot; snare (*for game*); trap, scheme (for persons); (*arch.*) knot *or* ornament; ***lazo corredizo,*** running knot; slipknot; ***caer en el lazo,*** to fall into the trap; ***tender un lazo a,*** to set a trap for; ***roer el lazo,*** to escape from danger.
lazulita, *n.f.* lazulite, lapis-lazuli.
le, *pers. pron. dative sing.* (*m.* or *f.*) to him, to her, to it. — *acc. m. sing.* him.
leal, *a.* loyal, faithful.
lealmente, *adv.* loyally, faithfully.
lealtad, *n.f.* loyalty, fidelity, fealty; ***según su leal saber y entender,*** to the best of his knowledge.
lebeche, *n.m.* a south-east wind (*in the Mediterranean*).
lebení, *n.m.* Moorish drink (*prepared with sour milk*).
lebrada, *n.f.* fricassee of hare.
lebratico, lebratillo, lebratito, lebrato, lebratón, *n.m.* young hare, leveret.
lebrel, *n.m.* whippet.
lebrela, *n.f.* whippet-bitch.
lebrero, -ra, *a.* hare-hunting. — *n.m.* harehound.
lebrillo, *n.m.* glazed earthenware tub.
lebrón, *n.m.* large hare; (*coll.*) poltroon.
lebroncillo, *n.m.* young hare.
lebruno, -na, *a.* leporine, harelike.
lección, *n.f.* lesson; ***dar lección,*** to teach; ***dar una lección (a),*** to teach a lesson (to); ***señalar lección,*** to assign the lesson; ***tomar lección,*** to take *or* hear a lesson.
leccionario, *n.m.* (*eccles.*) lectionary.
leccioncita, *n.f.* short lecture *or* lesson.
leccionista, *n.m.f.* private tutor.
lectisternio, *n.m.* banquet (*of the heathen gods*).
lectivo, -va, *a.* (of) school *or* university.
lector, -ra, *a.* reading. — *n.m.f.* reader; teaching assistant (teaching mother-tongue abroad).
lectorado, *n.m.* (*eccles.*) lectorate; teaching assistantship.
lectoral, *n.f.* (*eccles.*) prebend. — *n.m.* prebendary.
lectoría, *n.f.* (*eccles.*) lectorate.
lectura, *n.f.* reading; (*print.*) pica.
lecturita, *n.f.* (*print.*) small pica.
lecha, lechaza, *n.f.* milt.
lechada, *n.f.* grout; whitewash; pulp; lime-water.
lechal, *a.* sucking; (*bot.*) lactiferous, milky. — *n.m.* (*bot.*) milky juice.
lechar, *a.* suckling, nursing; promoting the secretion of milk in female mammals.
leche, *n.f.* milk; (*bot.*) milky juice; ***ama de leche,*** wet nurse; ***cochinillo de leche,*** sucking pig; ***estar con la leche en los labios,*** to be a greenhorn; ***estar en leche,*** to be immature *or* green; (*naut.*) to be calm; ***haber mamado una cosa en*** or ***con la leche,*** to have learned sth. at the breast, at one's mother's breast; ***hermano de leche,*** foster-brother; ***leche de canela,*** oil of cinnamon dissolved in wine; (*bot.*) ***leche de gallina*** or ***de pájaro,*** star of Bethlehem; ***leche desnatada,*** skim-milk; ***leche de tierra,*** magnesia; ***leche en polvo,*** powdered milk, milk powder; ***leche homogenizada,*** homogenized milk; ***leche manchada,*** very milky coffee; ***leche pasterizada,*** pasteurized milk; (*vulg.*) ***tener mala leche,*** to be damned nasty.
lechecillas, *n.f.pl.* sweetbread; livers and lights.
lechera (1), *a.* milch (*applied to animals*).
lechería, *n.f.* dairy.
lechero, -ra (2), *a.* milky. — *n.m.* milkman. — *n.f.* milkmaid, dairymaid; milk-can; milk-pot, milk-ewer.
lecherón, *n.m.* (*prov.*) milk-pail, milk-vessel; flannel wrap (*for new-born infants*).
lechetrezna, *n.f.* (*bot.*) spurge.
lechigada, *n.f.* brood, litter; gang, mob, crew.
lechiguana, *n.f.* (*Arg.*, *Bol.*) wasp.
lechín, *n.m.* olive-tree; olive; (*vet.*) tumour (*in horses*).
lechino, *n.m.* (*surg.*) tent; small tumour (*in horses*).
lecho, *n.m.* bed; couch; bottom; layer.
lechón, -chona, *a.* filthy. — *n.m.f.* sucking pig; pig, sow.
lechoso, -sa, *a.* milky.— *n.m.* papaw-tree. — *n.f.* papaw.
lechuga, *n.f.* (*bot.*) lettuce; (*sew.*) frill.
lechugado, -da, *a.* resembling lettuce.
lechuguero, -ra, *n.m.* lettuce seller.
lechuguilla, *n.f.* wild lettuce; frill, ruff.
lechuguina, *n.f.* (*coll.*) stylish young lady.
lechuguino, *n.m.* lettuce sprout; plot of small lettuces; (*coll.*) dandy, dude.
lechuzo, -za, *a.* (*fig.*) owlish; suckling (of a mule colt). — *n.m.* (*coll.*) bill-collector *or* summons server. — *n.f.* (*orn.*) owl; ugly old woman.
ledo, -da, *a.* (*poet.*) merry, cheerful.
leedor, -ra, *n.m.f.* reader.
leer [N], *v.t.*, *v.i.* to read; ***leer a uno la cartilla,*** to reprimand s.o.; ***leer cátedra,*** to occupy a university chair; ***leer entre líneas,*** to read between the lines; ***leer para sí,*** to read (for) o.s. — **leerse,** *v.r.* ***este libro se lee fácilmente,*** this book reads easily.
lega, *n.f.* [LEGO].
legacía, *n.f.* legateship; message entrusted to a legate; province *or* duration of a legateship.
legación, *n.f.* legation.
legado, *n.m.* (*law*) legacy; bequest; legate; legatus; ***legado a látere,*** pope's legate.
legador, *n.m.* labourer who ties the feet of sheep prior to shearing.
legadura [LIGADURA].
legajo, *n.m.* file, docket, bundle of papers.
legal, *a.* legal, lawful, legitimate.
legalidad, *n.f.* legality, lawfulness.
legalismo, *n.m.* legalism.
legalización, *n.f.* legalization, attestation, notary's certificate.
legalizar [C], *v.t.* to legalize; to attest the authenticity of.
légamo, *n.m.* slime; silt.
legamoso, -sa, *a.* slimy; silty.
legaña, *n.f.* bleariness of the eyes.
legañoso, -sa, *a.* blear-eyed.
legar [B], *v.t.* to depute; to send a legate; (*law*) to bequeath, legate.
legatario, -ria, *n.m.f.* (*law*) legatee.
legenda, *n.f.* (*eccles.*) history of saints, hagiology.
legendario, -ria, *a.* legendary. — *n.m.* legendary, book of legends.

legible, *a.* legible, readable.
legión, *n.f.* legion.
legionario, -ria, *a., n.m.* legionary.
legislación, *n.f.* legislation.
legislador, -ra, *a.* legislating, legislative. — *n.m.* legislator. — *n.f.* legislatress.
legislar, *v.t.* to legislate, enact laws.
legislativo, -va, *a.* legislative, law-making, law-giving.
legislatura, *n.f.* (term of) legislature.
legisperito, *n.m.* jurist.
legista, *n.m.f.* legist; professor of laws; student of laws.
legítima, *n.f.* [LEGÍTIMO].
legitimación, *n.f.* legitimation.
legitimar, *v.t.* to legitimate, legalize; to prove, establish in evidence.
legitimidad, *n.f.* legitimacy, legality; authenticity; genuineness.
legitimista, *a.* legitimistic, legitimist. — *n.m.f.* legitimist; Carlist.
legítimo, -ma, *a.* legitimate, lawful, right(ful); genuine, true. — *n.f.* (*law*) legitime.
lego, -ga, *a.* lay. — *n.m.f.* layman; lay brother; lay sister.
legón, *n.m.* (*agric.*) hoe.
legra, *n.f.* (*surg.*) periosteotome.
legración, legradura, *n.f.* (*surg.*) periosteotomy.
legrar, *v.t.* (*surg.*) perform periosteotomy on.
legrón, *n.m.* (veterinary's) periosteotomy.
legua, *n.f.* league; ***cómico de la legua,*** strolling player; ***se ve a la legua,*** you can see it from a mile off, you can see it a mile away.
leguario, -ria, *a.* relating to a league. — *n.m.* league post *or* stone.
leguleyo, *n.m.* petty lawyer, pettifogger.
legumbre, *n.f.* pulse; vegetable.
leguminoso, -sa, *a.* (*bot.*) leguminous.
leíble, *a.* legible, readable.
Leiden, *n.m.* Leiden; (*phys.*) ***botella de Leiden,*** Leiden jar.
leído, -da, *a.* well-read, book-learned; (*coll.*) ***leído y escribido,*** affectedly *or* supposedly learned.
leila, *n.f.* Morisco dance.
leima, *n.m.* (*mus.*) limma.
lejanía, *n.f.* distance, remoteness.
lejano, -na, *a.* distant, far-distant, far-off.
Lejano Oriente, *n.m.* Far East.
lejas, *a.pl.* far away; ***de lejas tierras,*** from far away lands.
lejía, *n.f.* bleach, lye; (*coll.*) severe reprimand, reproof.
lejío, *n.m.* lye.
lejitos, *adv.* quite a way off.
lejos, *adv.* far, far away, far off; far out; ***a lo lejos,*** in the distance; ***de*** or ***desde lejos,*** from afar, from a distance; ***lejos de,*** far from. — *n.m.* perspective, distant view, background; appearance at a distance; ***tener buen lejos,*** to look good from a distance.
lejuelos, *adv.* at some distance.
lelilí, *n.m.* Moorish war-whoop.
lelo, -la, *a.* daft, dim, thick, half-witted.
lema, *n.m.* lemma, theme; motto, slogan, watch-word.
lemanita, *n.f.* (*min.*) jade.
lemnáceo, -cea, *a.* (*bot.*) lemnaceous.
lemniscata, *n.f.* (*math.*) lemniscate.
lemosín, -sina, *a.* (of) Limousin. — *n.m.* Provençal, langue d'oc.
lémur, *n.m.* (*zool.*) lemur; (*pl.* **lémures**) lemures, ghosts.
len, *a.* soft, flossy (*of thread* or *silk*).
lena, *n.f.* spirit, vigour.
lencera, *n.f.* woman who deals in linen; linen-draper's wife.
lencería, *n.f.* linen goods; linen-draper's shop; linen-hall; linen-room; linen-trade; lingerie.
lencero, *n.m.* linen-draper, linen merchant.
lendel, *n.m.* track *or* circle (*described by a mill-horse*).
lendrera, *n.f.* fine comb for removing nits.
lendrero, *n.m.* place full of nits.
lendroso, -sa, *a.* nitty, verminous.
lene, *a.* soft; pleasant, kind; light.
lengua, *n.f.* tongue; language; clapper (*of a bell*); spit *or* strip (*of land*); index (*of a scale*); ***andar en lenguas,*** to be much talked about, be a subject of gossip; ***buscar la lengua a,*** to provoke to argument; ***con un palmo de lengua,*** panting, fagged out; ***de lengua en lengua,*** from mouth to mouth; ***hacerse lenguas de,*** to praise to the skies; (*bot.*) ***lengua canina*** or ***de perro,*** hound's tongue; (*bot.*) ***lengua cerval,*** hart's tongue; (*bot.*) ***lengua de buey,*** bugloss, alkanet; (*bot.*) ***lengua de vaca,*** sanseviera; ***ligero*** or ***suelto de lengua,*** free with one's tongue, outspoken; ***mala lengua,*** slanderer, backbiter; ***no morderse la lengua,*** not to mince words; ***sacar la lengua a,*** to stick one's tongue out at; ***se fue de la lengua,*** he said too much; ***se le fue la lengua,*** he let it slip out; ***tener en la punta de la lengua,*** to have on the tip of one's tongue; ***tener la lengua gorda*** or ***de trapo,*** to speak indistinctly; ***tirar de la lengua a alguien,*** to draw somebody out; ***tomar lengua(s),*** to seek information; ***trabársele a alguien la lengua,*** to get tongue-tied.
lenguado, *n.m.* (*ichth.*) sole.
lenguaje, *n.m.* language, parlance.
lenguaraz, *a.* free with one's tongue.
lenguaz, *a.* garrulous, talkative, loquacious.
lengüecica, lengüecilla, lengüecita, *n.f.* small tongue.
lengüeta, *n.f.* small tongue; (*anat.*) epiglottis; languet, barb; (*mus.*) languette; needle (*of a balance*); (*mech.*) feather, wedge, tongue, awl, bore; bit; bookbinder's cutting-knife; (*arch.*) buttress; moulding; catch (*of a trap* or *snare*); tongue (*of shoe*).
lengüetada, *n.f.* lick, licking.
lengüetería, *n.f.* reed-work (*of an organ*).
lengüezuela, *n.f.* small tongue.
lengüón, -guona (*C.R., Ec., Mex.*) [LENGUARAZ].
lenidad, *n.f.* lenity, lenience.
lenificar, *v.t.* to lenify, soften.
lenificativo, -va, *a.* mollifying, softening.
lenitivo, -va, *a.* lenitive. — *n.m.* lenitive, palliative.
lenocinio, *n.m.* pimping, pandering; (***casa de***) ***lenocinio,*** brothel.
lente [9], *n.f.* lens. — *n.m.pl.* (**lentes**) spectacles.
lentecer [9], *v.i.* to grow soft *or* tender.
lenteja, *n.f.* (*bot.*) lentil; disc (*of a pendulum*); (*bot.*) ***lenteja de agua,*** gibbous duck-weed.
lentejuela, *n.f.* spangle; sequin.
lenticular, *a.* lenticular, lentil-shaped.
lentiscal, *n.m.* thicket of mastic trees.
lentisco, *n.m.* (*bot.*) mastic tree, lentisk.
lentitud, *n.f.* slowness.
lento, -ta, *a.* slow, tardy; (*pharm.*) glutinous.
lentor, *n.m.* (*med.*) viscidity, tenacity (*of blood etc.*).
lenzuelo, *n.m.* (*agric.*) sheet (*for carrying straw*).
leña, *n.f.* firewood, kindling-wood; (*coll.*) drubbing, beating; ***del árbol caído todos hacen leña,*** everyone kicks a man when he's down; ***echar leña al fuego,*** to add fuel to the flames; ***llevar leña al monte,*** to carry coals to Newcastle.
leñador, *n.m.* woodman, wood-cutter; dealer in firewood.
leñame, *n.m.* wood; supply of firewood.
leñar, *v.t.* (*prov.*) to cut (*wood*).
leñazgo, *n.m.* pile of timber.
leñazo, *n.m.* clout with a cudgel.

leñera, *n.f.* woodshed, wood-bin.
leñero, *n.m.* timber-merchant, wood-dealer; log-man.
leño, *n.m.* log; (*fig.*) ship, vessel; (*coll.*) blockhead.
leñoso, -sa, *a.* woody, ligneous.
Leo, *n.m.* (*astron., astrol.*) Leo.
león, *n.m.* lion; lion ant; Leo, Leon; ***león marino,*** sea lion; ***parte del león,*** lion's share; ***no es tan fiero el león como pintan,*** his bark is worse than his bite.
leona, *n.f.* lioness.
leonado, -da, *a.* lion-coloured, tawny.
leoncico, leoncillo, leoncito, *n.m.* lion cub.
leonera, *n.f.* cage *or* den of lions; (*coll.*) gambling-den; (*fig.*) pig-sty; children's playroom.
leonero, *n.m.* keeper (*of lions*); master (*of a gambling house*).
leonés, -nesa, *a., n.m.f.* (native) of León.
leónica, *n.f.* (*anat.*) vein under the tongue.
leonino, -na, *a.* leonine; (*law*) one-sided, unfair. — *n.f.* (*med.*) leontiasis.
leontina, *n.f.*(*jewel.*) watch-chain.
leopardo, *n.m.* leopard.
leopoldina, *n.f.* (*jewel.*) fob-chain; (*mil.*) Spanish shako.
Lepe (saber más que), to be very smart and shrewd.
leperada, *n.f.* (*Hisp. Am.*) coarseness, vulgarity.
lépero, -ra, *a.* (*Hisp. Am.*) coarse, vulgar.
leperón, -rona, *a.* (*Hisp. Am.*) very coarse *or* vulgar.
lepidia, *n.f.* (*Chi.*) indigestion.
lepidio, *n.m.* (*bot.*) pepper-grass.
lepidóptero, -ra, *a.* (*ent.*) lepidopterous. — *n.m.pl.* (**lepidópteros**) lepidoptera.
lepisma, *n.f.* (*ent.*) lepisma; bristle-tail, silver-fish.
leporino, -na, *a.* like a hare; ***labio leporino,*** hare-lip.
lepra, *n.f.* leprosy.
leprosidad, *n.f.* leprosy, leprousness.
leproso, -sa, *a.* leprous. — *n.m.f.* leper.
lercha, *n.f.* reed (*for hanging fishes and birds*).
lerda (1), *n.f.* (*vet.*) tumour (*in a horse's pastern*).
lerdo, -da (2), *a.* slow, heavy; dull, obtuse, thick.
lerdón, *n.m.* (*vet.*) tumour (*in a horse's pastern*).
les, *pers. pron. dat. m.f.pl.* to *or* for them *or* you; from them *or* you; (*acc.*) them, you.
lesbiano, -na, *a.* Lesbian. — n.*f.* Lesbian.
lesbio, -bia, *a.* Lesbian.
lesión, *n.f.* lesion, injury; harm.
lesionar, *v.t.* to injure; to harm, hurt.
lesivo, -va, *a.* injurious, harmful.
lesna, *n.f.* awl.
lesnordeste, *n.m.* (*naut.*) east-north-east wind.
leso, -sa, *a.* injured; offended; ***lesa majestad,*** lese-majesty, high treason.
lessueste, *n.m.* (*naut.*) east-south-east wind.
leste, *n.m.* (*naut.*) east wind; east.
letal, *a.* deadly, lethal.
letame, *n.m.* mud fertilizer.
letanía, *n.f.* (*eccles.*) litany; (*coll.*) long string, rigmarole; (*pl.*) supplicatory procession.
letárgico, -ca, *a.* lethargic, lethargical.
letargo, *n.m.* lethargy.
letargoso, -sa, *a.* deadening, causing lethargy.
leteo, -tea, *a.* (*poet.*) Lethean.
letífero, -ra, *a.* deadly, lethal.
letificar [A], *v.t.* to make joyous.
letón, -tona, *a., n.m.f.* Latvian. — *n.m.* Latvian, Lettish (*language*).
Letonia, *n.f.* Latvia.
letra, *n.f.* letter; hand, handwriting; (*print.*) type; motto; rondeau; words (*of a song*); ***a la letra, al pie de la letra,*** to the letter, literally, strictly; (*com.*) ***a letra vista,*** at sight; ***despacito y buena letra,*** easy does it, gently; ***de su puño y letra,*** in his own hand; ***la letra con sangre entra,*** spare the rod and spoil the child; (*com.*) ***letra abierta,*** open credit; ***letra bastardilla, itálica*** or ***cursiva,*** italics; (*com.*) ***letra de cambio,*** bill of exchange; ***letra mayúscula,*** capital letter; ***letra minúscula,*** small letter; ***tener mucha letra,*** to be very cunning; (*pl.*) letters, learning; arts; ***letras humanas,*** litteræ humaniores, humanities; ***unas letras, cuatro letras,*** a few lines.
letrado, -da, *a.* learned, lettered; (*coll.*) presumptuous. — *n.m.* lawyer, counsellor; ***a lo letrado,*** as lawyer.
letrero, *n.m.* label; sign; notice.
letrilla, *n.f.* small letter; (*mus.*) rondelet.
letrina, *n.f.* latrine.
letrismo, *n.m.* letter-art; obession with letters.
leucina, *n.f.* (*chem.*) leucin.
leucocito, *n.m.* leucocyte.
leucorrea, *n.f.* (*med.*) leucorrhœa; whites.
leudar, *v.t.* to leaven. — **leudarse,** *v.r.* to yeast, rise.
leudo, -da, *a.* fermented, leavened (*bread*).
leva, *n.f.* (*naut.*) weighing anchor; (*mil.*) levy, press; (*naut.*) swell (*of the sea*); (*mech.*) lever, cog, tooth. cam, tappet; ***mar de leva,*** swell, ground swell.
levada, *n.f.* moving silk-worm; (*fenc.*) salute *or* flourish with the foil.
levadero, -ra, *a.* to be collected *or* levied.
levadizo, -za, *a.* that can be lifted *or* raised; ***puente levadizo,*** drawbridge.
levador, *n.m.* (paper-mills) piler; (*mech.*) cam, cog, tooth.
levadura, *n.f.* leaven, yeast; (*carp.*) sawn-off plank.
levantado, -da, *a.* raised, elevated, lofty.
levantador, -ra, *a.* raising, lifting. — *n.m.f.* lifter; disturber, rioter.
levantamiento, *n.m.* elevation, raising; sublimity; insurrection, rising, uprising; settlement (of accounts).
levantar, *v.t.* to raise; to lift (up); to elevate; to put *or* set up; to pick up; to rouse, stir (up); to adjourn; to weigh (*anchor*); to clear (*the table*); to break (*camp*); to strike, take down (*a tent*); to pack up (*house*); to draw up, make (*plans, surveys*); to bear (*false witness*); ***levantar acta,*** to draw up a formal statement, take proceedings; ***levantar el campo,*** to break *or* strike camp; ***levantar el vuelo,*** to fly off *or* away; (*fig.*) to clear *or* sheer off; ***levantar la sesión,*** to adjourn the proceedings, call the meeting closed; ***no levantar cabeza,*** not to get anywhere, find the going very heavy; to have to keep hard at it, have to keep one's nose to the grindstone. — **levantarse,** *v.r.* to rise; to get up; to start (*game*).
levante, *n.m.* east coast of Spain; east wind, levanter; Levant.
levantino, -na, *a.* of the east coast of Spain; Levantine.
levantisco, -ca, *a.* turbulent, restless; Levantine.
levar, *v.t.* (*naut.*) to weigh (*anchor*). — **levarse,** *v.r.* to set sail.
leve, *a.* light; slight, trifling.
levedad, *n.f.* lightness; slightness.
Leví, *n.m.* Levi.
leviatán, *n.m.* leviathan.
levigación, *n.f.* levigation.
levigar [B], *v.t.* to levigate.
levita, *n.m.* Levite. — *n.f.* frock-coat.
Levítico, *n.m.* Leviticus.
levítico, -ca, *a.* Levitical, priestly, ecclesiastical.
levitón, *n.m.* large *or* heavy frock-coat.
léxico, -ca, *a.* lexical. — *n.m.* lexicon; vocabulary.
lexicografía, *n.f.* lexicography.
lexicográfico, -ca, *a.* lexicographic, lexicographical.
lexicógrafo, *n.m.* lexicographer.

lexicología, *n.f.* lexicology.
lexicológico, -ca, *a.* lexicological.
lexicólogo, *n.m.* lexicologist.
ley, *n.f.* law; loyalty, devotion; norm, standard; fineness (*of a metal*); ***a ley de caballero,*** on the word of a gentleman; ***a toda ley,*** according to rule; ***con todas las de la ley,*** with every refinement, with everything fully covered; with full knowledge; ***de buena ley,*** sterling, good quality; ***de mala ley,*** disreputable; low, base; ***hecha la ley, hecha la trampa,*** rules are made to be broken; ***le mataron bajo la ley de fuga,*** he was shot while trying to escape; ***ley caldaria,*** ordeal by boiling water; (*coll.*) ***ley del embudo,*** one-sided law; ***ley del menor esfuerzo,*** line of least resistance; ***ley marcial,*** martial law; ***oro de ley,*** pure, fine gold; ***tener ley a,*** to be strongly attached to, be very fond of.
leyenda, *n.f.* legend; caption; reading.
leyente, *a.* reading.
lezda, *n.f.* ancient tax on merchandise.
lezna, *n.f.* awl.
lía, *n.f.* plaited bass-rope; lees, dregs; (*coll.*) ***estar hecho una lía,*** to be tipsy.
liar [L], *v.t.* to tie, bind, do up; (*coll.*) to involve, embroil; (*coll.*) ***liarlas,*** to clear off; to kick the bucket; ***estar liado con algo,*** to be all tied up with sth.; ***estar liado con alguien,*** to be having an affair with somebody; ***se lio a palos con él,*** he started to lay into him. — **liarse,** *v.r.* to join; to take up (***con,*** with), get involved (***con,*** with), start an affair (***con,*** with); ***liarse la manta a la cabeza,*** to plunge in, bash on regardless; ***la hemos liado,*** (now) we've done it!; ***no me líe usted,*** count *or* keep me out (of it).
liásico, -ca, *a.* (*geol.*) liassic.
liaza, *n.f.* hoops used by coopers.
libación, *n.f.* libation.
libamen, libamiento, *n.m.* offering in ancient sacrifices.
libanés, -nesa, *a., n.m.f.* Lebanese.
Líbano, *n.m.* Lebanon.
libar, *v.t.* to suck, sip, extract the juice of *or* from; to taste. — *v.i.* to perform a libation; to drink.
libatorio, *n.m.* libatory cup.
libelar, *v.t.* (*law*) to petition.
libelático, -ca, *a.* renegade (of persecuted early Christians).
libelista, *n.m.f.* lampooner.
libelo, *n.m.* lampoon; (*law*) petition.
libélula, *n.f.* libellula, dragonfly.
líber, *n.m.* (*bot.*) bast, liber, inner bark.
liberación, *n.f.* liberation; (*law*) quittance.
liberal, *a., n.m.f.* liberal.
liberalidad, *n.f.* liberality.
liberalismo, *n.m.* Liberalism, liberalism.
liberalizar [C], *v.t.* to liberalize.
libérrimo, -ma, *a. superl.* most free, extremely free.
libertad, *n.f.* liberty, freedom; ***libertad condicional,*** release on parole; ***libertad de comercio,*** free-trade; ***libertad de cultos,*** freedom of worship; ***libertad de imprenta*** or ***de prensa,*** freedom of the press; ***libertad de palabra,*** freedom of speech, free speech; ***libertad provisional,*** release on bail; ***poner en libertad,*** to set free; ***tomarse la libertad de,*** to take the liberty of.
libertadamente, *adv.* freely, impudently.
libertado, -da, *a.* free; bold, daring.
libertador, -ra, *a.* liberating. — *n.m.f.* deliverer, liberator.
libertar, *v.t.* to free, set at liberty, liberate.
libertario, -ria, *a.* libertarian, anarchistic. — *n.m.f.* libertarian, anarchist.
liberticida, *a., n.m.* liberticide.
libertinaje, *n.m.* libertinism, libertinage.
libertino, -na, *a., n.m.f.* libertine, profligate.
liberto, -ta, *n.m.f.* freed *or* emancipated slave.
Libia, *n.f.* Libya.
libidinal, *a.* (of the) libido.
libídine, *n.f.* lewdness, lust.
libidinoso, -sa, *a.* libidinous, lewd, lustful.
libido, *n.f.* libido.
libio, -bia, *a., n.m.f.* Libyan.
libra, *n.f.* pound; (*astron., astrol.*) Libra; ***libra esterlina,*** pound sterling; ***libra medicinal,*** pound troy; (*Cub.*) tobacco of superior quality.
libración, *n.f.* libration.
libraco, *n.m.* (*coll.*) wretched (old) book, tedious tome.
librado, *n.m.* (*com.*) drawee.
librador, -ra, *n.m.f.* deliverer; (*com.*) drawer (*of a cheque* or *draft*); storekeeper of the king's stables; grocer's scoop.
libramiento, *n.m.* delivery, delivering; warrant, order (*of payment*).
librancista, *n.m.f.* (*com.*) holder of a draft.
libranza, *n.f.* (*com.*) draft, bill of exchange; ***libranza postal,*** money order.
librar, *v.t.* to free, preserve, deliver; to expedite, despatch; to pass (sentence); to fight (*a battle*); to issue (*a decree*); (*com.*) to draw; ***librar sentencia,*** to give judgment. — *v.i.* to receive a visitor in the locutory (*of nuns*); to be delivered of a child; to expel the placenta; ***a bien*** or ***a buen librar,*** at best; ***librar bien*** or ***mal,*** to come off well *or* badly. — **librarse,** *v.r.* to get free (from), get out (of), dodge; to get rid (of), shake off; ***librarse por un pelo,*** to have a narrow escape *or* close shave; ***librarse de buena,*** to dodge *or* get out of a nasty *or* tedious business; ***librarse una batalla,*** to be fought (of a battle).
libratorio, *n.m.* locutory.
librazo, *n.m.* blow with a book; hefty great tome.
libre, *a.* free; detached, isolated; loose, fast, of easy virtue; ***al aire libre,*** in the open (*air*); ***entrada libre,*** free admission; (*com.*) ***libre a bordo*** (*or* ***l.a.b.***), free on board (*or* f.o.b.); ***libre cambio,*** free-trade; (*com.*) ***libre de derechos,*** duty free; ***libre de gastos,*** free of charge; ***libre pensador,*** freethinker; ***vía libre,*** clear line, line clear.
librea, *n.f.* livery.
librear, *v.t.* to weigh *or* sell by pounds.
librecambio, *n.m.* free-trade.
librecambismo, *n.m.* free-trade.
librecambista, *n.m.f.* free-trader.
librejo, *n.m.* wretched little book.
librepensador, -ra, *a.* free-thinking. — *n.m.f.* freethinker.
librepensamiento, *n.m.* freethought, freethinking.
librería, *n.f.* bookshop, bookseller's shop; book-trade; book-selling; bookcase.
libreril, *a.* relating to the book-trade.
librero, *n.m.* bookseller.
libresco, *a.* bookish.
libreta, *n.f.* one-pound loaf; book; notebook; bank book, savings book.
librete, *n.m.* small book; foot-stove.
libretista, *n.m.* libretto writer.
libreto, *n.m.* (*mus.*) libretto.
librillo, *n.m.* book of cigarette paper; ***librillo de cera,*** wax taper; ***librillo de oro,*** gold-leaf book.
libro, *n.m.* book; (*mus.*) libretto; (*zool.*) omasum; (*fig.*) tax; ***ahorcar los libros,*** to give up one's studies; ***hablar como un libro,*** to talk like a book; ***libro blanco,*** white paper; ***libro borrador,*** blotter, record book; ***libro de asiento*** or ***libro de cuentas,*** account book; ***libro de caja,*** cash book; ***libro de facturas,*** invoice book; ***libro de memoria,*** memorandum book; ***libro diario,*** journal; ***libro mayor,*** ledger; ***libro talonario,*** receipt book, cheque book.
librote, *n.m.* whacking great book, huge tome.
licantropía, *n.f.* (*med.*) lycanthropy.

licántropo, *n.m.* lycanthrope; werewolf.
liceísta, *n.m.f.* member of a lyceum.
licencia, *n.f.* licence; leave; degree of licentiate; (*mil.*) ***licencia absoluta,*** discharge.
licenciado, -da, *n.m.* bachelor, graduate; lawyer; (*mil.*) discharged soldier.
licenciamiento, *n.m.* graduation; (*mil.*) discharge.
licenciar, *v.t.* to permit, allow; to license; to confer a degree on; (*mil.*) to discharge. — **licenciarse,** *v.r.* to become dissolute; to graduate.
licenciatura, *n.f.* degree of licentiate; graduation.
licencioso, -sa, *a.* licentious, dissolute.
liceo, *n.m.* lyceum; literary society; secondary school.
licitación, *n.f.* bid (*at auction*).
licitador, *n.m.* bidder (*at auction*).
licitante, *n.m.f.* bidder.
licitar, *v.t.*, *v.i.* to bid (for).
lícito, -ta, *a.* licit; lawful; permissible.
licnobio, -bia, *n.m.f.* lychnobite; nocturnal person.
licopodio, *n.m.* (*bot.*) lycopodium.
licor, *n.m.* liquor; liqueur.
licorera, *n.f.* liquor-case, bottle-case.
licorista, *n.m.f.* liquor distiller *or* dealer.
licoroso, -sa, *a.* generous, spiritous.
licuable, *a.* liquable, liquefiable.
licuación, *n.f.* liquefaction; melting.
licuante, *a.* liquefying; melting.
licuar, *v.t.* to liquefy; to melt.
licuefacción, *n.f.* liquefaction.
licuefacer(**se**) [20], *v.t.* (*v.r.*) to liquefy.
licuefactible, *a.* liquefiable.
licurgo, -ga, *a.* smart, shrewd. — *n.m.* lawmaker.
lichera, *n.f.* woollen bed-cover.
lid, *n.f.* contest; fight; ***en buena lid,*** in fair fight, fairly.
líder, *n.m.* (*polit.*) leader.
liderato, liderazgo, *n.m.* leadership.
lidia, *n.f.* fight, contest; bullfight; ***toro de lidia,*** fighting bull.
lidiadero, -ra, *a.* in fighting condition.
lidiador, -ra, *n.m.f.* fighter, one who struggles; bullfighter.
lidiar, *v.t.*, *v.i.* to fight, to fight bulls; (*fig.*) ***lidiar con,*** to tackle, (try to) cope *or* deal with.
lidio, *a.*, *n.m.f.* Lydian.
liebrastón, liebratón, *n.m.* young hare; leveret.
liebre, *n.f.* hare; (*coll.*) lily-livered individual; ***coger una liebre,*** to come a cropper; ***dar gato por liebre,*** to sell a pig in a poke; ***levantar la liebre,*** to give the game away; ***donde menos se piensa salta la liebre,*** trouble *or* luck comes when you least expect it.
liebrecica, liebrecilla (1), **liebrecita, liebrezuela,** *n.f.* young *or* small hare.
liebrecilla (2), *n.f.* (*bot.*) bluebottle.
liendre, *n.f.* nit; (*coll.*) ***cascar a uno las liendres,*** to give s.o. a severe drubbing.
lientera, lientería, *n.f.* (*med.*) lientery.
lientérico, -ca, *a.* lienteric.
liento, -ta, *a.* damp, moist.
lienza, *n.f.* narrow strip of cloth.
lienzo, *n.m.* canvas; linen; hemp *or* cotton cloth; (*arch.*) face *or* front (*of a building*); (*fort.*) curtain; section (of wall).
liga, *n.f.* garter; league; (*coll.*) friendship; mistletoe; bird-lime; alloy.
ligación, *n.f.* ligation, tying, binding; union; mixture.
ligada, *n.f.* tying, binding; ligature.
ligado, *n.m.* (*mus.*) legato; tie.
ligadura, *n.f.* ligature; ligation; binding; tie; (*naut.*) seizing, lashing.
ligamaza, *n.f.* viscid matter (*surrounding the seeds of some fruits* or *plants*).
ligamen, *n.m.* spell (*causing impotency*).
ligamento, *n.m.* bond; ligament.
ligamentoso, -sa, *a.* ligamentous, ligamental.
ligamiento, *n.m.* union, uniting; tying, binding.
ligar [B], *v.t.* to tie, bind; to alloy (*gold* or *silver*); to league; to join, knit together; to render impotent by spells. — *v.i.* to combine cards of the same suit; (*coll.*) to chat up, pick up, hit it off with (the boys *or* the girls). — **ligarse,** *v.r.* to bind o.s.; to join together, link up.
ligazón, *n.f.* join, joining, link, linking, connection; (*naut.*) futtock.
ligereza, *n.f.* lightness; swiftness, fleetness; nimbleness; thoughtlessness, frivolousness.
ligero, -ra, *a.* light; swift, nimble; thoughtless, frivolous; ***a la ligera,*** carelessly, superficially; ***de ligero,*** rashly; ***ligera de cascos,*** of easy virtue; ***ligero de cascos,*** feather-brained; ***ligero de dedos,*** light-fingered; ***ligero de ropa,*** scantily clad.
ligio, -gia, *a.* liege, bound by feudal tenure.
lignario, -ria, *a.* ligneous.
lignito, *n.m.* (*min.*) lignite.
ligón, *n.m.* long-handled hoe; (*coll.*) one who chats up, picks up, hits it off with (a girl).
ligua, *n.f.* (*Philip.*) battle-axe.
liguano, -na, *a.* (*Chi.*) applied to a kind of sheep with thick and heavy wool.
ligue, *n.m.* (*fam.*) getting off with members of the opposite sex.
liguilla, *n.f.* narrow ribbon *or* garter.
lígula, *n.f.* (*bot.*) ligule.
ligur, ligurino, -na, *a.*, *n.m.f.* Ligurian.
ligustre, ligustro, *n.f.* (*bot.*) privet-flower, privet.
ligustrino, -na, *a.* relating to privet.
lija, *n.f.* (*ichth.*) dog-fish; skin of the dog-fish, shark-skin; sand-paper.
lijar, *v.t.* to sand-paper.
Lila, *n.f.* Lille.
lila, *a.* (*coll.*) silly, half-witted. — *n.m.f.* fool, half-wit, lemon. — *n.f.* (*bot.*) lilac (*flower and shrub*); lilac colour.
lilaila, *n.f.* thin woollen stuff; bunting; (*coll.*) trick, wile.
liliputiense, *a.*, *n.m.f.* Lilliputian.
lima, *n.f.* (*bot.*) sweet lime, lime-tree; file; polish, finish; (*arch.*) hip; ***lima de uñas,*** nail-file; (*coll.*) ***comer como una lima,*** to eat one's head off.
limadura, *n.f.* filing, limature; (*pl.*) filings.
limalla, *n.f.* filings.
limar, *v.t.* to file (down); to polish, touch up; to undermine, eat away.
limatón, *n.m.* coarse round file, rasp.
limaza, *n.f.* slug.
limazo, *n.m.* viscosity, sliminess.
limbo, *n.m.* limbo; hem, edge; (*astron.*) limb, border of sun *or* moon; protractor; graduated arc of a sextant, theodolite etc.
limeño, -ña, *a.*, *n.m.f.* (native) of Lima.
limera, *n.f.* (*naut.*) helmport, rudder-hole; woman file-seller *or* lime-seller.
limero, *n.m.* man who sells files *or* limes; (*bot.*) sweet lime-tree.
limeta, *n.f.* vial, small flask *or* bottle.
límiste, *n.m.* cloth of Segovia wool.
limitación, *n.f.* limitation.
limitáneo, -nea, *a.* limitary, limitaneous, bounding.
limitar, *v.t.* to limit, bound, set bounds to.
límite, *n.m.* limit; bound, boundary, border.
limítrofe, *a.* limiting, bounding, bordering.
limo, *n.m.* slime, mud.
limón, *n.m.* lemon; lemon-tree; shaft, thill.
limonado, -da *a.* lemon, lemon-coloured. — *n.f.* lemonade; ***limonada purgante,*** citrate of magnesia; ***limonada de vino,*** wine lemonade.

limonar, *n.m.* lemon grove; (*Guat.*) lemon tree.
limoncillo, *n.m.* small lemon.
limonero, -ra, *a.* shaft (*horse*). — *n.m.* lemon tree; lemon dealer. — *n.f.* woman lemon-seller; shaft, thrill.
limosidad, *n.f.* sliminess; tartar.
limosna, *n.f.* alms.
limosnear, *v.t.* to give alms to. — *v.i.* to beg (*for alms*).
limosnero, -ra, *a.* alms-giving. — *n.m.* almoner; (*Hisp. Am.*) beggar. — *n.f.* alms-bag, alms-box.
limoso, -sa, *a.* slimy, muddy.
limpia, *n.f.* cleaning.
limpiabarros, *n.m. inv.* foot-scraper.
limpiabotas, *n.m. inv.* shoe-black, boot-black.
limpiachimeneas, *n.m. inv.* chimney-sweep.
limpiadera, *n.f.* clothes-brush; comb-brush; plough-cleaner.
limpiadientes, *n.m. inv.* toothpick.
limpiador, -ra, *a.* cleaning. — *n.m.f.* cleaner.
limpiadura, *n.f.* cleaning, cleansing; (*pl.*) dirt, scourings, cleanings.
limpiamiento, *n.m.* cleaning.
limpiaplumas, *n.m. inv.* penwiper.
limpiar, *v.t.* to clean, cleanse; to clear; to clean out; to clean up; to mop up; to wipe, wipe up, wipe over; to weed *or* prune.
limpiaúñas, *n.m. inv.* nail-cleaner.
limpidez, *n.f.* limpidity.
límpido, -da, *a.* limpid, crystal-clear.
limpieza, *n.f.* cleanness, cleanliness; cleaning; mopping up; neatness; fairness; purity.
limpio, -pia, *a.* clean; clear; neat; fair; pure; ***juego limpio,*** fair play; ***limpio de polvo y paja,*** net, clear; free. — *adv.* cleanly; fair; ***a codazo limpio,*** shoving one's way violently; ***a grito limpio,*** shouting *or* yelling one's head off; (*fig.*) ***estar limpio,*** not to have a clue; ***jugar limpio,*** to play fair *or* fairly; ***no he sacado nada en limpio,*** I can't make head or tail of it; ***pasar a limpio,*** to make a clean copy of, copy out; ***poner en limpio,*** to copy out; to get clear; ***sacar en limpio,*** to get clear, get straight.
limpión, *n.m.* quick clean *or* wipe-over.
linaje, *n.m.* lineage, race, family; (*fig.*) class, kind; ***linaje humano,*** mankind.
linajista, *n.m.f.* genealogist.
linajudo, -da, *a.* of high lineage *or* degree, of very long and noble family tradition.
lináloe, *n.m.* (*bot.*) aloe.
linao, *n.m.* (*Chi.*) hand-ball game.
linar, *n.m.* flax-field.
linaria, *n.f.* (*bot.*) wild flax, yellow toad-flax.
linaza, *n.f.* linseed, flax-seed.
lince, *a.*, *n.m.f.* keen, shrewd (*person*). — *n.m.* (*zool.*) lynx.
lincear, *v.t.* (*coll.*) to see (*sth. not easily seem*).
linceo, *a.* (*poet.*) lyncean, lyncine; keen (*sight*).
lincurio, *n.m.* semi-precious stone.
linchamiento, *n.m.* lynching.
linchar, *v.t.* to lynch.
lindante, *a.* adjoining, bordering, contiguous.
lindar, *v.i.* — ***con,*** to border, verge, be contiguous.
linde, *n.m.f.* boundary, limit.
lindero, -ra, *a.* contiguous, bordering. — *n.m.* limit, boundary.
lindeza, lindura, *n.f.* prettiness, neatness, beauty, elegance; (*pl.*) (*iron.*) insults.
lindo, -da, *a.* neat, handsome, pretty, nice, fine; ***de lo lindo,*** a great deal, like fury. — *n.m.* beau, coxcomb, dude.
lindón, *n.m.* ridge in garden (*for asparagus etc.*).
lindura [LINDEZA].
línea (1), *n.f.* line; boundary, limit; class, order; (*fort.*) trench; (*mil.*) file, rank; ***en toda la línea,*** thoroughly, all along the line; ***línea aérea,*** airline; (*naut.*) ***línea de agua*** or ***de flotación,*** water-line; ***línea de puntos,*** dotted line; ***línea férrea,*** railway; ***línea quebrada,*** broken line.
lineal, *a.* lineal, linear.
lineamento, lineamiento, *n.m.* lineament, feature.
linear, *a.* linear. — *v.t.* to draw lines on; to sketch, outline.
líneo, -nea (2), *a.* (*bot.*) linaceous.
linero, -ra, *a.* (pertaining to) flax *or* linen. — *n.m.f.* linen draper.
linfa, *n.f.* lymph; (*poet.*) water.
linfático, -ca, *a.* lymphatic.
linfatismo, *n.m.* (*path.*) lymphatism.
lingote, *n.m.* (*min.*) ingot, pig.
lingual, *a.* lingual.
lingue, *n.m.* (*Chi.*) tree of the genus Laurus.
linguete, *n.m.* (*naut.*) pawl (*of the capstan*), ratchet.
lingüista, *n.m.f.* linguist.
lingüístico, -ca, *a.* linguistic. — *n.f.* linguistics.
linimento, linimiento, *n.m.* (*med.*) liniment.
linio, *n.m.* row of plants.
lino, *n.m.* (*bot.*) flax; linen; (*poet.*) sail.
linóleo, *n.m.* linoleum.
linón, *n.m.* lawn (*fabric*).
linotipia, *n.f.* linotype.
lintel, *n.m.* lintel.
linterna, *n.f.* lantern, lamp; (*electric*) torch; (*mech.*) lantern-wheel; (*naut.*) lighthouse; (*arch.*) lantern; ***linterna eléctrica,*** torch, (*Am.*) flashlight; ***linterna mágica,*** magic lantern; ***linterna sorda,*** dark lantern; ***linterna delantera,*** headlight; ***linterna trasera*** or ***de cola,*** tail-light.
linternazo, *n.m.* blow with a lantern.
linternero, *n.m.* lantern-maker.
linternón, *n.m.* large lantern; (*naut.*) poop-lantern.
liño, *n.m.* row of plants *or* trees; ridge between furrows.
liñuelo, *n.m.* strand (*of rope* or *cord*).
lío, *n.m.* bundle, parcel; muddle, mess, mix-up; trouble; affair, liaison; ***armar un lío,*** to get things muddled up; to raise a rumpus, create a furore; ***hacerse*** or ***armarse un lío,*** to get all mixed up.
lionés, -nesa, *a.*, *n.m.f.* (native) of Lyons.
Liorna, *n.f.* Leghorn.
liorna, *n.f.* (*coll.*) uproar, confusion, hubbub.
lioso, -sa, *a.* trouble-making; awkward, troublesome. — *n.m.f.* trouble-maker.
lipemanía, *n.f.* (*med.*) melancholia.
lipemaníaco, *a.* (*med.*) melancholic.
lipes, lipis, *n.f.* blue vitriol.
lipiria, *n.f.* (*med.*) continuous *or* remittent fever.
lipotimia, *n.f.* (*med.*) lipothymy.
liquefacción, *n.f.* liquefaction.
liquen, *n.m.* (*bot.*) lichen.
liquidable, *a.* liquefiable; liquidatable.
liquidación, *n.f.* liquefaction; liquidation; settlement; (bargain) sale.
liquidador, -ra, *a.* liquefying. — *n.m.f.* liquefier; liquidator.
liquidámbar, *n.m.* liquidambar.
líquidamente, *adv.* in a liquid state *or* manner.
liquidar, *v.t.* to liquefy; to liquidate; to settle; (*coll.*) to polish off.
liquidez, *n.f.* liquidness, liquidity.
líquido, -da, *a.* liquid; (*com.*) net. — *n.m.* liquid; (*com.*) net amount *or* profit, net; ***líquido imponible,*** taxable net. — *n.f.* liquid (*consonant*).
lira (1), *n.f.* lyre; inspiration, poetry; a poetic metre; (*astron.*) Lyra.
lira (2), *n.f.* lira.
lirado, -da, *a.* lyrate, lyre-shaped.
liria, *n.f.* bird-lime.
lírico, -ca, *a.* lyric, lyrical. — *n.m.f.* lyric poet. — *n.f.* lyric poetry.

lirio, *n.m.* (*bot.*) lily; iris.
lirismo, *n.m.* lyricism.
lirón, *n.m.* (*zool.*) dormouse; (*naut.*) jack-screw; (*bot.*) water plantain; ***dormir como un lirón,*** to sleep like a log.
lirondo, -da, *a.* (*coll.*) ***mondo y lirondo,*** bare, with nothing more; pure and simple.
lis, *n.f.* fleur-de-lis, lily, iris.
lisa (1), *n.f.* (*ichth.*) striped mullet.
lisamente, *adv.* smoothly; plainly; ***lisa y llanamente,*** plainly and simply.
Lisboa, *n.f.* Lisbon.
lisbonés, -nesa, lisbonense, *a.*, *n.m.f.* (native) of Lisbon.
lisera, *n.f.* berm.
lisiado, -da, *a.* injured, hurt; lame, crippled. — *n.m.f.* cripple, maimed person.
lisiar, *v.t.* to cripple, maim; (*coll.*) to make a mess of, make (to) look a sight.
lisimaquia, *n.f.* (*bot.*) loosestrife.
liso, -sa (2), *a.* smooth; plain; ***liso y llano,*** plain and simple. — *n.m.* smooth face (*of rock*); polishing stone.
lisol, *n.m.* lysol.
lisonja, *n.f.* adulation, flattery; (*her.*) lozenge.
lisonjeador, -ra, *a.* flattering. — *n.m.f.* flatterer.
lisonjear, *v.t.* to flatter.
lisonjero, -ra, *a.* flattering; pleasing. — *n.m.f.* flatterer.
lista (1), *n.f.* list; strip; stripe; band; roll, muster; (*naut.*) muster-book; ***a listas,*** striped; ***lista civil,*** civil list; ***lista de correos,*** poste restante; ***lista de platos,*** menu, bill of fare; ***pasar lista,*** to call the roll.
listado, -da, listeado, -da, *a.* striped.
listel, *n.m.* (*arch.*) fillet, listel, tringle.
listo, -ta (2), *a.* ready, prepared; finished; clever; (*coll.*) ***pasarse de listo,*** to be too clever, be too clever by half.
listón, *n.m.* ribbon, ferret; (*carp.*) lath, cleat; (*arch.*) fillet, listel.
listonado, -da, *a.* (*carp.*) made of laths. — *n.m.* laths, lathing.
listonar, *v.t.* (*carp.*) to batten, lath.
listonería, *n.f.* narrow ribbons; laths, lathing; ribbon shop; ribbon factory.
listonero, -ra, *n.m.f.* ribbon-maker.
listura, *n.f.* smartness, quickness.
lisura, *n.f.* smoothness, evenness; glibness; candour, sincerity; (*Hisp. Am.*) impudent *or* shameless behaviour.
lita, *n.f.* tongue-worm (*in dogs*).
litación, *n.f.* sacrificing.
litar, *v.t.* to sacrifice to the Deity.
litarge, litargirio, *n.m.* litharge.
lite, *n.m.* lawsuit, trial.
litera, *n.f.* litter; (*naut.*) berth, bunk bed.
literal, *a.* literal.
literalista, *n.m.f.* literalist, one who adheres to the letter.
literario, -ria, *a.* literary.
literato, -ta, *a.* literary (*person*). — *n.m.f* littérateur, literary person, writer.
literatura, *n.f.* literature.
literero, *n.m.* litter maker, litter driver.
lítico, -ca, *a.* (*med.*) lithic.
litigación, *n.f.* litigation, lawsuit.
litigante, *a.*, *n.m.f.* litigating, litigant, party in a lawsuit.
litigar [B], *v.t.* to fight in law. — *v.i.* to contend, dispute.
litigio, *n.m.* litigation, lawsuit; contest, dispute.
litigioso, -sa, *a.* litigious, contentious.
litina, *n.f.* (*chem.*) oxide of lithium.
litio, *n.m.* (*chem.*) lithium.
litis, *n.f. inv.* lawsuit.
litisconsorte, *n.m.f.* associate in a lawsuit, joint litigant.
litiscontestación, *n.f.* (*law*) litiscontestation.
litisexpensas, *n.f.pl.* (*law*) costs of lawsuit.
litispendencia, *n.f.* state of a lawsuit under judgment.
litocálamo, *n.m.* fossil reed.
litoclasa, *n.f.* (*geol.*) fissure, lithoclase.
litocola, *n.f.* lithocolla, lapidary's cement.
litófago, -ga, *a.* rock-boring.
litófito, *n.m.* lithophyte; coral.
litografía, *n.f.* lithography.
litografiar [L], *v.t.* to lithograph.
litográfico, -ca, *a.* lithographic.
litógrafo, *n.m.* lithographist.
litología, *n.f.* lithology.
litológico, -ca, *a.* lithological.
litólogo, *n.m.* lithologist.
litoral, *a.* littoral. — *n.m.* coast, shore.
litontrípico, -ca, *a.*, *n.m.f.* lithontriptic.
litote, *n.f.* (*rhet.*) litotes.
litotomía, *n.f.* lithotomy.
litre, *n.m.* (*bot.*) lithi.
litro, *n.m.* litre.
Lituania, *n.f.* Lithuania.
lituano, -na, *a.*, *n.m.f.* Lithuanian (*person*). — *n.m.* Lithuanian (*language*).
liturgia, *n.f.* liturgy.
litúrgico, -ca, *a.* liturgic, liturgical.
liudo, -da, *a.* (*Chi., Col.*) fermented, leavened.
liviandad, *n.f.* lightness; fickleness; triviality; lewdness.
liviano, -na, *a.* light; fickle; trivial; lewd. — *n.m.* leading donkey; (*pl.*) lights, lungs.
lividez, *n.f.* lividity, lividness.
lívido, -da, *a.* livid.
livor, *n.m.* livid colour; (*fig.*) malignity, perversity; envy, hatred.
lixiviar, *v.t.* (*chem.*) to lixiviate.
liza, *n.f.* lists (*for jousts*); combat, contest; (*ichth.*) mullet.
lizo, *n.m.* skein (*of silk*), warp-thread, heddle.
lizón, *n.m.* (*bot.*) water-plantain.
lo (1) [LOF].
lo (2), *def. art., neut.* the, that which is etc.; ***a lo español,*** in the Spanish manner; ***¡con lo alegre que estaba!*** and he was feeling so cheerful (too!); ***lo antes posible,*** as soon *or* early as possible; ***lo bello,*** the beautiful, what is beautiful; ***lo francés,*** things French; ***lo malo es que,*** the trouble is that; ***lo rápido del viaje,*** the speed of the journey; ***no sabe lo difícil que es,*** he doesn't know how difficult it is; ***verás lo bien que habla,*** you'll see how well he speaks. — *pers. pron. m. and neut.* him, you, it; ***a lo que veo,*** from *or* to judge by what I (can) see; ***¿lo viste?*** did you see him *or* it?; ***parece mayor, pero no lo es,*** he looks older, but he isn't; ***ya te lo dije,*** I told you so. — *demons. pron.* that; ***lo de ayer,*** that business yesterday; ***lo de siempre,*** the same old thing *or* story; (*coll.*) ***lo que es yo,*** as far as I'm concerned; ***todo lo que tiene,*** all *or* everything he has.
loa, *n.f.* praise; (*naut.*) lee; prologue (*of a play*); short dramatic panegyric.
loable, *a.* laudable, praiseworthy.
loador, -ra, *a.* praising. — *n.m.f.* praiser.
loanda, *n.f.* scurvy.
loar, *v.t.* to praise, eulogize.
loba (1), *n.f.* she-wolf; gown, cassock; ridge between furrows; (*coll.*) whore.
lobado, -da, *a.* (*bot., zool.*) lobate.
lobanillo, *n.m.* wen; gall.
lobato, *n.m.* young wolf, wolf cub.

lobero, -ra, *a.* wolf, wolfish. — *n.m.* wolf hunter. — *n.f.* wolf thicket *or* lair.
lobezno, *n.m.* young wolf, wolf cub.
lobina, *n.f.* (*ichth.*) bass.
lobo (1), *n.m.* wolf; (*anat., bot.*) lobe; (*ichth.*) loach; (*fam.*) drunkenness; (*coll.*) ***coger*** or ***pillar un lobo,*** to get plastered *or* pie-eyed; ***dormir*** or ***desollar el lobo,*** to sleep it off, sleep off the booze; ***el lobo está en la conseja,*** there's a spy in the camp; ***lobo cerval*** or ***cervario,*** lynx; (*coll.*) ***lobo de mar,*** sea dog, old salt; ***lobo marino,*** seal; ***lobos de una camada,*** birds of a feather; ***verle las orejas al lobo,*** to see trouble coming.
lobo (2), **-ba** (2), *a.* (*Chi.*) shy, unsociable.
loboso, -sa, *a.* full of wolves.
lóbrego, -ga, *a.* dark, gloomy, murky, dingy.
lobreguecer [9], *v.t.* to darken. — *v.i.* to grow dark.
lobreguez, *n.f.* darkness, gloominess.
lóbulo, *n.m.* lobe, lobule.
lobuno, -na, *a.* wolfish.
locación, *n.f.* (*law*) lease; ***locación y conducción,*** agreement to let.
locador, -ra, locatario, -ria, *n.m.f.* (*Ven.*) landlord; lessor.
local, *a.* local. — *n.m.* place, premises.
localidad, *n.f.* locality; location; seat (*theatre etc.*).
localización, *n.f.* localization.
localizar [C], *v.t.* to localize; to locate, spot.
locatis, *n.m. inv.* (*coll.*) madcap, nut case.
locativo, -va, *a., n.m.f.* (*gram.*) locative.
loción, *n.f.* lotion; wash.
loco, -ca, *a.* mad, insane; huge, excessive; ***estar loco de remate*** or ***de atar,*** to be stark staring mad; ***volver loco a,*** to drive mad; ***volverse loco,*** to go mad; ***a lo loco,*** wildly, without forethought, recklessly; ***a tontas y a locas,*** wildly. — *n.m.f.* madman, madwoman; ***cada loco con su tema,*** everyone has some bee or other in his bonnet; ***hacerse el loco,*** to pretend not to hear *or* understand, not to take the hint; ***la loca de la casa,*** crazy imagination; ***más sabe el loco en su casa que el cuerdo en la ajena,*** everyone is the best judge of his own business; ***una vena de loco,*** a strain of madness.
locomoción, *n.f.* (*phys.*) locomotion.
locomotor, -ra, *a.* locomotive. — *n.f.* locomotive, railway engine.
locomotriz, *n.f.* locomotive.
locomóvil, *a.* portable, movable.
locro, *n.m.* (*Hisp. Am.*) stew.
locuacidad, *n.f.* loquacity, talkativeness.
locuaz, *a.* loquacious, talkative.
locución, *n.f.* locution, manner of speech; expression, phrase.
locuelo, -la, *a.* frisky, madcap (*youngster*). — *n.m.f.* young madcap.
locura, *n.f.* madness, lunacy, insanity; folly; ***con locura,*** madly; ***hacer locuras,*** to act madly; ***ataque de locura,*** fit of madness.
locutor, -ra, *n.m.f.* radio announcer.
locutorio, *n.m.* locutory parlour (*place in convents, monasteries and prisons for receiving visitors*); public telephone box *or* booth.
locha, *n.f.,* **loche,** *n.m.* (*ichth.*) loach.
lodachar, lodazal, lodazar, *n.m.* quagmire.
lodo, *n.m.* mud, mire; ***cerrar a piedra y lodo,*** to bolt and bar, shut fast *or* tight.
lodoñero, *n.m.* lignum vitae tree.
lodoso, -sa, *a.* muddy, miry.
lof, lo, *n.m.* (*naut.*) luff.
logarítmico, -ca, *a.* (*math.*) logarithmic, logarithmical.
logaritmo, *n.m.* logarithm.
logia, *n.f.* (freemason's) lodge; loggia.
lógicamente, *adv.* logically, it stands to reason; naturally, of course.
lógico, -ca, *a.* logical, that stands to reason. — *n.m.f.* logician. — *n.f.* logic.
logística, *n.f.* logistics.
logogrifo, *n.m.* logogryph.
logomaquia, *n.f.* logomachy.
logrado, -da, *a.* successful, well executed.
lograr, *v.t.* to get, achieve, attain; to do *or* carry out successfully. — **lograrse,** *v.r.* to be achieved *or* carried out successfully, succeed; ***lograron entrar,*** they succeeded in getting in, managed to get in.
logrear, *v.i.* to lend at interest.
logrería, *n.f.* dealing in interest; usury.
logrero, -ra, *n.m.f.* lender at interest; usurer; profiteer.
logro, *n.m.* gain, profit; interest; usury; achievement, attainment; ***dar a logro,*** to put out (*money*) at usury.
logrón, -rona, *a.* profiteering. — *n.m.f.* profiteer.
logroñés, -ñesa, *a., n.m.f.* (native) of Logroño.
loica, *n.f.* (*Chi.*) singing bird.
lojeño, -ña, *a., n.m.f.* (native) of Loja.
loma, *n.f.* hillock, rise, slope.
lombarda (1), *n.f.* lombard, siege gun; (*bot.*) red cabbage.
lombardada, *n.f.* shot from a lombard (*gun*).
lombardear, *v.t.* to discharge lombard guns.
lombardería, *n.f.* park of lombard guns.
lombardero, *n.m.* lombard soldier.
lombárdico, -ca, lombardo, -da (2), *a., n.m.f.* (native) of Lombardy, Lombard.
lombriguera, *n.f.* hole made by worms; (*bot.*) southern-wood.
lombriz, *n.f.* earthworm, worm; ***lombriz solitaria,*** tapeworm.
lombrizal, *a.* vermiform.
lomear, *v.i.* to buck (*of horses*).
lomento, *n.m.* (*bot.*) loment.
lomera, *n.f.* main strap (*of harness*); (*arch.*) ridge (*of a roof*); (*bookbinding*) backing.
lomiancho, -cha, *a.* broad-backed.
lomillo, *n.m.* (*sew.*) cross-stitch; (*pl.*) pads (*of a packsaddle*).
lominhiesto, -ta, *a.* with high loins; presumptuous, arrogant, stiff-necked.
lomo, *n.m.* loin; back; chine; spine (*of book*); double (*of a cloth, leather etc.*); crease; ridge (*between furrows*); ***a lomo(s),*** on the back; ***de tomo y lomo,*** out and out, dyed in the wool; (*pl.*) ribs, loins.
lomoso, -sa, *a.* belonging to the loins.
lomudo, -da, *a.* broad-backed.
lona, *n.f.* canvas.
loncha, *n.f.* slab, flagstone; slice (*of meat*).
londinense, *a.* of *or* belonging to London. — ***n.m.f.*** Londoner.
Londres, *n.m.* London.
londrina, *n.f.* London woollen cloth.
londro, *n.m.* galley-like vessel.
loneta, *n.f.* ravens-duck, sail-cloth.
longa, *n.f.* (*mus.*) long (*two breves*).
longanimidad, *n.f.* forbearance, longanimity.
longánimo, -ma, *a.* forbearing, longanimous.
longaniza, *n.f.* long pork sausage.
longar, *a.* long (*honeycomb*).
longevidad, *n.f.* longevity.
longevo, -va, *a.* longeval, long-lived.
longincuo, -cua, *a.* distant, remote.
longísimo, -ma, *a. superl.* [LUENGO], very long, longest.
longitud, *n.f.* length; longitude.
longitudinal, *a.* longitudinal.
longuera, *n.f.* long, narrow strip of land.
longuetas, *n.f.pl.* (*surg.*) bandages.

lonja, *n.f.* exchange (*place for trading*); store-room (*for wool*); warehouse; grocer's shop; (*arch.*) portico; slice (*of meat*); leather strap.
lonjero, *n.m.* grocer.
lonjeta, *n.f.* small slice; small strap; pergola, arbour.
lonjista, *n.m.f.* grocer.
lontananza, *n.f.* distance; background; ***en lontananza,*** far away, far off, in the distance.
loor, *n.m.* (*poet.*) praise.
lopigia, *n.f.* baldness, alopecia.
lopista, *a.* relative to Lope de Vega. — *n.m.f.* Lope scholar.
loquear, *v.i.* to act the fool, talk nonsense; to frolic.
loquería, *n.f.* (*Chi., Per.*) madhouse.
loquero, -ra, *n.m.f.* warder *or* orderly in a madhouse. — *n.f.* lunatic's cage *or* cell; madhouse; (*Hisp. Am.*) folly.
loquesca, *n.f.* frantic behaviour of mad people.
loquesto, -ta, *a.* reckless, foolish.
loquillo, -lla, loquito, -ta, *a.* [LOCUELO].
loquios, *n.m.pl.* (*med.*) lochia, loches.
lora, *n.f.* [LORO].
lorantáceo, -cea, *a.* (*bot.*) lauraceous.
lord, *n.m.* lord (*English title*); ***la Cámara de los lores,*** the House of Lords.
Lorena, *n.f.* Lorraine.
lorenzana, *n.f.* linen.
Lorenzo, *n.m.* Laurence, Lawrence.
loriga, *n.f.* lorica (*cuirass*); horse armour; (*mech.*) nave-band.
lorigado, -da, *a.* loricate.
loriguillo, *n.m.* (*bot.*) spurge laurel, mezereon.
loro, -ra, *a.* tawny, dark brown. — *n.m.* parrot; (*bot.*) cherry laurel. — *n.f.* (*Col., C.R., Hond., Per.*) parrot; (*Chi.*) female parrot.
lorонés, -nesa, *a., n.m.f.* (native) of Lorraine.
los, *def. art. m. pl.* the; *pers. pros. m. acc. pl.* them.
losa, *n.f.* flagstone, slab; gravestone.
losado [ENLOSADO].
losange, *n.m.* lozenge; diamond.
losar [ENLOSAR].
loseta, *n.f.* (small) flagstone *or* tile.
lota, *n.f.* (*prov.*) fish sold by auction; place where auction is held.
lote, *n.m.* lot; share; prize; (*Hisp. Am.*) plot of land; (*coll.*) ***darse un lote,*** to get a bellyful, have a real blow-out, have a good tuck in, enjoy a good session.
lotería, *n.f.* lottery; lotto; ***le ha caído*** or ***tocado la lotería,*** he has won a lottery prize; (*coll., iron.*) he's in for it (now); he'll have his work cut out, he's got his work cut out; (***esto***) ***es una lotería,*** it's anybody's guess, anything can *or* may (could *or* might) happen.
lotero, -ra, *n.m.f.* seller of lottery tickets.
lotización, *n.f.* (*Hisp. Am.*) housing estate.
loto, *n.m.* lotus; lotus-tree; lotus-flower.
lotófago, -ga, *a.* lotus-eating. — *n.m.f.* lotus-eater.
loxodromia, *n.f.* (*naut.*) loxodrome.
loxodrómico, -ca, *a.* (*naut.*) loxodromic.
loza, *n.f.* china, crockery, earthenware.
lozanear, *v.i.* to be luxuriant; to be blooming with health.
lozanía, *n.f.* luxuriance, exuberant growth; exuberance, blooming health.
lozano, -na, *a.* luxuriant; exuberant, blooming with health, buxom.
lúa, *n.f.* esparto glove (*for cleaning horses*); (*naut.*) lee; (*prov.*) saffron bag.
lubricación, *n.f.* lubrication.
lubricán, *n.m.* dawn (*of day*).
lubricante, lubrificante, *a.* lubricant, lubricating. — *n.m.* lubricant.
lubricar [A], **lubrificar** [A], *v.t.* to lubricate.
lubricativo, -va, *a.* lubricant, lubricative.
lubricidad, *n.f.* lubricity; slipperiness; lewdness.
lúbrico, -ca, *a.* lubricious; slippery; lewd.
lucencia, *n.f.* brightness.
lucentísimo, -ma, *a. superl.* extremely bright.
lucera, *n.f.* skylight.
lucerna, *n.f.* chandelier; skylight; (*ichth.*) flying gurnard.
lucérnula, *n.f.* (*bot.*) lucern, sainfoin.
lucero, *n.m.* star; bright star; morning *or* evening star; brightness; light hole; (*coll.*) dear, darling; (*poet.*) eye; ***decirle una fresca al lucero del alba,*** to be no respecter of persons.
Lucía, *n.f.* Lucy, Lucia.
lucidez, *n.f.* lucidity.
lúcido, -da, *a.* lucid, crystal-clear; bright.
lucido, -da, *a.* brilliant, highly successful, showing to good effect, splendid.
lucidura, *n.f.* whitewashing.
luciente, *a.* shining, bright.
luciérnaga, *n.f.* glow-worm, fire-fly.
lucifer, *n.m.* Lucifer; morning star.
luciferino, -na, *a.* Luciferian.
lucífero, -ra, *a.* (*poet.*) resplendent, shining, luciferous. — *n.m.* morning star.
lucífugo, -ga, *a.* that shuns the light.
lucillo, *n.m.* tomb, sarcophagus.
lucimiento, *n.m.* brilliance, lustre, splendour; great success; ***con lucimiento,*** with great success, brilliantly, making an excellent show.
lucio, -cia, *a.* lucid, clear, bright.
lucir [9], *v.t.* to show, display; to light up; to plaster. — *v.i.* to shine; to show to good effect. — **lucirse,** *v.r.* to put up an excellent show; to show off; (*iron.*) to make a botch, put one's foot in it, make a fool of o.s.
lucrarse, *v.r.* (*fig.*) to line one's pockets.
lucrativo, -va, *a.* lucrative, profitable.
lucro, *n.m.* gain, profit, lucre; (*com.*) ***lucros y daños,*** profit and loss.
lucroso, -sa, *a.* lucrative, profitable.
luctuosa (1), *n.f.* feudal death tax.
luctuoso, -sa (2), *a.* mournful; tragic.
lucubración, *n.f.* lucubration.
lucubrar, *v.i.* to lucubrate; to burn the midnight oil.
lúcuma, *n.f.* fruit of the lucumo tree.
lúcumo, *n.m.* (*Chi., Per.*) lucumo tree.
lucha, *n.f.* fight, struggle; wrestling; (*fig.*) toil, heavy grind; ***lucha libre,*** all-in wrestling.
luchador, -ra, *a.* struggling. — *n.m.* fighter; wrestler.
luchar, *v.i.* to fight, struggle; to wrestle.
lucharniego, -ga, *a.* night-hunting (*dog*).
luche, *n.m.* (*Chi.*) edible seaweed.
luchillo, *n.m.* (*naut.*) goring, goring-cloth.
ludia, *n.f.* (*prov.*) ferment, yeast.
ludiar(se), *v.t.* (*v.r.*) (*prov.*) to ferment.
ludibrio, *n.m.* mockery, scorn, derision.
ludimiento, *n.m.* friction, rubbing.
ludión, *n.m.* (*phys.*) Cartesian devil.
ludir, *v.t., v.i.* to rub, rub together.
lúe, *n.f.* infection.
luego, *adv.* then, next, afterwards; presently, later; (*obs.*) immediately, at once; ***luego de,*** after; ***luego que,*** as soon as; ***desde luego,*** from the outset; of course; ***hasta luego,*** so long, see you later. — *conj.* so, therefore.
luello, *n.m.* (*prov.*) bad seed (*growing among grain* or *corn*).
luengo, -ga, *a.* (*obs.*) long; far.
lugano, *n.m.* (*orn.*) linnet.
lugar, *n.m.* place, spot; room; village; occasion, chance; cause, reason; ***dar lugar a,*** to give rise to; ***dejar en mal lugar,*** to let down; ***en lugar de,*** instead of, in lieu of; ***en primer lugar,*** in the

first place; ***en su lugar,*** in his, your etc. place; instead; (*mil.*) ***en su lugar, descanso,*** stand at ease; ***en último lugar,*** in the last resort; ***fuera de lugar,*** out of place; ***hacer lugar a,*** to make room for; ***lugares comunes,*** common places; ***lugar excusado,*** privy-house, water-closet; ***no deja lugar a dudas,*** it leaves no room for doubt; (*law*) ***no ha lugar,*** the petition is not granted; ***tener lugar,*** to take place.

lugarejo, *n.m.* wretched *or* miserable place *or* village.

lugareño, -ña, *a.* village. — *n.m.f.* villager, local.

lugarón, lugarote, *n.m.* ugly, overgrown *or* sprawling place *or* village.

lugartenencia, *n.f.* lieutenancy.

lugarteniente, *n.m.* deputy; lieutenant.

lugre, *n.m.* (*naut.*) lugger.

lúgubre, *a.* mournful, lugubrious, gloomy, dismal, dreary.

luir [O], *v.i.* (*naut.*) to gall, be galled *or* fretted, wear away by friction.

Luis, *n.m.* Louis, Lewis.

Luisa, *n.f.* Louise.

luisa, *n.f.* (*bot.*) lemon verbena.

lujación, *n.f.* (*surg.*) luxation.

lujar, *v.t.* (*Hisp. Am.*) to rub; to shine. — **lujarse,** *v.r.* to become luxated.

lujo, *n.m.* luxury; ***de lujo,*** de luxe, luxury; ***gastar mucho lujo,*** to live in great luxury *or* great style; ***lujo de,*** abundance of.

lujoso, -sa, *a.* luxurious.

lujuria, *n.f.* lust, lechery.

lujuriante, *a.* luxuriant, exuberant.

lujuriar, *v.i.* to lust, be lecherous; to couple (*of animals*).

lujurioso, -sa, *a.* lustful, lecherous.

luliano, -na, *a., n.m.f.* Lullian.

lulismo, *n.m.* system of Ramón Lull.

lumaquela, *n.f.* fire-marble.

lumbago, *n.m.* (*med.*) lumbago.

lumbar, *a.* lumbar, lumbal.

lumbrada, lumbrerada, *n.f.* great fire, fierce conflagration.

lumbre, *n.f.* fire; light; splendour, brightness; skylight; hammer (*of a flint-lock*); forepart (*of a horseshoe*); ***a lumbre de pajas,*** like a flash; ***ni por lumbre,*** not by a long shot, nothing like it; by no means; ***la lumbre de mis ojos,*** the apple of my eye; (*pl.*) tinder-box.

lumbrera, *n.f.* luminary; skylight, light shaft; vent, air duct; (*fig.*) leading light.

lumen, *n.m.* (*phys.*) lumen.

luminar, *n.m.* luminary.

luminaria, *n.f.* illumination, light(s).

lumínico, -ca, *a.* (of) light, lighting.

luminiscencia, *n.f.* luminescence.

luminiscente, *a.* luminescent.

luminoso, -sa, *a.* luminous; bright.

lumpo jibado, *n.m.* (*ichth.*) lump.

luna, *n.f.* moon; moonlight; plate glass, glass plate, mirror plate; glass, lens; (*ichth.*) moonfish; ***media luna,*** half moon, crescent (*moon*); ***luna de miel,*** honeymoon; ***quedarse a la luna de Valencia,*** to be none the wiser; ***estar de buena*** or ***mala luna,*** to be in a good *or* bad mood; ***tener lunas,*** to be moody.

lunación, *n.f.* lunation, revolution of the moon.

lunada (1), *n.f.* (*obs.*) ham, gammon.

lunado, -da (2), *a.* lunated, crescent-shaped.

lunanco, -ca, *a.* having one hind-quarter higher than the other (*horses etc.*)

lunar, *a.* lunar. — *n.m.* mole, beauty spot; flaw, blemish; (*pl.* **lunares**) polka dots.

lunarejo, -ja, *a.* (*Arg., Col., Per.*) having spots (*of animals*); having moles (*of persons*).

lunario, -ria, *a.* (pertaining to) lunation; lunarian, of the moon. — *n.m.* calendar.

lunático, -ca, *a., n.m.f.* lunatic, moonstruck (person).

lunecilla, *n.f.* crescent, crescent-shaped jewel.

lunes, *n.m. inv.* Monday; ***lunes de Carnaval,*** Shrove Monday.

luneta, *n.f.* lens, glass (*of spectacles*); lunette (*crescent-shaped ornament*); (*arch., fort.*) lunette; (*theat.*) stall; front tile (*in a roof*).

luneto, *n.m.* (*arch.*) lunette.

lunfardo, *n.m.* (*Arg.*) thief; underworld slang.

lunisolar, *a.* (*astron.*) lunisolar.

lunista, *n.m.* lunatic, madman.

lúnula, *n.f.* half-moon-shaped geometrical figure, lune; (*opt.*) meniscus.

lupanar, *n.m.* brothel.

lupia, *n.f.* (*med.*) cyst, wen.

lupino, -na, *a.* wolfish. — *n.m.* (*bot.*) lupin.

lúpulo, *n.m.* (*bot.*) hops.

lupus, *n.m.* (*med.*) lupus.

luquete, *n.m.* slice of orange dropped into wine; match, firebrand.

luquetera, *n.f.* match-girl.

Lurdes, *n.f.* Lourdes.

lurte, *n.m.* avalanche.

lusitanismo, *n.m.* Lusitanism, Portuguese idiom.

lusitano, -na, *a., n.m.f.* Lusitanian.

lustración, *n.f.* lustration.

lustrador, *n.m.* hot-press, mangler; polisher.

lustrar, *v.t.* to lustrate, purify; to polish, shine.

lustre, *n.m.* lustre; shine; shoe-polish.

lústrico, -ca, *a.* (*poet.*) lustral.

lustrina, *n.f.* lustring; (*Chi.*) shoeblacking.

lustro, *n.m.* lustrum, five-year period; chandelier.

lustroso, -sa, *a.* lustrous, shiny, glossy.

lutación, *n.f.* (*chem.*) lutation.

lútea (1), *n.f.* (*orn.*) golden oriole.

lúten, *n.m.* (*chem.*) lute.

lúteo, -tea (2), *a.* muddy, miry.

luteranismo, *n.m.* Lutheranism.

luterano, -na, *a., n.m.f.* Lutheran.

Lutero, *n.m.* Luther.

luto, *n.m.* mourning, grief, bereavement; ***estar*** or ***ir de luto,*** to be in mourning; (*pl.*) mourning drapery *or* clothes.

lutocar, *n.m.* (*Chi.*) refuse cart.

Luxemburgo, *n.m.* Luxembourg.

luxemburgués, -gesa, *a.* (of) Luxembourg. — *n.m.f.* Luxemburger.

luz, *n.f.* light; daylight; (*arch.*) span; light shaft; window, opening; ***a la luz de estos hechos,*** in the light of these facts, in view of these facts; ***a la luz del día,*** in the light of day, in broad daylight, openly; ***arrojar luz sobre,*** to cast *or* throw light on; ***a todas luces,*** clearly, evidently; ***dar a luz,*** to give birth; ***dar la luz,*** to put the light on; ***entre dos luces,*** at twilight, at dusk; at dawn, at day-break; ***luz de la razón,*** light of reason; ***llegamos con luz,*** we arrived while it was still light; ***rayar la luz,*** to dawn, break (*of day*); ***sacar a luz,*** to bring out, publish; ***salir a luz,*** to come out; ***ver la luz,*** to appear, come out; to be born; (*pl.* **luces**) ***el siglo de las luces, las luces,*** the Age of Reason, the Enlightenment.

Luzbel, *n.m.* Lucifer.

LL

Ll, ll, *n.f.* letter Ll, ll.

llábana, *n.f.* (*prov.*) smooth and slippery flagstone.

llaca, *n.f.* (*Arg., Chi.*) opossum.

llaga, *n.f.* sore, wound; ulcer; seam (*in masonry*); ***poner el dedo en la llaga,*** to put a finger on the *or* a sore spot, get on the raw; ***renovar la llaga,*** to open an old sore.

llagar, *v.t.* to make sore, ulcerate; to hurt, wound.

llama, *n.f.* flame; marshy ground; (*zool.*) llama.

llamadera, *n.f.* goad-stick.

llamado, -da, *a.* so-called. — *n.f.* call; calling; summons; knock, ring; sign, signal; reference mark; (*mil.*) chamade; ***llamada al servicio militar,*** conscription, (*Am.*) draft.

llamador, -ra, *n.m.f.* caller, one who calls; messenger; knocker (*of a door* or *at a door, if person is meant*); push button.

llamamiento, *n.m.* calling; call; summons; appeal; attraction of humours to one part of the body.

llamar, *v.t.* to call; to call upon, summon, invoke, appeal to; to name, term; to attract; ***llamar a filas,*** to call up (*for military service*); ***estar llamado a,*** to be destined *or* fated to; ***llamar la atención,*** to attract attention; ***llamar la atención a,*** to call to book, pull up (*for a misdemeanour*). — *v.i.* to knock; to ring; (*naut.*) to veer. — **llamarse,** *v.r.* to be called; ***¿cómo te llamas?*** what is your name?

llamarada, *n.f.* blaze; flash; flush, sudden blush; flare-up, outburst.

llamarón, *n.m.* (*Chi., Col., C.R.*) [LLAMARADA].

llamativo, -va, *a.* showy, flashy, loud.

llamazar, *n.m.* marsh, swamp.

llambria, *n.f.* steep face (*of a rock*).

llana, *n.f.* [LLANO].

llanada, *n.f.* plain, flat land, level ground.

llanamente, *adv.* simply, plainly, in a straightforward way.

llanca, *n.f.* (*Chi.*) bluish-green copper ore.

llanero, -ra, *n.m.f.* (*Hisp. Am.*) plainsman, plainswoman.

llaneza, *n.f.* simplicity; straightforwardness.

llano, -na, *a.* flat; plain; straightforward; (*gram.*) stressed on the penultimate syllable; ***canto llano,*** plain chant, plainsong; ***en canto llano,*** quite simply; ***de llano,*** plainly, openly; ***a (la pata) la llana,*** in a straightforward manner; ***estado llano,*** commons, common people. — *n.m.f.* plain, flat ground. — *n.f.* trowel; page of a book.

llanque, *n.m.* (*Per.*) sandal (*made of untanned leather*).

llanta, *n.f.* hoop, band (*of a wheel*); (*motor.*) rim; (*Hisp. Am.*) tyre; cabbage.

llantén, *n.m.* (*bot.*) plaintain, rib grass; ***llantén de agua,*** water plaintain, alisura.

llantería, *n.f.* (*Chi.*) general weeping.

llantina, *n.f.* fit of weeping.

llanto, *n.m.* crying, weeping, flood of tears; lament.

llanura, *n.f.* evenness, flatness; plain, flat land.

llapa, *n.f.* (*min.*) quicksilver.

llapar, *v.t.* to add quicksilver to.

llar, *n.m.* (*prov.*) [LAR]; *n.f.pl.* (**llares**) pot-hanger, chain with pot-hooks.

llatar, *n.m.* (*prov.*) fence with posts and railings.

llaullau, *n.m.* (*Chi.*) mushroom.

llave, *n.f.* key; wrench, spanner; water-cock; gunlock; clock winder; (*naut.*) knee; (*print.*) brace; piston (*of musical instrument*); hold, grip; ***llave maestra,*** master key, pass key; ***echar la llave,*** to lock; ***bajo llave,*** under lock and key; ***llave de paso,*** stop cock; ***llave de tuerca,*** set-screw spanner; ***llave inglesa,*** monkey wrench; ***llave de la mano,*** span of the hand; ***llave del pie,*** distance from heel to instep.

llavero, -ra, *n.m.f.* keeper of the keys; key-ring.

llavín, *n.m.* latch key.

lleco, -ca, *a.* virgin (*soil*).

llega, *n.f.* (*prov.*) gathering, collecting.

llegada, *n.f.* arrival, coming; ***a la llegada,*** on arrival.

llegar [B], *v.i.* to arrive, come, reach; to be enough, last; (*coll.*) to get there, be successful, make it; ***llegará un día en que,*** a time will come when; ***llegar hasta,*** to go as far as *or* as high as; ***no nos llega para vivir,*** it is not enough for us to live on; we haven't enough to live on; ***llegó a afirmar que,*** he went so far as to declare that; ***llegar a comprender,*** to come to understand *or* realize; ***llegar a ser,*** to become; ***llegar a más,*** to go up in the world; to go further; ***estar al llegar,*** to be about to arrive, due to arrive immediately *or* at any time (now); ***hasta ahí podíamos*** or ***podríamos llegar,*** that is *or* would be a fine thing, that is *or* would be the limit; ***llegar y topar, llegar y besar el santo,*** to strike lucky from the outset; ***llegar a las manos,*** to come to blows; ***no le llega la camisa al cuerpo,*** he is scared stiff, frightened out of his wits; ***llegar lejos,*** to go far (in the world). — **llegarse,** *v.r.* to draw near, come *or* go up (to); to pop *or* nip round (*to see s.o.*).

lleivún, *n.m.* (*Chi.*) bulrush.

llena, *n.f.* [LLENO].

llenar, *v.t.* to fill, fill in, fill up, fill out; to cover; to satisfy, content; to meet, comply with; (*fig.*) to overwhelm. — *v.i.* to be full (*of moon*). — **llenarse,** *v.r.* to fill, fill up; to get filled *or* covered; (*coll.*) to get fed up.

llenazo, *n.m.* packed house (*cine. theat.*).

llene, *n.m.* filling, filling up.

llenero, -ra, *a.* (*law*) full, complete, absolute.

llenito, -ta, *a.* plump(ish), nice and plump *or* chubby.

lleno, -na, *a.* full, full up; covered; complete; ***lleno de,*** full of; covered in; ***de lleno,*** fully, wholly, completely. — *n.m.* fill, plenty, abundance, perfection, completeness; fullness (*of the moon*); (*theat.*) full house. — *n.f.* overflow, flood.

llenura, *n.f.* fullness, plenty, abundance.

lleta, *n.f.* sprout, stalk.

lleudar, *v.t.* to leaven, ferment with leaven.

lleulle, *a.* (*Chi.*) inept, incompetent.

lleva, llevada, *n.f.* carriage, transport, means of carrying.

llevadero, -ra, *a.* tolerable, bearable.

llevador, -ra, *n.m.f.* carrier.

llevar, *v.t.* to carry, convey; to take; to take away, carry away; to lead; to bear; to wear; to keep (*accounts etc.*); to deal with; to charge; to cut off, sever; to manage; to have spent *or* been for (*a period of time*); ***llevar adelante,*** to carry on, keep up *or* going; ***llevar a cabo,*** to carry out *or* through; ***llevar calabazas,*** to get jilted *or* ploughed; ***llevar el compás,*** to keep time; ***llevar una caída,*** to get a fall; ***llevar la corriente a,*** to humour, keep happy, go along with; ***llevar la contraria a,*** to contradict, thwart, go against; ***llevar la cuenta (de),*** to keep an account (of), keep track (of); ***llevar la delantera,*** to lead, be in the lead; ***llevar a la práctica,*** to put into practice; ***llevar a cuestas,*** to carry on one's back *or* shoulders; ***lleva trabajando aquí mucho tiempo,*** he has been working here for a long time; ***llevo tres años aquí,*** I have been here three years; ***Juan me lleva tres años,*** John is three years older than I am; (*coll.*) ***lo llevaba bien estudiado,*** he had mugged it up well (beforehand). — **llevarse,** *v.r.* to take away; ***se lleva bien con su hermano,*** he gets on well with his brother;

llevarse una sorpresa, to get a surprise; ***te vas a llevar un chasco,*** you're in for a disappointment; ***llevarse la mejor parte,*** to take the biggest share.

lloica, *n.f.* (*Chi.*, *orn.*) robin readbreast.

lloradera, *n.f.* (*coll.*) blubber, weeping.

llorado, *n.m.* (*Col.*, *Ven.*) popular song of the Llaneros.

llorador, -ra, *a.* weeping. — *n.m.f.* weeper.

lloraduelos, *n.m. inv.* (*coll.*) weeper, moaner.

llorar, *v.t.*, *v.i.* to weep, cry; to lament, bewail one's lot; (*of eyes*) to water; to drip; ***quien bien te quiere, te hará llorar,*** he loves thee well that makes thee weep.

lloriquear, *v.t.* to whimper, snivel.

lloro, *n.m.* weeping, crying.

llorón, -rona, *a.* weepy. — *n.m.f.* cry baby; (one) much given to weeping and whining; ***sauce llorón,*** weeping willow. — *n.f.* hired mourner.

lloroso, -sa, *a.* tearful.

lloso, *n.f.* (*prov.*) enclosed estate.

llovediza, *a.* leaky; ***agua llovediza,*** rainwater.

llover [5], *v. impers.* to rain; ***llover a cántaros,*** to bucket with rain; ***llover chuzos,*** to rain cats and dogs, rain pitchforks; ***llueve sobre mojado,*** it isn't the first time; ***como quien oye llover,*** not paying the slightest attention; ***como llovido del cielo,*** out of the blue; ***a secas y sin llover,*** without preparation *or* warning; ***llueva o no*** (***llueva***), rain or shine. — **lloverse,** *v.r.* to leak (*of roofs*).

llovido, *n.m.* stowaway.

llovizna, *n.f.* drizzle.

lloviznar, *v. impers.* to drizzle.

llueca, *n.f.* brooding hen.

lluqui, *a.* (*Ec.*) left-handed.

lluvia, *n.f.* rain; (*fig.*) shower, flood.

lluvioso, -sa, *a.* rainy, wet.

M

M, m, *n.f.* letter M, m.
mabinga, *n.f.* (*Cub., Mex.*) inferior tobacco.
maca, *n.f.* bruise (*in fruit*); flaw, blemish; spot, stain; fraud, trick, deceit.
Macabeos, Libro(s) de los, *n.m.* Book(s) of the Maccabees.
macabro, -ra, *a.* macabre, gruesome.
macaco, -ca, *a.* (*Hisp. Am.*) ugly, misshapen. — *n.m.f.* monkey, macaque.
macadam, macadán, *n.m.* macadam.
macadamizar [C], *v.t.* to macadamize.
macagua, *n.f.* (*Ven.*) poisonous snake; (*Cub.*) macaw tree; (*orn.*) South American hawk.
macagüita, *n.f.* (*Ven.*) thorny palm tree.
macana, *n.f.* (*Hisp. Am.*) wooden sword *or* club; drug on the market; trick, lie; botch, bungle; nonsense, rubbish, piece of nonsense *or* rubbish.
macanazo, *n.m.* blow with a cudgel; (piece of) utter rubbish.
macano, *n.m.* (*Chi.*) dark dye.
macanudo, -da, *a.* (*coll.*) fine, dandy, first rate, smashing.
macareno, -na, *a.* of La Macarena (*Seville*); (*coll.*) bragging, boasting; gaudily dressed.
macarrón, *n.m.* piece of macaroni; macaroon; (*pl.* **macarrones**) macaroni; (*naut.*) stanchions.
macarronea, *n.f.* macaronics.
macarrónico, -ca, *a.* macaronic; (*coll.*) ghastly, frightful; (***un***) ***latín macarrónico,*** an apology for Latin.
macarronismo, *n.m.* macaronic style (*of poetry*).
macarse [A], *v.r.* to rot, be spoiled by a bruise *or* fall (*of fruit*).
macaurel, *n.f.* (*Ven.*) snake.
macazuchil, *n.m.* (*Mex.*) plant used to flavour chocolate.
maceador, *n.m.* beater, hammerer, mauler.
macear, *v.t.* to beat, hammer, pound, soften up. — *v.i.* to keep *or* harp on.
macedónico, -ca, macedonio, -nia, *a., n.m.f.* Macedonian.
macelo, *n.m.* slaughterhouse, abattoir.
maceración, *n.f.,* **maceramiento,** *n.m.* maceration, softening up; mortification.
macerar, *v.t.* to macerate, soften; to mortify.
macerina, *n.f.* saucer.
macero, *n.m.* mace-bearer.
maceta, *n.f.* (small) mace, mallet *or* maul; (*stonecutter's*) hammer; flower-pot; flower-vase; handle (*of a stick* or *tool*); haunch (*of mutton*).
macetero, *n.m.* flower-pot stand.
macia [MACIS].
macicez, *n.f.* solidity.
macilento, -ta, *a.* pallid, wan.
macillo, *n.m.* hammer (*of a piano*).
macis, *n.f.* mace (*kind of spice*).
macizar [C], *v.t.* to fill up, fill in, make solid.
macizo, -za, *a.* solid; massive. — *n.m.* flower bed; clump; mass; massif; bulk; (*build.*) solid wall. — *n.f.* (*fam.*) gorgeous bird, (*Am.*) broad.
macla, *n.f.* (*bot.*) water-caltrops; wooden flail.
macle, *n.m.* (*her.*) mascle.
macolla, *n.f.* bunch, cluster.
macón, *n.m.* dry brown honeycomb.
macona, *n.f.* basket without handles, hamper.
macrocefalia, *n.f.* macrocephalism, macrocephalia.
macrocéfalo, -la, *a.* macrocephalous.
macrocosmo, *n.m.* macrocosm.
macsura, *n.f.* reserved precinct in a mosque.
macuache, *n.m.* (*Mex.*) ignorant; illiterate Indian.
macuba, *n.f.* maccaboy (*Martinique tobacco*).
macuca (1), *n.f.* (*bot.*) wild pear, wild pear-tree.
macuco, -ca (2), *a.* (*Chi.*) cunning, sly. — *n.m.* (*Arg.*) overgrown boy.
mácula, *n.f.* stain, spot, blemish; (*astron.*) macula.
macular, *v.t.* (*print.*) to mackle; to stain, spot, mark.
maculatura, *n.f.* (*print.*) spoiled sheet.
maculoso, -sa, *a.* full of spots, stains, *or* blemishes.
macún, macuñ, *n.m.* (*Chi.*) poncho.
macuquero, *n.m.* unlawful worker of abandoned mines.
macuquino, -na, *a.* cut, clipped, edgeless (*of coin*).
macurije, *n.m.* (*Cub.*) medicinal tree (*Cupania opposifolia*).
macuteno, *n.m.* (*Mex.*) petty thief.
macuto, *n.m.* alms basket; (*mil.*) knapsack.
macha, *n.f.* (*Chi.*) edible sea mollusc.
machaca, *n.m.f.* (*coll.*) bore, tiresome person.
machacadera, *n.f.* instrument for pounding, crushing *or* breaking.
machacador, -ra, *a.* pounding, crushing. — *n.m.f.* pounder, crusher. — *n.f.* crushing machine.
machacante, *n.m.* sergeant's attendant; (*coll.*) 5-peseta coin.
machacar [A], *v.t., v.i.* to pound, crush, mash. — *v.i.* to harp on a subject, keep on and on.
machacón, -cona, *a.* importunate, monotonous, boring. — *n.m.f.* bore.
machaconería, *n.f.* tiresome insistence, tiresomeness.
machada, *n.f.* flock of he-goats; (*coll.*) stupidity.
machado, *n.m.* hatchet.
machaje, *n.m.* (*Arg., Chi.*) herd of male animals.
machamartillo, *adv.* ***a* —,** firmly, strongly, solidly; ***creer en Dios a machamartillo,*** to be a steadfast believer in God.
machango, *a.* (*Cub.*) coarse, unpolished.
machaqueo, *n.m.* pounding, crushing.
machar, *v.t.* to pound.
machear, *v.i.* to beget more males than females (*of animals*).
machera, *n.f.* cork-tree plantation.
machetazo, *n.m.* blow *or* cut with a machete.
machete, *n.m.* machete, matchet, cutlass.
machetear, *v.t.* to wound with a cutlass. — *v.i.* (*Col.*) to wrangle.
machetero, *n.m.* one who clears ground with a machete; sugar-cane cutter; (*Hisp. Am., coll.*) sabre rattler.
machi, *n.m.f.* (*Chi.*) quack, healer.
máchica, *n.f.* (*Per.*) toasted maize flower.
machihembrado, *n.m.* (*carp.*) dovetailing.
machihembrar, *v.t.* (*carp.*) to dovetail, feather, mortise.
machina, *n.f.* crane, derrick; pile-driver.
machinete, *n.m.* (*prov.*) chopping-knife.
machismo, *n.m.* glorification of masculinity; belief in male supremacy.
macho, *n.m.* male; (*engin.*) male piece *or* part; tap, screw tap; hook (*to catch hold in an eye*); bolt (*of a lock*); (*arch.*) spur, buttress, abutment; (*mech.*) sledge hammer; block (*in which an anvil is fixed*); mould (*for bells*); square anvil; (*coll.*) blockhead; (*naut.*) ***machos del timón,*** rudder-pintles; ***macho cabrío,*** he-goat.
machón, *n.m.* (*arch.*) buttress; pillar.
machorra, *n.f.* barren female.
machota, *n.f.* maul, mallet; (*coll.*) mannish woman.
machote, *n.m.* hammer; (*coll.*) (real) he-man, tough guy.
machucadura, *n.f.,* **machucamiento,** *n.m.* pounding; crushing; bruising.
machucar [A], *v.t.* to pound; to crush; to bruise.
machucho, -cha, *a.* mature; elderly; level-headed.

machuelo, *n.m.* small he-mule; heart (*of an onion*); clove (*of garlic*).
machuno, -na, *a.* mannish.
madama, *n.f.* madam.
madamisela, *n.f.* affected young lady.
madeja, *n.f.* hank, skein; shock (*of hair*); (*coll.*) slovenly fellow; ***madeja sin cuenda,*** hopeless tangle; muddlehead; sloppy fellow; ***hacer madeja,*** to go ropy, go off (*wine*); ***enredarse la madeja,*** to become involved.
madera (1), *n.m.* madeira wine.
madera (2), *n.f.* wood; timber; lumber; piece of wood, wooden part; horny part (*of hoof*); ***¡toca madera!*** touch wood! ***descubrir la madera,*** to show one's true colours; ***saber a la madera,*** to be a chip off the old block; ***tener madera de,*** to have the makings of, be made of the right stuff for.
maderada, *n.f.* lumber (floated downstream).
maderaje, maderamen, *n.m.* timber, timber work.
maderar, *v.t.* to plank, timber.
maderería, *n.f.* timber-yard, lumber-yard.
maderero, -ra, *a.* (of) wood, (of) timber. — *n.m.* timber-merchant, lumber-dealer; carpenter.
maderista, *n.m.* lumberman.
madero, *n.m.* beam; piece of timber; (*coll.*) block-head; (*fig.*) ship, vessel.
madrastra, *n.f.* step-mother; bad mother.
madraza, *n.f.* (*coll.*) doting mother.
madre, *n.f.* mother; bed (*of a river*); main sewer; main ditch; main piece; lees, dregs; ***madre de leche,*** wet nurse; ***salirse de madre,*** to overflow the banks; (*fig.*) to go beyond bounds, go too far, overdo it; ***ésta es la madre del cordero,*** this is the real reason; ***son (el) ciento y la madre,*** there's a whole mob of them; ***madre política,*** mother-in-law.
madrearse, *v.r.* to become *or* turn sour (*applied to wines* or *liquors*).
madrecilla, *n.f.* ovarium of birds.
madrecita, *n.f.* dear *or* darling mother.
madreclavo, *n.m.* clove of two years' growth.
madreperla, *n.f.* mother-of-pearl, pearl-oyster.
madrépora, *n.f.* madrepore, white coral.
madrero, -ra, *a.* (*coll.*) fondling, caressing a mother; attached to one's mother.
madreselva, *n.f.* (*bot.*) honeysuckle.
madrigada (1), *a.* twice married (*of a woman*).
madrigado, -da (2), *a.* bull that has been a sire; (*fig.*) practical, experienced.
madrigal, *n.m.* madrigal.
madrigaleja, *n.f.,* **madrigalete,** *n.m.* short madrigal.
madriguera, *n.f.* den; lurking-place; warren.
madrileño, -ña, *a., n.m.f.* (native) of Madrid.
madrilla, *n.f.* (*prov., ichth.*) small river-fish.
madrillera, *n.f.* (*prov.*) instrument for catching small fish.
madrina, *n.f.* godmother; patroness; prop, stanchion; straps *or* cords yoking two horses; (*Ven.*) small herd.
madrona, *n.f.* (*coll.*) mother who spoils her children; main irrigating ditch; (*bot.*) clandestine toothwort.
madroncillo, *n.m.* strawberry.
madroñal, *n.m.,* **madroñera,** *n.f.* grove of strawberry trees.
madroñero, *n.m.* (*bot.*) strawberry tree.
madroñito, *n.m.* small strawberry tree.
madroño, *n.m.* strawberry tree; strawberry fruit; silk tassel.
madrugada, *n.f.* early morning, small hours; ***de madrugada,*** in the small hours.
madrugador, -ra, *a.* early rising. — *n.m.f.* early riser.
madrugar [B], *v.i.* to rise *or* get up early; (*fig.*) to get a head-start; ***a quien madruga Dios le ayuda,*** the early bird catches the worm; ***no por mucho madrugar amanece más temprano,*** more haste, less speed.
madrugón, -gona, *a.* early rising. — *n.m.* rising very early; ***darse*** or ***pegarse un madrugón,*** to get up very early, at an ungodly hour.
maduración, *n.f.* ripeness, maturity.
maduradero, *n.m.* place for ripening fruits.
madurador, -ra, *n.m.f.* that which matures *or* ripens.
madurante, *a.* maturing, ripening.
madurar, *v.t.* to ripen, mature, mellow; (*med.*) to maturate. — *v.i.* to ripen, grow ripe, mature; (*med.*) to suppurate perfectly. — **madurarse,** *v.r.* to ripen, grow ripe.
madurativo, -va, *a.* maturative. — *n.m.* sth. that matures; (*med.*) maturant; means employed to make a person grant a request.
madurez, *n.f.* maturity, mellowness, ripeness; prudence, wisdom.
madurillo, -lla, *a,* beginning to ripen.
maduro, -ra, *a.* ripe; mature; middle-aged.
maese, *n.m.* (*obs.*) master.
maesillas, *n.f.pl.* cords (*used in making passementerie to raise* or *lower the skeins*).
maestra, *n.f.* [MAESTRO].
maestral, *a.* relating to a grand master (*of a military order*); north-west (*wind*). — ***n.m.*** cell (*of the queen-bee*).
maestralizar [C], *v.i.* (*naut.*) to decline to north-west.
maestramente, *adv.* dexterously, skilfully.
maestrante, *n.m.* member of a ***maestranza.***
maestranza, *n.f.* order *or* fraternity of knights *or* noblemen skilled in riding; dock-yard, naval storehouse, arsenal, armoury.
maestrazgo, *n.m.* dignity *or* jurisdiction of the grand-master (*of a military order*).
maestre, *n.m.* master (*of a military order*); (*naut.*) master, ship-master.
maestrear, *v.t.* to direct, conduct; to lop, trim, prune. — *v.i.* to behave domineeringly.
maestreescuela, maestrescuela, *n.m.* cathedral canon.
maestresala, *n.m.* chief waiter (*at a nobleman's table*).
maestría, *n.f.* mastery; mastership.
maestril, *n.m.* queen cell (*of beehives*).
maestro, -ra, *a.* master, main, chief; trained; ***abeja maestra,*** queen bee; ***llave maestra,*** master key; ***obra maestra,*** masterpiece; ***pared maestra,*** main wall; ***perro maestro,*** trained dog. — *n.m.* master; teacher; maestro; (*naut.*) mainmast; ***maestro de armas,*** fencing master; ***maestro de capilla,*** choirmaster; ***maestro de escuela,*** schoolmaster, school-teacher; ***maestro de obras,*** builder, building contractor; ***maestro de cocina,*** head cook, chef. — *n.f.* mistress; schoolmistress; master's wife; (*fig.*) teacher; (*build.*) guideline.
maga, *n.f.* [MAGO].
magancear, *v.i.* (*Chi., Col.*) to idle, loaf about.
magancés, *a.* traitorous, evil.
maganel, *n.m.* (*mil.*) battering-ram.
maganto, -ta, *a.* spiritless, dull, languid.
magaña, *n.f.* flaw (*in the bore of a gun*); (*coll.*) cunning trick.
magarza, *n.f.* (*bot.*) feverfew.
magarzuela, *n.f.* (*bot.*) mayweed.
magdalena, *n.f.* sponge cake, fairy cake.
magdaleón, *n.m.* (*pharm.*) roll of plaster.
magia, *n.f.* magic.
mágico, -ca, *a.* magic, magical. — *n.m.* magician; sorcerer. — *n.f.* enchantress, sorceress.
magín, *n.m.* fancy, imagination; ***se le ha metido en el magín,*** he has taken it into his head.

magisterial, *a.* magisterial.
magisterio, *n.m.* teaching, guidance; mastership; ministry; teaching profession; teachers; affected gravity; (*chem.*) precipitate.
magistrado, *n.m.* magistrate; justice, judge; member of a court of justice.
magistral, *a.* magisterial; masterly; pompous, pedantic. — *n.m.* title of a Roman Catholic prebendary; ***canónigo magistral,*** priest who enjoys the ***magistral.***
magistratura, *n.f.* magistracy, judicature; judgeship.
magnanimidad, *n.f.* magnanimity.
magnánimo, -ma, *a.* magnanimous.
magnate, *n.m.* magnate; tycoon; (*coll.*) baron.
magnesia, *n.f.* (*chem.*) magnesia.
magnesiano, -na, *a.* magnesian.
magnésico, -ca, *a.* magnesic.
magnesio, *n.m.* magnesium; (*photo.*) flashlight.
magnesita, *n.f.* meerschaum.
magnético, -ca, *a.* magnetic.
magnetismo, *n.m.* magnetism.
magnetización, *n.f.* magnetization.
magnetizador, -ra, *a.* magnetizing. — *n.m.f.* magnetizer.
magnetizar [C], *v.t.* to magnetize.
magneto, *n.f.* magneto.
magnificar [A], *v.t.* to magnify, extol, exalt.
magníficat, *n.m.* Magnificat; ***criticar*** (or ***corregir***) ***el magníficat,*** to criticize something that is perfect, carp.
magnificencia, *n.f.* magnificence, splendour, grandeur, gorgeousness.
magnífico, -ca, *a.* magnificent.
magnitud, *n.f.* magnitude, size; greatness.
magno, -na, *a.* great (*used as an epithet, as* ***Alejandro Magno,*** *Alexander the Great.*)
magnolia, *n.f.* (*bot.*) magnolia.
mago, -ga, *a.* skilled in magic. — *n.m.* Magus; magician, wizard. — *n.m.pl.* ***los Reyes Magos,*** the Magi, the Wise Men of the East. — *n.f.* enchantress.
magosto, *n.m.* bonfire (*to roast chestnuts*).
magrez, *n.f.* thinness, leanness.
magrica, magricilla, magricita, *n.f.* small rasher.
magro, -ra, *a.* lean; thin. — *n.m.* (*coll.*) lean meat. — *n.f.* rasher, slice of ham.
magrujo, -ja, *a.* meagre.
magrura, *n.f.* leanness, thinness.
magua, *n.f.* (*Cub.*) joke.
maguer, maguera, *conj.* although.
magüeto, -ta, *n.m.f.* young steer *or* heifer.
maguey, *n.m.* (*bot.*) American agave.
maguillo, *n.m.* wild apple tree.
magujo, *n.m.* (*naut.*) decaulking hook.
magulladura, *n.f.* bruise.
magullamiento, *n.m.* bruising.
magullar, *v.t.* to bruise.
Maguncia, *n.f.* Mainz.
Mahoma, *n.m.* Mohammed.
mahometano, -na, *a., n.m.f.* Mohammedan.
mahometismo, *n.m.* Mohammedanism.
mahometista, *n.m.f.* Mohammedan.
mahometizar, *v.t.* to convert to Islam. — *v.i.* to profess Islam.
mahón, *n.m.* nankeen.
mahona, *n.f.* Turkish transport vessel.
mahozmedín, *n.m.* gold maravedi.
maicena, *n.f.* (fine) cornflour, (*Am.*) cornstarch.
maicero, *n.m.* (*Cub.*) seller of maize.
maicillo, *n.m.* plant similar to millet.
maído, *n.m.* mewing, mew.
maimón, *n.m.* monkey; (*pl.* **maimones**) Andalusian soup made with olive oil.
maimona, *n.f.* beam (*of a horse-mill*).
maitencito, *n.m.* (*Chi.*) children's game resembling blindman's-buff.
maitinante, *n.m.* one who attends matins.
maitinario, *n.m.* book containing matins.
maitines, *n.m.pl.* matins.
maíz, *n.m.* (*bot.*) maize, Indian corn, (*Am.*) corn; ***harina de maíz,*** cornflour, (*Am.*) cornstarch.
maizal, *n.m.* maize-field.
maja, *a., n.f.* [MAJO].
majada, *n.f.* sheep-cote, sheep-fold; dung.
majadal, *n.m.* land used for a sheep-fold; good pasture-ground.
majadear, *v.i.* to take shelter in the night (*of sheep*). — *v.t.* to manure.
majadería, *n.f.* nonsense, piece of stupidity.
majaderillo, majaderito, *n.m.* bobbin (*for lace*).
majadero, -ra, *a.* stupid, half-witted. — *n.m.f.* idiot, dim-wit. — *n.m.* pestle, pounder; bobbin.
majador, -ra, *a.* crushing, pounding.
majadura, *n.f.* crushing; pounding.
majagranzas, *n.m. inv.* (*coll.*) stupid, ignorant fellow.
majagua, *n.f.* (*Cub., Hisp. Am.*) corkwood tree, majagua.
majagüero, *n.m.* (*Cub.*) maker *or* seller of majagua cordage.
majal, *n.m.* school (*of fishes*).
majano, *n.m.* heap of stones (*landmark*).
majar, *v.t.* to crush, pound; (*fig.*) to bore to death.
majencia [MAJEZA].
majestad, *n.f.* majesty; royalty; dignity, grandeur, gravity, loftiness; power, sovereignty, kingship; elevation.
majestuosamente, *adv.* majestically, in kingly fashion.
majestuosidad, *n.f.* majesty, dignity.
majestuoso, -sa, *a.* majestic, august, grand, stately, lofty; grave, solemn.
majeza, *n.f.* (*coll.*) flamboyant style, bold and uninhibited manner.
majo, -ja, *a., n.m.f.* (one) free and nonchalant in manner, gay and sporty in dress; boasting, blustering, swaggering, bullying; (*coll.*) (one) nice, genial, decent; handsome, smart.
majolar, *v.t.* (*obs.*) to put straps to (shoes). — *n.m.* white hawthorn grove.
majuela, *n.f.* fruit of the white hawthorn; shoelace made of leather.
majuelo, *n.m.* vine newly planted; white hawthorn.
mal, *a.* bad, evil. — *adv.* bad, badly, ill, wrongly; ***mal avenidos,*** on bad terms; ***anda mal,*** he walks badly; ***de mal en peor,*** from bad to worse; ***has hecho mal,*** it was wrong of you; ***las cosas andan mal,*** things are going badly; ***mal de mi*** (***su, tu***) ***grado,*** unwillingly, reluctantly; ***mal hecho,*** bad show; ***mal que bien,*** somehow or other; ***mal que le pese,*** in spite of him; ***menos mal,*** it's a good job; ***sentar mal,*** to upset, disagree with; to offend; ***tomar a mal,*** to take badly, take offence at. — *n.m.* evil, wrong, harm, injury; illness, disease; ***bien vengas mal, si vienes solo,*** welcome evil, if thou comest alone; ***del mal, el menos,*** the lesser of two evils; ***mal caduco,*** epilepsy; ***mal de muchos, consuelo de tontos,*** the bane of many is the consolation of fools; ***mal de ojo,*** evil eye; ***mal francés,*** syphilis; ***no hay mal que por bien no venga,*** it's an ill wind that blows nobody any good; ***un mal llama a otro,*** one misfortune breeds another.
mala (I), *n.f.* mail post, mail-bag; deuce of spades; manille.
malabar, *a.* ***juegos malabares,*** juggling.
malabarista, *n.m.f.* juggler; (*Chi.*) sly thief, confidence man.
Malaca, *n.f.* Malay Peninsula.

malacate, *n.m.* capstan, windlass; (*Mex., min.*) spindle.
malacia, *n.f.* (*med.*) depraved appetite.
malaconsejado, -da, *a.* ill-advised.
malacostumbrado, -da, *a.* having bad habits; spoiled.
malacuenda, *n.f.* sacking, oakum, tow.
málaga, *n.m.* Malaga wine.
malagana, *n.f.* (*coll.*) faintness, dizziness.
malagueño, -ña, *a., n.m.f.* (inhabitant) of Malaga. — *n.f.* popular song of Malaga.
malagueta, *n.f.* grains of Paradise.
malandante, *a.* unhappy, unfortunate.
malandanza, *n.f.* misfortune.
malandar, *n.m.* wild hog.
malandrín, *a.* wicked. — *n.m.* rascal, scoundrel.
malanga, *n.f.* arum.
malaquita, malaquites, *n.f.* (*min.*) malachite.
malar, *a.* (*anat.*) malar.
Malasia, *n.f.* Malaysia, Malaya.
malasiano, -na [MALASIO].
malasio, -sia, *a., n.m.f.* Malaysian.
malatía, *n.f.* leprosy.
malato (1), **-ta,** *a.* leprous.
malato (2), *n.m.* (*chem.*) malate.
malavenido, -da, *a.* at odds, in disagreement, at loggerheads.
malaventura, *n.f.* misfortune.
malaventurado, -da, *a.* ill-fated, luckless.
malaventuranza, *n.f.* unhappiness; misfortune.
malayo, *a., n.m.f.* Malay, Malayan (*person*). — *n.m.* Malay (*language*).
malbaratador, -ra, *a.* squandering; underselling.
malbaratar, *v.t.* to squander; to undersell.
malbaratillo, *n.m.* cheap second-hand shop.
malcarado, -da, *a.* grim-faced, evil-faced.
malcasado, -da, *a.* unfaithful, undutiful (*spouse*).
malcasar, *v.t.* to mismate; to make (*s.o.*) marry against his *or* her will. — **malcasarse,** *v.r.* to marry the wrong *or* an unsuitable person.
malcaso, *n.m.* treason, turpitude; crime.
malcocinado, *n.m.* entrails (*of an animal*); tripe-shop.
malcomer, *v.i.* to eat poorly.
malcomido, -da, *a.* ill-fed, undernourished.
malcontento, -ta, *a.* discontented. — *n.m.f.* malcontent.
malcriado, -da, *a.* ill-bred, unmannerly; spoilt; (*Hisp. Am.*) naughty.
malcriar [L], *v.t.* to spoil (*a child*).
maldad, *n.f.* wickedness, evil; (*coll.*) mischief.
maldadoso, -sa, *a.* wicked.
maldecido, -da, *a.* wicked.
maldecidor, -ra, *n.m.f.* swearer; calumniator, detractor.
maldecimiento, *n.m.* backbiting, calumny, censure.
maldecir [17, *p.p.* **maldecido, maldicho, maldito**; *imper. sing.*, **maldice**], *v.t.* to curse, accurse. — *v.i.* **maldecir,** to speak ill (**de**, of), backbite.
maldiciente, *a.* cursing; evil-speaking, slanderous, back-biting. — *n.m.f.* curser; evil-speaker, slanderer, backbiter.
maldición, *n.f.* malediction, curse.
maldicho, -cha, *a.* accursed, calumniated.
maldispuesto, -ta, *a.* indisposed; reluctant, unwilling.
maldito, -ta, *a.* accursed, damned; wicked; (not) the slightest, no; ***no sabe maldita la cosa,*** he knows nothing about it; ***maldito lo que me importa,*** I don't care a straw. — *n.m.* ***el Maldito,*** the Devil. — *n.f.* (*coll.*) tongue; (*coll.*) ***soltar la maldita,*** to give rein to one's tongue, to speak one's mind.
maleabilidad, *n.f.* malleability, malleableness
maleable, *a.* malleable.
maleador, -ra, *a,* spoiling; perverting, corrupting. — *n.m.f.* spoiler; perverter, corrupter.
maleante, *a.* corrupting, evil-doing. — *n.m.* crook.
malear, *v.t.* to damage, spoil; to pervert, corrupt. — **malearse,** *v.r.* to go wrong, turn bad; to get into evil ways, pick up all kinds of (evil) ideas and tricks, (*coll.*) get off the straight and narrow.
malecón *n.m.* levee, dyke, sea-wall.
maledicencia, *n.f.* evil talk, slander, backbiting.
maleficencia, *n.f.* maleficence.
maleficiar, *v.t.* to hurt, injure, harm, adulterate, corrupt, vitiate; to bewitch, harm by witchcraft.
maleficio, *n.m.* hurt, damage, injury; witchcraft, enchantment, charm, spell.
maléfico, -ca, *a.* mischievous, malicious; injuring others by witchcraft.
malejo, -ja, *a.* baddish, poorish.
malentrada, *n.f.* tax, fee.
malestar, *n.m.* malaise, uneasiness.
maleta, *n.f.* suitcase, valise, travelling bag; (*motor.*) boot, (*Am.*) trunk; (*coll.*) harlot; ***hacer la maleta,*** to pack up; (*Chi., coll.*) ***largar*** or ***soltar la maleta,*** to kick the bucket. — *n.m.* (*coll.*) bungler, ham bullfighter.
maletero, *n.m.* suitcase maker *or* seller; station porter.
maletía, *n.f.* (*obs.*) malice; injury to health.
maletín, *n.m.* small suitcase, travelling case.
maletón, *n.m.* large valise *or* suitcase.
malevo, -va (*Arg., Bol.*) [MALÉVOLO].
malevolencia, *n.f.* malevolence.
malévolo, -la, *a.* malevolent.
maleza, *n.f.* weeds; thicket, underbrush.
malformación, *n.f.* (*med.*) malformation.
malgastador, -ra, *a.* extravagant, squandering, wasteful. — *n.m.f.* squanderer, spendthrift, wastrel.
malgastar, *v.t.* to misspend, squander, waste.
malgenioso, -sa, *a.* (*Chi., Mex.*) wrathful, enraged.
malhablado, -da, *a.* foul-mouthed.
malhadado, -da, *a.* ill-starred.
malhecho, -cha, *a.* misshapen. — *n.m.* misdeed.
malhechor, -ra, *n.m.f.* malefactor, evil-doer.
malherido, -da, *a.* seriously injured, dangerously wounded.
malherir [6], *v.t.* to wound badly, injure seriously.
malhojo, *n.m.* refuse of plants; rubbish.
malhumorado, -da, *a.* ill-humoured, bad tempered.
malicia, *n.f.* slyness, artfulness; suspiciousness, distrust; knowingness, suggestiveness, innuendo.
maliciar, *v.t.* to suspect, get *or* have an inkling of. — **maliciarse,** *v.r.* to get *or* have an inkling *or* (shrewd) suspicion of.
malicioso, -sa, *a.* sly, artful; suspicious, mistrustful; knowing, suggestive, risqué.
malignar, *v.t.* to vitiate, corrupt, deprave.
malignidad, *n.f.* malignity.
maligno, -na, *a.* malignant, malign, evil, wicked.
malilla, *n.f.* manille.
malintencionado, -da, *a.* ill-meaning, evilly disposed.
malmandado, -da, *a.* (*coll.*) disobedient.
malmaridada, *a.* unfaithful (*of the wife*). — *n.f.* adulteress.
malmeter, *v.t.* (*coll.*) to incline, induce to evil; to estrange; to waste, misspend.
malmirado, -da, *a.* disliked; inconsiderate.
malo, -la (2), *a.* bad, evil; naughty, mischievous; ill, sick; hard, difficult; poor; wrong; ***mala fama,*** ill fame, evil reputation; ***dedo malo,*** sore finger; ***malo de resolver,*** hard to solve; ***por (las) malas o por (las) buenas,*** by fair means or foul, willy nilly; ***estar de malas,*** to be in a nasty mood; ***venir de malas,*** to have evil *or* bad

intentions, have a nasty look; ***andar a malas,*** to be on bad terms; ***ser malo,*** to be bad *or* naughty; ***estar malo,*** to be ill *or* rotten; ***lo malo es que,*** the trouble is that. — *n.m.* ***el Malo,*** the Evil One.

maloca, *n.f.* (*Hisp. Am.*) invasion of Indian lands.

malogrado, -da. *a.* unsuccessful, failed, ill-fated; late, deceased, having met an untimely death.

malogramiento [MALOGRO].

malograr, *v.t.* to miss, lose, waste, spoil. — **malograrse,** *v.r.* to fail, fall through, turn out badly, fail to fulfil (early) promise, come to nothing, come to grief, meet an untimely end; to die before one's time, die early *or* young; to go wrong, break down.

malogro, *n.m.* failure; loss, waste; disappointment; untimely end.

maloja, *n.f.* (*Cub.*) maize-leaves and stalks.

malojal, *n.m.* (*Ven.*) plantation of ***maloja.***

malojero, *n.m.* (*Cub.*) seller of ***maloja.***

malojo, *n.m.* (*Ven.*) [MALOJA].

malón, *n.m.* (*Hisp. Am.*) Indian raid; surprise attack.

maloquear, *v.i.* (*Hisp. Am.*) to raid, carry out raids.

malordenado, -da, *a.* ill-arranged.

malparado, -da, *a.* damaged, in a bad way.

malparar, *v.t.* to ill-treat, damage, put in a bad way.

malparida, *n.f.* woman who has miscarried.

malparir, *v.i.* to miscarry.

malparto, *n.m.* miscarriage.

malquerencia, *n.f.* ill-will, dislike.

malquerer, *v.t.* to dislike, hate, bear ill-will against.

malquistar, *v.t.* to estrange, set at odds; ***le malquistaron con su jefe,*** they set his boss against him; ***se malquistó con su amigo,*** he fell out with his friend.

malquisto, -ta, *a.* hated, disliked, unpopular.

malrotador -ra, *a.* squandering. — *n.m.f.* waster, squanderer, spendthrift.

malrotar, *v.t.* to misspend, squander, waste.

malsano, -na, *a.* unhealthy, unwholesome.

malsín, *n.m.* talebearer, mischief-maker, back-biter.

malsinante, *a.* backbiting.

malsinar, *v.t.* to speak ill of, gossip about, run down.

malsindad, malsinería, *n.f.* gossiping, backbiting.

malsonante, *a.* offensive to the ear.

malsufrido, -da, *a.* impatient, lacking in forbearance.

malta, *n.f.* malt.

maltés, -tesa, *a., n.m.f.* Maltese. — *n.m.* Maltese (*language*).

maltrabaja, *n.m.f.* (*coll.*) idler, lounger.

maltraer [34], *v.t.* to treat ill; ***lo trae*** (or ***tiene***) ***a maltraer,*** he's driving him to distraction.

maltratamiento, *n.m.* ill-treatment, ill usage.

maltratar, *v.t.* to ill-treat, treat roughly.

maltrato, *n.m.* ill-treatment.

maltrecho, -cha, *a.* in a bad way, down-at-heel; (*coll.*) tatty.

maluco, -ca, *a., n.m.f.* (native) of the Moluccas.

malucho, -cha, *a.* (*coll.*) sickly, groggy, off-colour.

malva, *n.f.* (*bot.*) mallow; ***como una malva,*** as meek as you please; ***estar criando malvas,*** to be pushing up daisies; ***malva real,*** hollyhock.

malváceo, -cea, *a.* (*bot.*) malvaceous.

malvado, -da, *a.* wicked, evil.

malvar (1), *n.m.* place covered with mallows.

malvar (2), *v.t.* to corrupt.

malvasía, *n.f.* malmsey (*grape* or *wine*).

malvavisco, *n.m.* (*bot.*) marsh-mallow.

malvender, *v.t.* to sell at a loss, sell off hastily.

malversación, *n.f.* malversation, misappropriation of funds, embezzlement.

malversador, -ra, *n.m.f.* one who misappropriates funds, embezzler.

malversar, *v.t.* to misappropriate (*funds*), embezzle.

Malvinas, Las Islas, *n.f.pl.* Falkland Islands.

malvís, malviz, *n.m.* (*orn.*) red-wing.

malla, *n.f.* mesh (*of a net*); mail (*of armour*); meshwork, meshed *or* netted fabric; tights; bathing suit.

mallar, *v.t.* to arm with a coat of mail. — *v.i.* to make mesh- *or* net-work; (*of fish*) to get caught in the mesh of a net.

mallero, *n.m.* mesh-, net- *or* mail-maker.

mallete, *n.m.* gavel, mallet; (*pl.*) (*naut.*) partners.

mallo, *n.m.* mall, pall-mall; (game of) bowls; mallet; (game of) croquet.

Mallorca, *n.f.* Majorca.

mallorquín, -quina, *a., n.m.f.* (native) of Majorca.

mamá, *n.f.* mum(my), mamma, mother.

mama, *n.f.* mamma, breast.

mamacallos, *n.m. inv.* (*coll.*) simpleton, dolt.

mamacona, *n.f.* (*Bol., Col., Per.*) religious virgin (*among the Incas*).

mamada, *n.f.* (*coll.*) suck, sucking.

mamadera, *n.f.* breast-pump; (*Hisp. Am.*) nipple; nursing bottle.

mamador, -ra, *a.* sucking. — *n.m.f.* sucker, one who sucks.

mamaluco, *n.m.* (*coll.*) dolt, simpleton, fool.

mamancia, *n.f.* (*coll.*) childishness, silliness.

mamancona, *n.f.* (*Chi.*) old and fat woman.

mamandurria, *n.f.* (*Hisp. Am., coll.*) sinecure.

mamante, *a.* sucking.

mamantón, -tona, *a.* sucking.

mamar, *v.t., v.i.* to suck. — **mamar**(**se**), *v.t., v.r.* to suck in *or* take in with one's mother's milk, learn at one's mother's breast; (*coll.*) to gulp down; to get, get hold of; (*coll.*) ***no mamarse el dedo,*** to be no fool. — **mamarse,** *v.r.* (*Hisp. Am.*) to get drunk; (*Hisp. Am.*) ***mamarse a alguien,*** to get the better of s.o.; to get rid of, rub out *or* eliminate s.o.

mamario, -ria, *a.* mammary.

mamarrachada, *n.f.* collection of ridiculous figures; ridiculous thing *or* object; grotesque thing to do; botch, bungle, daub.

mamarrachista, *n.m.f.* dauber, botcher.

mamarracho, *n.m.* grotesque ornament; figure of fun, ridiculous figure *or* object; botch, daub.

mambla, *n.f.* rounded hillock.

mameluco, *n.m.* Mameluke; mameluke; (*fig.*) dolt, blockhead.

mamellado, -da, *a.* mammillated.

mamífero, -ra, *a.* mammalian. — *n.m.* mammal.

mamila, *n.f.* part of breast round the nipple; mammilla (*of a man*).

mamilar, *a.* mammillary.

mamola, *n.f.* chuck under the chin.

mamón, -mona, *a.* sucking; fond of sucking. — *n.m.f.* suckling. — *n.m.* (*bot.*) shoot, sucker. — *n.f.* chuck under the chin.

mamoncillo, *n.m.* young *or* little suckling.

mamoso, -sa, *a.* sucking. — *n.m.* panic grass.

mamotreto, *n.m.* memorandum book; (*coll.*) hefty tome *or* bundle of papers; hefty object.

mampara, *n.f.* screen.

mamparo, *n.m.* (*naut.*) bulkhead.

mamperlán, mampernal, *n.m.* wooden guard (*on steps of a staircase*).

mamporro, *n.m.* (*coll.*) blow, thump, wallop.

mampostear, *v.t.* to build with rubble masonry.

mampostería, *n.f.* rubble-work.

mampostero, *n.m.* rubble mason.

mampresar, *v.t.* to begin to break in (*horses*).

mampuesta, *n.f.* (*build.*) course, row of bricks.

mampuesto, *n.m.* (*mas.*) rubble, rubblework stone; (*Hisp. Am.*) rest *or* support (***for a firearm in***

taking aim); parapet; ***de mampuesto***, set apart, extra.
mamujar, *v.t.* to suck on and off.
mamullar, *v.t.* to eat *or* chew as if sucking; (*coll.*) to mumble, mutter.
mamut, *n.m.* mammoth.
maná, *n.m.* manna.
manada, *n.f.* herd, drove, pack, flock; ***a manadas,*** in droves.
manadero, -ra, *a.* springing, issuing. — *n.m.* source, spring; shepherd, herdsman.
manadilla, *n.f.* small flock.
managerman, *n.m.* aggressive, go-getting executive.
manantial, *a.* flowing, running; ***agua manantial,*** spring water. — *n.m.* source; spring.
manar, *v.t.* to pour forth. — *v.i.* to spring (from), flow, run, issue; to abound.
manare, *n.m.* (*Ven.*) sieve (*for yucca starch*).
manatí, manato, *n.m.* (*ichth.*) manatee, manatus, sea-cow; whip made of sea-cow's hide.
manaza, *n.f.* (*fig.*) hefty great hand *or* paw, clumsy fist.
mancamiento, *n.m.* want, lack, deficiency; maimedness, maiming.
mancar [A], *v.t.* to maim, cripple, disable. — *v.i.* (*prov.*) to be lacking.
manceba, *n.f.* [MANCEBO].
mancebete, *n.m.* youth, lad.
mancebía, *n.f.* brothel, bawdy-house.
mancebo, -ba, *n.m.f.* lad, lass; shop-assistant, clerk, journeyman; bachelor. — *n.f.* concubine.
máncer, *n.m.* prostitute's son.
mancera, *n.f.* plough-tail, plough-handle.
mancerina, *n.f.* saucer with holder for chocolate cup.
mancilla, *n.f.* spot, stain, blemish; ***sin mancilla,*** pure, immaculate.
mancillar, *v.t.* to spot, stain, sully, soil, blemish.
mancipar, *v.t.* to enslave, subject.
manco, -ca, *a.* one-handed; one-armed; maimed; only half-complete. — *n.m.f.* person with only one hand *or* one arm; (*Chi.*) sorry nag; (*fig.*) ***no ser manco,*** to (have to) be reckoned with.
mancomún, *n.m.* concurrence; ***de mancomún*** (or ***mancomunadamente***), jointly, by common consent.
mancomunar, *v.t.* to unite, associate; (*law*) to make (*several persons*) pay the costs of a lawsuit.
mancomunidad, *n.f.* union, fellowship; commonwealth.
mancornar [4], *v.t.* to twist the neck of (*a steer etc.*) and hold down on the ground with the horns downwards; to join, couple, tie by the horns.
mancuerda, *n.f.* each turn of the rack bars (*torture*).
mancuerna, *n.f.* pair tied together; thong for tying two steers; (*Cub.*) tobacco stem with two leaves; (*Philip.*) pair of convicts chained together.
mancha, *n.f.* spot; speckle; stain; blot; blemish; discoloration; patch; ***mancha solar,*** sun spot; (*zool.*) ***mancha ocular,*** eyespot.
manchadizo, -za, *a.* easily stained *or* soiled.
manchado, -da, *a.* spotted, speckled.
manchar, *v.t.* to spot; to speckle; to stain; to blot; to dirty, soil, sully; to discolour; ***¡mancha!*** wet paint!
manchego, -ga, *a., n.m.f.* (native) of La Mancha.
manchón, *n.m.* large stain *or* spot; thick patch (*of vegetation*).
manda, *n.f.* legacy, bequest.
mandadero, -ra, *n.m.f.* messenger, errand-boy, errand-girl.
mandado, *n.m.* order, command; errand, message; (*coll.*) henchman, one under orders from another.
mandamás, *n.m.* (*coll.*) big boss, top man.
mandamiento, *n.m.* mandate, command, order; (*eccles.*) commandment; (*law.*) writ; (*pl.*) (*coll.*) five fingers of the hand.
mandanga, *n.f.* sluggishness, slowness.
mandante, *a.* commanding. — *n.m.* (*law*) mandator.
mandar, *v.t.* to command, order; to head, lead; to leave, bequeath; to send; ***mandar hacer algo,*** to have sth. done *or* made; to order sth. to be done *or* made; ***mandar decir que,*** to send word that; ***mandar venir,*** to order to come, call, summon; ***como Dios manda,*** properly, in the right way. — *v.i.* to be in command, give (the) orders; ***¡mande Vd!*** I'm at your disposal, what can I do for you? ***este barco manda bien,*** this vessel handles well, answers the helm well. — **mandarse,** *v.r.* to be able to get about (*of sick persons*); to be communicating (*of rooms*).
mandarín, -rina, *a.* mandarin. — *n.m.* mandarin. — *n.f.* mandarin (*orange*); Mandarin Chinese (*language*).
mandarria, *n.f.* (*naut.*) iron maul, sledge-hammer.
mandatario, *n.m.* (*law*) attorney, agent; mandatory.
mandato, *n.m.* mandate; order, injunction; (*eccles.*) maundy.
mandíbula, *n.f.* jaw-bone; jaw; mandible.
mandibular, *a.* (*med.*) mandibular, belonging to the jaw.
mandil, *n.m.* apron; leather apron; leather *or* coarse cloth; fine-meshed net.
mandilar, *v.t.* to wipe (*a horse*) with a coarse cloth.
mandilejo, *n.m.* small apron; ragged cloth *or* apron.
mandilete, *n.m.* (*artill.*) door of the port-hole of a battery.
mandilón, *n.m.* (*coll.*) coward, mean fellow.
mandioca, *n.f.* tapioca, manioc, cassava.
mando, *n.m.* command; (*mech.*) drive, control; ***alto mando,*** high command; ***don de mando,*** talent for commanding; ***voz de mando,*** military order; ***estar al mando de, tener el mando de,*** to be in command of; ***mando a distancia,*** remote control; ***mando doble,*** dual control; (*pl.*) (the) controls; ***cuadro de mandos,*** instrument panel.
mandoble, *n.m.* two-handed blow *or* swipe with a sword; large sword; (*coll.*) sharp ticking-off.
mandón, -dona, *a.* domineering, bossy. — *n.m.f.* domineering *or* bossy person. — *n.m.* (*Hisp. Am.*) foreman, boss, overseer.
mandrachero, *n.m.* proprietor of a gaming-house.
mandracho, *n.m.* gambling-house.
mandrágora, *n.f.* (*bot.*) mandrake.
mandria, *a., n.m.* lily-livered (*person*).
mandril, *n.m.* (*zool.*) baboon; (*mech.*) mandrel, chuck, spindle (*of a lathe*).
mandrón, *n.m.* stone ball (*used as a missile*).
manducación, *n.f.* (*coll.*) eating, noshing.
manducar [A], *v.t.* (*coll.*) to eat.
manducatoria, *n.f.* (*coll.*) food, grub.
manea, *n.f.* shackles, fetters, fetterlock.
manear, *v.t.* to chain, fetter, shackle, hobble.
manecica, manecita, *n.f.* small hand.
manecilla, *n.f.* small hand; mark; (*print.*) index, fist; book clasp; hand (*of clock* or *watch*); tendril (*of vines*).
manejable, *a.* manageable, easy to handle.
manejar, *v.t.* to manage; to handle; (*Hisp. Am.*) to drive.
manejo, *n.m.* handling, wielding; management, conduct; horsemanship; (*Hisp. Am.*) driving; manipulation, scheming.
maneota, *n.f.* shackles, fetters, hobbles.
manera (I), *n.f.* manner, way, fashion; ***a manera de,*** by way of; ***a la manera de,*** in the style of; ***de mala manera,*** any old how; ***de ninguna manera,*** by no means, certainly not; ***de todas maneras,*** in any case, anyway; ***no hay manera,*** it's hopeless; ***de manera que,*** in such a way that,

so that; ***en gran manera, sobre manera,*** extremely, exceedingly; (*pl.*) manners, behaviour.
manero, -ra (2), *a.* tame (*of hawks etc.*).
manes, *n.m.pl.* manes.
manezuela, *n.f.* small handle.
manfla, *n.f.* (*prov.*) old sow; (*coll.*) concubine.
manga, *n.f.* sleeve; arm (*of axletree*); portmanteau; hose; whirlwind; water spout; line of troops; piquet; mango; fishing-net; (*naut.*) beam; wind sail; straining bag; (*Mex.*) poncho; (*eccles.*) case for covering a cross; (*Arg., Chi., Cub.*) guide-rails (*for enclosing* or *shipping horses, cattle etc.*); ***manga de ángel,*** woman's wide sleeve; ***manga de agua,*** waterspout; ***en mangas de camisa,*** in shirt sleeves; ***estar manga por hombro,*** to be topsy-turvy, be in a mess *or* muddle; ***tener manga ancha,*** to be broad-minded, easy-going *or* lenient; ***hacer mangas y capirotes (de),*** to do just as one likes *or* pleases (with), play old Harry *or* the merry devil (with); ***sacarse algo de la manga,*** to make up, think up *or* concoct sth., come out with sth., trot sth. out; ***¡a buenas horas mangas verdes!*** (it's) about time!
mangachapuy, *n.m.* (*Philip.*) dipterad tree.
mangajarro, *n.m.* (*coll.*) long and ill-shaped sleeve.
mangana, *n.f.* lasso, lariat.
manganear, *v.t.* to lasso.
manganeo, *n.m.* lassoing.
manganesa, manganesia, *n.f.* peroxide of manganese.
manganeso, *n.m.* (*min.*) manganese.
manganilla, *n.f.* sleight of hand; trick, stratagem; (*prov.*) pole (*for gathering acorns*).
mangante, *n.m.* good-for-nothing, layabout; crook, sharp customer.
mangar, *v.i.* to live by one's wits.
mangla, *n.f.* gum (*exuding from certain plants*).
manglar, *n.m.* mangrove swamp.
mangle, *n.m.* (*bot.*) mangrove tree.
mango, *n.m.* handle; (*bot.*) mango; ***mango de pluma,*** penholder; ***mango de escoba,*** broomstick.
mangonada, *n.f.* push with the arm.
mangonear, *v.t.* (*coll.*) to handle, have control of, run, boss. — *v.i.* to have a big say; to run *or* boss the show, rule the roost, lord it.
mangoneo, *n.m.* running *or* bossing the show, ruling the roost.
mangorrero, -ra, *a.* wandering, roving, rambling; hafted (*of a knife*); worthless, useless.
mangosta, *n.f.* (*zool.*) mongoose.
mangote, *n.m.* (*coll.*) large wide sleeve; oversleeve.
mangual, *n.m.* war flail, morning star.
manguardia, *n.f.* (*Mex.*) buttress (*of a bridge*).
manguera, *n.f.* hose; tarred canvas; wind sail; waterspout; (*Arg.*) large corral; ***manguera de desinflar,*** deflating sleeve; ***manguera de inflar,*** inflating sleeve.
manguero, *n.m.* hoseman.
mangueta, *n.f.* jamb (*of a glass door*); pipe (*for clysters*); lever; neck (*of a water-closet hopper*).
manguilla, manguita, *n.f.* small sleeve.
manguitero, *n.m.* muff-maker, muff-seller; leather-dresser.
manguito, *n.m.* muff; closely fitting sleeve; wristlet; oversleeve; (*mech.*) bush, coupler, collar, sleeve.
maní, *n.m.* peanut.
manía, *n.f.* mania; fad, craze, obsession; ***tener manía a,*** to have a loathing for; ***tener manía por el teatro,*** to be crazy about the theatre; ***tener manía de ir descalzo,*** to be crazy about going barefoot; (*coll.*) to have a thing about going barefoot.
maníaco, -ca, *a.* maniacal, maniac. — *n.m.f.* maniac; fiend.
manialbo, -ba, *a.* white-footed (*of a horse*).
maniatar, *v.t.* to manacle, handcuff.
maniático, -ca, *a.* maniacal; crazy, faddish, terribly fussy. — *n.m.f.* maniac; faddy individual; one with crazy *or* weird likes and dislikes; fiend (***de algo,*** for sth.); ***es un maniático de la fotografía,*** he is a photography fiend, *or* a fiend for photography.
manicomio, *n.m.* lunatic asylum, madhouse; bedlam.
manicordio, *n.m.* manichord.
manicorto, -ta, *a.* tight-fisted.
manicuro, -ra, *n.m.f.* manicure.
manida (1), *n.f.* abode, haunt; den, lair.
manido, -da (2), *a.* (*cook.*) high, gamey; trite, hackneyed.
manifacero, -ra, *a.* intriguing, meddlesome, intrusive.
manifactura, *n.f.* [MANUFACTURA]; form, shape.
manifestación, *n.f.* manifestation; declaration, statement; demonstration; (*law*) writ.
manifestador, -ra, *a.* manifesting.
manifestante, *a.* manifesting. — *n.m.f.* demonstrator.
manifestar [1], *v.t.* to manifest, show; to state, declare; to expose (*the Sacrament*) for adoration. — **manifestarse,** *v.r.* to demonstrate.
manifiesto, *a.* manifest, evident. — *n.m.* exposition of the Blessed Sacrament; (*com.*) manifest; manifesto; ***poner de manifiesto,*** to show clearly.
manigua, *n.f.* (*Cub.*) jungle.
manigueta, *n.f.* haft, handle; (*pl.*) (*naut.*) kevels.
maniguetones, *n.m.pl.* (*naut.*) snatch-cleats.
manija, *n.f.* haft, handle; shackles, handcuffs; ring, brace, clamp, clasp.
manijero, *n.m.* (*prov.*) manager, foreman.
manilargo, -ga, *a.* long-handed; (*fig.*) light-fingered.
manilense, manileño, -ña, *a., n.m.f.* (native) of Manila.
maniluvio, *n.m.* bath for the hands.
manilla, *n.f.* bracelet; manacle, handcuff; hand (*of watch*).
maniobra, *n.f.* handling; working (*of a ship*); (*naut.*) gear, rigging, tackle; manoeuvre, manoeuvring; (*railw.*) shunting; (*pl.*) (*mil.*) manoeuvres.
maniobrar, *v.t., v.i.* to manoeuvre; to shunt.
maniobrero, -ra, *a.* easy to handle *or* manoeuvre; (*naut.*) that handles well.
maniobrista, *n.m.* (*naut.*) skilled manoeuvrer, manipulator.
maniota, *n.f.* fetterlock, manacles, shackles.
manipulación, *n.f.* manipulation.
manipulador, -ra, *a.* manipulating. — *n.m.f.* manipulator. — *n.m.* telegraph key.
manipular, *v.t.* (*coll.*) to manipulate, handle; to manage.
manípulo, *n.m.* maniple; standard.
maniqueísmo, *n.m.* oversimplification; tendency to assign absolute values.
maniquete, *n.m.* black lace; mitten.
maniquí, *n.m.* manikin, mannequin, dummy; model; puppet.
manir [Q], *v.t. defect.*, to keep meat *or* game until high; (*coll.*) to handle repeatedly, make hackneyed.
manirroto, -ta, *a.* extravagant, wasteful, spendthrift.
manirrotura, *n.f.* extravagance.
manita, *n.f.* little hand; mannitol.
manivacío, -cía, *a.* (*coll.*) empty-handed; idle, lazy.
manivela, *n.f.* (*mech.*) crank; (*motor.*) ***manivela de arranque,*** starting handle, crank.
manjar, *n.m.* food, dish; ***manjar blanco,*** blancmange; creamed chicken.
manjolar, *v.t.* to carry (*a hawk*).
manjorrada, *n.f.* pile of food.
manjúa, *n.f.* (*prov., Cub.*) sardine.

manlieva, *n.f.* tax collected from house to house.

mano, *n.f.* hand; forefoot, trotter; (elephant's) trunk; pestle; quire (*of paper*); (musical) scale; cylindrical stone (*for grinding cocoa*), round (*of a game*); coat (*of paint*); band, gang (*of reapers*); knack, skill; reprimand; (*coll.*) going over; ***a mano izquierda,*** on the left (*hand*); ***tener mano izquierda,*** to have tact and savoir faire, know how to handle things adroitly; ***a mano,*** to hand; by hand; ***hecho a mano,*** hand-made; ***a la mano,*** at hand, to hand, within reach; ***a mano airada,*** violently; ***a manos llenas,*** liberally, lavishly; ***mano a mano,*** alternatingly, alternately, first one then the other; together, between us, them etc.; ***bajo mano,*** underhandedly; ***mano de obra,*** labour, manpower; ***mano de santo,*** sure cure; ***buena(s) mano(s),*** skill, adroitness; ***mala(s) mano(s),*** awkwardness, clumsiness; ***tener de buena mano,*** to have on good authority; ***mala mano,*** bad luck; ***manos muertas,*** mortmain; ***poner manos a la obra,*** to put one's hand to the plough; ***¡manos a la, obra!*** to work! let's get cracking!; ***abrir la mano,*** to hold out one's hand (*for a tip etc.*); to be open-handed; to let up, ease up, become more lenient; ***alzar la mano,*** to raise one's hand; ***tener*** or ***llevar entre manos,*** to have on one's hands; ***coger con las manos en la masa,*** to catch in the act, catch red-handed; ***comerse las manos,*** to smack one's lips with relish; ***venir por su mano,*** to come inevitably, automatically *or* naturally; ***tratar con mano dura,*** to treat harshly; ***llevar de la mano,*** to lead by the hand; ***dar de mano,*** to pack up, leave off, knock off, stop work; ***estar mano sobre mano,*** to be *or* stand idle; ***dar en manos de,*** to fall into the hands of; ***dar la última mano,*** to give the finishing touch(es); ***darse la mano,*** to be very similar; ***dejado de la mano de Dios,*** God-forsaken; ***dejar de la mano,*** to forsake, abandon; ***de manos a boca,*** all of a sudden; ***echar mano a,*** to grab, take hold of; ***cargar la mano***, to overdo it, go too far; ***descargar la mano sobre,*** to unleash one's fury upon; ***echar mano de,*** to have recourse to, resort to; ***echar una mano,*** to lend a hand; ***ganar por la mano,*** to steal a march on, get in ahead of; ***manos blancas no ofenden,*** a lady's hand can cause no offence; ***meter mano a,*** to tackle; to go for, assault; (*coll.*) to paw; ***llegar a las manos,*** to come to blows; ***sentar la mano a,*** to beat, lay hands on; ***si a mano viene,*** should the occasion arise; ***traer(se) algo entre manos,*** to be up to sth.; ***se me vino a las manos,*** it came my way (*without any effort on my part*); ***con sus manos lavadas,*** without having made an effort; ***untar la mano a,*** to grease the palm of; ***vivir de*** (or ***por***) ***sus manos,*** to live by one's toil.

manobra, *n.f.* (*prov.*) raw material.

manobre, *n.m.* (*prov.*) hodman, hod-carrier.

manobrero, *n.m.* cleaner of fountains *or* aqueducts.

manojear, *v.t.* (*Chi. Cub.,*) to tie tobacco leaves in small bundles.

manojico, manojillo, manojito, *n.m.* small bundle, small faggot.

manojo, *n.m.* faggot, bundle of twigs *or* grass; bunch (*of keys etc.*); handful; ***a manojos,*** abundantly.

Manolo, *n.m.* (familiar form of) Manuel.

manolo, -la, *a., n.m.f.* flashy low-class Madrilenian.

manométrico, -ca, *a.* manometric.

manómetro, *n.m.* manometer.

manopla, *n.f.* gauntlet; coachman's whip; face-flannel, (*Am.*) washrag; (*Chi.*) knuckle-duster; ***tela de manoplas,*** silk ornamented with large flowers.

manosear, *v.t.* to handle, keep touching; (*coll.*) to paw, paw about; to rumple.

manoseo, *n.m.* handling; (*coll.*) pawing.

manota, *n.f.* large, ugly hand.

manotada, *n.f.,* **manotazo,** *n.m.* cuff, slap, blow with the hand.

manotear, *v.t.* to cuff, slap. — *v.i.* to flay about with the hands.

manoteo, *n.m.* slapping; waving about with the hands.

manquear, *v.i.* to be one-handed *or* handless; to affect the cripple, pretend to be maimed.

manquedad, manquera, *n.f.* lack of one *or* both arms *or* hands; (*fig.*) maimed state; defect.

mansalva, *adv.* ***a —,*** without risk *or* danger.

mansedumbre, *n.f.* meekness, mildness, gentleness; tameness.

mansejón, -jona, *a.* very tame.

manseque, *n.m.* (*Chi.*) children's dance.

mansera, *n.m.* (*Cub.*) vat (*for sugar-cane juice*).

mansión, *n.f.* stay, sojourn; abode, mansion, home; ***hacer mansión,*** to stop, stay.

manso (1), **-sa,** *a.* tame; meek, mild; gentle; ***una mansa brisa,*** a gentle breeze; ***un arroyuelo manso,*** a slow stream.

manso (2), *n.m.* manor, manor-house; manse; bell-wether.

manta (1), *n.m.* (*coll.*) good-for-nothing; botcher.

mansurrón, -rrona, *a.* meek, mild *or* tame to a fault.

manta (2), *n.f.* blanket; travelling rug; (*Mex.*) coarse cotton shirting; (*mil.*) mantelet; threshing, drubbing; tossing in a blanket; quill feathers (*of birds of prey*); (*Hisp. Am.*) bag of agave (*for carrying ore*); card game; ***manta de algodón,*** wadding; ***manta blanca,*** bleached cotton; ***manta prieta,*** unbleached cotton; (*coll.*) ***a manta (de Dios),*** in plenty, galore; ***liarse la manta a la cabeza,*** to take the plunge, (decide to) bash on, throw caution to the winds; ***tirar de la manta,*** to let the cat out of the bag, spill the beans, (start) to give the game away.

mantaterilla, *n.f.* coarse hempen cloth (*for horse blankets*).

manteador, -ra, *n.m.f.* tosser, one who tosses in a blanket.

manteamiento, *n.m.* tossing in a blanket.

mantear, *v.t.* to toss in a blanket. — *v.i.* (*prov.*) to gad about.

manteca, *n.f.* lard; grease, fat; pomade; (*prov.*) butter; ***manteca de cacao,*** cocoa butter.

mantecada, *n.f.* lard powder cake.

mantecado, *n.m.* lard short-bread lump; vanilla ice-cream.

mantecón, *n.m.* milksop.

mantecoso, -sa, *a.* greasy, fatty.

manteísta, *n.m.* day student in a seminary.

mantel, *n.m.* table-cloth; altar-cloth; ***levantar los manteles,*** to clear the table; ***tener a mesa y mantel,*** to treat like a lord.

mantelería, *n.f.* table-linen.

manteleta, *n.f.* mantelet, small scarf *or* mantle, lady's shawl.

mantelete, *n.m.* (*eccles.*) mantelet; bishop's mantle; (*fort.*) movable parapet; (*her.*) mantling.

mantelo, *n.m.* very wide apron.

mantellina, *n.f.* mantilla.

mantenedor, *n.m.* president of a tournament *or* jousts.

mantenencia, *n.f.* maintenance, support.

mantener [33], *v.t.* to maintain, support; to hold, keep, keep up; ***mantenerse en lo dicho,*** to abide by what one has said; ***mantenerse firme,*** to stand firm, hold one's ground.

manteniente, *n.m.* (*obs.*) violent blow with both hands; ***a manteniente,*** with all one's might, firmly.

mantenimiento, *n.m.* maintenance; support; sustenance; upkeep.

manteo, *n.m.* long cloak *or* mantle; woollen skirt; tossing in a blanket.

mantequería, *n.f.* grocer's shop.
mantequero, -ra, *a.* (pertaining to) butter. — *n.m.f.* butter maker *or* seller; butter-dish. — *n.f.* churn.
mantequilla, *n.f.* butter.
mantero, -ra, *n.m.f.* mantle maker *or* seller.
mantés, -tesa, *a., n.m.f.* (*coll.*) rogue, scoundrel.
mantilla, *n.f.* mantilla; saddlecloth; (*print.*) blanket; (*pl.*) swaddling-clothes; ***estar en mantillas,*** to be in one's *or* its infancy.
mantillo, *n.m.* (*agric.*) humus; manure.
mantillón, -llona, *a.* (*prov.*) dirty, slovenly.
mantisa, *n.f.* (*math.*) mantissa.
manto, *n.m.* mantle, large mantilla, cloak, robe; mantelpiece; (*min.*) stratum, layer.
mantón, -tona, *a.* having drooping wings (*of birds*). — *n.m.* large shawl; ***mantón de Manila,*** embroidered silk shawl.
mantudo, -da, *a.* [MANTÓN].
manuable, *a.* manageable, easily handled.
manual, *a.* hand, manual. — *n.m.* manual, handbook; notebook; (*eccles.*) ritual.
manubrio, *n.m.* handle, crank; manubrium.
manucodiata, *n.f.* (*orn.*) bird of paradise.
Manuel, *n.m.* Emmanuel.
Manuela, *n.f.* Emma.
manuela, *n.f.* open hackney-carriage.
manuella, *n.f.* (*naut.*) capstan bar, handspike.
manufactura, *n.f.* manufacture.
manufacturar, *v.t.* to manufacture.
manufacturero, -ra, *a.* manufacturing.
manumisión, *n.f.* manumission.
manumiso, -sa, *a.* emancipated, free.
manumisor, *n.m.* manumitter.
manumitir [*p.p.* **manumitido, manumiso**], *v.t.* to manumit, set free (*slaves*); emancipate.
manuscribir [*p.p.* **manuscrito**], *v.t.* to write by hand.
manuscrito, -ta, *a.* manuscript. — *n.m.* manuscript.
manutención, *n.f.* maintaining, maintenance, upkeep; support.
manutener [33], *v.t.* (*law*) to maintain, support.
manutigio, *n.m.* gentle friction with the hand.
manutisa, *n.f.* (*bot.*) sweet-william pink.
manvacío, -cía, *a.* (*coll.*) empty-handed.
manzana, *n.f.* (*bot.*) apple; pommel, knob; block (*of houses*); ***manzana de la discordia,*** bone of contention; ***manzana de Adán,*** Adam's apple.
manzanal, manzanar, *n.m.* (apple) orchard.
manzanil, *a.* apple, of apples.
manzanilla, *n.f.* (*bot.*) c(h)amomile; small ball *or* knob; olive; tip (*of the chin*); pad (*of animals' feet*); white sherry wine.
manzanillo, *n.m.* (*bot.*) manchineel.
manzanita, *n.f.* little apple.
manzano, *n.m.* (*bot.*) apple tree.
maña (1), *n.f.* skill, knack; cleverness; cunning; bad habit; bundle of hemp *or* flax; ***darse maña,*** to manage, contrive.
mañana, *adv.* tomorrow; ***pasado mañana,*** the day after tomorrow. — *n.m.* morrow, future; ***el día de mañana,*** some time in the future. — *n.f.* morning; ***de la noche a la mañana,*** overnight; ***mañana por la mañana,*** tomorrow morning; (***muy***) ***de mañana,*** (very) early in the morning; ***por la mañana,*** in the morning.
mañanear, *v.i.* to rise very early.
mañanero, -ra, *a.* morning; early-rising.
mañanica, mañanita, *n.f.* break of day, early morning; bed jacket.
mañear, *v.t., v.i.* to manage skilfully *or* craftily.
mañería, *n.f.* sterility; cunning; feudal right of inheriting from those who died without legitimate issue.
mañero, -ra, *a.* clever, skilful, artful; handy, easy.
maño, -ña (2), *a., n.m.f.* (*coll.*) Aragonese; (*Hisp. Am., dial.*) brother, sister; dear, darling.
mañoco, *n.m.* tapioca; (*Ven.*) Indian corn meal.
mañoso, -sa, *a.* skilful, clever with one's hands; crafty, cunning.
mañuela, *n.f.* mean trick, low cunning; (*pl.*) artful, cunning person.
mapa, *n.m.* map. — *n.f.* sth. of outstanding excellence; ***llevarse la mapa,*** to excel.
mapache, *n.m.* (*zool.*) raccoon.
mapamundi, *n.m.* map of the world; globe.
mapanare, *n.f.* (*Ven.*) poisonous snake.
mapurite, *n.m.* (*zool.*) skunk.
maque, *n.m.* (*Mex.*) sumac lacquer.
maquear, *v.t.* to lacquer with ***maque.***
maqueta, *n.f.* (scale) model.
maqui, *n.m.* (*Chi.*) ginger.
maquiavélico, -ca, *a.* Machiavellian.
maquiavelismo, *n.m.* Machiavellism.
maquiavelista, *n.m.f.* Machiavellian.
Maquiavelo, *n.m.* Machiavelli.
maquila, *n.f.* toll-corn; toll; corn-measure; (*Cent. Am.*) unit of weight (*about* 125 *lb.*).
maquilandero, *n.m.* (*prov.*) measure with which corn is tolled.
maquilar, *v.t.* to measure and take dues for (*grinding corn*).
maquilero, maquilón, *n.m.* one who measures *or* takes dues for grinding corn.
maquillaje, *n.m.* make-up.
maquillar(se), *v.t.* (*v.r.*) to make up.
máquina, *n.f.* machine; engine; ***máquina de afeitar,*** razor; ***máquina de componer,*** typesetter; ***máquina de coser,*** sewing machine; ***máquina de escribir,*** typewriter; ***máquina de sumar,*** adding machine; ***máquina de vapor,*** steam engine; ***máquina (fotográfica),*** camera; ***máquina herramienta,*** machine-tool; ***máquina tragaperras,*** slot machine; ***a toda máquina,*** at full speed; ***sala de máquinas,*** engine room.
maquinación, *n.f.* machination.
maquinador, -ra, *n.m.f.* contriver, schemer.
maquinal, *a.* mechanical; routine, automatic.
maquinante, *a.* planning, contriving, machinating.
maquinar, *v.t.* to machinate, contrive.
maquinaria, *n.f.* machinery; mechanics.
maquinete, *n.m.* (*prov.*) chopping-knife.
maquinista, *n.m.f.* machinist; engine-driver, (*Am.*) engineer.
mar, *n.m.f.* sea, ocean; swell of the sea; ***alta mar,*** high seas; ***mar alta,*** rough sea; ***baja mar,*** low water, ebb-tide; ***mar llena*** (or ***plena mar***), high water; (*naut.*) ***mar de través,*** sea on the beam; ***mar gruesa,*** heavy sea; ***mar de leva,*** high swelling sea; (*naut.*) ***correr con la mar en popa,*** to scud before the sea; ***hablar de la mar,*** to waste one's breath; ***la mar de cosas,*** masses of things; ***llover a mares,*** to pour down; ***echar a la mar,*** to launch; ***hacerse a la mar,*** to put out to sea; (*naut.*) ***ir con la proa a la mar,*** to head the sea; ***mar de fondo,*** swell; ***mar territorial,*** territorial waters; ***quien no se arriesga*** (or ***se aventura***), ***no pasa la mar,*** faint heart never won fair lady.
marabú, *n.m.* (*orn.*) marabou.
maracá, *n.m.* (*Hisp. Am.*) maraca.
maraca, *n.f.* (*Hisp. Am.*) maraca; game played with three dice marked with sun, diamond, heart, star, moon and anchor; harlot, prostitute.
maracure, *n.m.* (*bot.*) curare plant.
maragato, -ta, *a., n.m.f.* Maragato, (native) of the Maragatería.
maranata, *n.f.* maranatha, anathema.
maraña, *n.f.* thicket, undergrowth; tangle, entanglement; refuse of silk; perplexity, puzzle; fraud; (*bot.*) kermes oak.
marañar, *v.t.* to tangle, entangle.

marañero, -ra, marañoso, -sa, *a.* entangling, ensnaring.
marañón, *n.m.* (*Hisp. Am.*) cashew tree; cashew nut.
marasmo, *n.m.* (*med.*) marasmus; stagnation.
maravedí, *n.m.* old Spanish coin.
maravilla, *n.f.* marvel, wonder; (*bot.*) marigold; (*bot.*) marvel of Peru; (*bot.*) ivy-leaved morning glory; ***a maravilla, a las mil maravillas,*** wonderfully well; ***de maravilla,*** superbly; ***por maravilla,*** once in a blue moon.
maravillar, *v.t.* to amaze, astonish. — **maravillarse,** *v.r.* to be amazed *or* astonished (***de,*** at).
maravilloso, -sa, *a.* wonderful, marvellous.
marbete, *n.m.* label, tag, (*Am.*) sticker; ticket; fillet, border.
marca, *n.f.* mark; make, brand; standard (of size); gauge *or* rule (*for measuring*); marker, stencil; label, tag, ticket; (*geog.*) march; (*sport*) record; ***marca de fábrica,*** trade-mark; ***marca registrada,*** registered trade-mark; ***de marca*** (***mayor***), exceptional, outstanding; (*coll.*) ***canalla de marca mayor,*** first-rate swine.
marcación, *n.f.* (*naut.*) bearing; taking a ship's bearings.
marcador, -ra, *a.* marking; branding. — *n.m.f.* marker. — *n.m.* (*sport*) scorer; scoreboard; (*embroidery*) sampler; (*print.*) feeder.
marcar [A], *v.t.* to mark; to brand; to designate; to show (*the hour*); to dial (*a number*); to score (*a point, goal etc.*); to take the bearings of (*a ship*); ***marcar el compás,*** to beat time; ***marcar el paso,*** to mark time; ***lavar y marcar el pelo,*** to wash and set the hair; ***marcarse un tanto,*** to chalk up a point, chalk one up; ***marcarse un farol,*** to pull a fast one.
marcear, *v.t.* to shear (*animals*). — *v.i.* to be rough, March-like (*of the weather*).
marceo, *n.m.* trimming honeycombs in spring.
marcescente, *a.* (*bot.*) marcescent, withering.
marcial, *a.* martial, warlike, soldierly; (*pharm.*) chalybeate. — *n.m.* aromatic powder for dressing gloves.
marcialidad, *n.f.* martialness, military bearing.
marco, *n.m.* frame (*door, window, picture etc.*); mark (*coin*); standard; scantling and length of timber; size stick.
márcola, *n.f.* pruning-hook.
marconigrama, *n.m.* marconigram, wireless telegram.
Marcos, *n.m.* Mark.
marcha, *n.f.* march; progress, course; running; departure; (*motor.*) gear; movement (*of a watch*); (*prov.*) bonfire; (*naut.*) speed, headway; ***marchas forzadas,*** forced marches; ***a largas marchas,*** speedily; ***sobre la marcha,*** on the way, as we (they etc.) go; ***batir*** (***la***) ***marcha,*** to strike up a march; ***doblar las marchas,*** to go twice as fast; ***poner en marcha,*** to set going, put in motion; ***ponerse en marcha,*** to start off; ***a toda marcha,*** at full speed.
marchamar, *v.t.* to mark (*goods at the customs-house*).
marchamero, *n.m.* customs-house marker.
marchamo, *n.m.* customs-house mark on goods; lead seal.
marchante, *a.* mercantile, commercial, trading. — *n.m.* shopkeeper, dealer; (*Hisp. Am.*) customer.
marchapié, *n.m.* foot-board; (*naut.*) horse, foot-rope.
marchar, *v.i.* to march, walk; to go ahead, go well; to function, run, work; to depart; (*naut.*) to make headway. — **marcharse,** *v.r.* to go, go away, be off, leave, depart.
marchazo, *n.m.* boaster, bragger.
marchitable, *a.* perishable, liable to wither *or* fade.
marchitamiento, *n.m.* fading, withering.
marchitar, *v.t.* to wither, cause to fade. — **marchitarse,** *v.r.* to wither, fade; to languish.
marchitez, marchitura, *n.f.* withering, fading.
marchito, -ta, *a.* faded, withered.
marea, *n.f.* tide; gentle sea breeze; beach; dew, drizzle; street dirt washed away; ***marea muerta,*** neap tide; ***marea creciente,*** flood-tide; ***marea menguante,*** ebb-tide; ***ir contra marea,*** to sail against the tide; ***mareas vivas,*** spring-tides; ***la marea mengua,*** the tide ebbs; ***la marea crece,*** the tide comes up; ***contra viento y marea,*** in the teeth of all opposition.
mareado, -da, *a.* sick, sea-sick, air-sick, travel-sick; dizzy, giddy; in a dither.
mareaje, *n.m.* navigating of a ship, seamanship; course of a ship.
mareamiento [MAREO].
mareante, *a.* causing seasickness; making dizzy; driving crazy; navigating, sea-faring.
marear, *v.t.* to sail (*a ship*); to sell (*goods*); to make dizzy; to drive crazy.— *v.i.* to navigate. — **marearse,** *v.r.* to get sick, seasick etc.; to faint, come over sick *or* faint; to be damaged at sea.
marega [MARGA].
marejada, *n.f.* swell, surge.
marejadilla, *n.f.* slight swell.
maremágnum, *n.m.* pandemonium, chaos.
mareo, *n.m.* sickness, sea-, air-, travel-sickness; (*coll.*) thing to drive one crazy *or* make one dizzy.
marero, *a.* sea.
mareta, *n.f.* slight swell *or* surge; rumbling; growing *or* decreasing excitement.
maretazo, *n.m.* heavy surge, swell.
márfaga, *n.f.* (*prov.*) straw bed.
Marfil, Costa de, *n.f.* Ivory Coast.
marfil, *n.m.* ivory; ***marfil vegetal,*** ivory nut; ***torre de marfil,*** ivory tower.
marfileño, -ña, *a.* (of) ivory.
marfuz, -za, *a.* repudiated, rejected; deceitful, false.
marga, *n.f.* marl, loam; coarse cloth; burlap.
margajita, *n.f.* (*min.*) white pyrites.
margal, *n.m.* marl-pit.
margar, *v.t.* to manure with marl.
margarina, *n.f.* margarine.
Margarita, *n.f.* Margaret.
margarita, *n.f.* pearl; (*bot.*) daisy, marguerite; (*zool.*) periwinkle; (*min.*) margarite; ***echar margaritas a los cerdos,*** to cast pearls before swine.
margen, *n.m.* margin; border, edge, verge, (*Am.*) shoulder; fringe; marginal note; ***esta al margen,*** to be out of it; ***al margen de,*** in addition to; outside; ***margen de aproximación,*** margin of error; ***margen de ganancia,*** profit margin; ***dar margen,*** to give cause, occasion. — *n.f.* (river) bank; (sea) shore; (frontier) line; ***andarse por las márgenes,*** to beat about the bush.
marginar, *v.t.* to make marginal notes to; to leave a margin on; to margin; to leave out (in the cold), leave on the fringe (of society).
marginoso, -sa, *a.* wide-margined.
margoso, -sa, *a.* marly, loamy.
margrave, *n.m.* margrave.
margraviato, *n.m.* margraviate.
marguera, *n.f.* marl-pit.
María, *n.f.* Mary.
maría, *n.f.* (*coll.*) white wax taper.
mariache, mariachi, *n.m.* (*Mex.*) popular music; player of this music.
marial, *a.* [MARIANO].
mariano, -na, *a.* (*eccles.*) Marian.
marica, *n.f.* (*orn.*) magpie; thin asparagus; knave of diamonds. — *n.m.* (*coll.*) sissy; queer.
maricangalla, *n.f.* (*naut.*) driver, spanker.
Maricastaña, ***en tiempos de Maricastaña,*** in days of yore, long, long ago.
maricón, *n.m.* (*coll.*) pansy, queer; (*vulg.*) sod.

maridable, *a.* conjugal, matrimonial; marriageable.
maridaje, *n.m.* marriage, union.
maridar, *v.t.* to unite, join. — *v.i.* to marry; to live as man and wife.
maridazo, *n.m.* doting husband.
maridillo, *n.m.* pitiful husband, miserable specimen; foot-stove.
marido, *n.m.* husband.
mariguana, marihuana, *n.f.* marijuana, cannabis.
marimacho, *n.m.* mannish woman.
marimandona, *n.f.* bossy woman.
marimanta, *n.f.* bugbear, hob-goblin.
marimba, *n.f.* marimba.
marimoña, *n.f.* (*bot.*) crowfoot.
marimorena, *n.f.* (*coll.*) row, shindy.
marina, *n.f.* [MARINO].
marinaje, *n.m.* seamanship; sailors.
marinar, *v.t.* to marinate; to salt (*fish*); to man (*a ship*).
marinear, *v.i.* to be *or* work as a sailor.
marinerado, -da, *a.* manned.
marinería, *n.f.* seamanship, sailoring; sailors.
marinero, -ra, *a.* marine, sea, sailor; sailorlike; seaworthy; ready to sail; ***a la marinera,*** sailor-fashion. — *n.m.* mariner, sailor, seaman. — *n.f.* sailor blouse, middy.
marinesco, -ca, *a.* sailorly.
marinista, *a.* marine (painter). — *n.m.* seascapist.
marino, -na, *a.* marine, nautical, sea. — *n.m.* mariner, sailor; naval officer. — *n.f.* shore, sea coast; (*art.*) sea-piece; navy, marine; nautical art, seamanship; ***marina de guerra,*** navy; ***marina mercante,*** merchant marine.
marión, marón, *n.m.* (*ichth.*) sturgeon.
mariona, *n.f.* Spanish dance.
marioneta, *n.f.* puppet, marionette.
maripérez, *n.f.* servant-girl.
mariposa, *n.f.* butterfly; night-light, dimmed night-lamp; ***tuerca de mariposa,*** wing nut; ***válvula de mariposa,*** butterfly valve.
mariposear, *v.i.* (*fig.*) to be flighty; to flutter around.
mariquita, *n.f.* ladybird; (*fig.*) sissy.
marisabidilla, *n.f.* (*coll.*) blue-stocking, little know-it-all.
mariscal, *n.m.* marshal; blacksmith, farrier; ***mariscal de campo,*** field-marshal.
mariscala, *n.f.* marshal's wife.
mariscalato, *n.m.*, **mariscalía,** *n.f.* marshalship.
mariscar [A], *v.i.* to gather shellfish.
marisco, *n.m.* shellfish, seafood.
marisma, *n.f.* marsh, swamp, morass.
marital, *a.* marital.
maritata, *n.f.* (*Chi.*) trough lined with leather used to wash rich minerals.
marítimo, -ma, *a.* maritime, marine.
maritornes, *n.f. inv.* (*coll.*) ungainly, mannish maid of all work.
marjal, *n.m.* fen, marsh; a measure of land (5,650 sq. ft.).
marjoleto, *n.m.* (*bot.*) white hawthorn.
marlota, *n.f.* Moorish gown.
marmita, *n.f.* stew-pot, saucepan.
marmitón, *n.m.* scullion, dish-washer, kitchen boy.
mármol, *n.m.* marble; (*print.*) imposing-stone.
marmolejo, *n.m.* small marble column.
marmoleño, -ña, *a.* marbly, marble-like.
marmolería, *n.f.* marble-work, marbles; marble shop *or* works.
marmolillo, *n.m.* fender stone; (*fig.*) phlegmatic person, lump of pudding.
marmolista, *n.m.* marble worker *or* dealer.
marmoración, *n.f.* marbling, stucco.
marmóreo, -rea, marmoroso, -sa, *a.* marble, marbled, made of marble, marmorean.
marmosa, *n.f.* (*zool.*) marmose.
marmosete, *n.m.* (*print.*) vignette.
marmota, *n.f.* (*zool.*) marmot; (*fig.*) sleepy-head; (*coll.*) servant-girl.
marmotear, *v.i.* (*prov.*) to jabber.
maro, *n.m.* (*bot.*) germander, marum.
marojo, *n.m.* (*bot.*) red-berried mistletoe.
maroma, *n.f.* rope, cable; tightrope; (*Hisp. Am.*) acrobatics.
marón, *n.m.* (*ichth.*) sturgeon.
marqués, *n.m.* marquis.
marquesa, *n.f.* marchioness.
marquesado, *n.m.* marquisate.
marquesina, *n.f.* (glass) canopy; (glass) roof.
marquesita, *n.f.* (*min.*) marcasite.
marquesota, *n.f.* high white collar.
marquesote, *n.m.* (*Hond.*) corn cake.
marqueta, *n.f.* crude cake of wax.
marquetería, *n.f.* cabinet-work; marquetry, inlaid work.
marquida, marquisa, *n.f.* (*vulg.*) prostitute.
marquilla, *n.f.* demy (*paper*).
marquista, *n.m.* (*prov.*) wholesale dealer in sherry.
marra, *n.f.* gap; stone hammer.
márraga, *n.f.* coarse grogram, ticking.
marrajo, -ja, *a.* crafty, wily, tricky, treacherous. — *n.m.* (*ichth.*) shark.
marramao, marramáu, *n.m.* miaow (*cry of a cat*).
marranada, *n.f.* filthiness, filthy thing.
marranalla, *n.f.* rabble.
marrancho, *n.m.* pig, hog.
marranería [MARRANADA].
marranillo, *n.m.* little pig.
marrano, -na, *a.* filthy. — *n.m.* pig, swine; drum (*of water-wheel*); timber (*of shaft*). — *n.f.* sow. — *n.m.f.* (*coll.*) filthy creature.
marrar, *v.t.*, *v.i.* to miss, fail; to go astray.
marras, *adv.* long ago, long since; ***de marras,*** well-known, well-remembered, famous, notorious.
marrasquino, *n.m.* maraschino.
marrazo, *n.m.* mattock.
márrega, *n.f.*, **marregón,** *n.m.* straw bed.
marrido, -da, *a.* (*obs.*) melancholy.
marrillo, *n.m.* (*prov.*) short thick stick.
marro, *n.m.* quoits; twisting aside, dodging; failure, miss.
marrón, *a.* brown. — *n.m.* quoit.
marroquí, *a.*, *n.m.f.* Moroccan. — *n.m.* Morocco leather.
marroquinería, *n.f.* Morocco leather work *or* shop.
marrubio, *n.m.* (*bot.*) white horehound.
marrueco, -ca, *a.* Moroccan.
Marruecos, *n.m.* Morocco.
marrullería, *n.f.* cunning; artful tricks; wheedling, cajolery.
marrullero, -ra, *a.* crafty, cunning; wheedling, coaxing.
Marsella, *n.f.* Marseilles.
marsellés, -llesa, *a.*, *n.m.f.* (native) of Marseilles; ***la Marsellesa,*** the Marseillaise:
marsopa, marsopla, *n.f.* porpoise.
marsupial, *a.* (*zool.*) marsupial. — *n.m.pl.* (**marsupiales**) marsupials.
Marta, *n.f.* Martha.
marta, *n.f.* marten, pine marten; ***marta cebellina,*** sable.
martagón (1), **-gona,** *n.m.f.* (*coll.*) cunning, artful person.
martagón (2), *n.m.* (*bot.*) wild lily.
Marte, *n.m.* (*astron.*) Mars.
marte, *n.m.* iron.
martelo, *n.m.* jealousy, immoderate passion.
martellina, *n.f.* marteline, millstone hammer.

martes, *n.m. inv.* Tuesday; ***martes de carnestolendas,*** Shrove Tuesday.
martillada, *n.f.* hammer-stroke.
martillador, -ra, *a.* hammering. — *n.m.f.* hammerer.
martillar, *v.t.* to hammer; to keep on at.
martillazo, *n.m.* hammer-stroke.
martillejo, *n.m.* smith's hammer; little hammer.
martilleo, *n.m.* hammering; clatter.
martillero, *n.m.* (*Chi.*) owner *or* manager of an auction mart.
martillito, *n.m.* small hammer.
martillo, *n.m.* hammer; auction mart; (*anat.*) malleus; (*com.*) hardware shop; (*ichth.*) hammer-headed shark; ***a martillo,*** by hammering; ***de martillo,*** wrought (metal); ***a macha martillo,*** strongly but roughly made; ***martillo pilón,*** drop hammer; ***remate a martillo,*** sale by auction.
Martín, San, *n.m.* pig-slaughtering season; ***a cada puerco le llega su San Martín,*** everyone meets his Waterloo.
martín del río, (*orn.*) [MARTINETE].
martín pescador, *n.m.* (*orn.*) kingfisher.
martinete, *n.m.* (*orn.*) night heron; coppersmith's hammer; drive hammer; drop hammer; piano hammer.
martingala, *n.f.* trick; cunning; breeches worn under armour.
martinico, *n.m.* (*coll.*) goblin.
martiniega, *n.f.* tax payable on St. Martin's Day.
mártir, *n.m.* martyr.
martirio, *n.m.* martyrdom.
martirizador, -ra, *a.* martyrizing, tormenting, torturing. — *n.m.f.* martyrizer, tormentor.
martirizar [C], *v.t.* to martyr, martyrize; to torment, torture.
martirologio, *n.m.* martyrology.
marucho, *n.m.* (*Chi.*) castrated cock, capon.
Maruja, *n.f.* (*familiar form of*) Mary.
marullo, *n.m.* light swell.
marxismo, *n.m.* Marxism.
marxista, *a.*, *n.m.f.* Marxist, Marxian.
marzadga, *n.f.* tax payable in March.
marzal, *a.* (*belonging to*) March.
marzo, *n.m.* March.
más, *adv.* more; most; ***cada vez más,*** more and more; ***nada más,*** nothing else, nothing further; ***tanto más . . . cuanto que,*** all the more . . . because; ***es más,*** moreover, further, indeed; ***a lo más, todo lo más, cuando más,*** at (the) most, at the outside; ***ya no más,*** not any more, no longer; ***a más tardar,*** at the latest; ***a más de,*** besides; ***a más y mejor,*** for all one is worth; ***como el que más,*** as much as the best of them; ***de más,*** over, too much; ***cobrar de más,*** to overcharge; ***estar de más,*** not to be needed *or* wanted; ***más bien,*** rather; ***no . . . más que,*** only; ***no hay más que verlo,*** you have only to see it; ***me gusta más,*** I prefer it, I like it better; ***más vale así,*** it's better like that; ***por más que,*** however much; ***sin más ni más,*** all of a sudden; without more ado; ***¿que más da?*** what difference does it make?; ***los más,*** the majority. — *n.m.* plus; ***tener sus más y sus menos,*** to have one's good and bad points.
mas, *conj.* but, yet; ***mas que,*** although; ***mas si,*** perhaps, if. — *n.m.* (*prov.*) farmhouse.
masa, *n.f.* mass; dough; mortar; nature; ***en masa,*** mass, en masse, in the mass, in a body.
masada, *n.f.* farmhouse.
masadero, *n.m.* farmer.
masaje, *n.m.* massage.
mascabado, -da, *a.* raw, unrefined (*of sugar*).
mascada, *n.f.* (*Mex.*) silk handkerchief.
mascador, -ra, *a.* chewing.
mascadura, *n.f.* chewing.
mascar [A], *v.t.* to chew; (*coll.*) to mumble, pronounce indistinctly.
máscara, *n.f.* mask, masquerade. — *n.m.f.* masquerader.
mascarada, *n.f.* masquerade, mummery.
mascarero, *n.m.* dealer in masks.
mascarilla, *n.f.* mask; half mask; death-mask.
mascarón, *n.m.* large mask; (*fig.*) fright; ***mascarón de proa,*** figurehead.
mascujar [MASCULLAR].
masculinidad, *n.f.* masculinity.
masculino, -na, *a.* masculine, male.
mascullar, *v.t.*, *v.i.* to chew hurriedly; to mumble.
masecoral, masejicomar, *n.m.* sleight of hand, legerdemain.
masera, *n.f.* kneading-trough; cloth for covering the dough.
masería, masía, *n.f.* farmhouse.
masetero, *n.m.* masseter.
masilla, *n.f.* putty.
masita, *n.f.* (*mil.*) uniform allowance.
maslo, *n.m.* root of the tail (*of quadrupeds*).
masón (1), *n.m.* mess given to fowls.
masón (2), *n.m.* freemason.
masonería, *n.f.* freemasonry.
masónico, -ca, *a.* masonic.
masoquismo, *n.m.* masochism.
masoquista, *a.* masochistic. — *n.m.f.* masochist.
masora, *n.f.* Masorah.
masovero, *n.m.* farmer.
mass-media, *n.f.* bulk of society, general run of people. — *n.m. pl.* **(mass-media)** media.
mastelerillo, *n.m.* (*naut.*) topgallant mast.
mastelero, *n.m.* (*naut.*) top-mast.
masticación, *n.f.* mastication.
masticar [A], *v.t.* to chew, masticate; to ruminate, muse on.
masticatorio, -ria, *a.* masticatory.
mastigador, *n.m.* horse's bit.
mástil, *n.m.* mast; top-mast; upright pole *or* post; trunk, stem, stalk; shaft (*of feather*); neck (*of stringed instruments*); ***mástil de barrena,*** shank (*of an auger*).
mastín, *n.m.* mastiff.
mastina, *n.f.* mastiff bitch.
mastinazo, *n.m.* large mastiff.
mastinillo, *n.m.* little mastiff.
mástique, *n.m.* mastic; mastic tree.
masto, *n.m.* stock into which a scion is grafted; (*prov.*) male bird.
mastodonte, *n.m.* mastodon, mammoth.
mastoides, *a.* mastoid.
mastranto, mastranzo, *n.m.* (*bot.*) apple mint.
mastuerzo, *n.m.* (*bot.*) pepper cress, peppergrass; cress; (*coll.*) dolt, dunder-head.
masturbación, *n.f.* masturbation.
masturbarse, *v.r.* to masturbate.
mata, *n.f.* bush, shrub; blade, sprig; head of hair, crop of hair; brush, underbrush; grove; (*bot.*) mastic tree; (*metal.*) matte; ***saltar de la mata,*** to come out of hiding; ***mata parda,*** dwarf oak; ***mata rubia,*** kermes, kermes oak; ***a salto de mata,*** on the run and in hiding; hastily, in a rush and furtively.
matacabras, *n.m. inv.* north wind (*especially when it is strong and cold*).
matacán, *n.m.* dog-poison; old hare; (*bot.*) dogbane; nux vomica; pebble, stone; deuce of clubs (*in cards*); troublesome *or* painful business; (*fort.*) machicolation gallery.
matacandelas, *n.m. inv.* candle extinguisher, snuffer.
matacandil, *n.m.* (*bot.*) London rocket.
matacía, *n.f.* (*prov.*) havoc, slaughter.

matachín, *n.m.* merry-andrew; jack-pudding; grotesque dance; slaughterman, butcher; laughing-stock; (*coll.*) swashbuckler.
matadero, *n.m.* slaughterhouse; abattoir; (*coll.*) drudgery.
matador, -ra, *a.* killing. — *n.m.f.* killer. — *n.m.* (*tauro.*, *cards*) matador.
matadura, *n.f.* (*vet.*) harness-sore; gall.
matafuego, *n.m.* fire extinguisher.
matagallina, *n.f.* (*bot.*) flax-leaved daphne.
ma(ta)hambre, *n.m.* (*Cub.*) marzipan; (*Arg.*) big portion of meat.
matahombres, *n.m. inv.* black beetle with yellow stripes; oil beetle; Spanish fly, blister-fly.
matajudío, *n.m.* (*ichth.*) mullet.
matalahuga, matalahuva, *n.f.* (*bot.*) anise; aniseed.
mátalas callando, *n.m.f.* (*coll.*) hypocrite, sly dog.
matalobos, *n.m. inv.* (*bot.*) wolf's-bane, aconite.
matalón, matalote, *n.m. a.* skinny and covered in sores (*of horses*). — *n.m.f.* sorry old nag.
matalotaje, *n.m.* (*naut.*) ship's stores; mess, jumble.
matamoros, *n.m. inv.* (*coll.*) bully, braggart.
matamoscas, *n.m. inv.* fly-swatter.
matancero, -ra, *a.*, *n.m.f.* (native) of Matanzas.
matanza, *n.f.* killing; slaughter, butchery, massacre; swine slaughtering and its season; pork products; (*coll.*) worry, anxiety.
matapalo, *n.m.* (*Hisp. Am.*) matapalo tree.
mataperrada, *n.f.* mischievous prank.
mataperros, *n.m. inv.* (*coll.*) street urchin.
matapiojos, *n.m. inv.* (*Chi.*, *Col.*) dragonfly.
matapolvo, *n.m.* light rain.
matapulgas, *n.f. inv.* (*bot.*) round-leaved mint.
matar, *v.t.* to kill, slay, put to death, slaughter; (*carp.*) to bevel, round; to put out (*a light*); to extinguish (*a fire*); to slake (*lime*); to spot (*cards*); to bore *or* pester to death; to make sore (*of harness*); to subdue, tone down (*a colour*); to mat (*metal*); ***estar a matar,*** to be at daggers drawn; (*coll.*) ***¡que me maten!*** I'll stake my life on it!; ***¡no me mates!*** you're not serious!; ***matar de hambre,*** to starve to death; ***matarse de risa,*** to kill o.s. with laughter; ***las mata callando,*** he's a sly one; ***matarse por,*** to go to any lengths to.
matarife, *n.m.* slaughterman.
matarratas, *n.m. inv.* rat-poison; (*coll.*) rot-gut.
matasanos, *n.m. inv.* quack, charlatan.
matasellos, *n.m. inv.* postmark, cancellation stamp.
matasiete, *n.m.* bully, braggart.
mate, *a.* mat, dull, lustreless. — *n.m.* mate, checkmate; (*bot.*) maté; gourd; vessel; ***dar mate a,*** to checkmate; (*fig.*) to make fun of; ***mate ahogado,*** stalemate.
matear, *v.i.* to shoot up, grow up (*of wheat etc.*).
matemático, -ca, *a.* mathematical; (*fig.*) automatic, unfailing, like clock-work. — *n.m.f.* mathematician. — *n.f.*, *n.f.pl.* mathematics.
Mateo, *n.m.* Matthew.
materia, *n.f.* matter; material, stuff; subject; ***materia colorante,*** dye-stuff; ***materia prima, primera materia,*** raw material; ***en materia de,*** as regards; ***entrar en materia,*** to get (in)to the subject, get to the point *or* main issue.
material, *a.* material; coarse. — *n.m.* stuff, material(s); (*print.*) copy; (*railw.*) ***material fijo,*** permanent way; (*railw.*) ***material rodante,*** rolling-stock.
materialidad, *n.f.* materiality; coarseness; literalness; outward appearance.
materialismo, *n.m.* materialism.
materialista, *a.* materialistic. — *n.m.f.* materialist.
materializar [C], *v.t.* to materialize. — **materializarse,** *v.r.* to become *or* get obsessed with material things.
maternal, *a.* maternal, motherly.
maternidad, *n.f.* maternity; ***casa de maternidad,*** maternity hospital.
materno, -na, *a.* maternal, of one's mother; ***lengua materna,*** mother tongue.
matero, -ra, *a.*, *n.m.f.* (*Hisp. Am.*) maté drinker.
matidez, *n.f.* dullness (*of light* or *sound*).
matigüelo, matihuelo, *n.m.* tumbler (*a toy*).
matinal, *a.* matutine, morning.
matiné, *n.m.* matinée.
matiz, *n.m.* tint, hue; shade, nuance; blending of colours; shade of meaning.
matizado, -da, *a.* variegated; nuanced.
matizar [C], *v.t.* to give a hue, shade *or* nuance to; to go into fine detail over, introduce subtle distinctions into; to blend the colours of.
mato, *n.m.* brake, coppice.
matojo, *n.m.* bush; (*bot.*) glasswort; (*Cub.*) shoot, sucker, tiller.
matón, *n.m.* bully, hector.
matorral, *n.m.* bush, thicket; scrubland.
matoso, -sa, *a.* bushy, covered in scrub.
matraca, *n.f.* rattle; (*coll.*) pestering; jibing; ***dar matraca a,*** to pull the leg of, jibe at.
matraquear, *v.t.* to rattle; to pester, importune; to jibe at.
matraqueo, *n.m.* rattle; pestering; jibing.
matraquista, *n.m.f.* jiber, joker, tease.
matraz, *n.f.* (*chem.*) matrass.
matrería, *n.f.* shrewdness, slyness.
matrero, -ra, *a.* shrewd, cunning, sly. — *n.m.f.* shrewd person, sly dog. — *n.m.* (*Hisp. Am.*) tramp, thug.
matriarcado, *n.m.* matriarchate.
matricaria, *n.f.* (*bot.*) feverfew.
matricida, *a.* matricidal. — *n.m.f.* matricide (*person*).
matricidio, *n.m.* matricide (*deed*).
matrícula, *n.f.* register, list; matriculation; registration number (*of a car etc.*); enrolment; ***matrícula de mar,*** mariner's register.
matriculado, -da, *a.* matriculate, matriculated.
matriculador, *n.m.* one who matriculates.
matricular, *v.t.* to matriculate, register, enrol; enter on a list. — **matricularse,** *v.r.* to register; to enter (*a contest etc.*).
matrimonial, *a.* matrimonial.
matrimoniar, *v.t.* (*joc.*) to marry.
matrimonio, *n.m.* marriage, matrimony; (*coll.*) married couple; ***matrimonio rato,*** legal marriage not consummated.
matritense, *a.* (of) Madrid.
matriz, *a.* mother; first, chief, head; ***casa matriz,*** mother house, headquarters, main office; ***escritura matriz,*** original draft. — *n.f.* womb; matrix, mould; female screw, nut; stub (*of a cheque book*).
matrona, *n.f.* matron; midwife.
matronal, *a.* matronal.
matronaza, *n.f.* plump, respectable matron.
maturrango, -ga, *n.m.f.* (*Hisp. Am.*) bad horseman; (*Chi.*) clumsy, rough person.
Matusalén, *n.m.* Methuselah.
matute, *n.m.* smuggling, smuggled goods, contraband; gambling den.
matutear, *v.t.* to smuggle.
matutero, *n.m.f.* smuggler, contrabandist.
matutinal, matutino, -na, *a.* matutinal, matutine, morning.
maula, *n.f.* rubbish, trash; remnant, reject piece; deceitful trick. — *n.m.f.* trickster, cheat; bad payer; shirker.
maulería, *n.f.* shop where remnants are sold; trickery.
maulero, *n.m.* seller of remnants; trickster, cheat.
maulón, *n.m.* great cheat.
maullador, -ra, *a.* mewing, miauling (*of a cat*).

maullar, *v.i.* to miaow (*of a cat*).
maullido, maúllo, *n.m.* miaow.
mauraca, *n.f.* (*prov.*) roasting chestnuts over coals.
Mauricio, *n.m.* Maurice.
mausoleo, *n.m.* mausoleum.
mavorcio, -cia, *a.* (*poet.*) belonging to war.
maxilar, *a.* maxillary.
máxime, *adv.* principally; especially.
máximo, -ma, *a.* maximum, greatest, top. — *n.m.* maximum. — *n.f.* maxim.
máximum, *n.m.* maximum.
maya (I), *a., n.m.f.* Maya, Mayan.
maya (2), *n.f.* (*bot.*) daisy; may-queen.
mayador, -ra, *a.* mewing.
mayal, *n.m.* flail; lever (*in oil-mills*).
mayar, *v.i.* to mew.
mayestático, -ca, *a.* majestic, of majesty, royal; ***el nos mayestático,*** the royal plural, royal we.
mayeto, *n.m.* mallet (*for paper-beating*).
mayo, *n.m.* May; maypole; Mayday festivity.
mayólica, *n.f.* majolica ware.
mayonesa, *n.f.* mayonnaise.
mayor, *a.* greater; greatest; larger; older, elder; eldest, senior; of age; major, main, principal; (*eccles.*) high (*altar, mass*); (*mus.*) major; (*math.*) sign $>$; ***calle mayor,*** main *or* high street; ***ganado mayor,*** large livestock; ***mayor de edad,*** of age; ***sin dificultades mayores, sin mayores dificultades,*** without any (very) great difficulty *or* trouble; ***al por mayor,*** wholesale; ***aguas mayores,*** excrement, droppings. — *n.m.* (*mil.*) major; ***al por mayor,*** wholesale. — *n.f.* (*log.*) first proposition (*in a syllogism*); (*pl.* **mayores**) forefathers; grown-ups, adults.
mayoral, *n.m.* stage-coach driver; head shepherd; overseer, steward.
mayoralía, *n.f.* flock, herd; herdsman's wages.
mayorana, *n.f.* (*bot.*) sweet marjoram.
mayorazga, *n.f.* woman, *or* wife of a person, having an entailed estate.
mayorazgo, *n.m.* primogeniture; first-born son; heir to *or* owner of an entailed estate; entailed estate.
mayorazguista, *n.m.* author treating of entails.
mayordoma, *n.f.* steward's wife; stewardess.
mayordomear, *v.t.* to manage *or* administer (*an estate*).
mayordomía, *n.f.* stewardship.
mayordomo, *n.m.* butler, majordomo; steward.
mayoría, *n.f.* majority; coming of age; major's commission.
mayoridad, *n.f.* majority, full age; superiority.
mayorista, *n.m.* student of the highest class in a grammar school; wholesale merchant; wholesale trade.
mayoritario, *a.* (of the) majority.
mayormente, *adv.* principally, chiefly.
mayúsculo, -la, *a.* large, good-sized; (*coll.*) awful, tremendous; capital (*letter*). — *n.f.* capital, big letter.
maza, *n.f.* mace (*weapon, staff*); war club; flax *or* hemp brake; drumstick (*of a bass drum*); ram (*of a pile driver*); thick end (*of a billiard cue*); sth. noisy tied to a dog's tail; hub (*of a wheel*); (*fig.*) bore; person of great authority; ***la maza y la mona,*** constant companions; ***maza de fraga,*** drop-hammer; ***maza de gimnasia,*** Indian club; (*bot.*) ***maza sorda,*** reed mace.
mazacote, *n.m.* kali, barilla; concrete; crude piece of work; (*coll.*) thick, heavy (lump of) stuff; (*coll.*) bore.
mazada, *n.f.* blow with a mace *or* club; (*coll.*) ***dar mazada a,*** to hurt, injure.
mazagatos, *n.m. inv.* rumpus, row, wrangle.
mazagrán, *n.m.* cold coffee and rum.
mazamorra, *n.f.* bread-dust; bits, scraps; broken biscuit; (*Per.*) pap made of Indian corn with sugar *or* honey; (*Col.*) thick corn soup; (*Arg.*) divided maize boiled with milk; (*naut.*) mess made of broken tack.
mazaneta, *n.f.* apple-shaped ornament in jewels.
mazapán, *n.m.* marzipan, marchpane.
mazar [C], *v.t.* (*prov.*) to churn (*milk*).
mazarí, *n.m.* tile-shaped brick.
mazarota, *n.f.* (*metal.*) deadhead.
mazmodina, *n.f.* gold coin of the Spanish Moors.
mazmorra, *n.f.* dungeon.
maznar, *v.t.* to knead; to beat (*hot iron*).
mazo, *n.m.* mallet, maul; bundle, bunch; stack; (*prov.*) clapper (*of bell*); (*coll.*) bore.
mazonería, *n.f.* masonry, brickwork; relief-work.
mazorca, *n.f.* thick ear *or* spike; ear (*of Indian corn*); cocoa bean; spindleful; spindle; (*Chi.*) political clique.
mazorral, *a.* rude, uncouth, clownish; (*print.*) solid.
mazote, *n.m.* cement, mortar; blockhead.
mazotear, *v.t.* to strike with a club *or* mallet.
mazurca, *n.f.* mazourka, mazurka (*dance and tune*).
me, *pron. pers. and reflex.* me; to me, for me; from me; myself, to myself, for myself; from myself.
meada, *n.f.* urination; (*vulg.*) pissing; piss stain.
meadero, *n.m.* urinal; (*vulg.*) piss-house.
meados, *n.m.pl.* urine; (*vulg.*) piss.
meaja, *n.f.* crumb; ***meaja de huevo,*** tread (*of an egg*).
meajuela, *n.f.* small crumb; slavering chain (*of bit*).
meandro, *n.m.* meander.
meaperros, *n.m. inv.* (*bot.*) stinking goose-foot.
mear, *v.t., v.i.* (*vulg.*) to piss (on).
meato, *n.m.* (*anat.*) meatus.
meauca, *n.f.* (*orn.*) shearwater.
Meca, *n.f.* Mecca.
meca (I), *n.f.* mecca; ***andar de ceca en meca,*** to go from pillar to post, wander about.
¡mecachis! *interj.* 'struth!
mecanicista, *a.* mechanistic. — *n.m.f.* mechanist.
mecánico, -ca, *a.* mechanical; mean, servile. — *n.m.* mechanic; driver. — *n.f.* mechanics; machinery, works; (*mil.*) fatigue duty; (*coll.*) dirty trick.
mecanismo, *n.m.* mechanism.
mecanizar [C], *v.t.* to mechanize.
mecanografía, *n.f.* typewriting.
mecanografiar, *v.t.* to typewrite, type.
mecanográfico, -ca, *a.* typewriting.
mecanógrafo, -fa, *n.m.f.* typist.
mecapal, *n.f.* (*Mex.*) leather band with ropes (*used by porters*).
mecate, *n.m.* (*Hond., Mex., Philip.*) maguey-rope.
mecedero, *n.m.* stirrer.
mecedor, -ra, *a.* rocking; swinging. — *n.m.* stirrer, shaker; swing. — *n.f.* rocking chair.
mecedura, *n.f.* rocking.
mecenas, *n.m. inv.* patron (of art *or* literature).
mecenazgo, *n.m.* patronage.
mecer [D], *v.t.* to rock; to swing; to stir; to shake.
mecereón, *n.m.* (*bot.*) mezereon.
meco, -ca (2), *a.* (*Mex.*) blackish red. — *n.m.f.* (*Mex.*) wild Indian.
meconio, *n.m.* meconium; poppy juice.
mecha, *n.f.* wick; fuse, match, match-rope; roll of lint; bacon for larding; lock (*of hair*); bundle (*of threads*); ***a toda mecha,*** at full force; ***aguantar mecha,*** to stick it, stick it out.
mechar, *v.t.* to lard, force, stuff.
mechazo, *n.m.* (*min.*) fizzle (*of a blast fuse*).
mechera, *n.f.* larding-pin; shoplifter.
mechero, *n.m.* tube (*for lamp-wick*); candlestick-socket; lamp burner; gas burner; cigarette lighter.

mechinal, *n.m.* putlog hole; hovel.
mechoacán, *n.m.* (*bot.*) bindweed.
mechón, *n.m.* tuft, mop, shock (*of hair etc.*).
mechoso, -sa, *a.* thready, towy; shock-headed.
medalla, *n.f.* medal; medallion.
medallón, *n.m.* medallion; locket; (*coll.*) hefty great medal.
médano, medaño, *n.m.* sand-bank; dune.
media (I), *n.f.* stocking.
mediacaña, *n.f.* (*arch.*) fluted moulding; picture moulding; (*carp.*) gouge; half-round file; curling tongs.
mediación, *n.f.* mediation; intercession.
mediado, -da, *a.* half-full; half-over; ***iba mediada la tarde,*** the afternoon was half over. — *adv.* ***a mediados de,*** about the middle of.
mediador, *a.* mediating, interceding. — *n.m.f.* mediator, intercessor.
mediana (I), *n.f.* long billiard cue; top of a fishing rod; (*geom.*) median.
medianejo, -ja, *a.* (*coll.*) mediocre.
medianería, *n.f.* moiety; party wall; party-line fence *or* hedge.
medianero, -ra, *a.* middle, dividing; mediating, interceding; party (*wall*). — *n.m.f.* mediator, go-between; owner of a house having a common wall.
medianía, medianidad, *n.f.* mean; moderate circumstances; mediocrity.
medianil, *a.* (*agric.*) middle-piece of ground; (*print.*) crossbar of a chase.
medianista, *n.m.f.* student of the fourth class in grammar schools.
mediano, -na (2), *a.* middling, medium, moderate; mediocre; average.
medianoche, *n.f.* midnight; middle of the night; light savoury roll.
mediante, *a.* intervening; ***Dios mediante,*** God willing. — *adv.* by means of, by virtue of, through.
mediar, *v.t.* to half-fill. — *v.i.* to be at the middle, be half-over; to mediate, intervene; to elapse; to take place in the interim.
mediatizar [C], *v.t.* to mediatize; to tie down.
mediato, -ta, *a.* mediate.
mediator, *n.m.* ombre.
medicable, *a.* medicable.
medicación, *n.f.* medical treatment, medication.
medicamento, *n.m.* medicament, medicine.
medicar [A], *v.t.* to cure by medicine, administer medicine to.
medicastro, *n.m.* quack, medicaster.
medicina, *n.f.* medicine; ***medicina casera,*** home remedies.
medicinal, *a.* medicinal, healing.
medicinante, *n.m.* medical student who practises before taking his final degree.
medicinar, *v.t.* to medicine, administer medicines to, apply medicaments to.
medición, *n.f.* measurement, mensuration, measuring.
médico, -ca, *a.* medical, medicinal; medic. — *n.m.* doctor, physician; ***médico de cabecera,*** family doctor; ***médico de plaza,*** bullring doctor; ***médico forense,*** forensic expert; ***médico partero,*** obstetrician. — *n.f.* woman doctor; doctor's wife.
medicucho, *n.m.* quack; (*coll.*) third-rate doctor.
medida, *n.f.* measure, measurement; step; moderation; ***a medida de,*** according to; ***a medida que,*** as; in proportion as; ***en la medida que,*** to the extent that; (***hecho***) ***a*** (***la***) ***medida,*** (made) to measure, custom-made; ***tomarse las medidas,*** to have one's measurements taken; ***tomar medidas,*** to take steps; ***medida de longitud,*** linear, long measure; ***medida de superficie,*** square measure; ***medida para áridos,*** dry measure; ***colmar la medida,*** to be the last straw; ***pesos y medidas,*** weights and measures.
medidor, -ra, *a.* measuring. — *n.m.f.* measurer.
mediera, *n.f.* stocking-maker.
mediero, *n.m.* hosier, stocking-dealer, stocking-maker; co-partner.
medieval, medioeval, *a.* medieval.
medio, -dia (2), *a.* half, half a; middle; mean, average; medium; medial; median; mid; ***media libra,*** half a pound; ***dos libras y media,*** two and a half pounds; ***a media asta,*** at half-mast; ***a media noche,*** at midnight; in the middle of the night; ***clase media,*** middle class; ***distancia media,*** average *or* mean distance; ***término medio,*** middle of the way, middle course; ***medias tintas,*** half measures. — *adv.* half; part, partly; ***medio muerto,*** half dead; ***a medio hacer,*** half done; ***a medias,*** half; half and half; by halves. — *n.m.* half; middle, midst; means; medium; ***de medio a medio,*** smack in the middle; right through; completely; ***de por medio,*** in between, in the way; ***en medio,*** in the middle; in the way; meanwhile; ***por medio de,*** by means of; ***meterse de por medio,*** to interfere, intervene; ***quitar de en medio,*** to clear *or* get out of the way; ***medios bien informados,*** well-informed circles *or* quarters. — *n.f.* mean; ***media diferencial,*** arithmetical mean; ***media proporcional,*** geometrical mean, mean proportional.
mediocre, *a.* middling, mediocre.
mediocridad, *n.f.* mediocrity.
mediodía, *n.m.* midday; middle of the afternoon; south.
mediopaño, *n.m.* thin woollen cloth.
mediquillo, *n.m.* two penny ha'penny little doctor; (*fig.*, *pej.*) quack.
medir [8], *v.t.*, *v.i.* to measure; to scan. — **medirse,** *v.r.* to act with moderation.
meditabundo, -da, *a.* pensive, thoughtful, musing.
meditación, *n.f.* meditation.
meditar, *v.t.*, *v.i.* to meditate (on).
meditativo, -va, *a.* meditative.
mediterráneo, -nea, *a.* Mediterranean; land-locked; having no seaboard.
médium, *n.m.* medium.
medo, -da, *a.*, *n.m.f.* Mede.
medra, *n.f.* thriving, prosperity, improvement, growth.
medrar, *v.i.* to thrive, prosper, improve, grow.
medre, *n.m.* (*fam.*) rat-race.
medriñaque, *n.m.* material for lining and stiffening women's skirts; short skirt.
medro, *n.m.* progress, improvement, growth, prosperity.
medroso, -sa, *a.* fearful; timorous, faint-hearted; terrible.
medula, médula, *n.f.* marrow, medulla; ***médula espinal,*** spinal cord; ***hasta la médula,*** to the core.
medular, *a.* medullar, medullary.
meduloso, -sa, *a.* full of marrow, marrowy.
medusa, *n.f.* (*ichth.*) medusa, jellyfish.
megáfono, *n.m.* megaphone.
megalítico, -ca, *a.* megalithic.
megalito, *n.m.* megalith.
megalocéfalo, -la, *a.* megalocephalous.
megalomanía, *n.f.* megalomania.
megalómano, -na, *a.*, *n.m.f.* megalomaniac.
mégano, *n.m.* dune.
megaterio, *n.m.* megathere.
mego, -ga, *a.* gentle, mild, meek.
megohmio, *n.m.* (*elec.*) megohm.
mehala, *n.f.* (*Morocco*) corps of regular troops.
mejana, *n.f.* islet (*in a river*).
mejicanismo, *n.m.* Mexicanism.
mejicano, -na, *a.*, *n.m.f.* Mexican.

Méjico, *n.m.* Mexico.
mejido, -da, *a.* beaten with sugar and milk (*egg*).
mejilla, *n.f.* cheek.
mejillón, *n.m.* (*zool.*) mussel.
mejor, *a.* (*compar.* of **bueno**) better; best; ***a lo mejor,*** probably, very likely; ***lo mejor,*** the best (thing); ***el mejor día,*** some fine day; ***coger lo mejor,*** to take the best of sth.; ***mejor postor,*** higher bidder. — *adv.* (*compar.* of **bien**) better; best; rather; ***mejor que mejor,*** better still; a good job too; ***tanto mejor,*** so much the better; ***mejor dicho,*** rather; to be more precise.
mejora, *n.f.* improvement, melioration, betterment; higher bid; (*law*) special bequest to a lawful heir.
mejorable, *a.* improvable.
mejoramiento, *n.m.* improvement, amelioration.
mejorana, *n.f.* sweet marjoram.
mejorar, *v.t.* to ameliorate, improve, better; to surpass; to raise (*a bid*); (*law*) to leave a special bequest to (*an heir*); ***mejorando lo presente,*** present company excepted. — **mejorar(se),** *v.i.* (*v.r.*) to improve, grow better, get better.
mejoría, *n.f.* improvement, bettering, amelioration; advantage, superiority.
mejunje, *n.m.* medical mixture; concoction.
melado, -da, *a.* honey-coloured. — *n.m.* cane-juice syrup; honey-cake, treacle. — *n.f.* toast dipped in honey.
meladucha, *n.f.* coarse, mealy apple.
meladura, *n.f.* (*Hisp. Am.*) treacle; concentrated syrup.
melampo, *n.m.* (*theat.*) prompter's candle.
melancolía, *n.f.* melancholia, melancholy, gloom, gloominess.
melancólico, -ca, *a.* melancholy, gloomy.
melancolizar [C], *v.t.* to affect with melancholy, dispirit.
melandro, *n.m.* (*zool.*) badger.
melanesio, -sia, *a.*, *n.m.f.* Melanesian.
melanita, *n.f.* (*min.*) melanite.
melanosis, *n.f.* (*med.*) melanosis, black cancer.
melapia, *n.f.* pippin.
melar, *a.* sweet, honey-sweet (*of cane* or *fruit*). — [I], *v.t.* to fill with honey; to boil (sugar-cane juice) clear.
melaza(s), *n.f.* molasses; treacle.
melcocha, *n.f.* molasses; honey-cake.
melcochero, *n.m.* maker of honey cakes.
melena, *n.f.* long, dishevelled hair (*in men*); loose hair (*in women*); hair on the forehead (*of an animal*); mane (*of lion*); (*med.*) melaena.
melenera, *n.f.* crown of ox's head; fleecy skin put under a yoke.
melenudo, -da, *a.* hairy, long-haired.
melera, *n.f.* state of melons spoiled by rain *or* hail; (*bot.*) alkanet, bugloss.
melero, *n.m.* dealer in honey; storage place for honey.
melesa, *n.f.* candle-wood.
melgacho, *n.m.* dog-fish.
melgar, *n.m.* patch of wild alfalfa.
meliáceo, -cea, *a.* (*bot.*) of the cinnamon family.
mélico, -ca, *a.* melic.
melífero, -ra, *a.* melliferous.
melificado, -da, *a.* mellifluous.
melificar [A], *v.t.*, *v.i.* to make honey (from).
melifluidad, *n.f.* mellifluousness, mellifluence.
melifluo, -lua, *a.* mellifluous, mellifluent.
meliloto, -ta, *a.*, *n.m.f.* foolish, simpleton. — *n.m.* melilot, sweet clover.
melindre, *n.m.* honey fritter; lady-finger; narrow ribbon; mincing delicacy, over-nicety.
melindrear, *v.i.* to act in a mincing fashion.
melindrería, *n.f.* [MELINDRE].
melindrero, -ra [MELINDROSO].
melindroso, -sa, *a.* mincing, finicky, over-nice.
melinita, *n.f.* melinite.
melisa, *n.f.* bee balm.
melocotón, *n.m.* peach; peach tree.
melocotonero, *n.m.* peach tree; peach-seller.
melodía, *n.f.* melody; tune.
melodioso, -sa, *a.* melodious, harmonious, tuneful.
melodrama, *n.m.* melodrama.
melodramático, -ca, *a.* melodramatic.
meloe, *n.m.* meloe, oil-beetle.
melografía, *n.f.* art of writing music.
meloja, *n.f.* metheglin, mead.
melojo, *n.m.* white oak.
melomanía, *n.f.* melomania, music-mania.
melómano, -na, *n.m.f.* melomaniac, music-lover.
melón, *n.m.* melon; musk-melon; (*fig.*) lemon, fool; (*fig.*) ***calar el melón,*** to take a person's measure.
melonar, *n.m.* field *or* bed of melons.
meloncillo, *n.m.* ichneumon, mongoose.
melonero, -ra, *n.m.f.* melon-grower; melon-seller.
melopea, *n.f.* (*coll.*) drunkenness.
melopeya, *n.f.* melopœia.
melosidad, *n.f.* honey-sweetness; mildness.
meloso, -sa, *a.* honeyed; mild.
melote, *n.m.* dregs of molasses.
melsa, *n.f.* (*prov.*) phlegm, slowness.
mella, *n.f.* nick, notch, dent; gap; impression; ***hacer mella a,*** to make a deep impression on, leave a heavy imprint *or* mark on.
mellar, *v.t.* to nick, notch, dent, jag; to break a tooth *or* teeth from.
melliza (1), *n.f.* honey sausage.
mellizo, -za (2), *a.*, *n.m.f.* twin.
mellón, *n.m.* straw torch.
membrado, -da, *a.* (*her.*) membered.
membrana, *n.f.* membrane.
membranáceo, -cea, *a.* membranaceous.
membranoso, -sa, *a.* membraneous.
membrete, *n.m.* letterhead, heading (*on letter paper*); note, memo; invitation card.
membrilla, *n.f.* quince bud.
membrillar, *n.m.* quince tree orchard; quince tree.
membrillero, *n.m.* quince tree.
membrillo, *n.m.* quince; quince tree; (***carne de***) ***membrillo,*** quince jelly.
membrudo, -da, *a.* burly, sturdy, robust.
memela, *n.f.* (*Mex.*) pancake (*made of maize meal*).
memez, *n.f.* stupid thing to do *or* say.
memo, -ma, *a.* silly, foolish. — *n.m.f.* fool, idiot.
memorable, memorando, -da, *a.* memorable.
memorándum, *n.m. inv.* memorandum; notebook; diplomatic note; (*Hisp. Am.*) certificate of deposit.
memorar, *v.t.* to remember, record.
memoratísimo, -ma, *a. superl.* worthy of eternal memory.
memoria, *n.f.* memory; recollection; memoir, record, report; paper; ***borrarse de la memoria,*** to fade from (one's) memory; ***encomendar a la memoria,*** to commit to memory; ***ser flaco de memoria,*** to have a poor *or* short memory; ***traer a la memoria,*** to bring to mind; to recall; to remind; ***de memoria,*** by heart; ***hablar de memoria,*** to talk at random; ***hacer memoria,*** to try to remember; ***de feliz memoria,*** of happy memory; (*pl.*) memoirs; regards, compliments; ***memorias a su señora,*** my best regards to your wife.
memorial, *n.m.* memorial; petition; memorandum book.
memorialista, *n.m.* amanuensis.
memorión, *n.m.* phenomenal memory.
memorioso, -sa, *a.* retentive (*of the memory*); mindful.
mena, *n.f.* (*naut.*) girt of cordage; (*ichth.*) picarel; (*min.*) ore; (*Philip.*) size and shape of a cigar.

ménade, *n.f.* maenad.
menador, -ra, *n.m.f.* (*prov.*) winder (*of silk*).
menaje, *n.m.* household furniture; school equipment and supplies.
menar, *v.t.* (*prov.*) to wind (*silk*); (*coll.*) to contemplate.
mención, *n.f.* mention; ***hacer mención de,*** to mention, make mention of; ***mención honorífica,*** honourable mention.
mencionar, *v.t.* to mention, name.
menchevique, *n.m.f.* Menshevik.
mendacidad, *n.f.* mendacity.
mendaz, *a.* mendacious. — *n.m.f.* liar.
mendeliano, -na, *a.* Mendelian.
mendicación, *n.f.* begging, asking charity.
mendicante, *a.* mendicant, begging. — *n.m.* mendicant, beggar.
mendicidad, *n.f.* mendicity, mendicancy, beggary.
mendigante, -ta, *n.m.f.* mendicant, beggar.
mendigar [B], *v.t., v.i.* to beg.
mendigo, *n.m.* beggar.
mendiguez, *n.f.* beggary, mendicancy.
mendoso, -sa, *a.* mendacious.
mendrugo, *n.m.* crust of bread, piece of dry bread.
meneador, -ra, *a.* stirring, shaking.
menear, *v.t.* to stir, shake; to wag, waggle; to sway, move about; to manage, run; ***hay que menearse,*** we've got to make a move, got to shift, got to get cracking; ***más vale no menearlo*** or ***meneallo,*** it's better left alone, the least said the better.
meneo, *n.m.* shake, shaking; wag, wagging; shift, shifting; rearranging; going over.
menester, *n.m.* need, necessity, want; occupation; implement; ***haber menester,*** to need; ***ser menester,*** to be necessary.
menesteroso, -sa, *a.* needy, necessitous.
menestra, *n.f.* pottage; vegetable soup.
menestral, *n.m.* mechanic, artisan, handicraftsman, workman.
menestralería, *n.f.* artisanship.
menestralía, *n.f.* artisans, body of artisans.
menestrete, *n.m.* (*naut.*) nail puller.
menfita, *a., n.m.f.* (native) of Memphis. — *n.f.* (*min.*) onyx.
mengajo, *n.m.* (*prov.*) rag, tatter.
mengano, -na, *n.m.f.* so-and-so; Tom, Dick or Harry.
mengua, *n.f.* diminution, waning, decrease; decay, decline; poverty, need; disgrace; ***en mengua de,*** to the discredit *or* detriment of.
menguadamente, *adv.* ignominiously.
menguado, -da, *a.* impaired, diminished; cowardly, weak-spirited; mean; wretched, sorry; fatal, ill-starred. — *n.m.f.* wretch. — *n.m.* drop stitch.
menguante, *a.* diminishing, decreasing, waning. — *n.f.* ebb tide; low water; decline, decay.
menguar [H], *v.t.* to lessen, diminish; to detract from. — *v.i.* to lessen, diminish; to decline, decay, fall (off); to fall, go down (*of water*); to wane; to drop-stitch.
mengue, *n.m.* (*coll.*) deuce, devil.
meniantes, *n.m.* (*bot.*) marsh-trefoil.
menina, *n.f.* young lady-in-waiting, maid of honour.
meningitis, *n.f. inv.* (*med.*) meningitis.
menino, *n.m.* royal page.
menique, *n.m.* [MEÑIQUE].
menisco, *n.m.* (*phys.*) meniscus.
menologio, *n.m.* menology.
menopausia, *n.f.* (*med.*) menopause.
menor, *a.* minor; smaller, smallest; younger, youngest; less, lesser, least; junior; ***menor de edad,*** under age. — *n.m.f.* minor. — *n.m.* minorite; ***al por menor,*** retail. — *n.f.* minor (*premise*).
Menorca, *n.f.* Minorca.
menorete, *a.* (*coll.*) ***al menorete,*** at least.
menorquín, -quina, *a., n.m.f.* Minorcan.
menos, *adv.* less, lesser, least; fewer; except (for); minus; ***menos de, menos que,*** less than; ***al menos, a lo menos, por lo menos,*** at least; ***a menos que,*** unless; ***de menos,*** less; ***echar de menos,*** to miss; ***ni más ni menos,*** exactly; (***poco***) ***más o menos,*** more or less; ***venir a menos,*** to come down in the world; ***ni mucho menos,*** not at all, far from it, absolutely not; ***tiene menos amigos que antes,*** he has fewer friends than before; ***las dos menos cuarto,*** a quarter to two; ***¡menos mal!*** thank goodness!; ***menos mal que . . . ,*** it's a good job that. . . .
menoscabar, *v.t.* to lessen, detract from, impair.
menoscabo, *n.m.* lessening, reduction, impairing.
menoscuenta, *n.f.* discount.
menospreciable, *a.* despicable, contemptible.
menospreciador, -ra, *a.* contemptuous, despising. — *n.m.f.* contemner, despiser.
menospreciar, *v.t.* to undervalue, underrate, underestimate; to despise, slight.
menospreciativo, -va, *a.* contemptuous, despising, scornful.
menosprecio, *n.m.* contempt, scorn; undervaluing; underestimation.
mensaje, *n.m.* message.
mensajería, *n.f.* stage-coach, public conveyance; (*pl.*) transportation company; shipping line.
mensajero, -ra, *n.m.f.* messenger; ***paloma mensajera,*** carrier pigeon; (*naut.*) bull's-eye traveller.
menstruación, *n.f.* menstruation.
menstrual, *a.* menstrual.
menstruar [M], *v.i.* to menstruate.
menstruo, -rua, *a.* menstruous, monthly, menstrual. — *n.m.* menses; (*chem.*) menstruum.
mensual, *a.* monthly.
mensualidad, *n.f.* monthly salary, month's pay; monthly instalment, payment.
ménsula, *n.f.* brace, bracket; elbow rest; (*arch.*) corbel.
mensura, *n.f.* measure.
mensurabilidad, *n.f.* mensurability.
mensurador, -ra, *a.* measuring. — *n.m.f.* measurer.
mensural, *a.* measuring.
mensurar, *v.t.* to measure.
menta, *n.f.* (*bot.*) mint; peppermint.
mentado, -da, *a.* famous.
mental, *a.* mental, intellectual, ideal.
mentalidad, *n.f.* mentality.
mentalización, *n.f.* conditioning of the mind, indoctrination, brain-washing.
mentalizar, *v.t.* to condition the mind of, indoctrinate, brain-wash.
mentalmente, *adv.* mentally, intellectually, ideally.
mentar [I], *v.t.* to name, mention; (*coll.*) to abuse; (*coll.*) ***eso es mentar la bicha,*** that's taboo.
mente, *n.f.* mind; ***tener en la mente,*** to have in mind.
mentecatería, *n.f.* folly, absurdity, nonsense.
mentecatez, *n.f.* stupidity, dim-wittedness.
mentecato, -ta, *a., n.m.f.* simple, foolish (*person*).
mentidero, *n.m.* (*coll.*) tattling corner; centre *or* hive of gossip.
mentir [6], *v.t., v.i.* to lie; ***miento,*** I'm a liar; ***miente más que siete,*** he's an out-and-out liar; ***mentir con,*** to disagree, clash with.
mentira, *n.f.* lie, falsehood; error, mistake (*in writing*); (*coll.*) white spot (*on the nails*); ***mentira oficiosa*** or ***piadosa,*** white lie; ***coger en una mentira,*** to catch out in a lie; ***parece mentira,*** it's hard to believe; ***¡parece mentira que digas eso!*** how can you say such a thing?; ***¡mentira!*** nonsense! rubbish! no such thing!

mentirilla, mentirijilla, *n.f.* fib, white lie; ***de mentirilla(s), de mentirijilla(s),*** in fun, for fun.
mentirón, *n.m.* great lie, whopper.
mentiroso, -sa, *a.* lying. — *n.m.f.* liar.
mentís, *n.m. inv.* denial; ***dar un mentís a,*** to give the lie to.
mentol, *n.m.* (*pharm.*) menthol.
mentón, *n.m.* chin.
mentor, *n.m.* mentor.
menú, *n.m.* menu; set menu.
menudamente, *adv.* minutely; in detail.
menudear, *v.t.* to do *or* repeat often; to tell in detail. — *v.i.* to happen often, become common *or* frequent; to be frequently to be found, be *or* become a common occurrence; to go into detail.
menudencia, *n.f.* trifle; littleness, minuteness; minute detail; (*pl.*) offal; (*Hisp. Am.*) giblets.
menudeo, *n.m.* constant repetition *or* occurrence; retail.
menudero, -ra, *n.m.f.* dealer in tripe, giblets etc.
menudillo, *n.m.* fetlock joint; (*pl.*) giblets.
menudo, -da, *a.* small, minute, tiny; ***chica menuda,*** daintily built *or* petite girl; (*coll.*) ***¡menudo!, ¡menuda!*** a fine one!; ***¡menuda suerte!*** talk about luck!; ***a menudo,*** often; ***por menudo,*** in detail; retail; ***ganado menudo,*** young livestock; ***gente menuda,*** children, kids, small fry. — *n.m.pl.* small change; offal; giblets.
menura, *n.f.* lyre-bird.
meñique, *a.* little; tiny. — *n.m.* little finger.
meollada, *n.f.* (*prov.*) fry of animals' brains.
meollar, *n.m.* (*naut.*) spun yarn.
meollo, *n.m.* marrow; brain; brains; sense; substance, pith.
meón, meona, *a.* (*vulg.*) pissing; dripping, soaking.
meple, *n.m.* (*bot.*) maple; ***meple moteado,*** bird's-eye maple.
mequetrefe, *n.m.* whipper-snapper, coxcomb.
meramente, *adv.* merely, solely.
merar, *v.t.* to mix; to mix with water.
merca, *n.f.* (*coll.*) purchase.
mercachifle, *n.m.* pedlar, hawker; (*contempt.*) twopenny-halfpenny merchant; money-grabber.
mercadantesco, -ca, *a.* mercantile.
mercadear, *v.i.* to traffic, trade.
mercader, mercadante, *n.m.* merchant; ***hacer oídos de mercader,*** to lend a deaf ear.
mercadera, *n.f.* shopkeeper's wife, tradeswoman.
mercadería, *n.f.* merchandise, commodity.
mercado, *n.m.* market, mart.
mercadotecnia, *n.f.* marketing.
mercadotecnología, *n.f.* marketing.
mercaduría, *n.f.* merchandise.
mercal, *n.m.* ancient Spanish copper coin.
mercancía, *n.f.* merchandise, goods; ***tren de mercancías,*** goods train, (*Am.*) freight train.
mercante, *a.* merchant. — *n.m.* merchant ship.
mercantil, *a.* mercantile.
mercantilismo, *n.m.* mercantilism.
mercar [A], *v.t., v.i.* to purchase, buy.
Merced, *n.f.* Mercederian Order.
merced, *n.f.* favour, grace, mercy; ***vuestra*** or ***vuesa merced,*** your honour, your grace, your worship, sir; ***a merced de,*** at the mercy of; ***hágame usted la merced (de),*** be so kind (as to); ***merced a,*** thanks to.
mercenaria (1), *n.m.f.* Mercederian.
mercenario, -ria (2), *a., n.m.* mercenary.
mercería, *n.f.* haberdashery, drapery, (*Am.*) dry goods.
mercero, *n.m.* haberdasher.
merculino, -na, mercurino, -na, *a.* (*obs.*) belonging to Wednesday.
mercurial, *a.* mercurial. — *n.f.* (*bot.*) herb mercury.
mercúrico, -ca, *a.* mercuric.
Mercurio, *n.m.* (*astron.*) Mercury.
mercurio, *n.m.* mercury.
mercurioso, -sa, *a.* mercurous.
merchante, *a., n.m.* [MARCHANTE].
merdellón, -llona, *a.* (*coll.*) slovenly, dirty, unclean (*of a servant*).
merdoso, -sa, *a.* filthy.
merecedor, -ra, *a.* deserving; entitled.
merecer [9], *v.t., v.i.* to deserve, merit, be entitled to; (*coll.*) to try hard; ***merece la pena,*** it's worth it, worthwhile, worth the trouble.
merecido, -da, *a.* well-deserved; ***se lo tiene (bien) merecido,*** it serves him right. — *n.m.* (just) deserts.
merecimiento, *n.m.* merit.
merendar [1], *v.t.* to have for tea; to picnic on. — *v.i.* to have tea; to have a snack; to picnic; (*coll.*) ***merendarse a alguien,*** to make mincemeat of s.o., wipe the floor with s.o.
merendero, *n.m.* open-air café, refreshment kiosk, place to have tea.
merendona, *n.f.* (*coll.*) slap-up tea, grand spread.
merengue, *n.m.* meringue.
meretricio, -cia, *a.* meretricious.
meretriz, *n.f.* prostitute.
merey, *n.f.* cashew tree.
mergo, *n.m.* (*orn.*) diver.
meridiano, -na, *a.* meridian; bright, dazzling. — *n.m.* meridian. — *n.f.* couch; nap; meridian; ***a la meridiana,*** at noon.
meridional, *a.* southern; (*fig.*) Latin.
merienda, *n.f.* tea, afternoon snack; picnic; ***merienda campestre,*** picnic; (*coll.*) ***merienda de negros,*** chaos, hopeless mix-up; bedlam.
merino, -na, *a.* merino; thick and curly (*hair*). — *n.m.* merino; merino shepherd; royal judge.
meritísimo, -ma, *a. superl.* most worthy.
mérito, *n.m.* merit, worth; ***de mucho mérito,*** highly deserving, of great worth; ***hacer méritos,*** to make oneself deserving, build up one's credit; ***hacer mérito de,*** to mention.
meritorio, -ria, *a.* meritorious. — *n.m.* employee who begins with a small *or* no salary.
merla, *n.f.* blackbird.
Merlín, *n.m.* Merlin; ***saber más que Merlín,*** to be very shrewd *or* knowing.
merlín, *n.m.* (*naut.*) marline; magician.
merlón, *n.m.* (*fort.*) merlon.
merluza, *n.f.* hake; (*coll.*) ***coger una merluza,*** to get pie-eyed *or* sozzled.
merma, *n.f.* decrease; leakage.
mermar, *v.t., v.i.* to decrease, diminish, lessen, reduce.
mermelada, *n.f.* jam; ***mermelada de naranja,*** marmalade.
mero (1), **-ra,** *a.* mere, pure, simple.
mero (2), *n.m.* (*ichth.*) grouper, jewfish.
merodeador, -ra, *a.* marauding. — *n.m.* marauder.
merodear, *v.i.* to maraud; (*coll.*) to lie in wait, hang about.
merodeo, *n.m.* marauding.
merodista, *n.m.* marauder.
mes, *n.m.* month; menses, courses; monthly wages; ***meses mayores,*** last months of pregnancy; months immediately preceding harvest; ***al mes,*** a month, per month.
mesa, *n.f.* table; desk; table-land, plateau; landing (*of a staircase*); (*print.*) case (*of type*); board (*keep*); set, rubber (*of cards*); flat (*of a sword etc.*); executive board; incomes of cathedrals, churches, prelates *or* dignitaries in Spain; billiard table; billiard game; facet (*of diamond*); ***hacer mesa gallega,*** to make a clean sweep; ***mesa de cambios,*** bank; (*naut.*) ***mesas de guarnición,*** channels; ***mesa franca,*** open table; ***media mesa,*** servants' table; ***mesa de milanos,*** scanty table; ***mesa redonda,*** table d'hôte; round table;

levantar or ***alzar la mesa,*** to clear the table; ***mesa revuelta,*** medley; ***poner la mesa,*** to lay the table; ***a mesa puesta,*** at others' expense; ***a mesa y mantel,*** like a lord; ***mesa camilla,*** blanket-draped table equipped with a brazier.
mesada, *n.f.* monthly pay, wages.
mesadura, *n.f.* tearing the hair *or* beard.
mesana, *n.f.* mizzen-mast.
mesar, *v.t.* to tear *or* pull (the hair *or* beard).
mescal, mexcal, *n.m.* (*Mex.*) liquor made of maguey.
mescolanza, *n.f.* medley; mess, jumble.
meseguería, *n.f.* guard over fruits; money paid for watching the harvest.
meseguero, -ra, *a.* (pertaining to the) harvest. — *n.m.* harvest watchman; vineyard watchman.
mesentérico, -ca, *a.* mesenteric.
mesenterio, *n.m.* mesentery.
mesera, *n.f.* (*Mex.*) waitress.
mesero, *n.m.* journeyman paid by the month; (*Mex.*) waiter.
meseta, *n.f.* table-land, plateau; staircase-landing; (*naut.*) backstay-stool.
mesiánico, -ca, *a.* Messianic.
mesianismo, *n.m.* Messianism.
Mesías, *n.m.* Messiah.
mesiazgo, *n.m.* dignity of Messiah.
mesilla, *n.f.* small table; sideboard; screw; board wages; staircase-landing; (*arch.*) window sill; ***mesilla de noche,*** bedside table.
mesillo, *n.m.* first menses after parturition.
mesita, *n.f.* small table.
mesmedad, *n.f.* sameness; essential nature; ***por su misma mesmedad,*** by itself, by the very fact; (*obs.*) [MISMO].
mesmerismo, *n.m.* mesmerism.
mesmo, -ma, *a.* [MISMO].
mesnada, *n.f.* armed retinue.
mesnadería, *n.f.* wages of a ***mesnadero.***
mesnadero, *n.m.* member of a ***mesnada.***
mesón, *n.m.* inn, hostelry.
mesonaje, *n.m.* street full of inns.
mesoncillo, *n.m.* little inn.
mesonero, -ra, *a.* waiting, serving in an inn. — *n.m.f.* inn-keeper, publican, landlord *or* landlady; host *or* hostess.
mesonista, *n.m.* waiter in an inn.
mesta, *n.f.* body of sheep-owners.
mestal, *n.m.* piece of barren, uncultivated ground.
mestizar [C], *v.t.* to cross (*breeds of animals*).
mestizo, -za, *a.*, *n.m.f.* half-breed, half-caste.
mesto, *n.m.* prickly oak.
mestura, *n.f.* (*prov.*) meslin, mixed grain.
mesura, *n.f.* moderation, circumspection, restraint; dignity, gravity.
mesurado, -da, *a.* moderate, circumspect, restrained; dignified, grave.
mesurar, *v.t.* to moderate, restrain.
meta, *n.f.* goal; finishing line; aim.
metabolismo, *n.m.* metabolism.
metafísico, -ca, *a.* metaphysical. — *n.m.* metaphysician. — *n.f.* metaphysics.
metafonía, *n.f.* metaphony.
metáfora, *n.f.* metaphor.
metafórico, -ca, *a.* metaphorical.
metaforizar [C], *v.t.* to express metaphorically. — *v.i.* to use metaphors.
metal, *n.m.* metal; brass, latten; timbre (*of the voice*); quality, condition; (*mus.*) brass (*instruments*); ***el vil metal,*** filthy lucre.
metalario, *n.m.* metal-worker, metallist.
metalescente, *a.* of metallic lustre.
metálico, -ca, *a.* metallic; medallic. — *n.m.* metal-worker, metallurgist; cash. — *n.f.* metallurgy.
metalífero, -ra, *a.* metalliferous.
metalizar [C], *v.t.* to metallize. — **metalizarse,** *v.r.* to become metallized; to become obsessed with money.
metalografía, *n.f.* metallography.
metaloide, *n.m.* metalloid.
metalurgia, *n.f.* metallurgy.
metalúrgico, -ca, *a.* metallurgic, metallurgical. — *n.m.* metallurgist.
metalla, *n.f.* small pieces of gold leaf (*for mending*).
metamorfosear, *v.t.* to metamorphose, transform.
metamorfosis, *n.f. inv.* metamorphosis.
metano, *n.m.* (*chem.*) methane.
metaplasmo, *n.m.* (*gram., biol.*) metaplasm.
metástasis, *n.f. inv.* (*med.*) metastasis.
metate, *n.m.* (*Mex.*) grinding stone.
metátesis, *n.f. inv.* (*rhet.*) metathesis.
metedor, -ra, *n.m.f.* smuggler; one who brings *cr* puts in.
metedurı́a, *n.f.* smuggling.
metempsícosis, metempsicosis, *n.f. inv.* metempsychosis.
metemuertos, *n.m. inv.* (*theat.*) stage hand; busybody.
meteórico, -ca, *a.* meteoric.
meteorito, *n.m.* meteorite.
meteorización, *n.f.* influence of atmospheric phenomena on the soil.
meteorizar, *v.t.* to meteorize.
meteoro, *n.m.* meteor.
meteorología, *n.f.* meteorology.
meteorológico, -ca, *a.* meteorological.
meteorologista, *n.m.f.* meteorologist.
meter, *v.t.* to put, place, shove, stick in; to insert; to take in (*a seam*); to make (*noise, trouble*); to cause (*fear*); to start (*a rumour, a row*); to tell (*lies*); to stake (*money*); ***a todo meter,*** as fast as he, it, they etc. can go. — **meterse,** *v.r.* to butt in, meddle; to become; to project, extend; ***meterse a,*** to set o.s. up as; ***meterse a*** + *inf.*, to take it upon o.s. to + *inf.*; ***meterse con,*** to pick a quarrel with; to interfere with; to have a go, crack, dig, *or* poke at; ***meterse en,*** to get into, plunge into; ***meterse en sí mismo,*** to retire into one's shell.
metesillas y sacamuertos, *n.m. inv.* (*theat.*) stage hand.
meticón, -cona, *n.m.f.* busybody.
meticuloso, -sa, *a.* meticulous.
metido, -da, *a.* close, compressed; ***estar muy metido con,*** to be very close with; ***estar metido en,*** to be involved *or* engaged in ; ***estar metido en carnes,*** to be plump, fleshy, have got fat. — *n.m.* punch given below the ribs; baby's nappy; (*coll.*) dressing down, lecture.
metileno, *n.m.* (*chem.*) methylene.
metilo, *n.m.* (*chem.*) methyl.
metimiento, *n.m.* putting *or* getting in; interference; favoured position.
metódico, -ca, *a.* methodical, formal.
metodismo, *n.m.* systematic method; (*eccles.*) Methodism.
metodista, *n.m.f.* Methodist; one given to method and order.
método, *n.m.* method.
metonimia, *n.f.* metonymy.
metonímico, -ca, *a.* metonymical.
metoposcopia, *n.f.* metoposcopy.
metralla, *n.f.* grape-shot, shrapnel.
metrallar, *v.t.* to shoot with grape-shot.
metralleta, *n.f.* sub-machine gun.
metreta, *n.f.* a Greek and Roman liquid measure.
métricamente, *adv.* metrically.
métrico, -ca, *a.* metric, metrical. — *n.f.* metrical art, prosody; poesy.

metrificador, -ra, *n.m.f.* versifier.
metrificar, *v.t.* to versify, put into verse.
metro *n.m.* metre; (*coll.*) tube, underground (railway), (*Am.*) subway.
metrología, *n.f.* metrology.
metromanía, *n.f.* metromania, rhyming-madness.
metrónomo, *n.m.* (*mus.*) metronome.
metrópoli, *n.f.* metropolis; mother country; archiepiscopal church.
metropolitano, -na, *a.* metropolitan. — *n.m.* underground railway; metropolitan (*archbishop*).
mexcal [MESCAL].
meya, *n.f.* spider-crab.
mezcal, *n.m.* (*Hisp. Am.*) maguey; pulque.
mezcla, *n.f.* mixture, blend; medley; mortar; tweed cloth.
mezcladamente, *adv.* in a mixed manner.
mezclador, -ra, *a.* mixing, blending. — *n.m.f.* mixer, blender; (*obs.*) trouble-maker.
mezcladura, *n.f.*, **mezclamiento,** *n.m.* mixture, medley; mixing.
mezclar, *v.t.* to mix, mingle, blend. — **mezclarse,** *v.r.* to mix, mingle; to intermarry; to meddle.
mezclilla, *n.f.* tweed.
mezcolanza, *n.f.* mixture, medley, jumble.
mezquindad, *n.f.* meanness, niggardliness; wretchedness; paltriness; poverty.
mezquino, -na, *a.* mean, niggardly; wretched; paltry; penurious.
mezquita, *n.f.* mosque.
mezquital, *n.m.* clump of mesquite shrubs.
mezquite, *n.m.* mesquite shrub.
mí, *pers. pron.* me, myself.
mi (1), **mis,** *poss. pron.* my.
mi (2), *n.m.* (*mus.*) mi.
mía, *n.f.* contingent of Moroccan troops.
miaja, *n.f.* crumb.
miar [L], *v.i.* to mew.
miasma, *n.f.* miasma.
miasmático, -ca, *a.* miasmatic.
miau, *n.m.* mew.
mica, *n.f.* mica; female monkey; (*Guat.*) flirt.
micáceo, -cea, *a.* mica-like.
micción, *n.f.* micturition.
micénico, -ca, *a.* Mycenæan.
mico, *n.m.* monkey, long-tailed ape; (*coll.*) brat, kid, titch; (*coll.*) randy type; (*coll.*) ***volverse mico,*** to be at one's wit's end, go crazy.
micología, *n.f.* mycology.
micra, *n.f.* micron.
microbio, *n.m.* microbe, germ.
microbiología, *n.f.* microbiology.
microbiológico, -ca, *a.* microbiological.
microbiólogo, -ga, *n.m.f.* microbiologist.
microbús, *n.m.* minibus.
microcefalía, *n.f.* microcephaly.
microcéfalo, -la, *a.* microcephalic.
microcosmo, *n.m.* microcosm.
microfilm(e), *n.m.* microfilm.
micrófono, *n.m.* microphone.
micrografía, *n.f.* micrography.
micrómetro, *n.m.* micrometer.
micromilímetro, *n.m.* micron (*one-thousandth of a millimetre*).
microorganismo, *n.m.* micro-organism.
microscópico, -ca, *a.* microscopic, microscopical.
microscopio, *n.m.* microscope.
microsurco, *a.*, *n.m.* microgroove, long-playing (record).
micuré, *n.m.* (*Par.*) opossum.
michino, *n.m.* kitten, pussy.
micho, -cha, *n.m.f.* puss.
mida (1), *n.f.* plant louse.
mida (2), *pres. subj.* [MEDIR].
miedo, *n.m.* fear, dread; apprehension; ***miedo cerval,*** panic; ***dar miedo,*** to be dreadful, appalling; ***dar miedo a,*** to frighten; ***tener miedo,*** to be afraid; ***tener miedo a*** or ***de,*** to fear, be afraid of; (*coll.*) ***de miedo,*** terrific.
miedoso, -sa, *a.* fearful, timorous; apprehensive.
miel, *n.m.* honey; molasses, cane juice; ***miel de caña,*** molasses; ***hacerse de miel,*** to be too compliant; ***no hay miel sin hiel,*** nothing is ever totally perfect; ***miel sobre hojuelas,*** all this and heaven too; ***dejar a uno con la miel en los labios,*** to deprive s.o. of a thing which he was just beginning to enjoy; ***quedarse a media miel,*** to lose sth. one had just begun to enjoy.
mielgo, -ga, *a.*, *n.m.f.* twin. — *n.f.* strip of land marked for planting; winnowing fork; (*ichth.*) fox shark; (*bot.*) lucerne.
miembro, *n.m.* member; limb.
mienta (1), *n.f.* (*bot.*) mint.
mienta (2), *pres. subj.* [MENTIR].
mientes, *n.f.pl.* mind, thought; ***caer en mientes, en las mientes,*** to come to mind; ***parar*** or ***poner mientes en,*** to consider, reflect on; ***traer a las mientes,*** to bring *or* call to mind; ***venírsele a uno a las mientes,*** to come to one's mind, occur to one.
miento, *pres. indic.* [MENTAR], [MENTIR].
mientras, *adv.*, *conj.* while, whilst, when, meanwhile; ***mientras tanto,*** meanwhile; ***mientras que,*** while; whereas; ***mientras más*** (or ***menos***) ***. . . más*** (or ***menos***)***,*** the more (*or* less) . . . the more (*or* less); ***mientras no,*** until; unless.
miera, *n.f.* juniper oil, resin.
miércoles, *n.m. inv.* Wednesday; ***miércoles de ceniza*** or (*coll.*) ***miércoles de corvillo,*** Ash Wednesday.
mierda, *n.f.* (*obsc.*) shit; filth; (*fig.*) mess (up), muck (up); ***¡vete a la mierda!*** go to hell!
mierdacruz, *n.f.* (*bot.*) ciliate sparrow-wort.
mies, *n.f.* wheat, corn; crop; harvest time; (*fig.*) multitude converted *or* ripe for conversion; (*pl.* **mieses**) grain fields.
miga, *n.f.* crumb (*soft part of bread*); bit; substance, marrow; ***hacer buenas*** (or ***malas***) ***migas*** (***con***), to get along well (*or* badly) (with); ***hacerse migas,*** to be smashed to bits; (*coll.*) ***tener miga,*** to have sth. to it; (*pl.*) fried crumbs.
migaja, *n.f.* crumb; scrap.
migajada, migajica, migajilla, migajita, migajuela, *n.f.* small *or* mere crumb *or* scrap.
migajón, *n.m.* pap (of bread); (*fig.*) substance.
migar [B], *v.t.* to crumble, crumb, break into small particles.
migración, *n.f.* migration.
migraña, *n.f.* migraine.
migratorio, -ria, *a.* migrating, migratory.
Miguel, *n.m.* Michael; ***Miguel Angel,*** Michelangelo.
miguelete, *n.m.* miquelet.
miguero, -ra, *a.* relating to crumbs.
mijar, *n.m.* millet-field.
mijediega, *n.f.* (*bot.*) shrubby trefoil.
mijo, *n.m.* (*bot.*) millet.
mil, *a.*, *n.m.* thousand, a *or* one thousand; thousandth; ***a las mil y quinientas,*** at an unearthly hour, terribly late.
miladi, *n.f.* milady.
milagrero, -ra, *a.* miracle-working; superstitious.
milagro, *n.m.* miracle; wonder, marvel; votive offering; ***vida y milagros,*** life and times; ***hacer milagros,*** to work miracles; to do *or* perform wonders; ***escaparse*** or ***salvarse de milagro,*** to have a narrow escape *or* close shave; ***vivir de milagro,*** to have had a narrow escape; to scrape by; ***cogió el tren de milagro,*** he caught the train by the skin of his teeth; ***¡milagro sería!***

that'll be the day! some hope! you've got a hope!; ***se dice*** or ***se mienta el milagro, pero no el santo,*** that would be telling!
milagrón, *n.m.* (*coll.*) terrific fuss.
milagroso, -sa, *a.* miraculous; marvellous.
milamores, *n.f. inv.* valerian.
Milán, *n.m.* Milan.
milán, *n.m.* linen cloth.
milanés, -nesa, *a., n.m.f.* Milanese.
milano, *n.m.* (*orn.*) kite; (*ichth.*) flying gurnard; bur *or* down (*of the thistle*); ***esto parece una mesa de milanos,*** you'd think these people hadn't eaten for days!
mildeu, *n.m.* mildew.
milenario, -ria, *a.* millennial, thousand-year-old. — *n.m.f.* millenarian. — *n.m.* millennium.
milenrama, *n.f.* (*bot.*) milfoil, yarrow.
milépora, *n.f.* millepore.
milésimo, -ma, *a.* thousandth, millesimal.
milhojas, *n.m. inv.* puff pastry, flaky pastry (*cake*). — *n.f.* (*bot.*) milfoil.
mili, *n.f.* (*coll.*) national service.
miliamperio, *n.m.* (*elec.*) milliampere.
miliar, *a.* miliary.
miliárea, *n.f.* milliare.
milicia, *n.f.* militia; military service; art of warfare.
miliciano, -na, *a.* military. — *n.m.* militiaman.
miligramo, *n.m.* milligram.
mililitro, *n.m.* millilitre.
milímetro, *n.m.* millimetre.
militante, *a.* militant.
militar, *a.* army, military; soldierly. — *n.m.* officer, army man, soldier; ***los militares,*** the military. — *v.i.* to serve in the army; (*fig.*) to militate, stand (for); ***militar en,*** to be active in, be in *or* belong to (*a party etc.*).
militara, *n.f.* (*coll.*) wife, widow *or* daughter of a soldier.
militarada, *n.f.* military coup d'état, pronunciamiento.
militarismo, *n.m.* militarism.
militarista, *a.* militaristic, militarist. — *n.m.f.* militarist.
militarización, *n.f.* militarization.
militarizar [C], *v.t.* to militarize.
militarón, *n.m.* (*coll.*) old campaigner.
militarote, *n.m.* member of the thick-headed military caste, blimp.
milmillonésimo, -ma, *a.* billionth (*million-millionth, unit and* 12 *ciphers,* (*Am.*) *thousand-millionth, unit and nine ciphers*).
milo, *n.m.* (*prov.*) earthworm.
miloca, *n.f.* owl.
milocha, *n.f.* kite.
milonga, *n.f.* (*Arg., Bol.*) popular dance.
milonguero, -ra, *a.* (*Arg., Bol.*) dancing the ***milonga.***
milord, *n.m.* milord; my lord; (*pl.* **milores**) my lords.
milpa, *n.f.* (*Cent. Am., Mex.*) maize field.
milpiés, *n.m. inv.* wood-louse.
milla, *n.f.* mile; ***milla marina,*** nautical mile.
millar, *n.m.* thousand; ***a millares,*** by the thousand.
millarada, *n.f.* about a thousand; ***a millaradas,*** by the thousand; ***echar millaradas,*** to boast of wealth and riches.
millón, *n.m.* million; (*pl.* **millones**) ancient customs duties in Spain; ***sala de millones,*** board of excise.
millonada, *n.f.* huge sum of money; ***vale una millonada,*** it's worth a fortune.
millonario, *a., n.m.f.* millionaire; having *or* teeming with millions of inhabitants.
millonésimo, -ma, *a.* millionth.
mimado, -da, *a.* pampered; ***niño mimado,*** spoiled child.
mimador, *n.m.* coaxer.
mimar, *v.t.* to pet, fondle, cuddle; to spoil, pamper.
mimbral, *n.m.* osier bed.
mimbre, *n.m.* osier, willow; wicker.
mimbrear(se), *v.t.* (*v.r.*) to sway, bend (*in the breeze*).
mimbreño, -ña, *a.* osier-like.
mimbrera, *n.m.* osier.
mimbreral, *n.m.* osier bed.
mimbroso, -sa, *a.* made of osiers.
mimesis, *n.f.* mimesis, burlesque.
mimético, -a, *a.* mimetic.
mimetismo, *n.m.* mimesis, mimetism, mimicry.
mímico, -ca, *a.* mimic. — *n.f.* pantomime, language of signs.
mimo, *n.m.* mime (*actor and play*); caress, petting; pampering, indulgence.
mimoso, -sa, *a.* pampered, spoiled; finicky, fussy; wheedlingly affectionate. — *n.f.* (*bot.*) mimosa; ***mimosa púdica*** or ***vergonzosa,*** sensitive plant.
mina, *n.f.* (*mil., min.*) mine; (*min.*) gallery; lead *of a pencil*); harlot; (*fig.*) gold mine; ***beneficiar una mina,*** to work a mine; ***encontrar una mina,*** to strike a gold-mine; ***volar la mina,*** to let the cat out of the bag; ***voló la mina,*** the truth is out.
minador, -ra, *a.* mining; mine-laying. — *n.m.* miner; (*mil.*) sapper; mining engineer; (*naut.*) minelayer.
minal, *a.* (belonging to a) mine.
minar, *v.t.* to mine, burrow; (*fig.*) to sap, sap away, undermine. — *v.i.* to mine.
minarete, *n.m.* minaret.
mineraje, *n.m.* mining; ***mineraje a tajo abierto,*** open-cast mining.
mineral, *a.* mineral. — *n.m.* mineral; ore; mine; spring of water; fountain-head, source; ***mineral bruto,*** crude ore.
mineralogía, *n.f.* mineralogy.
mineralógico, -ca, *a.* mineralogical.
mineralogista, *n.m.f.* mineralogist.
minería, *n.f.* mining; body of miners; (area of) mines.
minero, -ra, *a.* mining. — *n.m.* miner; mine operator; mine owner; mine; source.
mingaco, *n.m.* (*Chi.*) communal work.
mingitorio, -ria, *a., n.m.* urinal.
mingo, *n.m.* red *or* object ball (*in billiards*).
mingón, *n.m.* (*Hisp. Am.*) spoilt brat.
miniar, *v.t.* to paint in miniature; to miniate, illuminate.
miniatura, *n.f.* miniature.
miniaturista, *n.m.f.* miniature-painter.
minifalda, *n.f.* miniskirt.
minifundio, *n.m.* small farm; tiny estate.
mínima (1), *n.f.* (*mus.*) minim.
minimizar [C], *v.t.* to minimize; to belittle.
mínimo, -ma (2), *a.* minimal, minimum; least, smallest, slightest; tiny. — *n.m.* minimum.
minino, mino, *n.m.* puss, pussy.
minio, *n.m.* minium, red lead.
ministerial, *a.* ministerial.
ministerio, *n.m.* ministry; ***ministerio de Asuntos Exteriores,*** Foreign Office, (*Am.*) State Department; ***ministerio de Hacienda,*** Treasury; ***ministerio de (la) Gobernación,*** Home Office; (*obs.*) ***ministerio del Ejército,*** War Office; ***ministerio de (la) Guerra,*** Ministry of Defence, (*Am.*) Defence Department.
ministrable, *n.m.* one in line for ministerial office.
ministrador, -ra, *a., n.m.f.* ministrant.
ministrante, *a., n.m.f.* ministrant.
ministrar, *v.t., v.i.* to minister. — *v.t.* to supply.

ministril, *n.m.* apparitor, tipstaff; minstrel; musician.
ministro, *n.m.* minister; head of a ministry; bailiff; ***ministro de Asuntos Exteriores,*** Foreign Secretary; ***ministro de Hacienda,*** Chancellor of the Exchequer; ***ministro sin cartera,*** minister without portfolio.
mino [MININO].
minoración, *n.f.* minoration.
minorar, *v.t.* to lessen, diminish.
minorativo, -va, *a.* lessening, decreasing; (*med.*) laxative.
minoría, *n.f.* minority.
minoridad, *n.f.* minority.
minoritario, -ria, *a.* (of) minority.
minotauro, *n.m.* Minotaur.
minucia, *n.f.* trifle, tiny point, extremely small consideration.
minuciosidad, *n.f.* minuteness; trifle; meticulousness.
minucioso, -sa, *a.* minute; meticulous, painstaking.
minué, *n.m.* minuet.
minúsculo, -la, *a.* minute, tiny. — *n.f.* small letter.
minuta (1) *n.f.* first draft; memo; statement of fees; menu; roll *or* list.
minutar, *v.t.* to make notes on *or* a first draft of.
minutario, *n.m.* minute-book.
minutero, *n.m.* minute-hand (*of a clock* or *watch*).
minutía, *n.f.* (*bot.*) pink, carnation.
minutisa, *n.f.* (*bot.*) sweet-william.
minuto, -ta (2), *a.*, *n.m.* minute.
miñón, *n.m.* light infantry, rural guard; minion.
miñona, *n.f.* (*print.*) minion type, 7-point type.
miñosa, *n.f.* (*prov.*) intestinal worm.
mío, mía, míos, mías, *pron. pers. poss.* my, mine; ***¡Dios mío!*** my God!; ***es muy amigo mío,*** he is a great friend of mine; ***ya he hecho otra de las mías,*** there I go again; ***ésta es la mía,*** this is where I come in, this is my chance.
mio, *n.m.* puss.
miodinia, *n.f.* (*med.*) myodinia, muscular pain.
miografía, *n.f.* myography.
miología, *n.f.* myology.
miope, *a.*, *n.m.f.* myopic, short- *or* near-sighted (*person*).
miopía, *n.f.* short-sightedness.
miosis, *n.f. inv.* (*med.*) myosis.
miosotis, *n.f. inv.* (*bot*). forget-me-not.
mira, *n.f.* sight; levelling-rod; watch-tower; care; design, aim; view; (*build.*) rule; ***estar a la mira,*** to be on the look-out; ***alteza de miras,*** high-mindedness; ***con miras a,*** with a view to.
mirabel, *n.m.* (*bot.*) cypress goose-foot; sunflower.
miradero, *n.m.* view-point, cynosure.
mirado, -da, *a.* considerate, thoughtful; circumspect; discreet; ***bien mirado,*** highly regarded. — *n.f.* look, glance; view; gaze; ***mirada fija,*** stare; ***echar una mirada,*** to take *or* have a look *or* glance.
mirador, *n.m.* balcony, gallery, belvedere, vantage-point.
miradura, *n.f.* looking.
miraguano, *n.m.* (*bot.*) fan palm.
miramiento, *n.m.* consideration, respect, circumspection; ***sin miramientos,*** without (due) consideration, unceremoniously.
miranda, *n.f.* height, elevated position, vantage-point.
mirante, *a.* looking. — *n.m.f.* onlooker.
mirar, *v.t.* to look at; to look on, upon; to watch; to gaze, glance at; to behold; to consider; to mind, watch; ***mirar con buenos ojos,*** to look upon favourably; ***mirar de hito en hito,*** to look up and down; ***mirar de reojo,*** to look askance at; ***mirar por encima,*** to give a cursory glance; ***mirar por encima del hombro,*** to look down on; ***los jóvenes no miran nada,*** young people don't stop to think, have no consideration (*for others*); ***mirándolo bien,*** all things considered, when you come to think of it; ***mira mucho la puntualidad,*** he sets great store by punctuality. — *v.i.* to look, glance; to look (on to); to face; ***mirar por,*** to look after, look out for; ***¡mira!*** well, well! you don't say! ***¡mira (que) si es mentira!*** supposing (that) it's not true!; ***mira que llegues pronto,*** see to it (that) you get there early. — **mirarse,** *v.r.* to look at o.s.; to look at each other; to take care, take an example (***en,*** from); ***mírate en él,*** take an example *or* warning from him; ***de mírame y no me toques,*** terribly fragile *or* delicate; ***si bien se mira,*** all things considered, when you come to think of it.
mirasol, *n.m.* (*bot.*) sunflower.
miriagramo, *n.m.* myriagram.
miriámetro, *n.m.* myriametre.
miriápodo, miriópodo, *n.m.* myriapod, centipede.
mirífico, -ca, *a.* marvellous, wonderful.
mirilla, *n.f.* spy-hole, peep-hole; target (*of a levelling rod*).
miriñaque, *n.m.* trinket, bauble; hoop-skirt; crinoline.
mirística, *n.f.* nutmeg tree.
mirla, *n.f.* blackbird.
mirlamiento, *n.m.* air of importance, affected gravity.
mirlarse, *v.r.* to assume an air of importance, affect gravity.
mirlo, *n.m.* blackbird; (*coll.*) air of importance, affected gravity; ***mirlo blanco,*** rara avis.
mirón, -rona, *a.* gazing, gawping. — *n.m.f.* looker-on; gazer, gawper.
mirra, *n.f.* myrrh.
mirrado, -da, *a.* myrrhic, of myrrh, scented with myrrh.
mirrauste, *n.m.* (*cook.*) timbale of pigeons; pigeon-sauce.
mirrino, -na, *a.* myrrhic.
mirtáceo, -cea, *a.* myrtaceous.
mirtídano, *n.m.* myrtle sprout.
mirtiforme, *a.* myrtiform.
mirtino, -na, *a.* resembling myrtle.
mirto, *n.m.* myrtle.
miruello, -lla, *n.m.f.* (*prov.*) blackbird.
misa, *n.f.* mass; ***misa del gallo,*** midnight mass; ***misa mayor,*** high mass; ***misa rezada,*** low mass; ***ayudar a misa,*** to serve mass; ***oír misa,*** to hear mass, go to church; ***no saber de la misa la media,*** not to know the first thing about it.
misacantano, *n.m.* celebrant (of a first mass).
misal, *n.m.* missal, mass-book; (*print.*) two-line pica.
misantropía, *n.f.* misanthropy.
misantrópico, -ca, *a.* misanthropic.
misántropo, *n.m.* misanthropist, misanthrope.
misar, *v.i.* (*coll.*) to say *or* hear mass.
misario, *n.m.* acolyte.
misceláneo, -nea, *a.* miscellaneous. — *n.f.* miscellany.
miscible, *a.* miscible.
miserable, *a.* miserable, wretched, unhappy; miserly, mean, stingy, close-fisted; wicked. — *n.m.f.* wretch.
miserear, *v.i.* to be niggardly, stingy.
miserere, *n.m.* Miserere; (*med.*) ileus; ***cólico miserere,*** iliac passion.
miseria, *n.f.* misery, wretchedness; privation, poverty; stinginess, meanness; (*coll.*) lice; pittance.
misericordia, *n.f.* mercy, mercifulness, pity; misericord (*dagger*); misericord (*on seat of choir-stall*).
misericordioso, -sa, *a.* merciful.

mísero, -ra, *a.* miserable, wretched, unhappy; miserly, stingy.
misero, -ra, *a.* (*coll.*) exaggeratedly church-going, sanctimonious.
misérrimo, -ma, *a. superl.* most miserable; very miserly; very short *or* scanty.
misión, *n.f.* mission.
misionar, *v.i.* to preach missions; to reprimand.
misionario, *n.m.* messenger, agent, missionary; (*pl.*) body of persons (*sent on a diplomatic mission*).
misionero, *n.m.* missionary.
Misisipí, *n.m.* Mississippi.
misivo, -va, *a.* missive, sent. — *n.f.* missive (*letter*).
mismamente, *adv.* (*coll.*) exactly, precisely.
mismísimo, -ma, *a. superl.* very same, self-same; (very) in person, himself, herself.
mismo, -ma, *adv.* right; ***ahora mismo,*** right now; ***desde mañana mismo,*** right from tomorrow; ***así mismo,*** likewise, also; ***lo vi ayer mismo,*** I saw him only yesterday; ***hoy mismo,*** this very day; today without fail; ***ha llegado hoy mismo,*** he's just arrived today. — *a.* same, self-same; very; ***el mismo hombre,*** the same man; ***su mismo hijo se ríe de él,*** his very son laughs at him; ***el mismo niño se dio cuenta,*** even the child noticed (it); ***eso mismo,*** that very thing; ***lo mismo,*** the same (thing); ***lo mismo da,*** it's all the same, it makes no difference; ***lo mismo me da,*** it's all the same to me; ***por lo mismo,*** for the same reason; for that very reason; ***lo haré yo mismo,*** I'll do it myself.
misoginia, *n.f.* misogyny.
misógino, *a.* misogynous. — *n.m.* misogynist.
mistagógico, -ca, *a.* mystagogic.
mistagogo, *n.m.* mystagogue.
mistar, *v.i.* to speak *or* mumble.
mistela, *n.f.* refreshing beverage (*made of aniseed, water, sugar and cinnamon*); (*Col.*) highly intoxicating liquor.
misterio, *n.m.* mystery.
misterioso, -sa, *a.* mysterious; eerie.
misticismo, *n.m.* mysticism.
místico (I), **-ca,** *a.* mystic, mystical; (*coll.*) dreamy, — *n.m.* mystic. — *n.f.* study of the contemplative life.
misticón, -cona, *a.* hopelessly mystical *or* dreamy.
mistilíneo, -nea, *a.* (*geom.*) mixtilinear.
mistión [MIXTIÓN].
misto [MIXTO].
misturera, *n.f.* (*Hisp. Am.*) flower-girl.
mita, *n.f.* (*Hisp. Am.*) enforced service (*of Indians*); tax (*paid by Indians*).
mitad, *n.f.* half; centre, middle; ***mitad y mitad,*** half and half; ***por mitades,*** by halves; ***a la mitad,*** half-way through; ***a mitad de camino,*** half-way there; ***por la mitad, mitad por mitad,*** down the middle; (*fig.*) ***cara mitad,*** better half; ***mentir por la mitad de la barba,*** to tell lies unashamedly.
mitadenco, *a.* (*law*) lease paid half in products, half in cash.
mitayo, *n.m.* (*Hisp. Am.*) Indian serving his ***mita***; Indian in charge of the accounts of the ***mita.***
mítico, -ca, *a.* mythical.
mitigación, *n.f.* mitigation.
mitigador, -ra, *a.* mitigating.
mitigante, *a.* mitigating.
mitigar [B], *v.t.* to mitigate, ease.
mitin, *n.m.* political meeting, rally; ***dar un*** or ***el mitin,*** to kick up a row *or* shindy.
mito, *n.m.* myth.
mitología, *n.f.* mythology.
mitológico, -ca, *a.* mythological. — *n.m.* mythologist.
mitóloto, *n.m.,* **mitologista,** *n.m.f.* mythologist.
mitón, *n.m.* mitten.
mitote, *n.m.* (*Hisp. Am.*) Indian dance; noisy party; riot, uproar; fastidiousness, affectedness.
mitotero, -ra, *a.* (*Hisp. Am.*) jolly, rollicking, finical, fastidious.
mitra, *n.f.* mitre.
mitrado, *a.* mitred. — *n.m.* bishop; archbishop.
mitrar, *v.i.* (*coll.*) to be mitred.
mitridato, *n.m.* mithridate.
mítulo, *n.m.* mytilus.
mixtela [MISTELA].
mixtifori, *n.m.* (*coll.*) medley, hotchpotch.
mixtión, *n.f.* mixture.
mixto, -ta, *a.* mixed, mingled; cross-bred; ***tren mixto,*** combined passenger and goods train. — *n.m.* compound; sulphur match; (*artill.*) explosive compound.
mixtura, *n.f.* mixture; compound.
mixturar, *v.t.* to mix, mingle.
mixturero, -ra, *a.* mixing.
miz, mizo, *n.m.* puss, pussy.
mizcal, *n.m.* (*Morocco*) small coin.
mízcalo, *n.m.* mushroom.
mnemónica, mnemotecnia, *n.f.* mnemonics.
moaré, *n.m.* moiré.
mobiliario, -ria, *a.* movable, personal (*property*). — *n.m.* furniture.
moblaje, *n.m.* furniture.
moblar [4], *v.t.* to furnish.
mocadero, mocador, *n.m.* handkerchief.
mocarro, *n.m.* (*coll.*) disgusting snot; ***tener mocarros,*** to have a disgustingly runny nose.
mocasín, -sina, *n.m.f.* moccasin.
mocear, *v.i.* to act as boys will; to sow wild oats.
mocedad, *n.f.* youth.
mocerío, *n.m.* young people; boys, lads.
mocero, *a.* lascivious, womanizing.
mocetón, -tona, *n.m.f.* strapping lad *or* lass.
moción, *n.f.* motion.
mocionar, *v.i.* (*Arg., Hond.*) to table a motion.
mocito, -ta, *n.m.f.* young lad *or* lass.
moco, *n.m.* nasal mucus; (candle) drippings; iron-slag; (*naut.*) martingale boom, dolphin striker; (*bot.*) love-lies-bleeding; (*coll.*) ***llorar a moco tendido,*** to cry one's eyes out; ***tener mocos,*** to have a running nose; ***no es moco de pavo,*** it is not to be sneezed at.
mococoa, *n.f.* (*Bol., Col.*) bad *or* ill temper.
mocora, *n.f.* (*Ec.*) small plant the fibre of which is used for hammocks and hats.
mocosidad, *n.f.* mucosity.
mocoso, -sa, *a.* (*coll.*) snotty-nosed, dirty-nosed. — *n.m.f.* kid, brat.
mocosuelo, -la, *n.m.f.* (*coll.*) kid, young shaver.
mochada, *n.f.* butt, buffet.
mochar, *v.t.* to butt, buffet.
mochazo, *n.m.* blow with the butt-end.
mocheta, *n.f.* (*arch.*) quoin; corner-stone; thick edge of tools.
mochete, *n.m.* sparrow-hawk.
mochil, *n.m.* farmer's boy.
mochila, *n.f.* rucksack, knapsack, haversack; ***hacer mochila,*** to prepare for a journey.
mochilero, *n.m.* baggage-carrier.
mochín, *n.m.* (*coll.*) hangman.
mocho, -cha, *a.* cut short, cropped off, lopped off; shorn; mutilitated, maimed; (*Mex., coll.*) hypocritical. — *n.m.* butt-end.
mochuelo, *n.m.* little owl; (*coll.*) ***cargar con el mochuelo,*** to take the rap, carry the can, be left holding the baby; ***cada mochuelo a su olivo,*** time to go home.
moda, *n.f.* fashion, mode, trend; habit; ***estar de moda,*** to be in fashion, be fashionable; ***a la última moda,*** in the latest fashion, (*coll.*) with

it, up-to-the-minute; ***pasado de moda,*** out of fashion.
modal, *a.* (*log.*) modal.
modales, *n.m.pl.* manners.
modalidad, *n.f.* kind, type; (*sport*) category.
modelar, *v.t.* to model, shape, form.
modelo, *n.m.* model; pattern. — *n.f.* fashion model.
moderación, *n.f.* moderation.
moderado, -da, *a.* moderate.
moderador, -ra, *a.* moderating. — *n.m.f.* moderator.
moderante, *a.* moderating.
moderar, *v.t.* to moderate, check, restrain.
moderativo, -va, *a.* moderating.
moderatorio, -ria, *a.* moderating.
modernamente, *adv.* in modern times; recently.
modernidad, *n.f.* modernness, modernity.
modernismo, *n.m.* modernism.
modernista, *a.* modernist, modernistic. — *n.m.f.* modernist.
modernizar [C], *v.t.* to modernize. — **modernizarse,** *v.r.* to get up to date, (*coll.*) get with the times, get with it.
moderno, -na, *a.* modern; recent. — *n.m.f.* modern.
modestia, *n.f.* modesty.
modesto, -ta, *a.* modest, unassuming.
modicidad, *n.f.* moderateness, reasonableness.
módico, -ca, *a.* moderate, reasonable.
modificable, *a.* modifiable.
modificación, *n.f.* modification; modifying.
modificador, -ra, *a.* modifying. — *n.m.f.* modifier.
modificar [A], *v.t.* to modify, alter.
modificativo, -va, *a.* modificative.
modificatorio, -ria, *a.* modificatory.
modillón, *n.m.* (*arch.*) bracket.
modismo, *n.m.* idiom.
modista, *n.m.f.* modiste, dressmaker; ***modista de sombreros,*** milliner.
modistería, *n.f.* dressmaking; fashion shop.
modistilla, *n.f.* (*coll.*) seamstress, midinette.
modo, *n.m.* mode; manner, way; (*gram.*) mood; moderation; courtesy; ***modo de ser,*** disposition; ***al modo de,*** in the manner of; ***a modo de,*** by way of; ***a modo,*** properly; ***de ese modo,*** in that case; like that; ***de modo que,*** so that; ***de ningún modo,*** certainly not; ***de otro modo,*** otherwise; ***de todos modos,*** anyhow, at any rate; ***en cierto modo,*** in a way; ***un a modo de sombrero,*** a sort of hat (arrangement); ***con malos modos,*** rudely, brusquely, roughly.
modorrar, *v.t.* to make drowsy *or* heavy.
modorrilla, *n.f.* (*mil.*) third night-watch.
modorro, -rra, *a.* drowsy, heavy; stupid, dull. — *n.f.* drowsiness, heaviness; (*vet.*) staggers.
modoso, -sa, *a.* unobtrusive, well-behaved.
modrego, *n.m.* awkward fellow.
modulación, *n.f.* modulation.
modulador, -ra, *a.* modulating. — *n.m.f.* modulator.
modular, *v.i.* to modulate.
módulo, *n.m.* (*arch.*) module; (*mus.*) modulation; (*numis.*) size of coins etc.; (*math.*) modulus; (*hydrost.*) unit of measure of running water.
modurria, *n.f.* (*obs.*) folly.
moeda, *n.f.* moidore (*Portuguese gold coin*).
mofa, *n.f.* scoffing, jeering, mockery; ***hacer mofa de,*** to jeer at.
mofador, -ra, *a.* scoffing, jeering, mocking. — *n.m.f.* scoffer, jeerer, mocker.
mofadura [MOFA].
mofante, *a.* [MOFADOR].
mofar, *v.i.* to scoff, jeer, mock. — **mofarse,** *v.r.* — ***de,*** to mock, jeer at.
mofeta, *n.f.* mofette; mephitis; (*zool.*) skunk; polecat.
mófler, *n.m.* (*Hisp. Am., motor.*) silencer, (*Am.*) muffler.
moflete, *n.m.* chubby-cheek.
mofletudo, -da, *a.* chubby-cheeked.
mogate, *n.m.* varnish, glazing; (*coll.*) ***a medio mogate,*** carelessly, heedlessly.
mogol, -la, *a., n.m.f.* Mongol, Mongolian (person). — *n.m.* Mongol, Mongolian (*language*).
Mogolia, *n.f.* Mongolia.
mogólico, -ca, *a.* Mongolian.
mogollón, *n.m.* hanger-on, sponger; ***comer de mogollón,*** to sponge.
mogón,[1] **-gona,** *a.* having one horn missing *or* broken.
mogote, *n.m.* hillock, hummock; rick *or* stack of corn; brocket's antler.
mogrollo, *n.m.* sponger; rustic, clod.
mohada, *n.f.* wetting.
moharra, *n.f.* head (*of a spear*).
moharrache, moharracho, *n.m.* jester, clown.
mohatra, *n.f.* sham sale; sharp practice, fraud.
mohatrar, *v.i.* to make a sham sale.
mohatrero, -ra, *n.m.f.* **mohatrón,** *n.m.* extortioner, trickster, swindler.
mohecer [9], *v.t.* to mildew.
moheda, *n.f.* woods covered in bramble and underbrush.
mohín, *n.m.* grimace, face, pouting.
mohino, -na, *a.* sulky, sullen; black (*horse* or *cattle*); begotten by a stallion and a she-ass. — *n.m.* one playing alone against several others (*at cards*); blue magpie. — *n.f.* grudge.
moho, *n.m.* (*bot.*) mould, mouldiness; ***no criar moho,*** to get no chance to grow stale *or* mouldy.
mohoso, -sa, *a.* mouldy, mildewed, musty.
Moisés, *n.m.* Moses.
mojada, *n.f.* wetting, moistening, sop; (*coll.*) stab.
mojador, -ra, *a.* wetting, soaking. — *n.m.f.* wetter, moistener, soaker.
mojadura, *n.f.* moistening, wetting, soaking.
mojama, *n.f.* dry salted tunny.
mojar, *v.t.* to wet, damp(en), soak; to dunk, dip; (*coll.*) to stab. — *v.i.* (*coll.*) to have a hand in. — **mojarse,** *v.r.* to get wet.
mojarra, *n.f.* mojarra fish; (*Hisp. Am.*) broad and short knife.
mojarrilla, *n.m.* (*coll.*) punster, jester, jolly person.
moje, *n.m.* broth, gravy.
mojel, *n.m.* (*naut.*) braided cord.
mojí, *n.m.* sponge-cake.
mojicón, *n.m.* sponge-cake; punch.
mojiganga, *n.f.* morris dance; masquerade, masque, mummery.
mojigatería, mojigatez, *n.f.* prudery, prudishness, grundyism.
mojigato, -ta, *a.* prudish. — *n.m.f.* prude.
mojón, *n.m.* landmark; boundary stone; heap, pile; wine-taster; (*vulg.*) turd; quoits.
mojona, *n.f.* retail wine-duty; survey of land, setting up of landmarks.
mojonera, *n.f.* landmark.
mojonero, *n.m.* gauger.
mola, *n.f.* (*med.*) mole, tumour (*in the womb*); salted flour.
molada, *n.f.* colours ground together.
molar, *a.* molar.
molcajete, *n.m.* (*Mex.*) mortar.
moldar, *v.t.* to mould.
molde, *n.m.* mould; matrix; pattern mould; model; form; ***letra de molde,*** printed letter, print; ***en letra de molde,*** in print; ***pan de molde,*** square sandwich loaf; ***venir de molde,*** to be perfect, just right *or* just the thing, fit the bill.

moldeador, *n.m.* moulder, cast-maker.
moldear, *v.t.* to mould; cast.
moldura, *n.f.* moulding.
moldurar, *v.t.* to make a moulding for.
mole, *a.* soft. — *n.m.* (*Mex.*) meat *or* turkey fricassee with chilli sauce. — *n.f.* mass, pile.
molécula, *n.f.* molecule.
molecular, *a.* molecular.
moledero, -ra, *a.* to be ground. — *n.f.* grinding stone; (*coll.*) botheration.
moledor, -ra, *a.* grinding, crushing; (*coll.*) boring. — *n.m.* grinder, crusher; roller. — *n.m.f.* (*coll.*) bore.
moledura, *n.f.* grinding.
molejón, *n.m.* (*Cub.*) ridge of rock (*near the surface of the water*).
molendero, *n.m.* miller, grinder; chocolate maker.
moleña, *n.f.* flint; millstone.
moler [5], *v.t.* to grind, crush; to mill; (*coll.*) to bore, weary, give the hump to; to wear out; (*coll.*) ***moler a palos,*** to thrash, give a drubbing (to); (*coll.*) ***estar molido,*** to be fagged out *or* knocked up, be whacked.
molero, *n.m.* maker *or* seller of millstones.
molestador, -ra, *n.m.f.* disturber, vexer, molester.
molestar, *v.t.* to disturb; to put to inconvenience; to annoy, irritate. — **molestarse,** *v.r.* to bother, go to trouble; to take offence; ***no se moleste usted,*** don't bother, don't go to any trouble, don't put yourself out; don't take offence.
molestia, *n.f.* disturbance, inconvenience, nuisance, bother, trouble; annoyance, irritation.
molesto, -ta, *a.* troublesome, bothersome, irritating, annoying; uncomfortable.
moleta, *n.f.* muller; polisher; (*print.*) ink-grinder.
molibdeno, *n.m.* molybdenum.
molicie, *n.f.* softness; soft living.
molienda, *n.f.* milling, grinding; grist; mill; milling season; [MOLIMIENTO].
moliente, *a.* grinding; ***corriente y moliente,*** run-of-the-mill, common-or-garden.
molificable, *a.* mollifiable.
molificación, *n.f.* mollification.
molificador, *n.m.* mollifier.
molificar [A], *v.t.* to mollify.
molificativo, -va, *a.* mollifying.
molimiento, *n.m.* grinding; (*fig.*) (state of) being exhausted *or* fagged out.
molinar, *n.m.* place where there are mills.
molinería, *n.f.* mill industry.
molinero, -ra, *a.* mill; to be ground. — *n.m.* miller, grinder. — *n.f.* miller's wife, mill-woman.
molinete, *n.m.* windlass; turnstile; pin-wheel; friction-roller; ventilating fan; old-fashioned dance; (act of) swinging *or* sweeping round (*a sword*); (*naut.*) winch.
molinillo, *n.m.* hand-mill; coffee-grinder.
molinismo, *n.m.* Molinism.
molinista, *n.m.f.* Molinist.
molino, *n.m.* mill; grinder; (*fig.*) fidget; ***molino de agua,*** water-mill; ***molino de mano,*** hand-mill; ***molino de sangre,*** mill turned by men *or* animals; ***molino de viento,*** windmill; ***llevar agua al molino,*** to have one's eye to the main chance; (*fig.*) ***comulgar con ruedas de molino,*** to swallow anything.
molitivo, -va, *a.* mollient.
mololoa, *n.f.* (*Hond.*) noisy conversation.
molondro, molondrón, *n.m.* layabout.
moloso, *n.m.* (*poet.*) molossus.
moltura, *n.f.* grinding.
molturar, *v.t.* to grind.
molusco, *n.m.* mollusc.
moly, *n.m.* great yellow garlic.
molla, *n.f.* juicy lump of meat *or* flesh; best cut of lean meat; (*coll.*) fat (*of a person*).
mollar, *a.* soft, tender, pulpous; (*fig.*) easy; easily taken in; ***la cosa se presenta mollar,*** it's a walk-over, a piece of cake.
molle, *n.m.* (*Hisp. Am.*) sacred tree of the Incas (*Schinus molle*).
mollear, *v.i.* to grow soft and pliable, soften, yield easily.
molledo, *n.m.* fleshy part of a limb.
molleja, *n.f.* gizzard; maw; sweetbread.
mollejón, *n.m.* grindstone; (*coll.*) fat slob.
mollera, *n.f.* crown (*of the head*); (*fig.*) head, brains, sense; ***cerrado*** or ***duro de mollera,*** thick-headed, dense; stubborn.
mollero, *n.m.* fleshy part (*of the arm*).
molleta, *n.f.* biscuit; brown bread; (*pl.*) snuffers.
mollete, *n.m.* manchet, French roll; fleshy part (*of the arm*); (*pl.*) plump cheeks.
molletero, -ra, *n.m.f.* baker of rolls.
molletudo, -da, *a.* chubby-cheeked.
mollina, mollizna, *n.f.* mist, drizzle.
molliznar, molliznear, *v.i.* to drizzle.
moma, *n.f.* (*Mex.*) blindman's-buff.
momentáneo, -nea, *a.* momentary.
momento, *n.m.* moment; minute; (*mech.*) momentum; ***al momento,*** immediately, at once; a few minutes *or* seconds later; ***de momento, por el momento,*** for the moment, for the time being; ***por momentos,*** constantly, continually, all the time; ***de un momento a otro,*** any minute *or* time now; ***en el momento menos pensado,*** when least expected.
momería, *n.f.* mummery.
momia (1), *n.f.* mummy.
momio, -mia (2), *a.* meagre, lean. — *n.m.* (*fig.*) extra; bargain; cushy job.
momificar [A], *v.t.* to mummify.
momo, *n.m.* buffoonery; grimacing; bogey-man.
mona, *n.f.* [MONO].
monacal, *a.* monastic, monkish.
monacato, *n.m.* monachism, monasticism.
monacillo, *n.m.* acolyte.
monacordio, *n.m.* spinet.
mónada, *n.f.* monad.
monada, *n.f.* monkey trick; grimace, face; pretty *or* cute child, girl *or* thing; (*iron.*) ***¡qué monada!*** what a sight *or* mess!; (*iron.*) ***¡es una monada!*** it's lovely!
monago, monaguillo, *n.m.* choir-boy, server.
monaquismo, *n.m.* monachism.
monarca, *n.m.* monarch.
monarquía, *n.f.* monarchy.
monárquico, -ca, *a.* monarchical, monarchist, royalist. — *n.m.f.* monarchist, royalist.
monasterial, *a.* monastic.
monasterio, *n.m.* monastery.
monástico, -ca, *a.* monastic.
monda, *n.f.* [MONDO].
mondadientes, *n.m. inv.* tooth-pick.
mondador, -ra, *a.* pruning, peeling, clearing. — *n.m.f.* pruner, peeler, clearer.
mondadura, *n.f.* pruning; peeling, paring.
mondaoídos, mondaorejas, *n.m. inv.* ear-pick.
mondar, *v.t.* to prune; to peel; to clear, clean; to shell, husk; to cut the hair of; (*fig.*) to fleece. — **mondarse,** *v.r.* — ***de risa,*** to split one's sides laughing.
mondejo, *n.m.* belly of a pig *or* sheep stuffed with mincemeat.
mondo, -da, *a.* bare, stripped clean; ***mondo y lirondo,*** bare, stripped clean, unadulterated. — *n.f.* peeling, peel, skinning, skin; pruning, trimming; (*coll., fig.*) ***es la monda,*** it's, he's, *or* she's the limit *or* a scream.
mondón, *n.m.* barkless tree-trunk.
mondongo, -ga, *n.m.* entrails, innards. — *n.f.* (*coll.*) kitchen wench.

mondonguería, *n.f.* place *or* shop where tripe is sold.
mondonguero, -ra, *n.m.f.* seller *or* cooker of tripe.
monear, *v.i.* to do pretty things *or* tricks; to pull faces.
moneda, *n.f.* coin; coinage, currency; loose change; ***casa de moneda,*** mint; ***moneda de vellón,*** debased currency; ***moneda suelta,*** small change; ***correr la moneda,*** to pass money; to circulate (*of money*); ***pagar a alguien con la misma moneda,*** to repay s.o. in the same coin; ***moneda falsa,*** forged money; ***ser moneda corriente,*** to be common usage; ***acuñar moneda,*** to mint money.
monedaje, *n.m.* coinage; seigniorage.
monedar, monedear, *v.t.* to coin.
monedería, *n.f.* mint, mintage.
monedero, *n.m.* purse; money-maker; ***monedero falso,*** counterfeiter.
monedilla, monedita, *n.f.* small coin.
monería, *n.f.* grimace; pretty ways (*of children*), mimicry; trifle, gewgaw, bauble.
monesco, -ca, *a.* apish, monkeyish.
monetario, -ria, *a.* monetary, financial. — *n.m.* (*obs.*) coin case.
monfí, *n.m.* a Moorish highwayman.
monforte, *n.m.* strong cloth.
monicaco, *n.m.* whipper-snapper, scamp.
monición, *n.f.* admonition; publication of banns.
monigote, *n.m.* lay-brother; puppet, rag figure; botch, scrawl; cartoon drawing; (*fig.*) nobody.
monillo, *n.m.* waist, bodice, corset.
Monipodio, *n.m.* ***patio de Monipodio,*** den of thieves.
monís, *n.f.* (*prov.*) cute thing; (*pl.* **monises**) (*coll.*) money.
monismo, *n.m.* (*phil.*) monism.
monista, *n.m.f.* monist.
mónita, *n.f.* artifice, cunning, suavity.
monitor, *n.m.* monitor.
monitorio, -ria, *a.* monitory, admonitory. — *n.f.* (*eccles.*) monition.
monja, *n.f.* nun.
monje, *n.m.* monk; (*orn.*) titmouse; ***el hábito no hace al monje,*** clothes don't make the man.
monjía, *n.f.* prebend (*of a monk in a convent*).
monjil, *a.* nun, nun-like; prudish.
monjío, *n.m.* nunship; taking of the veil.
monjita, *n.f.* little nun.
mono, -na, *a.* (*coll.*) cute, ducky, sweet. — *n.m.* monkey, ape; (*fig.*) scamp; (*coll.*) clumsy picture, daub; (*coll.*) copy-cat; overalls; ***mono sabio,*** trained monkey; picador's assistant; ***estar de monos,*** to be at odds; (*fig.*) ***quedarse hecho un mono,*** to get a flea in one's ear. — *n.f.* female monkey; copy-cat; (*coll.*) drunken bout; old maid (*cards*); protective leg pad *or* plate; Easter cake; (*coll.*) ***coger*** or ***pillar una mona,*** to get sozzled *or* pie-eyed; ***dormir la mona,*** to sleep it off; ***aunque la mona se vista de seda, mona se queda,*** you can't make a silk purse out of a sow's ear.
monobloque, *a.* in block.
monobsesivo, -va, *a.* having a one-track mind.
monocerote, monoceronte, *n.m.* unicorn.
monociclo, *a.* monocycle.
monocilíndrico, -ca, *a.* single-cylinder.
monocordio, *n.m.* monochord.
monocromata, *n.f.* monochrome.
monocromo, -ma, *a.* monochrome.
monóculo, -la, *a.* monoculous, monocular, one-eyed. — *n.m.* monocle.
monodía, *n.f.* (*mus.*) monody.
monogamia, *n.f.* monogamy.
monógamo, -ma, *a.* monogamous. — *n.m.f.* monogamist.
monografía, *n.f.* monograph.
monográfico, -ca, *a.* monographic.
monograma, *n.m.* monogram.
monolítico, -ca, *a.* monolithic.
monolito, *n.m.* monolith.
monologar [B], *v.i.* to soliloquize, talk in a monologue.
monólogo, *n.m.* monologue, soliloquy.
monomanía, *n.f.* monomania.
monomaquia, *n.f.* monomachy.
monona, *n.f.* (*coll.*) darling.
monopastos, *n.m. inv.* one-wheeled pulley.
monoplano, *n.m.* (*aer.*) monoplane.
monopolio, *n.m.* monopoly.
monopolista, *n.m.f.* monopolist, monopolizer.
monopolizar [C], *v.t.* to monopolize.
monosilábico, -ca, *a.* monosyllabic.
monosílabo, -ba, *a.*, *n.m.* monosyllable.
monote, *n.m.* one dumbfounded.
monoteísmo, *n.m.* monotheism.
monoteísta, *a.* monotheistic. — *n.m.f.* monotheist.
monotipia, *n.f.* monotype.
monotipista, *n.m.* monotyper.
monotonía, *n.f.* monotony.
monótono, -na, *a.* monotonous.
monseñor, *n.m.* monseigneur, monsignor.
monserga, *n.m.* (*coll.*) rigmarole; same old thing.
monstruo, *n.m.* monster; freak.
monstruosidad, *n.f.* monstrosity, hideous object.
monstruoso, -sa, *a.* monstrous, hideous.
monta, *n.f.* amount, sum; signal for cavalry to mount; mounting; stud farm; ***de poca monta,*** of small account.
montacargas, *n.f. inv.* hoist; goods-lift.
montadero, *n.m.* mounting-block.
montado, *n.m.* trooper, horseman.
montador, *n.m.* one who mounts; mounting-block, horse-block; (*elec.*, *motor. etc.*) installer, fitter.
montadura, *n.f.* trooper's accoutrements; mounting; (*jewel.*) setting.
montaje, *n.m.* setting up, installation; assembly; montage; décor.
montanera, *n.f.* oak forest.
montanero, *n.m.* forester, forest-keeper.
montano, -na, *a.* mountainous.
montantada, *n.f.* boasting, ostentation; multitude, crowd.
montante, *n.m.* broadsword; (*carp.*, *mech.*) upright, standard; post, strut, jamb; (*min.*) stempel; (*arch.*) transom; (*com.*) amount. — *n.f.* flood tide.
montantear, *v.i.* to wield the broadsword; (*fig.*) to vaunt, boast, brag; to interfere.
montantero, *n.m.* broadsword fighter.
montaña, *n.f.* mountain, mount; highland; (*Hisp. Am.*) forest *or* jungle area.
montañés, -nesa, *a.* mountain, highland; of La Montaña (*Santander*). — *n.m.f.* highlander, mountain dweller; native of La Montaña.
montañoso, -sa, *a.* mountainous.
montar, *v.t.* to mount; to set (*diamonds etc.*); to cover (*a mare*); to cock (*a gun*); to hang (*a rudder*); to assemble, set up, put up. — *v.i.* to mount; to ride, go on horseback; to have importance; to amount (**a,** to); ***montar en cólera,*** to fly into a rage; ***montar la guardia,*** to mount guard; ***montar en pelo,*** to ride bareback; ***tanto monta,*** it's all the same, it makes no odds.
montaraz, *a.* wild. — *n.m.* forester.
montazgar [B], *v.t.* to levy *or* collect (*toll on cattle*).
montazgo, *n.m.* toll on cattle.
monte, *n.m.* mountain, mount; hill; wood, woodland; pool (*in cards*); talon, cards left in the pack after dealing; ***monte alto,*** woodland, forest; ***monte bajo,*** thicket, brush; ***monte de piedad,*** savings bank; pawnbroker's shop; ***monte pío***

[MONTEPÍO]; ***se me hace un monte,*** it's an awful drag; ***echarse al monte,*** to take to the hills; ***tira al monte,*** Nature will out; ***no todo el monte es orégano,*** life is not all a bed of roses.

montea, *n.f.* hewing of stone; (*arch.*) working drawing; plan *or* profile of a building; versed sine of an arch; beating a wood for game; stone-cutting.

montear, *v.t.* to beat (*a wood*); to draw up the plan of (*a building*); (*arch.*) to vault, arch.

montecillo, *n.m.* small wood; hillock, hummock.

montepío, *n.m.* fund for widows and orphans.

montera, *n.f.* cloth cap; sky-light; condenser (*of a still*); hunter's wife; (*naut.*) skysail; (*coll.*) ***ponerse el mundo por montera,*** to cock a snook at society, not to give a damn for what people think.

monterería, *n.f.* cap-factory, cap-store.

monterero, *n.m.* seller *or* maker of caps.

montería, *n.f.* hunting; hunt.

montero, *n.m.* huntsman, hunter.

monterrey, *n.m.* (*cook.*) meat pie.

montés, -tesa, *a.* wild.

montescos, *n.m.pl.;* (***haber***) ***Montescos y Capuletos,*** a furore.

montesino, -na, *a.* wild.

montículo, *n.m.* monticle, mound.

monto, *n.m.* sum (*of money*); (*com.*) amount (*principal plus interest*).

montón, *n.m.* heap, pile, stack; ***a montones,*** galore; ***en montón,*** in a heap, all jumbled up together; ***ser del montón,*** to be run-of-the-mill, common or garden, just ordinary, one of the crowd.

montonera, *n.f.* (*Hisp. Am.*) group of mounted revolutionaries; large crowd; (*Col.*) rick.

montonero, *n.m.* (*Hisp. Am.*) guerrilla.

montuno, -na, *a.* mountain; wild.

montuosidad, *n.f.* hilliness.

montuoso, -sa, *a.* hilly; wooded.

montura, *n.f.* mount; saddle; trappings; (*spectacle*) frame; mounting, setting.

monumental, *a.* monumental.

monumento, *n.m.* monument.

monzón, *n.m.* monsoon.

moña, *n.f.* doll, puppet; badge (*on a bull's neck*); (*dressmaker's*) lay-figure; (*coll.*) drunkenness; ribbons; (*coll.*) ***coger una moña,*** to get plastered *or* sozzled.

moño, *n.m.* chignon, bun; topknot; crest, tuft of feathers; frippery; (*fig.*) ***ponerse moños,*** to put on airs; ***se le ha puesto en el moño ir,*** he has got it into his head to go.

moñón, -ñona, moñudo, -da, *a.* crested, topped; (*Col.*) sulky, sullen, morose.

moquear, *v.i.* to snivel; to run (*the nose*).

moquero, *n.m.* handkerchief.

moqueta, *n.f.* moquette, fitted carpet.

moquete, *n.m.* blow (*on the face* or *nose*).

moquetear, *v.t.* to punch on the nose. — *v.i.* to snivel.

moquillo, *n.m.* pip (*in fowls*); distemper (*of dogs and cats*).

moquita, *n.f.* running nose.

mor, *n.m.* aphæresis of ***amor***; (*coll.*) ***por mor de,*** for the love of, out of regard for, because of.

mora (1), *n.f.* (*bot.*) mulberry, blackberry.

mora (2), *n.f.* [MORO].

morabito, *n.m.* Mohammedan hermit.

moracho, -cha, *a.* light purple.

morada (1), *n.f.* abode, habitation, dwelling; mansion; stay, sojourn.

morado, -da (2), *a.* mulberry-coloured, purple.

morador, -ra, *n.m.f.* dweller.

moraga, *n.f.*, **morago,** *n.m.* handful, bunch; gleaner's bundle.

moral, *a.* moral. — *n.m.* (*bot.*) mulberry tree. — *n.f.* morals, morality; morale.

moraleja, *n.f.* moral.

moralidad, *n.f.* morality.

moralista, *n.m.f.* moralist.

moralización, *n.f.* moralization.

moralizador, -ra, *n.m.f.* moralizer, commentator, critic.

moralizar [C], *v.t.*, *v.i.* to moralize, speak *or* write on morals.

morar, *v.i.* to dwell.

moratoria, *n.f.* (*law.*, *com.*) moratorium.

morbidez, *n.f.* softness, delicacy; sensualness.

mórbido, -da, *a.* soft, delicate; sensual; (*med.*) morbid.

morbífico, -ca, *a.* morbific.

morbilidad, *n.f.* sick rate.

morbo, *n.m.* disease; ***morbo comicial,*** epilepsy; ***morbo gálico,*** venereal disease; ***morbo regio,*** jaundice.

morbosidad, *n.f.* morbidity; morbidness, morbid nature; (*med.*) disease rate.

morboso, -sa, *a.* morbid; (*med.*) diseased.

morcella, *n.f.* spark from a lamp.

morciguillo, *n.m.* (*orn.*) bat.

morcilla (1), *n.f.* black pudding; (*theat.*) stale gag; (*coll.*) ***meter morcilla,*** to stick sth. extra in; (*theat.*) to ad lib; ***dar morcilla,*** to poison.

morcillero, -ra, *n.m.f.* maker of black puddings; (*theat.*) gagger.

morcillo (1), **-lla** (2), *a.* reddish-black (*of horses*).

morcillo (2), *n.m.* fleshy *or* muscular part of the arm.

morcón, *n.m.* large black pudding; large sausage; (*coll.*) stocky individual; slovenly individual.

mordacidad, *n.f.* mordacity; mordant *or* biting nature.

mordante, *n.m.* (*print.*) guide, container.

mordaz, *a.* mordant, biting.

mordaza, *n.f.* gag; muzzle; clamp; stopper; (*railw.*) fish-plate.

mordedor, -ra, *a.* biting.

mordedura, *n.f.* bite.

mordente, *n.m.* (*mus.*) mordent.

morder [5], *v.t.*, *v.i.* to bite, bite into, nip, nip into; to nibble away, eat away, wear away; to back-bite; ***no se muerde la lengua,*** he doesn't mince his words.

mordicación, *n.f.* smarting, stinging.

mordicante, *a.* biting, pungent, mordicant, acrid, corrosive.

mordicar [A], *v.t.* to nibble, gnaw, sting, smart.

mordicativo, -va, *a.* biting, stinging, mordicant.

mordido, *n.m.* nibble, bite.

mordiente, *a.* biting. — *n.m.* mordant.

mordihuí, *n.m.* weevil.

mordimiento, *n.m.* bite; biting.

mordiscar [A], *v.t.* [MORDISQUEAR].

mordisco, *n.m.* bite; pinch.

mordisquear, *v.t.*, *v.i.* to nibble (at), gnaw (at), champ (at).

moreda, *n.f.* mulberry tree *or* grove.

morel de sal, *n.m.* (*art*) purple-red (*for fresco painting*).

morena (1), *n.f.* brown bread; (*bot.*) frog-bit; (*agric.*) rick (*of newly mown grain*); (*ichth.*) muræna; (*geol.*) moraine.

morenazo, -za, morenote, -ta, *a.* very dark, swarthy, dark and handsome.

morenillo, -lla, *a.* rather *or* a bit brown *or* dark. — *n.m.* charcoal and vinegar paste (*for cuts*).

moreno, -na (2), *a.* brown, dark-brown; dark, dark-complexioned; (*coll.*) coloured; (*Hisp. Am.*) mulatto. — *n.m.f.* (*coll.*) coloured person; (*Hisp. Am.*) mulatto. — *n.f.* brunette.

morera, *n.f.* (*bot.*) white mulberry tree.

moreral, *n.m.* plantation of white mulberry trees.

morería, *n.f.* Moorish quarter; Moorish land.
moretón, *n.m.* bruise, black and blue mark.
morfa, *n.f.* citrus scab.
morfema, *n.m.* morpheme.
Morfeo, *n.m.* (*myth.*) Morpheus.
morfina, *n.f.* morphine.
morfinismo, *n.m.* (*med.*) morphinism.
morfinómano, -na, *a.* addicted to morphine *or* drugs. — *n.m.f.* morphine *or* drug addict.
morfología, *n.f.* morphology.
morfológico, -ca, *a.* morphologic, morphological.
morga, *n.f.* juice oozing from a heap of olives.
morganático, -ca, *a.* morganatic.
moribundo, -da, *a.* moribund, dying.
moriche, *n.m.* palm tree.
moriego, -ga, *a.* Moorish.
morigeración, *n.f.* temperance, moderation.
morigerado, -da, *a.* temperate, moderate.
morigerar, *v.t.* to moderate, restrain.
morillo, *n.m.* andiron, firedog; little Moor; (*And.*) unbaptized child.
morir [7, *p.p.* **muerto**], *v.i.* to die, die away, die out; ***morir ahogado,*** to drown; ***morir helado,*** to freeze to death; ***morir de hambre,*** to starve to death; ***morir de viejo,*** to die of old age; ***morir como chinches,*** to die like flies. — **morirse,** *v.r.* to die, die away slowly, be dying.
morisco, -ca, *a.* Morisco; Moorish. — *n.m.f.* Morisco.
morisma, *n.f.* the Moorish faith; the Moorish people.
morisqueta, *n.f.* Moorish trick; (*coll.*) deception, trick, fraud; face, grimace.
morlaco, -ca, *a.* affecting ignorance.
morlés, *n.m.* kind of linen, lawn; ***morlés de morlés,*** all of a piece.
mormón, -mona, *n.m.f.* Mormon.
mormonismo, *n.m.* Mormonism.
mormullo, *n.m.* murmur.
moro, -ra (2), *a.* Moorish; Moslem; unbaptized; (*coll.*) unwatered (*wine*); black with a white spot on the forehead (*horses*). — *n.m.f.* Moor; Mohammedan; ***a más moros, más ganancias,*** the more, the merrier, *or* the more there is, the larger the shareout; ***hubo moros y cristianos,*** there was a great furore *or* rumpus; ***hay moros en la costa,*** there's sth. afoot, trouble in the offing; ***moro de paz,*** peaceful person; ***a moro muerto, gran lanzada,*** it is easy to kick a man when he's down.
morocada, *n.f.* butt of a ram.
morocho, -cha, *a.* (*Hisp. Am.*) vigorous.
morón, *n.m.* hill, hillock.
moroncho, -cha, morondo, -da, *a.* bald, bare.
morondanga, *n.f.* (*coll.*) medley, hodge-podge.
morosidad, *n.f.* tardiness, slowness.
moroso, -sa, *a.* tardy, slow, lingering; delinquent (*in payment*).
morquera, *n.f.* winter savoury.
morra, *n.f.* crown, top of head; mora (*game*).
morrada, *n.f.* butting with the head; slap, punch in the face.
morral, *n.m.* nose-bag; game-bag; knapsack; (*naut.*) boom-sail; (*coll.*) clod, boor.
morralla, *n.f.* small fry; rubbish, trash; rabble, riff-raff.
morrillo, *n.m.* pebble; fat of the nape (*of a sheep*).
morriña, *n.f.* murrain; (*coll.*) nostalgia, homesickness; melancholy, blues.
morrión, *n.m.* (*mil.*) morion; vertigo (*in hawks*).
morro (1), *n.m.* knob; snout; headland, head, bluff; pebble; thick lips; ***andar al morro,*** to be at daggers drawn; ***estar de morros,*** to be sulky *or* sullen.
morro (2), **-rra,** *a.* purring.
morrocotudo, -da, *a.* (*coll.*) terrific; tremendous.
morrocoyo, morrocoy, *n.m.* (*Cub.*) boxturtle.
morrón, *a.* knotted (*flag*); sweet (*red pepper*). — *n.m.* crash, smash; ***darse un morrón,*** to come a cropper.
morroncho, -cha, *a.* mild, meek, tame.
morrudo, -da, *a.* big-snouted.
morsa, *n.f.* walrus.
mortadela, *n.f.* mortadella.
mortaja, *n.f.* shroud, winding-sheet; mortise; (*Hisp. Am.*) cigarette paper.
mortal, *a.* mortal, fatal, deadly, lethal. — *n.m.* mortal.
mortalidad, *n.f.* mortality; death rate.
mortandad, *n.f.* slaughter; (*coll.*) crushing bore.
mortecino, -na, *a.* dying; weak, feeble; dull, dim.
morterada, *n.f.* bowlful; (*artill.*) grape-shot discharge.
morterete, *n.m.* small mortar; gun for firing salutes; maroon; broad candlestick.
mortero, *n.m.* mortar.
morteruelo, *n.m.* small mortar; toy; fricassee of hog's liver.
morticinio, *n.m.* carrion, carcass.
mortífero, -ra, *a.* lethal, death-dealing.
mortificación, *n.f.* mortification.
mortificar [A], *v.t.* to mortify.
mortuorio, -ria, *a.* of the dead. — *n.m.* funeral.
morucho, *n.m.* young bull with horns tipped.
morueco, *n.m.* ram.
moruno, -na, *a.* Moorish.
moruro, *n.m.* Cuban acacia.
morusa, *n.f.* (*coll.*) cash.
mosaico, -ca, *a.* Mosaic, of Moses. — *n.m.* mosaic; pattern.
mosaísmo, *n.m.* Mosaic law.
mosca, *n.f.* fly; tuft of hair under the lip; (*coll.*) cash, dough; ***mosca de burro*** or ***de caballo,*** horse-fly; (*fig.*) ***es una mosca muerta,*** he *or* she looks as if butter wouldn't melt in his *or* her mouth; (*fig.*) ***¿qué mosca le ha picado?*** what's biting him?; (*fig.*) ***estar con la mosca detrás de la oreja,*** to smell a rat; ***papar moscas,*** to gape; (*sl.*) ***aflojar*** or ***soltar la mosca,*** to cough up the cash, come across with the dibs; ***por si las moscas,*** just in case; (*pl.*) sparks
moscarda, *n.f.* gad-fly, horse-fly, blowfly.
moscardear, *v.i.* to lay eggs (*bee*).
moscardón, *n.m.* botfly; bluebottle; hornet, drone; bumble-bee.
moscareta, *n.f.* (*orn.*) fly-catcher.
moscatel, *a.* muscatel. — *n.m.* muscatel.
mosco, *n.m.* gnat, mosquito.
moscón, -cona, *a.* droning, buzzing. — *n.m.* big fly; bluebottle. — *n.f.* hussy.
mosconear, *v.t., v.i.* to pester, be a pest.
moscovita, *a., n.m.f.* Muscovite.
Moscú, *n.f.* Moscow.
mosén, *n.m.* sir; title given to clergymen in Aragon and Catalonia.
mosqueado, -da, *a.* spotted.
mosqueador, *n.m.* fly-flap; (*coll.*) tail.
mosquear, *v.t.* to shoo away; to answer sharply; to flog. — **mosquearse,** *v.r.* to shrug off bother; to get ratty, irritated.
mosqueo, *n.m.* fly-catching.
mosquero, *n.m.* fly-trap, fly-flap; (*Chi., Cub.*) swarm of flies.
mosquerola, mosqueruela, *n.f.* Muscadine pear.
mosqueta, *n.f.* white musk-rose.
mosquetazo, *n.m.* musket-shot.
mosquete, *n.m.* musket.
mosquetería, *n.f.* body of musketeers.
mosqueteril, *a.* (*coll.*) of *or* belonging to musketeers; (*coll., theat.*) belonging to the crowd in the pit.

mosquetero, *n.m.* musketeer; (*obs.*) spectator standing in the pit (*of a theatre*).
mosquetón, *n.m.* short carbine.
mosquil, mosquino, -na, *a.* belonging to flies.
mosquita, *n.f.* small fly; (*coll., fig.*) ***mosquita muerta,*** one who looks as if butter wouldn't melt in his mouth.
mosquitero, -ra, *n.m.f.* mosquito net.
mosquito, *n.m.* gnat; mosquito; tippler.
mostacero, -ra, *n.m.f.* mustard pot.
mostacilla, *n.f.* sparrow-shot; small bead.
mostacho, *n.m.* bushy moustache; spot on the face; (*naut.*) bowsprit shrouds.
mostachón, *n.m.* macaroon.
mostachoso, -sa, *a.* having a bushy moustache.
mostagán, *n.m.* (*coll.*) wine.
mostajo, *n.m.* (*bot.*) white beam tree.
mostaza, *n.f.* mustard; mustard-seed; grape-shot; ***hacer la mostaza,*** to draw blood from the nose by striking it.
mostazo, *n.m.* (*bot.*) mustard-plant; strong must.
mostear, *v.i.* to yield must; to put must into vats; to mix must with old wine.
mostela, *n.f.* (*agric.*) gavel, sheaf.
mostelera, *n.f.* place where sheaves are laid up.
mostellar, *n.m.* (*bot.*) white beam tree.
mostillo, *n.m.* must-cake; sauce made of must and mustard.
mosto, *n.m.* must; ***mosto agustín,*** must cake cooked with flour, fine spices, and various fruit.
mostrable, *a.* demonstrable.
mostrador, -ra, *a.* showing, pointing. — *n.m.* counter; dial (*of a clock* or *watch*).
mostrar [4], *v.t.* to show, ***mostrar las suelas de los zapatos,*** to show a clean pair of heels.
mostrenco, -ca, *a.* strayed, vagabond, homeless, unowned, masterless; nondescript; dense, stupid; bulky, fat; ***bienes mostrencos,*** unclaimed property.
mota, *n.f.* speck, mite, mote; small flaw; bank of earth, mound, hummock; (*Arg., Bol.*) tightly curled lock of hair.
motacila, *n.f.* (*orn.*) wagtail.
mote, *n.m.* motto; nickname; (*Hisp. Am.*) stewed corn.
motear, *v.t.* to speckle, mark with spots.
motejador, -ra, *n.m.f.* mocker, scoffer; name-caller.
motejar, *v.t.* to nickname.
motete, *n.m.* (*mus.*) motet; affront, abuse.
motil, *n.m.* farmer's boy.
motilar, *v.t.* to crop, cut the hair of.
motilón, *a.* having cropped hair. — *n.m.* lay-brother.
motín, *n.m.* mutiny; riot.
motivar, *v.t.* to motivate, cause; to give a reason for.
motivo, -va, *a.* motive. — *n.m.* cause, reason; ***con motivo de,*** because of; on the occasion of; on the pretext of; ***de su propio motivo,*** off his own bat; ***bajo ningún motivo,*** on no account.
moto, *n.m.* guide-post, landmark. — *n.f.* motor-cycle.
motocicleta, *n.f.* motor-cycle.
motociclista, *n.m.f.* motor-cyclist.
motolito, -ta, *a.* simple, easily deceived. — *n.f.* (*orn.*) wagtail.
motón, *n.m.* (*naut.*) block, pulley.
motonave, *n.f.* motor-ship.
motonería, *n.f.* (*naut.*) pulley-blocks.
motonero, *n.m.* pulley-block maker.
motor, -ra, *a.* motor, motive. — *n.m.* motor; engine; ***el primer motor,*** the prime mover, first cause; ***motor de explosión,*** internal combustion engine; ***motor de reacción a chorro, motor de reacción, motor a chorro,*** jet engine; ***motor de dos tiempos,*** two-stroke engine. — *n.f.* motor-boat; speedboat.
motorismo, *n.m.* motor-cycle riding.
motorista, *n.m.* motor-cyclist; motor-cycle policeman.
motril, *n.m.* apprentice.
motriz, *a.* motive, driving.
movedizo, -za, *a.* movable, easily moved; shifting; shaky, unsteady; ***arenas movedizas,*** quick-sands.
movedor, -ra, *a.* moving.
movedura, *n.f.* movement; miscarriage.
mover [5], *v.t.* to move; to stir, shake, wag; to drive, prompt; to stir up, excite. — *v.i.* to miscarry; (*arch.*) to spring; (*agric.*) to bud. — **moverse,** *v.r.* to move, stir, budge, shift, get a move on; (*naut.*) to heave.
movible, *a.* movable, mobile; changeable, fickle.
moviente, *a.* moving, motive.
móvil, *a.* movable, mobile, portable. — *n.m.* motive; moving body.
movilidad, *n.f.* mobility, movableness; fickleness, inconstancy.
movilización, *n.f.* mobilization.
movilizar [C], *v.t.* to mobilize.
movimiento, *n.m.* move; movement; motion; moving; life, liveliness, animation; comings and goings; traffic; (*mus.*) tempo; (*astron.*) clock error; (*naut.*) heaving, pitching; ***juguete de movimiento,*** mechanical toy; ***en movimiento,*** going, working; ***movimiento alternativo,*** reciprocating motion; ***movimiento continuo*** or ***perpetuo,*** perpetual movement; ***movimiento oratorio,*** oratorical gesture.
moxa, *n.f.* (*surg.*) moxa.
moyana, *n.f.* large culverin; (*coll.*) lie, falsehood; dog biscuit.
moyo, *n.m.* liquid measure of about 57 gallons.
moyuelo, *n.m.* very fine bran.
moza, *n.f.* [MOZO].
mozalbete, mozalbillo, *n.m.* lad, beardless youth.
mozallón, *n.m.* strapping lad.
mozárabe, *a.* Mozarabic. — *n.m.f.* Mozarab, Christian who lived among the Moors in Spain.
mozo, -za, *a.* young, youthful; single, unmarried. — *n.m.* youth, lad; servant-boy; waiter; porter; (*mil.*) conscript; ***buen, guapo*** or ***real mozo,*** handsome lad, lusty lad; ***mozo de cuadra,*** stable boy *or* groom; ***mozo de paja y cebada,*** ostler; ***mozo de cordel*** or ***de cuerda,*** porter, carrier; (*Cat.*) ***mozo de escuadra,*** local militiaman; ***mozo de estación,*** railway porter; ***mozo de labranza,*** farm-hand. — *n.f.* girl; lass; wench; maidservant; last *or* winning game (*at cards*); wash beetle; ***moza de fortuna*** or ***del partido,*** harlot; ***buena, guapa*** or ***real moza,*** buxom wench, handsome woman, fine figure of a woman.
mozuela, *n.f.* young girl *or* lass.
mozuelo, *n.m.* young boy *or* lad.
mu, *n.m.* moo, lowing; ***habló el buey y dijo mu,*** it turned out to be a flop. — *n.f.* ***hacer mu,*** to sleep; ***ir a la mu,*** to go bye-byes.
muaré, *n.m.* moiré, watered silk.
mucamo, -ma, *n.m.f.* (*Hisp. Am.*) servant.
muceta, *n.f.* (*eccles.*) mozetta.
mucilaginoso, -sa, *a.* mucilaginous, slimy.
mucílago, mucilago, *n.m.* mucilage, slime.
mucosidad, *n.f.* mucosity.
mucoso, -sa, *a.* mucous, viscous.
múcura, *n.m.* (*Ven.*) pitcher, ewer, gurglet; (*Col.*) blockhead.
muchacha, *n.f.* girl, lass; maid, maid-servant.
muchachada, *n.f.* boyish *or* girlish trick *or* prank; bunch of boys *or* boys and girls.
muchachear, *v.i.* to fool about; to get up to tricks *or* pranks.

muchachería [MUCHACHADA].
muchachez, *n.f.* childhood; puerility.
muchachil, *a.* youthful.
muchacho, *n.m.* boy, lad, chap; ***gran*** or ***buen muchacho,*** good chap, decent fellow, jolly good sort.
muchachote, *n.m.* (*coll.*) hefty lad; tom-boy.
muchedumbre, *n.f.* multitude, crowd; (*fig.*) masses, piles, a lot.
mucho, -cha, *a.* much, a good *or* great deal of, a lot of; (*pl.*) many, a lot of, lots of. — *adv. m.* much, a great deal, a lot, hard, far, long, often; ***llueve mucho,*** it is raining hard; ***mucho más,*** much more, a lot more, far more; ***ni mucho menos,*** far from it, nor anything like it, not by a long shot; ***por mucho que,*** however much. — *pron. and n.* much, a great deal; ***como mucho,*** at the outside, at the very most; ***con mucho,*** by far; ***guárdate muy mucho (de),*** take jolly good care not to; ***ni con mucho,*** not by a long shot; ***mucho será que . . .,*** it's unlikely that. . . .
muda (1), *n.f.* change of linen; mew; moulting-time; roost of birds of prey; cosmetic.
mudable, *a.* changeable, fickle.
mudanza, *n.f.* removal; change, mutation, inconstancy, levity; figure in dancing, motion.
mudar, *v.t.* to change; to move, remove; to moult, shed, cast off; to break (*voice*). — *v.i.* ***mudar de color,*** to turn *or* go white *or* pale; ***mudar de parecer,*** to change one's mind. — **mudarse,** *v.r.* to change; to move (*house*); to change (*clothes*).
mudéjar, *a.*, *n.m.f.* Mudejar (*Mohammedan under Christian rule, XIIIth to XVIth century*).
mudez, *n.f.* dumbness, silence, muteness.
mudo, -da (2), *a.* dumb, silent, mute.
mué, *n.m.* moiré.
mueblaje, *n.m.* furniture.
mueble, *n.m.* piece of furniture; (*pl.*) furniture.
mueblería, *n.f.* furniture factory *or* store.
mueblista, *n.m.f.* maker *or* seller of furniture.
mueca, *n.f.* grimace, wry face; ***hacer muecas,*** to pull faces.
muecín, *n.m.* muezzin.
muela, *n.f.* upper millstone; mill-dam; grindstone, whetstone; grinder, molar tooth; knoll, flat-topped hill; flat pea; ***muela del juicio,*** wisdom tooth; ***echar las muelas,*** to cut one's teeth; (*coll.*, *fig.*) ***está que echa las muelas,*** he's fuming, he's hopping mad.
muellaje, *n.m.* dues paid on entering a port.
muelle, *a.* soft; easy. — *n.m.* spring; mole, pier, jetty, quay, wharf, (*Am.*) dock; (*jewel.*) chatelaine; (*railw.*) goods platform.
muérdago, *n.m.* (*bot.*) mistletoe.
muérgano, *n.m.* (*Col.*) worthless *or* contemptible person *or* thing.
muergo, *n.m.* razor-fish.
muermo, *n.m.* (*vet.*) glanders.
muermoso, -sa, *a.* glandered, suffering from glanders.
muerte, *n.f.* death; murder; ***dar (la) muerte a,*** to put to death, kill; ***estar a la muerte,*** to be at death's door; ***odiar a muerte,*** to hate the guts of; ***perseguir de muerte,*** to hound relentlessly; ***guerra a muerte,*** war to the death; ***de mala muerte,*** rotten, tenth-rate, punk; (*coll.*, *fig.*) ***esto es una muerte*** or ***la muerte,*** it's ghastly *or* dreadful.
muerto, -ta, *p.p. irreg.* **morir** and *adj.* dead; faded, dull; (*coll.*, *fig.*) dead tired, fagged out. — *n.m.* dead person, dead body, corpse; ***muerto de curiosidad,*** dying *or* bursting with curiosity; ***muerto de frío,*** frozen stiff; ***muerto de hambre,*** starving, ravenous; ***muerto de miedo,*** scared stiff; ***muerto de risa,*** helpless with laughter; ***echar el muerto a,*** to put the blame on; ***hacerse el muerto,*** to lie doggo, play possum; ***hacer el muerto,*** to lie face up in the water; ***cargar con el muerto,*** to take the rap.
muesca, *n.f.* notch, nick; mortise, dovetail scarf.
muestra, *n.f.* sign-board; sample, specimen; end of a piece of cloth bearing manufacturer's name; sampler; sign, show, token; pattern, model; (*mil.*) muster-roll; ***dar muestras de,*** to show signs of; ***feria de muestras,*** industrial fair; ***es muestra de cariño,*** it is a token of affection.
mufla, *n.f.* muffle (*of a furnace*); kiln; (*pl.*) thick winter gloves.
muftí, *n.m.* mufti.
muga, *n.f.* boundary, landmark.
mugido, *n.m.* bellow, low.
mugiente, *a.* bellowing, lowing.
mugir [E], *v.i.* to bellow, low.
mugre, *n.f.* grime, filth, greasy dirt.
mugriento, -ta, *a.* grimy, filthy, greasy and dirty.
mugrón, *n.m.* (plant) shoot.
muguete, *n.m.* lily of the valley.
muharra, *n.f.* steel point (*of lance* or *spear*).
muir [O], *v.t.* (*prov.*) to milk.
mujalata, *n.f.* (*Morocco*) farming partnership between a Moroccan and a Christian *or* a Jew.
mujer, *n.f.* woman; wife; ***tomar mujer,*** to take a wife; ***mujer de su casa,*** dutiful housewife; ***mujer airada, de mala vida, del partido*** or ***pública,*** harlot, whore; ***mujer fatal,*** femme fatale; ***mujer galante,*** courtesan; ***¡mujer!*** good Lord, woman!
mujercilla, *n.f.* wretched (little) woman; miserable creature; slut.
mujerengo, *a.* (*Arg.*, *Cent. Am.*) effeminate.
mujeriego, *a.* keen on women, womanizing. — *n.m.* womanizer, (*fam.*) wolf.
mujeril, *a.* womanly, feminine; effeminate.
mujerío, *n.m.* women, mob of women.
mujerona, *n.f.* stout *or* lusty woman, hefty creature.
mujerzuela, *n.f.* worthless woman; prostitute.
mújol, *n.m.* (*ichth.*) mullet.
mula, *n.f.* she-mule; ancient Roman shoe worn now by the Pope on ceremonial occasions.
mulada, *n.f.* drove of mules; stupid thing to do *or* say.
muladar, *n.m.* dungheap; filth.
muladí, *n.m.f.* Spanish convert to Islam.
mulante, *n.m.* muleteer, mule-boy.
mular, *a.* of mules, mule; ***ganado mular,*** mules.
mulatero, *n.m.* muleteer, mule-driver.
mulato, -ta, *a.*, *n.m.f.* mulatto.
mulero, *n.m.* mule-boy.
muleta, *n.f.* crutch; prop, support; (*tauro.*) muleta; snack.
muletada, *n.f.* herd of mules.
muletero, *n.m.* muleteer, mule-driver.
muletilla, *n.f.* cross-handle cane; braid frog; pet word *or* phrase, tag; muleta.
muleto, *n.m.* young he-mule.
muletón, *n.m.* swanskin.
mulilla, *n.f.* small mule.
mulo, *n.m.* mule.
mulquía, *n.f.* (*Morocco*, *law*) title deed.
mulso, -sa, *a.* sweetened with honey *or* sugar.
multa, *n.f.* fine.
multar, *v.t.* to fine.
multicolor, *a.* many-coloured.
multicopista, *a.* duplicating. — *n.m.* duplicator.
multifloro, -ra, *a.* (*bot.*) multiflorous.
multiforme, *a.* multiform.
multilateral, multilátero, -ra, *a.* multilateral.
multimillionario, -ria, *a.*, *n.m.f.* multi-millionaire.
multinacional, *a.*, *n.f.* multinational (company).
multíparo, -ra, *a.* multiparous.
multiplicable, *a.* multipliable.
múltiple, *a.* multiple.
multiplicación, *n.f.* multiplication.

multiplicador, -ra, *a.* multiplying. — *n.m.f.* multiplier.
multiplicando, *n.m.* (*arith.*) multiplicand.
multiplicar [A], *v.t.* to multiply. — **multiplicarse,** *v.r.* to multiply, be multiplied; to be here, there and everywhere; ***no me puedo multiplicar,*** I can't be in more than one place at a time.
multíplice, *a.* multiple.
multiplicidad, *n.f.* multiplicity.
múltiplo, -la, *a.* multiple.
multitubular, *a.* multitubular.
multitud, *n.f.* multitude, crowd.
mulla, *n.f.* digging round vines.
mullido, -da, *a.* fluffed up, soft. — *n.m.* soft filling.
mullir [J], *v.t.* to fluff up, soften up, loosen up; to get ready, prepare. — **mullirse,** *v.r.* ***mullírselas a,*** to chastise, mortify.
mulló, *n.m.* (*ichth.*) surmullet; (*Hisp. Am.*) glass bead.
mundanal, *a.* of the world.
mundanalidad, *n.f.* wordliness.
mundanear, *v.i.* to be worldly-minded.
mundanería, *n.f.* worldliness, sophistication.
mundano, -na, *a.* mundane, worldly.
mundial, *a.* world-wide, world.
mundificar [A], *v.t.* to cleanse, make clean.
mundificativo, -va, *a.* mundificative, mundatory, cleansing.
mundillo, *n.m.* warming-pan; arched cloth dryer; (*bot.*) viburnum; cushion for lace-making; (*fig.*) world, circle; ***el mundillo del arte,*** the (limited *or* confined) world of art.
mundinovi, mundinuevo, *n.m.* rare-show, a spectacle.
mundo, *n.m.* world; (*coll.*) crowd, mob; large trunk; ***echar al mundo,*** to bring into the world; ***no ser de este mundo,*** to be very unworldly; ***el gran mundo,*** high life, high society; ***todo el mundo,*** everybody; ***medio mundo,*** nearly everybody; ***hacer mundo nuevo,*** to introduce changes *or* novelties, make a clean sweep; ***tener (mucho) mundo,*** to have savoir-faire; ***ver*** or ***correr mundo,*** to see the world; ***ha corrido mundo,*** he's been around; ***hombre de mundo,*** man of the world; ***no es cosa del otro mundo,*** it's nothing very wonderful; ***el mundo es un pañuelo,*** it's a small world; ***por esos mundos de Dios,*** out in the wilderness; ***aunque se hunda el mundo,*** even if the world comes to an end; ***no cabe en este mundo,*** he's too big for his boots; ***prometer este mundo y el otro,*** to promise the earth; ***creerse este mundo y el otro,*** to think o.s. the goods; ***valer un mundo,*** to be beyond price; ***anda el mundo al revés,*** the world is topsy-turvy.
mundología, *n.f.* savoir-faire; (*coll.*) know-how.
munición, *n.f.* munition, ammunition; supplies; charge (*of firearms*); ***de munición,*** government issued; (*pl.* **municiones**) provisions, victuals.
municionar, *v.t.* to store, supply with ammunition.
municipal, *a.* town, municipal. — *n.m.* urban policeman.
municipalidad, *n.f.* municipality, municipal corporation.
munícipe, *n.m.* citizen.
municipio, *n.m.* township; town hall.
munificencia, *n.f.* munificence, liberality.
munificentísimo, -ma, *a. superl.* most munificent.
munífico, -ca, *a.* munificent, liberal.
munitoria, *n.f.* art of fortification.
muñeca, *n.f.* (*anat.*) wrist; doll; polishing bag; dressmaker's dummy.
muñeco, *n.m.* puppet; doll; (*pl.*) (*coll.*) pictures.
muñeira, *n.f.* popular dance of Galicia.
muñequear, *v.i.* to play with the wrist in fencing.
muñequera, *n.f.* wrist-watch strap.
muñequería, *n.f.* effeminacy in dress; over-dressing.
muñequilla, *n.f.* (*Chi.*) young ear of corn.
muñidor, *n.m.* beadle; canvasser.
muñir [K], *v.t.* to summon, call, convoke.
muñón, *n.m.* stump (*of a limb*); (*mech.*) journal, gudgeon, pivot; (*artill.*) trunnion.
muñonera, *n.f.* trunnion plate; (*mech.*) gudgeon socket, journal box, bearing.
murajes, *n.m.pl.* (*bot.*) pimpernel.
mural, *a.*, *n.m.* mural.
muralla, *n.f.* wall, rampart.
murallón, *n.m.* (*fort.*) strong fortress wall.
murar, *v.t.* to wall, wall in, wall round.
murciélago, *n.m.* (*zool.*) bat.
murciglero, *n.m.* (*sl.*) prowling thief, night prowler.
murena, *n.f.* (*ichth.*) moray.
murete, *n.m.* small wall.
murga, *n.f.* lees (*of olives*); street band; (*coll.*) ***dar la murga,*** to kick up a rumpus, make a lot of fuss, be a pain in the neck.
murgón, *n.m.* (*ichth.*) parr.
muriático, -ca, *a.* (*chem.*) muriatic.
muriato, *n.m.* (*chem.*) muriate.
múrice, *n.m.* murex; (*poet.*) purple.
murmujear, *v.i.* (*coll.*) to mutter, murmur.
murmullo, *n.m.* mutter, murmur; whisper; ripple, purl; rustle.
murmuración, *n.f.* backbiting, gossiping.
murmurador, -ra, *a.* murmuring; gossiping. — *n.m.f.* murmurer; gossip (*person*).
murmurante, *a.* murmuring, purling.
murmurar, *v.i.* to mutter, murmur; to whisper; to ripple, purl; to rustle; to grumble; to gossip.
murmurio, *n.m.* murmuring.
muro, *n.m.* wall; (*fort.*) rampart; ***muro de contención,*** retaining wall.
murrio, -rria, *a.* melancholy, dejected, (*coll.*) blue. — *n.f.* melancholy, dejection, fit of blues.
murtilla, murtina, *n.f.* (*bot.*) Chilean myrtus.
murtón, *n.m.* myrtle-berry.
murucuyá, *n.f.* (*bot.*) purple passion-flower.
mus, *n.m.* card game.
musa, *n.f.* Muse; muse; (*fig.*) inspiration; (*fig.*) luck.
musaraña, *n.f.* shrew-mouse; creature; (*coll.*) floating speck (*in eye*); ***mirar a*** or ***pensar en las musarañas,*** to gaze vacantly into space *or* to have one's head in the clouds.
muscicapa, *n.f.* (*orn.*) fly-catcher.
musco, -ca, *a.* musk-colour. — *n.m.* moss; musk rat.
muscular, *a.* muscular.
musculatura, *n.f.* musculature.
músculo, *n.m.* muscle; (*fig.*) brawn; (*zool.*) finback, rorqual.
musculoso, -sa, *a.* muscular, brawny.
muselina, *n.f.* muslin, (*Am.*) cheesecloth.
museo, *n.m.* museum; art gallery.
muserola, *n.f.* noseband (*of a bridle*).
musgaño, *n.m.* shrew-mouse.
musgo, -ga, *a.* dark brown. — *n.m.* moss.
musgoso, -sa, *a.* mossy, moss-covered.
musical, *a.* musical.
músico, -ca, *a.* musical. — *n.m.f.* musician. — *n.f.* music; tune; band; ***hacer música,*** to make *or* play music, sing songs; ***dar música a un sordo,*** to waste one's breath; (*coll., fig.*) ***vete con la música a otra parte,*** clear off, go and give s.o. else a pain in the neck; (*coll., fig.*) ***eso es música celestial, eso son músicas,*** it's all hot air, just so much wind.
musicógrafo, -fa, *n.m.f.* musicographer.
musicómano, -na, *a.* music-loving. — *n.m.f.* music-lover.
musiquero, *n.m.* music cabinet.

musitar, *v.i.* to mutter, mumble, whisper.
muslera, *n.f.* cuisse, thigh-armour.
muslímico, -ca, *a.* Moslem.
muslo, *n.m.* (*anat.*) thigh.
musmón, *n.m.* (*zool.*) mouflon.
musquerola, *n.f.* muscadine pear.
mustaco, *n.m.* cake made of must.
mustela, *n.m.* (*ichth.*) dogfish.
mustio, -tia, *a.* withered, faded; sad, dejected.
musulmán, -mana, *a.*, *n.m.f.* Moslem.
muta, *n.f.* pack of hounds.
mutabilidad, *n.f.* mutability, fickleness.
mutable, *a.* changeable, fickle.
mutación, *n.f.* mutation, change; (*theat.*) change of scene; unseasonable weather.
mutilación, *n.f.* mutilation, maimedness.
mutilado, *n.m.* war-wounded, cripple.
mutilar, *v.t.* to mutilate, cripple, maim; to dock, cut short.
mutis, *n.m. inv.* (*theat.*) exit of an actor; ***¡mutis!*** silence!; ***hacer mutis,*** to go off; to keep silent.
mutismo, *n.m.* dumbness; silence.
mutual, *a.* mutual, reciprocal.
mutualidad, *n.f.* mutuality; (*com.*) mutual benefit society.
mutuante, *n.m.f.* lender, loaner.
mutuatario, -ria, *a.* (*law*) mutuary.
mutuo, -tua, *a.* mutual. — *n.m.* (*law*) mutuum, loan.
muy, *adv.* very, greatly; most; too; ***muy de mañana,*** very early; ***muy de noche,*** late at night; ***era muy tarde ya,*** by this time it was too late; ***muy hombre,*** very much (of) a man; ***muy señor mío,*** Dear Sir (*in letters*); ***¡el muy sinvergüenza!*** the nerve of the fellow! what a cheek the fellow's got!; ***ser muy dueño de,*** to be perfectly entitled to, have every right to.
muz, *n.m.* (*naut.*) extremity of the cutwater.

N

N, n, *n.f.* letter N, n; ***el Señor N,*** Mister X; for ***norte*** (*north*) and ***número*** (*number*).
naba, *n.f.* Swedish turnip.
nabab, *n.m.* nabob.
nabal, nabar, *a.* (pertaining to the) turnip. — *n.m.* turnip field.
nabería, *n.f.* turnip-pottage; heap of turnips.
nabí, *n.m.* Moorish prophet.
nabicol, *n.m.* (*bot.*) turnip.
nabina, *n.f.* turnip seed.
nabizas, *n.f.pl.* turnip tops.
nabla, *n.f.* (*mus.*) nabla (*psaltery*).
nabo, *n.m.* turnip.
naborí, *n.m.f.* (*Hisp. Am.*) free Indian servant.
naboría, *n.f.* (*Hisp. Am.*) allotment of Indian servants (*during the Spanish conquest*).
nácar, *n.m.* mother-of-pearl.
nácara, *n.f.* kettledrum.
nacarado, -da, *a.* mother-of-pearl (*colour*).
nacáreo, -rea, nacarino, -na, *a.* nacreous, nacrine.
nacarón, *n.m.* mother-of-pearl of low quality.
nacascolo, *n.m.* (*Cent. Am.*) dividivi tree.
nacatamal, *n.m.* (*Hond.*) tamale stuffed with pork.
nacatete, *n.m.* (*Mex.*) young cockerel.
nacencia, *n.f.* tumour, outgrowth; lineage, family.
nacer [9], *v.i.* to be born; to bud, shoot forth; to arise, spring up; to appear, come forth; to come (from); (*coll.*) ***nacer de pie,*** to be born lucky; ***acabas de nacer, has vuelto a nacer,*** you've had a narrow escape, you can count yourself lucky to be alive; (*coll., fig.*) ***no he nacido ayer,*** I wasn't born yesterday. — **nacerse,** *v.r.* to bud, shoot; to split.
nacido, -da, *a.* ***bien nacido,*** of noble birth, high-born; ***mal nacido,*** low-born; ***recién nacido,*** newly born. — *n.m.* human being; growth.
naciente, *a.* nascent; incipient; rising; (*her.*) naissant. — *n.m.* east.
nacimiento, *n.m.* birth; springing forth; source; origin; crib, nativity scene; ***de nacimiento,*** from birth.
nación, *n.f.* nation; (*Hisp. Am.*) race, tribe; ***de nación,*** by nationality.
nacional, *a.* national; home. — *n.m.f.* nationalist; militiaman.
nacionalidad, *n.f.* nationality.
nacionalismo, *n.m.* nationalism.
nacionalista, *a.* nationalist(ic). — *n.m.f.* nationalist.
nacionalización, *n.f.* nationalization.
nacionalizar [C], *v.t.* to nationalize.
naco, *n.m.* (*Arg., Bol.*) black chewing tobacco.
nada, *adv.* not at all, not in the least; ***no me gusta nada,*** I don't like it at all. — *pron.* nothing, not a bit, very little; ***nada de eso,*** nothing of the sort, certainly not; ***nada de pretextos,*** no excuses; ***nada más,*** nothing else; ***nada menos,*** nothing less, no less; ***¡ahí es nada!*** that's no mean thing!; ***antes de nada,*** first of all; ***casi nada,*** hardly anything; ***como si nada,*** as if nothing had happened *or* been said; ***de nada,*** not at all; ***con nada, por nada,*** over nothing, at the slightest provocation. — *n.f.* nothing, nothingness.
nadaderas, *n.f.pl.* water-wings.
nadadero, *n.m.* swimming-place.
nadador, -ra, *n.m.f.* swimmer.
nadar, *v.i.* to swim; ***nadar en la abundancia,*** to be rolling (in plenty); ***nadar y guardar la ropa,*** to get it both ways, have one's cake and eat it; ***nada en ese traje,*** that suit is very floppy on him, is a very loose fit.
nadie, *indef. pron.* nobody, no one.
nadir, *n.m.* (*astron.*) nadir.
nado, *adv.* ***a nado,*** swimming; ***pasar*** or ***cruzar a nado,*** to swim across.
nafa, *n.f.* orange flower.
nafta, *n.f.* naphtha; (*Hisp. Am.*) petrol.
naftalina, *n.f.* naphthaline.
naftol, *n.m.* naphthol.
nagual, *n.m.* (*Mex.*) sorcerer, conjurer, wizard; (*Hond.*) pet animal.
naguapate, *n.m.* (*Hond.*) cruciate plant used to cure, venereal diseases.
naguas, *n.f.pl.* under-petticoat.
naguatlato, -ta, *a.* (*Mex.*) Indian interpreter.
nagüela, *n.f.* (*obs.*) thatched cottage, hovel.
naife, *n.m.* diamond of superior quality.
naipe, *n.m.* playing-card; pack of cards; ***no se me da el naipe,*** my luck is not in; ***tener buen naipe, tener el naipe,*** to have good luck.
naire, *n.m.* elephant-keeper.
najarse, *v.r.* (*coll.*) to scram, beat it, clear out, clear off, do a bunk
nalca, *n.f.* (*Chi.*) edible leaf stalk.
nalga, *n.f.* buttock, rump.
nalgada, *n.f.* slap on the buttocks; blow with the buttocks; ham (*of pork*).
nalgatorio, *n.m.* (*coll.*) posterior, seat, buttocks.
nalgón, -gona (*Hond.*) [NALGUDO].
nalgudo, -da, *a.* having big buttocks.
nalguear, *v.i.* to wobble one's backside.
nalguilla, *n.f.* thick part of the hub of a wheel.
nambí, *n.m.f.* (*Arg.*) horse *or* mare with drooping ears.
nambimba, *n.f.* (*Mex.*) dish made of maize boiled with honey, cocoa and chilli.
nambira, *n.f.* (*Hond.*) half of a dried gourd used as a drinking vessel etc.
nana, *n.f.* (*coll.*) grandma; lullaby, cradlesong; (*Mex.*) child's nurse, nanny; (*Arg., Chi.*) [PUPA]; ***del año de la nana,*** donkey's years old; ***más viejo que la nana,*** as old as the hills; ***hacer nana,*** to go bye-byes; ***cantar la nana,*** to lull (a baby).
nanacate, *n.m.* (*Mex., bot.*) mushroom.
nance, *n.m.* (*Hond., bot.*) shrub and its fragrant fruit.
nancear, *v.i.* (*Hond.*) to catch; to fit, have room, reach.
nandú [ÑANDÚ].
nango, -ga, *a.* (*Mex.*) foreign; silly, foolish, stupid.
nanjea, *n.f.* (*Philip.*) tree largely used in making cabinets and musical instruments.
nanquín, *n.m.* nankeen.
nansa, *n.f.* fish-pond; fish trap.
nansú, nanzú, *n.m.* nainsook.
nao, *n.f.* ship, vessel; ***nao capitana,*** flag-ship.
naonato, -ta, *a.* born on board ship.
napea, *n.f.* (*myth.*) wood-nymph.
napelo, *n.m.* (*bot.*) monk's-hood, wolf's-bane.
napias, *n.f.pl.* (*sl.*) nose, conk.
Nápoles, *n.m.* Naples.
napolitano, -na, *a., n.m.f.* Neapolitan.
naque, *n.m.* two strolling comedians.
naranja, *n.f.* orange; (*arch.*) ***media naranja,*** cupola, (*coll.*) better half; alter ego; ***naranja agria*** or ***cajel,*** bitter orange; ***naranja sanguina,*** blood orange. — *interj.* ***¡naranjas!*** you've got a hope!
naranjado, -da, *a.* orange-coloured. — *n.f.* orange juice, orangeade; (*fig.*) rude speech *or* action.
naranjal, *n.m.* orangery, orange-grove.
naranjazo, *n.m.* blow with an orange.
naranjero, -ra, *a.* orange, orange-sized. — *n.m.f.* orange seller. — *n.m.* orange grower; (*prov.*) orange tree.
naranjilla, *n.f.* marmalade-orange.
naranjo, *n.m.* orange-tree; (*coll.*) booby.

narcisismo, *n.m.* narcissism.
narciso, *n.m.* (*bot.*) narcissus; fop; ***narciso (trompón),*** daffodil.
narcosis, *n.f.* (*path.*) narcosis.
narcótico, -ca, *a., n.m.f.* narcotic.
narcotina, *n.f.* (*chem.*) narcotine.
narcotismo, *n.m.* narcotism, drug addiction.
narcotizar [C], *v.t.* to drug, dope.
nardino, -na, *a.* (made of) spikenard.
nardo, *n.m.* spikenard; tuberose.
narguile, *n.m.* narghile, hookah.
narigada, *n.f.* (*Arg., Chi., Ec.*) portion of snuff.
narigón, -gona, narigudo, -da, *a.* big-nosed. — *n.m.f.* big-nosed person. — **narigón,** *n.m.* big nose.
nariguera, *n.f.* nose pendant.
narigueta, nariguita, *n.f.* small nose.
nariz, *n.f.* nose; nostril; sense of smell; bouquet (*of wine*); ***meter la nariz en,*** to stick one's nose into; ***darse de narices con,*** to bang *or* bump into; ***me da en la nariz que,*** I have a (shrewd) suspicion that; ***dejar con un palmo de narices,*** to leave crest-fallen, disappoint deeply; ***estar hasta las narices,*** to be browned off, be cheesed off; ***se le hincharon las narices,*** he got mad *or* ratty; ***esto le hinchó las narices,*** this got his goat; ***¡narices!*** tell that to the marines!; you've got a hope!
narizota, *n.f.* ugly great nose.
narizudo, -da, *a.* large-nosed.
narrable, *a.* capable of being narrated.
narración, *n.f.* narration, account.
narrador, -ra, *a.* narrating. — *n.m.f.* narrator.
narrar, *v.t.* to narrate.
narrativo, -va, narratorio, -ria, *a.* narrative, narratory. — **narrativa,** *n.f.* narrative.
narria, *n.f.* sledge, sled; heavy *or* fat woman.
narval, *n.m.* (*ichth.*) narwhal; sea-unicorn.
nasa, *n.f.* bow *or* bag net; fyke; basket.
nasal, *a.* nasal.
nasalizar [C], *v.t.* to nasalize.
nasardo, *n.m.* nasard.
nata (1), *n.f.* cream; skim; scum; (*fig.*) ***flor y nata,*** flower, cream, crème de la crème.
natación, *n.f.* swimming.
natal, *a.* natal, native. — *n.m.* birth; birthday.
natalicio, -cia, *a.* natal. — *n.m.* birthday.
natátil, *a.* floating.
natatorio, -ria, *a.* natatory.
naterón, *n.m.* cottage cheese.
natilla, *n.f.* (*usu. pl.*) custard.
natío, *a.* ***oro natío,*** native gold. — *n.m.* (*prov.*) birth; sprouting (*of plants*).
natividad, *n.f.* nativity; Yuletide, Christmas.
nativo, -va, *a.* native; vernacular; born, natural-born.
nato, -ta (2), *a.* born; ***ladrón nato,*** born thief.
natral, *n.m.* (*Chi.*) land planted with ***natris.***
natri, *n.m.* (*Chi.*) medicinal plant (*Solanum crispum*).
natrón, *n.m.* (*chem.*) natron.
natura, *n.f.* nature; genital parts; (*mus.*) major scale; ***contra natura,*** artificial, unnatural.
natural, *a.* natural; usual; artless, spontaneous; ***es natural,*** it stands to reason, it's understandable; ***es natural que,*** it's only natural that. — *a., n.m.f.* native; ***natural de Madrid,*** a native of Madrid. — *n.m.* temper, disposition, nature; ***al natural,*** without dressing; ***del natural,*** from life.
naturaleza, *n.f.* nature; temperament; nationality; citizenship, naturalization; ***adquirir carta de naturaleza,*** to take out naturalization papers; (*fig.*) to become standard *or* normal practice; (*art*) ***naturaleza muerta,*** still life; ***por naturaleza,*** by nature.
naturalidad, *n.f.* naturalness; ***con (la mayor) naturalidad,*** in a natural way, unaffectedly; as a matter of course, without turning a hair.
naturalismo, *n.m.* naturalism, exaggerated *or* thorough-going realism.
naturalista, *n.m.f.* naturalist.
naturalización, *n.f.* naturalization.
naturalizar [C], *v.t.* to naturalize.—**naturalizarse,** *v.r.* to be naturalized.
naturalmente, *adv.* naturally, of course; ***naturalmente que sí,*** I should think so too; ***naturalmente que no,*** I should think not indeed.
naturismo, *n.m.* naturism.
naturista, *n.m.f.* naturist.
naufragante, *a.* [NÁUFRAGO].
naufragar [B], *v.i.* to be *or* become wrecked, founder; (*fig.*) to sink, fall through.
naufragio, *n.m.* shipwreck.
náufrago, -ga, *a.* relating to shipwreck; wrecked. — *n.m.f.* shipwrecked person, survivor of a wreck.
naumaquia, *n.f.* naumachy.
náusea, *n.f.* nausea; sickness.
nauseabundo, -da, *a.* loathsome, nauseating.
nausear, *v.i.* to feel nausea.
nauseativo, -va [NAUSEABUNDO].
nauseoso, -sa [NAUSEABUNDO].
nauta, *n.m.* mariner.
náutico, -ca, *a.* nautical. — *n.f.* navigation, nautics.
nautilo, *n.m.* nautilus.
nava, *n.f.* high plain between mountains.
navacero, -ra, *n.m.f.* gardener who cultivates the sandy soil close to the shores of Andalusia.
navaja, *n.f.* razor; clasp-knife, folding-knife; wild boar's tusk; backbiter's tongue; ***navajas de gallo,*** cockspurs.
navajada, *n.f.,* **navajazo,** *n.m.* knife slash *or* gash.
navajero, *n.m.* razor-case; shaving-towel.
navajita, navajilla, *n.f.* penknife.
navajo, *n.m.* pool, puddle.
navajón, *n.m.* large knife.
naval, *a.* naval.
Navarra, *n.f.* Navarre.
navarro, -rra, *a., n.m.f.* Navarrese.
navazo, *n.m.* kitchen garden on a sandy shore.
nave, *n.f.* ship, vessel; nave (*of a church*), aisle; (factory) bay; ***quemar las naves,*** to burn one's boats.
navecilla, *n.f.* small ship; (*eccles.*) navicula.
navegable, *a.* navigable.
navegabilidad, *n.f.* navigability.
navegación, *n.f.* navigation; sailing; voyage, crossing.
navegador, -ra, *a.* navigating. — *n.m.f.* navigator.
navegante, *a.* navigating. — *n.m.f.* navigator.
navegar [B], *v.t., v.i.* to navigate, sail.
naveta, *n.f.* incense-boat; small drawer.
navícula, *n.f.* small ship; (*bot.*) navicula.
navicular, *a.* (*anat.*) navicular.
navichuelo, *n.m.* wretched little vessel.
navidad, *n.f.* nativity; Christmas; ***la Navidad*** or ***las Navidades,*** Christmas *or* Christmas-time.
navideño, -ña, *a.* (of) Christmas.
naviero, -ra, *a.* shipping, ship. — *n.m.* ship-owner.
navío, *n.m.* ship, vessel; ***navío de guerra,*** warship, man-of-war.
náyada, náyade, *n.f.* naïad, water-nymph.
nazareno, -na, *a., n.m.f.* Nazarene, (native) of Nazareth; Holy Week penitent.
nazareo, -rea, *a., n.m.f.* Nazarene.
nea, *n.f.* [NEO].
nébeda, *n.f.* (*bot.*) calamint, catmint.
nebladura, *n.f.* damage caused to crops by mist.
neblí, *n.m.* (*orn.*) falcon, merlin.
neblina, *n.f.* mist.
nebrina, *n.f.* juniper berry.

nebulón, *n.m.* hypocrite.
nebulosidad, *n.f.* nebulosity, nebulousness.
nebuloso, -sa, *a.* nebulous; misty, hazy. — *n.f.* nebula.
necear, *v.i.* to talk nonsense, play the fool.
necedad, *n.f.* stupidity, piece of nonsense.
necesariamente, *adv.* necessarily, of necessity.
necesario, -ria, *a.* necessary. — *n.f.* privy, water-closet.
neceser, *n.m.* sewing case; toilet case; ***neceser de costura,*** work basket.
necesidad, *n.f.* necessity; need, want; hunger; ***la necesidad carece de ley,*** necessity knows no bounds; (*pl.* **necesidades**) bodily functions.
necesitado, -da, *a.* necessitous, needy. — *n.m.f.* needy person.
necesitar, *v.t.* to need, want. — *v.i.* to need, be in need (***de,*** of).
necio, -cia, *a.* stupid, idiotic. — *n.m.f.* fool; ***a palabras necias, oídos sordos,*** pay no heed to the words of a fool.
necrología, *n.f.* necrology, obituary notice.
necrológico, -ca, *a.* necrological.
necrologio, *n.m.* necrology, mortuary.
necromancia, *n.f.* necromancy.
necrópolis, *n.m. inv.* necropolis, cemetery.
necropsia, necroscopia, *n.f.* post-mortem examination.
necrosis, *n.f. inv.* (*surg., path.*) necrobiosis.
néctar, *n.m.* nectar; exquisite drink.
nectáreo, -rea, *a.* nectareal, nectarean.
nectarífero, -ra, *a.* nectar-bearing.
neerlandés, -desa, *a.* Dutch. — *n.m.* Dutch (*language*). — *n.m.f.* Dutchman, Dutchwoman.
nefalista, *n.m.f.* total abstainer; prohibitionist.
nefando, -da, *a.* foul, abominable.
nefario, -ria, *a.* nefarious, abominable.
nefas, *adv.* ***por fas o por nefas,*** rightly or wrongly.
nefasto, -ta, *a.* ill-omened, ill-fated, unlucky; (*coll.*) ghastly.
nefrítico, -ca, *a.* nephritic.
nefritis, *n.f.* nephritis.
negable, *a.* deniable.
negación, *n.f.* negation; denial; want, privation; (*gram.*) negative.
negado, -da, *a.* (*coll.*) useless, hopeless. — *n.m.f.* dead loss.
negador, -ra, *n.m.f.* denier, disclaimer.
negante, *a.* denying, disclaiming.
negar [IB], *v.t.* to deny; to refuse; ***negar el saludo*** (***a***), to cut, cut dead. — **negarse,** *v.r.* to refuse (***a,*** to).
negativo, -va, *a.* negative. — *n.m.* (*photo.*) negative. — *n.f.* denial, refusal.
negligencia, *n.f.* negligence, neglect, carelessness.
negligente, *a.* negligent, careless.
negociabilidad, *n.f.* negotiability.
negociable, *a.* negotiable.
negociación, *n.f.* negotiation.
negociado, *n.m.* bureau, section, division.
negociador, *n.m.* negotiator.
negociante, *a.* dealing, trading. — *n.m.* dealer, trader; businessman.
negociar, *v.t., v.i.* to negotiate. — *v.i.* to deal, trade, do business.
negocio, *n.m.* trade; business; piece of business; profitable business; firm, concern; shop; ***hombre de negocios,*** businessman; ***encargado de negocios,*** chargé d'affaires.
negocioso, -sa, *a.* diligent, prompt, business-like.
negra, *n.f.* negress, black woman; (*fenc.*) foil; (*mus.*) crotchet; (*coll.*) foul luck; ***tener la negra,*** to be dead unlucky.
negrada, *n.f.* (*Cub.*) (crowd of) negroes.
negral, *a.* blackish.
negrear, *v.i.* to grow black; to be (seen) black, show up black, be a mass of black.
negrecer [9], *v.i.* to blacken, become black.
negrero, -ra, *a.* slave, slaving, slave-trading. — *n.m.* slave-trader; slave-driver; (*naut.*) slaver; ***barco negrero,*** slave-ship.
negreta, *n.f.* (*orn.*) black scoter.
negrilla, *n.f.* (*ichth.*) black conger eel; (*print.*) bold-face type.
negrillera, *n.f.* plantation of elms.
negrillo, *n.m.* (*bot.*) elm; (*min.*) black silver ore; (*Arg., Bol.*) linnet.
negrita, *n.f.* (*print.*) bold-face type.
negro, -ra, *a.* black; dark; deep-tanned; Negro; (*Hisp. Am.*) dear, darling. — *n.m.f.* Negro, Negress, black. — *n.m.* black; ***blanco y negro,*** black and white; (*coll.*) ***pasarlas negras,*** to have a terrible *or* grim time of it; (*coll.*) ***poner negro a,*** to drive crazy, get on the nerves of; (*coll.*) ***verse negro para,*** to have a hell of a job to; ***negro de humo,*** lamp-black, soot.
negror, *n.m.,* **negrura,** *n.f.* blackness.
negruzco, -ca, *a.* blackish.
neguijón, *n.m.* caries.
neguilla, *n.f.* (*bot.*) fennel-flower, love-in-a-mist; age mark (*in horse's teeth*).
neguillón, *n.m.* (*bot.*) campion, corn-rose.
nema, *n.f.* seal, sealing (*of a letter*).
nemoroso, -sa, *a.* sylvan.
nene, nena, *n.m.f.* (*coll.*) infant, baby, child.
neneque, *n.m.* helpless and weak person.
nenúfar, *n.m.* (*bot.*) white water-lily.
neo, nea, *a., n.m.f.* Neo-Catholic, Ultramontane.
neocatólico, -ca, *a., n.m.f.* Neo-Catholic.
neocelandés, -desa, *a.* (of) New Zealand. — *n.m.f.* New Zealander.
neófito, *n.m.* neophyte, convert; novice, beginner.
neolatino, -na, *a.* Neo-Latin.
neolítico, -ca, *a.* neolithic.
neología, *n.f.* neology.
neológico, -ca, *a.* neological.
neologismo, *n.m.* neologism.
neólogo, *n.m.* neologist.
neón, *n.m.* (*chem.*) neon.
neoplasma, *n.m.* (*med.*) neoplasm.
neoplatónico, -ca, *a., n.m.f.* Neoplatonic; Neoplatonist.
neoyorkino, -na, *a.* (of) New York. — *n.m.f.* New Yorker.
Nepal, *n.m.* Nepal.
nepalés, -lesa, *a., n.m.f.* Nepalese (person). — *n.m.* Nepali (*language*).
nepente, *n.m.* nepenthe.
nepotismo, *n.m.* nepotism.
neptuniano, -na, *a.* (*geol.*) Neptunian.
Neptuno, *n.m.* (*astron.*) Neptune.
nequáquam, *adv.* (*coll.*) by no means, nothing doing.
nequicia, *n.f.* perversity, iniquity.
nereida, *n.f.* nereid.
nerita, *n.f.* (*zool.*) nerita.
Nerón, *n.m.* Nero; (*fig.*) cruel person.
nervado, -da, *a.* nervate, nerved.
nervadura, *n.f.* (*arch.*) nervure, rib; (*carp.*) feather; (*min.*) leader; (*bot.*) nervation, nervure.
nérveo, -vea, *a.* nerval.
nervezuelo, *n.m.* nervule.
nervino, -na, *a.* nervine, nerve-strengthening.
nervio, *n.m.* nerve; vigour; stamina; gristle, sinew; tendon; string (*of a musical instrument*); (*bookb.*) rib, fillet; (*naut.*) span-rope, stay; ***nervio maestro,*** tendon; ***nervio óptico,*** optic nerve; ***nervio vago,*** vagus pneumogastric nerve; ***ataque de nervios,*** fit of nerves; ***me crispa*** or

ataca los nervios, it gets on my nerves; ***me pone los nervios de punta,*** it sets my nerves on edge.
nerviosidad, *n.f.* nervousness.
nerviosismo, *n.m.* nervousness, nerviness.
nervioso, -sa, *a.* nervous; nervy, jittery, edgy, excited; (*fig.*) ***no te pongas nervioso,*** don't get excited, don't panic.
nervosidad, *n.f.* strength, vigour; sinewyness, toughness.
nervosismo, *n.m.* neurosis.
nervoso, -sa, *a.* nervous.
nervudo, -da, *a.* strong, tough; sinewy, wiry.
nesciencia, *n.f.* ignorance, nescience.
nesciente, *a.* ignorant.
nesga, *n.f.* (*sew.*) gore; triangular piece.
néspera, *n.f.* medlar.
netamente, *adv.* clearly, distinctly, plainly; totally, thoroughly; ***esto es netamente español,*** this is thoroughly *or* typically Spanish.
neto, -ta, *a.* net, nett; bare; sharp, clear. — *n.m.* (*arch.*) dado (*cube of a pedestal*).
neuma, *n.m.* (*mus.*) neume. — *n.m.f.* (*rhet.*) affirmative *or* negative expression by signs or nods.
neumático, -ca, *a.* pneumatic. — *n.f.* pneumatics. — *n.m.* tyre.
neumonía, *n.f.* pneumonia.
neumónico, -ca, *a.* pneumonic.
neuralgia, *n.f.* (*med.*) neuralgia.
neurálgico, -ca, *a.* neuralgic.
neurastenia, *n.f.* neurasthenia.
neurasténico, -ca, *a.* neurasthenic.
neurítico, -ca, *a.* neurotic.
neuroesqueleto, *n.m.* (*zool.*) endoskeleton.
neurología, *n.f.* neurology.
neurólogo, *n.m.* neurologist.
neuropatía, *n.f.* neuropathology.
neurosis, *a.* neurosis.
neurótico, -ca, *a.* neurotic.
neurotomía, *n.f.* (*anat.*) neurotomy.
neutral, *a.* neutral; indifferent.
neutralidad, *n.f.* neutrality, indifference.
neutralizar [C], *v.t.* to neutralize; to check.
neutralmente, *adv.* neutrally.
neutro, -ra, *a.* neutral; neuter, sexless.
nevadilla, *n.f.* whitlow-wort, whittle-wort.
nevado, -da, *a.* snow-covered; snowy; snow-bound. — *n.f.* snowfall.
nevar [I], *v.t.* to cover in snow. — *v.i.* to snow.
nevasca, *n.f.* snow-storm, blizzard.
nevatilla, *n.f.* (*orn.*) wagtail.
nevazón, *n.f.* (*Arg., Chi., Ec.*) [NEVADA].
nevera, *n.f.* refrigerator, (*coll.*) fridge, (*Am.*) icebox.
nevería, *n.f.* place where ice is sold.
nevero, *n.m.* ice-seller; place of perpetual snow.
nevisca, *n.f.* light snowfall.
neviscar [A], *v.i.* to snow lightly.
nevoso, -sa, *a.* snowy.
nexo, *n.m.* nexus, link, connection.
ni, *conj.* neither, nor; or; not a; not even; ***ni siquiera,*** not even; ***no tengo ni idea,*** I haven't the faintest idea, notion *or* inkling; ***ni por asomo,*** by no stretch of the imagination; ***ni tanto ni tan calvo,*** the middle way is best, it's better not to run to extremes; ***no dice ni sí ni no,*** he is non-committal; ***ni que decir tiene que,*** needless to say; (*coll.*) ***¡ni hablar!*** no fear! not likely! not on your life!
niara, *n.f.* straw-rick; clamp.
nicaragüense, nicaragüeño, -ña, *a., n.m.f.* Nicaraguan.
nicociana, *n.f.* tobacco.
Nicolás, *n.m.* Nicholas.
nicotina, *n.f.* nicotine.
nicotismo, *n.m.* nicotinism.
nictagíneo, -nea, *a.* (*bot.*) nyctaginaceous, nyctitropic.
nictalopia, *n.f.* (*med.*) day-blindness.
nicho, *n.m.* niche; recess.
nidada, *n.f.* nest, clutch of eggs; brood, covey.
nidal, *n.m.* nest; nest-egg; (*coll.*) hangout, haunt; hiding place.
nidificación, *n.f.* nest-building.
nidificar [A], *v.i.* to nest, build a nest.
nido, *n.m.* nest; eyry; abode; den; (*coll.*) ***caerse de un nido,*** to be gullible.
niebla, *n.f.* fog; mist, haze; mildew.
niego, *a.* new-born (*falcon*).
niel, *n.m.* niello work.
nielar, *v.t.* to niello.
niéspera, *n.f.* (*bot.*) medlar.
nieta, *n.f.* granddaughter, grandchild.
nietastro, -ra, *a.* step-grandson, step-granddaughter.
nieto, *n.m.* grandson, grandchild; descendant.
nieve (1), *n.f.* snow; (*Hisp. Am.*) ice-sorbet.
nieve (2), *pres. subj.* [NEVAR].
Níger, *n.m.* (river) Niger; ***la República del Níger,*** the Republic of the Niger.
Nigeria, *n.f.* Nigeria.
nigromancia, *n.f.* necromancy.
nigromante, *n.m.* necromancer.
nigromántico, -ca, *a.* necromantic.
nigua, *n.f.* chigoe, jigger flea.
nihilismo, *n.m.* nihilism.
nihilista, *a.* nihilistic. — *n.m.f.* nihilist.
Nilo, *n.m.* Nile.
nimbo, *n.m.* halo, nimbus.
nimiedad, *n.f.* (*obs.*) prolixity, excessiveness; minuteness; insignificant thing, thing of no account, triviality.
nimio, -mia, *a.* (*obs.*) prolix, excessive; meticulous; insignificant, of no account, trivial.
ninfa, *n.f.* nymph; kell, chrysalis, pupa; young lady.
ninfea, *n.f.* (*bot.*) water-lily.
ninfo, *n.m.* (*coll.*) fop, beau, affected creature.
ninfómana, *n.f.* nymphomaniac.
ninfomanía, *n.f.* nymphomania.
ningún, *a.* (*contr. of* ***ninguno,*** *used only before m. nouns*), no, not one, not any; ***ningún hombre,*** no man; ***de ningún modo,*** by no means.
ninguno, -na, *a.* no, not one, not any; ***ninguna cosa,*** nothing; ***de ninguna manera,*** by no means, under no circumstances. — *indef. pron. m.f.* none, not any, neither; ***ninguno de ellos,*** not any of them; ***ninguno de estos dos,*** neither of these two; ***el tiene mucho dinero y yo ninguno,*** he has a lot of money and I have none. — *indef. pron. m.* nobody, no one.
niñada, *n.f.* childish thing to do *or* say.
niñato, *n.m.* unborn calf; (*coll.*) big baby.
niñear, *v.i.* to behave childishly.
niñera, *n.f.* nursemaid.
niñería, *n.f.* [NIÑADA]; bauble; plaything.
niñero, -ra, *a., n.m.f.* (one) fond of children.
niñez, *n.f.* childhood.
niñito, -ta, *n.m.f.* little boy, little girl.
niño, -ña, *a.* childish, childlike. — *n.m.* child, little boy; ***niño zangolotino,*** clumsy, overgrown youth; ***de niño,*** as a child; ***desde niño,*** from childhood; ***niño de teta,*** child in arms, suckling babe; ***como niño con zapatos nuevos,*** like a child with a new toy; (*pl.*) children (*boys and girls*). — *n.f.* girl, child; ***niña del ojo,*** pupil of the eye; ***niña de los ojos,*** apple of one's eye, darling; (*Hisp. Am.*) mistress (*title of respect given by servants*).
niobio, *n.m.* (*chem.*) niobium.
nioto, *n.m.* dogfish.
nipa, *n.f.* nipa.
nipis, *n.m.* (*Philip.*) fine cloth.

nipón, -pona, *a., n.m.f.* Nipponese, Japanese.
nipos, *n.m.pl.* (*coll.*) money.
níquel, *n.m.* (*chem.*) nickel.
niquelado, *n.m.* nickel-plating, nickel-plate.
niquelar, *v.t.* to nickel-plate.
niquelina, *n.f.* nickelite.
niquiscocio, *n.m.* (*coll.*) trifle; business of no account.
níspero, *n.m.* (*bot.*) medlar (*tree and fruit*); (*Hisp. Am., bot.*) sapodilla; ***níspero del Japón,*** loquat.
níspola, *n.f.* medlar (*fruit*).
nitidez, *n.f.* clarity, brightness; sharpness.
nítido, -da, *a.* clear; bright; sharply defined.
nitral, *n.m.* nitre-bed.
nitrato, *n.m.* (*chem.*) nitrate.
nitrería, *n.f.* saltpetre works.
nítrico, -ca, *a.* nitric.
nitrito, *n.m.* nitrite.
nitro, *n.m.* nitre, saltpetre.
nitrobencina, *n.f.* nitrobenzene.
nitrogenar, *v.t.* to nitrogenize.
nitrógeno, *n.m.* nitrogen.
nitroglicerina, *n.f.* nitroglycerine.
nitroso, -sa, *a.* nitrous.
nivel, *n.m.* level; levelness; standard; ***nivel de aire,*** spirit-level; ***nivel de (la) vida,*** standard of living; ***a nivel,*** flush, dead level; ***a nivel de,*** in the area *or* sphere of, as regards; ***paso a nivel,*** level-crossing.
nivelación, *n.f.* levelling.
nivelador, -ra, *a.* levelling. — *n.m.* (*surv.*) leveller.
nivelar, *v.t.* to level, level up *or* down; to make even; to grade; to balance. — **nivelarse,** *v.r.* to become level; ***nivelarse con,*** to get onto a level *or* even footing with.
nivoso, *a.* snowy.
no, *adv.* no; not; ***¿cómo no?*** of course, please do; ***creo que no,*** I don't think so; ***no más que,*** only; ***no bien,*** no sooner, barely; ***no sea que,*** lest; ***no . . . sino,*** only; ***si no,*** unless; otherwise; ***ya no,*** no longer, not any more; ***que no y que no,*** no and that's final; ***¿a que no?*** I bet you won't, will you? it isn't, is it?
nobiliario, -ria, *a.* nobiliary.
nobilísimo, -ma, *a. superl.* most noble.
noble, *a.* noble. — *n.m.* nobleman; noble.
nobleza, *n.f.* nobleness; nobility.
noca, *n.f.* crab.
nocente, *a.* harmful; guilty.
noción, *n.f.* notion; rudiment (usually in *pl.*).
nocional, *a.* notional.
nocivo, -va, *a.* noxious, harmful.
noctambulismo, *n.m.* sleep-walking.
noctámbulo, -la, *a., n.m.f.* sleep-walking; sleep-walker.
noctiluca, *n.f.* glow-worm.
nocturnal, *a.* nocturnal.
nocturnidad, *n.f.* (*law*) increased liability resulting from committing a crime by night.
nocturno, -na, *a.* nocturnal, night. — *n.m.* (*eccles.*) nocturn; (*mus.*) nocturne.
noche, *n.f.* night; evening; ***buenas noches,*** good night; good evening; ***a media noche,*** at mid-night; in the middle of the night; ***noche buena,*** Christmas Eve; ***noche vieja,*** New Year's Eve; ***noche toledana,*** sleepless night; ***de la noche a la mañana,*** over-night; ***de noche, por la noche,*** at night; ***hacerse de noche,*** to get dark; ***hacer noche en,*** to stay the night at, break one's journey at; ***muy de noche,*** very late at night.
Nochebuena, *n.f.* Christmas Eve.
nochebueno, *n.m.* Christmas cake; yule log.
nochecita, *n.f.* (*Hisp. Am.*) twilight, nightfall.
nocherniego, -ga, *a.* night-wandering.
nochizo, *n.m.* (*bot.*) wild hazel tree.
nodación, *n.f.* (*surg.*) impediment caused by a node.
nodal, *a.* nodal, nodical.
nodo, *n.m.* knot; node.
nodriza, *n.f.* wet-nurse; ***buque nodriza,*** supply ship.
nódulo, *n.m.* nodule.
Noé, *n.m.* Noah.
nogada, *n.f.* sauce of pounded walnuts and spice.
nogal, *n.m.* walnut tree; walnut wood.
noguera, *n.f.* walnut tree.
noguerado, -da, *a.* walnut (*colour*).
nogueral, *n.m.* walnut grove *or* plantation.
noguerela, *n.f.* (*bot.*) spurge.
noguerón, *n.m.* large walnut-tree.
nolición, *n.f.* (*phil.*) unwillingness.
noli me tángere, *n.m.* (*bot.*) touch-me-not.
noluntad, *n.f.* (*Lit.*) nolition.
nómada, nómade, *a.* nomad, nomadic. — *n.m.f.* nomad.
nomadismo, *n.m.* nomadism.
nombradamente, *adv.* expressly.
nombradía, *n.f.* fame, reputation, renown.
nombrado, -da, *a.* well-known, much talked-about.
nombrador, *a.* nominating; appointing. — *n.m.f.* nominator; appointer.
nombramiento, *n.m.* nomination, naming; appointment; (*mil.*) commission.
nombrar, *v.t.* to name, mention by name; to nominate; to appoint; to commission.
nombre, *n.m.* name; (*gram.*) noun; ***nombre de pila,*** Christian name; (*Am.*) given name; ***en nombre de,*** on behalf of; ***a nombre de,*** in the name of; ***de nombre,*** nominally; ***¡no tiene nombre!*** it's unspeakable.
nomenclador, *n.m.* nomenclator, gazetteer, glossary.
nomenclátor, *n.m.* nomenclator.
nomenclatura, *n.f.* nomenclature, terminology; catalogue.
nomeolvides, *n.f. inv.* (*bot.*) forget-me-not.
nómina, *n.f.* name-list; payroll.
nominación, *n.f.* nomination; appointment.
nominador, -ra, *a.* nominating; appointing. — *n.m.f.* nominator; appointer.
nominal, *a.* nominal, titular; (*com.*) face (value).
nominalismo, *n.m.* nominalism.
nominalista, *a.* nominalistic. — *n.m.f.* nominalist.
nominar [NOMBRAR].
nominativo, *a.* (*com.*) personal, registered (*as bonds, shares etc.*). — *n.m.* (*gram.*) nominative.
nominilla, *n.f.* pay warrant, voucher.
nómino, *n.m.* nominee.
nomo [GNOMO].
nomología, *n.f.* nomology.
nomparell, *n.f.* (*print.*) nonpareil.
non, *a.* odd, uneven; ***estar de non,*** to be odd man out; ***quedar de non,*** to get left out; to be odd man out. — *n.m.pl.* (**nones** (1)) odd number; ***pares y nones,*** odds and evens; ***andar de nones,*** to be idle.
nona (1), *n.f.* none.
nonada, *n.f.* trifle, mere nothing.
nonagenario, -ria, *a.* nonagenarian.
nonagésimo, -ma, *a.* ninetieth, nonagesimal.
nonagonal, *a.* nine-sided.
nonágono, *n.m.* nonagon.
nonato, -ta, *a.* not naturally born; unborn.
nones (2), *adv.* (*coll.*) no; ***decir nones,*** to say no; ***estar de nones,*** to be in a negative mood.
nonio, *n.m.* (*math.*) nonius, sliding gauge; vernier.
nono, -na (2), *a.* ninth.
nonuplo, -la, *a.* nonuple, nine-fold.
nopal, *n.m.* (*bot.*) nopal, prickly pear tree.

nopalera, *n.f.* plantation of nopals.
noque, *n.m.* tanning vat; heap *or* basket of bruised olives.
noquear, *v.t.* to knock out.
noquero, *n.m.* currier, leather-dresser.
norabuena, *adv.* by good fortune. — *n.f.* congratulation.
Noráfrica, *n.f.* North Africa.
noramala, *adv.* in an evil hour.
noray, *n.m.* (*naut.*) mooring.
nordestal, *a.* north-easterly.
nordeste, *n.m.* north-east.
nordestear, *v.i.* (*naut.*) to be north-easting.
nórdico, -ca, *a., n.m.f.* Nordic; Norse.
nordovestear, *v.i.* (*naut.*) to decline to north-west.
noria, *n.f.* water-wheel, draw-wheel; (*fig.*) treadmill, grind.
norma, *n.f.* square (*builder's* or *joiner's*); norm; rule; standard; pattern; ***normas de conducta,*** standards of behaviour.
normal, *a.* normal, usual; standard; (*geom.*) ***línea normal,*** perpendicular line; ***escuela normal,*** teachers' training college.
normalidad, *n.f.* normality; ***volver a la normalidad,*** to get back to normal.
normalista, *a.* of a teachers' training college. — *n.m.f.* student at a teachers' training college.
normalizar [C], *v.t.* to normalize, restore to normal.
Normandía, *n.f.* Normandy.
normando, -da, *a., n.m.f.* Norman; Norman-French; Norseman, Northman.
normano, -na, *n.m.f.* Norman, Northman.
nornordeste, *n.m.* north-north-east.
nornoroeste, nornorueste, *n.m.* north-north-west.
noroeste, *n.m.* north-west.
noroestear, *v.i.* (*naut.*) to decline to the north-west.
nortada, *n.f.* north gale, norther.
norte, *n.m.* north; north wind; pole-star; guide, direction; ***sin norte,*** aimless(ly).
norteamericano, -na, *a., n.m.f.* (North) American; (inhabitant) of the United States.
nortear, *v.i.* (*naut.*) to stand *or* steer to the northward; to decline to the north.
norteño, -ña, *a., n.m.f.* (native) of the north (*esp. of Spain*).
Noruega, *n.f.* Norway.
noruego, -ga, *a., n.m.f.* Norwegian (person). — *n.m.* Norwegian (*language*).
nos, *pers. pron.* us; to us, for us; ourselves; to ourselves; each other; to each other; (*high style*) we.
nosocomio, *n.m.* hospital.
nosografía, *n.f.* (*med.*) nosography.
nosología, *n.f.* nosology.
nosotros, -ras, *pers. pron.* we; us, ourselves.
nostalgia, *n.f.* nostalgia, homesickness.
nostramo, *n.m.* (*naut.*) master, boatswain.
nota (1), *n.f.* note; bill; statement; mark; censure.
notabilidad, *n.f.* notability.
notabilísimo, -ma, *a. superl.* most notable *or* remarkable.
notable, *a.* notable, remarkable; mark of 'very good', distinction mark.
notablemente, *adv.* notably, noticeably.
notación, *n.f.* note, annotation; (*math., mus.*) notation.
notar, *v.t.* to note, notice, mark; ***se nota que,*** it's obvious that.
notaría, *n.f.* profession *or* office of notary.
notariado, *n.m.* notary's title *or* profession.
notarial, *a.* notarial.
notariato, *n.m.* title *or* practice of a notary.
notario, *n.m.* notary; notary public.
noticia, *n.f.* news, news item, piece of news; knowledge, information; ***una noticia,*** an item of news; ***noticia bomba,*** bombshell (news), sensational news; ***¡noticia fresca!*** that's news to nobody!; ***noticias de última hora,*** late news; ***tener noticia de,*** to be informed *or* aware of.
noticiar, *v.t.* to give notice of, notify, make known.
noticiario, *n.m.* newsreel; newscast.
noticiero, *a.* news-bearing, news-giving. — *n.m.f.* newsman, reporter.
notición, *n.m.* (*coll.*) terrific *or* astonishing piece of news.
noticioso, -sa, *a.* well-informed; apprised.
notificación, *n.f.* notification, official notice.
notificar [A], *v.t.* to notify, inform.
notita, *n.f.* short note.
noto (1), **-ta** (2), *a.* known, notorious; bastard, illegitimate.
noto (2), *n.m.* Notus, south wind.
notomía, *n.f.* (*obs.*) skeleton; anatomy.
notoriedad, *n.f.* renown; well-known character.
notorio, -ria, *a.* well-known, known to all; evident.
nova, *n.f.* (*astron.*) nova.
novación, *n.f.* (*law*) novation.
novador, -ra, *n.m.f.* innovator.
noval, *a.* newly broken up (*of land*); fruit produced in such land.
novar, *v.t.* (*law*) to renew by novation.
novatada, *n.f.* ragging, prank played on a newcomer; beginner's blunder.
novato, -ta, *a.* (*coll.*) new, commencing. — *n.m.f.* new boy, newcomer, new arrival.
novator, -ra, *n.m.f.* innovator.
novecientos, -tas, *a.* nine hundred.
novedad, *n.f.* novelty, new thing, latest thing; latest news; ***estar sin novedad,*** to be the same, unchanged; ***no hay novedad,*** nothing new, nothing to report, all quiet; ***sin novedad,*** as usual; (*pl.* **novedades**) novelties, fancy goods.
novedoso, -sa, *a.* new, with it, trendy, in the latest fashion.
novel, *a.* new, inexperienced.
novela, *n.f.* novel; romance; made-up tale, yarn, fabrication; ***novela policíaca,*** detective story; ***novela de clave,*** roman à clef; ***novela por entregas,*** serial story.
novelador, -ra, *n.m.f.* novelist.
novelar, *v.t.* to novelize, turn into a novel. — *v.i.* to write novels; to make up *or* concoct yarns.
novelería, *n.f.* love of the latest fad *or* craze; curiosity; love of novels; trashy reading.
novelero, -ra, *a.* fond of the latest fad *or* craze; keen on novels; flighty.
novelesco, -ca, *a.* novelistic; like a novel *or* romance, romantic, wildly imaginative.
novelista, *n.m.f.* novelist.
novelón, *n.m.* tediously long novel, dreary third-rate novel.
novenario, *n.m.* (*eccles.*) novenary.
noveno, -na, *a.* ninth. — *n.m.* ninth part of tithes. — *n.f.* (*eccles.*) novena.
noventa, *n.m.* ninety.
noventavo, -va, *a.* ninetieth.
noventón, -tona, *n.m.f.* nonagenarian.
novia, *n.f.* [NOVIO].
noviazgo, *n.m.* engagement; courtship.
noviciado, *n.m.* novitiate; apprenticeship.
novicio, -cia, *a.* new, inexperienced. — *n.m.f.* novice; beginner.
noviembre, *n.m.* November.
novilunio, *n.m.* new moon.
novilla, *n.f.* young heifer.
novillada, *n.f.* drove of young bulls; bullfight with young animals.
novillero, *n.m.* herdsman for young cattle; pasture ground for young cattle; stable for young cattle; novice bullfighter; truant.
novillo, *n.m.* young bull; (*fam.*) cuckold; (*coll.*) ***hacer novillos,*** to play truant.

novio, -via, *n.m.f.* bridegroom; bride; fiancé; fiancée; boy-friend; girl-friend.
novísimo, -ma, *a. superl.* newest, most recent, latest; ***Novísima Recopilación,*** code of laws promulgated in Spain, July 15, 1805.
noyó, *n.m.* noyau.
nubada (1), **nubarrada** (1), *n.f.* shower of rain; crowd, mass.
nubado, -da (2), **nubarrado, -da** (2), *a.* clouded.
nubarrón, *n.m.* heavy black *or* threatening cloud.
nube, *n.f.* cloud; shadow; crowd, swarm; spot (*on cornea*); ***estar por las nubes,*** to be sky-high *or* soaring (*in price*); ***poner por las nubes,*** to praise to the skies; ***como caído de las nubes,*** out of the blue.
nubiense, *a.*, *n.m.f.* Nubian.
nubífero, -ra, *a.* (*poet.*) cloud-bringing.
núbil, *a.* nubile.
nubilidad, *n.f.* nubility.
nubiloso, -sa, *a.* (*poet.*) cloudy, nubilous.
nublado, -da, *a.* cloudy, overcast. — *n.m.* storm cloud; (*fig.*) storm; ***aguantar el nublado,*** to weather the storm.
nublar, *v.t.* to cloud over. — **nublarse,** *v.r.* to get cloudy *or* overcast.
nublo, -la, *a.* cloudy. — *n.m.* storm cloud; mildew.
nubloso, -sa, *a.* cloudy, overcast; ill-fated.
nuca, *n.f.* (*anat.*) nape of the neck.
nuclear, *a.* nuclear.
núcleo, *n.m.* nucleus; kernel, core.
nuco, *n.m.* (*Chi.*) owl.
nuche, *n.m.* (*Hisp. Am.*, *ent.*) gadfly, horsefly.
nudillo, *n.m.* knuckle; nodule; (*build.*) plug, dowel.
nudo (1), *n.m.* knot; joint; tie, bond, union; node; snag; crux; tumour; knotty point; ***nudo gordiano,*** Gordian knot; ***nudo en la garganta,*** lump in the throat.
nudo (2), **-da,** *a.* nude, naked.
nudoso, -sa, *a.* knotty, knotted.
nuecero, -ra, *n.m.f.* walnut-seller.
nuégado, *n.m.pl.* sweet paste.
nuera, *n.f.* daughter-in-law.
nuestramo, -ma, *n.m.f. contr. of* ***nuestro amo,*** our master, ***nuestra ama,*** our mistress; (*Hisp. Am.*) the Eucharist.
nuestro, -ra, *poss. pron.* our, ours; (*in literary* or *authoritative style*) my, mine.
nueva, *n.f.* [NUEVO].
Nueva Escocia, *n.f.* Nova Scotia.
Nueva Gales del Sur, *n.f.* New South Wales.
nuevamente, *adv.* again, anew.
Nueva Orleáns, *n.f.* New Orleans.
Nueva York, *n.f.* New York.
Nueva Zelanda, *n.f.* New Zealand.
nueve, *a.*, *n.m.* nine, ninth; ***las nueve,*** nine o'clock.
nuevecito, -ta, *a.* nice and new, spanking new, brand new.
nuevo, -va, *a.* new; ***de nuevo,*** again, anew; ***¿qué hay de nuevo?*** what's (the) news? what's new?; ***nuevo flamante,*** brand new, spanking new. — *n.f.* news, tidings; ***hacerse de nuevas,*** to pretend one does not know; ***no me coge de nuevas,*** it's no news to me.
nuez, *n.f.* walnut; Adam's apple; nut *or* kernel (*of coconuts, cocoa etc.*); notch (*of a crossbow*); (*mus.*) ferrule (*of a bow*).
nueza, *n.f.* (*bot.*) briony.
nugatorio, -ria, *a.* deceptive; disappointing.
nulidad, *n.f.* nullity; (*coll.*) useless object, hopeless individual, dead loss.
nulo, -la, *a.* null, void; (*coll.*) useless, hopeless.
numen, *n.m.* deity; (*poet.*) inspiration.
numerable, *a.* numerable.
numeración, *n.f.* numeration.
numerador, *n.m.* enumerator; numberer; numbering machine; (*arith.*) numerator.
numeral, *a.* numeral.
numerar, *v.t.* to number, put numbers to; to page.
numerario, -ria, *a.* numerary. — *n.m.* cash, coin, specie.
numérico, -ca, *a.* numerical.
número, *n.m.* number, figure; ***de número,*** one of a fixed number; ***sin número,*** numberless, innumerable; (*pl.*) Book of Numbers.
numerosidad, *n.f.* numerousness.
numeroso, -sa, *a.* numerous; harmonious; ***familia numerosa,*** large family.
númida, numídico, -ca, *a.*, *n.m.f.* Numidian.
numismático, -ca, *a.* numismatic. — *n.m.f.* numismatist. — *n.f.* numismatics.
numo, *n.m.* money; coin.
numulario, *n.m.* trade in money; banker, money broker.
nunca, *adv.* never; ***nunca jamás,*** never ever.
nunciatura, *n.f.* nunciature.
nuncio, *n.m.* nuncio; messenger; (*fig.*) forerunner, harbinger.
nuncupativo, -va, *a.* nuncupative.
nuncupatorio, -ria, *a.* nuncupatory.
nupcial, *a.* nuptial.
nupcialidad, *n.f.* marriage rate.
nupcias, *n.f.pl.* nuptials, wedding; ***casarse en segundas nupcias,*** to marry for the second time.
nutación, *n.f.* (*astron.*) nutation.
nutra, nutria, *n.f.* otter.
nutricio, -cia, *a.* nutritious, nourishing, nutritive.
nutrición, *n.f.* nutrition.
nutrido, -da, *a.* large, copious.
nutrimental, *a.* nutrimental, nourishing.
nutrimento, *n.m.* nutriment, nourishment.
nutrir, *v.t.* to nourish, feed.
nutritivo, -va, *a.* nutritive, nourishing.
nutriz, *n.f.* wet-nurse.

Ñ

Ñ, ñ, *n.f.* letter Ñ, ñ.
ña, *n.f.* [ÑO].
ñacanima, *n.f.* (*Arg.*) viper.
ñaco, *n.m.* (*Chi.*) porridge; pap.
ñacurutú, *n.m.* (*Arg., Ur.*) barn owl.
ñagaza, *n.f.* bird-call, decoy-call.
ñame, *n.m.* yam.
ñandú, *n.m.* American ostrich.
ñandubay, *n.m.* (*Hisp. Am.*) mimosa.
ñandutí, *n.m.* (*Arg., Par.*) hand-made cloth (*used for underwear*).
ñangotarse, *v.r.* (*P.R.*) to squat.
ñangué, *n.m.* (*Cub., bot.*) stramonium.
ñaño, -ña, *a.* (*Col.*) spoiled (*child*); (*Per.*) very close (*friend*). — *n.m.* (*Arg., Chi.*) elder brother. — *n.f.* (*Chi.*) children's nurse; (*Arg., Chi.*) elder sister.
ñapa, *n.f.* (*Hisp. Am.*) bonus, additional amount; ***de ñapa,*** to boot, into the bargain.
ñapango, -ga, *a.* (*Col.*) half-breed; mulatto.
ñapinda, *n.m.* (*Arg., bot.*) acacia.
ñapo, *n.m.* (*Chi.*) jonquil; reed; rattan.
ñaque, *n.m.* useless trifles, odds and ends.
ñaruso, -sa, *a.* (*Ec.*) pock-marked.
ñato, -ta, *a.* (*Hisp. Am.*) flat-nosed.
ñeque, *a.* (*C.R.*) energetic, strong, brave. — *n.m.* (*Chi., Per.*) energy, vim.
ñipe, *n.m.* (*Chi.*) shrub used for dyeing.
ñiqueñaque, *n.m.* (*coll.*) whipper-snapper; nick-nack; shoddy goods.
ñisñil, *n.m.* (*Chi., bot.*) reed-mace.
ño, ña, *n.m.f.* (*Hisp. Am., contr. of* ***señor, señora***) owner, boss.
ñocios, *n.m.pl.* sweetmeat.
ñocha, *n.f.* (*Chi.*) brome grass.
ñongo, -ga, *a.* (*Chi., coll.*) lazy, good-for-nothing. — *n.m.pl.* (**ñongos**) (*Col.*) loaded dice.
ñoñería, *n.f.* **ñoñez,** *n.f.* feebleness; prudishness; soppiness; fussiness.
ñoño, -ña, *a.* feeble-minded; characterless; prudish; soppy; fussy, finicky.
ñorbo, *n.m.* (*Ec., Per., bot.*) passion flower.
ñu, *n.m.* gnu.
ñublado, *n.m.*, **ñublar,** *v.t.*, **ñublo,** *n.m.* [NUBLADO] [NUBLAR] [NUBLO].
ñudo, *n.m.* [NUDO (I)].
ñuto, -ta, *a.* (*Ec.*) reduced to fine powder.

O

O, o, *n.f.* letter O, o. — *conj.* or, either; ***o sea,*** that is, in other words.
oasis, *n.m.* oasis.
obcecación, *n.f.* obfuscation, blindness; obduracy.
obcecado, -da, *a.* blind; obdurate.
obcecar [A], *v.t.* to obfuscate, blind. — **obcecarse,** *v.r.* to become obfuscated, blind; to get into a state in which the balance of one's mind is disturbed.
obduración, *n.f.* obduracy, obstinacy.
obedecedor, -ra, *a.* obeying. — *n.m.f.* obeyer.
obedecer [9], *v.t., v.i.* to obey; to be due (to), arise (from).
obedecimiento, *n.m.* obedience.
obediencia, *n.f.* obedience.
obediente, *a.* obedient.
obelisco, *n.m.* obelisk; (*print.*) dagger.
obenques, *n.m.pl.* (*naut.*) shrouds.
obertura, *n.f.* (*mus.*) overture.
obesidad, *n.f.* obesity, corpulence.
obeso, -sa, *a.* obese, fat.
óbice, *n.m.* obstacle, impediment, hindrance.
obispado, *n.m.* bishopric, episcopate.
obispal, *a.* episcopal.
obispalía, *n.f.* bishop's palace; bishopric.
obispar, *v.i.* to obtain a bishopric, be made a bishop.
obispillo, *n.m.* boy-bishop; little bishop; large black pudding; parson's nose (*of fowl*).
obispo, *n.m.* bishop.
óbito, *n.m.* death, decease, demise.
obituario, *n.m.* obituary.
objeción, *n.f.* objection.
objetal, *a.* (of an) object; (of) protest.
objetante, *a.* objecting. — *n.m.f.* objector.
objetar, *v.t.* to object, raise as an objection; ***¿quiere usted objetar algo?*** do you have any objections to make?
objetivo, -va, *a.* objective. — *n.m.* objective.
objeto, *n.m.* object; ***no tiene objeto,*** there is no point (in it).
oblación, *n.f.* oblation.
oblada, *n.f.* (*eccles.*) funeral offering of bread.
oblata, *n.f.* (*eccles.*) oblation; oblate.
oblato, *n.m.* (*eccles.*) oblate.
oblea, *n.f.* wafer (*for sealing letters*).
obleera, *n.f.* wafer-holder, wafer-case.
oblicuángulo, -la, *a.* oblique-angled.
oblicuar, *v.t.* to cant, slant. — *v.i.* to oblique.
oblicuidad, *n.f.* obliquity, slant.
oblicuo, -cua, *a.* oblique, slanting.
obligación, *n.f.* obligation, duty; bond; debenture; (*pl.* **obligaciones**) engagements; (*com.*) liabilities.
obligacionista, *n.m.f.* (*com.*) bondholder.
obligado, -da, *a.* tight, having little play; essential; ***es cosa obligada,*** it's a must. — *n.m.* public contractor; (*mus.*) obbligato.
obligante, *a.* obligating.
obligar [B], *v.t.* to oblige, force; to place under an obligation; ***verse obligado a,*** to be forced to.
obligatorio, -ria, *a.* obligatory, compulsory.
obliterar, *v.t.* to obstruct; to fill in; to forget; to obliterate.
oblongo, -ga, *a.* oblong.
oboe, *n.m.* oboe; oboe-player.
óbolo, *n.m.* obolus; mite; (*pharm.*) obole.
obra, *n.f.* work; piece of work, task; fabric (*of building*); play; agency, channel; hearth (*of blast furnace*); ***obra de,*** about, more *or* less; ***obra de romanos,*** colossal undertaking; ***obra maestra,*** masterpiece; (*naut.*) ***obra muerta,*** upper works; ***maestro de obras,*** clerk of works; ***mano de obra,*** labour, manpower; ***¡manos a la obra!*** let's get cracking!; ***a pie de obra,*** on the spot;

en obras, under repair; road up; ***por obra de,*** by virtue of, through; ***poner por obra,*** to put into effect; ***obras son amores y no buenas razones,*** deeds, not words.
obrada, *n.f.* day's work; land measure (*varies between* 1 *and* 1½ *acres*).
obrador, -ra, *a.* working. — *n.m.f.* workman, workwoman. — *n.m.* workshop, studio.
obradura, *n.f.* load of an olive-oil mill.
obraje, *n.m.* manufacture, handiwork, sth. made by art; manufactory, workshop.
obrajero, *n.m.* foreman, overseer, quarterman, superintendent.
obrante, *a.* acting, working.
obrar, *v.t.* to work, carry out, perform. — *v.i.* to act; to take effect; (*coll.*) to open one's bowels; ***obra en mi poder su carta,*** I am in receipt of your letter.
obrepción, *n.f.* (*law*) obreption.
obrepticio, -cia, *a.* (*law*) obreptitious.
obrería, *n.f.* workman's task; money for the repairs of a church.
obrerismo, *n.m.* (*polit., econ.*) labour movement.
obrero, -ra, *a.* working. — *n.m.f.* worker; missionary. — *n.m.* churchwarden.
obrita, *n.f.* small *or* short work.
obrizo, -za, *a.* pure, refined (*of gold*).
obscenidad, *n.f.* obscenity, lewdness.
obsceno, -na, *a.* obscene, lewd.
obscurantismo, *n.m.* obscurantism.
obscurantista, *a., n.m.f.* obscurantist.
obscuras (a) [OSCURAS].
obscurecer [9] [OSCURECER].
obscurecimiento [OSCURECIMIENTO].
obscuridad [OSCURIDAD].
obscuro, -ra [OSCURO].
obsequiante [OBSEQUIOSO].
obsequiar, *v.t.* to treat, entertain, lavish attention on; to honour (***con,*** with); to present (***con,*** with).
obsequias, *n.f.pl.* obsequies, funeral ceremony.
obsequio, *n.m.* civility, attention; present, gift; ***en obsequio de,*** in honour of.
obsequioso, -sa, *a.* attentive, obliging.
observable, *a.* observable, noticeable.
observación, *n.f.* observation; remark.
observador, -ra, *a.* observing, observant. — *n.m.f.* observer, remarker.
observancia, *n.f.* observance.
observante, *a.* observant; observing.
observar, *v.t.* to observe; ***le hice observar que,*** I pointed out to him that. — *v.i.* to observe, remark.
observatorio, *n.m.* observatory.
obsesión, *n.f.* obsession.
obsesionante, *a.* obsessive; haunting.
obsesionar, *v.t.* to obsess; to haunt.
obsesivo, -va, *a.* obsessive.
obseso, -sa, *a.* obsessed.
obsidiana, *n.f.* (*geol.*) obsidian.
obsidional, *a.* (*mil.*) obsidional; (pertaining to a) siege.
obsoleto, -ta, *a.* obsolete.
obstaculizar, *v.t.* to obstruct; to place obstacles, impediments *or* stumbling blocks in the way of.
obstáculo, *n.m.* obstacle; check, hindrance.
obstante, *a.* ***no obstante,*** nevertheless, notwithstanding.
obstar, *v.i.* to stand in the way, be an obstacle; ***esto no obsta para que lo siga haciendo,*** this does not prevent his continuing to do it.
obstetricia, *n.f.* (*med.*) obstetrics.
obstinación, *n.f.* obstinacy, stubbornness.
obstinado, -da, *a.* obstinate, stubborn.
obstinarse, *v.r.* to be obstinate (***en,*** about), persist (***en,*** in).
obstrucción, *n.f.* (*med.*) obstruction; stoppage.
obstruccionista, *a., n.m.f.* obstructionist.
obstructivo, -va, *a.* obstructive; obstruent.
obstruir [O], *v.t.* to obstruct, block; to block up, stop up, choke, clog. — **obstruirse,** *v.r.* to get blocked up.
obtemperar, *v.t.* to obey.
obtención, *n.f.* attainment, obtaining.
obtener [33], *v.t.* to obtain, attain, secure, get.
obtento, *n.m.* (*eccles.*) prebend.
obtentor, *n.m.* (*eccles.*) one who obtains a prebend.
obtestación, *n.f.* (*rhet.*) obtestation.
obturación, *n.f.* obturation, stopping up.
obturador, obturatriz, *a.* stopping-up, plugging. — *n.m.* stopper, plug; (*surg.*) obturator; (*photo.*) shutter; (*motor.*) choke, throttle.
obturar, *v.t.* (*surg.*) to obturate, stop up, plug; (*motor.*) to throttle.
obtusángulo, -la, *a.* obtuse-angled, obtuse-angular.
obtuso, -sa, *a.* obtuse.
obús, *n.m.* howitzer; shell; core (*of tyre-valve*).
obusera, *n.f.* gun-boat.
obvención, *n.f.* perquisite.
obviar [L *and regular*], *v.t.* to obviate, prevent. — *v.i.* to stand in the way.
obvio, -via, *a.* obvious, evident.
obyecto, *n.m.* objection, reply.
oca, *n.f.* goose; (*bot.*) oxalis; royal goose (*game*).
ocarina, *n.f.* ocarina.
ocasión, *n.f.* occasion; chance, opportunity; ***de ocasión,*** second-hand; ***con ocasión de,*** on the occasion of; ***coger la ocasión por los pelos,*** to take time by the forelock, seize one's opportunities; ***dar ocasión a,*** to give rise to; ***no hay ocasión,*** there is no cause; ***la ocasión hace al ladrón,*** opportunity makes the thief; ***quien quita la ocasión, quita el pecado,*** no temptation, no sin; ***a la ocasión la pintan calva,*** opportunities should not be missed.
ocasionado, -da, *a.* provoking, insolent, vexatious; perilous.
ocasionador, -ra, *a.* occasioning, causing, giving rise to.
ocasional, *a.* occasional; chance; ***mano de obra ocasional,*** casual labour.
ocasionalmente, *adv.* by chance.
ocasionar, *v.t.* to cause, occasion, give rise to.
ocaso, *n.m.* sunset; west; (*fig.*) decline, wane, waning.
occidental, *a.* occidental, western; west.
occidente, *n.m.* west, occident.
occiduo, -dua, *a.* occidental.
occipital, *a.* (*anat.*) occipital.
occipucio, *n.m.* occiput.
occisión, *n.f.* slaying, slaughter.
occiso, -sa, *a.* slain.
oceánico, -ca, *a.* oceanic, ocean; ocean-going.
oceánidas, *n.f.pl.* (*myth.*) oceanids, ocean-nymphs.
océano, *n.m.* ocean, sea.
oceanografía, *n.f.* oceanography.
oceanográfico, -ca, *a.* oceanographic(al).
ocelado, -da, *a.* having ocelli.
ocelo, *n.m.* (*biol.*) ocellus.
ocelote, *n.m.* ocelot.
ocena, *n.f.* (*med.*) ozena.
ociar, *v.i.* (*obs.*) to loiter, idle.
ocio, *n.m.* idleness; leisure.
ociosear, *v.i.* (*Arg., Chi.*) to be idle.
ociosidad, *n.f.* idleness, laziness; ***la ociosidad es madre de todos los vicios,*** the Devil finds work for idle hands.
ocioso, -sa, *a.* idle.
oclocracia, *n.f.* ochlocracy.
ocluir [O], *v.t.* (*med.*) to occlude, close.

oclusión, *n.f.* occlusion.
ocosial, *n.m.* (*Per.*) lowland, morass.
ocote, *n.m.* (*Mex.*) torch-pine.
ocozoal, *n.m.* (*Mex.*) rattlesnake.
ocozol, *n.m.* (*bot.*) sweet-gum.
ocre, *n.m.* ochre.
octacordio, *n.m.* octachord.
octaedro, *n.m.* (*geom.*) octahedron.
octagonal, *a.* octagonal, eight-sided.
octágono, *n.m.* (*geom.*) octagon.
octangular, *a.* octangular.
octante, *n.m.* (*naut.*) octant.
octava, *n.f.* [OCTAVO].
octavar, *v.i.* (*mus.*) to form octaves on stringed instruments; to deduct the eighth part.
octavario, *n.m.* eight-days' festival.
octavilla, *n.f.* the eighth part of a sheet of paper; (*poet.*) stanza of eight lines of octosyllabic verse; leaflet.
octavín, *n.m.* piccolo.
octavo, -va, *a.*, *n.m.* eighth; ***en octavo,*** octavo. — *n.f.* (*eccles.*) octave; eight days; (*poet.*) eight-line stanza.
octogenario, -ria, *a.*, *n.m.f.* octogenarian, eighty-year old.
octogésimo, -ma, *a.* eightieth.
octópodo, -da, *a.* octopod, having eight feet.
octosilábico, -ca, *a.* octosyllabic.
octóstilo, -la, *a.* octostyle.
octubre, *n.m.* October.
óctuplo, -la, *a.* octuple, eight-fold.
ocular, *a.* ocular; ***testigo ocular,*** eye-witness. — *n.m.* eye-glass, eye-piece.
oculista, *n.m.f.* oculist.
ocultación, *n.f.* concealment, hiding; (*astron.*) ocultation.
ocultador, -ra, *n.m.f.* concealer, hider.
ocultar, *v.t.* to conceal, hide, cloak; ***no se me oculta que,*** I am not unaware that.
ocultismo, *n.m.* occultism.
ocultista, *a.*, *n.m.f.* occultist.
oculto, -ta, *a.* hidden; occult; secret.
ocupación, *n.f.* occupation; (*rhet.*) prolepsis.
ocupado, -da, *a.* busy; engaged.
ocupador, -ra, *a.* occupying. — *n.m.f.* occupier.
ocupante, *a.* occupying. — *n.m.f.* occupant.
ocupar, *v.t.* to occupy; to employ; to hold (*a post*); to take up (*a post*); to take up (*time*); ***me ocupa mucho tiempo,*** it takes up a lot of my time. — **ocuparse,** *v.r.* to concern o.s., deal (***de,*** with), attend (***de,*** to).
ocurrencia, *n.f.* idea, notion; witty remark, witticism; occurrence.
ocurrente, *a.* witty, amusing, funny.
ocurrir, *v.i.* to occur, happen. — **ocurrirse,** *v.r.* to occur, strike (*the mind*); ***eso no se me había ocurrido,*** that hadn't occurred to me; ***no se te ocurra ir,*** don't even think of going, don't you dare go.
ocurso, *n.m.* (*Mex.*) petition, claim.
ochava, *n.f.* eighth part; (*eccles.*) octave; (*naut.*) ***ochavas del molinete,*** whelps of the windlass.
ochavado, -da, *a.* octagonal, eight-sided.
ochavar, *v.t.* to make octagonal.
ochavo, *n.m.* (*obs.*) farthing.
ochavón, -vona, *a.* octoroon.
ochenta, *a.*, *n.m.* eighty; eightieth.
ochentón, -tona, *a.*, *n.m.f.* eighty-year-old, octogenarian.
ocho, *a.*, *n.m.* eight, eighth. — *n.m.* card with eight spots; ***las ocho,*** eight o'clock.
ochocientos, -tas, *a.* eight-hundred.
oda, *n.f.* ode.
odalisca, *n.f.* odalisque.
odeón, *n.m.* odeon, odeum.
odiar, *v.t.* to hate, detest.
odio, *n.m.* hatred, odium, detestation; ***tener odio a,*** to hate, loathe.
odiosidad, *n.f.* hatefulness, odiousness.
odioso, -sa, *a.* odious, hateful, loathsome.
odisea, *n.f.* Odyssey.
odómetro, *n.m.* hodometer.
odontalgia, *n.f.* odontalgia, toothache.
odontología, *n.f.* (*med.*) odontology.
odontólogo, -ga, *a.*, *n.m.f.* odontologist.
odontorrea, *n.f.* (*med.*) odontorrhagia, bleeding of the gums.
odorante, *a.* odorous, fragrant.
odorífero, -ra, *a.* odoriferous, fragrant, perfumed.
odorífico, -ca [ODORÍFERO].
odre, *n.m.* wine-skin; (*joc.*) drunkard.
odrería, *n.f.* wine-skin works.
odrezuelo, *n.m.* small wine-skin.
odrina, *n.f.* ox-skin bag (*for wine*).
oesnorueste, *n.m.* west-north-west.
oessudueste, *n.m.* west-south-west.
oeste, *n.m.* west; west wind; ***oeste cuarta al norte*** (or ***sur***), west by north (*or* south).
ofendedor, -ra, *a.* offending. — *n.m.f.* offender; attacker.
ofender, *v.t.* to offend, slight, insult; to wrong. — **ofenderse,** *v.r.* to take offence, take umbrage, (*coll.*) get into a huff.
ofensa, *n.f.* offence, insult; wrong.
ofensivo, -va, *a.* offensive; attacking; insulting; unpleasant. — *n.f.* offensive.
ofensor, -ra, *a.* offending. — *n.m.f.* offender; attacker.
oferente, *a.* offering. — *n.m.f.* offerer.
oferta, *n.f.* offer; (*com.*) tender; (*Am.*) bid; (*com.*) ***oferta y demanda,*** supply and demand.
ofertorio, *n.m.* offertory.
off-side, *n.m.* (*fig.*) ***estar en off-side,*** to be out of play; to have one's head in the clouds, (*fam.*) not to be with it.
oficial, *a.* official. — *n.m.* officer; clerk; apprentice; ***oficial mayor,*** chief clerk.
oficiala, *n.f.* workwoman; forewoman; apprentice.
oficialía, *n.f.* clerk's place in an office; clerkship.
oficialidad, *n.f.* (body of) officers.
oficiar, *v.t.*, *v.i.* to officiate, minister; ***oficiar de,*** to act as.
oficina, *n.f.* office.
oficinal, *a.* (*med.*, *pharm.*) officinal.
oficinesco, -ca, *a.* (*pej.*, *coll.*) office.
oficinista, *n.m.f.* office worker, clerk.
oficio, *n.m.* work, occupation, job; official memo; (*pl.*) divine service; ***de oficio,*** by trade; officially; ***no tener ni oficio ni beneficio,*** to have no fixed occupation; ***por los buenos oficios de,*** through the good offices of; ***tomar por oficio,*** to get into the habit (of); ***gajes del oficio,*** perks; occupational hazards.
oficionario, *n.m.* canonical office-book.
oficiosidad, *n.f.* officiousness; diligence, alacrity.
oficioso, -sa, *a.* officious; unofficial, non-official; diligent; obliging, helpful; useful.
ofidio, -dia, *a.*, *n.m.* (*zool.*) ophidian.
ofiómaco, *n.m.* locust.
ofita, *n.f.* (*min.*) ophite.
ofrecedor, -ra, *n.m.f.* offerer.
ofrecer [9], *v.t.*, *v.i.* to offer. — *v.t.* to afford, present; to display, show. — **ofrecerse,** *v.r.* to offer o.s., volunteer (***a,*** to).
ofreciente, *a.* offering.
ofrecimiento, *n.m.* offer.
ofrenda, *n.f.* offering.
ofrendar, *v.t.* to proffer as an offering.
oftalmía, *n.f.* ophthalmia.
oftálmico, -ca, *a.* ophthalmic.

oftalmología, *n.f.* ophthalmology.
oftalmografía, *n.f.* ophthalmography.
oftalmoscopia, *n.f.* ophthalmoscopy.
ofuscación, *n.f.*, **ofuscamiento,** *n.m.* bewilderment; (*fig.*) blindness.
ofuscar [A], *v.t.* to bewilder; (*fig.*) to blind.
ogaño, *adv.* this present year; these days.
ogro, *n.m.* ogre; bogeyman.
¡oh! *interj.* oh!
ohm, ohmio, *n.m.* (*elec.*) ohm.
óhmico, -ca, *a.* (*elec.*) ohmic.
oíble, *a.* audible, that may be heard.
oída, *n.f.* hearing; ***de*** or ***por oídas,*** by hearsay.
oídio, *n.m.* (*bot.*) oidium.
oído, *n.m.* ear; hearing; (*artill.*) vent, priming-hole, touchhole; ***dolor de oídos,*** ear-ache; ***aguzar los oídos,*** to prick up one's ears; ***dar oídos a,*** to lend credence to; ***entrar por un oído y salir por el otro,*** to go in one ear and out the other; ***hacer oídos de mercader a,*** to turn a deaf ear to; ***pegarse al oído,*** to be catchy (*of music etc.*); ***tocar de oído,*** to play by ear.
oidor, -ra, *n.m.f.* hearer; judge.
oidoría, *n.f.* office *or* dignity of an ***oidor.***
oír [22], *v.t.*, *v.i.* to hear; to listen (to); ***le oí cantar,*** I heard him sing *or* singing; ***oír decir que,*** to hear that; ***oír hablar de,*** to hear of *or* about; ***¡oiga! ¡oígame!*** I say! hello there! look here!; ***como lo oye usted, como lo oyes,*** that's how it was, those were his very words, I'm not lying, I swear it's true; ***me oye como quien oye llover,*** he pays not the slightest attention to what I say, I'm wasting my breath.
oíslo, *n.m.f.* (*coll.*) beloved, wife.
ojal, *n.m.* button-hole; (*min*). loop.
¡ojalá! *interj.* would to God! that'll be the day!; ***¡ojalá que . . .!*** I wish *or* hope that . . .!
ojaladera, *n.f.* button-hole-maker
ojalador, -ra, *n.m.f.* button-hole-maker.
ojaladura, *n.f.* set of button-holes.
ojalar, *v.t.* to make button-holes in.
ojalatero, *n.m. a.* (*coll.*) armchair patriot.
ojaranzo, *n.m.* (*bot.*) common hornbeam; witch-hazel.
ojeada, *n.f.* glance, look.
ojeador, *n.m.* beater.
ojeadura, *n.f.* glazing of clothes.
ojear, *v.t.* to start (*game*); to take a look at; to cast the evil eye upon.
ojeo, *n.m.* starting (*of game*), hallooing.
ojera, *n.f.* dark ring round the eye; eye-bath.
ojeriza, *n.f.* spite, grudge, ill-will; ***me tiene ojeriza,*** he's got it in for me.
ojeroso, -sa, ojerudo, -da, *a.* hollow-eyed, having rings round the eyes.
ojete, *n.m.* eyelet-hole; (*coll.*) anus.
ojeteador, *n.m.* eyeleteer, stiletto.
ojetear, *v.t.* to make eyelet-holes in.
ojetera, *n.f.* piece of whalebone sown near eyelet-hole; eyelet-maker.
ojialegre, *a.* with sparkling eyes.
ojienjuto, -ta, *a.* dry-eyed.
ojimel, ojimiel, *n.m.* (*pharm.*) oxymel.
ojimoreno, -na, *a.* brown-eyed.
ojinegro, -ra, *a.* black-eyed.
ojito, *n.m.* small eye; cute little eye.
ojiva, *n.f.* (*arch.*) ogive.
ojival, *a.* ogival.
ojizaino, -na, *a.* (*coll.*) squint-eyed; moon-eyed.
ojizarco, -ca, *a.* (*coll.*) blue-eyed.
ojo, *n.m.* eye; hole; bow (*of a key*); well (*of stairs*); span, bay *or* arch (*of a bridge*); mesh-hole (*of a net*); ***ojo de buey,*** (*bot.*) ox-eye; port-hole; ***a ojo,*** roughly; ***a los ojos de,*** in the eyes of; in the presence of; ***a ojos vista,*** clearly, visibly; ***estar ojo alerta*** or ***avizor,*** to be on the look out; ***abrir tanto ojo,*** to open one's eyes wide; ***avivar el ojo,*** to keep a sharp watch; ***a ojos cerrados,*** without hesitation; ***clavar los ojos en,*** to fix one's gaze upon; ***comerse con los ojos,*** to devour with one's gaze; ***costar un ojo de la cara,*** to cost the earth; (*fig.*) ***dar en los ojos,*** to hit in the eye; ***le tiene echado el ojo,*** he's got his eye on it; ***le ha entrado por el ojo,*** he's taken a liking to it; ***en un abrir y cerrar de ojos,*** in the twinkling of an eye; ***estar con cien ojos,*** to be keeping a sharp look-out; ***hablar con los ojos,*** to make one's meaning clear by a look; ***hacer del ojo,*** to wink; ***empeñado hasta los ojos,*** up to one's eyes in debt; ***más ven cuatro ojos que dos,*** two heads are better than one; ***mal de ojo,*** evil eye; ***mirar con otros ojos,*** to look at in a new light; ***¡(mucho) ojo!*** watch out! take jolly good care!; ***no pegar ojo,*** not to sleep a wink; ***niña del ojo,*** pupil of the eye; ***ojos que no ven, corazón que no siente,*** what the eye does not see, the heart does not grieve over; ***pasar los ojos por,*** to cast one's eyes over; (*fig.*) ***sacar los ojos a,*** to tear to pieces; ***me tiene entre ojos,*** he's got it in for me, I'm in his bad books.
ojota, *n.f.* (*Hisp. Am.*) sandal.
ojuelo, *n.m.* small eye, beady little eye; (*pl.*) sparkling eyes; spectacles.
ola, *n.f.* wave, billow; ***ola de calor,*** heat-wave; ***ola de frío,*** cold spell *or* snap; ***ola de marea,*** tidal wave.
olaje, *n.m.* surge.
ole, *n.m.* Andalusian dancer.
¡olé! *interj.* bravo! well done!
oleáceo, -cea, *a.* oleaceous.
oleada, *n.f.* surge, swell; (*fig.*) wave; abundant oil-crop.
oleaginosidad, *n.f.* oleaginousness, oiliness.
oleaginoso, -sa, *a.* oleaginous, oily.
oleaje, *n.m.* surge.
oleandro, *n.m.* (*bot.*) oleander.
olear, *v.t.* to administer extreme unction to.
oleastro, *n.m.* (*bot.*) oleaster.
oleato, *n.m.* oleate.
oleaza, *n.f.* (*prov.*) refuse of oil-extraction.
oledero, -ra, *a.* odorous, fragrant.
oleína, *n.f.* olein.
óleo, *n.m.* oil; anointing, extreme unction; ***al óleo,*** in oils; ***cuadro*** or ***pintura al óleo,*** oil painting.
oleoducto, *n.m.* oil pipeline.
oleografía, *n.f.* oleography.
oleómetro, *n.m.* oleometer.
oleosidad, *n.f.* oleosity, oiliness.
oleoso, -sa, *a.* oily.
oler [5: **huelo** etc.] *v.t.*, *v.i.* to smell, scent, sniff; to pry (into); ***esto huele a traición,*** this smacks of treachery; ***se lo olieron en seguida,*** they got wind of it at once, they smelt a rat at once.
olfacción, *n.f.* smelling, olfaction.
olfatear, *v.t.* to smell, scent, sniff.
olfato, *n.m.* sense of smell.
olfatorio, -ria, *a.* olfactory.
olíbano, *n.m.* (*bot.*) gum-resin; incense.
oliente, *a.* smelling, odorous.
oliera, *n.f.* vessel for holy oil.
oligarca, *n.m.* oligarch.
oligarquía, *n.f.* oligarchy.
oligárquico, -ca, *a.* oligarchic(al).
olimpíada, *n.f.* Olympiad.
olímpico, -ca, *a.* Olympic.
olimpo, *n.m.* Olympus.
olingo, *n.m.* monkey.
olio, *n.m.* oil.
oliscar, *v.t.* to sniff; (*fig.*) to pry into. — *v.i.* to be tainted; to be *or* smell high.

oliva, *n.f.* olive; olive tree; owl; (*fig.*) olive branch.
olivar, *n.m.* olive grove. — *v.t.* to prune.
olivarda, *n.f.* (*orn.*) green goshawk; (*bot.*) elecampane.
olivarse, *v.r.* to form bubbles when baking (*of bread*).
olivera, *n.f.* olive tree.
olivífero, -ra, *a.* (*poet.*) olive-producing.
olivillo, *n.f.* (*bot.*) terebinth.
olivino, *n.m.* (*min.*) olivin, peridot.
olivo, *n.m.* olive tree.
olmeda, *n.f.*, **olmedo,** *n.m.* elm grove.
olmo, *n.m.* elm tree.
ológrafo, -fa, *a.* holograph.
olor, *n.m.* smell, odour, scent.
oloroso, -sa, *a.* odoriferous, fragrant, perfumed. — *n.m.* oloroso sherry.
olvidadizo, -za, *a.* forgetful; oblivious.
olvidar, *v.t.* to forget; to leave behind.
olvido, *n.m.* forgetfulness; oblivion; ***echar al*** or ***en olvido,*** to cast into oblivion; ***poner en olvido,*** to forget.
olla, *n.f.* stewpot; whirlpool; ***olla exprés*** or ***a presión,*** pressure cooker; ***olla podrida,*** stew, pot-pourri; (*artill.*) ***olla de fuego,*** stinkpot; ***olla de grillos,*** pandemonium, shindy, uproar.
ollao, *n.m.* (*naut.*) eyelet-hole.
ollar, *a.* soft (*stone*). — *n.m.* horse's nostril.
ollaza, *n.f.* large pot.
ollería, *n.f.* pottery; crockery-shop.
ollero, *n.m.* potter; earthenware dealer.
olleta, *n.f.* (*Ven.*) maize dish; (*Col.*) chocolate jug.
ollita, *n.f.* small pot.
ombligada, *n.f.* (*tannery*) part of skin corresponding to the navel.
ombligo, *n.m.* navel; (*fig.*) hub; (*bot.*) ***ombligo de Venus,*** Venus' navelwort.
ombliguero, *n.m.* bandage for baby's navel.
ombría, *n.f.* shade, shady place.
ombú, *n.m.* ombu tree.
omega, *n.f.* omega.
omental, *a.* belonging to the omentum.
omento, *n.m.* (*anat.*) omentum.
ominar, *v.t.* to augur, foretell, foretoken.
ominoso, -sa, *a.* ominous; ghastly.
omisión, *n.f.* omission, missing out.
omiso, -sa, *a.* careless; ***hacer caso omiso de,*** to ignore, leave out, pass over.
omitir [*p.p.* **omitido, omiso**], *v.t.* to omit, miss *or* leave out.
ómnibus, *n.m.* omnibus; slow *or* stopping train.
omnímodo, -da, *a.* all-embracing.
omnipotencia, *n.f.* omnipotence.
omnipotente, *a.* omnipotent, almighty.
omnipresencia, *n.f.* omnipresence.
omnipresente, *a.* omnipresent, ubiquitous.
omnisapiente, *a.* omniscient.
omnisciencia, *n.f.* omniscience.
omniscio, -cia, *a.* omniscient.
omnívoro, -ra, *a.* omnivorous.
omóplato, *n.m.* (*anat.*) omoplate, shoulder-blade.
onagra, *n.f.* (*bot.*) evening primrose.
onagro, *n.m.* onager, wild ass; crossbow.
onanismo, *n.m.* onanism.
once, *a.*, *n.m.* eleven; eleventh; ***las once,*** eleven o'clock; (*coll.*) ***tomar las once,*** to have elevenses.
oncear, *v.t.* to weigh out by ounces.
onceavo, -va, *a.* eleventh.
oncejera, *n.f.* snare.
oncejo, *n.m.* (*orn.*) swift, black-martin.
onceno, -na, *a.* eleventh.
onda, *n.f.* wave; ripple; flicker; (*sew.*) scallop; ***onda corta,*** short wave; ***onda larga,*** long wave; ***onda media,*** medium wave; ***onda de choque,*** shock wave; blast wave; ***onda luminosa,*** light wave; ***onda sonora,*** sound wave.
ondeado, *n.m.* scalloping.
ondeante, *a.* undulating, waving.
ondear, *v.i.* to wave; to flutter; to undulate; to fluctuate. — **ondearse,** *v.r.* to swing, sway.
ondeo, *n.m.* waving; fluttering.
ondina, *n.f.* undine, water-sprite.
ondisonante, *a.* pounding.
ondulación, *n.f.* undulation; ***ondulación permanente,*** permanent wave.
ondulado, -da, *a.* undulating, rolling; corrugated.
ondulante, *a.* waving; undulating.
ondular, *v.t.* to wave. — *v.i.* to wave, flutter; to undulate.
oneroso, -sa, *a.* burdensome, onerous.
onfacino, *n.m.* oil extracted from green olives.
onfacomeli, *n.m.* (*pharm.*) oxymel.
onfalismo, *n.m.* (*fig.*) thumb-twiddling.
ónice, ónique, ónix, *n.m.* (*min.*) onyx.
onírico, -ca, *a.* of dreams, dream.
onocrótalo, *n.m.* white pelican.
onomástico, -ca, *a.* onomastic. — *n.f.* saint's day; ***fiesta onomástica,*** saint's day.
onomatopeya, *n.f.* onomatopœia.
onomatopéyico, -ca, *a.* onomatopœic.
onoquiles, *n.f. inv.* (*bot.*) dyer's bugloss, alkanet.
onoto, *n.m.* (*Ven.*) arnotto tree.
ontogenia, *n.f.* (*biol.*) ontogenesis.
ontogénico, -ca, *a.* ontogenetic.
ontología, *n.f.* ontology.
ontológico, -ca, *a.* ontologic, ontological.
ontologista, *n.m.f.* ontologist.
ontólogo, *n.m.* ontologist.
onza, *n.f.* ounce; (*zool.*) ounce; ***por onzas,*** sparingly.
onzavo, -va, *a.* eleventh.
oolítico, -ca, *a.* oolitic.
oolito, *n.m.* (*geol.*) oolite.
opacidad, *n.f.* opacity; darkness, gloom.
opaco, -ca, *a.* opaque; dark, gloomy.
opalescencia, *n.f.* opalescence.
opalescente, *a.* opalescent.
ópalo, *n.m.* (*min.*) opal.
opción, *n.f.* option, choice; right.
ópera, *n.f.* opera.
operable, *a.* operable, feasible; operatable.
operación, *n.f.* operation.
operador, *n.m.* operator.
operante, *a.* operating, operative.
operar, *v.t.* (*med.*) to operate on. — *v.i.* to operate. — **operarse,** *v.r.* (*med.*) to have an operation *or* operations.
operario, -ria, *n.m.f.* workman, workwoman. — *n.m.* priest who assists sick *or* dying people.
operativo, -va, *a.* operative.
operatorio, -ria, *a.* operative; (*med.*) surgical.
opérculo, *n.m.* operculum, opercle.
opereta, *n.f.* operetta.
operista, *n.m.f.* opera singer.
operístico, -ca, *a.* operatic.
operoso, -sa, *a.* laborious, wearisome.
opiáceo, -cea, *a.* opiate; assuaging; soothing.
opiado, -da, *a.* opiate, narcotic.
opiato, -ta, *a.* opiate, narcotic. — *n.f.* opiate.
opilación, *n.f.* oppilation, obstruction; amenorrhœa.
opilar, *v.t.* to oppilate, obstruct. — **opilarse,** *v.r.* to have *or* get amenorrhœa.
opilativo, -va, *a.* obstructive, oppilative.
opimo, -ma, *a.* rich, fruitful, abundant.
opinable, *a.* questionable, debatable.
opinante, *a.*, *n.m.f.* (one) who gives his views.

opinar, *v.i.* to think, have an opinion; to express one's views.
opinión, *n.f.* opinion, view; ***hacerse*** or ***formarse una opinión,*** to form an opinion; ***cambiar*** or ***mudar de opinión,*** to change one's mind.
opio, *n.m.* opium.
opíparo, -ra, *a.* sumptuous, splendid, magnificent, lavish.
opobálsamo, *n.m.* opobalsam.
oponer [25], *v.t.* to oppose; to put up, offer (resistance) (***a,*** to). — **oponerse,** *v.r.* — ***a,*** to oppose; to be opposed to; to go against.
oponible, *a.* opposable.
opopónaca, opopónace, *n.f.* (*bot.*) rough parsnip.
opopónaco, opopánax, *n.m.* opoponax.
oporto, *n.m.* port wine.
oportunidad, *n.f.* opportunity.
oportunismo, *n.m.* opportunism.
oportunista, *a., n.m.f.* opportunist.
oportuno, -na, *a.* opportune, timely; suitable, fitting.
oposición, *n.f.* opposition; competitive examination; ***hacer oposiciones a,*** to compete (*by examination*) for.
opositor, -ra, *n.m.f.* opponent, competitor; candidate (*in a competitive examination*).
opresión, *n.f.* oppression.
opresivo, -va, *a.* oppressive.
opresor, -ra, *a.* oppressive. — *n.m.f.* oppressor.
oprimir [*p.p.* **oprimido, opreso**], *v.t.* to oppress; to press down on, weigh down on; ***oprimió el botón del timbre,*** he pressed the door-bell.
oprobiar, *v.t.* to defame, revile.
oprobio, *n.m.* opprobrium.
oprobioso, -sa, *a.* opprobrious.
optación, *n.f.* (*rhet.*) optation.
optar, *v.i.* to opt, choose; ***optar por,*** to choose, decide on; to choose to, decide to; ***optar a,*** to aspire to, aim at, be a candidate for.
optativo, *a., n.m.* optative.
óptico, -ca, *a.* optic, optical. — *n.m.* optician. — *n.f.* optics; optician's stereoscope.
optimismo, *n.m.* optimism.
optimista, *a.* optimistic. — *n.m.f.* optimist.
óptimo, -ma, *a.* best; first-class.
optómetro, *n.m.* optometer.
opuesto, -ta, *a.* opposite; contrary; against.
opugnación, *n.f.* attack; refutation.
opugnador, -ra, *a.* attacking.
opugnar, *v.t.* to oppugn; to attack.
opulencia, *n.f.* opulence, wealth.
opulento, -ta, *a.* opulent, wealthy.
opúsculo, *n.m.* opuscule, tract, short treatise.
oquedad, *n.f.* hollow, cavity; hollowness; emptiness.
oquedal, *n.m.* plantation of lofty trees.
oqueruela, *n.f.* kink (*in thread*).
ora, *conj.* now; ***ora . . . ora . . .,*** now . . . now . . .; ***tomando ora la espada, ora la pluma,*** taking now the sword and now the pen.
oración, *n.f.* oration; prayer; (*gram.*) sentence; (*gram.*) ***partes de la oración,*** parts of speech; (*pl.* **oraciones**) first part of catechism; angelus.
oracional, *a.* sentence. — *n.m.* prayer-book.
oráculo, *n.m.* oracle.
orador, *n.m.* orator.
oral, *a.* oral. — *n.m.* (*prov.*) soft breeze; oral (*examination*).
orangután, *n.m.* (*zool.*) orang-outang.
orante, *a.* praying.
orar, *v.i.* to pray; to make a speech.
orate, *n.m.f.* lunatic, madman; ***casa de orates,*** lunatic asylum.
oratorio, -ria, *a.* oratorial, oratorical. — *n.m.* oratory; (*mus.*) oratorio. — *n.f.* oratory.
orbe, *n.m.* orb; globe; (*ichth.*) globe fish.
orbicular, *a.* orbicular, circular.
órbita, *n.f.* (*astron.*) orbit; (*anat.*) eye-socket.
orbital, *a.* orbital.
orca, *n.f.* (*ichth.*) grampus, orca.
orcaneta, *n.f.* (*bot.*) dyer's bugloss, alkanet.
orcina, *n.f.* (*chem.*) orcein.
orco, *n.m.* (*ichth.*) grampus; (*poet.*) hell.
orchilla, *n.f.* (*Ec., bot.*) archil, orchil.
órdago, *n.m.* move in a game of cards; (*coll.*) ***de órdago,*** super, grand, smashing.
ordalías, *n.f.pl.* ordeal, trial by ordeal.
orden, *n.m.* order; ***por su orden,*** in order, successively; ***hombre de orden,*** law-abiding man; ***llamar al orden,*** to call to order, take to task; ***del orden de,*** of the order of, in the region of; ***en orden a,*** with regard to; ***orden del día,*** agenda; ***sin orden ni concierto,*** without system, in a disorganized manner. — *n.f.* order; command; ***a la orden de usted, a sus órdenes,*** at your command, at your disposal; ***a las órdenes de,*** under the command of; ***orden del día,*** order of the day; ***orden de batalla,*** battle array.
ordenación, *n.f.* disposition, array; layout; arrangement; ordination; ordinance; auditor's office.
ordenada, *n.f.* (*geom.*) ordinate.
ordenadamente, *adv.* in an orderly way, methodically.
ordenador, -ra, *a.* ordering, arranging; ordaining. — *n.m.f.* orderer, arranger; ordainer. — *n.m.* auditor, controller; computer.
ordenamiento, *n.m.* ordaining, regulating; ordinance, edict.
ordenancista, *n.m.f.* disciplinarian, martinet.
ordenando, ordenante, *n.m.* ordinand.
ordenanza, *n.f.* method, order; command; ordination; regulation, ordinance. — *n.m.* messenger; (*mil.*) orderly.
ordenar, *v.t.* to arrange, put in order, sort out, tidy up; to ordain; to order, command.
ordeñadero, *n.m.* milk-pail.
ordeñador, -ra, *n.m.f.* milker.
ordeñar, *v.t.* to milk; to pick (*olives*); (*fig.*) to squeeze dry, exploit.
ordinal, *a.* ordinal.
ordinariez, *n.f.* vulgarity, coarseness.
ordinario, -ria, *a.* ordinary, regular; vulgar; ***de ordinario,*** usually. — *n.m.* ordinary; ecclesiastical judge; daily household expense; bishop; regular mail *or* post; carrier, messenger.
ordinativo, -va, *a.* ordering, regulating, ordinative.
orea, oréada, oréade, *n.f.* oread, wood-nymph.
oreante, *a.* cooling, airing.
orear, *v.t.* to cool, refresh; to air, expose to the air, aerate, ventilate. — **orearse,** *v.r.* to go out for fresh air.
orégano, *n.m.* (*bot.*) wild marjoram; ***no todo el monte es orégano,*** life is not all a bed of roses.
oreja, *n.f.* ear; spy; (*mech.*) lug, flange; (*naut.*) fluke (*of an anchor*); (*bot.*) ***oreja de abad,*** Venus' navelwort; (*bot.*) ***oreja de ratón,*** mouse-ear; (*bot.*) ***oreja de oso,*** primrose; (*conch.*) ***oreja marina,*** gasteropod; (*coll.*) ***oreja de mercader,*** deaf ear; ***con las orejas gachas,*** crestfallen, with one's tail between one's legs; ***aguzar las orejas,*** to prick up one's ears; ***apearse por las orejas,*** to take a tumble; (*fig.*) to answer completely off the point; ***bajar las orejas,*** to knuckle under; ***calentar las orejas a alguien,*** to box s.o.'s ears; ***descubrir*** or ***enseñar la oreja,*** to show one's true colours, show the cloven hoof; ***verle las orejas al lobo,*** to see trouble coming.
orejano, -na, *a.* unbranded.
orejeado, -da, *a.* informed, warned.
orejear, *v.i.* to shake the ears; (*fig.*) to act reluctantly; to whisper.
orejera, *n.f.* ear-cap, oreillette; mould-board (*of a plough*).

orejeta, *n.f.* small ear.
orejón, *n.m.* pull *or* tug on ear; ring of dried fruit; hind part (*of a plough*); (*fort.*) orillon; (*Per.*) privileged nobleman; (*Hisp. Am.*) Orejon Indian.
orejudo, -da, *a.* flap-eared, long-eared.
oreo, *n.m.* breeze; fresh air; airing.
orfanato, *n.m.* orphanage.
orfandad, *n.f.* orphanhood; neglect; dearth.
orfebre, *n.m.* goldsmith; silversmith.
orfebrería, *n.f.* gold *or* silver work.
orfeón, *n.m.* choral society.
orfeonista, *n.m.f.* member of a choral society.
órfico, -ca, *a.* orphic.
orfo, *n.m.* (*ichth.*) orfe.
organdí, *n.m.* organdie.
organero, *n.m.* organ-maker.
orgánico, -ca, *a.* organic.
organillero, *n.m.* organ-grinder.
organillo, *n.m.* barrel-organ.
organismo, *n.m.* organism; organization.
organista, *n.m.f.* organist.
organizable, *a.* organizable.
organización, *n.f.* organization; arrangement, fixing up.
organizador, -ra, *a.* organizing; arranging. — *n.m.f.* organizer.
organizar [C], *v.t.* to organize; to arrange, fix, fix up. — **organizarse,** *v.r.* to organize one's life, get one's priorities right *or* in order.
órgano, *n.m.* organ; part; (*bot.*) organ-pipe cactus.
orgasmo, *n.m.* orgasm.
orgía, *n.f.* orgy; revel.
orgiástico, -ca, *a.* orgiastic.
orgullo, *n.m.* pride; haughtiness.
orgulloso, -sa, *a.* proud; haughty.
orientación, *n.f.* orientation; bearings; guidance.
orientador, -ra, *a.* guiding.
oriental, *a.* oriental; eastern.
orientalista, *n.m.f.* orientalist.
orientar, *v.t.* to orientate; to direct, give guidance to, set on the right road. — **orientarse,** *v.r.* to find one's bearings, find one's way.
oriente, *n.m.* orient; east; east wind; lustre (*of pearls*); (*fig.*) dawn, start.
orificación, *n.f.* (*dent.*) gold filling.
orificar [A], *v.t.* (*dent.*) to fill with gold.
orífice, *n.m.* goldsmith.
orificia, *n.m.* goldsmith's art *or* profession.
orificio, *n.m.* orifice, hole; (*artill.*) vent-hole.
oriflama, *n.f.* oriflamme; flag, banner.
origen, *n.m.* origin, source; extraction, stock.
original, *a.*, *n.m.* original.
originalidad, *n.f.* originality, originalness.
originar, *v.t.* to originate, occasion, give rise to. — **originarse,** *v.r.* to originate, spring, arise.
originario, -ria, *a.* original; native. — *n.m.f.* native.
orilla, *n.f.* bank, shore; edge; water's edge; (*prov.*) fresh breeze; ***a orillas de,*** on the banks of, beside, on; ***a orilla del mar,*** by the sea(side); ***salir a la orilla,*** to win through, make it; ***orilla de mi casa,*** next door.
orillar, *v.t.*, *v.i.* to leave a selvedge on (*cloth*); to border, skirt; (*fig.*) to dodge round.
orillo, *n.m.* selvedge.
orín (1), *n.m.* rust.
orín (2), *n.m.* (*usu.* in *pl.* **orines**) urine.
orina, *n.f.* urine.
orinal, *n.m.* chamber-pot.
orinar, *v.i.* to urinate, pass water.
oriniento, -ta, *a.* rusty.
orinque, *n.m.* (*naut.*) buoy-rope.
oriol, *n.m.* (*orn.*) golden thrush, oriole.
Orión, *n.m.* (*astron.*) Orion.
oriundo, -da, *a.* native (of), coming (from).
orla, *n.f.* border, edge, edging; (*her.*) orle; (*typ.*) ornamental border.
orlador, -ra, *n.m.f.* borderer.
orladura, *n.f.* border, edging.
orlar, *v.t.* to border, edge, garnish.
orlo, *n.m.* Alpine oboe; organ-stop; plinth.
ormesí, *n.m.* satin.
ormino, *n.m.* (*bot.*) annual clary sage.
ornabeque, *n.m.* (*fort.*) hornwork.
ornamentación, *n.f.* ornamentation.
ornamental, *a.* ornamental.
ornamentar, *v.t.* to ornament.
ornamento, *n.m.* ornament; (*pl.*) (*eccles.*) vestments; (*arch.*) frets, mouldings.
ornar, *v.t.* to adorn, ornament.
ornato, *n.m.* ornament, embellishment.
ornitología, *n.f.* ornithology.
ornitológico, -ca, *a.* ornithological.
ornitólogo, *n.m.* ornithologist.
oro, *n.m.* gold; ***de oro,*** (made of) gold; ***oro batido,*** gold leaf; ***oro en bruto,*** gold in nuggets; bullion; ***oro de ley,*** standard gold; upright person; ***oro en polvo,*** gold-dust; ***de oro y azul,*** splendidly attired; ***no es oro todo lo que reluce,*** all that glitters is not gold; ***costar el oro y el moro,*** to cost the earth; ***hacerse de oro,*** to make a mint of money; ***matar (a) la gallina de los huevos de oro,*** to kill the goose that lays the golden egg(s); (*pl.*) diamonds (*in cards*).
orobanca, *n.f.* (*bot.*) broom rape.
orobias, *n.m. inv.* fine incense.
orografía, *n.f.* orography.
orográfico, -ca, *a.* orographic.
orología, *n.f.* orology.
orondo, -da, *a.* fat; pot-bellied; fat and sleek; puffed up, pleased with o.s.
oropel, *n.m.* tinsel; flashy rubbish; (*fig.*) show.
oropelero, -ra, oropelesco, -ca, *a.* flashy, trashy. — *n.m.* tinsel maker.
oropéndola, *n.f.* (*orn.*) golden oriole.
oropimente, *n.m.* (*min.*) orpiment.
oroya, *n.f.* (*Hisp. Am.*) hanging basket (*for carrying passengers over rope bridges*).
orozuz, *n.m.* liquorice.
orquesta, *n.f.* orchestra; band.
orquestación, *n.f.* orchestration.
orquestar, *v.t.* to orchestrate.
orquídeo, -dea, *a.* orchidaceous. — *n.f.* orchid.
orquitis, *n.f.* (*med.*) orchitis.
orsay, *n.m.* [OFF-SIDE].
orre (en), *adv.* loose, in bulk.
ortega, *n.f.* (*orn.*) grouse.
ortiga, *n.f.* nettle, stinging-nettle.
ortigarse, *v.r.* to get stung by nettles, sting o.s. on nettles.
ortivo, -va, *a.* (*astron.*) ortive.
orto, *n.m.* rising (*of the sun* or *a star*).
ortodoxia, *n.f.* orthodoxy.
ortodoxo, -xa, *a.* orthodox; conventional.
ortodromia, *n.f.* (*naut.*) orthodromy.
ortogonal, ortogonio, -nia, *a.* orthogonal.
ortografía, *n.f.* orthography, spelling.
ortográfico, -ca, *a.* orthographic(al).
ortógrafo, *n.m.* orthographer.
ortología, *n.f.* orthoepy.
ortológico, -ca, *a.* orthoepic.
ortólogo, -ga, *n.m.f.* orthoepist.
ortopedia, *n.f.* (*med.*) orthopædy.
ortopédico, -ca, *a.* orthopædic.
ortopedista, *n.m.f.* orthopædist.
ortóptero, -ra, *a.* orthopterous. — *n.m.pl.* (*ent.*) orthoptera.
ortosa, *n.f.* (*min.*) orthoclase.

oruga, *n.f.* caterpillar; (*bot.*) rocket.
orujo, *n.m.* waste of grapes *or* olives.
orvalle, *n.m.* (*bot.*) clary sage.
orvallo, *n.m.* (*prov.*) drizzle.
orvietano, *n.m.* orvietan.
orza, *n.f.* gallipot, preserve-jar; (*naut.*) luff; (*yachting*) lead stabilizer.
orzada, *n.f.* (*naut.*) luffing.
orzaderas, *n.f.pl.* (*naut.*) leeboards.
orzaga, *n.f.* (*bot.*) orache.
orzar, *v.i.* (*naut.*) to luff.
orzaya, *n.f.* children's nurse.
orzuelo, *n.m.* (*med.*) sty; snare, trap (*for animals*).
orzura, *n.f.* (*chem.*) minimum.
os, *pron. pers. dative and accusative of* **vos** *and* **vosotros**: you, to you.
osa, *n.f.* she-bear; (*astron.*) ***Osa Mayor,*** Ursa Major, Dipper; ***Osa Menor,*** Ursa Minor.
osadía, *n.f.* audacity, boldness.
osado, -da, *a.* daring, audacious, bold.
osambre, *n.m.*; **osamenta,** *n.f.* bonework; framework.
osar (1), **osario,** *n.m.* ossuary, charnel-house.
osar (2), *v.i.* to dare.
oscarizar [C], *v.t.* to award an Oscar to.
oscilación, *n.f.* oscillation, fluctuation.
oscilador, *n.m.* (*phys.*) oscillator; oscillation valve.
oscilar, *v.i.* to oscillate, fluctuate.
oscilatorio, -ria, *a.* oscillatory.
oscitancia, *n.f.* carelessness, heedlessness.
ósculo, *n.m.* kiss.
oscuras (a), *adv.* in the dark.
oscurecer [9], *v.t.* to obscure, darken, dim; to shade. — *v.i. impers.* to grow dark. — **oscurecerse,** *v.r.* to become dark, darken over.
oscurecimiento, *n.m.* darkening, dimness; shading.
oscuridad, *n.f.* darkness; obscurity; shade.
oscuro, -ra, *a.* dark; obscure.
oseína, *n.f.* (*chem.*) ossein.
óseo, -sea, *a.* osseous, bony.
osera, *n.f.* bear den.
osero, *n.m.* charnel-house.
osezno, *n.m.* bear cub.
osificación, *n.f.* ossification.
osificarse [A], *v.r.* to ossify, become ossified.
osífico, -ca, *a.* ossific.
osífraga, *n.f.*; **osífrago,** *n.m.* (*orn.*) osprey, ossifrage.
osmio, *n.m.* (*min.*) osmium.
oso, *n.m.* bear; ***oso hormiguero,*** ant-eater; ***oso colmenero,*** honey-bear; ***oso blanco,*** polar bear; ***oso marino,*** fur seal; (*coll.*) ***hacer el oso,*** to make a fool of o.s.
ososo, -sa, *a.* osseous, bony.
osta, *n.f.* (*naut.*) lateen brace.
ostaga, *n.f.* (*naut.*) tie, runner.
ostensible, *a.* ostensible, visible.
ostensión, *n.f.* show, manifestation.
ostensivo, -va, *a.* ostensive, showing.
ostentación, *n.f.* ostentation, display, show.
ostentador, -ra, *a.* boastful, ostentatious. — *n.m.f.* boaster, ostentatious person.
ostentar, *v.t.* to show, display; to bear, have, hold.
ostentativo, -va, *a.* ostentatious.
ostento, *n.m.* prodigy, portent.
ostentoso, -sa, *a.* ostentatious.
osteolito, *n.m.* osteolite.
osteología, *n.f.* osteology.
osteomielitis, *n.f.* (*path.*) osteomyelitis.
ostiario, *n.m.* (*eccles.*) ostiary, door-keeper.
ostión, *n.m.* large oyster.
ostra, *n.f.* oyster.
ostraceo, -cea, *a.* ostraceous.
ostracismo, *n.m.* ostracism.
ostracita, *n.f.* (*palæont.*) ostracite.
ostral, *n.m.* oyster-bed.
ostrero, -ra, *a.* oyster. — *n.m.* oysterman; oyster-bed. — *n.f.* oyster-woman.
ostrícola, *a.* oyster-breeding.
ostricultura, *n.f.* oyster-culture, oyster-farming.
ostrífero, -ra, *a.* ostriferous, oyster-producing.
ostro, *n.m.* large oyster; south wind; purple-yielding mollusc; Sidonian purple.
ostrogodo, -da, *a.* Ostrogoth. — *n.m.f.* Ostrogothic.
ostugo, *n.m.* piece, bit; corner.
osudo, -da, *a.* bony.
osuno, -na, *a.* bearlike, bearish.
otalgia, *n.f.* (*med.*) ear-ache.
otario, -ria, *a.* (*Arg.*) silly, foolish, stupid.
oteador, -ra, *a.* watching, scanning.
otear, *v.t.* to watch, scan, sweep with one's gaze, search, survey from on high.
Otelo, *n.m.* Othello.
otero, *n.m.* hill, hillock, knoll.
oto, *n.m.* (*orn.*) tawny owl.
otoba, *n.f.* (*Hisp. Am.*) nutmeg tree.
otología, *n.f.* (*med.*) otology.
otólogo, *n.m.* otologist.
otomano, -na, *a., n.m.f.* Ottoman. — *n.f.* ottoman, divan.
otoñada, *n.f.* autumn season.
otoñal, *a.* autumnal.
otoñar, *v.i.* to spend the autumn; to grow in autumn. — **otoñarse,** *v.r.* to be seasoned.
otoñizo, -za, *a.* autumnal.
otoño, *n.m.* autumn, (*Am.*) fall.
otorgador, -ra, *a.* granting. — *n.m.f.* grantor.
otorgamiento, *n.m.* granting; awarding; consent; drawing up (*of a will, deed etc.*).
otorgante, *n.m.f.* grantor; maker (*of a deed*).
otorgar, *v.t.* to grant; to award; to consent to; to execute (*will etc.*); ***quien calla otorga,*** silence gives consent.
otorgo, *n.m.* marriage contract.
otorrinolaringología, *n.f.* (*path.*) study of the diseases of the ear, nose and throat.
otorrinolaringólogo, *n.m.* ear, nose and throat specialist.
otoscopia, *n.f.* otoscopy.
otoscopio, *n.m.* otoscope.
otramente, *adv.* otherwise; differently.
otro, -ra, *a.* other, another; ***otra cosa,*** sth. else; ***otra vez,*** another time; on another occasion; again; ***otros tantos,*** as many more, as many again; ***otro tanto,*** as much (again), the same (again); ***al otro día,*** the next day; ***por otra parte,*** on the other hand; moreover; ***como dijo el otro,*** as the saying goes. — *pron.* another (one); ***algún otro,*** some other, s.o. else, somebody else.
otrora, *adv.* in former days.
otrosí, *adv.* moreover, furthermore. — *n.m.* (*law*) every petition made after the principal.
ova, *n.f.* seawrack; (*arch.*) egg; (*pl.*) roe.
ovación, *n.f.* ovation.
ovacionar, *v.t.* to give an ovation to.
ovado, -da, *a.* ovate.
oval, *a.* oval.
ovalado, -da, *a.* egg-shaped, oval-shaped.
ovalar, *v.t.* to make oval.
óvalo, *n.m.* oval.
ovante, *a.* victorious, triumphant.
ovar, *v.i.* to lay eggs.
ovario, *n.m.* ovary, ovarium; (*arch.*) egg ornament.
oveja, *n.f.* ewe, sheep; ***cada oveja con su pareja,*** birds of a feather flock together.
ovejero, -ra, *n.m.f.* shepherd, shepherdess.
ovejuela, *n.f.* young ewe.
ovejuno, -na, *a.* (of) sheep.

overo, -ra, *a.* egg-coloured, speckled, blossom-coloured (*horse*); bulging (*eyes*). — *n.f.* ovary of birds.
ovezuelo, *n.m.* small egg.
óvidos, *n.m.pl.* (*zool.*) ovidæ.
oviducto, *n.m.* (*anat.*) oviduct.
ovil, *n.m.* sheep-cote.
ovillar, *v.i.* to wind (into a ball). — **ovillarse,** *v.r.* to curl up into a ball.
ovillo, *n.m.* clew; ball (*of wool etc.*); ***hacerse un ovillo,*** to curl up.
ovíparo, -ra, *a.* oviparous.
ovoide, *a.* ovoid.
óvolo, *n.m.* (*arch.*) ovolo.
ovoso, -sa, *a.* full of roe.
ovovivíparo, -ra, *a.* ovoviviparous.
ovulación, *n.f.* (*biol.*) ovulation.
óvulo, *n.m.* (*biol.*) ovule.
¡ox! *interj.* shoo!
oxalato, *n.m.* (*chem.*) oxalate.
oxálico, *a.* oxalic.
oxalídeo, -dea, *a.* (*bot.*) oxalis.
oxalme, *n.m.* acidulated brine.
oxear, *v.t.* to shoo (*birds*).
oxiacanta, *n.f.* (*bot.*) hawthorn, whitehorn.
oxidable, *a.* (*chem.*) oxidizable.
oxidación, *n.f.* oxidation; rusting.
oxidante, *a.* oxidant; rusting.
oxidar, *v.t.* to oxidize; to rust; ***tengo el español muy oxidado,*** my Spanish is very rusty. — **oxidarse,** *v.r.* to oxidize; to become *or* go rusty.
óxido, *n.m.* oxide; rust.
oxigenable, *a.* (*chem.*) oxygenizable.
oxigenar, *v.t.* to oxygenate. — **oxigenarse,** *v.t.* to get some fresh air.
oxígeno, *n.m.* oxygen.
oximel, oximiel, *n.m.* oxymel.
oxizacre, *n.m.* bitter-sweet beverage.
¡oxte! *interj.* keep off! shoo!; (*coll.*) ***sin decir oxte ni moxte,*** without so much as a by-your-leave.
oyente, *a.* hearing. — *n.m.* listener, hearer; non-graduating student.
ozonizar, *v.t.* ozonize.
ozono, *n.m.* ozone.

P

P, p, *n.f.* letter P, p.
pabellón, *n.m.* pavilion; bell tent; canopy; building; (*naut.*) colours, flag; bell of a wind instrument; (*mil.*) stack (of arms); (*anat.*) external ear, pinna.
pabilo, *n.m.* wick; snuff (*of a candle*); ***del hilo al pabilo,*** from beginning to end.
pabilón, *n.m.* bunch of silk, wool *or* oakum hanging from the distaff.
pablar, *v.i.* (*coll.*) to jabber; ***ni hablar ni pablar,*** to say never a word.
Pablo, *n.m.* Paul.
pábulo, *n.m.* pabulum, food; encouragement.
paca, *n.f.* spotted cavy; bundle, bale.
pacana, *n.f.* pecan tree; pecan nut.
pacato, -ta, *a.* timid; prudish.
pacay (*pl.* **pacayes** or **pacaes**), *n.m.* (*Hisp. Am., bot.*) pacay.
pacedero, -ra, *a.* pasturable, fit for pasture.
pacedura, *n.f.* pasture-ground.
paceño, -ña, *a., n.m.f.* (native) of La Paz.
pacer [9], *v.t., v.i.* to pasture, graze.
paciencia, *n.f.* patience, forbearance; (*fig.*) ***paciencia y barajar,*** have patience and shuffle the cards; ***armarse de paciencia,*** to possess one's soul in patience, fortify o.s. with patience.
paciente, *a.* patient, forbearing. — *n.m.* patient.
pacienzudo, -da, *a.* very patient, long-suffering.
pacificación, *n.f.* pacification.
pacificador, -ra, *a.* pacifying. — *n.m.f.* pacifier, peacemaker.
pacificar [A], *v.t.* to pacify. — *v.i.* to seek peace. — **pacificarse,** *v.r.* to become quiet *or* calm.
pacífico, -ca, *a.* pacific, peaceful; peaceable, peace-loving; ***el Pacífico,*** the Pacific Ocean.
pacifismo, *n.m.* pacifism.
pacifista, *a., n.m.f.* pacifist.
Paco, *n.m.* (*familiar form of* [FRANCISCO]) Frank.
paco, *n.m.* (*zool., min.*) paco; alpaca; sniper; (*Chi.*) policeman.
pacón, *n.m.* (*Hond.*) soapbark tree.
pacotilla, *n.f.* (*naut.*) venture; stock of goods; ***de pacotilla,*** flimsy, trashy, makeshift, jerry-built.
pactar, *v.t.* to agree to *or* upon. — *v.i.* to come to terms.
pacto, *n.m.* pact; ***pacto social,*** social contract.
pacú, *n.m.* (*Arg.*) pacu fish.
pachamanca, *n.f.* (*Per.*) barbecue.
pachocha, (*Chi.*) [PACHORRA].
pachón, *n.m.* pointer (*dog*); stolid individual.
pachorra, *n.f.* sluggishness, slowness, stolidness; ***tener pachorra,*** to be phlegmatic, stolid.
pachorrudo, -da, *a.* sluggish, phlegmatic, stolid, bovine.
pachulí, *n.m.* patchouli.
padecer [9], *v.t.* to suffer (from); to endure; (*fig.*) to suffer *or* labour under (*misconceptions etc.*). — *v.i.* to suffer; to get knocked about.
padecimiento, *n.m.* suffering; complaint, ailment.
padilla, *n.f.* small frying-pan; oven.
padrastro, *n.m.* step-father; (*fig.*) unnatural father; (*fig.*) hang-nail.
padrazo, *n.m.* (*coll.*) indulgent father.
padre, *n.m.* father; stallion, sire; author, source, origin; ***padre de familia,*** head of a family, family man; householder; ***padre nuestro,*** Lord's prayer; ***Padre Santo*** (or ***Santo Padre***), Pope; ***padre adoptivo,*** foster father; ***esto es el lío padre,*** this is a hell of a mess; ***cada uno de su padre y de su madre,*** no two alike, all different; ***de padre y muy señor mío,*** terrific; (*pl.*) father and mother; ancestors; elders, senators, leading men.
padrear, *v.i.* to resemble one's father; to breed, be kept for procreation.
padrenuestro, *n.m.* (*pl.* **padrenuestros**) Lord's Prayer.
padrinazgo, *n.m.* (baptismal) sponsorship; patronage.
padrino, *n.m.* godfather; second in a duel; patron, protector; best man.
padrón, *n.m.* census, electoral list; mark of infamy; pattern, model; (*coll.*) indulgent father; ***sacarle el padrón a alguien,*** to find out everything about somebody.
paella, *n.f.* paella; paella dish.
¡paf! *interj.* wallop!
paga, *n.f.* [PAGO (1)].
pagadero, -ra, *a.* payable. — *n.m.* time and place of payment.
pagado, -da, *a.* conceited; ***pagado de sí mismo,*** self-satisfied.
pagador, -ra, *n.m.f.* payer, paymaster; teller (*bank*); ***al buen pagador no le duelen prendas,*** a man who keeps his word doesn't mind giving it.
pagaduría, *n.f.* paymaster's office.
pagamento, pagamiento, *n.m.* payment.
paganismo, *n.m.* paganism.
pagano, -na, *a.* pagan, heathen. — *n.m.f.* pagan, heathen; (*coll.*) one who foots the bill.
pagar [B], *v.t.* to pay, pay for; to repay, return; ***pagar al contado,*** to pay cash (*down*); ***pagar un delito,*** to pay for a misdeed; ***pagar una visita,*** to return a visit; ***pagar en buena moneda,*** to give satisfaction; ***pagar con la misma moneda,*** to return like for like; ***pagar el pato*** or ***pagar los vidrios rotos,*** to take the rap, carry the can, face the music; ***estar muy pagado de sí mismo,*** to have a great opinion of o.s. — **pagarse,** *v.r.* — ***de,*** to be pleased with, be conceited about, pride o.s. on.
pagaré, *n.m.* promissory note, I.O.U.
página, *n.f.* page.
paginación, *n.f.* pagination.
paginar, *v.t.* to page, paginate.
pago (1), **-ga,** *a.* (*coll.*) paid. — *n.m.* payment; ***en pago,*** in *or* as payment; in return; (*com.*) ***suspender el pago,*** to stop payment. — *n.f.* pay, wages.
pago (2), *n.m.* rural district.
pagoda, *n.f.* pagoda.
pagote, *n.m.* (*coll.*) scapegoat.
pagro, *n.m.* (*ichth.*) braize.
paguro, *n.m.* small crab.
paico, *n.m.* (*Hisp. Am.*) saltwort.
paidología, *n.f.* pædeutics.
paila, *n.f.* large pan; (*Cub.*) evaporator, sugar pan.
pailebot, pailebote, *n.m.* (*naut.*) small schooner.
pailón, *n.m.* large copper.
painel, *n.m.* (*carp.*) panel.
paipai, *n.m.* (*Philip.*) large fan.
pairar, *v.i.* (*naut.*) to lie to.
pairo (al), *adv.* lying to.
país, *n.m.* country; region, district, area; (*art*) landscape; paper, cloth, etc. forming the cover of a hand fan; ***del país,*** home, national; local, from the local area.
paisaje, *n.m.* landscape; scenery.
paisajista, *n.m.f.* landscape-painter.
paisanaje, *n.m.* civilian population, civilians; peasantry; condition of coming from the same area as another.
paisano, -na, *a., n.m.f.* (one) from the same area *or* part of the country; civilian; peasant.— *n.f.* country dance.
Países Bajos, *n.m.pl.* Low Countries, Netherlands.
paisista, *n.m.f.* landscape-painter.
paja, *n.f.* straw; chaff; trash; ***echar pajas,*** to draw lots with straws; ***en un quítame allá esas pajas,*** in a twinkling; ***por un quítame***

allá esas pajas, about nothing, over a trifle; ***no dormirse en las pajas,*** not to let the grass grow under one's feet; (*fig.*) ***meter paja,*** to fill out with padding, stick in padding; (*com.*) ***limpio de polvo y paja,*** net.
pajado, -da, *a.* pale, straw-coloured. — *n.f.* moist straw with bran.
pajar, *n.m.* barn, straw-loft.
pájara, *n.f.* hen-bird; paper kite; (*coll.*) crafty creature, woman who needs watching; tart; ***pájara pinta,*** game of forfeits.
pajarear, *v.t.* to go bird catching; to loiter about.
pajarel, *n.m.* (*orn.*) linnet.
pajarería, *n.f.* large number of birds; bird-market.
pajarero, -ra, *a.* merry, gay, cheerful; showy, gaudy, loud. — *n.m.* bird-catcher; bird-fancier. — *n.f.* aviary; large bird cage.
pajarete, *n.m.* sherry wine liqueur.
pajaril, *adv.* (*naut.*) passarado.
pajarilla, *n.f.* (*bot.*) columbine; spleen.
pajarillo, *n.m.* small bird; frail little bird, miserable little bird.
pajarita, *n.f.* bow-tie; paper kite; ***corbata de pajarita,*** bow-tie; (*orn.*) ***pajarita de las nieves,*** wagtail.
pájaro, *n.m.* bird; crafty customer, chap who needs watching; (*coll.*) ***pájaro gordo,*** big noise, V.I.P.; ***tener la cabeza a pájaros,*** to be feather-brained; to be all of a dither; ***tener pájaros en la cabeza,*** to have bats in the belfry; ***matar dos pájaros de un tiro,*** to kill two birds with one stone; ***más vale pájaro en mano que ciento volando,*** a bird in the hand is worth two in the bush.
pajarota, pajarotada, *n.f.* idle rumour, hoax.
pajarote, *n.m.* clumsy great bird.
pajarraco, *n.m.* ugly (great) bird; (*coll.*) dodgy customer.
pajaza, *n.f.* stalks of horses' fodder left uneaten.
pajazo, *n.m.* prick of stubble.
paje, *n.m.* page, (*Am.*) bellhop; familiar (*of a bishop*); cabin boy; dressing table; ***paje de hacha,*** link-boy.
pajear, *v.i.* (*coll.*) to feed well; to behave.
pajecillo, *n.m.* little page; (*prov.*) washstand.
pajel, *n.m.* red sea bream.
pajera, *n.f.* straw-loft.
pajero, *n.m.* straw-dealer.
pajita, *n.f.* (drinking) straw.
pajizo, -za, *a.* made of straw, thatched with straw; straw-coloured.
pajo, *n.m.* mango.
pajón, *n.m.* coarse straw.
pajonal, *n.m.* (*Hisp. Am.*) field with tall grass.
pajoso, -sa, *a.* strawy.
pajote, *n.m.* straw interwoven with bulrush.
pajuela, *n.f.* sulphur match; short straw.
pajulí, *n.m.* (*P.R.*) cashew; cashew nut.
pajuncio, *n.m.* booby, ninny, fool.
pala, *n.f.* shovel, spade; scoop; (food) slice; dust-pan; racquet, bat (*for ball games*); (*shoe.*) upper; leaf (*of a hinge*); top (*of an epaulet*); flat surface (*of the teeth*); baker's peel; battledore; blade (*of an oar*).
palabra, *n.f.* word; ***de palabra,*** by word of mouth; ***dejar con la palabra en la boca,*** to leave standing; ***faltar a la palabra,*** to break one's word; ***medir las palabras,*** to choose one's words carefully; ***no tiene más que una palabra,*** he's very straightforward; ***no tiene palabra,*** he is very unreliable; ***palabras mayores,*** strong words; serious matter; ***a media palabra,*** at the slightest hint; ***empeñar la palabra,*** to pledge one's word; ***tener la palabra,*** to have the floor; ***comerse las palabras,*** to mutter *or* mumble, slur one's speech; (*fig.*) ***tragarse las palabras,*** to eat one's words; ***pedir la palabra,*** to ask permission to speak, request to take the floor; ***tomar la palabra,*** to (begin to) speak, take the floor; ***te tomaré la palabra,*** I'll take you at your word, I'll hold you to that. — *interj.* ***¡palabra!*** I promise!; I give you my word!
palabrada, *n.f.* verbiage; coarse expression.
palabreja, *n.f.* wretched *or* queer expression.
palabreo, *n.m.* empty talk, verbiage.
palabrería, *n.f.* verbiage; (*coll.*) waffle.
palabrero, -ra, *a.* talkative.
palabrimujer, *n.m.* (*coll.*) man with an effeminate voice.
palabrista, *n.m.f.* loquacious person, chatterbox.
palabrita, *n.f.* brief word; sweet *or* gentle word; charged *or* pointed expression.
palabrota, *n.f.* coarse expression, swear word.
palaciego, -ga, *a.* palace, court. — *n.m.* courtier.
palacio, *n.m.* palace; mansion; ***las cosas de palacio van despacio,*** officialdom takes its time; ***en palacio,*** at court.
palacra, palacrana, *n.f.* gold nugget.
palada (1), *n.f.* shovelful; (*naut.*) stroke (*of an oar*).
paladar, *n.m.* palate.
paladear, *v.t.* to taste; to relish, savour (the taste of). — *v.i.* to desire to suck. — **paladearse,** *v.r.* to relish, taste.
paladeo, *n.m.* tasting, relishing.
paladial, *a.* (*gram.*) palatal.
paladín, *n.m.* paladin, knight, champion.
paladino, -na, *a.* open, clear.
paladio, *n.m.* (*min.*) palladium.
paladión, *n.m.* palladium, safeguard.
palado, -da (2), *a.* (*her.*) paled.
palafito, *n.m.* primitive house *or* dwelling built upon stakes in a lake.
palafrén, *n.m.* palfrey; groom's horse.
palafrenero, *n.m.* groom, ostler, stable-boy.
palahierro, *n.m.* bushing (*of the spindle of the upper millstone*).
palamallo, *n.m.* pall-mall.
palamenta, *n.f.* oars (*of a galley*); (*naut.*) set of oars.
palanca, *n.f.* lever; bar, crowbar; cowl-staff; (*naut.*) stay-rope; (*naut.*) garnet-tackle; (*fort.*) outer fortification, palisade; (*fig.*) influence, pull; ***palanca de mando,*** control stick *or* column; (*naut.*) ***palanca del timón,*** tiller.
palancada, *n.f.* stroke with a lever.
palangana, *n.f.* basin, wash-hand basin.
palanganero, *n.m.* wash-stand.
palangre, *n.m.* paternoster (*fishing line*).
palanquera, *n.f.* enclosure with stakes *or* poles.
palanquero, *n.m.* leverman; blower of bellows.
palanqueta, *n.f.* (*artill.*) bar-shot *or* crossbar shot; small lever; dumb-bell.
palanquín, *n.m.* palanquin; porter, carrier; (*naut.*) double-tackle; clew-garnet.
Palas, *n.m.* (*astron.*) Pallas, the second asteroid.
palastro, *n.m.* iron plate; sheet-iron.
palatina (1), *n.f.* tippet, women's boa.
palatinado, *n.m.* palatinate.
palatino, -na (2), *a.* palatial; palatine; (*anat.*) palatal. — *n.m.* palatine.
palay, *n.m.* (*Philip.*) unhusked rice.
palazo, *n.m.* blow with a stick *or* shovel.
palazón, *n.m.* (*naut.*) masting; woodwork, timber.
palca, *n.f.* (*Bol.*) cross-road.
palco, *n.m.* theatre-box; ***palco escénico,*** stage box.
paleador, *n.m.* stoker, shoveller.
palear, *v.t.* to winnow, fan (*grain*).
palenque, *n.m.* palisade, paling, enclosure; (*theat.*) passage from pit to stage; arena.
paleografía, *n.f.* palæography.
paleográfico, -ca, *a.* palæographic.
paleógrafo, *n.m.* palæographer.
paleolítico, -ca, *a.* palæolithic.

paleólogo, *n.m.* palæologist.
paleontográfico, -ca, *a.* palæontographic.
paleontología, *n.f.* palæontology.
paleozoico, -ca, *a.* palæozoic.
palería, *n.f.* draining of marshy lands.
palero, *n.m.* shovel maker *or* seller; drainer (*of marshes*); sapper.
palestina (1), *n.f.* (*print.*) two-line small pica.
palestino, -na (2), *a.*, *n.m.f.* Palestinian.
palestra, *n.f.* palaestra, palestra; (*fig.*) lists, arena; (*fig.*) contest, tournament.
paléstrico, -ca, *a.* palæstric, palæstrical.
palestrita, *n.m.* athlete, wrestler.
paleta, *n.f.* fire-shovel; palette; iron ladle, small shovel, trowel; (*anat.*) shoulder-blade; (*aer.*, *mech.*, *naut.*) blade (*of a screw-propeller*); (*hydrost.*) paddle board; ***de paleta,*** opportunely; ***en dos paletas,*** briefly, shortly.
paletada, *n.f.* trowelful (*of mortar*).
paletazo, *n.m.* thrust with a bull's horn.
paletear, *v.t.* to row ineffectively.
paletilla, *n.f.* little fire-shovel; shoulder-blade; cartilage of the sternum *or* xiphoid; short candlestick.
paletó, *n.m.* paletot.
paleto, *n.m.* fallow-deer; (*coll.*) country bumpkin, yokel.
paletón, *n.m.* bit, web (*of a key*).
paletoque, *n.m.* dress like a scapulary; defensive jacket.
palhuén, *n.m.* (*Chi.*) thorny shrub.
palia, *n.f.* altar-cloth; veil before the tabernacle; pall, square piece of linen covering the chalice.
paliación, *n.f.* palliation, extenuation; alleviation.
paliadamente, *adv.* dissemblingly.
paliar, *v.t.* to palliate, mitigate, extenuate.
paliativo, -va, paliatorio, -ria, *a.* palliative, mitigating.
palidecer [9], *v.i.* to turn pale, pale.
palidez, *n.f.* paleness, wanness, pallor.
pálido, -da, *a.* pallid, pale, wan.
palillero, *n.m.* toothpick-case; maker *or* seller of toothpicks.
palillo, *n.m.* small stick; knitting-needle case; bobbin (*for lace*); toothpick; tobacco stem; drumstick; (*coll.*) table-talk, chit-chat; (*pl.*) castanets; knitting needles; chop-sticks; rudiments, first principles; trifles; small pins (*put on the centre of the billiard table in certain games*).
palimpsesto, *n.m.* palimpsest.
palingenesia, *n.f.* palingenesia.
palinodia, *n.f.* palinode, recantation.
palio, *n.m.* pallium, short mantle; canopy.
palique, *n.m.* (*coll.*) small talk, chit-chat.
palisandro, *n.m.* rosewood.
palito, *n.m.* little stick.
palitoque, palitroque, *n.m.* rough, ill-shaped stick.
paliza, *n.f.* beating.
palizada, *n.f.* palisade, stockade; paling.
palma, *n.f.* (*anat.*, *bot.*) palm; sole (*of hoof*); ***ganar*** or ***llevarse la palma,*** to take the palm; (*fig.*) to take the cake; (*pl.*) clapping; ***andar en palmas,*** to be generally applauded.
palmacristi, *n.f.* (*bot.*) castor-oil palm *or* plant.
palmada, *n.f.* slap; clap; (*pl.*) hand-clapping, applause.
palmar (1), *a.* palmar; clear, evident. — *n.m.* palm-grove; fuller's thistle.
palmar (2), *v.i.* (*coll.*) to kick the bucket; ***palmarla,*** (*coll.*) to kick the bucket, snuff it.
palmario, -ria, *a.* obvious, evident.
palmatoria, *n.f.* ferule; candlestick.
palmeado, -da, *a.* palmiped, web-footed; (*bot.*) palmate.
palmear, *v.t.* to slap. — *v.i.* to clap hands.
palmejar, *n.m.* (*naut.*) thick stuff.
palmeo, *n.m.* measuring by spans.
palmera, *n.f.* palm tree.
palmero, *n.m.* palmer, pilgrim; keeper of palms.
palmesano, -na, *a.*, *n.m.f.* (native) of Palma de Mallorca.
palmeta, *n.f.* ferule; cane; cane-stroke.
palmetazo, *n.m.* blow with a cane.
palmiche, *n.m.* royal palm; palm nut.
palmífero, -ra, *a.* palmiferous.
palmilla, *n.f.* blue woollen cloth; inner sole (*of a shoe*).
palmípedo, -da, *a.*, *n.m.f.* (*orn.*) palmiped, web-footed.
palmitieso, -sa, *a.* flat-hoofed.
palmito, *n.m.* (*bot.*) dwarf fan-palm, palmetto; palm sprout; (*fig.*, *coll.*) woman's face *or* figure.
palmo, *n.m.* (*anat.*) palm; span, hand-breadth; game of span-farthing; ***palmo a palmo,*** inch by inch; ***crecer a palmos,*** to shoot up, grow by leaps and bounds; ***dejar con un palmo de narices,*** to disappoint, leave crestfallen.
palmotear, *v.i.* to clap.
palmoteo, *n.m.* clapping, applause; caning.
palo, *n.m.* stick, pole; mast; swipe, clout, whack, wallop; gallows; garrote; stalk; suit (*cards*); stroke (*writing*); wood; ***palo de Campeche*** or ***de tinte,*** logwood; ***palo dulce,*** liquorice; (*naut.*) ***palo de marca,*** buoy; ***palo santo,*** lignum vitæ; ***de tal palo, tal astilla,*** like father, like son *or* a chip off the old block; ***dar un palo a,*** to give a pasting, clobber; ***estar del mismo palo,*** to be in the same boat; (*pl.*) blows, beating; billiard pins; ***dar de palos,*** to thrash, drub; ***liarse a palos,*** to begin to lay into one another.
paloma, *n.f.* (*orn.*) pigeon, dove; ***paloma buchona,*** pouter; ***paloma brava*** or ***silvestre,*** rock-dove; ***paloma torcaz,*** wood-pigeon; ***paloma zorita,*** stock dove; ***paloma mensajera,*** carrier pigeon; ***paloma casera,*** domestic pigeon. — *n.m.* (*fig.*) dove, soft-liner.
palomadura, *n.f.* (*naut.*) boltrope tie.
palomar, *n.m.* pigeon-house, dovecot; hard-twisted twine.
palomariego, -ga, *a.* domestic (of pigeons).
palomear, *v.i.* to shoot *or* breed pigeons.
palomera, *n.f.* small dovecot; bleak place.
palomería, *n.f.* pigeon-shooting.
palomero, *n.m.* dealer in doves *or* pigeons.
palometa, *n.f.* (*Hisp. Am.*) pomfret.
palomilla, *n.f.* young pigeon; grain moth; wing nut; wall bracket; (*print.*) galley rack; (*bot.*) common fumitory; horse's back; chrysalis; peak of a pack-saddle; milk-white horse; (*pl.*) white-caps.
palomina, *n.f.* pigeon dung; (*bot.*) fumitory.
palomino, *n.m.* young pigeon.
palomo, *n.m.* cock-pigeon.
palón, *n.m.* (*her.*) guidon.
palor, *n.m.* pallor, paleness.
palotada, *n.f.* stroke with a drumstick; ***no dar palotada,*** to do *or* say nothing right; not to do a stroke of work.
palote, *n.m.* stick, drumstick, ruler; downstroke in penmanship.
paloteado, *n.m.* rustic dance; scuffle.
palotear, *v.i.* to clash, scuffle; to wrangle.
paloteo, *n.m.* fight with sticks.
palpable, *a.* palpable; clear, obvious, evident.
palpadura, *n.f.*, **palpamiento,** *n.m.* (*med.*) feeling, touching, palpation, palpability, palpableness.
palpallén, *n.m.* (*Chi.*) flower-bearing shrub.
palpar, *v.t.* to touch, feel; to grope through; to see as self-evident; (*med.*) to palpate. — **palparse,** *v.r.* to be felt, make itself felt, be obvious.
pálpebra, *n.f.* eyelid.
palpitación, *n.f.* palpitation, throbbing.

palpitante, *a.* palpitating, vibrating; burning (*question*).
palpitar, *v.i.* to palpitate, pulsate, throb, vibrate; to be felt, make itself felt.
pálpito, *n.m.* (*Hisp. Am.*) thrill, excitement; (*Hisp. Am.*) premonition; (*coll.*) hunch.
palpos, *n.m.pl.* (*zool.*) palps, palpi.
palta, *n.f.* alligator pear, avocado pear.
palúdico, -ca, *a.* paludal, malarial.
paludismo, *n.m.* paludism, malaria.
paludoso, -sa, *a.* marshy, swampy.
palurdo, -da, *a.* rustic, boorish. — *n.m.f.* rustic, yokel, country bumpkin.
palustre, *a.* marshy, boggy, fenny. — *n.m.* trowel.
pallaco, *n.m.* (*Chi.*) pay-dirt (*recovered from a derelict mine*).
pallador, *n.m.* (*Hisp. Am.*) minstrel, roving singer.
pallar, *v.t.* (*Per.*) to extract the richest part from (*minerals*). — *n.m.* Peruvian bean.
pallete, *n.m.* (*naut.*) fender.
pallón, *n.m.* button of gold, assay of gold by cupellation.
pamamdabuán, *n.m.* (*Philip.*) snake boat, large dugout.
pambil, *n.m.* (*Ec.*) small palm tree.
pamela, *n.f.* straw hat.
pamema, *n.f.* (*coll.*) trifle, bagatelle; nonsense, rubbish.
pampa, *n.f.* (*Hisp. Am.*) pampa.
pámpana, *n.f.* vine leaf.
pampanada, *n.f.* juice of vine shoots.
pampanaje, *n.m.* abundance of vine shoots; (*fig.*) empty words.
pampanilla, *n.f.* loin-cloth.
pámpano, *n.m.* tendril, vine shoot; vine leaf; (*ichth.*) gilthead.
pampanoso, -sa, *a.* abounding in tendrils, shoots *or* leaves.
pampeano, -na, *a.*, *n.m.f.* (*Hisp. Am.*) (native) of *or* from the pampa.
pampear, *v.i.* (*Hisp. Am.*) to travel over the pampa.
pampero, -ra, *a.*, *n.m.f.* (native) of *or* from the pampa. — *n.m.* pampero wind.
pampirolada, *n.f.* garlic sauce; (*coll.*) silly thing.
pamplina, *n.f.* (*bot.*) chickweed; (*coll.*) trifle; nonsense, rubbish.
pamporcino, *n.m.* (*bot.*) sow-bread, cyclamen.
pamposado, -da, *a.* lazy, idle.
pampringada, *n.f.* dunked toast; (*coll.*, *fig.*) rubbish.
pan, *n.m.* bread; loaf; wafer; gold- *or* silver-leaf; ***pan ázimo,*** unleavened bread; ***pan de azúcar,*** sugar loaf; ***pan de oro,*** gold leaf; (*bot.*) ***pan y quesillo,*** shepherd's purse; ***pan tierno,*** fresh bread; ***pan duro,*** stale bread; ***tierras de pan llevar,*** wheat-growing land; ***es pan bendito, es más bueno que el pan,*** he's as good as gold; ***es pan comido,*** it's as easy as pie, it's a push-over, it's dead easy; ***contigo, pan y cebolla,*** love in a garret, love on a shoestring; ***llamar al pan pan y al vino vino,*** to call a spade a spade; ***con su pan se lo coma,*** let him stew in his own juice, he's made his bed—let him lie on it; ***hacer un pan con unas tortas,*** to make a botch; ***tener a pan y agua,*** to keep on bread and water; ***dame pan y dime tonto,*** as long as I get what I want you can say what you like.
pana, *n.f.* velveteen, corduroy; (*naut.*) limberboard.
pánace, *n.f.* (*bot.*) opopanax.
panacea, *n.f.* panacea.
panadear, *v.t.* to make (*flour*) into bread. — *v.i.* to make bread (*for sale*).
panadeo, *n.m.* baking bread.
panadería, *n.f.* baker's shop, bakery; baking business.
panadero, -ra, *a.* (pertaining to) bread. — *n.m.f.* baker. — *n.f.* baker's wife. — *n.m.pl.* (**panaderos**) Spanish dance.
panadizo, panarizo, *n.m.* whitlow; (*coll.*) pale and sickly person.
panado, -da, *a.* (bread) soaked in water for sick persons.
panal, *n.m.* honeycomb; hornet's nest; sponge sugar.
panamá, *n.m.* Panama hat.
panameño, -ña, *a.*, *n.m.f.* Panamanian.
panamericanismo, *n.m.* Pan-Americanism.
panamericano, -na, *a.* pan-American.
panarra, *n.m.* simpleton, blockhead, dolt.
panatela, *n.f.* sponge-cake.
panática, *n.f.* (*naut.*) provision of bread.
panca, *n.f.* (*Hisp. Am.*) corn husk; (*Philip.*) fishing boat.
pancada, *n.f.* wholesale disposal of goods.
pancarpia, *n.f.* garland.
pancarta, *n.f.* placard.
pancera, *n.f.* stomach-armour.
pancilla, *n.f.* (*print.*) roman.
pancista, *a.* (*coll.*, *polit.*) one who sits on the fence, one who runs with the hare and hunts with the hounds.
panco, *n.m.* (*Philip.*) coasting vessel.
páncreas, *n.m. inv.* (*anat.*) pancreas.
pancreático, -ca, *a.* pancreatic.
pancreatina, *n.f.* pancreatin.
Pancho, *n.m.* (*Hisp. Am.*) Frank.
pancho, *n.m.* (*ichth.*) spawn of the sea bream. — *a.* calm, unruffled; (*coll.*) ***quedarse tan pancho,*** to remain perfectly calm, quite unperturbed, not to turn a hair.
panda (1), *n.f.* cloister gallery.
panda (2), *n.f.* (*coll.*) gang, mob, crowd.
panda (3), *n.m.* (*zool.*) panda.
pandear, *v.i.* to warp, sag, bulge.
pandectas, *n.f.pl.* (*law*) pandects; (*com.*) index-book.
pandemonio, *n.m.* pandemonium.
pandeo, *n.m.* warping, sagging, bulging.
panderada, *n.f.* tambourines; stroke with a tambourine; (*coll.*) silly proposition, nonsense.
panderazo, *n.m.* blow with a tambourine.
pandereta, *n.f.* tambourine.
panderete, *n.m.* small tambourine; ***tabique de panderete,*** thin brick partition.
panderetear, *v.i.* to play on the tambourine.
pandereteo, *n.m.* beating of the tambourine; merriment.
panderetero, *n.m.* one who beats the tambourine; tambourine-maker.
pandero, *n.m.* tambourine; paper-kite; (*coll.*) jabberer, silly talker.
pandiculación, *n.f.* (*met.*) pandiculation, gaping.
pandilla, *n.f.* gang, band, party; clique.
pandillero, pandillista, *n.m.* fomenter of factions; gang leader.
pando, -da (4), *a.* bulgy; slow-moving.
pandorga, *n.f.* (*coll.*) fat, bulky woman; (*prov.*) kite.
panecillo, *n.m.* roll.
panegírico, -ca, *a.* panegyrical. — *n.m.* panegyric, eulogy.
panegirista, *n.m.f.* panegyrist, encomiast, eulogist.
panegirizar [C], *v.t.*, *v.i.* to panegyrize, eulogize, extol.
panel, *n.m.* panel.
panela, *n.f.* maize-cake; brown sugar; (*her.*) panel.
panera, *n.f.* pannier, bread-basket; granary.
panero, *n.m.* baker's basket.
paneslavismo, *n.m.* Pan-Slavism.
panetela, *n.f.* panada; (*Hisp. Am.*) sponge-cake; cigar.
panetería, *n.f.* pantry (*of royal palace*).
panetero, *n.m.* pantler.

pánfilo, -la, *a., n.m.f.* simple-minded (individual), foolish *or* gullible (fellow *or* creature).
panfleto, *n.m.* lampoon.
pangelín, *n.m.* angelin tree.
paniaguado, *n.m.* protegé.
pánico, -ca, *a.* of Pan; panic. — *n.m.* panic.
panícula, *n.f.* panicle.
panículo, *n.m.* panniculus.
paniego, -ga, *a.* wheat-producing; (*coll.*) keen on bread.
panificación, *n.f.* panification, bread-making.
panificadora, *n.f.* bakery.
panificar [A], *v.t.* to make into bread; to make into wheat land. — *v.i.* to make bread.
panislamista, *a., n.m.f.* Pan-Islamist.
panizo, *n.m.* panic-grass; Indian corn; (*Hisp. Am.*) mineral bed.
panocha, ponoja, *n.f.* ear (*of maize*); panicle; bunch.
panoli(s), *n.m.* nitwit.
panoplia, *n.f.* panoply; collection of arms.
panóptico, -ca, *a.* panoptic. — *n.m.* panopticon.
panorama, *n.m.* panorama.
panorámico, -ca, *a.* panoramic.
panormitano, -na, *a., n.m.f.* (native) of Palermo.
panoso, -sa, *a.* mealy.
pantagruélico, -ca, *a.* Pantagruelian; ***comida pantagruélica,*** Gargantuan meal.
pantalán, *n.m.* (*Philip.*) pier.
pantalón, *n.m.* pair of trousers; ***pantalón tejano*** or ***vaquero,*** jeans.
pantalla, *n.f.* lampshade; screen; ***pantalla de chimenea,*** fire-screen.
pantanal, *n.m.* swampy, marshy ground.
pantano, *n.m.* marsh, swamp; reservoir.
pantanoso, -sa, *a.* swampy, boggy, marshy, fenny.
pantasana, *n.f.* fishing seine.
panteísmo, *n.m.* pantheism.
panteísta, *n.m.f.* pantheist.
panteístico, -ca, *a.* pantheistic.
panteón, *n.m.* pantheon; mausoleum.
pantera, *n.f.* (*zool.*) panther; (*min.*) yellow agate.
pantógrafo, *n.m.* pantograph.
pantómetra, *n.f.* pantometer.
pantomima, *n.f.* pantomime, dumb show.
pantomímico, -ca, *a.* pantomimic.
pantomimo, *n.m.* pantomimist, mimic.
pantoque, *n.m.* (*naut.*) bilge.
pantorrilla, *n.f.* calf (*of the leg*).
pantorrillera, *n.f.* padded stocking.
pantorrilludo, -da, *a.* having large *or* thick calves.
pantuflazo, *n.m.* blow with a slipper.
pantuflo, *n.m.*, **pantufla,** *n.f.* slipper; babouche.
panuco, *n.m.* (*Chi.*) handful of toasted flour.
panucho, *n.m.* (*Mex.*) omelet of corn-meal crust with meat.
panudo, *a.* (*Cub.*) firm (*avocado pear*).
panul, *n.m.* (*Chi.*) celery.
panza, *n.f.* belly, paunch.
panzada, *n.f.* bellyful; (*coll.*) push with the belly.
panzón, -zona, *a.* big-bellied. — *n.m.f.* big-bellied *or* pot-bellied person.
panzudo, -da, *a.* big-bellied, pot-bellied.
pañal, *n.m.* swaddling-cloth; ***estar en pañales,*** to be in its infancy; (*fig.*) to be wet behind the ears.
pañería, *n.f.* draper's shop, drapery.
pañero, -ra, *a.* (pertaining to) drapery. — *n.m.f.* draper, woollen-draper, clothier.
pañete, *n.m.* inferior *or* light cloth; (*pl.*) fisherman's trunks; (*art.*) loincloth (*in representations of the Crucifixion*); (*Col.*) plastering.
pañil, *n.m.* (*Chi.*) small tree with yellow flowers and vulnerary leaves (*Buddleia globosa*).
pañito, pañizuelo, *n.m.* small cloth; (*Mex.*) small handkerchief.
paño, *n.m.* cloth; face flannel, (*Am.*) washrag; tapestry; small plot (*of land*); length, stretch, section (*of a wall*); (*sew.*) breadth; (*naut.*) sail-cloth; ***ser del mismo paño,*** to be of the same ilk; ***soy su paño de lagrimas,*** he cries on my shoulder; (*theat.*) ***al paño,*** off-stage; ***conocer el paño,*** to know one's business; to know the type; ***paños menores,*** underclothes; ***paños calientes,*** half-measures.
pañol, *n.m.* (*naut.*) store-room; ***pañol de proa,*** boatswain's store-room; ***pañol de pólvora,*** magazine.
pañolería, *n.f.* handkerchief shop *or* factory.
pañolero de Santabárbara, *n.m.* (*naut.*) gunner's yeoman.
pañoleta, *n.f.* triangular shawl.
pañolón, *n.m.* large square shawl.
pañoso, -sa, *a.* ragged, tattered. — *n.f.* (*coll.*) cloak.
pañuelo, *n.m.* handkerchief; neckcloth, kerchief; shawl.
papá, *n.m.* papa, daddy.
papa, *n.m.* pope. — *n.f.* (*coll.*) food, grub; fib, hoax; potato; (*orn.*) goldfinch.
papacho, *n.m.* (*Mex.*) cuddle, caress.
papada, *n.f.* double chin; dewlap.
papadilla, *n.f.* fleshy part under the chin.
papado, *n.m.* pontificate, papacy.
papafigo, *n.m.* (*orn.*) fig-pecker; golden oriole.
papagayo, -ya, *n.m.f.* parrot; (*ichth.*) rock bass; (*bot.*) three-coloured amaranth; white arum.
papahigo, *n.m.* winter cap; Balaclava helmet; (*naut.*) lower sail.
papahuevos, *n.m. inv.* simpleton.
papal, *a.* papal.
papalina, *n.f.* cap with ear-flaps; coif; drunken fit.
papalote, *n.m.* (*Mex.*) kite.
papamoscas, *n.m. inv.* (*orn.*) fly-catcher; simpleton.
papanatas, *n.m. inv.* ninny, simpleton.
papandujo, -ja, *a.* (*coll.*) over-ripe, mushy.
papar, *v.t.* to eat, swallow, gulp down; to pay little attention to; ***papar moscas,*** to gape.
páparo, *n.m.* simple-witted fellow.
paparrabias, *n.m.f. inv.* (*coll.*) testy, fretful, peevish person.
paparrasolla, *n.f.* hobgoblin.
paparrucha, *n.f.* humbug, hoax, fake; rubbish, drivel.
papasal, *n.m.* boy's game; bagatelle, trifle.
papaya, *n.f.* papaw.
papayo, *n.m.* (*bot.*) papaw tree.
papazgo, *n.m.* papacy, pontificate.
papel, *n.m.* paper; sheet of paper; role, part; ***papel (de) celo,*** transparent adhesive tape; ***papel esmeril,*** emery paper; ***papel de lija,*** sandpaper; ***papel de estraza,*** coarse wrapping paper; ***papel de forrar,*** brown paper; ***papel de fumar,*** cigarette paper; ***papel moneda,*** paper money; ***papel sellado*** or ***timbrado,*** stamped paper; ***papel del Estado,*** government bonds; ***papel secante,*** blotting paper; ***papel de seda,*** tissue paper; ***papel de estaño,*** tin-foil; ***papel higiénico,*** toilet paper; ***papel pintado,*** wallpaper; ***papel de tornasol,*** litmus paper; ***papel volante,*** small leaflet; ***papeles mojados,*** so much waste paper; ***hacer, desempeñar*** or ***jugar un papel,*** to play a part; ***hacer buen papel,*** to put up a good performance *or* show, cut a good figure; ***hacer un papel poco airoso,*** to cut a sorry figure; ***esto hará el papel,*** this will do the job *or* trick.
papelear, *v.i.* to search *or* rummage through papers; to cut a figure.
papeleo, *n.m.* paper work; red-tape.
papelera, *n.f.* [PAPELERO].
papelería, *n.f.* stationer's; untidy heap of papers.

papelero, -ra, *a.* (of) paper; boastful, ostentatious. — *n.m.f.* paper-maker; stationer. — *n.f.* waste paper basket, (*Am.*) waste basket; paper case.
papeleta, *n.f.* slip of paper; card; ticket; (*Hisp. Am.*) ticket (*for a motoring offence*); (examination) question *or* result paper; ballot paper; (*coll.*) tricky problem, tough proposition.
papelillo, *n.m.* scrap of paper; cigarette paper.
papelina, *n.f.* wine-glass; poplin; (*coll.*) bout of drunkenness.
papelista, *n.m.f.* scribbler; paper-maker; stationer; keeper of documents.
papelito, *n.m.* small paper; curl-paper.
papelón, -lona, *a.* (*coll.*) boastful; bluffing. — *n.m.* (*coll., fig.*) rubbish, trash; (*coll., fig.*) ***hacer un papelón,*** to cut a sorry figure, make a fool of o.s.
papelonear, *v.i.* (*coll.*) to boast; to bluff.
papelorio, *n.m.* wretched *or* trashy bit of paper.
papelote, papelucho, *n.m.* wretched *or* trashy bit of paper, rubbish; (*fig.*) rag, gutter press.
paperas, *n.f.pl.* mumps; goitre.
papero, *n.m.* pot in which pap is made.
papialbillo, *n.m.* (*zool.*) weasel.
papila, *n.f.* (*med.*) papilla.
papilar, *a.* papillary, papillous, papillose.
papilla, *n.f.* pap; guile, deceit, trick.
papillote, *n.m.* papillote, curl-paper.
papión, *n.m.* (*zool.*) papion.
papiro, *n.m.* (*bot.*) Egyptian papyrus.
papirolada, *n.f.* (*coll.*) garlic sauce; frivolity.
papirotada, *n.f.*, **papirotazo,** *n.m.* fillip, flick.
papirote, *n.m.* fillip.
papisa, *n.f. only in* ***la papisa Juana,*** Pope Joan.
papismo, *n.m.* papism.
papista, *n.m.f.* papist.
papo, *n.m.* double-chin; dewlap; thistledown; food (*given to a bird of prey*); (*fowl's*) gizzard; puff (in garments); ***hablar de papo,*** to speak idly *or* presumptuously; ***estar en papo de buitre,*** to be in s.o.'s grip; ***hablar papo a papo,*** to speak bluntly, plainly.
papudo, -da, *a.* double-chinned.
papujado, -da, *a.* swollen, full-gorged (*of birds*); (*fig.*) thick; swollen, puffed up.
paquear, *v.t., v.i.* to snipe (at).
paquebote, *n.m.* packet-boat, steamer.
paquete, *n.m.* packet, parcel; (*coll.*) ticket (*fine, penalty*); (*naut.*) packet-boat; ***paquete turístico,*** package tour.
paquetería, *n.f.* (*com.*) shop; retail trade.
paquidermo, *n.m.* (*zool.*) pachyderm.
Paquistán, *n.m.* Pakistan.
paquistaní, *a., n.m.f.* Pakistani.
par, *a.* even. — *n.m.* pair; couple; equal; peer; (*elec.*) cell; angle rafter; ***a pares,*** in pairs, in twos; ***al par con,*** on a level with; ***al par que,*** at the same time as *or* that; as well as; ***de par en par,*** wide open; ***pares y nones,*** odds and evens; (*elec., motor.*) ***par de torsión, par motor,*** torque; ***sin par,*** matchless, peerless. — *n.f.* par; ***a la par,*** at the same time; jointly; at par; ***ir a la par,*** to go halves; (*pl.*) placenta.
para, *prep.* for; to; in order to; ***tengo para mí,*** I hold, it's my view (that); ***¿para qué?*** what for? why?; ***para ser la primera vez, no está mal,*** it's not bad for the first attempt; ***para vergüenza suya,*** to his shame; ***para entonces,*** by then; ***es bueno para con él,*** he's kind to him; ***te lo digo para que vengas pronto,*** I'm telling you so that you get here early; ***para siempre,*** for ever; ***para siempre jamás,*** for ever and ever; ***decir para su capote,*** to say to o.s.
paraba, *n.f.* (*Bol.*) parrot.
parabién, *n.m.* congratulation.
paraboidal, *a.* (*geom.*) paraboliform.
parábola, *n.f.* parable; (*geom.*) parabola.
parabolano, *n.m.* priest of the orthodox primitive church; one who uses parables; hoaxer.
parabólico, -ca, *a.* parabolical.
paraboloide, *n.m.* paraboloid.
parabrisas, *n.m. inv.* windscreen, (*Am.*) windshield.
paraca, *n.m.* (*Hisp. Am.*) strong breeze.
paracaídas, *n.m. inv.* parachute.
paracaidista, *n.m.* parachutist, paratrooper.
paracleto, paráclito, *n.m.* Paraclete, Holy Ghost.
paracronismo, *n.m.* parachronism.
parachispas, *n.m. inv.* (*elec.*) suppressor.
parachoques, *n.m. inv.* bumper, (*Am.*) fender.
parada (I), *n.f.* stop; halt, pause; relay, post, stage; stud farm; dam; bid, stake; (*fenc.*) parry; (*mil.*) parade, review; (*sport*) catch, save; ***parada de taxis,*** taxi rank, stand *or* stance; ***parada en seco,*** dead stop, pulling-up dead.
paradera, *n.f.* sluice, floodgate; fishing-net.
paradero, *n.m.* whereabouts; halt; end.
paradeta, paradilla, *n.f.* short-stop (*in dancing*); (*pl.*) dance.
paradigma, *n.m.* paradigm; pattern.
paradigmático, -ca, *a.* paradigm; forming a pattern; characteristic; (*fig.*) typical.
paradina, *n.f.* round enclosure, corral.
paradisíaco, -ca, *a.* paradisiacal, like paradise, heavenly, out of this world.
paradislero, *n.m.* hunter waiting for his game; newsmonger.
parado, -da (2), *a.* slow, diffident, lifeless; out-of-work, unemployed.
paradójico, -ca, *a.* [PARADOJO]
paradojo, -ja, *a.* paradoxical. — *n.f.* paradox.
parador, *n.m.* hostelry; State-run hotel.
paraestatal, *a.* semi-official.
parafernales (bienes), *n.m.pl.* (*law*) paraphernalia.
parafina, *n.f.* paraffin.
parafrasear, *v.t.* to paraphrase.
paráfrasis, *n.f. inv.* paraphrase.
parafraste, *n.m.* paraphrast.
parafrástico, -ca, *a.* paraphrastic, paraphrastical.
paragolpes, *n.m. inv.* bumper, (*Am.*) fender.
paragonar, *v.t.* to compare.
paraguas, *n.m. inv.* umbrella.
paraguatán, *n.m.* (*bot.*) madder.
paraguay, *n.m.* (*orn.*) parrot.
paraguayano, -na, paraguayo, -ya, *a., n.m.f.* Paraguayan.
paragüería, *n.f.* umbrella shop.
paragüero, -ra, *n.m.f.* maker *or* seller of umbrellas. — *n.m.* umbrella stand.
parahuso, *n.m.* pump drill.
paraíso, *n.m.* paradise; (*theat.*) gods.
paraje, *n.m.* place, spot.
paral, *n.m.* scaffolding prop *or* pole; (*naut.*) launching-trough.
paraláctico, -ca, *a.* parallactic.
paralaje, *n.f.* (*astron.*) parallax.
paralelepípedo, *n.m.* (*geom.*) parallelepiped.
paralelismo, *n.m.* parallelism, parallel.
paralelizar [C], *v.t.* to parallel.
paralelo, -la, *a.* parallel. — *n.m.* parallel.
paralelogramo, *n.m.* parallelogram.
Paralipómenos, *n.m.pl.* Book of Chronicles.
parálisis, *n.f. inv.* paralysis.
paralítico, -ca, *a.* paralytic, palsied.
paralización, *n.f.* paralysation; (*com.*) stagnation.
paralizado, -da, *a.* (*com.*) dull, stagnant, flat; strike-bound.
paralizar [C], *v.t.* to paralyse; to stop, bring to a stop *or* halt.
paralogismo, *n.m.* (*log.*) paralogism, false reasoning.

paralogizar [C], *v.t.* to paralogize.
paramentar, *v.t.* to embellish, adorn, bedeck.
paramento, *n.m.* hanging, ornament, embellishment; caparison, trappings; (*arch.*) facing; (*eccles.*) ***paramentos sacerdotales,*** robes and ornaments.
paramera, *n.f.* high bleak tableland *or* heathland; bleak and barren country.
parámetro, *n.m.* (*geom.*) parameter.
paramilitar, *a.* paramilitary.
páramo, *n.m.* high bleak tableland *or* heathland, wilderness; (*fig.*) bleak windy spot.
parancero, *n.m.* bird-catcher.
parangón, *n.m.* comparison.
parangona, *n.f.* (*print.*) paragon type.
parangonar, *v.t.* to compare, place on a level (***con,*** with).
paranínfico, -ca, *a.* (*arch.*) having statues of nymphs.
paraninfo, *n.m.* best man at a wedding; hall, auditorium (*of university*).
paranomasia, *n.f.* paranomasia.
paranza, *n.f.* hut *or* hide for huntsmen.
parao, *n.m.* (*Philip.*) passenger vessel.
paraparo, *n.m.* (*Ven.*) soapbark tree.
parapetar, *v.t.* (*fort.*) to build a parapet round. — **parapetarse,** *v.r.* to shelter behind a parapet.
parapeto, *n.m.* (*fort.*) parapet, breastwork; railing.
parapoco, *n.m.f.* (*coll.*) timid person; numskull.
parar, *n.m.* lansquenet. — *v.t.* to stop, halt, check; to parry, ward off; to save; ***parar mientes en,*** to consider; to notice. — **parar(se),** *v.i.* (*v.r.*) to stop, halt; to stay; to end up, finish; ***parar de llover,*** to stop raining; ***fueron a parar a la comisaría,*** they ended up *or* landed in the police station; ***pararse a,*** to stop *or* pause to; (*fig.*) ***¿dónde va a parar?*** there's no comparison!; ***no parar,*** to be always on the go, always at it; ***sin parar,*** constantly, endlessly; ***salir bien*** (***mal***) ***parado,*** to come off well (badly).
pararrayos, *n.m. inv.* lightning rod.
parasceve, *n.f.* Good Friday.
paraselene, *n.f.* (*astron.*) mock-moon.
parasemo, *n.f.* figurehead of a galley.
parasismo, *n.m.* paroxysm.
parasítico, -ca, *a.* parasitic.
parásito, -ta, *a.* parasitic. — *n.m.f.* parasite, sponger.
parasol, *n.m.* parasol, sunshade.
parástade, *n.m.* (*arch.*) anta, pilaster.
parata, *n.f.* artificial land terrace (*on a steep slope*).
paratifoidea, *n.f.* paratyphoid.
paraulata, *n.f.* (*Ven.*) bird like the thrush.
parausar, *v.t.* to drill (*metals*).
parauso, *n.m.* jeweller's bow drill.
Parca, *n.f.* one of the Parcæ *or* fates; (*poet.*) death.
parce, *n.m.* certificate given to grammar-students.
parcela, *n.f.* plot (*of land*).
parcelar, *v.t.* to parcel out, divide up.
parcelario, -ria, *a.* of *or* in small lots *or* holdings.
parcial, *a.* partial; biased.
parcialidad, *n.f.* bias; faction.
parcidad, *n.f.* parsimony, frugality.
parcionero, *n.m.* partner; participant.
parcísimo, -ma, *a. superl.* [PARCO].
parco, -ca, *a.* frugal, sparing.
parcha, *n.f.* (*Hisp. Am.*) passion flower; genus.
parchazo, *n.m.* large plaster; (*naut.*) flapping of a sail; trick.
parche, *n.m.* plaster, sticking-plaster; drum-cover; drum-head; drum; patch; ***poner parches,*** to patch, patch up; (*fig.*) to plug *or* stop up holes.
pardal, *a.* rustic. — *n.m.* (*orn.*) sparrow; linnet; (*zool.*) camelopard; leopard; (*bot.*) wolf's-bane; (*coll.*) crafty fellow.
pardear, *v.i.* to be, look *or* show up dun-coloured.
¡pardiez! *interj.* heavens! by Jove! good gracious!
pardillo, -lla, *a.* dunnish. — *n.m.* (*orn.*) linnet; (*coll.*) clod, yokel, bumpkin.
pardo, -da, *a.* dun, dun-coloured; grey; dull, drab; (*Hisp. Am.*) mulatto. — *n.m.* (*zool.*) leopard; (*Hisp. Am.*) mulatto; ***gramática parda,*** shrewdness, worldly wisdom.
pardusco, -ca, *a.* dunnish.
pareado, -da, *a., n.m.* couplet.
parear, *v.t.* to mate, match, pair, couple.
parecer, *n.m.* opinion, view; look; ***variar de parecer,*** to alter one's opinion; ***soy de parecer que,*** I am of the view that; ***ser de buen parecer,*** to have a good appearance. — [9], *v.i.* to appear, seem, look; ***al parecer, a lo que parece, según parece,*** apparently; ***me parece que no,*** I don't think so; ***¿qué le parece?*** what do you think? how does it strike you? — **parecerse,** *v.r.* (**a**) to look like, resemble; ***se parecen mucho,*** they look very much alike.
parecido, -da, *a.* like, similar; (*pl.*) alike. — *n.m.* likeness, resemblance; ***bien*** (***mal***) ***parecido,*** well- (ill-) favoured.
pared, *n.f.* wall; ***entre cuatro paredes,*** confined; ***las paredes oyen,*** walls have ears; (*fig.*) ***darse contra las paredes,*** to bang one's head against a brick wall; (*fig.*) ***dejar pegado a la pared,*** to floor, knock for six; (*coll.*) ***subirse por las paredes,*** to go up the wall; ***vivir pared por medio con,*** to live next door to; ***pared maestra,*** main wall; ***pared medianera,*** party wall.
paredaño, -ña, *a.* having a wall between.
paredón, *n.m.* (ugly) big wall; stark isolated wall; execution wall; ***¡todos al paredón!*** shoot the lot of them!
parejo, -ja, *a.* equal; similar; even; ***por parejo,*** on equal terms, on a par. — *n.f.* pair; couple; team; brace; partner; ***por parejas,*** in pairs, in twos; ***correr parejas con,*** to be on a par with; ***la pareja,*** two Civil Guards.
parejura, *n.f.* equality; similarity.
paremiología, *n.f.* treatise on proverbs.
parentela, *n.f.* kindred, kinsfolk, relations.
parentesco, *n.m.* kinship, relationship.
paréntesis, *n.m. inv.* parenthesis; gap, pause; brackets; ***entre paréntesis,*** in brackets; (*fig.*) incidentally, in passing.
pareo, *n.m.* pairing, coupling, matching.
parergon, *n.m.* additional ornament.
pares, *n.f.pl.* (*anat.*) placenta.
paresa, *n.f.* peeress.
pargo, *n.m.* (*ichth.*) porgy.
parhelio, -lia, *n.m.f.* parhelion, mock sun.
parhilera, *n.f.* (*arch.*) ridgepole, ridgepiece.
paria, *n.f.* pariah, outcast; low caste.
parición, *n.f.* calving-time.
parida, *n.f.* woman lately delivered of a child.
paridad, *n.f.* parity.
paridera, *a.* fruitful, prolific. — *n.f.* parturition; time and place where cattle bring forth their young.
pariente, -ta, *n.m.f.* relative, kinsman, kinswoman. — *n.f.* (*coll.*) wife, missus.
parietal, *a.* (*anat.*) parietal; relating to walls.
parietaria, *n.f.* (*bot.*) pellitory.
parificar [A], *v.t.* to exemplify.
parihuela, *n.f.* stretcher.
parima, *n.f.* (*Arg.*) large heron of the pampas.
parir, *v.t., v.i.* to bring forth, give birth (to); to lay eggs, spawn; ***poner a parir,*** to call every name under the sun.
parisiena, *n.f.* (*print.*) five-point type.
parisiense, parisino, -na, *a., n.m.f.* Parisian.
paritario, -ria, *a.* based on equality.
parla, *n.f.* gab, chatter; speech.

parlador, -ra, *n.m.f.* chattering person.
parladuría, *n.f.* loquacity, impertinent speech.
parlaembalde, *n.m.f.* (*coll.*) chatterbox.
parlamental, *a.* parliamentary.
parlamentar, *v.i.* to parley.
parlamentario, -ria, *a.* parliamentary, parliamentarian. — *n.m.f.* member of parliament, parliamentarian. — *n.m.* parliamentary, flag of truce.
parlamentarismo, *n.m.* parliamentary system *or* government.
parlamento, *n.m.* parliament; (*theat.*) speech; (*mil.*) flag of truce; parley.
parlanchín, -china, *a.* chattering, babbling. — *n.m.f.* chatterer, babbler.
parlante, *a.* speaking, talking.
parlar, *v.i.* to chatter, babble.
parlatorio, *n.m.* parley; parlour.
parlería, *n.f.* chattering, jabbering.
parlero, -ra, *a.* loquacious, talkative, garrulous; (*poet.*) purling (*brook*); chirping (*birds*). — *n.m.f.* chatterer; tattler, tale-teller.
parleta, *n.f.* (*coll.*) chat; tale, gossip.
parlotear, *v.i.* to chatter, prattle, prate.
parloteo, *n.m.* prattle, talk.
Parnaso, *n.m.* (*poet.*) Parnassus, Helicon; collection of poems; company of poets.
parné, *n.m.* (*sl.*) cash, dibs, lolly.
paro, *n.m.* stop, stoppage; lock-out; unemployment; (*orn.*) tit, tit-mouse.
parodia, *n.f.* parody, travesty.
parodiar, *v.t.* to parody, travesty.
parola, *n.f.* (*coll.*) volubility, gift of the gab; chat, chatter, idle talk.
pároli, *n.m.* triple stakes.
parónimo, -ma, *a.* paronymous. — *n.m.* paronym.
parótida, *n.f.* parotid; mumps.
paroxismal, *a.* paroxysmal.
paroxismo, *n.m.* paroxysm.
parpadear, *v.i.* to blink; to wink.
parpadeo, *n.m.* blinking; winking.
párpado, *n.m.* eyelid.
parpar, *v.i.* to quack.
parque, *n.m.* park; (total) number of vehicles; ***parque de atracciones,*** amusement park, funfair, (*Am.*) carnival; ***parque de bomberos,*** fire station; ***parque zoológico,*** zoological gardens, zoo; ***parque móvil,*** vehicle depot.
parquedad, *n.f.* parsimony, frugality.
parra, *n.f.* vine; honey jar; (*fig.*) ***hoja de parra,*** fig leaf; ***subirse a la parra,*** to go off the deep end.
parrafada, *n.f.* chat; ***echar una parrafada,*** to have a chin-wag.
párrafo, *n.m.* paragraph.
parragón, *n.m.* standard silver for essayers.
parral, *n.m.* vine arbour; straggling vineyard; large earthen jar.
parranda, *n.f.* spree; carousing party.
parrandear, *v.i.* to go on a spree.
parrandista, *n.m.f.* reveller.
parrar, *v.i.* to extend, spread out (*in branches*).
parricida, *n.m.f.* parricide (*person*).
parricidio, *n.m.* parricide (*act*).
parrilla, *n.f.* grill; grill-room; hotel ballroom; ***a la parrilla,*** grilled.
parriza, *n.f.* wild vine.
parro, *n.m.* duck.
párroco, *n.m.* parish priest.
parrocha, *n.f.* sardine.
parroquia, *n.f.* parish; parish church; customers.
parroquial, *a.* parochial. — *n.f.* parish church.
parroquialidad, *n.f.* parochial right.
parroquiano, -na, *a.* parish. — *n.m.f.* (regular) customer.

parsi, *a.*, *n.m.f.* Parsee. — *n.m.* Parsee (*language*).
parsimonia, *n.f.* moderation; tedious slowness.
parsimonioso, -sa, *a.* moderate; tediously slow.
parta, *n.f.* [PARTO].
parte, *n.f.* part; share, lot; spot, place; side, party; ***parte del león,*** lion's share; ***llevar(se) la mejor parte,*** to get the best of it; ***a partes iguales,*** in equal parts; ***de parte a parte,*** right through, completely; ***de parte de,*** from, on behalf of; ***en parte,*** partly; ***por todas partes,*** on all sides, everywhere; ***hacer (las) partes,*** to make a share-out; ***ir a la parte,*** to share, go halves; ***no ser parte en,*** to have no say in; ***por todas partes se va a Roma,*** all roads lead to Rome; ***de ocho días a esta parte,*** within this last week; ***echar una cosa a buena*** or ***mala parte,*** to take a thing in a good *or* bad sense; ***parte de la oración,*** part of speech; ***por una parte,*** on the one hand, in a way; ***por otra parte,*** on the other hand; besides, moreover; ***ponerse de parte de,*** to side with. — *n.m.* bulletin; communiqué; ***parte meteorológico,*** weather report; ***dar parte (de),*** to report.
partear, *v.t.* to assist, deliver (*in childbirth*).
partenogénesis, *n.f.* parthenogenesis.
partera, *n.f.* midwife.
partería, *n.f.* midwifery.
partero, *n.m.* accoucheur.
parterre, *n.m.* flower-bed; garden.
partesana, *n.f.* partisan.
partible, *a.* divisible.
partición, *n.f.* share-out, sharing-out.
particionero, -ra, *a.* participant.
participación, *n.f.* participation; notification; (part) ticket; entry; (*com.*) co-partnership; ***cuenta en participación,*** joint account.
participante, *a.* participating. — *n.m.f.* participant; entrant.
participar, *v.t.* to inform, give notice of. — *v.i.* to participate, share.
partícipe, *a.* participant, sharing. — *n.m.* partner.
participial, *a.* (*gram.*) participial.
participio, *n.m.* participle.
partícula, *n.f.* particle.
particular, *a.* particular; special, peculiar, odd; private. — *n.m.* particular matter *or* subject; private individual; ***sobre este particular,*** on this point, issue; ***no tiene nada de particular,*** there's nothing special *or* surprising about it.
particularidad, *n.f.* particularity; peculiarity; special circumstance.
particularizar [C], *v.t.* to detail, particularize. — **particularizarse,** *v.r.* to make a name for o.s., get a name; to make o.s. conspicuous; to be (an *or* the) odd man out.
partida (I), *n.f.* departure; (*com.*) entry, item; certificate; game; (*mil.*) squad; guerrilla; party, band; (*com.*) shipment, lot, consignment; (*com.*) ***partida doble,*** double entry; ***partida simple,*** single entry; ***las siete partidas,*** the laws of Castile compiled by King Alfonso X; ***jugar una mala partida,*** to play a dirty trick (***a,*** on).
partidario, -ria, *a.* adhering, following, supporting. — *n.m.f.* partisan; adherent, follower, supporter; party-man; district physician; ***ser partidario de,*** to be in favour of; to be a supporter of.
partidismo, *n.m.* bias, party *or* partisan spirit.
partido (I), **-da** (2), *a.* (*her.*) party, parted, *or* parti per pale; free, liberal, munificent.
partido (2), *n.m.* party; profit, usefulness; game, match; district; ***mujer del partido,*** woman of the town; ***tomar partido,*** to resolve, embrace a resolution; to engage, join, enlist; ***sacar partido de,*** to get a lot out of; ***ser un (buen) partido,*** to be an eligible bachelor.
partija, *n.f.* partition.
partimento, partimiento, *n.m.* partition.

partir, *v.t.* to divide, split; to crack, break open; to cut; to share; ***partir por el eje,*** to muck up, throw out of gear. — *v.i.* to leave, start, set out; ***partir de la base de que,*** to work on the assumption that; ***a partir de,*** from, as from, starting from. — **partirse,** *v.r.* ***se me parte el alma de verlo,*** it breaks my heart to see it; (*coll., fig.*) ***no se te partirá el alma,*** you're not exactly killing yourself.

partitivo, -va, *a.* (*gram.*) partitive.

partitura, *n.f.* (*mus.*) score.

parto (1), **-ta,** *a., n.m.f.* Parthian; ***flecha del parto,*** Parthian shot.

parto (2), *n.m.* childbirth, delivery; creation, production; ***parto del ingenio,*** brain child; ***estar de parto,*** to be in labour; ***el parto de los montes,*** much ado about very little.

parturienta, parturiente, *a.* parturient.

párulis, *n.m. inv.* (*med.*) gumboil.

parva (1), *n.f.* unthreshed corn in heaps; threshing.

parvada, *n.f.* unthreshed corn.

parvedad, parvidad, *n.f.* minuteness, littleness; small amount, scantiness.

parvo, -va (2), *a.* small, little; scanty.

parvulario, *n.m.* nursery school, kindergarten.

parvulez, *n.f.* smallness, small size.

párvulo, -la, *a.* very small; innocent; humble, lowly. — *n.m.f.* infant.

pasa (1), *n.f.* raisin; kink (*of hair*); ***pasa de Corinto,*** currant.

pasa (2), *n.f.* (*naut.*) channel.

pasabalas, *n.m. inv.* (*mil.*) ball calibre gauge.

pasable, *a.* passable.

pasacaballo, *n.m.* horse ferry-boat.

pasacalle, *n.m.* lively march, passacaglia.

pasada (1), *n.f.* passage; step, pace; game; trick; ***de pasada,*** in passing; hastily, cursorily; (*coll.*) ***mala pasada,*** bad turn.

pasadero, -ra (1), *a.* supportable, sufferable; passable, fairly good.

pasadera (2), *n.f.* stepping-stone; (*naut.*) spun-yarn.

pasadillo, *n.m.* two-face embroidery.

pasadizo, *n.m.* passage; alley; corridor; hall; aisle.

pasado, -da (2), *a.* past; gone; worn, worn through *or* out; gone bad, rotten; out-of-date; ***pasado de moda,*** out of fashion; ***lo pasado, pasado,*** let bygones be bygones. — *n.m.* past.

pasador, *n.m.* smuggler; sharp arrow; brooch; bolt; clock-peg; linch-pin; fastener; pin, hatpin *or* hairpin; colander; (*naut.*) marline spike.

pasadura, *n.f.* passage; fit of crying.

pasagonzalo, *n.m.* (*coll.*) slight, sharp blow.

pasahilo, *n.m.* thread-guide.

pasaje, *n.m.* passage; ticket, fare; voyage, crossing; passengers.

pasajero, -ra, *a.* passing, transient, transitory. — *n.m.f.* passenger, traveller.

pasamanar, *v.t.* to trim with lace.

pasamanera, *n.f.* lace-woman, lace-maker.

pasamanería, *n.f.* lace-trade, lace-making; fancy trimming, passementerie.

pasamanero, *n.m.* lace-maker, ribbon-maker.

pasamano, *n.m.* hand-rail, banister; passementerie; (*naut.*) gangway.

pasamiento, *n.m.* passage, transit.

pasante, *n.m.* doctor's *or* lawyer's assistant; apprentice; tutor; (*her.*) passant; game of cards.

pasantía, *n.f.* student's profession (law *or* medicine).

pasapán, *n.m.* (*coll.*) throat, gullet.

pasapasa, *n.m.* legerdemain, hocus-pocus.

pasaporte, *n.m.* passport; (*mil.*) furlough.

pasar, *v.t.* to pass; to take *or* carry across; to cross, go across; to go through, undergo, suffer; to tolerate; to spend (*time*); ***pasar a cuchillo,*** to put to the sword; ***pasar de largo,*** to pass by (*on the other side*); ***pasar en claro,*** to omit mentioning; ***pasar las de Caín,*** to go through hell; ***pasar por agua (un huevo),*** to boil (an egg); ***pasar por alto,*** to omit, leave out; ***pasar por las armas,*** to shoot, execute; ***pasar revista a,*** to review; ***pasarlo bien (mal),*** to have a good (bad) time; ***un buen pasar,*** a fair living; ***¡eso no se lo paso!*** I'm not letting him get away with that! — *v.i.* to pass; to go *or* get through; to go by; to go in, enter; ***pasar a,*** to proceed; to go on to; ***pasar de,*** to go beyond; ***pasaré por tu casa,*** I'll call round to your place. — *v. impers.* to happen; ***pase lo que pase,*** come what may; ***¿qué pasa?*** what's up? — **pasarse,** *v.r.* to go over (to); to cross (*the mind*); to pass off; to lose force; to get spoilt *or* worn out; to get *or* work loose; to become stale; to get overcooked; to overdo it; ***pasarse con poco,*** to manage on little; ***pasarse de bueno,*** to be too good *or* kind; ***pasarse de listo,*** to be too clever by half; ***pasarse sin,*** to go without.

pasarela, *n.f.* footbridge; (*naut.*) gangplank; bridge (*on a ship*).

pasatiempo, *n.m.* pastime, amusement, hobby.

pasavante, *n.m.* safe-conduct, permit.

pasavolante, *n.m.* swift *or* hasty thing to do.

pascana, *n.f.* (*Arg., Bol., Ec., Per.*) inn; a halt during a long journey.

pascar [A], *v.i.* (*Bol.*) to encamp.

pascua, *n.f.* Passover; Easter; Christmas; Twelfth-day; Whitsun; ***Pascua de Resurrección, de flores, florida,*** Easter; (*coll.*) ***hacerle la pascua a,*** to mess things up for. — *n.f.pl.* Christmas; ***Pascua(s) de Navidad,*** Christmas; ***de Pascuas a Ramos,*** once in a blue moon; ***dar las pascuas a,*** to wish a Merry Christmas; ***estar como unas pascuas,*** to be as pleased as Punch; ***y santas pascuas,*** and that's that, and that's the lot, and there's an end to it; ***felices pascuas y próspero año nuevo,*** merry Christmas and a happy New Year.

pascual, *a.* paschal, Easter.

pascuilla, *n.f.* Low Sunday.

pase, *n.m.* pass.

paseadero, *n.m.* avenue, public walk.

paseador, -ra, *n.m.f.* walker, stroller.

paseante, *n.m.f.* stroller; ***paseante en corte,*** idler.

pasear, *v.t.* to take for a walk, stroll *or* ride. — **pasear(se),** *v.i., v.r.* to go for a walk, stroll *or* ride; ***pasear la(s) calle(s),*** to wander the streets *or* stroll around.

paseata, *n.f.* walk, drive.

paseo, *n.m.* walk, stroll; drive, ride; avenue, promenade; (*fig.*) walk-over; (*coll.*) ***¡vete a paseo!*** get lost!

pasera, *n.f.* (*prov.*) place where raisins are dried.

pasibilidad, *n.f.* susceptibility.

pasible, *a.* capable of suffering.

pasicorto, -ta, *a.* short-stepped.

pasiego, -ga, *a., n.m.f.* (native) of Pas. — *n.f.* Pas cow; wet nurse.

pasiflora, *n.f.* passion-flower.

pasilargo, -ga, *a.* long-stepped.

pasillo, *n.m.* corridor, passage, (*Am.*) aisle; basting stitch.

pasión, *n.f.* passion.

pasionaria, *n.f.* passion-flower.

pasionario, *n.m.* (*eccles.*) Passion-book.

pasionero, *n.m.* chorister who sings the Passion.

pasito, *adv.* gently, softly. — *n.m.* short step; ***pasito a pasito,*** very gently.

pasitrote, *n.m.* short trot.

pasivo, -va, *a.* passive; on pension; ***clases pasivas,*** old-age pensioners. — *n.m.* (*com.*) liabilities; debit side.

pasmar, *v.t.* to chill, frostbite; to strike dumb, stun, amaze. — **pasmarse,** *v.r.* to be astonished.

pasmarota, pasmarotada, *n.f.* (*coll.*) display of amazement *or* shock.

pasmo, *n.m.* astonishment, amazement; chill; (*med.*) tetanus, lockjaw.

pasmoso, -sa, *a.* marvellous, wonderful.
paso (1), **-sa** (3), *a.* dried (*fruit*).
paso (2), *adv.* softly, gently.
paso (3), *n.m.* pace; footstep, step; gait, walk; passing; passage; pass; chapter; situation; turn (*of screw*); float (*Holy Week etc.*); (*mech.*) pitch; (*theat.*) curtain-raiser, sketch; ***paso a nivel,*** level crossing, (*Am.*) grade crossing; ***paso a paso,*** step by step; ***¡paso!*** give way!; ***paso de tortuga,*** snail's pace; ***a buen paso,*** at a good rate; ***al paso,*** at a walking pace; ***al paso que,*** at the same time as; whilst; ***a dos pasos,*** at a stone's throw; ***a pocos pasos,*** at a short distance; ***a ese paso,*** at that rate; ***andar en malos pasos,*** to follow evil ways; ***dar paso,*** to give way; ***dejar paso,*** to let through; ***apretar el paso,*** to get a move on, hurry up; ***de paso,*** at the same time; while you're at it; in passing; ***salir del paso,*** to get out of a difficulty; ***para salir del paso,*** as a (mere) makeshift; ***salir al paso,*** to counter; to go to meet; ***salirse de su paso,*** to alter one's normal ways; ***marcar el paso,*** to mark time; ***a paso llano,*** smoothly, regularly; ***ceder el paso,*** to give way; ***cerrar el paso,*** to bar, block the way; ***por sus pasos contados,*** following the set pattern.
paspié, *n.m.* dance.
pasquín, *n.m.* lampoon.
pasquinada, *n.f.* pasquinade.
pasquinar, *v.t.* to lampoon.
pássim, *adv.* passim.
pasta, *n.f.* paste; batter; pastry; Italian pasta; dough; bullion; pie-crust; board-binding; (*bookb.*) cover; pulp; ***media pasta,*** half-leather binding; (*fig.*) ***buena pasta,*** good nature.
pastar, *v.t.* to graze. — *v.i.* to graze, pasture.
pasteca, *n.f.* (*naut.*) snatch-block.
pastel, *n.m.* cake, pastry; (*bot.*) woad; (*print.*) pie; type for recasting; (*art*) pastel; trick in card-dealing; (*coll.*) underhand arrangement, jiggery-pokery; ***pastel de carne,*** meat pie, pasty.
pastelear, *v.i.* (*coll.*) to make an undercover arrangement, indulge in jiggery-pokery.
pastelería, *n.f.* pastry-cook's shop; pastry, pies.
pastelero, -ra, *a.* (relating to) pastry; (*coll.*) given to jiggery-pokery. — *n.m.* confectioner. — *n.f.* confectioner's wife.
pastelillo, pastelito, *n.m.* small cake; meat-pasty; ***pastelillo de fruta,*** tart, (*Am.*) pie.
pastelón, *n.m.* pigeon *or* meat pie; big cake.
pasterización, *n.f.* pasteurization.
pasterizar [C], *v.t.* to pasteurize.
pastilla, *n.f.* tablet; bar (*of chocolate*); cake (*of soap*).
pastinaca, *n.f.* (*bot.*) parsnip; (*zool.*) sting-ray.
pasto, *n.m.* pasture, pasture-ground; food, nourishment; ***a pasto,*** galore; (*fig.*) ***pasto del fuego,*** fuel for the flames.
pastor, *n.m.* shepherd; (Protestant) pastor, clergyman.
pastora, *n.f.* shepherdess.
pastoral, *a.* pastoral. — *n.f.* pastoral letter; pastoral poem.
pastorear, *v.t.* to pasture, graze.
pastorela, *n.f.* shepherd's song; pastourelle.
pastoreo, *n.m.* pasturing.
pastoría, *n.f.* pastoral life; body of shepherds.
pastoril, pastoricio, -cia, *a.* pastoral.
pastosidad, *n.f.* pastiness, thickness.
pastoso, -sa, *a.* pasty, doughy, thick.
pastura, *n.f.* pasture, pasture-ground; fodder.
pasturaje, *n.m.* pasturage; duty (*for grazing of cattle*).
pata (1), *n.f.* foot; paw; leg; pocket flap; female duck; ***pata de cabra,*** crowbar; ***pata de gallina,*** crow's foot; ***pata de gallo,*** crow's foot, wrinkle; blunder; ***pata de banco,*** stupid *or* tactless thing to say, blunder; ***pata de palo,*** wooden *or* peg leg; ***a cuatro patas,*** on all fours; ***a pata(s),*** on foot; ***a la pata la llana,*** in straightforward fashion; ***patas arriba,*** upside down; topsy-turvy; (*fig.*) ***enseñar*** or ***sacar la pata,*** to show the cloven hoof *or* one's true colours; (*fig.*) ***estirar la pata,*** to kick the bucket; (*fig.*) ***meter la pata,*** to put one's foot in it; ***quedar*** or ***salir pata(s),*** to draw, tie; ***tener buena (mala) pata,*** to have good (bad) luck; (*fig.*) ***tirar*** or ***echar las patas por alto,*** to go off the deep end; ***jugar a la pata coja,*** to play hop-scotch.
patabán, *n.m.* (*Cub.*) mangrove.
pataca (1), *n.f.* Jerusalem artichoke; small copper coin.
pataco, - ca (2), *a.* boorish, churlish.
patacón, *n.m.* dollar; penny.
patache, *n.m.* (*naut.*) advice-boat.
patada, *n.f.* kick; stamp; step; ***a patadas,*** galore; ***dar*** or ***pegar la patada a, echar a patadas,*** to kick *or* chuck out; ***hacer en dos patadas,*** to do in two shakes; ***me da cien patadas,*** I can't stand it *or* him.
patagón, -gona, *a., n.m.f.* from *or* of Patagonia, Patagonian.
patagorrillo, *n.m.* hash of pork liver and lights.
patagua, *n.f.* Chile linden, whitewood.
pataje, *n.m.* (*naut.*) tender, advice-boat.
patalear, *v.i.* to kick; to stamp; to kick up a fuss.
pataleo, *n.m.* kicking; stamping; (*coll.*) grousing, grumbling; kicking up a fuss.
pataleta, *n.f.* (*coll.*) fit.
pataletilla, *n.f.* dance.
patán, -tana, *a.* churlish, boorish. — *n.m.* bumpkin, churl, lout.
patanería, *n.f.* churlishness, boorishness.
patarata, *n.f.* mincingness.
pataratero, -ra, *a.* mincing.
patarráez, *n.m.* (*naut.*) preventer-shroud.
patasca, *n.f.* (*Arg.*) dish made of pork and maize; (*Per.*) dispute, angry argument.
patata, *n.f.* potato; ***patatas fritas,*** chips; ***patatas a la inglesa,*** potato crisps, (*Am.*) chips; ***no saber ni una patata,*** not to know the first thing (***de,*** about).
patatal, *n.m.* potato-field.
patatero, -ra, *a.* potato; (*coll.*) keen on potatoes; (*coll.*) risen from the ranks (*of soldiers*).
patatús, *n.m.* (*coll.*) fit.
patay, *n.m.* (*Hisp. Am.*) dry paste made from carob beans.
pateadura, *n.f.* kicking, stamping; (*coll.*) dressing down.
pateamiento, *n.m.* kicking.
patear, *v.t., v.i.* (*coll.*) to kick, stamp; ***nos pateamos todo Madrid,*** we traipsed all over Madrid.
patena, *n.f.* paten, patina; large medal.
patentar, *v.t.* to patent.
patente, *a.* patent, evident. — *n.f.* patent; licence; (*naut.*) ***patente de sanidad,*** bill of health; ***patente de corso,*** letters of marque.
patentizar [C], *v.t.* to render evident, make obvious *or* plain, show clearly.
pateo, *n.m.* (*coll.*) kicking; stamping.
pátera, *n.f.* goblet.
paternal, *a.* (*fig.*) paternal, fatherly.
paternidad, *n.f.* paternity, fatherhood.
paterno, -na, *a.* (*lit.*) paternal, fatherly.
paternóster, *n.m.* paternoster, Lord's prayer; (*fig., coll.*) tight knot.
pateta, *n.f.* (*coll.*) lame person; (*coll.*) Devil, deuce, Old Nick.
patético, -ca, *a.* (deeply) moving.
patiabierto, -ta, *a.* (*coll.*) bow-legged.
patialbillo, *n.m.* genet.
patiblanco, -ca, *a.* white-footed.
patibulario, -ria, *a.* sinister; hang-dog.
patíbulo, *n.m.* gallows, scaffold.

paticojo, -ja, *a.* (*coll.*) lame.
patidifuso, -sa, *a.* (*coll.*) flabbergasted.
patiestevado, -da, *a.* bow-legged.
patihendido, -da, *a.* cloven-footed.
patilla, *n.f.* small foot; (*naut.*) rudder spike; trigger; chape of a buckle; pocket flap; (*carp.*) tenon; (*Ven.*) water-melon; (*pl.*) side-boards, side-burns; (*coll.*) the Devil, deuce.
patín, *n.m.* small courtyard; (*orn.*) goosander; skate; ***patín de ruedas,*** roller skate.
pátina, *n.f.* patina.
patinadero, *n.m.* skating rink; skating place.
patinador, -ra, *n.m.f.* skater.
patinar, *v.i.* to skate; to skid.
patinillo, *n.m.* small (back) courtyard.
patio, *n.m.* court, courtyard; (*theat.*) pit; ***patio de recreo,*** playground.
patita, *n.f.* small foot, leg (*of animals*), paw; ***poner de patitas en la calle,*** to throw out.
patitieso, -sa, *a.* (*coll.*) flabbergasted.
patito, *n.m.* duckling.
patituerto, -ta, *a.* crooked-legged.
patizambo, -ba, *a.* bandy-legged.
pato, -ta (2), *n.m.f.* (*orn.*) drake, duck; ***pagar el pato,*** to carry the can.
patochada, *n.f.* blunder; (*coll.*) clanger.
patogenia, *n.f.* (*med.*) pathogenesis.
patojo, -ja, *a.* waddling.
patología, *n.f.* pathology.
patológico, -ca, *a.* pathological.
patólogo, *n.m.* pathologist.
patón, -tona, *a.* large-footed; clumsy-footed.
patoso, -sa, *a.* clumsy; tactless.
patraña, *n.f.* cock-and-bull story, yarn.
patria, *n.f.* [PATRIO].
patriarca, *n.m.* patriarch.
patriarcado, *n.m.* patriarchate.
patriarcal, *a.* patriarchal.
patriciado, *n.m.* dignity of a patrician.
patricio, -cia, *a.*, *n.m.f.* patrician.
patrimonial, *a.* patrimonial.
patrimonialidad, *n.f.* birthright, right of patrimony.
patrimonio, *n.m.* patrimony; heritage, birthright.
patrio, -ria, *a.* native; paternal. — *n.f.* native land, fatherland; ***madre patria,*** mother country; ***patria chica,*** native region *or* area; ***hacer patria,*** to boast about one's country.
patriota, *a.* patriotic. — *n.m.f.* patriot.
patriotería, *n.f.* (*coll.*) jingoism.
patriotero, -ra, *a.* jingoistic.
patriótico, -ca, *a.* patriotic.
patriotismo, *n.m.* patriotism.
patrístico, -ca, *a.* patristic. — *n.f.* patristics.
patrocinador, -ra, *a.*, *n.m.f.* sponsoring; sponsor.
patrocinar, *v.t.* to patronize, sponsor; to give *or* lend one's patronage to, give one's support *or* backing to.
patrocinio, *n.m.* patronage, sponsorship.
patrología, *n.f.* patrology.
patrón, *n.m.* patron; boss, master; host, landlord; patron saint; standard; pattern; (*naut.*) skipper.
patrona, *n.f.* patroness; owner, mistress; hostess; landlady; patron saint; (*naut.*) galleon next after flagship.
patronado, -da, *a.* having a patron.
patronato, patronazgo, *n.m.* patronage, patronship; foundation; employers, bosses; board of trustees; ***patronato de turismo,*** State Tourist Office.
patronear, *v.t.* to captain, skipper.
patronía, *n.f.* mastership (*of a vessel*).
patronímico, -ca, *a.*, *n.m.* patronymic.
patrono, *n.m.* patron, protector; employer, boss, master.
patrulla, *n.f.* patrol; gang, band.
patrullar, *v.t.*, *v.i.* to patrol.
patrullero, *a.* patrolling. — *n.m.* (*Hisp. Am.*) mobile police.
patudo, -da, *a.* having large feet *or* paws.
patulea, *n.f.* band of disorderly soldiers; mob, gang; mob of brats.
patullar, *v.i.* to stamp *or* charge about; to kick up a rumpus; (*coll.*) to prattle.
paturro, *a.* (*Col.*) small; chubby.
paují, paujil, *n.m.* (*Per.*) guan.
paúl, paular, *n.m.* bog, marsh.
paulatino, -na, *a.* gradual.
paulina, *n.f.* degree of excommunication, interdict, reproof, objurgation; (*coll.*) anonymous letter.
paulinia, *n.f.* (*Hisp. Am.*) shrub (*Paullinia cupana*).
paulonia, *n.f.* (*bot.*) paulownia.
pauperismo, *n.m.* pauperism, abject poverty.
paupérrimo, -ma, *a. superl.* extremely poor.
pausa, *n.f.* pause, break; stop.
pausado, -da, *a.* slow, deliberate; calm.
pausar, *v.t.* to delay, halt. — *v.i.* to pause, slow down.
pauta, *n.f.* ruler; guidelines; model, standard, pattern; ***dar la pauta,*** to set the pattern.
pautador, *n.m.* marker of lines on paper.
pautar, *v.t.* to rule; to set standards for; (*mus.*) ***papel pautado,*** ruled paper.
pava, *n.f.* [PAVO].
pavada, *n.f.* flock of turkeys; (*Hisp. Am.*) (piece of) nonsense.
pavana, *n.f.* pavan.
pavería, *n.f.* turkey farm.
pavero, -ra, *n.m.f.* turkey breeder *or* dealer. — *n.m.* broad-brimmed hat. — *n.f.* (*Arg., Bol.*) kettle.
pavés, *n.m.* pavis, buckler.
pavesa, *n.f.* ash, cinder.
pavesadas, *n.f.pl.* (*naut.*) waistcloths.
pavesear, *v.i.* to flutter.
pavezno, *n.m.* young turkey.
pavía, *n.f.* clingstone peach.
pávido, -da, *a.* (*poet.*) timid, fearful.
pavimentación, *n.f.* paving.
pavimentar, *v.t.* to pave.
pavimento, *n.m.* tiled floor; paving.
paviota, *n.f.* seagull, mew.
pavipollo, *n.m.* young turkey.
pavo, -va, *a.* (*coll.*) soppy, silly. — *n.m.* (*orn.*) turkey; ***pavo real,*** peacock; (*ichth.*) peacock-fish; ***la edad del pavo,*** the teens; ***subírsele a alguien el pavo,*** to blush, flush; ***esto no es moco de pavo,*** this is not to be sneezed at. — *n.f.* turkey-hen, large furnace bellows; (*Hisp. Am.*) joke; (*Ven.*) large hat; (*Col.*) guan; ***pelar la pava,*** to flirt, court.
pavón, *n.m.* peacock; (*ent.*) peacock butterfly; bluing, blacking *or* browning (*of iron* or *steel*).
pavonada, *n.f.* strutting, showing off.
pavonar, *v.t.* to blue, black *or* brown (*iron* or *steel*).
pavonazo, *n.m.* crimson, purple pigment.
pavoncillo, pavoncito, *n.m.* little peacock.
pavonearse, *v.r.* to strut, show off.
pavor, *n.m.* fear, terror, dread.
pavorde, *n.m.* provost (*of a cathedral*); divinity professor.
pavordear, *v.i.* to swarm (*of bees*).
pavordía, *n.f.* office and dignity of a provost.
pavorido, -da, *a.* intimidated, terror-struck.
pavoroso, -sa, *a.* awful, dreadful, fearful.
pavura, *n.f.* dread, terror, fear.
paya (1), *n.f.* improvised song, calypso.
payacate, *n.m.* (*Mex.*) large handkerchief.
payada, *n.f.* (*Arg., Chi.*) song of the ***payador.***

payador, *n.m.* (*Arg., Chi.*) minstrel who accompanies himself with a guitar.
payasada, *n.f.* clownish thing to do *or* say.
payaso, *n.m.* clown.
payés, -yesa, *n.m.f.* Catalan *or* Balearic countryman (-woman).
payo, -ya (2), cloddish. — *n.m.f.* clod, churl, hoyden.
payuelas, *n.f.pl.* chicken-pox.
paz, *n.f.* peace; ***bandera de paz,*** flag of truce; ***gente de paz,*** friend (*answer to the challenge of a sentry*); ***en paz,*** quits, clear; ***a la paz de Dios,*** God be with you; ***dejar en paz,*** to leave alone; ***estar en paz,*** to be quits, even; ***hacer las paces,*** to make it up; ***poner paz, meter paz,*** to calm things down. — *interj.* hush!
pazguato, -ta, *n.m.f.* dolt, fool; prude.
pazote, *n.m.* (*bot.*) saltwort.
pazpuerca, *n.f.* (*coll.*) dirty, slovenly creature.
pe, *n.f.* letter P; ***de pe a pa,*** from beginning to end
pea, *n.f.* drunkenness; ***coger una pea,*** to get sozzled.
peaje, *n.m.* toll.
peajero, *n.m.* toll-gatherer.
peal, *n.m.* stocking-foot; legging; worthless person
peana, peaña, *n.f.* pedestal, base; (*mech.*) ground plate; step (*before an altar*).
peatón, *n.m.* pedestrian; rural postman.
peazgo, *n.m.* toll.
pebete, *n.m.* joss-stick; fuse; (*coll.*) stinker.
pebetero, *n.m.* censer.
pebrada, pebre, *n.f.* pepper sauce.
peca, *n.f.* freckle.
pecable, *a.* peccable, sinful.
pecadillo, *n.m.* peccadillo.
pecado, *n.m.* sin; ***pecado mortal,*** deadly sin; ***de mis pecados,*** of mine; ***por mis pecados,*** for my sins.
pecador, -ra, *a.* sinning. — *n.m.f.* sinner.
pecaminoso, -sa, *a.* sinful.
pecante, *a.* peccant; excessive.
pecar [A], *v.i.* to sin; to be excessive; ***peca de largo,*** it is too long.
pece, *n.f.* clay (*for making mud walls*); ridge (*between furrows*).
pececillo, pececito, *n.m.* little fish; ***pececillos,*** small fry.
peceño, -ña, *a.* pitch-coloured (*said of horses*); tasting of pitch.
pecera, *n.f.* fish bowl; aquarium.
pecezuela, *n.f.* small piece.
pecezuelo, *n.m.* small foot; small fish.
peciento, -ta, *a.* pitch-black.
peciluengo, -ga, *a.* long-stalked (*fruit*).
pecina, *n.f.* piscina; slime.
pecinal, *n.m.* slimy pool.
pecio, *n.m.* (*law*) jetsam, flotsam, ligan, wreckage.
pécora, *n.f.* sheep; (*coll.*) slut.
pecorea, *n.f.* marauding; rustling.
pecorear, *v.t.* to rustle. — *v.i.* to loot, maraud (*soldiers*).
pecoso, -sa, *a.* freckly, freckled.
pectiniforme, *a.* (*zool.*) pectiniform.
pectoral, *a.* pectoral. — *n.m.* pectoral cross (*worn by ecclesiastics*); breastplate.
pecuario, -ria, *a.* of *or* pertaining to cattle.
peculado, *n.m.* peculation; peculation of public funds.
peculiar, *a.* peculiar, appropriate, special.
peculiaridad, *n.f.* peculiarity.
peculiarmente, *adv.* peculiarly.
peculio, *n.m.* stock of money; (*law*) peculium; (*fig.*) pocket.
pecunia, *n.f.* (*coll.*) hard cash, specie.
pecuniario, -ria, *a.* pecuniary.
pecha, *n.f.* (*obs.*) tax, impost, tribute.
pechada, *n.f.* (*Hisp. Am.*) blow on the chest.
pechar, *v.t.* to pay (*taxes etc.*); ***pechar con,*** to take on, shoulder, to endure, suffer.
peche, *n.m.* pilgrim's shell.
pechera (1), *n.f.* stomacher; breast; shirt-front; chest protector; breast strap (*harness*); (*coll.*) bosom.
pechería, *n.f.* paying tax, toll *or* duty.
pechero, -ra (2), *n.m.f.* commoner, taxpayer. — *n.m.* bib.
pechiblanco, -ca, *a.* white-breasted.
pechicolorado, *n.m.* robin redbreast.
pechina, *n.f.* pilgrim's shell; (*arch.*) triangle formed by arches.
pechirrojo, *n.m.* robin redbreast.
pechisacado, -da, *a.* haughty, arrogant.
pecho, *n.m.* breast, chest, bosom; (*fig.*) valour, heart; slope, gradient; ancient tax; ***dar el pecho,*** to give suck; ***se echó entre pecho y espalda un pollo entero,*** he tucked a whole chicken away; ***hombre de pecho,*** firm, spirited man; ***hombre de pelo en pecho,*** he-man; ***el dolor no le cabía en el pecho,*** he couldn't contain his sorrow; ***tomar a pecho***(***s***), to take to heart; ***a pecho descubierto,*** unarmed, defenceless; ***a lo hecho, pecho,*** there's no use (in) crying over spilt milk.
pechuga, *n.f.* breast (*of a fowl*); (*coll.*) bosom.
pechugón, *n.m.* blow on the breast.
pechuguera, *n.f.* cough, hoarseness.
pedacico, pedacillo, pedacito, *n.m.* small bit, small piece.
pedagogía, *n.f.* pedagogy.
pedagógico, -ca, *a.* pedagogic.
pedagogo, *n.m.* pedagogue, educator.
pedaje, *n.m.* toll.
pedal, *n.m.* pedal.
pedalear, *v.i.* to pedal.
pedáneo, -nea, *a.* (*law*) petty.
pedante, *a.* pedantic. — *n.m.f.* pedant.
pedantear, *v.i.* to pedantize, play the pedant.
pedantería, *n.f.* pedantry.
pedantesco, -ca, *a.* (absurdly) pedantic.
pedantismo, *n.m.* pedantry.
pedantón, *n.m.* great pedant.
pedazo, *n.m.* piece, bit; lump; ***pedazo de animal,*** thick-headed nit-wit; ***a*** or ***en pedazos,*** in bits; ***hacerse pedazos,*** to fall to bits *or* be smashed to pieces; (*fig.*) ***me muero por tus pedazos,*** I'm crazy about you.
pederasta, *n.m.* paederast.
pederastia, *n.f.* paederasty.
pedernal, *n.m.* flint.
pedernalino, -na, *a.* (*poet.*) flinty.
pedestal, *n.m.* pedestal, base.
pedestre, *a.* pedestrian.
pedíatra, *n.m.f.* pediatrician.
pediatría, *n.f.* pediatrics.
pedicoj, *n.m.* hopping, jumping on one foot.
pedicular, *a.* pedicular.
pedículo, *n.m.* (*bot.*) pedicle.
pedicuro, *n.m.* chiropodist.
pedido, *n.m.* (*com.*) order; request.
pedidor, -ra, *a.* importunate.
pedidura, *n.m.f.* begging, petitioning.
pedigón, -gona, *n.m.f.* importuner.
pedigüeño, -ña, *a.* importuning, importunate.
pediluvio, *n.m.* (*med.*) pediluvium, foot-bath.
pedimento, *n.m.* petition; (*law*) claim, bill; ***a pedimento de,*** at the request of.
pedir [8], *v.t.* to ask, ask for; to call for; to order; ***pídeselo,*** ask him for it; ***pedir cuenta a,*** to call to account, ask for an explanation from; ***pedir la palabra,*** to ask leave to speak; ***pedir prestado,*** to borrow; ***no me lo pide el cuerpo,***

I don't feel like it. — *v.i.* to beg, ***pedir limosna,*** to ask (for) alms, beg; ***esto viene a pedir de boca,*** this is just what the doctor ordered.
pedo, *n.m.* (*vulg.*) fart; (*bot.*) ***pedo de lobo,*** puff-ball.
pedómetro, *n.m.* pedometer.
pedorrear, *v.i.* (*vulg.*) to fart.
pedorreras, *n.f. pl.* tights.
pedorrero, -ra, pedorro, -rra, *a.* (*vulg.*) farting; flatulent.
pedorreta, *n.f.* (*sl.*) raspberry.
pedrada, *n.f.* chucking *or* flinging of a stone; blow from a stone; snide dig; cockade bow; ***venir como pedrada en ojo de boticario,*** to be just what the doctor ordered.
pedrea, *n.f.* stone-throwing; hailstorm; (lottery) small prizes.
pedrecita, *n.f.* small stone.
pedregal, *n.m.* stony place *or* ground.
pedregoso, -sa, *a.* stony, rocky; (*med.*) afflicted with the gravel.
pedrejón, *n.m.* large, loose stone.
pedreñal, *n.m.* blunderbuss, flintlock.
pedrera, *n.f.* quarry, stone-pit.
pedrería, *n.f.* collection of jewels.
pedrero, *n.m.* stone-cutter; (*artill.*) stone mortar; slinger; lapidary; (*prov.*) foundling.
pedrezuela, *n.f.* pebble.
pedriscal, *n.m.* stony place.
pedrisco, *n.m.* hailstone; shower of hail; heap of loose stones.
pedriza, *n.f.* heap of loose stones.
Pedro, *n.m.* Peter.
pedro, *n.m.* (*sl.*) rough dress, night burglar's dress; (*sl.*) lock.
pedrojiménez, *n.m.* grape from Jerez; wine made with these grapes.
pedrusco, *n.m.* (*coll.*) rough chunk of rock.
pedunculillo, *n.m.* pedicel.
pedúnculo, *n.m.* peduncle.
peer, *v.i.* (*vulg.*) to fart.
pega, *n.f.* cementing *or* sticking; pitch, varnish; leather tanning; (*orn.*) magpie; (*ichth.*) remora; hoax, trick, fake; drawback, snag, catch; ***poner pegas,*** to find fault; to raise objections.
pegadizo, -za, *a.* sticky; catching; catchy.
pegado, -da, *a.* (*coll.*) floored, nonplussed; having no idea. — *n.m.* sticky, sticking-plaster.
pegador, -ra, *n.m.f.* bill-sticker, paper-hanger; (*min.*) blaster.
pegadura, *n.f.* pitching, daubing with pitch; sticking.
pegajoso, -sa, *a.* sticky; catching; hard to get rid of; (*med.*) infectious; (*fig.*) contagious.
pegamiento, *n.m.* cementing; sticking.
pegante, *a.* sticking.
pegar [B], *v.t.* to stick, glue; to bring *or* put close together; to hit; to give; ***pegar fuego a,*** to set fire to; ***pegar tumbos,*** to stagger, rock; ***pegar una paliza,*** to give a thrashing (***a,*** to); ***pegar un tiro,*** to fire a shot. — *v.i.* to stick; to take (*root*); to be suitable, fitting; to be next to; ***no pegar*** (***un***) ***ojo,*** not to sleep a wink; ***dale que te pego,*** keeping on and on, persisting; ***eso no pega,*** it's (quite) out of place. — **pegarse,** *v.r.* to stick; to get close; to attach o.s.; to be catching; ***pegársela a alguien,*** to take s.o. in, fool s.o., take s.o. for a ride, pull a fast one on s.o.; ***pegarse un tiro,*** to blow one's brains out.
pegáseo, -sea, *a.* (*poet.*) belonging to Pegasus.
Pegásides, *n.f.pl.* the Muses.
Pegaso, *n.m.* (*myth.*, *astron.*) Pegasus.
pegata, *n.f.* (*coll.*) trick, fraud.
pegatina, *n.f.* sticker.
pegatista, *n.m.f.* sponger.
pegmatita, *n.f.* (*min.*) pegmatite.
pego, *n.m.* cheating (*by sticking two cards together*); cheat, fraud; ***de pego,*** sham, mock; ***una cosa de pego,*** a put-up job; ***dar el pego,*** to cheat, fool, trick.
pegollo, *n.m.* (*prov.*) pillar, post.
pegote, *n.m.* pitch plaster; plaster; (*coll.*) lump, lumpy mess; (*coll.*) crude bit stuck on, out-of-place object; (*coll.*) sponger, hanger-on.
pegotear, *v.i.* (*coll.*) to sponge, cadge.
pegual, *n.m.* (*Hisp. Am.*) strap with rings.
peguera, *n.f.* pitch pit; place where sheep are marked with pitch.
peguero, *n.m.* pitch maker *or* dealer.
pegujal, pegujar, *n.m.* small fund; small farm *or* herd.
pegujalero, pegujarero, *n.m.* small farmer.
pegujón, *n.m.* pellet *or* ball of wool *or* hair.
pegunta, *n.f.* mark (on cattle, sheep etc.).
peguntar, *v.t.* to mark (*cattle etc.*) with pitch.
peinada, *n.f.* combing.
peinado, *n.m.* hair-do, hair-style.
peinador, *n.m.* hairdresser; combing-gown, dressing-gown.
peinadura, *n.f.* combing.
peinar, *v.t.* to comb, do the hair of; to graze; to eat away; to shuffle (*cards*); ***peinar canas,*** to be getting old.
peinazo, *n.m.* cross-piece (*of a door* or *window-frame*).
peine, *n.m.* comb; (weaver's) reed; wool-card; cartridge clip; (*coll.*) tricky customer.
peinería, *n.f.* comb-shop, comb-factory.
peinero, -ra, *n.m.f.* comb-maker, comb-seller.
peineta, *n.f.* curved comb, back comb.
peje, *n.m.* fish; crafty fellow; (*ichth.*) ***peje araña,*** stingbull; (*ichth.*) ***peje diablo,*** scorpene.
pejegallo, *n.m.* rooster-fish.
pejemuller, *n.f.* manatee.
pejepalo, *n.m.* stockfish.
pejerrey, *n.m.* atherine.
pejesapo, *n.m.* toad-fish.
pejiguera, *n.f.* (*coll.*) nuisance, bore, drag.
pela, *n.f.* peeling; shelling.
pelada, *n.f.* [PELADO].
peladera, *n.f.* shedding of the hair.
peladero, *n.m.* scalding-house; (*coll.*) sharper's den; (*Hisp. Am.*) barren spot.
peladilla, *n.f.* sugared almond; small pebble.
peladillo, *n.m.* clingstone peach; (*pl.*) wool.
pelado, -da, *a.* stripped bare, bare; hairless, featherless, treeless, leafless; (*coll.*) cleaned out, skint. — *n.m.* down and out. — *n.f.* pelt (*stripped skin of a sheep*).
pelador, -ra, *a.* peeling, stripping.
peladura, *n.f.* peeling, stripping.
pelafustán, pelagallos (*inv.*), **pelagatos** (*inv.*), *n.m.* good-for-nothing.
pelágico, -ca, *a.* pelagic.
pelagra, *n.f.* pellagra.
pelaire, *n.m.* wool-dresser.
pelairía, *n.f.* wool-comber's trade.
pelaje, *n.m.* coat, fur; (*fig.*) look; ilk, kind.
pelambrar, *v.t.* to flesh (*hides*).
pelambre, *n.m.* hides put into lime-pits. — ***n.f.*** (*coll.*) mop of hair; bald patch.
pelambrera, *n.f.* mop of hair; shedding of hair; place where hides are macerated in lime-pits.
pelambrero, *n.m.* tanner.
pelamesa, *n.f.* catfight.
pelámide, *n.f.* young brood of tunny fish.
pelandusca, *n.f.* strumpet.
pelantrín, *n.m.* small farmer.
pelar, *v.t.* to strip of hair; to strip, lay bare; to skin; to peel; to cut the hair of; to scald, blanch; ***eso es duro de pelar,*** that's a hard nut to crack; ***corre***

que se las pela, he's running like mad; ***hace un frío que pela,*** it's bitterly *or* bitingly cold. — **pelarse,** *v.r.* to have one's hair cut; to lose the *or* one's hair; ***pelarse de fino,*** to be very shrewd.

pelarruecas, *n.f. inv.* poor woman who lives by spinning.

pelásgico, -ca, *a.* Pelasgic.

pelasgo, -ga, *a., n.m.f.* Pelasgian.

pelaza, *n.f.* chopped *or* beaten straw; quarrel, affray; caterwauling; ***dejar en la pelaza,*** to leave in the lurch.

pelazga, *n.f.* quarrel, scuffle.

peldaño, *n.m.* step (*of stairs*); rung (*of ladder*).

pelea, *n.f.* fight; quarrel, row.

peleador, *n.m.* fighter.

peleante, *a.* fighting.

pelear, *v.i.* to fight. — **pelearse,** *v.r.* to fight, quarrel, row; ***pelearse con alguien,*** to fight somebody; to have a set-to with somebody.

pelechar, *v.i.* to grow a new coat, grow hair *or* feathers; (*fig.*) to pick up.

pelele, *n.m.* dummy; puppet.

pelendengue, *n.m.* frivolous foppery.

peleón, -leona, *a.* given to fighting; ordinary (*wine*). — *n.f.* quarrel, hell of a fight.

pelete, *n.m.* punter (*at cards*); poor man; ***en pelete,*** naked.

peletería, *n.f.* trade of furrier *or* skinner; (*Cub.*) leather goods, and shop.

peletero, *n.m.* furrier, skin-dealer.

pelgar, *n.m.* good-for-nothing.

peliagudo, -da, *a.* (*fig.*) hard, tough.

peliblanco, -ca, *a.* having white hair.

peliblando, -da, *a.* having soft, fine hair.

pelicabra, *n.f.* satyr.

pelícano, *n.m.* pelican.

pelicano, -na, *a.* grey-haired, hoary.

pelicorto, -ta, *a.* short-haired.

película, *n.f.* pellicle; film.

pelicular, *a.* pellicular.

peliculero, -ra, *a.* (*coll.*) of films. — *n.m.f.* person in films.

peliforra, *n.f.* (*coll.*) harlot, whore.

peligrar, *v.i.* to be in danger *or* jeopardy.

peligro, *n.m.* danger, peril; ***correr peligro,*** to be in peril.

peligroso, -sa, *a.* dangerous, perilous, hazardous.

pelilargo, -ga, *a.* long-haired.

pelillo, *n.m.* short weak hair; trifle; ***echar pelillos a la mar,*** to bury the hatchet, let bygones be bygones; ***reparar en pelillos,*** to fuss over trifles.

pelilloso, -sa, *a.* touchy.

pelinegro, -ra, *a.* black-haired.

pelirrojo, -ja, *a.* red-haired, ginger.

pelirrubio, -bia, *a.* fair-haired.

pelitieso, -sa, *a.* with strong, bushy hair.

pelitre, *n.m.* (*bot.*) pellitory of Spain.

pelitrique, *n.m.* trifle, fiddling matter.

pelmacería, *n.f.* tediousness.

pelmazo, *n.m.* heavy lump; hell of a bore *or* drag.

pelo, *n.m.* hair; down; hair's breadth; nap, pile (*of cloth*); raw silk; grain (*in wood*); colour (*of animal's coat*); hairspring (*of a watch* or *firearm*); flaw (*in a jewel* or *crystal*); split (*in metal, horse's hoof etc.*); abscess (*in a woman's breast*); splinter; trifle; kiss (*in billiards*); ***con pelos y señales,*** in full detail; ***montar a pelo*** or ***en pelo,*** to ride bareback; ***librarse por un pelo,*** to have a narrow escape; ***faltó un pelo para que se cayera,*** he very nearly fell; ***ser de pelo en pecho,*** to be a he-man; ***ser de medio pelo,*** to be low-class, be riff-raff; ***soltarse el pelo,*** to show one's true colours, throw restraint to the winds; ***tener el pelo de la dehesa,*** to be uncouth; ***no tener (ni) un pelo de tonto,*** to be all there, be no fool, have no flies on one; ***no tener pelos en la lengua,*** to be thoroughly outspoken; ***tomar el pelo a,*** to take in, trick; to pull the leg of; ***venir al pelo,*** to be just what the doctor ordered.

pelón, -lona, *a., n.m.f.* bald (person); (*coll.*) skint (individual). — *n.f.* baldness.

pelonía, *n.f.* baldness.

pelonería, *n.f.* (*coll.*) poverty.

peloponense, *a., n.m.f.* Peloponnesian.

pelosilla, *n.f.* (*bot.*) hawkweed, mouse-ear.

peloso, -sa, *a.* hairy.

pelota, *n.f.* ball; pelota; pile of debts; (*Hisp. Am.*) leather punt; ***en pelota(s),*** naked; (*fig.*) ***jugar a la pelota, echarse la pelota,*** to pass the buck; ***estar la pelota en el tejado,*** (things) to be in the melting pot, in an unresolved state.

pelotari, *n.m.f.* pelota player.

pelotazo, *n.m.* shot (with a ball); ***sistema del pelotazo,*** buck-passing.

pelote, *n.m.* goat's hair.

pelotear, *v.t.* to check, go over. — *v.i.* to throw a ball about; to wrangle.

pelotera, *n.f.* quarrel, row, wrangle.

pelotería, *n.f.* heap of balls; heap of goat's hair.

pelotero, *n.m.* ball-maker.

pelotilla, *n.f.* small ball; small ball of wax and pieces of glass fastened to a scourge; ***hacer pelotillas,*** to pick the nose; (*fig.*) ***hacer la pelotilla a,*** to butter up to.

pelotillero, -ra, *n.m.f.* toady.

pelotón, *n.m.* large ball; mass, mop; (*mil.*) platoon; crowd.

pelta, *n.f.* ancient buckler.

peltiforme, *a.* shield-shaped.

peltre, *n.m.* pewter.

peltrero, *n.m.* pewterer, pewter-worker.

pelú, *n.m.* (*Chi.*) pelu tree.

peluca, *n.f.* wig; (*coll.*) ticking-off, wigging.

pelucón, *n.m.* large wig.

pelucona, *n.f.* (*coll.*) double doubloon.

peludo, -da, *a.* hairy. — *n.m.* oval bass-mat; (*Hisp. Am.*) armadillo.

peluquera, *n.f.* hairdresser.

peluquería, *n.f.* hairdresser's (shop).

peluquero, *n.m.* wig-maker; hairdresser.

peluquín, *n.m.* bag-wig, top-wig.

pelusa, *n.f.* down; fluff, fuzz; nap; (*coll.*) childish jealousy; (*joc.*) ***gente de pelusa,*** the wealthy.

pella, *n.f.* ball; lump; fat, lard; mass of crude ore; head of cauliflower.

pellada, *n.f.* pat, dab, gentle blow; trowelful.

pelleja, *n.f.* hide *or* skin; (*fig.*) strumpet.

pellejería, *n.f.* shop, street *or* district where skins are dressed and sold.

pellejero, *n.m.* leather dresser, skinner.

pellejina, *n.f.* small skin.

pellejo, *n.m.* skin, hide, pelt; (*joc.*) tippler, drunkard; ***pagar con el pellejo,*** to pay (the penalty) with one's life; ***no caber en el pellejo,*** to be very fat; to be very pleased, proud; ***no quisiera estar en su pellejo,*** I wouldn't be in his shoes; ***jugarse el pellejo,*** to risk one's neck *or* skin.

pellejudo, -da, *a.* having a great quantity of skin.

pellejuela, *n.f.* small hide *or* skin.

pellejuelo, *n.m.* small skin.

pelleta, *n.f.* skin, hide.

pellica, *n.f.* coverlet of fine furs; small dressed skin.

pellico, *n.m.* shepherd's jacket; dress made of skins *or* furs.

pelliza, *n.f.* pelisse, sheepskin coat *or* jacket; (*mil.*) dolman.

pellizcar [A], *v.t.* to pinch, nip; to peck at.

pellizco, *n.m.* pinch, nip; ***pellizco de monja,*** pinch with a twist.

pello, *n.m.* fur jacket.

pellón, pellote, *n.m.* long robe of skin *or* fur; (*Hisp. Am.*) fur riding-cloak.

pelluzgón, *n.m.* handful of hair *or* wool.
pena, *n.f.* punishment, penalty, sentence; pain; hardship; grief, sorrow; effort, trouble; ***a penas,*** hardly, scarcely; ***a duras penas,*** with great difficulty; ***so pena de,*** on pain of; ***da pena,*** it's pitiful; ***¡qué pena!*** what a pity!; ***ahogar las penas,*** to drown one's sorrows; ***no merece*** or ***no vale la pena,*** it's not worth it, it's not worth while; ***vivir sin pena ni gloria,*** to live in humdrum *or* unspectacular fashion.
penable, *a.* punishable.
penachera, *n.f.* panache; crest, tuft, plume.
penacho, *n.m.* panache; crest, tuft, plume; (*fig.*) haughtiness.
penadamente, *adv.* painfully.
penadilla, *n.f.* narrow-mouthed vessel; blister.
penado, -da, *n.m.f.* convict.
penal, *a.* penal. — *n.m.* penitentiary, prison.
penalidad, *n.f.* hardship.
penalista, *n.m.f.* penologist.
penalty, *n.m.* ***casarse de penalty,*** to have a shotgun wedding.
penante, *a.* suffering; love-sick, love-lorn. — *n.m.* lover.
penar, *v.t.* to chastise, punish. — *v.i.* to suffer; to linger in death; ***penar por,*** to long, pine, sorrow for *or* after. — **penarse,** *v.r.* to grieve, sorrow.
penates, *n.m.pl.* penates, household gods.
penca, *n.f.* fleshy leaf; cactus leaf; cowhide; ***hacerse de pencas,*** to drive a tough bargain.
pencazo, *n.m.* lash.
penco, *n.m.* (*coll.*) jade, sorry nag.
pencudo, -da, *a.* with pulpy leaves.
pendanga, *n.f.* (*coll.*) tart, slut.
pendejo, *n.m.* pubic hair; (*fam.*) good-for-nothing.
pendencia, *n.f.* quarrel, brawl, row.
pendenciar, *v.i.* to wrangle, quarrel.
pendenciero, -ra, *a.* quarrelsome, wrangling.
pender, *v.i.* to hang, dangle; to depend; to be pending.
pendiente, *a.* pendent, hanging; pending; ***cuenta pendiente,*** outstanding *or* unsettled account; ***estar pendiente de,*** to depend on; to be waiting for, be in expectation over. — *n.m.* earring, pendant. — *n.f.* incline, slope; gradient, (*Am.*) grade; dip, pitch.
pendil, *n.m.* mantle; ***tomar el pendil,*** to go away.
pendingue, *n.m.* French leave.
pendol, *n.m.* (*naut.*) boot-topping.
péndola, *n.f.* pen; pendulum.
pendolaje, *n.m.* plunder (*of a captured vessel*).
pendolero, -ra, *a.* hanging.
pendolista, *n.m.* penman.
pendón, *n.m.* standard, banner, pennon, pennant; (*bot.*) tiller, shoot; (*coll.*) slut.
pendonista, *n.m.f.* standard bearer.
pendulazo, *n.m.* swing of the pendulum; ***los pendulazos políticos,*** veering from one extreme to the other.
péndulo, -la, *a.* pendent, hanging, pendulous. — *n.m.* pendulum; (*astron.*) ***péndulo sidéreo,*** standard clock.
pene, *n.m.* penis.
peneque, *n.m.* (*coll.*) drunkard.
penetrabilidad, *n.f.* penetrability.
penetrable, *a.* penetrable.
penetración, *n.f.* penetration; piercing; insight.
penetral, *n.m.* interior part, innermost recess.
penetrante, *a.* penetrating; piercing, acute.
penetrar, *v.t., v.i.* to penetrate; to fathom. — **penetrarse,** *v.r.* to become imbued (**de,** with); to grasp.
penetrativo, -va, *a.* penetrative, penetrant.
penicilina, *n.f.* penicillin.
penígero, -ra, *a.* (*poet.*) winged, feathered.
península, *n.f.* peninsula.
peninsular, *a.* peninsular.
penique, *n.m.* penny.
penisla, *n.f.* peninsula.
penitencia, *n.f.* penance, penitence; (*coll.*) ***hacer penitencia,*** to take pot-luck.
penitenciado, -da, *a.* punished by the Inquisition. — *n.m.f.* sentenced convict.
penitencial, *a.* penitential.
penitenciar, *v.t.* to impose a penance on.
penitenciaría, *n.f.* penitentiary (tribunal).
penitenciario, *n.m.* penitentiary.
penitenta, *n.f.* female penitent.
penitente, *a., n.m.f.* penitent.
penol, *n.m.* yard-arm.
penoso, -sa, *a.* painful; laborious, tedious.
pensador, -ra, *n.m.f.* thinker.
pensamiento, *n.m.* thought, thinking; intention; (*bot.*) heartsease, pansy; ***tener el pensamiento de,*** to intend to.
pensar [1], *v.t.* to think; to think of *or* about; to think over; to think out *or* up; to feed (*animals*); ***bien pensado, pensándolo bien,*** all things considered, when (you come) to think of it; ***¡ni pensarlo!*** not on your life!; ***lo pensó mejor,*** he thought better of it, he had second thoughts; ***cuando menos se piensa,*** when least expected. — *v.i.* to think; to intend; ***sin pensar,*** thoughtlessly; unintentionally; ***pensar en lo excusado,*** to attempt the impossible.
pensativo, -va, *a.* pensive, thoughtful.
penseque, *n.m.* careless *or* thoughtless error.
pensil, *a.* pensile, hanging. — *n.m.* hanging garden.
pensilvano, -na, *a., n.m.f.* Pennsylvanian.
pensión, *n.f.* pension; allowance; annuity; scholarship; boarding-house; board; (*coll.*) drawback; ***pensión completa,*** full board; ***pensión de bajísima categoría,*** doss house, (*Am.*) flophouse.
pensionado, -da, *a.* (*coll.*) burdensome. — ***n.m.f.*** pensioner; scholarship-holder. — *n.m.* boarding school; ***pensionado de señoritas,*** finishing school.
pensionar, *v.t.* to grant a pension *or* allowance to to impose a charge on.
pensionario, *n.m.* pensionary.
pensionista, *n.m.f.* pensioner; boarder; ***medio pensionista,*** day boarder.
pentacordio, *n.m.* pentachord.
pentadecágono, *n.m.* pentadecagon.
pentaedro, *n.m.* pentahedron.
pentagloto, -ta, *a.* in five languages.
pentagonal, *a.* pentagonal.
pentágono, *n.m.* pentagon.
pentagrama, *n.m.* musical staff.
pentámetro, *n.m.* pentameter.
pentasílabo, -ba, *a.* five-syllabled.
Pentateuco, *n.m.* Pentateuch.
Pentecostés, *n.m.* Whitsun(tide); Pentecost.
penúltimo, -ma, *a.* penultimate.
penumbra, *n.f.* penumbra, half-light.
penuria, *n.f.* penury, poverty.
peña, *n.f.* rock, crag, boulder; mount; circle, club.
peñascal, *n.m.* rocky place.
peñasco, *n.m.* boulder, rock; strong silk.
peñascoso, -sa, *a.* rocky, craggy; boulder-strewn.
peñol, *n.m.* yard-arm.
péñola, *n.f.* (*poet.*) pen.
peñón, *n.m.* rock.
peón, *n.m.* labourer, hand, navvy; foot-soldier; top, spinning-top; pawn (*in chess*); piece (*in draughts*); (*mech.*) spindle, axle; ***peón caminero,*** road mender; ***peón de albañil,*** bricklayer's mate.
peonada, *n.f.* labourer's day's work; gang of labourers.
peonaje, *n.m.* party of labourers; party of foot-soldiers.

peonería, *n.f.* day's ploughing.
peonía, *n.f.* peony; (*mil.*) land given to a soldier.
peonza, *n.f.* top, whipping-top; (*coll.*) ***a peonza,*** on foot.
peor, *a., adv. comp.* worse; ***peor que peor,*** even worse; ***tanto peor,*** so much the worse.
peoría, *n.f.* worsening.
pepinar, *n.m.* cucumber-field.
pepinillo, *n.m.* gherkin.
pepino, *n.m.* cucumber; (***no***) ***se le da un pepino,*** he doesn't care a rap.
pepita, *n.f.* pip, seed; nugget; (*vet.*) pip.
pepitoria, *n.f.* fricassee of chicken; medley; (*Mex.*) peanut butter.
pepitoso, -sa, *a.* full of pips *or* seeds; having the pip (*of fowls*).
pepla, *n.f.* bore, drag.
peplo, *n.m.* peplum.
pepón, *n.m.* water-melon.
pepona, *n.f.* large paper doll.
pepónide, *n.f.* pepo.
pepsina, *n.f.* pepsin.
peptona, *n.f.* peptone.
pequén, *n.m.* (*Chi.*) burrowing owl.
pequeñez, *n.f.* smallness, littleness; tender age; trifle, trifling matter; mean-spiritedness.
pequeño, -ña, *a.* little, small; young; (*fig.*) mean-spirited. — *n.m.f.* child.
pequeñuelo, -la, *a.* very little *or* young. — *n.m.f.* little one.
pequín, *n.m.* Chinese silk stuff.
pera, *n.f.* pear; goatee (*beard*); (*coll.*) sinecure; ***pedir peras al olmo,*** to ask the impossible; ***poner las peras a cuarto a,*** to bring to reason; to tick off; ***de uvas a peras,*** once in a blue moon.
perada, *n.f.* pear-juice; pear preserve.
peral, *n.m.* (*bot.*) pear tree.
peraleda, *n.f.* pear orchard.
peralejo, *n.m.* (*bot.*) white poplar.
peraltar, *v.t.* (*arch.*) to stilt (*an arch* or *vault*); (*railw.*) to raise, elevate, bank.
peralte, *n.m.* super elevation; raised edge; banking.
perantón, *n.m.* (*bot.*) marvel-plant; (*fig.*) very tall person.
peraza, *n.f.* fruit of an engrafted pear tree.
perca, *n.f.* (*ichth.*) perch.
percal, *n.m.* percale.
percalina, *n.f.* glazed calico; book muslin.
percance, *n.m.* mischance, mishap.
percarburo, *n.m.* (*chem.*) percarbide.
percatarse, *v.r.* to perceive; ***percatarse de,*** to notice, become aware of.
percebe, *n.m.* goose barnacle.
percepción, *n.f.* perception; collection (*money, taxes etc.*).
perceptibilidad, *n.f.* perceptibility.
perceptible, *a.* perceptible; collectable.
perceptivo, -va, *a.* perceptive.
perceptor, -ra, *a.* perceiving; collecting. — *n.m.f.* collector.
percibir, *v.t.* to perceive; to receive, earn, get; to collect.
percibo, *n.m.* receiving; collection; (*com.*) yield.
perclorato, *n.m.* perchlorate.
perclórico, -ca, *a.* perchloric.
percloruro, *n.m.* perchloride.
percocería, *n.f.* filigree *or* silver work.
percuciente, *a.* percutient, striking.
percudir, *v.t.* to begrime.
percusión, *n.f.* percussion.
percusor, *n.m.* striker; (*artill.*) percussion hammer.
percutir, *v.t.* to percuss, strike.
percha, *n.f.* perch; pole; snare (*for catching partridges*); coat-hanger; (*naut.*) spar, rough tree; head rail; ***de percha,*** off the peg; (*fig.*) ***estar en percha,*** to be in the bag.
perchador, -ra, *n.m.f.* one raising nap on cloth.
perchar, *v.t.* to raise the nap on (*cloth*).
perchero, *n.m.* hat- *or* clothes-rack.
percherón, -rona, *a., n.m.f.* Percheron (*horse*).
perchón, *n.m.* principal vine-shoot.
perchonar, *v.i.* to leave several important shoots on a vine-stock; to lay snares for catching game.
perdedero, *n.m.* occasion *or* cause of loss.
perdedor, -ra, *n.m.f.* loser.
perder [2], *v.t.* to lose; to forfeit; to waste; to miss; to ruin, spoil; to be the undoing of, (*coll.*) cause to come unstuck; to push *or* drive too far; ***le perdió la pereza,*** laziness was *or* proved his undoing; ***pierda cuidado,*** have no fear, set your mind at rest; ***perder los estribos,*** to fly off the handle; ***perder de vista,*** to lose sight of. — *v.i.* to lose; to fade; to go off, go down; ***echarse a perder,*** to go to wrack and ruin, go bad, go rotten. — **perderse,** *v.r.* to get lost; to lose the way, go astray; to go to the dogs; to disappear, vanish; to fall madly in love; ***no te lo pierdas,*** you mustn't miss it, it's too good to be missed; ***de la mano a la boca se pierde la sopa,*** there's many a slip 'twixt cup and lip.
perdición, *n.f.* perdition; loss; unbridled passion.
pérdida, *n.f.* losing; loss; waste; leak; leakage; ***pérdidas y ganancias,*** profit and loss; ***vender con pérdida(s),*** to sell at a loss; ***no tiene pérdida,*** you can't miss it.
perdidamente, *adv.* desperately.
perdidizo, -za, *a.* lost designedly *or* on purpose; ***hacerse perdidizo,*** to lose intentionally; ***hacerse el perdidizo,*** to sneak away, disappear.
perdido, -da, *a.* stray; profligate, wanton; confirmed, inveterate; spare, idle, free; ***ratos perdidos,*** free time; odd moments; ***fondo perdido,*** annuity; ***perdido por,*** crazy about, mad on; ***perdido por uno, perdido por todo*** or ***de perdidos, al río,*** in for a penny, in for a pound.
perdidoso, -sa, *a.* losing.
perdigana, *n.f.* young partridge.
perdigar [B], *v.t.* to broil (*partridges*) slightly; to brown (*meat*); to dispose, prepare.
perdigón, *n.m.* young partridge; decoy partridge; squanderer; reckless gambler; (*pl.* **perdigones**) small shot, buck-shot.
perdigonada, *n.f.* shot *or* wound with bird shot.
perdigonera, *n.f.* shot pouch.
perdiguero, -ra, *a., n.m.f.* setter (*dog*). — *n.m.* game dealer.
perdimiento, *n.m.* loss.
perdis, *n.m. inv.* rake.
perdiz, *n.f.* partridge.
perdón, *n.m.* pardon, forgiveness; drop of hot oil, wax etc.; ***con perdón,*** by your leave.
perdonable, *a.* pardonable, forgivable.
perdonador, *n.m.* pardoner.
perdonar, *v.t.* to pardon, forgive, excuse; to spare.
perdonavidas, *n.m. inv.* (*coll.*) bully.
perdulario, *n.m.* rake.
perdurable, *a.* everlasting, enduring.
perdurar, *v.i.* to last long; to endure.
perecear, *v.t.* to protract, delay, put off.
perecedero, -ra, *a.* perishable, doomed to perish. — *n.m.* extreme want.
perecer [9], *v.i.* to perish. — **perecerse,** *v.r.* — ***por*** to be dying (for), crave (for).
pereciente, *a.* perishing, dying.
perecimiento, *n.m.* perishing, end, death.
pereda, *n.f.* pear orchard.
peregrinación, *n.f.* peregrination; pilgrimage.
peregrina, *n.f.* [PEREGRINO].
peregrinaje, *n.m.* pilgrimage.

peregrinante, *a.* peregrinating, itinerant. — *n.m.f.* peregrinator.
peregrinar, *v.i.* to peregrinate, go on a pilgrimage.
peregrinidad, *n.f.* strangeness.
peregrino, -na, *a.* peregrinating, itinerant; strange, unusual. — *n.m.f.* pilgrim.
perejil, *n.m.* parsley.
perendeca, *n.f.* low wench, hussy, whore.
perendengue, *n.m.* earring, eardrop; bauble, trinket; small coin.
perengano, -na, *n.m.f.* so-and-so.
perennal, *a.* perennial.
perenne, *a.* perennial, everlasting.
perennidad, *n.f.* perenniality.
perentoriedad, *n.f.* peremptoriness; great urgency.
perentorio, -ria, *a.* peremptory; urgent, pressing.
perero, *n.m.* fruit-parer.
pereza, *n.f.* laziness, sloth; slowness.
perezoso, -sa, *a.* lazy, slothful. — *n.m.* (*zool.*) sloth.
perfección, *n.f.* perfection; faultlessness; ***a la perfección,*** perfectly, to perfection.
perfeccionador, *a.* perfecting. — *n.m.f.* perfecter.
perfeccionamiento, *n.m.* perfection; improvement, improving.
perfeccionar, *v.t.* to perfect; to improve; to finish off.
perfectamente, *adv.* perfectly; fine, excellent.
perfectibilidad, *n.f.* perfectibility.
perfectivo, -va, *a.* perfective.
perfecto, -ta, *a.* perfect, faultless; (*coll.*) fine, just right. — *n.m.* perfect (*tense*).
perficiente, *a.* that which perfects.
perfidia, *n.f.* perfidy, treachery.
pérfido, -da, *a.* perfidious, treacherous.
perfil, *n.m.* profile; outline; side-view; cross-section; thin stroke; trimming; ***de perfil,*** from the side, silhouetted; (*pl.* **perfiles**) finishing touches.
perfilado, -da, *a.* long and thin, delicate; well-formed; streamlined.
perfiladura, *n.f.* profiling, outlining; profile, outline.
perfilar, *v.t.* to profile, outline; to put the finishing touches to; to streamline. — **perfilarse,** *v.r.* to show up, stand out.
perfoliada (1), **perfoliata,** *n.f.* (*bot.*) hare's-ear.
perfoliado, -da (2), *a.* (*bot.*) perfoliated.
perfolla, *n.f.* (*prov.*) corn husk; shucks.
perforación, *n.f.* perforation; drilling, boring.
perforador, -ra, *a.* perforating; drilling, boring. — *n.m.f.* drill.
perforar, *v.t.* to perforate, pierce, drill (through), bore (through); to punch; to puncture.
perfumadero, *n.m.* perfumer; perfuming-pan.
perfumador, -ra, *a.* perfuming. — *n.m.f.* perfumer.
perfumar, *v.t.* to perfume.
perfume, *n.m.* perfume, scent.
perfumería, *n.f.* perfumer's shop.
perfumero, -ra, *n.m.f.* perfumer.
perfumista, *n.m.* perfumer.
perfunctorio, -ria, *a.* perfunctory.
perfusión, *n.f.* sprinkling.
pergal, *n.m.* leather paring (*for sandal straps*).
pergaminero, *n.m.* parchment-maker.
pergamino, *n.m.* parchment, vellum.
pergeñar, *v.t.* to outline; to think out, devise.
pergeño, *n.m.* look, looks.
pérgola, *n.f.* pergola; roof garden.
peri, *n.f.* (*myth.*) peri, fairy.
periancio, periantio, *n.m.* (*bot.*) perianth.
pericardio, *n.m.* (*anat.*) pericardium.
pericarpio, *n.m.* (*bot.*) pericarp.
pericia, *n.f.* skill, expertise, know-how.
pericial, *a.* expert.
periclitar, *v.i.* to be in danger *or* jeopardy; to be unsound, shaky; to become out-moded.
Perico, *n.m.* Pete; ***Perico de los palotes,*** John Jones.
perico, *n.m.* parakeet; woman's curls; (queen) of clubs; (*naut.*) mizzen top-gallant sail; large fan.
pericón, -cona, *a.* fit for all uses. — *n.m.* large fan; (queen) of clubs; quadrille dance.
pericote, *n.m.* (*Hisp. Am.*) large field rat.
pericráneo, *n.m.* (*anat.*) pericranium.
peridoto, *n.m.* (*min.*) chrysolite.
periferia, *n.f.* periphery; outskirts.
periférico, -ca, *a.* peripheral.
perifollo, *n.m.* common chervil; (*pl.*) frippery.
perifonear, *v.t.* to broadcast.
perifonía, *n.f.* broadcasting.
perífono, *n.m.* microphone.
perifrasear, *v.i.* to periphrase, use circumlocutions.
perífrasi, perífrasis (*inv.*), *n.f.* periphrasis.
perifrástico, -ca, *a.* periphrastic, round about, circumlocutory.
perigallo, *n.m.* skin hanging from the chin; ribbon; (*coll.*) tall, thin man; sling; (*naut.*) topping lift.
perigeo, *n.m.* (*astron.*) perigeum.
perigonio, *n.m.* (*bot.*) perianth.
perihelio, *n.m.* (*astron.*) perihelion.
perilustre, *a.* highly illustrious.
perilla, *n.f.* small pear; pear-shaped ornament; pommel, knob; goatee; ***venir de perilla,*** to be just what the doctor ordered.
perillán, *n.m.* knave.
perillo, *n.m.* gingerbread nut.
perímetro, *n.m.* perimeter.
períclito, -ta, *a.* highly illustrious.
perineo, *n.m.* (*anat.*) perinœum.
perinola, *n.f.* four-faced dice, teetotum; vivacious little woman.
períoca, *n.f.* synopsis.
periódico, -ca, *a.* periodic, periodical; regular. — *n.m.* newspaper; periodical, journal.
periodismo, *n.m.* journalism.
periodista, *n.m.f.* journalist.
periodístico, -ca, *a.* journalistic.
período, periodo, *n.m.* period; (*elec.*) cycle.
periostio, *n.m.* (*anat.*) periosteum.
peripatetico, -ca, *a.*, *n.m.f.* peripatetic.
peripecia, *n.f.* vicissitude, incident.
periplo, *n.m.* voyage, journey, wanderings.
peripuesto, -ta, *a.* (*coll.*) natty, spruce.
periquete, *n.m.* jiffy, instant, trice.
periquillo, *n.m.* sugar-plum.
periquito, *n.m.* (*naut.*) stay-sail; (*orn.*) budgie, budgerigar; (*orn.*) parakeet; ***periquito entre ellas,*** ladies' man.
periscios, *n.m.pl.* (*geog.*) periscii.
periscópico, -ca, *a.* periscopic.
periscopio, *n.m.* periscope.
perista, *n.m.* (*sl.*) fence.
peristáltico, -ca, *a.* peristaltic.
peristilo, *n.m.* (*arch.*) peristyle.
perita (1), *n.f.* small pear.
peritaje, *n.m.* appraisal; degree obtained in a technical college.
perito, -ta (2), *a.* skilful, experienced. — *n.m.* expert.
perjudicador, -ra, *a.* harmful, damaging, injurious. — *n.m.f.* harmer, injurer.
perjudicar [A], *v.t.* to damage, hurt, injure, impair.
perjudicial, *a.* harmful, hurtful.
perjuicio, *n.m.* detriment, damage, harm.
perjurador, -ra, *n.m.f.* perjurer, forswearer.
perjurar, *v.i.* to commit perjury; (*coll.*) to curse and swear. — **perjurarse,** *v.r.* to perjure o.s.
perjurio, *n.m.* perjury.
perjuro, -ra, *a.* perjured. — *n.m.f.* perjurer.

perla, *n.f.* pearl; ***venir de perlas,*** to be just the thing, just what the doctor ordered.
perlada, *a.* pearled (*barley*).
perlático, -ca, *a.* paralytic, palsied.
perlería, *n.f.* collection of pearls.
perlesía, *n.f.* paralysis, palsy.
perlino, -na, *a.* pearl-coloured.
perlita, *n.f.* small pearl; (*geol.*) phonolite, clinkstone.
perlongar [B], *v.i.* (*naut.*) to coast, sail along the coast; to pay out a cable.
permanecer [9], *v.i.* to stay, remain; to last, endure.
permaneciente, *a.* permanent, persisting.
permanencia, *n.f.* permanency; stay, sojourn.
permanente, *a.* permanent. — *n.f.* permanent wave.
permeabilidad, *n.f.* permeability.
permeable, *a.* permeable.
pérmico, *a.* (*geol.*) permian.
permisible, *a.* permissible.
permisión, *n.f.* permission; permissiveness.
permisivo, -va, *a.* permissive.
permiso, *n.m.* permission; leave; permit, licence; ***con permiso,*** by your leave, with your permission.
permitente, *a.* that grants *or* permits.
permitidero, -ra, *a.* that may be permitted.
permitidor, *n.m.* permitter.
permitir, *v.t.* to permit, allow; to enable; ***me permito recordarle que,*** I take the liberty of reminding you that, I venture to remind you that.
permuta, permutación, *n.f.* permutation.
permutador, *n.m.* permuter.
permutante, *a.* permutant, exchanging.
permutar, *v.t.* to permute, exchange.
pernada, *n.f.* kick; (*naut.*) leg.
pernaza, *n.f.* thick *or* big leg.
perneador, -ra, *a.* strong-legged.
pernear, *v.i.* to kick, shake the legs; to fret.
perneo, *n.m.* (*prov.*) sale of pigs.
pernera, *n.f.* trouser leg.
pernería, *n.f.* (*naut.*) collection of pins *or* bolts.
pernetas (en), *adv.* bare-legged.
pernete, *n.m.* (*naut.*) small pin, bolt, *or* peg.
perniabierto, -ta, *a.* bandy-legged.
pernicioso, -sa, *a.* pernicious.
pernigón, *n.m.* Genoese preserved plum.
pernil, *n.m.* ham; leg of pork; leg (*of trousers*).
pernio, *n.m.* door-hinge, window-hinge.
perniquebrar [1], *v.t.* to break the leg *or* legs of.
pernituerto, -ta, *a.* crooked-legged.
perno, *n.m.* spike; bolt; hook of a hinge; (*mech.*) joint-pin, crank-pin.
pernoctar, *v.i.* to spend the night.
pero (1), *n.m.* pear tree.
pero (2), *conj.* but; ***pero que muy bien,*** very good indeed. — *n.m.* (*fig.*) but, objection, fault; ***poner peros,*** to find fault, quibble.
perogrullada, *n.f.* (*col.*) truism, platitude.
perol, *n.m.* boiler, copper, kettle.
peroné, *n.m.* (*anat.*) fibula, perone.
peroración, *n.f.* peroration; long speech.
perorar, *v.i.* to deliver a speech; to speak at length.
perorata, *n.f.* speech; rigmarole.
peróxido, *n.m.* peroxide.
perpendicular, *a.*, *n.f.* perpendicular.
perpendículo, *n.m.* plumb, plummet; pendulum; altitude of a triangle.
perpetración, *n.f.* perpetration.
perpetrador, *n.m.* perpetrator.
perpetrar, *v.t.* to perpetrate.
perpetua (1), *n.f.* (*bot.*) immortelle.
perpetuación, *n.f.* perpetuation.
perpetuar, *v.t.* to perpetuate. — **perpetuarse,** *v.r.* to go on interminably, drag on and on.
perpetuidad, *n.f.* perpetuity.
perpetuo, -tua (2), *a.* perpetual, everlasting.
perplejidad, *n.f.* perplexity.
perplejo, -ja, *a.* perplexed, mystified.
perpunte, *n.m.* quilted under-waistcoat.
perquirir [3], *v.t.* to seek diligently.
perra, *n.f.* [PERRO].
perrada, *n.f.* pack of dogs; (*fig.*) dirty trick.
perrazo, *n.m.* hefty great dog *or* hound.
perrengue, *n.m.* short-tempered *or* surly person; (*fig.*) negro.
perrera, *n.f.* kennel; drudgery, toil.
perrería, *n.f.* pack of dogs; nest of rogues; (*coll.*) dirty trick; sth. that hurts like hell.
perrero, *n.m.* kennel-keeper; dog-fancier.
perrezno, -na, *n.m.f.* whelp, puppy.
perrillo, *n.m.* little dog; trigger of a gun; piece of horse's bridle; ***perrillo de falda,*** lap dog.
perrito, *n.m.* puppy; little dog.
perro, -rra, *a.* (*coll.*, *fig.*) lousy, wretched. — *n.m.* dog; ***perro alano,*** mastiff; ***perro braco,*** setter; ***perro cobrador,*** retriever; ***perro de aguas,*** spaniel; ***perro de lanas,*** poodle; ***perro chico,*** 5 céntimo coin; ***perro gordo,*** 10 céntimo coin; (*fig.*) ***perro viejo,*** old hand, old dog; ***a otro perro con ese hueso,*** try that on s.o. else; ***de perros,*** lousy; ***echar a perros,*** to give up as a dead loss; ***perro caliente,*** hot-dog. — *n.f.* bitch; (*coll.*) tantrum; fixation, obsession; (*coll.*) farthing, copper; ***para ti la perra gorda,*** you win.
perroquete, *n.m.* topmast.
perruno, -na, *a.* doggish, dog-like, canine. — *n.f.* dog-bread, dog-cake.
persa, *a.*, *n.m.f.* Persian (*person*). — *n.m.* Persian (*language*).
persecución, *n.f.* pursuit, chase; persecution, hounding.
perseguidor, *n.m.* pursuer; persecutor.
perseguimiento, *n.m.* pursuing, pursuit.
perseguir [8G], *v.t.* to pursue, chase; to persecute, hound.
Perseo, *n.m.* (*astron.*) Perseus.
persevante, *n.m.* pursuivant at arms.
perseverancia, *n.f.* perseverance.
perseverante, *a.* perseverant, persevering.
perseverar, *v.i.* to persevere.
persiana, *n.f.* venetian blind, (*Am.*) shade.
persicaria, *n.f.* (*bot.*) spotted snakeweed, lady's thumb.
pérsico (1), **pérsigo,** *n.m.* peach (*tree and fruit*).
pérsico (2), **-ca,** *a.* Persian.
persignarse, *v.r.* to make the sign of the cross.
persistencia, *n.f.* persistence.
persistente, *a.* persistent.
persistir, *v.i.* to persist.
persona, *n.f.* person; personage; human being; ***en persona*** or ***por su persona,*** in person; ***muchas personas,*** a lot of people; ***buena persona,*** decent person; ***mala persona,*** nasty individual.
personado, *n.m.* (*eccles.*) benefice without jurisdiction.
personaje, *n.m.* personage; character.
personal, *a.* personal; characteristic. — *n.m.* personnel, staff; (*coll.*) people.
personalidad, *n.f.* personality.
personalismo, *n.m.* favouritism, nepotism; personality cult.
personalizar [C], *v.t.* to personalize, make personal.
personarse, *v.r.* to present o.s., put in an appearance, show up, attend.
personería, *n.f.* agent's charge, solicitorship.
personero, -ra, *n.m.f.* deputy, agent, attorney, trustee.
personificar [A], *v.t.* to personify.

personilla, *n.f.* ridiculous little person.
perspectiva, *n.f.* perspective; view, vista; prospect, outlook; (*fig.*) horizon.
perspicacia, perspicacidad, *n.f.* perspicacity, perspicaciousness, clear-sightedness, discernment.
perspicaz, *a.* perspicacious, keen-sighted, discerning.
perspicuidad, *n.f.* perspicuity, transparency, clearness.
perspicuo, -cua, *a.* perspicuous.
persuadidor, -ra, *n.m.f.* persuader.
persuadir, *v.t.* to persuade. — **persuadirse,** *v.r.* to become convinced.
persuasible, *a.* persuasible, persuadible.
persuasión, *n.f.* persuasion.
persuasivo, -va, *a.* persuasive. — *n.f.* persuasiveness, persuasion.
persuasor, -ra, *n.m.f.* persuader.
pertenecer [9], *v.i.* to belong; to concern.
pertenecido, *n.m.* dependence.
perteneciente, *a.* belonging; appertaining.
pertenencia, *n.f.* belonging; property; province, domain; ***eso no es de mi pertenencia,*** that is not my province; (*min.*) claim (2½ acres).
pértica, *n.f.* (*geom.*) perch.
pértiga, pertigal, *n.f.* (*geom.*) pole.
pértigo, *n.m.* pole (*of waggon* or *cart*).
pertiguería, *n.f.* verger's office.
pertiguero, *n.m.* verger.
pertinacia, *n.f.* pertinacity, doggedness, stubbornness.
pertinaz, *a.* pertinacious, dogged.
pertinente, *a.* pertinent, relevant; (*law*) concerning, pertaining.
pertrechar, *v.t.* to equip.
pertrechos, *n.m.pl.* equipment.
perturbable, *a.* capable of being perturbed.
perturbación, *n.f.* perturbation, disorder.
perturbador, -ra, *a.* perturbing, disturbing, upsetting.
perturbar, *v.t.* to perturb, disturb, unsettle.
peruano, -na, *a., n.m.f.* Peruvian.
peruétano, *n.m.* wild pear tree.
perulero, -ra, *a.* Peruvian. — *n.m.* rich American uncle.
peruviano, -na, *a.* Peruvian; ***corteza peruviana,*** Peruvian bark, cinchona.
perversidad, *n.f.* perversity, perverseness, wickedness.
perversión, *n.f.* perversion; perverting; perverseness.
perverso, -sa, *a.* perverse, wicked.
pervertido, -da, *a.* perverted. — *n.m.f.* pervert.
pervertidor, -ra, *n.m.f.* perverter, corrupter.
pervertimiento, *n.m.* perversion, perverting.
pervertir [6], *v.t.* to pervert.
pervigilio, *n.m.* sleeplessness, wakefulness.
pervulgar [B], *v.t.* to divulge; to promulgate.
pesa, *n.f.* weight; ***pesas y medidas,*** weights and measures; ***según caigan las pesas,*** according to the way things work out.
pesacartas, *n.m. inv.* letter-scale.
pesada, *n.f.* [PESADO].
pesadez, *n.f.* heaviness; gravity; sluggishness; drowsiness; sultriness; tediousness; tedious business, bore.
pesadilla, *n.f.* nightmare.
pesado, -da, *a.* heavy; sluggish; sultry; tedious, wearisome; ***broma pesada,*** nasty joke, practical joke. — *n.m.f.* bore. — *n.f.* quantity weighed at one time.
pesador, -ra, *n.m.f.* weigher.
pesadumbre, *n.f.* grief, sorrow; heaviness.
pesalicores, *n.m. inv.* hydrometer.
pésame, *n.m.* (expression of) condolence, sympathy; ***dar el pésame,*** to offer one's condolences.
pesante, *a.* weighing. — *n.m.* half-drachm weight.
pesantez, *n.f.* gravity.
pesar, *v.t.* to weigh; to weigh up; to grieve; ***me pesa haberlo dicho,*** I regret saying it; ***ya te pesará,*** you'll live to regret it; ***mal que le pese,*** whether he likes it or not; ***pese a quien (le) pese,*** regardless of everybody; ***pese a,*** in spite of. — *v.i.* to weigh; to have weight. — *n.m.* sorrow; regret; ***a pesar de,*** in spite of.
pesario, *n.m.* (*med.*) pessary.
pesaroso, -sa, *a.* sad, sorrowful; repentant.
pesca, *n.f.* fishing; angling; haul, catch; ***toda la pesca,*** the whole caboodle; ***ir de pesca,*** to go fishing; ***andar a la pesca de,*** to fish *or* angle for.
pescada, *n.f.* (small) hake.
pescadería, *n.f.* fish-market; fishmonger's (shop).
pescadero, *n.m.* fishmonger, (*Am.*) fish dealer.
pescadilla, *n.f.* small hake.
pescado, *n.m.* fish, (*Am.*) seafood.
pescador, *n.m.* fisherman; angler.
pescadora, *n.f.* fishwoman, fishwife.
pescante, *n.m.* jib (*of a crane* or *derrick*); boom; driving-seat; coach-box; (*naut.*) davit; fish davit; (*theat.*) trapdoor.
pescar [A], *v.t.* to fish; to catch; to catch out; to get, manage to get. — *v.i.* to fish.
pescozada, *n.f.,* **pescozón,** *n.m.* slap (*on neck* or *head*).
pescozudo, -da, *a.* thick-necked.
pescuezo, *n.m.* neck; (*fig.*) stiff-neckedness, haughtiness; ***retorcer el pescuezo a,*** to wring the neck of.
pescuño, *n.m.* wedge (*of coulter*).
pesebre, *n.m.* crib, manger.
pesebrera, *n.f.* row (*of mangers*).
pesebrón, *n.m.* boot (*of a coach*).
peseta, *n.f.* peseta.
pésete, *n.m.* curse.
¡pesia! *interj.* curse it! curse you!
pesillo, *n.m.* small scales.
pesimismo, *n.m.* pessimism.
pesimista, *a.* pessimistic. — *n.m.f.* pessimist.
pésimo, -ma, *a.* atrocious, abominable.
pesita, *n.f.* small weight.
peso, *n.m.* weight; load; gravity; scales; peso; burden; weighing; ***en peso,*** held up, bodily; ***de peso,*** of (due) weight; ***a peso de oro,*** at a terrific price; ***caerse du su peso,*** to be obvious, self-evident; ***llevar el peso de,*** to bear the brunt of; ***peso muerto,*** dead weight; ***peso específico,*** specific gravity.
pésol, *n.m.* kind of pea.
pespuntador, -ra, *n.m.f.* (*sew.*) back-stitcher.
pespuntar, *v.t.* to back-stitch.
pespunte, *n.m.* back-stitching.
pesquera, *n.f.* fishery, fishing grounds.
pesquería, *n.f.* fisherman's trade; fishery.
pesquis, *n.m.* cleverness, acumen; ***tener muchó pesquis,*** to be quick on the up-take.
pesquisa, *n.f.* inquiry, investigation.
pesquisante, *a.* investigating, inquiring.
pesquisar, *v.t., v.i.* to enquire (into), investigate.
pesquisidor, -ra, *n.m.f.* examiner, inquirer.
pestaña, *n.f.* eyelash; edging, fringe; (*mech.*) flange, rib, rim; (*bot.*) hairs; sunshade.
pestañear, *v.i.* to wink, blink; (*fig.*) ***sin pestañear,*** without batting an eyelid.
pestañeo, *n.m.* winking, blinking.
peste, *n.f.* plague, pestilence; epidemic, stink; foul smell; (*fig., coll.*) plague, swarm; ***una peste de extranjeros,*** a plague of foreigners; ***decir*** or ***echar pestes de,*** to call every name under the sun.
pestífero, -ra. *a.* pestiferous, foul.

pestilencia, *n.f.* plague, pestilence; foulness, stench.
pestilencial, *a.* pestilential.
pestilencioso, -sa, *a.* pestilential.
pestilente, *a.* pestilent, foul.
pestillo, *n.m.* bolt, door-latch; catch, fastener.
pestiño, *n.m.* sweet fritter.
pestorejo, *n.m.* scruff of the neck.
pesuña [PEZUÑA].
pesuño [PEZUÑO].
petaca, *n.f.* tobacco-pouch; cigar-case; (*Hisp. Am.*) leather-covered trunk *or* chest.
petalismo, *n.m.* (*polit.*) banishment.
pétalo, *n.m.* petal.
petanque, *n.m.* (*min.*) native silver.
petaquita, *n.f.* (*Col.*) climbing rose tree.
petar, *v.t.* (*coll.*) to please, attract; ***no me peta,*** I don't fancy it.
petardear, *v.t.* (*mil.*) to blow up with petards; (*fig.*) to cheat, trick. — *v.i.* to backfire.
petardero, *n.m.* petardeer; (*fig.*) cheat, swindler.
petardista, *n.m.f.* cheat, swindler.
petardo, *n.m.* petard; squib, firecracker; trick, swindle; (*fig.*) damp squib, dud; (*fig.*) bore.
petate, *n.m.* sleeping-mat; bedding; luggage, goods and chattels; (*coll.*) liar, cheat; (*coll.*) good-for-nothing; (*coll.*) ***liar el petate,*** to clear out, pack up and scram; to kick the bucket.
petenera, *n.f.* Andalusian song.
petequia, *n.f.* (*med.*) petechiæ.
petequial, *a.* petechial.
petera, *n.f.* wrangle; fit of temper.
petertes, *n.m.pl.* titbits, sweets.
peticano, peticanón, *n.m.* (*print.*) petit-canon type.
petición, *n.f.* petition; request; claim; ***petición de mano,*** formal request for the hand of a woman in marriage.
peticionario, *n.m.* petitioner.
petifoque, *n.m.* (*naut.*) outer jib.
petigrís, *n.m.* squirrel pelt.
petillo, *n.m.* stomacher.
petimetra, *n.f.* stylish, affected lady.
petimetre, *n.m.* fop, beau.
petirrojo, *n.m.* robin redbreast.
petitorio, -ria, *a.* petitory, petitionary. — *n.f.* petition.
peto, *n.m.* breastplate; plastron; protective mattress (*for horses*).
petral, *n.m.* breast-leather.
petrarquista, *a.*, *n.m.f.* Petrarchist.
petrel, *n.m.* (*orn.*) petrel.
pétreo, -rea, *a.* stony, rocky.
petrificación, *n.f.* petrification.
petrificante, *a.* petrifying.
petrificar [A], *v.t.* to petrify, turn to stone.
petrífico, -ca, *a.* petrific.
petrografía, *n.f.* petrography.
petróleo, *n.m.* petroleum, oil; ***pozo de petróleo,*** oil well; ***petróleo crudo,*** crude oil; ***petróleo combustible,*** fuel oil.
petrolero, -ra, *a.* (of) petroleum *or* oil. — *n.m.* petroleum *or* oil man, dealer *or* seller; incendiarist, fire-raiser; (***barco***) ***petrolero,*** oil-tanker.
petrolífero, -ra, *a.* oil-bearing.
petroquímico, -ca, *a.* petrochemical.
petulancia, *n.f.* arrogance.
petulante, *a.* arrogant.
petunia, *n.f.* petunia.
peucédano, *n.m.* sulphurwort.
peyorativo, -va, *a.*, *n.m.* pejorative.
pez, *n.m.* fish; (*pl.* **peces**); ***pez de color,*** goldfish; (*coll.*) ***pez gordo,*** big shot, big noise; ***como el pez en el agua,*** in one's element; (*coll.*) ***estar pez,*** not to have a clue; ***pez sierra,*** sawfish; ***pez volador,*** flying fish; ***pez martillo,*** hammerfish. — *n.f.* pitch, tar; ***pez griega*** or ***rubia,*** rosin.
pezolada, *n.f.* end-threads.
pezón, *n.m.* stalk; stem; nipple; arm (*of an axle-tree*); end (*of a spindle*); cape *or* point (*of land*).
pezonera, *n.f.* linchpin; nipple-shield.
pezpalo, *n.m.* (*com.*) stockfish.
pezpita, *n.f.*, **pezpítalo,** *n.m.* wagtail.
pezuelo, *n.m.* beginning of cloth (*in weaving*).
pezuña, *n.f.* hoof, cloven-hoof.
pezuño, *n.m.* toe, digit (*half of cloven hoof*).
piache, (*fam.*) ***tarde piache,*** too late.
piada, *n.f.* chirping, puling.
piador, -ra, *n.m.f.* chirper, puler.
piadoso, -sa, *a.* pious, godly, clement, merciful; ***mentira piadosa,*** white lie.
piafar, *v.i.* to stamp, paw (*of horses*).
piale, *n.m.* (*Hisp. Am.*) casting the lasso.
piamáter, *n.f.* (*anat.*) pia mater.
piamontés, -tesa, *a.*, *n.m.f.* Piedmontese.
pian, *adv.* gently, softly, slowly.
pianino, *n.m.* upright piano.
pianista, *n.m.f.* pianist. — *n.m.* pianoforte dealer.
piano, *adv.* [PIAN]; *n.m.* [PIANOFORTE].
pianoforte, *n.m.* piano, pianoforte; ***piano de cola,*** grand piano; ***piano vertical,*** upright piano.
pianola, *n.f.* pianola.
piante, *a.* chirping, puling.
piar [L], *v.i.* to chirp, pule; (*coll.*) to whine, cry.
piara, *n.f.* herd (*of swine, mares* or *mules*); (*fig.*) mob.
piariego, -ga, *a.* owning a herd of swine *or* a drove of mules.
piastra, *n.f.* piastre.
pica, *n.f.* pike; bullfighter's goad; stone-cutter's hammer; a measure of depth (12¾ ft.); (*med.*) pica; ***poner una pica en Flandes,*** to do sth. great, set the Thames on fire.
picacureba, *n.f.* Brazilian pigeon.
picacho, *n.m.* crag, peak.
picada (1), *n.f.* puncture; pricking; bite (*of insects, snakes etc.*).
picadero, *n.m.* riding-school; (*naut.*) stocks, boat skid; stamping ground (*of a stag*); (*fig.*) bachelor flat.
picadillo, *n.m.* minced meat, hash; ***hacer picadillo,*** to make minced meat.
picado, -da (2), *a.* (*sew.*) pinked; pitted (*with smallpox*); vexed, smarting. — *n.m.* hash, minced meat; [PICADILLO]; (*aer.*) dive; ***bombardeo en picado,*** dive bombing.
picador, *n.m.* riding-master; horse-breaker; horseman armed with a goad; (*tauro.*) chopping-block; pinking-iron; file-cutter.
picadura, *n.f.* puncture; pricking, pinking; bite, sting; cut, slash; cut tobacco.
picaflor, *n.m.* humming-bird.
picajón, -jona, picajoso, -sa, *a.* easily offended, peevish.
picamaderos, *n.m. inv.* woodpecker.
picana, *n.f.* (*Hisp. Am.*) goad.
picanear, *v.t.* (*Hisp. Am.*) to goad.
picante, *a.* hot, piquant; highly seasoned, spicy; stinging. — *n.m.* piquancy, hot seasoning; cutting remark.
picaño, -ña, *a.* roguish, vagrant, lazy. — *n.m.* patch on a shoe.
picapedrero, *n.m.* stone-breaker.
picapica, *n.f.* itching powder.
picapleitos, *n.m. inv.* (*coll.*) pettifogging lawyer.
picaporte, *n.m.* latch; latchkey; (door-) knob; knocker.
picaposte, *n.m.* woodpecker.
picapuerco, *n.m.* spotted woodpecker.
picar [A], *v.t.* to prick, pierce, puncture; to punch, punch out; to pink, prick out; to sting; to bite; to itch; to burn, smart; to peck, peck at; to pick

(at), nibble (at); to pit, leave pock-marks on; to mince, chop up; to prod, goad; to spur (on); to harass; to train, tame; to stipple; to roughen; to get on the raw, raise the hackles of, pique, vex. — *v.i.* to itch, sting, smart; to burn, make itself felt; to bite, take the bait, rise to the bait; to nibble, eat bits and pieces; to dive; ***picar alto,*** to aim high, set one's sights high; ***picar muy*** or ***demasiado alto,*** to expect too much; ***pica en escritor,*** he is a bit of a writer, dabbles in writing. — **picarse,** *v.r.* to get moth-eaten; to go bad, rotten, sour *or* stale; to develop decay; to get choppy *or* rough; (*fig.*) to take offence; ***picarse de formal,*** to pride o.s. on one's reliability *or* on being reliable.

picaraza, *n.f.* (*orn.*) magpie.

picarazo, *n.m.f.* great rogue.

picardear, *v.i.* to play the knave; to make mischief.

picardía, *n.f.* knavery, roguery; roguish, cunning *or* sly trick; risqué *or* blue remark; saucy thing to do *or* say.

picarhihuela, *n.f.* prank, roguish trick.

picaresco, -ca, *a.* roguish, knavish; picaresque. — *n.f.* life of roguery.

picaril, *a.* [PICARESCO].

pícaro, -ra, *a.* knavish, roguish; mischievous; crafty, sly. — *n.m.f.* rogue, knave; scamp, rascal; ***pícaro de cocina,*** scullion, kitchen-boy.

picarón, *n.m.* great rogue.

picarona, *n.f.* jade.

picaronazo, -za, *n.m.f.* out-and-out rogue *or* jade.

picatoste, *n.m.* buttered toast; fried bread.

picazo, -za, *a.* piebald. — *n.m.* jab; peck; young magpie. — *n.f.* magpie; ***picaza marina,*** flamingo.

picazón, *n.m.* itching; peevishness; fretfulness.

picea, *n.f.* (*bot.*) spruce.

píceo, -cea, *a.* piceous, pitchy, tarry.

pico, *n.m.* beak, bill; pick, pickaxe; peak; spout; corner; (*orn.*) woodpecker; (*coll.*) mouth, trap; (*coll.*) odd bit; (*fig.*) ***pico de oro,*** fine speaker; one with the gift of the gab; ***tener mucho pico,*** to gab, talk too much; ***perderse por el pico,*** to talk too much; ***hablar de pico,*** to talk plenty (but do little); ***hincar el pico,*** to kick the bucket; ***andar de picos pardos,*** to go on the spree; ***las tres y pico,*** just after three o'clock; ***diez y pico,*** ten odd; ***nos salió por un pico,*** it worked out at a pretty penny.

picofeo, *n.m.* (*Col.*) toucan.

picolete, *n.m.* bolt staple.

picón, -cona, *a.* having the upper teeth projecting; touchy. — *n.m.* jest; small charcoal; broken rice.

piconero, -ra, *n.m.f.* charcoal maker.

picor, *n.m.* itch, itching; burning sensation *or* taste.

picoso, -sa, *a.* pitted with smallpox.

picota, *n.f.* pillory; (*naut.*) cheek of a pump; (*fig.*) peak, point, top, spire; children's game; ***poner en la picota,*** to pillory, hold up to ridicule.

picotada, *n.f.*, **picotazo,** *n.m.* (savage) peck; (sharp) bite; peck *or* bite mark.

picote, *n.m.* coarse stuff made of goat's hair; glossy silk stuff.

picotear, *v.t.* to peck, peck at. — *v.i.* to toss the head (*of horses*); to chatter, gab, prattle. — **picotearse,** *v.r.* to bandy sharp words.

picotería, *n.f.* gossip; loquacity, volubility.

picotero, -ra, *a.* wrangling; chattering, prattling.

picotillo, *n.m.* inferior goat's-hair cloth.

picotín, *n.m.* a dry measure of capacity, the fourth part of a ***cuartal*** (*about* 3 *pints*).

picrato, *n.m.* (*chem.*) picrate.

pícrico, *a.* picric.

pictografía, *n.f.* pictography.

pictórico, -ca, *a.* pictorial.

picudilla, *n.f.* olive; insectivorous bird.

picudo, -da, *a.* beaked, sharp-pointed; long-snouted; chattering, prattling. — *n.f.* (*Cub.*) barracuda.

pichana, *n.f.* (*Arg., Chi.*) broom.

pichanga, *n.f.* (*Col.*) broom.

pichel, *n.m.* pewter tankard; mug; pitcher.

pichelería, *n.f.* tankard factory.

pichelero, *n.m.* tankard maker.

pichelete, *n.m.* small mug *or* tankard.

pichi, *n.m.* (*Chi.*) a medicinal shrub.

pichihuén, *n.m.* (*Chi., Hisp. Am., ichth.*) umbra.

pichoa, *n.f.* (*Chi.*) cathartic plant.

pichola, *n.f.* Galician wine measure (*about* I *pint*).

pichón (I), *n.m.* young pigeon.

pichón (2), **-chona,** *n.m.f.* (*fig.*) darling; (*coll.*) ducky.

pidén, *n.f.* (*Chi.*) a bird resembling the coot with a melodious song.

pidientero, *n.m.* beggar.

pidón, -dona, *a.*, *n.m.f.* (one) always asking for sth.

pie, *n.m.* foot; leg; stand, base; footing; warped yarn; last player (*at cards*); (*theat.*) cue; cause; caption; first colour given in dyeing; ***a pie,*** on foot; ***de pie,*** standing; (*naut.*) ***pie derecho,*** stanchion; (*naut.*) ***pie de roda,*** forefoot, forepart of the keel; ***pie de cabra,*** crowbar; ***a pie enjuto,*** without bother; ***a pie firme,*** steadfastly; ***de pies a cabeza,*** from head to foot; ***haber nacido de pie,*** to be born lucky; ***soldado de a pie,*** foot-soldier; ***al pie del cañón,*** on the job; ***al pie de la obra,*** on the spot; ***al pie de,*** roughly; ***a pies juntillas,*** literally; ***tomar pie de,*** to use as a pretext; ***en pie de igualdad,*** on an equal footing; ***parar los pies a,*** to check; ***no hacer pie,*** to be out of one's depth; ***no tiene ni pies ni cabeza,*** I can't make head or tail of it; ***dar pie a,*** to give cause *or* encouragement to, lead on; ***entrar con buen pie,*** to start off on the right foot; ***hacer algo con los pies,*** to do sth. in a ham-fisted fashion, make a mess of sth.; ***no dar pie con bola,*** to be right off the mark; ***en pie de guerra,*** on a war footing.

piecezuela, *n.f.* little piece.

piecezuelo, *n.m.* little foot.

piedad, *n.f.* piety; mercy, pity.

piedra, *n.f.* stone; hail; gunflint; ***piedra de amolar*** or ***afilar,*** whetstone, grindstone; ***piedra angular,*** corner-stone; ***piedra berroqueña,*** granite stone; ***piedra de escándalo,*** subject of scandal; ***piedra fundamental,*** foundation-stone; corner-stone; ***piedra infernal,*** silver nitrate; ***piedra lipis,*** copper sulphate; ***piedra pómez,*** pumice-stone; ***piedra sepulcral,*** gravestone, headstone; ***piedra de toque,*** touch-stone; ***a piedra y lodo,*** fast *or* tight (shut); ***no dejar piedra por mover,*** to leave no stone unturned; ***no dejar piedra sobre piedra,*** to raze to the ground; ***quedarse de piedra,*** to be struck dumb, be flabbergasted, be stricken to the heart, be shaken to the core; ***piedra movediza, nunca moho la cobija,*** a rolling stone gathers no moss.

piedrezuela, *n.f.* little stone, pebble.

piel, *n.f.* skin; hide, pelt; leather; fur; peel, skin; ***piel de gallina,*** goose-flesh; ***abrigo de pieles,*** fur coat; ***los pieles rojas,*** the redskins; ***ser de la piel del diablo,*** to be of the Devil's brood, be the very Devil.

piélago, *n.m.* sea, ocean; vast number.

pienso (I), *n.m.* fodder.

pienso (2), ***¡ni por pienso!*** quite out of the question! the very idea!

pienso (3), *pres. indic.* [PENSAR].

Piérides, *n.f.pl.* (*poet.*) Muses.

pierna, *n.f.* leg; honey jar; unequal selvedge (*of cloth*); downstroke (*of a letter*); cheek (*of a printing press*); (*mech.*) shank, fork; section, part; lobe (*of a walnut*); ***en piernas,*** bare-legged;

dormir a pierna suelta or ***tendida,*** to sleep soundly *or* peacefully; ***estirar las piernas,*** to stretch one's legs.
piernas, *n.m. inv.* (*coll.*) good-for-nothing, creep, drip.
piernitendido, -da, *a.* with extended legs.
pietismo, *n.m.* pietism.
pietista, *a., n.m.f.* pietist.
pieza, *n.f.* piece, fragment, part; quarry, game; play; room; ***pieza de recambio*** or ***repuesto,*** spare part; ***quedarse de una pieza,*** to be nonplussed; ***¡buena pieza!*** a fine one! a fine specimen! a fine hussy!
piezgo, *n.m.* foot (*of a hide* or *skin*); dressed wine-skin.
pífano, *n.m.* (*mus.*) fife; fifer.
pifia, *n.f.* miscue (*at billiards*); blunder.
pifiar, *v.t., v.i.* to miscue; to blunder.
pigargo, *n.m.* pygarg, osprey; ringtail hawk.
pigmento, *n.m.* pigment.
pigmeo, -mea, *a., n.m.f.* pigmy.
pignoración, *n.f.* pawning.
pignorar, *v.t.* to pawn.
pigre, *a.* slothful.
pigricia, *n.f.* sloth.
pigro, -ra, *a.* slothful.
píhua, *n.f.* sandal.
pihuela, *n.f.* leash; obstruction, hindrance; (*pl.*) fetters, shackles.
pijama, *n.m.* pyjamas, (*Am.*) pajamas.
pijota, *n.f.* (*ichth.*) small hake.
pijote, *n.m.* (*naut.*) swivel-gun.
pila, *n.f.* basin; trough; font; sink; pile, heap; pillar; battery; parish church; ***nombre de pila,*** Christian name, (*Am.*) given name.
pilada, *n.f.* pile, heap; batch (*of mortar*); cloth fulled.
pilapila, *n.f.* (*Chi.*) medicinal plant of the genus *Malva.*
pilar (1), *n.m.* pillar, column, post; milestone; basin of a fountain; spur, support, abutment; pedestal; arbor of a press.
pilar (2), *v.t.* to hull (*grain*).
pilarejo, pilarito, *n.m.* small pillar.
pilastra, *n.f.* (*arch.*) pilaster, square column.
pilatero, *n.m.* worker employed fulling cloth.
pilca, *n.m.* (*Hisp. Am.*) mud and stone wall.
pilche, *n.m.* (*Per.*) wooden cup *or* bowl.
píldora, *n.f.* pill; pellet; (*fig.*) bad news; ***dorar la píldora,*** to sugar the pill; ***tragarse la píldora,*** to swallow the pill, take the medicine.
píleo, *n.m.* pileus; cardinal's red hat.
pileta, *n.f.* small basin; (*Hisp. Am.*) swimming-pool; (*min.*) place for drained water.
pilífero, -ra, *a.* (*bot.*) piliferous, hairy.
pilme, *n.m.* (*Chi.*) a coleopterous insect of the cantharides.
pilo, *n.m.* (*Chi.*) medicinal shrub used as an emetic.
pilón, *n.m.* watering-trough; basin (*of a fountain*); drop (*of a steelyard*); counterpoise (*in an olive-press*); heap of grapes ready to be pressed; pounding-mortar; loaf (*of sugar*); pylon; heap of mortar.
pilonero, -ra, *n.m.f.* newsmonger.
pilongo (1), **-ga** (1), *a.* peeled and dried (*chestnut*); weakly.
pilongo (2), **-ga** (2), *a.* of the *or* of a parish.
pilórico, -ca, *a.* (*anat.*) pyloric.
píloro, *n.m.* (*anat.*) pylorus.
piloso, -sa, *a.* pilous, hairy.
pilotaje (1), *n.m.* (*naut.*) pilotage.
pilotaje (2), *n.m.* pile-work, piling.
pilotar, *v.t.* to pilot; (*Hisp. Am.*) to drive (*racing cars*).
pilote, *n.m.* (*engin.*) pile.
pilotín, *n.m.* pilot's mate, second pilot.
piloto, *n.m.* pilot; mate; driver; ***piloto de altura,*** navigator; ***piloto de pruebas,*** test pilot.
pilpilén, *n.m.* (*Chi.*) wading bird (*Hæmatocus palliatus*).
piltraca, piltrafa, *n.f.* scrap, tatter.
pilvén, *n.m.* (*Chi.*) freshwater fish.
pilla, *n.f.* [PILLO].
pillada, *n.f.* knavish trick.
pillador, -ra, *n.m.f.* plunderer, pillager.
pillaje, *n.m.* pillage, plunder, plundering, looting.
pillar, *v.t.* to pillage, plunder, loot; (*coll.*) to get, catch, grab; to catch out.
pillastre, pillastro, pillastrón, *n.m.* roguish fellow, rascal.
pillear, *v.i.* (*coll.*) to play the rogue.
pillería, *n.f.* crowd of rogues; knavish trick.
pillete, *n.m.* little rogue; urchin.
pillo, -lla, *a.* roguish, rascally; shrewd, sly. — *n.m.f.* rogue, scamp, rascal. — *n.f.* pillage, plunder.
pilluelo, *n.m.* little rogue, urchin.
pimental, *n.m.* pepper plantation.
pimentero, *n.m.* pepper seller; pepper-box; (*bot.*) pepper-plant.
pimentón, *n.m.* red pepper; ***pimentón dulce,*** sweet red pepper; ***pimentón picante,*** cayenne pepper.
pimienta, *n.f.* (black) pepper.
pimiento, *n.m.* (vegetable) pepper.
pímpido, *n.m.* (*ichth.*) dogfish.
pimpín, *n.m.* child's game.
pimpina, *n.f.* (*Ven.*) earthenware bottle.
pimpinela, *n.f.* (*bot.*) burnet, pimpernel.
pimplar, *v.t., v.i.* (*coll.*) to tipple.
pimpleo, -lea, *a.* belonging to the Muses.
pimplón, *n.m.* (*prov.*) waterfall, cascade.
pimpollar, *n.m.* nursery (*of plants*).
pimpollecer, *v.i.* to sprout, bud.
pimpollo, *n.m.* sucker, sprout, shoot; rosebud; young tree; (handsome, healthy) youngster.
pimpolludo, -da, *a.* covered in sprouts *or* buds.
pina, *n.f.* [PINO (2)].
pinabete, *n.m.* fir tree.
pinacate, *n.m.* (*Mex.*) black beetle.
pinacoteca, *n.f.* picture gallery.
pináculo, *n.m.* pinnacle.
pinado, -da, *a.* (*bot.*) pinnate.
pinar, *n.m.* pine forest, pine grove.
pinariego, -ga, *a.* (of the) pine.
pinastro, *n.m.* wild pine.
pinatífido, -da, *a.* (*bot.*) pinnatifid.
pinaza, *n.f.* pinnace.
pincarrascal, *n.m.* grove of Aleppo pines.
pincarrasco, *n.m.* Aleppo pine.
pincel, *n.m.* (*artist's*) brush, paintbrush; pencil.
pincelada, *n.f.* brush-stroke; pencil-stroke; ***dar la última pincelada,*** to give the finishing touch.
pincelar, *v.t.* to paint; to draw.
pincelero, *n.m.* brush-maker; pencil-maker; brush-box.
pincelillo, pincelito, *n.m.* fine brush; camel-hair brush.
pincerna, *n.m.f.* cupbearer.
pinciano, -na, *a., n.m.f.* (native) of Valladolid.
pinchadura, *n.f.* pricking; puncture.
pinchar, *v.t.* to prick, puncture, pierce; to jab; to goad; ***ni pincha ni corta,*** he has no say (*in the matter*).
pinchaúvas, *n.m. inv.* good-for-nothing.
pinchazo, *n.m.* puncture; prick, jab.
pinche, *n.m.* scullion, kitchen-boy.
pinchito, *n.m.* savoury tit-bit.
pincho, *n.m.* thorn, prickle; skewer; goad.
pindárico, -ca, *a.* Pindaric.

pindonga, *n.f.* gadding, gossiping woman.
pindonguear, *v.i.* (*coll.*) to gad about.
pineda, *n.f.* braid for garters; pine grove.
pingajo, *n.m.* rag, tatter.
pinganitos (en), *adv.* (*coll.*) well up, well in.
pingar [B], *v.i.* to drip; ***estar pingando,*** to be soaking, soaking wet, sodden.
pingo, *n.m.* rag; ***ir, andar*** or ***estar de pingo,*** to gad about; (*pl.*) cheap clothes, duds.
pingorotudo, -da, *a.* (*coll.*) posh.
pingüe, *a.* fat, oily, greasy; rich, plentiful, abundant.
pingüedinoso, -sa, *a.* fatty, pinguid.
pingüino, *n.m.* penguin.
pinguosidad, *n.f.* fatness.
pinífero, -ra, *a.* (*poet.*) piniferous.
pinillo, *n.m.* (*bot.*) germander.
pinitos, *n.m.pl.* first steps; ***hacer pinitos,*** to take one's first steps; to have a try.
pinjante, *n.m.* (*arch.*) moulding of eaves; pendant.
pino (1), **-na** (1), *a.* steep. — *n.m.* (*pl.*) first steps.
pino (2), *n.m.* pine, pine tree. — **pina** (2), *n.f.* cone-shaped landmark; jaunt, felloe (*of a wheel*).
pinocha, *n.f.* pine-needle.
pinocho, *n.m.* pine-cone.
pinol, *n.m.* (*Hisp. Am.*) cereal meal.
pinole, *n.m.* (*Mex.*) aromatic powder to mix with chocolate.
pinoso, -sa, *a.* piny.
pinsapo, *n.m.* Spanish fir.
pinta, *n.f.* spot, mark; pint; look; (*coll.*) tart; ***tener buena pinta,*** to look good. — *n.m.* good-for-nothing.
pintacilgo, *n.m.* goldfinch.
pintada, *n.f.* [PINTADO].
pintadera, *n.f.* instrument for ornamenting bread.
pintadillo, *n.m.* goldfinch.
pintado, -da, *a.* spotted, mottled, speckled; ***el más pintado,*** the best (one), the cleverest (one); ***venir pintado,*** to fit just right, be just the thing. — *n.f.* guinea-hen; graffito; ***pintadas políticas,*** political graffiti.
pintamonas, *n.m. inv.* (*coll.*) dauber.
pintar, *v.t.* to paint; to scribble, scrawl; to depict, draw; ***no pintar nada,*** to be a nobody. — *v.i.* to begin to ripen; to show, look; ***pintar bien,*** to begin to look good *or* well. — **pintarse,** *v.r.* to use *or* put on make-up; ***pintarse solo para,*** to be great *or* first-rate at; ***se pinta mucho,*** she makes up very heavily, she uses a lot of make-up.
pintarrajar, pintarrajear, *v.t.* (*coll.*) to daub.
pintarrajo, *n.m.* (*coll.*) daub.
pintarrojo, *n.m.* linnet.
pintiparado, -da, *a.* identical, exactly alike; ideal, just the thing.
pintiparar, *v.t.* to compare.
pintojo, -ja, *a.* spotted, mottled, stained.
pintor, -ra, *n.m.f.* painter; ***pintor de brocha gorda,*** house painter; (*fig.*) dauber.
pintoresco, -ca, *a.* picturesque, colourful.
pintorrear, *v.t.* to daub.
pintorzuelo, *n.m.* wretched painter.
pintura, *n.f.* painting, picture; paint.
pinturero, -ra, *a.* showy, flashy.
pínula, *n.f.* sight (*of an optical instrument*).
pinzas, *n.f.pl.* pincers, nippers; tweezers; claws (*of lobsters etc.*); burling-iron.
pinzón, *n.m.* chaffinch.
pinzote, *n.m.* (*naut.*) whip-staff.
piña, *n.f.* pine-cone; pineapple; pool (*in billiards*); (*naut.*) wall-knot; cluster; (*min.*) virgin silver treated with mercury; (*coll.*) punch.
piñata, *n.f.* pot; suspended pot filled with sweet-meats; ***domingo de piñata,*** first Sunday in Lent.
piñón, *n.m.* pine-nut, pine-kernel; (*bot.*) nut-pine; (*orn.*) pinion; (*mech.*) pinion; spring catch (*of a gun*); ***estar a partir un piñón,*** to be as thick as thieves.
piñonata, *n.f.* shredded almond preserve.
piñonate, *n.m.* pine-nut paste.
piñoncico, piñoncillo, piñoncito, *n.m.* small pine kernel; pinion.
piñonear, *v.i.* to click (*of a gun being cocked*); to call (*of a male partridge in rut*).
piñoneo, *n.m.* cry (*of partridges in rut*).
piñuela, *n.f.* figured silk; cypress nut, cypress fruit; (*Ec.*) agave.
pío (1), **pía** (1), *a.* pious, devout; merciful.
pío (2), **pía** (2), *a.* pied, piebald (*horse*).
pío (3), *n.m.* chirping, cheep; anxious desire.
piocha, *n.f.* trinket (*for women's headdress*); flower made of feathers.
piojento, -ta, *a.* lousy.
piojería, *n.f.* lousiness; (*fig.*) poverty.
piojillo, *n.m.* small louse.
piojo, *n.m.* louse; (*coll., fig.*) ***piojo pegadizo,*** pest.
piojoso, -sa, *a.* lousy; filthy; stingy, mean.
piojuelo, *n.m.* small louse.
piola, *n.f.* (*naut.*) housing, house-line.
pión, piona, *a.* chirping, twittering.
pionía, *n.f.* bucare seeds.
piorno, *n.m.* (*bot.*) broom; cytisus.
piorrea, *n.f.* pyorrhœa.
pipa, *n.f.* cask, butt, hogshead; (tobacco) pipe; pip (*of fruit*); reed (*of a clarion*); (*artill.*) fusee.
pipar, *v.i.* to smoke a pipe.
pipería, *n.f.* collection of pipes *or* barrels.
pipeta, *n.f.* pipette.
pipí, *n.m.* (*orn.*) pit-pit, honey creeper.
pipián, *n.m.* (*Hisp. Am.*) fricassee.
pipiar [L], *v.i.* to chirp.
pipiolo, *n.m.* novice, beginner.
pipirigallo, *n.m.* (*bot.*) sainfoin.
pipirijaina, *n.f.* (*coll.*) band of strolling players.
pipiripao, *n.m.* (*coll.*) slap-up do.
pipiritaña, pipitaña, *n.f.* green-cane flute.
pipo, *n.m.* (*orn.*) fly-catcher.
piporro, *n.m.* bassoon.
pipote, *n.m.* keg.
piqué, *n.m.* pique.
pique, *n.m.* pique, resentment; spade (*cards*); chigoe, jigger flea; (*naut.*) sharp-cut cliff; (*naut.*) crutch; (*naut.*) ***echar a pique,*** to sink; send to the bottom; ***estar a pique de,*** to be on the point of, in danger of; (*naut.*) ***irse a pique,*** to founder sink, go to the bottom.
piquera, *n.f.* cock-hole; entrance-hole (*in a hive*); outlet (*of a smelting furnace*); lamp-burner.
piquero, *n.m.* pikeman; (*Chi., Per., orn.*) tern.
piqueta, *n.f.* pickaxe, mattock; (mason's) hammer.
piquete, *n.m.* prick, scratch, cut; small hole (*in clothes*); stake, picket; (*mil.*) piquet.
piquetero, *n.m.* (*min.*) pick *or* mattock carrier.
piquetilla, *n.f.* (bricklayer's) hammer.
piquituerto, *n.m.* (*orn.*) cross-bill.
pira, *n.f.* pyre.
piragua, *n.f.* (*naut.*) pirogue, canoe.
piragüero, *n.m.* canoeist.
piramidal, *a.* pyramidal.
pirámide, *n.f.* pyramid.
piraña, *n.f.* (*ichth.*) pirana.
pirata, *a.* piratical. — *n.m.* pirate; cruel devil.
piratear, *v.i.* to buccaneer, engage in piracy.
piratería, *n.f.* piracy.
pirático, -ca, *a.* piratic, piratical.
pirausta, *n.f.* fabulous firefly.
pirca, *n.f.* (*Hisp. Am.*) dry-stone wall.
pircar, *v.t.* (*Hisp. Am.*) to wall round.
pirco, *n.m.* (*Chi.*) succotash.
pirenaico, -ca, *a.* Pyrenean.

pírico, -ca, *a.* pyrotechnic.
piriforme, *a.* pear-shaped.
pirineo, -nea, *a.* Pyrenean.
Pirineos, *n.m.pl.* Pyrenees.
pirita, *n.f.* (*min.*) pyrite.
pirofilacio, *n.m.* subterraneous fire.
pirogálico, -ca, *a.* pyrogallic.
pirólatra, *n.m.* pyrolater, fire-worshipper.
pirolatría, *n.f.* pyrolatry, fire-worship.
piromancia, *n.f.* pyromancy.
piromántico, -ca, *a.* pyromantic.
pirómetro, *n.m.* pyrometer.
piropear, *v.t.* (*coll.*) to pass flattering *or* cheeky remarks on.
piropo, *n.m.* (*min.*) pyrope; carbuncle; (*coll.*) complimentary, flattering *or* cheeky remark.
piróscafo, *n.m.* steamboat.
piroscopio, *n.m.* pyroscope.
pirosis, *n.f.* (*med.*) pyrosis.
pirotecnia, *n.f.* pyrotechnics.
pirotécnico, -ca, *a.* pyrotechnical.
piroxilina, *n.f.* gun-cotton.
pirquén, (**al**), (*Chi.*) at will, without restrictions *or* method (*said of the right to work a leased mine*).
pirquinear, *v.i.* (*Chi.*) to work ***al pirquén.***
pirrarse, *v.r.* to be all eagerness; ***pirrarse por,*** to long for, be crazy about, mad on.
pírrico, -ca, *a.* Pyrrhic.
pirrónico, -ca, *a.* Pyrrhonic, sceptical. — *n.m.f.* Pyrrhonist, sceptic.
pirronismo, *n.m.* Pyrrhonism.
pirueta, *n.f.* pirouette, caper.
pirulí, *n.m.* lollypop.
pisa, *n.f.* tread, treading; portion of olives *or* grapes obtained in one pressing; kick.
pisada, *n.f.* footstep; footprint; ***seguir las pisadas de,*** to follow (in) the footsteps of.
pisador, -ra, *a.* treading; high-stepping, prancing. — *n.m.* grape treader.
pisadura, *n.f.* treading.
pisapapeles, *n.m. inv.* paper-weight.
pisar, *v.t.* to step *or* tread on; to press down; to overlap; to mate (*birds*). — *v.i.* to tread; ***pisar fuerte,*** to act with determination.
pisasfalto, *n.m.* mixture of bitumen and pitch.
pisaúvas, *n.m. inv.* grape treader.
pisaverde, *n.m.* (*coll.*) coxcomb, popinjay, fop.
piscator, *n.m.* almanac.
piscatorio, -ria, *a.* piscatory.
piscicultor, -ra, *n.m.f.* pisciculturist.
piscicultura, *n.f.* pisciculture, fish-culture.
pisciforme, *a.* pisciform, fish-shaped.
piscina, *n.f.* swimming-pool; (*eccles.*) piscina.
Piscis, *n.m.* (*astron.*, *astrol.*) Pisces.
piscívoro, -ra, *a.* piscivorous.
pisco, *n.m.* (*Chi.*, *Per.*) first-quality anisette made in Pisco (Peru).
piscolabis, *n.m. inv.* (*coll.*) snack.
piso, *n.m.* floor, flooring; storey; flat, apartment; ***piso bajo,*** ground floor.
pisón, *n.m.* rammer.
pisonear, *v.t.* to ram down.
pisotear, *v.t.* to trample, tread under foot.
pisoteo, *n.m.* trampling, treading under foot.
pista, *n.f.* track, trail; strip; clue; carriageway; ***pista de aterrizaje,*** runway; landing strip; ***pista de baile,*** dance floor; ***pista de despegue,*** take-off strip; ***estar sobre la pista,*** to be on the track; ***seguir la pista de,*** to be on the trail *or* track of.
pistacho, *n.m.* pistachio nut.
pistadero, *n.m.* pestle for pounding.
pistar, *v.t.* to pound with a pestle.
pistero, *n.m.* feeding-cup.
pistilo, *n.m.* (*bot.*) pistil.
pisto, *n.m.* tomato, marrow and egg-plant hash; (*coll.*) mess; (*coll.*) ***darse pisto,*** to put on airs.
pistola, *n.f.* pistol.
pistolera, *n.f.* holster.
pistolero, *n.m.* gunman; gangster.
pistoletazo, *n.m.* pistol-shot.
pistolete, *n.m.* pistolet, pocket-pistol.
pistón, *n.m.* piston; (percussion-) cap.
pistonear, *v.i.* to knock (*of engines*).
pistonudo, -da, *a.* (*coll.*) smashing, great.
pistoresa, *n.f.* short dagger.
pistraje, pistraque, *n.m.* concoction.
pistura, *n.f.* pounding, pestling.
pita, *n.f.* (*bot.*) aloe, pita; pita thread; (*coll.*) hissing, booing; marble.
pitaco, *n.m.* stem of aloe-plant.
pitada, *n.f.* whistle-blast; whistling.
pitagórico, -ca, *a.*, *n.m.f.* Pythagorean.
pitahaya, *n.f.* tree-cactus.
pitancería, *n.f.* distribution of doles *or* rations; dole *or* ration centre.
pitanciero, *n.m.* distributor of doles *or* rations.
pitanga, *n.f.* Surinam cherry.
pitanza, *n.f.* dole, ration; (*coll.*) grub, eats.
pitaña, *n.f.* bleariness.
pitañoso, -sa, *a.* blear-eyed.
pitar, *v.t.* to whistle at, cat-call, boo, hiss. — *v.i.* to whistle; to hoot, honk; (*coll.*) ***salir pitando,*** to go tearing off, tear *or* rush off.
pitarra, *n.f.* blearedness.
pitarroso, -sa, *a.* blear-eyed.
pitecántropo, *n.m.* pithecanthrope.
pitezna, *n.f.* bolt (*for stocks*); spring (*of a trap*).
pitido, *n.m.* whistle (-blast).
pitihue, *n.m.* (*Chi.*) woodpecker.
pitillera, *n.f.* woman cigarette-maker; cigarette-case.
pitillo, *n.m.* cigarette, fag.
pítima, *n.f.* (*pharm.*) plaster; (*coll.*) drunkenness.
pitío, *n.m.* whistling.
pitipié, *n.m.* (*math.*) scale.
pitirre, *n.m.* (*Cub.*) kingbird.
pito, *n.m.* whistle; fife; fifer; cat-call; (*zool.*) tick; (*orn.*) woodpecker; ***no vale un pito,*** it's not worth a straw; ***me importa un pito,*** I don't care a rap; ***no tocar pito en,*** to have no say in; ***pitos flautos,*** foolery.
pitoflero, -ra, *n.m.f.* (*coll.*) dud musician; gossip.
pitoitoy, *n.m.* (*Hisp. Am.*) wading-bird.
pitón, *n.m.* python; protuberance, lump; sprig, shoot; nozzle, spout; horn; sprouting horn; horn tip.
pitonisa, *n.f.* pythoness; witch, sorceress.
pitora, *n.f.* (*Col.*) poisonous snake.
pitorra, *n.f.* woodcock.
pitorrearse, *v.r.* to make fun.
pitorreo, *n.m.* jeering.
pitorro, *n.m.* spout, nozzle.
pitpit, *n.m.* (*orn.*) pit-pit.
pituita, *n.f.* pituita.
pituitario, -ria, pituitoso, -sa, *a.* pituitous, pituitary.
pituso, -sa, *a.* cute; tiny.
piular, *v.i.* to chirp, pule.
piune, *n.m.* (*Chi.*) medicinal tree.
piuquén, *n.m.* (*Chi.*) great bustard.
piure, *n.m.* (*Chi.*) edible mollusc.
píxide, *n.f.* (*eccles.*) pyx, ciborium.
piyama [PIJAMA].
pizarra, *n.f.* (*min.*) slate; shale; blackboard.
pizarral, *n.m.* slate quarry.
pizarreño, -ña, *a.* slate-coloured, slaty.
pizarrero, *n.m.* slater, slate-cutter; roofer.

pizarrín, *n.m.* slate pencil.
pizca, *n.f.* (*coll.*) mite, jot, whit; ***ni pizca,*** not one little bit.
pizcar, *v.t.* to pinch; (*Mex.*) to glean (*maize*).
pizco, *n.m.* pinch.
pizmiento, -ta, *a.* pitch-coloured.
pizote, *n.m.* (*C.R., Guat., Hond.*) squirrel.
pizpereta, pizpireta, *a.* brisk, lively, vivacious (*woman*).
pizpirigaña, *n.f.* boy's game.
pizpita, *n.f.*, **pizpitillo,** *n.m.* wagtail.
placa, *n.f.* plaque; plate; badge; (*Hisp. Am.*) scab, spot; (*elec.*) ***placa giratoria,*** turntable; ***placa de matrícula,*** number plate, (*Am.*) license plate.
placabilidad, *n.f.* placability.
placable, *a.* placable, easily soothed.
placarte, *n.m.* placard, poster.
placativo, -va, *a.* placable.
placear, *v.t.* to publish, post up, proclaim; to sell at retail (*provisions*).
placel, *n.m.* (*naut.*) sand-bank.
pláceme, *n.m.* congratulation.
placenta, *n.f.* (*anat., bot.*) placenta.
placentero, -ra, *a.* pleasant, enjoyable.
placer (1), *n.m.* pleasure, enjoyment. — [23], *defect. v.t.* to please, content, gratify.
placer (2), *n.m.* (*naut.*) sand-bank; (*Hisp. Am.*) pearl-fishing; (*min.*) placer.
placero, -ra, *a.* pertaining to the market-place. — *n.m.f.* marketer, seller at a market; gadabout, idler.
placeta, placetilla, *n.f.* small square *or* public place.
placibilidad, *n.f.* agreeableness.
placible, *a.* placid, agreeable, pleasant.
placidez, *n.f.* placidness, placidity, peacefulness.
plácido, -da, *a.* placid, calm.
placiente, *a.* pleasing, pleasant.
plafón, *n.m.* (*arch.*) soffit (*of an architrave*).
plaga, *n.f.* plague, scourge; pest; glut; clime; (*naut.*) cardinal point.
plagar [B], *v.t.* to plague, fill, infest; ***estar plagado de,*** to be seething with, full of.
plagiar, *v.t.* to plagiarize; (*Hisp. Am.*) to kidnap.
plagiario, -ria, *a.* plagiary. — *n.m.f.* plagiarist.
plagio, *n.m.* plagiarism; (*Hisp. Am.*) kidnapping.
plan, *n.m.* plan; scheme; level, height; diet; mine floor; (*naut.*) floor timber; ***plan de estudios,*** curriculum; (*coll.*) affair, love affair; (*coll.*) easy girl; (*coll.*) date; (*coll.*) ***no es plan,*** that's no game, fun *or* ploy; ***¡vaya (un) plan!*** what a lark! what a set-up!; (*coll.*) ***tener mucho plan,*** to have lots of dates *or* engagements; (*coll.*) ***no me hace plan,*** it doesn't suit me; ***estar en plan de,*** to be in a mood to, have it in mind to; ***a todo plan,*** in grand *or* lavish style.
plana, *n.f.* [PLANO].
planada, *n.f.* level ground, plain.
planador, *n.m.* planisher.
plancha, *n.f.* iron; ironing; plate, sheet; (*coll.*) blunder, gaffe, howler, (*Am.*) boner; tailor's goose; (paper making) mould; horizontal suspension (*in gymnastics*); (*naut.*) gang-plank, gang-board; (*naut.*) ***plancha de agua,*** floating stage; (*naut.*) ***plancha de viento,*** hanging stage; ***plancha de blindaje,*** armour plate; ***hacer*** or ***tirarse una plancha,*** to put one's foot in it, drop a brick.
planchada, *n.f.* (*naut.*) framing *or* apron of a gun.
planchado, *n.m.* ironing.
planchadora, *n.f.* ironer.
planchar, *v.t.* to iron; to press.
planchazo, *n.m.* blunder, gaffe.
planchear, *v.t.* to plate, sheathe, cover with metal.
plancheta, *n.f.* (*surv.*) plane table.
planchón, *n.m.* large plate.
planchuela, *n.f.* small plate; fluting-iron.
planeador, *n.m.* (*aer.*) glider.
planear, *v.t.* to plan. — *v.i.* (*aer.*) to glide.
planeo, *n.m.* (*aer.*) gliding.
planeta, *n.m.* planet.
planetario, -ria, *a.* planetary. — *n.m.* planetarium.
planetícola, *n.m.f.* inhabitant of another planet.
planga, *n.f.* gannet.
planicie, *n.f.* plane.
planimetría, *n.f.* planimetry.
planímetro, *n.m.* planimeter.
planisferio, *n.m.* planisphere.
plano, -na, *a.* plane, level, flat; smooth, even. — *n.m.* plane; level, position; plan, map; survey; flat; ***plano de nivel,*** datum plane; ***primer plano,*** foreground; ***caer de plano,*** to fall flat; ***cantar de plano,*** to make a clean breast of it; ***de plano,*** plainly, flatly; ***levantar un plano,*** to make a survey. — *n.f.* page; copy; plane, level ground; trowel; (*mil.*) ***plana mayor,*** staff; ***a toda plana,*** full page; ***en primera plana,*** on the front page; ***enmendar la plana a,*** to go one better than; to find fault with.
planta, *n.f.* plant; sole (*of foot*); foot; planting; plan; floor; floor *or* ground plan; roster; stance; ***planta baja,*** ground floor; ***buena planta,*** fine appearance; ***estar en planta,*** to be up and doing, be on the go.
plantación, *n.f.* plantation; planting.
plantador, -ra, *n.m.f.* planter.
plantaina, *n.f.* (*bot.*) plantain.
plantaje, *n.m.* collection of plants.
plantar, *v.t.* to plant; to set up; to throw, fling, chuck; to jilt; to pack in, throw up. — **plantarse,** *v.r.* to take a stand, make a stand; to balk; to land, get, arrive; ***en una hora se plantó en Madrid,*** he was in Madrid in an hour.
plantario, *n.m.* nursery.
plante, *n.m.* revolt.
planteamiento, *n.m.* planning; statement, framing approach; posing, raising.
plantear, *v.t.* to plan; to set up; to state, frame; to pose, raise; ***es una cuestión difícil de plantear de una forma sencilla,*** it is an issue that it is difficult to state in simple terms; ***vamos a planteárselo,*** let us put it to him.
plantel, *n.m.* nursery (*garden*); (*fig.*) training-ground.
plantífero, -ra, *a.* (*poet.*) plantiferous.
plantificar [A], *v.t.* to establish, set up; to plant; to deliver, land (*a blow*); to dump, plonk down.
plantígrado, -da, *a.* plantigrade.
plantilla, *n.f.* sock; first sole, insole; vamp; mould; model, pattern; (*mech.*) template, templet; (*med.*) plaster for the feet; plate of a gun-lock; (*astron.*) celestial configuration; (*Cub., P.R.*) lady-finger; ***de plantilla,*** established, permanent (*staff*).
plantillar, *v.t.* to vamp, sole (*shoes etc.*)
plantío, -tía, *a.* planted; ready to be planted; tillable (*land*). — *n.m.* planted ground; nursery (*for trees*); planting.
plantista, *n.m.* braggart; landscape-gardener.
plantón, *n.m.* scion, sprout, shoot; (*coll.*) long wait; watchman, door-keeper; (*mil.*) sentry doing long guard as a punishment; ***dar un plantón a alguien,*** to stand somebody up; ***estar de plantón,*** to cool one's heels; ***llevarse un plantón,*** to be kept waiting.
planudo, -da, *a.* (*naut.*) drawing little water, flat-bottomed.
plañidero, -ra, *a.* mourning, moaning, weeping. — *n.f.* hired mourner.
plañido, *n.m.* lamentation, crying, moan.
plañir [K], *v.t.* to lament, grieve over. — *v.i.* to lament.
plaqué, *n.m.* plated metal, plate, plating.
plaquín, *n.m.* hauberk, loose coat of mail.
plasma, *n.m.* (*biol.*) plasma.

plasmador, -ra, *a.* creative. — *n.m.f.* maker, creator, moulder, shaping agent.
plasmante, *a.* moulding, shaping.
plasmar, *v.t.* to mould, form; to create. — *v.i.* to take shape. — **plasmarse,** *v.r.* to take (solid) shape, appear in solid form, take visible *or* concrete form.
plasta, *n.f.* paste, soft clay; (*coll.*) mess, botch.
plaste, *n.m.* size *or* filler.
plastecer [9], *v.t.* to size, besmear with size.
plastecido, *n.m.* (*art*) sizing.
plasticidad, *n.f.* plasticity.
plástico, -ca, *a.*, *n.m.* plastic. — *n.f.* modelling, moulding.
plastrón, *n.m.* (*fenc.*) plastron; leather apron; large cravat.
plata, *n.f.* silver; silverware; (*Hisp. Am.*) money; (*her.*) white; ***plata agria,*** stephanite; ***plata alemana,*** German silver; ***plata córnea,*** cerargyrite; ***plata labrada,*** wrought silver; ***como una plata,*** clean, bright, shining; ***hablando en plata,*** to put it bluntly.
plataforma, *n.f.* platform; (*mach.*) index-plate, division plate; orlop; (*fig.*) springboard; pad.
platal, *n.m.* great wealth, riches.
platanal, platanar, *n.m.* plane-tree plantation; banana-tree plantation.
platanero, -ra, *a.* banana. — *n.m.* banana (*plant*); (*banana*) boat; owner of a banana plantation.
plátano, *n.m.* banana; (*bot.*) plane tree; plantain (*tree and fruit*); ***plátano falso,*** sycamore maple.
platazo, *n.m.* platter; blow with a plate *or* dish; large helping (*of food*).
platea, *n.f.* (*theat.*) orchestra, pit; (*theat.*) ***asiento*** or ***butaca de platea,*** stall.
plateado, -da, *a.* silvered, silver-plated, silver. — *n.m.* silver plating.
plateador, *n.m.* plater, silverer.
plateadura, *n.f.* silvering, silver-plating.
platear, *v.t.* to silver, plate with silver. — *v.i.* to be, show up, gleam *or* glitter (like) silver.
platel, *n.m.* platter, tray.
plateresco, -ca, *a.* (*arch.*) plateresque.
platería, *n.f.* silversmith's shop *or* trade.
platero, *n.m.* silversmith, plate-worker; jeweller; ***platero de oro,*** goldsmith.
plática, *n.f.* address, sermon; talk, conversation, chat.
platicar [A], *v.i.* to talk, converse, chat.
platija, *n.f.* (*ichth.*) plaice, flounder.
platilla, *n.f.* Silesian linen.
platillo, *n.m.* saucer; small dish; (balance-) pan, beef stew; valve (*of a chain pump*); (*cards*) kitty; (*mus.*) cymbal; (*fig.*) small talk, backbiting; ***platillo volante,*** flying saucer.
platina, *n.f.* slide (*of microscope*); plate (*of air-pump*); (*print.*) platen, bedplate; (*print.*) imposing table; (*min.*) ore of platinum.
platinado, *n.m.* platinum plating.
platinar, *v.t.* to plate, coat with platinum.
platinífero, -ra, *a.* platiniferous, platinum bearing.
platino, *n.m.* platinum.
plato, *n.m.* dish, (*Am.*) platter; plate; (balance-) pan; (*arch.*) metope; ***plato frutero,*** fruit dish; ***plato sopero,*** soup plate; ***plato giratorio,*** turntable; ***plato fuerte,*** main dish; (*fig.*) ***plato de segunda mano,*** cast-off; second-fiddle; ***tener cara de no haber roto un plato,*** to look as if butter would not melt in one's mouth; ***comer en el mismo plato,*** to be bosom pals; ***nada entre dos platos,*** much ado about nothing.
platónico, -ca, *a.* platonic.
platonismo, *n.m.* Platonism.
plausibilidad, *n.f.* praiseworthiness; reasonableness.
plausible, *a.* praiseworthy, laudable; reasonable.
plause, *n.m.* applause.
plaustro, *n.m.* cart.
playa, *n.f.* beach, strand, sandy shore; seaside resort.
playado, -da, *a.* with a beach, beach-lined.
playazo, *n.m.* long wide beach.
playero, -ra, *a.* beach. — *n.m.f.* fish-seller. — *n.f.* song; beach shoe.
playón, *n.m.* large beach.
plaza, *n.f.* square, place; market-place; market; fortified place *or* town; post, position, seat; ***¡plaza!*** make way!; ***hacer plaza,*** to make room; ***plaza fuerte,*** stronghold; ***plaza de armas,*** parade-ground; ***plaza de toros,*** bull-ring; ***sacar a (la) plaza,*** to make public; (*mil.*) ***sentar plaza,*** to join up; ***sentar plaza de,*** to set o.s. up as an authority on, lay down the law on.
plazo, *n.m.* term; space of time; day of payment; time limit; instalment; ***a corto plazo,*** short-term; ***a largo plazo,*** long-term; ***venta a plazos,*** hire-purchase (*system*), (*Am.*) instalment plan; ***comprar a plazos,*** to buy in instalments.
plazoleta, plazuela, *n.f.* small square.
ple, *n.m.* hand-ball game.
pleamar, *n.f.* highwater, high tide.
plébano, *n.m.* curate of a parish.
plebe, *n.f.* common people.
plebeyo, -ya, *a.* plebeian. — *n.m.f.* plebeian.
plebiscitar, *v.t.* to hold a plebiscite on.
plebiscito, *n.m.* plebiscite.
pleca, *n.f.* (*print.*) rule, straight line.
plectro, *n.m.* plectrum; (*poet.*) inspiration.
plegable, *a.* pliable, folding.
plegadera, *n.f.* paper folder; paper-knife.
plegadizo, -za, *a.* pliable, folding.
plegado, *n.m.* plaiting, folding.
plegador, -ra, *a.* folding. — *n.m.* folding instrument; weaving beam; warper's beam, yarn beam. — *n.f.* folding machine.
plegadura, *n.f.* fold, crease, plait, doubling, folding, plaiting.
plegar [1B], *v.t.* to fold, bend, plait, pleat; to pucker; to turn (*the warp*) on the yarn beam. — *v.i.* to pack up, pack in. — **plegarse,** *v.r.* to yield, give way.
plegaria, *n.f.* prayer.
pleguete, *n.m.* tendril of vines.
pleistoceno, *a.* (*geol.*) pleistocene.
pleita, *n.f.* plaited strand of bass.
pleiteador, -ra, *n.m.f.* pleader; wrangler.
pleiteante, *a.* litigating. — *n.m.f.* litigant.
pleitear, *v.t.* to plead, contend, litigate.
pleitista, *n.m.* pettifogger.
pleito, *n.m.* litigation, lawsuit; ***poner pleito a,*** to sue, bring suit against; ***pleito de acreedores*** insolvency proceedings.
plenamar, *n.f.* high water.
plenario, -ria, *a.* (*law*) plenary; ***indulgencia plenaria,*** plenary indulgence.
plenilunio, *n.m.* full moon.
plenipotencia, *n.f.* plenipotence.
plenipotenciario, -ria, *a.*, *n.m.f.* plenipotentiary.
plenitud, *n.f.* plenitude, fullness, abundance.
pleno, -na, *a.* full, complete; ***en pleno día,*** in broad daylight; ***en pleno invierno,*** in the middle *or* depths of winter. — *n.m.* plenary session.
pleonasmo, *n.m.* pleonasm.
pleonástico, -ca, *a.* pleonastic.
plepa, *n.f.* (*coll.*) pain-in-the-neck, bore; dud.
plesímetro, *n.m.* (*med.*) pleximeter.
plesiosauro, *n.m.* (*palæont.*) plesiosaurus.
pletina, *n.f.* small iron plate.
plétora, *n.f.* plethora, superabundance.
pletórico, -ca, *a.* plethoric.
pleuresía, pleuritis, *n.f.* pleurisy.
pleurítico, -ca, *a.* pleuritic, pleuritical.

pleurodinia, *n.f.* (*med.*) pleurodynia.
plexo, *n.m.* (*anat.*) plexus; network of veins, fibres, *or* nerves.
Pléyadas, *n.f.* (*astron.*) Pleiades.
plica, *n.f.* sealed will etc.; matted hair, plica.
pliego (1), *n.m.* sheet of paper; folded paper; sealed letter *or* document; ***pliego de condiciones,*** specifications, tender, bid; ***pliego de cargos,*** charge sheet; ***pliego de prensa,*** page proof.
pliego (2), **pliegue** (1), *pres. indic., pres. subj.* [PLEGAR].
pliegue (2), *n.m.* fold, crease; (*sew.*) pleat.
plieguecillo, *n.m.* half sheet of standard ***pliego*** (435 mm. × 315 mm.).
plinto, *n.m.* plinth.
plioceno, *a.* (*geol.*) pliocene.
plomada, *n.f.* blacklead pencil; plumb; plummet; (*naut.*) lead; apron (*of a cannon*); (fishing-net) sinker; scourge with lead balls, cat-o'-nine-tails.
plomar, *v.t.* to put a lead seal on.
plomazón, *n.m.* gilding cushion.
plombagina, *n.f.* plumbago.
plomería, *n.f.* plumber's trade; lead roofing; storehouse of lead goods.
plomero, *n.m.* lead-worker; plumber.
plomizo, -za, *a.* leaden.
plomo, *n.m.* lead; piece of lead; plumb, plummet, bob; bullet; sinker; fuse; (*coll.*) bore; ***andar con pies de plomo,*** to go gingerly, take it very easy; ***a plomo,*** straight down; down flat.
plomoso, -sa, *a.* leaden.
pluma, *n.f.* feather; quill; pen; down; ***buena pluma,*** good writer; ***pluma de agua,*** running water; ***pluma viva,*** eiderdown; ***pluma estilográfica,*** fountain-pen; ***dejar correr la pluma,*** to scribble away, write at length; ***a vuela pluma,*** speedily.
plumado, -da, *a.* feathered, feathery, plumy. — *n.f.* stroke, flourish of the pen.
plumaje, *n.m.* plumage.
plumajería, *n.f.* feather-trade.
plumajero, *n.m.* feather-seller, feather-dealer.
plumario, *n.m.* painter of birds; plume-maker.
plumazo, *n.m.* feather mattress; feather pillow; stroke of the pen; ***de un plumazo,*** with *or* at a stroke of the pen.
plumazón, *n.m.* plumage.
plúmbeo, -bea, plúmbico, -ca, *a.* leaden.
plumeado, *n.m.* (*art.*) lines in miniature painting.
plumear, *v.t.* (*art*) to shade, darken.
plúmeo, -mea, *a.* feathered, plumed.
plumería, *n.f.* feather-trade.
plumerilla, *n.f.* (*River Plate*) red-flowered mimosa.
plumero, *n.m.* plume, bunch of feathers; feather-duster; box for feathers *or* plumes.
plumífero, -ra, *a.* (*poet.*) feathered.
plumilla, *n.f.* small feather; (*bot.*) plumule; ***plumín plumilla,*** nib, (*Am.*) pen point.
plumista, *n.m.* pen-pusher, scrivener; plume-maker.
plumón, *n.m.* down; feather bed.
plumoso, -sa, *a.* feathered, plumy.
plúmula, *n.f.* (*bot.*) plumule.
plural, *a., n.m.* plural.
pluralidad, *n.f.* plurality; ***a pluralidad de votos,*** by a majority.
pluralizar, *v.t.* to pluralize.
pluriempleo, *n.m.* holding of more than one job.
plus, *n.m.* bonus; extra.
pluscuamperfecto, *n.m.* (*gram.*) pluperfect.
plusvalía, *n.f.* increased value, appreciation.
plúteo, *n.m.* bookshelf.
plutocracia, *n.f.* plutocracy.
plutócrata, *n.m.f.* plutocrat.
plutocrático, -ca, *a.* plutocratic.
Plutón, *n.m.* (*astron.*) Pluto.
plutónico, -ca, *a.* (*geol.*) plutonic.
plutonismo, *n.m.* (*geol.*) plutonism.
pluvia, *n.f.* (*poet.*) rain.
pluvial, *n.m.* (*eccles.*) pluvial.
pluvímetro, pluviómetro, *n.m.* (*phys.*) pluviometer.
pluvioso, -sa, *a.* rainy, wet.
poa, *n.f.* (*naut.*) bowline bridle.
pobeda, *n.f.* poplar grove.
población, *n.f.* population; town.
poblacho, poblachón, *n.m.* wretched *or* sprawling village *or* town.
poblado, *n.m.* town, village, settlement.
poblador, -ra, *a.* peopling, populating. — *n.m.f.* founder, settler.
poblano, -na, *a.* (*Hisp. Am.*) belonging to a village.
poblar [4], *v.t.* to inhabit, people, settle; to cover. — *v.i.* to found towns. — **poblarse,** *v.r.* to become peopled; to become filled *or* covered.
poblazo, *n.m.* large, ugly village.
poblezuelo, *n.m.* small village.
pobo, *n.m.* white poplar.
pobre, *a.* poor, ***más pobre que una rata,*** poor as a church mouse; ***pobre de solemnidad,*** desperately poor (*person*). — *n.m.f.* poor person, pauper; beggar.
pobrecico, -ca, pobrecillo, -lla, pobrecito, -ta, *a., n.m.f.* poor little (*fellow, thing, etc.*).
pobrería, pobretería, *n.f.* poverty; beggars, paupers, wretched people.
pobrero, *n.m.* distributor of alms.
pobrete, -ta, *a.* poor, wretched. — *n.m.f.* poor wretch. — *n.f.* prostitute, strumpet.
pobretear, *v.i.* to pretend poverty.
pobretón, -tona, *a., n.m.f.* wretchedly poor.
pobreza, *n.f.* poverty; want, lack.
pobrezuelo, -la, *a.* poorish. — *n.m.f.* poor little wretch.
pobrismo, *n.m.* poor people, beggars, pauperism.
pocero, *n.m.* well-sinker; sewer-man.
pocilga, *n.f.* pigsty; (*fig.*) filthy place.
pocillo, *n.m.* vessel sunk in the ground in oil mills; chocolate cup.
pócima, *n.f.* concoction.
poción, *n.f.* potion; drink, draught.
poco, -ca, *a.* little, not much; ***poco dinero,*** not much money; ***de poco tiempo acá,*** recently, of late; (*pl.*) few; ***unos pocos,*** a few, one or two; ***a los pocos días,*** a few days later. — *adv.* little; shortly; ***poco más o menos,*** more or less; ***poco antes,*** shortly before; ***tener en poco,*** to set little value on; to have a poor view of; ***a poco,*** shortly afterwards; ***dentro de poco,*** shortly, soon; ***en poco estuvo que,*** (it) almost (happened that); ***poco a poco,*** little by little, very gently, easy does it; ***por poco,*** very nearly; ***por poco se cae,*** he almost fell. — *n.m.* little amount; ***un poco de,*** a little, some.
póculo, *n.m.* drinking-cup.
pocho, -cha, *a.* faded; soft; off-colour.
poda, *n.f.* pruning; pruning season.
podadera, *n.f.* pruning-knife, pruning-hook; hedging-bill.
podador, -ra, *n.m.f.* pruner.
podagra, *n.f.* gout.
podar, *v.t.* to prune (*trees*); to head, lop, trim.
podazón, *n.f.* pruning-season.
podenco, *n.m.* hound.
poder, *n.m.* power, might; authority; command, influence; vigour, strength, force, mastery; faculty; power of attorney; military strength; proxy; possession, tenure; ***en mi poder,*** in my possession; (*pl.* **poderes**) power, written authority. — *v.t.* to be a match for, be more than a match for, get the better of; ***le pude,*** I proved a

match for him, I got the better of him. — [24] *v.i.* to be able; to have power *or* strength; to be possible; (*coll.*) ***este tío me puede,*** this bloke gets on my nerves; ***no podrá ir,*** he won't be able to go; ***podrá no ir,*** he may not go, he won't of necessity have to go, he'll be able to choose not to go; — ***No puedo.*** — ***Pues puede.*** —, 'I can't.' 'You'll just have to, I'm afraid'; ***no puedo (por) menos de reírme,*** I can't help laughing; ***lo haré como pueda,*** I'll do it as best I can; (*coll.*) ***no me puede ver,*** he can't stand the sight of me; ***no poder más,*** to be at the end of one's tether, be all in; ***no puedo con todo esto,*** I can't manage all this (lot); ***no puede con ese niño,*** she can't manage that child; she can't stand that child; ***¿se puede?*** may I come in?; ***poder mucho,*** to have power, influence; ***poder poco,*** to have little power, influence; ***a*** or ***hasta más no poder,*** to the utmost; ***puede que sea verdad,*** it may be true.

poderdante, *n.m.f.* (*law*) constituent.
poderhabiente, *n.m.* attorney.
poderío, *n.m.* power, might.
poderoso, -sa, *a.* powerful, mighty; rich, wealthy.
podio, *n.m.* (*arch.*) podium.
podómetro, *n.m.* podometer.
podón, *n.m.* bill-hook.
podre, *n.m.f.* pus; corrupted matter.
podrecer [9], *v.t.*, *v.i.* to rot.
podrecimiento, *n.m.* rottenness, putrefaction.
podredumbre, *n.f.* rottenness, putrefaction; decay, corruption; grief.
poema, *n.m.* poem; epic.
poesía, *n.f.* poetry, poesy; poem.
poeta, *n.m.* poet.
poetastro, *n.m.* poetaster.
poético, -ca, *a.* poetic, poetical. — *n.f.* poetry, poetics.
poetisa, *n.f.* poetess.
poetizar [C], *v.t.*, *v.i.* to poetize; to practise the art of poetry.
poíno, *n.m.* gantry, stilling.
polaco, -ca, *a.* Polish. — *n.m.f.* Pole.
polacra, *n.f.* (*naut.*) polacre.
polaina, *n.f.* legging, gaiter.
polar, *a.* polar.
polaridad, *n.f.* polarity.
polarización, *n.f.* polarization.
polarizar [C], *v.t.* to polarize. — **polarizarse,** *v.r.* to become polarized, polarize.
polca, *n.f.* polka.
polcar, *v.i.* to dance the polka.
polea, *n.f.* pulley; tackle-block, block-pulley; ***polea loca,*** loose pulley; ***polea motriz,*** driving-pulley.
poleadas, *n.f.pl.* pap.
poleame, *n.m.* collection of pulleys, tackle.
polémico, -ca, *a.* polemical, polemic. — *n.f.* polemics; dispute, controversy.
polemista, *n.m.f.* polemicist, controversialist.
polemizar [C], *v.i.* to engage in argument.
polemonio, *n.m.* (*bot.*) Jacob's ladder.
polen, *n.m.* pollen.
polenta, *n.f.* polenta.
poleo, *n.m.* (*bot.*) penny-royal: strutting gait; pompous style; strong cold wind.
poliandria, *n.f.* (*bot.*) polyandria.
poliantea, *n.f.* polyanthea.
poliarquía, *n.f.* polyarchy.
poliárquico, -ca, *a.* relating to polyarchy.
policarpo, *n.m.* (*bot.*) polycarpous.
pólice, *n.m.* thumb.
policía, *n.f.* police. — *n.m.* policeman; detective; ***policía municipal,*** city *or* town police; ***policía fluvial,*** river police.
policitación, *n.f.* pollicitation.
policlínica, *n.f.* (*med.*) polyclinic.
policopia, *n.f.* multigraph.
policromar, *v.t.* to polychrome.
policromía, *n.f.* polychromy.
polichinela, *n.m.f.* buffoon.
polidor, *n.m.* (*sl.*) seller of stolen goods.
poliédrico, -ca, *a.* polyhedral, polyhedric.
poliedro, *n.m.* polyhedron.
polifásica, *n.f.* (*elec.*) multiphase.
polifonía, *n.f.* polyphony.
polifónico, -ca, *a.* polyphonic.
polígala, *n.f.* milkwort.
poligamia, *n.f.* polygamy.
polígamo, -ma, *a.* polygamous. — *n.m.f.* polygamist.
polígloto, -ta, *a.*, *n.m.f.* polyglot.
poligonal, *a.* (*geom.*) polygonal. — *n.f.* (*surv.*) broken line.
polígono, *n.m.* polygon; (*artill.*) range.
poligrafía, *n.f.* polygraphy.
polígrafo, *n.m.* polygraph.
polihedro, *n.m.* polyhedron.
polilla, *n.f.* moth; (*fig.*) waster, destroyer.
polímita, *a.* made of many-coloured threads.
polimorfo, -fa, *a.* (*chem.*) polymorphous.
polín, *n.m.* wooden roller.
polinización, *n.f.* (*bot.*) pollination.
polinomio, *n.m.* (*alg.*) polynomial.
polipétalo, -la, *a.* (*bot.*) polypetalous.
pólipo, *n.m.* (*med.*) polypus; (*zool.*) polyp; octopus.
polipodio, *n.m.* fern.
polisílabo, -ba, *a.* polysyllabic. — *n.m.* polysyllable.
polisinodia, *n.f.* multiplicity of synods *or* councils.
polisón, *n.m.* bustle; pad, cushion *or* framework.
polispasto, *n.m.* burton, hoisting tackle.
polista, *n.m.* (*Philip.*) Indian serving in communal works; polo player.
politécnico, -ca, *a.* polytechnic.
politeísmo, *n.m.* polytheism.
politeísta, *n.m.f.* polytheist.
politicastro, *n.m.* politicaster, wretched politician.
político, -ca, *a.* politic, political; discreet, tactful; polite; ***padre político,*** father-in-law. — *n.m.* politician. — *n.f.* politics; policy; diplomacy; ***política-ficción,*** phoney politics.
politicón, -cona, *a.* intriguing, keen on politics; overpolite.
politiquear, *v.i.* (*coll.*) to dabble in politics.
politiqueo, *n.m.* dabbling in politics.
politiquero, -ra, *a.*, *n.m.f.* (one) fond of (low) politics; hack politician.
politizar, *v.t.* to politicize, give a political slant to.
polivalvo, -va, *a.* multivalve.
póliza, *n.f.* (*com.*) paybill; policy; excise stamp; customs-house permit.
polizón, *n.m.* gadabout, loafer; stowaway.
polizonte, *n.m.* (*coll.*) policeman, cop.
polo, *n.m.* (*geom.*, *astron.*) pole; polo (*game*); Andalusian song and dance; ice-lolly; water ice; ***polo de desarrollo,*** regional development centre.
polonés, -nesa, *a.* Polish. — *n.m.f.* Pole. — *n.m.* Polish (*language*).
Polonia, *n.f.* Poland.
poltrón, -rona, *a.* lazy, sluggish, work-shy. — *n.m.f.* work-shy individual, skiver. — *n.f.* easy chair.
poltronería, *n.f.* laziness, sluggishness.
poltronizarse [C], *v.r.* to become lazy *or* sluggish.
polución, *n.f.* pollution; masturbation; smog.
poluto, -ta, *a.* polluted, soiled.
polvareda, *n.f.* cloud of dust; (*fig.*) rumpus, outcry; (*coll.*) dust-up.
polvera, *n.f.* powder-case, compact.

polvificar [A], *v.t.* (*coll.*) to pulverize.
polvo, *n.m.* dust; powder; pinch of snuff; (*vulg.*) shot; (*com.*) ***limpio de polvo y paja,*** net; ***morder el polvo,*** to bite the dust; ***sacudir el polvo a,*** to give a beating to; ***hacer polvo,*** to wreck, smash up, make a mess of; to fag out, whack; to upset terribly; ***está hecho polvo,*** he's fagged out; he's terribly cut up (about it); (*pl.*) face powder.
pólvora, *n.f.* powder, gunpowder; fireworks; vivacity, liveliness, briskness; bad temper, irritability; ***pólvora de algodón,*** gun cotton; ***gastar la pólvora en salvas,*** to waste one's time *or* energy; ***no ha inventado la pólvora,*** he hasn't set the Thames on fire; ***ser una pólvora,*** to be a live wire.
polvoreamiento, *n.m.* pulverization, powdering.
polvorear, *v.t.* to powder, sprinkle with powder; to sprinkle *or* dust (***de,*** with).
polvoriento, -ta, *a.* dusty.
polvorín, *n.m.* very fine powder; powder-flask, priming-horn; powder magazine.
polvorista, *n.m.* maker of gunpowder; firework-maker.
polvorización, *n.f.* pulverization.
polvorizar [C], *v.t.* to pulverize.
polvorón, *n.m.* powder cake.
polvoroso, -sa, *a.* dusty; ***poner pies en polvorosa,*** to take to one's heels.
polla, *n.f.* pullet, chicken, young hen; (*coll.*) chick, girl; pool (*at cards*); (*orn.*) fulica, coot.
pollada, *n.f.* brood, hatch, covey; grapeshot.
pollancón, -cona, *n.m.f.* large chicken; (*coll.*) overgrown youth.
pollastra, *n.f.* pullet.
pollastre, *n.m.* (*fig.*) young blood.
pollastro, *n.m.* cockerel.
pollazón, *n.m.* hatch, brood; hatching and rearing (*fowls*).
pollera, *n.f.* chicken-rearer; hen-coop; go-cart; hooped skirt; (*Hisp. Am.*) skirt; (*astron.*) Pleiades.
pollería, *n.f.* poultry-shop; poultry-market; young people.
pollero, *n.m.* chicken-run; poulterer.
pollerón, *n.m.* (*Arg.*) riding-skirt.
pollina, *n.f.* young she-ass.
pollinar, *a.* (*coll.*) stupid.
pollino, *n.m.* ass, young ass, donkey.
pollita, *n.f.* chick, young chicken; (*coll.*) chick, bird, girl.
pollito, *n.m.* chick; (*coll.*) young lad *or* chap.
pollo, *n.m.* chicken; (*fig.*) young chap *or* fellow.
polluelo, -la, *n.m.f.* chick.
poma, *n.f.* apple; perfume-box; smelling-bottle; pomander box.
pomada, *n.f.* pomade; ointment; hair-cream.
pomar, *n.m.* apple orchard.
pomarada, *n.f.* apple plantation.
pomarrosa, *n.f.* rose apple.
pómez, *n.m.* pumice; ***piedra pómez,*** pumice-stone.
pomífero, -ra, *a.* apple-bearing.
pomo, *n.m.* pome, pomander; jar, vial; pommel; handle, knob.
pomol, *n.m.* (*Mex.*) maize omelet.
pompa (1), *n.f.* pomp, pageantry; ostentation; bubble; ballooning (*of clothes*); spread (*of peacock's tail*); (*naut.*) pump; ***pompas fúnebres,*** undertaker's (parlour); funeral ceremony; ***director de pompas fúnebres,*** undertaker, (*Am.*) mortician.
pompear, *v.t.* to pump. — *v.i.* to make a show. — **pompearse,** *v.r.* to make a show; to strut about.
pompo, -pa (2), *a.* (*Col.*) obtuse, blunt; flat-nosed.
pompón, *n.m.* (*mil.*) pompon.
pomposidad, *n.f.* grand style; pompousness.
pomposo, -sa, *a.* grand, in grand style; showy; pompous.
pómulo, *n.m.* cheekbone.
ponasí, *n.m.* (*Cub.*) poisonous shrub with deep-red flowers (*Hamelia patens*).
poncí, poncidre, poncil, *n.m.* bitter citron *or* lemon.
ponchada, *n.f.* bowlful of punch.
ponche, *n.m.* punch.
ponchera, *n.f.* punch-bowl.
poncho, -cha, *a.* soft, lazy, listless. — *n.m.* poncho.
ponderable, *a.* praiseworthy.
ponderación, *n.f.* weighing; circumspection; exaggeration; high praise.
ponderado, -da, *a.* circumspect; calm.
ponderador, -ra, *a.* weighing; exaggerating; emphasizing; praising. — *n.m.f.* weigher; exaggerator; praiser.
ponderal, *a.* relating to weight.
ponderar, *v.t.* to weigh; to exaggerate, emphasize; to praise to the skies.
ponderativo, -va, *a.* exaggerating; emphasizing, stressing; laudatory.
ponderosidad, *n.f.* ponderousness, weightiness; circumspection.
ponderoso, -sa, *a.* ponderous, weighty; circumspect.
ponedero, -ra, *a.* egg-laying. — *n.m.* nesting-box; nest egg.
ponedor, -ra, *a.* egg-laying. — *n.m.f.* bidder.
ponencia, *n.f.* paper, communication.
ponente, *n.m.* chairman of a committee of enquiry; one who reads a paper *or* communication; proposer of a bill *or* policy.
poner [25], *v.t.* to put, set, lay; to contribute; to suppose; to bet; to give; to put on, add; to impose; to put *or* set down; to name, call; ***pongamos diez, vamos a poner diez,*** let's say ten; ***poner una conferencia,*** to make a trunk-call; ***poner un telegrama,*** to send a telegram; ***poner unas letras a,*** to write a few lines to; ***poner el grito en el cielo,*** to raise Cain; ***poner los ojos en,*** to take a fancy to; ***poner los ojos en blanco,*** to turn up the whites of one's eyes; ***poner casa,*** to set up house; ***poner coto a,*** to set a limit to; ***poner peros a,*** to find fault with; ***poner como un trapo, poner de vuelta y media,*** to call every name under the sun; ***poner de relieve,*** to bring out sharply, emphasize; ***poner en claro,*** to make clear; ***poner en limpio,*** to make a fair copy of; ***poner en duda,*** to call in question; ***poner en ridículo,*** to make a fool of; ***poner en vigor,*** to bring into force; ***poner por escrito,*** to put in writing. — **ponerse,** *v.r.* to become, get, go, grow; to set, go down; ***ponerse a,*** to set about, start; ***ponerse de,*** to get a job as; ***ponerse en,*** to get to, arrive in, reach; ***¡cómo te has puesto!*** what a state you've got into! what a state *or* mess you're in!; ***ponerse colorado,*** to go red, blush crimson; (*fig.*) ***ponerse las botas,*** to have a good tuck-in; ***ponerse a bien con,*** to get right with, get on good terms with; ***ponerse de largo,*** to come out (in society); ***ponerse de parte de,*** to side with; ***ponerse en camino,*** to set *or* start out; ***se le ha puesto ir,*** he has got it firmly into his head to go.
pongo, *n.m.* (*zool.*) orang-outang; (*Bol., Per.*) Indian servant; (*Ec., Per.*) narrow and dangerous ford.
poniente, *n.m.* west; west wind; (***sol***) ***poniente,*** setting sun, sunset.
ponimiento, *n.m.* putting (on).
ponleví, *n.m.* high-heeled shoe.
ponqué, *n.m.* (*Cub., Ven.*) cake.
pontazgo, pontaje, *n.m.* bridge-toll, pontage.
pontear, *v.t.* to bridge.
pontezuelo, -la, *n.m.f.* small bridge.
pontificado, *n.m.* pontificate, papacy.

pontifical, *a.* pontifical, papal. — *n.m.* pontifical; pontifical robe; parochial tithes.
pontificar [A], *v.i.* to pontificate.
pontífice, *n.m.* pontiff.
pontificio, -cia, *a.* pontifical.
pontín, *n.m.* (*Philip.*) coasting vessel.
ponto, *n.m.* (*poet.*) sea.
pontón, *n.m.* (*mil.*) pontoon; dredge; hulk serving as store-ship, hospital *or* prison ship; log bridge.
pontonero, *n.m.* pontoneer.
ponzoña, *n.f.* poison, venom.
ponzoñosamente, *adv.* poisonously.
ponzoñoso, -sa, *a.* poisonous, venomous.
popa, *n.f.* (*naut.*) poop, stern; ***a popa, de popa,*** aft, abaft; (*naut.*) ***viento en popa,*** before the wind; (*fig.*) swimmingly, fine.
popamiento, *n.m.* despising; cajoling.
popar, *v.t.* to despise; to fondle, caress; to pamper.
popel, *a.* sternmost.
popelín, *n.m.* poplin, (*Am.*) broadcloth.
popés, *n.m.* mizzen-mast stay.
popocho, -cha, *a.* (*Col.*) very full, gorged, stuffed.
popote, *n.m.* (*Mex.*) Indian straw for brooms.
populación, *n.f.* population; populating.
populachería, *n.f.* vulgarity; playing to the gallery; (*pej.*) common people.
populachero, -ra, *a.* vulgar, common.
populacho, *n.m.* rabble, mob.
popular, *a.* popular; of the people.
popularidad, *n.f.* popularity.
popularizar [C], *v.t.* to popularize, make popular. — **popularizarse,** *v.r.* to become popular.
populazo, *n.m.* rabble, mob.
populeón, *n.m.* white poplar ointment.
populoso, -sa, *a.* populous, crowded.
popusa, *n.f.* (*E.S., Guat.*) maize omelet stuffed with cheese and meat.
poquedad, *n.f.* littleness, paucity; pusillanimity; trifle.
poquillo, -lla, *a.* [POQUITO].
poquísimo, -ma, *a. superl.* (miserably) little.
poquitico, -ca, poquitillo, -lla, poquitito, -ta, poquitín, *a. dim. of.* **poquito**; ***un poquitín de,*** a wee bit of.
poquito, -ta, *a.* very little; (*pl.*) very few. — *adv.* very little; ***poquito a poco,*** gently, slowly. — *n.m.* very small amount, very short time, little bit; ***un poquito,*** a little bit; ***a poquitos,*** in tiny bits, in dribs and drabs.
por, *prep.* for; for the sake of; on behalf of; because of, on account of; by; about; through, across; per; ***por otra parte,*** on the other hand; moreover; ***por ahí,*** thereabouts; out (there) somewhere; ***por la mañana,*** in the morning; ***por mayor,*** wholesale; ***por Navidad,*** about *or* at Christmas time; ***cuentas por cobrar,*** bills to be collected; ***por barba,*** per head; ***por carta de más,*** excessively; ***por carta de menos,*** insufficiently; ***por ce o por be,*** for one reason or another; (*law*) ***por cuanto,*** whereas; ***por mejor decir,*** to be more precise; ***por lo tanto,*** therefore; ***por ahora,*** for the present, for the time being; ***por cierto,*** incidentally, by the way; indeed; ***de por sí,*** in itself; ***por demás,*** overmuch; excessively; ***por encima,*** superficially; ***por ende,*** for that reason; ***por entre,*** through, between; ***por más que*** or ***por mucho que,*** however much; ***por las buenas o por las malas,*** like it or not; ***por el bien parecer,*** for appearances' sake; ***por si acaso,*** just in case; ***lo hizo por mí,*** he did it for me, for my sake *or* on my behalf; ***por mí, que se vaya,*** as far as I'm concerned, he can go; ***por completo,*** completely; ***por supuesto,*** of course; ***por junto,*** altogether; ***esto está por hacer,*** this has yet to be done; ***estoy por ir,*** I'm inclined to go; ***doce por tres,*** twelve times three; ***por ciento,*** per cent.
porca, *n.f.* earth between furrows.
porcachón, -chona, *a.* (*coll.*) filthy.
porcelana, *n.f.* porcelain, chinaware.
porcentaje, *n.m.* percentage.
porcino, -na, *a.* pig. — *n.m.* young pig; bruise, bump; ***ganado porcino,*** pigs, swine; (*bot.*) ***pan porcino,*** sow bread.
porción, *n.f.* portion, lot; allowance, allotment; share; ***porción de gente,*** crowd of people.
porcionero, -ra, *a.* apportioning; participating.
porcionista, *n.m.f.* shareholder; partner; co-owner.
porcipelo, *n.m.* (*coll.*) bristle.
porcuno, -na, *a.* pig.
porchada, *n.f.* stretcher (*in a paper-factory*).
porche, *n.m.* porch, portico.
pordiosear, *v.i.* to beg, ask alms.
pordioseo, *n.m.* begging.
pordiosería, *n.f.* begging, asking alms.
pordiosero, -ra, *n.m.f.* beggar.
porfía, *n.f.* tussle, dispute; obstinacy, stubbornness; importunity; ***a porfía,*** in rivalry.
porfiado, -da, *a.* obstinate, stubborn.
porfiador, -ra, *n.m.f.* persistent person.
porfiar, *v.i.* to persist; to argue insistently.
porfídico, -ca, *a.* porphyritic.
pórfido, *n.m.* porphyry.
porfirizar [C], *v.t.* (*pharm.*) to pound, reduce to powder.
porfolio, *n.m.* portfolio.
porgadero, *n.m.* (*prov.*) sieve.
pormenor, *n.m.* detail, particular.
pormenorizar [C], *v.t.* to detail, itemize, give in detail.
pornocracia, *n.f.* exercise of power through pornography, rule of the pornographer.
pornografía, *n.f.* pornography.
pornográfico, -ca, *a.* pornographic.
pornógrafo, *n.m.* pornographer.
poro, *n.m.* pore.
pororó, *n.m.* (*Hisp. Am.*) toasted corn.
pororoca, *n.m.* (*Arg.*) tide rip.
porosidad, *n.f.* porosity, porousness.
poroso, -sa, *a.* porous.
poroto, *n.m.* (*Hisp. Am.*) French bean.
porque, *conj.* because.
¿por qué? *interrog.* why? what for?
porqué, *n.m.* reason why, why and wherefore.
porquera, *n.f.* wild boar's lair
porquería, *n.f.* filthy *or* disgusting thing, revolting mess; (piece of) trash; muck.
porqueriza, *n.f.* pigsty.
porquerizo, porquero, *n.m.* swineherd.
porquerón, *n.m.* catchpoll, bumbailiff.
porqueta, *n.f.* woodlouse; cochineal insect.
porquezuelo, -la, *n.m.f.* young pig.
porra, *n.f.* stick, truncheon, (*Am.*) night stick, bludgeon; maul; 'it' (*in children's games*); (*fig.*) bore, pain-in-the-neck; ***¡porra(s)!*** blast! damn! ***¡vete a la porra!*** go to blazes!
porrada, *n.f.* swipe (*with a stick* or *bludgeon*); (*coll.*) stupid thing to do *or* say; ***una porrada de,*** a hell of a lot of.
porrazo, *n.m.* blow, knock; fall; ***darse un porrazo,*** to come a cropper; ***de golpe y porrazo,*** all of a sudden, out of the blue.
porrear, *v.i.* (*coll.*) to insist, persist, be importunate.
porrería, *n.f.* (*coll.*) obstinacy, tediousness, stupidity.
porreta, *n.f.* green leaf of leeks, garlic *or* onions; (*coll.*) ***en porreta,*** stark naked.
porrilla, *n.f.* forging hammer; small club-headed stick; (*vet.*) osseous tumour in joints.
porrillo (a), *adv.* (*coll.*) galore.
porrina, *n.f.* field of green corn.
porrino, *n.m.* tender leek-plant.

porrizo, *n.m.* leek-bed, leek-plot.
porro, -rra, *a.* dull, thick, stupid. — *n.m.* leek.
porrón (1), *n.m.* earthen jug, pitcher; wine bottle with long spout.
porrón (2), **-rrona,** *a.* (*coll.*) heavy, slow, sluggish.
porrudo, *n.m.* (*prov.*) shepherd's crook.
porta, *n.f.* porthole.
portaaguja, *n.f.* needle-holder.
portaaviones, *n.m. inv.* aircraft-carrier.
portabandera, *n.f.* flag-pole socket.
portabrocas, *n.m. inv.* drill chuck, drill holder.
portacaja, *n.f.* loom carrier; (*mil.*) drum sash *or* strap.
portacarabina, *n.f.* scabbard *or* sheath for a carbine.
portacartas, *n.m. inv.* mail-bag; postman.
portada (1), *n.f.* (*arch.*) front; front page, cover; division (*of warp*).
portadera, *n.f.* chest.
portado, -da (2), *a.* ***bien portado,*** well dressed *or* behaved; ***mal portado,*** poorly dressed, badly behaved.
portador, -ra, *a.* bearing, carrying. — *n.m.f.* bearer, holder; carrier.
portaequipajes, *n.m. inv.* boot, (*Am.*) trunk; luggage-rack.
portaestandarte, *n.m.* standard-bearer, colour-sergeant.
portafusil, *n.m.* rifle-strap.
portaguión, *n.m.* standard-bearer.
portaherramientas, *n.m. inv.* (*mech.*) chuck.
portal, *n.m.* doorway; town-gate; crib.
portalada, *n.f.* portal, large gate.
portalámparas, *n.m. inv.* socket, lamp holder.
portalápiz, *n.m.* pencil holder.
portaleña, *n.f.* (*fort.*, *naut.*) embrasure; plank for doors.
portalero, *n.m.* octroi officer.
portalibros, *n.m. inv.* book-strap, school satchel.
portalón, *n.m.* gangway; side-opening (*in a ship*).
portamantas, *n.m. inv.* rug-strap.
portamanteo, *n.m.* portmanteau.
portamira, *n.m.* (*surv.*) rodman.
portamonedas, *n.m. inv.* purse.
portaneumáticos, *n.m. inv.* (*motor.*) tyre rack.
portante, *n.m.* gait in which a horse raises the legs of one side simultaneously; (*coll.*) ***tomar el portante,*** to clear out, shove off.
portantillo, *n.m.* tiny rapid steps, pattering steps.
portanuevas, *n.m.f. inv.* newsmonger.
portañola, *n.f.* porthole.
portañuela, *n.f.* fly (*of trousers*).
portaobjetos, *n.m. inv.* slide (*of a microscope*).
portaparaguas, *n.m. inv.* umbrella stand.
portapaz, *n.m.f.* pax.
portaplacas, *n.m. inv.* plate-holder.
portapliegos, *n.m. inv.* portfolio, document-case.
portaplumas, *n.m. inv.* pen-holder.
portar, *v.t.* to bear, carry. — *v.i.* (*naut.*) to fill (*sails*). — **portarse,** *v.r.* to behave; ***portarse bien,*** to behave well; to do well, give a good account of o.s.; ***se ha portado bien conmigo,*** he's been good *or* kind to me.
portátil, *a.* portable.
portavasos, *n.m. inv.* glass rack.
portaventanero, *n.m.* carpenter specializing in making doors and windows.
portaviandas, *n.m. inv.* lunch basket; dinner pail.
portavoz, *n.m.* megaphone; spokesman.
portazgo, *n.m.* toll, turnpike-duty.
portazguero, *n.m.* toll-collector, toll-gatherer.
portazo, *n.m.* bang of a door; ***dar un portazo,*** to slam the door.
porte, *n.m.* portage, porterage; carriage, freight; (*naut.*) burden *or* tonnage; bearing, deportment; demeanour, behaviour; nobility, illustrious descent; size, capacity; ***porte franco,*** carriage free *or* prepaid.
portear, *v.t.* to carry, haul, convey. — *v.i.* to bang, slam. — **portearse,** *v.r.* to migrate.
portento, *n.m.* portent, prodigy, wonder.
portentoso, -sa, *a.* portentous, prodigious.
porteño, -ña, *a.*, *n.m.f.* (person) of *or* from Buenos Aires.
porteo, *n.m.* portage, cartage, haulage, conveyance.
portería, *n.f.* porter's lodge; employment of a porter; goal; goal area; (*naut.*) portholes.
portero, -ra, *a.* half-fired (*brick*). — *n.m.f.* porter, (*Am.*) janitor; (*sport*) goal-keeper; ***portero de estrados,*** court usher.
portezuela, *n.f.* little door; (carriage) door; flap, pocket-flap; (*Mex.*) narrow pass.
pórtico, *n.m.* portico, porch.
portier, *n.m.* portière, door-curtain.
portilla, *n.f.* track *or* path (*across a person's land*); (*naut.*) porthole.
portillo, *n.m.* opening, passage, breach, gap; gate, wicket; pass; chip (*in crockery etc.*); octroi gate (*of a town*).
portón, *n.m.* large door; inner door.
portorriqueño, -ña, *a.*, *n.m.f.* Puerto Rican.
portuario, -ria, *a.* of *or* relating to a dock, port *or* harbour. — *n.m.* dock-worker, docker, (*Am.*) longshoreman.
portugués, -guesa, *a.*, *n.m.f.* Portuguese. — *n.m.* Portuguese language.
portuguesada, *n.f.* typical piece of Portuguese behaviour; exaggeration, talking big.
portulano, *n.m.* sets of charts of ports and harbours.
porvenir, *n.m.* future, time to come.
¡porvida! *interj.* in God's name! in the name of God!
pos, (**en**), *adv.* after, behind, in pursuit.
posa, *n.f.* passing bell; (*eccles.*) halt to sing a response; (*pl.*) buttocks.
posada, *n.f.* inn.
posaderas, *n.f.pl.* buttocks.
posadero, *n.m.* inn-keeper, host; rope seat. — *n.f.* landlady, innkeeper's wife.
posante, *a.* reposing; (*naut.*) smooth sailing.
posar, *v.t.* to lay *or* set down. — *v.i.* to lodge, put up; to rest; to pose. — **posar**(**se**), *v.i.* (*v.r.*) to perch, alight; to settle (*of a liquid*).
posaverga, *n.f.* (*naut.*) yard prop; spare mast *or* yard.
posca, *n.f.* mixture of vinegar and water.
posdata, *n.f.* postscript.
poseedor, -ra, *a.* possessing, having, owning, holding. — *n.m.f.* possessor, owner, holder.
poseer [N, *p.p.* **poseído, poseso**], *v.t.* to possess, own, have, hold.
poseído, -da, *a.* conceited; possessed (**de,** by).
posesión, *n.f.* possession; property, holding; tenure, tenancy; ***dar posesión de,*** to give possession of, install in; ***tomar posesión*** (**de**), to take up (*a position, office etc.*), be sworn in.
posesional, *a.* including *or* belonging to possession; (*law*) ***acto posesional,*** act of possession.
posesionar, *v.t.* to put in possession, give possession to. — **posesionarse** (**de**), *v.r.* to take possession (of), be installed (in).
posesionero, *n.m.* cattle-keeper who owns pasturage.
posesivo, -va, *a.* possessive.
poseso, -sa, *a.* possessed. — *n.m.f.* person possessed by an evil spirit.
posesor, -ra, *n.m.f.* possessor, owner, holder.
posesorio, -ria, *a.* possessory.
poseyente, *a.* possessing, possessive.
posfecha, *n.f.* postdating, postdate.
posfechar, *v.t.* to postdate.

posguerra, *n.f.* postwar period.
posibilidad, *n.f.* possibility, feasibility; chance; means.
posibilitar, *v.t.* to make *or* render possible *or* feasible.
posible, *a.* possible, feasible; ***hacer lo posible*** or ***todo lo posible,*** to do one's (very) best; ***en lo posible,*** as far as possible. — *n.m.pl.* (**posibles**) substance, means.
posición, *n.f.* position; situation; pose; (*law*) questions and answers of a cross-examination.
positivismo, *n.m.* positivism.
positivista, *n.m.f.* positivist.
positivo, -va, *a.* positive; ***de positivo,*** certainly, without doubt.
pósito, *n.m.* public granary; (*econ.*) co-operative society.
positrón, *n.m.* (*phys.*) positron.
positura, *n.f.* posture, disposition, state.
posma, *n.f.* sluggishness, dullness, sloth. — *n.m.f.* (*coll.*) pain-in-the-neck, drag.
posó, *n.m.* (*Philip.*) chignon, hair knot.
poso, *n.m.* sediment, lees, dregs; repose, rest.
posón, *n.m.* round matted stool.
pospelo (a), *adv.* reluctantly, against the grain.
pospierna, *n.f.* horse's flank.
posponer [25], *v.t.* to subordinate; (*Hisp. Am.*) to postpone, put off.
pospositivo, -va, *a.* postpositive.
pospuesto, -ta, *a.* subordinated. — *p.p. irreg.* [POSPONER].
posta, *n.f.* post-house, stage-house; post-horses, relay, post; slug (*of lead*); slice, piece (*of meat* or *fish*); memorial tablet; stake (*at cards*); ***a posta,*** on purpose; ***correr la posta, ir en posta,*** to travel by post coach. — *n.m.* one who rides a post-horse; courier.
postal, *a.* postal; (*Hisp. Am.*) ***casilla postal,*** letterbox; ***giro postal,*** postal order. — *n.f.* postcard.
postdiluviano, -na, *a.* postdiluvian.
poste, *n.m.* post, pillar, pole; standing (*punishment*); ***dar poste a,*** to stand up, keep waiting; ***oler el poste,*** to smell a rat, to scent danger.
postear, *v.i.* to travel by post coach.
postelero, *n.m.* (*naut.*) skid.
postema, *n.f.* abscess; bore.
postemero, *n.m.* (*surg.*) large lancet.
postergación, *n.f.* passing over (*for promotion*); postponement.
postergar [B], *v.t.* to pass over (*for promotion*); to postpone.
posteridad, *n.f.* posterity.
posterior, *a.* later, subsequent; back, rear.
posterioridad, *n.f.* posteriority; ***con posterioridad,*** later, subsequently.
posteta, *n.f.* (*print.*) number of printed sheets stitched together.
postfijo, *n.m.* suffix.
postguerra, *n.f.* postwar (period).
postigo, *n.m.* wicket; (*fort.*) sally-port; postern, small gate; (window) shutter.
postila, *n.f.* postil, annotation, marginal note.
postilación, *n.f.* making annotations *or* marginal notes.
postilador, *n.m.* annotator.
postilar, *v.t.* to postillate, annotate.
postilla, *n.f.* scab.
postillón, *n.m.* postilion, post-boy.
postilloso, -sa, *a.* pustulous, scabby.
postín, *n.m.* airs; (*coll.*) poshness; ***darse postín,*** to put on airs; (*coll.*) ***de postín,*** posh; snooty.
postinero, -ra, *a.* (*coll.*) posh, snooty.
postizo, -za, *a.* artificial, false; ***dentadura postiza,*** false teeth. — *n.m.* toupet, wig. — *n.f.* upper works (*on galleys, for an additional tier of oars*).
postmeridiano, -na, *a.* postmeridian, afternoon.
postoperatorio, -ria, *a.* post-operative.
postor, *n.m.* bidder.
postración, *n.f.* prostration.
postrador, -ra, *n.m.f.* one who prostrates himself; foot-stool (*in choir*).
postrar, *v.t.* to prostrate. — **postrarse,** *v.r.* to prostrate o.s.
postre, *a.* last. — *n.m.* dessert, sweet; (*pl.*) dessert; ***llegar a los postres,*** to arrive (too) late. — *n.f.* ***a la postre,*** in the end, in the long run.
postremo, -ma, *a.* last.
postrer (*apocope of* POSTRERO *used before a masculine singular noun*).
postrero, -ra, *a.* (*shortened form* POSTRER), last, hindmost, hindermost.
postrimer (*apocope of* POSTRIMERO *used before a masculine singular noun*).
postrimerías, *n.f.pl.* last years of life; last period; (*theol.*) last stage of man.
postrimero, -ra, *a.* (*shortened form* POSTRIMER), last; hindmost, hindermost.
póstula, postulación, *n.f.* postulation, petition, request.
postulado, *n.m.* postulate.
postulanta, *n.f.* woman postulant.
postulante, *a.* postulating. — *n.m.f.* postulant.
postular, *v.t.* to postulate; to beg; to demand.
póstumo, -ma, *a.* posthumous.
postura, *n.f.* posture; attitude; (*com.*) bid; egg-laying, eggs laid; planting trees, trees planted; tree *or* plant transplanted; assize of provisions; agreement, convention.
potable, *a.* (for) drinking, drinkable.
potación, *n.f.* potation, drinking.
potador, -ra, *a.* drinking. — *n.m.f.* drinker. — *n.m.* inspector of weights and measures.
potaje, *n.m.* pottage; thick soup; stew of dry pulse; mixed drink; hodge-podge.
potajería, *n.f.* dry pulse; vegetable store.
potajier, *n.m.* keeper of the vegetables in the royal palace.
potala, *n.f.* stone anchor; (*coll.*) tub (*wretched boat*).
potar, *v.t.* to equalize (*weights and measures*); to drink, tipple.
potasa, *n.f.* potash.
potásico, -ca, *a.* potassic.
potasio, *n.m.* (*min.*) potassium.
pote, *n.m.* pot, jar; flower-pot; (*prov.*) stew; (*coll.*) ***a pote,*** galore.
potencia, *n.f.* power; dominion, sway; potency; potentiality; (*min.*) thickness (*of a vein*); (*artill.*) reach; ***en potencia,*** potential.
potencial, *a., n.m.* potential.
potencialidad, *n.f.* potentiality.
potenciar, *v.t.* to give strength, force *or* vigour to.
potentado, *n.m.* potentate, magnate.
potente, *a.* potent, mighty, powerful; strong, vigorous; (*coll.*) great, bulky, huge.
potentísimo, -ma, *a. superl.* most powerful.
poterna, *n.f.* (*mil.*) postern, sally-port.
potestad, *n.f.* power; dominion; authority; potentate.
potestativo, -va, *a.* optional.
potingue, *n.m.* (*coll.*) concoction; (*fig.*) make-up.
potísimo, -ma, *a. superl.* most powerful.
potista, *n.m.f.* (*coll.*) tippler, drunkard.
potoco, -ca, *a.* (*Chi.*) short, fat, stout.
potosí, *n.m.* (*Hisp. Am., fig.*) untold riches; (*fig.*) ***valer un potosí,*** to be worth a fortune.
potra, *n.f.* (*coll.*) filly; rupture, hernia; ***tener potra,*** to have good luck.
potrada, *n.f.* troop of colts.
potranca, *n.f.* filly, young mare.

potrear, *v.t.* (*coll.*) to tease, annoy.
potrera, *n.f.* head-stall.
potrero, *n.m.* herdsman of colts; pasture-ground; (*coll.*) rupture specialist; (*Hisp. Am.*) cattle farm.
potril, *a.* colt.
potrilla, *n.f.* filly. — *n.m.* (*coll.*) old fellow acting young.
potro, *n.m.* colt; foal; vaulting horse; rack; shoeing frame; pit (*for breaking open a beehive*); obstetrical chair.
potroso, -sa, *a.* having a rupture; (*coll.*) lucky.
poya, *n.f.* fee for baking (*in a public oven*); hemp bagasse.
poyal, *n.m.* striped cover (*for benches*); stone seat.
poyar, *v.i.* to pay the baking fee.
poyata, *n.f.* shelf; cupboard.
poyo, *n.m.* stone seat *or* bench; judge's fee.
poza, *n.f.* pool.
pozal, *n.m.* bucket, pail; coping (*of a well*).
pozanco, *n.m.* pool (*in a river bank*).
pozo, *n.m.* well; pit; deep hole (*in a river*); eddy, whirlpool; fish tank (*on ship*); (*min.*) shaft; (*naut.*) hold; ***pozo artesiano,*** artesian well; ***pozo negro,*** cesspool; ***es un pozo de ciencia,*** he's a mine of knowledge.
pozol, pozole, *n.m.* (*Hisp. Am.*) stew.
pozuela, *n.f.* small pond; puddle.
pozuelo, *n.m.* small well *or* pit.
práctica, *n.f.* [PRÁCTICO].
practicable, *a.* practicable; usable; that opens.
practicador, -ra, *n.m.f.* practiser, practitioner.
practicaje, *n.m.* (*naut.*) pilotage.
practicante, *a.* practising. — *n.m.* practiser, practitioner; hospital intern; hospital nurse; assistant chemist; medical assistant.
practicar [A], *v.t.* to practise; to perform, carry out; to make, cut (*holes etc.*)
práctico, -ca, *a.* practical; skilful, experienced. — *n.m.* practiser, practitioner; (*naut.*) pilot. — *n.f.* practice; training; ***poner en práctica, llevar a la práctica,*** to put into practice.
practicón, -cona, *n.m.f.* (*coll.*) hack, old plodder.
pradeño, -ña, *a.* meadow.
pradera, pradería, *n.f.* meadow, meadowland.
praderoso, -sa, pradial, *a.* meadow.
prado, *n.m.* meadow; ***el Prado,*** Madrid promenade.
pragmático, -ca, *a.* pragmatic, pragmatical. — *n.m.* commentator upon national laws. — *n.f.* pragmatic, pragmatic sanction, decree.
pragmatismo, *n.m.* pragmatism.
pragmatista, *a.* pragmatist, pragmatistic. — *n.m.f.* pragmatist.
prasio, *n.m.* (*min.*) prase.
prasma, *n.m.* (*min.*) dark green agate.
pratense, *a.* meadow.
pravedad, *n.f.* depravity, perversity.
praviana, *n.f.* Asturian song.
pravo, -va, *a.* depraved.
pre, *n.m.* soldier's daily pay.
preámbulo, *n.m.* preamble, preface; (*coll.*) circumlocution; ***sin más preámbulos,*** without more ado.
prebenda, *n.f.* prebend; (*fig.*) sinecure.
prebendado, *n.m.* prebendary.
prebendar, *v.t.* to confer a prebend *or* benefice on.
prebostal, *a.* provostal.
prebostazgo, *n.m.* provostship.
preboste, *n.m.* provost.
precario, -ria, *a.* precarious; shaky.
precaución, *n.f.* precaution, wariness.
precaucionarse, *v.r.* to be cautious, take precautions.
precautelar, *v.t.* to ward off, take precautions against.
precaver, *v.t.* to try to prevent, provide against. — **precaverse,** *v.r.* — ***de,*** to guard against.
precavido, -da, *a.* cautious, wary.
precedencia, *n.f.* precedence; primacy.
precedente, *a.* precedent, preceding, foregoing. — *n.m.* precedent.
preceder, *v.t., v.i.* to precede; to be in a higher position than.
preceptista, *n.m.f.* one who gives precepts.
preceptivo, -va, *a.* preceptive; obligatory.
precepto, *n.m.* precept, command; rule; ***de precepto,*** of obligation, obligatory.
preceptor, -ra, *a.* preceptor, (*private*) tutor.
preceptuar, *v.t.* to lay down as a precept *or* essential requirement.
preces, *n.f.pl.* prayers; supplication.
precesión, *n.f.* (*astron.*) precession; (*rhet.*) reticence.
preciado, -da, *a.* precious, valuable; boastful, vain.
preciador, -ra, *n.m.f.* appraiser.
preciar, *v.t.* to value, prize; to appraise. — **preciarse,** *v.r.* to pride o.s. (***de,*** on).
precinta, *n.f.* sealing bands; (*naut.*) parcelling.
precintar, *v.t.* to strap, band, hoop; to seal; (*naut.*) to parcel the seams of.
precinto, *n.m.* seal, sealing; strap, band.
precio, *n.m.* price; value, worth; esteem; ***no tener precio,*** to be priceless; ***tener en precio,*** to hold in esteem.
preciosa (1), *n.f.* (*eccles.*) allowance to prebendaries.
preciosidad, *n.f.* beauty, beautiful thing; preciousness.
preciosismo, *n.m.* preciosity, affectation.
precioso, -sa (2), *a.* precious; beautiful, lovely, glorious.
precipicio, *n.m.* precipice; chasm, abyss.
precipitación, *n.f.* precipitation; precipitancy, rash haste.
precipitadamente, *adv.* precipitately, hastily.
precipitadero, *n.m.* precipice, steep cliff.
precipitado, -da, *a.* precipitate, hasty. — *n.m.* (*chem.*) precipitate; ***precipitado blanco,*** white precipitate; ***precipitado rojo,*** red precipitate.
precipitante, *n.m.* precipitant.
precipitar, *v.t.* to precipitate; to fling headlong. — **precipitarse,** *v.r.* to rush headlong; to act rashly.
precípite, *a.* in danger of falling.
precipitoso, -sa, *a.* precipitous; rash.
precipuo, -pua, *a.* principal, chief.
precisamente, *adv.* precisely, exactly; just; indeed; ***precisamente en ese momento,*** at that very moment.
precisar, *v.t.* to specify; to need; to force.
precisión, *n.f.* preciseness, precision, accuracy; necessity, need; compulsion; ***verse en la precisión de,*** to find o.s. obliged to.
preciso, -sa, *a.* precise, accurate; just right; distinct, clear; necessary.
precitado, -da, *a.* fore-cited, above-quoted, aforesaid.
precito, -ta, *a.* damned (*condemned to Hell*).
preclaro, -ra, *a.* illustrious.
precocidad, *n.f.* precocity.
precognición, *n.f.* precognition.
precolombino, -na, *a.* pre-Columbian.
preconcebir [8], *v.t.* to preconceive.
preconización, *n.f.* preconization.
preconizador, *n.m.* extoller, eulogiser.
preconizar [C], *v.t.* to announce; to be in favour of, support, back.
preconocer [9], v.t. to foreknow.
precoz, *a.* precocious.
precursor, -ra, *a.* preceding. — *n.m.f.* precursor, forerunner, pioneer.
predecesor, -ra, *n.m.f.* predecessor, forerunner.
predecir [17], *v.t.* to foretell, predict, anticipate.

predefinición, *n.f.* (*theol.*) predetermination.
predefinir, *v.t.* (*theol.*) to predetermine.
predestinación, *n.f.* predestination.
predestinado, -da, *a.* foreordained. — *n.m.* predestinate.
predestinante, *a.* predestinating.
predestinar, *v.t.* to predestine, foreordain.
predeterminación, *n.f.* predetermination.
predeterminar, *v.t.* to predetermine.
predial, *a.* predial.
prédica, *n.f.* sermon.
predicable, *a.* fit *or* able to be preached; (*log.*) predicable.
predicación, *n.f.* preaching.
predicadera, *n.f.* pulpit; (*pl.*) (*coll.*) gift of preaching.
predicado, *n.m.* (*log.*) predicate.
predicador, -ra, *a.* preaching. — *n.m.f.* preacher.
predicamental, *a.* (*phil.*) predicamental.
predicamento, *n.m.* prestige, standing, influence.
predicante, *n.m.* sectarian preacher.
predicar [A], *v.t.* to preach; (*fig.*) to lecture, preach a sermon on *or* about. — *v.i.* to preach; ***predicar con el ejemplo,*** to practise what one preaches.
predicción, *n.f.* prediction, forecast.
predicho, -cha, *a.* predicted, foretold. — *p.p. irreg.* [PREDECIR].
predilección, *n.f.* predilection.
predilecto, -ta, *a.* preferred, favourite.
predio, *n.m.* landed property; farm.
predisponer [25], *v.t.* to predispose; to prejudice; to prearrange.
predisposición, *n.f.* predisposition.
predispuesto, -ta, *a.* predisposed, biased; conditioned.
predominación, *n.f.* predominance.
predominante, *a.* predominant; prevailing.
predominar, *v.t.* to tower over, rise above, overlook. — *v.i.* to predominate, prevail.
predominio, *n.m.* predominance.
preelegir [8E], *v.t.* to pre-elect.
preeminencia, *n.f.* pre-eminence.
preeminente, *a.* pre-eminent.
preexcelso, -sa, *a.* most illustrious.
preexistencia, *n.f.* pre-existence.
preexistente, *a.* pre-existent.
preexistir, *v.i.* to pre-exist.
prefacio, *n.m.* preface.
prefación, *n.f.* preface, introduction.
prefecto, *n.m.* prefect.
prefectura, *n.f.* prefecture.
preferencia, *n.f.* preference; priority.
preferente, *a.* preferring; preferential; preferable.
preferentemente, *adv.* preferably.
preferible, *a.* preferable.
preferir [6], *v.t.* to prefer.
prefiguración, *n.f.* prefiguration, foreshadowing.
prefigurar, *v.t.* to prefigure, foreshadow.
prefijar, *v.t.* prearrange, predetermine; to prefix.
prefijo, -ja, *a.* prefixed. — *n.m.* prefix; (telephone exchange) code.
prefinición, *n.f.* setting a time limit.
prefinir, *v.t.* to set a time limit on.
prefulgente, *a.* resplendent.
pregón, *n.m.* proclamation by crier; cry.
pregonar, *v.t.* to cry *or* proclaim publicly, cry about the streets, make publicly known.
pregoneo, *n.m.* cries of street hawkers; crying of goods.
pregonería, *n.f.* office of crier.
pregonero, -ra, *a.* proclamatory, proclaiming. — *n.m.* town crier; ***no dar tres cuartos al pregonero,*** to keep sth. quiet.
pregunta, *n.f.* question; query, inquiry; ***hacer una pregunta,*** to ask a question; ***estar a la cuarta pregunta,*** not to have a bean.
preguntador, -ra, *a.* questioning. — *n.m.f.* questioner, inquirer.
preguntante, *a.* inquiring.
preguntar, *v.t., v.i.* to ask, inquire; ***preguntar por,*** to ask after. — **preguntarse,** *v.r.* to wonder.
preguntón, -tona, *a., n.m.f.* (one) always asking questions.
prehistoria, *n.f.* prehistory.
prehistórico, -ca, *a.* prehistoric.
preinserto, -ta, *a.* previously-inserted.
prejudicial, *a.* (*law*) requiring judicial decision.
prejudicio, prejuicio, *n.m.* prejudice; bias; prejudgment.
prejuzgar [B], *v.t.* to prejudge.
prelacía, *n.f.* prelacy, prelature.
prelación, *n.f.* preference.
prelada, *n.f.* abbess, mother superior, prelatess.
prelado, *n.m.* prelate.
prelaticio, -cia, *a.* prelatic.
prelatura, *n.f.* prelacy, prelature.
preliminar, *a., n.m.* preliminary.
prelucir [9], *v.i.* to shine forth.
preludiar, *v.i.* to prelude; to herald.
preludio, *n.m.* prelude.
prelusión, *n.f.* prelude, prelusion.
prematuro, -ra, *a.* premature; unripe; (*law*) impuberal.
premeditación, *n.f.* premeditation, forethought.
premeditadamente, *adv.* premeditatedly, with malice aforethought.
premeditar, *v.t.* to premeditate.
premiador, -ra, *n.m.f.* rewarder.
premiar, *v.t.* to reward.
premio, *n.m.* reward; prize; premium.
premioso, -sa, *a.* pressing, urgent; tight, close; troublesome, burdensome; rigid, strict; slow, awkward.
premiso, -sa, *a.* premised; (*law.*) precedent. — *n.f.* (*log.*) premise; (*fig.*) mark, indication.
premoción, *n.f.* predisposition.
premonición, *n.f.* premonition.
premonitorio, -ria, *a.* premonitory.
premoriencia, *n.f.* (*law*) prior death, predecease.
premorir [7, *p.p.* **premuerto**], *v.i.* (*law*) to predecease s.o.
premura, *n.f.* tightness; hurry, haste; pressure, urgency.
prenatal, *a.* antenatal.
prenda, *n.f.* pledge, pawn, security; token; garment; (*fig.*) gem; (*fig.*) darling; (*pl.*) endowments, talents, accomplishments; game of forfeits.
prendador, *a.* pledging, pawning. — *n.m.f.* pledger, pawner.
prendamiento, *n.m.* pledging, pawning; falling in love, taking a liking (to).
prendar, *v.t.* to pledge, pawn; to charm, captivate. — **prendarse,** *v.r.* to become enamoured (***de,*** of *or* with), fall in love (***de,*** with).
prendedero, *n.m.* hook, brooch; fillet.
prendedor, *n.m.* catcher, apprehender; hook, brooch, breastpin; fillet, bandeau.
prender, *v.t.* to seize, grasp; to pin, clasp; to apprehend, arrest, capture; to light; to set light to; (*Hisp. Am.*) to turn on (*a light*); to mate (*animals*); to dress up, adorn (*women*). — *v.i.* to take root (*plants*); to catch, take (*fire*).
prendería, *n.f.* second-hand shop; pawnbroker's shop; frippery.
prendero, -ra, *n.m.f.* second-hand dealer; broker, pawnbroker.
prendido, *n.m.* women's headdress; pattern for bobbin-lace.
prendimiento, *n.m.* seizure, capture.

prenoción, *n.f.* (*phil.*) prenotion, first knowledge.
prenombre, *n.m.* Christian name, forename, (*Am.*) given name.
prenotar, *v.t.* to note in advance.
prensa, *n.f.* press; (photo) printing-frame; ***prensa de lagar,*** wine-press; ***prensa de paños,*** clothes-press; ***dar a la prensa,*** to publish.
prensado, *n.m.* pressing; lustre, gloss.
prensador, -ra, *a.* pressing.
prensadura, *n.f.* pressure.
prensar, *v.t.* to press; to pack tight.
prensero, *n.m.* (*Col.*) worker in a sugar mill.
prensil, *a.* prehensile.
prensista, *n.m.* (*print.*) pressman.
prensor, -ra, *a.* (*orn.*) psittacine. — *n.f.pl.* (**prensoras**) Psittaci.
prenunciar, *v.t.* to prognosticate, foretell.
prenuncio, *n.m.* prognostication, prediction.
preñado, -da, *a.* pregnant, full of, big with; fraught with. — *n.m.* pregnancy.
preñar, *v.t.* to impregnate, make pregnant; (*fig.*) to fill.
preñez, *n.f.* pregnancy; (*fig.*) gestation period.
preocupación, *n.f.* preoccupation, worry.
preocupar, *v.t.* to preoccupy, worry. — **preocuparse,** *v.r.* to worry (***de,*** about), get worried.
preopinante, *a., n.m.f.* last *or* previous speaker (*in a debate*).
preordinación, *n.f.* (*theol.*) pre-ordination.
preordinar, *v.t.* (*theol.*) to foreordain.
preparación, *n.f.* preparation, getting ready; readiness.
preparado, -da, *a.* prepared, ready. — *n.m.* preparation.
preparamiento, *n.m.* preparation; preparedness.
preparar, *v.t.* to prepare, make ready, get ready.
preparativo, -va, *a.* preparative, preparatory. — *n.m.* preparation.
preparatorio, -ria, *a.* preparatory, introductory.
preponderancia, *n.f.* preponderance.
preponderante, *a.* preponderant, overwhelming.
preponderar, *v.i.* to preponderate, prevail.
preponer [25], *v.t.* to put before, prefer.
preposición, *n.f.* (*gram.*) preposition.
prepósito, *n.m.* president, chairman; provost.
prepositura, *n.f.* dignity of provost.
preposteración, *n.f.* inversion of order.
preposterar, *v.t.* to invert the order of.
prepóstero, -ra, *a.* in inverted *or* wrong order.
prepotencia, *n.f.* prepotency.
prepotente, *a.* very powerful.
prepucio, *n.m.* (*anat.*) prepuce, foreskin.
prepuesto, -ta, *a.* preferred. — *p.p. irreg.* [PREPONER].
prerrafaelista, *a., n.m.f.* pre-Raphaelite.
prerrogativa, *n.f.* prerogative.
presa, *n.f.* [PRESO].
presada (1), *n.f.* dam, reservoir.
presado, -da (2), *a.* pale-green.
presagiar, *v.t.* to presage, forebode.
presagio, *n.m.* presage, omen, token.
presagioso, -sa, présago, -ga, *a.* presaging.
presbicia, *n.f.* (*med.*) presbyopia, long-sightedness.
présbita, présbite, *a.* long-sighted. — *n.m.f.* long-sighted person, presbyope, presbyte.
presbiterado, *n.m.* presbytership, priesthood.
presbiteral, *a.* sacerdotal.
presbiterianismo, *n.m.* Presbyterianism.
presbiteriano, -na, *a., n.m.f.* Presbyterian.
presbiteriato, *n.m.* rank of a presbyter.
presbiterio, *n.m.* presbytery, chancel.
presbítero, *n.m.* presbyter, priest.
presciencia, *n.f.* prescience, foreknowledge.
prescindible, *a.* expendable, able to be dispensed with.
prescindir, *v.i.* — ***de,*** to leave out *or* aside; to dispense with, do without.
prescribir [*p.p.* **prescri(p)to**], *v.t.* to prescribe, lay down. — *v.i.* to lapse.
prescripción, *n.f.* prescription; period laid down.
prescriptible, *a.* prescriptible.
prescripto, -ta, prescrito, -ta, *a.* prescribed. — *p.p. irreg.* [PRESCRIBIR].
presea, *n.f.* jewel, gem.
presencia, *n.f.* presence; ***presencia de ánimo,*** presence of mind; ***hacer acto de presencia,*** to put in an appearance; ***en presencia de,*** in the presence of.
presencial, *a.* relating to actual presence; ***testigo presencial,*** eyewitness.
presenciar, *v.t.* to witness, be present at.
presentación, *n.f.* presentation; display, lay-out; introduction.
presentado, *n.m.* (*eccles.*) presentee.
presentador, -ra, *a.* presenting. — *n.m.f.* presenter; compère; sponsor.
presentalla, *n.f.* votive offering.
presentáneo, -nea, *a.* quick-acting.
presentar, *v.t.* to present; to produce (*for scrutiny*); to introduce (*a person to another*); to show, display; (*eccles.*) to offer as candidate. — **presentarse,** *v.r.* to report; to appear, turn up; to volunteer, come forward; ***presentarse como candidato,*** to stand for election, (*Am.*) to run for election.
presente, *a.* present; ***hacer presente,*** to draw attention to, bring up, raise; ***tener presente,*** to bear in mind; ***mejorando lo presente,*** present company excepted; ***de cuerpo presente,*** lying in state. — *n.m.* present (*time*); present, gift; ***al presente,*** at present. — *interj.* here! present!; (*mil.*) attention!
presentemente, *adv.* at present, now.
presentero, *n.m.* (*eccles.*) presenter.
presentimiento, *n.m.* presentiment, foreboding, premonition.
presentir [6], *v.t.* to have a presentiment *or* foreboding of.
presepio, *n.m.* stable, manger.
presera, *n.f.* goose-grass, cleavers.
presero, *n.m.* dam-keeper; dike-keeper.
preservación, *n.f.* preservation, conservation.
preservador, -ra, *a.* preserving. — *n.m.f.* preserver.
preservar, *v.t.* to save, preserve, guard, keep.
preservativo, -va, *a.* preservative, preserving. — *n.m.* preservative, preventive; contraceptive.
presidario [PRESIDIARIO].
presidencia, *n.f.* presidency; chair; chairmanship; speakership; presidential term.
presidencial, *a.* presidential.
presidencialismo, *n.m.* presidentialism.
presidenta, *n.f.* president's wife; woman chairman; woman president.
presidente, *n.m.* president; chairman; speaker (*of a parliamentary body*); presiding officer *or* judge.
presidiar, *v.t.* to garrison.
presidiario, *n.m.* convict.
presidio, *n.m.* penitentiary; prison sentence; fortress, citadel; garrison; (*fig.*) help, aid.
presidir, *v.t.* to preside over; (*fig.*) to govern, dictate, determine.
presilla, *n.f.* fastening loop; (*sew.*) buttonhole stitching.
presión, *n.f.* pressure.
presionar, *v.t.* to put pressure on, bring pressure to bear on.
preso, -sa, *a.* arrested; in prison. — *n.m.f.* prisoner, convict. — *n.f.* capture, seizure; catch, hold; **prey;** dam, lock, weir; trench, conduit, **drain;** slice,

morsel, bit; fang, tusk, claw; ***ave de presa,*** bird of prey; ***hacer presa en,*** to lay hold on, seize on; ***ser presa de,*** to be a prey to.
prest, *n.m.* (*mil.*) daily pay.
presta (1), *n.f.* (*bot.*) mint.
prestación, *n.f.* lending, loan; service.
prestadizo, -za, *a.* that may be lent *or* borrowed.
prestado, -da, *a.* loaned, lent; ***de prestado,*** loaned; on a temporary basis; ***dar prestado,*** to lend; ***pedir*** or ***tomar prestado,*** to borrow. — *p.p.* [PRESTAR].
prestador, -ra, *n.m.f.* lender.
prestamera, *n.f.* (*eccles.*) benefice.
prestamero, *n.m.* incumbent of a benefice.
prestamista, *n.m.* pawnbroker; moneylender.
préstamo, *n.m.* loan; lending; borrowing; ***préstamo lingüístico,*** loan word, borrowing; ***dar a préstamo,*** to loan; ***recibir en préstamo, tomar a préstamo,*** to borrow, have on loan.
prestancia, *n.f.* fine presence *or* bearing.
prestante, *a.* fine.
prestar, *v.t.* to lend, loan; to render, perform; to give, pay; to take (*an oath*). — *v.i.* to be of use; to give.
prestatario, -ria, *a.* borrowing.
preste, *n.m.* celebrant at High Mass; ***Preste Juan,*** Prester John.
presteza, *n.f.* quickness, promptitude.
prestidigitación, *n.f.* juggling; sleight of hand, legerdemain, conjuring.
prestidigitador, *n.m.* juggler; conjurer.
prestigiador, *n.m.* trickster.
prestigiar, *v.t.* to give *or* lend prestige, distinction, status *or* standing to.
prestigio, *n.m.* prestige; spell, fascination.
prestigioso, -sa, *a.* prestigious; spellbinding.
presto, -ta (2), *a.* quick, prompt; ready. — *adv.* quickly; ***de presto,*** promptly, swiftly.
presumible, *a.* presumable, supposable.
presumido, -da, *a.* conceited.
presumir, *v.t.* to presume, assume. — *v.i.* to be conceited; to boast, show off; to over-dress; ***presume de listo,*** he considers himself very smart.
presunción, *n.f.* presumption, assumption; conceit.
presuntivo, -va, *a.* presumptive, supposed.
presunto, -ta, *a.* presumed; alleged, would-be; ***presunto heredero,*** heir-presumptive. — *p.p. irreg.* [PRESUMIR].
presuntuoso, -sa, *a.* presumptuous, conceited.
presuponer [25], *v.t.* to presuppose; to estimate for, budget for.
presuposición, *n.f.* presupposition.
presupuesto (1), *n.m.* motive, pretext; supposition; estimate; budget.
presupuesto (2), **-ta,** *p.p. irreg.* [PRESUPONER].
presura, *n.f.* hurry, haste; urgency.
presuroso, -sa, *a.* hasty, rushing, urgent, quick.
pretal, *n.m.* girth (*of saddle*).
pretender, *v.t.* to try, attempt, endeavour; to aspire to, aim at; to claim; (*coll.*) to court.
pretendiente, -ta, *n.m.f.* pretender, claimant; office-hunter; suitor, wooer.
pretensión, *n.f.* pretension; aim; claim.
pretenso, -sa, *a.* pretended. — *p.p. irreg.* [PRETENDER].
pretensor, -ra, *n.m.f.* pretender, claimant.
preterición, *n.f.* omission; (*rhet., law*) preterition.
preterir, *v.t.* to pass over, leave out, disregard; (*law*) to omit (*lawful heirs*) in a will.
pretérito, -ta, *a.* past, bygone. — *a., n.m.* past, preterite.
pretermisión, *n.f.* preterition, pretermission.
pretermitir, *v.t.* to omit, pass over.
preternatural, *a.* preternatural.
preternaturalizar [C], *v.t.* to alter the nature of.
pretextar, *v.t.* to plead, offer as an excuse; ***pretextar ignorancia,*** to plead ignorance.
pretexto, *n.m.* pretext, cover, excuse; ***bajo ningún pretexto,*** on no account.
pretil, *n.m.* railing, breastwork.
pretina, *n.f.* girdle, waistband, belt.
pretinazo, *n.m.* swipe with a belt, belting.
pretinero, *n.m.* maker of girdles.
pretor, *n.m.* prætor; blackness of the waters where tunny abound.
pretoría, *n.f.* prætorship.
pretorial, pretoriano, -na, *a.* prætorian.
pretoriense, *a.* belonging to the prætor's residence.
pretorio, -ria, *a.* prætorian. — *n.m.* prætorium.
pretura, *n.f.* prætorship.
prevalecer [9], *v.i.* to prevail; to take root; to thrive.
prevaleciente, *a.* prevalent, prevailing.
prevalente, *a.* prevalent.
prevaler [35], *v.i.* to prevail. — **prevalerse,** *v.r.* to avail o.s., take advantage.
prevaricación, *n.f.* breach of faith.
prevaricador, -ra, *n.m.f.* perverter, corrupter, one who causes breach of faith.
prevaricar [A], *v.i.* to fail in one's word, duty *or* obligation.
prevaricato, *n.m.* (*law*) breach of faith.
prevención, *n.f.* arrangement; foresight; prejudice; (*mil.*) guard-house; detention room.
prevenidamente, *adv.* beforehand.
prevenido, -da, *a.* ready, prepared; stocked, supplied; forewarned; cautious.
preventiente, *a.* predisposing; foreseeing.
prevenir [36], *v.t.* to prepare, make ready; to anticipate, foresee, forestall; to prevent, avoid, avert; to warn, caution; to prejudice. — **prevenirse,** *v.r.* to get ready; to take precautions; to provide o.s.
preventivo, -va, *a.* preventive.
prever [37], *v.t.* to foresee.
previo, -via, *a.* previous; ***previo aviso,*** subject to (previous) warning *or* notice.
previsible, *a.* foreseeable, predictable.
previsión, *n.f.* foresight; ***previsión social,*** social security.
previsor, -ra, *a.* provident.
prez, *n.m.* honour, worth.
priesa, *n.f.* haste, hurry.
prieto, -ta, *a.* black, dark; close-fisted, mean; tight, compressed.
prima, *n.f.* [PRIMO].
primacía, *n.f.* primacy; primateship.
primacial, *a.* primatial, relating to primacy.
primada (1), *n.f.* (*coll.*) foolish *or* stupid thing to do *or* say.
primado, -da (2), *a.* primatial. — *n.m.* primate; primacy.
primal, -la, *a.* yearling. — *n.m.* lace; silk cord.
primario, -ria, *a.* primary. — *n.m.* primary coil.
primate, *n.m.* worthy; (*zool.*) primate.
primavera, *n.f.* spring; flowered silk; (*bot.*) primrose.
primaveral, *a.* spring.
primazgo, *n.m.* cousinhood.
primearse, *v.r.* to treat each other as cousins.
primer, *a.* (*apocope of* PRIMERO *used before masculine singular noun*); (*theat.*) ***primer galán,*** lead; ***primer ministro,*** prime minister.
primerizo, -za, *a.* first; firstling. — *n.f.* woman who has borne her first child.
primero, -ra, *a.* (*shortened form* PRIMER) first; former; leading; early; primary; prime; ***primer paso,*** first step; ***primera cura,*** first aid; (*theat.*) ***primera dama,*** leading lady; ***primeras materias,*** raw material(s). — *adv.* first; ***de***

primero, at first, at the beginning; ***de buenas a primeras,*** all of a sudden; ***de primera,*** first class; ***a las primeras de cambio,*** at the first opportunity.
primevo, -va, *a.* primeval.
primicerio, -ria, *a.* principal, first in a line. — *n.m.* precentor, chanter.
primicia, *n.f.* first fruit; offering of the first fruits.
primicial, *a.* of the first fruits.
primichón, *n.m.* skein of fine soft silk.
primigenio, -nia, *a.* primigenial.
primilla, *n.f.* (*coll.*) pardon of a first offence.
primitivo, -va, *a.* primitive; original.
primo, -ma, *a.* first; excellent, superior; ***materia prima,*** raw material. — *n.m.f.* cousin; (*coll.*) simpleton, dupe; (*coll.*) ***hacer el primo,*** to do sth. stupid; to be taken in. — *n.f.* morning; (*eccles.*) prime; (*mus.*) treble chord; (*eccles.*) first tonsure; bonus; premium; (*mil.*) first quarter of the night.
primogénito, -ta, *a.*, *n.m.f.* first-born, eldest.
primogenitura, *n.m.f.* primogeniture.
primor, *n.m.* care, neatness; beauty, exquisite thing; ***hace primores con la aguja,*** she can do wonders with a needle; ***un guisado que es un primor,*** a stew cooked to perfection.
primordial, *a.* primordial, original, primal.
primorear, *v.i.* to perform neatly and elegantly.
primorosamente, *adv.* painstakingly, with great care; neatly.
primoroso, -sa, *a.* neat; exquisite; painstaking.
prímula, *n.f.* (*bot.*) primula.
princesa, *n.f.* princess; princesse (gown).
principada, *n.f.* high-handed action.
principado, *n.m.* princedom, principality; primacy; pre-eminence.
principal, *a.* principal, main, chief, capital; essential; illustrious, notable. — *n.m.* (*com.*) stock, principal, capital; first floor (*of a house*); (*theat.*) dress circle, (*Am.*) balcony; manager; (*law*) constituent; (*mil.*) main guard.
principalía, *n.f.* (*Philip.*) board of town officials, municipal council.
principalidad, *n.f.* principalness; nobility.
príncipe, *n.m.* prince; ruler; ***edición príncipe,*** editio princeps.
principela, *n.f.* light camlet.
principiador, -ra, *a.* beginning. — *n.m.f.* beginner.
principiante, -ta, *n.m.f.* beginner, learner; apprentice, novice.
principiar, *v.t.* to commence, begin.
principio, *n.m.* beginning, start; source, origin; principle; basis; (*cook.*) entrée; ***dar principio a,*** to begin, start; ***al principio,*** at first, in the beginning; ***a principios de mes,*** at the beginning of the month, early in the month; ***en un principio,*** at first; ***del principio al fin,*** from start to finish, from beginning to end; ***en principio,*** in principle: (*pl.*) rudiments; introductory matter.
pringada, *n.f.* bread dipped in fat.
pringamoza, *n.f.* (*Col.*, *Cub.*, *Hond.*) nettle.
pringar [B], *v.t.* to dip in grease *or* fat; to baste (*meat*); to spatter with grease; (*coll.*) to stab, wound; (*coll.*) to make a mess of. — *v.i.* to get mixed up (in); (*coll.*) to have had it. — **pringarse,** *v.r.* to get into a (greasy) mess; to get involved.
pringón, -gona, *a.* dirty, greasy. — *n.m.* (*coll.*) messer; stain of grease.
pringoso, -sa, *a.* greasy; sticky.
pringote, *n.m.* hodge-podge.
pringue, *n.m.f.* grease, fat; greasiness, oiliness, fattiness.
prionodonte, *n.m.* (*Hisp. Am.*) giant armadillo.
prior, *a.* prior, preceding. — *n.m.* prior; rector, parson.
priora, *n.f.* prioress.
prioral, *a.* belonging to a prior *or* prioress.
priorato, priorazgo, *n.m.* priorship; priory.
prioridad, *n.f.* priority, precedence.
prioste, *n.m.* steward (*of a confraternity*).
prisa, *n.f.* hurry, haste, speed; skirmish, hot fight; ***a prisa, de prisa,*** quickly, in a hurry; ***a toda prisa,*** with the greatest speed, with all despatch; ***no corre prisa,*** there's no hurry; ***date prisa,*** hurry up, get a move on; ***no me des prisa,*** don't rush me; ***tener prisa, estar de prisa,*** to be in a hurry.
priscal, *n.m.* cattle *or* sheep shelter.
prisco, *n.m.* peach.
prisión, *n.f.* seizure, capture; imprisonment; prison; bond, tie; (*pl.* **prisiones**) chains, shackles, fetters.
prisionero, *n.m.* prisoner (*of war*); captive.
prisma, *n.m.* prism.
prismático, -ca, *a.* prismatic. — *n.m.pl.* (**prismáticos**) field-glasses.
priste, *n.m.* saw-fish.
prístino, -na, *a.* pristine.
prisuelo, *n.m.* muzzle (*for ferrets*).
privación, *n.f.* privation, want; deprivation, loss.
privada, *n.f.* [PRIVADO].
privadero, *n.m.* cesspool-cleaner.
privado, -da, *a.* private. — *n.m.* favourite. — *n.f.* privy, water-closet; filth.
privanza, *n.f.* favour (*at court*); private life.
privar, *v.t.* to deprive; to forbid; ***privar del sentido,*** to stun; ***no se priva de nada,*** he goes without nothing, he denies himself nothing; ***no se prive usted,*** go ahead, by all means do. — *v.i.* to be in fashion; to prevail; to be in favour.
privativo, -va, *a.* exclusive, peculiar; ***privativo de,*** exclusive to, peculiar to.
privilegiadamente, *adv.* in a privileged manner.
privilegiar, *v.t.* to privilege, grant privilege to.
privilegiativo, -va, *a.* containing a privilege.
privilegio, *n.m.* privilege; patent, copyright.
pro, *n.m.f.* profit, benefit, advantage; ***¡buena pro!*** much good may it do you!; ***en pro de,*** in favour of, for the good *or* benefit of; ***en pro y en contra,*** for and against; ***el pro y el contra,*** pros and cons; ***hombre de pro,*** man of worth.
proa, *n.f.* (*naut.*) bow, prow; foreship, steerage; (*aer.*) nose; ***poner proa a,*** to head for; ***poner la proa a,*** to oppose, go against.
proal, *a.* belonging to the prow.
probabilidad, *n.f.* probability, likelihood, chance.
probabilísimo, -ma, *a. superl.* most probable.
probabilismo, *n.m.* (*theol.*) probabiliorism, probabilism.
probabilista, *n.m.* (*theol.*) probabilist.
probable, *a.* probable, likely.
probación, *n.f.* proof; probation time; trial.
probador, -ra, *n.m.f.* taster, sampler, trier; fitter. — *n.m.* fitting room.
probadura, *n.f.* trial; tasting, sampling.
probanza, *n.f.* proof, evidence.
probar [4], *v.t.* to prove; to test; to try, try on, try out; to taste, sample, touch; to suit, agree with; ***pruebe a callar,*** try keeping quiet.
probatorio, -ria, *a.* probatory, probationary. — *n.f.* time allowed for producing evidence.
probatura, *n.f.* (*coll.*) attempt, trial; fitting.
probeta, *n.f.* manometer, pressure gauge; (*artill.*) powder prover; (*chem.*) test tube; (*photo.*) developing tray.
probidad, *n.f.* probity, honesty, integrity.
problema, *n.m.* problem.
problemático, -ca, *a.* problematic, problematical.
problematizar, *v.t.* to fill, riddle *or* load down with problems, difficulties *or* snags; to give a problematic nature *or* air to.
probo, -ba, *a.* upright, honest.

proboscidio, -dia, *a.* (*zool.*) proboscidean, proboscidian. — *n.m.* proboscidian, (*pl.*) Proboscidea.
procacidad, *n.f.* procacity, lewdness; indecency.
procaz, *a.* procacious, lewd; indecent, foul.
procedencia, *n.f.* derivation, origin; place of sailing *or* departure.
procedente, *a.* coming (from); (*law*) fitting, proper.
proceder, *v.i.* to proceed; to behave; to be suitable, fitting, appropriate; ***no procede,*** not applicable. — *n.m.* conduct, behaviour.
procedimiento, *n.m.* proceeding, procedure; method, process; way, manner.
procela, *n.f.* (*poet.*) storm, tempest.
proceloso, -sa, *a.* tempestuous, stormy.
prócer, *a.* noble, eminent, distinguished. — *n.m.* nobleman, grandee; person of elevated rank *or* station; (*pl.* **próceres**) grandees and high nobility of Spain.
procerato, *n.m.* high station *or* rank.
proceridad, *n.f.* eminence, nobility; vigour, growth.
procesado, -da, *a.* (*law*) indicted, prosecuted. — *n.m.f.* accused, defendant.
procesal, *a.* belonging to a lawsuit.
procesamiento, *n.m.* indictment, institution of a criminal suit.
procesar, *v.t.* (*law*) to indict, sue, prosecute; to try.
procesión, *n.f.* procession.
procesional, *a.* processional.
proceso, *n.m.* process; progress, lapse of time; (*law*) proceedings; criminal case *or* suit; trial.
procinto, *n.m.* (*mil.*) readiness, preparedness.
proción, *n.m.* (*astron.*) procyon.
proclama, *n.f.* proclamation, address; marriage banns.
proclamación, *n.f.* proclamation; acclamation, applause.
proclamar, *v.t.* to proclaim; to announce publicly, promulgate; to acclaim, cheer.
proclive, *a.* inclined, disposed, prone (to).
proclividad, *n.f.* proclivity, propensity.
procomún, procomunal, *n.m.* public welfare.
procónsul, *n.m.* proconsul.
proconsulado, *n.m.* proconsulship.
proconsular, *a.* proconsular.
procreación, *n.f.* procreation, generation.
procreador, -ra, *a.* procreative. — *n.m.f.* procreator, begetter, generator.
procreante, *a.* procreating.
procrear, *v.t.* to procreate, generate, beget.
procura, *n.f.* power of attorney, proxy; procuracy; careful management.
procuración, *n.f.* care, careful management; power of attorney, proxy; employment of an attorney; attorney's office.
procurador, *n.m.* attorney, solicitor, proctor; procurator; representative at Cortes.
procuradora, *n.f.* procuratrix.
procuraduría, *n.f.* attorney's office; proctorship.
procurante, *a.* solicitant.
procurar, *v.t.* to try *or* endeavour to get; to get; to give, yield; to manage; ***procura ir,*** try to go, do your best to go.
procurrente, *n.m.* cape, headland, promontory, peninsula.
prodición, *n.f.* prodition, treason, treachery.
prodigalidad, *n.f.* prodigality; lavishness.
prodigar [B], *v.t.* to lavish; to squander. — **prodigarse,** *v.r.* to make a display of o.s.; to pay frequent visits; to give lavishly of one's time, energy etc.; to let people see plenty of one; ***no te prodigas, que digamos,*** we don't see much of you, to say the least of it.
prodigiador, *n.m.* soothsayer.
prodigio, *n.m.* prodigy; wonder, marvel.
prodigiosidad, *n.f.* prodigiousness.
prodigioso, -sa, *a.* prodigious; marvellous.
pródigo, -ga, *a.* prodigal; wasteful; lavish. — *n.m.f.* prodigal.
proditorio, -ria, *a.* treacherous.
pródromo, *n.m.* (*med.*) prodrome, prodromus.
producción, *n.f.* production; output; yield; crop; ***producción en masa,*** mass production.
producente, *a.* generating, producing.
producibilidad, *n.f.* (*phil.*) productiveness.
producible, *a.* (*phil.*) producible.
producidor, -ra, *n.m.f.* producer, procreator.
producir [16], *v.t.* to produce, bring forth; to bring in, yield; to bring about. — **producirse,** *v.r.* to come about, occur; to express o.s., behave.
productible, *a.* productile.
productividad, *n.f.* productivity.
productivo, -va, *a.* productive.
producto, *n.m.* product, produce; proceeds.
proejar, *v.i.* to row against the wind *or* current.
proel, *n.m.* (*naut.*) bows (*of a ship*); seaman at prow; bow hand.
proemial, *a.* proemial, introductory.
proemio, *n.m.* proem, introduction.
proeza, *n.f.* prowess; feat.
profanación, *n.f.* profanation, desecration.
profanador, -ra, *a.* profanatory. — *n.m.f.* profaner.
profanamiento, *n.m.* profanation.
profanar, *v.t.* to profane, desecrate.
profanidad, *n.f.* profanity, profaneness.
profano, -na, *a.* profane, secular; worldly; lay. — *n.m.f.* profane; worldly person; layman.
profecía, *n.f.* prophecy; (*pl.*, *Bibl.*) Prophets.
proferente, *a.* uttering.
proferir [6], *v.t.* to utter.
profesante, *a.* professing.
profesar, *v.t.* to profess, practise; to entertain (*friendship etc.*); harbour (*hatred etc.*). — *v.i.* to profess (*join a religious order*).
profesión, *n.f.* profession; occupation.
profesional, *a.* professional.
profeso, -sa, *a.* professed (*monk* or *nun*).
profesor, -ra, *n.m.f.* professor; lecturer; teacher; instructor.
profesorado, *n.m.* professorship; professorate; teaching staff; teaching profession.
profesoral, *a.* professorial; teaching.
profeta, *n.m.* prophet.
profético, -ca, *a.* prophetic.
profetisa, *n.f.* prophetess.
profetizador, -ra, *a.* prophesying. — *n.m.f.* prophesier.
profetizante, *a.* prophesying.
profetizar [C], *v.t.* to prophesy.
proficiente, *a.* proficient; progressing.
proficuo, -cua, *a.* advantageous, profitable, useful.
profiláctico, -ca, *a.* prophylactic, preventive. — *n.f.* hygiene.
profilaxis, *n.f.* (*med.*) prophylaxis.
prófugo, -ga, *a.* fugitive (*from justice*). — *n.m.* (*mil.*) deserter.
profundidad, *n.f.* profundity, profoundness; depth; (*geom.*) altitude, height.
profundizar [C], *v.t.* to deepen, make deeper; to fathom, go deep into, get to the bottom of. — *v.i.* to go deep (*into things*).
profundo, -da, *a.* profound; deep. — *n.m.* profundity; (*poet.*) the sea, the deep; (*poet.*) hell.
profusión, *n.f.* profusion, profuseness, lavishness.
profuso, -sa, *a.* profuse, lavish, abundant.
progenie, progenitura, *n.f.* descent, lineage, parentage.
progenitor, *n.m.* progenitor; ancestor.
progenitura, *n.f.* lineage, descent; primogeniture.

prognato, -ta, *a.* prognathous, prognathic. — *n.m.f.* prognathic person.
progne, *n.f.* (*poet.*) swallow.
prognosis, *n.f.* (weather) forecast; prognosis.
programa, *n.m.* programme.
progre, *a.*, *n.m.f.* (*fam.*) trendy, with it (person).
progresar, *v.i.* to progress, make progress; to advance.
progresía, *n.f.* (people of) advanced *or* (*fam.*) trendy ideas, (*fam.*) those politically with it.
progresión, *n.f.* progression.
progresista, *a.*, *n.m.f.* progressive.
progresivo, -va, *a.* progressive.
progreso, *n.m.* progress; ***hacer progresos,*** to make progress.
prohibición, *n.f.* prohibition.
prohibir, *v.t.* to prohibit, forbid; ***se prohíbe el paso,*** no thoroughfare.
prohibitivo, -va, *a.* prohibitory.
prohibitorio, -ria, *a.* prohibitory.
prohijación, *n.f.* adoption.
prohijar, *v.t.* to adopt.
prohombre, *n.m.* head man, top man, notable; master (*of a guild*).
proís, *n.m.* (*naut.*) hitching post, tying *or* fastening place; mooring berth.
prójima, *n.f.* (*coll.*) slut; tart.
prójimo, *n.m.* fellow-creature, fellow human-being; neighbour.
prolapso, *n.m.* (*med.*) prolapsus, prolapsion.
prole, *n.f.* issue, progeny, offspring.
prolegómenos, *n.m.pl.* prolegomena.
proletariado, *n.m.* proletariat, lower classes.
proletario, -ria, *a.*, *n.m.f.* proletary, proletarian, of the proletariat.
proletariocracia, *n.f.* rule of the proletariat.
proliferación, *n.f.* proliferation.
proliferar, *v.i.* to proliferate.
prolífico, -ca, prolific.
prolijidad, *n.f.* prolixity; tediousness.
prolijo, -ja, *a.* prolix; tedious.
prologar [B], *v.t.* to write a prologue *or* preface to *or* for.
prólogo, *n.m.* prologue, preface.
prologuista, *n.m.* prologue-writer, prefacer.
prolonga, *n.f.* (*artill.*) prolonge.
prolongación, *n.f.* prolongation, lengthening, extension.
prolongador, -ra, *a.* prolonging, extending.
prolongamiento, *n.m.* prolongation.
prolongar [B], *v.t.* to prolong, lengthen, extend.
proloquio, *n.m.* maxim, axiom, apothegm.
promanar, *v.i.* to issue, stem.
promediar, *v.t.* to divide into equal parts; to average. — *v.i.* to mediate; to be half over.
promedio, *n.m.* average, mean.
promesa, *n.f.* promise; pious vow.
prometedor, -ra, *a.* promising. — *n.m.f.* promiser
prometer, *v.t.* to promise; to betroth. — *v.i.* to promise, be promising. — **prometerse,** *v.r.* to expect confidently; to become betrothed; to give o.s. to God; ***se las prometía muy felices,*** he imagined that things were going to be just dandy.
prometido, -da, *a.* engaged, betrothed. — *n.m.f.* fiancé, fiancée, betrothed.
prometiente, *a.* promising.
prometimiento, *n.m.* promise, promising.
prominencia, *n.f.* prominence, protuberance.
prominente, *a.* prominent, protuberant, jutting out.
promiscuar, *v.i.* to eat meat with fish on fasting-days; to be promiscuous.
promiscuidad, *n.f.* promiscuity.
promiscuo, -cua, *a.* promiscuous.
promisión, *n.f.* promise; ***tierra de promisión,*** promised land.
promisorio, -ria, *a.* promissory.
promoción, *n.f.* promotion, advancement; class, year (group that gets degree, commission *or* appointment at the same time).
promocionar, *v.t.* to promote, boost, encourage; to improve *or* raise the status *or* standing of. — **promocionarse,** *v.r.* to better o.s.
promontorio, *n.m.* promontory, headland; height, elevation; (*coll.*) bulky, unwieldy thing.
promotor, -ra, *a.* promotive. — *n.m.f.* promoter, furtherer; instigator; ***promotor fiscal,*** district attorney; ***promotor de la fe,*** devil's advocate.
promovedor, -ra, *n.m.f.* promoter.
promover [5], *v.t.* to promote, further; to advance; to start, stir up.
promulgación, *n.f.* promulgation.
promulgador, -ra, *a.* promulgating. — *n.m.f.* promulgator.
promulgar [B], *v.t.* to promulgate, publish, proclaim.
prono, -na, *a.* prone; propense, inclined, disposed, bent.
pronombre, *n.m.* (*gram.*) pronoun.
pronominal, *a.* pronominal.
pronosticación, *n.f.* prognostication.
pronosticador, -ra, *a.* prognosticating, foretelling. — *n.m.f.* prognosticator, foreteller.
pronosticar [A], *v.t.* to prognosticate, foretell, forecast.
pronóstico, *n.m.* prognostic, prediction, forecast; (*med.*) prognosis; almanac; ***de pronóstico reservado,*** in a critical condition.
prontitud, *n.f.* promptitude, promptness; readiness; swiftness, diligence; dispatch.
pronto, -ta, *a.* prompt, quick; ready; willing. — *adv.* soon; promptly, quickly; early; ***lo más pronto posible*** as soon as possible; ***tan pronto como,*** as soon as; ***al pronto,*** at first; right off; ***de pronto,*** suddenly; ***por de pronto*** or ***por lo pronto,*** for the time being; to start with. — *n.m.* (sudden) impulse; fit of anger.
prontuario, *n.m.* memorandum book; compendium of rules.
prónuba, *n.f.* (*poet.*) bridesmaid.
pronunciación, *n.f.* pronunciation.
pronunciado, -da, *a.* marked, pronounced; sharp (*bend*); steep (*hill*). — *n.m.f.* rebel, insurgent.
pronunciador, -ra, *a.* pronouncing. — *n.m.f.* pronouncer.
pronunciamiento, *n.m.* (*law*) pronouncement of a sentence; military revolution, sedition, uprising.
pronunciar, *v.t.* to pronounce, utter, articulate; to deliver, make (*a speech*); to pronounce (judgment) and pass (sentence). — **pronunciarse,** *v.r.* to rise in insurrection; to rebel; to declare o.s.
propagación, *n.f.* propagation; spreading.
propagador, -ra, *a.* propagating. — *n.m.f.* propagator.
propaganda, *n.f.* propaganda; (*com.*) advertising.
propagandista, *n.m.f.* propagandist; advertiser.
propagar [B], *v.t.* to propagate, spread, disseminate.
propagativo, -va, *a.* propagating, propagative.
propalador, -ra, *n.m.f.* divulger.
propalar, *v.t.* to divulge, spread abroad; ***la prensa propaló los amores de la princesa,*** the press made public the love-affairs of the princess.
propao, *n.m.* (*naut.*) breastwork, bulkhead.
propartida, *n.f.* time preceding departure.
propasarse, *v.r.* to go too far, overstep the mark.
propender, *v.i.* to tend, be inclined.
propensión, *n.f.* inclination, tendency, bent.
propenso, -sa, *a.* propense, inclined, prone.
propiamente, *adv.* properly; ***Afganistán propiamente dicho,*** Afghanistan proper.

propiciación, *n.f.* propitiation.
propiciador, -ra, *a.* propitiating, appeasing. — *n.m.f.* propitiator.
propiciar, *v.t.* to propitiate; to create a propitious *or* favourable atmosphere for.
propiciatorio, -ria, *a.* propitiatory. — *n.m.* mercy-seat.
propicio, -cia, *a.* propitious, well-disposed.
propiedad, *n.f.* property; estate; ownership, proprietorship; likeness; suitability, fitness; propriety; correct use, accuracy; copyright, patent; ***hablar con propiedad,*** to speak properly, with exactitude.
propietariamente, *adv.* with right of ownership.
propietario, -ria, *n.m.f.* proprietor, proprietress, owner; landlord, landlady.
propina, *n.f.* tip; pocket money; ***de propina,*** into the bargain.
propinar, *v.t.* to give, administer; to deliver, land (*a blow etc.*).
propincuidad, *n.f.* propinquity, proximity.
propincuo, -cua, *a.* near; contiguous.
propio, -pia, *a.* one's own; proper; peculiar, typical; suitable, right; natural; accurate, exact, precise, strict; same; self; ***es lo propio,*** it's the natural thing, it's what is to be expected; ***de propio,*** specially. — *n.m.* messenger; (*pl.*) public lands *or* estates.
proponedor, -ra, *n.m.f.* proposer, proponent.
proponente, *a.* proposing.
proponer [25], *v.t.* to propose, suggest. — **proponerse,** *v.r.* to make up one's mind, become *or* be determined (to).
proporción, *n.f.* proportion; chance, opportunity; ***a proporción,*** proportionally.
proporcionable, *a.* proportionable.
proporcionablemente, proporcionadamente, *adv.* proportionably, in proportion.
proporcionado, -da, *a.* proportionate.
proporcional, *a.* proportional.
proporcionalidad, *n.f.* proportionality.
proporcionar, *v.t.* to proportion; to adapt, adjust; to afford, furnish, supply; ***le proporcionaron un empleo,*** they got him a job. — **proporcionarse,** *v.r.* to get, obtain.
proposición, *n.f.* proposition; proposal, overture, scheme; tender, (*Am.*) bid.
propósito, *n.m.* purpose, intention, aim; subject-matter; ***a propósito,*** suitable; by the way, incidentally; ***de propósito,*** on purpose, purposely; ***a propósito de,*** on the subject of; ***fuera de propósito,*** irrelevant, out of place.
propuesto, -ta, *a.* proposed. — *n.f.* proposal, proposition; offer; nomination. — *p.p. irreg.* [PROPONER].
propugnáculo, *n.m.* fortress; (*fig.*) bulwark.
propulsa [REPULSA].
propulsar, *v.t.* to propel, drive; [REPULSAR].
propulsión, *n.f.* propulsion; ***avión de propulsión a chorro,*** jet-propelled aircraft.
propulsor, -ra, *a.* propelling, driving. — *n.m.f.* propellent; instigator; promoter.
prora, *n.f.* (*poet.*) prow.
prorrata, *n.f.* quota, apportionment; (*com.*) ***a prorrata,*** pro rata.
prorratear, *v.t.* to apportion, divide into shares.
prorrateo, *n.m.* apportionment, pro-rata division.
prórroga, prorrogación, *n.f.* prorogation, prolongation, extension; deferment.
prorrogable, *a.* capable of prorogation.
prorrogar [B], *v.t.* to extend, prolong; to defer, postpone.
prorrumpir, *v.i.* to break forth, burst (***en,*** into).
prosa, *n.f.* prose; (*coll.*) verbiage.
prosador, *n.m.* prose-writer; (*coll.*) chatterer.
prosaico, -ca, *a.* prosaic.
prosaísmo, *n.m.* prosaic nature.
prosapia, *n.f.* line, ancestry, lineage.
proscenio, *n.m.* proscenium.
proscribir [*p.p.* **proscrito**], *v.t.* to outlaw, proscribe.
proscripción, *n.f.* proscription, outlawing.
proscrito, -ta, *a.* proscribed, outlawed. — *n.m.f.* outlaw, exile, proscribed person.
prosecución, *n.f.* prosecution; pursuit.
proseguimiento, *n.m.* prosecution; pursuit.
proseguir [8G], *v.t.*, *v.i.* to proceed (with), continue (with), go on (with); to pursue.
proselitismo, *n.m.* proselytism.
prosélito, *n.m.* proselyte.
prosificar [A], *v.t.* to prosify.
prosista, *n.m.* prose-writer.
prosodia, *n.f.* prosody.
prosopopeya, *n.f.* prosopopœia; (*coll.*) pompousness.
prospecto, *n.m.* prospectus, brochure.
prosperar, *v.i.* to prosper, thrive.
prosperidad, *n.f.* prosperity.
próspero, -ra, *a.* prosperous, flourishing.
próstata, *n.f.* prostate.
prostático, -ca, *a.* prostatic.
prosternarse, *v.r.* to prostrate o.s.
próstilo, *n.m.* (*arch.*) prostyle.
prostitución, *n.f.* prostitution.
prostituir [O], *v.t.* to prostitute.
prostituta, *n.f.* prostitute.
protagonismo, *n.m.* chief part, main role; top position; leadership.
protagonista, *n.m.f.* protagonist, hero, heroine; leading actor *or* actress.
protagonizar [C], *v.t.* to play the chief part *or* main role in; to hold the top position in; to be the leader of.
prótasis, *n.f. inv.* protasis.
protección, *n.f.* protection; favour, patronage.
proteccionismo, *n.m.* (*polit.*) protectionism.
proteccionista, *n.m.* (*polit.*) protectionist.
protector, -ra, *a.* protecting, protective; patronizing. — *n.m.f.* protector, protectress; patron, patroness.
protectorado, *n.m.* protectorate.
protectoría, *n.f.* protectorship, protectorate.
protectorio, -ria, *a.* protective.
protectriz, *n.f.* protectress.
proteger [O], *v.t.* to protect; to favour; to patronize.
protegido, -da, *n.m.f.* protégé *or* protégée.
proteína, *n.f.* protein.
proteo, *n.m.* fickle person.
protervia, protervidad, *n.f.* protervity, (stubborn) wickedness.
protervo, -va, *a.* (stubbornly) wicked.
prótesis, *n.f.* (*surg. and gram.*) prosthesis.
protesta, *n.f.* protest; protestation.
protestación, *n.f.* protestation.
protestante, *a.*, *n.m.f.* protestant; Protestant.
protestantismo, *n.m.* Protestantism.
protestar, *v.t.* to protest. — *v.i.* to protest, complain.
protestatario, -ria, *a.* (of) protest, (of) argument; bolshie.
protestativo, -va, *a.* protesting.
protesto, *n.m.* (*com., law*) refusal to pay a bill.
protestón, -tona, *a.* grumbling, grousing. — *n.m.f.* grumbler, grouser.
protético, -ca, *a.* prosthetic.
protoalbéitar, *n.m.* principal veterinary surgeon.
protocloruro, *n.m.* (*chem.*) protochloride.
protocolar, protocolizar [C], *v.t.* to protocol, record.
protocolario, -ria, *a.* in accord with protocol; formal.
protocolo, *n.m.* protocol; formality.

protomártir, *n.m.* protomartyr.
protomedicato, *n.m.* board of royal physicians; office of royal physician.
protomédico, *n.m.* royal physician.
protón, *n.m.* (*elec.*) proton.
protonotario, *n.m.* first notary.
protoplasma, *n.m.* protoplasm.
prototipo, *n.m.* prototype.
protráctil, *a.* protractile.
protuberancia, *n.f*, protuberance.
protuberante, *a.* jutting *or* sticking out.
provecto, -ta, *a.* advanced in years, learning *or* experience; mature.
provecho, *n.m.* advantage, benefit, good; ***¡buen provecho!*** bon appétit!; ***en provecho de,*** for the benefit of, to the good of, in the interest of; ***hombre de provecho,*** man of substance, useful man; ***no hacer nada de provecho,*** to do nothing useful.
provechoso, -sa, *a.* profitable, beneficial, useful, of use.
proveedor, -ra, *n.m.f.* supplier, purveyor, furnisher; ***proveedor de la Real Casa,*** (supplier) by appointment to His *or* Her Majesty.
proveeduría, *n.f.* store-house; purveyor's office.
proveer [N, *p.p.* **provisto**], *v.t.* to provide, furnish, supply, stock; to fill (*a post*); (*law*) to give (*a ruling*). — **proveerse,** *v.r.* to provide o.s. (**de,** with).
proveído, *n.m.* (*law*) ruling.
proveimiento, *n.m.* providing, provisioning, supply.
provena, *n.f.* layer of vine.
proveniente, *a.* deriving, arising (*from*).
provenir [36], *v.i.* to arise, originate, derive.
provento, *n.m.* product, rent, revenue.
Provenza, *n.f.* Provence.
provenzal, *a.*, *n.m.f.* (native) of Provence, Provençal. — *n.m.* Provençal (*language*).
proverbiador, *n.m.* collection of sayings.
proverbial, *a.* proverbial.
proverbio, *n.m.* saying; (*pl.* **Proverbios**) Book of Proverbs.
proverbista, *n.m.f.* (*coll.*) one much given to clichés.
providencia, *n.f.* providence, foresight, forethought; step, measure; (*law*) ruling.
providencial, *a.* providential.
providenciar, *v.t.* to give a ruling on; to take measures *or* steps concerning.
providente, *a.* provident.
próvido, -da, *a.* provident.
provincia, *n.f.* province.
provincial, *a.*, *n.m.f.* provincial.
provincialismo, *n.m.* provincialism.
provinciano, -na, *a.* of *or* from the provinces; provincial; having a provincial mentality. — *n.m.f.* one from the provinces.
provisión, *n.f.* provision; supply, stock; (precautionary) measure.
provisional, *a.* provisional, temporary.
proviso (al), *adv.* on the spot, immediately.
provisor, -ra, *n.m.f.* provider; vicar-general.
provisorato, *n.m.* office of provider.
provisoría, *n.f.* college (*or* convent) pantry; office of a ***provisor.***
provisorio, -ria, *a.* (*Hisp. Am.*) provisional, temporary.
provisto, -ta, *a.* provided (***de,*** with).
provocación, *n.f.* provocation.
provocador, -ra, *a.* provoking, provocative. — *n.m.f.* provoker.
provocante, *a.* provoking.
provocar [A], *v.t.* to provoke; to rouse, move; to dare. — *v.i.* to vomit.
provocativo, -va, *a.* provocative, provoking.
próximamente, *adv.* soon, shortly.
proximidad, *n.f.* proximity, vicinity, nearness.
próximo, -ma, *a.* next, nearest; neighbouring, near.
proyección, *n.f.* projection.
proyectar, *v.t.* to project; to show; to plan.
proyectil, *n.m.* projectile, missile; shell; ***proyectil dirigido,*** guided missile.
proyectista, *n.m.* projector, schemer.
proyecto, *n.m.* project; design; scheme, plan; draft; intention; ***proyecto de ley,*** bill.
proyector, -ra, *a.* projecting. — *n.m.* projector; searchlight; spotlight.
proyectura, *n.f.* projecture; (*arch.*) jut, projection.
prudencia, *n.f.* prudence, caution; moderation.
prudencial, *a.* prudential; sensible, reasonable.
prudente, *a.* prudent, cautious.
prueba, *n.f.* proof, (piece of) evidence; mark, token; trial, test; trying on, fitting; sample, taste; sampling, tasting; ordeal; (*sport*) heat; ***prueba de indicios*** or ***indiciaria,*** circumstantial evidence; ***a prueba,*** on trial, on approval; ***a prueba de,*** proof against; ***a prueba de bombas,*** bomb-proof; ***poner a prueba,*** to put to the test.
prurito, *n.m.* (*med.*) prurience, itching; strong urge.
Prusia, *n.f.* Prussia.
prusiano, -na, *a.*, *n.m.f.* Prussian.
prusiato, *n.m.* (*chem.*) prussiate.
prúsico, -ca, *a.* (*chem.*) prussic.
pseudónimo, *n.m.* [SEUDÓNIMO].
psicoanálisis, *n.m.inv.* psychoanalysis.
psicodélico, -ca, *a.* psychedelic.
psicología, *n.f.* psychology.
psicológico, -ca, *a.* psychological.
psicólogo, -ga, *n.m.f.* psychologist.
psicópata, *n.m.f.* psychopath.
psicopatía, *n.f.* psychopathy.
psicosis, *n.f. inv.* psychosis.
psicosomático, -ca, *a.* psychosomatic.
psicoterapia, *n.f.* psychotherapy.
psique, *n.f.* psyche.
psiquiatra, *n.m.f.* psychiatrist.
psiquiatría, *n.f.* psychiatry.
psíquico, -ca, *a.* psychical, psychic; mental.
psitacosis, *n.f.* (*med.*) psittacosis.
¡pu! *interj.* phew!
púa, *n.f.* prickle; prong; tooth (of a comb); graft, scion; spine *or* quill (*of a hedgehog etc.*); point (*of a spinning top*); (*mus.*) plectrum; (*fig.*) thorn; (*sl.*) peseta; (*coll.*) cunning, wily person.
puado, *n.m.* teeth (*of a comb*), set of prongs etc.
puar [M], *v.t.* to make teeth *or* prongs in.
púber, púbero, -ra, *a.* pubescent.
pubertad, *n.f.* puberty.
pubes, pubis, *n.m. inv.* (*anat.*) pubes.
pubescencia, *n.f.* pubescence, puberty.
pubescente, *a.* pubescent.
pubescer [9], *v.i.* to attain the age of puberty.
publicación, *n.f.* publication; proclamation.
publicador, -ra, *a.* publishing. — *n.m.f.* publisher; proclaimer.
publicano, *n.m.* publican, Roman tax-gatherer.
publicar [A], *v.t.* to publish; to publish abroad, publicize; to issue; to reveal.
publicata, *n.f.* certificate of publication.
publicidad, *n.f.* publicity, advertising.
publicista, *n.m.f.* writer, publicist.
público, -ca, *a.* public. — *n.m.* public; audience; ***en público,*** publicly. — *n.f.* (*univ.*) public debate before graduating.
pucelana, *n.f.* volcanic ash.
pucia, *n.f.* closed pharmaceutical vessel.
puchada, *n.f.* cataplasm; pigs' food, swill.
pucherazo, *n.m.* (*polit.*) rigging (*of elections*).

puchero, *n.m.* earthenware cooking pot; stew; (*fig.*) food; (*pl.*) pouting; ***hacer pucheros,*** to pout.
puches, *n.f.pl.* pap, gruel.
pucho, *n.m.* cigar stub.
pudelación, *n.f.* puddling.
pudelador, *n.m.* puddler.
pudelar, *v.t.* to puddle.
pudendo, -da, *a.* shameful, obscene; ***partes pudendas,*** private parts, pudenda.
pudibundo, -da, *a.* modest; bashful, shy.
pudicia, *n.f.* chastity, modesty.
púdico, -ca, *a.* chaste, modest; maidenly.
pudiente, *a.* wealthy, of means.
pudín, *n.m.* pudding; pie.
pudor, *n.m.* modesty, bashfulness, shame.
pudoroso, -sa, *a.* modest, bashful, shy.
pudrición, *n.f.* rottenness, putrefaction.
pudridero, *n.m.* temporary burial place; rubbish heap.
pudridor, *n.m.* steeping-vat (*for paper-making*).
pudrigorio, *n.m.* (*coll.*) sickly, infirm man.
pudrimiento, *n.m.* rotting, putrefaction.
pudrir, *v.t.* to rot; (*fig.*) to gnaw at. — **pudrirse,** *v.r.* to rot.
pudú, *n.m.* (*Chi.*) wild goat.
puebla, *n.f.* village; seed sown in gardens.
pueblada, *n.f.* (*Hisp. Am.*) mob; uprising; (*Arg.*) gathering of workers.
pueble (1), *n.m.* (*min.*) working gang.
pueblerino, -na, *a.* village, country; hick, provincial.
pueblo (1), *n.m.* town; village; settlement; people, nation.
pueblo (2), **pueble** (2), *pres. indic., pres. subj.* [POBLAR].
puelche, *n.m.* (*Chi.*) native of the eastern side of the Andes.
puente, *n.m.f.* bridge; (*carp.*) transom, lintel, cross-beam; (*naut.*) bridge; gun-deck; (*aut.*) rear axle; (*mus.*) tail-piece; ***puente giratorio,*** swing bridge; ***puente pivotante,*** swivel bridge; ***puente colgante,*** suspension bridge; ***puente levadizo,*** drawbridge; ***puente aéreo,*** air-lift; ***puente de engrase,*** grease lift *or* rack; (*fig.*) ***tender un puente a,*** to go some way to meet; ***hacer puente,*** to link up holidays.
puercada, *n.f.* (*Cent. Am. P.R.*) foul action.
puerco, -ca, *a.* filthy. — *n.m.* pig, hog; ***puerco espín,*** porcupine; ***puerco de mar,*** porpoise. — *n.f.* sow; (*zool.*) millepede; woodlouse; ring (*of hinge*); (*med.*) scrofulous swelling; slut.
puericia, *n.f.* childhood.
puericultura, *n.f.* child-care.
pueril, *a.* puerile, childish.
puerilidad *n.f.* puerility, childishness; trifle.
puérpera, *n.f.* woman lately delivered of a child.
puerperal, *a.* puerperal.
puerperio, *n.m.* puerpery.
puerro, *n.m.* leek.
puerta, *n.f.* door, doorway; gate, gateway; ***puerta excusada*** or ***falsa,*** back- *or* side-door; ***a puerta cerrada,*** behind closed doors, in camera; ***dar con la puerta en las narices a,*** to slam the door in the face of; ***poner puertas al campo,*** to waste one's time, attempt the impossible; ***tener algo en puertas,*** to have sth. ready *or* all lined up; ***estar en puerta para,*** to be next in line for; (*pl.*) octroi.
puertaventana, *n.f.* window shutter.
puertezuela, *n.f.* small door.
puertezuelo, *n.m.* small port.
puerto, *n.m.* port, harbour; haven; mountain-pass; ***puerto franco,*** free port.
Puerto Príncipe, *n.m.* Port-au-Prince.
puertorriqueño, -ña, *a., n.m.f.* (person) of *or* from Puerto Rico.
pues, *conj.* for, as, since. — *adv.* well, why; ***así pues,*** so then; ***pues bien,*** well now, well then; ***¿(y) pues?*** so what?
puesta, *n.f.* stake (*at cards*); (*astron.*) setting; ***puesta del sol,*** sunset; ***puesta de largo,*** coming out, social debut; ***puesta en escena,*** mise en scène; ***puesta a punto,*** tuning; tuning up.
puesto, *n.m.* place; stall, stand, booth; post, job.
puesto que, *conj.* since, inasmuch as.
¡puf! *interj.* phew!
púgil, *n.m.* pugilist; boxer, prizefighter.
pugilato, *n.m.* pugilism, boxing; struggle, tussle.
pugna, *n.f.* conflict, struggle.
pugnacidad, *n.f.* pugnacity, quarrelsomeness.
pugnante, *a.* fighting, struggling, conflicting.
pugnar, *v.i.* to fight, struggle, strive; to conflict.
pugnaz, *a.* pugnacious, quarrelsome.
puja, *n.f.* outbidding, overbidding; higher bid.
pujador, -ra, *n.m.f.* outbidder.
pujame, pujamen, *n.m.* (*naut.*) foot of a sail.
pujamiento, *n.m.* flow of blood *or* humours.
pujante, *a.* powerful; booming, flourishing, thriving.
pujanza, *n.f.* strength, force, drive.
pujar, *v.t.* to push; to bid up. — *v.i.* to struggle, strain, strive; to falter; to grope for words; to pout, snivel.
pujavante, *n.m.* butteris, hoof parer.
pujo, *n.m.* (*med.*) tenesmus; irresistible impulse (*to cry, laugh etc.*); powerful urge; eagerness; pretension.
pulcritud, *n.f.* neatness, tidiness; fastidiousness.
pulcro, -ra, *a.* neat and tidy, fastidious.
pulchinela, *n.m.* punchinello.
pulga, *n.f.* flea; small playing top; (*coll.*) ***tener malas pulgas,*** to be irritable, ill-tempered.
pulgada, *n.f.* inch.
pulgar, *n.m.* thumb; shoot left on vines.
pulgarada, *n.f.* fillip, pinch; inch.
pulgón, *n.m.* vine-fretter, vine-grub, green fly, aphis.
pulgoso, -sa, *a.* flea-ridden.
pulguera, *n.f.* flea-ridden place; (*bot.*) fleawort.
pulguillas, *n.m.pl.* (*coll.*) restless, fretful fellow.
pulicán, *n.m.* dentist's forceps.
pulicaria, *n.f.* (*bot.*) fleawort.
pulidero, *n.m.* polisher, glosser, burnisher.
pulidez, *n.f.* neatness, cleanliness.
pulido, -da, *a.* polished, neat, clean.
pulidor, *a.* polishing, furbishing. — *n.m.* polisher, furbisher. — *n.m.* polishing tool *or* machine.
pulimentar, *v.t.* to polish, gloss, burnish, make bright.
pulimento, *n.m.* polish, glossiness, gloss.
pulir, *v.t.* to polish, burnish, furbish; (*coll.*) to flog, sell.
pulmón, *n.m.* lung; ***pulmón de acero,*** iron lung.
pulmonar, *a.* pulmonary, lung.
pulmonaria, *n.f.* (*bot.*) lungwort.
pulmonía, *n.f.* pneumonia.
pulmoníaco, -ca, *a.* pulmonary, pulmonic, pneumonic.
pulpa, *n.f.* pulp, flesh.
pulpejo, *n.m.* soft fleshy part (*finger, ear etc.*); ball (*thumb*); heel (*of a horse's hoof*).
pulpería, *n.f.* (*Hisp. Am.*) grocer's shop, general store.
pulpero, *n.m.* octopus catcher; (*Hisp. Am.*) grocer, storekeeper.
pulpeta, *n.f.* slice of meat.
púlpito, *n.m.* pulpit.
pulpo, *n.m.* (*zool.*) octopus.

pulposo, -sa, *a.* pulpy, pulpous, fleshy.
pulque, *n.m.* (*Hisp. Am.*) pulque, fermented agave juice.
pulquería, *n.f.* (*Hisp. Am.*) pulque bar.
pulsación, *n.f.* pulsation; throb, beat; strum, striking.
pulsada, *n.f.* pulsation, throb.
pulsador, -ra, *a.* pulsating; striking. — *n.m.* push button.
pulsante, *a.* pulsating; striking; feeling.
pulsar, *v.t.* to push, press; to feel (the pulse of); to strike, strum, play. — *v.i.* to pulsate, throb, beat.
pulsátil, pulsativo, -va, *a.* pulsing, beating.
pulsatila, *n.f.* pasque-flower.
pulsear, *v.i.* to hand-wrestle.
pulsera, *n.f.* bracelet; wristlet; (*surg.*) wrist bandage; side lock (*of hair*); ***reloj de pulsera,*** wrist-watch.
pulsímetro, *n.m.* (*hydrost.*) pulsometer; (*med.*) pulsimeter.
pulsión, *n.f.* (*phys.*) pulsion.
pulsista, *n.m.* pulse specialist.
pulso, *n.m.* pulse; pulse-beat, throb; care, tact; steady hand; ***tomar el pulso a,*** to feel the pulse of; ***ganar algo a pulso,*** to get sth. by sheer (unaided) effort, achieve sth. the hard way.
pultáceo, -cea, *a.* pultaceous; (*med.*) gangrened.
pululante, *a.* pullulating; swarming.
pulular, *v.i.* to pullulate; to swarm, seethe, teem.
pulverizable, *a.* pulverizable.
pulverización, *n.f.* pulverization; spray(ing).
pulverizador, *n.m.* pulverizer; spray.
pulverizar, [C], *v.t.* to pulverize, grind *or* pound to dust *or* powder; to turn into spray.
pulverulento, -ta, *a.* pulverulent, dusty, powdery.
pulla, *n.f.* cutting remark, sharp dig *or* hint.
¡pum! *interj.* bang!
puma, *n.m.* puma, cougar.
pumita, *n.f.* pumice-stone.
puna, *n.f.* (*Hisp. Am.*) puna (*bleak, arid tableland*).
punción, *n.f.* (*surg.*) puncture.
puncha, *n.f.* thorn, prickle, sharp point.
punchar, *v.t.* to prick, puncture.
pundonor, *n.m.* point of honour, punctiliousness.
pundonorcillo, *n.m.* punctilio.
pundonoroso, -sa, *a.* punctilious; haughty, standing on one's honour.
pungente, *a.* pungent.
pungimiento, *n.m.* punching, pricking.
pungir [E], *v.t.* to punch, prick; to sting.
pungitivo, -va, *a.* punching, pricking.
punible, *a.* punishable.
punición, *n.f.* punishment, chastisement.
púnico, -ca, *a.* Punic, Carthaginian.
punitivo, -va, *a.* punitive.
punta, *n.f.* point, tip; pen-nib; sharp end; prong; top, head; prick; headland; (*print.*) bodkin; tack, nail; touch, suggestion; pointing (of game); tartness, sourish taste; ***estar de punta,*** to be at loggerheads; (*coll.*) ***tener puntas de loco,*** to be a bit peculiar; ***punta seda,*** point of dividers; ***de punta en blanco,*** dressed up to the nines; ***punta de diamante,*** glazier's diamond; ***de puntas,*** on tiptoe; ***a punta de lanza,*** meticulously; ***de punta a punta,*** from end to end; ***sacar punta a,*** to sharpen; (*fig.*) to twist the meaning of; to get the most out of; (*pl.*) bonelace, point lace; horns (*of a bull*); head (*of a river*).
punctación, *n.f.* punctuation.
puntada, *n.f.* stitch; hint, sharp dig; gore.
puntador, *n.m.* noter, observer; prompter.
puntal, *n.m.* stanchion, prop, support, stay; fulcrum; (*naut.*) depth of hold.
puntapié, *n.m.* kick; ***echar a puntapiés,*** to kick out; ***tratar a puntapiés,*** to treat like dirt.
puntar, *v.t.* to mark with points.
puntear, *v.t.* (*art*) to stipple; to strum; to mark, punctuate; to sew, stitch. — *v.i.* (*naut.*) to tack.
puntel, *n.m.* blowpipe, glass-blower's rod.
puntera (1), *n.f.* toe-cap; (*coll.*) kick.
puntería, *n.f.* aim.
puntero (1), **-ra** (2), *a.* good shot; (*fig.*) first rate.
puntero (2), *n.m.* farrier's punch; chisel; graver, style.
puntiagudo, -da, *a.* sharp-pointed.
puntilla, *n.f.* small point; narrow lace edging; brad, tack; tracing point; (*tauro.*) short dagger; ***dar la puntilla,*** to finish off; ***de puntillas,*** on tiptoe.
puntillazo, *n.m.* kick; (*fig.*) finishing stroke.
puntillero, *n.m.* (*tauro.*) bullfighter's attendant who administers coup de grâce to the bull.
puntillo, *n.m.* small point; punctilio.
puntillón, *n.m.* kick.
puntilloso, -sa, *a.* punctilious; touchy.
punto, *n.m.* point; state, degree; full stop, (*Am.*) period; dot; end, stop; stitch; tumbler (*of gunlock*); pen-nib; hole (*in stockings*); mesh (*of a net*); knitting; point in lace; punch-hole (*in straps*); polka dot; point of honour, punctilio; twelfth part (*of a line*); shoe size; ***punto en boca,*** silence, not a word; ***punto menos que imposible,*** barely possible; ***punto y coma,*** semi-colon; ***al punto,*** instantly; ***estar a punto de,*** to be about to; ***hacer punto,*** to knit; ***en punto,*** precisely, dead on; sharp; ***hasta cierto punto,*** to a certain extent; ***por punto general,*** as a rule; ***por puntos,*** on points; ***esta en su punto,*** it's just right, done to a turn; ***poner los puntos sobre las íes,*** to get things straight *or* clear; ***de todo punto,*** utterly, absolutely; ***coche de punto,*** cab; ***poner los puntos a,*** to get one's eye on, set one's cap at; ***dar en el punto,*** to put one's finger on the spot; ***estar a punto,*** to be ready.
puntoso, -sa, *a.* sharp-pointed; over-punctilious.
puntuación, *n.f.* punctuation; marks, points, score.
puntual, *a.* punctual; exact, precise, accurate; reliable.
puntualidad, *n.f.* punctuality; preciseness, accuracy.
puntualizar [C], *v.t.* to specify, detail, state in detail; to fix in the mind.
puntuar [M], *v.t.* to punctuate; to score.
puntura, *n.f.* puncture; (*print.*) register point.
punzada, *n.f.* prick; puncture; shooting *or* stabbing pain; pang.
punzador, -ra, *a.* pricking, stinging.
punzadura, *n.f.* prick, puncture.
punzante, *a.* sharp, stinging.
punzar [C], *v.t.* to punch, puncture; to prick; to sting.
punzó, *n.m.* bright scarlet.
punzón, *n.m.* punch, puncheon, puncher; graver; point, bodkin, pick, awl; countersink, counterdie; type mould; young horn (*of a deer*).
punzonería, *n.f.* collection of moulds for type-making.
puñada, *n.f.* punch, blow with the fist.
puñado, *n.m.* handful, fistful; ***a puñados,*** by the handful; galore.
puñal, *n.m.* poniard, dagger.
puñalada, *n.f.* stab; ***coser a puñaladas,*** to stab all over; ***puñalada por la espalda,*** stab in the back.
puñalejo, *n.m.* small dagger.
puñalero, *n.m.* maker *or* seller of daggers.
puñera, *n.f.* flour measure (*about a third of a peck*).
puñetazo, *n.m.* punch; thump.
puñete, *n.m.* blow with the fist; bracelet.
puñetería, *n.f.* (*vulg.*) bloody-mindedness.
puñetero, -ra, *a.* (*vulg.*) cantankerous, bloody-minded.

puño, *n.m.* fist; handful; cuff; handle; hilt; head (*of cane*); corner (*of sail*); ***hombre de puños,*** tough fellow, one with what it takes; ***de su puño y letra,*** in his own hand; ***apretar los puños,*** to clench one's fists, ***lo tiene metido en un puño,*** she's got him under her thumb; ***como un puño,*** tight-fisted; whopping big; tiny.
pupa, *n.f.* pimple, pustule; (*ent.*) pupa; hurt, pain.
pupila, *n.f.* pupil; ward; boarder, inmate.
pupilaje, *n.m.* pupilage, wardship; board, boarding; boarding-house.
pupilar, *a.* pupillary.
pupilero, -ra, *n.m.f.* master *or* mistress of a boarding-house.
pupilo, *n.m.* ward; boarder, inmate.
pupitre, *n.m.* desk.
puposo, -sa, *a.* pustulous.
puré, *n.m.* purée; ***puré de patata(s),*** mashed *or* creamed potatoes.
pureza, *n.f.* purity.
purga, *n.f.* purge; purgative; draining.
purgable, *a.* purgeable.
purgación, *n.f.* purgation; (*med.*) menstruation; (*pl.*) gonorrhœa.
purgador, -ra, *a.* purging.
purgante, *a., n.m.* purgative; laxative.
purgar [B], *v.t.* to purge; to atone for. — *v.i.* to suffer purgatory. — **purgarse,** *v.r.* to take a purge.
purgativo, -va, *a.* purgative.
purgatorio, *n.m.* purgatory.
puridad, *n.f.* purity; ***en puridad,*** strictly speaking; in secret.
purificación, *n.f.* purification, cleansing.
purificadero, -ra, *a.* cleansing, purifying.
purificador, -ra, *a.* cleansing, purifying.
purificar [A], *v.t.* to purify, cleanse, clean; to clarify, refine.
purificatorio, -ria, *a.* purificatory, purificative.
Purísima, la, *n.f.* the Holy Virgin.
purismo, *n.m.* purism.
purista, *n.m.* purist.
puritanismo, *n.m.* puritanism.
puritano, -na, *a.* puritanical. — *n.m.f.* puritan.
puro, -ra, *a.* pure; ***a puro trabajar,*** by sheer hard work; ***de puro bueno, parece tonto,*** he's so good he gives the impression of being a fool; ***de pura cepa,*** out and out, to the backbone, to the core; ***pura sangre,*** thoroughbred. — *n.m.* cigar.
púrpura, *n.f.* purple; (*med.*) purpura; (*zool.*) Purpura.
purpurado, *n.m.* cardinal.
purpurante, *a.* giving a purple colour.
purpurar, *v.t.* to purple; to dress in purple.
purpúreo, -rea, *a.* purple.
purpurino, -na, *a.* purplish. — *n.f.* purpurin; tinsel *or* metal powder, mock snow.
purrela, *n.f.* worthless wine.
purriela, *n.f.* (*coll.*) despicable *or* valueless object.
purulencia, *n.f.* purulence, purulency.
purulento, -ta, *a.* purulent.
pus, *n.m.* pus.
pusilánime, *a.* pusillanimous, faint-hearted.
pusilanimidad, *n.f.* pusillanimity.
pústula, *n.f.* pustule, scab.
puta, *n.f.* whore, harlot.
putaísmo, putanismo, *n.m.* whoredom, harlotry.
putañear, *v.i.* (*coll.*) to whore, go whoring.
putañero, *n.m.* whoremonger.
putativo, -va, *a.* putative, reputed.
putear, *v.i.* to whore, wench, womanize.
putería, *n.f.* (*vulg.*) harlotry; brothel.
putero, *n.m.* whoremonger.
putesco, -ca, *a.* whore, whorish.
puto, *n.m.* sodomite.
putput, *n.m.* hoopoe.
putrefacción, *n.f.* putrefaction, corruptness.
putrefactivo, -va, *a.* putrefactive.
putrefacto, -ta, *a.* putrefied, putrid, decayed, rotten.
putridez, *n.f.* putridity, rottenness.
pútrido, -da, *a.* rotten, putrid, decayed.
puya, *n.f.* goad; (*fig.*) dig; (*bot.*) puya.
puyazo, *n.m.* jab; (*fig.*) dig.
puyo, *n.m.* (*Arg.*) poncho (*made of coarse wool*).
puzol, *n.m.,* **puzolana,** *n.f.* pozzolana.

Q

Q, q, *n.f.* letter Q, q.
que, *rel. pron.* who, whom; that, which; ***el que lo diga,*** he who, the one who, anyone who says so. — *adv.* than. — *conj.* that; for, because; let; ***que pase,*** tell him to come in; ***¿a que no te gusta?*** I bet you don't like it.
qué, *interrog. pron., interj.* what, what a, how; ***no hay de qué,*** not at all, don't mention it; ***¿qué hay?, ¿qué tal?*** what's news, how are things?; ***¿qué ha sido de él?*** what's become of him?; ***¡qué de libros!*** what a lot of books!; ***sin qué ni para qué,*** without rhyme or reason.
quebracho, *n.m.* (*Hisp. Am.*) quebracho.
quebrada, *n.f.* ravine, gorge; (*Hisp. Am.*) brook; (*com.*) failure, bankruptcy.
quebradero, *n.m.* breaker; ***quebradero de cabeza,*** worry, poser.
quebradillo, *n.m.* wooden shoe-heel; flexure of the body (*in dancing*).
quebradizo, -za, *a.* brittle; crumbly; fragile.
quebrado, -da, *a.* broken; (*com.*) bankrupt. — *n.m.* (*arith.*) fraction; bankrupt; ruptured person; (*Cub.*) tobacco leaf full of holes.
quebrador, -ra, *a.* breaking.
quebradura, *n.f.* breaking; splitting; slit; (*med.*) fracture; rupture.
quebraja, *n.f.* crack, fissure, split.
quebrajar, *v.t.* to crack; to split.
quebrajoso, -sa, *a.* brittle, fragile; full of cracks; splintery.
quebramiento [QUEBRANTAMIENTO].
quebrantable, *a.* breakable.
quebrantador, -ra, *a.* breaking; crushing.
quebrantadura, *n.f.* [QUEBRANTAMIENTO].
quebrantahuesos, *n.m. inv.* (*orn.*) osprey; (*orn.*) lammergeier; (*coll.*) bore.
quebrantamiento, *n.m.* breaking; breach, infraction; fracture; rupture; fatigue, exhaustion.
quebrantanueces, *n.m. inv.* (*orn.*) nutcracker.
quebrantaolas, *n.m. inv.* breakwater; mooring buoy.
quebrantar, *v.t.* to break; to breach; to knock up; to weaken, undermine.
quebrantaterrones, *n.m. inv.* (*coll.*) clodhopper.
quebranto, *n.m.* break, breaking; fatigue; weakness; great loss; heavy damage; grief, affliction.
quebrar [1], *v.t.* to break; to bend; to crush; to overcome; to weaken. — *v.i.* (*com.*) to go bankrupt, bust *or* broke. — **quebrarse,** *v.r.* to become ruptured.
queche, *n.f.* ketch.
quechemarín, *n.m.* coasting lugger.
quechol, *n.m.* (*Mex.*) flamingo.
quechua, *a., n.m.f.* Quechua.
queda, *n.f.* [QUEDO].
quedada, *n.f.* sojourn, stay.
quedar, *v.i.* to remain, be left; to stay; to agree, arrange; to be, be situated; (*print.*) ***quede,*** stet; ***quedar en hacer algo,*** to agree to do sth.; ***quedar por hacer,*** to be still to be done; ***quedar atrás,*** to be left behind; ***quedar bien*** or ***mal,*** to make a good *or* bad impression; (*fig.*) ***me quedo,*** count me out, I'm sticking. — **quedarse,** *v.r.* to stay, remain; ***quedarse con,*** to keep; ***quedarse sin,*** to run out of; to get left without; to go without; ***quedarse frío,*** to be stunned.
quedito, -ta, *a., adv.* softly, gently.
quedo, -da, *a.* quiet, still; easy, soft, gentle. — *adv.* gently, softly, in a low voice. — *n.f.* curfew.
quehacer, *n.m.* job, task, chore.
queja, *n.f.* complaint, grumble, moan.
quejarse, *v.r.* to complain, grumble, moan.
quejica, *n.m.f.* (*coll.*) grumble-guts.
quejicoso, -sa, *a.* groaning, moaning.
quejido, *n.m.* moan, groan; ***dar quejidos,*** to moan.
quejigal, *n.m.* gall oak grove.
quejigo, *n.m.* gall oak.
quejigueta, *n.f.* dwarf oak.
quejoso, -sa, *a.* querulous, complaining; ***estoy quejoso contigo,*** I've got a bone to pick with you.
quejumbre, *n.f.* grumble, moan.
quejumbroso, -sa, *a.* plaintive, complaining, grumbling, moaning.
quema, *n.f.* burning, fire.
quemadero, -ra, *a.* for burning, inflammable. — *n.m.* stake; incinerator; burning place.
quemado, *n.m.* burn; thing burnt; (*fig., fam.*) ***estar quemado,*** to be finished, washed up.
quemador, -ra, *a.* burning. — *n.m.f.* burner. — *n.m.* (*gas*) burner.
quemadura, *n.f.* burn; scald; (*agric.*) blight.
quemajoso, -sa, *a.* pricking, burning.
quemar, *v.t.* to burn; to scald; to scorch; to nettle, irritate; to run through; to sell off cheap: ***quemar la sangre a,*** to nettle, irritate, needle; ***coger la cosa por donde quema,*** to go off the deep end. — *v.i.* to be burning hot. — **quemarse,** *v.r.* to burn; to get burnt; to be (burning) hot (*in games of finding*); to get nettled.
quemazón, *n.f.* burn; burning; intense heat; itch, smarting; burning desire; cutting remark; pique; bargain sale.
quena, *n.f.* (*Hisp. Am.*) Indian flute.
quepis, *n.m. inv.* kepi.
querella, *n.f.* complaint; (act of) suing, law-suit; quarrel, dispute.
querellador, -ra, *n.m.f.* complainant.
querellante, *a.* complaining. — *n.m.f.* complainant.
querellarse, *v.r.* to go to law.
querelloso, -sa, *a.* querulous.
querencia, *n.f.* homing instinct; affection, fondness; favourite *or* chosen spot, haunt, retreat.
querencioso, -sa, *a.* homing; affectionate; favourite, chosen.
querer, *n.m.* love, affection; will. — [26], *v.t.* to wish, want; to love; to be fond of; to will, be willing; to try, attempt; to expect; to accept; ***¿quieres callar?*** will you be silent?; ***quiso entrar,*** he tried to get in; ***no quiso entrar,*** he wouldn't come in, refused to come in; ***¿qué quieres que le haga?*** what do you expect me to do about it?; ***¿para qué quieres más?*** I'll spare you the details; you've had it; ***dejarse querer,*** condescendingly to accept adulation; ***querer más*** to prefer; ***querer decir,*** to mean; ***sin querer,*** unwillingly; unintentionally; ***como usted quiera,*** just as you like; ***quieras o no, quieras que no,*** willy nilly, like it or not; ***cuando quieras,*** any time you like, whenever you like; ***quiere llover,*** there's a threat *or* hint of rain; ***quien todo lo quiere, todo lo pierde,*** grasp all, lose all.
querido, -da, *a.* dear, darling. — *n.m.f.* darling; lover, mistress.
queriente, *a.* willing.
quermes, *n.m. inv.* (*ent.*) kermes.
querub, querube, querubín, *n.m.* cherub.
querva, *n.f.* (*bot.*) castor oil.
quesadilla, *n.f.* cheesecake.
quesear, *v.i.* to make cheese.
quesería, *n.f.* cheese-season; cheese factory; cheese dairy.
quesero, -ra, *a.* cheese. — *n.m.f.* maker *or* seller of cheese. — *n.f.* cheese board; cheese tub *or* mould; cheese dish; cheese factory.
queso, *n.m.* cheese; ***queso de bola,*** Dutch cheese.
quevedos, *n.m.pl.* pince-nez.
¡quiá! *interj.* not on your life!
quicial, *n.m.,* **quicialera,** *n.f.* side-post.

quicio, *n.m.* door-jamb: pivot-hole; ***sacar de quicio,*** to force, strain; (*coll.*) to drive up the wall; ***fuera de quicio,*** raving mad, beside o.s.
quiché, *a., n.m.f.* (*Guat.*) Indian tribe and language.
quichua [QUECHUA].
quid, *n.m.* crux of the matter.
quídam, *n.m.* (*coll.*) nobody.
quiebra, *n.f.* crack, break; failure, bankruptcy.
quiebrahacha, *n.m.* (*Cub., bot.*) breakaxe.
quiebro (1), *n.m.* (*mus.*) trill; twist, dodge (*of the body*).
quiebro (2), **quiebre,** *pres. indic.; pres. subj.* [QUEBRAR].
quien, *pron. rel.* (*pl.* **quienes**) who, whom. — (*interrog.* **¿quién?**).
quienquiera, *pron. rel.* (*pl.* **quienesquiera**), whosoever, whoever, whomsoever.
quietación, *n.f.* quieting, appeasing.
quietador, -ra, *n.m.f.* quieter, appeaser.
quietar, *v.t.* to quiet, appease.
quiete, *n.m.* repose, quiet.
quietismo, *n.m.* quietism.
quietista, *a., n.m.f.* quietist.
quieto, -ta, *a.* still, peaceful; undisturbed; ***¡estate quieto!*** keep still! stop fidgeting!
quietud, *n.f.* stillness, tranquillity.
quijada, *n.f.* jaw, jawbone.
quijal, quijar, *n.m.* grinder, back-tooth; jaw.
quijarudo, -da, *a.* large-jawed.
quijera, *n.f.* cheeks (*of a crossbow*); each of the two straps of a noseband.
quijero, *n.m.* sloping bank.
quijo, *n.m.* (*Hisp. Am.*) silver *or* gold ore.
quijones, *n.m.pl.* (*bot.*) dill.
quijongo, *n.m.* (*C.R.*) one-stringed Indian musical instrument.
quijotada, *n.f.* quixotic behaviour, idealistic action.
quijote, *n.m.* thigh-armour, cuisse; upper part of the haunch (*of horses*); (*fig.*) Don Quixote.
quijotería, *n.f.* quixotry.
quijotesco, -ca, *a.* quixotic.
quijotismo, *n.m.* quixotism.
quila, *n.f.* (*Hisp. Am.*) bamboo.
quilatador, *n.m.* assayer of gold *or* silver.
quilatar, *v.t.* to assay (*gold* or *silver*).
quilate, *n.m.* carat; ancient coin; ***honradez de muchos quilates,*** outstanding honesty.
quilatera, *n.f.* (*jewel.*) pearl sieve.
quilco, *n.m.* (*Chi.*) large basket *or* hamper.
quilífero, -ra, *a.* (*zool.*) chyliferous.
quilificación, *n.f.* chylification.
quilificar [A], *v.t.* to chylify, make chyle.
quilo (1), *n.m.* kilogramme.
quilo (2), *n.m.* chyle; ***sudar el quilo,*** to slave.
quilogramo, *n.m.* kilogramme.
quilombo, *n.m.* (*Ven.*) cabin, shanty; (*Arg., Chi.*) brothel, bawdy house.
quilómetro, *n.m.* kilometre.
quiloso, -sa, *a.* chylous, chylaceous.
quiltro, *n.m.* (*Chi.*) cur.
quilla, *n.f.* keel; (*orn.*) breastbone.
quillango, *n.m.* (*Arg.*) patchwork blanket.
quillay, *n.m.* (*Arg., Chi.*) soapbark tree.
quillotrar, *v.t.* to incite; to woo, enamour; to attract; to think over, consider; to adorn, deck. — **quillotrarse,** *v.r.* to fall in love; to complain.
quillotro, -ra, *n.m.f.* (*obs.*) incitement, urging; sign, indication; lovemaking, love affair; puzzling situation; dear friend; lover.
quimera, *n.f.* chimera; fancy; (*coll.*) suspicion.
quimérico, -ca, quimerino, -na, *a.* chimerical; fantastic, unreal.
quimerista, *n.m.* visionary; wrangler.
quimerizar [C], *v.i.* to indulge in wild fancy.
químico, -ca, *a.* chemical. — *n.m.f.* chemist; industrial chemist. — *n.f.* chemistry.
quimificar [A], *v.t.* to convert into chyme.
quimo, *n.m.* chyme.
quimón, *n.m.* chintz.
quimono, *n.m.* kimono.
quina, *n.f.* cinchona.
quinado, -da, *a.* prepared with cinchona.
quinal, *n.m.* (*naut.*) preventer shroud.
quinario, -ria, *a.* consisting of five.
quincalla, *n.f.* hardware.
quincallería, *n.f.* ironmongery; hardware trade.
quincallero, -ra, *a., n.m.f.* (maker *or* seller of) hardware *or* ironmongery; ironmonger, (*Am.*) hardware dealer.
quince, *a.* fifteen; fifteenth. — *n.m.* fifteen; card game; ***dar quince y raya a,*** to knock spots off, beat hollow.
quincena, *n.f.* [QUINCENO].
quincenal, *a.* fortnightly.
quincenario, *a.* fortnightly. — *n.m.f.* one who serves a fortnight *or* several fortnights in prison.
quinceno, -na, *a.* fifteenth. — *n.m.* mule fifteen months old. — *n.f.* fortnight; fortnight's pay; (*mus.*) fifteenth.
quincuagenario, -ria, *a.* fiftieth. — *n.m.f.* person fifty years old.
quincuagésimo, -ma, *a.* fiftieth. — *n.f.* Quinquagesima Sunday.
quindécimo, -ma, *a.* fifteenth. — *n.f.* fifteenth part.
quindenio, *n.m.* period of fifteen years.
quinete, *n.m.* camlet.
quinfa, *n.f.* (*Col.*) Indian sandal.
quingentésimo, -ma, *a.* five-hundredth.
quingombó, *n.m.* (*bot.*) gumbo, okra.
quingos, *n.m.* (*Hisp. Am.*) zigzag.
quiniela, *n.f.* (pools) coupon; (*pl.*) (football) pools.
quinientos, -tas, *a.* five hundred.
quinina, *n.f.* quinine.
quinismo, *n.m.* cinchonism.
quino, *n.m.* cinchona-tree; (*chem.*) quinine.
quinoa, *n.f.* (*Hisp. Am.*) goosefoot.
quínolas, *n.f.pl.* four of a kind (*card game*).
quinqué, *n.m.* oil *or* kerosene table lamp.
quinquefolio, *n.m.* (*bot.*) cinquefoil.
quinquenal, *a.* quinquennial.
quinquenervia, *n.f.* (*bot.*) rib-grass plantain.
quinquenio, *n.m.* quinquennium, lustrum.
quinquillería [QUINCALLERÍA].
quinquillero, *n.m.* [QUINCALLERO].
quinta, *n.f.* [QUINTO].
quintador, -ra, *n.m.f.* (*mil.*) one who draws lots in fives.
quintaesencia, *n.f.* quintessence.
quintal, *n.m.* quintal, hundred-weight; (*fig.*) ***pesa un quintal,*** it weighs a ton.
quintalada, *n.f.* (*naut.*) primage, hat money.
quintaleño, -ña, quintalero, -ra, *a.* capable of holding a quintal.
quintana, *n.f.* country house; fever occurring every fifth day.
quintante, *n.m.* quintant.
quintañón, -ñona, *a., n.m.f.* centenarian.
quintar, *v.t.* to draw (one) out of five; to draw lots for (*soldiers*); to draft (men) for service; to plough the fifth time. — *v.i.* to reach the fifth day (*of the moon*).
quintería, *n.f.* farm; grange.
quinterno, *n.m.* five sheets of paper; five numbers drawn.
quintero, *n.m.* farmer; farm-hand.
quinteto, *n.m.* (*mus.*) quintet.
quintilla, *n.f.* five-lined stanza; ***andar en quintillas con,*** to oppose obstinately.

quintillo, *n.m.* ombre, card game with five players.
Quintín, *n.m.* Quentin; ***armar la de San Quintín,*** to kick up a shindy.
quinto, -ta, *a.* fifth. — *n.m.* fifth; one-fifth; share of pasture-ground; duty of 20 per cent.; (*mil.*) conscript. — *n.f.* country house, country seat, villa; (*mil.*) draft; drawing lots; quint (*in piquet*); (*mus.*) fifth; (*fenc.*) quinte; (*mil.*) ***entrar en quintas,*** to be called up.
quintral, *n.m.* (*Chi.*) red-berried mistletoe; (*Chi.*) disease of watermelons and beans.
quintuplicar [A], *v.t.* to quintuple.
quíntuplo, -la, *a.* quintuple, fivefold.
quinua, *n.f.* (*Hisp. Am.*) quinoa.
quinzavo, -va, *a.* fifteenth. — *n.m.* fifteenth.
quiñón, *n.m.* share of partnership *or* profit; (*Philip.*) land measure (approx. 2 acres).
quiñonero, *n.m.* part-owner, shareholder.
quiosco, *n.m.* kiosk; pavilion; bandstand; newsstand.
quipo, *n.m.* quipu.
quique, *n.m.* (*Chi.*) weasel (*Galictis vittata*); (*Arg.*) ferret.
quiquiriquí, *n.m.* cock-a-doodle-do; (*coll.*) cock of the walk.
quiragra, *n.f.* chiragra.
quirófano, *n.m.* operating theatre.
quirógrafo, *n.m.*, *a.* chirograph; chirographic.
quiromancia, *n.f.* chiromancy, palmistry.
quiromántico, -ca, *a.* chiromantic, chiromantical. — *n.m.f.* chiromancer, palmist.
quirópteros, *n.m.pl.* Cheiroptera.
quiroteca, *n.f.* (*coll.*) glove.
quirquincho, *n.m.* (*Hisp. Am.*) armadillo.
quirúrgico, -ca, *a.* surgical; ***intervención quirúrgica,*** operation.
quirurgo, *n.m.* (*coll.*) surgeon.
quisa, *n.f.* (*Mex.*) black pepper; (*Bol.*) toasted banana.
quisicosa, *n.f.* (*coll.*) enigma, riddle, puzzle.
quisquemenil, *n.m.* (*Hisp. Am.*) short cloak.
quisquilla, *n.f.* trifle; shrimp. — *n.f.pl.* fuss, fussing, quibbling.
quisquilloso, -sa, *a.* trifling; touchy; fussing, quibbling.
quiste, *n.m.* (*surg.*) cyst.
quisto, *a.*, ***bien quisto,*** well-loved, popular; ***mal quisto,*** disliked, unpopular.
quita, *n.f.* [QUITO].
quitación, *n.f.* salary, income.
quitador, -ra, *n.m.f.* remover.
quitamanchas, *n.m. inv.* stain-remover.
quitameriendas, *n.f. inv.* (*bot.*) meadow-saffron.
quitamiento, *n.m.* acquittance.
quitamotas, *n.m.f. inv.* (*coll.*) servile flatterer.
quitanieve(s), *n.m.* snow-plough.
quitanza, *n.f.* (*law*) quittance; (*com.*) receipt in full, discharge.
quitapelillos, *n.m.f. inv.* (*coll.*) flatterer, fawner.
quitapesares, *n.m.f. inv.* comfort, consolation.
quitapón, *n.m.* ornament (*of the headstall of mules*).
quitar, *v.t.* to remove, take off, take away; to do away with; to get out of the way; to steal; to clear, free; to prevent, get *or* be in the way of; to parry; ***quitar de en medio,*** to get out of the way; ***me quita el sueño,*** it keeps me awake; ***quitando dos o tres,*** except for two *or* three; ***ni quito ni pongo rey,*** I'm not taking sides; ***sin quitar ni poner,*** without either omission *or* exaggeration; ***eso no quita para que seas cortés,*** that is no reason for not being polite; ***¡quítate de ahí!*** get out of it! get out of the way!; ***me he quitado del tabaco,*** I've given up smoking; ***de quita y pon,*** detachable.
quitasol, *n.m.* parasol, sunshade.
quite, *n.m.* hindrance, obstacle; (*fenc.*) parry; dodge; (*tauro.*) drawing off *or* away, feint.
quiteño, -ña, *a.*, *n.m.f.* (native) of Quito.
quito, -ta, *a.* exempt. — *n.f.* (*law*) acquittance, discharge, release (*from debt*).
quitrín, *n.m.* (*Cub.*) gig, light chaise.
quizá, quizás, *adv.* perhaps, maybe.
quórum, *n.m. inv.* quorum.

R

R, r, *n.f.* letter R, r.
raba, *n.f.* bait.
rabada, *n.f.* hind quarter, rump.
rabadán, *n.m.* chief shepherd.
rabadilla, *n.f.* coccyx; parson's nose.
rabanal, *n.m.* radish patch.
rabanero, -ra, *a.* (*coll.*) very short (*skirt*); forward. — *n.m.f.* radish seller. — *n.f.* indecent creature.
rabanillo, *n.m.* wild radish; sour taste (*of wine*); (*coll.*) sour temper; (*coll.*) itch, longing.
rabaniza, *n.f.* radish seed.
rábano, *n.m.* (*bot.*) radish; ***rábano picante,*** horseradish; ***rábano silvestre,*** jointed charlock; (*coll.*) ***tomar el rábano por las hojas,*** to get hold of the wrong end of the stick.
rabazuz, *n.m.* liquorice juice.
rabear, *v.i.* to wag the tail.
rabel, *n.m.* (*mus.*) rebec; (*vulg.*) backside.
rabeo, *n.m.* wagging of the tail.
rabera, *n.f.* tail, hind part; chaff, remains; handle (*of a crossbow*).
raberón, *n.m.* top of a felled tree.
rabí, *n.m.* rabbi.
rabia, *n.f.* rabies; rage, fury; grudge; ***le tengo mucha rabia,*** I hate his guts; ***tomar rabia a,*** to take a dislike to.
rabiar, *v.i.* to have rabies; to rage, be furious, be hopping mad; to be in agony; (*fig.*) to be dying (to).
rabiatar, *v.t.* to tie by the tail.
rabiazorras, *n.m. inv.* east wind.
rabicán, rabicano, -na, *a.* white-tailed (*of a horse*).
rabicorto, -ta, *a.* short-tailed; dock-tailed.
rábido, -da, *a.* rabid; raging.
rabieta, *n.f.* (*coll.*) tantrum.
rabihorcado, *n.m.* (*orn.*) frigate bird.
rabil, *n.m.* (*prov.*) crank; (*prov.*) wheat husker.
rabilargo, -ga, *a.* long-tailed. — *n.m.* (*orn.*) blue magpie.
rabillo, *n.m.* mildew; darnel; little tail, stem; corner (*of the eye*); ***mirar con el rabillo del ojo,*** to look out of the corner of one's eye (at).
rabínico, -ca, *a.* rabbinical.
rabinista, *n.m.* rabbinist.
rabino, *n.m.* rabbi.
rabión, *n.m.* rapids.
rabioso, -sa, *a.* rabid; furious, raging, hopping mad.
rabisalsera, *a.* (*coll.*) impudent, pert, forward.
rabiza, *n.f.* point of a fishing-rod; rope-end; point, end (*of a shoal*); tail (*of a block*).
rabo, *n.m.* tail; stalk, stem; corner (*of the eye*); (*naut.*) ***rabo de gallo,*** stern timbers; ***con el rabo entre las piernas,*** with one's tail between one's legs; ***mirar con el rabo del ojo,*** to look out of the corner of one's eye (*at*); ***falta el rabo por desollar,*** the worst is still to come; ***de cabo a rabo,*** from end to end.
rabón, -bona, *a.* docked, bob-tailed, short-tailed. — *n.f.* (*Hisp. Am.*) woman camp-follower; ***hacer rabona,*** to play truant.
raboseada, raboseadura, *n.f.* splashing; chafing, fraying.
rabosear, *v.t.* to spatter; to fray, fret, chafe.
raboso, -sa, *a.* ragged, tattered.
rabotada, *n.f.* harsh *or* ill-tempered remark.
rabotear, *v.t.* to crop the tail of.
raboteo, *n.m.* cropping (*of sheep's tails*).
rabudo, -da, *a.* long-tailed, thick-tailed; (*prov.*) bad-tempered.
rábula, *n.f.* pettifogger, petty lawyer.
racamenta, *n.f.,* **racamento,** *n.m.* (*naut.*) parral, parrel; cranse-iron.
racel, *n.m.* (*naut.*) run, rising of a ship.
racial, *a.* racial.
racima, *n.f.* raceme, grapes left on vines.
racimado, -da, *a.* in clusters *or* racemes.
racimar, *v.t.* to strip the last bunches from. — **racimarse,** *v.r.* to bunch together, cluster.
racimo, *n.m.* bunch; cluster; raceme.
racimoso, -sa, *a.* covered in bunches *or* clusters; racemose.
raciocinación, *n.f.* ratiocination, reasoning.
raciocinar, *v.i.* to reason, ponder.
raciocinio, *n.m.* reason(ing).
ración, *n.f.* ration; portion; allowance; cathedral prebend; ***poner a ración,*** to put on short commons; ***ración de hambre,*** starvation wages.
racionabilidad, *n.f.* reasoning capacity.
racional, *a.* rational. — *n.m.* (*eccles.*) rational.
racionalidad, *n.f.* rationality.
racionalismo, *n.m.* rationalism.
racionamiento, *n.m.* rationing.
racionar, *v.t.* to ration.
racionero, *n.m.* distributor of rations; prebendary.
racionista, *n.m.f.* one who receives daily allowances; (*theat.*) utility man.
racista, *a.*, *n.m.f.* racist.
racha, *n.f.* gust (*of wind*); run of luck; split, crack; ***mala racha,*** bad spell, run of bad luck.
racheado, -da, *a.* in gusts *or* bursts; ***viento racheado,*** gusting wind; ***fuego racheado,*** fire issued in bursts.
rachear, *v.t.* to issue in gusts; to fire in bursts.
rada, *n.f.* (*naut.*) roads, roadstead, anchorage.
radar, *n.m.* radar.
radiación, *n.f.* radiation.
radiactividad, *n.f.* radioactivity.
radiactivo, -va, *a.* radioactive.
radiador, *n.m.* radiator.
radial, *a.* (*anat.*) radial.
radiante, *a.* radiant.
radiar, *v.t.* to radio; to broadcast; to radiate, issue forth, give out. — *v.i.* to radiate.
radicación, *n.f.* radication, taking root; settling.
radical, *a.* radical; root. — *n.m.* radical; root.
radicalismo, *n.m.* radicalism.
radicar [A], *v.i.* to take root. — **radicarse,** *v.r.* to put *or* set down roots, make one's home (***en,*** in).
radicoso, -sa, *a.* radical.
radícula, *n.f.* (*bot.*) radicle.
radiestesista, *n.m.f.* water-diviner.
radífero, *a.* radium-bearing.
radio, *n.m.* radius; (*chem.*) radium; spoke. — *n.f.* radio, wireless.
radioactividad, *n.f.* radioactivity.
radioactivo, -va, *a.* radioactive.
radioaficionado, -da, *n.m.f.* radio enthusiast, ham.
radiodifusión, *n.f.* broadcasting.
radiodifusora, radioemisora, *n.f.* broadcasting station.
radioescucha, *n.m.f.* (radio) listener.
radiofonía, *n.f.* radiophony.
radiografía, *n.f.* radiography; X-ray photograph.
radiografiar, *v.t.* to X-ray, radiograph.
radiograma, *n.m.* radiogram.
radioguía, *n.f.* radio range beacon.
radiología, *n.f.* radiology.
radiólogo, *n.m.* radiologist.
radiómano, -na, *n.m.f.* radio fan.
radiómetro, *n.m.* radiometer.
radioperturbación, *n.f.* jamming, interference.
radiorreceptor, *n.m.* radio receiver.

radiorrevista, *n.f.* radio magazine.
radioscopia, *n.f.* radioscopy.
radioso, -sa, *a.* radiant.
radiotelefonía, *n.f.* radiotelephony.
radiotelegrafía, *n.f.* radio telegraphy.
radiotelegrafista, *n.m.f.* wireless operator.
radioterapia, *n.f.* radiotherapy.
radiotransmisor, *n.m.* radio transmitter.
radioyente, *n.m.f.* listener (*to radio*).
raedera, *n.f.* scraper.
raedizo, -za, *a.* easily scraped.
raedor, -ra, *a.* scraping. — *n.m.f.* scraper. — *n.m.* strickle, strike.
raedura, *n.f.* scraping; wearing out.
raer [27], *v.t.* to scrape, scrape off; to fret, wear out; to eradicate, wipe out; to strike.
rafa, *n.f.* (*arch.*) buttress; irrigating trench *or* ditch, small opening in a canal; (*vet.*) crack in the toe of hoofs; (*min.*) cut in a rock to anchor a supporting arch.
Rafael, *n.m.* Raphael.
ráfaga, *n.f.* gust of wind; flash of light; blast; small cloud; burst (*of gunfire*).
rafe, *n.m.* (*arch.*) caves; (*anat., bot.*) raphe.
rafear, *v.t.* to support with buttresses.
rafia, *n.f.* (*bot.*) raffia.
rahez, *a.* low, base.
raíble, *a.* that may be scraped.
raído, -da, *a.* frayed, threadbare; (*fig.*) impudent, shameless.
raigal, *a.* root, radical. — *n.m.* root (*of a tree*).
raigambre, *n.f.* intertwined roots; (*fig.*) long-standing tradition.
raigón, *n.m.* tough old root; root (*of a tooth*).
rail, *n.m.* rail.
raimiento, *n.m.* scraping; impudence, shamelessness.
Raimundo, *n.m.* Raymond.
raíz, *n.f.* root; ***a raíz de,*** as a result of; immediately following upon; ***arrancar de raíz,*** to root out, eradicate; ***de raíz,*** at the root; ***echar raíces,*** to take root; ***bienes raíces,*** landed property, real estate, (*Am.*) realty.
rajá, *n.m.* rajah.
raja, *n.f.* gash, split, rent, slash; slice; ***sacar raja,*** to get sth. out of it; ***a raja tabla,*** unswervingly, unfailingly, strictly.
rajable, *a.* easily split.
rajabroqueles, *n.m. inv.* (*coll.*) bully, brawler.
rajadillo, *n.m.* frangipane; sugared almonds.
rajadizo, -za, *a.* fissile, easily split.
rajador, *n.m.* wood-splitter.
rajadura, *n.f.* gash, split, rent, slash.
rajante, *a.* slashing, splitting.
rajar, *v.t.* to split, rend, slash; to slice. — *v.i.* to brag, chatter. — **rajarse,** *v.r.* (*coll.*) to back out.
rajatabla, (a), *adv.* without fail, strictly.
rajeta, *n.f.* coarse cloth.
rajuela, *n.f.* thin flagstone.
ralea, *n.f.* (*pej.*) race, breed, ilk; prey (*of predatory birds*).
ralear, *v.i.* to thin, become thin *or* sparse.
raleón, -leona, *a.* predatory (*of birds of prey*).
raleza, *n.f.* thinness, sparseness.
ralo, -la, *a.* thin, sparse.
ralladera, *n.f.*, **rallador,** *n.m.* grater.
ralladura, *n.f.* scratch, grating.
rallar, *v.t.* to grate; to vex, molest.
rallo, *n.m.* grater, rasp, scraper.
rallón, *n.m.* arrow with crosshead.
rama, *n.f.* (*bot.*) branch, bough; (*print.*) chase; rack (*in cloth-mills*); ***en rama,*** raw; crude; (in) leaf; unbound; ***andarse por las ramas,*** to beat about the bush.
ramada, *n.f.*, **ramaje,** *n.m.* arbour; mass of branches.
ramal, *n.m.* strand (*of a rope*); halter; branch, offshoot; branch line.
ramalazo, *n.m.* lash; mark, streak; shooting pain; sudden blow; ***ramalazo de locura,*** sudden outburst of madness.
ramalla, *n.f.* twigs, brushwood.
rambla, *n.f.* dry river-bed; boulevard, avenue; tenter *or* tentering machine.
ramblazo, *n.m.* torrent-bed.
rameado, -da, *a.* having a branch and flower pattern.
rameal, rámeo, -mea, *a.* branch.
ramera (1), *n.f.* whore, harlot.
ramería, *n.f.* brothel; prostitution.
ramero, -ra (2), *a.* (*orn.*) tree.
ramial, *n.m.* ramie plantation.
ramificación, *n.f.* ramification, branching out.
ramificarse [A], *v.r.* to ramify, branch out.
ramilla, ramita, *n.f.* sprig; twig.
ramillete, *n.m.* bouquet, bunch (*of flowers*), nosegay, posy; umbel, cluster; collection (*of choice objects*); (*table*) centre-piece.
ramilletera, *n.f.* flower-girl.
ramilletero, *n.m.* flower-vase.
ramillo, ramito, *n.m.* small branch, sprig, twig.
ramina, *n.f.* ramie yarn.
ramio, *n.m.* (*bot.*) ramie.
ramiza, *n.f.* lopped branches.
ramo, *n.m.* branch; bough; antler; cluster, bouquet; line (*of goods*); section, division, department; ***domingo de Ramos,*** Palm Sunday; ***de Pascuas a Ramos,*** once in a blue moon; ***ramo de olivo,*** olive branch.
ramojo, *n.m.* brushwood.
Ramón, *n.m.* Raymond.
ramón, *n.m.* browse, browsage.
ramonear, *v.i.* to cut *or* lop branches; to browse.
ramoneo, *n.m.* cutting *or* lopping branches.
ramoso, -sa, *a.* branchy, ramous.
rampa, *n.f.* ramp, slope.
rampante, *a.* (*her.*) rampant.
rampiñete, *n.m.* (*artill.*) vent-gimlet.
ramplón, -lona, *a.* heavy, clumsy; dull, uninspiring. — *n.m.* calk (*of a shoe*).
ramplonería, *n.f.* heaviness; dullness, mediocrity.
ramplonizar, *v.t.* to make *or* render commonplace, pedestrian, dull *or* uninspiring; to give a commonplace, pedestrian, dull *or* uninspiring character *or* air to.
rampojo, *n.m.* grape-stalk; (*mil.*) caltrop.
rampollo, *n.m.* cutting.
rana, *n.f.* frog; (*ichth.*) ***rana marina*** or ***pescadora,*** angler; (*fig.*) ***nos ha salido rana,*** he's turned out to be a handful *or* a wrong-'un; (*pl.*) frog tongue, ranula.
ranacuajo [RENACUAJO].
rancajado, -da, *a.* wounded by a splinter. — *n.f.* uprooting.
rancajo, *n.m.* splinter.
ranciarse, *v.r.* to grow rancid, stale.
rancidez, *n.f.* rancidness, staleness; oldness.
rancio, -cia, *a.* rancid, stale; musty; old; old-fashioned, out-dated. — *n.m.* rancidity, rankness; mustiness; pork fat.
rancioso, -sa, *a.* rancid, stale.
rancheadero, *n.m.* hut settlement.
ranchear, *v.i.* to build huts *or* shanties; to dwell in huts *or* shanties.
ranchería, *n.f.* hut *or* shanty settlement; (*mil.*) kitchen (*in barracks*).
ranchero, *n.m.* mess-steward; small farmer; (*Mex.*) rancher.

rancho, *n.m.* food (*in barracks, prisons etc.*); soldiers' mess; hut; hut *or* shanty settlement; coterie; (*Hisp. Am.*) board and lodging; cattle ranch; (*naut., fig.*) lower deck; ***asentar el rancho,*** to stop in a place to rest *or* have a meal; ***hacer rancho,*** to make room; (*coll.*) ***hacer rancho aparte,*** to go one's own way, be a lone wolf.
randa, *n.f.* lace. — *n.m.* (*coll.*) pickpocket.
randado, -da, *a.* lace, lace-trimmed.
randera, *n.f.* lace-maker (*woman*).
rangífero, *n.m.* reindeer.
rango, *n.m.* rank, class, position.
rangua, *n.f.* spindle-box, shaft-socket.
ranilla, *n.f.* frog (*of a horse's hoof*); (*vet.*) intestinal blood clot.
ranking, *n.m.* rating, order *or* scale of importance *or* merit, stakes.
ránula, *n.f.* (*med., vet.*) ranula.
ranúnculo, *n.m.* (*bot.*) ranunculus; crowfoot, buttercup.
ranura, *n.f.* groove, rabbet; slot.
raña, *n.f.* hook frame for catching cuttlefish; thicket.
raño, *n.m.* oyster-tongs; (*ichth.*) pike-perch.
rapa, *n.f.* flower of the olive tree.
rapacejo, *n.m.* border, edging; child, urchin.
rapacería, *n.f.* childish prank.
rapacidad, *n.f.* rapacity, greed.
rapador, -ra, *a.* scraping, shaving. — *n.m.f.* (*coll.*) barber.
rapadura, *n.f.* close hair-cut.
rapagón, *n.m.* beardless youth.
rapamiento, *n.m.* [RAPADURA].
rapante, *a.* shaving; snatching, pilfering; (*her.*) rampant.
rapapiés, *n.m. inv.* running squib; chaser.
rapapolvo, *n.m.* (*coll.*) dressing-down, scolding.
rapar, *v.t.* to shave, shave close; to crop (*the hair*); (*fig.*) to pilfer, snatch. — **raparse,** *v.r.* to shave one's head; (*Hisp. Am.*) to lead an easy life.
rapasa, *n.f.* wax-stone.
rapavelas, *n.m. inv.* (*coll.*) sexton; altar boy.
rapaz, -za, *a.* rapacious, predatory; of prey, raptorial; (*fig.*) thievish. — *n.m.* lad. — *n.f.* lass. — *n.f.pl.* (**rapaces**) (*orn.*) Raptores, birds of prey.
rapazada, *n.f.* childish thing to do *or* say; childish prank.
rapazuelo, -la, *n.m.f.* little boy, little girl.
rapé, *n.m.* snuff.
rape, *n.m.* (*coll.*) quick shave *or* hair-cut; (*ichth.*) angler; ***al rape,*** cropped (*hair*).
rapidez, *n.f.* rapidity, swiftness.
rápido, -da, *a.* rapid, quick, swift. — *n.m.* express train; (*pl.*) rapids.
rapiego, -ga, *a.* rapacious (*of birds*).
rapingancho, *n.m.* (*Col., Per.*) cheese omelet.
rapiña, *n.f.* rapine; plundering, looting; ***ave de rapiña,*** bird of prey.
rapiñador, -ra, *a.* plundering, predatory. — *n.m.f.* plunderer, robber.
rapiñar, *v.t.* (*coll.*) to plunder, rob.
rapista, *n.m.* (*coll.*) barber, shaver, scraper.
rapo, *n.m.* round-rooted turnip.
rapónchigo, *n.m.* (*bot.*) rampion, bellflower.
raposa, *n.f.* vixen; cunning, artful person.
raposear, *v.i.* to be fox-like, foxy, wily.
raposera, *n.f.* fox-hole.
raposería, *n.f.* foxiness, craftiness.
raposino, -na, *a.* vulpine, fox.
raposo, *n.m.* dog-fox.
raposuno, -na, *a.* vulpine, fox.
rapsoda, *n.m.* rhapsode.
rapsodia, *n.f.* rhapsody.
rapsodista, *n.m.* rhapsodist.
rapta, *a., n.f.* abducted, ravished (*woman*).
raptar, *v.t.* to abduct, kidnap.
rapto, *n.m.* abduction, kidnapping; rapture; fit; ***rapto de locura,*** fit of madness.
raptor, *n.m.* abductor.
raque, *n.m.* beachcombing.
raquear, *v.i.* to beachcomb.
Raquel, *n.f.* Rachel.
raquero, *n.m.* beachcomber; dock-thief.
raqueta, *n.f.* racket; battledore and shuttlecock; badminton; snowshoe; rake.
raquetero, *n.m.* racket-maker; racket-seller.
raquis, *n.m. inv.* (*anat.*) rachis; (*bot.*) stalk.
raquítico, -ca, *a.* rickety; having rickets, rachitic; flimsy, feeble; measly, scanty, skimpy.
raquitis, *n.f. inv.*, **raquitismo,** *n.m.* (*med.*) rachitis, rickets.
rara (1), *n.f.* (*Hisp. Am., orn.*) passerine.
rarefacción, *n.f.* rarefaction.
rarefacer [20], *v.t.* to rarefy.
rareza, *n.f.* rarity, rareness; oddity, freakishness, queerness; peculiarity, eccentricity; unpredictableness.
raridad, *n.f.* rarity.
rarificar [A], *v.t.* to rarefy.
rarificativo, -va, *a.* rarefying.
raro, -ra (2), *a.* rare; rarefied; odd, freakish, queer; peculiar, eccentric; unpredictable; ***rara vez,*** seldom.
ras, *n.m.* level; ***ras en ras, ras con ras,*** on an equal footing, on a par; flush; ***a ras de,*** flush with.
rasa, *n.f.* [RASO].
rasadura, *n.f.* levelling.
rasante, *a.* levelling. — *n.f.* grading line; (*motor.*) ***cambio de rasante,*** brow of a hill.
rasar, *v.t.* to graze, skim; to level. — *v.r.* to clear up.
rascacielos, *n.m. inv.* skyscraper.
rascadera, *n.f.* scraper; curry-comb.
rascador, *n.m.* scraper; rasp; bodkin, hatpin; huller, sheller.
rascadura, *n.f.* scratching; scraping; rasping; scratch.
rascalino, *n.m.* (*bot.*) dodder.
rascamiento, *n.m.* scratching; scraping.
rascamoño, *n.m.* head-pin, hatpin, bodkin.
rascar [A], *v.t.* to scratch; to scrape. — *v.i.* (*Hisp. Am.*) to itch.
rascatripas, *n.m.f. inv.* (*pej.*) gut-scraper.
rascazón, *n.f.* pricking, tickling, itching.
rascle, *n.m.* fishing net.
rascón, -cona, *a.* sour, sharp. — *n.m.* (*orn.*) water-rail; marsh-hen.
rasel, *n.m.* (*naut.*) entrance and run (*vessels*).
rasero, *n.m.* strickle; yardstick, measuring stick.
rasete, *n.m.* satinet, sateen.
rasgado, -da, *a.* rent, open, torn; ***ojos rasgados,*** almond eyes; ***boca rasgada,*** wide mouth.
rasgador, -ra, *a.* tearing, ripping, slitting.
rasgadura, *n.f.* rent, rip, tear; renting, ripping, tearing.
rasgar [B], *v.t.* to tear, rend, rip, slash, slit; ***de rompe y rasga,*** determined, forceful, dauntless.
rasgo, *n.m.* stroke; feature, trait; gesture, act; ***a grandes rasgos,*** in broad outline.
rasgón, *n.m.* rent, rip, tear, slash.
rasgueado, *n.m.* strumming.
rasguear, *v.t., v.i.* to strum. — *v.i.* to scribble.
rasgueo, *n.m.* strumming (*on the guitar*); flourishing (*with a pen*).
rasguillo, *n.m.* small dash (*with a pen*).
rasguñar, *v.t.* to scratch, scrape; to sketch, outline.
rasguño, *n.m.* scratch, scrape; outline, sketch.
rasilla, *n.f.* serge; fine flooring tile.
raso, -sa, *a.* clear, open; flat; ***al raso,*** in the open; ***tiempo raso,*** fine weather; ***cielo raso,*** clear sky; ceiling; ***soldado raso,*** private, ranker;

hacer tabla rasa, to make a clean sweep, a fresh start. — *n.m.* satin. — *n.f.* tease (*in textiles*); plateau, tableland.
raspa, *n.f.* rasp, coarse file; (*carp.*) wood-rasp, scraper, grater; grape-stalk; fruit-rind; fish-bone; hair on a pen-nib; beard (*of ear of wheat*); (*Hisp. Am., coll.*) lecture, sermon, dressing down; (*Mex.*) dance.
raspado, *n.m.* (*surg.*) scraping.
raspador, *n.m.* rasp, grater, scraper; eraser.
raspadura, *n.f.* erasure; rasping, filing; scraping; (*Cub.*) pan sugar.
raspajo, *n.m.* grape-stalk.
raspamiento, *n.m.* rasping, filing.
raspante, *a.* rasping, rough (*wine*).
raspar, *v.t.* to erase; to rasp, scrape, scrape out; to taste harsh *or* rough to; (*coll.*) to pinch, steal.
raspear, *v.i.* to sputter, scratch (*of a pen*).
raspilla, *n.f.* (*bot.*) forget-me-not.
raspón, *n.m.* (*Col.*) large straw hat; (*Chi.*) dressing-down.
rasqueta, *n.f.* (*naut.*) scraper; (*horse grooming*) curry-comb.
rastacuero, *n.m.* (*Hisp. Am.*) upstart; boaster, show-off; sharper, adventurer.
rastel, *n.m.* bar, lattice, railing.
rastra, *n.f.* sled, sledge; dray, brake; (*agric.*) harrow; dragging along; track, trail; string of dried fruit; reaping-machine; (*naut.*) drag, grapnel; (*fig.*) ***a la rastra, a rastra*** or ***a rastras,*** unwillingly; ***a rastras de,*** dragging behind.
rastrallar, *v.t.* to lash. — *v.i.* to crack (*a whip*).
rastreador, -ra, *a.* tracing, tracking, trailing; trawling. — *n.m.f.* tracer, tracker, trailer; trawler.
rastrear, *v.t.* to trace, scent, track, trail; (*agric.*) to harrow, rake; to drag, trawl; to sell (*carcasses*) wholesale; to fathom, go deep into. — *v.i.* to skim the ground; (*aer.*) to fly low.
rastreo, *n.m.* dragging, trawling.
rastrero (1), **-ra,** *a.* crawling, trailing; dragging, trawling; skimming the ground; scenting; grovelling, cringing.
rastrero (2), *n.m.* slaughterhouse employee.
rastrillada, *n.f.* rakeful.
rastrillador, -ra, *n.m.f.* hackler, hatcheller, flax-dresser; raker.
rastrillar, *v.t.* to hackle, hatchel, comb, dress (*flax*); to rake.
rastrillazo, *n.m.* blow from a rake.
rastrilleo, *n.m.* hackling; raking.
rastrillo, *n.m.* hackle, flax-comb; rake; ward (*of a key*); ward (*of a lock*); hammer (*of a gunlock*); rack (*of a manager*); (*fort.*) portcullis.
Rastro, el, *n.m.* Madrid flea market.
rastro, *n.m.* trace; track, trail; scent; sign; rake; harrow; slaughterhouse.
rastrojera, *n.f.* stubble-ground.
rastrojo, *n.m.* stubble.
rasura, *n.f.* shaving; scraping.
rasuración, *n.f.* shaving.
rasurar, *v.t.* to shave.
rata (1), *n.f.* rat.
ratafía, *n.f.* ratafia.
ratania, *n.f.* rhatany.
rataplán, *n.m.* rub-a-dub (*drum-beat*).
ratear, *v.t.* to lessen *or* distribute proportionally; to filch, pilfer. — *v.i.* to crawl, creep.
rateo, *n.m.* proportional distribution, apportionment.
ratería, *n.f.* petty thieving, pilfering; baseness.
ratero, -ra, *a.* creeping; flying low; thieving; despicable, mean. — *n.m.* petty thief, pickpocket.
ratificación, *n.f.* ratification.
ratificar [A], *v.t.* to ratify.
ratificatorio, -ria, *a.* ratificative.
ratigar [B], *v.t.* to secure the load (*on a cart*) with a rope.
rátigo, *n.m.* cart-load.
ratihabición, *n.f.* (*law*) ratification.
ratina, *n.f.* ratteen.
ratito, *n.m.* short time, little while.
rato (1), *n.m.* short time; while, little while; ***buen rato,*** quite a while, quite some time; ***mal rato,*** nasty time, nasty turn *or* experience; ***tenemos para rato,*** this is going to take some time; ***le gusta un rato largo,*** he's terribly keen on it; ***a ratos,*** every now and again, off and on; ***a ratos perdidos,*** in odd moments, in one's spare time; ***de rato en rato,*** from time to time; ***pasar el rato,*** to pass the time, to while the time away.
rato (2), **-ta** (2), *a.* (*law*) ratified.
ratón, *n.m.* mouse; (*fig.*) ***ratón de archivo*** or ***de biblioteca,*** book-worm.
ratona, *n.f.* female mouse.
ratonar, *v.t.* to gnaw. — **ratonarse,** *v.r.* to become sick from eating mice (*of cats*).
ratonero, -ra, *a.* mouse; mousy. — *n.f.* mouse-trap; mouse-hole; nest of mice; ***caer en la ratonera,*** to fall into the trap.
rauco, -ca, *a.* (*poet.*) raucous, hoarse, husky.
raudal, *n.m.* torrent, rapid stream; (*fig.*) abundance, plenty.
raudo, -da, *a.* rapid, swift, fleet.
raulí, *n.m.* (*Chi.*) large limber tree.
rauta, *n.f.* (*coll.*) road, way, route.
raya, *n.f.* stroke, dash; stripe; mark, score; line, boundary, frontier; parting (*of the hair*); spiral groove (*of a rifle*); (*ichth.*) ray, skate; ***a rayas,*** striped; ***a raya,*** within bounds; ***tener a raya,*** to keep at bay, at arm's length; (*fig.*) ***dar ciento y raya a,*** to knock into a cocked hat, knock spots off; ***pasar de la raya,*** to go too far, exceed bounds; ***hacer raya,*** to be outstanding, brilliant; ***tres en raya,*** noughts and crosses; ***cruz y raya,*** I'm finished with you, them etc.
rayado, -da, *a.* ruled; striped; (*artill.*) rifled, grooved. — *n.m.* ruling; stripes.
rayano, -na, *a.* bordering.
rayar, *v.t.* to rule, line; to scratch; to stripe; to strike out, cross out; to underline. — *v.i.* to stand out; to border; to break (*of day*).
rayo, *n.m.* beam, ray; spoke (*of a wheel*); radius; (*fig.*) genius; streak (*of light*); thunderbolt, lightning flash; ***¡rayo(s)!*** blazes!; ***echar rayos,*** to be fuming; ***¡que lo parta un rayo!*** to blazes with him!; ***esto sabe a rayos,*** this tastes ghastly.
rayoso, -sa, *a.* full of lines *or* rays.
rayuela, *n.f.* small lines; hop-scotch.
rayuelo, *n.m.* snipe.
raza, *n.f.* race, breed, stock; cleft in a horse's hoof; lightly woven stripe in fabrics; ray of light; crack, fissure; ***de raza,*** thoroughbred.
razado, -da, *a.* lightly-woven (*of stripes*).
rázago, *n.m.* coarse cloth, sackcloth, burlap.
razón, *n.f.* reason; right; word, speech; ratio; enquiry; ***razón social*** or ***comercial,*** trade name (*of a company*); ***a razón de,*** at a rate of, on a basis of; ***tiene razón, le asiste la razón,*** he is right; ***atender a razones,*** to listen to reason; ***¡con razón!*** rightly (so); ***dar razón de,*** to give an account *or* explanation of; ***dar la razón a alguien,*** to admit that somebody is right; ***entrar en razón,*** to see reason; ***ponerse en razón,*** to see reason; ***tomar razón,*** to take note; ***fuera de razón,*** unreasonable; ***perder la razón,*** to lose one's reason, go out of one's mind; ***ya está puesto en razón,*** you can reason with him now; ***uso de razón,*** understanding; ***razón en portería,*** details at porter's box.
razonable, *a.* reasonable.
razonador, -ra, *n.m.f.* reasoner.
razonamiento, *n.m.* reasoning.

razonante, *a.* reasoning.
razonar, *v.t.* to itemize, detail. — *v.i.* to reason, argue.
razzia, *n.f.* foraging expedition, raid, plundering, ravaging.
re, *n.m.* (*mus.*) re, second note of scale; D.
rea, *n.f.* accused woman.
reacción, *n.f.* reaction.
reaccionar, *v.i.* to react.
reaccionario, -ria, *a., n.m.f.* reactionary.
reacio, -cia, *a.* reluctant, unwilling.
reacomodo, *n.m.* readjustment.
reacondicionar, *v.t.* to recondition, overhaul.
reactivo, *n.m.* reagent; stimulant.
reagravación, *n.f.* reaggravation.
reagravar, *v.t.* to aggravate anew.
reagudo, -da, *a.* very acute.
reajuste, *n.m.* readjustment.
real, *a.* real, actual; royal; magnificent, splendid, fine, handsome; ***real sitio,*** royal country seat. — *n.m.* camp, encampment; king's tent; real (*quarter of a peseta*); fair-ground; ship of the line; royal galley; ***sentar*** or ***asentar los reales,*** to pitch camp; to settle down; ***alzar*** or ***levantar los reales,*** to break, strike camp.
realce, *n.m.* raised work, embossment; splendour, lustre; (*art*) high light.
realdad, *n.f.* royal office, sovereignty.
realegrarse, *v.r.* to be overjoyed.
realejo, *n.m.* chamber organ.
realengo, -ga, *a.* royal, kingly; unappropriated (*land*).
realera, *n.f.* queen-bee's cell.
realeza, *n.f.* royalty, regal dignity.
realidad, *n.f.* reality; truth; ***en realidad,*** actually, in actual fact.
realismo, *n.m.* realism; royalism.
realista, *a.* realistic; royalist. — *n.m.f.* realist; royalist.
realizable, *a.* realizable; practical, feasible; (*com.*) saleable.
realización, *n.f.* realization; fulfilment; (*com.*) sale.
realizar [C], *v.t.* to realize; to accomplish, carry out, do, make, perform; to sell off. — **realizarse,** *v.r.* to be realized; to come true, materialize.
realmente, *adv.* royally; in fact, actually.
realquilar, *v.t., v.i.* to sub-let.
realzar [C], *v.t.* to raise, elevate; to emboss; to heighten, enhance; to dignify; to emphasize.
reanimar, *v.t.* to reanimate, revive.
reanudar, *v.t.* to renew, resume.
reaparecer [9], *v.i.* to reappear.
reaparición, *n.f.* reappearance, reappearing.
reapretar [I], *v.t.* to press again; to squeeze hard.
rearar, *v.t.* to plough again.
rearme, *n.m.* rearmament.
reaseguro, *n.m.* (*com.*) reinsurance.
reasumir [*p.p.* **reasumido, reasunto**], *v.t.* to take up again.
reasunción, *n.f.* reassumption, resumption.
reata, *n.f.* rope (*to tie horses in single file*); string, file; leading mule; ***de reata,*** in single file.
reatadura, *n.f.* retying; tying animals in single file.
reatar, *v.t.* to tie again; to tie tight; to tie in a string *or* file.
reato, *n.m.* (*eccles.*) obligation of atonement.
reavivar, *v.t.* to revive; to heighten.
rebaba, *n.f.* (*mech.*) burr, fin, mould mark.
rebaja, *n.f.* reduction, diminution; (*com.*) rebate, discount; (*pl.*) bargain sales.
rebajado, -da, *a.* discharged from service (*soldier*); (*arch.*) depressed; reduced (*price*).
rebajamiento, *n.m.* lowering; (*art*) toning down; humiliation.
rebajar, *v.t.* to lower, reduce, cut down; (*carp.*) to rabbet, shave down, plane down; (*art*) to tone down. — **rebajarse,** *v.r.* to lower o.s.; (*mil.*) to be excused.
rebajo, *n.m.* (*carp.*) rabbet; groove (*in timber* or *stone*).
rebalaje, *n.m.* eddy; current, flow of water.
rebalsa, *n.f.* stagnation; stagnant water; puddle, pool, pond.
rebalsar, *v.t.* to dam *or* dam up. — **rebalsar(se),** *v.i.* (*v.r.*) to form a pool.
rebanada, *n.f.* slice.
rebanar, *v.t.* to slice; to cut through.
rebañadera, *n.f.* drag, drag-hook, grapnel.
rebañadura, *n.f.* (*coll.*) gleaning, picking up.
rebañar, *v.t.* to wipe round (*the plate*); to carry off.
rebañego, -ga, *a.* sheep-like, easily led.
rebaño, *n.m.* flock, herd, drove; (*fig.*) crowd.
rebasadero, *n.m.* (*naut.*) pass.
rebasar, *v.t., v.i.* to go beyond, exceed; (*naut.*) to sail past.
rebate, *n.m.* dispute, contention.
rebatible, *a.* refutable, rebuttable.
rebatimiento, *n.m.* rejection, refutation.
rebatiña, *n.f.* bounce-up; free-for-all, scramble; ***a la rebatiña,*** broadcast; ***andar a la rebatiña,*** to scramble, grab and snatch (*things from one another*).
rebatir, *v.t.* to refute, rebut; to ward off; to knock *or* force down; to turn down; (*com.*) to deduct.
rebato, *n.m.* (*mil.*) alarm, alarm bell; call to arms; surprise attack; ***tocar a rebato,*** to sound the alarm.
rebautización, *n.f.* rebaptism.
rebautizar [C], *v.t.* to rebaptize, rechristen; to rename.
rebeca, *n.f.* cardigan.
rebeco, *n.f.* (*zool.*) chamois.
rebelarse, *v.r.* to rebel, revolt.
rebelde, *a.* rebellious, rebel; stubborn, unmanageable. — *n.m.f.* rebel; (*law*) defaulter.
rebeldía, *n.f.* rebelliousness; obstinacy, stubbornness, disobedience; (*law*) default, non-appearance; ***en rebeldía,*** in *or* by default.
rebelión, *n.f.* rebellion, revolt.
rebelón, -lona, *a.* restive, stubborn (*of a horse*).
rebencazo, *n.m.* blow with a ratline; whiplash.
rebenque, *n.m.* (*naut.*) ratline; cross rope; (*Hisp. Am.*) whip, lash.
rebién, *adv.* (*coll.*) jolly well.
rebina, rebinadura, *n.f.* third ploughing.
rebisabuela, *n.f.* great-great-grandmother.
rebisabuelo, *n.m.* great-great-grandfather.
rebisnieta, *n.f.* great-great-granddaughter.
rebisnieto, *n.m.* great-great-grandson.
reblandecer [9], *v.t.* to soften.
reblandecimiento, *n.m.* softening; (*fig.*) ***reblandecimiento cerebral,*** softening of the brain.
rebocillo, rebociño, *n.m.* shawl.
rebolisco, *n.m.* (*Cub.*) commotion.
rebollar, rebolledo, *n.m.* thicket of oak saplings.
rebollidura, *n.f.* honeycomb flaw in a gun's bore.
rebollo, *n.m.* (*bot.*) Turkey oak; tree trunk.
rebolludo, -da, *a.* thick-set; ***diamante rebolludo,*** rough diamond.
rebombar, *v.i.* to resound.
reborde, *n.m.* rim, flange, collar, border.
rebosadero, *n.m.* (place of) overflow.
rebosadura, *n.f.,* **rebosamiento,** *n.m.* overflow, overflowing.
rebosar(se), *v.t., v.i.* (*v.r.*) to overflow, flow over, brim over, run over, burst (with).
rebotadera, *n.f.* nap-raiser.
rebotadura, *n.f.* rebounding; bouncing.

rebotar, *v.t., v.i.* to clinch, bend back *or* over; to raise the nap on; to drive back; to upset. — *v.i.* to rebound, ricochet; to bounce. — **rebotarse,** *v.r.* to turn colour, change; to get upset.
rebote, *n.m.* rebound, rebounding; ricochet; bounce, bound; ***de rebote,*** on the rebound.
rebotica, *n.f.* back shop.
rebotín, *n.m.* second growth (*of mulberry leaves*).
rebozar [C], *v.t.* (*cook.*) to dip in, cover with batter, baste; to muffle up.
rebozo, *n.m.* muffling; muffler; shawl; pretext; ***de rebozo,*** secretly, covertly; ***sin rebozo,*** openly, frankly.
rebramar, *v.i.* to bellow repeatedly *or* loudly.
rebramo, *n.m.* bellowing (*animals*).
rebudiar, *v.i.* to snuffle, grunt (*wild boar*).
rebufar, *v.i.* to blow *or* snort repeatedly.
rebufo, *n.m.* (*artill.*) muzzle-blast.
rebujado, -da, *a.* tangled, entangled.
rebujal, *n.m.* number of cattle above fifty; small piece of arable ground.
rebujiña, *n.f.* (*coll.*) wrangle, scuffle.
rebujo, *n.m.* muffler, wrapper, thick veil; clumsy bundle.
rebullicio, *n.m.* great bustle, uproar.
rebullir(**se**) [J], *v.i.* (*v.r.*) to begin to move, stir, show signs of life.
reburujar, *v.t.* (*coll.*) to wrap, pack in a bundle.
reburujón, *n.m.* clumsy bundle.
rebusca, *n.f.* searching; gleaning; refuse, remains.
rebuscado, -da, *a.* recherché, affected.
rebuscador, -ra, *n.m.f.* searcher; gleaner.
rebuscamiento, *n.m.* searching; affectation.
rebuscar [A], *v.t.* to search into; to seek after; to glean.
rebusco, *n.m.* search; gleaning.
rebutir, *v.t.* (*prov.*) to stuff, fill up.
rebuznador, -ra, *a.* braying.
rebuznar, *v.i.* to bray.
rebuzno, *n.m.* bray(ing).
recabar, *v.t.* to obtain by entreaty; to entreat; to claim.
recadero, -ra, *n.m.f.* one who runs errands; messenger.
recado, *n.m.* errand; message; regards, compliments, complimentary message; present, gift; outfit; supply; ***recado de escribir,*** writing materials; ***mandar recado,*** to send word.
recaer [14], *v.i.* to fall back, relapse; to fall (***en, sobre,*** to, upon); to come round (***en,*** to).
recaída, *n.f.* relapse; second fall *or* offence.
recalada, *n.f.* landfall; homing.
recalar, *v.t.* to soak, drench, saturate (slowly). — *v.i.* to sight *or* reach land, make landfall.
recalcadura, *n.f.* pressing, pressing tight; cramming, packing.
recalcar [A], *v.t.* to cram, stuff; to emphasize, stress. — *v.i.* (*naut.*) to heel, list. — **recalcarse,** *v.r.* to harp (on); to sprawl.
recalce, *n.m.* (*agric.*) hilling; (*arch.*) strengthening.
recalcitrante, *a.* recalcitrant.
recalcitrar, *v.i.* to baulk.
recalentamiento, *n.m.* reheating; overheating.
recalentar [I], *v.t.* to heat again, heat up; to overheat.
recalmón, *n.m.* (*naut.*) lull of the wind.
recalvastro, -ra, *a.* bald-headed.
recalzar [C], *v.t.* (*agric.*) to hill; (*arch.*) to strengthen the foundation of; (*art.*) to colour (*a drawing*).
recalzo, *n.m.* repairing, strengthening a foundation; outer felloe of a cart-wheel.
recalzón, *n.m.* outer felloe of a wheel.
recamado, *n.m.* raised work (*embroidery*).
recamador, -ra, *n.m.f.* embroiderer.
recamar, *v.t.* to embroider with raised work.
recámara, *n.f.* wardrobe, clothes room; dressing-room, boudoir; (*Mex.*) bedroom; (*min.*) explosives store; chamber (*of a gun*); (*coll., fig.*) reserve, cunning.
recambiar, *v.t.* to rechange, re-exchange; (*com.*) to redraw.
recambio, *n.m.* re-exchange; rechange; (*com.*) redrawing; (*mach.*) spare (part).
recamo, *n.m.* embroidery of raised work.
recancanilla, *n.f.* children's game, hobbling; (*coll.*) emphasis.
recantación, *n.f.* recantation, retraction.
recantón, *n.m.* corner-stone.
recapacitar, *v.t., v.i.* to think over; to think carefully.
recapitulación, *n.f.* recapitulation.
recapitular, *v.t.* to recapitulate.
recarga, *n.f.* second charge of firearms.
recargar [B], *v.t.* to reload, recharge; to overload, surcharge; (*law*) to increase (a sentence). — *v.i.* to charge again. — **recargarse,** *v.r.* (*med.*) to have an increase in temperature.
recargo, *n.m.* new charge *or* accusation; extra charge; surcharge; overload; increase of temperature; (*law*) increase of a sentence.
recata, *n.f.* tasting again.
recatado, -da, *a.* circumspect; retiring, modest.
recatar, *v.t.* to secrete, conceal; to taste again.
recato, *n.m.* circumspection, caution; secrecy; modesty, bashfulness, coyness; virtue, honour.
recatonazo, *n.m.* stroke with the butt of a lance.
recaudación, *n.f.* collection of taxes; recovery of debts; collector's office.
recaudador, *n.m.* tax-gatherer, collector.
recaudamiento, *n.m.* collection of taxes; collector's office *or* district.
recaudar, *v.t.* to collect, gather; to put in a safe place.
recaudo, *n.m.* collection (*of rents* or *taxes*); precaution, care; surety, security, bail, bond; ***a buen recaudo,*** well guarded, in a safe place, in safety.
recavar, *v.t.* to dig a second time.
recazo, *n.m.* guard (*of sword*); back (*of knife-blade*).
recebar, *v.t.* to gravel.
recebo, *n.m.* gravel.
recelador, *a., n.m.* (horse) for getting mare in heat.
recelar, *v.t.* to suspect, fear; to excite (*a mare*) sexually. — **recelar**(**se**), *v.i.* (*v.r.*) to have suspicions, fears *or* misgivings.
recelo, *n.m.* fear, suspicion, misgiving.
receloso, -sa, *a.* suspicious, mistrustful, having misgivings.
recensión, *n.f.* recension; (book) review.
recentadura, *n.f.* leaven.
recental, *a.* suckling.
recentar [I], *v.t.* to leaven. — **recentarse,** *v.r.* to be renewed.
recenir [8K], *v.t.* to regird.
recepción, *n.f.* reception; receiving; admission; (*law*) cross-examination.
recepta, *n.f.* record of fines.
receptáculo, *n.m.* receptacle; repository; refuge, shelter.
receptador, *n.m.* receiver of stolen goods; abettor.
receptar, *v.t.* to receive (*stolen goods*); to abet; to hide, shelter.
receptivo, -va, *a.* receptive.
recepto, *n.m.* asylum, shelter, refuge.
receptor, -ra, *a.* receiving, recipient. — *n.m.* receiver; abettor.
receptoría, *n.f.* receiver's office; receivership.
recercador, *n.m.* chaser (*of jewellery*).
recercar [A], *v.t.* to fence again; to fence in.
recésit, *n.m.* vacation, recess.
receso, *n.m.* recess, withdrawal, retirement, recession; (*astron.*) deviation.

receta, *n.f.* prescription; recipe; memorandum of orders; (*com.*) amount brought forward.
recetador, *n.m.* prescriber.
recetar, *v.t.* to prescribe.
recetario, *n.m.* register of physicians' prescriptions; pharmacopœia; apothecary's file; recipe book.
recetor, *n.m.* receiver; treasurer.
recetoría, *n.f.* treasury; sub-treasury.
recial, *n.m.* rapid (*in rivers*).
recibí, *n.m.* receipt.
recibidero, -ra, *a.* receivable.
recibidor, *n.m.* receiver; hall.
recibiente, *a.* receiving.
recibimiento, *n.m.* reception; reception *or* drawing room; ante-chamber; hall.
recibir, *v.t.* to receive; to take; to meet. — *v.i.* to receive calls, be at home to callers. — **recibirse,** *v.r.* to graduate (**de,** as), be admitted to the number (of); ***recibirse de abogado,*** to be called to the bar, (*Am.*) to be admitted to the bar.
recibo, *n.m.* (*com.*) receipt; reception; drawing-room; ***de recibo,*** fit for service; (*coll.*) standing on ceremony; ***día de recibo,*** at-home day; ***sala de recibo,*** reception room; (*com.*) ***acusar recibo,*** to acknowledge receipt; ***estar de recibo,*** to be at home to callers.
recidiva, *n.f.* relapse.
recién, *adv.* recently, just, lately, newly, new.
reciente, *a.* recent, new, fresh.
recinchar, *v.t.* to gird, bind with a girdle.
recinto, *n.m.* (enclosed) area, precinct; site.
recio, -cia, *a.* strong, tough, hardy; hard, severe; (*fig.*) heavy. — *adv.* strongly, hard; ***pisar recio,*** to tread firmly; ***de recio,*** strongly, hard; ***hablar recio,*** to talk loudly.
récipe, *n.m.* prescription; (*coll.*) dressing-down.
recipiendario, *n.m.* member received (*into an academy etc.*).
recipiente, *a.* receiving. — *n.m.* recipient; (*chem.*) receiver; receptacle, container; (*phys.*) bell (*of an air pump*).
reciprocación, *n.f.* reciprocation.
recíprocamente, *adv.* reciprocally, mutually; conversely.
reciprocar [A], *v.t.* to reciprocate. — *v.i.* to return, repay the favour. — **reciprocarse,** *v.r.* to correspond mutually.
reciprocidad, *n.f.* reciprocity.
recíproco, -ca, *a.* reciprocal, mutual; (*coll.*) ***a la recíproca,*** tit for tat; quits.
recisión, *n.f.* rescission, abrogation.
recitación, *n.f.* recitation.
recitado, *n.m.* recitation; recitative.
recitador, -ra, *n.m.f.* reciter.
recital, *n.m.* recital.
recitar, *v.t.* to recite.
recitativo, -va, *a.* recitative.
reciura, *n.f.* strength, force; rigour, severity.
reclamación, *n.f.* reclamation; objection, remonstrance; (*com.*) complaint; claim.
reclamante, *a.*, *n.m.* claimant.
reclamar, *v.t.* to claim; to call for; (*law*) to order to appear; (*law*) to reclaim; to decoy (*birds*). — *v.i.* to put in a claim.
reclame, *n.m.* sheave hole (*in a topmast head*).
reclamo, *n.m.* (*law*) reclamation; decoy-bird, lure, attraction; catch-word, slogan; blurb; (*naut.*) tie-block.
recle, *n.m.* (*eccles.*) vacation from choir duties.
reclinación, *n.f.* reclining.
reclinar, *v.t.* to lean. — **reclinarse,** *v.r.* to lean back, recline.
reclinatorio, *n.m.* prie-dieu.
recluir [O], *v.t.* to shut up, put away; to keep in.
reclusión, *n.f.* reclusion, seclusion; shutting up, putting away; imprisonment; ***reclusión perpetua,*** life imprisonment.
recluso, -sa, *n.m.f.* inmate, prisoner.
reclusorio, *n.m.* place of confinement.
recluta, *n.f.* recruiting, supply; (*Arg.*) herd (*of cattle*). — *n.m.* recruit.
reclutador, *n.m.* recruiting-officer.
reclutamiento, *n.m.* recruiting.
reclutar, *v.t.* to recruit; (*Arg.*) to round up (*cattle*).
recobrar, *v.t.* to recover; ***recobrar el tiempo perdido,*** to make up for lost time. — **recobrarse,** *v.r.* to recover.
recobro, *n.m.* recovery.
recocer [5D], *v.t.* to boil again; to over-boil; to anneal. — **recocerse,** *v.r.* to be consumed *or* eaten up (**de,** with).
recocido, -da, *n.m.f.* annealing.
recocina, *n.f.* back kitchen.
recochineo, *n.m.* malicious gloating.
recocho, -cha, *a.* over-boiled, over-done; over-fired (*bricks*).
recodadero, *n.m.* elbow-chair.
recodar(se), *v.i.* (*v.r.*) to lean on one's elbows; to twist, turn, wind.
recodo, *n.m.* elbow-bend; turn, twist.
recogeabuelos, *n.m. inv.* ring-comb.
recogedero, *n.m.* collector; catchment area, drainage area.
recogedor, *n.m.* gatherer; shelterer; dust-pan.
recoger [E], *v.t.* to pick up; to gather, gather up, gather in, gather together; to collect, collect up, collect together; to take in; to withdraw, call in; to seize, confiscate; to put away; to record; ***recoger velas,*** to ease up, climb down a bit, draw one's horns in. — **recogerse,** *v.r.* to take refuge; to withdraw; to retire; to go home, pack up.
recogido, -da, *a.* secluded; retiring; in retreat; abstracted from worldly thoughts. — *n.f.* gathering; collection; withdrawal; woman inmate (*of house of correction*).
recogimiento, *n.m.* devout abstraction, engrossment; devoutness; house of correction.
recolección, *n.f.* collection, compilation; summary; gathering, harvest; recollection, abstraction.
recolectar, *v.t.* to gather in, harvest.
recoleto, -ta, *a.* devout; in retreat; recollect.
recomendable, *a.* commendable, advisable.
recomendación, *n.f.* recommendation; ***carta de recomendación,*** letter of introduction; ***recomendación del alma,*** prayers for the dying.
recomendar, *v.t.* to recommend.
recomendatorio, -ria, *a.* recommendatory.
recompensa, *n.f.* recompense, reward.
recompensable, *a.* deserving reward.
recompensación, *n.f.* recompense, reward.
recompensar, *v.t.* to recompense, reward.
recomponer [25], *v.t.* to recompose; to mend, repair. — **recomponerse,** *v.r.* to take excessive care over one's appearance.
reconcentración, *n.f.*, **reconcentramiento,** *n.m.* deep concentration *or* thought.
reconcentrar, *v.t.* to concentrate. — **reconcentrarse,** *v.r.* to concentrate, sink deep into thought, become engrossed in thought.
reconciliable, *a.* reconcilable.
reconciliación, *n.f.* reconciliation, reconcilement.
reconciliador, -ra, *a.* reconciling. — *n.m.f.* reconciler.
reconciliar, *v.t.* to reconcile; to bring together again; (*eccles.*) to hear a short additional confession from. — **reconciliarse,** *v.r.* to be reconciled; to return to the faith, make peace with the Church.
reconcomerse [CONCOMERSE].
reconcomio, *n.m.* [CONCOMIO]; itching, desire; (*fam.*) fear, suspicion, misgiving.

reconditez, *n.f.* reconditeness.
recóndito, -ta, *a.* recondite, secret, hidden, concealed, abstruse.
reconducción, *n.f.* renewal of a lease.
reconducir, *v.t.* to renew (a lease *or* contract).
reconocedor, -ra, *a.* inspecting, examining. — *n.m.f.* examiner.
reconocer [9], *v.t.* to recognize; to acknowledge, admit; to examine; (*mil.*) to reconnoitre, scout. — **reconocerse,** *v.r.* to be known; to know o.s.
reconocido, -da, *a.* acknowledged; grateful, obliged.
reconociente, *a.* recognizing.
reconocimiento, *n.m.* recognition; gratitude; acknowledgement; admission; (*med.*) examination; (*mil.*) reconnoitring, reconnaissance.
reconquista, *n.f.* reconquest.
reconquistar, *v.t.* to reconquer.
reconstitución, *n.f.* reconstitution.
reconstituir [O], *v.t.* to reconstitute; (*med.*) to restore.
reconstituyente, *a.* reconstituent. — *n.m.* (*med.*) restorative, tonic.
reconstrucción, *n.f.* reconstruction.
reconstruir [O], *v.t.* to reconstruct, rebuild.
recontamiento, *n.m.* narration.
recontar, *v.t.* to re-count, count again; to recount, tell.
recontento, -ta, *a.* very pleased, greatly delighted. — *n.m.* deep satisfaction.
reconvalecer [9], *v.i.* to reconvalesce.
reconvención, *n.f.* reproach, recrimination; reprimand; counter-charge.
reconvenir [36], *v.t.* to reproach; to reprimand; (*law*) to counter-charge.
recopilación, *n.f.* compilation; compendium; abridgement; (*law*) digest.
recopilador, *n.m.* compiler, collector; abridger.
recopilar, *v.t.* to compile, collect; to abridge.
recoquín, *n.m.* short chubby fellow.
récord, *a. inv.* record. — *n.m.* record (*in sports*).
recordable, *a.* worthy of record, memorable.
recordación, *n.f.* memory, recollection.
recordador, -ra, *a.* remembering; reminding.
recordante, *a.* reminding.
recordar [4], *v.t.* to remind, recall; to remember; ***recordar algo a alguien,*** to remind s.o. of sth.; ***recuérdale que escriba,*** remind him to write. — *v.i.* to awaken.
recordativo, -va, *a.* reminding. — *n.m.* reminder.
recordatorio, *n.m.* memento, souvenir.
recorrer, *v.t.* to cross, traverse; to go over, through *or* across; to travel over, through *or* across; to run over, read through; to go round; to overhaul.
recorrido, *n.m.* run, trip; course, route, round; going over; stroke, travel; overhaul; (*coll.*) dressing-down.
recortado, -da, *a.* (*bot.*) incised. — *n.m.* (*figure*) cut-out.
recortador, -ra, *n.m.f.* cutter-out.
recortadura, *n.f.* cutting, cutting out; clipping.
recortar, *v.t.* to cut away, cut off; to cut down, cut back; to clip, trim; to cut out; to outline. — **recortarse,** *v.r.* to stand out.
recorte, *n.m.* cutting, clipping.
recorvar, *v.t.* to bend, arch, curve.
recoser, *v.t.* to sew again; to mend (*linen*).
recosido, *n.m.* mend(ing).
recostadero, *n.m.* resting-place.
recostar [4], *v.t.* to prop, lean. — **recostarse,** *v.r.* to recline; to lean back.
recova, *n.f.* dealing in eggs, poultry etc.; poultry market; pack of hounds.
recoveco, *n.m.* turning, winding; turn, bend; corner; trick; ***tener muchos recovecos,*** to be tortuous; ***sin recovecos,*** straightforward.
recovero, *n.m.* poultry-dealer.
recre, *n.m.* (*eccles.*) choristers' vacation.
recreación, *n.f.* recreation.
recrear, *v.t.* to delight, amuse, divert; to recreate.
recreativo, -va, *a.* recreative.
recrecer [9], *v.t.* to augment, increase. — *v.i.* to grow again. — **recrecerse,** *v.r.* to recover one's spirits.
recrecimiento, *n.m.* increase, growth.
recreído, -da, *a.* intractable, having recovered its native wildness.
recrementicio, -cia, *a.* recrementitious.
recremento, *n.m.* (*physiol.*) recrement.
recreo, *n.m.* recreation; amusement; recreation time, play-time; ***barco de recreo,*** pleasure boat; ***casa de recreo,*** country house, weekend residence.
recría, *n.f.* repasturing.
recriar [L], *v.t.* to improve with new pastures; to give new strength to; to redeem.
recriminación, *n.f.* recrimination.
recriminar, *v.t.* to reproach. — *v.i.* to recriminate.
recrudecer(se) [9], *v.i.* (*v.r.*) to break out again, flare up again.
recrudecimiento, *n.m.* recrudescence, fresh outbreak.
recrujir, *v.i.* to squeak.
recta, *n.f.* [RECTO (I)].
rectangular, *a.* rectangular.
rectángulo, -la, *a.* rectangular, rectangled. — *n.m.* rectangle.
rectificable, *a.* rectifiable.
rectificación, *n.f.* rectification.
rectificar [A], *v.t.* to rectify, put right, set straight. — *v.i.* to adjust one's attitude, change tactics. — **rectificarse,** *v.r.* to correct o.s.
rectificativo, -va, *a.* rectifying.
rectilíneo, -nea, *a.* rectilinear, rectilineal.
rectitud, *n.f.* rectitude; uprightness; straightness; correctness.
recto (I), **-ta,** *a.* straight; upright; right, precise; ***siga Vd. (la calle) todo recto,*** go straight down the road. — *n.f.* straight line *or* stretch.
recto (2), *n.m.* (*anat.*) rectum.
rector, -ra, *a.* ruling, governing. — *n.m.f.* rector, principal.
rectorado, *n.m.* rectorship.
rectoral, *a.* rectorial. — *n.f.* rectory.
rectorar, *v.i.* to attain the office of rector.
rectoría, *n.f.* rectory; rectorship.
recua, *n.f.* drove, string (*of mules etc.*).
recuadro, *n.m.* (*arch.*) square compartment, box.
recuaje, *n.m.* tribute, duty for the passing of cattle.
recuarta, *n.f.* additional fourth string (*lute*).
recudimento, recudimiento, *n.m.* power to collect rents, rates *or* taxes.
recudir, *v.t.* to pay (*money, dues etc.*). — *v.i.* to rebound, set out again, revert.
recuelo, *n.m.* strong bleach; weak warmed-up coffee.
recuento, *n.m.* recount; count; checking, going over.
recuerdo (I), *n.m.* memory, recollection; remembrance; souvenir; (*pl.*) regards.
recuerdo (2), **recuerde,** *pres. indic., pres. subj.* [RECORDAR].
recuero, *n.m.* muleteer, mule-driver.
recuesta, *n.f.* (*obs.*) request.
recuestar, *v.t.* (*obs.*) to request.
recuesto (I), *n.m.* slope.
recuesto (2), **recueste,** *pres. indic., pres. subj.* [RECOSTAR].

reculada, *n.f.* falling back; recoil, recoiling; (*naut.*) falling astern.
recular, *v.i.* to fall back, recoil; to reverse; (*naut.*) to fall astern; (*coll.*) to back down.
reculo, -la, *a.* tailless (*of poultry*).
reculones, (**a**), *adv.* (*coll.*) going backwards, edging back.
recuñar, *v.t.* (*min.*) to wedge, brake with wedges.
recuperable, *a.* recoverable.
recuperación, *n.f.* recovery, regain; recuperation, recovering.
recuperador, -ra, *a.* recovering. — *n.m.f.* recoverer. — *n.m.* recuperator.
recuperar, *v.t.* to recover, regain, retrieve. — **recuperarse,** *v.r.* to recuperate, recover.
recuperativo, -va, *a.* recuperative.
recura, *n.f.* comb-saw.
recurar, *v.t.* to make *or* open the teeth of (*combs*).
recurrente, *a.* (*bot.*) recurrent; (*law*) appellant.
recurrir, *v.i.* to appeal, resort (to), have recourse (to); to revert.
recurso, *n.m.* recourse, resort; resource; petition; reversion, return; (*law*) appeal; ***sin recurso,*** irremediably, inescapably; (*pl.*) means; ***de recursos,*** resourceful.
recusable, *a.* refusable, exceptionable; (*law*) challengeable.
recusación, *n.f.* recusation.
recusante, *a.* recusant.
recusar, *v.t.* to reject; to recuse.
rechazador, -ra, *a.* rejecting; repellent.
rechazamiento, *n.m.* rejection; repulsion.
rechazar [C], *v.t.* to reject; to repel, throw back.
rechazo, *n.m.* rebound, recoil; rejection; ***de rechazo,*** on the rebound; indirectly.
rechifla, *n.f.* hooting, jeering; derision.
rechiflar, *v.t.*, *v.i.* to hoot, jeer. — **rechiflarse,** *v.r.* to mock.
rechinador, -ra, rechinante, *a.* creaking, squeaking, grating.
rechinamiento, *n.m.* creaking, squeaking, grating.
rechinar, *v.i.* to creak, squeak, grate; to gnash (*the teeth*); to balk.
rechistar, *v.i.* to speak, open one's mouth.
rechoncho, -cha, *a.* (*coll.*) chubby.
rechupete, (**de**), *a.* (*coll.*) delicious; super, smashing.
red, *n.f.* net; net-work; netting; luggage-rack; grille; snare; system, grid; ***red de espías,*** spy ring; ***caer en la red,*** to fall into the trap; ***echar*** or ***tender la red,*** to cast the net; to lay the snare, set the trap.
redacción, *n.f.* editing; wording; editorial staff; editorial office; essay, composition.
redactar, *v.t.* to edit; to word; to draw up.
redactor, -ra, *n.m.f.* editor; subeditor, (*Am.*) copy editor.
redada, *n.f.* casting of a net; netful, haul, catch; round-up.
redaño, *n.m.* caul. — *n.m.pl.* grit, guts, mettle.
redar, *v.t.* to net.
redargución, *n.f.* retort; refutation.
redargüir [I], *v.t.* to retort; (*law*) to impugn.
redaya, *n.f.* net.
redecilla, *n.f.* small net, bag-net; mesh; hair-net; (*anat.*) reticulum.
rededor, *n.m.* surroundings, environs; ***al rededor,*** round about.
redel, *n.m.* (*naut.*) loof-frame.
redención, *n.f.* redemption; recovery; ransom.
redentor, -ra, *n.m.f.* redeemer.
redero, -ra, *a.* reticular, retiform, reticulated. — *n.m.* net-maker; one who catches with nets.
redescuento, *n.m.* (*com.*) rediscount.
redhibición, *n.f.* (*law*) redhibition.
redhibir, *v.t.* to use the right of redhibition on.
redhibitorio, -ria, *a.* redhibitory.
redición, *n.f.* reiteration, repetition.
redicho, -cha, *a.* affected, over-precise (*in speech*).
rediezmar, *v.t.* to tithe a second time.
rediezmo, *n.m.* extra tithe.
redil, *n.m.* sheepfold.
redimible, *a.* redeemable.
redimir, *v.t.* to redeem.
redingote, *n.m.* redingote, great-coat.
rédito, *n.m.* (*com.*) interest; revenue, proceeds, yield, income.
redituable, reditual, *a.* income-producing.
redituar [M], *v.t.* to yield, produce.
redivivo, -va, *a.* redivivous, alive once more.
redoblado, -da, *a.* double-lined; (*mil.*) double (*step*); stocky, heavy-built.
redobladura, *n.f.*, **redoblamiento,** *n.m.* redoubling; clinching (*a nail* or *rivet*).
redoblante, *a.* drumming. — *n.m.* long-framed drum.
redoblar, *v.t.* to redouble; to bend over, clinch, rivet; to double, repeat. — *v.i.* to roll a drum. — **redoblarse,** *v.r.* to grow louder and louder.
redoble, *n.m.* (*mil.*, *mus.*) redoubling; roll (*of a drum*).
redoblegar [B], *v.t.* to redouble; to bend, clinch.
redoblón, *n.m.* rivet, clinch-nail.
redoliente, *a.* smarting, aching.
redolino, *n.m.* wheel for drawing lots.
redolor, *n.m.* dull, lingering ache *or* pain.
redoma, *n.f.* phial, flask; (*chem.*) balloon.
redomado, -da, *a.* dyed-in-the-wool, inveterate, out-and-out.
redomón, -mona, *a.* (*Hisp. Am.*) half broken-in (*horse* or *mule*).
redonda, *n.f.* [REDONDO].
redondeado, -da, *a.* approaching a circular *or* spherical shape.
redondeador, *n.m.* rounding-tool.
redondear, *v.t.* to round, make round, round off; to clear (*debts and charges*). — **redondearse,** *v.r.* to fill out one's finances.
redondel, *n.m.* circle; bull-ring; roundabout, (*Am.*) traffic circle; circular mat; round cloak; (*mech.*) flange.
redondete, *a.* roundish.
redondez, *n.f.* roundness, rotundity; ***redondez de la tierra,*** face of the earth.
redondilla, *n.f.* stanza of four octosyllables, rhyming *abba*; ***letra redondilla,*** round hand (*writing*).
redondo, -da, *a.* round; (*print.*) Roman; flat, categorical; pasture (*land*); ***caer redondo,*** to fall flat; ***negarse en redondo,*** to refuse flatly; ***negocio redondo,*** first-rate business proposition; ***redondo de carne,*** joint; ***en redondo,*** all around. — *n.f.* district, neighbourhood; (*naut.*) square sail; pasture-ground; (*mus.*) semibreve; ***a la redonda,*** roundabout; ***en diez millas a la redonda,*** for ten miles round.
redondón, *n.m.* large sphere *or* circle.
redopelo, redropelo, *n.m.* rubbing the wrong way; (*coll.*) boys' wrangle *or* scuffle; ***a*** or ***al redopelo,*** against the grain; ***traer a redopelo,*** to drag about.
redor, *n.m.* round mat; (*poet.*) ***en redor,*** round about.
redro, *adv.* (*coll.*) backward, behind. — *n.m.* yearly ring on the horn (*sheep* or *goats*).
redrojo, redruejo, redrojuelo, *n.m.* after-vintage grapes, after-fruit; (*coll.*) titch, runt.
reducción, *n.f.* reduction, decrease, cut; (*Hisp. Am.*) settlement of Indians converted to Christianity.
reducible, *a.* reducible.
reducido, -da, *a.* small, compact.

reducimiento, *n.m.* reduction, reducing.
reducir [15], *v.t.* to reduce, cut down. — **reducirse,** *v.r.* to cut down one's expenses; ***reducirse a,*** to be reduced to, come to; to amount to, (*fig.*) boil down to.
reducto, *n.m.* redoubt.
reductor, -ra, *a.* reducing. — *n.m.* reducer.
redundancia, *n.f.* redundancy.
redundante, *a.* redundant.
redundar, *v.i.* to redound; to overflow; ***redundar en beneficio de,*** to redound to the benefit of.
reduplicación, *n.f.* reduplication.
reduplicado, -da, *a.* reduplicate.
reduplicar [A], *v.t.* to reduplicate.
reedificación, *n.f.* rebuilding.
reedificador, -ra, *n.m.f.* rebuilder.
reedificar [A], *v.t.* to rebuild.
reeditar, *v.t.* to reprint, republish.
reelección, *n.f.* re-election.
reelecto, -ta, *a.* re-elected. — *p.p. irreg.* [REELEGIR].
reelegible, *a.* re-eligible.
reelegir [8E, *p.p.* **reelegido**], *v.t.* to re-elect.
reembarcar [A], *v.t.* to re-embark, re-ship.
reembarco, reembarque, *n.m.* re-embarkation, reshipment.
reembargar [B], *v.t.* to seize *or* embargo a second time.
reembolsar, *v.t.* to reimburse, repay, refund. — **reembolsarse,** *v.r.* to recover money lent.
reembolso, *n.m.* reimbursement, refunding; refund; ***contra reembolso,*** cash on delivery.
reempacar [A], *v.t.* to re-pack.
reemplazar [C], *v.t.* to replace, supersede.
reemplazo, *n.m.* replacement; call-up of yearly draft; ***de reemplazo,*** (officer) on active service but without command.
reemprender, *v.t.* to undertake again.
reencarnación, *n.f.* reincarnation.
reencarnar, *v.t.* to reincarnate. — **reencarnar(se),** *v.i.* (*v.r.*) to be reincarnated.
reencuentro, *n.m.* collision; (fresh) encounter.
reenganchamiento, reenganche, *n.m.* re-enlisting, re-enlistment; re-enlistment bounty.
reenganchar, *v.t.* to re-enlist; to recouple.
reengendrador, *n.m.* regenerator.
reengendrar, *v.t.* to regenerate.
reensayar, *v.t.* to test *or* try again; to rehearse anew.
reensaye, *n.m.* re-assay.
reensayo, *n.m.* retrial, second *or* fresh test; fresh rehearsal.
reenvasar, *v.t.* to refill, repack.
reenviar [L], *v.t.* to forward, send on.
reenvío, *n.m.* forwarding, sending on.
reestreno, *n.m.* (*theat.*) revival.
reexaminación, *n.f.* re-examination.
reexaminar, *v.t.* to re-examine.
reexpedición, *n.f.* forwarding.
reexpedir [8], *v.t.* to forward, send on.
reexportación, *n.f.* re-export.
reexportar, *v.t.* to re-export.
refacción, *n.f.* refection; (*Hisp. Am.*) repair; financial aid.
refaccionar, *v.t.* (*Hisp. Am.*) to repair; (*Hisp. Am.*) to finance.
refaccionista, *n.m.* (*Cub.*) financial backer.
refajo, *n.m.* skirt; underskirt, slip.
refalsado, -da, *a.* false, deceitful.
refección, *n.f.* refection, light meal; repairs.
refectorio, *n.m.* refectory.
referencia, *n.f.* reference; account; testimonial.
referendario, *n.m.* countersigner.
referéndum, *n.m.* referendum.
referente, *a.* referring, relating.
referir [8], *v.t.* to refer; to relate, give an account of. — **referirse,** *v.r.* to refer (to), allude (to).
refertero, -ra, *a.* quarrelsome, wrangling.
refigurar, *v.t.* to refigure; to represent anew (*in the imagination*).
refilón, (**de**), *adv.* slanting; in passing.
refinación, *n.f.* refinement, refining.
refinadera, *n.f.* stone roller (*for refining chocolate*).
refinado, -da, *a.* refined; sophisticated; subtle. — *n.m.* refining.
refinador, *n.m.* refiner.
refinadura, *n.f.* refining.
refinamiento, *n.m.* refining, refinement; sophistication.
refinar, *v.t.* to refine; to make sophisticated; to polish.
refinería, *n.f.* refinery.
refino, -na, *a.* very fine *or* refined. — *n.m.* refining; coffee, cocoa and sugar exchange.
refirmar, *v.t.* to support; to confirm, ratify.
refitolero, -ra, *a.* dandified, foppish; meddlesome. — *n.m.f.* refectioner; (*coll.*) meddler, busybody. — *n.m.* dandy, fop.
reflectante, *a.* reflecting.
reflectar, *v.i.* to reflect.
reflector, -ra, *a.* reflecting, reflective. — *n.m.* reflector; searchlight.
refleja, *n.f.* [REFLEJO].
reflejar, *v.t.* to reflect; to show, reveal. — *v.i.* to reflect. — **reflejarse,** *v.r.* to be reflected.
reflejo, -ja, *a.* reflected; (*gram.*) reflexive; (*physiol.*) reflex. — *n.m.f.* reflection. — *n.m.* reflex; glare. — *n.f.* observation, remark.
reflexible, *a.* reflectible.
reflexión, *n.f.* reflection; remark.
reflexionar, *v.i.* to reflect, think it over.
reflexivo, -va, *a.* reflexive; reflective.
reflorecer [9], *v.i.* to flower anew, blossom again.
refluente, *a.* refluent; flowing back.
refluir [O], *v.i.* to flow back; to redound.
reflujo, *n.m.* reflux; ebb, ebb-tide.
refocilación, *n.f.* coarse enjoyment, wallowing.
refocilarse, *v.r.* to wallow, revel filthily.
refocilo, *n.m.* [REFOCILACIÓN].
reforma, *n.f.* reform; reformation; amendment.
reformable, *a.* reformable.
reformación, *n.f.* reformation, reshaping.
reformador, -ra, *a.* reforming. — *n.m.f.* reformer.
reformar, *v.t.* to reform, amend; to re-form, reshape.
reformatorio, -ria, *a.* corrective. — *n.m.* reformatory.
reformista, *a.*, *n.m.f.* reformer, reformist.
reforzada, *n.f.* narrow tape.
reforzar [C], *v.t.* to strengthen, reinforce.
refracción, *n.f.* refraction.
refractar, *v.t.* to refract.
refractario, -ria, *a.* refractory; heat-proof.
refracto, -ta, *a.* refracted.
refrán, *n.m.* proverb, adage, saying.
refranero, *n.m.* collection of proverbs.
refregadura, *n.f.* hard rubbing.
refregamiento, *n.m.* hard rubbing.
refregar [1B], *v.t.* to rub, scrub; (*coll.*) to reprove, scold.
refregón, *n.m.* rubbing, rub; gust.
refreír [28, *p.p.* **refrito**], *v.t.* to fry thoroughly; to fry again; (*fig.*) to rehash.
refrenable, *a.* capable of being restrained.
refrenamiento, *n.m.* restraining, curbing, checking.
refrenar, *v.t.* to restrain, curb, check.
refrendación, *n.f.* countersigning; endorsement; legalization, authentication.

refrendar, *v.t.* to countersign; to endorse, back, ratify; to legalize, authenticate.
refrendario, *n.m.* countersigner.
refrendata, *n.f.* countersignature.
refrendo, *n.m.* legalization, authentication.
refrescador, -ra, *a.* refreshing, cooling.
refrescadura, *n.f.* refreshing.
refrescamiento, *n.m.* refreshing, cooling.
refrescante, *a.* refreshing, cooling.
refrescar [A], *v.t.* to refresh, freshen, cool; to brush up. — *v.i.* to turn cool *or* chilly. — **refrescarse,** *v.r.* to get cool, cool off.
refresco, *n.m.* refreshment; cooling drink; ***de refresco,*** again, once more; fresh.
refriega, *n.f.* fray, affray, scuffle.
refrigeración, *n.f.* cooling; refrigeration.
refrigerador, -ra, *a.* cooling; refrigerating. — *n.m.* cooler; refrigerator; (*coll.*) fridge; (*Am.*) icebox.
refrigerante [REFRIGERADOR].
refrigerar, *v.t.* to cool; to refrigerate.
refrigerativo, -va, *a.* refrigerative, cooling.
refrigerio, *n.m.* coolness; refreshment, light repast; comfort, consolation.
refringente, *a.* refracting, refractive.
refringir(se) [E], *v.t.* (*v.r.*) to refract.
refrito, -ta, *p.p. irreg.* [REFREIR]. — *n.m.* (*fig.*) rehash.
refuerzo, *n.m.* reinforcement; strengthening; backing, bracing; welt (*of a shoe*).
refugiar, *v.t.* to shelter. — **refugiarse,** *v.r.* to take refuge *or* shelter.
refugio, *n.m.* refuge; shelter; traffic island; ***refugio antiaéreo,*** air-raid shelter.
refulgencia, *n.f.* refulgence, radiance.
refulgente, *a.* refulgent, gleaming.
refulgir [E], *v.i.* to shine, gleam.
refundición, *n.f.* recasting.
refundir, *v.t.* to recast.
refunfuñador, -ra, *a.* grumbling, grousing. — *n.m.f.* grumbler, grouser.
refunfuñadura, *n.f.* grumbling, grousing.
refunfuñar, *v.i.* to grumble, grouse.
refunfuño, *n.m.* grumble, grouse.
refutación, *n.f.* refutation.
refutable, *a.* refutable.
refutador, -ra, *n.m.f.* refuter.
refutar, *v.t.* to refute.
refutatorio, -ria, *a.* refutatory.
regadera, *n.f.* watering-can; ditch, channel; ***como una regadera,*** as crazy as a coot, mad as a hatter.
regadero, *n.m.* irrigation ditch.
regadío, *n.m.* irrigation; ***de regadío,*** irrigated.
regadizo, -za, *a.* irrigable.
regador, -ra, *n.m.f.* irrigator; comb maker's gauge.
regadura, *n.f.* irrigation.
regaifa, *n.f.* large cake, Easter cake; grooved stone of an oil-mill.
regajal, regajo, *n.m.* pool; brook.
regala, *n.f.* (*naut.*) gunwale, gunnel.
regalada, *n.f.* [REGALADO].
regaladamente, *adv.* in luxury, in ease and comfort.
regalado, -da, *a.* easy, of luxury. — *n.f.* king's stables; king's horses.
regalador, -ra, *n.m.f.* generous person, liberal entertainer; stick for cleaning wine-skins.
regalamiento, *n.m.* regalement.
regalar, *v.t.* to give away, give as a present; to treat, regale, entertain. — **regalarse,** *v.r.* to take good care of o.s.; to live lavishly.
regalero, *n.m.* royal purveyor of fruit and flowers.
regalía, *n.f.* privileges, royal rights; exemption, privilege; (*Cub.*) cigar of superior quality.
regalillo, *n.m.* small present; muff.
regalismo, *n.m.* regalism.
regalista, *a.*, *n.m.* (*hist.*) regalist.
regalito, *n.m.* small present; (*fig.*, *iron.*) gem.
regaliz, *n.m.*, **regaliza,** *n.f.* liquorice.
regalo, *n.m.* present, gift; delight; regalement, ease, luxury.
regalón, -lona, *a.* (*coll.*) luxury-loving; pampered, spoiled.
regamiento, *n.m.* irrigation.
reganar, *v.t.* to regain.
regante, *n.m.* irrigator, holder of irrigation rights.
regañadientes, (**a**), *adv.* reluctantly, grumblingly.
regañado, -da, *a.* split open (*of plums and bread*). — *n.f.* cake.
regañador, -ra, *a.* scolding; grumbling.
regañamiento, *n.m.* scolding; grumbling.
regañar, *v.t.* to scold. — *v.i.* to growl; to grumble; to quarrel; to crack, split open.
regañina, *n.f.* scolding, ticking off.
regañir [K], *v.i.* to yelp, howl.
regaño, *n.m.* scolding; snarling; (*fig.*) scorched bread.
regañón, -ñona, *a.* (given to) scolding; (given to) grousing, grumbling, snarling.
regar [I], *v.t.* to water, irrigate; to splash, wash; to sprinkle, strew.
regata, *n.f.* small channel for irrigation; (*naut.*) regatta.
regate, *n.m.* ducking; dodging, dodge.
regatear, *v.t.* to haggle over; to give grudgingly, give in dribs and drabs; to dodge; ***no regatea esfuerzos,*** he spares no effort; ***no le regateo inteligencia,*** I don't deny that he has intelligence. — *v.i.* to haggle, bargain; to dribble (*in football*); to dodge; to race (*in a regatta*).
regateo, *n.m.* haggling, bargaining.
regatería, *n.f.* retail.
regatero, -ra [REGATÓN].
regato, *n.m.* rivulet, brook.
regatón, -tona, *a.* haggling; retailing. — *n.m.f.* haggler; retailer.
regatonear, *v.i.* to huckster, sell (at) retail.
regatonería, *n.f.* huckster's shop; retail.
regazar [C], *v.t.* to tuck up.
regazo, *n.m.* lap.
regencia, *n.f.* regency; regentship.
regeneración, *n.f.* regeneration.
regenerador, -ra, *a.* regenerating. — *n.m.f.* regenerator.
regenerar, *v.t.* to regenerate.
regenerativo, -va, *a.* regenerative.
regenta, *n.f.* regent's wife; magistrate's wife; bossy woman.
regentar, *v.t.* to run, manage, boss; to hold.
regente, *a.* ruling. — *n.m.* regent; director, manager; president (*of a court of justice*), magistrate; (*print.*) foreman.
regentear, *v.t.*, *v.i.* to boss (over); to throw one's weight about.
regicida, *a.*, *n.m.f.* regicide.
regicidio, *n.m.* regicide.
regidor, *n.m.* alderman; governor.
regidora, *n.m.f.* alderman's wife; governor's wife.
regidoría, regiduría, *n.f.* office of alderman *or* councillor.
régimen, *n.m.* (*pl.* **regímenes**) system, government; pattern; regime; (*med.*) regimen, diet; rate.
regimentar [I], *v.t.* to regiment.
regimiento, *n.m.* administration, government; council-board; (*mil.*) regiment; (*naut.*) pilot's sailing book.
regio, -gia, *a.* royal, regal, kingly; (*coll.*) magnificent.

región, *n.f.* region; area.
regional, *a.* regional, of a region *or* district.
regionalismo, *n.m.* regionalism.
regionalista, *a.* regionalistic, regional. — *n.m.f.* regionalist.
regir [8E], *v.t.* to rule, govern; to manage, run. — *v.i.* to obtain; to be applicable; (*naut.*) to steer, obey the helm.
registrador, *n.m.* registrar, recorder; searcher; controller; toll-gatherer.
registrar, *v.t.* to search, examine; to register, record; to mark; (*min.*) to prospect.
registro, *n.m.* search, examination; register, record; registry, registrar's office; manhole; certificate of entry; census; regulator (*of a clock* or *watch*); (*print.*) correspondence of pages; marker (*of a book*); stop (*of an organ*); ***no sé por qué registro me va a salir,*** I don't know what line he's going to take.
regitivo, -va, *a.* ruling, governing.
regla, *n.f.* rule; ruler; measure; (*physiol.*) menstruation, period; ***en regla,*** in order, in due form; ***salirse de regla,*** to go too far; ***poner en regla,*** to put in order.
regladamente, *adv.* in an orderly way.
reglamentación, *n.f.* rules and regulations.
reglamentar, *v.t.* to lay down rules *or* provisions for.
reglamentario, -ria, *a.* obligatory.
reglamento, *n.m.* rules and regulations.
reglar, *a.* regular. — *v.t.* to rule; to regulate; to adjust.
reglero, *n.m.* ruler.
regleta, *n.f.* (*print.*) reglet; lead.
regletear, *v.t.* (*print.*) to lead.
reglón, *n.m.* mason's level.
regnícola, *a., n.m.f.* native. — *n.m.f.* writer on local subjects.
regocijado, -da, *a.* joyful, merry, rejoicing; cheering.
regocijador, -ra, *a.* rejoicing. — *n.m.f.* merry-maker.
regocijar, *v.t.* to gladden, cheer, delight. — **regocijarse,** *v.r.* to rejoice.
regocijo, *n.m.* joy, delight; mirth, merriment; rejoicing.
regodearse, *v.r.* (*coll.*) to delight, take delight (in); to gloat (over), revel (in).
regodeo, *n.m.* gross pleasure; gloating delight, pleasure *or* enjoyment.
regojo, *n.m.* crumb; puny boy.
regoldano, -na, *a.* wild (*chestnut*).
regoldar [10], *v.i.* to belch.
regoldo, *n.m.* wild chestnut tree.
regolfar(se), *v.i.* (*v.r.*) to flow back.
regolfo, *n.m.* flowing back; turning, deflection; eddy; inlet.
regona, *n.f.* irrigation canal.
regordete, -ta, *a.* (*coll.*) chubby, plump.
regostarse, *v.r.* to delight.
regraciar, *v.t.* to thank, show gratitude to.
regresar, *v.i.* to return.
regresión, *n.f.* regression.
regresivo, -va, *a.* regressive.
regreso, *n.m.* return; ***de regreso,*** back, back again.
regruñir [K], *v.i.* to growl, snarl fiercely.
reguardarse, *v.r.* to take good care of o.s.
regüeldo, *n.m.* belch.
reguera, *n.f.* irrigating canal.
reguero, *n.m.* trickle; stream; trail.
regulación, *n.f.* regulation; adjustment, control.
regulador, -ra, *a.* regulating; governing. — *n.m.* regulator; governor; throttle; ***regulador de fuerza centifruga,*** ball governor.
regular (1), *a.* regular; usual; average, fair, middling, so-so; poorish, weakish, not too good.
regular (2), *v.t.* to regulate, adjust, control.
regularidad, *n.f.* regularity; ***con regularidad,*** regularly, steadily.
regularizar [C], *v.t.* to regularize, systematize.
régulo, *n.m.* petty ruler; basilisk; (*orn.*) kinglet, golden-crested wren.
regurgitación, *n.f.* regurgitation.
regurgitar, *v.i.* to regurgitate.
regusto, *n.m.* after-taste; certain flavour.
rehabilitación, *n.f.* rehabilitation.
rehabilitar, *v.t.* to rehabilitate.
rehacer [20], *v.t.* to re-do, remake, recast, reshape, remodel; to repair. — **rehacerse,** *v.r.* to recover rally, pull o.s. together.
rehacimiento, *n.m.* redoing, remaking, recasting, reshaping, remodelling; repairing.
rehala, *n.f.* drove of sheep.
rehalero, *n.m.* (head) shepherd.
rehartar, *v.t.* to surfeit.
reharto, -ta, *a.* surfeited.
rehecho, -cha, *a.* stocky, thickset.
rehelear, *v.i.* to grieve, to become sad.
rehén, *n.m.* hostage.
rehenchidura, *n.f.* stuffing, refilling.
rehenchimiento, *n.m.* stuffing again, refilling.
rehenchir, *v.t.* to fill *or* stuff again.
rehendija [RENDIJA].
reherir [6], *v.t.* to repel, repulse, drive back.
reherrar [1], *v.t.* to reshoe (*a horse*).
rehervir [6], *v.t.* to boil again. — *v.i.* (*fig.*) to be blinded by passion; to be inflamed with love. — **rehervirse,** *v.r.* to ferment, become sour.
rehiladillo, *n.m.* ribbon.
rehilandera, *n.f.* pinwheel.
rehilar, *v.t.* to twist too hard. — *v.i.* to stagger, reel; to whiz, whir.
rehilete, rehilero, *n.m.* shuttlecock; dart; barbed dart, banderilla; (*fig.*) dig, cutting hint *or* remark.
rehilo, *n.m.* shivering, shaking.
rehogar [B], *v.t.* to give (*sth.*) a turn in the frying pan.
rehollar [4], *v.t.* to trample under foot, tread upon.
rehoya, *n.f.*, **rehoyo,** *n.m.* deep hole *or* pit.
rehoyar, *v.t.* to dig holes again in.
rehuída, *n.f.* shunning, shirking *or* shrinking (*from sth.*); backtracking (*of game*).
rehuir [O], *v.t.* to shun, shirk, shrink from; to backtrack.
rehumedecer(se) [9], *v.t.* (*v.r.*) to dampen well.
rehundir, *v.t.* to sink deeper; to deepen; to remelt recast; to squander.
rehurtarse, *v.r.* to feint (*animals*).
rehurto, *n.m.* feint, dodge; shrug.
rehusar, *v.t.* to refuse, decline, turn down.
reidero, -ra, *a.* inclined to laugh; laughable.
reidor, -ra, *a.* jolly, full of laughter. — *n.m.f.* laughter.
reimportar, *v.t.* to reimport.
reimpresión, *n.f.* reprint; reprinting.
reimpreso, -sa, *p.p.* [REIMPRIMIR].
reimprimir [*p.p.* **reimpreso**], *v.t.* to reprint.
reina, *n.f.* queen; ***reina de los prados,*** meadow-sweet; ***reina luisa,*** lemon verbena; ***reina mora*** hop-scotch.
reinado, *n.m.* reign.
reinal, *n.m.* strong hemp cord.
reinante, *a.* reigning; prevailing.
reinar, *v.i.* to reign; to prevail.
reincidencia, *n.f.* repetition; backsliding, relapsing; (*law*) recidivism.
reincidente, *a.* backsliding, relapsing; (*law* recividist.
reincidir, *v.i.* to backslide, relapse.
reincorporación, *n.f.* reincorporation; rejoining.

reincorporar, *v.t.* to reincorporate, reembody. — **reincorporarse,** *v.r.* to rejoin, be reunited (to).
reingresar, *v.i.* to re-enter.
reino, *n.m.* kingdom, realm.
reinstalación, *n.f.* reinstallation; reinstatement.
reinstalar, *v.t.* to reinstall; to reinstate; to resettle.
reintegrable, *a.* (*com.*) reimbursable, payable.
reintegración, *n.f.* reintegration; repayment.
reintegrar, *v.t.* to reintegrate; to return, repay; to pay stamp duty on. — **reintegrarse,** *v.r.* to get back, recover; to go back, return.
reintegro, *n.m.* reintegration; repayment; stamp duty; refund prize.
reír(se) [28] *v.i.* (*v.r.*) to laugh; ***reírse a carcajadas,*** to guffaw; ***reírse tontamente,*** to giggle, titter, snigger; ***reírle a alguien las gracias,*** to laugh at s.o.'s jokes *or* amusing tricks; ***reírse de,*** to laugh at, make fun of; ***reírse el último,*** to have the last laugh; ***reírse (un vestido),*** to begin to tear *or* go at the seams (*of a dress etc.*).
reiteración, *n.f.* reiteration.
reiteradamente, *adv.* repeatedly.
reiterar, *v.t.* to reiterate.
reiterativo, -va, *a.* reiterative.
reivindicable, *a.* (*law*) recoverable.
reivindicación, *n.f.* (*polit. and industry*) claim, demand for return.
reivindicar [A], *v.t.* to claim, claim back; to assert one's claim to, make a bid to recover *or* for the recovery of; to rehabilitate.
reivindicatorio, -ria, *a.* (of) claim.
reja, *n.f.* ploughshare, coulter; ploughing, tillage; grating, grille.
rejacar [A], *v.t.* to plough across (*for clearing weeds*).
rejada, *n.f.* paddle (*of a plough*).
rejado, *n.m.* grating, grille.
rejal, *n.m.* pile of bricks laid in a cross.
rejalgar, *n.m.* (*min.*) realgar.
rejazo, *n.m.* stroke with a ploughshare.
rejería, *n.f.* iron-grating.
rejero, *n.m.* iron-grating maker.
rejilla, *n.f.* lattice, latticework; lattice-window; grating, grille; grid; canework; luggage net *or* rack; foot stove.
rejo, *n.m.* iron spike; iron rim; goad-stick; (insect's) sting; hob (*for quoits*); strength, vigour; (*bot.*) caulicle.
rejón, *n.m.* dagger; lance, spear; spike.
rejonazo, *n.m.* dagger-thrust *or* dagger-wound.
rejoneador, *n.m.* mounted bullfighter.
rejonear, *v.i.* to fight bulls from horse-back.
rejoneo, *n.m.* mounted bullfighting.
rejuvenecer [9], *v.t.* to rejuvenate, make (look) younger. — **rejuvenecer(se),** *v.i.* (*v.r.*) to be rejuvenated, become younger (-looking).
relabrar, *v.t.* to re-cut (*precious stones*).
relación, *n.f.* relation; report, account; story, tale; connection, relationship; list, enumeration, statement; ratio; reference; speech, long passage; (*pl.* **relaciones**) engagement, betrothal.
relacionar, *v.t.* to relate, connect; to give an account of. — **relacionarse,** *v.r.* to make connections, mix, get known, get in the swim.
relacionero, *n.m.* ballad-singer, teller of tales.
relajación, *n.f.* relaxation; slackening, loosening; laxity; permissiveness; lowering of *or* fall in standards; (*eccles.*) relaxing to the secular arm; (*law*) release (*from an oath*); hernia, rupture.
relajadamente, *adv.* slackly, laxly.
relajador, -ra, *a.* slackening, loosening.
relajamiento, *n.m.* looseness, laxity, excessive permissiveness; slackening.
relajante, *a.* loosening.
relajar, *v.t.* to slacken, loosen; to release (*from an oath*); to relax to the secular arm; to corrupt; to distend, rupture; ***hablar relajado,*** to speak in a careless way (*pronunciation*).
relajo, *n.m.* degeneracy, depravity, shocking behaviour, loss of all decency.
relamer, *v.t.* to lick repeatedly. — **relamerse,** *v.r.* to lick *or* smack one's lips *or* chops; ***relamerse de gusto,*** to lick *or* smack one's lips with relish.
relamido, -da, *a.* over-fastidious in dress; over-nice, affected.
relámpago, *n.m.* lightning-flash; (*vet.*) blemish in the eyes of horses.
relampagueante, *a.* flashing with lightning; flashing.
relampaguear, *v.i.* to flash with lightning; to flash.
relampagueo, *n.m.* lightning; flashing.
relance, *n.m.* repeated casting of a net; chance, fortuitous event; repeated attempt; series of chances.
relancina, *n.f.* (*Ec.*) chance; chance event.
relanzar [C], *v.t.* to repulse, repel; to hurl *or* cast again.
relapso, -sa, *a.* backsliding. — *n.m.f.* backslider.
relatador, -ra, *n.m.f.* relater, narrator.
relatante, *a.* reporting; narrating.
relatar, *v.t.* to relate, narrate; to report, give an account of.
relativamente, *adv.* relatively, comparatively.
relatividad, *n.f.* relativity.
relativismo, *n.m.* relativism.
relativista, *a.*, *n.m.f.* relativist.
relativo, -va, *a.* relative, comparative.
relato, *n.m.* report, account; narrative, tale.
relator, *n.m.* relater, teller, narrator; court-reporter.
relatoría, *n.f.* court-reporter's office.
relavar, *v.t.* to re-wash.
relave, *n.m.* second washing (*of ore*).
relax, *n.m.* (*neol.*) time off, relaxation.
relazar, *v.t.* to tie repeatedly.
relé, *n.m.* (*elec.*) relay.
releer [N], *v.t.* to re-read.
relegación, *n.f.* relegation; exile, banishment.
relegar [B], *v.t.* to relegate; to banish, exile ***relegar al olvido,*** to consign to oblivion.
relej, releje, *n.m.* wheel-rut, track; (*artill.*) narrow chamber; (*arch.*) tapering (*of a wall*); burr (*in a cutting tool*).
relejar, *v.i.* (*arch.*) to taper, slope.
relente, *n.m.* (night) damp atmosphere; (*coll.* cheek, boldness.
relentecer(se) [9], *v.i.* (*v.r.*) to soften *or* be softened.
relevación, *n.f.* relief, release; removal (*from office*); remission, pardon; raising, lifting up.
relevante, *a.* outstanding.
relevar, *v.t.* to emboss, make stand out; to relieve; to free, release; to remove; to absolve; to exalt. — *v.i.* (*art*) to stand out in relief.
relevo, *n.m.* relief; relay; change, changing.
relicario, *n.m.* reliquary; locket.
relieve, *n.m.* relief, relievo, raised work, embossment; (*pl.*) leavings; ***bajo relieve,*** bas-relief; ***medio relieve,*** demi-relief; ***poner de relieve,*** to bring into relief, high-light, stress.
religar [B], *v.t.* to bind again *or* more tightly (*metal.*) to realloy.
religión, *n.f.* religion; ***entrar en religión,*** to enter the religious life.
religionario, -ria, religionista, *n.m.f.* religionist; Protestant.
religiosidad, *n.f.* religiousness, religiosity; ***con religiosidad,*** religiously, without fail.
religioso, -sa, *a.* religious; godly; scrupulous.
relimar, *v.t.* (*mech.*) to re-file.
relimpiar, *v.t.* to clean again; to shine (*sth.*) up.
relimpio, -pia, *a.* (*coll.*) shining (*with cleanness*).

relinchador, -ra, *a.* neighing, whinnying.
relinchante, *a.* neighing, whinnying.
relinchar, *v.i.* to neigh, whinny.
relincho, relinchido, *n.m.* neigh, neighing; whinny, whinnying.
relindo, -da, *a.* delightful.
relinga, *n.f.* (*naut.*) bolt-rope.
relingar [B], *v.t.* (*naut.*) to sew bolt-ropes on. — *v.i.* (*naut.*) to rustle.
reliquia, *n.f.* relic; (*fig.*) left-over, survival.
reliquiario, *n.m.* reliquary; locket.
reliz, *n.m.* (*Mex.*) landslide.
reloco, -ca, *a.* (*coll.*) raving mad, bonkers.
reloj, *n.m.* clock, watch, timepiece; ***reloj de arena,*** hour-glass; ***reloj de agua,*** water clock; ***reloj de sol,*** sun-dial; ***reloj de repetición,*** repeater; ***reloj de bolsillo,*** pocket watch; ***reloj de pulsera,*** wristwatch; ***reloj despertador,*** alarm clock; (*coll.*) ***como un reloj,*** like clock-work; ***contra reloj,*** against the clock, against time.
relojera, *n.f.* clock-case; watch-case; watch-stand; watch pocket.
relojería, *n.f.* clock-making; watchmaker's shop; ***bomba de relojería,*** time-bomb.
relojero, *n.m.* watchmaker, clockmaker.
reluciente, *a.* shining, glittering, glistening, gleaming; sleek.
relucir [9], *v.i.* to shine, glitter, glisten, gleam.
reluchar, *v.i.* to struggle, strive.
relumbrante, *a.* resplendent.
relumbrar, *v.i.* to shine brightly.
relumbre, *n.m.* lustre.
relumbrón, *n.m.* flash, glare; ***de relumbrón,*** flashy, tinselly, showy.
rellanar, *v.t.* to relevel. — **rellanarse,** *v.r.* [ARRELLANARSE].
rellano, *n.m.* landing (*of a staircase*).
rellenar, *v.t.* to refill, replenish; to stuff; to fill in, fill up.
relleno, -na, *a.* stuffed; padded. — *n.m.* (*cook.*) stuffing, forcemeat; filling, repletion; padding; (*mech.*) packing, gasket.
remachado, *n.m.* clinching, riveting, rivet-work; ***remachado alternado,*** staggered riveting; ***remachado de cadena,*** chain riveting.
remachar, *v.t.* to rivet, clinch; (*fig.*) to drive home, hammer in.
remache, *n.m.* clinching, riveting; rivet.
remachón, *a.* tedious, insistent. — *n.m.* buttress; (*fig.*) one who keeps on and on.
remador, *n.m.* rower.
remadura, *n.f.* rowing.
remallar, *v.t.* to mend.
remamiento, *n.m.* rowing.
remandar, *v.t.* to order several times.
remanecer [9], *v.i.* to appear, reappear unexpectedly *or* suddenly.
remaneciente, *a.* reappearing.
remanente, *a.* residual (*magnetism*). — *n.m.* remainder, remnant, residue.
remangadura, *n.f.* (*prov.*) tucking up.
remangar [B], *v.t.* to tuck up (*the sleeves etc.*). — **remangarse,** *v.r.* to roll one's sleeves up, get ready.
remango, *n.m.* tucking up.
remansarse, *v.r.* to become still *or* calm; to tarry.
remanso, *n.m.* backwater, dead water, still water; slowness; ***remanso de paz,*** haven of peace.
remante, *n.m.* rower.
remar, *v.i.* to row, paddle; to toil, labour.
remarcar [A], *v.t.* to mark again; to stress.
rematadamente, *adv.* totally, entirely, utterly.
rematado, -da, *a.* absolutely hopeless, utter; ***loco rematado,*** raving madman. — *n.f.* (*vulg.*) strumpet.
rematamiento, *n.m.* winding up, finishing off.
rematante, *n.m.* highest bidder.
rematar, *v.t.* to finish off, wind up; to clinch; to knock down (*at auction*). — *v.i.* to end up (***en,*** in).
remate, *n.m.* end, finish; edge, hem, border; (*com.*) auction, public sale; highest bid; (*print.*) vignette; abutment; (*arch.*) pinnacle; ***remate de cuentas,*** closing of accounts; ***de remate,*** utterly; ***loco de remate,*** stark staring mad; ***por remate,*** finally.
remecedor, *n.m.* olive-beater.
remecer [D], *v.t.* to rock, swing, move to and fro.
remedable, *a.* imitable.
remedador, -ra, *n.m.f.* imitator, mimic.
remedamiento, *n.m.* copy, imitation.
remedar, *v.t.* to copy, imitate, mimic; (*coll.*) to take off.
remediable, *a.* remediable.
remediador, -ra, *a.* remedial.
remediar, *v.t.* to remedy; to cure; to put to rights, set right; to help; to avoid; ***no se puede remediar,*** there's no help for it, it's hopeless; ***sin poderlo remediar,*** unable to avoid *or* help it; ***lo que no se puede remediar, se ha de aguantar,*** what can't be cured must be endured; ***urge remediarlo,*** it is a matter of urgency to put it right.
remedición, *n.f.* re-measuring.
remedio, *n.m.* remedy; cure; help; ***remedio casero,*** makeshift, Heath Robinson arrangement; ***como último remedio,*** as a last resort; ***no hay ni para un remedio,*** there's not one to be found; (*coll.*) not a sausage, not a hope; ***no hay más remedio,*** there's no help for it; ***no tener remedio,*** to be hopeless; ***sin remedio,*** inevitably; past redemption.
remedión, *n.m.* (*theat.*) makeshift performance.
remedir [8], *v.t.* to re-measure.
remedo, *n.m.* imitation, copy.
remellado, -da, *a.* dented, jagged.
remellar, *v.t.* to unhair (*hides*).
remellón, -llona, *a.* dented, jagged.
remembración, *n.f.* remembrance.
remembrar, *v.t.* to remember.
rememorar, *v.t.* to recall, remember.
rememorativo, -va, *a.* that reminds, recalls, brings to memory.
remendado, -da, *a.* spotted, patchy.
remendar [I], *v.t.* to patch, patch up, mend, repair, darn.
remendón, -dona, *a.* patching, mending; botching. — *n.m.* cobbler.
remeneo, *n.m.* rapid movement.
rementir [6], *v.i.* to lie like a trooper.
remera, *n.f.* flight feather (*of birds*).
remero, *n.m.* rower, oarsman.
remesa, *n.f.* (*com.*) sending; remittance; shipment; delivery.
remesar, *v.t.* to pull out (*hair*); to send, remit, ship.
remesón, *n.m.* plucking out of hair; hair pulled out; stopping a horse in full gallop; (*fenc.*) closing in, *corps-à-corps.*
remeter, *v.t.* to put back; to take in; to tuck in. — *v.i.* to keep on, make a nuisance of o.s.
remezón, *n.m.* (*Hisp. Am.*) slight earthquake.
remiche, *n.m.* space between benches (*in galleys*).
remiel, *n.m.* second extract of soft sugar (*from the cane*).
remiendo (I), *n.m.* patch; repair; mending-piece, darning; amendment; (*print.*) job-work; ***a remiendos,*** piecemeal, patchwork.
remiendo (2), **remiende,** *pres. indic.; pres. subj.* [REMENDAR].
remilgado, -da, *a.* mincing, prim and finicky, over-fastidious *or* fussy; squeamish.

remilgarse [B], *v.r.* to behave in a finnicky, fussy *or* mincing manner.
remilgo, *n.m.* finnickiness, fussiness, mincing attitude; ***no hacer remilgos*** (***a*** or ***ante***), not to turn one's nose up (at).
reminiscencia, *n.f.* reminiscence, recollection.
remirado, -da, *a.* thoughtful, considerate; wary.
remirar, *v.t.* to go over, check. — **remirarse,** *v.r.* to take great pains.
remisible, *a.* remissible.
remisión, *n.f.* remission; sending, remitting; abatement.
remisivo, -va, *a.* remitting; remissory, remissive.
remiso, -sa, *a.* remiss; reluctant.
remisoria (1), *n.f.* (*law*) reference of a case to another tribunal.
remisorio, -ria (2), *a.* remissory.
remitir, *v.t.* to remit; to send, forward; to refer. — *v.i.* to abate.
remo, *n.m.* oar; paddle; rowing; ***a*** or ***al remo,*** rowing; ***condenado al remo,*** condemned to the galleys; (*pl.*) limbs; wings.
remoción, *n.f.* removal, removing.
remojadero, *n.m.* steeping-tub.
remojar, *v.t.* to steep, soak; to drench.
remojo, *n.m.* steeping, soaking.
remolacha, *n.f.* beetroot, (*Am.*) beets; sugar beet.
remolar, *n.m.* master-carpenter; oar-maker; oar-shop.
remolcador, *n.m.* (*naut.*) tug.
remolcar [A], *v.t.* (*naut.*) to tow, take in tow; to haul.
remoler [5], *v.t.* to grind again *or* fine.
remolida, *n.f.* regrinding (*of sugar cane*).
remolimiento, *n.m.* regrinding.
remolinante, *a.* whirling.
remolinar, *v.i.* to whirl, whirl round, spin, spin round. — **remolinarse,** *v.r.* to whirl round, swirl, seethe.
remolinear, *v.t.* to whirl about. — *v.i.* to spin, eddy, whirl.
remolino, *n.m.* whirl, eddy; whirlpool; cowlick, twisted tuft of hair; disturbance; swirling mass (*of people*).
remolón (1), **-lona,** *a.* shirking, work-shy. — *n.m.f.* shirker, slacker; ***hacerse el remolón,*** to shirk; to put things off; to be slow and unwilling; to drag one's feet.
remolón (2), *n.m.* upper tusk of boar; horse's sharp tooth.
remolonear(se), *v.i.* (*v.r.*) to be slow *or* reluctant to move, dodge the column, shirk, hang back; to drag one's feet.
remolque, *n.m.* tow; towing; towage; tow-line, tow-rope; caravan, (*Am.*) trailer; ***llevar a remolque,*** to have *or* take in tow.
remondar, *v.t.* to clean *or* prune again *or* fully.
remono, -na, *a.* (*coll.*) delightful.
remonta, *n.f.* remount; remount cavalry; (*shoe.*) repairing, resoling; revamping; restuffing (*of saddle*).
remontamiento, *n.m.* remounting cavalry.
remontar, *v.t.* to frighten away; to remount; to repair; to restuff; to resole, revamp; to raise; to go up. — *v.i.* to go back (*in time*). — **remontarse,** *v.r.* to go back (*in time*); to rise, soar; to take to the forest.
remonte, *n.m.* remounting; repairing; soaring.
remontista, *n.m.* commissioner for the purchase of cavalry horses.
remoque, *n.m.* (*coll.*) sarcastic word.
remoquete, *n.m.* punch; nickname; quip, gibe; sky-larking.
rémora, *n.f.* (*ichth.*) sucking fish, remora; hindrance, burden, dead weight.
remordedor, -ra, *a.* causing remorse.
remorder [5], *v.t.* to bite repeatedly; to sting, cause remorse to. — **remorderse,** *v.r.* to show remorse, regret.
remordimiento, *n.m.* remorse.
remosquearse, *v.r.* (*print.*) to be smeared *or* blurred; to show suspicion.
remostar, *v.t.* to put must into (*old wine*). — **remostarse,** *v.r.* to grow sweet and must-like (*of wine*).
remostecerse [9], *v.r.* [REMOSTARSE].
remosto, *n.m.* putting of must into old wine.
remoto, -ta, *a.* remote; ***idea remota,*** vague *or* faint idea.
remover [5], *v.t.* to stir, stir up, stir round; to turn, turn up.
removimiento, *n.m.* stirring (up).
remozadura, *n.f.*, **remozamiento,** *n.m.* giving a new look to.
remozar [C], *v.t.* to renovate, renew; to give a face-lift *or* new look to. — **remozarse,** *v.r.* to be rejuvenated, get a younger *or* new look, get a face-lift.
rempujar, *v.t.* to push, jostle.
rempujo, *n.m.* push, thrust; (*naut.*) sailmaker's palm.
rempujón, *n.m.* push, thrust.
remuda, *n.f.* change; change of clothes.
remudamiento, *n.m.* change; change of clothing.
remudar, *v.t.* to change; to change again.
remugar, *v.t.* (*prov.*) to ruminate.
remullir, *v.t.* to soften *or* fluff up thoroughly.
remunerable, *a.* remunerable.
remuneración, *n.f.* remuneration.
remunerador, -ra, *a.* remunerating, remunerative. — *n.m.f.* remunerator.
remunerar, *v.t.* to remunerate.
remunerativo, -va, *a.* remunerative.
remuneratorio, -ria, *a.* remuneratory.
remusgar [B], *v.t.* to get wind of, scent, sense.
remusgo, *n.m.* guess, suspicion, sensing; sharp breeze.
remusguillo, *n.m.* vague suspicion *or* sense.
renacentista, *a.* (relating to the) Renaissance. — *n.m.f.* scholar of the Renaissance.
renacer [9], *v.i.* to be reborn *or* born again; (*fig.*) to spring up again.
renaciente, *a.* renascent, springing up anew.
Renacimiento, *n.m.* Renaissance.
renacimiento, *n.m.* rebirth; renewal; renascence.
renacuajo, *n.m.* tadpole; (*fig.*) shrimp, runt.
renadío, *n.m.* second crop.
renal, *a.* (*anat.*) renal.
rencilla, *n.f.* squabble; bickering; rancour.
rencilloso, -sa, *a.* quarrelsome; touchy.
rencionar, *v.t.* to set at odds.
renco, -ca, *a.* lame, halting.
rencor, *n.m.* rancour, grudge.
rencoroso, -sa, *a.* rancorous, spiteful, bearing a grudge.
renda, *n.f.* second dressing of vines.
rendaje, *n.m.* set of reins and bridles.
rendajo, *n.m.* (*orn.*) mocking-bird; (*coll.*) mimic.
rendar, *v.t.* to plough *or* dig a second time.
rendición, *n.f.* surrender; submission; rendering.
rendido, -da, *a.* whole-hearted, devoted.
rendija, *n.f.* split, slit, chink, cleft, crack.
rendimiento, *n.m.* yield; whole-hearted allegiance; (*coll.*) exhaustion, being fagged out.
rendir [8], *v.t.* to bring to submission; to yield; to give up, give back; (*naut.*) to spring (*a mast or yard*); ***rendir la guardia,*** to hand over the guard; ***rendir gracias,*** to give thanks; ***rendir honores,*** to do the honours; to do honour (to); ***rendir obsequios,*** to fête; ***rendir el alma,*** to give up the ghost. — **rendirse,** *v.r.* to surrender; to give up: (*coll.*) to get exhausted *or* worn out.

renegado, *a., n.m.f.* renegade, apostate. — *n.m.* ombre.
renegador, -ra, *a.* swearing, blasphemous. — *n.m.f.* swearer, blasphemer.
renegar [IB], *v.t.* to deny vigorously; to detest. — *v.i.* to apostatize; to swear, blaspheme; ***renegar de,*** to renounce; to disown; to abhor.
renegón, -gona, *n.m.f.* inveterate swearer.
renegrear, *v.i.* to look pitch black.
renegrido, -da, *a.* deeply livid (*said of bruises*); deeply begrimed.
rengífero, *n.m.* reindeer.
renglón, *n.m.* line; item; ***a renglón seguido,*** immediately after *or* following; ***leer entre renglones,*** to read between the lines; (*pl.* **renglones**) lines.
renglonadura, *n.f.* ruling (*of paper*).
rengo, -ga [RENCO].
renguear (*Arg., Col., Chi., Ec., Per.*) [RENQUEAR].
reniego, *n.m.* execration, blasphemy, curse.
renitencia, *n.f.* resistance.
renitente, *a.* reluctant.
reno, *n.m.* (*zool.*) reindeer.
renombrado, -da, *a.* renowned, celebrated, famous.
renombre, *n.m.* surname; renown, fame.
renovable, *a.* renewable.
renovación, *n.f.* renovation; renewal.
renovador, -ra, *a.* renovating; renewing. — *n.m.f.* renovator.
renovar [4], *v.t.* to renovate; to renew; to restore.
renovero, -ra, *n.m.f.* usurer.
renquear, *v.i.* to limp, hobble, shamble; to move along limpingly *or* haltingly.
renta, *n.f.* rent; income; ***rentas públicas,*** state revenues; (*coll.*) ***ser una renta,*** to be a drain (*on one's resources*).
rentabilidad, *n.f.* profitability.
rentable, *a.* income-yielding, paying, profitable; ***no es rentable,*** it's not a paying proposition.
rentado, -da, *a.* living on an income.
rentar, *v.t.* to yield, produce, bring in. — *v.i.* to pay, be a paying proposition.
rentería, *n.f.* productive land.
rentero, -ra, *a.* tax-paying. — *n.m.f.* tenant farmer.
rentilla, *n.f.* game of cards; game of dice.
rentista, *n.m.f.* financier; bondholder; one living on a private income.
rentístico, -ca, *a.* financial.
rento, *n.m.* annual rent, rental.
rentoso, -sa, *a.* producing income.
rentoy, *n.m.* game of cards.
renuencia, *n.f.* reluctance, unwillingness.
renuente, *a.* reluctant, unwilling.
renuevo, *n.m.* shoot, sprout; renovation, renewal.
renuncia, *n.f.* renunciation, giving up.
renunciable, *a.* that can be renounced.
renunciación, *n.f.* renunciation.
renunciamiento, *n.m.* renouncement.
renunciante, *a.* renouncer, renouncing.
renunciar, *v.t.* to renounce, resign, relinquish, give up; ***renunciar a,*** to give up, abandon (*all hope* or *intention of*). — *v.i.* to resign, leave, give up, give the idea up; to abdicate.
renunciatario, *n.m.* one to whom anything is resigned.
renuncio, *n.m.* revoke (*at cards*); (*coll.*) contradiction; lie.
renvalsar, *v.t.* (*carp.*) to rabbet the edge of (*a door* or *window*).
renvalso, *n.m.* rabbet (*along the edge of a door* or *window*).
reñidero, *n.m.* cockpit.
reñido, -da, *a.* at odds, on bad terms; bitter, hard-fought.
reñidor, -ra, *n.m.f.* quarreller.
reñir [8K], *v.t.* to scold, reprove. — *v.i.* to quarrel, fight, wrangle; ***están reñidos,*** they've had a quarrel, they've fallen out; ***lo uno no está reñido con lo otro,*** one thing is perfectly compatible with the other.
reo, *a.* guilty. — *n.m.f.* accused (*person*), prisoner; (*ichth.*) ray trout.
reojo, *n.m.*, ***mirar de reojo,*** to look askance.
reorganización, *n.f.* reorganization.
reorganizar [C], *v.t.* to reorganize.
reóstato, *n.m.* (*elec.*) rheostat.
repacer, *v.t.* to graze pasture bare.
repagar [B], *v.t.* to pay back and more.
repajo, *n.m.* enclosure for pasture.
repanocha, *n.f.* (*coll.*) end, limit.
repantigarse [B], **repanchigarse** [B], *v.r.* to sprawl.
repapilarse, *v.r.* to stuff o.s.
reparable, *a.* reparable, remediable; noticeable, remarkable.
reparación, *n.f.* reparation, compensation; repair.
reparado, -da, *a.* squint-eyed. — *n.f.* shying (*of a horse*).
reparador, -ra, *a.* repairing; restorative; fault-finding. — *n.m.f.* repairer, mender; fault-finder.
reparamiento, *n.m.* repair.
reparar, *v.t.* to repair, mend; to make reparation for; to notice, remark; to parry. — *v.i.* to stop, make a halt; ***reparar en,*** to notice, pay heed to. — **repararse,** *v.r.* to restrain o.s.; (*Mex.*) to rear (*of horses*).
reparativo, -va, *a.* reparative.
reparo, *n.m.* repair; reparation; misgiving, qualm; objection; parry; spot (*in the eye*); ***poner reparos a,*** to raise objections to, quibble over, find fault with; ***no tengas reparo en decirme lo que piensas,*** do not hesitate to tell me what you think.
reparón, -rona, *a.* carping, fault-finding. — *n.m.f.* carper, fault-finder.
repartible, *a.* distributable.
repartición, *n.f.* distribution, sharing *or* dealing out.
repartidamente, *adv.* in shares.
repartidero, -ra, *a.* for sharing out, to be distributed.
repartidor, -ra, *a.* distributing. — *n.m.f.* distributor, dealer. — *n.m.* delivery man; distributing point (*in an irrigation ditch*).
repartimiento, *n.m.* distribution, division, allotment; assessment (*of taxes etc.*).
repartir, *v.t.* to share out, split up.
reparto, *n.m.* (*theat.*) cast; casting; distribution, share-out.
repasadera, *n.f.* smoothing plane.
repasadora, *n.f.* woman carder (*of wool*).
repasar, *v.t., v.i.* to pass again. — *v.t.* to go over; to go over again; to revise; to mend, darn; to comb (*wool*); to amalgamate (*ore*).
repasata, *n.f.* dressing-down.
repaso, *n.m.* going over; revising; (*coll.*) dressing-down.
repastar, *v.t.* to feed *or* pasture a second time; to re-knead (*flour, clay etc.*).
repasto, *n.m.* increase of feed.
repatriación, *n.f.* repatriation, return home.
repatriar [L], *v.t.* to repatriate, send home. — **repatriar(se),** *v.i.* (*v.r.*) to be repatriated, return home.
repechar, *v.i.* to mount a slope, go uphill.
repecho, *n.m.* sharp rise, steep incline; (*adv.*) ***a repecho,*** uphill.
repelada, *n.f.* salad of herbs.
repeladura, *n.f.* re-stripping.

repelar, *v.t.* to pull out hair of; to nibble, crop; to clip, crop, lop off.
repelente, *a.* repellent; objectionable.
repeler, *v.t.* to repel, repulse.
repelo, *n.m.* twist *or* turn against the grain; cross fibre; scuffle; aversion, repugnance.
repelón, *n.m.* tug *or* yank on hair; bit torn off; kink; dash, spurt; ***a repelones,*** by fits and starts; ***de repelón,*** quickly.
repeloso, -sa, *a.* of bad grain (*wood*); peevish, touchy.
repeluzno, *n.m.* shiver.
repellar, *v.t.* (*build.*) to slap plaster on.
repensar [I], *v.t.* to reconsider, think over.
repente, *n.m.* sudden impulse; ***de repente,*** suddenly.
repentino, -na, *a.* sudden.
repentista, *n.m.* improviser.
repentizar [C], *v.i.* to sight-read (*music*); to improvise; to ad-lib.
repentón, *n.m.* sudden impulse.
repeor, *a., adv.* much worse.
repercudida, *n.f.* rebound.
repercudir, *v.i.* to rebound.
repercusión, *n.f.* repercussion.
repercusivo, -va, *a.* (*med.*) repercussive.
repercutir, *v.t.* (*med.*) to repel. — *v.i.* to rebound; to re-echo; to have repercussions; to boomerang.
repertorio, *n.m.* repertory; repertoire.
repesar, *v.t.* to weigh again; to weigh up carefully.
repeso, *n.m.* re-weighing; weighing office.
repetición, *n.f.* repetition; (*mus.*) repeat; repeater (*clock* or *watch*).
repetidor, -ra, *a.* repeating. — *n.m.f.* repeater.
repetir [8], *v.t.* to repeat, do *or* say again; to echo. — *v.i.* to have a second helping.
repicar [C], *v.t., v.i.* to mince finely; to ring (*bells*); to repique. — **repicarse,** *v.r.* to boast, brag.
repicotear, *v.t.* to scallop.
repinaldo, *n.m.* large apple.
repinarse, *v.r.* to rise, soar.
repintar, *v.t.* to repaint. — **repintarse,** *v.r.* to use too much make-up; (*print.*) to offset, set off.
repique, *n.m.* chopping, hashing, fine mincing; chime, peal; squabble.
repiquete, *n.m.* lively peal *or* ringing (*of bells*); (*naut.*) short tack.
repiquetear, *v.t., v.i.* to chime, ring, peal; to clatter, rattle. — **repiquetearse,** *v.r.* to bicker, quarrel, wrangle.
repiqueteo, *n.m.* lively ringing *or* pealing; rattle; bickering.
repisa, *n.f.* ledge, sill; shelf; ***repisa de la chimenea,*** mantelpiece.
repisar, *v.t.* to tread again; to pack, tamp down hard.
repiso, *n.m.* second press (*wine*).
repitiente, *a.* repeating.
repizcar [A], *v.t.* to pinch.
repizco, *n.m.* pinch, pinching.
replantación, *n.f.* replanting.
replantar, *v.t.* to replant.
replantear, *v.t.* (*arch.*) to lay out the ground-plan of; to bring up, raise again.
replanteo, *n.m.* re-raising, fresh look.
repleción, *n.f.* repletion.
replegar [IB], *v.t.* to redouble, replait, refold. — **replegarse,** *v.r.* (*mil.*) to fall back.
repleto, -ta, *a.* replete.
réplica, *n.f.* repartee; retort, answer back; (*art*) replica.
replicador, -ra, *n.m.f.* disputant, replier.
replicante, *a., n.m.f.* replying; replier, disputant.
replicar [A], *v.i.* to retort, answer back; to argue back; (*law*) to respond.
replicato, *n.m.* (*law*) answer, reply; objection.
replicón, -cona, *a.* (*coll.*) given to answering back.
repliegue, *n.m.* doubling; folding; fold, crease; (*mil.*) withdrawal, retreat.
repoblación, *n.f.* repopulation; ***repoblación forestal,*** reafforestation.
repoblar [4], *v.t.* to repeople, repopulate; to reafforest; to restock.
repodar, *v.t.* to prune back.
repodrir [REPUDRIR].
repollar, *v.i.* to head (*cabbages*).
repollo, *n.m.* head, round head (*of a cabbage*); cabbage.
repolludo, -da, *a.* cabbage-headed, round-headed; (*fig.*) stocky, thickset.
reponer [25], *v.t.* to replace, put back, restore; to answer, reply. — **reponerse,** *v.r.* to recover, get better; ***reponerse de,*** to get over.
reportación, *n.f.* moderation, forbearance.
reportado, -da, *a.* moderate, forbearing.
reportaje, *n.m.* report; reporting; article.
reportamiento, *n.m.* forbearance, restraint.
reportar, *v.t.* to restrain, check; to bring; to yield; to transfer (*lithography*); ***reportar beneficios,*** to have advantages; to yield profit. — **reportarse,** *v.r.* ***¡repórtate!*** behave properly! control yourself!
reporte, *n.m.* report; gossip; lithographic proof.
reporterismo, *n.m.* (newspaper) reporting.
reportero, -ra, *n.m.f.* reporter.
reportista, *n.m.* transferer (*lithography*).
reportorio, *n.m.* almanac, calendar.
reposadero, *n.m.* trough (*for molten metal*).
reposado, -da, *a.* peaceful, quiet, calm.
reposar, *v.t.* to (allow to) settle. — *v.i.* to rest, lie down.
reposición, *n.f.* replacing; recovery; revival.
repositorio, *n.m.* repository.
reposo, *n.m.* rest; repose.
repostada, *n.f.* (*Hisp. Am.*) discourteous answer.
repostar, *v.i.* to take on stores; to stock up; to refuel; to coal.
repostería, *n.f.* larder, pantry; plate-room; confectionery; pastry-shop, cake-shop.
repostero, *n.m.* pastrycook; ornamental cloth with coat of arms.
repregunta, *n.f.* (*law*) second question *or* demand; cross-examination.
repreguntar, *v.t.* (*law*) to question repeatedly, cross-examine.
reprender, reprehender, *v.t.* to reprehend, reprimand, reprove.
reprendiente, *a.* reprimanding.
reprensible, reprehensible, *a.* reprehensible.
reprensión, reprehensión, *n.f.* reprehension, reprimand, reproof.
reprensor, -ra, *n.m.f.* reprehender, reprover.
represa, *n.f.* dam; damming up; check; (*naut.*) recapture.
represalia, *n.f.* reprisal, retaliation.
represar, *v.t.* to dam, dam up; to check; (*naut.*) to recapture.
representable, *a.* representable; performable.
representación, *n.f.* representation; representatives, delegation; power, dignity; performance, production; (*law*) right of succession.
representador, -ra, *n.m.f.* representative; actor, player.
representante, *a.* representing. — *n.m.* representative; performer.
representar, *v.t.* to represent; to state, express; to be, signify; to perform; ***tiene cuarenta años, pero representa menos,*** he is forty (years old), but he looks younger.
representativo, -va, *a.* representative.
represión, *n.f.* repression, check, curbing.

represivo, -va, *a.* repressive.
reprimenda, *n.f.* reprimand, dressing down.
reprimir, *v.t.* to repress, check, curb.
reprobable, *a.* reprehensible, blameworthy.
reprobación, *n.f.* reproof, reprobation.
reprobado, -da, *a.* reprobate; failed in an examination.
reprobador, -ra, *a.* reproving. — *n.m.f.* reprover, condemner.
reprobar [4], *v.t.* to condemn; to reprove; to fail.
reprobatorio, -ria, *a.* reprobative, objurgatory.
réprobo, -ba, *a.*, *n.m.f.* reprobate, damned (*person*).
reprochar, *v.t.* to reproach.
reproche, *n.m.* reproach, upbraiding.
reproducción, *n.f.* reproduction; (*art*) copy, print.
reproducir [16], *v.t.* to reproduce.
reproductible, *a.* reproducible.
reproductividad, *n.f.* reproductiveness.
reproductivo, -va, *a.* reproductive, productive.
reproductor, -ra, *a.* reproducing, reproductive. — *n.m.f.* reproducer; breeding animal.
repromisión, *n.f.* repeated promise.
repropiarse, *v.r.* to shy, balk (*horses*).
repropio, -pia, *a.* skittish (*horses*).
reprueba, *n.f.* (*print.*) new proof.
reps, *n.m.* rep *or* reps (*cloth*).
reptar, *v.i.* to crawl, creep.
reptil, *a.*, *n.m.* reptile, reptilian. — *n.m.pl.* (**reptiles**) Reptilia.
república, *n.f.* republic, commonwealth.
republicanismo, *n.m.* republicanism.
republicano, -na, *a.*, *n.m.f.* republican.
repúblico, *n.m.* prominent citizen, statesman, good patriot.
repudiación, *n.f.* repudiation.
repudiar, *v.t.* to repudiate.
repudio, *n.m.* repudiation.
repudrir, *v.t.* to rot, eat into. — **repudrirse,** *v.r.* to rot away.
repuesto, -ta, *p.p. irreg.* [REPONER]. — *a.* secluded. — *n.m.* store, stock, supply; sideboard, dresser; spare part; pantry; ***de repuesto,*** spare, extra.
repugnancia, *n.f.* repugnance, aversion, loathing.
repugnante, *a.* repugnant, repulsive, loathsome.
repugnar, *v.t.*, *v.i.* to disgust, nauseate; to cause loathing (in), be loathsome (to); to reject, contradict.
repujado, *n.m.* repoussé, embossed work, embossing.
repujar, *v.t.* to do repoussé work on; to emboss.
repulgado, -da, *a.* affected.
repulgar [B], *v.t.* to border, hem, put an edging on.
repulgo, *n.m.* hem, border, fringe; (*coll.*) scruple, qualm.
repulido, -da, *a.* spruce.
repulir, *v.t.* to repolish; to polish up; to doll up.
repulsa, *n.f.* check; rebuff; rejection; rebuke.
repulsar, *v.t.* to check; to rebuff, rebuke; to reject.
repulsión, *n.f.* repulsion, loathing.
repulsivo, -va, *a.* repulsive, disgusting.
repullo, *n.m.* jerk, leap, bound, bounce; start, shock; small dart *or* arrow.
repunta, *n.f.* point, cape, headland; mark of displeasure; (*coll.*) dispute, disagreement.
repuntar, *v.i.* to begin to ebb *or* rise, turn. — **repuntarse,** *v.r.* to begin to turn sour; to fall out.
repunte, *n.m.* turn (*of the tide*).
repurgar [B], *v.t.* to clean *or* purify again *or* thoroughly.
reputación, *n.f.* reputation, repute.
reputar, *v.t.* to repute; to estimate, appraise.
requebrador, *n.m.* suitor, wooer, gallant.
requebrar [1], *v.t.* to woo, flatter, pay amorous compliments to.
requemado, *n.m.* black crêpe.
requemar, *v.t.* to burn up; to scorch; to inflame. — **requemarse,** *v.r.* to be consumed.
requemazón, *n.f.* pungency, bite.
requeridor, *n.m.* summons server; suitor.
requerimiento, *n.m.* request, requisition; summons, intimation; searching, hunting.
requerir [6], *v.t.* to require, demand; to summon; to call upon; to call for; to search for, hunt for, feel for, fumble for, grope for, reach for; to make amorous advances to.
requesón, *n.m.* second curds; cottage cheese.
requeté, *n.m.* Carlist volunteer.
requetebién, *adv.* (*coll.*) first rate, super.
requiebro, *n.m.* compliment, flattery; well-crushed ore.
réquiem, *n.m.* requiem.
requilorios, *n.m.pl.* (*coll.*) useless ceremony; beating about the bush.
requintador, -ra, *n.m.f.* outbidder.
requintar, *v.t.* to outbid by a fifth part; (*mus.*) to raise *or* lower the pitch by five tones; to exceed, surpass.
requinto, *n.m.* second fifth subtracted from a quantity; rise of a fifth in bidding; (*mus.*) treble clarinet; small guitar; treble clarinet player.
requisa, *n.f.* round, tour of inspection; (*mil.* requisition; confiscation.
requisar, *v.t.* (*mil.*) to requisition; to confiscate.
requisición, *n.f.* requisition.
requisito, -ta, *p.p. irreg.* [REQUERIR]. — *n.m.* requisite, requirement.
requisitorio, -ria, *a.* requisitory. — *n.f.* (*law*) requisition.
res, *n.f.* head of cattle; ***res brava,*** fighting bull.
resaber [30], *v.t.* to know only too well.
resabiado, -da, *a.* having ingrained bad habits *or* ways.
resabiar, *v.t.* to lead s.o. into evil ways. — **resabiarse,** *v.r.* to get into bad habits *or* artful ways.
resabido, -da, *a.* know-all.
resabio, *n.m.* bad habit, artful way; unpleasant aftertaste.
resabioso, -sa, *a.* (*Hisp. Am.*) ill-tempered.
resaca, *n.f.* (*naut.*) undertow; (*com.*) redraft; (*coll.*) hangover.
resacar [A], *v.t.* (*naut.*) to underrun, haul; (*com.*) to redraw.
resalado, -da, *a.* (*coll.*) charming; dear, darling; great fun, very amusing.
resalir [31], *v.i.* to jut out, stick out.
resaltar, *v.i.* to bounce, rebound; to jut out, stand out; ***hacer resaltar,*** to emphasize, bring into prominence.
resalte, *n.m.* sticking, standing out; prominence.
resalto, *n.m.* rebound; prominence, projection; (*railw.*) super-elevation of curves.
resaludar, *v.t.* to return a salute *or* greeting.
resalutación, *n.f.* return of a salute.
resalvo, *n.m.* tiller, sapling.
resallar, *v.t.* to weed again.
resanar, *v.t.* to regild defective spots in.
resarcimiento *n.m.* compensation; making amends, making good.
resarcir [D], *v.t.* to compensate, reimburse. — **resarcirse,** *v.r.* — ***de,*** to make up for.
resbaladero, -ra, *a.* slippery. — *n.m.* slippery place; chute, slide.
resbaladizo, -za, *a.* slippery; (*fig.*) treacherous.
resbalador, -ra, *a.* slipping, sliding. — *n.m.f.* slider; back-slider.
resbaladura, *n.f.* slip, slipping, slide, sliding; slippery track.

resbalamiento, *n.m.* slip; (*aer.*) ***resbalamiento de ala,*** side-slip; (*aer.*) ***resbalamiento de cola,*** tail slide.
resbalante, *a.* sliding, slipping.
resbalar, *v.i.*, slide, slip; to slip up. — **resbalarse,** *v.r.* to slip (up).
resbalo. *n.m.* (*Hisp. Am.*) steep incline.
resbalón, *n.m.* slip, slipping; slip (up).
resbaloso, -sa, *a.* slippery.
rescaldar, *v.t.* to scald.
rescaño, *n.m.* leavings, fragments, scraps.
rescatar, *v.t.* to ransom; to redeem; to rescue; to recover; to barter for; to make up for.
rescate, *n.m.* ransom; redemption; rescue; ransom money.
rescaza, *n.f.* (*ichth.*) grouper.
rescindir, *v.t.* to rescind, cancel.
rescisión, *n.f.* recission, cancellation.
rescisorio, -ria, *a.* rescissory, rescinding.
rescoldera, *n.f.* heartburn.
rescoldo, *n.m.* embers, hot ashes; scruple, doubt, qualm; ***avivar el rescoldo,*** to put new life into the thing, stir up the embers.
rescontrar [4], *v.t.* to offset, set off.
rescripto, *n.m.* rescript, mandate.
rescriptorio, -ria, *a.* rescriptive.
resecación, *n.f.* desiccation, drying out *or* up.
resecar [A], *v.t.* to dry out *or* up.
resección, *n.f.* (*surg.*) resection.
reseco, -ca, *a.* dried out *or* up, parched; spare, lean. — *n.m.* dry part.
reseda, *n.m.* reseda, mignonette.
resegar [IB], *v.t.* to mow again.
reseguir [8G], *v.t.* to put an edge to (*swords*).
resellante, *a.* recoining, restamping.
resellar, *v.t.* to reseal; to restamp; to recoin. — **resellarse,** *v.r.* to go over to the other side.
resello, *n.m.* recoinage; surcharge.
resembrar [I], *v.t.* to resow.
resentido, -da, *a.* resentful, bitter; surly.
resentimiento, *n.m.* resentment, bitterness.
resentirse [6], *v.r.* to begin to give way, show signs of giving way, show the ill effects (***de,*** of); to take offence, be hurt.
reseña, *n.f.* review; outline, description.
reseñar, *v.t.* to review; to sketch, outline, give a brief description of.
resequido, -da, *a.* dried up.
reserva, *n.f.* reserve; secretiveness; reservation; ***reserva mental,*** mental reservation; ***de reserva,*** extra, spare; ***bajo la mayor reserva,*** in strictest confidence.
reservación, *n.f.* reservation.
reservadamente, *adv.* secretly, reservedly.
reservado, -da, *a.* reserved; secret. — *n.m.* reserved compartment *or* cubicle.
reservar, *v.t.* to reserve; to exempt; to keep back; to keep secret. — **reservarse,** *v.r.* to husband one's strength; to bide one's time; to keep some spare room.
reservativo, -va, *a.* reserved.
reservatorio, *n.m.* reservoir; greenhouse, hothouse, conservatory.
reservista, *n.m.* (*mil.*) reservist.
reservón, -vona, *a.* very reserved, secretive *or* close.
resfriado, *n.m.* cold, chill.
resfriador, -ra, *a.* chilling.
resfriadura, *n.f.* cold.
resfriamiento, *n.m.* chilling; cold.
resfriante, *a.* chilling.
resfriar [L], *v.t.* to chill. — *v.i.* to turn chilly. — **resfriarse,** *v.r.* to catch cold.
resfrío, *n.m.* cold, chill.
resguardar, *v.t.* to defend, protect, shield. — **resguardarse,** *v.r.* to take shelter; to proceed with caution.
resguardo, *n.m.* guard, preservation, to safety; defence, shelter, protection; (*com.*) voucher, receipt; excise men; (*naut.*) sea room, wide berth.
resí, *adv.* yes , yes.
residencia, *n.f.* residence, domicile; residing, stay, sojourn; (*law*) impeachment.
residenciado, -da, *a.* resident, residentiary.
residencial, *a.* residential, residentiary.
residenciar, *v.t.* to call (*a public officer*) to account; to impeach.
residente, *a.* resident, residing, residentiary. — *n.m.* resident, minister at a foreign court.
residir, *v.i.* to reside; to be in residence; to lie, be.
residual, *a.* residual.
residuo, *n.m.* residue, remainder; (*chem.*) residuum; (*arith.*) difference; (*pl.*) left-over *or* waste material, fall-out.
resiembra, *n.f.* (*agric.*) resowing.
resigna, *n.f.* (*eccles.*) resignation.
resignación, *n.f.* resignation.
resignante, *a.* resigning.
resignar, *v.t.* to resign, hand over. — **resignarse,** *v.r.* to resign o.s., be resigned.
resignatorio, *n.m.* resignee.
resina, *n.f.* resin, rosin.
resinar, *v.t.* to draw resin from.
resinero, -ra, *a.* resinous, resin. — *n.m.* resin extractor.
resinífero, -ra, *a.* resin-bearing.
resinoso, -sa, *a.* resinous.
resisa, *n.f.* (*com.*) eighth part taken as duty.
resisar, *v.t.* to diminish further things taxed.
resistencia, *n.f.* resistance; reluctance; strength, stamina, endurance; (*elec.*) resistor; ***oponer resistencia,*** to offer resistance; (*aer.*) ***resistencia al avance,*** drag.
resistente, *a.* resistant, resisting; strong, tough, having stamina.
resistero, *n.m.* hottest part of the day; heat produced by reflection of the sun's rays; place where such heat is felt.
resistible, *a.* resistible.
resistidor, -ra, *a.* resistant.
resistir, *v.t.* to resist; to withstand, stand, bear. — *v.i.* to resist. — **resistirse,** *v.r.* to struggle; ***resistirse a,*** to be loath, reluctant *or* unwilling to.
resma, *n.f.* ream (*of paper*).
resmilla, *n.f.* four quires of paper.
resobrar, *v.i.* to be considerably over and above.
resobrino, -na, *n.m.* great-nephew. — *n.f.* great-niece.
resol, *n.m.* sun's glare.
resolano, -na, *a.* sunny and sheltered (*from wind*). — *n.f.* sunny and sheltered spot.
resoluble, *a.* resolvable, resoluble.
resolución, *n.f.* resolution, decision; resoluteness, determination; (*law*) nullification; ***en resolución,*** in short, in a word.
resolutivo, -va, *a.* analytical. — *n.m.* (*med.*) resolutive.
resoluto, -ta, *a.* resolute; brief, compendious.
resolutorio, -ria, *a.* resolute.
resolvente, *a.* resolvent, resolving.
resolver [5, *p.p.* **resuelto**], *v.t.* to resolve; to decide; to solve. — **resolverse,** *v.r.* to make up one's mind (***a,*** to); ***resolverse por,*** to decide on, settle on.
resollar [4], *v.i.* to breathe; to breathe heavily, puff and blow, pant; ***no resuella,*** he keeps mum.
resonación, *n.f.* resounding.

resonancia, *n.f.* resonance; repercussion; ***tener resonancia,*** to cause a stir.
resonante, *a.* resounding, resonant.
resonar [4], *v.i.* to resound; to echo.
resoplar, *v.i.* to breathe hard, puff and blow, pant; to snort.
resoplido, resoplo, *n.m.* hard breathing, puffing and blowing, panting; snorting.
resorber, *v.t.* to sip repeatedly.
resorte, *n.m.* spring; ***tener resortes,*** to have pull *or* ways and means.
respaldar, *n.m.* back. — *v.t.* to endorse; to back. — **respaldarse,** *v.r.* to lean back; to get backing; (*vet.*) to dislocate the backbone.
respaldo, *n.m.* back; backing; endorsement.
respectar, *v.i. defect.* to regard, concern; ***por lo que respecta a,*** as regards.
respectivo, -va, *a.* respective.
respecto, *n.m.* respect, connection; ***respecto a*** or ***de,*** with regard to; ***al respecto,*** on the subject.
résped, *n.m.* tongue (*of a snake*); wasp's *or* bee's sting; (*fig.*) viper's tongue.
respetabilidad, *n.f.* respectability, worthiness for respect *or* consideration.
respetable, *a.* worthy of respect; respectable, considerable.
respetar, *v.t.* to respect.
respeto, *n.m.* respect; consideration; ***de respeto,*** very special, to be treated with some awe; (*naut.*) ***velas de respeto,*** spare sails; ***campar por sus respetos,*** to do just as one pleases, answer to no one.
respetoso, -sa, respetuoso, -sa, *a.* respectful.
réspice, *n.m.* (*coll.*) retort; sharp reproof.
respigador, -ra, *n.m.f.* gleaner.
respigar [B], *v.t.* to glean.
respigón, *n.m.* hangnail; sore.
respingar [B], *v.i.* to balk; to shy; to start, jump; to ride up.
respingo, *n.m.* start, jump; part (of garment) that rides up.
respingón, -gona, *a.* snub (*nose*), turned up; (*Hisp. Am.*) surly, churlish.
respingoso, -sa, *a.* skittish, bouncy; (*coll.*) gruff, sour.
respirable, *a.* breathable.
respiración, *n.f.* respiration, breathing; ventilation; ***faltarle a alguien la respiración,*** to choke, get short of breath.
respiradero, *n.m.* vent, venthole, breathing-hole; (*arch.*) air-hole, ventilator; skylight, loophole; (*coll.*) breathing organ; (*fig.*) breather, respite.
respirador, -ra, *a.* breathing, respiratory. — *n.m.* respirator.
respirante, *a.* breathing.
respirar, *v.t.* to breathe, take in (*air*). — *v.i.* to breathe, get breath, take air; to rest, take rest; to open the lips, speak; to spread odours; ***sin respirar,*** quickly, with scarcely time to breathe; ***no tener por donde respirar,*** to have no satisfactory answer; ***respirar por la herida,*** to show where one's grievance lies; ***respirar a,*** to smell of.
respiratorio, -ria, *a.* respiratory.
respiro, *n.m.* breathing; breather, respite; reprieve, relief; (*com.*) extension of time (*for payment*).
resplandecencia, *n.f.* resplendency, splendour; fame, lustre.
resplandecer [9], *v.i.* to shine, gleam, glitter; (*fig.*) to stand out.
resplandeciente, *a.* gleaming, glittering, resplendent, luminous.
resplandecimiento, *n.m.* splendour, brilliancy, brightness, radiance; glare; (*obs., poet.*) make-up.
resplandina, *n.f.* (*coll.*) sharp reproof, dressing down.
resplandor, *n.m.* brilliance, radiance; glare; gleam, gleaming; (*obs.*) cosmetic.
respondedor, -ra, *n.m.f.* answerer.
responder, *v.t.* to answer, reply. — *v.i.* to re-echo; to respond; to answer back; to yield, produce; to give *or* do what's needed; ***responder de*** or ***por,*** to answer for; ***responder a,*** to answer; to match.
respondiente, *a.* respondent, answering. — *n.m.f.* answerer.
respondón, -dona, *a* (*coll.*) cheeky, saucy.
responsabilidad, *n.f.* responsibility, accountability, liability.
responsabilizarse, *v.r.* (***de***), to accept, take *or* claim responsibility (for).
responsable, *a.* responsible, accountable, liable, answerable.
responsar, responsear, *v.i.* to say prayers for the dead; (*coll.*) to scold.
responso, *n.m.* (*eccles.*) responsory for the dead; (*coll.*) dressing down.
responsorio, *n.m.* responsory.
respuesta, *n.f.* reply, answer; response; sound echoed back; ***respuesta aguda*** or ***picante,*** repartee.
resquebradura, resquebrajadura, *n.f.* crack, chink, split; crevice, fault.
resquebrajadizo, -za, *a.* easily cracked *or* split.
resquebrajar, *v.i.* to split, crack.
resquebrajo, *n.m.* cleft, crack.
resquebrajoso, -sa [RESQUEBRAJADIZO].
resquebrar [I], *v.t.* to begin to crack *or* split.
resquemar, *v.t., v.i.* to bite, sting (*the mouth*); to burn (*food*); (*fig.*) to smart. — **resquemarse,** *v.r.* to get parched *or* burnt; (*fig.*) to smoulder.
resquemo, *n.m.,* **resquemazón,** *n.f.* pungency; (*fig.*) burning passion; pricking of the conscience.
resquemor, *n.m.* smarting; vague fear; resentment.
resquicio, *n.m.* chink, cleft, crack, slit, crevice; chance, opportunity.
resta, *n.f.* (*arith.*) subtraction; rest, residue, remainder.
restablecedor, -ra, *a.* restoring. — *n.m.f.* restorer.
restablecer [9], *v.t.* to re-establish, restore, reinstate. — **restablecerse,** *v.r.* to recover.
restablecimiento, *n.m.* re-establishment, restoration; recovery.
restallar, *v.i.* to crack (*as a whip*); to crackle.
restante, *a.* remaining.
restañadero, *n.m.* estuary.
restañadura, *n.f.* retinning.
restañar, *v.t.* to stanch; stop (*blood*); to re-tin.
restañasangre, *n.f.* bloodstone.
restaño, *n.m.* stanching; stagnation.
restar, *v.t.* (*arith.*) to subtract, take away; to return (*a ball*). — *v.i.* to remain, be left.
restauración, *n.f.* restoration.
restaurador, -ra, *a.* restoring. — *n.m.f.* restorer.
restaurante, *a.* restoring. — *n.m.* restorer; restaurant.
restaurar, *v.t.* to restore.
restaurativo, -va, *a.* restorative.
restinga, *n.f.* shoal, bar.
restingar, *n.m.* place of shoals.
restitución, *n.f.* restitution, restoring.
restituible, *a.* restorable.
restituidor, -ra, *n.m.f.* restorer, re-establisher.
restituir [O], *v.t.* to restore, give back. — **restituirse,** *v.r.* to return to the place of departure.
restitutivo, -va, restitutorio, -ria, *a.* restitutive.
resto, *n.m.* remainder, residue, rest; limit for stakes (*at cards*); return (*of a ball*); player who returns the service-ball; ***restos mortales,*** mortal remains; ***a resto abierto,*** without limit; ***echar el resto,*** to give it everything one has got.
restorán, *n.m.* restaurant.

restregadura, *n.f.*, **restregamiento,** *n.m.* (hard) rubbing; scrubbing.
restregar [IB], *v.t.* to rub (hard); to scrub.
restregón, *n.m.* hard rubbing; scrubbing.
restribar, *v.i.* to lean heavily.
restricción, *n.f.* restriction; cut.
restrictivo, -va, *a.* restrictive.
restricto, -ta, *a.* restricted.
restringa, *n.f.* (*naut.*) shoal, bar.
restringente, *a.*, *n.m.* restringent.
restringible, *a.* limitable.
restringir [E], *v.t.* to restrict, limit; to contract, astringe.
restriñente, *a.* restringent, restricting.
restriñidor, -ra, *a.*, *n.m.f.* restringent.
restriñimiento, *n.m.* contraction, constriction.
restriñir [K], *v.t.* to contract, constrict.
restrojo [RASTROJO].
resucitador, -ra, *a.* resurrective, resuscitative, reviving. — *n.m.f.* resurrector, resuscitator, reviver.
resucitar, *v.t.*, *v.i.* to resuscitate, resurrect, revive.
resudación, *n.f.* slight perspiration, oozing.
resudar, *v.i.* to sweat *or* perspire slightly; to ooze, exude.
resudor, *n.m.* slight perspiration.
resuelto, -ta, *a.* resolute, bold; quick, prompt.
resuello, *n.m.* breathing, hard breathing; ***sin resuello,*** breathless, panting; ***meter el resuello a,*** to put the wind up, scare stiff.
resulta, *n.f.* result, outcome; vacancy; ***de resultas de,*** as a result of.
resultado, *n.m.* result, outcome, effect.
resultancia, *n.f.* result, resultance.
resultante, *a.* resulting, consequent, following. — *n.f.* (*mech.*) resultant (*force, velocity etc.*).
resultar, *v.i.* to result; to be, prove to be, turn out, turn out to be; to come out; to work out; (*coll.*) to be a good thing; (*coll.*) to look good.
resumen, *n.m.* abridgement, summary, précis, résumé; recapitulation; compendium; (*law*) brief; ***en resumen,*** in short, briefly, summing up.
resumido, -da, *a.* summarized; ***en resumidas cuentas,*** in short, to cut a long story short.
resumir, *v.t.* to sum up, summarize, abridge. — **resumirse,** *v.r.* to be reduced (***en,*** to).
resunción, *n.f.* summary, abridgement; repetition.
resurgimiento, *n.m.* resurgence, reappearance, revival; (*hist.*) risorgimento.
resurgir [E], *v.i.* to reappear, arise, spring up again.
resurrección, *n.f.* resurrection; revival; resuscitation.
resurtida, *n.f.* rebound, repercussion.
resurtir, *v.i.* to rebound, spring back.
retablo, *n.m.* altar-piece, reredos.
retacar, *v.t.* to hit (a billiard-ball) twice.
retacería, *n.f.* collection of remnants of cloth.
retaco, *n.m.* short musket; short cue; dumpy fellow, runt.
retador, -ra, *a.* challenging. — *n.m.f.* challenger.
retaguardia, *n.f.* rearguard; ***picar la retaguardia,*** to harass the retreating enemy; ***a (la) retaguardia,*** in the rear.
retahila, *n.f.* string, line, series, stream.
retajar, *v.t.* to cut round; to circumcise; to trim the nib of (*a quill pen*).
retal, *n.m.* clipping, remnant, piece.
retallar, *v.t.* to retouch (*an engraving*); (*arch.*) to build ledges in. — *v.i.* to shoot *or* sprout again.
retallecer [9], *v.i.* to shoot *or* sprout again.
retallo, *n.m.* new sprout; (*arch.*) jut.
retama, *n.f.* (*bot.*) genista; broom; ***retama negra*** or ***de escobas,*** furze, whin; ***retama de tintes,*** dyer's-broom, dyeweed.
retamal, retamar, *n.m.* land covered with broom; broom *or* gorse bush.
retamero, -ra, *a.* relating to broom *or* gorse.
retamilla, *n.f.* (*Mex.*) barberry tree.
retamo, *n.m.* (*Arg., Chi., Col.*) [RETAMA].
retamón, *n.m.* (*bot.*) purging broom.
retar, *v.t.* to challenge.
retardación, *n.f.* retardation, delay.
retardar, *v.t.* to retard; to slow down; to delay.
retardo, *n.m.* retardment, delay.
retasa, *n.f.* price reduction *or* assessment.
retasación, *n.f.* price reduction.
retasar, *v.t.* to reduce the price of; to re-assess, reappraise.
retazar [C], *v.t.* to tear in pieces.
retazo, *n.m.* remnant; piece, fragment, portion.
retejador, *n.m.* retiler.
retejar, *v.t.* to retile.
retejer, *v.t.* to weave closely.
retejo, *n.m.* retiling.
retemblar [I], *v.i.* to tremble, shake, quiver violently.
retén, *n.m.* stock, store; reserve; (*mil.*) reserve corps; (*mech.*) ratchet, catch.
retención, *n.f.*, retention, keeping back.
retener [33], *v.t.* to retain, withhold, keep back; to detain.
retenida, *n.f.* (*naut.*) preventer rope; (*aer.*) ***retenida de costado,*** side guy wire; (*aer.*) ***retenida de guiñada,*** yaw guy; (*naut.*) ***retenida de proa,*** headfast.
retentar, *v.t.* to threaten with a relapse.
retentivo, -va, *a.* retentive. — *n.f.* retentiveness, memory.
reteñir [8K], *v.t.* to dye again. — *v.i.* to ring, tinkle.
retesamiento, *n.m.* tightening.
retesar, *v.t.* to tighten.
reteso, *n.m.* tightening; brow of a hill, rise.
reticencia, *n.f.* innuendo, double-meaning, hidden meaning, hint, suggestion, implication.
reticente, *a.* hinting, suggesting, implying.
rético, -ca, *a.* Rhaetian. — *n.m.* Rhaeto-Romanic.
reticular, *a.* reticular, reticulate.
retín, *n.m.* tinkling, jingle, clink; (*coll.*) sarcastic tone.
retina, *n.f.* retina.
retinte, *n.m.* second dying; tinkling sound.
retintín, *n.m.* jingle, tinkling, clink; sarcastic tone.
retinto, -ta, *a.* dark reddish brown.
retiñir [K], *v.i.* to jingle, tinkle, ring, clink; to pitter-patter.
retirada, *n.f.* [RETIRADO].
retiradamente, *adv.* secretly; in seclusion.
retirado, -da, *a.* withdrawn, set back; off the beaten track, remote, secluded. — *n.f.* retreat, retirement, withdrawal; place of refuge; dry bed (*of river*); (*mil.*) ***tocar la retirada,*** to sound the retreat.
retiramiento, *n.m.* retirement.
retirar, *v.t.* to draw back, withdraw; to draw aside, pull back; to reserve, conceal; (*com.*) to withdraw, call in; (*print.*) to back. — **retirarse,** *v.r.* to withdraw, retreat, go back, move back, move away; to retire from active life, go into seclusion, go into retreat.
retiro, *n.m.* retreat; seclusion; retirement; (*mil.*) condition and salary of a retired officer.
reto, *n.m.* challenge, threat.
retobado, -da, *a.* (*Hisp. Am.*) given to grumbling; obstinate, unruly; (*Arg., Per.*) cunning, wily.
retobar, *v.t.* (*Arg.*) to cover with hides; (*Chi.*) to pack in hides *or* burlap. — **retobarse,** *v.r.* (*Arg.*) to become surly.
retobo, *n.m.* (*Col., Hond.*) refuse, useless thing; (*Chi.*) burlap; oilcloth; (*Arg.*) packing in hides.

retocador, *n.m.* (*photo.*) retoucher.
retocar [A], *v.t.* to retouch; to touch up, give the finishing touches to.
retoñar, retoñecer [9], *v.i.* to sprout again, shoot again; to reappear.
retoño, *n.m.* (*bot.*) sprout, shoot, sucker; offspring.
retoque, *n.m.* retouch, touching up; repeated beating; touch (*of a disease*).
rétor, *n.m.* rhetor; orator.
retor, *n.m.* twilled cotton fabric.
retorcedura, *n.f.* twisting, writhing.
retorcer [5D], *v.t.* to wring, twist; to contort; to twirl; to distort, misconstrue. — **retorcerse,** *v.r.* to double up, writhe, squirm; to wind around (*plants*).
retorcido, -da, *a.* involved; twisted, crafty. — *n.m.* sweetmeat; tutti-frutti.
retorcimiento, *n.m.* twisting, wreathing, wringing, writhing.
retórico, -ca, *a.* rhetorical. — *n.m.f.* rhetorician. — *n.f.* rhetoric; (*pl.*, *coll.*) sophistries, quibbling.
retornamiento, *n.m.* return.
retornante, *a.* returning.
retornar, *v.t.* to return, give back; to twist *or* bend back; to cause to go back. — *v.i.* to return, go *or* come back.
retorno, *n.m.* return; requital, repayment; coming back, home trip; traffic, exchange, barter; (*naut.*) leading block.
retorsión, *n.f.* twisting; retortion; retaliation; retort.
retorsivo, -va, *a.* bending back; retorting.
retorta, *n.f.* (*chem.*) retort; twilled linen fabric.
retortero, *n.m.* twirl, rotation; ***andar al retortero,*** to hover about; (*coll.*) ***traer al retortero,*** to push around, keep on the hop.
retortijar, *v.t.* to twist, curl.
retortijón, *n.m.* twisting, contortion, curlicue; ***retortijón de tripas,*** griping, cramp.
retostado, -da, *a.* brown-coloured.
retostar [4], *v.t.* to retoast, toast brown.
retozador, -ra, *a.* frisky frolicsome, pranky.
retozadura, *n.f.* friskiness.
retozar [C], *v.i.* to frolic, gambol, romp, frisk about.
retozo, *n.m.* gambol, frolic, romping, friskiness; ***retozo de la risa,*** giggle, titter.
retozón, -zona, *a.* frolicsome, frisky.
retracción, *n.f.* retraction.
retractable, *a.* retractable.
retractación, *n.f.* retractation.
retractar, *v.t.* to retract, withdraw; (*law*) to redeem. — **retractarse,** *v.r.* to recant, withdraw one's remarks *or* statements.
retráctil, *a.* retractile.
retracto, *n.m.* (*law*) prior right to purchase.
retraducir [15], *v.t.* to retranslate.
retraer [34], *v.t.* to bring back; to dissuade; (*law*) to redeem. — **retraerse,** *v.r.* to withdraw, retire.
retraído, -da, *a.* reserved, shy.
retraimiento, *n.m.* withdrawal, retirement; shyness, reserve; retreat, asylum, refuge; sanctum, private room.
retranca, *n.f.* crupper; (*Col.*, *Cub.*, *Mex.*) brake; ill will, ill intention.
retranquear, *v.t.* (*arch.*) to carve figures round.
retranquero, *n.m.* (*Col.*, *Cub.*, *Mex.*) brakeman.
retransmisión, *n.f.* (*rad.*) relay.
retransmitir, *v.t.* to relay.
retrasar, *v.t.* to delay; to put off; to set *or* turn back; to slow down. — *v.i.* to be slow; to get behind. — **retrasarse,** *v.r.* to delay; to be late; to be slow.
retraso, *n.m.* delay; slowness, lag; ***llevar retraso,*** to be late; to come through slowly, with a lag.
retratador, -ra, *n.m.f.* portrait painter; photographer.
retratar, *v.t.* to portray; to do *or* give a portrait *or* picture of; to paint; to photograph; (*coll.*) ***esto le retrata,*** this (*just*) shows what he is like, this is typical of him. — **retratarse,** *v.r.* to have one's portrait painted *or* picture taken; (*coll.*) to fork out (the) cash, let the colour of one's money be seen; ***a ver si te retratas,*** how about letting us see the colour of your money?
retratería, *n.f.* (*Guat.*, *Ur.*) photographer's studio.
retratista, *n.m.* portrait painter; photographer.
retrato, *n.m.* portrait; picture; likeness; photograph.
retrayente, *a.* retracting.
retrechar, *v.i.* to back, move backward.
retrechería, *n.f.* winsomeness; artfulness.
retrechero, -ra, *a.* charming, winsome, attractive; artful.
retrepado, -da, *a.* slanting backward.
retreparse, *v.r.* to lean back, recline.
retreta, *n.f.* (*mil.*) tattoo; retreat; (*Col.*) open-air concert (*by a military band*).
retrete, *n.m.* lavatory; private room; boudoir.
retribución, *n.f.* reward, payment.
retribuir [O], *v.t.* reward, pay.
retribuyente, *a.* retributory.
retrillar, *v.t.* (*agric.*) to thresh again.
retroacción, *n.f.* retroaction.
retroactivamente, *adv.* retroactively.
retroactividad, *n.f.* retroactivity.
retroactivo, -va, *a.* retroactive; back-dated.
retrobar, *v.t.* (*Chi.*) to reproach; to scold, chide.
retrobón, -bona, *a.*, *n.m.f.* (*Chi.*) scold, grumbler.
retrocarga, *n.f.* breech-loading (*of firearms*).
retroceder, *v.i.* to go back, back up, move backwards, recede, turn back, reverse.
retrocesión, *n.f.* retrocession, receding; going back; (*law*) recession.
retroceso, *n.m.* [RETROCESIÓN]; going back, backing up, backward motion, receding; (*med.*) aggravation; (*billiards*) draw; recoil (*of firearms*).
retrogradación, *n.f.* (*astron.*) retrogradation, retrogression.
retrogradar, *v.i.* (*astron.*) to retrograde; to recede.
retrógrado, -da, *a.* retrograde, retrogressive; (*polit.*) reactionary.
retronar [4], *v.i.* to make a thundering noise.
retrospectivo, -va, *a.* retrospective; flash-back.
retrotracción, *n.f.* (*law*) antedating.
retrotraer [34], *v.t.* to date back, antedate.
retrovendendo, *n.m.* (*law*) reversion sale.
retrovender, *v.t.* (*law*) to sell back to the first vendor.
retrovendición, *n.f.* selling back to the vendor.
retrovisor, *n.m.* driving mirror.
retrucar [A], *v.i.* (*billiards*) to kiss.
retruco, *n.m.* kiss (*billiards*).
retruécano, *n.m.* pun, play upon words.
retrueque, *n.m.* kiss (*of a rebounding ball*).
retuerto, -ta, *a.* twisted. — *p.p. irreg.* [RETORCER].
retumbante, *a.* sonorous, resonant; pompous, bombastic, high-flown.
retumbar, *v.i.* to resound, sound loudly, thunder, rumble.
retumbo, *n.m.* resounding, rumble, thunder.
retundir, *v.t.* (*build.*) to even (*a wall*); (*med.*) to repel.
reuma, *n.m.* rheumatism. — *n.f.* rheum.
reumático, -ca, *a.* rheumatic, rheumatical. — *n.m.f.* rheumatic.
reumatismo, *n.m.* rheumatism.
reunión, *n.f.* union, reunion; meeting, gathering, assembly; party.
reunir [P], *v.t.* to congregate, gather; to unite, reunite; to reconcile. — **reunirse,** *v.r.* to assemble, gather (together); (***con***) to join, meet.
reuntar [P], *v.t.* to oil again, grease again.
revacunación, *n.f.* revaccination.

revacunar, *v.t.* to revaccinate.
reválida, *n.f.* final university examination; university entrance exam.
revalidación, *n.f.* confirmation.
revalidar, *v.t.* to ratify, confirm. — **revalidarse,** *v.r.* to pass the final examination (*for a degree*).
revancha, *n.f.* revenge; return match *or* fight; ***en revancha,*** in return, in exchange.
revecero, -ra, *n.m.f.* farmhand tending oxen.
reveedor, *n.m.* revisor, censor, inspector.
revejecer [9], *v.i.* to grow prematurely old.
revejecido, -da, revejido, -da, *a.* prematurely old.
revelación, *n.f.* revelation; disclosure.
revelado, *n.m.* (*photo.*) developing.
revelador, -ra, *a.* revealing. — *n.m.f.* revealer; (*photo.*) developer.
revelamiento, *n.m.* revelation; (*photo.*) developing.
revelante, *a.* revealing.
revelar, *v.t.* to reveal, disclose; (*photo.*) to develop.
reveler, *v.t.* (*med.*) to cause revulsion in.
revellín, *n.m.* (*fort.*) ravelin.
revenar, *v.i.* to sprout (*plants, trees etc.*).
revendedor, *n.m.* retailer; ticket tout.
revender, *v.t.* to retail; re-sell.
revenimiento, *n.m.* going tough, hard *or* stale; (*min.*) cave-in.
revenirse [36], *v.r.* to harden, become stale *or* sour.
reveno, *n.m.* sprout, shoot.
reventa, *n.f.* retail; resale, second sale.
reventadero, *n.m.* rough piece of ground; painful work, drudgery.
reventar [1], *v.t.* to burst, explode; to crush, smash; to spoil, wreck; (*coll.*) to fag out, knock up; to get on the nerves of. — *v.i.* to burst, explode, blow out; to break; (*coll.*) to peg out, croak; ***está reventando por ir*** or ***de ganas de ir,*** he's dying to go; ***¡que reviente!*** let him go hang!
reventazón, *n.f.* bursting; burst, blow-out; dashing (*of waves*).
reventón, *a.* bursting; bulging; ***ojos reventones,*** bulging eyes. — *n.m.* burst, blow-out; steep hill; (*coll.*) fagging out; (*coll.*) ***pegar un reventón,*** to peg out; ***le dio un reventón al caballo para llegar a tiempo,*** he thrashed the horse unmercifully to arrive in time.
rever [37], *v.t.* to revise, review; (*law*) to retry.
reverberación, *n.f.* reverberation.
reverberar, *v.i.* to reverberate, shimmer.
reverbero, *n.m.* reverberation; reflector; street lamp; (*Arg., Cub., Ec., Hond.*) cooking stove, spirit stove.
reverdecer [9], *v.i.* to sprout again, grow green again; to acquire new vigour.
reverdeciente, *a.* growing fresh and green again.
reverencia, *n.f.* reverence; obeisance; curtsy; bow.
reverenciable, *a.* worthy of reverence.
reverenciador, -ra, *n.m.f.* reverencer.
reverencial, *a.* reverential.
reverenciar, *v.t.* to reverence.
reverendísimo, -ma, *a. superl.* Most Reverend.
reverendo, -da, *a.* reverend, worthy of reverence.
reverente, *a.* reverent, respectful.
reversibilidad, *n.f.* revertibility, reversibility.
reversible, *a.* (*law*) revertible; (*phys.*) reversible.
reversión, *n.f.* (*law*) reversion, return.
reverso, *n.m.* reverse (*of coins*); back, wrong side; ***el reverso de la medalla,*** the other side of the picture.
reverter [2], *v.i.* to overflow.
revertir [6], *v.i.* (*law*) to revert.
revés, *n.m.* back, wrong side, reverse; back-handed slap; setback; (*Cub.*) tobacco grub; ***al revés,*** on the contrary; the wrong way round; ***al revés de,*** contrary to; ***del revés,*** the wrong way round, back to front, inside out.
revesa, *n.f.* eddy, backwater.
revesado, -da, *a.* [ENREVESADO]; (*fig.*) mischievous, wayward.
revesar, *v.t.* to vomit.
revesino, *n.m.* reversis (*card game*); ***cortar el revesino,*** to thwart.
revestido, *n.m.* (*arch.*) facing.
revestimiento, *n.m.* (*build.*) revetment, covering, lining, facing (*on a surface, wall etc.*).
revestir [8], *v.t.* to clothe, cover; to line, face, revet; to give an air to; to have, take on, assume; ***revestir de,*** to clothe in. — **revestirse,** *v.r.* to clothe o.s. (***de,*** in); to adopt, take on.
revezar [C], *v.i.* to alternate, work in rotation, come in by turn.
revezo, *n.m.* working by shifts; shift, relay.
reviejo, -ja, *a.* very old. — *n.m.* withered branch of a tree.
revientacaballo, *n.m.* (*Cub., bot.*) dog's-bane.
reviernes, *n.m.* each of the first seven Fridays after Easter.
revindicar [A], *v.t.* to claim.
revirado, -da, *a.* (*bot.*) twisted.
revirar, *v.t.* to turn, twist; to roll (*one's eyes*). — *v.i.* (*naut.*) to veer again, retack.
revisada (*Chi.*) [REVISIÓN].
revisar, *v.t.* to revise, review, examine; to check, verify; ***revisar las cuentas,*** to audit accounts.
revisión, *n.f.* (*mil.*) revision, reviewing, revisal, revise; (*law*) new trial *or* hearing; check; audit.
revisita, *n.f.* revision; reinspection.
revisor, -ra, *a.* revising, revisory. — *n.m.f.* reviser, re-examiner. — *n.m.* inspector; auditor.
revisoría, *n.f.* office of censor *or* reviser.
revista (1), *n.f.* review; magazine, journal; parade, muster; revue, show; (*law*) fresh hearing; ***pasar revista,*** to review.
revistar, *v.t.* to revise (*a lawsuit*); to review, inspect (*troops*).
revistero, -ra, *n.m.f.* (*newsp.*) reporter.
revisto, -ta (2), *a., p.p. irreg.* [REVER].
revitalizar [C], *v.t.* to revitalize.
revividero, *n.m.* silkworm incubator.
revivificable, *a.* revivable.
revivificar [A], *v.t.* to revivify, revive.
revivir, *v.i.* to revive, return to life; to arise again, be renewed.
revocable, *a.* revocable, reversible.
revocación, *n.f.* revocation, abrogation.
revocador, -ra, *a.* revoking. — *n.m.f.* revoker. — *n.m.* plasterer.
revocadura, *n.f.* plaster, plastering; edge of canvas covered by the frame.
revocante, *a., n.m.f.* revoker, revoking.
revocar [A], *v.t.* to revoke; recall; to drive back; to plaster.
revocatorio, -ria, *a.* revocatory.
revoco, *n.m.* driving back; plastering; cover of broom for charcoal baskets.
revolante, *a.* fluttering.
revolar [4], *v.i.* to take a second flight; to fly again; to flutter around.
revolcadero, *n.m.* wallowing-place; mud-hole.
revolcadura, *n.f.* wallow.
revolcar [4A], *v.t.* to knock down, roll over; to floor, lay out; (*fig.*) to plough, fail. — **revolcarse,** *v.r.* to wallow (about), roll (around).
revolcón, *n.m.* tumble, spill; ploughing; ***dar un revolcón a,*** to wipe the floor with.
revolear, *v.t.* to swing round. — *v.i.* to fly about.
revolotear, *v.t.* to fling in the air. — *v.i.* to flutter round.
revoloteo, *n.m.* fluttering.
revoltijo, revoltillo, *n.m.* jumble, tangle; mess; tripe; ***revoltillo de huevos,*** scrambled eggs.
revoltón, *n.m.* vine-grub.

revoltoso, -sa, *a.* turbulent, rebellious; mischievous.
revoltura, *n.f.* (*min.*) mixture of fluxes.
revolución, *n.f.* revolution.
revolucionar, *v.t.* to revolutionize; to turn topsy-turvy *or* upside down.
revolucionario, -ria, *a., n.m.f.* revolutionary.
revolvedero, *n.m.* wallowing place.
revolvedor, -ra, *a.* stirring, mixing.
revólver, *n.m.* revolver.
revolver [5, *p.p.* **revuelto**], *v.t.* to stir, stir round; to stir up; to turn, turn over, turn upside down, upset; to swing round; ***revolver el cotarro,*** to set the cat among the pigeons. — *v.i.* to swing round. — **revolverse,** *v.r.* to turn round; to toss and turn; to turn, round (***contra,*** on).
revolvimiento, *n.m.* revolution, turn, turning round.
revoque, *n.m.* plastering.
revotarse, *v.r.* to reverse one's vote.
revuelco, *n.m.* rolling; wallowing; tumble; heave.
revuelo, *n.m.* second flight; flying round; commotion, rumpus; ***de revuelo,*** promptly, speedily.
revuelto, -ta, *a.* easily turned (*horse*); intricate; disordered, topsy-turvy; stormy (*weather*); ***huevos revueltos,*** scrambled eggs; ***mesa revuelta,*** medley. — *n.f.* stir, riot, to-do; return, second turn; turn, bend, winding.
revuelvepiedras, *n.m. inv.* (*orn.*) turnstone.
revulsión, *n.f.* (*med.*) revulsion.
revulsivo, *n.m.* revulvise, enema; nasty shock that does one good.
rey, *n.m.* king; ***rey de armas,*** king-at-arms; ***ni rey ni roque,*** nobody; ***tener el rey en el cuerpo,*** to be haughty; ***a rey muerto, rey puesto,*** nothing is irreplaceable; ***ni quito ni pongo rey,*** I'm not taking sides; (*pl.* **reyes**) monarchs, king and queen; ***los Reyes Magos,*** the Magi, the Three Wise Men; ***el día de Reyes,*** Epiphany, Twelfth Night.
reyerta, *n.f.* brawl, fight.
reyertar, *v.i.* to brawl.
reyezuelo, *n.m.* princeling, petty ruler; (*orn.*) kinglet.
rezado, *n.m.* prayer, divine service.
rezador, -ra, *a.* praying. — *n.m.f.* pious person, one who prays often.
rezagado, -da, *a.* straggling, lagging, left behind. — *n.m.f.* straggler, lagger, one who falls behind.
rezagante, *a.* straggling, lagging.
rezagar [B], *v.t.* to leave behind; to put off. — **rezagarse,** *v.r.* to lag, trail behind.
rezago, *n.m.* remainder, leftover.
rezar [C], *v.t.* to pray; to say. — *v.i.* to pray; to read, go; ***reza así,*** it reads *or* goes like this; ***eso no reza conmigo,*** that doesn't apply to me.
rezno, *n.m.* bot-fly; gadfly.
rezo, *n.m.* prayer, praying; devotions; divine office.
rezón, *n.m.* (*naut.*) grappling-iron, grapnel.
rezongador, -ra, *a.* grumbling, grousing. — *n.m.f.* grumbler, grouser.
rezongar [B], *v.i.* to grumble, grouse.
rezongón, -gona, *a.* grumbling, grousing.
rezumadero, *n.m.* dripping-place; cesspool.
rezumar(se), *v.t., v.i.* (*v.r.*) to ooze, seep, leak.
ría (1), *n.f.* estuary.
riachuelo, *n.m.* small stream; rivulet; pokey little stream.
riada, *n.f.* flood *or* rush of water, freshet.
riatillo, *n.m.* brook.
riba, *n.f.* sloping bank, embankment.
ribaldería, *n.f.* ribaldry, knavery.
ribaldo, -da, *a.* ribald, knavish. — *n.m.f.* ribald, knave.
ribazo, *n.m.* sharp slope, embankment.
ribera, *n.f.* shore; bank.
ribereño, -ña, *a.* riparian, riverside; coastal, bordering on the sea.
riberiego, -ga, *a.* grazing on the banks of rivers.
ribero, *n.m.* bank (*of a dam*); river-wall, levee.
ribete, *n.m.* edge, border, fringe, trimming; streak, touch; extra bit added on.
ribeteador, -ra, *n.m.f.* binder.
ribetear, *v.t.* to hem, border, fringe, trim.
ricacho, -cha, *n.m.f.* (*coll.*) filthy-rich individual, money-bags.
ricadueña, ricafembra, ricahembra, *n.f.* lady, nobleman's wife *or* daughter; (*pl.* **ricasdueñas, ricasfembras, ricashembras**).
ricamente, *adv.* richly; (*coll.*) nicely, fine and dandy, sitting pretty.
ricial, *a.* growing again, green, new.
ricino, *n.m.* (*bot.*) Palma Christi, castor-oil plant.
rico, -ca, *a.* rich, wealthy; delicious, lovely. — *n.m.f.* rich individual; love, dear, darling; ***nuevo rico,*** nouveau riche, upstart; (*iron.*) ***¡que rico!*** well, well! that's a fine thing! how do you like that!
ricohombre, *n.m.* nobleman, peer of the realm; (*pl.* **ricoshombres**).
rictus, *n.m. inv.* agonized grin, grimace.
ricura, *n.f.* (*coll.*) delightful, lovely *or* charming child, person *or* object.
ridiculez, *n.f.* ridiculousness, absurdity; ridiculous thing to do *or* say; trifle, mere trifle.
ridiculizar [C], *v.t.* to ridicule, mock at.
ridículo, -la, *a.* ridiculous, absurd. — *n.m.* ridicule; ***ponerse en ridículo, hacer el ridículo,*** to make a fool of o.s.
riego (1), *n.m.* irrigation.
riego (2), **riegue,** *pres. indic., pres. subj.* [REGAR].
riel, *n.m.* ingot; rail.
rielar, *v.i.* to shimmer, glimmer, gleam, shine.
rielera, *n.f.* ingot-mould.
rienda, *n.f.* rein; ***dar rienda suelta a,*** to give free rein to; ***soltar la rienda,*** to let go, let rip; ***a rienda suelta, a toda rienda,*** hell for leather.
riente, *a.* smiling; laughing.
riesgo, *n.m.* risk; ***correr riesgo,*** to run a risk, be in danger.
rifa, *n.f.* raffle; scuffle, wrangle.
rifador, *n.m.* raffler; disputer.
rifadura, *n.f.* brawl; (*naut.*) splitting (*sail*).
rifar, *v.t.* to raffle. — *v.i.* to quarrel, dispute. — **rifarse,** *v.r.* (*naut.*) to split.
rifeño, -ña, *a., n.m.f.* from the Rif.
rifirrafe, *n.m.* squabble, set-to.
rifle, *n.m.* rifle.
riflero, *n.m.* rifleman.
rigente, *a.* (*poet.*) rigid, rigescent.
rigidez, *n.f.* rigidity; inflexibility; ***rigidez cadavérica,*** rigor mortis.
rígido, -da, *a.* rigid, stiff.
rigodón, *n.m.* rigadoon.
rigor, *n.m.* rigour; ***de rigor,*** de rigueur, obligatory; ***en rigor,*** strictly speaking.
rigorismo, *n.m.* rigorousness; rigorism.
rigorista, *a., n.m.f.* rigorist.
rigoroso, -sa [RIGUROSO].
rigüe, *n.m.* (*Hond.*) omelet made of the ears of green corn.
riguridad, *n.f.* (*Chi.*) rigour; sternness; (*med.*) rigidity.
rigurosidad, *n.f.* rigour, rigorousness, severity.
riguroso, -sa, *a.* rigorous, strict; absolute.
rija (1), *n.f.* lachrymal fistula; quarrel, scuffle.
rijador, -ra, *a.* quarrelsome, litigious.
rijo (1), *n.m.* ruttishness (*animals*); lust.
rijo (2), **rija** (2), *pres. indic., pres. subj.* [REGIR].
rijoso, -sa, *a.* ruttish (*animals*); randy, lustful; quarrelsome.

rima, *n.f.* (*poet.*) rime, rhyme; heap, pile; (*poet.*) ***rima imperfecta,*** assonance.
rimador, -ra, *n.m.f.* rhymer, versifier.
rimar, *v.t., v.i.* to rhyme.
rimbombancia, *n.f.* resonance, thundering; bombast, pompousness.
rimbombante, *a.* resounding, resonant, thundering; bombastic, pompous, high-flown.
rimbombar, *v.i.* to resound, echo; to thunder.
rimbombe, rimbombo, *n.m.* resonance, echo; thundering.
rimero, *n.m.* heap, pile.
Rin, *n.m.* Rhine.
rincón, *n.m.* (*inside*) corner; place, spot.
rinconada, *n.f.* corner (*between buildings, boulders, cliffs etc.*).
rinconcillo, *n.m.* small corner.
rinconero, -ra, *a.* transverse, athwart (*honeycomb*). — *n.f.* corner cabinet, stand, bracket *or* table; spot.
ringla, *n.f.*, **ringle,** *n.m.*, **ringlera,** *n.f.* row, file, line, tier, series.
ringlero, *n.m.* ruled line.
ringorrango, *n.m.* (*coll.*) curlicue, flourish (*in writing*); frippery.
rinoceronte, *n.m.* (*zool.*) rhinoceros.
rinoplastia, *n.f.* (*surg.*) rhinoplasty.
riña (1), *n.f.* fight, quarrel, wrangle; dressing-down.
riño, riña (2), **él riñó,** *pres. indic., pres. subj., pret.* [REÑIR].
riñón, *n.m.* (*anat.*) kidney; (*arch.*) spandrel; (*min.*) nodule, kidney ore; (*fig.*) heart; ***costar un riñón,*** to cost the earth; ***tener cubierto el riñón,*** to be well off; (*pl.* **riñones**) loins; (*coll.*) ***tener riñones,*** to have guts.
riñonada, *n.f.* layer of fat about the kidneys; loins; dish of kidneys.
río (1), *n.m.* river, stream; ***cuando el río suena, agua lleva,*** there's no smoke without fire; ***pescar en río revuelto,*** to fish in troubled waters; ***a río revuelto, ganancia de pescadores,*** fishing in troubled waters.
río (2), **ría** (2), *pres. indic., pres. subj.* [REÍR].
riolada, *n.f.* stream, flood.
rioplatense, *a.* of *or* from the River Plate.
riostra, *n.f.* (*arch.*) brace, truss, strut, spur.
riostrar, *v.t.* to brace, stay.
ripia, *n.f.* shingle (*for roofing*).
ripiar, *v.t.* to fill with rubble.
ripio, *n.m.* rubbish, debris, rubble: (*fig.*) padding; ***no perder ripio,*** not to miss a word, chance *or* trick.
riqueza, *n.f.* riches; wealth.
risa, *n.f.* laugh, laughter; ***no es cosa de risa,*** it's no laughing matter; ***desternillarse de risa,*** to split one's sides laughing; ***echar*** or ***tomar a risa,*** to treat as a joke.
risada, *n.f.* horse-laugh, burst of laughter.
riscal, *n.m.* cliffy, craggy place.
risco, *n.m.* cliff, crag; honey fritter.
riscoso, -sa, *a.* rocky, craggy.
risibilidad, *n.f.* risibility.
risible, *a.* risible, ludicrous, laughable.
risica, risicilla, risicita, *n.f.* giggle, titter, snigger.
risotada, *n.f.* guffaw.
ríspido, -da, *a.* rough, harsh.
ristra, *n.f.* string (*of onions etc.*); row, file.
ristre, *n.m.* lance-rest.
ristrel, *n.m.* (*arch.*) wooden moulding.
risueño, -ña, *a.* smiling; pleasant.
rítmico, -ca, *a.* rhythmical, rhythmic. — *n.f.* rhythmics.
ritmo, *n.m.* rhythm; pace, rate.
rito, *n.m.* rite.
ritual, *a., n.m.* ritual.
ritualidad, *n.f.* ritualism.
ritualismo, *n.m.* ritualism.
ritualista, *a., n.m.f.* ritualist.
rival, *a., n.m.* rival.
rivalidad, *n.f.* rivalry.
rivalizar [C], *v.i.* to vie, compete; ***rivalizar con,*** to rival.
rivera, *n.f.* brook, stream.
riza (1), *n.f.* stubble; destruction, ravage.
rizado, -da, *a.* curly; frizzy. — *n.m.* curling; curliness; curls; crimping, frizzing.
rizador, *n.m.* curling-iron; (*sew.*) ruffler.
rizar [C], *v.t.* to curl, to crimp, frizzle; to ruffle; to ripple.
rizo, -za (2), *a.* curly. — *n.m.* curl; ripple; (*aer.*) loop; (*naut.*) reef; ***hacer*** or ***rizar el rizo,*** to loop the loop.
rizófago, -ga, *a.* (*zool.*) root-eating.
rizoma, *n.m.* (*bot.*) rhizome.
rizoso, -sa, *a.* curly.
roa, *n.f.* (*naut.*) stem.
roán, *n.m.* Rouen linen.
roanés, -nesa, *a., n.m.f.* native of Rouen.
roano, -na, *a.* sorrel, roan (*horse*).
rob, *n.m.* (*pharm.*) rob; fruit jelly.
robada, *n.f.* land measure (¼ acre).
robadera, *n.f.* (*agric.*) levelling harrow.
robador, -ra, *n.m.f.* robber, thief.
robaliza, *n.f.* (*ichth.*) female sea bass.
róbalo, robalo, *n.m.* (*ichth.*) sea bass; (*ichth.*) snook.
robar, *v.t., v.i.* to rob, steal, thieve, pilfer; to abduct; to sweep away, eat away; to draw (*cards*).
robellón, *n.m.* milk mushroom.
robezo, *n.m.* wild goat.
robín, *n.m.* rust (*of metal*).
robinia, *n.f.* locust-tree *or* false acacia.
robla, *n.f.* ancient pasturage fee.
robladero, -ra, *a.* made to be riveted.
robladura, *n.f.* clinching, riveting.
roblar, *v.t.* to clinch, rivet, make strong.
roble, *n.m.* oak, oak tree, oak wood; ***roble albar,*** durmast; ***roble carrasqueño,*** gall oak.
robleda, *n.f.* oak grove.
robledal, robledo, *n.m.* oak grove.
roblizo, -za, *a.* oaken; hard, strong.
roblón, *n.m.* rivet; ridge of tiles.
robo, *n.m.* theft, robbery, stealing; burglary; larceny; draw (*cards*).
roboración, *n.f.* corroboration, strengthening.
roborante, *a.* corroborant; (*med.*) roborant.
roborar, *v.t.* to corroborate; to strengthen.
roborativo, -va, *a.* corroborative.
robra, *n.f.* treat *or* tip (*given at the conclusion of a deal*); (*law*) deed.
robre, *n.m.* oak.
robredo, *n.m.* oak grove *or* wood.
robustecer [9], *v.t.* to strengthen, make strong.
robustez, *n.f.* robustness, strength, toughness.
robusto, -ta, *a.* robust, strong, tough.
roca, *n.f.* rock.
rocada, *n.f.* wool *or* cotton wound on the distaff.
rocadero, *n.m.* distaff-knob.
rocador, *n.m.* distaff-head.
rocalla, *n.f.* chippings of stone; riprap; glass beads.
rocalloso, -sa, *a.* rocky.
rocambola, *n.f.* (*bot.*) rocambole, leek.
rocambor, *n.m.* (*Hisp. Am.*) card game.
roce, *n.m.* rubbing, grazing; (*fig.*) brush; (*pl.*) friction.
rociado, -da, *a.* dewy, bedewed. — *n.f.* sprinkling, shower; (*naut.*) spray, squall; dew; upbraiding, rebuke.

rociador, *n.m.* sprinkler, sprayer.
rociadura, *n.f.* sprinkling.
rociadera, *n.f.* watering can, sprinkler.
rociamiento, *n.m.* sprinkling, bedewing.
rociar [L], *v.t.* to sprinkle, spray. — *v.i.* to fall (*dew*).
rocín, *n.m.* hack, jade, nag.
rocinal, *a.* (*belonging to a*) hack.
rocinante, *m.* sorry hack, nag.
rocino, *n.m.* hack, jade.
rocío, *n.m.* dew; spray, sprinkling; shower; spoon-drift.
roción, *n.m.* (*naut.*) breaker (*sea*).
rococó, *a.* rococo.
rocoso, -sa, *a.* rocky.
rocote, *n.m.* (*Hisp. Am.*) capsicum.
rocha, *n.f.* clearing.
rochela, *n.f.* (*Col., Ven.*) din, uproar.
rocho, *n.m.* roc (*a fabulous bird*).
roda, *n.f.* (*naut.*) stem.
rodaballo, *n.m.* (*ichth.*) turbot; ***rodaballo menor,*** brill.
rodada (1), *n.f.* rut, cart-track, wheel-track.
rodadero, -ra, *a.* rolling *or* wheeling easily.
rodadizo, -za [RODADERO].
rodado, -da (2), *a.* dapple, dappled; round; fluent, easy; (*min.*) scattered (*fragments of ore*); ***tráfico rodado,*** traffic, vehicles; ***la cosa vino rodada,*** the matter came up quite spontaneously *or* naturally; everything worked out beautifully.
rodador, -ra, *a.* rolling, rolling down. — *n.m.* mosquito; sun-fish.
rodadura, *n.f.* rolling; rut; tread (*of a wheel*).
rodaja, *n.f.* small wheel; disk; rowel (*of a spur*); castor; (round) slice.
rodaje, *n.m.* (*set of*) wheels; filming, shooting; running in; ***en rodaje,*** being filmed; (*motor.*) running in.
rodal, *n.m.* place, spot, patch.
rodamiento, *n.m.* (ball *or* roller) bearing.
Ródano, *n.m.* Rhone.
rodante, *a.* rolling; ***material rodante,*** rolling stock.
rodapelo, *n.m.* rubbing against the grain; (*coll.*) scuffle, affray.
rodapié, *n.m.* skirting; foot rail; fringe, dado.
rodaplancha, *n.f.* main ward (*of a key*).
rodar [4], *v.t.* to roll, roll along, roll down; to take, shoot, film; to run in; ***¡ruede la bola!*** on with the motley! — *v.i.* to roll, roll along, roll down; to go, run *or* tumble around; to wander *or* knock about; (*aer.*) to taxi; (*coll.*) ***echarlo todo a rodar,*** to spoil, ruin *or* wreck everything.
Rodas, *n.f.* Rhodes.
rodeabrazo, (a), *adv.* overarm.
rodeador, -ra, *a.* surrounding.
rodear, *v.t.* to surround; to encircle, enclose; to go round, skirt; to round up. — *v.i.* to go round, make a detour.
rodela, *n.f.* round shield, buckler.
rodelero, *n.m.* soldier bearing a buckler.
rodenal, *n.m.* spinney of red pines.
rodeno, -na, *a.* red, reddish.
rodeo, *n.m.* detour, roundabout way; rodeo, round-up; subterfuge; ***sin rodeos,*** straight to the point; ***andarse con rodeos,*** to beat about the bush.
rodeón, *n.m.* long detour; complete turn.
rodero (1), **-ra,** *a.* relating to wheels. — *n.f.* rut, cart-track.
rodero (2), *n.m.* collector of pasturage fee.
Rodesia, *n.f.* Rhodesia.
rodesiano, *a., n.m.f.* (native) of Rhodesia.
rodete, *n.m.* bun *or* knot of plaited hair; padded ring (*for carrying loads on the head*); fifth wheel (*of carriage*); band pulley; belt pulley, circular ward (*in a lock*); (*mech.*) horizontal water wheel.
rodezno, *n.m.* cogwheel; (*hydrost.*) turbine.
rodezuela, *n.f.* tiny wheel.
ródico, -ca, *a.* (*chem.*) rhœadic.
rodilla, *n.f.* knee; ward (*in a lock*); dusting cloth; ***de rodillas,*** on one's knees, kneeling; ***hincar*** or ***doblar la rodilla,*** to go down on one knee; ***hincarse de rodillas,*** to kneel down.
rodillada, *n.f.* push with the knee; kneeling position.
rodillazo, *n.m.* push with the knee.
rodillera, *n.f.* knee-cap, knee-guard, knee-patch; bagging of trousers at the knee; injury of the knees of horses.
rodillo, *n.m.* roller; rolling-pin; inking-roller; road-roller; platen (*of typewriter*).
rodilludo, -da, *a.* big-kneed.
rodio, *n.m.* (*chem.*) rhodium.
rodo, *n.m.* roller.
rododafne, *n.f.* (*bot.*) rosebay, daphne.
rododendro, *n.m.* (*bot.*) rhododendron.
Rodolfo, *n.m.* Rudolph, Ralph.
rodomiel, *n.m.* rose-juice with honey.
rodrigar [B], *v.t.* to prop up (*vines*).
rodrigazón, *n.m.* time for propping vines.
Rodrigo, *n.m.* Roderick.
rodrigón, *n.m.* vine-prop; stake; (*coll.*) old servant who waits upon ladies.
roedor, -ra, *a.* gnawing, rodent. — *n.m.* rodent.
roedura, *n.f.* gnawing, nibbling; eating away; place that has been nibbled.
roela, *n.f.* button of crude silver *or* gold.
roer [29], *v.t.* to gnaw, nibble, gnaw at; to eat away.
roete, *n.m.* pomegranate wine.
rogación, *n.f.* request, petition; (*pl.* **rogaciones**) litany, rogation.
rogador, -ra, *n.m.f.* supplicant, petitioner.
rogar [4B], *v.t., v.i.* to beg; to pray; ***no hacerse (de) rogar,*** not to have to be asked twice; ***a Dios rogando y con el mazo dando,*** pray to God and keep your powder dry.
rogativo, -va, *a.* supplicatory. — *n.f.* supplication, prayer; (*eccles.*) rogation.
rogatorio, -ria, *a.* rogatory.
rogo, *n.m.* fire, pyre.
roído, -da, *a.* stingy; rotten.
rojal, *a.* red, reddish. — *n.m.* red land *or* soil.
rojear, *v.i.* to redden; to blush.
rojete, *n.m.* rouge.
rojez, rojeza, *n.f.* redness.
rojizo, -za, *a.* reddish, ruddy.
rojo, -ja, *a.* red; ruddy; red, ginger (*hair*). — *n.m.* red colour; ***al rojo,*** red-hot; ***al rojo vivo,*** white hot.
rojura, *n.f.* redness.
rol, *n.m.* roll, list; (*naut.*) muster-roll.
rolar, *v.i.* (*naut.*) to veer around.
Rolando, Roldán, *n.m.* Roland.
roldana, *n.f.* (*naut.*) sheave.
rolde, *n.m.* (*prov.*) circle, knot (*of persons*).
rolla, *n.f.* collar (*of draught-horse*); (*Col.*) nurse.
rollar, *v.t.* to roll.
rollete, *n.m.* small roller.
rollizo, -za, *a.* plump, chubby. — *n.m.* log.
rollo, *n.m.* roller; rolling-pin; log; yoke-pad; column of stone, round stone, round pillar; (*law*) roll; (*coll.*) bore, pain-in-the-neck.
rollón, *n.m.* fine bran.
rollona, *n.f.* (*coll.*) nurse.
Roma, *n.f.* Rome; ***cuando a Roma fueres, haz como vieres,*** when in Rome, do as the Romans do.
romadizarse [C], *v.r.* to catch cold.
romadizo, *n.m.* cold.
romana (1), *n.f.* steelyard; scales.
romanador, *n.m.* weigh-master.

romanar, *v.t.* to weigh with a steelyard.
romance, *a.* Romance. — *n.m.* Spanish language; romance, tale of chivalry; (*historic*) ballad; poem in octosyllabic metre with alternate assonance; ***hablar en romance,*** to speak plainly; ***en buen romance,*** in honest-to-goodness language; (*pl.*) prattle, drivel.
romancear, *v.t.* to translate into the vernacular. — *v.i.* to take a Romance form.
romancero, *n.m.* collection of ballads *or* romances; romancer.
romancesco, -ca, *a.* romantic, novelistic.
romancillo, *n.m.* short romance *or* ballad.
romancista, *n.m.* author who writes in the vernacular.
romanear, *v.t.* to weigh with a steelyard; to shift part of (*the stowage*). — *v.i.* to weigh more.
romaneo, *n.m.* weighing with steelyard; (*naut.*) arranging the stowage.
romanero, *n.m.* weigh-master.
romanesco, *a.* Roman; novelistic.
romanía, (de), *adv.* crestfallen.
románico, -ca, *a.* Romanesque; Romance.
romanilla (1), *n.f.* (*Ven.*) dining-room screen.
romanillo, -lla (2), *a.* round-hand; (*print.*) ***letra romanilla,*** roman.
romanismo, *n.m.* Romanism; Romance philology.
romanista, *n.m.* Romanist; Romance philologist.
romanística, *n.f.* Romance scholarship.
romanizar [C], *v.t.* to Romanize; to Latinize. — **romanizarse,** *v.r.* to become Romanized *or* Latinized.
romano, -na (2), *a.* Roman; tabby (cat); ***a la romana,*** in the Roman fashion—*n.m.f.* Roman (*person*).
romanticismo, *n.m.* romanticism.
romántico, -ca, *a.* romantic.
romanza, *n.f.* (*mus.*) romance, romanza.
romanzar [C], *v.t.* to translate into the vernacular.
romanzón, *n.m.* long and tedious romance.
romaza, *n.f.* (*bot.*) sorrel.
rombal, *a.* rhombic.
rombo, *n.m.* rhomb; lozenge, diamond.
romboedro, *n.m.* (*geom.*) rhombohedron.
romboidal, *a.* rhomboidal.
romboide, *n.m.* (*geom.*) rhomboid.
romera, *n.f.* (*bot.*) rosemary-leaved cistus.
romeraje, *n.m.* pilgrimage.
romeral, *n.m.* growth of rosemary.
romería, *n.f.* pilgrimage; gathering at a shrine on saint's day; crowd, gathering.
romero, *n.m.* palmer, pilgrim; (*bot.*) rosemary; (*ichth.*) pilot-fish; whiting.
romo, -ma, *a.* blunt; flat-nosed; (*fig.*) dull, stupid.
rompecabezas, *n.m. inv.* puzzle, jigsaw puzzle; riddle; sling-shot.
rompecoches, *n.m. inv.* everlasting prunella.
rompedero, -ra, *a.* brittle, easily broken. — *n.f.* iron punch, blacksmith's punch; powder screen.
rompedor, -ra, *n.m.f.* breaker, destroyer, crusher.
rompedura, *n.f.* break, breaking, breakage.
rompegalas, *n.m. inv.* (*coll.*) slovenly person.
rompehielos, *n.m. inv.* icebreaker (*ship*).
rompenueces, *n.m. inv.* (*Hisp. Am.*) nut-cracker.
rompeolas, *n.m. inv.* breakwater, jetty, mole.
romper [*pres. p.* **rompiendo,** *p.p.* **roto**], *v.t.* to break, smash, cause breakage in; to tear, tear up; to break through; to plough for the first time; ***no se rompe, pero puede romper*** (***otras cosas***), it won't break itself, but it can cause damage in other things. — *v.i.* to break *or* burst open; ***de rompe y rasga,*** tough proposition, dauntless; ***rompió a cantar,*** he burst into song. — **romperse,** *v.r.* to break, smash; to tear, rip; to snap; to wear out; ***romperse la crisma,*** to break one's neck; ***romperse la cabeza,*** to rack one's brains.
rompesacos, *n.m. inv.* (*bot.*) goat grass.
rompesquinas, *n.m. inv.* bully, corner loafer.
rompezaragüelles, *n.m.* (*Hisp. Am.*) aromatic and medicinal plant.
rompible, *a.* breakable.
rompido, *n.m.* ground newly broken.
rompiente, *a.* breaking. — *n.f.* reef, shoal.
rompimiento, *n.m.* break, breaking, breaking off; (*theat.*) open drop scene; (*art*) opening in the background of a painting; (*min.*) drift, driftway.
ron, *n.m.* rum.
ronca (1), *n.f.* threat, menace, brag, boast; halberd; cry of a buck at rutting time; (*coll.*) ***echar roncas,*** to menace, threaten.
roncador, -ra (1), *a.* snoring. — *n.m.f.* snorer. — *n.m.* (*ichth.*) roncador, croaker.
roncadora (2), *n.f.* (*Arg., Bol., Ec.*) spur with large wheel.
roncal, *n.m.* (*orn.*) nightingale.
roncar [A], *v.i.* to snore; to roar; to cry (*rutting time of deer etc.*); to brag, boast; to threaten.
ronce, *n.m.* coaxing, cajoling.
roncear, *v.i.* to kill time, fool around; to wheedle, cajole; to sail slowly.
roncería, *n.f.* time-killing, fooling around; coaxing; cajoling, wheedling; sluggish sailing.
roncero, -ra, *a.* slow; unwilling, grumbling; wheedling, coaxing, cajoling; slow-sailing.
ronco, -ca (2), *a.* hoarse, husky.
roncón, *n.m.* drone (*of a bagpipe*).
roncha, *n.f.* weal; bruise; trick; round slice.
ronchar, *v.t.* to crunch (*food*), chew noisily. — *v.i.* to make weals.
ronchón, *n.m.* large weal, welt.
ronda, *n.f.* round; night-patrol; beat; night serenaders; ***coger la ronda a,*** to catch in the act.
rondador, *n.m.* watchman, night-guard; night wanderer; serenader.
rondalla, *n.f.* fable, story.
rondar, *v.t.* to go round; to patrol; to hang over (*as a threat*); to hang *or* hover round; to serenade. — *v.i.* to go round; to patrol, go the rounds; to hang *or* prowl around; to go serenading; ***las temperaturas rondan los 30 grados,*** you get temperatures of around 30 degrees.
rondel, *n.m.* (*poet.*) rondel.
rondeño, -ña, *a., n.m.f.* (native) of Ronda. — *n.f.* song *or* dance of Ronda.
rondí, rondiz, *n.m.* face *or* table (*of a precious stone*).
rondín, *n.m.* corporal's rounds; watchman (*in an arsenal*).
rondó, *n.m.* rondo.
rondón, (de), *adv.* abruptly, suddenly, without so much as a by-your-leave.
ronfea, *n.f.* broad sword.
rongigata, *n.f.* pinwheel.
ronquear, *v.i.* to be hoarse.
ronquedad, *n.f.* hoarseness.
ronquera, *n.f.* hoarseness.
ronquido, *n.m.* harsh, rough sound; snore.
ronquillo, -lla, *a.* slightly hoarse.
ronronear, *v.i.* to purr.
ronroneo, *n.m.* purr, purring.
ronza, *n.f.* (*naut.*) lee; ***a la ronza,*** to leeward.
ronzal, *n.m.* halter; (*naut.*) purchase rope.
ronzar [C], *v.t.* (*naut.*) to lever up *or* along; to crunch.
roña, *n.f.* scab, mange, manginess; crust of filth; (pine) bark; (plant) rust; (*coll.*) stinginess. — *n.m.f.* (*coll.*) stingy individual.
roñada, *n.f.* (*naut.*) garland.
ronería, roñosería, *n.f.* stinginess.
roñoso, -sa, *a.* scabby, mangy; filthy; rusty; (*coll.* stingy.

ropa, *n.f.* clothes, clothing; dry goods; ***ropa blanca,*** linen; ***ropa de cama,*** bed linen; bedclothes; ***ropa interior,*** underwear; ***ropa sucia,*** laundry; ***a quema ropa,*** point-blank; ***nadar y guardar la ropa,*** to (want to) have one's cake and eat it.
ropaje, *n.m.* clothes, clothing; garb; robe, gown; drapery.
ropavejería, *n.f.* old-clothes shop.
ropavejero, *n.m.* old-clothes man.
ropería, *n.f.* clothes-store; wardrobe, wardrobe-keeper.
ropero, *n.m.* vestiary, wardrobe-keeper; salesman; wardrobe, locker.
ropeta, *n.f.* short garment.
ropilla, *n.f.* doublet; (*fig., coll.*) ***dar una ropilla,*** to give a friendly reproof.
ropón, *n.m.* loose over-gown; (*Chi.*) lady's riding habit.
roque, *n.m.* rook (*in chess*); ***ni rey ni roque,*** not a soul.
roqueda, *n.f.* rocky place.
roquedo, *n.m.* rock, boulder.
roqueño, -ña, *a.* rocky, full of rocks; hard, flinty.
roquero, -ra, *a.* rocky, situated on rocks.
roqués, *n.m.* black falcon.
roqueta, *n.f.* turret in a fortress.
roquete, *n.m.* (*eccles.*) rochet; barbed spearhead; (*artill.*) ramrod, rammer.
rorcual, *n.m.* (*zool.*) rorqual (*whale*).
rorro, *n.m.* babe, infant.
ros, *n.m.* (*mil.*) shako.
rosa, *n.f.* [ROSO].
rosáceo, -cea, *a.* rosaceous. — *n.f.pl.* (**rosáceas**) Rosaceæ.
rosada (1), *n.f.* hoar-frost, rime.
rosado, -da (2), *a.* rose, rosy, pink; relating to *or* made up of roses; ***agua rosada,*** rose-water; ***miel rosada,*** honey of roses.
rosal, *n.m.* (*bot.*) rose bush; ***rosal castellano,*** red rose; ***rosal de cien hojas,*** cabbage-rose; ***rosal perruno,*** dog-rose.
rosariero, *n.m.* maker and seller of rosaries.
rosario, *n.m.* rosary; string; chain pump; (*coll.*) backbone; ***acabar como el rosario de la aurora,*** to break up in disorder, end in uproar.
rosbif, *n.m.* roast beef.
rosca, *n.f.* coil, ring; screw-thread; twist, spiral line *or* motion; circular badge of Spanish students; (*naut.*) flake of a cable; (*Chi.*) yoke-pad; ***rosca de pan,*** twisted loaf; ***hacer la rosca*** (***del galgo***), to curl up and go to sleep; ***hacer la rosca a,*** to wheedle; ***pasarse de rosca,*** to go too far.
roscado, -da, *a.* ring-shaped. — *n.m.* threading.
roscar [A], *v.t.* to cut a screw-thread in.
rosco, *n.m.* ring-shaped piece of pastry.
roscón, *n.m.* large screw; round loaf; large bun.
róseo, -sea, *a.* rosy, roseate.
roséola, *n.f.* (*med.*) roseola, German measles.
rosero, -ra, *n.m.f.* collector of saffron flowers; (*Ec.*) dessert on Corpus Christi day.
roseta, *n.f.* shoe-tassel; rosette; bloom of the cheeks; nozzle, watering-can rose; rose-shaped jewel; popcorn.
rosetón, *n.m.* (*arch.*) rose-window; rosette.
rosicler, *n.m.* pink of dawn; ruby silver.
rosillo, -lla, *a.* clear red; roan (*horse*).
rosmarino, -na, *a.* light red. — *n.m.* (*bot.*) rosemary.
rosmaro, *n.m.* (*zool.*) manatee, sea-cow.
roso, -sa, *a.* red, rosy; threadbare; ***a roso y velloso,*** without distinction. — *n.f.* rose; rose-colour; rose diamond; rosy appearance; (*arch.*) rose-window; rosette; flower of saffron; ***rosa náutica*** or ***rosa de los vientos,*** rose of a mariner's compass, compass.
rosoli, *n.m.* rosolio.
rosones, *n.m.pl.* bots.
rosqueado, -da, *a.* twisted.
rosquete, *n.m.* ring-shaped fritter.
rosquilla, *n.f.* ring-shaped fritter; (*ent.*) grub.
rostrado, -da, *a.* rostrated.
rostral, *a.* rostral.
rostrituerto, -ta, *a.* sullen-looking.
rostro, *n.m.* face; rostrum; beak; ***rostro a rostro,*** face to face; ***hacer rostro a,*** to face, face up to.
rota, *n.f.* [ROTO].
rotación, *n.f.* rotation; ***rotación de cultivos,*** rotation of crops.
rotante, *a.* revolving.
rotar, *v.i.* to revolve.
rotativo, -va, *a.* rotary. — *n.f.* (*print.*) rotary press; (*fig.*) the press.
rotatorio, -ria, *a.* rotatory.
roten, *n.m.* (*bot.*) rattan; rattan cane.
rotería, *n.f.* (*Chi.*) rabble.
roto, -ta, *a.* broken, shattered; torn, ragged; debauched, gone to the dogs. — *n.m.f.* down-and-out; good-for-nothing. — *n.f.* (*mil.*) rout, defeat; (*naut.*) course; (*eccles.*) rota; (*bot.*) rattan; ***de rota*** (***batida***), of a sudden; with total ruin.
rotonda, *n.f.* rotunda; back part of a coach; (*traffic*) roundabout.
rotoso, -sa, *a.* (*Arg., Chi.*) torn; ragged, in tatters.
rótula, *n.f.* (*anat.*) rotula, knee-cap; (*pharm.*) troche, lozenge.
rotulación, *n.f.* labelling, lettering.
rotular, *v.t.* to label, letter, give a title *or* heading to.
rotulata, *n.f.* label, title, mark; collection of labels.
rótulo, *n.m.* label, tag, (*Am.*) sticker; title, lettering; sign-board; poster.
rotunda, *n.f.* [ROTUNDO].
rotundamente, *adv.* categorically, roundly.
rotundidad, *n.f.* roundness; rotundity.
rotundo, -da, *a.* round; rotund; full, sonorous; flat, categorical. — *n.f.* rotunda.
rotura, *n.f.* breaking; breaking off; rupture; fracture; break, crack; rent, tear.
roturación, *n.f.* (*agric.*) breaking new ground.
roturar, *v.t.* (*agric.*) to break (*new ground*).
roya, *n.f.* (*bot.*) rust, red blight, mildew.
roza, *n.f.* stubbing; clearing, grubbing up; ground cleared of briers.
rozadero, *n.m.* stubbing-place; (*mech.*) bearing-plate.
rozado, -da, *a.* stubbed, cleared; chilled, frappé (*of a beverage*).
rozador, -ra, *n.m.f.* stubber, weeder.
rozadura, *n.f.* friction, rubbing; chafing; chafe, gall; (*bot.*) punkwood.
rozagante, *a.* showy, pompous; elegant, magnificent; strapping; in blooming health; flowing, sweeping (*gown, robe*); looking superb.
rozamiento, *n.m.* rubbing, friction, chafing.
rozar [C], *v.t.* to grub, stub, weed, clear; to cut and gather; to graze, browse; to scrape, rub, chafe, gall; to skim over. — **rozarse,** *v.r.* to interfere, knock one foot against another; to stammer, falter; to hobnob, be on close terms; to have a resemblance *or* connection; to fray; to graze oneself.
roznar, *v.t.* to crunch, crack with the teeth. — *v.i.* to bray.
roznido, *n.m.* braying; crunching noise.
rozno, *n.m.* little ass.
rozo, *n.m.* stubbing, weeding; chip of wood; brushwood.
rozón, *n.m.* short, broad and thick scythe.
rúa, *n.f.* street, road; highroad; ***hacer la rúa,*** to walk *or* ride around town.
ruán, *n.m.* printed cotton cloth made in Rouen (France).

ruana (1), *n.f.* (*Col.*, *Ven.*) square and heavy poncho.
ruano, -na (2), *a.* prancing; round, circular; sorrel-coloured, roan (*horse*).
ruante, *a.* walking through the streets.
ruar, *v.t.*, *v.i.* to ride *or* walk through the streets; to flirt, court in the street.
rubefacción, *n.f.* rubefaction.
rubefaciente, *a.* rubefying, rubefacient.
Rubén, *n.m.* Reuben.
rúbeo, -bea, *a.* ruby, reddish, ruddy.
rubéola, *n.f.* rubeola, German measles.
rubeta, *n.f.* toad.
rubí, *n.m.* ruby, (*Am.*) agate; red colour, redness of the lips.
rubia (1), *n.f.* (*bot.*) madder; (*motor.*, *coll.*) estate car, (*Am.*) station wagon; (*coll.*) peseta.
rubial, *a.* reddish. — *n.m.* madder field.
rubiales, *n.m.f. inv.* (*coll.*) blondie, blond-top.
rubicán, *a.* fairish.
rubicela, *n.f.* reddish topaz.
rubicundez, *n.f.* rubicundity, ruddiness.
rubicundo, -da, *a.* red, rubicund; blond(e), golden-red; rosy with health.
rubiera, *n.f.* (*Ven.*) mischief, tomfoolery; (*P.R.*) merry-making, carousal.
rubificar, *v.t.* to rubefy, make red.
rubín, rubinejo, *n.m.* ruby.
rubio, -bia (2), *a.* golden; blond(e), fair. — *n.m.f.* fair, blond(e) (*person*). — *n.m.* red gurnard.
rubión, *a.* reddish (*wheat*).
rublo, *n.m.* rouble.
rubor, *n.m.* blush, flush; bashfulness, shame.
ruborizar [C], *v.t.* to make blush. — **ruborizarse,** *v.r.* to blush, flush.
ruboroso, -sa, *a.* shameful, bashful.
rúbrica, *n.f.* red mark; rubric; flourish to a signature; (*coll.*) ***de rúbrica,*** according to rule *or* custom.
rubricante, *a.* signing.
rubricar, *v.t.* to add one's flourish to, sign with a flourish; to provide the finishing flourish to; to sign and seal; to certify to.
rubriquista, *n.m.* rubrician.
rubro, -ra, *a.* red, reddish. — *n.m.* (*Hisp. Am.*) title, heading; item.
ruc, *n.m.* roc (*a fabulous bird*).
ruca (1), *n.f.* (*Arg.*, *Chi.*) hut, cabin.
rucio, -cia, *a.* silver-grey; grey-haired.
ruco, -ca (2), *a.* (*Cent. Am.*) old, worthless.
rucho, *n.m.* donkey.
ruda (1), *n.f.* (*bot.*) rue.
rudeza, *n.f.* roughness; coarseness, crudeness; harshness, hardness.
rudimental, *a.* rudimental.
rudimentario, -ria, *a.* rudimentary.
rudimento, *n.m.* rudiment.
rudo, -da (2), *a.* rough; coarse, crude; harsh, hard.
rueca, *n.f.* distaff; twist, winding.
rueda, *n.f.* wheel; castor, roller; ring, circle (*of people*); (*ichth.*) sun-fish; (*peacock's*) spread tail; round slice; turn, time; hoop (*for a skirt*); three-handed billiard game; ***rueda de andar,*** treadmill; ***rueda de prensa,*** press conference; ***rueda de presos,*** line-up, identification parade; ***hacer la rueda a,*** to pay court to; ***comulgar con ruedas de molino,*** to swallow *or* believe anything.
ruedo (1), *n.m.* rotation, turn; circumference; circuit; edge, border; hem lining; circle, round, ring; bull-ring; round mat; ***a todo ruedo,*** at all events.
ruedo (2), **ruede,** *pres. indic.*, *pres. subj.* [RODAR].
ruego (1), *n.m.* prayer; request, petition; entreaty.
ruego (2), **ruegue,** *pres. indic.*, *pres. subj.* [ROGAR].
ruejo, *n.m.* mill-wheel; ground-roller.
ruello, *n.m.* (*prov.*) ground-roller.
rufián, *n.m.* pimp, procurer, pander; rascal.
rufianear, *v.t.* to pimp; to live a rogue's life.
rufianería, *n.f.* pimping; roguery.
rufianesco, -ca, *a.* of pimps; of scoundrels. — *n.f.* (*mob of*) pimps *or* scoundrels.
rufo, -fa, *a.* carroty, red-haired; frizzed, curled.
ruga, *n.f.* wrinkle.
rugar [B], *v.t.* to wrinkle.
rugido, *n.m.* roar; bellow; rumble.
rugiente, *a.* roaring.
ruginoso, -sa, *a.* rusty, covered with rust.
rugir [E], *v.i.* to roar; to bellow; to rumble; to be bruited abroad.
rugosidad, *n.f.* rugosity.
rugoso, -sa, *a.* rugose; wrinkled.
ruibarbo, *n.m.* (*bot.*) rhubarb.
ruido, *n.m.* noise; sound; fuss; ***hacer*** or ***meter ruido,*** to kick up a row; to create a stir; ***querer ruido,*** to be looking for a fight; ***mucho ruido y pocas nueces,*** much ado about nothing.
ruidoso, -sa, *a.* noisy, loud; sensational.
ruin, *a.* mean, low, base; poor, sorry; wretched; niggardly, stingy; treacherous, rascally; vicious (*of animals*). — *n.m.* rascal, scoundrel; tip (*of cat's tail*); ***en nombrando el ruin de Roma, luego asoma,*** talk of the Devil.
ruina, *n.f.* ruin, fall, downfall; wreck; ***amenazar ruina,*** to (appear to) be on the point of collapse, be in a shaky state; ***estar hecho una ruina,*** to be a wreck.
ruinar, *v.t.* to ruin, destroy. — **ruinarse,** *v.r.* to go to ruin.
ruindad, *n.f.* baseness, vileness; stinginess; viciousness (*of animals*); bad turn, mean *or* base action.
ruinoso, -sa, *a.* ruinous, dilapidated; baneful.
ruipóntico, *n.m.* garden rhubarb.
ruiseñor, *n.m.* (*orn.*) nightingale.
rujiada, *n.m.* (*prov.*) heavy shower; (*fig.*) reprimand.
rular, *v.i.* to roll.
ruleta, *n.f.* roulette.
ruló, *n.m.* (*print.*) inking roller; brayer.
rulo, *n.m.* ball, bowl; stone in oil-mills; road-roller hair-curler.
rulota, *n.f.* caravan, (*Am.*) trailer.
ruma, *n.f.* (*Arg.*, *Chi.*, *Ec.*) heap, pile, mass.
Rumania, *n.f.* Rumania *or* Romania.
rumano, -na, *a.*, *n.m.f.* Rumanian *or* Romanian— *n.m.* Rumanian *or* Romanian (*language*).
rumba, *n.m.* (*Hisp. Am.*) rumba.
rumbada, *n.f.* wale of a row galley.
rumbar, *v.i.* (*prov.*) to be lavish, magnificent; (*Col.*) to buzz, hum; (*Chi.*) to find one's bearings. — *v.t.* (*Hond.*) to throw, cast, fling.
rumbatela, *n.f.* (*Cub.*, *Mex.*, *coll.*) feast, blow-out, revelry.
rumbático, -ca, *a.* lavish.
rumbeador, *n.m.* (*Arg.*) guide.
rumbear, *v.i.* (*Arg.*) to find one's bearings; (*Cub.*) to carouse, revel.
rumbo, *n.m.* course, direction, bearing; road, route, way; (*coll.*) pomp, ostentation, show; generosity, lavishness; (*naut.*) scuttle; (*her.*) rustre; (*Gaut.*) revel, carousal; (*Col.*) small humming bird; ***abatir el rumbo,*** to fall to leeward; ***con rumbo a,*** bound for, in the direction of, heading for; ***hacer rumbo a,*** to sail for.
rumbón, -bona, *a.* (*coll.*) open-handed, lavish; (in) grand style.
rumboso, -sa, *a.* open-handed, lavish; (in) grand style.
rumí, *n.m.* (*hist.*) appellative given to the Christians by the Moors.
rumia, *n.f.* rumination, chewing the cud.
rumiador, -ra, *a.* ruminant.
rumiadura, *n.f.* rumination.

rumiante, *a.* ruminant; reflecting, musing. — *n.m.pl.* (**rumiantes**) Ruminantia, ruminants.
rumiar, *v.t.*, *v.i.* to ruminate; to meditate, muse.
rumión, -miona, *a.* ruminative, pondering.
rumo, *n.m.* first hoop of a cask.
rumor, *n.m.* rumbling sound, murmur; buzz, noise of voices; rumour.
rumoroso, -sa, *a.* murmurous.
rumpiata, *n.f.* (*Chi.*) shrub.
runa, *n.f.* [RUNO].
runcho, *n.m.* (*Col.*) opossum.
rundún, *n.m.* (*Arg.*) small humming-bird; toy.
runfla, runflada, *n.f.* series, succession (*of things*).
rúnico, -ca, *a.* runic.
runo, -na, *a.* runic.—*n.f.* rune, runic character.
runrún, *n.m.* (*coll.*) rumour, report; (*Arg.*, *Chi.*) rattle; horn call; (*Chi.*) wading-bird.
runrunearse, *v.r.* to be rumoured, be whispered abroad.
ruña, ruñadera, *n.f.* croze.
ruñar, *v.t.* to croze.
rupestre, *a.* rupestrian, rock (*plants, paintings*).
rupia, *n.f.* rupee; (*med.*) rupia.
rupicabra, *n.f.* chamois-goat.
ruptura, *n.f.* rupture, breaking off.
rural, *a.* rural.
rurrupata, *n.f.* (*Chi.*) lullaby.
rus, *n.m.* (*bot.*) sumach.
rusco, *n.m.* (*bot.*) butcher's-broom.
Rusia, *n.f.* Russia; ***la Rusia Soviética,*** Soviet Russia.
rusiente, *a.* reddish, becoming red-hot.
rusificar [A], *v.t.* to Russianize.
ruso, -sa, *a.*, *n.m.f.* Russian.—*n.m.* Russian (*language*).
rústica (1), (**en**), *a.* paper-covered, paper-backed.
rusticación, *n.f.* country life, retirement to the country.
rustical, *a.* rustic.
rusticano, -na, *a.* wild (*of plants*).
rusticar [A], *v.t.* to rusticate.
rusticidad, *n.f.* rusticity; uncouthness.
rústico, -ca (2), *a.* rustic; uncouth; vulgar (*Latin*).
rustiquez, rustiqueza, *n.f.* rusticity.
Rut, *n.f.* Ruth.
ruta, *n.f.* route.
rutenio, *n.m.* (*chem.*) ruthenium.
rutero, -ra, rutista, *n.m.f.* experienced driver; long-distance driver.
rutilante, *a.* brilliant, flashing.
rutilar, *v.i.* (*poet.*) to shine, glitter.
rútilo, -la, *a.* shining, sparkling.
rutina, *n.f.* routine; rut; ***por rutina,*** from (mere) force of habit, unthinkingly.
rutinario, -ria, *a.* routine; from mere force of habit, unthinking. — *n.m.f.* routinist.
rutinero, -ra, *a.* [RUTINARIO].
ruzafa, *n.f.* garden, park.

S

S, s, *n.f.* letter S, s.
sábado, *n.m.* Saturday; sabbath; ***sábado de gloria,*** Holy Saturday.
sabalar, *n.m.* net for catching shad.
sabalera, *n.f.* fire-grate (*of a furnace*); fishing-net.
sabalero, *n.m.* shad-fisher.
sábalo, *n.m.* (*ichth.*) shad.
sábana, *n.f.* sheet (*of a bed*); altar-cloth; ***pegársele a uno las sábanas,*** to oversleep, stay in bed until late.
sabana, *n.f.* (*Hisp. Am.*) savannah.
sabandija, *n.f.* grub, insect; vermin.
sabanero, -ra, *a.* (of the) savannah. — *n.m.f.* savannah dweller. — *n.m.* savannah lark; savannah snake.
sabanilla, *n.f.* small sheet; napkin; kerchief; altar-cloth; (*Chi.*) bedspread, coverlet.
sabañón, *n.m.* chilblain; ***comer como un sabañón,*** to eat like a horse.
sabara, *n.f.* (*Ven.*) very light fog.
sabatario, -ria, *a.* sabbatarian.
sabático, -ca, *a.* sabbatical.
sabatino, -na, *a.* sabbatine. — *n.f.* divine service of Saturday; (*Chi.*) flogging, drubbing.
sabedor, -ra, *a.* — ***de,*** aware (of), appraised (of), knowing (about).
saber, *n.m.* learning, knowledge, lore. — [80] *v.t.* to know, be aware of; to learn, hear (about); to be able to, know how to; ***sabe latín,*** he's as smart as they come; ***saber cuántas son cinco,*** to know what's what; ***lo supo después,*** he heard, learned about it later; ***no supo dominarse,*** he was unable to control himself, he failed to control himself; ***a saber,*** to wit, i.e., namely; ***que yo sepa,*** to my knowledge, as far as I know. — *v.i.* to taste (***a,*** of). — **saberse,** *v.r.* to know; ***saberse de memoria,*** to know off by heart, have off pat; ***sabérselas todas,*** to know all the answers.
sabicú, *n.m.* (*Cub., bot.*) sabicu, horseflesh mahogany.
sabidillo, -lla, *a., n.m.f.* little pedant, know-all. — *n.f.* blue-stocking.
sabido, -da, *a.* well-informed, learned; known.
sabiduría, *n.f.* learning, knowledge, wisdom.
sabiendas, (a), *adv.* knowingly, wittingly, consciously.
sabiente, *a.* knowledgeable, knowing.
sabihondez, *n.f.* (*coll.*) know-it-all attitude.
sabihondo, -da, *a., n.m.f.* know-it-all.
sabina, *n.f.* (*bot.*) savin.
sabinar, *n.m.* clump of savins.
sabio, -bia, *a., n.m.f.* sage, wise, learned (person).
sablazo, *n.m.* sabre-stroke; (*coll.*) ***dar un sablazo a,*** to touch for money.
sable, *a.* (*her.*) sable, black. — *n.m.* sabre, cutlass; (*Cub.*) a long, flat silvery fish.
sablista, *n.m.f.* sponger.
sablón, *n.m.* coarse sand.
saboga, *n.f.* (*ichth.*) shad.
sabogal, *n.m.* shad-catching net.
saboneta, *n.f.* hunting-case watch, hunter.
sabor, *n.m.* taste, flavour, relish, savour; dash, zest; ***a sabor,*** to one's liking; ***sabor local,*** local colour; (*pl.* **sabores**) beads on bit (*of bridle*).
saboreamiento, *n.m.* relish, relishing.
saborear, *v.t.* to savour, relish; to flavour. — **saborearse,** *v.r.* to take pleasure *or* relish (***en,*** in).
saboreo, *n.m.* savouring; relishing.
saborete, *n.m.* slight flavour *or* taste.
sabotaje, *n.m.* sabotage.
saboteador, -ra, *n.m.f.* saboteur.
sabotear, *v.t.* to sabotage.
Saboya, *n.f.* Savoy.
saboyana (1), *n.f.* apron; paste *or* pie.
saboyano, -na (2), *a., n.m.f.* Savoyard.
sabroso, -sa, *a.* palatable, tasty, delicious, luscious; (*fig.*) meaty; (*fig.*) saucy.
sabucal, sabugal, *n.m.* clump of elders.
sabuco, sabugo, *n.m.* (*bot.*) elder.
sabueso, *n.m.* bloodhound; (*fig.*) sleuth.
sábulo, *n.m.* gravel, coarse sand.
sabuloso, -sa, *a.* sabulous, sandy, gravelly.
saca, *n.f.* sack, bag; exportation; extraction, drawing out; authorized copy; ***estar de saca,*** to be on sale; (*coll.*) to be ready for marriage.
sacabalas, *n.m. inv.* bullet-extractor.
sacabotas, *n.m. inv.* boot-jack.
sacabrocas, *n.m. inv.* tack-drawer, pincers.
sacabuche, *n.m.* (*mus.*) sackbut; sackbut-player; (*naut.*) hand pump; nincompoop.
sacacorchos, *n.m. inv.* corkscrew.
sacada, *n.f.* district separated from a province.
sacadinero(s), *n.m.* (*coll.*) catch-penny.
sacador, -ra, *n.m.f.* extractor, drawer; (*print.* delivery table.
sacadura, *n.f.* sloping cut; (*Chi.*) taking out, extracting.
sacafilásticas, *n.f. inv.* (*artill.*) gun-spike, priming-wire.
sacaliña, *n.f.* trick, cunning.
sacamanchas, *n.m. inv.* stain-remover.
sacamantas, *n.m. inv.* (*coll.*) tax-collector.
sacamiento, *n.m.* taking out, drawing out.
sacamolero, sacamuelas (*inv.*), *n.m.* tooth-drawer, dentist; (*coll.*) quack.
sacanabo, *n.m.* (*artill.*) bomb extractor.
sacanete, *n.m.* lansquenet; card game.
sacapelotas, *n.m. inv.* bullet-screw.
sacaperras, *n.m. inv.* slot-machine.
sacapotras, *n.m. inv.* butcher (*surgeon*); quack.
sacar [A], *v.t.* to draw; to draw out, take out, pull out; to pick out; to bring out; to get out; to stick out; to find out; to get, obtain; to make (*copies*); to take (*photographs*); to work out (*problems etc.*); to win (*prizes*); to serve (*tennis*); ***sacar a luz,*** to bring out; ***sacar adelante,*** to bring up (*children*), to carry on, see through (*to a conclusion*); ***sacar a bailar,*** to ask for a dance, to take onto the floor for a dance; ***sacar a relucir,*** to bring *or* drag up, trot out; ***sacar un apodo a,*** to make up a nick-name for; ***sacar en claro*** or ***en limpio,*** to get clear, get straight; ***sacar la cara por,*** to stand up for; ***sacar de quicio,*** to force, strain; to drive to distraction; ***¿quién saca?*** who starts off *or* kicks off?
sacarímetro, *n.m.* saccharimeter.
sacarino, -na, *a., n.f.* saccharine.
sacasebo, *n.m.* (*Cub.*) fodder plant.
sacasillas, *n.m. inv.* (*theat.*) stage hand; (*fig.*) busybody.
sacatapón, *n.m.* corkscrew.
sacate, *n.m.* (*Mex.*) grass, herb, hay.
sacatinta, *n.m.* (*Cent. Am.*) shrub giving a dye.
sacatropos, *n.m. inv.* (*artill.*) wad hook, wormer.
sacaxquihuite, *n.m.* (*Mex.*) sapindaceous plant of the lowlands (*Cupania*).
sacayán, *n.m.* (*Philip.*) small boat.
sacerdocio, *n.m.* priesthood, ministry.
sacerdotal, *a.* of the priesthood, priestly.
sacerdote, *n.m.* priest, clergyman.
sacerdotisa, *n.f.* priestess.
saciable, *a.* satiable, that may be satisfied.
saciar, *v.t.* to satiate, sate; to quench.
saciedad, *n.f.* satiety.
saciña, *n.f.* (*bot.*) willow.
sacio, -cia, *a.* satiate, satiated.

saco, *n.m.* sack, bag; sackful, bagful; sackcloth; (*Hisp. Am.*) jacket; pillage, plunder; sagum; (*naut.*) cove, small bay; ***entrar a saco,*** to go in pillaging and plundering; (*coll.*) ***no echar en saco roto,*** not to forget, not to overlook.
sacral, *a.* (of) taboo, ritual(istic).
sacramentado, -da, *a.* (*eccles.*) transubstantiated; sacramented, having received the sacraments.
sacramental, *a.* sacramental.
sacramentar, *v.t.* to administer the sacraments to; (*fig.*) to conceal. — **sacramentarse,** *v.r.* to be transubstantiated.
sacramentario, -ria, *a.* sacramentarian.
sacramente, *adv.* in a sacred way.
sacramento, *n.m.* sacrament; ***hacer sacramento,*** to make a mystery; ***incapaz de sacramentos,*** an absolute fool.
sacratísimo, -ma, *a. superl.* [SAGRADO].
sacre, *n.m.* (*orn.*) saker; (*artill.*) small cannon.
sacrificadero, *n.m.* place of sacrifice.
sacrificador, *n.m.* sacrificer.
sacrificante, *a.* sacrificing, sacrificatory. — *n.m.f.* sacrificer.
sacrificar [A], *v.t.* to sacrifice; to slaughter (*animals*).
sacrificatorio, -ria, *a.* sacrificatory.
sacrificio, *n.m.* sacrifice; slaughter.
sacrilegio, *n.m.* sacrilege.
sacrílego, -ga, *a.* sacrilegious.
sacrismoche, -cho, *n.m.* (*coll.*) fellow dressed in shabby black clothes.
sacristán, *n.m.* sacristan, sexton, verger; hoop-skirt; ***ser gran sacristán,*** to be very sly.
sacristana, *n.f.* sexton's wife; nun in charge of the sacristy.
sacristanesco, -ca, *a.* sacristanlike; (*fig.*) artful, crafty.
sacristanía, *n.f.* sexton's office.
sacristía, *n.f.* sacristy, vestry; sacristan's office.
sacro, -ra, *a.* sacred, holy; (*anat.*) sacral. — *n.m.* sacrum. — *n.f.* (*eccles.*) sacring tablet.
sacrosanto, -ta, *a.* sacrosanct, most holy.
sacudida (1), *n.f.* shake, jerk, jolt; shock.
sacudido, -da (2), *a.* intractable; determined.
sacudidor, -ra, *a.* shaking. — *n.m.* shaker; beater; duster.
sacudidura, *n.f.* shaking; dusting.
sacudimiento, *n.m.* shake, jerk, jolt; shaking.
sacudión, *n.m.* sudden, violent shake *or* jerk.
sacudir(se), *v.t.* (*v.r.*) to shake, jerk, jolt, jar; to shake off; to beat; ***sacudirse una pesadez,*** to shake *or* throw off a bore.
sachadura, *n.f.* hoeing, weeding.
sachar, *v.t.* to hoe, weed.
sacho, *n.m.* hoe, weeder.
sádico, -ca, *a.* sadistic. — *n.m.f.* sadist.
sadismo, *n.m.* sadism.
saduceo, -cea, *a., n.m.f.* Sadducean, Sadducee.
saeta, *n.f.* arrow, shaft; bud (*of a vine*); hand (*of a clock*); magnetic needle; song addressed to the Virgin (*in Holy Week processions*); (*astron.*) Sagitta; ***echar saetas,*** to recite pious eulogies; to make innuendos.
saetada, *n.f.,* **saetazo,** *n.m.* arrow shot *or* wound.
saetear, *v.t.* to shoot with arrows.
saetera (1), *n.f.* loophole; small grated window.
saetero, -ra (2), *a.* relating to arrows, arrow. — *n.m.* archer, bowman.
saetí, *n.m.* sateen.
saetía, *n.f.* (*naut.*) settee; loophole.
saetilla, *n.f.* small arrow; hand (*of a watch*); (*bot.*) sagittaria.
saetín, *n.m.* mill-run, flume; brad; sateen.
sáfico, -ca, *a.* (*poet.*) sapphic.
safio, *n.m.* (*Cub.*) conger eel.
saga, *n.f.* witch; saga.
sagacidad, *n.f.* sagacity.
sagapeno, *n.m.* sagapenum (*gum*).
sagatí, *n.m.* silk and cotton fabric.
sagaz, *a.* sagacious; keen-scented.
sagita, *n.f.* (*geom.*) sagitta, segment.
sagital, *a.* sagittal, sagittated.
sagitaria, *n.f.* (*bot.*) sagittaria, arrowhead.
Sagitario, *n.m.* (*astron., astrol.*) Sagittarius.
sagitario, *n.m.* archer.
ságoma, *n.f.* (*arch.*) reglet, rule.
sagrado, -da, *a.* sacred. — *n.m.* sanctuary, asylum; ***acogerse a sagrado,*** to take sanctuary, seek asylum.
sagrario, *n.m.* tabernacle; sanctuary; ciborium.
sagú, *n.m.* sago-palm; sago.
saguaipe, *n.m.* (*Arg.*) parasitic worm.
ságula, *n.f.* small frock.
saguntino, -na, *a., n.m.f.* (native) of Sagunto.
Sahara, el, *n.m.* Sahara.
sahárico, -ca, *a.* Saharan, of the Sahara.
sahina [ZAHINA].
sahornarse, *v.r.* to chafe.
sahorno, *n.m.* chafe, chafing.
sahumado, -da, *a.* bettered; (*Hisp. Am.*) tipsy.
sahumador, *n.m.* perfuming pot, incensing pot; stretcher, clothes drier.
sahumadura, *n.f.* fumigation; perfuming.
sahumar, *v.t.* to perfume; to fumigate.
sahumerio, sahumo, *n.m.* perfuming; fumigation; odorous smoke; aromatics burnt as perfume.
saimiri, *n.m.* squirrel monkey.
saín, *n.m.* grease, dirt on clothes; fat, fatness; sardine fat used as lamp-oil.
sainar [P], *v.t.* to fatten (*animals*).
sainete, *n.m.* burlesque, one-act comedy; zest, flavour, relish; sauce, tit-bit; (*coll.*) rumpus.
sainetear, *v.i.* to play one-act comedies.
sainetero, *n.m.* writer of one-act comedies.
sainetesco, -ca, *a.* comical, burlesque.
saíno, *n.m.* (*Hisp. Am.*) boar.
saja, sajadura, *n.f.* cut, incision.
sajador, *n.m.* bleeder; (*surg.*) scarificator.
sajar, *v.t.* to slice open.
sajelar, *v.t.* to sift and clean (*clay*).
sajon, -jona, *a., n.m.f.* Saxon.—*n.m.* Saxon (*language*).
Sajonia, *n.f.* Saxony.
sajuriana, *n.f.* (*Chi., Per.*) ancient popular dance.
sal, *n.f.* salt; wit, wittiness; charm, winning ways; (*Hisp. Am.*) bad luck; ***sal de la Higuera,*** Epsom salts; ***sal gema,*** mineral salt; (*coll.*) ***echar en sal,*** to salt away.
sala, *n.f.* hall; drawing-room, parlour, lounge; court room; ward (*in hospitals*); ***hacer sala,*** to form a quorum; ***sala de batalla,*** sorting room (*post office*).
salabardo, *n.m.* scoop net, dip net.
salacidad, *n.f.* salacity, salaciousness.
salacot, *n.m.* sun-helmet, topee.
saladar, *n.m.* salt-marsh.
saladería, *n.f.* (*Arg.*) meat salting factory.
saladero, *n.m.* salting-place; salting tub.
saladillo, *n.m.* half-salted bacon.
salado, -da, *a.* salty, brackish, briny; (*fig.*) funny, amusing; genial, likeable; (*C.R., P.R.*) hapless; (*Arg., Chi.*) dear, costly. — *n.m.* (*bot.*) saltwort; saline land.
salador, -ra, *n.m.f.* salter, curer, salting-place.
saladura, *n.f.* salting, curing; pickled *or* salted meat, fish etc.; saltness.
salamanca, *n.m.* (*Chi.*) cave; (*Arg.*) salamander.
salamandra, *n.f.* salamander; stove; ***salamandra acuática,*** newt.
salamandria, *n.f.* [SALAMANQUESA].

salamanqués, -quesa, *a., n.m.f.* (native) of Salamanca. — *n.f.* star-lizard, tarente.
salamanquino, -na, *a., n.m.f.* [SALAMANQUÉS].
salangana, *n.f.* swift, swallow.
salar, *v.t.* to salt; ***esta sopa resulta muy salada,*** this soup has too much salt in it.
salarial, *a.* (of) wage *or* wages.
salariar, *v.t.* to pay a wage to.
salario, *n.m.* wage, wages, pay.
salaz, *a.* salacious, lustful.
salazón, *n.f.* salting; salted meats *or* fish.
salbanda, *n.f.* (*min.*) selvage.
salce, *n.m.* willow.
salceda, *n.f.*, **salcedo,** *n.m.* willow grove.
salcereta, *n.f.* dice-box.
salcochar, *v.t.* to boil in water and salt.
salcocho, *n.m.* (*Hisp. Am.*) food boiled in water and salt.
salchicha, *n.f.* sausage; (*mil.*) saucisse.
salchichería, *n.f.* sausage-shop.
salchichero, -ra, *n.m.f.* sausage-maker; sausage-seller.
salchichón, *n.m.* salame; (*fort.*) large fascine.
saldar, *v.t.* to liquidate, settle; to hold a sale of, sell off cheap.
saldista, *n.m.* liquidation broker; remnant dealer.
saldo, *n.m.* (*com.*) balance; settlement, liquidation; bargain-sale; ***saldo acreedor, deudor,*** credit, debit balance.
saledizo, *a.* jutting, salient. — *n.m.* [SALIDIZO].
salegar, *n.m.* salt-lick.
salema, *n.f.* (*ichth.*) gilt-head.
salera, *n.f.* salt-lick.
salero, *n.m.* salt-cellar; salt store; salt lick; (*coll.*) charm, wit, amusing and likeable nature.
saleroso, -sa, *a.* (*coll.*) charming, delightful, having a gay, amusing and likeable nature.
saleta, *n.f.* small reception room; royal antechamber; court of appeal.
salga (1), *n.f.* (*hist.*) salt tax (*in Aragon*).
salgar [B], *v.t.* to give salt to (*cattle*).
salgo, salga (2), *pres. indic., pres. subj.* [SALIR].
salguera, *n.f.*, **salguero,** *n.m.* osier, willow.
salicaria, *n.f.* purple loosestrife.
salicilato, *n.m.* (*chem.*) salicylate.
salicílico, -ca, *a.* salicylic.
salicina, *n.f.* (*chem.*) salicin.
sálico, -ca, *a.* Salic.
salicor, *n.m.* (*bot.*) saltwort.
salida (1), *n.f.* going *or* coming out; exit; way out; outlet; start, leaving, departure; outing; sally; discharge; sprouting forth; rise (*of sun etc.*); outlay; end; projection; (*naut.*) headway; (*mil.*) sally, sortie; (*games*) lead; ***salida de baño,*** bathrobe; ***salida de teatro,*** evening wrap; ***salida graciosa,*** witty remark *or* retort; ***salida de pie de banco,*** stupidly tactless *or* out of place remark; ***salida de tono,*** remark in bad taste; ***tener salida,*** to sell well, be popular.
salidizo, *n.m.* (*arch.*) projection, corbel.
salido, -da (2), *a.* projecting; on heat (*of female animals*).
saliente, *a.* jutting out, projecting, salient; outgoing.
salífero, -ra, *a.* (*chem.*) saliferous.
salificable, *a.* salifiable.
salín, *n.m.* salt magazine.
salina, *n.f.* [SALINO].
salinero, *n.m.* salter, salt-maker; dealer in salt.
salino, -na, *a.* saline. — *n.f.* salt-pit; salt-mine.
salir [31], *v.i.* to go out, come out, get out; to go *or* come forth; to leave; to set out; to lead on (to); to stand out; to turn out; (*theat.*) to enter, come on; to rise (*sun, moon etc.*); to be drawn, elected (*in a ballot*); (*naut.*) to pass another vessel (*in sailing*); ***salir a,*** to take after; ***sale por un ojo de la cara,*** it works out devilishly expensive; ***ya saldremos adelante,*** we'll make out somehow; ***nos salió con un pretexto,*** he came out with an excuse; ***eso salió de él,*** that was his idea; ***salir disparado, pitando,*** to rush off; ***salir a la mar,*** to put out to sea; ***salir al encuentro,*** to go to meet; ***salir a luz,*** to appear, come out; ***salga lo que saliere,*** come what may; ***salir con bien,*** to turn out well; ***salir ganado,*** to do better. — **salirse,** *v.r.* to leak; to boil over, spill over, overflow; to go off, fly off; ***el tren se salió de la vía,*** the train went off the rails; ***salirse de madre,*** to lose control; ***salirse con la suya,*** to get one's own way.
salisipan, *n.m.* (*Philip.*) swift boat.
salitrado, -da, *a.* saltpetrous.
salitral, *a.* nitrous. — *n.m.* saltpetre bed, saltpetre works.
salitre, *n.m.* (*chem.*) saltpetre.
salitrería, *n.f.* saltpetre works.
salitrero, -ra, *a.* saltpetre. — *n.m.f.* saltpetre worker; saltpetre refiner.
salitroso, -sa, *a.* nitrous, salinitrous, saltpetrous.
saliva, *n.f.* saliva, spittle; (*coll.*) ***gastar saliva en balde,*** to talk in vain; (*coll.*) ***tragar saliva,*** to suffer in silence, lump it, take it.
salivación, *n.f.* salivation.
salivadera, *n.f.* (*Arg., Chi.*) spittoon.
salival, *a.* salivous, salivary.
salivar, *v.i.* to spit, salivate.
salivera, *n.f.* round knob (*on a bridle*).
salivoso, -sa, *a.* salivous.
salma, *n.f.* ton-weight.
salmantino, -na, *a., n.m.f.* (native of) Salamanca.
salmear, *v.i.* to sing psalms.
salmerón, *a., n.m.* fanfaron wheat.
salmista, *n.m.* psalmist, psalm-singer.
salmo, *n.m.* psalm.
salmodia, *n.f.* psalmody; psalter.
salmodiar, *v.t., v.i.* to sing psalms; to sing monotonously, chant, drone.
salmón, *n.m.* (*ichth.*) salmon; ***salmón pequeño,*** samlet; ***salmón zancado,*** kelt.
salmonado, -da, *a.* salmon-like (*in colour, taste etc.*).
salmonera, *n.f.* salmon net.
salmonete, *n.m.* (*ichth.*) red mullet.
salmorejo, *n.m.* game sauce; cold soup.
salmuera, *n.f.* brine; pickle.
salmuerarse, *v.r.* to become sick from eating too much salt (*of cattle*).
salobral, *a.* salty, briny. — *n.m.* brine, briny ground.
salobre, *a.* brackish, saltish, briny.
salobreño, -ña, *a.* saltish, brackish.
salobridad, *n.f.* brackishness, saltiness.
saloma, *n.f.* (*naut.*) shanty.
salomar, *v.i.* to sing shanties.
Salomón, *n.m.* Solomon.
salón, *n.m.* drawing-room; large hall; assembly room.
salpa, *n.f.* (*ichth.*) gilt-head.
salpicadero, *n.m.* dashboard.
salpicadura, *n.f.* spattering, splash.
salpicar [A], *v.t.* to splash, spatter; to sprinkle, strew.
salpicón, *n.m.* bespattering, splashing; salmagundi; ***salpicón de mariscos,*** sea-food cocktail *or* medley.
salpimentar [1], *v.t.* to season with pepper and salt.
salpimienta, *n.f.* mixture of pepper and salt.
salpresar [*p.p.* **salpresado, salpreso**], *v.t.* to salt, preserve with salt.
salpullido, *n.m.* rash, eruption.
salpullir [J], *v.t.* to cause a rash in.

salsa, *n.f.* sauce; gravy; (*coll.*) ***salsa de San Bernardo,*** hunger.
salsedumbre, *n.f.* saltness.
salsera, *n.f.* gravy-dish.
salserilla, *n.f.* small saucer.
salsifí, *n.m.* (*bot.*) salsify; goat's-beard.
saltabanco(s), *n.m.* mountebank.
saltabardales, *n.m. inv.* (*coll.*) wild youth.
saltacaballo, *n.m.* (*arch.*) crossette.
saltación, *n.f.* leaping, hopping; dancing, dance.
saltacharquillos, *n.m. inv.* jaunty, tripping fellow.
saltadero, *n.m.* leaping-place; fountain.
saltadizo, -za, *a.* breaking, snapping.
saltador, -ra, *n.m.f.* jumper, leaper, hopper, springer. — *n.m.* skipping rope.
saltamontes, *n.m. inv.* grasshopper.
saltanejoso, *a.* (*Cub.*) undulating.
saltante, *a.* jumping, leaping, springing.
saltaojos, *n.m. inv.* peony.
saltaparedes, *n.m. inv.* (*coll.*) wild youth.
saltar, *v.t.* to leap, jump over; to skip; (*of animals*) to cover (*the female*). — *v.i.* to jump, leap, spring, bound, hop, skip; to shoot up, spurt; to fly up; to fly apart, snap, burst; to come off, fly off; to stand out, be evident; to burst out angrily; to shift about (*of wind*); ***saltar de alegría,*** to jump for *or* with joy; ***salta a la vista,*** it hits one in the eye; ***hicieron saltar el puente,*** they blew up the bridge; ***se saltó la tapa de los sesos,*** he blew his brains out; ***se saltó una línea,*** he skipped a line.
saltarelo, *n.m.* saltarello.
saltarén, *n.m.* tune on the guitar; grasshopper.
saltarín, -rina, *a.* hopping, skipping, jumping; dancing.
saltarregla, *n.f.* bevel square; sliding rule.
saltaterandate, *n.m.* embroidery.
saltatrás, *n.m. inv.* throw-back.
saltatriz, *n.f.* woman rope-dancer, ballet-girl.
saltatumbas, *n.m. inv.* (*contempt.*) clergyman who makes a living from funerals.
salteado, -da, *a.* in bits, here and there, all over the place, all mixed up; sauté.
salteador, *n.m.* footpad, highwayman.
salteadora, *n.f.* female footpad; woman living with highwaymen.
salteamiento, *n.m.* assault, attack, highway robbery; (*cook.*) frying.
saltear, *v.t.* to hold up, waylay; to assault, attack; to do by fits and starts; (*cook.*) to sauté.
salteo, *n.m.* highway assault, robbery.
salterio, *n.m.* psalter; rosary; psaltery.
saltero, *n.m.* highlander.
saltico, saltillo, saltito, *n.m.* little hop; ***a saltillos,*** hopping.
saltimbanco, saltimbanqui, *n.m.* mountebank; quack; trifler.
salto, *n.m.* jump, spring, leap, bound; hop, skip; gap; ***salto de altura,*** high jump; ***salto de agua,*** waterfall; ***salto de cama,*** dressing-gown, (*Am.*) bathrobe; ***salto del viento,*** sudden shift in the wind; ***salto mortal,*** somersault; ***salto del ángel,*** swallow dive, (*Am.*) swan dive; ***a saltos,*** by leaps, by fits and starts; ***de un salto,*** at one jump; ***en un salto,*** in a flash; ***dar un salto,*** to take a jump; ***vivir a salto de mata,*** to live on the run; to live from hand to mouth.
saltón, -tona, *a.* given to jumping *or* leaping about; protruding; ***ojos saltones,*** bulging, starting, goggle-eyes. — *n.m.* grasshopper.
salubérrimo, -ma, *a. superl.* most salubrious.
salubre, *a.* salubrious, healthy.
salubridad, *n.f.* salubrity, healthiness, wholesomeness, salutariness.
salud, *n.f.* health; welfare, good; ***¡salud!*** cheers!; ***¡a su salud!*** to your health!; ***beber a la salud de,*** to drink the health of; ***estar bien*** or ***mal de salud,*** to be in good *or* bad health; ***gastar salud,*** to enjoy excellent health. — *interj.* (*coll.*) hello!
saludable, *a.* salutary, healthy, wholesome.
saludador, *n.m.* greeter, saluter; quack.
saludar, *v.t., v.i.* to greet, hail, welcome; to salute; to say good-day *or* hello; ***saludar con la mano,*** to wave (to); ***saludar militarmente,*** to salute.
saludo, *n.m.* greeting; wave; salute; (*pl.*) compliments, regards.
salumbre, *n.f.* flower of salt.
salutación, *n.f.* salutation, greeting, salute; exordium of a sermon; ave Maria.
salutífero, -ra, *a.* healthful, salubrious.
salva (1), *n.f.* salute (*of firearms*), salvo; round (*of applause*); ordeal; oath, solemn promise, assurrance; salver, tray; pregustation.
salvación, *n.f.* salvation; deliverance.
salvachia, *n.f.* (*naut.*) salvage strap.
salvadera, *n.f.* sand-box.
salvado, *n.m.* bran.
Salvador, El, *n.m.* El Salvador.
salvador, -ra, *a.* saving; rescuing; delivering; redeeming. — *n.m.f.* saviour; rescuer; deliverer; redeemer.
salvadoreño, -ña, *a., n.m.f.* Salvadorean.
salvaguardia, *n.f.* safeguard; security; protection; safe-conduct. — *n.m.* watchman, guard.
salvajada, *n.f.* atrocity, bestial act; savage behaviour.
salvaje, *a.* savage, barbarous; wild. — *n.m.* savage, barbarian.
salvajería, *n.f.* savageness, savagery.
salvajez, *n.f.* savageness, savagery.
salvajino, -na, *a.* savage, wild; game (*meat*). — *n.f.* wild beasts; game; skins of wild beasts.
salvajismo, *n.m.* savagery.
salvamano, (a), *adv.* without danger *or* risk.
salvamanteles, *n.m. inv.* table-mat.
salvamento, salvamiento, *n.m.* salvage, salvaging; saving, life-saving, rescuing; place of safety.
salvar, *v.t.* to save, rescue; to salve; to overcome, surmount; to get over, clear, bridge; to get through, negotiate; to cover (*distance*); to make an exception of; ***salvar las apariencias,*** to save face, keep up appearances. — *v.i.* to taste food against fear of poisoning. — **salvarse,** *v.r.* to be saved; to win salvation; ***¡sálvese quien pueda!*** every man for himself!
salvavidas, *n.m. inv.* (*naut.*) life-jacket; fender, guard; (***bote***) ***salvavidas,*** lifeboat.
salve, *n.f.* salve.
¡salve! *interj.* hail!
salvedad, *n.f.* reservation, exception, qualification.
salvia, *n.f.* (*bot.*) sage, salvia.
salvilla, *n.f.* salves, tray; (*Chi.*) cruet-stand.
salvo, -va (2), *a.* saved; safe; ***a salvo,*** safe; ***en salvo,*** at liberty; safe; ***dejar a salvo,*** to leave aside *or* out; ***en salva sea la parte,*** in a delicate spot, in an unmentionable place. — *conj.* save, saving, except; ***salvo que,*** unless, only if.
salvoconducto, *n.m.* pass, safe-conduct.
salladura, *n.f.* weeding.
sallar, *v.t.* to weed; to stow (*logs and planks*).
sallete, *n.m.* weeder, weeding tool.
sámago, *n.m.* alburnum, alburn, sap-wood.
samán, *n.m.* (*bot.*) rain tree.
samaritano, -na, *a., n.m.f.* Samaritan.
samaruco, *n.m.* (*Chi.*) game bag.
samaruguera, *n.f.* fishing-net (*across streams*).
sambenitar, *v.t.* to dishonour publicly.
sambenito, *n.m.* sanbenito; note of infamy, disgrace.
samblaje, *n.m.* joinery.
sambuca, *n.f.* (*mus.*) sambuca, sambuke.

sambumbia, *n.f.* (*Cub.*) drink made from cane juice, water and chilli; (*Mex.*) drink made from pineapple, water and sugar.
samotana, *n.f.* (*C.R., Hond.*) merrymaking; din.
sampa, *n.f.* (*Arg., bot.*) ramose shrub.
sampaguita, *n.f.* tropical jasmine.
sampsuco, *n.m.* marjoram.
samuga, *n.f.* mule-chair.
samuro, *n.m.* (*Col., Ven.*) turkey-buzzard, turkey-vulture.
San, *a.* (*contraction of* SANTO) Saint (*before masculine proper nouns except* ***Tomás*** or ***Tomé, Toribio,*** *and* ***Domingo***).
sanable, *a.* healable, curable.
sanador, -ra, *n.m.f.* healer, curer.
sanalotodo, *n.m.* panacea, cure-all.
sanar, *v.t.* to heal, cure. — *v.i.* to heal.
sanativo, -va, *a.* sanative, curative.
sanatorio, *n.m.* sanatorium.
sanción, *n.f.* sanction; penalty.
sancionar, *v.t.* to sanction; to penalize.
sanco, *n.m.* (*Arg., Chi.*) kind of porridge; (*Chi.*) thick mud.
sancochar, *v.t.* to parboil; to cook badly.
sancocho, *n.m.* half-cooked meal; (*Hisp. Am.*) stew of meat, yucca, banana, etc.
sanctasanctórum, *n.m.* holy of holies; sanctum sanctorum.
sanctus, *n.m. inv.* sanctus (*in the Mass*).
sanchopancesco, -ca, *a.* like Sancho Panza; materialistic.
sandalia, *n.f.* sandal.
sandalino, -na, of *or* belonging to sandal-wood; tinctured with sanders.
sándalo, *n.m.* (*bot.*) bergamot mint; sandal-wood, sanders.
sandáraca, *n.f.* sandarach; (*min.*) realgar.
sandez, *n.f.* stupidity, silliness; foolish thing to do *or* say.
sandía, *n.f.* water-melon.
sandialahuén, *n.m.* (*Chi.*) verbenaceous plant.
sandiar, *n.m.* water-melon patch.
sandiego, *n.m.* (*Cub.*) amaranth.
sandilla, *n.f.* (*Chi.*) verbenaceous plant with a fruit resembling a small water-melon.
sandio, -dia, *a.* stupid, foolish, silly.
sandunga, *n.f.* winsomeness; charm; (*Chi., P.R.*) carousal, revelry.
sandunguero, -ra, *a.* (*coll.*) winsome, amusing and charming.
saneado, -da, *a.* free, clear, unencumbered.
saneamiento, *n.m.* (*law*) sanitation; drainage; reparation; (*law*) guarantee.
sanear, *v.t.* (*law*) to indemnify; to guarantee; to drain, give sanitation to; (*fig.*) to put right *or* straight.
sanedrín, *n.m.* Sanhedrin.
sanfrancia, *n.f.* (*coll.*) dispute, quarrel.
sangley, *n.m.* (*Philip.*) Chinese *or* Japanese trader.
sangradera, *n.f.* lancet; basin for blood-letting; lock, sluice, drain.
sangrador, *n.m.* phlebotomist, blood-letter; opening, outlet.
sangradura, *n.f.* (*surg.*) bleeding; (*anat.*) inner angle of the elbow; draining, drainage.
sangrar, *v.t., v.i.* to bleed. — *v.t.* (*print.*) to indent.
sangraza, *n.f.* thick *or* heavy blood.
sangre, *n.f.* blood; gore; ***tener (mucha) sangre fría,*** to be a cool customer, have plenty of sang-froid; (*coll.*) ***tener mala sangre,*** to be bloody-minded, a nasty piece of work; ***tener sangre de horchata,*** to be a milksop; ***me he hecho sangre,*** I've cut *or* pricked myself; ***me fríe la sangre,*** he needles me; ***a sangre fría,*** in cold blood; ***a sangre y fuego,*** with fire and sword; ***no llegó la sangre al río,*** they didn't come to blows, things didn't get too serious.
sangría, *n.f.* bleeding, blood-letting; drain, drainage; outlet; cut, tap, tapping; (*anat.*) inner angle of the elbow; (*print.*) indentation; sangaree, sangria; ***sangría intelectual,*** brain-drain.
sangriento, -ta, *a.* bloody, blood-stained; savage.
sanguaraña, *n.f.* (*Per.*) popular dance; (*pl.*) (*Ec., Per.*) beating about the bush.
sanguaza, *n.f.* gore; reddish fluid (*of fruits and vegetables*).
sangüeño, *n.m.* (*bot.*) dogberry tree, wild cornel.
sangüesa, *n.f.* (*bot.*) raspberry.
sangüeso, *n.m.* raspberry bush.
sanguífero, -ra, *a.* (*med.*) sanguiferous.
sanguificación, *n.f.* (*med.*) sanguification.
sanguificar [A], *v.t.* to sanguify.
sanguijuela, *n.f.* (*zool.*) leech.
sanguinaria (1), *n.f.* (*bot.*) knot-grass; blood-wort; (*min.*) bloodstone.
sanguinario, -ria (2), *a.* sanguinary, bloodthirsty.
sanguíneo, -nea, sanguino, -na, *a.* sanguine, ruddy, sanguineous, (of) blood.
sanguinolento, -ta, *a.* bloody, dripping blood.
sanguinoso, -sa, *a.* (of) blood; bloody; sanguinary.
sanguiñuelo, *n.m.* (*bot.*) dogberry tree, wild cornel.
sanguisorba, *n.f.* (*bot.*) great burnet.
sanícula, *n.f.* (*bot.*) sanicle.
sanidad, *n.f.* health; healthfulness; ***carta de sanidad,*** bill of health.
sanie(s), *n.f.* sanies.
sanioso, -sa, *a.* sanious.
sanitario, -ria, *a.* (of) health; sanitary.
sanjacado, sanjacato, *n.m.* sanjak.
sanjuanada, *n.f.* picnic on St. John's Day.
sanjuanero, -ra, *a.* ripe on St. John's Day (*of fruits*); of St. John's Day.
San Lorenzo, *n.m.* St. Lawrence (river).
sanmiguelada, *n.f.* Michaelmas-tide.
sanmigueleño, -ña, *a.* of Michaelmas.
sano, -na, *a.* sound; healthy; fit; wholesome; whole; ***sano y salvo,*** safe and sound; ***cortar por lo sano,*** to cut one's losses, to act drastically.
sánscrito, -ta, *a., n.m.* Sanskrit.
sansimonismo, *n.m.* St. Simonism.
Sansón, *n.m.* Samson.
sansón, *n.m.* (*fig.*) very strong man.
santa, *n.f.* [SANTO].
santabárbara, *n.f.* (*naut.*) magazine, powder-room.
Santa Elena, *n.f.* St. Helena.
santamente, *adv.* (*coll.*) quite right; ***has hecho santamente,*** you've done quite right.
Santelmo, *n.m.* St. Elmo's fire.
santero, -ra, *a.* over-devout to the saints. — *n.m.f.* caretaker of a sanctuary; alms collector.
Santiago, *n.m.* St. James.
santiago, *n.m.* war-cry of the Spaniards on engaging with Moors.
santiagueño, -ña, *a.* (*fruits*) ripe on St. James' Day; of *or* from Santiago del Estero (*Argentina*).
santiaguero, -ra, *a., n.m.f.* of Santiago (Cuba).
santiagués, -guesa, *a., n.m.f.* of Santiago (Galicia).
santiaguino, -na, *a., n.m.f.* of Santiago (Chile).
santiaguista, *a.* pertaining to the order of Santiago. — *n.m.* knight of Santiago.
santiamén, (en un), *n.m.* (*coll.*) in the twinkling of an eye, in a jiffy.
santico, -ca [SANTITO].
santidad, *n.f.* sanctity, saintliness, piety, holiness, godliness; ***su Santidad,*** his Holiness (the Pope).
santificación, *n.f.* sanctification, making holy; ***santificación de las fiestas,*** keeping of holy days.
santificador, -ra, *a.* sanctifying. — *n.m.f.* sanctifier.

santificante, *a.* blessing, sanctifying.
santificar [A], *v.t.* to sanctify, hallow; ***santificar las fiestas,*** to keep holy days. — **santificarse,** *v.r.* to become sanctified.
santiguada, *n.f.* sign of the cross.
santiguador, -ra, *n.m.f.* healer by signing with the cross.
santiguamiento, *n.m.* crossing, blessing by crossing.
santiguar [H], *v.t.* to bless, make the sign of the cross upon; to heal by blessing; (*coll.*) to beat, slap. — **santiguarse,** *v.r.* to cross o.s.
santimonia, *n.f.* sanctity, piousness, holiness; (*bot.*) corn, marigold, chrysanthemum.
santísimo, -ma, *a. superl.* most holy. — *n.m.* ***el Santísimo,*** the holy sacrament; (*coll.*) ***hacer la santísima a,*** to play a filthy trick on, jigger up.
santito, -ta, *n.m.f.* regular little saint; little image of a saint.
santo, -ta, *a.* saint, holy, blessed, sacred; righteous, saintly; (*coll.*) simple-minded; ***santo varón,*** simple, artless man; ***en el santo suelo,*** on the bare ground, on the floor; ***su santa voluntad,*** his own sweet will; ***todo el santo día,*** the whole blessed day; ***una santa bofetada,*** a fine slap. — *adv.* ***santo y bueno,*** well and good. — *n.m.* saint; saint's day; image of a saint; (*coll.*) picture (*in a book*); (*mil.*) watchword; ***santo titular,*** patron saint; ***no es santo de su devoción,*** he does not like him; it's not his cup of tea; ***alzarse con el santo y la limosna,*** to clear out with everything, walk off with the proceeds; ***desnudar a un santo para vestir a otro,*** to rob Peter to pay Paul; ***se me fue el santo al cielo,*** it went clean out of my mind; (*coll., fig.*) ***comerse los santos,*** to be a hot gospeller; (*coll.*) ***dar con el santo en tierra,*** to let sth. fall; ***dar el santo y seña,*** to give the watchword. — *n.m.f.* saintly *or* righteous person. — *n.f.* saint.
santol, *n.m.* sandal tree.
santón, *n.m.* holy man.
santónico, *n.m.* (*med.*) santonica.
santonina, *n.f.* (*chem.*) santonine.
santoral, *n.m.* church-choir book; collection of lives of the saints.
santuario, *n.m.* sanctuary; (*Col.*) treasure.
santucho, -cha, *n.m.f.* (*coll.*) hypocrite.
santurrón, -rrona, *a.* sanctimonious. — *n.m.f.* (*coll.*) sanctimonious individual.
santurronería, *n.f.* sanctimony.
saña, *n.f.* savage cruelty; fury.
sañoso, -sa [SAÑUDO].
sañudo, -da, *a.* savagely cruel; furious.
sao, *n.m.* (*bot.*) laburnum; (*Cub.*) small savannah.
sapajú, *n.m.* sapajou.
sapán, *n.m.* sapan wood; sapan tree.
sapenco, *n.m.* snail.
sápido, -da, *a.* sapid.
sapiencia, *n.f.* (*coll.*) wisdom, learning; Book of Wisdom.
sapiencial, *a.* belonging to wisdom, of wisdom.
sapiente, *a.* wise, learned.
sapillo, *n.m.* (*bot.*) glasswort; small tumour.
sapina, *n.f.* (*bot.*) glasswort.
sapino, *n.m.* fir tree.
sapo, *n.m.* toad; toadfish; ***sapo marino,*** angler fish; ***echar sapos y culebras,*** to curse and swear.
saponáceo, -cea, *a.* saponaceous.
saponaria, *n.f.* (*bot.*) soapwort.
saponia, *n.f.* (*chem.*) saponin.
saponificación, *n.f.* saponification.
saponificar, *v.t.* to saponify.
saporífero, -ra, *a.* saporific.
saque, *n.m.* (*tennis*) serve, service; (*football*) kick-off; (*coll.*) ***tener buen saque,*** to be a good trencherman.
saqueador, -ra, *a.* plundering.
saqueamiento, saqueo, *n.m.* sacking, plundering, pillaging, looting.
saquear, *v.t.* to sack, plunder, pillage, loot.
saquera (1), *n.f.* packing-needle.
saquería, *n.f.* manufacture of sacks; (*collection of*) sacks.
saquero, -ra (2), *n.m.f.* sack-maker.
saquete, *n.m.* cartridge bag.
saquilada, *n.f.* small quantity of grain for grinding.
saraguate, *n.m.* (*Cent. Am.*) monkey.
saragüete, *n.m.* informal party.
sarampión, *n.m.* measles.
sarandí, *n.m.* (*Arg.*) shrub.
sarangasti, *n.m.* (*naut.*) pitch-gum.
sarao, *n.m.* soirée.
sarape, *n.m.* (*Mex.*) blanket, shawl.
sarapia, *n.f.* tonka bean.
sarapico, *n.m.* (*orn.*) curlew.
sarasa, *n.m.* sissy.
saraviado, -da, *a.* (*Col., Ven.*) spotted, piebald.
sarazo, *a.* (*Col., Cub., Mex., Ven.*) ripening (*wheat*).
sarcasmo, *n.m.* sarcasm.
sarcástico, -ca, *a.* sarcastic.
sarcia, *n.f.* load, burden.
sarcocola, *n.f.* resinous gum.
sarcófago, *n.m.* sarcophagus.
sarda (1), *n.f.* (*ichth.*) horse mackerel.
sardana, *n.f.* national Catalonian dance.
sardesco, -ca, *a.* sardonic; crude; small (*ass*).
sardina, *n.f.* (*ichth.*) sardine; ***como sardinas en banasta*** or ***en barril,*** packed like sardines.
sardinal, *n.m.* sardine net.
sardinel, *n.m.* brickwork having the bricks set on edge.
sardinero, -ra, *a.* pertaining to sardines. — *n.m.f.* dealer in sardines.
sardineta, *n.f.* small sardine, sprat; part of cheese that overtops the cheese-vat; (*naut.*) knittle, lanyard; fillip with the wet finger; (*pl., mil.*) chevrons.
sardio, sardo (1), *n.m.* sardius, sard.
sardo (2), **-da** (2), *a.* Sardinian. — *n.m.f.* native of Sardinia, Sardinian.
sardo (3), **-da** (3), *a.* red, black and white (*cattle*).
sardonia, *n.f.* (*bot.*) crowfoot, spearwort.
sardónica (1), **sardónice,** *n.f.* sardonyx.
sardónico, -ca (2), *a.* sardonic.
sarga, *n.f.* serge, twill; fabric painted in distemper *or* oil, like tapestry; (*bot.*) willow, osier.
sargadilla, *n.f.* (*bot.*) soda-ash plant.
sargado, -da, *a.* serge-like.
sargal, *n.m.* osier bed.
sargazo, *n.m.* gulf-weed.
sargenta, *n.f.* sergeant's halberd; sergeant's wife.
sargentada, *n.f.* barrack-room mutiny.
sargentear, *v.t.* to bully. — *v.i.* to throw one's weight about.
sargentería, *n.f.* body of sergeants; sergeant's drill.
sargentía, *n.f.* sergeant's office, sergeantship.
sargento, *n.m.* sergeant; ***sargento primero,*** sergeant-major.
sargentona, *n.f.* (*fig., coll.*) (old) battle-axe.
sargo, *n.m.* (*ichth.*) sargo.
sargueta, *n.f.* thin serge.
sarilla, *n.f.* marjoram.
sarmentar [1], *v.t.* to gather pruned vine-shoots.
sarmentera, *n.f.* place for pruned vine-shoots.
sarmentillo, *n.m.* slender vine-shoot.
sarmentoso, -sa, *a.* covered in vine-shoots; dried up, wrinkled.
sarmiento, *n.m.* vine-shoot, runner.
sarna, *n.f.* itch, mange, scabies; ***más viejo que la sarna,*** as old as the hills.
sarnazo, *n.m.* malignant itch.

sarnoso, -sa, *a.* itchy, mangy, scabby.
sarpullido, *n.m.* rash; flea-bite.
sarpullir [J], *v.i.* to have a rash; to be flea-bitten.
sarracénico, -ca, *a.* Saracene, Saracenic.
sarraceno, -na, *n.m.f.* Saracen.
sarracina, *n.f.* fight, scuffle, brawl; (*fig.*) purge, massacre.
Sarre, *n.m.* Saar (river); Saar *or* Saarland.
sarria, *n.f.* rope net; large frail.
sarrillo, *n.m.* death-rattle; (*bot.*) arum.
sarro, *n.m.* crust, incrustation (*in vessels*); tartar (*on teeth*); (*bot.*) rust, mildew.
sarroso, -sa, *a.* crusty; covered in tartar.
sarta, *n.f.* string; (*fig.*) pack, load.
sartal, *a.* stringed. — *n.m.* string.
sartén, *n.f.* frying-pan; ***tener la sartén por el mango,*** to be firmly in the saddle, be in control; to have the upper hand.
sartenada, *n.f.* amount contained in frying-pan; frying-panful.
sartenazo, *n.m.* blow with a frying-pan; (*coll.*) hard blow.
sarteneja, *n.f.* small frying-pan.
sastra, sastresa, *n.f.* tailor's wife; tailoress.
sastre, *n.m.* tailor.
sastrería, *n.f.* tailoring, tailor's trade; tailor's shop.
Satán, Satanás, *n.m.* Satan.
satánico, -ca, *a.* satanic.
satelitario, -ria, *a.* satellite.
satélite, *n.m.* satellite.
satelizar [C], *v.t.* to put into orbit.
satén, satín, *n.m.* satin.
satinar, *v.t.* to satin, polish.
sátira, *n.f.* satire.
satírico, -ca, *a.* satirical. — *n.m.* satirist.
satirio, *n.m.* water-vole.
satirión, *n.m.* orchis.
satirizante, *a.* satirizing.
satirizar [C], *v.t.* to satirize.
sátiro, *n.m.* satyr.
satisfacción, *n.f.* satisfaction; self-satisfaction, complacency; ***a satisfacción,*** satisfactorily.
satisfacer [20], *v.t.* to satisfy; to meet.
satisfaciente, *a.* satisfying.
satisfactorio, -ria, *a.* satisfactory; satisfying.
satisfecho, -cha, *a.* self-satisfied, complacent, smug.
sativo, -va, *a.* sown, cultivated.
sátrapa, *n.m.* satrap; sly fellow.
satrapía, *n.f.* satrapy.
saturable, *a.* saturable.
saturación, *n.f.* saturation; glut.
saturar, *v.t.* to saturate; to glut.
saturnal, *a.* saturnalian. — *n.f.* saturnalia.
saturnino, -na, *a.* saturnine; gloomy, morose.
Saturno, *n.m.* (*astron.*) Saturn.
saturno, *n.m.* (*chem.*) lead.
sauce, *n.m.* (*bot.*) willow; ***sauce llorón,*** weeping-willow.
sauceda, *n.f.*, **saucedal,** *n.m.*, **saucera,** *n.f.* willow plantation.
saucillo, *n.m.* (*bot.*) knot-grass.
saúco, *n.m.* elder tree; second hoof of horses.
Saúl, *n.m.* (*Bibl.*) Saul.
sauquillo, *n.m.* dwarf elder.
saurio, -ria, *a.*, *n.m.* (*zool.*) saurian. — *n.m.pl.* (**saurios**) Saurian.
sausería, *n.f.* palace larder.
sausier, *n.m.* head of a palace larder.
sautor, *n.m.* (*her.*) saltire.
sauz, *n.m.* willow.
sauzal, *n.m.* willow plantation.
sauzgatillo, *n.m.* (*bot.*) agnus castus tree.
savia, *n.f.* sap; (*fig.*) vital fluid, strength, vigour.
saxátil, *a.* saxatile, saxicolous.
saxífraga, saxifragia, *n.f.* saxifrage.
saxofón, saxófono, *n.m.* saxophone.
saxoso, -sa, *a.* stony.
saya, *n.f.* skirt; petticoat; (ancient) tunic; dowry given by the Queen of Spain to her maids when marrying.
sayal, *n.m.* sackcloth; coarse woollen cloth; skirt.
sayalería, *n.f.* sackcloth trade.
sayalero, *n.m.* weaver of sackcloth.
sayalesco, -ca, *a.* (made of) sackcloth.
sayalete, *n.m.* light, thin stuff.
sayama, *n.f.* (*Ec.*) kind of snake.
sayo, *n.m.* smock, frock, tunic; (*coll.*) garment; (*coll.*) ***cortar un sayo a,*** to talk behind the back of; (*coll.*) ***decir para su sayo,*** to say to o.s., say in one's sleeve; (*coll.*) ***hacer de su capa un sayo,*** to do just as one pleases.
sayón, *n.m.* fierce-looking fellow; executioner.
sayuela, *n.f.* kind of fig tree; woollen shift; (*Cub.*) petticoat.
sayuelo, *n.m.* small dress; slit sleeves worn by peasant women of Leon.
sazón, *n.f.* maturity, ripeness; season; time, occasion; taste, seasoning; ***a la sazón,*** at that time; ***en sazón,*** ripe, in season; fittingly.
sazonado, -da, *a.* seasoned, mature, mellow, ripe; witty; apposite, pertinent.
sazonador, -ra, *n.m.f.* seasoner.
sazonar, *v.t.* to season; to ripen. — *v.i.* to ripen, mature.
scaléxtric, *n.m.* flyover and underpass complex, spaghetti junction.
se, *pron. m.f., s. and pl.* him(self), her(self), your(self), your(selves), them(selves), one(self); it(self); each other, one another; ***Pedro y María se quieren,*** Peter and Mary love each other; ***yo se lo di,*** I gave it to him; ***se lava las manos,*** he washes his hands; ***mi amigo se fue,*** my friend went away; ***se dice,*** they say, people say; ***no se puede negar,*** it cannot be denied.
sebáceo, -cea, *a.* sebaceous.
sebe, *n.f.* wattle, fence.
sebera, *n.f.* (*Chi.*) leather bag to carry tallow.
sebillo, *n.m.* tallow; suet paste; toilet soap.
sebiya, *n.f.* (*Cub.*) wading bird.
sebo, *n.m.* tallow, suet; candle grease; fat, grease.
seboro, *n.m.* (*Bol.*) freshwater crab.
seborrea, *n.f.* seborrhœa.
seboso, -sa, *a.* fat, greasy, tallowy, unctuous.
sebucán, *n.m.* (*Ven.*) manioc strainer.
seca, *n.f.* [SECO].
secadal, *n.m.* barren ground.
secadero, -ra, *a.* good for drying (*especially fruit or tobacco*). — *n.m.* drying-shed, drying-floor; drier; fruit-drier.
secadillo, *n.m.* almond meringue.
secador, -ra, *a.* drying. — *n.m.* drier; drying-room.
secamiento, *n.m.* drying.
secano, *n.m.* unirrigated land; dry sandbank; (*fig.*) anything very dry; ***cultivo de secano,*** dry farming.
secansa, *n.f.* sequence.
secante, *a.* drying; blotting; secant; (*fig.*) abrupt. — *n.m.* siccative; blotting paper. — *n.f.* secant.
secar [A], *v.t.* to dry; to wipe dry.
secaral, *n.m.* dryness, drought.
secatón, -tona, *a.* extremely curt, graceless.
secatura, *n.f.* flatness, vapidness, dullness.
sección, *n.f.* section; cross-section; department; cutting.
seccionado, -da, *a.* sectional, in sections.
seccionar, *v.t.* to section.
secesión, *n.f.* secession.

secesionista, *a., n.m.f.* secessionist.
seceso, *n.m.* excrement, stool.
seco, -ca, *a.* dry, dried up; lean, spare; bare, unadorned; cold, hard; curt, brusque; ***hojas secas,*** dead leaves; ***golpe seco,*** sharp, quick blow; ***a secas,*** just, plain, simply, merely; (*coll.*) ***dejar seco,*** to liquidate, bump off, shoot down; ***parar en seco,*** to stop dead; (*coll.*) ***a secas y sin llover,*** out of the blue, all of a sudden. — *n.f.* drought, dry season; dry sandbank; (*med.*) infarction of a gland; (*pl.*) sands, rocks.
secreción, *n.f.* (*med.*) secretion.
secreta, *n.f.* [SECRETO].
secretar, *v.t.* (*physiol.*) to secrete.
secretaría, *n.f.* secretariat; secretary's office; secretaryship.
secretaria, *n.f.* secretary.
secretario, *n.m.* secretary.
secretear, *v.i.* (*coll.*) to speak confidentially, whisper.
secreteo, *n.m.* (*coll.*) confidential whispering.
secreter, *n.m.* writing desk.
secretista, *n.m.* naturalist; dealer in secrets.
secreto, -ta, *a.* secret. — *n.m.* secret; secrecy; secret drawer *or* place; secret key *or* combination; (*mus.*) soundboard; ***secreto a voces,*** open secret; ***en secreto,*** secretly, confidentially. — *n.f.* private examination (*preceding graduation of licentiates*); (*eccles.*) secret; secret investigation; privy, closet.
secretorio, -ria, *a.* (*med.*) secretory.
secta, *n.f.* sect.
sectador, -ra, *n.m.f.* sectarist.
sectario, -ria, *a., n.m.f.* sectarian, sectary.
sectarismo, *n.m.* sectarianism.
sector, *n.m.* sector.
secuaz, *n.m.f.* follower; henchman.
secuela, *n.f.* sequel, outcome.
secuencia, *n.f.* sequence; (*gram.*) word-order, sequence.
secuestrable, *a.* sequestrable.
secuestración, *n.f.* sequestration; kidnapping, abduction.
secuestrador, *n.m.* sequestrator; kidnapper; ***secuestrador aéreo,*** aeroplane hijacker.
secuestrar, *v.t.* to sequester, sequestrate; to kidnap, abduct.
secuestro, *n.m.* sequestration; kidnapping, abduction; (*surg.*) sequestrum; ***secuestro aéreo,*** aeroplane hijacking.
sécula seculórum, *adv.* (for) ever and ever, world without end.
secular, *a.* secular; hundred-year-old; aged, age-old, time-honoured.
secularidad, *n.f.* secularity.
secularización, *n.f.* secularization.
secularizar [C], *v.t.* to secularize.
secundar, *v.t.* to second; to back.
secundario, -ria, *a.* secondary; high (*school*); subordinate, accessory, second-rank, subsidiary. — *n.m.* (*watch*) seconds hand.
secundinas, *n.f.pl.* afterbirth, secundines.
secura, *n.f.* dryness, drought.
sed, *n.f.* thirst; ***tener sed,*** to be thirsty; ***sed de,*** thirst for; ***apagar la sed,*** to quench the thirst.
seda, *n.f.* silk; wild boar's bristles; ***como una seda,*** smooth as silk; as meek as a lamb.
sedadera, *n.f.* hackle for dressing flax.
sedal, *n.m.* angling line; (*vet.*) rowel; (*surg.*) seton.
sedar, *v.t.* to allay; to quiet, soothe.
sedativo, -va, *a.* (*med.*) sedative.
sede, *n.f.* (*eccles.*) see; ***Santa Sede,*** Holy See, Papacy; ***sede social,*** headquarters (*of a firm, society etc.*), head office.
sedear, *v.t.* to clean (jewels) with a brush.
sedentario, -ria, *a.* sedentary.
sedente, *a.* sitting, seated.
sedeño, -ña, *a.* silky, silken, silk-like; made of hair. — *n.f.* flaxen tow.
sedería, *n.f.* silks, silk stuff; silk shop.
sedero, -ra, *a.* silk, silken; ***industria sedera,*** silk industry. — *n.m.f.* silk weaver; silk dealer. — *n.f.* bristle brush.
sedicente, *a.* self-styled, so-called.
sedición, *n.f.* sedition, insurrection, mutiny.
sedicioso, -sa, *a.* seditious. — *n.m.f.* seditious person, rebel, trouble-maker.
sediento, -ta, *a.* thirsty; ***sediento de,*** thirsty for.
sedimentación, *n.f.* sedimentation.
sedimentar, *v.t.* to deposit. — **sedimentarse,** *v.r.* to settle.
sedimentario, -ria, *a.* sedimentary.
sedimento, *n.m.* sediment, settlings, deposit(s).
sedoso, -sa, *a.* silky, silk-like, silken.
seducción, *n.f.* seduction, seducement; charm.
seducir [15], *v.t.* to seduce; to allure, tempt; to entice; ***no me seduce la idea,*** I don't find the idea tempting.
seductivo, -va, *a.* seductive, enticing.
seductor, -ra, *a.* seducing, seductive, alluring, tempting; charming, captivating. — *n.m.f.* seducer; charmer.
sefardí, sefardita, *a.* Sephardic. — *n.m.f.* Sephardi. — *n.m.* language of the Sephardim; (*pl.* **sefardíes**) Sephardim.
segable, *a.* fit to be reaped.
segada, *n.f.* harvest.
segadero, -ra, *a.* fit for reaping.— *n.f.* reaping-hook, sickle.
segador, -ra, *n.m.f.* mower, reaper, harvester, sickleman; ***segadora trilladora,*** combine harvester, (*Am.*) harvester. — *n.f.* mowing machine; ***segadora de césped,*** lawn-mower.
segar [1B], *v.t.* to harvest, reap, mow; to cut down, mow down.
segazón, *n.f.* reaping; reaping season.
seglar, *a.* secular, lay. — *n.m.* layman.
segmento, *n.m.* segment.
segregación, *n.f.* segregation; secretion.
segregar [B], *v.t.* to segregate; to secrete.
segregativo, -va, *a.* segregative; secreting.
segrí, *n.m.* heavy silk fabric.
segueta, *n.f.* fretsaw.
seguetear, *v.i.* to use a fretsaw.
seguida, *n.f.* [SEGUIDO].
seguidamente, *adv.* immediately after, following on.
seguidero, *n.m.* guidelines (*for writing*).
seguidilla, *n.f.* (*poet.*) stanza of four *or* seven lines; (*pl.*) lively tune and dance; (*coll.*) diarrhœa.
seguido, -da, *a.* successive, running, in a row, consecutive; straight, direct; ***a renglón seguido,*** immediately following on; ***acto seguido,*** at once. — *adv.* straight on *or* ahead, right on. — *n.m.* drop stitch. — *n.f.* following, continuation, succession; ***de seguida,*** in succession; at once; ***en seguida,*** at once, straight away.
seguidor, -ra, *n.m.f.* follower.
seguimiento, *n.m.* pursuit, chase, hunt; continuation.
seguir [8G], *v.t.* to follow, come after; to continue; ***seguirle a alguien la corriente,*** to go along with, row in with s.o. — *v.i.* to go on, continue; ***seguir adelante,*** to go on *or* ahead, press on, continue; ***sigue enfermo,*** he is still ill; ***suma y sigue,*** carry forward; (*coll.*) and what's more. — **seguirse,** *v.r.* to follow, be deduced.
según, *adv.* it (all) depends; ***según y como, según y conforme,*** just as; it (all) depends (on how). — *conj.* according as, as; depending on; so; ***según*** (***que***), it (all) depends on whether. — *prep.* according to.
segunda, *n.f.* [SEGUNDO].

segundar, *v.t.* to repeat. — *v.i.* to be second.
segundario, -ria, *a.* secondary.
segundero, -ra, *a.* (*agric.*) second (*crop in the same year*). — *n.m.* seconds hand (*of a watch*).
segundilla, *n.f.* call bell (*in convents*).
segundillo, *n.m.* second portion of bread; (*mus.*) accidental.
segundo, -da, *a.* second; double; secondary; ***segunda enseñanza,*** secondary education; ***de segunda mano,*** second hand; ***en segundo lugar,*** secondly. — *n.m.* second; (*naut.*) mate. — *n.f.* (*mus.*) second; double meaning; double turn (*of a key*).
segundogénito, -ta, *a.*, *n.m.f.* second-born.
segundón, *n.m.* second *or* younger son.
segur, *n.f.* axe; sickle.
segurador, *n.m.* security, surety, bondsman.
seguramente, *adv.* very likely, very probably; indeed.
segurar, *v.t.* [ASEGURAR].
segureja, *n.f.* small hatchet.
seguridad, *n.f.* security; surety; certainty; safety; sureness, confidence; assurance, guarantee.
seguro, -ra, *a.* secure, safe; sure, certain; constant, firm; steady, dependable. — *n.m.* assurance, insurance; safety; safety catch; ***a buen seguro,*** almost certainly; ***de seguro,*** for sure, very probably; ***sobre seguro,*** with every guarantee of success; ***seguro que sí,*** I suppose so, very probably; ***seguro social,*** social security.
segurón, *n.m.* large axe *or* hatchet.
seis, *a.* six. — *n.m.* six; sixth (*of the month*); six-spotted card, die *or* domino. — ***n.f.pl. las seis,*** six o'clock.
seisavado, -da, *a.* hexagonal.
seisavo, *n.m.* sixth, sixth part; hexagon.
seiscientos, -tas, *a.* six hundred, six hundredth.
seise, *n.m.* one of the six choirboys who sing and dance in some cathedrals.
seiseno, -na, *a.* sixth.
seisillo, *n.m.* sextolet.
séismico, *a.* seismic.
seje, *n.m.* (*Hisp. Am.*) palm tree.
selácio, -cia, *a.* (*ichth.*) selachian. — *n.m.pl.* (**selácios**) Selachii.
selección, *n.f.* selection, choice; ***selección natural,*** natural selection; (*sport*) ***selección nacional,*** national team *or* side.
seleccionador, -ra, *a.* selecting. — *n.m.f.* selector. — *n.m.* (*sport*) manager.
seleccionar, *v.t.* to select, choose, pick out.
selectas, *n.f.pl.* analects.
selecto, -ta, *a.* select, choice; excellent.
selenio, *n.m.* selenium.
selenita, *n.m.f.* Selenite. — *n.f.* (*min.*) selenite.
selenitoso, -sa, *a.* selenitic.
seleniuro, *n.m.* (*chem.*) selenide.
selenografía, *n.f.* selenography.
self (inducción), *n.f.* (*elec.*) self-induction coil.
selva, *n.f.* forest; tropical forest; jungle; ***Selva Negra,*** Black Forest.
selvático, -ca, *a.* (of the) forest, wild.
selvatiquez, *n.f.* uncouthness; wildness.
selvicultura, *n.f.* forestry, silviculture.
selvoso, -sa, *a.* silvan, sylvan; wooded, woody.
sellador, *n.m.* sealer.
selladura, *n.f.* sealing.
sellar, *v.t.* to seal; to stamp; ***sellar los labios,*** to seal one's lips; to seal the lips (of).
sello, *n.m.* seal; signet; stamp; (*pharm.*) cachet, wafer; ***sello de correos,*** postage stamp; ***sello de aduana,*** cocket.
semafórico, -ca, *a.* semaphoric.
semáforo, *n.m.* semaphore; traffic light.
semana, *n.f.* week; ***Semana Santa,*** Holy Week, Easter; ***entre semana,*** on weekdays; ***estar de semana,*** to be on duty (*for the week*).
semanal, *a.* weekly.
semanario, -ria, *a.* weekly. — *n.m.f.* weekly (*publication*); set of seven razors.
semanería, *n.f.* work done in the course of a week.
semanero, -ra, *a.* engaged by the week. — *n.m.f.* weekly worker.
semántico, -ca, *a.* semantic. — *n.f.* semantics, semasiology.
semasiología, *n.f.* semasiology, semantics.
semblante, *n.m.* countenance; look.
semblanza, *n.f.* biographical sketch, portrait.
sembradera, *n.f.* sowing machine, sower, seeder.
sembradío, -día, *a.* ready for sowing seed; arable.
sembrado, *n.m.* field, sown ground.
sembrador, *n.m.* sower.
sembradura, *n.f.* sowing, seeding.
sembrar [I], *v.t.* to sow; to seed; to scatter, disseminate, spread.
semeja, *n.f.* resemblance, likeness; mark, sign.
semejable, *a.* resembling, similar, like.
semejado, -da, *a.* like, resembling.
semejante, *a.* similar, like, alike, akin; such (a). — *n.m.* fellow-creature; likeness, resemblance.
semejanza, *n.f.* resemblance, similarity, likeness; ***a semejanza de,*** in the likeness of.
semejar, *v.i.* to resemble, be like.
semen, *n.m.* semen, sperm, seed.
semencera, *n.f.* sowing, seeding.
semencontra, *n.m.* (*pharm.*) vermifuge.
semental, *a.* seminal. — *n.m.* stallion, stud horse, sire; breeding animal.
sementera, *n.f.* sowing, seeding; seed-field, seed-bed, seed plot, land sown; seed-time; origin, beginning; (*fig.*) hotbed.
sementero, *n.m.* seed-bag; seed-bed, seed-plot.
sementino, -na, *a.* (belonging to) seed *or* seed-time.
semestral, *a.*, **semestralmente,** *adv.* half-yearly.
semestre, *n.m.* semester, half-year.
semibreve, *n.f.* (*mus.*) semibreve.
semicabrón, semicapro, *n.m.* satyr.
semicilindro, *n.m.* half-cylinder.
semicircular, *a.* semicircular.
semicírculo, *n.m.* semicircle.
semicopado, -da, *a.* syncopated.
semicorchea, *n.f.* semiquaver.
semidea, *n.f.* (*poet.*) demigoddess.
semideo, *n.m.* (*poet.*) demigod.
semidiáfano, -na, *a.* semi-diaphanous.
semidiámetro, *n.m.* semidiameter.
semidifunto, -ta, *a.* half-dead.
semidiós, *n.m.* demigod.
semidiosa, *n.f.* demigoddess.
semidítono, *n.m.* demi-ditone.
semidoble, *a.*, *n.m.* semidouble.
semidormido, -da, *a.* half-asleep.
semieje, *n.m.* (*geom.*) semiaxis; (*motor.*) half axle-tree.
semiesfera, *n.f.* hemisphere.
semiesférico, -ca, *a.* hemispherical.
semiflúido, -da, *a.* semifluid.
semiforme, *a.* half-formed.
semifusa, *n.f.* hemidemisemiquaver.
semigola, *n.f.* (*fort.*) demi-gorge.
semihombre, *n.m.* half-man.
semilunar, *a.* semilunar.
semilunio, *n.m.* half-moon.
semilla, *n.f.* seed.
semillero, *n.m.* seed-bed, seed-plot; nursery; (*fig.*) hotbed.
seminal, *a.* seminal.

seminario, *n.m.* seminary; seminar; seed-bed.
seminarista, *n.m.* seminarist, theological student.
semínima, *n.f.* crotchet.
semiología, semiótica, *n.f.* semeiology, semeiotics.
semiplena, *n.f.* (*law*) imperfect evidence.
semirrecto, -ta, *a.* (*geom.*) of forty-five degrees.
semirrubio, -bia, *a.* half-blond(e).
semita, *a.* Semitic. — *n.m.f.* Semite.
semitíco, -ca, *a.* Semitic. — *n.m.* Semitic (*group of languages*).
semitono, *n.m.* semitone.
semitransparente, *a.* almost transparent.
semivivo, -va, *a.* half-alive.
semivocal, *a.* semivocalic. — *n.f.* semivowel.
sémola, *n.f.* groats; semolina.
semoviente, *a.* self-moving; ***bienes semovientes,*** livestock.
sempiterno, -na, *a.* everlasting, sempiternal. — *n.f.* durance (*fabric*); (*bot.*) globe amaranth.
sen, *n.f.* senna.
Sena (**el**), *n.m.* Seine.
sena (1), *n.f.* six spots (*on dice*); (*pl.*) double sixes (*on dice*).
sena (2), *n.f.* senna.
senado, *n.m.* senate; senate house, town hall; audience.
senadoconsulto, *n.m.* senatus-consultum, senatorial decree.
senador, *n.m.* senator.
senaduría, *n.f.* senatorship.
senara, *n.f.* piece of ground (*assigned to servants as part of their wages*).
senario, -ria, *a.* senary. — *n.m.* (*poet.*) senarius.
senatorial, senatorio, -ria, *a.* senatorial.
sencillamente, *adv.* simply, just; in a straightforward manner.
sencillez, *n.f.* simplicity, straightforwardness.
sencillo, -lla, *a.* simple; plain; single; straightforward, uncomplicated.
senda, *n.f.* path, footpath, way.
senderar, senderear, *v.t.* to lead on a footpath; to cut a path through. — *v.i.* to adopt unusual measures.
sendero, *n.m.* path, footpath, by-way.
sendos, -das, *a.* one each; ***les dio sendos libros,*** he gave a book to each of them.
senectud, *n.f.* old age, senility.
senescal, *n.m.* seneschal.
Senegal (**el**), *n.m.* Senegal.
senegalés, -lesa, *a.*, *n.m.f.* Senegalese.
senescalía, *n.f.* office of a seneschal.
senil, *a.* senile. — *n.m.* (*astron.*) fourth quadrant.
seno, *n.m.* breast; bosom; womb; (*surg.*) sinus; bay; innermost recess; (*math.*) sine; (*arch.*) spandrel; (*naut.*) curvature of sail *or* line; ***murió en el seno de la Iglesia,*** he died in the bosom of the Church.
senojil, *n.m.* garter.
sensación, *n.f.* sensation; feeling, emotion.
sensacional, *a.* sensational.
sensatez, *n.f.* sense, sensibleness, good sense.
sensato, -ta, *a.* sensible, level-headed.
sensibilidad, *n.f.* sensitiveness, sensitivity.
sensibilizar [C], *v.t.* to sensitize, make sensitive.
sensible, *a.* sensitive; sentient; perceptible; appreciable, considerable; much lamented, deeply felt. — *n.f.* (*mus.*) seventh note.
sensiblería, *n.f.* sentimentality.
sensitivo, -va, *a.* sensitive, of the senses. — *n.f.* sensitive plant.
sensorio, -ria, *a.* sensorial, sensory. — *n.m.* sensorium.
sensorial, *a.* ***cine sensorial,*** (*fam.*) feelies.
sensual, *a.* sensual, sensuous.
sensualidad, *n.f.* sensuality, sensuousness.
sensualismo, *n.m.* sensualism; sensuality.
sensualista, *a.* sensualistic. — *n.m.f.* sensualist.
sentada (1), *n.f.* sitting; sit-in; ***de una sentada,*** at one sitting *or* go.
sentaderas, *n.f.pl.* seat, backside.
sentadero, *n.m.* place where one can sit.
sentadillas, (**a**), *adv.* side-saddle.
sentado, -da (2), *a.* steady; (*bot.*) sessile.
sentar [1], *v.t.* to seat; to establish, lay down; to suit, fit, agree with; ***sentar la cabeza,*** to settle down; ***sentar plaza,*** to join up; to lay down the law; ***le sentó como un tiro,*** it upset him violently; ***dar por sentado,*** to consider as settled, take for granted; ***lo tengo sentado en la boca del estómago,*** I can't stomach him. — **sentarse,** *v.r.* to sit (down); to settle (down).
sentencia, *n.f.* sentence, verdict, judgment; maxim; ***pronunciar la sentencia,*** to pass judgment.
sentenciador, -ra, *n.m.f.* one who passes judgment.
sentenciar, *v.t.* to sentence, condemn, pass judgment on; to consign. — *v.i.* to decide; to be sententious, lay down the law.
sentención, *n.m.* severe *or* excessive sentence.
sentencioso, -sa, *a.* sententious.
senticar, *n.m.* briary, thicket.
sentido, -da, *a.* sensitive; deep-felt, heart-felt, sincere. — *n.m.* sense; meaning; direction; consciousness; ***sentido común,*** common sense; ***no tiene sentido,*** it doesn't make sense; ***costar un sentido,*** to cost the earth; ***perder el sentido,*** to go off one's head; to lose consciousness; ***poner los cinco sentidos en,*** to pay the closest attention to; ***sin sentido,*** meaningless; unconscious.
sentimental, *a.* sentimental, emotional.
sentimentalismo, *n.m.* sentimentalism.
sentimiento, *n.m.* sentiment, feeling, emotion; sense; grief, sorrow, regret.
sentina, *n.f.* (*naut.*) bilge; (*fig.*) cesspool.
sentir, *n.m.* feeling. — [6], *v.t.* to feel; to sense, notice; to hear; to regret, be sorry about; ***lo siento,*** I'm sorry; ***sin sentir,*** imperceptibly, unnoticed.
seña, *n.f.* sign, mark, token; signal, motion, nod; (*mil.*) password; ***por más señas,*** to be (more) precise; ***por señas,*** by signs; ***santo y seña,*** password; (*pl.*) address; personal description.
señal, *n.f.* sign, mark, token; trace; signal; landmark; book-mark; deposit (*money*); traffic sign; ***en señal de,*** as a sign of, in token of; ***código de señales,*** signal code; ***ni señal de,*** not a sign of; ***prohibidas todas señales acústicas,*** sounding of horns forbidden.
señalado, -da, *a.* notable.
señalamiento, *n.m.* appointed day; marking with signs.
señalar, *v.t.* to mark out (*with signs*), signpost; to indicate, point out; to point to; to mark; to fix. — **señalarse,** *v.r.* to make a name for o.s., distinguish o.s.
señalizar, *v.t.* to signpost.
señera (1), *n.f.* ancient pendant *or* banner.
señero, -ra (2), *a.* solitary; unique.
señolear, *v.i.* to catch birds with a decoy.
señor, -ra, *a.* noble, grand; (*coll.*) some, quite, fine, super; ***un señor coche,*** quite a car. — *n.m.* sir; lord; master; Mr.; seigneur; ***muy señor mío,*** Dear Sir (*in letters*); ***una paliza de padre y muy señor mío,*** a monumental beating; ***un señor,*** a gentleman; ***sí, señor,*** certainly; ***no, señor,*** certainly not; ***todo un señor,*** perfect gentleman, every inch a gentleman. — *n.f.* lady; mistress; madam; dame; gentlewoman; ***nuestra Señora,*** our Lady.
señorada, *n.f.* grand gesture, gesture worthy of a gentleman.

señoraje, señoreaje, *n.m.* seigniorage.
señoreador, -ra, *a., n.m.f.* overbearing, domineering (*person*).
señoreante, *a.* domineering.
señorear, *v.t.* to dominate; to master; to tower over; (*coll.*) to lord it over; (*coll.*) to 'sir'.
señoría, *n.f.* lordship, seigniory; rule.
señorial, *a.* lordly, grand; manorial; feudal.
señoril, *a.* lordly.
señorío, *n.m.* fief; lordship; aristocracy, people of quality; grand manner *or* style.
señorita, *n.f.* Miss; young lady; (*coll.*) mistress of the house.
señoritingo, *n.m.* despicable young blood *or* parasite.
señorito, *n.m.* young gentleman; (*pej.*) young upper-class parasite; (*coll.*) master of the house.
señorón, -rona, *n.m.f.* great lord *or* lady; (*pej.*) one of the bloated upper classes *or* gentry.
señuelo, *n.m.* lure, enticement; decoy; ***caer en el señuelo,*** to fall into the trap.
seo (1), *n.f.* (*prov.*) cathedral church.
seo (2), **seor, seora,** (*contraction of* ***señor, señora***).
sepancuantos, *n.m. inv.* (*coll.*) spanking; scolding.
separable, *a.* separable.
separación, *n.f.* separation; splitting *or* breaking up; discharge, dismissal; secession.
separado, -da, *a.* separate; apart; ***por separado,*** separately; apart.
separador, -ra, separante, *a.* separating.
separar, *v.t.* to separate; to split *or* break up; to set asunder; to detach, remove; to lay aside, set apart; to dismiss. — **separarse,** *v.r.* to separate; to resign, leave; (*law*) to withdraw.
separata, *n.f.* off-print.
separatismo, *n.m.* separatism; secessionism.
separatista, *a., n.m.f.* separatist; secessionist.
separativo, -va, *a.* separatory.
sepedón, *n.m.* seps; lizard.
sepelio, *n.m.* interment, burial.
sepelir, *ant.* [SEPULTAR].
sepia, *n.f.* (*ichth.*) cuttle-fish; (*art*) sepia.
septembrino, -na, *a.* (of) September.
septena, *n.f.* septenary.
septenario, -ria, *a.* septenary.
septenio, *n.m.* (space of) seven years.
Septentrión, *n.m.* (*astron.*) Great Bear.
septentrión, *n.m.* septentrion, north.
septentrional, *a.* septentrional, northern.
septeto, *n.m.* (*mus.*) septet.
séptico, -ca, *a.* septic.
septiembre, *n.m.* September.
séptimo, -ma, *a.* seventh. — *n.f.* (*mus.*) seventh; sequence of seven cards.
septuagenario, -ria, *a.* septuagenary, seventy years of age.
septuagésimo, -ma, *a.* septuagesimal, seventieth. — *n.f.* third Sunday before Lent.
septuplicar [A], *v.t.* to multiply by seven.
séptuplo, -la, *a.* septuple, sevenfold.
sepulcral, *a.* sepulchral; deathly.
sepulcro, *n.m.* sepulchre, tomb, grave.
sepultador, *n.m.* burier, grave-digger.
sepultar, *v.t.* to inter, bury, entomb; to conceal, hide.
sepulto, -ta, *a.* buried. — *p.part. irreg. of* SEPULTAR, SEPELIR.
sepultura, *n.f.* sepulture, interment; tomb, grave; ***dar sepultura,*** to inter.
sepulturero, *n.m.* grave-digger, sexton.
sequedad, *n.f.* aridity, dryness; sterility, barrenness; asperity, gruffness, surliness; lack of irrigation.
sequedal, sequeral, *n.m.* dry, barren soil.
sequero, *n.m.* dry, arid, unirrigated land.
sequeroso, -sa, *a.* dry, moistureless.
sequete, *n.m.* dry crust; dry *or* stale bread *or* biscuit; curt, harsh answer; harshness; violent shock; stroke, blow.
sequía, *n.f.* dryness, drought; (*ant., prov.*) thirst.
sequillo, *n.m.* rusk, kind of biscuit.
sequío, *n.m.* unirrigated arable ground.
séquito, *n.m.* retinue, suite; train; followers.
sequizo, -za, *a.* dry (*fruits*); dryish.
ser [32], *v. subst.* to be. — *v. aux.* to be (*forming passives*). — *v.i.* to be, have one's being *or* essence; to become; to belong (to); ***un si es no es,*** a bit, somewhat; ***soy con usted,*** I agree with you; I'll be with you in a minute; ***sea lo que fuere,*** be that as it may; ***lo que fuere, sonará,*** wait and see; ***érase una vez,*** once upon a time; ***a*** or ***de no ser por,*** were it not for; ***no es para menos,*** well you might; ***para no ser menos,*** not to be outdone; ***la mujer que después fue su esposa,*** the woman who later became his wife; ***no sea que,*** lest, in case; ***o sea,*** that's to say, i.e.; ***¿qué ha sido de él?*** what's become of him?; ***es de ver,*** it's worth seeing; ***es para poco,*** it's *or* he's not much use. — *n.m.* life, being; essence.
sera, *n.f.* large pannier *or* basket, frail.
serado, *n.m.* number of panniers *or* baskets.
seráfico, -ca, *a.* seraphic, angelic; (*coll.*) poor, humble; ***hacer la seráfica,*** to affect virtue *or* modesty.
serafín, *n.m.* seraph; angel (*beautiful person*).
seraje [SERADO].
serba, *n.f.* fruit of the service tree.
serbal, serbo, *n.m.* service tree.
serena (1), *n.f.* evening dew; serenade.
serenar, *v.t.* to calm down; to clear the head of. — *v.i.* to become calm, clear up. — **serenarse,** *v.r.* to sober up.
serenata, *n.f.* (*mus.*) serenade.
serenero, *n.m.* nightrail, night-wrap; (*Arg.*) kerchief worn by peasant women.
serení, *n.m.* (*naut.*) jolly-boat; yawl.
serenidad, *n.f.* serenity; clearness; calmness, tranquillity, placidity; Serene Highness (*title*).
serenísimo, -ma, *a. superl.* Most Serene (*title of princes*).
sereno (1), **-na** (2), *a.* serene; calm; clear, fair; (*coll.*) sober.
sereno (2), *n.m.* night watchman; night dew; ***al sereno,*** in the night air.
sergas, *n.f.pl.* exploits, achievements.
sergenta, *n.f.* lay sister of the order of Santiago.
seriado, -da, *a.* mass-produced, stereotyped.
seriar, *v.t.* to produce a (whole) series of, mass-produce.
sérico, -ca, *a.* silk, silken.
serícula, *a.* sericultural.
sericultor, -ra, *n.m.f.* sericulturist.
sericultura, *n.f.* silk culture, sericulture.
serie, *n.f.* series; set; ***fabricar en serie,*** to mass-produce; ***coche de serie,*** mass-produced car; ***fuera de serie,*** out of the ordinary, exceptional.
seriedad, *n.f.* seriousness; earnestness; reliability; diligence.
serijo, serillo, *n.m.* small basket.
seringa, *n.f.* (*Hisp. Am.*) rubber tree.
serio, -ria, *a.* serious; earnest; solemn, dignified; reliable, dependable; considerable; ***una cosa seria,*** no light *or* small matter.
sermón, *n.m.* sermon; (*fig.*) lecture.
sermonario, -ria, *a.* relating to sermons. — *n.m.* collection of sermons.
sermonear, *v.t., v.i.* to sermonize, preach (to), lecture.
sermoneo, *n.m.* (*fig.*) preaching, lecturing.

serna, *n.f.* (cultivated) field.
seroja, *n.f.*, **serojo,** *n.m.* withered leaf; brushwood.
serón, *n.m.* hamper; pannier.
seronero, *n.m.* frail-maker; frail-seller.
serosidad, *n.f.* serosity.
seroso, -sa, *a.* serous.
serpa, *n.f.* provine, layer, runner.
serpear, *v.i.* to meander, wind; to wriggle, squirm.
serpentaria, *n.f.* (*bot.*) snake-root; ***serpentaria virginiana,*** Virginia snake-root.
Serpentario, *n.m.* (*astron.*) Ophiuchus.
serpentario, *n.m.* (*orn.*) secretary bird.
serpentear, *v.i.* to meander, wind; to wriggle, squirm.
serpentín, *n.m.* (*min.*) serpentine; cock, musket lock; (*chem.*) distilling worm; (*artill.*) twenty-four pounder.
serpentino, -na, *a.* serpentine, snake-like; winding; venomous. — *n.f.* (*paper*) streamer; cock (*of a gun*); (*min.*) serpentine.
serpentón, *n.m.* large snake; (*mus.*) serpent.
serpezuela, *n.f.* little snake.
Serpiente, *n.f.* (*astron.*) Serpens.
serpiente, *n.f.* serpent; snake; ***serpiente de cascabel,*** rattlesnake.
serpiginoso, -sa, *a.* serpiginous.
serpigo, *n.m.* ring-worm, tetter.
serpol, *n.m.* wild thyme.
serpollar, *v.i.* to shoot, sprout.
serpollo, *n.m.* shoot, sprout.
serradizo, -za, *a.* fit to be sawn.
serrado, -da, *a.* dentated, serrated.
serrador, *n.m.* sawer.
serraduras, *n.f.pl.* sawdust.
serrallo, *n.m.* seraglio.
serrana, *n.f.* [SERRANO].
serranía, *n.f.* range of hills *or* mountains; hilly *or* mountainous country.
serraniego, -ga, *a.* highland, hill, mountain.
serranil, *n.m.* knife; poniard.
serranilla, *n.f.* bucolic poem.
serrano, -na, *a.* mountain, highland. — *n.m.f.* mountain dweller, backwoodsman; (*Hisp. Am.*) Andean Indian. — *n.m.* (*ichth.*) sea bass. — *n.f.* bucolic poem.
serrar [1], *v.t.* to saw.
serrátil, *a.* (*med.*) irregular (*of pulse*).
serratilla, *n.f.* small mountain chain.
serrato, -ta, *a.* (*naut.*) denticulated, serrated. — *n.m.* serratus.
serreta, *n.f.* small saw; cavesson.
serretazo, *n.m.* jerk on the cavesson; dressing-down, reprimand.
serrezuela, *n.f.* small saw.
serrijón, *n.m.* short mountain chain.
serrín, *n.m.* sawdust.
serrino, -na, *a.* belonging to *or* like a saw; (*med.*) irregular (*of pulse*).
serruchar, *v.t.* (*Hisp. Am.*) to saw.
serrucho, *n.m.* hand-saw; ***serrucho braguero,*** pit-saw; (*Cub.*) saw-fish.
serum, *n.m.* (*med.*) serum.
servador, *n.m.* (*poet.*) guard, defender.
servato, *n.m.* hog-fennel, sulphur-weed.
serventesio, *n.m.* quatrain with rhyme *abab*; sirvente (*Provençal moral lay*).
serventía, *n.f.* (*Cub.*) path with right of way.
Servia, *n.f.* Serbia.
servible, *a.* serviceable, useful.
serviciador, *n.m.* collector of sheepwalk dues.
servicial, *a.* obliging, accommodating. — *n.m.* (*coll.*) clyster.
serviciar, *v.t.* to collect *or* pay (grazing dues).
servicio, *n.m.* service; duty; servants; tea, coffee *or* dinner set; toilet; ***de servicio,*** on duty; ***hacer un flaco servicio,*** to do a poor *or* scant service; ***servicio de mesa,*** table service.
servidero, -ra, *a.* fit for service, useful.
servidor, *n.m.* servant; wooer, gallant; privy-pan; ***servidor de Vd.,*** at your service.
servidora, *n.f.* maid, female servant.
servidumbre, *n.f.* servitude, serfdom, bondage; servants; unavoidable obligation; (*law*) easement, right; ***servidumbre de paso,*** right of way.
servil, *a.* servile, fawning, grovelling, menial, slavish; abject, mean, low, vile; (*Span. hist.*) partisan of absolute monarchy.
servilidad, *n.f.* servility; baseness.
servilismo, *n.m.* servility, servileness; (*Span. hist.*) absolutism.
servilla, *n.f.* pump (*shoe*).
servilleta, *n.f.* napkin, serviette; (*coll.*) ***doblar la servilleta,*** to snuff it.
servilletero, *n.m.* serviette-ring.
servio, -via, *a.*, *n.m.f.* Serbian. — *n.m.* Serbian (*language*).
serviola, *n.f.* cat-head, anchor beam.
servir [8], *v.t.* to serve; to help, serve with; to wait on; to tend (*a machine*); to fill (*an order*). — *v.i.* to serve; to be of use; ***servir de,*** to serve as, act as, be useful as; ***servir para,*** to serve for, be good *or* useful for; ***¿de*** or ***para qué sirve?*** what's the good of it?, what use is it?; ***no sirvió de nada,*** it was a waste of time and effort; (*coll.*) ***estar*** or ***ir servido,*** to have had it; ***para servir a Vd.,*** at your service; ***sirva de advertencia,*** let it be a warning; ***si Dios es servido,*** God willing. — **servirse,** *v.r.* to serve *or* help o.s.; to be so kind as to, deign to; (— ***de***), to make use of, avail o.s. of; ***sírvase*** (***Vd.***) ***entrar,*** please come in *or* go in.
servocroata, *a.*, *n.m.f.* Serbo-Croatian. — *n.m.* Serbo-Croat (*language*).
servodirección, *n.f.* power steering.
sesada, *n.f.* brains; fried brains.
sésamo, *n.m.* sesame.
sesear, *v.i.* to pronounce *c* (before *e*, *i*) and *z* as *s*.
sesenta, *a.* sixty, sixtieth.
sesentavo, -va, *a.* sixtieth.
sesentón, -tona, *a.*, *n.m.f.* (person) sixty years old, sixty-year-old.
seseo, *n.m.* pronouncing *c* (before *e*, *i*) and *z* as *s*.
sesera, *n.f.* brain; brain-pan.
sesga, *n.f.* [SESGO].
sesgado, -da, *a.* sloping, slanting, askew.
sesgadura, *n.f.* slope, slant, skew.
sesgar [B], *v.t.* to slope, slant, put askew; to cut on the bias. — *v.i.* to slant, be askew.
sesgo, -ga, *a.* sloped, slanting, oblique; placid, serene; severe, stern. — *n.m.* slope, slant, skew; dodge, twist; turn; ***al sesgo,*** slanting, askew. — *n.f.* (*sew.*) goring.
sesil, *a.* sessile.
sesión, *n.f.* session, sitting; meeting; ***sesión continua,*** continuous performance *or* showing; ***abrir*** (***levantar***) ***la sesión,*** to open (close) the meeting.
sesmo, *n.m.* division, administrative unit (*of territory*).
seso, *n.m.* brain; good sense; (steadying) block; ***devanarse los sesos,*** to rack one's brains; ***saltarse, levantarse la tapa de los sesos,*** to blow one's brains out; ***perder el seso,*** to lose one's wits; ***le tiene sorbido*** or ***bebido el seso, sorbidos*** or ***bebidos los sesos,*** he is completely under his influence; he is crazy about her.
sesquidoble, *a.* two and a half times.
sesteadero, *n.m.* resting-place (*for cattle*).
sestear, *v.i.* to take a siesta, nap, rest.

sesudo, -da, *a.* sensible *or* level-headed to a fault.
seta, *n.f.* bristle; mushroom.
setecientos, -tas, *a.* seven hundred.
setena, *n.f.* seven; ***pagar con las setenas,*** to suffer excessive punishment.
setenta, *a.* seventy, seventieth.
setenón, -tona, *a., n.m.f.* (person) seventy years old, seventy-year-old.
setentrión, *n.m.* septentrion, north.
setica, *n.f.* (*Per.*) tree (*Artocarpus genus*).
setiembre, *n.m.* September.
seto, *n.m.* fence, enclosure; hedge; (*P.R.*) wall; ***seto vivo,*** quickset hedge, hedgerow.
setuní, *n.m.* (*hist.*) rich oriental cloth; (*arch.*) arabesque work.
seudo, *a.* pseudo-, false.
seudónimo, -ma, *a.* pseudonymous. — *n.m.* pseudonym, nom-de-plume, pen name.
severidad, *n.f.* severity, strictness, sternness.
severo, -ra, *a.* severe, strict, stern.
sevicia, *n.f.* extreme cruelty.
seviche, *n.m.* (*Ec., Per.*) dish made of fish cooked with lemon juice.
sevillanas, *n.f.pl.* Sevillan air and dance.
sevillano, -na, *a.* of Seville. — *n.m.f.* Sevillan.
sexagenario, -ria, *a., n.m.f.* sexagenarian.
sexagesimal, *a.* sexagesimal.
sexagésimo, -ma, *a.* sixtieth, sexagesimal. — *n.f.* Sexagesima.
sexagonal, *a.* hexagonal.
sexángulo, -la, *a.* sexangular. — *n.m.* sexangle.
sexapel, *n.m.* sex-appeal.
sexenio, *n.m.* space of six years.
sexma, *n.f.* small coin; sixth part of a yard.
sexmo, *n.m.* administrative district.
sexo, *n.m.* sex; ***bello sexo,*** fair sex; ***sexo débil,*** weaker sex; ***sexo feo*** or ***fuerte,*** sterner *or* stronger sex.
sexta, *n.f.* [SEXTO (I)].
sextante, *n.m.* sextant; sextans.
sexteto, *n.m.* (*mus.*) sextet; group of six.
sextil, *a.* (*astrol.*) sextile.
sexto (I), **-ta,** *a.* sixth. — *n.f.* (*eccles.*) sext; sequence of six cards at piquet; (*mus.*) sixth; ancient Roman division of the day; afternoon.
sexto (2), *n.m.* book of canonical decrees.
sextuplicar [A], *v.t.* to sextuple.
séxtuplo, -la, *a.* sixfold.
sexual, *a.* sexual.
sexualidad, *n.f.* sexuality.
sexy, *a.* sexy. — *n.m.* sex-appeal.
show, *n.m.* (floor-)show; (*fig.*) scene, rumpus.
si, *conj.* if, whether; (*coll.*) but, why; (***por***) ***si acaso,*** in the event (that); if anything, if at all, at most, at best; ***por si acaso,*** (just) in case; ***si bien,*** although; ***si no,*** unless; if not, otherwise, or else; ***¡si será verdad!*** supposing it's true!; ***un si es no es,*** a bit, somewhat. — *n.m.* (*mus.*) B *or* si.
sí (I), *adv.* yes, yea. — *n.m.* yes; consent, acceptance; yea; ***dar el sí,*** to say yes; (***él***) ***sí lo sabe,*** he *does* know; ***te gusta mucho, ¿a qué sí?*** you like it a lot, don't you?; ***porque sí,*** for the hell of it, just because, for no reason.
sí (2), *pron.* (*reflexive form of the personal pronoun of the third person, in both genders and numbers*) himself, herself, yourself, itself, oneself, themselves; ***de sí, de por sí,*** in itself; ***volver en sí,*** to come to *or* round; ***fuera de sí,*** beside himself etc.; ***sobre sí,*** self-possessed.
sialismo, *n.m.* (*med.*) salivation.
siamés, -mesa, *a., n.m.f.* Siamese.—*n.m.* Siamese (*language*).
sibarita, *n.m.* Sybarite, voluptuary, epicure.
sibaritismo, *n.m.* Sybaritism.
sibil, *n.m.* cave, cellar.
sibila, *n.f.* sibyl.
sibilante, *a.* sibilant, hissing.
sibilino, -na, *a.* sibylline.
sicalíptico, -ca, *a.* suggestive, sexy.
sicario, *n.m.* hired assassin.
Sicilia, *n.f.* Sicily.
siciliano, -na, *a., n.m.f.* Sicilian.
siclo, *n.m.* shekel.
sicoanálisis [PSICOANÁLISIS].
sicofanta, sicofante, *n.m.* spy, informer; slanderer.
sicología [PSICOLOGÍA].
sicomoro, *n.m.* sycamore.
sideral, sidéreo, -rea, *a.* sidereal.
siderita, siderosa, *n.m.* (*min.*) siderite; (*bot.*) ironwort.
siderurgia, *n.f.* iron and steel industry.
siderúrgico, -ca, *a.* (relating to the) iron and steel (*industry*).
sidonio, -nia, *a., n.m.f.* Sidonian.
sidra, *n.f.* cider.
sidrería, *n.f.* cider shop.
siega, *n.f.* harvest, mowing, reaping.
siembra, *n.f.* sowing; seed-time; sown field.
siempre, *adv.* always; ever; ***las cosas de siempre,*** the usual things, the same old things as usual; ***para*** (***por***) ***siempre,*** forever; ***por siempre jamás,*** for ever and ever; ***desde siempre,*** since time immemorial; ***hasta siempre,*** so long, be seeing you; ***siempre que,*** (always) provided that.
siempreviva, *n.f.* (*bot.*) everlasting flower, immortelle; ***siempreviva menor,*** stone-crop; ***siempreviva mayor,*** houseleek.
sien, *n.f.* temple.
siento (I), **siente,** *pres. indic., pres. subj.* [SENTAR].
siento (2), **sienta, él sintió,** *pres. indic., pres. subj., pret.* [SENTIR].
sierpe, *n.f.* serpent; snake; (*fig.*) shrew; (*bot.*) sucker.
sierra, *n.f.* saw; mountain-range; range of hills; highlands; ***sierra abrazadera,*** frame-saw; ***sierra circular,*** circular saw, (*Am.*) buzz saw; ***sierra de cinta,*** bandsaw; ***sierra de mano,*** hand saw; ***sierra de punta,*** keyhole-saw; ***sierra de trasdós,*** tenon-saw; ***sierra de armero*** or ***de metal,*** hack-saw; ***sierra de marquetería,*** fret saw.
sierrecilla, *n.f.* small saw.
siervo, -va, *n.m.f.* slave; servant; serf; ***siervo de Dios,*** servant of God; (*coll.*) poor devil.
sieso, *n.m.* anus.
siesta, *n.f.* siesta; nap; hottest part of the day; ***echar la siesta,*** to take a nap.
siete, *a., n.m.* seven, seventh; v-shaped tear *or* gash; ***hablar más que siete,*** to talk nineteen to the dozen; ***de siete suelas,*** utter, dyed-in-the wool, out and out.
sieteañal, *a.* septennial.
sieteenrama, *n.f.* (*bot.*) tormentil.
sietemesino, -na, *a.* premature; born seven months after conception. — *n.m.* (*coll.*) stunted runt.
sieteñal, *a.* septennial.
sífilis, *n.f.* syphilis.
sifilítico, -ca, *a.* syphilitic.
sifón, *n.m.* syphon.
sifosis, *n.f.* hunch, crooked back.
sifué, *n.m.* surcingle.
sigilación, *n.f.* impression, mark, seal, stamp.
sigilar, *v.t.* to seal; to conceal, keep secret.
sigilo, *n.m.* seal; secret; reserve, concealment; ***sigilo profesional,*** professional secrecy; ***sigilo sacramental,*** secrecy of the confessional.
sigilosidad, *n.f.* quality of silence.
sigiloso, -sa, *a.* silent, reserved.
sigla, *n.f.* initials (*used as abbreviation*).

siglo, *n.m.* century; age; world; ***por los siglos de los siglos,*** for ever and ever; ***siglo de oro,*** Golden Age; ***siglos medios,*** Middle Ages; ***hace siglos que no te veo,*** I haven't seen you for ages.
signáculo, *n.m.* signet, seal.
signar, *v.t.* to sign, put a mark on; to make the sign of the cross over. — **signarse,** *v.r.* to cross o.s.
signatario, -ria, *a.* signing. — *n.m.f.* signatory.
signatura, *n.f.* sign, mark, signature; library number; (*eccles.*) rescript granting indulgence.
significación, *n.f.* significance; meaning.
significado, *a.* notable. — *n.m.* meaning.
significador, -ra, *a.* signifying. — *n.m.f.* signifier.
significante, *a.* meaningful.
significar [A], *v.t.* to signify, mean; to declare, state. — *v.i.* to mean, have significance. — **significarse,** *v.r.* to make a name for o.s.
significativo, -va, *a.* significant; meaning.
signo, *n.m.* sign; mark, symbol; hallmark; nod; (*mus.*) character; ***signo externo,*** status symbol.
sigua, *n.f.* (*Cub.*) tree resembling the ash tree.
siguapa, *n.f.* (*orn.*) Antillean gnome owl.
síguemepollo, *n.m.* ribbon adornment hanging down the back.
siguiente, *a.* following, next.
sijú, *n.m.* (*orn.*) Antillean gnome owl.
sil, *n.m.* yellow ochre.
sílaba, *n.f.* syllable.
silabar, *v.t.* to syllabicate.
silabario, *n.m.* spelling-book.
silabear, *n.m.* to syllabicate.
silabeo, *n.m.* syllabification.
silábico, -ca, *a.* syllabic.
sílabo, *n.m.* syllabus, index.
silanga, *n.f.* (*Philip.*) long and narrow inlet.
silba, *n.f.* hiss, hissing.
silbador, -ra, *a.* whistling, hissing. — *n.m.f.* whistler, hisser.
silbar, *v.t.* to whistle; to hiss, catcall. — *v.i.* to whistle; to hoot; to hiss; to whiz (*of a bullet*).
silbato, *n.m.* whistle; crack emitting hissing liquid *or* air.
silbido, *n.m.* whistle, whistling; hiss, hoot, hooting; whiz; ***silbido de oídos,*** ringing in the ears.
silbo, *n.m.* whistle, hiss, whiz.
silbón, *n.m.* (*orn.*) widgeon.
silboso, -sa, *a.* (*poet.*) whistling, hissing.
silenciador, *n.m.* (*motor.*) silencer, (*Am.*) muffler.
silenciar, *v.t.* to silence.
silenciario, -ria, *a.* observing silence.
silenciero, *n.m.* silentiary.
silencio, *n.m.* silence; (*mil.*) lights out, (*Am.*) taps; (*mus.*) rest; ***pasar en silencio,*** to pass over, omit, not to mention. — *interj.* hush! silence!
silencioso, -sa, *a.* silent, noiseless.
silente, *a.* silent; still.
silepsis, *n.f. inv.* (*gram.*) syllepsis.
silería, *n.f.* group of silos.
silero, *n.m.* (*agric.*) silo.
sílfide, *n.f.*, **silfo,** *n.m.* sylph.
silguero, *n.m.* linnet.
silicato, -ta, *a.* silicate.
sílice, *n.f.* (*chem.*) silica.
silicio, *n.m.* silicon.
silicua, *n.f.* siliqua; carat; (*bot.*) pod.
silo, *n.m.* silo.
silogismo, *n.m.* syllogism.
silogístico, -ca, *a.* syllogistic, syllogistical.
silogizar [C], *v.i.* to syllogize, argue, reason.
silueta, *n.f.* silhouette, outline.
silúrico, -ca, *a.* Silurian.
siluro, *n.m.* catfish; self-propelling torpedo.
silva, *n.f.* verse; miscellany, anthology.
silvestre, *a.* wild; uncivilized.
silvicultor, *n.m.* silviculturist, forester.
silvicultura, *n.f.* forestry.
silla, *n.f.* chair; see; ***silla de manos,*** sedan chair; ***silla de posta,*** postchaise; ***silla de tijera,*** folding chair; ***silla giratoria,*** swivel chair; ***silla de montar,*** saddle; ***silla de la reina,*** chair made by two persons' hands and wrists.
sillar, *n.m.* (square hewn) slab of stone; back (*of a horse*).
sillarejo, *n.m.* small ashlar.
sillera, *n.f.* place for parking sedan chairs.
sillería, *n.f.* set of chairs *or* seats; shop where chairs are made *or* sold; choir-stalls; stone-work.
sillero, *n.m.* saddler; chair-maker.
silleta, *n.f.* small chair; side-saddle; bed-pan; stone (*on which chocolate is ground*); (*pl.*) mule chairs.
silletazo, *n.m.* blow with a chair.
silletero, *n.m.* sedan-chair bearer; chair-maker; chair-seller.
sillico, *n.m.* basin (*of a close-stool*).
sillín, *n.m.* (light riding) saddle; (harness) saddle; (elaborate) mule chair; (cycle) seat.
sillita, *n.f.* small chair.
sillón, *n.m.* armchair; easy chair; side-saddle.
sima, *n.f.* abyss, chasm.
simado, -da, *a.* deep.
simbiosis, *n.f. inv.* symbiosis.
simbol, *n.m.* (*Arg.*) pampas grass.
simbólico, -ca, *a.* symbolic, symbolical.
simbolismo, *n.m.* symbolism.
simbolización, *n.f.* symbolization.
simbolizar [C], *v.i.* to symbolize, typify.
símbolo, *n.m.* symbol.
simetría, *n.f.* symmetry.
simétrico, -ca, *a.* symmetric, symmetrical.
simia, *n.f.* female ape.
simiente, *n.f.* seed, semen, sperm.
simiesco, -ca, *a.* simian, apelike, apish.
símil, *a.* similar. — *n.m.* simile.
similar, *a.* similar, like.
similicadencia, *n.f.* (*rhet.*) rhyming cadences.
similitud, *n.f.* similitude, similarity.
similitudinario, -ria, *a.* similar, similitudinary.
similor, *n.m.* similor; ***de similor,*** sham, fake.
simio, *n.m.* simian, ape.
simón, *n.m.* (*hansom*) cab; cabby (*in Madrid*).
simonía, *n.f.* simony.
simoníaco, -ca, simoniático, -ca, *a.* simoniacal.
simpa, *n.f.* (*Hisp. Am.*) braid, plait; (*Hisp. Am.*) tress.
simpar, *a.* unequalled, unmatched.
simpatía, *n.f.* sympathy, fellow-feeling; genialness, likeableness; ***tener simpatía por alguien,*** to like s.o.
simpático, -ca, *a.* genial, likeable, nice; (*anat.*) ***gran simpático,*** sympathetic nervous system.
simpatizante, *a.* favouring, supporting. — *n.m.f.* sympathizer; supporter.
simpatizar [C], *v.i.* to sympathize; (*coll.*) to hit it off (**con,** with); to take a liking (**con,** to).
simple, *a.* simple; mere; single; simple-minded; ***a simple vista,*** at first sight. — *n.m.f.* simpleton. — *n.m.* (*pharm.*) simple.
simpleza, *n.f.* silly *or* foolish thing to do *or* say; gullibility.
simplicidad, *n.f.* simplicity; ingenuousness.
simplificación, *n.f.* simplification.
simplificar [A], *v.t.* to simplify.
simplista, *a.* simplistic, oversimplifying. — *n.m.f.* simplist.
simplón, -lona, *n.m.f.* great simpleton.
simposio, *n.m.* symposium.

simulación, *n.f.* simulation, feigning; pretence.
simulacro, *n.m.* simulacrum; sham, mock-up; (*mil.*) sham battle.
simulado, -da, *a.* sham, mock.
simulador, -ra, *a.* dissembling, pretending. — *n.m.* simulator, dissembler.
simular, *v.t.* to simulate; to feign; to fake, sham.
simultaneidad, *n.f.* simultaneity.
simultáneo, -nea, *a.* simultaneous.
simún, *n.m.* sandstorm, sirocco.
sin, *prep.* without; besides, without counting; ***sin embargo,*** however, nevertheless; ***sin pies ni cabeza,*** without rhyme *or* reason; ***eso no tiene ni pies ni cabeza,*** I can't make head or tail of it; ***sin comerlo ni beberlo,*** undeservedly; without really trying; ***sin un cuarto,*** penniless; ***sin decir agua va,*** without giving warning; ***sin decir oxte ni moxte,*** without so much as a 'by your leave'; ***sin más ni más,*** without more ado; ***sin ton ni son,*** without rhyme or reason; ***sin terminar,*** unfinished; ***sin satisfacer,*** unsatisfied.
sinagoga, *n.f.* synagogue.
sinalagmático, -ca, *a.* (*law*) synallagmatic.
sinalefa, *n.f.* synaloepha.
sinapismo, *n.m.* sinapism; (*coll.*) bore.
sincerador, -ra, *n.m.f.* exculpator, excuser.
sincerar, *v.t.* to exculpate, vindicate. — **sincerarse,** *v.r.* to open one's heart *or* mind (**con,** to); to speak frankly (**con,** with).
sinceridad, *n.f.* sincerity.
sincero, -ra, *a.* sincere.
síncopa, syncope; syncopation.
sincopar, *v.t.* to syncopate; to abridge. — **sincoparse,** *v.r.* to miss a beat (*heart etc.*).
síncope, *n.f.* fainting-fit; syncope; ***síncope cardíaco,*** heart failure.
sincopizar [C], *v.t.* to cause a swoon *or* fainting-fit in. — **sincopizarse,** *v.r.* to faint; to have a fit; to miss a beat.
sincresis, *n.f. inv.* syncresis.
sincrónico, -ca, *a.* synchronous; synchronic.
sincronismo, *n.m.* synchronism.
sincronizar [C], *v.t., v.i.* to synchronize.
sindéresis, *n.f. inv.* discretion, good judgment.
sindicado, *n.m.* syndicate.
sindicadura, *n.f.* office of a syndic.
sindical, *a.* syndical; trade union.
sindicalismo, *n.m.* syndicalism; trade unionism.
sindicalista, *a., n.m.f.* syndicalist; trade unionist.
sindicar [A], *v.t.* to accuse; to syndicate. — **sindicarse,** *v.r.* to form *or* band into a (trade) union; to join a *or* the union.
sindicato, *n.m.* syndicate; trade union.
sindicatura, *n.f.* syndic's office.
síndico, *n.m.* receiver; syndic.
sindiós, *a.* godless. — *n.m.f. inv.* godless person, atheist.
síndrome, *n.m.* syndrome; ***síndrome de abstención,*** withdrawal symptoms.
sinécdoque, sinédoque, *n.f.* (*rhet.*) synecdoche.
sinecura, *n.f.* sinecure.
sinedrio, *n.m.* Sanhedrin.
sinéresis, *n.f. inv.* (*gram.*) synæresis.
sinfín, *n.m.* no end, endless number *or* amount; terrific number *or* amount.
sínfito, *n.m.* (*bot.*) comfrey.
sinfonía, *n.f.* symphony.
sinfónico, -ca, *a.* symphonic.
sinfonista, *n.m.f.* symphonist.
singa, *n.f.* sculling.
singar [B], *v.i.* to scull over the stern.
singladura, *n.f.* (*naut.*) day's run; voyage, trip.
singlar, *v.i.* to sail, voyage.
singlón, *n.m.* futtock.
singular, *a.* singular; single.
singularidad, *n.f.* singularity, peculiarity, oddity.
singularización, *n.f.* singularization; singling out.
singularizar [C], *v.t.* to singularize; to single out. — **singularizarse,** *v.r.* to make a name for o.s.; to make o.s. conspicuous; to be (an *or* the) odd man out.
singulto, *n.m.* sob; hiccough, singultus.
sinhueso, *n.f.* (*coll.*) ***la sinhueso,*** the tongue.
sínico, -ca, *a.* Chinese.
siniestrado, -da, *n.m.f.* victim; one rendered homeless (*by wreck, fire etc.*).
siniestro, -ra, *a.* sinister; left, left-hand; ill-omened. — *n.m.* perverseness; disaster, wreck; (*com.*) damage, loss. — *n.f.* left hand; left-hand side.
sinistrorso, sinistrorsum, *a.* (*bot.*) sinistrorse.
sinnúmero, *n.m.* endless succession; ***un sinnúmero de,*** no end of, countless.
sino, *conj.* but, except; only; ***no sólo . . . sino también,*** not only . . . but also. — *n.m.* fate, destiny.
sinoble, *a.* (*her.*) vert.
sinocal, sínoco, -ca, *a.* (*med.*) synochal.
sinodal, *a.* synodic, synodal.
sinodático, *n.m.* tax paid to the bishop.
sinódico, -ca, *a.* synodal, synodical; (*astron.*) synodic.
sínodo, *n.m.* synod; conjunction of the heavenly bodies.
sinología, *n.f.* Sinology.
sinonimia, *n.f.* synonymy.
sinónimo, -ma, *a.* synonymous. — *n.m.* synonym.
sinople, *a.* (*her.*) sinople, green.
sinopsis, *n.f. inv.* synopsis.
sinóptico, -ca, *a.* synoptic, synoptical.
sinovial, *a.* synovial.
sinrazón, *n.f.* wrong, injustice; unreason.
sinsabor, *n.m.* displeasure; sorrow; anxiety, trouble, worry.
sinsonte, *n.m.* (*orn.*) mocking-bird.
sinsostenismo, *n.m.* no-bra fashion.
sinsubstancia, *n.m.f.* blockhead.
sintáctico, -ca, *a.* syntactic, syntactical.
sintaxis, *n.f.* (*gram.*) syntax.
síntesis, *n.f. inv.* synthesis.
sintético, -ca, *a.* synthetical.
sintetizar [C], *v.t.* to synthesize.
síntoma, *n.m.* symptom.
sintomático, -ca, *a.* symptomatic(al).
sintonía, *n.f.* syntony; tuning, tune; theme song.
sintonización, *n.f.* (*rad.*) tuning.
sintonizador, *n.m.* (*rad.*) tuner.
sintonizar [Z], *v.t., v.i.* (*rad.*) to tune; ***sintonizar con,*** to tune in to.
sinuosidad, *n.f.* sinuosity; winding; deviousness.
sinuoso, -sa, *a.* sinuous; winding; wavy; devious.
sinvergüencería, *n.f.* (*coll.*) shamelessness, brazenness; caddish *or* rotten behaviour.
sinvergüenza, *n.m.f.* shameless individual; scoundrel, rascal, cad, rotter.
sinvergüenzada, *n.f.* (*Col.*) base action.
sionismo, *n.m.* Zionism.
sionista, *a., n.m.f.* Zionist.
sipedón, *n.m.* seps, a serpent-lizard.
siquiatría [PSIQUIATRÍA].
síquico, -ca [PSÍQUICO].
siquier, siquiera, *adv.* at least; even; ***ni siquiera,*** not even; ***dime siquiera dónde está,*** at least tell me where it is. — *conj.* although, even though; whether . . . or; ***siquera un poquito,*** even if it's only a wee bit.
sirena, *n.f.* syren, mermaid; siren, foghorn.
sirga, *n.f.* tow-line, tow-rope; line for hauling seines; ***a la sirga,*** tracking from the shore.

sirgadura, *n.f.* towing.
sirgar [B], *v.t.* (*naut.*) to tow, track.
sirgo, *n.m.* twisted silk.
sirguero, *n.m.* linnet.
Siria, *n.f.* Syria.
siríaco, -ca, *a.* Syrian.
Sirio, *n.m.* (*astron.*) Sirius.
sirio, -ria, *a.*, *n.m.f.* Syrian.
sirle, *n.f.* sheep's dung; goat's dung.
siroco, *n.m.* sirocco.
sirria, *n.f.* sheep-dung.
sirte, *n.f.* hidden sandbank, shoal.
sirvienta, *n.f.* servant, servant-girl, maid.
sirviente, *n.m.* servant, serving-man.
sisa, *n.f.* pilfering; size (*used by gilders*); excise; (*sew.*) dart.
sisador, -ra, *n.m.f.* filcher, pilferer; sizer.
sisallo, *n.m.* saltwort.
sisar, *v.t.* to filch, pilfer; to size (*for gilding*); to excise; (*sew.*) to take in. — *v.i.* to pilfer.
sisear, *v.i.* to hiss.
siseo, *n.m.* hissing.
sisero, *n.m.* exciseman, excise-collector.
sisimbrio, *n.m.* hedge-mustard.
sísmico, -ca, *a.* seismic.
sismógrafo, *n.m.* seismograph.
sismología, *n.f.* seismology.
sismológico, -ca, *a.* seismological.
sismómetro, *n.m.* seismometer.
sisón, -sona, *a.* pilfering. — *n.m.f.* pilferer. — *n.m.* (*orn.*) little bustard.
sistema, *n.m.* system; method, orderliness; ***el Sistema,*** the Established Order *or* Establishment.
sistemático, -ca, *a.* systematic; methodical.
sistematizar [C], *v.t.* to systematize.
sístilo, *n.m.* (*arch.*) systyle.
sístole, *n.f.* (*physiol. and rhet.*) systole.
sistólico, -ca, *a.* (*physiol.*) systolic.
sistro, *n.m.* (*mus.*) sistrum.
sitiador, -ra, *a.* besieging. — *n.m.* besieger.
sitial, *n.m.* (president's) chair, seat (*of honour*).
sitiar, *v.t.* to besiege, lay siege to; to hem in, surround.
sitibundo, -da, *a.* thirsty.
sitiero, *n.m.* (*Cuba*) petty farmer.
sitio, *n.m.* place, spot; room; site, location; siege; (*Hisp. Am.*) cattle ranch; ***real sitio,*** royal residence; ***dejar, hacer sitio a,*** to leave, make room for; ***poner sitio a,*** to lay siege to; ***quedarse en el sitio,*** to die on the spot; ***en cualquier sitio,*** anywhere.
sito, -ta, *a.* situated, lying, located.
situación, *n.f.* situation; position; location; ***situación activa,*** active service, position *or* office; ***situación pasiva,*** position of a retired *or* redundant person; ***en situación de,*** in a position to.
situar [M], *v.t.* to situate, locate, place. — **situarse,** *v.r.* to get *or* take a position.
sixtino, *a.* Sistine.
slip, *n.m.* briefs; knickers; swimming-trunks.
smoking, *n.m.* dinner-jacket, (*Am.*) tuxedo.
so (1), *prep.* under; ***so capa de, so color de,*** under pretext of, under pretence of; ***so pena de,*** on pain of, under penalty of.
¡so! (2), *interj.* whoa! stop!; ***¡so tonto!*** you fool!
soasar, *v.t.* to half roast; to cook lightly.
soata, *n.f.* (*Ven.*) kind of squash.
soba, *n.f.* beating, beating up; pawing, mussing about, petting.
sobacal, *a.* axillary.
sobaco, *n.m.* armpit; arm-hole; (*bot.*) axil.
sobadero, *n.m.* place where hides are tanned.
sobado, -da, *a.* hackneyed, done to death. — *n.m.* drubbing, beating; (*C.R.*) molasses made of inferior honey.
sobadura, *n.f.* kneading, rubbing.
sobajadura, *n.f.* kneading; scrubbing, friction.
sobajamiento, *n.m.* friction, rubbing.
sobajanero, *n.m.* (*coll.*) errand-boy.
sobajar, *v.t.* to squeeze, scrub, rub hard.
sobanda, *n.f.* end of a cask.
sobaquera, *n.f.* arm-hole, opening in clothes under the armpit.
sobaquina, *n.f.* underarm odour.
sobar, *v.t.* to knead; to finger, paw; (*coll.*) to neck, pet.
sobarba, *n.f.* noseband of a bridle.
sobarbada, *n.f.* sudden check; jerk; reprimand, scolding.
sobarcar [A], *v.t.* to draw up (clothes) to the arm-holes; to carry under the arm.
sobeo, *n.m.* leather thong for tying the yoke to the pole.
soberanear, *v.i.* to be domineering, lord it.
soberanía, *n.f.* sovereignty.
soberano, -na, *a.* sovereign, supreme; magnificent, great; ***una soberana tontería,*** egregious nonsense — *n.m.f.* sovereign.
soberbio, -bia, *a.* overproud, haughty; superb, magnificent; high-spirited. — *n.f.* (overweening) pride, arrogance.
sobina, *n.f.* peg, wooden pin.
sobón, -bona, *a.* much given to necking, petting *or* fondling; (*coll.*) slurpy.
sobordo, *n.m.* (*naut.*) check of a cargo with its manifest.
sobornación, *n.f.* subornation, bribery.
sobornador, -ra, *n.m.f.* briber, suborner.
sobornal, *n.m.* overload.
sobornar, *v.t.* to bribe, suborn.
soborno, *n.m.* subornation; bribe; bribery, graft; (*Arg., Bol., Chi.*) overload.
sobra, *n.f.* surplus, excess; left over, leaving; ***de sobra,*** more than enough, to spare, plenty; (*coll.*) ***está de sobra,*** he's not wanted.
sobradar, *v.t.* to add a loft to.
sobradillo, *n.m.* cockloft, penthouse.
sobrado, -da, *a.* more than enough, (in) plenty, (to) spare; (*Hisp. Am., coll.*) show-off, exaggerated. — *n.m.* attic, loft.
sobrancero, -ra, *a.* unemployed; surplus.
sobrante, *a.* left-over, remaining, surplus, excess. — *n.m.* surplus, excess.
sobrar, *v.i.* to be left over; to be surplus, over, in excess; to be more than enough, to spare, (in) plenty; not to be wanted *or* needed; ***le sobra razón,*** he has every reason *or* every right; he has every bit of right on his side.
sobrasada, *n.f.* sausage (*speciality of Majorca*).
sobrasar, *v.t.* to add fuel under (*a pot etc.*).
sobre, *prep.* on, upon; over, above; about, nearly; besides, in addition to; out of; ***estar sobre sí,*** to be in control of o.s.; to be on the lookout, on guard; ***sobre poco más o menos,*** more or less; ***sobre que,*** on top of the fact that. — *n.m.* envelope.
sobreabundancia, *n.f.* superabundance, glut.
sobreabundar, *v.i.* to superabound, be superabundant, be in glut.
sobreaguar [H], *v.i.* to float.
sobreagudo, *n.m.* (*mus.*) highest treble.
sobrealiento, *n.m.* difficult breathing.
sobrealimentar, *v.t.* to overfeed.
sobrealzar [C], *v.t.* over-praise.
sobreañadir, *v.t.* to superadd.
sobreañal, *a.* more than a year old.
sobreasada [SOBRASADA].
sobreasar, *v.t.* to roast again.
sobrebarato, -ta, *a.* extra cheap.

sobreboya, *n.f.* (*naut.*) marking buoy.
sobrecaja, *n.f.* outer case.
sobrecalza, *n.f.* leggings.
sobrecama, *n.f.* quilt, coverlet, bedspread.
sobrecaña, *n.f.* tumour.
sobrecarga, *n.f.* surcharge; overburden; additional trouble; overload; packing strap.
sobrecargar [B], *v.t.* to surcharge; to overload, overburden; to overcharge.
sobrecargo, *n.m.* supercargo; purser.
sobrecarta, *n.f.* envelope, cover of a letter; (*law*) second decree *or* warrant.
sobrecebadera, *n.f.* (*naut.*) sprit topsail.
sobrecédula, *n.f.* second decree.
sobreceja, *n.f.* forehead.
sobrecejo, *n.m.* frown.
sobreceño, *n.m.* frown.
sobrecercar [A], *v.t.* (*sew.*) to welt.
sobrecerco, *n.m.* (*sew.*) welt.
sobrecincho, -cha, *n.m.f.* surcingle.
sobrecoger [E], *v.t.* to overawe, fill with awe; to take by surprise.
sobrecogimiento, *n.m.* awe; apprehension.
sobrecomida, *n.f.* dessert.
sobrecopa, *n.f.* lid of a cup.
sobrecrecer [9], *v.i.* to grow out, grow on top.
sobrecreciente, *a.* outgrowing, growing on top.
sobrecruces, *n.m.pl.* (*carp.*) cross-joints.
sobrecubierta, *n.f.* double cover *or* wrapping; jacket (*of a book*); (*naut.*) upper deck.
sobrecuello, *n.m.* top collar; cravat.
sobredicho, -cha, *a.* above-mentioned, aforesaid.
sobredorar, *v.t.* to gold-plate (*metals*); (*fig.*) to gloss over.
sobreedificar [A], *v.t.* to build on *or* over (*an existing building*).
sobreempeine, *n.m.* covering for the instep.
sobreentender(se) [SOBRENTENDER].
sobreestadías, *n.f.pl.* (*com.*) extra lay days.
sobreexcitación, *n.f.* over-excitement.
sobreexcitar, *v.t.* to over-excite.
sobrefalda, *n.f.* overskirt.
sobrefaz, *n.f.* superficies, surface, outside; (*fort.*) face prolonged.
sobrefino, -na, *a.* superfine, overfine.
sobreflor, *n.f.* flower growing within another.
sobrefusión, *n.f.* (*phys.*, *chem.*) superfusion.
sobreguarda, *n.m.* second guard.
sobrehaz, *n.f.* surface; outside cover.
sobreherido, -da, *a.* slightly wounded.
sobrehilar, *v.t.* (*sew.*) to overcast.
sobrehueso, *n.m.* (*vet.*) splint; hard tumour (*on a bone*); (*fig.*) encumbrance, burden.
sobrehumano, -na, *a.* superhuman.
sobrehusa, *n.f.* stew of fried fish.
sobrejalma, *n.f.* cover of a packsaddle.
sobrejuanete, *n.m.* (*naut.*) royal (*sail*).
sobrellave, *n.f.* double key. — *n.m.* keeper of double keys in royal palace.
sobrellenar, *v.t.* to overfill, overflow, glut.
sobrelleno, -na, *a.* overfull, superabundant.
sobrellevar, *v.t.* to ease (another's burden); to bear, endure; to suffer patiently, bear with.
sobremanera, *adv.* exceedingly.
sobremano, *n.m.* bony tumour on fore-hoofs.
sobremesa, *n.f.* table cloth; dessert; table-talk, after-dinner conversation; ***de sobremesa,*** after dinner.
sobremesana, *n.f.* mizen topsail.
sobremuñonera, *n.f.* (*artill.*) clamp, cap-square.
sobrenadar, *v.i.* to float, stay on the surface.
sobrenatural, *a.* supernatural.
sobrenaturalmente, *adv.* supernaturally.
sobrenombre, *n.m.* surname; nickname.
sobrentender [2], *v.t.* to understand (*sth. implied*). — **sobrentenderse,** *v.r.* to be understood, go without saying; ***se sobrentiende que,*** it is understood, taken for granted, implied (that).
sobrepaga, *n.f.* increase of pay; bonus.
sobrepaño, *n.m.* upper cloth, wrapper.
sobreparto, *n.m.* (*med.*) after-birth; confinement after childbirth.
sobrepeine, *adv.* slightly, briefly. — *n.m.* hair-trimming.
sobrepelliz, *n.f.* surplice.
sobrepeso, *n.m.* overweight.
sobrepié, *n.m.* bony tumour on rear hoofs.
sobreplán, *n.m.* (*naut.*) rider.
sobreponer [25], *v.t.* to put over *or* above, on *or* upon, superimpose. — **sobreponerse,** *v.r.* to rise above, overcome; to pull o.s. together.
sobreprecio, *n.m.* extra charge, surcharge.
sobreproducción, *n.f.* over-production.
sobrepuerta, *n.f.* cornice; portière, door-curtain; pelmet.
sobrepuesto (1), *n.m.* honeycomb (*formed after the hive is full*).
sobrepuesto (2), **-ta,** *a.* superposed. — *p.p. irreg.* [SOBREPONER].
sobrepuja, *n.f.* outbidding.
sobrepujamiento, *n.m.* surpassing, excelling.
sobrepujante, *a.* surpassing, excelling.
sobrepujanza, *n.f.* great strength, exceeding vigour.
sobrepujar, *v.t.* to surpass, excel.
sobrequilla, *n.f.* keelson.
sobrerronda, *n.f.* (*mil.*) counter-round.
sobreropa, *n.f.* overcoat; overalls.
sobresaliente, *a.* outstanding, excellent; projecting. — *n.m.* distinction mark, mark of 'excellent'; substitute, understudy.
sobresalir [31], *v.i.* to stand out, protrude; to be outstanding *or* prominent.
sobresaltar, *v.t.* to startle. — *v.i.* to stand out. — **sobresaltarse,** *v.r.* to start, be startled.
sobresalto, *n.m.* start, fright, scare; ***de sobresalto,*** unexpectedly, suddenly.
sobresanar, *v.t.* to heal superficially; to palliate.
sobresano, *adv.* superficially healed; feignedly; affectedly. — *n.m.* (*naut.*) tabling, beach-lining.
sobrescribir [*p.p.* **sobrescri(p)to**], *v.t.* to superscribe; to address (*a letter*).
sobrescrito, *n.m.* address (*of a letter*).
sobresdrújulo, -la, *a.* accented on any syllable before the antepenultimate.
sobreseer [N], *v.t.* (*law*) to supersede; to stay. — *v.i.* to desist, yield.
sobreseguro, *adv.* safely, without risk.
sobreseimiento, *n.m.* suspension, discontinuance; (*law*) stay (*of proceedings*).
sobresello, *n.m.* second seal, double seal.
sobresembrar [1], *v.t.* to sow over again.
sobreseñal, *n.f.* (*her.*) (knight's) device.
sobresolar [4], *v.t.* to resole; to pave anew.
sobrestante, *n.m.* overseer, foreman.
sobresueldo, *n.m.* addition to pay, extra pay.
sobresuelo, *n.m.* overlaid floor.
sobretarde, *n.f.* dusk; hour before darkness.
sobretodo, *adv.* above all; especially. — *n.m.* greatcoat, overcoat, (*Am.*) topcoat.
sobreveedor, *n.m.* chief supervisor, overseer.
sobrevenida, *n.f.* supervention; unexpected arrival, sudden occurrence.
sobrevenir [36], *v.i.* to arrive, occur, happen *or* come about unexpectedly *or* suddenly.
sobreverterse [2], *v.r.* to run over, overflow.
sobrevesta, sobreveste, *n.f.* over-tunic.
sobrevestir [8], *v.t.* to put on over other clothes.
sobrevidriera, *n.f.* window-guard, window-grill; storm window.

sobrevienta, *n.f.* violent gust of wind; (*fig.*) onslaught, impetuous fury; surprise.
sobreviento, *n.m.* gust of wind; (*naut.*) ***estar a sobreviento,*** to have the wind of.
sobrevista, *n.f.* beaver (*of a helmet*).
sobreviviente, *a.* surviving. — *n.m.f.* survivor.
sobrevivir, *v.i.* to survive; ***sobrevivir a,*** to outlive.
sobrexcedente, *a.* surpassing, exceeding.
sobrexceder, *v.t.* to surpass, exceed.
sobrexcitación, *n.f.* overexcitement.
sobrexcitar, *v.t.* to overexcite.
sobriedad, *n.f.* sobriety, frugality, moderation.
sobrina, *n.f* niece.
sobrinazgo, *n.m.* relationship of a nephew *or* niece.
sobrino, *n.m.* nephew.
sobrio, -ria, *a.* sober, frugal, moderate, sparing.
soca, *n.f.* (*Hisp. Am.*) ratoon (*of the sugar cane*); (*Bol.*) bud (*of rice plant*).
socaire, *n.m.* (*naut.*) lee; ***al socaire de,*** under the shelter of; (*coll.*) ***estar*** or ***ponerse al socaire,*** to shirk work.
socairero, *n.m.* (*naut.*) skulker, lurker.
socaliña, *n.f.* cunning, trick.
socaliñar, *v.t.* to extort by cunning.
socalzar [C], *v.t.* (*arch.*) to underpin, underset.
socapa, *n.f.* pretext, pretence; ***a socapa,*** on the sly.
socapar, *v.t.* (*Bol., Ec., Mex.*) to hide, conceal; palliate another's faults and sins.
socarra, *n.f.* singe, singeing; cunning, craft.
socarrar, *v.t.* to singe, scorch.
socarrén, *n.m.* eave, gable end.
socarrena, *n.f.* hollow, cavity, interval, space between rafters.
socarrina, *n.f.* (*coll.*) scorching, singeing.
socarrón, -rrona, *a.* ironic, wryly humorous; sly.
socarronería, *n.f.* irony, wry humour; slyness.
socava, socavación, *n.f.* undermining; rooting *or* digging round trees.
socavar, *v.t.* to dig under, undermine.
socavón, *n.m.* cave, cavern; subsidence, caving in.
socaz, *n.m.* outlet of a mill.
sociabilidad, *n.f.* sociability, sociableness.
sociable, *a.* sociable.
social, *a.* social; ***razón social,*** trade name.
socialismo, *n.m.* socialism.
socialista, *a., n.m.f.* socialist.
socialistizante, *a., n.m.f.* (one) having socialist leanings.
socialistoide, *a., n.m.f.* (one) tainted *or* tinged with socialism; would-be socialist.
socialización, *n.f.* socialization.
socializar [C], *v.t.* to socialize.
sociedad, *n.f.* society; company; (*com.*) ***sociedad anónima,*** limited (liability) company; ***sociedad en comandita,*** partnership including sleeping partners; ***sociedad colectiva,*** joint-stock company; ***entrar en sociedad,*** to come out (in society).
societario, -ria, *a.* pertaining to associations *or* trade unions.
socio, *n.m.* partner; member, fellow; ***socio capitalista,*** financial partner; ***socio comanditario,*** sleeping partner, (*Am.*) silent partner; ***socio industrial,*** working partner.
sociología, *n.f.* sociology.
sociológico, -ca, *a.* sociological.
sociólogo, -ga, *n.m.f.* sociologist.
socolar, *v.t.* (*Ec., Hond.*) to clear (*land*).
socolor, *n.m.* pretence, pretext.
socollada, *n.f.* (*naut.*) flapping; pitching.
soconusco, *n.m.* (*Mex.*) cocoa (*from Soconusco*).
socoro, *n.m.* place under the choir.
socorredor, -ra, *a.* succouring, helping. — *n.m.f.* succourer, helper.
socorrer, *v.t.* to succour, help, aid; to give alms to; to pay on account.
socorrido, -da, *a.* ready to help; handy, useful, that comes in handy *or* useful; well-tried.
socorro, *n.m.* succour, aid, assistance, help; alms; part payment on account.
socrático, -ca, *a.* Socratic.
socrocio, *n.m.* (*pharm.*) saffron poultice.
socucho, *n.m.* (*Hisp. Am.*) poky place, den.
sochantre, *n.m.* (*eccles.*) choirmaster.
soda, *n.f.* soda; soda-water.
sódico, -ca, *a.* sodic.
sodio, *n.m.* sodium.
sodomía, *n.f.* sodomy.
sodomita, *a., n.m.* sodomite.
sodomítico, -ca, *a.* of *or* belonging to sodomy.
soez, *a.* filthy, foul, obscene.
sofá, *n.m.* couch, sofa, (*Am.*) davenport.
sofaldar, *v.t.* to raise up, lift up; to tuck up, truss up.
sofaldo, *n.m.* tucking up, trussing-up.
sofí, *n.m.* sufi.
sofión, *n.m.* snort; sharp refusal *or* dressing down.
sofisma, *n.m.* sophism.
sofista, *n.m.* sophist.
sofistería, *n.f.* sophistry.
sofisticación, *n.f.* sophistication; falsification, adulteration.
sofisticar [A], *v.t.* to sophisticate; to falsify, adulterate.
sofístico, -ca, *a.* sophistical.
sofito, *n.m.* (*arch.*) soffit.
soflama, *n.f.* low flame; glow, blush; flattery; demagoguery.
soflamar, *v.t.* to make blush; (*fig.*) to take in. — **soflamarse,** *v.r.* to get scorched.
soflamero, *n.m* trickster.
sofocación, *n.f.* suffocation, choking; upset.
sofocante, *a.* suffocating, stifling.
sofocar [A], *v.t.* to suffocate, stifle, choke, smother; to put out, extinguish, quench; to make blush; to make hot under the collar. — **sofocarse,** *v.r.* to suffocate, choke; to blush, get embarrassed; (*coll.*) to get all het up, get hot under the collar, get hot and bothered, get all stewed up.
sofoco, *n.m.* suffocation; annoyance, upset.
sofocón, *n.m.* annoyance, upset.
sofreír [28, *p.p.* **frito**], *v.t.* to fry lightly.
sofrenada, *n.f.* sudden check (*with the bridle*); severe reproof.
sofrenar, *v.t.* to check sharply.
sofrenazo, *n.m.* violent pull (*of the bridle*); severe reproof.
sofrito, -ta, *a.* lightly fried. — *n.m.* anything lightly fried.
soga (1), *n.f.* rope, cord, halter; (*mas.*) stretcher; (*mas.*) face (*of brick* or *stone*); ***dar soga a,*** to make fun of; ***echar la soga tras el caldero,*** to throw the whole thing up *or* over (*fig.*) ***con la soga al cuello*** or ***a la garganta,*** with the water up to one's neck; ***hacer soga,*** to lag behind; ***mentar la soga en casa del ahorcado,*** to be tactless; ***siempre se quiebra la soga por lo más delgado,*** a chain is only as strong as its weakest link; ***a soga,*** in a stretcher bond.
soga (2), *n.m.* (*coll.*) sly person.
soguear, *v.t.* to measure with a rope.
soguería, *n.f.* rope-making; ropeshop; ropes.
soguero, *n.m.* rope-maker; rope-dealer; street porter.
soguica, soguilla, soguita, *n.f.* small rope; small braid of hair.
soja, *n.f.* soy(a) bean.
sojuzgador, -ra, *a.* subjugating. — *n.m.f.* conqueror, subduer, subjugator.
sojuzgar [B], *v.t.* to subjugate, conquer, subdue.

sol, *n.m.* sun; sunlight; day; (*Per., numis.*) sol; (*mus.*) sol, G; ***sol de medianoche,*** midnight sun; ***sol medio,*** mean sun; ***baño de sol,*** sun bath; ***rayo de sol,*** sunbeam; ***arrimarse al sol que más calienta,*** to know on which side one's bread is buttered; ***hace sol,*** it is sunny; ***no dejar a sol ni a sombra,*** not to leave in peace; to keep a constant eye on; ***tomar el sol,*** to bask *or* walk in the sun, sunbathe; (*naut.*) to take bearings on the sun; ***al sol,*** in the sun; ***al salir el sol,*** at sunrise; ***al ponerse el sol,*** at sunset; ***a sol puesto,*** at nightfall; ***de sol a sol,*** from sunrise to sunset.
solacear [SOLAZAR].
solada, *n.f.* dregs, sediment, lees.
solado, *n.m.* tile floor, pavement; paving, flooring.
solador, *n.m.* tiler, paver.
soladura, *n.f.* paving, flooring; paving *or* flooring materials.
solamente, *adv.* only, solely, merely.
solampiar, *v.i.* (*Arg.*) to eat alone and hastily.
solana, *n.f.* sunny spot; sun gallery; worst heat of the day.
solanáceo, -cea, *a.* solanaceous. — *n.f.pl.* (**solanáceas**) (*bot.*) Solanaceæ.
solanera, *n.f.* sunstroke; hot, sunny place; hot sunshine.
solano, *n.m.* hot easterly wind; (*bot.*) nightshade.
solapa, *n.f.* lapel; pretence; dust jacket (*book*); (*vet.*) sinus (*of a wound*); ***de solapa,*** sneakingly; ***junta de solapa,*** lap joint.
solapado, -da, *a.* cunning, artful, crafty.
solapadura, *n.f.* overlap; ***obra de solapadura,*** clinker work.
solapar, *v.t.* to put lapels on; to overlap; to conceal, cover up. — *v.i.* to overlap.
solape, solapo, *n.m.* lapel; pretence; (*coll.*) ***a solapo,*** sneakingly.
solar, *a.* solar. — *n.m.* building site *or* plot, (*Am.*) lot; ancestral dwelling; noble lineage. — [4] *v.t.* to floor, pave; to sole (*shoes*).
solariego, -ga, *a.* manorial, ancestral; ***casa solariega,*** ancestral home.
solas, (a), *adv.* alone.
solaz, *n.m.* solace; relaxation; ***a solaz,*** pleasantly, agreeably.
solazar [C], *v.t.* to solace; to afford enjoyment to.
solazo, *n.m.* scorching sun.
solazoso, -sa, *a.* affording solace, comforting.
soldada, *n.f.* wages, service-pay.
soldadesco, -ca, *a.* soldier, of soldiers. — *n.f.* soldiery.
soldado, *n.m.* soldier; ***soldado raso,*** private soldier, ranker.
soldador, *n.m.* solderer; soldering-iron.
soldadote, *n.m.* (*coll.*) bluff soldier; blimp, one of the thick-headed military.
soldadura, *n.f.* soldering; solder; welding; amending, correction; ***soldadura autógena,*** welding.
soldán, *n.m.* sultan.
soldar [4], *v.t.* to solder, weld; (*fig.*) to amend, correct.
soleá, *n.f.* Andalusian dance, song and tune.
solear, *v.t.* to sun.
solecismo, *n.m.* solecism.
soledad, *n.f.* solitude; solitariness, loneliness; lonely place; (*mus.*) Andalusian dance, song and tune.
solejar, *n.m.* place exposed to the sun.
solemne, *a.* solemn; downright, arrant, utter.
solemnidad, *n.f.* solemnity, solemnness; ceremony; impressiveness; ***pobre de solemnidad,*** desperately poor, poor as a church mouse; (*pl.* **solemnidades**) formalities.
solemnizador, -ra, *n.m.f.* solemnizer, one who solemnizes.
solemnizar [C], *v.t.* to solemnize, celebrate.
solenoide, *n.m.* (*elec.*) solenoid.
sóleo, *n.m.* (*anat.*) soleus.
soler (1) [5; *used only in pres. and imperf. indicative*], *v.i.* to be wont to, be in the habit of; ***suele hablar poco,*** he usually has little to say.
soler (2), *n.m.* (*naut.*) under-flooring.
solera, *n.f.* entablature, cross-beam; rib, lintel; lower millstone; flat stone, stone slab; (*fig.*) long tradition; ***vino de solera,*** vintage (sherry) wine.
solercia, *n.f.* shrewdness.
solería, *n.f.* flooring; paving; sole leather.
solero, *n.m.* nether millstone.
solerte, *a.* shrewd.
soleta, *n.f.* additional sole; (*coll.*) brazen woman; (*Mex.*) iced cake; (*coll.*) ***tomar soleta,*** to scram, sheer off.
soletar, soletear, *v.t.* to resole, refoot (*stockings*).
soletero, -ra, *n.m.f.* vamper, refooter, resoler.
solevación, *n.f.,* **solevamiento,** *n.m.* rising, upheaval; revolt.
solevantado, -da, *a.* worried, perturbed.
solevantar, *v.t.* to raise up, lift; to incite to revolt.
solevar, *v.t.* to incite to revolt; to raise up, upheave.
solfa, *n.f.* sol-fa; solfeggio; solmization; musical annotation, notes; music harmony; (*coll.*) spanking; ***poner en solfa,*** to make a laughing stock of.
solfatara, *n.f.* (*geol.*) solfatara.
solfeador, *n.m.* sol-faer.
solfear, *v.t.* (*mus.*) to sol-fa; (*coll.*) to beat, spank; to dress down.
solfeo, *n.m.* (*mus.*) sol-fa, sol-faing, solmization; (*coll.*) beating, spanking.
solferino, -na, *a.* reddish-purple.
solfista, *n.m.f.* sol-faist.
solicitación, *n.f.* solicitation; request.
solicitado, -da, *a.* in demand, sought after.
solicitador, -ra, *a.* soliciting. — *n.m.* agent.
solicitante, *a.* soliciting. — *n.m.f.* applicant.
solicitar, *v.t.* to solicit, request; to apply for.
solícito, -ta, *a.* solicitous, eager *or* anxious to please *or* help.
solicitud, *n.f.* solicitude; request; application.
solidar, *v.t.* to make firm, make solid, consolidate; to establish.
solidaridad, *n.f.* solidarity, sympathy.
solidario, -ria, *a.* (*law*) jointly liable; ***hacerse solidario de*** or **con,** to express one's sympathy *or* support for.
solidarizar [C], *v.t.* solidarize, make jointly liable. — **solidarizarse,** *v.r.* to express sympathy and support (**con,** for); to make *or* form common cause (**con,** with).
solideo, *n.m.* (*eccles.*) calotte.
solidez, *n.f.* solidity, firmness, strength; soundness, solidness.
solidificación, *n.f.* solidification.
solidificar(**se**) [A], *v.t.* (*v.r.*) to solidify.
sólido, -da, *a.* solid, strong, firm, sound. — *n.m.* solid.
soliloquiar, *v.i.* to soliloquize.
soliloquio, *n.m.* soliloquy, monologue.
solimán, *n.m.* corrosive sublimate.
solio, *n.m.* canopied throne.
solípedo, -da, *a.* soliped.
solipsismo, *n.m.* (*phil.*) solipsism.
solista, *n.m.f.* soloist.
solitaria (1), *n.f.* post-chaise; tapeworm.
solitario, -ria (2), *a.* solitary, lone, lonely. — *n.m.f.* hermit, recluse. — *n.m.* patience (*card game*), (*Am.*) solitaire.
sólito, -ta, *a.* wonted, usual, customary.
solitud, *n.f.* (*poet.*) solitude, loneliness, loneness; lonely place.
soliviadura, *n.f.* raising *or* lifting slightly.

soliviantar, *v.t.* to stir up, incite to revolt.
soliviar, *v.t.* to raise up, prop up, lift up.
solivio, *n.m.* [SOLIVIADURA].
sólo, *adv.* only, solely, just.
solo, -la, *a.* alone, by one's self, on one's own; lone, lonely; only, sole; ***a solas,*** alone. — *n.m.* solo.
solomillo, solomo, *n.m.* sirloin; rump steak.
solsticial, *a.* solstitial.
solsticio, *n.m.* solstice.
soltadizo, -za, *a.* easily untied *or* loosened.
soltador, -ra, *a.* loosening.
soltar [4], *v.t.* to untie, unfasten, loosen; to release, set free, let out, let go; to cast off (*hawsers etc.*); to turn on (*water etc.*); to let have; (*fig.*) ***soltarle a alguien una andanada,*** to let s.o. have a broadside *or* give s.o. a blasting. — **soltarse,** *v.r.* to get *or* work loose, come undone *or* off; to begin to get the idea, begin to get the knack *or* hang of, begin to get proficient *or* fluent; ***soltarse el pelo,*** to let o.s. go, let rip, abandon all restraint.
soltería, *n.f.* bachelorhood; spinsterhood.
soltero, -ra, *a.* unmarried, single. — *n.m.* bachelor, unmarried man. — *n.f.* spinster, unmarried woman.
solterón, *n.m.* confirmed (old) bachelor.
solterona, *n.f.* old maid.
soltura, *n.f.* looseness; ease; fluency; release.
solubilidad, *n.f.* solubility, solubleness.
soluble, *a.* soluble.
solución, *n.f.* solution; loosening, untying; ***sin solución de continuidad,*** without a break, without interruption; ***no tiene solución,*** it's hopeless, a dead loss.
solucionar, *v.t.* to solve; to sort out.
solutivo, -va, *a.* (*med.*) solutive.
solvencia, *n.f.* solvency; reliability, trustworthiness.
solventar, *v.t.* to settle (*debts*); to solve.
solvente, *a.* solvent; reliable.
solver [5, *p.p.* **suelto**], *v.t.* (*obs.*) to solve; to loosen, untie.
sollado, *n.m.* (*naut.*) orlop.
sollamar, *v.t.* to scorch.
sollastre, *n.m.* scullion, kitchen boy; cunning knave.
sollastría, *n.f.* scullery.
sollo, *n.m.* sturgeon.
sollozar [C], *v.i.* to sob.
sollozo, *n.m.* sob.
soma, *n.f.* coarse flour.
somali, *a.*, *n.m.f.* Somali.—*n.m.* Somali (*language*).
Somalia, *n.f.* Somaliland.
somanta, *n.f.* beating.
somatar, *v.t.* (*Hond.*, *Mex.*) to misspend, waste, squander.
somatén, *n.m.* (Catalan) militia; alarm; (*coll.*) tumult, hubbub.
somatología, *n.f.* somatology.
somatológico, -ca, *a.* somatological.
sombra, *n.f.* shade; shadow; shelter; vague likeness; (*astron.*) umbra; (*art*) umber; ***ni por sombra,*** not by any stretch of the imagination, not in the slightest; ***hacer sombra a,*** to shade; to overshadow, outshine; ***tener buena sombra,*** to be likeable and amusing; ***tener mala sombra,*** to be dull *or* a drag; to be tactless; (*coll.*) ***poner a la sombra,*** to put inside *or* away.
sombraje, *n.m.* branch-covered hut *or* screen.
sombrajo, *n.m.* shed, hut; shadow cast by a person preventing the light from reaching another.
sombrar, *v.t.* to overshadow, get in the light of, shade.
sombreado, *n.m.* (*art*) shading; shady spot.
sombrear, *v.t.* (*lit. and art*) to shade.
sombrerazo, *n.m.* large hat; blow with a hat; doffing the hat (with a grand sweep).
sombrerera, *n.f.* hat-box; hatter's wife.
sombrerería, *n.f.* hat-shop; hat-factory; millinery shop; hat business.
sombrerero, *n.m.* hatter, hat-maker.
sombrerete, *n.m.* small hat; (*mech.*) cap, bonnet, cowl; spark catcher of a locomotive; (*arch.*) calotte.
sombrerillo, *n.m.* alms basket (*in prisons*); navelwort.
sombrero, *n.m.* hat; canopy (*of a pulpit*); cap (*of mushrooms*); (*naut.*) ***sombrero de cabrestante,*** capstan drum; ***sombrero apuntado,*** cocked hat; ***sombrero de tres picos,*** three-cornered hat; ***sombrero de copa,*** top-hat; ***sombrero gacho,*** slouch hat; ***sombrero de jipijapa,*** Panama hat; ***sombrero de pelo,*** silk hat; ***sombrero jarano,*** sombrero; ***sombrero hongo,*** bowler hat; (*naut.*) ***sombrero del patrón,*** hat money, primage.
sombría, *n.f.* [SOMBRÍO].
sombrilla, *n.f.* parasol, sunshade; slight shade.
sombrío, -ría, *a.* gloomy, sombre; dark, murky, sullen; (*art*) shaded. — *n.f.* shady place.
sombroso, -sa, *a.* shady.
somero, -ra, *a.* slight, superficial; shallow.
someter, *v.t.* to submit, subject, subdue. — **someterse,** *v.r.* to submit, yield, comply (***a,*** with), acquiesce.
sometimiento, *n.m.* submission, subduing, subjection.
somier, *n.m.* bedspring, spring mattress.
somnambulismo [SONAMBULISMO].
somnámbulo, -la [SONÁMBULO].
somnífero, -ra, *a.* somniferous, inducing sleep. — *n.m.* sleeping draught.
somnílocuo, -cua, *a.* somniloquous, talking in sleep.
somnolencia, *n.f.* somnolence, sleepiness, drowsiness.
somo, *n.m.* summit, peak.
somonte, (de), *a.* coarse, rough, shaggy.
somorgujador, *n.m.* diver.
somorgujar, *v.t.* to duck. — *v.i.* to dive.
somorgujo, somorgujón, somormujo, *n.m.* (*orn.*) grebe, diver; ***a lo somorgujo*** or ***a somormujo,*** under water; on the quiet.
sompesar, *v.t.* to weigh, heft.
son, *n.m.* sound; tune; rumour; pretext; way, manner; ***¿a qué son? ¿a son de qué?*** why on earth?; ***en son de,*** as; by way of; with a threat of; ***sin ton ni son,*** without rhyme or reason; ***bailar al son que le tocan,*** to dance to any tune (*as circumstances dictate*).
sonable, *a.* sonorous; loud; celebrated.
sonada (1), *n.f.* tune; (*obs.*) sonata.
sonadera, *n.f.* blowing the nose.
sonadero, *n.m.* handkerchief.
sonado, -da (2), *a.* much talked of, famous; crazy, cracked; ***hacer la sonada,*** to create a real stir.
sonador, -ra, *a.* that makes a noise. — *n.m.* handkerchief.
sonaja, *n.f.* timbrel; jingle.
sonajero, *n.m.* (baby's) rattle.
sonambulismo, *n.m.* somnambulism, sleep-walking.
sonámbulo, -la, *a.* sleep-walking. — *n.m.f.* sleep-walker, somnambulist.
sonante, *a.* sounding; ***dinero contante y sonante,*** ready cash.
sonar [4], *v.t.* to (make) sound, ring; to blow on; to blow the nose of. — *v.i.* to sound, be sounded, be heard; to ring, chime, tinkle; to ring a bell, have a familiar ring; to be reported; ***como suena,*** it's as true as I'm standing here; ***lo que sea, sonará,*** what will be will be; ***suena a mentira,*** it sounds like a lie. — **sonarse,** *v.r.* to blow one's nose.
sonata, *n.f.* sonata.
sonatina, *n.f.* sonatina.

sonda, *n.f.* sounding; lead, sounder, plummet; sound, probe; (annular) borer; (diamond) drill; (*surg.*) catheter; (*artill.*) proof stick.
sondable, *a.* which may be sounded.
sondaleza, *n.f.* lead-line, sounding line.
sondar, sondear, *v.t.* to sound; to sound out, fathom; (*naut.*) ***sondar la bomba,*** to sound the pump.
sondeo, *n.m.* sounding; sounding out, fathoming; (*min.*) boring; feeler, approach; (opinion) poll.
sonecillo, *n.m.* slight sound; little tune.
sonetico, *n.m.* tapping with the fingers.
sonetillo, *n.m.* short-line sonnet.
sonetista, *n.m.f.* sonnet writer.
soneto, *n.m.* sonnet.
sonido, *n.m.* sound.
soniquete, *n.m.* continuous little sound *or* noise.
sonochada, *n.f.* evening watch.
sonochar, *v.i.* to keep watch during the first hours of the night.
sonómetro, *n.m.* sonometer.
sonoridad, *n.f.* sonorousness; voiced quality.
sonorización, *n.f.* (*phon.*) voicing.
sonorizar, *v.t.* (*phon.*) to voice.
sonoro, -ra, sonoroso, -sa, *a.* sonorous; loud; (*phon.*) voiced.
sonreír(se) [28], *v.i.* (*v.r.*) to smile.
sonrisa, *n.f.* smile.
sonrisueño, -ña, *a.* smiling.
sonrodarse, *v.r.* to stick in the mud.
sonrojar, sonrojear, *v.t.* to make flush, cause to blush. — **sonrojarse, sonrojearse,** *v.r.* to blush, flush.
sonrojo, *n.m.* blush; word which causes a blush.
sonrosar, sonrosear, *v.t.* to dye rose-red. — **sonrosarse, sonrosearse,** *v.r.* to blush.
sonroseo, *n.m.* blush, flush.
sonsaca, *n.f.* wheedling; enticement; pilfering; drawing out.
sonsacador, -ra, *n.m.f.* wheedler, enticer, coaxer; petty thief.
sonsacamiento, *n.m.* wheedling, extortion.
sonsacar [A], *v.t.* to wheedle, wheedle out; to pilfer.
sonsaque, *n.m.* petty theft; wheedling; enticement.
sonsonete, *n.m.* sing-song tone; rhythmical tapping; scornful tone.
sonto, -ta, *a.* (*Guat.*, *Hond.*) with cropped ears (*of horses*).
soñador, -ra, *a.* dreamy. — *n.m.f.* dreamer.
soñante, *a.* dreaming.
soñar [4], *v.t.* to dream, dream about; ***ni soñarlo,*** not on your life, no fear; ***soñar despierto,*** to daydream. — *v.i.* to dream; ***soñar con*** or ***de,*** to dream of.
soñarrera, *n.f.* deep *or* heavy sleep; drowsiness.
soñera, *n.f.* sleepiness, drowsiness.
soñolencia, *n.f.* sleepiness, drowsiness, somnolence.
soñoliento, -ta, *a.* sleepy, dozy, drowsy; lazy, sluggish.
sopa, *n.f.* soup; sop; ***sopa de gato,*** thin soup; ***hecho una sopa,*** wet through, wet to the skin; (*coll.*) ***a la sopa boba,*** sponging.
sopaipa, *n.f.* honey fritter.
sopalancar, *v.t.* to raise with a lever.
sopalanda, *n.f.* student's gown.
sopanda, *n.f.* brace; lintel, joist, cross-beam.
sopapear, *v.t.* to slap; to call names.
sopapo, *n.m.* chuck under the chin; slap; (*mech.*) sucker, pump-valve.
sopar, sopear, *v.t.* to sop, dunk; to trample, tread; to maltreat.
sopeña, *n.f.* rock-formed cavity.
sopero, -ra, *a.* soup (*plate*); (*coll.*) fond of soup. — *n.m.* soup plate.— *n.f.* soup tureen.
sopesar, *v.t.* to weigh up.
sopetear, *v.t.* to sop, dunk; to maltreat.
sopeteo, *n.m.* sopping, dipping (bread).
sopetón, *adv.* ***de sopetón,*** suddenly. — *n.m.* toasted bread in oil; slap.
sopicaldo, *n.m.* watery soup.
sopista, *n.m.f.* person living on charity.
sopita, *n.f.* light soup; nice soup.
sopitipando, *n.m.* (*coll.*) swoon, fit.
¡sopla! *interj.* gracious me!
sopladero, *n.m.* blow-hole.
soplado, -da, *a.* (*coll.*) overnice; stuck up; (*coll.*) pie-eyed. — *n.m.* (*min.*) deep fissure.
soplador, -ra, *a.* blowing. — *n.m.* blowing fan. — *n.m.f.* blower.
sopladura, *n.f.* blowing; air hole.
soplamocos, *n.m. inv.* slap.
soplar, *v.t.* to blow, blow on, fan; to blow up; to blow out; to blow away; (*coll.*) to pinch, snitch; to huff (*at draughts*); to whisper, prompt; to drink up; (*coll.*) to knock off. — **soplarse,** *v.r.* (*coll.*) to polish *or* hog off; to guzzle down *or* booze up; to blow the gaff, spill the beans, squeal.
soplete, *n.m.* blowpipe; blow-lamp.
soplido, *n.m.* blowing, puff, blast.
soplillo, *n.m.* gauze, chiffon; blowing-fan; light sponge-cake.
soplo, *n.m.* blowing, blast; gust, puff, breath; (*coll.*) jiffy; tip-off; ***ir con el soplo,*** to blow the gaff, give a tip-off, give the game away, spill the beans.
soplón, -lona, *n.m.f.* informer, squealer; (*Cent. Am.*) prompter.
sopón, *n.m.* one living on charity soup.
soponcio, *n.m.* fainting; (nasty) upset.
sopor, *n.m.* drowsiness, lethargy.
soporífero, -ra, *a.* soporiferous.
soporífico, -ca, *a.* soporific; sleeping draught.
soporoso, -sa, *a.* soporiferous.
soportable, *a.* tolerable, supportable, bearable, endurable.
soportal, *n.m.* portico; arcade.
soportar, *v.t.* to tolerate, bear, endure; to support, carry.
soporte, *n.m.* support, stand, bracket, rest.
soprano, *n.m.f.* soprano.
sopuntar, *v.t.* to underscore with dots.
sor, *n.f.* (*eccles.*) sister.
sorba, *n.f.* sorb apple.
sorbedor, -ra, *a.* absorbing, sucking.
sorber, *v.t.* to sip, suck; to absorb, soak up, swallow up; to suck down *or* under.
sorbete, *n.m.* sherbet; water ice.
sorbetón, *n.m.* large draught.
sorbible, *a.* that can be sipped.
sorbo, *n.m.* sip, swallow, gulp, draught; sipping; (*bot.*) sorb tree.
sorda (1), *n.f.* woodcock; (*naut.*) stream-cable.
sordera, sordez, *n.f.* deafness.
sordidez, *n.f.* sordidness; squalor, squalidness; stinginess.
sórdido, -da, *a.* sordid; squalid; stingy.
sordina, *n.f.* mute, sordine; damper (*of a piano*); ***a la sordina,*** secretly, on the quiet.
sordino, *n.m.* kit, small fiddle.
sordo, -da (2), *a.* deaf; mute, noiseless; muffled, dull; unvoiced, unspoken, veiled; (*math.*) irrational; ***a la sorda, a lo sordo, a sordas,*** noiselessly; ***sordo como una tapia,*** as deaf as a post; ***no hay peor sordo que el que no quiere oír,*** there are none so deaf as those who will not hear; ***hacerse el sordo,*** to pretend not to hear.
sordomudez, *n.f.* deaf-mutism.
sordomudo, -da, *a.* deaf and dumb. — *n.m.f.* deaf-mute.
sordón, *n.m.* fagotto, double curtall.
sorgo, *n.m.* sorghum.

soriano, -na, *a.* of Soria. — *n.m.f.* native of Soria.
sorna, *n.f.* sarcasm, irony; slowness, sluggishness; sloth; malice.
sorocharse, *v.r.* (*Hisp. Am.*) to become mountain-sick.
soroche, *n.m.* (*Hisp. Am.*) mountain sickness; (*Bol., Chi., min.*) galena.
soroque, *n.f.* matrix of ores.
sorprendente, *a.* surprising.
sorprender, *v.t.* to surprise; to astonish; to come upon; to overhear.
sorpresa, *n.f.* surprise.
sorregar [IB], *v.t.* to irrigate by overflow.
sorriego, *n.m.* irrigation by overflowing; overflow water.
sorrostrada, *n.f.* insolence; bluntness; ***dar sorrostrada,*** to taunt, insult.
sorteable, *a.* (*mil.*) eligible to be drafted; that can be raffled; avoidable.
sorteador, *n.m.* one who draws lots; one who gets around.
sorteamiento, *n.m.* casting lots.
sortear, *v.t.* to draw *or* cast lots for; to choose by lot; to dodge, get round, manage to miss; (*tauro.*) to dodge away from. — *v.i.* to draw *or* cast lots.
sorteo, *n.m.* raffle; drawing *or* casting of lots; choosing by lots; dodging.
sortero, -ra, *n.m.f.* soothsayer, fortune-teller.
sortiaria, *n.f.* fortune-telling by cards.
sortija, *n.f.* ring; buckle, hoop; curl (*of hair*); ***sortija de sello,*** signet ring.
sortijero, *n.m.* jewel-case.
sortijita, sortijuela, *n.f.* little ring; ringlet.
sortilegio, *n.m.* sorcery.
sortílego, -ga, *n.m.f.* sorcerer, sorceress.
sosa (1), *n.f.* glass-wort, kelp, soda-ash; (*chem.*) soda.
sosaina, *a.*, *n.m.f.* dull, colourless (person).
sosal, *n.m.* soda-bearing field.
sosegado, -da, *a.* quiet, peaceful, calm, pacific.
sosegador, -ra, *a.* calming, quieting. — *n.m.f.* appeaser.
sosegar [IB], *v.t.* to calm, quiet. — *v.i.* to rest. — **sosegarse,** *v.r.* to become calm, calm down, lull.
sosera (1), **sosería, sosez,** *n.f.* insipidity, tastelessness; dullness, flatness, dreariness.
sosero, -ra (2), *a.* yielding soda.
sosia, *n.m.* sosia, double.
sosiega, *n.f.* rest after work; nightcap.
sosiego, *n.m.* calm, quiet, peace, rest.
soslayar, *v.t.* to place obliquely; to dodge, avoid.
soslayo, *a.* oblique, slanting; ***al*** or ***de soslayo,*** obliquely, slantingly, at a slant; askance.
soso, -sa (2), *a.* insipid, tasteless; dull, flat, dreary.
sospecha, *n.f.* suspicion.
sospechable, *a.* suspicious, suspect.
sospechar, *v.t.* to suspect; ***sospechar de,*** to suspect, distrust. — *v.i.* to suspect, be suspicious.
sospechoso, -sa, *a.* suspicious, suspect. — *n.m.f.* suspect.
sospesar, *v.t.* to try the weight of.
sosquín, *n.m.* treacherous blow, back-hander.
sostén, *n.m.* support; maintenance; brassière; steadiness (*of a ship*).
sostenedor, -ra, *a.* supporting. — *n.m.f.* supporter, upholder.
sostener [33], *v.t.* to support, hold up; to sustain, keep up; to uphold; to maintain.
sostenido (1), **-da,** *a.* constant, sustained.
sostenido (2), *n.m.* (*mus.*) sharp.
sosteniente, *a.* sustaining, supporting.
sostenimiento, *n.m.* maintenance; up-keep; support.
sota, *n.f.* jack, knave (*at cards*); jade, hussy; ***es sota, caballo y rey,*** there's no variation, variety *or* choice. — *n.m.* (*Hisp. Am.*) boss, foreman.
sotabanco, *n.m.* (*arch.*) pediment (*of an arch*); attic.
sotabraga, *n.f.* axle-tree band; yoke hoop.
sotacola, *n.f.* crupper.
sotacoro, *n.m.* place under the choir.
sotalugo, *n.m.* second hoop (*of a cask*).
sotana, *n.f.* cassock; (*coll.*) flogging, beating.
sotanear, *v.t.* to beat; to reprimand severely.
sotaní, *n.m.* short skirt without pleats.
sótano, *n.m.* cellar, basement.
sotaventarse, *v.r.* to fall to leeward.
sotavento, *n.m.* leeward, lee.
sotayuda, *n.m.* assistant steward.
sote, *n.m.* (*Col.*) jigger flea.
sotechado, *n.m.* covered place, roofed place, shed.
soteño, -ña, *a.* produced in forests.
soterramiento, *n.m.* burial.
soterraño, -ña, *a.* subterranean, underground.
soterrar [1], *v.t.* to bury; to hide, conceal.
sotil, sotileza (*obs.*) [SUTIL, SUTILEZA].
sotillo, *n.m.* little grove *or* copse.
soto, *prep.* under, beneath, below. — *n.m.* copse.
sotoministro, *n.m.* assistant steward.
sotreta, *n.f.* (*Hisp. Am.*) nag, hack.
sotrozo, *n.m.* linch-pin, axle-pin; (*mech.*) key; foot-hook staff.
sotuer, *n.m.* (*her.*) saltire.
soviet, *n.m.* soviet.
soviético, -ca, *a.* soviet.
sovoz, (a), *adv.* in a low tone, sotto voce.
soya, *n.f.* soya bean, soybean.
speech, *n.m.* address; harangue; sermon, talking-to.
spich, *n.m.* [SPEECH].
standing, *n.m.* (high) class, (top) quality).
striptisismo, *n.m.* (vogue for) strip-tease.
su, *pron. poss.* 3rd *pers. m. and f. sing.* (*pl.* **sus**) his, her, its, one's, their, your.
suabo, -ba, *a.*, *n.m.f.* Swabian.
suasorio, -ria, *a.* suasive, suasory.
suave, *a.* smooth; soft; mellow, mild; gentle.
suavidad, *n.f.* smoothness; softness; mellowness, mildness; gentleness.
suavizador, -ra, *a.* smoothing; softening; mollifying. — *n.m.* (razor) strop.
suavizar [C], *v.t.* to smooth; to soften; to mollify.
subácido, -da, *a.* sub-acid.
subacuático, -ca, *a.* underwater, subaquatic.
subafluente, *n.m.* tributary (*river*).
subalcaide, *n.m.* deputy-warden.
subalternante, *a.* subalternant.
subalternar, *v.t.* to subject, subdue.
subalterno, -na, *a.*, *n.m.f.* subaltern.
subarrendador, -ra, *n.m.f.* subletter, subleaser, subtenant.
subarrendamiento, *n.m.* subletting, sublease.
subarrendar [1], *v.t.* to sublet, sublease.
subarrendatario, -ria, *n.m.f.* sublessor, sublessee, subtenant.
subarriendo, *n.m.* subrenting, sublease, underlease.
subasta, subastación, *n.f.* auction, auction sale; ***sacar a pública subasta,*** to sell at auction.
subastador, *n.m.* auctioneer.
subastar, *v.t.* to auction, auction off, sell at auction.
subcinericio, -cia, *a.* baked under ashes.
subclase, *n.f.* (*biol.*) subclass.
subclavio, -via, *a.* (*anat.*) subclavian.
subcolector, *n.m.* assistant tax-collector.
subcomendador, *n.m.* deputy-commander.
subcomisión, *n.f.* subcommission, subcommittee.
subconsciencia, *n.f.* subconsciousness, subconscious.
subconsciente, *a.*, *n.m.* subconscious.
subcutáneo, -nea, *a.* subcutaneous.
subdelegable, *a.* that may be subdelegated.

subdelegación, *n.f.* subdelegation.
subdelegado, *n.m.* subdelegate.
subdelegar [B], *v.t.* to subdelegate.
subdiaconado, subdiaconato, *n.m.* subdeaconship.
subdiácono, *n.m.* subdeacon.
subdirector, *n.m.* assistant manager.
subdistinción, *n.f.* subdistinction.
subdistinguir [G], *v.t.* to make a subdistinction.
súbdito, -ta, *a.* subject, inferior. — *n.m.* subject.
subdividir, *v.t.* to subdivide.
subdivisión, *n.f.* subdivision.
subduplo, -la, *a.* subduple.
subejecutor, *n.m.* deputy executor, subagent.
subentender [SOBRENTENDER].
subérico, -ca, *a.* suberic.
suberina, *n.f.* suberin.
suberoso, -sa, *a.* suberose, corky.
subestimar, *v.t.* to underestimate, underrate.
subfiador, *n.m.* second surety, co-surety.
subforo, *n.m.* agreement of sublease.
subgénero, *n.m.* (*biol.*) subgenus.
subgobernador, -ra, *n.m.* deputy governor.
subida, *n.f.* [SUBIDO].
subidero, -ra, *a.* rising, mounting, climbing. — *n.m.* ladder; up-grade, uphill road; mounting-block.
subido, -da, *a.* high, fine, superior; bright, vivid (*colour*); spicy, risqué. — *n.f.* ascent, going up, climbing; accession; rise; rising; acclivity; (wage) rise, (*Am.*) raise.
subidor, *n.m.* porter; lift, elevator.
subiente, *a.* rising, ascending. — *n.m.* leaf-decoration rising around column.
subilla, *n.f.* awl.
subimiento, *n.m.* rising, ascending, climbing.
subinquilino, *n.m.* subtenant.
subinspector, *n.m.* subinspector, assistant inspector.
subintendente, *n.m.* subintendant.
subintración, *n.f.* (*med.*) subintrant fever; overlapping fracture.
subintrar, *v.i.* (*med.*) to overlap (*fevers* or *fractures*).
subir, *v.t.* to raise; to lift up; to carry up, bring up, take up; to go up. — *v.i.* to rise; to come up, go up, climb; to mount; to amount; to accede (*to throne*); to grow, increase. — **subirse,** *v.r.* to climb, mount, get on; ***el vino se le subió a la cabeza,*** the wine went to his head; ***se nos ha subido a las barbas,*** he has got (a bit) above himself.
subitáneo, -nea, *a.* sudden.
súbito (1), **-ta,** *a.* sudden.
súbito (2), *adv.* suddenly; ***de súbito,*** suddenly.
subjefe, *n.m.* second in command; assistant chief.
subjetividad, *n.f.* subjectivity.
subjetivismo, *n.m.* subjectivism.
subjetivo, -va, *a.* subjective.
subjuntivo, -va, *a., n.m.* subjunctive.
sublevación, *n.f.,* **sublevamiento,** *n.m.* rising, insurrection, revolt.
sublevado, -da, *n.m.f.* rebel.
sublevar, *v.t.* to rouse to rebellion, incite to revolt. — **sublevarse,** *v.r.* to rise in revolt, rebel.
sublimación, *n.f.* sublimation.
sublimado, *n.m.* sublimate.
sublimar, *v.t.* to sublimate.
sublimatorio, -ria, *a.* sublimatory.
sublime, *a.* sublime.
sublimidad, *n.f.* sublimity.
sublingual, *a.* sublingual.
sublunar, *a.* sublunar, sublunary.
submarino, -na, *a., n.m.* submarine.
submúltiplo, -la, *a., n.m.f.* (*math.*) submultiple.
suboficial, *n.m.* non-commissioned officer.
subordinación, *n.f.* subordination.
subordinado, -da, *a., n.m.f.* subordinate.
subordinar, *v.t.* to subordinate.
subpolar, *a.* subpolar.
subprefecto, *n.m.* sub-prefect, deputy prefect.
subprefectura, *n.f.* sub-prefecture.
subproducto, *n.m.* by-product.
subrayar, *v.t.* to underline; to emphasize, stress.
subrepción, *n.f.* subreption, underhand proceeding.
subrepticio, -cia, *a.* surreptitious, subreptitious.
subrogación, *n.f.* subrogation, surrogation, substitution.
subrogar [B], *v.t.* to subrogate, substitute.
subsanable, *a.* excusable; reparable, remediable.
subsanación, *n.f.* excusal, excusing; mending.
subsanar, *v.t.* to excuse, exculpate; to amend, correct, put right *or* to rights; to make up for, compensate for.
subscribir(se) [*p.p.* **subscri(p)to**], *v.t.* (*v.r.*) to subscribe (***a,*** to).
subscripción, *n.f.* subscription (*to club etc.*), (*Am.*) dues.
subscri(p)to, -ta, *a., p.p. irreg.* [SUBSCRIBIR].
subscriptor, -ra, *n.m.f.* subscriber.
subsecretario, *n.m.* under-secretary, assistant secretary.
subsecuente, *a.* subsequent.
subseguir(se) [8G], *v.i.* (*v.r.*) to follow next.
subséstuplo, -la, *a.* subsextuple.
subsidiario, -ria, *a.* subsidiary.
subsidio, *n.m.* subsidy; allowance, pension.
subsiguiente, *a.* subsequent, succeeding.
subsistencia, *n.f.* subsistence; livelihood, living.
subsistente, *a.* subsistent, subsisting.
subsistir, *v.i.* to subsist; to have means of livelihood.
subsolano, *n.m.* easterly wind.
substancia [SUSTANCIA].
substanciación [SUSTANCIACIÓN].
substancial [SUSTANCIAL].
substanciar [SUSTANCIAR].
substancioso, -sa [SUSTANCIOSO].
substantivar, *v.t.* to use as a substantive.
substantivo, -va, *a.* substantive. — *n.m.* substantive, noun.
substitución [SUSTITUCIÓN].
substituir [SUSTITUIR].
substituto (1), *n.m.* [SUSTITUTO].
substituto (2), *a.* substitute. — *p.p. irreg.* [SUSTITUIR].
substituyente, *a.* [SUSTITUYENTE].
substracción [SUSTRACCIÓN].
substraendo [SUSTRAENDO].
substraer [SUSTRAER].
subsuelo, *n.m.* subsoil, under-soil.
subtangente, *n.f.* subtangent.
subtender, *v.t.* (*geom.*) to subtend.
subteniente, *n.m.* sub-lieutenant, second lieutenant.
subtensa (1), *n.f.* (*geom.*) subtense (*chord*).
subtenso, -sa (2), *p.p. irreg.* [SUBTENDER].
subterfugio, *n.m.* subterfuge.
subterráneo, -nea, *a.* subterranean, underground. — *n.m.* underground passage *or* store.
subtítulo, *n.m.* subtitle.
suburbano, -na, *a.* suburban. — *n.m.* underground (*railway*), tube.
suburbial, *a.* slum.
suburbio, *n.m.* slum.
subvención, *n.f.* subvention, subsidy.
subvencionar, *v.t.* to subsidize, subvent.
subvenir [36], *v.i.* to provide (for); to meet, defray.
subversión, *n.f.* subversion.
subversivo, -va, *a.* subversive.
subversor, -ra, *a.* subverting.

subvertir [6], *v.t.* to subvert.
subyacente, *a.* underlying.
subyugación, *n.f.* subjugation, subjection.
subyugador, -ra, *a.* subjugating, subjecting.
subyugar [B], *v.t.* to subjugate, subject.
succino, *n.m.* succinite.
succión, *n.f.* suction.
succionar, *v.t.* to suck, suck in.
sucedáneo, -nea, *a., n.m.* ersatz; substitute.
suceder, *v.i.* to succeed, follow, follow upon. — *v.i.* to happen.
sucedido, *n.m.* event, happening.
sucediente, *a.* succeeding, following.
sucesible, *a.* capable of succession.
sucesión, *n.f.* succession; offspring; (*law*) estate.
sucesivamente, *adv.* successively; ***y así sucesivamente,*** and so on.
sucesivo, -va, *a.* successive; ***en lo sucesivo,*** hereafter, in future.
suceso, *n.m.* event, happening, incident; issue, outcome; course (*of time*).
sucesor, -ra, *n.m.f.* successor.
suciedad, *n.f.* dirtiness, filthiness, dirt, filth.
sucintarse, *v.r.* to be brief, be expressed with concision.
sucinto, -ta, *a.* succinct; concise.
sucio, -cia, *a.* dirty, filthy; foul, unclean.
suco, *n.m.* sap, juice; (*Bol., Chi., Ven.*) muddy land.
sucre, *n.m.* Ecuadorean monetary unit.
súcubo, *a.* succubine. — *n.m.* succubus.
sucucho, *n.m.* ship's store-room; hovel, den.
súcula, *n.f.* windlass, winch.
suculencia, *n.f.* succulence.
suculento, -ta, *a.* succulent, juicy.
sucumbir, *v.i.* to succumb; to give in, give way.
sucursal, *a.* subsidiary. — *n.f.* (*com.*) branch.
suche, *a.* (*Ven.*) green, unripe, sour. — *n.m.* (*Arg.*) mud; (*Chi.*) minor employee.
súchel, súchil, *n.m.* (*Cub., Mex.*) suche tree.
sud, *n.m.* south; south wind.
sudadero, *n.m.* handkerchief; horse's backcloth; sweating-place, sudatory, sweating-bath; moist ground.
sudado, -da, *a.* sweaty, sweating, bathed in sweat.
Sudáfrica, *n.f.* South Africa.
sudafricano, -na, *a., n.m.f.* South African.
Sudamérica, *n.f.* South America.
sudamericano, -na, *a., n.m.f.* South American.
sudante, *a.* sweating.
sudar, *v.t., v.i.* to sweat, perspire; to ooze; to soak with sweat; ***sudar la gota gorda,*** to sweat one's guts out; ***sudar tinta (china),*** to sweat blood; ***ha tenido que sudarlo,*** he's really had to work hard for it.
sudario, *n.m.* shroud, winding sheet.
sudatorio, -ria, *a.* sudorific.
sudeste, *n.m.* south-east; south-east wind.
sudoeste, *n.m.* south-west; south-west wind.
sudor, *n.m.* sweat, perspiration; ooze.
sudoriento, -ta, *a.* perspiring.
sudorífero, -ra, *a.* sudorific.
sudoroso, -sa, *a.* sweating, perspiring freely.
sudoso, -sa, *a.* sweaty, covered with sweat.
sudsudeste, *n.m.* south-south-east.
sudsudoeste, *n.m.* south-south-west.
sudueste, *n.m.* south-west.
Suecia, *n.f.* Sweden.
sueco, -ca, *a.* Swedish. — *n.m.f.* Swede; ***hacerse el sueco,*** to pretend not to realize. — *n.m.* Swedish (*language*).
suegra, *n.f.* mother-in-law.
suegro, *n.m.* father-in-law.
suela, *n.f.* shoe-sole; (*arch.*) base; tip of a billiard-cue; (*ichth.*) sole; horizontal rafter; washer; ***pícaro de siete suelas,*** dyed-in-the-wool *or* out-and-out rogue; ***no le llega (ni) a la suela del zapato,*** he can't hold a candle to him; (*pl.*) sandals.
suelda, *n.f.* comfrey.
sueldo (1), *n.m.* salary; wages, pay; sou.
sueldo (2), **suelde,** *pres. indic., pres. subj.* [SOLDAR].
suelo, *n.m.* ground; floor; soil; land; ***suelo natal,*** native soil; ***dar en el suelo con,*** to throw to the ground; ***venirse al suelo,*** to fall to the ground, collapse; ***medir el suelo,*** to fall head-long *or* full-length; ***le faltó el suelo,*** he tripped and fell; (*pl.*) grain remaining on threshing-floor after threshing; ***por los suelos,*** rock bottom; gone right off, dirt cheap; ***poner por los suelos,*** to give a rotten press to.
suelto (1), **-ta,** *a.* loose; free, easy; fluent; odd; single (*copy*); ***suelto de lengua,*** quick to speak out, free with one's tongue; ***dormir a pierna suelta,*** to sleep like a top. — *n.m.* small change; short report, item. — *n.f.* loosening, freeing; relay (*of oxen*); fetters.
suelto (2), **suelte,** *pres. indic., pres. subj.* [SOLTAR].
sueño (1), **sueñe,** *pres. indic., pres. subj.* [SOÑAR].
sueño (2), *n.m.* sleep; sleepiness; dream; ***tener sueño,*** to be sleepy *or* tired; ***coger el sueño,*** to get to sleep; ***conciliar el sueño,*** to try to go to sleep, woo sleep; ***caerse de sueño,*** to be dropping with sleep; ***descabezar un sueño,*** to have a snooze *or* nap; ***me quita el sueño,*** it keeps me awake at nights; ***entre sueños,*** half-asleep; ***ni por sueño,*** not on your life, out of the question.
suero, *n.m.* whey; serum.
sueroso, -sa, *a.* serous.
suerte, *n.f.* luck; good luck; fate, fortune, chance, lot; kind, sort; way, manner; trick; feat; phase, stage (*in bullfighting*); plot (*of land*); ***probar suerte,*** to try one's luck; ***echar suertes,*** to cast lots; ***la suerte está echada,*** the die is cast; ***eso no entra en suerte,*** there's no question of that; ***por suerte,*** luckily; ***de suerte que,*** so that.
suertero, -ra, *a.* (*Hisp. Am.*) lucky. — *n.m.* lottery seller.
sueste, *n.m.* south-east.
suevo, -va, *a.* of the Suevi; Swabian. — *n.m.f.* one of the Suevi; Swabian.
sufí, *n.m.* sufi.
suficiencia, *n.f.* sufficiency; competency; conceitedness; self-satisfaction, complacency.
suficiente, *a.* sufficient; competent; conceited, smug, self-satisfied, complacent.
sufijo, -ja, *a.* suffixed. — *n.m.* (*gram.*) suffix.
sufocación, *n.f.* suffocation.
sufocador, -ra, sufocante, *a.* suffocating.
sufocar [A], *v.t.* to choke, suffocate, smother.
sufra, *n.f.* ridge-band (*of a harness*).
sufragáneo, -nea, *a., n.m.* suffragan.
sufragar [B], *v.t.* to favour, aid; to defray, pay for; (*Hisp. Am.*) to vote for.
sufragio, *n.m.* suffrage; aid, assistance.
sufragismo, *n.m.* suffragism; suffragette movement.
sufragista, *a.* suffragistic. — *n.m.f.* suffragist. — *n.f.* suffragette.
sufrible, *a.* sufferable, bearable.
sufridera, (1), *n.f.* smith's puncher.
sufridero, -ra (2), *a.* supportable, tolerable.
sufrido, -da, *a.* long-suffering; hard-wearing; (*colour, clothes etc.*) that does not show the dirt; complacent (*husband*); ***mal sufrido,*** having little patience, who does not suffer fools gladly.
sufridor, -ra, *a.* suffering. — *n.m.f.* sufferer.
sufriente, *a.* suffering.
sufrimiento, *n.m.* suffering.
sufrir, *v.t.* to suffer; to endure, sustain; to undergo; to put up with. — *v.i.* to suffer, be in pain.

sufusión, *n.f.* suffusion.
sugerencia, *n.f.* suggestion.
sugerente, *a.* suggesting; thought-provoking.
sugeridor, -ra, *a.* suggesting.
sugerir [6], *v.t.* to suggest; to hint, imply.
sugestión, *n.f.* suggestion; auto-suggestion; hypnotic suggestion; prompting; fascination.
sugestionable, *a.* easily influenced *or* affected.
sugestionar, *v.t.* to hypnotize, fascinate.
sugestivo, -va, *a.* attractive; fascinating; thought-provoking, stimulating.
suicida, *a.* suicidal. — *n.m.f.* suicide (*person*).
suicidarse, *v.r.* to commit suicide.
suicidio, *n.m.* suicide.
suite, *n.m.* dwarf palm.
Suiza, *n.f.* Switzerland.
suiza (1), *n.f.* ancient military sport; (*coll.*) brawl, row.
suizo, -za (2), *a.* Swiss. — *n.m.f.* Swiss; (sugar) bun.
sujeción, *n.f.* subjection; attachment, fastening; ***con sujeción a,*** subject to.
sujetador, -ra, *a.* fastening. — *n.m.* fastener, clip; brassière, bra.
sujetapapeles, *n.m. inv.* paper clip.
sujetar [*p.p.* **sujetado, sujeto**], *v.t.* to subject; to fasten; to keep hold of, hold fast *or* tight. — **sujetarse,** *v.r.* — (***a***), to adhere, stick, conform (to).
sujeto, -ta, *a.* subject; held fast *or* tight. — *n.m.* subject; individual.
sulfatado, *n.m.* sulphating, sulphation.
sulfatador, -ra, *a.* sulphating. — *n.m.f.* sulphating machine.
sulfatar, *v.t.* to sulphate.
sulfato, *n.m.* sulphate.
sulfhidrato, *a.*, *n.m.* hydrosulphate.
sulfhídrico, *a.*, *n.m.* sulphydric.
sulfito, *n.m.* sulphite.
sulfurar, *v.t.* to make angry *or* mad. — **sulfurarse,** *v.r.* (*coll.*) to get steamed up *or* in a stew *or* ratty *or* hopping mad.
sulfúreo, -rea, *a.* sulphurous.
sulfúrico, -ca, *a.* sulphuric.
sulfuro, *n.m.* (*chem.*) sulphide.
sulfuroso, -sa, *a.* sulphurous.
sultán, *n.m.* sultan.
sultana, *n.f.* sultana; Turkish admiral's ship.
sultanato, *n.m.*, **sultanía,** *n.f.* sultanate.
suma (1), *n.f.* sum, addition; amount; compendium; ***suma y sigue,*** carried forward; (*coll.*) and so on and so forth, and so one could go on, and what's more; ***en suma,*** in short.
sumamente, *adv.* extremely.
sumando, *n.m.* (*math.*) addend.
sumar, *v.t.* to add; to add up, tot up; to add up to, tot up to, amount to; ***¿cuánto suma en total?*** how much does it come to all together? — **sumarse,** *v.r.* — ***a,*** to join; to support.
sumario, -ria, *a.* summary. — *n.m.f.* (*law*) indictment. — *n.m.* summary.
sumarísimo, -ma, *a. superl.* (*law*) swift, expeditious; ***consejo sumarísimo,*** drum-head court-martial.
sumergible, *a.* submersible, sinkable. — *n.m.* submarine.
sumergimiento, *n.m.* submersion, sinking.
sumergir [E], *v.t.* to submerge, immerse, sink; to plunge (under). — **sumergirse,** *v.r.* to submerge, sink, dive, plunge (under).
sumerio, -ria, *a.*, *n.m.f.* Sumerian. — *n.m.* Sumerian (*language*).
sumersión, *n.f.* submersion.
sumidad, *n.f.* top, summit, apex.
sumidero, *n.m.* drain; sink; sump, (*Am.*) oil-pan.
sumido, -da, *a.* sunken.
sumiller, *n.m.* chamberlain; ***sumiller de corps,*** gentleman of the bed-chamber.
sumillería, *n.f.* (lord) chamberlain's office.
suministración, *n.f.* provision, supply.
suministrador, -ra, *n.m.f.* provider, supplier.
suministrar, *v.t.* to provide, furnish, supply.
suministro, *n.m.* provision, furnishing, supply.
sumir, *v.t.* to sink, plunge; to take, consume.
sumisión, *n.f.* submission.
sumiso, -sa, *a.* submissive, meek.
sumista, *n.m.* abridger; computer, rapid adder.
sumo, -ma (2), *a.* highest, loftiest; greatest; utmost, extreme; ***a lo sumo,*** at most; ***en sumo grado,*** exceedingly; ***Sumo Pontífice,*** Pontifex Maximus; Supreme Pontiff.
sumoscapo, *n.m.* top of shaft (*of a column*).
sumulas, *n.f.pl.* compendium of the elements of logic.
sumulista, *n.m.* teacher *or* student of logic.
sunción, *n.f.* partaking of the Eucharist.
sundín, *n.m.* (*Arg.*) merry gathering.
sunsún, *n.m.* (*Cub.*) humming-bird.
suntuario, -ria, *a.* sumptuary.
suntuosidad, *n.f.* sumptuosity, sumptuousness.
suntuoso, -sa, *a.* sumptuous; lavish.
supedáneo, *n.m.* pedestal (*of a crucifix*).
supeditación, *n.f.* subjection; subordination.
supeditar, *v.t.* to subject; to subordinate.
superable, *a.* superable.
superabundancia, *n.f.*, superabundance, glut.
superabundante, *a.* superabundant, in glut.
superabundar, *v.i.* to superabound, be in glut.
superádito, -ta, *a.* superadded.
superante, *a.* surpassing, surmounting, exceeding.
superar, *v.t.* to surpass, excel; to overcome, surmount. — **superarse,** *v.r.* to set one's sights (ever) higher, aim (ever) higher.
superávit, *n.m.* surplus.
superchería, *n.f.* fraud, trick.
superchero, -ra, *a.* fraudulent, tricking. — *n.m.f.* trickster.
superdominante, *n.f.* (*mus.*) submediant.
supereminencia, *n.f.* supereminence.
supereminente, *a.* supereminent.
superentender [2], *v.t.* to superintend, inspect, oversee, supervise.
supererogación, *n.f.* supererogation.
supererogatorio, -ria, *a.* supererogatory.
superfetación, *n.f.* superfetation, superimpregnation.
superficial, *a.* surface; superficial; shallow.
superficialidad, *n.f.* superficiality; shallowness.
superficializar, *v.t.* to make *or* render superficial *or* shallow, give *or* lend an air of superficiality *or* shallowness to.
superficialmente, *adv.* superficially.
superficiario, -ria, *a.* (*law*) superficiary.
superficie, *n.f.* surface; area; ***superficie alabeada,*** warped surface; ***superficie de calefacción,*** heating surface; ***superficie de rodadura,*** tread of a wheel; ***superficie desarrollable,*** developable surface; ***superficie reglada,*** ruled surface.
superficionario, -ria, *a.* lease-holder.
superfino, -na, *a.* superfine, extra fine.
superfluidad, *n.f.* superfluity.
superfluo, -lua, *a.* superfluous, needless.
superfosfato, *n.m.* superphosphate.
superhombre, *n.m.* superman.
superhumeral, *n.m.* ephod, superhumeral.
superintendencia, *n.f.* superintendence; supervision.
superintendente, *n.m.f.* superintendent; supervisor, overseer; controller, comptroller.
superior, *a.* superior; upper, higher; better, finer; first class. — *n.m.* superior.

superiora, *n.f.* mother superior.
superiorato, *n.m.* office of a superior; term of office.
superioridad, *n.f.* superiority; pre-eminence; higher authority.
superlativo, -va, *a.* superlative; ***en grado superlativo,*** in the highest degree. — *n.m.* superlative.
superno, -na, *a.* supreme, highest, supernal.
supernumerario, -ria, *a.* supernumerary.
superponer [25], *v.t.* to superpose, superimpose.
superposición, *n.f.* superposing, superposition.
superpotencia, *n.f.* superpower.
superproducción, *n.f.* overproduction; superproduction.
superstición, *n.f.* superstition.
supersticioso, -sa, *a.* superstitious.
supérstite, *a.* surviving.
supersubstancial, *a.* supersubstantial.
supervacáneo, -nea, *a.* superfluous.
supervalorar, *v.t.* to over-rate.
superveniencia, *n.f.* supervention.
supervivencia, *n.f.* survival; (*law*) survivorship.
superviviente, *a.* surviving. — *n.m.f.* survivor.
supinador, *n.m.* supinator.
supino, -na, *a.* supine; ***ignorancia supina,*** crass ignorance. — *n.m.* (*gram.*) supine.
suplantación, *n.f.* supplanting.
suplantador, -ra, *a.* supplanting.
suplantar, *v.t.* to supplant; to alter fraudulently.
suplefaltas, *n.m. inv.* (*coll.*) scapegoat.
suplemental, *a.* supplemental.
suplementario, -ria, *a.* supplementary.
suplemento, *n.m.* supplement.
suplente, *a.* replacing, substituting, standing in, acting. — *n.m.* substitute.
supletorio, -ria, *a.* suppletory, supplementary.
súplica, *n.f.* petition, request; supplication, entreaty; ***a súplica,*** by request.
suplicación, *n.f.* supplication; (*law*) appeal; ***a suplicación,*** on petition, by request.
suplicacionero, -ra, *n.m.f.* waffle seller.
suplicante, *a.*, *n.m.f.* supplicant.
suplicar [A], *v.t.*, *v.i.* to entreat, supplicate, beg, implore; (*law*) to appeal (against).
suplicatoria, *n.f.*, **suplicatorio,** *n.m.* (*law*) letters rogatory.
suplicio, *n.m.* torment, torture; capital punishment, execution.
suplidor, -ra, *n.m.f.* substitute, deputy.
suplir, *v.t.* to supply, furnish; to replace, substitute; to stand in for; to make up for.
suponer [25], *v.t.* to suppose, assume; to mean, imply; to entail, involve; to give the benefit of the doubt concerning, take for granted. — *v.i.* to mean sth., carry weight.
suportar [SOPORTAR].
suposición, *n.f.* supposition, assumption.
supositicio, -cia, *a.* supposititious, supposed, assumed.
supositorio, *n.m.* suppository.
supremacía, *n.f.* supremacy.
supremo, -ma, *a.* supreme; final, last. — *n.f.* (*hist.*) Supreme Council of the Inquisition.
supresión, *n.f.* suppression; omission; elimination; cancellation; abolition; banning.
supresivo, -va, *a.* suppressive.
supreso, -sa, *a.* suppressed. — *p.p. irreg.* [SUPRIMIR].
suprimir [*p.p.* **suprimido, supreso**], *v.t.* to suppress; to omit, cut out, delete; to eliminate, remove, do away with, get rid of; to cancel, lift; to abolish; to ban.
suprior, -ra, *n.m.f.* sub-prior, sub-prioress.
supriorato, *n.m.* office of sub-prior *or* sub-prioress.
supuesto, -ta, *a.* would-be, so-called; ***dar por supuesto,*** to take for granted; ***esto supuesto,*** this being understood; ***por supuesto,*** of course naturally; ***supuesto que,*** granted that, assuming that. — *n.m.* supposition, assumption; premise.
supuración, *n.f.* suppuration.
supurante, *a.* suppurating.
supurar, *v.i.* to suppurate.
supurativo, -va; supuratorio, -ria, *a.* suppurative, suppurating.
suputación, *n.f.* computation, calculation, reckoning.
suputar, *v.t.* to compute, calculate, reckon.
sur, *n.m.* south; south wind.
sural, *a.* (*anat.*) sural.
Suramérica, *n.f.* South America.
surcador, -ra, *n.m.f.* plougher. — *n.m.* ploughman.
surcar [A], *v.t.* to furrow, plough; to fly *or* cleave through; ***surcar los mares,*** to plough the seas.
surco, *n.m.* furrow; rut; groove; wrinkle, line.
surculado, -da, *a.* (*bot.*) having only one stem.
súrculo, *n.m.* stem without branches.
surculoso, -sa, *a.* (*bot.*) having only one stem.
surgente, *a.* springing, spurting, arising; (*naut.*) anchoring.
surgidero, *n.m.* port, road, anchoring-place.
surgidor, *n.m.* one who anchors.
surgir [E, *p.p.* **surgido, surto**], *v.i.* to rise, spring *or* spurt up *or* forth; to arise, crop up; (*naut.*) to anchor.
suri, *n.m.* (*Arg.*) ostrich.
suripanta, *n.f.* (*obs.*) chorus girl; (*contempt.*) slut, hussy.
sursudoeste, *n.m.* south-south-west; south-south-west wind.
surtida (1), *n.f.* sally, sortie; back door; sally-port; (*naut.*) slipway.
surtidero, *n.m.* conduit, outlet; jet, fountain; ***surtidero de agua,*** reservoir.
surtido, -da (2), *a.* mixed, assorted. — *n.m.* stock; supply; assortment.
surtidor, -ra, *a.* supplying, furnishing. — *n.m.f.* supplier, purveyor. — *n.m.* jet, spout, spring; ***surtidor de gasolina,*** petrol pump.
surtimiento, *n.m.* supply; assortment; stock.
surtir, *v.t.* to furnish, supply, provide, stock. — *v.i.* to spout, spurt; ***surtir efecto,*** to have the desired effect, produce results.
surto, -ta, *a.* anchored; (*fig.*) quiet, calm. — *p.p. irreg.* [SURGIR].
súrtuba, *n.f.* (*C.R., bot.*) giant fern.
surumbiar, *v.t.* (*Arg.*) to punish, to whip, to beat.
surumpe, *n.m.* (*Per.*) snow-blindness.
sus (1), *pron. poss. pl. of* **su.**
¡sus! (2), *interj.* up!; on!; off with you!, away!
suscepción, *n.f.* susception; (*eccles.*) receiving holy orders.
susceptibilidad, *n.f.* susceptibility; touchiness; admitting *or* allowing (of).
susceptible, *a.* susceptible; touchy; admitting *or* allowing (of).
susceptivo, -va, *a.* susceptible.
suscitar, *v.t.* to stir up, excite, rouse, arouse, raise.
suscitación, *n.f.* stirring up.
suscribir(se) [*p.p.* **suscri(p)to**], *v.t.* (*v.r.*) to subscribe; to subscribe (to); to sign, endorse; to take out a subscription (for); ***subcribirse a una revista,*** to subscribe to *or* take out a subscription to a magazine.
suscripción, *n.f.* subscription.
suscriptor, -ra, *n.m.f.* subscriber.
suscri(p)to, -ta, *a.* subscribed, endorsed. — *p.p. irreg.* [SUSCRIBIR].
susidio, *n.m.* anxiety.
suso, *adv.* above.
susodicho, -cha, *a.* aforementioned, aforesaid.
suspendedor, -ra, *a.* suspending.

suspender [*p.p.* **suspendido, suspenso**], *v.t.* to suspend; to hang (up); to astonish; to adjourn; to postpone, call off. — *v.t., v.i.* to fail (in an examination).
suspense, *n.m.* suspense; cliff-hanging.
suspensión, *n.f.* suspension; astonishment; adjournment; postponement; suspense.
suspensivo, -va, *a.* suspensive; ***puntos suspensivos,*** suspension points, row of dots.
suspenso, -sa, *a.* hung, hanging, suspended; bewildered. — *n.m.* fail (mark). — *p.p. irreg.* [SUSPENDER].
suspensorio, -ria, *a.* suspensory. — *n.m.* suspensory bandage, truss, brace.
suspicacia, *n.f.* suspiciousness, mistrust.
suspicaz, *a.* suspicious, mistrustful.
suspirado, -da, *a.* longed for, desired.
suspirador, -ra, *a.* sighing.
suspirar, *v.i.* to sigh.
suspiro, *n.m.* sigh; glass whistle; meringue; (*mus.*) short pause; (*bot.*) heartsease.
suspirón, -rona, *a.* (much) given to sighing; wistful.
suspiroso, -sa, *a.* wheezy.
sustancia, *n.f.* substance; solidness, body; extract.
sustanciación, *n.f.* substantiation.
sustancial, *a.* substantial; solid, having body.
sustanciar, *v.t.* to abridge, condense.
sustancioso, -sa, *a.* (*fig.*) with body to it, having body; nourishing.
sustantivar, *v.t.* to use as a substantive.
sustantivo, *n.m.* (*gram.*) substantive, noun.
sustentable, *a.* sustainable, defensible.
sustentación, *n.f.* sustentation; support; sustenance.
sustentáculo, *n.m.* stay, prop, support.
sustentador, -ra, *n.m.f.* sustainer.
sustentamiento, *n.m.* sustenance.
sustentante, *a.* sustaining. — *n.m.* supporter, defender.
sustentar, *v.t.* to sustain, support; to nourish; to maintain.
sustento, *n.m.* sustenance; support; maintenance.
sustitución, *n.f.* substitution.
sustituidor, -ra, *a.* substituting. — *n.m.f.* one that substitutes.
sustituir [O], *v.t.* to substitute, replace, stand in for.
sustituto, -ta, *a., n.m.* substitute. — *p.p. irreg.* [SUSTITUIR].
sustituyente, *a.* substituting.
susto, *n.m.* fright, shock, scare.
sustracción, *n.f.* subtraction; stealing.
sustraendo, *n.m.* subtrahend.
sustraer [34], *v.t.* to remove, take away, steal. — **sustraerse (a),** *v.r.* to dodge, evade.
susurración, *n.f.* whispering.
susurrador, -ra, *a.* whispering. — *n.m.f.* whisperer.
susurrante, *a.* whispering.
susurrar, *v.i.* to whisper; (*poet.*) to purl (*of a stream*); to rustle (*of trees*); to murmur.
susurro, *n.m.* whisper, murmur, rustle, purl.
susurrón, -rrona, *a.* whispering, murmuring.
sutás, *n.m.* soutache, braid.
sute, *a.* (*Col., Ven.*) sickly, weak, thin. — *n.m.* (*Col.*) sucking pig; (*Hond.*) avocado, alligator pear.
sutil, *a.* subtle; sharp, keen; fine, slender, delicate.
sutileza, sutilidad, *n.f.* subtlety; fineness, slenderness; acuteness; nicety; splitting of hairs; ***sutileza de manos,*** lightfingeredness.
sutilización, *n.f.* subtilization.
sutilizador, -ra, *n.m.f.* one who subtilizes, subtilizer.
sutilizar [C], *v.t.* to subtilize; to render thin *or* slender; to refine, polish. — *v.i.* to subtilize, split hairs.
sutorio, -ria, *a.* shoe-making.
sutura, *n.f.* seam; suture.
suturar, *v.t.* to suture; to stitch.
suversión, *n.f.* subversion.
suversivo, -va, *a.* subversive.
suyo, -ya, *pron. poss., m.f.,* 3*rd person* (*pl.* **suyos, suyas**), his, hers, theirs, one's; his own, her own, its own, one's own, their own; ***los suyos,*** his (*or* her, *or* their) folk, people, supporters etc.; ***de suyo,*** by *or* in itself; ***una de las suyas,*** one of his (*or* her) tricks; ***salirse con la suya,*** to get one's own way.
suyru, *n.m.* (*Per.*) long robe used by the Incas.
suyuntu, *n.m.* (*Hisp. Am.*) [ZOPILOTE].

T

T, t, *n.f.* letter T, t.
¡ta! *interj.* ho-ho!
taba, *n.f.* anklebone, knucklebone.
tabacal, *n.m.* tobacco plantation.
tabacalero, -ra, *a.* tobacco, of tobacco. — *n.m.f.* tobacco-grower, tobacco-dealer.
tabaco, *n.m.* tobacco; cigarettes; snuff; dry rot; brown (*colour*).
tabacoso, -sa, *a.* tobacco-stained; snuffy; (*bot.*) blighted.
tabalada, *n.f.* (*coll.*) heavy fall.
tabalario, *n.m.* (*coll.*) posterior.
tabalear, *v.t.* to rock to and fro. — *v.i.* to drum with the fingers.
tabaleo, *n.m.* rocking, swinging; drumming with the fingers.
tabanazo, *n.m.* (*coll.*) blow, slap.
tabanco, *n.m.* market-stall; (*Mex.*) cock-loft.
tábano, *n.m.* gadfly, horse-fly.
tabanque, *n.m.* treadle (*of a potter's wheel*).
tabaola, *n.f.* clamour, hubbub.
tabaque, *n.m.* basket; large tack.
tabaquería, *n.f.* tobacco *or* snuff shop; tobacconist.
tabaquero, -ra, *a.* (of) tobacco. — *n.m.* tobacconist; cigar-maker. — *n.f.* snuff-box; pipe-case; tobacco-case; cigar-case; pipe-bowl.
tabaquismo, *n.m.* addiction to cigarettes.
tabaquista, *n.m.f.* one addicted to tobacco *or* snuff; tobacco expert.
tabardete, tabardillo, *n.m.* sunstroke; typhus; ***tabardillo pintado,*** spotted fever; (*coll.*) jitterbug.
tabardo, *n.m.* tabard.
tabarra, *n.f.* bore, pain in the neck.
tabasco, *n.m.* tabasco; banana.
tabellar, *v.t.* to fold (*cloth*) leaving the selvage visible; to mark (*fabrics*) with trade-mark.
taberna, *n.f.* tavern, public house, wine-shop.
tabernáculo, *n.m.* tabernacle.
tabernario, -ria, *a.* tavern; low, vulgar.
tabernera, *n.f.* innkeeper's wife; barmaid.
tabernero, *n.m.* innkeeper, tavern-keeper, barkeeper.
tabes, *n.f. inv.* tabes, consumption.
tabí, *n.m.* tabby, watered fabric.
tabica, *n.f.* lintel, panel, covering board.
tabicar [A], *v.t.* to wall up; to partition off.
tabicón, *n.m.* thick wall.
tábido, -da, *a.* tabid, wasted; putrid, corrupted.
tabinete, *n.m.* tabinet (*fabric*).
tabique, *n.m.* partition wall.
tabiquería, *n.f.* set of partition walls.
tabla, *n.f.* board; plank; bench; slab; tablet, plate; table; list; (*mus.*) tabla; box-pleat; panel; flat diamond; meat-stall; largest face (*of a piece of timber*); smooth, flat part (*of the body*); strip (*of land*); revenue office (*at frontier*); ***a raja tabla,*** strictly, with the utmost rigour, by the book; ***hacer tabla rasa,*** to make a clean sweep; ***hacer tablas,*** to draw; ***salvarse en una tabla,*** to have a narrow escape; (*fig.*) ***tener tablas,*** to know the ropes; (*pl.*, *theat.*) boards.
tablachina, *n.f.* wooden shield *or* buckler.
tablacho, *n.m.* floodgate, sluice-gate.
tablada, *n.f.* (*Arg.*) slaughterhouse corral.
tablado, *n.m.* stage; scaffold; platform; flooring; boards (*of a bedstead*); tableau; (*processions*) float; (*theat.*) boards; ***sacar al tablado,*** to publish, make known.
tablaje, *n.m.* planking, pile of boards; gaming-house.
tablajería, *n.f.* gaming, gambling; hire of the gaming-table; butcher's shop.
tablajero, *n.m.* scaffold-maker; stage carpenter; collector of taxes; gambler; keeper of a gaming house; (*prov.*, *iron.*) assistant resident surgeon in a hospital; butcher.
tablar, *n.m.* division of gardens into plots; set of garden plots.
tablazo, *n.m.* stroke with a board; shallow arm of a river *or* sea; sheet of water; (*Hisp. Am.*) sea-floor deposit.
tablazón, *n.f.* boards, planks, platform; planking, flooring; decks and sheathing of a ship; lumber; (*naut.*) ***tablazón de la cubierta,*** deck planks.
tablear, *v.t.* to divide (*a garden*) into beds; to plank, saw into boards; to hammer (*iron*) into plates; (*sew.*) to make box-pleats.
tableo, *n.m.* sawing (*timber*) into boards; dividing (*a garden*) into plots; levelling (*ground*); hammering (*iron*) into plates; making box-pleats in.
tablero, *n.m.* board; panel; gambling-house; gambling-table; money-table; shop-counter; timber for sawing up; dog-nail; stock of a cross-bow; chess board; (*tail.*) cutting-table; blackboard; (*Mex.*) backgammon board; planking of a bridge; skirts of a coat; compartment; ***tablero contador,*** abacus; ***tablero de cocina,*** dresser; (*elec.*) ***tablero de distribución,*** switchboard.
tableta, *n.f.* tablet; memorandum; writing-pad, clapper; ***estar en tabletas,*** to be in suspense.
tableteado, *n.m.* noise made by clappers.
tabletear, *v.i.* to move boards; to rattle.
tableteo, *n.m.* rattle; tapping; clatter.
tablica, tablita, *n.f.* small board, small table, tablet.
tablilla, *n.f.* tablet, slab; notice-board; (*surg.*) splint; ***tablilla de mesón,*** sign of an inn; kind of cake; ***por tablilla,*** indirectly.
tablón, *n.m.* plank, thick board; (*naut.*) ***tablón de aparadura,*** garboard strake; (*fig.*) ***llevar*** or ***tener un tablón,*** to be drunk; ***tablón de anuncios,*** notice board, (*Am.*) bulletin.
tabloncillo, *n.m.* flooring-board; last row of seats in a bullring.
tabloza, *n.f.* painter's palette.
tabo, *n.m.* (*Philip.*) cup made from coconut shell.
tabor, *n.m.* a unit of Moroccan troops in the Spanish Army.
tabora, *n.f.* (*prov.*) stagnant pool.
tabú, *n.m.* taboo.
tabuco, *n.m.* hut, hovel; narrow room.
tabuizar, *v.t.* to place a taboo on.
tabular, *a.* tabular.
tabuquillo, tabuquito, *n.m.* shack, shanty.
taburete, *n.m.* stool; (*pl.*, *theat.*) benches in the pit.
taca, *n.f.* cupboard, small pantry; (*prov.*) stain; (*min.*) plates (*of the crucible*).
tacada, *n.f.* stroke at billiards; (*naut.*) wedge.
tacamaca, *n.f.* balsam poplar.
tacana *n.m.* grey silver ore.
tacañear, *v.i.* to be stingy.
tacañería, *n.f.* niggardliness, stinginess, tight-fistedness.
tacaño, -ña, *a.* stingy, tight-fisted. — *n.m.f.* miser, (*Am.*) tightwad.
tacar [A], *v.t.* to mark. — *v.i.* to have one's turn (*at billiards*).
tacazo, *n.m.* stroke with a cue.
taceta, *n.f.* copper basin (*in oil-mills*).
tacica, tacilla, tacita, *n.f.* small cup.
tácito, -ta, *a.* tacit; silent.
taciturnidad, *n.f.* taciturnity, silence.
taciturno, -na, *a.* taciturn, silent.
taco, *n.m.* wad; plug; stopper; rammer; billiard cue; writing-pad; pop-gun; snack; swig, draught; swear-word; muddle, mess; ***armarse un taco,*** to get into a muddle, get all mixed up.
tacón, *n.m.* heel (*of a shoe*); ***tacón de aguja,*** stiletto heel, (*Am.*) spike heel.

taconazo, *n.m.* stamp with a heel; click of the heels.
taconear, *v.i.* to drum with the heels; (*fig.*) to strut.
taconeo, *n.m.* drumming, stamping made with the heels.
tacotal, *n.m.* (*C.R.*) dense thicket; (*Hond.*) marsh.
táctico, -ca, *a.* tactical. — *n.m.f.* tactician. — *n.f.* tactics.
táctil, *a.* tactile.
tacto, *n.m.* touch, feel; tact.
tacuacín, *n.m.* (*Cent. Am.*) opossum.
tacuará, *n.f.* (*Arg.*) hard bamboo.
tacurú, *n.m.* (*Arg.*) black ant.
tacuacha, *n.f.* (*Cub.*) skilful trick.
tacha, *n.f.* blemish, flaw; ***poner tacha a,*** to find fault with.
tachar, *v.t.* to call, accuse; to cross out, score out, strike through; (*law*) to challenge (*a witness*); ***le tachan de cobarde,*** they call *or* brand him a coward.
tachero, *n.m.* (*Hisp. Am.*) tinman, tinsmith.
tachigual, *n.m.* (*Mex.*) cheap cotton cloth.
tacho, *n.m.* (*Hisp. Am.*) boiler, evaporator, pan; tin; pot; bucket, pail.
tachón, *n.m.* crossing out, erasure; gilt-headed tack; (*sew.*) trimming.
tachonar, *v.t.* (*sew.*) to trim; to adorn with gilt tacks; to stud, spangle; ***tachonado de estrellas,*** star-spangled, star-studded.
tachonería, *n.f.* ornamental work with gilt tacks *or* studs.
tachoso, -sa, *a.* defective, faulty.
tachuela, *n.f.* tack, hobnail; (*Hisp. Am.*) tin cup; (*Hisp. Am.*) runt.
tael, *n.m.* (*Philip.*) tael (*coin and weight*).
tafanario, *n.m.* (*coll.*) buttocks, behind.
tafetán, *n.m.* taffeta, thin silk; ***tafetán inglés,*** court-plaster; (*pl.* **tafetanes**) flags, colours, standard, ensign.
tafia, *n.f.* (*Hisp. Am.*) tafia *or* taffia rum.
tafilete, *n.m.* tafilet *or* Moroccan leather.
tafiletear, *v.t.* to ornament with tafilet leather.
tafiletería, *n.f.* art of dressing tafilet leather.
tafurea, *n.f.* flat-bottomed boat (*for transporting horses*).
tagalo, -la, *a.*, *n.m.f.* (*Philip.*) Tagalog. — *n.m.* Tagalog language.
tagarino, -na, *n.m.f.* (*hist.*) Moor who lived among Christians.
tagarnina, *n.f.* (*bot.*) golden thistle; (*coll.*) poor cigar, stinker.
tagarote, *n.m.* (*orn.*) sparrow-hawk; quill-driver, scrivener; lanky, gawky fellow; (*coll.*) sponger; has-been.
tagarotear, *v.t.* (*coll.*) to write with a flourish.
tagua, *n.f.* (*Ec.*) tagua, ivory nut; (*Chi.*, *orn.*) moor hen.
taguán, *n.m.* (*Philip.*, *zool.*) flying squirrel.
taha, *n.f.* region, district.
taharal, *n.m.* tamarisk plantation.
taheño, *a.* red (*hair*); red-bearded.
Tahití, *n.m.* Tahiti.
tahona, *n.f.* flour-mill; bakehouse, bakery, baker's shop.
tahonero, *n.m.* miller; baker.
tahulla, *n.f.* (*prov.*) a measure of land (about ¼ acre).
tahur, -ra, *a.* gambling, given to gambling. — *n.m.f.* gambler; card-sharper.
tahurería, *n.f.* gambling; gaming-house; cheating at cards.
taifa, *n.f.* party, faction; (*coll.*) lot, mob, gang.
Tailandia, *n.f.* Thailand.
tailandés, -desa, *a.*, *n.m.f.* Thai (*person*). — *n.m.* Thai (*language*).
taima, *n.f.* (*Hisp. Am.*) sullenness, stubbornness.
taimado, -da, *a.* crafty, sly, cunning; (*Hisp. Am.*) sullen, stubborn.
taita, *n.m.* (*coll.*) daddy; (*Hisp. Am.*) old negro; (*Ven.*) family name for the head of the household; (*Arg.*, *Chi.*) child's name for father *or* as a term of courteous address; ***taita cura,*** reverend father; procurer.
Taití, *n.m.* Tahiti.
taitano, -na, *a.*, *n.m.f.* Tahitian.
taja, *n.f* cut; tally; tree (*of a packsaddle*).
tajada (1), *n.f.* cut, slice; hoarseness; (*Hisp. Am.*) slash, gash; (*coll.*) drunkenness; (*coll.*) ***hacer tajadas de,*** to slash up; ***sacar tajada,*** to get sth. out of it.
tajadera, *n.f.* chopping-knife; (*mech.*) gouge, round chisel; (*pl.*) sluice of a mill dam.
tajadero, *n.m.* chopping-block, trencher.
tajadilla, *n.f.* small slice; dish of lights.
tajado, -da (2), *a.* steep, sheer; (*her.*) divided diagonally.
tajador, -ra, *n.m.f.* cutter, chopper; cutting edge.
tajadura, *n.f.* cut; cutting, chopping.
tajalán, -lana, *a.* (*Cub.*) idle, lazy, indolent.
tajamar, *n.m.* cutwater; stem.
tajante, *a.* cutting; sweeping; categorical, uncompromising.
tajaplumas, *n.m. inv.* penknife.
tajar, *v.t.* to cut, chop, hew, hack, cleave, cut off.
tajea, *n.f.* channel, watercourse; drain.
Tajo, *n.m.* (river) Tagus.
tajo, *n.m.* cut, cutting; slice; slash; gorge, ravine; chopping-block; place of work; ***vamos al tajo,*** let's get cracking *or* get on with the grind.
tajón, *n.m.* chopping-block.
tajuela, *n.f.*, **tajuelo,** *n.m.* low stool.
tal, *a.* (*pl.* **tales**) such, such a; as, like; ***un tal Sánchez,*** a chap called Sánchez, one Sánchez; ***tal cual,*** the odd one or two. — *adv.* in such a way *or* state, so, thus; ***tal cual,*** just as it is; ***otro que tal,*** another of the same ilk; another in the same condition; ***¿qué tal?*** how goes it? how are things? — *conj.* ***con tal*** (***de***) ***que,*** on condition that. — *pron.* s.o.; such a thing; ***tal para cual,*** two of a kind; ***el tal*** (***Sánchez***), this chap (Sánchez).
tala, *n.f.* felling (*of trees*); havoc, destruction; stockade; tip-cat (*children's game*); cat (*in game*).
talabarte, *n.m.* sword-belt.
talabartería, *n.f.* saddlery.
talabartero, *n.m.* saddler.
talador, -ra, *a.* felling.
taladrador, -ra, *a.* drilling. — *n.m.f.* drilling machine.
taladrar, *v.t.* to drill, bore, pierce.
taladro, *n.m.* drill, borer, auger; drilling bit; drill-hole.
talaje, *n.m.* (*Chi.*) pasturage and duty paid for it.
talamera, *n.f.* tree used for decoying.
talamete, *n.m.* (*naut.*) foredeck planking.
tálamo, *n.m.* bridal bed *or* chamber; (*bot.*) thalamus.
talán, *n.m.* ding-dong.
talanquera, *n.f.* breastwork; ***hablar desde la talanquera,*** to speak from a safe place, without any risk.
talante, *n.m.* mood; disposition; look; grace; ***de buen*** or ***mal talante,*** in a good *or* bad mood; with a good *or* bad grace.
talar (1), *v.t.* to fell (*trees*); to lay waste, desolate; to prune.
talar (2), *a.* full length, reaching the heels.
talco, *n.m.* tinsel; talc(um).
talcoso, -sa, *a.* talcoid, talcose.
talcualillo, -lla, *a.* (*coll.*) middling, not too bad, so so, fairish.
talega, *n.f.* bag; small sack; money-bag; bagful; diaper.
talego, *n.m.* bag, sack; clumsy, dumpy fellow; ***tener talego,*** to have money.
taleguilla, *n.f.* small bag; bullfighter's breeches; (*coll.*) ***taleguilla de la sal,*** daily expenditure.

talento, *n.m.* talent; intelligence, cleverness.
talentoso, -sa, *a.* talented, able, clever; endowed with intelligence.
talentudo, -da, *a.* highly talented; overtalented, a bit too intelligent.
tálero, *n.m.* thaler.
talio, *n.m.* thallium.
talión, *n.m.* talion, retaliation.
talionar, *v.t.* to take retaliation on.
talismán, *n.m.* talisman, amulet, charm.
talma, *n.f.* long cape *or* cloak.
talmente, *adv.* (*coll.*) literally, positively.
talmud, *n.m.* Talmud.
talmúdico, -ca, *a.* Talmudical.
talmudista, *n.m.f.* Talmudist.
talofita, *a.* (*bot.*) thallophytic. — *n.f.* thallophyte.
talofítico, -ca, *a.* thallophytic.
talón, *n.m.* heel; standard (*in a monetary system*); cheque, voucher, coupon, ticket; ***apretar los talones,*** to hurry up, speed up; ***pisar los talones a,*** to be hard on the heels of.
talonada, *n.f.* kick with the heels.
talonario, -ria, *a.* counterfoil. — *n.m.* counterfoil book, cheque- *or* stub-book.
talonear, *v.i.* to be nimble, walk quickly, dash along.
talonera, *n.f.* (*Chi.*) spur support.
talonesco, -ca, *a.* (*coll.*) relating to the heels.
talque, *n.m.* refractory clay.
talqueza, *n.f.* (*C.R.*) grass used for thatching.
talquina, *n.f.* (*Chi.*) treason, ambush, artful trick.
talud, *n.m.* bank, embankment.
taludín, *n.m.* (*Guat.*) alligator.
talvina, *n.f.* almond-meal porridge.
talla, *v.f.* carving; ransom; price on a criminal's head; round (*of card games*); height, stature; size (*of shoes, garments etc.*); instrument for measuring height; (*naut.*) purchase block; (*surg.*) gallstone operation; ***media talla,*** half-relief; ***no dar la talla,*** not to be up to it, not to be up to scratch.
tallador, *n.m.* carver, engraver, die-sinker; (*Hisp. Am.*) dealer (*in a game*); croupier.
talladura, *n.f.* engraving.
tallar, *a.* ready for cutting. — *n.m.* forest ready for first cutting. — *v.t.* to carve, engrave; to cut (*a precious stone*); to appraise; to tax. — *v.i.* to deal (*at cards*); (*Arg.*) to chat; (*Chi.*) to court.
tallarín, *n.m.* noodle.
tallarola, *n.f.* knife for cutting velvet pile.
talle, *n.m.* figure; waist; fit.
tallecer [9], *v.i.* to sprout, shoot.
taller, *n.m.* workshop; studio, atelier; ***taller de reparaciones,*** repair shop.
tallista, *n.m.* engraver, carver in wood.
tallo, *n.m.* stem, stalk.
talludo, -da, *a.* grown into long stalks; grown, grown up; overgrown; (*coll.*) getting long in the tooth.
tamagás, *n.m.* (*Hisp. Am.*) poisonous snake.
tamango, *n.m.* (*Chi.*) sheepskin cover for the feet; (*Arg.*) coarse shoe worn by the gauchos.
tamañamente, *adv.* this *or* that size, long, big *etc.*
tamañito, -ta, *a.* so small, very small, cut down to size.
tamaño, -ña, *a.* so big, such a big; very big *or* very large; the size (of). — *n.m.* size; ***de tamaño natural,*** life-size; (*coll.*) huge.
támara, *n.f.* (*Canary Islands*) palm tree *or* palm field; (*pl.*) dates (*in a bunch*); faggots of wood.
tamarindo, *n.m.* tamarind tree; tamarind fruit.
tamarisco, tamariz, *n.m.* tamarisk.
tamba, *n.m.* (*Ec.*) loin-cloth.
tambalco, *n.m.* staggering, reeling, tottering.
tambaleante, *a.* staggering, tottering, reeling; wobbling, swaying.
tambalear(se), *v.i.* (*v.r.*) to stagger, totter, reel; to wobble, sway.
tambaleo, *n.m.* staggering, tottering, reeling; wobbling, swaying.
tambanillo, *n.m.* (*arch.*) tympanum.
tambarillo, *n.m.* chest with an arched cover.
tambarria, *n.f.* (*Col., Ec., Hond., Per.*) carousal; (*Chi.*) low tavern.
tambero, -ra, *a.* (*Arg.*) tame, gentle. — *n.m.f.* (*Per.*) innkeeper.
tambesco, *n.m.* (*prov.*) swing.
también, *adv.* also, too, as well; (*coll.*) ***¡también es mala suerte!*** that's bad luck if you like!
tambo, *n.m.* (*Chi., Col., Ec., Per.*) roadside lodging-house, hostelry; (*Arg.*) cowshed.
tambocha, *n.f.* (*Col.*) poisonous ant.
tambor, *n.m.* drum; drummer; chestnut roaster, coffee roaster; tambour frame; (*mech.*) band pulley; (*fort., arch.*) tambour; (*jewel.*) barrel; screen; thole; (*naut.*) capstan-drum; paddle-box; (*anat.*) eardrum; ***tambor mayor,*** drum-major; ***a tambor batiente,*** with drums beating.
tambora, *n.f.* bass drum.
tamborete, *n.m.* timbrel; (*naut.*) cap (*of the masthead*).
tamboril, *n.m.* tabour, timbrel.
tamborilada, *n.f.* (*coll.*) fall onto the backside; slap on the head *or* shoulders.
tamborilazo, *n.m.* [TAMBORILADA].
tamborilear, *v.i.* to drum; to patter, tap. — *v.t.* to praise, extol; (*print.*) to plane, level (*types*).
tamborileo, *n.m.* beating of a drum, drumming.
tamborilero, *n.m.* drummer.
tamborilete, *n.m.* taboret; (*print.*) planer.
tamborín, tamborino, *n.m.* tabour.
tamborón, *n.m.* large bass drum.
tambre, *n.m.* (*Col.*) dam; waterwheel.
tameme, *n.m.* (*Chi., Mex., Per.*) Indian porter, carrier.
Támesis, *n.m.* (river) Thames.
tamiz, *n.m.* sieve, sifter; ***pasar por tamiz,*** to sift.
tamizar [C], *v.t.* to sift.
tamo, *n.m.* fuzz, fluff; dust; chaff.
tamojo, *n.m.* (*bot.*) salt-wort.
tampoco, *adv.* neither, not either; ***tampoco voy yo*** or ***no voy yo tampoco,*** I'm not going either.
tamujal, *n.m.* buckthorn thicket.
tamujo, *n.m.* (*bot.*) buckthorn.
tan, *adv.* (*contraction of* **tanto**), so, as; ***tan siquiera,*** even if only, at least; ***tan sólo,*** only, just; ***qué . . . tan,*** what a. . . .
tanaceto, *n.m.* tansy.
tanate, *n.m.* (*C.R., Hond., Mex.*) bale made of hide *or* palm-leaf; (*Cent. Am.*) bundle, parcel.
tanatero, *n.m.* (*Mex.*) carrier in the mines.
tanato, *n.m.* tannate.
tanda, *n.f.* turn; shift, relay; task; layer, bed; game (*of billiards*); batch; series, round; (*Chi., theat.*) performance; ***una tanda de azotes,*** a flogging.
tándem, *n.m.* tandem.
tandeo, *n.m.* distribution of irrigating water by turns.
tangán, *n.m.* (*Ec.*) square board hung from the ceiling (*for storing food*).
tanganillas, (en), *adv.* waveringly, shaky, tottering.
tanganillo, *n.m.* small prop *or* stay.
tángano, *n.m.* hob (*child's game*).
tangencia, *n.f.* tangency.
tangente, *a., n.m.* tangent; ***escapar, escaparse, irse*** or ***salir por la tangente,*** to go off at a tangent; to dodge the issue.
Tánger, *n.m.* Tangier(s).
tangerino, -na, *a.* of Tangier(s). — *n.m.f.* native *or* inhabitant of Tangier(s). — *n.f.* tangerine (*fruit*).
tangible, *a.* tangible.
tangidera, *n.f.* stern-fast, cable.
tango, *n.m.* tango; hob (*boys' game*).

tanguear(se), *v.i.* (*v.r.*) (*Hisp. Am.*) to change parties.
tanguillo, *n.m.* (*prov.*) top (*toy*).
tánico, -ca, *a.* tannic.
tanino, *n.m.* tannin.
tanor, -ra, *a.*, *n.m.f.* (*Philip.*) Indian compelled to serve in Spanish households.
tanoría, *n.f.* (*Philip.*) obligatory and unpaid domestic service for the Spaniards.
tanque, *n.m.* tank; water tank; (*Hisp. Am.*) reservoir; bee-glue.
tanta (1), *n.f.* (*Per.*) bread made of maize.
tantalato, *n.m.* tantalate.
tantalio, *n.m.* tantalum.
tantarantán, *n.m.* tantarara, rub-a-dub-dub, double drum-beat.
tanteador, *n.m.* score board. — *n.m.f.* scorer, marker, scorekeeper.
tantear, *v.t.* to try; to test, test out, feel, sound; (*art*) to sketch, outline; to estimate at sight. — *v.i.* to keep the score. — **tantearse,** *v.r.* to think carefully.
tanteo, *n.m.* trial, test; feeling, sounding out; rough estimate; score.
tantico, tantillo, *adv.* (*coll.*) a little, somewhat. — *n.m.* (a) little, (a) little bit.
tanto, -ta (2), *a.* so much, as much, so great, as great, very great; (*pl.*) many; as many, so many. — *adv. m.* so, so much, as much, thus, so far, so hard, so long, so often, in such a way, to such an extent; ***tanto como,*** as much as, so much as; ***tanto el uno como el otro,*** both of them; ***un tanto, algún tanto,*** a little, somewhat; ***tanto más*** (or ***menos***) ***que,*** all the more (*or* the less) because, especially as; ***tanto mejor*** (***peor***), so much the better (the worse). — *pron.* so much, as much, that; ***no es para tanto,*** it's not so bad as all that; ***por lo tanto,*** therefore; ***¡tanto bueno!*** good to see you! — *n.m.* amount, sum; point (*in games*); counter, scorer; copy (*of a writing*); (*com.*) rate; ***tanto alzado,*** lump sum; ***tanto por ciento,*** percentage; ***otro tanto,*** as much again; ***¡y tanto!*** you're telling me! you can say that again!; ***apuntarse un tanto,*** to score a point, a success; ***estar al tanto,*** to be up to the minute, be in the picture; ***en*** or ***entre tanto,*** in the meantime.
tanza, *n.f.* (*prov.*) fishing-line.
tañedor, -ra, *n.m.f.* player (*on a musical instrument*).
tañente, *a.* playing (*on a musical instrument*).
tañer [K], *v.t.* to play (*a musical instrument*); to ring (*a bell*).
tañido, *n.m.* tune; sound; twang; ring.
tañimiento, *n.m.* playing (*on an instrument*).
tao, *n.m.* badge of the orders of St. Antony and St. John.
tapa, *n.f.* cover, cap, lid; horny part (*of hoof*); heel (*of shoe*); (*motor.*) cylinder head; board, book cover; knuckle (*of veal*); facing (*of lapel*); flap (*of pocket*); savoury tit-bit.
tapabalazo, *n.m.* shot-plug.
tapaboca, *n.f.* (*coll.*) slap on the mouth; muffler; silencer; (*artill.*) tampion.
tapacubo(s), *n.m.* hub-cap.
tapaculo, *n.m.* rose hip.
tapachiche, *n.m.* (*C.R.*) locust.
tapada, *n.f.* [TAPADO].
tapadera, *n.f.* cover, lid.
tapadero, *n.m.* stopper.
tapadillo, *n.m.* concealment (*of a woman's face*); flute-stop (*of an organ*); ***de tapadillo,*** secretly, under cover.
tapadizo, *n.m.* cover, shed.
tapado, -da, *a.* (*Hisp. Am.*) unspotted (*of horses*). — *n.m.* overcoat; buried treasure. — *n.f.* veiled woman.
tapador, -ra, *a.* covering. — *n.m.* plug, stopper; cover, lid.
tapadura, *n.f.* covering.
tapafunda, *n.f.* holster-flap.
tapagujeros, *n.m. inv.* (*coll.*) makeshift; botcher.
tapajuntas, *n.m. inv.* door strip (*covering joint with wall*); corner angle (*protecting plaster*).
tapalo, *n.m.* (*Mex.*) shawl.
tapamiento, *n.m.* covering.
tápana, *n.f.* (*bot.*) caper.
tapanca, *n.f.* (*Chi.*, *Ec.*) horse trappings.
tapaojo, *n.m.* (*Col.*, *Ven.*) blinkers (*for horses*).
tapapiés, *n.m. inv.* long skirt.
tapar, *v.t.* to cover (up); to stop (up), plug (up); to cap, cork; to bung; to close up; to wrap up.
tápara, *n.f.* (*bot.*) caper; (*Ven.*) gourd (*for drink*).
taparo, *n.m.* gourd tree.
taparrabo, *n.m.* loin cloth; bathing trunks.
tapayagua, *n.f.* (*Hond.*, *Mex.*) drizzle.
tapera, *n.f.* (*Bol.*, *Par.*) deserted village; (*Cent. Am.*) abandoned house.
taperujarse, *v.r.* (*coll.*) to cover up one's face.
taperujo, *n.m.* (*coll.*) ill-shaped stopper; awkward way of wrapping o.s. up *or* covering one's face.
tapetado, -da, *a.* dark brown.
tapete, *n.m.* small carpet, rug; table cover; ***tapete verde,*** gambling table; (*fig.*) ***estar sobre el tapete,*** to be under discussion.
tapia, *n.f.* enclosing wall (*made of mud*).
tapiador, *n.m.* enclosing-wall builder.
tapial, *n.m.* mould for making mud walls.
tapiar, *v.t.* to wall, wall in; to block up (sth.).
tapicería, *n.f.* tapestry; art of making tapestry; upholstery; tapestry-shop.
tapicero, *n.m.* tapestry-worker; carpet monger; upholsterer; ***tapicero mayor,*** tapestry keeper in the royal palace.
tapido, -da, *a.* closely woven.
tapioca, *n.f.* tapioca.
tapir, *n.m.* tapir.
tapis, *n.m.* (*Philip.*) sash used by women.
tapiscar, *v.t.* (*C.R.*, *Hond.*) to gather and thresh maize.
tapiz, *n.m.* tapestry.
tapizar [C], *v.t.* to hang with tapestry; to upholster.
tapón, *n.m.* cork, stopper; plug, bung; (*surg.*) tampon; (*coll.*) stocky bloke; ***al primer tapón, zurrapas,*** starting off on the wrong foot; ***estado tapón,*** buffer state.
taponamiento, *n.m.* tamponage; traffic jam.
taponar, *v.t.* to tampon; to plug, stop up.
taponazo, *n.m.* pop (*of a cork*).
taponería, *n.f.* corks; cork factory *or* industry; cork shop.
taponero, -ra, *a.* cork. — *n.m.f.* cork maker, cork cutter, cork seller.
tapsia, *n.f.* deadly carrot.
tapujarse, *v.r.* to muffle o.s.
tapujo, *n.m.* muffler; (*coll.*) jiggery-pokery.
taque, *n.m.* noise made by locking a door; rap, knock at a door.
taquera, *n.f.* stand *or* rack for billiard-cues.
taquichuela, *n.f.* (*Par.*) five-stones (*children's game*).
taquigrafía, *n.f.* stenography, shorthand.
taquigrafiar, *v.t.* to write in shorthand.
taquigráfico, -ca, *a.* stenographic.
taquígrafo, -fa, *n.m.f.* stenographer, shorthand writer.
taquilla, *n.f.* ticket rack; box office, ticket office, booking office; position, till; take, receipts.
taquillero, -ra, *n.m.f.* booking office clerk *or* attendant.
taquimeca, *n.f.* (*coll. abbrev.* **taquimecanógrafa**).
taquimecanógrafa, *n.f.* shorthand-typist.
taquimetría, *n.f.* tachymetry, tacheometry.
taquímetro, *n.m.* tachymeter, tacheometer.
taquín, *n.m.* knuckle-bone of a sheep.

tara, *n.f.* (*com.*) tare; tally; flaw, blemish; (*Ven*) green grasshopper; (*Col.*) poisonous snake; (*fig.*) ***menos la tara,*** allowing for exaggeration.
tarabilla, *n.f.* clapper; catch, latch, bolt; fastener *or* holder; pin *or* peg; (*Arg.*) rattle; (*coll.*) chatterbox; jabber, harping on the same old tune; ***soltar la tarabilla,*** to start to jabber away.
tarabita, *n.f.* (*Hisp. Am.*) main cable of a rope bridge.
taracea, *n.f.* marquetry, chequered work, inlaid work.
taracear, *v.t.* to inlay, make inlaid work in.
tarado, -da, *a.* defective, imperfect; impaired; suffering from a defect *or* disability.
taragallo, *n.m.* rod attached to a dog's collar.
taraje, *n.m.* tamarisk.
tarambana, *n.m.f.* (*coll.*) madcap.
tarando, *n.m.* reindeer.
tarángana, *n.f.* black pudding.
taranta, *n.f.* (*Hond.*) giddiness, dizziness; (*Arg.*, *C.R.*, *Ec.*) sudden impulse.
tarantela, *n.f.* (*mus.*) tarantella.
tarantín, *n.m.* (*Cent. Am.*, *Cub.*) useless stuff, rubbish, lumber.
tarántula, *n.f.* (*zool.*) tarantula.
tararear, *v.t.*, *v.i.* to hum (*a tune*).
tararira, *n.f.* noisy laughter. — *n.m.f.* noisy laughing person.
tarasca, *n.f.* termagant, virago; (*fig.*) shrew.
tarascada, *n.f.* bite; shrewish thing to do *or* say.
tarascar [A], *v.t.* to bite.
taray, *n.m.* tamarisk.
tarayal, *n.m.* tamarisk plantation.
tarazana, *n.m.f.* (*naut.*) arsenal; building-yard.
tarazar [C], *v.t.* to bite; to harass, mortify.
tarazón, *n.m.* large slice.
tarbea, *n.f.* large hall.
tardador, -ra, *n.m.f.* delayer.
tardanaos, *n.m. inv.* (*ichth.*) remora.
tardanza, *n.f.* delay.
tardar, *v.i.* to take a long time; ***¿cuánto tarda?*** how long does it take?; ***a más tardar,*** at the latest; ***tardó un año en hacerlo,*** he took a year to do it, he was a year doing it.
tarde, *adv.* late, too late; ***de tarde en tarde,*** not very often, at rare intervals; ***hacerse tarde,*** to get late; ***tarde o temprano,*** sooner or later; ***más vale tarde que nunca,*** better late than never. — *n.f.* afternoon; evening; ***buenas tardes,*** good afternoon; good evening.
tardecer [9], *v.i. impers.* to grow late; to come on (*of evening*).
tardecillo, tardecito, *adv.* a little late.
tardígrado, -da, *a.* (*zool.*) slow-moving, slow-paced.
tardío, -día, *a.* late; tardy, slow.
tardo, -da, *a.* tardy, slow; dull.
tardón, -dona, *a.* dead slow. — *n.m.f.* slow-coach.
tarea, *n.f.* task; toil; piece of work; homework.
tareco, *n.m.* (*Cub.*, *Ec.*, *Ven.*) implement, tool.
tareche, *n.m.* (*Bol.*, *orn.*) buzzard.
tarifa, *n.f.* tariff; price-list; fare, rate.
tarima, *n.f.* stand, dais, platform.
tarín barín, *adv.* (*coll.*) just about, more or less.
tarja, *n.f.* ancient Spanish coin; tally, check; tally-stick; shield, buckler; (*coll.*) ***beber sobre tarja,*** to get drink on credit; (*Hisp. Am.*) visiting card.
tarjador, -ra, *n.m.f.* tally-keeper.
tarjar, *v.t.* to tally.
tarjero, *n.m.* tally-keeper.
tarjeta, *n.f.* card; (*arch.*) label; tablet with inscription; ***tarjeta postal,*** postcard; ***tarjeta de visita,*** visiting card.
tarjeteo, *n.m.* (*coll.*) exchange of cards.
tarjetero, *n.m.* card-case.
tarjetón, *n.m.* large card, show-card.
tarlatana, *n.f.* tarlatan, transparent muslin.
tarma, *n.f.* wood-tick.
taropé, *n.m.* (*Arg.*, *Par.*) water-lily.
tarquín, *n.m.* mire, slime.
tarquinada, *n.f.* (*coll.*) rape.
tárraga, *n.f.* ancient Spanish dance.
tarraja, *n.f.* pipe-stock, screw-stock.
tarralí, *n.f.* (*Col.*) wild climbing plant.
tarraya, *n.f.* casting-net.
tarreña, *n.f.* piece of broken china (*used as castanets*).
tarrico, *n.m.* salt-wort.
tarro, *n.m.* jar; bottle.
tarsana, *n.f.* (*C.R.*, *Ec.*, *Per.*) bark of a Sapindaceæ tree (*used for washing*).
tarso, *n.m.* (*anat.*) tarsus; (*horses*) hock, cambrel; (*orn.*) shank.
tarta, *n.f.* cake; tart; ***tarta helada,*** ice-cream cake.
tártago, *n.m.* (*bot.*) spurge; unfortunate incident *or* event, misfortune; practical joke.
tartajear, *v.i.* to stutter, stammer.
tartajoso, -sa, *a.* stuttering, stammering.
tartalear, *v.i.* to stagger, reel; to be perplexed, dumbfounded.
tartamudear, *v.i.* to stutter, stammer, mumble; to fumble; to falter, halt.
tartamudeo, *n.m.*, **tartamudez,** *n.f.* stuttering, stammering.
tartamudo, -da, *a.* stuttering, stammering. — *n.m.f.* stutterer.
tartán, *n.m.* tartan.
tartana, *n.f.* round-topped two-wheeled carriage; (*naut.*) tartan.
tartáreo, -rea, *a.* (*poet.*) Tartarean, hellish.
tartarizar [C], *v.t.* to tartarize.
tártaro (1), *n.m.* (*dent.*) tartar; (*chem.*) cream of tartar, argol.
tártaro (2), *n.m.* (*poet.*) Tartarus, hell.
tártaro (3), **-ra,** *a.* Tartarian, of Tartary. — *n.m.f.* Tartar.
tarteleta, *n.f.* tart.
tartera, *n.f.* baking-pan; lunch-tin.
tartrato, *n.m.* tartrate.
tártrico, -ca, *a.* tartaric.
taruga, *n.f.* (*Hisp. Am.*) vicuña.
tarugo, *n.m.* wooden peg, stopper, plug, bung; (*coll.*) blockhead.
tarumba, *a.* ***volver a uno tarumba,*** to drive crazy.
tas, *n.m.* small anvil.
tasa, *n.f.* rate, price; appraisement, valuation; measure; ***sin tasa,*** without limit.
tasación, *n.f.* appraisement, valuation, (*Am.*) appraisal.
tasadamente, *adv.* barely, scantily.
tasador, *n.m.* appraiser, valuer.
tasajear, *v.t.* (*Hisp. Am.*) to jerk; to slash, cut to pieces.
tasajo, *n.m.* jerked beef, hung beef.
tasar, *v.t.* to value, appraise, price; to limit, keep within bounds; to give sparingly.
tasca, *n.f.* tavern; eating-house; den, dive.
tascador, *n.m.* brake (*for dressing flax*).
tascar [B], *v.t.* to brake *or* dress (*flax*); to crunch (*grass*); to champ (*bit*); ***tascar el freno,*** to champ at the bit, to hold o.s. reluctantly in check.
tasco, *n.m.* refuse (*of flax* or *hemp*); (*naut.*) topping (*of hemp*).
tasconio, *n.m.* refractory clay.
tasi, *n.m.* (*Arg.*) liana.
tasquera, *n.f.* wrangle, row.
tasquero, *n.m.* (*Per.*) Indian docker.
tasquil, *n.m.* chip (*of stone*).
tastana, *n.f.* hard crust (*on soil*); membrane (*inside fruit*).

tástara, *n.f.* coarse bran.
tastaz, *n.m.* polishing powder.
tasto, *n.m.* bad taste (*of stale food*).
tasugo, *n.m.* badger.
tata (1), *n.m.* (*Hisp. Am., coll.*) dad, daddy. — *n.f.* nanny; siss (*sister*); maid (*servant*); ***andar a tatas,*** to toddle; to go on all fours.
tatabro, *n.m.* (*Col.*) wild hog.
tatagua, *n.f.* (*Cub.*) giant butterfly.
tataibá, *n.m.* (*Arg., Par.*) mulberry tree.
tatarabuela, *n.f.* great-great-grandmother.
tatarabuelo, *n.m.* great-great-grandfather.
tataradeudo, -da, *n.m.f.* very distant relation.
tataranieta, *n.f.* great-great-granddaughter.
tataranieto, *n.m.* great-great-grandson.
¡tate! *interj.* so that's it! so that's the little game!
tato (1), *n.m.* (*Chi.*) younger brother.
tato (2), **-ta** (2), *a.* stammering and lisping.
tatú, *n.m.* (*Arg., Chi.*) giant armadillo.
tatuaje, *n.m.* tattooing, tattoo.
tatuar [M], *v.t.* to tattoo.
taujel, *n.m.* batten.
taumaturgia, *n.f.* thaumaturgy, miracle-working.
taumaturgo, *n.m.* thaumaturge, miracle-worker.
taurino, -na, *a.* taurine, bullfighting.
Tauro, *n.m.* (*astron., astrol.*) Taurus.
taurómaco, -ca, *a.* tauromachian. — *n.m.* bullfighter; expert on bullfighting.
tauromaquia, *n.f.* (art of) bullfighting, tauromachy.
tauromáquico, -ca, *a.* bullfighting, tauromachian.
tautología, *n.f.* tautology.
tautológico, -ca, *a.* tautological.
taxativo, -va, *a.* definite, precise; (*law*) limitative, restrictive.
taxi, *n.m.* taxi, taxicab.
taxidermia, *n.f.* taxidermy.
taxímetro, *n.m.* taximeter; taxicab, taxi.
taxista, *n.m.f.* taxi driver.
taxonomía, *n.f.* taxonomy.
taylorismo, *n.m.* Taylorism, industrial management.
tayuyá, *n.m.* (*Arg.*) creeping plant.
taz a taz, *adv.* on an even basis; (*Hisp. Am.*) ***taz con taz,*** even, tied.
taza, *n.f.* cup; cupful; basin (*of a fountain*); bowl (*of toilet*); cup guard (*of sword*).
tazar(se) [C], *v.t.* (*v.r.*) to fray.
tazmía, *n.f.* share of tithes, tithe register.
tazón, *n.m.* large basin, bowl.
te (1), *n.f.* letter T, t.
te (2), *pron. pers. and reflex.* you, to you; yourself, to yourself; ***te lo haré yo,*** I'll do it for you; ***lávate las manos,*** wash your hands.
té, *n.m.* tea.
tea, *n.f.* brand, firebrand, torch; hawser for raising the anchor.
teame, teamide, *n.f.* stone said to repel iron.
teatino, *n.m.* Theatin, Theatine.
teatralidad, *n.f.* (excessively) theatrical *or* dramatic quality.
teatrero, -ra, *n.m.f.* theatre-goer.
teátrico, -ca, teatral, *a.* (excessively) theatrical *or* dramatic.
teatro, *n.m.* theatre, playhouse; stage; drama; plays.
tebano, -na, *a.* Theban, of Thebes. — *n.m.f.* native of Thebes; a Boeotian.
tebeo, *n.m* comic (*magazine*).
teca, *n.f.* teak; teakwood; locket, reliquary.
tecali, *n.m.* Mexican onyx.
tecla, *n.f.* key (*of a pianoforte, typewriter etc.*); delicate point; ***dar en la tecla,*** to touch the right chord, hit the mark; ***tocar una tecla,*** to try sth.; to touch on a subject.
teclado, *n.m.* keyboard (*of a piano, typewriter etc.*).
tecle, *n.m.* (*naut.*) single purchase.
teclear, *v.t.* to test, try; to touch upon, tackle. — *v.i.* to strum, thrum, play a few chords; to drum with the fingers.
tecleo, *n.m.* fingering; tapping (*of a typewriter*); drumming with the fingers; (*fig.*) scheming, intrigue.
tecnicismo, *n.m.* technicality; technical term.
técnico, -ca, *a.* technical. — *n.m.* technician. — *n.f.* technics, technique.
tecnócrata, *n.m.f.* technocrat.
tecnología, *n.f.* technology.
tecnológico, -ca, *a.* technological.
tecol, *n.m.* (*Mex.*) caterpillar.
tecolote, *n.m.* (*Hond., Mex.*) owl.
tecomate, *n.m.* (*Mex.*) pot made of coarse clay.
techado, *n.m.* roof, roofing; ceiling; ***bajo techado,*** under cover, indoors.
techador, *n.m.* roofer, thatcher.
techar, *v.t.* to roof, put a roof on.
techo, *n.m.* roof; cover; ceiling.
techumbre, *n.f.* roof, roofing.
tedero, *n.m.* candlestick, torch-holder.
tediar, *v.t.* to hate, abhor, loathe.
tedio, *n.m.* ennui, world-weariness.
tedioso, -sa, *a.* tedious, wearisome.
tefe, *n.m.* (*Col., Ec.*) strip of cloth *or* leather.
tegue, *n.m.* (*Ven.*) plant with milky edible tubers.
teguillo, *n.m.* thin board, strip used for ceilings.
tegumento, *n.m.* tegument, covering.
teína, *n.f.* theine, cafeine.
teinada, *n.f.* cattle-shed.
teísmo, *n.m.* theism.
teísta, *n.m.f.* theist.
teja, *n.f.* roof-tile; linden tree; steel facings (*of a sword blade*); (*naut.*) hollow cut (*for scarfing*); ***sombrero de teja,*** shovel hat; ***a teja vana,*** with a plain tile roof; ***de tejas abajo,*** in this base world, here below; ***de tejas arriba,*** in the heavenly sphere, up above; ***a toca teja,*** spot cash, cash down, on the nail.
tejadillo, *n.m.* small roof; (coach) roof; shed; card sharper's trick.
tejado, *n.m.* roof; tiled roof.
tejamaní, tejamanil, *n.m.* (*Cub., Mex., P.R.*) shingle, wood roof-covering.
tejar, *n.m.* tile-works, tile-kiln. — *v.t.* to tile, cover with tiles.
tejaroz, *n.m.* eaves.
tejazo, *n.m.* blow with a tile.
tejedera, *n.f.* weaver; (*zool.*) water-skipper.
tejedor, -ra, *a.* weaving. — *n.m.f.* weaver; (*fig.*) schemer. — *n.m.* (*zool.*) water-flea.
tejedura, *n.f.* texture; weaving.
tejeduría, *n.f.* weaving; mill, factory.
tejemaneje, *n.m.* (*coll.*) jiggery-pokery.
tejer, *v.t., v.i.* to weave; to knit; to scheme (up).
tejera, tejería, *n.f.* tile-kiln.
tejero, *n.m.* tile-maker.
tejido, *n.m.* texture, weave; textile, material, cloth, fabric; tissue.
tejillo, *n.m.* girdle-band, plaited girdle.
tejo, *n.m.* quoit; disc, plate; hopscotch; (*bot.*) yew tree; (*mech.*) bush, pillow-block; piece of tile.
tejocote, *n.m.* (*Mex.*) sloe fruit.
tejoleta, *n.f.* tile; broken tile; brickbat; shuffle-board counter; clapper.
tejolote, *n.m.* (*Mex.*) stone pestle.
tejón, *n.m.* (*zool.*) badger; round gold ingot.
tejuela, *n.f.* small tile; brickbat; saddle-tree.
tejuelo, *n.m.* book-label; quoit; (*mech.*) bush, pillow-block, socket.
tela, *n.f.* fabric, cloth, material; film, pellicle, membrane; ***tela de araña,*** cobweb; ***tela***

encerada, buckram; ***tela de cebolla,*** onion-skin; ***tela de juicio,*** judicial proceeding; ***tela metálica,*** wire-netting; ***libro en tela,*** cloth-bound book; ***poner en tela de juicio,*** to call in doubt *or* in question; (*coll.*) ***aquí hay mucha tela,*** there's a lot in this (to be done, discussed etc.); (*coll.*) ***afloja la tela,*** cough up the dough.

telar, *n.m.* loom; frame; (*theat.*) gridiron.

telaraña, *n.f.* cobweb; (*coll.*) ***mirar las telarañas,*** to be in a brown study.

telarejo, *n.m.* small loom.

telecomunicación, *n.f.* telecommunication.

telefio, *n.m.* stone-crop.

telefonazo, *n.m.* telephone call, ring.

telefonear, *v.t.* to telephone, ring up.

telefonema, *n.m.* telephone message.

telefonía, *n.f.* telephony; ***telefonía sin hilos,*** wireless telephony.

telefónico, -ca, *a.* telephonic. — *n.f.* ***cabina telefónica,*** telephone kiosk, call-box, (*Am.*) phone-booth.

telefonista, *n.m.f.* telephonist, operator.

teléfono, *n.m.* telephone.

telefoto, *n.m.* telephoto (*apparatus*). — *n.f.* telephoto (*picture*).

telefotografía, *n.f.* telephotography; telephotograph.

telefotografiar [L], *v.t.*, *v.i.* to telephotograph.

telegrafía, *n.f.* telegraphy; ***telegrafía sin hilos,*** wireless telegraphy.

telegrafiar [L], *v.t.* to telegraph.

telegráfico, -ca, *a.* telegraphic.

telegrafista, *n.m.f.* telegraph operator, telegrapher, telegraphist.

telégrafo, *n.m.* telegraph; ***hacer telégrafos,*** to talk by signs; ***telégrafo sin hilos,*** wireless; ***telégrafo marino,*** nautical signals; ***telégrafo óptico,*** semaphore.

telegrama, *n.m.* telegram.

telele, *n.m.* fit; ***le va a dar un telele,*** he'll have a fit, he'll go up the wall.

telemando, *n.m.* remote control.

telemetría, *n.f.* telemetry.

telemétrico, -ca, *a.* telemetric.

telémetro, *n.m.* telemeter, rangefinder.

telendo, -da, *a.* lively, jaunty.

teleobjetivo, *n.m.* telephotographic object glass.

telépata, *n.m.f.* telepathist.

telepatía, *n.f.* telepathy.

telepático, -ca, *a.* telepathic.

telera, *n.f.* plough pin; cattle pen, corral; (*mech.*) cheek, jaw (*of a clamp, press etc.*); (*motor.*) body transom cross frame; (*artill.*) transom of a gun carriage; (*naut.*) rack block; loaf (*of bread*).

telescópico, -ca, *a.* telescopic.

telescopio, *n.m.* telescope.

telesilla, *n.m.f.* chair lift (*for skiers*).

telespectador, -ra, *n.m.f.* viewer, televiewer.

telestudio, *n.m.* television studio.

teleta, *n.f.* blotting-paper; sieve in paper-mills.

teletipo, *n.m.* teletype.

teletón, *n.m.* strong silken stuff.

televisar, *v.t.* to televise.

televisión, *n.f.* television.

televisivo, *a.* (of) television.

televisual, *a.* [TELEVISIVO].

telilla, *n.f.* light *or* flimsy cloth; rind of fruit; film on molten silver.

telina, *n.f.* clam.

telón, *n.m.* (*theat.*) curtain, drop-curtain; ***telón de fondo,*** back curtain, drop-scene; background; ***telón de acero,*** iron curtain.

telonio, *n.m.* customs-house, tax-office; ***a manera de telonio,*** disordered, jumbled up.

telúrico, -ca, *a.* telluric; ***tendencias telúricas,*** back-to-earth trends.

telurio, *n.m.* tellurium.

tellina, *n.f.* clam.

telliz, *n.m.* horse-cloth, saddle-cover.

telliza, *n.f.* bed-cover, bedspread, coverlet.

tema, *n.m.* theme; subject, topic; (*astrol.*) ***tema celeste,*** map of the heavens. — *n.f.* mania, fixed idea, obsession; grudge; ***cada loco con su tema,*** we all have our pet hobby-horse.

temario, *n.m.* agenda; list of topics.

temático, -ca, *a.* thematic, relating to a theme *or* subject; obstinate.

tembladal, *n.m.* quagmire.

tembladera, *n.f.* tankard; (*ichth.*) cramp-fish, electric ray; (*bot.*) quaking-grass; gem *or* ornament mounted on a spiral; (*Arg.*) horse disease; (*Hisp. Am.*) quagmire.

tembladero, *n.m.* quagmire.

temblador, -ra, *a.* trembling, shaking, quivering. — *n.m.f.* trembler.

temblante, *a.* trembling, quavering. — *n.m.* loose bracelet.

temblar [I], *v.i.* to tremble, shake, quiver; to thrill; (*coll.*) ***dejaron la botella temblando,*** they made the bottle look sorry.

tembleque, *n.m.* shaking fit, fit of the shakes; spiral spring jewel.

temblequear, tembletear, *v.i.* to tremble, shake, quiver, quake.

temblón, -lona, *a.* tremulous, shaking; (*bot.*) ***álamo temblón,*** aspen; ***hacer la temblona,*** to fake the shakes (*beggars and malingerers*).

temblor, *n.m.* trembling; ***temblor (de tierra),*** earth-tremor.

temblorcillo, *n.m.* slight tremor.

tembloroso, -sa, *a.* tremulous, shivering, shaking.

tembloso, -sa, *a.* tremulous, shivering, shaking.

temedero, -ra, *a.* dread, redoutable.

temedor, -ra, *a.* dreading, fearing.

temer, *v.t.*, *v.i.* to fear, be afraid (of); ***mucho me temo que no vendrá,*** I have a shrewd *or* nasty suspicion that he won't come; ***me temo que no,*** I fear not.

temerario, -ria, *a.* rash, foolhardy, reckless.

temeridad, *n.f.* temerity, rashness, foolhardiness.

temerón, -rona, *a.* blustering.

temeroso, -sa, *a.* fearful, apprehensive; ***temeroso de Dios,*** God-fearing.

temible, *a.* fearful, formidable.

temor, *n.m.* fear, dread, apprehension.

temoso, -sa, *a.* stubborn, obstinate.

tempanador, *n.m.* cutter (*for beehives*).

tempanar, *v.t.* to cover the tops of (*beehives*).

témpano, *n.m.* flitch (*of bacon*); kettle-drum, tabour, timbrel; tympan; drum-head, drum-skin; heading (*of a barrel*); cork dome (*of a beehive*); ***témpano de hielo,*** ice-floe; ***témpano(s) flotante(s),*** ice-pack, (*Am.*) pack ice.

temperación, *n.f.* tempering.

temperadamente, *adv.* temperately.

temperamento, *n.m.* temperament; compromise; weather.

temperancia, *n.f.* temperance, moderation.

temperante, *a.* tempering.

temperar, *v.t.* to temper, calm.

temperatura, *n.f.* temperature.

temperie, *n.f.* weather, atmospheric conditions.

tempero, *n.m.* seasonableness.

tempestad, *n.f.* tempest, storm.

tempestear, *v.i.* to storm, be stormy, rage.

tempestividad, *n.f.* opportuneness, timeliness.

tempestivo, -va, *a.* seasonable, opportune, timely.

tempestuoso, -sa, *a.* tempestuous, stormy.

templa (1), *n.f.* (*anat.*) temple; (*pl.*) temples.

templa (2), *n.f.* (*Cub.*) sugar-cane juice contained in evaporating pan.

templa (3), *n.f.* tempera, distemper, size (*for paints*).

templadera, *n.f.* sluice gate.
templado, -da, *a.* temperate; moderate; warm, lukewarm; firm, brave; level-headed, well-balanced; (*Hisp. Am.*) tipsy; (*Hisp. Am.*) frugal.
templador, -ra, *a.* tempering; tuning. — *n.m.f.* temperer; tuner. — *n.m.* tuning key.
templadura, *n.f.* tempering; tuning.
templanza, *n.f.* temperance, moderation; temperateness; (*art*) blend (*of colours*).
templar, *v.t.* to temper; to moderate, cool, calm; to tune; to assuage; (*naut.*) to trim (*the sails*); to train (*a hawk*); to anneal (*glass*); to blend (*colours*). — *v.i.* to ease up. — **templarse,** *v.r.* to use moderation.
templario, *n.m.* Knight Templar.
temple, *n.m.* temperature; temper (*of metals, glass*); frame of mind, mood; tuning, concord; resolution, determination; order of the Templars; distemper; ***al temple,*** painted with distemper.
templén, *n.m.* temple (*of a loom*).
templete, *n.m.* small temple; niche; ***templete de música,*** bandstand.
templista, *n.m.* painter in distemper.
templo, *n.m.* temple, church.
témpora, *n.f.* Ember Week, Ember Day.
temporada, *n.f.* season; spell (*of time*); while; duration; ***estar de temporada,*** to be holidaying.
temporal, *a.* temporary; temporal. — *n.m.* storm; spell of rainy weather; temporal zone.
temporalidad, *n.f.* temporality.
temporalizar [C], *v.t.* to make temporary; to secularize.
temporáneo, -nea, temporario, -ria, *a.* temporary, transient.
temporejar, *v.i.* (*naut.*) to lie to.
temporero, -ra, *a.*, *n.m.f.* (seasonal) labourer.
temporizador, *n.m.* temporizer.
temporizar [C], *v.i.* to temporize; to while away the time.
tempranal, *a.* producing early fruit.
tempranero, -ra, *a.* early, early-rising.
tempranilla, *n.f.* early grape.
temprano, -na, *a.* early. — *adv.* early. — *n.m.* early crops.
temulento, -ta, *a.* intoxicated, inebriated.
ten con ten, *n.m.* (*coll.*) compromise, tact, entente, understanding.
tena, *n.f.* shed (*for cattle*).
tenacear, *v.t.* to tear with pincers. — *v.i.* to be tenacious *or* obstinate.
tenacero, *n.m.* maker of pincers *or* tongs.
tenacidad, *n.f.* tenacity, tenaciousness.
tenacillas, *n.f.pl.* pincers, nippers; small tongs; curling irons; snuffers.
tenáculo, *n.m.* (*surg.*) tenaculum.
tenada, *n.f.* cattle-shed.
tenallas, *n.f.pl.* pair of tongs *or* pincers.
tenallón, *n.m.* (*fort.*) tenaillon.
tenante, *n.m.* (*her.*) supporter of a shield.
tenaz, *a.* tenacious.
tenaza, *n.f.* pincer, nipper, claw; (*fort.*) tenail; (*cards*) tenance; (*pl.*) pincers, nippers; tongs.
tenazada, *n.f.* gripping with tongs *or* pincers; gripping *or* biting hard.
tenazón, (a *or* **de),** *adv.* blindly, wildly; unexpectedly.
tenazuelas, *n.f.pl.* tweezers, pliers.
tenca, *n.f.* (*ichth.*) tench; (*Arg.*, *Chi.*, *orn.*) lark.
tención, *n.f.* holding, retaining.
tendajo, *n.m.* small and tumble-down shop.
tendal, *n.m.* awning; canvass; drying frame *or* clothes-line.
tendalera, *n.f.* (*coll.*) mess, muddle.
tendalero, *n.m.* drying place.
tendedero, *n.m.* clothes-line; drying frame.
tendedor, *n.m.* stretcher; tenter; spreader.
tendedura, *n.f.* extending, stretching; spreading out.
tendejón, *n.m.* sutler's tent; small shop.
tendel, *n.m.* plumb-line; layer (*of mortar*).
tendencia, *n.f.* tendency, bent, trend, leaning.
tendencioso, -sa, *a.* tendentious, biased.
tendente, *a.* aimed *or* aiming, tending.
ténder, *n.m.* tender (*of a locomotive*).
tender [2], *v.t.* to spread (out); to stretch (out); to extend; to hold out; to hang up; to lay, set; to throw, cast; to coat with plaster. — *v.i.* to tend. — **tenderse,** *v.r.* to lie down, stretch out; to lay one's cards on the table; to run full tilt; to let o.s. go slack.
tenderete, *n.m.* (ramshackle) stall *or* stand.
tendero, -ra, *n.m.f.* shopkeeper; tentmaker.
tendezuela, *n.f.* small shop.
tendido, -da, *a.* full tilt, headlong. — *n.m.* laying (down); spreading; hanging; wires; wash (hung up); batch (of bread); run (of lace); coat (of plaster); slope (of roof); stand, seats.
tendinoso, -sa, *a.* tendinous.
tendón, *n.m.* (*anat.*) tendon.
tenducha, *n.f.*, **tenducho,** *n.m.* wretched little shop, dump.
tenebrario (1), *n.m.* (*astron.*) Hyades.
tenebrario (2), *n.m.* candlestick.
tenebrosidad, *n.f.* darkness, obscurity, gloom.
tenebroso, -sa, *a.* dark, gloomy, shady.
tenedero, *n.m.* anchoring-ground.
tenedor, *n.m.* holder, bearer; keeper; fork; ***tenedor de libros,*** book-keeper; ***tenedor de póliza,*** policy-holder.
teneduría, *n.f.* position of book-keeper; ***teneduría de libros,*** book-keeping.
tenencia, *n.f.* holding; possession; tenancy, occupancy, tenure; lieutenancy, lieutenantship.
tener [33], *v.t.* to have; to own; to keep; to hold; to consider; to have gone wrong with one; ***tengo dicho,*** I have said; ***tengo leídas veinte páginas,*** I have read twenty pages; ***tener hambre, sed, sueño, razón*** etc., to be hungry, thirsty, sleepy, right etc.; ***tener lugar,*** to take place; ***tener por,*** to consider as; ***tener que,*** to have to; ***ahí tiene,*** there you are; ***tener a bien,*** to deem fit to; ***no tenerlas todas consigo,*** to be worried; not to be too sure; ***no tener nada que ver con,*** to have nothing to do with; ***tener para sí,*** to think, have as one's own opinion; ***tener que ver con,*** to have to do with, deal with; ***¿cuántos años tienes?*** how old are you?; ***tengo diez años,*** I am ten years old; ***¿con que ésas tenemos?*** so that's the game, is it?; ***¿qué tiene de particular?*** what's so special about it?; ***tenerla tomada con alguien,*** to have it in for s.o.; ***ya tengo,*** I have some already. — ***tenerse,*** *v.r.* to stop, halt; to hold fast; ***tenerse en pie,*** to stand; ***tenérselas con,*** to have it out with; ***tenérselas tiesas,*** to stick to one's guns; ***tenerse tieso,*** to stand firm.
tenería, *n.f.* tannery, tan yard.
tengue, *n.m.* (*Cub.*, *bot.*) acacia.
tenguerengue, (en), *adv.* (*coll.*) teetering, shaky, wobbly.
tenia, *n.f.* tape-worm; (*arch.*) fillet.
tenida, *n.f.* (*Hisp. Am.*) meeting, session.
tenientazgo, *n.m.* lieutenantship, lieutenant's office; office of deputy.
teniente, *a.* holding, having, owning; immature, unripe; mean, miserly; (*coll.*) hard of hearing. — *n.m.* lieutenant; deputy.
tenis, *n.m. inv.* tennis.
tenor, *n.m.* tenor; drift, purport; ***a tenor de,*** in accord with; ***a este tenor,*** at this rate, like this.
tenorio, *n.m.* Don Juan, rake.
tensión, *n.f.* tension; tenseness, tautness; strain, stress; blood pressure.

tenso, -sa, *a.* tense, taut.
tensón, *n.f.* (*poet.*) poetical polemic on love.
tensor, -ra, *a.* tensile. — *n.m.* tension; turnbuckle.
tentación, *n.f.* temptation.
tentaculado, -da, *a.* tentacled.
tentáculo, *n.m.* tentacle.
tentadero, *n.m.* corral (*in which young bulls suitable for fighting are tried out and selected*).
tentador, -ra, *a.* tempting. — *n.m.f.* tempter, temptress.
tentadura, *n.f.* alloy of silver ore and mercury.
tentalear, *v.t.* to feel, examine by touch.
tentar [2], *v.t.* to tempt; to feel, touch, grope over, probe; to try, test.
tentativo, -va, *a.* tentative. — *n.f.* attempt, trial, test.
tentemozo, *n.m.* prop, support; strap (*of noseband*); (*self-righting*) tumblerdoll.
tentempié, *n.m.* (*coll.*) snack.
tentenelaire, *n.m.f.* half-breed.
tentón, *n.m.* (*coll.*) touch; rough handling.
tenue, *a.* tenuous; slender; slight; subdued, faint, vague.
tenuidad, *n.f.* tenuousness; slenderness; faintness.
tenuta, *n.f.* provisional possession.
tenutario, -ria, *n.m.f.* provisional tenant.
teñidura, *n.f.* dyeing, tingeing.
teñir [8K], *v.t.* to dye, tinge, stain.
teobroma, *n.m.* cacao.
teocali, *n.m.* teocalli.
teocracia, *n.f.* theocracy.
teocrático, -ca, *a.* theocratic, theocratical.
teodicea, *n.f.* theodicy.
teodolito, *n.m.* theodolite.
teogonía, *n.f.* theogony.
teologal, *a.* theological.
teología, *n.f.* theology; (*coll.*) ***no meterse en teologías,*** not to meddle with intricate matters.
teológico, -ca, *a.* theological.
teologizar [C], *v.i.* to theologize.
teólogo, -ga, *a.* theological. — *n.m.* theologian.
teorema, *n.m.* theorem.
teoría, *n.f.* theory; speculation.
teórico, -ca, *a.* theoretical; speculative. — *n.f.* theory; speculation.
teorizar [C], *v.t., v.i.* to theorize.
teoso, -sa, *a.* resinous (*of wood*).
teosofía, *n.f.* theosophy.
teosófico, -ca, *a.* theosophical.
teósofo, -fa, *n.m.f.* theosophist.
tepache, *n.m.* (*Mex.*) drink made of pulque, water, pineapple and cloves.
tepalcate, *n.m.* (*Mex.*) potsherd.
tepe, *n.m.* sod, turf.
tepeguage, *a.* (*Mex.*) obstinate, stubborn. — *n.m.* (*Mex.*) very hard wood.
tepeizcuinte, *n.m.* (*C.R., Mex.*) paca.
tepemechín, *n.m.* (*C.R., Hond.*) freshwater fish.
tepexilote, *n.m.* (*Mex.*) palm nut used for beads.
tepozán, *n.m.* (*Mex.*) tepozan plant.
tepú, *n.m.* (*Chi.*) small tree of the Myrtaceous family.
tequiche, *n.m.* (*Ven.*) meal made of toasted maize, coconut milk and butter.
tequila, *n.f.* (*Mex.*) drink resembling gin.
tequio, *n.m.* (*Mex., obs.*) task, personal service imposed on Indians; bother, damage; ore dug per man-shift.
terapeuta, *n.m.f.* therapeutist.
terapéutico, -ca, *a.* therapeutic. — *n.f.* therapeutics.
tercena, *n.f.* wholesale tobacco warehouse.
tercenista, *n.m.* wholesale tobacco merchant.
tercer, *a,* [TERCERO].
tercera, *n.f.* [TERCERO].
tercería, *n.f.* arbitration, mediation; pandering; jiggery-pokery; (*law*) third party.
tercerilla, *n.f.* (*poet.*) triplet.
tercermundista, *a.* (of the) Third World.
tercero, -ra, *a.* (**tercer** *before masc. sing. noun*) third. — *n.m.* third party *or* person; go-between, pander, procurer; mediator, arbitrator; umpire; middleman; tithe-collector; (*eccles.*) tertiary; (*geom.*) sixtieth of a second; ***tercero en discordia,*** arbitrator. — *n.f.* piquet (*card game*); three-of-a-kind; triplets; (*mus.*) third; third string of a guitar; bawd, procuress.
tercerol, *n.m.* (*naut.*) third in order.
tercerola, *n.f.* short carbine; barrel, cask; tierce.
tercerón, -rona, *n.m.f.* (*Hisp. Am.*) mulatto.
terceto, *n.m.* tercet, terzet, tierce, triplet, trio.
tercia, *n.f.* third, third part; sequence of three cards; (*eccles.*) tierce; storehouse, barn; (*fenc.*) tierce.
terciado, -da, *a.* slanting, tilted; cross-wise; ***azúcar terciado,*** brown sugar; ***pan terciado,*** rent of ground paid in grain. — *n.m.* cutlass, broad sword; ribbon.
terciana, *n.f.* [TERCIANO].
tercianario, -ria, *a.* tertian, suffering from, *or* infested with, tertian fever. — *n.m.f.* person suffering from tertian fever.
tercianela, *n.f.* heavy silk fabric.
terciano, -na, *a.* tertian. — *n.f.* tertian ague.
terciar, *v.t.* to place slanting *or* diagonally; to divide into three parts; to plough the third time; to carry (*arms*). — *v.i.* to arbitrate, mediate; to take part. — **teciarse,** *v.r.* to crop up, arise; ***si se tercia,*** should the occasion arise *or* opportunity present itself.
terciario, -ria, *a.* tertiary.
terciazón, *n.m.* third ploughing.
tercio, *n.m.* third; (*mil.*) regiment of infantry; company *or* troop; (*bullfighting*) stage; pack; ***hacer buen tercio,*** to come in handy; ***irse al tercio,*** to join the (Foreign) Legion; ***mejorado en tercio y quinto,*** greatly-favoured; (*pl.*) strong limbs.
terciopelado, -da, *a.* velvet-like, velvety. — *n.m.* velvet-like stuff.
terciopelero, *n.m.* velvet-weaver.
terciopelo, *n.m.* velvet.
terco, -ca, *a.* obstinate, stubborn.
terebinto, *n.m.* turpentine tree, terebinth.
terebrante, *a.* piercing (*pain*).
tergiversación, *n.f.* twisting (*of facts*), distortion.
tergiversar, *v.t.* to twist, distort, misrepresent.
teriaca, *n.f.* (*obs., med.*) theriaca.
teriacal, *a.* theriacal.
teristro, *n.m.* thin shawl *or* veil.
terliz, *n.m.* tick, ticking; sackcloth, tent-cloth.
termal, *a.* thermal.
termas, *n.f.pl.* hot baths; hot springs.
termes, *n.m. inv.* termite.
térmico, -ca, *a.* thermic, thermal.
terminable, *a.* terminable.
terminación, *n.f.* termination; ending.
terminacho, *n.m.* (*coll.*) coarse *or* crude expression.
terminador, -ra, *a.* finishing, completing.
terminajo [TERMINACHO].
terminal, *a., n.m.f.* terminal.
terminante, *a.* flat, categorical, sweeping, final.
terminar(se), *v.t., v.i.* (*v.r.*) to terminate, end, finish.
terminativo, -va, *a.* terminative.
término, *n.m.* end, completion, term; limit, boundary; district; (*med.*) crisis (*of a disease*); (*arch.*) terminal, stay; (*mus.*) tone, pitch, note; ***en primer término,*** in the first place; in the foreground; ***en último término,*** in the last

place; in the last resort; in the background; ***término medio,*** average, compromise, happy medium; ***llevar a término,*** to carry through to a conclusion; ***poner término a,*** to put an end to.
terminología, *n.f.* terminology.
terminológico, -ca, *a.* terminological.
terminote, *n.m.* (*coll.*) big word.
termio, *n.m.* (*phys.*) therm.
termita, *n.f.* (*ent.*) termite; (*chem.*) thermit.
termite, *n.m.* (*ent.*) termite.
termo, *n.m.* vacuum flask.
termodinámica, *n.f.* thermodynamics.
termométrico, -ca, *a.* thermometric.
termómetro, *n.m.* thermometer.
termoscopio, *n.m.* thermoscope.
termostato, *n.m.* thermostat.
termostático, -ca, *a.* thermostatic.
terna, *n.f.* three names submitted for the election of a candidate; ternary number, triad; set of dice.
ternario, -ria, *a.* ternary; triple, three-part. — *n.m.* three days' devotion.
terne, *a.* tough; obstinate, stubborn; bullying. — *n.m.* bully, tough.
ternecico, -ca, ternecito, -ta, *a.* very tender.
ternejal, *a.* bullying.
ternejón, -jona, *a.* easily moved, sentimental. — *n.m.f.* easily moved person.
ternero, -ra, *n.m.f.* calf. — *n.f.* veal.
ternerón, -rona, *a.* easily moved, easily weeping, sentimental. — *n.m.f.* sentimental person.
terneruela, *n.f.* sucking calf.
terneza, *n.f.* softness; tenderness; endearment, sweet word.
ternilla, *n.f.* gristle, cartilage.
ternilloso, -sa, *a.* gristly, cartilaginous.
terno, *n.m.* ternary number; triad; three-piece suit; vestments (*for High Mass*); curse, oath; trio (*in lottery*); (*Cub.*, *P.R.*) set of jewellery; (*print.*) three printed sheets one within another; ***echar ternos,*** to swear, curse.
ternura, *n.f.* tenderness, gentleness.
terquedad, terquería, terqueza, *n.f.* stubbornness, obstinacy, pigheadedness.
terrada, *n.f.* bitumen.
terradillo, *n.m.* small terrace.
terrado, *n.m.* terrace; flat roof (*of a house*).
terraja, *n.f.* screw-plate, die-stock; modelling board.
terraje, *n.m.* rent paid for land.
terrajero, *n.m.* lessee of arable land.
terral, *a.*, *n.m.* land (*breeze*).
Terranova, *n.f.* Newfoundland.
terraplén, terrapleno, *n.m.* (*fort.*) terrace, mound; (*railw.*) embankment.
terraplenar, *v.t.* to terrace, raise, bank up; to level off; to fill in.
terráqueo, -quea, *a.* terraqueous; ***globo terráqueo,*** globe.
terrateniente, *n.m.* land-owner, land-holder.
terraza, *n.f.* terrace; garden border; two-handled jar; ***está sentado en la terraza del café,*** he is sitting at a table in front of the café.
terrazgo, *n.m.* arable land; land-rent.
terrazguero, *n.m.* lessee of arable land.
terrazo, *n.m.* landscape.
terrear, *v.i.* to be visible (*said of the soil showing through crops*).
terrecer [9], *v.t.* to terrify.
terregoso, -sa, *a.* full of clods.
terremoto, *n.m.* earthquake.
terrenal, *a.* terrestrial; earthly, worldly.
terrenidad, *n.f.* earthliness.
terreno, -na, *a.* terrestrial; earthly, worldly. — *n.m.* land, ground, terrain; piece of land *or* ground; ***ganar*** (***perder***) ***terreno,*** to gain (lose) ground; ***ceder terreno,*** to give ground; ***medir el terreno,*** to see how the land lies; ***sobre el terreno,*** on the spot.
térreo, -rrea, *a.* earthy, of earth.
terrero, -ra, *a.* of *or* for earth; lowly; (*orn.*) low-flying. — *n.m.* mound, heap *or* bank of earth; flat roof; terrace; alluvium; target; dump. — *n.f.* steep bare ground; (*orn.*) lark.
terrestre, *a.* terrestrial.
terrezuela, *n.f.* small wretched piece of ground.
terribilidad, *n.f.* terribleness, awfulness.
terrible, *a.* terrible, awful, dreadful.
terrícola, *n.m.f.* inhabitant of the earth.
terrífico, -ca, *a.* frightful.
terrígeno, -na, *a.* earthborn.
terrino, -na, *a.* of earth.
territorial, *a.* territorial.
territorialidad, *n.f.* territoriality.
territorio, *n.m.* territory; ground, soil.
terrizo, -za, *a.* of earth. — *n.m.* earthen tub.
terromontero, *n.m.* hill, hillock.
terrón, *n.m.* clod of earth; lump (*of sugar*); (*pl.* **terrones**) land, soil.
terroncillo, *n.m.* small clod, small lump.
terror, *n.m.* terror, dread.
terrorífico, -ca, *a.* horrific, bloodcurdling.
terrorismo, *n.m.* terrorism.
terrorista, *a.*, *n.m.f.* terrorist.
terrosidad, *n.f.* earthiness, cloddiness.
terroso, -sa, *a.* earthy, cloddy.
terruño, *n.m.* piece of ground; one's own part of the country.
tersar, *v.t.* to smooth.
tersidad, *n.f.* smoothness.
terso, -sa, *a.* smooth.
tersura, *n.f.* smoothness.
tertulia, *n.f.* [TERTULIO].
tertuliano, -na, *a.* of a conversation group. — *n.m.f.* member of a conversation group.
tertulio, -lia, *a.* of a conversation group. — *n.m.f.* member of a conversation group. — *n.f.* gathering, group, party (*that meets for conversation*); (*theat.*) gallery; billiards *or* card room; ***hacer tertulia,*** to sit around talking.
teruelo, *n.m.* ballot box *or* urn.
teruteru, *n.m.* (*Hisp. Am.*, *orn.*) Cayenne lapwing.
terzón, -zona, *a.*, *n.m.f.* three-year-old (bull *or* cow).
terzuelo, *n.m.* third part; (*orn.*) tiercel, male hawk.
tesar [*p.p.* **teso**], *v.t.* (*naut.*) to haul taut, tauten. — *v.i.* to back (*of oxen etc.*); (*naut.*) ***tesar un cabo,*** to haul a rope taut.
tesauro, *n.m.* thesaurus.
tesela, *n.f.* tessela, mosaic piece.
teselado, -da, *a.* tessellated.
tésera, *n.f.* tessera, countersign, token.
tesina, *n.f.* short thesis, dissertation.
tesis, *n.f. inv.* thesis, dissertation.
tesitura, *n.f.* (*mus.*) tessitura; state.
teso, -sa, *a.* taut, drawn tight. — *n.m.* flat-topped hill, kopje; small bulge *or* lump.
tesón, *n.m.* tenacity, doggedness; firmness.
tesonería, *n.f.* doggedness; obstinacy.
tesorería, *n.f.* treasury, exchequer, treasurer's office, treasurership.
tesorero, -ra, *n.m.f.* treasurer. — *n.m.* canon in charge of relics and jewels.
tesoro, *n.m.* treasure; treasury, exchequer; thesaurus.
tespíades, *n.f.pl.* (*poet.*) the Muses.
testa, *n.f.* head; forehead; front, forepart; (*coll.*) sense; cleverness; ***testa coronada,*** monarch, crowned head.
testáceo, -cea, *a.* testaceous.
testación, *n.f.* obliteration, erasure.

testada (1), *n.f.* stubbornness, obstinacy.
testado, -da (2), *a.* testate.
testador, *n.m.* testator.
testadora, *n.f.* testatrix.
testadura, *n.f.* obliteration, erasure.
testaférrea, testaferro, *n.m.* man of straw, dummy, figurehead.
testamentaría, *n.f.* testamentary execution; executrix; estate.
testamentario, -ria, *a.* testamentary. — *n.m.* executor. — *n.f.* executrix.
testamento, *n.m.* will, testament.
testar, *v.i.* to make a will, make a testament. — *v.t.* (*obs.*) to scratch out, blot.
testarada, *n.f.* blow with the head; (*fig.*) obstinacy, stubbornness.
testarazo, *n.m.* blow with the head.
testarrón, -rrona, *a.* (*coll.*) pig-headed.
testarronería, testarudez, *n.f.* (*coll.*) pig-headedness, stubbornness.
testarudo, -da, *a.* obstinate, inflexible, stubborn, pig-headed.
teste, *n.m.* (*anat.*) testis, testicle.
testera, *n.f.* front part, forepart; seat facing forward (*of a coach*); forehead of an animal; headpiece (*of a bridle*); wall.
testero, *n.m.* front part; ore rock showing vertical and horizontal faces; back plate (*of a fireplace*); big log; wall.
testicular, *a.* testicular.
testículo, *n.m.* (*anat.*) testicle.
testificación, *n.f.* testification, attestation.
testificante, *a.* attesting, witnessing.
testificar [A], *v.t.* to attest, witness, certify, testify.
testificata, *n.f.* affidavit.
testificativo, -va, *a.* attesting, testificatory.
testigo, *n.m.f.* witness; ***testigo de oídas,*** auricular witness; ***testigo ocular,*** eye witness; ***testigo de cargo,*** witness for the prosecution; ***testigo de descargo,*** witness for the defence. — *n.m.* witness, testimony.
testimonial, *a.* attesting, bearing witness.
testimoniales, *n.f.pl.* certificate of good character.
testimoniar, *v.t.* to attest, testify to, bear witness to.
testimoniero, -ra, *a.* calumniating; hypocritical.
testimonio, *n.m.* testimony, evidence; statement; affidavit; ***falso testimonio,*** false witness.
testón, *n.m.* silver coin.
testuz, testuzo, *n.m.* nape; forehead.
tesura, *n.f.* stiffness.
teta, *n.f.* teat; breast; hummock; ***dar la teta,*** to give suck (***a,*** to); ***niño de teta,*** child at the breast, babe in arms.
tetania, *n.f.* (*med.*) tetanus.
tetánico, -ca, *a.* (*med.*) tetanic.
tétano, tétanos, *n.m.* tetanus, lockjaw.
tetar, *v.t.* to suckle.
tetera, *n.f.* tea-pot; kettle; (*Hisp. Am.*) nipple, teat.
tetero, *n.m.* (*Hisp. Am.*) nursing bottle.
tetigonia, *n.f.* (*ent.*) cicada.
tetilla, *n.f.* small teat; (male) nipple.
tetón, *n.m.* stub (*of a pruned branch*).
tetona, *a.f.* with large teats.
tetracordio, *n.m.* tetrachord.
tetraedro, *n.m.* tetrahedron.
tetrágono, *n.m.* tetragon.
tetragrama, *n.m.* four-lined stave.
tetralogía, *n.f.* tetralogy.
tetramotor, *n.m.* four-engined aircraft.
tetrarca, *n.m.* tetrarch.
tetrarquía, *n.f.* tetrarchate, tetrarchy.
tétrico, -ca, *a.* gloomy, dark, grim.
tetro, -ra, *a.* (*obs.*) black.
tetuaní, *a., n.m.f.* (native) of Tetuan.
tetuda, *a.f.* with large breasts *or* nipples; (*coll.*) busty.
teucali, *n.m.* (*Mex.*) teocalli.
teucrio, *n.m.* germander.
teucro, -ra, *a., n.m.f.* Trojan.
teurgia, *n.f.* black magic.
teutón, -tona, *a., n.m.f.* Teuton.
teutónico, -ca, *a.,* Teutonic. — *n.m.* Teutonic (*language*).
teuvecracia, *n.f.* television rule *or* control.
textil, *a., n.m.* textile.
texto, *n.m.* text; textbook; (*print.*) great primer.
textorio, -ria, *a.* textorial.
textual, *a.* textual; (*coll.*) the very words used.
textualmente, *adv.* textually; ***dice textualmente que . . . ,*** he says, and these are his precise words, that. . . .
textura, *n.f.* texture; weaving; structure.
teyú, *n.m.* (*Arg., Par., Ur.*) iguana.
tez, *n.f.* complexion, skin.
tezado, -da, *a.* very black.
ti, *disj. pron.* you; ***hoy por ti y mañana por mí,*** you scratch my back and I'll scratch yours.
tía, *n.f.* aunt; old mother *or* wife; (*coll.*) tart; (*coll.*) ***una tía buena,*** a bit of all right, smashing bit of stuff; (*coll.*) ***cuéntaselo a tu tía,*** tell that to the marines; (*coll.*) ***no hay tu tía,*** nothing doing.
tialina, *n.f.* (*chem.*) ptyalin.
tialismo, *n.m.* (*med.*) ptyalism.
tianguis, *n.m.* (*Mex.*) market; market days.
tiara, *n.f.* tiara.
tibe, *n.m.* (*Col.*) corundum; (*Cub.*) whetstone.
Tíber, *n.m.* (river) Tiber.
tiberio, *n.m.* (*coll.*) uproar, rumpus.
tibia (1), *n.f.* shin-bone; flute.
tibieza, *n.f.* lukewarmness, coolness.
tibio, -bia (2), *a.* lukewarm; (*coll.*) ***poner tibio,*** to call every name under the sun; ***ponerse tibio (de comida),*** to stuff o.s. silly.
tibor, *n.m.* large china jar; (*Cub.*) chamber-pot.
tiburón, *n.m.* (*ichth.*) shark.
tic, *n.m.* tic.
tica, *n.f.* (*Hond.*) children's game with seeds.
tictac, *n.m.* ticking, tick-tock.
tichela, *n.f.* (*Bol.*) vessel for collecting rubber.
ticholo, *n.m.* (*Arg.*) snack of guava paste.
tiempo, *n.m.* time; season; age; weather; (*gram.*) tense; (*mus.*) tempo; ***a su tiempo,*** in due course; ***a tiempo,*** in time; ***con el tiempo,*** with the passing of time, in the course of time; ***a un tiempo,*** at one and the same time; ***a tiempo que,*** while; ***con tiempo,*** in good time; ***de tiempo en tiempo,*** from time to time; ***la carta llegó a su tiempo,*** the letter duly arrived; ***dar tiempo al tiempo,*** to let things take their course, let things come all in due time; ***haga buen o mal tiempo,*** rain or shine; ***engañar el tiempo,*** to while away the time; ***tomarse tiempo,*** to take one's time; ***del tiempo de Maricastaña,*** as old as the hills; ***en tiempos de Maricastaña,*** in days of yore, once upon a time; ***en tiempo hábil,*** within the appointed time; ***acomodarse al tiempo,*** to move with the times; ***dejar al tiempo una cosa,*** to let time do its work; ***al tiempo, el tiempo dirá,*** time will tell; ***hacer tiempo,*** to mark time; ***en otro tiempo,*** formerly; ***aquellos tiempos,*** the good old days.
tienda (1), *n.f.* tent; shop; (*naut.*) awning; tilt; ***tienda de ultramarinos,*** grocer's shop *or* store; ***tienda de campaña,*** tent; ***ir de tiendas,*** to go shopping; ***poner tienda,*** to open a shop.
tiendo, tienda (2), *pres. indic., pres. subj.* [TENDER].
tienta, *n.f.* testing (*of bulls*); shrewdness; sounding rod; probe; ***andar a tientas,*** to feel one's way.
tientaguja, *n.f.* boring-rod.

tientaparedes, *n.m.f. inv.* groper (*morally* or *materially*).

tiento, *n.m.* feel, careful touch, tact, care; halter (*of a mill horse*); (*coll.*) blow, cuff; (blind man's) stick; (tight-rope walker's) pole; (*zool.*) tentacle; maulstick; (*mus.*) preliminary flourish, tuning up; ***a tiento,*** by touch, feeling one's way; ***con tiento,*** carefully; ***andarse con tiento,*** to go carefully; ***dar un tiento a,*** to have a go *or* bash at; ***perder el tiento,*** to lose one's touch *or* grip.

tierno, -na, *a.* tender, soft; gentle, sweet; ***de edad tierna,*** of tender years.

tierra, *n.f.* earth; land, soil, ground; country; part of the country; ***tierra campa,*** treeless land; ***tierra de pan llevar,*** wheat-bearing land; ***tierra de año y vez,*** land cultivated in alternate years; ***tierra firme,*** continent; ***en cualquier*** or ***en toda tierra de garbanzos,*** everywhere, in every known place; ***le faltó la tierra,*** he slipped and fell; ***dar en tierra con,*** to throw down, throw to the ground; ***echar por tierra,*** to demolish, wreck; ***echar tierra a,*** to cover up, hush up; ***poner tierra por medio,*** to get out, clear out *or* off; ***tomar tierra,*** to land; ***ver tierra,*** to sight land; ***ver tierras,*** to see the world.

tieso, -sa, *a.* stiff; rigid; firm; stuck-up; ***tenerse tieso, tenérselas tiesas,*** to stick to one's guns; ***quedarse tieso,*** to get frozen stiff.

tiesto, *n.m.* pot; old pot, bit of junk.

tiesura, *n.f.* stiffness; rigidity.

tifo (1), *n.m.* (*med.*) typhus; ***tifo asiático,*** Asiatic cholera; ***tifo de América,*** yellow fever; ***tifo de Oriente,*** bubonic plague.

tifo (2), **-fa,** *a.* (*coll.*) sated, glutted.

tifoideo, -dea, *a.* typhoid.

tifón, *n.m.* typhoon.

tifus, *n.m. inv.* typhus.

tigra, *n.f.* (*Hisp. Am.*) female jaguar.

tigre, *n.m.* tiger; (*Hisp. Am.*) jaguar.

tigrida, tigridia, *n.f.* tiger-flower.

tigrillo, *n.m.* (*Hisp. Am.*) grey fox.

tija, *n.f.* shaft of a key.

tijera, *n.f.* scissors, shears; sawbuck, sawhorse; trench (*for draining land*); sheep-shearer; ***catre de tijera,*** folding cot; ***silla de tijera,*** folding chair, deck-chair; ***buena tijera,*** good cutter; great eater; (*coll.*) backbiter, gossip; ***hacer tijeras,*** to twist the mouth (*horses*); (*pl.*) boom (*to stop floating timber*).

tijereta, *n.f.* small scissors; (*ent.*) earwig; (*bot.*) small tendril of a vine; (*orn.*) skimmer.

tijeretada, *n.f.* clip, cut with scissors.

tijeretazo, *n.m.* cut with scissors.

tijeretear, *v.t.* to cut with scissors; (*fig.*) to meddle with.

tijereteo, *n.m.* clipping; snip-snap noise of scissors.

tijerica, tijerilla, tijerita, *n.f.* small scissors.

tijeruela, *n.f.* small tendril of a vine.

tijuil, *n.m.* (*Hond.*) black bird of the conirostrous order.

tila, *n.f.* (*bot.*) linden tree, lime tree; linden flower; infusion of linden flowers, linden tea.

tílburi, *n.m.* tilbury.

tildar, *v.t.* to put a tilde *or* dash over; to cancel, cross out; to find fault with; ***tildar de,*** to call, brand.

tilde, *n.f.* tilde, dash; fault, blemish; jot, tittle.

tildón, *n.m.* long dash *or* stroke.

tilia, *n.f.* (*bot.*) linden tree, lime tree.

tiliche, *n.m.* (*Cent. Am., Mex.*) trifle, trinket, knick-knack.

tilichero, *n.m.* (*Hisp. Am.*) pedlar.

tilín, *n.m.* chime, ring, ting-a-ling; ***tener tilín,*** to be winsome; ***no me hace tilín,*** I'm not very keen on it, I don't care for it; (*Hisp. Am.*) ***en un tilín,*** in a jiffy.

tilingo, -ga, *a.* (*Arg., Mex.*) silly, foolish; dull, stupid.

tilma, *n.f.* (*Mex.*) cotton blanket used as cloak.

tilo, *n.m.* (*bot.*) linden tree, lime tree.

tilla, *n.f.* midship, gangway.

tillado, *n.m.* wooden floor.

tillar, *v.t.* to floor; to plank.

timador, -ra, *n.m.f.* (*coll.*) swindler.

timalo, *n.m.* (*ichth.*) grayling.

timar, *v.t.* to cheat, swindle; (*coll.*) ***timarse con,*** to flirt with, make sheep's eyes at.

timba, *n.f.* (*coll.*) hand in a game; gambling-den; (*Cent. Am., Mex.*) belly.

timbal, *n.m.* kettledrum.

timbaleo, *n.m.* beat of kettledrum.

timbalero, *n.m.* kettledrummer.

timbiriche, *n.m.* (*Mex.*) a tree of the Rubiaceous family with edible fruit.

timbirimba, *n.f.* (*coll.*) game of chance; gaming house.

timbrador, *n.m.* stamper; stamping machine; rubber-stamp.

timbrar, *v.t.* to stamp.

timbrazo, *n.m.* (sharp) ring.

timbre, *n.m.* stamp; seal; duty *or* revenue stamp; bell, chime; timbre; ***timbre de gloria,*** source of pride.

timidez, *n.f.* timidity, shyness; diffidence.

tímido, -da, *a.* timid, shy; diffident.

timing, *n.m.* timing; rate of progress.

timo, *n.m.* grayling; (*anat.*) thymus gland; (*coll.*) cheat, swindle; ***dar un timo a,*** to cheat, swindle.

timón, *n.m.* helm; rudder; joy-stick; (rocket) stick; beam (*of a plough*); coach-pole; (*aer.*) ***timón de profundidad,*** elevator.

timonear, *v.i.* to steer.

timonel, *n.m.* helmsman.

timonera, *n.f.* helmsman's post, pilot-house, wheel-house; (*orn.*) rectricial.

timonero, *n.m.* helmsman.

timorato, -ta, *a.* timorous, pusilanimous.

timpa, *n.f.* bar of cast-iron (*in a furnace hearth*).

timpánico, -ca, *a.* (*med.*) tympanic.

timpanillo, *n.m.* small kettledrum; small tympano; (*print.*) inner tympan; (*arch.*) gablet.

tímpano, *n.m.* kettledrum; (*anat.*) tympanum, eardrum; (*arch., print.*) tympan.

tina, *n.f.* large earthen jar; vat, tub.

tinaco, *n.m.* wooden vat, tub.

tinada, *n.f.* woodstack; shed.

tinado, tinador, *n.m.* cattle-shed.

tinaja, *n.f.* large earthen jar.

tinajería, *n.f.* jar-shop.

tinajero, *n.m.* maker *or* seller of jars.

tinajita, tinajuela, *n.f.* small jar.

tinajón, *n.m.* large jar.

tincar [A], *v.t.* (*Hisp. Am.*) to fillip, flip.

tincazo, *n.m.* (*Hisp. Am.*) fillip, flip.

tinción, *n.f.* dyeing, tingeing.

tinelar, *a.* pertaining to the servants' dining-room.

tinelo, *n.m.* servants' dining-room.

tineta, *n.f.* small tub.

tinge, *n.m.* (*orn.*) black owl.

tingladillo, *n.m.* (*naut.*) clinker work.

tinglado, *n.m.* shed; temporary platform *or* stage; set-up.

tingle, *n.f.* (glaziers') lead opener.

tinicla, *n.f.* hauberk.

tiniebla, *n.f.* darkness, gloom; (*pl.*) darkness; (*eccles.*) tenebræ.

tinillo, *n.m.* tank for collecting must.

tino, *n.m.* skilful touch; good aim; right feel; tact; moderation; ***a tino,*** gropingly; ***a buen tino,*** at a guess; ***con tino,*** in moderation; well, successfully; ***sin tino,*** to excess; wildly; ***perder el tino,*** to lose one's touch *or* head; ***sacar de tino,*** to drive up the wall.

tinola, *n.f.* (*Philip.*) soup made of minced chicken, potatoes and pumpkins.

tinta, *n.f.* [TINTO].

tintar, *v.t.* to dye, tinge.

tinte, *n.m.* dyeing; dye, tint; dyer's, cleaner's; shade, hue; tinge.

tinterazo, *n.m.* blow with an inkstand.

tinterillada, *n.f.* (*Hisp. Am.*) trickery, tricky action; lie, fib.

tinterillo, *n.m.* small inkstand; (*Hisp. Am., coll.*) pettifogger.

tintero, *n.m.* inkstand, inkwell; (*print.*) ink-table; ***dejar algo en el tintero,*** to leave sth. unsaid.

tintilla, *n.f.* astringent sweet red wine of Rota (Cádiz).

tintillo, *n.m.* light-coloured wine.

tintín, *n.m.* clang, clink (*of metal*).

tintirintín, *n.m.* piercing sound (*as of a clarion*).

tinto, -ta, *a.* deep-coloured, dyed, tinged; red; ***vino tinto,*** red wine. — *n.f.* ink; tint, dye; ***tinta china,*** Indian ink; ***tinta simpática,*** invisible ink; ***saber de buena tinta,*** to know on good authority; ***recargar las tintas,*** to lay it on (too) thick, overdo it; ***medias tintas,*** half measures.

tintóreo, -rea, *a.* tinctorial.

tintorería, *n.f.* dyer's shop; dry cleaner's.

tintorera (1), *n.f.* (*ichth.*) female shark.

tintorero, -ra (2), *n.m.f.* dyer.

tintura, *n.f.* dyeing; make-up; tincture, dye, colour; stain, spot; smattering; extract of drugs.

tinturar, *v.t.* to dye, tinge, imbue; (*fig., teaching*) to give a smattering of.

tiña (1), *n.f.* scalp ringworm; (*beekeeping*) small spider damaging beehives; (*coll.*) poverty; niggardliness.

tiñería, *n.f.* (*coll.*) poverty; meanness.

tiño, él tiñó, tiña (2), *pres. indic., 3rd pers. sing. pret., pres. subj.* [TEÑIR].

tiñoso, -sa, *a.* mangy, scabby; stingy.

tiñuela, *n.f.* ship-worm; (*bot.*) common dodder.

tío, *n.m.* uncle; (*coll.*) chap, bloke, guy.

tiorba, *n.f.* theorbo.

tiovivo, *n.m.* merry-go-round.

tipa, *n.f.* (*Hisp. Am.*) hardwood tree; (*Arg.*) leather-pouch *or* bag; (*coll.*) tart.

tipiadora, *n.f.* typewriter; typist.

típico, -ca, *a.* typical.

tiple, *n.m.* treble *or* soprano voice; treble guitar; (*naut.*) one-piece mast. — *n.m.f.* soprano singer.

tiplisonante, *a.* (*coll.*) treble-toned.

tipo, *n.m.* type; figure; (*com.*) rate; (*coll.*) fellow, bloke, customer; ***tener buen tipo,*** to have a good figure.

tipografía, *n.f.* typography, typesetting.

tipográfico, -ca, *a.* typographical.

tipógrafo, *n.m.* typographer.

tipometría, *n.f.* typometry.

tipómetro, *n.m.* type-gauge, type measure.

tipoy, *n.m.* (*Arg., Par.*) tunic.

típula, *n.f.* (*ent.*) daddy-long-legs.

tiquismiquis, *n.m.pl.* fiddle-faddle, hair-splitting, fussiness.

tiquistiquis, *n.m.* (*Philip.*) bitterwood tree.

tira, *n.f.* strip; shred; thong; (*coll.*) ***la tira de cosas,*** a whole string *or* mass of things.

tirabala, *n.f.* popgun.

tirabeque, *n.m.* tender pea.

tirabotas, *n.m. inv.* boot-hook.

tirabotón, *n.m.* button-hook.

tirabraguero, *n.m.* truss.

tirabuzón, *n.m.* corkscrew; curl, ringlet.

tiracol, tiracuello, *n.m.* sword-belt.

tirada (1), *n.f.* throw, cast; distance, stretch; space, lapse (*of time*); series, run; printing, edition; circulation; shooting; (*mus.*) tirade; ***tirada aparte,*** reprint, extra printing; off-printing; ***de una tirada,*** at one go.

tiradera, *n.f.* strap; long Indian arrow; trace (*of harness*).

tiradero, *n.m.* (hunting *or* shooting) hide, cover.

tirado, -da (2), *a.* long and low (*ship*); flowing, running (*writing*); (*coll.*) dirt cheap, give-away (*in price*); walk-over, push-over; low, of the dregs *or* scum, trash. — *n.m.* drawing, pulling; printing.

tirador, -ra, *n.m.f.* drawer, thrower; sharpshooter; marksman; handle, pull, knob, button; bell-pull; (*print.*) pressman; ***tirador de oro,*** gold-wire drawer.

tirafondo, *n.m.* metal bolt; (*med.*) alphonsin (forceps).

tiralíneas, *n.m. inv.* ruling-pen, drawing-pen.

tiramiento, *n.m.* stretching, drawing.

tiramira, *n.f.* long ridge of mountains; long line (*of things* or *people*); long distance.

tiramollar, *v.t.* (*naut.*) to slacken, ease off; to overhaul.

tirana (1), *n.f.* song.

tiranía, *n.f.* tyranny.

tiranicida, *n.m.* tyrannicide.

tiranicidio, *n.m.* tyrannicide.

tiránico, -ca, *a.* tyrannical.

tiranización, *n.f.* tyrannizing.

tiranizadamente, *adv.* tyrannically.

tiranizar [C], *v.t.* to tyrannize.

tirano, -na (2), *a.* tyrannical. — *n.m.f.* tyrant.

tirante, *a.* taut; tense, strained. — *n.m.* trace (*of harness*); (*mech.*) brace; tie-rod, stay-rod; (*arch.*) anchor, truss-rod; ***a tirantes largos,*** with two horses and two coachmen; (*pl.*) braces, (*Am.*) suspenders.

tirantez, *n.f.* tenseness, tautness, tightness; tension, strained relations.

tiranuelo, -la, *n.m.f.* little tyrant, petty tyrant.

tirapié, *n.m.* shoemaker's strap.

tirar, *v.t.* to throw, cast, fling, pitch; to throw away, cast off; to fire (*a shot*); to give (*a kick*); to draw, stretch; to knock down, upset; to draw (*a line*); to squander; to print; ***tirar un tiro,*** to fire a shot; ***tirar coces,*** to kick. — *v.i.* to attract, excite (*love* or *interest*); to draw (*of a chimney*); to last, endure; ***tirar a,*** to shoot at; to turn to; to tend (toward), to seek, aim at; to have a tinge of (*of colours*); ***tirar de,*** to draw; to pull; to take out; ***tirar al blanco,*** to shoot at a target; ***tirar a la derecha,*** to turn to the right; ***tira a rojo,*** it is reddish; ***tirar de una cuerda,*** to pull a rope; ***tirar de un carro,*** to draw a cart; ***tiró de espada,*** he drew his sword; ***tiró de cartera,*** he took out his wallet; ***ir tirando,*** to get by, get along; ***tira y afloja,*** stop-go, yes-no situation; give and take; ***a todo tirar,*** at the most. — **tirarse,** *v.r.* to rush, throw o.s.; to jump; to lie down; to give o.s. over; (*vulg.*) to knock off.

tirela, *n.f.* striped stuff.

tireta, *n.f.* (*prov.*) lace, latch, thong.

tiricia, *n.f.* (*coll.*) jaundice.

tirilla, *n.f.* strip, frilling, edging; neckband.

tirio, -ria, *a., n.m.f.* Tyrian; ***tirios y troyanos,*** opposing factions.

tiritaña, *n.f.* thin cloth *or* silk; flimsy *or* unsubstantial thing, trifle.

tiritar, *v.i.* to shiver, shake with cold.

tiritón, *n.m.* shivering, chill.

tiritona, *n.f.* shivering (*affected*).

Tiro, *n.m.* Tyre.

tiro, *n.m.* cast, throw, fling; shot; charge, discharge, mark, aim; firing, report of firing; (*artill.*) piece of ordnance; target practice; shooting-ground, shooting-gallery; team of draught animals; trace (*of harness*); hoisting rope; flight of stairs;

theft; length of a piece of cloth; prank, trick; serious injury; (*min.*) shaft; depth of a shaft; draught of a chimney; (*pl.*) sword belts; ***a tiro,*** within range *or* reach; (*Hisp. Am.*) ***al tiro,*** at once; ***de tiros largos,*** dressed up to the nines; ***a un tiro de ballesta,*** at a stone's throw; ***a tiro hecho,*** on purpose; straight, direct; ***tiro al blanco,*** target-shooting; ***errar el tiro,*** to miss one's shot; ***salir el tiro por la culata,*** to backfire; ***no quiere hacerlo ni a tiros,*** wild horses won't *or* wouldn't make him do it; (*pl.*) swordbelt.

tirocinio, *n.m.* apprenticeship, novitiate, pupilage.

tiroides, *n.m. inv.* thyroid gland.

tirolés (1), **-lesa,** *a.*, *n.m.f.* Tyrolese, Tyrolean.

tirolés (2), *n.m.* pedlar, huckster.

tirón, *n.m.* pull, jerk, haul, tug; tyro, novice; ***de un tirón,*** with a pull; (*fig.*) in one go *or* stretch; ***ni a tirones,*** hopeless.

tirona, *n.f.* fishing-net, seine.

tiroriro, *n.m.* (*coll.*) sound of a wind instrument; (*pl.*, *coll.*) wind instruments.

tirotear, *v.t.* to shoot wildly at. — **tirotearse,** *v.r.* to exchange shots *or* fire.

tiroteo, *n.m.* wild shooting; exchange of shots *or* fire.

tirria, *n.f.* (*coll.*) dislike; ***tener tirria a,*** to have it in for.

tirso, *n.m.* thyrsus, wand.

tirulato, -ta, *a.* stupefied, astounded.

tirulo, *n.m.* tobacco leaf forming the core of a cigar.

tisana, *n.f.* decoction, infusion.

tísico, -ca, *a.*, *n.m.f.* phthisical, consumptive.

tisis, *n.f. inv.* phthisis, consumption.

tiste, *n.m.* (*Cent. Am.*) drink made of toasted maize flour, cacao, anatta and sugar.

tisú, *n.m.* gold *or* silver tissue.

Titán, *n.m.* Titan.

titánico, -ca, *a.* titanic.

titanio, -nia, *a.* Titanic. — *n.m.* titanium.

títere, *n.m.* puppet; ***no dejar títere con cabeza,*** to spare nothing *or* no one; (*pl.*) puppet show.

titeretada, *n.f.* mean trick.

tití, *n.m.* small monkey.

titilación, *n.f.* titillation; quivering; twinkling.

titilador, -ra, titilante, *a.* titillating; quivering; twinkling.

titilar, *v.t.* to titillate. — *v.i.* to quiver; to twinkle.

titímalo, *n.m.* (*bot.*) spurge.

titirimundi, *n.m.* peepshow.

titiritaina, *n.f.* (*coll.*) din, racket.

titiritar, *v.i.* to shiver, tremble.

titiritero, *n.m.* puppet-player, puppeteer.

tito, *n.m.* pea *or* bean.

titubeante, *a.* hesitating, vacillating.

titubear, *v.i.* to stammer; to hesitate, vacillate.

titubeo, *n.m.* hesitation, wavering.

titulado, *n.m.* titled person.

titular, *a.* titular; official. — *n.m.f.* bearer, holder; incumbent. — *n.m.* headline. — *n.f.* capital letter. — *v.t.* to title, entitle, call. — *v.i.* to obtain a title.

titulillo, *n.m.* petty title; (*print.*) page-heading; ***andar en titulillos,*** to split hairs.

título, *n.m.* title; titled person; (university) degree; title deed; qualification; foundation (*of a right* or *claim*); certificate, bond; cause, reason; ***a título de,*** as, by way of.

tiza, *n.f.* chalk.

tizna, *n.f.* blackening; lampblack.

tiznadura, *n.f.* smudginess.

tiznajo, *n.m.* (*coll.*) smudge, stain.

tiznar, *v.t.* to smut, smudge, begrime, blacken.

tizne, *n.m.* smut, soot, lampblack.

tiznón, *n.m.* smut, smudge; stain.

tizo, *n.m.* half-burnt charcoal.

tizón, *n.m.* brand, firebrand; half-burnt wood; blight, mildew; (*fig.*) disgrace; (*arch.*) header.

tizona, *n.f.* (*coll.*) sword.

tizonada, *n.f.*, **tizonazo,** *n.m.* stroke with a firebrand; (*coll.*) hell fire.

tizoncillo, *n.m.* small burning coal.

tizonear, *v.t.* to stir up (*a fire*).

tizonera, *n.f.* heap of half-burnt charcoal.

tizonero, *n.m.* fire poker.

tlazol, *n.m.* (*Mex.*) fodder of maize tops.

toa, *n.f.* (*Hisp. Am.*) rope, hawser.

toalla, *n.f.* towel; pillow-sham.

toallero, *n.m.* towel rack.

toalleta, *n.f.* small towel.

toar, *v.t.* to tow.

toba, *n.f.* (*min.*) tufa, travertin, calcsinter; (*dent.*) tartar; (*bot.*) cotton-thistle.

toballeta, tobelleta, *n.f.* napkin.

tobar, *n.m.* tufa quarry.

tobillera, *n.f.* flapper; (*sport*) ankle support.

tobillo, *n.m.* ankle.

tobogán, *n.m.* slide; chute.

toca, *n.f.* wimple; cornet; coif, bonnet; head-dress.

tocadiscos, *n.m. inv.* record player, gramophone, (*Am.*) phonograph.

tocado, -da, *a.* (*coll.*) daft, touched. — *n.m.* head-dress, headgear.

tocador, -ra, *n.m.f.* (*mus.*) player, performer. — *n.m.* dressing-table; toilet case; dressing room, toilet room; ***artículos de tocador,*** toilet articles.

tocadorcito, *n.m.* small toilet-table.

tocadura, *n.f.* coiffure, headgear.

tocamiento, *n.m.* touching.

tocante, *a.* touching; ***tocante a,*** concerning, as regards, regarding.

tocar [A], *v.t.* to touch; to feel; to strike (the hour); to try; to find, come to know; to touch upon; to play (*a musical instrument*); to move, inspire; ***tocar fondo,*** to strike ground; ***tocar diana,*** to beat the reveille; ***tocar a muerto,*** to toll, sound the knell. — *v.i.* to be one's turn *or* right; to be related *or* allied to; ***tocar a*** or ***en,*** to touch, touch at; to kiss (*in billiards*); ***tocar a,*** to appertain to, concern; to fall to; ***le tocó el premio,*** he won the prize; ***tocar de cerca,*** to affect closely; ***tocar a la puerta,*** to knock at the door; ***tocar en lo vivo,*** to wound to the quick; ***por lo que toca a,*** as regards, with regard to. — *v. impers.* ***toca,*** it is time for *or* to. — **tocarse,** *v.r.* to put on one's hat, cover one's head.

tocasalva, *n.f.* rack *or* tray for glasses.

tocata, *n.f.* (*mus.*) toccata; (*coll.*) drubbing, beating.

tocayo, -ya, *a.*, *n.m.f.* namesake.

tocia (1), *n.f.* (*min.*) tutty.

tocinero, -ra, *a.* of speck *or* streaky bacon.

tocino, *n.m.* speck; streaky bacon; fast skipping; ***tocino del cielo,*** egg-yolk confection.

tocio, -cia (2), *a.* low, dwarfish (oak tree).

tocología, *n.f.* tocology, obstetrics.

tocólogo, *n.m.* tocologist, obstetrician.

tocón, -cona, *a.* (much) given to touching. — *n.m.* stump.

toconal, *n.m.* olive-yard planted with stumps.

tocororo, *n.m.* (*orn.*) Cuban trogon.

tocotoco, *n.m.* (*Ven.*, *orn.*) pelican.

tocuyo, *n.m.* (*Hisp. Am.*) coarse cotton cloth.

tochedad, *n.f.* rusticity, coarseness.

tochimbo, *n.m.* (*Per.*) blast furnace.

tocho, -cha, *a.* rustic, uncouth, coarse. — *n.m.* (*metal.*) bloom, billet.

tochura [TOCHEDAD].

todabuena, todasana, *n.f.* St. John's-wort.

todavía, *adv.* still, ever, yet; ***todavía no,*** not yet.

todito, -ta, *a.* (*coll.*) absolutely all, every little bit (of).

todo, -da, *a.* all; entire, whole; each, every; ***de todo punto,*** completely, utterly; ***a todo correr,*** full tilt, flat out; ***de todas todas,*** for a (dead) certainty *or* cert; ***no tenerlas todas consigo,*** not to feel too sure. — *adv.* all, completely. — *pron.* everything, all; ***es todo uno,*** it's all the same thing, one and the same thing; ***todo incluido,*** inclusive terms, (*Am.*) American plan. — *n.m.* all; whole; everything; (*pl.*) all; everybody; ***ante todo,*** first of all, firstly; ***con todo,*** for all that, even so; ***de todo,*** a bit of everything; ***del todo,*** altogether; **no . . . del todo,** not . . . altogether; ***sobre todo,*** above all, particularly; ***jugarse el todo por el todo,*** to stake all; ***así y todo,*** even so, even then; ***tiene coche y todo,*** he's even got a car; ***viejo y todo,*** even though he is old, despite his age.

todopoderoso, -sa, *a.* all-powerful, almighty. — *n.m.* ***el Todopoderoso,*** the Almighty.

toesa, *n.f.* toise.

tofo, *n.m.* tumour.

toga, *n.f.* toga; robe, gown.

togado, -da, *a.* togaed; robed.

toisón de oro, *n.m.* Golden Fleece.

tojal, *n.m.* gorse patch.

tojino, *n.m.* (*naut.*) cleat.

tojo, *n.m.* gorse; (*Bol., orn.*) lark.

tojosita, *n.f.* (*Cub., orn.*) pigeon.

tola, *n.f.* (*Hisp. Am.*) shrub.

tolano, *n.m.* tumour (*in horse's gums*); (*pl.*) short hair (*on the neck*).

toldadura, *n.f.* hangings; awning.

toldar, *v.t.* to cover with an awning.

toldería, *n.f.* (*Arg.*) Indian camp.

toldero, *n.m.* (*prov.*) salt retailer.

toldilla, *n.f.* (*naut.*) round-house.

toldillo, *n.m.* covered sedan-chair; small awning.

toldo, *n.m.* awning; blinds, (*Am.*) shades; tilt; pomp, ostentation; (*Arg.*) Indian tent.

tole, *n.m.* (*coll.*) hubbub, uproar; outcry; ***tomar*** or ***coger el tole,*** to clear out, dash off.

toledano, -na, *a., n.m.f.* Toledan; ***noche toledana,*** sleepless night.

tolerable, *a.* tolerable, sufferable, bearable.

tolerancia, *n.f.* toleration; tolerance.

tolerante, *a.* tolerant; tolerationist.

tolerantismo, *n.m.* toleration, freedom of worship.

tolerar, *v.t.* to tolerate, bear, suffer.

tolete, *n.m.* thole, thole-pin; (*Cent. Am., Cub., Ven.*) cudgel, club; (*Col.*) large boat *or* canoe.

tolmo, *n.m.* tor, pillar of rock.

tolondro, -ra, *a.* scatterbrained, reckless, rash. — *n.m.f.* scatterbrain; ***a topa tolondro,*** headlong, recklessly. — *n.m.* bump.

tolondrón, -rona, *a.* scatterbrained, reckless, rash. — *n.m.* bump, swelling; ***a tolondrones,*** by fits and starts.

tolteca, *a., n.m.f.* (*Mex.*) relating to the Toltec tribe and language.

tolú, *n.m.* Peruvian balsam.

tolva, *n.f.* mill-hopper, chute.

tolvanera, *n.f.* cloud of dust, dust whirl.

tolla, *n.f.* bog; (*Cub.*) trough.

tollina, *n.f.* (*coll.*) beating, drubbing.

tollo, *n.m.* (*ichth.*) spotted dogfish; hide (*for hunting*); quagmire, bog.

tollón, *n.m.* gorge, narrow passage.

toma, *n.f.* taking; dose; capture; (*hydrost.*) inlet, intake; (*elec.*) current collector, tap; (*rad.*) terminal.

tomacorriente, *n.m.* (*Hisp. Am.*) socket, plug; (*Chi.*) trolley.

tomada, *n.f.* taking, capture.

tomadero, *n.m.* haft, handle; outlet, opening into a drain.

tomador, -ra, *a.* taking; retrieving (*dog*); (*Hisp. Am.*) drinking. — *n.m.f.* taker, receiver; setter, retriever; (*naut.*) gasket; (*Arg., Chi.*) drinker, tipler; (*com.*) drawee.

tomadura, *n.f.* taking; ***tomadura de pelo,*** leg-pull(-ing); taking for a ride.

tomaína, *n.f.* ptomaine.

tomajón, -jona, *a.* (*coll.*) light-fingered.

tomar, *v.t.* to take; to have; to take hold of; to take on *or* up; to get, gather; ***tomar a mal,*** to take offence *or* umbrage at; ***la cosa va tomando un cariz feo,*** the business is beginning to look nasty; ***tomar fuerzas,*** to get strength; ***tomar el sol,*** to sunbathe; ***tomar el fresco,*** to take the air; ***tomar tierra,*** to land; ***tomar puerto,*** to make port; ***tomar vuelo,*** to take flight, take off; ***tomar la delantera a,*** to get ahead of; ***tomar la puerta, tomar las de Villadiego,*** to clear out *or* off; ***tomar estado,*** to marry; to take holy orders; ***tomar lenguas,*** to make enquiries; ***tomarle a alguien el pelo,*** to pull s.o.'s leg; to take s.o. for a ride; ***la tiene tomada conmigo,*** he has it in for me. — *v.i.* to turn; ***toma y daca,*** tit for tat. — **tomarse,** *v.r.* to get rusty; to get hoarse (*voice*); (*Hisp. Am.*) to get drunk. — *interj.* ***¡toma!*** well, well! you don't say!

Tomás, *n.m.* Thomas.

tomatada, *n.f.* fry of tomatoes.

tomatal, *n.m.* tomato patch *or* field.

tomatazo, *n.m.* blow with a tomato.

tomate, *n.m.* (*bot.*) tomato; (*coll.*) hole (*in stockings etc.*); (*coll.*) ***aquí hay mucho tomate,*** there's plenty to be done here.

tomatero, -ra, *a.* of tomato *or* tomatoes; (*coll.*) keen on tomatoes. — *n.m.f.* tomato grower *or* seller. — *n.f.* (*bot.*) tomato plant.

tomaticán, *n.m.* (*Chi.*) dish of tomatoes.

tomavistas, *n.m. inv.* cine camera.

tómbola, *n.f.* (charity) raffle, tombola.

tome, *n.m.* (*Chi.*) reed mace.

tomeguín, *n.m.* (*Cub., orn.*) humming-bird.

tomento, *n.m.* coarse tow.

tomillar, *n.m.* thyme bed.

tomillo, *n.m.* (*bot.*) thyme; (*bot.*) ***tomillo salsero,*** Spanish thyme.

tomín, *n.m.* third part of a drachm; (*Hisp. Am.*) silver coin.

tominejo, -ja, *n.m.f.* (*orn.*) humming-bird.

tomismo, *n.m.* Thomism.

tomista, *a., n.m.f.* Thomist.

tomiza, *n.f:* bass-rope.

tomo, *n.m.* volume, tome; bulk; ***de tomo y lomo,*** utter, dyed-in-the-wool.

tomón, -mona, *a.* light-fingered. — *n.m.f.* thief.

ton, *n.m.* ***sin ton ni son,*** without rhyme or reason.

tonada, *n.f.* tune.

tonadilla, *n.f.* light tune; musical interlude.

tonadillero, *n.m.* writer of light tunes.

tonalidad, *n.f.* tonality; key; tone; shade.

tonante, *a.* (*poet.*) thundering.

tonar, *v.i.* (*poet.*) to thunder.

tonca, *n.f.* (*bot.*) tonka bean.

tondino, *n.m.* (*arch.*) astragal.

tondo, *n.m.* (*arch.*) round moulding.

tonel, *n.m.* cask, barrel.

tonelada, *n.f.* ton; tun (*measure*).

tonelaje, *n.m.* (*naut.*) tonnage; (*com.*) tonnage dues.

tonelería, *n.f.* cooper's shop, cooper's trade, cooperage, coopering; barrels, casks, *or* water-casks.

tonelero, *n.m.* cooper.

tonelete, *n.m.* small cask, keg; short skirt.

tonga, tongada, *n.f.* layer, stratum; (*Cub.*) lay, tier, row, ledge; (*Arg., Col.*) task.

tongo, *n.m.* (*sport*) fix; cheat.

tónico, -ca, *a.* tonic; (*mus.*) key (*note*). — *n.m.* tonic. — *n.f.* keynote.
tonificador, -ra, tonificante, *a.* tonic, strengthening.
tonificar [A], *v.t.* (*med.*) to tone up.
tonillo, *n.m.* monotonous tone, sing-song note.
tonina, *n.f.* fresh tunny; dolphin.
tono, *n.m.* tone; tune; (*med.*) vigour, strength; (*mus.*) key, pitch; ***darse tono,*** to give o.s. airs; ***bajar el tono,*** to lower one's tone; ***de buen*** or ***mal tono,*** in good *or* bad taste; ***a ese tono,*** at that rate; ***ir a tono con,*** to be in accord *or* in tune with; ***dar el tono,*** to set the standard; ***ponerse a tono,*** to get back on one's feet; to get in step *or* in line; ***subido de tono,*** bright; risqué; ***fuera de tono,*** out of place, inappropriate; ***salida de tono,*** tasteless remark; ***sin venir a tono,*** for no good reason.
tonsila, *n.f.* (*anat.*) tonsil.
tonsilitis, *n.f. inv.* (*med.*) tonsillitis.
tonsura, *n.f.* tonsure; cutting of hair *or* wool, shearing, fleecing.
tonsurar, *v.t.* to cut off hair *or* wool from; to give the tonsure; to shear, fleece.
tontada, *n.f.* nonsense, foolishness, silliness.
tontaina, *n.m.f.* (*coll.*) fool, dolt.
tontear, *v.i.* to fool about, act foolishly; to flirt.
tontería, *n.f.* foolishness, foolery, tomfoolery, nonsense.
tontico, *n.m.* little dolt, twit.
tontiloco, -ca, *a.* harebrained.
tontillo, *n.m.* hoop-skirt; bustle.
tontina, *n.f.* (*com.*) tontine.
tontito, *n.m.* (*Chi., orn.*) goatsucker (*Caprimulgus*).
tontivano, -na, *a.* foolishly conceited.
tonto, -ta, *a.* stupid, silly, foolish. — *n.m.f.* fool, nincompoop; (*Chi., Col., C.R.*) old maid (*at cards*); (*Chi.*) lariat with balls at one end; ***a tontas y a locas,*** any old how, without thinking; ***volver a uno tonto,*** to drive s.o. crazy; ***tonto de capirote,*** dunce; ***hacer el tonto,*** to play the fool; ***hacerse el tonto,*** to pretend not to understand, hear etc.
tontuelo, -la, *n.m.f.* little fool.
tontuna, *n.f.* foolishness.
toña, *n.f.* tip-cat; bat for this game; (*prov.*) big loaf of bread; (*prov.*) cake kneaded with oil and honey; (*coll.*) drunkenness.
toñina, *n.f.* (*prov.*) fresh tunny fish.
¡top! *interj.* (*naut.*) hold, stop.
topa, *n.f.* (*naut.*) pulley (*to hoist the mainsails*).
topacio, *n.m.* topaz.
topada, *n.f.* butt.
topador, *n.m.* butter (*an animal which butts*); ready gambler.
topar, *v.t.* to knock against; to run into; to butt. — *v.i.* to butt; ***topar*** or ***toparse con,*** to run *or* bump into, come across.
toparca, *n.m.* toparch.
toparquía, *n.f.* toparchy.
tope, *n.m.* top, butt, end; stop, stop device, stopper; obstacle; quarrel, scuffle; butt, knock, bump; (*railw.*) buffer; (*naut.*) mast-head, topmast-head; topman; ***a todo tope,*** at the very most *or* outside; ***al*** or ***a tope,*** full up; ***estar hasta el tope*** or ***los topes,*** to be packed, crammed *or* stuffed to the brim; ***sueldo tope,*** ceiling salary, salary limit.
topeadura, *n.f.* (*Chi.*) gaucho horse-play.
topera, *n.f.* mole-hole.
topetada, *n.f.* butt; bump.
topetar, *v.t., v.i.* to butt; to bump, strike, knock (against).
topetazo, topetón, *n.m.* collision, knock, bump; butt.
topetudo, -da, *a.* (much) given to butting.
tópico, -ca, *a.* local. — *n.m.* cliché.
topil, *n.m.* (*Mex.*) constable, policeman.
topinada, *n.f.* (*coll.*) awkwardness, clumsiness.
topinambur, *n.m.* (*Arg., Bol.*) sweet potato.
topinaria, *n.f.* (*surg.*) talpa, wen.
topinera, *n.f.* mole-hole, mole-hill.
topo, *n.m.* mole; (*coll.*) clumsy, blundering, half-blind individual; (*Hisp. Am.*) league and a half; (*Arg., Chi., Per.*) large scarf-pin.
topocho, -cha, *a.* (*Ven.*) plump.
topografía, *n.f.* topography; surveying.
topográfico, -ca, *a.* topographical.
topógrafo, *n.m.* topographer; surveyor.
toponímico, -ca, *a.* toponymic, of place-names. — *n.m.* place-name.
toque, *n.m.* touch; sounding, ringing, beat; call; trial, test; tap; hint, warning; ***toque a muerto, de ánimas*** or ***de difuntos,*** knell, toll; ***toque de corneta,*** bugle call; ***toque de diana,*** reveille; ***toque de queda,*** curfew; ***a toque de campana,*** at the double; ***ahí está el toque,*** there's the rub; ***dar un toque a,*** to drop a hint to; to put out a feeler to, sound out.
toqueado, *n.m.* rhythmical noise, clapping, stamping.
toquetear, *v.t.* to finger, paw, muss *or* mess about; to bash away on.
toquero, *n.m.* head-dress maker, veil-maker.
toqui, *n.m.* (*Chi.*) Araucanian war chief.
toquilla, *n.f.* shawl; kerchief.
tora (1), *n.f.* Torah.
tora (2), *n.f.* figure of a bull (*in fireworks*).
torada, *n.f.* drove of bulls.
toral, *a.* main, principal. — *n.m.* unbleached wax; mould (*for copper bars*); copper bar.
tórax, *n.m.* thorax; chest.
torbellino, *n.m.* whirlwind.
torca, *n.f.* cavern, deep hollow place in the earth.
torcal, *n.m.* cavernous region.
torcaz, torcazo, -za, *a.* wild (*pigeons*); (*orn.*) ***paloma torcaz,*** ring-dove.
torce, *n.f.* coil *or* turn of a chain around the neck.
torcecuello, *n.m.* (*orn.*) wryneck.
torcedero, -ra, *a.* twisted. — *n.m.* twisting implement.
torcedor, -ra, *a.* twisting. — *n.m.f.* twister. — *n.m.* twisting tool; (*fig.*) cause of grief *or* worry; ***torcedor de tabaco,*** cigar-maker.
torcedura, *n.f.* twisting, sprain; small wine.
torcer [5D], *v.t.* to twist, wrench; to twine; to turn, bend; to sprain; ***torcer el gesto,*** to pull a face, frown; ***no dar el brazo a torcer,*** not to give way (*in argument*); ***estar torcido con,*** to be on bad terms with. — *v.i.* to turn. — **torcerse,** *v.r.* to be *or* get twisted; to go wrong *or* awry, misfire; ***si no se tuerce,*** as long as sth. doesn't (crop up to) prevent *or* spoil it.
torcidillo, *n.m.* twisted silk.
torcido, -da, *a.* oblique, crooked, tortuous. — *n.m.* twist of candied fruit; twisted silk. — *n.f.* wick.
torcijón, *n.m.* twist, wrench; bellyache, cramps, gripes.
torcimiento, *n.m.* twist, twisting; bend, bending; warping; circumlocution.
torculado, -da, *a.* screw-shaped.
tórculo, *n.m.* (*print.*) small press; rolling-press.
tordella, *n.f.* (*orn.*) missel-thrush.
tórdiga, *n.f.* neat's leather.
tordillo, -lla, *a.* thrush-coloured, grizzled, greyish.
tordo, -da, *a.* speckled, dapple (*horse*). — *n.m.* thrush; ***tordo loco,*** solitary thrush; ***tordo de agua,*** reed-thrush.
toreador, *n.m.* bullfighter.
torear, *v.t.* to fight (*bulls*); (*coll.*) to lead a merry dance. — *v.i.* to fight (bulls), be a bullfighter.
toreo, *n.m.* bullfighting.
torería, *n.f.* (*Cub.*) boys' pranks.

torero, -ra, *a.* bullfighting; (*coll.*) smart, dapper. — *n.m.* bullfighter. — *n.f.* short and tight unbuttoned jacket; ***saltarse a la torera,*** to disregard, pay no heed to (*a rule, duty etc.*).

torete, *n.m.* bullock; current rumour; (*coll.*) puzzle, intricate business; absorbing topic.

torga, *n.f.* yoke for dogs *or* hogs.

toril, *n.f.* bull pen.

torillo, *n.m.* little bull; dowel; (*zool.*) raphe; (*ichth.*) a fish of the Acanthopterygian order.

torio, *n.m.* (*chem.*) thorium.

toriondez, *n.f.* rut (*of cattle*).

toriondo, -da, *a.* rutting (*of cattle*).

torito, *n.m.* small bull; bullock; (*Chi., orn.*) humming-bird; (*Arg., Per., ent.*) rhinoceros beetle; (*Ec.*) orchid.

torloroto, *n.m.* shepherd's flute *or* pipe.

tormagal, *n.m.*, **tormellera,** *n.f.* (*geol.*) place abounding in tors.

tormenta, *n.f.* storm.

tormentario, -ria, *a.* projectile. — *n.m.* gunnery.

tormentila, *n.f.* tormentil, septifoil.

tormentín, *n.m.* (*naut.*) jib-boom.

tormento, *n.m.* torment; torture; (*mil.*) battering ordnance; ***dar tormento a,*** to torture, put to torture, put on the rack.

tormentoso, -sa, *a.* stormy.

tormo, *n.m.* tor.

torna, *n.f.* restitution, return; ***volver las tornas a,*** to turn the tables on; ***se cambiaron las tornas,*** the tables are turned.

tornaboda, *n.f.* day after a wedding, first day of honeymoon; celebrations upon this day.

tornachile, *n.m.* (*Mex.*) thick pepper.

tornada, *n.f.* return; (*poet.*) envoy; (*vet.*) tape worm cyst.

tornadera, *n.f.* winnowing-fork.

tornadizo, -za, *a.* fickle, changeable. — *n.m.* turncoat, deserter.

tornado, *n.m.* tornado.

tornadura, *n.f.* return, recompense.

tornaguía, *n.f.* landing certificate.

tornalecho, *n.m.* bed canopy.

tornamiento, *n.m.* turn, change.

tornapunta, *n.f.* (*arch.*) chock, shoe, wedge; (*naut.*) stay, prop, brace.

tornar, *v.t.* to return, give back; to turn, change. — *v.i.* to return, go *or* come back; ***tornar a,*** to do again; ***tornar en sí,*** to come to *or* round. — **tornarse,** *v.r.* to turn, become.

tornasol, *n.m.* iridescence; sunflower; litmus.

tornasolado, -da, *a.* changing colours, iridescent.

tornasolar, *v.t.* to cause to iridesce.

tornátil, *a.* turned (*in a lathe*); changeable, fickle.

tornatrás, *n.m.f.* throw-back.

tornavía, *n.f.* turntable.

tornaviaje, *n.m.* return trip.

tornavirón, *n.m.* box, slap.

tornavoz, *n.m.* sounding-board.

torneador, *n.m.* turner; tilter.

torneadura, *n.f.* lathe shavings, swarf.

torneante, *n.m.* tilter at tournaments; turner.

tornear, *v.t.* to turn, shape by turning. — *v.i.* to turn, go round; to tilt at tournaments; (*fig.*) to meditate, muse.

torneo, *n.m.* tournament, tourney; turning.

tornera, *n.f.* door-keeper (*in a nunnery*).

tornería, *n.f.* turning; turnery.

tornero, *n.m.* turner.

tornillero, *n.m.* (*coll.*) deserter.

tornillo, *n.m.* screw; clamp, vice; ***tornillo de banco,*** vice; ***apretar los tornillos a,*** to put the screw on; ***hacer tornillo,*** to desert; (*coll.*) ***le falta un tornillo,*** he's a bit screwy, he's got a screw loose.

torniquete, *n.m.* tourniquet; turnpike, turnstile; swivel; bell-crank.

torniscón, *n.m.* box, slap, cuff.

torno, *n.m.* wheel, axle-tree; winch, windlass; lathe; carriage-brake; spinning-wheel, spindle; drill; serving hatch; ***en torno,*** round about; ***volver al torno,*** to go back to the grind.

toro, *n.m.* bull; ogee moulding; (*astron., astrol.*) Taurus; ***ciertos son los toros,*** so it's true; ***ver los toros desde la barrera,*** to sit on the fence; ***dejar en los cuernos del toro,*** to leave in the lurch; ***toro bravo*** or ***de lidia,*** fighting bull; ***toro corrido,*** old hand; ***toros y cañas,*** quarrel, set-to; (*pl.*) bullfight; bullfighting.

toronja, *n.f.* (*bot.*) grapefruit, shaddock.

toronjil, *n.m.*, **toronjina,** *n.f.* (*bot.*) balm-gentle.

toronjo, *n.m.* shaddock tree.

toroso, -sa, *a.* strong, robust.

torozón, *n.m.* gripes.

torpe, *a.* clumsy, awkward; dull-witted, thick; lewd.

torpedear, *v.t.* to torpedo; to wreck.

torpedeo, *n.m.* torpedoing.

torpedero, *n.m.* torpedo-boat.

torpedo, *n.m.* torpedo; (*ichth.*) electric ray cramp-fish; streamlined touring-car; ***torpedo automóvil,*** self-propelling torpedo; ***torpedo de botalón,*** spar torpedo; ***torpedo de fondo, durmiente*** or ***flotante,*** naval mine.

torpeza, *n.f.* clumsiness, awkwardness; blunder; stupidity.

torpor, *n.m.* torpor.

torrado, *n.m.* toasted chick-pea.

torrar, *v.t.* to toast.

torre, *n.f.* tower; turret; belfry, steeple; castle *or* rook (*chess*); ***torre de costa,*** watch-tower, Martello tower; ***torre de viento,*** castle in the air; (*naut.*) ***torre de luces,*** lighthouse.

torrear, *v.t.* to fortify with towers.

torrefacción, *n.f.* torrefaction, toasting.

torreja, *n.f.* (*Hisp. Am.*) [TORRIJA].

torrejón, *n.m.* ill-shaped turret.

torrencial, *a.* torrent-like, torrential; overpowering.

torrentada, *n.f.* sweep of a torrent, impetuous current.

torrente, *n.m.* torrent; avalanche, rush; mass, abundance.

torrentera, *n.f.* ravine made by a torrent.

torreón, *n.m.* round fortified tower.

torrero, *n.m.* tower-guard; (*prov.*) farmer; ***torrero de faro,*** lighthouse-keeper.

torreznada, *n.f.* large dish of rashers.

torreznero, *n.m.* (*coll.*) lazy fellow.

torrezno, *n.m.* fritter of streaky bacon.

tórrido, -da, *a.* torrid, parched, terribly hot.

torrija, *n.f.* sweet bread fritter.

torrontera, *n.f.*, **torrontero,** *n.m.* heap of earth left by a freshet.

tórsalo, *n.m.* (*Cent. Am.*) parasitic worm.

torsión, *n.f.* torsion, twist, twisting.

torso, *n.m.* (*anat.*) torso, trunk.

torta, *n.f.* cake; pancake; pie; (*print.*) font; (*print.*) forme; (*coll.*) slap, smack; ***tortas y pan pintado,*** trifles; child's play; ***costar la torta un pan,*** to work out *or* turn out damned expensive; ***hacer un pan con unas tortas,*** to make a mess-up *or* botch-up; ***tener mucha torta,*** to be as stolid as an ox; ***ser un torta,*** to be a stolid individual.

tortada, *n.f.* meat *or* chicken pie.

tortedad, *n.f.* twistedness.

tortel, *n.m.* flat bun.

tortero, -ra, *n.m.f.* whorl (*of a spindle*). — *n.f.* baking-pan; deep dish.

tortícolis, *n.f. inv.* stiff neck.

tortilla, *n.f.* omelet; (*Mex.*) pancake; ***tortilla española,*** potato omelet; ***tortilla francesa,*** plain omelet; ***hacerse tortilla,*** to get flattened *or* smashed; ***cuando se vuelva la tortilla,*** when the tables are turned, when the boot is on the other foot.

tortita, *n.f.* waffle.

tórtola, *n.f.* (*orn.*) turtle-dove.

tortolillo, -lla, tortolito, -ta, *n.m.f.* small turtle-dove; (*fig.*) little love-bird.

tórtolo, *n.m.* (*orn.*) turtle-dove; (*fig.*) love-bird.

tortor, *n.m.* (*naut.*) fraps.

tortuga, *n.f.* tortoise; turtle; ***paso de tortuga,*** snail's pace.

tortuosidad, *n.f.* tortuosity, tortuousness.

tortuoso, -sa, *a.* tortuous; winding.

tortura, *n.f.* torture; twistedness, torsion.

torturar, *v.t.* to torture, torment.

torva (1), *n.f.* whirl of snow *or* rain.

torvisca, *n.f.*, **torvisco,** *n.m.* (*bot.*) flax-leaved daphne.

torvo, -va (2), *a.* sullen, glowering, grim, sinister.

torzadillo, *n.m.* thin silk twist.

torzal, *n.m.* silk twist; cord.

torzón, *n.m.* (*vet.*) gripes.

torzonado, -da, *a.* contracted, twisted; (*vet.*) suffering from gripes.

tos, *n.f.* cough; ***tos ferina,*** whooping-cough; ***tos perruna,*** gruff cough.

tosca, *n.f.* [TOSCO].

Toscana, *n.f.* Tuscany.

toscano, -na, *a.*, *n.m.f.* Tuscan.

tosco, -ca, *a.* rough, coarse; crude, clumsy. — *n.f.* (*dent.*) tartar.

tosegoso, -sa, *a.* coughing.

toser, *v.i.* to cough. — *v.t.* (*coll.*) to tread on the toes of, needle.

tosidura, *n.f.* coughing.

tosigar [B], *v.t.* to poison.

tósigo, *n.m.* poison; (*fig.*) pain, grief.

tosigoso, -sa, *a.* poisonous; coughing.

tosquedad, *n.f.* coarseness; clumsiness.

tostada, *n.f.* (piece of) toast; (*fig.*, *coll.*) bore, drag.

tostador, -ra, *n.m.f.* toaster.

tostadura, *n.f.* toasting.

tostar [4], *v.t.* to toast; to roast; to tan, brown; ***tostarse al sol,*** to bask in the sun.

tostón, *n.m.* buttered toast; roasted pea; arrow with a burnt, sharpened point; sucking pig; (*Mex.*) silver coin of 50 cents; (*Bol.*) silver coin of 30 cents; (*coll.*) bore, drag.

total, *a.* total. — *adv.* in short, to sum up. — *n.m.* total, sum total, whole, totality.

totalidad, *n.f.* totality, aggregate, whole.

totalitario, -ria, *a.* totalitarian.

totem, *n.m.* totem.

totemismo, *n.m.* totem-worship.

totilimundi, *n.m.* raree-show.

totolate, *n.m.* (*C.R.*, *ent.*) chicken louse.

totoloque, *n.m.* (*Mex.*) Indian game of quoits.

totoposte, *n.m.* (*Cent. Am.*, *Mex.*) corn-cake *or* biscuit.

totora, *n.f.* (*Hisp. Am.*, *bot.*) cat-tail *or* red mace.

totuma, *n.f.* (*Hisp. Am.*) cup made from a calabash.

totumo, *n.m.* (*Hisp. Am.*, *bot.*) calabash tree.

toxicar [A], *v.t.* to poison.

tóxico, -ca, *a.* toxic, poisonous. — *n.m.* poison.

toxicología, *n.f.* toxicology.

toxicológico, -ca, *a.* toxicological.

toxicomanía, *n.f.* drug-addiction.

toxicómano, -na, *a.*, *n.m.* drug-addict(ed).

toxina, *n.f.* (*med.*) toxin.

tozalbo, -ba, *a.* white-faced (*cattle*).

tozar [C], *v.i.* to butt with the head.

tozo, -za, *a.* small, stumpy, dwarfy. — *n.f.* log, block of wood, stump; piece of bark.

tozolada, *n.f.*, **tozolón,** *n.m.* stroke *or* blow on the neck.

tozudo, -da, *a.* obstinate, stubborn, pig-headed.

tozuelo, *n.m.* (*anat.*) occiput (*animals*).

traba, *n.f.* binding, clasping; bond, tie, clasp; fetter, hobble, trammel; hindrance; wedge; ***sin trabas,*** unrestrained(ly); ***poner trabas,*** to hinder.

trabacuenta, *n.f.* slip, mistake, error (*in accounts*).

trabadero, *n.m.* pastern of a horse.

trabado, -da, *a.* thickened, inspissated; strong, robust; (*horse*) with two white fore-feet.

trabadura, *n.f.* bond, join, union, bracing.

trabajado, -da, *a.* carefully finished; elaborate; over-worked.

trabajador, -ra, *a.* industrious, hard-working; working. — *n.m.f.* worker.

trabajante, *a.* toiling, working.

trabajar, *v.t.* to work; to till; to elaborate; to train (*a horse*); to work at; to work on, to work out; to trouble, bother, prey on; to deal in; (*coll.*) do. —*v.i.* to work, labour.

trabajillo, *n.m.* small job; modest piece of work.

trabajo, *n.m.* work, labour, toil; job; task; exertion, trouble; hardship, drudgery; ***trabajo a destajo,*** piece-work; ***trabajos forzados,*** hard labour; ***tomarse el trabajo de,*** to take the trouble to; ***pasar trabajos,*** to undergo hardship, go through difficulties; ***cuesta trabajo,*** it's hard; ***dar trabajo,*** to make *or* create work; ***trabajo le mando,*** he'll have his work cut out.

trabajoso, -sa, *a.* laborious, toilsome; laboured.

trabal, *a.* clasping.

trabalenguas, *n.m. inv.* tongue-twister.

trabamiento, *n.m.* joining, uniting.

trabanco, *n.m.* piece of wood (*attached to a dog's collar*).

trabar, *v.t.* to join, clasp, brace, fasten, bind; to fetter, shackle, hobble, trammel, check; to begin, engage in, strike up; to thicken; to set (*a saw*); ***trabar amistad,*** to strike up a friendship, make friends; ***trabar batalla,*** to join battle; ***trabar conversación,*** to strike up a conversation; ***se le trabó la lengua,*** he got tongue-tied.

trabazón, *n.f.* joining, union; connection, cohesion; bond; consistency.

trabe, *n.f.* beam.

trabilla, *n.f.* strap; dropped stitch.

trabón, *n.m.* fetter.

trabuca, *n.f.* firecracker.

trabucación, *n.f.* confusion, mix-up.

trabucaire, *a.* bold, arrogant, blustering.

trabucante, *a.* confusing, muddling.

trabucar [A], *v.t.* to upset, confuse, mix up. — **trabucarse,** *v.r.* to get mixed up.

trabucazo, *n.m.* shot with a blunderbuss; report of a blunderbuss; (*coll.*) sudden shock.

trabuco, *n.m.* blunderbuss; catapult; ***trabuco naranjero,*** wide-mouthed blunderbuss; punt gun.

trabuquete, *n.m.* catapult; (*naut.*) seine.

traca, *n.f.* string of firecrackers; (*naut.*) strake.

trácala, *n.f.* (*Mex.*, *P.R.*) scheme, trick.

tracalada, *n.f.* (*Hisp. Am.*) mob.

tracalero, -ra, *a.* (*Mex.*) tricky, artful.

tracamundana, *n.f.* (*coll.*) barter; hubbub; bustle.

tracción, *n.f.* traction; drive.

tracería, *n.f.* (*arch.*) tracery.

tracio, -cia, *a.*, *n.m.f.* Thracian.

tracista, *n.m.f.* designer; schemer.

tracoma, *n.f.* trachoma.

tracto, *n.m.* stretch, lapse, space (*of time*); tract (*sung at Mass*).

tractocarril, *n.m.* car *or* train (*that can run on a road* or *on rails*).
tractor, *n.m.* tractor; traction engine; ***tractor oruga,*** caterpillar tractor.
tradición, *n.f.* tradition.
tradicional, *a.* traditional.
tradicionalismo, *n.m.* traditionalism.
tradicionalista, *n.m.f.* traditionalist.
traducción, *n.f.* translation.
traducible, *a.* translatable.
traducir [16], *v.t.* to translate; to change, convert. — **traducirse,** *v.r.* — ***en,*** to result in.
traductor, -ra, *n.m.f.* translator.
traedizo, -za, *a.* portable.
traedor, -ra, *n.m.f.* carrier, porter.
traer [34], *v.t.* to bring; to bring over, bring in; to carry, fetch; to bring about, result in; to make, keep; to wear; ***traer a mal traer*** or ***traer de cabeza,*** to treat roughly; to drive up the wall; ***traer y llevar,*** to bandy about; ***traer a colación,*** to bring up; ***traer a cuento,*** to mention; ***traer entre ojos,*** to be suspicious of; ***por la cuenta que le trae,*** for his own good, in his own interest. — **traerse,** *v.r.* ***traer(se) entre manos,*** to be currently occupied with, have going; ***algo se trae entre manos,*** he's up to sth.; ***se las trae,*** it's, he's, she's a tough proposition, to be reckoned with.
traeres, *n.m.pl.* ornaments, finery.
trafagador, *n.m.* trafficker, dealer, trader.
trafagante, *a.* trafficking, dealing, trading.
trafagar [B], *v.i.* to traffic, trade; to travel, roam; to bustle, hustle.
tráfago, *n.m.* traffic, trade; bustle, hustle, things going on.
trafagón, -gona, *a.* active, industrious. — *n.m.f.* hustler.
trafalgar, *n.m.* cotton lining.
trafalmeja(s), *a., n.m.f.* rowdy, noisy and silly (*person*).
traficación, *n.f.* traffic, trade, commerce.
traficante, *a.* trafficking, trading. — *n.m.f.* trafficker, trader.
traficar [A], *v.i.* to traffic, deal, trade; to travel, roam.
tráfico, *n.m.* commerce, trade; traffic.
trafulla, *n.f.* (*coll.*) cheating, swindling.
tragacanta, *n.f.* milk-vetch, goat's-thorn.
tragacanto, *n.m.* tragacanth.
tragacete, *n.m.* javelin, dart.
tragaderas, *n.f.pl.* gullet; ***tener buenas tragaderas,*** to be gullible.
tragadero, *n.m.* œsophagus, gullet; pit, gulf, vortex; (*naut.*) trough (*of the sea*).
tragador, -ra, *n.m.f.* glutton, gobbler.
tragahombres, *n.m. inv.* (*coll.*) bully, hector.
trágala, *n.m.* political song against absolutism; (*coll., fig.*) ***cantarle a alguien el trágala,*** to ram sth. down s.o.'s throat.
tragaldabas, *n.m. inv.* (*coll.*) glutton.
tragaleguas, *n.m. inv.* (*coll.*) great walker, brisk walker.
tragaluz, *n.f.* skylight.
tragamallas, *n.m. inv.* (*coll.*) gormandizer, glutton.
tragantada, *n.f.* big swig.
tragante, *a.* swallowing. — *n.m.* top opening (*of a furnace*).
tragantón, -tona, *a.* gluttonous. — *n.f.* (*coll.*) blow-out; swallowing.
tragar [B], *v.t.* to swallow, swallow down, gulp down; ***a ése no lo puedo tragar,*** I can't stand that fellow; ***eso no me lo trago,*** I'm not swallowing *or* having that; ***se tragó el insulto,*** he pocketed his pride; ***tragar quina,*** to lump it, grin and bear it; ***tragar aceite,*** to burn (a lot of) oil.
tragasantos, *n.m.f. inv.* (*contempt.*) Bible-puncher.
tragavenado, *n.f.* (*Ven.*) boa.
tragavirotes, *n.m. inv.* (*coll.*) 'stuffed shirt.'
tragazón, *n.f.* gluttony.
tragedia, *n.f.* tragedy.
trágico, -ca, *a.* tragic. — *n.m.f.* tragedian, tragedienne.
tragicomedia, *n.f.* tragi-comedy.
tragicómico, -ca, *a.* tragi-comical.
trago, *n.m.* swallow, gulp; drink, swig; tragus; ***a tragos,*** bit by bit; ***echar un trago,*** to have a drink; ***pasar malos tragos,*** to go through the mill.
tragón, -gona, *a.* greedy, gluttonous. — *n.m.f.* (*coll.*) greedy-guts.
tragonear, *v.t.* (*coll.*) to hog.
tragonería, *n.f.* hogging.
tragontina, *n.f.* (*bot.*) arum.
traguillo, traguito, *n.m.* short swig.
traición, *n.f.* treason, treachery, betrayal; ***a traición,*** treacherously; ***alta traición,*** high treason.
traicionar, *v.t.* to betray.
traicionero, -ra, *a.* treacherous; deceptive.
traída (1), *n.f.* carriage, bringing.
traído, -da (2), *a.* threadbare; ***traído y llevado,*** much bandied about.
traidor, -ra, *a.* treacherous, traitorous; disloyal, faithless. — *n.m.f.* traitor, traitress.
traílla, *n.f.* leash; lash; road-scraper, road-leveller.
traillar [P], *v.t.* to level (*ground*).
traína, *n.f.* seine.
trainera, *n.f.* fishing-smack; racing row-boat.
traíña, *n.f.* net.
traite, *n.m.* raising a nap (*on cloth*).
traje, *n.m.* dress; suit; lounge suit, (*Am.*) business suit; costume; ***traje de etiqueta,*** full dress *or* evening dress; ***traje de luces,*** bullfighter's garb; ***baile de trajes,*** fancy-dress ball; (*Mex.*) ***traje charro,*** showy riding costume.
trajear, *v.t.* to clothe.
trajín, *n.m.* carriage; bustle, hustle, toing and froing.
trajinante, *n.m.* carrier.
trajinar, *v.t.* to cart, transport. — *v.i.* to bustle, hustle about; to potter about.
trajinería, *n.f.* carrying, carting; bustling about.
trajinero, *n.m.* carrier.
tralla, *n.f.* cord, whip-lash.
trallazo, *n.m.* lash; crack (*of a whip*).
trama, *n.f.* weft, woof; tram (*twisted silk*); texture; plot; scheme; blossom(ing).
tramador, -ra, *a.* weaving; plotting, scheming. — *n.m.f.* weaver; plotter, schemer.
tramar, *v.t.* to weave; to plot, hatch. — *v.i.* to blossom (*of olive trees*).
tramilla, *n.f.* twine.
tramitación, *n.f.* procedure; steps, formalities, arrangements.
tramitar, *v.t.* to arrange, negotiate, put through.
trámite, *n.m.* step, arrangement, formality; procedure.
tramo, *n.m.* strip of ground; flight (*of stairs*); stretch, section (*of a canal, road etc.*); span (*of a bridge*).
tramojo, *n.m.* band (*for tying sheaf*); trouble; (*Hisp. Am.*) tether.
tramontano, -na, *a.* transmontane, ultramontane; north side. — *n.f.* north wind; (*fig.*) haughtiness; ***perder la tramontana,*** to lose one's head, lose control of o.s.
tramontar, *v.t.* to help escape, help get away. — *v.i.* to pass beyond the mountains; to sink behind the mountains (*of the sun*).
tramoya, *n.f.* stage machinery; (*fig.*) intrigue.

tramoyista, *n.m.* theatre machinist; scene-shifter; stage carpenter, stage hand; (*fig.*) schemer, intriguer.
trampa, *n.f.* trap, snare, pitfall; trap-door; flap *or* spring door; falling board (of a counter); fly (*of trousers*); bad debt; cheat; ***coger en la trampa,*** to trap; ***hacer trampas,*** to cheat; ***caer en la trampa,*** to fall into the trap; (*fig.*) ***se lo llevó la trampa,*** it all went down the drain; ***trampa adelante,*** living on borrowed money.
trampal, *n.m.* quagmire, bog.
trampantojo, *n.m.* (*coll.*) trick, deception.
trampazo, *n.m.* last twist of a cord (*in tortures*).
trampeador, -ra, *n.m.f.* borrower, swindler, sharper, cheat.
trampear, *v.i.* to live on borrowed money; to scrape by, just manage to make out, just last out. — *v.t.* to trick, deceive.
trampería, *n.f.* trickery, cheating, chicanery.
trampilla, *n.f.* peep-hole; door of a kitchen-stove; front flap of trousers.
trampista, *n.m.* cheat, swindler, card-sharper.
trampolín, *n.m.* springboard; jumping-off place.
tramposo, -sa, *a.* cheating, tricking, swindling. — *n.m.f.* cheat, swindler, trickster.
tranca, *n.f.* thick stick, club; cross-bar; (*coll.*) drunkenness; ***a trancas y barrancas,*** through hell and highwater, through thick and thin; (*coll.*) ***tener*** or ***llevar una tranca,*** to be drunk.
trancada, *n.f.* long stride; clout, wallop; ***en dos trancadas,*** in two shakes.
trancahilo, *n.m.* surgeon's knot.
trancanil, *n.m.* (*naut.*) waterway.
trancar [A], *v.t.* to bar (*a door*). — *v.i.* to stride along.
trancazo, *n.m.* clout, wallop; (*coll.*) flu.
trance, *n.m.* critical moment *or* situation; trance; (*law*) seizure; ***a todo trance,*** at all costs.
trancelín, *n.m.* hatband of gold *or* silver garnished with precious stones.
tranco, *n.m.* long stride; threshold; ***a trancos,*** in haste; ***en dos trancos,*** in two shakes.
tranchete, *n.m.* (*shoe.*) heel-knife.
trancho, *n.m.* shad.
tranquera, *n.f.* palisade; (*Hisp. Am.*) gate.
tranquero, *n.m.* angular stone (of a jamb *or* lintel).
tranquil, *n.m.* (*arch.*) plumb line.
tranquilar, *v.t.* to check off, balance (accounts).
tranquilidad, *n.f.* tranquillity, quiet, peace; calmness, reassurance, ease of mind.
tranquilizar [C], *v.t.* to tranquillize, calm, quiet, reassure; ***¡tranquilízate! ¡tranquilícese Vd!*** calm down! don't worry! put your mind at rest!
tranquilo, -la, *a.* tranquil, quiet, calm, peaceful; placid; reassured, easy in mind, at rest; ***¡tranquilo!*** calm down! take it easy!
tranquilla, *n.f.* bar; pin; lug; trap, snare, dodge.
tranquillo, *n.m.* knack, hang.
tranquillón, *n.m.* maslin.
transacción, *n.f.* transaction; accommodation, arrangement, compromise.
transalpino, -na, *a.* transalpine.
transandino, -na, *a.* trans-Andean.
transar, *v.i.* (*Hisp. Am.*) to compromise, settle.
transatlántico, -ca, *a.* transatlantic. — *n.m.* transatlantic liner.
transbordador, -ra, *a.* transhipping, transferring. — *n.m.* ferry.
transbordar, *v.t.*, *v.i.* to transfer, change.
transbordo, *n.m.* transfer, change; transhipment; ***hacer transbordo,*** to transfer, change.
transcendencia [TRASCENDENCIA].
transcendental [TRASCENDENTAL].
transcendentalismo, *n.m.* transcendentalism.
transcendente [TRASCENDENTE].
transcender [TRASCENDER].
transcribir [*p.p.* **transcri(p)to**], *v.t.* to transcribe.
transcripción, *n.f.* transcription; transcript.
transcurrir, *v.i.* to pass, elapse; to take place.
transcurso, *n.m.* lapse, course, passing (*of time*).
transeúnte, *a.* transient. — *n.m.f.* passer-by.
transferencia, *n.f.* transference, transfer.
transferible, *a.* transferable.
transferidor, -ra, *n.m.f.* transferrer.
transferir [6], *v.t.* to transfer.
transfigurable, *a.* transformable.
transfiguración, *n.f.* transfiguration.
transfigurar, *v.t.* to transfigure. — **transfigurarse,** *v.r.* to be transfigured.
transfijo, -ja, *a.* transfixed.
transfixión, *n.f.* transfixion.
transflor, *n.m.* enamel painting.
transflorar, *v.t.* to paint on metal; to copy *or* trace against the light. — *v.i.* to show through.
transflorear, *v.t.* to paint on metal.
transformable, *a.* transformable; convertible.
transformación, *n.f.* transformation.
transformador, -ra, *a.* transforming. — *n.m.f.* transformer. — *n.m.* (*elec.*) transformer; ***transformador de aceite,*** oil-cooled transformer; ***transformador de reducción,*** step-down transformer.
transformar, *v.t.* to transform. — **transformarse,** *v.r.* to be transformed, be turned into, change.
transformativo, -va, *a.* transformative.
transformista, *a.* transformistic. — *n.m.f.* transformist; (*theat.*) quick-change artist.
transfregar [B], *v.t.* to rub, scrub.
transfretano, -na, *a.* located across a strait.
transfretar, *v.t.* to cross (*the sea*). — *v.i.* to spread, extend.
tránsfuga, tránsfugo, *n.m.* deserter, fugitive, runaway, turncoat.
transfundición [TRANSFUSIÓN].
transfundir, *v.t.* to transfuse, pour (into); to transmit, spread.
transfusión, *n.f.* transfusion; transmission; (*med.*) ***transfusión de sangre,*** blood transfusion.
transfusor, *a.* transfusing. — *n.m.f.* transfuser.
transgredir [Q], *v.t. defect.* to transgress.
transgresión, *n.f.* transgression.
transgresor, -ra, *n.m.f.* transgressor, offender.
transición, *n.f.* transition.
transido, -da, *a.* overcome, overwhelmed, stricken; (*fig.*) mean, stingy.
transigencia, *n.f.* compromise, compromising; tolerance.
transigente, *a.* compromising, accommodating; broad-minded, tolerant.
transigir [E], *v.i.* to compromise; ***transigir en,*** to compromise on; ***transigir con,*** to countenance.
transistor, *n.m.* (*elec.*) transistor.
transitable, *a.* passable, practicable.
transitar, *v.i.* to go, pass, walk, journey (along *or* through).
transitivo, -va, *a.* (*gram.*) transitive; (*law*) transferable.
tránsito, *n.m.* traffic; passage, transit; transition; stopping-place; death; ***de tránsito,*** passing through, in transit; ***hacer tránsito,*** to make a stop; ***tránsito rodado,*** wheeled traffic.
transitorio, -ria, *a.* transitory.
translación [TRASLACIÓN].
translaticio, -cia [TRASLATICIO].
translimitación, *n.f.* trespass; armed intervention.
translimitar, *v.t.* to pass beyond the boundary of; to go beyond the limits of (*morality, reason etc.*).
translinear, *v.i.* (*law*) to pass from one line of heirs to another.
translucidez, *n.f.* translucence.
translúcido, -da, *a.* translucent.

transmarino, -na, *a.* transmarine.
transmigración, *n.f.* transmigration.
transmigrar, *v.i.* to transmigrate.
transminar [TRASMINAR].
transmisibilidad, *n.f.* transmissibility.
transmisible, *a.* transmissible.
transmisión, *n.f.* transmission; transference; transfer.
transmisor, -ra, *a.* transmitting. — *n.m.* transmitter.
transmitir, *v.t.* to transmit; to broadcast.
transmudación, transmudamiento, *n.m.f.* transmutation.
transmudar, *v.t.* to transfer; to change.
transmutable, *a.* transmutable, convertible.
transmutación, *n.f.* transmutation.
transmutar, *v.t.* to transmute.
transmutativo, -va, transmutatorio, -ria, *a.* transmitting.
transparencia, *n.f.* transparency.
transparentarse, *v.r.* to be transparent, show through.
transparente, *a.* transparent. — *n.m.* altar window; window-shade.
transpirable, *a.* perspirable.
transpiración, *n.f.* perspiration.
transpirar, *v.i.* to transpire, perspire.
transpirenaico, -ca, *a.* trans-Pyrenean.
transponedor, -ra, *a.* transposing. — *n.m.f.* transplanter, transposer.
transponer [25], *v.t.* to transpose; to transplant; to turn. — **transponerse,** *v.r.* to set, go down; to get sleepy, drop off to sleep.
transportable, *a.* transportable.
transportación, *n.f.* transportation, carriage, conveyance.
transportador, -ra, *a.* transporting, carrying. — *n.m.* transporter, carrier; (*geom.*) protractor; (*railw.*) ropeway.
transportamiento, *n.m.* transportation, carriage; transport, ecstasy.
transportar, *v.t.* to transport, convey; (*mus.*) to transpose. — **transportarse,** *v.r.* to fall into a transport, get carried away.
transporte, *n.m.* transport; transportation, conveyance; transport ship; fit.
transposición, *n.f.* transposition.
transpuesto, -ta, *p.p. irreg.* of TRANSPONER; ***quedarse transpuesto,*** to drop off to sleep, doze off.
transterminar, *v.t.* to transfer.
transubstanciación, *n.f.* transubstantiation.
transubstancial, *a.* transubstantial.
transubstanciar, *v.t.* to transubstantiate.
transvasar, *v.t.* to decant.
transverberación, *n.f.* transfixion.
transversal, *a.* transversal.
transverso, -sa, *a.* transverse.
tranvía, *n.m.* tram, (*Am.*) streetcar.
tranviario, -ria, tranviero, -ra, *a.* relating to tramways. — *n.m.f.* tramway employee.
tranza, *n.f.* (*law*) seizure.
tranzadera, *n.f.* knot of plaited cords *or* ribbons.
tranzar [C], *v.t.* to cut; to plait, braid.
tranzón, *n.m.* plot (*of land*).
Trapa, la, *n.f.* Trappist order.
trapa, *n.f.* tramp, tramping (*of feet*); shouting, uproar; (*naut.*) spilling line; (*pl., naut.*) relieving-tackle.
trapacear, *v.i.* to cheat, swindle.
trapacería, *n.f.* cheat, swindle; fraud, deceit.
trapacero, -ra, *a.* cheating, swindling. — *n.m.f.* cheat, swindler.
trapacete, *n.m.* daybook.
trapacista, *n.m.* cheater, sharper, deceiver.
trapajo, *n.m.* rag, tatter.
trapajoso, -sa, *a.* ragged, tattered; ***lengua trapajosa,*** thick speech.
trápala, *n.f.* stamping with the feet; galloping noise (*of a horse*); confusion; (*coll.*) deceit. — *n.m.* garrulity. — *n.m.f.* (*coll.*) prattler; cheat, humbug.
trapalear, *v.i.* to chatter, jabber; to lie, cheat; to clatter along.
trapalón, -lona, *a.* lying; cheating. — *n.m.f.* liar; cheat.
trapaza, *n.f.* fraud; trick.
trape, *n.m.* buckram.
trapecio, *n.m.* (*geom.*) trapezium; trapeze.
trapense, *n.m.* Trappist.
trapería, *n.f.* rags; rag shop.
trapero, -ra, *n.m.f.* rag-and-bone dealer; rag picker.
trapezoide, *n.m.* (*anat., geom.*) trapezoid.
trapico, *n.m.* little rag.
trapiche, *n.m.* sugar-mill; olive-press; ore-crusher.
trapichear, *v.i.* (*coll.*) to scheme, be on the fiddle; to deal retail.
trapicheo, *n.m.* (*coll.*) scheming, fiddling, shady dealing.
trapichero, -ra, *n.m.f.* shady operator.
trapiento, -ta, *a.* ragged, tattered.
trapillo, *n.m.* (*coll.*) sordid love affair; (*coll.*) nest-egg (*savings*); ***de trapillo,*** in (one's) casual clothes.
trapío, *n.m.* sails (*of a ship*); grand and spirited style.
trapisonda, *n.f.* (*coll.*) uproar, shindy; scheme, scheming; (*naut.*) white-caps.
trapisondear, *v.i.* (*coll.*) to scheme; to cause an uproar.
trapisondista, *n.m.f.* schemer, wrangler.
trapito, *n.m.* (small) rag; (*coll.*) ***trapitos de cristianar,*** Sunday best.
trapo, *n.m.* rag; cleaning rag; (*naut.*) canvas, sails; bullfighter's ***muleta***; ***a todo trapo,*** full tilt, all sails set; ***poner como un trapo,*** to haul over the coals; ***soltar el trapo,*** to burst out crying *or* laughing; ***lengua de trapo,*** thick speech; ***manos de trapo,*** butter-fingers.
traque, *n.m.* crack (*of a bursting rocket*); fuse (*of a firework*); (*coll.*) ***a traque barraque,*** at any time; for any reason.
tráquea, *n.f.* (*anat.*) trachea, windpipe.
traqueal, *a.* (*anat.*) tracheal.
traquear, *v.i.* [TRAQUETEAR].
traqueo, *n.m.* [TRAQUETEO].
traqueotomía, *n.f.* tracheotomy.
traquetear, *v.t.* to shift about; to shake up. — *v.i.* to rattle, jolt; to crackle.
traqueteo, *n.m.* rattling; jolting; crackling.
traquido, *n.m.* crack.
traquita, *n.m.* (*geol.*) trachyte.
trarigüe, *n.m.* (*Chi.*) Indian belt.
trarilongo, *n.m.* (*Chi.*) Indian head-band.
tras, *prep.* after; behind; beyond; besides; ***tras de,*** after; behind; in addition to, on top of. — *n.m.* (*coll.*) behind, backside; knock, rap.
trasalcoba, *n.f.* alcove (*off a bedroom*).
trasalpino, -na [TRANSALPINO].
trasaltar, *n.m.* altar-screen.
trasandino, -na [TRANSANDINO].
trasanteanoche, *adv.* three nights ago.
trasanteayer, *adv.* three days ago.
trasantier, *adv.* (*coll.*) three days ago.
trasañejo, -ja, *a.* three year(s) old.
trasatlántico, -ca [TRANSATLÁNTICO].
trasbordo [TRANSBORDO].
trasca, *n.f.* leather thong.
trascabo, *n.m.* leg-hold (*in wrestling*).

trascantón, *n.m.* corner curbstone; street porter; ***dar trascantón a,*** to dodge, give the slip.
trascartarse, *v.r.* to remain unplayed (*card*).
trascendencia, *n.f.* transcendency; importance, moment.
trascendental, *a.* transcendental; far-reaching, highly important.
trascendentalismo [TRANSCENDENTALISMO].
trascendente, *a.* transcendent.
trascender [2], *v.i.* to transcend; to leak out, spread; to have (wider) effects *or* consequences.
trascendido, -da, *a.* acute.
trascocina, *n.f.* back kitchen.
trascolar [4], *v.t.* to percolate, strain; (*coll.*) to pass over (*a mountain*).
trasconejarse, *v.r.* to squat (*of pursued game*); to get mislaid.
trascordarse [4], *v.r.* to forget.
trascoro, *n.m.* space behind the choir.
trascorral, *n.m.* backyard; (*coll.*) posterior.
trascribir [TRANSCRIBIR].
trascripción [TRANSCRIPCIÓN].
trascuarto, *n.m.* back room.
trascurso [TRANSCURSO].
trasdobladura, *n.f.* trebling.
trasdoblar, *v.t.* to treble.
trasdoblo, *n.m.* treble number.
trasdós, *n.m.* (*arch.*) extrados.
trasdosear, *v.t.* to strengthen the back of (*an arch*).
trasechador, *n.m.* waylayer.
trasechar, *v.t.* to waylay.
trasegar [1B], *v.t.* to turn upside down; to decant, transfer. — *v.i.* to tipple.
traseñalador, -ra, *n.m.f.* one who counter-marks.
traseñalar, *v.t.* to mark anew.
trasero, -ra, *a.* back, hind, rear. — *n.m.* behind, buttocks; (*pl.*) ancestors. — *n.f.* back (*of a house, door etc.*).
trasferidor [TRANSFERIDOR].
trasferir [TRANSFERIR].
trasfigurable [TRANSFIGURABLE].
trasfiguración [TRANSFIGURACIÓN].
trasfigurar [TRANSFIGURAR].
trasformación [TRANSFORMACIÓN].
trasformador [TRANSFORMADOR].
trasformamiento [TRANSFORMACIÓN].
trasformar [TRANSFORMAR].
trasfregar [1B], *v.t.* to rub.
trasfretano, -na [TRANSFRETANO].
trásfuga, trásfugo [TRÁNSFUGA].
trasfundición [TRANSFUNDICIÓN].
trasfundir [TRANSFUNDIR].
trasfusión [TRANSFUSIÓN].
trasgo, *n.m.* goblin, hobgoblin, sprite; (*fig.*) mischievous child.
trasgredir [Q] [TRANSGREDIR].
trasgresión [TRANSGRESIÓN].
trasgresor, -ra [TRANSGRESOR].
trasguear, *v.i.* to play the hobgoblin; to make mischief.
trashoguero, -ra, *a.* lazy, stay-at-home. — *n.m.* fireback; big log.
trashojar, *v.t.* to leaf through (*a book etc.*).
trashumancia, *n.f.* moving from winter to summer pasture *or* vice-versa.
trashumante, *a.* nomadic (*of flocks*).
trashumar, *v.t.* to move (*flocks*) from winter to summer pasture *or* vice-versa.
trasiego (1), *n.m.* upset, disorder; decanting; racking (*of wine*); moving (to and fro).
trasiego (2), **trasiegue,** *pres. indic., pres. subj.* [TRASEGAR].
trasijado, -da, *a.* lank, meagre; with sunken cheeks.
traslación, trasladación, *n.f.* moving, transfer; translation; postponement; transcription.
trasladador, -ra, *n.m.f.* mover, transferrer; translator.
trasladar, *v.t.* to move, remove, transfer; to translate; to postpone, adjourn; to copy.
traslado, *n.m.* moving, removal, transfer; copy, transcript; likeness; (*law*) notification.
traslapar, *v.t.* to superpose, overlap.
traslapo, *n.m.* overlapping.
traslaticio, -cia, *a.* metaphorical, figurative.
traslativo, -va, *a.* transferring, conveying.
traslato, -ta, *a.* metaphorical, figurative.
trasloar, *v.t.* to praise fulsomely.
traslucidez [TRANSLUCIDEZ].
traslúcido, -da [TRANSLÚCIDO].
trasluciente [TRANSLÚCIDO].
traslucirse [9], *v.r.* to shine *or* show through; to be revealed, plain to see; to leak out.
traslumbramiento, *n.m.* dazzling, dazzlement.
traslumbrar, *v.t.* to dazzle. — **traslumbrarse,** *v.r.* to pass swiftly; to vanish; to be dazzled.
trasluz, *n.m.* diffused *or* reflected light; ***al trasluz,*** against the light.
trasmallo, *n.m.* trammel net; hammer-handle; iron collar (*round a hammer head*).
trasmano, *n.m.* second player (*at cards*); ***a trasmano,*** out of the way, off the beaten track.
trasmañana, *n.f.* day after tomorrow.
trasmañanar, *v.t.* to put off.
trasmarino, -na [TRANSMARINO].
trasmatar, *v.t.* (*coll.*) to wish dead.
trasmigración [TRANSMIGRACIÓN].
trasmigrar [TRANSMIGRAR].
trasminar, *v.t.* to undermine; to penetrate, percolate.
trasmisible [TRANSMISIBLE].
trasmisión [TRANSMISIÓN].
trasmontar, *v.t.* to pass beyond.
trasmosto, *n.f.* wine of low quality.
trasmudar [TRANSMUDAR].
trasmutable [TRANSMUTABLE].
trasmutación [TRANSMUTACIÓN].
trasmutar [TRANSMUTAR].
trasmutativo, -va, trasmutatorio, -ria [TRANSMUTATIVO].
trasnochada (1), *n.f.* last night; sleeplessness; sleepless night; night attack.
trasnochado, -da (2), *a.* out-dated, out-moded, old-fashioned; stale; pale and wan.
trasnochador, -ra, *n.m.f.* one who stays up late, night bird.
trasnochar, *v.i.* to stay up late; to turn night into day; to sleep out.
trasnoche, trasnocho, *n.m.* staying up late.
trasnombrar, *v.t.* to mix up the name of.
trasoír [22], *v.t.* to misunderstand, mistake.
trasojado, -da, *a.* having sunken eyes.
trasoñar [4], *v.t.* to imagine wrongly, get all wrong.
trasovado, -da, *a.* (*bot.*) obovate.
traspalar, *v.t.* to remove with a shovel; to hoe, weed.
traspaleo, *n.m.* shovelling; hoeing, weeding.
traspapelarse, *v.r.* to get mislaid.
trasparencia [TRANSPARENCIA].
trasparentarse [TRANSPARENTARSE].
trasparente [TRANSPARENTE].
traspasador, -ra, *n.m.f.* trespasser, transgressor.
traspasamiento [TRASPASO].
traspasar, *v.t.* to transfer; to cross, go over, go beyond; to transfix, pierce; to transgress.
traspaso, *n.m.* transfer; crossing; transfixing piercing; transgressing; key money, payment for fittings and fixtures.

traspatio, *n.m.* (*Hisp. Am.*) backyard.
traspecho, *n.m.* bone ornament on a crossbow.
traspeinar, *v.t.* to touch up (*the hair with a comb*).
traspellar, *v.t.* to shut, close.
traspié, *n.m.* leg-hold (*in wrestling*); stumble, slip; ***dar traspiés,*** to slip; (*fig.*) to slip up.
traspillar, *v.t.* to close, shut. — **traspillarse,** *v.r.* to grow thin, become emaciated.
traspintar, *v.t.* to show one card and play another. — **traspintarse,** *v.r.* to show through; (*coll.*) to turn out contrary to one's expectations.
traspiración [TRANSPIRACIÓN].
traspirar [TRANSPIRAR].
trasplantar, *v.t.* to transplant. — **trasplantarse,** *v.r.* (*fig.*) to migrate.
trasplante, *n.m.* transplantation; migration; (*med.*) ***trasplante de corazón,*** heart transplant.
trasponer [25] [TRANSPONER].
traspontín, trasportín, *n.m.* under-mattress; (*motor.*) tip-seat; (*coll.*) buttocks.
trasportación [TRANSPORTACIÓN].
trasportamiento [TRANSPORTAMIENTO].
trasportar [TRANSPORTAR].
trasporte [TRANSPORTE].
trasposición [TRANSPOSICIÓN].
traspuesta (1), *n.f.* transport, removal; corner, nook, turning; concealment; disappearance, flight; lurking-place; back court, backyard, back-door; rear outbuilding.
traspuesto, -ta (2) [TRANSPUESTO].
traspunte, *n.m.* prompter.
traspuntín [TRASPONTÍN].
trasquero, *n.m.* leather-cutter.
trasquiladero, *n.m.* sheep-shearing place.
trasquilador, *n.m.* shearer.
trasquiladura, *n.f.* shearing, clipping, cropping; (*coll.*) botched haircut.
trasquilar, *v.t.* to shear (*sheep*); to snip, cut the hair irregularly; (*fig.*) to curtail, clip; to diminish.
trasquilimocho, -cha, *a.* (*coll.*) close-cropped.
trasquilón, *n.m.* cut of the shears; clipping, shearing; (*coll.*) money lost through trickery; ***a trasquilones,*** irregularly.
trastabillar, *v.i.* to reel; to waver; to stammer.
trastada, *n.f.* (*coll.*) bad turn, dirty trick.
trastazo, *n.m.* (*coll.*) blow, thump, hard whack.
traste, *n.m.* (*mus.*) fret (*of a guitar*); wine sampling glass; (*Hisp. Am.*) rubbish; ***dar al traste con,*** to scotch, demolish, explode, wreck; ruin, put paid to; to exhaust; (*pl.*) (*Hisp. Am.*) dishes.
trasteado, *n.m.* (*mus.*) set of stops *or* frets (*of a guitar etc.*).
trasteador, -ra, *a.* moving (things) around. — *n.m.f.* rummager.
trastear, *v.t.* to fret (*a guitar*); to play (*a guitar*); (*tauro.*) to wave the ***muleta*** at; (*coll.*) to manipulate (*people* or *things*). — *v.i.* to rummage about; to talk lively.
trastejador, *n.m.* roof tiler.
trastejar, *v.t.* to tile; to repair, overhaul.
trastejo, *n.m.* tiling; bustle.
trasteo, *n.m.* playing (*a bull*); tactful management (*of a person* or *business*).
trastería, *n.f.* heap of lumber; (*coll.*) dirty trick.
trastero, -ra, *a.* (of *or* for) lumber, furniture *or* other items not in use. — *n.m.* lumber(room).
trastesado, -da, *a.* stiff, hardened.
trastesón, *n.m.* superabundance of milk (*in cow's udder*).
trastienda, *n.f.* back-room (*of a shop*); (*fig.*) canniness, shrewdness.
trasto, *n.m.* piece of furniture; utensil, implement, tool, weapon, piece of tackle *or* equipment; piece of junk *or* lumber; (*theat.*) set-piece, trick-piece; (*coll.*) good-for-nothing; tricky customer; ***tirarse los trastos a la cabeza,*** to have a set-to *or* row.
trastornable, *a.* easily upset.
trastornador, -ra, *a.* upsetting.
trastornadura, *n.f.,* **trastornamiento,** *n.m.* upsetting.
trastornar, *v.t.* to upset, mess up, make topsy-turvy; to put in a daze, put in a crazed state; (*coll.*) ***le tiene trastornado,*** she's got him so that he doesn't know whether he's coming or going.
trastorno, *n.m.* upset, upheaval, mess-up, topsy-turvy state; disorder, trouble.
trastrabado, -da, *a.* having the far hind-foot and the near fore-foot white (*horse*).
trastrabarse, *v.r.* to become tied up.
trastrabillar, *v.i.* to stumble, to reel; to waver, hesitate; to stammer.
trastrás, *n.m.* last but one.
trastrocamiento, *n.m.* switching round.
trastrocar [4A], *v.t.* to switch round.
trastrueco, trastrueque, *n.m.* switching round.
trastulo, *n.m.* toy.
trastumbar, *v.t.* to drop; to upset.
trasudar, *v.i.* to sweat (gently).
trasudor, *n.m.* gentle sweat.
trasuntar, *v.t.* to copy; to abridge.
trasunto, *n.m.* copy, transcript; likeness, image.
trasvenarse, *v.r.* to be forced from the veins; to be spilled (*of blood*).
trasver [35], *v.t.* to see through, glimpse; to see erroneously.
trasversal [TRANSVERSAL].
trasverso, -sa [TRANSVERSO].
trasverter [2], *v.i.* to overflow, run over.
trasvinarse, *v.r.* to leak out (*of wine*); to be inferred, surmised.
trasvolar [4], *v.t.* to fly across.
trata, *n.f.* slave-trade; ***trata de blancas,*** white slavery.
tratable, *a.* tractable; approachable.
tratadista, *n.m.f.* author of treatises.
tratado, *n.m.* treaty; agreement; treatise.
tratador, -ra, *n.m.f.* mediator.
tratamiento, *n.m.* treatment; title; ***apear el tratamiento,*** to drop the title, cut the formality.
tratante, *n.m.* dealer, trader.
tratar, *v.t.* to treat; to deal with, discuss; ***tratar de tú,*** to be on first-name terms with; ***tratar de usted,*** to treat formally. — *v.i.* to deal (with); to try (to); ***¿de qué trata el libro?*** what's the book about? — **tratarse,** *v.r.* to deal; to behave, conduct o.s.; to live (*well* or *badly*); ***¿de qué se trata?*** what's it all about?; ***no me trato con,*** I'm not on speaking terms with.
trato, *n.m.* treatment; manner; deal; address; title, style; ***malos tratos,*** ill treatment; ***tener buen trato,*** to be well-mannered, pleasant; ***¡trato hecho!*** it's a deal; ***cerrar un trato,*** to clinch a deal; ***trato de gentes,*** ability to get on with people.
traumático, -ca, *a.* traumatic.
traumatismo, *n.m.* traumatism.
traumatizar, *v.t.* to traumatize, subject to a traumatic experience.
traumatología, *n.f.* traumatology.
traversa, *n.f.* (*naut.*) back-stay.
través, *n.m.* slant; (*arch.*) cross-beam; (*fort.*) traverse, screen; ***de través,*** crosswise, askew; ***mirar de través,*** to look askance; ***a través de,*** across, through; ***por el través,*** on the beam.
travesaño, *n.m.* cross-beam, transom, traverse, cross-bar, cross-piece; bolster (*of a bed*).
travesar [1], *v.t.* to cross.
travesear, *v.i.* to jest, joke; to be quick at repartee; to lead a vicious life; to skip, caper, frisk, romp; to be mischievous.

travesero, -ra, cross, transverse. — *n.m.* bolster (*of a bed*).
travesío, -sía, *a.* traversing; transverse, oblique (*wind*). — *n.m.* crossroad, crossing. — *n.f.* crossroad, cross street; crosswise position; crossing; (*fort.*) traverse works; (*naut.*) side-wind; sailor's pay for a voyage; (*Arg.*) waste land.
travestido, -da, *a.* disguised.
travesura, *n.f.* piece of mischief *or* naughtiness; mischievous trick, prank *or* escapade.
travieso, -sa, *a.* cross, transverse; naughty, mischievous. — *n.f.* distance across; (*railw.*) sleeper, cross-tie; (*arch.*) rafter; transverse wall; (*min.*) cross level *or* gallery.
trayecto, *n.m.* stretch; stage, fare stage; route.
trayectoria, *n.f.* trajectory; course, path.
trayente, *a.* bringing, carrying, conducting.
traza, *n.f.* design; scheme; means, way; look, mark, sign; (*geom.*) trace; ***darse trazas,*** to find a way, manage; ***llevar*** or ***tener trazas de,*** to look like, show signs of; ***por las trazas,*** by the looks of it, him etc.
trazado, *n.m.* plan, design, outline, layout.
trazador, -ra, *n.m.f.* planner, designer.
trazar [C], *v.t.* to plan, design, draw, outline, mark out, map out, lay out; to trace.
trazo, *n.m.* outline; line, stroke; (*art*) fold (*of drapery*); ***al trazo,*** drawn in outline.
trazumarse, *v.r.* to ooze.
trébedes, *n.m.f.pl.* trivet, tripod.
trebejo, *n.m.* toy, plaything; chess piece; (*pl.*) implements, tools.
trébol, *n.m.* (*bot.*) trefoil, clover, shamrock.
trece, *a.* thirteenth. — *n.m.* thirteen; ***seguir en sus trece,*** to dig one's heels in, refuse to budge, be adamant.
trecemesino, -na, *a.* of thirteen months.
trecenario, *n.m.* (space of) thirteen days.
treceno, -na, *a.* thirteenth.
trecésimo, -ma, *a.* thirtieth.
trecientos, -tas, *a.*, *n.m.f.* three hundred.
trechear, *v.t.* to pass from hand to hand.
trechel, *a.* spring (wheat).
trecho, *n.m.* stretch; ***un buen trecho,*** a good stretch *or* way, a long pull; ***a trechos, de trecho en trecho,*** here and there, at intervals, now and again; ***del dicho al hecho, hay gran trecho,*** sooner said than done.
tredécimo, -ma, *a.* thirteenth.
trefe, *a.* lean, thin; spurious.
tregua, *n.f.* truce; respite, let-up.
treinta, *a.*, *n.m.f.* thirty, thirtieth.
treintanario, *n.m.* (space of) thirty days.
treintañal, *a.* containing thirty years.
treintavo, -va, *a.* thirtieth.
treinteno, -na, *a.* thirtieth. — *n.f.* (some) thirty.
treja, *n.f.* cushion shot (*at billiards*).
tremebundo, -da, *a.* dreadful, fearful; (*coll.*) terrific.
tremedal, *n.m.* marsh, morass, quagmire.
tremendismo, *n.m.* sordidly *or* shockingly realistic literary style.
tremendo, -da, *a.* tremendous; fearful; (*coll.*) terrific.
tremente, *a.* trembling.
trementina, *n.f.* turpentine.
tremés, tremesino, -na, *a.* three-month-old.
tremielga, *n.f.* electric ray, torpedo.
tremó, tremol, *n.m.* frame (*of a wall-mirror*).
tremolante, *a.* waving, fluttering.
tremolar, *v.t.* to wave. — *v.i.* to flutter.
tremolina, *n.f.* rustling (*of the wind*); (*coll.*) hubbub, stir.
trémolo, *n.m.* tremolo.
tremor, *n.m.* trembling, tremor.
tremulante, tremulento, -ta, trémulo, -la, *a.* tremulous, trembling, quivering, shaking.
tren, *n.m.* train; outfit, gear; show, ostentation; (*sport*) speed, fury; ***a todo tren,*** expense no object; ***tren de recreo,*** excursion train; ***tren ascendente,*** up train; ***tren descendente,*** down train; ***tren correo,*** mail train; ***tren de carga*** or ***de mercancías,*** goods train; (*aer.*) ***tren de aterrizaje,*** undercarriage; ***tren de montaje,*** assembly line; ***tren de vida,*** pace of life, rate of spending; ***jefe de tren,*** guard, (*Am.*) brakeman.
trena, *n.f.* sash, scarf; (*sl.*) clink, nick; burnt silver; (*prov.*) twist bread.
trenado, -da, *a.* reticulated, mesh.
trenca, *n.f.* cross-tree (*in a beehive*); main root (*of a vine*); trench coat.
trencica, trencilla, trencita, *n.f.* braid, plait.
trencillar, *v.t.* to ornament with braid.
trencillo, *n.m.* jewelled hat-band of gold *or* silver.
treno, *n.m.* threnody, dirge.
trenque, *n.m.* (*prov.*) wall, dyke.
trenza, *n.f.* plait, braid; braided hair, tresses; plaited silk.
trenzadera, *n.f.* tape; knot of plaited cord.
trenzado, *n.m.* braided hair; caper (*in dance*); prance (*horse*).
trenzar [C], *v.t.* to braid, plait, tress. — *v.i.* to caper (*in dance*); to prance (*horse*).
treo, *n.m.* cross-jack sail.
trepa, *n.f.* climbing; perforating, boring, drilling; trimming *or* edging of clothes; grain *or* flake of polished wood; (*coll.*) flogging, beating; (*coll.*) fraud, artful trick; somersault.
trepado (1), **-da,** *a.* strong, robust (*animals*).
trepado (2), *n.m.* trimming *or* edging of clothes; perforation.
trepador, -ra, *a.* climbing, creeping. — *n.m.* climbing place. — *n.f.* climber.
trepajuncos, *n.m. inv.* (*orn.*) marsh warbler.
trepanar, *v.t.* to trepan, trephine.
trépano, *n.m.* trepan, trephine.
trepante, *a.* climbing; artful, crafty.
trepar, *v.t.* to bore, perforate; to put a wavy edging *or* trimming on. — *v.i.* to climb, clamber up.
trepatroncos, *n.m. inv.* (*orn.*) blue tit.
trepe, *n.m.* (*coll.*) reprimand, scolding.
trepidación, *n.f.* vibration, throbbing.
trepidar, *v.i.* to vibrate, throb.
tres, *a.* three, third. — *n.m.* three; third; trey (*cards*); ***como tres y dos son cinco,*** as sure as twice two are four. — *n.f.pl.* (**las tres**), three o'clock.
tresañal, tresañejo, -ja, *a.* three-year-old.
tresbolillo, (**al**), *adv.* (*agriculture*) quincunx; staggered.
trescientos, -tas, *a.*, *n.m.f.* three hundred.
tresdoblar, *v.t.* to triple, treble; to fold three times.
tresdoble, *n.m.* threefold.
tresillista, *n.m.f.* ombre player.
tresillo, *n.m.* ombre; (*mus.*) triplet; three-piece suite; three-stone ring.
tresmesino, -na [TREMESINO].
tresnal, *n.m.* stook.
trestanto, *adv.* three times as much. — *n.m.* triple amount *or* number.
treta, *n.f.* (*fenc.*) feint; trick, wile.
trezavo, -va, *a.* thirteenth.
tría, *n.f.* sorting out; tease (*in cloth*).
triaca, *n.f.* theriac; antidote.
triacal, *a.* theriacal.
triache, *n.m.* refuse (*of coffee beans*).
triangulación, *n.f.* triangulation.
triangulado, -da, triangular, *a.* triangular.
triángulo, -la, *a.* triangular. — *n.m.* triangle.

triar [L], *v.t.* to sort out. — *v.i.* to swarm in and out (*bees*). — **triarse,** *v.r.* to show teases (*cloth*).
tribu, *n.f.* tribe.
tribuente, *a.* attributing.
tribulación, *n.f.* tribulation.
tríbulo, *n.m.* (*bot.*) caltrop.
tribuna, *n.f.* tribune; platform, rostrum; gallery; grandstand; parliament, political life.
tribunado, *n.m.* tribuneship.
tribunal, *n.m.* tribunal; court (*of justice*); board (*of examiners*); ***tribunal tutelar de menores,*** juvenile court.
tribunicio, -cia, tribúnico, -ca, *a.* tribunitial.
tribuno, *n.m.* tribune; political orator.
tributación, *n.f.* tribute; contribution; (system of) taxation.
tributante, *n.m.* taxpayer.
tributar, *v.t.* to pay (*as tribute* or *tax*).
tributario, -ria, *a.* tributary; (of) tax.
tributo, *n.m.* tribute; tax.
tricahue, *n.m.* (*Chi., orn.*) large parrot.
tricenal, *a.* thirty year.
tricentésimo, -ma, *a.* three hundredth.
tricésimo, -ma, *a.* thirtieth.
triciclo, *n.m.* tricycle.
tricípite, *a.* three-headed.
tricolor, *a.* tri-coloured.
tricorne, *a.* three-horned.
tricornio, *n.m.* three-cornered hat.
tricotomía, *n.f.* trichotomy.
tridente, *a., n.m.* trident.
triduano, -na, *a.* tertian; three-day.
trienal, *a.* triennial.
trienio, *n.m.* triennium.
trieñal [TRIENAL].
trifásico, -ca, *a.* (*elec.*) three-phase.
trífido, -da, *a.* (*bot.*) trifid.
trifinio, *n.m.* meeting-place of three boundaries.
trifolio, *n.m.* (*bot.*) trifolium, clover.
triforme, *a.* triform.
trifulca, *n.f.* three levers for moving the bellows (*in a foundry*); (*coll.*) squabble, row.
trifurcado, -da, *a.* trifurcate.
triga, *n.f.* a three-horse cart; three horses in line.
trigal, *n.m.* wheat-field.
trigaza, *n.f.* short straw (*of wheat*).
trigémino, -na, *a.* trigeminal, trigeminous. — *n.m.* (*anat.*) terminal nerve.
trigésimo, -ma, *a.* thirtieth.
trigla, *n.f.* red mullet.
triglifo, *n.m.* triglyph.
trigo, *n.m.* (*bot.*) wheat; ***trigo alonso,*** bearded wheat; ***trigo candeal,*** summer wheat; ***trigo chamorro,*** winter wheat; ***trigo fanfarrón,*** Barbary wheat; (*pl.*) crops, cornfields.
trígono, *n.m.* (*astron.*) trigon; (*geom.*) triangle.
trigonometría, *n.f.* trigonometry.
trigonométrico, -ca, *a.* trigonometrical.
trigueño, -ña, *a.* (of) wheat colour; of light brown complexion.
triguero, -ra, *a.* wheaten, wheat-growing; growing among wheat. — *n.m.* sieve for corn; corn-merchant, grain-dealer; (*orn.*) fallow-finch. — *n.f.* Triticum.
trilátero, -ra, *a.* trilateral.
trile, *n.m.* (*Chi.*) blackbird with yellow markings (*Agelæus thilius*).
trilingüe, *a.* trilingual.
trilítero, -ra, *a.* triliteral.
trilogía, *n.f.* trilogy.
trilla, *n.f.* (*agric.*) threshing, threshing time; (*agric.*) spike-tooth harrow; (*ichth.*) red mullet.
trilladera, *n.f.* spike-tooth harrow.
trillado, -da, *a.* threshed, beaten; trite, stale, hackneyed; ***camino trillado,*** beaten track, common run.
trillador, *n.m.* thresher.
trilladora, *n.f.* threshing machine; ***trilladora segadora,*** combine harvester.
trilladura, *n.f.* threshing.
trillar, *v.t.* to thresh, tread out (*corn*), beat; to frequent, to repeat.
trillo, *n.m.* threshing harrow, threshing-machine; (*Hisp. Am.*) path.
trillón, *n.m.* (*British*) trillion; (*Am.*) quintillion.
trimestral, *a.* trimestral, trimensual, quarterly.
trimestre, *n.m.* term, quarter, space of three months; quarterly payment.
trimielga, *n.f.* (*ichth.*) electric ray, torpedo.
trimotor, *n.m.* three-engined aeroplane.
trinado, *n.m.* trill; twittering, warble.
trinar, *v.i.* to trill, quaver, warble; to twitter; (*coll.*) to get angry, be beside o.s.
trinca, *n.f.* group of three; (*naut.*) rope, cable; (*naut.*) lashing; (*coll.*) gang; (*naut.*) ***estar a la trinca,*** to lie to.
trincadura, *n.f.* large two-masted barge.
trincafía, *n.f.* (*naut.*) marline, woolding.
trincar [A], *v.t.* to break, chop; to skip, leap; to tie, bind, lash; (*naut.*) to fasten, gammon; (*coll.*) to pinch. — *v.i.* (*naut.*) to lie to; (*coll.*) to drink (liquor).
trincha, *n.f.* strap for buckling garments.
trinchador, -ra, *a.* carving. — *n.m.f.* carver.
trinchante, *a.* carving. — *n.m.* carver; carving-knife, (*Am.*) butcher's knife; stone-cutter's hammer.
trinchar, *v.t.* to carve.
trinche, *n.m.* (*Hisp. Am.*) table fork; (*Hisp. Am.*) sideboard.
trinchera, *n.f.* trench, entrenchment; deep cut, ditch; trench coat; ***abrir trincheras,*** to begin a siege.
trinchero, *n.m.* trencher; sideboard.
trincherón, *n.m.* large trench *or* ditch.
trinchete, *n.m.* paring-knife.
trineo, *n.m.* sledge, sled, sleigh, toboggan.
Trini, *n.f.* affectionate form of Trinidad.
Trinidad, *n.f.* Trinity.
trinitaria (1), *n.f.* (*bot.*) heartsease, pansy.
trinitario, -ria (2), *a., n.m.f.* Trinitarian.
trino, -na, *a.* triadic, trinal, trine. — *n.m.* (*astron.*) trine; (*mus.*) trill.
trinomio, *n.m.* trinomial.
trinquetada, *n.f.* sailing under foresail.
trinquete, *n.m.* foresail; foremast; main yard (*of the foremast*); (*mech.*) catch, pawl; (game of) squash; ***a cada trinquete,*** at every step.
trinquetilla, *n.f.* fore staysail.
trinquis, *n.m.* (*coll.*) drink.
trío, *n.m.* trio.
trióxido, *n.m.* trioxide.
tripa, *n.f.* gut, intestine, bowel; (*coll.*) belly; (sausage) skin; (cigar) filler; ***echar tripa,*** to get paunchy; ***hacer de tripas corazón,*** to pluck up courage; ***me revuelve las tripas,*** it turns my stomach up; ***tener malas tripas,*** to be hard-hearted.
tripada, *n.f.* (*coll.*) bellyful.
tripartir, *v.t.* to divide into three parts.
tripartito, -ta, *a.* tripartite.
tripe, *n.m.* shag (*cloth*).
tripería, *n.f.* tripe-shop.
tripero, -ra, *n.m.f.* tripe-seller. — *n.m.* belly-band.
tripicallero, -ra, *n.m.f.* (street) tripe-seller.
tripicallos, *n.m.pl.* tripe.
triplano, *n.m.* (*aer.*) triplane.
triple, *a.* triple, treble.

tríplica, *n.m.* (*law*) rejoinder.
triplicación, *n.f.* multiplication by three.
triplicado, -da, *a.* triplicate.
triplicar [A], *v.t.* to triple, treble; (*law*) to rejoin.
tríplice, *a.* triple, treble.
triplo, -la, *a.* triple, treble, triplicate.
trípode, *n.m.* tripod, trivet.
trípol, trípoli, *n.m.* tripoli, rottenstone.
tripolio, *n.m.* sea starwort.
tripón, -pona, *a.* (*coll.*) big-bellied, pot-bellied.
tríptico, *n.m.* triptych; document *or* book containing three folios.
triptongo, *n.m.* triphthong.
tripudiar, *v.i.* to dance.
tripudio, *n.m.* dance.
tripudo, -da, *a.* big-bellied.
tripulación, *n.f.* (*naut.*, *aer.*) crew.
tripulante, *n.m.* member of crew (*ship, aircraft*).
tripular, *v.t.* to man, crew; to fit out, equip.
trique, *n.m.* sharp noise, crack; (*Chi.*) medicinal plant.
triquete, *n.m.* (*fig.*) ***a cada triquete,*** at every step.
triquina, *n.f.* (*zool.*) trichina.
triquinosis, *n.f. inv.* trichinosis.
triquiñuela, *n.f.* (*coll.*) trick, wile, underhand game.
triquitraque, *n.m.* crack; clattering; firecracker.
trirreme, *n.m.* trireme.
tris, *n.m.* clink (*of breaking glass*); ace, hairbreadth; ***en un tris,*** within an ace, very nearly; ***tris tras,*** tedious repetition.
trisa, *n.f.* shad.
trisca, *n.f.* noise made by stamping the feet on nuts etc.; fun, uproar, merriment.
triscador, -ra, *a.* noisy, frisky. — *n.m.* saw set.
triscar [A], *v.t.* to mingle, mix; to set the teeth of a saw. — *v.i.* to stamp the feet; (*fig.*) to frisk, caper, frolic, romp about.
trisecar, *v.t.* to trisect.
trisección, *n.f.* trisection.
trisemanal, *a.* thrice weekly.
trisílabo, -ba, *a.* trisyllabic.
trismo, *n.m.* lockjaw.
trispasto, *n.m.* three-pulley tackle.
triste, *a.* sad, depressed, miserable; dismal, gloomy; mean, low; sorry (*figure*).
tristeza, *n.f.* sadness, depression; grief, sorrow.
tristón, -tona, *a.* saddish, rather sad; dull, dreary.
tristura [TRISTEZA].
trisulco, -ca, *a.* (*poet.*) three-pronged.
tritíceo, -ea, *a.* wheaten.
trítono, *n.m.* (*mus.*) minor third.
triturable, *a.* triturable, crushable.
trituración, *n.f.* trituration, crushing.
triturador, -ra, *a.* crushing. — *n.m.f.* crusher. — *n.f.* crushing machine.
triturar, *v.t.* to triturate, crush, mash, grind; to masticate; (*fig.*) to tear to pieces.
triunfador, -ra, *a.* triumphing, winning. — *n.m.f.* victor, winner, triumpher.
triunfal, *a.* triumphal.
triunfalismo, *n.m.* (*pol.*) 'everything-in-the-garden-is-lovely' attitude, 'you've-never-had-it-so-good' attitude, 'what-more-could-one-possibly-want?' attitude.
triunfante, *a.* triumphant, victorious, conquering.
triunfar, *v.i.* to triumph; to win the day; to conquer; to trump at cards.
triunfo, *n.m.* triumph, victory, conquest; spoils of war; trump card.
triunvirato, *n.m.* triumvirate.
triunviro, *n.m.* triumvir.
trivial, *a.* hackneyed, commonplace, trite; (pertaining to the) trivium.
trivialidad, *n.f.* trivialness, triviality; triteness.
trivio, *n.m.* (three-way) fork of a road; trivium.
triza, *n.f.* mite, bit, scrap, shred; (*naut.*) cord, rope; ***hacer trizas,*** to smash to smithereens.
trocable, *a.* changeable, exchangeable.
trocado, -da, *a.* changed, permuted; ***a la trocada,*** in exchange, in the contrary sense. — *n.m.* change, small coin. — *p.p.* [TROCAR].
trocador, -ra, *n.m.f.* exchanger, barterer; changer, alterer.
trocaico, -ca, *a.* trochaic.
trocamiento, *n.m.* change; exchange, barter.
trocante, *a.* bartering, exchanging; changing, altering.
trocar [4A], *v.t.* to exchange, barter; to change; to switch, switch over *or* round.
trocatinta, *n.f.* (*coll.*) confusing mistake.
trocear, *v.t.* to cut up in pieces.
troceo, *n.m.* cutting up in pieces.
trocisco, *n.m.* troche, lozenge.
trocla, *n.f.* pulley.
troco, *n.m.* (*ichth.*) sun-fish.
trocha, *n.f.* cross-path, narrow path, trail; (*Arg.*) gauge.
trochemoche, (a), *adv.* helter-skelter, pell-mell.
trofeo, *n.m.* trophy; spoils of war; military insignia.
troglodita, *n.m.f.* troglodyte, cave-dweller; (*fig.*) hog.
troj, troje, *n.m.* granary, barn.
trojero, *n.m.* granary-keeper.
trojezado, -da, *a.* shredded, minced.
trola, *n.f.* (*coll.*) fib.
trole, *n.m.* trolley.
trolebús, *n.m.* trolleybus.
tromba, *n.f.* waterspout; rush.
trombón, *n.m.* trombone; trombone player.
trombosis, *n.f. inv.* thrombosis.
trompa, *n.m.* horn player. — *n.f.* horn; (elephant's) trunk; proboscis; humming top; projecting arch; (*metal.*) trompe; ***trompa de Eustaquio,*** Eustachian tube; ***trompa de Falopio,*** Fallopian tube; ***trompa marina,*** trumpet marine; (*coll.*) ***estar trompa,*** to be sozzled.
trompada, *n.f.*, **trompazo,** *n.m.* (*coll.*) wallop, clout; bump, collision.
trompar, trompear, *v.i.* to spin a top.
trompero, -ra, *a.* deceitful. — *n.m.f.* top maker *or* seller.
trompeta, *n.f.* trumpet; bugle. — *n.m.* trumpeter, bugler; (*coll.*) noodle, nit.
trompetada, *n.f.* (*coll.*) foolish remark.
trompetazo, *n.m.* trumpet blast; wallop.
trompetear, *v.i.* (*coll.*) to sound the trumpet.
trompeteo, *n.m.* sounding the trumpet.
trompetería, *n.f.* trumpetry; trumpets.
trompetero, *n.m.* trumpeter.
trompetilla, *n.f.* small trumpet; ear-trumpet; (*ent.*) proboscis.
trompicar [A], *v.t.* to trip, trip up; (*coll.*) to promote over another. — *v.i.* to trip, trip up.
trompicón, *n.m.*, **trompilladura,** *n.f.* stumbling; stumble; ***a trompicones,*** stumblingly; by fits and starts.
trompillo, *n.m.* (*Hisp. Am., bot.*) bixa tree.
trompis, *n.m. inv.* (*coll.*) blow with the fist.
trompo, *n.m.* top; chessman; trochid; ***ponerse como un trompo,*** to eat *or* drink o.s. silly.
trompón, *n.m.* large top; bump, collision; daffodil; ***de trompón,*** in a disorderly way, helter-skelter.
tronado, -da, *a.* (*coll.*) worn-out; broke, skint. — *n.f.* thunderstorm.
tronador, -ra, *a.* thundering.
tronante, *a.* thundering.
tronar [4], *v.i.* to thunder; (*coll.*) to go broke *or* bust; ***tronar con,*** to break with; ***por lo que pueda tronar,*** just in case. — *v. impers.* to thunder.

tronca, *n.f.* truncation.
troncal, *a.* (relating to the) trunk; basic.
troncar [A], *v.t.* [TRUNCAR].
tronco, *n.m.* trunk; log; stem; stock; team (*of two horses*); (*geom.*) frustum; (*coll.*) fathead, sap; (*coll.*) ***estar hecho un tronco,*** to be knocked out; to be fast asleep.
tronchado, -da, *a.* (*her.*) having a diagonal bar.
tronchar, *v.t.* to split, break off; to cut short, cut down; to fag out. — **troncharse,** *v.r.* to split, fall down; (*coll.*) to tire o.s. out; ***troncharse de risa,*** to split one's sides laughing.
tronchazo, *n.m.* large stalk; blow with a stalk.
troncho, *n.m.* stalk, stem.
tronchudo, -da, *a.* stalky, having a long stalk *or* stem.
tronera, *n.f.* (*naut.*) loophole; porthole; (*fort.*) embrasure; dormer, small skylight; opening; pocket-hole in a billiards table; squib, cracker.
tronero, *n.m.* rake, mad-cap fellow.
tronerar, *v.t.* to make embrasures in.
tronga, *n.f.* (*vulg.*) concubine, mistress.
trónica, *n.f.* (*coll.*) gossip.
tronido, *n.m.* thunder, loud report.
tronío, *n.m.* (*coll., prov.*) show, ostentation.
tronitoso, -sa, *a.* (*coll.*) resounding, thundering.
trono, *n.m.* throne; (*eccles.*) shrine; (*pl.*) thrones (*third choir of angels*).
tronquista, *n.m.* coachman driving a pair.
tronzador, *n.m.* two-handed saw; crosscut saw; mechanical saw.
tronzar [C], *v.t.* to shatter, break to pieces; to crosscut; to wear out; (*sew.*) to pleat.
tronzo, -za, *a.* with cropped ears (*horses*).
tropa, *n.f.* troops, soldiers, men; mob, crowd; (*Hisp. Am.*) drove of cattle; (*Arg.*) fleet of carts *or* wagons; ***de tropa,*** in the army, in the ranks.
tropel, *n.m.* rush, stampede, mob; ***en tropel,*** in a throng.
tropelía, *n.f.* outrage; mad rush.
tropero, *n.m.* (*Arg.*) cowboy, cattle driver.
tropezadero, *n.m.* stumbling place.
tropezador, -ra, *a.* stumbling. — *n.m.f.* stumbler.
tropezadura, *n.f.* stumbling.
tropezar [C], *v.i.* to stumble, trip up; ***tropezar con,*** to bump into, stumble over, come up against. — **tropezarse,** *v.r.* — ***con,*** to stumble upon, light upon, bump into.
tropezón, -zona, *a.* stumbling, tripping often. — *n.m.* tripping, stumbling; solid piece of food, titbit; obstacle, difficulty; (*vet.*) interfering; (*coll.*) ***a tropezones,*** by fits and starts, falteringly, jerkily.
tropezoso, -sa, *a.* faltering.
tropical, *a.* tropical.
trópico, -ca, *a.* (*rhet.*) tropical. — *n.m.* tropic.
tropiezo, *n.m.* trip, stumble; slip, slip up; hitch, snag.
tropo, *n.m.* (*rhet.*) trope.
tropología, *n.f.* tropology.
tropológico, -ca, *a.* tropological.
troque, *n.m.* dyer's knot.
troquel, *n.m.* die (*for coins, medals etc.*).
troquelar, *v.t.* to coin, mint.
troqueo, *n.m.* trochee.
trotaconventos, *n.f. inv.* (*coll.*) procuress, bawd, go-between.
trotador, -ra, *a.* trotting.
trotamundos, *n.m.f. inv.* globe-trotter.
trotar, *v.i.* to trot; to hustle, shift fast.
trote, *n.m.* trot; hustle, bustle, go; ***al trote,*** at a trot, at the double; ***de trote,*** for hard *or* constant use *or* wear; ***para todo trote,*** all-purpose; ***viejo para estos trotes,*** (too) old for this sort of thing *or* lark, not up to it any more.
trotón, -tona, *a.* trotting; tough, hard-wearing. — *n.m.* trotter, horse. — *n.f.* chaperone; (*coll.*) street-walker.
trotonería, *n.f.* continual trot.
trova, *n.f.* verse; song.
trovador, -ra, *n.m.f.* troubadour, minstrel.
trovar, *v.t.* to misconstrue; to parody. — *v.i.* to write verse.
trovero, *n.m.* trouveur, trouvère.
trovista, *n.m.* versifier, ballad-writer, minstrel.
trovo, *n.m.* love-ballad.
Troya, *n.f.* Troy; ***aquí fue Troya,*** that's how it all started; ***¡arda Troya!*** damn the consequences!
troyano, -na, *a., n.m.f.* Trojan.
troza, *n.f.* parrel; tree-trunk *or* log.
trozar [C], *v.t.* to break up; to cut into logs.
trozo, *n.m.* piece, bit; chunk, lump.
trucaje, *n.m.* trick photography.
trucar [A], *v.i.* to use trickery; to pocket a ball (*at pool*).
truco, *n.m.* trick; dodge; knack; ***coger el truco,*** to get the knack.
truculento, -ta, *a.* blood-and-thunderish, horrific, gruesome.
trucha, *n.f.* trout; crane.
truchero, -ra, *n.m.f.* trout fisherman; trout-seller.
truchimán, -mana, *n.m.f.* dragoman; artful fellow *or* creature.
truchuela, *n.f.* small trout; dry codfish.
trueco, *n.m.* exchange; ***a*** or ***en trueco,*** in exchange. — *pres. indic.* [TROCAR].
trueno, *n.m.* thunderclap; (*coll.*) rake; (*coll.*) ***trueno gordo,*** big bang; (*pyr., fig.*) bombshell.
trueque, *n.m.* exchange, barter; ***a*** or ***en trueque,*** in exchange. — *pres. subj.* [TROCAR].
trufa, *n.f.* lie; (*bot.*) truffle.
trufador, -ra, *n.m.f.* liar, fibber.
trufar, *v.t.* to stuff with truffles. — *v.i.* to lie, fib.
truhán, *n.m.* rascal, scoundrel, knave; jester.
truhanada, *n.f.* knavish trick.
truhanear, *v.i.* to cheat, swindle; to play the buffoon, be clownish.
truhanería, *n.f.* rascality; rascals; buffoonery.
truhanesco, -ca, *a.* knavish, crooked; clownish.
truja, *n.f.* olive bin.
trujal, *n.m.* oil-press, wine-press; oil mill; soda vat.
trujamán, trujimán, *n.m.* dragoman, interpreter; expert buyer *or* trader.
trujamanear, *v.i.* to act as an interpreter; to act as broker; to exchange, barter, trade.
trujamanía, *n.f.* brokering, brokerage.
trulla, *n.f.* trowel; bustle, noise, hurly-burly; crowd.
trullo, *n.m.* teal; vat for the must.
trumao, *n.m.* (*Chi.*) volcanic dust.
trun, *n.m.* (*Chi.*) a variety of bur.
truncado, -da, *a.* truncate, truncated.
truncamiento, *n.m.* truncation, maiming.
truncar [A], *v.t.* to truncate; to cut, mutilate (*a speech etc.*); to cut off, leave unfinished.
truque, *n.m.* card game.
truquero, *n.m.* keeper of a pool table.
truquiflor, *n.m.* card game.
trusas, *n.f.pl.* breeches.
tsetsé, *n.f.* (*ent.*) tsetse fly.
tú, *pron. pers. 2nd person, m.f.* you; (*obs.*) thou; ***de tú por tú,*** intimately; ***tratar de tú,*** to be on first-name terms (with).
tu, *pron. poss.* your; (*obs.*) thy, thine; (*pl.* **tus**).
tuatúa, *n.f.* American spurge.
tuáutem, *n.m.* (*coll.*) indispensable person; sine qua non.
tuba, *n.f.* (*Philip.*) palm wine; (*mus.*) tuba.
tuberculina, *n.f.* (*med.*) tuberculine.
tuberculización, *n.f.* tuberculosis, tuberculization.

tubérculo, *n.m.* tubercle; tuber.
tuberculosis, *n.f. inv.* tuberculosis.
tuberculoso, -sa, *a.* tuberculous, tubercular. — *n.m.f.* tubercular (*person*).
tubería, *n.f.* tubing, piping; tube, pipe; drains.
tuberosa, *n.f.* [TUBEROSO].
tuberosidad, *n.f.* tuberosity, protuberance, swelling.
tuberoso, -sa, *a.* tuberous. — *n.f.* tuberose.
tubífero, -ra, *a.* provided with tubes.
tubo, *n.m.* tube, pipe, duct; lamp-chimney; ***tubo acústico,*** speaking tube; ***tubo de ensayo,*** test tube; ***tubo lanzallamas,*** flame-thrower; ***tubo lanzatorpedos,*** torpedo-tube.
tubular, *a.* tubular, tube-shaped.
tucán, *n.m.* (*orn.*) toucan.
tucía, *n.f.* tutty.
tuco, -ca, *a.* (*Hisp. Am.*) one-armed, armless. — *n.m.* stump; (*Arg.*) glow-worm; (*Per., orn.*) owl.
tucúquere, *n.m.* (*Chi.*) large owl.
tucuso, *n.m.* (*Ven.*) humming-bird.
tucutuco, *n.m.* (*Arg.*) mole.
tudel, *n.m.* mouth-piece of a bassoon.
tudesco (1), **-ca,** *a.* Germanic, Teutonic. — *n.m.f.* German.
tudesco (2), *n.m.* broad cloak.
tueca, tueco, *n.m.f.* stump, stub; hole left by woodworm in wood.
tuera, *n.f.* (*prov.*) colocynth, bitter apple.
tuerca, *n.f.* nut, female screw.
tuerce, *n.m.* twisting, sprain.
tuero, *n.m.* dry wood, fuel, brushwood; spignel.
tuerto, -ta, *a.* one-eyed; ***a tuertas o a derechas, a tuerto o a derecho,*** rightly or wrongly. — *n.m.* injury, wrong; (*pl.* **tuertos**) birth pains, after-pains.
tueste (1), *n.m.* toast, toasting.
tuesto, tueste (2), *pres. indic., pres. subj.* [TOSTAR].
tuétano, *n.m.* (bone) marrow; pith (*of trees*); ***hasta los tuétanos,*** to the marrow, to the core.
tufarada, *n.f.* (*coll.*) bad smell, pong.
tufo, *n.m.* fume, vapour; offensive *or* foul smell, stink; (*coll.*) pong; sidelock; (*geol.*) tufa; (*pl.*) airs, conceit.
tugurio, *n.m.* shepherd's hut; (*coll.*) hole, den, dive, joint.
tuición, *n.f.* (*law*) protection, guardianship.
tuina, *n.f.* long loose jacket.
tuitivo, -va, *a.* (*law*) protective.
tul, *n.m.* tulle.
tule, *n.m.* (*Mex.*) rush, reed.
tulipa, *n.f.* (*bot.*) small tulip; (tulip-shaped) lamp-shade.
tulipán, *n.m.* (*bot.*) tulip.
tullidez, *n.f.* crippled state.
tullidura, *n.f.* dung (*of birds of prey*).
tullimiento, *n.m.* crippled state.
tullir [J], *v.t.* to cripple, maim, break; (*coll.*) to knock up. — *v.i.* to drop dung.
tumba, *n.f.* tomb, grave; roof (*of a coach*); driver's seat (*in state coaches*); tumble, somersault; Andalusian dance.
tumbacuartillos, *n.m. inv.* (*coll.*) sot, boozer.
tumbadero, *n.m.* tumbling-place.
tumbadillo, *n.m.* (*naut.*) companion.
tumbado, -da, *a.* vaulted, arched.
tumbaga, *n.f.* alloy of gold and copper; ring.
tumbar, *v.t.* to knock down, throw down, lay flat, lay out. — *v.i.* to tumble, fall down, roll down; (*naut.*) to heel, heel over. — **tumbarse,** *v.r.* to lie down; to (start to) take it easy, put one's feet up.
tumbilla, *n.f.* bed-warming frame.
tumbo, *n.m.* tumble, fall; rise and fall; boom, rumble; deed-book; ***tumbo de dado,*** imminent danger; ***dar tumbos,*** to stagger.
tumbón, -bona, *a.* lazy, slack, idle. — *n.m.f.* lazy-bones. — *n.m.* coach with rounded roof; trunk with arched lid. — *n.f.* easy-chair.
tumefacción, *n.f.* tumefaction, swelling.
túmido, -da, *a.* swollen, tumid; pompous, high-flown; (*arch.*) domed.
tumor, *n.m.* tumour.
tumorcico, tumorcillo, tumorcito, *n.m.* small tumour.
tumulario, -ria, *a.* tumulary.
túmulo, *n.m.* tomb, sepulchre, monument; catafalque; tumulus; funeral pile.
tumulto, *n.m.* tumult, uproar, riot, commotion.
tumultuante, *a.* fomenting sedition.
tumultuar [M], *v.i.* to mob, raise a tumult. — **tumultuarse,** *v.r.* to rise in arms.
tumultuario, -ria, *a.* tumultuary, tumultuous.
tumultuoso, -sa, *a.* tumultuous.
tuna, *n.f.* [TUNO].
tunal, *n.m.* (*bot.*) Indian fig-tree; growth of prickly pears.
tunantada, *n.f.* rascally trick.
tunante, *a.* loafing; crooked, tricky. — *n.m.* loafer; rogue, scamp.
tunantear, *v.i.* to loaf; to act the rascal.
tunantería, *n.f.* vagrancy; rascality.
tunantuelo, -la, *n.m.f.* (*coll.*) little rascal, scamp.
tunar, *v.i.* to loiter about; to loaf, stroll; to lead a loose life.
tunata, *a.f.* (*coll.*) shrewd, rascally woman.
tunco, *n.m.* (*Hond., Mex.*) hog, swine.
tunda, *n.f.* shearing of cloth; beating, drubbing.
tundente, *a.* beating, whipping.
tundición, *n.f.* shearing of cloth.
tundidor, *n.m.* cloth-shearer.
tundidora, *n.f.* cloth-shearing machine.
tundidura, *n.f.* shearing.
tundir, *v.t.* to shear (*cloth*); (*coll.*) to beat, drub, thrash.
tundizno, *n.m.* shearings from cloth.
tunduque, *n.m.* (*Chi.*) mouse.
tunear, *v.i.* to act the rogue.
tunecino, -na, *a., n.m.f.* Tunisian.
túnel, *n.m.* tunnel.
Túnez, *n.f.* Tunis; Tunisia.
tungstato, *n.m.* tungstate.
tungsteno, *n.m.* tungsten.
túnica, *n.f.* tunic, robe, gown; (*anat., bot.*) tunicle, pellicle; (*bot.*) ***túnica de Cristo,*** stramonium.
tunicela, *n.f.* tunic; (*eccles.*) tunicle.
túnico, *n.m.* gown, tunic, robe; (*Cub.*) frock, dress; (*Col., C.R., Hond., Ven.*) women's tunic; (*Chi.*) woollen monastic dress.
tuno, -na, *a.* crooked, rascally. — *n.m.f.* crook, rascal. — *n.f.* (*Hisp. Am., bot.*) prickly pear, Indian fig; (*coll.*) loafing; strolling musical band of students; ***correr la tuna,*** to loaf around.
tuntún, (al buen), *adv.* (*coll.*) heedlessly, thoughtlessly.
tupa, *n.f.* tight packing; (*coll.*) repletion, satiety.
tupamaro, *n.m.* (*neol.*) Uruguayan urban guerrilla.
tupaya, *n.f.* (*Philip.*) insectivorous squirrel.
tupé, *n.m.* toupee, forelock; (*coll.*) cheek, nerve.
tupido, -da, *a.* dense, thick; close-woven; dull, stupid.
tupinambo, *n.m.* Jerusalem artichoke.
tupir, *v.t.* to pack tight, make compact. — **tupirse,** *v.r.* to stuff o.s., eat too much.
turba, *n.f.* crowd, mob, rabble; peat.
turbación, *n.f.* upset; confusion, embarrassment.
turbadamente, *adv.* in a confused *or* flustered way.
turbador, -ra, *a.* troubling *or* flustering.
turbal, *n.m.* peat-bog, peat-bed.
turbamulta, *n.f.* crowd, mob, rabble.

turbante, *n.m.* turban.
turbar, *v.t.* to alarm, disturb, trouble, upset; to confuse, fluster, embarrass. — **turbarse,** *v.r.* to become troubled *or* flustered.
turbativo, -va, *a.* alarming.
turbera, *n.f.* peat-bog.
turbia, *n.f.* [TURBIO].
turbidez, *n.f.* turbidity.
túrbido, -da, *a.* turbid.
turbiedad, turbieza, *n.f.* turbidness, turbidity; muddiness; obscurity; dubious nature.
turbina, *n.f.* turbine.
turbino, *n.m.* (*bot.*) pulverized turpeth.
turbinto, (*bot.*) *n.m.* terebinth.
turbio, -bia, *a.* turbid; troubled; cloudy, muddy; obscure; dubious. — *n.m.pl.* (**turbios**) dregs. — *n.f.* muddiness.
turbión, *n.m.* squall, heavy rain shower; whirlwind; sweep, rush.
turbit, *n.m.* (*bot.*) turpeth; (*pharm.*) ***turbit mineral,*** turpeth mineral.
turbonada, *n.f.* storm and whirlwind.
turbulencia, *n.f.* turbidness; turbulence.
turbulento, -ta, *a.* turbid; turbulent.
turca (1), *n.f. coll.* binge; ***coger una turca,*** to get sozzled.
turco, -ca (2), *a.* Turkish. — *n.m.f.* Turk. — *n.m.* Turkish (*language*).
túrdiga, *n.f.* strip of hide *or* leather.
turdión, *n.m.* dance.
turgencia, *n.f.* turgescence, swelling.
turgente, *a.* turgent, turgescent, swollen; prominent.
turibular, *v.t.* (*eccles.*) to cense with a thurible.
turibulario, turiferario, *n.m.* thurifer, censer bearer.
turíbulo, *n.m.* thurible, censer.
turífero, -ra, *a.* thuriferous, incense-bearing.
turingio, -gia, *a.*, *n.m.f.* Thuringian.
turismo, *n.m.* tourism; touring; (*motor.*) saloon (car), (*Am.*) sedan.
turista, *n.m.f.* tourist.
turístico, -ca, *a.* tourist.
turma, *n.f.* testicle; (lamb's) fry; ***turma de tierra,*** truffle.
turmalina, *n.f.* (*min.*) tourmaline.
turnar, *v.i.* to alternate; to take turns.
turnio, -nia, *a.* squint-eyed.
turno, *n.m.* turn; shift; ***el*** or ***la de turno,*** the one (happening to be) on duty, to hand at the time, in use *or* favour at the time.
turón, *n.m.* fitch.
turquesa, *n.f.* turquoise; bullet-mould.
turquesado, -da, *a.* turquoise.
turquesco, -ca, *a.* Turkish.
turquí, turquino, -na, *a.* deep blue.
Turquía, *n.f.* Turkey.
turrar, *v.t.* to roast, toast, broil.
turrón, *n.m.* nougat *or* almond paste; (*coll.*) soft berth; ***comer del turrón,*** to have a plum job.
turronero, *n.m.* maker *or* seller of ***turrón.***
turulato, -ta, *a.* (*coll.*) stunned, dumbfounded.
turumbón, *n.m.* bump on the head.
¡tus! *interj.* here! here! (*to call dogs*); (*coll., fig.*) ***sin decir tus ni mus,*** not daring to say boo to a goose.
tusílago, *n.m.* (*bot.*) colt's-foot.
¡tuso! (1), *interj.* come here! get away! (*dogs*).
tuso (2), **-sa,** *a.* (*Col.*) pitted by smallpox; (*P.R.*) bobtailed. — *n.f.* (*Hisp. Am.*) husks (*of maize* or *wheat*); (*Chi.*) horse's mane; (*Col.*) pock-mark; trollop.
tusón (1), *n.m.* sheep's fleece.
tusón (2), **-sona,** *n.m.* (*prov.*) colt under two years old. — *n.f.* (*prov.*) filly under two years old; (*coll.*) strumpet.
tute, *n.m.* card game.
tutear, *v.t.* to be on first-name terms with.
tutela, *n.f.* tutelage, tutorage, guardianship, protection.
tutelar, *a.* tutelar, tutelary.
tuteo, *n.m.* being on first-name terms with.
tutía, *n.f.* tutty.
tutiplén, (**a**), *adv.* galore.
tutor, -ra, tutriz, *n.m.f.* guardian, protector. — *n.m.* prop (*for plants*).
tutoría, *n.f.* tutelage, guardianship.
tuya (1), *n.f.* thuya.
tuyo, tuya (2), **tuyos, tuyas,** *pron. poss. 2nd pers. m. and f., sing. and pl.* yours; (*obs.*) thine; ***lo tuyo,*** (what is) yours; ***los tuyos,*** yours, your people.

U

U, u, *n.f.* letter U, u; ***en U,*** U-shaped.
u, *disj. conj.* used in place of ***o,*** to avoid cacophony, before words beginning with ***o*** or ***ho,*** as in ***diez u once,*** ten *or* eleven.
uacari, *n.m.* (*Hisp. Am.*) monkey (*Cebid family*).
ubajay, *n.m.* (*Arg.*) tree (*Myrtaceæ family*).
ube, *n.m.* (*Philip.*) plant (*Dioscoreaceæ family*).
ubérrimo, -ma, *a. superl.* very fruitful, very abundant.
ubí, *n.m.* (*Chi.*) plant (*Ampelidæ family*).
ubicación, *n.f.* situation, position, location.
ubicar [A], *v.t.* to situate, locate, place. — **ubicar(se),** *v.i.* (*v.r.*) to be situated, located, placed.
ubicuidad, *n.f.* ubiquity.
ubicuo, -cua, *a.* ubiquitous, omnipresent.
ubiquitario, *n.m.* (*theol.*) Ubiquitarian.
ubre, *n.f.* (*anat.*) udder.
ubrera, *n.f.* (*med.*) thrush.
ucase, *n.m.* ukase.
uchú, *n m.* (*Per.*) fruit of a shrub (*Capsicum genus*).
Ucrania, *n.f.* Ukraine.
ucranio, -nia, *a., n.m.f.* Ukrainian.
udómetro, *n.m.* udometer, rain-gauge.
uesnorueste, *n.m.* west-north-west.
uessudueste, *n.m.* west-south-west.
ueste, *n.m.* west.
¡uf! *interj.* ugh! phew! ouch!
ufanarse, *v.r.* to boast; ***ufanarse de,*** to boast about, pride o.s. on.
ufanía, *n.f.* pride, conceit, haughtiness; satisfaction, pleasure.
ufano, -na, *a.* proud, haughty; pleased as Punch, delighted.
ufo, (a), *adv.* parasitically.
uisque, *n.m.* whisky; ***uisque con soda,*** whisky and soda, (*Am.*) highball.
ujier, *n.m.* usher, doorkeeper.
ulala, *n.f.* (*Bol.*) cactus.
ulano, *n.m.* (*mil.*) uhlan.
úlcera, *n.f.* (*med.*) ulcer; (*bot.*) rot; (*fig.*) sore.
ulceración, *n.f.* ulceration.
ulcerante, *a.* ulcerating.
ulcerar, *v.t.* to ulcerate.
ulcerativo, -va, *a.* causing ulcers.
ulceroso, -sa, *a.* ulcerous.
ulcoate, *n.m.* (*Mex.*) poisonous snake.
Ulises, *n.m.* Ulysses.
ulpo, *n.m.* (*Chi., Per.*) gruel.
ulterior, *a.* farther; subsequent.
ulteriormente, *adv.* farther, beyond; subsequently.
últimamente, *adv.* lastly, finally, ultimately; recently, of late; in the final analysis.
ultimar, *v.t.* to finish.
ultimátum, *n.m.* ultimatum.
ultimidad, *n.f.* ultimateness; finality.
último, -ma, *a.* last; latest; latter; ultimate, final; farthest; utmost, most extreme, highest, lowest; ***a última hora,*** at the last minute; ***a últimos de,*** at the end of; ***estar a lo último,*** to be up with the latest developments; ***estar a la última,*** to be in the latest fashion; ***estar en las últimas,*** to be on one's last legs; ***en último caso,*** in the final resort, as a final resort; ***por último,*** finally.
ultra, *a., n.m.f.* (member) (of the) extreme right.
ultrajador, -ra, *n.m.f.* outrageous *or* offensive person; criminal.
ultrajamiento, *n.m.* outrage, affront; outraging, affronting.
ultrajar, *v.t.* to outrage, affront.
ultraje, *n.m.* outrage, affront.
ultrajoso, -sa, *a.* outrageous, insulting.
ultramar, *n.m.* lands beyond the sea, overseas.
ultramarino, -na, *a.* ultramarine. — *n.m.* ultramarine, finest blue; (*pl.*) oversea goods; grocer's shop.
ultramaro, *n.m.* ultramarine colour.
ultramicroscopio, *n.m.* ultramicroscope.
ultramontanismo, *n.m.* ultramontanism.
ultramontano, -na, *a.* ultramontane.
ultranza, (a), *adv.* at all costs, to the death; out and out.
ultrarrojo, *a.* infra-red.
ultratumba, *n.f.* what lies beyond the grave.
ultraviolado, -da, ultravioleta, *a.* ultraviolet.
úlula, *n.f.* (*orn.*) tawny owl.
ulular, *v.i.* to hoot, howl.
ululato, *n.m.* screech, howl.
ulva, *n.f.* (*Arg.*) cactus.
ulluco, *n.m.* (*Bol., Ec., Per.*) original potato (*Ullusus tuberosus*).
umareo, *n.m.* (*Per.*) first irrigation of a field recently sown.
umbela, *n.f.* (*bot.*) umbel.
umbelíferas, *n.f.pl.* (*bot.*) umbelliferæ.
umbelífero, -ra, *a.* umbelliferous.
umbilicado, -da, *a.* navel-shaped.
umbilical, *a.* umbilical.
umbráculo, *n.m.* shaded, airy place for plants.
umbral, *n.m.* threshold; (*arch.*) lintel.
umbralado, *n.m.* (*Hisp. Am.*) threshold; lintelled opening.
umbralar, *v.t.* (*arch.*) to put a lintel in.
umbrátil, *a.* umbratile, shady.
umbrío, -ría, *a.* umbrageous, shady. — *n.f.* shady place, grove.
umbroso, -sa, *a.* shady.
un, *indef. article* a, an. — *a.* one (*apocope of* ***uno***).
una, *n.f.* [UNO].
unánime, *a.* unanimous.
unanimidad, *n.f.* unanimity; ***por unanimidad,*** unanimously.
uncial, *a.* uncial.
unciforme, *a.* unciform.
unción, *n.f.* unction, anointing; (*eccles.*) extreme unction; devotion; (*naut.*) storm try-sail; (*pl.* **unciones**) treatment by unctions of mercury.
uncionario, -ria, *a.* being under mercurial treatment. — *n.m.* place where mercurial treatment is taken.
uncir [D], *v.t.* to yoke.
undante, *a.* (*poet.*) waving, undulating.
undecágono, *n.m.* undecagon.
undécimo, -ma, *a., n.m.* eleventh.
undécuplo, -la, *a.* eleven times as much.
undísono, -na, *a.* (*poet.*) pounding (*of the sea*).
undívago, -ga, *a.* (*poet.*) billowy, wavy.
undoso, -sa, *a.* wavy, undulating, undulatory.
undulación, *n.f.* undulation, wave motion.
undular, *v.i.* to rise in waves; to undulate; to wriggle.
undulatorio, -ria, *a.* undulatory.
ungido, *n.m.* anointed priest *or* king.
ungimiento, *n.m.* unction.
ungir [G], *v.t.* to anoint, consecrate.
ungüentario, -ria, *a.* sweet-scented; unguentary. — *n.m.* perfume-box; preparer of ointment.
ungüento, *n.m.* ointment, salve.
unguiculado, -da, *a.* (*zool.*) unguiculate.
ungulado, -da, *a.* ungulate.
unible, *a.* that may be united *or* joined.
únicamente, *adv.* only, solely, just.
único, -ca, *a.* only, sole; unique, unmatched, unequalled.
unicornio, *n.m.* unicorn; (*zool.*) rhinoceros; (*zool.*) ***unicornio de mar,*** narwhal.

unidad, *n.f.* unity; unit.
unificación, *n.f.* unification.
unificar [A], *v.t.* to unify.
uniformación, *n.f.* standardization, uniformity.
uniformador, -ra, *a.* standardizing, making uniform.
uniformar, *v.t.* to standardize, make uniform; to put into uniform.
uniforme, *a.* uniform, standard. — *n.m.* uniform; regimentals.
uniformidad, *n.f.* uniformity.
unigénito, -ta, *a.* only-begotten.
unilateral, *a.* unilateral, one-sided.
unión, *n.f.* union; unity; joint; joining; ring; ***Unión de Repúblicas Socialistas Soviéticas,*** Union of Soviet Socialist Republics.
unionista, *a., n.m.f.* unionist.
unípara, *a.f.* uniparous.
unipersonal, *a.* unipersonal, for one (person).
unipolar, *a.* (*elec.*) unipolar.
unir(se), *v.t.* (*v.r.*) to unite, join; to couple, attach, connect; ***unirse a,*** to join.
unisexual, *a.* unisexual.
unisón, *n.m.* unison.
unisonancia, *n.f.* unisonance; monotony.
unísono, -na, *a.* unison; ***al unisono,*** in unison.
unitario, -ria, *a.* Unitarian; unitary. — *n.m.f.* Unitarian.
unitarismo, *n.m.* Unitarianism.
unitivo, -va, *a.* unitive.
univalvo, -va, *a.* univalve.
universal, *a.* universal.
universalidad, *n.f.* universality.
universalizar [C], *v.t.* to universalize.
universidad, *n.f.* university.
universitario, -ria, *a.* university. — *n.m.f.* university student, university man *or* woman.
universo, -sa, *a.* universal. — *n.m.* universe.
univocación, *n.f.* univocation.
univocarse [A], *v.r.* to have the same meaning.
unívoco, -ca, *a.* univocal; unanimous.
uno, una, *a.* a, an, one. — *n.m.* (number) one. — *n.f.* ***la una,*** one o'clock. — *pron. indef.* one, s.o.; (*coll.*) a bloke; ***cada uno,*** each one; ***uno a uno, de uno en uno*** or ***uno por uno,*** one by one; ***una cosa,*** sth.; ***a una,*** in unison; ***uno y otro,*** both; ***es todo uno,*** it's all the same; ***uno que otro,*** one or two; (*pl.*) some people, a few; about; ***unos . . . otros,*** some . . . others.
untador, -ra, *a.* oiling, greasing, smearing. — *n.m.f.* oiler, greaser, smearer.
untadura, *n.f.* anointing, oiling, greasing; ointment.
untamiento, *n.m.* unction, anointing.
untar, *v.t.* to anoint; to spread; to smear, oil, grease; (*coll.*) to grease the palm of, bribe. — **untarse,** *v.r.* (*coll.*) to line one's pocket.
untaza, *n.f.* grease.
unto, *n.m.* grease, fat; ointment, unguent; (*coll.*) ***unto amarillo*** or ***unto de rana,*** bribe.
untuosidad, *n.f.* unctuosity, greasiness.
untuoso, -sa, *a.* unctuous, greasy.
untura, *n.f.* ointment, unction, liniment.
uña, *n.f.* nail, fingernail, toenail; nail hole; claw, hoof, talon; sting (*of scorpion*); thorn; scab; short tree stump; plectrum; (*mech.*) claw, gripper; fluke, bill (*of an anchor*); ***a uña de caballo,*** hell-for-leather, hurriedly; ***hincar la uña,*** to overcharge; ***mostrar*** or ***enseñar las uñas,*** to show one's claws; ***ser uña y carne,*** to be as thick as thieves; ***caer en las uñas de,*** to fall into the clutches of; ***cortarse las uñas con,*** to pick a quarrel with; ***largo de uñas,*** light-fingered; ***mirarse las uñas,*** to twiddle one's thumbs; ***recibir de uñas,*** to give a hostile *or* nasty reception to.
uñada, *n.f.* scratch, nip, mark (*with fingernails*).
uñarada, *n.f.* scratch (*with fingernails*).
uñate, *n.m.* pinch (*with fingernails*); chuck-farthing.
uñero, *n.m.* ingrowing nail; (*med.*) felon.
uñeta, *n.f.* little nail; chuck-farthing; stonecutter's chisel; (*Chi.*) plectrum.
uñi, *n.m.* (*Chi.*) shrub (*Myrtaceæ family*).
uñidura, *n.f.* yoking.
uñir [K], *v.t.* to yoke.
uñoso, -sa, *a.* having long nails.
¡upa! *interj.* hoop-la! up, up!
upupa, *n.f.* hoopoe.
ura, *n.f.* (*Arg.*) maggot.
uránico, -ca, *a.* (*chem.*) uranic.
uranio, *n.m.* (*chem.*) uranium.
uranita, *n.f.* uranite.
uranografía, *n.f.* uranography.
uranometría, *n.f.* uranometry.
urao, *n.m.* (*Hisp. Am.*) hydrous carbonate of soda.
urape, *n.m.* (*Ven.*) leguminous shrub.
uraquear, *v.t.* (*Arg.*) to perforate, bore; burrow.
urato, *n.m.* urate.
urbanidad, *n.f.* urbanity, civility.
urbanismo, *n.m.* town-planning.
urbanista, *n.m.f.* town-planner.
urbanístico, -ca, *a.* (of) town-planning.
urbanización, *n.f.* urbanization; housing estate.
urbanizar [C], *v.t.* to urbanize; build up; ***zona urbanizada,*** built-up area.
urbano, -na, *a.* urban; town; urbane, civil. — *n.m.* traffic policeman.
urbe, *n.f.* city.
urca, *n.f.* (*naut.*) hooker, dogger; (*ichth.*) killer whale.
urce, *n.m.* heath.
urchilla, *n.f.* (*bot.*) orchil; orchil dye.
urdidera, *n.f.* warper (*woman*); warping-frame.
urdidor, -ra, *a.* warping; scheming, hatching. — *n.m.f.* warper; warping-frame.
urdidura, *n.f.* warping.
urdiembre, urdimbre, *n.f.* warp; warping-chain; mesh (*of a plot*).
urdir, *v.t.* to warp; (*fig.*) to contrive, plot, scheme, hatch (up), cook (up).
urea, *n.f.* (*chem.*) urea.
uremia, *n.f.* (*med.*) uræmia.
urémico, -ca, *a.* (*med.*) uræmic.
urente, *a.* hot, burning.
uréter, *n.m.* (*anat.*) ureter.
urético, -ca, *a.* (*anat.*) urethral.
uretra, *n.f.* (*anat.*) urethra.
uretritis, *n.f. inv.* urethritis.
urgencia, *n.f.* urgency; emergency; special delivery.
urgente, *a.* urgent, pressing.
urgir [E], *v.i.* to be urgent, be pressing; ***me urge,*** I need it urgently, I am in urgent need of it.
úrico, -ca, *a.* uric.
urinal, *n.m.* urinal.
urinario, -ria, *a.* urinary. — *n.m.* urinal.
urna, *n.f.* urn; case; ballot-box; ***acudir a las urnas,*** to go to the polls.
uro, *n.m.* (*zool.*) aurochs.
urogallo, *n.m.* (*orn.*) capercaillie.
uromancía, *n.f.* uromancy.
uroscopia, *n.f.* uroscopy.
urpila, *n.f.* (*Arg.*) small dove.
urraca, *n.f.* (*orn.*) magpie.
ursa, *n.f.* (*astron.*) ***Ursa Mayor,*** Great Bear; ***Ursa Menor,*** Little Bear.
ursulina, *n.f.* Ursuline nun.
urticáceo, -cea, *a.* urticaceous.
urticaria, *n.f.* nettle-rash.
urú, *n.m.* (*Arg.*) partridge.
urubú, *n.m.* (*Hisp. Am.*) black vulture.

Uruguay (el), *n.m.* Uruguay.
uruguayo, -ya, *a., n.m.f.* Uruguayan.
urundey, *n.m.* (*Arg.*) urunday tree.
urutaú, *n.m.* (*Arg.*) owl.
usadamente, *adv.* according to custom.
usado, -da, *a.* threadbare, worn out; usual, common.
usagre, *n.m.* (*med.*) infantile eczema; (*vet.*) scald-head.
usanza, *n.f.* use, usage, custom.
usar, *v.t.* to use, make use of; to wear; ***eso ya no se usa,*** that's out of fashion now. — *v.i.* ***usar de,*** to make use of, call upon.
usarcé, usarced, *n.m.f.* (*obs.*) (*contraction of* ***vuesa merced***) your honour.
usencia, *n.m.f.* (*contraction of* ***vuesa reverencia***) (*eccles.*) your reverence.
useñoría, *n.m.f.* (*contraction of* ***vuestra señoría***) your lordship *or* ladyship.
usgo, *n.m.* lothing.
usía, *n.m.f.* (*contraction of* ***vuestra señoría***) your excellency, your lordship, your ladyship.
usina, *n.f.* (*Arg., Hisp. Am.*) plant, factory; power-house.
uso, *n.m.* use; usage; custom, habit, practice; wear and tear; ***al uso,*** according to custom; contemporary; ***en buen uso,*** in good working order; ***uso de razón,*** ability to reason *or* think for o.s.
ustaga, *n.f.* (*naut.*) tie.
usted, *pron. m.f.* (*pl.* **ustedes**) you (*written* **V.,** or **Vd.,** *pl.* **VV.** or **Vds.**).
ustible, *a.* easily burnt.
ustión, *n.f.* burning.
ustorio, -ria, *a.* burning (*glass*).
usual, *a.* usual, ordinary, customary, current, general; tractable, social.
usuario, -ria, *a.* (*law*) usuary; user.
usucapión, *n.f.* (*law*) usucapion.
usucapir, *v.t.* to usucapt.
usufructo, *n.m.* (*law*) usufruct; enjoyment, profit.
usufructuar [M], *v.t.* to usufruct, enjoy the use of. — *v.i.* to yield, be profitable.
usufructuario, -ria, *a., n.m.f.* usufructuary.
usura, *n.f.* usury.
usurar [USUREAR].
usurario, -ria, *a.* usurious.
usurear, *v.i.* to practise usury; to lend *or* borrow money on interest; to reap great profit.
usurero, -ra, *n.m.f.* usurer, money-lender.
usurpación, *n.f.* usurpation.
usurpador, -ra, *n.m.f.* usurper.
usurpar, *v.t.* to usurp.
usuta, *n.f.* (*Arg., Bol., Chi.*) sandal worn by Indian women.
uta, *n.f.* (*Per.*) facial ulcers common in the Andes.
utensilio, *n.m.* utensil, tool.
uterino, -na, *a.* uterine.
útero, *n.m.* (*anat.*) uterus, womb.
uteroscopio, *n.m.* (*med.*) hysteroscope.
útil, *a.* useful, serviceable; handy, convenient; (*law*) operative (*applied to time*). — *n.m.* utensil, tool.
utilero, -ra, *n.m.f.* (*Hisp. Am., theat.*) property man.
utilidad, *n.f.* utility; profit; usefulness; ***de gran*** or ***mucha utilidad,*** extremely useful.
utilitario, -ria, *a., n.m.f.* utilitarian.
utilitarismo, *n.m.* utilitarianism.
utilitarista, *a., n.m.f.* utilitarian.
utilizable, *a.* usable, utilizable.
utilizar [C], *v.t.* to utilize, use; ***utilizarse de,*** to turn to account.
utopía, utopia, *n.f.* utopia.
utópico, -ca, *a.* utopian.
utopismo, *n.m.* wishful-thinking, 'pie-in-the-sky' attitude.
utopista, *a., n.m.f.* utopian.
utrero, -ra, *n.m.f.* bull *or* heifer from two to three years old.
uva, *n.f.* grape; barberry; berry; wart; tumour; ***uva pasa,*** raisin; ***uva de Corinto,*** currant; (*bot.*) ***uva crespa,*** gooseberry; (*bot.*) ***uva lupina,*** wolf's-bane; (*bot.*) ***uva de raposa,*** nightshade; (*fig.*) ***uvas verdes,*** sour grapes; (*coll.*) ***hecho una uva,*** sozzled; ***de uvas a peras,*** once in a blue moon; ***tener mala uva,*** to be bloody-minded.
uvada, *n.f.* glut of grapes.
uvaduz, *n.f.* (*bot.*) bearberry.
uval, *a.* grape-like.
uvate, *n.m.* conserve of grapes.
uvayema, *n.f.* (*bot.*) wild vine.
uve, *n.f.* name of the letter V.
uvero, -ra, *a.* (of) grape. — *n.m.f.* grape-seller. — *n.m.* sea-grape.
úvula, *n.f.* uvula.
uxoricida, *a.* uxoricidal. — *n.m.* uxoricide, wife-murderer.
uxoricidio, *n.m.* wife-murder, uxoricide (*act*).

V

V, v, *n.f.* letter V, v.
vaca, *n.f.* [VACO].
vacación, *n.f.* vacation, holiday; ***estar de vacaciones,*** to be on holiday; ***marcharse de vacaciones,*** to go away on holiday; ***vacaciones retribuidas,*** holidays with pay.
vacada, *n.f.* drove *or* herd of cows.
vacancia, *n.f.* vacancy.
vacante, *a.* vacant, empty, free, available. — *n.f.* vacancy; vacation.
vacar [A], *v.i.* to resign from a job, leave a post; to take a vacation; to fall *or* become vacant; to devote o.s. (*a*, to); ***vacar de,*** to lack.
vacarí, *a.* leathern *or* leather-covered.
vacatura, *n.f.* period of vacancy.
vaciada, *n.f.* (*metal.*) melt.
vaciadero, *n.m.* drain, sink, sewer; dumping-place.
vaciadizo, -za, *a.* cast, moulded.
vaciado, *n.m.* cast, casting; (*arch.*) excavation; (*arch.*) sunken part (*in the dado of a pedestal*); sharpenings (*of razors*).
vaciador, *n.m.* moulder, caster; dumper, emptier, pourer; ***vaciador de navajas,*** razor grinder.
vaciamiento, *n.m.* casting, moulding; evacuating, emptying, hollowing.
vaciar [L *and regular*], *v.t.* to empty; to hollow out, dig out; to cast; to sharpen; to exhaust (*a subject*); to transfer. — *v.i.* to flow into (*rivers*); to decrease. — **vaciarse,** *v.r.* (*fig.*) to blab, spill the beans.
vaciedad, *n.f.* emptiness; nonsense, hot air.
vaciero, *n.m.* shepherd of barren sheep.
vacilación, *n.f.* vacillation; staggering, reeling; hesitation, irresolution.
vacilante, *a.* vacillating, wavering; staggering, unsteady; hesitating.
vacilar, *v.i.* to vacillate, falter, waver, hesitate; to stagger, reel.
vacío, -cía, *a.* empty, void; idle; hollow; empty-headed; barren (*of cattle*). — *n.m.* void, vacuum; casting-mould; gap; flank (*of animals*); dancing step; ***de vacío,*** empty-handed; unloaded; ***en vacío,*** in vacuo; ***caer en el vacío,*** to fall flat; ***hacer el vacío a,*** to cold-shoulder, send to Coventry.
vaco, -ca, *a.* vacant. — *n.m.* (*coll.*) ox. — *n.f.* cow; beef; cow-hide; (gambling) pool; ***vaca de leche,*** milch cow; ***vaca lechera,*** dairy cow; ***vaca de San Antón,*** ladybird; ***vaca marina,*** sea cow; (*fig.*) ***vacas gordas*** (***flacas***), good (bad) times.
vacuidad, *n.f.* vacuity, emptiness.
vacuna, *n.f.* [VACUNO].
vacunación, *n.f.* (*med.*) vaccination.
vacunar, *v.t.* (*med.*) to vaccinate.
vacuno, -na, *a.* bovine, (belonging to) cattle. — *n.f.* (*med.*) vaccine; cow-pox.
vacuo, -cua, *a.* unoccupied, vacant, empty. — *n.m.* vacuum.
vacuómetro, *n.m.* vacuum gauge.
vade, *n.m.* portfolio, vade-mecum; satchel.
vadeable, *a.* fordable; conquerable.
vadear, *v.t.* to wade, ford; to surmount, conquer; to try, sound. — **vadearse,** *v.r.* to conduct o.s., behave.
vademécum, *n.m.* vade-mecum; case, portfolio.
vadera, *n.f.* wide ford.
¡vade retro! *interj.* (*obs.*) avaunt! away! get you gone!
vado, *n.m.* ford; resource, expedient; ***no hallar vado,*** to be at a loss, see no way out; ***al vado o a la puente,*** you can't have it both ways.
vadoso, -sa, *a.* shallow, shoaly.
vafe, *n.m.* (*prov.*) bold undertaking.
vagabundear, *v.i.* to rove about, loiter about.
vagabundo, -da, *a.* vagabond, vagrant. — *n.m.f.* vagabond, vagrant, tramp, roamer.
vagamundear [VAGABUNDEAR].
vagamundo, -da [VAGABUNDO].
vagancia, *n.f.* vagrancy; idleness.
vagante, *a.* vagrant; wandering.
vagar [B], *v.i.* to wander (about), roam (about), rove (about); to idle (about). — *n.m.* wandering; idling.
vagaroso, -sa, *a.* wandering.
vagido, *n.m.* squall, wail.
vagina, *n.f.* (*anat.*) vagina.
vaginal, *a.* (*anat.*) vaginal.
vago, -ga, *a.* wandering; lazy, idle; vague, indistinct, hazy; ***en vago,*** vaguely; unsteadily, insecurely. — *n.m.f.* lazy individual, idler. — *n.m.* uncultivated plot; vagus.
vagón, *n.m.* waggon; carriage; goods van, (*Am.*) box-car; ***vagón cama,*** sleeping-car; ***vagón restaurante,*** dining-car.
vagonada, *n.f.* wagon-load, car-load.
vagoneta, *n.f.* truck; trolley.
vaguada, *n.f.* water-course.
vagueación, *n.f.* flight of fancy.
vagueante, *a.* wandering.
vaguear, *v.i.* to wander, rove, roam; to idle.
vaguedad, *n.f.* vagueness, haziness; vague statement.
vaguemaestre, *n.m.* (*mil.*) transport master.
vaguido, -da, *a.* dizzy. — *n.m.* [VAHÍDO].
vahaje, *n.m.* gentle breeze.
vahar, *v.i.* to exhale, emit, give out.
vaharada, *n.f.* vapour, breath; breathing, exhalation.
vaharera, *n.f.* (*med.*) thrush.
vaharina, *n.f.* (*coll.*) mist, vapour.
vahear [VAHAR].
vahído, *n.m.* vertigo, giddiness, dizziness, giddy *or* dizzy spell.
vaho, *n.m.* steam, vapour; breath.
vaina, *n.m.* (*coll.*) twerp, nit. — *n.f.* scabbard; sheath; (*bot.*) pod; (*naut.*) tabling (*of a flag*); (*naut.*) bolt-rope tabling; (*Col.*, *C.R.*, *Pan.*) annoyance, bother.
vainazas, *n.m. inv.* (*coll.*) slob.
vainero, *n.m.* scabbard-maker.
vainica, *n.f.* back-stitch, hem-stitch.
vainilla, *n.f.* vanilla; heliotrope.
vainiquera, *n.f.* hemstitch worker.
vaivén, *n.m.* fluctuation; sway, swaying; swing, swinging, see-saw motion; to-and-fro motion, rolling; (*mech.*) reciprocating movement; (*naut.*) line, cord, rope.
vajilla, *n.f.* table-service, dinner-service; (set of) china; (*Mex.*) tax (*on jewellery*); ***vajilla de oro,*** gold plate; ***vajilla de plata,*** silver plate, silverware.
val, *n.m.* (*contraction of* VALLE) vale, valley, dale; (*prov.*) drain, sink, sewer.
valaco, -ca, *a.*, *n.m.f.* Wallachian.
valais, *n.m.* board, a piece of timber about 4 yards long.
valar, *a.* relating to an enclosure.
valdiviano, *n.m.* (*Chi.*, *cook.*) beef stew.
vale, *n.m.* promissory note, I.O.U.; voucher; receipt; coupon; token; farewell, adieu.
valedero, -ra, *a.* valid.
valedor, -ra, *n.m.f.* protector, defender.
valentía, *n.f.* valour, courage, gallantry, bravery; exploit, feat; boastfulness; great effort; (*art*) dash, fire, imagination; second-hand shoe shop; ***hambre y valentía,*** poverty and pride; ***pisar de valentía,*** to swagger *or* strut about.
Valentín, *n.m.* Valentine.

valentísimo, -ma, *a. superl.* most valiant; most perfect.
valentón, -tona, *a.* blustering, arrogant. — *n.m.f.* bully, hector, blusterer.
valentonada, *n.f.* brag, boast; piece of arrogance.
valer, *n.m.* value, worth, merit. — [36], *v.t.* to help, help out; to produce, yield, give; to bring in; to cause to get; to cost, be worth; to amount to, add up to; ***¡válgame Dios!*** God help me! good Heavens!; ***valer un ojo de la cara,*** to cost the earth; ***eso le valió una condecoración,*** he got a decoration for that; ***valer la pena,*** to be worthwhile; ***vale lo que pesa,*** he's worth his weight in gold; ***éste vale más que el otro,*** this one is better than the other. — *v.i.* to be worth, worthwhile, useful, of worth *or* value, of use; to be good (for); to be valid; (*coll.*) ***¡vale!*** all right, that'll do, O.K.; ***valga la comparación,*** if I may be allowed the analogy; ***eso no vale,*** that's not fair; ***más vale*** or ***más valiera,*** it is *or* it would be better; ***más vale tarde que nunca,*** better late than never. — **valerse,** *v.r.* to hold one's own; to manage (by one's self); to make use (***de,*** of).
valeriana, *n.f.* valerian.
valerianato, *n.m.* (*chem.*) valerianate.
valeriánico, -ca, *a.* (*chem.*) valeric.
valerosidad, *n.f.* courage, bravery, valour.
valeroso, -sa, *a.* valiant, courageous, brave, heroic, gallant; powerful, active, strong.
valet, *n.m.* jack, knave (*cards*).
valetudinario, -ria, *a.* valetudinarian, infirm, invalid.
valí, *n.m.* Moslem governor.
valía, *n.f.* value, worth; favour, influence (*at court*); ***de gran valía,*** of great worth; ***a las valías,*** at the highest price.
validación, *n.f.* validation.
validar, *v.t.* to validate.
validez, *n.f.* validity.
válido, -da, *a.* valid; sound.
valido, *n.m.* (*polit.*) favourite; (royal) minister.
valiente, *a.* valiant, brave, courageous; striking. — *n.m.* brave fellow; bully-boy; (*coll., iron.*) ***¡valiente amigo!*** a fine friend!
valija, *n.f.* valise; mail-bag; ***valija diplomática,*** diplomatic bag.
valijero, *n.m.* letter-carrier.
valimiento, *n.m.* favour (*at court*), influence (*at court*); protection, patronage.
valioso, -sa, *a.* esteemed; valuable; wealthy, rich.
valisoletano, -na, *a., n.m.f.* (native) of Valladolid.
valón, -lona (1), *a.* Walloon; ***u valona,*** letter W. — *n.m.f.* Walloon. — *n.m.pl.* (**valones**) bloomers.
valona (2), *n.f.* boy's shirt-collar, vandyke collar.
valor, *n.m.* value, worth; force, validity; valour, bravery, courage; audacity, nerve; ***valor adquisitivo,*** purchasing value *or* power; ***objetos de valor,*** valuables; ***armarse de valor,*** to pluck up courage; ***quitar valor a,*** to play down, belittle; (*pl.*) securities.
valorar, valorear, *v.t.* to value, appraise, price; to appreciate.
valoría, *n.f.* worth, value.
valorización, *n.f.* valuation, (*Am.*) appraisal.
valorizar, *v.t.* to price, fix a price for.
valquiria, *n.f.* valkyrie.
vals, *n.m.* waltz.
valsar, *v.i.* to waltz.
valsón, *n.m.* (*coll.*) ***dar valsones,*** to waltz about, barge around.
valuación, *n.f.* valuation, (*Am.*) appraisal.
valuador, -ra, *n.m.f.* valuer, appraiser.
valuar, *v.t.* to value, appraise, estimate.
valva, *n.f.* (*zool.*) valve.
valvasor, *n.m.* lesser nobleman.
válvula, *n.f.* valve; (*rad.*) valve, (*Am.*) tube; ***válvula de seguridad,*** safety valve; ***válvula de escape,*** exhaust valve; outlet.
valvular, *a.* valvular.
valla, *n.f.* fence; hurdle; ***romper*** or ***saltar la valla,*** to break the rules.
valladar, vallado, *n.m.* fence; barrier; obstacle.
valladear, vallar, *v.t.* to fence, enclose with stakes.
valle, *n.m.* valley; vale; glen; ***valle de lágrimas,*** vale of tears.
vallejo, *n.m.* small valley.
vallejuelo, *n.m.* tiny valley, dell.
vallico, *n.m.* (*bot.*) rye-grass.
vallisoletano, -na, *a., n.m.f.* (native) of Valladolid.
¡vamos! *interj.* come now! well! go on! come, come! let's stop!
vampiro, *n.m.* vampire; usurer, skinflint, miser; ghoul.
vanadio, *n.m.* (*chem.*) vanadium.
vanagloria, *n.f.* vaingloriousness, boastfulness.
vanagloriarse, *v.r.* to boast.
vanaglorioso, -sa, *a.* vainglorious, boastful, conceited.
vandálico, -ca, *a.* Vandalic; loutish.
vandalismo, *n.m.* vandalism.
vándalo, -la, *n.m.f.* Vandal; vandal.
vanear, *v.i.* to talk nonsense.
vanguardia, *n.f.* van, vanguard; avant-garde.
vanidad, *n.f.* vanity; idle nonsense; ***hacer vanidad de,*** to boast about.
vanidoso, -sa, *a., n.m.f.* vain (*person*).
vanilocuencia, *n.f.* verbosity, pomposity, empty talk.
vanílocuo, -cua, vanilocuente, *a.* empty (*talker*).
vaniloquio, *n.m.* empty prattle; (*coll.*) blether.
vanistorio, *n.m.* (*coll.*) ridiculous *or* affected vanity; affected fellow.
vano, -na, *a.* vain; idle; ***en vano,*** in vain. — ***n.m.*** opening (*in a wall*).
vánova, *n.f.* coverlet, bedspread.
vapor, *n.m.* vapour; steam; mist; (*naut.*) steamer, steamboat.
vaporable, *a.* evaporable ,volatile.
vaporación, vaporización, *n.f.* evaporation, vaporization.
vaporar, vaporear, vaporizar [C], *v.i.* to evaporate. — *v.t.* to vaporize.
vaporoso, -sa, *a.* vaporous, vapourish; ethereal, cloudy.
vapulación, *n.f.*, **vapulamiento,** *n.m.* whipping, flogging.
vapular, vapulear, *v.t.* to whip, flog.
vapuleamiento, vapuleo, *n.m.* whipping, flogging, thrashing.
vaquear, *v.t.* to serve (cows) (*said of bulls*).
vaquería, *n.f.* herd of cattle; dairy.
vaquerizo, -za, *a.* relating to cattle. — *n.m.f.* herdsman. — *n.f.* winter cattle-shed.
vaquero, -ra, *a.* pertaining to cowherds. — *n.m.f.* cowherd.
vaqueta, *n.f.* cow-hide, sole-leather.
vaquetear, *v.t.* to flog with leather thongs.
vaqueteo, *n.m.* flogging; running the gauntlet.
vaquilla, vaquita, *n.f.* small cow; (*Arg., Chi.*) heifer under two years.
vara, *n.f.* rod; pole, staff; yard; yardstick; wand (*of office*); switch, birch; shaft (*of carts*); goad; ***tener vara alta,*** to have a big say, be a big shot; ***meterse en camisa de once varas,*** to stick one's nose into other people's business.
varada, *n.f.* (*naut.*) stranding; (*agric.*) gang of farm hands; job on a farm; (*min.*) three months' work; (*min.*) quarterly profit and dividend.
varadera, *n.f.* (*naut.*) skid.
varadero, *n.m.* shipyard; dry-dock.
varadura, *n.f.* running aground.

varal, *n.m.* long pole; (*theat.*) side-lights; tall, gangling fellow.
varapalo, *n.m.* long pole; blow with a pole; (*fig.*) grief, trouble, damage.
varar, *v.t.* (*naut.*) to beach. — *v.i.* to run aground.
varaseto, *n.m.* espalier.
varazo, *n.m.* swipe *or* blow with a pole *or* stick.
varbasco, *n.m.* (*bot.*) verbascum, mullein.
vardasca, *n.f.* thin twig.
vareador, *n.m.* beater (*fruit-picking*).
vareaje, *n.m.* retail-trade; selling *or* measuring by the yard; beating down (*the fruit of trees*).
varear, *v.t.* to beat down (*fruit*); to cudgel; to measure *or* sell by the yard; to wound with the goad. — **varearse,** *v.r.* to grow thin *or* lean.
varejón, *n.m.* thick pole *or* staff.
varenga, *n.f.* (*naut.*) floor-timber.
vareo [VAREAJE].
vareta, *n.f.* small rod; lime-twig; stripe; dig, nasty crack *or* hint.
varetazo, *n.m.* blow from a horn.
varetear, *v.t.* to variegate.
varga, *n.f.* steepest part (*of a hill*).
varganal, *n.m.* enclosure, stockade.
várgano, *n.m.* railing *or* stake (*of a fence*).
varí, *n.m.* (*Chi., Per., orn.*) harrier.
variabilidad, *n.f.* variableness.
variable, *a.* variable, changeable; fickle.
variación, *n.f.* variation.
variado, -da, *a.* varied; variegated.
variante, *a., n.f.* variant.
variar [L], *v.t., v.i.* to vary, change; ***variar de idea,*** to change one's mind.
várice, varice, *n.f.* (*surg.*) varix; varicose vein.
varicela, *n.f.* (*med.*) chicken-pox.
varicocele, *n.f.* varicocele.
varicoso, -sa, *a.* varicose.
variedad, *n.f.* variety; (*pl.* **variedades**) miscellany; ***teatro de variedades,*** variety theatre, vaudeville.
varilarguero, *n.m.* picador.
varilla, *n.f.* (small) rod; spindle, pivot; switch; rib *or* stick (*of a fan* or *umbrella*); whalebone (*of corset*); dipstick, (*Am.*) bayonet; (*coll.*) jawbone; (*pl.*) frame (*of a sieve*); whisk.
varillaje, *n.m.* rib-work, ribbing (*umbrellas, corsets, fans etc.*).
varillar, *n.m.* (*Chi.*) shrubbery.
vario, -ria, *a.* various, different, diverse; changeable, unsteady; variegated; (*pl.*) several, various.
varioloso, -sa, *a.* variolous, variolar.
varita, *n.f.* switch; wand; (*Hond., bot.*) ***varita de San José,*** hollyhock.
varón, *n.m.* man, male; man of worth; male child; (*naut.*) pendant (*of rudder*); (*coll.*) ***santo varón,*** extremely worthy man; ***hijo varón,*** son.
varona, varonesa, *n.f.* woman; mannish woman.
varonía, male issue.
varonil, *a.* manly.
Varsovia, *n.f.* Warsaw.
varraco, *n.m.* boar.
varraquear, *v.i.* (*coll.*) to grunt; to squall (*of children*).
varraquera, *n.f.* (*coll.*) tantrum.
vasallaje, *n.m.* vassalage, servitude, subjection; dependence; liege-money.
vasallo, -lla, *a.* subject, dependant, feudatory. — *n.m.f.* vassal, subject.
vasar, *n.m.* kitchen-shelf.
vasco, -ca, vascongado, -da, *a., n.m.f.* Basque.
vascuence, *n.m.* Basque language; (*coll.*) jargon, gibberish.
vascular, vasculoso, -sa, *a.* vascular, vasculose.
vase, *n.m.* (*theat.*) exit. — *3rd pers. sing. pres. indic. of* IRSE.
vaselina, *n.f.* Vaseline (*reg. trade name*), petroleum jelly.
vasera, *n.f.* glass-rack.
vasico, *n.m.* small glass.
vasija, *n.f.* vessel; butt, cask; bowl, dish.
vasillo, *n.m.* honeycomb cell.
vaso, *n.m.* vessel; glass, tumbler; tumblerful; (*naut.*) hull; (*arch.*) vase; duct; hoof (*of a horse*); Crater (*constellation*).
vástago, *n.m.* stem; shoot, sapling; scion, offspring; (*mech.*) ***vástago del émbolo,*** piston rod; ***vástago de válvula,*** valve stem.
vastedad, *n.f.* vastness; huge expanse.
vasto, -ta, *a.* vast, immense, huge.
vate, *n.m.* (*poet.*) bard, poet; diviner, seer.
Vaticano, *n.m.* Vatican.
vaticano, -na, *a.* (of the) Vatican.
vaticinador, -ra, *a.* prophesying, vaticinating. — *n.m.f.* prophet, vaticinator.
vaticinar, *v.t.* to prophesy, vaticinate.
vaticinio, *n.m.* prophesy, vaticination.
vatídico, -ca, *a.* (*poet.*) prophetical.
vatio, *n.m.* watt; ***vatio-hora,*** watt-hour.
vaya, *n.f.* jest, scoff. — *interj.* well, well! you don't say! good Lord!; ***¡vaya por Dios!*** good Heavens!; ***¡vaya una ocurrencia!*** what a notion!
ve, *n.f.* name of the letter V.
véase, see, vide.
vecero, -ra, *a.* alternate; fruit-bearing in alternate years. — *n.m.f.* one waiting his turn; regular customer. — *n.f.* herd, drove.
vecinal, *a.* belonging to the neighbourhood, local.
vecindad, *n.f.* vicinity, neighbourhood; neighbours; tenants, inhabitants.
vecindario, *n.m.* neighbours; tenants, inhabitants; vicinity, neighbourhood.
vecino, -na, *a.* neighbouring; nearby; next. — *n.m.f.* neighbour; tenant, inhabitant, resident.
vectación, *n.f.* riding.
vector, *n.m.* vector.
Veda, *n.m.* Veda.
veda, *n.f.* prohibition; close season (*game*).
vedado, *n.m.* enclosure, park, game preserve.
vedamiento, *n.m.* prohibition.
vedar, *v.t.* to prohibit, forbid; to impede, hinder, obstruct; to veto.
vedegambre, *n.m.* (*bot.*) hellebore.
vedeja, *n.f.* long lock of hair; forelock; (*lion's*) mane.
vedija, *n.f.* tangled lock of wool; tuft of tangled hair.
vedijero, -ra, *n.m.f.* collector of loose locks (*at shearing*).
vedijoso, -sa, vedijudo, -da, *a.* shaggy.
veduño, *n.m.* quality (*of vines*).
veedor, -ra, *n.m.f.* spy, prier; inspector, overseer.
veeduría, *n.f.* office of inspector *or* overseer.
vega, *n.f.* fertile lowland *or* plain; (*Cub.*) tobacco-plantation; (*Chi.*) low and swampy ground.
vegetabilidad, *n.f.* vegetability.
vegetación, *n.f.* vegetation; (*pl.*) ***vegetaciones (adenoideas),*** adenoids.
vegetal, *a., n.m.* vegetable.
vegetante, *a.* vegetating.
vegetar, *v.i.* to vegetate.
vegetarianismo, *n.m.* vegetarianism.
vegetariano, -na, *a., n.m.f.* vegetarian.
vegetativo, -va, *a.* vegetative.
vegoso, -sa, *a.* (*Chi.*) damp (*ground*).
veguer, *n.m.* magistrate.
veguería, *n.f.,* **veguerío,** *n.m.* jurisdiction and office of magistrate.
veguero, -ra, *a.* of a fertile plain. — *n.m.* cigar; (*Hisp. Am.*) tobacco-planter.
vehemencia, *n.f.* vehemence.

vehemente, *a.* vehement.
vehículo, *n.m.* vehicle.
veintavo, *n.m.* twentieth part.
veinte, *a.*, *n.m.* twenty, twentieth; ***a las veinte,*** unseasonably.
veintén, *n.m.* gold dollar.
veintena, *n.f.*, **veintenar,** *n.m.* score, set of twenty.
veintenario, -ria, *a.* twenty years old.
veinteñal, *a.* lasting twenty years.
veinteocheno, -na, veintiocheno, -na, *a.* twenty-eighth. — *n.m.* cloth with 2,800 threads of warp.
veinteseiseno, -na, *a.* twenty-sixth.
veintésimo, -ma, *a.* twentieth.
veinticinco, *a.* twenty-five.
veinticuatreno, -na, *a.* twenty-fourth. — *n.m.* cloth with 2,400 threads of warp.
veinticuatro, *a.* twenty-four, twenty-fourth. — *n.m.* twenty-four, twenty-fourth; alderman in some Andalusian cities.
veintidós, *a.*, *n.m.* twenty-two.
veintidoseno, -na, *a.* twenty-second.
veintinueve, *a.*, *n.m.* twenty-nine, twenty-ninth.
veintiocho, *a.*, *n.m.* twenty-eight, twenty-eighth.
veintiséis, *a.*, *n.m.* *inv.* twenty-six, twenty-sixth.
veintiseiseno, -na, *a.* twenty-sixth.
veintisiete, *a.*, *n.m.* twenty-seven, twenty-seventh.
veintitrés, *a.*, *n.m.* twenty-three, twenty-third.
veintiún, *a.m.* twenty-one (*apocope of* ***veintiuno***).
veintiuno, -na, *a.*, *n.m.* twenty-one. — *n.f.* vingt-et-un, pontoon (*card game*).
vejación, *n.f.* molestation, humiliation, ill-treatment.
vejador, -ra, *a.* molesting, ill-treating. — *n.m.f.* molester, ill-treater.
vejamen, *n.m.* taunt; lampoon; ill-treatment.
vejaminista, *n.m.f.* lampooner.
vejancón, -cona, *a.*, *n.m.f.* old, decrepit (person).
vejar, *v.t.* to vex, molest, tease, annoy, harass; to scoff at; to censure.
vejarrón, -rrona, *a.*, *n.m.f.* very old (person).
vejatorio, -ria, *a.* vexatious.
vejazo, -za, *a.*, *n.m.f.* very old (person).
vejestorio, *n.m.* ancient object *or* character.
vejeta, *n.f.* (*orn.*) crested lark.
vejete, *n.m.* (sprightly) old codger.
vejez, *n.f.* oldness; old age; old thing; ***a la vejez, viruelas,*** there's no fool like an old fool.
vejezuelo, -la, *a.* oldish. — *n.m.f.* little old man *or* woman.
vejiga, *n.f.* bladder, gall-bladder; blister, pustule; (*bot.*) ***vejiga de perro,*** common winter cherry.
vejigatorio, -ria, *a.* blistering, raising blisters. — *n.m.* blistering plaster, vesicatory.
vejigón, *n.m.* large bladder, large blister.
vejigüela, vejiguica, vejiguilla, vejiguita, *n.f.* small bladder.
vela (1), *n.f.* watch; vigil; wakefulness; pilgrimage; candle; ***una noche en vela,*** a sleepless night; (*pl.*) runny *or* running nose; (*coll.*) ***¿quién le ha dado vela en este entierro?*** who asked you to butt in?
vela (2), *n.f.* sail; awning; nuptial mass and veiling; ***vela mayor,*** mainsail; ***vela de trinquete,*** foresail; ***vela de mesana,*** mizzen-sail; ***hacerse a la vela,*** to set sail; ***hacer fuerza de vela,*** to crowd on sail; ***alzar velas,*** to hoist sails; (*coll.*) ***recoger velas,*** to (start to) soft-pedal, rein in, pull in one's horns.
velación (1), *n.f.* watch, watching, vigil, wake.
velación (2), *n.f.* nuptial mass and veiling.
velacho, *n.m.* (*naut.*) fore-topsail.
velado, -da (1), *a.* veiled, hidden. — *n.m.* husband. — *n.f.* wife.
velada (2), *n.f.* watch; social evening, soirée.
velador, -ra, *a.* watching. — *n.m.* watchman, night-guard; wooden candlestick; small table with one leg.
velaje, velamen, *n.m.* canvas, sails, set of sails.
velante, *a.* watching.
velar (1), *v.t.* to watch, watch over; to guard; to keep. — *v.i.* to watch, keep watch, keep vigil; to stay awake, stay up late at night; to show above water; ***velar por,*** to be vigilant in the interests of, look after the interests of.
velar (2), *v.t.* to veil; (*photo.*) to fog.
velarte, *n.m.* broadcloth.
velatorio, *n.m.* wake (*watch by corpse before burial*).
veleidad, *n.f.* fickleness, inconstancy; whim.
veleidoso, -sa, *a.* fickle, inconstant, flighty.
velejar, *v.i.* to make use of sails.
velería, *n.f.* tallow-chandler's shop.
velero (1), **-ra** (1), *a.* fond of pilgrimages *or* vigils. — *n.m.* tallow chandler.
velero (2), **-ra** (2), *a.* swift-sailing. — *n.m.* sail-maker; sailing vessel.
veleta, *n.f.* vane; weather-cock; pennant, streamer; bob, float *or* cork (*of a fishing line*); fickle person; ***veleta de manga,*** wind-sleeve, wind-sock.
velete, *n.f.* light, thin veil.
velicación, *n.f.* (*med.*) lancing, opening.
velicar [A], *v.t.* (*med.*) to lance, open.
velico, velillo, velito, *n.m.* small veil; embroidered gauze.
velicomen, *n.m.* large glass used for toasts.
velilla, velita, *n.f.* small candle.
velis nolis, *adv.* willy-nilly, by hook or by crook.
velmez, *n.m.* tunic (*worn under armour*).
velo, *n.m.* veil; taking the veil; (*anat.*) velum; (*photo.*) fog; ***velo del paladar,*** velum, soft palate; ***correr el velo,*** to draw back the veil; ***correr*** or ***echar un velo sobre,*** to draw a veil over; ***tomar el velo,*** to take the veil.
velocidad, *n.f.* velocity, speed; gear; ***en gran velocidad,*** express, by passenger train; ***en pequeña velocidad,*** by goods train.
velocímetro, *n.m.* speedometer.
velocipédico, -ca, *a.* relating to bicycles.
velocipedismo, *n.m.* cycling.
velocipedista, *n.m.f.* velocipedist, cyclist.
velocípedo, *n.m.* velocipede, bicycle, tricycle.
velódromo, *n.m.* cycle-track.
velomotor, *n.m.* motor vehicle (*especially motor-cycle*).
velón, *n.m.* oil-lamp.
velonera, *n.f.* lamp-stand.
velonero, *n.m.* lamp-maker.
velorio, *n.m.* evening party; wake.
veloz, *a.* swift, fast, fleet, quick.
vellera, *n.f.* beautician.
vello, *n.m.* down, nap, soft hair; gossamer.
vellocino, *n.m.* fleece; ***Vellocino de oro,*** the Golden Fleece.
vellón, *n.m.* fleece; unsheared sheepskin; lock of wool; copper and silver alloy; ***real de vellón,*** copper coin.
vellonero, *n.m.* shearer's assistant.
vellora, *n.f.* curl in woollen cloth.
vellorí, vellorín, *n.m.* undyed broadcloth.
vellorita, *n.f.* (*bot.*) cowslip.
vellosidad, *n.f.* downiness, hairiness.
vellosilla, *n.f.* (*bot.*) mouse-ear.
velloso, -sa, *a.* hairy, downy.
velludillo, *n.m.* velveteen.
velludo, -da, *a.* shaggy, downy, hairy, woolly. — *n.m.* velvet; shag.
vellutero, -ra, *n.m.* velvet worker.
vena, *n.f.* vein; grain; fibre; (*min.*) seam, lode; subterranean flow of water; mood; leaning, streak; ***dar en la vena,*** to hit upon the right means; ***estar de vena*** or ***en vena,*** to be in the mood, in the right mood; ***le dio la vena por el deporte,*** he got very keen on sport.

venablo, *n.m.* javelin, dart; ***echar venablos,*** to be violently angry.
venadero, *n.m.* place where deer shelter; (*Col.*, *Ec.*) deer hound.
venado, *n.m.* deer, stag; venison.
venaje, *n.m.* sources of a river.
venal (1), *a.* venous, of the veins.
venal (2), *a.* saleable; venal.
venalidad, *n.f.* venality, mercenariness.
venático, -ca, *a.* cranky.
venatorio, -ria, *a.* (of) hunting, venatorial.
vencedor, -ra, *a.* vanquishing, conquering. — *n.m.f.* vanquisher, conqueror, victor, winner.
vencejo, *n.m.* band, string; (*orn.*) swift, black-martin.
vencer [D], *v.t.* to vanquish, conquer, overcome, beat, defeat; to clear. — *v.i.* to conquer, win, succeed; (*com.*) to fall due. — **vencerse,** *v.r.* to control o.s.; to give way, sag, lean over.
vencetósigo, *n.m.* (*bot.*) swallow-wort, milk-weed.
vencible, *a.* conquerable, superable, vincible.
vencido, -da, *a.* overdue; due; ***ir de vencida,*** to be on the wane, past its height; ***le pagan por meses vencidos,*** he is paid at the end of the month.
vencimiento, *n.m.* victory, conquest; vanquishment; sagging, giving way, leaning over; (*com.*) expiration, maturity.
venda, *n.f.* band; bandage; fillet; blindfold.
vendaje, *n.m.* bandage; bandaging; binding with a fillet; (*C.R.*, *Col.*, *Ec.*, *Per.*) gratuity, tip.
vendar, *v.t.* to bandage; to blindfold; to hoodwink, blind.
vendaval, *n.m.* gale, hurricane.
vendavalada, *n.f.* gale, hurricane.
vendedor, -ra, *a.* selling, vending. — *n.m.f.* seller, vendor, salesman, saleswoman, salesgirl; ***aparato vendedor,*** slot machine, (*Am.*) vending machine.
vendehúmos, *n.m.f. inv.* courtier who trades on his *or* her influence.
vendeja, *n.f.* public sale.
vender, *v.t.* to sell, vend; (*coll.*, *fig.*) to sell out, sell down the river; ***vender salud,*** to be bursting with health; ***vamos vendidos,*** we're taking our life in our hands. — **venderse,** *v.r.* to be sold, be for sale, be on sale, be on the market; ***venderse caro,*** to sell one's life dearly; to play hard to get, be seldom seen.
vendí, *n.m.* receipt.
vendible, *a.* saleable, marketable.
vendiente, *a.* selling.
vendimia, *n.f.* vintage, grape harvest; (*coll.*, *fig.*) pile; windfall; ***hacer vendimia,*** to make a pile, strike it rich.
vendimiador, -ra, *n.m.f.* vintager.
vendimiar, *v.t.* to gather (*vintage*); (*fig.*) to reap (*benefits*); (*coll.*) to kill, murder.
vendo, *n.m.* selvage (*of cloth*).
venduta, *n.f.* (*Hisp. Am.*) auction.
vendutero, *n.m.* auctioneer.
Venecia, *n.f.* Venice; ***tierra de venecia,*** yellow ochre.
veneciano, -na, *a.*, *n.m.f.* Venetian.
venencia, *n.f.* tube (*for sampling sherry*).
venenífero, -ra, *a.* (*poet.*) poisonous.
veneno, *n.m.* poison; venom.
venenosidad, *n.f.* poisonousness; venomousness.
venenoso, -sa, *a.* poisonous; venomous.
venera, *n.f.* scallop shell; badge, emblem; spring (*of water*); ***empeñar la venera,*** to spare no expense.
venerabilísimo, -ma, *a. superl.* most venerable.
venerable, *a.* venerable.
veneración, *n.f.* veneration, worship.
venerador, -ra, *n.m.f.* worshipper.
venerando, -da, *a.* venerable.
venerante, *a.* worshipping.
venerar, *v.t.* to venerate, worship, reverence.
venéreo, -rea, *a.* venereous, venereal. — *n.m.* (*med.*) venereal disease.
venero, *n.m.* (*min.*) vein, lode, seam; radius (*of sundial*); spring (*of water*); origin, source.
véneto, -ta, *a.*, *n.m.f.* Venetian.
venezolanismo, *n.m.* word *or* phrase peculiar to Venezuela.
venezolano, -na, *a.*, *n.m.f.* Venezuelan.
vengable, *a.* worthy of revenge; that can be avenged.
vengador, -ra, *a.* avenging, revengeful. — *n.m.f.* avenger.
venganza, *n.f.* revenge, vengeance; retaliation.
vengar [B], *v.t.* to avenge. — **vengarse,** *v.r.* to take revence (***de,*** for *or* on).
vengativo, -va, *a.* revengeful, vindictive.
venia, *n.f.* permission, leave; pardon; nod; (*Hisp. Am.*) military salute; (*law*) licence to a minor to manage his own estate.
venial, *a.* venial.
venialidad, *n.f.* veniality.
venida, *n.f.* coming, arrival; return; flood, freshet; (*fenc.*) attack; (*fig.*) rashness.
venidero, -ra, *a.* coming, future; ***en lo venidero,*** in the future.
venimécum, *n.m.* vade-mecum.
venir [36], *v.i.* to come; to come back; ***que viene,*** next, coming; ***venir bien,*** to suit, be convenient; ***ni me va ni me viene,*** it is no concern of mine; ***vino a parar aquí,*** he ended up here; ***viene a ser lo mismo,*** it amounts to the same thing; ***venir a las manos,*** to come to blows; ***venir al caso,*** to be relevant; ***venir a menos,*** to come down in the world; ***venir a pelo, al pelo,*** to come in the nick of time; to be opportune; ***¿a qué viene eso?*** what has that to do with it?; ***venga lo que viniere,*** come what may; ***le viene pequeño*** (***grande***), it is too small (big) for him; ***si a mano viene,*** if the occasion arises; ***no me vengas con ésas,*** don't give me that (stuff); ***¿de dónde vienes?*** where have you been? *or* where have you come from? — **venirse,** *v.r.* to come, return; to ferment (*of bread* or *wine*); ***venirse abajo, a tierra,*** to collapse, tumble; ***venirse al suelo,*** to fall to the ground; to fall through.
venoso, -sa, *a.* venous, veiny, veined.
venta, *n.f.* sale; market; selling; roadside inn; ***de venta*** or ***en venta,*** on sale; ***poner a la venta,*** to put on sale *or* up for sale.
ventada, *n.f.* gust, blast of wind.
ventaja, *n.f.* advantage; good point; odds; gain, profit.
ventajismo, *n.m.* (*esp. pol.*) one-upmanship.
ventajoso, -sa, *a.* advantageous.
ventalla, *n.f.* valve; (*bot.*) pod.
ventalle, *n.m.* fan.
ventana, *n.f.* window; window-shutter; window-frame; ***ventana de la nariz,*** nostril; ***echar por la ventana,*** to throw away, squander; ***tirar la casa por la ventana,*** to spare no expense.
ventanaje, *n.m.* number *or* row of windows.
ventanal, *n.m.* large window.
ventanazo, *n.m.* slamming of a window.
ventanear, *v.i.* (*coll.*) to gaze out of the window.
ventaneo, *n.m.* window-gazing.
ventanera, *n.f.* window-gazer.
ventanero, *n.m.* glazier, window-maker; window-gazer; window-cleaner.
ventanico, *n.m.* small window-shutter.
ventanilla, *n.f.* small window, opening; window (*of car, train etc.*); ticket window; (counter) position; nostril.
ventanillo, *n.m.* small window; peep-hole.

ventar [I], *v.t.* to smell, scent, sniff; to find, discover. — *v.i.* to blow (*of wind*).
ventarrón, *n.m.* violent gust; gale.
venteadura, *n.f.* anemosis *or* splitting of timber.
ventear, *v.t.* to scent, sniff, smell; to air, dry out; to pry into. — *v.i.* to blow (*of wind*); to pry about. — **ventearse,** *v.r.* to split, blister, crack open; to break wind.
venteo, *n.m.* vent-hole.
venteril, *a.* of *or* typical of an inn *or* inns.
ventero, -ra, *n.m.f.* inn-keeper; scenting-dog.
ventilación, *n.f.* ventilation; airing.
ventilador, *n.m.* ventilator.
ventilar, *v.t.* to ventilate; to air.
ventisca, *n.f.* blizzard.
ventiscar [A], *v. impers.* to snow hard.
ventisco, *n.m.* snow-storm; snow-drift.
ventiscoso, -sa, *a.* stormy and snowy; full of snow-drifts.
ventisquear, *v. impers.* [VENTISCAR].
ventisquero, *n.m.* snow-drift; snow-storm; glacier; snow-capped mountain.
ventola, *n.f.* strong blast of wind.
ventolera, *n.f.* gust of wind; (*coll.*) vanity, haughtiness, pride; whim, crazy notion.
ventolina, *n.f.* light wind.
ventor, -ra, *a.* pointer (*dog*).
ventorrero, *n.m.* exposed, windy place.
ventorrillo, ventorro, *n.m.* wretched, pokey little inn.
ventosa, *n.f.* [VENTOSO].
ventosear(se), *v.i.* (*v.r.*) to break wind.
ventosidad, *n.f.* wind.
ventoso, -sa, *a.* windy; flatulent. — *n.f.* vent, air-hole; (*med.*) cupping-glass; (*zool.*) sucker; ***pegar una ventosa,*** to swindle.
ventral, *a.* ventral, (of the) belly.
ventrecha, *n.f.* belly (*of fish*).
ventregada, *n.f.* litter, brood.
ventrera, *n.f.* belly-girdle, sash, cummerbund.
ventrezuelo, *n.m.* small belly.
ventrículo, *n.m.* (*anat.*) ventricle.
ventril, *n.m.* cinch strap (*saddle*); counterpoise (*olive-oil mill*).
ventrílocuo, *n.m.* ventriloquist.
ventriloquia, *n.f.* ventriloquism.
ventrón, *n.m.* large belly; tripe.
ventroso, -sa, ventrudo, -da, *a.* big-bellied.
ventura (I), *n.f.* luck, fortune; chance, hazard; venture; ***probar ventura,*** to try one's luck; ***a la (buena) ventura,*** taking whatever luck offers; ***por ventura,*** perhaps.
venturado, -da, *a.* fortunate, lucky.
venturanza, *n.f.* happiness.
venturero, -ra, *a.* casual; lucky; vagrant. — *n.m.* fortune-hunter, adventurer.
venturilla, *n.f.* good luck.
venturina, *n.f.* aventurine, avanturine.
venturo, -ra (2), *a.* future, coming.
venturoso, -sa, *a.* happy, lucky, fortunate.
Venus (I), *n.f.* Venus (*goddess*).
Venus (2), *n.m.* (*astron.*) Venus.
venus, *n.f.* beautiful woman; sensual pleasure, venery; (*alch.*) copper.
venustidad, *n.f.* beauty, grace.
venusto, -ta, *a.* beautiful, graceful.
ver, *n.m.* sight, seeing; appearance, looks; ***tener buen ver,*** to be good-looking; ***a mi ver,*** in my opinion. — [37], *v.t.* to see; to have a look at; to hear (*a case*); to meet; ***a ver,*** let's see; ***a ver si no,*** what else can we do?; ***ver el cielo abierto,*** to see one's chance; ***ver las estrellas,*** to see stars; ***ver mundo,*** to see the world; ***ver visiones,*** to see things; ***ver y creer,*** seeing is believing; ***estar por ver,*** to remain to be seen; ***hacer ver,*** to show; to pretend; ***ser de ver,*** to be worth seeing; ***ya veremos,*** time will tell; ***a más ver, hasta más ver,*** be seeing you; ***si te vi no me acuerdo,*** out of sight, out of mind; ***lo veo venir,*** I know what he's after; ***no poder ver a,*** not to be able to stand the sight of; ***no tener que ver con,*** to have nothing to do with; ***veremos de arreglarlo,*** we'll see if we can fix it. — **verse,** *v.r.* to be seen; to be obvious; to meet; to find o.s.; ***ya se ve,*** you can see that; ***verse apurado,*** to find o.s. in trouble; ***verse con,*** to meet, have a talk with; ***véase,*** see.
vera (I), *n.f.* border, side; ***a la vera de,*** at the side of, beside.
veracidad, *n.f.* veracity, truthfulness.
vera efigies, *Lat.* true likeness, faithful portrait.
veranada, *n.f.* summer season (*livestock*).
veranadero, *n.m.* summer pasture.
veraneante, *n.m.* summer resident *or* holiday-maker.
veranear, *v.i.* to summer, spend the summer; to go on *or* spend one's summer holidays.
veraneo, *n.m.* summer holiday(s).
veranero, *n.m.* spot where cattle graze in summer.
veraniego, -ga, *a.* summer; weak, light; sickly.
veranillo, *n.m.* late *or* untimely summer; ***veranillo de San Martín,*** Indian summer.
verano, *n.m.* summer (season).
veras, *n.f.pl.* truth; earnestness; ***de veras,*** really; ***con muchas veras,*** very earnestly; ***va de veras,*** I really mean it, he really means it etc.
verascopio, *n.m.* stereoscope.
veratro, *n.m.* (*bot.*) hellebore.
veraz, *a.* veracious, truthful.
verba, *n.f.* loquacity, talkativeness.
verbal, *a.* verbal, oral.
verbalismo, *n.m.* verbalism.
verbasco, *n.m.* (*bot.*) mullein.
verbena, *n.f.* (*bot.*) verbena, vervain; fair; festival; fête.
verbenear, *v.i.* to abound; to swarm.
verberación, *n.f.* verberation.
verberar, *v.t.* to verberate, whip (up).
verbigracia, *adv.* for instance, for example.
verbo, *n.m.* word; (*gram.*) verb; ***echar verbos,*** to curse, swear.
verborrea, verbosidad, *n.f.* verbosity, wordiness.
verboso, -sa, *a.* verbose.
verdacho, *n.m.* (*ceram.*) green earth.
verdad, *n.f.* truth; ***verdad de Perogrullo,*** truism; ***de verdad,*** really, honestly; real, actual; ***en verdad,*** verily; ***a decir verdad,*** to tell the truth, truth to tell; ***decir cuatro verdades,*** to speak one's mind; ***faltar a la verdad,*** to lie; ***la verdad es que,*** the truth of the matter is that; ***es verdad,*** it's *or* that's true *or* so; so it is, so they were, so we shall etc.; ***¿verdad? ¿no es verdad?*** isn't it? didn't he? won't you? etc.
verdadero, -ra, *a.* true; real; actual.
verdal, *a.* applied to certain fruits which keep their green colour when ripe, as ***ciruela verdal,*** greengage.
verdasca, *n.f.* green branch, bough, twig.
verde, *a.* green; young, blooming; unripe; unseasoned, callow; dirty, smutty; ***chiste verde,*** blue joke; ***viejo verde,*** dirty old man; ***¡están verdes!*** it's envy *or* thwarted desire talking; ***poner verde,*** to call every name under the sun; to criticize savagely. — *n.m.* green; verdure, foliage; ***darse un verde,*** to have a fling.
verdea, *n.f.* greenish wine.
verdear, *v.i.* to grow *or* show green; to be a mass of green.
verdeceledón, *n.m.* pale sea-green; celadon.
verdecer [9], *v.i.* to grow *or* show green.
verdecico, -ca, *a.* greenish.

verdicillo, -lla, *a.* greenish. — *n.m.* (*orn.*) greenfinch.
verdecito, -ta, *a.* greenish.
verdeesmeralda, *a.* emerald green.
verdegal, *n.m.* green field.
verdegay, *a.*, *n.m.* light green.
verdeguear, *v.i.* to grow *or* show green.
verdemar, *a.*, *n.m.* sea-green.
verdemontaña, *n.f.* mountain-green.
verderol, *n.m.* (*zool.*) cockle.
verderón, *n.m.* (*orn.*) greenfinch.
verdete, *n.m.* verdigris.
verdevejiga, *n.f.* sap-green, deep green.
verdezuelo, *n.m.* (*orn.*) greenfinch.
verdín, *n.m.* pond-scums, pond-weed; copper oxide, verdigris; mildew, mould, green snuff; verdure.
verdina, *n.f.* [VERDINO].
verdinal, *n.m.* patch of greenery.
verdinegro, -gra, *a.* deep green, dark green.
verdino, -na, *a.* bright green. — *n.f.* verdure, greenness (*of plants and fruit*).
verdiseco, -ca, *a.* pale green; half dry.
verdolaga, *n.f.* (*bot.*) purslane; ***como verdolaga en huerto,*** at one's ease.
verdón, *n.m.* (*orn.*) greenfinch.
verdor, *n.m.* verdure, greenness, herbage; (*fig.*) strength, freshness, physical vigour; (*pl.* **verdores**) youth, vigorous age.
verdoso, -sa, *a.* greenish; verdant.
verdoyo, *n.m.* green mould; pond-scum.
verdugada, *n.f.* layer of bricks.
verdugado, *n.m.* hoopskirt.
verdugal, *n.m.* young shoots growing after a wood has been burned *or* cut down.
verdugazo, *n.m.* stroke with a twig.
verdugo, *n.m.* executioner, hangman; (*fig.*) butcher, sadist; shoot, sucker; slender rapier; scourge, lash; switch; weal, welt; (*arch.*) layer of bricks; (*jewel.*) hoop (*of a ring*).
verdugón, *n.m.* long shoot; weal, welt.
verduguillo, *n.m.* small shoot; blight, mildew; rust; small razor; duelling rapier; (*naut.*) sheer-rail.
verdulera, *n.f.* market woman; (*coll.*) coarse, low woman.
verdulería, *n.f.* greengrocer's shop; (*coll.*) obscenity.
verdulero, *n.m.* greengrocer.
verdura, *n.f.* greenness, green colour; verdure, verdancy; foliage; obscenity; (*pl.*) greens, vegetables.
verdusco, -ca, *a.* greenish.
verecundo, -da, *a.* bashful, modest, shy.
vereda, *n.f.* path, footpath, trail; (*Hisp. Am.*) pavement; ***hacer entrar en vereda,*** to bring to heel.
veredero, *n.m.* messenger.
veredicto, *n.m.* (*law*) verdict.
verga, *n.f.* (*naut.*) yard; (*coll., animals*) penis; steel bow (*crossbow*); ***verga seca,*** crossjack yard; ***vergas en alto,*** ready to sail; ***vergas en cruz,*** with squared yards.
vergajo, *n.m.* pizzle.
vergel, *n.m.* orchard; garden.
vergeta, *n.f.* small twig.
vergeteado, -da, *a.* (*her.*) vergette, paley.
vergonzante, *a.* shamefaced, bashful. — *n.m.f.* honest poor person, shy beggar.
vergonzoso, -sa, *a.* shameful, disgraceful; private (*parts*); bashful, shamefaced. — *n.m.f.* bashful person. — *n.m.* (*zool.*) armadillo.
verguear, *v.t.* to beat with a rod.
vergüenza, *n.f.* shame; shyness, bashfulness; embarrassment; disgrace; ***¡qué vergüenza!*** what a disgrace!; ***es una (mala) vergüenza,*** it's (utterly) disgraceful; ***no tiene vergüenza,*** he has no shame; he's a rotter; he isn't shy; ***perder la vergüenza,*** to lose all sense of shame; (*pl.*) nakedness, private parts.
verguero, *n.m.* (*prov.*) high constable.
vergueta, *n.f.* small rod *or* switch.
verguío, -guía, *a.* tough and flexible, leathery (*of wood*).
vericueto, *n.m.* by-way; ***por vericuetos,*** along the by-ways, up hill and down dale.
verídico, -ca, *a.* true, actual, that actually happened.
verificación, *n.f.* verification; carrying out; inspection.
verificador, -ra, *n.m.f.* inspector.
verificar [A], *v.t.* to verify; to carry out; to inspect. — **verificarse,** *v.r.* to take place.
verificativo, -va, *a.* verifying.
verija, *n.f.* region of the genitals.
veril, *n.m.* edge of a sand-bank.
verilear, *v.i.* to coast around a bank.
verisímil, *a.* probable, likely.
verisimilitud, *n.f.* verisimilitude, probability, likelihood.
verismo, *n.m.* authentic nature; realism.
verja, *n.f.* door-grating, window-grating, iron railing, grille.
vermicida, *a.* vermicidal. — *n.m.* vermicide.
vermicular, *a.* vermiculous, vermicular, full of worms *or* grubs.
vermiforme, *a.* vermiform, worm-like.
vermífugo, *n.m.* vermifuge.
verminoso, -sa, *a.* verminous.
vermut, *n.m.* vermouth.
vernáculo, -la, *a.* vernacular, native.
vernal, *a.* vernal, spring, spring-like.
vero (1), **-ra** (2), *a.* true.
vero (2), *n.m.* ermine (*fur*); (*her.*) vair.
verónica, *n.f.* speedwell; pass in bullfighting.
verosímil, *a.* probable, likely.
verosimilitud, *n.f.* verisimilitude, probability, likelihood.
verraco, *n.m.* boar.
verraquear, *v.i.* (*coll.*) to grunt (like a boar); to yell, squall.
verriondez, *n.f.* rutting-time (*of boars*); withered state (*of herbs*); over-cooking, toughness.
verriondo, -da, *a.* ruttish, in rut; withered; badly cooked (*of greens*).
verrón, *n.m.* boar.
verruga, *n.f.* wart.
verrugo, *n.m.* (*coll.*) miser.
verrugoso, -sa, *a.* warty.
versado, -da, *a.* versed, experienced, knowledgeable; ***versado en,*** conversant with.
versal, *a.*, *n.f.* capital (*letter*).
versar, *v.i.* to go round, turn; ***versar sobre,*** to deal with, treat of.
versátil, *a.* changeable, fickle, moody.
versatilidad, *n.f.* fickleness.
versear, *v.i.* (*coll.*) to versify, to improvise verses.
versecillo, *n.m.* little verse, verselet.
versería, *n.f.* compilation of poems.
versícula, *n.f.* stand for choir-books.
versiculario, *n.m.* chanter of versicles; keeper of the choir books.
versículo, *n.m.* versicle, verse.
versificación, *n.f.* versification.
versificador, -ra, *n.m.f.* versifier.
versificar [A], *v.i.* to versify, make verses. — *v.t.* to turn into verse.
versión, *n.f.* version; translation.
versista, *n.m.* (*coll.*) versifier, poetaster.
verso, *a.* (*trig.*) versed. — *n.m.* verse; line; versicle; ***verso blanco, libre*** or ***suelto,*** blank verse; ***versos pareados,*** verses in couplets.

vértebra, *n.f.* (*anat.*) vertebra.
vertebrado, -da, *a.* vertebrate. — *n.m.pl.* (**vertebrados**) Vertebrata, vertebrates.
vertebral, *a.* vertebral.
vertedera, *n.f.* mouldboard (*of a plough*).
vertedero, *n.m.* sink; dumping place; spillway.
vertedor, -ra, *a.* pouring; emptying; dumping. — *n.m.* spillway, drain; grocer's scoop; (*naut.*) scoop, bailer.
verter [Z], *v.t.* to pour; to shed, spill; to cast; to translate; to utter. — *v.i.* to run, flow.
vertibilidad, *n.f.* changeableness.
vertible, *a.* changeable.
vertical, *a.* vertical, upright. — *n.m.* (*astron.*) vertical circle. — *n.f.* vertical line.
verticalidad, *n.f.* verticalness.
vértice, *n.m.* vertex, apex; top.
verticidad, *n.f.* rotation.
verticilado, -da, *a.* verticillate.
verticillo, *n.m.* verticil, whorl.
vertiente, *a.* pouring, flowing. — *n.f.* watershed; slope.
vertiginoso, -sa, *a.* vertiginous, giddy, dizzy.
vértigo, *n.m.* giddiness, dizziness, vertigo; fit of madness.
vertimiento, *n.m.* shedding, effusion; pouring; dumping.
vesania, *n.f.* madness, insanity.
vesánico, -ca, *a.*, *n.m.f.* insane (*person*).
vesícula, *n.f.* (*anat.*) vesicle; (*anat.*) ***vesícula aérea,*** air vesicle of the lungs; (*anat.*) ***vesícula biliar,*** gall bladder; (*biol.*) ***vesícula elemental,*** cell; (*zool.*) ***vesícula ovárica,*** Graffian follicle; (*anat.*) ***vesícula seminal,*** sperm sac.
vesicular, *a.* vesicular.
vesiculoso, -sa, *a.* vesiculate.
véspero, *n.m.* vesper, evening star.
vespertillo, *n.m.* (*zool.*) bat.
vespertino, -na, *a.* vespertine, evening. — *n.f.* evening discourse in universities; evening sermon.
vestal, *a.*, *n.f.* vestal.
veste, *n.f.* (*poet.*) clothes, dress.
vestíbulo, *n.m.* vestibule, lobby, hall.
vestido, *n.m.* dress; garments, clothes, clothing, wearing apparel, garb.
vestidura, *n.f.* dress, clothing, garb, wearing-apparel; (*pl.*) vestments.
vestigio, *n.m.* vestige, sign, trace.
vestiglo, *n.m.* ghoul, monster.
vestimenta, *n.f.* clothes, garments; robes, vestments.
vestir [8], *v.t.* to clothe, dress; to don, put on; to wear; to adorn, deck; to cover, cloak; to rough-cast. — *v.i.* to dress; to look well, formal *or* right; ***viste muy bien,*** he dresses very well. — **vestirse,** *v.r.* to dress; to be covered; ***vístete bien,*** dress properly.
vestuario, *n.m.* wardrobe; apparel, costumes; dressing-room; cloakroom; (*mil.*) uniform.
vestugo, *n.m.* olive-stem, olive-bud.
veta, *n.f.* vein; seam; lode; stripe; grain; ***descubrir la veta de,*** to get the measure of.
vetado, -da, veteado, -da, *a.* veined, striped, streaky.
vetear, *v.t.* to variegate; to grain.
veterano, -na, *a.*, *n.m.* veteran.
veterinaria, *n.f.* veterinary science.
veterinario, *n.m.* veterinary surgeon.
veto, *n.m.* veto.
vetustez, *n.f.* age, oldness, antiquity.
vetusto, -ta, *a.* ancient, very old.
vez, *n.f.* turn; time; occasion; ***a la vez,*** at the same time; ***a la vez que,*** at the same time as; ***a su vez,*** in its turn, in his turn etc.; ***a veces,*** at times, sometimes; ***cada vez más,*** more and more; ***cada vez (que),*** every time; ***¿cuántas veces?*** how often?; ***muchas veces,*** often; ***pocas veces,*** seldom; ***de una vez,*** at one go; once (and) for all; ***de vez en cuando,*** from time to time; ***en vez de,*** instead of; ***dos veces más grande,*** twice as big; ***tal cual vez,*** once in a while; ***tal vez,*** perhaps; ***guárdame la vez,*** keep my place; ***hacer las veces de,*** to stand in for; ***tomar la vez a,*** to cut in ahead of; ***una que otra vez,*** every now and then, occasionally; ***una vez,*** once; ***otra vez,*** again; ***alguna vez,*** on the odd occasion; ever.
veza, *n.f.* (*bot.*) vetch.
vezar [C], *v.t.* to accustom, habituate.
vía, *n.f.* way; road; route; rail; track; gauge; tract, canal, passage; channel; ***en vías de,*** in the process of; ***por la vía de,*** via; ***por vía de,*** by way of; ***vía acuática,*** waterway; ***vía de agua,*** waterway; leak; ***vía ancha (estrecha),*** broad (narrow) gauge; ***vía férrea,*** iron road, railway; ***Vía Láctea,*** Milky Way; ***vía muerta,*** dead end; siding.
viabilidad, *n.f.* viability, feasibility, practicability.
viable, *a.* viable.
viadera, *n.f.* harness shaft (*of a loom*).
viador, *n.m.* (*theol.*) traveller.
viaducto, *n.m.* viaduct.
viajador, -ra, *a.* travelling. — *n.m.f.* traveller.
viajante, *a.* travelling. — *n.m.f.* traveller; commercial traveller.
viajar, *v.i.* to travel, journey, voyage.
viajata, *n.f.* long trek.
viaje, *n.m.* travel; journey; voyage; trip; passage; water supply; (*arch.*) obliquity; ***viaje de ida y vuelta*** or ***redondo,*** return journey, round trip; ***billete de ida y vuelta,*** return ticket; ***de viaje,*** on a trip, travelling; ***¡buen viaje!*** have a good journey!
viajero, -ra, *a.* travelling, that travels. — *n.m.f.* traveller, passenger. — *n.m.pl.* (**viajeros**) boarding house.
vial, *a.* (of the) road, relating to roads. — *n.m.* garden-path, lane, avenue.
vialidad, *n.f.* highway department; engineering department.
vianda, *n.f.* food, viands, fare, victuals, meat.
viandante, *n.m.* traveller, passenger; tramp.
viaraza, *n.f.* (*med.*) diarrhœa.
viaticar [A], *v.t.* to administer the viaticum to.
viático, *n.m.* viaticum; provisions for a journey; travelling expenses.
víbora, *n.f.* (*zool.*) viper.
viborezno, -na, *a.* viperine, viperous. — *n.m.* young viper, small viper.
vibración, *n.f.* vibration, shaking, quivering.
vibrador, -ra, *a.* vibrating. — *n.m.* (*elec.*) vibrator.
vibrante, *a.* vibrating, shaking; (*phon.*) trilled.
vibrar, *v.i.* to vibrate, shake, quiver, rattle, throb, pulsate.
vibratorio, -ria, *a.* vibratory.
viburno, *n.m.* viburnum.
vicaría, *n.f.* vicarship, vicarage; curacy.
vicariato, *n.m.* vicarship, vicarage.
vicario, -ria, *a.* vicarial, vicarious. — *n.m.* vicar, curate, deputy. — *n.f.* assistant superior in a convent.
vicealmiranta, *n.f.* vessel next in order to the admiral's.
vicealmirantazgo, *n.m.* vice-admiralship.
vicealmirante, *n.m.* vice-admiral.
vicecanciller, *n.m.* vice-chancellor.
viceconsiliario, *n.m.* vice-councillor.
vicecónsul, *n.m.* vice-consul.
viceconsulado, *n.m.* vice-consulate.
vicecristo, vicediós, *n.m.* honorific title of the Pope.
vicegerente, *a.* assistant manager.
vicenal, *a.* of twenty years' duration *or* occurrence.

vicepresidencia, *n.f.* vice-presidency.
vicepresidente, *n.m.* vice-president.
viceprovincia, *n.f.* (*eccles.*) religious houses enjoying the rank of a province.
viceprovincial, *n.m.* (*eccles.*) the superior of a vice-province.
vicerrector, *n.m.* vice-rector; assistant director.
vicesecretaría, *n.f.* under-secretaryship.
vicesecretario, *n.m.* under-secretary.
vicesimario, -ria, *a.* vicenary.
vicésimo, -ma, *a.* twentieth.
viceversa, *adv.* vice versa.
vicia, *n.f.* carob bean.
viciado, -da, *a.* foul, contaminated.
viciar, *v.t.* to vitiate; to adulterate, falsify; to annul, make void. — **viciarse,** *v.r.* to give o.s. up to vice; to become vitiated; to get twisted, become warped.
vicio, *n.m.* vice; defect; bad habit; waywardness; excessive growth; twist, warp; ***de vicio,*** from force of habit; for the sake of it.
vicioso, -sa, *a.* viscious; faulty, defective; excessive, luxuriant; spoiled, unruly (*child*).
vicisitud, *n.f.* vicissitude.
vicisitudinario, -ria, *a.* subject to vicissitude.
víctima, *n.f.* victim; sacrifice; casualty.
victimario, *n.m.* (*eccles.*) server.
victo, *n.m.* day's sustenance.
¡víctor! ¡vítor! *interj.* hurrah!
victorear, *v.t.* to acclaim.
victoria, *n.f.* victory; triumph; ***cantar (la) victoria,*** to cry victory.
victorial, *a.* relating to victory.
victorioso, -sa, *a.* victorious.
vicuña, *n.f.* (*zool.*) vicuña.
vichoco, -ca, *a.* (*Arg., Chi.*) weak, feeble; disabled.
vid, *n.f.* vine, grape-vine.
vida, *n.f.* life; living; livelihood; life-time; ***coste*** or ***costo de (la) vida,*** cost of living; ***darse buena vida,*** to live well, enjoy life; ***de por vida,*** for life; ***en vida de,*** during the life-time of; ***en mi vida, en la vida,*** never; ***ganarse la vida,*** to earn one's living; ***hacer vida marital,*** to live together as man and wife; ***jugarse la vida,*** to risk one's life; ***tener siete vidas,*** to have nine lives; ***vida airada, mala vida,*** life of vice; ***vida de familia,*** home life.
vidalita, *n.f.* (*Arg.*) sad love-song.
vidarra, *n.f.* climbing plant.
videncia, *n.f.* clear-sightedness; clairvoyance.
vidente, *a.* seeing; sighted. — *n.m.* sighted person; seer.
vidorra, *n.f.* (*coll.*) great life, life of ease, pleasure and plenty; ***pegarse*** or ***darse una vidorra,*** to live it up.
vidriado, *n.m.* crockery, glazed earthenware.
vidriar [L], *v.t.* to varnish, glaze.
vidriera, *n.f.* stained-glass window; glass door *or* partition; (*Hisp. Am.*) shop window; showcase.
vidriería, *n.f.* glass factory; glazier's shop; glassware.
vidriero, *n.m.* glazier; glass-dealer; glass-blower.
vidrio, *n.m.* glass; ***pagar los vidrios rotos,*** to carry the can, face the music, foot the bill.
vidrioso, -sa, *a.* vitreous; glassy, touchy; delicate.
vidual, *a.* belonging to widowhood.
vidueño, viduño, *n.m.* variety of vine.
viejarrón, viejazo, *n.m.* very old man.
viejecito, -ta, viejezuelo, -la, *a.* little old man (woman).
viejo, -ja, *a.* old, aged; ***perro viejo,*** old dog. — *n.m.f.* old man, woman; ***cuentos de viejas,*** old wives' tales; ***viejo verde,*** dirty old man.
Viena, *n.f.* Vienna; Vienne.
vienés, -nesa, *a., n.m.f.* Viennese.
vientecillo, *n.m.* light wind, breeze.
viento, *n.m.* wind; (*artill.*) windage; (*naut.*) course; scent, smell; guy, bracing-rope; vanity; ***viento escaso,*** slack wind; ***viento terral,*** land breeze; ***afirmarse el viento,*** to blow steadily; ***refrescarse el viento,*** (*wind*) to freshen; ***viento contrario,*** adverse wind; ***vientos alisios,*** trade winds; ***contra viento y marea de,*** in the teeth of; ***beber(se) los vientos por,*** to be crazy about; ***rosa de los vientos,*** compass; ***ir viento en popa,*** to run before the wind; (*fig.*) to go great guns.
vientre, *n.m.* abdomen, belly, stomach; bowels; womb; ***reses de vientre,*** breeding cattle; ***hacer de vientre,*** to have a movement of the bowels.
viernes, *n.m. inv.* Friday; fast day; ***Viernes Santo,*** Good Friday; ***cara de viernes,*** wan, thin face.
vierteaguas, *n.m. inv.* (*arch.*) flashing.
Vietnam (el), *n.m.* Vietnam.
vietnamita, *a., n.m.f.* Vietnamese.
viga, *n.f.* beam, rafter; girder; joist; baulk; bridge truss; quantity of olives produced in one pressing; ***viga de aire,*** joist; ***viga maestra,*** continuous girder.
vigencia, *n.f.* (*law*) state of being in force.
vigente, *a.* (*law*) in force; prevailing.
vigesimal, *a.* vigesimal.
vigésimo, -ma, *a.* twentieth.
vigía, *n.m.* lookout, watch. — *n.f.* watchtower; watch, watching; (*naut.*) shoal, rock.
vigiar, *v.i.* to watch, keep a look out.
vigilancia, *n.f.* vigilance, watchfulness.
vigilante, *a.* vigilant, watchful. — *n.m.* watchman, guard; shopwalker, (*Am.*) floorwalker.
vigilar, *v.t., v.i.* to watch (over), keep guard (over); ***vigilar de cerca,*** to keep a close watch upon.
vigilativo, -va, *a.* causing wakefulness.
vigilia, *n.f.* wakefulness; watchfulness; nocturnal study; vigil; fast; eve; (*mil.*) watch, guard; ***comer de vigilia,*** to fast, abstain from meat.
vigitano, -na, *a., n.m.f.* (native) of Vich.
vigor, *n.m.* vigour, strength; force; ***entrar en vigor,*** to come into force *or* effect.
vigorar, vigorizar [C], *v.t.* to invigorate, strengthen; to encourage.
vigorosidad, *n.f.* vigour, strength.
vigoroso, -sa, *a.* vigorous, strong.
vigota, *n.f.* (*naut.*) dead-eye; plank of wood.
viguería, *n.f.* (*naut.*) timber-work; set of beams *or* girders.
vigués, -guesa, *a., n.m.f.* (native) of Vigo.
vigueta, *n.f.* small beam *or* girder.
vihuela, *n.f.* cithern.
vihuelista, *n.m.f.* cithern-player.
vil, *a.* base, vile, dastardly.
vilano, *n.m.* (*bot.*) thistledown.
vileza, *n.f.* baseness, dastardliness; base *or* dastardly act.
vilipendiar, *v.t.* to revile.
vilipendio, *n.m.* vilification; contempt, disdain.
vilipendioso, -sa, *a.* contemptible.
vilo, (en), *adv.* in the air.
vilordo, -da, *a.* slothful, heavy, lazy.
vilorta, *n.f.* willow-ring; game resembling lacrosse; clasp ring (*of a plough*); washer.
vilorto, *n.m.* reed; reed hoop; crosse for playing ***vilorta***; (*bot.*) clematis, liana.
vilote, *a.* (*Arg., Chi.*) cowardly, fainthearted.
viltrotear, *v.i.* (*coll.*) to gad about.
villa, *n.f.* town; villa; municipal council; ***casa de la villa,*** town hall; ***la Villa y Corte,*** Madrid.
Villadiego, *n.m.* (*coll.*) ***tomar*** (or ***coger***) ***las de Villadiego,*** to clear out; to run away.
villaje, *n.m.* village, hamlet.
villanada, *n.f.* villainous act.
villanaje, *n.m.* (*obs.*) villainage, peasantry.

villancejo, villancete, villancico, *n.m.* Christmas carol.
villanciquero, *n.m.* carol singer *or* writer.
villanchón, -chona, *a.* boorish, rustic.
villanería, *n.f.* lowness of birth; villainy; vile deed.
villanesco, -ca, *a.* rustic, boorish, rude. — *n.f.* ancient Spanish song and dance.
villanía, *n.f.* meanness, lowness of birth; (*obs.*) villainage, rusticity; vulgar remark *or* action; villainy.
villano, -na, *a.* rustic, boorish, low-class; unworthy, worthless; villainous, wicked. — *n.m.* villain, peasant, rustic; old Spanish melody and dance; ***el villano en su rincón,*** typical unsociable wary rustic.
villanote, *a.* great villain.
villar, *n.m.* village, hamlet.
villazgo, *n.m.* charter of a town; tax laid on towns.
villeta, *n.f.* small town *or* borough.
villoría, *n.f.* farm-house; hamlet.
villorín, *n.m.* undyed wool, broadcloth.
villorrio, *n.m.* mean little village.
vimbre, *n.m.* (*bot.*) osier, willow.
vinagrada, *n.f.* refreshment of water, vinegar and sugar.
vinagre, *n.m.* vinegar; (*coll.*) ***cara de vinagre,*** sour-puss.
vinagrera, *n.f.* vinegar cruet; (*bot.*) sorrel; (*Hisp. Am.*) heartburn; (*pl.*) cruet stand.
vinagrero, *n.m.* vinegar-seller.
vinagreta, *n.f.* vinaigrette sauce.
vinagrillo, *n.m.* weak vinegar; cosmetic lotion; rose-vinegar.
vinagroso, -sa, *a.* vinegary, sour; (*coll.*) vinegarish, peevish.
vinagrón, *n.m.* vinegary wine.
vinajera, *n.f.* (*eccles.*) cruet; (*pl.*) set of two cruets and a tray.
vinariego, *n.m.* vine-grower.
vinario, -ria, *a.* (belonging to) wine.
vinatera (1), *n.f.* (*naut.*) strop, tricing line.
vinatería, *n.f.* vintnery, wine-trade; wine-shop.
vinatero, -ra (2), *a.* pertaining to wine. — *n.m.* wine-merchant, vintner.
vinaza, *n.f.* wine drawn from the lees.
vinazo, *n.m.* strong, heavy wine.
vincapervinca, *n.f.* (*bot.*) periwinkle.
vinculable, *a.* that can be tied *or* bound; (*law*) entailable.
vinculación, *n.f.* tying; (*law*) entailment.
vincular, *v.t.* to tie, bind; to ground, found (*hopes etc.*); to entail.
vínculo, *n.m.* tie, vinculum, link, chain, bond (of union); foundation; entail.
vincha, *n.f.* (*Arg.*, *Bol.*, *Chi.*, *Per.*) ribbon, handkerchief for the head *or* hair.
vinchuca, *n.f.* (*Arg.*, *Chi.*, *Per.*) winged bed-bug.
vindicación, *n.f.* vindication; revenge.
vindicar [A], *v.t.* to vindicate; to avenge.
vindicativo, -va, *a.* vindictive, revengeful.
vindicatorio, -ria, *a.* vindicatory.
vindicta, *n.f.* revenge; ***vindicta pública,*** public punishment.
vínico, -ca, *a.* vinic.
vinícola, *a.* (of) wine; vine-growing. — *n.m.* vine-grower.
vinicultor, *n.m.* vine-grower.
vinicultura, *n.f.* viniculture.
viniebla, *n.f.* (*bot.*) hound's tongue.
vinificación, *n.f.* wine-making, wine-fermentation.
vinillo, *n.m.* weak wine.
vino, *n.m.* wine; wine *or* sherry party; ***vino bautizado,*** watered wine; ***vino moro,*** unadulterated wine; ***vino de cuerpo,*** strong-bodied wine; ***vino tinto,*** red wine; ***vino peleón,*** ordinary wine; ***vino de Jerez,*** sherry; ***vino de Oporto,*** port wine; ***vino de coco,*** coconut milk; ***vino generoso,*** vintage, select *or* well-aged wine; ***dormir el vino,*** to sleep it off.
vinolencia, *n.f.* inebriation, excess in drinking.
vinolento, -ta, *a.* fond of drink, given to excess in drinking.
vinosidad, *n.f.* vinosity.
vinoso, -sa, *a.* vinous, vinose.
vinote, *n.m.* coarse wine; wine residue.
vintén, *n.m.* (*Ur.*) small copper coin.
viña, *n.f.* vineyard.
viñadero, *n.m.* vineyard-keeper.
viñador, *n.m.* wine-grower.
viñatero, *n.m.* vine-grower.
viñedo, *n.m.* vineyard; vineyard-country.
viñero, *n.m.* vintager.
viñeta, *n.f.* vignette.
viñuela, *n.f.* small vineyard.
viola, *n.m.f.* viola player. — *n.f.* viola; viol.
violáceo, -cea, *a.* violaceous; violet coloured.
violación, *n.f.* violation; rape.
violado, -da, *a.* violet-coloured.
violador, -ra, *n.m.f.* violator; raper.
violar, *v.t.* to violate; to rape.
violencia, *n.f.* violence; embarrassment; embarrassing business.
violentar, *v.t.* to force. — **violentarse,** *v.r.* to force o.s., take a firm hold of o.s., make a deliberate *or* conscious effort.
violento, -ta, *a.* violent; embarrassing, awkward.
violero, *n.m.* (*obs.*) viol player.
violeta, *n.f.* (*bot.*) violet.
violeto, *n.m.* clingstone peach.
violín, *n.m.* violin; fiddle; violinist; (*Arg.*, *Ven.*, *coll.*) ***embolsar el violín,*** to be crestfallen, dejected; ***violín de Ingres,*** hobby.
violinista, *n.m.f.* violinist.
violón, *n.m.* bass-viol, double bass; double bass player; ***tocar el violón,*** to talk rot.
violoncelo, violonchelo, *n.m.* violoncello.
violonchelista, *n.m.f.* violoncellist, cellist.
viperino, -na, *a.* viperine, viperous.
vira, *n.f.* dart; welt (*of a shoe*).
viracocha, *n.m.f.* (*obs.*, *Chi.*, *Per.*) Spaniard.
virada, *n.f.* (*naut.*) tack, tacking; (*motor.*) turn.
virador, *n.m.* top-rope; (*naut.*) viol; (*photo.*) fixative.
virago, *n.f.* virago.
viraje, *n.m.* (*photo.*) toning; (*motor.*) turn, twist, swerve.
virar, *v.t.* (*photo.*) to tone; (*naut.*) to turn, heave (*the capstan*). — *v.t.*, *v.i.* (*naut.*) to tack, veer, put about. — *v.i.* (*motor.*) to turn, twist, swerve.
viratón, *n.m.* bolt (*arrow*).
viravira, *n.f.* (*Arg.*, *Chi.*, *Per.*, *Ven.*) medicinal plant.
virazones, *n.m.pl.* alternate land and sea breezes.
virgen, *a.*, *n.m.f.* virgin. — *n.f.* maiden, maid; beam standard (*in olive-oil mills*); (*astron.*) Virgin, Virgo; Blessed Virgin.
virgiliano, *a.* Virgilian.
virginal, *a.* virginal, virgin, maidenly. — *n.m.* (*mus.*) virginal.
virgíneo, -nea, *a.* virginal, virgin, maidenly.
virginia, *n.f.* Virginia tobacco.
virginiano, -na, *a.*, *n.m.f.* Virginian.
virginidad, *n.f.* virginity, maidenhood.
Virgo, *n.m.* (*astron.*, *astrol.*) Virgo.
virgo, *n.m.* virginity; (*anat.*) hymen.
vírgula, *n.f.* small rod, thin line; cholera germ.
virgulilla, *n.f.* small *or* fine stroke; very thin line; comma, apostrophe, diacritical sign.
viril, *a.* virile, manly. — *n.m.* clear glass; (*eccles.*) monstrance.
virilidad, *n.f.* virility, manhood.

virio, *n.m.* loriot, golden oriole.
viripotente, *a.* marriageable, nubile (*of women*); vigorous, strong.
virola, *n.f.* collar, hoop; knob of a curtain-rod; check-ring of a goad.
virolento, -ta, *a.* having smallpox; pock-marked.
virón, *n.m.* large dart.
virotazo, *n.m.* wound caused by shaft, dart *or* arrow.
virote, *n.m.* shaft, dart, arrow; iron rod on a slave's collar; (*coll.*) beau, young blood; (*coll.*) stuffed shirt; (*coll.*) April fool's trick; ***cada uno mire por el virote,*** let everyone see to his own business.
virotillo, *n.m.* (*arch.*) strut, intertie; (*pl.*) (*arch.*) braces.
virotismo, *n.m.* conceit, pride, airs.
virotón, *n.m.* large arrow *or* dart.
virreina, *n.f.* vicereine; viceroy's wife.
virreinato, virreino, *n.m.* viceroyship; viceroyalty.
virrey, *n.m.* viceroy.
virtual, *a.* virtual.
virtualidad, *n.f.* virtuality, efficacy.
virtud, *n.f.* virtue; ***en virtud de,*** by virtue of.
virtuoso, -sa, *a.* virtuous. — *n.m.f.* virtuoso.
viruela, *n.f.* smallpox; pock-mark; ***viruelas locas,*** chicken-pox; ***picado de viruela,*** pock-marked; ***a la vejez, viruelas,*** there's no fool like an old fool.
virulencia, *n.f.* virulence.
virulento, -ta, *a.* virulent.
virus, *n.m. inv.* virus.
viruta, *n.f.* wood shaving, cutting, chip.
vis, *n.f.* (*theat.*) ***vis cómica,*** verve.
visaje, *n.m.* grimace, wry face.
visajero, -ra, *n.m.f.* grimacer.
visar, *v.t.* to visa, mark with a visa; to countersign; (*artill., topog.*) to sight.
víscera, *n.f.* viscera.
visceral, *a.* visceral.
visco, *n.m.* bird-lime.
viscosidad, *n.f.* viscosity.
viscoso, -sa, *a.* viscous.
visera, *n.f.* visor; eye-shade.
visibilidad, *n.f.* visibility.
visible, *a.* visible; presentable, fit to be seen.
visigodo, -da, *a., n.m.f.* Visigoth.
visigótico, -ca, *a.* Visigothic.
visillo, *n.m.* lace curtain.
visión, *n.f.* sight; vision; view; ***ver visiones,*** to see things.
visionario, -ria, *a., n.m.f.* visionary.
visir, *n.m.* vizier.
visita, *n.f.* visit; visitor, caller; visitors, callers; social call; inspection; ***derecho de visita,*** right of search; ***tener visita,*** to have visitors *or* company; ***hacer una visita,*** to pay a call; ***pagar una visita,*** to repay *or* return a visit *or* call.
visitación, *n.f.* visitation; visiting; visit.
visitador, -ra (1), *n.m.f.* visitor, inspector.
visitadora (2), *n.f.* (*Hond., Ven.*) clyster, enema.
visitar, *v.t.* to visit, call upon; to search; to inspect; to go round (*town, museum, etc.*) sight-seeing.
visiteo, *n.m.* frequent calling *or* visiting.
visitero, -ra, *a.* fond of visiting.
visitón, *n.m.* tedious *or* unwelcome visit, visitor, caller.
visivo, -va, *a.* visual.
vislumbrar, *v.t.* to glimpse, catch a glimpse of, see indistinctly.
vislumbre, *n.f.* glimpse; glimmer; surmise, inkling.
viso, *n.m.* elevated spot; prospect, outlook; gleam, sheen; coloured slip worn under a transparent frock; appearance; moiré; ***a dos visos,*** in two ways, from two (*different*) points of view; ***hacer viso,*** to attract attention; ***de viso,*** of importance; ***no tiene visos de despejar,*** it doesn't look as if it's going to clear up (*weather*).
visogodo, -da, *a., n.m.f.* Visigoth.
visón, *n.m.* (*zool.*) mink.
visor, *n.m.* (*photo.*) view-finder; (*aer.*) bomb sight.
visorio, -ria, *a.* visual, optic. — *n.m.* expert examination.
víspera, *n.f.* eve, day before; (*pl.*) (*eccles.*) vespers; ***en vísperas de,*** on the eve of.
vista (1), *n.m.* customs inspector; (*pl.*) meeting, encounter; wedding presents; front, collar and cuffs (*shirts*); openings *or* windows (*of a building*). — *n.f.* view; sight; seeing, vision; eye, eyesight; look, appearance; prospect, vista; (*law*) hearing; ***alzar la vista,*** to look up; ***a primera vista,*** at first sight; ***a vista de pájaro,*** from a bird's-eye view; ***a la vista,*** in sight; on view; ***bajar la vista,*** to look down; ***estar a la vista,*** to be plain, obvious; ***con vistas a,*** with a view to; ***aguzar la vista,*** to sharpen one's eyes; ***apartar la vista,*** to turn one's eyes away; (*fig.*) to look the other way; ***comerse con la vista,*** to devour with one's eyes; ***conocer de vista,*** to know by sight; ***echar una vista a,*** to take a look at; ***echar la vista a,*** to get one's eyes on; ***le tiene echada la vista,*** he's got his eye on it; ***en vista de,*** in view of; ***hacer la vista gorda*** (***ante***), to wink (at), turn a blind eye (to); ***¡hasta la vista!*** good-bye!; ***pasar la vista por,*** to look over, glance over; ***perder de vista,*** to lose sight of; ***perderse de vista,*** to go out of sight; ***salta a la vista,*** it strikes you at once; ***tener vista,*** to look good; to be sharp, smart; ***volver la vista atrás,*** to look back.
vistazo, *n.m.* glance; ***echar un vistazo,*** to take a look.
vistillas, *n.f.pl.* heights; ***irse a las vistillas,*** to take a surreptitious peep.
visto, -ta (2), *a.* clear, obvious, evident; (*law*) whereas; ***está bien*** (***mal***) ***visto,*** he is (not) looked upon favourably; ***está visto que,*** it is obvious that; ***una cosa nunca vista,*** sth. extraordinary *or* unheard of; ***vista bueno*** (*abbreviation* ***V⁰ B⁰***), correct, approved. O.K. — *p.p. irreg.* [VER].
vistosidad, *n.f.* fine *or* grand look, appearance; showiness.
vistoso, -sa, *a.* fine, grand; showy.
visual, *a.* visual. — *n.f.* line of sight; glance.
visualidad, *n.f.* visuality.
visura, *n.f.* ocular inspection, expert examination.
vital, *a.* vital, belonging to life; necessary, essential.
vitalicio, -cia, *a.* life-long, (lasting for) life; ***pensión vitalicia,*** life pension. — *n.m.* life-insurance policy.
vitalicista, *n.m.f.* person who enjoys a life pension.
vitalidad, *n.f.* vitality.
vitalismo, *n.m.* vitalism.
vitalista, *n.m.f.* vitalist.
vitando, -da, *a.* that ought to be shunned; infamous.
vitela, *n.f.* vellum, parchment.
vitelina, *a.* vitelline.
vitícola, *a.* viticultural, grape-growing. — *n.m.* grape-grower.
viticultura, *n.f.* viticulture, vine cultivation.
vito, *n.m.* Andalusian folksong and dance.
vitola, *n.f.* (*mil.*) ball calibre, standard gauge; cigar-band; standard shape and size for cigars; (*naut.*) templet; appearance, looks, aspect.
vítor, *n.m.* triumphal pageant; commemorative tablet. — *interj.* hurrah! long live!
vitorear, *v.t.* to cheer, acclaim.
vitoriano, -na, *a., n.m.f.* (native) of Vitoria.

vitre, *n.m.* (*naut.*) thin canvas.
vítreo, -rea, *a.* vitreous, glassy.
vitrificable, *a.* vitrificable.
vitrificación, *n.f.* vitrification.
vitrificar [A], *v.t.* to vitrify.
vitrina, *n.f.* glasscase, showcase.
vitriólico, -ca, *a.* (*chem.*) vitriolic.
vitriolo, *n.m.* vitriol.
vitualla, *n.f.* victuals, provisions, viands.
vituallar, *v.t.* to victual.
vítulo marino, *n.m.* (*zool.*) sea calf.
vituperable, *a.* vituperable.
vituperación, *n.f.* vituperation.
vituperador, -ra, *a.* vituperating. — *n.m.f.* vituperator.
vituperante, *a.* vituperating.
vituperar, *v.t.* to vituperate.
vituperio, *n.m.* vituperation.
vituperioso, -sa, *a.* vituperative.
viuda, *n.f.* widow; dowager; (*bot.*) mourning bride; ***condesa viuda,*** dowager countess.
viudal, *a.* belonging to a widow *or* widower.
viudedad, *n.f.* widowhood; widow's pension.
viudez, *n.f.* widowhood.
viudita, *n.f.* merry (little) widow; sprightly widow.
viudo, *n.m.* widower; widower bird.
viva (I), *n.m.* hurrah, cry of acclamation. — *interj.* long live.
vivac, *n.m.* bivouac.
vivacidad, *n.f.* vivacity, liveliness, briskness; brilliancy; energy, vigour.
vivales, *n.m.* (*coll.*) smart *or* smooth operator, wily bird, clever customer.
vivandero, *n.m.* sutler.
vivaque, *n.m.* bivouac.
vivaquear, *v.i.* to bivouac.
vivaqueo, *n.m.* bivouacking.
vivar, *n.m.* warren, burrow; vivarium.
vivaracho, -cha, *a.* (*coll.*) lively, sprightly, frisky.
vivaz, *a.* lively; active, vigorous, energetic; bright, witty; perennial, evergreen.
vivencia, *n.f.* experience, piece of life.
vivencial, *a.* (of) experience (of life).
viveral, *n.m.* (*hort.*) nursery.
víveres, *n.m.pl.* provisions, eatables; (*mil.*) stores.
vivero, *n.m.* fish-pond; (*hort.*) nursery; (*fig.*) hot-bed.
viveza, *n.f.* liveliness; sprightliness, briskness; keenness; sharpness; brightness.
vividero, -ra, *a.* habitable; (*coll.*) bearable.
vívido, -da, *a.* vivid, bright.
vividor, -ra, *n.m.f.* bon viveur.
vivienda, *n.f.* dwelling; housing; ***problema de la vivienda,*** housing problem.
viviente, *a.* living, alive.
vivificación, *n.f.* vivification, enlivening.
vivificador, -ra, *n.m.f.* vivifier, life-giver, animator.
vivificante, *a.* vivifying, life-giving.
vivificar [A], *v.t.* to vivify, animate, enliven; to refresh, comfort.
vivificativo, -va, *a.* life-giving; comforting.
vivífico, -ca, *a.* vivific.
vivíparo, -ra, *a.* viviparous.
vivir, *n.m.* life, living; ***gente de mal vivir,*** loose-living people. — *v.i.* to live; to be alive; ***¿quién vive?*** who goes there?; ***vivir de,*** to live on.
vivisección, *n.f.* vivisection.
vivo, -va (2), *a.* alive, living, live; quick, sharp, smart; lively; bright; ***al vivo*** or ***a lo vivo,*** true to life, vividly; ***cal viva,*** quicklime; ***carne viva,*** quick flesh (*in a wound*); ***herir en lo vivo,*** to cut to the quick, get on the raw; ***a viva voz,*** by word of mouth. — *n.m.* raw (*flesh*); (*vet.*) inflamed swelling on the back; (*arch.*) sharp corner, angle, edge; edging, border; corded seam.

vizcacha, *n.f.* (*Hisp. Am.*) rock rabbit.
vizcaíno, -na, *n.m.f.* Biscayan.
vizcaitarra, *a.*, *n.m.f.* Basque nationalist.
Vizcaya, *n.f.* Biscay.
vizcondado, *n.m.* viscountship, viscountcy.
vizconde, *n.m.* viscount.
vizcondesa, *n.f.* viscountess.
vocablo, *n.m.* word, term.
vocabulario, *n.m.* vocabulary.
vocabulista, *n.m.f.* lexicographer; student of words.
vocación, *n.f.* vocation, calling.
vocal, *a.* vocal, oral. — *n.m.* voter; member (*of a committee* or *governing body*). — *n.f.* vowel.
vocalización, *n.f.* (*mus.*) vocalization.
vocalizar [C], *v.i.* (*mus.*) to vocalize, articulate.
vocativo, *n.m.* vocative case.
voceador, -ra, *n.m.f.* vociferator; town crier.
vocear, *v.t.*, *v.i.* to yell, bawl; to cry out.
vocejón, *n.m.* harsh voice.
vocería, *n.f.* clamour, hallooing, outcry.
vocerío, *n.m.* bawling, shouting.
vocero, *n.m.* spokesman.
vociferación, *n.f.* vociferation, outcry.
vociferador, -ra, *a.* shouting. — *n.m.f.* vociferator.
vociferante, *a.* vociferating.
vociferar, *v.t.*, *v.i.* to vociferate. — *v.t.* to boast of.
vocinglería, *n.f.* clamour, outcry.
vocinglero, -ra, *a.* bawling, yelling, screaming.
volada, *n.f.* [VOLADO].
voladero, -ra, *a.* volatile, fleeting, flying. — *n.m.* precipice, abyss. — *n.f.* float (*of a water-wheel*).
voladizo, -za, *a.* projecting, jutting out. — *n.m.* corbel.
volado, -da, *a.* (*print.*) superior; (*coll.*) furious, wild. — *n.m.* sweetmeat. — *n.f.* short flight; (*Mex.*) story, lie.
volador, -ra, *a.* flying; hanging; swift. — *n.m.* (*ichth.*) flying-fish; sky-rocket. — *n.f.* fly-wheel (*of an engine*).
voladura, *n.f.* explosion, blasting, blowing up.
volandas, (en), *adv.* in the air; flying; fleeting, swiftly.
volandero, -ra, *a.* ready to fly; fluttering in the air; suspended in the air; chance, fortuitous; fleeting, unsettled, volatile, variable; (*naut.*) ***vapor volandero,*** tramp steamer. — *n.f.* runner (*in oil-mills*); (*coll.*) lie; (*print.*) old-fashioned galley-slice; (*mech.*) washer.
volanta, *n.f.* (*W. Indies*) two-wheeled cab.
volante, *a.* flying. — *n.m.* shuttlecock; shuttlecock and battledore; balance beam; fly-wheel; balance-wheel; steering-wheel; flounce; (*coiner's*) stamping-mill; footman, lackey, flunkey; linen coat; receipt, note, form.
volantín, *n.m.* fishing-line; (*Arg.*, *Chi.*, *Cub.*, *P.R.*) kite.
volantista, *n.m.f.* driver, speed-merchant.
volantón, *n.m.* fledgling.
volapié, *n.m.* (*tauro.*) running and wounding thrust.
volar [4], *v.t.* to fly; to blow up; to start (*game*); to make furious *or* wild; to blow, fan; (*print.*) to raise. — *v.i.* to fly; to fly away; to jut out; to soar up; ***volando,*** double quick. — **volarse,** *v.r.* to get blown away; to get furious *or* wild.
volateo, (al), *adv.* shooting (birds) on the wing.
volatería, *n.f.* fowling; sporting with hawks; fowls, flock of birds; (*fig.*) wool-gathering, dreaming; ***de volatería,*** at random.
volátil, *a.* volatile.
volatilidad, *n.f.* volatility.
volatilización, *n.f.* volatilization.
volatilizar [C], *v.t.* to volatilize. — **volatilizarse,** *v.r.* to vaporize; (*coll.*) to disappear.
volatín, volatinero, *n.m.* tight-rope walker, acrobat; acrobatic feat; (*Per.*) acrobatic show.
volatizar [C], *v.t.* (*chem.*) to volatilize.

volcán, *n.m.* volcano; (*Col.*) precipice, steep and broken ground.
volcánico, -ca, *a.* volcanic.
volcar [A], *v.t.* to upset, overturn; to capsize; to dump, empty; to tip over; to spill. — *v.i.* to overturn; to capsize. — **volcarse,** *v.r.* (*fig.*) to go out of one's way, go to great lengths, spare no expense *or* trouble, consider nothing too much trouble.
volea, *n.f.* swingle-tree; volley (*of a ball*).
volear, *v.t.* to volley; (*agric.*) to sow broadcast.
voleo, *n.m.* volley; high step (*Spanish dance*); swipe; ***de un voleo,*** at one go *or* stroke; ***al voleo,*** broadcast.
volframio, *n.m.* (*chem.*) wolfram.
volframita, *n.f.* (*chem.*) wolframite.
volición, *n.f.* volition.
volitar, *v.i.* to twirl; to flutter.
volitivo, -va, *a.* volitional, volitive.
volquearse, *v.r.* to tumble; to wallow.
volquete, *n.m.* tip-car, tip-cart, dump-truck, tip-up lorry.
voltaico, -ca, *a.* voltaic.
voltaísmo, *n.m.* (*elec.*) voltaism.
voltaje, *n.m.* voltage.
voltámetro, *n.m.* (*phys.*) voltameter.
voltariedad, *n.f.* fickleness, inconstancy.
voltario, -ria, *a.* fickle, inconstant.
volteador, *n.m.* tumbler, vaulter, acrobat.
voltear, *v.t.* to whirl around, revolve; to overturn, upset; (*arch.*) to arch, vault. — *v.i.* to tumble, roll over. — **voltearse,** *v.r.* (*Hisp. Am.*) to turn round.
voltejear, *v.t.* to whirl; (*naut.*) to tack.
volteo, *n.m.* whirling round.
voltereta, *n.f.* tumble, handspring, somersault.
volteriano, -na, *a., n.m.f.* Voltairean; (*coll.*) subverter (*of the social order*).
voltímetro, *n.m.* voltmeter.
voltio, *n.m.* volt.
voltizo, -za, *a.* twisted; fickle, inconstant.
volubilidad, *n.f.* inconstancy, fickleness.
voluble, *a.* fickle, inconstant, moody; (*bot.*) twining.
volumen, *n.m.* volume; bulk, mass.
voluminoso, -sa, *a.* voluminous, bulky.
voluntad, *n.f.* will; will-power; willingness; affection; ***a voluntad,*** at will; ***de voluntad,*** willingly; ***deme la voluntad,*** give me whatever you like; ***tener mucha voluntad,*** to be very willing, try hard.
voluntariedad, *n.f.* voluntariness; wilfulness.
voluntario, -ria, *a.* voluntary. — *n.m.* volunteer.
voluntarioso, -sa, *a.* self-willed, wilful.
voluptuosidad, *n.f.* voluptuousness.
voluptuoso, -sa, *a.* voluptuous.
voluta, *n.f.* volute, spiral ring.
volvedor, *n.m.* tap-wrench, turn-screw; (*Arg., Col.*) horse that flees back home.
volver [5; *p.p.* **vuelto**], *v.t.* to turn; to turn over; to turn upside down; to turn inside out; to return; ***volver loco,*** to drive mad. — *v.i.* to turn; to return, come back, go back; ***volver a hacer una cosa,*** to do sth. again; ***volver en sí,*** to come to, come round; ***volver sobre sí,*** to pull o.s. together; ***volver sobre sus pasos,*** to retrace one's steps. — **volverse,** *v.r.* to turn, become; to turn round; to go back; ***volverse loco,*** to go mad; ***volverse atrás,*** to go back on what one has said, back down, back out; ***cuando se vuelva la tortilla,*** when the tables are turned, when the boot is on the other foot.
volvible, *a.* revolving, that may be turned.
volvo, vólvulo, *n.m.* (*med.*) volvulus, iliac passion.
vómico, -ca, *a.* vomitive, emetic, causing vomiting.
vomipurgante, vomipurgativo, *a.* (said of) purgatives and emetics. — *n.m.* purgative and emetic.
vomitado, -da, *a.* (*coll.*) palefaced, thin.
vomitador, -ra, *a.* vomiting.
vomitar, *v.t.* to vomit; (*fig.*) to cough up.
vomitivo, -va, *a., n.m.f.* vomitive, emetic.
vómito, *n.m.* vomiting, vomit; ***provocar a vómito,*** to nauseate.
vomitón, -tona, *a.* given to throwing up. — *n.f.* (*coll.*) violent vomiting.
vomitorio, -ria, *a.* vomitive, vomitory, emetic.
voquible, *n.m.* word, expression.
voracidad, *n.f.* voracity, voraciousness.
vorágine, *n.f.* vortex, whirlpool.
voraginoso, -sa, *a.* voraginous, full of whirlpools.
vorahunda, *n.f.* turmoil.
voraz, *a.* voracious.
vormela, *n.f.* (*zool.*) spotted weasel.
vórtice, *n.m.* vortex; whirlpool; whirlwind, centre of a cyclone.
vortiginoso, -sa, *a.* vortical.
vos, *pers. pron. 2nd pers. sing. and pl.* (*always with the plural form of the verb*), ye, you (*obsolete except in poetic, devotional and official styles*); *in some Spanish American countries it is used instead of* ***tú*** or ***ustedes.***
vosear, *v.t.* to use ***vos*** (*in addressing a person*).
vosotros, -ras, *pers. pron. 2nd pers. pl.,* you (familiar); ye.
votación, *n.f.* voting, balloting; vote.
votador, -ra, *a.* voting; swearing. — *n.m.f.* voter; swearer.
votante, *n.m.f.* voter.
votar, *v.i.* to vote; to vow; to give an opinion; to curse, swear; ***¡voto a Dios!*** 'struth!; (*archaic*) egad!
votivo, -va, *a.* votive.
voto, *n.m.* vow; wish; vote, ballot; prayer; oath, swear word; (*eccles.*) votive offering; ***hacer votos por,*** to pray for; ***voto de calidad*** or ***decisivo,*** casting vote; ***voto de amén,*** blind vote; ***ser*** or ***tener voto,*** to have a right to vote; ***a pluralidad de votos,*** by a majority of votes; ***no tener ni voz ni voto,*** to have no say.
voz, *n.f.* voice; shout; term, word; vote; rumour; (*mil.*) order; (*law*) life; ***dar voces,*** to shout, yell, call out; ***es voz común,*** it is generally rumoured; ***a media voz,*** in a whisper; ***a una voz,*** unanimously; ***a voces,*** shouting; ***a voz en cuello*** or ***en grito,*** at the top of one's voice; ***correr la voz,*** to be rumoured; to spread the rumour; ***tener la voz tomada,*** to have a husky voice, be a bit hoarse; ***aclarar la voz,*** to clear one's throat.
vozarrón, *n.m.* loud voice, strong voice.
voznar, *v.i.* to cackle like geese, cry like swans.
vuchén, *n.m.* (*Chi.*) legitimate son; potato that grows wild.
vuecelencia, vuecencia, *n.m.f.* (*contraction of* ***vuestra excelencia***) Your Excellency.
vuelco, *n.m.* overturning; tumble; upset.
vuelillo, *n.m.* lace cuff trimming.
vuelo, *n.m.* flight, flying; fullness (*of clothes*); (*sew.*) flounce, ruffle, frill; leap (*in pantomimes*); (*arch.*) projection, jutting; ***vuelo sin motor,*** gliding; ***alzar*** or ***levantar el vuelo,*** to take flight, get off the ground; ***al vuelo,*** quickly, on the wing; ***coger al vuelo,*** to cotton on to at once; ***cogerlas al vuelo,*** to be quick on the uptake; ***tomar vuelo,*** to get under way; ***en un vuelo,*** in a jiffy; (*pl.*) quills, wings (*of a bird*); ***cortar los vuelos a,*** to clip s.o.'s wings. — *pres. indic.* [VOLAR].
vuelto, -ta, *p.p. irreg.* [VOLVER]. — *n.f.* turn; revolution; round; going round, detour; return (ticket), (*Am.*) round trip; lap, leg; change; return; reverse, other side; repetition; going over; cuff; turn-up; ***a la vuelta,*** on coming *or* going back; over, please turn over; ***a la vuelta de,*** round; after; ***andar a vueltas con,*** to be at grips with; ***dar la vuelta,*** to turn round; ***dar una vuelta,*** to take a stroll *or*

ride; ***dar vueltas,*** to go round and round; ***estar de vuelta,*** to be back; ***no hay que darle vueltas,*** it's no use going over and over it; ***no tiene vuelta de hoja,*** there's no other way out, there are no two ways about it; ***coger las vueltas a,*** to get the hang of; (*fig.*) ***poner de vuelta y media,*** to tear to pieces; ***¡y vuelta con lo mismo!*** there we are, off again on the same tack!

vuesa, *a.f. contraction of* VUESTRA *used before* ***eminencia, merced,*** Your Eminence etc.

vuesamerced, (*obs.*) **vuesarced,** *n.f.* Your Honour, Your Worship, Your Grace.

vueseñoría, *n.f. contraction of* ***vuestra señoría,*** Your Lordship, Your Ladyship.

vuestro, -ra, *a., pron. poss.* your, yours.

vulcanio, -nia, *a.* vulcanian.

vulcanización, *n.f.* vulcanization.

vulcanizar [C], *v.t.* to vulcanize.

vulgacho, *n.m.* populace, mob, rabble.

vulgar, *a.* ordinary, commonplace; ***latín vulgar,*** vulgar Latin.

vulgaridad, *n.f.* ordinariness, commonplaceness; commonplace, trite remark.

vulgarización, *n.f.* popularization.

vulgarizar [C], *v.t.* to popularize; to translate into the vernacular.

vulgata, *n.f.* Vulgate.

vulgo, *n.m.* common people; (*coll.*) great unwashed.

vulnerable, *a.* vulnerable.

vulneración, *n.f.* wounding.

vulnerar, *v.t.* to injure.

vulnerario, -ria, *a., n.m.* vulnerary. — *n.f.* (*med.*) vulnerary.

vulpécula, vulpeja, *n.f.* vixen.

vulpino, -na, *a.* vulpine, of wolves.

vultuoso, -sa, *a.* (*med.*) bloated.

vulvario, -ria, *a.* vulvar.

W

W, w, *letter not belonging to the Spanish alphabet, and found only in adopted words.*

wat, *n.m.* (*elec.*) watt.

water, *n.m.* water-closet, lavatory.

whisky, whiskey, *n.m.* whisky.

whist, *n.m.* whist (*card game*).

X

X, x, *n.f.* letter X, x. — *n.m.pl.* ***rayos X,*** X-rays.

xana, *n.f.* nymph of the springs and mountains in Asturias.

xantato, *n.m.* (*chem.*) xanthate.

xapoípa, *n.f.* pancake.

xaquellas, *n.m.pl.* (*Par.*) an Indian tribe.

xara, *n.f.* Moslem law derived from the Koran.

xenofobia, *n.f.* xenophobia.

xenófobo, -ba, *a.* xenophobic. — *n.m.f.* xenophobe.

xilófono, *n.m.* xylophone.

xilografía, *n.f.* xylography.

xilográfico, -ca, *a.* xylographic.

xilógrafo, *n.m.* xylographer.

xilotila, *n.f.* (*Ec.*) hydrous silicate of magnesia and iron.

Y

Y, y, *n.f.* letter Y, y (*called* ***i griega*** or ***ye***).

y, *conj.* and; but, yet; ***y bien,*** well, now then; ***y eso que,*** although; ***¿y si . . . ?*** what if . . . ? ***¿y qué?*** so what?

ya, *adv.* already; now; yet; later, sooner or later, all in good time; ***ya voy,*** just coming; ***ya caigo,*** now I get it; ***ya . . . ya,*** now . . . now; ***ya que,*** since; ***ya se ve,*** that's obvious, I can see that; ***ya no,*** no longer, no more; ***¿lo has hecho ya?*** have you done it yet?; ***ya no por mí, sino por ti,*** not so much for my sake as for yours. — *conj.* whether; ***ya . . . ya,*** whether . . . or. — *interj.* oh, yes; I see; of course!

yaacabó, *n.m.* (*Ven.*) insectivorous bird.

yaba, *n.f.* (*Cub.*) yaba tree and bark.

yabuna, *n.f.* (*Cub.*) long creeping grass *or* weed.

yaca, *n.f.* (*bot.*) yacca tree.

yacal, *n.m.* (*Philip.*) yacal tree.

yacaré, *n.m.* (*Arg.*) cayman, alligator.

yacedor, *n.m.* boy who leads horses to graze.
yacente, *a.* jacent, lying.
yacer [38], *v.i.* to lie; to be lying (down); ***yacer con,*** to lie *or* sleep with.
yaciente, *a.* extended, stretched (*honeycomb*).
yacija, *n.f.* rough bed *or* couch; tomb, grave; ***ser de mala yacija,*** to be restless at night; to be a vagrant.
yacimiento, *n.m.* (*ore, oil etc.*) deposit, field, bed.
yacio, *n.m.* (*bot.*) India-rubber tree.
yactura, *n.f.* loss, damage.
yagua, *n.f.* bark of the royal palm.
yagual, *n.m.* (*C.R., Hond., Mex.*) padded ring (*for carrying weights on the head*).
yaguar, *n.m.* (*zool.*) jaguar.
yaguasa, *n.f.* (*Cub., Hond.*) tree duck.
yaguré, *n.m.* (*Hisp. Am.*) skunk.
yámbico, -ca, *a.* iambic.
yambo, *n.m.* iambic foot; (*bot.*) jamboo.
yanacona, *a., n.m.f.* (*Hisp. Am.*) Indian bondsman; (*Bol., Per.*) Indian partner in husbandry.
yanilla, *n.f.* (*Cub.*) mangrove tree.
yanqui, *a., n.m.f.* Yankee.
yantar, *n.m.* viands, food. — *v.t., v.i.* to eat, sup.
yapa, *n.f.* (*Hisp. Am.*) mercury mixed with silver; extra, bonus.
yapú, *n.m.* (*Arg.*) thrush.
yarará, *n.m.* (*Arg., Bol., Par.*) viper.
yaraví, *n.m.* (*Hisp. Am.*) Indian song.
yarda, *n.f.* yard.
yare, *n.m.* yucca juice; yucca bread.
yarey, *n.m.* (*Cub.*) palm tree.
yaro, *n.m.* (*bot.*) arum.
yatay, *n.m.* (*Arg., Par.*) tall palm tree.
yate, *n.m.* yacht; motor cruiser.
yaya, *n.f.* (*Cub.*) lancewood; (*Per., zool.*) acarus.
yayero, *n.m.* (*Cub.*) busybody.
ye, *n.f.* name of the letter Y.
yeco, *n.m.* (*Chi., zool.*) sea-crow.
yedra, *n.f.* ivy.
yegua, *n.f.* mare; (*Cent. Am.*) cigar stub.
yeguada, yegüería, *n.f.* stud, herd of breeding mares and stallions.
yeguar, *a.* belonging to mares.
yegüero, yegüerizo, *n.m.* keeper of mares.
yeísmo, *n.m.* pronunciation of ***ll*** as ***y.***
yelmo, *n.m.* helmet.
yema, *n.f.* bud, button; yolk (*of an egg*); heart, centre; (*fig.*) cream; ***yema del dedo,*** tip of the finger; ***yema del invierno,*** depth of winter; ***dar en la yema,*** to hit the nail on the head.
yente, *a.* ***yentes y vinientes,*** passers-by.
yerba [HIERBA].
yerbatear, *v.i.* (*Hisp. Am.*) to take maté.
yerbatero, *a.* (*Hisp. Am.*) fodder grass seller.
yermar, *v.t.* to lay waste; to leave uncultivated.
yermo, -ma, *a.* waste, barren; ***tierra yerma,*** uncultivated land. — *n.m.* desert; waste-land.
yerno, *n.m.* son-in-law.
yernocracia, *n.f.* (*jocular*) nepotism, system of family favouratism, jobs for those in the family.
yero, *n.m.* (*bot.*) tare, vetch.
yerro (1), *n.m.* error, fault, mistake.
yerro (2), **yerre,** *pres. indic.; pres. subj.* [ERRAR].
yerto, -ta, *a.* stiff, rigid; ***quedarse yerto,*** to get frozen stiff.
yervo, *n.m.* (*bot.*) tare, bitter vetch.
yesal, yesar, *n.m.* gypsum-pit.
yesca, *n.f.* tinder, spunk, touchwood; (*fig.*) fuel, stimulus; (*pl.*) tinder-box.
yesera, *n.f.* [YESERO].
yesería, *n.f.* gypsum-kiln; plasterer's shop; plaster-work.
yesero, -ra, *a.* gypsum. — *n.m.f.* plasterer, plaster-burner. — *n.f.* gypsum-pit; (female) seller of gypsum.
yeso, *n.m.* gypsum, plaster; plaster cast; ***yeso mate,*** plaster of Paris; ***yeso blanco,*** whiting; ***yeso negro,*** grey plaster.
yesón, *n.m.* plaster rubbish.
yesoso, -sa, *a.* gypseous.
yesquero, *n.m.* tinder-box; tinder-maker, tinder-seller.
yeta, *n.f.* (*Hisp. Am.*) bad luck; misfortune.
yeyuno, *n.m.* (*anat.*) jejunum.
yezgo, *n.m.* dwarf elder.
yista, *n.f.* (*Bol.*) a kind of bread.
yo, *pron.* I, myself. — *n.m.* (*phil.*) ego, I, me.
yocalla, *n.m.* (*Bol.*) ragamuffin.
yodado, -da, *a.* iodized.
yodo, *n.m.* (*chem.*) iodine.
yodoformo, *n.m.* (*chem.*) iodoform.
yoduración, *n.f.* iodization.
yodurar, *v.t.* to iodize.
yoduro, *n.m.* (*chem.*) iodide.
yogur, *n.m.* yogurt.
yol, *n.m.* (*Chi.*) leather saddlebag.
yola, *n.f.* (*naut.*) yawl.
yolero, -ra, *n.m.f.* (*P.R.*) person who mans the ***yola.***
yolillo, *n.m.* (*C.R., Nic.*) small palm tree.
yos, *n.m.* (*C.R.*) a plant of the *Euphorbia* genus.
yubarta, *n.f.* (*ichth.*) finback, rorqual.
yuca, *n.f.* (*bot.*) yucca; cassava.
yucal, *n.m.* yucca field.
yugada, *n.f.* yoke of land.
yugo, *n.m.* yoke; nuptial veil; (*naut.*) transom; frame (*of a church-bell*); ***sacudir(se) el yugo,*** to shake off the yoke.
Yugoslavia, *n.f.* Yugoslavia.
yugoslavo, -va, *a., n.m.f.* Yugoslav(ian).
yuguero, *n.m.* ploughman, plough-boy.
yugular, *a.* jugular.
yumbo, -ba, *a., n.m.f.* (*Ec.*) Indian.
yunque, *n.m.* anvil; (*anat.*) incus; ***estar al yunque,*** to stick it out.
yunta, *n.f.* [YUNTO].
yuntería, *n.f.* place where draught-oxen are fed; herd of draught-oxen.
yuntero, *n.m.* plough-boy.
yunto, -ta, *a.* joined, close; ***arar yunto,*** to plough close. — *n.f.* pair, yoke of oxen.
yuraguano, *n.m.* (*Cub.*) fan palm.
yuré, *n.m.* (*C.R.*) small pigeon.
yuruma, *n.f.* (*Ven.*) palm pith.
yusera, *n.f.* stone base (*in oil mills*).
yusión, *n.f.* (*law*) command, precept, mandate.
yute, *n.m.* (*bot.*) jute.
yuxtalineal, *a.* in juxtaposition.
yuxtaponer [25], *v.t.* to juxtapose.
yuxtaposición, *n.f.* juxtaposition.
yúyere, *n.m.* (*Cub.*) panic.
yuyo, *n.m.* (*Hisp. Am.*) yuyo weed; toe blister.
yuyuba, *n.f.* jujube.

Z

Z, z, *n.f.* letter Z, z (*called* ***zeda*** or ***zeta***).
¡za! *interj.* scram! skidaddle!
zabarcera, *n.f.* (female) greengrocer.
zábida, zábila, *n.f.* (*bot.*) common aloe.
zaborda, *n.f.*, **zabordamiento,** *n.m.* (*naut.*) stranding.
zabordar, *v.i.* (*naut.*) to run aground.
zabordo, *n.m.* stranding.
zaborro, -rra, *n.m.f.* (*coll.*) fatty.
zabra, *n.f.* brig.
zabucar [A], *v.t.* to shake.
zabullida [ZAMBULLIDA].
zabullidor, -ra [ZAMBULLIDOR].
zabullidura [ZAMBULLIDA].
zabullimiento, *n.m.* [ZAMBULLIDA].
zabullir [J], *v.t.* [ZAMBULLIR].
zaca, *n.f.* leather bucket.
zacapela, zacapella, *n.f.* uproar.
zacate, *n.m.* (*Hisp. Am.*) hay, fodder.
zacateca, *n.m.* (*Cub.*) undertaker; sexton.
zacatín, *n.m.* bazaar, market.
zacatón, *n.m.* (*Mex.*) fodder grass.
zacear, *v.t.* to shoo away.
zadorija, *n.f.* (*bot.*) yellow poppy.
zafa (1), *n.f.* (*prov.*) basin, bowl.
zafacoca, *n.f.* (*Hisp. Am.*) squabble, row, fight.
zafada (1), *n.f.*, **zafamiento,** *n.m.* loosening; dodging away *or* out; lightening (*a ship*).
zafado, -da (2), *a.* (*Hisp. Am.*) impudent, insolent.
zafar, *v.t.* to adorn; to loosen; to free, clear; to lighten (*a ship*). — **zafarse,** *v.r.* to slip off, slip away, come loose; ***zafarse de,*** to dodge, get out of.
zafareche, *n.m.* (*prov.*) tank.
zafariche, *n.m.* (*prov.*) shelf for water jars.
zafarrancho, *n.m.* (*naut.*) clearing for action; clearing of decks; (*coll.*) shambles, shindy.
zafiedad, *n.f.* boorishness, uncouthness, cloddishness.
zafío, *n.m.* (*ichth.*) conger eel.
zafio, -fia, *a.* boorish, uncouth, cloddish.
zafir, zafiro, *n.m.* sapphire.
zafíreo, -rea, zafirino, -na, *a.* sapphire, sapphirine.
zafo, -fa (2), *a.* free, disentangled; exempt from danger; (*naut.*) free and clear.
zafones [ZAHONES].
zafra, *n.f.* olive-oil jar; drip pan; crop; (*Cub.*) sugar-cane cutting; sugar making; sugar-making season; (*min.*) dross, slag.
zafrero, *n.m.* (*min.*) dross-clearer; sugar-cane cutter.
zaga, *n.m.* last player (*in a game*). — *n.f.* rear, back; load (*in the rear of a carriage*); ***a la zaga, en zaga,*** behind, in the rear; ***ir a la zaga,*** to bring up the rear; ***no irle en zaga a nadie,*** to be second to none.
zagal, *n.m.* lad, youth; shepherd lad; strapping lad, swain; assistant driver (*in a stagecoach*); underskirt.
zagala, *n.f.* young shepherdess; (*coll.*) lass, wench.
zagaleja, *n.f.* young lass.
zagalejo, *n.m.* young lad; underskirt.
zagalón, -lona, *n.m.f.* hefty *or* sturdy lad *or* lass.
zagua, *n.f.* (*bot.*) saltwort.
zagual, *n.m.* paddle.
zaguán, *n.m.* entrance, entrance hall *or* way.
zaguanete, *n.m.* small vestibule *or* entrance, small party of the king's life-guards.
zaguero, -ra, *a.* rear, hind; lagging behind. — *n.m.* (*sport*) back.
zahareño, -ña, *a.* unsociable, standoffish, wild.
zaharí, *n.f.* (*bot.*) variety of pomegranate.
zaharrón, *n.m.* clown, motley fool; motley.
zahén, zahena, *n.m.f.* Moorish coin of very fine gold.
zaheridor, -ra, *a.* taunting.
zaherimiento, *n.m.* taunt.
zaherir [6], *v.t.* to taunt, wound, hurt.
zahina, *n.f.* (*bot.*) sorghum.
zahinar, *n.m.* land sown with sorghum.
zahinas, *n.f.pl.* (*prov.*) thin porridge.
zahonado, -da, *a.* brownish, dark brown (*of animals' legs*).
zahondar, *v.t.* to dig (into). — *v.i.* to sink into soft ground.
zahones, *n.m.pl.* overalls; chaps.
zahora, *n.f.* rollicking meal.
zahorar, *v.i.* (*obs.*) to have a second supper; to have a noisy meal.
zahorí, *n.m.* seer; water diviner.
zahoriar, *v.t.* to scrutinize, look deeply into.
zahorra, *n.f.* ballast.
zahurda, *n.f.* pig-sty.
zaida, *n.f.* heron.
zaino, -na, *a.* chestnut-coloured (*horse*); black (*cattle*); vicious, wicked, treacherous; ***mirar de zaino,*** to look sideways *or* slyly.
zalá, *n.f.* salaam; (*coll.*) ***hacer la zalá,*** to wheedle.
zalagarda, *n.f.* ambush; snare, trap; skirmish; uproar, hullabaloo.
zalama, zalamería, *n.f.* flattery, adulation.
zalamear, *v.t.* to flatter.
zalamero, -ra, *a.* flattering, wheedling, fawning.
zalea, *n.f.* (undressed) sheepskin.
zalear, *v.t.* to shake, shake out; to frighten (*dogs*) away.
zalema, *n.f.* salaam.
zaleo, *n.m.* sheepskin (*used as proof of loss of sheep*); shaking.
zalmedina, *n.m.* magistrate (*Aragon*).
zalona, *n.f.* (*prov.*) large earthen jar.
zallar, *v.t.* to outrig.
zamacuco, *n.m.* (*coll.*) dolt; sullen fellow; sozzled state.
zamacueca, *n.f.* (*Chi., Per.*) Indian folksong and dance.
zamanca, *n.f.* drubbing, flogging.
zamarra, *n.f.* sheepskin jacket *or* coat.
zamarrear, *v.t.* to shake, pull *or* drag to and fro, drag about.
zamarreo, *n.m.* dragging, pulling, shaking about.
zamarrico, *n.m.* bag of sheepskin.
zamarrilla, *n.f.* mountain germander.
zamarro, *n.m.* sheepskin coat; sheepskin, lambskin; (*coll.*) dolt; (*pl.*) (*Col., Ven.*) chaps.
zamarrón, *n.m.* large sheepskin jacket.
zambaigo, -ga, *a., n.m.f.* (*Mex.*) Indian and Chinese half-breed.
zambapalo, *n.m.* ancient dance.
Zambia, *n.f.* Zambia.
zámbigo, -ga, *a.* knock-kneed.
zambo, -ba, *a.* knock-kneed; half-breed (*Indian and Negro*). — *n.m.* monkey.
zamboa, *n.f.* quince tree.
zambomba, *n.f.* sounding-box, drum. — *interj.* gosh!
zambombazo, *n.m.* wallop, thump *or* clout.
zambombo, *n.m.* boor.
zamborondón, -dona, zamborotudo, -da, *a.* big, boorish and clumsy; ill-shaped.
zambra, *n.f.* (Moorish) singing and dancing; gypsy do; uproar, din.
zambucar [A], *v.t.* to hide.
zambuco, *n.m.* hiding.

zambullida, *n.f.* diving, plunging in *or* under; (*fenc.*) breast-thrust.
zambullidor, -ra, *a.*, *n.m.f.* plunger, diver.
zambullir [J], *v.t.* to plunge in *or* under, duck. — **zambullirse,** *v.r.* to dive *or* plunge in *or* under.
zambullo, *n.m.* chamber pot; (*prov.*) wild olive tree.
Zamora, *n.f.* ***no se ganó Zamora en una hora,*** Rome wasn't built in a day.
zamorano, -na, *a.*, *n.m.f.* (native) of Zamora.
zampabodigos (*inv.*), **zampabollos** (*inv.*), *n.m.* (*coll.*) glutton.
zampalimosnas, *n.m. inv.* (*coll.*) importunate beggar.
zampapalo, zampatortas (*inv.*), *n.m.* glutton; clodhopper.
zampar, *v.t.* to stick *or* shove in; to polish off, hog down. — **zamparse,** *v.r.* to rush in, thrust o.s. in; (*coll.*) to polish off, hog down; (*Hisp. Am.*) ***zamparse la cola,*** to jump the queue.
zampeado, *n.m.* (*arch.*) grillage of timber, steel *or* masonry.
zampear, *v.t.* to strengthen with a grillage of timber, steel *or* masonry.
zampón, -pona, *a.* gluttonous. — *n.m.f.* glutton; (*coll.*) hog-belly; (*Hisp. Am.*) queue-jumper.
zampoña, *n.f.* pan-pipes, rustic flute; (*coll.*) frivolity.
zampuzar [C], *v.t.* to dip, plunge, dive; [ZAMPAR].
zampuzo, *n.m.* dive, plunge, ducking.
zamuro, *n.m.* (*Col.*, *Ven.*, *bot.*) turkey buzzard.
zanahoria, *n.f.* (*bot.*) carrot.
zanca, *n.f.* shank; long leg; large pin; (*min.*) shore, prop; string-piece of a staircase; ***por zancas o por barrancas,*** by hook or by crook.
zancada, *n.f.* long stride; ***en dos zancadas,*** in two shakes.
zancadilla, *n.f.* trip, tripping up; trick; ***echar*** or ***poner la zancadilla a alguien,*** to trip s.o. up.
zancado, -da, *a.* insipid (*said of salmon*).
zancajear, *v.i.* to hurry about, rush around.
zancajera, *n.f.* running-board.
zancajiento, -ta, *a.* bandy-legged.
zancajo, *n.m.* heel-bone; shoe-heel; heel-piece of a stocking; (*coll.*) ill-shaped person; (*fig.*) ***no llegar a los zancajos a,*** not to be able to hold a candle to.
zancajoso, -sa, *a.* bandy-legged; wearing holed and dirty stockings.
zancarrón, *n.m.* large heel-bone; large, fleshless, ugly, withered person; (*coll.*) quack, fraud.
zanco, *n.m.* stilt; (*naut.*) sliding-gunter mast; (*fig.*) ***en zancos,*** high up.
zancón, -cona, *a.* long-shanked.
zancudo, -da, *a.* long-legged, long-shanked; wading. — *n.m.* (*Hisp. Am.*) mosquito. — *n.f.pl.* **zancudas,** wading birds.
zandía [SANDÍA].
zandunga [SANDUNGA].
zandunguero, -ra, (*coll.*) [SANDUNGUERO].
zanfonía, *n.f.* hurdy-gurdy.
zanga, *n.f.* four-hand ombre.
zangala, *n.f.* buckram.
zangamanga, *n.f.* falsehood, trick, deceit.
zanganada, *n.f.* rude, impertinent word *or* deed.
zangandongo, zangandullo, zangandungo, *n.m.* idler, loafer.
zanganear, *v.i.* to loaf about.
zángano, *n.m.* drone; parasite, loafer.
zangarilla, *n.f.* (*prov.*) small millpond.
zangarilleja, *n.f.* dirty, lazy girl.
zangarrear, *v.i.* (*coll.*) to scrape a guitar.
zangarriana, *n.f.* (*coll.*) slight ailment; sadness, blues.
zangarrullón, *n.m.* tall, idle lad.
zangolotear, *v.t.* to shove about. — **zangolotear(se),** *v.i.* (*v.r.*) to fidget about; to wobble about.
zangoloteo, *n.m.* jigging, fidgeting (about); wobbling about.
zangolotino, -na, *a.* gangling, over-grown. — *n.m.f.* gangling *or* over-grown child.
zangón, *n.m.* lazy fellow, lout.
zanguanga, *n.f.* (*coll.*) malingering; fawning, wheedling.
zanguango, *n.m.* (*coll.*) loafer, lout.
zanguayo, *n.m.* (*coll.*) lanky fool.
zanja, *n.f.* ditch, trench; ***abrir las zanjas,*** to lay the foundations.
zanjar, *v.t.* to dig, dig ditches in; to settle, fix.
zanjón, *n.m.* deep ditch; large drain.
zanqueador, -ra, *n.m.f.* awkward walker; great walker.
zanqueamiento, *n.m.* waddling.
zanquear, *v.i.* to waddle; to run about.
zanquilargo, -ga, *a.* long-shanked, long-legged.
zanquilla, *n.m.f.* short little fellow *or* woman.
zanquituerto, -ta, *a.* bandy-legged.
zanquivano, -na, *a.* spindle-shanked.
zapa, *n.f.* spade; (*mil.*) sap, trenching; sharkskin; shagreen; ***labor de zapa,*** undermining.
zapador, *n.m.* sapper.
zapallo, *n.m.* (*Hisp. Am.*) calabash tree; pumpkin; (*Arg.*, *Chi.*) chance, unexpected event, stroke of good luck.
zapapico, *n.m.* pickaxe, mattock.
zapar, *v.t.*, *v.i.* to sap, mine.
zaparrada, *n.f.* heavy fall.
zaparrastrar, *v.i.* to trail (*of dress*).
zaparrastroso, -sa [ZARRAPASTROSO].
zaparrazo, *n.m.* thud, violent fall.
zapata, *n.f.* shoe (*of an anchor*); shoe (*of a brake*); buskin, half-boot; false keel; washer.
zapatazo, *n.m.* large shoe; blow with a shoe; thud; drumming (*of foot* or *hoof*); (*sail*) flapping; ***tratar a zapatazos,*** to treat like dirt.
zapateado, *n.m.* tap dance.
zapateador, -ra, *n.m.f.* tap-dancer.
zapatear, *v.t.* to kick with the shoe; (*fenc.*) to strike frequently; to ill-treat. — *v.i.* to flap (*sails*); to tap-dance. — **zapatearse,** *v.r.* to hold out, stick it out.
zapateo, *n.m.* beating the foot, tapping.
zapatería, *n.f.* shoemaker's trade; shoemaker's shop; ***zapatería de viejo,*** cobbler's.
zapatero, -ra, *a.* shoemaking. — *n.m.* shoemaker; seller of shoes; (*ichth.*) thread-fish; (*coll.*) card-player who takes no tricks; ***zapatero de viejo,*** cobbler; ***zapatero, a tus zapatos,*** mind your own business, the cobbler should stick to his last. — *n.f.* shoemaker's wife.
zapateta, *n.f.* caper, jump, leap; slap on the sole of a shoe.— *interj.* oh! good gracious!
zapatilla, *n.f.* slipper; little shoe, pump; button (*of a foil*); animal's hoof; leather washer.
zapatillero, *n.m.* slipper-maker.
zapato, *n.m.* shoe; ***meter en un zapato,*** to cow; ***zapatos papales,*** overshoes, galoshes; ***como tres en un zapato,*** like sardines in a tin; ***saber donde aprieta el zapato,*** to know which side one's bread is buttered (on); ***ser más necio que su zapato,*** to be more stupid than a bat; ***andar con zapatos de fieltro,*** to go very cunningly *or* quietly.
zapatudo, -da, *a.* wearing large shoes; large-hoofed, large-clawed; (*of meat*) tough, leathery.
¡zape! *interj.* shoo! gosh! phew!
zapear, *v.t.* to shoo away.
zapito, *n.m.*, **zapita,** *n.f.* (*prov.*) milk-pail.
zapote, *n.m.* (*bot.*) sapota; sapodilla (*tree and fruit*).
zapotero, *n.m.* (*bot.*) sapota tree.

zapotillo, *n.m.* (*bot.*) sapodilla and its fruit.
zapoyol, *n.m.* (*C.R.*, *Hond.*) kernel of the sapodilla fruit.
zapoyolito, *n.m.* (*Cent. Am.*) small parakeet.
zapuzar, *v.t.* to duck. — **zapuzar(se),** *v.i.* (*v.r.*) to duck, dive.
zaque, *n.m.* leather bottle, leather wine-bag; (*coll.*) tippler, drunkard; (*Col.*) chief of Chibcha tribe.
zaquear, *v.t.* to rack, draw off liquors.
zaquizamí, *n.m.* garret, loft; hovel, dump.
zar, *n.m.* czar, tsar.
zara, *n.f.* maize, Indian corn.
zarabanda, *n.f.* saraband; noise, bustle; (*Mex.*) beating.
zarabandista, *n.m.f.* saraband dancer; merry person.
zaragata, *n.f.* turmoil, quarrel, scuffle.
zaragate, *n.m.* (*Cent. Am.*, *Mex.*, *Per.*, *Ven.*) contemptible *or* despicable person.
zaragatona, *n.f.* ribgrass, ribwort.
zaragocí, *n.m.* kind of plum.
Zaragoza, *n.f.* Saragossa.
zaragozano, -na, *a.*, *n.m.f.* (native) of Saragossa.
zaragüelles, *n.m.pl.* breeches; (*bot.*) reed-grass.
zaragutear, *v.t.* (*coll.*) to bungle.
zaragutero, -ra, *a.* bungling. — *n.m.f.* bungler.
zaramagullón, *n.m.* (*orn.*) didapper.
zarambeque, *n.m.* Negro folksong and dance.
zaramullo, *n.m.* (*Per.*, *Ven.*) busybody.
zaranda, *n.f.* sifter, sieve; (*Ven.*) humming-top.
zarandador, *n.m.* sifter of wheat.
zarandajas, *n.f.pl.* trifles.
zarandar, zarandear, *v.t.* to sift, winnow (*corn*); to strain; to pick out; to shake, shake up. — **zarandearse,** *v.r.* to swagger.
zarandeo, *n.m.* sifting, winnowing, shaking up.
zarandillo, *n.m.* small sieve; (*coll.*) live wire; ***traer como un zarandillo,*** to keep on the go, give no rest to.
zarapatel, *n.m.* salmagundi.
zarapito, *n.m.* curlew.
zaratán, *n.m.* cancer of the breast.
zaraza (1), *n.f.* chintz; (*pl.*) rat-poison.
zarazo, -za (2), *a.* (*Hisp. Am.*) half-ripe (*fruit*).
zarcear, *v.t.* to clean (*pipes* or *conduits*) with briers. — *v.i.* to move to and fro; to pursue game into briers (*in hunting*).
zarceño, -ña, *a.* pertaining to briers.
zarcero, -ra, *a.*, *n.m.f.* retriever.
zarceta, *n.f.* (*orn.*) widgeon.
zarcillitos, *n.m.pl.* quaking-grass.
zarcillo, *n.m.* (vine) tendril; drop earring; hoop (*of a barrel*); hoe.
zarco, -ca, *a.* light-blue (*of eyes*).
zargatona, *n.f.* (*bot.*) ribgrass, ribwort.
zariano, -na, *a.* belonging to the tsar.
zarigüeya, *n.f.* (*Hisp. Am.*) opossum.
zarina, *n.f.* tsarina.
zaroche, *n.m.* (*Ec.*) mountain sickness.
zarpa, *n.f.* claw, paw; weighing anchor; dirt *or* mud (*on clothes*); footing; ***echar la zarpa a,*** to lay hands on, grab.
zarpada, *n.f.* claw, gash, slash.
zarpar, *v.t.* to weigh anchor. — *v.i.* to sail.
zarpazo, *n.m.* claw, gash, slash.
zarpear, *v.t.* (*C.R.*, *Hond.*) to bespatter, to bemire.
zarposo, -sa, *a.* bespattered with dirt.
zarracatería, *n.f.* lure, deception.
zarracatín, *n.m.* (*coll.*) haggler; miser.
zarramplín, *n.m.* (*coll.*) bungler, botcher.
zarramplinada, *n.f.* bungle, botch.
zarrapastra, *n.f.* dirt *or* mud (*on clothes*).
zarrapastrón, -rona, *n.m.f.* tatterdemalion.
zarrapastroso, -sa, *a.* ragged, slovenly, shabby.
zarria, *n.f.* dirt (*sticking to clothes*); leather thong.
zarriento, -ta, *a.* besmirched, bespattered.
zarza, *n.f.* (*bot.*) bramble, blackberry-bush.
zarzagán, *n.m.* cold north-east wind.
zarzaganillo, *n.m.* violent north-easterly storm.
zarzahán, *n.m.* striped silk.
zarzaidea, *n.f.* raspberry-bush.
zarzal, *n.m.* brier-patch, bramble-patch.
zarzamora, *n.f.* (*bot.*) blackberry bush; blackberry.
zarzaparrilla, *n.f.* (*bot.*) sarsaparilla.
zarzaperruna, zarzarrosa, *n.f.* (*bot.*) dog-rose.
zarzo, *n.m.* hurdle, wattle.
zarzoso, -sa, *a.* brambly, briery.
zarzuela, *n.f.* light *or* comic opera; ***zarzuela de mariscos,*** sea-food pot-pourri.
zarzuelero, -ra, *a.* (of) light opera.
zarzuelista, *n.m.f.* writer *or* composer of light opera.
¡zas! *interj.* whack! wham! bang!
zascandil, *n.m.* (*coll.*) jitter-bug, restless individual; busybody.
zata, zatara, *n.f.* river raft.
zatico, *n.m.* small bit of bread.
zato, *n.m.* piece of bread.
zazoso, -sa, *a.* lisping. — *n.m.f.* lisper.
zeda [ZETA].
zedilla, *n.f.* cedilla.
zejel, *n.m.* Hispano-Arabic verse form.
Zeland(i)a, (la), *n.f.* Zeeland; ***Nueva Zeland(i)a,*** New Zealand.
zenit, *n.m.* zenith [CENIT].
zeta, *n.f.* name of the letter Z, zed, (*Am.*) zee.
zigzag, *n.m.* zigzag.
zigzaguear, *v.i.* to zigzag.
zigzagueo, *n.m.* zigzagging.
zinc, *n.m.* zinc [CINC].
zipizape, *n.m.* shindy, set-to, scrap.
¡zis, zas! *interj.* slap, bang, wallop!
ziszás, *n.m.* zigzag.
zoca (1), *n.f.* square.
zócalo, *n.m.* socle; wainscotting.
zocato (1), **-ta** (1), *a.* over-ripe.
zocato (2), **-ta** (2), *a.* left-handed.
zoclo, *n.m.* clog; over-shoe.
zoco (1), **-ca** (2), *a.* left-handed.
zoco (2), *n.m.* clog; plinth; market; market-place; ***andar de zocos en colodros,*** to fall out of the frying-pan into the fire.
zodiacal, *a.* zodiacal.
zodíaco, *n.m.* zodiac.
zofra, *n.f.* Moorish carpet.
zolocho, -cha, *a.* (*coll.*) stupid, silly.
zollipar, *v.i.* (*coll.*) to sob, blub.
zollipo, *n.m.* sob, sobbing.
zoma, *n.f.* coarse flour.
zompo, -pa, *a.* maimed, deformed, crippled.
zona, *n.f.* zone; area; belt; (*med.*) shingles.
zoncería, *n.f.* silliness.
zonchiche, *n.m.* (*C.R.*, *Hond.*, *orn.*) red-headed vulture.
zonote, *n.m.* (*Mex.*) underground lake *or* water.
zonzo, -za, *a.* (*coll.*) dull, silly; soppy.
zonzorrión, -rriona, *n.m.f.* very dull *or* stupid person.
zoo, *n.m.* (*coll.*) zoo.
zoografía, *n.f.* zoography.
zoolito, *n.m.* zoolite.
zoología, *n.f.* zoology.
zoológico, -ca, *a.* zoological.
zoólogo, *n.m.* zoologist.
zootomía, *n.f.* zootomy.
zootropo, *n.m.* zoetrope, wheel of life.

zopas (*inv.*), **zopitas** (*inv.*), *n.m.f.* (*coll.*) one who lisps.
zope, *n.m.* (*C.R.*) buzzard.
zopenco, -ca, *a.* (*coll.*) doltish. — *n.m.f.* dolt, blockhead.
zopilote, *n.m.* (*C.R.*, *Hond.*, *Mex.*) buzzard.
zopisa, *n.f.* pitch; pitch and wax mixed.
zopo, -pa, *a.*, *n.m.f.* cripple.
zoqueta, *n.f.* a kind of wooden glove used by reapers.
zoquete, *n.m.* block, chunk; short, ugly fellow; blockhead, thickhead.
zoquetero, -ra, *a.* beggarly.
zoquetudo, -da, *a.* rough, coarse, crude.
zorcico, *n.m.* Basque folksong and dance.
zorita, *n.f.* (*orn.*) wood-pigeon.
zorollo, *a.* reaped but not ripe (*wheat*).
zorongo, *n.m.* folksong and dance (*Andalusia*); kerchief (*worn by Aragonese and Navarrese*); flat wide chignon.
zorra, *n.f.* [ZORRO].
zorrastrón, -rona, *a.* crafty, cunning.
zorrear, *v.i.* to street-walk, be a whore.
zorrera, *n.f.* [ZORRERO].
zorrería, *n.f.* artfulness; cunning.
zorrero, -ra, *a.* fox-hunting; foxy, cunning; slow, heavy. — *n.m.* terrier dog; game warden. — *n.f.* fox hole; room full of smoke; drowsiness, heaviness.
zorrilla, zorrita, *n.f.* little vixen; (*Arg.*, *Guat.*, *Hond.*) polecat; skunk.
zorro, -rra, *a.* foxy, cunning; (*coll.*) ***no tiene ni zorra idea,*** he hasn't the foggiest idea, hasn't a clue. — *n.m.* fox; (*fig.*) foxy fellow; (*pl.*) duster.— *n.f.* vixen; whore, street-walker; foxy creature; ***pillar una zorra,*** to get sozzled *or* pie-eyed.
zorrocloco, *n.m.* (*coll.*) sly customer who looks a drip; caress.
zorronglón, -lona, *a.* sulky, muttering.
zorruno, -na, *a.* foxy, fox-like.
zorzal, *n.m.* (*orn.*) thrush; artful, cunning fellow.
zoster, *n.m.* shingles.
zote, *n.m.* (*coll.*) dunce, dolt.
zozobra, *n.f.* anxiety, state of tenterhooks; foundering, sinking.
zozobrar, *v.t.* to sink; to wreck; to throw into a state of anxiety.— *v.i.* to capsize, founder, sink; to go on the rocks; to worry.
zuaca, *n.f.* (*C.R.*) practical joke; (*Mex.*) drubbing, flogging.
zubia, *n.f.* drain; channel.
zucarino, -na, *a.* sugary.
zúchil, *n.m.* (*Mex.*) bouquet.
zueco, *n.m.* clog; galosh.
zuindá, *n.m.* (*Arg.*) brown owl.
zuiza, *n.f.* tournament; quarrel.
zuizón, *n.m.* spear; (*naut.*) half pike.
zulacar [A], *v.t.* to cover with bitumen.
zulaque, *n.m.* (*hydraulics*) packing stuff; (*naut.*) oakum.
zulú, *a.* Zulu. — *n.m.f.* Zulu; (*fig.*) yahoo, barbarian.
zulla, *n.f.* (*bot.*) French honeysuckle.
zullarse, *v.r.* (*obsc.*) to shit; to fart.
zullenco, -ca, *a.* windy, flatulent.
zullón, -llona, *a.* windy, flatulent. — *n.m.* flatulence.
zumacal, *n.m.* sumach plantation.
zumacar *n.m.* sumach plantation. — [A], *v.t.* to dress (*hides* or *pelts*) with sumach.
zumacaya, *n.f.* (*orn.*) secretary bird.
zumaque, *n.m.* sumach tree; (*coll.*) wine.
zumaya, *n.f.* (*orn.*) barn-owl; goatsucker.
zumba, *n.f.* bell (*of the leading mule* or *ox of a drove*); rattle; jest, joke, raillery; (*Chi.*, *Col.*, *P.R.*) beating; flogging.
zumbador, -ra, *a.* humming, buzzing, whizzing. — *n.m.* (*elec.*) buzzer; (*P.R.*) humming-bird.
zumbar, *v.t.* to hit, strike, whack. — *v.i.* to buzz, hum; to ring (*in the ears*); ***salir zumbando,*** to tear *or* rush off. — **zumbarse,** *v.r.* to make fun (***de,*** of).
zumbel, *n.m.* frown, angry look; (*coll.*) cord for spinning tops.
zumbido, zumbo, *n.m.* humming, buzzing; ping (*of a bullet*); ringing (*in the ears*); blow, box, cuff.
zumbilín, *n.m.* (*Philip.*) dart, javelin.
zumbón, -bona, *a.* waggish, joking, facetious. — *n.m.f.* mocker, jester, wag.—*n.m.* (*prov.*) pigeon.
zumiento, -ta, *a.* juicy.
zumillo, *n.m.* deadly carrot; dragon's arum; Aaron's beard.
zumo, *n.m.* juice; (*fig.*) profit.
zumoso, -sa, *a.* juicy.
zuna, *n.f.* sunna (Islam); (*prov.*) trickery, treachery; viciousness (*of horses*).
zuncuya, *n.f.* (*Hond.*) bitter-sweet fruit.
zunchar, *v.t.* to strengthen with a hoop *or* band.
zuncho, *n.m.* hoop, band, collar; ferrule.
zunteco, *n.m.* (*Hond.*) black wasp.
zunzún, *n.m.* (*Cub.*) humming-bird.
zuño, *n.m.* frown, angry mien.
zupay, *n.m.* (*Arg.*) nickname of the Devil.
zupia, *n.f.* wine dregs; (*coll.*) slops; (*coll.*) scum, trash.
zurano, -na, *n.m.f.* stock-dove, wood-pigeon.
zurcidera, *n.f.* darner; (*coll.*) ***zurcidera de voluntades,*** pimp, bawd.
zurcido, *n.m.* darn, darning.
zurcidor, -ra, *n.m.f.* darner, fine-drawer.
zurcidura, *n.f.* darn, darning.
zurcir [D], *v.t.* to darn; to fine-draw; (*coll.*) ***¡que te zurzan!*** get stuffed!
zurdería, *n.f.* left-handedness.
zurdo, -da, *a.*, *n.m.f.* left-handed (person).
zurear, *v.i.* to bill and coo (*of doves*).
zureo, *n.m.* cooing.
zurita, *n.f.* stock-dove.
zuriza, *n.f.* dispute, quarrel.
zuro (1), **-ra,** *a.* belonging to a stock-dove. — *n.m.* stock-dove, wild pigeon.
zuro (2), *n.m.* corn-cob.
zurra, *n.f.* (*lit.*, *fig.*) tanning.
zurrador, *n.m.* currier, tanner, leather-dresser.
zurrapa, *n.f.* lees, dregs.
zurrapelo, *n.m.* (*coll.*) dressing-down.
zurrapiento, -ta, zurraposo, -sa, *a.* dreggy.
zurrapilla, *n.f.* small lees.
zurrar, *v.t.* to curry, dress (*leather*); to thrash; to dress down; ***zurrar la badana a,*** to tan the hide of, give a good thrashing to. — **zurrarse,** *v.r.* (*obsc.*) to shit o.s.
zurriaga, *n.f.* whip, thong; (*orn.*) lark.
zurriagar [B], *v.t.* to flog, horsewhip.
zurriagazo, *n.m.* whipping; stroke of lash; whip-lash.
zurriago, *n.m.* whip.
zurriar [L], *v.i.* to hum, buzz; to rattle.
zurribanda, *n.f.* horsewhipping; drubbing, thrashing; row, rumpus.
zurriburri, *n.m.* (*coll.*) ragamuffin, scamp; rabble, rowdies; (*pl.*) uproar.
zurrido, *n.m.* humming, buzzing, rattling noise; blow *or* stroke with a stick.
zurrir, *v.i.* to hum, buzz; to rattle.
zurrón, *n.m.* shepherd's pouch; game bag; leather bag; (*bot.*) husk; (*anat.*) fœtal sac.
zurrona, *n.f.* harlot.
zurronada, *n.f.* bagful.
zurroncillo, *n.m.* small shepherd's pouch; small game bag.

zurrusco, *n.m.* (*coll.*) burnt piece of bread.
zurullo, *n.m.* (*coll.*) soft roll; (*coll.*) turd.
zurumbático, -ca, *a.* stunned, dumbfounded.
zurumbela, *n.f.* (*Hisp. Am.*) singing bird.
zurupa, *n.f.* (*Ven.*) cockroach.
zurupeto, *n.m.* illegal stockbroker.
zutano, -na, *n.m.f.* so-and-so; ***fulano, zutano y mengano,*** Tom, Dick and Harry.
¡zuzo! *interj.* expression used to call a dog.
zuzón, *n.m.* (*bot.*) ragwort, groundsel.

Reference Books
Libros de consulta

SPANISH LANGUAGE
LENGUA ESPAÑOLA

I. Peninsular and general
Peninsular y general

A. Monolingual Dictionaries
Diccionarios monolingües

Real Academia Española *Diccionario de la lengua española.* Madrid, 19th ed. 1970.
Alfaro, R. J. *Diccionario de anglicismos.* Madrid, Gredos, 1964.
Alonso, M. *Enciclopedia del idioma.* Madrid, Aguilar, 1968.
Casarés, J. *Diccionario ideológico de la lengua española.* Barcelona, Gustavo Gili, 2nd ed. 1963.
Corominas, J. *Diccionario crítico etimológico de la lengua castellana.* Berne, Gredos, 1954–57.
Gili Gaya, S. *Diccionario general ilustrado de la lengua española.* Barcelona, Biblograf, 2nd ed. 1961.
Gili Gaya, S. *Diccionario Vox de sinónimos.* Barcelona, Biblograf, 3rd ed. 1968.
Moliner, M. *Diccionario de uso del español.* Madrid, Gredos, 1966–67.
Seco, M. *Diccionario de dudas y dificultades de la lengua española.* Madrid, Aguilar, 5th ed. 1967.

B. Allied Works
Obras afines

Alonso, M. *Ciencia del lenguaje y arte del estilo.* Madrid, Aguilar, 6th ed. 1964.
Beinhauer, W. *El español coloquial.* Madrid, Gredos, 2nd ed. 1968 (translation of *Spanische Umgangssprache*).
Bryson Gerrard, A. *Beyond the Dictionary in Spanish.* London, Cassell, revised ed. 1972.
Calvo Sotelo, J. *La bolsa de las palabras.* Madrid, Prensa Española, 1975.
Carnicer, R. *Sobre el lenguaje de hoy.* Madrid, Prensa Española, 1969.
Carnicer, R. *Nuevas reflexiones sobre el lenguaje.* Madrid, Prensa Española, 1972.
Criado de Val, M. *Así hablamos.* Madrid, Prensa Española, 1974.
Gooch, A. *Diminutive, Augmentative and Pejorative Suffixes in Modern Spanish.* Oxford, Pergamon, 2nd ed. 1970.
Lorenzo, E. *El español de hoy, lengua en ebullición.* Madrid, Gredos, 2nd ed. 1971.
Lyon, J. E. *Pitfalls of Spanish Vocabulary.* London, Harrap, 1961.
Náñez, E. *La lengua que hablamos: creación y sistema.* Santander, Gonzalo Bedia, 1973.

C. Grammar
Gramática

Alonso, M. *Gramática del español contemporáneo.* Madrid, Aguilar, 1968.
Harmer, L. C. and Norton, F. J. *A Manual of Modern Spanish.* London, University Tutorial Press, 2nd ed. 1957.
Ramsey, M. M. and Spaulding, R. K. *A Textbook of Modern Spanish.* New York, Holt Rinehart, 1965.
Stockwell, R. P., Bowen, J. D. and Martin, J. W. *The Grammatical Structures of English and Spanish.* Chicago, University of Chicago Press, 1965.

D. Phonetics
Fonética

Alarcos Llorach, E. *Fonología española.* Madrid, Gredos, 4th ed. 1968.
Navarro Tomás, T. *Manual de pronunciación española.* Madrid, C.S.I.C. (Consejo Superior de Investigaciones Científicas), 18th ed. 1974.
Stockwell, R. P. and Bowen, J. D. *The Sounds of English and Spanish.* Chicago, University of Chicago Press, 5th ed. 1970.

II. Latin-American
Hispanoamericano

A. Dictionaries
Diccionarios

Malaret, A. *Diccionario de americanismos.* Buenos Aires, Emecé, 3rd ed. 1946.
Malaret, A. *Lexicón de fauna y flora.* Bogotá, Instituto Caro y Cuervo, 1970.
Morínigo, M. A. *Diccionario manual de americanismos.* Buenos Aires, Muchnik, 1966.

B. Allied Works
Obras afines

Aguero Chaves, A. *El español en América.* San José de Costa Rica, 1960.
Canfield, D. L. *La pronunciación del español en América.* Bogotá, Instituto Caro y Cuervo, 1962.
Kany, C. E. *American-Spanish Euphemisms.* Berkeley/Los Angeles, University of California Press, 1960.
Kany, C. E. *American-Spanish Semantics.* Berkeley/Los Angeles, University of California Press, 1960.
Lope Blanch, J. L. *El español de América.* Madrid, Alcalá, 1968.
Rosenblat, A. *El castellano de España y el castellano de América.* Caracas, Universidad Central de Venezuela, 1962.

ENGLISH LANGUAGE
LENGUA INGLESA

I. British Works
Obras británicas

A. Dictionaries
Diccionarios

Oxford English Dictionary. London, Oxford University Press, 1928; supplements 1933, 1972–).

Shorter Oxford English Dictionary. London, Oxford University Press, 3rd ed. 1973.

Concise Oxford Dictionary of Current English. London, Oxford University Press, 4th ed. 1964.

Oxford Dictionary of English Etymology. London, Oxford University Press, 1966.

Fowler, H. W., rev. Gowers, Sir E. *Dictionary of Modern English Usage*. London, Oxford University Press, 2nd ed. 1965.

The Advanced Learner's Dictionary of Current English. London, Oxford University Press, 2nd ed. 1963.

Chambers Twentieth Century Dictionary. Edinburgh, Chambers, rev. ed. with new supplement 1977.

Jones, D. *English Pronouncing Dictionary*. London, Dent, 13th ed. 1967.

B. Allied Works
Obras afines

Partridge, E. *Usage and Abusage*. London, Hamish Hamilton, rev. ed. 1946.

Roget, P. M. *Thesaurus of English Words and Phrases*. London, Dent, 1952.

II. American Works
Obras norteamericanas

A. Dictionaries
Diccionarios

American Heritage Dictionary of the English Language. Boston, Houghton Mifflin, 1969.

Random House Dictionary of the English Language. New York, Random House, 1967.

Webster's Third New International Dictionary. Springfield, Mass., Merriam-Webster, 1961; (supplement 6000 *Words* 1976).

Webster's Seventh New Collegiate Dictionary. Springfield, Mass., Merriam-Webster, 1973.

B. Allied Works
Obras afines

Webster's New World Thesaurus. Springfield, Mass., Merriam-Webster, 1976.

Follett, W. *Modern American Usage*. London, Longman, 1966.

BILINGUAL TECHNICAL DICTIONARIES
DICCIONARIOS TÉCNICOS BILINGÜES

A. General
Generales

Diccionario politécnico de las lenguas española e inglesa. Madrid, Castilla, 3rd ed. 1965.

Duden español *Diccionario por la imagen*. Mannheim, Duden; London, Harrap, 2nd ed. 1963.

Sell, L. L. *Comprehensive Technical Dictionary, English–Spanish*. New York, McGraw-Hill, 1944/1959.

B. Specialized
Especializados

Accountancy, Business/Commerce
Contabilidad, Comercio

Macías, R. *Terminología contable; lexicografía y vocabulario inglés–español*. Mexico City, Trillas, 1967.

Reyes Orozco, C. *Spanish–English and English–Spanish Commercial Dictionary*. Oxford, Pergamon, 1969.

Sell, L. L. *Spanish–English Comprehensive Specialists' Dictionary for Insurance, Law, Labor, Politics, Business*. New York, McKay, 1957.

Aeronautics
Aeronáutica

Klein Serrallés, J. *English–Spanish and Spanish–English Dictionary of Aeronautical Terms*. New York/London, McGraw-Hill, 1944.

Chemistry and Medicine
Química y medicina

Goldberg, M. *English–Spanish and Spanish–English Chemical and Medical Dictionary*. New York, McGraw-Hill, 1947/1952.

Ruiz Torres, F. *Diccionario inglés–español y español–inglés de medicina*. Madrid, Alhambra, 3rd ed. 1965.

Communications and Electronics
Comunicaciones y electrónica

Freeman, R. L. *English–Spanish and Spanish–English Dictionary of Communications and Electronic Terms.* Cambridge, Cambridge University Press, 1972.

Piraux, H. *Diccionario inglés–español de la terminología relativa a electrotecnia y electrónica.* Madrid, Editores Técnicos Asociados, 1966.

Earth Sciences and Oil
Ciencias de la tierra y el petróleo

Ortellana Silva, E. *Diccionario inglés-español de ciencias de la tierra.* Madrid, Interciencia, 1967.

Cabra Fernández, A. and Varela Colmeiro, F. *Vocabulario del petróleo y de productos petroquímicos.* Madrid, Interciencia, 1963.

Engineering
Ingeniería

Robb, L. A. *Engineers' Dictionary, Spanish–English and English–Spanish.* New York, Wiley, 1949.

Law
Derecho

Robb, L. A. *Dictionary of Legal Terms, Spanish–English and English–Spanish.* New York, Wiley, 3rd printing 1966.

Library Science and Printing
Biblioteconomía y tipografía

Massa de Gil, B. *Diccionario técnico de biblioteconomía español–inglés, inglés–español.* Mexico City, Trillas, 1965.

Pepper, W. M. *Dictionary of Newspaper and Printing Terms, English–Spanish, Spanish–English.* New York, Columbia University Press, 1959.

Mathematics and Statistics
Matemáticas y estadística

García Rodríguez, M. *Diccionario matemático, español–inglés, inglés–español.* New York, Hobbs & Dorman, 1965.

Barceló, J. L. *Vocabulario de estadística.* Barcelona, Hispano–Europea, 1964.

Note: The Elsevier Publishing Co. (Amsterdam, London, New York) has published a wide range of specialized multilingual technical dictionaries with Spanish sections.

Guía para el lector

blank [blæŋk], *a.* blanco, suelto; en blanco; sin adorno; sin interés; confuso, desconcertado; ***blank cartridge,*** cartucho sin bala; ***blank look*** o ***stare,*** mirada *o* cara inexpresiva. — *s.* blanco, hueco; papel en blanco; cospel; tejo; ***to draw a blank,*** no encontrar *o* no conseguir nada. — *v.t.* borrar, cancelar; cerrar, obstruir; estampar.

public [ˈpʌblik], *a.* público; ***public address system,*** sistema acústico amplificador; ***public enemy,*** enemigo público; ***public house,*** taberna; ***public school,*** colegio interno (privado); (*Am.*) escuela (pública), instituto; ***public spirit,*** civismo, espíritu cívico. — *s.* público; ***in public,*** en público.

punish [ˈpʌniʃ], *v.t.* castigar; (*fig.*) fustigar; tratar con dureza.

punt (1) [pʌnt], *s.* batea. — *v.i.* ir en batea.

punt (2) [pʌnt], *v.i.* jugar, hacer apuestas.

punt (3) [pʌnt], *s.* puntapié (*a la pelota*). — *v.t.* dar un puntapié a (*la pelota*).

resistance [riˈzistəns], *s.* resistencia; oposición; (*elec.*) ***resistance box,*** caja de resistencias; ***resistance coil,*** bobina de resistencia; ***to offer resistance,*** oponer resistencia.

scraper [ˈskreipə], *s.* raspador, raedera; ***shoe-scraper,*** limpiabarros, *m.inv.*; (*fam.*) ***violin-scraper,*** rascatripas, *m.f.inv.*

scrumptious [ˈskrʌmpʃəs], *a.* (*fam.*) exquisito, delicioso.

seat [siːt], *s.* asiento; silla; (*teat.*) localidad; (*en el Parlamento*) escaño; residencia; sede (*del gobierno*); fondillos (*del pantalón*), *m.pl.*; (*fig.*) ***to take a back seat,*** hacer un papel secundario, pintar poco; ***country seat,*** casa solariega; ***seat back,*** respaldo; ***seat belt,*** cinturón de seguridad; ***seat of learning,*** centro de erudición, universidad; ***to have a seat in Parliament,*** ser diputado. — *v.t.* sentar; asentar; poner asiento a; tener asientos *o* cabida para; ***be seated,*** sentarse; estar sentado.

Pronunciación

Vocablo

Modismo

Traducción

Homógrafos

Acento

Categoría gramatical

Tema

Ejemplo ilustrativo

Significados distintos

Categorías gramaticales distintas

Uso regional

Contexto adecuado

Género en español

Nivel estilístico

Uso figurado

Guía para la pronunciación inglesa

Vocales

[i:]	m*i*sa
[i]	entre t*e*ngo y s*i*lba
[e]	p*e*rro
[æ]	más abierto que l*e*rdo
[a:]	p*a*to
[ɔ]	t*o*rre
[ɔ:]	[ɔ] alargada
[u]	entre p*o*ngo y p*u*nta
[u:]	l*u*na
[ʌ]	entre m*o*nte y p*a*to
[ə]	parecido al francés l*e*
[ə:]	[ə] alargada

Diptongos

[ei]	s*ei*s
[ou]	S*ou*za
[ai]	c*ae*
[au]	c*ao*s
[ɔi]	r*oe*
[iə]	m*ía*
[ɛə]	f*ea*
[uə]	p*úa*

Consonantes

[p]	*p*aso
[b]	*b*ajo
[t]	al*t*o
[d]	*d*ardo
[k]	*k*ilo
[g]	*g*ano
[m]	*m*ás
[n]	*n*o
[ŋ]	ta*n*go
[f]	*f*ino
[v]	*v*alencia
[θ]	*c*in*c*o (España)
[ð]	na*d*a
[s]	*s*al
[z]	mi*s*mo
[ʃ]	*ch*ile (Chile)
[ʒ]	ca*ll*e (Argentina)
[r]	pasa*r*
[h]	*j*ota (suave)
[x]	*j*arro (fuerte)
[j]	va*y*a
[w]	h*u*evo

Verbos ingleses

Presente	*Pronunciación*	*Pretérito*	*Participio Pasado*	*Español*

VERBOS IRREGULARES INGLESES

be

I am (I'm)	[ai æm, aim]	was	been	ser, estar
you are (you're)	[ju: ɑ:; jɔ:, juə]	were		
he is (he's)	[hi: iz, hi:z]	was		
she is (she's)	[ʃi: iz, ʃi:z]	was		
it is (it's)	[it iz, its]	was		
we are (we're)	[wi: ɑ:, wiə]	were		
you are *véase arriba*		were		
they are (they're)	[ðei ɑ:, ðεə]	were		

have

I have (I've)	[ai hæv, aiv]	had	had	haber, tener
you have (you've)	[ju: hæv, ju:v]	had		
he has (he's)	[hi: hæz, hi:z]	had		
she has (she's)	[ʃi: hæz, ʃi:z]	had		
we have (we've)	[wi: hæv, wi:v]	had		
they have (they've)	[ðei hæv, ðeiv]	had		

Infinitivo	*Pretérito*	*Participio Pasado*	*Español*
abide	***abode***	***abode***	morar
awake	***awoke***	***awoken, awakened***	despertar
bear	***bore***	***borne***	llevar; parir
beat	***beat***	***beaten***	batir
begin	***began***	***begun***	empezar
bend	***bent***	***bent***	doblar(se)
bereave	bereaved (***bereft***)	bereaved (***bereft***)	despojar
beseech	***besought***	***besought***	impetrar
bid	***bade, bid***	***bidden, bid***	mandar
bind	***bound***	***bound***	ligar
bite	***bit***	***bitten***	morder
bleed	***bled***	***bled***	sangrar
blow	***blew***	***blown***	soplar
break	***broke***	***broken***	quebrar
breed	***bred***	***bred***	criar
bring	***brought***	***brought***	traer
build	***built***	***built***	edificar
burn	***burned, burnt***	***burned, burnt***	quemar(se)
burst	***burst***	***burst***	reventar(se)
buy	***bought***	***bought***	comprar
cast	***cast***	***cast***	arrojar
catch	***caught***	***caught***	coger
chide	***chid***	***chid, chidden***	regañar
choose	***chose***	***chosen***	escoger
cleave	cleaved, ***cleft, clove***	cleaved, ***cleft, cloven***[1]	hender

[1] *Cloven* hoof.

Infinitivo	*Pretérito*	*Participio Pasado*	*Español*
cling	***clung***	***clung***	adherirse
clothe	clothed (*obs.* ***clad***)	***clad,*** clothed	vestir
come	***came***	***come***	venir
cost	***cost***	***cost***	costar
creep	***crept***	***crept***	arrastrarse
crow	crowed, ***crew***	crowed	cacarear
cut	***cut***	***cut***	cortar
dare	dared (*obs.* ***durst***)	dared	osar
deal	***dealt***	***dealt***	repartir
dig	***dug***	***dug***	cavar
do	***did***	***done***	hacer
draw	***drew***	***drawn***	tirar; dibujar
dream	dreamed, ***dreamt***	dreamed, ***dreamt***	soñar
drink	***drank***	***drunk***	beber
drive	***drove***	***driven***	conducir
dwell	***dwelt***	***dwelt***	morar
eat	***ate***	***eaten***	comer
fall	***fell***	***fallen***	caer
feed	***fed***	***fed***	(dar de) comer
feel	***felt***	***felt***	sentir
fight	***fought***	***fought***	combatir
find	***found***	***found***	encontrar
flee	***fled***	***fled***	huir
fling	***flung***	***flung***	arrojar
fly	***flew***	***flown***	volar
forbear	***forbore***	***forborne***	abstenerse
forbid	***forbad***(*e*)	***forbidden***	vedar
forget	***forgot***	***forgotten***	olvidar
forsake	***forsook***	***forsaken***	abandonar
freeze	***froze***	***frozen***	helar(se)
get	***got***	***got*** (*U.S.A.* ***gotten***)	obtener
gird	girded, ***girt***	girded, ***girt***	ceñir
give	***gave***	***given***	dar
go	***went***	***gone***	ir
grind	***ground***	***ground***	moler
grow	***grew***	***grown***	cultivar; crecer
hang[1]	***hung***	***hung***	colgar
hear	***heard***	***heard***	oír
heave	heaved, ***hove***	heaved, ***hove***	alzar
hew	hewed	hewed, ***hewn***	talar

[1] *Colgar.* Es regular en el sentido de *ahorcar*.

Verbos ingleses

Infinitivo	*Pretérito*	*Participio Pasado*	*Español*
hide	***hid***	***hidden***	esconder
hit	***hit***	***hit***	golpear
hold	***held***	***held***	(sos)tener
hurt	***hurt***	***hurt***	dañar
keep	***kept***	***kept***	guardar
kneel	***knelt***	***knelt***	arrodillarse
knit	***knit,*** knitted	knitted	hacer punto
know	***knew***	***known***	saber, conocer
lay	***laid***	***laid***	poner
lead	***led***	***led***	conducir
lean	***leant,*** leaned	***leant,*** leaned	apoyar(se)
leap	leaped, ***leapt***	leaped, ***leapt***	saltar
learn	learned, ***learnt***	learned, ***learnt***	aprender
leave	***left***	***left***	dejar
lend	***lent***	***lent***	prestar
let	***let***	***let***	dejar
lie[1]	***lay***	***lain***	yacer
light	***lit,*** lighted	***lit,*** lighted	iluminar
lose	***lost***	***lost***	perder
make	***made***	***made***	hacer
mean	***meant***	***meant***	querer decir
meet	***met***	***met***	encontrar(se)
melt	melted	melted, ***molten***	fundir
mow	mowed	***mown***	segar
pay	***paid***	***paid***	pagar
put	***put***	***put***	poner
quit	***quit,*** quitted	***quit,*** quitted	abandonar
read	***read***	***read***	leer
rend	***rent***	***rent***	desgarrar
rid	***rid***	***rid***	dezembarazar
ride	***rode***	***ridden***	montar
ring[2]	***rang***	***rung***	sonar
rise	***rose***	***risen***	levantarse
run	***ran***	***run***	correr
saw	sawed	***sawn***	aserrar
say	***said***	***said***	decir
see	***saw***	***seen***	ver
seek	***sought***	***sought***	buscar
sell	***sold***	***sold***	vender

[1] *Estar acostado*. En el sentido de *mentir* es regular.
[2] *Resonar*. En el sentido de *circundar* es regular.

Infinitivo	*Pretérito*	*Participio Pasado*	*Español*
send	***sent***	***sent***	enviar
set	***set***	***set***	fijar
sew	sewed	***sewn,*** sewed	coser
shake	***shook***	***shaken***	sacudir
shear	sheared	***shorn,*** sheared	esquilar
shed	***shed***	***shed***	despojarse de
shine	***shone***	***shone***	relucir
shoe	***shod***	***shod***	herrar
shoot	***shot***	***shot***	disparar
show	showed	***shown***	indicar
shrink	***shrank***	***shrunk***	encoger(se)
shut	***shut***	***shut***	cerrar(se)
sing	***sang***	***sung***	cantar
sink	***sank***	***sunk, sunken***[1]	hundir(se)
sit	***sat***	***sat***	sentarse
slay	***slew***	***slain***	matar
sleep	***slept***	***slept***	dormir
slide	***slid***	***slid***	resbalar
sling	***slung***	***slung***	lanzar
slink	***slunk***	***slunk***	escabullirse
slit	***slit***	***slit***	cortar
smell	***smelt,*** smelled	***smelt***	oler
smite (*obs.*)	***smote***	***smitten***	herir
sow	sowed	***sown***	sembrar
speak	***spoke***	***spoken***	hablar
speed	***sped***	***sped***	correr
spell	***spelt,*** spelled	***spelt***, spelled	deletrear
spend	***spent***	***spent***	gastar
spill	spilled, ***spilt***	spilled, ***spilt***	derramar
spin	***spun, span***	***spun***	hilar
spit	***spat***	***spat***	escupir
split	***split***	***split***	hender, partir
spoil	***spoilt,*** spoiled	***spoilt,*** spoiled	estropear(se)
spread	***spread***	***spread***	tender
spring	***sprang***	***sprung***	brincar
stand	***stood***	***stood***	estar (de pie)
steal	***stole***	***stolen***	robar
stick	***stuck***	***stuck***	hincar; pegar
sting	***stung***	***stung***	picar

[1] *Sunken* cheeks.

Verbos ingleses

Infinitivo	*Pretérito*	*Participio Pasado*	*Español*
stink	***stank, stunk***	***stunk***	heder
strew	strewed	***strewn,*** strewed	esparcir
stride	***strode***	***stridden***	andar a pasos largos
strike	***struck***	***struck***	golpear
string	***strung***	***strung***	ensartar
strive	***strove***	***striven***	esforzarse
swear	***swore***	***sworn***	jurar
sweep	***swept***	***swept***	barrer
swell	swelled	***swollen***, swelled	hinchar(se)
swim	***swam***	***swum***	nadar
swing	***swung***	***swung***	oscilar
take	***took***	***taken***	tomar
teach	***taught***	***taught***	enseñar
tear	***tore***	***torn***	romper
tell	***told***	***told***	contar
think	***thought***	***thought***	pensar
thrive	***throve,*** thrived	thrived, ***thriven***	prosperar
throw	***threw***	***thrown***	echar
thrust	***thrust***	***thrust***	empujar
tread	***trod***	***trodden***	pisar
wake	***woke***	***woken***	despertar(se)
wear	***wore***	***worn***	llevar
weave	***wove***	***woven***	tejer
weep	***wept***	***wept***	llorar
wet	wetted, ***wet***	wetted, ***wet***	mojar
win	***won***	***won***	ganar
wind	***wound***	***wound***	devanar
work	worked (*obs.* ***wrought***)	worked (*obs.* ***wrought***)	trabajar
wring	***wrung***	***wrung***	torcer
write	***wrote***	***written***	escribir

VERBOS DEFECTIVOS

Presente	*Pretérito*	*Participio Pasado*	*Español*
can	***could***	—	poder
may	***might***	—	tener permiso; poder
must	—	—	deber
shall	***should***	—	ir a (*futuro*)
will	***would***	—	querer; ir a (*futuro*)

Abreviaturas españolas usadas en el Diccionario

a.	adjetivo
abrev.	abreviatura
adv.	adverbio, adverbial
aer.	aeronáutica
agric.	agricultura
alb.	albañilería
álg.	álgebra
Am.	América
anat.	anatomía
ant.	anticuado
anglo-ind.	anglo-indio
apl.	aplícase
aprox.	aproximadamente
arit.	aritmética
arq.	arquitectura
art.	artículo
artill.	artillería
astrol.	astrología
astron.	astronomía
aut.	automovilismo
aux.	auxiliar
avia.	aviación
azu.	industria azucarera
b.a.	bellas artes
bact.	bacteriología
bíb.	bíblico
biol.	biología
blas.	blasón
brit.	británico
bot.	botánica
cant.	cantería
carp.	carpintería
carr.	carruajería
caz.	caza
célt.	céltico
cerá.	cerámica
cine.	cinematografía
cir.	cirugía
coc.	cocina
com.	comercio
compar.	comparativo
conj.	conjunción
constr.	construcción
contr.	contracción
cost.	costura
cristal.	cristalografía
danz.	danza
defec.	defectivo
dem.	demostrativo
dep.	deporte
der.	derecho
despec.	despectivo
dial.	dialecto
dib.	dibujo
dim.	diminutivo
dip.	diplomacia
econ.	economía
educ.	educación
EE.UU.	Estados Unidos
elec.	electricidad
enc.	encuadernación
ent.	entomología
e.p.	economía política
equit.	equitación
esc.	escultura
Esco.	Escocia, escocés
esgr.	esgrima
esp.	especialmente
etc.	et cetera
f.	femenino
fam.	familiar
farm.	farmacología
f.c.	ferrocarril
fig.	figurado
filos.	filosofía
fís.	física
fisiol.	fisiología
fonét.	fonética
for.	forense
fort.	fortificación
foto.	fotografía
fr.	francés
frenol.	frenología
fund.	fundición
gen.	generalmente
geog.	geografía
geol.	geología
geom.	geometría
ger.	gerundio
gram.	gramática
herr.	herraduría
hidr.	hidráulica
Hisp. Am.	Hispano-América
hist.	historia
hist. nat.	historia natural
hort.	horticultura
ict.	ictiología
igl.	iglesia
imper.	imperativo
impers.	impersonal
impr.	imprenta
ind.	industria
indef.	indefinido
indic.	indicativo
inf.	infinitivo
ing.	ingeniería
Ingl.	Inglaterra
interj.	interjección
interr.	interrogativo
inv.	invariable
irón.	irónico
irr.	irregular
joc.	jocoso
joy.	joyería
lat.	latín
lit.	literal
lóg.	lógica
ll.	llámase
m.	masculino
magn.	magnetismo
mar.	marina
mat.	matemáticas
mec.	mecánica
med.	medicina
Méj.	Méjico
metal.	metalurgia
meteorol.	meteorología
Méx.	México
mil.	milicia
min.	minería
mit.	mitología
mús.	música
neut.	neutro
numis.	numismática
obsc.	obsceno
obst.	obstetricia
odont.	odontología
ópt.	óptica
orn.	ornitología
p.a.	participio activo
pal.	paleontología
pat.	patología
pers.	persona, personal
pey.	peyorativo

pint.	pintura
piro.	pirotecnia
pl.	plural
poét.	poético, poética
pol.	política
pos.	posesivo
p.p.	participio pasado
prep.	preposición
pret.	pretérito
P. Rico	Puerto Rico
pron.	pronombre
prov.	proverbio
psic.	psicología
quím.	química
rad.	radio
radtlf.	radiotelefonía
radtlg.	radiotelegrafía
refl.	reflexivo
reg.	regular
rel.	relativo
relig.	religión
ret.	retórica
s.	substantivo
sast.	sastrería
sider.	siderurgía
sing.	singular
somb.	sombrerería
subj.	subjuntivo
superl.	superlativo
t.	también
teat.	teatro
tec.	tecnología
tej.	tejidos
tele.	telefonía
ten.	tenería
teo.	teología
tint.	tintorería
tip.	tipografía
tlg.	telegrafía
top.	topografía
T.V.	televisión
ú.	úsase
univ.	universidad
u. ref.	usado reflexivamente
v.	véase
Vd(s).	usted(es)
vet.	veterinaria
v.i.	verbo intransitivo
v.irr.	verbo irregular
v.r.	verbo reflexivo
v.t.	verbo transitivo
zap.	zapatería
zool.	zoologia
[. . .]	véase

A, a (1) [ei], primera letra del alfabeto; **A,** (*mús.*) la.
a (2) [ə, æ, ei], **an** [ən, æn] (*antes de una vocal o hache muda*), *art. indef.* un, una; el, la; ***sixpence a pound,*** seis peniques la libra; ***ten pounds a day,*** diez libras por día, diez libras diarias.
a (3) [ə, æ], *prep.* por (*se halla a veces delante del participio activo, para denotar la acción de un verbo*); ***a-hunting we will go,*** iremos a cazar.
Aachen [ˈɑːxən]. Aquisgrán.
Aaron [ˈɛərən]. Arón; (*bot.*) ***Aaron's beard,*** hiedra de Kenilworth; hierba china; saxífraga sarmentosa.
abaca [ˈæbəkə], *s.* (*bot.*) abacá, *m.*
aback [əˈbæk], *adv.* atrás; (*mar.*) en facha; ***to take aback,*** desconcertar.
abacus [ˈæbəkəs], *s.* ábaco.
abaft [əˈbɑːft], *adv.* (*mar.*) a popa, en popa, hacia la popa.
abaisance [əˈbeisəns], *s.* reverencia.
abalienation [æbeiliəˈneiʃən], *s.* enajenación, traspaso.
abandon [əˈbændən], *s.* abandono; desamparo; desenfreno; ***with gay abandon,*** alegremente, deportivamente. — *v.t.* abandonar; desamparar; ***they abandoned the enterprise,*** desistieron de la empresa.
abandoned [əˈbændənd], *a.* vicioso; ***an abandoned woman,*** una mujer perdida.
abandonee [əbændəˈniː], *s.* (*for.*) cesionario.
abandoning [əˈbændəniŋ], *s.* abandono; desamparo; (*for.*) cesión, renuncia.
abandonment [əˈbændənmənt], *s.* abandono; desamparo; (*for., com.*) cesión, dejación.
abase [əˈbeis], *v.t.* rebajar, humillar, envilecer, degradar.
abasement [əˈbeismənt], *s.* envilecimiento, humillación, degradación.
abash [əˈbæʃ], *v.t.* avergonzar, sonrojar.
abashment [əˈbæʃmənt], *s.* confusión, rubor, vergüenza.
abasing [əˈbeisiŋ], *a.* humillante; vergonzoso.
abate [əˈbeit], *v.t.* disminuir, debilitar; (*for.*) revocar, anular. — *v.i.* disminuir, amainar.
abatement [əˈbeitmənt], *s.* disminución, amaine; anulación.
abatis, abattis [əˈbætis], *s.* (*fort.*) tala, estacada.
abattoir [ˈæbətwaː], *s.* matadero.
abbacy [ˈæbəsi], *s.* abadía; abadiato; abadengo.
abbatial [əˈbeiʃəl], *a.* abacial, abadengo.
abbess [ˈæbes], *s.* abadesa.
abbey [ˈæbi], *s.* abadía, monasterio.
abbot [ˈæbət], *s.* abad.
abbotship [ˈæbətʃip], *s.* abadiato.
abbreviate [əˈbriːvieit], *v.t.* abreviar.
abbreviation [əbriːviˈeiʃən], *s.* abreviatura; abreviación; (*mat.*) reducción.
abbreviator [əˈbriːvieitə], *s.* abreviador.
abbreviatory [əˈbriːvieitəri], *a.* abreviatorio.
abbreviature [əˈbriːviətʃə], *s.* abreviatura.
ABC [ˈeiˈbiːˈsiː], *s.* abecé; guía alfabética de ferrocarriles.
abdicant [ˈæbdikənt], *a.* abdicante, renunciante.
abdicate [ˈæbdikeit], *v.t., v.i.* abdicar, renunciar (a); ***abdicate in favour of,*** abdicar en.
abdication [æbdiˈkeiʃən], *s.* abdicación, renuncia; (*for.*) denegación de paternidad; (*mar.*) abandono.
abdomen [æbˈdoumen], *s.* (*anat.*) abdomen, vientre.
abdominal [æbˈdɔminəl], *a.* abdominal.
abdominous [æbˈdɔminəs], *a.* ventrudo.
abducent [æbˈdjuːsənt], *a.* (*anat.*) abductor.
abduct [æbˈdʌkt], *v.t.* raptar, secuestrar; (*fisiol.*) producir la abducción de.
abduction [æbˈdʌkʃən], *s.* (*anat.*) abducción; (*for.*) rapto, secuestro.
abductor [æbˈdʌktə], *s.* (*anat.*) abductor; (*for.*) raptor, secuestrador.
abeam [əˈbiːm], *adv.* (*mar.*) por el través, de través.
abed [əˈbed], *adv.* acostado, en cama, en la cama.
aberrant [æˈberənt], *a.* aberrante, anormal; extraviado.
aberrate [ˈæbəreit], *v.i.* aberrar.
aberration [æbəˈreiʃən], *s.* aberración, extravío.
abet [əˈbet], *v.t.* alentar, instigar, incitar.
abetment [əˈbetmənt], *s.* instigación, incitación.
abetter, abettor [əˈbetə], *s.* instigador, incitador.
abeyance [əˈbeiəns], *s.* suspensión; ***in abeyance,*** en suspenso; ***lands in abeyance,*** bienes mostrencos.
abeyant [əˈbeiənt], *a.* en suspenso.
abhor [əbˈhɔː], *v.t.* aborrecer, detestar.
abhorrence, abhorrency [əbˈhɔrəns, -i], *s.* aborrecimiento, detestación, execración.
abhorrent [əbˈhɔrənt], *a.* detestable, aborrecible, execrable.
abhorring [əbˈhɔːriŋ], *s.* aborrecimiento.
abide [əˈbaid], *v.t.* sufrir, soportar. — *v.i. irr.* habitar, morar, residir; ***abide by,*** atenerse a, observar, respetar.
abiding [əˈbaidiŋ], *a.* permanente; perdurable.
abigail [ˈæbigeil], *s.* doncella.
ability [əˈbiliti], *s.* facultad, capacidad, aptitud; ***man of abilities,*** hombre de dotes; ***to the best of my ability,*** en la medida de mi capacidad, lo mejor que pueda.
abject [ˈæbdʒekt], *a.* abyecto, vil.
abjection, abjectness [æbˈdʒekʃən, ˈæbdʒektnis], *s.* abyección, vileza, bajeza.
abjuration [æbdʒuəˈreiʃən], *s.* abjuración.
abjuratory [æbdʒuəˈreitəri], *a.* abjuratorio.
abjure [æbˈdʒuə], *v.t.* abjurar de, renunciar a.
abjurer [æbˈdʒuərə], *s.* renunciante.
abjuring [æbˈdʒuəriŋ], *s.* abjuración, renuncia.
ablactate [æbˈlækteit], *v.t.* destetar.
ablactation [æblækˈteiʃən], *s.* destete.
ablation [æbˈleiʃən], *s.* (*cir.*) ablación.
ablative [ˈæblətiv], *a., s.* (*gram.*) ablativo.
ablaze [əˈbleiz], *a.* encendido, brillante. — *adv.* en llamas, ardiendo.
able [eibl], *a.* capaz; ***to be able,*** ser capaz (de), poder.
able-bodied [ˈeibl-ˈbɔdid], *a.* sano, robusto; ***able-bodied seaman,*** marinero de primera (clase).
able-minded [ˈeibl-ˈmaindid], *a.* inteligente.
ableness [ˈeiblnis], *s.* capacidad; poder.
ablest [ˈeiblist], *a. superl.* [ABLE]; el *o* la más capaz.
ablet [ˈæblit], *s.* (*ict.*) breca.
abloom [əˈbluːm], *a., adv.* en flor, floreciente.
abluent [ˈæbluənt], *a., s.* (*med.*) detersivo, detergente.
ablush [əˈblʌʃ], *a.* sonrojado, abochornado.
ablution [æbˈluːʃən], *s.* ablución.
ably [ˈeibli], *adv.* de una manera capaz.
abnegate [ˈæbnigeit], *v.t.* renunciar (a); abnegar.
abnegation [æbniˈgeiʃən], *s.* abnegación, renuncia.

abnormal [æb'nɔːməl], *a.* anormal.
abnormality [æbnɔː'mæliti], *s.* anormalidad.
aboard [ə'bɔːd], *adv.* (*mar.*) a bordo; ***to go aboard,*** embarcarse, ir a bordo; ***to take aboard,*** embarcar, llevar a bordo.
abode [ə'boud], *s.* domicilio, residencia, morada; ***to take up one's abode,*** fijar su residencia, domiciliarse.
abolish [ə'bɔliʃ], *v.t.* abolir, anular, revocar; suprimir.
abolishable [ə'bɔliʃəbl], *a.* abolible.
abolishment [ə'bɔliʃmənt] [ABOLITION].
abolition [æbə'liʃən], *s.* abolición.
abolitionism [æbə'liʃənizəm], *s.* abolicionismo.
abolitionist [æbə'liʃənist], *s.* abolicionista, *m.f.*
A-bomb ['eibɔm], *s.* *abrev.* ***atom(ic) bomb*** [BOMB].
abominable [ə'bɔminəbl], *a.* abominable.
abominableness [ə'bɔminəblnis], *s.* abominación.
abominate [ə'bɔmineit], *v.t.* abominar (de).
abomination [əbɔmin'eiʃən], *s.* abominación.
aboriginal [æbə'ridʒinəl], *a.*, *s.* aborigen.
aborigine [æbə'ridʒini], *s.* aborigen.
abort [ə'bɔːt], *v.t.* hacer abortar. — *v.i.* abortar.
abortion [ə'bɔːʃən], *s.* aborto; aborto provocado.
abortionist [ə'bɔːʃənist], *s.* abortador, abortadora.
abortive [ə'bɔːtiv], *a.* abortivo; abortado, malogrado.
abortiveness [ə'bɔːtivnis], *s.* aborto, malogro.
abound [ə'baund], *v.i.* abundar; ***abound with,*** abundar en.
abounding [ə'baundiŋ], *a.* abundante (***in, with,*** en).
about [ə'baut], *adv.* aproximadamente; por aquí, por ahí; en el aire, en el ambiente; en dirección contraria; ***about how many?*** ¿cuántos aproximadamente?; ***about time too!*** ¡ya es hora! ¡ya era hora!; (*mil.*) ***about turn!*** ¡media vuelta!; ***to bring about,*** ocasionar, originar. — *prep.* acerca de, sobre; alrededor de, por; hacia, a eso de (*tiempo*); ***about one o'clock,*** sobre, hacia, a eso de la una; ***what's this book about?*** ¿de qué trata este libro?; ***he's about to arrive,*** está a punto de llegar, está al llegar; ***there are no two ways about it,*** no hay que darle vueltas.
above [ə'bʌv], *adv.* arriba, encima; ***above board,*** abiertamente, a la vista de todos; ***from above,*** de arriba, desde lo alto; ***above-mentioned,*** ya citado, ya mencionado, susodicho. — *prep.* sobre, superior a, encima de; ***above all,*** sobre todo; ***he is above that sort of thing,*** no se rebaja a hacer semejantes cosas.
abrade [ə'breid], *v.t.* raer.
abrasion [ə'breiʒən], *s.* abrasión.
abrasive [ə'breisiv], *a.* abrasivo.
abreast [ə'brest], *adv.* a la par; (*mar.*) por el través; ***abreast of,*** al corriente de; a la altura de; ***four abreast,*** cuatro de frente, de cuatro en fondo.
abridge [ə'bridʒ], *v.t.* abreviar, compendiar; (*álg.*) reducir.
abridgment [ə'bridʒmənt], *s.* compendio, resumen; (*álg.*) reducción.
abroad [ə'brɔːd], *adv.* en el extranjero; al extranjero; ***to go abroad,*** ir al extranjero; ***there is a rumour abroad,*** corre la voz; ***to spread abroad,*** divulgar, publicar.
abrogate ['æbrogeit], *v.t.* abrogar, anular, revocar.
abrogation [æbro'geiʃən], *s.* abrogación, anulación, revocación.
abrupt [ə'brʌpt], *a.* brusco; seco.
abruption [æb'rʌpʃən], *s.* rotura; (*cir.*) fractura.
abruptness [ə'brʌptnis], *s.* sequedad; brusquedad.
abscess ['æbses], *s.* absceso.
abscind [æb'sind], *v.t.* cortar, tajar.
abscissa [æb'sisə], *s.* (*pl.* **abscissæ** [-i]) (*geom.*) abscisa.
abscission [æb'siʒən], *s.* (*cir.*) abcisión.
abscond [əb'skɔnd], *v.i.* fugarse; ***abscond with (the) money,*** alzarse con el santo y la limosna.
absconder [əb'skɔndə], *s.* fugitivo; prófugo.
absconding [əb'skɔndiŋ], *s.* huída, fuga.
absence ['æbsəns], *s.* ausencia; ***absence of mind,*** distracción; ***in the absence of,*** a falta de; ***leave of absence,*** permiso, licencia temporal, excedencia.
absent ['æbsənt], *a.* ausente; distraído, absorto. — **absent o.s.** [æb'sent], *v.r.* ausentarse.
absentee [æbsən'tiː], *a.* ausente; absentista, *m.f.*
absenteeism [æbsən'tiːizəm], *s.* absentismo.
absenter [æb'sentə], *s.* ausente.
absent-minded ['æbsənt-'maindid], *a.* absorto, abstraído, distraído, despistado.
absent-mindedness ['æbsənt-'maindidnis], *s.* distracción, despiste.
absinthe ['æbsinθ], *s.* ajenjo, absintio.
absinthium [æb'sinθiəm], *s.* (*bot.*) ajenjo, *Artemisia absinthium.*
absolute ['æbsəluːt], *a.* absoluto; incondicional. — *s.* ***the Absolute,*** lo absoluto.
absoluteness ['æbsəluːtnis], *s.* poder absoluto, calidad de absoluto, (lo) absoluto.
absolution [æbsə'luːʃən], *s.* absolución.
absolutism [æbsə'luːtizəm], *s.* absolutismo.
absolutist [æbsə'luːtist], *s.* absolutista, *m.f.*
absolutory, absolvatory [æbsə'luːtəri, əb'zɔlvətəri], *a.* absolutorio.
absolve [əb'zɔlv], *v.t.* absolver.
absolver [əb'zɔlvə], *s.* absolvedor.
absolving [əb'zɔlviŋ], *a.* absolutorio.
absorb [əb'sɔːb], *v.t.* absorber, tener absorto; ***to be absorbed in a book,*** estar absorto en un libro; ***to become absorbed,*** ensimismarse, enfrascarse.
absorbability [əbsɔːbə'biliti], *s.* absorbencia.
absorbable [əb'sɔːbəbl], *a.* absorbible, asimilable.
absorbency [əb'sɔːbənsi], *s.* absorbencia.
absorbent [əb'sɔːbənt], *a.*, *s.* absorbente; (*Am.*) ***absorbent cotton*** [COTTON WOOL].
absorbing [əb'sɔːbiŋ], *a.* absorbente, fascinante.
absorption [əb'sɔːpʃən], *s.* absorción; ensimismamiento.
absorptive [əb'sɔːptiv], *a.* absorbente.
abstain [əb'stein], *v.i.* abstenerse (de).
abstainer [əb'steinə], *s.* abstinente.
abstaining [əb'steiniŋ], *a.* abstinente. — *s.* abstinencia.
abstemious [əb'stiːmiəs], *a.* abstemio; sobrio, abstinente.
abstemiousness [əb'stiːmiəsnis], *s.* sobriedad; abstinencia.
abstention [əb'stenʃən], *s.* abstención.
absterge [əb'stəːdʒ], *v.t.* absterger, deterger.
abstergent, abstersive [əb'stəːdʒənt, -siv], *a.*, *s.* abstergente.
abstersion [əb'stəːʃən], *s.* (*med.*) abstersión.
abstinence, abstinency ['æbstinəns, -i], *s.* abstinencia.
abstinent ['æbstinənt], *a.* abstinente; sobrio.
abstract ['æbstrækt], *a.* abstracto. — *s.* extracto, resumen. — [æb'strækt], *v.t.* abstraer, extraer.
abstracted [æb'stræktid], *a.* abstraído.
abstractedness [æb'stræktidnis], *s.* abstracción.
abstraction [æb'strækʃən], *s.* abstracción.
abstractive [æb'stræktiv], *a.* abstractivo.
abstractness ['æbstræktnis], *s.* (lo) abstracto (de).
abstruse [æb'struːs], *a.* abstruso.
abstruseness, abstrusity [æb'struːsnis, -iti], *s.* (lo) abstruso (de).
absurd [əb'səːd], *a.* absurdo.
absurdity, absurdness [əb'səːditi, -nis], *s.* absurdo; despropósito, disparate; ***height of absurdity,*** colmo de lo absurdo.

abundance [əˈbʌndəns], *s.* abundancia, copia.
abundant [əˈbʌndənt], *a.* abundante, copioso.
abuse [əˈbjuːs], *s.* insulto, injuria, denuesto; abuso. — [əˈbjuːz], *v.t.* insultar, injuriar, denostar; abusar (de).
abuser [əˈbjuːzə], *s.* abusador; insultador.
abusive [əˈbjuːsiv], *a.* abusivo; injurioso, ofensivo, insultante.
abusiveness [əˈbjuːsivnis], *s.* insulto(s), injuria(s); (lo) injurioso (de).
abut [əˈbʌt], *v.i.* terminar; confinar; ***abut upon,*** confinar con, terminar en.
abutment [əˈbʌtmənt], *s.* linde, confín; (*arq.*) estribo, contrafuerte; botarel; (*carp.*) empalme.
abuttal [əˈbʌtəl], *s.* límite.
abutting [əˈbʌtiŋ], *a.* lindante, confinante.
abysm, abyss [əˈbizm, əˈbis], *s.* abismo, sima; (*blas.*) centro (del escudo).
abysmal [əˈbizməl], *a.* abismal; ***abysmal ignorance,*** ignorancia crasa *o* supina.
Abyssinia [æbiˈsinjə]. Abisinia.
Abyssinian [æbiˈsinjən], *a.*, *s.* abisinio.
acacia [əˈkeiʃə], *s.* (*bot.*) acacia.
academic [ækəˈdemik], *a.*, *s.* académico, erudito.
academician, academist [əkædəˈmiʃan, əˈkædəmist], *s.* académico.
academy [əˈkædəmi], *s.* academia.
acantha, acanthus [əˈkænθə, -θəs], *s.* (*bot.*) acanto, branca ursina.
acanthine [əˈkænθain], *a.* (*bot.*) de acanto.
acarus [ˈækərəs], *s.* (*zool.*) ácaro; arador, género de los ácaridos.
acatalectic [əkætəˈlektik], *s.* (*poét.*) acataléctico.
acatalepsy [əˈkætəlepsi], *s.* (*med.*) acatalepsis, *f.*
acataleptic [əkætəˈleptik], *a.* acataléptico.
acaulescent, acauline, acaulous [ækɔːˈlesənt, əˈkɔːlain, -ləs], *a.* acaule.
accede [ækˈsiːd], *v.i.* acceder, asentir; ascender; adherirse.
accelerate [ækˈseləreit], *v.t.*, *v.i.* acelerar.
accelerating [ækˈseləreitiŋ], *a.* acelerador, acelerante.
acceleration [ækseləˈreiʃən], *s.* aceleración.
accelerative [ækˈselərətiv], *a.* acelerador.
accelerator [ækˈseləreitə], *s.* acelerador.
acceleratory [ækˈseləreitəri], *a.* acelerador.
accent [ˈæksent], *s.* acento; dejo. — [ækˈsent], *v.t.* acentuar.
accentuate [ækˈsentjueit], *v.t.* acentuar; (*fig.*) recalcar.
accentuation [æksentjuˈeiʃən], *s.* acentuación.
accept [ækˈsept], *v.t.* aceptar; admitir; recibir, acoger; ***in the accepted sense,*** con su sentido normal.
acceptability, acceptableness [ækseptəˈbiliti, ækˈseptəblnis], *s.* aceptabilidad; (lo) aceptable.
acceptable [ækˈseptəbl], *a.* aceptable, admisible.
acceptance [ækˈseptəns], *s.* aceptación.
acceptant [ækˈseptənt], *a.*, *s.* aceptador, aceptante.
acceptation [æksepˈteiʃən], *s.* aceptación.
accepter, acceptor [ækˈseptə], *s.* aceptador; (*com.*) aceptante.
acception [ækˈsepʃən], *s.* acepción.
access [ˈækses], *s.* acceso, entrada; ingreso; (*med.*) accesión.
accessibility [æksesiˈbiliti], *s.* accesibilidad.
accessible [ækˈsesibl], *a.* accesible, asequible.
accession [ækˈseʃən], *s.* accesión; advenimiento; ***list of accessions,*** libros recién adquiridos.
accessory [ækˈsesəri], *a.* accesorio, adicional, adjunto. — *s.* accesorio; cómplice.
accidence [ˈæksidəns], *s.* (*gram.*) accidente.
accident [ˈæksidənt], *s.* accidente; casualidad; siniestro; ***by accident,*** por casualidad, casualmente, accidentalmente, sin querer; ***industrial accident,*** accidente de trabajo.
accidental [æksiˈdentəl], *a.* accidental; casual.
accidentality [æksidenˈtæliti], *s.* accidencia.
accidentalness [æksiˈdentəlnis], *s.* (lo) casual (de).
acclaim [əˈkleim], *s.* [ACCLAMATION]. — *v.t.* aclamar, aplaudir. — *v.i.* vitorear.
acclamation [ækləˈmeiʃən], *s.* aclamación.
acclimate [ˈæklimeit], (*Am.*) [ACCLIMATIZE].
acclimatization [əklaimətaiˈzeiʃən], *s.* aclimatación.
acclimatize [əˈklaimətaiz], *v.t.* aclimatar. — **acclimatize o.s.,** *v.r.* aclimatarse.
acclivity [əˈkliviti], *s.* declive.
accolade [ækoˈleid], *s.* acolada; espaldarazo.
accommodate [əˈkɔmədeit], *v.t.* acomodar; hospedar, alojar; servir, complacer. — **accommodate o.s.,** *v.r.* ***accommodate o.s. to the circumstances,*** adaptarse a las circunstancias.
accommodating [əˈkɔmədeitiŋ], *a.* obsequioso, servicial, complaciente.
accommodation [əkɔməˈdeiʃən], *s.* acomodación; habitaciones, *f.pl.*, alojamiento, hospedaje.
accommodator [əˈkɔmədeitə], *s.* el que acomoda.
accompaniment [əˈkʌmpənimənt], *s.* acompañamiento.
accompanist [əˈkʌmpənist], *s.* acompañante; acompañador.
accompany [əˈkʌmpəni], *v.t.* acompañar.
accomplice [əˈkʌmplis], *s.* cómplice.
accomplish [əˈkʌmpliʃ], *v.t.* realizar, efectuar, llevar a cabo; lograr.
accomplished [əˈkʌmpliʃt], *a.* cabal, consumado; culto, distinguido, elegante; habilidoso.
accomplishing [əˈkʌmpliʃiŋ], *s.* realización, ejecución.
accomplishment [əˈkʌmpliʃmənt], *s.* cumplimiento; realización, logro; talento, dote, habilidad; (*pl.*) talentos, prendas, dotes.
accord [əˈkɔːd], *s.* acuerdo, concierto, armonía; ***in accord,*** de acuerdo; ***of one's own accord,*** espontáneamente, por su (propia) cuenta; ***with one accord,*** de común acuerdo, unánimemente. — *v.t.* conciliar; acordar; otorgar, conceder. — *v.i.* concordar.
accordance, accordancy [əˈkɔːdəns, -i], *s.* acuerdo, conformidad; ***in accordance with,*** de acuerdo con, con arreglo a.
accordant [əˈkɔːdənt], *a.* acorde; conforme a.
according [əˈkɔːdiŋ], *a.* conforme. — *conj.* — ***as,*** conforme. — *prep.* — ***to,*** según, conforme a.
accordingly [əˈkɔːdiŋli], *adv.* en consecuencia, consiguientemente.
accordion [əˈkɔːdiən], *s.* (*mús.*) acordeón, *m.*
accordionist [əˈkɔːdiənist], *s.* acordeonista, *m.f.*
accost [əˈkɔst], *v.t.* abordar; dirigirse a.
account [əˈkaunt], *s.* cuenta; relato; reseña; modo, manera; ***account-book,*** libro de cuentas; ***current account,*** cuenta corriente; ***deposit account, savings account,*** cuenta de ahorro; ***expense account,*** cuenta de gastos; ***joint account,*** cuenta en participación; ***to keep an account,*** llevar la cuenta; ***persons of no account,*** personas sin importancia, *f.pl.*; ***on account of,*** por motivo de, a causa de; ***on no account,*** de ninguna manera; ***on your account,*** por Vd.; ***to pay on account,*** pagar a cuenta; ***profit and loss account,*** cuenta de ganancias y pérdidas; ***to settle accounts,*** ajustar cuentas; ***to take into account,*** tener en cuenta, tomar en consideración; ***to turn to account,*** sacar partido de. — *v.t.* juzgar, contar; considerar. — *v.i.* — ***for,*** dar razón de, responder de; dar una explicación de; ***there's no accounting for tastes,*** sobre gustos no hay nada escrito.
accountability, accountableness [əkauntəˈbiliti, əˈkauntəblnis], *s.* responsabilidad.
accountable [əˈkauntəbl], *a.* responsable.
accountancy [əˈkauntənsi], *s.* contabilidad, contaduría.

accountant [ə'kauntənt], *s.* habilitado; contable, contador; demandado (*en un juicio*).
accounting [ə'kauntiŋ], *s.* contabilidad; ***accounting-day,*** día de ajuste de cuentas, día de vencimiento.
accoutre [ə'ku:tə], *v.t.* aviar, ataviar; equipar; enjaezar.
accoutrement [ə'ku:təmənt], *s.* avío, atavío; pertrechos, *m.pl.*; equipo; jaeces, *m.pl.*
accredit [ə'kredit], *v.t.* acreditar.
accreditation [əkredi'teiʃən], *s.* credencial.
accrescence [ə'kresəns], *s.* acrecencia; acrecentamiento.
accrescent [ə'kresənt], *a.* creciente.
accretion [ə'kri:ʃən], *s.* acrecentamiento, aumento; (*for.*) (derecho de) acrecencia.
accretive [ə'kri:tiv], *a.* aumentativo; acrecentado, aumentado.
accrue [ə'kru:], *v.i.* resultar; acumularse; ***accrued interest,*** interés acumulado.
accumbency [ə'kʌmbənsi], *s.* reclinación.
accumbent [ə'kʌmbənt], *a.* reclinado, apoyado sobre el codo.
accumulate [ə'kju:mjuleit], *v.t.* acumular. — *v.i.* acumularse.
accumulation [əkju:mju'leiʃən], *s.* acumulación, amontonamiento.
accumulative [ə'kju:mjulətiv], *a.* acumulativo.
accumulator [ə'kju:mjuleitə], *s.* acumulador; amontonador; (*hidr.*) condensador.
accuracy ['ækjurisi], *s.* exactitud, precisión.
accurate ['ækjurit], *a.* exacto, preciso.
accurateness ['ækjuritnis], *s.* exactitud, precisión.
accursed [ə'kə:sid], *a.* maldito; detestable, execrable.
accusable [ə'kju:zəbl], *a.* acusable.
accusation [ækju'zeiʃən], *s.* acusación.
accusative [ə'kju:zətiv], *a.*, *s.* acusativo.
accusatory [ə'kju:zətəri], *a.* acusatorio.
accuse [ə'kju:z], *v.t.* acusar.
accuser [ə'kju:zə], *s.* acusador.
accustom [ə'kʌstəm], *v.t.* acostumbrar, habituar; ***to be accustomed to,*** estar acostumbrado a.
accustomed [ə'kʌstəmd], *a.* acostumbrado, avezado; que acostumbra.
ace [eis], *s.* as; ***within an ace of,*** en un tris de, a pique de.
acentric [ei'sentrik], *a.* sin centro.
acephalous [ei'sefələs], *a.* acéfalo.
acer ['eisə], *s.* (*bot.*) arce.
acerate, acerated ['æsəreit, -id], *a.* puntiagudo.
acerb [ə'sə:b], *a.* acerbo.
acerbate ['æsəbeit], *v.t.* agriar, exasperar.
acerbity [ə'sə:biti], *s.* acerbidad; desabrimiento.
aceric, acerous [ə'serik, 'æsərəs], *a.* acerado; espinoso.
acervate ['æsəveit], *a.* (*hist. nat.*) arracimado.
acervation [æsə'veiʃən], *s.* acervo.
acetabulum [æsi'tæbjuləm], *s.* acetábulo.
acetate ['æsiteit], *s.* (*quím.*) acetato; ***acetate of copper,*** cardenillo, verdigris.
acetated ['æsiteitid], *a.* acetoso, agrio.
acetic [ə'si:tik], *a.* acético; (*quím.*) ***acetic acid,*** ácido acético.
acetification [əsetifi'keiʃən], *s.* acetificación.
acetify [ə'setifai], *v.t.* acedar, acetificar.
acetimeter [æsi'timitə], *s.* (*quím.*) acetímetro.
acetimetry [æsi'timitri], *s.* (*quím.*) acetometría.
acetone ['æsitoun], *s.* (*quím.*) acetona.
acetous, acetose ['æsitəs, -ous], *a.* agrio, acedo, acetoso.
acetylene [ə'setili:n], *s.* acetileno.
Achaean [ə'ki:ən], *a.* aqueo.
ache [eik], *s.* dolor. — *v.i.* doler; ***my head aches,*** me duele la cabeza.
achievable [ə'tʃi:vəbl], *a.* hacedero, factible, realizable, lograble.
achieve [ə'tʃi:v], *v.t.* llevar a cabo, realizar; lograr, alcanzar, conseguir.
achievement [ə'tʃi:vmənt], *s.* consecución; logro; acierto.
Achilles [ə'kili:z]. Aquiles, *m.*
aching ['eikiŋ], *a.* dolorido. — *s.* dolor; desazón.
achromatic [ækro'mætik], *a.* acromático.
achromatism [ə'kroumətizəm], *s.* acromatismo.
achromatize [ə'kroumətaiz], *v.t.* acromatizar.
acicular [ə'sikjulə], *a.* acicular, alesnado.
acid ['æsid], *a.*, *s.* ácido.
acidifiable [ə'sidifaiəbl], *a.* acidificable.
acidification [əsidifi'keiʃən], *s.* acidificación.
acidify [ə'sidifai], *v.t.* acedar, acidular, agriar.
acidifying [ə'sidifaiiŋ], *a.* acidificante.
acidimeter [æsi'dimitə], *s.* acidímetro.
acidimetry [æsi'dimitri], *s.* acetometría.
acidity, acidness [ə'siditi, 'æsidnis], *s.* acidez.
acidulate [ə'sidjuleit], *v.t.* acidular.
acidulous [ə'sidjuləs], *a.* acídulo, acidulado.
acierate ['æsiəreit], *v.t.* acerar; convertir en acero.
acinose, acinous ['æsinous, -əs], *a.* granuloso.
ack-ack ['æk-'æk], *s.* (*mil.*) fuego antiaéreo; artillería antiaérea.
acknowledge [æk'nɔlidʒ], *v.t.* reconocer; confesar; agradecer; declarar; ***acknowledge receipt,*** acusar recibo.
acknowledg(e)ment [æk'nɔlidʒmənt], *s.* reconocimiento; confesión; agradecimiento; acuse de recibo.
aclinic [ə'klinik], *a.* aclínico.
acme ['ækmi], *s.* colmo, (lo) último; esencia, personificación.
acne ['ækni], *s.* acné.
acolyte ['ækolait], *s.* acólito.
aconite ['ækonait], *s.* (*bot.*) acónito.
acorn ['eikɔ:n], *s.* (*bot.*) bellota; (*naut.*) bola de madera.
acorned ['eikɔ:nd], *a.* cargado, alimentado *o* cebado con bellotas.
acotyledon [əkɔti'li:dən], *s.* (*bot.*) acotiledón.
acotyledonous [əkɔti'li:dənəs], *a.* acotiledóneo.
acoustic [ə'ku:stik], *a.* acústico.
acoustics [ə'ku:stiks], *s. pl.* (*fís.*) acústica.
acquaint [ə'kweint], *v.t.* informar, poner al corriente; ***to be acquainted with,*** conocer; estar familiarizado con; ***to get acquainted with,*** conocer; familiarizarse con.
acquaintance [ə'kweintəns], *s.* conocimiento; conocido; ***to make the acquaintance of,*** conocer.
acquaintanceship [ə'kweintənsʃip], *s.* conocimiento; trato.
acquaintedness [ə'kweintidnis], *s.* conocimiento.
acquest [ə'kwest], *s.* (*for.*) adquisición; propiedad no heredada.
acquiesce [ækwi'es], *v.i.* consentir, asentir.
acquiescence [ækwi'esəns], *s.* aquiescencia, consentimiento, conformidad.
acquiescent [ækwi'esənt], *a.* condescendiente, acomodadizo; conforme, aquiescente.
acquirable [ə'kwaiərabl], *a.* adquirible.
acquire [ə'kwaiə], *v.t.* adquirir; aprender.
acquirement [ə'kwaiəmənt], *s.* adquisición; (*pl.*) conocimientos.
acquirer [ə'kwaiərə], *s.* (*for.*) adquirente, adquiridor.
acquisition [ækwi'ziʃən], *s.* adquisición.
acquisitive [ə'kwizitiv], *a.* adquisitivo.
acquisitiveness [ə'kwizitivnis], *s.* adquisividad.
acquit [ə'kwit], *v.t.* descargar, absolver; exonerar, exculpar. — **acquit o.s.,** *v.r.* ***acquit o.s. well,*** portarse, conducirse de una manera loable; ***he***

acquitted himself well in the oral, estuvo muy bien en el (examen) oral.
acquittal [ə'kwitəl], *s.* descargo; pago, quitanza; desempeño; (*for.*) absolución.
acquittance [ə'kwitəns], *s.* descargo; recibo, quitanza; (*for.*) finiquito; ***acquittance roll,*** nómina del ejercito.
acquitted [ə'kwitid], *a.* absuelto.
acre ['eikə], *s.* acre (40,47 áreas).
acreage ['eikərid3], *s.* área, superficie medida en acres.
acred ['eikəd], *a.* hacendado.
acrid ['ækrid], *a.* acre; mordaz, áspero.
acridian [æ'kridiən], *a.*, *s.* (*ent.*) acridio.
acridity, acridness [æ'kriditi, 'ækridnis], *s.* acritud.
acrimonious [ækri'mouniəs], *a.* áspero, mordaz, sarcástico, acerbo.
acrimony, acrimoniousness ['ækriməni, ækri'mouniəsnis], *s.* acrimonia, acritud, aspereza, mordacidad, acerbidad.
acritical [ei'kritikəl], *a.* acrítico.
acrobat ['ækrobæt], *s.* acróbata, *m.f.*, volatín.
acrobatic [ækro'bætik], *a.* acrobático.
acrobatics [ækro'bætiks], *s.* acrobacia, ejercicios acrobáticos, *m.pl.*
acrobatism ['ækrobætizəm], *s.* acrobacia, acrobatismo.
acrogen ['ækrod3ən], *s.* (*bot.*) acrógeno.
acromegaly [ækro'megəli], *s.* (*med.*) acromegalia.
acromion [ə'kroumi:ən], *s.* (*anat.*) acromio.
acronycal [ə'krɔnikəl], *a.* (*astron.*) acrónico.
acropolis [ə'krɔpəlis], *s.* acrópolis, *f.*, ciudadela.
across [ə'krɔs], *adv.* de través, al través; al otro lado, cruzado; transversalmente; (*elec.*) en paralelo. — *prep.* a través de, por, sobre, de una parte a otra de; al otro lado de; ***across country,*** a campo traviesa; ***to come, to run across,*** encontrarse con; ***to place across,*** atravesar.
acrostic [ə'krɔstik], *a.* acróstico. — *s.* poema acróstico.
act [ækt], *s.* acto, hecho, acción; ley, decreto, disposición; acta; ***act of faith,*** acto de fe; ***act of God,*** caso fortuito, fuerza mayor; ***Acts of the Apostles,*** Hechos de los Apóstoles; ***by act and right,*** de hecho y derecho; ***to catch in the act,*** coger con las manos en la masa; ***to pass an act,*** votar una ley. — *v.t.* interpretar, desempeñar; representar (*un papel*); interinar; mover, actuar; ***act the fool*** (*horseplay*), hacer el tonto; (*incomprehension*) hacerse el tonto; ***act the part,*** desempeñar el papel (***of,*** de). — *v.i.* obrar, actuar; funcionar; trabajar; fingir, simular, hacer comedia; ***act as,*** actuar de; ***act openly,*** andar con la cara descubierta.
acting ['æktiŋ], *a.* que actúa *o* está en funciones; interino, suplente; que finge. — *s.* acción; (*teat.*) representación; interpretación; fingimiento.
actinic [æk'tinik], *a.* actínico.
actinism [æ'ktinizəm], *s.* (*fís.*) actinismo.
actinium [æk'tiniəm], *s.* actinio.
actinograph [æk'tinogræf], *s.* actinógrafo.
actinometer [ækti'nɔmitə], *s.* actinómetro.
actinometric [æktino'metrik], *a.* actinométrico.
action ['ækʃən], *s.* acción; marcha, funcionamiento; combate, batalla; proceso, litigio; (*der.*) ***to bring an action,*** entablar un pleito; ***to bring into action,*** (empezar a) usar, poner en uso, en movimiento, en marcha, en juego; ***to take action,*** tomar medidas.
actionable ['ækʃənəbl], *a.* procesable.
active ['æktiv], *a.* activo; enérgico.
activeness ['æktivnis], *s.* agilidad, energía.
activity [æk'tiviti], *s.* actividad.
actor ['æktə], *s.* actor; comediante.
actress ['æktris], *s.* actriz, *f.*, comedianta.
actual ['æktʃuəl], *a.* real, efectivo.
actuality [æktʃu'æliti], *s*, realidad.
actualize ['æktʃuəlaiz], *v.t.* realizar, llevar a la práctica.
actually ['æktʃuəli], *adv.* en (la) realidad; de hecho.
actuary ['æktjuəri], *s.* actuario.
actuate ['æktjueit], *v.t.* activar; poner en acción.
acuity [ə'kju:iti], *s.* agudeza, sutileza.
aculeate [ə'kju:lieit], *a.* (*hist. nat.*) erizado; (*bot.*) espinoso.
aculeiform [ə'kju:liifɔ:m], *a.* aculeiforme.
aculeous [ə'kju:liəs], *a.* (*bot.*) espinoso.
acumen [ə'kju:mən], *s.* perspicacia, vista; (*coll.*) pesquis.
acuminate [ə'kju:mineit], *a.* acuminado. — *v.t.* afilar, aguzar. — *v.i.* terminar en punta.
acute [ə'kju:t], *a.* agudo; penetrante; perspicaz; (*geom.*) ***acute-angled,*** acutángulo.
acutely [ə'kju:tli], *adv.* agudamente, con agudeza.
acuteness [ə'kju:tnis], *s.* agudeza; perspicacia; penetración; (*med.*) gravedad.
adage ['ædid3], *s.* adagio, refrán, dicho.
Adam ['ædəm]. Adán; (*fam.*) ***Adam's ale,*** agua; (*fam.*) ***Adam's apple,*** nuez de la garganta, manzana de Adán; ***I don't know him from Adam,*** no me suena nada.
adamant ['ædəmənt], *a.* diamantino; categórico, tajante, inflexible.
adamantine [ædə'mæntain], *a.* adamantino.
adapt [ə'dæpt], *v.t.* adaptar, adecuar; (*teat.*) arreglar, refundir. — *v.i.* adaptarse.
adaptability [ədæptə'biliti], *s.* adaptabilidad.
adaptable, adaptive [ə'dæptəbl, -iv], *a.* adaptable.
adaptation, adaption [ædæp'teiʃən, a'dæpʃən], *s.* adaptación; arreglo, refundición.
adaptedness [ə'dæptidnis], *s.* adaptación.
adapter [ə'dæptə], *s.* adaptador; refundidor; (*quím.*) alargadera; (*mec.*) ajustador.
add [æd], *v.t.* añadir, agregar, adicionar; ***add up,*** sumar; ***add up to,*** ascender a; venir a ser.
addendum [ə'dendəm], *s.* (*pl.* **addenda** [-də]) adición, aditamento, apéndice.
adder ['ædə], *s.* víbora.
adder's-grass, adder's wort ['ædəz-grɑ:s, -wə:t], *s.* (*bot.*) escorzonera.
adder's-tongue ['ædəz-tʌŋ], *s.* (*bot.*) lengua de sierpe, *Ophioglossum vulgatum.*
addict ['ædikt], *s.* maniático, forofo; ***drug-addict,*** toxicómano. — *v.t.* dedicar, consagrar.
addicted [ə'diktid], *a.* dado, propenso, entregado, aficionado (a); partidario (de); ***to become addicted to,*** aficionarse a, darse a.
addictedness [ə'diktidnis], *s.* inclinación, propensión, apego, afición.
addiction [ə'dikʃən], *s.* adhesión.
addition [ə'diʃən], *s.* adición, añadidura; (*arit.*) suma; ***in addition (to),*** además (de), por añadidura.
additional [ə'diʃənəl], *a.* adicional.
additive ['æditiv], *a.*, *s.* aumentativo.
addle [ædl], *a.* podrido; (*fig.*) huero, tontivano, vacío. — *v.t.* podrir, enhuerar; embrollar. — *v.i.* echarse a perder, podrirse.
address [ə'dres], *s.* discurso, alocución; proclama, *f.*; dedicatoria; dirección, señas, sobrescrito; destreza, maña, donaire; (*com.*) consignación; (*der.*) ***of no fixed address,*** sin domicilio fijo; ***to pay one's addresses to,*** hacer la corte a, cortejar a. — *v.t.* dirigir; (*com.*) consignar; dirigirse a; obsequiar; poner señas a.
addressee [ædre'si:], *s.* destinatario.
addresser [ə'dresə], *s.* suplicante, exponente.
adduce [ə'dju:s], *v.t.* alegar, aducir.
adducent [ə'dju:sənt], *a.* (*anat.*) aductor.
adducible [ə'dju:sibl], *a.* aducible.
adduction [ə'dʌkʃən], *s.* (*anat.*) aducción; alegación.
adductive [ə'dʌktiv], *a.* aductivo.
adductor [ə'dʌktə], *s.* (*anat.*) aductor.

ademption [ə'dempʃən], *s.* (*for.*) privación, revocación.

Aden [eidn]. Adén.

adeniform [ə'denifɔːm], *a.* glandiforme.

adenitis [ædə'naitis], *s.* adenitis, *f.inv.*

adenography [ædən'ɔgrəfi], *s.* adenografía.

adenoid ['ædənɔid], *a.* (*anat.*) adenoideo. — *s. pl.* vegetaciones (adenoideas).

adenology [ædə'nɔlədʒi], *s.* adenología.

adept [ə'dept], *a.* versado, consumado. — ['ædept], *s.* adepto; perito, experto, maestro.

adequacy ['ædikwisi], *s.* suficiencia; (lo) adecuado, (lo) apropiado.

adequate ['ædikwit], *a.* adecuado; suficiente.

adequateness ['ædikwitnis], *s.* idoneidad; suficiencia.

adhere [əd'hiə], *v.i.* adherirse; pegarse; ***adhere to the rules,*** atenerse al reglamento.

adherence [əd'hiərəns], *s.* adherencia; adhesión.

adherent [əd'hiərənt], *a.* adherente; adhesivo. — *s.* adherente, secuaz, partidario.

adherer [əd'hiərə], *s.* adherente, partidario.

adhesion [əd'hiːʒən], *s.* adhesión, adherencia.

adhesive [əd'hiːsiv], *a.* adhesivo; ***adhesive stamps,*** sellos engomados, *m.pl.*

adhesiveness [əd'hiːsivnis], *s.* adherencia, adhesividad.

adhibit [əd'hibit], *v.t.* aplicar.

adhibition [ædhi'biʃən], *s.* aplicación.

ad hoc ['æd 'hɔk], *adv.* ad hoc; ***ad hoc committee (for),*** junta constituida adrede (para).

adhortatory [ædhɔː'teitəri], *a.* exhortativo.

adieu [ə'djuː], *s.* adiós; ***to bid adieu,*** despedirse (de) — *interj.* adiós.

ad infinitum [æd infi'naitəm], *adv.* hasta lo infinito.

adipose ['ædipous], *a.* adiposo.

adiposity [ædi'pɔsiti], *s.* adiposidad.

adit ['ædit], *s.* acceso, entrada; socavón.

adjacence, adjacency [ə'dʒeisəns, -i], *s.* adyacencia, proximidad, contigüidad.

adjacent [ə'dʒeisənt], *a.* adyacente, contiguo.

adject [ə'dʒekt], *v.t.* añadir.

adjection [ə'dʒekʃən], *s.* añadidura.

adjectival [ædʒik'taivəl], *a.* adjetival.

adjective ['ædʒiktiv], *s.* adjetivo. — *v.t.* adjetivar.

adjoin [ə'dʒɔin], *v.t.* juntar; colindar con. — *v.i.* colindar.

adjoining [ə'dʒɔiniŋ], *a.* contiguo, inmediato, adyacente, colindante.

adjourn [ə'dʒəːn], *v.t.* suspender, prorrogar, aplazar; ***adjourn the session,*** levantar la sesión.

adjournment [ə'dʒəːnmənt], *s.* suspensión; aplazamiento.

adjudge [ə'dʒʌdʒ], *v.t.* juzgar; decretar; sentenciar; adjudicar.

adjudg(e)ment [ə'dʒʌdʒmənt], *s.* adjudicación.

adjudicate [ə'dʒuːdikeit], *v.t.* adjudicar; juzgar. — *v.i.* mediar.

adjudication [ədʒuːdi'keiʃən], *s.* adjudicación; sentencia; juicio.

adjudicative [ə'dʒuːdikeitiv], *a.* adjudicativo.

adjudicator [ə'dʒuːdikeitə], *s.* adjudicador; juez.

adjunct ['ædʒʌŋkt], *a.*, *s.* adjunto; auxiliar.

adjunction [ə'dʒʌŋkʃən], *s.* adjunción.

adjunctive [ə'dʒʌŋktiv], *a.* adjunto.

adjuration [ædʒuə'reiʃən], *s.* adjuración.

adjure [ə'dʒuə], *v.t.* implorar, impetrar; juramentar.

adjust [ə'dʒʌst], *v.t.* ajustar; acomodar, adaptar, graduar; modificar.

adjustable [ə'dʒʌstəbl], *a.* graduable, regulable.

adjuster [ə'dʒʌstə], *s.* ajustador; (*mec.*) regulador.

adjustment [ə'dʒʌstmənt], *s.* ajuste, ajustamiento; arreglo; adaptación; modificación.

adjutancy ['ædʒutənsi], *s.* ayudantía; grado *o* funciones de capitán adjunto mayor.

adjutant ['ædʒutənt], *s.* (*mil.*) ayudante.

adjuvant ['ædʒuvənt], *a.* adyuvante. — *s.* (*med.*) coadyuvante.

admeasurement [əd'meʒəmənt], *s.* repartimiento; medición.

adminicle [əd'minikl], *s.* adminículo; (*der.*) prueba corroborante.

administer [əd'ministə], *v.t.* administrar; propinar; dirigir, regir; ejercer; aplicar, poner en práctica; ***administer an oath,*** tomar juramento (a). — *v.i.* tender, contribuir (a).

administrable [əd'ministrəbl], *a.* administrable.

administrant [əd'ministrənt], *s.* director, administrador.

administration [ədminis'treiʃən], *s.* administración; dirección, gobierno, gestión; régimen, período de gobierno *o* de mandato.

administrative [əd'ministrətiv], *a.* administrativo.

administrator [əd'ministreitə], *s.* administrador; gobernante; testamentario; (*for.*) tenedor de bienes; (*der.*) curador.

administratorship [əd'ministreitəʃip], *s.* administración; curaduría.

administratrix [əd'ministreitriks], *s.* administradora, curadora.

admirable ['ædmirəbl], *a.* admirable.

admirableness, admirability ['ædmirəblnis, ædmirə'biliti], *s.* excelencia; (lo) admirable.

admiral ['ædmirəl], *s.* almirante; ***rear-admiral,*** contraalmirante; ***vice-admiral,*** vicealmirante.

admiralship ['ædmirəlʃip], *s.* almirantía.

admiralty ['ædmirəlti], *s.* almirantazgo; consejo superior de la armada; ***admiralty law,*** derecho marítimo, código marítimo; (*Ingl.*) ***First Lord of the Admiralty,*** primer lor del almirantazgo.

admiration [ædmi'reiʃən], *s.* admiración.

admire [əd'maiə], *v.t.* admirar.

admirer [əd'maiərə], *s.* admirador; adorador.

admiring [əd'maiəriŋ], *a.* admirativo, de admiración.

admissibility [ədmisi'biliti], *s.* admisibilidad.

admissible [əd'misibl], *a.* admisible, aceptable; lícito, permitido.

admission [əd'miʃən], *s.* admisión; entrada, acceso, ingreso; reconocimiento, confesión; ***admission ticket,*** entrada; boleto.

admissive, admissory [əd'misiv, -əri], *a.* que implica admisión.

admit [əd'mit], *v.t.* admitir; dar entrada a; reconocer, confesar; ***admit defeat,*** darse por vencido. — *v.i.* — ***of,*** admitir, permitir.

admittance, [əd'mitəns], *s.* admisión; acceso, entrada; precio de entrada; derecho de entrar; ***no admittance,*** prohibida la entrada.

admix [əd'miks], *v.t.* mezclar, juntar, incorporar.

admixture [əd'mikstʃə], *s.* mezcla.

admonish [əd'mɔniʃ], *v.t.* amonestar, reprender; exhortar.

admonisher [əd'mɔniʃə], *s.* amonestador, reprendedor.

admonishment [əd'mɔniʃmənt], *s.* amonestación, reprensión.

admonition [ædmo'niʃən], s. amonestación.

admonitive [əd'mɔnitiv], *a.* admonitivo.

admonitor [əd'mɔnitə], *s.* admonitor, censor.

admonitory [əd'mɔnitəri], *a.* admonitorio.

adnate ['ædneit], *a.* (*bot.*) adnato.

ad nauseam [æd 'nɔːziæm], *adv.* hasta la saciedad; a machamartillo.

ado [ə'duː], *s.* bullicio, aspaviento, baraúnda, ruido; ***much ado about nothing,*** mucho ruido y pocas nueces; ***without more ado,*** sin más ni más.

adobe [ə'doubi], *s.* adobe.

adolescence [ædo'lesəns], *s.* adolescencia.

adolescent [ædo'lesənt], ***a.***, *s.* adolescente.

Adolf [ˈædolf]. Adolfo.
adonis [əˈdounis], *s.* (*ict.*) adonis.
adopt [əˈdɔpt], *v.t.* adoptar; prohijar, ahijar; elegir, escoger.
adopted [əˈdɔptid], *a.* adoptivo.
adopter [əˈdoptə], *s.* adoptador; prohijador.
adoption [əˈdɔpʃən], *s.* adopción; prohijamiento; elección.
adoptive [əˈdoptiv], *a.* adoptivo.
adorability, adorableness [ədɔ:rəˈbiliti, əˈdɔ:rəblnis], *s.* (lo) adorable (de).
adorable [əˈdɔ:rəbl], *a.* adorable.
adoration [ædɔ:ˈreiʃən], *s.* adoración.
adore [əˈdɔ:], *v.t.* adorar; dar culto a.
adorer [əˈdɔ:rə], *s.* adorador.
adoring [əˈdɔ:riŋ], *a.* adorante, adorador, mimador.
adorn [əˈdɔ:n], *v.t.* adornar; ornar; embellecer.
adorning [əˈdɔ:niŋ], *s.* ornamento; decoración.
adornment [əˈdɔ:nmənt], *s.* adorno, ornamento, aderezo.
adrenal [əˈdri:nəl], *a.* (*anat.*) suprarrenal.
adrenalin [əˈdrenəlin], *s.* adrenalina.
Adriatic (Sea) [eidriˈætik (ˈsi:)], *s.* el (Mar) Adriático.
adrift [əˈdrift], *adv.* (*mar.*) a la deriva, al garete; a la ventura; a merced de las olas; ***to break adrift,*** (empezar a) ir a la deriva.
adroit [əˈdrɔit], *a.* hábil, diestro, mañoso.
adroitness [əˈdrɔitnis], *s.* destreza, habilidad, maña.
adscript [ˈædskript], *a.* adscrito; escrito después. — *s.* añadido; siervo de la gleba.
adulate [ˈædjuleit], *v.t.* adular.
adulation [ædjuˈleiʃən], *s.* adulación.
adulator [ˈædjuleitə], *s.* adulador, lisonjero.
adulatory [ˈædjuleitəri], *a.* adulador, adulatorio, lisonjero.
adult [ˈædʌlt, əˈdʌlt], *a.*, *s.* adulto, mayor.
adulterant [əˈdʌltərənt], *s.* adulterador, adulterante.
adulterate [əˈdʌltəreit], *v.t.* adulterar; falsear, viciar.
adulterated [əˈdʌltəreitid], *a.* adulterino, adulterado, espurio.
adulteration [ədʌltəˈreiʃən], *s.* adulteración, falsificación.
adulterer [əˈdʌltərə], *s.* adúltero.
adulteress [əˈdʌltəris], *s.* adúltera.
adulterine [əˈdʌltəri:n], *a.* adulterino; espurio.
adulterous [əˈdʌltərəs], *a.* adúltero, adulterino, espurio.
adultery [əˈdʌltəri], *s.* adulterio.
adultness [əˈdʌltnis], *s.* edad adulta, adultez.
adumbrant [əˈdʌmbrənt], *a.* bosquejado, trazado, sombreado ligeramente.
adumbrate [ˈædʌmbreit], *v.t.* bosquejar, esquiciar; sombrear; (*fig.*) augurar, presagiar.
adumbration [ædʌmˈbreiʃən], *s.* esquicio, trazo, esbozo, bosquejo, diseño; (*pint.*) adumbración; anuncio, presagio, barrunto.
adust [əˈdʌst], *a.* adusto, requemado, abrasado, desecado; moreno, curtido.
adustion [əˈdʌstʃən], *s.* adustión, quemadura; inflamación; cauterización.
ad valorem [æd vəˈlɔ:rem], *adv.* (*com.*) por avalúo.
advance [ədˈvɑ:ns], *a.* adelantado; (*mil.*) ***advance guard,*** avanzada; (*com.*) ***advance payment,*** anticipo, adelanto. — *s.* avance, adelanto, mejora, progreso; (*com.*) alza, encarecimiento; anticipo; proposición; insinuación; ***in advance,*** de antemano, por anticipado; ***to make advances,*** requerir de amores. — *v.t.* adelantar, avanzar; ascender; mejorar; acrecentar; anticipar; proponer. — *v.i.* adelantar, progresar; ascender; elevarse.
advanced [ədˈvɑ:nst], *a.* avanzado; precoz, adelantado; ***advanced mathematics,*** matemáticas superiores; ***advanced in years,*** entrado en años.
advancement [ədˈvɑ:nsmənt], *s.* fomento, mejora; ascenso; progreso; subida, alza; prosperidad; adelanto, anticipo.
advancer [ədˈvɑ:nsə], *s.* promotor; protector; impulsor; adelantador.
advantage [ədˈvɑ:ntidʒ], *s.* ventaja; superioridad; provecho; ***to advantage,*** ventajosamente, con provecho; ***to have the advantage of,*** llevar la ventaja a; ***to take (fair*** o ***proper) advantage of,*** aprovechar; ***to take (unfair) advantage of,*** aprovecharse de, abusar de. — *v.t.* aventajar.
advantageous [ædvənˈteidʒəs], *a.* ventajoso, provechoso, interesante.
advantageousness [ædvənˈteidʒəsnis], *s.* (lo) ventajoso, (lo) provechoso (de).
Advent [ˈædvənt], *s.* (*igl.*) Adviento.
advent [ˈædvənt], *s.* advenimiento, llegada.
adventitious [ædvenˈtiʃəs], *a.* adventicio.
adventual [ædˈventʃuəl], *a.* adventual.
adventure [ədˈventʃə], *s.* aventura. — *v.t.* aventurar, arriesgar. — *v.i.* aventurarse, arriesgarse.
adventurer [ədˈventʃərə], *s.* aventurero.
adventuresome [ədˈventʃəsəm], *a.* aventurero, emprendedor.
adventuress [ədˈventʃəris], *s.* (*despec.*) vampiresa.
adventurous [ədˈventʃərəs], *a.* aventurero, emprendedor.
adventurousness, adventuresomeness [ədˈventʃərəsnis, -səmnis], *s.* audacia, espíritu aventurero, espíritu emprendedor.
adverb [ˈædvə:b], *s.* adverbio.
adverbial [ædˈvə:biəl], *a.* adverbial.
adversary [ˈædvəsəri], *a.* adversario; contrincante.
adverse [ˈædvə:s], *a.* adverso, contrario.
adverseness [ədˈvə:snis], *s.* signo adverso.
adversity [ædˈvə:siti], *s.* adversidad, desgracia, infortunio.
advert [ˈædve:t], *s.* (*fam.*) [ADVERTISEMENT] — [ədˈvə:t], *v.t.* advertir.
advertence, advertency [ədˈvə:təns, -i], *s.* advertencia.
advertent [ədˈvə:tənt], *a.* atento.
advertise [ˈædvətaiz], *v.t.* anunciar, dar publicidad a. — *v.i.* anunciar.
advertisement [ədˈvə:tismənt], *s.* anuncio; ***classified advertisement,*** anuncio por palabras.
advertiser [ˈædvətaizə], *s.* anunciador, anunciante; diario de anuncios.
advertising [ˈædvətaiziŋ], *a.* que anuncia; ***advertising agent,*** agente de publicidad. — *s.* publicidad, propaganda.
advice [ədˈvais], *s.* consejos; admonición, advertencia; aviso, noticia; parecer, opinión; (*naut.*) ***advice-boat,*** patache, aviso; ***to give advice of,*** dar aviso de; ***letter of advice,*** carta de aviso; ***a piece of advice,*** un consejo; ***to take, get advice,*** tomar *o* pedir consejo, aconsejarse, asesorarse.
advisability, advisableness [ədvaizəˈbiliti, ədˈvaizəblnis], *s.* conveniencia, (lo) aconsejable.
advise, [ədˈvaiz], *v.t.* aconsejar, dar consejo a; asesorar; avisar, notificar.
advisedly [ədˈvaizidli], *adv.* adrede, de propósito.
advisedness [ədˈvaizidnis], *s,* cordura, juicio, reflexión, sensatez.
adviser [ədˈvaizə], *s.* aconsejador, consejero, consultor, asesor; avisador.
advisory [ədˈvaizəri], *a.* asesor, consultivo.
advocacy [ˈædvokəsi], *s.* abogacía; defensa, propugnación.
advocate [ˈædvokit], *s.* abogado, letrado; defensor, partidario; ***devil's advocate,*** abogado del diablo. — [ˈædvokeit], *v.t.* abogar por; defender, propugnar.
advocation [ædvoˈkeiʃən], *s.* defensa; apología; intercesión; vindicación, apelación.

advowee [ædvauˈiː], *s.* (*igl.*) patrón, colador.
advowson [ədˈvauzən], *s.* (*igl.*) patronato; colación.
adynamia [eidaiˈneimiə], *s.* (*med.*) adinamia.
adynamic [eidaiˈnæmik], *a.* adinámico, débil.
adze [ædz], *s.* azuela. — *v.t.* azolar, desbastar.
ædile [ˈiːdail], *s.* edil.
ædileship [ˈiːdailʃip], *s.* edilidad.
Aegean (**Sea**) [iˈdʒiːən (ˈsiː)], *s.* el (Mar) Egeo.
ægis [ˈiːdʒis], *s.* égida; tutela; patronicío.
ægyptiacum [iːdʒipˈtaiəkəm], *s.* (*vet.*) egipciaco.
æon [ˈiːən], *s.* eón; eternidad.
aerate [ˈɛəreit], *v.t.* airear, orear; saturar de aire; oxigenar.
aerated [ˈɛəreitid], *a.* gaseoso; ***aerated water,*** gaseosa, agua gaseosa.
aeration [ɛəˈreiʃən], *s.* ventilación; aerificación, aeración.
aerator [ˈɛəreitə], *s.* aparato para la aeración.
aerial [ˈɛəriəl], *a.* aéreo; etéreo; atmosférico. — *s.* (*elec.*) antena.
aerie, aery [ˈɛəri, ˈiəri] [EYRIE].
aeriform [ˈɛərifɔːm], *a.* aeriforme.
aerify [ˈɛərifai], *v.t.* (*quím.*) aerificar.
aerobatics [ɛəroˈbætiks], *s.* acrobacia aérea.
aeroboat [ˈɛərobout], *s.* hidroplano.
aerodrome [ˈɛərodroum], *s.* aeródromo, campo de aviación.
aerodynamics [ɛərodaiˈnæmiks], *s.* aerodinámica.
aerography [ɛəˈrogrəfi], *s.* aerografía.
aerolite, aerolith [ˈɛərolait, ˈɛəroliθ], *s.* aerolito.
aerological [ɛəroˈlɔdʒikəl], *a.* aerological.
aerologist [ɛərˈɔlədʒist], *s.* aerólogo.
aerology [ɛərˈɔlədʒi], *s.* aerología.
aeromancy [ˈɛəromænsi], *s.* aeromancia.
aerometer [ɛərˈɔmitə], *s.* aerómetro.
aerometric [ɛəroˈmetrik], *a.* aerométrico.
aerometry [ɛərˈɔmitri], *s.* aerometría.
aeronaut [ˈɛəronɔːt], *s.* aeronauta, *m.f.*
aeronautic(al) [ɛəroˈnɔːtik(əl)], *a.* aeronáutico.
aeronautics [ɛəroˈnɔːtiks], *s.* aeronáutica.
aerophoby [ɛərˈɔfəbi], *s.* (*med.*) aerofobia.
aerophone [ˈɛərofoun], *s.* aerófono.
aeroplane [ˈɛəroplein], *s.* aeroplano, avión.
aeroscopy [ɛərˈɔskəpi], *s.* aeroscopia.
aerostat [ˈɛərostæt], *s.* aerostático.
aerostatic [ɛəroˈstætik], *a.* aerostático.
aerostatics [ɛəroˈstætiks], *s.* aerostática.
aerostation [ˈɛərosteiʃən], *s.* aerostación.
aeruginous [ɛəˈruːdʒinəs], *a.* eruginoso, herrumbroso.
aerugo [ɛəˈruːgou], *s.* orín, óxido.
Aeschylus [ˈiːskiləs]. Esquilo.
æsculapian [eskjuˈleipiən], *a.* de Esculapio; medicinal.
Aesop [ˈiːsɔp]. Esopo.
æsthete [ˈiːsθiːt], *s.* esteta, *m.f.*
æsthetic [iːsˈθetik], *a.* estético.
æsthetics [iːsˈθetiks], *s.* estética.
æstival, estival [esˈtaivəl], *a.* estival.
ætiology [iːtiˈɔlədʒi], *s.* etiología.
aetites [iːˈtaitiːz], *s.* (*min.*) etites, *f.inv.*
afar [əˈfaː], *adv.* lejos, a gran distancia; ***afar off,*** a lo lejos, en lontananza; ***from afar,*** de lejos, desde lejos.
afeard [əˈfiəd], *a.* (*ant.*) atemorizado, temeroso.
affability, affableness [æfəˈbiliti, ˈæfəblnis], *s.* afabilidad, amabilidad.
affable [ˈæfəbl], *a.* afable, amable, bonachón.
affair [əˈfɛə], *s.* asunto; negocio; lance, episodio; aventura, lío amoroso; ***affair of honour,*** lance de honor; ***affair of the heart,*** asunto sentimental; ***it's no affair of yours,*** no es asunto tuyo; ***that's your affair,*** allá tú, ésa es cuestión tuya.
affect [əˈfekt], *v.t.* afectar a, influir en; fingir, simular; conmover, enternecer.
affectation, affectedness [æfekˈteiʃən, əˈfektidnis], *s.* afectación.
affected [əˈfektid], *a.* afectado.
affecting [əˈfektiŋ], *a.* patético, conmovedor.
affection [əˈfekʃən], *s.* afecto; cariño; afección.
affectionate [əˈfekʃənit], *a.* afectuoso, cariñoso.
affectionateness [əˈfekʃənitnis], *s.* afecto, cariño.
affectioned [əˈfekʃənd], *a.* (*ant.*) afectado, vanidoso.
affective [əˈfektiv], *a.* afectivo, emotivo.
afferent [ˈæfərənt], *a.* (*biol.*) aferente.
affiance [əˈfaiəns], *s.* esponsales, *m.pl.*, confianza, fe, *f.* — *v.t.* afianzar.
affianced [əˈfaiənst], *a.*, *s.* prometido; ***to become affianced to,*** comprometerse con.
affiant [əˈfaiənt], *s.* (*for.*) deponente, declarante.
affidavit [æfiˈdeivit], *s.* (*for.*) declaración jurada; atestación, certificación; afidávit.
affiliable [əˈfiliəbl], *a.* afiliable.
affiliate [əˈfilieit], *v.t.* adoptar; afiliar; (*der.*) determinar la paternidad de. — *v.i.* afiliarse (***with, to,*** a).
affiliated [əˈfilieitid], *a.* prohijado; reconocido; afiliado.
affiliation [əfiliˈeiʃən], *s.* adopción; afiliación; (*for.*) legitimación de un hijo.
affined [əˈfaind], *a.* pariente por afinidad.
affinity [əˈfiniti], *s.* afinidad.
affirm [əˈfəːm], *v.t.* afirmar, aseverar; confirmar, ratificar; declarar.
affirmable [əˈfəːməbl], *a.* que se puede afirmar.
affirmant [əˈfəːmənt], *s.* afirmador, afirmante; (*for.*) declarante.
affirmation [æfəˈmeiʃən], *s.* afirmación, aserción, aserto, declaración.
affirmative [əˈfəːmətiv], *a.* afirmativo. — *s.* aserción, afirmativa; ***to reply in the affirmative,*** contestar afirmativamente.
affirmatory [əˈfəːmətəri], *a.* asertorio, afirmativo.
affirmer [əˈfəːmə], *s.* afirmante.
affix [ˈæfiks], *s.* añadido; (*gram.*) afijo. — [əˈfiks], *v.t.* fijar, pegar; añadir; aplicar; poner (*firma, sello, etc.*).
affixer [əˈfiksə], *s.* pegador.
affixture [əˈfikstʃə], *s.* ligatura, adición.
afflation [əˈfleiʃən], *s.* aliento, respiración, inspiración, resuello.
afflatus [əˈfleitəs], *s.* hálito, aliento; (*fig.*) estro, aflato, inspiración, numen.
afflict [əˈflikt], *v.t.* afligir, aquejar; apenar, contristar; ***to be afflicted with,*** estar aquejado de; padecer de.
afflicting [əˈfliktiŋ], *a.* penoso, doloroso, aflictivo.
affliction [əˈflikʃən], *s.* aflicción, dolor; achaque; luto, duelo; azote.
afflictive [əˈfliktiv], *a.* aflictivo, lastimoso, penoso, gravoso, molesto.
affluence [ˈæfluəns], *s.* afluencia, aflujo; abundancia, opulencia, prosperidad.
affluent [ˈæfluənt], *a.* (*med.*) fluente; afluente; abundante, copioso, rico, opulento, próspero. — *s.* afluente.
afflux [ˈæflʌks], *s.* fluxión, flujo; afluencia, aflujo; gentío, concurrencia.
afford [əˈfɔːd], *v.t.* dar, deparar, proporcionar, ofrecer; permitirse; ***I can't afford those things,*** no me puedo permitir esos lujos.
afforest [əˈfɔrist], *v.t.* repoblar con árboles.
afforestation [əfɔrisˈteiʃən], *s.* repoblación forestal.
affranchise [əˈfræntʃaiz] [ENFRANCHISE].
affray [əˈfrei], *s.* refriega, combate; pelea.
affreight [əˈfreit], *v.t.* fletar.
affreighter [əˈfreitə], *s.* fletador.
affreightment [əˈfreitmənt], *s.* fletamiento.
affricate [ˈæfrikit], *a.* africado. — *s.* africada.

affright [ə'frait], *v.t.* espantar, asustar.
affrightment [ə'fraitmənt], *s.* espanto.
affront [ə'frʌnt], *s.* afrenta, insulto, denuesto. — *v.t.* afrentar, insultar, denostar; arrostrar.
affronting [ə'frʌntiŋ], *a.* afrentoso, ofensivo.
affusion [ə'fju:ʒən], *s.* afusión.
Afghan ['æfgæn], *a.*, *s.* afgano.
Afghanistan [æf'gænistɑ:n]. (el) Afganistán.
afield [ə'fi:ld], *adv.* en el campo; lejos; ***to go far afield,*** ir muy lejos, alejarse mucho; ***to look further afield,*** buscar más lejos *o* con más ahinco.
afire [ə'faiə], *adv.* en llamas, ardiendo; encendido, inflamado.
aflame [ə'fleim], *adv.* en llamas.
afloat [ə'flout], *adv.* (*mar.*) flotante, a flote.
afoot [ə'fut], *adv.* a pie; ***there's sth. afoot,*** se está tramando *o* fraguando algo.
aforehand [ə'fɔ:hænd], *adv.* de antemano.
aforementioned, aforenamed, aforesaid [ə'fɔ:-menʃənd, -neimd, -sed], *a.* susodicho, ya dicho, ya mencionado, sobredicho, antedicho, supracitado, precitado.
aforethought [ə'fɔ:θɔ:t], *a.* premeditado; ***with malice aforethought,*** con premeditación y alevosía.
afoul [ə'faul], *adv.* (*mar.*) en colisión, enredado; ***to run afoul of,*** chocar con, enredarse con.
afraid [ə'freid], *a.* asustado; ***to be afraid,*** tener miedo (***of,*** de, a); ***to be afraid,*** tener miedo (***to,*** de).
afresh [ə'freʃ], *adv.* de nuevo, nuevamente.
Africa ['æfrikə]. África.
African ['æfrikən], *a.*, *s.* africano.
Afrikaaner [æfri'kɑ:nə], *s.* habitante blanco de habla africaans.
Afrikaans [æfri'kɑ:nz], *s.* africaans, *m.*
Afro-Asian [æfrou-'eiʃən], *a.*, *s.* (*pol.*) afro-asiático.
aft [ɑ:ft], *adv.* (*mar.*) a popa, en popa.
after ['ɑ:ftə], *a.* posterior; (*mar.*) de popa. — *adv.* después. — *conj.* después (de) que. — *prep.* después de; detrás de; ***after all,*** al fin y al cabo; ***after you!*** ¡Vd. primero!; ***day after day,*** día tras día; ***the day after tomorrow,*** pasado mañana; ***the police are after the criminal,*** la policía persigue al responsable; ***to run after,*** correr tras; ***to take after,*** salir a.
afterbirth ['ɑ:ftə-bə:θ], *s.* secundinas, *f.pl.*; placenta.
after-care ['ɑ:ftə-kɛə], *s.* cuidados posteriores.
after-damp ['ɑ:ftə-dæmp], *s.* (*min.*) mofeta.
after-dinner ['ɑ:ftə-dinə], *a.* de sobremesa; ***after-dinner sleep,*** siesta; ***after-dinner speech,*** discurso de sobremesa. — *s.* sobremesa.
after-effect ['ɑ:ftə(r)-ifekt], *s.* resultado, efecto, consecuencia.
afterglow ['ɑ:ftəglou], *s.* resplandor crepuscular.
after-grass ['ɑ:ftə-grɑ:s], *s.* segunda yerba, segunda cosecha de heno.
after-life ['ɑ:ftə-laif], *s.* (el) resto de la vida; vida venidera.
aftermath ['ɑ:ftəmæθ], *s.* segunda siega; (*fig.*) consecuencia(s).
aftermost ['ɑ:ftəmoust], *a.* (*mar.*) último, postrero.
afternoon [ɑ:ftə'nu:n], *s.* tarde; ***every afternoon,*** todas las tardes; ***good afternoon,*** (*early*) buenos días; (*late*) buenas tardes; ***at half-past two in the afternoon,*** a las dos y media de la tarde; ***on Tuesday afternoon,*** el martes por la tarde.
after-pains ['ɑ:ftə-peinz], *s.pl.* (*med.*) entuertos, *m.pl.*, dolores de sobreparto, *m.pl.*
afterpiece ['ɑ:ftəpi:s], *s.* (*teat.*) sainete, entremés.
afters ['ɑ:ftəz], *s.pl.* (*fam.*) postre.
after-shave lotion [ɑ:ftə-'ʃeiv 'louʃən], *s.* loción facial.
after-taste ['ɑ:ftə-teist], *s.* resabio, dejo, gustillo; (*fam.*) sinsabor, pesar, disgusto.
afterthought ['ɑ:ftəθɔ:t], *s.* reflexión tardía; nueva idea; reparo.
afterwards ['ɑ:ftəwədz], *adv.* después, luego, más tarde; ***soon afterwards,*** poco después.
again [ə'gein], *adv.* otra vez, nuevamente, de nuevo; además, asimismo, por otra parte, del mismo modo; ***again and again,*** una y otra vez; ***as much again,*** otro tanto (más); (*fam.*) ***come again,*** ¿cómo dice?; ***to do again,*** volver a hacer; ***give it to me again,*** devuélvamelo; ***never again,*** nunca más; ***now and again,*** a veces, de vez en cuando.
against [ə'geinst], *prep.* contra; junto a, cerca de; a diferencia de; comparado con; ***against the grain,*** a contrapelo; ***against time,*** contra reloj; ***to be against,*** oponerse a; ***to run up against,*** tropezar con.
agamous ['ægəməs], *a.* (*biol.*) asexual.
agape (1) [ə'geip], *adv.* boquiabierto.
agape (2) ['ægəpi], *s.* ágape.
agaric ['ægərik], *s.* (*bot.*) agárico, garzo.
agate ['ægit], *s.* (*min.*) ágata; (*impr.*) carácter de letra de 5½ puntos; se llama ***ruby*** en Inglaterra.
agave [ə'geivi], *s.* (*bot.*) agave, pita, maguey.
age [eidʒ], *s.* edad; siglo; época; vejez; ***age-group,*** grupo de edad; (*mil.*) quinta; ***ages ago,*** hace siglos *o* una eternidad; ***to come of age,*** alcanzar la mayoría de edad; ***golden age,*** edad de oro; siglo de oro; ***of age,*** mayor de edad; ***under age,*** menor de edad. — *v.t.*, *v.i.* envejecer.
aged ['eidʒid], *a.* viejo, envejecido, anciano, cargado de años; añejo; [eidʒd] ***aged 20,*** de 20 años de edad.
ageless ['eidʒlis], *a.* eternamente joven; perenne.
agelong ['eidʒlɔŋ], *a.* eterno, secular.
agency ['eidʒənsi], *s.* agencia; organismo; mediación, medio; ***free agency,*** libre albedrío.
agenda [ə'dʒendə], *s.* orden del día, temario.
agent ['eidʒənt], *s.* agente; mediador; concesionario; ***to be a free agent,*** obrar independientemente.
agentship ['eidʒəntʃip], *s.* agencia; oficio de agente.
agglomerate [ə'glɔmərit], *a.* (*geol.*) aglomerado. — [ə'glɔməreit], *v.t.* aglomerar. — *v.i.* aglomerarse.
agglomeration [əglɔmə'reiʃən], *s.* aglomeración, amontonamiento.
agglutinant [ə'glu:tinənt], *a.*, *s.* aglutinante.
agglutinate [ə'glu:tineit], *v.t.* aglutinar, conglutinar. — *v.i.* aglutinarse.
agglutination [əglu:ti'neiʃən], *s.* aglutinación, conglutinación.
agglutinative [ə'glu:tinətiv], *a.* aglutinativo, conglutinativo, aglutinante.
aggrandize ['ægrəndaiz], *v.t.* engrandecer.
aggrandizement [ə'grændizmənt], *s.* engrandecimiento.
aggravate ['ægrəveit], *v.t.* agravar; exasperar.
aggravating ['ægrəveitiŋ], *a.* agravante; exasperante.
aggravation [ægrə'veiʃən], *s.* agravación, agravamiento; deterioro; exasperación.
aggregate ['ægrigit], *a.* agregado. — *s.* agregado; total; ***in the aggregate,*** en total, colectivamente, globalmente. — ['ægrigeit], *v.t.* agregar, juntar; ascender a, sumar.
aggregation [ægri'geiʃən], *s.* agregación, agregado.
aggression [ə'greʃən], *s.* agresión.
aggressive [ə'gresiv], *a.* agresivo.
aggressiveness [ə'gresivnis], *s.* carácter agresivo.
aggressor [ə'gresə], *s.* agresor.
aggrieve [ə'gri:v], *v.t.* apenar, afligir; vejar, oprimir; molestar, ofender.
aggro ['ægrou], *s.* (*pol.*, *fam.*) disturbio.
aggroup [ə'gru:p], *v.t.* agrupar.
aghast [ə'gɑ:st], *a.* horrorizado, estupefacto.
agile ['ædʒail], *a.* ágil, rápido.
agility, agileness [ə'dʒiliti, 'ædʒailnis], *s.* agilidad, soltura, prontitud, expedición.

agio [ˈædʒiou], *s.* (*com.*) agio, agiotaje.
agitable [ˈædʒitəbl], *a.* agitable; discutible.
agitate [ˈædʒiteit], *v.t.* agitar; inquietar. — *v.i.* discutir, debatir; ***agitate for,*** hacer propaganda a favor de, presionar para que.
agitation [ædʒiˈteiʃən], *s.* agitación, inquietud, desasosiego; discusión, debate.
agitator [ˈædʒiteitə], *s.* agitador.
agleam [əˈgli:m], *a.* (*poét.*) fulguroso, centelleante.
aglow [əˈglou], *a.* encendido en llamas; incandescente; ardiente, brillante.
agnail [ˈægneil], *s.* panadizo, uñero.
agnate [ˈægneit], *s.* (*for.*) agnado.
agnatic [ægˈnætik], *a.* agnaticio.
agnation [ægˈneiʃən], *s.* agnación, parentesco por la línea masculina.
Agnes [ˈægnis]. Inés, *f.*
agnomination [ægnɔmiˈneiʃən], *s.* sobrenombre; agnominación; (*ret.*) aliteración, paronomasia.
agnostic [ægˈnɔstik], *a.*, *s.* agnóstico.
agnosticism [ægˈnɔstisizəm], *s.* agnosticismo.
ago [əˈgou], *adv.* hace; ***long ago,*** hace mucho tiempo; ***how long ago?*** ¿cuánto hace?; ***some time ago,*** hace (algún) tiempo; ***a good while ago,*** hace ya bastante tiempo.
agog [əˈgɔg], *a.* anhelante, consumido por la curiosidad. — *adv.* anhelosamente, ansiosamente.
agoing [əˈgouiŋ], *adv.* en acción, en marcha, en movimiento; ***to set agoing,*** poner en marcha.
agometer [æˈgɔmitə], *s.* (*elec.*) agómetro.
agonic [æˈgɔnik], *a.* ágono.
agonism [ˈægənizəm], *s.* agonística; lucha.
agonist, agonistes [ˈægənist, ægəˈnisti:z], *s.* atleta, *m.f.*, combatiente, competidor.
agonistics [ægəˈnistiks], *s.* agonística.
agonize [ˈægənaiz], *v.t.* atormentar, angustiar. — *v.i.* angustiarse, sufrir, padecer.
agonizing [ˈægənaiziŋ], *a.* angustioso; atroz.
agony [ˈægəni], *s.* angustia; agonía; dolor atroz; ***agony column,*** sección de anuncios personales.
agouti [əˈgu:ti], *s.* (*zool.*) agutí.
agraffe [əˈgræf], *s.* broche, grapa.
agrarian [əˈgrɛəriən], *a.*, *s.* agrario; ***agrarian reform,*** reforma agrícola.
agree [əˈgri:], *v.t.* acordar, concertar. — *v.i.* estar de acuerdo; ponerse de acuerdo; convenir, quedar; (*gram.*) concordar; sentar bien; ***agree on*** o ***to,*** convenir en, quedar en; ***the fish did not agree with him,*** no le sentó bien *o* le sentó mal el pescado.
agreeable [əˈgri:əbl], *a.* agradable, grato; conforme.
agreeableness [əˈgriəblnis], *s.* (lo) agradable (de); (lo) amable (de); conformidad; simpatía.
agreed [əˈgri:d], *a.* convenido, acordado. — *adv.* de acuerdo, perfectamente.
agreement [əˈgri:mənt], *s.* acuerdo, convenio; conformidad; (*gram.*) concordancia; ***by mutual agreement,*** de mutuo acuerdo; ***to reach an agreement,*** llegar a un acuerdo.
agricultor [ˈægrikʌltə], *s.* agricultor.
agricultural [ægriˈkʌltʃərəl], *a.* agrícola; de la agricultura.
agricultur(al)ist [ægriˈkʌltʃər(al)ist], *s.* agricultor; agrónomo.
agriculture [ˈægrikʌltʃə], *s.* agricultura.
agrimony [ˈægriməni], *s.* (*bot.*) agrimonia.
agronomic [ægrəˈnɔmik], *a.* agronómico.
agronomy [æˈgrɔnəmi], *s.* agronomía.
agrope [əˈgroup], *adv.* a tientas.
aground [əˈgraund], *a.*, *adv.* varado, encallado; ***to run aground,*** varar, encallar.
ague [ˈeigju:], *s.* (*med.*) fiebre intermitente, *f.*; escalofrío; ***tertian ague,*** fiebre terciana.
ague-tree [ˈeigju:-tri:], *s.* (*bot.*) sasafrás.
aguish [ˈeigju:iʃ], *a.* febricitante, calenturiento; palúdico.
ah! [ɑ:], *interj.* ¡ah!
aha! [ɑˈhɑ:], *interj.* ¡ajá!
ahead [əˈhed], *adv.* adelante; por delante; (*mar.*) por la proa, avante; ***to be ahead,*** ir delante *o* por delante; ***to cut in ahead of,*** adelantarse a; ***to get ahead,*** adelantar, avanzar; progresar, medrar; ***to go ahead,*** continuar, seguir adelante; ***straight ahead,*** todo seguido.
ahem! [əˈhəm], *interj.* ¡perdón! ¿molesto? ¡por favor!
ahoy! [əˈhɔi], *interj.* (*mar.*) ¡ah! ¡hola!; ***ship ahoy!*** ¡ah del barco!
ahull [əˈhʌl], *adv.* (*mar.*) con las velas recogidas y el timón amarrado al viento.
aid [eid], *s.* ayuda, auxilio, socorro; ayudante; ***first aid,*** primeros auxilios; ***first-aid post,*** casa de socorro; ***economic aid,*** ayuda económica; ***what is this in aid of?*** ¿de qué sirve esto? — *v.t.* ayudar, auxiliar, socorrer; apoyar; subvenir; (*der.*) ***to aid and abet,*** ser cómplice de.
aide-de-camp [ˈeid-də-kã], *s.* (*mil.*) ayudante de campo, edecán.
aider [ˈeidə], *s.* (*ant.*) auxiliante, auxiliador.
aidless [ˈeidlis], *a.* (*ant.*) desvalido, desamparado.
aiglet [ˈeiglit], *s.* herrete de agujeta *o* franja.
aigret, aigrette [ˈeigret], *s.* penacho, cresta, airón; (*orn.*) garceta.
ail [eil], *v.t.* afligir, aquejar, apenar; ***what ails you?*** ¿qué le pasa? ¿qué tiene usted? — *v.i.* estar enfermo.
aileron [ˈeilərən], *s.* (*avia.*) alerón.
ailing [ˈeiliŋ], *a.* doliente, achacoso, enfermo.
ailment [ˈeilmənt], *s.* dolencia, dolor, enfermedad, achaque.
aim [eim], *s.* puntería; designio, objeto, mira, fin; ***to take aim,*** apuntar. — *v.t.* apuntar; asestar; dirigir. — *v.i.* ***aim at,*** aspirar a, pretender.
aimer [ˈeimə], *s.* (*artill.*) puntero.
aimless [ˈeimlis], *a.* sin objeto, sin designio; a la ventura.
ain't [eint], *contr. fam.* de ***am not, is not,*** o ***are not.***
air [ɛə], *a.* de aire, neumático; de aviación. — *s.* aire; ***air-to-air,*** aire-aire; ***foul air,*** aire viciado; ***to give o.s. airs,*** darse tono; ***ground-to-air,*** tierra-aire; ***there is sth. in the air,*** algo se está tramando; ***in the open air,*** al aire libre, al raso; ***on the air,*** en la radio; ***to take the air,*** tomar el fresco. — *v.t.* airear, orear, ventilar.
air-balloon [ˈɛə-bəlu:n], *s.* globo aerostático.
air-bladder [ˈɛə-blædə], *s.* vejiga llena de aire.
air-born [ˈɛə-bɔ:n], *a.* aeronato.
airborne [ˈɛəbɔ:n], *a.* llevado por el aire; aerotransportado; ***to become airborne,*** despegar.
air-brake [ˈɛə-breik], *s.* freno neumático.
air-cell [ˈɛə-sel], *s.* (*bot.*) célula llena de aire.
air-chamber [ˈɛə-tʃeimbə], *s.* cámara de aire.
air-condition [ˈɛə-kənˈdiʃən], *v.t.* proveer de aire acondicionado, climatizar.
air-conditioning [ˈɛə-kənˈdiʃəniŋ], *s.* acondicionamiento de aire, climatización.
air-cool [ˈɛə-ku:l], *v.t.* enfriar por aire, refrigerar.
aircraft [ˈɛəkrɑ:ft], *s.* avión; (*mar.*) ***aircraft carrier,*** (buque) portaaviones.
air-crew [ˈɛə-kru:], *s.* tripulación de avión.
air-cushion [ˈɛə-kuʃn], *s.* cojín de aire.
air-drill [ˈɛə-dril], *s.* taladro de aire comprimido, taladro neumático.
airfield [ˈɛəfi:ld], *s.* campo de aviación, aeródromo.
air force [ˈɛə fɔ:s], *s.* fuerzas aéreas, *f.pl.*
air-gun [ˈɛə-gʌn], *s.* escopeta de aire comprimido.
air-hole [ˈɛə-houl], *s.* respiradero, resolladero, zarcera; registro de hornillo.
air-hostess [ˈɛə-houstis], *s.* azafata, aeromoza.
airified [ˈɛərifaid], *a.* aéreo; ligero, fútil.

airily [ˈɛərili], *adv.* alegremente, a la ligera.
airiness [ˈɛərinis], *s.* ventilación, oreo; ligereza, deportividad.
airing [ˈɛəriŋ], *s.* ventilación; paseo; ***to take an airing,*** salir a dar un paseo *o* a tomar un poco de aire.
air-jacket [ˈɛə-dʒækit], *s.* chaqueta salvavidas, *m. inv.*
air-lane [ˈɛə-lein], *s.* ruta aérea.
airless [ˈɛəlis], *a.* falto de ventilación, ahogado; quieto.
air-lift [ˈɛə-lift], *s.* puente aéreo. — *v.t.* transportar por puente aérea.
air-like [ˈɛə-laik], *a.* como el aire, etéreo.
airline [ˈɛəlain], *s.* línea aérea.
air-mail [ˈɛə-mail], *s.* correo aéreo, correo por avión.
airman [ˈɛəmən], *s.* aviador.
Air Ministry [ˈɛə ministri], *s.* Ministerio del Aire.
air-pipe [ˈɛə-paip], *s.* tubo de ventilación.
air-pocket [ˈɛə-pɔkit], *s.* bache (aéreo).
airport [ˈɛəpɔ:t], *s.* aeropuerto.
air-pump [ˈɛə-pʌmp], *s.* bomba de aire, bomba neumática.
air-raid [ˈɛə-reid], *s.* bombardeo aéreo.
air-raid shelter [ˈɛə-reid ʃeltə], *s.* refugio antiaéreo.
air-shaft [ˈɛə-ʃɑ:ft], *s.* respiradero.
airship [ˈɛəʃip], *s.* aeronave, *f.*
air-sickness [ˈɛə-siknis], *s.* mareo (del aire).
air-sleeve o **-sock** [ˈɛə-sli:v, -sɔk], *s.* veleta de manga.
airstrip [ˈɛəstrip], *s.* pista de despegue *o* de aterrizaje.
air supremacy [ˈɛə suˈpreməsi], *s.* dominio del aire.
air-tight [ˈɛə-tait], *a.* herméticamente cerrado.
air-trap [ˈɛə-træp], *s.* ventilador, válvula de inodoro.
air-waves [ˈɛə-weivz], *s.* ondas de radio, *f.pl.*
airway [ˈɛəwei], *s.* vía aerea.
airworthy [ˈɛəwə:ði], *a.* en condiciones de vuelo.
airy [ˈɛəri], *a.* aireado, lleno de aire; despreocupado, deportivo; (*fam.*) ***airy-fairy,*** de iluso, quimérico, nebuloso.
aisle [ail], *s.* nave; pasillo; (*Am.*) [CORRIDOR].
aisled [aild], *a.* que tiene pasillos *o* naves.
aitch [eitʃ], *s.* ***to drop one's aitches,*** (*en inglés*) no pronunciar la hache.
Aix-la-Chapelle [eiks-lɑ:-ʃəˈpel]. Aquisgrán.
ajar [əˈdʒɑ:], *a.* entreabierto, entornado.
Ajax [ˈeidʒæks]. Ayax.
akimbo [əˈkimbou], *adv.* en jarras; ***to place one's arms akimbo,*** ponerse en jarras.
akin [əˈkin], *a.* consanguíneo, emparentado; análogo, afín.
alabaster [ˈæləbæstə], *a.* alabastrino. — *s.* alabastro.
alack! [əˈlæk], **alack-alas** [əˈlæk-əˈlɑ:s], *interj.* ¡ay! ¡ay de mí!
alacrity [əˈlækriti], *s.* presteza, prontitud.
Aladdin [əˈlædin]. Aladino.
alarm [əˈlɑ:m], *s.* alarma; sobresalto; rebato; ***to sound the alarm,*** dar la alarma; ***to spread alarm and despondency,*** sembrar (la) desconfianza. — *v.t.* alarmar, asustar.
alarm-bell [əˈlɑ:m-bel], *s.* campana de rebato.
alarm-clock [əˈlɑ:m-klɔk], *s.* despertador.
alarm-gun [əˈlɑ:m-gʌn], *s.* cañon de rebato.
alarming [əˈlɑ:miŋ], *a.* alarmante.
alarmist [əˈlɑ:mist], *s.* alarmista, *m.f.*
alarm-post [əˈlɑ:m-poust], *s.* punto de reunión (*en caso de rebato*).
alarum [əˈlærəm], *s.* rebato; despertador.
alas! [əˈlɑ:s], *interj.* ¡ay!
alate, alated [ˈeileit, -id], *a.* alado.
alb [ælb], *s.* (*igl.*) alba.
Albania, [ælˈbeinjə]. Albania.
Albanian [ælˈbeinjən], *a., s.* albanés, -nesa.
albatross [ˈælbətrɔs], *s.* (*orn.*) albatros.
albeit [ɔ:lˈbi:it], *adv., conj.* aunque, bien que.
Albert [ˈælbət]. Alberto.
albino [ælˈbi:nou], *s.* albino.
albinism [ˈælbinizəm], *s.* albinismo.
album [ˈælbəm], *s.* álbum.
albumen, albumin [ælˈbju:min], *s.* (*quim.*) albúmina; (*bot.*) albumen.
albuminoid [ælˈbju:minɔid], *a.* (*med.*) albuminoideo. — *s.pl.* albuminoides, *m.pl.*
albuminose, albuminous [ælˈbju:minous, -əs], *a.* albuminado, albuminoso.
alburnum [ælˈbə:nəm], *s.* (*bot.*) alburno, albura.
alcaic [ælˈkeiik], *a., s.* alcaico.
alcayde [ælˈkeid], *s.* alcaide.
alchemic(al) [ælˈkemik(al)], *a.* alquímico.
alchemist [ˈælkimist], *s.* alquimista, *m.f.*
alchemize [ˈælkimaiz], *v.t.* transmutar, convertir.
alchemy [ˈælkimi], *s.* alquimia, crisopeya.
alcohol [ˈælkəhɔl], *s.* alcohol; (*Am.*) ***alcohol lamp*** [SPIRIT LAMP]; (*Am.*) ***denatured alcohol*** [METHYLATED SPIRIT].
alcoholate [ˈælkəhɔleit], *a.* (*med.*) alcoholato.
alcoholic [ælkəˈhɔlik], *a., s.* alcohólico.
alcoholism [ˈælkəhɔlizəm], *s.* alcoholismo.
alcoholization [ælkəhɔlaiˈzeiʃən], *s.* alcoholización.
alcoholize [ˈalkəhɔlaiz], *v.t.* alcoholar, alcoholizar.
alcoholometer [ælkəhɔˈlɔmitə], *s.* alcoholímetro.
Alcoran [ALKORAN].
alcove [ˈælkouv], *s.* hueco, nicho; cenador.
aldehyde [ˈældihaid], *s.* (*quim.*) aldehido.
aldehydic [ˈældihaidik], *a.* aldehídrico.
alder [ˈɔ:ldə], *s.* (*bot.*) aliso.
alderman [ˈɔ:ldəmən], *s.* (*pl.* **aldermen** [-men]) concejal, regidor.
ale [eil], *s.* cerveza; ***ale-house,*** cervecería, taberna; ***pale ale,*** cerveza rubia.
aleak [əˈli:k], *adv.* goteando, derramándose.
ale-bench [ˈeil-bentʃ], *s.* mostrador de taberna.
Alec [ˈælik], *s. apodo de* ***Alexander; smart Alec,*** vivales, *m.inv.*
ale-conner [ˈeil-kɔnə], *s.* inspector de cervecerías.
a-lee [əˈli:], *adv.* (*mar.*) a sotavento.
ale-fed [ˈeil-fed], *a.* alimentado con cerveza.
alembic [əˈlembik], *s.* alambique.
ale-pot [ˈeil-pɔt], *s.* jarro de cerveza.
alert [əˈlə:t], *a.* alerta, vigilante; despierto; sobre aviso; dispuesto. — *s.* (*mil.*) sorpresa; alarma; ***on the alert,*** sobre aviso. — *v.t.* alertar.
alertness [əˈlə:tnis], *s.* vigilancia; diligencia, presteza, prontitud; viveza.
ale-vat [ˈeil-væt], *s.* cuba en que fermenta la cerveza.
ale-wife [ˈeil-waif], *s.* cervecera; pez norteamericano parecido a un sábalo.
Alexander [ælikˈsɑ:ndə]. Alejandro.
alexanders [ælikˈsændəz], *s.* (*bot.*) esmirnio, apio caballar.
Alexandra [ælikˈsɑ:ndrə]. Alejandra.
Alexandria [ælikˈsɑ:ndriə]. Alejandría.
Alexandrine [ælikˈsændrin], *a., s.* alejandrino.
alga [ˈælgə], *s.* (*pl.* **algæ** [-gi]), (*bot.*) alga.
algal [ˈælgəl], *a.* algaceo.
algebra [ˈældʒibrə], *s.* álgebra.
algebraic [ældʒiˈbreiik], *a.* algebraico.
algebraist [ældʒiˈbreiist], *s.* algebrista, *m.f.*
Algeria [ælˈdʒiəriə]. Argelia.
Algerian [ælˈdʒiəriən], *a., s.* argelino.
algid [ˈældʒid], *a.* (*med.*) álgido.
algidity [ælˈdʒiditi], *s.* (*med.*) algidez.
Algiers [ælˈdʒiəz]. Argel.
algoid [ˈælgɔid], *a.* de forma de alga.
algorism [ˈælgərizəm], *s.* algoritmia.

algorithm [ˈælgɔriðəm], *s.* algoritmo.
algous [ˈælgəs], *a.* algoso, lleno de algas.
alguazil [ælgwaˈzil], *s.* alguacil.
alias [ˈeiliəs], *adv.* alias, por otro nombre. — *s.* alias.
alibi [ˈælibai], *s.* (*for.*) coartada; ***to prove an alibi,*** probar la coartada.
Alice [ˈælis]. Alicia.
alien [ˈeiliən], *a.* ajeno, extraño; extranjero. — *s.* extranjero.
alienable [ˈeiliənəbl], *a.* enajenable; alienable.
alienate [ˈeiliəneit], *v.t.* enajenar; alienar; ***he alienated the friendship of all of them,*** se enajenó la amistad de todos.
alienation [eiliəˈneiʃən], *s.* enajenamiento; enajenación; alienación; desvío.
alienator [ˈeiliəneitə], *s.* enajenador.
alienism [ˈeiliənizəm], *s.* (*med.*) alienismo; extranjería.
alienist [ˈeiliənist], *s.* (*med.*) alienista, *m.f.*
aliform [ˈeilifɔːm], *a.* aliforme.
aligerous [əˈlidʒərəs], *a.* alígero, alado.
alight (1) [əˈlait], *v.i.* apearse; posarse.
alight (2) [əˈlait], *a.* encendido, iluminado.
align [əˈlain], *v.t.* alinear.
alignment [əˈlainmənt], *s.* alineamiento, alineación.
alike [əˈlaik], *a.* semejante, parecido; ***they look very alike,*** se parecen mucho.
aliment [ˈælimənt], *s.* alimento, sustento.
alimentary [æliˈmentəri], *a.* alimenticio; ***alimentary canal,*** tubo digestivo.
alimentation [ælimenˈteiʃən], *s.* alimentación.
alimony [ˈæliməni], *s.* (*for.*) alimentos, *m.pl.*
aline [ALIGN].
aliped [ˈæliped], *a.*, *s.* (*hist. nat.*) alípedo.
aliquant [ˈælikwənt], *a.* (*mat.*) alicuanta.
aliquot [ˈælikwɔt], *a.* (*mat.*) alícuota.
alisma [əˈlizmə], *s.* (*bot.*) alisma.
alive [əˈlaiv], *a.* vivo, viviente; en vida; activo, animado; ***alive to,*** despierto para, consciente de; ***alive with,*** hormigueante de; ***to be alive,*** estar vivo, vivir; ***he is still alive,*** vive aún; ***look alive!*** ¡de prisa! ¡muévete!
alkalescence [ælkəˈlesəns], *s.* (*quím.*) alcalescencia.
alkalescent [ælkəˈlesənt], *a.* alcalescente.
alkali [ˈælkəlai], *s.* álcali.
alkalify [ˈælkəlifai], *v.t.* alcalizar, alcalificar. — *v.i.* alcalizarse, alcalificarse.
alkalimeter [ælkəˈlimitə], *s.* (*quím.*) alcalímetro.
alkalimetry [ælkəˈlimitri], *s.* (*quím.*) alcalimetría.
alkaline [ˈælkəlain], *a.* (*quím.*) alcalino.
alkalinity [ælkəˈliniti], *s.* alcalinidad.
alkalization [ælkəlaiˈzeiʃən], *s.* alcalización.
alkalize [ˈælkalaiz], *v.t.* alcalizar.
alkaloid [ˈælkəlɔid], *s.* (*quím.*) *a.*, *s.* alcaloide.
alkanet [ˈælkənet], *s.* (*bot.*) alcama (*o* alheña) orcaneta; ancusa; onoquiles.
Alkoran [ælkɔˈrɑːn], *s.* Alcorán, Corán.
all [ɔːl], *a.* todo, toda, todos, todas; ***all day,*** todo el día; ***All Fools' Day,*** día de los Inocentes; ***on all fours,*** a cuatro patas; ***All Hallows,*** día de Todos los Santos; ***at all times,*** en todo momento; ***by all means,*** no faltaba más, por supuesto; ***All Saints' Day,*** día de Todos los Santos; ***All Souls' Day,*** día de los Difuntos; ***and all that,*** y todo lo demás; ***for all that,*** con todo, a pesar de eso. — *adv.* del todo, completamente, muy; ***all the better,*** tanto mejor; ***all at once,*** de golpe, de repente; ***all right!*** ¡está bien! vale; ***all of a sudden,*** de repente. — *s.* todo, conjunto, totalidad; ***after all,*** después de todo, al fin y al cabo; ***all aboard!*** ¡los señores pasajeros al tren!; ***all in all,*** bien mirado; ***all and sundry,*** todo el mundo; ***first of all,*** ante todo; ***for all I know,*** que yo sepa; ***not at all,*** en absoluto; de ninguna manera; no hay de qué; ***once and for all,*** de una vez para siempre.
Allah [ˈællə]. Alá.
all-American [ˈɔːl-əˈmerikən], *a.* auténticamente norteamericano.
all-atoning [ˈɔːl-əˈtouniŋ], *a.* que lo expía todo.
allay [əˈlei], *v.t.* aliviar, aquietar, calmar, apaciguar, suavizar, tranquilizar, mitigar, templar.
allayer [əˈleiə], *s.* aliviador, apaciguador, calmante, mitigante.
allayment [əˈleimənt], *s*, alivio, descanso, desahogo.
all-commanding [ˈɔːl-kəmɑːndiŋ], *a.* que manda en todas partes.
all-consuming [ˈɔːl-kənˈsjuːmiŋ], *a.* que lo gasta todo, lo consume todo.
all-destroying [ˈɔːl-diˈstrɔiiŋ], *a.* que lo arruina todo.
allegation [æliˈgeiʃən], *s.* alegación, alegato.
allege [əˈledʒ], *v.t.* alegar, sostener.
allegeable [əˈledʒəbl], *a.* (*for.*) alegable.
alleged [əˈledʒd], *a.* (*der.*) presunto.
allegement [əˈledʒmənt], *s.* alegación, alegato.
alleger [əˈledʒə], *s.* alegador, afirmante, declarante.
allegiance [əˈliːdʒəns], *s.* lealtad, fidelidad.
allegoric(al) [æliˈgɔrik(əl)], *a.* alegórico.
allegorist [ˈæligərist], *s.* alegorista, *m.f.*
allegorize [ˈæligəraiz], *v.t.* alegorizar; interpretar alegóricamente.
allegory [ˈæligəri], *s.* alegoría.
allegretto [æleiˈgretou], *s.* (*mús.*) alegreto.
allegro [æˈleigrou], *s.* (*mús.*) alegro.
alleluia [æliˈluːjə], *s.* aleluya. — *interj.* ¡aleluya!
allergic [əˈləːdʒik], *a.* alérgico.
allergy [ˈælədʒi], *s.* alergia.
alleviate [əˈliːvieit], *v.t.* aliviar, calmar, mitigar; (*fig.*) atenuar.
alleviation [əliːviˈeiʃən], *s.* alivio, mitigación; atenuación.
alleviative [əˈliːviətiv], *s.* paliativo.
alley [ˈæli], *s.* callejuela, callejón; pasadizo; ***alleyway,*** callejuela; ***blind alley,*** callejón sin salida; ***bowling-alley,*** bolera.
all hail! [ˈɔːl ˈheil], *interj.* ¡salud!
alliaceous [æliˈeiʃəs], *a.* aliáceo.
alliance [əˈlaiəns], *s.* alianza; liga.
allied [əˈlaid], *a.* aliado; afín.
allies [ALLY].
alligator [ˈæligeitə], *s.* caimán.
alligator-apple [ˈæligeitə(r)-ˈæpl], *s.* anona.
alligator-pear [ˈæligeitə-ˈpɛə], *s.* aguacate; (*Hisp. Am.*) palta.
alligator-tree [ˈæligeitə-triː], *s.* ocozol.
all-important [ˈɔːl-imˈpɔːtənt], *a.* de capital importancia, fundamental.
all-in [ˈɔːl-in], *a.* global. — **all in** [ˈɔːl ˈin], *adv.* todo incluido; (*fig.*) rendido.
all-in wrestling [ˈɔːl-in ˈresliŋ], *s.* lucha libre.
alliteration [əlitəˈreiʃən], *s.* aliteración.
alliterative [əˈlitərətiv], *a.* aliterado.
all-knowing [ˈɔːl-ˈnouiŋ], *a.* omnisciente.
allocate [ˈælokeit], *v.t.* asignar, adjudicar; distribuir.
allocation [æloˈkeiʃən], *s.* distribución.
allocution [æloˈkjuːʃən], *s.* alocución.
allodial [əˈloudiəl], *a.* (*for.*) alodial.
allodium [əˈloudiəm], *s.* alodio.
allonge [əˈlɔndʒ], *s.* (*esgr.*) bote, botonazo, estocada.
allopathic [æloˈpæθik], *a.* (*med.*) alopático.
allopathist [əˈlɔpəθist], *s.* alópata, *m.f.*
allopathy [əˈlɔpəθi], *s.* alopatía.
allophone [ˈælofoun], *s.* alófono.
allot [əˈlɔt], *v.t.* asignar, adjudicar; repartir.
allotment [əˈlɔtmənt], *s.* lote, porción, parte, *f.*; asignación; parcela (de terreno).
allotropic [ælɔˈtrɔpik], *a.* (*quím.*) alotrópico.

allotropism, allotropy [æ'lɔtrəpizəm, -i], *s.* (*quím.*) alotropía.
allottable [ə'lɔtəbl], *a.* repartible.
allotting [ə'lɔtiŋ], *s.* reparto, repartimiento.
all-out ['ɔ:l-aut], *a.* total; ***all-out effort,*** esfuerzo supremo.
allow [ə'lau], *v.t.* admitir; conceder; consentir, permitir; ***allow for,*** tener en cuenta; ***allow of,*** admitir; ***allow to,*** permitir + *inf.*; ***I can't allow you to do that,*** no te puedo permitir que hagas eso, no puedo consentir (en) que hagas eso.
allowable [ə'lauəbl], *a.* admisible; permisible, lícito.
allowance [ə'lauəns], *s.* concesión; asignación; permiso, autorización; paga, propina; indulgencia; tolerancia; pensión, subsidio; ración; descuento, bonificación; ***family allowance,*** subsidio familiar; ***to keep on allowance,*** tener a ración; ***to make allowances for,*** hacerse cargo de, ser indulgente con.
alloxanate [ə'lɔksəneit], *s.* (*quím.*) aloxanato.
alloxanic [əlɔk'sænik], *a.* aloxánico.
alloy [ə'lɔi], *s.* aleación, liga; ley; amalgama, impureza. — *v.t.* alear, ligar; desvirtuar; mezclar.
alloyed [ə'lɔid], *a.* ligado, mezclado; alterado, falsificado.
all-penetrating ['ɔ:l-'penitreitiŋ], *a.* que lo penetra todo.
all-powerful ['ɔ:l-'pauəful], *a.* omnipotente, todopoderoso.
allspice ['ɔ:lspais], *s.* (*bot.*) baya *o* fruta del pimiento de Jamaica.
allude [ə'lju:d], *v.i.* (***to***), aludir (a), referirse (a).
allure [ə'ljuə], *v.t.* seducir, atraer, fascinar, tentar.
allurement [ə'ljuəmənt], *s.* seducción, tentación, fascinación; atractivo; incentivo.
allurer [ə'ljuərə], *s.* seductor.
alluring [ə'ljuəriŋ], *a.* seductor, engañador, atractivo, atrayente, tentador.
alluringness [ə'ljuəriŋnis], *s.* atractivo, aliciente, incentivo.
allusion [ə'lju:ʒən], *s.* alusión; reticencia, insinuación.
allusive [ə'lju:siv], *a.* alusivo.
allusiveness [ə'lju'sivnis], *s.* (lo) alusivo.
alluvial [ə'lu:viəl], *a.* aluvial.
alluvion [ə'lu:viən], *s.* aluvión; inundación; avenida; derrubio.
alluvium [ə'lu:viəm], *s.* terreno aluvial, derrubio.
all-weather ['ɔ:l-'weðə], *a.* de todo tiempo.
ally ['ælai], *s.* (*pl.* **allies** ['ælaiz]) aliado; cosa afín; allegado. — [ə'læi], *v.t.* aliar, unir. — **ally o.s.,** *v.r.* aliarse, coligarse (***with*** o ***to,*** con).
almagra [æl'mægrə], *a.* almagre.
almanac ['ælmənæk], *s.* almanaque.
almanac-maker ['ælmənæk-meikə], *s.* almanaquero.
almandine ['ælməndin], *s.* (*min.*) almandina.
almightiness [ɔ:l'maitinis], *s.* omnipotencia.
almighty [ɔ:l'maiti], *a.* omnipotente, todopoderoso; ***the Almighty,*** el Todopoderoso.
almond ['ɑ:mənd], *s.* almendra, alloza; almendro, allozo; (*anat.*) ***almonds of the throat,*** amígdalas, *f.pl.*; ***sugar almonds,*** almendras garapiñadas.
almond-oil ['ɑ:mənd-ɔil], *s.* aceite de almendras.
almond-paste ['ɑ:mənd-'peist], *s.* pasta de almendras.
almond-teee ['ɑ:mənd-tri:], *s.* (*bot.*) almendro, allozo.
almoner ['ælmənə], *s.* limosnero.
almonry ['ælmənri], *s.* sitio donde se distribuye limosna.
almost ['ɔ:lmoust], *adv.* casi.
alms [ɑ:mz], *s.* limosna; caridad; ***alms-box,*** cepillo (de la limosna).
almsdeed ['ɑ:mzdi:d], *s.* obra de caridad.
almsgiver ['ɑ:mzgivə], *s.* limosnero.
almsgiving ['ɑ:mzgiviŋ], *s.* caridad.
almshouse ['ɑ:mzhaus], *s.* hospicio, casa de caridad.
almsman ['ɑ:mzmən], *s.* pordiosero.
almug-tree ['ælmʌg-tri:], *s.* (*bot.*) sándalo.
aloe ['ælou], *s.* áloe.
aloes ['ælouz], *s.* áloe; acíbar.
aloetic [ælou'etik], *a.* aloético.
aloft [ə'lɔft], *adv.* arriba, en alto; por los aires; (*naut.*) en la arboladura; (*aer.*) en vuelo.
alone [ə'loun], *a.* solo. — *adv.* a solas; ***to be alone,*** estar solo *o* a solas; ***he was alone with her,*** estaba a solas con ella; ***to leave o let alone,*** dejar en paz, no molestar, no tocar, no meterse con; ***let alone,*** sin hablar de, y no hablemos de, y mucho menos.
along [ə'lɔŋ], *adv.* a lo largo; adelante; ***all along,*** desde el principio, desde el primer momento, todo el tiempo; ***come along!*** ¡venga! ¡anda!; ***come along with me,*** vente conmigo; ***to get along,*** ir tirando, defenderse; ***to get along well with,*** llevarse bien con. — *prep.* por, a lo largo de; ***along the road,*** por la carretera; ***all along the road,*** a (todo) lo largo de la carretera.
alongshore [ə'lɔŋ'ʃɔ:], *adv.* a lo largo de la costa.
alongside [ə'lɔŋ'said], *adv.* al lado, al costado, costado con costado. — *prep.* al lado de, al costado de, a lo largo de; (*mar.*) ***to come alongside,*** acostarse.
aloof [ə'lu:f], *a.* altivo, altanero, fatuo, reservado; apartado. — *adv.* ***to stand aloof,*** mantenerse apartado *o* a distancia; considerarse superior.
aloofness [ə'lu:fnis], *s.* altivez, engreimiento, soberbia, reserva.
alopecia [ælo'pi:siə], *s.* (*med.*) alopecia.
aloud [ə'laud], *adv.* en voz alta.
alp [ælp], *s.* montaña muy alta; [ALPS].
alpaca [æl'pækə], *s.* alpaca.
alpenstock ['ælpənstɔk], *s.* alpenstock, bastón montañero.
alpha ['ælfə], *s.* alfa; ***alpha and omega,*** alfa y omega.
alphabet ['ælfəbet], *s.* alfabeto.
alphabetical [ælfə'betikəl], *a.* alfabético.
alpine ['ælpain], *a.* alpino; alpestre.
alpinist ['ælpinist], *s.* alpinista, *m.f.*
Alps [ælps], **the.** los Alpes.
alquifou ['ælkwifu:], *s.* alquifol.
already [ɔ:l'redi], *adv.* ya.
Alsace ['ælsæs]. Alsacia.
Alsace-Lorraine ['ælsæs-lɔ'rein]. Alsacia-Lorena.
also ['ɔ:lsou], *adv.* también.
altar ['ɔ:ltə], *s.* altar; ara; ***high altar,*** altar mayor.
altarage ['ɔ:ltəridʒ], *s.* pie de altar.
altar-boy ['ɔ:ltə-bɔi], *s.* monaguillo.
altar-cloth ['ɔ:ltə-klɔθ], *s.* paño de altar.
altar-piece ['ɔ:ltə-pi:s], *s.* retablo.
altar-rail ['ɔ:ltə-reil], *s.* comulgatorio.
altar-table ['ɔ:ltə-teibl], *s.* mesa del altar.
alter ['ɔ:ltə], *v.t.* cambiar, modificar; (*mar.*) ***alter course,*** cambiar el rumbo. — *v.i.* cambiar.
alterability [ɔ:ltərə'biliti], *s.* (lo) modificable.
alterable ['ɔ:ltəeəbl], *a.* modificable.
alterableness ['ɔ:ltərəblnis], *s.* (lo) modificable.
alterant ['ɔ:ltərənt], *a.* (*med.*) alterante.
alteration [ɔ:ltə'reiʃən], *s.* modificación; arreglo.
alterative ['ɔ:ltərətiv], *a.* (*med.*) alterativo. — *s.* alterante.
altercate ['ɔ:ltəkeit], *v.i.* altercar, disputar.
altercation [ɔ:ltə'keiʃən], *s.* altercado, disputa, agarrada.
alternancy [ɔ:l'tə:nənsi], *s.* alternación, alternancia, turno.
alternate [ɔ:l'tə:nit], *a.* alterno, alternado. — ['ɔ:ltəneit], *v.t.* alternar, variar. — *v.i.* alternar, turnar.

alternateness [ɔ:lˈtə:nitnis], *s.* alternación.
alternating [ˈɔ:ltəneitiŋ], *a.* alternante, por turno; alterna (*corriente, función*).
alternation [ɔ:ltəˈneiʃən], *s.* alternación, turno, vez; vicisitud; (*mat.*) permutación; (*igl.*) responsorio, responso.
alternative [ɔ:lˈtə:nətiv], *a.* alternativo; (*gram.*) disyuntivo. — *s.* alternativa, opción, posibilidad.
alternativeness [ɔ:lˈtə:nətivnis], *s.* vicisitud; reciprocidad; turno.
alternator [ˈɔ:ltəneitə], *s.* (*elec.*) alternador.
althea [ælˈθiə], *s.* (*bot.*) malvavisco.
although [ɔ:lˈðou], *conj.* aunque, si bien, aun cuando, bien que, a pesar de que.
altiloquence [ælˈtilokwəns], *s.* altilocuencia.
altiloquent [ælˈtilokwənt], *a.* altilocuente.
altimeter [ælˈtimitə], *s.* altímetro.
altimetry [ælˈtimitri], *s.* altimetría.
altisonant [æltiˈsounənt], *a.* altisonante, altísono, pomposo.
altitude [ˈæltitju:d], *s.* altura, altitud; elevación.
alto [ˈæltou], *s.* (*mús.*) contralto (*de la voz*); contralto (*cantante*) *m.f.*
altogether [ɔ:ltuˈgeðə], *adv.* enteramente, por completo; en total, en conjunto; (*fam.*) ***in the altogether,*** en cueros vivos.
alto-relievo [æltou-riˈli:vou], *s.* (*esc.*) alto relieve.
altruism [ˈæltruizəm], *s.* altruismo.
altruist [ˈæltruist], *s.* altruista, *m.f.*
altruistic [æltruˈistik], *a.* altruista.
alum [ˈæləm], *s.* alumbre, *m.*; ***alum-stone,*** aluminita; ***alum-water,*** agua de alumbre; ***alum-works,*** alumbrera. — *v.t.* (*tint.*) alumbrar.
alumina [əˈlju:minə], *s.* (*min.*) alumina.
aluminiferous [əlju:miˈnifərəs], *a.* (*min.*) aluminífero.
aluminite [æˈlju:minait], *s.* aluminita.
aluminium [æljuˈminiəm], *s.* (*min.*) aluminio.
aluminous [æˈlju:minəs], *a.* aluminoso.
aluminum [eˈlu:minəm], (*Am.*) [ALUMINIUM].
alumnus [əˈlʌmnəs], *s.* alumno; (*Am.*) graduado, licenciado.
alveary [ˈælviəri], *s.* (*anat.*) alveario.
alveolar [ælviˈoulə], *a.* (*anat.*) alveolar.
alveolate [ˈælvioleit], *a.* alveolado.
alveolus [ælviˈouləs], *s.* alvéolo.
alveus [ˈælviəs], *s.* álveo.
alvine [ˈælvin], *a.* (*anat.*) alvino.
always [ˈɔ:lwəz], *adv.* siempre.
alyssum [ˈælisəm], *s.* (*bot.*) alhelí.
amain [əˈmein], *adv.* vigorosamente, violentamente, con fuerza, con vehemencia; (*mar.*) en banda.
amalgam [əˈmælgəm], *s.* amalgama.
amalgamate [əˈmælgəmeit], *v.t.* amalgamar. — *v.i.* amalgamarse.
amalgamation [əmælgəˈmeiʃən], *s.* amalgamado.
amalgamator [əˈmælgəmeitə], *s.* amalgamador.
amanuensis [əmænjuˈensis], *s.* amanuense.
amaranth [ˈæmərænθ], *s.* (*bot.*) amaranto.
amaranthine [æməˈrænθin], *a.* amarantino; inmarcesible.
amaryllis [æməˈrilis], *s.* (*bot.*) amarilis, *f.*
amass [əˈmæs], *v.t.* acumular, amontonar.
amateur [ˈæmətə:], *s.* aficionado; (*despec.*) chapucero.
amateurish [æməˈtə:riʃ], *a.* poco experto, poco exacto; chapucero.
amateurishness [æməˈtə:riʃnis], *s.* (lo) poco experto (de), (lo) poco exacto (de); (lo) chapucero (de).
amateurism [æməˈtə:rizəm], *s.* culto de lo no-profesional; diletantismo.
amative [ˈæmətiv], *a.* amativo.
amatory [ˈæmətəri], *a.* amatorio.
amaze [əˈmeiz], *v.t.* asombrar, pasmar; ***to be amazed at*** o ***by,*** asombrarse de, maravillarse de, admirarse de.
amazedness, amazement [əˈmeizidnis, -mənt], *s.* asombro, pasmo, admiración.
amazing [əˈmeiziŋ], *a.* asombroso, pasmoso.
Amazon [ˈæməzən], *s.* amazona; ***River Amazon,*** Río Amazonas.
Amazonian [æməˈzouniən], *a.* amazónico.
ambassador [æmˈbæsədə], *s.* embajador.
ambassadorial [æmbæsəˈdɔ:riəl], *a.* embajatorio.
ambassadress [æmˈbæsədris], *s.* embajadora.
amber [ˈæmbə], *a.* ambarino. — *s.* ámbar.
ambergris [ˈæmbəgri:s], *s.* ámbar gris.
amber-tree [ˈæmbə-tri:], *s.* (*bot.*) escobilla de ámbar.
ambidexter [æmbiˈdekstə], *a., s.* ambidextro; falso, engañoso; prevaricador.
ambidexterity [æmbideksˈteriti], *s.* ambidexteridad; doblez, *f.*, simulación.
ambidextrous [æmbiˈdekstrəs], *a.* ambidextro; falso, hipócrita.
ambidextrousness [æmbiˈdekstrəsnis], *s.* ambidexteridad.
ambience [ˈæmbiəns], *s.* ambiente.
ambient [ˈæmbiənt], *a.* ambiente.
ambiguity [æmbiˈgju:iti], *s.* ambigüedad.
ambiguous [æmˈbigjuəs], *a.* ambiguo.
ambiguousness [æmˈbigjuəsnis], *s.* ambigüedad.
ambit [ˈæmbit], *s.* ámbito, recinto, contorno.
ambition [æmˈbiʃən], *s.* ambición (**to, for,** de, por).
ambitionless [æmˈbiʃənlis], *a.* sin ambición.
ambitious [æmˈbiʃəs], *a.* que tiene ambición *o* ambiciones; ***to be ambitious for,*** ambicionar.
ambitiousness [æmˈbiʃəsnis], *s.* ambición, (lo) ambicioso.
amble [æmbl], *s.* paso de andadura. — *v.i.* (*equit.*) amblar; (*pers.*) andar muy despacio; ***he ambled up to her,*** se acercó despacio a ella.
ambler [ˈæmblə], *s.* paseante.
ambling [ˈæmbliŋ], *s.* ambladura; paso lento.
amblyopia [æmbliˈoupiə], *s.* (*med.*) ambliopía.
ambrosia [æmˈbrouziə], *s.* ambrosía.
ambrosial [æmˈbrouziəl], *a.* ambrosíaco, delicioso.
ambrosian [æmˈbrouziən], *a.* ambrosiano.
ambry [ˈæmbri], *s.* repostería.
ambs-ace [ˈæmbz-eis], *s.* (*juego*) ases, *m.pl.*, ambos ases; (*fig.*) mala suerte.
ambulance [ˈæmbjuləns], *s.* ambulancia.
ambulant [ˈæmbjulənt], *a.* ambulante.
ambulate [ˈæmbjuleit], *v.i.* ambular.
ambulation [æmbjuˈleiʃən], *s.* paseo; ambulación.
ambulatory [ˈæmbjulətəri], *a.* ambulante; (*med.*) que puede andar.—*s.* paseo, galería, deambulatorio.
ambury [ˈæmbəri], *s.* (*vet.*) furúnculo, tumor blando.
ambuscade [æmbəsˈkeid], *s.* emboscada, celada. — *v.t.* atacar desde una emboscada.
ambush [ˈæmbuʃ], *s.* emboscada, celada, acecho; ***to lay an ambush,*** tender una celada; ***to lie in ambush,*** estar emboscado, estar al acecho.— *v.t.* atacar en emboscada.
Amelia [əˈmi:ljə]. Amalia.
ameliorable [əˈmi:liərəbl], *a.* mejorable.
ameliorate [əˈmi:liəreit], *v.t.* mejorar, adelantar, bonificar.—*v.i.* mejorarse.
amelioration [əmi:liəˈreiʃən], *s.* mejora, mejoramiento; medro; adelanto.
ameliorative [əˈmi:liəreitiv], *a.* mejorador, aumentador.
amen [ɑ:ˈmen], *adv.* amén, así sea.
amenability, amenableness [əmi:nəˈbiliti, əˈmi:nəblnis], docilidad, flexibilidad, (lo) razonable (de).
amenable [əˈmi:nəbl], *a.* dócil, razonable, flexible.

amend [ə'mend], *s.* [AMENDS]. — *v.t.* enmendar, modificar; ***to amend the law,*** reformar la ley.
amendable [ə'mendəbl], *a.* enmendable, modificable.
amender [ə'mendə], *s.* enmendador.
amendment [ə'mendmənt], *s.* enmienda, modificación; (*pol.*) ***to move an amendment,*** proponer una enmienda.
amends [ə'mendz], *s.pl.* desagravio, recompensa, satisfacción, indemnización; ***to make amends (for),*** compensar (de), hacer penitencia (en desagravio de).
amenity [ə'mi:niti], *s.* ***public amenity,*** servicio público.
amenorrhœa [əmenə'riə], *s.* (*med.*) amenorrea.
ament [ə'ment], *s.* (*bot.*) amento
amentaceous [æmen'teiʃəs], *a.* amentáceo.
amentia [ə'menʃə], *s.* demencia.
amerce [ə'mə:s], *v.t.* multar.
amercement [ə'mə:smənt], *s.* multa.
America [ə'merikə]. América; ***United States of America,*** Estados Unidos de América.
American [ə'merikən], *a., s.* americano; norteamericano; (*Am.*) ***American plan,*** todo incluido.
Americanism [ə'merikənizəm], *s.* americanismo.
Americanize [ə'merikənaiz], *v.t.* americanizar.
Amerindian [æmər'indjən], *a., s.* amerindio.
amethyst ['æməθist], *s.* (*min.*) amatista.
amethystine [æmə'θistain], *a.* de amatista; parecido *o* semejante a la amatista.
amiability, amiableness [aimjə'biliti, 'eimjəblnis], *s.* amabilidad, campechanía.
amiable ['eimjəbl], *a.* amable, campechano, bonachón.
amianthus [æmi'ænθəs], *s.* amianto.
amicability, amicableness [æmikə'biliti, 'æmikəblnis], *s.* cordialidad, disposición amistosa.
amicable ['æmikəbl], *a.* amigable, amistoso.
amice ['æmis], *s.* (*igl.*) amito.
amid, amidst [ə'mid, -st], *prep.* entre, en medio de, rodeado por.
amidin ['æmidin], *s.* (*quím.*) almidina.
amidship(s) [ə'midʃip(s)], *adv.* (*mar.*) en medio del navío.
amiss [ə'mis], *adv.* mal; ***to be amiss,*** estar mal; ***is sth. amiss?*** ¿pasa algo? ¿algo no marcha? ¿algo está mal?; ***to take amiss,*** tomar a mal; ***don't take it amiss,*** no lo tomes a mal, no te ofendas (por ello).
amity ['æmiti], *s.* amistad, concordia, bienquerencia.
ammeter ['æmitə], *s.* (*elec.*) amperímetro.
ammonia [ə'mouniə], *s.* (*quím.*) amoníaco.
ammoniac [ə'mounjæk], *s.* amoníaco, sal amoníaca.
ammoniacal [æmo'naiəkəl], *a.* amoniacal, amónico.
ammonite ['æmənait], *s.* (*zool.*) amonita.
ammonium [ə'mounjəm], *s.* amonio, radical alcalino hipotético.
ammunition [æmju'niʃən], *s.* (*mil.*) munición; municiones, balas; ***ammunition bread,*** pan de munición; ***round of ammunition,*** cartucho, bala; ***sporting ammunition,*** municiones de caza.
amnesia [æm'ni:ziə], *s.* (*med.*) amnesia.
amnesty ['æmnesti], *s.* amnistía.—*v.t.* amnistiar.
amnion ['æmniən], *s.* (*zool.*) amnios.
amœba [ə'mi:bə], *s.* amiba *o* ameba.
amœboid [e'mi:bɔid], *a.* amebeo.
amok [ə'mʌk] [AMUCK].
amomum [ə'moumәm], *s.* (*bot.*) amomo.
among, amongst [ə'mʌŋ, -st], *prep.* entre, en medio de; en el número de.
amorist ['æmərist], *s.* amante, galán.
amorous ['æmərəs], *a.* amoroso; amatorio; querendón.
amorousness ['æmərəsnis], *s.* amor, inclinación amorosa; terneza.
amorphism [ə'mɔ:fizəm], *s.* amorfia; (*pol.*) anarquismo.
amorphous [ə'mɔ:fəs], *a.* amorfo, informe.
amort [ə'mɔ:t], *a.* exánime.
amortization, amortizement [əmɔ:ti'zeiʃən, ə'mɔ:tizmənt], *s.* (*for.*) amortización.
amortize [ə'mɔ:taiz], *v.t.* amortizar.
amount [ə'maunt], *s.* cantidad, suma; importe; monta, monto, montante; cuantía, valor; ***to the amount of,*** por valor de, por la suma de.—*v.i.* — ***to,*** sumar, importar, ascender *o* subir a; equivaler a, venir a ser lo mismo que.
amour [ə'muə], *s.* amores, amoríos
amperage ['æmpəridʒ], *s.* (*elec.*) amperaje.
ampère ['æmpɛə], *s.* amperio.
ampersand ['æmpəsænd], *s.* el signo & (*y*).
amphibia [æm'fibiə], *s. pl.* anfibios.
amphibious [æm'fibiəs], *a.* anfibio; (*fig.*) híbrido.
amphibiousness [æm'fibiəsnis], *s.* naturaleza anfibia, (lo) anfibio.
amphibole ['æmfiboul], *s.* (*min.*) anfíbol.
amphibolite [æm'fibolait], *s.* anfibolita.
amphibological [æmfibo'lɔdʒikəl], *a.* anfibológico, dudoso, obscuro.
amphibology [æmfi'bɔlədʒi], *s.* anfibología, doble sentido.
amphiboly [æm'fibəli], *s.* anfibología; ambigüedad.
amphibrach ['æmfibræk], *s.* anfíbraco.
Amphipoda [æm'fipɔdə], *s.pl.* anfípodos, *m.pl.*
amphisbæna [æmfis'bi:nə], *s.* anfisbena.
amphitheatre ['æmfiθiətə], *s.* anfiteatro.
amphitheatrical [æmfiθi'ætrikəl], *a.* anfiteatral.
amphitryon [æm'fitriən], *s.* anfitrión.
amphora ['æmfərə], *s.* ánfora.
amphoric [æm'fɔrik], *a.* anfóreo.
ample [æmpl], *a.* amplio, extenso; holgado.
amplification [æmplifi'keiʃən], *s.* amplificación.
amplifier ['æmplifaiə], *s.* amplificador.
amplify ['æmplifai], *v.t.* amplificar, ampliar, aumentar. — *v.i.* extenderse.
amplifying ['æmplifaiiŋ], *a.* amplificador.
amplitude, ampleness ['æmplitju:d, 'æmplnis], *s.* amplitud; (*fís.*) ***amplitude of swing,*** amplitud de oscilación.
ampoule ['æmpu:l], *s.* (*med.*) ampolla.
ampulla [æm'pulə], *s.* ampolla.
ampullaceous [æmpu'leiʃəs], *a.* ampuláceo, ampollar.
amputate ['æmpjuteit], *v.t.* amputar.
amputation [æmpju'teiʃən], *s.* amputación.
amuck [ə'mʌk], *adv.* ***to run amuck,*** entrarle a alguien una locura *o* furia asesina.
amulet ['æmjulit], *s.* amuleto.
amuse [ə'mju:z], *v.t.* divertir, entretener.
amusement [ə'mju:zmənt], *s.* diversión, entretenimiento, pasatiempo; ***amusement guide,*** guía de espectáculos; ***amusement park,*** parque de atracciones.
amusing [ə'mju:ziŋ], *a.* divertido, entretenido; gracioso.
amygdala [æ'migdələ], *s.* (*anat.*) amígdala.
amygdalic [æmig'dælik], *a.* amigdalino.
amygdalin [æ'migdəlin], *s.* (*quím.*) amigdalina.
amygdaline [æ'migdəlain], *a.* almendrado amigdalino.
amygdaloid [æ'migdəlɔid], *a.* amigdaloide.
amyl ['æmil], *s.* (*quím.*) amilo.
amylaceous [æmi'leiʃəs], *a.* amiláceo.
amylene ['æmili:n], *s.* amileno.
amylic [æ'milik], *a.* amílico.
amyloid ['æmilɔid], *a.* amiloide.
an [A(2)], (*ante sonido vocálico*): ***an hour,*** una hora.

ana [ˈænə], *s.* (*med.*) ana.
anabaptism [ænəˈbæptizəm], *s.* anabaptismo.
anabaptist [ænaˈbæptist], *s.* anabaptista, *m.f.*
anabolism [əˈnæbəlizəm], *s.* (*biol.*) anabolismo.
anacardium [ænəˈkɑ:diəm], *s.* (*bot.*) anacardo.
anacathartic [ænəkəˈθɑ:tik], *s.* anacatártico.
anachronic(al) [ænəˈkrɔnik(əl)], *a.* anacrónico.
anachronism [əˈnækronizəm], *s.* anacronismo.
anachronistic [ənækroˈnistik], *a.* anacrónico.
anaclastics [ænəˈklæstiks], *s.* (*ópt.*) dióptrica.
anaconda [ænəˈkɔndə], *s.* (*zool.*) anaconda.
anacreontic [ənækriˈɔntik], *a.* anacreóntico.—*s.* anacreóntica.
anadromous [əˈnædroməs], *a.* anadromo.
anæmia [əˈni:miə], *s.* (*med.*) anemia.
anæmic [əˈni:mik], *a.* anémico.
anæthesia [ænəsˈθi:ziə], *s.* (*med.*) anestesia.
anæsthetic [ænəsˈθetik], *a.* anestésico.
anæsthetist [əˈni:sθətist], *s.* anestesiador.
anæsthetize [əˈni:sθətaiz], *v.t.* anestesiar.
anaglyph [ˈænəglif], *s.* anáglifo.
anagogical [ænəˈgɔdʒikəl], *a.* anagógico, misterioso.
anagogics [ænəˈgɔdʒiks], *s.* anagogía.
anagram [ˈænəgræm], *s.* anagrama, *m.*
anagrammatical [ænəgrəˈmætikəl], *a.* anagramático.
anal [ˈeinəl], *a.* (*anat.*) anal.
analecta [ænəˈlektə], *s.pl.* analectas, *f.pl.*
analectic [ænəˈlektik], *a.* analéctico.
analemma [ænəˈlemə], *s.* analema.
analepsis, analepsy [ænəˈlepsis, ˈænəlepsi], *s.* (*med.*) analepsia.
analeptic [ænəˈleptik], *a.*, *s.* analéptico.
analogical [ænəˈlɔdʒikəl] *a.* analógico.
analogism [əˈnælədʒizm], *s.* analogismo.
analogize [əˈnælədʒaiz], *v.t.* analogizar, explicar por analogía.
analogous [əˈnæləgəs], *a.* análogo, parecido, semejante.
analogue [ˈænəlɔg], *s.* cosa análoga.
analogy [əˈnælədʒi], *s.* analogía.
analysable [ˈænəlaizəbl], *a.* analizable.
analysableness [ˈænəlaizəblnis], *s.* calidad de ser analizable.
analyse [ˈænəlaiz], *v.t.* analizar, hacer análisis de.
analysis [əˈnælisis], *s.* análisis, *m.*; ***in the last analysis,*** en última instancia, últimamente.
analyst, analyser [ˈænəlist, ˈænəlaizə], *s.* analizador, analista, *m.f.*
analytic(al) [ænəˈlitik(əl)], *a.* analítico.
analytics [ænəˈlitiks], *s.* analítica.
anamnesis [ænəmˈni:sis], *s.* anamnesis, anamnesia.
anamorphosis [ænəmɔ:ˈfousis], *s.* anamorfosis, *f. inv.*
anandrous [əˈnændrəs], *a.* (*bot.*) destituto de estambre.
anapæst [ˈænəpi:st], *s.* anapesto.
anapæstic(al) [ænəˈpi:stik(əl)], *a.* anapéstico.
anaphora [əˈnæfərə], *s.* (*ret.*) anáfora.
anaphrodisiac [ænæfroˈdiziæk], *s.* (*med.*) antiafrodisíaco.
anarchic(al) [əˈnɑ:kik(əl)], *a.* anárquico.
anarchism [ˈænəkizəm], *s.* anarquismo.
anarchist [ˈænəkist], *s.* anarquista, *m.f.*
anarchy [ˈænəki], *s.* anarquía.
anastasis [ænəˈsteisis], *s.* (*med.*) convalecencia.
anastatic [ænəˈstætik], *a.* (*art.*) anastático, en relieve.
anastigmatic [ænæstigˈmætik], *a.* (*ópt.*) anastigmático.
anastomosis [ənæstoˈmousis], *s.* anastomosis, *f.*
anastrophe [əˈnæstrəfi], *s.* (*gram.*) anástrofe, *f.*
anathema [əˈnæθəmə], *s.* anatema, *m.*
anathematization [ənæθəmətaiˈzeiʃən], *s.* anatematización.
anathematize [əˈnæθəmətaiz], *v.t.* anatematizar.
anatomical [ænəˈtɔmikəl], *a.* anatómico.
anatomist [əˈnætəmist], *s.* anatomista, *m.f.* anatómico.
anatomize [əˈnætəmaiz], *v.t.* anatomizar.
anatomy [əˈnætəmi], *s.* anatomía.
anbury [ˈænbəri], *s.* (*vet.*) furúnculo.
ancestor [ˈænsistə], *s.* antepasado.
ancestral [ænˈsestrəl], *a.* ancestral.
ancestry [ˈænsistri], *s.* linaje, prosapia, abolengo.
anchor [ˈæŋkə], *s.* ancla; áncora; ***anchor back,*** galga del ancla; ***anchor beam,*** serviola; ***anchor bill,*** pico del ancla; ***anchor chocks,*** calzos del ancla; ***anchor flukes,*** orejas del ancla; ***anchor ground,*** fondeadero; ***anchor stock,*** cepo del ancla; ***to cast anchor,*** echar anclas; ***kedge anchor,*** anclote; ***to ride at anchor,*** estar anclado, fondeado, surto; ***sheet anchor,*** ancla grande, ancla de la esperanza; ***to weigh anchor,*** levar anclas.—*v.t.* anclar; sujetar (con ancla). —*v.i.* anclar.
anchorage [ˈæŋkəridʒ], *s.* (*mar.*) anclaje; fondeadero.
anchoress [ˈæŋkəris], *s.* anacoreta, *f.*
anchorite [ˈæŋkərait], *s.* anacoreta, *m.f.*
anchorless [ˈæŋkəlis], *a.* sin ancla; a la deriva.
anchorsmith [ˈæŋkəsmiθ], *s.* ancorero.
anchovy [ˈæntʃəvi], *s.* (*ict.*) anchoa; ***fresh anchovy,*** boquerón.
ancient [ˈeinʃənt], *a.* antiguo, vetusto; ***the ancients,*** los antiguos.
ancillary [ænˈsiləri], *a.* auxiliar.
ancipital [ænˈsipitəl], *a.* de dos caras, de dos cortes.
ancon [ˈæŋkən], *s.* ancón.
and [ænd], *conj.* y; e; ***and so on,*** y así sucesivamente; ***and son,*** e hijo; ***and he did more,*** e hizo más; ***and yet,*** sin embargo; ***better and better,*** cada vez mejor; ***bread and butter,*** pan con mantequilla; ***by and by,*** luego; ***go and see,*** vaya, ve a mirar; ***ifs and ands,*** dimes y diretes; ***now and then,*** de vez en cuando.
Andalusia [ændəˈlu:ziə]. Andalucía.
Andalusian [ændəˈlu:ziən], *a.*, *s.* andaluz, andaluza.
Andean [ˈændiən], *a.*, *s.* andino.
Andes [ˈændi:z], **the.** (la Cordillera de) los Andes.
andirons [ˈændaiənz], *s.pl.* morillos, *m.pl.*
Andorra [ænˈdɔrə]. Andorra.
Andorran [ænˈdɔrən], *a.*, *s.* andorrano.
Andrew [ˈændru:]. Andrés, *m.*
androgynous [ænˈdrɔdʒinəs], *a.* andrógino, hermafrodita, *m.f.*
android [ˈændrɔid], *a.* de figura humana.—*s.* androide; autómata, *m.*
androphagous [ænˈdrɔfəgəs], *a.* antropófago.
Andy [ˈændi], *forma cariñosa de* [ANDREW].
anecdotal [ænikˈdoutəl], *a.* anecdótico.
anecdote [ˈænikdout], *s.* anécdota.
anele [əˈni:l], *v.t.* administrar la extremaunción (a).
anelectric [æniˈlektrik], *a.* (*fís.*) aneléctrico.
anemometer [æniˈmɔmitə], *s.* anemómetro.
anemone [əˈneməni], *s.* anémona, anémone.
anemoscope [əˈnemoskoup], *s.* anemoscopio.
anent [əˈnent], *prep.*, *ant.* tocante, concerniente a.
aneroid [ˈænərɔid], *a.* aneroide, aneroideo.
aneuria [əˈnju:riə], *s.* (*med.*) aneuria.
aneurism [ˈænjurizəm], *s.* aneurisma, *m.f.*
aneurismal [ænjuˈrizməl], *a.* aneurismal.
anew [əˈnju:], *adv.* de nuevo, otra vez (más), nuevamente; ***to read anew,*** volver a leer.
anfractuose, anfractuous [ænˈfræktjuous, -əs], *a.* anfractuoso, sinuoso, quebrado.
anfractuosity, anfractuousness [ænfræktjuˈɔsiti, ænˈfræktjuəsnis], *s.* anfractuosidad, sinuosidad.

angel [ˈeindʒəl], *s.* ángel; moneda antigua de oro; (*ict.*) ***angel fish,*** peje angelote; ***guardian angel,*** ángel de la guarda.
angelhood [ˈeindʒəlhud], *s.* condición de ángel.
angelic(al) [ænˈdʒelik(əl)], *a.* angelical, angélico, seráfico.
angelica [ænˈdʒelikə], *s.* (*bot.*) angélica.
angelicalness [ænˈdʒelikəlnis], *s.* (lo) angelical, (lo) angélico.
angel-shot [ˈeindʒəl-ʃɔt], *s.* (*mar.*) balas enramadas, *f.pl.*, palanquetas, *f.pl.*
angel-worship [ˈeindʒəl-wə:ʃip], *s.* angelolatría, culto de los ángeles.
anger [ˈæŋgə], *s.* ira, cólera; enojo; ***a fit of anger,*** un acceso de cólera; ***to provoke to anger,*** encolerizar, irritar. — *v.t.* enfurecer, irritar, enojar, encolerizar, airar, enrabiar.
angered [ˈæŋgəd], *a.* encolerizado.—*p.p.* [ANGER].
Angevin [ˈændʒəvin], *a.* (*hist.*) angevino.
angina [ænˈdʒainə], *s.* (*med.*) angina; ***angina pectoris,*** angina de pecho.
angiography [ændʒiˈɔgrəfi], *s.* angiografía.
angiology [ændʒiˈɔlədʒi], *s.* (*med.*) angiología.
angiosperm [ˈændʒiospə:m], *s.* angiosperma.
angiotomy [ændʒiˈɔtəmi], *s.* angiotomía.
angle [æŋgl], *s.* ángulo; punto de vista, aspecto; ***acute angle,*** ángulo agudo; ***angle-brace,*** cuadral, riostra; ***angle-bracket,*** ménsula; ***angle-rafter,*** alfarda; ***obtuse angle,*** ángulo obtuso; ***right angle,*** ángulo recto; ***to be at right angles to,*** hacer ángulo recto con; ***visual angle,*** ángulo óptico. — *v.i.* pescar con caña.
angled [æŋgld], *a.* de ángulo(s); ***many-angled,*** a polígono; ***right-angled,*** rectangular; ***three angled,*** triangular.
angler [ˈæŋglə], *s.* pescador de caña.
Angles [æŋglz], *s.pl.* (*hist.*) anglos, *m.pl.*
Anglican [ˈæŋglikən], *a.*, *s.* anglicano.
Anglicanism [ˈæŋglikənizəm], *s.* anglicanismo.
anglicism [ˈæŋglisizəm], *s.* (*gram.*) anglicismo.
anglicize [ˈæŋglisaiz], *v.t.* dar carácter inglés a.
angling [ˈæŋgliŋ], *s.* pesca con caña, pesca de caña.
Anglo-American [ˈæŋglou-əˈmerikən], *a.*, *s.* anglo-americano.
Anglo-Indian [ˈæŋglou-ˈindjən], *a.*, *s.* angloindio.
anglomania [æŋgloˈmeiniə], *s.* anglomanía.
anglomaniac [æŋgloˈmeiniæk], *s.* anglómano.
Anglo-Norman [ˈæŋglou-ˈnɔ:mən], *a.*, *s.* anglo-normando.
anglophile [ˈæŋglofail], *a.*, *s.* anglófilo,
anglophobe [ˈæŋglofoub], *a.*, *s.* anglófobo.
anglophobia [æŋgloˈfoubiə], *s.* anglofobia.
Anglo-Saxon [ˈæŋglouˈ-sæksən], *a.*, *s.* anglosajón.
Angoulême [ɑ̃guˈlɛ:m]. Angulema.
angry [ˈæŋgri], *a.* enfadado, airado, irritado; inflamado, enconado; ***angry wound,*** herida enconada; ***angry young man,*** joven airado; ***to be very angry,*** estar muy enfadado, estar furioso *o* colérico; ***to get angry,*** enfadarse, airarse, irritarse; ***to make angry,*** exasperar.
anguiliform [æŋˈgwilifɔ:m], *a.* de forma de anguila.
anguish [ˈæŋgwiʃ], *s.* angustia, congoja.—*v.t.* angustiar, acongojar.
angular [ˈæŋgjulə], *a.* angular; anguloso; huesudo.
angularity, angularnesss [æŋgjuˈlæriti, ˈæŋgjulənis], *s.* angularidad; angulosidad.
angulate, angulated [ˈæŋgjuleit, -id], *a.* (*bot.*) angular.
anhydride [ænˈhaidraid], *s.* anhídrido.
anhydrite [ænˈhaidrait], *s.* anhidrita.
anhydrous [ænˈhaidrəs], *a.* anhidro.
anight [əˈnait], *adv.* de noche, por la noche, por las noches.
anil [ˈænil], *s.* (*bot.*) añil.
anile [ˈænail], *a.* senil.
aniline [ˈænilain], *s.* anilina.
anility [əˈniliti], *s.* senilidad.
animadversion [ænimædˈvə:ʃən], *s.* animadversión; censura, reproche, reprensión.
animadvert [ænimædˈvə:t], *v.t.* advertir, observar; censurar, reprochar.
animal [ˈæniməl], *a.*, *s.* animal.
animalcular [æniˈmælkjulə], *a.* animalcular.
animalcule [æniˈmælkju:l], *s.* animálculo.
animalism [ˈænimәlizәm], *s.* animalismo.
animalist [ˈænimәlist], *s.* animalista, *m.f.*
animality [æniˈmæliti], *s.* animalidad.
animalization [ænimәlaiˈzeiʃәn], *s.* animalización.
animalize [ˈænimәlaiz], *v.t.* animalizar.
animate [ˈænimit], *a.* animado, viviente.—[ˈænimeit], *v.t.* animar, alentar.
animated [ˈænimeitid], *a.* animadó, vigoroso, vivo; ***animated cartoon,*** dibujo animado.
animating [ˈænimeitiŋ], *a.* vivificante, que anima, animador.
animation [æniˈmeiʃən], *s.* animación, viveza.
animator [ˈænimeitə], *s.* animador, alentador.
anime [ˈænimi], *s.* anime, goma del curbaril (*árbol de Cayena*); goma copal.
animism [ˈænimizəm], *s.* animismo.
animist [ˈænimist], *s.* animista, *m.f.*
animosity [æniˈmɔsiti], *s.* animosidad, antipatía, hostilidad, rencor.
animus [ˈæniməs], *s.* ánimo, designio, intención.
anise [ˈænis], *s.* (*bot.*) anís.
aniseed [ˈænisi:d], *s.* simiente de anís.
anisette [æniˈset], *s.* anisete, licor de anís.
anisometric [ænisoˈmetrik], *a.* que no es isómero; de proporciones distintas.
Anjou [ɑ̃ˈʒu]. Anjeo.
anker [ˈæŋkə], *s.* medida de líquidos de cerca de 41 litros.
ankle [æŋkl], *s.* tobillo.
ankle-bone [ˈæŋkl-boun], *s.* astrágalo, hueso del tobillo.
anklet [ˈæŋklit], *s.* brazalete para el tobillo.
anna [ˈænə], *s.* moneda de la India equivalente a $\frac{1}{16}$ de rupia.
annalist [ˈænəlist], *s.* analista, *m.f.*, cronista, *m.f.*
annals [ˈænəlz], *s.pl.* anales, *m.pl.*, crónica; (*igl.*) misas celebradas durante el año.
annates [ˈæneits], *s.* anata.
Ann(e) [æn]. Ana.
anneal [əˈni:l], *v.t.* templar, atemperar, recocer (*metales* o *cristal*).
annelid [ˈænəlid], *a.*, *s.* anillado.
annex [ˈæneks], *s.* anexo, dependencia; aditamento, apéndice. — [æˈneks], *v.t.* anexar, anexionar; unir, agregar; juntar, adjuntar.
annexary [əˈneksəri], *s.* adición.
annexation [ænekˈseiʃən], *s.* anexión.
annihilable [əˈnaiələbl], *a.* aniquilable, destructible.
annihilate [əˈnaiəleit], *v.t.* aniquilar, anonadar.
annihilation [ənaiəˈleiʃən], *s.* aniquilación, aniquilamiento, anulación, anonadación.
anniversary [æniˈvə:səri], *a.* aniversario, anual.—*s.* aniversario, cumpleaños.
annotate [ˈænoteit], *v.t.* anotar, glosar. — *v.i.* anotar, comentar.
annotation [ænoˈteiʃən], *s.* anotación, apunte, acotación.
annotationist, annotator [ænoˈteiʃənist, ˈænoteitə], *s.* anotador, comentador.
announce [əˈnauns], *v.t.* anunciar, proclamar, declarar, participar.
announcement [əˈnaunsmənt], *s.* aviso, anuncio; declaración.
announcer [əˈnaunsə], *s.* anunciador, avisador; (*rad.*) locutor, locutora.

annoy [ə'nɔi], *v.t.* molestar, incomodar, fastidiar, fatigar, aburrir, cargar.
annoyance [ə'nɔiəns], *s.* molestia, incomodidad, disgusto, fastidio.
annoyer [ə'nɔiə], *s.* molestador, chinchorrero.
annoying [ə'nɔiiŋ], *a.* fastidioso, molesto.
annual ['ænjuəl], *a.* anual.—*s.* (*bot.*) planta anual; publicación anual.
annuitant [ə'njuitənt], *s.* rentista, *m.f.*, censualista, *m.f.*
annuity [ə'njuiti], *s.* anualidad; renta vitalicia; ***deferred annuity,*** renta diferida; ***life annuity,*** renta vitalicia; ***to settle an annuity on,*** señalar una renta a; ***terminable annuity,*** renta reembolsable.
annul [ə'nʌl], *v.t.* anular, invalidar; revocar.
annular ['ænjulə], *a.* anular.
annulate(d) ['ænjuleit(id)], *a.* anillado.
annulet ['ænjulit], *s.* anillejo, sortijilla; (*arq.*) anillo.
annulment [ə'nʌlmənt], *s.* anulación; revocación.
annulose ['ænjulouz], *a.* anuloso.
annunciate [ə'nʌnsieit], *v.t.* anunciar.
annunciation [ənʌnsi'eiʃən], *s.* anunciación.
annunciator [ə'nʌnsieitə], *s.* anunciador; indicador.
anode ['ænoud], *s.* ánodo.
anodyne ['ænodain], *a.* anodino.
anoint [ə'nɔint], *v.t.* ungir; untar.
anointed [ə'nɔintid], *a.* ungido.
anointing, anointment [ə'nɔintiŋ, -mənt], *s.* ungimiento; untamiento.
anomalistic [ənɔmə'listik], *a.* anomalístico.
anomalous [ə'nɔmələs], *a.* anómalo.
anomaly [ə'nɔməli], *s.* anomalía, irregularidad.
anon (1) [ə'nɔn] [ANONYMOUS].
anon (2) [ə'nɔn], *adv.* ya, luego; ***ever and anon,*** una y otra vez.
anonym ['ænɔnim], *s.* anónimo.
anonymity [ænɔ'nimiti], *s.* anonimato, anónimo; ***to preserve one's anonymity,*** guardar *o* conservar el anónimo.
anonymous [ə'nɔniməs], *a.* anónimo.
anorak ['ænəræk], *s.* anorak.
anorexia [æno'reksiə], *s.* (*med.*) anorexia.
anosmia [ə'nɔzmiə], *s.* (*med.*) anosmia.
another [ə'nʌðə], *a., pron.* otro; ***one another,*** uno a otro, el uno al otro, (los) unos a (los) otros.
anserine ['ænsərain], *a.* anserino; tonto, necio.
answer ['ɑ:nsə], *s.* contestación, respuesta; solución; refutación; ***this answers our purpose,*** esto nos resuelve el problema; ***to answer the door,*** abrir (la puerta); ***to answer the 'phone,*** coger el teléfono; ***to answer for,*** responder de; ***to answer to the name of,*** atender por; ***don't answer back!*** ¡no contestes!—*v.t., v.i.* contestar (a), responder (a).—*v.t.* solucionar, resolver.
answerable ['ɑ:nsərəbl], *a.* responsable; correspondiente, conforme; discutible, refutable.
answerableness ['ɑ:nsərəblnis], *s.* responsabilidad; correspondencia, correlación; calidad de discutible *o* refutable.
answerer ['ɑ:nsərə], *s.* fiador, caucionero, respondedor.
answering ['ɑ:nsəriŋ], *a* correspondiente, proporcionado.
answerless ['ɑ:nsəlis], *a.* que no tiene solución.
ant [ænt], *s.* hormiga.
anta ['æntə], *s.* (*zool.*) danta, tapir.
antacid [ænt'æsid], *a.* antiácido, álcali.—*s.* remedio para la acidez del estómago.
antagonism [æn'tægənizəm], *s.* antagonismo.
antagonist [æn'tægənist], *s.* antagonista, *m.f.*, adversario.
antagonistic [æntægə'nistik], *a.* contrario, antagónico.
antagonize [æn'tægənaiz], *v.t.* provocar la enemistad de, enemistarse con.
antalgic [æn'tældʒik], *a.* antálgico, anodino, calmante.
antaphrodisiac [æntæfrə'diziæk], *a., s.* antiafrodisíaco.
antapoplectic [æntæpə'plektik], *a.* (*med.*) anti-apopléctico.
Antarctic [ænt'ɑ:ktik], *a.* antártico; ***Antarctic Circle,*** el Círculo Polar Antártico.
Antarctica [ænt'ɑ:ktikə]. la Antártica.
antarthritic [æntɑ:'θritik], *a.* (*med.*) antiartrítico.
antasthmatic [æntæs(θ)'mætik], *a.* (*med.*) antiasmático.
ant-bear ['ænt-bɛə], *s.* (*zool.*) tamandoá.
ant-eater ['ænt-i:tə], *s.* (*zool.*) oso hormiguero; tamandoá.
antecede [ænti'si:d], *v.t.* anteceder, preceder (a).
antecedence [ænti'si:dəns], *s.* precedencia, antecedencia.
antecedent [ænti'si:dənt], *a., s.* antecedente, precedente.
antechamber ['æntitʃeimbə], *s.* antecámara, antesala.
antedate ['ænti'deit], *s.* antedata; antelación.—*v.t.* antedatar; ser anterior a.
antediluvian [æntidi'lju:viən], *a., s.* antediluviano.
ant-egg ['ænt-eg], *s.* huevo de hormiga.
antelope ['æntiloup], *s.* (*zool.*) antílope.
antemeridiem [æntimə'ridiem], *adv.* (*abrev.* **a.m.** ['ei'em]) de la mañana, antes del mediodía.
antemetic [ænti'metik], *a., s.* antiemético.
antemundane [ænti'mʌndein], *a.* anterior a la creación del mundo.
antenatal [ænti'neitəl], *a.* prenatal.
antenna [æn'tenə], *s.* antena.
antenuptial [ænti'nʌpʃəl], *a.* antenupcial.
antepenult [æntipi'nʌlt], *s.* (*gram.*) antepenúltima.
antepenultimate [æntipi'nʌltimit], *a., s.* ántepenúltimo.
antepileptic [æntepi'leptik], *a.* (*med.*) antiepiléptico.
anterior [æn'tiəriə], *a.* anterior.
anteriority [æntiəri'ɔriti], *s.* anterioridad.
anteroom ['æntiru:m], *s.* antesala, vestíbulo.
anthelmintic [ænθel'mintik], *a.* (*med.*) antielmíntico.
anthem ['ænθəm], *s.* antífona; ***national anthem,*** himno nacional.
anther ['ænθə], *s.* (*bot.*) antera.
antheral ['ænθərəl], *a.* anteral, referente a anteras.
antheriferous [ænθər'ifərəs], *a.* anterífero.
ant-hill ['ænt-hil], *s.* hormiguero.
anthological [ænθə'lɔdʒikəl], *a.* antológico.
anthologist [æn'θɔlədʒist], *s.* antólogo.
anthology [æn'θɔlədʒi], *s.* antología.
anthophagous [æn'θɔfəgəs], *a.* antófago.
Anthony ['æntəni]. Antonio; ***Saint Anthony's fire,*** fuego de San Antón; (*med.*) erisipela.
Anthozoa [ænθə'zouə], *s.pl.* antozoarios, *m.pl.*
anthracite ['ænθrəsait], *s.* antracita.
anthrax ['ænθræks], *s.* ántrax.
anthropoid ['ænθrəpɔid], *a., s.* antropoide, antropoideo.
anthropography [ænθrə'pɔgrəfi], *s.* antropografía.
anthropolite [æn'θrɔpəlait], *s.* antropolito.
anthropological [ænθrəpə'lɔdʒikəl], *a.* antropológico.
anthropology [ænθrə'pɔlədʒi], *s.* antropología.
anthropometer [ænθrə'pɔmitə], *s.* antropómetro.
anthropometrical [ænθrəpo'metrikəl], *a.* antropométrico.
anthropometry [ænθrə'pɔmitri], *s.* antropometría.

anthropomorphism [ænθrəpo'mɔ:fizəm], *s.* antropomorfismo.
anthropomorphist [ænθrəpo'mɔ:fist], *s.* antropomorfista, *m.f.*
anthropomorphous [ænθrəpo'mɔ:fəs], *a.* antropomorfo.
Anthropophagi [ænθrə'pɔfədʒai], *s.pl.* antropófagos, *m.pl.*
anthropophagous [ænθrə'pɔfəgəs], *a.* antropófago.
anthroposophy [ænθrə'pɔsəfi], *s.* antroposofía.
anthropotomy [ænθrə'pɔtəmi], *s.* antropotomía.
anti ['ænti], *prefijo.* anti.
anti-aircraft [ænti-'ɛəkrɑ:ft], *a.* antiaéreo.
antiarthritic [æntiɑ:θ'ritik], *a.* antiartrítico.
anti-bacterial [ænti-bæk'tiəriəl], *a.* antibactérico.
antibilious [ænti'biliəs], *a.* antibilioso.
antibiotic [æntibai'ɔtik], *a.*, *s.* antibiótico.
antibrachial [ænti'breikiəl], *a.* anti-braquial.
antic ['æntik], *s.* (*ú. más. en pl.*) cabriola, gracia; locura, travesura, bufonada; ***he's up to his old antics,*** ha vuelto a las andadas.
anticatarrhal [æntikə'tɑ:rəl], *a.* anticatarral.
Antichrist ['æntikraist], *s.* Anticristo.
antichristian [ænti'kristjən], *a.*, *s.* anticristiano.
anticipate [æn'tisipeit], *v.t.* esperar(se), contar con, prever; temerse (algo desagradable); prometerse (algo agradable); anticiparse a, adelantarse a, prevenir; anticipar, hacer de antemano; ***I did not anticipate so much trouble,*** no contaba con tantas dificultades.
anticipation [æntisi'peiʃən], *s.* anticipación; expectación, esperanza; previsión.
anticipative [æn'tisipətiv], *a.* anticipativo.
anticipator [æn'tisipeitə], *a.*, *s.* anticipador.
anticipatory [æn'tisipeitəri], *a.* anticipado, que anticipa.
anticlerical [ænti'klerikəl], *a.* anticlerical.
anticlimax [ænti'klaimæks], *s.* anticlímax; (*fam.*) petardo.
anticlinal [ænti'klainəl], *a.* (*geol.*) anticlinal.
anticonstitutional [æntikɔnsti'tju:ʃənəl], *a.* anticonstitucional.
anti-contagious [ænti-kən'teidʒəs], *a.* anticontagioso.
anti-convulsive [ænti-kən'vʌlsiv], *a.* anticonvulsivo.
anticyclone [ænti'saikloun], *s.* anticiclón.
antidote ['æntidout], *s.* antídoto; contraveneno.
antifebrile [ænti'febrail], *a.*, *s.* antifebril.
anti-freeze [ænti-'fri:z], *s.* anticongelante.
anti-galactic [ænti-gə'læktik], *a.* antigaláctico.
anti-glare [ænti-'glɛə], *a.* antideslumbrante.
antihistamine [ænti'histəmi:n], *a.*, *s.* antihistamínico.
antihysteric [æntihis'terik], *a.* antihistérico.
anti-inflationary [ænti-in'fleiʃənəri], *a.* antiinflacionista.
antiliberal [ænti'libərəl], *a.*, *s.* antiliberal.
Antilles [æn'tili:z], **the.** las Antillas.
antilog ['æntilɔg] [ANTILOGARITHM].
antilogarithm [ænti'lɔgeriθəm], *s.* (*mat.*) antilogaritmo.
antimacassar [æntimə'kæsə], *s.* antimacasar.
antimagnetic [æntimæg'netik], *a.* (*elec.*, *fís.*) antimagnético.
antimonarchist [ænti'mɔnəkist], *a.*, *s.* antimonárquico.
antimonial [ænti'mouniəl], *a.* antimonial. — *s.* preparación antimonial.
antimonic [ænti'mɔnik], *a.* antimónico.
antimony ['æntiməni], *s.* (*min.*) antimonio.
antinomian [ænti'noumiən], *a.*, *s.* antinomiano.
antinomianism [ænti'noumiənizəm], *s.* antinomia.
antinomy [æn'tinəmi], *s.* antinomia, paradoja.
Antioch ['æntiɔk]. Antioquía.

antipapal, antipapistical [ænti'peipəl,-pə'pistikəl], *a.* antipapal.
antipathetic [æntipə'θetik], *a.* antagónico, contrario, opuesto; antipático.
antipathy [æn'tipəθi], *s.* antipatía, aversión.
antipatriotic [æntipætri'ɔtik], *a.* antipatriótico.
antiperistaltic [æntiperi'stæltik], *a.* (*med.*) antiperistáltico.
antiphlogistic [æntiflə'dʒistik], *a.*, *s.* antiflogístico.
antiphon ['æntifən], *s.* antífona.
antiphonal, antiphonical [æn'tifənəl, ænti'fɔnikəl], *a.* antifonal.
antiphonary [æn'tifənəri], *s.* antifonal, antifonario.
antiphony [æn'tifəni], *s.* antífona.
antiphrasis [æn'tifrəsis], *s.* antífrasis, *f.*
antipodal [æn'tipədəl], *a.* antipodal.
antipodes [æn'tipədi:z], *s.pl.* antípodas, *f.pl.*; (*fig.*) opuesto, contrario.
antipope ['æntipoup], *s.* antipapa, *m.*
antipyretic [æntipai'retik], *a.* (*med.*) antipirético, febrífugo.
antiquarian [ænti'kwɛəriən], *a.*, *s.* anticuario.
antiquarianism [ænti'kwɛəriənizəm], *s.* afición a las antigüedades.
antiquary ['æntikwəri], *s.* anticuario.
antiquate ['æntikweit], *v.t.* anticuar.
antiquated ['æntikweitid], *a.* anticuado, desusado, pasado de moda.
antiquatedness ['æntikweitidnis], *s.* (lo) anticuado.
antique [æn'ti:k], *a.* antiguo. — *s.* antigüedad; antigualla; ***after the antique,*** a la antigua.
antiqueness [æn'ti:knis], *s.* antigüedad, vetustez.
antiquity [æn'tikwiti], *s.* antigüedad; vetustez, vejez.
antirepublican [æntiri'pʌblikən], *a.*, *s.* antirrepublicano.
antirevolutionary [æntirevə'lu:ʃənəri], *a.*, *s.* antirrevolucionario.
antirheumatic [æntiru:'mætik], *a.* antirreumático.
antirrhinum [ænti'rainəm], *s.* (*bot.*) antirrino.
antiscorbutic [æntiskɔ:'bu:tik], *a.* antiescorbútico, depurativo.
antisemite [ænti'si:mait], *s.* antisemita, *m.f.*
antisemitic [æntisə'mitik], *a.* antisemita.
antisemitism [ænti'semitizəm], *s.* antisemitismo.
antisepsis [ænti'sepsis], *s.* (*med.*) antisepsia.
antiseptic [ænti'septik], *a.* antiséptico, antipútrido, desinfectante.
antislavery [ænti'sleivəri], *s.* antiesclavismo.
antisocial [ænti'souʃəl], *a.* antisocial.
antispasmodic [æntispæz'mɔdik], *a.*, *s.* antiespasmódico.
antisplenetic [æntisplə'netik], *a.* (*med.*) antiesplenético.
antistrophe [æn'tistrəfi], *s.* antistrofa, antistrofe, *f.*
anti-submarine [ænti-'sʌbməri:n], *a.* antisubmarino; ***anti-submarine warfare,*** guerra antisubmarina.
antisyphilitic [æntisifi'litik], *a.*, *s.* antisifilítico.
antithesis [æn'tiθisis], *s.* (*filos.*) antítesis, *f. inv.*
antithetical [ænti'θetikəl], *a.* antitético.
antitoxin [ænti'tɔksin], *s.* antitoxina.
antitrinitarian [æntitrini'təriən], *s.* antitrinitario.
antitype ['æntitaip], *s.* antitipo, prototipo.
antitypical [ænti'tipikəl], *a.* antitípico.
anti-venereal [ænti-vi'niəriəl], *a.*, *s.* antivenéreo.
anti-vivisection [ænti-vivi'sekʃən], *s.* antivivisección.
anti-war [ænti-wɔ:], *a.* antiguerra.
antlered ['æntləd], *a.* con cornamenta.
antlers ['æntləz], *s.pl.* cornamenta.
antonomasia [æntɔnə'meiziə], *s.* antonomasia.

antonomastically [æntɔnə'mæstikəli], *adv.* antonomásticamente, por antonomasia.
antonym ['æntənim], *s.* antónimo.
antrum ['æntrəm], *s.* antro.
Antwerp ['æntwə:p]. Amberes.
anus ['einəs], *s.* (*anat.*) ano.
anvil ['ænvil], *s.* yunque; bigornia; ***hand-anvil,*** bigorneta; ***stock of an anvil,*** cepo de yunque.
anxiety [æŋ'zaiəti], *s.* angustia; inquietud, desasosiego; afán, (gran) interés; ***anxiety to please,*** afán de agradar.
anxious ['æŋkʃəs], *a.* angustioso; inquieto, desasosegado; deseoso, con afán (de); ***he is very anxious to please,*** tiene mucho interés en agradar.
anxiousness ['æŋkʃəsnis] [ANXIETY].
any ['eni], *a. pron.* cualquier, cualquiera; algún, alguno, alguna; todo; ***any time,*** en cualquier momento, cuando usted quiera; (*fam.*) de nada, encantado; ***not any longer, not any more,*** ya no.
anybody, anyone ['enibɔdi, -wʌn], *pron.* cualquiera, cualquier persona, quienquiera; alguien, alguna persona; ***not anybody,*** nadie.
anyhow ['enihau], *adv.* de todos modos, de todas maneras, de todas formas; ***any (old) how,*** de cualquier manera, a lo loco.
anything ['eniθiŋ], *pron.* cualquier cosa; algo, alguna cosa; ***not anything,*** nada.
anyway ['eniwei] [ANYHOW].
anywhere ['eniwɛə], *adv.* en *o* a cualquier sitio, donde sea; en *o* a todas partes; ***not anywhere,*** en *o* a ninguna parte, ningún lado.
aorist ['eiərist], *s.* (*gram.*) aoristo.
aorta [ei'ɔ:tə], *s.* (*anat.*) aorta.
aortal, aortic [ei'ɔ:təl, -ik], *a.* aórtico.
apace [ə'peis], *adv.* rápidamente, con rapidez *o* celeridad.
apanage ['æpənidʒ], *s.* infantazgo, dependencia.
apart [ə'pɑ:t], *adv.* aparte; separados; a distancia; ***apart from,*** aparte (de); ***to come*** o ***fall apart,*** deshacerse, descuajaringarse; ***to pull*** o ***tear apart,*** deshacer, destrozar; romper en dos; ***to set apart,*** dejar *o* poner a un lado; ***to take apart,*** desmontar, desarmar; ***I can't tell them apart,*** separados no los distingo.
apartheid [ə'pɑ:theit], *s.* (*pol., Africa del Sur*) segregación de (las) razas, aparteid.
apartment [ə'pɑ:tmənt], *s.* habitación, aposento; piso, apartamento.
apathetic [æpə'θetik], *a.* apático.
apathy ['æpəθi], *s.* apatía.
apatite ['æpətait], *s.* (*min.*) apatita.
ape [eip], *s.* mono, simio. — *v.t.* imitar, remedar.
apeak, apeek [ə'pi:k], *adv.* verticalmente; (*mar.*) a pique.
Apennines ['æpinainz], **the.** los Apeninos.
apepsia, apepsy [ə'pepsiə, -i], *s.* (*med.*) apepsia.
aper ['eipə], *s.* imitador.
aperitive [ə'peritiv], *a., s.* laxante; aperitivo.
aperture ['æpətʃe], *s.* abertura, orificio.
apery ['eipəri], *s.* remedo; monería; jaula de monos.
apetalous [ei'petələs], *a.* (*bot.*) apétalo.
apex ['eipeks], *s.* (*pl.* **apexes** ['eipeksiz] o **apices** ['æpisi:z]) ápice, cima, cúspide, *f.*, punta.
aphæresis [ə'fiərəsis], *s.* (*gram.*) aféresis, *f.*
aphasia [ə'feiziə], *s.* (*med.*) afasia.
aphelion [ə'fi:liən], *s.* (*astron.*) afelio.
aphesis ['æfəsis], *s.* (*gram.*) aféresis, *f.*
aphis ['eifis], *s.* áfido, pulgón.
aphonia, aphony [ə'founiə, 'æfəni], *s.* afonía.
aphonic [æ'fɔnik], *a.* afónico, áfono; muda (letra).
aphorism ['æfərizəm], *s.* aforismo.
aphoristic [æfə'ristik], *a.* aforístico, sentencioso.
aphrodisiac [æfrou'diziæk], *a., s.* afrodisíaco.
aphthous ['æfθəs], *a.* (*med.*) aftoso.
aphyllous [ə'filəs], *a.* (*bot.*) afilo.
apiary ['eipiəri], *s.* colmenar, abejar.
apical ['æpikəl], *a.* apical.
apiculture ['eipikʌltʃə], *s.* apicultura.
apiece [ə'pi:s], *adv.* cada uno, por cabeza, por persona, por pieza.
apish ['eipiʃ], *a.* simiesco, monesco; remedador; necio.
apishness ['eipiʃnis], *s.* monería, monada; remedo; imitación servil.
apium ['eipiəm], *s.* (*bot.*) apio.
aplanatic [æplə'nætik], *a.* (*ópt.*) aplanático.
aplenty [ə'plenti], *adv.* en abundancia, a manta.
aplomb [ə'plɔ̃], *s.* aplomo; seguridad.
apocalypse [ə'pɔkəlips], *s.* apocalipsis, *m. inv.*
apocalyptic(al) [əpɔkə'liptik(əl)], *a.* apocalíptico.
apocopate [ə'pɔkəpeit], *v.t.* (*gram.*) apocopar.
apocope [ə'pɔkəpi], *s.* apócope, *f.*
Apocrypha [ə'pɔkrifə], *s.pl.* libros apócrifos, *m.pl.*
apocryphal [ə'pɔkrifəl], *a.* apócrifo.
apodal ['æpɔdəl], *a.* ápodo.
apodictic [æpə'diktik], *a.* apodíctico.
apodosis [ə'pɔdəsis], *s.* (*gram.*) apódosis, *f. inv.*
apodous ['æpədəs] [APODAL].
apogee ['æpədʒi:], *s.* (*astron.*) apogeo.
apograph ['æpougrɑ:f], *s.* apógrafo.
apolaustic [æpə'lɔ:stik], *a.* entregado a los placeres; abandonado a los vicios.
apologetic(al) [əpɔlə'dʒetik(əl)], *a.* apologético; lleno de excusas, con ánimo de pedir perdón, que tiene ademán de pedir perdón.
apologetics [əpɔlə'dʒetiks], *s.* apologética.
apologist [ə'pɔlədʒist], *s.* apologista, *m.f.*
apologize [ə'pɔlədʒaiz], *v.i.* apologizar; excusarse, disculparse; ***apologize for,*** disculparse de.
apologue ['æpəlɔg], *s.* apólogo, fábula.
apology [ə'pɔlədʒi], *s.* apología; excusa, disculpa; (*fam.*) ***an apology for a car,*** un cochecillo de mala muerte.
aponeurotic [æpənju:'rɔtik], *a.* (*med.*) aponeurótico.
apophasis [ə'pɔfəsis], *s.* (*ret.*) apófasis, *f.*
apophlegmatic [æpofleg'mætik], *a.* (*med.*) apoflemático.
apophthegm ['æpəθem], *s.* apotegma, *m.*
apophysis [ə'pɔfisis], *s.* (*anat.*) apófisis, *f. inv.*
apoplectic [æpə'plektik], *a.* apoplético.
apoplexy ['æpəpleksi], *s.* (*med.*) apoplejía.
apostasis [ə'pɔstəsis], *s.* (*med.*) apóstasis, *f. inv.*
apostasy [ə'pɔstəsi], *s.* apostasía.
apostate [ə'pɔsteit], *a.* falso, pérfido. — *s.* apóstata, *m.f.*
apostatize [ə'pɔstətaiz], *v.i.* apostatar, renegar.
apostemate [ə'pɔstəmeit], *v.i.* (*med.*) apostemar.
apostle [ə'pɔsl], *s.* apóstol; ***the Apostles' Creed,*** el Símbolo de los Apóstoles.
apostleship, apostolate [ə'pɔslʃip, -təlit], *s.* apostolado.
apostolic [æpəs'tɔlik], *a.* apostólico.
apostrophe (1) [ə'pɔstrəfi], *s.* (*gram.*) apóstrofo.
apostrophe (2) [ə'pɔstrəfi], *s.* apóstrofe, *m.f.*
apostrophize [ə'pɔstrəfaiz], *v.t.* apostrofar.
apothecary [ə'pɔθəkəri], *s.* boticario, farmacéutico; ***apothecary's shop,*** botica, farmacia.
apothegm [APOPHTHEGM].
apotheosis [əpɔθi'ousis], *s.* apoteosis, *f.*
apotheosize [ə'pɔθiousaiz], *v.t.* deificar, divinizar.
apozem ['æpɔzəm], *s.* pócima.
Appalachians [æpə'leiʃiənz], **the.** los (Montes) Apalaches.
appal [ə'pɔ:l], *v.t.* espantar, aterrar; ***to be appalled,*** quedar espantado *o* aterrado.
appalling [ə'pɔ:liŋ], *a.* espantoso, aterrador.
appanage [APANAGE].

apparatus [æpə'reitəs], *s.* aparato(s); instrumento(s), instrumental; útiles, *m.pl.*, herramientas, *f.pl.*, equipo.
apparel [ə'pærəl], *s.* ropa, vestido(s), traje(s), atuendo, atavío(s); (*mar.*) aparejo. — *v.t.* vestir, ataviar; (*mar.*) aparejar.
apparent [ə'pærənt], *a.* aparente; teórico; que se da oficialmente; evidente, manifiesto; ***heir apparent,*** heredero forzoso.
apparently [ə'pærəntli], *adv.* aparentemente; al parecer, por lo visto, a lo que parece.
apparition [æpə'riʃən], *s.* aparición.
apparitor [ə'pæritə], *s.* portero, bedel.
appeach [ə'pi:tʃ], *v.t.* acusar, denunciar.
appeal [ə'pi:l], *s.* apelación, recurso; reclamación; súplica, instancia; llamamiento; atracción, interés. — *v.i.* apelar; reclamar; ***appeal for,*** suplicar, pedir (con súplicas); (*fig.*) ***appeal to,*** atraer, gustar, apetecer.
appealable [ə'pi:ləbl], *a.* apelable.
appealer [ə'pi:lə], *s.* apelante.
appealing [ə'pi:liŋ], *a.* suplicante; atrayente, atractivo.
appear [ə'piə], *v.i.* aparecer; aparecerse; mostrarse, asomar; salir; comparecer, personarse; parecer.
appearance [ə'piərəns], *s.* aparición; presencia; (*for.*) comparecencia; apariencia; aspecto, traza, porte, ver; viso, vislumbre; ***appearances are deceptive,*** las apariencias engañan; ***first appearance,*** estreno; ***for appearances' sake,*** por el bien parecer; ***to all appearances,*** a lo que parece, según las apariencias; ***to keep up appearances,*** guardar las apariencias.
appearer [ə'piərə], *s.* (*for.*) compareciente.
appearing [ə'piəriŋ], *s.* aparición; (*for.*) comparecencia.
appeasable [ə'pi:zəbl], *a.* aplacable, mitigable.
appeasableness [ə'pi:zəblnis], *s.* aplacabilidad, aplacamiento.
appease [ə'pi:z], *v.t.* aplacar, calmar, mitigar; apaciguar, pacificar; aquietar, sosegar; desenfadar, desenojar.
appeasement [ə'pi:zmənt], *s.* apaciguamiento; aquietamiento, sosiego; alivio; desenojo.
appeaser [ə'pi:zə], *s.* aplacador, apaciguador, pacificador.
appeasing [ə'pi:ziŋ], *a.* apaciguador, aplacador; sosegador.
appellant [ə'pelənt], *s.* apelante, demandante.
appellate [ə'pelit], *a.* de apelación, a que se puede recurrir.
appellation [æpə'leiʃən], *s.* denominación, título, nombre; apelativo, apelación.
appellative [ə'pelətiv], *a.* apelativo; común. — *s.* apelativo; (*fam.*) apellido.
appellee [æpe'li:], *s.* (*for.*) demandado; apelado, acusado.
append [ə'pend], *v.t.* colgar, atar; añadir; anexar; poner, fijar, ligar.
appendage [ə'pendidʒ], *s.* dependencia, accesorio, pertenencia; heredamiento, dote; (*bot.*, *zool.*) apéndice.
appendant [ə'pendənt], *a.* pendiente, colgante; dependiente, anexo; pegado, unido; accesorio. — *s.* adjunto, subordinado; cosa adjunta *o* dependiente.
appendicitis [əpendi'saitis], *s.* apendicitis, *f. inv.*
appendicle [ə'pendikəl], *s.* (*bot.*) apendículo.
appendix [ə'pendiks], *s.* (*pl.* **appendixes** [ə'pendiksiz] o **appendices** [ə'pendisi:z]), apéndice.
apperception [æpə'sepʃən], *s.* (*filos.*) apercepción.
appertain [æpə'tein], *v.i.* pertenecer, competer, atañer.
appetence, appetency ['æpətəns, -i], *s.* apetencia; deseo, avidez, *f.*; inclinación, afinidad, atracción.
appetite ['æpitait], *s.* apetito; apetencia.
appetizer ['æpitaizə], *s.* aperitivo; ***to take an appetizer,*** tomar el aperitivo.
appetizing ['æpitaiziŋ], *a.* apetitoso.
Appian Way ['æpiən 'wei]. Vía Apia.
applaud [ə'plɔ:d], *v.t.* aplaudir; alabar, celebrar. — *v.i.* aplaudir.
applause [ə'plɔ:z], *s.* aplauso(s); alabanza, aprobación; ***round of applause,*** salva de aplausos.
apple [æpl], *s.* manzana; ***apple of discord,*** manzana de la discordia; ***apple of one's eye,*** niña de los ojos; ***to upset the apple-cart,*** estropear las cosas, alterar el plan; ***apple-jack,*** aguardiente de manzana; ***apple orchard,*** manzanal; ***apple-pie,*** empanada de manzana; ***in apple-pie order,*** en perfecto orden; ***apple tart,*** tarteleta de manzana; ***apple tree,*** manzano; ***cider-apple,*** manzana para sidra; ***crab-apple,*** manzana silvestre; ***oak-apple,*** agalla de roble.
appliance [ə'plaiəns], *s.* instrumento, aparato, dispositivo.
applicability, applicableness [æplikə'biliti, 'æplikəblnis], *s.* aplicabilidad; (lo) aplicable; (lo) conveniente.
applicable ['æplikəbl], *a.* aplicable; pertinente.
applicant ['æplikənt], *s.* solicitante, aspirante.
application [æpli'keiʃən], *s.* aplicación; solicitud, petición; ***to make application to,*** dirigirse a; ***written application,*** solicitud por escrito.
apply [ə'plai], *v.t.* aplicar; adaptar; introducir; dar; pegar. — *v.i.* poder aplicarse, ser aplicable; presentarse; ***apply for,*** solicitar, pedir; ***it doesn't apply in this case,*** en este caso no vale *o* no rige. — **apply o.s.** *v.r.* — **to,** aplicarse a, dedicarse a, ocuparse de.
appoint [ə'pɔint], *v.t.* designar, nombrar; prescribir, fijar, señalar, indicar; amueblar, ataviar, equipar, enjaezar.
appointee [əpɔin'ti:], *s.* funcionario nombrado, designado.
appointment [ə'pɔintmənt], *s.* cita, hora (dada *o* convenida); nombramiento, designación; empleo, cargo, destino; ***to break an appointment,*** faltar a una cita; (*pl.*) equipo, aparejo; pertrechos, *m.pl.*; adornos, *m.pl.*, mobiliario.
apportion [ə'pɔ:ʃən], *v.t.* repartir; prorratear.
apportionment [ə'pɔ:ʃənmənt], *s.* distribución, reparto; rateo, prorrateo.
apposite ['æpəzait], *a.* apropiado, a propósito, conveniente, oportuno; yuxtapuesto.
appositeness ['æpəzaitnis], *s.* propiedad, conveniencia, oportunidad.
apposition [æpə'ziʃən], *s.* añadidura, adición; yuxtaposición; (*gram.*) aposición.
appositive [ə'pɔzitiv], *a.* (*gram.*) apositivo.
appraisable [ə'preizəbl], *a.* tasable, estimable, apreciable.
appraisal, appraisement [ə'preizəl, -mənt], *s.* apreciación; valorización; valuación, avalúo; tasación, estimación.
appraise [ə'preiz], *v.t.* apreciar; valuar; valorar; poner precio a, tasar; estimar, ponderar.
appraiser [ə'preizə], *s.* apreciador; evaluador, tasador, justipreciador.
appreciable [ə'pri:ʃəbl], *a.* apreciable, estimable, notable, sensible, perceptible.
appreciate [ə'pri:ʃieit], *v.t.* apreciar; agradecer; hacerse cargo de, darse cuenta de. — *v.i.* subir de precio *o* en valor.
appreciater [ə'pri:ʃieitə], *s.* apreciador, estimador; tasador, valuador.
appreciation [əpri:ʃi'eiʃən], *s.* apreciación, estimación; valuación; aprecio; agradecimiento; encarecimiento; estimativa.
appreciative [ə'pri:ʃiətiv], *a.* apreciativo.
apprehend [æpri'hend], *v.t.* aprehender; prender, asir, detener; comprender, percibir, sentir, oír; temer, recelar.
apprehender [æpri'hendə], *s.* aprehensor.
apprehensible [æpri'hensibl], *a.* comprensible, concebible.

apprehension [æpri'henʃən], *s.* aprehensión; percepción, comprensión; captura, prendimiento; temor, miedo, recelo.
apprehensive [æpri'hensiv], *a.* aprensivo; temeroso, receloso.
apprehensiveness [æpri'hensivnis], *s.* aprehensibilidad; temor, recelo.
apprentice [ə'prentis], *s.* aprendiz; mancebo de botica; novicio; ***to place as apprentice,*** poner en aprendizaje (***to,*** con). — *v.t.* poner de aprendiz.
apprenticeship [ə'prentisʃip], *s.* aprendizaje, noviciado; ***to serve one's apprenticeship,*** hacer *o* pasar el aprendizaje.
apprise [ə'praiz], *v.t.* informar, instruir, avisar, comunicar, dar parte.
approach [ə'proutʃ], *s.* acceso, avenida de acceso, entrada; proximidad; enfoque, planteamiento; (*pl.*) cercanías, alrededores; (*mil.*) aproches. — *v.t.* acercarse (a), aproximarse (a), avecinarse (a); acercar; abordar; rayar en; (*fig.*) ***not to approach,*** no poder compararse con. — *v.i.* acercarse, aproximarse, avecinarse.
approachability [ə'proutʃəbiliti], *s.* accesibilidad.
approachable [ə'proutʃəbl], *a.* accesible, abordable.
approaching [ə'proutʃiŋ], *a.* cercano, que se acerca, se acercaba.
approbation [æprə'beiʃən], *s.* aprobación, beneplácito.
approbatory ['æprəbeitəri], *a.* aprobativo, aprobatorio.
appropriable [ə'proupriəbl], *a.* apropiable.
appropriate [ə'proupriit], *a.* apropiado, adecuado. — [ə'prouprieit], *v.t.* apropiarse (de); aplicar, destinar.
appropriateness [ə'proupriitnis], *s.* conveniencia, (lo) apropiado.
appropriation [əproupri'eiʃən], *s.* apropiación.
approval [ə'pru:vəl], *s.* aprobación; ***on approval,*** a prueba.
approve [ə'pru:v], *v.t.* aprobar, dar el visto bueno (a). — *v.i.* — ***of,*** aprobar.
approved [ə'pru:vd], *a.* acreditado; aprobado; ***approved school,*** reformatorio.
approving [ə'pru:viŋ], *a.* aprobador, aprobante.
approvingly [ə'pru:viŋli], *adv.* con aprobación.
approximate [ə'prɔksimit], *a.* aproximado. — [ə'prɔksimeit], *v.t.* aproximar. — *v.i.* aproximarse.
approximately [ə'prɔksimitli], *adv.* aproximadamente.
approximation [əprɔksi'meiʃən], *s.* aproximación; cálculo aproximado.
approximative [ə'prɔksimətiv], *a.* aproximativo.
appulse [ə'pʌls], *s.* choque, encuentro.
appurtenance [ə'pə:tinəns], *s.* accesorio, pertenencia.
appurtenant [ə'pə:tinənt], *s.* accesorio, perteneciente.
apricot ['eiprikɔt], *s.* albaricoque.
April ['eipril], *s.* abril; ***April Fool's Day,*** día de los Inocentes.
apron ['eiprən], *s.* delantal; mandil; (*artill.*) planchada *o* plomada (*de cañón*); batiente (*de un dique*); antepecho; (*fig.*) ***tied to the apron strings of,*** pegado a las faldas de.
aproned ['eiprənd], *a.* vestido con delantal.
apse [æps], *s.* (*arq.*) ábside.
apsis ['æpsis], *s.* (*astron.*) ápside.
apt [æpt], *a.* apto; apropiado, adecuado; propenso, inclinado; ***apt to break,*** frágil; ***to be apt to,*** tener propensión a; estar expuesto a.
aptera ['æptərə], *s.pl.* (*zool.*) ápteros.
apterous ['æptərəs], *a.* (*ent.*) áptero; (*arq.*) sin columnas a los lados.
aptitude ['æptiju:d], *s.* aptitud.
aptote ['æptout], *s.* (*gram.*) nombre indeclinable.
apyretic [æpai'retik], *a.* (*med.*) apirético.
apyrexy ['æpireksi], *s.* (*med.*) apirexia.
apyrous [æ'pairəs], *a.* (*quím., min.*) no alterado por el calor.
aquafortis [ækwə'fɔ:tis], *s.* agua fuerte.
aquamarine ['ækwəməri:n], *s.* aguamarina.
aquaregia [ækwə'ri:dʒiə], *s.* agua regia.
aquarelle [ækwə'rel], *s.* (*art.*) acuarela.
aquarium [ə'kwɛəriəm], *s.* acuario, pecera.
Aquarius [ə'kwɛəriəs], *s.* (*astron., astrol.*) Acuario.
aquatic [ə'kwætik], *a.* acuático.
aquatint ['ækwətint], *s.* acuatinta.
aqueduct ['ækwidʌkt], *s.* acueducto.
aqueous ['eikwiəs], *a.* ácueo, acuoso.
aqueousness ['eikwiəsnis], *s.* acuosidad.
aquiferous [æ'kwiferəs], *a.* aquífero.
aquiline ['ækwilain], *a.* aquilino.
Aquinas [ə'kwainəs]. Aquino.
Arab, Arabian ['ærəb, ə'reibiən], *a., s.* árabe, arábico, natural de Arabia; ***street Arab,*** pilluelo, pillete.
Arabia [ə'reibiə]. Arabia; ***Saudi Arabia,*** la Arabia Saudita.
arabesque [ærə'besk], *a., s.* arabesco.
Arabic ['ærəbik], *a.* árabe; ***Arabic figures,*** cifras árabes. — *s.* (*lengua*) árabe.
Arabist ['ærəbist], *s.* arabista, *m.f.*
arable ['ærəbl], *a.* labrantío, labradero, cultivable.
Arachnida [ə'ræknidə], *s.pl.* (*zool.*) arácnidos, *m.pl.*, aracneidos, *m.pl.*
arbalest ['ɑ:bəlest], *s.* ballesta.
arbiter ['ɑ:bitə], *s.* arbitrador, árbitro, compromisario; (*prov.*) ***every man is the arbiter of his fortune,*** cada uno es artífice de su sino.
arbitrable ['ɑ:bitrəbl], *a.* arbitrable.
arbitrage ['ɑ:bitridʒ], *s.* (*com.*) arbitraje.
arbitrament, arbitrement [ɑ:'bitrəmənt], *s.* arbitramento, arbitrio.
arbitrariness ['ɑ:bitrərinis], *s.* arbitrariedad.
arbitrary ['ɑ:bitrəri], *a.* arbitrario.
arbitrate ['ɑ:bitreit], *v.t.* arbitrar, juzgar, decidir, resolver; someter a arbitraje.
arbitration [ɑ:bi'treiʃən], *s.* arbitramento; liquidación; arbitraje; ***arbitration tribunal,*** tribunal *o* junta de arbitraje.
arbitrator ['ɑ:bitreitər], *s.* arbitrador, árbitro.
arbitress ['ɑ:bitris], *s.* arbitradora.
arbor ['ɑ:bə], *s.* (*mec.*) árbol.
arboreal [ɑ:'bɔ:riəl], *a.* arbóreo.
arborescence [ɑ:bə'resəns], *s.* (*bot.*) arborescencia; (*min.*) arborización.
arborescent [ɑ:bə'resənt], *a.* arborescente.
arboretum [ɑ:bə'ri:təm], *s.* almáciga (*o* criadero) de árboles.
arboricultural [ɑ:bɔri'kʌltʃərəl], *a.* relativo a la arboricultura.
arboriculture ['ɑ:bɔrikʌltʃə], *s.* arboricultura.
arboriculturist [ɑ:bɔri'kʌltʃərist], *s.* arboricultor.
arborization [ɑ:bɔrai'zeiʃən], *s.* arborización.
arborized ['ɑ:bɔraizd], *a.* arborizado.
arbour ['ɑ:bə], *s.* emparrado, glorieta.
arbutus [ɑ:'bju:təs], *s.* (*bot.*) madroño.
arc [ɑ:k], *s.* arco; ***arc-lamp,*** arco voltaico; ***arc-light,*** arco galvánico.
arcade [ɑ:'keid], *s.* arcada; pasaje, galería (comercial).
Arcadian [ɑ:'keidiən], *a., s.* arcadio, árcade; (*fig.*) arcádico.
arcane [ɑ:'kein], *a.* arcano.
arcanum [ɑ:'keinəm], *s.* (*pl.* **arcana** [-nə]) arcano.
arch (1) [ɑ:tʃ], *a.* arqueado. — *s.* arco; bóveda; curvatura; ***arch of the aorta,*** curvatura de la aorta; ***the arch of heaven,*** la bóveda celeste; ***Gothic arch, pointed arch,*** arco gótico, arco ojival; ***segmental arch,*** arco abocinado;

semicircular arch, arco de medio punto. — *v.t.* abovedar; arquear, enarcar. — *v.i.* formar bóveda.
arch (2) [ɑːtʃ], *prefijo.* declarado, notable, de primer orden; travieso, malicioso; ***arch-enemy,*** archienemigo.
arch (3) [ɑːtʃ], *a.* picaresco, socarrón.
archaeological [ɑːkiəˈlɔdʒikəl], *a.* arqueológico.
archaeologist [ɑːkiˈɔlədʒist], *s.* arqueólogo.
archaeology [ɑːkiˈɔlədʒi], *s.* arqueología.
archaic [ɑːˈkeiik], *a.* arcaico, anticuado.
archaism [ˈɑːkeiizəm], *s.* arcaísmo.
archangel [ˈɑːkeindʒəl], *s.* arcángel; (*bot.*) ortiga muerta.
archangelic [ɑːkænˈdʒelik], *a.* arcangélico.
archbishop [ɑːtʃˈbiʃəp], *s.* arzobispo.
archbishopric [ɑːtʃˈbiʃəprik], *s.* arzobispado.
archdeacon [ɑːtʃˈdiːkən], *s.* arcediano.
archdeaconry, archdeaconship [ɑːtʃˈdiːkənri, -ʃip], *s.* arcedianato.
archdiocese [ɑːtʃˈdaiəsis], *s.* archidiócesis, *f. inv.*
archducal [ɑːtʃˈdjuːkəl], *a.* archiducal.
archduchess [ɑːtʃˈdʌtʃis], *s.* archiduquesa.
archduchy, archdukedom [ɑːtʃˈdʌtʃi, -ˈdjuːkdəm], *s.* archiducado.
archduke [ɑːtʃˈdjuːk], *s.* archiduque.
archer [ˈɑːtʃə], *s.* arquero, flechero.
archery [ˈɑːtʃəri], *s.* tiro de arco.
archetypal [ˈɑːkitaipəl], *a.* perteneciente al arquetipo, arquetípico.
archetype [ˈɑːkitaip], *s.* arquetipo, patrón.
arch-foe [ˈɑːtʃ-ˈfou], *s.* enemigo principal.
arch-hypocrite [ˈɑːtʃ-ˈhipəkrit], *s.* hipocritón.
archidiaconal [ɑːkidiˈækənəl], *a.* perteneciente al arcediano.
archiepiscopacy [ɑːkiəˈpiskəpəsi], *s.* arzobispado.
archiepiscopal [ɑːkiəˈpiskəpəl], *a.* arquiepiscopal, arzobispal.
archiepiscopate [ɑːkiəˈpiskəpeit], *s.* arzobispado.
archil [ˈɑːkil], *s.* (*bot.*) orchilla.
archimandrite [ɑːkiˈmændrait], *s.* archimandrita, *m.*
Archimedean [ɑːkiˈmiːdiən], *a.* de Arquímedes.
Archimedes [ɑːkiˈmiːdiːz]. Arquímedes, *m.*
arching [ˈɑːtʃiŋ], *a.* arqueado, en forma de arco. — *s.* arqueo, curvatura.
archipelago [ɑːkiˈpeləgou], *s.* archipiélago.
architect [ˈɑːkitekt], *s.* arquitecto; (*fig.*) artífice.
architectonic [ɑːkitekˈtɔnik], *a.* arquitectónico.
architectonics [ɑːkitekˈtɔniks], *s.* arquitectura, arte arquitectónico.
architectural [ɑːkiˈtektʃərəl], *a.* arquitectónico.
architecture [ˈɑːkitektʃə], *s.* arquitectura.
architrave [ˈɑːkitreiv], *s.* arquitrabe.
archive [ˈɑːkaiv], *s.* archivo.
archivist [ˈɑːkivist], *s.* archivero, archivista, *m.f.*
archlike [ˈɑːtʃlaik], *a.* arqueado, en forma de arco, abovedado.
archness [ˈɑːtʃnis], *s.* travesura, coquetería, picardía, malicia; astucia, sutileza.
archon [ˈɑːkən], *s.* (*pl.* **archontes** [ɑːˈkɔntiːz]) arconte.
archpriest [ˈɑːtʃˈpriːst], *s.* gran sacerdote; arcipreste; (*fig.*) santón.
archstone [ˈɑːtʃstoun], *s.* clave (*f.*) de bóveda.
arch-traitor [ˈɑːtʃ-ˈtreitə], *s.* architraidor.
arch-villain [ˈɑːtʃ-ˈvilən], *s.* bellaconazo, picarón.
arch-villainy [ˈɑːtʃ-ˈviləni], *s.* gran bellaquería.
archway [ˈɑːtʃwei], *s.* arco, arcada; pasaje abovedado.
archwork [ˈɑːtʃwəːk], *s.* construcción de arcos.
Arctic [ɑːktik], *a.* ártico; ***Arctic Circle,*** círculo polar ártico; (*zool.*) ***Arctic fox,*** zorro azul. — *s.* el Ártico.

arcuation [ˈɑːkjuˈeiʃən], *s.* arqueo, curvatura, encorvamiento.
Ardennes [ɑːˈden], *s.pl.* las Ardenas.
ardent [ˈɑːdənt], *a.* ardiente, vehemente, encendido.
ardour, ardency [ˈɑːdə, ˈɑːdənsi], *s.* ardor, vehemencia, calor; anhelo, ansia; pasión, celo; entusiasmo.
arduous [ˈɑːdjuəs], *a.* arduo; riguroso; difícil, penoso, puntiagudo.
arduousness [ˈɑːdjuəsnis], *s.* (lo) arduo; (lo) difícil.
area [ˈɛəriə], *s.* área; zona; superficie, *f.*
arena [əˈriːnə], *s.* arena; liza; redondel, ruedo; palestra.
arenaceous [æriˈneiʃəs], *a.* arenisco, arenoso, arenáceo.
arenation [æriˈneiʃən], *s.* (*med.*) arenación.
areometer [æriˈɔmitə], *s.* areómetro.
areometrical [æriəˈmetrikəl], *a.* areométrico.
areometry [æriˈɔmitri], *s.* areometría.
argal [ˈɑːgəl], *s.* tártaro.
argent [ˈɑːdʒənt], *a.* (*blas.*) argén, argento, argénteo.
argentation [ɑːdʒenˈteiʃən], *s.* plateadura, baño de plata.
argentiferous [ɑːdʒenˈtifərəs], *a.* (*min.*) argentífero.
Argentina [ɑːdʒenˈtiːnə]. (la) Argentina.
Argentine [ˈɑːdʒentain], *a.* argentino. — *s.* argentino; ***the Argentine,*** (la) Argentina.
argentine [ˈɑːdʒentain], *a.* argentino, argénteo, argentoso. — *s.* metal blanco plateado.
Argentinian [ɑːdʒenˈtiniən], *a., s.* argentino.
argil [ˈɑːdʒil], *s.* arcilla, alfar.
argillaceous [ɑːdʒiˈleiʃəs], *a.* arcilloso.
argon [ˈɑːgən], *s.* (*quím.*) argo.
argonaut [ˈɑːgənɔːt], *s.* (*ict., mit.*) argonauta, *m.*
argosy [ˈɑːgəsi], *s.* buque con rico cargamento.
argue [ˈɑːgjuː], *v.t.* argüir, demostrar; sostener; ***to argue into,*** convencer para que; ***to argue out of,*** disuadir de. — *v.i.* discutir, disputar; argüir, argumentar; ***it argues well for him,*** habla en su favor, dice bien de él.
arguer [ˈɑːgjuə], *s.* discutidor; argumentador.
arguing [ˈɑːgjuiŋ], *s.* discusión, discusiones; razonamiento.
argument [ˈɑːgjumənt], *s.* discusión; argumento.
argumentation [ɑːgjumenˈteiʃən], *s.* argumentación, raciocino.
argumentative [ɑːgjuˈmentətiv], *a.* discutidor; argumentativo, argumentador.
Argus [ɑːˈgəs]. (*mit.*) Argos.
aria [ˈɑːriə], *s.* (*mús.*) aria.
Arian [ˈɛəriən], *s.* arriano.
Arianism [ˈɛəriənizəm], *s.* arrianismo.
arid [ˈærid], *a.* árido.
aridity, aridness [əˈriditi, ˈæridnis], *s.* aridez.
arietta [æriˈetə], *s.* (*mús.*) arieta, aria corta.
aright [əˈrait], *adv.* acertadamente; rectamente; ***to set aright,*** poner bien, poner remedio a, rectificar.
aril [ˈæril], *s.* (*bot.*) arila.
arise [əˈraiz], *irr. v.i.* levantarse, alzarse; surgir, presentarse; provenir (de), originarse (en).
aristocracy [ærisˈtɔkrəsi], *s.* aristocracia.
aristocrat [ˈæristəkræt], *s.* aristócrata.
aristocratic [æristəˈkrætik], *a.* aristocrático.
Aristophanes [ærisˈtɔfəniːz]. Aristófanes.
Aristotelian [æristəˈtiːljən], *a.* aristotélico.
Aristotelianism [æristəˈtiːljənizəm], *s.* aristotelismo.
Aristotle [ˈæristɔtl]. Aristóteles.
arithmancy [ˈæriθmænsi], *s.* aritmancia.
arithmetic [əˈriθmətik], *s.* aritmética.
arithmetical [æriθˈmetikəl], *a.* aritmético.
arithmetician [æriθmiˈtiʃən], *s.* aritmético.
arithmometer [æriθˈmɔmitə], *s.* aritmómetro.

ark [ɑ:k], *s.* arca; (*mar.*) lanchón; ***ark of the Covenant,*** arca de la alianza; ***Noah's ark,*** arca de Noé.
arm [ɑ:m], *s.* brazo; arma; ***arm in arm,*** cogidos del brazo; ***arms race,*** carrera de (los) armamentos; ***babe in arms,*** niño de pecho; ***to keep at arm's length,*** mantener(se) a distancia; ***to lay down one's arms,*** rendir las armas; ***to rise up in arms,*** alzarse en armas; ***to take up arms,*** tomar las armas; ***to arms!*** ¡a las armas!; ***with folded arms,*** con los brazos cruzados; ***with open arms,*** con los brazos abiertos. — *v.t.* armar; aprestar, equipar. — *v.i.* tomar las armas, armarse.
armada [ɑ:ˈmɑ:də], *s.* armada, flota.
armadillo [ɑ:məˈdilou], *s.* armadillo, cachicamo.
Armageddon [ɑ:məˈgedn], *s.* (*bib.*) Armagedón; conflicto cataclísmico.
armament [ˈɑ:məmənt], *s.* armamento.
armature [ˈɑ:mətʃə], *s.* armadura, armazón; armas defensivas; (*elec.*) inducido (*de dínamo*).
armchair [ˈɑ:mˈtʃɛə], *s.* sillón, silla de brazos, butaca.
armed [ɑ:md], *a.* armado, provisto de (armas); (*bot.*) espinoso; ***armed forces,*** fuerzas armadas.
Armenian [ɑ:ˈmi:niən], *a., s.* armenio.
armful [ˈɑ:mful], *s.* brazada.
armhole [ˈɑ:mhoul], *s.* sobaquera, sisa.
armiger [ˈɑ:midʒə], *s.* armígero; escudero.
armillary [ɑ:ˈmiləri], *a.* armilar.
arming [ˈɑ:miŋ], *s.* armamento, acción de armar *o* armarse; armadura (*de un imán*); (*pl.*) (*mar.*) empavesadas, *f. pl.*
arming-press [ˈɑ:miŋ-pres], *s.* prensa de estampar.
armistice [ˈɑ:mistis], *s.* armisticio.
armless, [ˈɑ:mlis], *a.* sin brazos.
armlet [ˈɑ:mlit], *s.* brazal, brazalete.
armorial [ɑ:ˈmɔ:riəl], *a.* heráldico; ***armorial bearings,*** escudo de armas.
armorist [ˈɑ:mərist], *s.* heráldico.
armour [ˈɑ:mə], *s.* armadura; ***coat-armour,*** cota de malla. — *v.t.* (*mar.*) acorazar, blindar.
armour-bearer [ˈɑ:mə-bɛərə], *s.* escudero.
armoured [ˈɑ:məd], *a.* blindado; ***armoured car,*** carro blindado.
armourer [ˈɑ:mərə], *s.* armero.
armour-plating [ˈɑ:mə-ˈpleitiŋ], *s.* acorazamiento, blindaje.
armoury [ˈɑ:məri], *s.* armería, arsenal; heráldica.
armpit [ˈɑ:mpit], *s.* axila, sobaco.
army [ˈɑ:mi], *a.* del ejército, militar; ***army list,*** escalafón del ejército. — *s.* ejército; tropa.
arnatto [ɑ:ˈnætou], *s.* (*bot.*) bija, achiote.
arnica [ˈɑ:nikə], *s.* (*bot.*) árnica.
aroma [əˈroumə], *s.* aroma; fragancia.
aromatic [æroˈmætik], *a.* aromático, fragante.
aromatization [əroumətaiˈzeiʃən], *s.* aromatización.
aromatize [əˈroumətaiz], *v.t.* aromatizar.
aromatizer [əˈroumətaizə], *s.* aromatizador.
around [əˈraund], *adv.* alrededor, en derredor, en torno, a la redonda; ***all around,*** por todas partes; ***around somewhere,*** por ahí; ***the other way around,*** al contrario, al revés. — *prep.* alrededor de, en torno a; ***around the corner,*** a la vuelta de la esquina.
arouse [əˈrauz], *v.t.* despertar; mover, excitar; incitar.
arpeggio [ɑ:ˈpedʒiou], *s.* (*mús.*) arpegio.
arquebus [ˈɑ:kwibəs], *s.* arcabuz.
arquebusier [ɑ:kwibəˈsiə], *s.* arcabucero.
arrack [ˈærək], *s.* arak.
arraign [əˈrein], *v.t.* citar, emplazar; acusar, denunciar.
arraignment [əˈreinmənt], *s.* (*for.*) emplazo, emplazamiento; denuncia, acusación.
arrange [əˈreindʒ], *v.t.* arreglar; disponer; colocar; clasificar, ordenar; concertar.
arrangement [əˈreindʒmənt], *s.* arreglo; disposición; colocación; clasificación; medida; gestión, trámite.
arrant [ˈærənt], *a.* consumado, redomado; ***arrant fool,*** tonto de siete suelas.
arras [ˈærəs], *s.* tapicería de Arrás.
array [əˈrei], *s.* formación, orden; atavío, adorno, ornato, gala. — *v.t.* colocar, poner en orden, formar; ataviar, adornar, engalanar.
arrear [əˈriə], *s.* (*ú. más en pl.*) atrasos, *m.pl.*; ***in arrears,*** atrasado.
arrearage [əˈriəridʒ], *s.* atrasos; retraso.
arrest [əˈrest], *s.* detención, arresto, prisión; parada, cesación; ***under arrest,*** preso. — *v.t.* detener, prender, arrestar; parar, contrarrestar; atraer, llamar (*la atención*).
arrestation [æresˈteiʃən], *s.* detención.
arresting [əˈrestiŋ], *a.* (*fig.*) fascinante, que llama la atención.
arris [ˈæris], *s.* (*arq.*) arista.
arrival [əˈraivəl], *s.* llegada; arribo; ***a new arrival,*** un recién llegado.
arrive [əˈraiv], *v.i.* llegar; arribar; triunfar.
arrogance [ˈærəgəns], *s.* petulancia, soberbia, altanería.
arrogant [ˈærəgənt], *a.* petulante, soberbio, altanero.
arrogate [ˈærəgeit], *v.t.* arrogarse.
arrogation [ærəˈgeiʃən], *s.* arrogación.
arrow [ˈærou], *s.* flecha; saeta; ***arrow-grass,*** trigloquín; ***arrow-head,*** punta de flecha; ***arrow-root,*** arrurruz; ***arrow-shaped,*** aflechado, sagital.
arrowy [ˈæroui], *a.* de flecha, en forma de flecha; veloz.
arse [ɑ:s], *s.* (*obsc.*) culo.
arsenal [ˈɑ:sənəl], *s.* arsenal, atarazana.
arsenic [ˈɑ:sənik], *s.* (*quím.*) arsénico.
arsenical [ɑ:ˈsenikəl], *a.* arsenical, de arsénico.
arsenite [ˈɑ:sənait], *s.* arsenito.
arson [ˈɑ:sən], *s.* incendio premeditado; incendiarismo.
art (1) [ɑ:t], *s.* arte; maña, astucia, habilidad; ***arts and crafts,*** artes y oficios; ***Arts Faculty,*** Facultad de Letras; ***fine arts,*** bellas artes.
art (2) [ɑ:t] [BE].
arterial [ɑ:ˈtiəriəl], *a.* arterial.
arterialization [ɑ:tiəriəlaiˈzeiʃən], *s.* arterialización.
arterialize [ɑ:ˈtiəriəlaiz], *v.t.* arterializar.
arteriole [ɑ:ˈtiərioul], *s.* arteriola.
arteriology [ɑ:tiəriˈɔlədʒi], *s.* arteriología.
arteriotomy [ɑ:tiəriˈɔtəmi], *s.* arteriotomía.
artery [ˈɑ:təri], *s.* arteria.
artesian [ɑ:ˈti:ziən], *a., s.* artesiano; ***artesian well,*** pozo artesiano.
artful [ˈɑ:tful], *a.* artero, astuto, taimado, solapado.
artfulness [ˈɑ:tfulnis], *s.* astucia, artería, artes.
arthritic [ɑ:ˈθritik], *a.* (*med.*) artrítico, artético.
arthriticism [ɑ:ˈθritisizəm], *s.* (*med.*) artritismo.
arthritis [ɑ:ˈθraitis], *s.* (*med.*) artritis, *f.*, artética.
arthrology [ɑ:ˈθrɔlədʒi], *s.* artrología.
arthrosis [ɑ:ˈθrousis], *s.* (*anat.*) artrosis, *f.*, articulación.
Arthur [ˈɑ:θə]. Arturo; ***King Arthur,*** El Rey Artús *o* Arturo.
artichoke [ˈɑ:titʃouk], *s.* (*bot.*) alcachofa; ***Jerusalem artichoke,*** cotufa.
article [ˈɑ:tikl], *s.* artículo; cláusula; prenda; cosa, objeto; (*zool.*) artejo; ***articles of war,*** código militar, ordenanzas militares; ***leading article,*** artículo de fondo; ***to sign articles,*** escriturarse; ***trifling articles,*** bagatelas; ***to be under articles,***

estar escriturado. — *v.t.* detallar; escriturar, contratar; (*for.*) hacer cargos; ***article (an apprentice)***, poner en aprendizaje.
articular [ɑː'tikjulə], *a.* articular.
articulate [ɑː'tikjulit], *a.* articulado, hábil en expresarse. — *s.* animal articulado. — [ɑː'tikjuleit], *v.t.*, *v.i.* articular, enunciar.
articulateness [ɑː'tikjulitnis], *s.* calidad de ser articulado; capacidad para expresarse.
articulation [ɑːtikju'leiʃən], *s.* articulación.
artifice ['ɑːtifis], *s.* artificio, treta, ardid.
artificer [ɑː'tifisə], *s.* artífice.
artificial [ɑːti'fiʃəl], *a.* artificial; artificioso.
artificiality, artificialness, [ɑːtifiʃi'æliti, -'fiʃlnis], *s.* (lo) artificial; (lo) artificioso.
artillerist [ɑː'tilərist], *s.* artillero.
artillery [ɑː'tiləri], *s.* artillería; ***artillery-man,*** artillero; ***artillery-practice,*** ejercicio de cañón.
artisan [ɑːti'zæn], *s.* artesano.
artist ['ɑːtist], *s.* artista, *m.f.*
artistic [ɑː'tistik], *a.* artístico.
artistry ['ɑːtistri], *s.* maestría.
artless ['ɑːtlis], *a.* cándido, inocente, simple, ingenuo.
artlessness ['ɑːtlisnis], *s.* candidez, inocencia, simplicidad, ingenuidad.
arty ['ɑːti], *a.* (*fam.*) ostentoso, exagerado; ***arty-crafty,*** cursi; taimado, solapado.
arum ['ɛərəm], *s.* (*bot.*) aro.
Aryan ['ɛəriən], *a.*, *s.* ario.
as [æz], *adv.*, *conj.*, *prep.*, *pron.* como; ya que, puesto que; cuando, mientras, al; que; tan; ***as far as,*** hasta; por lo que toca a; ***as far as I know,*** que yo sepa; ***as for, as to,*** en cuanto a; ***as if, as though,*** como si; ***as if to,*** como para; ***as it is,*** dadas las circunstancias, dado el caso; ***as it seems,*** según parece; ***as it were,*** por decirlo así; ***as long as,*** mientras (que); siempre que; ***as much as,*** tanto como; ***as a rule,*** por regla general; ***as soon as,*** tan pronto como, en cuanto; ***as soon as possible,*** cuanto antes, lo antes posible; ***as well,*** también; ***not as yet,*** todavía no; ***as he was coming in,*** cuando entraba, al entrar; ***the same as,*** lo mismo que; ***so as to,*** de manera que, para; ***such as,*** (tal) como.
asafœtida [æsə'fiːtidə], *s.* asafétida.
asbestic [æz'bestik], *a.* asbestino.
asbestos [æz'bestɔs], *s.* amianto, asbesto.
ascend [ə'send], *v.t.*, *v.i.* ascender, subir; ***ascend the throne,*** subir al trono.
ascendancy, ascendency [ə'sendənsi], *s.* ascendiente.
ascendant, ascendent [ə'sendənt], *a.* ascendente; predominante. — *s.* ascendiente; ***in the ascendent,*** en auge, cada vez más poderoso.
ascending [ə'sendiŋ], *a.* ascendente.
ascension [ə'senʃən], (*Am.*) [ASCENT].
ascensional [ə'senʃənəl], *a.* (*astron.*) ascensional.
Ascension Day [ə'senʃən dei]. Día de la Ascensión.
ascent [ə'sent], *s.* subida, ascensión.
ascertain [æsə'tein], *v.t.* averiguar, enterarse (de), cerciorarse (de).
ascertainable [æsə'teinəbl], *a.* averiguable.
ascertainment [æsə'teinmənt], *s.* averiguación.
ascetic [ə'setik], *a.* ascético. — *s.* asceta, *m.f.*
asceticism [ə'setisizəm], *s.* ascetismo.
ascites [æ'saitiːz], *s.* (*med.*) ascitis, *f.*
ascitic(al) [ə'saitik(əl)], *a.* ascítico.
ascribe [ə'skraib], *v.t.* atribuir, achacar.
ascription [ə'skripʃən], *s.* atribución; imputación.
asepsis [æ'sepsis], *s.* (*med.*) asepsia.
aseptic [æ'septik], *a.* aséptico.
asexual [æ'seksjuəl], *a.* (*biol.*) asexual.
ash (1) [æʃ], *s.* ceniza; ***ash-colour,*** color de ceniza, ceniciento; ***ash-tray,*** cenicero; ***Ash Wednesday,*** miércoles de ceniza; (*pl.*) restos mortales, *m.pl.*
ash (2) [æʃ], *s.* (*bot.*) fresno; ***ash grove,*** fresneda; ***mountain ash,*** serbal.
ashamed [ə'ʃeimd], *a.* avergonzado, corrido; ***to be ashamed,*** tener vergüenza, avergonzarse (de).
ashen (1) ['æʃən], *a.* ceniciento; pálido.
ashen (2) ['æʃən], *a.* de fresno.
ashlar ['æʃlə], *s.* sillar, morillo.
ashlaring ['æʃləriŋ], *s.* ligazones a los cabríos del techo en guardillas, *f.pl.*; sillería, cantería.
ashore [ə'ʃɔː], *adv.* a tierra, en tierra; ***to go ashore,*** desembarcar; ***to run ashore,*** encallar, varar, embarrancar.
ashweed ['æʃwiːd], *s.* (*bot.*) angélica.
ashy ['æʃi], *a.* cenizoso, ceniciento.
Asia ['eiʃə]. Asia; ***Asia Minor,*** Asia Menor.
Asian, Asiatic ['eiʒn, eiʃi'ætik], *a.*, *s.* asiático, de Asia.
aside [ə'said], *adv.* a un lado, aparte; (*Am.*) ***aside from this,*** esto aparte, fuera de esto; ***to lay aside,*** dejar a un lado, apartar; desechar; ***to move aside,*** apartarse, echarse a un lado; ***to set aside,*** reservar; apartar; (*for*) anular; ***to turn aside,*** desviar(se). — *s.* (*teat.*) aparte.
asinine ['æsinain], *a.* asinino, asnal.
ask [ɑːsk], *v.t.* preguntar; pedir, solicitar; rogar (que); requerir, exigir; invitar; amonestar. — *v.i.* ***after, for*** o ***about,*** preguntar por; ***ask for,*** pedir (*una cosa*); (*fam.*) ***ask for it,*** buscársela.
askance [ə'skæns], *adv.* de reojo; al sesgo, de soslayo, oblicuamente; con desdén, con recelo.
askew [ə'skjuː], *adv.* torcido; de lado, al través, de través.
asking ['ɑːskiŋ], *s.* súplica, ruego, demanda, acción de pedir; publicación (*de amonestaciones*); ***this is the third time of asking,*** ésta es la tercera amonestación.
aslant [ə'slɑːnt], *a.* sesgado, ladeado. — *adv.*, *prep.* al sesgo, inclinado, oblicuamente.
asleep [ə'sliːp], *adv.* dormido, durmiendo; ***to fall asleep,*** dormirse, quedarse dormido.
aslope [ə'sloup], *adv.* en declive, en pendiente.
asp (1) [æsp], *s.* (*zool.*) áspid.
asp (2) [æsp], *s.* [ASPEN].
asparagus [əs'pærəgəs], *s.* (*bot.*) espárrago.
aspect ['æspekt], *s.* aspecto.
aspen ['æspən], *a.* perteneciente al álamo temblón. — *s.* (*bot.*) tiemblo; álamo temblón.
asper ['æspə], *s.* aspro.
aspergillus [æspə'dʒiləs], *s.* (*biol.*) aspersorio, hisopo.
asperifolious [æspəri'fouliəs], *a.* (*bot.*) asperfoliado.
asperity [æs'periti], *s.* aspereza.
asperse [æs'pəːs], *v.t.* asperjar, hisopar, rociar; (*fig.*) calumniar, difamar, denigrar.
asperser [æs'pəːsə], *s.* calumniador, infamador.
aspersion [æs'pəːʃən], *s.* aspersión; calumnia, difamación; mancha, mácula, tacha; deshonra; rociadura; (*fam.*) rociada, reprensión; (*igl.*) asperges; ***to cast aspersions on,*** difamar, calumniar.
aspersive [æs'pəːsiv], *a.* difamatorio, calumnioso.
asphalt ['æsfælt], *s.* asfalto. — *v.t.* asfaltar.
asphaltic [æs'fæltik], *a.* asfáltico.
asphodel ['æsfədel], *s.* (*bot.*) asfodelo.
asphyxia, asphyxiation [æs'fiksiə, æsfiksi'eiʃən], *s.* asfixia.
asphyxiate [æs'fiksieit], *v.t.* asfixiar.
aspic (1) ['æspik], *s.* (*zool.*) áspid.
aspic (2) ['æspik], *s.* gelatina.
aspirant [ə'spairənt], *s.* aspirante; candidato, pretendiente.
aspirate ['æspirit], *a.* (*gram.*) aspirado. — *s.* letra aspirada. — ['æspireit], *v.t.* aspirar.
aspiration [æspi'reiʃən], *s.* aspiración.
aspirator ['æspireitə], *s.* aspirador.
aspiratory ['æspireitəri], *a.* aspiratorio.

aspire [ə'spaiə], *v.i.* aspirar; ***aspire to,*** aspirar a, pretender.
aspirin ['æsprin], *s.* aspirina.
aspiring [ə'spaiəriŋ], *a.* ambicioso.
asquint [ə'skwint], *adv.* oblicuamente; ***to look asquint,*** mirar de soslayo.
ass [æs], *s.* asno; burro; (*fig.*) tonto, bestia; ***ass-driver,*** arriero; ***she-ass,*** burra; ***young ass,*** pollino.
assail [ə'seil], *v.t.* acometer, asaltar.
assailable [ə'seiləbl], *a.* que puede ser asaltado.
assailant [ə'seilənt], *s.* asaltador.
assailment [ə'seilmənt], *s.* asalto.
assassin [ə'sæsin], *s.* asesino.
assassinate [ə'sæsineit], *v.t.* asesinar.
assassination [əsæsi'neiʃən], *s.* asesinato.
assault [ə'sɔ:lt], *s.* asalto, ataque; atentado; violación; ***assault and battery,*** acometimiento *o* asalto con lesiones. — *v.t.* asaltar, atacar; violar.
assaultable [ə'sɔ:ltəbl], *a.* (*mil.*) que puede ser asaltado.
assaulter [ə'sɔ:ltə], *a.* agresor, asaltador.
assay [ə'sei], *s.* ensayo, ensaye, prueba. — *v.t.* ensayar; probar.
assayer [ə'seiə], *s.* ensayador.
assaying [ə'seiŋ], *s.* ensayo, ensaye.
assegai ['æsigai], *s.* azagaya.
assemblage [ə'semblidʒ], *s.* colección; asamblea, reunión; (*mec.*) montaje.
assemblance [ə'sembləns], *s.* apariencia.
assemble [ə'sembl], *v.t.* congregar, allegar, juntar, reunir, convocar. — *v.i.* juntarse, reunirse.
assembler [ə'semblə], *s.* convocador; (*mec.*) montador, armador.
assembling [ə'sembliŋ], *s.* reunión, *f.*, asamblea, junta; acción de convocar *o* de juntarse.
assembly [ə'sembli], *s.* asamblea, junta; concurso; concurrencia; montaje; armazón; juego, conjunto de piezas; ***assembly-line,*** cadena *o* tren de montaje; ***assembly-plant*** o ***shop,*** taller de montaje; ***assembly-room,*** congreso, asamblea, sala de sesiones *o* de juntas.
assent [ə'sent], *s.* asentimiento, asenso; beneplácito, aquiescencia. — *v.i.* asentir, convenir, obtemperar.
assenter [ə'sentə], *s.* consentidor
assentient [ə'senʃiənt], *a.* consentidor.
assentingly [ə'sentiŋli], *adv.* con asenso, con aprobación; en signo de aprobación *o* asentimiento.
assert [ə'sə:t], *v.t.* sostener, mantener, defender, hacer valer; afirmar, asegurar, aseverar; ***assert one's dignity,*** sostener su dignidad; ***assert one's rights,*** hacer valer sus derechos. — **assert o.s.,** *v.r.* imponerse, hacerse valer.
assertion [ə'sə:ʃən], *s.* aserción, aserto, aseveración, afirmación; defensa.
assertive [ə'sə:tiv], *a.* afirmativo, asertivo.
assess [ə'ses], *v.t.* apreciar, hacer una apreciación de; valorar, calcular, tasar; fijar; gravar.
assessable [ə'sesəbl], *a.* tasable, imponible.
assessment [ə'sesmənt], *s.* apreciación; tasación; imposición, tasa de impuestos; valoración, avalúo; (*for.*) fijación de daños y perjuicios.
assessor [ə'sesə], *s.* asesor; tasador de impuestos, imponedor de contribuciones.
assessorial [æse'sɔ:riəl], *a.* relativo a la asesoría.
asset ['æset], *s.* posesión; ventaja; (*pl.*) (*com.*) (crédito) activo, caudal en caja, haber, capital; fondos, valores; ***personal assets,*** bienes muebles; ***real assets,*** bienes raíces.
asseverate [ə'sevəreit], *v.t.* aseverar, afirmar, asegurar con solemnidad.
asseveration [əsevə'reiʃən], *s.* aseveración, afirmación.
assibilate [ə'sibileit], *v.t.* asibilar.
assiduity, assiduousness [æsi'dju:iti, ə'sidjuəsnis], *s.* asiduidad, constancia.
assiduous [ə'sidjuəs], *a.* asiduo, constante.
assign [ə'sain], *v.t.* asignar, señalar, fijar; adscribir, atribuir; transferir, ceder. — *v.i.* hacer cesión de bienes.
assignable [ə'sainəbl], *a.* asignable; transferible, negociable; cesible.
assignat [æsi'ŋɑ:], *s.* asignado.
assignation [æsig'neiʃən], *s.* asignación, señalamiento; designación; adscripción; cesión; cita.
assignee [æsai'ni:], *s.* poderhabiente, apoderado; (*derecho común*) cesionario; síndico.
assigner [ə'sainə], *s.* asignante, transferidor, transferente, cedente, comitente, cesionista, *m.f*
assignment [ə'sainmənt], *s.* asignación, señalamiento, cesión; (*for.*) traslación de dominio; escritura de cesión de bienes; tarea, misión.
assimilability [əsimilə'biliti], *s.* asimilabilidad.
assimilable [ə'similəbl], *a.* asimilable.
assimilate [ə'simileit], *v.t.* asimilar(se). — *v.i.* asimilar.
assimilation [əsimi'leiʃən], *s.* asimilación.
assimilative [ə'similətiv], *a.* asimilativo.
assist [ə'sist], *v.t.*, *v.i.* ayudar, auxiliar; asistir.
assistance [ə'sistəns], *s.* ayuda, auxilio; asistencia.
assistant [ə'sistənt], *s.* auxiliar; ayudante; ***shop assistant,*** dependiente; ***assistant manager,*** subdirector.
assize [ə'saiz], *s.* (*ú. más en pl.* **assizes** [-iz]) tribunal de justicia; sesión de tribunal.
associate [ə'souʃiit], *a.* asociado; coligado. — *s.* asociado, socio; colega, compañero. — [ə'souʃieit], *v.t.* asociar; relacionar. — *v.i.* asociarse; alternar, convivir.
association [əsousi'eiʃən], *s.* asociación; sociedad.
associative [ə'souʃiətiv], *a.* asociativo.
assonance ['æsənəns], *s.* asonancia.
assonant ['æsənənt], *a.* asonante.
assort [ə'sɔ:t], *v.t.* ordenar, clasificar.
assorted [ə'sɔ:tid], *a.* surtido, variado, mezclado.
assortment [ə'sɔ:tmənt], *s.* surtido, selección.
assuage [ə'sweidʒ], *v.t.* mitigar, suavizar, calmar, aliviar; apagar.
assuagement [ə'sweidʒmənt], *s.* mitigación, alivio.
assuasive [ə'sweisiv], *a.* lenitivo, mitigativo, calmante.
assuetude ['æswitju:d], *s.* hábito, costumbre.
assume [ə'sju:m], *v.t.* asumir, tomar; presumir, suponer; ***assume an air,*** tomar un aire.
assumed [ə'sju:md], *a.* fingido, falso.
assuming [ə'sju:miŋ], *a.* presuntuoso.
assumption [ə'sʌmpʃən], *s.* asunción; toma; suposición, supuesto.
assurance [ə'ʃuərəns], *s.* seguridad; confianza, aplomo; (*com.*) seguro.
assure [ə'ʃuə], *v.t.* asegurar.
assured [ə'ʃuəd], *a.* seguro; asegurado.
assuredly [ə'ʃuəridli], *adv.* con toda seguridad, indudablemente.
assuredness [ə'ʃuəridnis], *s.* seguridad, confianza, aplomo.
assurer [ə'ʃuərə], *s.* asegurador.
assurgent [ə'sə:dʒənt], *a.* surgente.
assuring [ə'ʃuəriŋ], *a.* que asegura.
Assyria [ə'siriə]. (*hist.*) Asiria.
Assyrian [ə'siriən], *a.*, *s.* asirio.
astatic [æs'tætik], *a.* astático.
aster ['æstə], *s.* (*bot.*) áster.
asteriated [æs'terieitid], *a.* asteriado, estrellado.
asterisk ['æstərisk], *s.* asterisco.
asterism ['æstərizəm], *s.* (*astron.*) asterismo, constelación; (*impr.*) grupo de asteriscos.
astern [ə'stə:n], *adv.* (*mar.*) por la popa, a popa; ***to go astern,*** ir hacia atrás.
asteroid ['æstərɔid], *s.* asteroide.

asthenia [æs'θi:niə], *s.* (*med.*) astenia.
asthenic [æs'θenik], *a.* asténico.
asthma [æs(θ)mə], *s.* (*med.*) asma.
asthmatic [æs(θ)'mætik], *a., s.* asmático.
astigmatic [æstig'mætik], *a.* (*ópt.*) astigmático.
astigmatism [æ'stigmətizəm], *s.* astigmatismo.
astir [ə'stə:], *adv.* en movimiento.
astonish [ə'stɔniʃ], *v.t.* asombrar, pasmar, sorprender; ***to be astonished,*** asombrarse.
astonishing [ə'stɔniʃiŋ], *a.* asombroso, pasmoso, sorprendente.
astonishment [ə'stɔniʃmənt], *s.* asombro, pasmo, admiración.
astound [ə'staund], *v.t.* asombrar, pasmar.
astounding [ə'staundiŋ], *a.* asombroso, pasmoso.
astraddle [ə'strædl], *adv.* a horcajadas.
astragal ['æstrəgəl], *s.* (*arq., bot.*) astrágalo; (*anat.*) astrágalo, chita.
astrakhan [æstrə'kæn], *s.* astracán.
astral ['æstrəl], *a.* astral, sideral.
astrand [ə'strænd], *adv.* (*mar.*) encallado, varado.
astray [ə'strei], *adv.* perdido, extraviado; ***to go astray,*** perderse, extraviarse; ***to lead astray,*** descaminar, descarriar, extraviar, llevar por mal camino.
astrict [ə'strikt], *v.t.* astringir, astreñir.
astriction [ə'strikʃən], *s.* astricción; (*med.*) astreñimiento.
astride [ə'straid], *adv.* a horcajadas, a caballo.
astringe [ə'strindʒ], *v.t.* (*med.*) astringir, astreñir.
astringency [ə'strindʒənsi], *s.* astringencia.
astringent [ə'strindʒənt], *a., s.* astringente; severo.
astrography [æs'trɔgrəfi], *s.* astrografía.
astrolabe ['æstrəleib], *s.* astrolabio.
astrologer [ə'strɔlədʒə], *s.* astrólogo.
astrological [æstrə'lɔdʒikəl], *a.* astrológico.
astrology [ə'strɔlədʒi], *s.* astrología.
astronaut ['æstrənɔ:t], *s.* astronauta, *m.f.*
astronautics [æstrə'nɔ:tiks], *s. pl.* astronáutica.
astronomer [ə'strɔnəmə], *s.* astrónomo.
astronomic(al) [æstrə'nɔmik(əl)], *a.* astronómico.
astronomy [ə'strɔnəmi], *s.* astronomía.
astrophotometry [æstroufo'tɔmitri], *s.* (*astron.*) astrofotometría.
astrophysics [æstrou'fiziks], *s. pl.* astrofísica.
astute [ə'stju:t], *a.* astuto; sagaz.
astuteness [ə'stju:tnis], *s.* astucia; sagacidad.
asunder [ə'sʌndə], *adv.* en dos; ***to set asunder,*** separar; ***to split asunder,*** partir (en dos), hender (en dos).
asylum [ə'sailəm], *s.* asilo; manicomio.
asymmetrical [æsi'metrikəl], *a.* asimétrico.
asymmetry [ə'simitri], *s.* asimetría.
asymptote ['æsimptout], *s.* (*geom.*) asíntota.
asymptotic [æsimp'tɔtik], *a.* asintótico.
asyndeton [ə'sindətən], *s.* (*ret.*) asíndeton.
at [æt], *prep.* en; a; ***at all costs,*** cueste lo que cueste, como sea; ***at all events,*** de todas maneras; ***at best,*** en el mejor de los casos; ***to come*** o ***go in at the door,*** entrar por la puerta; ***at home,*** en casa; en su propio país; (*fig.*) a gusto; ***at least,*** por lo menos; ***at most,*** a lo sumo, como mucho; ***at one,*** en armonía, a una; ***at a pinch,*** apurando mucho; ***at play,*** jugando; ***at the station,*** en la estación; ***at that time,*** (en aquel) entonces; ***at work,*** trabajando; ***at worst,*** en el peor de los casos; ***not at all,*** en absoluto; de nada.
ataraxy ['ætəræksi], *s.* ataraxia.
atavism ['ætəvizəm], *s.* atavismo.
atavistic [ætə'vistik], *a.* atávico.
ataxia, ataxy [ə'tæksiə, ə'tæksi], *s.* ataxia.
ataxic [ə'tæksik], *a.* atáxico.
atelier [æ'teljei], *s.* estudio, taller.
Athanasian [æθə'neiʃən], *a., s.* atanasiano.
Athenian [ə'θi:niən], *a., s.* ateniense.
Athens ['æθənz]. Atenas, *f.*
atheism ['eiθiizəm], *s.* ateísmo.
atheist ['eiθiist], *s.* ateo.
atheistic [eiθi'istik], *a.* ateo, impío.
athenæum [æθi'ni:əm], *s.* ateneo.
athirst [ə'θə:st], *a.* sediento.
athlete ['æθli:t], *s.* atleta, *m.f.*
athletic [æθ'letik], *a.* atlético.
athletics [æθ'letiks], *s.* atletismo.
athwart [ə'θwɔ:t], *adv.* de través. — *prep.* por el través de, a través de.
atilt [ə'tilt], *adv.* en postura inclinada; en ristre.
Atlantean [ætlæn'tiən], *a.* atlántido, atlántico.
Atlantic (Ocean) [ət'læntik ('ouʃən)]. el (Océano) Atlántico.
Atlantis [ət'læntis]. (*mit.*) Atlántida.
Atlas Mountains ['ætləs mauntinz]. el Atlas.
atlas ['ætləs], *s.* atlas; (*arq.*) atlante, telamón.
atmosphere ['ætməsfiə], *s.* atmósfera; ambiente.
atmospheric [ætməs'ferik], *a.* atmosférico.
atoll ['ætɔl], *s.* atolón.
atom ['ætəm], *s.* átomo; (*fig.*) pizca; ***atom bomb,*** bomba atómica; ***atom splitting,*** fisión del átomo.
atomic [ə'tɔmik], *a.* atómico; (*quím.*) atomístico.
atomism ['ætəmizəm], *s.* atomismo.
atomist ['ætəmist], *s.* atomista, *m.f.*
atomize ['ætəmaiz], *v.t.* reducir a átomos; pulverizar, rociar.
atomizer ['ætəmaizə], *s.* pulverizador, aromatizador.
atomy (1) ['ætəmi], *s.* átomo; (*fig.*) pigmeo, enano.
atomy (2) ['ætəmi], *s.* esqueleto, preparación anatómica.
atone [ə'toun], *v.i.* dar reparación *o* satisfacción; ***atone for,*** expiar.
atonement [ə'tounmənt], *s.* expiación; reparación, compensación; redención.
atonic [ə'tɔnik], *a.* débil; (*gram.*) atónico.
atony ['ætəni], *s.* (*med.*) atonía.
atop [ə'tɔp], *adv.* encima.
atoxic [æ'tɔksik], *a.* atóxico.
atrabilarian, atrabilarious [ætrəbi'lɛəriən, -iəs], *a.* (*med.*) atrabiliario, atrabilioso; melancólico, hipocondríaco.
atrabilariousness [ætrəbi'lɛəriəsnis], *s.* (*med.*) atrabilis, *f.*; melancolía.
atrabilis [æ'træbilis], *s.* (*med.*) atrabilis, *f.*
atrip [ə'trip], *adv.* (*mar.*) apeada el ancla; izado en lo más alto de las vergas (*velas*); vergas en alto.
atrium ['eitriəm], *s.* (*pl.* **atria** [-ə]) atrio.
atrocious [ə'trouʃəs], *a.* atroz.
atrociousness, atrocity [ə'trouʃəsnis, ə'trɔsiti], *s.* atrocidad; enormidad.
atrophic [æ'trɔfik], *a.* atrófico.
atrophy ['ætrəfi], *s.* (*med.*) atrofia. — ['ætrəfai], *v.t.* producir atrofia. — *v.i.* atrofiarse.
atropine ['ætrəpain], *s.* (*quím.*) atropina.
attach [ə'tætʃ], *v.t.* atar, ligar; pegar, adherir, sujetar, prender; atraer (a sí); agregar, adscribir; dar, conceder (*importancia etc.*); (*for.*) embargar, secuestrar; ***to get attached to,*** apegarse a; cobrar afecto a. — *v.i.* acompañar, ser inherente.
attachable [ə'tætʃəbl], *a.* agregable, enganchable, pegable; (*for.*) secuestrable, embargable.
attaché [ə'tæʃei], *s.* agregado.
attachment [ə'tætʃmənt], *s.* enlace, atadura, ligazón, unión, conexión; fijación; accesorio; apego, afecto; (*for.*) embargo, secuestro.
attack [ə'tæk], *s.* ataque; (*med.*) acceso. — *v.t.* atacar, agredir; acometer, abordar.
attacker [ə'tækə], *s.* agresor, atacador, acometedor.
attain [ə'tein], *v.t.* lograr, obtener, conseguir, alcanzar. — *v.i.* llegar a.

attainability [ə'teinə'biliti], *s.* (lo) alcanzable, (lo) factible.
attainable [ə'teinəbl], *a.* alcanzable, factible, asequible, realizable.
attainder [ə'teində], *s.* deshonra; (*for.*) proscripción; (*for.*) muerte civil; ***bill of attainder,*** decreto de proscripción.
attainment [ə'teinmənt], *s.* logro, consecución; (*pl.*) conocimientos, habilidades adquiridas, méritos.
attaint [ə'teint], *s.* mancha, baldón; muerte civil. — *v.t.* deshonrar; (*for.*) condenar; proscribir.
attar ['ætə], *s.* esencia de rosas.
attemper [ə'tempə], *v.t.* atemperar.
attempt [ə'tempt], *s.* intento, tentativa, conato; atentado; ***to make an attempt on the life of,*** atentar contra. — *v.t.* intentar; ***attempt the impossible,*** intentar lo imposible. — *v.i.* — ***to,*** tratar de, intentar, procurar, pretender.
attend [ə'tend], *v.t.* asistir (a); acompañar; ***attend lectures,*** asistir a clase. — *v.i.* asistir (a); ***attend to,*** atender a, ocuparse de.
attendance [ə'tendəns], *s.* asistencia; acompañamiento; concurrencia; público; (*for.*) comparecencia; ***to be in attendance,*** estar de servicio; estar presente; ***to dance attendance,*** hacer antesala; estar de plantón; ***lady in attendance,*** camarera mayor.
attendant [ə'tendənt], *a.* concomitante, acompañante. — *s.* sirviente, criado; mozo; acompañante.
attention [ə'tenʃən], *s.* atención; (*pl.*) atenciones, detalles; (*mil.*) ***attention!*** ¡atención! ¡firmes!; ***to attract attention,*** llamar la atención; ***to call attention to,*** llamar la atención sobre; (*mil.*) ***to come*** o ***stand to attention,*** cuadrarse; (*com.*) ***for the attention of,*** para atención de; ***to pay attention,*** prestar atención.
attentive [ə'tentiv], *a.* atento; considerado.
attentiveness [ə'tentivnis], *s.* consideración, cortesía.
attenuant [ə'tenjuənt], *a.* atenuante.
attenuate [ə'tenjueit], *v.t.* atenuar.
attenuating [ə'tenjueitiŋ], *a.* atenuante.
attenuation [ətenju'eiʃən], *s.* atenuación.
attest [ə'test], *v.t.* atestiguar, certificar, dar fe de; autenticar. — *v.i.* — ***to,*** dar fe de.
attestation [ætes'teiʃən], *s.* atestación, deposición, testimonio, testificación; autenticación; certificado, certificación.
attester, attestor [ə'testə], *s.* testigo, certificador.
Attic ['ætik], *a.* ático; ***Attic wit,*** sal ática.
attic ['ætik], *s.* desván, guardilla, buhardilla; (*arq.*) ático.
Atticism ['ætisizəm], *s.* aticismo.
atticize ['ætisaiz], *v.t.* emplear el dialecto ático en. — *v.i.* emplear aticismos.
attire [ə'taiə], *s.* atavío, atuendo. — *v.t.* ataviar. — **attire o.s.,** *v.r.* ataviarse.
attitude ['ætitju:d], *s.* actitud, postura.
attitudinize [æti'tju:dinaiz], *v.i.* pavonearse, tomar posturas afectadas.
attollent [ə'tɔlənt], *a.*, *s.* (*anat.*) elevador.
attorney [ə'tə:ni], *s.* procurador, agente, apoderado, poderhabiente, delegado, comisionado; (*Am.*) abogado; ***letter of attorney,*** poder, procuración.
attorney-general [ə'tə:ni-'dʒenərəl], *s.* fiscal, procurador, síndico general.
attorneyship [ə'tə:niʃip], *s.* fiscalía, procuraduría, oficio de procurador, agencia, poder.
attract [ə'trækt], *v.t.* atraer; llamar, captar; granjear, interesar.
attractability [ətræktə'biliti], *s.* atractabilidad, cualidad de atraíble.
attractable [ə'træktəbl], *a.* atraíble.
attractile [ə'træktail], *a.* atractivo.
attraction [ə'trækʃən], *s.* atracción; atractivo, aliciente.
attractive [ə'træktiv], *a.* atrayente, atractivo; interesante.
attractiveness [ə'træktivnis], *s.* atractivo, fuerza atractiva; gracia.
attractor [ə'træktə], *s.* persona *o* cosa que atrae.
attrahent ['ætrəhənt], *a.*, *s.* (*med.*) atrayante, supurativo.
attributable [ə'tribjutəbl], *a.* imputable.
attribute ['ætribju:t], *s.* atributo, cualidad, característica. — [ə'tribju:t], *v.t.* atribuir, achacar, imputar.
attribution [ætri'bju:ʃən], *s.* atribución, atributo.
attributive [ə'tribjutiv], *a.* atributivo.
attrite [ə'trait], *a.* estregado, frotado; (*teo.*) atrito, pesaroso.
attrition [ə'triʃən], *s.* atrición; roce, desgaste; ***war of attrition,*** guerra de desgaste.
attune [ə'tju:n], *v.t.* acordar, armonizar, afinar.
atwist [ə'twist], *adv.* torcidamente, al través, sesgado.
aubergine ['oubədʒi:n], *s.* berenjena.
auburn ['ɔ:bən], *a.* castaño, moreno rojizo.
auction ['ɔ:kʃən], *s.* subasta, almoneda. — *v.t.* subastar, vender en almoneda.
auctioneer [ɔ:kʃə'niə], *s.* subastador. — *v.t.* vender en subasta.
auction-room ['ɔ:kʃən-ru:m], *s.* sala de subastas.
audacious [ɔ:'deiʃəs], *a.* audaz, osado; atrevido, descarado.
audaciousness, audacity [ɔ:'deiʃəsnis, ɔ:'dæsiti], *s.* audacia, osadía; denuedo; descaro.
audibility, audibleness [ɔ:di'biliti, 'ɔ:diblnis], *s.* audibilidad.
audible ['ɔ:dibl], *a.* audible, oíble, perceptible (*al oído*).
audience ['ɔ:diəns], *s.* audiencia; auditorio, público; ***audience-chamber,*** audiencia.
audiphone ['ɔ:difoun], *s.* audífono.
audit ['ɔ:dit], *s.* revisión, ajuste, intervención. — *v.t.* revisar, intervenir.
audition [ɔ:'diʃən], *s.* audición; prueba.
auditive ['ɔ:ditiv], *a.* auditivo.
auditor ['ɔ:ditə], *s.* oyente; revisor, interventor.
auditorium [ɔ:di'tɔ:riəm], *s.* sala de conciertos, de conferencias, paraninfo.
auditorship ['ɔ:ditəʃip], *s.* auditoría; intervención.
auditory ['ɔ:ditəri], *a.* auditivo; ***auditory canal,*** conducto auditivo.
Augean [ɔ:'dʒiən], *a.* de Augías; (*fig.*) sucísimo; ***Augean stables,*** los establos de Augías.
auger ['ɔ:gə], *s.* barrena, taladro; ***auger-shank,*** vástago de barrena; (*mar.*) ***bolting auger,*** barrena de empernar.
aught [ɔ:t], *pron. indef.* alguna cosa; cualquier cosa.
augite ['ɔ:dʒait], *s.* (*min.*) augita.
augment [ɔ:g'ment], *v.t.* aumentar, incrementar. — *v.i.* aumentar.
augmentable [ɔ:g'mentəbl], *a.* aumentable.
augmentation [ɔ:gmen'teiʃən], *s.* aumento, acrecentamiento.
augmentative [ɔ:g'mentətiv], *a.*, *s.* aumentativo.
augur (1), ['ɔ:gə], *v.t.* augurar, pronosticar, predecir. — *v.i.* ***well, ill,*** ser de buen, mal agüero.
augur (2), **augurer** ['ɔ:gə, 'ɔ:gjuərə], *s.* augur, agorero, adivino.
augural ['ɔ:gjuərəl], *a.* augural.
augury ['ɔ:gjuəri], *s.* augurio, agüero, presagio, pronóstico.
August ['ɔ:gəst], *s.* agosto.
august [ɔ:'gʌst], *a.* augusto.
Augustan [ɔ:'gʌstən], *a.* de Augusto, augustal.
Augustine, Augustinian [ɔ:'gʌsti:n, ɔ:gʌs'tiniən], *s.* agustino.
augustness [ɔ:'gʌstnis], *s.* majestad, majestuosidad, grandeza.
auk [ɔ:k], *s.* (*orn.*) alca.

auld [ɔ:ld], *a.* (*Esco.*) viejo, antiguo; ***auld lang syne,*** por los dichosos tiempos pasados; (*fam.*) ***Auld Reekie,*** vieja humeante (*la ciudad de Edimburgo*).
aulic [ˈɔ:lik], *a.* áulico, palaciego.
aunt [ɑ:nt], *s.* tía.
auntie [ˈɑ:nti], *s.* (*fam.*) tía, tita.
au pair (**girl**) [ou ˈpɛə (gə:l)], *s.* chica au pair.
aura [ˈɔ:rə], *s.* aura, céfiro; efluvio, emanación; magnetismo animal; (*pat.*) vaho.
aural [ˈɔ:rəl], *a.* auditivo, auricular, del oído.
aurate [ˈɔ:reit], *s.* (*quím.*) auratón, aurato, sal de oro.
aurated [ɔ:ˈreitid], *a.* dorado; (*quím.*) aureado.
aurelia [ɔ:ˈri:liə], *s.* (*zool.*) crisálida, ninfa.
aureole [ˈɔ:rioul], *s.* aureola.
Aurelius [ɔ:ˈri:liəs]. Aurelio, Aureliano.
auricle [ˈɔ:rikl], *s.* aurícula, pabellón de la oreja.
auricula [ɔ:ˈrikjulə], *s.* (*bot.*) oreja de oso.
auricular [ɔ:ˈrikjulə], *a.* auricular; confidencial, secreto.
auriculate [ɔ:ˈrikjuleit], *a.* auriculado, que tiene aurículas *u* orejillas.
auriferous [ɔ:ˈrifərəs], *a.* (*poét.*) aurífero, aurígero.
auriga [ɔ:ˈri:gə], *s.* auriga, *m.*
auriscalp [ˈɔ:riskælp], *s.* (*cir.*) auriscalpo.
auriscope [ˈɔ:riskoup], *s.* auriscopio.
aurist [ˈɔ:rist], *s.* otólogo.
aurochs [ˈɔ:rɔks], *s.* (*zool.*) uro.
aurora [ɔ:ˈrɔ:rə], *s.* aurora, alborada, alba; (*meteorol.*) ***aurora borealis,*** aurora boreal.
auroral [ɔ:ˈrɔ:rəl], *a.* perteneciente a la aurora, auroral; matutino; rosáceo.
auscultate [ˈɔ:skəlteit], *v.t.* (*med.*) auscultar.
auscultation [ɔ:skəlˈteiʃən], *s.* auscultación; atención.
auscultatory [ɔ:skəlˈteitəri], *a.* relativo a la auscultación.
auspicate [ˈɔ:spikeit], *v.t.*, *v.i.* pronosticar, predecir, presagiar, augurar.
auspice [ˈɔ:spis], *s.* auspicio; agüero; ***under the auspices of,*** bajo los auspicios de.
auspicious [ɔ:ˈspiʃəs], *a.* favorable, propicio.
auspiciousness [ɔ:ˈspiʃəsnis], *s.* (lo) favorable, (lo) propicio.
Aussie [ˈɔsi], *s.* apodo de [AUSTRALIAN].
auster [ˈɔ:stə], *s.* austro.
austere [ɔ:sˈtiə], *a.* austero, severo, grave.
austerity, austereness [ɔ:sˈteriti, ɔ:sˈtiənis], *s.* austeridad, severidad.
Austin [ˈɔstin]. Agustín.
austral [ɔ:strəl], *a.* austral.
Australasia [ɔstrəˈleiʃə]. Australasia.
Australia [ɔsˈtreiliə]. Australia.
Australian [ɔsˈtreiliən], *a.*, *s.* australiano.
Austria [ˈɔstriə]. Austria.
Austrian [ˈɔstriən], *a.*, *s.* austríaco.
Austro-Hungarian [ˈɔstrou-hʌŋˈgɛəriən], *a.*, *s.* (*hist.*) austro-húngaro.
autarchic [ɔ:ˈtɑ:kik], *a.* autárquico.
autarchy [ˈɔ:tɑ:ki], *s.* autarquía.
authentic [ɔ:ˈθentik], *a.* auténtico; fehaciente.
authenticate [ɔ:ˈθentikeit], *v.t.* autenticar, legalizar, autorizar; certificar la autenticidad de.
authentication [ɔ:θentiˈkeiʃən], *s.* autenticación.
authenticity [ɔ:θenˈtisiti], *s.* autenticidad.
author [ˈɔ:θə], *s.* autor.
authoress [ɔ:θəˈres], *s.* autora.
authoritarian [ɔ:θɔriˈtɛəriən], *a.* autoritario.
authoritarianism [ɔ:θɔriˈtɛəriənizəm], *s.* autoritarismo.
authoritative [ɔ:ˈθɔritətiv], *a.* autorizado; de autoridad.
authoritativeness [ɔ:ˈθɔritətivnis], *s.* (lo) autorizado; actitud de autoridad.
authority [ɔ:ˈθɔriti], *s.* autoridad; (*impr.*) ***by authority,*** con licencia; ***on good authority,*** de fuente(s) fidedigna(s); (*fam.*) de buena tinta.
authorizable [ˈɔ:θəraizəbl], *a.* autorizable.
authorization [ɔ:θəraiˈzeiʃən], *s.* autorización, legalización.
authorize [ˈɔ:θəraiz], *v.t.* autorizar, sancionar, facultar, legalizar.
authorless [ˈɔ:θəlis], *a.* sin autor.
authorship [ˈɔ:θəʃip], *s.* profesión de escritor; calidad de autor; paternidad literaria; (*fig.*) origen.
auto [ˈɔ:tou], *s.* (*Am.*) automóvil, coche; ***auto industry,*** industria automovilística.
autobiographer [ɔ:tobaiˈɔgrəfə], *s.* autobiógrafo.
autobiographical [ɔ:tobaioˈgræfikəl], *a.* autobiográfico.
autobiography [ɔ:tobaiˈɔgrəfi], *s.* autobiografía.
auto-bus [ˈɔ:to-bʌs], (*Am.*) [BUS].
auto-car [ˈɔ:to-kɑ:], *s.* automóvil.
autocracy [ɔ:ˈtɔkrəsi], *s.* autocracia.
autocrat [ˈɔ:tokræt], *s.* autócrata, *m.f.*
autocratic [ɔ:toˈkrætik], *a.* autocrático.
autograph [ˈɔ:togrɑ:f], *s.* autógrafo.
autographic(**al**) [ɔ:toˈgræfik(əl)], *a.* autógrafo, autográfico.
autographometer [ɔ:togrəˈfɔmitə], *s.* autografómetro.
autography [ɔ:ˈtɔgrəfi], *s.* autografía.
automat [ɔ:toˈmæt], *s.* máquina expendedora.
automatic [ɔ:toˈmætik], *a.* automático.
automation [ɔ:toˈmeiʃən], *s.* automatización.
automaton [ɔ:ˈtɔmətən], *s.* (*pl.* **automata** [-tə]) autómata, *m.*
automatous [ɔ:ˈtɔmətəs], *a.* automático.
automobile [ˈɔ:tomobi:l], (*Am.*) [CAR].
autonomic [ɔ:toˈnɔmik], *a.* autonómico.
autonomist [ɔ:ˈtɔnəmist], *s.* autonomista, *m.f.*
autonomous [ɔ:ˈtɔnəməs], *a.* autónomo.
autonomy [ɔ:ˈtɔnəmi], *s.* autonomía.
autopathic [ɔ:toˈpæθik], *a.* autopático.
autopsy [ˈɔ:tɔpsi], *s.* (*med.*) autopsia, post-mortem.
autoscopy [ɔ:ˈtɔskəpi], *s.* autoscopia.
autotomy [ɔ:ˈtɔtəmi], *s.* autotomía.
autotype [ˈɔ:totaip], *s.* facsímil, autotipo, copia exacta.
autumn [ˈɔ:təm], *s.* otoño.
autumnal [ɔ:ˈtʌmnəl], *a.* otoñal, autumnal.
auxiliary [ɔ:gˈziljəri], *a.* auxiliar, subsidiario.
avail [əˈveil], *s.* provecho, utilidad; ***to no avail,*** en vano, inútilmente. — *v.t.* aprovechar, ser útil a, servir. — *v.i.* servir, ser útil. — **avail o.s.,** *v.r.* — ***of,*** servirse de, aprovechar, valerse de.
availability, availableness [əveiləˈbiliti, əˈveiləblnis], *s.* disponibilidad.
available [əˈveiləbl], *a.* disponible; obtenible; (*com.*) ***available assets,*** activo disponible.
avalanche [ˈævəlɑ:nʃ], *s.* alud; (*fig.*) avalancha.
avarice [ˈævəris], *s.* avaricia, codicia.
avaricious, avariciousness [ævəˈriʃəs, -nis], *a.* avaro, avariento, codicioso. — *s.* avaricia, codicia.
avast [əˈvɑ:st], *adv.* (*mar.*) forte. — *interj.* ¡forte! ¡basta! ¡no más!; ***avast heaving!*** (*mar.*) forte al virar.
avaunt! [əˈvɔ:nt], *interj.* (*ant.*) ¡fuera! ¡fuera de aquí! ¡quita allá!
avenaceous [ævəˈneiʃəs], *a.* aveníceo, avenáceo.
avenge [əˈvendʒ], *v.t.* vengar, vengarse de, vindicar.
avenger [əˈvendʒə], *s.* vengador.
avenging [əˈvendʒiŋ], *a.* vengador.
avens [ˈævənz], *s.* (*bot.*) gariofilea.
aventail, aventayle [ˈævənteil], *s.* (*blas.*) ventalla, abertura de la visera de la celada.
aventurine [əˈventjurin], *s.* venturina.

avenue [ˈævənjuː], *s.* avenida, alameda, paseo; camino, entrada; ***avenue of trade,*** ruta comercial.
aver [əˈvəː], *v.t.* asegurar, afirmar; verificar, certificar.
average [ˈævəridʒ], *a.* medio, de promedio; normal, corriente. — *s.* promedio, término medio; prorrata; (lo) corriente, (lo) común; (*mar.*) avería; (*for.*) servicio, carga. — *v.t.* determinar el promedio de; prorratear. — *v.i.* sumar por término medio.
averment [əˈvəːmənt], *s.* afirmación, aseveración.
averruncate [ævəˈrʌŋkeit], *v.t.* desarraigar, arrancar de raíz, extirpar.
averse [əˈvəːs], *a.* contrario, opuesto, renuente; ***to be averse to,*** sentir repugnancia por.
aversion, averseness [əˈvəːʃən, əˈvəːsnis], *s.* aversión, aborrecimiento, repugnancia; renuencia, mala gana.
avert [əˈvəːt], *v.t.* desviar, apartar; impedir, evitar, conjurar.
aviary [ˈeiviəri], *s.* pajarera.
aviate [ˈeivieit], *v.i.* volar.
aviation [eiviˈeiʃən], *s.* aviación.
aviator [ˈeivieitə], *s.* aviador.
avicultural [eiviˈkʌltʃərəl], *a.* avícola.
aviculture [ˈeivikʌltʃə], *s.* avicultura.
aviculturist [eiviˈkʌltʃərist], *s.* avicultor.
avid [ˈævid], *a.* ávido, ansioso, codicioso.
avidity [əˈviditi], *s.* avidez, ansia, codicia.
avocado [ævoˈkɑːdou], *s.* aguacate; (*Hisp.Am.*) palta.
avocation [ævoˈkeiʃən], *s.* ocupación; pasatiempo, diversión.
avocet [ˈævoset], *s.* (*orn.*) avoceta.
avoid [əˈvɔid], *v.t.* evitar, esquivar, eludir; (*for.*) anular.
avoidable [əˈvɔidəbl], *a.* evitable, eludible; (*for.*) revocable.
avoidance [əˈvɔidəns], *s.* evitación; anulación.
avoirdupois [ævədəˈpɔiz], *s.* sistema de pesos; (*fig.*) peso, gordura.
avouch [əˈvautʃ], *v.t.* afirmar, sostener; garantizar; reconocer.
avow [əˈvau], *v.t.* confesar; declarar.
avowable [əˈvauəbl], *a.* confesable.
avowal [əˈvauəl], *s.* confesión; declaración.
avowedly [əˈvauidli], *adv.* declaradamente, abiertamente.
avulsion [əˈvʌlʃən], *s.* arrancamiento, separación; (*cir.*) avulsión.
avuncular [əˈvʌŋkjulə], *a.* de un tío *o* parecido a un tío; protector.
await [əˈweit], *v.t.* esperar, aguardar.
awake [əˈweik], *a.* despierto; ***to keep awake,*** desvelar; (*fig.*) ***wide-awake,*** alerta, listo. — *v.t.* despertar. — *v.i.* despertar, despertarse.
awaken [əˈweikən], *v.t.*, *v.i.* [AWAKE].
awak(en)ing [əˈweik(ən)iŋ], *s.* despertar, despertamiento; ***rude awakening,*** desilusión amarga, escopetazo.
award [əˈwɔːd], *s.* sentencia, fallo, decisión; concesión, adjudicación; premio, galardón. — *v.t.* conceder, adjudicar, otorgar (*un premio*); conferir.
awardable [əˈwɔːdəbl], *a.* adjudicable.
awarder [əˈwɔːdə], *s.* sentenciador; adjudicador.
aware [əˈwɛə], *a.* sabedor, enterado, informado, consciente (de); ***to be aware of,*** estar enterado de, saber, darse cuenta de, tener noticia(s) de.
awareness [əˈwɛənis], *s.* conocimiento, conciencia.
awash [əˈwɔʃ], *adv.* (*mar.*) bajo el agua; inundado.
away [əˈwei], *adv.* fuera; ausente; continuamente; ***to play (an) away (match),*** jugar fuera (de casa); ***away from home,*** fuera, lejos de casa; ***to do away with,*** suprimir; ***to do away with o.s.,*** suicidarse; ***far and away the best,*** el mejor con mucho; ***to get away,*** escaparse; ***to get away with,*** conseguir; ***to go away,*** irse, marcharse; ***a long way away, far away,*** muy lejos, a mucha distancia; ***right away,*** ahora mismo, en sequida; ***to run away,*** escaparse; ***to send away,*** (*people*) despedir; ***to send away for,*** pedir por correo; ***to take away,*** quitar; ***he was singing away,*** estaba canta que te canta; ***five kilometres away,*** a cinco kilómetros. — *interj.* ¡fuera! ¡fuera de aquí!; ***away with you!*** ¡fuera! ¡tonterías!
awe [ɔː], *s.* temor (reverencial); ***to be awe-struck,*** quedarse atemorizado; ***to stand in awe of,*** tener temor de; ***to strike with awe,*** inspirar terror. — *v.t.* aterrar, amedrentar, atemorizar, imponer.
aweather [əˈweðə], *adv.* (*mar.*) a barlovento.
aweigh [əˈwei], *adv.* (*mar.*) pendiente, a plomo.
awesome [ˈɔːsəm], *a.* terrible, temible, aterrador, pavoroso.
awful [ˈɔːful], *a.* atroz, espantoso, terrible; muy malo, muy feo, infame.
awfully [ˈɔːfuli], *adv.* atrozmente, terriblemente; muy, muchísmo; ***thanks awfully,*** un millón de gracias.
awfulness [ˈɔːfulnis], *s.* solemnidad; veneración; temor reverencial.
awhile [əˈwail], *adv.* un rato; algún tiempo; ***not yet awhile,*** todavía no, por ahora no.
awkward [ˈɔːkwəd], *a.* torpe, desmañado; embarazoso, difícil, engorroso; mal hecho; de manejo difícil.
awkwardness [ˈɔːkwədnis], *s.* torpeza, desmaña; cortedad; (lo) embarazoso o difícil.
awl [ɔːl], *s.* lesna, lezna, alesna, subilla, punzón; ***awl-shaped,*** alesnado.
awn [ɔːn], *s.* (*bot.*) arista, raspa.
awning [ˈɔːniŋ], *s.* pabellón; toldo; marquesina; abrigaña; (*mar.*) toldilla.
awry [əˈrai], *a.* oblicuo, sesgado, torcido. — *adv.* oblicuamente, torcidamente, de través; ***to go awry,*** torcerse; (*fig.*) malograrse.
axe [æks], *s.* hacha, segur, *f.*; (*fam.*) ***an axe to grind,*** un fin interesado; ***cooper's axe,*** doladera; ***pick-axe,*** piqueta, zapapico. — *v.t.* hachear; (*fig.*) suprimir, dar al traste con.
axial [ˈæksiəl], *a.* axial, axil.
axiferous [ækˈsifərəs], *a.* axífero.
axil [ˈæksil], *s.* (*bot.*) axila.
axilla [ækˈsilə], *s.* (*anat.*, *bot.*, *zool.*) axila.
axillar(y) [ækˈsilə(ri)], *a.* axilar.
axinite [ˈæksinait], *s.* (*min.*) axinita.
axiom [ˈæksiəm], *s.* axioma, *m.*
axiomatic [æksiəˈmætik], *a.* axiomático.
axis [ˈæksis], *s.* (*pl.* **axes** [ˈæksiːz]) eje; (*anat.*) axis.
axle [æksl], *s.* eje; ***axle-tree,*** árbol.
axometer [ækˈsomətə], *s.* axómetro; (*mar.*) axiómetro.
ay, aye (1) [ai], *adv.* sí; seguramente; desde luego; — *interj.* ¡ay!; ***thirty ayes and forty noes,*** treinta votos a favor y cuarenta votos en contra.
aye (2) [ei], *adv.* (*ant.*) siempre, para siempre jamás.
azalea [əˈzeiliə], *s.* (*bot.*) azalea.
azerole [ˈæzəroul], *s.* (*bot.*) acerola.
azimuth [ˈæziməθ], *s.* (*astron.*) acimut.
azoic [əˈzouik], *a.* azoico.
Azores [əˈzɔːz], **the.** las Azores.
azote [əˈzout], *s.* (*quím.*) ázoe, nitrógeno.
azotic [əˈzɔtik], *a.* azoico, nítrico.
Aztec [ˈæztek], *a.*, *s.* azteca, *m.f.*
azure [ˈæʒuə], *a.* azul celeste, azulado. — *s.* azul (celeste); (*blas.*) azur.
azurine [ˈæʒurain], *a.* azulado.
azurite [ˈæʒurait], *s.* azurita.
azyme [ˈæzim], *s.* pan ázimo.
azymous [ˈæziməs], *a.* ázimo.

B

B, b [biː], segunda letra del alfabeto; ***not to know A from B,*** no saber cuántas son cinco; ***B,*** (*mús.*) si.
baa [bɑː], *s.* be, balido. — *v.i.* balar, dar balidos.
babbit (metal) [ˈbæbit (metl)], *s.* metal de antifricción.
babble [bæbl], *s.* balbuceo(s); charloteo(s), parloteo(s); palabrería; murmullo. — *v.t.* decir balbuceando *o* con incoherencia. — *v.i.* charlotear, parlotear; desbarrar; murmurar.
babbler [ˈbæblə], *s.* hablador, charlatán.
babbling [ˈbæbliŋ], *a.* hablador, charlatán; murmurador, murmurante; incoherente. — *s.* [BABBLE].
babe [beib], *s.* criatura, bebé, nene; (*fig.*) niño.
babel [ˈbeibəl], *s.* babel.
baboon [bəˈbuːn], *s.* (*zool.*) babuino, mandril.
baby [ˈbeibi], *a.* infantil; ***baby eel,*** angula; ***baby grand (piano),*** piano de media cola; ***baby marrow,*** calabacín. — *s.* bebé, criatura, niño pequeño; pequeño (*animal*); benjamín (*menor de la familia*). — *v.t.* mimar.
baby carriage [ˈbeibi kæridʒ], (*Am.*) [PERAMBULATOR].
babyhood [ˈbeibihud], *s.* niñez, primera infancia.
babyish [ˈbeibiiʃ], *a.* infantil.
babyishness [ˈbeibiiʃnis], *s.* puerilidad, infantilismo.
Babylonian [bæbiˈlouniən], *a.* babilonio; babilónico. — *s.* babilonio.
baby-sit [ˈbeibi-sit], *v.i.* vigilar a los niños (dormidos) en ausencia de los padres.
baby-sitter [ˈbeibi-sitə], *s.* persona que vigila a los niños (dormidos) en ausencia de los padres.
baccalaureate [bækəˈlɔriit], *s.* bachillerato.
baccarat [ˈbækərɑː], *s.* bacarrat, bacará.
baccate [ˈbækeit], *a.* (*bot.*) que se parece a una baya.
bacchanal, bacchanalian [ˈbækənəl, bækəˈneiliən], *a.* bacanal, báquico. — *s.* discípulo de Baco; calavera.
bacchanalia, *s.pl.* bacanales, *f.pl.*; (*fig.*) bacanal.
bacchic(al) [ˈbækik(əl)], *a.* báquico.
Bacchus [ˈbækəs]. (*mit.*) Baco.
bacciferous [bækˈsifərəs], *a.* (*bot.*) bacífero.
bachelor [ˈbætʃələ], *s.* soltero; bachiller; mancebo; ***bachelor of arts,*** licenciado en artes; (*bot.*) ***bachelor's button,*** botón de oro, azulejo; ***old bachelor,*** solterón.
bachelorship [ˈbætʃələʃip], *s.* celibato, soltería; bachillerato.
bacillary [bəˈsiləri], *a.* bacilar, perteneciente a un bacilo.
bacilliform [bəˈsilifɔːm], *a.* (*med.*) baciliforme.
bacillus [bəˈsiləs], *s.* (*pl.* **bacilli** [bəˈsilai]) bacilo.
back [bæk], *a.* trasero, posterior, de atrás, de detrás, atrasado; ***back number,*** número atrasado; ***back room,*** cuarto trasero; ***back shop,*** trastienda; ***back street,*** calle apartada. — *adv.* atrás, detrás; de vuelta, de retorno; ***to beat back,*** rechazar; ***to bring back,*** volver a traer; ***to come back,*** volver, regresar; ***to give back,*** devolver; ***to hold back,*** retener; ***to stand back,*** hacerse *o* echarse atrás; ***some time back,*** hace algún tiempo; ***years back,*** hace años, años atrás. — *s.* espalda, dorso; lomo; revés, reverso; fondo, parte posterior; respaldo (*de una silla*); trasera (*de un coche*); (*mar.*) galga de ancla; (*fútbol*) zaguero, defensa; foro (*de un teatro*); ***back to back,*** espalda con espalda; ***behind one's back,*** a espaldas de uno; ***to break one's back,*** deslomarse; ***to carry on one's back,*** llevar a cuestas; ***to cast behind one's back,*** dar al olvido; ***to see the back of,*** perder de vista, librarse de; ***to turn one's back,*** volver las espaldas; ***to have a pain in one's back,*** tener dolor de espaldas *o* riñones; ***on horseback,*** a caballo. — *v.t.* apoyar, respaldar; apostar a; ***back up,*** apoyar, respaldar. — *v.i.* retroceder, recular, dar marcha atrás; ***back down,*** volverse *o* echarse atrás, desdecirse; ***back out of,*** retractarse de, desdecirse de. — *interj.* ¡vuélvase Vd.! ¡vuélvanse Vds.! ¡atrás!
back-bencher [ˈbæk-ˈbentʃə], *s.* (*pol.*) diputado que no es ministro.
backbite [ˈbækbait], *v.i.* murmurar.
backbiter [ˈbækbaitə], *s.* maldiciente, murmurador.
backbiting [ˈbækbaitiŋ], *s.* murmuración, maledicencia.
back-board [ˈbæk-bɔːd], *s.* respaldo; espaldar.
backbone [ˈbækboun], *s.* espinazo, espina dorsal; (*fam., fig.*) firmeza, decisión; ***to the backbone,*** hasta los tuétanos, hasta la médula.
back-breaking [ˈbæk-breikiŋ], *a.* deslomador.
backdoor [ˈbækˈdɔː], *s.* puerta trasera; (*fig.*) pretexto, escapatoria.
back-drop [ˈbæk-drɔp], *s.* telón de foro.
backer [ˈbækə], *s.* el que apoya, partidario; (*com.*) comanditario; apostador.
backfire [ˈbækˈfaiə], *v.i.* petardear; (*fig.*) salir el tiro por la culata.
backgammon [bækˈgæmən], *s.* chaquete; ***backgammon board,*** tablas reales.
background [ˈbækgraund], *s.* fondo; trasfondo; último término; ambiente, antecedentes, educación; olvido, oscuridad; ***in the background,*** al fondo; en la oscuridad; entre bastidores.
backhanded [bækˈhændid], *a.* dado con el revés de la mano; (*fig.*) falto de sinceridad; ***backhanded blow,*** revés, golpe de revés.
backhouse [ˈbækhaus], *s.* trascuarto; retrete.
backing [ˈbækiŋ], *s.* apoyo, ayuda, sostén, garantía; refuerzo; respaldo; espaldar; forro; retroceso.
back-lash [ˈbæk-læʃ], *s.* (*pol.*) reacción violenta.
back-log [ˈbæk-lɔg], *s.* atraso.
backpiece [ˈbækpiːs], *s.* espaldar.
backside [ˈbækˈsaid], *s.* (*fam.*) trasero, posaderas, *f.pl.*, nalgas, *f.pl.*
backslide [ˈbækˈslaid], *v.i.* reincidir.
backslider [ˈbækˈslaidə], *s.* reincidente.
backsliding [ˈbækˈslaidiŋ], *s.* reincidencia.
backstaff [ˈbækstɑːf], *s.* (*mar.*) cuarto de cuadrante.
backstair(s) [ˈbækstɛə(z)], *a.* secreto, clandestino, oculto, de intriga(s). — [ˈbækˈstɛəz], *s.pl.* escalera excusada; (*fig.*) vías indirectas, *f.pl.*
backstays [ˈbæksteiz], *s.pl.* (*mar.*) brandales, *m.pl.*, traversas, *f.pl.*
backstitch [ˈbækstitʃ], *s.* pespunte. — *v.t., v.i.* pespuntar.
backward [ˈbækwəd], *a.* atrasado; retrógrado; retraído, corto; ***backward and forward motion,*** vaivén. — *adv.* [BACKWARDS].
backwardness [ˈbækwədnis], *s.* atraso; retraso; retraimiento, cortedad.
backwards [ˈbækwədz], *adv.* atrás, hacia atrás; de espaldas; al revés, en sentido contrario; ***to go backwards and forwards,*** ir y venir; ***to know sth. backwards,*** saberse al dedillo; ***to read backwards,*** leer al revés; ***to walk backwards,*** andar de espaldas; caminar hacia atrás.
back-wash [ˈbæk-wɔʃ], *s.* agua de rechazo; (*fig.*) consecuencias.
backwater [ˈbækwɔːtə], *s.* remanso; sitio apartado (de la vida).
backwoods [bækwuds], *s.* región apartada, monte; ***to be from the backwoods,*** ser paleto, palurdo.
backwoodsman [ˈbækwudsmən], *s.* patán; (*pol.*) miembro de la cámara de los lores que sólo vota al ver amenazados sus privilegios heredados.
back-yard [ˈbæk-ˈjɑːd], *s.* corral.
bacon [ˈbeikən], *s.* jamón; (*fam.*) ***to save one's bacon,*** salvar el pellejo.
bacteria [bækˈtiəriə], *s.pl.* [BACTERIUM].

bacterial [bæk'tiəriəl], *a.* bacterial, bactérico.
bacteriologist [bæktiəri'ɔlədʒist], *s.* (*med.*) bacteriólogo.
bacteriology [bæktiəri'ɔlədʒi], *s.* bacteriología.
bacterium [bæk'tiəriəm], *s.* (*pl.* **bacteria**) bacteria, microbio.
bad (1) [bæd], *a.* mal, malo; podrido (huevo); incobrable (deuda); ***with a bad grace,*** de mal grado; ***in a bad way,*** malamente; en mal estado; muy enfermo. — *adv.* mal; ***bad looking,*** feo, de mal aspecto, de mal cariz. — *s.* mal, (lo) malo; ***from bad to worse,*** de mal en peor.
bad (2), **bade** [bæd], *pret.* [BID].
badge [bædʒ], *s.* divisa; emblema, *m.*; distintivo; insignia; escarapela; condecoración; (*mar.*) ***badges of the stern and quarters,*** escudos de popa.
badgeless ['bædʒlis], *a.* sin divisa.
badger ['bædʒə], *s.* (*zool.*) tejón. — *v.t.* dar el tostón a, importunar, molestar, fastidiar.
badger-legged ['bædʒə-legd], *a.* patituerto, este vado.
badiane ['bædiæn], *s.* (*bot.*) badiena.
badinage ['bædinɑ:ʒ], *s.* burla, chanza, cháchara, jocosidad.
badly ['bædli], *adv.* mal; muy, mucho; ***badly off,*** mal de dinero; ***badly off for,*** mal de, con mucha necesidad de.
badminton ['bædmintən], *s.* (juego del) volante, bádminton.
badness ['bædnis], *s.* maldad, ruindad; mala calidad, (lo) malo.
baffle [bæfl], *s.* (*mec.*) pantalla, deflector. — *v.t.* confundir, desconcertar; burlar; frustar.
baffler ['bæflə], *s.* engañador; impedimento, contrariedad.
baffling ['bæfliŋ], *adj.* desconcertante.
baft [bɑ:ft], *s.* tejido grosero de algodón; (*mar.*) atrás, hacia la popa, en popa, a popa.
bag [bæg], *s.* bolsa; bolso; saco; talega; costal; (*fam.*) vieja fea; ***game bag,*** morral, zurrón; ***hand-bag,*** bolso; ***money bag,*** talega, saco de dinero; ***sleeping bag,*** saco de dormir; ***work bag,*** saquito de costura. — *v.t.* ensacar, entalegar, enzurronar; llenar; coger, cazar, capturar. — *v.i.* abotagarse, hincharse; hacer bolsa *o* pliegue (*la ropa*); (*mar.*) desviarse del rumbo.
bagasse [bæ'gæs], *s.* bagazo, gabazo.
bagatelle [bægə'tel], *s.* bagatela, futesa, pamema.
baggage ['bægidʒ], *s.* equipaje, bagaje; (*fam.*) zorra, pelleja.
bagging ['bægiŋ], *s.* arpillera.
baggy ['bægi], *a.* muy holgado; que tiene rodilleras.
bagpipe ['bægpaip], *s.* gaita, cornamusa.
bagpiper ['bægpaipə], *s.* gaitero.
Bahamas [bə'hɑ:məz], **the.** Islas Bahamas, *f.pl.*; las Bahamas.
bail (1) [beil], *s.* caución, fianza; fiador; agarradera, asa; ***to be on bail,*** estar en libertad bajo fianza; ***stand bail for,*** salir fiador por. — *v.t.* caucionar, fiar, dar fianzas, salir fiador; poner en libertad bajo caución *o* fianza.
bail (2) [beil], *s.* achicador. — *v.t.* desaguar, achicar el agua de, vaciar.
bailable ['beiləbl], *a.* (*for.*) caucionable, admisible con caución *o* fianza.
bail-bond ['beil-bɔnd], *s.* (*for.*) fianza, caución.
bailee [bei'li:], *s.* (*for.*) depositario.
bailer, bailor ['beilə], *s.* (*for.*) fiador.
bailie ['beili], *s.* regidor.
bailiff ['beilif], *s.* alguacil, corchete; gobernador; baile, ministril; mayordomo.
bailiwick ['beiliwik], *s.* bailía; alguacilazgo.
bairn [bɛən], *s.* (*Esco.*) niño, hijo.
bait [beit], *s.* cebo, carnada; anzuelo; añagaza, señuelo; ***to take the bait,*** tragar el anzuelo. — *v.t.* cebar; azuzar, atormentar, hostigar, hacer rabiar.
baiting ['beitiŋ], *s.* (el) cebar, (el) poner cebo; ***bull-baiting,*** lidia de toros con perros.
baize [beiz], *s.* bayeta; ***green baize,*** tapete verde.
bake [beik], *v.t.* cocer (en horno); asar; ***baked potato,*** patata asada.
bakehouse ['beikhaus], *s.* horno; panadería, tahona.
bakelite ['beikəlait], *s.* baquelita.
baker ['beikə], *s.* panadero; hornero; ***baker's dozen,*** trece; ***baker's shop,*** panadería, tahona.
bakery ['beikəri], *s.* panadería, tahona.
baking ['beikiŋ], *s.* hornada; (el) cocer; (el) asar; ***baking pan,*** tortera; ***baking-powder,*** levadura.
bakshish, baksheesh [bæk'ʃi:ʃ], *s.* propina, gratificación.
balance ['bæləns], *s.* balanza; equilibrio; balance; volante (*de reloj*); (*astron.*, *astrol.*) Libra; (*com.*) saldo (*de una cuenta*); ***balance-beam,*** balancín, fiel de balanza; ***balance-sheet,*** balance; ***balance-weight,*** contrapeso; ***balance-wheel,*** volante; ***balance of payments,*** balanza de pagos; ***balance of power,*** equilibrio político; ***balance of trade,*** balanza de comercio; ***to lose (one's) balance,*** perder el equilibrio; ***to strike a balance,*** lograr el equilibrio. — *v.t.* pesar en balanza; contrapesar; equilibrar; saldar; sopesar. — *v.i.* equilibrarse; mantenerse en equilibrio.
balancer ['bælənsə], *s.* pesador; fiel de balanza; equilibrista, *m.f.*
balancing ['bælənsiŋ], *s.* equilibrio; (el) equilibrar; ***balancing pole,*** balancín.
balcony ['bælkəni], *s.* balcón; galería; (*teat.*) anfiteatro; (*mar.*) galería de popa.
bald [bɔ:ld], *a.* calvo, pelado; escueto.
baldachin ['bɔ:ldəkin], *s.* (*arq.*) baldaquín, dosel.
bald buzzard ['bɔ:ld 'bʌzəd], *s.* (*zool.*) sangual, halieto.
balderdash ['bɔ:ldədæʃ], *s.* (*fam.*) galimatías; sandeces, tonterías. — *v.t.* falsificar, adulterar.
baldhead ['bɔ:ldhed], *s.* calvo.
baldness ['bɔ:ldnis], *s.* calvez, calvicie, *f.*; desnudez.
bald-pated ['bɔ:ld-'peitid], *a.* tonsurado, calvo.
baldric ['bɔ:ldrik], *s.* banda, cinturón terciado; tahalí; (*fig.*) zodíaco.
bale (1) [beil], [BAIL (2)]. — *v.i.* — ***out,*** tirarse en paracaídas (*de un avión*).
bale (2) [beil], *s.* bala, fardo, paca. — *v.t.* embalar, empacar, enfardar.
bale (3) [beil], *s.* calamidad, siniestro.
balefire ['beilfaiə], *s.* almenara, hoguera, lumbrada.
baleful ['beilful], *a.* siniestro; funesto; ceñudo, sombrío, torvo.
balefulness ['beilfulnis], *s.* (lo) siniestro; (lo) sombrío.
baling ['beiliŋ], *s.* achique.
balister ['bælistə], *s.* ballesta.
balize [bæ'li:z], *s.* (*mar.*) boya, baliza.
balk [bɔ:k], *s.* (*agric.*) caballón, haza de barbecho; yerro, desliz; fracaso, chasco; obstáculo, estorbo; viga, madero. — *v.t.* burlar, frustrar, desbaratar; impedir. — *v.i.* plantarse (*el caballo*); ***to balk at,*** resistirse a.
ball (1) [bɔ:l], *s.* bola; pelota; globo, esfera; ovillo; pella; bala; ***ball bearings,*** cojinete de bolas; ***pneumatic ball,*** pera de aire comprimido. — *v.t.* apelotonar; ovillar. — *v.i.* apelotonarse.
ball (2) [bɔ:l], *s.* baile; ***fancy dress ball,*** baile de disfraces; ***masked ball,*** baile de máscaras.
ballad ['bæləd], *s.* balada; romance.
ballad-monger ['bæləd-mʌŋgə], *s.* coplero, vendedor de baladas *o* romances.
ballad-singer ['bæləd-siŋə], *s.* cantor de coplas *o* romances, coplero.
ballast ['bæləst], *s.* (*mar.*) lastre; casquijo, balasto. — *v.t.* (*mar.*) lastrar, echar lastre; contrabalancear.
ballasting ['bæləstiŋ], *s.* lastre, materiales para lastrar, *m.pl.*; lastraje; terraplenaje.
ballet ['bælei], *s.* ballet.

ballista [bəˈlistə], *s.* ballesta; balista.
ballister [ˈbælistə], *s.* balaustre.
ballistic [bəˈlistik], *a.* balístico; ***ballistic missile,*** cohete *o* proyectil balístico.
ballistics [bəˈlistiks], *s. pl.* balística.
balloon [bəˈlu:n], *s.* globo; balón; (*aer.*) globo aerostático; (*quím.*) redoma; (*arq.*) bola de columna; ***balloon tyre,*** neumático balón.
ballooning [bəˈlu:niŋ], *s.* aerostación.
balloonist [bəˈlu:nist], *s.* aeronauta, *m.f.*
ballot [ˈbælət], *s.* balota, papeleta para votar; votación; escrutinio; ***ballot-box,*** urna de escrutinio, urna electoral. — *v.t.* balotar, votar con balotas; insacular.
ball-point pen [ˈbɔ:l-pɔint ˈpen], *s.* bolígrafo.
ballroom [ˈbɔ:lru:m], *s.* salón de baile, sala de fiestas.
bally [ˈbæli], *a.* (*fam.*) muy; ***bally rotten,*** malísimo, pésimo; puñetero.
balm [bɑ:m], *s.* bálsamo; (*bot.*) toronjil. — *v.t.* embalsamar; (*fig.*) mitigar, suavizar, calmar.
balmy [ˈbɑ:mi], *a.* balsámico; embalsamado, perfumado, fragrante; suave, templado.
balsam [ˈbɔ:lsəm], *s.* bálsamo.
balsam-apple [ˈbɔ:lsəm-æpl], *s.* (*bot.*) balsamina.
balsamic [bɔ:lˈsæmik], *a.* balsámico.
balsamiferous [bɔ:lsəˈmifərəs], *a.* balsamífero.
baluster [ˈbæləstə], *s.* balaustre.
balustered [ˈbæləstəd], *a.* balaustrado.
balustrade [bæləsˈtreid], *s.* balaustrada.
bamboo [bæmˈbu:], *s.* bambú.
bamboozle [bæmˈbu:zl], *v.t.* (*fam.*) engañar, embaucar.
bamboozler [bæmˈbu:zlə], *s.* engañador, embaucador.
ban [bæn], *s.* prohibición, proscripción; excomunión; bando; edicto. — *v.t.* prohibir, proscribir.
banal [bəˈnɑ:l], *a.* trivial, vulgar.
banality [bæˈnæliti], *s.* trivialidad, vulgaridad.
banana [bəˈnɑ:nə], *s.* plátano; ***banana tree,*** plátano.
band (1) [bænd], *s.* banda; faja; venda; tira; cinta; lista; franja; fleje; (*arq.*) filete, listón; ***cigar band,*** vitola; ***elastic band,*** goma, gomilla; ***machine band,*** correa; ***metal band,*** zuncho; (*fig.*) lazo, vínculo; (*Am.*) anillo.—*v.t.* atar; zunchar;
band (2) [bænd], *s.* banda, cuadrilla; banda (*de música*); ***dance band,*** orquesta; (*Antillas*) ***steel band,*** orquesta de instrumentos de acero; ***street-band,*** charanga. — *v.t.* juntar, (re)unir. — *v.i* (***together***), juntarse, (re)unirse.
bandage [ˈbændidʒ], *s.* venda, vendaje. — *v.t.* vendar.
bandanna [bænˈdænə], *s.* pañuelo de hierbas.
bandbox [ˈbændbɔks], *s.* sombrerera.
bandelet [ˈbændəlit], *s.* fajita, cintilla; (*arq.*) cordoncillo.
banderole [ˈbændəroul], *s.* banderola.
bandit [ˈbændit], *s.* bandido, bandolero.
bandlet [ˈbændlit], *s.* (*arq.*) filete, listón.
bandmaster [ˈbændmɑ:stə], *s.* músico mayor.
bandog [ˈbændɔg], *s.* mastín.
bandoleer, bandolier [bændəˈliə], *s.* bandolera.
bandoline [ˈbændəlin], *s.* bandolina.
bandwagon [ˈbændwægən], *s.* carro de música; (*fig.*) ***to jump on the bandwagon,*** unirse a los que triunfan; seguir lo que está de moda.
bandy (1) [ˈbændi], *v.t.* tirar de un lado a otro; pasar de uno(s) a otro(s); ***bandy words,*** cambiar palabras, discutir, andar en dimes y diretes (***with,*** con).
bandy (2) [ˈbændi], *a.* arqueado, combado, estevado.
bandy-legged [ˈbændi-legd], *a.* estevado, patizambo.
bane [bein], *s.* veneno, tósigo; (*fig.*) daño, ruina, destrucción, perdición, castigo, muerte, *f.*, peste, *f.*; ***henbane,*** beleño; ***rat's bane,*** arsénico; ***wolf's bane,*** acónito. — *v.t.* envenenar, dañar.
baneful [ˈbeinful], *a.* venenoso; pernicioso, destructivo, mortal, funesto; malvado.
banefulness [ˈbeinfulnis], *s.* (lo) pernicioso.
banewort [ˈbeinwɔ:t], *s.* (*bot.*) belladonna; hierba mora; francesilla.
bang [bæŋ], *adv.* con estrépito; de un golpe; ***bang on time,*** como un clavo. — *s.* golpe, porrazo; portazo; estallido, detonación, estampido; flequillo. — *v.t.* golpear; aporrear; ***bang the door,*** dar un portazo. — *v.i.* golpear, aporrear; (*fam.*) ***bang on,*** machacar. — *interj.* ¡pan! ¡pum!
banging [ˈbæŋiŋ], *s.* (*fam.*) paliza, tunda; golpeteo.
Bangladesh [bæŋgləˈdeʃ]. Bangla Desh, *m.*
bangle [bæŋgl], *s.* ajorca.
bang on [ˈbæŋ ˈɔn], *a.* (*fam.*) estupendo, de primera.
banish [ˈbæniʃ], *v.t.* desterrar; extrañar, alejar; ahuyentar.
banishment [ˈbæniʃmənt], *s.* destierro; expulsión, extrañación.
banister [ˈbænistə], *s.* baranda, pasamano.
banjo [ˈbændʒou], *s.* banjo.
bank (1) [bæŋk], *s.* orilla, margen, *f.*; talud, terraplén; lomo; hilera, serie, batería; banda (*del billar*); (*aer.*) inclinación al virar; (*mar.*) bajo, alfaque, bajío; (*mús.*) teclado; ***sand-bank,*** banco de arena. — *v.t.* represar *o* estancar con dique *o* reparo; contener (*agua*) con diques; cubrir con cenizas (*un fuego*); ***bank up,*** amontonar. — *v.i.* (*aer.*) inclinarse al virar.
bank (2) [bæŋk], *s.* banco; casa de banca; banca (*en el juego*); ***bank-note,*** billete de banco; ***to break the bank,*** hacer saltar la banca; ***savings bank,*** caja de ahorros. — *v.t.* depositar en el banco. — *v.i.* trabajar (***with,*** con); ***bank on,*** contar con, confiar en.
bankable [ˈbæŋkəbl], *a.* que se puede descontar *o* depositar.
bankbill [ˈbæŋkbil], *s.* billete de banco; cédula de banco.
banker [ˈbæŋkə], *s.* banquero.
banking [ˈbæŋkiŋ], *a.* bancario. — *s.* (*com.*) banca.
banking-house [ˈbæŋkiŋ-haus], *s.* casa de banca.
bankrupt [ˈbæŋkrʌpt], *a.*, *s.* insolvente; ***to go bankrupt,*** hacer bancarrota, quebrar.
bankruptcy [ˈbæŋkrʌptsi], *s.* bancarrota, quiebra.
banner [ˈbænə], *s.* bandera, estandarte, insignia, pendón, gonfalón.
bannered [ˈbænəd], *a.* con bandera, provisto de bandera.
banneret [ˈbænəret], *s.* mesnadero.
bannock [ˈbænək], *s.* torta, pan de harina de avena.
banns [bænz], *s.pl.* amonestaciones; ***to publish the banns (of marriage),*** decir las amonestaciones.
banquet [ˈbæŋkwit], *s.* banquete. — *v.t.*, *v.i.* banquetear.
banqueter [ˈbæŋkwitə], *s.* comensal, *m.*
banqueting [ˈbæŋkwitiŋ], *s.* (el) banquetear, *m.*
banquette [bæŋˈket], *s.* (*fort.*) banqueta, *f.*
banshee [ˈbænʃi:], *s.* espíritu de mal agüero, *m.*
bantam [ˈbæntəm], *a.* pequeño, ligero. — *s.* gallina pequeña de Bantam; persona pequeña.
bantamweight [ˈbæntəmweit], *s.* (*dep.*) peso gallo.
banter [ˈbæntə], *s.* burla(s), mofa, chanza(s), *f.* — *v.t.*, *v.i.* burlarse (de), mofarse (de), chancearse (de).
banterer [ˈbæntərə], *s.* zumbón, burlón.
bantling [ˈbæntliŋ], *s.* chicuelo, chicuela.
Bantu [bænˈtu:], *a.*, *s.* bantú.
banyan [ˈbænjən], *s.* (*bot.*) baniano.
baptism [ˈbæptizəm], *s.* bautismo; bautizo; ***baptism of fire,*** bautismo de fuego; ***baptism party*** o ***reception,*** bautizo; ***certificate of baptism,*** fe de bautismo.

baptismal [bæp'tizməl], *a.* bautismal.
Baptist ['bæptist], *s.* baptista, *m.f.*
baptist ['bæptist], *a.*, *s.* bautista, *m.f.*; ***St. John the Baptist,*** San Juan Bautista.
baptist(e)ry ['bæptistri], *s.* bautisterio, baptisterio.
baptize [bæp'taiz], *v.t.* bautizar; cristianar; poner por nombre. — *v.i.* administrar el bautismo.
baptizing [bæp'taiziŋ], *a.* bautizante. — *s.* bautismo.
bar (1) [bɑ:], *prep.* [BARRING].
bar (2) [bɑ:], *s.* barra; tranca (*de puerta* o *de ventana*); (*mar.*) caña (*del timón*); barrote; reja; barrera; obstáculo, impedimento; foro, tribunal; raya, lista; compás; (*for.*) excepción; ***bar gold,*** oro en barra(s); ***bar iron,*** hierro en barra(s); (*mar.*) ***bar-lock,*** escálamo; ***bar loom,*** telar de barras; ***to be called to the bar,*** recibirse de abogado; (*Am.*) ***to be admitted to the bar,*** recibirse de abogado. — *v.t.* atrancar, cerrar con barras; impedir; excluir; exceptuar.
barb [bɑ:b], *s.* barba, arista; púa; lengüeta; caballo berberisco. — *v.t.* armar con púas; hacer mordaz.
Barbadian [bɑ:'beidiən], *a.*, *s.* barbadense.
Barbados [bɑ:'beidɔs]. Barbados, *m.*
barbarian [bɑ:'bɛəriən], *a.*, *s.* bárbaro.
barbaric [bɑ:'bærik], *a.* bárbaro; barbárico.
barbarism ['bɑ:bərizəm], *s.* barbarismo; barbaridad; barbarie, *f.*, salvajismo.
barbarity [bɑ:'bæriti], *s.* barbaridad, crueldad, salvajada; estilo bárbaro.
barbarize ['bɑ:bəraiz], *v.t.* volver bárbaro. — *v.i.* barbarizar(se).
barbarous ['bɑ:bərəs], *a.* bárbaro; áspero; bronco.
barbarousness ['bɑ:bərəsnis], *s.* barbarie, *f.*
barbate(d) ['bɑ:beit(id)], *a.* barbado.
barbecue ['bɑ:bəkju:], *s.* barbacoa. — *v.t.* asar (un animal) entero; churrasquear.
barbed [bɑ:bd], *a.* con púas *o* lengüetas; mordaz, ferroz; ***barbed wire,*** alambre de púas, espino artificial; ***barbed wire entanglement,*** alambrada.
barbel ['bɑ:bəl], *s.* (*ict.*) barbo, comiza; (*vet.*) tolano.
barber ['bɑ:bə], *s.* barbero, peluquero. — *v.t.* afeitar, cortar el pelo a.
barberry, berberis ['bɑ:bəri, 'bə:bəris], *s.* (*bot.*) berberís, bérbero, agracejo, arlo.
barbet ['bɑ:bət], *s.* (*orn.*) barbudo.
barbican ['bɑ:bikən], *s.* (*for.*) barbacana.
barcarole ['bɑ:kəroul], *s.* barcarola.
bard [bɑ:d], *s.* vate; bardo; barda. — *v.t.* poner barda a; albardillar.
barded ['bɑ:did], *a.* (*blas.*) bardado.
bardic ['bɑ:dik], *a.* del bardo *o* poeta.
bardism ['bɑ:dizəm], *s.* bardismo.
bare [bɛə], *a.* desnudo; pelado; raso; descubierto, expuesto a la vista; desprovisto de; mero, puro, solo; liso, llano, sencillo; raído, gastado; ***to lay bare,*** desnudar, descubrir, poner al desnudo; (*equit.*) ***bareback,*** en pelo, sin silla; ***barehanded,*** con las manos. — *v.t.* desnudar, descubrir.
barebone ['bɛəboun], *s.* esqueleto; persona muy flaca.
bareboned ['bɛə'bound], *a.* descarnado, acecinado, muy flaco.
barefaced ['bɛəfeist], *a.* descarado, desvergonzado, atrevido, desfachatado.
barefacedness ['bɛə'feisidnis], *s.* desvergüenza, descaro, desfachatez.
barefoot(ed) ['bɛə'fut(id)], *a.* descalzo.
bareheaded ['bɛə'hedid], *a.* descubierto, sin sombrero.
barelegged ['bɛə'legd], *a.* en pernetas, sin medias.
barely ['bɛəli], *adv.* difícilmente, apenas.
barenecked ['bɛə'nekt], *a.* (d)escotado.
bareness ['bɛənis], *s.* desnudez; (lo) pelado; escasez.
bareribbed ['bɛə'ribd], *a.* demacrado.
bargain ['bɑ:gin], *s.* trato, negocio, acuerdo; ganga; ***bargain driver,*** regatón; ***bargain sale,*** saldo, liquidación; ***at a bargain,*** muy barato; ***it's a bargain!*** ¡trato hecho!; ***into the bargain,*** además, encima; ***to strike a bargain,*** cerrar un trato. — *v.i.* negociar; regatear; ***I didn't bargain on that,*** no me esperaba eso, no contaba con eso.
bargaining ['bɑ:giniŋ], *s.* regateo.
barge [bɑ:dʒ], *s.* barcaza, lanchón, gabarra. — *v.i.* — ***in,*** entrarse brusca *o* violentemente.
bargee, bargeman ['bɑ:dʒi:, bɑ:dʒmæn], *s.* barquero, lanchero, gabarrero.
baric ['bɛərik], *a.* bárico; barométrico.
barilla [bə'rilə], *s.* barrilla.
baritone ['bæritoun], *a.*, *s.* barítono.
barium ['bɛəriəm], *s.* (*quím.*) bario.
bark (1) [bɑ:k], *s.* corteza; ***angostura bark,*** corteza de angostura; ***Peruvian bark,*** quina. — *v.t.* descortezar; desollar.
bark (2) [bɑ:k], *s.* ladrido; estampido; ***his bark is worse than his bite,*** perro que ladra no muerde. — *v.i.* ladrar; ***bark up the wrong tree,*** andar descaminado.
bark (3) [bɑ:k], *s.* barca; barco.
barkbared ['bɑ:kbɛəd], *a.* descortezado.
barkery ['bɑ:kəri], *s.* tenería.
barking ['bɑ:kiŋ], *s.* descortezamiento; ladridos, *m.pl.*
barky ['bɑ:ki], *a.* cortezudo.
barley ['bɑ:li], *s.* cebada; alcacer; ***barley-bin,*** cebadera; ***barley bread,*** pan de cebada; ***barley-corn,*** grano de cebada; ***barley sugar,*** azúcar candi; ***barley water,*** hordiate; ***pearl barley,*** cebada perlada.
barm [bɑ:m], *s.* levadura, jiste.
barmaid ['bɑ:meid], *s.* moza de bar.
barman ['bɑ:mən], *s.* barman.
barmy ['bɑ:mi], *a.* espumoso; (*fam.*) chalado, mochales.
barn [bɑ:n], *s.* granero; hórreo; pajar, henil; ***barn-owl,*** lechuza; ***barn-yard,*** patio; (*Am.*) [COW-SHED].
barnabite ['bɑ:nəbait], *s.* barnabita.
barnacle ['bɑ:nəkl], *s.* acial; (*orn.*) barnacla; ***goose barnacle,*** percebe.
barograph ['bærogræf], *s.* barógrafo.
barometer [bə'rɔmitə], *s.* barómetro.
barometric(al) [bæro'metrik(əl)], *s.* barométrico.
barometrograph [bæro'metrogræf], *a.* barometrógrafo.
baron ['bærən], *s.* barón; (*fig.*) magnate.
baronage ['bærənidʒ], *s.* baronía.
baroness ['bærənis], *s.* baronesa.
baronet ['bærənit], *s.* baronet.
baronetage ['bærənitidʒ], *s.* dignidad de baronet.
baronetcy ['bærənitsi], *s.* rango *o* condición de baronet.
baronial [bə'rouniəl], *a.* baronial.
barony ['bærəni], *s.* baronía.
baroque [bə'rɔk], *a.* barroco; extravagante; ***baroque pearl,*** barrueco.
baroscope ['bærəskoup], *s.* (*fís.*) baróscopo.
barouche [bə'ru:ʃ], *s.* cabriolé; birlocho.
barracan ['bærəkæn], *s.* barragán.
barrack ['bærək], *s.* (*mil.*) cuartel; ***barrack-master,*** jefe de cuartel; (*pl.*) cuartel. — *v.t.*, *v.i.* abuchear.
barracoon [bærə'ku:n], *s.* barracón.
barrage ['bærɑ:ʒ], *s.* presa de contención; (*mil.*) cortina de fuego; interceptación, barrera.
barrator [bæ'reitə], *s.* trapacero, altercador, camorrista, *m.f.*; (*der.*, *mar.*) patrón de barco culpable de baratería.
barratrous ['bærətrəs], *a.* (*der.*, *mar.*) manchado de baratería.

barratry [ˈbærətri], *s.* (*for.*) embrollo; engaño, trapacería; (*der.*, *mar.*) baratería.
barrel [ˈbærəl], *s.* barril, tonel; cañón (*de fusil*); cañón (*de pluma*); caja (*del tímpano del oído*); caja (*de tambor*); cilindro; (*mar.*) eje (*de cabrestante* o *molinete*); ***barrel-maker,*** barrilero; ***barrel-organ,*** organillo; ***barrel-stand,*** poíno; ***barrel-chested,*** pechudo. — *v.t.* embarrilar, entonelar.
barrelled [ˈbærəld], *a.* embarrilado, entonelado; embanastado, encerrado en banasta; cilíndrico, en forma de barril; albardillado, arqueado; ***double-barrelled gun,*** escopeta de dos cañones.
barren [ˈbærən], *a.* estéril, infecundo; árido, erial, yermo; falto, desprovisto de.
barrenness [ˈbærənnis], *s.* esterilidad, infecundidad; aridez.
barrenworth [ˈbærənwəːθ], *s.* (*bot.*) epimedio.
barricade [bæriˈkeid], *s.* barricada. — *v.t.* barrear, cerrar con barricadas; obstruir, atrancar.
barrier [ˈbæriə], *s.* barrera; (*fig.*) obstáculo.
barring [ˈbɑːriŋ], *prep.* salvo, excepto, quitando.
barrister [ˈbæristə], *s.* abogado; curial letrado.
barrow (1) [ˈbærou], *s.* angarillas, parihuela; carretilla; ***hand barrow,*** angarillas; ***wheel barrow,*** carretilla de mano.
barrow (2) [ˈbærou], *s.* túmulo.
barse [bɑːs], *s.* (*ict.*) pértiga.
barshot [ˈbɑːʃɔt], *s.* (*mar.*) bala enramada; (*artill.*) palanqueta.
bartender [ˈbɑːtendə], *s.* barman.
barter [ˈbɑːtə], *s.* trueque, canje, cambalache. — *v.t.* cambiar, trocar, cambalachear, canjear. — *v.i.* trujamanear, cambalachear.
barterer [ˈbɑːtərə], *s.* traficante.
Bartholomew [bɑːˈθɔləmju]. Bartolomé.
bartizan [bɑːtiˈzæn], *s.* (*fort.*) torrecilla.
barwood [ˈbɑːwud], *s.* palo campeche.
baryphonia [bæriˈfouniə], *s.* (*med.*) barifonía.
baryta, barytes [bəˈraitə, -tiːz], *s.* (*quím.*) barita, baritina.
barytone [BARITONE].
basalt [bəˈsɔːlt], *s.* (*geol.*) basalto.
basaltic [bəˈsɔːltik], *a.* basáltico.
basanite [ˈbæsənait], *s.* basanita.
bascule bridge [ˈbæskjuːl bridʒ], *s.* puente basculante.
base [beis], *a.* bajo; ruin, vil; de baja ley, de baja calidad; de base. — *s.* base; fundamento; (*arq.*) basa, basamento, zócalo; pie (*de máquina*); (*mús.*) bajo. — *v.t.* basar, fundamentar; ***to be based on,*** basarse en, inspirarse en.
baseball [ˈbeisbɔːl], *s.* (*dep.*) béisbol.
baseless [ˈbeislis], *a.* infundado, sin fundamento.
basement [ˈbeismənt], *s.* sótano.
baseness [ˈbeisnis], *s.* bajeza, ruindad, vileza, infamia; baja ley.
bash [bæʃ], *s.* (*fam.*) golpe; ***to have a bash at sth.,*** intentarlo. — *v.t.* (*fam.*) golpear fuertemente; ***to bash in,*** romper a golpes, hundir a golpes; ***bash on*** (***regardless***), tirar por la calle de en medio.
bashaw [ˈbæʃɔː], *s.* bajá.
bashful [ˈbæʃful], *a.* vergonzoso, corto, tímido.
bashfulness [ˈbæʃfulnis], *s.* vergüenza, cortedad, timidez, encogimiento, apocamiento.
basic [ˈbeisik], *a.* básico, fundamental.
basil [ˈbæzil], *s.* (*bot.*) albahaca; (*carp.*) filo (*de escoplo* o *cepillo*); (*enc.*) badana. — *v.t.* achaflanar, biselar.
basilica [bəˈsilikə], *s.* basílica.
basilical [bəˈsilikəl], *a.* de basílica; regio.
basilicon [bəˈsilikən], *s.* (*farm.*) basilicón.
basilisk [ˈbæzilisk], *s.* (*zool.*) basilisco.
basin [ˈbeisən], *s.* jofaina; dársena (*de puerto*); cuenca (*de río*); tazón, pilón (*de fuente*); platillo (*de balanza*).
basinet [ˈbæsinet], *s.* bacinete.
basis [ˈbeisis], *s.* (*pl.* **bases** [ˈbeisiːz]) base, *f.*
bask [bɑːsk], *v.i.* calentarse; ***bask in the sun,*** tomar el sol.
basket [ˈbɑːskit], *s.* cesto; cesta; canasta; banasta; espuerta; cuévano; capazo; capacho.
basket-ball [ˈbɑːskit-bɔːl], *s.* baloncesto.
basketful [ˈbɑːskitful], *s.* cestada, canastada.
basket-maker, [ˈbɑːskit-meikə], *s.* cestero.
basket-making [ˈbɑːskit-meikiŋ], *s.* cestería.
basket-work [ˈbɑːskitˈwəːk], *s.* trabajo de cestería; (*mil.*) cestón, cestonada.
bason [ˈbeisən], *s.* banco *o* banqueta de sombrero.
Basque [bæsk], *a.*, *s.* vasco; vascongado; vascuence.
bas-relief [bɑː-rəˈliːf], *s.* bajo relieve.
bass (1) [bæs], *s.* (*ict.*) róbalo, lubina.
bass (2) [bæs], *s.* (*bot.*) tilo; líber; esparto, atocha.
bass (3) [beis], *a.*, *s.* (*mús.*) bajo, grave.
basset (1) [ˈbæsit], *s.* (— ***hound***) perro zarcero.
basset (2) [ˈbæsit], *s.* (*min.*) cabeza de filón.
bassinet [bæsiˈnet], *s.* cuna; bacinete.
basso [ˈbæsou], *s.* (*mús.*) bajo.
bassock [ˈbæsək], *s.* estera, felpudo.
bassoon [bəˈsuːn], *s.* (*mús.*) bajón.
bassoonist [bəˈsuːnist], *s.* bajonista, *m.f.*
basswood [ˈbæswud], *s.* tilo americano.
bast [bæst], [BASS (2)].
bastard [ˈbæstəd], *a.*, *s.* bastardo; (*obsc.*) [ˈbɑːstəd], cabrón, puñetero.
bastardism [ˈbæstədizəm], [BASTARDY].
bastardize [ˈbæstədaiz], *v.t.* bastardear, declarar bastardo.
bastardy [ˈbæstədi], *s.* bastardía.
baste [beist], *v.t.* pringar, untar; hilvanar, bastear, embastar; (*fam.*) dar de palos.
basting [ˈbeistiŋ], *s.* untadura, (el) untar; basta, embaste, hilván.
bastion [ˈbæstiən], *s.* (*fort.*) bastión, baluarte.
basyle [ˈbeisil], *s.* (*quím.*) radical, básico.
bat (1) [bæt], *s.* pala; paleta; bate; pedazo de ladrillo; (*fam.*) ***off his own bat,*** por su cuenta, espontáneamente; sin ayuda. — *v.t.* golpear con un bate, batear; ***without batting an eye-lid,*** sin pestañear. — *v.i.* batear (*cricket*).
bat (2) [bæt], *s.* (*zool.*) murciélago; ***blind as a bat,*** más ciego que un topo.
Batavian [bəˈteiviən], *a.*, *s.* bátavo, de Batavia.
batch [bætʃ], *s.* hornada; lote, tanda; serie, *f.*, conjunto.
bate (1) [beit] *s.* (*ant.*) contienda, debate.
bate (2) [beit], *v.t.* disminuir; ***with bated breath,*** casi sin atreverse a respirar.
Bath [bɑːθ], *a.* ***Bath chair,*** silla de ruedas (para inválidos).
bath [bɑːθ], *s.* baño; bañera; ***bath house,*** casa de baños; ***foot bath,*** pediluvio, baño de pies; ***to have a bath,*** bañarse, tomar un baño; ***hip bath,*** baño de asiento; ***public baths,*** piscina pública *o* baños públicos; ***shower bath,*** ducha. — *v.t.* bañar.
bathe [beið], *s.* baño (*de mar*); ***to go for a bathe,*** ir a bañarse. — *v.t.*, *v.i.* bañar(se).
bather [ˈbeiðə], *s.* bañista, *m.f.*
bathing [ˈbeiðiŋ], *s.* baño(s); ***bathing-cap,*** gorro de baño; ***bathing-costume,*** traje de baño, bañador; ***bathing-hut,*** caseta; ***bathing-wrap,*** albornoz.
bathos [ˈbeiθɔs], *s.* paso de lo sublime a lo ridículo *o* vulgar.
bathrobe [ˈbɑːθroub], (*Am.*) [DRESSING-GOWN].
bathroom [ˈbɑːθrum], *s.* cuarto de baño.
bathtub [ˈbɑːθtʌb], (*Am.*) [BATH].
bathyscaphe [ˈbæθiskæf], *s.* batiscafo.
batiste [bəˈtiːst], *s.* batista.
batlet [ˈbætlit], *s.* batidera.

batman [ˈbætmən], *s.* (*mil.*) asistente.
baton [ˈbætən], *s.* bastón (*de mando*); (*mús.*) batuta.
batrachian [bəˈtreikiən], *a.* batracio.
batsman [ˈbætsmən], *s.* batsman, bateador.
Batswana [bætsˈwɑːnə], *a.* botswanés, botswanesa. — *s.* botswanés, *m.*; ***the Batswana,*** los botswaneses; (*sing.*) [MOTSWANA].
battalion [bəˈtæliən], *s.* batallón.
batten [bætn], *s.* lata, tabla (*de chilla*), listón (*de madera*); tablilla. — *v.t.* cebar; asegurar con listones; listonar; (*mar.*) ***batten down the hatches,*** cerrar las escotillas (asegurándolas con listones de madera); (*fig.*) ***batten on (to),*** cebarse en, ensañarse con; abalanzarse sobre.
batter (1) [ˈbætə], *s.* pasta; bateador.
batter (2) [ˈbætə], *v.t.* apalear, golpear; cañonear; ***batter down,*** derribar, echar abajo.
batter (3) [ˈbætə], *s.* (*arq.*) talud.
battered [ˈbætəd], *a.* maltrecho; estropeado; magullado.
batterer [ˈbætərə], *s.* apaleador.
battering [ˈbætəriŋ], *s.* (*mil.*) cañoneo; ***battering-ram,*** ariete; ***battering-train,*** tren de artillería de sitio.
battery [ˈbætəri], *s.* batería; (*elec.*) pila, batería, acumulador; (*for.*) agresión, violencia.
batting [ˈbætiŋ], *s.* espadillaje, agramaje; (*cerá.*) moldeaje; algodón *o* lana en hojas; ***cotton batting,*** algodón en rama.
battle [bætl], *s.* batalla; combate, lucha; ***battle array,*** orden de batalla; ***battle axe,*** hacha de combate; (*fam.*) sargentona; ***to do battle, to fight a battle,*** dar, librar (una) batalla; ***pitched battle,*** batalla campal. — *v.i.* batallar, luchar; ***battle against adversity,*** luchar contra la mala fortuna.
battled [bætld], *a.* almenado.
battledore [ˈbætldɔː], *s.* pala, raqueta; ***battledore and shuttlecock,*** raqueta y volante.
battlements [ˈbætlmənts], *s.* almenas, *f.pl.*, almenaje; crestería; muro almenado.
battleship [ˈbætlʃip], *s.* (*mar.*) acorazado.
battling [ˈbætliŋ], *a.* batallador. — *s.* luchas, (el) batallar.
battue [bæˈtuː], *s.* montería de caza mayor; (*fig.*) matanza.
batty [ˈbæti], *a.* loco, chiflado.
baubee, bawbee [ˈbɔːbi], *s.* (*Esco.*, *ant.*) medio penique.
bauble [BAWBLE].
baulk [BALK].
bauson [ˈbɔːsən], *s.* (*zool.*) tejón.
bauxite [ˈbouzait, ˈbɔːksait], *s.* (*min.*) bauxita.
Bavaria [bəˈvɛəriə]. Baviera.
Bavarian [bəˈvɛəriən], *a.*, *s.* bávaro.
bawble [bɔːbl], *s.* cetro de bufón; chuchería, fruslería, futesa.
bawcock [ˈbɔːkɔk], *s.* guapo, hombre bien formado.
bawd [bɔːd], *s.* alcahueta. — *v.i.* alcahuetear.
bawdiness [ˈbɔːdinis], *s.* obscenidad; tono soez; alcahuetería.
bawdrick [ˈbɔːdrik], *s.* cinturón; tahalí; cuerda.
bawdry [ˈbɔːdri], *s.* alcahuetería, rufianería; obscenidad; tono soez.
bawdy [ˈbɔːdi], *a.* obsceno, soez.
bawdy-house [ˈbɔːdi-haus], *s.* burdel, mancebía, lupanar.
bawl [ˈbɔːl], *s.* grito, voz. — *v.t.*, *v.i.* vocear; pregonar.
bawler [ˈbɔːlə], *s.* voceador, alborotador, vocinglero, gritador, chillón.
bawling [ˈbɔːliŋ], *a.* gritador, chillador. — *s.* gritos, *m.pl.*, vocerío.
bay (1) [bei], *a.*, *s.* bayo (*caballo*).
bay (2) [bei], *s.* bahía, golfo; seno, entrante; compuerta (de un dique).
bay (3) [bei], *s.* vano, parte saliente (*de un mirador*); nave; ojo, tramo (*de un puente*); pajar, henil; ***bay-window,*** mirador, cierro.
bay (4) [bei], *s.* (*bot.*) laurel; ***bay-leaf,*** hoja de laurel.
bay (5) [bei], *s.* acorralamiento; ***at bay,*** acorralado; ***to be at bay,*** estar acosado. — *v.i.* ladrar.
bayberry [ˈbeibəri], *s.* (*bot.*) fruto del laurel.
bayed [beid], *a.* a rejas.
baying [ˈbeiiŋ], *s.* ladridos, aullidos.
bayonet [ˈbeiənət], *s.* bayoneta; (*Am.*) [DIPSTICK]. — *v.t.* atravesar de un bayonetazo, herir con bayoneta.
bayou [ˈbaijuː], *s.* canalizo, desagüe de un lago, con escasa corriente, casi estancada.
bay-salt [ˈbei-sɔːlt], *s.* sal marina.
bazaar, bazar [bəˈzɑː], *s.* bazar.
bdellium [ˈdeliəm], *s.* bedelio.
be [biː], *v.i.* ser; estar; existir; haber; constituir, representar; resultar; ir, andar; encontrarse, hallarse; aparecer; verse; presentarse, ofrecerse; tratarse de; ***he is an invalid,*** es un enfermo; ***he is ill,*** está enfermo; ***he was followed,*** fue seguido; ***he was shocked,*** se escandalizó; ***he was astonished,*** quedó asombrado; ***the door is shut,*** la puerta está cerrada; ***there are several,*** hay *o* existen varios; ***I am working,*** trabajo, estoy trabajando; ***I am going tomorrow,*** voy *o* voy a ir mañana; ***it is a problem,*** es, constituye *o* representa un problema; ***it was difficult,*** era (fue) *o* resultaba (resultó) difícil; ***he is worried,*** está *o* anda preocupado; ***he was in Mainz,*** estaba, se encontraba *o* se hallaba en Maguncia; ***it is nowhere to be seen,*** no aparece por ningún sitio; ***he was forced to go,*** se vio obligado a ir; ***there are few opportunities,*** se presentan *o* se ofrecen pocas ocasiones; ***it is an exceptional book,*** se trata de un libro excepcional; ***so be it,*** así sea; ***be that as it may,*** sea como fuere; ***to be in,*** estar (en casa); ***to be out,*** no estar, estar en la calle; ***to be away,*** estar fuera; ***it is hot,*** hace calor; ***I am hot,*** tengo calor; ***to be right,*** tener razón; ***to be ashamed,*** tener vergüenza; ***I'm off,*** me voy; ***what can he be up to?*** ¿en qué andará? ¿qué estará tramando?; ***it's up to you,*** depende de ti; ***he's not up to it,*** no está en condiciones de hacerlo, no está para eso, no vale lo suficiente para eso.
beach [biːtʃ], *s.* playa; ***beach-comber,*** raquero, azotaplayas; ***beach-head,*** cabeza de playa; ***beach-robe,*** albornoz. — *v.t.* encallar, varar.
beachy [ˈbiːtʃi], *a.* playado, con playas.
beacon [ˈbiːkən], *s.* faro; almenara; hacho; baliza. — *v.t.* alumbrar, iluminar; (*fig.*) guiar.
bead [biːd], *s.* cuenta; abalorio; mostacilla; gota; perla; (*arq.*) astrágalo; (*carp.*) filete, nervio; (*pl.*) (sarta de) cuentas, rosario; ***to say*** o ***tell one's beads,*** rezar el rosario. — *v.t.* adornar con abalorios. — *v.i.* ensartar cuentas.
beading [ˈbiːdiŋ], *s.* astrágalo; listón, borde.
beadle [biːdl], *s.* pertiguero; bedel.
beadsman [ˈbiːdzmən], *s.* beato.
beadswoman [ˈbiːdzwumən], *s.* beata.
bead-tree [ˈbiːd-triː], *s.* (*bot.*) coco de Indias.
beagle [biːgl], *s.* sabueso; alguacil.
beak [biːk], *s.* pico; (*fam.*) narizota; (*mar.*) rostro; (*fam.*) magistrado, juez; director (*de colegio*).
beaked [biːkt], *a.* picudo, encorvado.
beaker [ˈbiːkə], *s.* jícara; tazón.
beakhead [ˈbiːkhed], *s.* (*mar.*) proa.
beam [biːm], *s.* viga; timón (del arado); (*naut.*) bao; (*naut.*) manga; (*naut.*) través; astil; balancín; rayo, haz; ***on (the) beam,*** siguiendo el haz; (*naut.*) por el través; (*fam.*) bien encaminado, acertado; ***to be on one's beam ends,*** estar de capa caída. — *v.t.* emitir. — *v.i.* brillar; sonreír alegremente.
beaming [ˈbiːmiŋ], *a.* radiante, alegre.
beam-tree [ˈbiːm-triː], *s.* (*bot.*) serbal silvestre.

beamy [ˈbi:mi], *a.* radiante; alegre; (*mar.*) ancho de baos; enorme, pesado.
bean [bi:n], *s.* haba; habichuela; judía; alubia; grano (de café); ***broad bean,*** haba verde; ***French bean,*** judía verde.
bear (1) [bɛə], *s.* oso, osa; (*com., Bolsa*) bajista, *m.*; (*fam.*) ***bear garden,*** merienda de negros; ***bear-hug,*** achuchón fuerte; (*bot.*) ***bear's breech,*** branca ursina, acanto; (*bot.*) ***bear's ear,*** oreja de oso; (*bot.*) ***bear's foot,*** eléboro negro; (*astron.*) ***Great Bear and Little Bear,*** osa mayor y menor.
bear (2) [bɛə], *v.t.* llevar; soportar, aguantar; tolerar, sufrir; sostener; rendir, producir; pagar, costear; parir; experimentar, sentir, tener; ***bear arms,*** portar armas; ***bear the charges,*** pagar los gastos; ***bear fruit,*** dar fruto; ***bear a grudge against,*** guardar rencor a; ***bear in mind,*** tener presente; ***bear interest,*** devengar interés; ***bear out,*** confirmar, corroborar; ***bear witness,*** dar testimonio; ***I can't bear him,*** no le aguanto; ***bear away,*** llevarse. — *v.i.* ***bear down on,*** abalanzarse sobre; ***bear up,*** mantenerse firme; animarse; ir tirando; ***bear with,*** tener paciencia con, ser indulgente con.
bearable [ˈbɛərəbl], *a.* soportable, sufrible.
bearberry [ˈbɛəbəri], *s.* gayuba.
bearbinder [ˈbɛəbaində], *s.* correhuela.
beard [biəd], *s.* barba; barbillas (*de peces*); (*bot.*) brizna, raspa, arista (*de espiga*); lengüeta (*de flecha*); barbas (*de pluma*); ***grey beard,*** barba cana; (*fig.*) anciano. — *v.t.* desbarbar, arrancar la barba a; agarrar por la barba; subirse a las barbas a; (*fig.*) ***beard the lion in his den,*** enfrentarse con el adversario en su propio terreno.
bearded [ˈbiədid], *a.* barbado, barbudo; aristado.
beardless [ˈbiədlis], *a.* imberbe, barbilampiño, desbarbado; (*bot.*) derraspado.
bearer [ˈbɛərə], *s.* portador; dador; faquín, mozo de cordel; árbol fructífero; (*mec.*) chumacera, sostén, apoyo, soporte, gancho; (*impr.*) calzo; ***cross-bearer,*** crucífero *o* crucero; ***ensign-bearer,*** porta-estandarte, abanderado.
bearing [ˈbɛəriŋ], *s.* porte; aire, continente; conducta, maneras; aguante, paciencia; (*arq.*) soporte, apoyo, sostén; (*mec.*) manga (*de eje*), chumacera; producción; situación, orientación; rumbo; relación; parto; línea de flotación; (*blas.*) armas, blasón; (*mec.*) ***ball bearing,*** cojinete; ***beyond bearing,*** insufrible; ***to lose one's bearings,*** desorientarse; ***to take bearings,*** orientarse.
bearish [ˈbɛəriʃ], *a.* osuno; rudo, zafio; (*com., Bolsa*) bajista.
bearlike [ˈbɛəlaik], *a.* semejante al oso.
bearskin [ˈbɛəskin], *s.* piel de oso.
beast [bi:st], *s.* bestia; bruto; ***beast of burden,*** acémila.
beastlike [ˈbi:stlaik], *a.* bestial, brutal, abrutado.
beastliness [ˈbi:stlinis], *s.* bestialidad, brutalidad.
beastly [ˈbi:stli], *a.* bestial, brutal; horrible, espantoso. — *adv.* bestialmente, brutalmente; enormemente.
beat [bi:t], *s.* golpe; pulsación; latido; redoble, toque (*de tambor*); ronda (*de policía*); (*mús.*) compás. — *v.t.* batir; (*Am.*) [WHISK]; golpear; apalear; azotar; sacudir; vencer; superar; ganar, aventajar; ***beat back, off,*** rechazar; ***beat black and blue,*** moler a palos; ***beat to death,*** matar a golpes; ***beat down,*** abatir, derribar; rebajar con regateos; (*fig.*) ***beat hollow*** o ***into a cocked hat,*** dar quince y raya a; ***beat in,*** hundir a golpes; (*fam.*) ***beat it!*** ¡lárgate!; ***beat a retreat,*** batirse en retirada, retirarse; ***beat time,*** marcar el compás; (*fam.*) ***beat up,*** dar una paliza a; ***beat one's way,*** abrirse camino; (*fam.*) ***dead beat,*** agotado, rendido; ***the beat generation,*** la generación ye-yé; ***off the beaten track,*** fuera del camino trillado; fuera de lo corriente. — *v.i.* batir; latir; ***beat about the bush,*** andarse con rodeos y ambages.
beater [ˈbi:tə], *s.* sacudidor; batidor; golpeador, apaleador; (*caz.*) ojeador.
beatific(al) [bi:əˈtifik(əl)], *a.* beatífico.
beatification [bi:ætifiˈkeiʃən], *s.* beatificación.
beatify [bi:ˈætifai], *v.t.* beatificar.
beating [ˈbi:tiŋ], *s.* golpeo; paliza, zurra, tunda; pulsación, (el) latir; toque (*de tambor*).
beatitude [bi:ˈætitju:d], *s.* beatitud.
Beatrice, Beatrix [ˈbiətris, -triks]. Beatriz.
beau [bou], *s.* (*pl.* **beaus, beaux** [bouz]) petimetre; galán; pretendiente; majo.
beau-ideal [bou-aiˈdiəl], *s.* bello ideal.
beauteous [ˈbju:tiəs], *a.* bello, hermoso.
beauteousness [ˈbju:tiəsnis], *s.* belleza, hermosura.
beautification [bju:tifiˈkeiʃən], *s.* embellecimiento.
beautiful [ˈbju:tiful], *a.* hermoso, bello; precioso.
beautifulness [ˈbju:tifulnis], *s.* hermosura, belleza.
beautify [ˈbju:tifai], *v.t.* hermosear, embellecer.
beautifying [ˈbju:tifaiiŋ], *s.* embellecimiento.
beauty [ˈbju:ti], *s.* hermosura; belleza; beldad; preciosidad; (*fam.*) ***the beauty of the thing,*** lo estupendo de la cosa.
beauty-contest [ˈbju:ti-kɔntest], *s.* concurso de belleza.
beauty-parlour [ˈbju:ti-pɑ:lə], *s.* salón de belleza.
beauty-spot [ˈbju:ti-spɔt], *s.* lunar (postizo); sitio de belleza natural.
beaver [ˈbi:və], *s.* (*zool.*) castor; babera.
beavered [ˈbi:vəd], *a.* que lleva visera *o* babera; acastorado.
beaverteen [ˈbi:vəti:n], *s.* (*tej.*) fustán.
becalm [biˈkɑ:m], *v.t.* calmar, sosegar, serenar; (*mar.*) ***to be becalmed,*** quedarse sin viento, estar encalmado.
because [biˈkɔz], *conj.* porque; ***because of,*** a causa de, por causa de, por.
beccafico [bekəˈfi:kou], *s.* (*orn.*) papafigo.
bechance [biˈtʃɑ:ns], *adv.* acaso. — *v.i.* acaecer, suceder, acontecer.
becharm [biˈtʃɑ:m], *v.t.* encantar, hechizar.
bechic [ˈbekik], *a.* (*med.*) béquico, pectoral.
beck (1) [bek], *s.* seña, ademán, indicación; (*tint.*) cubeta; ***at s.o.'s beck and call,*** a la completa disposición de alquien. — *v.t.* indicar por señas. — *v.i.* hacer una seña (*con la cabeza* o *la mano*).
beck (2) [bek], *s.* arroyuelo.
becket [ˈbekit], *s.* (*mar.*) tojino, cornuza, taco; (*mar.*) vinatera, manzanillo de aparejo.
beckon [ˈbekən], *v.t.* llamar con señas. — *v.i.* hacer señas, llamar, atraer.
becloud [biˈklaud], *v.t.* obscurecer, anublar.
become [biˈkʌm], *v.t.* caer, sentar *o* ir bien a; ser propio *o* decoroso. — *v.i.* hacerse; volverse; convertirse; ponerse; meterse; (llegar a) ser, pasar a ser; (*filos.*) devenir; ***become angry,*** enfadarse; ***become worse,*** empeorar; ***what has become of him?*** ¿qué ha sido de él?
becoming [biˈkʌmiŋ], *a.* que sienta, va *o* está bien; decoroso.
becomingness [biˈkʌmiŋnis], *s.* decencia, decoro, corrección, compostura.
bed [bed], *s.* cama; lecho; yacija; álveo, cauce; macizo, cuadro, tabla, tablar (*de jardín* o *huerto*); asiento, base; bancada (*de máquinas*); basada; hilada; camada, tongada; capa, estrato, yacimiento; ***bed and breakfast,*** media pensión; ***bed of state,*** cama de respeto; ***to be brought to bed,*** parir; ***death bed,*** lecho de muerte; ***double bed,*** cama de matrimonio; ***feather bed,*** colchón de plumas; ***folding bed,*** cama plegable; (*fig.*) ***to get out of bed (on) the wrong side,*** levantarse por los pies de la cama; ***to go to bed,*** acostarse; ***to keep to one's bed,*** guardar cama; ***to put to bed,*** acostar; ***river bed,*** lecho, cauce (de río). — *v.t.* acostar, meter en la cama; plantar, sembrar; poner (una cosa) en tongadas *o* capas. — *v.i.* acostarse; cohabitar.

bedabble [bi'dæbl], *v.t.* rociar, mojar.
bedarken ['bi'dɑ:kən], *v.t.* obscurecer, sombrear.
bedaub [bi'dɔ:b], *v.t.* salpicar; ensuciar, embadurnar; vilipendiar.
bedazzle [bi'dæzl], *v.t.* deslumbrar, desvistar.
bed-bug ['bed-bʌg], *s.* chinche.
bedchamber ['bedtʃeimbə], *s.* dormitorio, alcoba.
bedclothes ['bedklouðz], *s.pl.* ropa de cama.
bedcover ['bedkʌvə], *s.* colcha, cubrecama.
bedding ['bediŋ], *s.* ropa de cama.
bedeck [bi'dek], *v.t.* adornar, engalanar, ataviar.
bedevil [bi'devəl], *v.t.* endiablar; hechizar; enmarañar, hacer dificilísimo.
bedew [bi'dju:], *v.t.* humedecer, rociar.
bedfellow ['bedfelou], *s.* compañero *o* compañera de cama; (*fig.*) ***they make strange bedfellows,*** hacen una pareja chocante.
bedhead ['bedhed], *s.* cabecera (de cama).
bedight [bi'dait], *a.* (*poét.*) adornado.
bedim [bi'dim], *v.t.* obscurecer.
bedizen [bi'daizən], *v.t.* adornar, aderezar.
bedlam ['bedləm], *s.* manicomio; belén, babel.
bedlamite ['bedləmait], *s.* loco, loca, orate.
Bedouin ['bedwin], *a., s.* beduino.
bedpan ['bedpæn], *s.* silleta.
bedplate ['bedpleit], *s.* (*mec.*) cama, bancaza.
bedraggle [bi'drægl], *v.t.* ensuciar, manchar.
bedraggled [bi'drægld], *a.* desaliñado, desordenado.
bedrench [bi'drentʃ], *v.t.* empapar.
bedridden ['bedridn], *a.* postrado en cama.
bedrock ['bedrɔk], *s.* (*min.*) lecho de roca; base, fundamento.
bedroom ['bedru:m], *s.* alcoba, dormitorio.
bedside ['bedsaid], *a.* de cabecera; ***bedside manner,*** comportamiento de cabecera (*de médico*). — *s.* lado de cama; cabecera.
bedside table ['bedsaid 'teibl], *s.* mesita, mesilla de noche.
bedsore ['bedsɔ:], *s.* úlcera de decúbito.
bedspread ['bedspred], *s.* colcha, cubrecama.
bedstead ['bedsted], *s.* armazón, armadura de cama.
bedstraw ['bedstrɔ:], *s.* (*bot.*) gallete, cardo lechero, cuajaleche; paja para jergón.
bedtime ['bedtaim], *s.* hora de acostarse.
bedung [bi'dʌŋ], *v.t.* cubrir *o* llenar de estiércol.
bedust [bi'dʌst], *v.t.* empolvar, polvorear.
bedwarf [bi'dwɔ:f], *v.t.* empequeñecer; asombrar.
bedye [bi'dai], *v.t.* teñir.
bee [bi:], *s.* abeja; (*fig.*) reunión, *f.*; (*orn.*) ***bee-bird,*** papamoscas; ***bee-bread,*** panal de miel; ***bee-culture,*** apicultura; (*orn.*) ***bee-eater,*** abejaruco; ***bee-garden,*** abejar; ***bee-hive,*** colmena; ***bee-keeper,*** colmenero; ***bee-line,*** línea recta; ***bumble-bee,*** abejorro; (*fig.*) ***busy little bee,*** hormiguita; ***to have a bee in one's bonnet,*** tener una idea fija, obsesión, manía; estar chiflado; ***queen bee,*** abeja reina.
beech [bi:tʃ], *s.* (*bot.*) haya.
beechen ['bi:tʃən], *a.* de haya.
beef [bi:f], *s.* carne de vaca, buey *o* toro; res de matadero, *f.*; (*fig.*) carne, músculo, peso; robustez; ***beef cattle,*** ganado vacuno de engorde; ***beef-steak,*** biftec; ***corned beef,*** vaca en conserva; ***dry beef,*** cecina; ***jerked beef,*** tasajo; ***roast beef,*** rosbif, vaca asada; ***salt beef,*** vaca salada. — *v.i.* (*fam.*) quejarse, protestar.
beefeater ['bi:fi:tə], *s.* alabardero.
beefy ['bi:fi], *a.* fornido, membrudo, corpulento.
beer [biə], *s.* cerveza; ***pale beer,*** cerveza rubia; (*fig.*) ***to be small beer,*** ser cosa de poca monta; ***stale beer,*** cerveza agriada.
beer-house, beer-saloon ['biə-haus, -səlu:n], *s.* cervecería.
beestings ['bi:stiŋz], *s. pl.* calostro.
beeswax ['bi:zwæks], *s.* cera de abejas.
beet [bi:t], *s.* (*bot.*) remolacha, betarraga; ***beet-sugar,*** azúcar de remolacha.
beetle (1) [bi:tl], *s.* (*ent.*) escarabajo; ***Colorado beetle,*** escarabajo de la patata; ***horn beetle, stag beetle,*** ciervo volante.
beetle (2) [bi:tl], *s.* pisón, maza, aplanadera; martinete; mallo; batón.
beetle (3) [bi:tl], *v.i.* combar; avanzar; salir.
beetle-browed ['bi:tl-braud], *a.* cejudo.
beetling ['bi:tliŋ], *a.* prominente, saliente; colgante, pendiente. — *s.* (*tej.*) batanee.
beetroot ['bi:tru:t], *s.* (raíz de) remolacha.
beets [bi:ts], *s. pl.* (*Am.*) [BEETROOT].
befall [bi'fɔ:l], *v.t.* suceder a; ocurrir a. — *v.i.* suceder, acontecer, sobrevenir; ***whatever befalls,*** suceda lo que suceda.
befit [bi'fit], *v.t.* convenir, venir bien a, ser propio *o* digno de.
befitting [bi'fitiŋ], *a.* propio, decoroso, digno.
befog [bi'fɔg], *v.t.* envolver en niebla; obscurecer; confundir.
befool [bi'fu:l], *v.t.* engañar, embaucar.
before [bi:'fɔ:], *adv.* anteriormente, antes, más pronto, primero; ***a little before,*** un poco antes; ***the night before,*** la noche anterior. — *conj.* antes que, antes de que. — *prep.* delante de, ante, en presencia de; enfrente de; antes de.
beforehand [bi'fɔ:hænd], *adv.* anticipadamente, con anticipación, de antemano, previamente, con antelación; ***to be beforehand with,*** anticiparse a; ***to pay beforehand,*** pagar por adelantado.
beforetime [bi'fɔ:taim], *adv.* en tiempo pasado, en otro tiempo, tiempo atrás.
befoul [bi'faul], *v.t.* ensuciar, emporcar; enredar.
befriend [bi'frend], *v.t.* favorecer, patrocinar, proteger, amparar.
befringe [bi'frindʒ], *v.t.* guarnecer con franjas.
befuddle [bi'fʌdl], *v.t.* aturdir, turbar; encalabrinar.
beg [beg], *v.t.* rogar, pedir, suplicar, implorar; (*log.*) ***to beg the question,*** cometer petición de principio. — *v.i.* mendigar, pordiosear, vivir de limosna; pedir.
beget [bi'get], *v.t.* engendrar, procrear.
begetter [bi'getə], *s.* engendrador, procreador.
beggar ['begə], *s.* mendigo, pordiosero, pobre; ***beggars can't be choosers,*** a caballo regalado no le mires el diente. — *v.t.* empobrecer, arruinar; agotar, apurar; ***it beggars all description,*** no hay palabras para describirlo.
beggarliness ['begəlinis], *s.* miseria, indigencia, pobreza; mendicidad; mezquindad.
beggarly ['begəli], *a.* miserable, pobre; mezquino.
begging ['begiŋ], *a.* mendicante. — *s.* mendicación, pordioseo.
begin [bi'gin], *v.t.* empezar, comenzar; iniciar. — *v.i.* empezar, comenzar; ***begin at the beginning,*** empezar por el principio; ***begin to,*** empezar a, comenzar a, ponerse a; ***begin with,*** empezar con *o* por; ***he began by singing,*** empezó por cantar; ***he began singing,*** se puso a cantar; ***to begin with,*** en primer lugar, para empezar.
beginner [bi'ginə], *s.* originador; principiante.
beginning [bi'giniŋ], *s.* principio, comienzo; génesis, *f.*; ***at the beginning of,*** al principio de; a principios de; ***from the beginning,*** desde el *o* un principio; ***from small beginnings,*** de antecedentes humildes, de origen humilde.
begird [bi'gə:d], *v.t.* ceñir.
begone! [bi'gɔn], *interj.* ¡fuera! ¡vete! ¡largo de aquí!
begonia [bi'gouniə], *s.* (*bot.*) begonia.
begrime [bi'graim], *v.t.* percudir, tiznar, llenar de mugre.
begrimed [bi'graimd], *a.* percudido, mugriento.
begrudge [bi'grʌdʒ], *v.t.* envidiar; dar de mala gana, resistirse a dar.

beguile [bi'gail], *v.t.* engañar, seducir; distraer, entretener; ***beguile the time,*** entretener el tiempo.
beguiler [bi'gailə], *s.* engañador, seductor.
behalf [bi'hɑ:f], *s.* favor, patrocinio; ***in*** o ***on behalf of,*** a favor de; ***on behalf of,*** en nombre de.
behave [bi'heiv], *v.i.* proceder, obrar, conducirse, portarse; funcionar; ***behave yourself (properly)!*** ¡pórtate bien!
behaviour [bi'heivjə], *s.* proceder; conducta, comportamiento; funcionamiento.
behavioural [bi'heivjərəl], *a.* del behaviorismo; ***behavioural scientist,*** estudioso del behaviorismo.
behaviourism [bi'heivjərizəm], *s.* behaviorismo.
behead [bi'hed], *v.t.* decapitar, descabezar.
beheader [bi'hedə], *s.* verdugo; matarife.
beheading [bi'hediŋ], *s.* decapitación, descabezamiento.
behest [bi'hest], *s.* petición, ruego, requerimiento.
behind [bi'haind], *adv.* (por) detrás, (hacia) atrás; con atraso, con retraso; ***to get left behind,*** quedarse atrás *o* a la zaga. — *prep.* detrás de, tras (de); ***behind the back of,*** a espaldas de; ***behind the times,*** atrasado, trasnochado, anticuado. — *s.* (*fam.*) trasero.
behindhand [bi'haindhænd], *adv.* atrasado, con atraso.
behold [bi'hould], *v.t.* mirar; contemplar; observar. — *interj.* (*ant.*) ¡he aquí! ¡mirad!
beholden [bi'houldən], *a.* deudor, en deuda, obligado. — *p.p.* [BEHOLD].
beholder [bi'houldə], *s.* espectador, observador.
behove [bi'houv], *v.t. impers.* atañer, incumbir; ser preciso, ser fuerza; ***to be behoven to,*** estar en deuda con.
beige [beiʒ], *s.* tejido de lana sin teñir ni blanquear; sarga; beige, color beige.
being ['bi:iŋ], *s.* ser, ente; existencia; ***well-being,*** bienestar. — *ger.* [BE].
belabour [bi'leibə], *v.t.* apalear.
belaced [bi'leist], *a.* guarnecido, galoneado, adornado con encaje.
belated [bi'leitid], *a.* tardío; retrasado.
belatedness [bi'leitidnis], *s.* retardo, tardanza.
belay [bi'lei], *v.t.* (*mar.*) amarrar.
belaying-pins [bi'leiiŋ-pinz], *s.* (*mar.*) cabillas, *f.pl.*
belch [beltʃ], *s.* eructo, regüeldo. — *v.t.* arrojar de sí, vomitar. — *v.i.* eructar, regoldar; ***belch out*** o ***forth,*** arrojar, vomitar.
beldam ['beldəm], *s.* vieja, bruja, arpía.
beleaguer [bi'li:gə], *v.t.* sitiar, bloquear.
beleaguerer [bi'li:gərə], *s.* sitiador.
beleaguering [bi'li:gəriŋ], *a.* sitiador.
belee [bi'li:], *v.t.* (*mar.*) sotaventar.
belemnite ['beləmnait], *s.* (*min.*) belemnita.
belfry ['belfri], *s.* campanario, campanil, torre; ***to have bats in the belfry,*** estar chalado.
Belgian ['beldʒən], *a.* belga. — *s.* belga, *m.f.*
Belgic ['beldʒik], *a.* bélgico.
Belgium ['beldʒəm]. Bélgica.
Belial ['bi:liəl]. Satanás; Belial.
belie [bi'lai], *v.t.* desmentir; defraudar.
belied [bi'laid], *a.* desmentido.
belief [bi'li:f], *s.* creencia.
believable [bi'li:vəbl], *a.* creíble.
believe [bi'li:v], *v.t., v.i.* creer; ***make-believe,*** pretexto.
believer [bi'li:və], *s.* creyente.
belike [bi'laik], *adv.* tal vez, acaso.
belime [bi'laim], *v.t.* enligar, enviscar.
belittle [bi'litl], *v.t.* empequeñecer; quitar *o* restar importancia a.
Belize [bə'li:z]. Belice.
Belizian [bə'liziən], *a., s.* beliceño.
bell [bel], *s.* campana; campanilla; timbre; cascabel; cencerro, esquila; (*bot.*) cáliz; (*arq.*) tambor (*del capitel*); ***bell gable,*** espadaña; ***bell stroke,*** campanada; ***diving bell,*** campana de buzo; (*mar.*) ***one bell,*** espacio de media hora; ***passing bell,*** doble (*por los difuntos*). — *v.t.* acampanar; encascabelar; ***to bell the cat,*** poner el cascabel al gato. — *v.i.* bramar (*el ciervo*); crecer en forma de campana.
belladonna [belə'dɔnə], *s.* belladona.
bell-boy ['bel-bɔi], *s.* botones, *m.sing.*
bell-buoy ['bel-bɔi], *s.* boya de campana.
bell-crank ['bel-kræŋk], *s.* torniquete.
belle [bel], *s.* mujer bella, guapa, beldad.
belles-lettres ['bel-'letr], *s.* bellas letras, *f.pl.*
bellflower ['belflauə], *s.* (*bot.*) campanilla, campánula.
bell-founder ['bel-faundə], *s.* campanero.
bell-glass ['bel-glɑ:s], *s.* campana de cristal.
bell-hanger ['bel-hæŋə], *s.* campanillero.
bellhop ['belhɔp], *s.* (*Am.*) [PAGE (I)].
bellicose ['belikous], *a.* belicoso; chulo.
bellicosity [beli'kɔsiti], *s.* belicosidad; chulería.
bellied ['belid], *a.* panzudo, ventrudo; convexo, combado.
belligerence [bi'lidʒərəns], *s.* beligerancia.
belligerent [bi'lidʒərənt], *a., s.* beligerante.
bellman ['belmən], *s.* pregonero de campana.
bell-mule ['bel-mju:l], *s.* cebadero.
bellow ['belou], *s.* bramido, rugido. — *v.t.* gritar a voz en cuello. — *v.i.* bramar, rugir.
bellower ['belouə], *s.* bramador.
bellowing ['belouiŋ], *a.* rugiente. — *s.* bramido(s) rugido(s).
bellows ['belouz], *s.pl.* fuelle.
bellows-fish ['belouz-fiʃ], (*ict.*) centrisco.
bellows-maker ['belouz-meikə], *s.* barquinero.
bell-pull ['bel-pul], *s.* botón, tirador (*de campanilla*).
bellringer ['belriŋə], *s.* campanero.
bell-rope ['bel-roup], *s.* cuerda de campana.
bell-shaped ['bel-ʃeipt], *a.* acampanado.
bell-tower [bel-tauə], *s.* campanario.
bell-tree ['bel-tri:], *s.* (*mús.*) chinescos.
belly ['beli], *s.* vientre, panza, barriga, bandullo, andorga. — *v.i.* hacer barriga; combarse, pandearse; (*mar.*) hacer bolso.
belly-ache ['beli-eik], *s.* dolor de vientre; (*fig.*) pataleo, queja(s). — *v.i.* quejarse.
belly-band ['beli-bænd], *s.* ventrera, cincha.
belly-button ['beli-bʌtn], *s.* (*fam.*) ombligo.
bellyful ['beliful], *s.* panzada, hartura, hartazgo, atracón; ***I've had a bellyful,*** estoy harto.
belly-worm ['beli-wə:m], *s.* lombriz, *f.*
belong [bi'lɔŋ], *v.i.* pertenecer, corresponder (a).
belongings [bi'lɔŋiŋz], *s.pl.* bártulos, *m.pl.*, cosas, *f.pl.*
beloved [bi'lʌv(i)d], *a., s.* amado, amada; caro, dilecto.
below [bi'lou], *adv.* abajo, debajo. — *prep.* debajo de; bajo; inferior a; ***below zero,*** bajo cero; ***here below,*** aquí abajo.
Belshazzar [bel'ʃæzə]. (*bíb.*) Baltasar.
belt [belt], *s.* cinturón; cinto; (*geog.*) faja, franja; (*mec.*) correa; (*fig.*) ***below the belt,*** no justo, no limpio; ***cross belt,*** bandolera; ***shoulder belt,*** tahalí; ***sword belt,*** biricú; ***to tighten one's belt,*** apretarse el cinturón. — *v.t.* ceñir; poner correa a; pegar con correa. — *v.i.* (*fam.*) ***belt along,*** ir a todo meter.
belvedere [belvi'diə], *s.* mirador, belvedere.
bemire [bi'maiə], *v.t.* enlodar, encenagar.
bemoan [bi'moun], *v.t.* lamentar, deplorar.
bemoaner [bi'mounə], *s.* lamentador, plañidor.
bemoaning [bi'mouniŋ], *s.* lamentación, lamento.
bemourn [bi'mɔ:n], *v.t.* deplorar, sentir, llorar (sobre).
bemuse [bi'mju:z], *v.t.* atontar, aturdir.
Ben [ben], *apodo de* [BENJAMIN].

bench [bentʃ], *s.* banco; escaño; banqueta; escabel; asiento (*de los jueces*); bancada; ***bench cover,*** bancal; ***bench vice,*** tornillo de banco; ***Queen's Bench,*** Tribunal supremo de justicia. — *v.t.* proveer de bancos; poner en un tribunal.
bencher [ˈbentʃə], *s.* miembro de un colegio de abogados.
bend [bend], *s.* curva, recodo; codo, ángulo; curvatura; inclinación; (*pl., mar.*) nudo, ligazón; (*mar.*) costillaje; (*blas.*) bandas, *f.pl.*, barra. — *v.t.* doblar, enarcar, encorvar, combar, torcer; armar (*el arco*); tensar; inclinar; dirigir; aplicar; doblegar, someter; entalingar, envergar; ***bend one's endeavours,*** dirigir sus esfuerzos; ***bend the knee,*** doblar la rodilla. — *v.i.* encorvarse, combarse; desviarse, torcer; inclinarse; dirigirse, tender; aplicarse con ahinco; ***bend back,*** doblarse hacia atrás; ***better bend than break,*** más vale doblarse que quebrarse.
bendable [ˈbendəbl], *a.* flexible, plegable.
bender [ˈbendə], *s.* el que encorva; tirador de arco; (*anat.*) flexor; torcedor, doblador; (*fam.*) curda.
bending [ˈbendiŋ], *s.* pliegue, doblez; comba, encorvadura; pendiente, *f.*, declive; recodo(s); vuelta; flexión, cimbreo.
bendy [ˈbendi], *s.* (*blas.*) banda.
beneath [biˈni:θ], *adv.* abajo, debajo. — *prep.* bajo, debajo de, por debajo de.
Benedict [ˈbenidikt]. Benito.
benedict [ˈbenidikt], *s.* benito; hombre casado.
Benedictine [beniˈdiktin], *a., s.* benedictino, benito.
benedictine [beniˈdikti:n], *s.* benedictino (*licor*).
benediction [beniˈdikʃən], *s.* bendición.
benefaction [beniˈfækʃən], *s.* beneficio, favor, gracia, merced.
benefactor [ˈbenifæktə], *s.* bienhechor, benefactor.
benefactress [ˈbenifæktris], *s.* bienhechora.
benefice [ˈbenifis], *s.* beneficio, prebenda.
beneficed [ˈbenifist], *a.* beneficiado, prebendado.
beneficence [biˈnefisəns], *s.* beneficencia.
beneficent [biˈnefisənt], *a.* benéfico.
beneficial [beniˈfiʃəl], *a.* beneficioso, provechoso.
beneficiary [beniˈfiʃəri], *a., s.* beneficiario, beneficiado.
benefit [ˈbenifit], *s.* beneficio, provecho, utilidad; ***for the benefit of,*** a beneficio de, en provecho de. — *v.t.* beneficiar, aprovechar. — *v.i.* sacar provecho *o* partido (de).
benevolence [biˈnevələns], *s.* benevolencia.
benevolent [biˈnevələnt], *a.* benévolo, benigno.
Bengal [benˈgɔ:l]. Bengala; ***Bay of Bengal,*** Golfo de Bengala; ***Bengal light*** (luz de) bengala.
Bengali [benˈgɔ:li], *a., s.* bengalí.
benighted [biˈnaitid], *a.* envuelto en tinieblas; sumido en ignorancia.
benign [biˈnain], *a.* benigno; suave.
benignant [biˈnignənt], *a.* benigno.
benignity [biˈnigniti], *s.* benignidad.
benison [ˈbenizn], *s.* bendición.
Benjamin [ˈbendʒəmin]. Benjamín.
bennet [ˈbenit], *s.* (*bot.*) gariofilata.
bent [bent], *a.* encorvado; doblado; torcido; ***bent on,*** empeñado en. — *s.* propensión, inclinación, tendencia; ***to follow one's own bent,*** seguir sus (propias) inclinaciones; campar por sus respetos.
bent-grass [ˈbent-grɑ:s], *s.* (*bot.*) agróstida.
benumb [biˈnʌm], *v.t.* entumecer, aterir de frío.
benumbed [biˈnʌmd], *a.* entumecido, aterido, yerto.
benumbedness [biˈnʌmdnis], *s.* insensibilidad, entumecimiento.
benzamide [ˈbenzəmaid], *s.* (*quím.*) benzámida,
benzedrine [ˈbenzidri:n], *s.* bencedrina.
benzene [ˈbenzi:n], *s.* benceno.
benzine [ˈbenzi:n], *s.* (*quím.*) benzina, bencina.
benzoic [benˈzouik], *a.* (*quím.*) benzoico.
benzoin [ˈbenzɔin], *s.* benjuí; benzoína.
benzol [ˈbenzɔl], *s.* benzol.
bepowder [biˈpaudə], *v.t.* empolvar.
bepurple [biˈpə:pl], *v.t.* purpurar, teñir de púrpura.
bequeath [biˈkwi:θ], *v.t.* legar.
bequeather [biˈkwi:θə], *s.* testador, testadora.
bequeathment [biˈkwi:θmənt], *s.* testamento, acto de testar; legado, manda.
bequest [biˈkwest], *s.* legado, manda.
berate [biˈreit], *v.t.* reprender severamente.
Berber [ˈbə:bə], *a., s.* bereber.
berberin [ˈbə:bərin], *s.* (*quím.*) berberina.
berberis [ˈbə:beris], [BARBERRY].
bereave [biˈri:v], *v.t.* desposeer, privar de; afligir.
bereavement [biˈri:vmənt], *s.* privación, despojo; desgracia, aflicción, luto, duelo; ***to express condolences on bereavement,*** acompañar en el sentimiento.
beret [ˈberei], *s.* boina.
berg [bə:g], *s.* témpano de hielo.
bergamot [ˈbə:gəmɔt], *s.* (*bot.*) bergamota; bergamoto.
Berlin [bə:ˈlin], *a.* berlinense, de Berlín. — *s.* Berlín.
berlin [ˈbə lin], *s.* berlina.
berm [bə:m], *s.* (*fort.*) berma, lisera.
Bermuda [bə:ˈmju:də]. las (Islas) Bermudas.
Bernard [ˈbə:nəd]. Bernardo.
Berne [bə:n]. Berna.
berret [ˈberit] [BERET].
berry [ˈberi], *s.* baya, bolita. — *v.i.* producir bayas *o* bolitas.
berry-bearing [ˈberi-bɛəriŋ], *a.* que produce bayas.
berserk [bəˈsə:k], *a.* frenético; ***to go berserk,*** ponerse furioso, volverse loco.
berth [bə:θ], *s.* (*mar.*) amarradero, anclaje; litera; camarote; (*fam.*) empleo, destino; ***to give a wide berth to,*** evitar, mantenerse lejos de. — *v.t.* dar anclaje a, amarrar; dar litera *o* empleo a.
Bertha [ˈbə:θə]. Berta.
berthage [ˈbə:θidʒ], *s.* anclaje.
bertram [ˈbə:trəm], *s.* (*bot.*) pelitre.
beryl [ˈberil], *s.* (*min.*) berilo, aguamarina.
berylline [ˈberilain], *a.* berilino, de color de berilo.
beryllium [biˈriliəm], *s.* (*quím.*) glucinio.
bescrawl [biˈskrɔ:l], *v.t.* garabatear, escarabajear.
beseech [biˈsi:tʃ], *v.t.* suplicar, rogar, pedir, implorar.
beseecher [biˈsi:tʃə], *s.* rogador, suplicante, implorante.
beseeching [biˈsi:tʃiŋ], *s.* ruego, súplica, instancia.
beseem [biˈsi:m], *v.t.* cuadrar, convenir. — *v.i.* ser decoroso.
beseeming [biˈsi:miŋ], *a.* decoroso.
beset [biˈset], *v.t.* asediar, rodear; engastar, tachonar.
besetting [biˈsetiŋ], *a.* habitual; ***besetting sin,*** punto flaco, vicio dominante.
beshrew [biˈʃru:], *v.t.* depravar.
beside [biˈsaid], *adv.* cerca, al lado, junto; además. — *prep.* al lado de, cerca de, junto a; en comparación de; además de; fuera de; ***beside o.s.,*** fuera de sí; ***beside the point,*** que no viene al caso.
besides [biˈsaidz], *adv.* además, por otra parte; asimismo. — *prep.* además de, amén de, sobre; aparte, excepto, fuera de.
besiege [biˈsi:dʒ], *v.t.* sitiar, asediar.
besieger [biˈsi:dʒə], *s.* sitiador, asediador.
beslaver [biˈslævə], *v.t.* babosear, rociar de babas.
besmear [biˈsmiə], *v.t.* embadurnar.
besmearer [biˈsmiərə], *s.* embadurnador.
besmirch [biˈsmə:tʃ], *v.t.* manchar, mancillar.
besmoke [biˈsmouk], *v.t.* ahumar.
besmut [biˈsmʌt], *v.t.* tiznar, llenar de hollín.
besom [ˈbi:zəm], *s.* escoba; (*fig., fam.*) ***old besom,*** sargentona, bruja.

besot [bi'sɔt], *v.t.* entontecer, embrutecer; emborrachar.
besotted [bi'sɔtid], *a.* entontecido, embrutecido; emborrachado; (*fig.*) amartelado.
besottedness [bi'sɔtidnis], *s.* entontecimiento, embrutecimiento; emborrachamiento.
bespangle [bi'spæŋgl], *v.t.* adornar con *o* de lentejuelas.
bespatter [bi'spætə], *v.t.* salpicar.
bespeak [bi'spi:k], *v.t.* encargar, apalabrar; indicar, anunciar.
bespeckle [bi'spekl], *v.t.* salpicar.
bespoke [bi'spouk], *a.* hecho de encargo. — *pret., p.p.* [BESPEAK].
bespot [bi'spɔt], *v.t.* salpicar.
bespread [bi'spred], *v.t.* sembrar, esparcir; cubrir; tender.
besprinkle [bi'spriŋkl], *v.t.* rociar, esparcir; regar.
Bess, Bessie, Bessy ['bes(i)]. Isabelita; [ELIZABETH]; (*hist.*) ***Good Queen Bess,*** Isabel I.
best [best], *a. superl.* [GOOD]; mejor; óptimo; ***at (the) best,*** a lo sumo, cuando más, en el mejor de los casos; ***best man,*** padrino de boda; ***best-seller,*** éxito de venta; ***to do one's best,*** hacer lo mejor posible, hacer todo lo posible; ***for the best,*** para bien; con la mejor intención; ***to get the best of,*** vencer, superar; ***to make the best of a bad job,*** sacar el mejor partido posible de un mal negocio; sacar fuerzas de flaqueza; ***second best,*** accésit, mejor después del primero; ***to the best of my knowledge,*** que yo sepa. — *adv.* mejor; ***we had best go,*** conviene que nos vayamos, debemos irnos; ***the best known,*** el más conocido.
bestain [bi'stein], *v.t.* manchar.
bestead [bi'sted], *v.t.* rodear, cercar.
bestial ['bestiəl], *a.* bestial, salvaje.
bestiality [besti'æliti], *s.* bestialidad, salvajismo.
bestiary ['bestiəri], *s.* bestiario.
bestir [bi'stə:], *v.t.* menear; incitar.
bestow [bi'stou], *v.t.* conferir, otorgar, conceder; ***bestow compliments,*** dedicar finezas.
bestowal [bi'stouəl], *s.* otorgamiento.
bestraddle [bi'strædl], *v.t.* atravesar, estar atravesado en.
bestraught [bi'strɔ:t], *a.* fuera de sí.
bestrew [bi'stru:], *v.t.* esparcir, derramar; sembrar.
bestride [bi'straid], *v.t.* cabalgar, montar a horcajadas; zanquear; atravesar.
bestud [bi'stʌd], *v.t.* tachonar.
bet [bet], *s.* apuesta; ***it's a good bet,*** es cosa bastante segura. — *v.t.* apostar(se); ***bet on,*** apostar a *o* por; ***what do you bet?*** ¿qué te apuestas? ¿cuánto va?; (*fig.*) ***you bet!*** ¡ya lo creo!
betake [bi'teik], *v.t., v.r.* recurrir, acudir; irse, trasladarse; darse, entregarse (a).
betel ['bi:təl], *s.* (*bot.*) betel.
bethel ['beθəl], *s.* capilla (*de secta protestante*).
bethink [bi'θiŋk], *v.i.* recordar, hacer memoria; recapacitar, pensar. — **bethink o.s.,** *v.r.*, ***bethink o.s. of,*** acordarse de.
bethrall [bi'θrɔ:l], *v.t.* sojuzgar, esclavizar.
betide [bi'taid], *v.t., v.i.* (*ant.*) suceder, acontecer, pasar, acaecer, efectuarse, verificarse; indicar, presagiar; ***whate'er betide,*** suceda lo que suceda; ***woe betide thee,*** ¡ay de ti!
betime(s) [bi'taim(z)], *adv.* (*ant.*) con tiempo; en sazón; pronto, temprano; ***to rise betimes,*** tomar la mañana.
betoken [bi'toukən], *v.t.* presagiar, anunciar; indicar, denotar.
betony ['betoni], *s.* (*bot.*) betónica.
betray [bi'trei], *v.t.* traicionar, hacer traición a; delatar, revelar.
betrayal [bi'treiəl], *s.* traición, perfidia, alevosía; abuso de confianza.
betrayer [bi'treiə], *s.* traidor.
betroth [bi'trouð], *v.t.* desposar, prometer; ***to be*** o ***become betrothed,*** prometerse, desposarse.
betrothal, betrothment [bi'trouðəl, -mənt], *s.* esponsales, *m. pl.*, desposorio.
betrothed [bi'trouðd], *a., s.* desposado; prometido.
better (1) ['betə], *a. compar.* [GOOD], mejor; mayor, más; ***better half,*** media naranja, cara mitad. — *adv. compar.* [WELL (2)], mejor; ***to get better,*** mejorar(se). — *s.* (lo) mejor; ventaja, superioridad; ***to get the better of,*** vencer, derrotar; ***so much the better,*** tanto mejor; (*pl.*) superiores. — *v.t.* mejorar; adelantar, favorecer. — *v.i.* mejorar; mejorarse.
better (2) ['betə], *s.* apostador, apostante.
bettering ['betəriŋ], *s.* mejoría, mejora, adelanto.
betterment ['betəmənt], *s.* mejora, mejoramiento, mejoría, adelanto.
betting ['betiŋ], *s.* acción de apostar; juego; ***what is the betting that he will 'arrive drunk?*** ¿qué te apuestas a que llega borracho?
Betty ['beti]. Isabelita.
between [bi'twi:n], *prep.* entre; (*mar.*) ***between decks,*** entrepuentes; ***between the devil and the deep blue sea,*** entre la espada y la pared; ***between now and then,*** de aquí a allá; ***between ourselves,*** entre nosotros dos; (*mar.*) ***between wind and water,*** entre dos aguas; ***between you and me,*** entre Vd. y yo.
betwixt [bi'twikst], *adv.* en medio; ***betwixt and between,*** entre lo uno y lo otro; ni fu ni fa. — *prep.* entre.
bevel ['bevəl], *a.* biselado, en bisel. — *s.* cartabón; chaflán; bisel. — *v.t.* achaflanar, biselar.
bevelled ['bevəld], *a.* biselado.
beverage ['bevəridʒ], *s.* bebida.
bevy ['bevi], *s.* bandada; grupo.
bewail [bi'weil], *v.t.* llorar, lamentar. — *v.i.* llorar, lamentarse, plañir.
bewailing [bi'weiliŋ], *s.* lamentación, lloro(s).
beware [bi'wɛə], *v.t.* guardarse de, precaverse de. — *v.i.* tener cuidado, andarse con cuidado; ***beware of,*** tener *o* andarse con cuidado con. — *interj.* ¡cuidado! ¡atención!
bewhiskered [bi'wiskəd], *a.* que tiene patillas *o* bigotes.
bewilder [bi'wildə], *v.t.* desconcertar, dejar perplejo, aturdir.
bewilderment [bi'wildəmənt], *s.* desconcierto, perplejidad, aturdimiento.
bewitch [bi'witʃ], *v.t.* hechizar, embrujar; fascinar, embelesar.
bewitcher [bi'witʃə], *s.* encantador; brujo, hechicero.
bewitching [bi'witʃiŋ], *a.* encantador, hechicero; fascinador.
bewitchment [bi'witʃmənt], *s.* encantamiento, hechizo; fascinación.
bey [bei], *s.* bey.
beyond [bi'jɔnd], *adv.* más allá, más lejos. — *prep.* más allá de, allende, al otro lado de; además de, fuera de; ***beyond dispute,*** indiscutible; ***beyond doubt,*** indudable; ***beyond measure,*** inconmensurable. — *s.* ***the (great) beyond,*** el más allá.
bezel [bezl], *s.* bisel; engaste. — *v.t.* biselar.
bezoar ['bi:zouə], *s.* (*biol.*) bezoar.
Bhutan [bu'tɑ:n]. Bhután.
biangular [bai'æŋgjulə], *a.* biangular.
bias ['baiəs], *s.* sesgo, oblicuidad, diagonal, *f.*; inclinación, predisposición; parcialidad, prejuicio; ***on the bias,*** al sesgo. — *v.t.* inclinar, predisponer; ***to be bias(s)ed,*** ser parcial *o* partidista, tener prejuicio.
bias(s)ed ['baiəst], *a.* parcial.
biaxial [bai'æksiəl], *a.* biáxico.
bib [bib], *s.* babero. — *v.t., v.i.* beber, pimplar.
bibasic [bai'beisik], *a.* (*quím.*) bibásico.
Bible [baibl], *s.* biblia.
biblical ['biblikəl], *a.* bíblico.

bibliographer [bibliˈɔgrəfə], *s.* bibliógrafo.
bibliographic(al) [biblioˈgræfik(əl)], *a.* bibliográfico.
bibliography [bibliˈɔgrəfi], *s.* bibliografía.
bibliomania [biblioˈmeiniə], *s.* bibliomanía.
bibliomaniac [biblioˈmeiniæk], *s.* bibliomaníaco, biblíómano.
bibliophile [ˈbibliofail], *s.* bibliófilo.
bibliopolist [bibliˈɔpəlist], *s.* librero, vendedor de libros raros.
bibulous [ˈbibjuləs], *a.* poroso, absorbente; borrachín, beodo.
bicapsular [baiˈkæpsjulə], *a.* (*bot.*) bicapsular.
bicarbonate [baiˈkɑ:bənit], *s.* (*quím.*) bicarbonato.
bice [bais], *s.* (*pint.*) azul de Armenia.
bicephalous [baiˈsefələs], *a.* bicéfalo.
biceps [ˈbaiseps], *s.* (*anat.*) bíceps.
bichloride [baiˈklɔ:raid], *s.* (*quím.*) bicloruro.
bichromate [baiˈkroumeit], *s.* (*quím.*) bicromato.
bicipital [baiˈsipitəl], *a.* (*anat.*) bicipital.
bicker [ˈbikə], *v.i.* discutir, pelearse (*por tonterías*); golpetear; parlar, gorjear; chisporrotear.
bickerer [ˈbikərə], *s.* camorrista, *m.f.*, discutidor.
bickering [ˈbikəriŋ], *s.* discusiones, *f.pl.*, riñas, *f.pl.*
bicornous [baiˈkɔ:nəs], *a.* bicorne.
bicorporal [baiˈkɔ:pərəl], *a.* bicorpóreo.
bicycle [ˈbaisikl], *s.* bicicleta. — *v.i.* andar en bicicleta.
bicycling [ˈbaisikliŋ], *s.* ciclismo.
bicyclist [ˈbaisiklist], *s.* biciclista, *m.f.*
bid [bid], *s.* oferta, postura; intento, esfuerzo. — *v.t.* decir; ofrecer; ordenar, mandar; pedir, rogar; invitar; anunciar; ***bid adieu*** o ***farewell,*** decir adiós; ***bid defiance to,*** retar, desafiar; ***bid welcome,*** dar la bienvenida. — *v.i.* hacer una oferta, licitar; ***bid fair to,*** ofrecer muchas probabilidades de.
bidder [ˈbidə], *s.* postor, pujador; ***the highest bidder,*** el mejor postor.
bidding [ˈbidiŋ], *s.* orden, mandato; oferta, puja, postura.
biddy (1) [ˈbidi], *s.* (*fam.*) gallina; pollo, pollito.
biddy (2) [ˈbidi], *s.* criada; (*fam.*) vieja, comadre, bruja.
bide [baid], *v.t.* sufrir, aguantar; esperar, aguardar; ***bide one's time,*** dar tiempo al tiempo.
bidental [baiˈdentl], *a.* bidente, bidentado.
bidentate [baiˈdenteit], *a.* (*bot.*) bidente.
bidet [ˈbi:dei], *s.* caballito, jaca; bidé.
biennial [baiˈeniəl], *a.* bienal. — *s.* planta bienal.
bier [biə], *s.* féretro.
bifarious [baiˈfɛəriəs], *a.* (*bot.*) bifollado.
biferous [ˈbaifərəs], *a.* (*bot.*) bífero.
biff [bif], *s.* (*fam.*) puñetazo. — *v.t.* dar un puñetazo a.
bifid [ˈbaifid], *a.* (*bot.*) bífido.
bifocal [baiˈfoukəl], *a.* (*ópt.*) bifocal; (*pl.*) (gafas de lentes) bifocales.
bifold [ˈbaifould], *a.* doble.
biform [ˈbaifɔ:m], *a.* biforme.
bifurcate [ˈbaifə:keit], *a.* bifurcado. — *v.t.* bifurcar; — *v.i.* bifurcarse.
bifurcation [baifə:ˈkeiʃən], *s.* bifurcación.
big [big], *a.* grande; abultado, voluminoso; importante; engreído; ***big with child,*** encinta; ***big-bellied,*** ventrudo, barrigón; ***big-boned,*** huesudo; (*mec.*) ***big end,*** cabeza de biela; ***big game,*** caza mayor; ***big-headed,*** cabezudo; creído; ***big-nosed,*** narigudo; (*fam.*) ***big shot, big-wig,*** pájaro gordo; ***big-time,*** de gran éxito, de primera clase, de campanillas; ***to talk big,*** ser bocazas, echar bravatas.
bigamist [ˈbigəmist], *s.* bígamo.
bigamy [ˈbigəmi], *s.* bigamia.
bigger, biggest [ˈbigə, -ist], *a. compar., superl.* [BIG].
biggish [ˈbigiʃ], *a.* grandecito.
bight [bait], *s.* caleta, ensenada.
bigness [ˈbignis], *s.* gran tamaño, grandor, grosor, volumen; importancia.
bigot [ˈbigət], *s. a.* fanático, intolerante, intransigente.
bigotry [ˈbigətri], *s.* fanatismo, intolerancia, intransigencia.
bike [baik], *s.* (*fam.*) bici, *f.*, bicicleta.
bilabiate [baiˈleibieit], *a.* (*bot.*) bilabiado.
bilamellate [baiˈlæməleit], *a.* (*bot.*) bilamelado.
bilander [ˈbailəndə], *s.* (*mar.*) balandra.
bilateral [baiˈlætərəl], *a.* bilateral.
bilberry [ˈbilbəri], *s.* (*bot.*) arándano.
bilbo [ˈbilbou], *s.* (*poét.*) espada, estoque.
bilboes [ˈbilbouz], *s.pl.* (*mar.*) cepo con grillos.
bile [bail], *s.* bilis, *f.*; hiel, *f.*
bile-duct [ˈbail-dʌkt], *s.* (*méd.*) conducto biliar.
bile-stone [ˈbail-stoun], *s.* cálculo biliar.
bilge [bildʒ], *s.* (*mar.*) pantoque, sentina; ***bilge-water,*** agua de pantoque; (*fam.*) sandeces.
biliary [ˈbiliəri], *a.* biliar.
bilingual [baiˈliŋgwəl], *a.* bilingüe.
bilious [ˈbiljəs], *a.* bilioso.
biliousness [ˈbiljəsnis], *s.* exceso de bilis.
bilk [bilk], *s.* estafa, timo; tramposo, estafador. — *v.t.* estafar, timar; eludir.
Bill [bil]. *forma cariñosa de* [WILLIAM].
bill (1) [bil], *s.* pico (*de ave*). — *v.i.* juntar los picos (*las palomas*); (*fig.*) ***bill and coo,*** arrullar(se).
bill (2) [bil], *s.* pica *o* alabarda; (*agric.*) hocino, podón, honcejo.
bill (3) [bil], *s.* cuenta; (*Am.*) billete de banco; nota; lista, cédula, relación; (*com.*) letra; (*com.*) billete, documento; patente, certificado; cartel, aviso; prospecto, hoja; (*der.*) escrito, petición; proyecto de ley; ***bill-book,*** registro de cuentas, letras etc. a cobrar *o* a pagar; ***bill-broker,*** corredor de cambios; ***bill of credit,*** carta de crédito; ***bill of entry,*** relación de mercancías entradas en aduana; ***bill of exchange,*** letra de cambio; ***bill of fare,*** minuta, carta, lista de platos; ***bill of health,*** patente de sanidad; ***bill of lading,*** conocimiento de embarque; ***bill of rights,*** declaración de derechos; ***bills payable,*** efectos a pagar; ***hand bill,*** octavilla. — *v.t.* anotar, facturar, cargar en cuenta; hacer una lista de; poner *o* fijar carteles de; anunciar (*por medio de carteles*).
billboard [ˈbilbɔ:d], *s.* cartelera; (*mar.*) apeadero de la uña del ancla.
billed [bild], *a.* picudo, en forma de pico; ***long-billed,*** de pico largo; ***short-billed,*** de pico corto.
billet [ˈbilit], *s.* billete, esquela; (*mil.*) boleta (*de alojamiento*); zoquete; ***billet-doux,*** billete amoroso. — *v.t.* (*mil.*) alojar; aposentar, colocar. — *v.i.* alojarse, estar aposentado.
billfold [ˈbilfould], (*Am.*) [WALLET].
billiard [ˈbiljəd], *a.* de billar, relativo al juego de billar; ***billiard ball,*** bola de billar; ***billiard cloth,*** paño de billar; ***billiard cue,*** taco; ***billiard pocket,*** tronera de billar; ***billiard table,*** mesa de billar.
billiards [ˈbiljədz], *s.* billar.
billing and cooing [ˈbiliŋ ənd ˈku:iŋ], *s.* arrullos, *m.pl.*
billion [ˈbiliən], *s.* (*arit.*) billón; mil millones (EE. UU.); millón de millones (*en Inglaterra, Francia y España*).
billionth [ˈbiliənθ], *a., s.* billonésimo.
billow [ˈbilou], *s.* ola, onda. — *v.i.* hincharse, crecer como una ola.
billowy [ˈbiloui], *a.* agitado; hinchado (*como las olas*).
billy [ˈbili], *s.* porra, palitroque.
billy-goat [ˈbili-gout], *s.* macho cabrío.

bilobate [bai'loubeit], *a.* (*bot.*) dicotiledóneo; de dos lóbulos.
bimana ['baimənə], *s.pl.* (*zool.*) bimanos, *m.pl.*
bimetallic [baimi'tælik], *a.* bimetálico.
bimetallism [bai'metəlizəm], *s.* bimetalismo.
bimonthly ['bai'mʌnθli], *a.* bimestral; bimensual, quincenal.
bin [bin], *s.* arcón; recipiente; ***coal-bin,*** carbonera; ***dust-bin,*** cubo de la basura. — *v.t.* guardar en arcón; poner en un recipiente.
binary ['bainəri], *a.* binario.
bind [baind], *v.t.* atar, ligar, trabar; ribetear, guarnecer; encuadernar; vendar; trabar, dar consistencia a; vincular, obligar; escriturar; ***bind over,*** obligar a comparecer ante el juez. — *v.i.* fraguar, trabarse; obligar, ser obligatorio. — **bind o.s.,** *v.r.* obligarse, comprometerse.
binder ['baində], *s.* encuadernador; atadero, atador; (*carp.*) ligazón; carpeta, cubierta (*para papeles*); atadora, agavilladora; ribeteador.
bindery ['baindəri], *s.* taller de encuadernador.
binding ['baindiŋ], *a.* obligatorio; astringente. — *s.* ligadura, ligazón, *f.*, ligamiento; ribete; encuadernación.
bindweed ['baindwi:d], *s.* (*bot.*) enredadera.
bine [bain], *s.* vástago.
bing [biŋ], *s.* montón de quijo *o* ganga.
binge [bindʒ], *s.* (*fam.*) jarana, juerga, borrachera; ***to go on a binge,*** irse de juerga.
bingo ['biŋgou], *s.* lotería de cartones.
binnacle ['binəkl], *s.* (*mar.*) bitácora.
binocle ['binəkl], *s.* (*ópt.*) binóculo.
binocular [bi'nɔkjulə], *a.* binocular. — *s.* (*pl.*) prismáticos.
binomial [bai'noumiəl], *a.*, *s.* (*álg.*) binomio.
binoxalate [bin'ɔksəleit], *s.* (*quím.*) bioxalato.
binoxide [bin'ɔksaid], *s.* bióxido.
biochemical [baio'kemikəl], *a.* bioquímico.
biochemist [baio'kemist], *s.* bioquímico.
biochemistry [baio'kemistri], *s.* bioquímica.
biodynamics [baioudai'næmiks], *s.* biodinámica.
biogenesis [baio'dʒenəsis], *s.* biogénesis, *f. inv.*
biographer [bai'ɔgrəfə], *s.* biógrafo.
biographic(al) [baio'græfik(əl)], *a.* biográfico.
biography [bai'ɔgrəfi], *s.* biografía.
biological [baiə'lɔdʒikəl], *a.* biológico.
biologist [bai'ɔlədʒist], *s.* biólogo.
biology [bai'ɔlədʒi], *s.* biología.
bionomy [bai'ɔnəmi], *s.* bionomía.
biophysics [baio'fiziks], *s.* biofísica.
bioplasm ['baioplæzəm], *s.* (*fisiol.*) bioplasma.
bioplasmic [baio'plæzmik], *a.* bioplásmico.
biparous ['bipərəs], *a.* bíparo.
bipartisan [baipɑ:ti'zæn], *a.* de (los) dos partidos.
bipartite [bai'pɑ:tait], *a.* bipartido, bipartito.
biped ['baiped], *s.* bípedo.
bipennate [bai'peneit], *a.* (*zool.*) bipeno.
bipetalous [bai'petələs], *a.* (*bot.*) bipétalo.
biplane ['baiplein], *s.* (*aer.*) biplano.
biquadratic [baikwɔ'drætik], *a.*, *s.* bicuadrado.
birch [bə:tʃ], *s.* (*bot.*) abedul; vara, férula. — *v.t.* varear.
birchen ['bə:tʃən], *a.* de abedul, abedulino.
bird [bə:d], *s.* ave, *f.*, pájaro; (*fam.*) chavala; ***cock-bird,*** ave macho; ***hen-bird,*** ave hembra; ***bird of Paradise,*** ave del Paraíso; ***bird of passage,*** ave de paso; ***bird of prey,*** ave de rapiña; ***singing bird,*** pájaro cantor; (*fam.*) ***jail-bird,*** presidiario; ***birds of a feather,*** gente de la misma calaña; ***birds of a feather flock together,*** Dios los cría y ellos se juntan; (*fig.*) ***to kill two birds with one stone,*** matar dos pájaros de un tiro; ***a bird in the hand is worth two in the bush,*** más vale pájaro en mano que ciento volando; ***bird's-eye view,*** (a) vista de pájaro; ***bird's nest,*** nido de pájaros; ***the early bird catches the worm,*** a quien madruga, Dios le ayuda.
bird-brained ['bə:d-breind], *a.* casquivano.
bird-cage ['bə:d-keidʒ], *s.* jaula.
bird-call ['bə:d-kɔ:l], *s.* reclamo; añagaza.
birdcatcher ['bə:dkætʃə], *s.* pajarero.
bird-fancier ['bə:d-fænsiə], *s.* pajarero.
birdlike ['bə:dlaik], *a.* como de pájaro, pajaril; ***to have a birdlike appetite,*** comer como un pajarito.
bird-lime ['bə:d-laim], *s.* liga.
bird-organ ['bə:d-ɔ:gən], *s.* organillo para enseñar a los canarios.
bird's-foot ['bə:dz-fut], *s.* (*bot.*) pie de pájaro.
biretta [bi'retə], *s.* (*igl.*) birreta.
birth [bə:θ], *s.* nacimiento; parto; origen, orto; ***birth control,*** limitación de la natalidad; ***birth-rate,*** natalidad; ***by birth,*** de nacimiento; ***to give birth to,*** parir, dar a luz; ***of noble birth,*** de alcurnia, de estirpe.
birthday ['bə:θdei], *s.* cumpleaños, *m. sing.*
birthmark ['bə:θmɑ:k], *s.* antojo, lunar; marca de nacimiento.
birthplace ['bə:θpleis], *s.* suelo nativo, lugar de nacimiento.
birthright ['bə:θrait], *s.* derecho natural; primogenitura.
Biscay ['biskei]. Vizcaya; ***Bay of Biscay,*** Mar Cantábrico.
Biscayan [bis'keiən], *a.*, *s.* vizcaíno.
biscuit ['biskit], *s.* galleta; ***ship's biscuit,*** bizcocho; (*Am.*) [SCONE].
bisect [bai'sekt], *v.t.* (*geom.*) bisecar.
bisection [bai'sekʃən], *s.* bisección.
bisector [bai'sektə], *s.* bisectriz.
bisexual [bai'seksjuəl], *a.* (*bot.*) bisexual.
bishop ['biʃəp], *s.* obispo; alfil.
bishopric ['biʃəprik], *s.* obispado; episcopado; diócesis, *f.*
bismuth ['bizməθ], *s.* (*quím.*) bismuto.
bison [baisn], *s.* (*zool.*) bisonte.
bisque [bisk], *s.* sopa de pescado, marisco *o* aves.
bissextile [bi'sekstail], *a.*, *s.* bisiesto.
bistre ['bistə], *s.* (*pint.*) bistre.
bistort ['bistɔ:t], *s.* (*bot.*) dragúnculo, bistorta.
bistoury [bis'tu:ri], *s.* (*cir.*) bisturí.
bisulcous [bai'sʌlkəs], *a.* bisulco.
bisulphide [bai'sʌlfaid], *s.* (*quím.*) bisulfuro.
bisulphite [bai'sʌlfait], *s.* bisulfito.
bit (1) [bit], *s.* pedazo, trozo, pedacito, trocito; ***tit-bit,*** tapa; ***not a bit,*** ni pizca, nada, en absoluto; ***wait a bit,*** espere un momentito *o* ratito; ***to do one's bit,*** aportar su grano de arena.
bit (2) [bit], *s.* bocado (*del freno*); paletón (*de la llave*); broca, taladro; ***to champ at the bit,*** tascar el freno; ***to take the bit between one's teeth,*** desbocarse, desmandarse.
bit (3) [bit], *pret.* [BITE].
bitartrate [bai'tɑ:treit], *s.* (*quím.*) bitartrato.
bitch [bitʃ], *s.* perra; (*fam.*, *despec.*) puñetera.
bitchy ['bitʃi], *a.* (*fam.*, *despec.*) puñetero.
bite [bait], *s.* mordedura, mordisco; picada, picadura; bocado, tentempié; resquemo (*en el paladar*). — *v.t.* morder, mordiscar; picar (*un insecto*); picar, resquemar, escocer; raspar (*el vino*); cortar (*el frío, el aire*); corroer, atacar (*ácidos*); tascar (*el freno*); ***bite the dust,*** morder el polvo; ***once bitten, twice shy,*** gato escaldado, del agua fría huye. — *v.i.* picar (*el anzuelo*).
biter ['baitə], *s.* mordedor.
biting ['baitiŋ], *a.* mordaz, cáustico; áspero, picante; penetrante.
bitt [bit], *s.* (*mar.*) bit (*ú. más en pl.*) — *v.t.* (*mar.*) abitar.

bitter [ˈbitə], *a.* amargo; feroz, atroz; enconado; encarnizado; crudo; ***bitter-sweet,*** agridulce; ***to the bitter end,*** hasta el final. — *s.* amargo, amargura; (*fam.*) cerveza; (*pl.*) bítter.
bitterish [ˈbitəriʃ], *s.* amarguillo.
bitterly [ˈbitəli], *adv.* amargamente; ***to weep bitterly,*** llorar desconsoladamente *o* a lágrima viva.
bittern [ˈbitə:n], *s.* (*orn.*) avetoro.
bitterness [ˈbitənis], *s,* amargor; amargura; encono; (lo) encarnizado.
bitumen [biˈtju:mən], *s.* betún.
bituminate [biˈtju:mineit], *v.t.* embetunar.
bituminiferous [bitju:miˈnifərəs], *a.* bituminífero.
bituminize [biˈtju:minaiz], *v.t.* embetunar.
bituminous [biˈtju:minəs], *a.* bituminoso.
bivalve, bivalvular [ˈbaivælv, baiˈvælvjulə], *a.* bivalvo.
bivaulted [ˈbaivɔ:ltid], *a.* de doble bóveda.
bivious [ˈbiviəs], *a.* bivial.
bivouac [ˈbivuæk], *s.* vivaque. — *v.i.* (*mil.*) vivaquear.
biweekly [baiˈwi:kli], *a.* quincenal; bisemanal.
bizarre [biˈzɑ:], *a.* extravagante, estrafalario, grotesco.
blab [blæb], *s.* parloteo; chismería. — *v.t.* soltar. — *v.i.* parlotear; chismear.
blabber [ˈblæbə], *s.* parloteador; chismoso.
black [blæk], *a.* negro; sombrío; ceñudo; ***black and blue,*** lívido, acardenalado, amoratado; ***black and blue mark,*** cardenal; ***black and white,*** blanco y negro; ***black art,*** nigromancia; ***to look black at,*** mirar con ceño; (*fig.*) ***it is looking black,*** la cosa se presenta negra. — *s.* negro (*persona*); negro, color negro; (*blas.*) sable; luto; ***to put in black and white,*** poner por escrito; ***to wear black,*** ir de luto. — *v.t.* ennegrecer; teñir de negro; (*fig.*) denigrar; boicotear.
blackamoor [ˈblækəmɔ:], *s.* negro; moro.
black-ball [ˈblæk-bɔ:l], *s.* bola negra. — *v.t.* dar bola negra a.
blackberry [ˈblækbəri], *s.* (*bot.*) zarza; zarzamora.
blackbird [ˈblækbə:d], *s.* (*orn.*) mirlo.
blackboard [ˈblækbɔ:d], *s.* pizarra, encerado.
black-browed [ˈblæk-braud], *a.* cejinegro.
black-cap [ˈblæk-kæp], *s.* (*orn.*) alondra; (*bot.*) frambuesa negra; espadaña.
black-cock [ˈblæk-kɔk], *s.* (*orn.*) urogallo.
black-currant [ˈblæk-kʌrənt], *s.* grosella negra.
Black Death [ˈblæk ˈdeθ], *s.* peste negra.
blacken [ˈblækən], *v.t.* ennegrecer, poner negro; embetunar; atezar; difamar, denigrar. — *v.i.* ennegrecerse.
blackening [ˈblækəniŋ], *s.* ennegrecimiento; atezamiento.
black-eyed [ˈblæk-aid], *a.* ojinegro.
blackface [ˈblækfeis], *a.* carinegro. — *s.* (*impr.*) letra negrilla.
blackguard [ˈblægɑ:d], *s.* (*fam.*) canalla, *m.*, bribón, sinvergüenza, *m.*
blackhaired [ˈblækhɛəd], *a.* pelinegro.
black-head [ˈblæk-hed], *s.* espinilla, comedón.
blacking [ˈblækiŋ], *s.* betún, lustre.
blackish [ˈblækiʃ], *a.* negruzco.
black-jack [ˈblæk-dʒæk], *s.* bandera pirata; porra; (*min.*) blenda.
black-leg [ˈblæk-leg], *s.* petardista, *m.f.*; fullero; (*vet.*) morriña negra; esquirol (*obrerismo*).
blackmail [ˈblækmeil], *s.* chantaje. — *v.t.* hacer chantaje a.
blackmailer [ˈblækmeilə], *s.* chantajista, *m.f.*
Black Maria [ˈblæk məˈraiə], *s.* coche celular.
blackmouthed [ˈblækmauðd], *a.* boquinegro; grosero, vil.
blackness [ˈblæknis], *s.* negrura.
black-out [ˈblæk-aut], *s.* apagón; amnesia. — *v.t.* apagar las luces de. — *v.i.* perder el conocimiento.
black-pudding [ˈblæk-ˈpudiŋ], *s.* morcilla.
Black Sea [ˈblæk ˈsi:]. Mar Negro.
blacksmith [ˈblæksmiθ], *s.* herrero.
blackthorn [ˈblækθɔ:n], *s.* (*bot.*) endrino.
black-vomit [ˈblæk-ˈvɔmit], *s.* vómito negro.
blad [blæd], *s.* manotada, golpe con la mano. — *v.t.* herir, dar una bofetada, golpear.
bladder [ˈblædə], *s.* (*anat.*) vejiga; ampolla.
bladderwort [ˈblædəwə:t], *s.* (*bot.*) utricularia.
bladdery [ˈblædəri], *a.* vesicular.
blade [bleid], *s.* hoja (*de arma blanca, de herramienta*); pala, paleta (*de turbina etc.*); lámina; (*bot.*) limbo; brizna; cuchilla (*de interruptor*); ***razor-blade,*** hoja *o* cuchilla de afeitar; (*anat.*) ***shoulder blade,*** paletilla.
blade-bone [ˈbleid-boun], *s.* (*anat.*) escápula, espaldilla, omóplato.
bladed [ˈbleidid], *a.* entallecido; guarnecido de hojas; armado con hojas; (*min.*) laminado.
blain [blein], *s.* ampolla, llaga.
blamable [ˈbleiməbl], *a.* culpable, vituperable, reprensible.
blame [bleim], *s.* culpa; tacha, censura, reprobación. — *v.t.* culpar, echar la culpa a; reprobar, censurar; ***he's to blame,*** él tiene la culpa.
blameful [ˈbleimful], *a.* censurable.
blameless [ˈbleimlis], *a.* intachable, irreprochable, sin culpa.
blamelessness [ˈbleimlisnis], *s.* inocencia, carencia de culpa.
blamer [ˈbleimə], *s.* reprensor, censurador.
blameworthiness [ˈbleimwə:ðinis], *s.* culpabilidad; (lo) censurable.
blameworthy [ˈbleimwə:ði], *a.* culpable; censurable.
blanch [blɑ:ntʃ], *v.t.* blanquear; hacer palidecer; emblanquecer (*las plantas*); escaldar (*la carne*); pelar, mondar; blanquear (*metales*). — *v.i.* palidecer, demudarse.
blancher [ˈblɑ:ntʃə], *s.* blanqueador
blanching [ˈblɑ:ntʃiŋ], *s.* blanqueo, blanquición, blanquimiento.
blanc-mange [bləˈmɔnʒ], *s.* (*coc.*) crema.
bland [blænd], *a.* suave, untuoso, meloso.
blandish [ˈblændiʃ], *v.t.* engatusar, halagar, lisonjear.
blandishment [ˈblændiʃmənt], *s.* halago, lisonja, engatusamiento.
blandness [ˈblændnis], *s.* dulzura, suavidad, amabilidad.
blank [blæŋk], *a.* blanco, suelto; en blanco; sin adorno; sin interés; confuso, desconcertado; ***blank cartridge,*** cartucho sin bala; ***blank look*** o ***stare,*** mirada *o* cara inexpresiva. — *s.* blanco, hueco; papel en blanco; cospel; tejo; ***to draw a blank,*** no encontrar *o* no conseguir nada. — *v.t.* borrar, cancelar; cerrar, obstruir; estampar.
blanket [ˈblæŋkit], *a.* global, que lo abarca todo. — *s.* manta; (*fig.*) capa, manto; (*fig.*) ***wet blanket,*** aguafiestas, *m.f. inv.*; jarro de agua fría. — *v.t.* cubrir (con manta); envolver; mantear; proteger; neutralizar.
blankly [ˈblæŋkli], *adv.* con cara inexpresiva.
blankness [ˈblæŋknis], *s.* (lo) inexpresivo.
blare [blɛə], *s.* estruendo: — *v.t.* emitir con estruendo. — *v.i.* sonar con estruendo.
blarney [ˈblɑ:ni], *s.* coba; labia.
blasé [ˈblɑ:zei], *a.* hastiado; que nunca se entusiasma.
blaspheme [blæsˈfi:m], *v.t.*, *v.i.* blasfemar (contra).
blasphemer [blæsˈfi:mə], *s.* blasfemo, blasfemador.
blasphemous [ˈblæsfəməs], *a.* blasfemo.
blasphemy, blaspheming [ˈblæsfəmi, blæsˈfi:mi *s.* blasfemia.

blast [blɑ:st], *s.* ráfaga, golpe de viento; bocanada de aire; soplo; chorro; carga; explosión, voladura; tizón; ***blast furnace,*** alto horno; ***in full blast,*** en plena marcha. — *v.t.* marchitar, agostar; (*agric.*) añublar; arruinar, destruir; volar, barrenar.
blasted [ˈblɑ:stid], *a.* (*fam.*) maldito, condenado.
blasting [ˈblɑ:stiŋ], *s.* destrucción, ruina; voladura; marchitamiento.
blast-off [ˈblɑ:st-ɔf], *s.* lanzamiento.
blatant [ˈbleitənt], *a.* vocinglero; descarado, desvergonzado.
blather [ˈblæðə], *s.* parloteo. — *v.i.* parlotear.
blaze (1) [bleiz], *s.* llamarada; fuego; fogata; hoguera; incendio; resplandor; explosión; ramalazo; estrella *o* mancha blanca (*en la frente del caballo*); ***in a blaze,*** en llamas. — *v.t.* ***blaze a trail,*** abrir *o* señalar un camino. — *v.i.* arder (furiosamente); resplandecer; ***blaze away,*** disparar furiosamente.
blaze (2) [bleiz], *v.t.* ***blaze abroad,*** proclamar *o* divulgar con mucho aparato de publicidad.
blazer [ˈbleizə], *s.* chaqueta (*de colegio* o *club*).
blazing [ˈbleiziŋ], *a.* flameante, llameante, brillante; abrasador; violento.
blazon [ˈbleizən], *s.* blasón; divulgación, publicación. — *v.t.* blasonar; proclamar, divulgar.
blazonry [ˈblaizənri], *s.* blasón; boato.
bleaberry [ˈbli:beri], *s.* (*bot.*) mírtilo.
bleach [bli:tʃ], *s.* blanqueo; lejía. — *v.t.* blanquear; descolorar; aclarar (*el pelo*); colar (*la ropa*). — *v.i.* ponerse blanco, palidecer.
bleacher [ˈbli:tʃə], *s.* blanqueador.
bleachery [ˈbli:tʃəri], *s.* blanqueo.
bleaching [ˈbli:tʃiŋ], *s.* blanqueadura, blanqueamiento, blanqueo; ***bleaching powder,*** blanquimento, cloruro de calcio.
bleak (1) [bli:k], *a.* yermo, desolado, desolador, adusto, helado.
bleak (2) [bli:k], *s.* (*ict.*) albur, breca.
bleakish [ˈbli:kiʃ], *a.* frío, glacial.
bleakness [ˈbli:knis], *s.* desolación, adustez, frío, frialdad.
blear [bliə], *a.* legañoso, lagañoso; pitarroso, cegajoso; (*fig.*) engañoso, falaz.
blearedness [ˈbliədnis], *s.* legaña, lagaña; turbación *u* ofuscación de la vista.
bleary [ˈbliəri], *a.* legañoso; ***bleary-eyed,*** legañoso.
bleat [bli:t], *v.t.* balar. — *v.i.* balar, dar balidos.
bleating [ˈbli:tiŋ], *a.* balante. — *s.* balidos.
bleb [bleb], *s.* ampolla, vejiga.
bleed [bli:d], *v.t.* sangrar; (*fig.*) ***bleed white,*** desangrar. — *v.i.* sangrar; ***bleed to death,*** desangrarse, morir desangrado.
bleeding [ˈbli:diŋ], *a.* sangrante, sangriento; (*fam.*) condenado, maldito. — *s.* sangría, sangradura; hemorragia, flujo de sangre.
bleeding-heart [ˈbli:diŋ-ˈhɑ:t], *s.* (*bot.*) dicentra, alhelí doble.
blemish [ˈblemiʃ], *s.* defecto, tacha, falta, imperfección; mancha, mácula, mancilla. — *v.t.* manchar, afear, empañar; mancillar.
blemishless [ˈblemiʃlis], *a.* sin tacha, defecto *o* falta.
blench [blentʃ], *v.i.* retroceder, recular, arredrarse.
blenching [ˈblentʃiŋ], *s.* retroceso.
blend [blend], *s.* mezcla, mixtura, combinación; (*pint.*) gradación. — *v.t.* mezclar, fundir, combinar; (*pint.*) matizar, armonizar, templar, casar. — *v.i.* combinarse, mezclarse, fundirse.
blende [blend], *s.* (*min.*) blenda (*sulfuro de cinc*).
blending [ˈblendiŋ], *a.* concordante, armonizado. — *s.* casamiento; combinación.
blennorrhœa [blenɔˈriə], *s.* (*med.*) blenorrea.
bless [bles], *v.t.* bendecir; ***bless my soul,*** válgame Dios; ***God bless you,*** Dios te bendiga.
blessed [ˈblesid], *a.* bendito, bienaventurado; santo; (*fam.*) ***the whole blessed day,*** todo el santo día.
blessedness [ˈblesidnis], *s.* bienaventuranza; santidad.
blessing [ˈblesiŋ], *s.* bendición; beneficio.
blest [blest], *a.* [BLESSED]. — *p.p.* [BLESS].
blethering [ˈbleðəriŋ], *a.* parloteo.
blight [blait], *s.* tizón; añublo; plaga. — *v.t.* atizonar, añublar; (*fig.*) marchitar, frustrar.
Blighty [ˈblaiti]. (*fam., mil.*) Inglaterra.
blind [blaind], *a.* ciego; oculto; ***blind alley,*** callejón sin salida; ***blind in one eye,*** tuerto; ***to turn a blind eye,*** hacer la vista gorda; ***blind man's buff,*** gallina ciega; ***blind side,*** lado flaco. — *s.* store; venda; (*fig.*) pantalla (*persona*); (*fig.*) pretexto; subterfugio; simulacro; (*pl., fort.*) blinda, blindajes; ***Venetian blinds,*** persianas. — *v.t.* cegar; deslumbrar, ofuscar, obcecar; velar; (*mil.*) blindar.
blindage [ˈblaindidʒ], *s.* (*mil.*) blindaje.
blindfold [ˈblaindfould], *adv.* con los ojos vendados; (*fig.*) a ciegas. — *v.t.* vendar los ojos a.
blindly [ˈblaindli], *adv.* ciegamente, a ciegas, a ojos cerrados.
blindness [ˈblaindnis], *s.* ceguedad; ceguera; obcecación, ofuscación.
blindworm [ˈblaindwə:m], *s.* (*zool.*) cecilia.
blink [bliŋk], *s.* pestañeo; guiño; guiñada; parpadeo; destello, reflejo. — *v.t.* guiñar (*el ojo*). — *v.i.* parpadear, pestañear; fulgurar, destellar.
blinkers [ˈbliŋkəz], *s.pl.* anteojeras, *f.pl.*
blinking [ˈbliŋkiŋ], *a.* (*fam.*) maldito.
bliss [blis], *s.* bienaventuranza; dicha, felicidad; deleite.
blissful [ˈblisful], *a.* bienaventurado; feliz, dichoso.
blissfully [ˈblisfuli], *adv.* felizmente; ***blissfully ignorant,*** sumido en la mayor inconsciencia.
blissfulness [ˈblisfulnis], *s.* bienaventuranza; dicha.
blister [ˈblistə], *s.* ampolla, vejiga. — ampollar; (*fig.*) fustigar. — *v.i.* ampollarse, avejigarse; ***blister off,*** desconcharse.
blister-fly [ˈblistə-flai], *s.* cantárida.
blistering [ˈblistəriŋ], *a.* (*fig.*) cáustico, despiadado, feroz; ***blistering heat,*** calor achicharrante.
blistery [ˈblistəri], *a.* cubierto de ampollas; desconchado.
blite [blait], *s.* (*bot.*) bledo.
blithe [blaið], *a.* alegre, gozoso.
blitheness [ˈblaiðnis], *s.* alegría, júbilo, contento, gozo, jovialidad.
blithesome [ˈblaiðsəm], *a.* alegre, vivo, divertido.
blithesomeness [ˈblaiðsəmnis], *s.* alegría, animación, júbilo, contento, gozo, jovialidad.
blizzard [ˈblizəd], *s.* ventisca, tempestad *o* temporal de nieve(s).
bloat [blout], *v.t.* hinchar, henchir; poner abotargado; curar (*arenques*); inflar, engreír. — *v.i.* hincharse, abotargarse; engreírse.
bloated [ˈbloutid], *a.* hinchado, abotargado; engreído.
bloatedness [ˈbloutidnis], *s.* hinchazón.
bloater [ˈbloutə], *s.* arenque ahumado.
blob [blɔb], *s.* gota, gotón, mancha (*de tinta, pintura etc.*).
blobberlip [ˈblɔbəlip], *s.* bezo.
block [blɔk], *s.* bloque; tarugo, zoquete; tajo (*de madera*); horma (*de sombrero*); dado, cubo; (*mar.*) motón, polea (*de aparejo*), garrucha; cuadernal; cepo (*de yunque*); zapata (*de freno*); manzana, cuadra (*de casas*); paquete, lote, partida; obstáculo, pega; (*mec.*) tope; (*dep.*) parada, blocaje; ***stumbling-block,*** escollo, obstáculo, pega; ***block booking,*** reserva en bloque. — *v.t.* bloquear, obstruir, cerrar; (*alb.*) tapiar, cegar, condenar; (*dep.*) parar (*la pelota*); (*tip.*) montar (*una plancha*); (*carp.*) reforzar (*un ángulo*); ahormar (*un sombrero*).

blockade [blɔ'keid], s. bloqueo. — *v.t.* bloquear.
blockader [blɔ'keidə], *s.* bloqueador.
blockhead ['blɔkhed], *s.* (*fam.*) zoquete, (pedazo de) alcornoque.
blockheaded [blɔk'hedid], *a.* (*fam.*) lerdo.
block-house ['blɔk-haus], *s.* blocao, fortín.
blockish ['blɔkiʃ], *a.* tonto, estúpido, necio.
bloke [blouk], *s.* (*fam.*) fulano, tío.
blomary, bloomary ['blu:məri], *s.* (*metal.*) horno de refinación.
blond(e) [blɔnd], *a.*, *s.* rubio; ***blonde lace,*** blonda (de seda).
blood [blʌd], *a.* de sangre, sanguíneo. — *s.* sangre; ***bad blood,*** encono; ***my blood is up,*** me hierve la sangre; ***to make one's blood run cold,*** helarle la sangre a alguien; ***in cold blood,*** a sangre fría; ***young blood,*** pollastre.; ***blood-and-thunder,*** *a.* de folletín, melodramático; — *v.t.* sangrar; ensañar.
blood-bank ['blʌd-bæŋk], *s.* banco de sangre.
blood-count ['blʌd-kaunt], *s.* recuento sanguíneo.
bloodcurdling ['blʌdkə:dliŋ], *a.* terrorífico, horripilante, espeluznante.
blood-group ['blʌd-gru:p], *s.* grupo sanguíneo.
blood-heat ['blʌd-'hi:t], *s.* calor natural de la sangre.
bloodhorse ['blʌdhɔ:s], *s.* caballo de pura sangre.
bloodhound ['blʌdhaund], *s.* sabueso.
bloodiness ['blʌdinis], *s.* ensangrentamiento, (lo) ensangrentado; (lo) sanguinolento; (lo) sanguinario.
bloodless ['blʌdlis], *a.* exangüe; incruento.
blood-letter ['blʌd-letə], *s.* sangrador, flebotomista, *m.f.*
blood-letting ['blʌd-letiŋ], s. sangría, flebotomía; (*fig.*) derramamiento de sangre.
blood-money ['blʌd-mʌni], *s.* precio pagado por el derramamiento de sangre, por la comisión de un homicidio *o* por el descubrimiento del homicida.
blood-orange ['blʌd-ɔrindʒ], *s.* naranja sanguínea, naranja de sangre.
blood-poisoning ['blʌd-pɔizəniŋ], *s.* envenenamiento de la sangre.
blood-pressure ['blʌd-preʃə], *s.* (*med.*) tensión arterial; ***high blood-pressure,*** hipertensión.
blood-red ['blʌd-red], *a.* rojo sangre.
blood-relation ['blʌd-ri'leiʃən], *s.* pariente consanguíneo.
blood-root ['blʌd-ru:t], *s.* (*bot.*) sanguinaria.
blood-sausage ['blʌd-sɔsidʒ], *s.* morcilla.
bloodshed ['blʌdʃed], *s.* efusión de sangre; matanza.
bloodshot ['blʌdʃɔt], *a.* inyectado de sangre.
blood-spavin ['blʌd-spævin], *s.* (*vet.*) esparaván.
blood-stain ['blʌd-stein], *s.* mancha de sangre.
blood-stained ['blʌd-steind], *a.* manchado de sangre.
bloodstone ['blʌdstoun], *s.* (*min.*) hematites, *f.*, albín, alaqueca.
bloodstream ['blʌdstri:m], *s.* corriente sanguínea.
bloodsucker ['blʌdsʌkə], *s.* sanguijuela; (*fig.*) chupóptero.
blood-test ['blʌd-test], *s.* análisis de sangre.
bloodthirstiness ['blʌdθə:stinis], *s.* sed de sangre, *f.*
bloodthirsty ['blʌdθə:sti], *a.* sanguinario.
blood-transfusion ['blʌd-trænz'fju:ʒən], *s.* transfusión de sangre.
bloodvessel ['blʌdvesəl], *s.* vaso sanguíneo; (*t. fig.*) ***to burst a bloodvessel,*** reventarse una vena.
bloodwort ['blʌdwə:t], *s.* (*bot.*) sanguinaria.
bloody ['blʌdi], *s.* sangriento, cruento; ensangrentado; sanguinolento; (*fam.*) puñetero; ***bloody-minded,*** puñetero, que tiene mala idea.
bloom [blu:m], *s.* flor, *f.*; florecimiento; lozanía; (*metal.*) changote; pelusilla (*frutos y hojas*). — *v.i.* florecer; lozanear.
bloomer ['blu:mə], *s.* (*fam.*) pifia, gazapo; (*pl.*) bragas, *f.pl.*
blooming ['blu:miŋ], *a.* floreciente; lozano; (*fam.*) maldito.
bloomy ['blu:mi], *a.* florido.
blossom ['blɔsəm], *s.* flor, *f.*, flores; brote(s). — *v.i.* florecer, echar flor.
blossoming ['blɔsəmiŋ], *s.* florecimiento.
blot [blɔt], *s.* borrón, mancha de tinta; ***to make a blot,*** echar un borrón; ***blot on one's escutcheon,*** baldón. — *v.t.* emborronar; manchar; secar; (*fig.*) ***blot one's copy-book,*** ponerse en entredicho; ***blot out,*** borrar. — *v.i.* echar borrones.
blotch [blɔtʃ], *s.* erupción; mancha, borrón. — *v.t.* cubrir de erupciones; emborronar.
blotchy ['blɔtʃi], *a.* lleno de erupciones.
blotter ['blɔtə], *s.* papel secante.
blotting-paper ['blɔtiŋ-peipə], *s.* (papel) secante.
blouse [blauz], *s.* blusa.
blow (1) [blou], *s.* golpe, porrazo; ***at one blow,*** de un golpe; ***blow on the face,*** bofetada; ***blow with the fist,*** puñetazo; ***to come to blows,*** venir a las manos; ***to strike a blow,*** asestar un golpe; ***without striking a blow,*** sin dar un golpe.
blow (2) [blou], *s.* soplo, soplido. — *v.t.* soplar; tocar (*la trompeta*); hacer sonar; pregonar; fundir; ***blow away,*** quitar soplando; ***blow down,*** derribar; ***blow the gaff,*** descubrir el pastel; ***blow (s.o.) a kiss,*** echar *o* enviar un beso; (*fam.*) ***blow one's mind,*** exaltarse (por medio de drogas, alcohol etc.), ponerse en estado de frenesí; ***blow one's money,*** tirar el dinero; ***blow one's nose,*** sonarse (la nariz); ***blow off steam,*** expulsar el vapor; (*fig.*) desahogarse; ***blow out,*** apagar a soplos; inflar; ***blow one's brains out,*** saltarse la tapa de los sesos; ***blow one's own trumpet,*** darse bombo, ponerse moños; ***blow up,*** hinchar, inflar; volar, hacer saltar; exagerar; ampliar (*una foto*); (*fam., fig.*) ***blow s.o. up,*** echar una bronca a. — *v.i.* soplar; correr (*el viento*), ventear; sonar, silbar, pitar; resoplar, bufar; volarse, levantarse; ***blow away,*** volarse (con el viento); ***blow hot and cold,*** titubear, vacilar; ***blow over,*** pasar; quedarse en nada.
blower [blouə], *s.* soplador; tapadera de chimenea; ventilador, aventador, fuelle; (*fam.*) teléfono.
blow-fly ['blou-flai], *s.* (*ent.*) moscarda.
blow-gun ['blou-gʌn], *s.* cerbatana, bodoquera.
blow-hole ['blou-houl], *s.* respiradero.
blow-out ['blou-aut], *s.* reventón; (*fam.*) comilona, atracón.
blow-pipe ['blou-paip], *s.* soplete; cerbatana.
blowtorch ['bloutɔ:tʃ], *s.* lámpara de soldar, soplete.
blowup ['blouʌp], *s.* voladura, explosión; ataque de ira; (*foto.*) ampliación.
blowzy ['blauzi], *a.* desaliñado; coloradote.
blubber ['blʌbə], *s.* esperma *o* grasa de ballena; ortiga marina; burbuja, ampolla. — *v.i.* llorar a lágrima viva; berrear.
bludgeon ['blʌdʒən], *s.* cachiporra.
blue [blu:], *a.* azul; azulado, cerúleo, amoratado; (*fig.*) triste, melancólico; (*fam.*) verde; (*bot.*) ***blue gum,*** eucalipto; ***once in a blue moon,*** de higos a brevas, una vez al cabo de cuando; (*mar.*) ***Blue Peter,*** gallardete de marcha; ***to look blue,*** tener cara triste; ***sky-blue,*** celeste. — *s.* azul; (*blas.*) azur; (*pl.*) murria; ***true blue,*** tradicionalista empedernido. — *v.t.* azular, teñir de azul; pavonar.
Bluebeard ['blu:biəd]. Barba Azul.
bluebell ['blu:bel], *s.* (*bot.*) campanilla azul.
blue-bird ['blu:-bə:d], *s.* pájaro azul, azulejo.
blue-bottle ['blu:bɔtl], *s.* (*bot.*) aciano, liebrecilla; (*ent.*) moscón.
blue-copper ['blu:-kɔpə], *s.* (*min.*) azurita.
blue-devils ['blu:-devilz], *s.pl.* vapores negros; *m.pl.*, melancolía.
blue-eyed ['blu:-aid], *a.* ojizarco, ojiazul, de ojos azules *o* zarcos; ***blue-eyed boy,*** paniaguado, favorito, protegido.

blueing [ˈblu:iŋ], *s.* pavonaje.

blue-jacket [ˈblu:-dʒækit], *s.* marinero (de la Marina Real).

blueness [ˈblu:nis], *s.* azul; (*fig.*, *fam.*) verdez, (lo) verde; tristeza.

blue-pencil [blu:-ˈpensil], *v.t.* (*fig.*) tachar, rechazar.

blue-print [ˈblu:-print], *s.* cianotipo; (ante) proyecto.

blue-stocking [ˈblu:-stɔkiŋ], *s.* marisabidilla; literata, bachillera.

blue-stone [ˈblu:-stoun], *s.* (*min.*) sulfato de cobre.

bluey [blu:i], *a.* azulado.

bluff (1) [blʌf], *a.* escarpado; francote, bruscote. — *s.* acantilado, risco.

bluff (2) [blʌf], *s.* farol, truco; ***to call s.o.'s bluff,*** demostrar que alguien es farolero *o* farolón. — *v.t.* engañar con faroles. — *v.i.* farolear, marcarse faroles, tirarse un farol.

bluffer [ˈblʌfə], *s.* farolero.

bluffing [ˈblʌfiŋ], *s.* farolero, farolón.

bluffness [ˈblʌfnis], *s.* brusquedad campechana.

bluish [ˈblu:iʃ], *a.* azulado.

bluishness [ˈblu:iʃnis], *s.* color azulado.

blunder [ˈblʌndə], *s.* torpeza, coladura, patinazo, metedura de pata, pifia. — *v.i.* cometer una torpeza, colarse, pegar un patinazo, meter la pata.

blunderbuss [ˈblʌndəbʌs], *s.* trabuco.

blunderer [ˈblʌndərə], *s.* torpe, torpón.

blunt [blʌnt], *a.* embotado, romo, sin punta, sin filo, desafilado; muy franco, brusco. — *v.t.* embotar, desafilar.

blunting [ˈblʌntiŋ], *s.* embotadura.

bluntly [ˈblʌntli], *adv.* bruscamente.

bluntness [ˈblʌntnis], *s.* embotadura, embotamiento; brusquedad, franqueza excesiva.

blunt-witted [ˈblʌnt-witid], *a.* lerdo.

blur [blə:], *s.* cosa borrosa. — *v.t.* poner *o* volver borroso. — *v.i.* ponerse *o* volverse borroso.

blurb [blə:b], *s.* palabrería; autopropaganda (*de un libro*).

blurt [blə:t], *v.t.* ***blurt out,*** soltar sin pensar *o* sin querer.

blush [blʌʃ], *s.* sonrojo, rubor; tono rojo. — *v.i.* ruborizarse, sonrojarse, ponerse colorado.

blushful [ˈblʌʃful], *a.* ruboroso, vergonzoso.

blushing [ˈblʌʃiŋ], *a.* ruboroso, vergonzoso.

bluster [ˈblʌstə], *s.* borrasca; jactancia y faroleo. — *v.i.* soplar borrascosamente; jactarse y farolear, echar bravatas y farolear.

blusterer [ˈblʌstərə], *s.* matasiete, tipo jactancioso y farolón.

blustering [ˈblʌstəriŋ], *a.* borrascoso; jactancioso y farolero.

blustery [ˈblʌstəri], *a.* ventoso, borrascoso; de ráfaga; fanfarrón.

boa [bouə], *s.* (*zool.*) boa.

boar [bɔ:], *s.* verraco; ***wild boar,*** jabalí.

board [bɔ:d], *s.* tabla; tablero; mesa; tribunal; junta, consejo; comida; pensión, pupilaje; (*mar.*) bordo, borda; (*mar.*) bordada; cartón; (*elec.*) cuadro; canto, orilla; tablón (*de anuncios*); ***across the board,*** global; ***full board and lodging,*** pensión completa; ***Board of Admiralty,*** Consejo Superior de Marina; ***board of directors, trustees*** o ***governors,*** junta directiva; consejo de administración; ***free on board (f.o.b.),*** franco a bordo; ***to go on board,*** ir a bordo, embarcar(se); ***to go by the board,*** caerse por la borda; (*fig.*) abandonarse; perderse; (*pl.*) tablazón; (*teat.*) tablas, escena. — *v.t.* entablar, entarimar, enmaderar; hospedar, tomar a pupilaje; abordar; embarcar en, subir a (*un tren, autobús et.*). — *v.i.* estar a pupilaje.

boardable [ˈbɔ̃:dəbl], *a.* (*mar.*) abordable; accesible.

boarder [ˈbɔ:də], *s.* pensionista, *m.f.*, huésped; pupilo; (*mar.*) abordador.

boarding [ˈbɔ:diŋ], *s.* entabladura, tablazón, *f.*; pupilaje, pensión; (*mar.*) abordaje; (*mar.*) ***boarding-pikes,*** chuzos.

boarding-house [ˈbɔ:diŋ-haus], *s.* casa de huéspedes, pensión.

boarding-pupil [ˈbɔ:diŋ-pju:pil], *s.* interno, pensionista, *m.f.*

boarding-school [ˈbɔ:diŋ-sku:l], *s.* colegio interno, internado, pensionado.

boarish [ˈbɔ:riʃ], *a.* jabaluno.

boast [boust], *s.* jactancia, vanagloria, alarde. — *v.t.* ponderar; ostentar, tener. — *v.i.* jactarse, alardear; ***boast of,*** presumir de, alardear de.

boaster [ˈboustə], *s.* fanfarrón.

boastful [ˈboustful], *a.* jactancioso, baladrón.

boastfulness, boasting [ˈboustfulnis, -iŋ], *s.* fanfarronería, jactancia.

boat [bout], *s.* buque; barco; bote, barca, lancha; (*mar.*) ***ballast boat,*** bote de lastrar; ***fishing boat,*** barca de pesca; pesquero; ***life-boat,*** lancha de socorro, bote salvavidas; ***packet boat,*** paquebote; ***tow-boat,*** remolcador; ***to be in the same boat,*** encontrarse en la misma situación. — *v.t.* llevar *o* pasar en barco, bote etc.; ***to boat oars,*** desarmar los remos. — *v.i.* ir *o* pasear en bote, lancha *etc.*

boatable [ˈboutəbl], *a.* navegable para botes.

boat-hook [ˈbout-huk], *s.* bichero, botador.

boathouse [ˈbouthaus], *s.* cobertizo para botes.

boating [ˈboutiŋ], *s.* transporte por agua, batelaje; paseo en un bote; manejo de un bote.

boat(s)man [ˈbout(s)mən], *s.* barquero, lanchero, botero, batelero.

boatswain [bousn], *s.* contramaestre.

bob (1) [bɔb], *s.* borla; cola cortada; pelo cortado; corcho flotador; lenteja (*de péndulo*); volante; balancín (*de bomba* o *máquina de vapor*). — *v.t.* agitar, sacudir, menear; cortar corto (*pelo*). — *v.i.* menearse, bambolear; fluctuar.

bob (2) [bɔb], *s.* (*fam.*) chelín.

bobbin [ˈbɔbin], *s.* bolillo; broca, canilla; bobina; carrete.

bobbinet [bɔbiˈnet], *s.* bobiné.

bobby [ˈbɔbi], *s.* (*fam.*) guardia, *m.*, guindilla, *m.*

bobbysoxer [ˈbɔbi-sɔksə], *s.* (*fam.*, *Am.*) tobillera.

bobsleigh, bob-sled [ˈbɔbslei, -sled], *s.* trineo.

bob-stay [ˈbɔb-stei], *s.* (*mar.*) barbiquejo.

bobtail [ˈbɔb-teil], *s.* rabo mocho, cola corta.

bobtailed [ˈbɔb-teild], *a.* rabón.

bocasine [ˈbɔkəsin], *s.* bocací.

bode [boud], *v.t.* presagiar. — *v.i.* ***bode well*** o ***ill,*** ser de buen *o* mal agüero.

bodice [ˈbɔdis], *s.* corsé, corpiño.

bodied [ˈbɔdid], *a.* corpóreo.

bodiless [ˈbɔdilis], *a.* incorpóreo.

bodiliness [ˈbɔdilinis], *s.* corporalidad, corporeidad.

bodily [ˈbɔdili], *a.* corpóreo; corporal; material. — *adv.* corporalmente: enteramente, completamente; ***to lift bodily,*** levantar en peso.

boding [ˈboudiŋ], *a.* ominoso, presagioso. — *s.* presagio.

bodkin [ˈbɔdkin], *s.* punzón; agujeta, aguja de jareta; puñal, daga; horquilla.

body [ˈbɔdi], *s.* cuerpo; tronco; persona; (*igl.*) nave, *f.*; corporación; solidez, densidad, consistencia; materia, substancia; (*aut.*) carrocería; ***body politic,*** entidad política; ***dead body,*** cadáver; ***in a body,*** corporativamente, en bloque; ***wine of good body,*** vino generoso; ***main body,*** grueso; ***to keep body and soul together,*** seguir viviendo, ir tirando. — *v.t.* dar cuerpo a.

bodyguard [ˈbodigɑ:d], *s.* guardaespaldas, *m.inv.*

body-snatcher [ˈbɔdi-snætʃə], *s.* ladrón de cadáveres.

Boeotian [biˈouʃən], *a.*, *s.* beocio.

bog [bɔg], *s.* pantano, lodazal, barrizal; (*fam.*) meódromo. — *v.t.* ***to get bogged down,*** empantanarse, atollarse.
bogey [ˈbougi], *s.* coco; (*f.c*) bogie.
boggle [bɔgl], *v.i.* estar boquiabierto; querer salirse de las órbitas (*los ojos*); ***the mind boggles,*** es inconcebible.
boggy [ˈbɔgi], *a.* pantanoso.
bogie [ˈbougi], *s.* (*f.c.*) bogie.
bogus [ˈbougəs], *a.* falso; falsificado; fingido; hipócrita; de impostor.
bogy [BOGEY].
bohea [boˈhi:], *s.* té de clase inferior.
Bohemia [boˈhi:miə]. Bohemia.
Bohemian [boˈhi:miən], *a.*, *s.* bohemio.
boil [bɔil], *s.* hervor, ebullición; (*med.*) furúnculo, divieso. — *v.t.* hervir; cocer; pasar por agua. — *v.i.* hervir; bullir; ***boil away,*** consumirse; ***it all boils down to this,*** todo se reduce a esto; ***boil fast,*** hervir a borbotones; ***boil over,*** salirse; ***boil up,*** borbollar; (*fig.*) fraguarse.
boiler [ˈbɔilə], *s.* caldera; termosifón; ***boiler-house,*** sala de calderas; ***boiler-maker,*** calderero; ***boiler-suit,*** mono.
boiling [ˈbɔiliŋ], *s.* ebullición, hervor; cocción; ***boiling-point,*** punto de ebullición.
boisterous [ˈbɔistrəs], *a.* borrascoso; alborotador, bullicioso, estrepitoso; vocinglero.
boisterousness [ˈbɔistrəsnis], *s.* turbulencia, tumulto, bulla, alboroto, vocinglería.
bold [bould], *a.* atrevido, osado; audaz, arrojado; descarado; ***to be so bold as to*** o ***to make bold to,*** tomarse la libertad de, atreverse a.
boldfaced [ˈbouldfeist], *a.* descarado, desvergonzado; (*impr.*) ***boldfaced type,*** negrita.
boldness [ˈbouldnis], *s.* atrevimiento, osadía; audacia, arrojo; descaro, desfachatez.
bole [boul], *s.* tronco de un árbol; (*min.*) bol, bolo.
bolide [ˈbɔlaid], *s.* (*astron.*) bólido.
Bolivia [bəˈliviə]. Bolivia.
Bolivian [bəˈliviən], *a.*, *s.* boliviano.
boll [boul], *s.* bodoque; cápsula. — *v.t.* granar.
Bologna [bəˈlɔnjə]. Bolonia.
Bolognese [bɔləˈneiz], *a.*, *s.* boloñés.
bolster [ˈboulstə], *s.* travesero, larguero, almohadón; cojín, cojinete; (*cir.*) cabezal; (*mar.*) almohada; (*f.c.*) solera de carro; (*mec.*) travesaño. — *v.t.* (*fig.*) ***bolster up,*** apoyar, apuntalar, sostener; animar, alentar.
bolt (1) [boult], *s.* dardo, azagaya; rayo; cerrojo, pasador; pestillo de cerradura; borrón, mancha; (*mar.*) perno, clavillas, *f.pl.*; (*carp.*) perno, clavija, tolete; salto rápido; fuga; rollo (*de tela*); ***bolt upright,*** erguido, enhiesto; ***to shoot one's bolt,*** hacer el último esfuerzo, echar el resto; (*pl.*) grillos, *m.pl.* — *v.t.* acerrojar; empernar; zampar(se); cribar. —*v.i.* escaparse: desbocarse; ***bolt off,*** salir de estampía.
bolt (2) [boult], *s.* tamiz. — *v.t.* cerner, tamizar.
bolter [ˈboultə], *s.* cedazo, criba.
bolus [ˈbouləs], *s.* (*med.*) bolo.
bomb [bɔm], *s.* bomba; ***A-bomb,*** bomba A; ***atom(ic) bomb,*** bomba atómica; ***hydrogen bomb,*** bomba de hidrógeno. — *v.t.* bombardear.
bombard [bɔmˈbɑ:d], *v.t.* bombardear; ***bombard with questions,*** asediar de preguntas.
bombardier [bɔmbəˈdiə], *s.* bombardero.
bombardment [bɔmˈbɑ:dmənt], *s.* bombardeo.
bombast [ˈbɔmbæst], *s.* ampulosidad, rimbombancia, énfasis.
bombastic [bɔmˈbæstik], *a.* ampuloso, rimbombante, enfático.
bombazine, bombasine [bɔmbəˈzi:n], *s.* bombasín.
bomb-bay [ˈbɔm-bei], *s.* compartimiento de las bombas.
bomber [ˈbɔmə], *s.* bombardero.
bomb(-)proof [ˈbɔm(-)pru:f], *a.* a prueba de bomba(s).
bombshell [ˈbɔmʃel], *s.* bomba; (*fig.*) noticia bomba.
bombyx [ˈbɔmbiks], *s.* (*ent.*) bómbice.
bona-fide [ˈbounə-ˈfaidi], *a.* (*lat.*) de confianza.
bonanza [bəˈnænzə], *s.* (*min.*) bonanza, mina.
bonbon [ˈbɔnbɔn], *s.* confite.
bond [bɔnd], *s.* lazo, atadura; vínculo; unión, *f.*; (*com.*) obligación; depósito; ***in bond,*** en depósito, en almacén; (*pl.*) grillos, *m.pl.*, cadenas, *f.pl.* — *v.t.* obligar por fianza; depositar en almacén.
bondage [ˈbɔndidʒ], *s.* cautiverio; esclavitud; servidumbre.
bonded [ˈbɔndid], *a.* almacenado, depositado, en depósito; ***bonded warehouse,*** almacén de depósito.
bondmaid [ˈbɔndmeid], *s.* joven esclava *o* sierva.
bondman [ˈbɔndmən], *s.* esclavo, siervo; vasallo.
bondslave [ˈbɔndsleiv], *s.* esclavo.
bondsman (1) [ˈbɔndzmən], *s.* fiador.
bondsman (2) [ˈbɔndzmən], [BONDMAN].
bone [boun], *s.* hueso; raspa *o* espina (*del pez*); barba (*de ballena*); ***jaw-bone,*** quijada; ***whalebone,*** ballena; ***bone setter,*** algebrista, *m.f.*, curandero; ***bone black,*** negro animal; ***to pick a bone,*** roer un hueso; ***to make no bones about it,*** no tener pelos en la lengua, no andarse con chiquitas; (*fig.*) ***to have a bone to pick with,*** tener que habérselas con, tener un asunto que ventilar con; ***bone of contention,*** piedra de toque, manzana de la discordia. — *v.t.* deshuesar; desraspar; emballenar, poner ballenas a; (*fam.*) ***bone up on,*** empollar(se).
boned [bound], *a.* osudo, huesudo.
bonelace [ˈbounleis], *s.* encaje de hilo.
boneless [ˈbounlis], *s.* pulposo, mollar, sin huesos; deshuesado.
boner [ˈbounə], (*Am.*) [HOWLER].
bonfire [ˈbɔnfaiə], *s.* hoguera, fogata.
bonhomie [ˈbɔnɔmi:], *s.* afabilidad.
boning [ˈbouniŋ], *s.* acción de deshuesar; nivelación de tierras.
bonito [boˈni:tou], *s.* (*ict.*) bonito.
bonnet [ˈbɔnit], *s.* gorro, gorra; capota; toca; sombrero de mujer; (*fort.*) bonete; (*mec.*) sombrerete; (*mar.*) boneta; (*aut.*) capo.
bonny [ˈbɔni], *a.* (*esco.*) bonito, hermoso, lindo. — *s.* (*min.*) filón.
bonus [ˈbounəs], *s.* prima, plus; adehala; dividendo extraordinario.
bony [ˈbouni], *a.* huesudo, flaco.
boo (1), [bu:], *s.* silbido. — *v.t.* abuchear.
boo (2), [bu:], *s.* ***not to say boo (to a goose),*** no decir ni pío.
booing, [ˈbu:iŋ], *s.* abucheo.
booby [ˈbu:bi], *s.* memo, bobo; (*orn.*) bobo.
boodle [bu:dl], *s.* (*fam.*) pasta, telángana, parné; dinero de soborno.
book [buk], *s.* libro; libreta, cuaderno; libro de asiento; ***account book,*** libro de cuentas corrientes; talonario; ***cash book,*** libro de caja; ***day book,*** diario; ***invoice book,*** libro de facturas; ***memorandum-book,*** libro de memoria; ***pocket-book,*** cartera; ***school book,*** libro de enseñanza; ***second-hand book,*** libro de ocasión; ***waste book,*** borrador; ***book-keeper,*** tenedor de libros; ***book-keeping,*** teneduría de libros; ***book-learning,*** erudición; ***book post,*** servicio de impresos; ***that does not suit my book,*** no me conviene; ***to be in s.o.'s good books,*** estar a bien con. — *v.t.* asentar; reservar (*localidades, billetes etc.*); apalabrar, contratar; denunciar, multar.
bookbinder [ˈbukbaində], *s.* encuadernador de libros.
bookbindery [ˈbukbaindəri], *s.* taller de encuadernación.
bookbinding [ˈbukbaindiŋ], *s.* encuadernación.
book-case [ˈbuk-keis], *s.* armario *o* estante para libros.

booking [ˈbukiŋ], *s.* reserva(ción); ***booking-clerk,*** vendedor de billetes de pasaje, teatro etc.; ***booking-office,*** despacho de billetes.
bookish [ˈbukiʃ], *a.* estudioso, dado al estudio, versado en libros; pedante, teórico, libresco.
bookishness [ˈbukiʃnis], *s.* estudiosidad; (lo) libresco.
bookmaker [ˈbukmeikə], *s.* el que compila, imprime *o* encuaderna libros; corredor de apuestas, apostador profesional.
bookmark [ˈbukmɑ:k], *s.* señal *o* marcador de libros.
bookseller [ˈbukselə], *s.* librero; ***bookseller and publisher,*** librero editor.
bookshop [ˈbukʃɔp], *s.* librería.
bookstall [ˈbukstɔ:l], *s.* puesto de libros.
bookstand [ˈbukstænd], *s.* estante de libros; puesto de libros.
bookstore [ˈbukstɔ:], *s.* librería.
bookworm [ˈbukwə:m], *s.* polilla; (*fig.*) ratón de biblioteca.
boom (1) [bu:m], *s.* (*mar.*) botalón; botavara; cadena (*para cerrar un puerto*).
boom (2) [bu:m], *s.* trueno, estampido; bramido (*de olas*); auge; (*com.*) alza fuerte, prosperidad repentina. — *v.i.* tronar, sonar con estruendo, resonar, retumbar; estar en auge, estar en alza, ir viento en popa.
boomerang [ˈbu:məræŋ], *s.* bumerang; (*fig.*) cosa contraproducente.
boom-sail [ˈbu:m-seil], *s.* (*mar.*) cangreja.
boon [bu:n], *s.* gracia, merced; bendición; ***boon companion,*** compañero entañable.
boor [buə], *s.* patán, zoquete.
boorish [ˈbuəriʃ], *a.* cerril, zoquetudo; grosero.
boost [bu:st], *s.* empujón, estímulo, promoción. — *v.t.* empujar, estimular, promocionar.
booster [ˈbu:stə], *a., s.* reforzador.
boot (1) [bu:t], *s.* bota; (*aut.*) maleta, maletero; ***to die with one's boots on,*** morir con las botas puestas; ***to lick the boots of,*** dar coba a; ***the boot is on the other foot,*** es *o* pasa todo lo contrario; ***you can bet your boots on it,*** puedes estar seguro de ello; (*fam.*) ***he got the boot,*** le echaron, le despidieron con cajas destempladas. — *v.t.* calzar; dar una patada a; ***boot about,*** patear; ***boot out,*** echar a patadas, dar la patada a.
boot (2) [bu:t], *s.* (*sólo en la frase*) ***to boot,*** por añadidura, encima, además.
booth [bu:ð], *s.* caseta; puesto; cabina (*de teléfono*).
bootlegger [ˈbu:tlegə], *s.* contrabandista (de bebidas alcohólicas), *m.f.*
bootless (1) [ˈbu:tlis], *a.* descalzo.
bootless (2) [ˈbu:tlis], *a.* inútil, sin provecho.
boots [bu:ts], *s.inv.* limpiabotas, *m.inv.*
boot-tree [ˈbu:t-tri:], *s.* horma.
booty [ˈbu:ti], *s.* botín.
booze [bu:z], *s.* (*fam.*) bebida, bebistrajo. — *v.i.* empinar el codo, trincar.
boozer [ˈbu:zə], *s.* (*fam.*) borrachín; taberna.
boozy [ˈbu:zi], *a.* borracho.
boracic [bəˈræsik], *a.* (*quím.*) borácico.
boracite [ˈbɔrəsait], *s.* (*min.*) boracita.
borage [ˈbɔridʒ], *s.* (*bot.*) borraja.
borate [ˈbɔ:reit], *s.* (*quím.*) borato.
borax [ˈbɔ:ræks], *s.* (*quím.*) bórax.
Bordeaux [bɔ:ˈdou]. Burdeos; (vino de) Burdeos.
border [ˈbɔ:də], *s.* frontera, raya, límite, confín; orla, ribete, cenefa; borde, orilla, margen; lomo (*de jardín*); ***border ballads,*** romances fronterizos; (*teat.*) ***borders,*** bambalinas. — *v.t.* orlar; orillar, ribetear; tocar, estar en el borde de. — *v.i.* ***border on,*** confinar *o* lindar con; rayar *o* frisar en.
borderer [ˈbɔ:dərə], *s.* habitante de la frontera.
bordering [ˈbɔ:dəriŋ], *a.* lindante, fronterizo. — *s.* orladura.
borderline [ˈbɔ:dəlain], *a.* dudoso, discutible. — *s.* frontera, límite.
bore (1) [bɔ:], *s.* taladro, barreno; calibre (de un cañon); (*fig.*) pesadez, lata; pesado, pelmazo; ola de marea, ola gigantesca. — *v.t.* taladrar, barrenar, perforar; (*fig.*) aburrir. — *v.i.* agujerear.
bore (2) [bɔ:], *pret.* [BEAR (2)].
boreal [ˈbɔ:riəl], *a.* boreal, septentrional.
boreas [ˈbɔ:riæs], *s.* bóreas, aquilón, cierzo.
boredom [ˈbɔ:dəm], *s.* aburrimiento, hastío, tedio.
boreshaft [ˈbɔ:ʃɑ:ft], *s.* (*min.*) pozo de indagación.
borer [ˈbɔ:rə], *s.* barreno, taladro; sonda.
boric [ˈbɔrik], *a.* (*quim.*) bórico.
boring [ˈbɔ:riŋ], *a.* penetrante, que perfora, taladra *o* barrena; (*fam.*) aburrido, pesado. — *s.* horadamiento, horadación; sondeo.
born (1) [bɔ:n], *a.* nacido; ***to be born,*** nacer; ***first-born,*** primogénito; ***high-born,*** de elevado nacimiento; ***low-born,*** de humilde nacimiento; ***new-born,*** recién nacido; ***still-born,*** nacido muerto; ***to be born with a silver spoon in one's mouth,*** nacer en buena cuna, en familia privilegiada, para ser rico; ***to be born lucky,*** nacer de pies; ***to be born and bred in Madrid,*** ser madrileño de casta y cuna.
born (2) [bɔ:n], **borne,** *p.p.* [BEAR (2)].
borough [ˈbʌrə], *s.* municipio; ciudad, villa grande.
borrow [ˈbɔrou], *v.t.* tomar *o* pedir prestado; apropiarse; copiar.
borrowed [ˈbɔroud], *a.* prestado, tomado en préstamo.
borrower [ˈbɔrouə], *s.* prestatario; el que toma *o* pide prestado.
borrowing [ˈbɔrouiŋ], *s.* préstamo; empréstito.
boscage [ˈbɔskidʒ], *s.* soto, floresta; boscaje.
bosh [bɔʃ], *s.* (*fam.*) necedad, tontería, palabrería, galimatías, *m. sing.*
bosk [bɔsk], *s.* matorral.
bosky [ˈbɔski], *a.* arbolado, frondoso, nemoroso.
Bosnian [ˈbɔzniən], *a., s.* bosnio.
bosom [ˈbuzəm], *s.* seno, pecho; fondo; cariño; (*cost.*) pechera; ***bosom friend,*** amigo del alma *o* íntimo; ***in the bosom of,*** en el seno de.
boss (1) [bɔs], *s.* clavo, tachón; joroba, corcova, giba, protuberancia; abolladura; (*arq.*) pinjante. — *v.t.* trabajar in relieve.
boss (2) [bɔs], *s.* jefe, amo; patrón; capataz. — *v.t.* (*fam.*) mandar, dominar, mangonear.
bossy [ˈbɔsi], *a.* (*fam.*) mandón.
bosun [BOATSWAIN].
botanic(al) [boˈtænik(əl)], *a.* botánico.
botanize [ˈbɔtənaiz], *v.i.* herborizar.
botanist [ˈbɔtənist], *s.* botánico.
botany [ˈbɔtəni], *s.* botánica.
botch [bɔtʃ], *s.* chapucería. — *v.t., v.i.* chapucear, hacer una chapucería (de).
botcher [ˈbɔtʃə], *s.* chapucero.
botchy [ˈbɔtʃi], *a.* chapucero.
bot-fly [ˈbɔtflai], *s.* (*ent.*) estro.
both [bouθ], *a.* ambos; ***on both sides,*** por ambos lados, de uno y otro lado. — *adv.* ***both he and I,*** tanto él como yo. — *pron.* ambos, los dos; ***both (of) his friends,*** sus dos amigos; ***both of them,*** los dos, ambos.
bother [ˈbɔðə], *s.* molestia, incomodidad, fastidio, trastorno — *v.t.* incomodar, molestar; (*fam.*) marear.
botheration! [bɔðəˈreiʃən], *interj.* ¡maldita sea!
bothersome [ˈbɔðəsəm], *a.* molesto, fastidioso.
Bothnian [ˈbɔθniən], *a., s.* botniano.
Botswana [bɔˈtswɑ:nə]. Botswana.
bottle [bɔtl], *s.* botella; frasco; ***baby's bottle,*** biberón; ***water-bottle,*** cantimplora; ***to hit the bottle,*** darse a la bebida. — *v.t.* embotellar; ***to bottle up,*** contener; acorralar.
bottle-green [ˈbɔtl-ˈgri:n], *a., s.* verde botella.
bottle-neck [ˈbɔtl-nek], *s.* cuello de botella; embotellamiento, atasco.

bottler [ˈbɔtlə], *s.* embotellador.
bottle-rack [ˈbɔtl-ræk], *s.* botellero.
bottling [ˈbɔtliŋ], *s.* embottellado.
bottom [ˈbɔtəm], *a.* mas bájo; ***rock-bottom,*** ínfimo. — *s.* fondo; asiento (*de silla*); final, pie (*de página*); (*naut.*) quilla; casco; (*fam.*) culo, trasero; ***at bottom,*** en el fondo; ***at the bottom,*** en el fondo; al final; ***to be at the bottom of,*** ser la causa *o* el motivo de; ***to get to the bottom of,*** enterarse a fondo de, investigar hasta el final; ***to go to the bottom,*** irse a pique; ***to start at the bottom,*** empezar por lo más bajo.
bottomless [ˈbɔtəmlis], *a.* sin fondo; insondable; inagotable; ***bottomless pit,*** abismo, sima.
bottomry [ˈbɔtəmri], *s.* (*mar.*) casco y quilla.
boudoir [ˈbu:dwɑ:], *s.* gabinete, tocador.
bough [bau], *s.* rama.
bougie [ˈbu:ʒi], *s.* bujía; (*cir.*) candelilla.
boulder [ˈbouldə], *s.* roca, canto, pedrejón, galga, peña.
boulevard [ˈbu:lvɑ:d], *s.* paseo, avenida, bulevar.
bounce [bauns], *s.* bote, rebote; salto, brinco. — *v.t.* lanzar; hacer chocar *o* botar; hacer saltar; despedir, poner de patitas en la calle. — *v.i.* botar, rebotar; saltar, brincar; lanzarse.
bouncer [ˈbaunsə], *s.* fanfarrón; embustero; expulsador.
bouncing [ˈbaunsiŋ], *a.* (*fam.*) fuerte, vigoroso, bien formado.
bound (1) [baund], *s.* término, límite, confín, lindero. — *v.t.* poner límites a; confinar; limitar.
bound (2) [baund], *s.* bote, brinco, salto, respingo. — *v.i.* saltar, brincar, resaltar, botar, corretear.
bound (3) [baund], *a.* atado, ligado; encuadernado; obligado, forzado; ***to be bound to,*** tener forzosamente que; ***to be bound up with,*** estar vinculado con; ***to be bound up in,*** estar absorto, enfrascado en; estar metido en; estar invertido en.
bound (4) [baund], *a.* (*mar.*) destinado a, cargado para; ***to be bound for,*** ir con destino a.
boundary [ˈbaundəri], *s.* término, límite, linde, frontera, confín.
bounden [ˈbaundən], *a.* obligado, precisado; obligatorio.
bounder [ˈbaundə], *s.* (*fam.*) sinvergüenza, *m.*, pillo.
boundless [ˈbaundlis], *a.* ilimitado, infinito.
boundlessly [ˈbaundlisli], *adv.* sin límites.
boundlessness [ˈbaundlisnis], *s.* inmensidad, infinidad, vastedad.
bounteous [ˈbauntiəs], *a.* liberal, bondadoso, generoso; abundante.
bounteousness [ˈbauntiəsnis], *s.* munificencia, liberalidad, bondad, generosidad.
bountiful [ˈbauntiful], *a.* generoso, liberal, dadivoso; abundante; bueno; fecundo.
bounty [ˈbaunti], *s.* generosidad, liberalidad, munificencia; (*com.*) premio; merced, gracia; concesión, subvención; ***bounty money,*** paga especial *o* extraordinaria.
bouquet [ˈbukei], *s.* ramo, ramillete; (*vino*) aroma.
Bourbon [ˈbɔ:bən], *a.* borbónico. — *s.* Borbón; ***House of Bourbon,*** Casa de Borbón; (*Am.*) whisky.
bourdon [buədən], *s.* bordón.
bourgeois (1) [ˈbuəʒwɑ:], *s.* burgués.
bourgeois (2) [bə:ˈdʒɔis], *s.* (*impr.*) tipo de nueve puntos.
bourgeoisie [buəʒwɑˈzi:], *s.* burguesía.
bourn [bɔ:n], *s.* límite, linde; arroyo, riachuelo.
bourse [buəs], *s.* (*com.*) bolsa, lonja.
bout [baut], *s.* vez; turno; golpe; ataque; (*esgrima*) asalto; broma, diversión; lucha, combate (*boxeo, lucha libre*); ***at one bout,*** de una sola vez; ***drinking bout,*** juerga, borrachera.
bovine [ˈbouvain], *a.* bovino, vacuno.
bow (1) [bau], *s.* reverencia. — *v.t.* doblar, inclinar; agobiar, oprimir; arquear, encorvar; bajar. — *v.i.* inclinarse, hacer una reverencia, saludar; doblarse; agobiarse; someterse, ceder; ***bow to a decision,*** acatar una decisión; ***bow out,*** retirarse.
bow (2) [bau], *s.* (*mar.*) proa, amura; ***on the bow,*** por la amura.
bow (3) [bou], *s.* arco; lazo; arzón (*de silla*); anillo (*de llave, de reloj etc.*); ***to have several strings to one's bow,*** tener varios recursos, varias actividades. — *v.t.* arquear.
bowdlerize [ˈbaudləraiz], *v.t.* expurgar.
bowel [ˈbauəl], *s.* intestino; vientre; (*pl.*) intestinos; vientre; (*fig.*) entrañas, *f.pl.*; ***bowel movement,*** deposición.
bower [bauə], *s.* enramada; cenador; morada; (*mar.*) ***bower-anchor,*** ancla de servidumbre.
bowery [ˈbauəri], *a.* frondoso, cubierto de enramadas.
bowie-knife [ˈbui-naif], *s.* cuchillo de monte.
bowl [boul], *s.* escudilla, cuenco; taza; tazón (*de fuente*); hornillo (*de pipa*); copa (*de vino*); paleta (*de cuchara*); concavidad; cuenca; palangana; bola, bocha; (*pl.*) bolos, juego de bolos. — *v.t.* tirar, arrojar; rodar; ***bowl down,*** derribar; ***bowl over,*** tumbar; dejar turulato, desconcertar. — *v.i.* rodar; ***bowl along,*** rodar, ir de prisa *o* con velocidad.
bow-legged [bou-ˈlegid], *a.* patiestevado.
bowler (1) [ˈboulə], *s.* jugador de bolos.
bowler (2) [ˈboulə], *s.* sombrero hongo.
bowline [ˈboulain], *s.* (*mar.*) bolina.
bowling [ˈbouliŋ], *s.* juego de bolos.
bowling alley [ˈbouliŋ æli], *s.* bolera.
bowman [ˈboumən], *s.* arquero, flechero.
bowse [bauz], *v.t.* (*mar.*) halar a un tiempo.
bow-shot [ˈbou-ʃɔt], *s.* tiro de flecha; ***within bow-shot,*** a tiro de ballesta.
bowsprit [ˈbousprit], *s.* (*mar.*) bauprés.
bowstring [ˈboustriŋ], *s.* cuerda de arco.
bow-window [ˈbou-ˈwindou], *s.* ventana salediza.
bow-wow [ˈbau-wau], *s.* guau guau.
box (1) [bɔks], *s.* caja; arca, cofre; palco (*de teatro*); pescante (*de coche*); (*impr.*) cajetín; (*mar.*) bitácora; (*bot.*) boj; (*mec.*) buje, manguito, émbolo; (*teat.*) ***box-office,*** taquilla; ***good box-office film,*** película taquillera; ***alms box,*** cepillo (*de limosna*); ***Christmas box,*** aguinaldo; ***dice box,*** cubilete; ***hat box,*** sombrerera; ***hunting*** o ***shooting box,*** casita de caza; ***jewel-box,*** joyelero, guardajoyas, *m.*; ***letter box,*** buzón (*del correo*); ***poor box,*** cepillo de limosnas; ***post office box,*** apartado de correos; ***snuff box,*** tabaquera; ***strong box,*** cofre fuerte, caja de caudales. — *v.t.* encajonar; (*mar.*) ***box the compass,*** cuartear.
box (2) [bɔks], *s.* bofetada. — *v.t.* abofetear. — *v.i.* boxear.
boxcar [ˈbɔkskɑ:], (*Am., f.c.*) [WAG(G)ON].
boxer [ˈbɔksə], *s.* boxeador.
boxing (1) [ˈbɔksiŋ], *s.* envase; ***Boxing Day,*** 26 de diciembre, día de los aguinaldos.
boxing (2) [ˈbɔksiŋ], *s.* boxeo; ***boxing-gloves,*** guantes de boxeo; ***boxing-match,*** combate de boxeo.
boxthorn [ˈbɔksθɔ:n], *s.* (*bot.*) licio, tamujo.
boxwood [ˈbɔkswud], *s.* boj, madera de boj.
boy [bɔi], *s.* niño; chico, muchacho; mozo, criado; ***cabin-boy,*** grumete; ***choir boy,*** niño de coro; ***boy scout,*** explorador; ***school boy,*** colegial.
boycott [ˈbɔikɔt], *s.* boicot. — *v.t.* boicotear; aislar; hacer el vacío a.
boycotting [ˈbɔikɔtiŋ], *s.* boicoteo.
boyhood [ˈbɔihud], *s.* niñez, muchachez.
boyish [ˈbɔiiʃ], *a.* aniñado; muchachil, amuchachado.
boyishness [ˈbɔiiʃnis], *s.* (lo) juvenil.
bra [brɑ:], (*fam.*) [BRASSIÈRE].
Brabantine [brəˈbæntain], *a.* brabanzón, de Brabante.

brace [breis], *s.* lazo, atadura; abrazadera, laña, grapón; brazal; (*arq.*) tirante; sopanda (*de coche*); (*impr.*) corchete; (*carp.*) berbiquí; par (de perdices, pistolas *etc.*); (*cir.*) braguero; (*pl.*) tirantes; (*mar.*) ***braces of a rudder,*** hembras de timón, *f.pl.* — *v.t.* atar, ligar, trabar; (*carp.*) enxamblar; vigorizar, fortificar; templar (*un tambor*); (*mar.*) bracear, halar las brazas.
bracelet [ˈbreislit], *s.* pulsera, ajorca.
bracer [ˈbreisə], *s.* brazal, abrazadera, laña; cinto, venda; braguero; (*med.*) tónico.
brach [brætʃ], *s.* braca.
brachial [ˈbreikiəl], *a.* braquial.
brachiopod [ˈbrækiəpɔd], *s.* (*zool.*) braquiópodo.
brachium [ˈbreikiəm], *a.* (*pl.* **brachia** [-kiə]) (*zool.*) brazo superior.
bracing [ˈbreisiŋ], *a.* fortificante, tónico. — *s.* amarra, trabazón, *f.*, ligazón, *f.*, refuerzo.
bracken [ˈbrækən], *s.* (*bot.*) helecho; helechal.
bracket [ˈbrækit], *s.* ménsula, repisa; can, modillón; puntal, soporte; brazo (de lámpara); (*impr.*) paréntesis, *m.inv.*; ***square bracket,*** corchete; clase, grupo, categoría; (*mar.*) ***cat-head bracket,*** aletas de serviola, *f.pl.* — *v.t.* poner entre paréntesis, corchetes; sostener, soportar; juntar, poner en el mismo grupo, catalogar juntos.
brackish [ˈbrækiʃ], *a.* salobre.
brackishness [ˈbrækiʃnis], *s.* saladura, salobridad, calidad de salobre.
bract [brækt], *s.* (*bot.*) bráctea.
bracteole [ˈbræktioul], *s.* bractéola.
brad [bræd], *s.* tachuela; clavo de ala de mosca.
bradawl [ˈbrædɔ:l], *s.* lesna, punzón.
brae [brei], *s.* (*esco.*) falda, ladera; colina, loma.
brag [bræg], *s.* fanfarronada, alarde; fanfarrón, farolero. — *v.i.* fanfarronear, jactarse, baladronar; ***brag about,*** alardear de; ***brag of one's riches,*** escupir doblones.
braggadocio [brægəˈdouʃiou], *s.* fanfarrón, baladrón.
braggart [ˈbrægət], *s.* fanfarrón, bravucón.
bragger [ˈbrægə], *s.* fanfarrón, matasiete.
bragget [ˈbrægit], *s.* aguamiel, *f.*
bragging [ˈbrægiŋ], *a.* fanfarrón. — *s.* fanfarronería.
Brahma [ˈbrɑ:mə], *s.* Brahma.
Brahmin [ˈbrɑ:min], *s.* brahmán.
Brahminical [brɑ:ˈminikəl], *a.* brahmánico.
Brahminism [ˈbrɑ:minizəm], *s.* brahmanismo.
braid [breid], *s.* trenza, trencilla; galón. — *v.t.* trenzar; galonear.
brail [breil], *v.t.* (*mar.*) cargar (*las velas*); halar con las candelizas.
brails [breilz], *s.pl.* (*mar.*) cargaderas, *f.pl.*, candelizas, *f.pl.*
brain [brein], *s.* cerebro; seso; inteligencia; (*pl.*) sesos; ***to cudgel*** o ***beat*** o ***rack one's brains,*** devanarse los sesos; ***to have sth. on the brain,*** estar obsesionado con algo; ***to pick the brains of,*** aprovechar la inteligencia de *o* los conocimientos de. — *v.t.* descerebrar; romper la crisma a.
brain-child [ˈbrein-tʃaild], *s.* parto del ingenio.
brain-fag [ˈbrein-fæg], *s.* fatiga cerebral.
brainless [ˈbreinlis], *a.* tonto, insensato, sin seso.
brainpan [ˈbreinpæn], *s.* (*fam.*) cráneo.
brains-trust [ˈbreinz-trʌst], *s.* consultorio intelectual.
brain-washing [ˈbrein-wɔʃiŋ], *s.* lavado de cerebro.
brain-wave [ˈbrein-weiv], *s.* idea luminosa.
brain-work [ˈbrein-wə:k], *s.* trabajo intelectual.
brainy [ˈbreini], *a.* (*fam.*) listo, talentudo.
braise [breiz], *v.t.* cocer en cazuela con poca agua.
brake (1) [breik], *s.* freno; amasadera; ***handbrake,*** freno de mano; (*aut.*) ***brake-lining,*** cinta de freno; (*aut.*) ***brake-shoe,*** zapata de freno.
brake (2) [breik], *s.* (*bot.*) helecho; agramadera; matorral, maleza.
brake (3) [breik], *s.* (*aut.*) ***shooting brake,*** furgoneta.
brakeman [ˈbreikmən], *s.* (*Am.*, *f.c.*) [GUARD].
bramble [bræmbl], *s.* (*bot.*) zarza.
brambly [ˈbræmbli], *a.* zarzoso.
bran [bræn], *s.* salvado.
branch [brɑ:ntʃ], *s.* rama; ramo; ramal; brazo; sucursal, *f.* — *v.i.* ramificarse; ***branch off,*** bifurcarse; desviarse; ***branch out,*** ramificarse; extenderse; ***branch out on one's own,*** independizarse.
branchiæ [ˈbræŋkii], *s.pl.* (*ict.*) branquias, *f.pl.*
branchial [ˈbræŋkiəl], *a.* branquial.
branch-line [ˈbrɑ:ntʃ-lain], *s.* (*f.c.*) ramal.
branch-office [ˈbrɑ:ntʃ-ɔfis], *s.* sucursal, *f.*
brand [brænd], *s.* tizón, tea; (*poét.*) rayo; (*poét.*) acero, espada; hierro (de marcar); marca; baldón, estigma; calidad, clase. — *v.t.* marcar (*con hierro*); tildar, infamar, estigmatizar; poner marca *o* sello de fábrica.
brandiron [ˈbrændaiən], *s.* hierro de marcar.
brandish [ˈbrændiʃ], *s.* floreo, molinete (*de la espada*). — *v.t.* blandir, esgrimir.
brand-name [ˈbrænd-neim], *s.* marca (registrada).
brand-new [ˈbrænd-ˈnju:], *a.* nuevecito, (nuevo) flamante.
brandy [ˈbrændi], aguardiente; coñac.
brasier, brazier [ˈbreiziə], *s.* brasero; latonero.
brass [brɑ:s], *s.* latón, cobre amarillo; (*fam.*) plata, dinero; (*mús.*) metal; (*fig.*) descaro, desvergüenza; (*fig.*) ***brass-hat,*** militarote, espadón; ***bold as brass,*** descarado; ***to come*** o ***get down to brass tacks,*** entrar en materia, ir al grano; ***red brass,*** tumbaga; ***yellow brass,*** latón. — *v.t.* revestir de latón.
brassart [ˈbræsɑ:t], *s.* brazal.
brass-band [ˈbrɑ:s-ˈbænd], *s.* banda, charanga.
brassfounder [ˈbrɑ:sfaundə], *s.* fundidor de bronce *o* latón.
brassière [ˈbræzjɛə], *s.* sostén.
brassiness [ˈbrɑ:sinis], *s.* bronceadura; (*fig.*) desfachatez.
brassy [ˈbrɑ:si], *a.* de latón, de bronce; (*fig.*) descarado.
brat [bræt], *s.* rapaz, mocoso.
bravado [brəˈvɑ:dou], *s.* bravatas, baladronadas.
brave [breiv], *a.* valiente; denodado. — *s.* valiente; (*Am.*) guerrero piel roja. — *v.t.* arrostrar, desafiar.
bravery [ˈbreivəri], *s.* valor, valentía; bravura; denuedo; gallardía.
bravo [ˈbrɑ:vou], *s.* asesino asalariado. — [brɑ:ˈvou], *interj.* ¡olé! ¡bravo!
bravura [brəˈvuərə], *s.* (*mús.*) bravura.
brawl [brɔ:l], *s.* reyerta, camorra. — *v.i.* reñir, alborotar, armar camorra, gresca *o* pendencia.
brawler [ˈbrɔ:lə], *s.* camorrista, alborotador, pendenciero.
brawling [ˌbrɔ:liŋ], *a.* pendenciero, reñidor. — *s.* pendencia(s), alboroto(s).
brawn [brɔ:n], *s.* músculo, carne dura; carne en gelatina.
brawniness [ˈbrɔ:ninis], *s.* (*fig.*) fuerza, músculo, musculatura.
brawny [ˈbrɔ:ni], *a.* membrudo, musculoso; fornido.
braxy [ˈbræksi], *a.* atacado por la fiebre carbuncular. — *s.* fiebre carbuncular (de los carneros y ovejas); res atacada de esta enfermedad.
bray (1) [brei], *s.* rebuzno. — *v.i.* rebuznar.
bray (2) [brei], *v.t.* majar, triturar.
braying [ˈbreiiŋ], *s.* rebuzno(s), rebuznar.
braze [breiz], *v.t.* soldar con latón; broncear.

brazen [ˈbreizən], *a.* bronceado, (*hecho*) de bronce, (*hecho*) de latón; (*fig.*) descarado, desvergonzado. — *v.t.* ***brazen out,*** arrostrar con descaro, llevar a cabo con descaro.

brazen-faced [ˈbreizən-feist], *a.* descarado, desvergonzado.

brazenness [ˈbreizənnis], *s.* descaro, desvergüenza, descoco.

brazier [ˈbreiziə], *s.* brasero; latonero.

Brazil [brəˈzil]. el Brasil.

Brazilian [brəˈziliən], *a., s.* brasileño.

Brazil-wood [brəˈzil-wud], *s.* madera *o* palo del Brasil.

breach [bri:tʃ], *s.* brecha; abertura; rotura, rompimiento; infracción, violación, contravención; ***breach of faith,*** abuso de confianza; (*der.*) ***breach of the peace,*** perturbación del orden público; ***breach of promise,*** incumplimiento de promesa. — *v.t.* abrir (una) brecha en.

bread [bred], *s.* pan; (*fam.*) pan (*dinero*); ***bread and butter,*** pan con mantequilla; (*fig.*) pan; ***to earn one's bread and butter,*** ganarse el pan; ***bread-basket,*** cesto del pan; (*bot.*) ***bread-fruit,*** árbol del pan; ***bread crumbs,*** pan rallado; ***bread-winner,*** sostén de la familia; ***to break bread with,*** comer con; ***brown bread,*** pan moreno; ***home-made bread,*** pan casero; ***new bread,*** pan tierno; ***rye-bread,*** pan de centeno; ***stale bread,*** pan duro; ***unleavened bread,*** pan ázimo; ***white bread,*** pan blanco; ***he knows (on) which side his bread is buttered,*** sabe dónde le aprieta el zapato.

bread-and-butter [ˈbred-ən(d)-ˈbʌtə], *a.* práctico; fundamental, de finalidad práctica; ***bread-and-butter letter,*** carta de gracias.

breaded [ˈbredid], *a.* empanado.

breadstuff [ˈbredstʌf], *s.* cereales, *m.f.pl.*, harina.

breadth [bredθ], *s.* anchura; ancho; liberalidad; ***throughout its length and breadth,*** por todas partes, a lo ancho y a lo largo

breadthwise [ˈbredθwaiz], *adv.* a lo ancho.

break [breik], *s.* brecha; abertura; rompimiento; rotura; alba; pausa, descanso; hueco; carruaje; puntos suspensivos, *m.pl.*; interrupción; (*com.*) baja; ***break of day,*** (el) rayar del día. — *irr. v.t.* romper; quebrar; quebrantar; infringir, violar; domar; cambiar; comunicar; amortiguar; moderar; suspender; faltar a; degradar; batir; cortar; interrumpir; ***break asunder,*** partir, escindir; ***break the bank,*** (hacer) saltar la banca; ***break cover,*** salir, desemboscarse; ***break down,*** demoler, derribar; desglosar; ***break one's fast,*** romper el ayuno; ***break (new) ground,*** hacer algo nuevo; ***break one's health,*** quebrantarse la salud; ***break one's heart,*** desgarrar el corazón, romper el alma; ***break in,*** domar; ***break the law,*** infringir la ley; ***break one's oath,*** quebrar el juramento; ***break off,*** desprender; (*fig.*) abandonar; ***break open,*** abrir a la fuerza; ***break a record,*** batir una marca; ***break a rule,*** infringir una regla; ***break silence,*** romper el silencio; ***break up,*** deshacer; desguazar; ***break wind,*** ventosear, pe(d)er. — *v.i.* romper(se); quebrar(se); quebrantarse; reventar(se), abrirse; prorrumpir; estallar; brotar; apuntar; mudarse; ***break down,*** perder la salud; deshacerse en lágrimas; desfondarse; ***break forth,*** prorrumpir (en), romper (en); ***break in,*** forzar la entrada; ***break into a run,*** echar a correr; ***break off,*** interrumpirse; ***break out,*** estallar; fugarse; ***break through,*** abrirse camino; ***break up,*** deshacerse, terminar, acabar; ***break with,*** romper con.

breakable [ˈbreikəbl], *a.* quebradizo, frágil.

breakage [ˈbreikidʒ], *s.* fractura, rotura, quebrantamiento.

breakdown [ˈbreikdaun], *s.* avería; surmenaje, crisis nerviosa; desglose.

breaker [ˈbreikə], *s.* infractor; roturador; rompedor; (*mar.*) ola rompiente.

breakfast [ˈbrekfəst], *s.* desayuno. — *v.i.* desayunar.

breaking [ˈbreikiŋ], *s.* rompimiento, fractura; quebrantamiento; quiebra; irrupción; interrupción; infracción; (*min.*) arranque; ***breaking up,*** disolución, desmembramiento.

breakneck [ˈbreiknek], *a.* precipitado, rápido, vertiginoso; ***at breakneck speed,*** a uña de caballo, a velocidad vertiginosa. — *s.* precipicio.

breakthrough [ˈbreikθru:], *s.* ruptura, brecha; rompimiento; invento *o* descubrimiento importante.

break-up [ˈbreik-ʌp], *s.* disolución; disgregación; dispersión; ruptura.

breakwater [ˈbreikwɔ:tə], *s.* rompeolas, *m.inv.*, escollera, espigón.

bream (1) [bri:m], *s.* (*ict.*) sargo; ***sea-bream,*** besugo.

bream (2) [bri:m], *v.t.* (*mar.*) carenar.

breast [brest], *s.* pecho; pechuga; ***to make a clean breast of it,*** confesarlo todo, desembuchar. — *v.t.* acometer; dar el pecho a; ***to breast the rise,*** coronar la cima.

breastbone [ˈbrestboun], *s.* (*anat.*) esternón.

breastdeep, breasthigh [ˈbrestˈdi:p, ˈhai], *a.* (alto) hasta el pecho.

breastpin [ˈbrestpin], *s.* prendedor, broche.

breastplate [ˈbrestpleit], *s.* peto, coraza, armadura del pecho.

breastrail [ˈbrestreil], *s.* (*mar.*) antepecho.

breastwork [ˈbrestwə:k], *s.* (*fort.*) terraplén, parapeto; (*mar.*) propao.

breath [breθ], *s.* respiración; aliento, resuello; hálito; ***foul breath,*** mal aliento; ***in the same breath,*** a renglón seguido; ***out of breath, short of breath,*** sin aliento, jadeante; ***under one's breath,*** en voz baja, entre dientes.

breathable [ˈbri:ðəbl], *a.* respirable.

breathe [bri:ð], *v.t., v.i.* repirar; ***breathe in,*** aspirar; ***breathe out,*** espirar, exhalar; ***breathe into,*** alentar, inspirar, infundir; (*fig.*) ***breathe freely,*** respirar; ***breathe heavily,*** resollar; ***breathe one's last,*** dar el último suspiro.

breather [ˈbri:ðə], *s.* (*fam.*) respiro, tregua; ***to take a breather,*** hacer una pausa, descansar un poco.

breathing [ˈbri:ðiŋ], *a.* respiratorio. — *s.* respiración; soplo; inspiración; aspiración.

breathing-hole [ˈbri:ðiŋ-houl], *s.* respiradero.

breathing-space [ˈbri:ðiŋ-speis], *s.* respiro, pausa, tregua.

breathing-time [ˈbri:ðiŋ-taim], *s.* respiro, pausa.

breathless [ˈbreθlis], *a.* desalentado, sin aliento, jadeante.

breathlessness [ˈbreθlisnis], *s.* falta de aliento.

breath-taking [ˈbreθ-teikiŋ], *a.* asombroso, emocionante.

breech [bri:tʃ], *s.* trasero; recámara; ***breech-loader,*** arma de retrocarga; (*pl.* **breeches** [ˈbritʃiz]) calzones, pantalones; ***to wear the breeches,*** llevar los calzones *o* pantalones.

breechings [ˈbri:tʃiŋz], *s.pl.* (*mar.*) bragueros (*de cañón*), *m.pl.*; grupera (*del arnés*).

breed [bri:d], *s.* raza, casta; progenie, *f.* — *v.t.* criar, procrear, engendrar; ocasionar, causar; educar; ***well bred,*** (bien) educado. — *v.i.* criarse, reproducirse, multiplicarse.

breeder [ˈbri:də], *s.* criador; progenitor; paridera; ***cattle breeder,*** ganadero.

breeding [ˈbri:diŋ], *s.* cría; crianza; educación; (*fisiol.*) gestación; ***good breeding,*** (buena) educación; ***bad breeding,*** mala educación; ***cross breeding,*** cruzamiento de razas.

breeding-ground, -place [ˈbri:diŋ-graund, -pleis], *s.* criadero; vivero.

breeze [bri:z], *s.* brisa, airecillo, vientecillo. — *v.i.* — ***in,*** entrar alegre y deportivamente.

breezy [ˈbri:zi], *a.* ventoso; (*fig.*) alegre, animado, deportivo.

Bren gun [ˈbren gʌn], *s.* ametralladora (Bren).

brest [brest], *s.* (*arq.*) toro.

bret [bret], *s.* (*ict.*) rombo.
brethren [ˈbreðrən], *s.pl.* hermanos, *m.pl.*; (*pl.*) [BROTHER].
Breton [ˈbretən], *a.*, *s.* bretón.
breve [bri:v], *s.* (*mús.*) breve.
brevet [ˈbrevit], *s.* (*mil.*) graduación, comisión honoraria.
breviary [ˈbri:viəri], *s.* compendio; breviario.
brevier [breˈviə], *s.* (*impr.*) breviario.
brevity [ˈbreviti], *s.* brevedad; concisión.
brew [bru:], *s.* braceaje (*de cerveza*); mezcla. — *v.t.* batir, bracear (*la cerveza*); preparar (*una bebida*); cocer; fraguar, tramar, urdir. — *v.i.* cocer, fermentar; ***a storm is brewing,*** se está fraguando una tormenta.
brewer [bru:ə], *s.* cervecero, bracero.
brewery [ˈbru:əri], *s.* cervecería, fábrica de cerveza.
brewing [ˈbru:iŋ], *s.* elaboración de cerveza.
bribe [braib], *s.* soborno; cohecho. — *v.t.* sobornar; cohechar.
briber [ˈbraibə], *s.* sobornador; cohechador.
bribery [ˈbraibəri], *s.* soborno; cohecho.
bric-a-brac [ˈbrik-ə-bræk], *s.* cachivaches.
brick [brik], *a.* de ladrillo. — *s.* ladrillo; ladrillos; (*fam.*) persona estupenda; (*fam.*) ***to drop a brick,*** hacer una plancha. — *v.t.* enladrillar; ***brick up,*** tapar con ladrillos.
brickbat [ˈbrikbæt], *s.* pedazo de ladrillo; (*fam.*) palabra hiriente, crítica.
brickdust [ˈbrikdʌst], *s.* ladrillo molido.
brick-kiln [ˈbrik-kiln], *s.* horno de cocer ladrillos.
bricklayer [ˈbrikleiə], *s.* albañil, enladrillador.
brick-maker [ˈbrik-meikə], *s.* ladrillero.
brickwork [ˈbrikwə:k], *s.* enladrillado.
bricky [ˈbriki], *a.* ladrilloso.
brickyard [ˈbrikjɑ:d], *s.* ladrillal, adobería.
bridal [braidl], *a.* nupcial; ***bridal song,*** epitalamio.
bride [braid], *s.* novia; (***the***) ***bride and groom,*** (los) novios, (los) recién casados.
bridecake [ˈbraidkeik], *s.* pastel de boda.
bridegroom [ˈbraidgru:m], *s.* novio.
bridesmaid [ˈbraidzmeid], *s.* dama de honor.
bridewell [ˈbraidwel], *s.* correccional.
bridge [bridʒ], *s.* puente; caballete (*de la nariz*); ***suspension bridge,*** puente colgante; (*elec.*) ***in bridge,*** en paralelo. — *v.t.* tender un puente sobre; salvar (*un obstáculo, una distancia*).
bridge-board [ˈbridʒ-bɔ:d], *s.* (*arq.*) gualdera, larguero de escalera.
bridge-head [ˈbridʒ-hed], *s.* cabeza de puente.
bridle [braidl], *s.* brida; freno; (*fisiol.*) frenillo; (*pl.*) (*mar.*) poas, *f.pl.* — *v.t.* embridar, enfrenar; reprimir, refrenar, poner (el) freno a. — *v.i.* levantar, erguir la cabeza, erguirse; ***bridle at,*** resistirse a aceptar.
bridle-path [ˈbraidl-pɑ:θ], *s.* camino de herradura.
bridoon [briˈdu:n], *s.* bridón, filete.
brief [bri:f], *a.* breve; efímero; fugaz. — *s.* escrito, memorial; epítome; breve; ***I hold no brief for him,*** no le defiendo; (*pl.*) calzoncillos, *m.pl.* — *v.t.* dar instrucciones a.
briefless [ˈbri:flis], *a.* sin pleitos, sin clientes (*un abogado*).
briefly [ˈbri:fli], *adv.* brevemente, sucintamente, en resumen, en pocas palabras, en una palabra.
briefness [ˈbri:fnis], *s.* brevedad, concisión.
brier [braiə], *s.* zarza; rosal silvestre; escaramujo.
briery [ˈbraiəri], *a.* zarzoso, lleno de zarzas.
brig [brig], *s. abrev.* [BRIGANTINE].
brigade [briˈgeid], *s.* brigada.
brigadier [brigəˈdiə], *s.* (*mil.*) brigadier.
brigand [ˈbrigənd], *s.* bandido, bandolero.
brigandage [ˈbrigəndidʒ], *s.* bandolerismo.
brigandine [ˈbrigəndi:n], *s.* cota de malla.
brigantine [ˈbrigənti:n], *s.* (*mar.*) bergantín.
bright [brait], *a.* claro; lustroso; brillante, reluciente; flamante; luminoso; subido (*color*); despejado, listo; ilustre, esclarecido; ***bright and early,*** temprano y con sol; tempranito.
brighten [braitn], *v.t.* abrillantar, dar brillo *o* lustre a; avivar, animar; despejar. — *v.i.* aclarar(se), despejar(se); animarse, despabilarse.
brightness [ˈbraitnis], *s.* lustre, brillo; brillantez; resplandor, claridad; (*fig.*) viveza; (lo) subido (*color*).
brill [bril], *s.* (*ict.*) rodaballo.
brilliance, brilliancy [ˈbriljəns, -i], *s.* brillantez; brillo, lustre; esplendor; resplandor, fulgor.
brilliant [ˈbriljənt], *a.* brillante; refulgente. — *s.* (*min.*) brillante.
brilliantine [ˈbriljənti:n], *s.* brillantina.
brim [brim], *s.* borde; orilla; labio (*de un vaso*); ala (*de un sombrero*). — *v.i.* ***brim over,*** rebosar (***with,*** de).
brimful [ˈbrimˈful], *a.* lleno hasta el borde, rebosante.
brimless [ˈbrimlis], *a.* sin borde; sin ala.
brimming [ˈbrimiŋ], *a.* lleno hasta el borde, rebosante.
brimstone [ˈbrimstən], *s.* azufre vivo.
brine [brain], *s.* salmuera; agua salobre. — *v.t.* salar, poner en salmuera.
bring [briŋ], *irr. v.t.* traer; llevar; conducir; hacer venir; aportar; causar, producir; atraer; acarrear; inducir; ***bring about,*** ocasionar, originar; ***bring away,*** traerse; llevarse; ***bring back,*** traer (de vuelta); devolver; ***bring down,*** bajar; abatir; derribar; ***it brought the house down,*** se vino abajo el teatro; ***bring forth,*** producir; parir; dar a luz, publicar; ***bring forward,*** (hacer) avanzar; presentar; (*com.*) llevar (*una suma*) a otra cuenta; ***brought forward,*** suma anterior, suma y sigue; ***bring home,*** traer a casa; demostrar (con energía); ***bring in,*** producir, reportar; sacar *o* traer a colación; ***bring off,*** lograr; rescatar; ***bring on,*** ocasionar, acarrear; ***bring out,*** sacar a la luz, descubrir; poner de relieve; ***bring over,*** persuadir, ganarse, atraerse; ***bring suit,*** poner pleito; ***bring to,*** hacer volver en sí; ***bring o.s. to,*** resignarse a; ***bring influence to bear on,*** influir en; ***bring together,*** reunir, juntar; ***bring to light,*** descubrir, revelar, hacer público; ***bring under,*** sojuzgar, someter; ***bring up,*** subir; criar, educar; arrimar, acercar; sacar a relucir; (*fam.*) devolver; ***bring upon o.s.,*** atraerse (*una desgracia etc.*).
brink [briŋk], *s.* borde, margen, límite, extremo; ***on the brink of,*** al borde de.
brinkmanship [ˈbriŋkmənʃip], *s.* (*pol.*) diplomacia consistente en llegar hasta el límite.
briny [ˈbraini], *a.* salobre, salado. — *s.* (*fam.*) ***the briny,*** el mar, el océano.
brisk [brisk], *a.* vivo, activo; alegre; despejado; animado; rápido; fuerte, vigoroso, enérgico.
brisket [ˈbriskit], *s.* pecho (*de un animal*).
briskness [ˈbrisknis], *s.* viveza.
bristle [brisl], *s.* cerda; porcipelo, pelusa. — *v.t.*, *v.i.* erizar, erizarse.
Britain [ˈbritən]. Gran Bretaña, *f.*
Britannia [briˈtænjə]. Britania.
British [ˈbritiʃ], *a.* británico.
British Honduras [ˈbritiʃ hɔnˈdjuərəs]. Honduras británica, *f.*
Briton [ˈbritən], *s.* británico; (*hist.*) ***Ancient Briton,*** britano.
Brittany [ˈbritəni]. Bretaña.
brittle [britl], *a.* quebradizo, frágil.
brittleness [ˈbritlnis], *s.* fragilidad.
broach [broutʃ], *s.* asador, espetón; espita; broche, prendedor; (*mec.*) broca, mandril; (*arq.*) aguja, chapitel. — *v.t.* ensartar, espetar; decantar, trasegar (*un líquido*); brochar, barrenar; ***broach***

the subject, plantear la cuestión, sacar el tema. — *v.i.* emerger; (*mar.*) ***broach to,*** tomar por avante.
broad [brɔ:d], *a.* ancho; amplio, extenso; comprensivo; tolerante, liberal; indecente, indecoroso; atrevido, descomedido; ***broad hint,*** insinuación clara, indirecta bastante directa; ***in broad daylight,*** en pleno día; ***broad-minded,*** de manga ancha; tolerante, liberal; ***broad accent,*** acento cerrado; ***it's as broad as it is long,*** tanto da, igual da; ***to grow broad,*** ensancharse.
broad-axe [ˈbrɔ:d-æks], *s.* hacha de carpintero.
broadcast [ˈbrɔ:dkɑ:st], *s.* (*agric.*) siembra al vuelo; emisión (*de radio*). — *v.t.* sembrar al vuelo; emitir, radiar; difundir, diseminar. — *v.i.* hablar por la radio.
broadcasting [ˈbrɔ:dkɑ:stiŋ], *s.* radiodifusión; ***broadcasting station,*** emisora.
broadcloth [ˈbrɔ:dklɔθ], *s.* velarte; (*Am.*) popelina.
broaden [ˈbrɔ:dn], *v.t.* ensanchar; ampliar.
broadness [ˈbrɔ:dnis], *s.* anchura; amplitud.
broadside [ˈbrɔ:dsaid], *s.* (*mar.*) costado (*de navío*); (*mar.*) andanada; (*impr.*) lado (*de un pliego de papel*).
broadsword [ˈbrɔ:dsɔ:d], *s.* espada ancha; chafarote.
broadwise [ˈbrɔ:dwaiz], *adv.* a lo ancho, por lo ancho.
brocade [broˈkeid], *s.* brocado. — *v.t.* decorar con brocado.
broccoli [ˈbrɔkəli], *s.* (*bot.*) bróculi, brécol.
brochure [ˈbrouʃə *or* brɔˈʃuə], *s.* folleto.
brock [brɔk], *s.* tejón.
brodekin [ˈbrɔdəkin], *s.* borceguí.
brogan [ˈbrougən], *s.* zapato basto.
brogue [broug], *s.* acento, dejo *o* deje (irlandés); zapato picado.
broil [brɔil], *s.* camorra, pendencia, riña. — *v.t.* asar, tostar. — *v.i.* asarse.
broiler [ˈbrɔilə], *s.* parrilla; pollo para asar.
broke [brouk], *a.* (*fam.*) ***to be broke,*** no tener ni cinco, estar sin cuartos. — *pret.* [BREAK].
broken [ˈbroukən], *a.* roto; quebrado; accidentado; ***broken sleep,*** sueño interrumpido; ***broken spirit,*** espíritu deshecho; ***broken set,*** serie incompleta; ***broken voice,*** voz cascada; ***to speak broken English,*** chapurrear el inglés.
broken-down [ˈbroukən-daun], *a.* desvencijado, arruinado; descompuesto, averiado.
broken-hearted [ˈbroukən-ˈhɑ:tid], *a.* desolado, destrozado, desfondado.
brokenwinded [ˈbroukən-ˈwindid], *a.* asmático; falto de aliento.
broker [ˈbroukə], *s.* corredor; agente.
brokerage [ˈbroukəridʒ], *s.* corretaje.
bromal [ˈbrouməl], *s.* (*quím.*) bromal.
bromate [ˈbroumeit], *s.* (*quím.*) bromato.
bromide [ˈbroumaid], *s.* bromuro; (*fam.*) perogrullada.
bromine [ˈbroumi:n], *s.* (*quím.*) bromo.
bronchi [ˈbrɔŋkai], *s.pl.* (*anat.*) bronquios, *m.pl.*
bronchial [ˈbrɔŋkiəl], *a.* (*anat.*) bronquial; (*med.*) ***bronchial pneumonia,*** bronconeumonía.
bronchitis [brɔŋˈkaitis], *s.* (*med.*) bronquitis, *f.inv.*
bronchocele [ˈbrɔŋkəsi:l], *s.* (*cir.*) broncocele.
bronchotomy [brɔŋˈkɔtəmi], *s.* (*cir.*) broncotomía.
bronco [ˈbrɔŋkou], *s.* (*Am.*) potro cerril.
brontograph [ˈbrɔntogræf], *s.* brontógrafo.
brontometer [brɔnˈtɔmitə], *s.* brontómetro.
brontosaurus [brɔntoˈsɔ:rəs], *s.* (*pal.*) brontosauro.
bronze [brɔnz], *a.* de bronce, hecho de bronce; bronceado. — *s.* bronce. — *v.t.* broncear. — *v.i.* broncearse.
bronzing [ˈbrɔnziŋ], *s.* bronceado.
brooch [broutʃ], *s.* broche, alfiler, prendedor.
brood [bru:d], *s.* camada; ralea; progenie; nidada; cría. — *v.t.* empollar, cobijar. — *v.i.* enclocar; ***brood over,*** rumiar, cavilar, obsesionarse con.
brooder [ˈbru:də], *s.* clueca; incubadora.
broodmare [ˈbru:dmɛə], *s.* yegua.
broody [ˈbru:di], *a.* clueca; (*fig.*) caviloso, meditabundo.
brook (1) [bruk], *s.* regato, riatillo.
brook (2) [bruk], *v.t.* tolerar, aguantar, admitir.
brooklet [ˈbruklit], *s.* arroyuelo.
brookmint [ˈbrukmint], *s.* (*bot.*) menta de agua.
broom [bru:m], *s.* escoba; (*bot.*) hiniesta, retama.
broom-maker [ˈbru:m-meikə], *s.* escobero.
broomstick [ˈbru:mstik], *s.* palo *o* mango de escoba.
broomy [ˈbru:mi], *a.* retamoso.
broth [brɔθ], *s.* caldo.
brothel [ˈbrɔθəl], *s.* casa de trato, casa de putas; burdel.
brother [ˈbrʌðə], *s.* hermano; cofrade; ***brother-in-law,*** cuñado; ***foster-brother,*** hermano de leche; ***half-brother,*** medio hermano.
brotherhood [ˈbrʌðəhud], *s.* hermandad; fraternidad; cofradía.
brotherless [ˈbrʌðəlis], *a.* sin hermanos.
brotherly [ˈbrʌðəli], *a.* fraternal; fraterno.
brougham [bru:m], *s.* coche simón.
brow [brau], *s.* ceja; frente; semblante, rostro; cresta, cima; ***to knit one's brow,*** fruncir el entrecejo; ***brow of hill,*** cambio de rasante.
browbeat [ˈbraubi:t], *v.t.* intimidar.
browbeating [ˈbraubi:tiŋ], *a.* avasallante. — *s.* intimidación, avasallamiento.
brown [braun], *a.* marrón, moreno, castaño; ***brown bread,*** pan moreno; ***brown paper,*** papel de envolver; ***brown sugar,*** azúcar moreno; ***brown bear,*** oso pardo; ***brown linnet,*** pardillo; ***brown owl,*** autillo. — *s.* color moreno, pardo *etc.* — *v.t.* poner moreno, poner tostado; (*coc.*) tostar.
brownie [ˈbrauni], *s.* (*Esco.*) duende benigno; exploradora.
browning [ˈbrauniŋ], *s.* bruñido, pulimento.
brownish [ˈbrauniʃ], *a.* pardusco.
brownness [ˈbraunnis], *s.* color moreno *o* pardo.
browse [brauz], *v.t.* ramonear; hojear (*un libro*); curiosear.
browsing [ˈbrauziŋ], *s.* ramoneo; curioseo.
brucite [ˈbru:sait], *s.* (*min.*) brucita.
Bruin [ˈbru:in], *s.* oso.
bruise [bru:z], *s.* magulladura, contusión, golpe, cardenal. — *v.t.* magullar, golpear.
bruiser [ˈbru:zə], *s.* (*fam.*) boxeador; matón.
bruit [bru:t], *v.t.* ***bruit abroad,*** divulgar, pregonar.
Brunei [ˈbru:nai]. Brunei.
brunette [bru:ˈnet], *s.* morena.
brunt [brʌnt], *s.* choque, embate; ***to bear the brunt,*** llevar el peso, soportar lo más duro.
brush [brʌʃ], *s.* cepillo; escoba; escobilla; brocha; pincel; roce; pelea, escaramuza; hojarasca; matorral, monte bajo; rabo, cola. — *v.t.* cepillar; rozar; ***brush aside,*** echar bruscamente a un lado, rechazar bruscamente; ***brush away*** o ***off,*** quitar con cepillo, quitar (bruscamente) con la mano; (*fig.*) ***brush up,*** repasar, refrescar. — *v.i.* ***brush by*** o ***past,*** rozar, pasar rozando; ***he brushed against me,*** me rozó.
brushing [ˈbrʌʃiŋ], *s.* cepillamiento, cepillado.
brush-off [ˈbrʌʃ-ɔf], *s.* desaire; ***to give s.o. the brush-off,*** sacudirse de mala manera a alguien.
brushwood [ˈbrʌʃwud], *s.* matorral, breñal; broza, ramojos, *m.pl.*
brushy [ˈbrʌʃi], *a.* cerdoso; velludo; cubierto de matojos.
brusque [bru:sk], *a.* brusco.
brusqueness [ˈbru:sknis], *s.* brusquedad.
Brussels [brʌslz]. Bruselas; ***brussels sprouts,*** coles de Bruselas, *f.pl.*

brutal [bru:tl], *a.* brutal, bestial, salvaje.
brutality [bru:ˈtæliti], *s.* brutalidad, ferocidad.
brutalize [ˈbru:təlaiz], *v.t.* embrutecer.
brute [bru:t], *s.* bruto, animal, salvaje, monstruo.
brutish [ˈbru:tiʃ], *a.* brutal, bestial; embrutecido.
brutishness [ˈbru:tiʃnis], *s.* brutalidad.
bryony [ˈbraiəni], *s.* (*bot.*) brionia.
bubble [bʌbl], *s.* burbuja; pompa; (*med.*) ampolla; engañifa; globo; quimera; (*coc.*) ***bubble and squeak,*** (plato de) patata con repollo. — *v.i.* burbujear, borbotar; ***boil and bubble,*** hervir a borbotones *o* a borbollones; ***bubble over,*** desbordarse, rebosar (***with,*** de).
bubble-gum [ˈbʌbl-gʌm], *s.* chicle hinchable.
bubbly [ˈbʌbli], *a.* espumoso. — *s.* (*fam.*) champaña.
bubo [ˈbju:bou], *s.* (*med.*) bubón.
bubonic [bju:ˈbɔnik], *a.* bubónico.
buccal [bʌkl], *a.* bucal.
buccaneer [bʌkəˈniə], *s.* bucanero.
Bucephalus [bju:ˈsefələs]. Bucéfalo.
buck [bʌk], *s.* cabrón, macho cabrío; macho (*de ciervo, gamo, conejo etc.*); petimetre, pisaverde; lejía; (*Am., fam.,*) dólar; (*fam.*) ***to pass the buck,*** echar a carga (a otro). — *v.t.* (*Am., fam.*) hacer frente a, embestir; colar (la ropa). — *v.i.* encorvarse, caracolear; ***buck against,*** embestir contra; ***buck up,*** animarse, cobrar ánimo.
buckbasket [ˈbʌkbɑ:skit], *s.* cesto de la colada.
bucket [ˈbʌkit], *s.* cubo, balde, pozal; paleta (*de rueda*); canjilón (*de noria*); cucharón *o* pala (*de excavadora*); ***drop in the bucket,*** fruslería, miseria; (*fam.*) ***to kick the bucket,*** estirar la pata.
bucketful [ˈbʌkitful], *s.* cubo (lleno).
buckeye [ˈbʌkai], *s.* (*bot.*) castaña de Indias.
buckle [bʌkl], *s.* hebilla; pandeo. — *v.t.* hebillar. — *v.i.* pandear; doblarse, encorvarse; ***buckle*** (***down***) ***to,*** dedicarse con empeño a, ponerse de codos a.
buckler [ˈbʌklə], *s.* rodela, adarga, broquel.
buckmast [ˈbʌkmɑ:st], *s.* hayuco.
buckram [ˈbʌkrəm], *a.* almidonado, engomado, aderezado; tieso, estirado. — *s.* bocací *o* bucarán.
bucksaw [ˈbʌksɔ:], *s.* sierra de bastidor.
buckskin [ˈbʌkskin], *s.* piel de ante, *f.*; coturno.
buckthorn [ˈbʌkθɔ:n], *s.* (*bot.*) ladierno, tamujo.
buckwheat [ˈbʌkwi:t], *s.* (*bot.*) trigo negro.
bucolic [bju:ˈkɔlik], *a.* bucólico. — *s.* bucólica.
bud [bʌd], *s.* pimpollo, brote, botón, yema; capullo; (*fam.*) niño, niña; ***to nip in the bud,*** cortar en flor; agostar. — *v.t.* injertar. — *v.i.* brotar, germinar; abotonar.
Buddha [ˈbudə]. Budha, Buda.
Buddhism [ˈbudizəm], *s.* budismo.
Buddhist [ˈbudist], *a., s.* budista, *m.f.*
budding [ˈbʌdiŋ], *a.* en capullo, en ciernes, ***budding lawyer,*** un abogado que promete. — *s.* injerto de esudete; brotadura.
buddy [bʌdi], *s.* (*Am., fam.*) compinche, compadre.
budge [bʌdʒ], *v.t.* (*fam.*) mover. — *v.i.* (*fam.*) moverse, menearse.
budget [ˈbʌdʒit], *s.* presupuesto. — *v.t., v.i.* hacer presupuesto (de), presupuestar.
buff [bʌf], *a.* de color de ante, amarillo claro. — *s.* ante; ***in buff,*** en cueros. — *v.t.* pulimentar con ante.
buffalo [ˈbʌfəlou], *s.* búfalo, piel de búfalo, *f.*
buffer [ˈbʌfə], *s.* tope; amortiguador; pulidora; ***buffer state,*** estado tapón; (*fig., fam.*) ***old buffer,*** mastuerzo; vejestorio.
buffet (1) [ˈbʌfit], *s.* embate; bofetada, sopapo. — *v.t.* abofetear; azotar.
buffet (2) [ˈbu:fei], *s.* bufé, ambigú.
buffeting [ˈbʌfitiŋ], *s.* mano de bofetadas.
buffing-block [ˈbʌfiŋ-blɔk], *s.* (*f.c.*) cojinete, tope.
buffing-spring [ˈbʌfiŋ-spriŋ], *s.* (*f.c.*) resorte de tope.
buffoon [bəˈfu:n], *s.* bufón.
buffoonery [bəˈfu:nəri], *s.* bufonada(s), bufonería.
bug [bʌg], *s.* bicho, sabandija, insecto; (*Am.*) insecto; microbio; (*fig.*) maniático, forofo; (*fig.*) manía; (*fig.*) ***big bug,*** pájaro gordo; (*mec., fig.*) defecto; ***bed bug,*** chinche; (*Am.*) ***lady-bug,*** mariquita. — *v.t.* intervenir (*el teléfono*); (*Am., fam.*) jorobar.
bugbear [ˈbʌgbɛə], *s.* (*fam.*) coco; pesadilla.
bugger [ˈbʌgə], *s.* (*obsc.*) sodomita, *m.*; (*fig., obsc.*) cabrón.
bugging device [ˈbʌgiŋ diˈvais], *s.* aparato audífono (*espionaje*).
buggy [ˈbʌgi], *s.* calesa.
bugle [bju:gl], *s.* corneta; (*bot.*) búgula.
bugler [ˈbju:glə], *s.* corneta, *m.*
bugloss [ˈbju:glɔs], *s.* (*bot.*) buglosa.
buhl [bu:l], *s.* taracea, marquetería.
build [bild], *s.* estructura; talle.— *irr. v.t.* construir, edificar; fabricar; fundar, establecer; componer; ***build up,*** armar; componer; desarrollar; urbanizar; ***build*** (***up***)***on,*** edificar sobre. — *v.i.* — ***up,*** crearse; acumularse; aumentar.
builder [ˈbildə], *s.* arquitecto; maestro de obras; constructor.
building [ˈbildiŋ], *s.* construcción; edificio; ***shipbuilding,*** construcción de barcos.
building lot [ˈbildiŋ lɔt], *s.* solar.
built-in [ˈbilt-ˈin], *a.* (*arq.*) incorporado; empotrado.
built-up [ˈbilt-ˈʌp], *a.* urbanizado.
bulb [bʌlb], *s.* (*bot.*) bulbo; (*elec.*) bombilla; cubeta (del barómetro); ampolleta (del termómetro).
bulbous [ˈbʌlbəs], *a.* bulboso.
Bulgaria [bʌlˈgɛəriə]. Bulgaria.
Bulgarian [bʌlˈgɛəriən], *a., s.* búlgaro.
bulge [bʌldʒ], *s.* pandeo, comba, bombeo, protuberancia, bulto. — *v.i.* pandearse, combarse, bombearse; saltar, sobresalir.
bulginess [ˈbʌldʒinis], *s.* pandeo, combadura; (lo) abultado.
bulging [ˈbʌldʒiŋ], *a.,* protuberante, abultado; (*ojos*) saltones.
bulk [bʌlk], *s.* bulto, volumen, grueso, grosor; corpulencia; carga; mayor parte; ***in bulk,*** a granel; ***bulk goods,*** mercancías sueltas. — *v.i.* ***bulk*** (***large***), abultar (mucho); tener (mucha) importancia.
bulkhead [ˈbʌlkhed], *s.* (*mar.*) mamparo.
bulkiness [ˈbʌlkinis], *s.* volumen, bulto.
bulky [ˈbʌlki], *a.* voluminoso; abultado; corpulento; grueso; grandote.
bull [bul], *s.* toro; macho; bula; (*com.*) alcista, *m.*; (*fam.*) pijada(s); ***to take the bull by the horns,*** irse a la cabeza del toro, coger al toro por los cuernos. — *v.t.* (*com.*) ***bull the market,*** jugar al alza.
bull-baiting [ˈbul-beitiŋ], *s.* combate de toros y perros.
bull-calf [ˈbul-kɑ:f], *s.* ternero.
bulldog [ˈbuldɔg], *a.* porfiado, terco. — *s.* bulldog, dogo; revólver de gran calibre.
bulldoze [ˈbuldouz], *v.t.* (*Am.*) intimidar, coaccionar, avasallar.
bulldozer [ˈbuldouzə], *s.* (máquina) niveladora, excavadora.
bullet [ˈbulit], *s.* bala; plomada de pescador.
bulletin [ˈbulitin], *s.* boletín; parte, comunicado; (*Am.*) tablón de anuncios.
bullet-proof [ˈbulit-pru:f], *a.* a prueba de balas.
bullfight [ˈbulfait], *s.* corrida de toros, lidia.
bullfighter [ˈbulfaitə], *s.* torero; diestro; ***bullfighter's garb,*** traje de luces.
bullfighting [ˈbulfaitiŋ], *a.* tauromáquico. — *s.* tauromaquia; toreo, toros, *m.pl.*
bullfinch [ˈbulfintʃ], *s.* (*orn.*) pinzón real.
bullhead [ˈbulhed], *s.* (*ict.*) chorlito, zote.
bull-headed [ˈbul-ˈhedid], *a.* obstinado, terco.

bullion [ˈbuljən], *s.* oro *o* plata en barras; (*com.*) metálico; ***bullion-office,*** oficina de cambios.

bullish [ˈbuliʃ], *a.* de toro; disparatado; (*com.*) en alza, alcista.

bull-necked [ˈbul-nekt], *a.* de cuello grueso; (*fig.*) de cerviz gruesa.

bullock [ˈbulək], *s.* novillo castrado.

bull's eye [ˈbulz ai], *s.* claraboya, tragaluz; linterna sorda; diana (*de un blanco*); tiro que da en el blanco; (*mar.*) ojo de buey; motón ciego.

bully [ˈbuli], *a.* (*Am., fam.*) magnífico, excelente. — *s.* matón, valentón, matasiete; ***bully beef,*** carne de vaca en conserva. — *v.t.* amedrentar, avasallar, maltratar. — *v.i.* bravear, avasallar, hacer el matón.

bullying [ˈbuliiŋ], *s.* avasallamiento; novatada.

bulrush [ˈbulrʌʃ], *s.* (*bot.*) junco, enea.

bulrushy [ˈbulrʌʃi], *a.* juncoso.

bulwark [ˈbulwək], *s.* baluarte; (*mar.*) amurada. — *v.t.* abaluartar, fortificar con baluartes.

bum [bʌm], *a.* (*Am., fam.*) malo, de mala calidad; ***to feel bum,*** sentirse malucho. — *s.* (*Am., fam.*) juerga, parranda; (*Am., fam.*) gandul, borrachín; gorrón, sablista, *m.*; (*obsc.*) trasero, culo. — *v.t.* (*Am., fam.*) conseguir (algo) de gorra. — *v.i.* holgazanear; emborracharse; vivir a costa ajena; ir de parranda; sablear, gorronear.

bumbailiff [ˈbʌmˈbeilif], *s.* corchete; alguacil.

bumble-bee [ˈbʌmbl-bi:], *s.* abejorro.

bumboat [ˈbʌmbout], *s.* (*mar.*) bote vivandero.

bummer [ˈbʌmə], *s.* (*Am., fam.*) holgazán, gandul; gorrón.

bump [bʌmp], *s.* chichón; golpe. — *v.t.* golpear, tropezar *o* dar contra; (*fam.*) ***bump off,*** eliminar, liquidar, despachar.

bumper [ˈbʌmpə], *a.* abundante; grande. — *s.* lo que da golpes; copa *o* vaso lleno; tope; parachoques, *m.inv.*

bumpkin [ˈbʌmpkin], *s.* palurdo, paleto, patán; (*mar.*) pescante, tangón; botalón de proa.

bumptious [ˈbʌmpʃəs], *a.* (*fam.*) presuntuoso, engreído, petulante.

bumptiousness [ˈbʌmpʃəsnis], *s.* presunción, engreimiento, petulancia.

bumpy [ˈbʌmpi], *a.* abollado; desigual; con baches; agitado (*aire*).

bun [bʌn], *s.* bollo, torta; gazapo; rabo de liebre; moño.

bunch [bʌntʃ], *s.* manojo; ramillete; haz; racimo; grupo, manada, hato; chichón, bollo; giba. — *v.t.* arracimar, amanojar. — *v.i.* juntarse; arracimarse; formar giba.

bunchy [ˈbʌntʃi], *a.* racimoso, arracimado; corcovado, giboso.

bundle [bʌndl], *s.* atado, lío, mazo, manojo, haz, fardel, bulto, envoltorio, paquete. — *v.t.* liar, atar; envolver, empaquetar, enfardelar; ***bundle up,*** liar; arropar bien; ***bundle off*** o ***out,*** despedir sin ceremonias.

bung [bʌŋ], *s.* tapón; tarugo; bitoque. — *v.t.* tapar; atarugar; cerrar; ***bung up,*** tapar, obstruir.

bungalow [ˈbʌŋgəlou], *s.* bungalow.

bunghole [ˈbʌŋhoul], *s.* boca de tonel.

bungle [bʌŋgl], *s.* chapucería, chafallo; torpeza. — *v.t.* chapucear, chafallar; echar a perder, estropear. — *v.i.* chapucear.

bungler [ˈbuŋglə], *s.* chapucero.

bungling [ˈbʌŋgliŋ], *a.* torpe, chapucero.

bunion [ˈbʌnjən], *s.* (*med.*) juanete.

bunk [bʌŋk], *s.* litera; (*fam.*) (***a lot of***) ***bunk,*** palabrería, sandeces; (*fam.*) ***to do a bunk,*** guillárselas, najárselas, salir de naja.

bunker [ˈbʌŋkə], *s.* carbonera; (*mar.*) pañol del carbón; (*golf*) bunker, hoya de arena; (*mil.*) bunker, fortín.

bunkum [ˈbʌŋkʌm], *s.* gaitas, *f.pl.*, tonterías, *f.pl.*

bunny [ˈbʌni], *s.* (*fam.*) conejito, gazapo.

bunt [bʌnt], *s.* hinchazón, *f.*, inflación; (*mar.*) fondo (*de vela*); batidero (*de vela*); (*agric.*) añublo, tizón; empellón, empujón, topetazo; hongo parásito. — *v.t.* topetar, golpear. — *v.i.* hincharse.

bunting [ˈbʌntiŋ], *s.* (*mar.*) lanilla (*para banderas*); estameña; banderas, *f.pl.*, empavesado; (*orn.*) escribano, triguero.

buntline [ˈbʌntlain], *s.* (*mar.*) briol.

buoy [bɔi], *s.* (*mar.*) boya; baliza; ***life-buoy,*** boya salvavidas, guindola. — *v.t.* abalizar, señalar con boyas; ***buoy up,*** mantener a flote, sostener; animar.

buoyancy [ˈbɔiənsi], *s.* flotación; fuerza ascensional; ligereza.

buoyant [ˈbɔiənt], *a.* boyante; ligero.

bur [bə:], *s.* (*bot.*) erizo; (*tej.*) mota. — *v.t.* (*tej.*) desmotar.

burbot [ˈbə:bət], *s.* (*ict.*) lota.

burden [bə:dn], *s.* carga; gravamen; peso; (*mar.*) arqueo; (*mar.*) peso del cargamento; tema; estribillo; ***beast of burden,*** bestia de carga, acémila. — *v.t.* cargar; agobiar; gravar.

burdensome [ˈbə:dnsəm], *a.* gravoso, oneroso, pesado.

burdock [ˈbə:dɔk], *s.* (*bot.*) bardana.

bureau [bjuəˈrou], *s.* escritorio; oficina, agencia; departamento; (*Am.*) [CHEST OF DRAWERS].

bureaucracy [bjuəˈrɔkrəsi], *s.* burocracia.

bureaucrat [ˈbjuərokræt], *s.* burócrata, *m.f.*

bureaucratic [bjuəroˈkrætik], *a.* burocrático.

burette [bjuəˈret], *s.* bureta, probeta.

burg [ˈbə:g], *s.* burgo; pueblo.

burgee [ˈbə:dʒi:], *s.* (bandera de) corneta.

burgeon [ˈbə:dʒən], *s.* retoño. — *v.i.* retoñar; (*fig.*) prosperar.

burgeoning [ˈbə:dʒəniŋ], *a.* pujante.

burgess [ˈbə:dʒis], *s.* vecino; concejal; diputado.

burgher [ˈbə:gə], *s.* habitante, ciudadano; vecino.

burglar [ˈbə:glə], *s.* ladrón.

burglary [ˈbə:gləri], *s.* robo (*de una casa*); allanamiento de morada.

burgle [bə:gl], *v.i.* robar (*en una casa*).

burgomaster [ˈbə:gomɑ:stə], *s.* burgomaestre.

Burgundian [bə:ˈgʌndiən], *a., s,* borgoñón.

Burgundy [ˈbə:gəndi]. Borgoña.

burgundy [ˈbə:gəndi], *s.* vino de Borgoña.

burial [ˈberiəl], *s.* entierro, sepelio; ***burial-ground, burial-place,*** cementerio, camposanto; ***burial-service,*** oficio de difuntos.

burin [ˈbjuərin], *s.* buril, cincel.

burl [bə:l], *s.* borra, mota, nudillo; nudo (*en la madera*). — *v.t.* batanar; desmotar, desborrar.

burlap [ˈbə:læp], *s.* arpillera, rázago; tela basta.

burlesque [bə:ˈlesk], *a.* burlesco, cómico. — *s.* parodia. — *v.t.* parodiar, poner en ridículo.

burletta [bə:ˈletə], *s.* opereta burlesca.

burliness [ˈbə:linis], *s.* corpulencia.

burly [ˈbə:li], *a.* corpulento, membrudo, fornido.

Burma [ˈbə:mə]. Birmania.

Burmese [bə:ˈmi:z], *a., s.* birmano.

burn (1) [bə:n], *s.* quemadura. — *irr. v.t.* quemar; ***burn down,*** arrasar con fuego, quemar de arriba abajo; (*fig.*) ***burn one's fingers,*** pillarse los dedos; (*fig.*) ***burn the midnight oil,*** quemarse las cejas; ***he has money to burn,*** le sobra dinero; ***burn up,*** consumir. — *v.i.* arder, quemarse; ***burn out,*** reducirse a cenizas; consumirse, apagarse; ***burn up,*** quemarse del todo; ***burn with impatience,*** arder de impaciencia.

burn (2) [bə:n], *s.* (*Esco.*) arroyo.

burnable [ˈbə:nəbl], *a.* combustible.

burner [ˈbə:nə], *s.* quemador, abrasador, incendiario; piquera, mechero (*de gas* o *lámpara*).

burnet [ˈbə:net], *s.* (*bot.*) sanguisorba, pimpinela.

burning [ˈbə:niŋ], *a.* abrasador; ardiente; ***burning issue,*** cuestión candente. — *s.* combustión;

quema; ***there is a smell of burning,*** huele a quemado.

burnish [ˈbəːniʃ], *s.* bruñido. — *v.t.* bruñir, pulir, satinar. — *v.i.* tomar lustre.

burnous [bəːˈnuːs], *s.* albornoz.

burnt-offering, burnt-sacrifice [bəːnt-ˈɔfəriŋ, -ˈsækrifais], *s.* holocausto.

burr (1) [bəː], *s.* [BUR].

burr (2) [bəː], *s.* dejo; pronunciación gutural de la *r*; ***to speak with a burr,*** tener un dejo *o* deje.

burrow [ˈbʌrou], *s.* madriguera; conejera; (*min.*) cata. — *v.t.* socavar. — *v.i.* — ***into, through,*** cavar, horadar.

bursar [ˈbəːsə], *s.* tesorero; becario.

bursarship [ˈbəːsəʃip], *s.* tesorería.

bursary [ˈbəːsəri], *s.* caja, tesorería; beca.

burst [bəːst], *s.* reventón; estallido; explosión; ráfaga; arranque. — *irr. v.t.* reventar. — *v.i.* reventar(se), estallar, explotar; ***burst into,*** irrumpir en; prorrumpir en; desatarse en, deshacerse en; ***burst out,*** salir como un loco; brotar; romper a, echarse a; ***burst with,*** reventar de; rebosar de.

burton (1) [bəːtn], *s.* (*mar.*) palanquín de polea.

burton (2) [bəːtn], *s.* (*fam.*) ***to go for a burton,*** estropearse; perderse, irse por la trampa.

Burundi [buˈrundiː], *a.* burundiano. — *s.* (*país*) Burundi; (*pers.*) burundiano.

bury [ˈberi], *v.t.* enterrar, sepultar; ocultar; ***bury the hatchet,*** echar pelillos a la mar, hacer las paces; ***bury in oblivion,*** echar en olvido.

burying [ˈberiiŋ], *s.* entierro.

bus [bʌs], *s.* autobús; ***long-distance bus,*** autocar; (*fig.*) ***to miss the bus,*** perder la ocasión.

busby [ˈbʌzbi], *s.* gorra, chacó (*de los húsares*).

bush [buʃ], *s.* arbusto; mata; matojo; maleza, matorral; cola de zorra; (*mec.*) buje, tejuelo; forro de metal; ***to beat about the bush,*** andarse por las ramas; andarse con rodeos.

bushed [buʃt], *a.* (*fam.*) chiflado; ***to be bushed about sth.,*** tener manía de algo.

bushel [ˈbuʃəl], *s.* medida de áridos; fanega.

bushiness [ˈbuʃinis], *s.* (lo) espeso, (lo) peludo.

bushing [ˈbuʃiŋ], *s.* (*mec.*) forro de metal; buje, tejuelo.

bushman [ˈbuʃmən], *s.* bosquimano; colonizador.

bushranger [ˈbuʃreindʒə], *s.* bandido.

bushy [ˈbuʃi], *a.* lleno de arbustos; espeso, poblado.

business [ˈbiznis], *s.* negocio(s), asunto, comercio; ***business hours,*** horas de despacho, *f.pl.*; ***I'll make it my business to find out,*** ya me cuidaré yo de averiguarlo; ***it is not my business,*** no es cosa mía; ***mind your own business,*** no se meta en lo que no le importa; zapatero, a tus zapatos; ***to do business for,*** trabajar para; ***to mean business,*** hablar *o* actuar en serio; ***what is your business here?*** ¿qué le trae a usted por aquí?; ***what's your line of business?*** ¿a qué se dedica usted?

businesslike [ˈbiznislaik], *a.* ordenado, sistemático, metódico, eficaz.

businessman [ˈbiznismæn], *s.* hombre de negocios.

business suit [ˈbiznis s(j)uːt], *s.* (*Am.*) [LOUNGE SUIT].

busk [bʌsk], *s.* ballena de corsé.

buskin [ˈbʌskin], *s.* borceguí; coturno; (*fig.*) tragedia.

busman [ˈbʌsmən], *s.* conductor de autobús.

bust (1) [bʌst], *s.* busto; pecho (de mujer).

bust (2) [bʌst], *v.t.* (*fam.*) reventar, romper; dar un puñetazo a. — *v.i.* ***go bust,*** arruinarse, quebrar.

bustard [ˈbʌstəd], *s.* (*orn.*) avutarda.

bustle [bʌsl], *s.* trajín, bullicio; prisa, bulla; polisón. — *v.i.* bullir, menearse, afanarse.

bustling [ˈbʌsliŋ], *a.* activo, vivo, diligente; afanado.

busy [ˈbizi], *a.* ocupado, atareado; bullicioso; concurrido (*calle etc.*). — *v.t.* ocupar, emplear, atarear; ***busy o.s.,*** afanarse, atarearse.

busybody [ˈbizibɔdi], *s.* entrometido.

but [bʌt], *adv.* sólo, solamente, no más que; ***he is but a child,*** no es más que un niño; ***he all but fell,*** por poco se cae; ***but few,*** sólo pocos; ***but for,*** a no ser por; ***but little,*** sólo poco, muy poco; ***but yesterday,*** ayer mismo. — *conj.* pero, mas; ***he's clever but poor,*** es listo pero pobre; ***I never go out but I meet him,*** nunca salgo a la calle sin encontrármelo *o* sin que me lo encuentre; ***he cannot but do it,*** no puede menos de hacerlo. — *prep.* y *conj.* excepto, fuera de, menos, sino, más que; ***last but one,*** penúltimo; ***no one but you,*** nadie más que tú, nadie sino usted. — *s.* pero; ***but me no buts,*** no me pongas peros.

butcher [ˈbutʃə], *s.* carnicero; matarife; (*fig.*) verdugo; ***butcher's shop,*** carnicería; ***butcher's knife,*** jifero; (*Am.*) trinchante. — *v.t.* matar, sacrificar (*reses*); matar atrozmente, hacer una carnicería de.

butcher-bird [ˈbutʃə-bəːd], *s.* (*orn.*) alcaudón.

butcher's broom [ˈbutʃəz bruːm], *s.* (*bot.*) brusco.

butchery [ˈbutʃəri], *s.* carnicería; matanza.

butler [ˈbʌtlə], *s.* mayordomo, despensero.

butment [ˈbʌtmənt], *s.* contrafuerte; estribo de un arco.

butt [bʌt], *s.* cabo, extremo; culata, mocho; cabeza (*de biela*); cepa, tocón; punta *o* colilla (*de cigarrillo*); blanco (*de tiro*); hazmerreír; estocada, botonazo; empalme *o* tope; (*fam.*) culo. — *v.t.* topar, topetar; empalmar a tope. — *v.i.* topar, topetar; ***butt against,*** topar con; ***butt in*** o ***into,*** meter baza en, meter la cuchara en.

butt-end [ˈbʌt-end], *s.* pie (*de árbol*); culata (*de un fusil*).

butter [ˈbʌtə], *s.* mantequilla; ***cocoa-butter,*** manteca de cacao. — *v.t.* untar con mantequilla; (*fam., fig.*) ***butter up,*** dar coba a, hacer la pelotilla a.

buttercup [ˈbʌtəkʌp], *s.* (*bot.*) ranúnculo, botón de oro.

butter-dish [ˈbʌtə-diʃ], *s.* mantequillera.

butterfingers [ˈbʌtəfiŋgəz], *s.* (*fam.*) desmanotado, torpe; manos de trapo. — *interj.* ¡premio!

butterfly [ˈbʌtəflai], *s.* mariposa.

buttermilk [ˈbʌtəmilk], *s.* leche de manteca.

butternut [ˈbʌtənʌt], *s.* nogal blanco.

butterwort [ˈbʌtəwəːt], *s.* (*bot.*) sanícula.

buttery [ˈbʌtəri], *a.* mantecoso. — *s.* despensa.

buttock(s) [ˈbʌtək(s)], *s.* nalga(s), posadera(s).

button [bʌtn], *s.* botón; (*agric.*) capullo; (*artill.*) cascabel; tope (*de un florete*). — *v.t.* abotonar; poner botones a. — *v.i.* — ***up,*** abotonar(se).

button-hole [ˈbʌtn-houl], *s.* ojal. — *v.t.* (*fig.*) abordar, coger.

button-hook [ˈbʌtn-huk], *s.* abotonador.

button-maker [ˈbʌtn-meikə], *s.* botonero.

buttons [bʌtnz], *s.* botones, *m. sing.*

buttress [ˈbʌtris], *s.* contrafuerte; arbotante; (*fig.*) apoyo, sostén. — *v.t.* apuntalar; (*fig.*) apoyar, reforzar.

butyric [bjuːˈtirik], *a.* butírico.

buxom [ˈbʌksəm], *a.* (*mujer*) frescachona, lozana, rolliza, regordeta.

buy [bai], *s.* (*fam.*) compra; ***a good buy,*** una ganga. — *v.t.* comprar; ***buy for,*** comprar para *o* a; ***buy from,*** comprar a; ***buy off,*** comprar, sobornar; ***buy out,*** comprar la parte de; ***buy up,*** acaparar.

buyable [ˈbaiəbl], *a.* comprable.

buyer [baiə], *s.* comprador.

buzz [bʌz], *s.* zumbido; ***buzz saw,*** sierra circular. — *v.t.* (*aer.*) acercarse mucho para molestar *o* atemorizar. — *v.i.* zumbar. — *interj.* (*fam.*) ***buzz off!*** ¡lárgate!

buzzard [ˈbʌzəd], *s.* (*orn.*) busardo; zopilote.
buzzer [ˈbʌzə], *s.* zumbador.
by [bai], *adv.* cerca; ***by and by,*** luego, ya, al poco rato; ***by and large,*** por lo general; ***hard by,*** muy cerca, al lado. — *prep.* por; de; según; ***by all means,*** por supuesto, no faltaba más; ***by day*** (***night***), de día (noche); ***by the dozen,*** a docenas; ***by far,*** con mucho; ***by moonlight,*** a la luz de la luna; ***by no means,*** de ninguna manera; ni mucho menos; ***by now,*** ya; ***by o.s.,*** solo; a solas; ***by then,*** ya, para entonces; ***by twos,*** de dos en dos; ***by us,*** cerca de nosotros, a nuestro lado; ***by the way, by the by***(***e***), a propósito, por cierto; ***side by side,*** lado a lado.
by-bidder [ˈbai-bidə], *s.* postor simulado.
bye [bai], *s.* jugador *o* equipo que queda de non (*torneos etc.*); ***by the bye,*** entre paréntesis, a propósito.
bye-bye (1) [ˈbai-bai], *s.* (*infantil*) (el) mimir; ***to go to bye-byes,*** ir a mimir.
bye-bye! (2) [ˈbai-ˈbai], *interj.* ¡adiós!
by-election [ˈbai-ilekʃən], *s.* elecciones parciales, *f.pl.*
Byelorussia [ˈbjeloˈrʌʃə]. Rusia Blanca.
Byelorussian [ˈbjeloˈrʌʃən], *a.* bieloruso; (***the***) ***Byelorussian Soviet Socialist Republic,*** (la) República Socialista Soviética de Bielorusia. — *s.* bieloroso, ruso blanco.

bygone [ˈbaigɔn], *a.* pasado, transcurrido. — *s.* (lo) pasado, (lo) transcurrido; ***let bygones be bygones,*** olvidemos lo pasado, lo pasado pasado, pelillos a la mar.
by-lane [ˈbai-lein], *s.* sendero, vereda.
by-law [ˈbai-lɔ:], *s.* reglamento; ley privada.
bypass [ˈbaipɑ:s], *a.* de paso, auxiliar *o* de derivación. — *s.* camino *o* canal secundario *o* de derivación; carretera de circunvalación. — *v.t.* desviar, derivar; rodear; saltar(se).
by-path [ˈbai-pɑ:θ], *s.* senda, vereda.
by-product [ˈbai-prɔdʌkt], *s.* subproducto, producto accesorio, derivado.
byre [baiə], *s.* establo, casa de vacas.
by-road [ˈbai-roud], *s.* camino vecinal.
bystander [ˈbaistændə], *s.* espectador; (*pl.*) circunstantes, *m.pl.*
by-view [ˈbai-vju:], *s.* fin particular, mira interesada.
by-way [ˈbai-wei], *s.* camino desviado.
byword [ˈbaiwə:d], *s.* comidilla; apodo, mote; dicho, muletilla; ***to be a byword for,*** ser notorio por.
Byzantine [biˈzæntain], *a.*, *s.* bizantino.

C

C, c [siː]. tercera letra del alfabeto. — *s.* (*mús.*) do.
cab [kæb], *s.* cabriolé, coche de punto, simón; taxi; (*f.c.*) casilla (*del maquinista*); ***cab-driver,*** cochero de punto; taxista, *m.*; ***cab-stand,*** punto de coches *o* parada de taxis.
cabal [kəˈbæl], *s.* cábala, intriga, trama, maquinación. — *v.i.* maquinar, tramar.
cabaret [ˈkæbərei], *s.* cabaret, café cantante; atracciones, espectáculo.
cabbage [ˈkæbidʒ], *s.* repollo, col, *f.*, berza; sisa; (*fig.*) ***cabbage-head,*** berzotas; ***cabbage-heart,*** cogollo de berza; ***cabbage-stalk, cabbage-stump,*** troncho de col; ***savoy cabbage,*** berza rizada; (*fig.*) ***to become a cabbage,*** vegetar. — *v.t.* sisar. — *v.i.* (*agric.*) repollar, acogollarse.
Cabbalah [kəˈbɑːlə], *s.* cábala de los judíos.
cabby [ˈkæbi], *s.* (*fam.*) cochero de punto; taxista, *m.*
cabin [ˈkæbin], *s.* cabaña; (*mar.*) camarote; cabina; ***cabin-boy,*** grumete. — *v.t.* encerrar, limitar, restringir.
cabinet [ˈkæbinet], *s.* gabinete; armario; vitrina; caja; (*pol.*) gabinete, ministerio; ***cabinet council,*** consejo de ministros; ***cabinet maker,*** ebanista, *m.*; ***cabinet making, cabinet work,*** ebanistería; ***medicine cabinet,*** botiquín.
cable [keibl], *s.* (*mar.*) cable; cable eléctrico; cablegrama, *m.* — *v.t.*, *v.i.* cablegrafiar.
cablegram [ˈkeiblgræm], *s.* cablegrama, *m.*
cable ship [ˈkeibl ʃip], *s.* buque cablero.
cabman [ˈkæbmən], *s.* cochero; taxista, *m.*
caboodle [kəˈbuːdl], *s.* (*fam.*) partida, cuadrilla; (*fam.*) ***the whole caboodle,*** toda la pesca.
caboose [kəˈbuːs], *s.* (*mar.*) fogón, cocina.
cabotage [ˈkæbətidʒ], *s.* (*mar.*) cabotaje.
cabriolet [kæbrioˈlei], *s.* cabriolé.
cabstand [ˈkæbstænd], *s.* parada de taxis.
cacao [kəˈkɑːou], *s.* (*bot.*) cacao.
cachalot [ˈkæʃəlou], *s.* cachalote.
cache [kæʃ], *s.* escondite, escondrijo; alijo. — *v.t.* — (***away***), meter en un escondrijo, esconder.
cachexy [kəˈkeksi], *s.* (*med.*) caquexia.
cachinnation [kækiˈneiʃən], *s.* carcajada, risotada.
cachou [kæˈʃuː], *s.* cachú, cato.
cackle [kækl], *s.* cacareo; cloqueo; cháchara; carcajada áspera. — *v.i.* cacarear; cloquear; (*fig.*) chacharear; reírse ásperamente.
cackler [ˈkæklə], *s.* cacareador; hablador, parlanchín.
cacography [kæˈkɔgrəfi], *s.* cacografía.
cacophonic [kækoˈfɔnik], *a.* cacofónico.
cacophony [kəˈkɔfəni], *s.* cacofonía.
cactus [ˈkæktəs], *s.* (*pl.* **cacti** [-ai]) (*bot.*) cactus, cacto.
cacumen [kəˈkjuːmən], *s.* ápice, cumbre.
cad [kæd], *s.* (*fam.*) canalla.
cadastral [kəˈdæstrəl], *a.* catastral.
cadastre [kəˈdæstə], *s.* catastro.
cadaver [kəˈdeivə], *s.* cadáver.
cadaverous [kəˈdævərəs], *a.* cadavérico.
cadaverousness [kəˈdævərəsnis], *s.* estado *o* aspecto cadavérico.
caddie [ˈkædi], *s.* caddie.
caddis [ˈkædis], *s.* jerguilla de lana; trencilla de estambre.
caddish [ˈkædiʃ], *a.* canallesco.
caddishness [ˈkædiʃnis], *s.* canallada(s).
caddow [ˈkædou], *s.* (*orn.*) chova.
caddy [ˈkædi], *s.* lata *o* cajita para té; [CADDIE].
cade [keid], *s.* animal manso, domesticado; niño mimado.
cadence [ˈkeidəns], *s.* cadencia, ritmo, modulación. — *v.t.* modular.
cadency [ˈkeidənsi], *s.* cadencia; acento, entonación.
cadent [ˈkeidənt], *a.* cadente; cadencioso.
cadet [kəˈdet], *s.* cadete.
cadge [kædʒ], *v.t.* conseguir de gorra; ***cadge money off,*** sablear, dar sablazos a. — *v.i.* sablear, gorronear.
cadger [ˈkædʒə], *s.* placero, revendedor; sablista, *m.f.*, gorrón.
cadi [ˈkɑːdi], *s.* cadí.
Cadmean, -ian [kædˈmiːən], *a.* de Cadmio.
cadmium [ˈkædmiəm], *s.* (*quím.*) cadmio.
cadre [kɑːdr], *s.* armazón; plan, esquema; (*mil.*) cuadro, mandos.
caducity [kəˈdjuːsiti], *s.* caducidad.
cæcum [ˈsiːkəm], *s.* (*anat.*) intestino ciego.
Cæsarean [siˈzɛəriən], *a.* cesáreo.
cæsura [siˈzjuərə], *s.* (*poét.*) cesura.
cæsural [siˈzjuərəl], *a.* que pertenece a la cesura.
café [ˈkæfei], *s.* café, cantina.
cafeteria [kæfiˈtiəriə], *s.* cafetería; restaurante de autoservicio.
caffeine [ˈkæfiːn], *s.* (*farm.*) cafeína.
caftan [ˈkæftən], *s.* caftán.
cage [keidʒ], *s.* jaula; camarín (*de ascensor*); fogaril. — *v.t.* enjaular.
cageling [ˈkeidʒliŋ], *s.* ave enjaulada.
cagey [ˈkeidʒi], *a.* (*fam.*) taimado, reservón.
cagmag [ˈkægmæg], *s.* carne dura.
cahoots [kəˈhuːts], *s.pl.* (*Am.*, *fam.*) acuerdo, arreglo, combinación; ***to go cahoots,*** asociarse, compincharse; ***in cahoots,*** compinchados, confabulados.
caic, caique [kɑːˈik], *s.* (*mar.*) caique.
cairn [kɛən], *s.* montón de piedras.
caisson [ˈkeisən], *s.* cajón; arcón; (*mil.*) carro de municiones; furgón de artillería; (*mar.*) camello; compuerta de dique; (*arq.*) artesón, casetón.
caitiff [ˈkeitif], *a.* ruin, bellaco. — *s.* miserable, canalla, *m.*
cajole [kəˈdʒoul], *v.t.* engatusar, enlabiar, camelar; lisonjear, halagar; ***cajole a person into doing sth.,*** conseguir con zalamerías que una persona haga algo.
cajoler [kəˈdʒoulə], *s.* engatusador, zalamero; lisonjeador.
cajolery [kəˈdʒouləri], *s.* engatusamiento, zalamería; halago, lisonja.
cake [keik], *s.* pastel; tarta; ***cake of soap,*** pastilla de jabón; (*fam.*) ***a piece of cake,*** pan comido; (*fig.*) ***to sell like hot cakes,*** venderse de miedo; (*fig.*) ***that takes the cake,*** es el colmo; ***you cannot have your cake and eat it,*** no se puede nadar y guardar la ropa. — *v.i.* hacerse una costra.
caking-coal [ˈkeikiŋ-koul], *s.* (*min.*) hulla grasa.
calabash [ˈkæləbæʃ], *s.* calabaza curada.
calabash tree [ˈkæləbæʃ triː], *s.* calabazo.
Calabrian [kəˈlæbriən], *a.*, *s.* calabrés.
caladium [kəˈleidiəm], *s.* (*bot.*) caladio.
calamine [ˈkæləmain], *s.* calamina.
calamint [ˈkæləmint], *s.* (*bot.*) calamento.
calamitous [kəˈlæmitəs], *a.* calamitoso, desastroso.
calamity [kəˈlæmiti], *s.* calamidad, desastre.
calamus [ˈkæləməs], *s.* (*bot.*) cálamo.
calander [kəˈlændə], *s.* (*orn.*) calandria.
calash [kəˈlæʃ], *s.* calesa.
calcareous [kælˈkɛəriəs], *a.* calcáreo, calizo.
calceolaria [kælsiəˈlɛəriə], *s.* (*bot.*) calceolaria.
calcic [ˈkælsik], *a.* cálcico.
calciferous [kælˈsifərəs], *a.* calcífero.
calcinable [ˈkælsinəbl], *a.* calcinable.
calcinate [ˈkælsineit], *v.t.* calcinar.
calcination [kælsiˈneiʃən], *s.* calcinación.
calcine [ˈkælsain], *v.t.* calcinar. — *v.i.* calcinarse.
calcining-furnace [ˈkælsainiŋ-ˈfəːnis], *s.* horno de calcinación.

calcite [ˈkælsait], *s.* (*quím.*) calcites.
calcium [ˈkælsiəm], *s.* (*quím.*) calcio.
calcographer [kælˈkɔgrəfə], *s.* calcógrafo.
calc-spar [ˈkælk-ˈspɑ:], *s.* espato calcáreo.
calculable [ˈkælkjuləbl], *a.* calculable.
calculary [ˈkælkjuləri], *a.* (*med.*) calculoso.
calculate [ˈkælkjuleit], *v.t.* calcular; computar. — *v.i.* calcular; ***calculate on,*** contar con.
calculated [ˈkælkjuleitid], *a.* calculado; premeditado, intencionado.
calculating [ˈkælkjuleitiŋ], *a.* calculador; cerebral, frío; ***calculating machine,*** (máquina) calculadora, computadora.
calculation [kælkjuˈleiʃən], *s.* cálculo, cómputo.
calculative [ˈkælkjuleitiv], *a.* calculatorio.
calculator [ˈkælkjuleitə], *s.* calculador.
calculatory [ˈkælkjuleitəri], *a.* calculatorio.
calculose, calculous [ˈkælkjulous, -əs], *a.* (*med.*) calculoso.
calculus [ˈkælkjuləs], *s.* (*med.*, *mat.*) cálculo.
caldron [ˈkɔ:ldrən], *s.* caldero, caldera.
Caledonian [kæliˈdouniən], *a.*, *s.* caledonio.
calefacient [kæliˈfeiʃənt], *a.*, *s.* calefaciente.
calefaction [kæliˈfækʃən], *s.* calefacción.
calefactive, calefactory [kæliˈfæktiv, -təri], *a.* calefactorio.
calefy [ˈkælifai], *v.t.* calentar.
calendar [ˈkæləndə], *s.* calendario; lista.
calender [ˈkæləndə], *s.* calandria. — *v.t.* calandrar.
calenderer [kæˈlendərə], *s.* calandrador, satinador.
calendering [ˈkæləndriŋ], *s.* acción de calandrar *o* satinar.
calends [ˈkæləndz], *s.pl.* calendas, *f.pl.*
calenture [ˈkæləntʃə], *s.* calentura, fiebre violenta.
calf [kɑ:f], *s.* (*pl.* **calves** [kɑ:vz]) becerro, ternero, ternera; cervatillo; piel de becerro; pantorrilla; ***calf-love,*** amores primerizos, *m.pl.*; (*fig.*) ***to kill the fatted calf,*** agasajar *o* festejar opíparamente.
calf-like [ˈkɑ:f-laik], *a.* aternerado, semejante a un ternero.
calfskin [ˈkɑ:fskin], *s.* becerrillo, becerro *o* piel de ternero.
calibrate [ˈkælibreit], *v.t.* calibrar, graduar.
calibration [kæliˈbreiʃən], *s.* calibración, graduación.
calibre [ˈkælibə], *s.* calibre; (*fig.*) capacidad; aptitud; valer, categoría.
calico [ˈkælikou], *s.* calicó; percal.
calidity [kəˈliditi], *s.* calor, encendimiento.
caligation [kæliˈgeiʃən], *s.* (*med.*) caligo.
caliginous [kəˈlidʒinəs], *a.* caliginoso, oscuro.
caliginousness [kəˈlidʒinəsnis], *s.* oscuridad.
caliper(s) [ˈkælipə(z)], [CALLIPERS].
caliph [ˈkeilif], *s.* califa, *m.*
caliphate [ˈkælifit], *s.* califato.
calix [CALYX].
calk (1) [kɔ:k], *v.t.* (*vet.*) herrar a ramplón.
calk (2) [CAULK].
calk (3) [kɔ:k], *v.t.* calcar.
calkin [ˈkælkin], *s.* (*vet.*) ramplón de herradura.
calking-iron [ˈkɔ:lkiŋ-ˈaiən], *s.* esclopo de calafate.
call [kɔ:l], *s.* llamada; grito; invitación; visita; escala (*barco, avión*); (*for.*) citación; reclamo (*pájaro*); (*caz.*) chilla; obligación; petición, demanda; llamamiento; vocación; ***call-boy,*** botones, mozo; ***call-box,*** cabina telefónica; ***call-girl,*** chica de cita; ***on call,*** disponible; ***within call,*** al alcance de la voz. — *v.t.* llamar; convocar; anunciar, proclamar, pregonar; nombrar; apelar, invocar; ***call it ten miles,*** digamos (que) unas diez millas; ***call attention to,*** llamar la atención sobre; ***call away,*** llamar a otro sitio; ***call back,*** hacer volver; (*tele.*) volver a llamar; ***call a bluff,*** descubrir un farol; ***call down,*** hacer bajar; ***call forth,*** hacer venir *o* salir; suscitar; provocar; ***call in,*** hacer entrar; retirar; hacer venir; ***call names,*** injuriar, insultar; ***call off,*** cancelar, suspender; retirar; ***call out,*** hacer salir; ***call together,*** reunir, convocar; ***call to mind,*** recordar; ***call up,*** hacer subir; evocar, recordar; llamar a filas; ***to be called upon,*** ser llamado. — *v.i.* gritar, vocear; hacer una visita, pasar, ir (a ver); ***call again,*** volver a pasar; ***call at,*** ir a, visitar, pasarse por; hacer escala en; ***call for,*** pedir, exigir, requerir; ***call on,*** visitar; pedir ayuda a; ***call out,*** gritar, vocear.
caller [ˈkɔ:lə], *s.* llamador; visita.
calligrapher, calligraphist [kəˈligrəfə, -ist], *s.* calígrafo.
calligraphic [kæliˈgræfik], *a.* caligráfico.
calligraphy [kəˈligrəfi], *s.* caligrafía.
calling [ˈkɔ:liŋ], *s.* profesión, vocación; (el) llamar.
callipers [ˈkælipəz], *s.pl.* calibrador; ***inside callipers,*** compás de calibres; ***outside callipers,*** compás de espesores; ***callipers gauge,*** calibrador.
callisthenics [kælisˈθeniks], *s.pl.* calistenia.
callose [kæˈlous], *a.* calloso.
callosity [kəˈlɔsiti], *s.* callosidad.
callous [ˈkæləs], *a.* calloso; insensible, duro, despiadado.
callousness [ˈkæləsnis], *s.* callosidad; insensibilidad, dureza.
callow [ˈkælou], *a.* inexperto, joven, ingenuo.
callus [ˈkæləs], *s.* callo.
calm [kɑ:m], *a.* tranquilo, sosegado, sereno; bonancible. — *s.* calma; sosiego, serenidad, tranquilidad; bonanza; (*mar.*) ***dead calm,*** calma chicha. — *v.t.*, *v.i.* — ***down,*** calmar(se), tranquilizar(se), sosegar(se).
calmly [ˈkɑ:mli], *adv.* sosegadamente, tranquilamente, con calma, con tranquilidad.
calmness [ˈkɑ:mnis], *s.* calma, serenidad, tranquilidad, sosiego.
calomel [ˈkæləmel], *s.* (*med.*) calomel.
caloric [kəˈlɔrik], *s.* (*fís.*) calórico.
calorific [kæləˈrifik], *a.* (*fís.*) calorífico.
calorimeter [kæləˈrimətə], *s.* (*fís.*) calorímetro.
calorimetric [ˈkæləriˈmetrik], *a.* calorimétrico.
calorimetry [kæləˈrimitri], *s.* calorimetría.
calory, calorie [ˈkæləri], *s.* caloría.
calotte [kəˈlɔt], *s.* bonete, casquete.
caltha [ˈkælθə], *s.* (*bot.*) calta, hierba centella.
caltrop [ˈkæltrəp], *s.* abrojo.
calumba [kəˈlʌmbə], *s.* (*bot.*) columbo.
calumniate [kəˈlʌmnieit], *v.t.* calumniar.
calumniation [kəlʌmniˈeiʃən], *s.* calumnia.
calumniator [kəˈlʌmnieitə], *s.* calumniador.
calumnious [kəˈlʌmniəs], *a.* calumnioso.
calumny [ˈkæləmni], *s.* calumnia, difamación.
calvary [ˈkælvəri], *s.* calvario.
calve [kɑ:v], *v.i.* parir (*la vaca*).
Calvinism [ˈkælvinizəm], *s.* calvinismo.
Calvinist [ˈkælvinist], *s.* calvinista, *m.f.*
Calvinistic [kælviˈnistik], *a.* calvinista.
calx [kælks], *s.* (*quím.*) (*pl.* **calxes, calces** [ˈkælksi:z, ˈkælsi:z]) cal, *f.*, yeso.
calycle, calycule, calyculus [ˈkælikl, -kju:l, kəˈlikjuləs], *s.* (*bot.*) calículo.
calyx [ˈkeiliks], (*pl.* **calyxes, calices** [ˈkeiliksi:z, -isi:z]) *s.* (*bot.*) cáliz.
cam [kæm], *s.* (*mec.*) leva, excéntrica; ***cam shaft,*** árbol de levas.
camber [ˈkæmbə], *s.* comba, combadura, bombeo; peralte; (*aut.*) inclinación (*de las ruedas*). — *v.t.* combar, peraltar, abombar. — *v.i.* tener comba, combarse.
cambered [ˈkæmbəd], *a.* combado, arqueado.
cambering [ˈkæmbəriŋ], *s.* comba, combadura, abombamiento.
cambial [ˈkæmbiəl], *a.* que se refiere al giro de letras.
cambist [ˈkæmbist], *s.* (*com.*) cambista, *m.f.*

cambium [ˈkæmbiəm], *s.* (*bot.*) cambium.
Cambodia [kæmˈboudiə]. Camboya.
Cambodian [kæmˈboudiən], *a.*, *s.* camboyano.
cambrel [ˈkæmbrəl], *s.* garfio de carnicería.
cambric [ˈkeimbrik], *s.* batista, holán.
came (1) [keim], *p.p.* [COME].
came (2) [keim], *s.* plomo de vidriera.
camel [ˈkæməl], *s.* camello; ***camel-driver,*** camellero; ***camel's hair,*** pelo de camello; ***she-camel,*** camella.
camellia [kəˈmi:liə], *s.* (*bot.*) camelia.
camelopard [kæˈmeləpɑ:d], *s.* camello pardal, jirafa.
cameo [ˈkæmiou], *s.* camafeo.
camera [ˈkæmərə], *s.* cámara (obscura); máquina (fotográfica); (*anat.*) cavidad; ***in camera,*** a puerta cerrada.
Cameroon [kæməˈru:n]. (el) Camerún.
Cameroonian [kæməˈru:niən], *a.*, *s.* camerunés, *m.*
camisade [kæmiˈseid], *s.* (*mil.*) encamisada.
camisole [ˈkæmisoul], *s.* camiseta, cubrecorsé.
camlet [ˈkæmlit], *s.* camelote, barragán.
camomile [ˈkæməmail], *s.* (*bot.*) manzanilla, camomila.
camouflage [ˈkæmuflɑ:ʒ], *s.* camuflaje. — *v.t.* camuflar.
camp (1) [kæmp], *a.* de campamento; de campaña; ***camp bed,*** catre de campaña; ***camp follower,*** prostituta que sigue a un ejército en campaña; (*fig.*) simpatizante, secuaz; ***camp stool,*** taburete plegable. — *s.* campamento; campo; ***to break camp,*** levantar el campo, alzar el real; ***to pitch camp,*** acampar, asentar los reales. — *v.t.*, *v.i.* acampar.
camp (2) [kæmp], *a.* (*fam.*) camp; cursi.
campaign [kæmˈpein], *s.* (*mil.*) campaña. — *v.i.* salir a campaña; hacer campaña *o* propaganda.
campaigner [kæmˈpeinə], *s.* (*mil.*) veterano; propagandista, *m.f.*
campanile [kæmpəˈni:li], *s.* campanil, campanario.
campanology [kæmpəˈnɔlədʒi], *s.* campanalogía.
campanula [kæmˈpænjulə], *s.* (*bot.*) campánula.
campanulate [kæmˈpænjuleit], *a.* campaniforme.
campeachy [kæmˈpi:tʃi], *s.* palo de Campeche.
camper [ˈkæmpə], *s.* acampador.
camphine [ˈkæmfi:n], *s.* espíritu de trementina.
camphor [ˈkæmfə], *s.* alcanfor. — *v.t.* alcanforar.
camphorate [ˈkæmfəreit], *a.* alcanforado. — *s.* canforato. — *v.t.* alcanforar.
camphorated oil [ˈkæmfəreitid ˈɔil], *s.* ungüento alcanforado.
camphor-tree [ˈkæmfə-tri:], *s.* alcanforero.
camping [ˈkæmpiŋ], *s.* camping; ***camping-site,*** camping; ***to go camping,*** hacer camping.
campion [ˈkæmpiən], *s.* (*bot.*) colleja.
campshed [ˈkæmpʃed], *v.t.* reforzar con estacados.
campus [ˈkæmpəs], *s.* campus, recinto.
can (1) [kæn], *s.* lata, bote; envase; (*fam.*, *fig.*) ***to carry the can,*** pagar el pato. — *v.t.* conservar (en lata), enlatar; (*fam.*) ***can it!*** ¡cállate!
can (2) [kæn], *pres. ind. v. defec. aux.* poder; saber.
Canaanite [ˈkeinənait], *a.*, *s.* cananeo.
Canada [ˈkænədə]. (el) Canadá.
Canadian [kəˈneidiən], *a.*, *s.* canadiense.
canal [kəˈnæl], *s.* canal; acequia; (*arq.*) estría.
canalage [ˈkænəlidʒ], *s.* sistema de canales, *m.*
canalization [kænəlaiˈzeiʃən], *s.* canalización.
canapé [ˈkænəpei], *s.* (*coc.*) tapa.
canard [kæˈnɑ:d], *s.* (*fam.*, *fig.*) bola.
Canaries [kəˈnɛəriz], **the.** [CANARY ISLANDS].
canary [kəˈnɛəri], *s.* canario; ***canary seed,*** alpiste.
Canary Islands [kəˈnɛəri ˈailəndz]. (las) Canarias.
cancel [ˈkænsəl], *v.t.* cancelar, suprimir, anular; matar.
cancellation [kænsəˈleiʃən], *s.* cancelación, supresión, anulación; (el) matar; matasellos.
Cancer [ˈkænsə], *s.* (*astron.*, *astrol.*) Cáncer.
cancer [ˈkænsə], *s.* cáncer.
cancerate [ˈkænsəreit], *v.i.* cancerarse, encancerarse.
canceration [kænsəˈreiʃən], *s.* ulceración cancerosa.
cancerous [ˈkænsərəs], *a.* canceroso.
cancriform [ˈkæŋkrifɔ:m], *a.* cancriforme.
cancrine [ˈkæŋkri:n], *a.* cancriforme.
cancrinite [ˈkænkrinait], *s.* (*min.*) cancrinita.
cancrite [ˈkæŋkrait], *s.* (*zool.*) cancrito.
candelabrum [kændəˈlɑ:brəm], *s.* (*pl.* **candelabra** [-brə]) candelabro.
candent [ˈkændənt], *a.* candente.
Candian [ˈkændiən], *a.*, *s.* candiota.
candid [ˈkændid], *a.* franco.
candidate [ˈkændideit], *s.* candidato; aspirante; examinando; opositor; pretendiente.
candidateship, candidature [ˈkændidətʃip, -tʃə], *s.* candidatura.
candidly [ˈkændidli], *adv.* francamente, a decir verdad, con toda franqueza.
candidness [ˈkændidnis], [CANDOUR].
candied [ˈkændid], *a.* azucarado, almibarado.
candle [kændl], *s.* vela; candela, bujía; cirio; ***candle-end,*** cabo de vela; ***candle-holder,*** portavela, *m.*; ***candle-snuffer,*** despabilador; ***candle-stick,*** candelero; palmatoria; ***candle-wick,*** pabilo, mecha; ***to burn the candle at both ends,*** agotarse; ***he can't hold a candle to him,*** no le llega (ni) a la suela del zapato; (*fam.*) ***not to be worth the candle,*** no valer *o* merecer la pena.
Candlemas [ˈkændlməs], *s.* Candelaria.
canned [kænd], *a.* en conserva, en lata; (*fam.*) bebido; ***canned music,*** música grabada.
candour [ˈkændə], *s.* franqueza.
candy [ˈkændi], *s.* azúcar cande, cande; (*Am.*) dulce, confite, bombón, caramelo. — *v.t.* confitar, escarchar, garapiñar. — *v.i.* confitarse, garapiñarse.
candyfloss [ˈkændiflɔs], *s.* algodón dulce *o* de caramelo *o* de azúcar.
candytuft [ˈkænditʌft], *s.* (*bot.*) carraspique.
cane [kein], *s.* caña; rota; junco de Indias; bastón; vara, palmeta; urdimbre (*de la seda*); ***cane sugar,*** azúcar de caña; ***sugar cane,*** caña de azúcar. — *v.t.* dar con la palmeta a, varear.
canella [kəˈnelə], *s.* (*bot.*) canelo, canela.
canescence [kəˈnesəns], *s.* blancura.
canescent [kəˈnesənt], *a.* canoso, que blanquea, blanquecino.
Canicula [kəˈnikjulə]. (*astron.*) Canícula, Sirio.
canicular [kəˈnikjulə], *a.* canicular.
canine [ˈkænain], *a.* canino. — *s.* (diente) canino, colmillo.
caning [ˈkeiniŋ], *s.* paliza, vareo; trenzado de juncos *o* cañas.
canister [ˈkænistə], *s.* lata, bote; ***canister-shot,*** metralla.
canker [ˈkæŋkə], *s.* úlcera maligna; cancro; corrosión, gangrena. — *v.t.* gangrenar, ulcerar. — *v.i.* gangrenarse, ulcerarse, corroerse.
cankered [ˈkæŋkəd], *a.* ulcerado, gangrenado; (*fig.*) agriado, virulento.
cankerous [ˈkæŋkərəs], *a.* gangrenoso, canceroso; corrosivo.
cankerworm [ˈkæŋkəwə:m], *s.* oruga dañina.
cankery [ˈkænkəri], *a.* gangrenado.
cannabis [ˈkænəbis], *s.* (*bot.*) cáñamo.
cannel-coal [ˈkænəl-coul], *s.* hulla grasa.
cannery [ˈkænəri], *s.* fábrica de conservas.
cannibal [ˈkænibəl], *s.* caníbal, antropófago.
cannibalism [ˈkænibəlizəm], *s.* canibalismo.
cannibalize [ˈkænibəlaiz], *v.t.* someter al canibalismo, practicar el canibalismo en; (*mec.*) desmontar (maquinaria) para alargar la vida de otra.
cannikin [ˈkænikin], *s.* cubo, balde; vaso de metal.

canning [ˈkæniŋ], *s.* envasado, enlatado.
cannon [ˈkænən], *s.* cañón (de artillería); (billar) carambola; ***cannon fodder,*** carne de cañón; ***cannon shot,*** cañonazo, tiro de cañón. — *v.i.* hacer carambolas; entrechocar.
cannon-ball [ˈkænən-bɔ:l], *s.* bala de cañón.
cannon-foundry [ˈkænən-ˈfaundri], *s.* fundición de cañones.
cannon-hole [ˈkænən-houl], *s.* (*mar.*) tronera.
cannon-proof [ˈkænən-pru:f], *a.* a prueba de cañón.
cannonade [kænəˈneid], *s.* cañoneo. — *v.t.* cañonear.
cannot [ˈkænət], *contr. de* **can** *y* **not.** [CAN (2)].
cannula [ˈkænjulə], *s.* (*med.*) cánula.
cannular [ˈkænjulə], *a.* canular.
canny [ˈkæni], *a.* (*Esco.*) sagaz, astuto; cuco.
canoe [kəˈnu:], *s.* piragua; canoa. — *v.i.* ir en canoa.
canoeing [kəˈnu:iŋ], *s.* piragüismo.
canon [ˈkænən], *s.* canónigo; canon, regla, precepto; ***canon law,*** cánones, derecho canónico.
canoness [ˈkænənes], *s.* canonesa.
canonical [kəˈnɔnikəl], *a.* canónico.
canonicals [kəˈnɔnikəlz], *s.pl.* hábito eclesiástico.
canonicate [kəˈnɔnikit], *s.* canonicato.
canonist [ˈkænənist], *s.* canonista, *m.*
canonization [kænənaiˈzeiʃən], *s.* canonización.
canonize [ˈkænənaiz], *v.t.* canonizar.
canonry [ˈkænənri], *s.* canonjía, canonicato.
Canopus [kəˈnoupəs], *s.* (*astron.*) Canopea.
canopy [ˈkænəpi], *s.* dosel; palio; bóveda; cielo (*de cama*); ***canopy of heaven,*** bóveda del cielo. — *v.t.* endoselar, cubrir con dosel.
canorous [kəˈnɔ:rəs], *a.* canoro.
cant (1) [kænt], *s.* fariseísmo, hipocresía; jerga, germanía. — *v.i.* camandulear, hablar con hipocresía.
cant (2) [kænt], *s.* sesgo, inclinación. — *v.t.* ladear, inclinar, poner al sesgo; volcar. — *v.t., v.i.* — ***over,*** ladear(se), volcar(se).
can't [kɑ:nt], *contr. de* **can** *y* **not.** [CAN (2)].
Cantabrian [kənˈtæbriən], *a.* cantábrico. — *s.* cántabro.
Cantabrigian [kæntəˈbridʒiən], *a., s.* (natural) de Cambridge.
cantaloup [ˈkæntəlu:p], *s.* melón de Cantalú.
cantankerous [kænˈtæŋkərəs], *a.* (*fam.*) atravesado, difícil, contreras, puñetero; malhumorado.
cantata [kænˈtɑ:tə], *s.* (*mús.*) cantata.
canteen [kænˈti:n], *s.* cantina; cantimplora.
canter [ˈkæntə], *s.* medio galope. — *v.i.* andar a medio galope.
cantharides [kænˈθæridi:z], *s.pl.* cantáridas, *f.pl.*
canticle [ˈkæntikl], *s.* cántico.
cantilever [ˈkæntili:və], *s.* viga voladiza; puente voladizo.
cantillate [ˈkæntileit], *v.t.* canturrear.
cantillation [kæntiˈleiʃən], *s.* canturreo.
canting [ˈkæntiŋ], *a.* hipócrita. — *s.* hipocresía.
cantle [kæntl], *s.* arzón (*de la silla de montar*).
canto [ˈkæntou], *s.* canto.
canton [ˈkæntən], *s.* cantón. — *v.t.* acantonar, acuartelar.
cantonal [ˈkæntənəl], *a.* cantonal.
cantonize [ˈkæntənaiz], *v.t.* acantonar.
cantonment [kənˈtɔnmənt, -ˈtu:nmənt], *s.* acantonamiento; cuartel, campamento.
cantor [ˈkæntə], *s.* chantre.
canula [ˈkænjulə], *s.* cánula.
canvas [ˈkænvəs], *s.* lona; cañamazo; (*pint.*) tela, lienzo; (*mar.*) velamen, trapo; toldo; tienda; (*fig.*) carpa, circo.
canvass [ˈkænvəs], *s.* recorrido en busca de votos; examen, inspección, escrutinio. — *v.t.* escudriñar. — *v.i.* solicitar votos.
canvasser [ˈkænvəsə], *s.* solicitador; agente electoral.
cany [ˈkeini], *a.* encañado; lleno de juncos.
canyon [ˈkænjən], *s.* cañón, garganta, desfiladero, barranca.
canzonet [kænzəˈnet], *s.* cantilena, cancioncilla.
caoutchouc [ˈkautʃu:k], *s.* caucho, gutapercha, goma elástica.
cap [kæp], *s.* gorro, gorra; birrete, solideo; casquete; birreta, capelo; cofia; cima, cumbre; colmo; (*arq.*) chapitel; (*mec.*) casquillo, sombrerete; (*mec.*) tapa; detonador, pistón; cápsula; ***percussion cap,*** detonante, fulminante; ***cap in hand,*** humildemente; ***if the cap fits,*** si te sientes aludido, si es tu caso; ***to put on one's thinking cap,*** ponerse a reflexionar; ***to set one's cap at,*** poner los puntos a. — *v.t.* cubrir; capsular, poner tapa, casquillo etc. a; poner cima *o* remate a; coronar; superar; dar el espaldarazo a; ***to cap it all,*** para remate. — *v.i.* descubrirse (*para saludar*).
capability [keipəˈbiliti], *s.* capacidad; competencia.
capable [ˈkeipəbl], *a.* capaz; apto, competente.
capacious [kəˈpeiʃəs], *a.* capaz; amplio, espacioso.
capaciousness [kəˈpeiʃəsnis], *s.* capacidad, cabida.
capacitate [kəˈpæsiteit], *v.t.* habilitar, hacer capaz; autorizar.
capacity [kəˈpæsiti], *s.* capacidad; cabida; poder, facultad; ***in the capacity of,*** en calidad de.
caparison [kəˈpærizn], *s.* caparazón, gualdrapa; jaeces, avíos. — *v.t.* engualdrapar, enjaezar; ataviar.
cape (1) [keip], *s.* cabo, promontorio; ***to round a cape,*** doblar un cabo.
cape (2) [keip], *s.* capa, esclavina, manteleta.
capelin [ˈkæpəlin], *s.* (*ict.*) capelán.
capeline [ˈkæpəlin], *s.* (*cir.*) capellina.
Capella [kəˈpelə], *s.* (*astron.*) cabrilla.
capellet [ˈkæpəlit], *s.* (*vet.*) esparaván.
caper (1) [ˈkeipə], *s.* cabriola, zapateta, travesura; ***to cut a caper,*** hacer una cabriola. — *v.i.* cabriolar, triscar, hacer cabriolas.
caper (2) [ˈkeipə], *s.* (*bot.*) alcaparra; ***caper-bush,*** alcaparro.
capercaillie, capercailzie [kæpəˈkeilji, -ˈkeilzi], *s.* (*orn.*) urogallo.
caperer [ˈkeipərə], *s.* saltarín, retozón.
capias [ˈkeipiæs], *s.* (*for.*) orden de arresto.
capillaceous [kæpiˈleiʃəs], *a.* (*bot.*) capiláceo.
capillament [kəˈpiləmənt], *s.* (*bot.*) hebra de flor; (*anat.*) fibra.
capillarity [kæpiˈlæriti], *s.* capilaridad.
capillary [kəˈpiləri], *a.* capilar.
capital [ˈkæpitl], *a.* capital; magnífico, excelente; (*for.*) ***capital punishment,*** pena de muerte; (*for.*) ***capital sentence,*** sentencia de muerte. — *s.* (*com.*) capital, *m.*; capital (*city*), *f.*; (*arq.*) capitel; (*gram.*) mayúscula; ***to make capital out of,*** sacar partido de, aprovecharse de.
capitalist [ˈkæpitəlist], *s.* capitalista, *m.f.*
capitalistic [kæpitəˈlistik], *a.* capitalista.
capitalization [kæpitələiˈzeiʃən], *s.* capitalización.
capitalize [ˈkæpitəlaiz], *v.t.* capitalizar; poner con mayúscula. — *v.i.* capitalizar; ***capitalize on,*** aprovecharse de.
capital ship [ˈkæpitəl ˈʃip], *s.* acorazado grande.
capitate [ˈkæpiteit], *a.* (*bot.*) capitado.
capitation [kæpiˈteiʃən], *s.* capitación.
Capitol [ˈkæpitɔl], *s.* Capitolio.
capitular [kəˈpitjulə], *a., s.* capitular.
capitulary [kəˈpitjuləri], *a.* capitular.
capitulate [kəˈpitjuleit], *v.i.* capitular.
capitulation [kəpitjuˈleiʃən], *s.* capitulación.
capon [ˈkeipən], *s.* capón. — *v.t.* capar.
caponet [ˈkeipənet], *s.* caponcillo.
caponiere [keipəˈniə], *s.* (*fort.*) caponera.
capote [kəˈpout], *s.* capote; capota.
capric [ˈkæprik], *a.* cáprico.

caprice [kə'pri:s], *s.* capricho, antojo; veleidad.
capricious [kə'priʃəs], *a.* caprichoso, antojadizo; veleidoso.
capriciousness [kə'priʃəsnis], *s.* (lo) caprichoso, (lo) veleidoso.
Capricorn ['kæprikɔ:n]. (*atron.*, *astrol.*) Capricornio.
capriole ['kæprioul], *s.* cabriola. — *v.i.* cabriolar.
capsicum ['kæpsikəm], *s.* (*bot.*) pimiento.
capsize [kæp'saiz], *v.t.*, *v.i.* volcar.
capstan ['kæpstən], *s.* cabrestante.
capstone ['kæpstoun], *s.* (*arq.*) coronamiento.
capsular ['kæpsjulə], *a.* capsular.
capsule ['kæpsju:l], *s.* cápsula.
captain ['kæptin], *s.* capitán. — *v.t.* capitanear.
captaincy, captainship ['kæptinsi, -ʃip], *s.* capitanía.
caption ['kæpʃən], *s.* pie, leyenda; texto; encabezamiento; subtítulo.
captious ['kæpʃəs], *a.* reparón, criticón; quisquilloso.
captiousness ['kæpʃəsnis], *s.* condición de reparón.
captivate ['kæptiveit], *v.t.* cautivar.
captivating ['kæptiveitiŋ], *a.* cautivador, encantador, seductor.
captivation [kæpti'veiʃən], *s.* encanto, fascinación, seducción.
captive ['kæptiv], *a.*, *s.* cautivo.
captivity [kæp'tiviti], *s.* cautiverio, cautividad.
captor ['kæptə], *s.* captor, apresador.
capture ['kæptʃə], *s.* captura; apresamiento; toma; presa, botín. — *v.t.* apresar, prender, capturar; (*mil.*) tomar.
capuchin ['kæpjutʃin], *s.* capuchino; capucho, capuchón.
capulet ['kæpjulit], *s.* (*vet.*) esparaván.
car [kɑ:], *s.* coche, automóvil; carro; camarín, caja (*de ascensor*); barquilla (*de globo*); ***dining-car,*** coche restaurante; ***sleeping-car,*** coche cama; ***tram-car,*** tranvía.
carabine ['kærəbain], *s.* [CARBINE].
carabineer, carabinier [kærəbi'niə], *s.* carabinero.
caracal ['kærəkl], *s.* lince de Persia, caracal.
caracole ['kærəkəl], *s.* caracol; (*equit.*) caracoleo; escalera caracol. — *v.i.* caracolear.
carafe [kə'ræf], *s.* garrafa.
caramel ['kærəmel], *s.* caramelo, azúcar quemado.
caramelize ['kærəməlaiz], *v.t.* acaramelar.
carapace ['kærəpeis], *s.* carapacho, caparazón.
carat ['kærət], *s.* quilate (*peso*).
caravan ['kærəvæn], *s.* caravana; carricoche; remolque, roulotte.
caravaneer [kærəvə'niə], *s.* caravanero; miembro de una caravana.
caravanserai, caravansary, caravansery [kærə'vænsərai, -i, -i], *s.* caravanera, caravanseray.
caravel ['kærəvel], *s.* (*mar.*) carabela.
caraway ['kærəwei], *s.* (*bot.*) alcaravea; ***caraway-seed,*** carvi.
carbide ['kɑ:baid], *s.* (*quím.*) carburo.
carbine ['kɑ:bain], *s.* carabina.
carbolic [kɑ:'bɔlik], *a.* carbólico.
carbon ['kɑ:bən], *s.* (*quím.*) carbono; (*aut.*) carboncilla; ***carbon copy,*** copia en papel carbón.
carbonaceous [kɑ:bə'neiʃəs], *a.* carbonoso.
carbonarism [kɑ:bə'nɑ:rizəm], *s.* carbonarismo.
carbonaro [kɑ:bə'nɑ:rou], *s.* carbonario.
carbonate ['kɑ:bəneit], *s.* (*quím.*) carbonato. — *v.t.* carbonatar.
carbonic [kɑ:'bɔnik], *a.* carbónico.
carboniferous [kɑ:bə'nifərəs], *a.* carbonífero.
carbonization [kɑ:bənai'zeiʃən], *s.* carbonización.
carbonize ['kɑ:bənaiz], *v.t.* carbonizar.
carboy ['kɑ:bɔi], *s.* damajuana, garrafón, bombona.
carbuncle ['kɑ:bʌŋkl], s. carbunclo, carbúnculo; (*med.*) carbunco.
carbuncled ['kɑ:bʌŋkld], *a.* con carbunclos; (*med.*) carbuncoso.
carbuncular [kɑ:'bʌŋkjulə], *a.* carbuncal.
carburet ['kɑ:bjuret], *v.t.*, *v.i.* carburar.
carburettor ['kɑ:bjuretə], *s.* carburador.
carburometer [kɑ:bju'rɔmitə], *s.* carburómetro.
carcanet ['kɑ:kənet], *s.* gargantilla.
carcass, carcase ['kɑ:kəs], *s.* cadáver; res muerta, canal; armazón, esqueleto; (*mil.*) carcasa; (*fam.*) corpacho.
carcinoma [kɑ:si'noumə], *s.* (*med.*) carcinoma.
carcinomatous [kɑ:si'noumətəs], *a.* (*med.*) carcinomatoso.
card (1) [kɑ:d], *s.* tarjeta; carta; ficha; rosa náutica; (*fam.*) tío *o* tipo salado *u* ocurrente; ***post-card,*** (tarjeta) postal; ***visiting-card,*** tarjeta de visita; ***pack of cards,*** baraja de cartas *o* de naipes; ***card game,*** juego de cartas; ***game of cards,*** partida de cartas; ***card-case,*** tarjetero; (***index-***) ***card catalogue,*** catálogo de fichas, fichero; ***it's on the cards,*** es probable, a lo mejor; ***to have a card up one's sleeve,*** querdarle a uno un recurso; ***to put one's cards on the table,*** poner las cartas boca arriba; ***like a pack of cards,*** como un castillo de naipes.
card (2) [kɑ:d], *s.* carda, cardencha. — *v.t.* cardar.
cardamine ['kɑ:dəmain], *s.* (*bot.*) mastuerzo de prado.
cardamom ['kɑ:dəməm], *s.* (*bot.*) cardamomo.
cardboard ['kɑ:dbɔ:d], *s.* cartón.
carder ['kɑ:də], *s.* cardador.
cardiac ['kɑ:diæk], *a.* cardíaco.
cardialgia [kɑ:di'ældʒə], *s.* cardialegia.
cardigan ['kɑ:digən], *s.* chaqueta de punto, rebeca.
cardinal ['kɑ:dinəl], *a.* cardinal. — *s.* cardenal.
cardinalate, cardinalship ['kɑ:dinəlit, -ʃip], *s.* cardenalato.
carding ['kɑ:diŋ], *s.* cardadura.
cardiogram ['kɑ:diogræm], *s.* cardiograma, *m.*
cardiograph ['kɑ:diogræf], *s.* cardiógrafo.
cardiology [kɑ:di'ɔlədʒi], *s.* cardiología.
carditis [kɑ:'daitis], *s.* (*med.*) carditis, *f. inv.*
cardmaker ['kɑ:dmeikə], *s.* fabricante de cartas (*de juego*).
cardoon [kɑ:'du:n], *s.* (*bot.*) cardo silvestre.
card-sharper ['kɑ:d-ʃɑ:pə], *s.* fullero, tahur.
care [kɛə], *s.* cuidado, atención; cuita, inquietud, preocupación; cargo, custodia; ***great*** *o* ***meticulous care,*** esmero; ***to take care,*** tener cuidado; ***to take care of,*** cuidar (de); ocuparse de, atender a; ***take care not to get wet!*** ¡(mucho) cuidado con mojarse! — *v.i.* cuidar, tener cuidado; ***care about,*** preocuparse de *o* por; ***care*** (***deeply***) ***for,*** querer; ***I don't care for him,*** no me gusta; ***would you care for a drink?*** ¿quiere una copa? ¿le apetece una copa?; ***he doesn't care,*** le trae sin cuidado.
careen [kə'ri:n], *s.* (*mar.*) carena. — *v.t.*, *v.i.* (*mar.*) carenar.
careenage [kə'ri:nidʒ], *s.* (*mar.*) carena, carenadura; carenaje; carenero.
career [kə'riə], *a.* de carrera; ***career diplomat,*** diplomático de carrera. — *s.* carrera; profesión. — *v.i.* ir a todo correr, correr a carrera tendida.
carefree ['kɛəfri:], *a.* libre de cuidados; despreocupado.
careful ['kɛəful], *a.* cuidadoso; esmerado; prudente; ***to be careful,*** tener cuidado.
carefulness ['kɛəfulnis], *s.* cuidado, cautela, vigilancia, atención.
careless ['kɛəlis], *a.* descuidado, negligente; falto de cuidado; dejado.
carelessness ['kɛəlisnis], *s.* descuido, incuria, negligencia, falta de cuidado.
caress [kə'res], *s.* caricia. — *v.t.* acariciar.

caressing [kə'resiŋ], *a.* acariciante, acariciador.
caret ['kærət], *s.* (*impr.*) signo de intercalación.
caretaker ['kɛəteikə], *s.* custodio; conserje, portero, portera.
cargo ['kɑ:gou], *s.* carga, cargamento; consignación.
Caribbean ['kæri'biən], *a.* caribe; ***Caribbean Sea,*** Mar Caribe.
caribou ['kæribu:], *s.* (*zool.*) caribú, reno norteamericano.
caricature ['kærikətʃuə], *s.* caricatura. — *v.t.* caricaturizar.
caricaturist ['kærikətʃuərist], *s.* caricaturista, *m.f.*
caried ['kɛəri:d], *a.* cariado.
caries ['kɛəri:z], *s.* (*med.*) caries, *f. inv.*
carillon [kə'riljən], *s.* carillón; toque *o* repique de carillón. — *v.i.* tocar el carillón.
carina [kə'ri:nə], *s.* (*bot.*) carena.
carinate, carinated ['kærineit, -id], *a.* carenado.
cariosity [kæri'ɔsiti], *s.* (*med.*) caries, *f. inv.*
carious ['kɛəriəs], *a.* cariado.
carking ['kɑ:kiŋ], *a.* molesto, penoso, inquietante.
carline ['kɑ:lin], *s.* carlín; (*bot.*) carlina.
carling ['kɑ:liŋ], *s.* (*mar.*) carlinga.
Carlism ['kɑ:lizəm], *s.* carlismo.
Carlist ['kɑ:list], *s.* carlista, *m.f.*
car-load ['kɑ:-loud], *s.* carretada; carga de un vagón.
Carlovingian [kɑ:lo'vindʒiən], *a.*, *s.* carlovingio [CAROLINGIAN].
carman ['kɑ:mən], *s.* carretero, carretonero.
Carmelite ['kɑ:məlait], *a.*, *s.* carmelita.
carmine ['kɑ:main], *s.* carmín, carmesí.
carnage ['kɑ:nidʒ], *s.* carnicería, matanza.
carnal ['kɑ:nəl], *s.* carnal.
carnality [kɑ:'næliti], *s.* carnalidad.
carnalize ['kɑ:nəlaiz], *v.t.* hacer carnal, excitar la sensualidad de.
carnallite ['kɑ:nəlait], *s.* carnalita.
carnation [kɑ:'neiʃən], *a.* encarnado. — *s.* (*bot.*) clavel.
carneous ['kɑ:niəs], *a.* carnoso.
carnification [kɑ:nifi'keiʃən], *s.* (*med.*) carnificación.
carnify ['kɑ:nifai], *v.i.* carnificarse.
carnival ['kɑ:nivl], *s.* carnaval; feria; (*Am.*) parque de atracciones, *m.*
Carnivora [kɑ:'nivərə], *s.pl.* (*zool.*) carnívoros, *m.pl.*
carnivorous [kɑ:'nivərəs], *a.* carnívoro.
carnous ['kɑ:nəs], *a.* carnoso.
carob ['kærəb], *s.* (*bot.*) algarroba; ***carob tree,*** algarrobo.
carol ['kærəl], *s.* villancico; canción alegre; gorjeo, trino (*de las aves*). — *v.i.* cantar, villancicos; gorjear.
Carolingian [kæro'lindʒiən], *a.*, *s.* carolingio.
carolling ['kærəliŋ], *s.* (el) cantar villancicos; gorjeo.
carom ['kærəm], *s.* carambola. — *v.i.* hacer carambola.
carotid [kə'rɔtid], *a.*, *s.* (*anat.*) carótida.
carousal [kə'rauzəl], *s.* jarana, juerga.
carouse [kə'rauz], *v.i.* jaranear, andar de parranda, correr una juerga, juerguearse.
carouser [kə'rauzə], *s.* jaranero, juerguista.
carp [kɑ:p], *s.* (*ict.*) carpa. — *v.i.* (*fam.*) criticar, censurar, poner pegas *o* reparos.
Carpathian [kɑ:'peiθjən], *a.* de los Cárpatos.
carpel ['kɑ:pəl], *s.* (*bot.*) carpelo.
carpenter ['kɑ:pintə], *s.* carpintero.
carpentry ['kɑ:pintri], *s.* carpintería.
carper ['kɑ:pə], *s.* (*fam.*) censurador, criticón, reparón.
carpet ['kɑ:pit], *s.* alfombra; ***to be on the carpet,*** recibir una bronca. — *v.t.* alfombrar; entapizar; (*fig.*) echar un rapapolvo a.
carpet-bag ['kɑ:pit-bæg], *s.* talega *o* saco de viaje.
carpet-bagger ['kɑ:pit-bægə], *s.* (*Am.*) aventurero (político).
carpet-beater ['kɑ:pit-bi:tə], *s.* sacudidor.
carpet-beetle ['kɑ:pit-bi:tl], *s.* (*ent.*) antreno.
carpeting ['kɑ:pitiŋ], *s.* tela de alfombra; alfombrado.
carpet-layer ['kɑ:pit-leiə], *s.* alfombrista, *m.f.*
carpet-maker ['kɑ:pit-meikə], *s.* alfombrero.
carpet-slipper ['kɑ:pit-slipə], *s.* zapatilla (de fieltro).
carping ['kɑ:piŋ], *a.* (*fam.*) criticón, reparón.
carpus ['kɑ:pəs], *s.* (*anat.*) carpo.
carrageen ['kærəgi:n], *s.* musgo.
carriage ['kæridʒ], *s.* porte; conducción, transporte, acarreo; carruaje; coche; vagón; (*artill.*) cureña; (*mec.*) carro; continente; ***carriage builder,*** maestro cochero; ***carriage door,*** portezuela; ***carriage free,*** franco de porte; ***carriage paid,*** porte pagado; ***carriage and pair,*** coche de dos caballos; ***railway carriage,*** coche, vagón de tren.
carriageable ['kæridʒəbl], *a.* transportable.
carrier ['kæriə], *s.* porteador; transportista, *m.f.*; portador; mandadero; ordinario, cosario; (*mec.*) carro; (*rad.*) onda portadora; (*med.*) agente transmisor de gérmenes; ***carrier pigeon,*** paloma mensajera.
carriole ['kærioul], *s.* carruaje pequeño; (*Canadá*) trineo ornamentado.
carrion ['kæriən], *a.* podrido. — *s.* carroña.
carronade [kærə'neid], *s.* (*mil.*) carronada.
carrot ['kærət], *s.* (*bot.*) zanahoria.
carroty ['kærəti], *a.* pelirrojo, bermejo, rufo.
carry ['kæri], *v.t.* llevar; traer; llevar encima; sostener, soportar; entrañar, incluir, comprender; dirigir, impulsar; arrebatar, arrastrar; ganar (*una elección, votación*); aprobar (*una moción*); dar *o* producir (fruto); (*com.*) tener surtido de; (*mar.*) arbolar; ***carry about,*** llevar de un lado para otro; ***carry all before one,*** vencer todos los obstáculos; llevarse de calle a la gente; ***carry away,*** arrebatar, arrastrar, llevarse; (*fig.*) ***be carried away,*** entusiasmarse; ***carry coals to Newcastle,*** llevar hierro a Vizcaya; ***carry the day,*** salir victorioso, vencer; ***carry forward,*** llevar adelante; (*com.*) pasar a cuenta nueva; (*fig.*) ***carry it off,*** ganar; ***carry off,*** llevarse; ***carry on,*** llevar adelante, proseguir; ***carry out,*** llevar a cabo, realizar; (*com.*) ***carry over,*** pasar a otra columna, página *o* cuenta; ***carried over,*** suma y sigue; ***carry one's point,*** salirse con la suya; ***carry through,*** llevar a término; ***carry up,*** elevar, (hacer) subir; ***carry weight,*** tener peso, influir. — *v.i.* alcanzar, llegar, tener alcance; oírse; ***carry on,*** proseguir, continuar; persistir, perseverar; portarse; ***carry on with*** (***s.o.***), flirtear con; estar liado con; ***carry over,*** persistir, durar.
carry-over ['kæri-ouvə], *s.* sobrante, excedente, reserva; (*com.*) suma *o* saldo anterior.
carrying ['kæriiŋ], *s.* transporte.
cart [kɑ:t], *s.* carro, carreta, carretón; ***cart-wheel,*** rueda de carro; ***to put the cart before the horse,*** empezar la casa por el tejado. — *v.t.* carretear, acarrear.
cartage ['kɑ:tidʒ], *s.* carretaje, porteo, carreteo, acarreo.
carte-blanche ['kɑ:t-'blɑ:ʃ], *s.* carta blanca.
cartel [kɑ:'tel], *s.* cartel; cartel de desafío.
carter ['kɑ:tə], *s.* carretero, carromatero.
Cartesian [kɑ:'ti:ʒən], *a.*, *s.* cartesiano.
Cartesianism [kɑ:'ti:ʒənizəm], *s.* cartesianismo.
cartful ['kɑ:tful], *s.* carretada.
Carthaginian [kɑ:θə'dʒiniən], *a.*, *s.* cartaginés.

carthamus [ˈkɑːθəməs], *s.* (*bot.*) cártamo, azafrán rumí.
Carthusian [kɑːˈθjuːziən], *a.*, *s.* cartujo.
cartilage [ˈkɑːtilidʒ], *s.* (*anat.*) cartílago, ternilla.
cartilaginous [kɑːtiˈlædʒinəs], *a.* cartilaginoso; cartilagíneo.
carting [ˈkɑːtiŋ], *s.* carreteo; acarreo.
cartload [ˈkɑːtloud], *s.* carretada.
cartman [ˈkɑːtmən], *s.* carretero.
cartographer [kɑːˈtɔgrəfə], *s.* cartógrafo.
cartographic(al) [kɑːtəˈgræfik(əl)], *a.* cartográfico.
cartography [kɑːˈtɔgrəfi], *s.* cartografía.
cartomancer [ˈkɑːtomænsə], *s.* cartomántico.
cartomancy [ˈkɑːtomænsi], *s.* cartomancia.
carton [ˈkɑːtən], *s.* caja de cartón.
cartoon [kɑːˈtuːn], (*arte*) *s.* caricatura; dibujo; dibujo animado; cartón; ***strip-cartoon,*** historieta. — *v.t.* caricaturizar.
cartoonist [kɑːˈtuːnist], *s.* caricaturista, *m.f.*
cartouche [kɑːˈtuːʃ], *s.* cartucho; cartela.
cartridge [ˈkɑːtridʒ], *s.* cartucho; ***blank cartridge,*** cartucho sin bala; ***cartridge-belt, cartridge-box,*** cartuchera; ***cartridge-case,*** casco de cartucho; ***cartridge-clip,*** peine de balas.
cart-rut [ˈkɑːt-rʌt], *s.* carril, rodada.
cartulary [ˈkɑːtjuləri], *s.* cartulario.
cartwright [ˈkɑːtrait], *s.* carretero.
caruncle [ˈkærəŋkl], *s.* (*med.*) carúncula.
carve [kɑːv], *v.t.* esculpir; trinchar; grabar; tallar; cincelar.
carvel [ˈkɑːvəl], *s.* (*mar.*) carabela.
carver [ˈkɑːvə], *s.* escultor; grabador; tallista, *m.f.*; cuchillo de trinchar; trinchante; trinchador.
carving [ˈkɑːviŋ], *s.* escultura; talladura; obra de talla; arte de trinchar; (el) trinchar; ***carving knife,*** trinchante, cuchillo de trinchar; ***carving table,*** trinchero.
caryatid [kæriˈætid], *s.* cariátide, *f.*
caryophyllaceous [kæriɔfiˈleiʃəs], *a.* (*bot.*) cariofiláceo.
cascade [kæsˈkeid], *s.* cascada, catarata.
case (1) [keis], *s.* caso (*t. gram.*); argumento; (*for.*) pleito, causa; ***as the case may be,*** según los casos; ***the case in point,*** el caso en cuestión; (*gram.*) ***case ending,*** desinencia casual; ***in case, just in case,*** por si (acaso); (*fam.*) por si las moscas; ***in case of,*** en caso de; ***in any case,*** de todas maneras *o* formas, de todos modos; ***to make one's case,*** demostrar su tesis; (*fig.*) ***strong case,*** argumento fuerte *o* convincente.
case (2) [keis], *s.* caja; estuche; vaina; cubierta; funda; (*carp.*) bastidor, marco; ***book-case,*** librería; ***dressing-case,*** tocador; ***jewel case,*** joyelero; ***glass case,*** vitrina; (*impr.*) ***lower case,*** caja baja; ***needle case,*** alfiletero; ***pillow case,*** funda de almohada; ***pistol case,*** pistolera; (*impr.*) ***upper case,*** caja alta. — *v.t.* encajonar, enfundar.
caseharden [ˈkeishɑːdn], *v.t.* endurecer; volver insensible.
casein [ˈkeisiːn], *s.* caseína.
casemate [ˈkeismeit], *s.* (*fort.*) casamata.
casement [ˈkeismənt], *s.* puerta ventana; (*fort.*) barbacana; caja, cubierta.
cash [kæʃ], *s.* dinero contante, metálico, efectivo; pago al contado; caja; ***cash account,*** cuenta de caja; ***cash book,*** libro de caja; ***cash down,*** dinero en mano, al contado, a toca teja; ***cash on delivery,*** entrega contra reembolso; ***cash register,*** caja registradora; ***in cash,*** en efectivo. — *v.t.* cambiar, convertir en dinero contante; hacer efectivo; cobrar; ***cash a cheque,*** cobrar un cheque. — *v.i.* ***cash in on,*** sacar partido *o* provecho de.
cashew [kəˈʃuː], *s.* (*bot.*) anacardo.
cashier [kæˈʃiə], *s.* cajero; contador. — *v.t.* destituir; (*mil.*) degradar.
cashiering [kæˈʃiəriŋ], *s.* destitución; (*mil.*) degradación.
cashmere [ˈkæʃmiə], *a.* de cachemira. — *s.* cachemira.
cashoo [kəˈʃuː], *s.* cachunde, *f.*
casing [ˈkeisiŋ], *s.* cubierta, envoltura; revestimiento.
casino [kəˈsiːnou], *s.* casino (*de juego*); [CASSINO].
cask [kɑːsk], *s.* barril, tonel, pipa; cuba. — *v.t.* entonelar, envasar.
casket [ˈkɑːskit], *s.* arquita, joyero; cofrecito, estuche; (*Am.*) ataúd.
casking [ˈkɑːskiŋ], *s.* embarrilado.
Caspian [ˈkæspiən], *a.* caspio.
casque [kæsk], *s.* casquete, capacete, almete, casco.
cass [kæs], *v.t.* (*for.*) casar, anular.
cassation [kæˈseiʃən], *s.* (*for.*) casación, anulación.
cassava [kəˈsɑːvə], *s.* mandioca.
casserole [ˈkæsəroul], *s.* cacerola; timbal.
cassia [ˈkæsiə], *s.* casia.
cassimere [ˈkæsimiə], *s.* casimir.
cassino [kəˈsiːnou], *s.* juego de naipes para cuatro jugadores.
cassiterite [kəˈsitərait], *s.* (*min.*) casiterita.
cassock [ˈkæsək], *s.* sotana, balandrán.
cassowary [ˈkæsəwəri], *s.* (*orn.*) casuario.
cast [kɑːst], *s.* echada, lanzamiento, tirada; ojeada; forma, molde; pieza fundida; (*teat.*) reparto, elenco; (*fig.*) aspecto; tono, tinte, matiz; ***at one cast,*** de un golpe, de una tirada; ***to have a cast in one's eye,*** bizcar, torcer la vista. — *irr. v.t.* tirar, arrojar, lanzar; verter, vaciar; despedir, desechar; repartir (*los papeles*); ***cast about,*** esparcir; ***cast anchor,*** echar ancla(s), fondear; ***cast aside,*** desechar; ***cast away,*** abandonar; ***cast down,*** abatir, echar por tierra; ***cast lots,*** echar suertes; ***cast off,*** abandonar; sacudir(se); ***cast out,*** echar fuera, arrojar; ***cast a spell on,*** hechizar; ***cast a vote,*** depositar un voto. — *v.i.* lanzar; echar a suertes; ***cast about,*** buscar alrededor; ***cast off,*** soltar amarras.
castanea [kæsˈteiniə], *s.* (*bot.*) castaño de Indias.
castanets [kæstəˈnets], *s.pl.* castañuelas, *f.pl.*
castaway [ˈkɑːstəwei], *s.* náufrago; réprobo.
caste [kɑːst], *s.* casta; ***to lose caste,*** desprestigiarse.
castellan [ˈkæstələn], *s.* castellano, alcaide.
castellated [ˈkæstəleitid], *a.* encastillado.
caster [ˈkɑːstə], *s.* tirador, echador; rueda, ruedecilla.
castigate [ˈkæstigeit], *v.t.* castigar; fustigar.
castigation [kæstiˈgeiʃən], *s.* castigo; fustigación.
castigator [ˈkæstigeitə], *s.* castigador.
castigatory [ˈkæstigeitəri], *a.* castigador; fustigante.
Castilian [kəsˈtiliən], *a.*, *s.* castellano.
casting [ˈkɑːstiŋ], *s.* fundición; pieza fundida; (*teat.*) reparto; ***casting vote,*** voto decisivo.
cast-iron [ˈkɑːst-ˈaiən], *a.* (*fig.*) fuerte, duro; perfecto. — *s.* hierro colado *o* fundido.
castle [kɑːsl], *s.* castillo; torre, roque (*ajedrez*); ***castles in the air,*** castillos en el aire; ***an Englishman's home is his castle,*** mientras en mi casa estoy, rey me soy. — *v.t.*, *v.i.* enrocar (*ajedrez*).
castlet [ˈkɑːslit], *s.* castillejo.
castling [ˈkɑːsliŋ], *s.* enroque.
cast-off [ˈkɑːst-ɔf], *a.* desechado. — *s.* cosa desechada, prenda desechada.
castor [ˈkɑːstə], *s.* rueda, ruedecilla; ***castor sugar,*** azúcar extrafino.
castor oil [ˈkɑːstər ˈɔil], *s.* aceite de ricino.
castrametation [kæstrəmiˈteiʃən], *s.* (*fort.*) castrametación.
castrate [ˈkæstreit], *v.t.* castrar.
castration [kæsˈtreiʃən], *s.* castración.
castrato [kæsˈtrɑːtou], *s.* (*mús.*) castrado.
castrel [ˈkæstrəl], *s.* (*orn.*) alfaneque.

casual [ˈkæʒjuəl], *a.* despreocupado; deportivo; indiferente; casual; provisional.
casualness [ˈkæʒjuəlnis], *s.* despreocupación; aire deportivo; indiferencia.
casualty [ˈkæʒjuəlti], *s.* baja; víctima; herido; muerto; desgracia personal.
casuist [ˈkæzjuist], *s.* casuista, *m.f.*
casuistic(al) [kæzjuˈistik(əl)], *a.* casuístico.
casuistry [ˈkæzjuistri], *s.* casuística; sofistería.
cat [kæt], *s.* gato, gata; felino; (*bot.*) ***cat's-foot,*** hiedra terrestre; (*min.*) ***cat's eye,*** cimófana; ***to make a cat's paw of,*** usar de cabeza de turco; ***cat o' nine tails,*** azote de nueve ramales; ***to bell the cat,*** poner el cascabel al gato; ***to rain cats and dogs,*** llover a cántaros; ***to see which way the cat will jump,*** ver qué sesgo toma el asunto; ***when the cat's away, the mice will play,*** donde no está el dueño, ahí está su duelo; ***to let the cat out of the bag,*** tirar de la manta, descubrir el pastel.
catacathartic [kætəkəˈθɑːtik], *a., s.* catacatártico.
catachresis [kætəˈkriːsis], *s.* (*ret.*) catacresis, *f.inv.*
catachrestic(al) [kætəˈkrestik(əl)], *a.* catacréstico.
cataclysm [ˈkætəklizəm], *s.* cataclismo.
catacomb [ˈkætəkuːm], *s.* catacumba.
catacoustic [kætəˈkuːstik], *a.* (*fís.*) catacústico.
catacoustics [kætəˈkuːstiks], *s.* catacústica.
catadioptric [kætədaiˈɔptrik], *a.* (*fís.*) catadióptrico.
catafalque [ˈkætəfælk], *s.* catafalco.
Catalan [ˈkætəlæn], *a., s.* catalán.
catalectic [kætəˈlektik], *a.* (*ret.*) cataléctico.
catalepsy [ˈkætəlepsi], *s.* (*med.*) catalepsia.
cataleptic [kætəˈleptik], *a.* cataléptico.
catalogue [ˈkætəlɔg], *s.* catálogo. — *v.t.* catalogar.
Catalonia [kætəˈlouniə]. Cataluña.
catalpa [kəˈtælpə], *s.* (*bot.*) catalpa.
catalysis [kəˈtælisis], *s.* (*quím.*) catálisis, *f.inv.*
catalytic [kætəˈlitik], *a.* catalítico.
catamaran [kætəməˈræn], *s.* (*mar.*) catamarán.
catamenia [kætəˈmiːniə], *s.* menstruación.
cataphonic [kætəˈfɔnik], *a.* catacústico.
cataphonics [kætəˈfɔniks], *s.* ciencia de los sonidos reflejos.
cataplasm [ˈkætəplæzəm], *s.* cataplasma.
catapult [ˈkætəpʌlt], *s.* catapulta.
cataract [ˈkætərækt], *s.* catarata; cascada.
catarrh [kəˈtɑː], *s.* catarro.
catarrhal [kəˈtɑːrəl], *a.* catarral; catarroso.
catastrophe [kəˈtæstrəfi], *s.* catástrofe, *f.*
catastrophic [kætəˈstrɔfik], *a.* catastrófico.
catbird [ˈkætbəːd], *s.* tordo mimo.
catcall [ˈkætkɔːl], *s.* silbo, silbido; reclamo.
catch [kætʃ], *s.* presa; captura; (*dep.*) parada; pega, trampa; corchete, gancho; pestillo, pasador; reclamo. — *irr. v.t.* coger; prender; atrapar, pillar; cazar, pescar; sorprender; contener; atraer (*la atención*); engranar, engarzar; ***catch at,*** intentar agarrar; ***catch cold,*** constiparse, acatarrarse, coger un resfriado; ***catch fire,*** incendiarse, prenderse; ***catch hold of,*** agarrar(se a); ***catch it,*** ganársela, cargársela; ***catch sight of,*** avistar, vislumbrar; ***catch up*** (***with***), alcanzar (a). — *v.i.* engancharse, enredarse, trabarse; contagiarse, ser pegadizo; ***catch up,*** ponerse al corriente *o* al día.
catching [ˈkætʃiŋ], *a.* contagioso; ***eye-catching,*** atractivo, que llama la atención.
catchment [ˈkætʃmənt], *s.* captación.
catchpenny [ˈkætʃpeni], *a.* de pacotilla, barato. — *s.* engañifa; baratija.
catch-phrase [ˈkætʃ-freiz], *s.* muletilla.
catch-word [ˈkætʃ-wəːd], *s.* reclamo; (*teat.*) pie; palabra de efecto.
catchy [ˈkætʃi], *a.* (*fam.*) pegadizo.
catechetics [kætiˈketiks], *s.* catequismo.
catechism [ˈkætikizəm], *s.* catecismo.
catechistic [kætiˈkistik], *a.* catequístico.
catechize [ˈkætikaiz], *v.t.* catequizar.
catechumen [kætiˈkjuːmən], *s.* catecúmeno.
categoric(al) [kætiˈgɔrik(əl)], *a.* categórico.
categorize [ˈkætigəraiz], *v.t.* clasificar, ordenar por categorías.
category [ˈkætigəri], *s.* categoría.
catenarian, catenary [kætəˈnɛəriən, kəˈtiːnəri], *a.* catenario.
catenary [kəˈtiːnəri], *s.* (*geom.*) catenaria.
catenate [ˈkatineit], *v.t.* encadenar.
catenation [kætiˈneiʃən], *s.* encadenamiento.
cater [ˈkeitə], *v.i.* abastecer, proveer; ***cater for*** o ***to,*** abastecer, proveer (a); atender (a).
caterer [ˈkeitərə], *s.* abastecedor, proveedor.
caterpillar [ˈkætəpilə], *s.* oruga; ***caterpillar tractor,*** tractor de oruga.
caterwaul [ˈkætəwɔːl], *s.* (*fam.*) maullido; aullido. — *v.i.* maullar; aullar.
caterwauling [ˈkætəwɔːliŋ], *s.* maullido(s), aullido(s).
catfish [ˈkætfiʃ], *s.* (*ict.*) siluro.
catgut [ˈkætgʌt], *s.* cuerda de tripa.
catharsis [kəˈθɑːsis], *s.* catarsis, *f.inv.*
cathartic [kəˈθɑːtik], *a., s.* catártico.
cathedra [kəˈθiːdrə], *s.* cátedra.
cathedral [kəˈθiːdrəl], *a.* catedralicio. — *s.* catedral, *f.*
Catherine wheel [ˈkæθərin hwiːl], *s.* (*piro.*) rueda catalina; (*arq.*) rosa *o* ventana circular.
catheter [ˈkæθitə], *s.* (*cir.*) catéter.
cathetometer [kæθiˈtɔmitə], *s.* catetómetro.
cathetus [ˈkæθitəs], *s.* (*geom.*) cateto.
cathodal, cathodic [ˈkæθoudəl, -ik], *a.* catódico.
cathode [ˈkæθoud], *a.* catódico; ***cathode ray,*** rayo catódico; ***cathode ray tube,*** tubo *o* válvula de rayos catódicos. — *s.* cátodo.
catholic [ˈkæθəlik], *a.* católico; amplio; ***catholic tastes,*** gustos omnímodos, *m.pl.* — *s.* católico.
catholicism [ˈkəˈθɔlisizəm], *s.* catolicismo.
catholicity [kæθəˈlisiti], *s.* catolicidad, universalidad.
catholicize [kəˈθɔlisaiz], *v.t.* convertir al catolicismo.
catholicon [kəˈθɔlikən], *s.* (*med.*) catolicón, panacea.
cation [ˈkætaiən], *s.* (*elec.*) catión.
catkin [ˈkætkin], *s.* (*bot.*) candeda, amento.
catlike [ˈkætlaik], *a.* gatesco, gatuno.
catling [ˈkætliŋ], *s.* (*cir.*) legra; gatito.
catmint, catnip [ˈkætmint, ˈkætnip], *s.* (*bot.*) calamento, calaminta.
catoptric(al) [kəˈtɔptrik(əl)], *a.* catóptrico.
catoptrics [kəˈtɔptriks], *s.* (*fís.*) catóptrica.
catstail [ˈkætsteil], *s.* (*bot.*) espadaña.
catsup [ˈkætsʌp], [KETCHUP].
cattish [ˈkætiʃ], *a.* gatuno, gatesco.
cattle [kætl], *s.* ganado (vacuno); reses.
cattle-ranch [ˈkætl-rɑːntʃ], *s.* ganadería.
cattle-rancher [ˈkætl-rɑːntʃə], *s.* ganadero.
cattle-shed [ˈkætl-ʃed], *s.* establo.
cattle-show [ˈkætl-ʃou], *s.* exposición de ganados, feria (ganadera).
cattle-thief [ˈkætl-θiːf], *s.* cuatrero.
cattle-trade [ˈkætl-treid], *s.* comercio de ganado.
cattle-truck [kætl-trʌk], *s.* vagón de ganados.
catty [ˈkæti], *a.* gatuno; arisco; rencoroso, chismoso.
Caucasian [kɔːˈkeiziən], *a.* caucásio (raza); caucáseo (cordillera); caucasiano. — *s.* caucasiano.
caucus [ˈkɔːkəs], *s.* (*pol.*) junta secreta, conventículo.
caudal [kɔːdl], *a.* caudal.
caudate [ˈkɔːdeit], *a.* caudato, raboso.
caudicle [ˈkɔːdikl], *s.* (*bot.*) apéndice.
caudle [ˈkɔːdl], *s.* pisto; yema mejida.
caul [kɔːl], *s.* redecilla; fondo de cofia; (*anat.*) membrana.

cauldrife [ˈkɔ:ldraif], *a.* frío, friolento.
cauldron [ˈkɔ:ldrən], *s.* caldero, calderón.
caulescent [kɔ:ˈlesənt], *a.* (*bot.*) caulescente.
cauliferous [kɔ:ˈlifərəs], *a.* colífero.
cauliflower [ˈkɔliflauə], *s.* coliflor, *f.*
cauline [ˈkɔ:lain], *a.* caulinario.
caulk [kɔ:k], *v.t.* calafatear.
caulker [ˈkɔ:kə], *s.* calafate.
caulking [ˈkɔ:kiŋ], *s.* calafateo.
causal [ˈkɔ:zəl], *a.* causal. — *s.* conjunción causativa.
causality, causation [kɔ:ˈzæliti, kɔ:ˈzeiʃən], *s.* causa, causalidad, principio, origen.
causally [ˈkɔ:zəli], *adv.* de un modo causal.
causative [ˈkɔ:zətiv], *a.* causativo, causante.
cause [kɔ:z], *s.* causa; motivo; ***there's no cause for alarm,*** no hay por qué alarmarse; ***without cause,*** sin motivo; sin qué ni por qué. — *v.t.* causar, ocasionar, originar; producir; ***cause to fall,*** hacer caer.
causeless [ˈkɔ:zlis], *a.* infundado, inmotivado, injusto, sin razón.
causelessness [ˈkɔ:zlisnis], *s.* falta de fundamento, motivo *o* causa.
causeway [ˈkɔ:zwei], *s.* calzada (elevada); arrecife.
caustic [ˈkɔ:stik], *a.* cáustico. — *s.* cáustico; ***lunar caustic,*** piedra infernal.
causticity [kɔ:sˈtisiti], *s.* causticidad; mordacidad.
cauterization [kɔ:tərai'zeiʃən], *s.* cauterización.
cauterize [ˈkɔ:teraiz], *v.t.* cauterizar.
cautery [ˈkɔ:təri], *s.* cauterio.
caution [ˈkɔ:ʃən], *s.* cautela, precaución; advertencia, amonestación. — *v.t.* advertir, amonestar.
cautionary [ˈkɔ:ʃənri], *a.* amonestador; aleccionador.
cautious [ˈkɔ:ʃəs], *a.* cauto, cauteloso, precavido, prudente, circunspecto.
cautiousness [ˈkɔ:ʃəsnis], *s.* cautela, circunspección, prudencia.
cavalcade [kævəlˈkeid], *s.* cabalgata.
cavalier [kævəˈliə], *a.* autoritario; altivo; desenvuelto. — *s.* caballero; galán.
cavalry [ˈkævəlri], *s.* caballería; ***cavalryman,*** soldado de caballería.
cave [keiv], *s.* cueva, caverna. — *v.i.* — ***in,*** hundirse, derrumbarse.
caveat [ˈkeiviæt], *s.* advertencia; aviso de suspensión.
cave-dweller *o* -man [ˈkeiv-dwelə, -mæn], *s.* cavernícola, *m.f.*, troglodita, *m.f.*
cave-in [ˈkeiv-in], *s.* hundimiento, derrumbe, socavón.
cavern [ˈkævən], *s.* caverna.
cavernous [ˈkævənəs], *a.* cavernoso.
caviar(e) [kæviˈɑ:], *s.* caviar.
cavil [ˈkævil], *s.* cavilación; reparo. — *v.i.* cavilar; sutilizar; ***cavil at, about*** o ***over,*** poner reparos a.
caviller [ˈkævilə], *s.* hombre caviloso; reparón.
cavilling [ˈkæviliŋ], *s.* cavilación, cavilosidad; (el) poner reparos.
cavillous [ˈkævibəs], *a.* caviloso; capcioso; reparón.
cavity [ˈkæviti], *s.* cavidad; agujero, orificio.
cavort [kəˈvɔ:t], *v.i.* cabriolar; (*fig.*) hacer tonterías.
caw [kɔ:], *s.* graznido(s). — *v.i.* graznar.
cawing [ˈkɔ:iŋ], *s.* [CAW].
cawk [kɔ:k], *s.* sulfato de barita.
cay [kei], *s.* cayo.
cayenne pepper [keiˈen ˈpepə], *s.* pimentón (picante).
cayman [ˈkeimən], *s.* (*zool.*) caimán.
cease [si:s], *s.* cese; cesación; ***without cease,*** sin cesar; ***cease fire,*** alto el fuego. — *v.t.* acabar, poner fin a. — *v.i.* cesar; ***cease working,*** dejar de trabajar.
ceaseless [ˈsi:slis], *a.* incesante, constante, continuo.
ceasing [ˈsi:siŋ], *s.* cese, cesación; pausa, descanso.
cecity [ˈsesiti], *s.* ceguedad, ceguera.
cedar [ˈsi:də], *s.* (*bot.*) cedro; ***cedar cone,*** cédride; ***cedar oil,*** cedreleón.
cedarn [ˈsi:dən], *a.* cedrino.
cede (si:d], *v.t.* ceder, traspasar, transferir.
cedilla [siˈdilə], *s.* cedilla, virgulilla.
cedrate [ˈsi:dreit], *s.* (*bot.*) cedrón.
ceil [si:l], *v.t.* revestir el techo de, poner cielo raso a.
ceiling [ˈsi:liŋ], *s.* techo, cielo raso; cima, tope; (*mar.*) tablazón interior, vágara; (*aer.*) altura máxima, techo.
celadon [ˈselədən], *s.* verde claro.
celandine [ˈseləndain], *s.* (*bot.*) celidonia.
celebrant [ˈselibrənt], *s.* celebrante.
celebrate [ˈselibreit], *v.t.* celebrar, solemnizar; alabar, aplaudir; festejar.
celebrated [ˈselibreitid], *a.* celebrado; célebre, famoso, afamado.
celebration [seliˈbreiʃən], *s.* celebración, conmemoración, solemnidad; fiesta, festividad, festejo.
celebrator [ˈselibreitə], *s.* celebrador, panegirista, *m.*
celebrity [siˈlebriti], *s.* celebridad, fama; persona célebre, personalidad.
celeriac [siˈleriæk], *s.* (*bot.*) apio napiforme.
celerity [siˈleriti], *s.* celeridad.
celery [ˈseləri], *s.* (*bot.*) apio.
celestial [siˈlestjəl], *a.* celeste; celestial; célico; divino.
celestine, celestite [ˈselistain, ˈselistait], *s.* (*min.*) celestina.
celibacy [ˈselibəsi], *s.* celibato, soltería.
celibate [ˈselibit], *a.*, *s.* celibato, célibe, soltero.
cell [sel], *s.* celda; célula; celdilla, vasillo; alvéolo, nicho, cavidad; (*elec.*) par, elemento; pila simple; (*impr.*) cajetín; ***dry cell,*** pila seca; ***wet cell,*** pila hidroeléctrica.
cellar [ˈselə], *s.* sótano; cueva, bodega.
cellarage [ˈseləridʒ], *s.* cueva, sótano; almacenaje *o* gastos de almacenaje.
cellarer [ˈselərə], *s.* cillerero de un monasterio.
cellaret [ˈselərit], *s.* frasquera, caja de licores.
celliferous [seˈlifərəs], *a.* (*bot.*) celulífero.
cello [ˈtʃelou], *s.* (*mús.*) violoncelo.
cellular [ˈseljulə], *a.* celular; celulario, celuloso.
cellule [ˈselju:l], *s.* celdilla, celdita.
celluloid [ˈseljulɔid], *s.* celuloide.
cellulose [ˈseljulous], *a.* (*bot.*) celuloso. — *s.* (*quím.*) celulosa.
Celt [kelt], *s.* celta.
Celtiberian [keltaiˈbiəriən], *a.*, *s.* celtibérico, celtíbero.
Celtic [ˈkeltik], *a.* céltico, celta.
Celticism [ˈkeltisizəm], *s.* celtismo.
cement [siˈment], *s.* cemento. — *v.t.* cementar; (*fig.*) consolidar.
cementation [si:menˈteiʃən], *s.* cementación.
cemetery [ˈsemitri], *s.* cementerio.
cenobite [CŒNOBITE].
cenotaph [ˈsenotæf], *s.* cenotafio.
cense [sens], *v.t.* incensar.
censer [ˈsensə], *s.* incensario.
censor [ˈsensə], *s.* censor. — *v.t.* censurar.
censorial [senˈsɔ:riəl], *a.* censorio.
censorious [senˈsɔ:riəs], *a.* hipercrítico.
censoriousness [senˈsɔ:riəsnis], *s.* (lo) hipercrítico.
censorship [ˈsensəʃip], *s.* censura.
censurable [ˈsenʃurəbl], *a.* censurable.
censurableness [ˈsenʃurəblnis], *s.* (lo) censurable.
censure [ˈsenʃə], *s.* censura. — *v.t.* censurar.
censurer [ˈsenʃərə], *s.* censurador.
census [ˈsensəs], *s.* censo; empadronamiento.
cent [sent], *s.* céntimo; (*Hisp. Am.*) centavo; ***per cent,*** por ciento.
centaur [ˈsentɔ:], *s.* centauro.

centaurea, centaury [sen'tɔ:riə, 'sentɔ:ri], *s.* (*bot.*) centaura.
centenarian [senti'nɛəriən], *a.*, *s.* centenario.
centenary [sen'ti:nəri], *a.*, *s.* centenario.
centennial [sen'tenjəl], *a.*, *s.* centenario.
centesimal [sen'tesiməl], *a.* (*arit.*) centésimo.
centifolious [senti'fouliəs], *a.* centifolio.
centigrade ['sentigreid], *a.* centígrado.
centigramme ['sentigræm], *s.* centigramo.
centilitre ['sentili:tə], *s.* centilitro.
centimetre ['sentimi:tə], *s.* centímetro.
centipede ['sentipi:d], *s.* (*zool.*) ciempiés.
cento ['sentou], *s.* (*poét.*) centón.
central ['sentrəl], *a.* central; céntrico; (***the***) ***Central African Empire,*** (el) Imperio Centroafricano.
centralism ['sentrəlizəm], *s.* centralismo.
centralist ['sentrəlist], *s.* centralista, *m.f.*
centrality [sen'træliti], *s.* centralidad.
centralization [sentrəlai'zeiʃən], *s.* centralización.
centralize ['sentrəlaiz], *v.t.* centralizar.
centre ['sentə], *a.* central; céntrico. — *s.* centro; (*mar.*) ***centre-board,*** orza de deriva; (*dep.*) ***centre-forward,*** delantero centro; ***centre-half,*** delantero medio. — *v.t.* centrar; concentrar; marcar el centro de; (*arq.*) cimbrar. — *v.i.* estar centrado (en); ***centre round,*** girar en torno a, tener como centro *o* foco (principal), tener como elemento principal.
centrepiece ['sentəpi:s], *s.* centro (*de mesa*); (*arq.*) rosetón (*de techo*).
centric(al) ['sentrik(əl)], *a.* céntrico; central.
centricalness, centricity ['sentrikəlnis, sen'trisiti], *s.* (lo) céntrico; (lo) central.
centrifugal [sen'trifjugəl], *a.* centrífugo. — *s.* centrifugador, centrifugadora.
centripetal [sen'tripətəl], *a.* centrípeto.
centring ['sentriŋ], *s.* acción de centrar; determinación del centro; ajuste, enfocamiento; (*arq.*) cimbra.
centumvir [sen'tʌmvə], *s.* (*pl.* **centumviri** [sen'tʌmviri:], centunviro.
centumvirate [sen'tʌmvirit], *s.* centunvirato.
centuple ['sentjupl], *a.* céntuplo, centuplicado.
centurial [sen'tjuəriəl], *a.* secular.
centurion [sen'tjuəriən], *s.* centurión.
century ['sentʃuri], *s.* siglo, centuria.
cephalalgia [sefə'lældʒə], *s.* (*med.*) cefalalgia.
cephalic [si'fælik], *a.* cefálico. — *s.* medicamento cefálico.
cephalitis [sefə'laitis], *s.* (*med.*) cefalitis, *f.inv.*
Cepheus ['si:fiəs], *s.* (*astron.*) Cefeo.
ceraceous [siə'reiʃəs], *a.* ceráceo.
ceramic [si'ræmik], *a.* cerámico.
ceramics [si'ræmiks], *s.* cerámica.
cerate ['siəreit], *s.* (*farm.*) cerato.
cerated ['siəreitid], *a.* encerado.
cereal ['siəriəl], *a.*, *s.* cereal.
cerebellum [seri'beləm], *s.* cerebelo.
cerebral ['seribrəl], *a.* cerebral.
cerebrate ['seribreit], *v.i.* trabajar mentalmente, pensar.
cerebration [seri'breiʃən], *s.* función cerebral; actividad cerebral.
cerebrum ['seribrəm], *s.* cerebro, celebro; encéfalo.
cerecloth, cerement ['siəklɔθ, 'siəmənt], *s.* encerado, hule.
ceremonial [seri'mouniəl], *a.*, *s.* ceremonial; rito externo.
ceremonious [seri'mounjəs], *a.* ceremonioso, cumplimentero, etiquetero; ceremonial.
ceremoniousness [seri'mounjəsnis], *s.* ceremoniosidad; etiqueta.
ceremony ['seriməni], *s.* ceremonia; cumplidos; etiqueta; ***don't stand on ceremony,*** no haga cumplidos, no se ande con cumplidos.
cereous ['siəriəs], *a.* ceroso, de cera.
cerite ['siərait], *s.* (*min.*) cerita.
cerium ['siəriəm], *s.* (*min.*) cerio.
ceroon [si'ru:n], *s.* (*com.*) coracha.
cert [sə:t], (*fam.*) [CERTAINTY].
certain ['sə:tin], *a.* cierto; seguro; fijo, determinado; (un) tal; convencido; ***at a certain hour,*** a una hora determinada; ***a certain Mr. Smith,*** un tal Mr. Smith; ***it is certain that,*** es seguro *o* indudable que; ***he is certain to come,*** es seguro que vendrá; ***for certain,*** (de) seguro, de fijo.
certainly ['sə:tənli], *adv.* ciertamente; seguramente; indudablemente, no hay duda; sin duda; desde luego; no faltaba más.
certainty ['sə:tənti], *s.* certidumbre, certeza; ***of a certainty,*** a cosa hecha.
certificate [sə:'tifikit], *s.* certificado; ***certificate of baptism, marriage, death,*** partida de bautismo, matrimonio, defunción; (***copy***) fe de bautismo *etc.* — [-eit], *v.t.* certificar.
certifier ['sə:tifaiə], *s.* certificador.
certify ['sə:tifai], *v.t.* certificar; garantizar.
certitude ['sə:titju:d], *s.* certidumbre.
cerulean [si'ru:liən], *a.* cerúleo.
ceruse ['siəru:s], *s.* cerusa.
cervical ['sə:vikəl], *a.* cervical.
Cesarean [CÆSAREAN].
cessation [se'seiʃən], *s.* cesación, cese; ***cessation of hostilities,*** suspensión de hostilidades.
cession ['seʃən], *s.* cesión.
cessionary ['seʃənəri], *s.* cesionista, *m.f.*, cesionario.
cesspool ['sespu:l], *s.* pozo negro; (*fig.*) sentina.
cestus ['sestəs], *s.* cesto; ceñidor de Venus, cinturón.
Cetacea [si'teisiə], *s.pl.* (*zool.*) cetáceos, *m.pl.*
cetacean [si'teisiən], *a.*, *s.* (*zool.*) cetáceo.
cetaceous [si'teisiəs], *a.* cetáceo.
Ceylon [si'lɔn]. (*isla*) Ceilán.
Ceylonese [silə'ni:z], *a.*, *s.* ceilanés, *m.*; cingalés, *m.*
Chad [tʃæd], *a.* chadiano. — *s.* (*país*) (el) Chad; (*pers.*) chadiano.
chad [ʃæd], *s.* (*ict.*) sábalo.
chafe [tʃeif], *s.* roce. — *v.t.* frotar, rozar; enojar, irritar. — *v.i.* (***against the bit***), tascar (el freno), impacientarse.
chaff [tʃɑ:f], *s.* aechadura(s), barcia; paja menuda; (*fig.*) chanza, zumba, burla. — *v.t.* chancearse de.
chaffer ['tʃæfə], *s.* regateo; burlón.
chaffinch ['tʃæfintʃ], *s.* (*orn.*) pinzón.
chafing ['tʃeifiŋ], *s.* desolladura, roce; impaciencia.
chagrin [ʃə'grin], *s.* mortificación, pesadumbre, desazón. — *v.t.* mortificar, apesadumbrar, desazonar.
chain [tʃein], *s.* cadena; ***chain-pump,*** noria; ***chain stitch,*** punto de cadenilla *o* cadeneta; ***chain-gang,*** cuerda de presos; (*mar.*) ***chain plates,*** cadenas de las vigotas; (*artill.*) ***chain-shot,*** balas enramadas, *f.pl.* — *v.t.* encadenar; ***chain up,*** atar con cadenas.
chainless ['tʃeinlis], *a.* desencadenado.
chair [tʃɛə], *s.* silla; sillón; sitial; cátedra; presidencia; (*f.c.*) cojinete; ***arm-chair,*** butaca; ***chair-rail,*** guardasilla; ***easy chair,*** poltrona; ***folding chair,*** silla plegable, de tijera; ***rocking-chair,*** mecedora; ***sedan-chair,*** silla de manos; ***swivel chair,*** silla giratoria; ***to take the chair, be in the chair,*** presidir, ocupar la presidencia; ***to put in the chair,*** eligir como presidente. — *v.t.* proveer de sillas; (*fig.*) instalar en puesto de autoridad; ***chair a meeting,*** presidir una reunión.
chairman ['tʃɛəmən], *s.* presidente; silletero, sillero.
chairmanship ['tʃɛəmənʃip], *s.* presidencia.
chaise [ʃeiz], *s.* silla volante; calesín; coche de cuatro ruedas; ***chaise longue,*** meridiana; ***post chaise,*** silla de posta.
chalcedony [kæl'sedəni], *s.* (*min.*) calcedonia.

chalcographer [kæl'kɔgrəfə], *s.* calcógrafo.
chalcography [kæl'kɔgrəfi], *s.* calcografía.
Chaldaic [kæl'deiik], *a.* caldaico, caldeo. — *s.* caldeo, lengua caldaica.
Chaldean [kæl'di:ən], *a.*, *s.* caldeo.
chalet ['ʃælei], *s.* chalet.
chalice ['tʃælis], *s.* cáliz.
chalk [tʃɔ:k], *s.* creta; tiza; ***chalk for cheese,*** gato por liebre; ***french chalk,*** jaboncillo de sastre; ***red chalk,*** lápiz rojo. — *v.t.* dibujar *o* marcar con tiza; (*agric.*) margar; ***chalk out,*** trazar; ***chalk up,*** apuntar, anotar en cuenta; (*fam.*) ***chalk up a victory,*** apuntarse un triunfo.
chalkiness ['tʃɔ:kinis], *s.* (lo) cretoso.
chalky ['tʃɔ:ki], *a.* cretoso.
challenge ['tʃælindʒ], *s.* desafío, reto; impugnación; incitación, acicate; recusación; (*mil.*) quién vive. — *v.t.* desafiar, retar; impugnar, poner en duda; recusar; dar el quién vive a.
challengeable ['tʃælindʒəbl], *a.* sujeto *o* expuesto a desafío *o* acusación; recusable.
challenger ['tʃælindʒə], *s.* desafiador, retador; duelista, *m.f.*; agresor.
challis ['ʃæli], *s.* (*com.*) chalí.
chalybeate [kə'libiət], *a.* ferruginoso, calibeado, impregnado de hierro o acero. — *s.* agua ferruginosa.
chamber ['tʃeimbə], *s.* cámara; aposento; sala; gabinete; bufete (*de un abogado*); despacho (*de un juez*); cilindro, cuerpo (*de bomba*); recámara (*de una mina*); ***chamber-maid,*** doncella; ***chamber music,*** música de cámara; ***chamber organ,*** órgano portátil; ***chamber pot,*** orinal; ***condensing chamber,*** condensador. — *v.t.* encerrar en cámara *o* aposento.
chamberlain ['tʃeimbəlin], *s.* chambelán, camarlengo.
chameleon [kə'mi:liən], *s.* camaleón.
chamfer ['tʃæmfə], *s.* chaflán. — *v.t.* chaflanar; estriar, acanalar.
chamois ['ʃæmwɑ:], *s.* gamuza; ['ʃæmi] gamuza (*piel*).
champ [tʃæmp], *v.t.* morder, mordiscar; ***champ the bit,*** morder, tascar el freno. — *v.i.* tascar.
champagne [ʃæm'pein], *s.* champaña.
champaign [tʃæm'pein], *a.* (*ant.*) abierto, llano. — *s.* campiña.
champion ['tʃæmpiən], *s.* campeón; paladín. — *v.t.* defender, abogar por.
championess [tʃæmpiə'nes], *s.* campeona.
championship ['tʃæmpiənʃip], *s.* campeonato.
chance [tʃɑ:ns], *a.* casual, fortuito. — *s.* ocasión, oportunidad; posibilidad; probabilidad; casualidad, azar; suerte; riesgo; ***by chance,*** por casualidad; ***the chances are that,*** lo más probable es que, según todas las probabilidades, a lo mejor; ***to let the chance slip,*** perder la ocasión; ***to have one's eye to the main chance,*** mirar por el interés *o* los intereses de uno (mismo); ***on the chance that,*** a ver si (acaso); ***it doesn't stand a chance,*** no hay esperanzas, no hay la más mínima posibilidad; ***to take a chance,*** probar suerte *o* fortuna; arriesgarse, aventurarse. — *v.t.* arriesgar; ***chance one's arm,*** arriesgarse. — *v.i.* acaecer; ***he chanced to pass that way,*** acertó a pasar por allí; ***chance upon,*** encontrar(se) casualmente (con).
chancel ['tʃɑ:nsəl], *s.* presbiterio.
chancellor ['tʃɑ:nsələ], *s.* canciller; ***Chancellor of the Exchequer,*** Ministro de Hacienda.
chancellorship ['tʃɑ:nsələʃip], *s.* cancillería.
chancery ['tʃɑ:nsəri], *s.* chancillería; cancillería.
chancre ['ʃæŋkə], *s.* (*med.*) chancro.
chancrous ['ʃæŋkrəs], *a.* chancroso.
chancy ['tʃɑ:nsi], *a.* (*fam.*) expuesto.
chandelier [ʃændə'liə], *s.* araña (*de luces*).
chandler ['tʃɑ:ndlə], *s.* cerero, velero; ***chandler's shop,*** abacería; ***corn-chandler,*** tratante en granos y semillas; ***ship-chandler,*** abastecedor de barcos; ***wax-chandler,*** cerero.
chandlery ['tʃɑ:ndləri], *s.* cerería, velería.
change [tʃeindʒ], *s.* cambio; transformación; muda (de ropa); (*dinero*) vuelta; ***change of heart,*** cambio de sentimiento; (*fig.*) ***change of scene,*** cambio de aire(s); ***for a change,*** para cambiar *o* por variar; ***keep the change,*** quédese con la vuelta; (***small***) ***change,*** suelto. — *v.t.* cambiar, mudar; transformar; sustituir; ***change colour,*** demudarse; ***change hands,*** cambiar de dueño; ***change one's mind,*** cambiar de opinión, variar de parecer; ***change the subject,*** cambiar de tema; ***change*** (***trains***), transbordar; ***change one's tune,*** cambiar de postura, recoger velas; ***I'm going to change*** (***my clothes***), me voy a cambiar. — *v.i.* cambiar; mudar; transbordar.
changeable ['tʃeindʒəbl], *a.* variable, mudable, cambiable, cambiante; tornasolado.
changeableness, changeability, changefulness ['tʃeindʒəblnis, tʃeindʒə'biliti, 'tʃeindʒfulnis], *s.* mutabilidad, versatilidad, inconstancia, volubilidad.
changeful ['tʃeindʒful], *a.* inconstante, variable, mudable, veleidoso.
changeless ['tʃeindʒlis], *a.* inmutable, constante.
changeling ['tʃeindʒliŋ], *s.* niño sustituido por otro.
changer ['tʃeindʒə], *s.* cambista, *m.f.*; cambiador.
changing ['tʃeindʒiŋ], *a.* cambiante; tornasolado. — *s.* cambio.
channel ['tʃænəl], *s.* canal (*t. rad. y T.V.*); álveo; cauce; (*arq.*) estría, mediacaña; estrecho; conducto, vía; ***English Channel,*** Canal de la Mancha; ***irrigation channel,*** acequia. — *v.t.* acanalar; canalizar; estriar; conducir, encauzar.
chant [tʃɑ:nt], *s.* canto; salmodia, sonsonete. — *v.t.*, *v.i.* cantar, discantar; salmodiar.
chanter ['tʃɑ:ntə], *s.* cantor; chantre.
chantlate ['tʃɑ:ntleit], *s.* (*arq.*) alero.
chantress ['tʃɑ:ntris], *s.* (*ant.*) cantora, cantatriz.
chantry ['tʃɑ:ntri], *s.* capilla.
chaos ['keiɔs], *s.* caos.
chaotic [kei'ɔtik], *a.* caótico.
chap (1) [tʃæp], *s.* (*fam.*) chico, muchacho; (*fam.*) tío, sujeto. — *v.t.* agrietar. — *v.i.* agrietarse, cuartearse.
chap (2) [tʃæp], *s.* grieta.
chap (3) [tʃæp], *s.* (*ú. más en pl.*) mandíbulas, *f.pl.*, quijadas, *f.pl.*; hocicos, *m.pl.*
chap-book ['tʃæpbuk], *s.* pliego suelto.
chape [tʃeip], *s.* chapa *o* charnela de cinturón; contera de espada.
chapel ['tʃæpl], *s.* capilla; templo (protestante); personal (*de una imprenta*); ***chapel of ease,*** capilla sufragánea; ***chapel master,*** maestro de capilla; ***chapel royal,*** capilla real.
chapeless ['tʃeiplis], *a.* sin chapa *o* contera.
chapelet ['tʃæpəlit], *s.* (*equit.*) doble estribo; (*hidr.*) draga de cubos.
chaperon ['ʃæpəroun], *s.* caperuza; carabina. — *v.t.* servir de carabina a.
chapfallen ['tʃæpfɔ:lən], *a.* abatido, alicaído.
chapiter ['tʃæpitə], *s.* (*arq.*) capitel.
chaplain ['tʃæplin], *s.* capellán.
chaplaincy, chaplainship ['tʃæplinsi, -ʃip], *s.* capellanía.
chaplet ['tʃæplit], *s.* guirnalda; sarta (*de cuentas*); rosario; gargantilla; (*arq.*) moldura de cuentas.
chapman ['tʃæpmən], *s.* buhonero.
chappie ['tʃæpi], *s.* (*fam.*) tipo; hombrecito.
chappy ['tʃæpi], *a.* agrietado.
chapter ['tʃæptə], *s.* capítulo; (*igl.*) cabildo; ***chapter-house,*** sala capitular; ***to quote chapter and verse*** (***for***), dar (con) pelos y señales.
chaptrel ['tʃæptrəl], *s.* (*arq.*) imposta.
char (1) [tʃɑ:], *s.* (*ict.*) umbra.
char (2) [tʃɑ:], *s.* (*fam.*) asistenta, (*abrev.*) [CHARWOMAN]. — *v.i.* limpiar, fregar (*en una casa*).

char (3) [tʃɑ:], *v.t.* carbonizar; chamuscar. — *v.i.* carbonizarse.
charabanc [ˈʃærəbæŋ], *s.* autocar.
character [ˈkærəktə], *s.* carácter; índole, *f.*; reputación, fama; personaje; (*teat.*) papel; (*fam.*) tipo, sujeto; tipo gracioso *o* estrafalario; ***in character,*** conforme al tipo; ***out of character,*** contrario al tipo; ***character study,*** retrato literario.
characteristic [kærəktəˈristik], *a.* característico, propio. — *s.* característica, rasgo propio.
characterize [ˈkærəktəraiz], *v.t.* caracterizar.
characterless [ˈkærəktəlis], *a.* sin carácter.
charade [ʃəˈrɑ:d], *s.* charada.
charcoal [ˈtʃɑ:koul], *s.* carbón de leña; (*arte*) carboncillo.
chard [tʃɑ:d], *s.* acelga.
charge [tʃɑ:dʒ], *s.* carga; cargo; precio, coste, gasto; encargo; orden, mandato; acusación; (*blas.*) blasón; ***to give in charge,*** entregar a la justicia; ***in charge of,*** encargado de; ***to leave in s.o.'s charge,*** dejar a alguien en depósito *o* en custodia; (*mil.*) ***to put on a charge,*** levantar acta a; ***to take charge of,*** encargarse de, hacerse cargo de; ***what are your charges?*** ¿cuánto cobra usted? — *v.t.* cargar; cobrar; encargar; ordenar, mandar; acusar; ***charge to s.o.'s account,*** cargarle a alguien en cuenta; ***charge with,*** acusar de; ***how much do you charge?*** ¿cuánto cobra usted? — *v.i.* cargar.
chargeable [ˈtʃɑ:dʒəbl], *a.* cobradero; acusable, imputable.
charger [ˈtʃɑ:dʒə], *s.* corcel, caballo de batalla; cargador.
charily [ˈtʃɛərili], *adv.* cautamente; parcamente.
chariness [ˈtʃɛərinis], *s.* cautela; parquedad.
chariot [ˈtʃæriət], *s.* carro de guerra; carroza ligera.
charioteer [tʃæriəˈtiə], *s.* cochero, carretero, auriga, *m.*
charism [ˈkærizəm, kəˈrizmə], *s.* carisma.
charismatic [kærizˈmætik], *a.* carismático.
charitable [ˈtʃæritəbl], *a.* caritativo, benéfico.
charitableness [ˈtʃæritəblnis], *s.* caridad, (lo) caritativo.
charity [ˈtʃæriti], *s.* caridad; limosna; beneficencia; ***charity begins at home,*** la caridad bien ordenada empieza por uno mismo.
charivari [ʃɑ:riˈvɑ:ri], *s.* cencerrada.
charlatan [ˈʃɑ:lətən], *s.* charlatán; curandero.
charlatanic [ʃɑ:ləˈtænik], *a.* charlatánico; propio de un curandero.
charlatanism, charlatanry [ˈʃɑ:lətənizəm, -ri], *s.* charlatanismo, charlatanería.
Charles's Wain [ˈtʃɑ:lziz ˈwein], *s.* (*astron.*) osa mayor.
charlock [ˈtʃɑ:lək], *s.* (*bot.*) mostaza silvestre.
charlotte [ˈʃɑ:lət], *s.* carlota rusa.
charm [tʃɑ:m], *s.* encanto, atractivo, gracia; hechizo, encantamiento, ensalmo; amuleto, talismán; dije. — *v.t.* encantar, hechizar; cautivar.
charmer [ˈtʃɑ:mə], *s.* encantador, hechicero.
charming [ˈtʃɑ:miŋ], *a.* encantador; hechicero; delicioso.
charnel [ˈtʃɑ:nəl], *a.* sepulcral. — *s.* (*o* — ***house***), osario.
chart [tʃɑ:t], *s.* carta de marear *o* de navegar; mapa (*militar, hidrográfico etc.*); plano (*topográfico*); cuadro, gráfico, esquema, *m.* — *v.t.* incluir, anotar en una carta *o* mapa; trazar en el mapa.
charter [ˈtʃɑ:tə], *s.* carta (*constitucional*), estatuto; cédula, título; privilegio; escritura; (*com.*) fletamento. — *v.t.* estatuir; conceder privilegio *o* patente a; fletar (*un barco* o *avión*); aquilar (*un vehículo*); ***chartered accountant,*** contable colegiado *o* titulado.
chartography [tʃɑ:ˈtɔgrəfi], [CARTOGRAPHY].
charwoman [ˈtʃɑ:wumən], *s.* asistenta.

chary [ˈtʃɛəri], *a.* cauto; receloso, circunspecto; parco.
chase [tʃeis], *s.* caza; persecución; montería; partida de caza; cosa que se persigue; cazadero; (*mec.*) ranura, muesca; (*impr.*) rama; ***wild goose chase,*** caza de ilusiones, pretensión disparatada. — *v.t.* cazar, dar caza a, perseguir; cincelar, labrar; engastar; acanalar, abrir una ranura en; ***chase away,*** ahuyentar; espantar; disipar.
chaser [ˈtʃeisə], *s.* cazador; cincelador; engastador; (*fam.*) bebida que se toma después de los licores fuertes.
chasing [ˈtʃeisiŋ], *s.* cinceladura; caza, seguimiento.
chasm [ˈkæzəm], *s.* sima, abismo.
chasseur [ʃæˈsə:], *s.* (*mil.*) cazador.
chassis [ˈʃæsi], *s.* chasis.
chaste [tʃeist], *a.* casto; puro; sencillo.
chasten [ˈtʃeisən], *v.t.* castigar; depurar.
chastener [ˈtʃeisənə], *s.* castigador; depurador.
chasteness [ˈtʃeistnis], *s.* castidad; pureza.
chastening [ˈtʃeisəniŋ], *a.* que hace pensar seriamente, aleccionador. — *s.* castigo.
chaste-tree [ˈtʃeist-tri:], *s.* (*bot.*) agnocasto, sauzgatillo.
chastise [tʃæsˈtaiz], *v.t.* castigar.
chastisement [ˈtʃæstizmənt], *s.* castigo.
chastity [ˈtʃæstiti], *s.* castidad.
chasuble [ˈtʃæzjubl], *s.* casulla.
chat [tʃæt], *s.* charla; cháchara; palique. — *v.i.* charlar.
chattels [ˈtʃætəlz], *s.pl.* bienes (muebles), *m.pl.*; enseres, *m.pl.*; (*fam.*) bártulos, *m.pl.*
chatter [ˈtʃatə], *s.* charla(s), charloteo, parloteo; chirrido(s); piar; castañeteo. — *v.i.* charlar, parlotear; chirriar; piar; ***his teeth were chattering,*** le castañeteaban los dientes, daba diente con diente.
chatterbox [ˈtʃætəbɔks], *s.* parlanchín, cotorra, tarabilla.
chatterer [ˈtʃætərə], *s.* [CHATTERBOX].
chattering [ˈʃætəriŋ], *s.* [CHATTER].
chatty [ˈtʃæti], *a.* hablador; lleno de noticias.
chauffeur [ˈʃoufə], *s.* chófer.
chauvinism [ˈʃouvinizəm], *s.* chauvinismo, patriotería.
chauvinist [ˈʃouvinist], *a., s.* chauvinista, *m.f.*, patriotero.
chauvinistic [ʃouviˈnistik], *a.* chauvinista.
chaw [tʃɔ:], *v.t.* (*fam.*) masticar.
cheap [tʃi:p], *a.* barato; baratero; de mal gusto, chabacano, de medio pelo; ***on the cheap,*** barato, con poco dinero *o* esfuerzo; ***to feel cheap,*** sentirse avergonzado; ***to hold cheap,*** dar poco valor a.
cheapen [ˈtʃi:pən], *v.t.* abaratar; rebajar; desprestigiar; ***cheapen o.s.,*** rebajarse.
cheapjack [ˈtʃi:pdʒæk], *s.* vendedor ambulante.
cheaply [ˈtʃi:pli], *adv.* barato, a precio bajo.
cheapness [ˈtʃi:pnis], *s.* baratura; economía.
cheat [tʃi:t], *s.* trampa, engaño, fraude, estafa, timo; tramposo, estafador, timador. — *v.t.* engañar, defraudar, estafar, timar. — *v.i.* hacer trampa, trampear.
cheating [ˈtʃi:tiŋ], *s.* engaño, trampa.
check [tʃek], *s.* rechazo; freno; represión; tope; contratiempo; derrota; control; comprobación; repaso; marca, señal; talón, contraseña; cuadro, escaque; (*teat.*) billete de salida; (*com.*) talón; (*Am.*) [CHEQUE]; (*Am.*) [BILL (3)]; jaque (*en ajedrez*); ***check-point,*** control; (*Am.*) ***check room,*** consigna; ***to hold in check,*** contener; ***to keep a check on,*** controlar, tener controlado; tener vigilado. — *v.t.* contener, refrenar, reprimir; detener, parar; comprobar; marcar; (*Am.*) facturar, depositar (*equipajes*); hacer *o* dibujar cuadros en; dar jaque a; ***check off,*** marcar para

indicar una comprobación; ***check up,*** comprobar. — *v.i.* — ***in,*** inscribirse (*en un hotel*); ***check out,*** despedirse y pagar la cuenta (*en un hotel*); ***check up on,*** combrobar.

checker [ˈtʃekə], *s.* inspector; reprensor; (*Am.*) ***checker-board,*** tablero de damas; ***checker-work,*** dibujo a cuadros; (*pl., Am.*) (*juego de*) damas. — *v.t.* taracear, ataracear; diversificar.

checkered [ˈtʃekəd], *a.* ajedrezado, escaqueado, jaquelado, a cuadros; accidentado, agitado.

checkmate [ˈtʃekmeit], *s.* mate, jaque mate; (*fig.*) callejón sin salida. — *v.t.* dar jaque mate a; (*fig.*) meter en un callejón sin salida.

check-up [ˈtʃek-ʌp], *s.* reconocimiento (médico), chequeo.

cheek [tʃi:k], *s.* mejilla, carrillo; cachete; (*artill.*) gualdera (de cureña); (*fam.*) cara dura, descaro, desfachatez, desvergüenza; caja de balanza; (*mec.*) quijada, montante, larguero; (*fam.*) ***to have a lot of cheek,*** tener mucha cara dura; ***to go cheek by jowl with,*** ser uña y carne de; ***with one's tongue in one's cheek,*** con sorna, irónicamente.

cheek-bone [ˈtʃi:k-boun], *s.* (*anat.*) pómulo.

cheeky [ˈtʃi:ki], *a.* descarado.

cheep [tʃi:p], *s.* pío, gorjeo. — *v.i.* piar, gorjear.

cheer [tʃiə], *s.* estado de ánimo; viandas, *f.pl.*, comida; ***cheers,*** vivas, *m.pl.*, vítores, *m.pl.*; salud; ***words of cheer,*** palabras (*f.*) de aliento, de ánimo. — *v.t.* alentar, animar; vitorear, aplaudir, dar vivas a; ***cheer on,*** animar, alentar. — *v.i.* — ***up,*** animarse; ***cheer up!*** ¡ánimo!

cheerer [ˈtʃiərə], *s.* regocijador; vitoreador.

cheerful, cheery [ˈtʃiəful, -ri], *a.* alegre, animado.

cheerfulness [ˈtʃiəfulnis], *s.* alegría, jovialidad, buen humor.

cheerio! [tʃiəriˈou], *interj.* ¡adiós!

cheerless [ˈtʃiəlis], *a.* triste.

cheese [tʃi:z], *s.* queso; ***cream cheese,*** queso fresco, requesón; (*fam.*) ***hard cheese,*** mala suerte.

cheesecake [ˈtʃi:zkeik], *s.* quesadilla, tarta de queso; (*fam.*) pornofrafía, (lo) pornográfico.

cheesecloth [ˈtʃi:zklɔθ], *s.* (*Am.*) [MUSLIN].

cheese-curds [ˈtʃi:z-kə:dz], *s.* cuajadas. *f.pl.*

cheesemonger [ˈtʃi:zmʌŋgə], *s.* quesero.

cheese-rennet [ˈtʃi:z-renit], *s.* cuajeleche.

cheese-vat [ˈtʃi:z-væt], *s.* quesera.

cheesy [ˈtʃi:zi], *a.* caseoso.

cheetah [ˈtʃi:tə], *s.* leopardo indio.

chef [ʃef], *s.* cocinero.

cheirology [kaiˈrɔlədʒi], *s.* quirología.

Cheiroptera [kaiˈrɔptərə], *s.pl.* (*zool.*) (orden de los mamíferos) quirópteros.

chela [ˈki:lə], *s.* pinza terminal (de algunos crustáceos y arácnidos).

chelonian [kiˈlouniən], *a.* quelonio.

chemical [ˈkemikəl], *a.* químico. — *s.* substancia química; (*pl.*) productos químicos, *m.pl.*

chemise [ʃəˈmi:z], *s.* camisa de mujer; (*fort.*) camisa.

chemist [ˈkemist], *s.* químico; farmacéutico; ***chemist's*** (***shop***), farmacia.

chemistry [ˈkemistri], *s.* química.

chenille [ʃəˈni:l], *s.* felpilla.

cheque [tʃek], *s.* cheque; ***cheque book,*** talonario de cheques.

cherish [ˈtʃeriʃ], *v.t.* querer, apreciar; tratar *o* recordar con profundo cariño *o* amor; (*fig.*) abrigar (*esperanzas etc.*).

cheroot [ʃəˈru:t], *s.* (cigarro) puro corto.

cherry [ˈtʃeri], *a.* de cereza; de cerezo; de color de cereza. — *s.* cereza; guinda; ***cherry tree,*** cerezo.

cherub [ˈtʃerəb], *s.* (*pl.* **cherubim** [-im]) querubín; (*fam.*) angelote.

cherubic [tʃəˈru:bik], *a.* querúbico.

chervil [ˈtʃə:vil], *s.* (*bot.*) perifollo.

chess [tʃes], *s.* ajedrez.

chess-board [ˈtʃes-bɔ:d], *s.* tablero de ajedrez.

chessman [ˈtʃesmæn], *s.* ficha, pieza de ajedrez.

chess-player [ˈtʃes-pleiə], *s.* ajedrecista, *m.f.*

chest [tʃest], *s.* arca, cofre, cajón; caja; pecho, tórax; ***chest of drawers,*** cómoda; ***to get sth. off one's chest,*** desahogarse.

chested [ˈtʃestid], *a.* de pecho; ***narrow-chested,*** estrecho de pecho.

chestnut [ˈtʃesnʌt], *a.* castaña; alazán. — *s.* castaña; ***chestnut tree,*** castaño; ***horse chestnut,*** castaña de Indias; (*fam.*) chiste viejo.

chesty [ˈtʃesti], *a.* (algo) enfermo del pecho.

chevalier [ʃevəˈliə], *s.* caballero.

cheviot [ˈtʃi:viət], *s.* (paño) cheviot.

chevron [ˈʃevrən], *s.* (*blas.*) cheurón; (*mil. etc.*) galón, sardineta.

chew [tʃu:], *v.t.* masticar; ***chew the cud,*** rumiar; (*fam.*) ***chew over,*** pensar despacio, meditar sobre. — *v.i.* masticar; rumiar.

chewing [ˈtʃu:iŋ], *s.* masticación; ***chewing gum,*** chicle.

chiaroscuro [kjɑ:rəˈsku:ro], *s.* claroscuro.

chic [ʃi:k], *a.* elegante, mono. — *s.* chic, elegancia, estilo, estilín.

chicane [ʃiˈkein], *s.* triquiñuela; argucia. — *v.i.* trapacear, usar *o* engañar con triquiñuelas; embrollar.

chicaner [ʃiˈkeinə], *s.* trapacero, enredador.

chicanery [ʃiˈkeinəri], *s.* trapacería, supercheria.

chick [tʃik], *s.* pollito, polluelo; (*fig.*) jovencita.

chicken [ˈtʃikin], *s.* pollo; (*fig.*) gallina, cobarde; ***chicken-coop*** (o ***-run***), gallinero; ***chicken-wire,*** tela metálica.

chicken-hearted [ˈtʃikin-ˈhɑ:tid], *a.* cobarde, gallina.

chicken-pox [ˈtʃikin-pɔks], *s.* (*med.*) varicela, viruelas locas.

chickpea [ˈtʃikpi:], *s.* (*bot.*) garbanzo.

chickweed [ˈtʃikwi:d], *s.* (*bot.*) morgelina, pamplina.

chicory [ˈtʃikəri], *s.* (*bot.*) achicoria.

chide [tʃaid], *irr. v.t.* regañar, reñir.

chider [ˈtʃaidə], *s.* regañador, regañón.

chiding [ˈtʃaidiŋ], *s.* regañina.

chidingly [ˈtʃaidiŋli], *adv.* con reprimenda, con reprensión.

chief [tʃi:f], *a.* principal; en jefe; primero; superior, mayor; capital; supremo; ***chief clerk,*** oficial mayor; ***chief justice,*** presidente de sala; ***chief town,*** capital, ciudad principal. — *s.* jefe; cacique; ***chief of staff,*** jefe de estado mayor.

chiefdom [ˈtʃi:fdəm], *s.* jefatura; cacicato.

chieftain [ˈtʃi:ftin], *s.* jefe; cacique; alidad, caudillo.

chieftaincy [ˈtʃi:ftinsi], *s.* jefatura, caudillaje.

chiffon [ˈʃifɔn], *s.* gasa, soplillo.

chiffonier [ʃifɔˈniə], *s.* armario de salón; gabinete, guardarropa; trapero.

chignon [ˈʃi:njɔŋ], *s.* moño, penca *o* castaña (*aderezo del pelo*).

chilblain [ˈtʃilblein], *s.* sabañón.

child [tʃaild], *s.* (*pl.* **children** [ˈtʃildrən]) niño, niña; hijo, hija; ***child-bearing,*** parto; ***child-bed,*** sobreparto; (*fam.*) ***child's play,*** pan comido, facilón; ***with child,*** encinta, embarazada.

childhood [ˈtʃaildhud], *s.* niñez, infancia.

childish [ˈtʃaildiʃ], *a.* infantil, pueril; aniñado; ***childish action,*** niñería, niñada, chiquillada.

childishness [ˈtʃaildiʃnis], *s.* puerilidad, niñada.

childless [ˈtʃaildlis], *a.* sin hijos.

childlike [ˈtʃaildlaik], *a.* pueril, infantil, propio de niño.

children [ˈtʃildrən], *s.pl.* [CHILD].

Chile [ˈtʃili]. Chile.

Chilean [ˈtʃiliən], *a., s.* chileno.

chill [tʃil], *a.* frío. — *s.* frío, escalofrío; enfriamiento; frialdad; ***to take the chill off,*** quitar del frío. — *v.t.* enfriar, helar; escalofriar; (*metal.*) templar, endurecer. — *v.i.* enfriarse, calofriarse.

chilli [ˈtʃili], *s.* pimentón, chile.
chill(i)ness [ˈtʃil(i)nis], *s.* frialdad; frío; fresquete.
chilling [ˈtʃiliŋ], *a.* resfriador.
chilly [ˈtʃili], *a.* frío; ***it is chilly,*** hace fresquillo *o* fresquete.
chime [tʃaim], *s.* juego *o* repique de campanas, campaneo, repiquete; conformidad; armonía. — *v.t., v.i.* repicar, sonar; ***chime the hour,*** dar la hora; (*fam.*) ***chime in,*** meter baza.
chimera [kiˈmiərə], *s.* quimera.
chimerical [kiˈmerikəl], *a.* quimérico.
chimney [ˈtʃimni], *s.* chimenea; tubo (*de lámpara*).
chimney-corner [ˈtʃimni-kɔ:nə], *s.* rincón del fuego.
chimney-piece [ˈtʃimni-pi:s], *s.* marco de chimenea.
chimney-pot [ˈtʃimni-pɔt], *s.* cañón de chimenea.
chimney-sweep [ˈtʃimni-swi:p], *s.* deshollinador, limpiachimeneas, *m.inv.*
chimpanzee [tʃimpænˈzi:], *s.* chimpancé.
chin [tʃin], *s.* barbilla; ***chin-strap,*** carrillera, barboquejo; (*fam.*) ***chin-wag,*** palique; ***double chin,*** papada; ***to keep one's chin up,*** no desanimarse; ***to take it on the chin,*** encajar bien el golpe.
China [ˈtʃainə]. China; (*pol.*) ***(mainland) China,*** China continental; ***People's Republic of China,*** República Popular de China; (*pol.*) ***China (Taiwan),*** China (Taiwán); ***Republic of China,*** (la) República de China.
china [ˈtʃainə], *s.* porcelana; loza; vajilla; ***set of china,*** vajilla.
china-ware [ˈtʃainə-wɛə], *s.* porcelana; vajilla.
chinchilla [tʃinˈtʃilə], *s.* (*zool.*) chinchilla.
Chinese [tʃaiˈni:z], *a., s.* chino.
chink (1) [tʃiŋk], *s.* raja, grieta, hendedura, resquicio.
chink (2) [tʃiŋk], *s.* ruidillo metálico, tintineo. — *v.i.* sonar metálicamente.
chintz [tʃints], *s.* quimón, zaraza.
chip [tʃip], *s.* astilla; brizna; saltadura, desportilladura; patata frita; (*Am.*) patata a la inglesa; (*póker*) ficha; pedacito; ***a chip off the old block,*** de tal palo, tal astilla; ***to have a chip on one's shoulder,*** ser un resentido. — *v.t.* astillar, desportillar, descascarillar, desconchar. — *v.i.* astillarse, desportillarse, descascarillarse; ***chip in,*** meter baza; interrumpir; aportar; contribuir.
chipping [ˈtʃipiŋ], *s.* pedazo, trozo, fragmento; astilla; brizna.
chirographer [kaiəˈrɔgrəfə], *s.* quirógrafo.
chiropodist [kiˈrɔpədist], *s.* pedicuro, callista, *m.f.*
chirp [tʃə:p], *s.* gorjeo, pío. — *v.i.* gorjear, piar.
chirping [ˈtʃə:piŋ], *s.* chirrido, piada.
chirrup [ˈtʃirəp], *s.* gorjeo, trino. — *v.t.* animar, excitar. — *v.i.* animarse; (*fam.*) actuar de claque.
chisel [ˈtʃizəl], *s.* cincel, escoplo; formón; ***cold chisel,*** cortafrío. — *v.t.* cincelar, escoplear; (*fam.*) timar, estafar.
chiseller [ˈtʃizələ], *s.* (*fam.*) timador, estafador.
chiselling [ˈtʃizəliŋ], *s.* cinceladura; estafa.
chit (1) [tʃit], *s.* vale, nota.
chit (2) [tʃit], *s.* ***a chit of a girl,*** un escuerzo.
chit-chat [ˈtʃit-tʃæt], *s.* charla, cháchara, palique.
chitterlings [ˈtʃitəliŋz], *s.pl.* mondongo de cerdo.
chitty [ˈtʃiti], [CHIT (1)].
chivalrous, chivalric [ˈʃivəlrəs, -rik], *a.* caballeresco, caballeroso.
chivalry [ˈʃivəlri], *s.* caballerosidad, hidalguía.
chives [tʃaivz], *s.pl.* (*bot.*) cebollino.
chloral [ˈklɔ:rəl], *s.* (*quím.*) cloral.
chlorate [ˈklɔ:reit], *s.* clorato.
chloric [ˈklɔ:rik], *a.* (*quím.*) clórico.
chloride [ˈklɔ:raid], *s.* (*quím.*) cloruro.
chlorine [ˈklɔ:ri:n], *s.* (*quím.*) cloro.
chloroform [ˈklɔrəfɔ:m], *s.* cloroformo. — *v.t.* cloroformizar.
chlorophyll [ˈklɔrəfil], *s.* (*bot.*) clorofila.
chlorosis [klɔ:ˈrousis], *s.* (*med.*) clorosis, *f. inv.*
chlorotic [klɔˈrɔtik], *a.* clorótico.
chlorous [ˈklɔ:rəs], *a.* cloroso.
chock [tʃɔk], *adv.* enteramente, por completo; ***chock full,*** atestado. — *s.* calza, cuña; (*mar.*) taco; cornamusa de guía. — *v.t.* calzar, acuñar, afianzar; tapar (*un hueco*); colmar, atestar.
chocolate [ˈtʃɔkəlit], *s.* chocolate; ***chocolate-cup,*** jícara; ***chocolate-pot,*** chocolatera; ***box of chocolates,*** caja de bombones.
choice [tʃɔis], *a.* escogido, selecto. — *s.* elección, selección; opción, posibilidad; cosa escogida; (la) flor, (lo) más escogido; variedad; ***Hobson's choice,*** tomarlo o dejarlo, o eso o nada.
choiceless [ˈtʃɔislis], *a.* sin (posibilidad de) elección.
choicely [ˈtʃɔisli], *adv.* escogidamente, primorosamente.
choiceness [ˈtʃɔisnis], *s.* superioridad, excelencia; discernimiento; delicadeza.
choir [kwaiə], *s.* coro.
choke [tʃouk], *s.* (*aut.*) obturador; (*fam.*) aire. — *v.t.* ahogar; sofocar; estrangular; tapar, atascar, obstruir; ***choke back*** o ***down,*** retener, aguantarse; ***choke off,*** desanimar, disuadir; ***choke up,*** tapar, obstruir. — *v.i.* ahogarse; atragantarse.
choker [ˈtʃoukə], *s.* (*mech.*) obturador; (*fig., fam.*) tapaboca.
choler [ˈkɔlə], *s.* cólera, ira.
cholera [ˈkɔlərə], *s.* (*med.*) cólera, *m.*
choleric [ˈkɔlərik], *a.* colérico, irascible.
cholesterine [kɔˈlestərin], *s.* colesterina.
cholesterol [kɔˈlestərɔl], *s.* (*med.*) colesterol.
choose [tʃu:z], *v.t., v.i.* escoger, elegir, seleccionar, optar (por); ***choose between,*** elegir entre; ***choose to,*** optar por.
choosing [ˈtʃu:ziŋ], *s.* escogimiento, elección.
choosy [ˈtʃu:zi], *a.* (*fam.*) escogido, exigentón.
chop [tʃɔp], *s.* golpe cortante; hachazo; tajada; chuleta; (*fam.*) despido; cambio; (*pl., fam.*) boca, labios, *m.pl.*, hocicos, *m.pl.*; (*fam.*) ***to get the chop,*** ser despedido. — *v.t.* tajar, cortar; ***chop off,*** tronchar, cercenar; ***chop up (small),*** picar, desmenuzar. — *v.i.* ***chop about, chop and change,*** cambiar, variar; cambiar de idea, vacilar; virar.
chop-chop! [ˈtʃɔp-ˈtʃɔp], *interj.* ¡rápido! ¡espabílate!
chop-house [ˈtʃɔp-haus], *s.* tasca.
chopper [ˈtʃɔpə], *s.* hacha, hacheta; cuchilla (*de carnicero*).
chopping [ˈtʃɔpiŋ], *s.* (el) tajar, cortar; ***chopping block,*** tajo.
choppy [ˈtʃɔpi], *a.* ***choppy sea,*** mar picada.
chopsticks [ˈtʃɔpstiks], *s. pl.* palillos, *m.pl.*
choral [ˈkɔ:rəl], *a.* coral; ***choral society,*** orfeón. — [kəˈrɑ:l], *s.* coral.
choralist [ˈkɔ:rəlist], *s.* corista, *m.f.*
chorally [ˈkɔ:rəli], *adv.* en coro.
chord [kɔ:d], *s.* cuerda; (*mús.*) acorde; (*med.*) cordón; (*fig.*) ***to strike the right chord,*** caer bien.
chore [tʃɔ:], *s.* tarea pesada; faena doméstica.
chorea [kəˈri:ə], *s.* (*med.*) corea.
choreographer [kɔriˈɔgrəfə], *s.* coreógrafo.
choreographic [kɔrioˈgræfik], *a.* coreográfico.
choreography [kɔriˈɔgrəfi], *s.* coreografía.
chorion [ˈkɔ:riən], *s.* (*anat.*) corión.
chorist, chorister [ˈkɔ:rist, ˈkɔristə], *s.* corista, *m.f.*
choroid [ˈkɔ:rɔid], *a., s.* (*anat.*) coroideo.
chortle [tʃɔ:tl], *v.i.* decir con tono alegre *o* jovial.
chorus [ˈkɔ:rəs], *s.* coro; estribillo; ***to sing in chorus,*** cantar en coro; ***chorus-girl,*** corista, vicetiple. — *v.t., v.i.* decir al unísono, corear.
chough [tʃʌf], *s.* (*orn.*) chova.

chow [tʃau], *s.* perro chino.
chowder [ˈtʃaudə], *s.* pitanza; mezcla, potaje.
chrism [ˈkrizəm], *s.* crisma, *m.f.*
chrismatory [ˈkrizmətəri], *s.* crismera.
chrisom [ˈkrizəm], *s.* capillo de cristianar; ropaje de bautismo.
Christ [kraist], *s.* Cristo, Jesucristo.
christen [krisn], *v.t.* bautizar, cristianar.
Christendom [ˈkrisəndəm], *s.* cristiandad.
christening [ˈkrisəniŋ], *a.* bautismal. — *s.* bautismo, bautizo.
Christian [ˈkristjən], *a.*, *s.* cristiano; ***Christian name,*** nombre de bautismo, nombre de pila.
Christianity [kristiˈæniti], *s.* cristianismo.
Christianize [ˈkristjənaiz], *v.t.* cristianizar, cristianar.
Christianlike [ˈkristjənlaik], *a.* propio de cristiano.
Christmas [ˈkrisməs], *a.* de Navidad; ***Christmas box,*** aguinaldo; ***Christmas carol,*** villancico; ***Christmas Eve,*** Nochebuena, *f.*; día de Nochebuena; ***Christmas tree,*** árbol de Navidad. — *s.* Navidad, Navidades, pascuas de Navidad, *f.pl.*; ***Merry Christmas!*** ¡Felices Navidades *o* Pascuas!
chromate [ˈkroumeit], *s.* (*quím.*) cromato.
chromatic [kroˈmætik], *a.*, *s.* cromático.
chrome [kroum], *s.* cromo; bicromato potásico; ***chrome steel,*** acero al cromo. — *v.t.* cromar.
chromium [ˈkroumiəm], *s.* cromo; ***chromium plating,*** cromado.
chromolithography [kroumoliˈθɔgrəfi], *s.* cromolitografía.
chromophotography [kroumofəˈtɔgrafi], *s.* cromofotografía.
chromophotographic [kroumofoutoˈgræfik], *a.* cromofotográfico.
chromoptometer [kroumɔpˈtɔmitə], *s.* cromoptómetro.
chromous [ˈkrouməs], *a.* cromoso.
chronic [ˈkrɔnik], *a.* crónico; inveterado.
chronicle [ˈkrɔnikl], *s.* crónica. — *v.t.* escribir una crónica de.
chronicler [ˈkrɔniklə], *s.* cronista, *m.f.*
chronique [krɔˈni:k], *s.* crónica, anales, *m.pl.*
chronogram [ˈkrɔnogræm], *s.* cronograma, *m.*
chronograph [ˈkrɔnogræf], *s.* cronógrafo.
chronographer [krəˈnɔgrəfə], *s.* cronógrafo.
chronologer, chronologist [krəˈnɔlədʒə, -ist], *s.* cronologista, *m.f.*, cronólogo.
chronological [krɔnəˈlɔdʒikəl], *a.* cronológico.
chronology [krəˈnɔlədʒi] *s.* cronología.
chronometer [krəˈnɔmitə] *s.* cronómetro.
chronometric(al) [krɔnəˈmetrik(əl)], *a.* cronométrico.
chronometry [krəˈnɔmitri], *s.* cronometría.
chrysalis [ˈkrisəlis], *s.* (*pl.* **chrysalides** [kriˈsælidi:z]), crisálida.
chrysanthemum [kriˈsænθəməm], *s.* (*bot.*) crisantemo.
chrysolite [ˈkrisolait], *s.* (*min.*) crisólito.
chub [tʃʌb], *s.* (*ict.*) cacho.
chubby [ˈtʃʌbi], *a.* regordete, rechoncho, gordinflón; ***chubby-faced, chubby-cheeked,*** mofletudo.
chuck [tʃʌk], *s.* cloqueo; mamola; echada; (*mec.*) mandril, mangote, plato de torno; cuña, calzo. — *v.t.* (*fam.*) echar, tirar; hacer la mamola, dar una sobarbada a; (*fam.*) ***chuck it!*** ¡déjate de eso!
chuckle [tʃʌkl], *s.* risa ahogada, risita; cloqueo. — *v.i.* reírse entre dientes; reírse de satisfacción; cloquear.
chuckle-head [ˈtʃʌkl-hed], *s.* cabeza de chorlito.
chuffed [tʃʌft], *a.* (*fam.*) ***to be chuffed*** (***with o.s.***), estar encantado de la vida.
chuffer [ˈtʃʌfə], *s.* (*infantil*) trenecito.
chuffy [ˈtʃʌfi], *a.* rechoncho, gordote; grosero.
chug [tʃʌg], *v.i.* (*mec.*, *fam.*) resoplar (sordamente); (*fam.*) ***chug along,*** avanzar despacito.
chum [tʃʌm], *s.* (*fam.*) compinche, compañero, amigo íntimo. — *v.i.* (*fam.*) — ***up,*** compartir el cuarto; hacerse amigos.
chump [tʃʌmp], *s.* tarugo, zoquete; majadero; (*fam.*) ***off one's chump,*** chalado.
chunk [tʃʌŋk], *s.* pedazo, trozote, cacho.
chunky [ˈtʃʌŋki], *a.* pesadote, cuadradote.
church [tʃə:tʃ], *s.* iglesia; ***Church of England,*** Iglesia Anglicana; ***church music,*** música sacra; ***to go to church,*** ir a misa. — *v.t.* purificar.
church-goer [ˈtʃə:tʃ-gouə], *s.* devoto; (*despec.*) beato, iglesiero.
churching [ˈtʃə:tʃiŋ], *s.* purificación.
churchman [ˈtʃə:tʃmən], *s.* eclesiástico, sacerdote; miembro de una iglesia.
churchwarden [ˈtʃə:tʃˈwɔ:dn], *s.* capiller.
churchyard [ˈtʃə:tʃjɑ:d], *s.* cementerio.
churl [tʃə:l], *s.* patán, paleto, palurdo.
churlish [ˈtʃə:liʃ], *a.* grosero, descortés, zafio.
churlishness [ˈtʃə:liʃnis], *s.* grosería, zafiedad.
churn [tʃə:n], *s.* mantequera. — *v.t.* mazar, batir; agitar, revolver.
churn-owl [ˈtʃə:n-aul], *s.* (*orn.*) chotacabras, *f.inv.*
churn-staff [ˈtʃə:n-ˈstɑ:f], *s.* batidera.
chute [ʃu:t], *s.* salto de agua; canalón; tolva; tobogán.
chylaceous [kaiˈleiʃəs], *a.* quilar, quiloso.
chyle [kail], *s.* quilo.
chylifaction [kailiˈfækʃən], *s.* quilificación.
chylous [ˈkailəs], *s.* quiloso.
chyme [kaim], *s.* (*fisiol.*) quimo.
chymify [ˈkaimifai], *v.t.* quimificar.
chymous [ˈkaiməs], *a.* quimoso.
ciborium [siˈbɔ:riəm], *s.* copón; dosel de altar, ciborio.
cicada [siˈkɑ:də], *s.* (*ent.*) cigarra, chicharra.
cicatrice, cicatrix [ˈsikətris, -ks], *s.* (*pat.*) cicatriz, *f.*
cicatricle, cicatricule [siˈkætrikl, -kju:l], *s.* (*biol.*) galladura.
cicatrize [ˈsikətraiz], *v.t.* cicatrizar. — *v.i.* cicatrizarse.
cicely [ˈsisəli], *s.* (*bot.*) perifollo, cerafollo.
cicerone [tʃitʃəˈrouni], *s.* cicerone, guía, *m.f.*
Ciceronian [sisəˈrouniən], *a.* ciceroniano.
cicisbeo [tʃitʃizˈbeiou], *s.* chichisbeo; amante de una mujer casada.
cider [ˈsaidə], *s.* sidra.
cierge [sə:dʒ], *s.* cirio.
cigar [siˈgɑ:], *s.* (cigarro) puro; ***cigar case,*** petaca, cigarrera; ***cigar holder,*** boquilla; ***cigar shop,*** cigarrería, estanco.
cigarette [sigəˈret], *s.* cigarrillo, pitillo; ***cigarette case,*** pitillera; ***cigarette paper,*** papel de fumar.
ciliary [ˈsiliəri], *a.* ciliar.
ciliate [ˈsilieit], *a.* (*bot.*) ciliado, pestañoso.
cilicious [siˈliʃəs], *a.* cerdoso, hecho de cerdas *o* crin.
cimeter [ˈsimitə], [SCIMITAR].
Cimmerian [siˈmiəriən], *a.* cimerio, cimeriano.
cinch [sintʃ], *s.* (*Am.*) cincha; ganga; (*fam.*) ***it's a cinch,*** es pan comido. — *v.t.* cinchar; ceñir.
cinchona [sinˈkounə], *s.* (*bot.*) cinchona, quina.
cincture [ˈsiŋktʃə], *s.* cinto, ceñidor, cíngulo, cercado; cerca. — *v.t.* ceñir, cercar, rodear.
cinder [ˈsində], *s.* ceniza; (*dep.*) ***cinder-track,*** pista de cenizas; (*pl.*) cenizas, pavesas.
Cinderella [sindəˈrelə]. (La) Cenicienta.
cine-camera [ˈsini-ˈkæmərə], *s.* (cámara) tomavistas, *f.inv.*
cinema [ˈsinimə], *s.* cine.
cinematograph [siniˈmætəgræf], *s.* cinematógrafo.
cine-projector [ˈsini-prəˈdʒektə], *s.* proyector cinematográfico.

cineraria [sinəˈrɛəriə], *s.* (*bot.*) cineraria.
cinerary [ˈsinərəri], *a.* cinerario.
cineration [sinəˈreiʃən], *s.* incineración.
Cingalese [ˈsiŋəli:z], *a.*, *s.* cingalés, *m.*
cinnabar [ˈsinəbɑ:], *s.* cinabrio.
cinnamic [siˈnæmik], *a.* de canela.
cinnamon [ˈsinəmən], *s.* (*bot.*) canela.
cinquefoil [ˈsiŋkfɔil], *s.* (*bot.*) quinquefolio, cincoenrama; (*arq.*) pentalóbulo.
cipher [ˈsaifə], *a.* cifrado, en cifra. — *s.* cifra, clave; cero; nulidad, don nadie; ***he's a mere cipher,*** es un cero a la izquierda. — *v.t.* cifrar, escribir en cifra; calcular. — *v.i.* hacer cálculos.
circinate [ˈsə:sineit], *a.* (*bot.*) circinado.
Circinus [ˈsə:sinəs], *s.* (*astron.*) Compás.
circle [sə:kl], *s.* círculo; corro, corrillo, grupo. *v.t.* dar la vuelta a, rodear, circundar. — *v.i.* dar vueltas, girar.
circlet [ˈsə:klit], *s.* círculo; pequeño anillo; corona.
circuit [ˈsə:kit], *s.* circuito; ***closed circuit television,*** televisión de circuito cerrado; ***to go on circuit,*** hacer un itinerario. — *v.t.*, *v.i.* dar la vuelta (a), hacer un rodeo (alrededor de), rodear.
circuit-breaker [ˈsə:kit-breikə], *s.* (*elec.*) cortacircuitos, *m.inv.*
circuitous [sə:ˈkju:itəs], *a.* indirecto; tortuoso.
circular [ˈsə:kjulə], *a.* circular. — *s.* (carta) circular.
circularize [ˈsə:kjuləraiz], *v.t.* mandar circulares a.
circulate [ˈsə:kjuleit], *v.t.* (hacer) circular; propagar, distribuir. — *v.i.* circular; propagarse.
circulating [ˈsə:kjuleitiŋ], *a.* circulante; (*mat.*) (fracción) continua, periódica; ***circulating medium,*** moneda corriente.
circulation [sə:kjuˈleiʃən], *s.* circulación, distribución; tirada (*de periódico*).
circulative [ˈsə:kjulətiv], *a.* circulatorio.
circulatory [ˈsə:kjuleitəri], *a.* circulatorio.
circumambient [sə:kəmˈæmbiənt], *a.* circumambiente.
circumcise [ˈsə:kəmsaiz], *v.t.* circuncidar.
circumcision [sə:kəmˈsiʒən], *s.* circuncisión.
circumference [səˈkʌmfərəns], *s.* circunferencia.
circumflex [ˈsə:kəmfleks], *a.*, *s.* circunflejo.
circumfuse [sə:kəmˈfju:z], *v.t.* difundir en derredor.
circumfusion [sə:kəmˈfju:ʒən], *s.* difusión.
circumjacent [sə:kəmˈdʒeisənt], *a.* circunyacente.
circumlocution [sə:kəmləˈkju:ʃən], *s.* circunlocución, circunloquio.
circumnavigable [sə:kəmˈnævigəbl], *a.* (*mar.*) circunnavegable.
circumnavigate [sə:kəmˈnævigeit], *v.t.* circunnavegar.
circumnavigation [sə:kəmnæviˈgeiʃən], *s.* circunnavegación.
circumnavigator [sə:kəmˈnævigeitə], *s.* circunnavegante.
circumscribe [ˈsə:kəmskraib], *v.t.* circunscribir.
circumscription [sə:kəmˈskripʃən], *s.* circunscripción.
circumscriptive [sə:kəmˈskriptiv], *a.* circunscriptivo.
circumspect [ˈsə:kəmspekt], *a.* circunspecto, prudente.
circumspection [sə:kəmˈspekʃən], *s.* circunspección, prudencia.
circumspective [sə:kəmˈspektiv], *a.* circunspecto, mirado.
circumspectness [ˈsə:kəmspektnis], *s.* cautela, prudencia.
circumstance [ˈsə:kəmstæns], *s.* circunstancia; pormenor, detalle; ceremonia; ***to act according to circumstances,*** obrar de acuerdo con las circunstancias; ***in the circumstances,*** dadas las circunstancias; ***in easy circumstances,*** holgado, acomodado; ***pomp and circumstance,*** pompa(s) y ceremonia(s); ***under no circumstances,*** de ninguna manera, bajo ningún concepto.
circumstantial [sə:kəmˈstænʃəl], *a.* circunstancial; circunstanciado; (*der.*) indiciario; ***circumstantial evidence,*** prueba(s) indiciaria(s).
circumstantiality [sə:kəmstænʃiˈæliti], *s.* (lo) circunstancial; detalle, pormenor.
circumstantiate [sə:kəmˈstænʃieit], *v.t.* circunstanciar, detallar; apoyar con pruebas.
circumvallate [sə:kʌmvəleit], *v.t.* circunvalar.
circumvallation [sə:kəmvəˈleiʃən], *s.* circunvalación.
circumvent [sə:kəmˈvent], *v.t.* salvar; burlar (*dificultades*).
circumvention [sə:kəmˈvenʃən], *s.* (el) salvar; (el) burlar.
circumventive [sə:kəmˈventiv], *a.* que salva; que burla.
circumvest [sə:kəmˈvest], *v.t.* circundar, rodear, cercar.
circumvolution [sə:kəmvəˈlju:ʃən], *s.* circunvolución; (*arq.*) voluta; vuelta, rodeo.
circumvolve [sə:kəmˈvɔlv], *v.t.* enrollar, envolver; dar un movimiento circular a.
circus [ˈsə:kəs], *s.* circo; glorieta, plaza circular.
cirque [ˈsə:k], *s.* espacio circular; (*poét.*) circo, arena; (*geol.*) anfiteatro natural.
cirrhosis [siˈrousis], *s.* (*med.*) cirrosis, *f.inv.*
cirrus [ˈsirəs], *s.* cirro.
Cisalpine [sisˈælpain], *a.* cisalpino.
Cisatlantic [sisətˈlæntik], *a.* cisatlántico.
cist [sist], *s.* arquilla; cámara sepulcral.
Cistercian [sisˈtə:ʃən], *a.*, *s.* cisterciense.
cistern [ˈsistən], *s.* cisterna.
cistus [ˈsistəs], *s.* (*bot.*) cisto, jara.
citable [ˈsaitəbl], *a.* citable.
citadel [ˈsitədl], *s.* ciudadela.
citation [seiˈteiʃən], *s.* citación; mención.
cite [sait], *v.t.* citar; mencionar.
cithara [ˈsiθərə], *s.* (*mús.*) cítara.
citharist [ˈsiθərist], *s.* citarista, *m.f.*
cithern [ˈsiθə:n], *s.* (*mús.*) vihuela de péndola.
citizen [ˈsitizən], *a.* ciudadano. — *s.* ciudadano; vecino; ***fellow-citizen,*** conciudadano.
citizenship [ˈsitizənʃip], *s.* ciudadanía.
citrate [ˈsitreit], *s.* citrato.
citric [ˈsitrik], *a.* cítrico.
citrine [ˈsitri:n], *a.* cetrino.
citron [ˈsitrən], *s.* cidra; ***citron tree,*** cidro.
citrus [ˈsitrəs], *a.* (*bot.*) auranciáceo; ***citrus fruit(s),*** agrios, *m.pl.*
city [ˈsiti], *a.* de la ciudad, ciudadano, municipal; ***city council,*** ayuntamiento. — *s.* ciudad; (*Londres*) centro comercial y bancario.
civet [ˈsivit], *s.* civeto; algalia; ***civet-cat,*** gato de algalia.
civic [ˈsivik], *a.* cívico; municipal; ***civic centre,*** conjunto de edificios municipales. — *s.* (*pl.*) ciencia de los derechos del ciudadano.
civil [ˈsivəl], *a.* civil; amable, urbano, cortés; ***Civil List,*** presupuesto de la Casa Real; ***civil defence,*** defensa pasiva; ***civil servant,*** funcionario público; ***civil service,*** burocracia (estatal).
civilian [siˈviljən], *s.* paisano.
civility [siˈviliti], *s.* amabilidad, urbanidad, cortesía.
civilizable [ˈsivilaizəbl], *a.* civilizable.
civilization [sivilaiˈzeiʃən], *s.* civilización.
civilize [ˈsivilaiz], *v.t.* civilizar.
civilizer [ˈsivilaizə], *s.* civilizador.
civism [ˈsivizəm], *s.* civismo.
civvy [ˈsivi], *a.*, *s.* (*fam.*, *mil.*) [CIVILIAN]; ***civvy street,*** la vida de paisano; ***in civvies,*** vestido de paisano.

clack [klæk], *s.* chasquido; tarabilla; ***clack valve,*** chapaleta. — *v.i.* hacer chasquido; sonar.
claim [kleim], *s.* reclamación; demanda; pretensión; reivindicación; (*min.*) pertenencia; ***lay claim to,*** reclamar; reivindicar. — *v.t.* reclamar; demandar; pretender; reivindicar; afirmar, alegar; ***claim*** (***the***) ***attention,*** llamar la atención.
claimant, claimer [ˈkleimənt, -ə], *s.* demandante; reclamante.
clairvoyance [klɛəˈvɔiəns], *s.* clarividencia.
clairvoyant [klɛəˈvɔiənt], *a.*, *s.* clarividente; adivino.
clam [klæm], *s.* almeja; peine (*de molusco*); telina, chirla; ***to shut up like a clam,*** no decir ni mu.
clamber [ˈklæmbə], *v.i.* gatear, trepar, encaramarse.
clamminess [ˈklæminis], *s.* humedad pegajosa.
clammy [ˈklæmi], *a.* húmedo y pegajoso.
clamorous [ˈklæmərəs], *a.* clamoroso, tumultuoso.
clamorousness [ˈklæmərəsnis], *s.* (lo) clamoroso.
clamour [ˈklæmə], *s.* clamor, clamoreo; tumulto; gritería, vocería. — *v.i.* clamar, gritar, vociferar.
clamp [klæmp], *s.* cárcel, tornillo de sujeción; abrazadera; mordaza; laña; borne; tenazas; (*mar.*) durmiente; (*agric.*) silo, silero. — *v.t.* lañar; afianzar, sujetar; ***clamp together,*** juntar fuertemente. — *v.i.* — ***down on,*** ponerse en plan duro *o* estricto con, apretar los tornillos a.
clamping [ˈklæmpiŋ], *s.* empalme.
clan [klæn], *s.* clan; camarilla; grupo cerrado.
clandestine [klænˈdestain], *a.* clandestino.
clandestinity [klændəsˈtiniti], *s.* clandestinidad.
clang [klæŋ], *s.* estruendo metálico. — *v.i.* sonar *o* resonar con sonido metálico. — *v.t.* hacer resonar.
clanger [ˈklæŋə], *s.* (*fam.*) ***to drop a clanger,*** hacer una plancha.
clangorous [ˈklæŋgərəs], *a.* estruendoso, estrepitoso.
clangour [ˈklæŋə], *s.* estruendo, estrépito.
clank [klæŋk], *s.* fuerte sonido metálico. — *v.i.* sonar, resonar (*al chocar*), entrechocar. — *v.t.* hacer resonar.
clannish [ˈklæniʃ], *a.* de clan; cerrado.
clanship [ˈklænʃip], *s.* asociación, unión bajo un jefe.
clansman [ˈklænzmən], *s.* miembro de un clan.
clap (1) [klæp], *s.* golpe seco; palmada; aplauso. — *v.t.* batir, golpear; aplaudir; dar una palmada a; cerrar de golpe; ***clap eyes on,*** echarle la vista encima a; ***clap in jail,*** meter en la cárcel. — *v.i.* cerrarse ruidosamente; aplaudir, dar palmadas; guachapear.
clap (2) [klæp], *s.* (*fam.*) gonorrea.
clap-board [ˈklæp-bɔ:d], *s.* duela de barril *o* tonel; (*Am.*) tabla de chilla.
clapper [ˈklæpə], *s.* palmoteador; badajo; tarabilla de molino; cítola; aldaba; (*mar.*) chapaleta; tableta, tejoleta.
clapperclaw [ˈklæpəklɔ:], *v.t.* regañar, maltratar de palabra.
clapping [ˈklæpiŋ], *s.* aleteo; palmoteo; palmadas; aplausos, *m.pl.*
claptrap [ˈklæptræp], *s.* golpe de teatro; charlatanería; (*fam.*) sandeces, *f.pl.*
clarabella [klærəˈbelə], *s.* clarabella, registro melodioso del órgano.
clarence [ˈklærəns], *s.* (coche) clarens, *m.inv.*
claret [ˈklærit], *s.* clarete.
clarification [klærifiˈkeiʃən], *s.* clarificación; aclaración.
clarify [ˈklærifai], *v.t.* clarificar; aclarar; esclarecer.
clarinet [klæriˈnet], *s.* (*mús.*) clarinete.
clarinettist [klæriˈnetist], *s.* clarinete.
clarion [ˈklæriən], *s.* (*mús.*) clarín.
clarity [ˈklæriti], *s.* claridad.
clary [ˈklɛəri], *s.* (*bot.*) salvia silvestre.
clash [klæʃ], *s.* choque; fragor; golpe violento. — *v.t.* batir; golpear. — *v.i.* chocar, entrechocar; desentonar.
clasp [klɑ:sp], *s.* broche; corchete; cierre; hebilla; abrazo; presilla; abrazadera; (*mec.*) grapa; apretón; ***clasp-knife,*** navaja; ***hand-clasp,*** apretón de manos. — *v.t.* abrochar, encorchetar; abrazar, apretar.
class [klɑ:s], *s.* clase, *f.*; (*fam.*) elegancia, buen tono, estilo; ***class books,*** libros de clase; (*pol.*) ***class struggle,*** lucha de clases. — *v.t.* clasificar, ordenar.
classic(**al**) [ˈklæsik(əl)], *a.* clásico. — *s.* obra clásica; ***the classics,*** las obras clásicas; las humanidades.
classicism [ˈklæsisizəm], *s.* clasicismo.
classicist [ˈklæsisist], *s.* clasicista, *m.f.*, humanista, *m.f.*
classification [klæsifiˈkeiʃən], *s.* clasificación.
classify [ˈklæsifai], *v.t.* clasificar.
classmate [ˈklɑ:smeit], *s.* condiscípulo, compañero de clase.
classroom [ˈklɑ:sru:m], *s.* (sala de) clase, aula.
clatter [ˈklætə], *s.* ruido, estruendo, choque ruidoso; chacoloteo; traqueteo. — *v.t.* mover *o* chocar ruidosamente. — *v.i.* hacer ruido *o* estruendo, chocar *o* entrechocar ruidosamente; chacolotear; traquetear.
clause [klɔ:z], *s.* cláusula.
claustral [ˈklɔ:strəl], *a.* claustral.
clavate [ˈkleiveit], *a.* (*bot.*) claviforme.
clavichord [ˈklævikɔ:d], *s.* (*mús.*) clavicordio.
clavicle [ˈklævikl], *s.* (*anat.*) clavícula.
clavicular [klæˈvikjulə], *a.* clavicular.
clavier [kləˈviə], *s.* (*mús.*) teclado; pianoforte.
claw [klɔ:], *s.* garra, uña, garfa; gancho, garfio; (*mar.*) uña de espeque; (*bot.*) pecíolo; ***claw hammer,*** martillo de orejas. — *v.t.* agarrar; desgarrar; arañar. — *v.i.* arañar.
clay [klei], *s.* arcilla, barro, greda; ***baked clay,*** tierra cocida; ***clay pigeon shooting,*** tiro al plato; ***clay pit,*** gredal, barrera; ***potter's clay,*** barro de olleros. — *v.t.* engredar, arcillar; embarrar.
clayey, clayish [ˈkleii, -iʃ], *a.* arcilloso.
claymore [ˈkleimɔ:], *s.* espada escocesa.
clean [kli:n], *a.* limpio; despejado; completo; bien formado; ***clean bill of health,*** patente de buena salud; ***clean-shaven,*** recién afeitado; ***to come clean,*** confesar (lo todo); ***to make clean,*** limpiar; ***to make a clean breast of it,*** cantar de plano; ***to show a clean pair of heels,*** escapar a toda prisa, poner pies en polvorosa. — *v.t.* limpiar; asear; mondar; ***clean out,*** vaciar, limpiar; (*fam.*) ***I have been cleaned out,*** me han desplumado; ***clean one's teeth,*** lavarse los dientes. — *v.i.* limpiar, fregar.
clean-cut [ˈkli:n-ˈkʌt], *a.* preciso, definido.
cleaner [kli:nə], *s.* mujer de la limpieza; quitamanchas, *m.inv.*; ***cleaner's*** (***shop***), tintorería.
cleaning [ˈkli:niŋ], *a.* de limpieza; ***cleaning rag,*** trapo de limpiar. — *s.* limpia, limpieza; aseo; monda.
cleanliness [ˈklenlinis], *s.* limpieza, aseo.
cleanly [ˈklenli], *a.* limpio, aseado; puro.
cleanness [ˈkli:nnis], *s.* limpieza; aseo, inocencia, pureza.
cleansable [ˈklenzəbl], *a.* limpiable, purificable.
cleanse [klenz], *v.t.* limpiar, purificar, purgar, lavar.
cleanser [ˈklenzə], *s.* depurativo; limpiador, purificador; detergente.
cleansing [ˈklenziŋ], *a.* detersorio, mundificativo. — *s.* purificación, depuración, detersión, limpieza.
clear [kliə], *a.* claro; limpio; puro; despejado; terso; libre; ***clear-headed,*** inteligente, despejado; ***clear profit,*** beneficio líquido; ganancia limpia; ***clear-sighted,*** perspicaz, clarividente; ***clear track,*** vía libre; ***the coast is clear,*** no hay

peligro. — *adv.* claramente; enteramente; ***clear-cut,*** bien definido, claramente delimitado; ***to keep clear of,*** evitar, mantenerse a distancia de. — *s.* ***in the clear,*** no comprometido. — *v.t.* disipar; despejar; aclarar; cancelar (*una hipoteca*); absolver; liquidar; purgar; justificar; saltar; franquear, salvar; clarificar, purificar; (*agric.*) desbrozar; despachar (*en la aduana*); ***clear accounts,*** liquidar cuentas; ***clear the air,*** despejar el ambiente; ***clear away,*** quitar, despejar; ***clear the decks for action,*** hacer zafarrancho de combate; ***clear the headland,*** doblar el cabo; ***clear a lot of money,*** ganar *o* sacar mucho dinero; ***clear out,*** sacar; desocupar; ***clear a path,*** abrir calle; ***clear the table,*** levantar, quitar, despejar la mesa; ***clear up,*** despejar, ordenar; esclarecer, dilucidar; ***clear the way,*** despejar el camino, allanar las dificultades. — *v.i.* aclararse; despejarse; clarear; despacharse (*en la aduana*); liquidar cuentas; ***clear off*** o ***out,*** marcharse, largarse; ***clear up,*** aclarar(se), despejar(se); arreglarse (*una situación*).

clearance [ˈkliərəns], *s.* espacio libre *o* muerto; acreditación; negociación, tramitación; despacho; liquidación; ***clearance sale,*** liquidación, saldo.

clearing [ˈkliəriŋ], *s.* claro (*de bosque*); (*com.*) compensación; ***clearing-house*** banco de compensación; (*f.c.*) ***clearing-iron,*** barredera; ***clearing-up,*** (el) limpiar, ordenar; despeje.

clearly [ˈkliəli], *adv.* claramente, evidentemente; libremente; llanamente, abiertamente, sin reserva.

clearness [ˈkliənis], *s.* claridad.

cleat [kliːt], *s.* (*mar.*) tojino; estaquita, tachuela.

cleavage [ˈkliːvidʒ], *s.* hendedura; división, escisión; escote.

cleave [kliːv], *irr. v.t.* hender, partir; dividir; penetrar, abrirse paso en. — *v.i.* pegarse; adherirse.

cleaver [ˈkliːvə], *s.* cuchilla.

cleavers [ˈkliːvəz], *s.pl.* (*bot.*) presera, galio.

clef [klef], *s.* (*mús.*) clave, *f.*; ***treble clef,*** clave de sol; ***bass clef,*** clave de fa.

cleft [kleft], *a.* hendido. — *pret., p.p.* [CLEAVE]. — *s.* hendedura, rajadura, cuarteadura, grieta, fisura.

clematis [ˈklemətis], *s.* (*bot.*) clemátide, *f.*

clemency [ˈklemənsi], *s.* clemencia, misericordia; benignidad, suavidad.

clement [ˈklemənt], *a.* clemente, misericordioso; benigno, suave.

clench [klentʃ], *v.t.* cerrar, apretar.

clepsydra [ˈklepsidrə], *s.* clepsidra.

clerestory [ˈkliəstəri], *s.* (*arq.*) claraboya.

clergy [ˈkləːdʒi], *s.* clero.

clergyman [ˈkləːdʒimən], *s.* clérigo, eclesiástico; sacerdote, cura, *m.*; pastor (protestante).

cleric [ˈklerik], *a.* clerical. — *s.* clérigo.

clerical [ˈklerikəl], *a.* clerical; de oficina, oficinesco; ***clerical error,*** error de pluma *o* de máquina.

clericalism [ˈklerikəlizəm], *s.* clericalismo.

clerk [klɑːk], *s.* empleado; escribiente, oficinista, *m.f.*; amanuense; escribano; clérigo.

clerkship [ˈklɑːkʃip], *s.* empleo de oficinista; escribanía, secretaría.

clever [ˈklevə], *a.* listo; hábil; mañoso.

cleverness [ˈklevənis], *s.* inteligencia; maña, habilidad.

clevis [ˈklevis], *s.* abrazadera en forma de U.

clew [kluː], *s.* ovillo; (*mar.*) puño de escota; pista, indicio. — *v.t.* (*mar.*) cargar los puños de (las velas); ovillar; indicar, señalar (*una pista*); seguir (*por una pista* o *indicio*).

cliché [ˈkliːʃei], *s.* clisé; tópico.

click [klik], *s.* golpecito seco; chasquido; taconazo; tecleo; seguro, fiador. — *v.t.* hacer sonar; ***click the heels,*** taconear; cuadrarse; chascar. — *v.i.* sonar (con un golpecito seco); piñonear (*el gatillo de un arma*); (*fam.*) cuajar; ligar; ***suddenly it clicked,*** de pronto caí.

clicker [ˈklikə], *s.* pestillo de puerta; (*impr.*) compaginador.

clicket [ˈklikit], *s.* llamador, aldaba de puerta.

clicking [ˈklikiŋ], *s.* rudillo(s) seco(s).

client [ˈklaiənt], *s.* cliente.

clientele [kliːɑ̃ˈtel], *s.* clientela.

cliff [klif], *s.* risco, acantilado, farallón.

cliffy [ˈklifi], *a.* acantilado, escarpado.

climacteric [klaimækˈterik], *s.* año climatérico.

climacteric(al) [klaimækˈterik(əl)], *a.* climatérico.

climate [ˈklaimət], *s.* clima, *m.*

climatic [klaiˈmætik], *a.* climático.

climatize [ˈklaimətaiz], *v.t.* aclimatar.

climatology [klaiməˈtɔlədʒi], *s.* climatología.

climax [ˈklaimæks], *s.* clímax; culminación; cenit; punto crítico, álgido *o* culminante; crisis.

climb [klaim], *s.* subida, ascensión. — *v.t.* trepar, subir, escalar. — *v.i.* trepar, subir, encaramarse; ***climb down,*** bajar (a gatas); volverse atrás, retractarse, recoger velas.

climbable [ˈklaiməbl], *a.* accesible, que se puede subir.

climber [ˈklaimə], *s.* montañista, *m.f.*; escalador; (*bot.*) enredadera; (*zool.*) trepadora (*pájaros*).

climbing [ˈklaimiŋ], *a.* trepante, trepador. — *s.* subida, trepa; montañismo.

clime [klaim], *s.* (*poét.*) clima, *m.*; región, sitio.

clinch [klintʃ], *s.* remache; roblón; grapa; argumento irrebatible; agarro, lucha cuerpo a cuerpo. — *v.t.* remachar; agarrar, afianzar; (*mar.*) entalingar; ***clinch a deal,*** cerrar un trato. — *v.i.* agarrarse, asirse fuertemente.

clinching [ˈklintʃiŋ], *s.* remache, robladura; (*mar.*) solapadura.

cling [kliŋ], *irr. v.i.* aferrarse, adherirse, pegarse; persistir (*un olor etc.*); ***cling to,*** agarrarse *o* cogerse a; adherirse *o* pegarse a.

clinging [ˈkliŋiŋ], *a.* pegajoso, adhesivo; ceñido.

clinic [ˈklinik], *s.* clínica.

clinical [ˈklinikəl], *a.* clínico.

clink [kliŋk], *s.* tintín; (*fam.*) chirona. — *v.t.* hacer tintinear; ***clink the glasses,*** chocar las copas. — *v.i.* retiñir, tintinear.

clinker [ˈkliŋkə], *s.* ladrillo refractario; escoria.

clinker-built [ˈkliŋkə-bilt], *a.* de tingladillo.

clinkstone [ˈkliŋkstoun], *s.* perleta, fonolita.

clinometer [kliˈnɔmitə], *s.* clinómetro.

clinometric [klinoˈmetrik], *a.* clinométrico.

clip [klip], *s.* tijeretada, tijeretazo; esquileo, trasquila; grapa, pinza, sujetapapeles, *m.inv.*; sujetador, presilla, alfiler, broche, clip; golpecito (seco), bofetoncito; (*fig., fam.*) ***clip joint,*** desplumadero. — *v.t.* cortar con tijeras; esquilar, trasquilar, cercenar; recortar; podar, mondar; pellizcar; acortar; sujetar; dar un bofetoncito a, dar un golpecito seco a.

clipper [ˈklipə], *s.* cizalla; (*mar., aer.*) clíper; (*s.pl.*) cizalla; (tijeras) podadoras; maquinilla (del pelo).

clipping [ˈklipiŋ], *s.* trasquilón; recorte; retal; tijereteo.

clique [kliːk], *s.* pandilla; camarilla.

cloak [klouk], *s.* capa; capote; manto; (*fig.*) pretexto. — *v.t.* encapotar; ocultar, encubrir.

cloak-and-dagger [ˈklouk-ənd-ˈdægə], *a.* de capa y espada; de agente secreto, jemsbondesco.

cloak-room [ˈklouk-ruːm], *s.* guardarropa; servicios, *m.pl.*

clock [klɔk], *s.* reloj; (*dep.*) cronómetro; ***alarm clock,*** despertador; ***against the clock,*** contra reloj; ***clock-case,*** caja de reloj; ***clock-maker,*** relojero; (*fig.*) ***to turn the clock back,*** volver al pasado *o* a lo de antes. — *v.t.* cronometrar; consignar. — *v.i.* — ***in, out,*** fichar, consignar la entrada, la salida.

clock-work [ˈklɔk-wəːk], *s.* (aparato de) relojería; ***like clock-work,*** matemático, automático, como un reloj, cual clavo.

clod [klɔd], *s.* terrón; gleba; zoquete, paleto, patán.
cloddish [ˈklɔdiʃ], *a.* paleto.
clodhopper [ˈklɔdhɔpə], *s.* patán, destripaterrones, *m.inv.*; (*pl.*) zapatones, *m.pl.*
clog (1) [klɔg], *s.* atasco, obstrucción; estorbo. — *v.t.* atascar, obstruir; estorbar.
clog (2) [klɔg], *s.* zueco.
cloister [ˈklɔistə], *s.* claustro. — *v.t.* enclaustrar.
cloistered [ˈklɔistəd], *a.* enclaustrado; ***to lead a cloistered existence,*** vivir aislado del mundo.
close (1) [klouz], *s.* fin, conclusión; clausura; cierre; caída; cercado; pasaje; ***the close of the day,*** la caída de la tarde; ***to bring to a close,*** llevar a término. — *v.t.* cerrar; tapar; concluir; saldar. — *v.i.* cerrar(se); terminar(se); concluir(se); convenirse; cicatrizarse; ***close down,*** cerrar(se) (por completo *o* definitivamente); ***close in,*** encerrar, cercar; irse acercando; ***close in on,*** ir acorralando cada vez más; ***close up,*** cerrar (por completo *o* definitivamente); acercar(se), apretar(se), correr(se); cicatrizarse.
close (2) [klous], *a.* cerrado; acotado; estrecho, ajustado; pesado, sofocante; espeso, tupido; inmediato, contiguo; reñido; exacto, fiel; estrecho, íntimo; cuidadoso, detenido; ***close fight,*** combate reñido; ***close-fisted,*** tacaño, agarrado; ***close-fitting,*** ajustado, ceñido; ***close season,*** veda; ***close shave,*** escape por un pelo; ***to have a close shave,*** librarse por un pelo, librarse de buena; ***close study,*** estudio minucioso; ***close weather,*** tiempo bochornoso. — *adv.* muy cerca; de cerca; ***close by,*** muy cerca; ***close to,*** cerca de, junto a. — *s.* recinto.
closely [ˈklousli], *adv.* estrechamente; cuidadosamente; ***closely packed,*** muy apretado; ***to be closely related,*** ser parientes cercanos.
closeness [ˈklousnis], *s.* (lo) estrecho, (lo) íntimo; reserva; apiñamiento; tacañería; proximidad; (lo) pesado; (lo) reñido.
closet [ˈklɔzit], *s.* gabinete; armario, alacena; retrete, lugar excusado. — *v.t.* guardar en un armario; ***to be closeted with,*** estar encerrado con, tener una conferencia secreta con.
close-up [ˈklous-ʌp], *s.* primer plano, fotografía tomada de cerca.
closing [ˈklouziŋ], *a.* de cierre; ***closing price,*** última cotización. — *s.* cierre; final, clausura.
closure [ˈklouʒə], *s.* cierre; final, conclusión, clausura; (*fon.*) oclusión.
clot [klɔt], *s.* grumo, coágulo, cuajarón; necio, zopenco; (*fig.*, *fam.*) lerdo. — *v.i.* coagularse, cuajarse.
cloth [klɔθ], *s.* tela, paño, tejido; trapo; (el) clero; ***packing-cloth,*** arpillera; ***table-cloth,*** mantel.
clothe [klouð], *v.t.* vestir, revestir, cubrir, arropar; trajear.
clothes [clouðz], *s.pl.* ropa; vestidos, *m.pl.*; ***cast-off clothes*** o ***old clothes,*** ropa usada; ***clothes-brush,*** cepillo para la ropa; ***clothes-hanger,*** percha; ***clothes-horse,*** tendal, enjugador (*para secar la ropa*); ***clothes-line,*** cuerda para tender la ropa; ***clothes-peg,*** pinza de la ropa; ***suit of clothes,*** traje.
clothier [ˈklouðiə], *s.* pañero, ropero.
clothing [ˈklouðiŋ], *s.* vestidos, ropa; revestimiento.
clotted [ˈklɔtid], *a.* grumoso, coagulado; ***clotted cheese,*** requesón.
cloud [klaud], *s.* nube; nublado; borrón; ***cloud-capped,*** coronado de nubes; ***storm cloud,*** nubarrón; ***in the clouds,*** en las nubes, distraído; ***under a cloud,*** sospechoso, desacreditado, en desgracia; ***cloud-burst,*** aguacero. — *v.t.* (a)nublar; envolver. — *v.i.* nublar(se).
cloudiness [ˈklaudinis], *s.* nubosidad, nebulosidad.
cloudless [ˈklaudlis], *a.* sin nubes, despejado.
cloudy [ˈklaudi], *a.* nublado, nuboso; turbio; oscuro, sombrío; (*foto.*) velado.
clough [klʌf], *s.* cañada; garganta, desfiladero.
clout [klaut], *s.* bofetada; trapo, sayo. — *v.t.* dar una bofetada a.
clove (1) [klouv], *s.* clavo (*de especia*); diente (*de ajo*).
clove (2) [klouv], *pret.* [CLEAVE].
cloven [klouvən], *a.* hendido; ***cloven-hoofed*** o ***footed,*** patihendido; (*fig.*) ***to show the cloven foot,*** enseñar la oreja. — *p.p.* [CLEAVE].
clover [ˈklouvə], *s.* (*bot.*) trébol; (*fig.*) ***to live in clover,*** vivir como un rey.
clovered [ˈklouvəd], *a.* lleno de tréboles.
clown [klaun], *s.* payaso. — *v.i.* hacer el payaso.
clownery [ˈklaunəri], *s.* payasada(s).
clowning [ˈklauniŋ], *s.* payasada(s).
clownish [ˈklauniʃ], *a.* bufonesco.
cloy [klɔi], *v.t.* empalagar.
cloying [ˈklɔiiŋ], *a.* empalagoso, dulzón.
club [klʌb], *s.* porra, cachiporra; palo; club, casino; (*pl.*) (*naipes*) bastos, *m.pl.* — *v.t.* aporrear. — *v.i.* — ***together,*** unirse; pagar a escote.
club-foot [ˈklʌb-ˈfut], *s.* pie calcáneo.
club-man [ˈklʌb-mən], *s.* clubista, *m.*
cluck (1) [klʌk], *v.i.* cloquear.
cluck (2), **clucking** [klʌk, ˈklʌkiŋ], *s.* cloqueo.
clue [klu:], *s.* dato; indicio; pista, rastro.
clump [klʌmp], *s.* grupo, masa, manchón. — *v.i.* andar pesada y torpemente.
clumsiness [ˈklʌmzinis], *s.* torpeza; tosquedad.
clumsy [ˈklʌmzi], *a.* torpe; desmañado, desmanotado; tosco; chapucero; burdo.
cluster [ˈklʌstə], *s.* racimo; grupo. — *v.t.* agrupar, apiñar. — *v.i.* arracimarse; agruparse, apiñarse.
clutch [klʌtʃ], *s.* garra; agarre, agarro; embrague; ***to fall into the clutches of,*** caer en las garras de; (*aut.*) ***to engage the clutch,*** embragar. — *v.t.* agarrar; empuñar, apretar.
clutter [ˈklʌtə], *s.* hacinamiento; lio, confusión, desorden. — *v.t.* poner en desorden; ***clutter up,*** atestar *o* llenar desordenadamente; estorbar, obstaculizar.
clyster [ˈklistə], *s.* clístel, enema.
co [kou], *pref.* co.
coach [koutʃ], *s.* coche; carroza; carruaje; autocar; coche de línea; (*f.c.*) vagón; (*dep.*) entrenador; ***coach box,*** pescante; ***coach-house,*** cochera; ***coach-maker,*** carrocero; ***stage-coach,*** diligencia. — *v.t.* entrenar; preparar para un examen. — *v.i.* pasear(se) en coche; estudiar con (un) profesor particular.
coachful [ˈkoutʃful], *s.* coche lleno de gente.
coaching [ˈkoutʃiŋ], *s.* entrenamiento; lecciones *o* clases particulares, *f.pl.*
coachman [ˈkoutʃmən], *s.* cochero.
coact [kouˈækt], *v.i.* cooperar, obrar de acuerdo *o* de consuno.
coaction [kouˈækʃən], *s.* coacción.
coactive [kouˈæktiv], *a.* coactivo, cooperante.
coadjutant [kouˈædʒutənt], *a.* coadyuvante, auxiliar. — *s.* auxiliar, asistente.
coadjutor [kouˈædʒutə], *s.* coadjutor; compañero.
coadministrator [kouədˈministreitə], *s.* coadministrador.
coadunate [kouˈædjuneit], *a.* (*fisiol.*) coadunado.
coagent [kouˈeidʒənt], *s.* coagente, cooperador.
coagulable [kouˈægjuləbl], *a.* coagulable.
coagulate [kouˈægjuleit], *v.t.* coagular, cuajar. — *v.i.* coagularse, cuajarse.
coagulation [kouægjuˈleiʃən], *s.* coagulación.
coagulator [kouˈagjuleitə], *s.* coágulo.
coagulatory [kouˈægjuleitəri], *a.* coagulante, coagulatorio.
coagulum [kouˈægjuləm], *s.* (*med.*) cuágulo, cuajarón.
coal [koul], *s.* carbón; ***coal-bunker*** o ***coal-cellar,*** carbonera; ***coal-field,*** yacimiento carbonífero; ***coal gas,*** gas de alumbrado; ***coal-hole,*** pañol del carbón, carbonera; ***coal-merchant,*** carbonero; ***coal-mine,*** mina de carbón; ***coal-miner,*** minero de carbón; ***coal-tar,*** alquitrán; ***coal-yard,***

carbonería; ***to call*** o ***haul over the coals,*** echar una bronca a; ***to carry coals to Newcastle,*** llevar hierro a Vizcaya. — *v.t.* carbonear. — *v.i.* proveerse de carbón.
coaler [ˈkoulə], *s.* carbonero.
coalesce [kouəˈles], *v.i.* juntarse, unirse, fundirse.
coalescence [kouəˈlesəns], *s.* fusión, unión; (*med.*) coalescencia.
coaling [ˈkouliŋ], *a.* carbonero.
coalition [kouəˈliʃən], *s.* coalición, alianza, unión.
coalitionist [kouəˈliʃənist], *s.* coalicionista, *m.f.*
coaly [ˈkouli], *a.* carbonífero, carbonoso.
coaming [ˈkoumiŋ], *s.* (*mar.*) brazola.
coaptation [kouæpˈteiʃən], *s.* coaptación.
coarse [kɔːs], *a.* basto; tosco; grosero; burdo.
coarse-grained [ˈkɔːs-ˈgreind], *a.* de grano grueso; (*fig.*) basto; tosco.
coarsen [ˈkɔːsən], *v.t.* embrutecer, volver basto.
coarseness [ˈkɔːsnis], *s.* tosquedad; grosería; (lo) basto; (lo) burdo.
coast [koust] *s.* costa; litoral; ***the coast is clear,*** ha pasado el peligro, no hay moros en la costa. — *v.i.* costear; navegar en cabotaje; deslizarse cuesta abajo; ir en punto muerto; avanzar sin esfuerzo.
coastal [ˈkoustəl], *a.* costero.
coaster [ˈkoustə], *s.* buque costero.
coastguard [ˈkoustgɑːd], *s.* guardacostas, *m.inv.*
coasting [ˈkoustiŋ], *s.* cabotaje.
coastwise [ˈkoustwaiz], *adv.* a lo largo de la costa.
coat [kout], *s.* chaqueta, americana; abrigo; capa, mano, *f.*; pelo; ***coat of arms,*** escudo de armas; ***dress-coat,*** frac; ***frock coat,*** levita; ***great-coat, overcoat,*** abrigo; ***to turn coat,*** volverse la casaca. — *v.t.* cubrir; revestir; bañar, dar una mano (de pintura) a.
coati [kouˈɑːti], *s.* cuati.
coating [ˈkoutiŋ], *s.* revestimiento; capa, mano, *f.*
coax [kouks], *v.t.* engatusar, halagar; instar; conseguir *o* sacar con lisonjas *o* halagos.
coaxing [ˈkouksiŋ], *s.* engatusamiento; halago(s), lisonja(s).
cob [kɔb], *s.* mazorca (*de maíz*); jaca; cisne macho.
cobalt [ˈkoubɔːlt], *s.* (*quím.*) cobalto.
cobaltic [kouˈbɔːltik], *a.* cobáltico.
cobble [kɔbl], *s.* guijarro; ***cobble-stone,*** adoquín. — *v.t.* empedrar, enguijarrar; remendar (*zapatos*); chapucear.
cobbler [ˈkɔblə], *s.* remendón, zapatero de viejo; ***cobbler's wax,*** cerote.
coble [koubl], *s.* barca de pescador (*de fondo chato*).
cobnut [ˈkɔbnʌt], *s.* avellana grande.
cobra [ˈkoubrə], *s.* cobra.
cobweb [ˈkɔbweb], *s.* telaraña.
cobwebby [ˈkɔbwebi], *a.* lleno de telarañas, telarañoso.
coca [ˈkoukə], *s.* (*bot.*) coca, hayo.
cocaine [kəˈkein], *s.* (*farm.*) cocaína.
coccinella [kɔksiˈnelə], *s.* (*ent.*) cocinela.
coccus [ˈkɔkəs], *s.* (*zool.*) coco, cóccido.
coccyx [ˈkɔksiks], *s.* (*anat.*) cóccix.
cochineal [ˈkɔtʃiniːl], *s.* cochinilla; grana.
cochlearia [kɔkliˈɛəriə], *s.* (*bot.*) coclearia.
cock [kɔk], *s.* gallo; macho de ave; espita, llave, *f.*; estilo *o* gnomon de reloj de sol; veleta, giraldilla; pie de gato de escopeta; can amartillado; ***cock-a-doodle-do,*** quiquiriquí; ***cock-a-hoop,*** eufórico; ***cock-and-bull story,*** cuento chino; ***cock-crow(ing),*** canto del gallo; aurora; ***cock-eyed,*** bizco; (*fig.*) torcido; disparatado; ***cock-fight,*** riña de gallos; ***cock-horse,*** caballito mecedor; ***cock-loft,*** desván, zaquizamí; ***cock of the walk*** o ***the roost,*** (el) gallito del lugar; ***cock's comb,*** cresta de gallo; ***cocksparrow,*** gorrión macho; ***cock-spurs,*** navajas de gallo, *f.pl.*; ***turkey cock,*** pavo; (*fam.*) ***hello, old cock,*** ¡hola, viejo! — *v.t.* montar, amartillar; hacinar *o* amontonar (*heno*); levantar, erguir, enderezar; encandilar (*el sombrero*); ***cock an eye,*** cucar el ojo; ***cock a snook at,*** desairar, reírse de; ***cock a snook at society,*** ponerse el mundo por montera.
cockade [kɔˈkeid], *s.* cucarda, escarapela.
Cockaigne [kɔˈkein], *s.* país de Jauja.
cockatoo [kɔkəˈtuː], *s.* (*orn.*) cacatúa.
cockatrice [ˈkɔkətris], *s.* basilisco.
cockboat [ˈkɔkbout], *s.* (*mar.*) barquilla.
cockchafer [ˈkɔktʃeifə], *s.* (*ent.*) abejorro.
cocker [ˈkɔkə], *s.* aficionado a las riñas de gallo; ***cocker spaniel,*** cócker. — *v.t.* mimar, acariciar.
cockerel [ˈkɔkrəl], *s.* gallipollo, gallito.
cocket [ˈkɔkit], *s.* sello (*de la aduana*); certificación de pago (*de la aduana*).
cockle [kɔkl], *s.* berberecho; barquichuelo; (*bot.*) vallico, cizaña; arruga, bolsa, pliegue; (*fam.*) ***it warms the cockles of your heart,*** te alegra el corazón. — *v.t.* arrugar. — *v.i.* rizarse (*el mar*).
cockney [ˈkɔkni], *a.*, *s.* londinense (*de clase popular*), castizo.
cockpit [ˈkɔkpit], *s.* gallera, reñidero de gallos; (*aer.*) carlinga; (*naut.*) recámara; (*fig.*) centro, escenario, teatro; ***cockpit of Europe,*** Flandes, *f.*, (los) Países Bajos.
cockroach [ˈkɔkroutʃ], *s.* (*ent.*) cucaracha.
cocksure [ˈkɔkʃuə], *a.* demasiado seguro; presumido, satisfecho.
cocktail [ˈkɔkteil], *s.* cocktail, cóctel, combinación; ***cocktail party,*** cocktail, cóctel; ***cocktail-shaker,*** coctelera.
cocky [ˈkɔki], *a.* presumido, presuntuoso, engreído.
cocoa [ˈkoukou], *s.* cacao.
coco(a)nut [ˈkoukənʌt], *s.* coco.
cocoon [kəˈkuːn], *s.* capullo.
coction [ˈkɔkʃən], *s.* cocción.
cod (1) [kɔd], *s.* bacalao; abadejo.
cod (2) [kɔd], *s.* escroto.
coda [ˈkoudə], *s.* (*mús.*) coda.
coddle [kɔdl], *v.t.* mimar.
code [koud], *s.* código; cifra, clave, *f.*; ***highway code,*** código de la circulación. — *v.t.* poner en clave.
codeine [ˈkoudiːn], *s.* codeína.
codex [ˈkoudeks], *s.* códice.
codfish [ˈkɔdfiʃ], *s.* bacalao; abadejo.
codger [ˈkɔdʒə], *s.* (*fam.*) tipo; ***old codger,*** vejete; (*despec.*) vejestorio.
codicil [ˈkɔdisil], *s.* codicilo.
codicillary [kɔdiˈsiləri], *a.* codicilar.
codification [koudifiˈkeiʃən], *s.* codificación.
codify [ˈkoudifai], *v.t.* codificar.
codling [ˈkɔdliŋ], *s.* pescadilla.
codliver-oil [ˈkɔdlivər-ɔil], *s.* aceite de hígado de bacalao.
co-education [ˈkouedjuːˈkeiʃən], *s.* coeducación.
coefficiency [kouiˈfiʃənsi], *s.* coeficiencia.
coefficient [kouiˈfiʃənt], *a.*, *s.* coeficiente.
cœlenterate [siːˈlentəreit], *a.*, *s.* celenterado.
cœliac [ˈsiːliæk], *a.* celíaco.
cœnobite [ˈsiːnobait], *s.* cenobita, *m.*
cœnobitic [siːnoˈbitik], *a.* cenobítico.
coequal [kouˈiːkwəl], *a.* coigual.
coerce [kouˈeːs], *v.t.* coercer; coaccionar, obligar, forzar.
coercible [kouˈəːsibl], *a.* coercible.
coercibleness [kouˈəːsiblnis], *s.* coercibilidad.
coercion [kouˈəːʃən], *s.* coerción; coacción.
coercive [kouˈəːsiv], *a.* coercitivo, coactivo.
coessential [kouiˈsenʃəl], *a.* coesencial.
coetaneous [kouiˈteiniəs], *a.* coetáneo.
coeval [kouˈiːvəl], *a.* coevo, contemporáneo.
coexist [kouigˈzist], *v.i.* coexistir.
coexistence [kouigˈzistəns], *s.* coexistencia, convivencia.

coexistent, coexisting [kouig'zistənt, -iŋ], *a.* coexistente.
coextensive [kouiks'tensiv], *a.* coextensivo.
coffee ['kɔfi], *s.* café; ***black coffee,*** café solo; ***coffee-bean, coffee-berry,*** grano de café; ***coffee-colour,*** color de café; ***coffee-cup,*** taza para café; ***coffee-house,*** café; ***coffee-mill,*** molinillo de café; ***coffee-plantation,*** cafetal; ***coffee-pot,*** cafetera; ***coffee-roaster,*** tostador de café; ***coffee-table,*** mesilla; ***coffee-table book,*** volúmen ilustrado (ligero); ***coffee-tree,*** café (*árbol*), cafeto; ***white coffee,*** café con leche.
coffer ['kɔfə], *s.* arca, cofre; artesón hondo; (*pl.*) arcas, *f.pl.*, tesoro, hacienda. — *v.t.* poner *o* guardar en cofre; artesonar; encofrar.
coffer-dam ['kɔfə-dæm], *s.* represa encofrada, ataguía; caja dique.
coffin ['kɔfin], *s.* ataúd, féretro, caja. — *v.t.* meter en (el) ataúd.
cog [kɔg], *s.* diente (*de engranaje*); espiga; lengüeta; botequín; fullería, fraude; ***cog-rail,*** cremallera; ***cog-wheel,*** rueda dentada; ***to slip a cog,*** equivocarse. — *v.t.* dentar (*una rueda*); ensamblar con lengüeta.
cogency ['koudʒənsi], *s.* fuerza lógica *o* moral; evidencia.
cogent ['koudʒənt], *a.* lógico, concluyente, convincente.
cogged [kɔgd], *a.* dentado, engranado.
cogitate ['kɔdʒiteit], *v.i.* cogitar, meditar.
cogitation [kɔdʒi'teiʃən], *s.* reflexión, meditación, cogitación.
cogitative ['kɔdʒitətiv], *a.* cogitabundo, cogitativo.
cognac ['kɔnjæk], *s.* coñac.
cognate ['kɔgneit], *a.* cognado, afín.
cognatic [kɔg'nætik], *a.* cognaticio.
cognation [kɔg'neiʃən], *s.* cognación, afinidad.
cognition [kɔg'niʃən], *s.* cognición.
cognitive ['kɔgnitiv], *a.* cognoscitivo.
cognizable ['kɔgnizəbl], *a.* cognoscible.
cognizance ['kɔgnizəns], *s.* cognición; conocimiento; ***to take cognizance of,*** tener en cuenta, tener presente.
cognomen [kɔg'noumən], *s.* apellido; apodo.
cognoscible [kɔg'nɔsibl], *a.* cognoscible.
cognoscitive [kɔg'nɔsitiv], *a.* cognoscitivo.
coguardian ['kou'gɑ:diən], *s.* cotutor.
cohabit [kou'hæbit], *v.i.* cohabitar.
cohabitant [kou'hæbitənt], *s.* cohabitante.
cohabitation [kouhæbi'teiʃən], *s.* cohabitación.
coheir ['kou'ɛə], *s.* coheredero.
coheiress ['kou'ɛəris], *s.* coheredera.
cohere [kou'hiə], *v.i.* adherirse.
coherence, coherency [kou'hiərəns, -i], *s.* coherencia.
coherent [kou'hiərənt], *a.* coherente.
cohesion [kou'hi:ʒən], *s.* cohesión.
cohesive [kou'hi:siv], *a.* cohesivo.
cohort ['kouhɔ:t], *s.* cohorte.
coif [kɔif], *s.* cofia. — *v.t.* cubrir con una cofia.
coiffure ['kwɑ:'fjuə], *s.* peinado.
coign [kɔin], *s.* esquina, ángulo saliente; ***coign of vantage,*** posición ventajosa; atalaya.
coil [kɔil], *s.* rollo; vuelta; espiral, *f.*; carrete; serpentín; (*naut.*) aduja, adujada; rizo. — *v.t.* enrollar. — *v.i.* serpentear; enrollarse.
coin [kɔin], *s.* moneda; cuña; ***to pay in the same coin, in his own coin,*** pagar en *o* con la misma moneda. — *v.t.* acuñar; inventar, forjar; (*fig.*) ***coin money,*** hacer dinero a espuertas.
coinage ['kɔinidʒ], *s.* acuñación; sistema monetario, *m.*; invención.
coincide [kouin'said], *v.i.* coincidir.
coincidence [kou'insidəns], *s.* casualidad; coincidencia.
coincident [kou'insidənt], *a.* coincidente.
coiner ['kɔinə], *s.* acuñador de moneda; monedero falso; inventor.
coining ['kɔiniŋ], *s.* acuñación.
coir [kɔiə], *s.* estopa de coco; cuerda de estopa; bonote.
coition [kou'iʃən], *s.* coito.
coke (1) [kouk], *s.* cok, coque; ***coke oven,*** horno de cok. — *v.t.* convertir en cok.
coke (2) [kouk], *s.* (*Am.*, *fam.*) coca-cola (*marca registrada*).
cola-nut ['koulə-nʌt], *s.* nuez de cola.
colander ['kʌləndə], *s.* colador, escurridor.
colcannon [kɔl'kænən], *s.* (*coc. irlandesa*) cocido (*de patatas y verduras*).
colchicum ['kɔlkikəm], *s.* (*bot.*) cólquico.
colcothar ['kɔlkəθɑ:], *s.* (*quím.*) colcótar.
cold [kould], *a.* frío; enfriado; ***cold-blooded,*** de sangre fría; ***cold-hearted,*** insensible; ***to be cold,*** tener frío; hacer frío; ***in cold blood,*** a sangre fría; ***cold cream,*** pomada para suavizar el cutis; colcrén; ***cold meat,*** fiambre; ***to give the cold shoulder,*** hacer el vacío a; ***cold snap,*** racha de frío; ***to throw cold water on,*** echar un jarro de agua fría a. — *s.* frío; resfriado, constipado; ***to catch (a) cold,*** acatarrarse, constiparse, resfriarse; ***to leave out in the cold,*** dejar colgado; excluir; hacer el vacío a.
cold-chisel ['kould-'tʃiʒəl], *s.* cortafrío.
coldish ['kouldiʃ], *a.* un poco frío, fresquito.
coldly ['kouldli], *adv.* fríamente, indiferentemente.
coldness ['kouldnis], *s.* frialdad; frío.
Coleoptera [kɔli'ɔptərə], *s.pl.* (*ent.*) coleópteros, *m.pl.*
co-lessee ['kou-le'si:], *s.* mediero.
colewort ['koulwə:t], *s.* (*bot.*) col verde, colza, berza.
colic ['kɔlik], *s.* (*med.*) cólico.
Coliseum, Colosseum [kɔli'si:əm, kɔlə'si:əm], *s.* Coliseo.
collaborate [kə'læbəreit], *v.t.* colaborar.
collaboration [kəlæbə'reiʃən], *s.* colaboración.
collaborator [kə'læbəreitə], *s.* colaborador; (*despec.*) colaboracionista, *m.f.*
collapse [kə'læps], *s.* derrumbamiento, desplome, hundimiento; (*med.*) colapso; fracaso. — *v.i.* derrumbarse, desplomarse, hundirse; fracasar.
collapsible [kə'læpsibl], *a.* plegable.
collar ['kɔlə], *s.* collar; cuello; (*mec.*) argolla; (*mar.*) encapilladura; ***collar-bone,*** clavícula, islilla; ***to slip the collar,*** escaparse. — *v.t.* poner cuello *o* collar a; (*fam.*) apercollar; agarrar, coger por el cuello.
collared ['kɔləd], *a.* engolado.
collate [kɔ'leit], *v.t.* compulsar, cotejar; colacionar.
collateral [kɔ'lætərəl], *a.* colateral; accesorio, indirecto; paralelo; recíproco; subsidiario, subordinado; (*for.*) ***collateral security,*** garantía subsidiaria. — *s.* pariente colateral; (*com.*) resguardo, garantía; (*Am.*) fianza.
collateralness [kɔ'lætərəlnis], *s.* colateralidad, coordinación.
collation [kɔ'leiʃən], *s.* colación; comparación, cotejo; refacción.
collative ['kɔlətiv], *a.* colativo.
collator [kɔ'leitə], *s.* colador de beneficio.
colleague ['kɔli:g], *s.* colega, *m.*, compañero.
collect (1) ['kɔlikt], *s.* colecta.
collect (2) [kə'lekt], *v.t.* recoger; reunir; coleccionar; recaudar; cobrar; ***collect o.s.*** o ***collect one's wits,*** serenarse; concentrarse. — *v.i.* acumularse.
collectable [kə'lektəbl], *a.* cobrable.
collected [kə'lektid], *a.* sosegado, tranquilo.
collection [kə'lekʃən], *s.* colección; compilación; cuestación; cobro; recaudación; recogida (*del correo*); colecta.
collective [kə'lektiv], *a.* colectivo; ***collective bargaining,*** trato colectivo; ***collective farming,*** agricultura colectiva. — *s.* colectivo.

collectiveness [kə'lektivnis], *s.* colectividad.
collector [kə'lektə], *s.* coleccionista, *m.f.*; recaudador (*de contribuciones*).
colleen ['kɔli:n], *s.* muchacha.
college ['kɔlidʒ], *s.* colegio; colegio universitario, facultad.
collegial [kɔ'li:dʒiəl], *a.* colegial.
collegian, collegiate [kɔ'li:dʒiən, -ieit], *a.* colegiado. — *s.* colegial.
collet ['kɔlit], *s.* (*mec.*) collar; (*joy.*) engaste; (*bot.*) cerco.
collide [kə'laid], *v.i.* chocar.
collie ['kɔli], *s.* perro pastor.
collier ['kɔliə], *s.* minero; (*mar.*) barco carbonero.
colliery ['kɔliəri], *s.* mina de carbón.
collimation [kɔli'meiʃən], *s.* (*ópt.*) colimación.
collineation [kɔlini'eiʃən], *s.* alineación.
colliquate ['kɔlikweit], *v.t.* colicuar. — *v.i.* colicuarse.
colliquation [kɔli'kweiʃən], *s.* colicuación.
collision [kə'liʒən], *s.* colisión, choque; (*coll.*) encontronazo, topetazo, trompazo.
collocate ['kɔləkeit], *a.* (*ant.*) colocado. — *v.t.* colocar.
collodion [kə'loudiən], *s.* colodión.
colloid ['kɔlɔid], *a., s.* coloide.
collop ['kɔləp], *s.* tajada; pedacito.
colloquial [kə'loukwiəl], *a.* familiar, coloquial.
colloquialism [kə'loukwiəlizəm], *s.* expresión familiar, coloquialismo.
colloquy ['kɔləkwi], *s.* coloquio.
collude [kə'lu:d], *v.i.* coludir, confabularse.
collusion [kə'lu:ʒən], *s.* colusión, contubernio.
collusive [kə'lu:siv], *a.* colusorio, confabulado.
collusiveness [kə'lu:sivnis], *s.* colusión.
colly ['kɔli], *s.* hollín. — *v.t.* ennegrecer.
collyrium [kə'liriəm], *s.* (*farm.*) colirio.
collywobbles ['kɔliwɔblz], *s.pl.* (*fam.*) retortijones, *m.pl.*
colocynth ['kɔləsinθ], *s.* (*bot.*) coloquíntida.
Colombia [kə'lɔmbiə]. Colombia.
Colombian [kə'lɔmbiən], *a., s.* colombiano.
colon (1) ['koulən], *s.* (*gram.*) dos puntos.
colon (2) ['koulən], *s.* (*anat.*) colon.
colonel ['kə:nəl], *s.* coronel.
colonelcy, colonelship ['kə:nəlsi, -ʃip], *s.* coronelía, coronelato.
colonial [kə'louniəl], *a.* colonial.
colonist ['kɔlənist], *s.* colono; colonizador.
colonization [kɔlənai'zeiʃən], *s.* colonización.
colonize ['kɔlənaiz], *v.t.* colonizar. — *v.i.* establecerse en colonia.
colonizer ['kɔlənaizə], *s.* colonizador.
colonnade [kɔlə'neid], *s.* (*arq.*) columnata.
colony ['kɔləni], *s.* colonia.
colophon ['kɔləfən], *s.* colofón.
colophony [kə'lɔfəni], *s.* colofonia.
coloration [kʌlə'reiʃən], *s.* coloración; (*farm.*) colorización, colorido.
coloratura [[kɔlərə'tjuərə], *s.* (*mús.*) floreos, *m.pl.*, cadencias, *f.pl.*
colorific [kʌlə'rifik], *a.* colorativo.
colorimeter [kʌlə'rimitə], *s.* (*tec.*) colorímetro.
colossal [kə'lɔsəl], *a.* colosal.
colossus [kə'lɔsəs], *s.* coloso.
colostomy [kə'lɔstəmi], *s.* (*cir.*) collotomía.
colostrum [kə'lɔstrəm], *s.* calostro.
colour ['kʌlə], *s.* color; colorido; (*pl.*) bandera; ***colour blindness,*** daltonismo; ***colour-sergeant,*** portaestandarte; ***fast colour,*** color sólido; ***with flying colours,*** a banderas desplegadas; ***water colour,*** acuarela; ***to call to the colours,*** llamar a filas; ***to hoist the colours,*** enarbolar *o* izar la bandera; ***to lose one's colour,*** perder el color; ***to nail one's colours to the mast,*** luchar hasta el final; (*fig.*) resolver seguir hasta el final; ***to see things in their true colours,*** ver las cosas como son; ***to show one's true colours,*** quitarse la careta, enseñar la oreja; ***to strike the colours,*** amainar el pabellón. — *v.t.* dar color(es) a, colorear. — *v.i.* ponerse colorado, ruborizarse.
coloured ['kʌləd], *a.* de *o* en color; de *o* en colores; de color (*de raza negra*); (*fig.*) parcial, tendencioso.
colourful ['kʌləful], *a.* lleno de color; pintoresco.
colouring ['kʌləriŋ], *s.* color, tez; colorante; colorido.
colourless ['kʌləlis], *a.* descolorido; incoloro; sin color; anodino.
Colt [koult], *s.* revólver.
colt [koult], *s.* potro; mozuelo; (*bot.*) ***colt's foot,*** uña de caballo.
colter ['koultə], *s.* reja (de arado).
coltish ['koultiʃ], *a.* juguetón, retozón.
columbary ['kɔləmbəri], *s.* palomar; columbario.
columbate [kə'lʌmbeit], *s.* (*quím.*) tantalita.
Columbian [kə'lʌmbiən], *a., s.* colombino.
Columbine ['kɔləmbain], *s.* (*teat.*) Colombina.
columbine (1) ['kɔləmbain], *a.* columbino.
columbine (2) ['kɔləmbain], *s.* (*bot.*) aguileña.
columella [kɔlju'melə], *s.* columela.
column ['kɔləm], *s.* columna.
columnar [kə'lʌmnə], *a.* columnario, de columna.
colza ['kɔlzə], *s.* colza.
coma (1) ['koumə], *s.* (*med.*) coma, *m.*
coma (2) ['koumə], *s.* (*astron.*) caballera; (*bot.*) manojito (de hebras).
comatose ['koumətous], *a.* comatoso.
comb [koum], *s.* peine; almohaza; carda; cresta (*de gallo*); cresta (*de ola*); ***curry-comb,*** almohaza. — *v.t.* peinar; cardar (*lana*); rastrillar (*lino*); (*fig.*) examinar *o* registrar exhaustivamente. — *v.i.* encresparse y romper (*las olas*).
combat ['kɔmbæt], *s.* combate; ***combat duty,*** servicio de frente; ***single combat,*** combate singular. — *v.t.* combatir. — *v.i.* combatir(se).
combatable ['kɔmbətəbl], *a.* combatible.
combatant ['kɔmbətənt], *a.* combatiente. — *s.* combatiente, combativo.
combativeness ['kɔmbətivnis], *s.* combatividad.
combe [ku:m], *s.* hondonada; vallecito.
comber ['koumə], *s.* peinador; cardador (*de lana*); ola encrestada, cabrilla.
combinable [[kəm'bainəbl], *a.* combinable.
combination [kɔmbi'neiʃən], *s.* combinación; concurso (*de circunstancias*).
combine ['kɔmbain], *s.* combinación; monopolio; ***combine harvester,*** trilladora segadora, cosechadora. — *v.t.* combinar. — *v.i.* combinarse, unirse.
combing ['koumiŋ], *s.* peinado, peinadura; cardadura; ***combing-cloth,*** peinador; ***combing-machine,*** peinadora.
combustibility [kəmbʌsti'biliti], *s.* combustibilidad.
combustible [kəm'bʌstibl], *a., s.* combustible.
combustibleness [kəm'bʌstiblnis], *s.* combustibilidad.
combustion [kəm'bʌstʃən], *s.* combustión; (*aut.*) ***combustion chamber,*** cámara de combustión; ***internal combustion engine,*** motor de combustión (interna).
come [kʌm], *irr. v.i.* venir; ir; llegar; ***come! come!*** ¡vamos! ¡vamos!; ***come in!*** ¡pase! ¡adelante! ¡entre!; ***come what may,*** pase lo que pase; ***come about,*** acaecer, suceder; ***come across,*** encontrarse con, tropezar con; ***come after,*** seguir, venir detrás (de); ***come again,*** volver, regresar; ***come apart,*** deshacerse; ***come at,*** atacar, agredir; ***come away,*** quitarse; alejarse; desprenderse; ***come back,*** volver; ***come before,*** preceder; comparecer ante; ***come between,*** interponerse entre; ***come by,*** hacerse con; pasar; ***come down,*** bajar; venir a menos; ***come for,***

venir por, venir a buscar; ***come forth,*** salir; ***come forward,*** adelantarse; ofrecerse; ***come home,*** volver a casa; ***come in,*** entrar; llegar; ***come in for,*** recibir; ***come into the world,*** venir al mundo, nacer; ***come near,*** acercarse; ***come next,*** seguir, venir después; ***come of,*** resultar de, proceder de; ***come of age,*** llegar a la mayoría de edad; ***come off,*** cuajar; desprenderse; ***come off a loser,*** salir perdiendo; ***come off without a scratch,*** salir ileso, incólume; ***come off well,*** salir bien; ***come on,*** avanzar; ***come on!*** ¡vamos! ¡venga!; ***come out,*** entrar en sociedad; ***come out with,*** salir con; dejar escapar; sacar a relucir; ***come over,*** pasar por encima; pasar(se), venir(se); ***come round,*** volver en sí; avenirse, transigir; pasar(se), venir(se); ***come short of,*** no llegar a, decepcionar; ***come to,*** llegar a; volver en sí; ***come to blows,*** llegar a las manos; ***come to grief,*** acabar mal, salir mal parado; ***come to hand,*** venir, llegar a mano; ***come to nothing,*** quedar(se) en nada; ***come to pass,*** acaecer, acontecer, suceder; ***come to terms with,*** avenirse, contemporizar con; ***come together,*** juntarse; ***come true,*** realizarse; ***come up to,*** llegar(se) a, acercarse a; ***come up with,*** alcanzar, dar con; salir con, proponer; ***come upon,*** encontrarse con.

come-back [ˈkʌm-bæk], *s.* reaparición; ***to make a come-back,*** volver a figurar, a primer plano, a ser actualidad.

comedian [kəˈmi:diən], *s.* cómico.

comedienne [kəmi:diˈen], *s.* cómica.

come-down [ˈkʌm-daun], *s.* cambio para peor.

comedy [ˈkɔmidi], *s.* comedia, obra ligera, humorística.

comeliness [ˈkʌmlinis], *s.* donaire, donosura.

comely [ˈkʌmli], *a.* gentil, donoso.

comer [ˈkʌmə], *s.* (*fam.*) persona que promete; ***the first comer,*** el primero que llegue *o* que se presente; ***all comers,*** todos los contendientes, contrincantes *o* adversarios; ***newcomer,*** recién llegado; novato; advenedizo.

comestible [kəˈmestibl], *a., s.* comestible.

comet [ˈkɔmit], *s.* cometa, *m.*

cometography [kɔmiˈtɔgrəfi], *s.* cometografía.

comfit [ˈkʌmfit], *s.* confite; ***comfit-maker,*** confitero.

comfort [ˈkʌmfət], *s.* comodidad, confort; consuelo, alivio; bienestar. — *v.t.* confortar, consolar aliviar; (*for.*) ayudar, apoyar.

comfortable [ˈkʌmfətəbl], *a.* cómodo; confortable; ***to feel comfortable,*** estar a gusto; ***to be in comfortable circumstances,*** vivir con desahogo.

comfortableness [ˈkʌmfətəblnis], *s.* comodidad; bienestar.

comfortably [ˈkʌmfətəbli], *adv.* cómodamente; desahogadamente; ***to be comfortably off,*** vivir con desahogo, con (cierta) holgura.

comforter [ˈkʌmfətə], *s.* consolador; bufanda, tapaboca, *m.*, chupete; (*Am.*) [EIDERDOWN].

comfortless [ˈkʌmfətlis], *a.* desconsolado, inconsolable; sin consuelo; incómodo, sin comodidad.

comfrey [ˈkʌmfri], *s.* (*bot.*) consuelda.

comfy [ˈkʌmfi], (*fam.*) [COMFORTABLE].

comic(al) [ˈkɔmik(əl)], *a.* cómico. — *s.* cómico; (*fam.*) tebeo, revista infantil.

comicalness [ˈkɔmikəlnis], *s.* carácter cómico.

coming [ˈkʌmiŋ], *a.* próximo, venidero, futuro. — *s.* venida, llegada, advenimiento; ***coming-on,*** proximidad, llegada; ***coming-out,*** salida; puesta de largo, entrada en sociedad.

comitia [koˈmiʃiə], *s.pl.* comicios, *m.pl.*

comity [ˈkɔmiti], *s.* cortesía; amistad.

comma [ˈkɔmə], *s.* coma.

command [kəˈmɑ:nd], *s.* mando; dominio; mandato, orden; comandancia; ***to be in command,*** mandar, tener el mando, estar al mando; ***to have command of o.s.,*** tener dominio de uno mismo; ***to have at one's command,*** tener a su disposición; ***to have a (good) command of a language,*** dominar un idioma. — *v.t.* mandar; ordenar; dominar; merecer, imponer. — *v.i.* mandar.

commandant [kɔmənˈdænt], *s.* comandante.

commandeer [kɔmənˈdiə], *v.t.* requisar.

commander [kəˈmɑ:ndə], *s.* jefe; caudillo; capitán; comendador; ***commander-in-chief,*** generalísimo.

commanding [kəˈmɑ:ndiŋ], *a.* dominante; ***commanding officer,*** jefe.

commandingly [kəˈmɑ:ndiŋli], *adv.* imperativamente; con tono de mando.

commandment [kəˈmɑ:ndmənt], *s* mandamiento; mandato, precepto.

commando [kəˈmɑ:ndou], *s.* comando.

commeasurable [kəˈmeʒjurəbl], *a.* conmensurable.

commemorable [kəˈmemərəbl], *a.* conmemorable, memorando.

commemorate [kəˈmeməreit], *v.t.* conmemorar.

commemoration [kəmeməˈreiʃən], *s.* conmemoración.

commemorative, commemoratory [kəˈmemərətiv, -reitəri], *a.* conmemorativo.

commence [kəˈmens], *v.t.* comenzar, iniciar. — *v.i.* comenzar, principiar.

commencement [kəˈmensmənt], *s.* principio, comienzo.

commend ([kəˈmend], *v.t.* recomendar; encarecer.

commendable [kəˈmendəbl], *a.* recomendable, loable; aconsejable.

commendableness [kəˈmendəblnis], *s.* mérito.

commendam [kəˈmendæm], *s.* beneficio tenido en encomienda.

commendation [kɔmenˈdeiʃən], *s.* recomendación; alabanza, encomio.

commendatory [kəˈmendətəri], *a.* comendatorio, laudatorio; comendaticio.

commensal [kəˈmensəl], *s.* comensal.

commensalism, commensality [kəˈmensəlizəm, kɔmenˈsæliti], *s.* comensalía.

commensurability, commensurableness [kəmenʃərəˈbiliti, kəˈmenʃərəblnis], *s.* conmensurabilidad.

commensurable [kəˈmenʃərəbl], *a.* conmensurable, proporcionado.

commensurate [kəˈmenʃərit], *a.* conmensurado, proporcionado; conmensurativo. — [kəˈmenʃəreit], *v.t.* conmensurar.

commensuration [kəmenʃəˈreiʃən], *s.* conmensuración, proporción.

comment [ˈkɔment], *s.* comentario, observación. — *v.i.* comentar, observar, ***comment on,*** hacer observaciones sobre, comentar.

commentary [ˈkɔməntri], *s.* comentario; comento.

commentate [ˈkɔmənteit], *v.i.* comentar.

commentator [ˈkɔmənteitə], *s.* comentador; comentarista, *m.f.*

commerce [ˈkɔmə:s], *s.* comercio; trato. — *v.i.* comerciar, traficar.

commercial [kəˈmə:ʃəl], *a.* comercial; mercantil; ***commercial law,*** derecho mercantil; ***commercial traveller,*** viajante de comercio. — *s.* anuncio *o* propaganda comercial.

commercialism [kəˈmə:ʃəlizəm], *s.* comercialismo; mercantilismo.

commercialize [kəˈmə:ʃəlaiz], *v.t.* comercializar; lanzar (*un producto*) al mercado.

commerge [kəˈmə:dʒ], *v.i.* mezclarse, unirse.

commination [kɔmiˈneiʃən], *s.* conminación.

comminatory [ˈkɔmineitəri], *a.* conminatorio.

commingle [kəˈmiŋgl], *v.t.* entremezclar. — *v.i.* entremezclarse.

comminute [ˈkɔminju:t], *v.t.* moler, desmenuzar, pulverizar.

commiserate [kəˈmizəreit], *v.i.* — ***with,*** acompañar en el sentimiento.
commiseration [kəmizəˈreiʃən], *s.* conmiseración.
commissarial [kɔmiˈsɛəriəl], *a.* de comisario.
commissariat [kɔmiˈsɛəriət], *s.* comisaría, comisariato.
commissary [ˈkɔmisəri], *s.* comisario.
commission [kəˈmiʃən], *s.* comisión; encargo; patente; nombramiento; perpetración (*de un delito*); ***to put into commission,*** poner en servicio; (*fig.*) ***to put out of commission,*** poner fuera de combate. — *v.t.* comisionar; autorizar; encargar; nombrar; poner en servicio.
commissioner [kəˈmiʃənə], *s.* comisionado; comisario.
commissure [ˈkɔmisjuə], *s.* comisura.
commit [kəˈmit], *v.t.* cometer; perpetrar; encomendar; confiar; entregar; encarcelar; ***commit to memory,*** aprender de memoria; ***commit o.s.,*** comprometerse; ***commit to paper,*** poner por escrito.
commitment [kəˈmitmənt], *s.* obligación, compromiso; auto de prisión; encierro, encarcelamiento.
committal [kəˈmitəl], *s.* comisión; entierro; encierro, encarcelamiento.
committee [kəˈmiti], *s.* junta; comité; ***executive committee,*** junta ejecutiva; ***joint committee,*** comisión colectiva; ***standing committee,*** comisión permanente.
commix [kəˈmiks], *v.t.* mezclar. — *v.i.* mezclarse.
commode [kəˈmoud], *s.* cómoda; inodoro; lavabo cubierto.
commodious [kəˈmoudiəs], *a.* amplio, de mucha capacidad.
commodity [kəˈmɔditi], *s.* artículo, producto; (*pl.* **commodities** [-z]) artículos, géneros de consumo, *m.pl.*
commodore [ˈkɔmədɔ:], *s.* (*mar.*) comodoro, jefe de escuadra.
common [ˈkɔmən], *a.* común, corriente; frecuente; ordinario; ***common crier,*** pregonero; ***common fraction,*** quebrado; ***common ground,*** coincidencia(s); ***common law,*** derecho consuetudinario; ***the common man,*** el hombre medio; ***the Common Market,*** el Mercado Común; ***common people,*** pueblo, vulgo; ***common sense,*** sentido común; ***common soldier,*** soldado raso; ***in common,*** en común, de común; ***to be out of the common,*** ser fuera de serie; ***it's nothing out of the common,*** no es cosa del otro jueves. — *s.* (lo) común; refectorio (*de colegio*); tierras comunales, ejido; parque; (*pl.*) el común, el pueblo, el estado llano; ***the Commons,*** la Cámara de los Comunes, la Cámara Baja.
commonable [ˈkɔmənəbl], *a.* común, comunal.
commonage [ˈkɔmənidʒ], *s.* derecho de pastar (ganados).
commonalty [ˈkɔmənəlti], *s.* pueblo, sociedad, comunidad.
commoner [ˈkɔmənə], *s.* plebeyo, comunero; miembro de la cámara baja; partícipe.
commonness [ˈkɔmənnis], *s.* (lo) común, (lo) frecuente; ordinariez.
commonplace [ˈkɔmənpleis], *a.* común, vulgar, adocenado. — *s.* lugar común, tópico, vulgaridad.
commonweal [ˈkɔmənwi:l], *s.* bien común.
commonwealth [ˈkɔmənwelθ], *s.* estado, nación, república, res pública; comunidad; federación; ***the Commonwealth,*** La Mancomunidad de naciones británica.
commotion [kəˈmouʃən], *s.* conmoción; alboroto.
communal [ˈkɔmjunəl], *a.* comunal, público.
commune [ˈkɔmju:n], *s.* comuna. — [kəˈmju:n], *v.i.* estar en comunión con.
communicability [kəmju:nikəˈbiliti], *s.* comunicabilidad.
communicable [kəˈmju:nikəbl], *a.* comunicable, comunicativo, contagioso.
communicant [kəˈmju:nikənt], *s.* comunicante; comulgante.
communicate [kəˈmju:nikeit], *v.t.* comunicar. — *v.i.* comunicar(se); estar en contacto con.
communication [kəmju:niˈkeiʃən], *s.* comunicación.
communicative [kəˈmju:nikətiv], *a.* comunicativo; expansivo.
communicativeness [kəˈmju:nikətivnis], *s.* (lo) comunicativo.
communicator [kəˈmju:nikeitə], *s.* comunicador.
communion [kəˈmju:njən], *s.* comunión.
communiqué [kəˈmju:nikei], *s.* comunicado, parte, *m.*
communism [ˈkɔmjunizəm], *s.* comunismo.
communist [ˈkɔmjunist], *a.*, *s.* comunista, *m.f.*
community [kəˈmju:niti], *s.* comunidad; sociedad; vecindario; ***community centre,*** centro social; ***community spirit,*** civismo.
commutability [kəmju:təˈbiliti], *s.* conmutabilidad.
commutable [kəˈmju:təbl], *a.* conmutable.
commutation [kɔmjuˈteiʃən], *s.* conmutación; (*Am.*) ***commutation ticket,*** (billete de) abono.
commutative [kəˈmju:tətiv], *a.* conmutativo.
commutator [ˈkɔmjuteitə], *s.* conmutador.
commute [kəˈmju:t], *v.t.* conmutar. — *v.i.* viajar con billete de abono; viajar a diario.
commuter [kəˈmju:tə], *s.* el que viaja diariamente desde las afueras hasta el centro de la ciudad.
comose [ˈkoumous], *a.* (*bot.*) peludo.
compact [kəmˈpækt], *a.* compacto; breve, compendioso; repartido con economía y aprovechamiento de(l) espacio *o* de(l) sitio. — [ˈkɔmpækt], *s.* pacto, convenio; estuche de maquillaje, polvera. — [kəmˈpækt], *v.t.* hacer compacto, condensar, consolidar; componer.
companion [kəmˈpænjən], *s.* compañero; acompañante; caballero (*de una orden*); (*mar.*) lumbrera; chupeta; ***companion way,*** escalerilla. — *v.t.* acompañar.
companionable [kəmˈpænjəbl], *a.* sociable, simpático.
companionship [kəmˈpænjənʃip], *s.* compañía, compañerismo.
company [ˈkʌmpəni], *s.* compañía; empresa; visita(s); (*mar.*) tripulación; ***good company,*** compañero simpático *o* divertido, compañera simpática *o* divertida; ***bad company,*** mala(s) compañía(s); ***to have company,*** tener visita; ***to keep company,*** hacer compañía a; ***to keep company with,*** frecuentar la compañía *o* sociedad de; ***to part company*** (***with***), separarse (de), tirar por caminos distintos.
comparable [ˈkɔmpərəbl], *a.* comparable.
comparative [kəmˈpærətiv], *a.* comparativo; relativo.
compare [kəmˈpɛə], *s.* comparación; ***beyond compare,*** sin comparación. — *v.t.* comparar; confrontar, cotejar; equiparar, paragonar; ***it is not to be compared,*** no se puede (ni) comparar.
comparing [kəmˈpɛəriŋ], *s.* comparación.
comparison [kəmˈpærisən], *s.* comparación; confrontación, cotejo; ***in*** o ***by comparison with,*** en comparación con, comparado con.
compartment [kəmˈpɑ:tmənt], *s.* compartimiento; (*f.c.*) departamento.
compass [ˈkʌmpəs], *s.* brújula; alcance; ámbito; (*pl.* **compasses** [-iz]) compás. — *v.t.* cercar, rodear; abarcar; conseguir, alcanzar.
compassion [kəmˈpæʃən], *s.* compasión, misericordia.
compassionable [kəmˈpæʃənəbl], *a.* digno de compasión.
compassionate [kəmˈpæʃənit], *a.* compasivo.
compaternity [kɔmpəˈtə:niti], *s.* compadrazgo.

compatibility, compatibleness [kəmpæti'biliti, kəm'pætiblnis], *s.* compatibilidad.
compatible [kəm'pætibl], *a.* compatible.
compatriot [kəm'pætriət], *s.* compatriota, *m.f.*
compeer [kəm'piə], *s.* compañero, compadre, colega, *m.* — *v.t.* igualar con, ser igual a.
compel [kəm'pel], *v.t.* compeler, constreñir, obligar, forzar; ***he compels respect,*** impone respeto.
compelling [kəm'peliŋ], *a.* apasionante.
compend [kəm'pend], [COMPENDIUM].
compendious [kəm'pendiəs], *a.* compendioso, sucinto.
compendium [kəm'pendiəm], *s.* compendio, resumen, epítome.
compensate ['kɔmpenseit], *v.t.* compensar; indemnizar; resarcir. — *v.i.* compensar.
compensation [kɔmpen'seiʃən], *s.* compensación; reparación; resarcimiento; desagravio; (*for.*) indemnización; ***compensation balance, bar*** o ***pendulum,*** volante, balanza, barra *o* péndulo de compensación.
compensative [kəm'pensətiv], *a.* compensativo, compensador.
compensator ['kɔmpenseitə], *s.* compensador.
compensatory ['kɔmpenseitəri], *a.* compensatorio.
compesce [kəm'pes], *v.t.* (*ant.*) refrenar, contener, restringir, limitar.
compete [kəm'pi:t], *v.i.* competir, contender, rivalizar.
competence, competency ['kɔmpitəns, -i], *s.* aptitud, capacidad; competencia.
competent ['kɔmpitənt], *a.* competente; capaz, apto, calificado.
competition [kɔmpi'tiʃən], *s.* competición; competencia; oposición; concurso.
competitive [kəm'petitiv], *a.* de competencia, de concurso; ***competitive examination,*** examen de concurso *u* oposición.
competitor [kəm'petitə], *s.* competidor, rival, opositor.
compilation [kɔmpi'leiʃən], *s.* compilación, recopilación.
compile [kəm'pail], *v.t.* compilar, recopilar.
compiler [kəm'pailə], *s.* compilador, recopilador.
complacence, complacency [kəm'pleisens, -i], *s.* satisfacción (de uno mismo).
complacent [kəm'pleisənt], *a.* satisfecho (de uno mismo).
complacently [kəm'pleisəntli], *adv.* con aire de satisfacción.
complain [kəm'plein], *v.i.* quejarse; protestar.
complainant [kəm'pleinənt], *s.* querellante, demandante.
complainer [kəm'pleinə], *s.* protestón.
complaining [kəm'pleiniŋ], *a.* quejoso. — *s.* queja(s); protesta(s).
complaint [kəm'pleint], *s.* queja; protesta; querella, demanda; mal, dolencia, enfermedad; ***to lodge a complaint,*** formular una protesta.
complaisance [kəm'pleizəns], *s.* condescendencia; consentimiento.
complaisant [kəm'pleizənt], *a.* condescendiente; consentido.
complement ['kɔmplimənt], *s.* complemento; (*mar.*) dotación, tripulación. — *v.t.* complementar.
complemental [kɔmpli'mentəl], *a.* completivo.
complementary [kɔmpli'mentəri], *a.* complementario.
complete [kəm'pli:t], *a.* completo; consumado. — *v.t.* completar; consumar.
completely [kəm'pli:tli], *adv.* por completo, completamente.
completeness [kəm'pli:tnis], *s.* (lo) completo: (lo) perfecto.
completion [kəm'pli:ʃən], *s.* terminación; consumación.
completive [kəm'pli:tiv], *a.* completivo.
completory [kəm'pli:təri], *a.* complementario. — *s.* (*igl.*) completas, *f.pl.*
complex ['kɔmpleks], *a.* complejo, complicado. — *s.* complejo; ***inferiority complex,*** complejo de inferioridad.
complexion [kəm'plekʃən], *s.* color, tez; naturaleza, carácter.
complexity, complexness [kəm'pleksiti, 'kɔmpleksnis], *s.* (lo) complejo, complejidad.
compliance [kəm'plaiəns], *s.* sumisión, obediencia; cumplimiento; consentimiento; ***in compliance with,*** en cumplimiento de, accediendo a, de acuerdo con.
compliant [kəm'plaiənt], *a.* sumiso, obediente, condescendiente.
complicate ['kɔmplikit], *a.* complicado. — ['kɔmplikeit], *v.t.* complicar. — *v.i.* complicarse.
complicated ['kɔmplikeitid], *a.* complicado.
complication [kɔmpli'keiʃən], *s.* complicación.
complicity [kəm'plisiti], *s.* complicidad; complicación.
complier [kəm'plaiə], *s.* consentidor, contemporizador, hombre condescendiente.
compliment ['kɔmplimənt], *s.* cumplido; lisonja, requiebro; cumplimiento; (*pl.*) saludos, *m.pl.*, respetos, *m.pl.* — [-ent], *v.t.* cumplimentar, felicitar; ***compliment on,*** felicitar por; ***compliment with,*** obsequiar con. — *v.i.* hacer cumplidos.
complimentary [kɔmpli'mentəri], *a.* ceremonioso, lisonjero; cumplido, obsequioso; gratuito, de obsequio, regalo *o* favor.
compline ['kɔmplin], *s.* (*igl.*) completas, *f.pl.*
complot ['kɔmplɔt], *s.* complot, intriga, trama. — *v.t.* tramar, maquinar, conspirar.
complotter [kɔm'plɔtə], *s.* conspirador, conjurado.
comply [kəm'plai], *v.i.* acceder, consentir; ***comply with,*** cumplir con; satisfacer, llenar, conformarse a.
component [kəm'pounənt], *a.* componente. — *s.* parte constitutiva.
comport o.s. [kəm'pɔ:t], *v.r.* comportarse, conducirse.
comportment [kəm'pɔ:tmənt], *s.* comportamiento, conducta; porte.
compose [kəm'pouz], *v.t.* componer. — **compose o.s.,** *v.r.* sosegarse, serenarse.
composed [kəm'pouzd], *a.* compuesto (de); sosegado, sereno, entero.
composedness [kəm'pouzidnis], [COMPOSURE].
composer [kəm'pouzə], *s.* compositor; autor; cajista, *m.*
composing [kəm'pouziŋ], *s.* (*impr.*) composición; (*impr.*) ***composing-stick,*** componedor.
compositæ [kəm'pɔsiti], *s.pl.* (*bot.*) compuestas, *f.pl.*
composite ['kɔmpəzit, -zait], *a.* compuesto, mixto; (*arit.*) múltiplo. — *s.* compuesto, mezcla, mixtura; (*bot.*) planta compuesta.
composition [kɔmpə'ziʃən], *s.* composición; redacción; arreglo, componenda.
compositive [kəm'pɔzitiv], *a.* compuesto, compositivo.
compositor [kəm'pɔzitə], *s.* (*impr.*) cajista. *m.*
compossible [kəm'pɔsibl], *a.* (*filos.*) capaz de existir.
compost ['kɔmpɔst], *s.* (*agric.*) abono. — *v.t.* abonar.
composure [kəm'pouʒə], *s.* compostura; serenidad, calma; entereza.
compote ['kɔmpɔt], *s.* compota.
compound ['kɔmpaund], *a.* compuesto; ***compound fracture,*** fractura múltiple. — *s.* compuesto. — [kɔm'paund], *v.t.* componer, combinar. — *v.i.* capitular (con); ponerse de acuerdo (con).
comprehend [kɔmpri'hend], *v.t.* comprender; colegir, deducir.

comprehensibility, comprehensibleness [kɔmprihensiˈbiliti, -ˈhensiblnis], *s.* comprensibilidad.
comprehensible [kɔmpriˈhensibl], *a.* comprensible.
comprehension [kɔmpriˈhenʃən], *s.* comprensión.
comprehensive [kɔmpriˈhensiv], *a.* exhaustivo, completo.
comprehensiveness [kɔmpriˈhensivnis], *s.* (lo) exhaustivo, (lo) completo.
compress [ˈkɔmpres], *s.* compresa; (*cir.*) cabezal. — [kəmˈpres], *v.t.* comprimir, condensar.
compressible [kəmˈpresibl], *a.* comprimible.
compression [kəmˈpreʃən], *s.* compresión.
compressor [kəmˈpresə], *s.* compresor.
comprise [kəmˈpraiz], *v.t.* comprender, contener, abarcar; constar de.
compromise [ˈkɔmprəmaiz], *s.* transacción, componenda; término medio. — *v.t.* comprometer. — *v.i.* transigir.
compromiser [ˈkɔmprəmaizə], *s.* pancista, *m.*
comptroller [kənˈtroulə], *s.* contralor, interventor.
compulsion [kəmˈpʌlʃən], *s.* compulsión, obligación.
compulsive [kəmˈpʌlsiv], *a.* compulsivo.
compulsory [kəmˈpʌlsəri], *a.* obligatorio, reglamentario.
compunction [kəmˈpʌŋkʃən], *s.* compunción.
compurgation [kɔmpəːˈgeiʃən], *s.* compurgación.
computable [kəmˈpjuːtəbl], *a.* computable.
computation [kɔmpjuˈteiʃən], *s.* computación; cómputo.
compute [kəmˈpjuːt], *v.t.* computar.
computer [kəmˈpjuːtə], *s.* (*mec.*) calculador, calculadora, computador, computadora.
comrade [ˈkɔmreid], *s.* camarada, *m.f.*, compañero.
con (1) [kɔn], *adv. s.* contra, *m.*; ***the pros and the cons,*** el pro y el contra; ***neither pro nor con,*** ni a favor ni en contra.
con (2) [kɔn], *v.t.* aprender de memoria.
con (3) [kɔn], *v.t.* (*mar.*) gobernar.
con (4) [kɔn], *v.t.* (*fam.*) timar.
conatus [kouˈneitəs], *s.* conato, tentativa.
concameration [kənkæməˈreiʃən], *s.* arco, bóveda; pieza abovedada; división en cámaras.
concatenate [kənˈkætineit], *a.* eslabonado, concatenado. — *v.t.* concatenar, encadenar.
concatenation [kənkætiˈneiʃən], *s.* concatenación, encadenamiento.
concave [ˈkɔnkeiv], *a.* cóncavo. — *s.* concavidad, cóncavo.
concavity, concaveness [kɔnˈkæviti, ˈkɔnkeivnis], *s.* concavidad, calidad de cóncavo.
concavo-concave [kɔnˈkeivou-ˈkɔnkeiv], *a.* bicóncavo.
concavo-convex [kɔnˈkeivou-ˈkɔnveks], *a.* cóncavo-convexo.
conceal [kənˈsiːl], *v.t.* tapar, ocultar, disimular, encubrir.
concealable [kənˈsiːləbl], *a.* ocultable.
concealedness [kənˈsiːlidnis], *s.* encubrimiento.
concealment [kənˈsiːlmənt], *s.* ocultación, encubrimiento; escondrijo, escondite.
concede [kənˈsiːd], *v.t.* conceder, admitir. — *v.i.* ceder; asentir, convenir.
conceit [kənˈsiːt], *s.* concepto, idea; presunción, engreimiento, fatuidad.
conceited [kənˈsiːtid], *a.* engreído, fatuo, presumido.
conceitedness [kənˈsiːtidnis] *s.* presunción, engreimiento, fatuidad.
conceivable [kənˈsiːvəbl], *a.* concebible.
conceivableness [kənˈsiːvəblnis], *s.* (lo) concebible.
conceive [kənˈsiːv], *v.t.* concebir; crear, idear; formular, expresar. — *v.i.* concebir; ***conceive of,*** concebir, imaginarse; ***I can't conceive of it,*** no me cabe en la cabeza.
conceiver [kənˈsiːvə], *s.* el que concibe.
concent [kənˈsent], *s.* concento, armonía.
concentrate [ˈkɔnsəntreit], *a.*, *s.* concentrado. — *v.t.* concentrar. — *v.i.* concentrarse; ***concentrate on,*** concentrar la atención en, concentrarse en.
concentration [kɔnsənˈtreiʃən], *s.* concentración.
concentre [kɔnˈsentə], *v.t.* reunir en un centro común. — *v.i.* concentrarse; tener un centro común.
concentric [kɔnˈsentrik], *a.* concéntrico.
concentricity [kɔnsenˈtrisiti], *s.* concentricidad.
concentus [kənˈsentəs], [CONCENT].
concept [ˈkɔnsept], *s.* concepto.
conception [kənˈsepʃən], *s.* concepción; concepto.
conceptive [kənˈseptiv], *a.* conceptivo.
conceptual [kənˈseptjuəl], *a.* conceptual.
concern [kənˈsəːn], *s.* negocio, asunto; interés; incumbencia; casa (comercial), firma, empresa; preocupación, inquietud; ***it is of concern,*** es de interés *o* de importancia; es una cosa que preocupa; ***that's your concern,*** allá tú. — *v.t.* concernir; tocar, importar, interesar; atañer; incumbir; inquietar, preocupar; ***as far as X is concerned,*** en cuanto a X, por lo que a X respecta; ***to be concerned,*** estar preocupado; ***to be concerned in,*** estar interesado *o* metido en; ***I am concerned not to waste time,*** tengo interés en no perder el tiempo. — **concern o.s.,** *v.r.* — ***with*** o ***about,*** interesarse por, preocuparse de *o* por.
concerned [kənˈsəːnd], *a.* interesado; complicado; ***those concerned,*** los interesados; los complicados.
concerning [kənˈsəːniŋ], *prep.* en cuanto a, respecto a.
concernment [kənˈsəːnmənt], *s.* interés; importancia.
concert (1) [ˈkɔnsəːt], *s.* concierto; acuerdo; ***to act in concert with,*** obrar de inteligencia con, de acuerdo con.
concert (2) [kɔnˈsəːt], *v.t.*, *v.i.* concertar.
concerted [kənˈsəːtid], *a.* conjunto.
concertina [kɔnsəˈtiːnə], *s.* concertina.
concerto [kənˈtʃəːtou], *s.* concierto.
concession [kənˈseʃən], *s.* concesión.
concessionary [kənˈseʃənəri], *a.*, *s.* concesionario.
concessive [kənˈsesiv], *a.* concesivo.
conch [kɔŋk], *s.* caracola; (*arq.*) concha.
concha [ˈkɔŋkə], *s.* concha.
conchiferous [kɔŋˈkifərəs], *a.* conchífero.
conchiform [ˈkɔŋkifɔːm], *a.* conquiforme.
conchoid [ˈkɔŋkɔid], *a.* (*geom.*) concoideo.
conchological [kɔŋkəˈlɔdʒikəl], *a.* conquiliológico.
conchologist [kɔŋˈkɔlədʒist], *s.* conquiliólogo.
conchology [kɔŋˈkɔlədʒi], *s.* conquiliología.
conciliable [kənˈsiliəbl], *a.* conciliable. — *s.* conciliábulo.
conciliar [kənˈsiliə], *a.* conciliar.
conciliate [kənˈsilieit], *v.t.* conciliar; reconciliar.
conciliation [kənsiliˈeiʃən], *s.* conciliación; reconciliación.
conciliator [kənˈsilieitə], *s.* conciliador.
conciliatory [kənˈsiliətəri], *a.* conciliativo; reconciliatorio.
concise [kənˈsais], *a.* conciso.
conciseness [kənˈsaisnis], *s.* concisión.
concision [kənˈsiʒən], *s.* concisión.
conclave [ˈkɔnkleiv], *s.* conclave.
conclavist [ˈkɔnkleivist], *s.* conclavista, *m.*
conclude [kənˈkluːd], *v.t.* concluir; inferir, deducir. — *v.i.* concluir, finalizar.
concluding [kənˈkluːdiŋ], *a.* final.
conclusion [kənˈkluːʒən], *s.* conclusión; inferencia, deducción; ***to bring to a conclusion,*** terminar, llevar a su término; ***to draw the conclusion that,*** sacar la conclusión de que; ***it is a foregone conclusion,*** ya se sabe cuál será el resultado; ***to try conclusions with,*** probar la habilidad con.
conclusive [kənˈkluːsiv], *a.* concluyente, terminante.

conclusiveness [kən'klu:sivnis], *s.* calidad de concluyente.
concoct [kən'kɔkt], *v.t.* mezclar; tramar, fraguar, inventar(se).
concoction [kən'kɔkʃən], *s.* mixtura, mezcla; mezcolanza; bebistrajo, comistrajo; invención.
concolorous [kən'kʌlərəs], *a.* (*hist. nat.*) uniforme en el color.
concomitance [kən'kɔmitəns], *s.* concomitancia.
concomitant [kən'kɔmitənt], *a.*, *s.* correspondiente, concomitante; ***to be a concomitant of,*** concomitar.
concord ['kɔnkɔ:d], *s.* concordia; conformidad; (*gram.*) concordancia; (*mús.*) acorde.
concordance [kən'kɔ:dəns], *s.* concordancia, conformidad.
concordant [kən'kɔ:dənt], *a.* concordante, concorde, conforme, consonante.
concordat [kən'kɔ:dət], *s.* concordato.
concorporate [kən'kɔ:pəreit], *v.t.* incorporar.
concourse ['kɔŋkɔ:s], *s.* concurso, concurrencia; confluencia.
concreate ['kɔnkrieit], *v.t.* crear al mismo tiempo.
concrement ['kɔnkrimənt], *s.* concremento.
concrescence [kən'kresəns], *s.* crecimiento, concrescencia.
concrete ['kɔŋkri:t], *a.* concreto; de hormigón. — *s.* hormigón; (lo) concreto; ***concrete mixer,*** hormigonera; ***reinforced concrete,*** hormigón armado. — *v.t.* concretar; concrecionar; cubrir con hormigón.
concreteness ['kɔŋkri:tnis], *s.* concreción.
concretion [kən'kri:ʃən], *s.* concreción.
concretionary [kən'kri:ʃənəri], *a.* (*geol.*) concrecionario.
concubinage [kɔn'kju:binidʒ], *s.* concubinato, amancebamiento.
concubine ['kɔŋkjubain], *s.* concubina, manceba.
concupiscence [kən'kju:pisəns], *s.* concupiscencia.
concupiscent [kən'kju:pisənt], *a.* concupiscente.
concur [kən'kə:], *v.i.* concurrir; convenir; asentir; consentir.
concurrence [kən'kʌrəns], *s.* concurrencia; convenio, acuerdo; asentimiento; consentimiento.
concurrent [kən'kʌrənt], *a.* concurrente; coexistente, simultáneo.
concuss [kən'kʌs], *v.t.* privar del conocimiento por concusión.
concussion [kən'kʌʃən], *s.* concusión, conmoción cerebral.
concussive [kən'kʌsiv], *a.* de (la) conmoción cerebral.
condemn [kən'dem], *v.t.* condenar; censurar; declarar ruinoso *o* insano; ***condemned cell,*** celda de los reos de muerte.
condemnable [kən'demnəbl], *a.* condenable; censurable.
condemnation [kɔndem'neiʃən], *s.* condenación; censura.
condemnatory [kɔn'demnətəri], *a.* condenatorio.
condensable [kən'densəbl], *a.* condensable.
condensation [kɔnden'seiʃən], *s.* condensación; compendio.
condensative [kən'densətiv], *a.* condensativo.
condense [kən'dens], *v.t.* condensar; abreviar. — *v.i.* condensarse.
condenser [kən'densə], *s.* condensador.
condescend [kɔndi'send], *v.i.* dignarse.
condescension [kɔndi'senʃən], *s.* condescendencia; postura protectora, aire protector.
condescending [kɔndi'sendiŋ], *a.* condescendiente; protector; ***he has a condescending manner,*** lo hace todo con aire protector *o* aire de superioridad.
condign [kən'dain], *a.* condigno, merecido.
condiment ['kɔndimənt], *s.* condimento; (*pl.*) sal y pimienta.

condition [kən'diʃən], *s.* condición; rango, categoría; ***on condition that,*** a condición de que; ***on one condition,*** con una condición. — *v.t.* condicionar, determinar; mentalizar.
conditional [kən'diʃənəl], *a.* condicional; ***conditional discharge,*** licencia condicional.
conditionally [kən'diʃənəli], *adv.* con (ciertas) condiciones *o* reservas.
condole [kən'doul], *v.i.* condolerse; ***condole with,*** acompañar en el sentimiento.
condolence [kən'douləns], *s.* condolencia, pésame; ***to express one's condolence,*** dar el pésame.
condone [kən'doun], *v.t.* condonar; remitir; perdonar; consentir, tolerar.
condonement [kən'dounmənt], *s.* condonación, indulto, perdón; toleración.
condor ['kɔndə], *s.* (*orn.*) cóndor.
conduce [kən'dju:s], *v.i.* conducir, tender (a).
conducive [kən'dju:siv], *a.* conducente; favorable, propicio; ***not to be conducive to,*** no favorecer.
conduciveness [kən'dju:sivnis], *s.* conducencia; (lo) propicio.
conduct ['kɔndʌkt], *s.* conducta, comportamiento, proceder; dirección, gestión. — [kən'dʌkt], *v.t.* conducir, guiar, llevar; dirigir, gestionar.
conductibility [kəndʌkti'biliti], *s.* (*fís.*) conductibilidad.
conductible [kən'dʌktibl], *a.* conductible.
conduction [kən'dʌkʃən], *s.* conducción; traída.
conductive [kən'dʌktiv], *a.* conductivo, que conduce.
conductivity [kɔndʌk'tiviti], *s.* conductividad, conductibilidad.
conductor [kən'dʌktə], *s.* conductor, guía; director (de orquesta); ***lightning conductor,*** pararrayo(s); ***bus conductor,*** cobrador.
conductress [kən'dʌktris], *s.* conductora; directora; ductriz; ***bus conductress,*** cobradora.
conduit ['kɔndit], *s.* conducto, tubo, tubería, arcaduz.
conduplicate [kən'dju:plikit], *a.* (*bot.*) duplicado, replegado.
condyle ['kɔndil], *s.* (*anat.*) cóndilo.
cone [koun], *s.* (*geom.*) cono; (*bot.*) piña; pilón (*de azúcar*); cucurucho; (*mec.*) ***cone wheel,*** rueda cónica; (*mec.*) ***friction cone,*** cono de fricción.
cone-shaped ['koun-ʃeipt], *a.* cónico, coniforme.
coney ['kouni], *s.* (*fam.*) conejo, gazapo.
confabulate [kən'fæbjuleit], *v.i.* confabular(se); platicar.
confabulation [kɔnfæbju'leiʃən], *s.* confabulación; plática.
confection [kən'fekʃən], *s.* confite, dulce; confección.
confectioner [kən'fekʃənə], *s.* confitero, dulcero, repostero; confeccionador.
confectionery [kən'fekʃənri], *s.* confitería, dulcería, repostería; confites, dulces; ***confectionery shop,*** confitería, dulcería.
confederacy [kən'fedərəsi], *s.* confederación, coalición, liga; complicidad.
confederate [kən'fedərit], *a.*, *s.* confederado; (*fam.*) compinche, cómplice. — *v.t.* confederar, coaligar. — *v.i* confederarse, coaligarse
confederation [kənfedə'reiʃən], *s.* confederación.
confer [kən'fə:], *v.t.* conferir, otorgar; ***confer a favour,*** hacer merced. — *v.i.* conferir, conferenciar, deliberar.
conference ['kɔnfərəns], *s.* conferencia, congreso, asamblea (anual).
confess [kən'fes], *v.t.* confesar; reconocer. — *v.i.* confesar(se).
confessedly [kən'fesidli], *adv.* por confesión propia.
confession [kən'feʃən], *s.* confesión; credo.
confessional [kən'feʃənəl], *a.* confesional. — *s.* confesonario.
confessor [kən'fesə], *s.* confesor; confesante.

confetti [kən'feti], *s.* confettis, *m.pl.*, confetis, *m.pl.*, carnavalina(s).
confidant [kɔnfi'dænt], *s.* confidente.
confide [kən'faid], *v.t.* confiar. — *v.i.* — ***in,*** confiarse a.
confidence ['kɔnfidəns], *s.* confianza; confidencia; ***in confidence,*** en confianza; ***confidence trick,*** timo.
confident ['kɔnfidənt], *a.* seguro; ***over-confident,*** confiado. — *s.* confidente.
confidential [kɔnfi'denʃəl], *a.* confidencial.
confidently ['kɔnfidəntli], *adv.* con confianza, lleno de confianza.
confiding [kən'faidiŋ], *a.* de secreto, íntimo.
configurate [kən'figəreit], *v.i.* configurar.
configuration [kənfigjuə'reiʃən], *s.* configuración.
configure [kən'figə], *v.t.* configurar.
confinable [kən'fainəbl], *a.* limitable.
confine ['kɔnfain], *s.* confín, límite, término. — [kən'fain], *v.t.* confinar; limitar; encerrar; ***to be confined,*** estar de parto; ***to be confined to one's bed,*** tener que guardar cama. — *v.i.* lindar. — **confine o.s.,** *v.r.* — ***to,*** atenerse a, limitarse a.
confinement [kən'fainmənt], *s.* confinamiento; encarcelamiento; encierro; parto, sobreparto.
confirm [kən'fə:m], *v.t.* confirmar; comprobar; ratificar.
confirmable [kən'fə:məbl], *a.* que puede ser confirmado *o* comprobado.
confirmation [kɔnfə'meiʃən], *s.* confirmación; comprobación.
confirmative [kən'fə:mətiv], *a.* confirmativo.
confirmatory [kɔn'fə:mətəri], *a.* confirmatorio.
confirmed [[kən:fə:md], *a.* inveterado, empedernido; ***confirmed bachelor,*** solterón.
confiscate ['kɔnfiskeit], *v.t.* confiscar.
confiscation [kɔnfis'keiʃən], *s.* confiscación.
confiscator ['kɔnfiskeitə], *s.* confiscador.
confix [kən'fiks], *v.t.* fijar, enclavar.
conflagration [kɔnflə'greiʃən], *s.* conflagración.
conflict ['kɔnflikt], *s.* conflicto, pugna; choque. — [kən'flikt], *v.i.* estar en conflicto, pugnar; chocar.
conflicting [kən'fliktiŋ], *a.* en conflicto, contradictorio, encontrado.
confluence ['kɔnfluəns], *s.* confluencia.
confluent ['kɔnfluənt], *a.* confluente. — *s.* confluente; afluente.
conflux ['kɔnflʌks], *s.* confluencia.
conform [kən'fɔ:m], *v.t.* conformar; ajustar. — *v.i.* conformarse; ajustarse; cumplir, obedecer; ***conform with the age,*** ir con la época.
conformability [kənfɔ:mə'biliti], *s.* conformidad.
conformable [kən'fɔ:məbl], *a.* conforme; concordable; sumiso; proporcionado.
conformation [kɔnfɔ:'meiʃən], *s.* conformación.
conformer [kən'fɔ:mə], *s.* el que se conforma.
conformist [kən'fɔ:mist], *s.* conformista, *m.f.*
conformity [kən'fɔ:miti], *s.* conformidad; ***in conformity with,*** con arreglo a, en consonancia con.
confound [kən'faund], *v.t.* confundir; desconcertar. — *interj.* **confound it!** ¡demonio! ¡maldita sea!
confounded [kən'faundid], *a.* (*fam.*) maldito, condenado.
confoundedness [kən'faundidnis], *s.* confusión, abatimiento.
confounder [kən'faundə], *s.* (*ant.*) enredador, desolador.
confraternity [kɔnfrə'tə:niti], *s.* cofradía, confraternidad, hermandad.
confrère ['kɔnfrɛə], *s.* colega, *m.*, compañero.
confrication [kɔnfri'keiʃən], *s.* confricación.
confront [kən'frʌnt], *v.t.* confrontar; afrontar; arrostrar; hacer frente a; carear.
confrontation [kɔnfrʌn'teiʃən], *s.* confrontación; enfrentamiento; careo.
confuse [kən'fju:z], *v.t.* confundir; desconcertar; aturdir; dejar perplejo a; embrollar, enmarañar.
confused [kən'fju:zd], *a.* confuso; perplejo; borroso.
confusedness [kən'fju:zidnis], *s.* confusión; perplejidad.
confusion [kən'fju:ʒən], *s.* confusión; desorden; embrollo; aturdimiento.
confutation [kɔnfju'teiʃən], *s.* refutación, confutación.
confute [kən'fju:t], *v.t.* refutar, confutar.
congeal [kən'dʒi:l], *v.t.* coagular, cuajar. — *v.i.* coagularse, cuajarse.
congealable [kən'dʒi:ləbl], *a.* coagulable.
congealment, congelation [kɔn'dʒi:lmənt, kɔndʒi'leiʃən], *s.* coagulación.
congener, congeneric ['kɔndʒinə, kɔndʒi'nerik], *a., s.* congénere.
congenial [kən'dʒi:niəl], *a.* simpático, agradable; compatible.
congeniality [kəndʒi:ni'æliti], *s.* simpatía, agrado; compatibilidad.
congenital [kən'dʒenitəl], *a.* congénito.
conger, conger-eel ['kɔŋgə, -r-i:l], *s.* (*ict.*) congrio.
congeries [kən'dʒiəri:z], *s.inv.* congerie, *f.*
congest [kən'dʒest], *v.t.* (*med.*) congestionar; atestar; superpoblar.
congested [kən'dʒestid], *a.* atestado, abarrotado; superpoblado; superconcurrido.
congestion [kən'dʒestʃən], *s.* congestión; superpoblación; aglomeración (*de tráfico*).
congestive [kən'dʒestiv], *a.* congestivo.
conglobate ['kɔnglobeit], *a.* conglobado. — *v.t.* conglobar.
conglomerate [kən'glɔmərit], *a., s.* conglomerado. — [kən'glɔməreit], *v.t.* conglomerar.
conglomeration [kənglɔmə'reiʃən], *s.* conglomeración; aglomeración; amontonamiento, hacinamiento; acumulación, montón.
conglutinate [kən'glu:tinit], *a.* conglutinado. — [kən'glu:tineit], *v.t.* conglutinar. — *v.i.* conglutinarse.
Congo ['kɔŋgou]. (*río*) Congo; (*país*) (***the***) ***Congo,*** (el) Congo; (***the***) ***Republic of the Congo,*** la República del Congo.
Congolese [kɔŋgo'li:z], *a., s.* congoleño.
congratulate [kən'grætʃuleit], *v.t.* felicitar; dar la enhorabuena a (***on, upon,*** por).
congratulation [kəngrætʃu'leiʃən], *s.* felicitación; enhorabuena, pláceme. — *interj.* ***congratulations!*** ¡enhorabuena!
congratulatory [kən'grætʃuleitəri], *a.* congratulatorio.
congregate ['kɔŋgrigeit], *v.t.* congregar. — *v.i.* congregarse.
congregation [kɔŋgri'geiʃən], *s.* congregación; feligreses, *m.pl.*
congregational [kɔŋgri'geiʃənəl], *a.* congregacionalista.
Congregationalism [kɔŋgri'geiʃənəlizəm], *s.* congregacionalismo.
Congregationalist [kɔŋgri'geiʃənəlist], *a., s.* congregacionalista, *m.f.*
congress ['kɔŋgres], *s.* congreso.
congressional [kən'greʃənəl], *a.* del congreso.
Congressman ['kɔŋgresmən], *s.* (*Am., pol.*) miembro del Congreso; diputado.
congrue [kən'gru:], *v.t.* concordar, adecuar, hacer corresponder.
congruence, congruency ['kɔŋgruəns, -i], *s.* congruencia; consonancia; correspondencia; superponibilidad, coincidencia.
congruent ['kɔŋgruənt], *a.* congruente, consonante; superponible, coincidente.
congruity [kɔŋ'gru:iti], *s.* congruidad; superponibilidad, coincidencia.
congruous ['kɔŋgruəs], *a.* congruo, congruente.

conical [ˈkɔnikəl], *a.* cónico, coniforme.
conics [ˈkɔniks], *s.pl.* (*geom.*) teoría de las secciones cónicas.
conifer [ˈkɔnifə], *s.* (*bot.*) conífera.
coniferous [kəˈnifərəs], *a.* conífero.
coniform [ˈkounifɔ:m], *a.* coniforme, cónico.
conium [kouˈnaiəm], *s.* (*bot.*) cicuta.
conjecturable [kənˈdʒektʃərəbl], *a.* conjeturable.
conjectural [kənˈdʒektʃərəl], *a.* conjetural.
conjecture [kənˈdʒektʃə], *s.* conjetura, presunción. — *v.t.*, *v.i.* conjeturar, presumir.
conjecturer [kənˈdʒektʃərə], *s.* conjeturador.
conjoin [kənˈdʒɔin], *v.t.* juntar, unir, asociar, conectar, casar. — *v.i.* confederarse, ligarse, unirse.
conjoint [ˈkɔndʒɔint], *a.* unido, aunado. — *s.* aliado, asociado; (*pl.*) consortes, *m.pl.*, cónyuges, *m.pl.*
conjugal [ˈkɔndʒugəl], *a.* conyugal.
conjugate [ˈkɔndʒugit], *a.* conjugado. — *s.* sinónimo. — [ˈkɔndʒugeit], *v.t.* conjugar. — *v.i.* conjugarse.
conjugation [kɔndʒuˈgeiʃən], *s.* (*gram.*) conjugación; conjunción; unión, adunamiento.
conjunct [kənˈdʒʌŋkt], *a.* conjunto, unido, allegado.
conjunction [kənˈdʒʌŋkʃən], *s.* conjunción.
conjunctiva [kɔndʒʌŋkˈtaivə], *s.* (*anat.*) conjuntiva.
conjunctive [kənˈdʒʌŋktiv], *a.* conjuntivo; conjunto.
conjunctivitis [kəndʒʌŋktiˈvaitis], *s.* (*pat.*) conjuntivitis, *f.inv.*
conjuncture [kənˈdʒʌŋktʃə], *s.* coyuntura; circunstancia.
conjuration [kɔndʒuəˈreiʃən], *s.* conjuración; conjuro.
conjure (1) [kənˈdʒuə], *v.t.* conjurar, pedir, rogar con instancia.
conjure (2) [ˈkʌndʒə], *v.t.* conjurar, exorcizar; ***conjure away,*** conjurar, exorcizar, hacer desaparecer; ***conjure up,*** evocar; hacer aparecer. — *v.i.* hacer juegos de manos; practicar las artes mágicas.
conjurer [ˈkʌndʒərə], *s.* prestidigitador; mago.
conjuring [ˈkʌndʒəriŋ], *s.* prestidigitación.
conjuror [CONJURER].
conk [kɔŋk], *s.* (*fam.*) narizota. — *v.i.* (*fam.*) — ***out,*** parar(se), fallar.
connatural [kəˈnætʃərəl], *a.* connatural.
connect [kəˈnekt], *v.t.* relacionar; conectar, conexionar; enlazar, asociar. — *v.i.* relacionarse; conectarse; asociarse; (*f.c. etc.*) enlazar, empalmar.
connected [kəˈnektid], *a.* conexo; relacionado; ***to be well connected,*** tener muchas relaciones; (*fam.*) estar muy enchufado.
connecting [kəˈnektiŋ], *a.* que une; ***connecting-rod,*** biela.
connection [kəˈnekʃən], *s.* relación; conexión; parentesco; unión, enlace; (*f.c.*) combinación, correspondencia, enlace, empalme; (*mec.*) acoplamiento; ***in connection with,*** en relación con, con respecto a; ***in this connection,*** a este respecto.
connective [kəˈnektiv], *a.* conexivo; conjuntivo. — *s.* palabra conjuntiva.
connector [kəˈnektə], *s.* conectador.
connexion [CONNECTION].
conning-tower [ˈkɔniŋ-tauə], *s.* (*mar.*) torreta.
connivance [kəˈnaivəns], *s.* connivencia; confabulación; consentimiento.
connive [kəˈnaiv], *v.i.* hacer la vista gorda; (***with***), confabularse (con).
conniver [kəˈnaivə], *s.* cómplice.
connoisseur [kɔnəˈsə:ə], *s.* conocedor.
connotation [kɔnoˈteiʃən], *s.* connotación; contexto; respecto.
connote [kəˈnout], *v.t.* (*lóg.*) connotar.
connubial [kəˈnju:biəl], *a.* connubial.
conoid [ˈkounɔid], *s.* conoide.
conoidal, conoidic(al) [kouˈnɔidəl, -ik(əl)], *a.* conoidal.
conquer [ˈkɔŋkə], *v.t.* vencer; conquistar. — *v.i.* vencer, triunfar.
conquerable [ˈkɔŋkərəbl], *a.* vencible; conquistable.
conquering [ˈkɔŋkəriŋ], *a.* vencedor, conquistador.
conqueror [ˈkɔŋkərə], *s.* vencedor, conquistador.
conquest [ˈkɔŋkwest], *s.* conquista.
consanguineous [kɔnsæŋˈgwiniəs], *a.* consanguíneo.
consanguinity [kɔnsæŋˈgwiniti], *s.* consanguinidad.
conscience [ˈkɔnʃəns], *s.* conciencia; ***conscience money,*** dinero que se paga por remordimientos; ***to have a clear, easy conscience,*** tener la conciencia limpia, tranquila; ***in all conscience,*** honradamente.
conscienceless [ˈkɔnʃənslis], *a.* sin conciencia, desalmado.
conscience-stricken [ˈkɔnʃəns-ˈstrikən], *a.* atormentado por remordimientos.
conscient [ˈkɔnʃiənt], *a.* consciente.
conscientious [kɔnʃiˈenʃəs], *a.* concienzudo, escrupuloso.
conscientiousness [kɔnʃiˈenʃəsnis], *s.* escrupulosidad; formalidad.
conscious [ˈkɔnʃəs], *a.* consciente; sabedor; ***to be conscious of,*** ser consciente de, darse cuenta de; ***to become conscious,*** recobrar el sentido, volver en sí.
consciously [ˈkɔnʃəsli], *adv.* conscientemente, con conocimiento, a sabiendas.
consciousness [ˈkɔnʃəsnis], *s.* conocimiento; sentido; ***to lose consciousness,*** perder el sentido; ***to recover*** o ***regain consciousness,*** recobrar el sentido *o* el conocimiento, volver en sí.
conscript [ˈkɔnskript], *a.* conscripto; reclutado; ***conscript army,*** ejército de reclutas involuntarios; ***conscript fathers,*** padres conscriptos. — *s.* recluta, *m.*, quinto. — [kənˈskript], *v.t.* reclutar.
conscription [kənˈskripʃən], *s.* reclutamiento; servicio militar obligatorio.
consecrate [ˈkɔnsikrit], *a.* consagrado. — [ˈkɔnsikreit], *v.t.*, *v.i.* consagrar.
consecration [kɔnsiˈkreiʃən], *s.* consagración; dedicación.
consecratory [ˈkɔnsikreitəri], *a.* sacramental.
consectary [kənˈsektəri], *s.* corolario, deducción obligada.
consecution [kɔnsiˈkju:ʃən], *s.* ilación; serie, *f.*, secuencia; (*astron.*) consecución.
consecutive [kənˈsekjutiv], *a.* consecutivo, seguido, sucesivo.
consecutiveness [kənˈsekjutivnis], *s.* carácter consecutivo.
consensus [kənˈsensəs], *s.* consenso; unanimidad, acuerdo; (*fís.*) simpatía.
consent [kənˈsent], *s.* consentimiento, aquiescencia; ***by common*** o ***mutual consent,*** de común acuerdo; ***silence gives consent,*** quien calla, otorga. — *v.i.* consentir (en, *to*).
consentaneous [kɔnsenˈteiniəs], *a.* consentáneo, acorde, conforme.
consentient [kənˈsenʃənt], *a.* consintiente, anuente; acorde, unánime.
consequence [ˈkɔnsikwəns], *s.* consecuencia; ***of no consequence,*** sin importancia; ***man of consequence,*** hombre de predicamento.
consequent [ˈkɔnsikwənt], *a.* consiguiente; lógico. — *s.* consecuencia; (*filos.*) consiguiente.
consequential [kɔnsiˈkwenʃəl], *a.* consiguiente; importante.
consequently [ˈkɔnsikwəntli], *adv.* por consiguiente, en consecuencia, consiguientemente.
conservancy [kənˈsə:vənsi], *s.* conservación.
conservation [kɔnsəˈveiʃən], *s.* conservación; preservación.
Conservatism [kənˈsə:vətizəm], *s.* (*pol.*) tradicionalismo, conservadurismo, conservatismo.
Conservative [kənˈsə:vətiv], *a.*, *s.* (*pol.*) tradicionalista, *m.f.*, conservador.

conservative [kən'sə:vətiv], *a.* conservativo, conservador; moderado.
conservatoire [kən'sə:vətwa:], *s.* (*mús.*) conservatorio.
conservator ['kɔnsəveitə, kən'sə:vətə], *s.* conservador.
conservatory [kən'sə:vətəri], *a.* conservatorio. — *s.* (*mús.*) conservatorio; invernadero.
conserve [kən'sə:v], *v.t.* conservar; preservar; ***to conserve (one's) strength,*** conservar las fuerzas, reservarse. — *s.* conserva.
consider [kən'sidə], *v.t.* considerar, tener en cuenta. — *v.i.* reflexionar; ***I consider that,*** estimo que.
considerable [kən'sidərəbl], *a.* considerable, apreciable, importante, cuantioso.
considerate [kən'sidərit], *a.* considerado, atento, solícito, delicado; ***how considerate!*** ¡qué detalle!
considerateness [kən'sidəritnis], *s.* solicitud.
consideration [kənsidə'reiʃən], *s.* consideración; deliberación; remuneración; ***in consideration of,*** en consideración a; ***to take into consideration,*** tomar en consideración; ***under consideration,*** sobre el tapete; ***without due consideration,*** inconsideradamente.
considering [kən'sidəriŋ], *prep.* en consideración a, en atención a; teniendo en cuenta; dadas las circunstancias.
consign [kən'sain], *v.t.* consignar; ***consign to oblivion,*** echar en olvido.
consignation [kɔnsig'neiʃən], *s.* consignación.
consignatory [kən'sainətəri], *s.* consignatario.
consignee [kɔnsai'ni:], *s.* consignatorio.
consigner [kən'sainə], *s.* consignador.
consignment [kən'sainmənt], *s.* consignación; remesa, envío.
consignor [kən'sainə], *s.* consignador.
consist [kən'sist], *v.i.* consistir (***in, of,*** en); constar (de).
consistence, consistency [kən'sistəns, -i], *s.* consecuencia; punto; (*fís.*) consistencia.
consistent [kən'sistənt], *a.* consecuente; uniforme, regular; conforme (***with,*** con).
consistently [kən'sistəntli], *adv.* consecuentemente; (*fam.*) habitualmente.
consistorial [kɔnsis'tɔ:riəl], *a.* consistorial.
consistory [kən'sistəri], *s.* consistorio; tribunal de una curia eclesiástica.
consociate [kən'souʃiit], *a.* unido, asociado. — *s.* consocio; cómplice. — [kən'souʃieit], *v.t.* asociar, aliar. — *v.i.* asociarse, aliarse.
consociation [kənsousi'eiʃən], *s.* asociación, alianza, liga.
consolable [kən'souləbl], *a.* consolable.
consolation [kɔnsə'leiʃən], *s.* consuelo; consolación; ***consolation prize,*** premio de consolación.
consolatory [kən'sɔlətəri], *a.* consolatorio, consolador.
console (1) ['kɔnsoul], *s.* consola; (*arq.*) ménsula, repisa.
console (2) [kən'soul], *v.t.* consolar, confortar.
consoler [kən'soulə], *s.* consolador.
consolidant [kən'sɔlidənt], *a.* consolidativo.
consolidate [kən'sɔlideit], *v.t.* consolidar; fusionar. — *v.i.* consolidarse; fusionarse.
consolidated [kən'sɔlideitid], *a.* consolidado; ***consolidated funds*** [CONSOLS].
consolidation [kənsɔli'deiʃən], *s.* consolidación.
consolidative [kən'sɔlideitiv], *a.* consolidativo.
consoling [kən'souliŋ], *a.* consolador, confortador.
consols ['kɔnsɔlz], *s.pl.* (*Ingl.*) consolidados.
consommé [kən'sɔmei], *s.* consomé.
consonance, consonancy ['kɔnsənəns, -i], *s.* conformidad, consonancia; armonía, concordancia.
consonant ['kɔnsənənt], *a.* consonante, cónsono, conforme. — *s.* (*gram.*) consonante, *f.*
consonantly ['kɔnsənəntli], *adv.* conformemente, en conformidad (con), consonantemente.
consonantness ['kɔnsənəntnis], *s.* consonancia, conformidad.
consonous ['kɔnsənəs], *a.* (*mús.*) cónsono, acorde, armonioso.
consort ['kɔnsɔ:t], *s.* consorte; cónyuge; compañía. — [kən'sɔ:t], *v.t.* casar, unir, juntar, asociar; acompañar. — *v.i.* asociarse; ***consort with,*** tratar con.
consortium [kən'sɔ:tjəm], *s.* consorcio.
consound [kən'saund], *s.* (*bot.*) consuelda.
conspectus [kən'spektəs], *s.* ojeada, vista general; compendio, sinopsis, *f.inv.*
conspicuous [kən'spikjuəs], *a.* conspicuo; sobresaliente; que (se) destaca; ***to be conspicuous by one's absence,*** brillar por su ausencia.
conspicuously [kən'spikjuəsli], *adv.* claramente, visiblemente, manifiestamente, notablemente.
conspicuousness [kən'spikjuəsnis], *s.* evidencia; nombradía, celebridad.
conspiracy [kən'spirəsi], *s.* conspiración, conjura.
conspirator [kən'spirətə], *s.* conspirado, conspirador.
conspire [kən'spaiə], *v.t.* maquinar. — *v.i.* conspirar; ***conspire to,*** conspirar a.
conspirer [kəns'paiərə], *s.* conspirador.
conspiring [kəns'paiəriŋ], *a.* conspirante.
constable ['kʌnstəbl], *s.* guardia, *m.*; condestable; alguacil.
constabulary [kən'stæbjuləri], *s.* policía; guardia civil.
constancy ['kɔnstənsi], *s.* constancia, perseverancia; fidelidad.
constant ['kɔnstənt], *a.* constante; continuo, incesante; fiel.
constellation [kɔnstə'leiʃən], *s.* (*astron.*, *astrol.*) constelación; (*fig.*) pléyade, *f.*
consternation [kɔnstə'neiʃən], *s.* consternación, asombro.
constipate ['kɔnstipeit], *v.t.* estreñir.
constipation [kɔnsti'peiʃən], *s.* estreñimiento.
constituency [kən'stitjuənsi], *s.* distrito (*electoral*).
constituent [kən'stitjuənt], *a.* constitutivo; constituyente; ***constituent assembly,*** cortes constituyentes, *f.pl.* — *s.* elector; comitente; poderdante.
constitute ['kɔnstitju:t], *v.t.* constituir.
constitution [kɔnsti'tju:ʃən], *s.* constitución.
constitutional [kɔnsti'tju:ʃənəl], *a.* constitucional. — *s.* (*fam.*) paseo, ejercicio.
constitutionalism [kɔnsti'tju:ʃənəlizəm], *s.* constitucionalismo.
constitutionalist [kɔnsti'tju:ʃənəlist], *s.* constitucional, constitucionalista, *m.f.*
constitutionality [kɔnstitju:ʃə'næliti], *s.* constitucionalidad.
constitutionist [kɔnsti'tju:ʃənist], *s.* constitucional.
constitutive [kən'stitjutiv], *a.* constitutivo; constituidor.
constrain [kən'strein], *v.t.* constreñir, obligar; impedir; restringir; detener.
constrainable [kən'streinəbl], *a.* constreñible.
constrained [kən'streind], *a.* (*sonrisa*) forzada.
constrainedly [kən'streinidli], *adv.* constreñidamente, por fuerza.
constraint [kən'streint], *s.* constreñimiento, coacción; sujeción; encogimiento.
constrict [kən'strikt], *v.t.* apretar; estrechar; encoger.
constriction [kən'strikʃən], *s.* constricción; contracción; encogimiento.
constrictive [kən'striktiv], *a.* constrictivo.
constrictor [kən'striktə], *s.* (*anat.*) constrictor.
constringent [kən'strindʒənt], *a.* constringente, constrictivo.

construct [ˈkɔnstrʌkt], *s.* invención conceptual. — [kənˈstrʌkt], *v.t.* construir; edificar; idear, componer.
constructer [kənˈstrʌktə], *s.* constructor; edificador.
construction [kənˈstrʌkʃən], *s.* construcción; edificación; interpretación; ***under construction,*** en construcción.
constructional [kənˈstrʌkʃənəl], *a.* estructural; interpretativo.
constructive [kənˈstrʌktiv], *a.* constructivo.
constructiveness [kənˈstrʌktivnis], *s.* (lo) constructivo.
constructor [CONSTRUCTER].
construe [kənˈstru:], *v.t.* interpretar; analizar; construir.
consubstantial [kɔnsəbˈstænʃəl], *a.* consubstancial.
consubstantiality [kɔnsəbstænʃiˈæliti], *s.* consubstancialidad.
consubstantiate [kɔnsəbˈstænʃieit], *v.t.* unir en una misma substancia.
consubstantiation [kɔnsəbstænʃiˈeiʃən], *s.* consubstanciación.
consuetudinary [kɔnswiˈtju:dinəri], *a.* consuetudinario, habitual.
consul [ˈkɔnsəl], *s.* cónsul.
consular [ˈkɔnsjulə], *a.* consular.
consulate [ˈkɔnsjulit], *s.* consulado.
consult [kənˈsʌlt], *v.t.*, *v.i.* consultar.
consultant [kənˈsʌltənt], *a.*, *s.* consultante; asesor; especialista, *m.f.*
consultary [kənˈsʌltəri], *a.* relativo a la consultación.
consultation [kɔnsəlˈteiʃən], *s.* consulta, consultación; deliberación; junta.
consultative [kənˈsʌltətiv], *a.* consultivo.
consulting [kənˈsʌltiŋ], *a.* consultante, de consulta; asesor; ***consulting hours,*** horas de consulta; ***consulting room,*** consultorio.
consumable [kənˈsju:məbl], *a.* consumible.
consume [kənˈsju:m], *v.t.* consumir; gastar. — *v.i.* consumirse.
consumer [kənˈsju:mə], *s.* consumidor; ***consumer goods,*** artículos de consumo.
consuming [kənˈsju:miŋ], *a.* consumidor; consuntivo.
consummate [kənˈsʌmit], *a.* consumado, acabado. — [ˈkɔnsəmeit], *v.t.* consumar.
consummation [kɔnsəˈmeiʃən], *s.* consumación, acabamiento.
consumption [kənˈsʌmpʃən], *s.* consumo; consumimiento; consunción; (*med.*) tisis, *f.inv.*
consumptive [kənˈsʌmptiv], *a.* consuntivo; consumidor; (*med.*) hético, tísico.
consumptiveness [kənˈsʌmptivnis], *s.* calidad de consuntivo.
contabescence [kɔntəˈbesəns], *s.* (*med.*) contabescencia.
contact [ˈkɔntækt], *s.* contacto; (*fam.*) enchufe; (*elec.*) ***contact-breaker,*** cortacorriente, interruptor; (*ópt.*) ***contact lenses,*** microlentillas (de contacto); (*elec.*) ***contact-pin,*** formón de contacto; (*elec.*) ***contact-plug,*** tarugo de presa corriente. — *v.t.* estar *o* ponerse en contacto con.
contagion [kənˈteidʒən], *s.* contagio.
contagious [kənˈteidʒəs], *a.* contagioso.
contagiousness [kənˈteidʒəsnis], *s.* carácter contagioso, (lo) contagioso (de).
contagium [kənˈteidʒiəm], *s.* contagio.
contain [kənˈtein], *v.t.* contener; incluir, encerrar; abarcar; (*mat.*) ser exactamente divisible por; ***to be (able to be) contained in,*** caber en. — **contain o.s.,** *v.r.* contenerse, refrenarse.
containable [kənˈteinəbl], *s.* contenible; que cabe.
container [kənˈteinə], *s.* continente; envase; contenedor, contáiner.
contaminate [kənˈtæmineit], *v.t.* contaminar; ***to be*** o ***get contaminated by,*** contaminarse con.
contamination [kəntæmiˈneiʃən], *s.* contaminación.
contango [kənˈtæŋgou], *s.* (*bolsa, cambio*) comisión pagada por el comprador en consideración del derecho de aplazar una liquidación de compra.
contemn [kənˈtem], *v.t.* desacatar, desestimar, despreciar.
contemplate [ˈkɔntəmpleit], *v.t.*, *v.i.* contemplar; pensar (en); pensar en la posibilidad de.
contemplation [kɔntəmˈpleiʃən], *s.* contemplación.
contemplative [kənˈtemplətiv], *a.* contemplativo; pensador.
contemplativeness [kənˈtemplətivnis], *s.* propensión a la contemplación.
contemplator [ˈkɔntəmpleitə], *s.* contemplador.
contemporaneity [kəntempəˈrəni:iti], s. contemporaneidad.
contemporaneous [kəntempəˈreinjəs], *a.* contemporáneo.
contemporaneousness [kəntempəˈreinjəsnis], *s.* contemporaneidad.
contemporariness [kənˈtempərərinis], *s.* contemporaneidad.
contemporary [kɔnˈtempərəri], *a.*, *s.* contemporáneo; coetáneo.
contempt [kənˈtempt], *s.* desprecio, desdén; desacato; (*for.*) ***contempt of court,*** contumacia, rebeldía.
contemptibility, contemptibleness [kəntemptiˈbiliti, kənˈtemptiblnis], *s.* (lo) despreciable, (lo) vil (de).
contemptible [kənˈtemptibl], *a.* despreciable, vil.
contemptuous [kənˈtemptjuəs], *a.* desdeñoso, despreciativo, despectivo.
contemptuousness [kənˈtemptjuəsnis], *s.* desdén, desprecio.
contend [kənˈtend], *v.t.* sostener, afirmar; disputar. — *v.i.* contender; porfiar.
contendent, contender [kənˈtendənt, -ə], *s.* competidor; concurrente; pretendiente.
contending [kənˈtendiŋ], *a.* contrario, opuesto.
content (1) [kənˈtent], *a.* contento; satisfecho. — *s.* contento; satisfacción; ***to be content to,*** contenarse con; ***to one's heart's content,*** cuanto se quiere *o* quiera. — *v.t.* contentar; satisfacer; complacer.
content (2) [ˈkɔntent], *s.* contenido; cabida; (*pl.*) tabla de materias.
contented [kənˈtentid], *a.* contento; satisfecho.
contentedly [kənˈtentidli], *adv.* a gusto; tranquilamente.
contentedness [kənˈtentidnis], *s.* contento, satisfacción.
contention [kənˈtenʃən], *s.* contención; contienda, disputa; aseveración, aserto; ***bone of contention,*** manzana de la discordia; ***it is my contention that,*** yo sostengo que.
contentious [kənˈtenʃəs], *a.* contencioso, litigioso.
contentiousness [kənˈtenʃəsnis], *s.* espíritu contencioso, espíritu de contradicción.
contentment [kənˈtentmənt], *s.* contento, contentamiento, satisfacción.
conterminal, conterminous [kɔnˈtə:minəl, -əs], *a.* contérmino, limítrofe; coextensivo.
contest [ˈkɔntest], *s.* contienda; lucha, combate; certamen, concurso. — [kənˈtest], *v.t.* disputar; negar, impugnar. — *v.i.* contender.
contestable [kənˈtestəbl], *a.* contestable, discutible.
contestant [kənˈtestənt], *s.* contendiente, contrincante; concursante; litigante.
contestation [kɔntesˈteiʃən], *s.* altercación; disputa.
context [ˈkɔntekst], *s.* contexto; ***out of context,*** fuera de (su) contexto.
contextual [kɔnˈtekstjuəl], *a.* relativo al contexto.
contextural [kənˈtekstʃurəl], *a.* relativo a la contextura.
contexture [kənˈtekstʃə], *s.* contextura; entretejido, enlazamiento.

contiguity [kɔnti'gju:iti], *s.* contigüidad.
contiguous [kən'tigjuəs], *a.* contiguo, adyacente, inmediato.
continence ['kɔntinəns], *s.* continencia; templanza.
continent (1) ['kɔntinənt], *a.* continente; moderado, templado.
continent (2) ['kɔntinənt], *s.* continente; (*fam.*) ***the Continent,*** Europa.
continental [kɔnti'nentl], *a., s.* continental; ***continental breakfast,*** desayuno (normal).
contingence, contingency [kən'tindʒəns, -i], *s.* contingencia, eventualidad, caso imprevisto.
contingent [kən'tindʒənt], *a., s.* contingente.
continual [kən'tinjuəl], *a.* continuo, constante.
continuance [kən'tinjuəns], *s.* continuación; persistencia; (*for.*) aplazamiento.
continuate [kən'tinjuit], *a.* (*ant.*) continuado.
continuation [kəntinju'eiʃən], *s.* continuación; prolongación.
continue [kən'tinju:], *v.t.* continuar; prolongar. — *v.i.* continuar, seguir, proseguir, durar; ***he continues to do it,*** sigue *o* continúa haciéndolo.
continued [kən'tinju:d], *a.* continuo, continuado, prolongado; ***to be continued,*** sigue.
continuity [kɔnti'nju:iti], *s.* continuidad; serie ininterrumpida; (*cine.*) guión; (*rad.*) secuencia; comentarios entre partes de un programa, *m.pl.*
continuous [kən'tinjuəs], *a.* continuo; continuado; ***continuous performance,*** sesión continua.
continuum [kən'tinjuəm], *s.* continuo.
contort [kən'tɔ:t], *v.t.* retorcer; deformar.
contortion [kən'tɔ:ʃən], *s.* contorsión; retorcimiento.
contortionist [kən'tɔ:ʃənist], *s.* contorsionista, *m.f.*
contour ['kɔntuə], *s.* contorno; perfil; ***contour line,*** curva de nivel.
contra ['kɔntrə], *prep.* contra.
contraband ['kɔntrəbænd], *a.* de contrabando. — *s.* contrabando.
contrabandist ['kɔntrəbændist], *s.* contrabandista, *m.f.*, matutero.
contrabass ['kɔntrə'beis], *s.* contrabajo.
contraception [kɔntrə'sepʃən], *s.* anticoncepcionismo.
contraceptive [kɔntrə'septiv], *a.* anticonceptivo. — *s.* preservativo, contraceptivo.
contract ['kɔntrækt], *s.* contrato; contrata; ***contract work,*** trabajo a destajo. — [kən'trækt], *v.t.* contraer; contratar. — *v.i.* contraerse; ***contract to,*** comprometerse por contrato a.
contracted [kən'træktid], *a.* (*gram.*) contracto; encogido; escaso.
contractedness [kən'træktidnis], *s.* contracción.
contractability, contractibleness [kəntrækti'biliti, kən'træktiblnis], *s.* contractibilidad.
contractible [kən'træktibl], *a.* contractible.
contractile [kən'træktail], *a.* contráctil.
contracting [kən'træktiŋ], *a.* contratante; contrayente; ***contracting party,*** contratante.
contraction [kən'trækʃən], *s.* contracción.
contractive [kən'træktiv], *a.* contrativo.
contractor [kən'træktə], *s.* contratante, contratista, *m.f.*; empresario.
contradict [kɔntrə'dikt], *v.t.* contradecir; desmentir.
contradiction [kɔntrə'dikʃən], *s.* contradicción; ***contradiction in terms,*** contrasentido.
contradictive [kɔntrə'diktiv], *a.* contradictorio.
contradictoriness [kɔntrə'diktərinis], *s.* espíritu de contradicción.
contradictory [kɔntrə'diktəri], *a.* contradictorio. — *s.* (*lóg.*) contradictoria.
contradistinction [kɔntrədis'tiŋkʃən], *s.* distinción por oposición, contraste; ***in contradistinction to,*** en contraste con, a diferencia de.
contra-indicate ['kɔntrə-'indikeit], *v.t.* (*med.*) contraindicar.
contra-indication ['kɔntrə-indi'keiʃən], *s.* contraindicación.
contralto [kən'træltou], *s.* (*mús.*) contralto.
contraplex ['kɔntrəpleks], *a.* (*tele.*) de transmisión simultánea en direcciones opuestas.
contraption [kən'træpʃən], *s.* artefacto; armatoste.
contrariety [kɔntrə'raiiti], *s.* contrariedad, oposición; discrepancia.
contrariness ['kɔntrərinis], *s.* contrariedad; espíritu de contradicción.
contrariwise ['kɔntrəriwaiz], *adv.* a la inversa.
contrary ['kɔntrəri], *a.* contrario, opuesto; [kən'trɛəri], que lleva la contraria; ***contrary to,*** en contra de, al contrario de. — *s.* contrario; ***on the contrary,*** al contrario; ***quite the contrary,*** todo lo contrario; ***to the contrary,*** en contrario.
contrast ['kɔntrɑ:st], *s.* contraste. — *v.t.* contrastar. — [kən'trɑ:st], *v.i.* contrastar, hacer contraste.
contrate ['kɔntreit], *a.* (relojería) con dientes *o* punto en ángulo recto al plano de la rueda.
contravallation [kɔntrəvə'leiʃən], *s.* (*fort.*) contravalación.
contravene [kɔntrə'vi:n], *v.t.* contravenir, infringir.
contravener [kɔntrə'vi:nə], *s.* contraventor, infractor.
contravention [kɔntrə'venʃən], *s.* contravención, infracción.
contributary [kən'tribjutəri], *a.* contribuyente, contributario.
contribute ['kɔntribju:t], *v.t.* contribuir; aportar; ***he's contributed £5,*** ha contribuido con 5 libras. — *v.i.* contribuir.
contribution [kɔntri'bju:ʃən], *s.* contribución; aportación; colaboración.
contributive [kən'tribjutiv], *a.* contributivo.
contributor [kən'tribjutə], *s.* contribuidor; contribuyente; colaborador.
contributory [kən'tribjutəri], *a.* contribuidor.
contrite ['kɔntrait], *a.* contrito.
contriteness, contrition ['kəntraitnis, kən'triʃən], *s.* contrición.
contrivable [kən'traivəbl], *a.* imaginable.
contrivance [kən'traivəns], *s.* inventiva; artificio, ingenio; dispositivo, mecanismo; plan, estratagema.
contrive [kən'traiv], *v.t.* inventar, ingeniar; maquinar, tramar. — *v.i.* lograr, darse maña; ***contrive to,*** ingeniárselas para.
contriver [kən'traivə], *s.* maquinador.
control [kən'troul], *a.* de mando, de control; ***control column,*** palanca de mando; ***control panel,*** tablero de mandos; ***control room,*** sala de control; ***control station,*** puesto de mando. — *s.* mando, gobierno; dirección, dominio, manejo; inspección, intervención; verificación, comprobación; control; ***to be at the controls,*** estar a los mandos; ***to be in control,*** mandar, tener el mando; ***to get out of control,*** desmandarse; ***to get under control,*** conseguir dominar; ***remote control,*** telecontrol. — *v.t.* mandar, gobernar; controlar; manejar, dirigir; dominar, reprimir; intervenir, revisar; regular. — **control o.s.,** *v.r.* dominarse.
controllable [kən'trouləbl], *a.* gobernable, dominable; dirigible, manejable.
controller [kən'troulə], *s.* inspector; interventor; director; regulador; contralor, superintendente.
controllership [kən'trouləʃip], *s.* contraloría; dirección.
controlling [kən'trouliŋ], *a.* predominante, decisivo; (*com.*) ***controlling interest,*** interés predominante.
controversial [kɔntro'və:ʃəl], *a.* polémico; debatido; discutible.
controversialist [kɔntro'və:ʃəlist], *s.* controversista *m.f.*, polemista, *m.f.*
controversy ['kɔntrovə:si], *s.* controversia, polémica, disputa.

controvert [ˈkɔntrovəːt], *v.t.* controvertir.
controvertible [kɔntroˈvəːtibl], *a.* controvertible.
contumacious [kɔntjuˈmeiʃəs], *a.* contumaz.
contumaciousness, contumacy [kɔntjuˈmeiʃəsnis, ˈkɔntjuməsi], *s.* contumacia.
contumelious [kɔntjuˈmiːliəs], *a.* contumelioso.
contumely [kənˈtjuːməli], *s.* contumelia.
contuse [kənˈtjuːz], *v.t.* contundir, contusionar.
contusion [kənˈtjuːʒən], *s.* contusión.
conundrum [kəˈnʌndrəm], *s.* adivinanza, acertijo.
convalesce [kɔnvəˈles], *v.i.* convalecer, estar convaleciente.
convalescence [kɔnvəˈlesəns], *s.* convalecencia.
convalescent [kɔnvəˈlesənt], *a.* convaleciente; ***convalescent home,*** clínica de reposo; ***to be convalescent,*** estar convaleciente.
convection [kənˈvekʃən], *s.* (acto de) transportar; (*fís.*)convección.
convene [kənˈviːn], *v.t.* convocar. — *v.i.* juntarse, reunirse.
convener [kənˈviːnə], *s.* convocador.
convenience [kənˈviːniəns], *s.* conveniencia; comodidad; oportunidad; ***at your earliest convenience,*** a la mayor brevedad; ***public conveniences,*** aseos, *m.pl.*, urinarios, *m.pl.*
convenient [kənˈviːniənt], *a.* conveniente; cómodo; oportuno; ***it's not convenient for me just now,*** no me conviene ahora mismo; ***will tomorrow be convenient?*** ¿le conviene *o* le viene bien mañana?
convent [ˈkɔnvənt], *s.* convento (*de monjas*).
conventicle [kənˈventikl], *s.* conventículo.
convention [kənˈvenʃən], *s.* convención; congreso asamblea.
conventional [kənˈvenʃənəl], *a.* convencional; tradicional.
conventionalism [kənˈvenʃənəlizəm], *s.* convencionalismo.
conventual [kənˈventjuəl], *a.* conventual. — *s.* conventual.
converge [kənˈvəːdʒ], *v.i.* converger; dirigirse.
convergence [kənˈvəːdʒəns], *s.* convergencia.
convergent, converging [kənˈvəːdʒənt, -iŋ], *a.* convergente.
conversable [kənˈvəːsəbl], *a.* conversable.
conversant [kənˈvəːsənt], *a.* (***with***), enterado (de); versado (en); ***to become conversant with,*** familiarizarse con.
conversation [kɔnvəˈseiʃən], *s.* conversación; plática.
conversational [kɔnvəˈseiʃənəl], *a.* familiar, coloquial, conversacional; dado a la conversación.
conversationalist [kɔnvəˈseiʃənəlist], *s.* conversador.
converse [ˈkɔnvəːs], *a.* inverso, contrario, opuesto. — *s.* conversación; (*mat.*) recíproca, inversa. — [kənˈvəːs], *v.i.* conversar; departir.
conversely [ˈkɔnvəːsli], *adv.* contrariamente, a la inversa.
conversible [kənˈvəːsibl] [CONVERTIBLE].
conversion [kənˈvəːʃən], *s.* conversión; cambio, modificación; apropiación ilícita.
convert [ˈkɔnvəːt], *s.* converso, convertido, neófito. — [kənˈvəːt], *v.t.* convertir; transformar; apropiarse ilícitamente. — *v.i.* convertirse.
converter [kənˈvəːtə], *s.* convertidor.
convertibility [kənvəːtiˈbiliti], *s.* convertibilidad.
convertible [kənˈvəːtibl], *a.* convertible, transformable; (*aut.*) descapotable; ***convertible currency,*** divisa cambiable.
convex [ˈkɔnveks], *a.* convexo. — *s.* convexidad; cuerpo convexo.
convexity [kɔnˈveksiti], *s.* convexidad.
convexo-concave [kɔnˈveksou-ˈkɔnkeiv], *a.* convexo-cóncavo.
convey [kənˈvei], *v.t.* llevar, transportar; transmitir; comunicar; expresar, dar a entender; (*for.*) traspasar.
conveyable [kənˈveiəbl], *a.* conductible, transportable.
conveyance [kənˈveiəns], *s.* conducción, transporte; vehículo; cesión, entrega, traspaso; escritura de traspaso.
conveyancing [kənˈveiənsiŋ], *s.* escritura de traspaso.
conveyer, conveyor [kənˈveiə], *s.* portador, mensajero; cedente; transportador; ***conveyor belt,*** correa transportadora.
convict [ˈkɔnvikt], *s.* reo convicto; sentenciado; presidiario. — [kənˈvikt], *v.t.* declarar culpable, condenar; probar la culpabilidad de.
conviction [kənˈvikʃən], *s.* convicción, convencimiento; prueba *o* declaración de culpabilidad; fallo condenatorio; condena.
convince [kənˈvins], *v.t.* convencer.
convincible [kənˈvinsibl], *a.* convencible.
convincing [kənˈvinsiŋ], *a.* convincente.
convincingness [kənˈvinsiŋnis], *s.* (lo) convincente.
convivial [kənˈviviəl], *a.* alegre, jovial, festivo.
conviviality [kənviviˈæliti], *s.* buen humor, jovialidad.
convocate [ˈkɔnvokeit], *v.t.* convocar, citar.
convocation [kɔnvoˈkeiʃən], *s.* convocación; asamblea.
convoke [kənˈvouk], *v.t.* convocar.
convoluted [kɔnvəˈljuːtid], *a.* convoluto. — *s.* enroscadura, convolución.
convolution [kɔnvəˈljuːʃən], *s.* convolución; repliegue; (*anat.*) sinuosidad.
convolve [kənˈvɔlv], *v.t.* arrollar, enroscar; retorcer. — *v.i.* retorcerse, enroscarse.
Convolvulaceæ [kənvɔlvjuˈleisiiː], *s.pl.* (*bot.*) convolvuláceas, *f.pl.*
convolvulus [kənˈvɔlvjuləs], *s.* convólvulo.
convoy [ˈkɔnvɔi], *s.* convoy; escolta. — *v.t.* convoyar; escoltar.
convulse [kənˈvʌls], *v.t.* convulsionar; crispar; agitar; ***to be convulsed with laughter,*** desternillarse de risa.
convulsion [kənˈvʌlʃən], *s.* convulsión; paroxismo.
convulsionary, convulsive [kənˈvʌlʃənəri, -siv], *a.* convulsivo; convulso.
cony [CONEY].
coo [kuː], *s.* arrullo, arrullos. — *v.i.* arrullar; gorjear (*niños*).
cooing [ˈkuːiŋ], *s.* [COO].
cook [kuk], *s.* cocinero, cocinera. — *v.t.* guisar, cocinar, preparar; (*fam.*) falsificar; (*fam.*) ***cook up,*** maquinar, tramar, urdir. — *v.i.* guisar, cocinar.
cooker [ˈkukə], *s.* cocina; fogón.
cookery [ˈkukəri], *s.* (arte de) cocina.
cook-house [ˈkuk-haus], *s.* cocina; fogón.
cookie [ˈkuki], *s.* pasta; pastelito; (*Am.*) [BISCUIT].
cooking [ˈkukiŋ], *s.* cocina, arte culinario.
cookshop [ˈkukʃɔp], *s.* tasca.
cool [kuːl], *a.* fresco; (*fig.*) sereno, tranquilo; (*fig.*) frío, indiferente, tibio; (*fig.*) descarado; ***as cool as you please*** o ***as a cucumber,*** tan tranquilo; ***a cool thousand pesetas,*** mil pesetas del ala. — *s.* fresco, frescor. — *v.t.* enfriar; refrescar; (*fig.*) ***cool down,*** calmar, tranquilizar. — *v.i.* refrescar (*tiempo*); ***cool down*** o ***off,*** enfriarse; refrescarse; (*fig.*) calmarse, serenarse, tranquilizarse.
cooler [ˈkuːlə], *s.* refrigerador; refrigerante; (*fam.*) chirona.
cool-headed [ˈkuːl-ˈhedid], *a.* sereno; sensato.
coolie [ˈkuːli], *s.* culí.
cooling [ˈkuːliŋ], *a.* refrigerante; refrescante. — *s.* refrigeración.
coolish [ˈkuːliʃ], *a.* fresquito.

coolness [ˈku:lnis], *s.* fresco, frescor; tibieza, frialdad; serenidad, calma.
coon [ku:n], *s.* (*zool.*) mapache.
coop [ku:p], *s.* gallinero; caponera; tonel. — *v.t.* — ***in*** o ***up,*** encerrar; enjaular.
cooper [ˈku:pə], *s.* tonelero. — *v.t.* fabricar (*barriles*).
cooperage, coopering [ˈku:pəridʒ, -iŋ], *s.* tonelería.
co-operate [kou-ˈɔpəreit], *v.i.* cooperar.
co-operation [kou-ɔpəˈreiʃən], *s.* cooperación.
co-operative [kou-ˈɔpərətiv], *a.* cooperativo. — *s.* cooperativa.
co-operator [kou-ˈɔpəreitə], *s.* cooperador.
co-opt [kou-ˈɔpt], *v.t.* cooptar.
co-ordinate [kou-ˈɔ:dinit], *a.* coordinado; coordenado. — *s.* coordenada. — [kouˈɔ:dineit], *v.t.* coordinar.
co-ordination [kou-ɔ:diˈneiʃən], *s.* coordinación.
coot [ku:t], *s.* (*orn.*) fúlica; foja.
cop [kɔp], *s.* copete; (*fam.*) policía, *m.*, polizonte. — *v.t.* (*fam.*) coger, pescar; ***cop it,*** ganársela, cobrar.
copaiba, copaiva [koˈpeibə, -və], *s.* copaiba.
copal [ˈkoupəl], *s.* goma copal.
coparcener [kouˈpɑ:sənə], *s.* (*for.*) coheredero.
co-partner [kou-ˈpɑ:tnə], *s.* consocio, copartícipe.
co-partnership [kou-ˈpɑ:tnəʃip], *s.* asociación, coparticipación.
cope (1) [koup], *s.* caperuza, tocado; capa pluvial; albardilla; bóveda. — *v.t.* vestir con capa pluvial; poner albardilla a.
cope (2) [koup], *v.i.* poder hacerlo; poder con; hacer frente a; ***they can't cope with so many customers,*** no dan abasto a servir a tantos clientes.
Copernican [kəˈpə:nikən], *a.* copernicano.
cope-stone [ˈkoup-stoun], *s.* piedra de albardilla.
copier [ˈkɔpiə], *s.* copista, *m.f.*, copiante; copiador; plagiario.
coping [ˈkoupiŋ], *s.* cumbre, *f.*; albardilla.
coping-stone [ˈkoupiŋ-stoun], [COPE-STONE].
copious [ˈkoupiəs], *a.* copioso, abundante.
copiousness [ˈkoupiəsnis], *s.* copia, profusión, abundancia.
copped [kɔpt], *a.* copado, copetudo.
copper (1) [ˈkɔpə], *a.* de cobre, cobrizo, cobreño. — *s.* cobre; calderilla; vellón, centavo, penique etc. (de cobre); perol; ***copper-plate,*** lámina de cobre; ***copper-smith,*** caldero; ***copper-sulphate,*** sulfato de cobre. — *v.t.* encobrar, forrar de cobre.
copper (2) [ˈkɔpə], *s.* (*fam.*) policía, guindilla, *m.*
copperas [ˈkɔpərəs], *s.* (*quím.*) caparrosa.
copper-worm [ˈkɔpə-wə:m], *s.* polilla; broma, taraza.
coppery [ˈkɔpəri], *a.* cobreño, cobrizo, encobrado.
coppice [ˈkɔpis], *s.* soto, sotillo, bosquecillo; maleza, matorral.
coproprietor [kouprəˈpraiətə], *s.* copropietario.
copse [kɔps], *s.* [COPPICE].
Copt [kɔpt], *s.* copto.
Coptic [ˈkɔptik], *a.* cóptico. — *s.* copto.
copula [ˈkɔpjulə], *s.* (*lóg.*) cópula; (*anat.*) ligamiento.
copulate [ˈkɔpjuleit], *v.t.* copular, juntar, unir. — *v.i.* copularse; ayuntarse.
copulation [kɔpjuˈleiʃən], *s.* cópula, coito; ayuntamiento.
copulative [ˈkɔpjulətiv], *a.* (*gram.*) copulativo, conjuntivo.
copulatory [ˈkɔpjuleitəri], *a.* copulativo.
copy [ˈkɔpi], *s.* copia; ejemplar; número (*de un periódico*); reproducción; modelo, pauta; ***copy-book,*** cuaderno de escritura; ***copy-cat,*** copión, imitamonos, *m.inv.*; (*Am.*) ***copy-editor*** [SUB-EDITOR]; ***copy writer,*** escritor publicitario; ***fair copy,*** copia en limpio; versión definitiva; ***to make a fair copy of,*** pasar a limpio; ***rough copy,*** borrador. — *v.t.* copiar; imitar. — *v.i.* copiar.
copyhold [ˈkɔpihould], *s.* (*for.*) enfiteusis, *f.inv.*
copyholder [ˈkɔpihouldə], *s.* enfiteuta, *m.f.*; arrendador.
copying [ˈkɔpiiŋ], *s.* transcripción, imitación, acción de copiar; ***copying ink,*** tinta de copiar; ***copying press,*** prensa de copiar.
copyist [ˈkɔpiist], *s.* copista, *m.f.*
copyright [ˈkɔpirait], *s.* propiedad literaria; derechos de autor, *m.pl.*; ***copyright reserved,*** reservados todos los derechos.
coquet, coquette (1) [kɔˈket], *v.t.*, *v.i.* coquetear.
coquetry [ˈkoukitri], *s.* coquetería, coqueteo.
coquette (2) [kɔˈket], *s.* coqueta.
coquettish [kɔˈketiʃ], *a.* coquetón, de coqueta.
cor [kɔ:], *s.* ***cor anglais,*** oboe tenor.
coracite [ˈkɔrəsait], *s.* (*min.*) coracita.
coracle [ˈkɔrəkl], *s.* barquilla.
coracoid [ˈkɔrəkɔid], *a.*, *s.* (*anat.*) coracoides, *m.pl.*
coral [ˈkɔrəl], *a.* coralino, de coral. — *s.* coral; ***coral-fisher,*** coralero; ***coral-reef,*** arrecife de coral.
coralline [ˈkɔrəlain], *a.* coralino. — *s.* coralina.
corbel, corbil [ˈkɔ:bəl], *s.* (*arq.*) ménsula, repisa; sostén.
corbie [ˈkɔ:bi], *s.* (*fam.*) cuervo.
cord [kɔ:d], *s.* cuerda; cordón; pana; ***spinal cord,*** médula espinal. — *v.t.* encordelar; atar con cuerdas.
cordage [ˈkɔ:didʒ], *s.* cordaje, cordelería.
cordate, cordated [ˈkɔ:deit, -id], *a.* (*bot.*) cordiforme.
cordial [ˈkɔ:diəl], *a.* cordial. — *s.* cordial.
cordiality, cordialness [kɔ:diˈæliti, ˈkɔ:diəlnis], *s.* cordialidad.
cordite [ˈkɔ:dait], *s.* cordita.
cordon [ˈkɔ:dən], *s.* cordón. — *v.t.* — ***off,*** acordonar.
Cordovan [ˈkɔ:dəvən], *a.*, *s.* cordobés.
cordovan [ˈkɔ:dəvən], *s.* cuero (de Córdoba).
corduroy [ˈkɔ:djurɔi], *s.* pana.
core [kɔ:], *s.* corazón; centro; núcleo; esencia, quid; (*med.*) foco; (*cable*) alma; ***core of the matter,*** quid de la cuestión; ***heart's core,*** fondo del corazón. — *v.t.* quitar el corazón a.
co-regent [kou-ˈri:dʒənt], *s.* corregente.
co-religionist [kou-riˈlidʒənist], *s.* correligionario.
co-respondent [kou-risˈpɔndənt], *s.* (*for.*) cómplice del demandado en una causa de divorcio.
coriaceous [kɔriˈeiʃəs], *a.* coriáceo.
coriander [kɔriˈændə], *s.* (*bot.*) culantro, coriandro.
Corinthian [kəˈrinθiən], *a.*, *s.* corintio.
co-rival [kou-ˈraivəl], *s.* competidor, rival.
cork [kɔ:k], *a.* corchero. — *s.* corcho; tapón; ***cork jacket,*** salvavidas de corcho; (*bot.*) ***cork oak,*** alcornoque; ***cork tip,*** filtro (de cigarrillo). — *v.t.* tapar con corcho.
corker [ˈkɔ:kə], *s.* (*fam.*) mentirona.
corking [ˈkɔ:kiŋ], *a.* (*fam.*) estupendo.
corkscrew [ˈkɔ:kskru:], *a.* en espiral de caracol. — *s.* sacacorchos, *m.inv.*, tirabuzón. — *v.i.* zigzaguear.
corky [ˈkɔ:ki], *a.* corchoso.
cormorant [ˈkɔ:mərənt], *s.* (*orn.*) cormorán.
corn (1) [kɔ:n], *s.* grano; trigo; ***corn-chandler,*** revendedor de cereales; ***corn-cob,*** mazorca de maíz; (*orn.*) ***corn-crake,*** guion *o* rey de codornices; ***corn-crops,*** cereales; ***corn-factor,*** mercante en trigos; (*bot.*) ***corn-flag,*** gladiolo, espadaña; ***corn-flour,*** harina de maíz; (*bot.*) ***corn-flower,*** aciano, coronilla; ***corn-meal,*** harina de maíz; ***corn-mill,*** molino; (*bot.*) ***corn-poppy,*** ababol, amapola; ***Indian corn,*** maíz.
corn (2) [kɔ:n], *s.* callo; ***corn-cutter,*** pedicuro, callista, *m.f.*; ***corn-plaster,*** emplasto (*de callos*); ***soft corn,*** callosidad.

cornaceous [kɔːˈneiʃəs], *a.* cornáceo.
cornea [ˈkɔːniə], *s.* (*anat.*) córnea.
corned [kɔːnd], *a.* salado; ***corned beef,*** cecina; carne de lata.
cornel [ˈkɔːnəl], *s.* (*bot.*) cornejo; (*joy.*) cornalina.
cornelian [kɔːˈniːliən], *s.* (*min.*) cornerina, cornalina.
corneous [ˈkɔːniəs], *a.* córneo; calloso.
corner [ˈkɔːnə], *s.* ángulo; esquina; rincón; recodo; escondrijo; pico (*del sombrero*); rabillo (*del ojo*); cantonera; aprieto, apuro; ***corner-stone,*** piedra angular; ***to cut corners,*** atajar; ahorrar tiempo, trabajo etc.; ***round the corner,*** a la vuelta de la esquina; ***to drive into a corner,*** arrinconar; poner en un aprieto. — *v.t.* arrinconar; acorralar; poner en un aprieto; (*com.*) acaparar. — *v.i.* (*aut.*) virar, tomar (las) curvas.
cornered [ˈkɔːnəd], *a.* angulado, esquinado; ***three-cornered hat,*** sombrero de tres picos; ***to be cornered,*** verse entre la espada y la pared.
cornering [ˈkɔːnəriŋ], *s.* acaparamiento; (*aut.*) capacidad para tomar las curvas.
cornet [ˈkɔːnit], *s.* corneta; portaestandarte; cucurucho; corona del casco; toca de mujer; (*mús.*) cornetín, corneta de llaves.
cornettist [kɔːˈnetist], *s.* cornetín.
cornfield [ˈkɔːnfiːld], *s.* trigal; maizal.
cornice [ˈkɔːnis], *s.* (*arq.*) cornisa.
cornicle [ˈkɔːnikl], *s.* cuernecico, cuernecillo.
cornific [kɔːˈnifik], *a.* cornífico.
Cornish [ˈkɔːniʃ], *a.* de Cornualles. — *s.* dialecto céltico de Cornualles.
cornist [ˈkɔːnist], *s.* corneta, *m.f.*
cornland [ˈkɔːnlənd], *s.* tierra de pan llevar; tierra de maíz.
cornopean [kɔːˈnoupiən], *s.* corneta de llaves.
cornstarch [ˈkɔːnstɑːtʃ], *s.* (*Am.*) harina de maíz.
cornucopia [kɔːnjuˈkoupiə], *s.* cornucopia.
corny [ˈkɔːni], *a.* (*fam.*) cursi.
corolla [kəˈrɔlə], *s.* (*bot.*) corola.
corollary [kəˈrɔləri], *s.* corolario; sobrante.
corona [kəˈrounə], *s.* (*astron.*, *arq.*) corona.
coronal [ˈkɔrənəl], *a.* coronal. — *s.* (*anat.*) coronal; corona, guirnalda.
coronary [ˈkɔrənəri], *a.* (*anat.*) coronario; (*pat.*) ***coronary thrombosis,*** trombosis coronaria. — *s.* (*fam.*) infarto (de miocardio).
coronation [kɔrəˈneiʃən], *s.* coronación.
coroner [ˈkɔrənə], *s.* oficial de la Corona que indaga las circunstancias de muertes violentas *o* repentinas, juez de primera instancia.
coronet [ˈkɔrənit], *s.* corona (*de título nobiliario*); diadema.
corporal (1) [ˈkɔːpərəl], *a.* corporal.
corporal (2) [ˈkɔːpərəl], *s.* (*mil.*) cabo.
corporality [kɔːpəˈræliti], *s.* corporalidad, corporeidad.
corporate [ˈkɔːpərit], *a.* corporativo.
corporation [kɔːpəˈreiʃən], *s.* corporación; ayuntamiento; sociedad anónima; (*fam.*) barriga.
corporeal [kɔːˈpɔːriəl], *a.* corpóreo; material, tangible.
corporeity [kɔːpɔːˈriːiti], *s.* corporeidad.
corporeous [kɔːˈpɔːriəs], *a.* corpóreo.
corposant [ˈkɔːpozænt], *s.* (*mar.*) fuego de Santelmo.
corps [kɔː], *s.inv.* cuerpo; ***army corps,*** cuerpo de ejército; ***ballet corps,*** cuerpo de baile.
corpse [kɔːps], *s.* cadáver.
corpulence, corpulency [ˈkɔːpjuləns, -i], *s.* obesidad.
corpulent [ˈkɔːpjulənt], *a.* grueso, obeso.
corpus [ˈkɔːpəs], *s.* (*pl.* **corpora** [ˈkɔːpərə]) cuerpo.
corpus delicti [ˈkɔːpəs diˈlikti], *s.* cuerpo del delito.
corpuscle [ˈkɔːpʌsl], *s.* corpúsculo; (*biol.*) glóbulo.
corpuscular [kɔːˈpʌskjulə], *a.* corpuscular.
corral [kəˈræl], *s.* corral. — *v.t.* acorralar, encerrar.
correct [kəˈrekt], *a.* correcto; exacto; ***to be correct,*** estar en lo cierto; ser cierto. — *v.t.* corregir; ***to stand corrected,*** reconocer el error.
correction [kəˈrekʃən], *s.* corrección.
correctional [kəˈrekʃənəl], *a.* correccional.
corrective [kəˈrektiv], *a.* correctivo. — *s.* correctivo.
correctness [kəˈrektnis], *s.* corrección; exactitud.
corrector [kəˈrektə], *s.* corrector.
correlate [ˈkɔrileit], *v.t.* correlacionar. — *v.i.* correlacionarse.
correlation [kɔriˈleiʃən], *s.* correlación.
correlative [kɔˈrelətiv], *a.*, *s.* correlativo.
correlativeness [kɔˈrelətivnis], *s.* correlación.
correspond [kɔrisˈpɔnd], *v.i.* corresponder; corresponderse, cartearse.
correspondence [kɔrisˈpɔndəns], *s.* correspondencia; epistolario.
correspondent [kɔrisˈpɔndənt], *a.* correspondiente. — *s.* corresponsal (*de periódico*); correspondiente.
corresponding [kɔrisˈpɔndiŋ], *a.* correspondiente.
corridor [ˈkɔridɔː], *s.* pasillo, corredor.
corroborant [kəˈrɔbərənt], *a.*, *s.* corroborante.
corroborate [kəˈrɔbəreit], *v.t.* corroborar.
corroboration [kərɔbəˈreiʃən], *s.* corroboración, confirmación.
corroborative [kəˈrɔbərətiv], *a.* corroborativo, corroborante, confirmatorio.
corrode [kəˈroud], *v.t.* corroer. — *v.i.* corroerse.
corrodent [kəˈroudənt], *a.* corrosivo.
corrodibility [kəroudiˈbiliti], *s.* (lo) corrosible.
corrodible [kəˈroudibl], *a.* corrosible.
corrosion [kəˈrouʒən], *s.* corrosión.
corrosive [kəˈrousiv], *a.* corrosivo.
corrosiveness [kəˈrousivnis], *s.* (lo) corrosivo.
corrugant [ˈkɔrugənt], *a.* que hace arrugas; (*med.*) astringente.
corrugate [ˈkɔrugit], *a.* [CORRUGATED]. — [ˈkɔrugeit], *v.t.* ondular, acanalar.
corrugated [ˈkɔrugeitid], *a.* ondulado, acanalado; ***corrugated iron,*** chapa ondulada, uralita.
corrugation [kɔruˈgeiʃən], *s.* corrugación, ondulación.
corrupt [kəˈrʌpt], *a.* corrompido; corrupto; viciado; estragado. — *v.t.* corromper; falsear. — *v.i.* corromperse.
corrupter [kəˈrʌptə], *s.* corruptor.
corruptibility, corruptibleness [kərʌptiˈbiliti, kəˈrʌptiblnis], *s.* corruptibilidad.
corruptible [kəˈrʌptibl], *a.* corruptible.
corrupting [kəˈrʌptiŋ], *a.* corruptor. — *s.* corrupción.
corruption [kəˈrʌpʃən], *s.* corrupción; influencia corruptora.
corruptive [kəˈrʌptiv], *a.* corruptivo.
corruptness [kəˈrʌptnis], *s.* estado de lo corrompido; corrupción.
corruptress [kəˈrʌptris], *s.* corrompedora, corruptora.
corsage [kɔːˈsɑːʒ], *s.* corpiño; ramillete.
corsair [ˈkɔːsɛə], *s.* corsario.
corselet [ˈkɔːslit], *s.* coselete; peto; corsé ligero.
corset [ˈkɔːsit], *s.* corsé, *m.*, faja.
corset-maker [ˈkɔːsit-meikə], *s.* corsetera.
Corsican [ˈkɔːsikən], *a.*, *s.* corso.
cortège [kɔːˈteiʒ], *s.* comitiva, cortejo, séquito.
cortex [ˈkɔːteks], *s.* corteza.
cortical [ˈkɔːtikəl], *a.* cortical.
corticate [ˈkɔːtikit], *a.* corticoso, cortezudo.
corundum [kəˈrʌndəm], *s.* (*min.*) corindón.
coruscant [kɔˈrʌskənt], *a.* coruscante, fulgurante.
coruscate [ˈkɔrəskeit], *v.i.* coruscar, fulgurar, relucir.
coruscation [kɔrəsˈkeiʃən], *s.* coruscación, fulguración, centelleo.
corvette [kɔːˈvet], *s.* (*mar.*) corbeta.

corybantic [kɔri'bæntik], *a.* coribántico.
corymb ['kɔrimb], *s.* (*bot.*) corimbo.
corymbiate [kə'rimbiit], *a.* (*bot.*) corímbeo.
corypheus [kɔri'fi:əs], *s.* corifeo.
coryza [kə'raizə], *s.* (*med.*) coriza.
cosecant [kou'si:kənt], *s.* (*geom.*) cosecante, *f.*
cosentient [kou'senʃənt], *a.* consintiente.
cosh [kɔʃ], *s.* (cachi)porra.
cosignatory [kou'signətəri], *a.*, *s.* cosignatario.
cosine ['kousain], *s.* (*geom.*) coseno.
cosiness ['kouzinis], *s.* (lo) cómodo; (lo) acogedor; (lo) abrigado.
cosmetic [kɔz'metik], *a.*, *s.* cosmético; (*pl.*) cosmética.
cosmic ['kɔzmik], *a.* cósmico.
cosmogonal [kɔz'mɔgənəl], *a.* cosmogónico.
cosmogony [kɔz'mɔgəni], *s.* cosmogonía.
cosmographer [kɔz'mɔgrəfə], *s.* cosmógrafo.
cosmographic(al) [kɔzmo'græfik(əl)], *a.* cosmográfico.
cosmography [kɔz'mɔgrəfi], *s.* cosmografía.
cosmological [kɔzmo'lɔdʒikəl], *a.* cosmológico.
cosmologist [kɔz'mɔlədʒist], *s.* cosmólogo.
cosmology [kɔz'mɔlədʒi], *s.* cosmología.
cosmometry [kɔz'mɔmitri], *s.* cosmometría.
cosmonaut ['kɔzmonɔ:t], *s.* cosmonauta, *m.f.*
cosmopolitan [kɔzmo'pɔlitən], *a.*, *s.* cosmopolita, *m.f.*
cosmopolitanism [kɔzmo'pɔlitənizəm], *s.* cosmopolitismo.
cosmorama [kɔzmo'rɑ:mə], *s.* cosmorama, *m.*
cosmos ['kɔzmos], *s.inv.* cosmos, *m.inv.*
Cossack ['kɔsæk], *a.*, *s.* cosaco.
cosset ['kɔsit], *s.* cordero criado con mimo; favorito, niño mimado. — *v.t.* mimar, acariciar.
cost [kɔst], *s.* coste, costo; costa; precio; ***at cost,*** al costo, a precio de coste; ***cost free,*** libre de gastos; ***to his cost,*** a expensas suyas; para su daño; con pesar suyo; ***at all costs, cost what it may,*** a toda costa, cueste lo que cueste; ***cost of living,*** coste *o* costo de (la) vida. — *v.i.* costar, valer.
costa ['kɔstə], *s.* (*zool.*, *fisiol.*) costilla.
costal ['kɔstəl], *a.* costal.
costard ['kɔstəd], *s.* manzana grande; (*vulg.*) cabeza.
Costa Rica ['kɔstə 'ri:kə]. Costa Rica.
Costa Rican ['kɔstə 'ri:kən], *a.*, *s.* costarricense.
costermonger ['kɔstəmʌngə], *s.* vendedor ambulante de fruta etc.
costive ['kɔstiv], *a.* estreñido.
costiveness ['kɔstivnis], *s.* estreñimiento.
costliness ['kɔstlinis], *s.* carestía, (lo) caro, (lo) costoso; suntuosidad.
costly ['kɔstli], *a.* caro, costoso; suntuoso.
costmary ['kɔstməri], *s.* (*bot.*) tanaceto.
costume ['kɔstju:m], *s.* traje, vestido; disfraz. — *v.t.* vestir.
costum(i)er [kɔs'tju:m(i)ə], *s.* sastre de teatro.
cosy ['kouzi], *a.* (*fam.*) cómodo; acogedor; (*vestido*) abrigado. — *s.* cubierta de tetera.
cot [kɔt], *s.* cuna; camita (*de niño*); catre; (*mar.*) coy.
co-tangent [kou-'tændʒənt], *s.* (*geom.*) cotangente, *f.*
cote [kout], *s.* (*ovejas*) aprisco; ***dove-cote,*** palomar.
co-tenant [kou-'tenənt], *s.* coinquilino.
coterie ['koutəri], *s.* corrillo; tertulia.
cothurnus [kə'θə:nəs], *s.* coturno.
cotillion [kə'tiljən], *s.* cotillón.
cotta ['kɔtə], *s.* (*igl.*) cota, sobrepelliz, *f.*
cottage ['kɔtidʒ], *s.* cabaña; casita de campo; ***cottage cheese,*** requesón.
cottager ['kɔtidʒə], *s.* habitante de una cabaña.
cotter ['kɔtə], *s.* chaveta.
cotton [kɔtn], *a.* algodonero, de algodón. — *s.* algodón; (*pl.*) géneros de algodón, *m.pl.*; ***cotton-gin,*** almarrá, *m.*; (*bot.*) ***cotton-plant,*** algodonero; ***cotton-waste,*** desperdicios de algodón, *m.pl.*; ***cotton-wool,*** algodón hidrófilo; ***cotton-yarn,*** hilado de algodón. — *v.t.* algodonar, mimar. — *v.i.* — ***on(to),*** caer, darse cuenta (de); ***he cottons on quick(ly),*** las caza al vuelo.
cottonwood ['kɔtnwud], *s.* álamo.
cottony ['kɔtni], *a.* algodonoso.
cotyle ['kɔtili:], *s.* (*anat.*) cotila.
cotyledon [kɔti'li:dən], *s.* (*bot.*) cotiledón.
cotyledonous [kɔti'li:dənəs], *a.* (*bot.*) cotiledóneo.
couch [kautʃ], *s.* sofá, diván. — *v.t.* expresar (*una idea*); acostar, tender; enristrar (*la lanza*). — *v.i.* acostarse; agacharse.
couchant ['kautʃənt], *a.* (*blas.*) acostado.
couch-grass ['kautʃ-grɑ:s], *s.* (*bot.*) grama.
cougar ['ku:gə], *s.* (*zool.*) puma.
cough [kɔf], *s.* tos, *f.*; ***whooping cough,*** tos ferina. — *v.t.* — ***up,*** expectorar; (*fam.*) aflojar (la pasta). — *v.i.* toser; (*fam.*) aflojar.
coughing ['kɔfiŋ], *s.* tos, tosidura; ***fit of coughing,*** acceso de tos.
coulisse [ku'li:s], *s.* corredera; (*teat.*) bastidores, *m.pl.*
coulter ['koultə], *s.* reja de arado.
council ['kaunsil], *s.* junta, consejo; concilio; concejo, ayuntamiento.
councillor ['kaunsilə], *s.* concejal; consejero.
counsel ['kaunsəl], *s.* consejo(s); dictamen, parecer; deliberación, consulta; sigilo, secreto; abogado; ***counsel for the defence,*** defensor; ***counsel for the prosecution,*** fiscal; ***to keep one's counsel,*** guardar silencio; ***to take counsel with,*** consultar, aconsejarse *o* asesorarse con. — *v.t.* aconsejar, asesorar.
counsellable ['kaunsələbl], *a.* aconsejable.
counsellor ['kaunsələ], *s.* consejero; consiliario; abogado; causídico.
counsellorship ['kaunsələʃip], *s.* dignidad de consejero.
count (1) [kaunt] *s.* cuenta; recuento; ***to lose count,*** perder la cuenta; ***to keep count,*** llevar la cuenta. — *v.t.* contar; ***count heads*** o ***noses,*** contar las personas presentes; ***count out,*** excluir, no contar con, no tener en cuenta; ***count o.s. happy,*** tenerse por dichoso. — *v.i.* contar; valer; ***count on*** o ***upon,*** contar con, confiar en; ***count on one's fingers,*** contar con los dedos.
count (2) [kaunt], *s.* conde.
countable [kauntəbl], *a.* contable, contadero.
countenance ['kauntinəns], *s.* semblante, rostro, continente, figura; aprobación, apoyo; ***to give countenance to*** [COUNTENANCE, *v.t.*]; ***to keep one's countenance,*** no alterarse, no inmutarse; ***to lose one's countenance,*** alterarse, inmutarse, desconcertarse; no poder contener la risa; ***to put out of countenance,*** alterar, desconcertar. — *v.t.* apoyar, aprobar, dar apoyo *o* aprobación a; admitir.
counter (1) ['kauntə], *s.* contador; mostrador; ficha; ***under the counter,*** bajo cuerda.
counter (2) ['kauntə], *adv.* en contra (***to,*** de), contrario (a); ***to go*** o ***run counter to,*** oponerse a. — *s.* (*mar.*) bovedilla; (lo) opuesto, (lo) contrario; pecho (*del caballo*); (*dep.*) contra, contragolpe. — *v.t.* oponerse a; contrarrestar; parar; (***with***), contestar (con).
counteract [kauntə'rækt], *v.t.* contrarrestar; neutralizar.
counteraction ['kauntərækʃən], *s.* oposición; contrarresto; acción contraria; neutralización.
counteractive [kauntə'ræktiv], *a.* contrario.
counter-attack ['kauntə-ə'tæk], *s.* contraataque. — *v.t.*, *v.i.* contraatacar.
counter-attraction ['kauntər-ə'trækʃən], *s.* attracción rival.

counterbalance [ˈkauntəˈbæləns], *s.* contrapeso; equilibrio; compensación. — *v.t.* contrabalancear, contrapesar; equilibrar; compensar.
counter-battery [ˈkauntə-ˈbætəri], *s.* contrabatería.
counter-blast [ˈkauntə-blɑːst], *s.* respuesta enérgica.
countercharge [ˈkauntətʃɑːdʒ], *s.* recriminación, acusación del acusado contra el acusador.
countercheck [ˈkauntəˈtʃek], *s.* oposición, contrarresto; segunda comprobación. — *v.t.* contrarrestar; comprobar por segunda vez.
counter-current [ˈkauntə-ˈkʌrənt], *s.* contracorriente, *f.*
counter-espionage [ˈkauntər-ˈespiənɑːʒ], *s.* contraespionaje.
counter-evidence [ˈkauntər-ˈevidəns], *s.* contraprueba.
counterfeit [ˈkauntəfiːt], *a.* falsificado, falso, contrahecho. — *s.* falsificación; moneda falsa. — *v.t.* falsificar; contrahacer.
counterfeiter [ˈkauntəfiːtə], *s.* falsificador, falsario, falseador.
counterfeiting [ˈkauntəfiːtiŋ], *s.* falsificación.
counterfoil [ˈkauntəfɔil], *s.* talón.
counterfort [ˈkauntəfɔːt], *s.* contrafuerte.
counter-guard [ˈkauntə-gɑːd], *s.* (*fort.*) contraguardia.
counter-intelligence [ˈkauntər-inˈtelidʒəns], *s.* contrainteligencia.
counter-irritant [ˈkauntər-ˈiritənt], *s.* (*med.*) contrairritante.
counterjumper [ˈkauntədʒʌmpə], *s.* (*despec.*) hortera.
countermand [kauntəˈmɑːnd], *s.* contramandato, contraorden, *f.* — *v.t.* contramandar; revocar.
counter-march [ˈkauntə-mɑːtʃ], *s.* contramarcha. — *v.i.* contramarchar.
counter-measure [ˈkauntə-ˈmeʒə], *s.* contramedida.
countermine [ˈkauntəmain], *s.* contramina. — *v.t.* contraminar.
counter-motion [ˈkauntə-ˈmouʃən], *s.* movimiento contrario; (*fig.*) proposición contraria.
counter-movement [ˈkauntə-ˈmuːvmənt], *s.* movimiento contrario.
counteroffensive [ˈkauntərəˈfensiv], *s.* contraofensiva.
counteroffer [ˈkauntərˈɔfə], *s.* contraoferta.
counterpace [ˈkauntəpeis], *s.* contrapaso.
counterpane [ˈkauntəpein], *s.* cobertor; colcha de cama, cubrecama, *m.*
counterpart [ˈkauntəpɑːt], *s.* igual, equivalente; persona correspondiente; (*mús.*) contraparte.
counter-petition [ˈkauntə-piˈtiʃən], *s.* petición opuesta. — *v.t.* hacer una petición contraria a otra.
counter-plea [ˈkauntə-ˈpliː], *s.* (*for.*) réplica, reconvención.
counter-plot [ˈkauntə-ˈplɔt], *s.* contratreta. — *v.t.* contraminar.
counterpoint [ˈkauntəpɔint], *s.* (*mús.*) contrapunto.
counterpoise [ˈkauntəpɔiz], *s.* contrapeso, equilibrio. — *v.t.* contrapesar, contrabalancear, equilibrar.
counterpoison [ˈkauntəpɔizən], *s.* contraveneno.
counter-pressure [ˈkauntə-ˈpreʃə], *s.* contrapresión.
counter-productive [ˈkauntə-prəˈdʌktiv], *a.* contraproducente.
counter-project [ˈkauntə-ˈprɔdʒekt], *s.* contraproyecto.
counter-proof [ˈkauntə-pruːf], *s.* contraprueba.
counterproposal [ˈkauntəprɔˈpouzəl], *s.* contrapropuesta.
counter-proposition [ˈkauntə-prɔpəˈziʃən], *s.* contraproposición.
Counter-Reformation [ˈkauntə-refəˈmeiʃən], *s.* Contrarreforma.
counter-revolution [ˈkauntə-revəˈl(j)uːʃən], *s.* contrarrevolución.
counter-revolutionary [ˈkauntə-revəˈl(j)uːʃənəri], *a.* contrarrevolucionario.
counter-seal [ˈkauntə-siːl], *v.i.* contrasellar.
counter-security [ˈkauntə-siˈkjuəriti], *s.* subgarantía.
countersign [ˈkauntəsain], *s.* refrendata; contraseña, consigna; (*mil.*) santo y seña. — *v.t.* refrendar, visar.
counter-signature [ˈkauntə-ˈsignətʃə], *s.* refrendata.
countersink [ˈkauntəsiŋk], *s.* avellanado; avellanador, broca de avellanar. — *v.t.* avellanar, abocardar.
counter-stroke [ˈkauntə-strouk], *s.* contragolpe, revés.
counter-tenor [ˈkauntə-ˈtenə], *s.* (*mús.*) contralto.
counter-tide [ˈkauntə-taid], *s.* (*mar.*) contramarea.
countervail [ˈkauntəveil], *v.t.* contrapesar, compensar, equivaler.
counter-vallation [ˈkauntə-vəˈleiʃən], *s.* (*fort.*) contravalación.
counter-valuation [ˈkauntə-væljuˈeiʃən], *s.* contravaluación.
counterview [ˈkauntəvjuː], *s.* opinión opuesta.
counter-weight [ˈkauntə-weit], *s.* contrapeso.
counter-work [ˈkauntə-wəːk], *v.t.* contrarrestar; neutralizar.
countess [ˈkauntis], *s.* condesa.
counting-house [ˈkauntiŋ-haus], *s.* despacho; contaduría.
countless [ˈkauntlis], *a.* incontable, sin cuento.
countrified [ˈkʌntrifaid], *a.* (*fam.*) rústico, rural.
countrify [ˈkʌntrifai], *v.t.* hacer rústico *o* rural.
country [ˈkʌntri], *a.* rural, campesino, campestre; provincial; del campo; ***country club,*** club de campo; ***country cousin,*** pariente paleto; ***country dance,*** baile campestre, contradanza; ***country estate,*** finca (rústica); ***country gentleman,*** propietario rural; ***country house,*** quinta, casa de campo; ***country life,*** vida rural; ***country road,*** camino vecinal; ***country seat,*** casa solariega. — *s.* campo; país, patria; comarca, provincia.
countryfolk [ˈkʌntrifouk], *s.* gente del campo, campesinos, *m.pl.*
countryman [ˈkʌntrimən], *s.* (*pl.* **countrymen** [-men]) campesino, hombre del campo; ***fellow countryman,*** compatriota, *m.f.*
countryside [ˈkʌntrisaid], *s.* campiña, campo; paisaje.
countrywoman [ˈkʌntriwumən], *s.* campesina mujer del campo, *f.*
county [ˈkaunti], *a.* del condado, perteneciente al condado. — *s.* condado; provincia; ***county town*** o ***seat,*** capital de provincia.
coup [kuː], *s.* golpe; ***coup d'état,*** golpe de estado; ***coup de grâce,*** golpe de gracia.
coupé [ˈkuːpei], *s.* cupé.
couple [kʌpl], *s.* par; (*dos personas*) pareja; ***married couple,*** matrimonio. — *v.t.* acoplar; aparear; juntar, unir; casar; enganchar. — *v.i.* juntarse.
coupler [ˈkʌplə], *s.* acoplador; enganche.
couplet [ˈkʌplit], *s.* pareado; par.
coupling [ˈkʌpliŋ], *s.* acoplamiento; enganche; junta, unión; ***coupling-iron,*** grapón; ***coupling-pin,*** pasador de enganche.
coupon [ˈkuːpɔn], *s.* cupón.
courage [ˈkʌridʒ], *s.* valor, valentía; ánimo; ***courage!*** ¡ánimo!; ***to pluck up courage,*** armarse de valor, hacer de tripas corazón.
courageous [kəˈreidʒəs], *a.* valeroso.
courageousness [kəˈreidʒəsnis], *s.* valerosidad.

courier [ˈkuriə], *s.* correo, estafeta; agente de turismo.

course [kɔ:s], *s.* curso; trayectoria; (*mar.*) rumbo, derrota; transcurso, decurso, paso (*del tiempo*); (*fig.*) proceder, camino, posibilidad; plato; hilada (*de ladrillos*); corriente (*de agua*); campo (*de golf*); ***race course,*** hipódromo; ***in due course,*** en su día, en su (debido) momento; ***in the course of,*** en el curso *o* decurso de, durante; ***of course,*** desde luego, por supuesto; ***to give course to,*** dar curso a. — *v.t.* cazar, perseguir; hacer correr. — *v.i.* correr; corretear.

courser [ˈkɔ:sə], *s.* corcel.

coursing [ˈkɔ:siŋ], *s.* caza de la liebre.

court [kɔ:t], *s.* patio, atrio; corte; tribunal, juzgado; ***court chaplain,*** capellán del rey; ***court day,*** día de besamanos; (*for.*) día hábil; ***court dress,*** traje de corte; ***court of appeal,*** tribunal de apelación; ***court plaster,*** tafetán inglés; ***pelota court,*** frontón; ***tennis court,*** cancha de tenis. — *v.t.* cortejar, hacer la corte a; (*fig.*) solicitar, buscar.

courteous [ˈkə:tiəs], *a.* cortés; fino; atento; cumplido; urbano.

courteousness [ˈkə:tiəsnis], *s.* cortesía; urbanidad.

courtesan [kɔ:tiˈʒæn], *s.* cortesana.

courtesy [ˈkə:tisi], *s.* cortesía; finura.

court-house [ˈkɔ:t-haus], *s.* audiencia; palacio de justicia.

courtier [ˈkɔ:tiə], *s.* cortesano, palaciego.

courtliness [ˈkɔ:tlinis], *s.* cortesanía; urbanidad; elegancia.

courtly [ˈkɔ:tli], *a.* cortesano; cortés; elegante; ***courtly love,*** amor cortés.

court-martial [ˈkɔ:t-ˈmɑ:ʃəl], *s.* (*pl.* **courts-martial** [-s-ˈmɑ:ʃəl]) consejo de guerra. — *v.t.* someter a consejo de guerra.

court-room [ˈkɔ:t-ru:m], *s.* sala de justicia.

courtship [ˈkɔ:tʃip], *s.* noviazgo; galanteo; cortejo.

courtyard [ˈkɔ:tjɑ:d], *s.* patio.

cousin [kʌzn], *s.* primo, prima.

cousinhood [ˈkʌznhud], *s.* primazgo.

cove (1) [kouv], *s.* cala, caleta, ensenada, ancón, abra; (*arq.*) bovedilla. — *v.t.* abovedar.

cove (2) [kouv], *s.* (*fam.*) tipo.

covenant [ˈkʌvənənt], *s.* convenio, pacto; alianza; ***Ark of the Covenant,*** Arca de la Alianza; ***Covenant of the League of Nations,*** Pacto de la Sociedad de Naciones; ***the New Covenant,*** el Nuevo Testamento. — *v.t., v.i.* pactar, convenir(se).

covenantee [kʌvənənˈti:], *s.* contratante.

covenanter [ˈkʌvənəntə], *s.* contratante; covenantario.

cover [ˈkʌvə], *s.* cubierta; tapa, funda, forro; sobre; portada; abrigo; techado; capa, pretexto; cubierto; guarida, maleza; (*com.*) provisión de fondos; ***to break cover,*** salir al descubierto; ***cover charge,*** cubierto; ***to take cover,*** refugiarse, buscar abrigo; ***under cover,*** bajo techado; secretamente; ***under cover of,*** so pretexto de; ***under separate cover,*** por separado, bajo cubierta separada. — *v.t.* cubrir, recubrir; tapar, forrar; abrigar, arropar; encubrir, disimular; recorrer; incluir, abarcar; ***cover up,*** cubrir completamente; disimular, encubrir. — *v.i.* cubrirse; hacer provisión de fondos.

coverage [ˈkʌvəridʒ], *s.* reportaje; riesgos que cubre una póliza.

covering [ˈkʌvəriŋ], *s.* acción de cubrir; cubierta, envoltura.

coverlet [ˈkʌvəlit], *s.* colcha, cobertura de cama, cubrecama, *m.*, sobrecama, *m.*, cobertor.

covert [ˈkʌvə:t], *a.* cubierto, tapado, oculto, secreto; (*for.*) bajo protección. — *s.* cubierto, cubierta; refugio, guarida, huidero; bandada (*en la caza de aves*).

covertness [ˈkʌvə:tnis], *s.* obscuridad; secreto.

coverture [ˈkʌvə:tʃə], *s.* cubierta; defensa, abrigo.

covert-way [ˈkʌvə:t-wei], *s.* (*fort.*) camino cubierto.

covet [ˈkʌvit], *v.t., v.i.* codiciar.

covetable [ˈkʌvitəbl], *a.* codiciable.

covetous [ˈkʌvitəs], *a.* codicioso.

covetousness [ˈkʌvitəsnis], *s.* codicia.

covey [ˈkʌvi], *s.* pollada, nidada; banda, bandada.

cow (1) [kau], *s.* vaca; hembra (*elefante, cetáceo etc.*); ***cow-bell,*** cencerro, esquila; (*Am., f.c.*) ***cow-catcher,*** quitapiedras, *m.inv.*; ***cow-dung,*** boñiga; ***cow-herd, cow-keeper,*** vaquero, boyero.

cow (2) [kau], *v.t.* acobardar, intimidar.

coward [ˈkauəd], *a., s.* cobarde.

cowardice, cowardliness [ˈkauədis, -linis], *s.* cobardía.

cowardly [ˈkauədli], *a.* cobarde, pusilánime.

cowboy [ˈkaubɔi], *s.* vaquero.

cower [kauə], *v.i.* acurrucarse, agacharse, alebrarse, agazaparse, acobardarse.

cowhide [ˈkauhaid], *s.* cuero; zurriago.

cowl [kaul], *s.* cogulla; capucha; cubierta (*de motor*); sombrerete (de chimenea); (*mec.*) caperuza. — *v.t.* poner cogulla a, cubrir con tapa etc.

cowling [ˈkauliŋ], *s.* cubierta (de motor).

cowman [ˈkaumən], *s.* vaquero.

co-worker [ˈkou-ˈwə:kə], *s.* coadjutor; colaborador.

cowpox [ˈkaupɔks], *s.* (*med.*) vacuna.

cowrie, cowry [ˈkauri], *s.* cauri.

cowshed [ˈkauʃed], *s.* establo.

cowslip [ˈkauslip], *s.* (*bot.*) primavera.

coxa [ˈkɔksə], *s.* (*anat., zool.*) coxa.

coxalgic [kɔkˈsældʒik], *a.* (*med.*) coxálgico.

coxcomb [ˈkɔkskoum], *s.* cresta de gallo; (*fig.*) mequetrefe, pisaverde.

coxswain [ˈkɔksn], *s.* (*mar.*) timonel.

coy [kɔi], *a.* vergonzoso, tímido, recatado.

coyly [ˈkɔili], *adv.* tímidamente; con coquetería.

coyness [ˈkɔinis], *s.* vergüenza, timidez, recato.

cozen [kʌzn], *v.t.* (*ant.*) engañar.

crab [kræb], *s.* cangrejo; buey de Francia; grúa; cabria; ***spider-crab,*** centollo, centolla; (*fig.*) ***to catch a crab,*** fallar al remar. — *v.t.* poner pegas a; poner la zancadilla a.

crab-apple [ˈkræb-æpl], *s.* manzana silvestre.

crabbed [kræbd], *a.* avinagrado, desabrido, malhumorado; (letra) mal formada, apretada.

crabbedness [ˈkræbidnis], *s.* desabrimiento, mal humor.

crabby [ˈkræbi], *a.* desabrido, malhumorado.

crabstone [ˈkræbstoun], *s.* ojo de cangrejo.

crack [kræk], *a.* (*fam.*) de primera categoría, escogido; (*puntería*) certero. — *s.* crujido; estallido; chasquido; estampido; hendedura, grieta, rendija; resquicio; rotura; chiste, gracia; ***at the crack of dawn,*** al romper el alba. — *v.t.* agrietar, hender; romper; quebrar; chasquear; restallar; (*botella*) abrir; (*chiste*) contar; (*nuez*) cascar; (*fam.*) ***crack up,*** alabar. — *v.i.* agrietarse; crujir; estallar; (*voz*) cascarse; (*fam.*) ceder, fallar, hundirse; ***crack down on,*** ponerse en plan duro con, usar mano dura con; (*fam.*) ***crack up,*** hundirse, desfondarse, deshacerse, desbaratarse.

cracker [ˈkrækə], *s.* petardo; traca; galleta; (*fiesta*) sorpresa.

cracking [ˈkrækiŋ], *s.* [CRACK].

crackle [krækl], *s.* crujido; crepitación. — *v.i.* crujir; crepitar.

crackling [ˈkrækliŋ], *s.* [CRACKLE]; chicharrón.

cracknel [ˈkræknəl], *s.* hojaldre; galletica.

cracksman [ˈkræksmən], *s.* (*fam.*) ladrón de cajas fuertes.

cradle [kreidl], *s.* cuna; (*cir.*) tablilla; (*agric.*) hoz de rastra; (*min.*) artesa móvil; ***cradle song,*** canción de cuna. — *v.t.* acunar.

craft (1) [krɑ:ft], *s.* oficio; maña, destreza; astucia.

craft (2) [krɑ:ft], *s.* embarcación.

craftiness [ˈkrɑ:ftinis], *s.* astucia, artería; (lo) taimado, (lo) solapado.
craftsman [ˈkrɑ:ftsmən], *s.* artesano.
craftsmanship [ˈkrɑ:ftsmənʃip], *s.* artesanía.
craftsmaster [ˈkrɑ:ftsmɑ:stə], *s.* artífice, maestro.
crafty [ˈkrɑ:fti], *a.* astuto, taimado, solapado, artero.
crag [kræg], *s.* peñasco, peña, risco.
cragginess [ˈkræginis], *s.* (lo) fragoso.
craggy [ˈkrægi], *a.* peñascoso, fragoso.
cram [kræm], *v.t.* atestar, atiborrar, atracar, embutir; preparar precipitadamente para un examen; ***cram up,*** empollar(se). — *v.i.* atracarse de comida.
crambo [ˈkræmbou], *s.* juego que consiste en hallar consonante a una palabra dada.
crammer [ˈkræmə], *s.* (*fam.*) profesor que prepara para exámenes; empollón.
cramming [ˈkræmiŋ], *s.* atiborramiento, atracón; preparación intensiva; empollamiento.
cramp [kræmp], *s.* (*med.*) calambre; (*med.*) entumecimiento; sujeción, aprieto, estrechez; laña; grapa; ***he got cramp,*** le dio un calambre. — *v.t.* dar calambre a; lañar, engrapar; apretar, sujetar; (*fig.*) ***to cramp the style of,*** estropear el juego a, poner la zancadilla a.
cramped [kræmpt], *a.* estrecho; apretado; incómodo.
crampit [ˈkræmpit], *s.* contera de espada.
crampon [ˈkræmpɔn], *s.* tenazas, *f.pl.*, garfios, *m.pl.*
cranage [ˈkreinidʒ], *s.* gruaje, derechos (*m.pl.*) *o* alquiler de grúa en los muelles.
cranberry [ˈkrænbəri], *s.* (*bot.*) arándano agrio.
crance [krɑ:ns], *s.* (*mar.*) suncho de botalón.
crane [krein], *s.* (*orn.*) grulla; (*mec.*) grúa; árgana; pescante; sifón; (*mar.*) abanico; arbotante; ***wheel-crane,*** grúa de ruedas. — *v.t.* levantar con grúa; ***crane the neck,*** estirar el cuello.
crane-fly [ˈkrein-flai], *s.* (*ent.*) típula.
crane's bill [ˈkreinz bil], *s.* (*bot.*) geranio; (*cir.*) fórceps.
cranial [ˈkreiniəl], *a.* craneal, craneano.
craniognomy [kreiniˈɔnəmi], *s.* craneología.
craniograph [ˈkreiniəgræf], *s.* craneógrafo.
craniology [kreiniˈɔlədʒi], *s.* craneología.
cranioscopy [kreiniˈɔskəpi], *s.* craneoscopia.
cranium [ˈkreiniəm], *s.* (*anat.*) cráneo.
crank [kræŋk], *a.* inestable, inseguro; (*mar.*) celoso. — *s.* hierro de farol; (*aut.*, *mec.*) manivela, manubrio, cigüeña; gancho; biela; maniático, chiflado; (*aut.*) ***crank-case,*** cárter del cigüeñal; ***crank-shaft,*** eje del cigüeñal. — *v.t.* poner en marcha con manivela; hacer virar.
crankiness [ˈkræŋkinis], *s.* chifladura.
crankle [kræŋkl], *s.* recodo, repliegue, vuelta. — *v.t.*, *v.i.* serpentear, culubrear.
cranky [ˈkræŋki], *a.* chiflado, extravagante; maniático.
crannied [ˈkrænid], *a.* hendido, grietoso.
cranny [ˈkræni], *s.* hendedura, grieta, raja; rincón.
crape [kreip], *s.* crespón. — *v.t.* encrespar, rizar; poner crespón a.
crapulence [ˈkræpjuləns], *s.* crápula.
crapulent, crapulous [ˈkræpjulənt, -ləs], *a.* crapuloso.
crash [kræʃ], *s.* estrépito; estallido; estampido; choque, encontronazo; desplome (estrepitoso); (*com.*) quiebra; fracaso; crac; ***crash-helmet,*** casco protector; ***crash-course,*** curso intensivo; ***crash-landing,*** aterrizaje violento forzoso. — *v.t.* estrellar; romper estrepitosamente. — *v.i.* estrellarse, chocar; romperse con estrépito; desplomarse con estrépito; estallar, dar un estallido; (*com.*) quebrar; fracasar.
crasis [ˈkreisis], *s.* (*gram.*) sinéresis, *f.inv.*
crass [kræs], *a.* craso.
crassitude, crassness [ˈkræsitju:d, -nis], *s.* crasitud; (lo) craso, (lo) elemental.
crate [kreit], *s.* caja, cajón (de embalaje); cesto grande, canasto, cuévano, banasta.
crater [ˈkreitə], *s.* cráter.
cravat [krəˈvæt], *s.* corbata.
crave [kreiv], *v.t.* suplicar, rogar, implorar; anhelar, ansiar. — *v.i.* — ***for*** o ***after,*** ansiar; tener antojo de.
craven [ˈkreivən], *a.* cobarde, pusilánime. — *s.* cobarde.
craver [ˈkreivə], *s.* uno que ansía (algo).
craving [ˈkreiviŋ], *s.* ansia, sed (***for,*** de); antojo.
craw [krɔ:], *s.* (*anat.*, *orn.*) buche.
crawfish [ˈkrɔ:fiʃ], [CRAYFISH].
crawl [krɔ:l], *s.* arrastramiento; gateamiento, (el) ir a gatas; (*natación*) crawl, crol; corral (de peces). — *v.i.* arrastrarse, serpear; gatear, ir a gatas; (*fig.*) ***crawl along,*** ir a paso de tortuga; ***to make s.o. crawl,*** hacer bajar la cerviz a alguien.
crawling [ˈkrɔ:liŋ], *a.* (*fam.*) atestado (***with,*** de); ***to be crawling with,*** pulular con, hormiguear con.
crayfish [ˈkreifiʃ], *s.* cigala.
crayon [ˈkreiən], *s.* creyón, tizna.
craze [kreiz], *s.* manía; locura; antojo, capricho; moda; (*fam.*) ***to be all the craze,*** estilarse muchísimo. — *v.t.* enloquecer.
crazed [kreizd], *a.* grietoso; demente.
crazily [ˈkreizili], *adv.* insensatamente, locamente.
craziness [ˈkreizinis], *s.* locura, chiflamiento, chifladura.
crazy [ˈkreizi], *a.* loco, chiflado, chalado; disparatado; ***crazy-paving,*** enlosado asimétrico.
creak [kri:k], *s.* crujido, chirrido, rechinamiento. — *v.i.* crujir, chirriar, rechinar.
creaking [ˈkri:kiŋ], *s.* [CREAK].
creaky [ˈkri:ki], *a.* rechinador.
cream [kri:m], *s.* crema; nata; (*fig.*) flor y nata; ***cream of tartar,*** crémor; ***whipped cream,*** nata batida. — *v.t.* desnatar. — *v.i.* criar nata.
creamery [ˈkri:məri], *s.* lechería.
creamy [ˈkri:mi], *a.* cremoso.
crease [kri:s], *s.* pliegue; arruga; (*pantalones*) raya; ***crease-resistant,*** inarrugable. — *v.t.* plegar; arrugar. — *v.i.* plegarse; arrugarse. — ***crease o.s.,*** *v.r.* (***with laughter***), desternillarse de risa.
creaser [ˈkri:sə], *s.* (*cost.*) repulgador.
create [kriˈeit], *v.t.* crear; originar; ***create a disturbance,*** revolver la feria, armar un cisco.
creation [kriˈeiʃən], *s.* creación.
creative [kriˈeitiv], *a.* creador, creativo.
creativeness [kriˈeitivnis], *s.* inventiva, facultad creadora.
creator [kriˈeitə], *s.* creador.
creatress [kriˈeitris], *s.* creadora.
creature [ˈkri:tʃə], *s.* criatura; hechura; (*fam.*) animal, bicho; ***fellow creature,*** semejante.
creatureliness [ˈkri:tʃəlinis], *s.* estado de animal; estado de todo ser creado.
credence [ˈkri:dəns], *s.* crédito; credencia; ***letters of credence,*** (cartas) credenciales; ***give credence to,*** dar crédito a.
credent [ˈkri:dənt], *a.* creyente.
credential [kriˈdenʃəl], *a.* credencial. — *s.* (*pl.*) (cartas) credenciales.
credibility, credibleness [krediˈbiliti, ˈkrediblnis], *s.* credibilidad; veracidad; ***credibility gap,*** falta de credibilidad.
credible [ˈkredibl], *a.* creíble, verosímil.
credit [ˈkredit], *a.* del haber, acreedor; ***credit balance,*** saldo acreedor. — *s.* crédito; ***on credit,*** a crédito; ***this does him credit,*** esto le honra; ***to give a person credit for,*** reconocerle a una persona el mérito de; ***to take credit for,*** atribuirse el mérito de. — *v.t.* creer; acreditar;

dar crédito a; ***credit a sum to,*** abonar una cantidad a; ***credit s.o. with,*** conceder a uno el mérito de.

creditable [ˈkreditəbl], *a.* loable, meritorio.

creditably [ˈkreditəbli], *adv.* honorablemente, honrosamente; ***to acquit o.s. creditably,*** salir airosamente.

creditor [ˈkreditə], *s.* acreedor; (*com.*) haber.

credo [ˈkriːdou], *s.* credo.

credulity, credulousness [kreˈdjuːliti, ˈkredjuləsnis], *s.* credulidad.

credulous [ˈkredjuləs], *a.* crédulo.

creed [kriːd], *s.* credo; creencia.

creek [kriːk], *s.* cala, abra; (*Am.*) arroyo; recodo.

creel [kriːl], *s.* cesta de pescador.

creep [kriːp], *s.* arrastramiento; (*fam.*) cobista, *m.f.*; (*pl.*) hormigueo; ***it gives me the creeps,*** me da grima. — *irr. v.i.* deslizarse; serpear; andar a hurtadillas; sentir hormigueo; ***creep in,*** entrar furtivamente; ***creep out,*** escabullirse; ***creep up,*** trepar; ***creep up on,*** acercarse a hurtadillas a; ***it makes my flesh creep,*** me da grima.

creeper [ˈkriːpə], *s.* reptil; (*orn.*) trepadora; (*bot.*) enredadera; ramplón de zapato; (*mar.*) garfio, garabato.

creephole [ˈkriːphoul], *s.* huronera; (*fig.*) pretexto, escapatoria.

creeping [ˈkriːpiŋ], *a.* lento; insidioso; ***creeping paralysis,*** parálisis progresiva. — *s.* arrastramiento; movimiento(s) subrepticio(s); (*fig.*) servilismo.

creepingly [ˈkriːpiŋli], *adv.* a paso de tortuga.

creese [kriːs], *s.* cris.

cremate [kriˈmeit], *v.t.* incinerar.

cremation [kriˈmeiʃən], *s.* cremación, incineración.

cremationist [kriˈmeiʃənist], *s.* partidario de la cremación.

crematorium [kreməˈtɔːriəm], *s.* (horno) crematorio.

crematory [ˈkremətəri], *a.* crematorio. — *s.* (horno) crematorio.

crenated [ˈkriːneitid], *a.* (*bot.*) dentado.

crenel(l)ate [ˈkrenileit], *v.t.* (*fort.*) almenar.

Creole [ˈkriːoul], *a.*, *s.* criollo.

creosote [ˈkriːəsout], *s.* creosota.

crepitate [ˈkrepiteit], *v.i.* crepitar, chisporrotear.

crepitation [krepiˈteiʃən], *s.* crepitación, chisporroteo.

crepuscular [kriˈpʌskjulə], *a.* crepuscular.

crescendo [kriˈʃendou], *s.* (*mús.*) crescendo.

crescent [ˈkresənt], *a.* creciente. — *s.* creciente; cuarto creciente; calle semicircular; (*aproximación*) glorieta.

cress [kres], *s.* (*bot.*) lepidio, mastuerzo; ***water-cress,*** berro(s).

cresset [ˈkresit], *s.* antorcha; antorchero, tedero.

crest [krest], *s.* cresta; penacho, copete; escudo; divisa, lema. — *v.t.* coronar. — *v.i.* encrestarse, encresparse.

crested [ˈkrestid], *a.* crestado; coronado, encopetado.

crestfallen [ˈkrestfɔːlən], *a.* cabizbajo, alicaído, con las orejas gachas.

cretaceous [kriˈteiʃəs], *a.* cretáceo, gredoso.

Cretan [ˈkriːtən], *a.*, *s.* cretense.

cretin [ˈkretin], *s.* cretino.

cretinism [ˈkretinizəm], *s.* cretinismo.

cretonne [ˈkretɔn], *s.* cretona.

crevasse [kriˈvæs], *s.* grieta profunda (*en un ventisquero*); (*Am.*) brecha (*en el terraplén de un río*).

crevice [ˈkrevis], *s.* hendedura, raja, grieta, resquicio.

crew [kruː], *s.* tripulación, dotación; (*fig.*) pandilla.

crewel [ˈkruːəl], *s.* ovillo (*de lana etc.*).

crib [krib], *s.* pesebre; camita; cuna; casucha, choza; jaula; arcón; cofre; cajón; (*min.*) brocal; estribo flotante; mimbrera; (*fam. escolar*) chuleta; (*fam.*) plagio; (*fam.*) ***to crack a crib,*** hacer un robo. — *v.i.* usar una chuleta; plagiar.

cribbage [ˈkribidʒ], *s.* juego de naipes.

cribble [kribl], *s.* criba, harnero; aventador. — *v.t.* cerner; agujerear; puntear.

cribriform [ˈkribrifɔːm], *a.* (*anat.*, *bot.*) cribiforme, en forma de criba.

crick [krik], *s.* chirrido; calambre; ***crick in the neck,*** tortícolis.

cricket (1) [ˈkrikit], *s.* cricket; (*fig.*) juego limpio.

cricket (2) [ˈkrikit], *s.* grillo; ***to be as cheery as a cricket,*** estar alegre como unas castañuelas.

cricketer [ˈkrikitə], *s.* jugador de cricket.

cricoid [ˈkraikɔid], *a.*, *s.* (*anat.*) cricoides, *m.inv.*

crier [kraiə], *s.* pregonero.

crikey! [ˈkraiki], *interj.* ¡diantre! ¡caray!

crime [kraim], *s.* crimen, delito.

Crimean [kraiˈmiːən], *a.* de Crimea.

crimeless [ˈkraimlis], *a.* inocente.

criminal [ˈkriminəl], *a.* criminal, delictivo. — *s.* criminal, delincuente.

criminality [krimiˈnæliti], *s.* criminalidad.

criminate [ˈkrimineit], *v.t.* acriminar, acusar.

crimination [krimiˈneiʃən], *s.* criminación, acriminación.

criminative, criminatory [ˈkrimineitiv, -ətəri], *a.* acriminatorio.

criminology [krimiˈnɔlədʒi], *s.* criminología.

criminous [ˈkriminəs], *a.* delictuoso, criminoso.

crimp [krimp], *a.* rizado; quebradizo. — *s.* rizador; enganchador, reclutador; ***to put a crimp in,*** estorbar. — *v.t.* rizar, encrespar; enganchar, reclutar (*a la fuerza*).

crimpage [ˈkrimpidʒ], *s.* rizaje; rizadura; estampado en relieve.

crimping-iron [ˈkrimpiŋ-ˈaiən], *s.* tenacillas de rizar.

crimple [krimpl], *s.* arruga, pliegue. — *v.t.* arrugar; rizar. — *v.i.* arrugarse; encogerse.

crimson [ˈkrimzən], *a.*, *s.* carmesí; ***to go*** o ***turn crimson,*** ruborizarse. — *v.t.* teñir de carmesí. — *v.i.* ruborizarse.

crinal [ˈkrainəl], *a.* perteneciente *o* relativo al cabello.

cringe [krindʒ], *s.* servilismo; bajeza. — *v.i.* encogerse; arrastrarse; conducirse servilmente.

cringer [ˈkrindʒə], *s.* adulón.

cringing [ˈkrindʒiŋ], *a.* servil.

cringle [kriŋgl], *s.* (*mar.*) ojo.

crinite [ˈkrainait], *a.* (*bot.*, *zool.*) crinito, peludo.

crinkle [kriŋkl], *s.* arruga; sinuosidad; susurro. — *v.t.* arrugar; ondular. — *v.t.* arrugarse; ondularse; susurrar, crujir (*la seda*).

crinoid [ˈkrainɔid], *s.* crinóideo.

crinoline [ˈkrinəlin], *s.* crinolina, miriñaque, ahuecador.

cripple [kripl], *a.* tullido, lisiado; desmantelado, desarbolado (*buque*). — *s.* tullido, lisiado. — *v.t.* lisiar, tullir, baldar; desarbolar, desmantelar.

crisis [ˈkraisis], *s.* crisis, *f.inv.*

crisp [krisp], *a.* crespo, rizado; terso; crujiente; fresco, despejado; tostado. — *s.* (*pl.*) patatas fritas a la inglesa, *f.pl.* — *v.t.* encrespar, rizar; tostar. — *v.i.* crujir.

crispate [ˈkrispeit], *s.* (*bot.*, *zool.*) arrugado, rizado.

crispness [ˈkrispnis], *s.* (lo) tostado, (lo) crujiente, etc.

crispy [ˈkrispi], *a.* [CRISP].

criss-cross [ˈkris-ˈkrɔs], *a.* cruzado, entrecruzado. — *v.t.* llenar de líneas cruzadas. — *v.i.* entrecruzarse.

criterion [kraiˈtiəriən], *s.* (*pl.* **criteria** [-riə]), criterio.

critic [ˈkritik], *s.* crítico; censor; criticón.

critical [ˈkritikəl], *a.* crítico.
criticalness [ˈkritikəlnis], *s.* (lo) crítico.
criticism [ˈkritisizəm], *s.* crítica; censura; (*filos.*) criticismo.
criticize [ˈkritisaiz], *v.t.*, *v.i.* criticar; censurar.
critique [kriˈti:k], *s.* crítica, reseña, ensayo crítico.
croak [krouk], *s.* graznido; (el) croar; canto; gruñido. — *v.i.* graznar; croar; gruñir; (*fam.*, *fig.*) reventar, diñarla, estirar la pata.
croaker [ˈkroukə], *s.* gruñidor.
croaking [ˈkroukiŋ], *s.* [CROAK].
crochet [ˈkrouʃei], *s.* crochet, croché, labor de croché *o* de ganchillo; ***crochet hook,*** ganchillo. — *v.i.* hacer croché *o* labor de ganchillo.
crock [krɔk], *s.* (*fam.*) cacharro; ***old crock,*** carcamal, vejestorio; (*aut.*) cacharro, fotingo. — *v.t.* poner fuera de combate.
crockery [ˈkrɔkəri], *s.inv.* loza, cacharros.
crocodile [ˈkrɔkədail], *s.* (*zool.*) cocodrilo; ***crocodile tears,*** lágrimas de cocodrilo, *f.pl.*
crocus [ˈkroukəs], *s.* (*bot.*) azafrán.
croft [krɔft], *s.* heredad; finca muy modesta.
crofter [ˈkrɔftə], *s.* colono, labrador.
cromlech [ˈkrɔmlek], *s.* crónlech.
crone [kroun], *s.* bruja; vieja; fea.
crony [ˈkrouni], *s.* compinche, compadre.
crook [kruk], *s.* curva; gancho; cayado (*de pastor*); delincuente, maleante; fullero. — *v.t.* encorvar. — *v.i.* encorvarse.
crookbacked [ˈkrukbækd], *a.* giboso, gibado, jorobado, corcovado.
crooked [ˈkrukid], *a.* encorvado; torcido; oblicuo; ladeado; (*fig.*) torcido; delincuente, maleante; ***to go crooked,*** torcerse; malearse.
crookedness [ˈkrukidnis], *s.* (lo) torcido; perversidad.
crooklegged [ˈkrukˈlegid], *a.* patituerto.
croon [kru:n], *v.t.*, *v.i.* canturrear, cantar en tono bajo.
crooner [ˈkru:nə], *s.* (*fam.*) cantante (sentimental).
crop [krɔp], *s.* cosecha; cabellera; pelo rapado; látigo mocho; buche (*de ave*); (*fig.*) hornada. — *v.t.* cortar, rapar; desorejar; desmochar; trasquilar; pacer; cosechar. — *v.i.* (*min.*) — ***up,*** aflorar; (*fig.*) asomar, surgir; terciarse.
cropper [ˈkrɔpə], *s.* (*fam.*) ***to come a cropper,*** caerse violentamente; darse una morrada; (*fig.*) meter la pata, lucirse, liársela.
cropping [ˈkrɔpiŋ], *s.* rapado; siega.
croquet [ˈkroukei], *s.* (juego de) croquet.
croquette [kroˈket], *s.* croqueta.
crosier [ˈkrouziə], *s.* (*igl.*) báculo.
cross [krɔs], *a.* en cruz; atravesado; transversal; contrario, opuesto; cruzado (*cheque*); enfadado. — *s.* cruz; cruce, cruzamiento; mezcla. — *v.t.* atravesar, cruzar; contrariar; ***to be crossed,*** ser chafado; ***cross your fingers,*** que haya suerte; ***cross one's mind,*** ocurrírsele a uno, pasársele a uno por la cabeza; ***cross o.s.,*** santiguarse; ***cross out,*** tachar. — *v.i.* cruzar; ***cross over,*** atravesar la calle, pasar a la otra acera, cruzar (la calle).
cross-armed [ˈkrɔs-ɑ:md], *a.* con los brazos cruzados.
cross-bar [ˈkrɔs-bɑ:], *s.* tranca, travesaño.
cross-bearer [ˈkrɔs-bɛərə], *s.* crucífero.
cross-bow [ˈkrɔs-bou], *s.* ballesta.
cross-breed [ˈkrɔs-bri:d], *s.* raza cruzada.
cross-breeding [ˈkrɔs-bri:diŋ], *s.* cruzamiento de razas.
cross-country [ˈkrɔs-ˈkʌntri], *a.* a campo traviesa; ***cross-country race,*** cross.
cross-cut [ˈkrɔs-kʌt], *a.* cortado al través. — *s.* corte transversal; atajo.
cross-examination [ˈkrɔs-igzæmiˈneiʃən], *s.* (*for.*) repregunta; interrogatorio.
cross-examine [ˈkrɔs-igˈzæmin], *v.t.* repreguntar; interrogar.
cross-eyed [ˈkrɔs-aid], *a.* bizco.
cross-fire [ˈkrɔs-faiə], *s.* fuego cruzado; tiroteo.
cross-grained [ˈkrɔs-greind], *a.* de contrafibra; desabrido, áspero; ***to be cross-grained,*** tener mala uva.
crossing [ˈkrɔsiŋ], *s.* travesía; paso; cruce; ***level crossing,*** paso a nivel.
cross-legged [ˈkrɔs-ˈlegid], *a.* con las piernas cruzadas.
crosslet [ˈkrɔslit], *s.* crucecita.
crossly [ˈkrɔsli], *adv.* con malhumor *o* enfado.
crossness [ˈkrɔsnis], *s.* enfado; mal humor.
cross-piece [ˈkrɔs-pi:s], *s.* (*carp.*) travesaño, cruceta.
cross-purpose [ˈkrɔs-ˈpə:pəs], *s.* despropósito; ***we are at cross-purposes,*** esto es el juego de los despropósitos.
cross-road [ˈkrɔs-roud], *s.* encrucijada, cruce.
cross-section [ˈkrɔs-ˈsekʃən], *s.* corte transversal; sección representativa.
cross-spur [ˈkrɔs-spə:], *s.* (*min.*) crucero de cuarzo.
cross-way [ˈkrɔs-wei], *s.* encrucijada, cruce.
cross-wind [ˈkrɔs-wind], *s.* viento contrario.
cross-wise [ˈkrɔs-waiz], *adv.* de través; en cruz.
crossword [ˈkrɔswə:d], *s.* crucigrama, *m.*
cross-wort [ˈkrɔs-wə:t], *s.* (*bot.*) cruciata.
crotalum [ˈkrɔtələm], *s.* crótalo.
crotch [krɔtʃ], *s.* horca, horquilla; bifurcación; (*mar.*) cabria.
crotchet [ˈkrɔtʃit], *s.* (*mús.*) negra, semínima; capricho, antojo; ganchillo.
crotchety [ˈkrɔtʃiti], *a.* irritable, desabrido.
crouch [krautʃ], *v.i.* agacharse, agazaparse, acuclillarse.
croup (1) [kru:p], *s.* anca, grupa.
croup (2) [kru:p], *s.* (*med.*) crup, garrotillo.
croupier [ˈkru:piə], *s.* crupier.
crow (1) [krou], *s.* cuervo; palanca; ***as the crow flies,*** en derechura, en línea recta; ***crow's foot,*** pata de gallo; ***to eat crow,*** cantar la palinodia; ***to have a crow to pluck with,*** tener que habérselas con.
crow (2) [krou], *s.* quiquiriquí. — *v.i.* cantar (*gallos*); ***crow over,*** jactarse de, alardear de; cantar victoria sobre.
crowbar [ˈkroubɑ:], *s.* pie de cabra.
crowd [kraud], *s.* gentío, muchedumbre, *f.*, multitud; vulgo; espectadores; ***to pass in a crowd,*** no descollar. — *v.t.* amontonar, atestar; (*mar.*) ***crowd sail,*** hacer fuerza de vela; ***to be crowded,*** estar atestado; estar concurrido; ***to be crowded out,*** estar de bote en bote; verse excluido. — *v.i.* agolparse, arremolinarse; apiñarse.
crowfoot [ˈkroufut], *s.* (*bot.*) ranúnculo; (*mar.*) araña; (*mil.*) abrojo.
crown [kraun], *s.* corona; cima; copa; cruz (de ancla); (*arq.*) coronamiento. — *v.t.* coronar; completar, terminar; abovedar.
crowning [ˈkrauniŋ], *s.* (*arq.*) coronamiento; remate.
crown prince [ˈkraun ˈprins], *s.* príncipe heredero.
crozier [ˈkrouziə], *s.* (*igl.*) báculo.
crucial [ˈkru:ʃəl], *a.* crucial; decisivo.
cruciate [ˈkru:ʃiit], *a.* (*bot.*) cruciforme.
crucible [ˈkru:sibl], *s.* crisol.
cruciferous [kru:ˈsifərəs], *a.* crucífero.
crucifix [ˈkru:sifiks], *s.* crucifijo, cruz.
crucifixion [kru:siˈfikʃən], *s.* crucifixión.
cruciform [ˈkru:sifɔ:m], *a.* cruciforme.
crucify [ˈkru:sifai], *v.t.* crucificar; (*fig.*) mortificar.
crude [kru:d], *a.* crudo; grosero; tosco.
crudeness, crudity [ˈkru:dnis, -iti], *s.* crudeza; grosería; tosquedad.
cruel [ˈkru:əl], *a.* cruel.
cruelty, cruelness [ˈkru:əlti, -nis], *s.* crueldad.

cruet [ˈkru:it], *s.* vinagrera; ***cruet stand,*** vinagreras, *f.pl.*
cruise [kru:z], *s.* viaje por mar, crucero. — *v.t.* cruzar. — *v.i.* llevar *o* ir con velocidad de crucero; ***cruise around,*** pasearse (por); (*policía*) patrullar (por).
cruiser [ˈkru:zə], *s.* (*mar.*) crucero.
cruising [ˈkru:ziŋ], *s.* (*mar.*) crucero(s); ***cruising speed,*** velocidad económica.
cruller [ˈkrʌlə], *s.* (*Am.*) buñuelo.
crumb [krʌm], *s.* miga, migaja. — *v.t.* migar, desmigajar; empanar.
crumble [krʌmbl], *v.t.* migar, desmigajar; desmenuzar. — *v.i.* desmigajarse; desmenuzarse; desmoronarse.
crumby [ˈkrʌmi], *a.* migajoso.
crummy [ˈkrʌmi], *a.* (*fam.*) costroso; cursi.
crumpet [ˈkrʌmpit], *s.* crumpet.
crumple [krʌmpl], *v.t.* arrugar, plegar. — *v.i.* arrugarse, plegarse; (*fig.*) ***crumple up,*** derrumbarse, desplomarse, hundirse.
crunch [krʌntʃ], *s.* crujido; choque decisivo; momento de la verdad. — *v.t.* triturar; ronzar; hacer crujir. — *v.i.* crujir.
crupper [ˈkrʌpə], *s.* grupa; grupera, baticola.
crural [ˈkruərəl], *a.* crural.
crusade [kru:ˈseid], *s.* cruzada. — *v.i.* tomar parte en una cruzada; hacer una cruzada.
crusader [kru:ˈseidə], *s.* cruzado.
cruse [kru:z], *s.* frasco, redomita, botellita.
crush [krʌʃ], *s.* apretura, aglomeración; (*fam.*) ***she's got a crush on him,*** le ha dado fuerte por él. — *v.t.* machacar; aplastar; triturar; majar; estrujar; despachurrar.
crusher [ˈkrʌʃə], *s.* machacadora, trituradora.
crushing [ˈkrʌʃiŋ], *a.* aplastante; triturador; ***crushing defeat,*** derrota aplastante. — *s.* molienda; trituración; machacamiento.
crust [krʌst], *s.* corteza; costra; mendrugo; escara. — *v.t.* encostrar. — *v.i.* encostrarse.
crustacea [krʌsˈteiʃiə], *s.pl.* crustáceos, *m.pl.*
crustaceous [krʌsˈteiʃiəs], *a.* crustáceo.
crustation [krʌsˈteiʃən], *s.* incrustación.
crustily [ˈkrʌstili], *adv.* (*fam.*) bruscamente, ásperamente.
crustiness [ˈkrʌstinis], *s.* dureza de la costra; (*fam.*) mal genio, aspereza.
crusty [ˈkrʌsti], *a.* costroso; crujiente, tostado; (*fam.*) áspero, desabrido.
crutch [krʌtʃ], *s.* muleta; horca, horquilla; horcajadura; puntal; bragadura. — *v.t.* ahorquillar; apuntalar.
crux [krʌks], *s.* (lo) esencial, (el) quid.
cry [krai], *s.* grito; lloro; pregón; ***to be a far cry,*** estar muy lejos; distar mucho; haber mucha diferencia; ***in full cry,*** acosando de cerca; ***to have a good cry,*** desahogarse llorando. — *v.t.* gritar; vocear; exclamar; pregonar; ***cry down,*** hacer callar a gritos; quitar importancia a; ***cry one's eyes out,*** llorar a lágrima viva; ***cry out,*** vociferar; proclamar; ***cry up,*** alabar, encarecer. — *v.i.* gritar; llorar; pregonar; ***cry for joy,*** llorar de alegría; ***cry off,*** renunciar, desistir, echarse atrás; ***cry out,*** vociferar; ***cry out for,*** clamar por.
cry-baby [ˈkrai-beibi], *s.* llorón, llorica, *m.f.*
crying [ˈkraiiŋ], *a.* atroz, enorme; ***a crying shame,*** una mala vergüenza, cosa que clama al cielo. — *s.* llanto, lloro; gritos, *m.pl.*
crypt [kript], *s.* cripta.
cryptic [ˈkriptik], *a.* críptico; oculto; enigmático.
cryptogamia [kriptoˈgeimiə], *s. pl.* (*bot.*) criptógamas, *f.pl.*
cryptogamous [kripˈtɔgəməs], *a.* criptógamo, acotiledóneo.
cryptogamy [kripˈtɔgəmi], *s.* criptogamia.
cryptogram [ˈkriptogræm], *s.* cifra.
cryptography [kripˈtɔgrəfi], *s.* criptografía.
cryptology [kripˈtɔlədʒi], *s.* criptología.
crysoscopy [kriˈsɔskəpi], *s.* (*fís.*) crisoscopía.
crystal [ˈkristəl], *a.* diáfano, transparente. — *s.* cristal (*de roca*); (*rad.*) galena; ***crystal clear,*** transparente; ***crystal-gazer,*** el que pronostica el futuro; ***crystal-gazing,*** previsión, pronosticación; ***as clear as crystal,*** más claro que el agua.
crystalline [ˈkristəlain], *a.* cristalino; transparente.
crystallization [kristəlaiˈzeiʃən], *s.* cristalización.
crystallize [ˈkristəlaiz], *v.t.* cristalizar. — *v.i.* cristalizarse.
crystallography [kristəˈlɔgrəfi], *s.* cristalografía.
crystalloid [ˈkristəlɔid], *s.* cristaloide.
cub [kʌb], *s.* cachorro; (*fig.*) rapaz.
Cuba [ˈkju:bə]. Cuba.
cubage, cubature [ˈkju:bidʒ, -ətʃə], *s.* (*geom.*) cubicación.
Cuban [ˈkju:bən], *a., s.* cubano.
cube [kju:b], *s.* (*geom.*) cubo; ***cube root,*** raíz cúbica; ***cube of sugar,*** cuadradillo. — *v.t.* (*mat.*) cubicar.
cubic(al) [ˈkju:bik(əl)], *a.* cúbico.
cubicle [ˈkju:bikl], *s.* cubículo; reservado.
cubit [ˈkju:bit], *s.* codo.
cubital [ˈkju:bitəl], *a.* cubital.
cuboid [ˈkju:bɔid], *a.* cuboide, cuboideo.
cuckold [ˈkʌkəld], *s.* (marido) cornudo. — *v.t.* poner los cuernos a.
cuckoo [ˈkuku:], *a.* (*fam.*) chalado. — *s.* (*orn.*) cuclillo; cucú (*el canto*); ***cuckoo-clock,*** reloj de cuclillo.
cucullate(d) [ˈkju:kəleit(id)], *a.* encapillado.
cucumber [ˈkju:kʌmbə], *s.* (*bot.*) pepino; ***cool as a cucumber,*** tan tranquilo.
cucurbit [kju:ˈkə:bit], *s.* (*bot.*) cucúrbita.
cucurbitaceous [kju:kə:biˈteiʃəs], *a.* cucurbitáceo.
cud [kʌd], *s.* bolo alimenticio; ***to chew the cud,*** rumiar.
cuddle [kʌdl], *s.* abrazo amoroso. — *v.t.* abrazar, acariciar.
cuddy [ˈkʌdi], *s.* (*mar.*) camarote (*de proa*); pañol (*del cocinero*).
cudgel [ˈkʌdʒəl], *s.* garrote, palo, porra; ***take up the cudgels for,*** romper una lanza por, salir en defensa de. — *v.t.* apalear, aporrear; ***cudgel one's brains,*** devanarse los sesos.
cue [kju:], *s.* taco (*de billar*); (*teat.*) apunte; pie; ***to take one's cue from,*** seguir el ejemplo de.
cuff [kʌf], *s.* puño (*de camisa*); bofetón, bofetada; ***cuff-links,*** gemelos, *m.pl.*; ***hand-cuffs,*** esposas, *f.pl.* — *v.t.* abofetear.
cuirass [kwiˈræs], *s.* coraza.
cuirassier [kwiˈræsiə], *s.* coracero.
cuisine [kwi:ˈzi:n], *s.* cocina.
cul-de-sac [ˈkʌl-də-sæk], *s.* callejón sin salida.
culex [ˈkju:leks], *s.* (*ent.*) mosquito.
culinary [ˈkʌlinəri], *a.* culinario.
cull [kʌl], *v.t.* coger, recoger, entresacar, espigar.
cullender [COLANDER].
cullet [ˈkʌlit], *s.* cristal desmenuzado.
cullis [ˈkʌlis], *s.* canalón.
culm [kʌlm], *s.* cisco; (*bot.*) caña.
culmiferous [kʌlˈmifərəs], *a.* (*bot.*) culmífero.
culminant [ˈkʌlminənt], *a.* culminante.
culminate [ˈkʌlmineit], *v.i.* culminar; ***culminate in,*** culminar en, acabar en, rematar en.
culmination [kʌlmiˈneiʃən], *s.* culminación.
culpability [kʌlpəˈbiliti], *s.* culpabilidad.
culpable [ˈkʌlpəbl], *a.* culpable.
culpableness [ˈkʌlpəblnis], *s.* culpa, (lo) culpable.
culprit [ˈkʌlprit], *s.* culpable, responsable.
cult [kʌlt], *s.* culto.
cultism [ˈkʌltizəm], *s.* cultismo, culteranismo.
cultist [ˈkʌltist], *s.* culterano.

cultivable [ˈkʌltivəbl], *a.* cultivable.
cultivate [ˈkʌltiveit], *v.t.* cultivar.
cultivated [ˈkʌltiveitid], *a.* culto, instruido, de estudios, que ha estudiado.
cultivation [kʌltiˈveiʃən], *s.* cultivo.
cultivator [ˈkʌltiveitə], *s.* cultivador.
culture [ˈkʌltʃə], *s.* cultura; cultivo. — *v.t.* culturar; educar.
culver [ˈkʌlvə], *s.* (*orn.*) paloma torcaz.
culverin [ˈkʌlvərin], *s.* (*mil.*) culebrina.
culvert [ˈkʌlvəːt], *s.* alcantarilla, cloaca.
cumber [ˈkʌmbə], *v.t.* estorbar, molestar.
cumbersome [ˈkʌmbəsəm], *a.* pesado, molesto, incómodo (*de manejar*); ***cumbersome object,*** armatoste.
cumbersomeness [ˈkʌmbəsəmnis], *s.* (lo) pesado, (lo) incómodo.
cumbrous [ˈkʌmbrəs], *a.* pesado, incómodo.
cumbrousness [ˈkʌmbrəsnis], *s.* pesadez, incomodidad.
cumin [ˈkʌmin], *s.* (*bot.*) comino.
cummerbund [ˈkʌməbʌnd], *s.* faja (*de etiqueta*).
cumulate [ˈkjuːmjuleit], *v.t.* acumular.
cumulation [kjuːmjuˈleiʃən], *s.* acumulación.
cumulative [ˈkjuːmjulətiv], *a.* cumulativo.
cumulo-cirrus [ˈkjuːmjulo-ˈsirəs], *a.* (*meteorol.*) cumulocirro.
cumulo-nimbus [ˈkjuːmjulo-ˈnimbəs], *a.* (*meteorol.*) cumulonimbo.
cumulo-stratus [ˈkjuːmjulo-ˈstrɑːtəs], *a.* (*meteorol.*) cumulostrato.
cumulus [ˈkjuːmjuləs], *a.* cúmulus; cúmulo.
cuneal, cuneate, cuneiform [ˈkjuːniəl, -it, -ifɔːm], *a.* cuneiforme.
cunning [ˈkʌniŋ], *a.* astuto, artero, solapado; (*fig.*) ingenioso. — *s.* astucia, artería.
cunningness [ˈkʌniŋnis], *s.* [CUNNING].
cup [kʌp], *s.* taza; copa; cáliz; (*med.*) ventosa; suerte, destino; (*fam.*) ***in one's cups,*** bebido; ***that's not my cup of tea,*** eso no es para mí; ***there's many a slip 'twixt cup and lip,*** de la mano a la boca se pierde la sopa. — *v.t.* (*med.*) aplicar ventosas a; ahuecar; (*golf*) meter (*la pelota*) en el hoyo. — *v.i.* (*golf*) hacer un hoyo en (*el suelo*).
cupbearer [ˈkʌpbɛərə], *s.* copero, escanciador.
cupboard [ˈkʌbəd], *s.* alacena, armario; ***cupboard love,*** amor interesado.
cupel [ˈkjuːpəl], *s.* copela.
cupellation [kjuːpəˈleiʃən], *s.* (*quím.*) copelación.
cupful [ˈkʌpful], *s.* (*contenido de una*) taza.
Cupid [ˈkjuːpid]. Cupido.
cupid [ˈkjuːpid], *s.* amorcillo.
cupidity [kjuːˈpiditi], *s.* codicia.
cupola [ˈkjuːpələ], *s.* (*arq.*) cúpula.
cupping [ˈkʌpiŋ], *s.* (*cir.*) aplicación de ventosas; ***cupping-glass,*** ventosa.
cupreous [ˈkjuːpriəs], *a.* cobrizo; cobreño.
cupriferous [kjuːˈprifərəs], *a.* cuprífero.
cupro-nickel [ˈkjuːpro-ˈnikəl], *s.* (*min.*) cuproníquel.
cupule [ˈkjuːpjuːl], *s.* (*bot.*) cúpula.
cur [kəː], *s.* perro de mala casta; (*fig.*) canalla.
curability [kjuərəˈbiliti], *s.* curabilidad.
curable [ˈkjuərəbl], *a.* curable, sanable.
curableness [ˈkjuərəblnis], *s.* curabilidad.
curaçao [kjuərəˈsou], *s.* curasao.
curacy [ˈkjuərəsi], *s.* vicariato, vicaría.
curate [ˈkjuərit], *s.* vicario, pastor protestante coadjutor.
curative [ˈkjuərətiv], *a.* curativo.
curator [kjuəˈreitə], *s.* conservador; encargado.
curb [kəːb], *s.* barbada; brocal (*de pozo*); bordillo, encintado (de una acera); (*vet.*) corva; (*fig.*) freno, restricción. — *v.t.* refrenar, contener.
curd [kəːd], *s.* cuajada. — *v.t.* cuajar.
curdle [kəːdl], *v.t.* cuajar, coagular; (*fig.*) ***curdle the blood of,*** helar la sangre a. — *v.i.* cuajarse, coagularse.
curd(l)y [ˈkəːd(l)i], *a.* cuajado.
cure [kjuə], *s.* cura; curación. — *v.t.* curar; sanar.
cure-all [ˈkjuər-ɔːl], *s.* panacea, curalotodo.
cureless [ˈkjuəlis], *a.* incurable.
curer [ˈkjuərə], *s.* curador.
curfew [ˈkəːfjuː], *s.* queda, toque de queda.
curia [ˈkjuəriə], *s.* curia.
curio [ˈkjuəriou], *s.* objeto curioso.
curiosity [kjuəriˈɔsiti], *s.* curiosidad.
curious [ˈkjuəriəs], *a.* curioso; (*ant.*) cuidadoso, delicado.
curiousness [ˈkjuəriəsnis], *s.* curiosidad.
curl [kəːl], *s.* rizo, bucle; sinuosidad, ondulación; espiral, *f.* — *v.t.* rizar, encrespar; ondular; fruncir. — *v.i.* rizarse, encresparse; ondularse; fruncirse; ***curl up,*** enroscarse, hacerse un ovillo.
curlew [ˈkəːljuː], *s.* (*orn.*) zarapito.
curliness [ˈkəːlinis], *s.* (lo) rizoso *etc.*
curling [ˈkəːliŋ], *s.* (*dep.*) curling; ***curling-iron(s),*** encrespador, rizador.
curly [ˈkəːli], *a.* ensortijado; rizado, crespo.
curmudgeon [kəˈmʌdʒən], *s.* tacaño; cicatero; erizo (*persona intratable*).
currant [ˈkʌrənt], *s.* grosella; uva *o* pasa de Corinto; ***currant bush,*** grosellero; ***black-currant,*** grosella negra; ***red-currant,*** grosella colorada.
currency [ˈkʌrənsi], *s.* curso, circulación; uso corriente; dinero, moneda; ***paper currency,*** papel moneda; ***foreign currency,*** divisas, *f.pl.*; ***legal currency,*** (de) curso legal.
current [ˈkʌrənt], *a.* corriente; común, general; presente, actual, en curso; ***current account,*** cuenta corriente; ***current events,*** actualidades, *f.pl.* — *s.* corriente; curso, marcha.
currently [ˈkʌrəntli], *adv.* corrientemente, generalmente; actualmente.
curricle [ˈkʌrikl], *s.* carriola.
curriculum [kəˈrikjuləm], *s.* plan de estudios; ***curriculum vitae,*** currículum (vitae).
currier [ˈkʌriə], *s.* curtidor, zurrador.
currish [ˈkəːriʃ], *a.* perruno; arisco; (*fig.*) regañón.
curry (1) [ˈkʌri], *s.* (*coc.*) cari, curry. — *v.t.* preparar con cari.
curry (2) [ˈkʌri], *v.t.* curtir; almohazar; ***curry favour,*** buscar favores.
curry-comb [ˈkʌri-koum], *s.* almohaza.
currying [ˈkʌriiŋ], *s.* zurra; lisonjeo, servilismo.
curse [kəːs], *s.* maldición; blasfemia, palabrota. — *v.t.* maldecir de, echar pestes de; ***to be cursed with,*** padecer, tener que aguantar. — *v.i.* jurar, soltar palabrotas.
cursed [ˈkəːsid], *a.* maldito, abominable.
cursedness [ˈkəːsidnis], *s.* (lo) abominable, (lo) maldito (de una cosa).
cursing [ˈkəːsiŋ], *s.* maldición, execración.
cursive [ˈkəːsiv], *a.* cursivo, corriente.
cursor [ˈkəːsə], *s.* cursor.
cursoriness [ˈkəːsərinis], *s.* precipitación, prisa; descuido, (lo) superficial.
cursory [ˈkəːsəri], *a.* superficial; rápido.
curt [kəːt], *a.* brusco, áspero, seco; corto.
curtail [kəːteil], *v.t.* cercenar, reducir; privar; restringir, escatimar.
curtailing [kəːˈteiliŋ], *s.* corte, *m.*; mutilación; cercenamiento; abreviatura.
curtailment [kəːˈteilmənt], *s.* cercenamiento, reducción; privación.
curtain [ˈkəːtin], *s.* cortina; telón; (*teat.*) ***curtain call,*** aplauso de llamamiento; ***curtain speech,*** discurso pronunciado al final de una obra teatral; ***iron curtain,*** telón de acero; ***behind the curtain,*** en secreto, de escondidas; ***to draw the curtain,*** correr la cortina; (*fig.*) correr un velo,

ocultar; ***to drop the curtain,*** bajar el telón. — *v.t.* encortinar; ***curtain off,*** separar con cortinas.
curtain-lecture [ˈkəːtin-lektʃə], *s.* reconvención conyugal.
curtain-raiser [ˈkəːtin-reizə], *s.* entremés, loa, paso.
curtness [ˈkəːtnis], *s.* brevedad, concisión; brusquedad, sequedad.
curts(e)y [ˈkəːtsi], *s.* reverencia. — *v.i.* hacer una reverencia.
curvated [kəːˈveitid], *a.* corvo, encorvado.
curvation [kəːˈveiʃən], *s.* curvatura.
curvature [ˈkəːvətʃə], *s.* curvatura.
curve [kəːv], *a.* curvo. — *s.* curva; recodo; combadura. — *v.t.* encorvar. — *v.i.* encorvarse; combarse; voltear en curva.
curvet [kəːˈvet], *s.* corveta. — *v.i.* corvetear, cabriolar.
curvilinear [kəːvəˈliniə], *a.* curvilíneo.
curving [ˈkəːviŋ], *s.* curvatura; comba.
cushat [ˈkuʃət], *s.* (*Esco.*) paloma torcaz.
cushion [ˈkuʃən], *s.* cojín; almohadilla, almohadón; banda (*de mesa de billar*); colchón. — *v.t.* proteger con cojines; (*fig.*) amortiguar; acolchonar.
cushy [ˈkuʃi], *a.* fácil, facilito, facilón; ***cushy berth,*** enchufe, enchufazo.
cusp, cuspid [kʌsp, ˈkʌspid], *s.* cúspide; punta.
cuspidate(d) [ˈkʌspideit(id)], *a.* puntiagudo, terminado en punta; cuspidada, apuntillada.
cuspidor [ˈkʌspidɔː], *s.* escupidera.
cuss [kʌs], *s.* (*fam.*) taco, ajo; (*fam.*) tío puñetero; tipo tozudo; ***it's not worth a tinker's cuss,*** no vale tres gordas.
cussed [ˈkʌsid], *a.* (*fam.*) maldito, condenado; puñetero; tozudo.
custard [ˈkʌstəd], *s.* natillas, *f.pl.*; ***caramel custard,*** flan; (*fam.*) ***cowardy custard,*** cobardica, *m.f.*
custodian [kʌsˈtoudiən], *s.* custodio; conservador; guardián.
custody [ˈkʌstədi], *s.* custodia; prisión; ***to take into custody,*** arrestar, detener.
custom [ˈkʌstəm], *s.* costumbre; clientela (*de una tienda*); ***custom-duties,*** derechos de aduana, *m.pl.*; ***custom house,*** aduana, oficinas de aduana, *f.pl.*
customable [ˈkʌstəməbl], *a.* sujeto al derecho de aduanas.
customary [ˈkʌstəmri], *a.* usual, habitual, acostumbrado.
custom-built [ˈkʌstəm-bilt], *a.* (*Am.*) de encargo.
customer [ˈkʌstəmə], *s.* parroquiano, cliente; (*fam.*) tipo, individuo; (***an***) ***ugly customer,*** pajarraco de mala catadura; tipo de cuidado.
cut [kʌt], *a.* cortado, labrado, tallado; ***cut and dried,*** concreto, sin dudas; ***cut off,*** aislado, incomunicado. — *s.* corte; cortadura; tajada; ***cut with a whip,*** latigazo; ***short cut,*** atajo. — *v.t.* cortar; acortar; tallar; segar; dividir, partir; (*fam.*) negar el saludo a; ***cut across,*** cortar al través; atajar; ***cut asunder,*** escindir, hender; ***cut away,*** cortar; ***cut a caper,*** hacer una cabriola; ***cut a dash,*** hacer un papel airoso; ***cut down,*** abatir, derribar; reducir, rebajar; ***cut in on,*** interrumpir, meterse en; ***cut it fine,*** salvarse por un pelo; llegar por los pelos; ***cut off,*** cortar, separar, amputar; interrumpir, desconectar; ***cut out,*** recortar; suprimir; ***cut it out!*** ¡déjate de eso!; ***to be cut out for,*** estar hecho para; ***you'll have your work cut out,*** trabajo te mando; ***cut short,*** acortar, abreviar, atajar; ***cut up,*** trinchar; trocear; descuartizar; (*fig.*) ***to be cut up,*** estar desolado, desfondado. — *v.i.* cortar; ser cortante; ***cut in,*** interrumpir, interponerse.
cutaneous [kjuːˈteiniəs], *a.* cutáneo.
cute [kjuːt], *a.* listo; mono.
cuticle [ˈkjuːtikl], *s.* cutícula.
cuticular [kjuːˈtikjulə], *a.* cuticular.
cutlass [ˈkʌtləs], *s.* chafarote; (*mar.*) sable de abordaje.
cutler [ˈkʌtlə], *s.* cuchillero.
cutlery [ˈkʌtləri], *s.* cuchillería, cubiertos.
cutlet [ˈkʌtlit], *s.* chuleta.
cut-off [ˈkʌt-ɔf], *s.* (*mec.*) cortavapor; (*elec.*) cortacircuito, atajo, trocha; (*Am.*) carretera de circunvalación.
cut-out [ˈkʌt-aut], *s.* recorte; (*elec.*) cortacircuito; (*mec.*) válvula de escape.
cut-price [ˈkʌt-prais], *s.* reducción, rebaja.
cutpurse [ˈkʌtpəːs], *s.* cortabolsas, *m.inv.*
cutter [ˈkʌtə], *s.* cortador; grabador, tallador; (*mar.*) cúter; (*Am.*) escampavía.
cut-throat [ˈkʌt-θrout], *a.* asesino; ***cut-throat competition,*** competencia feroz. — *s.* forajido.
cutting [ˈkʌtiŋ], *a.* cortante; incisivo, mordaz. — *s.* corte, cortadura; recorte; trinchera, zanja.
cuttle(-fish) [ˈkʌtl(-fiʃ)], *s.* jibia, sepia.
cuttle-bone [ˈkʌtl-boun], *s.* jibión.
cutwater [ˈkʌtwɔːtə], *s.* (*mar.*) tajamar.
cuvette [kjuːˈvet], *s.* cubeta.
cyanate [ˈsaiəneit], *s.* (*quím.*) cianato.
cyanic [saiˈænik], *a.* ciánico.
cyanide [ˈsaiənaid], *s.* cianuro.
cyanogen [saiˈænədʒən], *s.* cianógeno.
cyanometer [saiəˈnɔmitə], *s.* cianómetro.
cyanotic [saiəˈnɔtik], *a.* cianótico.
cyclamen [ˈsikləmən], *s.* (*bot.*) ciclamino; artanita.
cycle [saikl], *s.* ciclo; período; bicicleta. — *v.i.* ir *o* montar en bicicleta.
cyclic, cyclical [ˈsaiklik, ˈsiklikəl], *a.* cíclico.
cycling [ˈsaikliŋ], *s.* ciclismo.
cyclist [ˈsaiklist], *s.* ciclista, *m.f.*
cycloid [ˈsaiklɔid], *s.* (*geom.*) cicloide.
cycloidal [saiˈklɔidəl], *a.* cicloidal.
cyclometer [saiˈklɔmitə], *s.* ciclómetro.
cyclometry [saiˈklɔmitri], *s.* ciclometría.
cyclone [ˈsaikloun], *s.* ciclón, huracán.
cyclonic [saiˈklɔnik], *a.* ciclónico.
cyclopean [saikloˈpiːən], *a.* ciclópico, ciclópeo.
cyclopædia [saikloˈpiːdiə], [ENCYCLOPÆDIA].
cyclops [ˈsaiklɔps], *s.* cíclope.
cyclorama [saikloˈrɑːmə], *s.* ciclorama, *m.f.*
cyclostyle [ˈsaiklostail], *s.* ciclóstilo.
cygnet [ˈsignit], *s.* pollo del cisne; cisnecito.
cylinder [ˈsilində], *s.* cilindro; (*mec.*) ***cylinder block,*** bloque de cilindros; (*mec.*) ***cylinder capacity,*** cilindrada; (*mec.*) ***cylinder head,*** culata.
cylindrical [siˈlindrikəl], *a.* cilíndrico.
cymbal [ˈsimbəl], *s.* címbalo.
cyme [saim], *s.* (*bot.*) cima.
cymose [ˈsaimous], *a.* (*bot.*) cimoso.
cynic [ˈsinik], *s.* cínico; escéptico.
cynical [ˈsinikəl], *a.* cínico; escéptico.
cynicism [ˈsinisizəm], *s.* cinismo; escepticismo.
cynosure [ˈsainəʃuə], *s.* (*astron.*) cinosura; miradero; centro de atención.
cypher [ˈsaifə], *s.* [CIPHER].
cypress [ˈsaiprəs], *s.* (*bot.*) ciprés.
Cypriot [ˈsipriət], *a.*, *s.* chipriota, *m.f.*
Cyprus [ˈsaiprəs]. Chipre.
cyst [sist], *s.* (*anat.*) quiste.
cystic [ˈsistik], *a.* cístico.
cystoscope [ˈsistoskoup], *s.* cistoscopio.
cystotomy [sisˈtɔtəmi], *s.* cistotomía.
cytisus [ˈsitisəs], *s.* (*bot.*) citiso.
czar [zɑː], *s.* zar.
czarevitch [ˈzɑːrəvitʃ], *s.* zarevitz.
czarina [zɑːˈriːnə], *s.* zarina.
Czech [tʃek], *a.*, *s.* checo.
Czechoslovak [tʃekoˈslouvæk], *a.*, *s.* checoslovaco.
Czechoslovakia [tʃekosloˈvækjə]. Checoslovaquia.

D

D, d [di:], cuarta letra del alfabeto. — *s.* (*mús.*) re.
dab [dæb], *s.* golpecito, toque ligero; brochazo; pizca; (*ict.*) lenguado, platija. — *v.t.* dar golpecitos *o* toques ligeros en; untar; embadurnar ligeramente.
dabble [dæbl], *v.i.* — ***in,*** practicar en plan diletante, dedicarse en plan de aficionado a; jugar a (*la bolsa*), especular en.
dabbler [ˈdæblə], *s.* diletante, aficionado.
dab-chick [ˈdæb-tʃik], *s.* (*orn.*) somormujo.
dab-hand [ˈdæb-ˈhænd], *s.* (*fam.*) hacha, *m.*
dace [deis], *s.* (*ict.*) albur.
dactyl [ˈdæktil], *s.* dáctilo.
dactylic [dækˈtilik], *a.* dactílico.
dactylography [dæktiˈlɔgrəfi], *s.* dactilografía.
dactylology [dæktiˈlɔlədʒi], *s.* dactilología.
dad, daddie, daddy [dæd, ˈdædi], *s.* (*fam.*) papá, papaíto.
daddy-long-legs [dædi-ˈlɔŋ-legz], *s.* típula.
daffodil [ˈdæfədil], *s.* (*bot.*) narciso trompón; (*fam.*) narciso.
daft [dɑ:ft], *a.* tonto, loco, bobo, memo.
dagger [ˈdægə], *s.* daga, puñal; ***to be at daggers drawn,*** estar a matar; (*fam.*) ***to look daggers at,*** fulminar con la mirada.
daggle [dægl], *v.t.* embarrar, enlodar. — *v.i.* embarrarse, enlodarse.
daggle-tail [ˈdægl-teil], *s.* mujer desaliñada.
daguerreotype [dəˈgerotaip], *s.* daguerrotipo.
dahlia [ˈdeiliə], *s.* (*bot.*) dalia.
Dahomean [dəˈhoumiən], *a.*, *s.* dahomeyano.
Dahomey [dəˈhoumi]. (el) Dahomey.
daily [ˈdeili], *a.* diario, cotidiano; (*astron.*, *astrol.*) diurno. — *adv.* diariamente, todos los días. — *s.* (*periódico*) diario.
daintiness [ˈdeintinis], *s.* primor, exquisitez, delicadeza; ligereza.
dainty [ˈdeinti], *a.* primoroso, exquisito, delicado; menudito, ligero. — *s.* golosina, manjar delicado.
dairy [ˈdɛəri], *s.* lechería, vaquería; ***dairy-maid,*** lechera; ***dairy-man,*** lechero.
dais [ˈdeiis], *s.* tarima, estrado.
daisy [ˈdeizi], *s.* margarita, vellorita.
dale [deil], *s.* valle, cañada.
dalliance [ˈdæliəns], *s.* entretenimiento, escarceos, *m.pl.*; dilación.
dally [ˈdæli], *v.t.* ***dally away the time,*** entretener *o* matar el tiempo. — *v.i.* entretenerse; coquetear; tardar, retardarse; ***dally with,*** jugar con (*un tema etc.*), entretenerse con.
Dalmatian [dælˈmeiʃən], *a.* dálmata. — *s.* dálmata, *m.f.*; perro dalmático.
dalmatic [dælˈmætik], *s.* dalmático, dalmática.
dam (1) [dæm], *s.* dique, presa, represa, azud; embalse, pantano. — *v.t.* represar, embalsar; ***dam up,*** contener.
dam (2) [dæm], *s.* yegua; hembra.
damage [ˈdæmidʒ], *s.* daño, perjuicio, detrimento; menoscabo, pérdida; avería; (*pl.*, *for.*) daños y perjuicios. — *v.t.* dañar, perjudicar. — *v.i.* averiarse, dañarse.
damageable [ˈdæmidʒəbl], *a.* susceptible de daño; indemnizable.
damask [ˈdæməsk], *a.* damasquinado, adamascado. — *s.* damasco; ***damask-plum,*** ciruela damascena; ***damask-rose,*** rosa de damasco *o* encarnada. — *v.t.* adamascar; matizar.
dame [deim], *s.* dama; dueña, ama.
damn [dæm], *a.* maldito. — *adv.* ***he is doing damn all,*** no hace nada en absoluto. — *s.* maldición; ***I don't care a damn,*** me importa un bledo. — *v.t.* condenar; maldecir; ***damn it!*** ¡maldita sea!
damnable [ˈdæmnəbl], *a.* infame, abominable.
damnably [ˈdæmnəbli], *adv.* detestablemente.
damnation [dæmˈneiʃən], *s.* condenación, maldición; damnación.
damnatory [ˈdæmnətəri], *a.* condenatorio.
damned [dæmd], *a.* condenado; maldito, detestable. — *adv.* mucho, muy; ***damned good,*** estupendo.
damnify [ˈdæmnifai], *v.t.* dañar, perjudicar, lastimar.
damp [dæmp], *a.* húmedo. — *s.* humedad. — (*t.* **dampen** [-ən]), *v.t.* mojar, humedecer; (*fig.*) amortiguar; sofocar.
damp(en)ing [ˈdæmp(ən)iŋ], *s.* humectación.
damper [ˈdæmpə], *s.* registro, regulador (*de tiro*); apagador de piano, sordina.
dampish [ˈdæmpiʃ], *a.* humedillo.
dampness [dæmpnis], *s.* humedad.
damposcope [ˈdæmposkoup], *s.* (*min.*) damposcopio.
damsel [ˈdæmzəl], *s.* damisela; señorita; muchacha.
damson [ˈdæmzən], *s.* (*bot.*) ciruela damascena.
dance [dɑ:ns], *a.* de baile, para bailar, bailable. — *s.* baile; danza; ***dance of death,*** danza de la muerte; ***dance-floor,*** pista de baile; ***formal dance,*** baile de etiqueta; (*fam.*) ***to lead a dance,*** dar una marcha a, traer al retortero. — *v.i.* bailar; danzar.
danceable [ˈdɑ:nsəbl], *a.* bailable.
dancer [ˈdɑ:nsə], *s.* bailarín; (*flamenco*) bailaor.
dancing [ˈdɑ:nsiŋ], *s.* baile; danza; ***dancing-master,*** maestro de baile; ***dancing-partner,*** pareja de baile.
dandelion [ˈdændilaiən], *s.* (*bot.*) diente de león.
dander [ˈdændə], *s.* mal humor; ***to get one's dander up,*** malhumorarse, impacientarse.
dandle [dændl], *v.t.* hacer saltar sobre las rodillas.
dandruff [ˈdændrʌf], *s.* caspa.
dandy [ˈdændi], *a.* (*fam.*) estupendo, perfecto; pintiparado. — *s.* petimetre, currutaco, pisaverde, lechuguino, dandi.
dandyish [ˈdændiiʃ], *a.* elegantito, atildadillo.
dandyism [ˈdændiizəm], *s.* dandismo.
Dane [dein], *s.* danés, *m.*; dinamarqués, *m.*
danewort [ˈdeinwə:t], *s.* (*bot.*) yezgo.
danger [ˈdeindʒə], *s.* peligro; riesgo; ***to be in danger,*** correr peligro; ***to be on the danger list,*** estar grave; ***danger-money,*** paga extraordinaria (por peligro); ***out of danger,*** fuera de peligro.
dangerous [ˈdeindʒərəs], *a.* peligroso, arriesgado, expuesto.
dangerousness [ˈdeindʒərəsnis], *s.* (lo) peligroso.
dangle [dæŋgl], *v.t.* colgar, dejar colgar, columpiar. — *v.i.* colgar, colgar en el aire, bambolearse.
Danish [ˈdeiniʃ], *a.* danés. — *s.* (*idioma*) danés, *m.*
dank [dæŋk], *a.* húmedo, liento.
dankness [ˈdænknis], *s.* humedad.
Daphne [ˈdæfni]. Dafne, *f.*
dapper [ˈdæpə], *a.* peripuesto, elegantito; pinturero.
dapple [dæpl], *a.* rucio. — *v.t.* salpicar de manchas, motear.
dappled [dæpld], *a.* rodado.
dare [dɛə], *s.* (*fam.*) reto, desafío. — *v.t.* arrostrar, hacer frente a, desafiar, retar. — *v.i.* atreverse, arriesgarse, osar; ***I dare say,*** puede, puede ser.
dare-devil [ˈdɛə-devil], *s.* atrevido, temerario, osado.
daring [ˈdɛəriŋ], *a.* osado, arriesgado; intrépido; emprendedor. — *s.* atrevimiento, osadía; intrepidez.
dark [dɑ:k], *a.* oscuro, sombrío; moreno, negro; misterioso; tétrico, tenebroso, fúnebre; ***dark lantern,*** linterna sorda; (*foto.*) ***dark-room,*** cuarto oscuro; ***it is growing dark,*** está anocheciendo. — *s.* oscuridad; tinieblas, *f.pl.*; ignorancia; ***in the dark,*** a oscuras; ***to be*** *o* ***to be left in the dark,*** estar *o* quedarse a oscuras.

darken [ˈdɑ:kən], *v.t.* oscurecer; anublar; ennegrecer; embrollar, confundir; entristecer; manchar, denigrar. — *v.i.* obscurecerse.
darkening [ˈdɑ:kəniŋ], *s.* oscurecimiento; ennegrecimiento.
dark-eyed [ˈdɑ:k-aid], *a.* ojinegro.
darkish [ˈdɑ:kiʃ], *a.* algo oscuro.
darkle [dɑ:kl], *v.t.* oscurecer. — *v.i.* oscurecerse; parecer oscuro.
darkly [ˈdɑ:kli], *adv.* oscuramente; (*fig.*) ceñudamente.
darkness [ˈdɑ:knis], *s.* oscuridad, lobreguez, tinieblas, *f.pl.*, tenebrosidad, opacidad, densidad; obcecación, ofuscación; ignorancia; secreto; (*fig.*) maldad.
darling [ˈdɑ:liŋ], *a.* amado, querido. — *s.* ser predilecto, favorito; amor, pichón; ***to be a darling,*** ser un encanto; ***darling of the people,*** ídolo del pueblo.
darn (1) [dɑ:n], *s.* zurcido. — *v.t.* zurcir.
darn (2), **darned** [dɑ:n, -d], *a.* (*Am.*, *fam.*) maldito.
darnel [ˈdɑ:nəl], *s.* (*bot.*) cizaña.
darner [ˈdɑ:nə], *s.* zurcidor, zurcidora.
darning [ˈdɑ:niŋ], *a.* de zurcir. — *s.* zurcidura, zurcido; ***darning needle,*** aguja de zurcir.
dart [dɑ:t], *s.* dardo; saeta; flechilla; aguijón; sisa. — *v.t.* flechar, despedir. — *v.i.* lanzarse, precipitarse; ***dart out*** o ***off,*** salir disparado.
dartre [ˈdɑ:tə], *s.* roña *o* llaga que padecen los corderos, herpes, *m.pl.*
Darwinism [ˈdɑ:winizəm], *s.* darvinismo, doctrinas de Darwin, *f.pl.*
dash [dæʃ], *s.* choque; rociada; pizca; raya, guión; arrojo, brío; carrera corta; ***to cut a dash,*** hacer un gran papel. — *v.t.* arrojar, lanzar; golpear, batir; estrellar; truncar, dar al traste con; salpicar; ***dash off,*** hacer *o* escribir rápidamente; ***dash to pieces,*** hacer añicos, estrellar; ***dash one's hopes to the ground,*** dar al traste con las esperanzas de uno. — *v.i.* precipitarse, lanzarse; chocar, estrellarse; ***dash in*** o ***out, off,*** entrar *o* salir disparado.
dashing [ˈdæʃiŋ], *a.* arrojado, brioso; apuesto, gallardo. — *s.* embate(s).
dastard [ˈdæstəd], *s.* cobarde.
dastardly [ˈdæstədli], *a.* vil, miserable, abominable.
data [ˈdeitə], *s.pl.* datos, *m.pl.*; ***piece of data,*** dato. [DATUM].
datary [ˈdeitəri], *s.* datario.
date (1) [deit], *s.* fecha; (*fam.*) cita; ***date-line,*** línea de cambio de fecha; fecha tope; ***to bring up to date,*** poner al día; ***make a date with,*** arreglar una cita con; ***out of date,*** anticuado, trasnochado, pasado de moda; ***to date,*** hasta la fecha; ***what is the date?*** ¿cuál es la fecha? ¿a cuántos estamos? — *v.t.* fechar; citar. — *v.i.* datar (***from,*** de); ***date back to,*** remontarse a.
date (2) [deit], *s.* (*bot.*) dátil; ***date-palm,*** datilera, palmera.
dated [ˈdeitid], *a.* anticuado, trasnochado.
dative [ˈdeitiv], *a.*, *s.* dativo.
datum [ˈdeitəm], *s.* (*pl.* **data**) dato. [DATA].
datura [dəˈtjuərə], *s.* (*bot.*) dativia.
daub [dɔ:b], *s.* embadurnamiento; pintarrajo. — *v.t.*, *v.i.* embadurnar; pintarrajear.
dauber [ˈdɔ:bə], *s.* pintamonas, *m.f.inv.*, pintor de brocha gorda.
daughter [ˈdɔ:tə], *s.* hija; ***daughter-in-law,*** nuera, hija política.
daughterly [ˈdɔ:təli], *a.* filial.
daunt [dɔ:nt], *v.t.* arredrar, atemorizar; ***not to be daunted by,*** no arredrarse ante.
dauntless [ˈdɔ:ntlis], *a.* intrépido; impávido.
dauphin [dɔ:fin], *s.* delfín.
dauphiness [dɔ:finis], *s.* delfina.
davenport [ˈdævnpɔ:t], (*Am.*) [SOFA].
davit [ˈdævit], *s.* (*mar.*) pescante, grúa.
Davy Jones [ˈdeivi ˈdʒounz], *s.* espíritu marítimo maligno; ***Davy Jones's locker,*** el fondo de la *o* del mar.
Davy lamp [ˈdeivi læmp], *s.* (*min.*) lámpara de seguridad.
daw [dɔ:], [JACKDAW].
dawdle [dɔ:dl], *v.i.* hacerse el remolón, tardar mucho, andar muy despacio.
dawdler [ˈdɔ:dlə], *s.* tardón.
dawn [dɔ:n], *s.* amanecer; ***from dawn to dusk,*** de sol a sol; ***red dawn,*** aurora; ***white dawn,*** alba. — *v.i.* amanecer; (*fig.*) ***suddenly it dawned on him,*** de pronto comprendió *o* se dio cuenta *o* cayó.
dawning [ˈdɔ:niŋ], *s.* alba, alborada, amanecer.
day [dei], *s.* día, *m.*; jornada; (*fig.*) tiempo, época; victoria; ***day-book,*** diario, dietario; ***day-boy,*** alumno externo; ***day-school,*** colegio para externos; ***day-work,*** jornada, jornal; ***all day long,*** todo el día; ***by day,*** de día; ***day after day,*** día tras día; ***day after tomorrow,*** pasado mañana; ***day before,*** día anterior, víspera; ***day before yesterday,*** anteayer; ***day to day,*** cotidiano; ***dog-days,*** canícula; ***every other day,*** cada dos días, un día sí y otro no; ***fast-day,*** día de ayuno; ***for ever and a day,*** para siempre jamás; ***from day to day,*** de día en día; ***good day,*** buenos días; ***next day,*** al día siguiente; ***one of these days,*** algún día; ***this day week,*** de hoy en ocho días; ***to this day,*** hasta (el día de) hoy; ***working day,*** día laborable, día de trabajo; ***to call it a day,*** levantar la sesión, decir que basta; ***to carry the day,*** vencer, triunfar; ***to have seen better days,*** estar venido a menos.
daybreak [ˈdeibreik], *s.* amanecer, alba.
daydream [ˈdeidri:m], *s.* ensueño.
daylight [ˈdeilait], *s.* luz de día; ***in broad daylight,*** en pleno día; ***daylight saving time,*** (*Am.*) [SUMMER TIME].
dayspring [ˈdeispriŋ], *s.* albor.
daystar [ˈdeistɑ:], *s.* lucero del alba.
daze [deiz], *s.* aturdimiento; ***in a daze,*** aturdido. — *v.t.* aturdir.
dazzle [dæzl], *s.* deslumbramiento. — *v.t.* deslumbrar, ofuscar. — *v.i.* delumbrarse, ofuscarse.
dazzling [ˈdæzliŋ], *a.* deslumbrante.
deacon [ˈdi:kən], *s.* diácono.
deaconess [ˈdi:kənes], *s.* diaconisa.
deaconry, deaconship [ˈdi:kənri,-ʃip], *s.* diaconato, diaconía.
dead [ded], *a.* muerto; difunto; entumecido; sordo, apagado; estéril; marchito; (*elec.*) inactivo; inerte; ***dead calm,*** calma chicha; ***dead end,*** callejón sin salida; punto muerto; (*mil.*) ***dead ground,*** terreno oculto; (*fam.*) ***dead head,*** gorrón; ***dead letter,*** carta no reclamada; (*fig.*) letra muerta; ***dead loss,*** pérdida total; inutilidad total; ***dead sound,*** ruido sordo; ***dead water,*** aguas muertas, *f.pl.*; (*fig.*) ***dead wood,*** cosas superfluas, *f.pl.*; personal superfluo. — *adv.* enteramente, del todo, muy; ***dead against,*** totalmente en contra; (*fam.*) ***dead beat,*** rendido, agotado; ***dead drunk,*** borracho perdido; ***dead slow,*** muy despacio; (*fam.*) ***dead sure,*** completamente seguro; ***dead tired,*** muerto de cansancio. — *s.* ***in the*** o ***at dead of night,*** en el silencio de la noche; ***in the dead of winter,*** en lo más crudo *o* recio del invierno; (*pl.*) ***the dead,*** los muertos; los caídos.
deaden [dedn], *v.t.* amortiguar, amortecer; desvirtuar, adormecer; apagar; hacer insípido.
deadline [ˈdedlain], *s.* fecha tope; plazo.
deadliness [ˈdedlinis], *s.* (lo) mortífero.
deadlock [ˈdedlɔk], *s.* punto muerto.
deadly [ˈdedli], *a.* mortal, mortífero, letal; fatal; ***deadly sins,*** pecados capitales, *m.pl.* — *adv.* sumamente; mortalmente.
deadness [ˈdednis], *s.* (lo) muerto, (lo) silencioso.
deadnettle [ˈdednetl], *s.* (*bot.*) ortiga muerta.

deaf [def], *a.* sordo; apagado; ***deaf-mute,*** sordomudo; ***as deaf as a post,*** sordo como una tapia; ***to turn a deaf ear,*** hacerse el sordo, hacer oídos de mercader.
deafen [ˈdefən], *v.t.* ensordecer, asordar; apagar (*un sonido*); aturdir.
deafening [ˈdefəniŋ], *a.* ensordecedor.
deafness [ˈdefnis], *s.* sordera.
deal (1) [di:l], *s.* cantidad, porción, parte, *f.*; mano (*en el juego de naipes*); (*com.*) negocio, trato; ***a great deal, a good deal,*** mucho, bastante. — *v.t.* distribuir, repartir; dar, asestar. — *v.i.* negociar, comerciar, traficar; portarse; ser mano (*en juegos de cartas*); ***deal with,*** tratar con (*personas*); tratar de (*temas*); ocuparse de (*asuntos*).
deal (2) [di:l], *s.* madera de pino *o* abeto.
dealer [ˈdi:lə], *s.* comerciante, traficante; (*juego*) repartidor, mano; ***double dealer,*** (*Am.*) ***wheeler dealer,*** hombre de dobleces; ***plain dealer,*** hombre sin dobleces.
dealing [ˈdi:liŋ], *s.* proceder, modo de proceder, comportamiento, conducta; negocio, comercio; trato, relaciones; repartición.
deambulatory [di:ˈæmbjulətəri], *a.* deambulatorio.
dean [di:n], *s.* deán; decano.
deanery, deanship [ˈdi:nəri, -ʃip], *s.* deanato; decanato.
dear [diə], *a.* querido; caro; costoso; carero. — *s.* querido; ***dear!, dear dear!, oh dear!, dear me!*** ¡por Dios!, ¡Dios mío!; ***my dear,*** querido.
dearly [ˈdiəli], *adv.* caro; entrañablemente, tiernamente.
dearness [ˈdiənis], *s.* cariño; carestía.
dearth [də:θ], *s.* escasez, orfandad.
death [deθ], *s.* muerte, *f.*, fallecimiento, defunción; ***on pain of death,*** so pena de muerte; ***to be at death's door,*** estar a la muerte; ***to bore to death,*** matar de aburrimiento; ***to do*** o ***put to death,*** dar (la) muerte a; ***to freeze to death,*** matar de frío; morir(se) helado; ***to starve to death,*** matar de hambre; morir(se) de hambre.
death-bed [ˈdeθ-bed], *s.* lecho de muerte.
death-blow [ˈdeθ-blou], *s.* golpe mortal.
death-certificate [ˈdeθ-səˈtifikit], *s.* partida de defunción.
death-chamber [ˈdeθ-tʃeimbə], *s.* cámara mortuoria.
death-duties [ˈdeθ-dju:ti:z], *s.pl.* derechos sucesorios, *m.pl.*
deathless [ˈdeθlis], *a.* inmortal, inmarcesible.
deathlike, deathly [deθlaik, -li], *a.* mortal; cadavérico.
death-mask [ˈdeθ-mɑ:sk], *s.* mascarilla.
death-rate [ˈdeθ-reit], *s.* mortalidad.
death-rattle [ˈdeθ-rætl], *s.* estertor.
death's head [ˈdeθs hed], *s.* calavera.
death-toll [ˈdeθ-toul], *s.* toque de difuntos; balance.
death-trap [ˈdeθ-træp], *s.* sitio peligrosísimo.
death-warrant [ˈdeθ-wɔrənt], *s.* sentencia de muerte.
death-watch [ˈdeθ-wɔtʃ], *s.* vela; velorio; (*ent.*) ***death-watch beetle,*** anobio; (*fam.*) reloj de la muerte.
debacle [deiˈbɑ:kl], *s.* caída; ruina; desastre, cataclismo.
debar [diˈbɑ:], *v.t.* excluir; prohibir.
debark [diˈbɑ:k], *v.t., v.i.* desembarcar.
debarkation, debarcation [di:bɑ:ˈkeiʃən], *s.* desembarco; desembarque.
debase [diˈbeis], *v.t.* rebajar, envilecer, degradar; adulterar, falsificar.
debasement [diˈbeismənt], *s.* degradación; falsificación, adulteración.
debatable [diˈbeitəbl], *a.* discutible.
debate [diˈbeit], *s.* debate; discusión. — *v.t.* debatir, disputar. — *v.i.* deliberar, debatir, reflexionar.
debater [diˈbeitə], *s.* controversista, *m.f.*, polemista *m.f.*
debauch [diˈbɔ:tʃ], *s.* libertinaje, crápula. — *v.t.* corromper, viciar; seducir.
debauched [diˈbɔ:tʃt], *a.* libertino, disoluto.
debauchee [diˈbɔ:tʃi:], *s.* libertino, calavera, disoluto.
debaucher [diˈbɔ:tʃə], *s.* seductor.
debauchery [diˈbɔ:tʃəri], *s.* libertinaje; crápula.
debauchment [diˈbɔ:tʃmənt], *s.* corrupción.
debenture [diˈbentʃə], *s.* (*com.*) obligación, bono, vale, acción.
debilitate [diˈbiliteit], *v.t.* debilitar.
debilitation [dibiliˈteiʃən], *s.* debilitación.
debility [diˈbiliti], *s.* debilidad; languidez, atonía.
debit [ˈdebit], *s.* débito, cargo, adeudo; saldo deudor. — *v.t.* cargar, adeudar.
debonair [debəˈnɛə], *a.* gallardo.
debouch [diˈbautʃ], *v.t., v.i.* desembocar.
debris [ˈdebri:], *s.inv.* escombros, *m.pl.*, cascajos, *m.pl.*; despojos, *m.pl.*
debt [det], *s.* deuda; débito; obligación; ***bad debt,*** deuda incobrable; (***deeply***) ***in debt,*** entrampado; ***to get into debt,*** entramparse.
debtee [ˈdeti:], *s.* acreedor.
debtor [ˈdetə], *s.* deudor; cargo.
debunk [di:ˈbʌŋk], *v.t.* desmitificar.
debut [deiˈbju:], *s.* (*teat.*) estreno; debut; entrada en (la) sociedad; ***to make one's debut,*** debutar; entrar en sociedad.
debutante [ˈdebjutɑ:nt], *s.* debutante, chica que se pone de largo.
decade [ˈdekeid], *s.* década, decenio.
decadence [ˈdekədəns], *s.* decadencia, ocaso.
decadent [ˈdekədənt], *a.* decadente, decadentista.
decagon [ˈdekəgən], *s.* (*geom.*) decágono.
decagramme [ˈdekəgræm], *s.* decagramo.
decahedron [dekəˈhi:drən], *s.* decaedro.
decalitre [ˈdekəli:tə], *s.* decalitro.
decalogue [ˈdekəlɔg], *s.* decálogo.
decametre [ˈdekəmi:tə], *s.* decámetro.
decamp [di:ˈkæmp], *v.i.* largarse; decampar.
decampment [di:ˈkæmpmənt], *s.* acción de decampar.
decanal [diˈkeinəl], *a.* lo que pertenece al decanato.
decant [diˈkænt], *v.t.* decantar, trasegar.
decantation [di:kænˈteiʃən], *s.* decantación, trasiego.
decanter [diˈkæntə], *s.* garrafa; ampolla.
decapitate [diˈkæpiteit], *v.t.* decapitar.
decapitation [dikæpiˈteiʃən], *s.* decapitación.
decapod [ˈdekəpɔd], *s.* (*zool.*) decápodo.
decarbonization [di:kɑ:bənaiˈzeiʃən], *s.* descarburación.
decarbonize [di:ˈkɑ:bənaiz], *v.t.* quitar el carbono, descarburar.
decastich [ˈdekəstik], *s.* décima.
decastyle [ˈdekəstail], *s.* (*arq.*) decástilo.
decasyllable [ˈdekəsiləbl], *s.* decasílabo.
decay [diˈkei], *s.* decadencia, decaimiento, declinación; caries, *f.* — *v.i.* decaer, declinar; cariarse.
decease [diˈsi:s], *s.* fallecimiento, defunción. — *v.i.* fallecer.
deceased [diˈsi:st], *a.* fallecido, difunto, finado.
deceit [diˈsi:t], *s.* engaño; fraude; superchería; falsedad.
deceitful [diˈsi:tful], *a.* engañoso; mentiroso.
deceitfulness [diˈsi:tfulnis], *s.* falsedad, duplicidad, dobleces.
deceive [diˈsi:v], *v.t.* engañar; embaucar; ***to be deceived,*** engañarse.
deceiver [diˈsi:və], *s.* engañador; impostor.
December [diˈsembə], *s.* diciembre.
decency [ˈdi:sənsi], *s.* decencia; decoro; recato; honestidad.

decennary [di'senəri], *s.* decenario.
decennial [di'seniəl], *a.* decenal.
decent ['di:sənt], *a.* decente; honesto; ***he was decent to me,*** se portó bien conmigo.
decentness ['di:səntnis]. [DECENCY].
decentralization [di:sentrəlai'zeiʃən], *s.* descentralización.
decentralize [di:'sentrəlaiz], *v.t.* descentralizar.
deception [di'sepʃən], *s.* engaño, superchería, fraude.
deceptive [di'septiv], *a.* engañoso; ilusorio.
decide [di'said], *v.t.* decidir, resolver. — *v.i.* decidir, decidirse (a), resolverse (a); ***decide on,*** decidir.
decided [di'saidid], *a.* marcado, acusado.
deciduous [di'sidjuəs], *a.* caedizo.
decigram(me) ['desigræm], *s.* decigramo.
decilitre ['desili:tə], *s.* decilitro.
decimal ['desiməl], *a.*, *s.* decimal.
decimalize ['desiməlaiz], *v.t.* decimalizar. — *v.i.* adoptar el sistema decimal.
decimalization [desiməlai'zeiʃən], *s.* decimalización.
decimate ['desimeit], *v.t.* diezmar.
decimation [desi'meiʃən], *s.* (el) diezmar; estrago(s), mortandad.
decimetre ['desimi:tə], *s.* decímetro.
decipher [di'saifə], *v.t.* descifrar.
decipherable [di'saifərəbl], *a.* descifrable.
decipherer [di'saifərə], *s.* descifrador.
deciphering [di'saifəriŋ], *s.* desciframiento.
decision [di'siʒən], *s.* decisión, determinación, resolución.
decisive [di'saisiv], *a.* decisivo, concluyente, terminante; decidido.
decisiveness [di'saisivnis], *s.* decisión, firmeza; (lo) decisivo.
deck [dek], *s.* (*mar.*) cubierta; suelo; piso; baceta, monte (*naipes*); (*Am.*, *naipes*) [PACK]; ***deck-chair,*** hamaca; ***deck-hand,*** marinero (común); (*mar.*) ***lower deck,*** marinería. — *v.t.* ataviar, adornar, engalanar, revestir; (*fam.*) ***decked out in his Sunday best,*** emperejilado en sus trapitos de cristianar.
decker ['dekə], *s.* cubridor; ataviador, adornador; ***double-decker*** o ***two-decker,*** navío de dos cubiertas; de dos pisos (autobús etc.).
deckle [dekl], *s.* bastidor (*para hacer papel*); ***deckle edge,*** barba del papel.
declaim [di'kleim], *v.t.*, *v.i.* declamar, recitar.
declaimant, declaimer [di'kleimənt, -ə], *s.* declamador.
declamation [deklə'meiʃən], *s.* declamación; peroración; arenga.
declamatory [di'klæmətəri], *a.* declamatorio.
declaration [deklə'reiʃən], *s.* declaración; manifiesto; proclamación; aserto, aserción; publicación; exposición.
declarative [di'klærətiv], *a.* declarativo; expositivo.
declaratory [di'klærətəri], *a.* declaratorio, afirmativo.
declare [di'klɛə], *v.t.* declarar; manifestar; proclamar; confesar; asegurar, afirmar. — *v.i.* declarar(se), testificar, deponer.
declass ['di:'klɑ:s], *v.t.* degradar, bajar de categoría social.
declension [di'klenʃən], *s.* declinación.
declinable [di'klainəbl], *a.* declinable.
declination [dekli'neiʃən], *s.* declinación, declive, descenso, decadencia; decremento, deterioro; desviación, desvío; descarrío.
decline [di'klain], *s.* declinación, descenso, disminución; decaimiento, decadencia; ocaso; debilitación; ***in,*** *o* ***on the, decline,*** en decadencia. — *v.t.* declinar; inclinar; desviar; rehusar. — *v.i.* declinar; inclinarse; menguar; ***decline to,*** negarse a.
declining [di'klainiŋ], *a.* declinante; inclinante; pendiente; de decadencia, de ocaso.
declivity [di'kliviti], *s.* inclinación; declive, pendiente.
declutch [di:'klʌtʃ], *v.i.* desembragar.
decoct [di'kɔkt], *v.t.* cocer; extraer por decocción.
decoction [di'kɔkʃən], *s.* decocción, cocimiento.
decode [di:'koud], *v.t.* descifrar.
decollation [dəkɔ'leiʃən], *s.* degollación.
décolletage [dei'kɔletɑ:ʒ], *s.* escote.
décolleté(e) [dei'kɔltei], *a.* escotado; en traje escotado.
decolorant [di:'kʌlərənt], *s.* descolorante.
decoloration [di:kʌlə'reiʃən], *s.* descoloramiento.
decolour [di:'kʌlə], *v.t.* descolorar, blanquear; refinar, clarificar.
decomposable [di:kəm'pouzəbl], *a.* descomponible, corruptible.
decompose [di:kəm'pouz], *v.t.* descomponer, pudrir. — *v.i.* descomponerse, corromperse.
decomposition [di:kɔmpə'ziʃən], *s.* descomposición.
decontaminate [di:kən'tæmineit], *v.t.* descontaminar.
decorate ['dekəreit], v.t. decorar, adornar; empapelar; pintar; condecorar.
decoration [dekə'reiʃən], *s.* decoración; ornato, adorno; condecoración.
decorator ['dekəreitə], *s.* decorador.
decorous ['dekərəs], *a.* decoroso.
decorticate [di:'kɔ:tikeit], *v.t.* descortezar.
decorticator [di:'kɔ:tikeitə], *s.* descortezador.
decorum, decorousness [di'kɔ:rəm, 'dekərəsnis], *s.* decoro.
decoy [di'kɔi], *s.* señuelo, añagaza; reclamo; trampa; entruchón. — *v.t.* atraer con señuelo.
decrease ['di:kri:s], *s.* disminución, decrecimiento. —[di'kri:s], *v.t.* disminuir. — *v.i.* disminuir, decrecer.
decreasingly [di'kri:siŋli], *adv.* en disminución, cada vez menos.
decree [di'kri:], *s.* decreto. — *v.t.*, *v.i.* decretar.
decrement ['dekrimənt], *s.* decremento.
decrepit [di'krepit], *a.* decrépito.
decrepitate [di'krepiteit], *v.t.*, *v.i.* decrepitar.
decrepitation [dikrepi'teiʃən], *s.* decrepitación.
decrepitude, decrepitness [di'krepitju:d, -nis], *s.* decrepitud.
decrescent [di'kresənt], *a.* decreciente.
decretal [di'kri:təl], *a.* decretal. — *s.* decretal.
decretion [di'kri:ʃən], *s.* disminución, merma.
decretory [di'kri:təri], *a.* decretorio; definitivo, decisivo.
decrial [di'kraiəl], *s.* vituperio; censura.
decrier [di'kraiə], *s.* vituperador.
decrown [di:'kraun], *v.t.* destronar.
decry [di'krai], *v.t.* vituperar, censurar; desacreditar.
decumbent [di'kʌmbənt], *a.* (*bot.*) recostado, reclinado.
decuple ['dekjupl], *a.* décuplo. — *v.t.* decuplicar.
decurion [di'kjuəriən], *s.* decurión.
decussation [dekə'seiʃən], *s.* cruzamiento.
dedicate ['dedikeit], *v.t.* dedicar; consagrar.
dedicated ['dedikeitid], *a.* dedicado; consagrado.
dedication [dedi'keiʃən], *s.* dedicación; consagración; dedicatoria.
dedicator ['dedikeitə], *s.* dedicante.
dedicatory ['dedikeitəri], *a.* dedicatorio.
deduce [di'dju:s], *v.t.* deducir, sacar, derivar, inferir, concluir, colegir.
deducement [di'dju:smənt], [DEDUCTION].
deducible [di'dju:sibl], *a.* deducible.
deducive [di'dju:siv], *a.* deductivo.

deduct [di'dʌkt], *v.t.* deducir, sustraer; restar, descontar, rebajar.
deduction [di'dʌkʃən], *s.* deducción; corolario, consecuencia; descuento, rebaja; resta.
deductive [di'dʌktiv], *a.* deductivo.
deductively [di'dʌktivli], *adv.* por inferencia, por deducción.
deed [di:d], *s.* hecho, acto; proeza, hazaña; (*for.*) escritura.
deem [di:m], *v.t., v.i.* juzgar, estimar.
deep [di:p], *a.* hondo, profundo; intenso; ***deep in thought,*** ensimismado; ***deep in politics,*** muy metido en política; ***deep in trouble,*** con unos líos espantosos; ***ten inches deep,*** de diez pulgadas de espesor; ***deep in debt,*** entrampadísimo; (*Am.*) ***deep pie,*** empanada; ***deep sea,*** alta mar; ***deep mourning,*** luto riguroso. — *adv.* profundamente; intensamente; muy adentro; ***deep into the night,*** (hasta) muy entrada la noche. — *s.* abismo; mar.
deepen ['di:pən], *v.t.* profundizar, ahondar; oscurecer; hacer más grave (*un sonido*). — *v.i.* ahondarse; intensificarse; hacerse más grave.
deeply ['di:pli], *adv.* hondamente, profundamente; intensamente; gravemente; completamente; sumamente.
deepness ['di:pnis], *s.* profundidad; intensidad; gravedad.
deer [diə], *s.* ciervo, venado; ***fallow deer,*** gamo.
deerhound ['diəhaund], *s.* galgo.
deerskin ['diəskin], *s.* gamuza.
deer-stalker ['diə-stɔ:kə], *s.* cazador de ciervos al acecho; gorro de cazador.
deer-stalking ['diə-stɔ:kiŋ], *s.* caza de ciervos al acecho.
deface [di'feis], *v.t.* desfigurar; afear.
defacement [di'feismənt], *s.* desfiguración; afeamiento.
defalcate [di'fælkeit], *v.t.* descabalar, deducir, rebajar. — *v.i.* desfalcar, malversar.
defalcation [di:fæl'keiʃən], *s.* desfalco, malversación.
defamation [defə'meiʃən], *s.* difamación, calumnia.
defamatory [di'fæmətəri], *a.* infamatorio, difamatorio, calumnioso.
defame [di'feim], *v.t.* difamar, deshonrar, denigrar, desacreditar, calumniar.
defamer [di'feimə], *s.* difamador, calumniador.
default [di'fɔ:lt], *s.* falta, defecto, deficiencia; descuido; (*for.*) rebeldía, contumacia; ***by default,*** por omisión. — *v.t., v.i.* dejar de cumplir; faltar; no pagar; no comparecer.
defaulter [di'fɔ:ltə], *s.* desfalcador, malversador; contumaz, rebelde.
defeat [di'fi:t], *s.* derrota; vencimiento. — *v.t.* derrotar; vencer; frustar; ***defeat its own object,*** ser contraproducente.
defeatism [di'fi:tizəm], *s.* derrotismo.
defeatist [di'fi:tist], *a., s.* derrotista, *m.f.*
defecate ['defikeit], *v.t., v.i.* defecar.
defecation [defi'keiʃən], *s.* defecación.
defect [di'fekt], *s.* defecto; imperfección; mácula. — *v.i.* desertar.
defection [di'fekʃən], *s.* defección; deserción.
defective [di'fektiv], *a.* defectuoso; defectivo; falto, deficiente.
defectiveness [di'fektivnis], *s.* (lo) defectuoso *etc.*
defector [di'fektə], *s.* desertor.
defence [di'fens], *s.* defensa; protección; ***Ministry of Defence,*** ministerio de la guerra.
defenceless [di'fenslis], *a.* indefenso; sin defensa; a pecho descubierto.
defencelessness [di'fenslisnis], *s.* desvalimiento.
defend [di'fend], *v.t.* defender; amparar.
defendable [di'fendəbl], *a.* defendible.
defendant [di'fendənt], *s.* demandado, acusado.
defender [di'fendə], *s.* defensor.
defense (*Am.*) [DEFENCE].
defensive [di'fensiv], *a.* defensivo. — *s.* defensiva; ***on the defensive,*** a la defensiva.
defer [di'fə:], *v.t.* diferir, aplazar. — *v.i.* deferir, ceder (***to,*** a, ante).
deference ['defərəns], *s.* deferencia; ***in*** o ***out of deference to,*** por respeto a; en cumplimiento de.
deferent ['defərənt], *a.* deferente.
deferential [defə'renʃəl], *a.* deferente, respetuoso.
deferring [di'fə:riŋ], *s.* aplazamiento.
defiance [di'faiəns], *s.* desafío; insolencia; desobediencia; ***in defiance of,*** a despecho de; ***to bid defiance to, set at defiance,*** desafiar.
defiant [di'faiənt], *a.* desafiador.
deficience, deficiency [di'fiʃəns, -i], *s.* deficiencia, insuficiencia, carencia; ***deficiency disease,*** enfermedad carencial.
deficient [di'fiʃənt], *a.* deficiente, insuficiente; defectuoso.
deficit ['defisit], *s.* déficit.
defilade [defi'leid], *v.t.* (*mar., mil.*) desenfilar.
defile [di'fail], *s.* desfiladero. — *v.t.* manchar, mancillar, profanar. — *v.i.* desfilar.
defilement [di'failmənt], *s.* corrupción, profanación.
defiler [di'failə], *s.* corruptor, profanador.
definable [di'fainəbl], *a.* definible.
definably [di'fainəbli], *adv.* determinadamente.
define [di'fain], *v.t.* definir; delimitar, determinar.
definite ['definit], *a.* concreto, determinado; ***quite definite,*** indudable; tajante, terminante, categórico.
definitely ['definitli], *adv.* seguro; desde luego; sin lugar a dudas; categóricamente.
definiteness ['definitnis], *s.* (lo) concreto, (lo) determinado; (lo) seguro; (lo) categórico.
definition [defi'niʃən], *s.* definición; claridad (*de un lente etc.*).
definitive [di'finitiv], *a.* definitivo; que define.
definitiveness [di'finitivnis], *s.* (lo) definitivo.
deflagration [deflə'greiʃən], *s.* (*fís.*) deflagración.
deflagrator ['defləgreitə], *s.* (*elec.*) deflagrador.
deflate [di'fleit], *v.t.* desinflar; deflacionar.
deflation [di'fleiʃən], *s.* desinflamiento; deflación.
deflationary [di'fleiʃənəri], *a.* deflacionista.
deflect [di'flekt], *v.t.* desviar. — *v.i.* desviarse.
deflection [di'flekʃən], *s.* desvío, desviación, declinación de la aguja; (*mec.*) flexión; (*ópt.*) deflexión.
deflective [di'flektiv], *a.* que desvía.
deflorate [di:'flɔ:reit], *a.* (*bot.*) desflorado.
defloration [di:flɔ:'reiʃən], *s.* desfloración; desfloramiento.
deflower [di:'flauə], *v.t.* desflorar; desflorecer; ajar, deslustrar.
deflux, defluxion ['di:flʌks, di'flʌkʃən], *s.* fluxión.
defoliate [di:'foulieit], *a.* deshojado. — *v.t.* deshojar. — *v.i.* deshojarse.
defoliation [di:fouli'eiʃən], *s.* desfoliación; deshoje.
deforest [di:'fɔrist], *v.t.* desaforestar.
deforestation [di:fɔris'teiʃən], *s.* desaforestación.
deform [di'fɔ:m], *v.t.* deformar, desfigurar.
deformation [di:fɔ:'meiʃən], *s.* deformación, desfiguración.
deformed [di'fɔ:md], *a.* deformado, desfigurado.
deformity [di'fɔ:miti], *s.* deformidad.
defraud [di'frɔ:d], *v.t.* defraudar.
defraudation, defraudment [di:frɔ:'deiʃən, di'frɔ:dmənt], *s.* defraudación.
defrauder [di'frɔ:də], *s.* defraudador, estafador.
defray [di'frei], *v.t.* costear, sufragar, subvenir a.
defrayment [di'freimənt], *s.* gasto.
defreeze ['di:'fri:z], *v.t.* descongelar.
defrock ['di:'frɔk], *v.t.* exclaustrar.
defrost ['di:'frɔst], *v.t.* descongelar.

deft [deft], *a.* primoroso, delicado; hábil.
deftly [ˈdeftli], *adv.* con primor *o* delicadeza.
deftness [ˈdeftnis], *s.* primorosidad, delicadeza.
defunct [diˈfʌŋkt], *a.* difunto, muerto; desaparecido.
defy [diˈfai], *v.t.* desafiar; oponerse a; ***it defies description,*** no hay palabras para describirlo.
degeneracy [diˈdʒenərəsi], *s.* degeneración; depravación.
degenerate [diˈdʒenərit], *a., s.* degenerado. — [diˈdʒenəreit], *v.i.* degenerar.
degeneration, degenerateness [didʒenəˈreiʃən, diˈdʒenəritnis], *s.* degeneración.
deglutition [di:glu:ˈtiʃən], *s.* deglución.
degradation [degrəˈdeiʃən], *s.* degradación, envilecimiento.
degrade [diˈgreid], *v.t.* degradar, envilecer.
degrading [diˈgreidiŋ], *a.* degradante, envilecedor.
degree [diˈgri:], *s.* grado; rango, condición; título (universitario); ***by degrees,*** poco a poco; ***in some degree,*** en cierto modo; hasta cierto punto; ***to the highest degree,*** en sumo grado; ***to take a degree,*** licenciarse, graduarse; ***to a degree,*** algo, un tanto.
dehisce [diˈhis], *v.i.* entreabrirse, hendirse.
dehiscent [diˈhisənt], *a.* dehiscente.
dehumanize [di:ˈhju:mənaiz], *v.t.* deshumanizar.
dehydrate [di:ˈhaidreit], *v.t.* deshidratar.
de-ice [ˈdi:-ˈais], *v.t.* deshelar.
deification [di:ifiˈkeiʃən], *s.* deificación.
deiform [ˈdi:ifɔ:m], *a.* deiforme.
deify [ˈdi:ifai], *v.t.* deificar, endiosar.
deign [dein], *v.i.* dignarse; ***he does not deign to speak,*** no se digna hablar.
deism [ˈdi:izəm], *s.* deísmo.
deist [ˈdi:ist], *s.* deísta, *m.f.*
deistic(al) [di:ˈistik(əl)], *a.* deístico.
deity [ˈdi:iti], *s.* deidad, numen.
deject [diˈdʒekt], *v.t.* abatir, desalentar, desanimar.
dejected [diˈdʒektid], *a.* abatido, desanimado, cabizbajo, triste.
dejectedness [diˈdʒektidnis], *s.* abatimiento, desaliento, tristeza.
dejection [diˈdʒekʃən], *s.* abatimiento, tristeza; deyección.
dekko [ˈdekou], *s.* (*fam.*) ***to take a dekko,*** echar un vistazo (***at,*** a).
delay [diˈlei], *s.* dilación, tardanza, retraso, demora. — *v.t.* aplazar, diferir, retrasar. — *v.i.* demorarse, tardar.
delayed-action [diˈleid-ˈækʃən], *a.* de efecto retardado.
delectable [diˈlektəbl], *a.* deleitable, delicioso.
delectableness, delectation [diˈlektəblnis, delekˈteiʃən], *s.* (lo) deleitable; fruición.
delegate [ˈdeligit], *s.* delegado; diputado. — [ˈdeligeit], *v.t.* delegar; diputar.
delegation [deliˈgeiʃən], *s.* delegación; diputación.
delete [diˈli:t], *v.t.* borrar, tachar, suprimir.
deleterious [deliˈtiəriəs], *a.* deletéreo.
deletion [diˈli:ʃən], *s.* borradura, supresión.
delf [delf], *s.* zanja, desaguadero.
delft [delft], *s.* loza fina de Delft.
deliberate (1) [diˈlibərit], *a.* deliberado, intencionado, premeditado; reflexionado; cauto; lento, pausado.
deliberate (2) [diˈlibəreit], *v.t.* reflexionar, meditar (en). — *v.i.* deliberar.
deliberately [diˈlibəritli], *adv.* intencionadamente premeditadamente.
deliberation [dilibəˈreiʃən], *s.* deliberación; reflexión, premeditación.
deliberative [diˈlibərətiv], *a.* deliberativo, deliberante.
deliberator [diˈlibəreitə], *s.* deliberante.
delible [ˈdelibl], *a.* deleble, borrable.
delicacy [ˈdelikəsi], *s.* delicadeza; finura; cosa delicada; golosina.
delicate [ˈdelikit], *a.* delicado, exquisito.
delicately [ˈdelikitli], *adv.* delicadamente, sutilmente.
delicateness [ˈdelikitnis], *s.* delicadeza.
delicatessen [delikəˈtesən], *s.* tienda en que se venden manjares exquisitos.
delicious [diˈliʃəs], *a.* delicioso, exquisito, rico.
deliciousness [diˈliʃəsnis], *s.* (lo) delicioso.
delict [ˈdi:likt], *s.* (*der.*) delito.
deligation [deliˈgeiʃən], *s.* (*cir.*) vendaje, ligadura.
delight [diˈlait], *s.* deleite, delicia; ***to take delight in,*** deleitarse en *o* con; regodearse con. — *v.t.* deleitar. — *v.i.* deleitarse.
delightful [diˈlaitful], *a.* delicioso, deleitoso, exquisito.
delightfulness [diˈlaitfulnis], *s.* delicia, deleite, encanto.
delimit [di:ˈlimit], *v.t.* deslindar, delimitar.
delimitation [di:limiˈteiʃən], *s.* deslinde, delimitación.
delineament [diˈliniəmənt], *s.* delineamiento, delineación.
delineate [diˈlinieit], *v.t.* delinear, trazar.
delineation [diliniˈeiʃən], *s.* delineación, delineamiento.
delineator [diˈlinieitə], *s.* delineador.
delinquency [diˈliŋkwənsi], *s.* delincuencia.
delinquent [diˈliŋkwənt], *a., s.* delincuente.
deliquesce [deliˈkwes], *v.i.* liquidarse, hacerse líquido poco a poco.
deliquescence [deliˈkwesəns], *s.* delicuescencia, licuación.
deliquium [diˈlikwiəm], *s.* licuación; deliquio.
delirious [diˈliriəs], *a.* delirante.
deliriously [diˈliriəsli], *adv.* de una manera delirante.
deliriousness, delirium [diˈliriəsnis, diˈliriəm], *s.* delirio.
delitescence [deliˈtesəns], *s.* delitescencia.
deliver [diˈlivə], *v.t.* librar (***from,*** de); entregar; distribuir, repartir; pronunciar (*un discurso*); asestar (*un golpe*); comunicar; lanzar (*una pelota*); partear; ***deliver up*** o ***over,*** entregar; ***to be delivered of (child),*** parir, dar a luz.
deliverable [diˈlivərəbl], *a.* (*com.*) disponible.
deliverance [diˈlivərəns], *s.* liberación; salvación; rescate; (*for.*) absolución.
deliverer [diˈlivərə], *s.* libertador, salvador.
delivery [diˈlivəri], *s.* liberación; salvación; reparto; entrega; remesa; parto, alumbramiento; modo de expresarse, declamación; ***delivery service,*** servicio a domicilio.
deliveryman [diˈlivərimən], *s.* repartidor.
dell [del], *s.* vallecito.
Delphic [ˈdelfik], *a.* délfico.
delta [ˈdeltə], *s.* delta; (*aer.*) ***delta-wing,*** ala en delta.
deltoid [ˈdeltɔid], *a., s.* deltoide.
delouse [di:ˈlaus], *v.t.* despiojar.
delude [diˈl(j)u:d], *v.t.* engañar, embaucar; ***to be deluded,*** engañarse, hacerse ilusiones; ***easily deluded,*** iluso.
deluder [diˈl(j)u:də], *s.* engañador.
deluge [ˈdelju:dʒ], *s.* diluvio; inundación. — *v.t.* inundar (***with,*** de).
delusion [diˈl(j)u:ʒen], *s.* engaño, ilusión, espejismo.
delusive, delusory [diˈl(j)u:siv, -əri], *a.* engañoso, ilusorio.
de luxe [də ˈluks], *a.* de lujo.
delve [delv], *s.* hoyo, barranco, zanja; madriguera. — *v.t., v.i.* cavar; sondear; ahondar; ***delve into,*** investigar, indagar.
delver [ˈdelvə], *s.* cavador; el que ahonda.
demagnetize [di:ˈmægnitaiz], *v.t.* desmagnetizar.

demagogic [demə'gɔgik], *a.* demagógico.
demagogue ['deməgɔg], *s.* demagogo.
demain [də'mein], *s.* dominio; tierra solariega.
demand [di'mɑːnd], *s.* demanda; exigencia; petición, solicitud; ***to be in demand,*** estar (muy) solicitado. — *v.t.* demandar; reclamar; exigir.
demandable [di'mɑːndəbl], *a.* exigible.
demandant [di'mɑːndənt], *s.* (*for.*) demandador, demandante.
demander [di'mɑːndə], *s.* demandador; exactor.
demarcation [diːmɑː'keiʃən], *s.* demarcación; deslinde.
demean [di'miːn], *v.t.* degradar, rebajar. — **demean o.s.,** *v.r.* conducirse; degradarse, rebajarse.
demeanour [di'miːnə], *s.* conducta; porte, continente.
dement [di'ment], *v.t.* enloquecer.
demented [di'mentid], *a.* demente.
demerit [diː'merit], *s.* demérito.
demesne [DEMAIN].
demi ['demi], *prefijo.* medio, semi.
demigod ['demigɔd], *s.* semidiós.
demijohn ['demidʒɔn], *s.* damajuana, bombona.
demilitarization [diːmilitərai'zeiʃən], *s.* desmilitarización.
demilitarize [diː'militəraiz], *v.t.* desmilitarizar.
demise [di'miːz], *s.* fallecimiento, defunción; traspaso.
demisemiquaver ['demisemikweivə], *s.* (*mús.*) fusa.
demissive [di'misiv], *a.* humilde.
demit [di'mit], *v.t.* dimitir; renunciar.
demob [diː'mɔb], *s.* (*fam.*) licenciamiento. — *v.t.* licenciar.
demobilization [diːmoubilai'zeiʃən], *s.* desmovilización.
demobilize [diː'moubilaiz], *v.t.* desmovilizar.
democracy [di'mɔkrəsi], *s.* democracia.
democrat ['deməkræt], *s.* demócrata, *m.f.*
democratic [demə'krætik], *a.* democrático.
democratize [di'mɔkrətaiz], *v.t.* democratizar.
demography [diː'mɔgrəfi], *s.* demografía.
demolish [di'mɔliʃ], *v.t.* demoler, derribar; dar al traste con.
demolisher [di'mɔliʃə], *s.* demoledor.
demolishing [di'mɔliʃiŋ], *a.* demoledor.
demolition [demə'liʃən], *s.* demolición, derribo.
demon ['diːmən], *s.* demonio, diablo.
demonetize [diː'mʌnitaiz], *v.t.* desmonetizar.
demoniac [di'mouniæk], *a.* demoníaco, endemoniado. — *s.* energúmeno.
demoniacal [diːmo'naiəkəl], *a.* demoníaco, endemoniado.
demonology [diːmə'nɔlədʒi], *s.* demonología.
demonstrability [demənstrə'biliti], *s.* demostrabilidad.
demonstrable ['demənstrəbl], *a.* demostrable.
demonstrably ['demənstrəbli], *adv.* manifiestamente.
demonstrate ['demənstreit], *v.t.* demostrar. — *v.i.* manifestarse.
demonstration [demən'streiʃən], *s.* demostración; (*pol.*) manifestación.
demonstrative [di'mɔnstrətiv], *a.* demostrativo.
demonstrator ['demənstreitə], *s.* demostrador; manifestante.
demoralization [diːmɔrəlai'zeiʃən], *s.* desmoralización.
demoralize [diː'mɔrəlaiz], *v.t.* desmoralizar.
demoralizer [diː'mɔrəlaizə], *s.* desmoralizador.
demoralizing [diː'mɔrəlaiziŋ], *a.* desmoralizador.
demote [diː'mout], *v.t.* degradar.
demotic [di'mɔtik], *a.* demótico.
demotion [diː'mouʃən], *s.* degradación.
demur [di'məː], *s.* objeción, reparo; vacilación, irresolución. — *v.i.* objetar, poner reparos; vacilar.
demure [di'mjuə], *a.* recatado; modoso.
demureness [di'mjuənis], *s.* recato; modosidad.
demurrage [di'mʌridʒ], *s.* demora, detención; (*com.*) estadía.
demurrer [di'mʌrə], *s.* objeción; persona que objeta; (*for.*) exepción.
demy [di'mai], *s.* marquilla (*papelería*).
den [den], *s.* cubil, guarida, madriguera; antro; cuchitril; ***opium den,*** fumadero de opio.
denary ['diːnəri], *a.* decimal; lo que contiene diez.
denationalize [diː'næʃənəlaiz], *v.t.* desnacionalizar.
denaturalize [diː'nætʃərəlaiz], *v.t.* desnaturalizar; desfigurar.
denatured alcohol [diː'neitʃəd 'ælkəhɔl], (*Am.*) [METHYLATED SPIRIT].
dendriform ['dendrifɔːm], *a.* (*zool.*) dendrítico.
dendrite ['dendrait], *s.* (*min.*) dendrita.
dendrology [den'drɔlədʒi], *s.* dendrología.
denegation [diːni'geiʃən], *s.* denegación.
deniable [di'naiəbl], *a.* negable.
denial [di'naiəl], *s.* negación; negativa; denegación; ***self-denial,*** abnegación.
denier (1) [di'naiə], *s.* negador.
denier (2) ['deniə], *s.* dinero (*medida*).
denigrate ['denigreit], *v.t.* denigrar.
denigration [deni'greiʃən], *s.* denigración.
denim ['denim], *s.* dril de algodón.
denizen ['denizn], *s.* habitante; ciudadano, residente; (*for.*) extranjero naturalizado; voz naturalizada. — *v.t.* naturalizar.
Denmark ['denmɑːk]. Dinamarca.
denominate [di'nɔmineit], *v.t.* denominar.
denomination [dinɔmi'neiʃən], *s.* denominación; designación; título; secta; valor.
denominative [di'nɔminətiv], *a.* denominativo.
denominator [di'nɔmineitə], *s.* denominador; ***common denominator,*** denominador común.
denotable [di'noutəbl], *a.* capaz de ser notado.
denotation [diːno'teiʃən], *s.* denotación; significación; designación.
denote [di'nout], *v.t.* denotar; significar; designar, señalar.
denotement [di'noutmənt], *s.* denotación.
denouement [dei'nuːmɑ̃], *s.* desenlace.
denounce [di'nauns], *v.t.* denunciar; censurar.
denouncement [di'naunsmənt], [DENUNCIATION].
denouncer [di'naunsə], *s.* denunciador.
dense [dens], *a.* denso; espeso; cerrado, apretado, compacto, tupido; (*fam.*) estúpido, duro de mollera.
density ['densiti], *s.* densidad.
dent [dent], *s.* abolladura; mella. — *v.t.* abollar; mellar.
dental ['dentəl], *a.* dental, odontológico; ***dental surgeon,*** odontólogo.
dentate ['denteit], *a.* dentado; (*blas.*) dentellado, endentado.
denticle ['dentikl], *s.* dientecillo, dentículo.
denticulate [den'tikjulit], *a.* dentado, dentellado.
denticulation [dentikju'leiʃen], *s.* denticulación.
denticule ['dentikjuːl], [DENTICLE].
dentifrice ['dentifris], *s.* dentífrico.
dentil ['dentil], *s.* (*arq.*) dentículo, dentellón.
dentist ['dentist], *s.* dentista, *m.f.*, odontólogo.
dentistry ['dentistri], *s.* odontología.
dentition [den'tiʃən], *s.* dentición; dentadura.
denture ['dentʃə], *s.* dentadura; (*pl.*) dentadura postiza.
denudate ['denjudeit], *a.* desnudo; despojado. — *v.t.* desnudar.
denudation [denju'deiʃən], *s.* denudación; despojo.
denude [di'njuːd], *v.t.* denudar; despojar.

denunciate [di'nʌnsieit], *v.t.* denunciar.
denunciation [dinʌnsi'eiʃən], *s.* denuncia; denunciación.
denunciator [di:'nʌnsieitə], *s.* denunciador, denunciante.
deny [di'nai], *v.t.* negar; denegar; desmentir. — *v.i.* negar. — **deny o.s.,** *v.r.* negarse a sí mismo; privarse; ***deny o.s. to callers,*** negarse a recibir visitas.
deobstruct [di:əb'strʌkt], *v.t.* (*med.*) deobstruir.
deobstruent [di'ɔbstruənt], *a., s.* desobstruente.
deodorant [di:'oudərənt], *a., s.* desodorante.
deodorize [di:'oudəraiz], *v.t.* desodorizar.
deodorizer [di:'oudəraizə], *s.* aparato desodorizante.
deoppilate [di:'ɔpileit], *v.t.* (*med.*) desopilar.
deoxidize [di:'ɔksidaiz], *v.t.* (*quím.*) desoxigenar; desoxidar.
deoxidization [di:ɔksidai'zeiʃən], *s.* desoxigenación.
depart [di'pɑ:t], *v.i.* partir, salir, irse, marcharse; (*fig.*) fallecer; desviarse, apartarse; ***the departed,*** los difuntos. — *v.t.* abandonar; ***depart this life,*** abandonar este mundo.
department [di'pɑ:tmənt], *s.* departamento, sección, subdivisión; ramo; despacho; ministerio, negociado; distrito, provincia; ***department store,*** (grandes) almacenes.
departmental [di:pɑ:t'mentəl], *a.* departamental, de un ramo, negociado *o* departamento.
departure [di'pɑ:tʃə], *s.* marcha, salida, partida; fallecimiento; desviación; (*mar.*) diferencia de meridiano; ***new departure,*** rumbo nuevo, nueva orientación.
depauperate [di:'pɔ:pəreit], *v.t.* empobrecer, depauperar.
depauperation [di:pɔ:pə'reiʃən], *s.* empobrecimiento, depauperación.
depend [di'pend], *v.i.* pender, colgar; depender; ***depend on*** o ***upon,*** depender de; confiar en, contar con; ***it*** o ***that depends,*** depende, según (y conforme).
dependable [di'pendəbl], *a.* confiable, seguro, formal.
dependant [di'pendənt], *s.* dependiente; familiar; subalterno.
dependence [di'pendəns], *s.* dependencia; confianza; apoyo.
dependency [di'pendənsi], *s.* dependencia, posesión, colonia; pertenencia.
dependent [di'pendənt], *a.* dependiente, sujeto, subordinado, subalterno; contingente, condicional; necesitado; colgante, pendiente.
depending [di'pendiŋ], *a.* pendiente, colgante, dependiente; ***depending upon,*** según.
depersonalize [di:'pə:sənəlaiz], *v.t.* despersonalizar.
dephase [di:'feiz], *v.t.* (*elec.*) defasar.
depict [di'pikt], *v.t.* pintar, retratar, representar; describir.
depilate ['depileit], *v.t.* depilar.
depilation [depi'leiʃən], *s.* depilación.
depilatory [di'pilətəri], *a., s.* depilatorio.
deplete [di'pli:t], *v.t.* agotar; vaciar.
depletion [di'pli:ʃən], *s.* agotamiento; vaciamiento; (*med.*) depleción.
deplorable [di'plɔ:rəbl], *a.* deplorable, lamentable, lastimoso.
deplorableness [di'plɔ:rəblnis], *s.* estado deplorable; (lo) deplorable.
deplore [di'plɔ:], *v.t.* deplorar, lamentar, dolerse de.
deploy [di'plɔi], *v.t., v.i.* (*mil.*) desplegar(se).
deployment [di'plɔimənt], *s.* (*mil.*) despliegue.
deplumation [di:plu:'meiʃən], *s.* desplumadura.
deplume [di:'plu:m], *v.t.* desplumar.
depolarize [di:'pouləraiz], *v.t.* (*quím., fís.*) despolarizar.
deponent [di'pounənt], *a., s.* deponente; declarante.
depopulate [di:'pɔpjuleit], *v.t.* despoblar, deshabitar. — *v.i.* despoblarse.
depopulating [di:'pɔpjuleitiŋ], *a.* despoblador.
depopulation [di:pɔpju'leiʃən], *s.* despoblación, despueble.
deport [di'pɔ:t], *v.t.* deportar. — **deport o.s.,** *v.r.* portarse, conducirse.
deportation [di:pɔ:'teiʃən], *s.* deportación.
deportee [di:pɔ:'ti:], *s.* deportado.
deportment [di'pɔ:tmənt], *s.* porte; conducta, comportamiento, proceder.
deposal [di'pouzəl], *s.* deposición, destitución, degradación.
depose [di'pouz], *v.t.* deponer, destituir, derribar, destronar. — *v.i.* deponer.
deposer [di'pouzə], *s.* desposeedor; (*for.*) deponente.
deposit [di'pɔzit], *s.* depósito; sedimento, poso; yacimiento; señal; (*com.*) desembolso inicial. — *v.t.* depositar; sedimentar; dar como señal.
depositary [di'pɔzitəri], *s.* depositario; almacén, depósito.
deposition [di:pə'ziʃən], *s.* deposición; declaración.
depositor [di'pɔzitə], *s.* depositador; imponente.
depository [di'pɔzitəri], *s.* depósito, almacén.
depot ['depou], *s.* depósito, almacén; (*Am., f.c.*) [RAILWAY STATION].
depravation [deprə'veiʃən], *s.* depravación, perversión.
deprave [di'preiv], *v.t.* depravar, pervertir.
depravity, depravement [di'præviti, di'preivmənt], *s.* depravación.
deprecate ['deprikeit], *v.t.* desaprobar, censurar; lamentar.
deprecation [depri'keiʃən], *s.* desaprobación, censura.
deprecative, deprecatory ['deprikeitiv, -əri], *a.* reprobador, de desaprobación.
deprecator ['deprikeitə], *s.* crítico.
depreciate [di'pri:ʃieit], *v.t.* desestimar; abaratar. — *v.i.* bajar de precio, abaratarse.
depreciation [dipri:ʃi'eiʃən], *s.* depreciación; desestimación.
depreciatory [di'pri:ʃieitəri], *a.* despreciativo, despectivo.
depredate ['deprideit], *v.t.* depredar.
depredation [depri'deiʃən], *s.* depredación.
depredator ['deprideitə], *s.* depredador.
depredatory [di'predətəri], *a.* depredador.
depress [di'pres], *v.t.* deprimir; hacer bajar.
depressed [di'prest], *a.* deprimido, triste; ***depressed area,*** zona deprimida.
depressing [di'presiŋ], *a.* deprimente, triste.
depression [di'preʃən], *s.* depresión; abatimiento; crisis.
depressive [di'presiv], *a.* depresivo.
depressor [di'presə], *s.* depresor.
deprivable [di'praivəbl], *a.* amovible, separable.
deprivation [depri'veiʃən], *s.* privación; desposesión; pérdida.
deprive [di'praiv], *v.t.* privar, despojar, desposeer.
deprivement [di'praivmənt], [DEPRIVATION].
depth [depθ], *s.* profundidad, hondura; fondo; grueso, espesor; intensidad; (*mar.*) ***depth charge,*** carga de profundidad; ***in the depth of,*** en lo más recio de, en pleno; (*lit.*) ***to be out of one's depth,*** no hacer pie; (*fig.*) ***to get out of one's depth,*** meterse en muchas honduras.
depurate ['depjureit], *v.t.* depurar.
depuration [depju'reiʃən], *s.* depuración.
depurative [di'pjuərətiv], *a.* depurativo.
deputation [depju'teiʃən], *s.* delegación.
depute [di'pju:t], *v.t.* diputar, delegar.
deputy ['depjuti], *s.* diputado, delegado, comisario, comisionado, enviado, agente, lugarteniente;

deputy chairman, vice-presidente; ***deputy governor,*** teniente gobernador.
deracinate [di:ˈræsineit], *v.t.* desarraigar.
derail [diˈreil], *v.t., v.i.* descarrilar.
derailment [diˈreilmənt], *s.* descarrilamiento.
derange [diˈreindʒ], *v.t.* desarreglar; trastornar, perturbar.
deranged [diˈreindʒd], *a.* desarreglado; trastornado.
derangement [diˈreindʒmənt], *s.* desarreglo; trastorno (mental), desvarío.
Derby [ˈdɑ:bi], *s.* carrera de caballos; (*dep.*) encuentro entre dos equipos vecinos.
derby [ˈdə:bi], *s.* (*Am.*) [BOWLER (2)].
derelict [ˈderilikt], *a.* abandonado; desamparado; derrelicto. — *s.* (*mar.*) derrelicto.
dereliction [deriˈlikʃən], *s.* abandono; desamparo, dejación.
deride [diˈraid], *v.t.* ridiculizar, escarnecer, burlarse de, mofarse de.
derider [diˈraidə], *s.* escarnecedor, el que se burla *o* mofa.
deridingly [diˈraidiŋli], *adv.* con burla(s).
derision [diˈriʒən], *s.* irrisión, escarnio, burla, mofa.
derisive, derisory [diˈraisiv, -əri], *a.* irrisorio.
derivable [diˈraivəbl], *a.* derivable; deducible.
derivate [ˈderivit], *s.* derivado.
derivation [deriˈveiʃən], *s.* derivación; deducción, inferencia.
derivative [diˈrivətiv], *a.* derivativo. — *s.* derivado.
derive [diˈraiv], *v.t.* derivar, hacer derivar; obtener, sacar; deducir. — *v.i.* derivar(se); provenir, emanar.
derm [də:m], *s.* (*anat.*) dermis, *f.inv.*
dermal, dermic [ˈdə:məl, -ik], *a.* dérmico.
dermatography [də:məˈtɔgrəfi], *s.* dermatografía.
dermatoid [ˈdə:mətɔid], *a.* dermoide.
dermatologist [də:məˈtɔlədʒist], *s.* dermatólogo.
dermatology [də:məˈtɔlədʒi], *s.* dermatología.
dermatopathy [də:məˈtɔpəθi], *s.* dermatosis, *f.inv.*
derogate [ˈderogeit], *v.t., v.i.* derogar; detraer, detractar.
derogation [deroˈgeiʃən], *s.* derogación; detracción, menosprecio.
derogative [diˈrɔgətiv], [DEROGATORY].
derogatory [diˈrɔgətəri], *a.* despreciativo, despectivo.
derrick [ˈderik], *s.* grúa, cabria; cabrestante; torre de perforación.
dervish [ˈdə:viʃ], *s.* derviche.
descant [ˈdeskænt], *s.* (*mús.*) discante. — [desˈkænt], *v.i.* (*mús.*) discantar.
descend [diˈsend], *v.i.* descender, bajar; caer; rebajarse (a); ***to be descended from,*** descender de.
descendant [diˈsendənt], *s.* descendiente.
descendent [diˈsendənt], *a.* descendente.
descension [diˈsenʃən], *s.* descendimiento; descenso.
descent [diˈsent], *s.* descenso; descendimiento; descendencia; declive; (*for.*) herencia; (*mil.*) invasión.
describable [disˈkraibəbl], *a.* descriptible.
describe [disˈkraib], *v.t.* describir; ***to describe as,*** describir como; calificar de.
description [disˈkripʃən], *s.* descripción; género, clase, *f.*
descriptive [disˈkriptiv], *a.* descriptivo.
descry [disˈkrai], *v.t.* avistar, divisar, columbrar, alcanzar a ver.
desecrate [ˈdesikreit], *v.t.* profanar.
desecration [desiˈkreiʃən], *s.* profanación.
desegregate [di:ˈsegrigeit], *v.t.* (*pol.*) desegregar.
desegregation [di:segriˈgeiʃən], *s.* desegregación.
desert (1) [ˈdezət], *a.* desierto, yermo, despoblado, inhabitado. — *s.* desierto, yermo.
desert (2) [diˈzə:t], *v.t.* desamparar, abandonar; (*mil.*) desertar de. — *v.i.* (*mil.*) desertar.
desert (3) [diˈzə:t], *s.* merecido; ***to get one's (just) deserts,*** llevar su merecido.
deserter [diˈzə:tə], *s.* desertor, tránsfuga, *m.f.*
desertion [diˈzə:ʃən], *s.* deserción; abandono; defección.
deserve [diˈzə:v], *v.t.* merecer(se), ser *o* hacerse acreedor a, ser digno de, tener derecho a.
deservedly [diˈzə:vidli], *adv.* merecidamente; condignamente.
deserving [diˈzə:viŋ], *a.* meritorio; merecedor, acreedor, digno (***of,*** de).
deservingly [diˈzə:viŋli], *adv.* dignamente, merecidamente.
desiccant [deˈsikənt], *a., s.* desecante.
desiccate [ˈdesikeit], *v.t.* desecar, resecar.
desiccation [desiˈkeiʃən], *s.* desecación.
desiccative [deˈsikətiv], *a.* desecativo.
desiderate [diˈzidəreit], *v.t.* desear.
desideratum [dizidəˈreitəm], *s.* (*pl.* **desiderata** [-tə]) desiderátum.
design [diˈzain], *s.* diseño, dibujo; designio, intención, idea; ***by design,*** de intento, adrede; ***to have designs on,*** planear, proponerse algo contra; tenerle echado el ojo a; ***modern design,*** estilo moderno. — *v.t.* diseñar, dibujar; idear, proyectar, planear. — *v.i.* diseñar; proponerse, tener intención de.
designable [diˈzainəbl], *a.* que se puede dibujar *o* diseñar.
designate [ˈdezignit], *a.* titular. — [ˈdezigneit], *v.t.* señalar, designar.
designation [dezigˈneiʃən], *s.* designación; nombramiento; denominación.
designedly [diˈzainidli], *adv.* de propósito, adrede, aposta.
designer [diˈzainə], *s.* dibujante, diseñador, delineador; intrigante, proyectista, *m.f.*, maquinador.
designing [diˈzainiŋ], *a.* insidioso, traidor, astuto, intrigante. — *s.* dibujo.
designingly [diˈzainiŋli], *adv.* insidiosamente.
desinence [ˈdesinəns], *s.* desinencia.
desirable [diˈzaiərəbl], *a.* deseable, apetecible.
desirableness [diˈzaiərəblnis], *s.* (lo) deseable.
desire [diˈzaiə], *s.* deseo, anhelo; apetito. — *v.t.* desear, anhelar, apetecer, tener gana(s) de; rogar, suplicar.
desirous [diˈzaiərəs], *a.* deseoso, ansioso, ganoso; ***to be desirous,*** tener gana(s), estar deseoso.
desirousness [diˈzaiərəsnis], *s.* anhelo, deseo vivo.
desist [diˈzist], *v.i.* desistir (***from,*** de).
desistance [diˈzistəns], *s.* desistencia, desistimiento.
desk [desk], *s.* pupitre; escritorio, mesa, buró.
desolate [ˈdesəlit], *a.* desolado, desierto, despoblado, solitario. — [ˈdesəleit], *v.t.* desolar; asolar, devastar; entristecer.
desolately [ˈdesəlitli], *adv.* de un modo desolador.
desolateness [ˈdesəlitnis], *s.* desolación.
desolater, desolator [ˈdesəleitə], *s.* desolador; asolador.
desolation [desəˈleiʃən], *s.* desolación; soledad.
despair [disˈpɛə], *s.* desesperación; (*poet.*) desesperanza. — *v.i.* desesperar, desesperanzarse, perder la esperanza (***of,*** de).
despairing [disˈpɛəriŋ], *a.* desesperado, sin esperanza.
despairingly [disˈpɛəriŋli], *adv.* desesperadamente.
despatch [DISPATCH].
desperado [despəˈreidou], *s.* (*fam.*) forajido; bandido.
desperate [ˈdespərit], *a.* desesperado; grave; temerario.
desperately [ˈdespəritli], *adv.* desesperadamente; extremadamente, perdidamente, furiosamente.

desperateness [ˈdespəritnis], *s.* desesperación; temeridad; (lo) desesperado.
desperation [despəˈreiʃən], *s.* desesperación.
despicable [desˈpikəbl], *a.* despreciable, vil, ruin.
despicableness [desˈpikəblnis], *s.* bajeza, vileza.
despise [disˈpaiz], *v.t.* despreciar, menospreciar, desdeñar.
despiser [disˈpaizə], *s.* despreciador.
despisingly [disˈpaiziŋli], *adv.* desdeñosamente.
despite [disˈpait], *prep.* a pesar de, a despecho de, no obstante. — *s.* despecho.
despoil [disˈpɔil], *v.t.* despojar; robar.
despoiler [disˈpɔilə], *s.* despojador, robador, saqueador.
despoliation [despouliˈeiʃən], *s.* despojo.
despond [disˈpɔnd], *s.* desaliento. — *v.i.* desalentarse, abatirse.
despondence, despondency [disˈpɔndəns(i)], *s.* desaliento, abatimiento, melancolía.
despondent [disˈpɔndənt], *a.* desalentado, abatido, melancólico.
despot [ˈdespɔt], *s.* déspota, *m.*
despotic [desˈpɔtik], *a.* despótico.
despotism [ˈdespətizəm], *s.* despotismo.
despumation [despju:ˈmeiʃən], *s.* despumación.
desquamate [ˈdeskwəmeit], *v.i.* descamarse; exfoliarse.
desquamation [deskwəˈmeiʃən], *s.* descamación.
dessert [diˈzə:t], *s.* postre; ***dessert-spoon,*** cuchara de postre; ***dessert-wine,*** vino de Málaga.
destalinization [di:stɑ:linaiˈzeiʃən], *s.* (*pol.*) desestalinación.
destinate [ˈdestineit], *v.t.* destinar.
destination [destiˈneiʃən], *s.* destino.
destine [ˈdestin], *v.t.* destinar; consagrar, dedicar; ***to be destined to,*** haber de, estar llamado a.
destiny [ˈdestini], *s.* destino, sino, suerte.
destitute [ˈdestitju:t], *a.* indigente; desprovisto (de).
destitution [destiˈtju:ʃən], *s.* indigencia.
destroy [disˈtrɔi], *v.t.* destruir; aniquilar; acabar con; dar al traste con.
destroyable [disˈtrɔiəbl], *a.* destruible.
destroyer [disˈtrɔiə], *s.* destructor.
destructibility [distrʌktiˈbiliti], *s.* destructibilidad.
destructible [diˈstrʌktibl], *a.* destructible, destruible.
destruction [disˈtrʌkʃən], *s.* destrucción, ruina.
destructive [disˈtrʌktiv], *a.* destructivo, destructor; destrozón.
destructiveness [disˈtrʌktivnis], *s.* (lo) destructivo, (lo) destructor.
desuetude [ˈdeswitju:d], *s.* desuso.
desultoriness [ˈdesəltərinəs], *s.* (lo) esporádico *o* intermitente; (lo) parsimonioso.
desultory [ˈdesəltəri], *a.* esporádico, intermitente; parsimonioso.
detach [diˈtatʃ], *v.t.* separar, desprender; destacar.
detachable [diˈtætʃəbl], *a.* separable.
detachment [diˈtætʃmənt], *s.* desinterés; (*mil.*) destacamento; ***to view with detachment,*** considerar desinteresadamente *u* objetivamente.
detail [ˈdi:teil], *s.* detalle, pormenor. — [diˈteil], *v.t.* detallar, pormenorizar, particularizar; ***detail s.o. to do sth.,*** destacar *o* destinar a alguien a hacer algo.
detain [diˈtein], *v.t.* detener; retener, entretener; demorar, retardar.
detainee [di:teiˈni:], *s.* (*pol.*) detenido, recluido.
detainer [diˈteinə], *s.* (*for.*) detención, orden de arresto; detentador; retenedor.
detainment [diˈteinmənt], *s.* detención.
detect [diˈtekt], *v.t.* descubrir, averiguar; detectar.
detectable [diˈtektəbl], *a.* detectable.
detection [diˈtekʃən], *s.* averiguación; detección.
detective [diˈtektiv], *a.* de detective, policíaco; ***detective story,*** novela policíaca. — *s.* detective.
detector [diˈtektə], *s.* descubridor, averiguador; detector.
detent [diˈtent], *s.* retén; fiador, seguro; escape de un reloj.
détente [deiˈtɑ:nt], *s.* (*pol.*) distensión.
detention [diˈtenʃən], *s.* detención, arresto; retraso; retención.
deter [diˈtə:], *v.t.* disuadir.
deterge [dəˈtə:dʒ], *v.t.* deterger.
detergent [diˈtə:dʒənt], *a.*, *s.* detergente; detersivo, detersorio.
deteriorate [diˈtiəriəreit], *v.t.* deteriorar, desmejorar, empeorar. — *v.i.* deteriorarse, desmejorarse, empeorar.
deterioration [ditiəriəˈreiʃən], *s.* deterioro, deterioración, empeoramiento, desmejoramiento, menoscabo.
determent [diˈtə:mənt], *s.* impedimento, obstáculo; disuasión.
determinable [diˈtə:minəbl], *a.* determinable.
determinant [diˈtə:minənt], *a.*, *s.* determinante.
determinate [diˈtə:minit], *a.* determinado, definido; (*bot.*) ***determinate inflorescence,*** de inflorescencia limitida. — [diˈtə:mineit], *v.t.* limitar.
determination [ditə:miˈneiʃən], *s.* determinación, decisión, resolución; (*for.*) auto definitivo; (*lóg.*) especificación; (*med.*) congestión.
determinative [diˈtə:minətiv], *a.* determinativo.
determine [diˈtə:min], *v.t.* determinar, decidir. — *v.i.* determinarse, decidirse; ***he determined to go,*** determinó ir, se determinó a ir.
determined [diˈtə:mind], *a.* decidido, resuelto.
deterrent [diˈterənt], *a.* disuasivo. — *s.* (*fig.*) freno; amenaza; ***nuclear deterrent,*** fuerza disuasiva nuclear.
detersion [diˈtə:ʃən], *s.* (*med.*) detersión.
detersive [diˈtə:siv], *a.* detersivo, detersorio, detergente.
detest [diˈtest], *v.t.* detestar, abominar.
detestable [diˈtestəbl], *a.* detestable, aborrecible.
detestableness [diˈtestəblnis], *s.* (lo) detestable.
detestation [di:tesˈteiʃən], *s.* detestación, aborrecimiento.
dethrone [diˈθroun], *v.t.* destronar.
dethronement [diˈθrounmənt], *s.* destronamiento.
detonate [ˈdetoneit], *v.t.* hacer estallar *o* detonar. — *v.i.* detonar, estallar.
detonation [detoˈneiʃən], *s.* detonación.
detour [diˈtuə], *s.* rodeo; desvío.
detract [diˈtrækt], *v.t.* detraer, disminuir, quitar. — *v.i.* — ***from,*** quitar *o* restar valor, mérito *o* atractivo a.
detractingly [diˈtræktiŋli], *adv.* denigrativamente.
detraction [diˈtrækʃən], *s.* calumnia, denigración.
detractive [diˈtræktiv], *a.* denigrativo.
detractor [diˈtræktə], *s.* calumniador.
detractory [diˈtræktəri], *a.* denigrativo.
detrain [di:ˈtrein], *v.t.* (hacer) bajar de un tren. — *v.i.* bajar(se) del tren.
detriment [ˈdetrimənt], *s.* detrimento, perjuicio; ***to the detriment of,*** en detrimento de, en perjuicio de.
detrimental [detriˈmentəl], *a.* perjudicial.
detrition [diˈtriʃən], *s.* desgaste (*por frotamiento*).
detritus [diˈtraitəs], *s.* detrito.
detruncate [di:ˈtrʌŋkeit], *v.t.* destroncar.
detruncation [di:trʌŋˈkeiʃən], *s.* destroncamiento.
detrusion [diˈtru:ʒən], *s.* impulsión, empuje.
deuce [dju:s], *s.* diantre, demonio; dos; ***what the deuce?*** ¿qué diablos?
deuced [dju:st], *a.* (*fam.*) endiablado, maldito.
deuterogamist [dju:təˈrɔgəmist], *s.* deuterógamo.
deuterogamy [dju:təˈrɔgəmi], *s.* deuterogamia.
deuteropathy [dju:təˈrɔpəθi], *s.* deuteropatía.

devaluate [di:'væljueit], *v.t.* devaluar, desvalorizar.
devaluation [di:vælju'eiʃən], *s.* devaluación, desvalorización.
devastate ['devəsteit], *v.t.* devastar, asolar.
devastation [devəs'teiʃən], *s.* devastación, desolación.
develop [di'veləp], *v.t.* desarrollar, desenvolver; fomentar, explotar; urbanizar; (*foto.*) revelar. — *v.i.* desarrollarse; evolucionar; progresar, adelantar.
developer [di'veləpə], *s.* (*foto.*) revelador.
development [di'veləpmənt], *s.* desarrollo; evolución; progreso(s), adelanto(s); fomento, explotación; urbanización; (*foto.*) revelado; acontecimiento nuevo, novedad; ***development area,*** zona de desarrollo; ***development plan,*** plan de desarrollo.
devest [di'vest], *v.t.* (*for.*) privar de los bienes.
deviate ['di:vieit], *v.i.* desviarse.
deviation [di:vi'eiʃən], *s.* desviación, desvío; extravío; digresión; divagación.
device [di'vais], *s.* dispositivo, artefacto; recurso, ardid; divisa, lema; ***war device,*** ingenio bélico; ***to leave to one's own devices,*** abandonar a alguien a sus propios recursos, dejar que alguien se las bandee solo.
devil ['devəl], *s.* diablo, demonio; (*fam.*) arrojo, brío; ***the Devil!*** ¡demonio! ¡diablos!; ***between the devil and the deep blue sea,*** entre la espada y la pared; ***to give the devil his due,*** ser justo hasta con el diablo; ***poor devil,*** pobre diablo; ***talk of the devil!*** ¡en nombrando al ruin de Roma, luego asoma!; ***there'll be the devil to pay, they'll raise the (merry) devil,*** la van a armar, van a armarla gorda. — *v.t.* (*coc.*) asar con mucho picante.
devilish ['deviliʃ], *a.* diabólico, demoníaco.
devilishness ['dəvliʃnis], *s.* diablura; (lo) diabólico.
devil-may-care ['devəl-mei-kεə], *a.* ***devil-may-care attitude,*** postura de viva la Virgen.
devilment ['devəlmənt], *s.* diablura, pillería.
devilry ['devəlri], *s.* diablería, diablura; perversidad.
devious ['di:viəs], *a.* tortuoso; enrevesado, complicado, laberíntico.
deviously ['di:viəsli], *adv.* tortuosamente.
deviousness ['di:viəsnis], *s.* (lo) tortuoso; (lo) enrevesado.
devisable [di'vaizəbl], *a.* inventable, planeable; (*for.*) legable.
devise [di'vaiz], *s.* legado; bienes legados, *m.pl.* — *v.t.* proyectar, idear, inventar, discurrir; legar. — *v.i.* formar planes.
devisee [divai'zi:], *s.* legatario.
deviser [di'vaizə], *s.* inventor, autor; legador, testador.
devisor [di'vaizə], *s.* testador.
devitalize [di:'vaitəlaiz], *v.t.* desvitalizar.
devoid [di'vɔid], *a.* desprovisto, exento, falto.
devoir [də'vwɑ:], *s.* obsequio, homenaje.
devolution [di:və'l(j)u:ʃən], *s.* transferencia, transmisión; (*pol.*) delegación; (*for.*) devolución; derecho devoluto; (*biol.*) degeneración de especies.
devolve [di'vɔlv], *v.t.* transmitir, entregar, traspasar. — *v.i.* recaer; incumbir, tocar.
Devonian [di'vouniən], *a.*, *s.* devoniano, devónico.
Devonshire ['devənʃə], *a.* ***Devonshire cream,*** nata grumosa.
devote [di'vout], *v.t.* dedicar, consagrar. — **devote o.s.,** *v.r.* — **to,** dedicarse a, consagrarse a, entregarse a.
devoted [di'voutid], *a.* devoto, ferviente; leal; afecto, adicto.
devotedness [di'voutidnis], *s.* devoción; lealtad; afecto.
devotee [devo'ti:], *s.* devoto; adepto, adicto; aficionado.
devotion [di'vouʃən], *s.* devoción; dedicación.
devotional [di'vouʃənəl], *a.* devoto; piadoso, religioso.
devour [di'vauə], *v.t.* devorar(se).
devouring [di'vauəriŋ], *a.* devorante, devorador.
devout [di'vaut], *a.* devoto, piadoso, pío, religioso, fervoroso.
devoutness [di'vautnis], *s.* devoción, piedad.
dew [dju:], *s.* rocío; ***dew-bespangled,*** esmaltado de rocío. — *v.t.* rociar, refrescar. — *v.i.* rociar, formarse el rocío.
dewberry ['dju:bəri], *s.* (*bot.*) zarzamora.
dewdrop ['dju:drɔp], *s.* gota de rocío.
dewiness ['dju:inis], *s.* estado rociado.
dewlap ['dju:læp], *s.* papada de buey.
dew-worm ['dju:-wə:m], *s.* lombriz de tierra.
dewy ['dju:i], *a.* rociado; húmedo.
dexter ['dekstə], *a.* diestro; propicio.
dexterity [deks'teriti], *s.* destreza, maña, habilidad.
dexterous ['dekstrəs], *a.* diestro, mañoso, hábil.
dexterousness ['dekstrəsnis], *s.* destreza.
dextral ['dekstrəl], *a.* derecho; diestro.
dextrine ['dekstrin], *s.* (*quím.*) dextrina.
dextrose ['dekstrous], *s.* dextrosa.
dey [dei], *s.* dey.
diabetes [daiə'bi:ti:z], *s.* diabetes, *f.*
diabetic [daiə'betik], *a.*, *s.* diabético.
diabolic(al) [daiə'bɔlik(əl)], *a.* diabólico.
diabolicalness [daiə'bɔlikəlnis], *s.* (lo) diabólico.
diabolism [dai'æbəlizəm], *s.* diabolismo.
diachylon, diachylum [dai'ækilən, -ləm], *s.* diaquilón.
diacodium [daiə'koudiəm], *s.* diacodio.
diaconal [dai'ækənəl], *a.* diaconal.
diaconate [dai'ækənit], *s.* diaconato.
diacoustics [daiə'ku:stiks], *s.pl.* diacústica.
diacritical [daiə'kritikəl], *a.* diacrítico.
diadelphia [daiə'delfiə], *s.* (*bot.*) diadelfia.
diadem ['daiədem], *s.* diadema.
diæresis [dai'iərisis], *s.* diéresis, *f.*, crema.
diagnose [daiəg'nouz], *v.t.* diagnosticar.
diagnosis [daiəg'nousis], *s.* diagnosis, *f.*, diagnóstico.
diagnostic [daiəg'nɔstik], *a.*, *s.* diagnóstico.
diagonal [dai'ægənəl], *a.*, *s.* diagonal.
diagram ['daiəgræm], *s.* (*geom.*) diagrama, *m.*; esquema.
diagrammatic [daiəgrə'mætik], *a.* esquemático.
diagraph ['daiəgræf], *s.* diágrafo.
diagraphic(al) [daiə:græfik(əl)], *a.* diagráfico.
dial [daiəl], *s.* cuadrante; esfera; reloj; brújula; disco (*de teléfono*). — *v.t.*, *v.i.* (*tele.*) marcar; ***dialling tone,*** tono de marcar.
dialect ['daiəlekt], *s.* dialecto.
dialectic(al) [daiə'lektik(əl)], *a.* dialéctico.
dialectician [daiəlek'tiʃən], *s.* dialéctico.
dialectics [daiə'lektiks], *s.pl.* dialéctica.
dialogically [daiə'lɔdʒikəli], *adv.* en forma de diálogo.
dialogist [dai'ælədʒist], *s.* dialoguista, *m.f.*
dialogue ['daiəlɔg], *s.* diálogo. — *v.t.*, *v.i.* dialogar.
dialysis [dai'ælisis], *s.* diálisis, *f.*
dialytic [daiə'litik], *a.* dialítico.
diamagnetic [daiəmæg'netik], *a.*, *s.* diamagnético.
diameter [dai'æmitə], *s.* diámetro.
diametral [dai'æmitrəl], *a.* diametral.
diametrical [daiə'metrikəl], *a.* diametral; ***diametrically opposed to,*** diametralmente opuesto a.
diamond ['daiəmənd], *a.* diamantino. — *s.* diamante; brillante; losange; (*pl.*, *naipes*) oros; ***cut diamond,*** diamante tallado; ***rough diamond,*** diamante en bruto; ***diamond cutter,*** diamantista, *m.f.*; ***diamond jubilee,*** aniversario sexagésimo; ***diamond necklace,*** collar de diamantes; ***diamond wedding,*** bodas de diamante, *f.pl.*

diapason [daiə'peizən], *s.* diapasón.
diaper ['daiəpə], *s.* lienzo adamascado; (*Am.*) [NAPKIN]. — *v.t.* adamascar.
diaphanous [dai'æfənəs], *a.* diáfano.
diaphoretic [daiəfɔ'retik], *a.* diaforético.
diaphragm ['daiəfræm], *s.* diafragma, *m.*
diaphragmatic [daiəfræg'mætik], *a.* diafragmático.
diarist ['daiərist], *s.* diarista, *m.f.*
diarrhœa [daiə'riə], *s.* diarrea.
diarrhœic [daiə'riik], *a.* diarreico.
diarthrosis [daiɑː'θrousis], *s.* diartrosis, *f.inv.*
diary ['daiəri], *s.* diario, dietario.
diaspore ['daiəspɔː], *s.* diásporo.
diastase ['daiəsteis], *s.* diastasia.
diastole [daiə'stoul], *s.* diástole, *f.*
diastolic [daiə'stɔlik], *a.* diastólico.
diatomic [daiə'tɔmik], *a.* diatómico.
diatonic [daiə'tɔnik], *a.* diatónico.
diatribe ['daiətraib], *s.* diatriba.
dib [dib], *s.* (*ú. más en pl.*) tejo; taba; *s.pl.* (*fam.*) guita, parné.
dibble [dibl], *s.* plantador, almocafre. — *v.t.* plantar con plantador; escarbar. — *v.i.* sumergir.
dibstone ['dibstoun], *s.* tejo; taba.
dice (1) [dais], *s.pl.* dados, *m.pl.*, partida de dados; ***to load the dice,*** cargar los dados. [DIE (1)]. — *v.i.* jugar a los dados; ***dice with death,*** desafiar (a) la muerte.
dice (2) [dais], *v.t.* (*coc.*) cortar en cuadradillos.
dice-box ['dais-bɔks], *s.* cubilete de dados.
dicer ['daisə], *s.* jugador de dados.
dicey ['daisi], *a.* (*fam.*) aleatorio; dudoso; expuesto.
dichotomize [dai'kɔtəmaiz], *v.t.* separar *o* dividir en dos partes.
dichotomy [dai'kɔtəmi], *s.* dicotomía.
dichromatic [daikrou'mætik], *a.* dicromático.
dichromic [dai'kroumik], *a.* dicromático.
dick [dik], *s.* (*fam.*) policía, *m.*
dickens ['dikinz], *s.* (*fam.*) diantre.
dicker ['dikə], *v.i.* (*Am.*) [HAGGLE].
dickie-bird ['diki-bəːd], *s.* pajarito.
dicky (1) ['diki], *s.* (*fam.*) pechera postiza (de la camisa); asiento trasero, trasportín.
dicky (2) ['diki], *a.* (*fam.*) malucho, debilucho.
dicotyledon [daikɔti'liːdən], *s.* (*bot.*) dicotiledóneo.
dicotyledonous [daikɔti'liːdənəs], *a.* dicotiledóneo.
dictaphone ['diktəfoun], *s.* (*marca de fábrica*) dictáfono.
dictate ['dikteit], *s.* mandato, precepto. — [dik'teit], *v.t.*, *v.i.* dictar; mandar.
dictation [dik'teiʃən], *s.* dictado; ***to take dictation,*** escribir al dictado.
dictator [dik'teitə], *s.* dictador.
dictatorial [diktə'tɔːriəl], *a.* dictatorio, dictatorial.
dictatorship [dik'teitəʃip], *s.* dictadura.
dictatory [dik'teitəri], *a.* dictatorio, dictatorial.
diction ['dikʃən], *s.* dicción; estilo, lenguaje.
dictionary ['dikʃənri], *s.* diccionario, léxico.
dictograph ['diktogræf], *s.* (*marca de fábrica*) dictógrafo.
dictum ['diktəm], *s.* (*pl.* **dicta** [-tə]) sentencia, aforismo; dictamen judicial.
didactic [di'dæktik], *a.* didáctico.
didactics [dai'dæktiks], *s. pl.* didáctica.
didactylous, didactyl(e) [dai'dæktiləs, -il], *a.* (*zool.*) didáctilo.
diddle [didl], *v.t.* (*fam.*) embaucar, engañar, tomar el pelo a.
die (1) [dai], *s.* (*pl.* [DICE (1), (dais)]) dado (*para jugar*); cubito; suerte, azar; ***the die is cast,*** la suerte está echada.
die (2) [dai], *s.* (*pl.* **dies** [daiz]) (*arq.*) dado, neto; (*mec.*) estampa, troquel, cuño, matriz. — *v.t.* troquelar, estampar.
die (3) [dai], *v.i.* morir, fallecer, expirar; extinguirse; marchitarse; ***die away*** o ***out,*** desvanecerse; irse extinguiendo; ***die hard,*** resistirse a morir; ser difícil de suprimir, vencer; ***never say die,*** no rendirse; no hay que desanimarse; ***be dying for*** o ***to,*** morirse de ganas de; ***die with one's boots on,*** morir con las botas puestas.
diesis ['daiisis], *s.* (*mús.*) diesi, *f.*
diet ['daiət], *s.* dieta; régimen; ***to put on a diet,*** poner a régimen; ***to be on a diet*** [DIET, *v.i.*]. — *v.i.* hacer (un) régimen, estar a régimen.
dietary ['daiətəri], *a.* dietético.
dietetic(al) [daiə'tetik(əl)], *a.* dietético.
dietetics [daiə'tetiks], *s.pl.* dietética.
dietician [daiə'tiʃən], *s.* dietético.
differ ['difə], *v.i.* diferenciarse, distinguirse; diferir; disentir, discrepar; ***differ from,*** diferir de.
difference ['difərəns], *s.* diferencia; discrepancia; ***he doesn't know the difference,*** no se da cuenta (de que no es lo mismo), se cree que da igual; ***it makes no difference,*** lo mismo da, da lo mismo, igual da, da igual; ***what difference does it make?*** ¿qué más da?; ***to split the difference,*** partir la diferencia.
different ['difərənt], *a.* distinto, diferente; ***different from,*** diferente de.
differential [difə'renʃəl], *a.* diferencial. — *s.* diferencial, *f.*
differentiate [difə'renʃieit], *v.t.* diferenciar, distinguir. — *v.i.* distinguir (***between,*** entre).
differing ['difəriŋ], *a.* diverso, distinto; encontrado, opuesto.
difficult ['difikəlt], *a.* difícil; dificultoso.
difficulty ['difikəlti], *s.* dificultad; ***to be in difficulties,*** verse apurado, en un apuro *o* aprieto; ***to make difficulties for,*** crear dificultades para *o* a.
diffidence ['difidəns], *s.* timidez, cortedad.
diffident ['difidənt], *a.* tímido, corto.
diffluent ['difluənt], *a.* difluente.
diffraction [di'frækʃən], *s.* difracción.
diffuse [di'fjuːs], *a.* difuso. — [di'fjuːz], *v.t.* difundir, esparcir. — *v.i.* difundirse, esparcirse.
diffusedly [di'fjuːzidli], *adv.* difusamente.
diffusedness [di'fjuːzidnis], *s.* (lo) difuso.
diffusible [di'fjuːzibl], *a.* difusible.
diffusion [di'fjuːʒən], *s.* difusión.
diffusive [di'fjuːsiv], *a.* difusivo; difuso.
dig [dig], *s.* empujón, codazo; pulla. — *irr. v.t.* cavar; excavar; sacar, extraer, minar; escarbar; ***dig up,*** desarraigar; descubrir. — *v.i.* cavar; excavar; escarbar; (*mil.*) ***dig in,*** atrincherarse; ***dig into,*** emplearse en; ***dig deeply,*** profundizar.
digastric [dai'gæstrik], *a.* digástrico.
digest ['daidʒest], *s.* (*for.*) digesto; resumen, compendio. — [di'dʒest], *v.t.* digerir; resumir, compendiar. — *v.i.* digerir.
digester [di'dʒestə], *s.* digeridor, digestor.
digestibility [didʒesti'biliti], *s.* digestibilidad.
digestible [di'dʒestibl], *a.* digerible, digestible.
digestion [di'dʒestʃən], *s.* digestión.
digestive [di'dʒestiv], *a.* digestivo.
digger (1) ['digə], *s.* cavador; azada; cavadora.
digger (2) ['digə], *s.* (*Australia, fam.*) tío, tipo.
digging ['digiŋ], *s.* cava; (*pl.*) excavaciones, *f.pl.*
dight [dait], *a.* adornado, embellecido. — *v.t.* adornar, embellecer.
digit ['didʒit], *s.* dedo; dígito; cifra.
digital ['didʒitəl], *a.* digital, dactilar. — *s.* tecla (*de órgano*).
digitalis [didʒi'teilis], *s.* (*bot.*) digital, *f.*, dedalera.
digitated ['didʒiteitid], *a.* digitado.
diglyph ['daiglif], *s.* (*arq.*) diglifo.
dignified ['dignifaid], *a.* digno; grave, solemne; majestuoso; decoroso.
dignify ['dignifai], *v.t.* dignificar; enaltecer, honrar.
dignitary ['dignitəri], *s.* dignatario; dignidad.

dignity [ˈdigniti], *s.* dignidad; elevación; rango: ***to stand on one's dignity,*** adoptar una postura orgullosa, andarse con solemnidades.
digress [daiˈgres], *v.i.* hacer digresión, divagar.
digression [daiˈgreʃən], *s.* digresión, divagación.
digressional [daiˈgreʃənəl], *a.* divagatorio; secundario, accesorio.
digressive [daiˈgresiv], *a.* digresivo, discursivo.
digs [digz], *s.pl.* (*abrev.* **diggings**) (*fam.*) pensión.
dihedral [daiˈhi:drəl], *a.* (*geom.*) diedro.
dijudication [daidʒu:diˈkeiʃən], *s.* juicio decisivo.
dike [daik], *s.* dique; canal, acequia; contraveta. — *v.t.* contener (*con diques*); avenar, desaguar.
dilacerate [daiˈlæsəreit], *v.t.* dilacerar; desgarrar.
dilaceration [dailæsəˈreiʃən], *s.* dilaceración; desgarramiento.
dilapidate [diˈlæpideit], *v.t.* desmantelar, desmoronar. — *v.i.* desmantelarse, desmoronarse.
dilapidated [diˈlæpideitid], *a.* desvencijado; ruinoso, desmoronado.
dilapidation [dilæpiˈdeiʃən], *s.* desvencijamiento; estado ruinoso.
dilatability [daileitəˈbiliti], *s.* dilatabilidad.
dilatable [daiˈleitəbl], *a.* dilatable.
dilatant [daiˈleitənt], *a.*, *s.* dilatador.
dilatation [daileiˈteiʃən], *s.* dilatación.
dilate [daiˈleit], *v.t.* dilatar; extender, alargar, amplificar. — *v.i.* dilatarse; extenderse.
dilated [daiˈleitid], *a.* difuso, prolijo; *p.p.* [DILATE].
dilator [diˈleitə], *s.* (*med.*) dilatador.
dilatorily [ˈdilətrəli], *adv.* lentamente; detenidamente; con retardo.
dilatoriness [ˈdilətrinis], *s.* tardanza; lentitud; morosidad.
dilatory [ˈdilətri], *a.* tardo; lento; perezoso; pesado; (*for.*) dilatorio.
dilemma [diˈlemə], *s.* dilema, *m.*; ***to be in a dilemma,*** estar en un dilema.
dilettante [diliˈtænti], *s.* aficionado, diletante.
diligence [ˈdilidʒəns], *s.* diligencia, asiduidad.
diligent [ˈdilidʒənt], *a.* diligente, asiduo.
dill [dil], *s.* (*bot.*) eneldo.
dilly-dally [ˈdili-ˈdæli], *v.i.* entretenerse en tonterías.
dilucid [daiˈl(j)u:sid], *a.* lúcido, diáfano.
diluent [ˈdiljuənt], *a.*, *s.* diluente.
dilute [daiˈl(j)u:t], *a.* diluido. — *v.t.* diluir; deshacer, disolver.
dilution [daiˈl(j)u:ʃən], *s.* dilución.
diluvial, diluvian [daiˈl(j)u:viəl, -iən], *a.* diluviano.
diluvium [daiˈl(j)u:viəm], *s.* (*geol.*) diluvio.
dim [dim], *a.* débil, tenue, mortecino; opaco; poco claro, confuso, indistinto; lento, lerdo. — *v.t.* amortiguar; poner a media luz; oscurecer; empañar.
dime [daim], *s.* (*Am.*) 10 centavos.
dimension [diˈmenʃən], *s.* dimensión.
dimidiate [diˈmidieit], *v.t.* dimidiar.
diminish [diˈminiʃ], *v.t.* disminuir. — *v.i.* disminuir(se).
diminishing [diˈminiʃiŋ], *a.* que va en disminución; ***law of diminishing returns,*** ley del rendimiento descendente.
diminution [dimiˈnju:ʃən], *s.* disminución.
diminutive [diˈminjutiv], *a.*, *s.* diminutivo; diminuto.
diminutiveness [diˈminjutivnis], *s.* (lo) diminuto.
dimissory [ˈdimisəri], *a.* dimisorio.
dimity [ˈdimiti], *s.* fustán.
dimness [ˈdimnis], *s.* (lo) débil *etc.*
dimorphism [daiˈmɔ:fizəm], *s.* dimorfismo.
dimorphous [daiˈmɔ:fəs], *a.* dimorfo.
dimple [dimpl], *s.* hoyuelo. — *v.i.* formarse hoyuelos (en).
dimpled, dimply [dimpld, ˈdimpli], *a.* que tiene hoyuelos.
dim-sighted [ˈdim-ˈsaitid], *a.* cegato.
dim-witted [ˈdim-ˈwitid], *a.* (*fam.*) lerdo, necio.
din [din], *s.* estruendo, ruidazo; barahúnda. — *v.t.* ensordecer, asordar, aturdir; ***din sth. into s.o.,*** machacarle algo a alguien.
dine [dain], *v.t.* dar de cenar *o* almorzar a, convidar. — *v.i.* cenar; almorzar; ***dine out,*** cenar, almorzar en la calle.
diner [ˈdainə], *s.* comensal; (*Am.*) [DINING CAR].
ding [diŋ], *v.i.* (re)sonar, repicar.
ding-dong [ˈdiŋ-ˈdɔŋ], *s.* din-dán, tintín, repique; ***ding-dong contest,*** concurso, certamen reñido.
dinghy, dingey [ˈdiŋgi], *s.* bote.
dinginess [ˈdindʒinis], *s.* (lo) oscuro y tétrico.
dingle [diŋgl], *s.* vallecito.
dingy [ˈdindʒi], *a.* oscuro, sombrío, empañado; tétrico, tristón.
dining [ˈdainiŋ], *a.* de la comida; ***dining-car,*** coche-comedor; ***dining-hall,*** refectorio; ***dining-room,*** comedor; ***dining-table,*** mesa de comedor. — *s.* (el) comer, comida.
dinner [ˈdinə], *s.* cena; almuerzo; ***dinner-jacket,*** esmoquin; ***dinner-napkin,*** servilleta; ***dinner-party,*** convite; ***dinner-service,*** vajilla; ***dinner-time,*** hora de comer.
dinosaur [ˈdainəsɔ:], *s.* dinosaurio.
dint [dint], *s.* marca; ***by dint of,*** a fuerza de.
diocesan [daiˈɔsisən], *a.*, *s.* diocesano.
diocese [ˈdaiəsis], *s.* diócesis, *f.*
dioptric(al) [daiˈɔptrik(əl)], *a.* dióptrico.
dioptrics [daiˈɔptriks], *s.pl.* dióptrica.
diorama [daioˈrɑ:mə], *s.* diorama, *m.*
dioramic [daioˈræmik], *a.* diorámico.
dioxide [daiˈɔksaid], *s.* dióxido.
dip [dip], *s.* zambullida; inmersión; caída; pendiente; grado de inclinación; baño; (*geol.*) buzamiento; (*mec.*) cuchara (de lubricación). — *v.t.* zambullir, sumergir; bañar, mojar; sacar, achicar; (*aut.*) bajar, bascular (faros); ***dip the flag,*** batir banderas. — *v.i.* zambullirse, sumergirse; meter la cuchara; bajar, hundirse; (*geol.*) buzar; meterse; ***dip into a book,*** hojear un libro.
dipetalous [daiˈpetələs], *a.* dipétalo.
diphtheria [difˈθiəriə], *s.* difteria.
diphtheritic [difθəˈritik], *a.* diftérico.
diphtheritis [difθəˈraitis], *s.* difteritis, *f.inv.*
diphthong [ˈdifθɔŋ], *s.* diptongo.
diphthongize [ˈdifθɔŋgaiz], *v.t.* diptongar. — *v.i.* diptongarse.
diplograph [ˈdiplogræf], *s.* diplógrafo.
diploma [diˈploumə], *s.* diploma, *m.*
diplomacy [diˈplouməsi], *s.* diplomacia; diplomática.
diplomat [ˈdiplomæt], *s.* diplomático.
diplomatic [diploˈmætik], *a.* diplomático; ***diplomatic cold,*** resfriado de circunstancias; ***diplomatic corps,*** cuerpo diplomático.
diplomatist [diˈploumətist], *s.* diplomático.
dipolar [daiˈpoulə], *a.* que tiene dos polos.
dipper [ˈdipə], *s.* cucharón; (*orn.*) mirlo acuátilo; ***big dipper,*** montaña rusa.
dipping [ˈdipiŋ], *a.* que sumerge *o* zambulle; que inclina, de inclinación; ***dipping needle,*** aguja magnética. — *s.* inmersión; inclinación.
dipsomania [dipsoˈmeiniə], *s.* dipsomanía.
dipsomaniac [dipsoˈmeiniæk], *a.* dipsomaníaco. — *s.* dipsómano, dipsomaníaco.
dipstick [ˈdipstik], *s.* varilla del aceite.
dipterous [ˈdiptərəs], *a.* (*ent.*) díptero.
diptych [ˈdiptik], *s.* díptica.
dire [daiə], *a.* horrendo, espantoso; de mal agüero.
direct [diˈrekt], *a.* directo; claro, franco; ***direct hit,*** impacto directo; ***direct object,*** objeto *o* complemento directo; ***direct speech,*** discurso directo. — *v.t.* dirigir; ordenar, mandar.

direction [di'rekʃən], *s.* dirección; instrucción; (*pl.*) modo de empleo; ***direction-finder,*** radiogeniómetro.
directive [di'rektiv], *a.* directivo. — *s.* instrucción, orden.
directly [di'rektli], *adv.* directamente, en línea recta; inmediatamente, al instante, enseguida; precisamente, exactamente; con franqueza.
directness [di'rektnis], *s.* franqueza.
director [di'rektə], *s.* director; jefe; ***board of directors,*** consejo de administración, junta directiva.
directorial [dairek'tɔ:riəl], *a.* directorio, directorial, directivo.
directorship [di'rektəʃip], *s.* cargo de director.
directory [di'rektəri], *s.* directorio; guía; (*igl.*) añalejo; ***telephone directory,*** guía telefónica; ***trade directory,*** guía comercial.
directress [di'rektris], *s.* directora.
direful ['daiəful], *a.* tremebundo, horrendo.
direness, direfulness ['daiənis, -fulnis], *s.* horror, espanto.
dirge [də:dʒ], *s.* canto fúnebre; endecha, treno; elegía.
dirigible ['diridʒibl], *s.* dirigible.
dirk [də:k], *s.* daga, puñal.
dirt [də:t], *s.* suciedad, mugre, *f.*; barro; polvo; tierra; obscenidad; (*fam.*) ***dirt-cheap,*** tirado; ***dirt-track,*** pista de ceniza; ***to fling dirt at,*** calumniar; ***to treat like dirt,*** tratar a patadas.
dirtiness ['də:tinis], *s.* suciedad, mugre, *f.*; indecencia, obscenidad.
dirty ['də:ti], *a.* sucio, mugriento; manchado; obsceno, indecente; ***dirty trick,*** mala partida; ***dirty weather,*** tiempo infame. — *v.t.* ensuciar, enlodar, manchar.
disability [dísə'biliti], *s.* incapacidad; desventaja; impedimento.
disable [dis'eibl], *v.t.* mutilar; inhabilitar, inutilizar, incapacitar, imposibilitar; desmantelar, desaparejar.
disabled [dis'eibld], *a.*, *s.* inválido, mutilado.
disablement [dis'eiblmənt], *s.* invalidez, mutilación; inhabilitación.
disabuse [disə'bju:z], *v.t.* desengañar.
disaccord [disə'kɔ:d], *s.* desacuerdo, desavenencia. — *v.i.* discordar.
disaccustom [disə'kʌstəm], *v.t.* desacostumbrar.
disadjust [disə'dʒʌst], *v.t.* desarreglar.
disadvantage [disæd'vɑ:ntidʒ], *s.* desventaja; ***to be at a disadvantage,*** encontrarse en (una) situación desventajosa. — *v.t.* dañar, perjudicar.
disadvantageous [disædvən'teidʒəs], *a.* desventajoso.
disaffect [disə'fekt], *v.t.* malquistar.
disaffected [disə'fektid], *a.* desafecto.
disaffectedly [disə'fektidli], *adv.* con desafecto.
disaffection [disə'fekʃən], *s.* desafecto, desamor; malquerencia; descontento.
disagree [disə'gri:], *v.i.* disentir, discrepar; desavenirse; estar en desacuerdo; altercar; sentar mal (***with,*** a); ***I disagree with you,*** no estoy de acuerdo con usted, discrepamos.
disagreeable [disə'gri:əbl], *a.* desagradable; desabrido.
disagreeableness [disə'gri:əblnis], *s.* (lo) desagradable; desabrimiento.
disagreement [disə'gri:mənt], *s.* discrepancia, discordia, desacuerdo, disconformidad; desavenencia; altercado.
disallow [disə'lau], *v.t.* denegar, no admitir; anular (*un gol*).
disallowance [disə'lauəns], *s.* denegación.
disanimate [dis'ænimeit], *v.t.* desanimar.
disanimation [disæni'meiʃən], *s.* desaliento.
disappear [disə'piə], *v.i.* desaparecer.
disappearance [disə'piərəns], *s.* desaparición.
disappearing [disə'piəriŋ], *a.* que desaparece.
disappoint [disə'pɔint], *v.t.* decepcionar, desilusionar, defraudar, chasquear.
disappointing [disə'pɔintiŋ], *a.* decepcionante.
disappointment [disə'pɔintmənt], *s.* decepción, desilusión, desengaño, chasco; contrariedad.
disapprobation [disæpro'beiʃən], *s.* desaprobación.
disapprobatory [disæpro'beitəri], *a.* desaprobador.
disapproval [disə'pru:vəl], *s.* desaprobación.
disapprove [disə'pru:v], *v.t.* desaprobar, no aprobar. — *v.i.* — ***of,*** desaprobar.
disapprovingly [disə'pru:viŋli], *adv.* con desaprobación.
disarm [dis'ɑ:m], *v.t.* desarmar. — *v.i.* desarmarse.
disarmament [dis'ɑ:məmənt], *s.* desarmamiento, desarme.
disarmer [dis'ɑ:mə], *s.* desarmador.
disarming [dis'ɑ:miŋ], *a.* que desarma; que sabe congraciarse. — *s.* desarme; desarmadura.
disarrange [disə'reindʒ], *v.t.* desarreglar, descomponer, desordenar.
disarrangement [disə'reindʒmənt], *s.* desorden, desarreglo.
disarray [disə'rei], *s.* desorden, confusión; descompostura, desatavío. — *v.t.* desarreglar, desordenar; derrotar; desaliñar.
disarticulate [disɑ:'tikuleit], *v.t.* desarticular, descoyuntar. — *v.i.* desarticularse, descoyuntarse.
disassociate [disə'souʃieit], *v.t.* disociar. — **disassociate o.s.,** *v.r.* — ***from,*** desentenderse de, desligarse de.
disaster [di'zɑ:stə], *s.* desastre, catástrofe, siniestro.
disastrous [di'zɑ:strəs], *a.* desastroso, calamitoso; funesto.
disavow [disə'vau], *v.t.* negar, denegar; desaprobar, desconocer, desautorizar.
disavowal [disə'vauəl], *s.* denegación; retractación; repudiación.
disband [dis'bænd], *v.t.* licenciar; despedir; disolver. — *v.i.* dispersarse, desbandarse.
disbanding, disbandment [dis'bændiŋ, -mənt], *s.* licenciamiento; dispersión, desbandada.
disbar [dis'bɑ:], *v.t.* excluir del colegio de abogados; expulsar.
disbark [dis'bɑ:k], *v.t.* descortezar (*un árbol*).
disbelief [disbi'li:f], *s.* incredulidad, descreimiento.
disbelieve [disbi'li:v], *v.t.*, *v.i.* descreer, dudar.
disbeliever [disbi'li:və], *s.* incrédulo, descreído.
disbench [dis'bentʃ], *v.t.* desbancar.
disbud [dis'bʌd], *v.t.* desyemar.
disburden [dis'bə:dn], *v.t.*, *v.i.* descargar(se), aligerar(se).
disburse [dis'bə:s], *v.t.* desembolsar.
disbursement [dis'bə:smənt], *s.* desembolso.
disburser [dis'bə:sə], *s.* desembolsador.
disc [disk], *s.* disco; ***disc-brakes,*** frenos de disco, *m.pl.*; ***disc-harrow,*** grada de discos; ***disc-jockey,*** presentador de discos; ***to have a slipped disc,*** tener un disco descolocado.
discard [dis'kɑ:d], *s.* descarte; desecho. — *v.t.* desechar, descartar. — *v.i.* descartarse.
discern [di'sə:n], *v.t.* discernir, distinguir, percibir.
discerner [di'sə:nə], *s.* discernidor.
discernible [di'sə:nibl], *a.* discernible, perceptible, visible.
discerning [di'sə:niŋ], *a.* perspicaz, discernidor, de buen criterio.
discernment [di'sə:nmənt], *s.* discernimiento, criterio.
discharge [dis'tʃɑ:dʒ], *s.* descarga; descargo; desempeño; despedida; licenciamiento; (*med.*) supuración. — *v.t.* descargar; echar, despedir; (*mil.*) licenciar; (*med.*) dar de alta; (*deber etc.*) cumplir (con), desempeñar; (*med.*) sajar. — *v.i.* descargar; supurar.
discharger [dis'tʃɑ:dʒə], *s.* descargador.

disciple [di'saipl], *s.* discípulo.
discipleship ['disaiplʃip], *s.* discipulado.
disciplinable ['disiplinəbl], *a.* disciplinable.
disciplinarian [disipli'nɛəriən], *s.* ordenancista, *m.f.*
disciplinary ['disiplinəri], *a.* disciplinario.
discipline ['disiplin], *s.* disciplina; castigo; ***to enforce discipline,*** imponer una disciplina. — *v.t.* disciplinar; castigar.
disclaim [dis'kleim], *v.t.* negar, desconocer; (*for.*) denegar, renunciar a.
disclaimer [dis'kleimə], *s.* negación; (*for.*) renuncia.
disclose [dis'klouz], *v.t.* descubrir, revelar.
disclosure [dis'klouʒə], *s.* revelación.
discoidal [dis'kɔidəl], *a.* discoidal.
discoloration [diskʌlə'reiʃən], *s.* descoloración, descoloramiento.
discolour [dis'kʌlə], *v.t.* descolorar, manchar.
discomfit [dis'kʌmfit], *v.t.* derrotar; desazonar; desconcertar.
discomfiture [dis'kʌmfitʃə], *s.* desazón; desconcierto; derrota.
discomfort [dis'kʌmfət], *s.* incomodidad. — *v.t.* incomodar; desconsolar, desazonar.
discompose [diskəm'pouz], *v.t.* perturbar, descomponer, desconcertar.
discomposure [diskəm'pouʒə], *s.* descomposición, descompostura, agitación.
disconcert [diskən'sə:t], *v.t.* desconcertar.
disconcerting [diskən'sə:tiŋ], *a.* desconcertante.
disconnect [diskə'nekt], *v.t.* desunir; separar; desacoplar; desconectar.
disconnection [diskə'nekʃən], *s.* desunión, separación, desconexión.
disconsolate [dis'kɔnsəlit], *a.* desconsolado.
disconsolateness [dis'kɔnsəlitnis], *s.* desconsuelo, desconsolación.
discontent [diskən'tent], *a.*, *s.* descontento. — *v.t.* descontentar.
discontented [diskən'tentid], *a.* descontento.
discontentedly [diskən'tentidli], *adv.* de mala gana.
discontentedness, discontentment [diskən'tentidnis, -mənt], *s.* descontento.
discontinuance, discontinuation [diskən'tinjuəns, diskəntinju'eiʃən], *s.* discontinuación, interrupción; suspensión.
discontinue [diskən'tinju:], *v.t.*, *v.i.* discontinuar, interrumpir; dejar de; suspender.
discontinuity [diskɔnti'nju:iti], *s.* discontinuidad, solución de continuidad.
discontinuous [diskən'tinjuəs], *a.* discontinuo.
discord ['diskɔ:d], *s.* discordia; desavenencia. — [dis'kɔ:d], *v.i.* discordar.
discordance, discordancy [dis'kɔ:dəns, -i], *s.* discordancia, disensión; disonancia.
discordant [dis'kɔ:dənt], *a.* discorde; discordante, disonante.
discount ['diskaunt], *s.* descuento; rebaja; ***at a discount,*** al descuento; ***to be at a discount,*** no valorarse en su justo precio. — [dis'kaunt], *v.t.* descontar; rebajar; desestimar.
discountable [dis'kauntəbl], *a.* descontable.
discountenance [dis'kauntənəns], *s.* desaprobación. — *v.t.* desaprobar; desconcertar, turbar, avergonzar.
discounter [dis'kauntə], *s.* corredor de cambio.
discourage [dis'kʌridʒ], *v.t.* desalentar, desanimar; ***discourage from,*** disuadir de.
discouragement [dis'kʌridʒmənt], *s.* desaliento, desánimo; disuasión; desaprobación.
discourager [dis'kʌridʒə], *s.* desalentador, desanimador.
discourse ['diskɔ:s], *s.* discurso; disertación. — [dis'kɔ:s], *v.i.* discursar, discurrir; conversar.
discourser [dis'kɔ:sə], *s.* orador; conversador.
discourteous [dis'kə:tiəs], *a.* descortés, desatento.
discourtesy [dis'kə:tisi], *s.* descortesía, desatención.
discover [dis'kʌvə], *v.t.* descubrir, revelar; manifestar.
discoverable [dis'kʌvərəbl], *a.* que se puede descubrir.
discoverer [dis'kʌvərə], *s.* descubridor.
discovery [dis'kʌvəri], *s.* descubrimiento; hallazgo; revelación.
discredit [dis'kredit], *s.* descrédito; desprestigio; ***to bring into discredit,*** desacreditar. — *v.t.* desacreditar; desprestigiar.
discreditable [dis'kreditəbl], *a.* deshonroso, vergonzoso, ignominioso.
discreet [dis'kri:t], *a.* discreto, prudente, mirado.
discreetness [dis'kri:tnis], *s.* discreción, prudencia.
discrepancy [dis'krepənsi], *s.* discrepancia.
discrepant [dis'krepənt], *a.* discrepante.
discrete [dis'kri:t], *a.* discreto.
discretion [dis'kreʃən], *s.* discreción, prudencia, miramiento; ***discretion is the better part of valour,*** lo prudente no quita lo valiente; ***at*** (***one's***) ***discretion,*** a discreción; ***age of discretion,*** edad de discreción, discernimiento.
discretional, discretionary [dis'kreʃənəl, -əri], *a.* discrecional.
discriminate [dis'krimineit], *v.t.*, *v.i.* discriminar; ***discriminate against,*** hacer distinciones en detrimento de, discriminar contra; ***discriminate between,*** distinguir entre.
discriminating [dis'krimineitiŋ], *a.* discernidor, perspicaz; de (buen) criterio.
discrimination [diskrimi'neiʃən], *s.* discernimiento, (buen) criterio; discriminación.
discriminatory [dis'krimineitəri], *a.* discriminatorio; parcial, injusto.
discrown [dis'kraun], *v.t.* destronar.
discursive [dis'kə:siv], *a.* discursivo; digresivo.
discursiveness [dis'kə:sivnis], *s.* ilación; (lo) digresivo.
discus ['diskəs], *s.* disco; ***discus-thrower,*** discóbolo.
discuss [dis'kʌs], *v.t.* comentar, hablar de, tratar de.
discussion [dis'kʌʃən], *s.* conversación; ***the question under discussion,*** el asunto en cuestión; la cuestión que se debate; ***to start a discussion,*** plantear una conversación.
disdain [dis'dein], *s.* desdén, desprecio, menosprecio. — *v.t.* desdeñar, despeciar, menospreciar.
disdainful [dis'deinful], *a.* desdeñoso.
disdainfulness [dis'deinfulnis], *s.* desdén, displicencia.
disease [di'zi:z], *s.* enfermedad, morbo. — *v.t.* enfermar, contagiar.
diseased [di'zi:zd], *a.* enfermo; morboso.
diseasedness [di'zi:zidnis], *s.* (lo) enfermo; (lo) morboso.
disembark [disem'bɑ:k], *v.t.*, *v.i.* desembarcar.
disembarkation [disembɑ:'keiʃən], *s.* desembarco; desembarque.
disembarrass [disem'bærəs], *v.t.* desembarazar.
disembodied ['disim'bɔdid], *a.* incorpóreo, separado del cuerpo; desbandado.
disembody ['disim'bɔdi], *v.t.* separar del cuerpo; (*mil.*) licenciar.
disembogue [disim'boug], *v.t.*, *v.i.* desembocar, desaguar.
disemboguement [disim'bougmənt], *s.* desemboque, desagüe, salida al mar.
disembowel [disim'bauəl], *v.t.* destripar.
disembroil [disim'brɔil], *v.t.* desembrollar, desenredar.
disenable [disi'neibl], *v.t.* incapacitar.
disenchant [disin'tʃɑ:nt], *v.t.* desencantar; deshechizar.
disenchanting [disin'tʃɑ:ntiŋ], *a.* desencantador.

disenchantment [disin'tʃɑ:ntmənt], *s.* desilusión, desencanto.
disencumber [disin'kʌmbə], *v.t.* desembarazar, descombrar.
disencumbrance [disin'kʌmbrəns], *s.* desembarazo.
disendow [disin'dau], *v.t.* desamortizar.
disendowment [disin'daumənt], *s.* desamortización.
disengage [disin'geidʒ], *v.t.* soltar, librar; desenganchar, desembarazar; (*com.*) desempeñar; (*mil.*) retirar. — *v.i.* (*com.*) desempeñarse; (*mil.*) retirarse.
disengaged [disin'geidʒd], *a.* desembarazado, suelto, libre; desunido; desocupado, vacante.
disengagement [disin'geidʒmənt], *s.* desunión; desempeño; retirada; desembrague.
disennoble [disin'noubl], *v.t.* degradar, envilecer.
disentangle [disin'tæŋgl], *v.t.* desenredar, desembrollar, desenmarañar.
disentanglement [disin'tæŋglmənt], *s.* desenredo, desembarazo.
disenthral [disin'θrɑ:l], *v.t.* emancipar, manumitir.
disenthralment [disin'θrɑ:lmənt], *s.* emancipación, manumisión.
disenthrone [disin'θroun], *v.t.* destronar.
disentitle [disin'taitl], *v.t.* privar de un título.
disentomb [disin'tu:m], *v.t.* exhumar, desenterrar.
disestablish [disis'tæbliʃ], *v.t.* secularizar.
disestablishment [disis'tæbliʃmənt], *s.* secularización.
disesteem [disis'ti:m], *s.* desestima, falta de aprecio. — *v.t.* desestimar, no apreciar.
disfavour [dis'feivə], *s.* disfavor; desaprobación; ***to fall into disfavour,*** caer en desgracia. — *v.t.* desfavorecer, desairar.
disfiguration, disfigurement [disfigjuə'reiʃən, dis'figəmənt], *s.* desfiguración, afeamiento.
disfigure [dis'figə], *v.t.* desfigurar, afear.
disfranchise [dis'fræntʃaiz], *v.t.* privar del derecho de ciudadanía.
disfranchisement [dis'fræntʃaizmənt], *s.* privación del derecho de ciudadanía.
disfrock [dis'frɔk], [UNFROCK].
disgorge [dis'gɔ:dʒ], *v.t.* vomitar, arrojar, desembuchar. — *v.i.* desembocar.
disgorgement [dis'gɔ:dʒmənt], *s.* vómito; devolución.
disgrace [dis'greis], *s.* vergüenza; deshonra, baldón; desgracia; ***what a disgrace!*** ¡qué vergüenza!; ***to fall into disgrace,*** caer en desgracia. — *v.t.* deshonrar, desacreditar.
disgraceful [dis'greisful], *a.* vergonzoso; deshonroso.
disgracefulness [dis'greisfulnis], *s.* vergüenza, deshonra; (lo) vergonzoso, (lo) deshonroso.
disgregation [disgri'geiʃən], *s.* disgregación.
disgruntle [dis'grʌntl], *v.t.* descontentar, enfadar, disgustar.
disgruntled [dis'grʌntld], *a.* descontento, disgustado, refunfuñador.
disguise [dis'gaiz], *s.* disfraz; ***it's a blessing in disguise,*** no hay mal que por bien no venga. — *v.t.* disfrazar; tapar, ocultar; ***disguise one's feelings,*** disimular los sentimientos; ***there is no disguising the fact,*** no hay que engañarnos, el hecho es que.
disgust [dis'gʌst], *s.* asco, aversión, repugnancia. — *v.t.* repugnar, dar asco a; ***I'm disgusted with him,*** me da asco, es asqueroso lo que ha hecho.
disgusting [dis'gʌstiŋ], *a.* repugnante, asqueroso.
dish [diʃ], *s.* plato; fuente; concavidad; ***to wash the dishes,*** fregar los platos; (*fam.*) ***she's a dish,*** es un bombón. — *v.t.* servir en plato; (*fam.*) fastidiar; ***dish up,*** servir, sacar; ***that's dished it!*** ¡estamos aviados!
dishabille [disə'bi:l], *s.* deshabillé, trapillo.
disharmony [dis'hɑ:məni], *s.* disonancia; discordia.
dish-cloth ['diʃ-klɔθ], *s.* paño de cocina.
dish-cover ['diʃ-kʌvə], *s.* cubreplatos, *m.inv.*
dishearten [dis'hɑ:tn], *v.t.* descorazonar, desanimar, desalentar.
dishevel [di'ʃevəl], *v.t.* desgreñar, desmelenar.
dishevelled [di'ʃevəld], *a.* despeinado; desaliñado.
dishful ['diʃful], *s.* plato lleno; (*fam.*) mujer que está como un tren.
dishonest [dis'ɔnist], *a.* fraudulento; no honrado.
dishonesty [dis'ɔnisti], *s.* fraude; falta de honradez.
dishonour [dis'ɔnə], *s.* deshonra, deshonor. — *v.t.* deshonrar; (*com.*) negarse a pagar *o* a aceptar (*un cheque*).
dishonourable [dis'ɔnərəbl], *a.* deshonroso, indigno.
dishorn [dis'hɔ:n], *v.t.* descornar.
dish-washer ['diʃ-wɔʃə], *s.* lavaplatos, *m.*; friegaplatos, *m.f.*
dish-water ['diʃ-wɔ:tə], *s.* lavazas, *f.pl.*; (*fam.*) ***the soup is like dish-water,*** esta sopa es un calducho.
disillusion [disi'l(j)u:ʒən], *s.* desilusión. — *v.t.* desilusionar.
disinclination [disinkli'neiʃən], *s.* desgana.
disincline [disin'klain], *v.t.* desinclinar; ***be disinclined to,*** estar poco dispuesto a.
disincorporate [disin'kɔ:pəreit], *v.t.* desincorporar.
disinfect [disin'fekt], *v.t.* desinfectar.
disinfectant [disin'fektənt], *a., s.* desinfectante.
disinfection [disin'fekʃən], *s.* desinfección.
disinfector [disin'fektə], *s.* desinfectador.
disingenuous [disin'dʒenjuəs], *a.* falso, disimulado, insincero; de dos caras.
disingenuousness [disin'dʒenjuəsnis], *s.* doblez, astucia, mala fe.
disinherit [disin'herit], *v.t.* desheredar, exheredar.
disinheritance [disin'heritəns], *s.* desheredación.
disintegrate [dis'intigreit], *v.t.* desintegrar, deshacer. — *v.i.* desintegrarse, deshacerse.
disintegration [disinti'greiʃən], *s.* desintegración.
disinter [disin'tə:], *v.t.* desenterrar, exhumar.
disinterest [dis'intrəst], *s.* desinterés; indiferencia; desventaja.
disinterested [dis'intrəstid], *a.* desinteresado; imparcial.
disinterestedness [dis'intrəstidnis], *s.* desinterés; imparcialidad.
disinterment [disin'tə:mənt], *s.* desenterramiento, exhumación.
disinvolve [disin'vɔlv], *v.t.* desenredar, desembrollar.
disjoin [dis'dʒɔin], *v.t.* desunir, separar. — *v.i.* desunirse, separarse.
disjoint [dis'dʒɔint], *v.t.* desunir, separar; dislocar, desquiciar, desencajar; desarticular, descoyuntar; trinchar.
disjointed [dis'dʒɔintid], *a.* dislocado, desarticulado; inconexo, incoherente.
disjointedness [dis'dʒɔintidnis], *s.* descoyuntamiento; incoherencia.
disjunct [dis'dʒʌŋkt], *a.* descoyuntado, dislocado.
disjunction [dis'dʒʌŋkʃən], *s.* disyunción, dislocación, descoyuntamiento.
disjunctive [dis'dʒʌŋktiv], *a.* disyuntivo.
disk [DISC].
dislike [dis'laik], *s.* antipatía. — *v.t.* tener antipatía a; ***I dislike driving,*** no me gusta conducir; ***I dislike him,*** me es antipático.
dislocate ['dislokeit], *v.t.* dislocar, descoyuntar.
dislocation [dislo'keiʃən], *s.* dislocación.
dislodge [dis'lɔdʒ], *v.t., v.i.* desalojar.
disloyal [dis'lɔiəl], *a.* desleal.
disloyalty [dis'lɔiəlti], *s.* deslealtad.
dismal ['dizməl], *a.* tristón, lúgubre, gris, tétrico; (*fam.*) ***dismal Desmond,*** pesimista, *m.f.*
dismalness ['dizməlnis], *s.* lobreguez; tristeza.

dismantle [dis'mæntl], *v.t.* desarmar; desmontar; desmantelar, desguarnecer; (*mar.*) desaparejar.
dismask [dis'mɑ:sk], *v.t.* desenmascarar.
dismast [dis'mɑ:st], *v.t.* desarbolar.
dismay [dis'mei], *s.* consternación. — *v.t.* consternar.
dismember [dis'membə], *v.t.* desmembrar.
dismemberment [dis'membəmənt], *s.* desmembramiento.
dismiss [dis'mis], *v.t.* despedir; destituir; licenciar; rechazar, desechar; dar permiso a (para irse); ***dismiss sth. from one's mind,*** rechazar una idea, echar de la cabeza una idea.
dismissal [dis'misəl], *s.* despedida; destitución; licenciamiento; rechazamiento; permiso (para irse).
dismount [dis'maunt], *v.t.* desmontar, desarmar; (*artill.*) desplantar. — *v.i.* desmontar, apearse.
disobedience [diso'bi:diəns], *s.* desobediencia, inobediencia.
disobedient [diso'bi:diənt], *a.* desobediente.
disobey [diso'bei], *v.t.* desobedecer.
disoblige [diso'blaidʒ], *v.t.* hacer un flaco servicio a.
disobliging [diso'blaidʒiŋ], *a.* desatento, poco servicial.
disorder [dis'ɔ:də], *s.* desorden; desarreglo; desconcierto; trastorno; alboroto, tumulto. — *v.t.* desordenar, desarreglar; trastornar.
disorderliness [dis'ɔ:dəlinis], *s.* desorden.
disorderly [dis'ɔ:dəli], *a.* desordenado; alborotador, escandaloso.
disorganization [disɔ:gənai'zeiʃən], *s.* desorganización.
disorganize [dis'ɔ:gənaiz], *v.t.* desorganizar.
disorientate [dis'ɔ:riənteit], *v.t.* desorientar.
disorientation [disɔ:riən'teiʃən], *s.* desorientación.
disown [dis'oun], *v.t.* desconocer; repudiar.
disparage [dis'pæridʒ], *v.t.* desacreditar; desdorar; menospreciar, hablar mal de.
disparagement [dis'pæridʒmənt], *s.* desdoro; menosprecio.
disparaging [dis'pæridʒiŋ], *a.* desfavorable; desdeñoso.
disparate ['dispərit], *a.* dispar.
disparity [dis'pæriti], *s.* disparidad.
dispart [dis'pɑ:t], *s.* vivo de un cañón; (*artill.*) ***dispart-sight,*** mira de un cañón. — *v.t.* despartir; separar, apartar, dividir. — *v.i.* partirse, dividirse, rajarse.
dispassionate [dis'pæʃənit], *a.* desapasionado; imparcial.
dispatch [dis'pætʃ], *s.* despacho; expedición, prontitud; consignación; ***dispatch-rider,*** correo de moto. — *v.t.* despachar; apresurar; concluir; expedir.
dispel [dis'pel], *v.t.* disipar, despejar, dispersar.
dispensable [dis'pensəbl], *a.* dispensable, prescindible.
dispensary [dis'pensəri], *s.* dispensario.
dispensation [dispen'seiʃən], *s.* dispensa; designio divino.
dispensator ['dispenseitə], *s.* dispensador.
dispensatory [dis'pensətəri], *a.* dispensativo, dispensador. — *s.* farmacopea.
dispense [dis'pens], *v.t.* dispensar; despachar, administrar; preparar (*una medicina, receta*); ***dispense from,*** eximir de. — *v.i.* — ***with,*** prescindir de.
dispenser [dis'pensə], *s.* dispensador; expendecuchillas, *m.f.inv.*
dispensing [dis'pensiŋ], *a.* dispensativo; ***dispensing chemist,*** farmacéutico; ***dispensing chemist's,*** farmacia.
disperse [dis'pə:s], *v.t.* dispersar; disipar. — *v.i.* dispersarse; disiparse.
dispersion [dis'pə:ʃən], *s.* dispersión; desviación; difusión.
dispersive [dis'pə:siv], *a.* dispersivo.
dispirit [dis'pirit], *v.t.* desanimar, desalentar, descorazonar.
dispiritedly [dis'piritidli], *adv.* con desaliento.
dispiritedness [dis'piritidnis], *s.* desaliento, desánimo.
displace [dis'pleis], *v.t.* sacar de su sitio; destituir; desplazar; ***displaced person,*** persona desplazada *o* expatriada.
displacement [dis'pleismənt], *s.* desplazamiento; destitución (***by,*** por.)
displant [dis'plɑ:nt], *v.t.* desplantar.
displantation [displɑ:n'teiʃən], *s.* desplantación.
display [dis'plei], *s.* despliegue; exhibición; manifestación; exposición, presentación; alarde; pompa; ***display cabinet,*** vitrina; ***display window,*** escaparate; ***on display,*** expuesto. — *v.t.* desplegar; exhibir; manifestar; exponer, presentar; lucir; (*mar.*) enarbolar (*el pabellón* o *la bandera*).
displease [dis'pli:z], *v.t.* desagradar, desplacer, disgustar.
displeased [dis'pli:zd], *a.* disgustado.
displeasing [dis'pli:ziŋ], *a.* desagradable.
displeasure [dis'pleʒə], *s.* desplacer, desagrado, disgusto.
displume [dis'plu:m], *v.t.* desplumar.
disport [dis'pɔ:t], **disport o.s.,** *v.r.* retozar, juguetear, expansionarse, esparcirse.
disposable [dis'pouzəbl], *a.* que se puede tirar.
disposal [dis'pouzəl], *s.* disposición; arreglo; eliminación, (acto de) deshacerse (de); ***at your disposal,*** a su disposición.
dispose [dis'pouz], *v.t.* disponer, arreglar; inducir, decidir (***to,*** a); ***to be disposed to,*** estar dispuesto a; ***to be well disposed towards,*** querer bien; tener buenas intenciones en relación con. — *v.i.* — ***of,*** deshacerse de, eliminar, liquidar; enajenar; disponer de; ***man proposes and God disposes,*** el hombre propone y Dios dispone.
disposition [dispə'ziʃən], *s.* disposición; natural, temperamento, carácter.
dispossess [dispə'zes], *v.t.* desposeer; desahuciar.
dispossession [dispə'zeʃən], *s.* desposeimiento, despojo; desahucio.
dispraise [dis'preiz], *s.* censura. — *v.t.* censurar.
disproof [dis'pru:f], *s.* refutación, confutación.
disproportion [disprə'pɔ:ʃən], *s.* desproporción. — *v.t.* desproporcionar.
disproportionate [disprə'pɔ:ʃənit], *a.* desproporcionado.
disproportionateness [disprə'pɔ:ʃənitnis], *s.* desproporción, (lo) desproporcionado.
disprovable [dis'pru:vəbl], *a.* refutable.
disproval [dis'pru:vəl], *s.* refutación.
disprove [dis'pru:v], *v.t.* refutar, confutar.
disputable [dis'pju:təbl], *a.* disputable, discutible.
disputant [dis'pju:tənt], *s.* disputador, controversista, *m.f.*
disputation [dispju'teiʃən], *s.* disputa, controversia.
disputatious [dispju'teiʃəs], *a.* disputador.
dispute [dis'pju:t], *s.* disputa, controversia; contienda; ***beyond all dispute,*** sin disputa *o* duda alguna; ***in dispute,*** disputado, discutido, cuestionado. — *v.t.*, *v.i.* disputar, discutir, cuestionar.
disputer [dis'pju:tə], *s.* disputador; controversista, *m.f.*
disqualification [diskwɔlifi'keiʃən], *s.* inhabilitación; incapacidad; descalificación.
disqualify [dis'kwɔlifai], *v.t.* inhabilitar; incapacitar; descalificar.
disquiet [dis'kwaiet], *s.* (*t.* ***disquietude*** [-tju:d]) inquietud, desasosiego. — *v.t.* inquietar, intranquilizar, desasosegar.
disquisition [diskwi'ziʃən], *s.* disquisición.

disregard [disri'gɑ:d], *s.* desatención; descuido, incuria; indiferencia (*for,* ante). — *v.t.* no hacer caso de, desatender, desoír; descuidar.
disrelish [dis'reliʃ], *s.* repugnancia, aversión; desabor. — *v.t.* repugnar, sentir aversión por.
disrepair [disri'pɛə], *s.* mal estado, deterioro; ***to be in disrepair,*** estar en mal estado, desvencijado, deteriorado.
disreputable [dis'repjutəbl], *a.* de mala fama, mal reputado; desacreditado, despreciable; vergonzoso.
disrepute [disri'pju:t], *s.* mala fama, descrédito; deshonra; ***to bring into disrepute,*** desacreditar.
disrespect [disri'spekt], *s.* desacato, falta de respeto. — *v.t.* desacatar, faltar al respeto a.
disrespectful [disri'spektful], *a.* irrespetuoso, desatento.
disrespectfulness [disri'spektfulnis], *s.* irreverencia.
disrobe [dis'roub], *v.t.* desnudar, desvestir. — *v.i.* desnudarse.
disroot [dis'ru:t], *v.t.* desarraigar.
disrupt [dis'rʌpt], *v.t.* romper, desbaratar; interrumpir, trastornar, desorganizar; alborotar.
disruption [dis'rʌpʃən], *s.* ruptura; trastorno, alboroto; desorganización.
disruptive [dis'rʌptiv], *a.* quebrantador; disruptivo.
dissatisfaction [dissætis'fækʃən], *s.* descontento; ***to spread dissatisfaction,*** sembrar el descontento.
dissatisfied [dis'sætisfaid], *a.* disgustado, descontento (***with, at,*** con).
dissatisfy [dis'sætisfai], *v.t.* descontentar, desagradar.
dissect [di'sekt], *v.t.* hacer la disección de, anatomizar.
dissection [di'sekʃən], *s.* disección, anatomía.
dissector [di'sektə], *s.* disector, disecador.
disseisin [dis'si:zin], *s.* despojo, usurpación.
disseisor [dis'si:zə], *s.* usurpador.
dissemble [di'sembl], *v.t.* disimular, encubrir. — *v.i.* disimular.
dissembler [di'semblə], *s.* disimulador, fingidor, hipócrita, *m.f.*
dissembling [di'semb'liŋ], *a.* disimulado. — *s.* disimulación, disimulo.
disseminate [di'semineit], *v.t.* diseminar; difundir, propagar.
dissemination [disemi'neiʃən], *s.* diseminación; difusión, divulgación.
disseminator [di'semineitə], *s.* propagador, diseminador.
dissension [di'senʃən], *s.* disensión, discordia.
dissent [di'sent], *s.* disensión, disentimiento, disidencia. — *v.i.* disentir, disidir, diferir.
dissenter [di'sentə], *s.* disidente.
dissentient [di'senʃiənt], *a.* disconforme, opuesto. — *s.* disidente.
dissenting [di'sentiŋ], *a.* disidente.
dissertation [disə:'teiʃən], *s.* disertación.
dissertator ['disəteitə], *s.* disertador.
disservice [dis'sə:vis], *s.* flaco servicio.
dissever [dis'sevə], *v.t.* desunir, separar.
dissident ['disidənt], *a., s.* disidente.
dissimilar [dis'similə], *a.* diferente, disímil.
dissimilarity, dissimilitude [dissimi'læriti, dissi'militju:d], *s.* disimilitud, disparidad.
dissimulate [di'simjuleit], *v.t., v.i.* disimular.
dissimulation [disimju'leiʃən], *s.* disimulación, disimulo.
dissipate ['disipeit], *v.t.* disipar; despilfarrar. — *v.i.* disiparse; entregarse a la vida disoluta.
dissipation [disi'peiʃən], *s.* disipación; despilfarro.
dissociate [di'souʃieit], *v.t.* disociar. — **dissociate o.s.,** *v.r.* hacerse insolidario (***from,*** de).
dissociation [disousi'eiʃən], *s.* disociación.
dissolubility [disɔlju'biliti], *s.* disolubilidad.
dissoluble [di'sɔljubl], *a.* disoluble.
dissolute ['disol(j)u:t], *a.* disoluto.
dissoluteness ['disol(j)u:tnis], *s.* (lo) disoluto.
dissolution [diso'l(j)u:ʃən], *s.* disolución.
dissolvable [di'zɔlvəbl], *a.* disoluble.
dissolve [di'zɔlv], *v.t.* disolver; deshacer; desleír. — *v.i.* disolverse; deshacerse; desvanecerse; ***dissolve into tears,*** deshacerse en lágrimas; ***dissolve into thin air,*** desvanecerse.
dissolvent [di'zɔlvənt], *a., s.* disolvente.
dissolver [di'zɔlvə], *s.* disolvente.
dissonance ['disənəns], *s.* disonancia.
dissonant ['disənənt], *a.* disonante.
dissuade [di'sweid], *v.t.* disuadir.
dissuasion [di'sweiʒən], *s.* disuasión.
dissuasive [di'sweisiv], *a.* disuasivo.
dissyllabic [DISYLLABIC].
distaff ['distɑ:f], *s.* rueca; ***on the distaff side,*** por parte de la mujer.
distance ['distəns], *s.* distancia; lejanía, lontananza; trecho; (*mús.*) intervalo; ***from a distance,*** desde lejos; ***in the distance,*** a lo lejos; ***to keep at a distance,*** mantener a distancia; ***to keep one's distance,*** mantenerse a distancia, guardar las distancias. — *v.t.* distanciar, espaciar.
distant ['distənt], *a.* distante, lejano; remoto; frío, reservado; ***to be distant with,*** tratar con frialdad *o* con indiferencia.
distantly ['distəntli], *adv.* a distancia, de lejos; reservadamente.
distaste [dis'teist], *s.* desagrado, disgusto.
distasteful [dis'teistful], *a.* desagradable.
distastefulness [dis'teistfulnis], *s.* (lo) desagradable.
distemper [dis'tempə], *s.* destemplanza; (*pat.*) moquillo; pintura al temple. — *v.t.* pintar al temple.
distemperature [dis'tempərətʃə], *s.* [DISTEMPER].
distempering [dis'tempəriŋ], *s.* pintura al temple.
distend [dis'tend], *v.t.* dilatar, distender. — *v.i.* dilatarse, distenderse.
distensible [dis'tensibl], *a.* dilatable.
distension [dis'tenʃən], *s.* dilatación, distensión.
distich ['distik], *s.* dístico.
distil [dis'til], *v.t., v.i.* destilar.
distillate ['distilit], *s.* destilado.
distillation [disti'leiʃən], *s.* destilación.
distillatory [dis'tilətəri], *a.* destilatorio.
distiller [dis'tilə], *s.* destilador.
distillery [dis'tiləri], *s.* destilería.
distinct [dis'tiŋkt], *a.* distinto; preciso, claro, definido, nítido; ***as distinct from,*** a diferencia de, en contraste con.
distinction [dis'tiŋkʃən], *s.* distinción; (*examen*) sobresaliente; ***to draw a distinction between,*** hacer una distinción entre.
distinctive [dis'tiŋktiv], *a.* distintivo, característico, personal.
distinctness [dis'tiŋktnis], *s.* distinción, clarida d nitidez.
distinguish [dis'tiŋgwiʃ], *v.t., v.i.* distinguir.
distinguishable [dis'tiŋgwiʃəbl], *a.* distinguible, perceptible.
distinguished [dis'tiŋgwiʃt], *a.* distinguido, señalado, caracterizado.
distinguishing [dis'tiŋgwiʃiŋ], *a.* distintivo.
distinguishment [dis'tiŋgwiʃmənt], *s.* distinción.
distort [dis'tɔ:t], *v.t.* deformar, falsear, tergiversar.
distorted [dis'tɔ:tid], *a.* deformado, falseado, tergiversado; torcido.
distortion [dis'tɔ:ʃən], *s.* deformación, falseamiento; distorsión.
distract [dis'trækt], *v.t.* distraer; aturdir, enloquecer.
distracting [dis'træktiŋ], *a.* que distrae.

distraction [dis'trækʃən], *s.* distracción; confusión, perturbación; locura; diversión, pasatiempo; ***to drive s.o. to distraction,*** volver loco, sacar de quicio.
distractive [dis'træktiv], *a.* perturbador.
distrain [dis'trein], *v.t., v.i.* (*for.*) embargar, secuestrar.
distrainable [dis'treinəbl], *a.* secuestrable.
distraught [dis'trɔ:t], *a.* agitado, perturbado, inquietísimo.
distress [dis'tres], *s.* dolor, pena, aflicción; angustia; apuro, peligro; (*for.*) embargo, secuestro; ***distress signal,*** señal de peligro *o* de socorro; (*mar.*) ***to put in in distress,*** entrar de arribada forzosa. — *v.t.* afligir, acongojar; angustiar; (*for.*) embargar, secuestrar.
distressful [dis'tresful], *a.* afligido, acongojado.
distressing [dis'tresiŋ], *a.* que da pena *o* tristeza.
distributable [dis'tribjutəbl], *a.* repartible.
distributary [dis'tribjutəri], *a.* distributivo.
distribute [dis'tribju:t], *v.t.* distribuir; repartir.
distributor, distributer [dis'tribjutə], *s.* distribuidor; repartidor; (*com.*) concesionario.
distribution [distri'bju:ʃən], *s.* distribución; reparto.
distributive [dis'tribjutiv], *a.* distributivo.
district ['distrikt], *s.* comarca, región; barrio, zona; jurisdicción; ***electoral district,*** distrito electoral; ***postal district,*** distrito postal.
distrust [dis'trʌst], *s.* desconfianza, recelo. — *v.t.* desconfiar de, recelar de.
distrustful [dis'trʌstful], *a.* desconfiado, receloso.
distrustfulness [dis'trʌstfulnis], *s.* desconfianza.
disturb [dis'tə:b], *v.t.* molestar, incomodar; distraer, interrumpir; desasosegar, inquietar; perturbar, trastornar; alborotar.
disturbance [dis'tə:bəns], *s.* disturbio; alboroto; desasosiego; trastorno.
disunion [dis'ju:niən], *s.* desunión.
disunite [disju'nait], *v.t.* desunir. — *v.i.* desunirse.
disunity [dis'ju:niti], *s.* desunión.
disusage [dis'ju:zidʒ], *s.* desuso.
disuse [dis'ju:s], *s.* desuso; ***to fall into disuse,*** caer en desuso.
disyllabic [disi'læbik], *a.* disílabo.
disyllable [di'siləbl], *s.* disílabo.
disyoke [dis'youk], *v.t.* desuncir.
ditch [ditʃ], *s.* zanja; (*carretera*) cuneta; (*mil.*) foso; ***to make a last-ditch stand,*** echar el resto; ***to the last ditch,*** hasta quemar el último cartucho. — *v.t.* (*fam.*) deshacerse de, liquidar, abandonar. — *v.i.* hacer (un) aterrizaje *o* amerizaje forzoso.
dither ['diðə], *s.* aturdimiento, azoramiento, azaramiento; ***to be in a dither, all of a dither,*** estar aturdido, azorado, azarado. — *v.i.* vacilar, titubear.
dithyramb ['diθiræmb], *s.* ditirambo.
dithyrambic [diθi'ræmbik], *a.* ditirámbico.
ditone ['daitoun], *s.* (*mús.*) dítono.
dittany ['ditəni], *s.* (*bot.*) díctamo, marrubio.
ditto ['ditou], *adv., s.* ídem.
ditty (1) ['diti], *s.* cancioncilla.
ditty (2) **bag, ditty box** ['diti bæg, 'diti bɔks], *s.* (*mar.*) bolsa *o* caja de hilos, agujas etc.
diuresis [daijuə'ri:sis], *s.* (*med.*) diuresis, *f.inv.*
diuretic [daijuə'retik], *a., s.* diurético.
diurnal [dai'ə:nəl], *a.* diurno, cotidiano, diario. — *s.* diurno, diurnal.
divagate ['daivəgeit], *v.i.* divagar.
divagation [daivə'geiʃən], *s.* divagación.
divan [di'væn], *s.* diván; ***divan bed,*** cama turca.
divaricate [dai'værikeit], *a.* divergente, bifurcado. — *v.t.* bifurcar. — *v.i.* bifurcarse.
dive [daiv], *s.* zambullida; buceo; sumersión, inmersión; (*natación*) salto; (*aer.*) picado; (*fam.*) antro. — *v.i.* zambullirse; sumergirse; bucear; (*aer.*) picar; enfrascarse; meterse (en).
dive-bomb ['daiv-'bɔm], *v.t.* bombardear en picado.
dive-bomber ['daiv-bɔmə], *s.* bombardero en picado.
divellent [dai'velənt], *a.* (*quím.*) dividente.
diver ['daivə], *s.* buzo; (*orn.*) somorgujo.
diverge [dai'və:dʒ], *v.i.* divergir, diferir, apartarse.
divergence, divergency [dai'və:dʒəns, -i], *s.* divergencia.
divergent [dai'və:dʒənt], *a.* divergente.
divers ['daivəz], *a.pl.* diversos, varios.
diverse [dai'və:s], *a.* diverso, distinto, diferente; multiforme.
diversification [daivə:sifi'keiʃən], *s.* diversificación; variación.
diversify [dai'və:sifai], *v.t.* diversificar; matizar. — *v.i.* mudar, cambiar.
diversion [dai'və:ʃən], *s.* diversión; desvío, desviación; ***to create a diversion,*** distraer *o* desviar la atención (de).
diversity [dai'və:siti], *s.* diversidad; variedad.
divert [dai'və:t], *v.t.* desviar; divertir.
diverting [dai'və:tiŋ], *a.* divertido.
divest [dai'vest], *v.t.* despojar, desnudar; (*for*) desposeer.
divestiture [dai'vestitʃə], *s.* despojo; (*for.*) desposeimiento.
dividable [di'vaidəbl], *a.* divisible.
divide [di'vaid], *s.* divisoria de aguas. — *v.t.* dividir, partir; ***divide out,*** repartir. — *v.i.* dividirse; (*pol.*) pasar a una *o* la votación.
dividend ['dividənd], *s.* dividendo.
divider [di'vaidə], *s.* partidor; repartidor, distribuidor; (*arit.*) divisor; (*pl.*) compás de división.
divination [divi'neiʃən], *s.* adivinación.
divinatory [di'vinətəri], *a.* divinatorio.
divine [di'vain], *a.* divino. — *s.* teólogo. — *v.t., v.i.* adivinar; alumbrar.
divineness [di'vainnis], *s.* divinidad; perfección.
diviner [di'vainə], adivino, augur; zahorí.
diving ['daiviŋ], *s.* buceo; ***diving-bell,*** campana de buzo; ***diving-dress, diving-suit,*** escafandra.
divinity [di'viniti], *s.* divinidad; teología; (*escuela*) religión.
divisibility [divizi'biliti], *s.* divisibilidad.
divisible [di'vizibl], *a.* divisible.
division [di'viʒən], *s.* división; repartición, distribución; sección; discordia; votación; ***to force a division,*** exigir una *o* la votación.
divisional [di'viʒənəl], *a.* divisional.
divisive [di'vaisiv], *a.* divisivo.
divisor [di'vaizə], *s.* divisor.
divorce [di'vɔ:s], *s.* divorcio; separación; divergencia; ***to get a divorce,*** divorciarse. — *v.t.* divorciar; divorciarse de; separar. — *v.i.* divorciarse.
divorcee [divɔ:'si:], *s.* persona divorciada.
divorcement [di'vɔ:smənt], *s.* divorcio.
divulgate [di'vʌlgeit], *v.t.* divulgar.
divulge [di'vʌldʒ], *v.t.* divulgar; descubrir, revelar.
dizen ['daizən], *v.t.* endomingar.
dizziness ['dizinis], *s.* vértigo; vertiginosidad.
dizzy ['dizi], *a.* vertiginoso; aturdido, confuso; que produce vértigo; (*fam.*) casquivano; ***to feel dizzy,*** tener vértigo; tener vahidos; ***to make dizzy,*** dar vértigo a.
do (1) [du:], *s.* (*fam.*) fiesta, guateque, juerga; ***do's and don'ts,*** lo lícito y lo ilícito. — *irr. v.t.* hacer; (*fam.*) ***they did Europe in a week,*** se hicieron Europa en una semana; (*fam.*) ***they've done us,*** nos han tomado el pelo; ***do away with,*** eliminar; ***do a distance,*** recorrer *o* cubrir *o* hacerse una distancia; ***do one's duty,*** cumplir con su deber; ***do for s.o.,*** limpiarle la casa a alguien; (*fam.*) ***to be done for,*** estar listo; ***do***

German, estudiar el alemán; ***do one's hair,*** peinarse; hacerse el pelo; ***do homage,*** tributar *o* rendir homenaje; (*fam.*) ***do in,*** cargarse; (*fam.*) ***do s.o. out of sth.,*** pisarle algo a alguien; ***do to death,*** matar; repetir hasta la saciedad; ***do up,*** decorar; apañar; atar, liar, empaquetar; (*fam.*) ***to be done up*** o ***done in,*** estar rendido; (*carne*) ***well done,*** (bien) pasado. — *v.i.* estar, portarse; servir, valer; ***do badly,*** estar mal; ***do for o.s.,*** arreglárselas solo; ***do well,*** estar (muy) bien; tener éxito; ***I could do with,*** me vendría bien; ***to make do with,*** valerse con; conformarse con; ***to have nothing to do with,*** no tener nada que ver con; ***do without,*** pasarse sin, prescindir de; ***how do you do?*** mucho gusto; ***that will do,*** eso sirve *o* vale; basta ya; ***to have done with,*** haber terminado con; ***speak and have done with it,*** habla de una vez. — **do o.s.,** *v.r.* — ***well,*** darse buena vida. — *v.aux.* ***do come,*** no dejes de venir; ***do be silent,*** calla, por Dios; ***I do see it,*** sí que lo veo; ***I don't see his point. Well, I do,*** No sé qué quiere decir. Pues, yo sí.

do (2) [dou], *s.* (*mús.*) do.

dobbin [ˈdɔbin], *s.* buen caballo.

docile [ˈdousail], *a.* dócil.

docility [douˈsiliti], *s.* docilidad.

dock (1) [dɔk], *s.* dique; dársena; (*Am.*) [WHARF]; (*pl.*) puerto, (los) muelles; ***dry dock,*** dique seco; ***floating dock,*** dique flotante. — *v.t.* hacer entrar en dique *o* en muelle. — *v.i.* entrar en dique; atracar (en el muelle).

dock (2) [dɔk], *s.* (*for.*) banquillo (del acusado).

dock (3) [dɔk], *v.t.* derrabar, descolar; quitar, restar.

dock (4) [dɔk], *s.* (*bot.*) acedera, romeza.

dockage [ˈdɔkidʒ], *s.* entrada en dique; derechos de dique, *m.pl.*, muellaje.

docker [ˈdɔkə], *s.* obrero portuario, cargador.

docket [ˈdɔkit], *s.* rótulo, marbete; minuta, sumario; recibo; (*for.*) lista de causas pendientes; (*for.*) apuntamiento; ***on the docket,*** entre manos, bajo estudio. — *v.t.* rotular; anotar en el dorso de; poner en la lista de causas pendientes.

dockyard [ˈdɔkjɑːd], *s.* (*mar.*) arsenal, astillero.

doctor [ˈdɔktə], *s.* médico, doctor; (***woman***) ***doctor,*** (mujer) médico. — *v.t.* doctorar; medicinar; componer, reparar; ***doctor up,*** apañar. — *v.i.* ejercer la medicina.

doctoral [ˈdɔktərəl], *a.* doctoral.

doctorate [ˈdɔktərit], *s.* doctorado.

doctorship [ˈdɔktəʃip], *s.* doctorado.

doctrinal [dɔkˈtrainəl], *a.* doctrinal; didáctico.

doctrinaire [dɔktriˈnɛə], *a.* doctrinario.

doctrinarianism [dɔktriˈnɛəriənizəm], *s.* doctrinarismo.

doctrine [ˈdɔktrin], *s.* doctrina.

document [ˈdɔkjumənt], *s.* documento. — [ˈdɔkjument], *v.t.* documentar.

documentary [dɔkjuˈmentəri], *a.* documental, documentario. — *s.* documental.

dodder (1) [ˈdɔdə], *s.* (*bot.*) cuscuta.

dodder (2) [ˈdɔdə], *v.i.* tambalear; chochear.

doddering [ˈdɔdəriŋ], *a.* tambaleante; chocho.

dodecagon [douˈdekəgən], *s.* dodecágono.

dodecahedron [doudekəˈhiːdrən], *s.* dodecaedro.

dodge [dɔdʒ], *s.* regate; truco; esquinazo; evasiva. — *v.t.* esquivar, soslayar; dar esquinazo a. — *v.i.* zafarse.

dodgem [ˈdɔdʒəm], *s.* coche de choque.

dodger [ˈdɔdʒə], *s.* gandul; tramposo.

dodgy [ˈdɔdʒi], *a.* (*fam.*) dudoso, expuesto.

dodo [ˈdoudou], *s.* (*orn.*) dodo, dodó.

doe [dou], *s.* gama; hembra (*conejo, liebre, etc.*).

doer [ˈduːə], *s.* hacedor; actor; agente.

doeskin [ˈdouskin], *s.* ante, piel de gama.

doff [dɔf], *v.t.* quitarse (el sombrero); despojarse de.

dog [dɔg], *s.* perro; can; morillo; zorro; (*mar.*) pie de cabra; gatillo (de arma de fuego); (*despec.*) animal; (*despec.*) canalla; (*bot.*) ***dog-bane,*** matacán; ***dog-berry,*** cornizola; ***dog-cart,*** coche de dos ruedas; ***dog-days,*** canícula; ***dog-eared,*** estropeado, sobado, costroso; ***dog-fancier,*** perrero; ***dog-fight,*** pelea de perros; (*aer.*) duelo *o* combate aéreo; ***dog-fish,*** cazón; ***dog-fox,*** zorro; ***dog-grass,*** grama; (*fam.*) ***to be in the dog-house,*** haber caído en desgracia; ***dog in the manger,*** perro del hortelano; ***dog-kennel,*** perrera; ***dog-Latin,*** latinajo, latinajos, latín macarrónico; ***dog-licence,*** permiso para tener perro; ***dog-rose,*** escaramujo; ***dog-show,*** exposición canina; ***dog-star,*** Sirio; ***dog-teeth,*** dientes caninos, colmillos; ***dog-tired,*** rendido, agotado; ***dog-track,*** canódromo; ***dog-trot,*** trote de perro; (*mar.*) ***dog-vane,*** cataviento; (*mar.*) ***dog-watch,*** guardia de cuartillo; ***lap dog,*** perrito faldero; ***watch dog,*** perro de guardia; ***to go to the dogs,*** arruinarse, ir de cabeza. — *v.t.* cazar; acosar; (*mec.*) afianzar con grapas.

doge [doudʒ], *s.* dux.

dogged [ˈdɔgid], *a.* tozudo, terco; tenaz.

doggedly [ˈdɔgidli], *adv.* con tozudez, con terquedad; tenazmente.

doggedness [ˈdɔgidnis], *s.* terquedad; tenacidad.

dogger [ˈdɔgə], *s.* (*mar.*) dogre.

doggerel [ˈdɔgərəl], *a.* burlesco. — *s.* coplas de ciego, *f.pl.*, aleluyas, *f.pl.*, versos ramplones, *m.pl.*

doggish [ˈdɔgiʃ], *a.* perruno.

doggo [ˈdɔgou], *adv.* (*fam.*) ***to lie doggo,*** estarse escondido *o* quieto.

doggy [ˈdɔgi], *a.* (*fam.*) perruno. — *s.* (*fam.*) perrito.

dogma [ˈdɔgmə], *s.* dogma, *m.*

dogmatic [dɔgˈmætik], *a.* dogmático.

dogmatics [dɔgˈmætiks], *s.pl.* dogmática.

dogmatism [ˈdɔgmətizəm], *s.* dogmatismo.

dogmatist [ˈdɔgmətist], *s.* dogmatista, *m.f.*, dogmatizador.

dogmatize [ˈdɔgmətaiz], *v.i.* dogmatizar.

dogmatizer [ˈdɔgmətaizə], *s.* dogmatizador.

dogwood [ˈdɔgwud], *s.* (*bot.*) cornejo.

doings [ˈduːiŋz], *s.pl.* hechos, *m.pl.*, hazañas, *f.pl.*, andanzas, *f.pl.*

doldrums [ˈdɔldrəmz], *s.pl.* (*mar.*) calmas ecuatoriales; calma chicha; (*fig.*) estancamiento, bache, desánimo.

dole [doul], *s.* limosna; subsidio de paro; ***to be on the dole,*** estar parado *o* sin trabajo. — *v.t.* — ***out,*** repartir, hacer reparto de.

doleful, dolesome [ˈdoulful, -səm], *a.* lúgubre, triste, melancólico; lastimero.

dolefulness [ˈdoulfulnis], *s.* tristeza, melancolía.

dolerite [ˈdɔlərait], *s.* dolerita.

dolichocephalic [dɔlikousiˈfælik], *a.* dolicéfalo.

doll [dɔl], *s.* muñeca; (*fam.*) gachí, niña; ***guys and dolls,*** ellos y ellas. — **doll o.s.,** *v.r.* — ***up,*** emperejilarse, ponerse de punta en blanco.

dollar [ˈdɔlə], *s.* dólar.

dolly [ˈdɔli], *s.* muñequita; (*fam.*) ***dolly-bird,*** chica casquivana.

dolman [ˈdɔlmən], *s.* dolmán.

dolmen [ˈdɔlmen], *s.* dolmen.

dolomite [ˈdɔlomait], *s.* dolomía, dolomita.

dolorous [ˈdɔlərəs], *a.* doloroso, triste.

dolorousness [ˈdɔlərəsnis], *s.* dolor, desolación, aflicción, pena.

dolose [doˈlous], *a.* (*for.*) doloso.

dolphin [ˈdɔlfin], *s.* delfín; (*mar.*) poste de amarra.

dolt [doult], *s.* necio, lerdo.

doltish [ˈdoultiʃ], *a.* necio, lerdo.

doltishness [ˈdoultiʃnis], *s.* necedad, lerdez.

domain [doˈmein], *s.* dominio; (*fig.*) campo.

dome [doum], *s* cúpula, domo, cimborio.

domesday [DOOMSDAY].

domestic [do'mestik], *a.* doméstico; casero; interno, nacional; ***domestic commerce,*** comercio interior. — *s.* doméstico, sirviente, criado.
domesticate [do'mestikeit], *v.t.* domesticar; naturalizar.
domestication [domesti'keiʃən], *s.* domesticación.
domesticity [domes'tisiti], *s.* domesticidad.
domicile ['dɔmisail], *s.* (*for.*) domicilio. — *v.t.* domiciliar. — *v.i.* domiciliarse, estar domiciliado.
domiciliary [dɔmi'siliəri], *a.* domiciliario.
dominant ['dɔminənt], *a.* dominante. — *s.* (*mús.*) dominante, *f.*
dominate ['dɔmineit], *v.t.*, *v.i.* dominar, mandar.
domination [dɔmi'neiʃən], *s.* dominación.
dominator ['dɔmineitə], *s.* dominador.
domineer [dɔmi'niə], *v.t.*, *v.i.* dominar, mandar.
domineering [dɔmi'niəriŋ], *a.* dominante, mandón.
dominical [do'minikəl], *a.* dominical.
Dominican [do'minikən], *a.*, *s.* dominicano.
Dominican Republic [do'minikən ri'pʌblik], **the.** (la) República Dominicana.
dominie ['dɔmini], *s.* dómine.
dominion [do'miniən], *s.* dominio; ***the Dominions,*** los dominios británicos.
domino ['dɔminou], *s.* dominó; (*pl.* **dominoes** [-z]) dominó (*juego*).
don (1) [dɔn], *s.* noble español; profesor universitario.
don (2) [dɔn], *v.t.* vestirse. ponerse; investirse de.
donate [do'neit], *v.t.* donar.
donation [do'neiʃən], *s.* donativo; donación.
donator [do'neitə], *s.* donador.
done [dʌn], *p.p.* [DO (1)]. — *a.* hecho, acabado; ***the done thing,*** lo convencional; ***done for,*** desahuciado, listo. — *interj.* ¡hecho!; ***well done!*** ¡bien hecho!
donee [do'ni:], *s.* (*for.*) donatario.
donjon ['dʌndʒən], *s.* torre del homenaje.
donkey ['dɔŋki], *s.* burro, asno, borrico; ***donkey-work,*** trabajo duro, rutinario; ***it's donkey's years since I last saw you,*** hace un siglo que no le veo; ***to talk the hind leg off a donkey,*** hablar por los codos.
donnish ['dɔniʃ], *a.* pedante, pedantesco; académico, erudito.
donor ['dounə], *s.* donante, donador.
don't [dount], (*abrev.*, *fam.*) **do not** [DO(1)].
doodle [du:dl], *s.* garabato. — *v.i.* garabatear, garrapatear.
doom [du:m], *s.* sino, hado; juicio; condena; perdición; ***the crack of doom,*** (señal del) juicio final. — *v.t.* condenar, sentenciar; predestinar; desahuciar; ***to be doomed to disappear,*** estar llamado a desaparecer.
doomsday ['du:mzdei], *s.* día del juicio universal.
door [dɔ:], *s.* puerta; portal; (*vehículo*) puerta *o* portezuela; ***behind closed doors,*** a puerta(s) cerrada(s); ***door-bell,*** timbre; ***door-catch,*** picaporte; pestillo; ***door-chain,*** cadena de puerta; ***door-handle,*** tirador; picaporte; ***door-head,*** dintel; ***door-keeper,*** portero; ***door-knob,*** pomo, tirador de puerta; ***door-latch,*** picaporte; pestillo; ***door-mat,*** felpudo, esterilla; ***dead as a door-nail,*** más muerto que la abuela; ***door-post,*** jamba de puerta; ***door-way,*** entrada, portal; ***front*** o ***main door,*** puerta principal; ***next door,*** en la casa de al lado; ***next door to,*** al lado de; (*fig.*) que raya en, que le falta poco para llegar a; ***street door,*** portal; ***to close the door on,*** excluir la posibilidad de; ***to lay the blame at the door of,*** echarle la culpa a; ***to sell from door to door,*** vender de puerta en puerta; ***to show the door to,*** poner en la calle; ***to show to the door,*** acompañar hasta la puerta.
dope [doup], *s.* (*fam.*) estupefaciente(s); (*fam.*) informe(s), dato(s); tonto, memo. — *v.t.* narcotizar.
dor [dɔ:], *s.* (*fam.*) escarabajo estercolero.
doree [DORY].
Dorian, Doric ['dɔ:riən, 'dɔrik], *a.* dorio; dórico.
dormancy ['dɔ:mənsi], *s.* latencia; inactividad, letargo.
dormant ['dɔ:mənt], *a.* durmiente; latente; inactivo.
dormer ['dɔ:mə], *s.* ***dormer window,*** buharda, buhardilla.
dormitive ['dɔ:mitiv], *a.*, *s.* dormitivo.
dormitory ['dɔ:mitri], *s.* dormitorio; (*Am.*) residencia estudiantil.
dormouse ['dɔ:maus], *s.* (*zool.*) lirón.
dorsal ['dɔ:səl], *a.* dorsal.
dorsum ['dɔ:səm], *s.* dorso.
dory ['dɔ:ri], *s.* (*ict.*) ceo, gallo.
dosage ['dousidʒ], *s.* dosificación.
dose [dous], *s.* dosis, *f.inv.*; (*fig.*) mal trago. — *v.t.* dosificar; medicinar; administrar una dosis a.
doss [dɔs], *s.* (*fam.*) camastro; ***doss-house,*** hogar, refugio. — *v.i.* (*fam.*) ***doss down,*** dormir.
dossal ['dɔsəl], *s.* retablo.
dossier ['dɔsiei], *s.* expediente.
dossil ['dɔsil], *s.* (*cir.*) lechino.
dot [dɔt], *s.* punto; (*pl.*, *gram.*) puntos suspensivos; ***on the dot,*** en punto. — *v.t.* puntear, salpicar (de puntos); poner punto a; ***dot about,*** esparcir, desparramar; ***dot one's i's,*** poner los puntos sobre las íes; (*fam.*) ***dot s.o. one,*** dar una bofetada a. — *v.i.* hacer puntos, poner (los) puntos.
dotage ['doutidʒ], *s.* chochez; ***to be in one's dotage,*** chochear, estar chocho.
dotal ['doutəl], *a.* dotal.
dotard ['doutəd], *s.* viejo chocho.
dote [dout], *v.i.* chochear; ***to dote upon,*** mimar; estar loco con *o* por, idolatrar.
dotingly ['doutiŋli], *adv.* apasionadamente, con ceguera.
dotterel ['dɔtərəl], *s.* (*orn.*) calandria marina.
dotty ['dɔti], *a.* (*fam.*) chiflado.
double [dʌbl], *a.* doble, duplo, de dos; doblado, duplicado; ***double entry,*** partida doble; ***double track,*** vía doble. — *adv.* doblemente, dos veces; en par. — *s.* doble, duplo, duplicado; copia; doblez, pliegue; engaño. — *v.t.*, *v.i.* doblar, duplicar; redoblar, repetir; escapar, dar un rodeo a; forrar. — *v.i.* doblarse, duplicarse; encorvarse; ***double for,*** substituir a; ***double up,*** doblarse.
double-barrelled ['dʌbl-'bærəld], *a.* de dos cañones; ***double-barrelled surname,*** apellido altisonante.
double-bass ['dʌbl-'beis], *s.* contrabajo.
double-bed ['dʌbl-'bed], *s.* cama de matrimonio.
double-biting ['dʌbl-'baitiŋ], *a.* de dos filos.
double-bottomed ['dʌbl-'bɔtəmd], *a.* (*mar.*) de dos fondos.
double-breasted ['dʌbl-'brestid], *a.* cruzado.
double-chin ['dʌbl-'tʃin], *s.* papada.
double-cross ['dʌbl-'krɔs], *v.t.* traicionar (*a un cómplice*), delatar; chivarse contra; engañar, pegársela a.
double-dealing ['dʌbl-'di:liŋ], *s.* duplicidad, trato doble.
double-decker ['dʌbl-'dekə], *a.* de dos pisos; ***double-decker bus,*** autobus de dos pisos.
double-edged ['dʌbl-'edʒd], *a.* de doble filo.
double-faced ['dʌbl-'feist], *a.* de dos caras; que tiene muchas dobleces.
double-jointed ['dʌbl-'dʒɔintid], *a.* de doble unión.
double-lock ['dʌbl-'lɔk], *v.t.* echar la llave dos veces.
doubleness ['dʌblnis], *s.* doblez, dobladura; duplicidad.
doublet ['dʌblit], *s.* jubón, justillo; par, pareja; doblete.
doubling ['dʌbliŋ], *s.* dobladura, pliegue; vuelta, rodeo.

doubloon [dʌb'lu:n], *s.* doblón.
doubt [daut], *s.* duda; ***to call in doubt,*** poner en duda; ***if in doubt,*** en caso de duda; ***in doubt,*** dudoso; ***there can be no doubt,*** no cabe duda; ***no doubt, without doubt,*** sin duda, indudablemente. — *v.t., v.i.* dudar (de).
doubtable ['dautəbl], *a.* dudable.
doubter ['dautə], *s.* desconfiado, escéptico.
doubtful ['dautful], *a.* dudoso, incierto.
doubtfulness ['dautfulnis], *s.* duda; irresolución; incertidumbre, *f.*
doubtingly ['dautiŋli], *adv.* dudosamente.
doubtless(ly) ['dautlis(li)], *adv.* indudablemente, indubitablemente, sin duda.
douche [du:ʃ], *s.* ducha, regadera. — *v.t.* duchar.
dough [dou], *s.* masa, pasta; (*fam.*) pasta, guita; ***dough-nut,*** buñuelo, donú.
doughtiness ['dautinis], *s.* valentía, denuedo.
doughty ['dauti], *a.* bravo, valeroso.
doughy [doui], *a.* pastoso, crudo, blando.
douse [daus], *v.t.* zambullir, chapuzar; mojar, remojar; dar, golpear; (*mar.*) recoger, arriar. — *v.i.* zambullirse, chapuzarse.
dove [dʌv], *s.* palomo, paloma; ***dove-coloured,*** tornasolado; ***dove-cot(e),*** palomar; ***ring-dove,*** paloma torcaz; ***turtle-dove,*** tórtola.
dovetail ['dʌvteil], *s.* (*carp.*) cola de milano *o* de pato. — *v.t.* ensamblar a cola de milano; machihembrar.
dowager ['dauədʒə], *s.* viuda; ***dowager duchess,*** duquesa viuda.
dowdy ['daudi], *a.* que no tiene estilo ni gracia.
dowel ['dauəl], *s.* clavija, macho de madera, espiga de pie derecho.
dower ['dauə], *s.* dote; viudedad; prendas personales, *f.pl.*
dowerless ['dauəlis], *a.* sin dote.
down (1) [daun], *s.* plumón; vello, bozo.
down (2) [daun], *s.* (*ú. más en pl.*) loma, terreno en cuesta suave.
down (3) [daun], *a.* descendente; pendiente; (*fig.*) alicaído, abatido. — *adv.* abajo, hacia *o* para abajo; bajo; por tierra, en tierra; en la parte inferior; al contado; ***to be down,*** haber bajado; estar abatido *o* agotado; quedarse atrás; (*fam.*) ***to be down on,*** tenerla tomada con; ***to be down and out,*** estar en la indigencia; ***cash down,*** al contado; ***down below,*** allá abajo; ***down from,*** desde; ***down in the mouth,*** cariacontecido; ***down stream,*** río abajo; ***down to,*** hasta; ***down with the government!*** ¡abajo el gobierno! ***to take down,*** bajar, descolgar; apuntar, anotar; ***up and down,*** de arriba abajo; ***upside down,*** patas arriba. — *s.* (*fam.*) ***have a down on,*** tenerla tomada con; ***ups and downs,*** altibajos, *m.pl.* — *v.t.* derribar; trager(se); ***down tools,*** declararse en huelga.
downcast ['daunkɑ:st], *a.* abatido, alicaído.
downfall ['daunfɔ:l], *s.* caída, ruina, hundimiento.
downfallen ['daun'fɔ:lən], *a.* caído, arruinado.
down-grade ['daun-greid], *s.* ***to be on the down-grade,*** ir para abajo.
down-hearted ['daun-'hɑ:tid], *a.* abatido, desanimado.
downhill ['daun'hil], *a.* pendiente, en declive. — *adv.* cuesta abajo.
downiness ['dauninis], *s.* vellosidad.
down-payment ['daun-'peimənt], *s.* entrada.
downpour ['daunpɔ:], *s.* aguacero.
downright ['daunrait], *a.* abierto, franco; manifiesto, patente; categórico, absoluto, total. — *adv.* absolutamente, totalmente.
downstairs ['daun'stɛəz], *a.* de abajo. — *adv.* abajo; en el piso de abajo.
down-stroke ['daun-strouk], *s.* carrera descendente.
down-to-earth ['daun-tu-'ə:θ], *a.* práctico, realista.
down-town ['daun-taun], *a.* (*Am.*) del centro, céntrico. — *adv.* al centro. — *s.* centro (*comercial de una ciudad*).
downtrodden ['dauntrɔdn], *a.* pisoteado, oprimido, tiranizado.
downward ['daunwəd], *a.* descendente.
downward(s) ['daunwəd(z)], *adv.* hacia abajo.
downy ['dauni], *a.* velloso; plumoso.
dowry ['dauəri], *s.* dote, *f.*
dowse [dauz], *v.t.* apagar.
doxology [dɔk'sɔlədʒi], *s.* doxología.
doyen ['dɔijən], *s.* decano.
doze [douz], *s.* sueñecito, siestecita; ***to have a doze*** echar un sueñecito. — *v.i.* dormitar; ***doze off,*** quedarse traspuesto.
dozen ['dʌzən], *s.* docena; ***baker's dozen,*** docena de fraile; ***to do one's daily dozen,*** hacer un poco de ejercicio diario; ***to talk nineteen to the dozen,*** hablar por los codos.
doziness ['douzinis], *s.* somnolencia, modorra.
dozy ['douzi], *a.* soñoliento, amodorrado.
drab [dræb], *a.* pardusco; gris, triste, monótono. — *s.* mujerzuela.
drabble [dræbl], *v.t.* enlodar.
drachma ['drækmə], *s.* dracma.
Draco ['drækou], *s.* (*astron.*) dragón.
draconian, draconic [drə'kouniən, drə'kɔnik], *a.* draconiano.
draff [dræf], *s.* posos, *m.pl.*
draft [drɑ:ft], *s.* giro, letra de cambio; (*mil.*) quinta; (*Am., mil.*) [CONSCRIPTION]; bosquejo, esbozo; borrador, versión preliminar; [DRAUGHT]. — *v.t.* bosquejar, esbozar; hacer un borrador de, redactar provisionalmente; quintar.
drag [dræg], *s.* rastra; calzadera; traba, rémora; (*fam.*) petardo; (*fam.*) pitillo; (*aer.*) resistencia al avance; ***drag-boat,*** draga; ***drag-chain,*** cadena para enrayar; ***drag-hook,*** enrayador, garfio; ***drag-net,*** red barredera, brancada; redada. — *v.t.* arrastrar; rastrear; dragar; ***drag the anchor,*** garrear el ancla; (*fig.*) ***drag one's feet,*** hacerse el remolón; ***drag out,*** prolongar; dar largas a; ***drag sth. out of s.o.,*** sonsacarle algo a alguien. — *v.i.* arrastrarse; rastrear; pasar (muy) lentamente; ***drag on*** o ***on and on,*** prolongarse, hacerse interminable, eternizarse.
draggle [drægl], *v.t.* enlodar *o* ensuciar arrastrando. — *v.i.* enlodarse, emporcarse.
draggle-tailed ['drægl-teild], *a.* enlodado, sucio.
dragoman ['drægoumən], *s.* (*pl.* **dragomans** [-z]) dragomán.
dragon ['drægən], *s.* dragón; (*fam.*) bruja, tarasca.
dragonet ['drægənit], *s.* dragonete.
dragon-fly ['drægən-flai], *s.* libélula, (*fam.*) caballito del diablo.
dragonish ['drægəniʃ], *a.* dragontino.
dragon-like ['drægən-laik], *a.* fiero.
dragonnade [drægə'neid], *s.* dragonada, saqueo.
dragon-tree ['drægən-tri:], *s.* (*bot.*) drago.
dragoon [drə'gu:n], *s.* (*mil.*) dragón. — *v.t.* intimidar; ***dragoon into,*** obligar (por intimidación) a, forzar a.
drain [drein], *s.* desagüe; desaguadero; alcantarilla, albañal, sumidero; consumo, pérdida; ***brain-drain,*** fuga de cerebros; ***drain-pipe,*** tubo de desagüe. — *v.t.* desaguar; avenar; drenar, secar; escurrir. — *v.i.* desaguar; agotar, apurar.
drainable ['dreinəbl], *a.* desaguable.
drainage ['dreinidʒ], *s.* desagüe; avenamiento; desecamiento; saneamiento; drenaje.
drainer ['dreinə], *s.* colador, coladero; secadero.
draining ['dreiniŋ], *s.* desagüe; desecación; drenaje; agotamiento; ***draining-board,*** escurreplatos, *m.inv.*, escurridor.
drake [dreik], *s.* pato (*macho*).
dram [dræm], *s.* dracma; (*fig.*) grano, gota; (*fam.*) trago, copita; ***dram shop,*** taberna.

drama [ˈdrɑːmə], *s.* drama, *m.*
dramatic [drəˈmætik], *a.* dramático.
dramatis personæ [ˈdræmətis pəːˈsounai], *s.pl.* personajes, *m.pl.*
dramatist [ˈdræmətist], *s.* dramaturgo.
dramatization [dræmətaiˈzeiʃən], *s.* dramatización.
dramatize [ˈdræmətaiz], *v.t.* dramatizar.
dramaturgist [ˈdræmətəːdʒist], *s.* dramaturgo.
dramaturgy [ˈdræmətəːdʒi], *s.* dramática.
drape [dreip], *s.* colgadura. — *v.t.* vestir, colgar, poner colgaduras a; entapizar.
draper [ˈdreipə], *s.* pañero; ***linen draper,*** lencero.
drapery [ˈdreipəri], *s.* pañería; ropaje, cortinas, *f.pl.*, colgaduras, *f.pl.*, tapicería.
drastic [ˈdræstik], *a.* drástico.
drat! [dræt], *interj.* ¡diantre! ¡maldito sea!
draught [drɑːft], *s.* tiro (*de chimenea*); corriente de aire; trago; (*mar.*) calado; rastreo; borrador, proyecto; trazado, dibujo; (*pl.*) (juego de) damas; ***draught beer,*** cerveza al grifo; ***draught-board,*** tablero de damas; ***draught-horse,*** caballo de tiro.
draughtsman [ˈdrɑːftsmən], *s.* dibujante; delineante; peón (*del juego de damas*).
draughty [ˈdrɑːfti], *a.* expuesto a corrientes de aire.
draw [drɔː], *s.* tiro; arrastre; (*dep.*) empate; (*ajedrez*) tablas; sorteo; función taquillera *o* de mucho éxito. — *v.t.* arrastrar, tirar de; sacar; atraer(se); tender; aspirar (*aliento*); cobrar (*sueldo*); destripar (*aves*); dibujar, trazar (*diseño*); echar (*suertes*); (*mar.*) calar; ***draw aside,*** apartar; ***draw attention,*** llamar la atención; ***draw back,*** retirar; ***draw a blank,*** no conseguir nada; ***draw a comparison,*** hacer una comparación; ***draw the curtains,*** correr las cortinas; ***draw back the curtains,*** descorrer las cortinas; ***draw the enemy's fire,*** atraer el fuego del enemigo; ***draw forth,*** provocar; hacer salir; ***draw in,*** atraer(se); ***draw off,*** sacar, extraer; quitar; ***draw (s.o.) on,*** atraer(se); incitar, dar pie a; ***draw out,*** sacar; sonsacar; prolongar; ***draw up,*** redactar; acercar; ordenar; ***to refuse to be drawn,*** cerrarse en el mutismo. — *v.i.* tirar; dibujar; (*dep.*) empatar; ***draw aside,*** apartarse, hacerse a un lado; ***draw back,*** retirarse, retroceder, recular, volverse atrás; ***draw in,*** parar; ***the days are drawing in,*** los días se van acortando; ***draw near,*** acercarse; ***draw off,*** retirarse; ***draw on,*** aproximarse; (*recursos*) utilizar, servirse de; ***draw to a close,*** tocar a su fin; ***draw up (sharply),*** pararse (en seco).
drawback [ˈdrɔːbæk], *s.* desventaja, inconveniente; pega.
drawbridge [ˈdrɔːbridʒ], *s.* puente levadizo.
drawee [drɔːˈiː], *s.* (*com.*) girado, librado.
drawer [ˈdrɔːə], *s.* cajón, gaveta; dibujante; (*com.*) girador, librador; (*pl.*) calzoncillos, *m.pl.*; bragas, *f.pl.*; ***chest of drawers,*** cómoda.
drawing [ˈdrɔːiŋ], *s.* dibujo; sorteo; (*Am.*) ***drawing-account*** [CURRENT ACCOUNT]; ***drawing-board,*** tablero de dibujar; ***to be on the drawing-board,*** estar sobre el tapete *o* en vías de planearse; ***to go back to the drawing-board,*** volver al principio; ***drawing-frame,*** estirador; ***drawing-paper,*** papel de dibujar; ***drawing-pen,*** tiralíneas, *m.inv.*; ***drawing-pin,*** chincheta; ***drawing-room,*** salón.
drawl [drɔːl], *s.* habla lenta y pesada. — *v.i.* arrastrar las palabras.
drawling [ˈdrɔːliŋ], *s.* [DRAWL].
drawn [drɔːn], *a.* en tensión, desencajado, ojeroso; ***long drawn out,*** larguísimo, interminable. — *p.p.* [DRAW].
dray [drei], *s.* carro, carromato; ***dray-horse,*** caballo de carro; ***dray-man,*** carretero, carromatero.
drayage [ˈdreiidʒ], *s.* carretaje, acarreo.
dread [dred], *a.* espantoso, terrible. — *s.* espanto, terror, pavor; ***to fill with dread,*** infundir pavor *o* temor a. — *v.t., v.i.* temer; ***I dread to think of it,*** me da pavor *o* espanto pensarlo.
dreadful [ˈdredful], *a.* terrible, espantoso; infame.
dreadfulness [ˈdredfulnis], *s.* espanto, (lo) espantoso.
dreadnought [ˈdrednɔːt], *s.* tela muy doble; capote y capucha hecho de esta tela; (*mar.*) acorazado de combate.
dream [driːm], *s.* sueño; ensueño. — *irr. v.t.* soñar. — *v.i.* — ***of,*** soñar con *o* en.
dreamer [ˈdriːmə], *s.* soñador, iluso, utopista.
dreamily, dreamingly [ˈdriːmili, -iŋli], *adv.* como en sueños.
dreamlike [ˈdriːmlaik], *a.* como soñado, irreal.
dreamy [ˈdriːmi], *a.* soñador; de ensueño.
drear [driə], [DREARY].
drearily [driərili], *adv.* tristemente.
dreariness [ˈdriərinis], *s.* tristeza, melancolía.
dreary [ˈdriəri], *a.* tristón, melancólico; lúgubre; monótono.
dredge [dredʒ], *s.* draga, rastra. — *v.t.* dragar; rastrear; espolvorear.
dredger [ˈdredʒə], *s.* draga; dragador; espolvoreador.
dredging [ˈdredʒiŋ], *s.* dragado; acción de rastrear. — *a.* de dragar, rastrear *etc.*
dreg [dreg], *s.* (*fam.*) nulidad, cero a la izquierda; (*pl.*) hez, heces; madres (*del vino*), *f.pl.*, zupia; sedimento; escoria, desperdicio.
dregginess [ˈdreginis], *s.* turbiedad, heces, *f.pl.*, poso.
dreggish, dreggy [ˈdregiʃ,- i], *a.* zurraposo, turbio.
drench [drentʃ], *s.* poción; chaparrón; remojón. — *v.t.* mojar, empapar, calar.
dress [dres], *a.* de vestir, de gala; ***dress ball,*** baile de etiqueta; ***dress rehearsal,*** ensayo general; ***dress circle,*** anfiteatro. — *s.* vestido, traje, atavío; aderezo; tocado; ***evening dress,*** traje de noche; ***full dress,*** traje de ceremonia; ***winter dress,*** plumaje de invierno (*pájaros*). — *v.t.* vestir; ataviar, adornar; peinar; curar (*una herida*); almohazar; aderezar, aliñar; zurrar (*las pieles*); desbastar (*madera*); enlucir, revocar; (*mil.*) alinear; ***dress (a dead body),*** amortajar; ***dressed in black,*** vestido de negro; ***to get dressed,*** vestirse; ***dress down,*** echar un rapapolvo a; ***dress (a ship),*** empavesar. — *v.i.* vestirse; ***dress up,*** acicalarse; vestirse de etiqueta.
dresser [ˈdresə], *s.* aparador; (*Am.*) [CHEST OF DRAWERS]; moza de cámara; mesa de cocina; zurrador, adobador.
dressing [ˈdresiŋ], *s.* adorno; condimento, aliño; (*cir.*) cura; (*agric.*) bina, renda; encoladura (de paños); aderezamiento, aderezo; adobo; (*agric.*) abono, estercoladura; corta; (*fam.*) ***dressing-down,*** rapapolvo; ***dressing-case,*** neceser; ***dressing-gown,*** peinador, bata, batín; ***dressing-room,*** tocador, cuarto de vestir; camerino.
dressmaker [ˈdresmeikə], *s.* modista.
dressmaking [ˈdresmeikiŋ], *s.* modistería.
dressy [ˈdresi], *a.* (*fam.*) vistoso, llamativo.
dribble [dribl], *s.* babeo, babas, *f.pl.*; goteo. — *v.t.* hacer caer gota a gota; (*fútbol*) driblar. — *v.i.* babear; gotear; (*fútbol*) driblar.
driblet [ˈdriblit], *s.* gotita; adarme.
dried [draid], *a.* desecado; seco; (*fruta*) paso.
drier [draiə], *s.* secadora (*máquina*).
drift [drift], *s.* (impulso de una) corriente; (*mar.*) deriva; rumbo, dirección; sentido, giro, tendencia; acumulación; (*geol.*) terrenos de acarreo, *m.pl.*; ***drift from the land,*** despoblación del campo; ***snow-drift,*** montón de nieve; ventisquero. — *v.i.* ir a la deriva.
driftage [ˈdriftidʒ], *s.* (*mar.*) deriva; (*artill.*) desviación.
drifting [ˈdriftiŋ], *s.* (el) ir a la deriva.

driftway [ˈdriftwei], *s.* (*mar.*) deriva; (*min.*) galería.
driftwood [ˈdriftwud], *s.* leña de playa.
drill (1) [dril], *s.* taladro, perforador(a); sembradora; (*semilla*) hilera; (*mil.*) instrucción; (*fig.*) disciplina; (*fig.*) plan. — *v.t.* taladrar, perforar; (*mil.*) enseñar (la) instrucción a; disciplinar; sembrar en hilera(s). — *v.i.* hacer instrucción.
drill (2) [dril], *s.* dril (*tela*).
drilling [ˈdriliŋ], *s.* perforación.
drink [driŋk], *s.* bebida; alcohol; copa; ***to have a drink,*** beber algo; tomar una copa. — *irr. v.t.* beber; ***drink down*** o ***up,*** beberse; ***drink in,*** absorber, embeber; escuchar con avidez. — *v.i.* beber; ***drink out of,*** beber de; ***drink to*** (***the health of***), brindar por.
drinkable [ˈdriŋkəbl], *a.* potable.
drinker [ˈdriŋkə], *s.* bebedor.
drinking [ˈdriŋkiŋ], *a.* bebedor. — *s.* (el) beber; ***drinking bout,*** borrachera; ***drinking song,*** canción para beber *o* de taberna; ***drinking water,*** agua potable.
drip [drip], *s.* gotera; goteo; (*fam.*) mastuerzo; (*arq.*) alero. — *v.i.* gotear, caer gota a gota.
drip-dry [ˈdrip-ˈdrai], *a.* que no requiere plancha.
dripping [ˈdripiŋ], *s.* chorreo; (*coc.*) pringue.
drive [draiv], *s.* paseo (*en coche*); (avenida de) acceso; (*dep.*) golpe fuerte; vigor, energía; campaña vigorosa; (*caz.*) batida; mecanismo de transmisión; (*aut.*) conducción; ***left*** (***right***) ***hand drive,*** conducción a la izquierda (derecha). — *irr. v.t.* mover; empujar, impeler, impulsar; llevar, conducir, guiar; forzar, obligar; ***drive away*** o ***off,*** ahuyentar; ***drive back,*** rechazar, obligar a retroceder, ***drive a good bargain,*** hacer un buen negocio; ***drive in*** o ***home,*** hincar; remachar; (*fam.*) ***drive mad*** o ***up the wall,*** volver loco, sacar de quicio; ***drive on,*** estimular, aguijonear; ***drive out,*** echar, expulsar; ***what are you driving at?*** ¿qué quiere Vd. dar a entender? — *v.i.* conducir; (*dep.*) ***drive off,*** iniciar el juego; (*aut.*) ***drive off*** o ***away,*** marcharse *o* irse en coche; (*aut.*) ***drive on,*** seguir; ***drive on the right,*** circular por la derecha.
drive-in [ˈdraiv-in], *s.* (*Am.*) motocine.
drivel [ˈdrivəl], *s.* baba(s); (*fig.*) músicas, *f.pl.*, gaitas, *f.pl.*, monsergas, *f.pl.* — *v.i.* babear; decir tonterías, *f.pl.*
drivelling [ˈdrivəliŋ], *a.* baboso.
driver [ˈdraivə], *s.* conductor; cochero; maquinista, *m.f.*
driving [ˈdraiviŋ], *a.* motor, motriz; recio, violento. — *s.* conducción (*de vehículos*); impulso, tendencia; ***driving licence,*** permiso de conducir; ***driving school,*** autoescuela; ***driving shaft,*** árbol motor; ***driving wheel,*** rueda motriz.
drizzle [drizl], *s.* llovizna. — *v.t.* rociar, salpicar. — *v.i.* lloviznar.
drizzly [ˈdrizli], *a.* lloviznoso.
droit [drɔit], *s.* (*for.*) derecho, impuesto.
droll [droul], *a.* gracioso, ocurrente.
drollery [ˈdrouləri], *s.* chuscada(s), ocurrencia(s).
drollish [ˈdrouliʃ], *a.* divertido.
dromedary [ˈdrʌmədəri], *s.* dromedario.
drone (1) [droun], *s.* zángano, abejón. — *v.i.* zanganear, haraganear.
drone (2) [droun], *v.i.* zumbar.
droning [ˈdrouniŋ], *s.* zumbido(s).
dronish [ˈdrouniʃ], *a.* (de) zángano.
droop [dru:p], *s.* decaimiento. — *v.i.* caer, colgar, pender; decaer; languidecer; encamarse.
drooping [ˈdru:piŋ], *a.* bajo, caído, gacho; lánguido.
drop [drɔp], *s.* gota; pizca; pendiente, zarcillo; pastilla; trago; caída, baja; lanzamiento; declive; trampa, escotilla; ***drop-curtain,*** telón de boca; ***drop-hammer,*** martinete; (*fam.*) ***drop-out,*** uno que se raja (de la sociedad, universidad etc.); ***to have*** o ***to get the drop on,*** coger la delantera a, adelantarse a; (*fig.*) ***it's a drop in the ocean,*** es una miseria, no es nada. — *v.t.* dejar caer, soltar, echar; parir (*un animal*); verter; rociar; omitir, comerse; tumbar, derribar; desprenderse de; ***drop a curtsy,*** hacer una reverencia; ***drop a hint,*** soltar una indirecta; ***drop a line,*** poner unas líneas; ***drop a subject,*** dejar un asunto; cambiar de tema. — *v.i.* gotear, chorrear; caer (*sin sentido* o *muerto*); bajar; agacharse; cesar; ***drop behind,*** quedarse atrás; ***drop dead,*** caerse muerto; ***drop in,*** pasarse (por), dejarse caer (por), descolgarse (por); ***drop off,*** quedarse dormido *o* traspuesto; ***drop out,*** rajarse, darse de baja, retirarse.
droplet [ˈdrɔplit], *s.* gotita.
dropping [ˈdrɔpiŋ], *s.* goteo; (*farm.*) ***dropping-bottle,*** cuentagotas, *m.inv.*; (*pl.*) excrementos de animales, *m.pl.*, cagada.
dropsical [ˈdrɔpsikəl], *a.* hidrópico.
dropsy [ˈdrɔpsi], *s.* hidropesía.
dropwort [ˈdrɔpwə:t], *s.* (*bot.*) filipéndula.
dross [drɔs], *s.* (*lit.*, *fig.*) escoria; (*fig.*) horrura; hez, turbiedad.
drossy [ˈdrɔsi], *a.* lleno de escoria; impuro.
drought [draut], *s.* sequía, seca.
drove [drouv], *s.* manada, rebaño, recua, piara, hato; (*fig.*) muchedumbre, *f.*, gentío.
drover [ˈdrouvə], *s.* ganadero; boyero; pastor.
drown [draun], *v.t.* ahogar; anegar; apagar, sofocar; ***drown one's sorrows,*** matar el gusanillo. — *v.i.* ahogarse; morir ahogado; anegarse.
drowse [drauz], *v.t.* adormecer. — *v.i.* adormecerse, amodorrarse, adormitarse.
drowsiness [ˈdrauzinis], *s.* somnolencia, adormecimiento, modorra.
drowsy [ˈdrauzi], *a.* soñoliento, adormecido, amodorrado.
drub [drʌb], *v.t.* apalear, tundir.
drubbing [ˈdrʌbiŋ], *s.* paliza, tunda, zurra.
drudge [drʌdʒ], *s.* ganapán, esclavo del trabajo; acémila. — *v.i.* trabajar mucho, afanarse, sudar.
drudgery [ˈdrʌdʒəri], *s.* faena dura, trabajo duro *o* penoso.
drug [drʌg], *s.* droga, medicamento; estupefaciente, narcótico; (*fig.*) petardo, cosa de poca venta; ***drug addict,*** toxicómano; ***drug addiction,*** toxicomanía; (*Am.*) ***drug store,*** farmacia. — *v.t.* narcotizar; administrar drogas a.
drugget [ˈdrʌgit], *s.* droguete.
druggist [ˈdrʌgist], *s.* droguista, *m.f.*, droguero; boticario.
Druid [ˈdru:id], *s.* druida, *m.*
Druidic(al) [dru:ˈidik(əl)], *a.* druídico.
Druidism [ˈdru:idizəm], *s.* druidismo.
drum [drʌm], *s.* tambor; cilindro; barril, bidón; tímpano (*del oído*); ***big drum,*** bombo; ***drum-major,*** tambor mayor; ***kettle-drum,*** timbal. — *v.t.* ***drum out,*** expulsar a toque de tambor; ***drum sth. into s.o.,*** meterle a alguien algo en la cabeza, remacharle algo a alguien. — *v.i.* tocar el tambor; tamborilear; teclear.
drummer [ˈdrʌmə], *s.* tambor.
drumstick [ˈdrʌmstik], *s.* palillo (*de tambor*).
drunk [drʌŋk], *a.* borracho; ***a bit drunk,*** bebido; ***to get drunk,*** emborracharse; ***to make drunk,*** emborrachar. — *s.* borracho. — *p.p.* [DRINK].
drunkard [ˈdrʌŋkəd], *s.* borrachín.
drunken [ˈdrʌŋkən], *a.* borracho.
drunkenness [ˈdrʌŋkənnis], *s.* borrachera.
drupe [dru:p], *s.* (*bot.*) drupa.
druse [dru:z], *s.* drusa.
dry [drai], *a.* seco; árido; enjuto; adusto; mordaz, áspero; de ley seca; ***dry bread,*** pan sin mantequilla; ***dry-dock,*** dique seco; ***dry goods,*** lencería; ***dry humour,*** humor seco; ***dry ice,*** hielo carbónico; ***dry land,*** tierra firme; ***dry nurse,*** niñera, ama seca; ***dry rot,*** putrefacción fungoide; (*fam.*) carcoma; ***dry season,*** estación

de la seca; ***dry-stone,*** de piedra sin argamasa. — *v.t.* secar; enjugar. — *v.i.* secarse; (*fam.*) ***dry up,*** callar(se).
dryad [ˈdraiəd], *s.* (*mit.*) dríada.
dry-clean [ˈdrai-ˈkli:n], *s.* limpieza en seco. — *v.t.* limpiar en seco.
dry-cleaning [ˈdrai-ˈkli:niŋ], *s.* limpieza en seco.
dryer [DRIER].
drying [ˈdraiiŋ], *a.* desecativo.
dryness [ˈdrainis], *s.* sequedad; (lo) seco; aridez; (*humor*) (lo) discreto y agudo.
dryshod [ˈdraiˈʃɔd], *a.* a pie enjuto.
dual [djuəl], *a.* dual, doble.
dualism [ˈdjuəlizəm], *s.* dualidad, dualismo.
dualist [ˈdjuəlist], *s.* dualista, *m.f.*
duality [djuˈæliti], *s.* dualidad.
dub (1) [dʌb], *v.t.* armar caballero; apodar.
dub (2) [dʌb], *v.t.* doblar (*una película*).
dubbing (1) [ˈdʌbiŋ], *s.* armar caballero; (el) apodar.
dubbing (2) [ˈdʌbiŋ], *s.* (*cine.*) doblaje.
dubious [ˈdju:biəs], *a.* dudoso, problemático; equívoco; sospechoso.
dubiousness, dubiety [ˈdju:biəsnis, dju:ˈbaiəti], *s.* incertidumbre, *f.*, duda.
dubitable [ˈdju:bitəbl], *a.* dudable.
ducal [ˈdju:kəl], *a.* ducal.
ducat [ˈdʌkət], *s.* ducado.
ducatoon [dʌkəˈtu:n], *s.* ducado de plata.
duchess [ˈdʌtʃis], *s.* duquesa.
duchy [ˈdʌtʃi], *s.* ducado.
duck (1) [dʌk], *s.* pato, pata, ánade; (*fam.*) querida, pichona; chapuz, zambullida; agachada; ***duck-legged,*** corto de piernas; ***ducks and drakes,*** juego de hacer rebotar piedras sobre el agua; ***insults roll off him like water off a duck's back,*** los insultos no le hacen mella alguna. — *v.i.* zambullirse; agacharse, agachar rápidamente la cabeza; ***duck out,*** escabullirse.
duck (2) [dʌk], *s.* dril, brin; (*pl.*) pantalones de dril, *m.pl.*
ducking [ˈdʌkiŋ], *s.* zambullida; chapuz.
duckling [ˈdʌkliŋ], *s.* anadón; patito.
ducky [ˈdʌki], *s.* (*fam.*) queridito.
duct [dʌkt], *s.* conducto.
ductile [ˈdʌktail], *a.* dúctil.
ductileness, ductility [ˈdʌktailnis, -ˈtiliti], *s.* ductilidad.
dud [dʌd], *a.* fallido, huero; falso. — *s.* granada fallida; fallo, fracaso; petardo; filfa; (*pl.*) (*fam.*) ropa vieja, trapos, *m.pl.*, andrajos, *m.pl.*
dude [dju:d], *s.* petimetre, currutaco.
dudgeon [ˈdʌdʒən], *s.* enojo; ***in high dudgeon,*** muy enojado.
due [dju:], *a.* debido; vencido, devengado, pagadero; ***due to,*** debido a; ***to fall due,*** vencer (*un pagaré etc.*); ***he is due to arrive at five o'clock,*** se espera que llegue a las cinco; ***in due course,*** en su día; oportunamente; ***in due time,*** a su debido tiempo. — *adv.* derecho, exactamente; ***due west,*** poniente derecho. — *s.* derecho, merecido, (lo) debido; deuda; ***to get one's due,*** llevar su merecido; (*pl.*) derechos, tributos, *m.pl.*; (*Am.*) abono.
duel [ˈdjuəl], *s.* duelo, desafío; ***to fight a duel,*** batirse en duelo. — *v.i.* batirse en duelo.
dueller [ˈdjuələ], *s.* duelista, *m.*
duelling [ˈdjuəliŋ], *s.* duelos, desafíos, (el) desafiarse.
duellist [ˈdjuəlist], *s.* duelista, *m.f.*
duenna [djuˈenə], *s.* dueña.
duet [djuˈet], *s.* (*mús.*) duo, dueto.
duff (1) [dʌf], *s.* pudin(g).
duff (2) [dʌf], *v.t.* amañar, estafar.
duffel [ˈdʌfəl], *s.* ***duffel-bag,*** bolsa cerrada por una cuerda; ***duffel-coat,*** comando, gredos, *m.inv.*
duffer [ˈdʌfə], *s.* (*fam.*) burro.
dug (1) [dʌg], *s.* teta.
dug (2) [dʌg], *pret.* y *p.p.* [DIG].
dug-out [ˈdʌg-aut], *s.* (*mil.*) refugio (subterráneo); piragua.
duke [dju:k], *s.* duque.
dukedom [ˈdju:kdəm], *s.* ducado.
dulcet [ˈdʌlsit], *a.* dulce, suave.
dulcification [dʌlsifiˈkeiʃən], *s.* dulcificación.
dulcify [ˈdʌlsifai], *v.t.* dulcificar.
dulcimer [ˈdʌlsimə], *s.* (*mús.*) dulcémele.
dull [dʌl], *a.* lerdo, obtuso; embotado, romo; insensible; insulso, soso; apagado; opaco, gris, nublado; sordo; deslustrado, mate; flojo, muerto; ***dull of hearing,*** duro de oído; ***dull-sighted,*** cegato; ***dull-witted,*** lerdo. — *v.t.* embotar; deslustrar; apagar, amortiguar; enfriar; entorpecer.
dullard [ˈdʌləd], *a.*, *s.* lerdo, burro.
dullness [ˈdʌlnis], *s.* embotamiento; (lo) lerdo *etc.*
dulse [dʌls], *s.* alga marina.
duly [dju:li], *adv.* debidamente; a su debido tiempo; en debida forma.
dumb [dʌm], *a.* mudo; callado; (*fam.*) lerdo, poco avispado; ***to strike dumb,*** dejar sin habla; ***dumb show,*** pantomima; ***dumb waiter,*** montaplatos, *m.inv.*
dumb-bell [ˈdʌm-bel], *s.* pesa; tonto, lerdo.
dumbfound [dʌmˈfaund], *v.t.* dejar sin habla, pasmar, asombrar.
dumbness [ˈdʌmnis], *s.* mudez.
dummy [ˈdʌmi], *a.* simulado, fingido, postizo; (*aer.*) ***dummy run,*** ataque simulado, simulacro de ataque; prueba. — *s.* pelele; (*de niño*) chupete; (*naipes*) muerto; ***tailor's dummy,*** maniquí.
dump [dʌmp], *s.* basurero; depósito; sitio de tercera categoría; poblachón; cinucho; ***to be down in the dumps,*** tener murria, tener las murrias, estar deprimido. — *v.t.* descargar, vaciar de golpe; deshacerse de; (*com.*) inundar el mercado con; ***dump down,*** soltar, plantificar.
dumpling [ˈdʌmpliŋ], *s.* bola de masa.
dumpy [ˈdʌmpi], *a.* rechoncho, regordete.
dun (1) [dʌn], *a.* pardo.
dun (2) [dʌn], *s.* acreedor importuno; apremio. — *v.t.* importunar.
dunce [dʌns], *s.* tonto, burro.
dunderhead [ˈdʌndəhed], *s.* tonto, zopenco.
dune [dju:n], *s.* duna.
dung [dʌŋ], *s.* estiércol, fiemo; cagada; ***dung-beetle,*** escarabajo bolero; ***cow-dung,*** boñiga; ***hen-dung,*** gallinaza; ***horse-dung,*** cagajón. — *v.t.*, *v.i.* estercolar.
dungeon [ˈdʌndʒən], *s.* mazmorra, calabozo.
dunghill [ˈdʌŋhil], *s.* muladar, estercolero, basurero.
dungy [ˈdʌŋi], *a.* lleno de estiércol, puerco, sucio.
dunnage [ˈdʌnidʒ], *s.* (*mar.*) abarrote.
dunnish [ˈdʌniʃ], *a.* pardo.
duo [ˈdju:ou], *s.* dúo.
duodecimal [dju:ouˈdesiməl], *a.* duodecimal.
duodecimo [dju:ouˈdesimou], *s.* libro en dozavo.
duodenal [dju:ouˈdi:nəl], *s.* duodenal; ***duodenal ulcer,*** úlcera duodenal.
duodenum [dju:oˈdi:nəm], *s.* duodeno.
dupe [dju:p], *s.* engañado, primo, incauto. — *v.t.* embaucar.
duple [dju:pl], *a.* duplo, doble. — *v.t.* duplicar; doblar.
duplex [ˈdju:pleks], *a.* duplo, doble, dúplice; (*tele.*) duplex.
duplicate [ˈdju:plikit], *a.* duplicado, doble. — *s.* duplicado, copia. — [ˈdju:plikeit], *v.t.* duplicar, reproducir, copiar.
duplication [dju:pliˈkeiʃən], *s.* duplicación.
duplicator [ˈdju:plikeitə], *s.* duplicador, copiador.
duplicity [dju:ˈplisiti], *s.* duplicidad, doblez.
durability [djuərəˈbiliti], *s.* durabilidad.

durable [ˈdjuərəbl], *a.* durable, duradero; permanente, estable.
durableness [ˈdjuərəblnis], *s.* durabilidad.
durance [ˈdjuərəns], *s.* prisión, cautividad, encierro.
duration [djuəˈreiʃən], *s.* duración.
duress [djuəˈres], *s.* encierro, prisión; compulsión, coacción.
during [ˈdjuəriŋ], *prep.* durante.
dusk [dʌsk], *a.* obscuro, obscurecido. — *s.* obscuridad; crepúsculo, nochecita; ***at dusk,*** entre dos luces.
duskiness [ˈdʌskinis], *s.* obscuridad; (lo) obscuro; morenez; (lo) moreno.
dusky [ˈdʌski], *a.* obscuro; fusco; pardo; moreno.
dust [dʌst], *a.* de polvo, para el polvo. — *s.* polvo; cenizas, *f.pl.*; basura; ***dust-brush,*** plumero; (*aut.*) ***dust-cap,*** sombrerete de válvula, tapa guardapolvo; ***dust-cart,*** carro de la basura; ***dust-cover*** o ***dust-jacket,*** sobrecubierta (*libro*); ***dust-hole,*** basurero; ***dust-sheet,*** guardapolvo; ***dust-up,*** pelea, bronca; ***to raise a dust,*** armar un alboroto; ***to throw dust in s.o.'s eyes,*** engañar a alguien. — *v.t.* desempolvar, quitar *o* sacudir el polvo de; espolvorear.
dustbin [ˈdʌstbin], *s.* cubo de la basura.
duster [ˈdʌstə], *s.* plumero, guardapolvo; paño para el polvo.
dustiness [ˈdʌstinis], *s.* estado polvoriento, (lo) polvoriento.
dustman [ˈdʌstmən], *s.* basurero; barrendero.
dustpan [ˈdʌstpæn], *s.* recogedor.
dusty [ˈdʌsti], *a.* polvoriento, lleno de polvo; ***dusty answer,*** respuesta brusca.
Dutch [dʌtʃ], *a.*, *s.* holandés, *m.*; ***double Dutch,*** jerigonza, monserga, galimatías; ***to go Dutch,*** pagar a escote; ***the Dutch,*** los holandeses.
duteous [ˈdju:tiəs], *a.* obediente, respetuoso, obsequioso, sumiso.
dutiable [ˈdju:tiəbl], *a.* imponible.
dutiful [ˈdju:tiful], *a.* obediente, respetuoso.
dutifulness [ˈdju:tifulnis], *s.* obediencia, respeto.
duty [ˈdju:ti], *s.* deber, obligación; servicio; derecho; ***duty free,*** libre de derechos; franco de servicio; ***in duty bound to,*** con obligación de; ***off duty,*** libre; ***to be on duty,*** estar de servicio; estar de guardia; ***to do duty for,*** servir (en lugar) de; ***to take up one's duties,*** entrar en funciones; incorporarse al trabajo.
duumvir [dju:ˈʌmvə], *s.* duunviro.
duumvirate [dju:ˈʌmvirit], *s.* duunvirato.
dwale [dweil], *s.* belladona; (*blas.*) sable.
dwarf [dwɔ:f], *a.* enano; diminuto. — *s.* enano, enana. — *v.t.* achicar, empequeñecer; impedir el crecimiento de. — *v.i.* achicarse, empequeñecerse.
dwarfish [ˈdwɔ:fiʃ], *a.* enano, diminuto.
dwell [dwel], *v.i.* habitar, residir, morar; explayarse (***upon,*** en).
dweller [ˈdwelə], *s.* morador, habitante.
dwelling [ˈdweliŋ], *s.* morada; vivienda.
dwindle [dwindl], *v.i.* disminuir(se), menguar; ir consumiéndose, ir desapareciendo.
dye [dai], *s.* tinte; color, matiz; ***dye-stuff,*** tinte, colorante; ***dye-wood,*** madera de tinte; ***dye-works,*** tintorería; ***of the deepest dye,*** de la peor calaña.
dyeing [ˈdaiiŋ], *s.* tintura.
dyer [ˈdaiə], *s.* tintorero; (*bot.*) ***dyer's broom,*** ginesta.
dying [ˈdaiiŋ], *a.* moribundo, agonizante; ***dying words,*** últimas palabras; ***to be dying for,*** estar muerto por, estar deseando.
dynam [ˈdainæm], *s.* dinamia.
dynameter [daiˈnæmitə], *s.* dinámetro.
dynamic [daiˈnæmik], *a.* dinámico.
dynamics [daiˈnæmiks], *s.pl.* dinámica.
dynamite [ˈdainəmait], *s.* dinamita. — *v.t.* dinamitar.
dynamiter [ˈdainəmaitə], *s.* dinamitero.
dynamo [ˈdainəmou], *s.* dínamo, *f.*
dynamometer [dainəˈmɔmitə], *s.* dinamómetro.
dynamometric(al) [dainəmoˈmetrik(əl)], *a.* dinamométrico.
dynast [ˈdainæst], *s.* dinasta, *m.*
dynastic [diˈnæstik], *a.* dinástico.
dynasty [ˈdinəsti], *s.* dinastía.
dyne [dain], *s.* (*fís.*) dina.
dysenteric [disənˈterik], *a.* disentérico.
dysentery [ˈdisəntri], *s.* disentería.
dyspepsia [disˈpepsiə], *s.* dispepsia.
dyspeptic [disˈpeptik], *a.*, *s.* dispéptico; melancólico.
dysphagia [disˈfeidʒiə], *s.* disfagia.
dysphonia [disˈfouniə], *s.* disfonía.
dyspnœa [dispˈniə], *s.* disnea.
dysuria [disˈjuəriə], *s.* disuria.

E

E, e [iː], quinta letra del alfabeto. — *s.* (*mús.*) mi.
each [iːtʃ], *a.* cada, todo. — *adv.* cada uno, por persona, por cabeza. — *pron.* cada uno, cada cual; ***each other,*** uno(s) a otro(s).
eager [ˈiːgə], *a.* ansioso, anhelante; impaciente; afanoso.
eagerness [ˈiːgənis], *s.* ansia, anhelo; afán.
eagle [iːgl], *s.* (*orn.*) águila; ***eagle-eyed,*** de vista de lince; ***eagle-winged,*** alado como águila.
eagless [ˈiːglis], *s.* hembra del águila.
eaglet [ˈiːglit], *s.* aguilucho.
ear (1) [iə], *s.* oreja; oído; asa; ***to be all ears,*** ser todo oídos; ***by ear,*** de oído; ***to give ear to,*** prestar oído a; ***to have a good ear,*** tener buen oído; ***to have s.o.'s ear,*** gozar del favor de alguien; ***to prick up one's ears,*** aguzar el oído; ***to turn a deaf ear,*** hacerse el sordo, hacer oídos de mercader; ***up to the ears,*** (metido) hasta los ojos.
ear (2) [iə], *s.* espiga. — *v.i.* espigar.
earache [ˈiəreik], *s.* dolor de oídos.
eardrop [ˈiədrɔp], *s.* pendiente, zarcillo, arete.
eardrum [ˈiədrʌm], *s.* tímpano del oído.
eared [iəd], *a.* (*bot.*) espigado; ***long-eared,*** orejudo.
earing [ˈiəriŋ], *s.* (*mar.*) empuñidura de una vela; (*mar.*) ***reef-earings,*** empuñiduras de rizas.
earl [əːl], *s.* conde.
earlap [ˈiəlæp], *s.* lóbulo de la oreja.
earldom [ˈəːldəm], *s.* condado.
earless [ˈiəlis], *a.* desorejado.
earliness [ˈəːlinis], *s.* precocidad; prontitud, presteza; anticipación, antelación.
early [ˈəːli], *a.* temprano; primero, primitivo; pronto; precoz; ***early bird,*** madrugador; ***at an early date,*** en fecha próxima. — *adv.* temprano; pronto; al principio; con tiempo; ***as early as possible,*** lo más pronto posible; ***early in the morning,*** por la mañana temprano; de madrugada; ***early in the year,*** a comienzos del año; ***to arrive five minutes early,*** llegar cinco minutos antes *o* con cinco minutos de anticipación; ***to be early,*** llegar pronto.
earmark [ˈiəmɑːk], *s.* marca en la oreja; marca, contraseña. — *v.t.* marcar, traseñalar; destinar.
earn [əːn], *v.t.* merecer, ganar; devengar.
earnest (1) [ˈəːnist], *a.* serio, formal; grave; sincero, honrado; de veras. — *s.* veras, *f.pl.*, seriedad, buena fe; ***in (real) earnest,*** en serio, de veras.
earnest (2) [ˈəːnist], *s.* prenda, señal; ***earnest money,*** arras, *f.pl.*; paga y señal.
earnestness [ˈəːnistnis], *s.* seriedad, formalidad; gravedad.
earnings [ˈəːniŋz], *s.pl.* paga, jornal; (*com.*) ingresos, *m.pl.*, ganancias, *f.pl.*
earphone [ˈiəfoun], *s.* auricular.
earpiece [ˈiəpiːs], *s.* (*tele.*) auricular.
earring [ˈiəriŋ], *s.* zarcillo, pendiente, arete.
earshot [ˈiəʃɔt], *s.* alcance del oído; ***within earshot,*** al alcance del oído.
ear-splitting [ˈiə-splitiŋ], *a.* ensordecedor; que rompe el tímpano.
earth [əːθ], *s.* tierra; barro; madriguera; ***to cost the earth,*** valer un dineral; ***to run to earth,*** dar con; ***to the four corners of the earth,*** a las cinco partes del mundo; ***what on earth . . .?*** ¿qué demonios . . .? — *v.t.* enterrar; conectar a tierra; ***earth up,*** acollar, aporcar.
earth-bank [ˈəːθ-bæŋk], *s.* terraplén.
earth-board [ˈəːθ-bɔːd], *s.* orejera (del arado).
earth-born [ˈəːθ-bɔːn], *a.* terrígeno; humano, mortal; de nacimiento humilde.
earthen [ˈəːθən], *a.* térreo, terroso; de barro.
earthenware [ˈəːθənwɛə], *s.* loza (de barro).
earthiness [ˈəːθinis], *s.* (lo) terroso; (lo) grosero; (lo) sensual.
earthly [ˈəːθli], *a.* terrenal, mundano; ***he hasn't an earthly (chance),*** no tiene ni la menor posibilidad *o* esperanza; ***it's no earthly use,*** no sirve absolutamente para nada.
earth-nut [ˈəːθ-nʌt], *s.* chufa.
earthquake [ˈəːθkweik], *s.* terremoto.
earth-worm [ˈəːθ-wəːm], *s.* lombriz de tierra.
earthy [ˈəːθi], *a.* terroso; grosero, basto; sensual, carnal.
ear-trumpet [ˈiəː-trʌmpit], *s.* trompetilla.
earwig [ˈiəwig], *s.* (*ent.*) tijereta.
ease [iːz], *s.* facilidad; soltura, desenvoltura, desembarazo; comodidad, holgura, desahogo; alivio; naturalidad; ***at ease,*** cómodo, a gusto, a sus anchas; ***ill at ease,*** incómodo; ***life of ease,*** vida desahogada *o* descansada; ***put your mind at ease!*** ¡tranquilícese!; ***stand at ease!*** ¡en su lugar, descansen!; ***to take one's ease,*** descansar, ponerse a sus anchas; ***with ease,*** con facilidad, fácilmente. — *v.t.* aliviar; suavizar; aligerar; aflojar, soltar; tranquilizar. — *v.i.* amainar; moderarse.
easel [ˈiːzəl], *s.* caballete.
easement [ˈiːzmənt], *s.* comodidad; alivio; (*for.*) servidumbre, *f.*
easiness [ˈiːzinis], *s.* facilidad; soltura, desembarazo.
east [iːst], *a.* del este, oriental; levantino. — *s.* este, oriente; levante.
Easter [ˈiːstə], *s.* Pascua de Resurrección, Pascua florida; semana santa; ***Easter Sunday,*** Domingo de Resurrección.
easterly [ˈiːstəli], *a., adv.* del este; hacia el este.
eastern [ˈiːstən], *a.* oriental.
eastward [ˈiːstwəd], *adv.* hacia el este.
easy [ˈiːzi], *a.* fácil; desenvuelto, desembarazado; cómodo; holgado, desahogado, acomodado; natural, accesible, asequible; lento, pausado; ***easy-chair,*** sillón, butaca; ***easy-going,*** poco exigente, de manga ancha; despreocupado; ***easy to get on with,*** de trato fácil; ***to take it easy,*** tomar las cosas con calma *o* con filosofía; ir despacio *o* despacito; descansar.
eat [iːt], *irr. v.t., v.i.* comer; ***eat away*** o ***into,*** corroer; carcomer; ***eat one's heart out,*** consumirse; ***eat humble pie,*** humillarse, achantarse, ***eat up,*** comerse; ***eat one's words,*** retractarse; desdecirse; ***what's eating you?*** ¿qué mosca te ha picado? — *v.i.* comer; (*fig.*) ***he can't eat,*** no tiene ganas; ***to have s.o. eating out of one's hand,*** tener a alguien en un puño.
eatable [ˈiːtəbl], *a.* comestible. — *s.pl.* comestibles, *m.pl.*
eater [ˈiːtə], *s.* ***to be a big eater,*** ser comilón.
eating-house [ˈiːtiŋ-haus], *s.* tasca.
eaves [iːvz], *s.pl.* alero.
eavesdrop [ˈiːvzdrɔp], *v.i.* escuchar clandestinamente, escuchar a las puertas; fisgonear.
eavesdropper [ˈiːvzdrɔpə], *s.* el que escucha clandestinamente *o* a escondidas.
ebb [eb], *s.* menguante, reflujo; (*fig.*) decadencia; ***at a low ebb,*** decaído; ***ebb tide,*** marea menguante; ***ebb of life,*** vejez. — *v.i.* menguar (la marea); decaer, disminuir.
ebbing [ˈebiŋ], *s.* reflujo.
ebon [ˈebən], *a.* de ébano.
ebonist [ˈebənist], *s.* ebanista, *m.f.*
ebonite [ˈebənait], *s.* ebonita.
ebonize [ˈebənaiz], *v.t.* ebonizar.
ebony [ˈebəni], *s.* ébano.
ebriety [iˈbraiəti], *s.* ebriedad, embriaguez.
ebullience [iˈbʌliəns], *s.* ebullición, hervor; entusiasmo, euforia.
ebullient [iˈbʌliənt], *a.* entusiasta, eufórico.

ebullition [ebə'liʃən], *s.* hervor, ebullición; (*fig.*) viva emoción, euforia; (*quím.*) efervescencia.
eccentric [ik'sentrik], *a.* excéntrico; extravagante, estrafalario, estrambótico. — *s.* excéntrico, estrafalario; (*mec.*) rueda excéntrica; desvío del centro.
eccentricity [eksen'trisiti], *s.* excentricidad.
ecchymosis [eki'mousis], *s.* equimosis, *f.inv.*
ecclesiastic(al) ['ikli:zi'æstik(əl)], *a.* eclesiástico. — **ecclesiastic,** *s.* eclesiástico.
ecclesiology [ekli:zi'ɔlədʒi], *s.* ciencia de la arquitectura y decoración eclesiásticas; grado.
echelon ['eʃəlɔn], *s.* (*mil.*) escalón. — *v.t.* escalonar.
echinoderm [e'kainodə:m], *s.* (*zool.*) equinodermo.
echinus [e'kainəs], *s.* erizo de mar, equino, estrellamar; (*arq.*) cuarto bocel, miembro de moldura.
echo ['ekou], *s.* eco; ***echo sounder,*** sonda acústica. — *v.t.* repetir, hacerse eco de; ***echo s.o.'s opinions,*** hacerse eco de la opinión de alguien. — *v.i.* resonar, repercutir.
echometer [e'kɔmitə], *s.* ecómetro.
echometry [e'kɔmitri], *s.* ecometría.
eclat [ei'klɑ:], *s.* esplendor, magnificiencia, lustre; aclamación, aplauso; celebridad, renombre.
eclectic [i'klektik], *a.* ecléctico.
eclecticism [i'klektisizəm], *s.* eclecticismo.
eclipse [i'klips], *s.* eclipse. — *v.t.* eclipsar. — *v.i.* eclipsarse.
ecliptic [i'kliptik], *a.* eclíptico. — *s.* eclíptica.
eclogue ['eklɔg], *s.* égloga.
economic(al) [i:kə'nɔmik(əl)], *a.* económico.
economics [i:kə'nɔmiks], *s.pl.* (ciencias) económicas; economía política.
economist [i'kɔnəmist], *s.* economista, *m.f.*
economize [i'kɔnəmaiz], *v.t.*, *v.i.* economizar.
economy [i'kɔnəmi], *s.* economía.
ecstasy ['ekstəsi], *s.* éxtasis, arrobamiento; ***to go into ecstasies,*** extasiarse. — *v.t.* extasiar, arrobar.
ecstatic [eks'tætik], *a.* extático.
Ecuador ['ekwədɔ:]. (el) Ecuador.
Ecuadorian [ekwə'dɔ:riən], *a.*, *s.* ecuatoriano.
ecumenic(al) [i:kju'menik(əl)], *a.* ecuménico.
eczema ['eksimə], *s.* eczema, *m.*
eddy ['edi], *s.* remolino. — *v.t.* arremolinar, remolinear. — *v.i.* arremolinarse, remolinear.
edema [ŒDEMA].
edematous [ŒDEMATOUS].
Eden ['i:dən], *s.* (el) edén, Edén.
edentate [i'denteit], *a.* desdentado.
edge [edʒ], *s.* borde, margen, orilla; canto; extremidad; filo, corte; ribete; punta, acrimonia; ventaja; ***to have the edge on,*** llevar ventaja a; ***on edge,*** de canto; nervioso; ***to put an edge on,*** sacar filo a; ***to set the teeth on edge,*** dar dentera; ***to take the edge off,*** embotar. — *v.t.* afilar; orlar; ribetear; ***edge out,*** ir excluyendo poco a poco. — *v.i.* ***edge in,*** irse colando poco a poco; ***edge out,*** ir saliendo poco a poco.
edgeways, edgewise ['edʒweiz, -waiz], *adv.* de filo, de canto, de lado; ***I couldn't get a word in edgeways,*** no pude *o* no logré meter baza.
edging ['edʒiŋ], *s.* orla, ribete.
edgy ['edʒi], *a.* (*fam.*) nervioso.
edible ['edibl], *a.* comestible.
edict ['i:dikt], *s.* edicto.
edification [edifi'keiʃən], *s.* edificación.
edifice ['edifis], *s.* edificio.
edify ['edifai], *v.t.* edificar.
edifying ['edifaiiŋ], *a.* edificante.
edit ['edit], *v.t.* redactar; editar; preparar para la imprenta.
edition [i'diʃən], *s.* edición; tirada.
editor ['editə], *s.* redactor; editor.
editorial [edi'tɔ:riəl], *a.* editorial; ***editorial staff,*** redacción. — *s.* artículo de fondo, editorial.
editorship ['editəʃip], *s.* cargo de redactor.
educate ['edjukeit], *v.t.* educar; instruir.
educated ['edjukeitid], *a.* culto.
education [edju'keiʃən], *s.* educación; instrucción; enseñanza, pedagogía.
educational [edju'keiʃənəl], *a.* educativo; educacional; docente.
educator ['edjukeitə], *s.* educador.
educe [i'dju:s], *v.t.* educir, extraer.
edulcorate [i'dʌlkəreit], *v.t.* edulcorar, endulzar, dulzurar.
edulcoration [idʌlkə'reiʃən], *s.* edulcoración, dulcificación.
eel [i:l], *s.* anguila; ***electric eel,*** gimnoto.
e'en [i:n], *adv. contr.* [EVEN (2)].
e'er [ɛə], *adv. contr.* [EVER].
eerie, eery ['iəri], *a.* misterioso, sobrenatural, espectral; que infunde miedo *o* inquietud.
eeriness ['iərinis], *s.* (lo) misterioso, (lo) espectral.
efface [i'feis], *v.t.* borrar.
effaceable [i'feisəbl], *a.* deleble.
effacement [i'feismənt], *s.* (el) borrar.
effect [i'fekt], *s.* efecto; consecuencia, resultado; cumplimiento, vigencia, vigor; realidad; eficacia; (*pl.*) efectos, bienes; ***for effect,*** para impresionar; ***in effect,*** en realidad; vigente; ***of no effect,*** inútil, vano; ***to this effect,*** con este fin, propósito; ***to the effect that,*** en el sentido de que; ***to carry into effect,*** poner en ejecución; ***to give effect to,*** poner en efecto; ***to put into effect,*** poner en vigor; ***to take effect,*** ponerse en vigor; (empezar a) tener vigencia; surtir efecto. — *v.t.* efectuar, llevar a cabo, ejecutar.
effective [i'fektiv], *a.* eficaz; efectivo; potente, impresionante; útil (*para el servicio*); real; ***to become effective,*** entrar en vigor; ***effective capacity,*** capacidad útil; ***effective power,*** potencia real. — *s.*(*pl.*) efectivos, *m.pl.*
effectiveness [i'fektivnis], *s.* eficiencia, eficacia.
effectless [i'fektlis], *a.* ineficaz, sin efecto.
effector [i'fektə], *s.* causa eficiente; causador.
effectual [i'fektjuəl], *a.* eficaz, activo, eficiente.
effectualness [i'fektjuəlnis], *s.* eficacia.
effectuate [i'fektjueit], *v.t.* efectuar, ejecutar.
effeminacy, effeminateness [i'feminəsi, -itnis], *s.* afeminación, molicie, *f.*
effeminate [i'feminit], *a.* afeminado. — *s.* (hombre) afeminado.
effeminize [i'feminaiz], *v.t.* afeminar.
effervesce [efə'ves], *v.t.* bullir, estar (*o* entrar) en efervescencia.
effervescence [efə'vesəns], *s.* efervescencia.
effervescent [efə'vesənt], *a.* efervescente.
effervescing [efə'vesiŋ], *a.* gaseoso.
effete [i'fi:t], *a.* desvitalizado, lánguido, decadente; infructuoso, estéril.
efficacious [efi'keiʃəs], *a.* eficaz, eficiente; activo, vivo, fuerte, poderoso.
efficaciousness, efficacy [efi'keiʃəsnis, 'efikəsi], *s.* eficacia, eficiencia.
efficiency [i'fiʃənsi], *s.* eficacia; eficiencia; capacidad; rendimiento.
efficient [i'fiʃənt], *a.* eficaz; eficiente; capaz, activo. — *s.* causa eficiente.
effigy ['efidʒi], *s.* efigie, *f.*, imagen, *f.*, retrato.
effloresce [eflɔ:'res], *v.i.* (*quím.*) eflorescer(se).
efflorescence [eflɔ:'resəns], *s.* eflorescencia, florescencia.
efflorescent [eflɔ:'resənt], *a.* eflorescente, en flor.
effluence ['efluəns], *s.* emanación, efusión, efluxión.
effluent ['efluənt], *a.* efluente. — *s.* aguas residuales, *f.pl.*, residuos, *m.pl.*
effluvium [i'flu:viəm], *s.* (*pl.* **effluvia** [-viə]) efluvio, emanación, tufo.
efflux ['eflʌks], *s.* flujo, derrame; efusión, emanación.

effort [ˈefət], *s.* esfuerzo; trabajo; ***to make efforts,*** hacer esfuerzos, esforzarse; ***to make every effort to,*** hacer todo lo posible por.
effortless [ˈefətlis], *a.* sin esfuerzos; fácil.
effrontery [iˈfrʌntəri], *s.* desvergüenza, descaro, desfachatez, insolencia.
effulgent [iˈfʌldʒənt], *a.* resplandeciente, refulgente.
effuse [iˈfju:z], *v.t.* derramar, verter, efundir. — *v.i.* derramarse; emanar.
effusion [iˈfju:ʒən], *s.* efusión.
effusive [iˈfju:siv], *a.* efusivo; expansivo, demostrativo, comunicativo.
eft [eft], *s.* lagartija; tritón.
egad! [iˈgæd], *interj.* (*ant.*) ¡pardiez!
egalitarian [igæliˈtɛəriən], *a.* igualitario.
egalitarianism [igæliˈtɛəriənizəm], *s.* igualitarismo.
egg [eg], *s.* huevo; (*fam., fig.*) ***bad egg,*** tío de cuidado, mala persona; ***boiled egg,*** huevo pasado por agua; ***egg-cup,*** huevero; (*fam.*) ***egg-head,*** intelectualón, intelectualote; ***egg-merchant,*** huevero; ***egg-plant,*** berenjena; ***egg-shaped,*** oviforme; ***egg-shell,*** cascarón; ***fried egg,*** huevo frito; ***to kill the goose that lays the golden eggs,*** matar la gallina de los huevos de oro; (*fam., fig.*) ***good egg,*** buen chico; ***new-laid egg,*** huevo fresco; ***scrambled eggs,*** huevos revueltos; ***to put all one's eggs in one basket,*** jugarlo todo a una sola carta. — *v.t.* — ***on,*** incitar, animar.
egis [ÆGIS].
eglantine [ˈegləntain], *s.* (*bot.*) eglantina.
ego [ˈegou], *s.* (el) yo.
egocentric [egoˈsentrik], *a.* egocéntrico.
egoism [ˈegouizəm], *s.* egoísmo.
egoist [ˈegouist], *s.* egoísta, *m.f.*
egoistic(al) [egouˈistik(əl)], *a.* egoísta, *m.f.*
egotism [ˈegotizəm], *s.* egotismo.
egotist [ˈegotist], *s.* egotista, *m.f.*; egoísta, *m.f.*
egotistic(al) [egoˈtistik(əl)], *a.* egotista, *m.f.*; egoísta, *m.f.*
egregious [iˈgri:dʒəs], *a.* infame; insigne; ***egregious piece of nonsense,*** soberana tontería.
egregiousness [iˈgri:dʒəsnis], *s.* notoriedad; eminencia.
egress, egression [ˈi:gres, iˈgreʃən], *s.* salida.
egret [ˈi:gret], *s.* (*orn.*) [AIGRET].
Egypt [ˈi:dʒipt]. Egipto.
Egyptian [iˈdʒipʃən], *a., s.* egipcio.
Egyptologist [i:dʒipˈtɔlədʒist], *s.* egiptólogo.
eider(-duck) [ˈaidə(-dʌk)], *s.* (*orn.*) pato de flojel.
eiderdown [ˈaidədaun], *s.* edredón; plumazón.
eidograph [ˈaidogræf], *s.* eidógrafo.
eight [eit], *a.* ocho. — *s.* ocho; (*dep.*) tripulación de ocho; (*fam.*) ***to have one over the eight,*** coger una merluza.
eighteen [ˈeiˈti:n], *a., s.* dieciocho, diez y ocho.
eighteenth [ˈeiˈti:nθ], *a.* decimoctavo; dieciocho (*títulos*). — *s.* decimoctavo, dieciochavo; dieciocho (*fechas*).
eightfold [ˈeitfould], *a.* óctuplo, óctuple. — *adv.* ocho veces.
eighth [eitθ], *a.* octavo; ***Henry the Eighth,*** Enrique Octavo. — *s.* octavo; ocho (*fechas*).
eightieth [ˈeitiəθ], *a.* octogésimo. — *s.* octogésimo, ochentavo.
eight-sided [ˈeit-ˈsaidid], *a.* octagonal; ochavado.
eighty [ˈeiti], *a., s.* ochenta, *m.*
either [ˈaiðə], *a.* uno u otro; uno y otro; cualquier (a) (de dos). — *adv.* tampoco; también. — *conj.* o, ya; ***either he goes or I do,*** o va él o voy yo. — *pron.* uno *o* cualquiera de los dos; el uno o el otro.
ejaculate [iˈdʒækjuleit], *v.t.* proferir, exclamar; eyacular. — *v.i.* exclamar.
ejaculation [idʒækjuˈleiʃən], *s.* exclamación; eyaculación; jaculatoria.
ejaculatory [iˈdʒækjuleitəri], *a.* exclamativo; jaculatorio.
eject [iˈdʒekt], *v.t.* lanzar, despedir, echar, expulsar; desahuciar.
ejection [iˈdʒekʃən], *s.* expulsión; desahucio.
ejector [iˈdʒektə], *s.* eyector, expulsor; desposeedor; (*aer.*) ***ejector seat,*** asiento expulsor.
eke [i:k], *v.t.* — ***out,*** estirar; ganar a duras penas.
elaborate [iˈlæbərit], *a.* complicado; rebuscado; minucioso. — [iˈlæbəreit], *v.t.* elaborar, labrar minuciosamente. — *v.i.* explayarse; ***elaborate on,*** ampliar.
elaborately [iˈlæbəritli], *adv.* cuidadosamente, primorosamente; con muchos detalles.
elaborateness [iˈlæbəritnis], *s.* (lo) complicado; (lo) rebuscado.
elaboration [ilæbəˈreiʃən], *s.* elaboración, realización.
elaborator [iˈlæbəreitə], *s.* artífice.
elapse [iˈlæps], *v.i.* pasar, transcurrir.
elastic [iˈlæstik], *a., s.* elástico.
elasticity [elæsˈtisiti], *s.* elasticidad.
elate [iˈleit], *v.t.* alborozar, regocijar, llenar de euforia.
elated [iˈleitid], *a.* gozoso, alborozado, eufórico.
elation [iˈleiʃən], *s.* júbilo, alborozo, euforia.
elbow [ˈelbou], *s.* codo; recodo, codillo; brazo (de sillón); ***at one's elbow,*** a la mano; ***out at elbows,*** con los codos rotos, raído; ***to crook the elbow,*** empinar el codo; ***elbow-grease,*** trabajo duro. — *v.t.* empujar con el codo; ***elbow one's way (through),*** abrirse paso a codazos. — *v.i.* codear, dar codazos; formar codo.
elder (1) [ˈeldə], *a. compar.* mayor, más viejo, más anciano, de más edad. — *s.* anciano, mayor, jefe de familia; dignatario, funcionario, eclesiástico; (*pl.*) ancianos, *m.pl.*, antepasados, *m.pl.*
elder (2) [ˈeldə], *s.* (*bot.*) saúco; ***elder-berry,*** baya de saúco.
elderly [ˈeldəli], *a.* mayor, de edad.
eldership [ˈeldəʃip], *s.* ancianidad; primogenitura; presbiterato.
eldest [ˈeldist], *a. superl.* (el) más anciano; (el) mayor; primogénito.
elecampane [elikæmˈpein], *s.* (*bot.*) enula campana.
elect [iˈlekt], *a., s.* elegido, escogido, electo; (*teo.*) predestinado. — *v.t.* elegir, escoger.
election [iˈlekʃən], *s.* elección; (*teo.*) predestinación.
electioneer [ilekʃəˈniə], *v.i.* hacer propaganda electoral, solicitar (*votos*).
electioneering [ilekʃəˈniəriŋ], *s.* maniobras electorales, *f.pl.*; ***electioneering agent,*** cacique.
elective [iˈlektiv], *a.* electivo.
elector [iˈlektə], *s.* elector.
electoral [iˈlektərəl], *a.* electoral.
electorate [iˈlektərit], *s.* electorado.
electorship [iˈlektəʃip], *s.* electorado.
electoress, electress [iˈlektris], *s.* electriz, *f.*
electric(al) [iˈlektrik(əl)], *a.* eléctrico; (*fig.*) cargado de electricidad; ***electrical engineer,*** ingeniero electricista.
electrician [ilekˈtriʃən], *s.* electricista, *m.f.*
electricity [ilekˈtrisiti], *s.* electricidad.
electrification [ilektrifiˈkeiʃən], *s.* electrificación.
electrify [iˈlektrifai], *v.t.* electrificar; electrizar.
electrize [iˈlektraiz], *v.t.* electrizar.
electro-biology [iˈlektrou-baiˈɔlədʒi], *s.* electrobiología.
electro-chemical [iˈlektrou-ˈkemikəl], *a.* electroquímico.
electro-chemistry [iˈlektrou-ˈkemistri], *s.* electroquímica.
electrocute [iˈlektrokju:t], *v.t.* electrocutar.
electrocution [elektroˈkju:ʃən], *s.* electrocución.
electrode [iˈlektroud], *s.* electrodo.
electro-dynamic [iˈlektrou-daiˈnæmik], *a.* electrodinámico.
electrology [ilekˈtrɔlədʒi], *s.* electrología.

electrolysis [ilek'trɔlisis], *s.* electrólisis, *f.inv.*
electrolyte [i'lektrolait], *s.* electrolito.
electrolytic [ilektro'litik], *a.* electrolítico.
electrolyzation [ilektrolai'zeiʃən], *s.* electrolización.
electrolyze [i'lektrolaiz], *v.t.* electrolizar.
electro-magnet [i'lektrou-'mægnit], *s.* electroimán.
electro-magnetic [i'lektrou-mæg'netik], *a.* electromagnético.
electro-magnetism [i'lektrou-'mægnitizəm], *s.* electromagnetismo.
electro-metallurgy [i'lektrou-me'tælədʒi], *s.* electrometalurgia.
electrometer [ilek'trɔmitə], *s.* electrómetro.
electrometrical [ilektro'metrikəl], *a.* electrométrico.
electrometry [ilek'trɔmitri], *s.* electrometría.
electro-motion [i'lektrou-'mouʃən], *s.* electrodinamismo.
electro-motive [i'lektrou-'moutiv], *a.* electromotor, electromotriz.
electro-motor [i'lektrou-'moutə], *s.* electromotor, motor eléctrico.
electron [i'lektrɔn], *s.* (*fís.*) electrón.
electro-negative [i'lektrou-'negətiv], *a.* electronegativo.
electronic [ilek'trɔnik], *a.* electrónico.
electropathy [ilek'trɔpəθi], *s.* electroterapia.
electrophorus [ilek'trɔfərəs], *s.* electróforo.
electro-plate [i'lektrou-'pleit], *v.t.* galvanizar.
electro-positive [i'lektrou-'pɔzitiv], *a.* electropositivo.
electroscope [i'lektroskoup], *s.* electroscopio.
electrostatic [ilektro'stætik], *a.* electrostático.
electrostatics [ilektro'stætiks], *s.pl.* electrostática.
electrotechnics [ilektro'tekniks], *s.pl.* electrotecnia.
electro-telegraphy [i'lektrou-ti'legrəfi], *s.* telegrafía eléctrica.
electrotype [i'lektrotaip], *s.* electrotipia. — *v.t.* electrotipar.
electuary [i'lektjuəri], *s.* electuario.
eleemosynary [elii:'mɔsinəri], *a.* limosnero; mendicante.
elegance ['eligəns], *s.* elegancia.
elegant ['eligənt], *a.* elegante.
elegiac [eli'dʒaiək], *a.* elegíaco.
elegiast, elegist [e'li:dʒiæst, 'elidʒist], *s.* elegíaco.
elegize ['elidʒaiz], *v.t.*, *v.i.* lamentar, deplorar; hacer una elegía.
elegy ['elidʒi], *s.* elegía.
element ['elimənt], *s.* elemento; (*pl.*) principios, *m.pl.*, nociones, *f.pl.*, rudimentos, *m.pl.*; (los) elementos; (*igl.*) pan y vino de la misa; (*fig.*) ***to be in one's element,*** estar como pez en (el) agua.
elemental [eli'mentəl], *a.* elemental.
elementary [eli'mentəri], *a.* elemental; ***elementary school,*** escuela.
elephant ['elifənt], *s.* elefante; (*fig.*) ***white elephant,*** inutilidad (costosa), maula.
elephantiasis [elifən'taiəsis], *s.* (*med.*) elefantiasis, *f.inv.*
elephantine [eli'fæntain], *a.* elefantino.
elevate ['eliveit], *v.t.* elevar, levantar, ascender, exaltar.
elevated ['eliveitid], *a.* elevado.
elevation [eli'veiʃən], *s.* elevación; altura, eminencia; (*arq.*) alzado; (*astron.*) altura.
elevator ['eliveitə], *s.* escalera móvil; elevador; noria; (*Am.*) [LIFT].
elevatory ['eliveitəri], *a.* que eleva. — *s.* (*cir.*) elevatorio.
eleven [i'levən], *a.*, *s.* once.
elevenses [i'levənziz], *s.pl.* (*fam.*) tentempié (*matutino*).
eleventh [i'levənθ], *a.* onceno, undécimo; once (*títulos*); ***at the eleventh hour,*** a última hora. — *s.* onzavo, undécima parte.
elf [elf], *s.* (*pl.* **elves** [elvz]) duende, alarbio, trasgo; diablillo; enano.
elfin ['elfin], *a.* de duendes; fantástico. — *s.* diablillo, niño travieso.
elfish ['elfiʃ], *a.* aduendado; (*fam.*) travieso.
elicit [i'lisit], *v.t.* sacar; provocar; sonsacar.
elide [i'laid], *v.t.* elidir.
eligibility, eligibleness [elidʒi'biliti, 'elidʒiblnis], *s.* elegibilidad.
eligible ['elidʒibl], *a.* elegible; aceptable, adecuado; casadero; ***to be highly eligible (for marriage),*** ser un buen partido.
eliminate [i'limineit], *v.t.* eliminar.
elimination [ilimi'neiʃən], *s.* eliminación.
elision [i'liʒən], *s.* elisión.
élite [ei'li:t], *s.* (lo) mejor, (lo) escogido, (lo) selecto, (la) flor y nata.
elixate [e'likseit], *v.t.* extraer por decocción.
elixation [elik'seiʃən], *s.* decocción, ebullición.
elixir [i'liksə], *s.* elixir.
Elizabeth [i'lizəbəθ]. Isabel, *f.*
Elizabethan [ilizə'bi:θən], *a.*, *s.* isabelino.
elk [elk], *s.* (*zool.*) anta, alce.
ellipse [i'lips], *s.* elipse, *f.*
ellipsis [i'lipsis], *s.* (*pl.* **ellipses** [-i:z]) (*gram.*) elipsis, *f.inv.*
ellipsoid [i'lipsɔid], *s.* elipsoide.
ellipsoidal [ilip'sɔidəl], *a.* elipsoidal, elipsidal.
elliptic(al) [i'liptik(əl)], *a.* elíptico.
elm [elm], *s.* (*bot.*) olmo; ***elm-grove,*** olmedo.
elocution [elə'kju:ʃən], *s.* elocución; declamación.
elocutionist [elə'kju:ʃənist], *s.* declamador; profesor de elocución.
elongate ['i:lɔŋgeit], *v.t.* alargar, extender.
elongated ['i:lɔŋgeitid], *a.* alargado, estirado.
elongation [i:lɔŋ'geiʃən], *s.* alargamiento, extensión; (*med.*) elongación.
elope [i'loup], *v.i.* fugarse (*con un amante*).
elopement [i'loupmənt], *s.* fuga.
eloquence ['eləkwəns], *s.* elocuencia.
eloquent ['eləkwənt], *a.* elocuente.
El Salvador [el'sælvədɔ:]. El Salvador.
else [els], *adv.* otro; más; demás; (de) otro modo; ***all else,*** todo lo demás; ***anyone else,*** (cualquier) otro, otro cualquiera; ***no one else,*** ningún otro; ***nothing else,*** nada más; ***or else,*** de otro modo, de lo contrario; si no; o bien; ***what else?*** ¿qué más?
elsewhere ['els'wɛə], *adv.* en otra parte, en otro lado, en otro sitio.
elucidate [i'l(j)u:sideit], *v.t.* elucidar, dilucidar, aclarar.
elucidation [il(j)u:si'deiʃən], *s.* elucidación, dilucidación, aclaración.
elucidative, elucidatory [i'l(j)u:sideitiv, -əri], *a.* explicativo.
elude [i'l(j)u:d], *v.t.* eludir, evitar, esquivar; ***it eludes me,*** se me escapa; no se me alcanza.
elusive [i'l(j)u:siv], *a.* evasivo; fugaz; difícil de localizar.
elver ['elvə], *s.* angula.
elves [elvz], *s.pl.* [ELF].
Elysian [i'liziən], *a.* elíseo.
emaciate [i'meiʃieit], *v.t.* demacrar, enflaquecer; extenuar.
emaciated [i'meiʃieitid], *a.* demacrado, escuálido.
emaciation [imeiʃi'eiʃən], *s.* demacración; extenuación.
emanate ['eməneit], *v.i.* emanar.
emanation [emə'neiʃən], *s.* emanación.
emanative ['eməneitiv], *a.* emanante.

emancipate [i'mænsipit], *a.* emancipado; manumitido. — [i'mænsipeit], *v.t.* emancipar; libertar, manumitir.
emancipation [imænsi'peiʃən], *s.* emancipación; manumisión.
emasculate [i'mæskjulit], *a.* castrado; afeminado. — [i'mæskjuleit], *v.t.* castrar, capar; afeminar; (*fig.*) debilitar; empobrecer; mutilar.
emasculation [imæskju'leiʃən], *s.* emasculación; afeminamiento; debilitación.
embalm [im'bɑ:m], *v.t.* embalsamar.
embalmer [im'bɑ:mə], *s.* embalsamador.
embalming [im'bɑ:miŋ], *s.* embalsamamiento.
embank [im'bæŋk], *v.t.* represar; terraplenar.
embankment [im'bæŋkmənt], *s.* terraplén; dique; ribera.
embargo [em'bɑ:gou], *s.* embargo; detención (*de buques*); prohibición; ***to lay an embargo on,*** embargar. — *v.t.* embargar; detener (*buques*).
embark [im'bɑ:k], *v.t.* embarcar. — *v.i.* embarcarse; ***embark on,*** emprender.
embarkation [embɑ:'keiʃən], *s.* embarque, embarco; embarcación.
embarrass [im'bærəs], *v.t.* desconcertar, turbar; embarazar, estorbar; avergonzar, azorar; poner en un apuro; ***I am embarrassed,*** me da apuro, es violento (para mí), me es violento; me encuentro en un apuro.
embarrassing [im'bærəsiŋ], *a.* violento; embarazoso; que da vergüenza *o* apuro; ***how embarrassing!*** ¡qué violencia!
embarrassment [im'bærəsmənt], *s.* vergüenza; compromiso; violencia; apuro.
embassy ['embəsi], *s.* embajada.
embattle [im'bætl], *v.t.* formar en orden de batalla; (*fig.*) fortificar, almenar. — *v.i.* ponerse en orden de batalla.
embattled [im'bætld], *a.* en orden de batalla; (*fig.*) arriscado; sitiado.
embed [im'bed], *v.t.* encajar, encajonar; incrustar, empotrar.
embellish [im'beliʃ], *v.t.* embellecer, hermosear; adornar.
embellishment [im'beliʃmənt], *s.* adorno, ornato; embellecimiento.
ember ['embə], *s.* ascua, pavesa; (*pl.*) rescoldos, *m.pl.*, brasas, *f.pl.*
Ember-week ['embə-wi:k], *s.* semana de témporas.
embezzle [im'bezl], *v.t.* malversar, desfalcar.
embezzlement [im'bezlmənt], *s.* malversación, desfalco.
embezzler [im'bezlə], *s.* malversador; desfalcador.
embitter [im'bitə], *v.t.* amargar, agriar; (*fig.*) envenenar.
emblazon [im'bleizən], *v.t.* blasonar; alabar, ensalzar.
emblazoner [im'bleizənə], *s.* blasonador; heraldo.
emblazonry [im'bleizənri], *s.* blasón.
emblem ['embləm], *s.* emblema, *m.*, símbolo, signo, cifra, divisa. — *v.t.* simbolizar.
emblematic(al) [emblə'mætik(əl)], *a.* emblemático.
emblements ['emblmənts], *s.pl.* (*for.*) derecho del arrendatario a su cosecha.
embodiment [im'bɔdimənt], *s.* encarnación; personificación.
embody [im'bɔdi], *v.t.* encarnar; personificar; incorporar.
embolden [im'bouldən], *v.t.* envalentonar.
embolism ['embəlizəm], *s.* (*astron.*) embolismo; (*med.*) embolia.
embolus ['embələs], *s.* (*pl.* **emboli** [-ai]) émbolo.
emboss [im'bɔs], *v.t.* repujar, realzar.
embossment [im'bɔsmənt], *s.* repujado, realce.
embottle [im'bɔtl], *v.t.* embotellar.
embow [im'bau], *v.t.* (*arq.*) abovedar.
embower [im'bauə], *v.t.* emparrar, enramar.
embrace [im'breis], *s.* abrazo. — *v.t.* abrazar; abarcar; ceñir; aceptar.
embrasure [im'breiʒə], *s.* (*fort.*) aspillera, tronera.
embrocate ['embrokeit], *v.t.* embrocar.
embrocation [embro'keiʃən], *s.* embrocación.
embroider [im'brɔidə], *v.t.* bordar; recamar.
embroiderer [im'brɔidərə], *s.* bordador; recamador.
embroidery [im'brɔidəri], *s.* bordado; bordados; recamado.
embroil [im'brɔil], *v.t.* embrollar, enredar (***with,*** con).
embroilment [im'brɔilmənt], *s.* embrollo, enredo.
embryo ['embriou], *a.* embrionario, en embrión. — *s.* embrión.
embryologist [embri'ɔlədʒist], *s.* embriólogo.
embryology [embri'ɔlədʒi], *s.* embriología.
embryonic [embri'ɔnik], *a.* embrionario.
emend [i'mend], *v.t.* enmendar.
emendation [i:men'deiʃən], *s.* enmienda.
emendator ['i:mendeitə], *s.* enmendador.
emendatory [i'mendətəri], *a.* enmendador.
emerald ['emərəld], *a.* de esmeralda; (*fam.*) ***the Emerald Isle,*** Irlanda. — *s.* esmeralda.
emerge [i'mə:dʒ], *v.i.* salir, surgir, emerger; aparecer; resultar.
emergence [i'mə:dʒəns], *s.* salida, aparición.
emergency [i'mə:dʒənsi], *a.* de urgencia; de emergencia; de auxilio. — *s.* urgencia; estado *o* caso de urgencia; emergencia.
emergent [i'mə:dʒənt], *a.* naciente.
emeritus [i'meritəs], *a.* emérito.
emersion [i'mə:ʃən], *s.* emersión.
emery ['eməri], *s.* esmeril; ***emery-paper,*** papel de esmeril.
emetic [i'metik], *a.*, *s.* emético.
emigrant ['emigrənt], *a.*, *s.* emigrante.
emigrate ['emigreit], *v.i.* emigrar.
emigration [emi'greiʃən], *s.* emigración.
émigré ['emigrei], *a.*, *s.* emigrado.
eminence ['eminəns], *s.* eminencia; (*fig.*) distinción.
eminent ['eminənt], *a.* eminente; distinguido.
emir [e'miə], *s.* emir.
emissary ['emisəri], *s.* emisario.
emission [i'miʃən], *s.* emisión; escape (*de vapor*).
emissory [i'misəri], *a.* excretor; que emite.
emit [i'mit], *v.t.* emitir; arrojar, despedir; (*quím.*) exhalar.
emmet ['emit], *s.* hormiga.
emollescence [emɔ'lesəns], *s.* (*metal.*) ablandamiento, reblandecimiento.
emolliate [i'mɔlieit], *v.t.* ablandar.
emollient [i'mɔliənt], *a.*, *s.* emoliente.
emolument [i'mɔljumənt], *s.* emolumento.
emotion [i'mouʃən], *s.* emoción; sentimiento; ***to appeal to the emotions,*** halagar los sentimientos.
emotional [i'mouʃənəl], *a.* emotivo; emocional; sentimental; impresionable muy sensible.
emotive [i'moutiv], *a.* emotivo.
empanel [im'pænəl], *v.t.* (*for.*) elegir (un jurado).
empathy ['empəθi], *s.* empatía.
emperor ['empərə], *s.* emperador.
emphasis ['emfəsis], *s.* énfasis, *m.*; ***to lay emphasis on*** [EMPHASIZE].
emphasize ['emfəsaiz], *v.t.* acentuar, subrayar, recalcar, hacer resaltar, hacer hincapié en, poner de relieve, ponderar.
emphatic [im'fætik], *a.* enfático, categórico, enérgico.
emphysema [emfi'si:mə], *s.* (*med.*) enfisema, *m.*
emphyteutic [emfi'tju:tik], *a.* enfitéutico.
empire ['empaiə], *s.* imperio.
empiric(al) [im'pirik(əl)], *a.* empírico. — **empiric,** *s.* empírico.

empiricism [im'pirisizəm], *s.* empirismo.
emplacement [im'pleismənt], *s.* emplazamiento.
employ [im'plɔi], *s.* empleo; ***in the employ of,*** empleado por. — *v.t.* emplear, servirse de; dar trabajo a.
employable [im'plɔiəbl], *a.* empleable.
employee [im'plɔii:], *s.* empleado, dependiente.
employer [im'plɔiə], *s.* patrón.
employment [im'plɔimənt], *s.* empleo; ocupación, servicio; ***employment agency,*** agencia de colocaciones; ***full employment,*** pleno empleo; ***level of employment,*** nivel de trabajo.
emporium [em'pɔ:riəm], *s.* emporio.
empower [im'pauə], *v.t.* autorizar, facultar, habilitar.
empress ['empris], *s.* emperatriz.
emptiness ['emptinis], *s.* vacío; vaciedad, vacuidad.
empty ['empti], *a.* vacío; vacuo, hueco; desocupado; vacante; vano; ***empty-handed,*** con las manos vacías; (*fam.*) ***empty-headed,*** casquivano. — *s.* casco. — *v.t.* vaciar; desocupar; descargar. — *v.i.* vaciarse; desaguar.
empurple [im'pə:pl], *v.t.* purpurar, teñir de púrpura.
empyreal, empyrean [empai'riəl, -'riən], *a.*, *s.* empíreo.
emu ['i:mju:], *s.* (*orn.*) emú.
emulate ['emjuleit], *v.t.* emular.
emulation [emju'leiʃən], *s.* emulación.
emulative ['emjulətiv], *a.* emulador.
emulator ['emjuleitə], *s.* émulo, emulador.
emulgent [i'mʌldʒənt], *a.*, *s.* (*med.*) emulgente.
emulous ['emjuləs], *a.* émulo, emulador.
emulously ['emjuləsli], *adv.* (*ant.*) a porfía, con emulación.
emulsion [i'mʌlʃən], *s.* emulsión.
emulsive [i'mʌlsiv], *a.* emulsivo.
emunctory [i'mʌŋktəri], *s.* (*med.*) emuntorio.
enable [i'neibl], *v.t.* permitir, habilitar (para), poner en condiciones (de), hacer posible (que).
enact [i'nækt], *v.t.* efectuar, poner en ejecución; dar, promulgar; decretar; hacer el papel de.
enactment [i'næktmənt], *s.* decreto; estatuto; promulgación.
enactor [i'næktə], *s.* ejecutor.
enamel [i'næməl], *s.* esmalte. — *v.t.* esmaltar.
enameller [i'næmələ], *s.* esmaltador.
enamelling [i'næməliŋ], *s.* esmaltadura.
enamour [i'næmə], *v.t.* enamorar; ***to become enamoured of*** o ***with,*** enamorarse de, prendarse de; encapricharse con.
encage [in'keidʒ], *v.t.* enjaular.
encamp [in'kæmp], *v.t.* acampar. — *v.i.* acamparse.
encampment [in'kæmpmənt], *s.* campamento.
encase [in'keis], *v.t.* encajonar; encerrar.
encash [in'kæʃ], *v.t.* cobrar.
encashment [in'kæʃmənt], *s.* cobro.
encaustic [in'kɔ:stik], *a.* encáustico. — *s.* (*pint.*) encausto.
enceinte [ɑ̃'sɛ̃:t], *s.* (*fort.*) recinto.
encephalic [ensi'fælik], *a.* encefálico.
encephalitis [ensefə'laitis], *s.* encefalitis, *f.inv.*
encephalon [en'sefəlɔn], *s.* encéfalo.
enchain [in'tʃein], *v.t.* encadenar.
enchainment [in'tʃeinmənt], *s.* encadenamiento.
enchant [in'tʃɑ:nt], *v.t.* encantar, hechizar.
enchanter [in'tʃɑ:ntə], *s.* encantador, hechicero.
enchanting [in'tʃɑ:ntiŋ], *a.* encantador.
enchantress [in'tʃɑ:ntris], *s.* encantadora, seductora.
encharge [in'tʃɑ:dʒ], *v.t.* fiar, encargar, encomendar.
enchase [in'tʃeis], *v.t.* engastar, cincelar.
enchasing [in'tʃeisiŋ], *s.* obra de cinceladura.

encircle [in'sə:kl], *v.t.* ceñir, cercar, rodear; circunvalar.
encirclement [in'sə:klmənt], *s.* envolvimiento.
enclave ['enkleiv], *s.* enclave.
enclitic [in'klitik], *a.* (*gram.*) enclítico. — *s.* enclítica.
enclose [in'klouz], *v.t.* cercar, encerrar; incluir, remitir adjunto, adjuntar.
enclosed [in'klouzd], *a.* adjunto.
enclosure [in'klouʒə], *s.* vallado, cercado, recinto; encerramiento; (lo) incluido.
encomiast [en'koumiæst], *s.* encomiasta, *m.f.*
encomium [en'koumiəm], *s.* encomio, elogio.
encompass [in'kʌmpəs], *v.t.* cercar, circundar, rodear; abarcar; llevar a cabo.
encompassment [in'kʌmpəsmənt], *s.* cerco, sitio; rodeo, vuelta; circunlocución.
encore [ɔŋ'kɔ:], *adv.* bis. — *s.* repetición, bis, *m.* — *v.t.* pedir la repetición de.
encounter [in'kauntə], *s.* encuentro. — *v.t.* encontrar, tropezar con, encontrarse con.
encourage [in'kʌridʒ], *v.t.* animar, alentar; fomentar, estimular.
encouragement [in'kʌridʒmənt], *s.* ánimo, aliento; fomento, estímulo, incentivo.
encourager [in'kʌridʒə], *s.* protector, fomentador.
encouraging [in'kʌridʒiŋ], *a.* alentador, esperanzador; fomentador, estimulante.
encroach [in'kroutʃ], *v.i.* — ***on*** o ***upon,*** insinuarse en, introducirse en; invadir, usurpar.
encroachment [in'kroutʃmənt], *s.* usurpación, intrusión.
encrust [in'krʌst], *v.t.* incrustar. — *v.i.* incrustarse.
encumber [in'kʌmbə], *v.t.* embarazar, estorbar, abrumar; sobrecargar, poner trabas a.
encumbrance, encumberment [in'kʌmbrəns, -bəmənt], *s.* embarazo, obstáculo, impedimento, estorbo, traba, carga, gravamen.
encyclical [in'siklikəl], *s.* encíclica.
encyclopædia, encyclopedia [insaiklo'pi:diə], *s.* enciclopedia.
encyclopædic(al) [insaiklo'pi:dik(əl)], *a.* enciclopédico.
encyclopædism [insaiklo'pi:dizəm], *s.* enciclopedismo.
encyclopædist [insaiklo'pi:dist], *s.* enciclopedista, *m.f.*
encyst [in'sist], *v.t.* enquistar. — *v.i.* enquistarse.
end [end], *s.* fin, final; extremo, cabo; remate; límite; acabamiento, término; objeto, finalidad; desenlace; fondo; consecuencia, resultado; ***at the end of,*** al fin de, al final de, al cabo de; a fines *o* finales de; ***from end to end,*** de cabo a cabo, de punta a punta, de cabo a rabo; ***in the end,*** al fin, al final; ***no end of,*** un sinfín de; ***on end,*** de punta; ***for days on end,*** durante días y (más) días; ***two hours on end,*** dos horas enteras; ***to the end that,*** a fin de que; ***to be at an end,*** estar terminado, haberse terminado; (*fam.*) ***to be at the end of one's tether,*** estar al final de su aguante; ***to come to an end,*** concluir(se), terminar(se), llegar a (su) término; (*fam.*) ***to get hold of the wrong end of the stick,*** coger el rábano por las hojas; (*fam.*) ***to go off at the deep end,*** subirse por las paredes; (*fam.*) ***to keep one's end up,*** cumplir (con) su cometido *o* (con) la parte que le corresponde; ***to make an end of,*** acabar con; (*fam.*) ***to make ends meet,*** cubrir las necesidades con el dinero disponible, estirar el dinero de forma que cubra las necesidades; ***to meet end on,*** chocar de frente; ***to set on end,*** poner de punta. — *v.t.* acabar, concluir, terminar. — *v.i.* terminar(se) *etc.*; morir; ***he ended up*** (***by***) ***shouting,*** acabó gritando, acabó por gritar.
endanger [in'deindʒə], *v.t.* poner en peligro; comprometer.

endear [in'diə], *v.t.* hacer querer, hacer simpático. — **endear o.s.,** *v.r.* — ***to,*** hacerse querer de, hacerse simpático a.
endearing [in'diəriŋ], *a.* atractivo, simpático.
endearment [in'diəmənt], *s.* ternura, terneza.
endeavour [in'devə], *s.* esfuerzo; conato; empeño. — *v.i.* esforzarse (por), intentar, procurar.
endecagon [en'dekəgən], *s.* endecágono.
endemic [en'demik], *a.* endémico.
endermic [en'də:mik], *a.* endérmico.
ending ['endiŋ], *s.* fin, conclusión; desenlace; terminación; desinencia.
endive ['endiv], *s.* (*bot.*) endibia, escarola.
endless ['endlis], *a.* interminable, inacabable, sin fin.
endlessness ['endlisnis], *s.* (lo) interminable.
endocardiac [endou'kɑ:diæk], *a.* endocardíaco.
endocardium [endou'kɑ:diəm], *s.* endocardio.
endocarp ['endoukɑ:p], *s.* endocarpio.
endometry [en'dɔmitri], *s.* endometría.
endorse [in'dɔ:s], *v.t.* endosar; (*com.*) firmar al dorso; avalar, refrendar, autorizar, aprobar; ***endorse a driving licence,*** poner nota de inhabilitación en el permiso de conducir.
endorsee [endɔ:'si:], *s.* endorsatorio.
endow [in'dau], *v.t.* dotar; fundar; ***endow with,*** dotar de.
endowment [in'daumənt], *s.* dotación; fundación; dote(s), prenda(s).
endue [in'dju:], *v.t.* ponerse (*vestidos etc.*), vestir; dotar, investir.
endurable [in'djuərəbl], *a.* soportable, tolerable, sufrible, resistible.
endurably [in'djuərəbli], *adv.* de un modo soportable.
endurance [in'djuərəns], *s.* resistencia, paciencia, aguante; duración; ***beyond*** o ***past endurance,*** insoportable.
endure [in'djuə], *v.t.* aguantar, soportar, tolerar. — *v.i.* perdurar.
endurer [in'djuərə], *s.* paciente, sufridor.
enduring [in'djuəriŋ], *a.* paciente, sufrido, tolerante; perdurable.
endways, endwise ['endweiz, -waiz], *adv.* de punta, de pie, derecho.
enema ['enimə], *s.* enema, *m.*
enemy ['enimi], *s.* enemigo; ***he is his own worst enemy,*** a quien perjudica es sobre todo a sí mismo.
energetic [enə'dʒetik], *a.* enérgico, vigoroso.
energize ['enədʒaiz], *v.t.* dar energía, dar vigor a. — *v.i.* obrar con energía.
energy ['enədʒi], *s.* energía.
enervate ['enəveit], *v.t.* debilitar, aplanar; enervar.
enervating ['enəveitiŋ], *a.* aplanador; enervante, enervador.
enervation [enə'veiʃən], *s.* debilidad; enervación.
enfeeble [in'fi:bl], *v.t.* debilitar, enervar.
enfeeblement [in'fi:blmənt], *s.* debilitación, debilidad.
enfeebling [in'fi:bliŋ], *a.* debilitante.
enfeoff [in'fef], *v.t.* enfeudar.
enfeoffment [in'fefmənt], *s.* enfeudación.
enfilade [enfi'leid], *s.* doble hilera; (*mil.*) enfilada. — *v.t.* enfilar; disponer en doble hilera.
enfold [in'fould], *v.t.* envolver, abrazar.
enforce [in'fɔ:s], *v.t.* hacer cumplir; dar cumplimiento a; obtener por fuerza; imponer; hacer efectivo.
enforceable [in'fɔ:səbl], *a.* ejecutable.
enforcement [in'fɔ:smənt], *s.* ejecución, puesta en vigor; compulsión, coacción.
enforcer [in'fɔ:sə], *s.* el que impone *o* hace cumplir.
enfranchise [in'fræntʃaiz], *v.t.* franquear; libertar, manumitir; dar carta de naturaleza a; conceder derechos políticos a.
enfranchisement [in'fræntʃaizmənt], *s.* franquicia; derecho de ciudadano; emancipación; manumisión.
enfranchiser [en'fræntʃaizə], *s.* libertador.
engage [in'geidʒ], *v.t.* empeñar, comprometer; ajustar, apalabrar, contratar; alistar; alquilar; atraer; trabar (*batalla*); trabar (*conversación*) con; (*mec.*) endentar, encajar, engranar. — *v.i.* — ***in,*** tomar parte en; ocuparse de, dedicarse a; practicar; trabar (*conversación, combate etc.*); (*mec.*) engranar, encajar.
engaged [in'geidʒd], *a.* ocupado; prometido (*para casarse*).
engagement [in'geidʒmənt], *s.* compromiso, cita; noviazgo; palabra *o* promesa de casamiento; ajuste, contrato; combate, batalla.
engaging [in'geidʒiŋ], *a.* atractivo, simpático.
engender [in'dʒendə], *v.t.* engendrar. — *v.i.* engendrarse.
engine ['endʒin], *s.* motor; máquina; locomotora; ***engine of war,*** ingenio bélico; ***engine-driver,*** maquinista, *m.*; ***engine-room,*** sala de máquinas.
engineer [endʒi'niə], *s.* ingeniero; mecánico; maquinista, *m.*; (*Am., f.c.*) [ENGINE-DRIVER]. — *v.t.* organizar; maquinar, tramar.
engineering [endʒi'niəriŋ], *a.* de ingeniería, ingenieril. — *s.* ingeniería.
English ['iŋgliʃ], *a.* inglés. — *s.* inglés, *m.*; ***the English,*** los ingleses.
Englishman ['iŋgliʃmən], *s.* inglés, *m.*
Englishwoman ['iŋgliʃwumən], *s.* inglesa.
engorge [in'gɔ:dʒ], *v.t* engullir. — *v.i.* atracarse.
engraft [in'grɑ:ft], *v.t.* injertar; implantar.
engrain [in'grein], *v.t.* [INGRAIN].
engrave [in'greiv], *v.t.* grabar; burilar; imprimir.
engraver [in'greivə], *s.* grabador.
engraving [in'greiviŋ], *s.* grabado.
engross [in'grous], *v.t.* absorber; copiar, poner en limpio, hacer una transcripción legal de; ***to be engrossed (in),*** estar absorto, estar ensimismado; estar absorbido por, estar enfrascado en.
engrossment [in'grousmənt], *s.* absorción, ensimismamiento, embebecimiento.
engulf [in'gʌlf], *v.t.* inundar, tragarse.
enhance [in'hɑ:ns], *v.t.* realzar; aumentar.
enhancement [in'hɑ:nsmənt], *s.* realce.
enharmonic [enhɑ:'mɔnik], *a.* enarmónico.
enigma [i'nigmə], *s.* enigma, *m.*
enigmatic [enig'mætik], *a.* enigmático.
enigmatist [i'nigmətist], *s.* enigmatista, *m.f.*
enjoin [in'dʒɔin], *v.t.* encargar, ordenar, mandar; imponer; (*for.*) prescribir, prohibir.
enjoy [in'dʒɔi], *v.t.* disfrutar de, gozar de; ***do you enjoy his books?*** ¿le gustan sus libros? — **enjoy o.s.,** *v.r.* divertirse, disfrutar, gozar, pasarlo bien.
enjoyable [in'dʒɔiəbl], *a.* agradable.
enjoyment [in'dʒɔimənt], *s.* goce, disfrute; fruición; gusto.
enkindle [in'kindl], *v.t.* encender; (*fig.*) inflamar.
enlace [in'leis], *v.t.* ceñir, enlazar, entrelazar.
enlarge [in'lɑ:dʒ], *v.t.* agrandar; aumentar; ensanchar; abultar; explayar; ampliar. — *v.i.* — ***upon,*** extenderse, explayarse (*sobre un tema etc.*).
enlargement [in'lɑ:dʒmənt], *s.* agrandamiento; ensanchamiento; ampliación.
enlighten [in'laitən], *v.t.* alumbrar, iluminar; ilustrar.
enlightened [in'laitənd], *a.* ilustrado; ***enlightened despotism,*** despotismo ilustrado.
enlightenment [in'laitənmənt], *s.* ilustración; esclarecimiento; ***the Enlightenment,*** (el siglo de) las Luces, la Ilustración.
enlink [in'liŋk], *v.t.* eslabonar.

enlist [in'list], *v.t.* (*mil.*) enganchar, reclutar, alistar; conseguir. — *v.i.* alistarse, sentar plaza, engancharse.
enlisting, enlistment [in'listiŋ, -mənt], *s.* alistamiento; enganche.
enliven [in'laivən], *v.t.* avivar, animar, alegrar.
enlivener [in'laivənə], *s.* vivificador, animador.
enlivenment [in'laivənmənt], *s.* animación.
enmesh [in'meʃ], *v.t.* enredar, enmarañar. — *v.i.* engranar, endentar.
enmity ['enmiti], *s.* enemistad, hostilidad.
ennead ['eniæd], *s.* grupo de nueve.
ennoble [i'noubl], *v.t.* ennoblecer.
ennoblement [i'noublmənt], *s.* ennoblecimiento.
ennui [ɔ'nwi:], *s.* tedio, hastío.
enormity [i'nɔ:miti], *s.* enormidad; demasía.
enormous [i'nɔ:məs], *a.* enorme.
enormousness [i'nɔ:məsnis], *s.* enormidad, inmensidad.
enough [i'nʌf], *a.* bastante, suficiente; ***that's enough,*** basta. — *adv.* bastante, suficientemente; harto; ***curiously enough,*** es curioso que, no deja de ser curioso que; por casualidad; ***would you be kind enough to . . .?*** ¿quiere Vd. tener la bondad de . . .? — *s.* (lo) bastante. — *interj.* ¡basta! ¡vale ya!
enounce [i'nauns], *v.t.* enunciar; declarar.
enquire [INQUIRE].
enquirer [INQUIRER].
enrage [in'reidʒ], *v.t.* enrabiar, hacer rabiar, enfurecer.
enrapt [in'ræpt], *a.* extasiado, arrebatado.
enrapture [in'ræptʃə], *v.t.* arrebatar, arrobar, embelesar, extasiar.
enrich [in'ritʃ], *v.t.* enriquecer.
enrichment [in'ritʃmənt], *s.* enriquecimiento.
enring [in'riŋ], *v.t.* cercar; anillar.
enrobe [in'roub], *v.t.* vestir, adornar.
enrol(l) [in'roul], *v.t.* alistar; inscribir; matricular. — *v.i.* alistarse; inscribirse; matricularse.
enrol(l)ment [in'roulmənt], *s.* matrícula, inscripción; alistamiento.
ensanguine [in'sæŋgwin], *v.t.* ensangrentar.
ensconce [in'skɔns], **o.s.,** *v.r.* instalarse, acomodarse.
ensemble [ɔ:n'sɔ:mbl], *s.* conjunto.
enshrine [in'ʃrain], *v.t.* guardar como reliquia; guardar *o* consignar con respeto y amor.
enshroud [in'ʃraud], *v.t.* amortajar; envolver.
ensiform ['ensifɔ:m], *a.* ensiforme.
ensign ['ensain], *s.* bandera, enseña; divisa, insignia; alférez, abanderado; ['ensən], (*mar.*) pabellón.
ensilage ['ensilidʒ], *s.* (*agric.*) ensilaje. — *v.t.* ensilar.
enslave [in'sleiv], *v.t.* esclavizar; avasallar.
enslavement [in'sleivmənt], *s.* esclavitud; avasallamiento.
enslaver [in'sleivə], *s.* esclavizador.
ensnare [in'snɛə], *v.t.* coger en una trampa, hacer caer en una trampa.
ensue [in'sju:], *v.i.* seguir; resultar.
ensuing [in'sju:iŋ], *a.* siguiente, próximo; consiguiente.
ensure [in'ʃuə], *v.t.* asegurar; garantizar; procurar; ***try to ensure that there is no repetition of this,*** procure que (esto) no vuelva a ocurrir.
entablature [in'tæblətʃə], *s.* (*arq.*) entablamento.
entail [in'teil], *s.* (*for.*) vínculo; mayorazgo. — *v.t.* vincular; suponer, comportar, implicar, entrañar; ocasionar, originar, acarrear.
entailment [in'teilmənt], *s.* (*for.*) vinculación.
entangle [in'tæŋgl], *v.t.* enmarañar, enredar, embrollar, liar; ***to become entangled,*** enmarañarse etc.
entanglement [in'tæŋglmənt], *s.* maraña, enredo, embrollo, lío; ***barbed-wire entanglement,*** alambrada.
enter ['entə], *v.t.* entrar en, ingresar en; penetrar en; asentar; anotar, registrar; inscribir, matricular; formular; inscribirse en, matricularse en; presentarse a *o* para; participar en; comprometerse a; entablar, establecer; ***enter a protest,*** formular una protesta. — *v.i.* entrar (en), ingresar (en); penetrar (en); (*teat.*) salir; ***enter into,*** (empezar a) participar en; (*acuerdo*) comprometerse a; ***enter into the spirit of,*** compenetrarse de, participar plenamente en; ***enter on*** o ***upon,*** emprender, iniciar; tomar posesión de.
enteric [en'terik], *a.* entérico.
entering ['entəriŋ], *s.* entrada.
enteritis [entə'raitis], *s.* (*pat.*) enteritis, *f.inv.*
enterprise ['entəpraiz], *s.* empresa; iniciativa, espíritu emprendedor.
enterprising ['entəpraiziŋ], *a.* emprendedor; aventurero.
entertain [entə'tein], *v.t.* festejar, agasajar; divertir, entretener; abrigar, albergar; considerar, tomar en consideración. — *v.i.* recibir gente (en casa).
entertainer [entə'teinə], *s.* animador; anfitrión, festejador.
entertaining [entə'teiniŋ], *a.* entretenido, divertido.
entertainment [entə'teinmənt], *s.* agasajo; entretenimiento, diversión; función, espectáculo.
enthrall [in'θrɔ:l], *v.t.* cautivar, hechizar; sojuzgar; apasionar.
enthralling [in'θrɔ:liŋ], *a.* cautivador, fascinante, apasionante.
enthrone [in'θroun], *v.t.* entronizar.
enthronement [in'θrounmənt], *s.* entronización.
enthusiasm [in'θju:ziæzəm], *s.* entusiasmo.
enthusiast [in'θju:ziæst], *s.* entusiasta, *m.f.*; aficionado.
enthusiastic [inθju:zi'æstik], *a.* entusiástico, entusiasta, caluroso; entusiasmado.
entice [in'tais], *v.t.* halagar, seducir, inducir, tentar, atraer.
enticement [in'taismənt], *s.* incitación, incitamiento; seducción.
enticer [in'taisə], *s.* incitador, tentador, seductor.
enticing [in'taisiŋ], *a.* atrayente, seductor.
entire [in'taiə], *a.* entero, cabal, íntegro, intacto.
entirely [in'taiəli], *adv.* enteramente, totalmente, por completo, por entero.
entirety, entireness [in'tai(ər)əti, -'taiənis], *s.* totalidad, integridad, entereza.
entitle [in'taitl], *v.t.* titular, intitular; calificar; dar derecho a, autorizar.
entity ['entiti], *s.* entidad, ente.
entoil [in'tɔil], *v.t.* enredar, coger en la trampa.
entomb [in'tu:m], *v.t.* enterrar, sepultar.
entombment [in'tu:mmənt], *s.* sepultura, entierro.
entomological [entəmə'lɔdʒikəl], *a.* entomológico.
entomologist [ento'mɔlədʒist], *s.* entomólogo.
entomology [ento'mɔlədʒi], *s.* entomología.
entourage [ɔntu'rɑ:ʒ], *s.* séquito, cortejo.
entrails ['entreilz], *s.pl.* intestinos, *m.pl.*; (*fig.*) entrañas, *f.pl.*
entrance (1) ['entrəns], *s.* entrada; acceso; ingreso; (*teat.*) salida; ***entrance-fee,*** cuota de entrada; ***entrance-hall,*** vestíbulo.
entrance (2) [in'trɑ:ns], *v.t.* arrobar, extasiar, transportar, hechizar, fascinar, cautivar.
entrant ['entrənt], *s.* aspirante; concursante; opositor; examinando.
entrap [in'træp], *v.t.* entrampar, atrapar.
entreat [in'tri:t], *v.t.* suplicar, rogar, implorar, instar.
entreaty [in'tri:ti], *s.* súplica, ruego, instancia.
entrée ['ɔntrei], *s.* derecho de acceso *o* entrada; (*coc.*) entrada, principio.

entrench [inˈtrentʃ], *v.t.* atrincherar; — ***o.s.,*** atrincherarse.
entrenchment [inˈtrentʃmənt], *s.* atrincheramiento, trinchera.
entrepôt [ˈɔntrəpou], *s.* almacén; centro comercial.
entrust [inˈtrʌst], *v.t.* confiar.
entry [ˈentri], *s.* entrada; ingreso; toma de posesión; (*dep.*) participación; participante; (*obra de consulta*) artículo; (*com.*) partida; ***entry permit,*** permiso de entrada; ***no entry,*** prohibido el paso.
entwine [inˈtwain], *v.t.* entrelazar, entretejer.
entwist [inˈtwist], *v.t.* enroscar, ensortijar.
enucleate [iˈnju:klieit], *v.t.* enuclear.
enucleation [inju:kliˈeiʃən], *s.* enucleación.
enumerate [iˈnju:məreit], *v.t.* enumerar.
enumeration [inju:məˈreiʃən], *s.* enumeración.
enumerative [iˈnju:mərətiv], *a.* enumerativo.
enunciate [eˈnʌnsieit], *v.t., v.i.* enunciar; pronunciar.
enunciation [enʌnsiˈeiʃən], *s.* enunciación; pronunciación.
enunciative [iˈnʌnsieitiv], *a.* enunciativo.
envelop [inˈveləp], *v.t.* envolver.
envelope [ˈenviloup], *s.* sobre; envoltura.
enveloping [inˈveləpiŋ], *a.* envolvente.
envelopment [inˈveləpmənt], *s.* envolvimiento.
envenom [inˈvenəm], *v.t.* envenenar, emponzoñar.
enviable [ˈenviəbl], *a.* envidiable.
envious [ˈenviəs], *a.* envidioso.
enviousness [ˈenviəsnis], *s.* envidia.
environment [inˈvaiərənmənt], *s.* ambiente, medio ambiente, entorno.
environs [inˈvaiərənz], *s.pl.* alrededores, *m.pl.*, cercanías, *f.pl.*, inmediaciones, *f.pl.*; afueras, *f.pl.*
envisage [inˈvizidʒ], *v.t.* prever, esperar(se); considerar.
envoy [ˈenvɔi], *s.* enviado.
envy [ˈenvi], *s.* envidia; ***he is the envy of all his friends,*** le envidian todos sus amigos. — *v.t.* envidiar, tener envidia a.
enwrap [inˈræp], *v.t.* envolver.
enwreathe [inˈri:ð], *v.t.* enguirnaldar.
enzyme [ˈenzaim], *s.* enzima.
Eolian [i:ˈouliən], *a.* eólico.
epact [ˈi:pækt], *s.* epacta.
epaule [iˈpɔ:l], *s.* (*fort.*) espaldón.
epaulement [iˈpɔ:lmənt], *s.* espaldón.
epaulette [ˈepɔ:let], *s.* (*mil.*) charretera, hombrera.
epenthesis [eˈpenθisis], *s.* (*gram.*) epéntesis, *f.inv.*
epenthetic(al) [epenˈθetik(əl)], *a.* epentético.
epergne [eˈpə:n], *s.* centro de mesa.
ephemeral [iˈfemərəl], *a.* efímero.
ephemerides [efiˈmeridi:z], *s.pl.* efemérides, *f.pl.*
Ephesian [eˈfi:ʒən], *a., s.* efesino.
ephod [ˈi:fɔd], *s.* efod, superhumeral.
epic [ˈepik], *a.* épico. — *s.* epopeya, poema épico.
epicardium [epiˈkɑ:diəm], *s.* epicardio.
epicarp [ˈepikɑ:p], *s.* epicarpo.
epicene [ˈepisi:n], *a.* epiceno.
epicure [ˈepikjuə], *s.* epicúreo, gastrónomo, sibarita, *m.f.*
epicurean [epikjuəˈriən], *a., s.* epicúreo.
epicurism [ˈepikjuərizəm], *s.* epicureísmo.
epicycle [ˈepisaikl], *s.* epiciclo.
epidemic [epiˈdemik], *a.* epidémico, epidemial. — *s.* epidemia.
epidermic [epiˈdə:mik], *a.* epidérmico.
epidermis [epiˈdə:mis], *s.* epidermis, *f.inv.*, cutícula.
epigastric [epiˈgæstrik], *a.* epigástrico.
epigastrium [epiˈgæstriəm], *s.* epigastrio.
epiglottis [epiˈglɔtis], *s.* epiglotis, *f.inv.*
epigram [ˈepigræm], *s.* epigrama, *m.*
epigrammatic(al) [epigrəˈmætik(əl)], *a.* epigramático.
epigrammatist [epiˈgræmətist], *s.* epigramatista, *m.f.*, epigramatario.
epigraph [ˈepigræf], *s.* epígrafe; inscripción.
epilepsy [ˈepilepsi], *s.* epilepsia, alferecía.
epileptic [epiˈleptik], *a., s.* epiléptico.
epilogize [eˈpilodʒaiz], *v.t., v.i.* epilogar.
epilogue [ˈepilɔg], *s.* epílogo.
Epiphany [iˈpifəni]. Epifanía.
episcopacy [iˈpiskəpəsi], *s.* episcopado.
Episcopal [iˈpiskəpəl], *a.* episcopal.
episcopal [iˈpiskəpəl], *a.* episcopal, obispal.
Episcopalian [ipiskəˈpeiliən], *a., s.* episcopalista, *m.f.*
episcopalian [ipiskəˈpeiliən], *a.* episcopal.
episcopate [iˈpiskəpit], *s.* episcopado, obispado.
episode [ˈepisoud], *s.* episodio.
episodic(al) [epiˈsɔdik(əl)] *a.* episódico.
epispastic [epiˈspæstik], *a.* epispástico, vejigatorio.
episperm [ˈepispə:m], *s.* episperma.
epistaxis [episˈtæksis], *s.* epistaxis, *f.inv.*
epistemology [ipistiˈmɔlədʒi], *s.* epistemología.
epistle [iˈpisl], *s.* epístola; carta.
epistolary [iˈpistələri], *a.* epistolar.
epistolic(al) [episˈtɔlik(əl)], *a.* epistolar.
epistolography [ipistoˈlɔgrəfi], *s.* ciencia epistolar.
epistrophe [eˈpistrəfi], *s.* epístrofe, *f.*
epistyle [ˈepistail], *s.* (*arq.*) arquitrabe.
epitaph [ˈepitæf], *s.* epitafio.
epithalamium [epiθəˈleimiəm], *s.* epitalamio.
epithelium [epiˈθi:liəm], *s.* epitelio.
epithet [ˈepiθet], *s.* epíteto.
epithetic [epiˈθetik], *a.* calificativo.
epitome [iˈpitəmi], *s.* epítome, muestra, compendio.
epitomist [iˈpitəmist], *s.* compendiador.
epitomize [iˈpitəmaiz], *v.t.* epitomar, compendiar.
epitomizer [iˈpitəmaizə], *s.* epitomador.
epoch [ˈi:pɔk], *s.* época, era; ***epoch-making,*** memorable, que hace época.
epode [ˈepoud], *s.* epodo.
Epsom salts [ˈepsəm ˈsɔ:lts], *s.pl.* sal de Epsom, sal de la Higuera.
equability [ekwəˈbiliti], *s.* uniformidad, igualdad; ecuanimidad.
equable [ˈekwəbl], *a.* uniforme, igual; ecuánime.
equal [ˈi:kwəl], *a.* igual; ***equal to,*** igual a; (*fig.*) con fuerzas para, a la altura de, suficiente *o* adecuado para. — *s.* igual; ***between equals,*** de igual a igual; ***without equal,*** sin igual, sin par. — *v.t.* igualar, igualarse a *o* con; ***six minus four equals two,*** seis menos cuatro da dos.
equality [iˈkwɔliti], *s.* igualdad.
equalization [i:kwəlaiˈzeiʃən], *s.* igualación, igualamiento.
equalize [ˈi:kwəlaiz], *v.t.* igualar. — *v.i.* lograr el empate.
equally [ˈi:kwəli], *adv.* igualmente; uniformemente.
equalness [ˈi:kwəlnis], *s.* igualdad; uniformidad.
equanimity [ekwəˈnimiti], *s.* ecuanimidad.
equanimous [eˈkwænimәs], *a.* ecuánime.
equate [iˈkweit], *v.t.* igualar; equiparar.
equation [iˈkweiʒən], *s.* ecuación.
equator [iˈkweitə], *s.* ecuador.
equatorial [ekwəˈtɔ:riəl], *a.* ecuatorial; ***Equatorial Guinea,*** Guinea Ecuatorial.
equerry [iˈkweri], *s.* caballerizo del rey.
equestrian [iˈkwestriən], *a.* ecuestre. — *s.* jinete.
equestrianism [iˈkwestriənizəm], *s.* equitación.
equiangular [i:kwiˈæŋgjulə], *a.* equiángulo.
equidistance [i:kwiˈdistəns], *s.* equidistancia.
equidistant [i:kwiˈdistənt], *a.* equidistante.
equilateral [i:kwiˈlætərəl], *a.* equilátero.
equilibrate [i:kwiˈlaibreit], *v.t.* equilibrar.
equilibration [i:kwilaiˈbreiʃən], *s.* equilibración.

equilibrist [i:ˈkwilibrist], *s.* equilibrista, *m.f.*
equilibrium [i:kwiˈlibriəm], *s.* equilibrio.
equine [ˈi:kwain], *a.* equino, caballar, hípico.
equinoctial [i:kwiˈnɔkʃəl], *a.* equinoccial. — *s.* línea equinoccial.
equinox [ˈi:kwinɔks], *s.* equinoccio.
equip [iˈkwip], *v.t.* equipar, pertrechar; aprestar, aparejar; ***to be well equipped to,*** estar bien dotado para.
equipage [ˈekwipidʒ], *s.* bagaje, equipo, bártulos, *m.pl.*; séquito.
equipment [iˈkwipmənt], *s.* equipo; pertrechos, *m.pl.*; material; avíos, *m.pl.*; capacidad.
equipoise [ˈi:kwipɔiz], *s.* contrapeso; equilibrio.
equipollence, equipollency [i:kwiˈpɔləns, -i], *s.* equipolencia.
equipollent [i:kwiˈpɔlənt], *a.* equipolente.
equiponderance [i:kwiˈpɔndərəns], *s.* equiponderancia.
equiponderant [i:kwiˈpɔndərənt], *a.* equiponderante.
equitable [ˈekwitəbl], *a.* equitativo.
equitableness [ˈekwitəblnis], *s.* equidad.
equitation [ekwiˈteiʃən], *s.* equitación.
equity [ˈekwiti], *s.* equidad.
equivalence, equivalency [iˈkwivələns, -i], *s.* equivalencia.
equivalent [iˈkwivələnt], *a.*, *s.* equivalente.
equivocal [iˈkwivəkəl], *a.* equívoco, ambiguo.
equivocalness, equivocacy [iˈkwivəkəlnis, -kəsi], *s.* carácter equívoco, ambigüedad.
equivocate [iˈkwivəkeit], *v.i.* usar de equívocos.
equivocation [ikwivəˈkeiʃən], *s.* equívoco, anfibología.
equivocator [iˈkwivəkeitə], *s.* equivoquista, *m.f.*
era [ˈiərə], *s.* era.
eradiate [iˈreidieit], *v.i.* radiar, irradiar.
eradiation [ireidiˈeiʃən], *s.* radiación; brillo.
eradicate [iˈrædikeit], *v.t.* desarraigar, extirpar.
eradication [irædiˈkeiʃən], *s.* extirpación.
eradicative [iˈrædikətiv], *a.* erradicativo; radical.
erasable [iˈreizəbl], *a.* borrable.
erase [iˈreiz], *v.t.* borrar.
erasement [iˈreizmənt], *s.* borradura.
eraser [iˈreizə], *s.* borrador, raspador.
erasure [iˈreiʒə], *s.* borradura, raspadura.
ere [ɛə], *adv.*, *conj.* antes, antes (de) que. — *prep.* antes de; ***long ere now,*** hace ya mucho tiempo.
erect [iˈrekt], *a.* erecto; erguido, enhiesto. — *v.t.* erigir, elevar; erguir; montar, formular.
erectable [iˈrektəbl], *a.* que se puede erigir.
erectile [iˈrektail], *a.* eréctil.
erection [iˈrekʃən], *s.* (*med.*) erección; fundación, construcción (*de edificios*); montaje, instalación; estructura, elevación, edificación.
erectly [iˈrektli], *adv.* perpendicularmente.
erectness [iˈrektnis], *s.* erección, erguimiento; (lo) erguido.
erector [iˈrektə], *s.* erector.
erelong [ɛəˈlɔŋ], *adv.* (*ant.*) dentro de poco tiempo.
eremite [ˈerimait], *s.* ermitaño.
erethism [ˈeriθizəm], *s.* eretismo.
erg [ə:g], *s.* (*fís.*) ergio.
ergograph [ˈə:gogræf], *s.* ergógrafo.
ergot [ˈə:gɔt], *s.* cornezuelo de centeno.
ergotism [ˈə:gətizəm], *s.* ergotismo.
ermine [ˈə:min], *s.* (*zool.*) armiño; (*fig.*) judicatura.
ermined [ˈə:mind], *a.* armiñado.
erode [iˈroud], *v.t.* corroer, roer, desgastar; gastar, desnudar. — *v.i.* corroerse, desgastarse.
erosion [iˈrouʒən], *s.* erosión; corrosión, desgaste.
erotic [iˈrɔtik], *a.* erótico.
erotomania [irɔtoˈmeiniə], *s.* erotomanía.
erpetology [ə:piˈtɔlədʒi], [HERPETOLOGY].
err [ə:r], *v.i.* errar.
errand [ˈerənd], *s.* recado, mandado; ***to run an errand,*** hacer un recado *o* mandado.
errant [ˈerənt], *a.* errante; ***knight errant,*** caballero andante.
errantry [ˈerəntri], *s.* caballería andante.
errata [eˈrɑ:tə], *s.pl.* [ERRATUM].
erratic [iˈrætik], *a.* errático; inconstante, irregular, desigual.
erratum [eˈrɑ:təm], *s.* errata; (*pl.* **errata** [-tə]) erratas, *f.pl.*, fe de erratas.
erroneous [iˈrouniəs], *a.* erróneo.
erroneousness [iˈrouniəsnis], *s.* (lo) erróneo, (lo) equivocado.
error [ˈerə], *s.* error; equivocación; ***in error,*** por equivocación, equivocadamente.
ersatz [ɛəˈzæts], *a.* artificial, sucedáneo.
Erse [ˈə:s], *s.* celta irlandés.
erstwhile [ˈə:stwail], *a.* antiguo; de otro tiempo.
erubescence [eruˈbesəns], *s.* erubescencia.
erubescent [eruˈbesənt], *a.* erubescente.
eructate [iˈrʌkteit], *v.i.* eructar.
eructation [i:rʌkˈteiʃən], *s.* eructación; eructo.
erudite [ˈerudait], *a.* erudito.
erudition, eruditeness [eruˈdiʃən, ˈerudaitnis], *s.* erudición.
erupt [iˈrʌpt], *v.i.* entrar en erupción; hacer erupción; estar en erupción; estallar; irrumpir (***into***, en). — *v.t.* arrojar.
eruption [iˈrʌpʃən], *s.* erupción.
eruptive [iˈrʌptiv], *a.* eruptivo.
erysipelas [eriˈsipələs], *s.* (*pat.*) erisipela.
erysipelatous [erisiˈpelətəs], *a.* erisipelatoso.
escalade [eskəˈleid], *s.* escalada. — *v.t.* escalar.
escalate [ˈeskəleit], *v.t.* aumentar; ampliar; escalar. — *v.i.* ir en aumento; ampliarse; escalarse.
escalation [eskəˈleiʃən], *s.* escalación, aumento.
escalator [ˈeskəleitə], *s.* escalera mecánica.
escallop [isˈkɔləp], *s.* [SCALLOP].
escapade [ˈeskəpeid], *s.* aventura, travesura, calaverada.
escape [isˈkeip], *s.* escape; evasión; fuga; escapatoria; ***he had a narrow escape,*** se libró por un pelo *o* por los pelos. — *v.t.* eludir, evitar; burlar; ***escape death,*** escapar a la muerte; (*fig.*) ***it escapes me,*** se me escapa; no se me alcanza; ***a cry escaped him,*** se le salió un grito; ***escape notice,*** pasar inadvertido, desapercibido; ***he escaped his pursuers,*** se libró de sus perseguidores. — *v.i.* escapar(se); evadirse; fugarse.
escapism [isˈkeipizəm], *s.* evasionismo.
escapist [isˈkeipist], *a.*, *s.* evasionista, *m.f.*
escarp [isˈkɑ:p], *v.t.* escarpar.
escarpment [isˈkɑ:pmənt], *s.* escarpa.
eschalot [ˈeʃəlɔt], [SHALLOT].
eschatology [eskəˈtɔlədʒi], *s.* escatología.
escheat [isˈtʃi:t], *s.* reversión al fisco. — *v.t.* confiscar; transferir. — *v.i.* revertir.
eschew [isˈtʃu:], *v.t.* rehuir.
escort [ˈeskɔ:t], *s.* escolta; acompañante. — [isˈkɔ:t], *v.t.* escoltar; acompañar.
escritoire [eskriˈtwɑ:], *s.* escritorio.
escutcheon [isˈkʌtʃən], *s.* escudo de armas, blasón.
escutcheoned [isˈkʌtʃənd], *a.* blasonado.
Eskimo [ˈeskimou], *a.*, *s.* esquimal, *m.f.*
esophagus [ŒSOPHAGUS].
esoteric [esoˈterik], *a.* esotérico.
espalier [isˈpæljə], *s.* (*horticultura*) espaldar, espaldera. — *v.t.* hacer espalderas a.
esparto [esˈpɑ:tou], *s.* (*bot.*) esparto.
especial [isˈpeʃəl], *a.* especial; particular, peculiar, notable.
especialness [isˈpeʃəlnis], *s.* (lo) especial.
Esperanto [espəˈræntou], *a.*, *s.* esperanto.
espial [isˈpaiəl], *s.* espionaje, acecho.

espionage [ˈespiənɑːʒ], *s.* espionaje.
esplanade [espləˈneid], *s.* explanada; glacis, *m.inv.*; ribera.
espousal [isˈpauzəl], *s.* desposorio, esponsales, *m.pl.*; adhesión.
espouse [isˈpauz], *v.t.* desposarse con, casarse con; (*fig.*) abrazar, defender (*una causa etc.*).
espy [isˈpai], *v.t.* divisar, percibir, columbrar. — *v.i.* vigilar, otear, mirar en derredor.
esquire [isˈkwaiə], *s.* (*abrev.* **Esq.**) escudero; don; ***William Brown, Esq.,*** Señor Don William Brown.
essay [ˈesei], *s.* ensayo; redacción, composición. — [eˈsei], *v.t.* ensayar, probar. — *v.i.* — ***to,*** intentar, probar a.
essayist [ˈeseiist], *s.* ensayista, *m.f.*
essence [ˈesəns], *s.* esencia.
essential [iˈsenʃəl], *a.* esencial, fundamental. — *s.* (*pl.*) (lo) fundamental, (lo) esencial; fundamentos, *m.pl.*
essentiality, essentialness [isenʃiˈæliti, iˈsenʃəlnis], *s.* esencialidad, (lo) esencial.
establish [isˈtæbliʃ], *v.t.* establecer, instituir, fundar, sentar, fijar, erigir; demostrar, probar.
establishment [isˈtæbliʃmənt], *s.* establecimiento; los que mandan en el sistema social; fundación; renta vitalicia; (*mil.*) nómina; plantilla.
estate [isˈteit], *s.* estado, estamento; bienes, *m.pl.*, patrimonio; hacienda, heredad; finca, fundo; ***estate agent,*** corredor de fincas; ***estate car,*** furgoneta, rubia; ***personal estate,*** bienes muebles, *m.pl.*; (*Am.*) ***real estate,*** bienes raíces, *m.pl.*; ***third estate,*** estado llano.
esteem [isˈtiːm], *s.* estima, estimación, aprecio. — *v.t.* estimar, apreciar.
ester [ˈestə], *s.* (*quím.*) éster.
estimable [ˈestiməbl], *a.* estimable, apreciable; evaluable.
estimableness [ˈestiməblnis], *s.* estimabilidad; aprecio.
estimate [ˈestimit], *s.* estimación, tasa, avalúo; presupuesto. — [ˈestimeit], *v.t.* estimar, apreciar, tasar, evaluar; presupuestar.
estimation [estiˈmeiʃən], *s.* estimación, aprecio; evaluación.
estimative [ˈestimətiv], *a.* estimativo; apreciativo.
estimator [ˈestimeitə], *s.* estimador; apreciador; tasador.
estival [iːsˈtaivəl], *a.* estival.
estivation [iːstiˈveiʃən], *s.* veraneo.
Estonia, Esthonia [esˈtouniə]. Estonia.
Estonian, Esthonian [esˈtouniən], *a.*, *s.* estonio.
estrange [isˈtreindʒ], *v.t.* enajenarse; ***to become estranged,*** distanciarse.
estrangement [isˈtreindʒmənt], *s.* distanciamiento, desvío, apartamiento.
estuary [ˈestjuəri], *s.* estuario; ría.
etcetera [itˈsetrə], (*abrev.* **etc.**) etcétera, etc.
etch [etʃ], *v.t.* grabar al agua fuerte.
etcher [ˈetʃə], *s.* aguafortista, *m.f.*
etching [ˈetʃiŋ], *s.* aguafuerte, *f.*
etching-needle [ˈetʃiŋ-niːdl], *s.* buril de grabador.
eternal [iˈtəːnəl], *a.* eterno.
eternity [iˈtəːniti], *s.* eternidad.
eternize [iˈtəːnaiz], *v.t.* eternizar.
etesian [iˈtiːʒən], *a.* etesio.
ether [ˈiːθə], *s.* éter.
ethereal [iˈθiəriəl], *a.* etéreo.
etherealize [iˈθiəriəlaiz], *v.t.* eterificar.
etheric [iːˈθerik], *a.* (*quím.*) etérico.
etherification [iːθerifiˈkeiʃən], *s.* eterificación.
etherize [ˈiːθəraiz], *v.t.* eterificar, eterizar.
ethic [ˈeθik], *a.* ético; honrado. — *s.* credo; (*pl.*) ética; moralidad; ***puritan ethic,*** el credo puritano.
ethical [ˈeθikəl], *a.* ético; honrado.
Ethiopia [iːθiˈoupiə]. Etiopía.
Ethiopian [iːθiˈoupiən], *a.*, *s.* etíope.
ethnic [ˈeθnik], *a.* étnico.
ethnogeny [eθˈnɔdʒəni], *s.* etnogenia.
ethnographer [eθˈnɔgrəfə], *s.* etnógrafo.
ethnographic(al) [eθnoˈgræfik(əl)], *a.* etnográfico.
ethnography [eθˈnɔgrəfi], *s.* etnografía.
ethnology [eθˈnɔlədʒi], *s.* etnología.
ethological [iːθoˈlɔdʒikəl], *a.* etológico.
ethology [iːˈθɔlədʒi], *s.* etología.
ethyl [ˈeθil], *s.* etilo.
ethylene [ˈəθiliːn], *s.* etileno.
etiology [iːtiˈɔlədʒi], *s.* etiología.
etiquette [ˈetiket], *s.* etiqueta; cánones profesionales, *m.pl.*
etui [eˈtwiː], *s.* estuche.
etymologist [etiˈmɔlədʒist], *s.* etimologista, *m.f.*, etimólogo.
etymological [etiməˈlɔdʒikəl], *a.* etimológico.
etymologize [etiˈmɔlədʒaiz], *v.t.* etimologizar.
etymology [etiˈmɔlədʒi], *s.* etimología.
etymon [ˈetimɔn], *s.* forma primitiva *o* radical de una palabra.
eucalyptus [juːkəˈliptəs], *s.* (*bot.*) eucalipto.
eucharist [ˈjuːkərist], *s.* eucaristía.
eucharistic [juːkəˈristik], *a.* eucarístico.
euchology [juːˈkɔlədʒi], *s.* eucologio.
eudemonism [juːˈdiːmənizəm], *s.* eudemonismo.
eudiometer [juːdiˈɔmitə], *s.* (*fís.*) eudiómetro.
eudiometric [juːdioˈmetrik], *a.* eudiométrico.
eugenic [juːˈdʒenik], *a.* eugenésico.
eugenics [juːˈdʒeniks], *s.pl.* eugenesia.
eulogist [ˈjuːlədʒist], *s.* elogiador, panegirista, *m.f.*
eulogistic [juːləˈdʒistik], *a.* laudatorio.
eulogize [ˈjuːlədʒaiz], *v.t.* elogiar, encomiar, loar.
eulogy [ˈjuːlədʒi], *s.* elogio, encomio, panegírico.
eunuch [ˈjuːnək], *s.* eunuco.
eupepsy [juːˈpepsi], *s.* (*med.*) eupepsia.
eupeptic [juːˈpeptik], *a.* eupéptico.
euphemism [ˈjuːfimizəm], *s.* eufemismo.
euphemistic [juːfiˈmistik], *a.* eufemístico.
euphonic, euphonious [juːˈfɔnik, -ˈfouniəs], *a.* eufónico.
euphonium [juːˈfouniəm], *s.* (*mús.*) eufono.
euphony [ˈjuːfəni], *s.* eufonía.
euphorbia [juːˈfɔːbiə], *s.* (*bot.*) euforbio.
euphoria [juːˈfɔːriə], *s.* euforia.
euphoric [juːˈfɔrik], *a.* eufórico.
euphuism [ˈjuːfjuːizəm], *s.* (*ret.*) eufuismo.
Eurasian [juːˈreiʒən], *a.*, *s.* eurasiático.
eureka! [juːˈriːkə], *interj.* ¡eureka!
European [juərəˈpiən], *a.* europeo; (*Am.*) ***European plan,*** a la carta. — *s.* europeo.
Europeanism [juərəˈpiənizəm], *s.* europeísmo.
Europeanize [juərəˈpiənaiz], *v.t.* europeizar.
Eustachian tube [juːsˈteiʃiən tjuːb], *s.* (*anat.*) trompa de Eustaquio.
eustyle [ˈjuːstail], *s.* (*arq.*) éustilo.
euthanasia [juːθəˈneiziə], *s.* eutanasia.
evacuant [iˈvækjuənt], *a.* (*med.*) evacuante, evacuativo.
evacuate [iˈvækjueit], *v.t.* evacuar, vaciar, desocupar.
evacuation [ivækjuˈeiʃən], *s.* evacuación.
evacuative [iˈvækjuətiv], *a.* evacuativo, purgativo.
evade [iˈveid], *v.t.* eludir, evitar, esquivar, soslayar.
evaluate [iˈvæljueit], *v.t.* evaluar, tasar.
evaluation [ivæljuˈeiʃən], *s.* evaluación, tasación.
evanesce [evəˈnes], *v.i.* esfumarse, disiparse, desvanecerse.
evanescence [evəˈnesəns], *s.* desvanecimiento, disipación.
evanescent [evəˈnesənt], *a.* evanescente; fugaz.

evangelical [i:væn'dʒelikəl], *a.* evangélico.
evangelism [i'vændʒəlizəm], *s.* evangelismo.
evangelist [i'vændʒəlist], *s.* evangelista, *m.f.*; evangelizador.
evangelization [ivændʒəlai'zeiʃən], *s.* evangelización.
evangelize [i'vændʒəlaiz], *v.t.* evangelizar. — *v.i.* predicar el evangelio.
evaporable [i'væpərəbl], *a.* evaporable.
evaporate [i'væpəreit], *v.t.* evaporar, evaporizar. — *v.i.* evaporarse; esfumarse.
evaporation [ivæpə'reiʃən], *s.* evaporación.
evaporative [i'væpərətiv], *a.* evaporativo.
evasion [i'veiʒən], *s.* evasión; evasiva.
evasive [i'veisiv], *a.* evasivo; ***to be evasive,*** contestar con evasivas.
eve [i:v], *s.* víspera; ***on the eve of,*** la víspera de, en vísperas de.
evection [i'vekʃən], *s.* (*astron.*) evección.
even (1) ['i:vən], *a.* llano, plano, igual, uniforme, liso; par; constante; imparcial; sereno; invariable; ***even-handed,*** justo, imparcial; ***even-tempered,*** ecuánime; ***to be even,*** estar en paz; ***to break even,*** salir en paz; ***to get even with,*** desquitarse con; vengarse de; ***to make even,*** igualar, nivelar; ***that makes us even,*** ya estamos en paz, eso iguala el tanteo. — *adv.* aun, hasta, incluso; ***even as,*** justo cuando, en el preciso momento en que; ***even if,*** aunque, aun cuando; ***even so,*** aun así, no obstante; ***not even,*** ni (siquiera). — *v.t.* igualar; nivelar; allanar; ***even out*** o ***up,*** igualar, nivelar; allanar; (*fig.*) ***even*** (***up***) ***the score,*** ajustar cuentas.
even (2) ['i:vən], [EVE].
evening ['i:vniŋ], *a.* vespertino; ***evening dress,*** traje de etiqueta; ***evening star,*** véspero, estrella vespertina. — *s.* tarde; noche; anochecer; ***good evening!*** ¡buenas tardes!; ¡buenas noches!
evenness ['i:vənnis], *s.* igualdad; uniformidad; lisura; imparcialidad.
evensong ['i:vənsɔŋ], *s.* vísperas, *f.pl.*
event [i'vent], *s.* acontecimiento, suceso; caso; (*dep.*) prueba, carrera; acto; (*pl.*, *dep.*) programa, *m.*; ***at all events, in any event,*** de todos modos; ***in the event,*** después de todo; ***in the event of,*** en (el) caso de que.
eventful [i'ventful], *a.* azaroso, accidentado; memorable, notable; lleno de incidentes.
eventual [e'ventʃuəl], *a.* final.
ever ['evə], *adv.* siempre; alguna vez; nunca, jamás; ***as ever,*** como siempre; ***better than ever,*** mejor que nunca; ***ever since,*** desde entonces; después ya; (*fam.*) ***ever so*** (***much***), muy, muchísimo; ***for ever*** (***and ever***), para siempre; por siempre jamás; ***hardly*** o ***scarcely ever,*** casi nunca; ***have you ever been?*** ¿ha ido usted alguna vez?
evergreen ['evəgri:n], *a.* siempre verde; de hoja perenne. — *s.* (*bot.*) siempreviva.
everlasting [evə'la:stiŋ], *a.* eterno, sempiterno, perdurable, perpetuo. — *s.* eternidad; ser eterno; sempiterna.
evermore [evə'mɔ:], *adv.* eternamente, siempre; ***for evermore,*** para siempre jamás.
eversion [i'və:ʃən], *s.* eversión.
evert [i'və:t], *v.t.* volver de dentro afuera.
every ['evri], *a.* cada, todo, todos, todas, todos los, todas las; ***every day,*** todos los días; ***each and every day,*** cada día; ***every other day,*** cada dos días, un día sí y otro no; ***I have every confidence in him,*** tengo plena confianza en él; ***every now and then, every so often,*** de vez en cuando, cada cierto tiempo.
everybody ['evribɔdi], *pron.* todo el mundo, todos, *m.pl.*
everyday ['evridei], *a.* cotidiano.
everyone ['evriwʌn], *pron.* todos, *m.pl.*, todo el mundo, cada uno.
everything ['evriθiŋ], *pron.* todo.
everywhere ['evriwɛə], *adv.* por *o* en todas partes; a todas partes.
evict [i'vikt], *v.t.* desposeer; desahuciar; expulsar.
eviction [i'vikʃən], *s.* (*der.*) desahucio.
evidence ['evidəns], *s.* testimonio(s), prueba(s); deposición; indicio; evidencia; ***circumstantial evidence,*** prueba indiciaria; ***to give evidence,*** deponer, declarar; ***to turn Queen's*** o ***State's evidence,*** testimoniar a favor del Estado. — *v.t.* evidenciar, patentizar.
evident ['evidənt], *a.* evidente, obvio, patente, manifiesto.
evidential [evi'denʃəl], *a.* indiciario, probatorio.
evidentness ['evidəntnis], *s.* (lo) evidente.
evil ['i:vil], *a.* malo, malvado, perverso, pernicioso, maligno; ***evil eye,*** mal de ojo; ***evil-minded,*** malicioso, mal intencionado; ***the Evil One,*** el Malo. — *adv.* mal; ***to speak evil of,*** hablar mal de. — *s.* mal, maldad; ***evil-doer,*** malhechor; ***evil-speaker,*** mala lengua; ***evil-speaking,*** maledicencia; ***evil-starred,*** malhadado; ***king's evil,*** escrófula, lamparones, *m.pl.*
evilness ['i:vilnis], *s.* malignidad.
evince [i'vins], *v.t.* patentizar, dar señales de, manifestar.
evincible [i'vinsibl], *a.* demostrable.
eviscerate [i'visəreit], *v.t.* destripar, desentrañar.
evitable ['evitəbl], *a.* evitable.
evocation [i:vo'keiʃən], *s.* evocación; (*for.*) avocación.
evocative [i'vɔkətiv], *a.* evocativo, sugestivo.
evoke [i'vouk], *v.t.* evocar; provocar; (*for.*) avocar.
evolute ['i:vəl(j)u:t], *s.* (*geom.*) voluta, evoluta.
evolution [i:və'l(j)u:ʃən], *s.* evolución; desenvolvimiento; (*mat.*) extracción de una raíz; (*mil.*, *mar.*) maniobra.
evolutionary [i:və'l(j)u:ʃənri], *a.* evolucionario; evolutivo.
evolutionism [ivə'l(j)u:ʃənizəm], *s.* evolucionismo.
evolutionist [i:və'l(j)u:ʃənist], *s.* táctico, estratégico; evolucionista, *m.f.*
evolve [i'vɔlv], *v.t.* desarrollar. — *v.i.* evolucionar.
evulsion [i'vʌlʃən], *s.* evulsión.
ewe [ju:], *s.* oveja.
ewer ['ju:ə], *s.* aguamanil.
ex [eks], *prefijo.* ex; antiguo; ***ex dividend,*** sin participación en; ***ex officio,*** de oficio; ***ex works,*** de la fábrica.
exacerbate [eks'æsəbeit], *v.t.* exacerbar.
exacerbation [eksæsə'beiʃən], *s.* exacerbación.
exact [ig'zækt], *a.* exacto, preciso; puntual. — *v.t.* exigir; imponer; ***exact sth. from s.o.,*** exigir, imponer algo a alguien.
exacting [ig'zæktiŋ], *a.* exigente; severo, duro.
exaction [ig'zækʃən], *s.* exacción.
exactitude [ig'zæktitjud], *s.* exactitud; puntualidad.
exactness [ig'zæktnis], *s.* exactitud, precisión.
exaggerate [ig'zædʒəreit], *v.t.* exagerar.
exaggeration [igzædʒə'reiʃən], *s.* exageración.
exaggeratory [ig'zædʒəreitəri], *a.* exagerativo.
exalt [ig'zɔ:lt], *v.t.* exaltar; ensalzar, enaltecer.
exaltation [egzɔ:l'teiʃən], *s.* exaltación; ensalzamiento; euforia.
exalted [ig'zɔ:ltid], *a.* exaltado, encumbrado, excelso, sublime.
examination [igzæmi'neiʃən], *s.* examen; reconocimiento; investigación; interrogatorio; inspección.
examine [ig'zæmin], *v.t.* examinar; reconocer; investigar; interrogar; inspeccionar.
examinee [igzæmi'ni:], *s.* examinando.
examiner [ig'zæminə], *s.* examinador.
example [ig'za:mpl], *s.* ejemplo; ***for example,*** por ejemplo; ***to make an example of,*** castigar de modo ejemplar *o* para que sirva de escarmiento; ***to set an example,*** dar ejemplo.
exanimate [eg'zænimeit], *a.* exánime.

exarch [ˈeksɑːk], *s.* exarca, *m.*
exarchate [ˈeksɑːkeit], *s.* exarcado.
exasperate [igˈzæspəreit], *v.t.* exasperar, sacar de quicio, desesperar.
exasperation [igzæspəˈreiʃən], *s.* exasperación, desesperación.
exasperating [igˈzæspəreitiŋ], *a.* desesperante.
excavate [ˈekskəveit], *v.t.* excavar.
excavation [ekskəˈveiʃən], *s.* excavación.
excavator [ˈekskəveitə], *s.* excavador; (*mec.*) excavadora.
exceed [ikˈsiːd], *v.t.* exceder de, sobrepasar, rebasar, superar; ***exceed one's brief,*** excederse, extralimitarse; ***exceed the speed limit,*** pasar de la velocidad máxima. — **exceed o.s.,** *v.r.* excederse.
exceeding [ikˈsiːdiŋ], *a.* excesivo; excedente, superante.
exceedingly [ikˈsiːdiŋli], *adv.* sumamente.
excel [ikˈsel], *v.t.* sobrepujar, aventajar, superar. — *v.i.* sobresalir, destacar, descollar.
excellence [ˈeksələns], *s.* excelencia; calidad excelente.
excellency [ˈeksələnsi], *s.* excelencia.
excellent [ˈeksələnt], *a.* excelente; selecto.
except [ikˈsept], *conj.* ***except that,*** sólo que. — *prep.* excepto, salvo, menos; ***except for,*** con excepción de. — *v.t.* exceptuar.
excepting [ikˈseptiŋ], *prep.* a excepción de, salvo.
exception [ikˈsepʃən], *s.* excepción; salvedad; ***to take exception (to),*** ofenderse (por), sentirse molesto (por).
exceptionable [ikˈsepʃənəbl], *a.* recusable.
exceptional [ikˈsepʃənəl], *a.* excepcional.
excerpt [ˈeksəːpt], *s.* fragmento *o* trozo escogido.
excerption [ekˈsəːpʃən], *s.* selección; extracto.
excess [ikˈses], *a.* excedente, sobrante. — *s.* exceso, demasía; desmán, desafuero.
excessive [ikˈsesiv], *a.* excesivo, desmesurado, desmedido.
excessiveness [ikˈsesivnis], *s.* (lo) excesivo.
exchange [iksˈtʃeindʒ], *s.* cambio; intercambio; canje; (*com.*) bolsa, lonja; central (*de teléfonos*); ***bill of exchange,*** letra de cambio; ***exchange-broker,*** cambista, *m.f.*; ***exchange rate,*** tipo de cambio. — *v.t.* cambiar; intercambiar; canjear.
exchangeable [iksˈtʃeindʒəbl], *a.* cambiable.
exchequer [iksˈtʃekə], *s.* Hacienda; tesorería; erario; ***Chancellor of the Exchequer,*** Ministro de Hacienda.
excisable [ekˈsaizəbl], *a.* imponible.
excise (1) [ekˈsaiz], *s.* impuesto interior. — *v.t.* aforar; gravar.
excise (2) [ekˈsaiz], *v.t.* cortar, extirpar.
exciseman [ekˈsaizmən], *s.* aforador; aduanero.
excision [ekˈsiʒən], *s.* excisión; corte.
excitability [iksaitəˈbiliti], *s.* excitabilidad; exaltación.
excitable [ikˈsaitəbl], *a.* excitable; exaltado; nervioso.
excitant [ˈeksitənt], *a.*, *s.* excitante.
excitation [eksiˈteiʃən], *s.* excitación.
excite [ikˈsait], *v.t.* excitar; provocar, estimular; emocionar.
excitedly [ikˈsaitidli], *adv.* agitadamente; con emoción.
excitement [ikˈsaitmənt], *s.* excitación; agitación, emoción.
exciter [ikˈsaitə], *s.* (*med.*) excitante.
exciting [ikˈsaitiŋ], *a.* emocionante, apasionante; excitante.
exclaim [iksˈkleim], *v.t.* exclamar. — *v.i.* ***exclaim against,*** clamar contra.
exclamation [eksklə ˈmeiʃən], *s.* exclamación; ***exclamation mark,*** (punto de) admiración.
exclamatory [iksˈklæmətəri], *a.* exclamatorio.
exclude [iksˈkluːd], *v.t.* excluir; exceptuar.
exclusion [iksˈkluːʒən], *s.* exclusión; ***to the exclusion of,*** con exclusión de.
exclusive [iksˈkluːsiv], *a.* exclusivo; exclusivista; selecto; único; ***exclusive of,*** sin incluir; ***exclusive to,*** privativo de.
exclusively [iksˈkluːsivli], *adv.* exclusivamente.
exclusiveness [iksˈkluːsivnis], *s.* carácter exclusivo; (lo) selecto.
excogitate [eksˈkɔdʒiteit], *v.t.* excogitar, idear.
excogitation [ekskɔdʒiˈteiʃən], *s.* meditación, reflexión.
excommunicable [ekskəˈmjuːnikəbl], *a.* digno de excomunión.
excommunicate [ekskəˈmjuːnikeit], *v.t.* excomulgar.
excommunication [ekskəmjuːniˈkeiʃən], *s.* excomunión.
excoriate [eksˈkɔːrieit], *v.t.* excoriar, desollar.
excoriation [ekskɔːriˈeiʃən], *s.* excoriación, desolladura.
excortication [ekskɔːtiˈkeiʃən], *s.* descortezamiento, descortezadura.
excrement [ˈekskrimənt], *s.* excremento.
excremental [ekskriˈmentəl], *a.* excremental.
excrescence [iksˈkresəns], *s.* excrecencia.
excrescent [iksˈkresənt], *a.* excrecente.
excrete [iksˈkriːt], *v.t.* excretar.
excretion [iksˈkriːʃən], *s.* excreción; excremento.
excretive [iksˈkriːtiv], *a.* excretorio.
excretory [iksˈkriːtəri], *a.* excretorio. — *s.* emuntorio.
excruciate [iksˈkruːʃieit], *v.t.* atormentar, dar suplicio a.
excruciating [iksˈkruːʃieitiŋ], *a.* agudísimo; dolorosísimo.
excruciation [ikskruːʃiˈeiʃən], *s.* suplicio.
exculpate [ˈekskʌlpeit], *v.t.* disculpar, excusar, justificar.
exculpation [ekskʌlˈpeiʃən], *s.* disculpa.
exculpatory [ˈekskʌlpeitəri], *a.* justificativo, disculpador.
excursion [iksˈkəːʃən], *s.* excursión; divagación; correría; (*mec.*) oscilación, amplitud; ***excursion train,*** tren botijo.
excursionism [iksˈkəːʃənizəm], *s.* excursionismo.
excursionist [iksˈkəːʃənist], *s.* excursionista, *m.f.*
excursive [iksˈkəːsiv], *a.* errante, errático; digresivo.
excursiveness [iksˈkəːsivnis], *s.* calidad de errante *o* digresivo.
excusable [iksˈkjuːzəbl], *a.* excusable, disculpable.
excusableness [iksˈkjuːzəblnis], *s.* (lo) excusable, (lo) disculpable.
excusatory [iksˈkjuːzətəri], *a.* justificativo; apologético.
excuse [iksˈkjuːs], *s.* disculpa, excusa; ***to make excuses for,*** justificar. — [iksˈkjuːz], *v.t.* disculpar, dispensar (***from,*** de); excusar; perdonar.
exeat [ˈeksiæt], *s.* (*igl.*) exeat.
execrable [ˈeksikrəbl], *a.* execrable, aborrecible, abominable.
execrate [ˈeksikreit], *v.t.* execrar, abominar de.
execration [eksiˈkreiʃən], *s.* execración.
execratory [ˈeksikreitəri], *a.* execratorio.
executable [ˈeksikjuːtəbl], *a.* ejecutable.
executant [igˈzekjutənt], *s.* ejecutante.
execute [ˈeksikjuːt], *v.t.* ejecutar, efectuar, llevar a cabo; cumplir, desempeñar; (*for.*) formalizar, legalizar; ajusticiar.
execution [eksiˈkjuːʃən], *s.* ejecución; desempeño, cumplimiento, realización; fusilamiento; ***stay of execution,*** indulto provisional.
executioner [eksiˈkjuːʃənə], *s.* ejecutor, verdugo.
executive [igˈzekjutiv], *a.* ejecutivo. — *s.* poder ejecutivo; director, gerente, dirigente; (***Am.***) ejecutivo.

executor [igˈzekjutə], *s.* ejecutor; albacea, testamentario.
executorship [igˈzekjutəʃip], *s.* albaceazgo.
executory [igˈzekjutəri], *a.* ejecutorio, ejecutivo, administrativo.
executrix [igˈzekjutriks], *s.* albacea, testamentaria.
exegesis [eksiˈdʒi:sis], *s.* exégesis, *f.inv.*
exegete [ˈeksidʒi:t], *s.* exégeta, *m.f.*
exegetical [eksiˈdʒetikəl], *a.* exegético.
exemplar [igˈzemplə], *s.* modelo, pauta.
exemplariness [igˈzemplərinis], *s.* ejemplaridad.
exemplary [igˈzempləri], *a.* ejemplar.
exemplification [igzemplifiˈkeiʃən], *s.* ejemplificación; (*for.*) copia certificada.
exemplify [igˈzemplifai], *v.t.* ejemplificar.
exempt [igˈzempt], *a.* exento, libre, franco. — *v.t.* exentar, eximir; exceptuar, dispensar.
exemptible [igˈzemptibl], *a.* exento.
exemption [igˈzempʃən], *s.* exención; franquicia.
exequatur [eksiˈkweitə], *s.* exequátur.
exequies [ˈeksikwiz], *s.pl.* exequias, *f.pl.*
exercisable [eksəsaizəbl], *a.* ejercitativo.
exercise [ˈeksəsaiz], *s.* ejercicio; (*pl.*, *mil.*) maniobras, *f.pl.*; ***exercise-book,*** cuaderno; ***to take exercise,*** hacer ejercicio. — *v.t.* ejercer; ejercitar; preocupar; dar ejercicio a, llevar de paseo; ***exercise care,*** tener cuidado.
exergue [ekˈsə:g], *s.* exergo.
exert [igˈzə:t], *v.t.* ejercer. — **exert o.s.,** *v.r.* hacer un esfuerzo.
exertion [igˈzə:ʃən], *s.* esfuerzo; mucho esfuerzo.
exeunt [ˈeksiʌnt], *v.i.* (*teat.*) vanse.
exfoliate [eksˈfoulieit], *v.t.* exfoliar. — *v.i.* exfoliarse.
exfoliation [eksfouliˈeiʃən], *s.* exfoliación.
exhalable [eksˈheiləbl], *a.* exhalable.
exhalation [ekshəˈleiʃən], *s.* exhalación; espiración.
exhale [eksˈheil], *v.t.* exhalar; espirar.
exhaust [igˈzɔ:st], *s.* (*mec.*) escape; vapor (*m.*) *o* gases (*m.pl.*) de escape; ***exhaust pipe,*** tubo de escape. — *v.t.* agotar; apurar.
exhaustible [igˈzɔ:stibl], *a.* agotable.
exhausting [igˈzɔ:stiŋ], *a.* agotador.
exhaustion [igˈzɔ:stʃən], *s.* agotamiento; postración.
exhaustive [igˈzɔ:stiv], *a.* exhaustivo.
exhibit [igˈzibit], *s.* objeto expuesto; pieza; prueba. — *v.t.* exhibir, presentar, exponer, mostrar.
exhibition [eksiˈbiʃən], *s.* exposición; exhibición; beca (*de universidad*); ***to make an exhibition of o.s.,*** ponerse en ridículo.
exhibitioner [eksiˈbiʃənə], *s.* becario.
exhibitionism [eksiˈbiʃənizəm], *s.* exhibicionismo.
exhibitionist [eksiˈbiʃənist], *s.* exhibicionista, *m.f.*
exhibitor [igˈzibitə], *s.* exponente, expositor.
exhibitory [igˈzibitəri], *a.* (*der.*) exhibitorio; que exhibe.
exhilarate [igˈziləreit], *v.t.* animar, estimular; tonificar, vigorizar.
exhilarating [igˈziləreitiŋ], *a.* estimulante; tonificante, vigorizante.
exhilaration [igziləˈreiʃən], *s.* animación, emoción, euforia.
exhort [igˈzɔ:t], *v.t.* exhortar.
exhortation [igzɔ:ˈteiʃən], *s.* exhortación.
exhortative [igˈzɔ:tətiv], *a.* exhortativo.
exhortatory [igˈzɔ:tətəri], *a.* exhortatorio.
exhumation [ekshu:ˈmeiʃən], *s.* exhumación.
exhume [eksˈhju:m], *v.t.* exhumar.
exigence, exigency [ˈeksidʒəns, -i], *s.* exigencia; urgencia.
exigent [ˈeksidʒənt], *a.* exigente; apremiante.
exiguity, exiguousness [eksiˈgju:iti, igˈzigjuəsnis], *s.* exigüidad.
exiguous [igˈzigjuəs], *a.* exiguo.

exile [ˈekzail], *s.* exilio, destierro; exilado, exiliado. — *v.t.* exilar, desterrar.
exist [igˈzist], *v.i.* existir.
existence [igˈzistəns], *s.* existencia.
existential [egzisˈtenʃəl], *a.* existencial.
existentialism [egzisˈtenʃəlizəm], *s.* (*filos.*) existencialismo.
existentialist [egzisˈtenʃəlist], *a.*, *s.* existencialista, *m.f.*
exit [ˈeksit], *s.* salida; partida; (*teat.*) ***to make an exit,*** hacer mutis. — *v.i.* (*teat.*) hacer mutis.
exodus [ˈeksədəs], *s.* éxodo.
exonerate [igˈzɔnəreit], *v.t.* exonerar.
exoneration [igzɔnəˈreiʃən], *s.* exoneración.
exonerative [igˈzɔnərətiv], *a.* que puede exonerar.
exorbitance [igˈzɔ:bitəns], *s.* exorbitancia, enormidad.
exorbitant [igˈzɔ:bitənt], *a.* exorbitante.
exorcise [ˈeksɔ:saiz], *v.t.* exorcizar.
exorciser [ˈeksɔ:saizə], [EXORCIST].
exorcism [ˈeksɔ:sizəm], *s.* exorcismo.
exorcist [ˈeksɔ:sist], *s.* exorcista, *m.f.*, conjurador.
exordial [egˈzɔ:diəl], *a.* previo, preliminar.
exordium [egˈzɔ:diəm], *s.* exordio.
exosmose [ˈeksosmouz], *s.* (*fís.*) exósmosis, *f.inv.*
exosmotic [eksosˈmɔtik], *a.* exosmótico.
exoteric(al) [eksoˈterik(əl)], *a.* exotérico.
exothermic [eksoˈθə:mik], *a.* exotérmico.
exotic [igˈzɔtik], *a.* exótico.
expand [iksˈpænd], *v.t.* extender; dilatar, ensanchar; ampliar. — *v.i.* extenderse; dilatarse, ensancharse; hincharse; ampliarse.
expanse [iksˈpæns], *s.* extensión, espacio.
expansibility, expansibleness [ikspænsiˈbiliti, iksˈpænsiblnis], *s.* expansibilidad.
expansible [iksˈpænsibl], *a.* expansible; afable.
expansion [iksˈpænʃən], *s.* expansión; dilatación, ensanche; ***economic expansion,*** desarrollo económico.
expansive [iksˈpænsiv], *a.* expansivo.
expansiveness [iksˈpænsivinis], *s.* (lo) expansivo; campechanía.
expatiate [eksˈpeiʃieit], *v.i.* espaciarse; extenderse, explayarse (***on,*** sobre).
expatiation [ekspeiʃiˈeiʃən], *s.* explayamiento; prolijidad.
expatiatory [eksˈpeiʃiətəri], *a.* prolijo.
expatriate [eksˈpætriit], *a.*, *s.* expatriado. — [-eit], *v.t.* expatriar.
expatriation [ekspætriˈeiʃən], *s.* expatriación.
expect [iksˈpekt], *v.t.* esperar(se); prometerse; contar con; querer; suponer, figurarse; ***just as I expected,*** ya me lo figuraba, ya lo sabía yo.
expectancy [iksˈpektənsi], *s.* expectación; expectativa.
expectant [iksˈpektənt], *a.* expectante; ***expectant mother,*** futura madre.
expectantly [iksˈpektəntli], *adv.* con expectación.
expectation [ekspekˈteiʃən], *s.* expectación; expectativa; esperanza; ***beyond all expectation,*** infinitamente mejor de lo que se esperaba; ***expectation of life,*** índice vital; ***in expectation of,*** en espera de, con la esperanza de; ***to live up to expectations,*** realizar (alguien) todo lo que prometía.
expectorant [iksˈpektərənt], *a.*, *s.* expectorante.
expectorate [iksˈpektəreit], *v.t.* expectorar. — *v.i.* escupir.
expectoration [ikspektəˈreiʃən], *s.* expectoración; esputo, gargajo.
expedience, expediency [iksˈpi:diəns, -i], *s.* conveniencia, (lo) oportuno.
expedient [iksˈpi:diənt], *a.* conveniente, oportuno. — *s.* medio, recurso.
expedite [ˈekspidait], *v.t.* acelerar; facilitar; despachar.

expedition [ekspi'diʃən], *s.* expedición; prontitud.
expeditionary [ekspi'diʃənəri], *a.* expedicionario.
expeditious [ekspi'diʃəs], *a.* expeditivo.
expel [iks'pel], *v.t.* expulsar; expeler, despedir.
expeller [iks'pelə], *s.* expulsor.
expend [iks'pend], *v.t.* expender, gastar, desembolsar.
expenditure [iks'penditʃə], *s.* gasto, desembolso.
expense [iks'pens], *s.* gasto, desembolso; expensas, costa; ***at the expense of,*** a expensas de; ***at any expense,*** a todo coste; a toda costa; ***expense account,*** cuenta de gastos; ***expense no object,*** a todo tren; ***free of expense,*** franco de gastos; ***to go to expense,*** meterse en gastos; ***petty expenses,*** gastos menudos; ***running expenses,*** gastos de funcionamiento.
expensive [iks'pensiv], *a.* caro, costoso.
expensiveness [iks'pensivnis], *s.* (lo) caro, (lo) costoso.
experience [iks'piəriəns], *s.* experiencia; vivencia; ***by experience,*** por experiencia. — *v.t.* experimentar.
experienced [iks'piəriənst], *a.* experimentado.
experiment [iks'perimənt], *s.* experimento, experiencia, ensayo; ***by way of experiment,*** en plan de experimento; ***to carry out an experiment in,*** realizar un experimento de. — [-ent], *v.t., v.i.* experimentar; hacer experimentos (***with,*** con, ***on,*** en).
experimental [iksperi'mentəl], *a.* experimental; ***experimental psychology,*** psicología experimental.
experimentalist [iksperi'mentəlist], *s.* experimentador.
experimentally [iksperi'mentəli], *adv.* experimentalmente, por experiencia.
experimentation [iksperimen'teiʃən], *s.* experimentación.
experimenter [iks'perimentə], *s.* experimentador.
expert [iks'pə:t, 'ekspə:t], *a.* experto, experimentado, práctico, diestro, hábil. — ['ekspə:t], *s.* experto; perito.
expertise [ekspə:'ti:z], *s.* pericia; habilidad; técnica.
expertness ['ekspə:tnis], *s.* destreza, habilidad, pericia.
expiable ['ekspiəbl], *a.* expiable.
expiate ['ekspieit], *v.t.* expiar.
expiation [ekspi'eiʃən], *s.* expiación.
expiator ['ekspieitə], *s.* el que expía.
expiatory ['ekspieitəri], *a.* expiatorio.
expirable [iks'paiərəbl], *a.* expirable.
expiration [ekspaiə'reiʃən], *s.* expiración; término, vencimiento; espiración.
expire [iks'paiə], *v.t.* espirar, expeler. — *v.i.* espirar; expirar; vencer, caducar, cumplirse.
expiry [iks'paiəri], *s.* expiración; caducidad, vencimiento; ***expiry date,*** plazo.
explain [iks'plein], *v.t.* explicar. — *v.i.* explicarse, dar una explicación. — **explain o.s.,** *v.r.* dar explicaciones, explicarse.
explainable [iks'pleinəbl], *a.* explicable; justificable.
explainer [iks'pleinə], *s.* exponente; intérprete; comentador.
explanation [eksplə'neiʃən], *s.* explicación; explanación; aclaración.
explanative, explanatory [iks'plænətiv, -təri], *a.* explicativo.
expletive [iks'pli:tiv], *a.* expletivo. — *s.* voz expletiva; exclamación.
explicable [eks'plikəbl], *a.* explicable.
explicative, explicatory [eks'plikətiv, -təri], *a.* explicativo, explicatorio.
explicit [iks'plisit], *a.* explícito, concreto.
explicitness [iks'plisitnis], *s.* (lo) explícito, (lo) concreto, concreción.
explode [iks'ploud], *v.t.* hacer explotar; dar al traste con. — *v.i.* explotar, estallar; ***explode with*** o ***into laughter,*** estallar en risas, romper a reír.
exploit ['eksplɔit], *s.* hazaña, proeza. — [iks'plɔit], *v.t.* explotar; sacar partido de.
exploitation [eksplɔi'teiʃən], *s.* explotación.
exploiter [iks'plɔitə], *s.* explotador.
exploration [eksplɔ:'reiʃən], *s.* exploración.
exploratory [iks'plɔ:rətəri], *a.* exploratorio; de sondeo.
explore [iks'plɔ:], *v.t.* explorar; examinar, sondear. — *v.i.* explorar; hacer sondeos.
explorer [iks'plɔ:rə], *s.* explorador.
explosion [iks'plouʒən], *s.* explosión; estallido.
explosive [iks'plousiv], *a., s.* explosivo.
exponent [iks'pounənt], *s.* (*mat.*) exponente; expositor, representante.
export ['ekspɔ:t], *s.* exportación; ***export licence,*** permiso de exportación; ***export trade,*** comercio de exportación. — [iks'pɔ:t], *v.t.* exportar.
exportable [iks'pɔ:təbl], *a.* exportable.
exportation [ekspɔ:'teiʃən], *s.* exportación.
exporter [iks'pɔ:tə], *s.* exportador.
expose [iks'pouz], *v.t.* exponer; descubrir, revelar; ***to be exposed,*** verse expuesto; quedar al descubierto.
exposé [iks'pouzei], *s.* revelación, desenmascaramiento.
exposed [iks'pouzd], *a.* expuesto, al descubierto; desabrigado.
exposedness [iks'pouzidnis], *s.* (lo) expuesto; (lo) desabrigado, (lo) desamparado.
exposition [ekspo'ziʃən], *s.* exposición.
expositor [iks'pɔzitə], *s.* expositor.
expository, expositive [iks'pɔzitəri, -tiv], *a.* expositivo.
expostulate [iks'pɔstjuleit], *v.i.* protestar; reconvenir (***with,*** a).
expostulation [ikspɔstju'leiʃən], *s.* protesta; reconvención.
expostulator [iks'pɔstjuleitə], *s.* amonestador.
expostulatory [iks'pɔstjulətəri], *a.* amonestador.
exposure [iks'pouʒə], *s.* revelación; ***to die of exposure,*** morir(se) de frío; ***exposure meter,*** fotómetro.
expound [iks'paund], *v.t.* exponer.
expounder [iks'paundə], *s.* expositor.
express [iks'pres], *a., s.* expreso; exprés, rápido; ***express delivery,*** correo urgente; ***express train,*** rápido. — *v.t.* expresar; enviar por expreso. — **express o.s.,** *v.r.* expresarse.
expressible [iks'presibl], *a.* expresable.
expression [iks'preʃən], *s.* expresión.
expressionless [iks'preʃənlis], *a.* sin expresión.
expressive [iks'presiv], *a.* expresivo; significativo.
expressiveness [iks'presivnis], *s.* (lo) expresivo; fuerza de expresión, energía.
expressly [iks'presli], *adv.* expresamente.
expressness [iks'presnis], *s.* (lo) explícito.
expropriate [eks'prouprieit], *v.t.* expropriar, enajenar.
expropriation [eksproupri'eiʃən], *s.* expropriación, enajenamiento.
expugn [eks'pju:n], *v.t.* expugnar.
expugnable [eks'pʌgnəbl], *a.* expugnable.
expulsion [iks'pʌlʃən], *s.* expulsión.
expulsive [iks'pʌlsiv], *a.* expulsivo.
expunction [iks'pʌŋkʃən], *s.* canceladura, borradura, raspadura.
expunge [iks'pʌndʒ], *v.t.* borrar, tachar, cancelar, expurgar.
expurgate ['ekspəgeit], *v.t.* expurgar.
expurgation [ekspə:'geiʃən], *s.* (*med.*) purgante, purga; expurgación, expurgo.
expurgator ['ekspəgeitə], *s.* expurgador.
expurgatory [iks'pə:gətəri], *a.* expurgatorio.

exquisite [ˈekskwizit], *a.* exquisito; rico; precioso, primoroso, delicado.
exquisiteness [ˈekskwizitnis], *s.* exquisitez.
exsanguine [ekˈsæŋgwin], *a.* exangüe.
exscind [ekˈsind], *v.t.* cortar, excluir, extirpar.
ex-serviceman [eks-ˈsəːvismən], *s.* excombatiente.
exsiccate [ˈeksikeit], *v.t.* secar, desecar.
exsiccation [eksiˈkeiʃən], *s.* desecación.
extant [eksˈtænt], *a.* existente.
extemporaneous [ekstempəˈreiniəs], *a.* improvisado, sin preparación.
extemporariness [eksˈtempərərinis], *s.* (lo) improvisado.
extemporary [eksˈtempərəri], *a.* improvisado.
extempore [eksˈtempəri], *a.* improvisado. — *adv.* de improviso, sin preparación; ***to speak extempore,*** improvisar.
extemporize [eksˈtempəraiz], *v.i.* improvisar.
extemporizer [eksˈtempəraizə], *s.* improvisador.
extend [iksˈtend], *v.t.* extender; tender; prolongar; prorrogar; ofrecer, dar, facilitar, proporcionar; (*fondos, recursos etc.*) estirar hasta lo máximo; ***extend a welcome to,*** brindar una (calurosa) acogida a. — *v.i.* extenderse; prolongarse; estirarse.
extendible [iksˈtendibl], *a.* extensivo.
extensibility, extensibleness [ikstensiˈbiliti, iksˈtensiblnis], *s.* extensibilidad.
extensible [iksˈtensibl], *a.* extensible, extensivo.
extension [iksˈtenʃən], *s.* extensión; ampliación; anexo; prolongación; prórroga; (*Am., elec.*) ***extension cord*** [FLEX].
extensive [iksˈtensiv], *a.* extenso; amplio; dilatado.
extensiveness [iksˈtensivnis], *s.* (lo) extenso; (lo) dilatado.
extensor [iksˈtensɔː], *s.* extensor.
extent [iksˈtent], *s.* extensión; amplitud; alcance; punto, grado; ***to a certain extent,*** hasta cierto punto; ***to the full extent,*** en toda su extensión; ***to a great extent,*** en gran parte; ***to a lesser extent,*** en menor grado; ***to such an extent that,*** hasta tal punto que; ***to what extent?*** ¿hasta qué punto?
extenuate [iksˈtenjueit], *v.t.* extenuar; atenuar.
extenuating [iksˈtenjueitiŋ], *a.* atenuante.
extenuation [ikstenjuˈeiʃən], *s.* extenuación; atenuación.
exterior [iksˈtiəriə], *a.* exterior; externo. — *s.* exterior; exterioridad.
exteriority [ikstiəriˈɔriti], *s.* exterioridad.
exterminate [iksˈtəːmineit], *v.t.* exterminar.
extermination [ikstəːmiˈneiʃən], *s.* exterminio.
exterminator [iksˈtəːmineitə], *s.* exterminador.
exterminatory [iksˈtəːminətəri], *a.* exterminador.
external [iksˈtəːnəl], *a.* externo; exterior. — *s.(pl.)* formas exteriores, *f.pl.*, exterioridad.
externality [ekstəːˈnæliti], *s.* exterioridad.
externalize [iksˈtəːnəlaiz], *v.t.* exteriorizar.
extinct [iksˈtiŋkt], *a.* extinto; extinguido; apagado; abolido; ***to become extinct,*** extinguirse.
extinction, extinguishment [iksˈtiŋkʃən, -gwiʃmənt], *s.* extinción; apagamiento; abolición.
extine [ˈekstin], *s.* (*bot.*) exina *o* extina del polen.
extinguish [iksˈtiŋgwiʃ], *v.t.* extinguir; apagar.
extinguishable [iksˈtiŋgwiʃəbl], *a.* extinguible; apagable.
extinguisher [iksˈtiŋgwiʃə], *s.* apagador, matacandelas, *m. inv.*; ***fire extinguisher,*** extintor, matafuego.
extirpate [ˈekstəːpeit], *v.t.* extirpar; (*cir.*) escindir.
extirpation [ekstəːˈpeiʃən], *s.* extirpación; (*cir.*) escisión.
extirpator [ˈekstəːpeitə], *s.* extirpador.
extol [iksˈtoul], *v.t.* alabar, ensalzar.
extort [iksˈtɔːt], *v.t.* arrancar, arrebatar, obtener por fuerza *o* con amenazas.
extorter [iksˈtɔːtə], *s.* el que causa extorsión; concusionario.
extortion [iksˈtɔːʃən], *s.* extorsión, exacción.
extortionary [iksˈtɔːʃənəri], *a.* contra derecho *o* de acto ilegal.
extortionate [iksˈtɔːʃənit], *a.* exorbitante.
extortioner [iksˈtəːʃənə], *s.* concusionario; opresor.
extra [ˈekstrə], *a.* extra, extraordinario; adicional, (de) más, suplementario; aparte; de repuesto; ***extra charge,*** recargo; ***extra pay,*** paga extraordinaria; ***service is extra,*** el servicio se paga aparte. — *adv.* extra, especial; ***extra fine,*** extrafino. — *s.* exceso, recargo, suplemento; extra; plus.
extract [ˈekstrækt], *s.* trozo, pasaje, cita; excerpta; (*quím.*) tintura. — [iksˈtrækt], *v.t.* extraer; sacar.
extraction [iksˈtrækʃən], *s.* extracción; origen, descendencia.
extractive [iksˈtræktiv], *a.* extractivo.
extractor [iksˈtræktə], *s.* extractor, extractador; (*cir.*) fórceps.
extradite [ˈekstrədait], *v.t.* conceder *o* pedir la extradición de.
extradition [ekstrəˈdiʃən], *s.* extradición.
extrados [eksˈtreidɔs], *s.* (*arq.*) trasdós.
extra-judicial [ekstrə-dʒuːˈdiʃəl], *a.* extrajudicial.
extramural [ekstrəˈmjuərəl], *a.* de fuera del recinto, de extramuros; externo.
extraneous [iksˈtreiniəs], *a.* superfluo; extrínseco.
extraordinariness [iksˈtrɔːdnərinis], *s.* carácter extraordinario, (lo) extraordinario.
extraordinary [iksˈtrɔːdnəri], *a.* extraordinario.
extraterritorial [ekstrəteriˈtɔːriəl], *a.* extraterritorial.
extravagance, extravagancy [iksˈtrævəgəns, -i], *s.* prodigalidad, derroche; exceso, despilfarro; extravagancia.
extravagant [iksˈtrævəgənt], *a.* pródigo, gastador, derrochador, manirroto; desmedido, exagerado; disparatado; extravagante.
extravagantness [iksˈtrævəgəntnis], *s.* (lo) exorbitante; (lo) pródigo.
extravaganza [ikstrævəˈgænzə], *s.* obra extravagante y fantástica.
extravasate [eksˈtrævəseit], *v.t.* (*med.*) extravasar; extravenar.
extravasation [ekstrævəˈseiʃən], *s.* extravasación.
extreme [iksˈtriːm], *a.* extremo; postrero; extremado, riguroso. — *s.* extremo, situación extrema; ***in the extreme,*** en extremo, en sumo grado; ***to go to extremes,*** extremar las cosas.
extremity [iksˈtremiti], *s.* extremidad; aprieto, situación apurada.
extricate [ˈekstrikeit], *v.t.* sacar, librar, extraer. — **extricate o.s.,** *v.r.* — ***from,*** librarse de.
extrication [ekstriˈkeiʃən], *s.* (el) sacar.
extrinisic(al) [iksˈtrinisik(əl)], *a.* extrínseco.
extrorse [iksˈtrɔːs], *a.* (*bot.*) extrorso.
extrovert [ˈekstrovəːt], *a., s.* extrovertido.
extrude [iksˈtruːd], *v.t.* expulsar, empujar hacia fuera. — *v.i.* sobresalir.
extrusion [iksˈtruːʒən], *s.* expulsión.
exuberance [igˈzjuːbərəns], *s.* exuberancia; euforia.
exuberant [igˈzjuːbərənt], *a.* exuberante; eufórico.
exudation [ekzjuːˈdeiʃən], *s.* exudación.
exude [igˈzjuːd], *v.t., v.i.* exudar, rezumar.
exult [igˈzʌlt], *v.i.* exultar, regocijarse.
exultant [igˈzʌltənt], *a.* eufórico.
exultation [egzʌlˈteiʃən], *s.* exultación, regocijo, euforia.
exultingly [igˈzʌltiŋli], *adv.* con exultación.
eyas [ˈaiəs], *a.* implume. — *s.* halcón niego, halconcillo.
eye [ai], *s.* ojo; (*cost.*) corchete; (*bot.*) yema; ***eye of the storm,*** remanso de paz en medio de un torbellino; ***black eye,*** ojo amoratado, morado;

blind in one eye, tuerto; ***eye-bath,*** baño de ojos; ***eye-doctor,*** médico oculista; ***eye-drops,*** colirio; ***eye-flap,*** anteojera; ***eye-glass,*** anteojo; ocular; ***eye-glasses,*** lentes, *m.pl.*, quevedos, *m.pl.*; (*cost.*) ***eye-hole,*** ojete; ***eye-lash,*** pestaña; ***eye-lid,*** párpado; (*fam.*) ***eye-opener,*** sorpresa, revelación; ***eye-piece,*** ocular; ***eye-shade,*** guardavista, visera; ***eye-strain,*** cansancio de la vista; ***to have eye-strain,*** tener la vista cansada; ***eye-tooth,*** diente canino, colmillo; ***eye-witness,*** testigo ocular *o* presencial; ***in the eyes of,*** a los ojos de; ***visible to the naked eye,*** que puede verse a simple vista; ***to catch the eye,*** llamar la atención; ***to catch s.o.'s eye,*** atraer la atención de alguien; ***to cry one's eyes out,*** llorar a lágrima viva; ***to give the glad eye,*** dar pie (a), mirar con ojos golositos; ***to have eyes at the back of one's head,*** ver crecer la hierba; ***to have an eye for,*** tener mucha idea de, saber apreciar; ***to have one's eye on,*** tener echado el ojo a; tener vigilado; ***to have an eye to the main chance,*** barrer para dentro; ***to keep an eye on,*** vigilar, controlar; ***to make eyes at,*** hacer guiños a, mirar con ojos golositos; ***to see eye to eye,*** estar completamente de acuerdo, tener el mismo punto de vista; ***to set*** o ***clap eyes on,*** ponerle los ojos encima a, ver; ***to shut one's eyes (to), turn a blind eye (to),*** hacer la vista gorda (ante); ***to be up to the eyes in,*** estar hasta arriba de; ***to undertake to do sth. with one's eyes open,*** comprometerse a hacer algo con los ojos abiertos; ***with an eye to,*** con idea de. — *v.t.* ojear; mirar, contemplar.

eyeball [ˈaibɔːl], *s.* globo del ojo.

eyebright [ˈaibrait], *s.* (*bot.*) eufrasia.

eyebrow [ˈaibrau], *s.* ceja.

eyed [aid], *a.* ***bleary-eyed,*** legañoso; ***blue-eyed,*** ojiazul, ojizarco.

eyeful [ˈaiful], *s.* ojeada; (*fam.*) ***to get an eyeful,*** ver más de la cuenta; ***she's an eyeful!*** ¡es un monumento!

eyeless [ˈailis], *a.* ciego, sin ojos.

eyelet [ˈailit], *s.* resquicio, ojete, abertura; (*mar.*) ***eyelet-holes of the reefs,*** ollados de los drizos.

eyesight [ˈaisait], *s.* vista.

eyesore [ˈaisɔː], *s.* cosa que hiere la vista, fealdad.

eyestring [ˈaistriŋ], *s.* tendón del ojo.

eyot [eit], *s.* islote, isleta.

eyre [ɛə], *s.* (*for.*) vuelta, circuito.

eyrie [ˈaiəri], *s.* nido de ave de rapiña, aguilera.

F

F, f [ef], sexta letra del alfabeto. — *s.* (*mús.*) fa.
fa [fɑ:], *s.* (*mús.*) fa.
fable [feibl], *s.* fábula; mentira. — *v.t.* inventar. — *v.i.* inventar *o* contar fábulas, mentir.
fabler [ˈfeiblə], *s.* fabulista, *m.f.*; cuentero, mentiroso.
fabric [ˈfæbrik], *s.* tejido; textura; fábrica, obra.
fabricate [ˈfæbrikeit], *v.t.* inventar; fabricar, construir.
fabrication [fæbriˈkeiʃən], *s.* invención, embuste; fabricación.
fabricator [ˈfæbrikeitə], *s.* inventor, embustero; fabricador.
fabulist [ˈfæbjulist], *s.* fabulista, *m.f.*
fabulous [ˈfæbjuləs], *a.* fabuloso.
fabulousness [ˈfæbjuləsnis], *s.* fabulosidad, (lo) fabuloso.
façade [fəˈsɑ:d], *s.* fachada, frente.
face [feis], *s.* cara; rostro; faz; (*reloj*) esfera; ***face to face,*** cara a cara; ***face value,*** valor nominal; (*fig.*) valor *o* sentido aparente; ***in the face of,*** ante, frente a; a pesar de; ***on the face of it,*** a primera vista, según las apariencias; ***to keep a straight face,*** no alterar (ni) un músculo (de la cara), no inmutarse; ***to lose face,*** desprestigiarse; ***to make faces,*** hacer muecas; ***to save face,*** salvar las apariencias; ***to set one's face against,*** mostrarse contrario *o* reacio a; ***to show one's face,*** dejarse ver; ***to show*** o ***pull a long face,*** tener *o* poner cara de ajo. — *v.t.* arrostrar, hacer frente a, afrontar; mirar hacia, dar a; (*mec.*) revestir; forrar; alisar; ***to be faced with,*** encontrarse con; ***face it out,*** aguantar hasta el final. — *v.i.* — ***about,*** dar media vuelta; ***face onto,*** dar a *o* sobre; ***face up to,*** enfrentarse con, afrontar resueltamente.
face-cloth [ˈfeis-klɔθ], *s.* paño de la cara.
faced [feist], *a.* ***full-faced,*** carrilludo, mofletudo; ***double-faced*** o ***two-faced,*** que tiene dos caras, falso.
faceless [ˈfeislis], *a.* sin cara.
face-lift(ing) [ˈfeis-lift(iŋ)], *s.* cirugía estética (facial); (*fig.*) ***to give a face-lift to,*** remozar.
facer [ˈfeisə], *s.* puñetazo; problemón.
facet [ˈfæsit], *s.* faceta.
facetious [fəˈsi:ʃəs], *a.* chistoso, guasón.
facetiousness [fəˈsi:ʃəsnis], *s.* guasa.
facial [ˈfeiʃəl], *a.* facial.
facile [ˈfæsail], *a.* fácil; superficial.
facilitate [fəˈsiliteit], *v.t.* facilitar.
facilitation [fəsiliˈteiʃən], *s.* facilitación.
facility [fəˈsiliti], *s.* facilidad; habilidad, facultad, don; (*pl.* **facilities** [-z]) servicios; ***not to have facilities for,*** no tener servicio para; no disponer de lo preciso para.
facing [ˈfeisiŋ], *s.* paramento, revestimiento.
facsimile [fækˈsimili], *s.* facsímil.
fact [fækt], *s.* hecho; realidad; dato; ***a matter of fact,*** un hecho; ***in*** (***actual***) ***fact,*** de hecho; en realidad; ***fact-finding mission,*** misión de investigación; ***the fact of the matter is that,*** (ello) es que; ***the facts of life,*** las realidades de la vida.
faction [ˈfækʃən], *s.* facción, bando; disensiones, *f.pl.*
factional [ˈfækʃənəl], *a.* faccionario.
factionist [ˈfækʃənist], *s.* faccioso.
factious [ˈfækʃəs], *a.* faccioso; de facción; de partido; partidista.
factitious [fækˈtiʃəs], *a.* facticio.
factor [ˈfæktə], *s.* factor; ***the human factor,*** el elemento *o* factor humano.
factorage [ˈfæktəridʒ], *s.* comisión; factoraje.
factory [ˈfæktəri], *s.* fábrica.
factotum [fækˈtoutəm], *s.* factótum.
factual [ˈfæktʃuəl], *a.* objetivo, basado en hechos.
facultative [ˈfækəltətiv], *a.* facultativo.
faculty [ˈfækəlti], *s.* facultad; (*Am.*, *educ.*) [STAFF].
fad [fæd], *s.* capricho, manía, chifladura, obsesión.
faddist [ˈfædist], *s.* maniático (***for,*** de).
faddy [ˈfædi], *a.* (*fam.*) caprichoso, novelero.
fade [feid], *v.t.* disminuir poco a poco, ir desvaneciendo *o* esfumando. — *v.i.* — ***out*** o ***away,*** disminuir poco a poco, irse desvaneciendo *o* esfumando.
faded [ˈfeidid], *a.* marchito, descolorido; desvanecido, desaparecido.
fadeless [ˈfeidlis], *a.* que no se descolora.
fading [ˈfeidiŋ], *a.* decaído, flojo; que desaparece. — *s.* descolorimiento; decadencia, flojedad; desaparición.
fæcal [ˈfi:kəl], *a.* fecal.
fæces [ˈfi:si:z], *s.pl.* excrementos, *m.pl.*
fæcula [ˈfækjulə], *s.* fecula.
faerie, faery [FAIRY].
fag [fæg], *s.* (*fam.*) pitillo; (*colegio privado selecto*) alumno menor; tarea penosa, fatiga; ***fag-end,*** colilla (*de cigarrillo*). — *v.t.* fatigar, reventar, agotar; ***fagged out,*** rendido, agotado — *v.i.* fatigarse, agotarse; servir a un estudiante mayor.
faggot [ˈfægət], *s.* haz, gavilla de leña; manojo; (*fort.*) fajina; albóndiga. — *v.t.* liar, hacer líos de; recaudar, recoger.
fagotto [fəˈgɔtou], *s.* (*mús.*) fagot.
faience [faiˈɑ̃:ns], *s.* loza fina.
fail [feil], *s.* suspenso; ***without fail,*** sin falta. — *v.t.* faltar (a); no cumplir, no corresponder (a); errar, marrar, no alcanzar; suspender (*un examen*). — *v.i.* faltar; estar escaso (de); menguar, decaer; fallar; no poder, no saber; no lograr, dejar de; fracasar, salir mal; malograrse; suspender (*en un examen*); quebrar, hacer bancarrota; ***do not fail to do it,*** no deje de hacerlo; ***I fail to understand,*** no logro entender.
failing [ˈfeiliŋ], *a.* menguante, decadente. — *prep.* a falta de. — *s.* falta, defecto; malogro.
failure [ˈfeiljə], *s.* fracaso, malogro, fallo; fracasado; falta; paro (*de una máquina etc.*); (*com.*) bancarrota, quiebra; ***heart failure,*** colapso cardíaco; ***failure of issue,*** falta de descendencia; ***failure to keep one's word,*** falta de cumplimiento de la palabra.
fain [fein], *a.* (*ant.*) dispuesto. — *adv.* de buena gana, gustosamente.
faint [feint], *a.* débil, tenue; desfallecido. — *s.* desmayo, deliquio; desfallecimiento. — *v.i.* desmayarse; desfallecer.
faint-hearted [feint-ˈhɑ:tid], *a.* cobarde, pusilánime, medroso, apocado.
faint-heartedness [feint-ˈhɑ:tidnis], *s.* pusilanimidad, cobardía.
fainting [ˈfeintiŋ], *s.* [FAINT]; ***fainting-fit,*** síncope, desmayo; (*med.*) lipotimia.
faintness [ˈfeintnis], *s.* debilidad, desfallecimiento, desmayo; tenuidad, (lo) tenue.
fair (I) [fɛə], *a.* sereno, despejado; rubio, blanco; favorable, propicio; imparcial, justo, equitativo; bueno; hermoso, bello; honrado; razonable; corriente, mediano, regular; ***fair and square,*** honrado, a carta cabal; ***fair-complexioned,*** de tez blanca; ***to make a fair copy,*** poner en limpio, pasar a limpio; ***fair dealing,*** honradez; ***fair game,*** caza legal; (*fig.*) objeto lícito; ***fair-haired,*** de pelo rubio; ***to give a fair hearing,*** oír con imparcialidad; ***by fair means,*** por medios rectos *o* honrados; ***fair name,*** nombre honrado, sin tacha; ***fair play,*** equidad, proceder leal, juego limpio; ***fair sex,*** bello sexo; ***fair to middling,*** mediano, regular, decentito, discretito; ***to be in a fair way to succeed,*** llevar buen camino para triunfar, llevar trazas de triunfar; ***fair weather,*** buen tiempo; ***fair-weather friend,*** amigo en la

prosperidad; ***fair wind,*** viento favorable; ***it's not fair,*** no hay derecho. — *adv.* honradamente; imparcialmente; cortésmente; decentemente; felizmente; ***to play fair,*** jugar limpio.

fair (2) [fɛə], *s.* feria; verbena, parque de atracciones.

fairly [ˈfɛəli], *adv.* imparcialmente, rectamente; medianamente; bastante.

fairness [ˈfɛənis], *s.* hermosura, belleza; imparcialidad, rectitud, equidad, justicia; color rubio; ***in all fairness,*** para ser justo.

fairway [ˈfɛəwei], *s.* (*mar.*) canalizo.

fairy [ˈfɛəri], *a.* de hada, feérico, de ensueño. — *s.* hada; ***fairy-godmother,*** hada madrina; ***fairy-land,*** país de las hadas; ***fairy-tale,*** cuento de hadas; (*fig.*) mentira.

fairylike [ˈfɛərilaik], *a.* parecido a una hada.

faith [feiθ], *s.* fe, *f.*; confianza; ***in good (bad) faith,*** de buena (mala) fe; ***in faith,*** en verdad; ***to break faith,*** faltar a la palabra dada, incumplir su palabra; ***to keep faith,*** cumplir la palabra dada; ***to pin one's faith on,*** tener puestas las esperanzas en.

faithful [ˈfeiθful], *a.* fiel, leal; puntual.

faithfully [ˈfeiθfuli], *adv.* fielmente; puntualmente; ***yours faithfully,*** le saluda atentamente.

faithfulness [ˈfeiθfulnis], *s.* fidelidad, lealtad.

faithless [ˈfeiθlis], *a.* sin fe; desleal, pérfido.

faithlessness [ˈfeiθlisnis], *s.* deslealtad, infidelidad.

fake [feik], *a.* falso, falsificado. — *s.* falsificación, cosa falsificada; impostura; impostor, farsante. — *v.t.* falsificar.

faker [ˈfeikə], *s.* falsificador, amañador; (*fam.*) buhonero.

fakir [ˈfeikiə, fəˈkiə], *s.* fakir, faquir, alfaquí.

falcate [ˈfælkeit], *a.* falcado.

falchion [ˈfɔːltʃən], *s.* cimitarra; falce, *f.*

falcon [ˈfɔː(l)kən], *s.* (*orn.*) halcón; (*artill.*) falcón.

falconer [ˈfɔː(l)kənə], *s.* halconero, cetrero.

falconet [ˈfɔː(l)kənet], *s.* (*artill.*) falconete.

falconry [ˈfɔː(l)kənri], *s.* halconería, cetrería.

faldstool [ˈfɔːldstuːl], *s.* facistol, atril; faldistorio; silla de tijera.

fall [fɔːl], *s.* caída; baja; (*Am.*) otoño; (*mil.*) caída, pérdida; declive; (*pl.*) salto de agua; ***the Fall,*** la Caída. — *irr. v.i.* caer, caerse; bajar, descender; echarse (*el viento*); ***fall asleep,*** dormirse; ***fall away,*** desmoronarse; fallar; apostatar; desertar; desaparecer; ***fall back,*** retroceder; retirarse; echarse atrás; replegarse; ***fall back on*** o ***upon,*** recurrir a, echar mano de; (*mil.*) replegarse sobre *o* hacia; ***fall behind,*** rezagarse, quedarse atrás; ***fall down,*** caer(se), caer(se) al suelo; postrarse; (*com.*) ***fall due,*** vencer; ***fall flat,*** caer tendido, caer cuan largo se es; fracasar; caer en el vacío; ***fall for,*** prendarse de; dejarse engañar por; ***fall in,*** desplomarse, hundirse; expirar, caducar; (*mil.*) alinear(se); ***fall in line,*** alinearse; conformarse; ***fall in love with,*** enamorarse de; ***fall in with,*** conformarse a, ponerse de acuerdo con, avenirse a; ***fall into the habit of,*** caer en la costumbre de; ***fall off,*** caerse; bajar; deteriorarse; ***fall on,*** echarse, abalanzarse sobre; ***fall on Monday,*** caer en lunes; ***fall out,*** caer(se); reñir, pelearse (***with,*** con); ***fall over,*** caer(se); ***fall over backwards*** o ***over o.s. to,*** desvivirse por; ***fall short,*** venir escaso; no llegar, no alcanzar (a); defraudar; ***fall through,*** fallar, no cuajar; ***fall to,*** empezar, ponerse a; tocar, corresponder (a); ***fall to pieces,*** deshacerse; ***fall under,*** caer dentro *o* bajo, estar comprendido en; venir por; ***fall upon,*** abalanzarse, caer sobre; incumbir, tocar a; ***fall within,*** estar comprendido en.

fallacious [fəˈleiʃəs], *a.* falaz; erróneo.

fallaciousness [fəˈleiʃəsnis], *s.* falacia; error.

fallacy [ˈfæləsi], *s.* falacia; error.

fallen [ˈfɔːlən], *a.* caído. — *p.p.* [FALL].

fallibility [fæliˈbiliti], *s.* falibilidad.

fallible [ˈfælibl], *a.* falible.

falling [ˈfɔːliŋ], *a.* que cae, que disminuye; ***falling star,*** estrella fugaz. — *s.* [FALL]; ***falling away,*** defección; ***falling in,*** derrumbamiento, desmoronamiento; ***falling off,*** disminución; ***falling sickness,*** mal caduco.

Fallopian tubes [fəˈloupiən ˈtjuːbz], *s.pl.* (*anat.*) trompas de Falopio, *f.pl.*

fallow (1) [ˈfælou], *a.* barbecho; ***to allow to lie fallow,*** dejar en barbecho. — *v.t.* barbechar.

fallow (2) [ˈfælou], *a.* (*ent.*) rojizo; ***fallow-deer,*** gamo.

fallowing [ˈfælouiŋ], *s.* (*agric.*) barbechera.

fallowness [ˈfælounis], *s.* (*agric.*) barbechada.

false [fɔːls], *a.* falso; postizo; ***false alarm,*** falsa alarma; ***false bottom,*** doble fondo; ***false-hearted,*** traidor, pérfido; ***false teeth,*** dentadura postiza; ***to play false, be false to,*** hacer traición a.

falsehood [ˈfɔːlshud], *s.* mentira; falsedad.

falseness [ˈfɔːlsnis], *s.* falsedad; perfidia.

falsetto [fɔːlˈsetou], *a.* (*mús.*) de falsete. — *s.* (*mús.*) falsete.

falsifiable [ˈfɔːlsifaiəbl], *a.* falsificable.

falsification [fɔːlsifiˈkeiʃən], *s.* falsificación.

falsifier [ˈfɔːlsifaiə], *s.* falsificador.

falsify [ˈfɔːlsifai], *v.t.* falsificar; falsear.

falsity [ˈfɔːlsiti], *s.* falsedad.

falter [ˈfɔːltə], *s.* vacilación, titubeo. — *v.i.* vacilar, titubear; quebrarse (la voz).

faltering [ˈfɔːltəriŋ], *s.* [FALTER].

falteringly [ˈfɔːltəriŋli], *adv.* de una manera vacilante *o* titubeante.

fame [feim], *s.* fama, renombre.

famed [feimd], *a.* famoso, renombrado.

familiar [fəˈmiljə], *a.* familiar; conocido; confianzudo; ***to be familiar with,*** conocer, estar familiarizado con; tomarse (demasiadas) confianzas con. — *s.* familiar.

familiarity [fəmiliˈæriti], *s.* familiaridad, confianza, llaneza; trato confianzudo; ***familiarity breeds contempt,*** la confianza da asco.

familiarize [fəˈmiljəraiz], *v.t.* familiarizar. — **familiarize o.s.,** *v.r.* familiarizarse (***with,*** con).

family [ˈfæmili], *a.* familiar, de(la) familia; casero; ***family allowance,*** subsidio familiar; ***family man,*** padre de familia; (*Am.*) ***family name,*** [SURNAME]; ***family tree,*** árbol genealógico; ***in the family way,*** en estado. — *s.* familia.

famine [ˈfæmin], *s.* hambre, *f.*

famish [ˈfæmiʃ], *v.t.* hambrear; matar de hambre. — *v.i.* morirse de hambre.

famished [ˈfæmiʃt], *a.* hambriento.

famous [ˈfeiməs], *a.* famoso, célebre.

fan (1) [fæn], *s.* abanico; (*agric.*) aventador; (*mec.*) ventilador; volante (*de molino de viento*); (*f.c.*) bifurcación en abanico; paleta (*de hélice*); ***fan-belt,*** correa de ventilador; ***fan-blast,*** tiro de fuelle; ***fan-blower,*** aventador, soplador; (*bot.*) ***fan-palm,*** miraguano; ***fan-shaped,*** en forma de abanico; ***fan-vaulting,*** bóveda de abanico. — *v.t.* abanicar; soplar; ventilar; (*agric.*) aventar.

fan (2) [fæn], *s.* aficionado, forofo; ***fan-mail,*** cartas de aficionados, *f.pl.*

fanatic [fəˈnætik], *a., s.* fanático.

fanatical [fəˈnætikəl], *a.* fanático.

fanaticism [fəˈnætisizəm], *s.* fanatismo.

fancied [ˈfænsid], *a.* imaginado, imaginario; que tiene probabilidades de ganar *o* de salir bien.

fancier [ˈfænsiə], *s.* criador (*de animales* o *aves*); fantaseador.

fanciful [ˈfænsiful], *a.* fantástico, fantasioso.

fancifulness [ˈfænsifulnis], *s.* antojo, capricho.

fancy [ˈfænsi], *a.* caprichoso, imaginario; extravagante, fantástico; elegante, bello; (*com.*) de gusto de capricho; ***fancy dress,*** disfraz, traje de capricho; ***fancy goods,*** objetos *o* artículos de fantasía; ***fancy man, fancy woman,*** amante, *m.f.*; ***fancy work,*** labor. — *s.* fantasía, imaginación; capricho, antojo, ventolera; gusto; afición; idea, imagen, *f.*, concepción; (*fam.*) ***fancy-free,*** sin trabas sentimentales; ***to take a fancy to,*** encapricharse con. — *v.t.* imaginar, suponer; antojarse; figurarse; apetecerle (a uno); ***fancy meeting you!*** ¡qué casualidad encontrarle a Vd!; (*ironía*) ***fancy that now!*** ¡no me digas!

fane [fein], *s.* templo, fano.

fanfare [ˈfænfɛə], *s.* toque de trompetas, fanfarria.

fanfaron [ˈfænfærɔn], *s.* fanfarrón.

fanfaronade [fænfærəˈneid], *s.* fanfarronada. — *v.i.* fanfarronear.

fang [fæŋ], *s.* colmillo.

fanged [fæŋd], *a.* que tiene colmillos.

fangless [ˈfæŋlis], *a.* descolmillado, sin colmillos.

fanion [ˈfæniən], *s.* banderola.

fanlight [ˈfænlait], *s.* (*arq.*) abanico.

fanlike [ˈfænlaik], *a.* en forma de abanico.

fannel [ˈfænəl], *s.* manípulo.

fanon [ˈfænɔn], *s.* (*igl.*) manípulo.

fantail [ˈfænteil], *s.* cola en forma de abanico; (*orn.*) colipava; (*carp.*) cola de milano; ***fantail burner,*** mechero de abanico (*gas*).

fantailed [ˈfænteild], *a.* de cola en forma de abanico; de cola de milano.

fantasia [fæntəˈsiə], *s.* (*mús.*) fantasía.

fantasm [ˈfæntæzəm], *s.* fantasma, *m.*

fantastic(al) [fænˈtæstik(əl)], *a.* fantástico; funambulesco.

fantasticalness [fænˈtæstikəlnis], *s.* (lo) fantástico; (lo) funambulesco.

fantasy [ˈfæntəsi], *s.* fantasía.

fanwheel [ˈfænwi:l], *s.* rueda aventadora; rueda de paletas.

faquir [FAKIR].

far [fɑ:], *a.* lejano, distante, remoto. — *adv.* lejos; a lo lejos; muy, mucho; ***as far as,*** hasta; hasta donde; tan lejos como; ***as far as I am concerned,*** por lo que a mí respecta; ***as far as I can see, so far as I know,*** que yo sepa, según parece; ***by far,*** en mucho; con mucho; ***far and away the best,*** el mejor con mucho; ***far and wide,*** por todas partes; ***far away, far off,*** a lo lejos, a gran distancia; ***far be it from me,*** lejos de mí, lejos de mi ánimo, no permita Dios; ***far beyond,*** mucho más allá (de); ***far from it,*** nada de eso, lejos de eso; ni mucho menos; ***far into the night,*** hasta muy entrada *o* avanzada la noche; ***to go far towards,*** contribuir mucho a; ***to go too far,*** (pro)pasarse, excederse; ***how far is it to Madrid?*** ¿qué distancia hay de aquí a Madrid?; ***in so far as,*** por cuanto; ***so far, thus far,*** hasta ahora, hasta aquí; ***so far this year,*** en lo que va del año.

farad [ˈfærəd], *s.* (*elec.*) faradio.

faradic [fəˈrædik], *a.* (*elec.*) farádico.

faradism [ˈfærədizəm], *s.* faradismo.

faradization [færədaiˈzeiʃən], *s.* faradización.

far-away [ˈfɑ:r-əwei], *a.* lejano; distraído, en las nubes.

farce [fɑ:s], *s.* farsa; absurdo, cosa ridícula, disparate.

farcical [ˈfɑ:sikəl], *a.* absurdo, ridículo, disparatado.

fare [fɛə], *s.* precio, tarifa, pasaje, billete; pasajero; comida, alimento; ***bill of fare,*** lista de platos. — *v.i.* — ***well*** (***ill***), irle bien (mal) a alguien; ***how did you fare?*** ¿qué tal te fue?

farewell [ˈfɛəwel], *a.* de despedida. — [fɛəˈwel], *s.* despedida; ***to bid farewell,*** despedirse de, decir adiós a. — *interj.* adiós, ¡vaya Vd. con Dios!

far-fetched [ˈfɑ:-fetʃt], *a.* inverosímil, disparatado.

far-flung [ˈfɑ:-ˈflʌŋ], *a.* muy extenso, desperdigado por el mundo.

farina [fəˈri:nə], *s.* harina; fécula; almidón.

farinaceous [færiˈneiʃəs], *a.* farináceo.

farinose [ˈfærinous], *a.* farináceo.

farm [fɑ:m], *s.* finca de labranza; granja; hacienda; arrendamiento; ***farm-hand, farm-labourer,*** mozo de labranza, labriego; peón; ***farm-house,*** casa de labranza; alquería; granja. — *v.t.* cultivar, labrar (*la tierra*); ***farm out,*** arrendar. — *v.i.* dedicarse a la agricultura, ser agricultor.

farmable [ˈfɑ:məbl], *a.* arrendable; cultivable.

farmer [ˈfɑ:mə], *s.* labrador, granjero, agricultor, rentero; arrendatario; ***small farmer,*** labriego.

farming [ˈfɑ:miŋ], *s.* cultivo, agricultura, labranza; arrendamiento.

farmstead [ˈfɑ:msted], *s.* cortijada; alquería.

farmyard [ˈfɑ:mjɑ:d], *s.* corral de una granja.

farness [ˈfɑ:nis], *s.* distancia.

faro [ˈfɛərou], *s.* faraón (*juego de naipes*).

farrago [fəˈrɑ:gou], *s.* fárrago.

far-reaching [ˈfɑ:-ˈri:tʃiŋ], *a.* de gran alcance *o* trascendencia.

farrier [ˈfæriə], *s.* herrador; albéitar.

farriery [ˈfæriəri], *s.* albeitería; taller de herrador.

farrow [ˈfærou], *s.* lechigada de cerdos. — *v.t., v.i.* parir (*la cerda*).

far-seeing [ˈfɑ:-ˈsi:iŋ], *a.* previsor, precavido; que ve a gran distancia.

far-sighted [ˈfɑ:-ˈsaitid], *a.* que ve a distancia; perspicaz, sagaz; (*med.*) présbita.

farther [ˈfɑ:ðə], *a.* más remoto, ulterior. — *adv.* más lejos; más allá; además; ***farther on,*** más adelante.

farthermost [ˈfɑ:ðəmoust], [FARTHEST].

farthest [ˈfɑ:ðist], *a.* más lejano, más remoto; ***in farthest Siberia,*** en lo más remoto de Siberia.

farthing [ˈfɑ:ðiŋ], *s.* (*ant.*) cuarto de penique; perra chica, ardite; ***I don't care a farthing,*** no se me da un ardite.

farthingale [ˈfɑ:ðiŋgeil], *s.* verdugado, guardainfante.

fasces [ˈfæsi:z], *s.pl.* fasces, *f.*

fascia [ˈfæʃiə], *s.* (*anat.*) aponeurosis, *f. inv.*; [ˈfeiʃiə], (*astron.*) faja (alrededor de un planeta); (*arq.*) faja, banda (de arquitrabe); cinturón, venda; (*aut.*) salpicadero.

fascial [ˈfæʃiəl], *a.* (*anat.*) fascial.

fasciate(d) [ˈfæʃieit(id)], *a.* fajado, vendado.

fasciation [fæʃiˈeiʃən], *s.* vendaje.

fascicle [ˈfæsikl], *s.* fascículo; hacecillo; (*bot.*) glomérulo.

fascicled [ˈfæsikld], *a.* arracimado, fasciculado.

fascicular [fæˈsikulə], *a.* fascicular.

fascinate [ˈfæsineit], *v.t.* fascinar, alucinar, hechizar.

fascination [fæsiˈneiʃən], *s.* fascinación, encanto, hechizo.

fascine [fæˈsi:n], *s.* (*fort.*) fajina; haz.

fascism [ˈfæʃizəm], *s.* fascismo.

fascist [ˈfæʃist], *a., s.* fascista, *m.f.*

fashion [ˈfæʃən], *s.* modo, manera; moda, uso, estilo; clase, suerte; forma, hechura; ***after the fashion of,*** a la manera de; ***to be the fashion,*** estar de moda; ***fashion-designer,*** modisto; ***fashion-model,*** modelo, *m.f.*; ***fashion-shop,*** tienda de modas; ***in fashion,*** de moda; ***man of fashion,*** hombre elegante *o* del gran mundo; ***out of fashion,*** pasado de moda; ***to go out of fashion,*** pasar de moda; ***shipshape and Bristol fashion,*** en perfecto orden. — *v.t.* formar, hacer; amoldar.

fashionable [ˈfæʃənəbl], *a.* de moda, de estilo, elegante.

fashionableness [ˈfæʃənəblnis], *s.* elegancia, estilo.

fashionably [ˈfæʃənəbli], *adv.* a la moda, según la moda.

fashioner [ˈfæʃənə], *s.* hacedor.

fast (I) [fɑ:st], *a.* rápido, de mucha velocidad; firme, fuerte, seguro; (*reloj*) ***to be fast,*** ir adelantado; ***fast colour,*** color sólido; ***fast friend,*** amigo fiel, constante; ***fast living,*** vida disoluta; ***fast woman,*** mujer ligera de cascos, fresca; (*mar.*) ***to make fast,*** amarrar; (*fam.*) ***to pull a fast one on s.o.,*** tomarle a alguien el pelo. — *adv.* rápidamente, de prisa; firmemente fuertemente; ***fast asleep,*** profundamente dormido; ***to follow fast on the heels of,*** seguir muy de cerca, pisarle a alguien los talones; ***to play fast and loose with,*** dar la marcha a.

fast (2) [fɑ:st], *s.* ayuno; ***fast-day,*** día de ayuno; ***to break one's fast,*** romper el ayuno. — *v.i.* ayunar.

fasten [ˈfɑ:sən], *v.t.* atar; asegurar; sujetar; amarrar; pegar, fijar; cerrar; abrochar; ***fasten blame on,*** achacar *o* cargar la culpa a; ***fasten one's eyes upon,*** fijar los ojos en. — *v.i.* fijarse; agarrarse; pegarse; ***fasten on*** o ***upon,*** sujetarse a, fijarse a, pegarse a.

fastener [ˈfɑ:sənə], *s.* cerrojo; cierre; broche; (*vestido*) corchete; (*papel*) grapa.

fastening [ˈfɑ:səniŋ], [FASTENER].

faster (1) [ˈfɑ:stə], *a. compar.* [FAST (1)].

faster (2) [ˈfɑ:stə], *s.* ayunador.

fastidious [fəsˈtidiəs], *a.* meticuloso, esmerado; exigente; pulcro.

fastidiousness [fəsˈtidiəsnis], *s.* meticulosidad, esmero; exigencia; pulcritud.

fasting [ˈfɑ:stiŋ], *s.* ayuno; ***fasting day,*** día de ayuno.

fastness [ˈfɑ:stnis], *s.* rapidez; firmeza; solidez; (*reloj*) adelanto; plaza fuerte, fortaleza; (lo) más intrincado, (lo) más fragoso.

fat [fæt], *a.* gordo, grueso; graso, enjundioso; pingüe; (*tierras*) feraz; (*carne*) de mucha grasa; (*ironía*) ***a fat lot of help!*** ¡valiente ayuda!; ***to get fat,*** ponerse gordo, engordar. — *s.* gordo; grasa; sebo; enjundia; (*fig.*) (lo) más rico; ***to live off the fat of the land,*** vivir con mucho regalo *o* como un príncipe; ***now the fat is in the fire*** (***properly***), ahora sí que se va a armar la gorda (a base de bien); ***to put on fat,*** ponerse gordo, engordar.

fatal (ˈfeitəl], *a.* fatal; mortal, mortífero.

fatalism [ˈfeitəlizəm], *s.* fatalismo.

fatalist [ˈfeitəlist], *s.* fatalista, *m.f.*

fatality [fəˈtæliti], *s.* fatalidad; desgracia; siniestro.

fatalness [ˈfeitəlnis], *s.* (lo) fatal; (lo) mortal.

fate [feit], *s.* sino, destino; suerte, hado; (*pl.*) ***the Fates,*** las Parcas, *f.pl.*

fated [ˈfeitid], *a.* fatal, predestinado.

fateful [ˈfeitful], *a.* fatal, funesto, nefasto.

fat-head [ˈfæt-hed], *s.* idiota, *m.f.*

fat-headed [ˈfæt-ˈhedid], *a.* lerdo, estúpido.

father [ˈfɑ:ðə], *s.* padre; (*pl.*) ***the City Fathers,*** los concejales de la ciudad, *m.pl.*; ***Father Christmas,*** Papá Noel; ***father confessor,*** padre espiritual; (*pol.*) ***father of the House,*** decano de la Cámara; ***father-in-law,*** suegro; ***father-like,*** paternal; ***like father, like son,*** de tal palo tal astilla. — *v.t.* engendrar; prohijar; servir de padre a; ***father*** (***sth.***) ***on*** (***s.o.***), achacar (algo) a (alguien), atribuir (algo) a (alguien).

fatherhood [ˈfɑ:ðəhud], *s.* paternidad.

fatherland [ˈfɑ:ðəlænd], *s.* patria.

fatherless [ˈfɑ:ðəlis], *a.* huérfano de padre.

fatherliness [ˈfɑ:ðəlinis], *s.* ternura *o* amor paternal.

fatherly [ˈfɑ:ðəli], *a.* paternal; paterno. — *adv.* paternalmente.

fathom [ˈfæðəm], *s.* braza. — *v.t.* sondar, sondear; penetrar.

fathomable [ˈfæðəməbl], *a.* sondable.

fathomless [ˈfæðəmlis], *a.* insondable.

fatidical [fəˈtidikəl], *a.* fatídico.

fatigue [fəˈti:g], *s.* fatiga, cansancio; desgaste; ***fatigue-dress,*** traje de fajina; (*mil.*) ***fatigue duty,*** faena, fajina; ***fatigue-party,*** pelotón de castigo. — *v.t.* fatigar, cansar, agotar.

fatiguing [fəˈti:giŋ], *a.* cansado, agotador.

fatling [ˈfætliŋ], *s.* cebón, ceboncillo.

fatness [ˈfætnis], *s.* gordura; obesidad.

fatten [fætn], *v.t.* engordar, cebar; (*agric.*) abonar. — *v.i.* engordar, echar carnes.

fattener [ˈfætnə], *s.* cebo.

fattiness [ˈfætinis], *s.* gordura.

fattish [ˈfætiʃ], *a.* gordinflón, regordete.

fatty [ˈfæti], *a.* graso; gordo; grasiento; ***fatty tissue,*** tejido adiposo; ***fatty acid,*** ácido graso.

fatuous [ˈfætjuəs], *a.* necio, estúpido.

fatuity [fəˈtju:iti], *s.* necedad.

fauces [ˈfɔ:si:z], *s.pl.* (*anat.*) fauces, *f.pl.*

faucet [ˈfɔ:sit], *s.* espita, canilla; grifo; (*Am.*) [TAP].

fault [fɔ:lt], *s.* falta; culpa; defecto, desperfecto; (*elec.*) avería; (*geol.*) falla; ***at fault,*** responsable; ***it's your fault,*** tú tienes la culpa; ***to find fault,*** poner pegas (***with,*** a); poner faltas (a). — *v.t.* quitar puntos a; ***this work cannot be faulted,*** este trabajo no tiene defectos. — *v.i.* (*geol.*) producirse una falla.

fault-finder [ˈfɔ:lt-ˈfaində], *s.* criticón, reparón.

fault-finding [ˈfɔ:lt-ˈfaindiŋ], *a.* criticón, reparón, chinche. — *s.* manía de criticar, chinchorrería.

faultily [ˈfɔ:ltili], *adv.* defectuosamente.

faultiness [ˈfɔ:ltinis], *s.* (lo) defectuoso.

faultless [ˈfɔ:ltlis], *a.* impecable; intachable; perfecto.

faultlessness [ˈfɔ:ltlisnis], *s.* (lo) impecable; (lo) intachable; (lo) perfecto.

faulty [ˈfɔ:lti], *a.* defectuoso, imperfecto.

faun [fɔ:n], *s.* fauno.

fauna [ˈfɔ:nə], *s.* (*zool.*) fauna.

favor [FAVOUR].

favour [ˈfeivə], *s.* favor; apoyo; aprobación; privanza; prenda; (*carta*) atenta, grata; ***to be in favour*** (***with***), tener aceptación (con, entre); gozar de favor (con, entre); tener el apoyo (de); ***to be in favour of,*** ser partidario de; estar por; ***to curry favour with,*** congraciarse con; ***to decide in s.o.'s favour,*** resolver a favor de alguien; ***to fall out of favour with,*** caer en desgracia con; ***to find favour with,*** caerle en gracia a; ***in favour of,*** a favor de; ***without fear or favour,*** imparcialmente. — *v.t.* favorecer; apoyar.

favourable [ˈfeivərəbl], *a.* favorable, propicio.

favoured [ˈfeivəd], *a.* agraciado; ***ill-favoured,*** poco agraciado; ***well-favoured,*** (muy) agraciado.

favourer [ˈfeivərə], *s.* favorecedor.

favourite [ˈfeivərit], *a.* favorito, predilecto, preferido. — *s.* valido, privado, protegido.

favouritism [ˈfeivəritizəm], *s.* favoritismo.

fawn (1) [fɔ:n], *a.* beige. — *s.* cervato; beige.

fawn (2) [fɔ:n], *v.i.* — ***on,*** adular.

fawner [ˈfɔ:nə], *s.* adulador, adulón, lisonjero.

fawning [ˈfɔ:niŋ], *a.* adulador, adulón, lisonjero, servil. — *s.* adulación, lisonjas, *f.pl.*, servilismo.

fealty [ˈfiəlti], *s.* homenaje, lealtad, fidelidad.

fear [fiə], *s.* miedo, temor; ***for fear of,*** por miedo de, por temor a; ***for fear that,*** por miedo de que; ***to go in fear of one's life,*** temer por su vida; (*fam.*) ***no fear!*** ¡ni hablar! ¡ni pensarlo! — *v.t.* temer, tener miedo de. — *v.i.* temer, tener miedo; ***fear for,*** temer por.

fearful [ˈfiəful], *a.* medroso, temeroso; espantoso, tremebundo, pavoroso.

fearfulness [ˈfiəfulnis], *s.* (lo) terrible, (lo) espantoso.

fearless [ˈfiəlis], *a.* intrépido.

fearlessness [ˈfiəlisnis], *s.* intrepidez.

fearsome [ˈfiəsəm], *a.* espantoso, pavoroso.

feasibility, feasibleness [fi:ziˈbiliti, ˈfi:ziblnis], *s.* (lo) factible, viabilidad.

feasible [ˈfi:zibl], *a.* factible, viable.

feasibly [ˈfi:zibli], *adv.* posiblemente.

feast [fi:st], *s.* banquete, festín; fiesta; agasajo; regalo; abundancia. — *v.t.* banquetear; festejar, agasajar; ***feast one's eyes,*** recrear(se) la vista. — *v.i.* banquetear; ***feast on,*** regalarse con.

feaster [ˈfi:stə], *s.* festejador, anfitrión; comensal.

feasting [ˈfi:stiŋ], *s.* banquete, fiesta.

feat [fi:t], *s.* hazaña, proeza; ***feat of arms,*** hecho de armas, lance.

feather [ˈfeðə], *s.* pluma; lengüeta; cuña; ***in fine feather,*** de buen talante; hecho un brazo de mar; ***to show the white feather,*** volver las espaldas, mostrarse cobarde; ***feather in one's cap,*** timbre de honor, triunfo personal; ***birds of a feather,*** gente de la misma calaña; ***birds of a feather flock together,*** cada oveja con su pareja, Dios los cría y ellos se juntan; ***feather-bed,*** colchón de plumas; ***feather-brain,*** casquivano; ***feather-duster,*** plumero; (*carp.*) ***feather joint,*** encaje de barbilla y farda; (*dep.*) ***feather-weight,*** peso pluma. — *v.t.* emplumar; cubrir *o* adornar con plumas; (*carp.*) machihembrar; ***feather one's nest,*** forrarse, lucrarse. — *v.i.* (*orn.*) cubrirse con plumas.

feathered [ˈfeðəd], *a.* plumado; alado; ***feathered friends,*** pájaros.

feathering-wheel [ˈfeðəriŋ-wi:l], *s.* rueda de paletas movibles.

featherless [ˈfeðəlis], *a.* desplumado; implume.

feathery [ˈfəðəri], *a.* plumoso, cubierto de plumas; ligero como una pluma.

feature [ˈfi:tʃə], *s.* facción; rasgo, rasgo distintivo, característica, nota característica, nota distintiva; atracción; artículo. — *v.t.* delinear, representar; ofrecer; destacar, hacer resaltar; presentar como atracción principal.

featured [ˈfi:tʃəd], *a.* anunciado de modo destacado; ***well-featured,*** de facciones regulares.

featureless [ˈfi:tʃəlis], *a.* sin rasgos característicos; anodino.

febrifugal [feˈbrifjugəl], *a.* febrífugo.

febrifuge [ˈfebrifju:dʒ], *s.* febrífugo.

febrile [ˈfi:brail], *a.* febril.

February [ˈfebruəri], *s.* febrero.

fecal [FÆCAL].

feces [FÆCES].

feckless [ˈfeklis], *a.* irreflexivo, que no reflexiona.

fecula [ˈfekjulə], *s.* fécula.

feculence, feculency [ˈfekjuləns, -si], *s.* feculencia.

feculent [ˈfekjulənt], *a.* feculento.

fecund [ˈfi:kənd], *a.* fecundo.

fecundate [ˈfi:kəndeit], *v.t.* fecundar.

fecundation [fi:kənˈdeiʃən], *s.* fecundación.

fecundity [fiˈkʌnditi], *s.* fecundidad.

fed [fed], *a.* (*fam.*) ***fed-up,*** harto (***with,*** de). — *pret., p.p.* [FEED].

federal [ˈfedərəl], *a.* federal.

federalism [ˈfedərəlizəm], *s.* federalismo.

federalist [ˈfedərəlist], *s.* federalista, *m.f.*

federalize [ˈfedərəlaiz], *v.t.* federalizar, (con)federar. — *v.i.* federalizarse, (con)federarse.

federate, federated [ˈfedərət, -reitid], *a.* (con)federado, federal. — *v.t.* (con)federar, aliar. — *v.i.* (con)federarse, aliarse.

federation [fedəˈreiʃən], *s.* (con)federación.

federative [ˈfedərətiv], *a.* federativo, federal.

fee [fi:], *s.* honorario; derecho; cuota; gratificación; (*pl.*) honorarios; cuota de enseñanza; ***to hold in fee,*** tener a sueldo; ***entrance fee,*** cuota de entrada. — *v.t.* pagar.

feeble [fi:bl], *a.* débil; flojo, endeble; irresoluto; ***to grow feeble,*** debilitarse.

feeble-minded [ˈfi:bl-ˈmaindid], *a.* imbécil; irresoluto.

feeble-mindedness [ˈfi:bl-ˈmaindidnis], *s.* debilidad mental; irresolución.

feebleness [ˈfi:blnis], *s.* debilidad; flojedad, endeblez.

feed [fi:d], *s.* comida; alimento; pasto; pienso; alimentación; (*fam.*) comilona; (*elec.*) ***feed-back,*** realimentación, regeneración; ***feed-pipe,*** tubo *o* válvula de alimentación; ***feed-pump,*** bomba de alimentación; ***to be off its feed,*** estar desganado. — *irr. v.t.* dar de comer a, alimentar; ***feed up,*** cebar, engordar. — *v.i.* comer, alimentarse; pacer.

feeder [ˈfi:də], *s.* alimentador; afluente; (*f.c.*) ramal; (*elec.*) conductor de alimentación; (*mec.*) avanzador; ***feeder line,*** ramal tributario.

feeding [ˈfi:diŋ], *s.* alimentación; (el) comer *o* pastar.

feeding-bottle [ˈfi:diŋ-bɔtl], *s.* biberón.

feel [fi:l], *s.* sensación; tacto. — *v.t.* sentir; tentar, palpar, tocar; sondear; tomar (el pulso); ***feel one's way,*** tantear el camino; ***to feel out,*** tantear, sondear; ***to feel that,*** creer que, parecerle a uno que. — *v.i.* sentirse; estar; notarse; tener; ***feel happy,*** estar contento; ***feel cold,*** tener frío; ***it feels cold,*** está frío, lo encuentro frío; ***how do you feel?*** ¿cómo está usted? ¿cómo se siente usted?; ***how do you feel about it?*** ¿qué le parece a usted?; ***feel for,*** requerir, buscar tentando; compadecerse de; ***feel like,*** tener ganas de.

feeler [ˈfí:lə], *s.* antena; tentáculo; sondeo; tentativa; ***to put out feelers,*** sondear.

feeling [ˈfi:liŋ], *a.* sensible, compasivo. — *s.* tacto; sensación; sentimiento; sensibilidad; compasión; pasión; ***to touch the feelings of,*** conmover.

feelingly [ˈfi:liŋli], *adv.* de un modo conmovedor; emocionadamente.

feet [fi:t], *s.pl.* [FOOT].

feetless [ˈfi:tlis], *a.* sin pies.

feign [fein], *v.t.* fingir, simular; ***feign ignorance,*** hacerse el desentendido. — *v.i.* fingir, simular.

feignedness [ˈfeinidnis], *s.* disimulo.

feigning [ˈfeiniŋ], *s.* fingimiento, simulación.

feint [feint], *s.* treta; (*esgr.*) finta. — *v.i.* hacer una finta.

feldspar [ˈfel(d)spɑ:], *s.* (*min.*) feldespato.

feldspathic [fel(d)ˈspæθik], *a.* feldespático, de feldespato.

felicitate [fiˈlisiteit], *v.t.* felicitar, dar el parabién a.

felicitation [filisiˈteiʃən], *s.* felicitación, parabién.

felicitous [fiˈlisitəs], *a.* feliz, acertado.

felicity [fiˈlisiti], *s.* felicidad, dicha; expresión feliz.

felid [ˈfi:lid], *s.* (*zool.*) félido.

feline [ˈfi:lain], *a., s.* felino.

fell (1) [fel], *s.* páramo; risco.

fell (2) [fel], *a.* cruel, feroz, sañudo; ***in one fell swoop,*** de un golpe.

fell (3) [fel], *s.* tala (*de árboles*). — *v.t.* derribar; talar (*árboles*); acogotar, abatir (*reses*).

fell (4) [fel], *pret.* [FALL].

feller [ˈfelə], *s.* máquina taladora.

felling [ˈfeliŋ], *s.* tala.

felloe [ˈfelou], *s.* pina (*de la rueda*).

fellow [ˈfelou], *s.* compañero; prójimo; igual; pareja; miembro, socio; becario; (*fam.*) tío, individuo, sujeto; chico, muchacho, hombre; ***brave fellow,*** valiente, muchacho echado para adelante; ***clever young fellow,*** muchacho listo; ***fellow-being,*** prójimo; semejante; ***fellow-citizen,*** conciudadano; ***fellow-countryman,*** compatriota, *m.*; (*local*) paisano; ***fellow-creature,*** prójimo; semejante; ***fellow-feeling,*** simpatía; afinidad; solidaridad; ***fellow-heir,*** coheredero; ***fellow-member, fellow-partner,*** consocio; ***fellow-student,*** condiscípulo; ***fellow-traveller,*** compañero de viaje; simpatizante; comunistizante; ***school-fellow,*** condiscípulo; ***young fellow,*** joven muchacho; ***to be hail-fellow-well-met (with),*** tratar con campechanía, ser campechano (con).

fellowship [ˈfelouʃip], *s.* compañerismo; confraternidad; compañía; plaza pensionada; beca.
felly [ˈfeli], [FELLOE].
felon [ˈfelən], *s.* reo, criminal, delincuente; felón.
felonious [fiˈlouniəs], *a.* criminal, delincuente; perverso.
felony [ˈfeləni], *s.* crimen, delito, fechoría; felonía.
felsite [ˈfelsait], *s.* felsita.
felspar [FELDSPAR].
felstone [ˈfelstoun], [FELSITE].
felt (1) [felt], *s.* fieltro. — *v.t.* cubrir con fieltro.
felt (2) [felt], *p.p.*, *pret.* [FEEL].
felting [ˈfeltiŋ], *s.* fieltro.
felucca [feˈlʌkə], *s.* falucho.
female [ˈfi:meil], *a.* femenino; ***female screw,*** tuerca, hembra de tornillo. — *s.* hembra.
feminine [ˈfeminin], *a.* femenino.
femininity [femiˈniniti], *s.* feminidad, femineidad.
feminism [ˈfeminizəm], *s.* feminismo.
feminist [ˈfeminist], *s.* feminista, *m.f.*
femoral [ˈfemərəl], *a.* femoral.
femur [ˈfi:mə], *s.* (*anat.*) fémur.
fen [fen], *s.* marjal, pantano, paúl; ***fen-duck,*** ánade silvestre; ***fen-fire,*** fuego fatuo.
fence [fens], *s.* cerca, valla, vallado; (*mec.*) guarda, *m.f.*, guía *m.f.*; perista, *m.*, comprador de objetos robados; ***to sit on the fence,*** ver los toros desde la barrera, estar a ver venir; ***wire fence,*** cerca de alambre. — *v.t.* cercar; proteger; ***fence in,*** cercar; ***fence off,*** cercar, separar con vallas. — *v.i.* esgrimir; defenderse con evasivas.
fenceless [ˈfenslis], *a.* abierto, no cercado.
fence-month [ˈfens-mʌnθ], *s.* tiempo de veda.
fencer [ˈfensə], *s.* esgrimidor; tirador de florete; caballo ágil para saltar cercas.
fencing [ˈfensiŋ], *s.* esgrima; material para cercas; valladar; ***fencing-bout,*** asalto de armas; ***fencing-master,*** maestro de esgrima, maestro de armas; ***fencing-school,*** escuela de esgrima.
fend [fend], *v.t.* — ***off,*** rechazar. — *v.i.* esgrimir; ***fend for o.s.,*** apañárselas, bandeárselas (por su cuenta).
fender [ˈfendə], *s.* guardafuegos, *m.pl.*; (*pl.*, *mar.*) defensas, *f.pl.*, pallete, andullo; (*Am.*, *aut.*) [BUMPER].
fenestration [fenisˈtreiʃən], *s.* (*arq.*) ventanaje.
Fenian [ˈfi:njən], *a.* perteneciente *o* relativo a los fenianos. — *s.* feniano.
fenland [ˈfenlənd], *s.* tierra pantanosa.
fennel [ˈfenəl], *s.* (*bot.*) hinojo; (*bot.*) ***giant fennel,*** cañaheja, férula.
fenny [ˈfeni], *a.* pantanoso.
fenugreek [ˈfenjugri:k], *s.* (*bot.*) fenogreco, alholva.
feoff [fef], *s.* feudo. — *v.t.* enfeudar.
feral [ˈfiərəl], *a.* feral.
ferial [ˈfiəriəl], *a.* (*igl.*) ferial.
ferine [ˈfiərain], *a.* ferino.
ferment [ˈfə:ment], *s.* fermento, fermentación; (*fig.*) agitación. — *v.t.* [fə:ˈment] (hacer) fermentar. — *v.i.* fermentar.
fermentable [fəˈmentəbl], *a.* fermentable.
fermentation [fə:menˈteiʃən], *s.* fermentación.
fermentative [fəˈmentətiv], *a.* fermentativo.
fern [fə:n], *s.* (*bot.*) helecho.
ferny [ˈfə:ni], *a.* abundante en helechos, lleno de helechos.
ferocious [fəˈrouʃəs], *a.* feroz; fiero.
ferociousness, ferocity [fəˈrouʃəsnis, fəˈrɔsiti], *s.* ferocidad; fiereza.
ferrate [ˈfereit], *s.* ferrato.
ferreous [ˈferiəs], *a.* férreo.
ferret [ˈferit], *s.* hurón. — *v.t.* — ***out,*** buscar tercamente, sonsacar. — *v.i.* — ***about,*** huronear; fisgonear, husmear.
ferric [ˈferik], *a.* férrico.
ferrocalcite [ferouˈkælsait], *s.* ferrocalcita.
ferrocyanide, ferricyanide [ferouˈsaiənaid, feriˈsaiənaid], *s.* ferrocianuro.
ferroprussiate [ferouˈprʌsieit], *s.* ferroprusiato.
ferrotype [ˈferoutaip], *s.* ferrotipo.
ferrous [ˈferəs], *a.* ferroso.
ferruginous [fəˈru:dʒinəs], *a.* ferruginoso.
ferrule [ˈferu:l], *s.* regatón, virola, contera; casquillo; cantonera (*de libro*).
ferry [ˈferi], *s.* pasaje, balsadero; balsa, barca (*de pasaje*); transbordador; ***ferry-boat,*** barca de pasaje, balsa; transbordador. — *v.t.* pasar, balsear, transportar. — *v.i.* pasar en barca.
ferryman [ˈferimən], *s.* barquero.
fertile [ˈfə:tail], *a.* fértil, fecundo, feraz.
fertility, fertileness [fə:ˈtiliti, ˈfə:tailnis], *s.* fertilidad, fecundidad, feracidad.
fertilization [fə:tilaiˈzeiʃən], *s.* (*biol.*) fertilización, fecundación; (*agric.*) abono.
fertilize [ˈfə:tilaiz], *v.t.* fertilizar, fecundar; abonar.
fertilizer [ˈfə:tilaizə], *s.* (*agric.*) abono, fertilizante.
ferula [ˈferulə], *s.* (*bot.*) férula, cañaheja.
ferule [ˈferu:l], *s.* férula, palmeta. — *v.t.* dar palmetazos, castigar con la férula.
fervency [ˈfə:vənsi], [FERVOUR].
fervent [ˈfə:vənt], *a.* ferviente, fervoroso.
fervid [ˈfə:vid], *a.* férvido, fogoso, ardiente, vehemente.
fervour [ˈfə:v:], *s.* fervor, calor, ardor; devoción, celo.
Fescennine [ˈfesenain], *a.* fescenino; obsceno, licencioso; ***Fescennine verses,*** versos obscenos, *m.pl.*
fescue [ˈfeskju:], *s.* puntero; (*bot.*) festuca; (*bot.*) ***fescue-grass,*** cañuela.
fesse [fes], *s.* (*blas.*) faja.
festal [ˈfestəl], *a.* festivo.
fester [ˈfestə], *s.* llaga, úlcera. — *v.i.* ulcerarse, enconarse.
festival [ˈfestivəl], *a.* festivo. — *s.* fiesta, festividad, festejo; festival.
festive [ˈfestiv], *a.* festivo, alegre.
festivity [fesˈtiviti], *s.* fiesta, festividad, festejo.
festoon [fesˈtu:n], *s.* festón, guirnalda. — *v.t.* festonear.
festooned [fesˈtu:nd], *a.* afestonado.
fetal [FŒTAL].
fetch [fetʃ], *v.t.* traer; ir por, ir a buscar; hacer venir; dar, pegar (*un golpe*); (*precios*) venderse por; atraer; ***fetch down,*** hacer bajar; derribar; ***fetch in,*** entrar, meter; ***fetch up,*** subir; vomitar. — *v.i.* ***fetch and carry,*** trajinar, traer y llevar; ***fetch up at,*** ir a parar a, llegar por fin a.
fetching [ˈfetʃiŋ], *a.* atrayente; simpático.
fête [feit], *s.* fiesta; ***fête-day,*** día de fiesta. — *v.t.* festejar, agasajar.
fetid [ˈfetid], *a.* fétido; hediondo.
fetidness [ˈfetidnis], *s.* fetidez; hediondez.
fetish [ˈfetiʃ], *s.* fetiche; manía.
fetishism [ˈfetiʃizəm], *s.* fetichismo.
fetlock [ˈfetlɔk], *s.* cerneja; espolón.
fetter [ˈfetə], *s.* (*pl.*) grillos, *m.pl.*, grilletes, *m.pl.*; trabas, *f.pl.* — *v.t.* engrillar; encadenar, trabar; estorbar.
fettle [fetl], *s.* condición, estado; ***in (fine) fettle,*** en forma; en (muy) buenas condiciones, estupendamente; de (muy) buen humor.
fetus [FŒTUS].
feud [fju:d], *s.* enemistad, enemiga, odio; feudo; ***family feud,*** desavenencia familiar.
feudal [ˈfju:dəl], *a.* feudal.
feudalism [ˈfju:dəlizəm], *s.* feudalismo.
feudality [fju:ˈdæliti], *s.* feudalidad; feudo.
feudalize [ˈfju:dəlaiz], *v.t.* enfeudar.
feudary [ˈfju:dəri], *a.* feudal, feudatario. — *s.* feudatario.

feudatory [ˈfjuːdətəri], *a.*, *s.* feudatario.
feudist [ˈfjuːdist], *s.* feudista, *m.*
feuilleton [ˈfəːitɔːn], *s.* folletín.
fever [ˈfiːvə], *s.* (*med.*) fiebre, *f.*; calentura; ***scarlet fever,*** escarlatina; ***spotted fever,*** tabardillo pintado; ***typhoid fever,*** fiebre tifoidea; ***typhus fever,*** tifus; ***to set in a fever,*** poner febril.
fevered [ˈfiːvəd], *a.* febril.
feverfew [ˈfiːvəfjuː], *s.* (*bot.*) matricaria.
feverish [ˈfiːvəriʃ], *a.* febril, calenturiento; (*fig.*) afanado.
feverishly [ˈfiːvəriʃli], *adv.* de un modo febril; afanadamente.
feverishness [ˈfiːvəriʃnis], *s.* estado febril.
few [fjuː], *a.* pocos, *m.pl.*; ***a few,*** algunos, *m.pl.*, unos cuantos, *m.pl.*; ***the few,*** la minoría; ***few and far between,*** contados, *m.pl.*, poco frecuentes, *m.pl.*; ***quite a few, a good few,*** bastantes, *m.pl.*, no pocos, *m.pl.*
fewness [ˈfjuːnis], *s.* escasez, corto número, número reducido.
fez [fez], *s.* fez, *m.*
fiancé [fiˈɑ̃ːnsei], *s.* novio, prometido.
fiancée [fiˈɑ̃ːnsei], *s.* novia, prometida.
fiasco [fiˈæskou], *s.* fracaso (lastimoso); fiasco.
fiat [ˈfiət], *s.* fíat, orden, mandato.
fib [fib], *s.* (*fam.*) embuste, bola, trola. — *v.i.* mentir, embustear.
fibber [ˈfibə], *s.* embustero, trapalón.
fibre [ˈfaibə], *a.* de fibra. — *s.* fibra; (*fig.*) carácter, nervio; ***fibre-glass,*** fibra vidrio.
fibril [ˈfaibril], *s.* fibrita.
fibrin [ˈfaibrin], *s.* fibrina.
fibrinous [ˈfaibrinəs], *a.* fibrinoso.
fibroid [ˈfaibrɔid], *a.* fibroso.
fibroma [fiˈbroumə], *s.* (*med.*) fibroma, tumor fibroso.
fibrous [ˈfaibrəs], *a.* fibroso.
fibula [ˈfibjulə], *s.* (*anat.*) peroné; (*ant.*) fíbula.
fibular [ˈfibjulə], *a.* peroneo.
fichu [ˈfiʃuː], *s.* fichú, pañoleta.
fickle [ˈfikl], *a.* voluble, veleidoso, versátil.
fickleness [ˈfiklnis], *s.* volubilidad, veleidad, versatilidad.
fictile [ˈfiktail], *a.* plástico, moldeable.
fiction [ˈfikʃən], *s.* ficción, invención; novelas, *f.pl.*, género novelístico.
fictional [ˈfikʃənəl], *a.* novelesco, de ficción.
fictitious [fikˈtiʃəs], *a.* ficticio, fingido; imaginario.
fictitiousness [fikˈtiʃəsnis], *s.* representación fingida.
fid [fid], *s.* (*mar.*) barra de sostén; pasador; ***fid of a topmast,*** cuña de mastelero.
fiddle [fidl], *s.* violín; timo, estafa; apaño; ***fiddle-block,*** motón de poleas diferenciales; ***fiddle-bow,*** arco de violín; ***fiddle-string,*** cuerda de violín; ***fit as a fiddle,*** como un reloj; (*fig.*) ***to play second fiddle,*** hacer un papel secundario. — *v.t.* estafar, timar; apañar; (*fam.*) ***fiddle the books,*** falsificar las cuentas. — *v.i.* tocar el violín; hacer chanchullos; (*fam.*) ***fiddle away,*** desperdiciar; (*fam.*) ***fiddle with,*** jugar con, manosear; andar en.
fiddle-de-dee [ˈfidl-di-ˈdiː], *s.* necedad, disparate. — *interj.* ¡quiá! ¡tonterías!
fiddle-faddle [ˈfidl-fædl], *s.* tonterías, *f.pl.*; simplezas, *f.pl.*; fruslerías, *f.pl.*; tiquismiquis, *m.pl.* — *v.i.* decir *u* ocuparse en tonterías.
fiddler [ˈfidlə], *s.* violinista, *m.f.*
fiddlestick [ˈfidlstik], *s.* arco de violín; bagatela. — *interj.* (*pl.*) ¡qué disparate! ¡tonterías!
fiddling [ˈfidliŋ], *a.* (*fam.*) fútil, insignificante; engorroso.
fidelity [fiˈdeliti], *s.* fidelidad, lealtad.
fidget [ˈfidʒit], *s.* (*fam.*) culo inquieto; (***the***) ***fidgets,*** desasosiego; ***to have the fidgets,*** no poder estarse quieto. — *v.t.* incordiar. — *v.i.* estar inquieto, agitarse nerviosamente; ***fidget with,*** manosear, jugar con; ***stop fidgeting!*** ¡estate quieto!
fidgety [ˈfidʒiti], *a.* (*fam.*) inquieto.
fiducial [fiˈdjuːʃiəl], *a.* fiduciario; de confianza; lleno de confianza; (*mat.*) fiducial.
fiduciary [fiˈdjuːʃiəri], *a.* fiduciario.
fie! [fai], *interj.* ¡qué vergüenza!
fief [fiːf], *s.* feudo.
field [fiːld], *s.* campo; sembrado; esfera, orden; (*dep.*, *fig.*) aspirantes, *m.f.pl.*, opositores, *m.pl.*, pretendientes, *m.pl.*, competidores, *m.pl.*; ***field-artillery,*** artillería de campaña; (*bot.*) ***field-basil,*** albahaca silvestre; ***field-book,*** manual de agrimensor; ***field-day,*** día de maniobras, *m.*; día de mucha actividad *o* de mucho éxito, *m.*; ***field-glasses,*** prismáticos, *m.pl.*; ***field-gun,*** cañón de campaña; ***field-hospital,*** hospital de campaña *o* de sangre; ***field-kitchen,*** cocina de campaña; ***field-marshal,*** mariscal de campo; capitán general de ejército; ***field-mouse,*** ratón de campo; ***to take the field,*** salir a palestra, entrar en liza. — *v.t.* recoger y devolver (*la pelota*); presentar (*un equipo*); ***field the same side,*** presentar el mismo equipo. — *v.i.* (*dep.*) jugar de recogepelota.
fielder [ˈfiːldə], *s.* (*dep.*) el que recoge la pelota.
fieldfare [ˈfiːldfɛə), *s.* (*orn.*) zorzal.
fiend [fiːnd], *s.* demonio; sádico; (*fam.*) fanático, maniático (***for,*** de); (*fam.*) pelmazo; ***dope-fiend, drug-fiend,*** toxicómano.
fiendish [ˈfiːndiʃ], *a.* diabólico; sádico.
fiendishness [ˈfiːndiʃnis], *s.* (lo) diabólico; (lo) sádico.
fierce [ˈfiəs], *a.* feroz; furioso; violento, intenso, recio.
fierceness [ˈfiəsnis], *s.* ferocidad; furia; violencia, intensidad.
fieriness [ˈfaiərinis], *s.* fogosidad, ardor, pasión.
fiery [ˈfaiəri], *a.* fogoso, ardiente, apasionado, vehemente.
fife [faif], *s.* pífano.
fifer [ˈfaifə], *s.* pífano.
fifteen [fifˈtiːn], *a.*, *s.* quince; ***to be fifteen,*** tener quince años.
fifteenth [ˈfifˈtiːnθ], *a.* decimoquinto, quinceno; quince (*títulos*). — *s.* decimoquinta (parte); quince (*fechas*).
fifth [fifθ], *a.* quinto (*también títulos*). — *s.* quinta (parte); (*mús.*) quinta; cinco (*fechas*).
fifthly [ˈfifθli], *adv.* en quinto lugar.
fiftieth [ˈfiftəθ], *a.*, *s.* quincuagésimo.
fifty [ˈfifti], *a.*, *s.* cincuenta; ***fifty-fifty,*** mitad y mitad.
fig [fig], *s.* higo; breva; (*fig.*) ***fig-leaf,*** hoja de parra; ***fig-tree,*** higuera; (*fam.*) ***I don't care a fig,*** no se me da un higo.
fight [fait], *s.* pelea, combate; lucha; lidia; ***in fair fight,*** en buena lid; ***to pick a fight with,*** buscar camorra a; ***to put up a good fight,*** luchar con denuedo; estar valiente; ***to show fight,*** mostrarse dispuesto a luchar. — *irr. v.t.* combatir, luchar con *o* contra; dar *o* librar (*una batalla*); (*toros*) lidiar; ***fight off,*** rechazar; ***fight it out,*** decidir, zanzar la cuestión luchando; ***fight one's way through,*** abrirse paso luchando. — *v.i.* combatir, luchar, pelear; ***fight against the odds,*** luchar con desventaja; ***fight back,*** contraatacar; ***fight shy of,*** esquivar, soslayar, rehuir; ***fight to a finish,*** luchar hasta el fin.
fighter [ˈfaitə], *s.* luchador, combatiente, peleador; duelista, *m.f.*; (*aer.*) caza, *m.*; ***fighter-bomber,*** caza bombardero.
fighting [ˈfaitiŋ], *a.* aguerrido, combatiente; de combate; ***fighting cock,*** gallo de pelea. — *s.* combate, combates, (el) luchar; ***street fighting,*** luchas callejeras.
figment [ˈfigmənt], *s.* ficción, invención; ***figment of the imagination,*** quimera; entelequia.
figurable [ˈfigjurəbl], *a.* figurable.

figurant [ˈfigjurənt], *s.* (*teat.*) figurante.
figurante [figjuˈrænti], *s.* figuranta.
figuration [figjuˈreiʃən], *s.* figuración; figura.
figurative [ˈfigjurətiv], *a.* figurado; figurativo; ***figurative sense,*** sentido figurado.
figurativeness [ˈfigjurətivnis], *s.* (lo) figurado *o* metafórico.
figure [ˈfigə], *s.* figura, hechura; cifra, número; facha, tipo; dibujo; ***central figure,*** protagonista, *m.f.*; ***figure dance,*** baile de figuras; ***figure of fun,*** hazmerreír; ***figure skating,*** patinaje artístico; ***figure of speech,*** tropo; ***fine figure of a woman,*** buena moza; ***in round figures,*** en cifras redondas; ***to cut a poor figure,*** hacer mal papel; ***to keep one's figure,*** guardar la línea. — *v.t.* figurar, representar; imaginar; calcular; (*fam.*) ***figure out,*** entender; descifrar. — *v.i.* figurar; hacer viso; calcular, planear.
figured [ˈfigəd], *a.* adornado, labrado, floreado, estampado; (*mús.*) ***figured bass,*** bajo cifrado.
figurehead [ˈfigəhed], *s.* (*mar.*) mascarón de proa; figurón.
figurine [ˈfigjuri:n], *s.* figurilla.
figuring [ˈfigəriŋ], *s.* computación.
figwort [ˈfigwɔ:t], *s.* (*bot.*) escrofularia.
Fiji [ˈfi:ˈdʒi:]. Fiji.
Fijian [fi:ˈdʒi:ən], *a.* de Fiji. — *s.* habitante *o* lengua de las Islas Fiji.
filaceous [fiˈleiʃəs], *a.* hebroso, fibroso, estoposo, filamentoso.
filament [ˈfiləmənt], *s.* filamento.
filamentous [filəˈmentəs], *a.* filamentoso, hilachoso; fibroso.
filature [ˈfilətʃə], *s.* hilandería; fábrica de hilados.
filbert [ˈfilbət], *s.* (*bot.*) avellana; ***filbert-tree,*** avellano.
filch [filtʃ], *v.t.* (*fam.*) ratear, sisar.
filcher [ˈfiltʃə], *s.* (*fam.*) garduño, ratero, sisón, ladroncillo.
file (1) [fail], *s.* ficha; expediente; fichero; archivo; fila, hilera. — *v.t.* fichar; archivar; ***file away,*** archivar. — *v.i.* — ***by*** o ***past,*** desfilar; ***file out,*** salir en fila.
file (2) [fail], *s.* lima; ***file-cutter,*** picador de limas; (*ict.*) ***file-fish,*** liga. — *v.t.* — ***down,*** limar.
filer [ˈfailə], *s.* limador.
filial [ˈfiliəl], *a.* filial.
filiation [filiˈeiʃən], *s.* filiación.
filibuster [ˈfilibʌstə], *s.* (*pol.*) filibustero; obstruccionista, *m.f.*; obstrucción. — *v.i.* filibustear; usar de maniobras obstruccionistas.
filibusterism [ˈfilibʌstərizəm], *s.* filibusterismo.
filiform [ˈfilifɔ:m], *a.* filiforme.
filigree [ˈfiligri:], *s.* filigrana.
filigreed [ˈfiligri:d], *a.* afiligranado.
filing-cabinet [ˈfailiŋ-ˈkæbinit], *s.* archivador.
filings [ˈfailiŋz], *s.pl.* limaduras, *f.pl.*
fill [fil], *s.* hartazgo; pipa; ***to eat*** o ***have one's fill,*** hartarse. — *v.t.* llenar; rellenar; ocupar, desempeñar, cubrir; hinchar, inflar; (*dientes*) empastar; satisfacer; completar; ***fill the bill,*** valer, servir, ser (justo) lo que hace falta; ***fill in,*** rellenar; completar; (*espacio*) obliterar; (*fam.*) informar (***on,*** de); ***fill out,*** ampliar, redondear; ***fill the place of,*** ocupar el puesto de, sustituir; ***fill up,*** (re)llenar, colmar. — *v.i.* llenarse; ***fill out,*** engordar.
filler [ˈfilə], *s.* relleno.
fillet [ˈfilit], *s.* filete; prendedero; cinta, lista, tira. — *v.t.* desraspar; partir en filetes.
filling [ˈfiliŋ], *a.* que llena. — *s.* relleno; (*dientes*) empaste; ***filling-station,*** estación de servicio, gasolinera.
fillip [ˈfilip], *s.* capirotazo; estímulo.
fillister [ˈfilistə], *s.* (*carp.*) guillame.
filly [ˈfili], *s.* potra; (*fam.*) muchacha, chavala.

film [film], *s.* película; membrana; (*en el ojo*) nube, *f.*; ***documentary film,*** documental, *m.*; ***film rights,*** derechos de cine; ***film-star,*** estrella (de cine), astro, vedette; ***silent film,*** película muda; ***talking film,*** película sonora; ***to shoot a film,*** rodar una película; ***covered in a film of grease,*** cubierto *o* lleno de una capa de grasa. — *v.t.* cubrir con una película; filmar. — *v.i.* formarse película; cubrirse de una película; ***film over,*** empañarse.
filminess [ˈfilminis], *s.* diafanidad.
filmy [ˈfilmi], *a.* diáfano; membranoso, pelicular.
filose [ˈfailous], *a.* (*anat.*, *bot.*) filiforme.
filter [ˈfiltə], *s.* filtro. — *v.t.* filtrar. — *v.i.* filtrarse; ***filter in*** o ***through,*** (in)filtrarse; introducirse.
filth [filθ], *s.* inmundicia, suciedad, mugre.
filthiness [ˈfilθinis], *s.* inmundicia, asquerosidad, suciedad.
filthy [ˈfilθi], *a.* sucio, inmundo, mugriento; ***filthy language,*** lenguaje soez.
filtrate [ˈfiltreit], *s.* líquido filtrado. — *v.t.* filtrar. — *v.i.* filtrarse.
filtration [filˈtreiʃən], *s.* filtración.
fimbriate [ˈfimbrieit], *a.* franjeado, lacinado. — *v.t.* franjear; ribetear.
fin [fin], *s.* aleta (*de pez*); barba (*de ballena*); (*mec.*) rebaba, apéndice (*en forma de aleta*); (*fam.*) mano.
finable [ˈfainəbl], *a.* multable.
final [ˈfainəl], *a.* final, último; definitivo; decisivo; tajante, terminante; ***final call,*** último aviso. — *s.* final.
finale [fiˈnɑ:li], *s.* (*mús.*) final.
finalist [ˈfainəlist], *s.* finalista, *m.f.*
finality [faiˈnæliti], *s.* finalidad; (lo) definitivo; decisión; ***tone of finality,*** tono resuelto.
finally [ˈfainəli], *adv.* finalmente, en conclusión, por último.
finance [faiˈnæns], *s.* ciencia financiera, ciencia rentística; (*pl.*) asuntos financieros, *m.pl.*, finanzas, *f.pl.*; hacienda, rentas, *f.pl.*, fondos, *m.pl.* — *v.t.* suministrar fondos para, financiar.
financial [faiˈnænʃəl], *a.* financiero, rentístico, monetario, económico; ***financial year,*** ejercicio económico.
financially [faiˈnænʃəli], *adv.* rentísticamente, económicamente.
financier [faiˈnænsiə], *s.* financiero; hacendista, *m.*
finback [ˈfinbæk], *s.* (*ict.*) yubarta, rorcual.
finch [fintʃ], *s.* (*orn.*) pinzón, picogordo, fringílido; ***bull-finch,*** pinzón real; ***gold-finch,*** acanta.
find [faind], *s.* hallazgo. — *irr. v.t.* encontrar, hallar; dar con, descubrir; enterarse de; averiguar; ***find favour with,*** caer en gracia de; (*for.*) ***find guilty,*** declarar culpable; ***I find it impossible to,*** me veo en la imposibilidad de; ***find it in one's heart to,*** tener (el) valor de *o* entrañas para; ***find its mark,*** dar en el blanco; ***find out,*** averiguar; ***he has been found out,*** le han pescado; le han descubierto el juego; ***find one's way home,*** (poder) llegar a casa. — *v.i.* (*der.*) pronunciar, declarar; ***find out*** o ***out about,*** enterarse de.
finder [ˈfaində], *s.* hallador; inventor; descubridor; (*ópt.*) buscador; (*foto.*) visor.
finding [ˈfaindiŋ], *s.* descubrimiento; invención; fallo, decisión, sentencia; (*pl.*) conclusiones, *f.pl.*, recomendaciones, *f.pl.*
fine (1) [fain], *a.* fino; refinado; hermoso, bello; escogido, selecto, primoroso; magnífico, estupendo, soberbio; (*ironía*) bueno; ***fine!*** ¡estupendo! ¡estupendamente!; ***fine arts,*** bellas artes; ***fine-drawn,*** muy fino, muy sutil; ***he's a fine fellow,*** es un chico estupendo; (*ironía*) ***you're a fine one!*** ¡bueno estás tú!; (*fig.*) ***fine-spun,*** alambicado; (*ironía*) ***that'd be a fine thing!*** ¡estaría bueno!; ***to have a fine time,*** pasárselo en grande; ***fine weather,*** buen tiempo. — ***adv.***

estupendamente, estupendo; ***to cut it fine,*** dejarse muy poco tiempo *o* muy poco margen, dejar una cosa para última hora. — *s.* ***in fine,*** en resumen.

fine (2) [fain], *s.* multa. — *v.t.* multar.

fineness [ˈfainnis], *s.* excelencia, excelente calidad, primor; sutileza; finura; perfección; pureza; ley (*de un metal*).

finery [ˈfainəri], *s.* galas, *f.pl.*, adornos, *m.pl.*; perifollos, *m.pl.*

finesse [fiˈnes], *s.* sutileza; delicadeza; tacto, tino, diplomacia.

finger [ˈfiŋgə], *s.* dedo; ***finger-board,*** teclado; ***finger-bowl,*** lavafrutas, *m. inv.*; ***finger mark,*** mancha hecha con el dedo; ***finger-nail,*** uña; ***finger-post,*** poste indicador; ***finger-print,*** impresión dactilar, huella dactilar; ***to have sth. at one's finger-tips,*** saberse una cosa al dedillo; ***index finger,*** dedo índice; ***little finger,*** dedo meñique; ***to twist round one's little finger,*** tener metido en un puño, dominar *o* manejar totalmente; ***middle finger,*** dedo del corazón; ***ring finger,*** dedo anular; (*fig.*) ***he has burnt his fingers,*** se ha cogido los dedos; ***to have a finger in every pie,*** mangonearlo todo; estar metido en todo; ***he would not lift a finger to help you,*** no se molestaría en absoluto para ayudarle; ***to put one's finger on,*** señalar acertadamente; ***to put one's finger on the sore spot,*** poner el dedo en la llaga; ***it slipped through his fingers,*** se le fue de entre las manos. — *v.t.* tocar, manosear; (*mús.*) teclear, pulsar.

fingered [ˈfiŋgəd], *a.* que tiene dedos; (*bot.*, *zool.*) digitado; sobado.

fingering [ˈfiŋgəriŋ], *s.* (el) tocar ligeramente; manoseo; (*mús.*) digitación.

finial [ˈfiniəl], *s.* (*arq.*) florón.

finical, finicky [ˈfinikəl, -i], *a.* delicado, escogido, melindroso, remilgado.

finish [ˈfiniʃ], *s.* fin, final, término; remate, conclusión; acabado; (*dep.*) llegada. — *v.t.* acabar, terminar; ***finish off,*** rematar; completar; acabar con; ***finish up,*** acabar. — *v.i.* acabar; ***finish (up) by,*** acabar por; ***finish with,*** reñir, terminar con.

finisher [ˈfiniʃə], *s.* acabador.

finishing [ˈfiniʃiŋ], *a.* de acabado; ***finishing blow,*** golpe de gracia; ***finishing touch,*** última mano, retoque. — *s.* acabado; ***finishing-line,*** meta; ***finishing-school,*** colegio (de formación social) para señoritas.

finite [ˈfainait], *a.* finito; limitado.

finiteness [ˈfainaitnis], *s.* (lo) finito.

Finland [ˈfinlənd]. Finlandia.

finless [ˈfinlis], *a.* sin aletas.

finlike [ˈfinlaik], *a.* aleteado.

Finn [fin], *s.* finlandés.

finned [find], *a.* que tiene aletas.

Finnic [ˈfinik], *a.* finés (*raza*).

Finnish [ˈfiniʃ], *a.* finlandés. — *s.* finlandés (*lengua*); lengua finesa.

fiord [fjɔːd], *s.* fiord, fiordo, ría.

fir [fəː], *s.* (*bot.*) abeto; ***fir-cone,*** piña; ***Scotch fir,*** pino albar; ***spruce fir,*** pinabete.

fire [faiə], *s.* fuego; lumbre; incendio, quema; fogosidad; ardor, viveza; ***fire-alarm,*** alarma de incendios; ***fire-arm,*** arma de fuego; ***fire-ball,*** bola de fuego; ***fire-brand,*** tea, tizón; ***fire-brick,*** ladrillo refractario; ***fire-brigade,*** cuerpo de bomberos; (*mil.*) ***fire-control,*** dirección del fuego; ***fire-dog,*** morillo de hogar; ***fire-drill,*** ejercicio para caso de incendio; ***fire-eater,*** matamoros, *m.inv.*, fierabrás, *m.*; ***fire-engine,*** coche de bomberos; ***fire-escape,*** escalera de incendios; ***fire-extinguisher,*** extintor, matafuego; (*ent.*) ***fire-fly,*** luciérnaga; ***fire-guard,*** guardafuegos, *m. inv.*; ***fire-hydrant,*** boca de riego; ***fire-insurance,*** seguro contra incendios; ***fire-pan,*** brasero; ***fire-proof,*** incombustible, a prueba de incendios; ***fire-raiser,*** incendiario; ***fire-screen,*** pantalla de chimenea; ***fire-ship,*** brulote; ***fire-shovel,*** badil, paleta; ***fire-station,*** parque de bomberos; ***fire-water,*** aguardiente; ***fire-worshipper,*** adorador del fuego, ignícola, *m.f.*; ***fire is a good servant, but a bad master,*** sírvete del fuego, mas guárdate de él; ***to be on fire,*** arder, estar ardiendo; ***to breathe fire and brimstone,*** echar chispas; ***to catch fire,*** incendiarse, encenderse, inflamarse; ***to get on like a house on fire,*** ir viento en popa; ***to go through fire and water,*** enfrentarse con lo que sea, aguantarlo todo ;***to hang fire,*** tardar en explotar (*un cañón*); (*fig.*) estar estancado; ***to put out the fire,*** apagar el fuego; ***to set fire to, to set on fire,*** pegar fuego a, incendiar; ***to set the Thames on fire,*** inventar la pólvora; ***St. Anthony's fire,*** erisipela; ***St. Elmo's fire,*** fuego de Santelmo; ***under fire,*** expuesto al fuego; atacado, censurado; ***with fire and sword,*** a sangre y fuego. — *v.t.* encender; inflamar; (*fam.*) despedir, echar a la calle; disparar; cocer. — *v.i.* encenderse; hacer fuego, disparar, tirar. — *interj.* ***fire away!*** ¡adelante! ¡venga!

firelock [ˈfaiəlɔk], *s.* escopeta de pedernal.

fireman [ˈfaiəmən], *s.* bombero; fogonero.

fireplace [ˈfaiəpleis], *s.* chimenea; hogar.

firewood [ˈfaiəwud], *s.* leña.

fireworks [ˈfaiəwəːks], *s.pl.* fuegos artificiales, *m.pl.*; (*fig.*) jaleo, cisco.

firing [ˈfaiəriŋ], *s.* combustible; (*tec.*) cocción; encendido; disparos, *m.pl.*, tiroteo; (*fam.*) despedida; ***firing-line,*** frente de batalla; ***firing-squad,*** pelotón de fusilamiento.

firkin [ˈfəːkin], *s.* cuñete.

firm (1) [fəːm], *a.* firme; duro.

firm (2) [fəːm], *s.* (*com.*) firma, razón social, casa (de comercio), empresa.

firmament [ˈfəːməmənt], *s.* firmamento.

firmness [ˈfəːmnis], *s.* firmeza; dureza.

first [fəːst], *a.* primero; ***Charles the First,*** Carlos Primero; ***first-class,*** excelente; de primera clase; ***first cousin,*** primo hermano, prima hermana; ***first-fruits,*** frutos primerizos, *m.pl.*; (*fig.*) primicias, *f.pl.*; ***first hand,*** de primera mano; ***first night,*** estreno; ***first-rate,*** excelente, de primera (clase). — *adv.* primero, en primer lugar; ***first of all, first and foremost,*** ante todo; ***to go first,*** pasar (el) primero; (*fam.*) viajar en primera (clase). — *s.* primero; principio; ***at first,*** al principio, en un principio; ***to be the first to,*** ser el primero en; ***from the first,*** desde el *o* un principio; ***from first to last,*** desde el principio hasta el final.

firstborn [ˈfəːstbɔːn], *a.*, *s.* primogénito.

firstling [ˈfəːstliŋ], *a.*, *s.* primogénito; primerizo.

firstly [ˈfəːstli], *adv.* primero, en primer lugar.

firth [fəːθ], *s.* estuario, ría.

firwood [ˈfəːwud], *s.* madera de abeto.

fisc [fisk], *s.* fisco.

fiscal [ˈfiskəl], *a.* fiscal; económico, monetario.

fish [fiʃ], *s.* pez, *m.*; pescado; ***fish-bone,*** espina, raspa; ***fish-day,*** día de abstinencia, *m.*; (*Am.*) ***fish dealer*** [FISHMONGER]; ***fish-glue,*** colapez, cola de pescado; ***fish-hook,*** anzuelo; ***fish-pond,*** estero, nansa, vivero; ***fish-wife,*** pescadera; ***to be like a fish out of water,*** estar como gallina en corral ajeno; ***to have other fish to fry,*** tener otras cosas más importantes que hacer; ***a different kettle of fish,*** harina de otro costal; (*fig.*) ***a queer fish,*** un tipo raro. — *v.t.* pescar; ***fish out,*** sacar; agotar la pesca de. — *v.i.* pescar; ***fish for,*** tratar de pescar; andar a la pesca de; ***fish in troubled waters,*** pescar en río revuelto.

fisher(man) [ˈfiʃə(mən)], *s.* pescador.

fishery [ˈfiʃəri], *s.* pesquera, pesquería.

fishiness [ˈfiʃinis], *s.* olor *o* sabor a pescado; (*fam.*) (lo) sospechoso.

fishing [ˈfiʃiŋ], *s.* pesca; (el) pescar; ***fishing-bait*** cebo; ***fishing-boat,*** barca de pesca; barco pesquero; ***fishing-fly,*** mosca artificial; ***fishing-grounds,*** pesquería, pesquera; ***fishing-line,*** sedal; ***fishing net,*** red de pesca; ***fishing-rod,*** caña de pescar; ***fishing-reel,*** carretel; ***fishing-smack,*** barco de pesca; ***fishing-tackle,*** avíos (*m.pl.*) *o* aparejo de pescar.

fishmonger [ˈfiʃmʌŋgə], *s.* pescadero; (*fam.*) ***fishmonger's,*** pescadería.

fishplate [ˈfiʃpleit], *s.* (*f.c.*) eclisa.

fishy [ˈfiʃi], *a.* que huele *o* sabe a pescado; (*fam.*) sospechoso, que escama.

fissate [ˈfiseit], *a.* hendido.

fissile [ˈfisail], *a.* hendible.

fission [ˈfiʃən], *s.* hendimiento; (*biol.*) escisión; (*fís.*) fisión.

fissiped [ˈfisiped], *a.*, *s.* fisípedo, bisulco.

fissure [ˈfiʃə], *s.* hendimiento; hendidura, grieta; fisura. — *v.t.* hender, agrietar. — *v.i.* henderse, agrietarse.

fist [fist], *s.* puño; escritura; (*impr.*) manecilla; ***with clenched fists,*** a puño cerrado. — *v.t.* apuñear, apuñar, dar puñetazos a.

fisticuff [ˈfistikʌf], *s.* puñada; puñetazo; (*pl.*) riña a puñadas.

fistula [ˈfistjulə], *s.* (*cir.*) fístula.

fistular [ˈfistjulə], *a.* fistular, afistolado, fistuloso.

fistulous [ˈfistjuləs], *a.* fistuloso.

fit (1) [fit], *a.* apto, propio, adecuado, a propósito; en (buena) forma (física); ***to be fit to,*** ser adecuado, a propósito para; ser digno de; estar en forma, en condiciones de; ***to keep fit,*** mantenerse en forma; ***to see*** o ***think fit,*** tener a bien. — *s.* ajuste; encaje; (*vestidos*) ***easy fit,*** holgado; ***tight fit,*** estrecho. — *v.t.* adaptar, adecuar; ajustar, encajar; entallar; probar (*un vestido*); ***fit out,*** proveer, equipar, armar; ***fit together,*** montar; ***fit up,*** proveer, equipar. — *v.i.* adaptarse, ajustarse; cuadrar; caer, ir, venir, sentar bien *o* mal; ***fit in,*** encajar, caber (en); ***fit in with,*** concordar con, compaginar con; adaptarse a; ***fit like a glove,*** sentar como un anillo; ***fit together,*** corresponderse, encajar.

fit (2) [fit], *s.* ataque, acceso; arranque, arrebato; (*fam.*) patatús, telele; ***by fits and starts,*** a empellones; esporádicamente; ***fainting fit,*** desmayo, síncope, soponcio; ***to go into fits of laughter,*** desternillarse de risa; ***fit of passion,*** corajina, berrinche; ***if the fit takes me,*** si me da por ahí; ***he'll have a fit,*** le dará un patatús.

fitchew [ˈfitʃuː], *s.* (*zool.*) veso.

fitful [ˈfitful], *a.* espasmódico; caprichoso; inquieto.

fitment [ˈfitmənt], *s.* mueble; accesorio; dispositivo.

fitness [ˈfitnis], *s.* propiedad; conveniencia; aptitud; buena salud; buena forma (*física*).

fitter [ˈfitə], *s.* ajustador; mecánico.

fitting [ˈfitiŋ], *a.* propio, adecuado; conveniente. — *s.* ajuste; (*cost.*) prueba; medida, corte. — (*pl.*) guarniciones, *f.pl.*; avíos, *m.pl.*; herrajes, *m.pl.*; muebles, *m.pl.*; accesorios, *m.pl.*

five [faiv], *a.*, *s.* cinco; (*bot.*) ***five-finger, five-leaf,*** cincoenrama; ***five-year plan,*** plan quinquenal.

fivefold [ˈfaivfould], *a.* quíntuplo. — *adv.* cinco veces.

fiver [ˈfaivə], *s.* (*fam.*) billete de cinco libras.

fives [faivz], *s.* juego de pelota; ***fives-court,*** frontón.

fix [fiks], *s.* aprieto, apuro; (*fam.*) dosis de estupefaciente; (*fam.*) ***to be in a fix,*** verse en un aprieto *o* apuro. — *v.t.* fijar; clavar; asegurar; decidir, determinar, precisar; señalar; arreglar, apañar; ocuparse de; (*bayoneta*) calar; (*culpa*) colgar (**on**, a); ***fix up,*** arreglar, apañar; ***fix up with,*** proporcionar, buscar, encontrar; ***how are we fixed for time?*** ¿qué tal vamos de hora? — *v.i.* — ***upon,*** elegir, escoger.

fixation [fikˈseiʃən], *s.* fijación; obsesión.

fixative [ˈfiksətiv], *a.*, *s.* fijativo; fijador.

fixed [fikst], *a.* fijo; sujeto.

fixedness, fixity [ˈfiksidnis, -iti], *s.* fijeza; fijación.

fixing [ˈfiksiŋ], *s.* fijación; (*pl.*) accesorios, *m.pl.*

fixture [ˈfikstʃə], *s.* objeto fijo, mueble fijo, instalación fija, aparato fijo; (*dep.*) fecha concertada; (*fam.*) pegote; ***fixture list,*** programa, *m.*

fizz [fiz], *s.* siseo; (*fam.*) gaseosa; champaña. — *v.i.* sisear; (*fam.*) ***fizz out,*** apagarse; quedarse en agua de borrajas.

fizzle [fizl], *s.* chisporroteo. — *v.i.* chisporrotear; (*fam.*) ***fizzle out,*** apagarse; quedarse en agua de borrajas.

flabbergast [ˈflæbəgɑːst], *v.t.* asombrar, pasmar, dejar turulato.

flabby [ˈflæbi], *a.* fláccido, blanducho.

flabellate, flabelliform [flæˈbeleit, -ˈbelifɔːm], *a.* flabeliforme.

flaccid [ˈflæksid], *a.* fláccido.

flaccidity [flækˈsiditi], *s.* flaccidez.

flag (1) [flæg], *s.* bandera; pabellón; insignia; ***black flag,*** bandera pirata; ***flag-day,*** cuestación, día de la banderita, *m.* (*mar.*) ***flag-officer,*** jefe de (una) escuadra; (*mar.*) ***flag-ship,*** capitana, almiranta, buque insignia; ***flag-waver,*** patriotero; (*mar.*) ***flag of convenience,*** pabellón de convenienca; ***flag of truce,*** bandera de parlamento; ***to hoist the flag,*** izar la bandera; ***to lower*** o ***strike the flag,*** arriar la bandera. — *v.t.* embanderar; hacer señales a.

flag (2) [flæg], *s.* (*bot.*) espadaña; ácoro falso.

flag (3) [flæg], *s.* baldosa, losa. — *v.t.* enlosar, embaldosar.

flag (4) [flæg], *v.i.* flaquear; decaer, debilitarse.

flagellant [ˈflædʒilənt], *a.*, *s.* flagelante.

flagellate [ˈflædʒileit], *v.t.* azotar, flagelar.

flagellation [fladʒiˈleiʃən], *s.* flagelación, disciplina.

flageolet (1) [flædʒoˈlet], *s.* caramillo, dulzaina, octavín.

flageolet (2) [flædʒoˈlet], *s.* judía verde.

flagging (1) [ˈflægiŋ], *s.* enlosado.

flagging (2) [ˈflægiŋ], *a.* flojo, lánguido; cada vez más débil, cada vez menor; que flaquea.

flagitious [fləˈdʒiʃəs], *a.* malvado, facineroso.

flagitiousness [fləˈdʒiʃəsnis], *s.* maldad, perversidad.

flagon [ˈflægən], *s.* garrafa.

flagrance, flagrancy [ˈfleigrəns, -i], *s.* insolencia, descaro.

flagrant [ˈfleigrənt], *a.* insolente, descarado.

flagstaff [ˈflægstɑːf], *s.* (*mar.*) asta de bandera.

flagstone [ˈflægstoun], *s.* losa, baldosa; lastra, laja; (*geol.*) asperón.

flail [fleil], *s.* (*agric.*) mayal; (*mil.*) mangual. — *v.t.* desgranar (con mayal); azotar. — *v.i.* dar sacudidas; ***flail about,*** debatirse.

flair [flɛə], *s.* olfato; instinto; don, aptitud, facilidad. — *v.t.* sentir, olfatear.

flake [fleik], *s.* escama, hojuela, laminilla; copo (*de nieve*); ***flake of fire,*** chispa, centella; ***flake white,*** albayalde. — *v.i.* — ***off*** o ***away,*** desconcharse, descascarillarse, descascararse (*a pedacitos*).

flaky [ˈfleiki], *a.* hecho de copos, hojuelas *o* escamas; escamoso; hojaldrado; ***flaky pastry,*** hojaldre.

flamboyant [flæmˈbɔiənt], *a.* exagerado; llamativo, chillón; chulesco; exageradamente extrovertido.

flame [fleim], *s.* llama; fuego; (*fam.*) amorío; ***flame-thrower,*** lanzallamas, *m.inv.*; (*fam.*) ***old flame,*** ex-novio, ex-novia, ex. — *v.i.* llamear; arder; brillar; ***flame up, out, forth,*** estallar, inflamarse.

flameless [ˈfleimlis], *a.* sin llamas.

flamen [ˈfleimən], *s.* flamen.

flaming [ˈfleimiŋ], *a.* llameante. — *adv.* ***he's flaming mad,*** está furioso, está que arde.

flamingo [fləˈmiŋgou], *s.* (*orn.*) flamenco.

flan [flæn], *s.* tarta de fruta.

flange [flændʒ], *s.* (*mec.*) reborde, pestaña; ***flange-joint,*** junta de pestañas; ***flange-pipe,*** tubo con reborde; ***flange-wheel,*** rueda con pestaña. — *v.t.* proveer de reborde *o* de pestaña.

flank [flæŋk], *a.* por el flanco, lateral; de costado. — *s.* ijar, ijada; costado; flanco. — *v.t.* flanquear; escoltar.

flannel [ˈflænəl], *s.* franela.

flap [flæp], *s.* cartera; tapa (*de bolsillo*); falda, faldilla (*de vestido*); hoja plegadiza (*de mesa*); ala (*de sombrero*); oreja (*de zapato*); solapa (*de sobre*); trampa (*de mostrador*); golpe (*de la lengua*); (*pájaros*) aletazo; (*fam.*) ***to get into a flap*** [FLAP, *v.i.* (*fam.*)]. — *v.t.* batir; sacudir; agitar. — *v.i.* aletear; moverse, agitarse ruidosamente; (*fam.*) aturdirse, atolondrarse, azorarse, azararse.

flapjack [ˈflæpdʒæk], *s.* tortita (de sartén).

flapper [ˈflæpə], *s.* volantón; (*fam.*) tobillera.

flapping [ˈflæpiŋ], *s.* aleteo, aletazos, *m.pl.*; movimiento agitado; sacudimiento.

flare [flɛə], *s.* bengala; cohete de señales; llamarada(s); nesga, vuelo (*de falda*); ***flare-up,*** estallido. — *v.t.* nesgar. — *v.i.* llamear, destellar; arder con aparato de llamaradas; ***flare up,*** inflamarse; estallar; montar en cólera.

flash [flæʃ], *a.* llamativo, de relumbrón, charro; ***flash bulb,*** lámpara de magnesio; ***flash language,*** germanía. — *s.* relámpago; (*luz*) destello, ráfaga; (*fusil*) fogonazo; (*esperanza*) rayo; (*foto.*) flash; noticia urgente; ***flash in the pan,*** cosa que se da por chiripa; ***flash of lightning,*** relámpago; ***flash of wit,*** rasgo de ingenio. — *v.t.* hacer brillar; despedir (*luz*); lanzar (*una mirada*); enviar rápidamente (*un mensaje*); hacer ostentación de. — *v.i.* relampaguear, destellar; pasar como un relámpago.

flashback [ˈflæʃbæk], *s.* (*cine*) escena retrospectiva.

flashily [ˈflæʃili], *adv.* con ostentación, con colores chillones; superficialmente.

flashing [ˈflæʃiŋ], *s.* centelleo; soplado (*del vidrio*); golpe de agua.

flashlight [ˈflæʃlait], *s.* linterna (eléctrica); luz de magnesio.

flashy [ˈflæʃi], *a.* llamativo; superficial.

flask [flɑːsk], *s.* frasco, redoma; (*fund.*) caja de moldear; ***vacuum flask,*** termo.

flat [flæt], *a.* llano, plano; liso; raso; tendido, de plano; (*fig.*) categórico, terminante; insulso, insípido; sin vida, sin gracia; mate, sin lustre; (*com.*) paralizado; (*precio*) fijo, alzado, monótono; desafinado, bemol, flojo; (*neumático*) desinflado; (*pila*) descargada; ***flat-bottomed,*** de fondo plano; ***flat-footed,*** de pies planos; (*fam.*) torpe, desmañado; ***flat-nosed,*** chato; ***flat roof,*** azotea, terrado; ***400 metres flat,*** 400 metros lisos. — *adv.* enteramente, del todo; ***flat broke,*** tronado; (*fam.*) ***to go flat out,*** ir *o* correr a todo gas. — *s.* llanura; plano; piso; (*mano*) palma; bemol; banco, bajío; ***flat-mate,*** compañero de piso. — *v.t.* achatar; abemolar; evaporar; acuartelar (*las velas*). — *v.i.* aplanarse; perder sabor; desafinar (por bajo).

flatly [ˈflætli], *adv.* llanamente; absolutamente; sin animación ni interés; ***to deny flatly,*** negar de plano, rotundamente.

flatness [ˈflætnis], *s.* (lo) llano, (lo) liso, (lo) chato; insipidez, insulsez; abatimiento.

flatten [flætn], *v.t.* allanar, aplastar, aplanar. — *v.i.* aplanarse; perder el sabor; ***flatten out,*** enderezarse (*un avión*).

flatter [ˈflætə], *v.t.* adular, lisonjear; favorecer. — *v.i.* valerse de lisonjas, ser adulador — **flatter o.s.,** *v.r.* — ***that,*** hacerse la ilusión de que, congratularse de que; ***you flatter yourself!*** ¡eso se cree usted! ¡eso te crees tú!

flatterer [ˈflætərə], *s.* adulador, lisonjero.

flattering [ˈflætəriŋ], *a.* lisonjero, halagüeño.

flattery [ˈflætəri], *s.* adulación, halagos, lisonjas.

flattish [ˈflætiʃ], *a.* chatillo; algo insípido.

flatulence [ˈflætjuləns], *s.* flatulencia.

flatulent [ˈflætjulənt], *a.* flatulento.

flaunt [flɔːnt], *v.t.* ostentar, lucir. — *v.i.* pavonearse.

flautist [ˈflɔːtist], *s.* flautista, *m.f.*

flavour [ˈfleivə], *s.* sabor; gusto; condimento. — *v.t.* sazonar, condimentar; dar sabor a.

flavoured [ˈfleivəd], *a.* con sabor *o* gusto (a).

flavouring [ˈfleivəriŋ], *s.* sabor, condimento.

flavourless [ˈfleivəlis], *a.* sin sabor, insípido, soso.

flaw [flɔː], *s.* tacha, defecto, desperfecto, imperfección, mácula; grieta. — *v.t.* afear, estropear.

flawed [flɔːd], *a.* defectuoso, que tiene un desperfecto.

flawless [ˈflɔːlis], *a.* sin tacha, sin imperfecciones, impecable.

flawy [ˈflɔːi], *a.* lleno de desperfectos.

flax [flæks], *s.* lino; ***flax-brake,*** agramadera; ***flax-comb,*** rastrillo; ***flax-dresser,*** rastrillador; ***flax-seed,*** linaza; (*bot.*) ***flax-weed,*** linaria.

flaxen [ˈflæksən], *a.* de lino; ***flaxen-haired,*** rubio.

flay [flei], *v.t.* desollar, despellejar; (*fig.*) fustigar.

flea [fliː], *s.* pulga; ***he left with a flea in his ear,*** salió con el rabo entre piernas; ***flea-bite,*** picadura de pulga; (*fig.*) friolera, nada; ***a mere flea-bite,*** una miseria, una cantidad insignificante; ***flea-bitten,*** picado de pulgas; (*fam.*) ***flea-market,*** mercado de trastos viejos; (*fam.*) ***flea-pit,*** teatrucho, cinucho.

fleabane [ˈfliːbein], *s.* (*bot.*) coniza, pulguera.

fleawort [ˈfliːwəːt], *s.* (*bot.*) pulguera, zaragatona.

fleck [flek], *s.* mancha, punto de color; vedija. — *v.t.* manchar, salpicar de puntos de color.

flection [FLEXION].

flector [ˈflektə], *s.* músculo flexor.

fledge [fledʒ], *v.t.* emplumar. — *v.i.* emplumar, emplumecer.

fledged [fledʒd], *a.* plumado; ***fully fledged,*** totalmente plumado; (*fig.*) hecho y derecho.

fledg(e)ling [ˈfledʒliŋ], *s.* volantón; (*fig.*) novato.

flee [fliː], *irr. v.t., v.i.* huir (de).

fleece [fliːs], *s.* vellón; lana; ***Golden Fleece,*** Vellocino de Oro; ***Order of the Golden Fleece,*** orden del Toisón de Oro. — *v.t.* esquilar, trasquilar; (*fig.*) desplumar.

fleecy [ˈfliːsi], *a.* lanudo; ***fleecy clouds,*** nubes aborregadas.

fleet [fliːt], *a.* veloz, raudo; ***fleet-footed,*** alípede, veloz. — *s.* flota, armada, escuadra; parque (*coches, camiones etc.*). — *v.i.* pasar rápidamente.

fleeting [ˈfliːtiŋ], *a.* fugaz, transitorio, efímero, pasajero.

fleetness [ˈfliːtnis], *s.* velocidad, celeridad.

Fleming [ˈflemiŋ], *s.* flamenco, de Flandes.

Flemish [ˈflemiʃ], *a., s.* flamenco.

flesh [fleʃ], *s.* carne; pulpa (*de la fruta*); ***flesh wound,*** herida superficial; ***his own flesh and blood,*** su propia sangre; ***in the flesh,*** en persona; ***of flesh and blood,*** de carne y hueso; ***to put on flesh,*** echar carnes. — *v.t.* descarnar; encarnizar; avezar.

fleshed [fleʃt], *a.* carnoso, carnudo.

fleshiness [ˈfleʃinis], *s.* carnosidad.

fleshings [ˈfleʃiŋz], *s.pl.* descarnaduras, *f.pl.*, piltrafas, *f.pl.*; (*teat.*) mallas, *f.pl.*, calzones de punto de color de carne, *m.pl.*

fleshless [ˈfleʃlis], *a.* descarnado.

fleshliness [ˈfleʃlinis], *s.* carnalidad.

fleshly [ˈfleʃli], *a.* carnal.

fleshmonger [ˈfleʃmʌŋgə], *s.* (*ant.*) carnicero; alcahuete.

fleshpot [ˈfleʃpɔt], *s.* olla; (*pl., fig.*) vida regalada *o* de molicie.

fleshy [ˈfleʃi], *a.* gordo, carnoso; pulposo; suculento.

fletcher [ˈfletʃə], *s.* flechero.

fleur-de-lis [fləː-də-ˈliː], *s.* (*pl.* **fleurs-de-lis** [fləː-də-ˈliː]) flor de lis, *f.*

fleuret [ˈfləːret], *s.* florete; ornamento en forma de pequeña flor.

flex [fleks], *s.* doblez, encorvadura; (*elec.*) cordón eléctrico. — *v.t.* doblar, doblegar, encorvar.
flexibility [fleksiˈbiliti], *s.* flexibilidad.
flexible [ˈfleksibl], *a.* flexible.
flexion [ˈflekʃən], *s.* flexión; corvadura.
flexor [ˈfleksə], *s.* (*anat.*) músculo flexor.
flexuose, flexuous [ˈfleksjuous, -əs], *a.* tortuoso; (*bot.*) flexuoso.
flexure [ˈflekʃə], *s.* flexión, corvadura.
flibbertigibbet [ˈflibətiˈdʒibit], *s.* (*fam.*) veleta, persona voluble, casquivana.
flick [flik], *s.* capirotazo; chasquido; golpecito rápido; (*pl., fam.*) cine. — *v.t.* dar un capirotazo a; chasquear; ***flick away,*** apartar de un capirotazo.
flicker [ˈflikə], *s.* vacilación; parpadeo; oscilación; estremecimiento. — *v.i.* vacilar; parpadear; oscilar; estremecerse.
flier [FLYER].
flight [flait], *s.* vuelo, recorrido; escuadrilla (*de aviones*); trayectoria (*de bala etc.*); bandada (*de pájaros*); huida, fuga; tramo (*de escalones*); (*aer.*) ***flight-deck,*** cubierta de aterrizaje *o* de despegue; ***flights of fancy,*** imaginaciones, *f.pl.*, sueños, *m.pl.*, utopías, *f.pl.*; ***to put to flight,*** poner en fuga; ***to take (to) flight,*** darse a la fuga, huir; ***to take flight,*** levantar el vuelo.
flightiness [ˈflaitinis], *s.* veleidad, inconstancia, caprichosidad.
flighty [ˈflaiti], *a.* veleidoso, inconstante, caprichoso.
flimflam [ˈflimflæm], *s.* (*fam.*) soflama, supercheria, embuste. — *v.t.* soflamar, engañar con astucia.
flimsiness [ˈflimzinis], *s.* endeblez, falta de solidez.
flimsy [ˈflimzi], *a.* débil, endeble; delgaducho, delgadillo; flojucho, flojillo; fútil, poco sólido. — *s.* papel de copiar.
flinch [flintʃ], *v.i.* acusar visiblemente el golpe; echarse atrás; ***flinch from,*** no tener valor para, no atreverse a, echarse atrás ante, sentir espanto *u* horror ante; ***to cause to flinch*** o ***make flinch,*** herir visiblemente en lo vivo; ***without flinching,*** sin inmutarse, sin alterar un músculo.
flinder [ˈflində], *s.* astilla, fragmento.
fling [fliŋ], *s.* baile escocés; ***to have one's fling,*** correrla, echar una canita al aire. — *irr. v.t.* echar, tirar, arrojar, lanzar; ***fling about,*** echar violentamente de un lado a otro; ***fling away,*** tirar, arrojar con fuerza; desparramar; ***fling down,*** echar *o* tirar violentamente al suelo; ***fling open,*** abrir con violencia. — *v.i.* — ***off, fling out of the room,*** salir disparado, airadamente.
flint [flint], *s.* pedernal; ***flint-hearted,*** duro de corazón; ***flint-lock,*** llave de chispa.
flintiness [ˈflintinis], *s.* dureza.
flinty [ˈflinti], *a.* de pedernal, pedernalino; (*fig.*) empedernido, duro.
flip [flip], *s.* capirotazo; (*fam.*) vuelo (*en avión*). — *v.t.* echar de un capirotazo; mover de un tirón; ***flip shut,*** cerrar de golpe; ***flip up,*** echar a cara *o* cruz. — *v.i.* — ***through,*** hojear.
flip-flap [ˈflip-flæp], *s.* zis-zas; buscapiés; tiovivo.
flip-flop [ˈflip-flɔp], *s.* trapa trapa.
flippancy [ˈflipənsi], *s.* ligereza, frivolidad; guasa.
flippant [ˈflipənt], *a.* ligero, frívolo; guasón.
flipper [ˈflipə], *s.* aleta; (*fam.*) mano.
flipping [ˈflipiŋ], *a.* (*fam.*) dichoso.
flirt [flə:t], *s.* coqueta; flirteador. — *v.i.* flirtear, coquetear, mariposear; ***flirt with death,*** jugar con la muerte; ***flirt with an idea,*** acariciar una idea.
flirtation, flirting [flə:ˈteiʃən, ˈflə:tiŋ], *s.* flirteo, coqueteo.
flit [flit], *s.* ***to do a flit*** [FLIT, *v.i.* (*fam.*)]. — *v.i.* volar, revolotear; pasar rápidamente, deslizarse; (*fam.*) mudarse a la chita callando.
flitch [flitʃ], *s.* hoja de tocino; lonja ahumada; (*carp.*) costera, costanera.
flitter [ˈflitə], *s.* jirón, pedazo; lentejuela. — *v.i.* [FLUTTER].
flitting [ˈflitiŋ], *a.* pasajero, fugitivo; ligero. — *s.* fuga; vuelo rápido.
flix [fliks], *s.* borra, borrilla, pelusa, pelusilla.
float [flout], *s.* flotador; cosa flotante; boya; corcho; salvavidas, *m.inv.*, nadadera; balsa, armadía; carroza, paso. — *v.t.* poner a flote; inundar; (*com.*) emitir; (*com.*) lanzar; enlucir con talocha. — *v.i.* flotar, sobrenadar; hacer la plancha; cenerse; fluctuar; (*com.*) tener buena acogida.
floatable [ˈfloutəbl], *a.* flotable, flotante.
floatage [ˈfloutidʒ], *s.* flotante.
floater [ˈfloutə], *s.* flotador, flotante.
floating [ˈfloutiŋ], *a.* flotante; indeciso; ***floating population,*** población flotante *o* de tránsito; ***floating vote,*** votadores *o* votantes indecisos. — *s.* flote, flotación; enlucido, revestimiento.
floccose [ˈflɔkous], *a.* (*bot.*) velludo.
flocculence [ˈflɔkjuləns], *s.* vellosidad.
flocculent [ˈflɔkjulənt], *a.* velludo, lanudo; (*orn.*) parecido al flojel, al plumón; (*ent.*) cubierto con una substancia viscosa.
flocculose [ˈflɔkjulous], *a.* que tiene pelusa.
flock (1) [flɔk], *s.* (*pájaros*) bandada; (*ovejas*) rebaño; (*igl.*) grey, congregación; gentío, tropel. — *v.i.* congregarse; atroparse; ***to come flocking,*** llegar en tropel.
flock (2) [flɔk], *s.* borra, tamo, pelusa; ***flock-paper,*** papel aterciopelado.
floe [flou], *s.* témpano de hielo.
flog [flɔg], *v.t.* azotar, tundir, vapulear; (*fam.*) vender, pulir; ***flog a dead horse,*** machacar en hierro frío.
flogging [ˈflɔgiŋ], *s.* vapuleo, tunda, azotaina, zurra.
flood [flʌd], *s.* inundación; diluvio; avenida, riada; (*fig.*) torrente, avalancha; ***flood-gate,*** compuerta; esclusa; ***flood-tide,*** pleamar; ***in flood,*** crecido; ***the Flood,*** el Diluvio. — *v.t.* inundar; (*fig.*) abrumar. — *v.i.* desbordar(se); ***flood in,*** entrar a raudales.
flooding [ˈflʌdiŋ], *s.* inundación; inundaciones, *f.pl.*
floodlight [ˈflʌdlait], *s.* foco. — *v.t.* iluminar con foco(s).
floor [flɔ:], *s.* suelo; piso; (*mar.*) fondo; (*asamblea*) hemiciclo; ***first floor,*** primer piso; ***floor-cloth,*** trapo del suelo; ***floor-show,*** show, atracciones, *f.pl.*; (*mar.*) ***floor-timbers,*** varengas, *f.pl.*; ***ground floor,*** piso bajo; ***to have, hold the floor,*** tener la palabra; ***to take the floor,*** tomar la palabra; salir a actuar; (*fam.*) ***to wipe the floor with s.o.,*** merendarse a alguien, hacer fosfatina a alguien. — *v.t.* poner suelo a; derribar, tender por el suelo; (*fig.*) dejar turulato *o* totalmente perplejo, confundir.
flooring [ˈflɔ:riŋ], *s.* suelo, piso.
floorwalker [ˈflɔ:wɔ:kə], *s.* (*Am.*) [SHOPWALKER].
flop [flɔp], *s.* fracaso lamentable *o* lastimoso; (*Am.*) ***flop-house*** [DOSS-HOUSE]. — *v.i.* fracasar lastimosamente; ***flop about,*** moverse, agitarse pesadamente; ***flop down,*** caerse *o* tirarse pesadamente, desplomarse.
floppy [ˈflɔpi], *a.* flojucho; que cuelga pesada y desgarbadamente.
flora [ˈflɔ:rə], *s.* flora.
floral [ˈflɔ:rəl], *a.* floral.
Florentine [ˈflɔrentain], *a., s.* florentino.
florescence [flɔˈresəns], *s.* florescencia.
florescent [flɔˈresənt], *a.* floreciente.
floret [ˈflɔ:ret], *s.* (*bot.*) flósculo; florecilla.
floriculture [ˈflɔ:rikʌltʃə], *s.* floricultura.
floriculturist [flɔ:riˈkʌltʃərist], *s.* floricultor.
florid [ˈflɔrid], *a.* florido; coloradote.
floridness [ˈflɔridnis], *s.* (lo) florido; (lo) coloradote.
florin [ˈflɔrin], *s.* (*ant.*) florín.
florist [ˈflɔrist], *s.* florista, *m.f.*
floscule [ˈflɔskju:l], *s.* (*bot.*) flósculo.

flosculous [ˈflɔskjuləs], *a* flosculoso.
floss [flɔs], *s.* seda floja; penacho (*del maíz*); ***floss-silk,*** seda floja.
flossy [ˈflɔsi], *a.* len; lene.
flotation [floˈteiʃən], *s.* flotación.
flotilla [floˈtilə], *s.* flotilla.
flotsam [ˈflɔtsəm], *s.* pecio, pecios, *m.pl.*, objetos flotantes, *m.pl.*
flounce (1) [flauns], *s.* (*cost.*) volante. — *v.t.* adornar con volantes.
flounce (2) [flauns], *v.i.* — ***out,*** salir airado y displicente.
flounder (1) [ˈflaundə], *s.* (*ict.*) platija.
flounder (2) [ˈflaundə], *v.i.* — ***about,*** vacilar; tener dificultades; avanzar con mucha dificultad, lenta y torpemente; debatirse torpemente; no dar pie con bola.
flour [flauə], *s.* harina; ***flour-bolt,*** tamiz, cedazo; ***flour-mill,*** molino harinero. — *v.t.* (*coc.*) enharinar.
flourish [ˈflʌriʃ], *s.* rúbrica; rasgo, plumada; (*esgr.*) molinete; (*mús.*) floreo, toque; ademán. — *v.t.* blandir; (*espada*) esgrimir; (*bastón*) menear; hacer alarde de. — *v.i.* prosperar, medrar, florecer; florear.
flourishing [ˈflʌriʃiŋ], *a.* floreciente; pujante, próspero.
floury [ˈflauəri], *a.* harinoso.
flout [flaut], *s.* mofa, befa, escarnio. — *v.t.* mofarse de, escarnecer; desdeñar; hacer caso omiso de.
flouter [ˈflautə], *s.* burlador, mofador.
flow [flou], *s.* corriente; flujo; caudal; gasto; curso; torrente; afluencia; movimiento (fuerte, suave, elegante). — *v.i.* fluir, manar, correr; subir, (*marea*) crecer; flotar, ondear; dimanar, proceder; derramarse; ***flow away,*** deslizarse; ***flow into,*** desembocar en, desaguar en, afluir a; ***flow over,*** rebosar; ***flow with,*** abundar en.
flower [flauə], *s.* (*bot.*) flor, *f.*; (*fig.*) flor y nata; (*pl.*, *quím.*) flor; ***flower-bed,*** macizo; ***flower-bud,*** capullo, botón de flor; ***flower-garden,*** jardín, pensil; ***flower-girl,*** florera, ramilletera, florista; ***flower-piece,*** ramillete; (*pint.*) florero; ***flower-pot,*** tiesto, maceta de flores; ***flower-stand,*** jardinera; ***flower-vase,*** florero; ***in full flower,*** en plena flor. — *v.i.* florecer, dar flor, florar.
flowered [ˈflauəd], *a.* floreado.
floweret [ˈflauəret], *s.* florecilla, florecita.
floweriness [ˈflauərinis], *s.* abundancia de flores; floreo de palabras, ampulosidad.
flowering [ˈflauəriŋ], *a.* (*bot.*) fanerógamo; floreciente. — *s.* florecimiento; floración.
flowerless [ˈflauəlis], *a.* sin flores, que no tiene flores.
flowery [ˈflauəri], *a.* florido, lleno de flores; (*fig.*) altisonante.
flowing [ˈflouiŋ], *a.* corriente, fluente; fluido suelto; ondeante, fluctuoso. — *s.* derrame, flujo, manantial, creciente, *f.*, fluidez.
flowingly [ˈflouiŋli], *adv.* abundantemente, copiosamente.
flowingness [ˈflouiŋnis], *s.* dicción fluida, soltura.
flown [floun], *a.* ***high-flown,*** ampuloso, altisonante. — *p.p.* [FLY].
flu [flu:], *s.* (*abrev. fam.*) [INFLUENZA].
fluctuant [ˈflʌktjuənt], *a.* fluctuoso, fluctuante, vacilante.
fluctuate [ˈflʌktjueit], *v.i.* fluctuar, oscilar.
fluctuation [flʌktjuˈeiʃən], *s.* fluctuación, oscilación.
flue (1) [flu:], *s.* humero, cañón (*de chimenea*); tubo (*de humos*); (*mús.*) cañón (*de órgano*).
flue (2) [flu:], *s.* pelusa, tamo.
fluency [ˈflu:ənsi], *s.* fluidez; soltura.
fluent [ˈflu:ənt], *a.* fluido; ***to be fluent in Spanish,*** hablar el español con soltura, dominar el español.
fluently [ˈflu:əntli], *adv.* con soltura.
fluff [flʌf], *s.* pelusa; lanilla; plumón; tamo; (*fam.*) ***a bit of fluff,*** una chavala. — *v.t.* (*fam.*) — ***it,*** equivocarse, meter la pata, estropear la cosa; ***fluff up,*** mullir.
fluffiness [ˈflʌfinis], *s.* (lo) velloso, plumoso, sedoso.
fluffy [ˈflʌfi], *a.* que tiene pelusa, velloso, plumoso, sedoso.
fluid [ˈflu:id], *a.*, *s.* fluido.
fluidity, fluidness [flu:ˈiditi, ˈflu:idnis], *s.* fluidez.
fluke (1) [flu:k], *s.* (*mar.*) uña; aleta (*de la cola de la ballena*).
fluke (2) [flu:k], *s.* (*ict.*) platija; (*zool.*) trematodo.
fluke (3) [flu:k], *s.* (*fam.*) casualidad, chiripa; ***by a fluke, by a sheer fluke,*** por chiripa, por pura casualidad.
flume [flu:m], *s.* caz, canalizo, canal.
flummery [ˈflʌməri], *s.* manjar blanco; (*fig.*) lisonjas, *f.pl.*; sandeces, *f.pl.*
flunk [flʌŋk], *v.t.* (*fam.*) — ***it,*** rajarse, echarse atrás, fallar. — *v.i.* suspender.
flunkey [ˈflʌŋki], *s.* lacayo; adulón.
fluor, fluor-spar [ˈflu:ɔ:-spɑ:], *s.* (*min.*) espato flúor.
fluorescence [fluəˈresəns], *s.* fluorescencia.
fluorescent [fluəˈresənt], *a.* fluorescente.
fluoric [flu:ˈɔrik], *a.* fluórico.
fluoride [ˈfluəraid], *s.* (*quím.*) fluoruro.
fluorine [ˈfluəri:n], *s.* flúor.
flurry [ˈflʌri], *s.* perturbación, agitación, aturdimiento, azoramiento; barullo; ráfaga, racha; ***to get into a flurry,*** aturdirse, azararse, atolondrarse. — *v.t.* aturdir, atolondrar.
flush (1) [flʌʃ], *a.* igual, parejo, a nivel, nivelado, a ras; abundante, copioso; lleno de vigor; (*fam.*) adinerado, rico. — *s.* rubor, sonrojo; copia, abundancia; flujo rápido *o* copioso; (*naipes*) flux. — *v.t.* sonrojar, poner colorado; igualar, nivelar; limpiar con un chorro de agua; (*mil.*) ***flush out,*** desalojar. — *v.i.* derramarse repentinamente, llenarse de agua; sonrojarse; ruborizarse, ponerse colorado.
flush (2) [flʌʃ], *s.* vuelo súbito (*de pájaros*); bandada de pájaros espantados. — *v.t.* levantar (*aves de caza*).
flushing [ˈflʌʃiŋ], *s.* limpieza a base de chorros de agua.
fluster [ˈflʌstə], *s.* ***to be in a fluster,*** estar aturdido *o* atolondrado. — *v.t.* aturdir, azarar, azorar, atolondrar, poner nervioso.
flustered [ˈflʌstəd], *a.* aturdido, aturrullado, azorado, azarado.
flute [flu:t], *s.* (*mús.*) flauta; rizado, pliegue; (*arq.*) estría. — *v.t.* estriar, acanalar, encanutar; (*cost.*) alechugar, plegar, rizar. — *v.i.* tocar la flauta.
fluter, flutist [ˈflu:tə, -ist], *s.* flautista, *m.f.*
fluting [ˈflu:tiŋ], *s.* (*arq.*) estriadura, acanaladura, estría; (*cost.*) rizado, alechugado, pliegue; ***fluting-iron,*** hierro de rizar; ***fluting-plane,*** cepillo bocel.
flutter [ˈflʌtə], *s.* revoloteo; palpitación, emoción; agitación; (*fam.*) apuesta; (*bolsa*) jugada. — *v.t.* hacer tremolar. — *v.i.* aletear, revolotear; tremolar, agitarse.
fluvial [ˈflu:viəl], *a.* fluvial.
flux [flʌks], *s.* flujo; mudanza continua; (*med.*) fluxión; (*quím.*) fundente. — *v.t.* fundir, derretir, mezclar (con fundente). — *v.i.* fundirse.
fluxion [ˈflʌkʃən], *s.* flujo; (*med.*) fluxión, congestión; (el) fluir; fusión, derretimiento; (*mat.*) cálculo diferencial.
fly [flai], *a.* (*fam.*) despabilado. — *s.* mosca; bragueta; calesín, volanta; vuelo; (*pl.*, *teat.*) bambalinas; ***fly-bitten,*** manchado por las moscas; ***fly-by-night,*** de poca confianza, informal; (*orn.*) ***fly-catcher,*** doral, papamoscas, *m. inv.*, moscareta; ***fly-fishing,*** pesca con moscas artificiales; (*impr.*) ***fly-leaf,*** (hoja de) guarda; ***fly-net,*** mosquitero; ***fly-paper,*** papel de moscas; (*aer.*)

fly-past, desfile aéreo; ***fly-swatter,*** matamoscas, *m.inv.*; ***fly-trap,*** mosqueador, mosquero, espantamoscas, *m.inv.*; (*dep.*) ***fly-weight,*** peso mosca; ***fly-wheel,*** (rueda) volante; (*fig.*) ***fly in the ointment,*** clavito, clavico; (*fam.*) ***to catch flies,*** papar moscas; ***to die like flies,*** morir como chinches; ***she wouldn't hurt a fly,*** es incapaz de matar una mosca; ***there are no flies on him,*** ve crecer la hierba; ***Spanish fly,*** cantárida. — *irr. v.t.* hacer volar; dirigir (*un avión*); elevar (*una cometa*); transportar en avión; atravesar, sobrevolar; recorrer (*en avión*); enarbolar, izar (*bandera*); huir de, abandonar. — *v.i.* volar; huir; lanzarse, precipitarse; dispararse (*un muelle*); ***fly about,*** circular (*noticias*); ***fly around,*** volar de un lado a otro; ***fly at,*** lanzarse sobre; ***fly away,*** volar, escaparse; ***fly down,*** bajar volando; ***fly in the face of,*** desacatar descaradamente; ***fly into a passion*** o ***rage,*** montar en cólera; ***fly off,*** salir volando; desprenderse; ***fly off the handle,*** perder los estribos; ***fly open,*** abrirse de repente; ***fly to arms,*** recurrir a las armas; ***to let fly,*** descargar.

flyblow [ˈflaiblou], *s.* cresa, huevo de mosca.

flyblown [ˈflaibloun], *a.* lleno de cresas; (*fig.*) carcomido.

flyboat [ˈflaibout], *s.* (*mar.*) flibote.

flyer [flaiə], *s.* aviador, piloto; (*fam.*) ***high flyer,*** arribista, *m.f.*, ambicioso; (*bolsa*) acción que va en alza.

flying [ˈflaiiŋ], *a.* volador, volante; veloz, rápido; ***flying-boat,*** hidroavión; (*arq.*) ***flying buttress,*** arbotante; ***flying circus,*** escuadrilla de acrobacias; ***flying field,*** campo de aviación; ***flying fish,*** pez volador; ***flying fortress,*** fortaleza volante; (*mar.*) ***flying jib,*** petifoque; ***flying machine,*** máquina de volar, avión; ***flying saucer,*** platillo volante; ***flying squad,*** escuadra ligera; ***flying visit,*** visita relámpago; ***to come off with flying colours,*** salir airoso; ***to get off to a flying start,*** empezar estupendamente, con mucho brío. — *s.* vuelo; (el) volar; aviación; ***blind flying,*** vuelo a ciegas.

foal [foul], *s.* potro. — *v.t., v.i.* parir.

foam [foum], *s.* espuma; ***foam rubber,*** gomaespuma. — *v.i.* espumar; ***foam at the mouth,*** echar espumarajos.

foamy [ˈfoumi], *a.* espumoso.

fob [fɔb], *s.* faltriquera (del reloj). — *v.t.* — ***off with excuses,*** intentar conformar con pretextos; ***to fob sth. off on s.o.,*** encajarle, endilgarle algo a alguien.

focal [ˈfoukəl], *a.* focal.

fo'c'sle [FORECASTLE].

focus [ˈfoukəs], *s.* foco; punto céntrico; ***in focus,*** enfocado; ***out of focus,*** desenfocado. — *v.t.* enfocar; concentrar.

fodder [ˈfɔdə], *s.* forraje. — *v.t.* dar forraje a.

foe [fou], *s.* enemigo; adversario.

foelike [ˈfoulaik], *a.* hostil, como enemigo.

fœtal [ˈfiːtəl], *a.* fetal.

fœtid [FETID].

fœtus [ˈfiːtəs], *s.* feto.

fog [fɔg]. *s.* niebla; (*foto.*) velo; (*fig.*) confusión; ***fog-bound,*** envuelto en *o* inmovilizado por la niebla; ***fog-horn,*** sirena. — *v.t.* envolver en niebla; empañar; oscurecer, entenebrecer; (*foto.*) velar.

fogginess [ˈfɔginis], *s.* nebulosidad.

foggy [ˈfɔgi], *a.* nebuloso, brumoso, envuelto en niebla; (*foto.*) velado; (*fam.*) ***not to have the foggiest idea,*** no tener ni idea.

fogy [ˈfougi], *s.* vejestorio, antigualla.

foible [fɔibl], *s.* debilidad, flaqueza, punto flaco.

foil (1) [fɔil], *v.t.* frustrar, hacer nulo *o* vano, burlar, impedir.

foil (2) [fɔil], *s.* hojuela (de metal); contraste, realce; ***to act as foil to,*** servir de contraste para, dar realce a, realzar.

foil (3) [fɔil], *s.* florete.

foist [fɔist], *v.t.* — ***on,*** encajar, endilgar a. — **foist o.s.,** *v.r.* — ***on s.o.,*** abusar de, pegarse a alguien.

fold (1) [fould], *s.* (*agric.*) redil, aprisco; (*fig.*) rebaño, grey.

fold (2) [fould], *s.* (*t. geog.*) pliegue, doblez; arruga; hoja (*de puerta*); abrazo. — *v.t.* plegar, doblar; envolver; ***fold one's arms,*** cruzar los brazos; ***fold down,*** doblar hacia abajo. — *v.i.* doblarse, plegarse, cerrarse; (*coc.*) ***fold in,*** mezclar; ***fold up,*** encogerse; abarquillarse; (*com.*) quebrar.

folder [ˈfouldə], *s.* plegador, plegadera; prospecto; carpeta.

folderol [ˈfɔldərɔl], *a.* absurdo, desatinado. — *s.* pampirolada.

folding [ˈfouldiŋ], *a.* plegador, plegadizo, plegable; ***folding-bed,*** cama plegable; ***folding-chair,*** silla plegable *o* de tijera; ***folding-cot,*** catre de tijera; ***folding-door,*** puerta plegadiza; ***folding-machine,*** plegadora mecánica; ***folding-ruler,*** metro plegable; ***folding-seat,*** asiento levadizo; traspontín. — *s.* plegado, plegadura.

foliaceous [fouliˈeiʃəs], *a.* foliáceo; laminado.

foliage [ˈfouliidʒ], *s.* follaje, frondosidad, verdor; ramillete de hojas y flores.

foliate [[ˈfouliit], *a.* frondoso; laminado, batido. — [ˈfoulieit], *v.t.* (*metal.*) batir (*hojas*); azogar (*un espejo*).

foliated [ˈfoulieitid], *a.* (*metal.*) batido, laminado; chapeado; (*arq.*) lobulado; azogado.

foliation, foliature [fouliˈeiʃən, ˈfouliətʃə], *s.* (*metal.*) batimiento; laminación; azogamiento; exfoliación; (*bot.*) foliación.

folio [ˈfouliou], *s.* infolio, página, folio; cartera (*para grabados o documentos*). — *v.t.* foliar.

foliole [ˈfoulioul], *s.* hojuela.

folk [fouk], *s.* gente, *f.*; nación, pueblo, raza; (*pl., fam.*) familia; ***folk-song,*** canción popular *o* tradicional; ***folk-speech,*** lenguaje popular; (*fam.*) ***old folks,*** los viejos.

folklore [ˈfouklɔː], *s.* tradiciones, *f.pl.*, saber popular, folklore.

folksy [ˈfouksi], *a.* (*Am.*) empalagoso; cursi.

follicle [ˈfɔlikl], *s.* (*bot.*) folículo, hollejo; (*anat.*) folículo; (*ent.*) capullo.

follicular [fɔˈlikjulə], *a.* folicular, foliculoso.

follow [ˈfɔlou], *v.t.* seguir; suceder; ***follow suit,*** seguir el ejemplo, hacer lo mismo; ***follow up,*** llevar hasta el fin; proseguir. — *v.i.* seguir(se); deducirse, resultar; ***as follows,*** como sigue; ***I don't follow,*** no entiendo; ***it follows that,*** síguese que; ***follow on,*** seguir la misma línea; ***follow on from,*** ser la consecuencia lógica de.

follower [ˈfɔlouə], *s.* seguidor; partidario; discípulo; imitador; (*pl.*) séquito.

following [ˈfɔlouiŋ], *a.* siguiente; próximo. — *s.* séquito, cortejo; adherentes, *m.pl.*, partidarios, *m.pl.*, secuaces, *m.pl.*; (*toros*) afición; aficionados, *m.pl.*

folly [ˈfɔli], *s.* locura, insensatez, desatino.

foment [foˈment], *v.t.* fomentar; ***foment a quarrel,*** echar leña al fuego.

fomentation [foumenˈteiʃən], *s.* fomentación; fomento.

fomenter [foˈmentə], *s.* fomentador.

fond [fɔnd], *a.* aficionado; afectuoso, cariñoso; ***to be fond of,*** ser aficionado a (*una cosa*), ser amigo de (*una cosa*); tener afecto *o* cariño a (*una persona*).

fondle [fɔndl], *v.t.* acariciar.

fondling [ˈfɔndliŋ], *s.* caricias, *f.pl.*

fondness [ˈfɔndnis], *s.* afición (***for,*** a); afecto *o* cariño (***for,*** a).

font [fɔnt], *s.* pila de bautismo; fuente, *f.*

fontanel [fɔntəˈnel], *s.* (*anat.*) fontanela.

food [fuːd], *s.* comida; alimento, alimentación; pasto; pábulo; ***food-poisoning,*** intoxicación; ***food-stuffs,*** comestibles, *m.pl.*, artículos *o* productos alimenticios, *m.pl.*; ***food-value,*** valor alimenticio; ***to give food for thought,*** dar que pensar.

fool [fu:l], *s.* tonto; bufón; ***All Fools' Day,*** día de (los) Inocentes, *m.*; ***fool's errand,*** empresa descabellada; ***fool's paradise,*** utopía(s), ilusión, ilusiones, *f.pl.*, espejismo(s); ***to make a fool of o.s.,*** ponerse en ridículo; ***to play the fool,*** hacer el tonto, el primo. — *v.t.* engañar embaucar. — *v.i.* tontear; divertirse; bromear.

foolery [ˈfu:ləri], *s.* tontería(s), bufonada(s).

foolhardiness [fu:lˈhɑ:dinis], *s.* temeridad, locura.

foolhardy [ˈfu:lhɑ:di], *a.* temerario, arrojado, osado.

foolish [ˈfu:liʃ], *a.* tonto; imprudente.

foolishness [ˈfu:liʃnis], *s.* tontería, tonterías, *f.pl.*; imprudencia.

foolproof [ˈfu:lpru:f], *a.* infalible, que no falla.

foolscap [ˈfu:lzkæp], *s.* papel folio.

foot [fut], *s.* (*pl.* **feet** [fi:t]) pie; pata; base, *f.*; (*mil.*) infantería; ***by foot,*** a pie; ***foot-board,*** estribo; ***foot-brake,*** pedal del freno; freno de pie; ***foot-bridge,*** puente para peatones; ***from head to foot,*** de pies a cabeza; ***on foot,*** a pie; ***to get cold feet,*** entrarle a alguien la cagueta; (*fig.*) ***to fall*** o ***land on one's feet,*** caer de pie; ***to have one foot in the grave,*** tener un pie en la tumba; ***to keep one's feet,*** mantenerse en pie; ***to put one's foot down,*** (*lit.*) pisar a fondo; (*fig.*) plantarse; ***to put one's best foot forward,*** hacer todo lo posible; ***to put one's foot in it,*** meter la pata; ***to put one's feet up,*** descansar. — *v.t.* — ***it,*** ir andando; ***foot the bill,*** pagar la cuenta; (*fam.*) pagar el pato.

football [ˈfutbɔ:l], *s.* balón; fútbol, balonpié; ***football-player,*** futbolista, *m.*; ***football pools,*** quinielas, *f.pl.*

footboy [ˈfutbɔi], *s.* lacayo niño.

footcloth [ˈfutklɔθ], *s.* gualdrapa.

footed [ˈfutid], *a.* que tiene pies *o* patas; sumado.

footfall [ˈfutfɔ:l], *s.* paso, pisada; ruido de un paso.

foothills [ˈfuthilz], *s.pl.* estribaciones, *f.pl.*

foothold [ˈfuthould], *s.* asidero para el pie; pie firme.

footing [ˈfutiŋ], *s.* posición; pie, base, fundamento; condición; ***on an equal footing,*** en pie de igualdad; ***on a war footing,*** en pie de guerra; ***to be on a friendly footing with,*** estar en relaciones amistosas con; ***to gain a footing,*** conseguir *o* tener un pie dentro.

footlights [ˈfutlaits], *s.pl.* (*teat.*) candilejas, *f.pl.*, luces de proscenio, *f.pl.*

footling [ˈfu:tliŋ], *a.* (*fam.*) baladí.

footloose [ˈfutlu:s], *a.* libre, suelto; andariego.

footman [ˈfutmən], *s.* lacayo.

footmark [ˈfutmɑ:k], *s.* huella, pisada.

footnote [ˈfutnout], *s.* nota, apostilla.

footpace [ˈfutpeis], *s.* descanso de escalera; paso lento *o* corto.

footpath [ˈfutpɑ:θ], *s.* senda, vereda, acera.

footprint [ˈfutprint], *s.* huella, pisada.

footrest [ˈfutrest], *s.* apoyapié.

footrule [ˈfutru:l], *s.* regla de doce pulgadas.

footsore [ˈfutsɔ:], *a.* con los pies doloridos, despeado.

footstalk [ˈfutstɔ:k], *s.* (*bot.*) pedúnculo.

footstep [ˈfutstep], *s.* paso, pisada; vestigio, huella; ***to follow in the footsteps of,*** seguir las huellas de, ir en pos de.

footstool [ˈfutstu:l], *s.* escabel.

footway [ˈfutwei], *s.* sendero.

footwear [ˈfutwɛə], *s.* calzado.

footwork [ˈfutwə:k], *s.* juego *o* ejercicios (*m.pl.*) de piernas; (*fig.*) manipulaciones, *f.pl.*

fop [fɔp], *s.* petimetre, currutaco, pisaverde; lechuguino.

foppery [ˈfɔpəri], *s.* afectación; perifollos, *m.pl.*

foppish [ˈfɔpiʃ], *a.* afectado, presumido.

foppishness [ˈfɔpiʃnis], *s.* afectación.

for [fɔ:], *conj.* porque, puesto que, ya que, pues. — *prep.* por; para; a; de; ***to be for,*** estar por, ser partidario de, estar de parte de; ***I'm all for it,*** lo apruebo sin reservas; ***what for?*** ¿para qué?; ***it's easy for him,*** le es fácil; ***open the door for me,*** ábreme la puerta; ***he's tall for his age,*** es alto para la edad que tiene; ***for fuel,*** como combustible; ***a cheque for £20,*** un cheque de 20 libras; ***time for lunch,*** hora de comer; ***to cry for joy,*** llorar de alegría; ***it is for you to decide,*** a usted le toca decidir; ***but for,*** a no ser por; ***for all,*** a pesar de; ***for all that,*** pese a todo, con todo; ***for all his money,*** a pesar del dinero que tiene; ***not for the world,*** por nada del mundo; ***for ever,*** para siempre; ***for good,*** definitivamente; para no volver; ***for short,*** para abreviar; ***there is nothing for it but,*** no hay más remedio que; ***O, for . . .!*** ¡quién tuviera . . .!; ***for three days,*** (durante) tres días; ***as for,*** en cuanto a; ***as for me,*** por mi parte; ***if it were not for him,*** si no fuera por él; ***were it not for that,*** de no ser por eso.

forage [ˈfɔridʒ], *s.* forraje. — *v.t., v.i.* forrajear, proveer de forraje, buscar forraje; saquear, pillar, hurtar.

forager [ˈfɔridʒə], *s.* forrajeador.

foramen [fɔˈreimen], *s.* foramen.

forasmuch [fɔ:reəzˈmʌʃ], *conj.* — ***as,*** puesto que; visto que.

foray [ˈfɔrei], *s.* correría, incursión, algara.

forbear (1) [FOREBEAR].

forbear (2) [fɔ:ˈbɛə], *irr. v.i.* tener paciencia, abstenerse, contenerse; ***I cannot forbear laughing,*** no puedo menos de reírme.

forbearance [fɔ:ˈbɛərəns], *s.* paciencia, indulgencia.

forbearing [fɔ:ˈbɛəriŋ], *a.* paciente, indulgente.

forbid [fəˈbid], *irr. v.t.* prohibir, vedar; ***God forbid,*** no lo quiera *o* no lo permita Dios.

forbiddenly [fəˈbidənli], *adv.* ilícitamente.

forbidding [fəˈbidiŋ], *a.* temible, que infunde temor *o* espanto; adusto, ceñudo.

force [fɔ:s], *s.* fuerza; ***by force,*** a la fuerza; ***by force of,*** a fuerza de; ***in force,*** en gran número; en vigor, vigente; ***to be in force,*** estar en vigor, regir; ***main force,*** fuerza mayor. — *v.t.* forzar; obligar; violentar; hacer madurar pronto; rellenar, embutir; ***to be forced to,*** verse obligado a; ***force back,*** hacer retroceder, rechazar violentamente; ***force down,*** obligar a bajar; obligar a aterrizar; (*comida*) tragar(se) haciendo un esfuerzo; ***force the issue,*** forzar la solución (*de un asunto*); ***force out,*** obligar a salir; echar violentamente; ***force the pace,*** apretar el paso; ***force a passage,*** abrirse camino. — **force o.s.,** *v.r.* obligarse a; violentarse.

forced [fɔ:st], *a.* forzado; forzoso; de, a, *o* por presión; ***forced landing,*** aterrizaje forzoso.

forcedness [ˈfɔ:sidnis], *s.* (lo) forzado; falta de naturalidad.

forceful [ˈfɔ:sful], *a.* enérgico, vigoroso.

forcemeat [ˈfɔ:smi:t], *s.* (*coc.*) relleno.

forceps [ˈfɔ:seps], *s.* (*cir.*) fórceps, *m. inv.*, pinzas, *f.pl.*

forcible [ˈfɔ:sibl], *a.* forzado, violento; contundente, convincente.

forcibly [ˈfɔ:sibli], *adv.* por fuerza, a la fuerza, violentamente.

forcing-bed [ˈfɔ:siŋ-bed], *s.* almajara.

forcing-house [ˈfɔ:siŋ-haus], *s.* invernadero.

forcing-pump [ˈfɔ:siŋ-pʌmp], *s.* bomba impelente.

ford [fɔ:d], *s.* vado. — *v.t.* vadear.

fordable [ˈfɔ:dəbl], *a.* vadeable.

fore [fɔ:], *a.* anterior, delantero; (*mar.*) proel. — *adv.* anteriormente, antes, delante; (*mar.*) de proa; ***fore and aft,*** de popa a proa.

forearm (1) [ˈfɔ:rɑ:m], *s.* antebrazo.

forearm (2) [fɔ:rˈɑ:m], *v.t.* armar de antemano; ***forewarned is forearmed,*** hombre prevenido vale por dos.

forebear [ˈfɔ:bɛə], *s.* antepasado.
forebode [fɔ:ˈboud], *v.t.*, *v.i.* presagiar, pronosticar.
foreboding [fɔ:ˈboudiŋ], *s.* presentimiento; presagio.
forecast [ˈfɔ:kɑ:st], *s.* pronóstico; previsión. — *v.t.* pronosticar, predecir.
forecastle [fouksl], *s.* (*mar.*) castillo de proa.
foreclose [fɔ:ˈklouz], *v.t.* excluir; (*for.*) extinguir el derecho de redimir.
foreclosure [fɔ:ˈklouʒə], *s.* (*for.*) extinción del derecho de redimir.
foredoom [fɔ:ˈdu:m], *v.t.* predestinar, predeterminar.
fore-end [ˈfɔ:r-end], *s.* delantera.
forefather [ˈfɔ:fɑ:ðə], *s.* abuelo, antecesor; (*pl.*) antepasados, *m.pl.*
forefinger [ˈfɔ:fiŋgə], *s.* dedo índice.
forefoot [ˈfɔ:fut], *s.* mano *o* pata delantera, pie delantero (*de un cuadrúpedo*); (*mar.*) gorja, tajamar.
forefront [ˈfɔ:frʌnt], *s.* delantera, vanguardia.
forego (1) [FORGO].
forego (2) [fɔ:ˈgou], *v.i.* preceder.
foregoing [ˈfɔ:gouiŋ], *a.* precedente, anterior.
foregone [ˈfɔ:gɔn], *a.* predeterminado, decidido de antemano. — [fɔ:ˈgɔn], *p.p.* [FOREGO (2)].
foreground [ˈfɔ:graund], *s.* primer plano *o* término.
forehand [ˈfɔ:hænd], *s.* cuarto delantero del caballo.
forehanded [ˈfɔ:ˈhændid], *a.* temprano.
forehead [ˈfɔrid], *s.* frente, *f.*
foreign [ˈfɔrin], *a.* extranjero, exterior; ajeno; extraño; ***foreign body,*** cuerpo extraño; ***foreign currency,*** divisas, *f.pl.*; ***foreign-made,*** fabricado en el extranjero; ***Foreign Office,*** Ministerio de Asuntos Exteriores; ***foreign parts,*** el extranjero.
foreigner [ˈfɔrinə], *s.* extranjero.
foreignness [ˈfɔrinnis], *s.* calidad de extranjero; (lo) extranjero.
forejudgment [fɔ:ˈdʒʌdʒmənt], *s.* prejuicio.
foreknow [fɔ:ˈnou], *v.t.* preconocer, saber *o* conocer de antemano, tener presciencia de.
foreknowledge [fɔ:ˈnɔlidʒ], *s.* presciencia.
foreland [ˈfɔ:lənd], *s.* promontorio, cabo.
foreleg [ˈfɔ:leg], *s.* pata delantera.
forelock [ˈfɔ:lɔk], *s.* guedeja; copete; (*mec.*) chaveta; ***forelock bolts,*** pernos de chaveta, *m.pl.*; ***to take time by the forelock,*** asir la ocasión por los cabellos.
foreman [ˈfɔ:mən], *s.* capataz, encargado; (*for.*) presidente (*del jurado*).
foremast [ˈfɔ:mɑ:st], *s.* (*mar.*) palo de trinquete.
forementioned [ˈfɔ:menʃənd], *a.* susodicho, antedicho, precitado, ya citado.
foremost [ˈfɔ:moust], *a.* delantero; primero; principal, más destacado. — *adv.* primero; ***first and foremost,*** en primer lugar.
forename [ˈfɔ:neim], *s.* nombre de pila.
forenamed [ˈfɔ:neimd], *a.* susodicho, antedicho, ya citado.
forenoon [ˈfɔ:nu:n], *s.* (la) mañana.
forensic [fɔˈrensik], *a.* forense.
foreordain [fɔ:rɔ:ˈdein], *v.t.* preordinar, predestinar.
forepart [ˈfɔ:pɑ:t], *s.* delantera; primera parte.
forepaw [ˈfɔ:pɔ:], *s.* pata delantera.
forerun [fɔ:ˈrʌn], *irr. v.t.* preceder; anunciar.
forerunner [ˈfɔ:rʌnə], *s.* precursor; antecessor; presagio, anuncio.
foresaid [ˈfɔ:sed], *a.* antedicho, susodicho.
foresail [ˈfɔ:səl], *s.* (*mar.*) trinquete.
foresee [fɔ:ˈsi:], *irr. v.t.* prever; anunciar.
foreseeable [fɔ:ˈsiəbl], *a.* previsible.
foreseer [fɔ:ˈsiə], *s.* previsor.
foreshadow [fɔ:ˈʃædou], *v.t.* presagiar, anunciar. — *v.i.* configurarse (el futuro).
foreship [ˈfɔ:ʃip], *s.* (*mar.*) proa.
foreshore [ˈfɔ:ʃɔ:], *s.* playa.
foreshorten [fɔ:ˈʃɔ:tn], *v.t.* (*pint.*) escorzar.
foreshortening [fɔ:ˈʃɔ:tniŋ], *s.* (*pint.*) escorzo.
foreshow [fɔ:ˈʃou], *v.t.* pronosticar, anunciar.
foresight [ˈfɔ:sait], *s.* previsión, presciencia.
foresignify [fɔ:ˈsignifai], *v.t.* prefigurar, presagiar.
foreskin [ˈfɔ:skin], *s.* (*anat.*) prepucio.
forespeak [fɔ:ˈspi:k], *v.t.* predecir.
forest [ˈfɔrist], *a.* de bosque, forestal. — *s.* bosque.
forestal [ˈfɔristəl], *a.* forestal.
forestall [fɔ:ˈstɔ:l], *v.t.* anticipar; prevenir.
forestalling [fɔ:ˈstɔ:liŋ], *s.* anticipación.
forestay [ˈfɔ:stei], *s.* (*mar.*) estay del trinquete.
forested [ˈfɔristid], *a.* cubierto de bosque(s).
forester [ˈfɔristə], *s.* silvicultor; guardabosque, *m.*
forestry [ˈfɔristri], *s.* silvicultura.
foretaste [ˈfɔ:teist], *s.* anticipo. — *v.t.* gustar *o* conocer de antemano.
foretell [fɔ:ˈtel], *irr. v.t.* predecir, pronosticar, vaticinar.
foreteller [fɔ:ˈtelə], *s.* vaticinador.
foretelling [fɔ:ˈteliŋ], *s.* predicción, pronóstico.
forethought [ˈfɔ:θɔ:t], *a.* premeditado. — *s.* premeditación; providencia, prevención.
foretoken [ˈfɔ:toukən], *s.* anuncio, presagio. — [fɔ:ˈtoukən], *v.t.* presagiar, anunciar, prefigurar.
foretop [ˈfɔ:tɔp], *s.* (*mar.*) cofa de trinquete.
forever [fɔ:rˈevə], *adv.* siempre; para siempre.
forewarn [fɔ:ˈwɔ:n], *v.t.* prevenir, avisar, advertir, poner sobre aviso; ***to be forewarned,*** estar advertido, tener aviso.
forewarning [fɔ:ˈwɔ:niŋ], *s.* advertencia, aviso.
forewent [fɔ:ˈwent], *pret.* [FOREGO (2)].
forewind [ˈfɔ:wind], *s.* viento favorable.
forewoman [ˈfɔ:wumən], *s.* primera oficiala; encargada.
foreword [ˈfɔ:wə:d], *s.* prefacio.
foreyard [ˈfɔ:jɑ:d], *s.* (*mar.*) verga del trinquete.
forfeit [ˈfɔ:fit], *a.* perdido, confiscado. — *s.* pena; decomiso; gaje, prenda; ***game of forfeits,*** juego de prendas. — *v.t.* perder el título *o* derecho a.
forfeitable [ˈfɔ:fitəbl], *a.* confiscable.
forfeiture [ˈfɔ:fitʃə], *s.* confiscación, decomiso, pérdida de bienes.
forfend [fɔ:ˈfend], *v.t.* (*ant.*) impedir; desviar; asegurar; ***heaven forfend!*** ¡líbreme el cielo!
forgather [fɔ:ˈgæðə], *v.i.* congregarse, reunirse.
forge [fɔ:dʒ], *s.* fragua; herrería; forja; ***forge-hearth,*** atrio, hogar de fábrica; ***forge-train,*** fragua de laminar. — *v.t.* forjar, fraguar; inventar; falsificar. — *v.i.* — ***ahead,*** avanzar rápidamente, hacer muchos progresos.
forger [ˈfɔ:dʒə], *s.* forjador, fraguador; falseador, falsificador, falsario.
forgery [ˈfɔ:dʒəri], *s.* falsificación.
forget [fəˈget], *irr. v.t.* olvidar, olvidarse de, descuidar; ***forget it!*** ¡déjelo! — *v.i.* olvidar(se); ***I have forgotten to write,*** se me ha olvidado escribir. — **forget o.s.,** *v.r.* olvidarse de sí mismo; propasarse.
forgetful [fəˈgetful], *a.* olvidadizo, desmemoriado.
forgetfulness [fəˈgetfulnis], *s.* olvido, descuido.
forget-me-not [fəˈget-mi-nɔt], *s.* (*bot.*) nomeolvides, *f.inv.*, miosotis, *f.inv.*
forgetter [fəˈgetə], *s.* olvidadizo.
forgetting [fəˈgetiŋ], *s.* descuido, negligencia.
forging [ˈfɔ:dʒiŋ], *s.* forja, forjadura.
forgivable [fəˈgivəbl], *a.* perdonable, remisible.
forgive [fəˈgiv], *irr. v.t.* perdonar, dispensar, disculpar; remitir; ***forgive and forget,*** echar pelillos a la mar.
forgiveness [fəˈgivnis], *s.* perdón; misericordia, clemencia.

forgiving [fə'giviŋ], *a.* perdonador, clemente, magnánimo.
forgo [fɔː'gou], *irr. v.t.* privarse de, renunciar a.
fork [fɔːk], *s.* tenedor; (*agric.*) horca, horqueta, horquilla; horcajo, confluencia (*de ríos*); ramal, bifurcación; (*árbol*) horcadura; (*anat.*) horcajadura, entrepierna. — *v.t.* ahorquillar; cargar *o* hacinar con horca; (*ajedrez*) atacar dos piezas a la vez; (*fam.*) ***fork out,*** entregar, desembolsar. — *v.i.* bifurcarse.
forked [fɔːkt], *a.* bifurcado, ahorquillado; hendido; ***forked lightning,*** relámpago en zigzag.
forlorn [fə'lɔːn], *a.* abandonado, desamparado; desesperado; triste, mustio, tétrico, lúgubre; ***forlorn hope,*** esperanza muy remota.
forlornness [fə'lɔːnnis], *s.* desamparo, soledad, abandono, tristeza.
form [fɔːm], *s.* forma; figura; estado; impreso; formulario; formulismo; banco; clase; (*calzado*) horma; ***it is bad form,*** no es de buena educación, es de mal gusto; ***for form's sake,*** por guardar las formas; ***to be in*** o ***on form,*** estar en forma; estar de vena, estar inspirado; ***in due form,*** en debida forma; ***it's purely a matter of form,*** es puro formulismo. — *v.t.* formar. — *v.i.* formarse; ***form up,*** alinearse. — **form o.s.,** *v.r.* (***into***) constituirse en.
formal ['fɔːməl], *a.* ceremonioso, etiquetero, formalista; (*visita*) de cumplido; (*vestido*) de etiqueta; formal.
formaldehyde [fɔː'mældihaid], *s.* (*quím.*) formaldehido.
formalin ['fɔːməlin], *s.* (*quím.*) formalina.
formalism ['fɔːməlizəm], *s.* formalismo.
formalist ['fɔːməlist], *s.* formalista, *m.f.*
formality [fɔː'mæliti], *s.* ceremonia, ceremoniosidad, etiqueta; formulismo; (*pl.* **formalities** [-z]), requisitos, *m.pl.*, trámites, *m.pl.*, gestiones, *f.pl.*
formally ['fɔːməli], *adv.* con ceremoniosidad; oficialmente.
format ['fɔːmæt], *s.* formato.
formate ['fɔːmeit], *s.* (*quím.*) formiato.
formation [fɔː'meiʃən], *s.* formación; (*aer.*) ***to fly in formation,*** volar en formación.
formative ['fɔːmətiv], *a.* formativo; ***formative years,*** años de formación, *m.pl.*
forme [fɔːm], *s.* (*impr.*) forma, molde.
former ['fɔːmə], *a.* antiguo; anterior, precedente; primero. — *pron.* aquél *etc.*
formerly ['fɔːməli], *adv.* antiguamente, en otro tiempo.
formic ['fɔːmik], *a.* (*quím.*) fórmico.
formicant ['fɔːmikənt], *a.* formicante.
formidable ['fɔːmidəbl], *a.* temible, que infunde pavor.
formless ['fɔːmlis], *a.* informe.
Formosa [fɔː'mouzə]. Formosa.
formula ['fɔːmjulə], *s.* (*pl.* **formulæ** [-liː], **formulas** [-z]) fórmula.
formulary ['fɔːmjuləri], *a., s.* formulario.
formulate ['fɔːmjuleit], *v.t.* formular.
formulize ['fɔːmjulaiz], *v.t.* formalizar.
fornicate ['fɔːnikeit], *v.i.* fornicar.
fornication [fɔːni'keiʃən], *s.* fornicación.
fornicator ['fɔːnikeitə], *s.* fornicador.
forsake [fə'seik], *irr. v.t.* abandonar, desamparar; renegar de.
forsaken [fə'seikən], *a.* abandonado, desamparado; ***God-forsaken,*** dejado de la mano de Dios. — *p.p.* [FORSAKE].
forsaking [fə'seikiŋ], *s.* abandono.
forsooth [fə'suːθ], *adv.* (*ant.*) en verdad. — *interj.* (*ant.*) ¡de veras! ¡vaya!
forswear [fɔː'swεə], *irr. v.t.* abjurar, renegar de. — **forswear o.s.,** *v.r.* perjurarse.
fort [fɔːt], *s.* fuerte, fortín.

fortalice ['fɔːtəlis], *s.* fortín.
forte (1) ['fɔːti], *s.* fuerte.
forte (2) ['fɔːti], *a., adv., s.* (*mús.*) forte.
forth [fɔːθ], *adv.* (a)delante, (a)fuera; ***and so on and so forth,*** y así sucesivamente; ***from that day forth,*** desde aquel día en adelante; ***to go forth,*** salir; ***to step forth,*** avanzar, adelantarse.
forthcoming [fɔːθ'kʌmiŋ], *a.* venidero, próximo; disponible; abierto, comunicativo.
forthright ['fɔːθrait], *a.* directo, franco; terminante.
forthwith ['fɔːθ'wiθ], *adv.* inmediatamente, en el acto, acto seguido.
fortieth ['fɔːtiəθ], *a.* cuadragésimo; cuarenta. — *s.* cuarentavo.
fortifiable ['fɔːtifaiəbl], *a.* fortificable.
fortification [fɔːtifi'keiʃən], *s.* fortificación; (*pl.*) defensas.
fortifier ['fɔːtifaiə], *s.* fortificador; fortalecedor; fautor.
fortify ['fɔːtifai], *v.t.* fortificar; fortalecer; reconfortar; corroborar, confirmar, reforzar. — *v.i.* construir fortificaciones.
fortissimo [fɔː'tisimou], *a., adv., s.* (*mús.*) fortísimo.
fortitude ['fɔːtitjuːd], *s.* fortaleza, entereza.
fortnight ['fɔːtnait], *s.* quincena, quince días, dos semanas.
fortnightly ['fɔːtnaitli], *a.* quincenal, una vez cada quince días. — *adv.* quincenalmente. — *s.* (publicación) quincenal.
fortress ['fɔːtris], *s.* fortaleza, alcázar.
fortuitous [fɔː'tjuːitəs], *a.* fortuito, casual.
fortuitousness [fɔː'tjuːitəsnis], *s.* (lo) fortuito.
fortuity [fɔː'tjuːiti], *s.* caso fortuito; accidente.
fortunate ['fɔːtʃənit], *a.* afortunado, venturoso, que tiene suerte.
fortune ['fɔːʃuːn], *s.* fortuna; suerte; ***to cost a fortune,*** costar un dineral; ***fortune-hunter,*** aventurero; cazadotes, *m.inv.*; ***fortune-teller,*** adivino, adivina; ***soldier of fortune,*** mercenario; ***to tell s.o.'s fortune,*** decirle a uno la buenaventura.
fortuneless ['fɔːtʃuːnlis], *a.* sin fortuna.
forty ['fɔːti], *a., s.* cuarenta; (*pl.*) ***the forties,*** los años cuarenta; (*fam.*) ***forty winks,*** sueñecito.
forum ['fɔːrəm], *s.* foro; tribunal.
forward ['fɔːwəd], *a.* delantero; precoz; desenvuelto, atrevido; vivo, listo. — *adv.* adelante; hacia adelante; ***from this time forward,*** (de aquí) en adelante, en lo venidero; ***from that time forward,*** desde entonces; a partir de entonces; ***to bring forward,*** adelantar; ***to carry forward,*** sumar y seguir; ***to come*** o ***go forward,*** adelantar(se); ***to look forward to,*** esperar con ilusión, tener (mucha) ilusión por, estar deseando que llegue; ***to step forward,*** dar un paso hacia adelante. — *s.* (*dep.*) delantero. — *v.t.* hacer seguir, reexpedir; fomentar, favorecer; ***forwarding address,*** dirección para reexpedición de cartas.
forwardness ['fɔːwədnis], *s.* precocidad; desenvoltura, descaro, atrevimiento.
forwards ['fɔːwədz], *adv.* [FORWARD, *adv.*].
fossa ['fɔsə], *s.* (*anat.*) fosa.
fosse [fɔs], *s.* (*fort.*) foso.
fossil ['fɔsil], *a., s.* fósil; (*fam.*) vejestorio.
fossiliferous [fɔsil'ifərəs], *a.* fosilífero.
fossilization [fɔsilai'zeiʃən], *s.* fosilización.
fossilize ['fɔsilaiz], *v.t.* fosilizar, convertir en fósil. — *v.i.* fosilizarse.
fossorial [fɔ'sɔːriəl], *a.* cavador; (*ent.*) ***fossorial wasp,*** avispa cavadora.
foster ['fɔstə], *v.t.* criar; fomentar, favorecer.
foster-brother ['fɔstə-brʌðə], *s.* hermano de leche; ***foster-child,*** hijo, hija de leche; ***foster-father,*** padre adoptivo; ***foster-home,*** hogar adoptivo, casa adoptiva; país de adopción.
fostering ['fɔstəriŋ], *s.* (el) fomentar, fomento.

fosterling [ˈfɔstəliŋ], *s.* hijo *o* hija de leche.
foster-mother [ˈfɔstə-mʌðə], *s.* madre adoptiva; ***foster-nurse,*** nodriza, ama de leche; ***foster-sister,*** hermana de leche.
foul [faul], *a.* sucio; asqueroso; inmundo; fétido, mefítico; (*aire*) viciado; soez; atascado, enredado, obstruido; detestable, vil; (*fam.*) malo, atroz; ***foul-mouthed,*** mal hablado, deslenguado; ***foul weather,*** tiempo atroz *o* infame; ***by fair means or foul,*** por las buenas o por las malas; ***to fall*** o ***run foul of,*** enredarse en *o* con; ponerse a malas con. — *s.* falta; juego sucio. — *v.t.* ensuciar, emporcar; chocar con, enredarse en; (*dep.*) cometer una falta contra. — *v.i.* ensuciarse; (*mar.*) enredarse, enceparse; (*dep.*) jugar sucio.
foulard [ˈfu:lɑ:d], *s.* fular.
foulness [ˈfaulnis], *s.* suciedad, asquerosidad.
found (1) [faund], *pret., p.p.* [FIND].
found (2) [faund], *v.t.* fundar; fundamentar; cimentar; basar; asentar.
found (3) [faund], *v.t.* (*fund.*) fundir.
foundation [faunˈdeiʃən], *s.* fundación; fundamento, base; (*cost.*) forro, refuerzo; (*ing.*) firme; fundamento, entibo; (*arq.*) cimiento; (*mec.*) asiento, pie, lecho; ***foundation garment,*** corsé; ***foundation school,*** escuela dotada; ***foundation-stone,*** piedra fundamental; ***to lay the foundations,*** cimentar, poner los cimientos.
foundationless [faunˈdeiʃənlis], *a.* sin fundamento.
founder (1) [ˈfaundə], *s.* fundador.
founder (2) [ˈfaundə], *s.* (*fund.*) fundidor.
founder (3) [ˈfaundə], *s.* (*vet.*) despeadura. — *v.i.* irse a pique, zozobrar; (*fig.*) fracasar.
founding [ˈfaundiŋ], *s.* fundición.
foundling [ˈfaundliŋ], *s.* (niño) expósito, cunero; ***foundling hospital,*** casa de expósitos, inclusa.
foundry [ˈfaundri], *s.* fundición; fundería.
fount (1) [faunt], *s.* fuente, pila.
fount (2) [faunt], *s.* (*impr.*) fundición.
fountain [ˈfauntin], *s.* fuente, surtidor; ***fountain-head,*** fuente, origen; ***fountain-pen,*** (pluma) estilográfica.
four [fɔ:], *a., s.* cuatro; ***four-cornered,*** cuadrangular; ***four-engined,*** cuatrimotor; ***four-footed,*** cuadrúpedo; ***four in hand, coach and four,*** carruaje tirado por cuatro caballos; ***four-letter word,*** palabra soez; (*bot.*) ***four-o'clock,*** dondiego de noche; ***four-square,*** sólido, sólidamente; ***on all fours,*** a gatas.
fourfold [ˈfɔ:fould], *a., adv.* cuádruplo.
fourpence [ˈfɔ:pəns], *s.* cuatro peniques.
fourscore [ˈfɔ:skɔ:], *a., s.* (*ant.*) ochenta; octogenario.
fourteen [ˈfɔ:ˈti:n], *a., s.* catorce.
fourteenth [ˈfɔ:ˈti:nθ], *a.* catorceno, decimocuarto; catorce (*títulos*). — *s.* decimocuarta parte; catorce (*fechas*).
fourth [fɔ:θ], *a.* cuarto. — *s.* cuarta parte; cuatro (*fechas*).
fourthly [ˈfɔ:θli], *adv.* en cuarto lugar.
fowl [faul], *s.* ave (*de corral*), *f.*; ***fowl pest,*** peste aviar, *f.*; (*pl.*) aves, volatería. — *v.i.* cazar aves.
fowler [ˈfaulə], *s.* cazador (*de aves*).
fowling [ˈfauliŋ], *s.* volatería, caza (de aves); ***fowling-net,*** red (para cazar pájaros); ***fowling-piece,*** escopeta.
fox [fɔks], *s.* zorro, zorra, raposa; (*mar.*) rebenque; (*mil.*) ***fox-hole,*** pozo de lobo; ***fox-hound,*** perro zorrero *o* raposero; ***fox-hunter,*** montero; ***fox-like,*** zorruno; ***fox-trot,*** fox. — *v.t.* desconcertar, dejar perplejo.
foxglove [ˈfɔksglʌv], *s.* (*bot.*) dedalera.
foxiness [ˈfɔksinis], *s.* astucia.
foxish [ˈfɔksiʃ], *a.* zorruno.
foxtail [ˈfɔksteil], *s.* (*bot.*) cola de zorra, carricera.
foxy [ˈfɔksi], *a.* raposuno, zorruno; astuto, taimado.
foyer [ˈfɔijei], *s.* vestíbulo; (*teat.*) salón de descanso.
fracas [ˈfrækɑ:], *s.* pelea, zipizape; batahola.
fraction [ˈfrækʃən], *s.* parte muy pequeña; (*arit.*) fracción, quebrado; ***to escape by a fraction of an inch,*** salvarse por un pelo.
fractional [ˈfrækʃənəl], *a.* fraccionario.
fractious [ˈfrækʃəs], *a.* reacio, rebelde, díscolo.
fracture [ˈfræktʃə], *s.* fractura; ***compound fracture,*** fractura conminuta. — *v.t.* fracturar. — *v.i.* fracturarse.
fragile [ˈfrædʒail], *a.* frágil; quebradizo; delicado.
fragility, fragileness [frəˈdʒiliti, ˈfrædʒailnis], *s.* fragilidad.
fragment [ˈfrægmənt], *s.* fragmento; trozo; ***to break into fragments,*** fragmentar; destrozar.
fragmentary [ˈfrægməntəri], *a.* fragmentario.
fragrance, fragrancy [ˈfreigrəns, -i], *s.* fragancia, aroma, *m.*
fragrant [ˈfreigrənt], *a.* fragante, aromático, aromoso.
fragrantly [ˈfreigrəntli], *adv.* con fragancia.
frail (1) [freil], *a.* frágil, deleznable, quebradizo; endeble, débil, delicado.
frail (2) [freil], *s.* capacho, espuerta.
frailness, frailty [ˈfreilnis, -ti], *s.* fragilidad, debilidad; (lo) endeble.
frame [freim], *s.* armazón, *f.*; esqueleto; estructura; marco (*de cuadro, espejo*); armadura, montura (*de gafas*); bastidor (*de bordar*); (*mar.*) cuaderna; encuadre; forma, figura; ***man with a big frame,*** hombre corpulento. — *v.t.* enmarcar, poner (un) marco a; formular, expresar; formar, forjar; (*fam.*) hacer que (*una persona*) pague el pato.
framer [ˈfreimə], *s.* constructor; armador; inventor, autor, forjador; fabricante de marcos.
framework [ˈfreimwə:k], *s.* armazón, esqueleto, armadura; entramado; estructura; sistema, *m.*, organización.
framing [ˈfreimiŋ], *s.* armadura, armazón, *f.*
franc [fræŋk], *s.* franco (*moneda*).
France [frɑ:ns]. Francia.
franchise [ˈfræntʃaiz], *s.* derecho de voto, sufragio; franquicia; exención. — *v.t.* exentar; conceder franquicias.
franchisement [ˈfræntʃizmənt], *s.* franquicia; exención.
Franciscan [frænˈsiskən], *a., s.* franciscano.
Frank [fræŋk], *s.* franco; ***the Franks,*** los francos.
frank [fræŋk], *a.* franco. — *v.t.* franquear.
frankincense [ˈfræŋkinsens], *s.* incienso.
Frankish [ˈfræŋkiʃ], *a., s.* franco.
frankness [ˈfræŋknis], *s.* franqueza, sinceridad.
frantic [ˈfræntik], *a.* frenético; furioso; desquiciado.
frap [fræp], *v.t.* (*mar.*) atortorar.
frass [fræs], *s.* excremento (de la larva).
fraternal [frəˈtə:nəl], *a.* fraternal.
fraternity [frəˈtə:niti], *s.* fraternidad, hermandad.
fraternization [frætənaiˈzeiʃən], *s.* fraternización.
fraternize [ˈfrætənaiz], *v.i.* fraternizar; hermanarse.
fratricidal [frætriˈsaidəl], *a.* fratricida.
fratricide [ˈfrætrisaid], *s.* (*acto*) fratricidio; (*pers.*) fratricida, *m.f.*
fratry, fratery [ˈfrætri], *s.* refectorio (en un convento *o* monasterio).
fraud [frɔ:d], *s.* fraude; impostor, farsante.
fraudulence, fraudulency [ˈfrɔ:djuləns, -i], *s.* fraude, engaño, fraudulencia.
fraudulent [ˈfrɔ:djulənt], *a.* fraudulento, engañoso.
fraught [frɔ:t], *a.* cargado; erizado; ***situation fraught with difficulties,*** situación erizada de dificultades.
fraxinella [fræksiˈnelə], *s.* (*bot.*) fresnillo.
fray (1) [frei], *s.* lucha, combate, refriega, riña; ***in the thick of the fray,*** en lo más recio del combate.
fray (2) [frei], *v.t.* desgastar; refregar. — *v.i.* deshilacharse.

fraying ['freiiŋ], *s.* rozamiento, raedura, desgaste, deshiladura.
freak [fri:k], *s.* tipo raro; cosa rara; monstruo; ***freak of nature,*** aborto de la naturaleza.
freakish ['fri:kiʃ], *a.* caprichoso; raro, extravagante; monstruoso; imprevisible; ***freakish weather,*** tiempo disparatado.
freakishness ['fri:kiʃnis], *s.* (lo) raro; (lo) monstruoso; (lo) caprichoso.
freckle [frekl], *s.* peca; ***freckle-faced,*** pecoso. — *v.t.* motear. — *v.i.* ponerse pecoso.
freckled, freckly [frekld, 'frekli], *a.* pecoso.
free [fri:], *a.* libre; despejado; franco; vacante; desocupado; exento; gratuito; suelto; ***free-born,*** nacido libre; ***free enterprise,*** libertad de empresa; ***free-for-all,*** marimorena, zipizape; ***free hand,*** carta blanca, plena libertad (para todo); ***free-spoken,*** franco; dicho sin reserva; ***free style,*** estilo a discreción; ***free-thinker,*** librepensador; ***free-thinking,*** librepensamiento; ***free-trade,*** libre cambio; ***free-trader,*** librecambista, *m.f.*; ***free verse,*** poesía libre de toda traba; ***free-wheeling,*** marcha a rueda libre; ***free will,*** libre albedrío; ***of one's own free will,*** por voluntad propia, espontáneamente; ***free and easy,*** de trato fácil, campechano; desenvuelto, que tiene desparpajo; ***free on board (f.o.b.),*** franco a bordo; ***free of charge,*** gratis; ***free with money,*** espléndido, que gasta con liberalidad; ***to be free to,*** ser libre de; ***to be free with,*** usar *o* gastar libremente; ***to make free with,*** tomarse muchas confianzas con; ***to set free,*** libertar; liberar. — *v.t.* libertar, poner en libertad, liberar; librar; exentar, eximir; despejar; soltar. — **free o.s.,** *v.r.* librarse (***from,*** de).
freebooter ['fri:bu:tə], *s.* pirata, *m.*, filibustero.
freebooting ['fri:bu:tiŋ], *s.* piratería.
freedman ['fri:dmən], *s.* liberto.
freedom ['fri'dəm], *s.* libertad; exención; ***freedom of the city,*** ciudadanía de honor; ***freedom of the press,*** libertad de prensa; ***freedom of worship,*** libertad de cultos; ***freedom of speech,*** libertad de palabra.
freehold ['fri:hould], *s.* feudo franco.
freeholder ['fri:houldə], *s.* poseedor de feudo franco.
freelance ['fri:lɑ:ns], *a., s.* (*mil.*) mercenario; (*fig.*) independiente; ***freelance journalist,*** periodista que trabaja por cuenta propia, *m.f.*
freeman ['fri:mən], *s.* hombre independiente, hombre libre; ciudadano de honor.
freemason ['fri:'meisən], *s.* francmasón.
freemasonry ['fri:'meisənri], *s.* masonería, francmasonería.
freeness ['fri:nis], *s.* libertad; franqueza.
freestone ['fri:stoun], *s.* piedra franca; (*bot.*) abridero.
freeway ['fri:wei], (*Am.*) [MOTORWAY].
freeze [fri:z], *s.* helada; congelación. — *irr. v.t.* helar; congelar; (*fam.*) ***freeze out,*** eliminar; hacer el vacío a. — *v.i.* helarse, congelarse; ***freeze to death,*** morir(se) helado *o* de frío.
freezer ['fri:zə], *s.* nevera, congelador.
freezing ['fri:ziŋ], *a.* glacial, helador. — *s.* congelación, helamiento; ***freezing-point,*** punto de congelación.
freight [freit], *s.* flete; carga, porte; (*Am.*) ***freight train*** [GOODS TRAIN]. — *v.t.* fletar; cargar.
freightage ['freitidʒ], *s.* cargamento; flete; porte.
freighter ['freitə], *s.* fletador, cargador; buque de carga, carguero.
French [frentʃ], *a.* francés; ***French bean,*** judía; ***French chalk,*** blanco de Meudón; ***French horn,*** trompa de armonía; (*arq.*) ***French roof,*** mansarda; ***French window,*** puerta ventana; ***in the French fashion,*** a la francesa; ***to take French leave,*** despedirse a la francesa. — *s.* (*idioma*) francés, *m.*; ***the French,*** los franceses.
frenchify ['frentʃifai], *v.t.* afrancesar.
Frenchified ['frentʃifaid], *a.* afrancesado.
Frenchman ['frentʃmən], *s.* francés, *m.*
Frenchwoman ['frentʃwumən], *s.* francesa.
frenetic [fre'netik], *a.* frenético; furioso.
frenzied ['frenzid], *a.* frenético.
frenzy ['frenzi], *s.* frenesí, delirio, desvarío.
frequence, frequency ['fri:kwəns, -i], *s.* frecuencia; (*estadística*) ***frequency distribution,*** distribución de frecuencias; ***high frequency,*** alta frecuencia.
frequent ['fri:kwənt], *a.* frecuente. — [fri'kwent], *v.t.* frecuentar.
frequentation [fri:kwen'teiʃən], *s.* frecuentación.
frequentative [fri'kwentətiv], *a.* frecuentativo.
frequenter [fri'kwentə], *s.* frecuentador.
fresco ['freskou], *s.* (*pl.* **frescoes**) fresco (*pintura al fresco*). — *v.t.* pintar al fresco.
fresh [freʃ], *a.* fresco; nuevo; reciente; (*fig.*) descarado; ***fresh air,*** aire puro; ***fresh hand,*** novicio, novato; ***fresh paint!*** ¡mancha!; ***fresh water,*** agua dulce; ***fresh from,*** recién salido de.
freshen ['freʃən], *v.t.* refrescar. — *v.i.* refrescarse.
freshet ['freʃit], *s.* crecida, riada.
freshman ['freʃmən], *s.* estudiante de primer año; novato.
freshness ['freʃnis], *s.* frescor; (*despec.*) frescura; (*fig.*) lozanía; novedad.
fret (1) [fret], *s.* greca, calado; (*mús.*) traste.
fret (2) [fret], *s.* estado inquieto, nerviosidad. — *v.t.* raer, rozar. — *v.i.* inquietarse, impacientarse.
fretful ['fretful] *a.* inquieto; preocupón; desazonado; sobresaltado; irritable; enojadizo; descontentadizo.
fretfully ['fretfuli], *adv.* con mal humor; con impaciencia.
fretfulness ['fretfulnis], *s.* mal humor; impaciencia.
fretsaw ['fretsɔ:], *s.* sierra de calados.
fretted ['fretid], *a.* calado.
fretwork ['fretwə:k], *s.* (*carp.*) calado.
friability [fraiə'biliti], *s.* friabilidad.
friable ['fraiəbl], *a.* friable, desmenuzable.
friar ['fraiə], *s.* fraile; (*título*) fray; ***black friar,*** dominico; ***friar-like,*** frailesco; ***grey friar,*** franciscano; ***white friar,*** carmelita, *m.*
friary ['fraiəri], *s.* convento de frailes.
fricandeau [frikən'dou], *s.* (*coc.*) fricandó.
fricassee [frikə'si:], *s.* (*coc.*) fricasé. — *v.t.* hacer fricasé de.
fricative ['frikətiv], *a.* (*gram.*) fricativo. — *s.* fricativa.
friction ['frikʃən], *s.* fricción; roce(s), rozamiento(s).
Friday ['fraidi], *s.* viernes; ***Good Friday,*** viernes santo; ***Man Friday,*** Viernes.
fried [fraid], *a.* frito.
friend [frend], *s.* amigo, amiga; (*relig.*) cuáquero; ***bosom friend,*** amigo de corazón, amigo íntimo; ***friend!*** ¡gente de paz!; ***friend at court,*** amigo influyente; ***a friend in need is a friend indeed,*** amigo de mal tiempo, amigo de verdad; ***to be friends again,*** reconciliarse, hacer las paces; ***to be friends with,*** ser amigo de, tener amistad con; ***to have a lot of friends,*** tener muchos amigos *o* muchas amistades; ***to make friends with,*** hacerse amigo de, trabar amistad con.
friendless ['frendlis], *a.* desamparado, desvalido, sin amigos.
friendly ['frendli], *a.* amistoso; simpático, cordial; acogedor; (*dep.*) ***friendly match,*** partido amistoso; ***friendly society,*** mutualidad.
friendliness ['frendlinis], *s.* simpatía, cordialidad.
friendship ['frendʃip], *s.* amistad.
frieze [fri:z], *s.* (*arq.*) friso; (*tej.*) frisa.
frigate ['frigit], *s.* (*mar.*) fragata; (*orn.*) ***frigate bird,*** rabihorcado.
fright [frait], *s.* susto, sobresalto; (persona) esperpento, espantajo; ***to take fright,*** asustarse, sobresaltarse.

frighten [fraitn], *v.t.* asustar, dar miedo a; ***frighten away*** o ***off,*** ahuyentar, espantar; ***frighten s.o. out of their wits,*** dar un susto de muerte a alguien; ***to be frightened (of),*** tener miedo (a).
frightful [ˈfraitful], *a.* espantoso, horroroso, pavoroso, terrible; feísimo.
frightfulness [ˈfraitfulnis], *s.* horror, espanto.
frigid [ˈfridʒid], *a.* frío; frígido; gélido.
frigidity [friˈdʒiditi], *s.* frialdad, frío; frigidez.
frigidly [ˈfridʒidli], *adv.* fríamente, con frialdad.
frigorific [frigəˈrifik], *a.* frigorífico.
frill [fril], *s.* (*cost.*) escarola, lechuga; volante, faralá; (*pl.*) perifollos, *m.pl.*; (*fam.*) ***with all the frills,*** sin faltar detalle. — *v.t.* (*cost.*) alechugar, escarolar.
fringe [frindʒ], *s.* borde; orla; franja; periferia; (*pelo*) flequillo; ***fringe benefits,*** beneficios accesorios, *m.pl.*; ***fringe-maker,*** fabricante de franjas. — *v.t.* orlar (***with,*** de).
fringeless [ˈfrindʒlis], *a.* sin fleco, sin ribete, sin franjas.
fringy [ˈfrindʒi], *a.* floqueado.
fripperer [ˈfripərə], *s.* ropavejero, baratillero, prendero.
frippery [ˈfripəri], *s.* perifollos, *m.pl.*; frivolidades, *f.pl.*
friseur [friːˈzəː], *s.* peluquero.
frisk [frisk], *s.* brinco, retozo; cacheo. — *v.t.* cachear, registrar. — *v.i.* retozar, triscar, cabriolar.
frisket [ˈfriskit], *s.* (*impr.*) frasqueta.
friskiness [ˈfriskinis], *s.* retozo, viveza, vivacidad.
frisky [ˈfriski], *a.* juguetón, retozón, vivaracho; (*caballo*) fogoso.
frit [frit], *s.* (*vidrio*) frita. — *v.t.* derretir.
frith [friθ], *s.* estuario.
fritillary [friˈtiləri], *s.* (*bot.*, *ent.*) fritilaria.
fritter [ˈfritə], *s.* buñuelo; fruta de sartén; torrezno. — *v.t.* desmenuzar; ***fritter away,*** malgastar, disipar.
frivolity, frivolousness [friˈvɔliti, ˈfrivələsnis], *s.* frivolidad.
frivolous [ˈfrivələs], *a.* frívolo.
frizz(le) [friz(l)], *s.* bucle, rizo. — *v.t.* frisar, encrespar, rizar.
frizzler [ˈfrizlə], *s.* frisador, rizador.
fro [frou], *adv.* atrás, hacia atrás; ***to and fro,*** de un lado a otro, de aquí para allá; de arriba para abajo; ***to go to and fro,*** ir y venir.
frock [frɔk], *s.* (*cost.*) vestido (*de mujer* o *de niña*); sotana (*de cura*); ***frock-coat,*** levita; ***smock frock,*** sayo.
frog [frɔg], *s.* rana; (*sast.*) alamar, recamo; (*f.c.*) corazón, rana; (*vet.*) ranilla del caballo; (*fam.*) gabacho; ***frog in the throat,*** carraspera; (*bot.*) ***frog-lettuce,*** espiga de agua; (*fam.*) ***to frog-march s.o.,*** llevar (*dos personas*) rápidamente y a la fuerza al alguien, llevar codo con codo.
frogman [ˈfrɔgmən], *s.* (*pl.* **-men** [-men]) hombre-rana.
frolic [ˈfrɔlik], *s.* juego, travesura, retozo. — *v.i.* retozar, juguetear.
frolicsome [ˈfrɔliksəm], *a.* juguetón, retozón, travieso.
from [frɔm], *prep.* de, desde; de parte de; por, a causa de; a; según; ***from above,*** desde encima; de lo alto; ***from afar,*** desde lejos; ***from head to toe,*** de pies a cabeza; ***from long ago,*** de hace mucho tiempo; ***from memory,*** de memoria; ***from now on,*** de ahora en adelante; ***from what you say,*** por, según lo que usted dice; ***judging from,*** a juzgar por; ***to take sth. away from s.o.,*** quitarle algo a alguien.
frond [frɔnd], *s.* fronda; hoja.
frondage [ˈfrɔndidʒ], *s.* frondosidad.
front [frʌnt], *a.* (*pol.*) ***front bench,*** los dirigentes del gobierno *o* de la oposición; ***front door,*** puerta principal; (*mil.*) ***front line,*** primera línea, línea del frente; ***front page,*** primera plana; de primera plana; ***front row,*** primera fila; ***front seat,*** asiento de delante; ***front view,*** vista hacia adelante. — *s.* frente; parte delantera; fachada; pechera (*de camisa*); principio; (*fam.*, *fig.*) afectación, pos(e); ***in front of,*** delante de; ***to come to the front,*** (empezar a) destacar; ***to put on a bold front,*** armarse de valor. — *v.t.* hacer frente a, afrontar. — *v.i.* — ***on, onto,*** dar (a), mirar (hacia).
frontage [ˈfrʌntidʒ], *s.* fachada; terreno frontero.
frontal [ˈfrʌntəl], *a.*, *s.* frontal.
fronted [ˈfrʌntid], *a.* que tiene fachada.
frontier [ˈfrʌntiə], *a.* fronterizo. — *s.* frontera.
frontiersman [ˈfrʌntiəzmən], *s.* (*pl.* **-men** [-men]) (*Am.*) pionero.
frontispiece [ˈfrʌntispiːs], *s.* (*impr.*) portada; (*arq.*) fachada, frontispicio.
frontlet [ˈfrʌntlit], *s.* venda (para la frente).
frost [frɔst], *s.* helada; ***frost-bite,*** congelación; ***frost-bitten,*** congelado, helado; ***white frost, hoar frost,*** escarcha; (*fam.*) petardo. — *v.t.* cubrir de escarcha; (*confituras*) escarchar; (*plantas*) quemar; (*vidrios*) esmerilar; (*alimentos*) congelar.
frostiness [ˈfrɔstinis], *s.* gelidez.
frosting [ˈfrɔstiŋ], *s.* capa de clara de huevo.
frosty [ˈfrɔsti], *a.* que tiene escarcha; helado; canoso; gélido, glacial.
froth [frɔθ], *s.* espuma; (*fig.*) frivolidad. — *v.i.* espumar, echar espuma(s) *o* espumarajos.
frothiness [ˈfrɔθinis], *s.* espumosidad.
frothy [ˈfrɔθi], *a.* espumoso.
frouzy [FROWZY].
froward [ˈfrouəd], *a.* indócil, díscolo.
frown [fraun], *s.* ceño, entrecejo; desagrado, enojo; ***frowns of fortune,*** reveses de la fortuna. —*v.i.* fruncir el entrecejo, ponerse ceñudo, poner mal gesto, enfurruñarse; ***frown at*** o ***upon,*** mirar con ceño; mirar con malos ojos, no mirar con buenos ojos.
frowning [ˈfrauniŋ], *a.* torvo, ceñudo.
frowningly [ˈfrauniŋli], *adv.* con ceño, ceñudo, enojadamente.
frowst [fraust], *s.* aire cargado, tufo.
frowzy [ˈfrauzi], *a.* (*fam.*) desaseado, desaliñado, desgreñado; maloliente.
frozen [ˈfrouzən], *a.* congelado; ***frozen foods,*** alimentos congelados, *m.pl.* — *p.p.* [FREEZE].
fructiferous [frʌkˈtifərəs], *a.* fructífero.
fructification [frʌktifiˈkeiʃən], *s.* (*bot.*) fructificación.
fructify [ˈfrʌktifai], *v.t.* fertilizar, fecundar. — *v.i.* fructificar, dar fruto.
frugal [ˈfruːgəl], *a.* frugal, parco.
frugality [fruːˈgæliti], *s.* frugalidad, parquedad.
fruit [fruːt], *s.* (*lit.*) fruta, frutas; (*lit.*, *fig.*) fruto; ***first fruits,*** (frutas) primicias; ***fruit-bearing,*** frutal; ***fruit-cake,*** plumcake; ***fruit-drier,*** secadero de frutas; ***fruit-parer,*** mondafruta, *m.*; (*pint.*) ***fruit-piece,*** frutaje; ***fruit-tree,*** frutal; (*fig.*) ***fruits of his labours,*** fruto de su trabajo. — *v.i.* dar fruto, frutar.
fruitage [ˈfruːtidʒ], *s.* fruta; fruto, efecto.
fruiter [ˈfruːtə], *s.* árbol frutero; (*mar.*) buque frutero.
fruiterer [ˈfruːtərə], *s.* frutero.
fruitery [ˈfruːtəri], *s.* fruta; frutería.
fruitful [ˈfruːtful], *a.* fructífero; provechoso, ventajoso, fructuoso; fecundo, abundante.
fruitfulness [ˈfruːtfulnis], *s.* fertilidad, fecundidad.
fruition [fruˈiʃən], *s.* fruición; realización; ***to come to fruition,*** fructificar, verse logrado.
fruitless [ˈfruːtlis], *a.* estéril, infructuoso; vano, ocioso, inútil.
fruitlessness [ˈfruːtlisnis], *s.* esterilidad; infructuosidad.
fruity [ˈfruːti], *a.* de olor *o* de sabor de fruta; (*fam.*) verde; (*voz*) pastosa.

frumentaceous [fruːmen'teiʃəs], *a.* frumenticio.
frumenty ['fruːminti], *s.* manjar hecho de trigo y leche.
frump [frʌmp], *s.* facha; mujer desaliñada.
frustrate [frʌs'treit], *v.t.* frustrar, cohibir, inhibir; limitar, restringir; burlar.
frustrated [frʌs'treitid], *a.* frustrado; inhibido, cohibido; sin horizontes; sin posibilidades, sin alicientes.
frustration [frʌs'treiʃən], *s.* frustración; defraudación; contratiempo.
frustum ['frʌstəm], *s.* (*geom.*) tronco; cono truncado.
fry (1) [frai], *s.* (*pl.* **fries** [-z]) (*coc.*) fritada. — *v.t.* freír. — *v.i.* freírse; ***I have other fish to fry,*** tengo otras cosas en que pensar.
fry (2) [frai], *s.* cría (*de animales, peces etc.*); (*fam.*) ***small fry,*** gente menuda; morralla.
frying-pan ['fraiiŋ-pæn], *s.* sartén, *f.*; ***to jump out of the frying-pan into the fire,*** huir del fuego y caer en las brasas.
fuchsia ['fjuːʃə], *s.* fucsia.
fucoid ['fjuːkɔid], *a.* fucóideo.
fucus ['fjuːkəs], *s.* fuco.
fuddle [fʌdl], *v.t.* aturdir; ***to be fuddled,*** no tener la cabeza despejada.
fuddy-duddy ['fʌdi-dʌdi], *s.* (*fam.*) vejestorio, antigualla; chinche; aguafiestas, *m.f.inv.*
fudge [fʌdʒ], *s.* dulce blando. — *v.t.* hacer mal *o* de modo chapucero, estropear.
fuel ['fjuːəl], *s.* combustible; carburante; pábulo; ***to add fuel to the flames,*** echar leña al fuego. —*v.t.* aprovisionar de combustible *o* de carburante. — *v.i.* aprovisionarse de combustible *o* de carburante.
fug [fʌg], *s.* (*fam.*) ambiente ahogado, malventilado.
fugacious [fjuː'geiʃəs], *a.* fugaz.
fugaciousness, fugacity [fjuː'geiʃəsnis, fjuː'gæsiti], *s.* fugacidad.
fuggy ['fʌgi], *a.* (*fam.*) ahogado, malventilado.
fugitive ['fjuːdʒitiv], *a.* fugitivo; pasajero. — *s.* fugitivo, evadido, prófugo.
fugleman ['fjuːgəlmən], *s.* (*pl.* **-men** [-men]) (*mil.*) jefe de fila.
fugue [fjuːg], *s.* (*mús.*) fuga.
fulcrum ['fʌlkrəm], *s.* (*mec.*) fulcro.
fulfil [ful'fil], *v.t.* cumplir (con); llenar; realizar.
fulfilment [ful'filmənt], *s.* cumplimiento; ejecución; realización.
fulgency ['fʌldʒənsi], *s.* fulgor, resplandor.
fulgent ['fʌldʒənt], *a.* fulgente, fúlgido.
fulgurate ['fʌlgjuəreit], *v.i.* fulgurar.
fuliginous [fjuː'lidʒinəs], *a.* fuliginoso.
full (1) [ful], *a.* lleno; pleno; plenario; cabal, íntegro; completo; (*miembro*) de número; amplio, holgado; abundante, copioso; ***full-back,*** defensa, *m.*; ***full-blooded,*** pletórico, vigoroso, viril; generoso; ***full details,*** (con) todos los detalles; información completa; ***full dress,*** (traje) de etiqueta *o* de gala; ***full employment,*** pleno empleo; ***full-faced,*** carilleno; ***a full hour,*** una buena hora (o más), una hora larga *o* entera; ***full length,*** de cuerpo entero; de largo metraje; ***full moon,*** luna llena, plenilunio; ***full powers,*** plenos poderes, *m.pl.*; ***full speed, full blast,*** (a) toda velocidad, marcha *o* máquina, (a) velocidad máxima; ***full speed ahead,*** toda máquina; ***full stop,*** punto; ***in full swing,*** en pleno funcionamiento; en pleno desarrollo; viento en popa; ***full-time,*** de plena dedicación; (*dep.*) final; ***full up,*** (*comida*) repleto, ahito; (*autobús*) completo. — *adv.* completamente; de lleno; ***full-blown,*** (*flor*) abierta; (*vela*) llena; (*fam.*) hecho y derecho; con todas las de la ley; ***full-bodied,*** generoso; ***full-grown,*** crecido; hecho y derecho; ***full well,*** perfectamente; de sobra. — *s.* ***in full,*** en su totalidad, por completo; ***to the full,*** totalmente, hasta el máximo. — *v.t.* dar amplitud a.
full (2) [ful], *v.t.* (*tej.*) abatanar.
fuller ['fulə], *s.* batanero; (*tej.*) ***fuller's-earth,*** tierra de batán; ***fuller's thistle,*** cardencha, cardo de bataneros.
fullery ['fuləri], *s.* batán.
fulling-mill ['fuliŋ-mil], *s.* batán.
fullness ['fulnis], *s.* plenitud, abundancia; (lo) lleno; (***all***) ***in the fullness of time,*** (todo) a su debido tiempo, con el tiempo, en su momento.
fully ['fuli], *adv.* totalmente, de lleno.
fulminant ['fʌlminənt], *a.* fulminante.
fulminate (1) ['fʌlmineit], *v.t.* fulminar. — *v.i.* tronar; ***fulminate against,*** despotricar de *o* contra.
fulminate (2) ['fʌlmineit], *s.* (*quím.*) fulminato.
fulminating, fulminatory ['fʌlmineitiŋ, -əri], *a.* fulminante, fulmíneo, fulminoso.
fulmination [fʌlmi'neiʃən], *s.* fulminación, detonación, trueno.
fulmine ['fʌlmin], *v.t.* fulminar, lanzar con explosión. — *v.i.* tronar.
fulminic [fʌl'minik], *a.* (*quím.*) fulmínico.
fulsome ['fulsəm], *a.* insincero, hipócrita; empalagoso; servil, adulador.
fulsomeness ['fulsəmnis], *s.* insinceridad, hipocresía.
fulvous ['fʌlvəs], *a.* color leonado, amarillo rojizo.
fumble [fʌmbl], *v.t.* marrar. — *v.i.* — ***for,*** requerir, buscar a tientas *o* con torpeza; ***fumble with,*** tratar desmañadamente de hacer (algo).
fumbler ['fʌmblə], *s.* chapucero.
fumbling ['fʌmbliŋ], *a.* desmañado, torpe.
fume [fjuːm], *s.* vapor, gas, emanación; tufo; acaloramiento. — *v.i.* humear; echar pestes; ***he's fuming with rage,*** está que trina, está que arde.
fumigate ['fjuːmigeit], *v.t.* fumigar; sahumar.
fumigation [fjuːmi'geiʃən], *s.* fumigación; sahumerio.
fumigator ['fjuːmigeitə], *s.* fumigador.
fumigatory ['fjuːmigeitəri], *a.*, *s.* fumigatorio.
fuming ['fjuːmiŋ], *a.* humeante, fumante; encolerizado, furioso. — *s.* sahumerio.
fumitory ['fjuːmitəri], *s.* (*bot.*) fumaria.
fumy ['fjuːmi], *a.* humoso, fumoso.
fun [fʌn], *s.* diversión; ***for fun,*** en broma; ***fun-fair,*** parque de atracciones; ***to be good*** (***great***) ***fun*** o ***full of fun,*** ser muy divertido; ***to have fun,*** divertirse; ***in fun,*** en broma; ***just for fun,*** de sport; ***to make fun of, to poke fun at,*** burlarse de; ***we'll see some fun then,*** entonces será ella; ***it's real fun!*** ¡es el disfrute!
funambulatory [fjuː'næmbjuleitəri], *a.* funambulesco, de volatinero.
funambulist [fjuː'næmbjulist], *s.* funámbulo.
function ['fʌŋkʃən], *s.* función; ceremonia, acto. — *v.i.* funcionar.
functional ['fʌŋkʃənəl], *a.* funcional.
functionary ['fʌŋkʃənəri], *s.* funcionario.
fund [fʌnd], *s.* fondo; (*pl.*) fondos; ***sinking fund,*** fondo de amortización; ***to be in funds,*** estar en fondos. — *v.t.* consolidar (*una deuda*).
fundable ['fʌndəbl], *a.* consolidable.
fundament ['fʌndəmənt], *s.* fundamento, cimiento, principio; ano.
fundamental [fʌndə'mentəl], *a.* fundamental, esencial. — *s.* fundamento, cosa fundamental *o* esencial; (lo) fundamental, (lo) esencial.
fundus ['fʌndəs], *s.* fondo.
funeral ['fjuːnərəl], *a.* funeral, fúnebre, funerario; ***funeral director,*** director de pompas fúnebres. — *s.* entierro; ***funeral march,*** marcha fúnebre; ***funeral parlour,*** funeraria; ***funeral service,*** funeral, funerales, *m.pl.*
funereal [fjuː'niəriəl], *a.* fúnebre, funéreo, funerario.
fungoid ['fʌŋgɔid], *a.* fungoideo.

fungosity [fʌŋˈgɔsiti], *s.* fungosidad.
fungous [ˈfʌŋgəs], *a.* fungoso.
fungus [ˈfʌŋgəs], *s.* (*pl.* **fungi** [ˈfʌŋgai]) hongo; excrecencia.
funicle [ˈfju:nikl], *s.* funículo.
funicular [fju:ˈnikjulə], *a.*, *s.* funicular.
funk [fʌŋk], *s.* (*fam.*) canguelo, mieditis; (*persona*) gallina; ***to be in a (blue) funk,*** tener canguelo *o* mieditis. — *v.t.*, *v.i.* (*fam.*) — ***it,*** rajarse por miedo, no tener agallas (para una cosa).
funnel [ˈfʌnəl], *s.* embudo; (*mar.*) chimenea (*de un vapor*); ***funnel-shaped,*** de forma de embudo.
funny [ˈfʌni], *a.* cómico, gracioso, divertido; chistoso; curioso, raro, extraño; ***funny-bone,*** hueso de risa; (*fam.*) ***funny ha-ha or funny peculiar?*** ¿gracioso o raro?; ***the funny thing (about it) is that,*** lo gracioso *o* lo raro (del caso) es que; ***I find it funny that,*** me hace gracia que; me parece curioso que; ***it struck him as funny that,*** le hizo gracia que; le pareció extraño que.
fur [fə:], *s.* piel, *f.*; pelo; sarro; saburra (*de la lengua*); ***fur-coat,*** abrigo de pieles; ***to make the fur fly,*** armar una marimorena. — *v.t.* cubrir con pieles; ***fur up,*** llenar de sarro. — *v.i.* — ***up,*** llenarse de sarro, incrustarse.
furbelow [ˈfə:bilou], *s.* farfalá, volante. — *v.t.* adornar con volantes *o* con perifollos.
furbish [ˈfə:biʃ], *v.t.* bruñir, pulir, limpiar.
furbishable [ˈfə:biʃəbl], *a.* capaz de ser pulido.
furcate [ˈfə:keit], *a.* ahorquillado, hendido.
furcation [fə:ˈkeiʃən], *s.* bifurcación, horcajadura.
furcular [ˈfə:kjulə], *a.* horcado.
furfur [ˈfə:fə], *s.* (*med.*) caspa, escamitas, *f.pl.*
furfuraceous [fə:fjuˈreiʃəs], *a.* furfuráceo.
furious [ˈfjuəriəs], *a.* furioso, furibundo.
furiousness [ˈfjuəriəsnis], *s.* frenesí, furia.
furl [fə:l], *v.t.* plegar, recoger; (*mar.*) aferrar; ***furling lines,*** aferravelas.
furlong [ˈfə:lɔŋ], *s.* estadio.
furlough [ˈfə:lou], *s.* (*mil.*) licencia, permiso. — *v.t.* dar licencia a.
furnace [ˈfə:nis], *s.* horno; hogar (*de caldera*); ***blast furnace,*** alto horno; ***furnace bar,*** botador; ***furnace charger,*** cebadera; ***furnace hoist,*** cabria de horno; ***oil-fired furnace,*** horno que funciona a base de petróleo.
furnish [ˈfə:niʃ], *v.t.* suministrar, proporcionar; equipar, dotar; aviar, amueblar, decorar; aducir; ***furnish s.o. with sth.,*** proporcionarle *o* suministrarle algo a alguien.
furnisher [ˈfə:niʃə], *s.* equipador, guarnecedor, decorador; proveedor, aparejador.
furnishing [ˈfə:niʃiŋ], *s.* habilitación, equipo, suministro; (*pl.*) accesorios, *m.pl.*, mueblaje, mobiliario, avíos, *m.pl.*
furnishment [ˈfə:niʃmənt], *s.* surtimiento, surtido.
furniture [ˈfə:nitʃə], *s.* muebles, *m.pl.*, mobiliario; mueblaje; equipo, aderezo; útiles, *m.pl.*; (*mar.*) aparejo; (*impr.*) fornitura; ***furniture depository,*** guardamuebles, *m.inv.*; ***furniture van,*** camión de mudanzas; ***piece of furniture,*** mueble.
furore [fjuˈrɔ:ri], *s.* furor.
furred [fə:d], *a.* forrado, cubierto de piel; cargado, cubierto con sarro.
furrier [ˈfʌriə], *s.* peletero.
furriery [ˈfʌriəri], *s.* peletería.
furring [ˈfə:riŋ], *s.* forro *o* guarnición de pieles; tabletas (para enlucidos), *f.pl.*; incrustaciones (de una caldera), *f.pl.*; operación de limpiar una caldera; sarro; contrapar de armadura falsa.
furrow [ˈfʌrou], *s.* (*agric.*) surco; tajea; (*fig.*) arruga, señal, *f.*; ***furrow-faced,*** (con la) cara arrugada. — *v.t.* surcar, hacer surcos en; estriar; ***to plough one's own furrow,*** seguir su propio camino.
furry [ˈfə:ri], *a.* hecho de pieles, adornado con pieles; peludo; sarroso.
further [ˈfə:ðə], *a. compar.* [FAR] más lejano, más distante; más adelantado; ulterior, adicional, nuevo, otro; más, más amplio; ***the further end,*** el extremo más lejano; ***till further orders,*** hasta nueva orden; ***without further delay,*** sin más demora. — *adv.* más lejos, más allá; además. — *v.t.* promover, fomentar; adelantar.
furtherance [ˈfə:ðərəns], *s.* promoción, fomento; adelantamiento.
furtherer [ˈfə:ðərə], *s.* promotor, fomentador; patrón, protector.
furthermore [fə:ðə:ˈmɔ:], *adv.* además, por otra parte.
furthermost [ˈfə:ðəmoust], *a.* más lejano, más remoto.
furthest [ˈfə:ðist], *a.* más lejano, más remoto; extremo. — *adv.* más lejos.
furtive [ˈfə:tiv], *a.* furtivo.
furuncle [ˈfjuərʌŋkl], *s.* furúnculo, divieso.
furuncular [fjuəˈrʌŋkjulə], *a.* furunculoso.
fury [ˈfjuəri], *s.* furia; furor; frenesí; ***to be in a fury,*** estar furioso.
furze [fə:z], *s.* (*bot.*) aulaga, tojo; retama.
fuse [fju:z], *s.* plomo, fusible; (*mil.*) espoleta, mecha; ***fuse-box,*** caja de (los) plomos *o* fusibles; ***fuse-extractor,*** sacaespoletas, *m.inv.* — *v.t.* fundir; fusionar. — *v.i.* fundirse; fusionarse; ***it has fused, the light has fused,*** se ha fundido el plomo.
fusee [fju:ˈzi:], *s.* fósforo; caracol, husillo (de reloj); (*artill.*) espoleta, espiga, pipa.
fuselage [ˈfju:zilɑ:ʒ], *s.* (*aer.*) fuselaje.
fusibility [fju:ziˈbiliti], *s.* fusibilidad.
fusible [ˈfju:zibl], *a.* fusible, fundible.
fusiform [ˈfju:zifɔ:m], *a.* fusiforme.
fusilier [fju:ziˈliə], *s.* (*mil.*) fusilero.
fusillade [fju:ziˈleid], *s.* descarga cerrada.
fusing [ˈfju:ziŋ], *a.* fundente. — *s.* de fusión; ***fusing point,*** punto de fusión.
fusion [ˈfju:ʒən], *s.* fusión; fundición.
fuss [fʌs], *s.* bulla; aspavientos, *m.pl.*; cisco; trámites, *m.pl.*; (*fam.*) ***fuss-pot,*** melindroso; mimoso; protestón; ***to make*** o ***kick up a fuss,*** armar un cisco, poner el grito en el cielo, organizar una protesta; ***to make a fuss of,*** mimar, hacer mimos a; agasajar; ***there's no call for so much fuss,*** no es para tanto. — *v.i.* inquietarse, preocuparse; ser pesado; ***fuss over s.o.,*** mimar, preocuparse excesivamente por.
fussy [ˈfʌsi], *a.* remilgado, melindroso; entrometido, pesado; exigente, minucioso, meticuloso.
fust [fʌst], *s.* fuste.
fustian [ˈfʌstiən], *a.* hecho de fustán; altisonante, enfático. — *s.* (*tej.*) fustán; (*fig.*) énfasis.
fustic [ˈfʌstik], *s.* fustete.
fusty [ˈfʌsti], *a.* mohoso, rancio; que huele a cerrado.
futile [ˈfju:tail], *a.* vano, inútil, infructuoso.
futility [fju:ˈtiliti], *s.* inutilidad, (lo) inútil.
futtock [ˈfʌtək], *s.* (*mar.*) genol; ***futtock-shrouds,*** pernadas de las arraigadas, *f.pl.*
future [ˈfju:tʃə], *a.* futuro, venidero. — *s.* porvenir, futuro; ***in (the) future,*** en el futuro *o* porvenir, en lo sucesivo; ***in the near future,*** en fecha próxima, en un futuro próximo.
futurism [ˈfju:tʃərizəm], *s.* futurismo.
futurist [ˈfju:tʃərist], *s.* futurista, *m.f.*
futurity [fju:ˈtjuəriti], *s.* estado futuro.
fuzz (1) [fʌz], *s.* pelusa, tamo; (*bot.*) ***fuzz-ball,*** bejín.
fuzz (2) [fʌz], *s.* (*fam.*) bofia, madán, *f.*
fuzziness [ˈfʌzinis], *s.* vellosidad.
fuzzy [ˈfʌzi], *a.* velloso; borroso, confuso; rizoso, crespo.
fyke [faik], *s.* nasa.

G

G, g [dʒiː], séptima letra del alfabeto. — *s.* (*mús.*) *G*, sol; ***G clef***, clave de sol.
gab (1) [gæb], *s.* (*fam.*) cháchara, parloteo; ***to have the gift of the gab***, tener mucha labia, tener pico de oro. — *v.i.* parlotear, charlar.
gab (2) [gæb], *s.* (*mec.*) gancho, horquilla.
gabardine [ˈgæbədiːn], *s.* gabardina (*tela*).
gabble [gæbl], *s.* algarabía, cotorreo, parloteo. — *v.t.* farfullar, decir atropelladamente. — *v.i.* parlotear, picotear, farfullar, cotorrear.
gabbler [ˈgæblə], *s.* charlador, hablador, parlador, chacharero, picotero.
gabbro [ˈgæbrou], *s.* (*geol.*) roca compuesta de feldespato y diálaga.
gabion [ˈgeibiən], *s.* (*fort.*) gavión, cestón.
gable [geibl], *s.* (*arq.*) faldón; gablete; ***gable-end***, socarrén, alero.
Gabon [gæˈbɔn]. (el) Gabón.
Gabonese [gæbɔˈniːz], *a.*, *s.* gabonés, *m.*
gad (1) [gæd], *s.* chuzo; barra, lingote; ***gad-fly***, tábano.
gad (2) [gæd], *s.* (*fam.*) ***to be on the gad***, andar callejeando *o* de pendoneo. — *v.i.* andorrear, callejear; ***gad about***, pendonear, corretear.
gadabout [ˈgædəbaut], *a.* callejero, vagabundo. — *s.* persona callejera.
gadder [ˈgædə], *s.* callejero, andorrero, correntón; mujer cantonera.
gadding [ˈgædiŋ], *s.* vagancia, callejeo.
gadget [ˈgædʒit], *s.* artefacto, dispositivo, chisme.
gadgetry [ˈgædʒitri], *s.* chismería.
gadwall [ˈgædwɔːl], *s.* (*orn.*) ánade silvestre grande.
Gael [geil], *s.* celta, *m.f.*, escocés.
Gaelic [ˈgeilik], *a.*, *s.* gaélico, céltico.
gaff (1) [gæf], *s.* garfio, gancho; bichero; (*mar.*) botavara; (*mar.*) ***gaff-boom***, verga de cangreja; ***gaff sail***, cangreja.
gaff (2) [gæf], *s.* ***to blow the gaff***, chivarse.
gaffe [gæf], *s.* (*fam.*) metedura de pata, plancha.
gaffer [ˈgæfə], *s.* tío; capataz; jefe; ***old gaffer***, vejete.
gaffle [gæfl], *s.* espolón, navaja de gallo.
gag [gæg], *s.* mordaza; (*teat.*) morcilla, chiste. — *v.t.* amordazar. — *v.i.* (*teat.*) meter morcilla; chunguearse, bromear.
gage [geidʒ], *s.* prenda, caución; guante, reto, gaje. — *v.t.* (*ant.*) empeñar, dar en prenda; apostar.
gaggle [gægl], *s.* bandada (*gansos*). — *v.i.* graznar.
gaiety [ˈgeiiti], *s.* alegría; regocijo.
gaily [ˈgeili], *adv.* alegremente.
gain [gein], *s.* ganancia; provecho; aumento; (*carp.*) gárgol, ranura. — *v.t.* ganar; conseguir; alcanzar; ***to gain the day***, vencer, triunfar. — *v.i.* medrar, mejorar, crecer; aumentar; ganar terreno; (*reloj*) adelantar; ***gain on***, ir alcanzando.
gainer [ˈgeinə], *s.* ganador; ***to be the gainer***, salir ganando.
gainful [ˈgeinful], *a.* ganancioso, provechoso; ***gainful employment***, trabajo remunerado.
gainfulness [ˈgeinfulnis], *s.* provecho.
gainsay [geinˈsei], *irr.* *v.t.* negar; contradecir; contrariar.
gainsaying [geinˈseiiŋ], *s.* oposición; contradicción.
gait [geit], *s.* paso; modo de andar; andares, *m.pl.*
gaiter [ˈgeitə], *s.* polaina.
gala [ˈgɑːlə], *a.* de fiesta; de gala. — *s.* fiesta.
galactic [gəˈlæktik], *a.* galáctico.
galactometer [gæləkˈtɔmitə], *s.* galactómetro.
galangal [gəˈlæŋgəl], *s.* (*bot.*) galanga.
galantine [ˈgælənti:n], *s.* galantina.
galaxy [ˈgæləksi], *s.* (*astron.*) galaxia; (*fig.*) pléyade, *f.*
galbanum [ˈgælbənəm], *s.* gálbano.
gale [geil], *s.* galerna; vendaval.
galenic(al) [geiˈlenik(əl)], *a.* galénico.
Galenist [ˈgeilənist], *s.* galenista, *m.f.*
Galilean [gæliˈliən], *a.*, *s.* galileo.
galiot [GALLIOT].
galipot [ˈgælipɔt], *s.* galipote.
gall (1) [gɔːl], *s.* hiel, *f.*, bilis, *f.inv.*; rencor; (*fam.*) descaro; (*vet.*) rozadura, matadura; ***gall-stone***, cálculo biliario; ***to vent one's gall on***, ensañarse con. — *v.t.* lastimar rozando; mortificar.
gall (2) [gɔːl], *s.* (*bot.*) ***gall-apple***, ***gall-nut***, agalla; ***gall-fly***, cinípido.
gallant [ˈgælənt], *a.* valiente, animoso; denodado; gallardo, bizarro; galante. — *s.* galán.
gallantry, gallantness [ˈgæləntri, -nis], *s.* valentía, valor; gallardía, bizarría; galantería, galanteo; bizarría, elegancia.
galleon [ˈgæljən], *s.* (*mar.*) galeón.
gallery [ˈgæləri], *s.* galería; ***art gallery***, museo de arte; ***to play to the gallery***, hablar para la galería.
galley [ˈgæli], *s.* (*mar.*) galera; falúa; cocina, fogón; (*impr.*) galera; (*impr.*) ***galley-proof***, galerada; ***galley-slave***, galeote; ***galley-tiles***, azulejos, *m.pl.*
galliard [ˈgæljɑːd], *a.* (*ant.*) vivo, alegre. — *s.* gallarda.
Gallic(an) [ˈgælik(ən)], *a.* galo, galicano.
gallic [ˈgælik], *a.* (*bot.*) agálico; ***gallic acid***, ácido agálico.
gallicism [ˈgælisizəm], *s.* galicismo.
gallicize [ˈgælisaiz], *v.t.* afrancesar. — *v.i.* afrancesarse.
galligaskins [gæliˈgæskinz], *s.pl.* calzacalzones, gregüescos.
gallimaufry [gæliˈmɔːfri], *s.* gigote, picadillo; (*fig.*) mezcolanza.
gallinaceous [gæliˈneiʃəs], *a.* gallináceo.
gallinule [ˈgælinjuːl], *s.* gallineta, fúlica.
galliot [ˈgæliət], *s.* (*mar.*) galeota.
gallipot [ˈgælipɔt], *s.* orza, bote, pote, vasija de barro vidriada.
gallium [ˈgæliəm], *s.* (*quím.*) galio.
gallivant [ˈgælivænt], *v.i.* (*fam.*) callejear; viajar por placer; pindonguear.
gallon [ˈgælən], *s.* galón.
galloon [gəˈluːn], *s.* (*tej.*) galón; trencilla; ribecillo.
gallop [ˈgæləp], *s.* galope; galopada; ***at full gallop***, a galope tendido, a uña de caballo; ***to break into a gallop***, echar a galope. — *v.t.* hacer galopar. — *v.i.* galopar; ***gallop through sth.***, hacer algo al galope.
gallopade [gæləˈpeid], *s.* caracoleo; (*mús.*) galop.
galloping [ˈgæləpiŋ], *a.* galopante; ***galloping consumption***, tisis galopante.
gallows [ˈgælouz], *s.* horca, patíbulo; armazón, *f.* ***gallows-bird***, carne de horca.
galop [ˈgæləp], *s.* (*baile*) galop.
galore [gəˈlɔː], *adv.* a porrillo, a manta.
galosh [gəˈlɔʃ], *s.* chanclo.
galvanic [gælˈvænik], *a.* galvánico.
galvanism [ˈgælvənizəm], *s.* galvanismo.
galvanization [gælvənaiˈzeiʃən], *s.* galvanización.
galvanize [ˈgælvənaiz], *v.t.* galvanizar; ***galvanize s.o. into action***, impulsar violentamente a la acción a alguien.
galvanometer [gælvəˈnɔmitə], *s.* galvanómetro.
galvanometric [gælvənoˈmetrik], *a.* galvanométrico.
galvanometry [gælvəˈnɔmitri], *s.* galvanometría.
Gambia [ˈgæmbiə], **The.** Gambia.
Gambian [ˈgæmbiən], *a.*, *s.* gambiano.
gambit [ˈgæmbit], *s.* (*ajedrez*) gambito; (*fig.*) táctica
gamble [gæmbl], *s.* empresa arriesgada, aventura, cosa aleatoria. — *v.t.* jugar; aventurar; ***gamble***

away, perder *o* desperdiciar en el juego *o* jugando. — *v.i.* jugar; aventurarse.
gambler [ˈgæmblə], *s.* jugador; garitero, tahur.
gambling [ˈgæmbliŋ], *s.* juego; ***gambling-den*** o ***house,*** garito, casa de juego.
gamboge [gæmˈboudʒ], *s.* gomaguta.
gambol [gæmbl], *s.* brinco, retozo. — *v.i.* brincar, triscar, retozar.
gambrel [ˈgæmbrəl], *s.* corvejón; (*arq.*) ***gambrel roof,*** techo a la holandesa.
game (1) [geim], *a.* animoso, valiente; dispuesto; ***to be game for,*** estar dispuesto a. — *s.* juego; partida; (*dep.*) partido; deporte; caza, piezas (de caza); (*bridge*) manga; ***big game,*** caza mayor; ***fair game,*** presa legítima; ***game-bag,*** zurrón, morral; ***game-bird,*** ave de caza; ***game-cock,*** gallo de pelea; ***game-keeper,*** guardabosque, guarda de coto, *m.*; ***game-preserve,*** coto *o* vedado de caza; (*fig.*) ***the game's up,*** estamos perdidos *o* aviados, nos han calado, nos tienen calados; ***to beat s.o. at his own game,*** vencer a alguien con sus propias armas; ***to make game of,*** burlarse de; ***to be out of the game,*** haber(se) quedado fuera de combate; ***to play the game,*** jugar limpio. — *v.i.* jugar.
game (2) [geim], *a.* cojo.
gamesome [ˈgeimsəm], *a.* juguetón, retozón.
gamester [ˈgeimstə], *s.* jugador, tahur.
gaming [ˈgeimiŋ], *s.* juego; ***gaming house,*** casa de juego, garito; ***gaming table,*** mesa de juego.
gamma [ˈgæmə], *s.* gama; ***gamma rays,*** rayos gama, *m.pl.*
gammer [ˈgæmə], *s.* vieja, abuelita.
gammon (1) [ˈgæmən], *s.* jamón. — *v.t.* curar.
gammon (2) [ˈgæmən], *s.* añagaza. — *v.t.* engañar.
gammon (3) [ˈgæmən], *s.* lance del juego de chaquete. — *v.t.* ganar doble partida de chaquete (*a alguien*).
gamopetalous [gæmouˈpetələs], *a.* (*bot.*) gamopétalo.
gamosepalous [gæmouˈsepələs], *a.* (*bot.*) gamosépalo.
gamut [ˈgæmət], *s.* gama.
gamy [ˈgeimi], *a.* manido, salvajino.
gander [ˈgændə], *s.* ánsar, ganso.
gang [gæŋ], *s.* pandilla; cuadrilla; brigada; banda; juego (*de herramientas*); (*min.*) ganga; (*mar.*) ***gang-board,*** plancha, andamio; (*elec.*) ***gang condenser,*** condensador múltiple; ***gang-plank,*** pasamano; plancha; ***gang-plough,*** arado de reja múltiple; ***gang-saw,*** sierra múltiple. — *v.i.* — ***up,*** juntarse, agavillarse; ***gang up against,*** conchabarse contra, unirse contra.
ganglion [ˈgæŋgliən], *s.* (*anat.*) ganglio.
ganglionic [gæŋgliˈɔnik], *a.* ganglionar.
gangrene [ˈgæŋgri:n], *s.* gangrena. — *v.t.* gangrenar. — *v.i.* gangrenarse.
gangrenous [ˈgæŋgrinəs], *a.* gangrenoso.
gangster [ˈgæŋstə], *s.* gángster, atracador.
gangway [ˈgæŋwei], *s.* (*mar.*) pasamano, pasarela, escalerilla; pasadizo, corredor. — *interj.* ¡paso!
gannet [ˈgænit], *s.* (*orn.*) bubia.
ganoid [ˈgænɔid], *a.* (*ict.*) ganoideo.
gantry [ˈgæntri], *s.* grúa corrediza; caballete.
gaol [dʒeil], *s.* cárcel, *f.*; (*fam.*) ***gaol-bird,*** delincuente empedernido.
gaoler [ˈdʒeilə], *s.* carcelero.
gap [gæp], *s.* portillo, abertura; brecha, boquete; hueco, vacío; claro, laguna; quebrada; distancia; espacio; intervalo; resquicio; ***generation gap,*** problema *o* enfrentamiento generacional.
gape [geip], *s.* bostezo; abertura, boquete. — *v.i.* bostezar; embobarse, quedarse embobado, ***gape at,*** mirar boquiabierto.
gaper [ˈgeipə], *s.* bostezador; papamoscas, *m.inv.*, bobalicón.
gar [gɑ:], *s.* (*ict.*) sollo.
garage [ˈgærɑ:dʒ], *s.* garaje. — *v.t.* dejar en garaje.
garb [gɑ:b], *s.* traje, atuendo. — *v.t.* vestir, ataviar.
garbage [ˈgɑ:bidʒ], *s.* basura, desperdicios, *m.pl.*, inmundicias, *f.pl.*; (*Am.*) [RUBBISH]; (*Am.*) ***garbage can*** [DUSTBIN]; (*Am.*) ***garbage man*** [DUSTMAN].
garbel [gɑ:bl], *s.* (*mar.*) aparadura.
garble [gɑ:bl], *v.t.* alterar, falsificar, falsear; escoger, entresacar.
garbler [ˈgɑ:blə], *s.* garbillador; falsificador, alterador.
garboard [ˈgɑ:bɔ:d], *s.* (*mar.*) aparadura, tablón de aparadura.
garden [gɑ:dn], *s.* jardín; huerta; huerto; ***garden city,*** ciudad jardín; ***garden-mould,*** abono vegetal; ***garden party,*** fiesta de jardín. — *v.t.* trabajar en, cultivar. — *v.i.* trabajar en el huerto *o* jardín.
gardener [ˈgɑ:dnə], *s.* jardinero; hortelano.
gardenia [gɑ:ˈdi:niə], *s.* (*bot.*) gardenia.
gardening [ˈgɑ:dniŋ], *s.* horticultura; jardinería.
garfish [ˈgɑ:fiʃ], *s.* (*ict.*) belona.
gargantuan [gɑ:ˈgæntjuən], *a.* pantagruélico.
gargarism [ˈgɑ:gərizəm], *s.* gargarismo.
gargarize [ˈgɑ:gəraiz], *v.t., v.i.* gargarizar, hacer gárgaras.
garget [ˈgɑ:git], *s.* (*vet.*) inflamación de la garganta del ganado; enfermedad de las ubres.
gargle [gɑ:gl], *s.* gárgara, gargarismo. — *v.t., v.i.* gargarizar, hacer gárgaras.
gargoyle [ˈgɑ:gɔil], *s.* (*arq.*) gárgola.
garish [ˈgɛəriʃ], *a.* llamativo; chillón; ostentoso.
garishness [ˈgɛəriʃnis], *s.* (lo) llamativo, (lo) chillón; (lo) ostentoso.
garland [ˈgɑ:lənd], *s.* guirnalda; (*mar.*) roñada. — *v.t.* enguirnaldar.
garlic [ˈgɑ:lik], *s.* ajo.
garlicky [ˈgɑ:liki], *a.* que huele *o* sabe a ajo.
garment [ˈgɑ:mənt], *s.* prenda (*de vestir*).
garner [ˈgɑ:nə], *s.* granero; acopio. — *v.t.* entrojar, almacenar; recoger.
garnet [ˈgɑ:nit], *s.* granate.
garnish [ˈgɑ:niʃ], *s.* aderezo; adorno; guarnición. — *v.t.* aderezar; adornar; guarnecer; aprestar; ***garnished with vegetables,*** con guarnición de verduras.
garnisher [ˈgɑ:niʃə], *s.* aderezador; guarnecedor.
garnishment [ˈgɑ:niʃmənt], *s.* ornamento, adorno; (*for.*) entredicho.
garniture [ˈgɑ:nitʃə], *s.* guarnición, adorno.
garret [ˈgærət], *s.* guardilla, desván.
garrison [ˈgærisən], *s.* (*mil.*) guarnición. — *v.t.* guarnecer; guarnicionar; poner en guarnición.
garrotte [gəˈrɔt], *s.* garrote. — *v.t.* dar garrote a, agarrotar.
garrulity [gəˈru:liti], *s.* garrulidad, locuacidad.
garrulous [ˈgærələs], *a.* gárrulo, locuaz, charlatán.
garter [ˈgɑ:tə], *s.* liga; ***Order of the Garter,*** Orden de la Jarretera.
garth [gɑ:θ], *s.* patio.
gas (1) [gæs], *s.* gas, *m.*; charloteo; (*fam.*) ***gas-bag,*** charlatán; ***gas-burner,*** mechero de gas; ***gas-fitter,*** gasista, *m.*; ***gas-fitting,*** instalación de gas; ***gas-holder,*** gasómetro; ***gas-light,*** luz de gas; mechero de gas; ***gas-main,*** cañería principal *o* maestra de gas; ***gas-mask,*** careta antigás; ***gas-meter,*** contador de(l) gas; ***gas-oven,*** cocina de gas; ***gas-works,*** fábrica de gas; ***poison gas,*** gas asfixiante. — *v.t.* asfixiar con gas; atacar con gas; gasear.
gas (2) [gæs], *s.* [GASOLINE]; (*fam.*) ***to step on the gas,*** acelerar (la marcha).
gasconade [gæskəˈneid], *s.* gasconada, fanfarronada. — *v.i.* jactarse, fanfarronear.
gaseous [ˈgæsiəs], *a.* gaseoso.
gash (1) [gæʃ], *s.* cuchillada, raja. — *v.t.* acuchillar, dar una cuchillada a, rajar.
gash (2) [gæʃ], *a.* (*fam.*) que sobra *o* sobre.

gasification [gæsifi'keiʃən], *s.* gasificación.
gasify ['gæsifai], *v.t.* gasificar.
gasket ['gæskit], *s.* (*mec.*) junta, empaquetadura; (*pl.*, *mar.*) tomadores, *m.pl.*; (*fam.*) ***to blow a gasket,*** subirse por las paredes.
gaskin ['gæskin], *s.* empaquetadura.
gasogene [GAZOGENE].
gasolene ['gæsoli:n], *s.* gasoleno, gasolina.
gasolier [gæso'liə], *s.* candelabro colgante (*para gas*).
gasoline ['gæsoli:n], (*Am.*) [PETROL].
gasometer [gæ'sɔmitə], *s.* gasómetro.
gasometry [gæ'sɔmitri], *s.* gasometría.
gasoscope ['gæsoskoup], *s.* gasoscopio.
gasp [gɑ:sp], *s.* boqueada; grito entrecortado; ***to be at one's last gasp,*** estar dando las boqueadas. — *v.i.* boquear; ***gasp for,*** anhelar; ***gasp for breath,*** jadear.
gasper ['gɑ:spə], *s.* (*fam.*) pitillo.
gassy ['gæsi], *a.* gaseoso.
gasteropod ['gæstərəpɔd], *a.*, *s.* gasterópodo.
gastralgia [gæs'trældʒə], *s.* gastralgia.
gastric ['gæstrik], *a.* gástrico.
gastritis [gæs'traitis], *s.* gastritis, *f.inv.*
gastronome ['gæstronoum], *s.* gastrónomo.
gastronomic(al) [gæstrə'nɔmik(əl)], *a.* gastronómico.
gastronomy [gæs'trɔnəmi], *s.* gastronomía.
gastropod [GASTEROPOD].
gate [geit], *s.* puerta; verja, cancela; portal, portillo; barrera; entrada; ***gate-crash,*** meterse de rondón en; ***gate-crasher,*** intruso; ***gate-keeper,*** portero; (*f.c.*) guardabarrera, *m.*; (*dep.*) ***gate-money,*** taquilla, ingresos de entrada, *m.pl.*; ***gate-post,*** poste; ***between you, me and the gate-post,*** entre nosotros. — *v.t.* poner puertas a; castigar (*a un alumno*) haciéndole quedarse en el colegio.
gated ['geitid], *a.* que tiene puertas.
gateway ['geitwei], *s.* puerta, entrada; paso.
gather ['gæðə], *s.* (*cost.*) frunce. — *v.t.* reunir, allegar, acumular; recolectar, cosechar; coger; congregar, juntar; recaudar; (*cost.*) fruncir; (*impr.*) alzar; colegir, deducir, inferir; ***gather breath,*** tomar aliento; ***gather the crops,*** recoger *o* levantar las cosechas; ***gather dust,*** cubrirse de polvo; ***gather flesh,*** echar, criar carnes; ***gather grapes,*** vendimiar; ***gather in,*** recoger; ***gather money,*** recaudar dinero; ***gather speed,*** ir tomando velocidad; ***gather strength,*** cobrar fuerzas; ***gather one's thoughts,*** concentrarse; ***gather together,*** juntar; ***gather up,*** recoger. — *v.i.* reunirse, juntarse, congregarse; acumularse; condensarse; amontonarse; formar pus. — **gather o.s.,** *v.r.* — ***together,*** recobrarse, serenarse, sobreponerse.
gatherable ['gæðərəbl], *a.* deducible; que puede juntarse *o* cosecharse.
gatherer ['gæðərə], *s.* cogedor; recolector; recaudador; fruncidor; alzador.
gathering ['gæðəriŋ], *s.* recolección; recaudación; reunión, asamblea, muchedumbre; alzado; supuración; fruncido.
gauche [gouʃ], *a.* torpe.
gaucherie ['gouʃəri], *s.* torpeza.
gaud [gɔ:d], *s.* objeto charro.
gaudery ['gɔ:dəri], *s.* lujo ostentoso; (*fam.*) charrada.
gaudiness ['gɔ:dinis], *s.* lo chillón *o* llamativo; charrada.
gaudy ['gɔ:di], *a.* chillón, llamativo, vistoso; charro.
gauge [geidʒ], *s.* regla, norma de medir; medida; calibre; aforo; indicador; manómetro; (*mar.*) calibrador, gramil; calado; (*f.c.*) entrevía, ancho. — *v.t.* medir, graduar, calibrar, escantillar, aforar; (*mar.*) arquear; estimar, calcular.
gauging ['geidʒiŋ], *s.* (el) calcular, (el) calibrar, (el) medir.
Gaul [gɔ:l], *s.* Galia (*país*); galo (*hombre*).
Gaulish ['gɔ:liʃ], *a.* galo.
gaultheria [gæl'tiəriə], *s.* (*bot.*) gualteria.
gaunt ['gɔ:nt], *a.* escuálido, demacrado; macilento.
gauntlet ['gɔ:ntlit], *s.* guantelete; guante; ***to fling*** o ***throw down the gauntlet,*** arrojar el guante; ***to run the gauntlet,*** correr baquetas, pasar por baquetas; ***to take up the gauntlet,*** recoger el guante.
gauze [gɔ:z], *s.* gasa, cendal; ***silk gauze,*** gasa de seda.
gauziness ['gɔ:zinis], *s.* diafanidad.
gauzy ['gɔ:zi], *a.* diáfano.
gavel ['gævəl], *s.* mazo, martillo.
gavotte [gə'vɔt], *s.* gavota.
gawk [gɔ:k], *s.* páparo, bobo. — *v.i.* mirar boquiabierto, papar moscas.
gawky ['gɔ:ki], *a.* desgarbado.
gay [gei], *a.* alegre; festivo.
gayness ['geinis], *s.* alegría; (lo) festivo.
gaze [geiz], *s.* mirada fija. — *v.i.* — ***at,*** mirar con fijeza, contemplar.
gazebo [gə'zi:bou], *s.* mirador.
gazelle [gə'zel], *s.* gacela.
gazer ['geizə], *s.* mirón.
gazette [gə'zet], *s.* gaceta. — *v.t.* publicar en (la) gaceta.
gazetteer [gæzi'tiə], *s.* gacetero; diccionario geográfico.
gazogene ['gæzodʒi:n], *s.* aparato para la fabricación de bebidas gaseosas.
gear [giə], *s.* (*mec.*) engranaje; rueda dentada; marcha, velocidad; pertrechos, *m.pl.*, avíos, *m.pl.*, bártulos, *m.pl.*; aparejo; arreos, *m.pl.*, arneses, *m.pl.*; herramientas, *f.pl.*, utensilios, *m.pl.*; aparato, mecanismo; ***gear-box, gear-case,*** caja de engranajes *o* de velocidades; ***gear-lever,*** (palanca de) cambio de marchas; ***gear-ratio,*** razón de engranajes; ***in gear,*** engranado; en juego; ***low, bottom gear,*** primera (velocidad); ***neutral (gear),*** punto muerto; ***out of gear,*** desengranado; (*fig.*) alterado; ***second gear,*** segunda; ***top gear,*** tercera, cuarta; ***to engage first gear,*** meter (la) primera; ***to put in gear,*** engranar; (*fig.*) ***to throw out of gear,*** alterar. — *v.t.* engranar; aparejar, pertrechar; ***to be geared to,*** estar organizado *o* ideado para. — *v.i.* engranar.
gearing ['giəriŋ], *s.* (*mec.*) engranaje.
gee [dʒi:], *interj.* ***gee up!*** ¡arre!; (*Am.*) ***gee(whiz)!*** ¡hombre! ¡por Dios!
gee-gee ['dʒi:-dʒi:], *s.* (*infantil*) caballito.
geese [gi:s], *s.pl.* [GOOSE].
geezer ['gi:zə], *s.* (*fam.*) ***old geezer,*** vejestorio, carcamal.
Gehenna [gi'henə], *s.* Gehena, infierno.
gelatine ['dʒeləti:n], *s.* gelatina.
gelatinate, gelatinize [dʒe'lætineit, -aiz], *v.t.* gelatinizar. — *v.i.* gelatinizarse.
gelatinous [dʒe'lætinəs], *a.* gelatinoso.
gelation [dʒe'leiʃən], *s.* congelación.
geld (1) [geld], *v.t.* castrar, capar.
geld (2) [geld], *s.* tributo antiguo.
gelder ['geldə], *s.* castrador, capador.
gelding ['geldiŋ], *s.* caballo capado; capón.
gelignite ['dʒelignait], *s.* gelignita.
gem [dʒem], *s.* gema, piedra preciosa; (*lit.*, *fig.*) joya, alhaja, dije.
gemel ['dʒeməl], *a.*, *s.* gemelo; ***gemel ring,*** sortija de alianza.
geminate ['dʒemineit], *s.* (*bot.*) geminado. — *v.t.* geminar.
gemination [dʒemi'neiʃən], *s.* geminación.
Gemini ['dʒeminai], *s.* (*astron.*, *astrol.*) Géminis, *m.*
gemma ['dʒemə], *s.* (*bot.*) botón; (*zool.*) yema.
gemmate ['dʒemeit], *a.* (*bot.*, *zool.*) que tiene yemas *o* botones.
gemmation [dʒe'meiʃən], *s.* (*bot.*, *zool.*) gemación; vernación.

gemmule [ˈdʒemjuːl], *s.* (*bot.*) botoncillo, botón pequeño.
gender [ˈdʒendə], *s.* género.
gene [dʒiːn], *s.* (*biol.*) gen.
genealogical [dʒiːniəˈlɔdʒikəl], *a.* genealógico.
genealogist [dʒiːniˈælədʒist], *s.* genealogista, *m.f.*
genealogy [dʒiːniˈælədʒi], *s.* genealogía.
generable [ˈdʒenərəbl], *a.* generable.
general [ˈdʒenərəl], *a.* general; ***to become general,*** generalizarse; ***general election,*** elecciones generales, *f.pl.*; ***general factotum,*** criado para todo; ***general practitioner,*** médico no especializado, de medicina general; ***as a general rule,*** por regla general; ***the general run of,*** la generalidad de; ***general staff,*** estado mayor general; ***in general,*** en general, por lo general; en términos generales. — *s.* general.
generalissimo [dʒenərəˈlisimou], *s.* generalísimo.
generality [dʒenəˈræliti], *s.* generalidad.
generalization [dʒenərəlaiˈzeiʃən], *s.* generalización.
generalize [ˈdʒenərəlaiz], *v.t.*, *v.i.* generalizar.
generalness [ˈdʒenərəlnis], *s.* extensión, frecuencia.
generalship [ˈdʒenərəlʃip], *s.* generalato; don de mando; estrategia, dirección.
generant [ˈdʒenərənt], *a.* generativo, generador, generatriz.
generate [ˈdʒenəreit], *v.t.* engendrar, generar. — *v.i.* procrear; engendrarse, originarse.
generation [dʒenəˈreiʃən], *s.* generación.
generative [ˈdʒenərətiv], *a.* generativo.
generator [ˈdʒenəreitə], *s.* generador; (*Am.*) [DYNAMO]; ***generator unit,*** grupo electrógeno.
generatrix [ˈdʒenəreitriks], *s.* generatriz, *f.*
generic(al) [dʒeˈnerik(əl)], *a.* genérico.
generosity, generousness [dʒenəˈrɔsiti, ˈdʒenərəsnis], *s.* generosidad; liberalidad, largueza, esplendidez.
generous [ˈdʒenərəs], *a.* generoso; liberal, desprendido, espléndido; amplio, abundante.
Genesis [ˈdʒenisis]. (*bíb.*) el Génesis, *m.inv.*
genesis [ˈdʒenisis], *s.* génesis, *f.inv.*
genet [ˈdʒenit], *s.* jineta; jaca.
genetic [dʒiˈnetik], *a.* genésico, genético.
genetics [dʒiˈnetiks], *s.* genética.
Genevan [dʒiˈniːvən], *a.*, *s.* ginebriño, ginebrés; calvinista, *m.f.*
genial [ˈdʒiːniəl], *a.* afable, cordial, simpático.
geniality [dʒiːniˈæliti], *s.* afabilidad, cordialidad, simpatía.
genii [ˈdʒiːniai], *s.pl.* [GENIUS].
genista [dʒiˈnistə], *s.* retama.
genital [ˈdʒenitəl], *a.* genital. — *s.pl.* genitales, *m.pl.*
genitive [ˈdʒenitiv], *a.*, *s.* (*gram.*) genitivo.
genius [ˈdʒiːniəs], *s.* (*pl.* **genii** [ˈdʒiːniai]) genio; (*pl.* **geniuses** [ˈdʒiːniəsiz]) genio, talento, superdotado; ***to have a genius for,*** tener el don de.
Genoese [dʒenouˈiːz], *a.*, *s.* genovés.
gent [dʒent], *s.* (*fam.*) [GENTLEMAN]; (*fam.*) ***the gents',*** el váter.
genteel [dʒenˈtiːl], *a.* finísimo, excesivamente fino, cursi.
gentian [ˈdʒenʃən], *s.* genciana.
Gentile [ˈdʒentail], *a.*, *s.* gentil.
gentile [ˈdʒentail], *a.* (*gram.*) gentilicio.
gentility, genteelness [dʒenˈtiliti, -ˈtiːlnis], *s.* nobleza; gentileza; delicadeza; finura exagerada, cursilería.
gentle [dʒentl], *a.* suave, dulce; benigno; manso, dócil; moderado; ligero; bien nacido; ***gentle reader,*** querido lector; ***gentle sex,*** bello sexo, sexo débil.
gentlefolk [ˈdʒentlfouk], *s.* gente bien nacida.
gentleman [ˈdʒentlmən], *s.* caballero, señor; gentilhombre; ***gentleman farmer,*** hacendado; ***gentleman of fortune,*** caballero de industria; ***gentleman of leisure,*** persona que vive de sus rentas; ***gentleman of the road,*** salteador de caminos; vagabundo; ***gentlemen's agreement,*** pacto de caballeros, acuerdo verbal.
gentlemanliness [ˈdʒentlmənlinis], *s.* caballerosidad.
gentlemanly [ˈdʒentlmənli], *a.* caballeroso.
gentleness [ˈdʒentlnis], *s.* dulzura, suavidad; docilidad, mansedumbre.
gentlewoman [ˈdʒentlwumən], *s.* señora, dama.
gentry [ˈdʒentri], *s.* señorío; gente bien nacida; pequeña aristocracia; (*ironía*) gentecilla; ***light-fingered gentry,*** rateros, *m.pl.*, descuideros, *m.pl.*
genuflection [dʒenjuˈflekʃən], *s.* genuflexión.
genuine [ˈdʒenjuin], *a.* auténtico, verdadero, genuino; sincero.
genuineness [ˈdʒenjuinnis], *s.* autenticidad, legitimidad.
genus [ˈdʒiːnəs, ˈdʒenəs], *s.* (*pl.* **genera** [ˈdʒenərə]) género.
geocentric [dʒioˈsentrik], *a.* geocéntrico.
geodesy [dʒiˈɔdisi], *s.* geodesia, topografía.
geodetic(al) [dʒioˈdetik(əl)], *a.* geodésico.
geogenic [dʒioˈdʒenik], *a.* geogénico, geogónico.
geognosy [dʒiˈɔgnəsi], *s.* geognosia.
geographer [dʒiˈɔgrəfə], *s.* geógrafo.
geographic(al) [dʒioˈgræfik(əl)], *a.* geográfico.
geography [dʒiˈɔgrəfi], *s.* geografía.
geologic(al) [dʒioˈlɔdʒik(əl)], *a.* geológico.
geologist [dʒiˈɔlədʒist], *s.* geólogo.
geologize [dʒiˈɔlədʒaiz], *v.i.* estudiar (la) geología.
geology [dʒiˈɔlədʒi], *s.* geología.
geomancy [ˈdʒiːomænsi], *s.* geomancia.
geometer [dʒiˈɔmitə], *s.* geómetra, *m.*
geometric(al) [dʒioˈmetrik(əl)], *a.* geométrico, geometral.
geometrician [dʒiɔmiˈtriʃən], *s.* geómetra, *m.f.*
geometrize [dʒiˈɔmitraiz], *v.i.* geometrizar.
geometry [dʒiˈɔmitri], *s.* geometría.
geonomic [dʒioˈnɔmik], *a.* geonómico.
geonomy [dʒiˈɔnəmi], *s.* geonomía.
geophysics [dʒioˈfiziks], *s.* geofísica.
georama [dʒioˈrɑːmə], *s.* georama, *m.*, globo geográfico.
Geordie [ˈdʒɔːdi], *a.*, *s.* (*fam.*) natural de Newcastle.
Georgian [ˈdʒɔːdʒən], *a.*, *s.* georgiano.
georgic(al) [ˈdʒɔːdʒik(əl)], *a.* geórgico.
geoscopy [dʒiˈɔskəpi], *s.* geoscopia.
geranium [dʒiˈreiniəm], *s.* geranio.
gerfalcon [ˈdʒəːfɔː(l)kən], *s.* (*orn.*) gerifalte.
geriatric [dʒeriˈætrik], *a.* geriátrico.
geriatrics [dʒeriˈætriks], *s.* geriatría.
germ [dʒəːm], *s.* microbio; germen; (*bot.*) yema, simiente; ***germ-carrier,*** portador de microbios; ***germ cell,*** célula embrionaria; ***germ warfare,*** guerra bacteriológica.
German [ˈdʒəːmən], *a.*, *s.* alemán; germánico; ***German measles,*** rubéola; ***German silver,*** alpaca, metal blanco, plata alemana; ***German tinder,*** yesca.
german [ˈdʒəːmən], *a.* carnal; ***brother-german,*** hermano carnal; ***cousin-german,*** primo carnal.
germander [dʒəːˈmændə], *s.* pinillo, maro.
germane [dʒəːˈmein], *a.* afín, relacionado; ***germane to,*** pertinente a, oportuno para.
Germanic [dʒəːˈmænik], *a.* germánico.
Germanism [ˈdʒəːmənizəm], *s.* germanismo.
germanium [dʒəːˈmeiniəm], *s.* germanio.
Germanophile, Germanophil [dʒəːˈmænofail, -fil], *s.* germanófilo.
Germanophobe [dʒəːˈmænofoub], *s.* germanófobo.
Germanophobia [dʒəːmænoˈfoubiə], *s.* germanofobia.

germicidal [ˈdʒəːmisaidəl], *a.* germicida, *m.f.*
germicide [ˈdʒəːmisaid], *s.* germicida, *m.*
germinal [ˈdʒəːminəl], *a.* germinal.
germinate [ˈdʒəːmineit], *v.t.* hacer germinar. — *v.i.* germinar.
germination [dʒəːmiˈneiʃən], *s.* germinación.
germinative [ˈdʒəːminətiv], *a.* germinativo.
gerontology [dʒerɔnˈtɔlədʒi], *s.* gerontología.
gerrymander [dʒeriˈmændə], *v.t.* (*fam.*, *pol.*) dar pucherazo.
gerund [ˈdʒerʌnd], *s.* (*gram.*) gerundio.
gerundive [dʒiˈrʌndiv], *s.* (*gram.*) gerundio adjetivado.
gest(e) [dʒest], *s.* (*ant.*) gesta.
gestation [dʒesˈteiʃən], *s.* gestación.
gestatory [ˈdʒestətəri], *a.* gestatorio.
gesticulate [dʒesˈtikjuleit], *v.i.* gesticular, accionar.
gesticulation [dʒestikjuˈleiʃən], *s.* gesticulación.
gesticulator [dʒesˈtikjuleitə], *s.* (el) que gesticula.
gesticulatory [dʒesˈtikjulətəri], *a.* gesticular.
gesture [ˈdʒestʃə], *s.* ademán; gesto; demostración; rasgo, detalle; ***empty gesture,*** puro formulismo, vaciedad; ***nice gesture,*** rasgo bonito, detalle bonito.
get [get], *irr. v.t.* conseguir, lograr; coger; recibir; cobrar; dar a *o* en; comprender; cazar; alcanzar; buscar, traer; sacar; engendrar; (*fam.*) ***get across,*** expresar, hacer entender; ***get away,*** quitar (de en medio); separar; conseguir que (*una persona*) se vaya *o* se escape; ***get back,*** recobrar, recuperar; ***get down,*** bajar; tragarse; apuntar, escribir; deprimir, abatir; ***get going,*** poner en marcha; ***get in,*** hacer entrar; introducir; meter; recoger; dar (un golpe); (*fam.*) ***get a move on,*** darse prisa, moverse; ***get off,*** quitar(se); librarse de; aprenderse de memoria; ***get on,*** ponerse (*traje*); ***get out,*** sacar; publicar; ***get over,*** hacer pasar por encima de; expresar, hacer entender; terminar, acabar; ***get through,*** (conseguir) pasar *o* introducir; meter; ***get up,*** levantar; (hacer) subir; montar; organizar; ataviar, disfrazar; (*fam.*) ***get it*** (***in the neck***), cobrar; (*fam.*) ***get it bad,*** enamorarse fuerte; ***I'll get you for this!*** ¡ya ajustaremos las cuentas!; ***that's what gets me!*** ¡eso es lo que me saca de quicio! — *v.i.* hacerse, llegar a ser, ponerse, volverse, quedarse; ir; llegar; (*fam.*) largarse; ***get about,*** moverse; divulgarse; ***get across,*** pasar, cruzar; surtir efecto, tener éxito, ser entendido; ***get ahead,*** avanzar, hacer progresos, medrar; ***get along,*** ir tirando; ***get along well with,*** llevarse bien con; ***get along with you!*** ¡no digas tonterías!; ***get along without,*** pasarse sin, prescindir de; ***get angry,*** enfadarse; ***I'll get around to it sometime,*** ya lo haré; ***get at,*** alcanzar, llegar a; atacar; meterse con; averiguar; querer decir; sobornar; ***get away,*** escaparse; irse; ***get away with it,*** (conseguir) hacerlo impunemente; ***get behind,*** atrasarse; rezagarse; ***get by,*** pasar; defenderse; ***get down to,*** ponerse a; ***get fat,*** engordar; ***get going,*** ponerse en marcha; ponerse con ello; menearse; ***get in,*** entrar; volver a casa; ser elegido; ***get into,*** entrar en; subir(se) a (*un coche etc.*); meterse en; (*fam.*) ***get in with,*** hacerse aceptar por; ***get killed,*** ser muerto, matarse; ***get lost!*** ¡lárgate!; ***get off,*** bajar(se) (de); irse; librarse, zafarse; despegar; (*fam.*) ***get off with,*** ligar con; ***get on,*** subir a; ponerse encima de; medrar; ***get on well with,*** llevarse bien con, congeniar con; ***get out,*** salir; escaparse; bajarse; ***get out of,*** librarse de, zafarse de; ***get over,*** pasar; superar; reponerse de; sobreponerse a; ***get around,*** dar la vuelta a; soslayar, evitar; convencer; ***get run over,*** ser atropellado; ***get through,*** pasar; llegar; pasar por; gastar(se); terminar; aprobar (*un examen*); ***get through to,*** ponerse en contacto con; ***get together,*** reunirse; ***get up,*** levantarse; ponerse de pie; subir; ponerse más fuerte, arreciar; (*fam.*) ***get up to sth.,*** hacer alguna maldad.
get-away [ˈget-əwei], *s.* escape; ***to make one's get-away,*** conseguir escaparse, fugarse.
gettable [ˈgetəbl], *a.* asequible, obtenible.
getting [ˈgetiŋ], *s.* adquisición; ganancia; engendramiento.
get-up [ˈget-ʌp], *s.* atavío; presentación.
gewgaw [ˈgju:gɔ:], *s.* chuchería, fruslería, baratija.
geyser [ˈgi:zə], *s.* géiser; calentador (de agua).
Ghana [ˈgɑ:nə]. Ghana.
Ghanaian [gɑ:ˈneiən], *a.*, *s.* ghanés, *m.*
ghastliness [ˈgɑ:stlinis], *s.* (lo) espantoso.
ghastly [ˈgɑ:stli], *a.* lívido, cadavérico; horrible, espantoso; lúgubre.
gherkin [ˈgə:kin], *s.* pepinillo, cohombrillo; encurtido.
Ghibelline [ˈgibəli:n], *s.* gibelino.
ghost [goust], *s.* aparecido, espectro, fantasma, *m.*; alma, espíritu; ánima en pena; (*foto.*, *ópt.*) imagen falsa; mancha; traza leve; ***ghost-like,*** espectral; ***ghost-writer,*** el que compone los escritos para otro; ***the Holy Ghost,*** el Espíritu Santo; ***to give up the ghost,*** entregar el alma; ***not a ghost of,*** ni una sombra de, ni la más leve traza de. — *v.t.* componer (*escritos para otra persona*).
ghostliness [ˈgoustlinis], *s.* (lo) espectral *o* fantasmal.
ghostly [ˈgoustli], *a.* fantasmal, espectral.
ghoul [gu:l], *s.* demonio necrófago; (*fig.*) persona de gustos inhumanos; vampiro.
ghoulish [ˈgu:liʃ], *a.* necrófago; macabro, granguiñolesco; sádico.
giant [ˈdʒaiənt], *a.* gigante, gigantesco. — *s.* gigante; ***giant-like,*** gigantesco.
giantess [ˈdʒaiəntes], *s.* giganta.
giaour [ˈdʒauə], *s.* infiel.
gib (1) [dʒib], *s.* (*mec.*) chaveta, cuña, contraclavija. — *v.t.* afianzar con chaveta, cuña etc.
gib (2) [gib], *s.* (*fam.*) gato; ***gib-cat,*** gato castrado.
gibber [ˈdʒibə], *v.i.* farfullar.
gibberish [ˈdʒibəriʃ], *s.* galimatías, *m. inv.*, jerigonza.
gibbet [ˈdʒibit], *s.* horca, patíbulo. — *v.t.* ahorcar; poner en la picota.
gibbon [ˈgibən], *s.* (*zool.*) gibón.
gibbosity [giˈbɔsiti], *s.* giba, gibosidad.
gibbous [ˈgibəs], *a.* giboso; convexo.
gibbousness [ˈgibəsnis], *s.* (lo) giboso.
gibe [dʒaib], *s.* escarnio, mofa. — *v.t.* escarnecer; ***gibe at,*** mofarse de.
giber [ˈdʒaibə], *s.* escarnecedor, mofador.
gibingly [ˈdʒaibiŋli], *adv.* con burla(s), con mofa.
giblets [ˈdʒiblits], *s.pl.* menudillos, *m.pl.*
Gibraltar [dʒiˈbrɔ:ltə]. Gibraltar.
giddiness [ˈgidinis], *s.* vértigo, mareo; atolondramiento, aturdimiento.
giddy [ˈgidi], *a.* vertiginoso; mareante; que siente vértigo, mareado; casquivano, atolondrado; ***giddy-headed,*** casquivano.
gift [gift], *s.* regalo, obsequio, dádiva, presente; don; dote, *f.*, talento; ofrenda; (*fam.*) cosa regalada, ganga; (*for.*) donación; ***I wouldn't take it*** (***even***) ***as a gift,*** no lo aceptaría ni regalado; ***never look a gift horse in the mouth,*** a caballo regalado no hay que mirarle el diente; ***he has a gift for causing offence,*** tiene el don de ofender. — *v.t.* obsequiar; dotar.
gifted [ˈgiftid], *a.* talentoso, de mucho talento.
gig [gig], *s.* calesa, calesín; (*mar.*) bote, falúa, lancha.
gigantic [dʒaiˈgæntik], *a.* gigantesco.
giggle [gigl], *s.* risita *o* risilla tonta. — *v.i.* reírse tontamente.
gigolo [ˈdʒigəlou], *s.* gigoló.
gigot [ˈdʒigət], *s.* pierna de cordero.
Gilbertian [gilˈbə:tiən], *a.* zarzuelero.
gild [gild], *irr. v.t.* dorar; dar brillo *o* lustre a.
gilder [ˈgildə], *s.* dorador.
gilding [ˈgildiŋ], *s.* doradura.
gilia [ˈdʒiliə], *s.* (*bot.*) gilia.
gill (1) [dʒil], *s.* medida de líquidos (¼ pinta).

gill (2) [gil], *s.* (*ict.*) agalla; (*fam.*) papada; (*fam.*) ***to look green about the gills,*** tener mala cara.
gillie [ˈgili], *s.* (*Esco.*) criado; ayudante (de caza).
gillyflower [ˈdʒiliflauə], *s.* (*bot.*) alhelí.
gilt [gilt], *a.* dorado. — *s.* dorado; falso brillo, oropel; (*fig.*) ***gilt-edged,*** de toda confianza. — *pret., p.p.* [GILD].
gilthead [ˈgilthed], *s.* (*ict.*) dorada.
gimbals [ˈdʒimbəlz], *s.pl.* (*mar.*) balancines de la brújula, *m.pl.*
gimcrack [ˈdʒimkræk], *a.* de baratillo; chapucero. — *s.* fruslería; chuchería.
gimlet [ˈgimlit], *s.* barrena de mano; ***gimlet eyes,*** ojos de lince, *m.pl.*
gimmal [ˈdʒiməl], *s.* par *o* serie de eslabones.
gimmick [ˈgimik], *s.* artilugio; treta, truco; camelo.
gin (1) [dʒin], *s.* desmotadora (*de algodón*); trampa, armadijo; cabria, malacate; ***roller gin,*** almarrá. — *v.t.* coger con trampa; desmotar (*algodón*).
gin (2) [dʒin], *s.* ginebra; ***gin-fizz,*** ginebra con azúcar y seltz.
ginger [ˈdʒindʒə], *a.* rojo, rufo. — *s.* jengibre; brío, viveza; ***ginger-bread,*** bizcocho melado; ***ginger-snap,*** galletita de jengibre. — *v.t.* — ***up,*** espabilar.
gingerliness [ˈdʒindʒəlinis], *s.* sumo cuidado, cautela.
gingerly [ˈdʒindʒəli], *a.* cauteloso. — *adv.* con tiento, con pies de plomo; ***to go gingerly,*** ir (como) pisando huevos.
gingham [ˈgiŋəm], *s.* carranclán, guinga.
gingival [dʒinˈdʒaivəl], *a.* gingival.
gingivitis [dʒindʒiˈvaitis], *s.* (*pat.*) gingivitis, *f.inv.*
ginseng [dʒinˈseŋ], *s.* ginseng.
gip [dʒip], *v.t.* destripar (pescados).
gipsy [ˈdʒipsi], *a., s.* gitano.
gipsyism [ˈdʒipsiizəm], *s.* gitanismo; gitanería; vida gitanesca.
giraffe [dʒiˈrɑːf], *s.* jirafa; (*astron.*) constelación Camelopardalis.
girandole [ˈdʒirəndoul], *s.* candelabro; girándula; (*joy.*) pendiente.
girasol [ˈdʒirəsɔl], *s.* heliotropo, girasol; (*min.*) ópalo girasol.
gird [gəːd], *irr. v.t.* ceñir; cercar; ***gird on a sword,*** ceñir espada. — **gird o.s.,** *v.r.* — ***for,*** aprestarse a.
girder [ˈgəːdə], *s.* (*arq.*) viga.
girding [ˈgəːdiŋ], *s.* ceñidura.
girdle [gəːdl], *s.* cinto; cinturón; faja; cincho; cíngulo; cerco; ***girdle-belt,*** ceñidor; ***pectoral girdle,*** cinturón escapular; ***pelvic girdle,*** cinturón pélvico. — *v.t.* ceñir, fajar; cercar.
girl [gəːl], *s.* muchacha, niña, chica; ***girl-friend,*** amiga, amiguita, novia.
girlhood [ˈgəːlhud], *s.* niñez, mocedad, juventud.
girlish [ˈgəːliʃ], *a.* de niña, juvenil, infantil; ***girlish prank,*** niñada.
Girondist [dʒiˈrɔndist], *a., s.* girondino.
girt [gəːt], *pret., p.p.* [GIRD].
girt-line [ˈgəːt-lain], *s.* andarivel.
girth [gəːθ], *s.* cincha; cintura; mucha barriga, gordura; ***girth-straps,*** correas de cincha, *f.pl.* — *v.t.* — ***up,*** cinchar.
gist [dʒist], *s.* sustancia; (lo) esencial; resumen.
give [giv], *s.* elasticidad, flexibilidad; ***give-and-take,*** (de) toma y daca, (de) tira y afloja; ***give-away,*** de regalo, de ganga; revelación, delación. — *irr. v.t.* dar; proporcionar; ofrecer; regalar; (*enfermedad*) pegar; (*castigo*) imponer; dar por resultado, arrojar; causar, ocasionar; dedicar; pronunciar; representar; ***give away,*** dar, regalar; revelar, delatar; ***give away the bride,*** ser padrino de boda; ***give back,*** devolver; ***give forth,*** publicar, divulgar; emitir; ***give ground*** o ***way,*** ceder; retroceder; ***give in,*** entregar; ***give off,*** despedir, echar, emitir; ***give out,*** distribuir, repartir; anunciar; divulgar; despedir, emitir; ***give over,*** entregar; ***give up,*** entregar; ceder; renunciar (a); desahuciar; dar por perdido; (*fam.*) ***give s.o. what for,*** poner de vuelta y media. — *v.i.* dar; ceder; cejar; flaquear; romperse; dar de sí; ***give as good as one gets,*** contestar con la misma moneda; ***give in,*** rendirse, darse por vencido; ceder; consentir; ***give out,*** acabarse, agotarse; fallar, romperse, estropearse; (*fam.*) ***give over,*** dejarse de tonterías; ***give up,*** dejar (de); renunciar, desistir; darse por vencido. — **give o.s.,** *v.r.* — ***up to,*** darse a, entregarse a, dedicarse a.
given [ˈgivən], *a.* (*Am.*) ***given name*** [CHRISTIAN NAME]; ***given to,*** dado a. — *conj.* ***given that,*** dado que. — *p.p.* [GIVE].
giver [ˈgivə], *s.* donador, dador.
gizzard [ˈgizəd], *s.* molleja de ave; ***it sticks in my gizzard,*** no puedo con ello, no lo puedo tragar *o* soportar.
glabrous [ˈgleibrəs], *a.* glabro.
glacial [ˈgleisiəl], *a.* glacial.
glaciate [ˈgleisieit], *v.t.* (*geol.*) cubrir con hielo glacial.
glaciation [gleisiˈeiʃən], *s.* glaciación.
glacier [ˈglæsiə], *s.* ventisquero, glaciar.
glacis [ˈgleisis], *s.* (*fort.*) glacis.
glad [glæd], *a.* contento, satisfecho; alegre, gozoso; ***to be glad that,*** alegrarse de que; ***to be glad to,*** tener mucho gusto en.
gladden [glædn], *v.t.* alegrar, regocijar.
glade [gleid], *s.* claro, calvero (*bosque*).
gladiator [ˈglædieitə], *s.* gladiador.
gladiatorial [glædiəˈtɔːriəl], *a.* gladiatorio.
gladiolus [glædiˈouləs], *s.* (*pl.* **gladioli, gladioluses** [glædiˈoulai, -ˈouləsiz]) (*bot.*) gladíolo, estoque.
gladly [ˈglædli], *adv.* de buena gana, de buen grado, con mucho gusto.
gladness [ˈglædnis], *s.* alegría, contento, gozo.
gladsome [ˈglædsəm], *a.* alegre, contento.
gladsomeness [ˈglædsəmnis], *s.* contento; alegría, regocijo.
Gladstone [ˈglædstən], *s.* portamantas, *m.inv.*
glair [glɛə], *s.* clara de huevo. — *v.t.* untar con clara de huevo.
glairy [ˈglɛəri], *a.* viscoso, pegajoso.
glamorize [ˈglæməraiz], *v.t.* dar una aureola a.
glamorous [ˈglæmərəs], *a.* atractivo, encantador, fascinador.
glamour [ˈglæmə], *s.* encanto, hechizo.
glance [glɑːns], *s.* mirada, ojeada, vistazo; destello (*de luz*); vislumbre; golpe oblicuo; (*min.*) mineral lustroso; rebote; ***at a glance,*** de una ojeada; ***at first glance,*** a primera vista. — *v.i.* — ***at,*** ojear, echar un vistazo a; mirar de soslayo; lanzar una mirada a; mirar por encima; ***glance off,*** desviarse, rebotar de soslayo; destellar; ***glance over,*** ojear, echar un vistazo a.
glancing [ˈglɑːnsiŋ], *a.* oblicuo, de refilón.
gland (1) [glænd], *s.* (*anat., bot.*) glándula.
gland (2) [glænd], *s.* (*mec.*) prensaestopas, *m.inv.*
glandered, glanderous [ˈglɑːndəd, -rəs], *a.* muermoso, amormado.
glanders [ˈglɑːndəz], *s.* (*vet.*) muermo.
glandiferous [glænˈdifərəs], *a.* glandífero.
glandiform [ˈglændifɔːm], *a.* glandiforme.
glandular [ˈglændjulə], *a.* glanduloso, glandular.
glandule [ˈglændjuːl], *s.* glandulilla.
glandulosity [glændjuˈlɔsiti], *s.* calidad de glanduloso; conjunto de glándulas.
glandulous [ˈglændjuləs], [GLANDULAR].
glans [glænz], *s.* (*pl.* **glandes** [ˈglændiːz]) (*anat.*) glande, bálano; clítoris; (*bot.*) bellota.
glare [glɛə], *s.* luz intensa, resplandor; deslumbramiento; mirada penetrante; ***in the glare of***

publicity, en el foco de la publicidad. — *v.i.* relumbrar, deslumbrar, resplandecer; ser vivo *o* chillón; echar miradas feroces.
glaring [ˈglɛəriŋ], *a.* deslumbrador; chillón; de mirada feroz; notorio, que salta a la vista; garrafal.
glass [glɑːs], *s.* vidrio, cristal; vaso, copa, caña; barómetro; reloj de arena; (contenido de) vaso *o* copa; (*pl.*) **glasses,** gafas, *f.pl.*, lentes, espejuelos, *m.pl.*; ***cut glass,*** cristal tallado; ***glass-blower,*** vidriero; ***glass-case,*** vitrina; ***glass-cutter,*** cortavidrios, *m.inv.*; ***glass door,*** puerta vidriera; ***glass-house,*** invernadero; cárcel militar; ***people in glass houses shouldn't throw stones,*** hay que tener mucha seguridad para poder tirar la primera piedra; ***glass-maker,*** vidriero; ***glass-shop,*** vidriería; ***ground glass,*** vidrio deslustrado *o* esmerilado.
glassful [ˈglɑːsful], *s.* (contenido de un) vaso.
glassiness [ˈglɑːsinis], *s.* (lo) vidrioso.
glassware [ˈglɑːswɛə], *s.* cristalería; vajilla de cristal.
glasswork [ˈglɑːswəːk], *s.* vidriería, cristalería; (*pl.*) fábrica de cristal *o* de vidrios.
glasswort [ˈglɑːswəːt], *s.* almarjo.
glassy [ˈglɑːsi], *a.* vítreo; vidrioso; cristalino.
Glaswegian [glæsˈwiːdʒən], *a.*, *s.* (natural) de Glasgow.
glaucoma [glɔːˈkoumə], *s.* glaucoma.
glaucous [ˈglɔːkəs], *a.* glauco.
glaucus [ˈglɔːkəs], *s.* (*zool.*) glauco.
glaze [gleiz], *s.* superficie lisa y lustrosa; vidriado; esmalte; barniz; lustre. — *v.t.* vidriar; poner vidrios a; dar una apariencia vidriosa a; satinar; glasear; barnizar.
glazed [gleizd], *a.* vidriado; ***with a glazed look,*** con los ojos vidriosos; ***glazed paper,*** papel satinado.
glazier [ˈgleiziə], *s.* vidriero.
glazing [ˈgleiziŋ], *s.* vidriado; satinado; barnizado; superficie lustrosa; lustre; barniz.
gleam [gliːm], *s.* destello, rayo, brillo, centelleo, vislumbre, luz tenue. — *v.i.* centellear, brillar, destellar.
gleaming [ˈgliːmiŋ], *a.* reluciente, resplandeciente.
glean [gliːn], *v.t.* espigar; recoger.
gleaner [ˈgliːnə], *s.* espigador; rebuscador.
gleaning [ˈgliːniŋ], *s.* rebusca; moraga; (*pl.*) fragmentos recogidos, *m.pl.*, cosas recopiladas, *f.pl.*
glebe [gliːb], *s.* gleba; tierras beneficiales (*de un cura*), *f.pl.*
glee [gliː], *s.* alegría, júbilo, regocijo; (*mús.*) canción para voces solas; ***glee club,*** orfeón.
gleeful [ˈgliːful], *a.* alegre, jubiloso, regocijado.
glen [glen], *s.* cañada, vaguada, vallecito.
glengarry [glenˈgæri], *s.* gorra escocesa.
glenoid [ˈglenɔid], *a.* glenoideo.
glib [glib], *a.* de mucha labia, de palabra fácil; charlatán.
glibness [ˈglibnis], *s.* labia, facilidad de palabra; charlatanería.
glide [glaid], *s.* deslizamiento; (*aer.*) planeo. — *v.i.* deslizarse; (*aer.*) planear; ***glide by*** o ***past,*** pasar deslizando *o* deslizándose.
glider [ˈglaidə], *s.* (*aer.*) planeador.
gliding [ˈglaidiŋ], *s.* vuelo sin motor.
glimmer [ˈglimə], *s.* vislumbre, resplandor tenue; luz débil. — *v.i.* vislumbrarse; brillar débilmente *o* con luz débil y vacilante.
glimmering [ˈglimәriŋ], *a.* luciente, rielante. — *s.* luz trémula; viso, vislumbre.
glimpse [glimps], *s.* vistazo, vislumbre; ***to catch a glimpse of,*** vislumbrar, divisar. — *v.t.* vislumbrar, divisar, entrever, ver brevemente.
glint [glint], *s.* fulgor, destello; reflejo. — *v.i.* destellar, rielar.
glissade [gliˈːsɑːd, gliˈseid], *s.* (*alpinismo*) resbalada.
glisten [ˈglisən], *v.i.* relucir, brillar, relumbrar, rielar.
glister [ˈglistə], *v.i.* chispear, rutilar.
glistering [ˈglistəriŋ], *a.* brillante, rutilante.
glitter [ˈglitə], *s.* resplandor, brillo, lustre. — *v.i.* resplandecer, rutilar; ***all that glitters is not gold,*** no es oro todo lo que reluce.
glittering [ˈglitəriŋ], *a.* resplandeciente, rutilante, reluciente.
gloaming [ˈgloumiŋ], *s.* crepúsculo (vespertino), anochecida, (el) anochecer.
gloat [glout], *v.i.* — ***over,*** deleitarse, regodearse en; relamerse.
global [ˈgloubəl], *a.* esférico; mundial.
globate [ˈgloubeit], *a.* esférico, globular.
globe [gloub], *s.* esfera, bola, globo; mundo; pecera globular; ***globe-fish,*** orbe; ***globe-trotter,*** trotamundos, *m.f.inv.*
globose [ˈgloubous], *a.* globoso, esférico.
globosity [glouˈbɔsiti], *s.* esfericidad, redondez.
globular [ˈglɔbjulə], *a.* esférico, globular.
globule [ˈglɔbjuːl], *s.* glóbulo, globulillo.
globulous [ˈglɔbjuləs], *a.* globuloso.
glomerate [ˈglɔmərit], *a.* aglomerado, globulado.
glomeration [glɔməˈreiʃən], *s.* conglobación.
glomerule [ˈglɔməruːl], *s.* glomérula.
gloom [gluːm], *s.* oscuridad, lobreguez; melancolía, abatimiento; ***to cast a pall of gloom over,*** entenebrecer, ensombrear. — *v.t.* encapotar, oscurecer. — *v.i.* oscurecerse, encapotarse; entristecerse, abatirse.
gloominess [ˈgluːminis], *s.* oscuridad, lobreguez; melancolía, abatimiento.
gloomy [ˈgluːmi], *a.* oscuro, tenebroso, lóbrego, sombrío; abatido, melancólico.
glorification [glɔːrifiˈkeiʃən], *s.* glorificación, ensalzamiento, apoteosis, *f.inv.*
glorified [ˈglɔːrifaid], *a.* ilustrado.
glorify [ˈglɔːrifai], *v.t.* glorificar.
gloriole [ˈglɔːrioul], *s.* aureola.
glorious [ˈglɔːriəs], *a.* glorioso; magnífico, espléndido.
gloriousness [ˈglɔːriəsnis], *s.* gloria, esplendor.
glory [ˈglɔːri], *s.* gloria; ***to be in one's glory,*** estar en sus glorias; ***to be at the height of its glory,*** estar en el apogeo de su grandeza. — *v.i.* — ***in,*** gozar con; gloriarse en; gloriarse de; ***he glories in it,*** le encanta.
gloss (1) [glɔs], *s.* lustre, brillo; apariencia superficial; barniz; ***to put a gloss on the truth,*** dorar la píldora; ***to put a gloss of truth on,*** dar un barnicillo de verdad a. — *v.t.* dar brillo a, lustrar; barnizar; paliar. — *v.i.* — ***over,*** paliar, quitar importancia a.
gloss (2) [glɔs], *s.* glosa, escolio. — *v.t.* glosar.
glossa [ˈglɔsə], *s.* glosis, *f.inv.*
glossarial [glɔˈsɛəriəl], *a.* de glosario.
glossarist [ˈglɔsərist], *s.* glosador, comentador.
glossary [ˈglɔsəri], *s.* glosario.
glossiness [ˈglɔsinis], *s.* lustre, (lo) lustroso.
glossy [ˈglɔsi], *a.* lustroso, brillante; satinado; superficial, engañoso.
glottal [glɔtl], *a.* glótico.
glottis [ˈglɔtis], *s.* (*anat.*) glotis, *f.inv.*
glove [glʌv], *s.* guante; ***glove-money,*** gratificación, propina; ***glove-stretcher,*** abridor de guantes; (*fig.*) ***the gloves are off,*** se acabaron las contemplaciones; ***to fit like a glove,*** encajar *o* sentar a la perfección; ***to be hand in glove,*** estar conchabados.
gloved [glʌvd], *a.* enguantado.
glover [ˈglʌvə], *s.* guantero.
glow [glou], *s.* resplandor; arrebol; incandescencia; (sensación de) calor, calorcillo agradable; color (vivo), colorcete; (*ent.*) ***glow-worm,*** luciérnaga,

gusano de luz. — *v.i.* resplandecer; estar candente *o* encendido; arder; dar *o* tener sensación de calorcillo; tener un aspecto colorado y sano.

glower [glauə], *v.i.* mirar con ceño, mirar ceñudamente.

glowing [ˈglouiŋ], *a.* resplandeciente; ardiente; encendido; colorado; radiante; ***to speak in glowing terms of,*** elogiar, encarecer.

glowingly [ˈglouiŋli], *adv.* ***to speak glowingly of,*** elogiar, encarecer, ponderar.

glucina [glu:ˈsainə], *s.* (*quím.*) glucina.

glucinum [glu:ˈsainəm], *s.* glucinio.

glucose [ˈglu:kous], *s.* glucosa.

glue [glu:], *s.* cola, pegamento; ***glue-pot,*** bote de cola; ***fish-glue,*** colapez. — *v.t.* encolar, pegar.

gluey [ˈglu:i], *a.* pegajoso, lleno de cola *o* de pegamento.

glum [glʌm], *a.* sombrío, triste, mustio.

glumaceous [glu:ˈmeiʃəs], *a.* glumáceo.

glume [glu:m], *s.* (*bot.*) gluma.

glut (1) [glʌt], *s.* hartura, hartazgo; superabundancia. — *v.t.* hartar, colmar, abarrotar; ***glut the market,*** inundar, saturar el mercado.

glut (2) [glʌt], *s.* ripio (*de ladrillo*); caña de madera.

gluteal [ˈglu:tiəl], *a.* glúteo, nalgar.

gluten [ˈglu:tən], *s.* gluten.

gluteus [ˈglu:tiəs], *s.* músculo glúteo.

glutinous [ˈglu:tinəs], *a.* glutinoso, pegajoso, viscoso, gelatinoso.

glutinousness [ˈglu:tinəsnis], *s.* glutinosidad, viscosidad.

glutton [glʌtn], *s.* glotón; tragón; (*zool.*) carcajú.

gluttonize [ˈglʌtənaiz], *v.i.* glotonear.

gluttonous [ˈglʌtənəs], *a.* glotón.

gluttony [ˈglʌtəni], *s.* glotonería, gula.

glyceric [gliˈserik], *a.* de glicerina.

glycerin(e) [ˈglisərin], *s.* glicerina.

glycogen [ˈglaikodʒən], *s.* glicógeno.

glycol [ˈglaikɔl], *s.* glicol.

glyph [glif], *s.* (*arq.*) glifo; estría.

glyptics [ˈgliptiks], *s.* glíptica.

glyptography [glipˈtɔgrəfi], *s.* gliptografía.

gnarl [nɑ:l], *s.* nudo (*en el árbol* o *la madera*). — *v.t.* torcer.

gnarled [nɑ:ld], *a.* nudoso, retorcido.

gnash [næʃ], *v.t.* rechinar, crujir (*los dientes*).

gnat [næt], *s.* mosquito, cínife.

gnaw [nɔ:], *v.t.* roer; carcomer.

gnawer [nɔ:ə], *s.* roedor.

gneiss [nais], *s.* gneis, *m.inv.*

gnome [noum], *s.* gnomo; ***gnome owl,*** mochuelo pequeño.

gnomic(al) [ˈnoumik(əl)], *a.* sentencioso, gnómico, críptico, oculto.

gnomon [ˈnoumɔn], *s.* gnomon.

gnomonic [nouˈmɔnik], *a.* sentencioso, gnómico.

gnomonics [nouˈmɔniks], *s.* gnomónica.

gnostic [ˈnɔstik], *s.* gnóstico.

gnosticism [ˈnɔstisizəm], *s.* gnosticismo.

gnu [n(j)u:], *s.* ñu.

go [gou], *a.* (*fam.*) ***go-ahead,*** emprendedor, enérgico, activo. — *s.* energía, brío; turno; ***to be always on the go,*** no parar; ***to have a go,*** probar suerte; ***it's your go,*** te toca a ti; ***it's no go,*** es inútil, nada; ***to make a go of it,*** conseguir que sea un éxito; ***right from the word go,*** desde el primer momento; ***to give s.o. the go-ahead,*** dar el visto bueno a alguien; ***go-between,*** mediador; alcahuete; tercero; ***go-by,*** desaire, menosprecio; ***to give s.o. the go-by,*** hacer el vacío a alguien; ***go-cart,*** carretilla, carricoche; ***go-getter,*** buscavidas, *m.f. inv.*, persona emprendedora; ***go-slow*** huelga de brazos caídos, *f.* — *irr. v.i.* ir; andar, marchar; irse, marcharse; (*manchas etc.*) quitarse; ceder, romperse; (*gestos, ademanes*) hacer; hacerse, ponerse, volverse; venderse; (*tiempo*) pasar; entrar, encajar; resultar bien; hacer juego (con); salir, resultar; ***go about,*** abordar, acometer, emprender; andar de un lado para otro; circular; (*mar.*) virar; ***go abroad,*** ir(se) al extranjero; ***go against,*** ir en contra de; oponerse a; ***go ahead,*** seguir; proseguir; ***go and see,*** ir a ver; ***go at,*** abalanzarse sobre; ***go away,*** marcharse, irse; desaparecer; ***go back,*** volver, regresar; retroceder; ***go back (on),*** desdecirse (de); rajarse; ***go back to,*** datar de, remontarse a; ***go before,*** anteceder; comparecer ante; ***go blind,*** quedarse ciego; ***go by,*** pasar (por); atenerse a; regirse por; juzgar por; ***go by car,*** ir en coche; ***go by the name of,*** conocerse con el nombre de; ***go down,*** bajar; hundirse; sucumbir; ponerse (*el sol*); (*fam.*) aceptarse, tragarse; ***go for,*** ir por; atacar; ***go great guns,*** ir viento en popa; ***go halves with,*** ir a medias; ***go hungry,*** quedarse sin comer; ***go hunting,*** ir de caza; ***go in,*** entrar (en); encajar (en); ***go in for,*** ser aficionado a; presentarse para; ***go into,*** entrar en; investigar; ***go in with,*** hacerse socio de; (*fam.*) ***go it,*** echar el resto; pisar a fondo; (*fam.*) ***go it alone,*** resolver las cosas por su cuenta, tirar por la calle de en medio, liarse la manta a la cabeza; ***go off,*** irse; dispararse; estallar; (*leche*) cortarse; (*carne*) pasarse, deteriorarse, estropearse; ***go on,*** seguir (adelante); durar; (*fam.*) machacar; dar la lata; ***go on foot,*** ir a pie; ***go on to say,*** pasar a decir, decir a continuación; ***go one better than,*** superar; ***go out,*** salir; apagarse; ***go over,*** recorrer; pasar; repasar; pasarse (a); (*fam.*) ***go phut,*** pegar un estallido; ***go places,*** ir lejos; ver mundo; ***go round,*** dar la vuelta (a); girar; circular; alcanzar para todos; ***go slow,*** hacer huelga de brazos caídos; (*fam.*) ***go steady with,*** hacerse novio *o* novia formal de; ***go through,*** pasar por; sufrir; gastar(se); ***go through thick and thin with,*** acompañar a traves de todas las vicisitudes; ***go through with it,*** seguir hasta el final; (*fig.*) ***go to the dogs, to pot,*** ir de cabeza; ***go to sea,*** hacerse marinero; ***go to show,*** servir para demostrar; ***go under,*** hundirse; ***go up,*** subir; estallar, saltar; ***go with,*** acompañar; hacer juego con; ***go without,*** pasarse sin, prescindir de; ***as far as it goes,*** dentro de lo que cabe; ***here goes!*** ¡ahí va!; ***how goes it?*** ¿qué tal?; ***it goes without saying,*** huelga decirlo; ***it's going on for one o'clock,*** es casi la una; ***to keep going,*** seguir, continuar; no cejar; ***to set going,*** poner en marcha; ***the story goes,*** según cuentan; ***there goes the bell,*** ya suena el timbre; ***who goes there?*** ¿quién vive? — *interj.* ¡váyase! ¡vete!; (*aut.*) ¡paso!; ***all systems go!*** ¡en marcha todo!; (*dep.*) ***on your marks, get set, go!*** ¡preparados, listos, ya!

goad [goud], *s.* aguijada; aguijón; ***goad-stick,*** garrocha. — *v.t.* aguijar, aguijonear; incitar, estimular; provocar.

goal [goul], *s.* meta; (*dep.*) portería; gol, tanto.

goalkeeper [ˈgoulki:pə], *s.* guardameta, *m.*, portero.

goat [gout], *s.* cabra, cabrón, chivo, chiva; (*bot.*) ***goat-beard,*** barba cabruna; ***goat-buck*** o ***he-goat,*** cabrón, macho cabrío; (*bot.*) ***goat's rue,*** gálega, ruda cabruña; (*bot.*) ***goat's thorn,*** tragacanto, alquitira; ***he gets my goat,*** me saca de quicio.

goatee [gouˈti:], *s.* perilla.

goatherd [ˈgouthə:d], *s.* cabrero.

goatish [ˈgoutiʃ], *a.* cabruno; lascivo, rijoso.

goatskin [ˈgoutskin], *s.* piel de cabra.

goatsucker [ˈgoutsʌkə], *s.* (*orn.*) caprimulga, chotacabras, *f.inv.*

gob [gɔb], *s.* (*fam.*) boca, pico; pedazo, grumo.

gobbet [ˈgɔbit], *s.* bocado, pedazo.

gobble [gɔbl], *s.* gluglú. — *v.t.* engullir, zampar. — *v.i.* gluglutear.

gobbler [ˈgɔblə], *s.* engullidor, tragón; (*fam.*) pavo.

goblet [ˈgɔblit], *s.* copa.

goblin [ˈgɔblin], *s.* trasgo, duende.

God [gɔd]. Dios; ***God-fearing,*** reverente, temeroso de Dios; ***God forbid,*** no lo quiera Dios; ***God-forsaken,*** dejado de la mano de Dios; ***God-given knowledge,*** ciencia infusa; (*ant.*) ***God speed!*** ¡que tenga buen viaje!; ***thank God,*** gracias a Dios.
godchild [ˈgɔdtʃaild], *s.* ahijado, ahijada.
goddaughter [ˈgɔddɔːtə], *s.* ahijada.
goddess [ˈgɔdes], *s.* diosa; diva.
godfather [ˈgɔdfɑːðə], *s.* padrino.
Godhead [ˈgɔdhed], *s.* deidad, divinidad.
godless [ˈgɔdlis], *a.* ateo, sin Dios.
godlessness [ˈgɔdlisnis], *s.* ateísmo.
godlike [ˈgɔdlaik], *a.* divino; deiforme.
godliness [ˈgɔdlinis], *s.* piedad, santidad, devoción.
godly [ˈgɔdli], *a.* piadoso, religioso, devoto.
godmother [ˈgɔdmʌðə], *s.* madrina.
godsend [ˈgɔdsend], *s.* bendición; maná, *m.*, cosa llovida del cielo.
godson [ˈgɔdsʌn], *s.* ahijado.
godwit [ˈgɔdwit], *s.* (*orn.*) francolín.
goer [gouə], *s.* andador; corredor; ***good goer,*** buen andador.
goffer [ˈgɔfə], *s.* rizado. — *v.t.* rizar, encrespar; estampar (cuero).
goggle [gɔgl], *a.* ***goggle-eyed,*** de ojos saltones; ***goggle-eyes,*** ojos saltones. — *s.* (*pl.*) gafas, *f.pl.*, anteojos, *m.pl.* — *v.i.* abrir un palmo de ojos, mirar con (los) ojos desorbitados.
going [ˈgouiŋ], *a.* que va; en marcha; funcionando; (*fam.*) disponible, que hay; (*fam.*) en venta; ***going concern,*** empresa en pleno funcionamiento *o* que marcha bien. — *s.* ida, salida, partida; marcha, velocidad; estado del camino *o* hipódromo; ***comings and goings,*** idas y venidas; (*fam.*) ***goings-on,*** tejemaneje, ciscos, *m.pl.*, líos, *m.pl.*; ***good going!*** ¡muy bien! — *interj.* ***going, going, gone!*** [GONE].
goitre [ˈgɔitə], *s.* bocio.
goitrous [ˈgɔitrəs], *a.* que tiene bocio.
gold [gould], *s.* oro; ***gold-bearing,*** aurífero; ***gold-beater,*** batihoja, batidor de oro; (*fam.*) ***gold-digger,*** aventurera, vampiresa; ***gold-dust,*** oro en polvo; ***gold-leaf,*** oro batido; ***gold-mine,*** mina de oro; (*fig.*) mina, Potosí; ***gold-rush,*** fiebre del oro; ***gold-standard,*** patrón oro.
golden [ˈgouldən], *a.* áureo, de oro; dorado; brillante, floreciente, feliz; ***golden mean,*** justo medio; ***golden number,*** número áureo; (*bot.*) ***golden thistle,*** cardillo; ***golden wedding,*** bodas de oro, *f.pl.*
goldfinch [ˈgouldfintʃ], *s.* jilguero.
goldfish [ˈgouldfiʃ], *s.* pez de colores.
goldsmith [ˈgouldsmiθ], *s.* orfebre.
goldy-locks [ˈgouldi-lɔks], *s.* (*coll.*) rubiales, *m.f.pl.*
golf [gɔlf], *s.* golf; ***golf-club,*** palo de golf; club de golf; ***golf-links,*** campo de golf.
golliwog [ˈgɔliwɔg], *s.* muñeco negro de trapo.
gondola [ˈgɔndələ], *s.* góndola.
gondolier [gɔndəˈliə], *s.* gondolero.
gone [gɔn], *a.* ido; pasado; desaparecido; arruinado; perdido; agotado; muerto; (*fam.*) chiflado, ido; ***be gone!*** ¡vete!; (*fam.*) ***far gone,*** muy adelantado *o* avanzado; casi muerto; muy bebido; ***gone four o'clock,*** las cuatro pasadas; (*fam.*) ***gone on,*** encaprichado con, enamorado de. — *interj.* ***going, going, gone!*** ¡a la de una, a la de dos, a la de tres! — *p.p.* [GO].
goner [ˈgɔnə], *s.* (*fam.*) persona (casi) muerta.
gonfalon [ˈgɔnfəlɔn], *s.* gonfalón, pendón.
gonfalonier [gɔnfəlɔˈniə], *s.* gonfalonero.
gong [gɔŋ], *s.* gong, batintín.
goniometer [gɔniˈɔmitə], *s.* goniómetro.
goniometric [gɔniəˈmetrik], *a.* goniométrico.
goniometry [gɔniˈɔmitri], *s.* goniometría.
gonorrhœa [gɔnəˈriə], *s.* gonorrea.
gonorrhœal [gɔnəˈriəl], *a.* gonorréico.
good [gud], *a.* bueno; útil; válido; ***as good as,*** tan bueno como; igual que; ***as good as done,*** cosa hecha; ***to be as good as one's word,*** cumplir lo prometido; ***good at,*** fuerte en, hábil en; ***good-bye,*** adiós; ***good day,*** buenos días; ***a good deal,*** mucho, bastante; ***in good earnest,*** seriamente, de veras; ***he is good for nothing,*** no sirve *o* no vale para nada; ***good fortune,*** buena fortuna, dicha, suerte; ***Good Friday,*** Viernes Santo; ***good humour,*** jovialidad, buen humor; ***good-humoured,*** alegre, bienhumorado; ***good-looking,*** guapo, bien parecido; ***good morning,*** buenos días; ***good-natured,*** bonachón, afable; ***good-naturedly,*** amistosamente; ***good night,*** buenas noches; ***in good time,*** con tiempo (de sobra); ***all in good time,*** ya, en su momento; ***good turn,*** favor; ***a good while,*** un buen rato; ***to hold good,*** ser válido, valer; ***to make good,*** cumplir, llevar a cabo; compensar; reparar; triunfar, prosperar. — *adv.* bien. — *s.* bien, provecho; (*pl.*) géneros, *m.pl.*; mercancías, *f.pl.*; ***for good (and all),*** (de una vez) para siempre, definitivamente; ***it's for your own good,*** es por tu bien; ***much good may it do you,*** buen provecho le haga; ***it's no good,*** no vale; es inútil; ***he's up to no good,*** no está en nada bueno; ***to return good for evil,*** volver bien por mal; ***it's all to the good,*** tanto mejor; ***what's the good of it?*** ¿de qué sirve? ¿para qué sirve?; ***goods shed,*** almacén, depósito, cobertizo; ***goods train,*** tren de mercancías; ***goods van*** *o* ***wagon,*** vagón de mercancías, furgón. — *interj.* ¡bueno! ¡bien!
goodies [ˈgudiz], *s.pl.* (*fam.*) confitura, dulce; golosinas, *f.pl.*
goodish [ˈgudiʃ], *a.* bastante bueno; bastante grande, regular, apreciable.
goodliness [ˈgudlinis], *s.* (lo) bello, (lo) hermoso.
goodly [ˈgudli], *a.* hermoso, bien parecido; apreciable.
goodman [ˈgudmən], *s.* (*pl.* **-men** [-men]) (*ant.*) señor, dueño, amo; marido.
goodness [ˈgudnis], *s.* bondad; sustancia. — *interj.* ¡por Dios!
goodwill [gudˈwil], *s.* buena voluntad, buena gana; benevolencia; (*com.*) clientela, parroquia, buen crédito.
goody (1) [ˈgudi], *a.*, *s.* bonachón; ***goody-goody,*** mojigato, santurrón. — *interj.* ¡qué bien!
goody (2) [ˈgudi], *s.* (*fam.*) comadre.
goosander [guːˈsændə], *s.* (*orn.*) mergánsar, mergo.
goose (1) [guːs], *s.* (*pl.* **geese** [giːs]) ganso *o* gansa, ánsar; oca; juego de la oca; bobo, necio; ***goose-cap,*** bobo, tonto, pazguato, ganso; (*fig.*) ***goose-flesh,*** carne de gallina, *f.*; (*bot.*) ***goose-foot,*** chual; ***goose-herd,*** ansarero; (*mar.*) ***goose-neck,*** gancho de botalones; arbotante; pescante de bote; cuello de cisne; ***goose-quill,*** pluma de ganso, cañón; (*mil.*) ***goose-step,*** paso de ganso; (*mar.*) ***goose-wings,*** calzones, *m.pl.*; ***that cooked his goose,*** esto dio al trasto con sus proyectos; ***to kill the goose that lays the golden eggs,*** matar la gallina de los huevos de oro; ***all his geese are swans,*** tiene mucha fantasía.
goose (2) [guːs], *s.* (*pl.* **gooses** [-iz]) (***tailor's***) ***goose,*** plancha de sastre.
gooseberry [ˈguzbəri], *s.* (*bot.*) grosella blanca *o* verde; (*fig.*) carabina.
gooseflesh [ˈguːsfleʃ], *s.* carne de gallina.
gopher [ˈgoufə], *s.* geomís; (*bot.*) ***gopher-wood,*** árbol de madera amarilla.
Gordian [ˈgɔːdiən], *a.* gordiano; ***Gordian knot,*** nudo gordiano.
gore (1) [gɔː], *s.* sangre, *f.*, sangre cuajada, cruor. — *v.t.* herir con los cuernos, cornear, coger.
gore (2) [gɔː], *s.* (*cost.*) cuchillo, nesga; (*mar.*) tabla triangular.
gorge [gɔːdʒ], *s.* garganta; gaznate; barranco, desfiladero. — *v.t.* atiborrar, cebar, hartar. — *v.i.* atiborrarse, atracarse. — **gorge o.s.,** *v.r.* darse un atracón, cebarse.

gorgeous [ˈgɔ:dʒəs], *a.* hermoso, precioso, soberbio, espléndido, suntuoso.
gorgeousness [ˈgɔ:dʒəsnis], *s.* (lo) hermoso etc.
gorget [ˈgɔ:dʒit], *s.* (*mil.*) gola, golilla, gorguera, gorjal; (*cost.*) gorguera; (*orn.*) collar, mancha (de color); (*cir.*) cuchilla.
gorilla [gəˈrilə], *s.* gorila.
gormand [ˈgɔ:mənd], [GOURMAND].
gormandize [ˈgɔ:məndaiz], [GOURMANDIZE].
gormandizer [ˈgɔ:məndaizə], *s.* glotón.
gorse [gɔ:s], *s.* (*bot.*) aulaga(s), tojo(s).
gory [ˈgɔ:ri], *a.* sangriento, ensangrentado, cruento.
goshawk [ˈgɔshɔ:k], *s.* (*orn.*) azor.
gosling [ˈgɔzliŋ], *s.* (*orn.*) ansarino.
gospel [ˈgɔspəl], *s.* evangelio; (*fam.*) ***it's gospel (truth),*** es el evangelio.
gospeller [ˈgɔspələ], *s.* evangelista, *m.f.*; evangelistero.
gospellize [ˈgɔspəlaiz], *v.t.* evangelizar.
gossamer [ˈgɔsəmə], *s.* hilo finísimo; telaraña; tela impermeable; gasa sutilísima.
gossamery [ˈgɔsəməri], *a.* sutil, finísimo, ligerísimo.
gossip [ˈgɔsip], *s.* chisme(s), chismería, hablilla(s), habladuría(s), murmuración; chismoso, murmurador; comadre; ***piece of gossip,*** hablilla; ***subject for*** o ***of gossip,*** comidilla. — *v.i.* chismear, murmurar.
gossiping [ˈgɔsipiŋ], *s.* [GOSSIP].
Goth [gɔθ], *s.* godo.
Gothic [ˈgɔθik], *a.* gótico; godo; bárbaro. — *s.* (*idioma*) gótico; (*letra*) gótica.
Gothicism [ˈgɔθisizəm], *s.* goticismo; barbarie.
gotten [ˈgɔtən], (*Am.*, *ant.*) *p.p.* [GET].
gouge [gaudʒ], *s.* (*carp.*) gubia. — *v.t.* excavar, escoplear con (una) gubia; sacar, arrancar; ***to gouge out the eyes of,*** sacarle los ojos a.
gourd [guəd], *s.* calabaza; calabacera; ***bottle-gourd,*** calabaza vinatera.
gourmand [ˈguəmənd], [GOURMET].
gourmandize [ˈguəməndaiz], *v.i.* glotonear; comer con gula.
gourmet [ˈguəmei], *s.* gastrónomo.
gout [gaut], *s.* (*med.*) gota.
goutiness [ˈgautinis], *s.* afección gotosa.
goutwort [ˈgautwə:t], *s.* (*bot.*) angélica.
gouty [ˈgauti], *a.* gotoso.
govern [ˈgʌvən], *v.t.* gobernar, regir; dominar. — *v.i.* gobernar.
governable [ˈgʌvənəbl], *a.* gobernable, dócil.
governance [ˈgʌvənəns], *s.* gobierno, gobernación.
governess [ˈgʌvənis], *s.* institutriz, *f.*; gobernadora.
government [ˈgʌvənmənt], *s.* gobierno; administración pública; (*gram.*) régimen.
governmental [gʌvənˈmentəl], *a.* gubernamental, gubernativo, del gobierno.
governor [ˈgʌvənə], *s.* gobernador; director; alcaide; (*fam.*) padre; (*fam.*) jefe; (*mec.*) regulador.
gowan [ˈgauən], *s.* margarita.
gown [gaun], *s.* vestido; bata; toga, traje talar; ***dressing gown,*** bata, batín. — *v.t.* vestir (*con toga*).
gowned [gaund], *a.* vestido, vestido con toga, togado.
gownsman [ˈgaunzmən], *s.* togado; paisano, civil; clérigo; concejal.
grab [græb], *s.* agarro; presa; arrebatiña; captura; robo, sisa; (*mec.*) gancho, garfio, grapa; ***grab bucket,*** cucharón de quijadas; ***smash and grab robbery,*** atraco. — *v.t.* agarrar, coger; arrebatar; apropiarse violentamente de. — *v.i.* — ***at,*** tratar de coger.
grabber [ˈgræbə], *s.* avaro; ladrón.
grabble [græbl], *v.i.* ir a tientas; postrarse.
grace [greis], *s.* gracia; garbo, donaire; donosura; elegancia; talante; margen, *m.*; (*mús.*) adorno; ***with a good*** o ***an ill grace,*** de buen *o* mal talante; ***to say grace,*** dar gracias, bendecir la mesa; (*pl.*) juego con aros y palillos; ***good graces,*** favor, amistad; (*mit.*) [GRACES]. — *v.t.* adornar; agraciar, favorecer; honrar.
graceful [ˈgreisful], *a.* agraciado; garboso, airoso, elegante.
gracefully [ˈgreisfuli], *adv.* con gracia, con garbo, airosamente, donosamente, elegantemente.
gracefulness [ˈgreisfulnis], *s.* gracia; donaire, airosidad; gallardía, gentileza, elegancia, garbo.
graceless [ˈgreislis], *a.* réprobo; sin gracia, desgarbado, sin garbo, torpe.
gracelessly [ˈgreislisli], *adv.* sin gracia; desgarbadamente, sin garbo, sin elegancia.
gracelessness [ˈgreislisnis], *s.* falta de gracia, de garbo *o* de airosidad.
Graces [ˈgreisiz], *s.pl.* (las tres) Gracias.
gracile [ˈgræsail], *a.* grácil.
gracious [ˈgreiʃəs], *a.* benigno, benévolo; cortés, afable; ***His*** o ***Her Gracious Majesty,*** Su Graciosa Majestad. — *interj.* ***gracious me! goodness gracious!*** ¡válgame Dios!
graciousness [ˈgreiʃəsnis], *s.* benevolencia; afabilidad.
grackle [grækl], *s.* estornino.
gradate [grəˈdeit], *v.t.* graduar.
gradation [grəˈdeiʃən], *s.* gradación.
grade [greid], *s.* grado; nivel; clase, calidad; nota, calificación; pendiente, cuesta; (*Am.*) [GRADIENT]; ***down grade,*** cuesta abajo; (*Am.*) ***grade-school,*** escuela; (*Am.*) ***grade crossing*** [LEVEL-CROSSING]; ***to make the grade,*** dar la talla, alcanzar el nivel preciso; ***up grade,*** cuesta arriba. — *v.t.* clasificar; calificar, dar (una) calificación a; nivelar; ***grade as,*** clasificar como, calificar de.
grader [ˈgreidə], *s.* (*ing.*) nivelador.
gradient [ˈgreidiənt], *a.* en disnivel, pendiente. — *s.* desnivel, rampa, declive, pendiente, *f.*; inclinación.
gradin [ˈgreidin], *s.* grada.
grading [ˈgreidiŋ], *s.* clasificación; nivelación.
gradual [ˈgrædjuəl], *a.* gradual; insensible, imperceptible, paulatino. — *s.* (*igl.*) gradual.
graduate [ˈgrædjuit], *a.*, *s.* graduado; licenciado. — [ˈgrædjueit], *v.t.* graduar; licenciar. — *v.i.* graduarse, licenciarse.
graduation [grædjuˈeiʃən], *s.* colación de grados; (el) licenciarse.
graduator [ˈgrædjueitə], *s.* graduador.
graecism [ˈgri:sizəm], *s.* grecismo.
graecize [ˈgri:saiz], *v.t.* grecizar. — *v.i.* grecizarse.
Graeco-Latin [ˈgri:kou-ˈlætin], *a.* grecolatino.
Graeco-Roman [ˈgri:kou-ˈroumən], *a.* grecorromano.
graffito [grəˈfi:tou], *s.* (*pl.* **graffiti** [grəˈfi:ti:]) grafito.
graft (1) [grɑ:ft], *s.* injerto. — *v.t.*, *v.i.* injertar (***onto,*** en *o* a).
graft (2) [grɑ:ft], *s.* corrupción, soborno, chanchullos, *m.pl.*; (*fam.*) ***to be on the graft,*** hacer chanchullos.
graft (3) [grɑ:ft], *s.* (*fam.*) ***hard graft,*** trabajo duro.
grafting [ˈgrɑ:ftiŋ], *s.* injerto; (*carp.*) empalme; remiendo; ***grafting knife,*** abridor; ***grafting twig,*** estaca.
grail [greil], *s.* grial; ***the Holy Grail,*** el Santo Grial.
grain [grein], *s.* grano; cereales, *m.pl.*; pizca; (*madera*) fibra, hebra; (*piedra*) vena, veta; (*cuero*) flor; (*tela*) granilla; ***against the grain,*** a contrapelo; ***it goes against the grain with me,*** se me hace cuesta arriba; ***dyed in the grain,*** teñido en rama; empedernido; ***grain-fork,*** bieldo; ***grain-moth, grain-weevil,*** gorgojo; ***to saw with the grain,*** (a)serrar a hebra; ***to take with a grain of salt,*** creer hasta cierto punto nada más, aceptar

con reservas; ***there is not a grain of truth in it,*** no tiene la más mínima base de verdad. — *v.t.* vetear; granear.

graining [ˈgreiniŋ], *s.* graneladura, graneo.

grainy [ˈgreini], *a.* granado, graneado, granoso.

gram(me) [græm], *s.* gramo.

grama-grass [ˈgrɑːmə-grɑːs], *s.* (*ant.*) grama.

graminaceous, gramineous [græmiˈneiʃəs, græˈminiəs], *a.* gramíneo.

graminivorous [græmiˈnivərəs], *a.* graminívoro.

grammar [ˈgræmə], *s.* gramática; ***grammar school,*** colegio de segunda enseñanza.

grammarian, grammatist [grəˈmɛəriən, ˈgræmətist], *s.* gramático.

grammatical [grəˈmætikəl], *a.* gramatical.

grammaticalness [grəˈmætikəlnis], *s.* corrección gramatical.

gramophone [ˈgræməfoun], *s.* gramófono.

grampus [ˈgræmpəs], *s.* orco, orca.

granary [ˈgrænəri], *s.* granero.

grand [grænd], *a.* gran, grande; grandioso; magnífico, imponente; espléndido, soberbio; admirable; majestuoso, magno; ***grand-aunt,*** tía abuela; ***grand-daughter,*** nieta; ***grand-duke,*** granduque; archiduque; (*orn.*) duque, buho (maximus); ***grand opera,*** ópera seria; ***grand-piano,*** piano de cola; (*ant.*) ***grand-sire,*** abuelo; ***grand strategy,*** alta estrategia; ***grand total,*** suma de totales; ***grand-uncle,*** tío abuelo.

grandad [ˈgrændæd], *s.* (*fam.*) abuelito.

grandam [ˈgrændæm], *s.* (*ant.*) abuela; anciana.

grandchild [ˈgræntʃaild], *s.* nieto, nieta.

grandee [grænˈdiː], *s.* grande (de España); prócer.

grandeur [ˈgrændjə], *s.* grandeza; magnificencia, grandiosidad, majestuosidad.

grandfather [ˈgrændfɑːðə], *s.* abuelo; ***grandfather-clock,*** reloj de péndulo.

grandiloquence [grænˈdiləkwəns], *s.* grandilocuencia.

grandiloquent [grænˈdiləkwənt], *a.* grandílocuo.

grandiose [ˈgrændious], *a.* grandioso; ampuloso.

grandma [ˈgrænmɑː], *s.* (*fam.*) abuelita.

grandmother [ˈgrænmʌðə], *s.* abuela.

grandness [ˈgrændnis], *s.* grandiosidad.

grandpa [ˈgrænpɑː], *s.* (*fam.*) abuelito.

grandparent [ˈgrænpɛərənt], *s.* abuelo.

grandson [ˈgrænsʌn], *s.* nieto.

grandstand [ˈgrændstænd], *s.* tribuna.

grange [greindʒ], *s.* granja; casa de campo.

graniferous [grəˈnifərəs], *a.* granífero.

granite [ˈgrænit], *s.* granito, piedra berroqueña.

granitic [græˈnitik], *a.* granítico.

granivorous [grəˈnivərəs], *a.* granívoro.

granny [ˈgræni], *s.* (*fam.*) abuelita; ***granny-knot,*** nudo hecho a lo loco.

grant [grɑːnt], *s.* concesión; donativo; subvención; subsidio; beca. — *v.t.* conceder, otorgar; donar; admitir; ***granted!*** ¡cierto!; ***granted that,*** dado que; ***granting this,*** dado que sea así, en el supuesto de que sea así; ***I'll grant you that,*** eso lo admito; ***to take for granted,*** dar por supuesto *o* por sentado *o* por descontado; tratar con indiferencia, no hacer caso de, no tener en cuenta.

grantee [grɑːnˈtiː], *s.* cesionario; donatario.

grantor [ˈgrɑːntɔː], *s.* cesionista, *m.f.*, donador.

granular [ˈgrænjulə], *a.* granular; granuloso.

granulate [ˈgrænjuleit], *v.t.* granular. — *v.i.* granularse.

granulated [ˈgrænjuleitid], *a.* granulado; ***granulated sugar,*** azúcar granulado. — *p.p.* [GRANULATE].

granulation [grænjuˈleiʃən], *s.* granulación.

granule [ˈgrænjuːl], *s.* gránulo.

granulous [ˈgrænjuləs], *a.* granuloso.

grape [greip], *s.* uva; ***grape-hyacinth,*** almizcleña; ***grape-juice,*** zumo de uva; ***unfermented grape-juice,*** mosto; (*mil.*) ***grape-shot,*** metralla; ***grape-skin,*** hollejo; ***grape-sugar,*** glucosa; ***grape-vine,*** parra; ***sour grapes!*** ¡están verdes!

grapefruit [ˈgreipfruːt], *s.* pomelo, toronja.

graph [grɑːf], *s.* gráfico, gráfica, diagrama, *m.*; ***graph paper,*** papel cuadriculado.

graphic(al) [ˈgræfik(əl)], *a.* gráfico; ***graphic art,*** arte gráfica.

graphically [ˈgræfikəli], *adv.* gráficamente, de un modo gráfico *o* pintoresco.

graphite [ˈgræfait], *s.* (*min.*) grafito, plombagina; lápiz.

graphitic [græˈfitik], *a.* grafítico.

grapholite [ˈgræfolait], *s.* pizarra.

graphometer [græˈfɔmitə], *s.* grafómetro.

graphophone [ˈgræfofoun], *s.* fonógrafo.

grapnel [ˈgræpnəl], *s.* (*mar.*) anclote, rezón; arpeo, gancho, garabato, cloque, rastra, rebanadera.

grapple [græpl], *s.* (*mar.*) arpeo, rezón; asimiento; (*lucha libre*) presa; (*mec.*) garfio. — *v.t.* aferrar; asir, agarrar. — *v.i.* agarrarse, luchar cuerpo a cuerpo; ***grapple with,*** luchar con, habérselas con; esforzarse por resolver.

grappling [ˈgræpliŋ], *s.* (*mar.*) rezón; aferramiento; ***grappling-iron,*** cloque, arpeo de abordaje.

grapy [ˈgreipi], *a.* lleno *o* hecho de uvas.

grasp [grɑːsp], *s.* agarro, asimiento; apretón; poder; alcance; comprensión; ***within the grasp of,*** al alcance de; ***to have a good grasp of,*** tener bastante idea de. — *v.t.* agarrar, coger, asir; empuñar; estrechar; comprender, captar; ***grasp all, lose all,*** quien mucho abarca poco aprieta. — *v.i.* — ***at,*** hacer por coger, asir etc.

grasper [ˈgrɑːspə], *s.* agarrador.

grasping [ˈgrɑːspiŋ], *a.* codicioso, avaro.

grass [grɑːs], *s.* hierba; pasto; césped; ***grass-green,*** verde como la hierba; ***grass-grown,*** cubierto de hierba; ***grass-mower,*** dallador; (*pol.*) ***grass-roots,*** (la) gran masa de los partidarios; ***to get to the grass-roots of the problem,*** ir al grano del problema; ***grass-widow,*** mujer separada temporalmente de su marido; ***grass-widower,*** marido separado temporalmente de su mujer; ***to let the grass grow under one's feet,*** perder el tiempo, dormirse en las pajas; ***to put out to grass,*** jubilar. — *v.t.* cubrir de hierba; apacentar; blanquear (*lino*). — *v.i.* criar hierba.

grasshopper [ˈgrɑːshɔpə], *s.* saltamontes, *m. inv.*

grassiness [ˈgrɑːsinis], *s.* abundancia de hierba.

grassless [ˈgrɑːslis], *a.* sin hierba.

grassy [ˈgrɑːsi], *a.* herboso, lleno de hierba; herbáceo.

grate (1) [greit], *s.* reja, verja; parrilla; hogar, rejilla.

grate (2) [greit], *v.t.* rallar; raspar; hacer rechinar; irritar; enrejar. — *v.i.* rechinar; ***grate against*** o ***upon,*** ludir, rozar (con); (*fig.*) ***grate on*** o ***upon,*** irritar; (*fig.*) ***grate on the ear,*** herir el oído.

grateful [ˈgreitful], *a.* agradecido, reconocido; grato; ***to be grateful for,*** agradecer.

gratefulness [ˈgreitfulnis], *s.* gratitud, reconocimiento, agradecimiento; gusto, agrado.

grater [ˈgreitə], *s.* rallo, rallador, raspador.

graticulate [grəˈtikjuleit], *v.t.* cuadricular.

gratification [grætifiˈkeiʃən], *s.* satisfacción, placer, complacencia.

gratify [ˈgrætifai], *v.t.* satisfacer, complacer, dar gusto a.

grating (1) [ˈgreitiŋ], *s.* reja, verja; rejilla, retícula.

grating (2) [ˈgreitiŋ], *a.* que raspa; rechinador, rechinante; áspero, irritante; discordante. — *s.* rechinamiento; (*pl.*) ralladuras, *f.pl.*

gratitude [ˈgrætitjuːd], *s.* gratitud, reconocimiento, agradecimiento.

gratuitous [grəˈtjuːitəs], *a.* gratuito, injustificado, innecesario.

gratuity [grəˈtjuːiti], *s.* gratificación.

gravamen [grə'veimən], *s.* agravio; causa *o* parte más grave.

grave (1) [greiv], *s.* sepultura, sepulcro, tumba; ***grave-clothes,*** mortaja; ***grave-digger,*** sepulturero. — *irr. v.t., v.i.* grabar.

grave (2) [greiv], *a.* grave, serio, solemne; [grɑːv] (*mús.*) grave, bajo; [grɑːv] (*gram.*) grave. — [grɑːv], *s.* acento grave.

grave (3) [greiv], *v.t.* (*mar.*) despalmar.

gravel ['grævəl], *s.* grava; (*pat.*) arenillas, *f.pl.*; ***gravel-pit,*** yacimiento de grava. — *v.t.* cubrir de grava.

graveless ['greivlis], *a.* insepulto.

gravelly ['grævəli], *a.* lleno de grava, arenoso.

graven ['greivən], *a.* ***graven image,*** ídolo. — *p.p.* [GRAVE (1)].

graveness ['greivnis], *s.* gravedad, seriedad, (lo) solemne.

graver ['greivə], *s.* buril, punzón.

gravestone ['greivstoun], *s.* lápida (sepulcral).

graveyard ['greivjɑːd], *s.* cementerio, camposanto.

gravid ['grævid], *a.* grávido.

gravimeter ['grævimiːtə], *s.* gravímetro.

graving ['greiviŋ], *s.* grabado; (*mar.*) carena; ***graving-dock,*** dique de carena.

gravitate ['græviteit], *v.i.* gravitar; ***gravitate towards,*** tender *o* propender a ir hacia *o* a congregarse alrededor de, ser *o* verse atraído a.

gravitation [grævi'teiʃən], *s.* gravitación; tendencia, atracción.

gravity ['græviti], *s.* gravedad; ***centre of gravity,*** centro de gravedad; ***law of gravity,*** ley de la gravedad; ***specific gravity,*** peso específico.

gravure [grə'vjuə], *s.* fotograbado.

gravy ['greivi], *s.* salsa, jugo; ***gravy-boat,*** salsera.

gray [GREY].

grayling ['greiliŋ], *s.* (*ict.*) umbla.

graze [greiz], *s.* roce; abrasión; desolladura. — *v.t.* pacer; apacentar, pastar; rozar, raspar. — *v.i.* pacer.

grazier ['greiziə], *s.* ganadero.

grease [griːs], *s.* grasa; pringue; unto, sebo; (*fig.*) soborno; (*mec.*) ***grease-box,*** caja de sebo; (*aut.*) ***grease-gun,*** engrasador; ***grease-proof,*** a prueba de grasa. — *v.t.* engrasar; untar; ***grease the palm of,*** untar la mano a.

greaser ['griːzə], *s.* engrasador; lubricante; lubricador; (*Am., despec.*) mejicano *o* hispanoamericano.

greasily ['griːzili], *adv.* crasamente.

greasiness ['griːzinis], *s.* pringue; (lo) resbaladizo; (lo) grasiento.

greasy ['griːzi], *a.* grasiento, pringoso; resbaladizo; (*fig.*) suavón.

great [greit], *a.* gran, grande; magno; mayor; soberbio, estupendo; ***great at, great on,*** fuerte en; ***great-bellied,*** barrigudo; preñada; ***great-coat,*** abrigo, capote; ***great-grandfather,*** bisabuelo; ***Greater London,*** el Gran Londres; ***great-grandmother,*** bisabuela; ***great-great-grandfather,*** tatarabuelo; ***great-great-grandmother,*** tatarabuela; ***great-hearted,*** magnánimo, de alma grande; ***Great War,*** Primera Guerra Mundial.

greaten ['greitən], *v.t.* (*ant.*) agrandar, engrandecer. — *v.i.* crecer, aumentar.

greatly ['greitli], *adv.* muy, mucho; sumamente.

greatness ['greitnis], *s.* grandeza; amplitud, magnitud, extensión.

greaves (1) [griːvz], *s. pl.* (*mil.*) grebas, *f.pl.*

greaves (2) [griːvz], *s.pl.* (*coc.*) chicharrones, *m.pl.*

grebe [griːb], *s.* colimbo.

Grecian ['griːʃən], *a., s.* griego.

Greece [griːs]. Grecia.

greed, greediness [griːd, 'griːdinis], *s.* voracidad, gula; codicia, avaricia; ansia.

greedy ['griːdi], *a.* voraz; codicioso; ansioso.

Greek [griːk], *a., s.* griego; (*fam.*) ***it's all Greek to me,*** para mí (es) como si fuera chino.

green [griːn], *a.* verde; (*fig.*) nuevo, novato; (*fig.*) ***green light,*** permiso para seguir adelante; ***to be, look*** *o* ***show up green,*** verdear; ***to be green with envy,*** ponérsele a alguien los dientes largos de envidia; (*fig.*) ***to go green,*** demudarse; ***to have green fingers,*** tener mucha maña para *o* con las plantas. — *s.* verde; verdor; prado, (terreno de) césped; (*pl.*) verdura(s), col, repollo; ***bottle green,*** verde botella; ***dark green,*** verde oscuro.

greenback ['griːnbæk], *s.* (*Am., fam.*) billete de banco.

greenery ['griːnəri], *s.* verdor, verde; follaje, espesura.

greenfinch ['griːnfintʃ], *s.* (*orn.*) verderón.

greenfly ['griːnflai], *s.* pulgón.

greengage ['griːngeidʒ], *s.* (ciruela) claudia.

greengrocer ['griːngrousə], *s.* verdulero.

greengrocery ['griːngrousəri], *s.* verdulería.

greenhorn ['griːnhɔːn], *s.* (*fam.*) novato, bisoño.

greenhouse ['griːnhaus], *s.* invernáculo, invernadero.

greening ['griːniŋ], *s.* manzana verdosa.

greenish ['griːniʃ], *a.* verdoso.

greenness ['griːnnis], *s.* verdor; falta de experiencia.

greenroom ['griːnrum], *s.* (*teat.*) sala de espera (*de los actores*); almacén.

greensand ['griːnsænd], *s.* arenisca verde.

greenstuff ['griːnstʌf], *s.* verdura(s).

greensward ['griːnswɔːd], *s.* césped.

greenwood ['griːnwud], *s.* bosque frondoso.

greet [griːt], *v.t.* saludar; recibir; dar la bienvenida a; presentarse a.

greeting ['griːtiŋ], *s.* saludo; (buena) acogida; bienvenida.

gregarious [gri'gɛəriəs], *a.* gregario; sociable.

gregariousness [gri'gɛəriəsnis], *s.* tendencia a congregarse; sociabilidad.

Gregorian [gri'gɔːriən], *a.* gregoriano.

gremial ['griːmiəl], *a.* gremial.

Grenada [gre'neidə]. Granada.

grenade [gri'neid], *s.*granada; bomba de mano.

Grenadian [gre'neidiən], *a., s.* granadino.

grenadier [grenə'diə], *s.* granadero.

grenadine ['grenədiːn], *s.* (*tej.*) granadina.

grey [grei], *a.* gris; canoso, encanecido; rucio; ***grey-beard,*** anciano; ***grey-bearded,*** barbicano; ***grey-fish,*** trompetilla, mosca gris; ***grey hairs,*** canas; ***grey-headed,*** canoso; ***grey (horse),*** (caballo) rucio; ***grey matter,*** materia gris. — *s.* gris, *m.*; rucio; ***dark grey,*** gris oscuro. — *v.t.* poner, volver gris. — *v.i.* ponerse, volverse gris.

greyhound ['greihaund], *s.* galgo, lebrel.

greyish ['greiiʃ], *a.* agrisado, grisáceo; entrecano.

greyness ['greinis], *s.* (lo) gris; encanecimiento.

grid [grid], *s.* parrilla, rejilla; (*elec.*) red.

griddle [gridl], *s.* (*coc.*) tartera; tapadera de fogón; ***griddle cake,*** pastelillo, fritura de harina.

gridiron ['gridaiən], *s.* parrilla; (*teat.*) telar; (*mar.*) andamiada.

grief [griːf], *s.* dolor, pesar, aflicción; ***to come to grief,*** acabar mal; desgraciarse; malograrse.

grievance ['griːvəns], *s.* agravio, injusticia, motivo de queja; ***to air one's grievances,*** dar expresión a las quejas.

grieve [griːv], *v.t.* afligir, apesadumbrar. — *v.i.* afligirse, acongojarse; ***grieve over,*** dolerse de.

grievingly ['griːviŋli], *adv.* apesaradamente.

grievous ['griːvəs], *a.* gravoso, aflictivo; grave; sensible, doloroso, penoso, lamentable.

grievousness ['griːvəsnis], *s.* gravedad; dolor; opresión.

griffin ['grifin], *s.* grifo.

griffon ['grifən], *s.* perro zorrero; (*orn.*) ***griffon-vulture,*** buitre común.

grig [grig], *s.* (*ent.*) cigarra, grillo; (*ict.*) anguila pequeña; ***as merry as a grig,*** alegre como un grillo.

grill [gril], *s.* parrilla; asado a la parrilla; ***mixed grill,*** mezcla de asados. — *v.t.* asar a la parrilla; (*fam.*) atormentar, interrogar.

grillage ['grilidʒ], *s.* emparrillado.

grille [gril], *s.* verja; reja; enrejado; calado de adorno.

grilse [grils], *s.* salmón joven (cuando regresa por primera vez del mar).

grim [grim], *a.* torvo, severo, adusto, ceñudo; (*fam.*) siniestro, fatal.

grimace [gri'meis], *s.* mueca, visaje. — *v.i.* hacer muecas.

grimalkin [gri'mælkin], *s.* gatazo, gata vieja; (*fig.*) vieja de mal genio, bruja, arpía.

grime [graim], *s.* tizne, mugre, *f.* — *v.t.* ensuciar, tiznar, llenar de mugre.

grimness ['grimnis], *s.* horror, espanto.

grimy ['graimi], *a.* tiznado, mugriento.

grin [grin], *s.* sonrisa (de felicidad). — *v.i.* sonreír (feliz, contento); ***grin and bear it,*** reírse y aguantar, poner al mal tiempo buena cara.

grind [graind], *s.* molienda; rutina. — *irr. v.t.* moler; triturar, pulverizar; amolar, afilar; gravar; pulir, bruñir; hacer rechinar; desgastar; oprimir, agobiar; ***grind out,*** producir mecánicamente. — *v.i.* molerse; trabajar *o* estudiar laboriosamente; quemarse las cejas; mover el manubrio.

grinder ['graində], *s.* amolador, afilador; molinillo.

grinding ['graindiŋ], *s.* pulverización; molienda, (el) moler; (*dientes*) rechinamiento; (*odontología*) desgaste.

grindstone ['graindstoun], *s.* muela, piedra de moler *o* amolar; ***to keep one's nose to the grindstone,*** batir el yunque.

grip [grip], *s.* asimiento, agarro; agarradero, empuñadura; garras, *f.pl.*; apretón (*de manos*); (*fig.*) dominio, comprensión; (*equipaje*) maletín; ***to come*** o ***get to grips with,*** enfrentarse resueltamente con, abordar resueltamente, luchar (a brazo partido) con; ***to lose one's grip,*** perder facultades, perder fuerzas, decaer, no ser ya como antes, empezar a flaquear *o* a fallar. — *v.t.* asir, agarrar, coger fuerte; apretar; agarrarse a; absorber la atención de *o* a.

gripe [graip], *s.* retortijón, dolor de tripas. — *v.i.* (*fam.*) quejarse, protestar, refunfuñar.

griper ['graipə], *s.* (*fam.*) protestón.

griping ['graipiŋ], *s.* (*fam.*) protestas, *f.pl.*

gripping ['gripiŋ], *a.* (*fam.*) absorbente, apasionante.

grisly ['grizli], *a.* espantoso, espeluznante.

grist [grist], *s.* molienda; ***it's all grist to the mill,*** de todo ello se puede sacar partido.

gristle [grisl], *s.* cartílago, ternilla; nervio(s).

gristly ['grisli], *a.* cartilaginoso; que tiene nervio(s).

grit [grit], *s.* arena; cascajo; (*geol.*) arenisca; (*pl.*) sémola, farro; (*fam.*) ***to have grit,*** tener agallas. — *v.t.* cerrar fuertemente *o* hacer rechinar (*los dientes*).

gritty ['griti], *a.* arenoso, arenisco; duro.

grizzle [grizl], *v.i.* (*fam.*) lloriquear.

grizzled, grizzly [grizld, 'grizli], *a.* gris, grisáceo; canoso; ***grizzly bear,*** oso gris.

groan [groun], *s.* gemido, quejido. — *v.i.* gemir, quejarse; crujir.

groaning ['grouniŋ], *s.* gemidos, *m.pl.*, quejidos, *m.pl.*; crujir.

groat [grout], *s.* (*ant.*) ardite.

groats [grouts], *s.pl.* avena a medio moler.

grocer ['grousə], *s.* tendero (de ultramarinos); abacero; ***grocer's shop,*** tienda (de ultramarinos); mantequería; abacería, colmado.

groceries ['grousəriz], *s.pl.* comestibles, *m.pl.*, ultramarinos, *m.pl.*

grog ['grɔg], *s.* grog (*ron y agua*); ***grog-shop,*** taberna.

groggy ['grɔgi], *a.* calamocano; malucho, flojo; (*dep.*) grogui.

grogram ['grɔgrəm], *s.* (*tej.*) gorgorán.

groin [grɔin], *s.* ingle, *f.*; (*arq.*) arista de encuentro. — *v.t.* (*arq.*) formar aristas.

groom ['gru:m], *s.* mozo de cuadra; gentilhombre; lacayo; novio; ***groom of the bedchamber,*** ayuda de cámara del rey; ***groom in waiting,*** camarero de semana. — *v.t.* cuidar, almohazar (*caballos*); arreglar (*con esmero*); preparar (*para una profesión*).

grooming ['gru:miŋ], *s.* acicalamiento, aseo; (el) almohazar.

groove [gru:v], *s.* surco; ranura, estría, acanaladura. — *v.t.* acanalar, estriar.

grope [group], *v.t.* ***grope one's way,*** tentar el camino; avanzar a tientas. — *v.i.* andar a tientas; ***grope for,*** requerir, buscar a tientas.

grosbeak ['grousbi:k], *s.* (*orn.*) cardenal, loxia; picogordo.

grosgrain ['grougrein], *s.* (*tej.*) gro.

gross ['grous], *a.* gordo, pesado; craso; bruto, total. — *s.* gruesa; ***by the gross,*** en gruesas; ***in (the) gross,*** en grueso, al por mayor.

grossly ['grousli], *adv.* en bruto; groseramente, crasamente, toscamente.

grossness ['grousnis], *s.* gordura; grosería; enormidad.

grossular ['grɔsjulə], *s.* (*min*). grosularia.

grot [grɔt], *s.* (*poet.*) gruta.

grotesque [gro'tesk], *a.* grotesco.

grotto ['grɔtou], *s.* gruta.

grouch [grautʃ], *s.* mal humor. — *v.i.* estar de mal humor, refunfuñar.

grouchy ['grautʃi], *a.* malhumorado, refunfuñador.

ground (1) [graund], *s.* suelo, piso; tierra, terreno; campo; fondo; causa, motivo; base, fundamento; (*pint.*) primera capa; (*pl.*) fundamento, motivo; sedimento, posos, *m.pl.*; terrenos, *m.pl.*, jardines, *m.pl.*; ***ground-floor,*** piso bajo; ***ground-ivy,*** hiedra terrestre; ***ground-pine,*** pinillo; ***ground-plan,*** planta, primer proyecto; ***ground-plot,*** solar; ***ground-rent,*** alquiler (*por el terreno en que se levanta un edificio*); ***ground-staff,*** personal de tierra; ***ground swell,*** mar de fondo; (*mar.*) ***ground-tackle,*** amarrazón de ancla; ***ground-work,*** fundamento, cimiento; trabajo fundamental *o* básico; ***on the grounds of,*** con motivo de; ***to be on one's own ground,*** estar en su elemento; ***to burn to the ground,*** arrasar; ***to cut the ground from under s.o.'s feet,*** minar a alguien, dejar a alguien en tenguerengue; ***to fall to the ground,*** venirse al suelo; fracasar; ***to gain ground,*** ganar terreno; ***to give ground,*** ceder terreno; ***to hold*** o ***stand one's ground,*** mantenerse firme; ***to run to ground,*** dar con; (*fam.*) ***to suit s.o. down to the ground,*** venirle a alguien de perillas *o* de perlas. — *v.t.* hacer varar; conectar con tierra; basar, cimentar, fundamentar; establecer; (*aer.*) prohibir el vuelo a; ***ground s.o. in sth.,*** enseñarle a alguien los rudimentos de algo. — *v.i.* basarse; encallar, embarrancar.

ground (2) [graund], *a.* molido. — *p.p.* [GRIND].

groundage ['graundidʒ], *s.* (*mar.*) derecho de puerto, derecho de anclaje.

grounded ['graundid], *a.* ***well grounded (in),*** muy versado (en), bien fundado (en).

grounding ['graundiŋ], *s.* (*mar.*) (el) encallar *o* varar; (*aer.*) prohibición de todo vuelo; (*fig.*) fundamento, base.

groundless ['graundlis], *a.* infundado, falto de motivo *o* de razón.

groundlessness ['graundlisnis], *s.* falta de fundamento, de motivo *o* de razón.

groundling [ˈgraundliŋ], *s.* animal terrestre; (*ict.*) loche, loja.
groundnut [ˈgraundnʌt], *s.* cacahuete; chufa.
groundsel [ˈgraundsəl] *s.* (*bot.*) zuzón, hierba cana.
ground-work [ˈgraund-wəːk], *s.* trabajo fundamental *o* básico.
group [gruːp], *a.* colectivo. — *s.* grupo; agrupación; corrillo. — *v.t.* agrupar. — *v.i.* agruparse.
grouse (1) [graus], *s.* (*orn.*) ***sand grouse,*** ortega; (*orn.*) ***black grouse,*** gallo de bosque; (*orn.*) ***red grouse,*** lagópodo escocés.
grouse (2) [graus], *s.* (*fam.*) queja(s), protesta(s), pataleo; ***to have a grouse against,*** tener motivo de queja contra. — *v.i.* quejarse, protestar, patalear, refunfuñar.
grout [graut], *s.* mezcla, lechada. — *v.t.* llenar *o* rellenar con mezcla *o* lechada.
grove [grouv], *s.* arboleda, soto, boscaje, bosquecillo.
grovel [ˈgrɔvəl], *v.i.* arrastrarse; (*fig.*) envilecerse.
groveller [ˈgrɔvələ], *s.* hombre servil y rastrero.
grovelling [ˈgrɔvəliŋ], *a.* servil, rastrero. — *s.* servilismo.
grow [grou], *irr. v.t.* cultivar. — *v.i.* crecer; cultivarse; aumentar, desarrollarse; hacerse, ponerse, volverse; ***grow angry,*** enfadarse; ***grow cold,*** enfriarse; ***grow dark,*** oscurecer(se); ***grow fat,*** engordar; ***grow old,*** envejecer; ***grow into,*** hacerse, llegar a ser; ***it grows on one,*** con el tiempo le va gustando a uno; ***grow out of,*** resultar de, ser consecuencia de; ***he grew out of his shoes,*** se le quedaron pequeños los zapatos; ***grow up,*** hacerse mayor; crearse, llegar a imponerse.
grower [ˈgrouə], *s.* cultivador; cosechero; criador.
growl [graul], *s.* gruñido; rezongo, refunfuño. — *v.t.* decir gruñendo. — *v.i.* gruñir, rezongar, refunfuñar.
growler [ˈgraulə], *s.* perro gruñidor.
grown [groun], *a.* crecido, hecho; adulto, maduro; desarrollado; ***grown over with,*** cubierto de (*hierba, maleza etc.*); ***fully grown,*** crecido del todo, hecho y derecho; ***grown up,*** adulto, (persona) mayor.
growth [grouθ], *s.* crecimiento, desarrollo; vegetación; producción, producto; aumento; estatura completa; (*med.*) tumor; (*fam.*) ***a week's growth,*** barba de una semana.
grub [grʌb], *s.* larva, gusano; gorgojo; (*fam.*) pitanza. — *v.t.* desmalezar; arrancar, descuajar; (*fam.*) alimentar. — *v.i.* cavar, azadonar; (*fam.*) alimentarse; ***grub about for,*** lampar por; ***grub away,*** afanarse tristemente; ***grub for,*** buscar (con trabajo).
grubber [ˈgrʌbə], *s.* desyerbador; arrancador de raíces.
grubby [ˈgrʌbi], *a.* sucio, mugriento.
Grub Street [ˈgrʌb striːt], *s.* (los) escritores de mala muerte.
grudge [grʌdʒ], *s.* rencor, inquina; ***to bear, have*** o ***nurse a grudge against,*** tener rencor a. — *v.t.* escatimar, dar de mala gana; envidiar; ***grudge no pains,*** no escatimar esfuerzos.
grudging [ˈgrʌdʒiŋ], *a.* reacio, renuente, mezquino.
grudgingly [ˈgrʌdʒiŋli], *adv.* con repugnancia, de mala gana.
gruel [ˈgruːəl], *s.* gachas, *f.pl.*; (*Hisp. Am.*) atole.
gruel(l)ing [ˈgruːəliŋ], *a.* agotador; riguroso, penoso.
gruesome [ˈgruːsəm], *a.* horrendo, espantoso.
gruff [grʌf], *a.* bronco, brusco, áspero, arisco.
gruffness [ˈgrʌfnis], *s.* brusquedad, aspereza.
grumble [grʌmbl], *s.* queja, rezongo, refunfuño; ruido sordo. — *v.i.* — ***about,*** quejarse, protestar, de *o* por; (*fig.*) retumbar.
grumbler [ˈgrʌmblə], *s.* refunfuñador, gruñidor, gruñón, rezongador.
grumbling [ˈgrʌmbliŋ], *a.* refunfuñón. — *s.* refunfuño, quejas, *f.pl.*
grumblingly [ˈgrʌmbliŋli], *adv.* refunfuñando.
grume [gruːm], *s.* grumo, cuajarón; masa viscosa.
grumous [ˈgruːməs], *a.* grumoso.
grumpy [ˈgrʌmpi], *a.* (*fam.*) gruñón, malhumorado.
grunt [grʌnt], *s.* gruñido. — *v.t.* decir entre gruñidos. — *v.i.* gruñir.
grunting [ˈgrʌntiŋ], *s.* gruñido(s), (el) gruñir.
grunter [ˈgrʌntə], *s.* gruñidor.
guaco [ˈgwɑːkou], *s.* (*bot.*) guaco.
guaiacum [ˈgwaiəkəm], *s.* (*bot.*) guayaco, guayacán.
guanaco [gwəˈnɑːkou], *s.* guanaco.
guano [ˈgwɑːnou], *s.* guano.
guarantee [gærənˈtiː], *s.* garantía; garante, fiador; (*for.*) persona por quien otra responde. — *v.t.* garantizar; asegurar.
guarantor [gærənˈtɔː], *s.* garante, fiador.
guaranty [ˈgærənti], *s.* (*for.*) garantía, fianza.
guard [gɑːd], *s.* guardia; guarda; protección, defensa; coraza, peto; resguardo; (*f.c.*) jefe de tren; ***guard-rail,*** baranda, barandilla; (*f.c.*) contracarril; (*mil.*) ***guard-room,*** cuarto de guardia; ***guard-ship,*** navío de guardia; ***to mount guard,*** montar (la) guardia; ***off one's guard,*** desprevenido; ***to be one of the old guard,*** ser del antiguo régimen; ***to be on guard,*** estar de guardia; (*fig.*) ***to be on (one's) guard,*** estar en guardia, estar ojo avizor, estar alerta, estar sobre aviso; ***under careful guard,*** a buen recaudo. — *v.t.* guardar; proteger, defender; vigilar. — *v.i.*—***against,*** guardarse de, prevenirse contra.
guarded [ˈgɑːdid], *a.* cauteloso, cauto, reservado, circunspecto.
guardedness [ˈgɑːdidnis], *s.* cautela, circunspección, precaución.
guardhouse [ˈgɑːdhaus], *s.* cuartel de la guardia; cárcel (militar).
guardian [ˈgɑːdiən], *a.* tutelar; ***guardian angel,*** angel de la guarda. — *s.* tutor; protector; guardián.
guardianship [ˈgɑːdiənʃip], *s.* tutela; protección; guardianía.
guardsman [ˈgɑːdzmən], *s.* (*pl.* **-men** [-men]) soldado de la guardia (real).
Guatemala [gwætiˈmɑːlə]. Guatemala.
Guatemalan [gwætiˈmɑːlən], *a., s.* guatemalteco.
guava [ˈgwɑːvə], *s.* (*bot.*) guayabo; guayaba.
gubernatorial [gjuːbənəˈtɔːriəl], *a.* gubernativo.
gudgeon (1) [ˈgʌdʒən], *s.* (*ict.*) gobio; (*fig.*) chiripa, ganga; (*fig.*) mentecato, bobo.
gudgeon (2) [ˈgʌdʒən], *s.* (*mar.*) hembra (*del timón*); (*mec.*) gorrón; perno; cuello (de eje).
guelder-rose [ˈgeldə-rouz], *s.* (*bot.*) viburno.
Guelph [gwelf], *s.* güelfo.
guerdon [ˈgəːdən], *s.* galardón.
guerite [ˈgeiriːt], *s.* (*mil.*) garita.
guernsey [ˈgəːnzi], *s.* jersey (originario de Guernsey).
guerrilla [gəˈrilə], *s.* guerrilla, partida; guerrillero; ***guerrilla-fighter,*** guerrillero; ***guerrilla-warfare,*** guerra de guerrillas.
guess [ges], *s.* conjetura, suposición. — *v.t.* adivinar. — *v.i.* suponer, imaginar; creer; ***guess right(ly),*** acertar; ***guess at,*** conjeturar, estimar; ***I guess so,*** creo que sí, me parece que sí.
guesser [ˈgesə], *s.* conjeturador, adivinador.
guesswork [ˈgeswəːk], *s.* conjeturas, *f.pl.*, suposiciones, *f.pl.*
guest [gest], *s.* huésped; invitado, convidado; ***guest-house,*** casa de huéspedes; (*mar.*) ***guest-rope,*** guía de falsa amarra; ***guest-room,*** cuarto de huéspedes.
guffaw [gʌˈfɔː], *s.* carcajada, risotada. — *v.i.* reírse a carcajadas.
guidable [ˈgaidəbl], *a.* dócil, manejable.

guidance [ˈgaidəns], *s.* gobierno, dirección, orientación; ***for your guidance,*** para su gobierno.
guide [gaid], *s.* guía, *m.f.*; guía; pauta; (*impr.*) mordante; ***guide-board,*** hito; ***guide-book,*** guía (*de turistas*); ***guide-lines,*** falsilla; líneas directrices, *f.pl.*; ***guide-post,*** hito, poste indicador. — *v.t.* guiar, encaminar, orientar.
guideless [ˈgaidlis], *a.* sin guía; sin gobierno.
guidon [ˈgaidən], *s.* (*mil.*) guión; portaguión.
guild [gild], *s.* gremio, cofradía, hermandad.
guilder [ˈgildə], *s.* florín holandés.
guildhall [ˈgildhɔːl], *s.* casa de ayuntamiento, casa consistorial.
guile [gail], *s.* astucia; maña, malicia, engaño; treta.
guileful [ˈgailful], *a.* astuto; engañoso.
guilefulness [ˈgailfulnis], [GUILE].
guileless [ˈgaillis], *a.* cándido, ingenuo, inocente.
guilelessness [ˈgaillisnis], *s.* inocencia, ingenuidad.
guillemot [ˈgilimɔt], *s.* (*orn.*) alca, uria.
guillotine [ˈgilətiːn], *s.* guillotina. — *v.t.* guillotinar; ***guillotine a bill,*** votar la clausura del debate de un proyecto de ley.
guilt [gilt], *s.* culpa; culpabilidad.
guiltiness [ˈgiltinis], *s.* culpabilidad.
guiltless [ˈgiltlis], *a.* inocente, libre de culpa.
guiltlessness [ˈgiltlisnis], *s.* inocencia, inculpabilidad.
guilty [ˈgilti], *a.* culpable; ***to be found guilty,*** ser declarado culpable; ***to have a guilty conscience,*** remorderle a uno la conciencia; ***to plead guilty,*** confesarse culpable.
Guinea [ˈgini]. Guinea.
guinea [ˈgini], *s.* (*ant.*) guinea (21 chelines); (*orn.*) ***guinea-fowl,*** gallina de Guinea; (*zool.*) ***guinea-pig,*** conejillo de Indias, cobayo; (*fig.*) conejillo de Indias.
Guinean [ˈginiən], *a.*, *s.* guineo.
guise [gaiz], *s.* atuendo; aspecto; manera, guisa; ***in the guise of,*** disfrazado de; ***under the guise of,*** so capa de.
guitar [giˈtɑː], *s.* guitarra; ***guitar-player,*** guitarrista, *m.f.*
gulch [gʌltʃ], (*Am.*) *s.* quebrada, barranco.
gules [gjuːlz], *s.* (*blas.*) gules, *m.pl.*
gulf [gʌlf], *s.* golfo; abismo; vorágine, *f.*; ***gulf-weed,*** sargazo, sargazos.
gull [gʌl], *s.* (*orn.*) gaviota; bobo, primo. — *v.t.* engañar.
gullet [ˈgʌlit], *s.* gaznate; (*anat.*) esófago.
gullibility [gʌliˈbiliti], *s.* tragaderas, *f.pl.*, credulidad.
gullible [ˈgʌlibl], *a.* simple, crédulo; ***to be terribly gullible,*** comulgar con ruedas de molino.
gully [ˈgʌli], *s.* barranca, hondonada; zanja honda; ***gully-hole,*** albañal, sumidero.
gulp [gʌlp], *s.* trago, sorbo; ***at one gulp,*** de un (solo) trago. — *v.t.* engullir, tragar; ***to gulp down,*** engullirse, tragarse, zamparse; ahogar (*sollozos etc.*). — *v.i.* ahogarse momentáneamente, tragar saliva.
gum (1) [gʌm], *s.* (*anat.*) encía; ***gum-boil,*** flemón.
gum (2) [gʌm], *s.* goma; cola, pegamento; ***gum-arabic,*** goma arábiga; ***gum-boots,*** botas de agua, *f.pl.*; ***gum-elastic,*** goma elástica; ***gum-lac,*** goma laca; ***gum-tree,*** eucalipto; (*fam.*) ***to be up a gum-tree,*** estar en un aprieto; ***gum-water,*** aguagoma. — *v.t.* engomar, pegar con cola; (*fam.*) ***gum up the works,*** jeringar el asunto.
gumbo [ˈgʌmbou], *s.* (*bot.*) quingombó, quimbombó; sopa de quimbombó.
gummiferous [gʌˈmifərəs], *a.* gomífero.
gummy [ˈgʌmi], *a.* gomoso, pegajoso.
gump [gʌmp], *s.* (*fam.*) simplón.
gumption [ˈgʌmpʃən], *s.* (*fam.*) sentido común; inventiva, iniciativa.
gun [gʌn], *s.* arma de fuego; fusil; cañón; pistola, revólver; escopeta; (*fig.*) ***big gun,*** pájaro gordo; ***to go great guns,*** ir viento en popa; ***gun-barrel,*** cañón (de fusil); ***gun-carriage,*** cureña; ***gun-cotton,*** pólvora de algodón; ***gun-runner,*** contrabandista de armas, *m.f.*; ***gun-running,*** contrabando de armas; ***twenty-one gun salute,*** salva de veintiún cañonazos; ***to stick to one's guns,*** no dar su brazo a torcer; ***to spike s.o.'s guns,*** inutilizar, chafar a uno. — *v.t.* — ***down,*** matar a balazos. — *v.i.* — ***for,*** buscar para matar.
gunboat [ˈgʌnbout], *s.* (*mar.*) cañonero.
gunner [ˈgʌnə], *s.* artillero.
gunnery [ˈgʌnəri], *s.* artillería.
gunning [ˈgʌniŋ], *s.* caza.
gunport [ˈgʌnpɔːt], *s.* (*mar.*) porta.
gunpowder [ˈgʌnpaudə], *s.* pólvora.
gunshot [ˈgʌnʃɔt], *s.* cañonazo; escopetazo, tiro de fusil; ***within gunshot,*** a tiro de fusil.
gunsmith [ˈgʌnsmiθ], *s.* armero.
gunwale [ˈgʌnəl], *s.* borda, regala.
gurgitation [gəːdʒiˈteiʃən], *s.* hervor, agitación; remolino.
gurgle [gəːgl], *s.* gorgoteo, gluglú. — *v.i.* borbotar, gorgotear, borbollear.
gurnard [ˈgəːnəd], *s.* (*ict.*) rubio; golondrina; ***flying gurnard,*** alcotán.
gush [gʌʃ], *s.* chorro; borbotón; efusión, extremo. — *v.t.* echar, derramar a borbotones. — *v.i.* borbotar, manar a borbotones; hacer extremos, ser extremoso.
gusher [ˈgʌʃə], *s.* pozo de petróleo que sale a chorro.
gushing [ˈgʌʃiŋ], *a.* extremoso; efusivo.
gusset [ˈgʌsit], *s.* (*cost.*) escudete, contrete; codo de hierro, hierro angular.
gust [gʌst], *s.* ráfaga, racha, golpe (de viento); acceso, arrebato.
gustation [gʌsˈteiʃən], *s.* gustadura, gustación.
gustatory, gustative [ˈgʌstətəri, -tiv], *a.* gustativo.
gusto [ˈgʌstou], *s.* fruición; brío, rejo.
gusty [ˈgʌsti], *a.* borrascoso.
gut [gʌt], *s.* intestino, tripa; cuerda de tripa; (*pl.*) agallas, *f.pl.* — *v.t.* destripar; saquear *o* destruir el interior de.
gutta [ˈgʌtə], *s.* (*farm.*) gota.
gutta-percha [gʌtəˈpəːtʃə], *s.* gutapercha.
gutter [ˈgʌtə], *s.* arroyo; canalón; ***gutter-press,*** periodicuchos de baja estofa, *m.pl.*; ***to rise from the gutter,*** salir de la nada. — *v.t.* acanalar. — *v.i.* acanalarse; correrse, gotear.
guttersnipe [ˈgʌtəsnaip], *s.* golfillo, pillete.
guttural [ˈgʌtərəl], *a.*, *s.* gutural.
gutturalness [ˈgʌtərəlnis], *s.* (lo) gutural.
guy (1) [gai], *s.* (*mar.*) tirante.
guy (2) [gai], *s.* muñeco, mamarracho; (*fam.*) tío, tipo; ***guys and dolls,*** ellos y ellas. — *v.t.* ridiculizar.
Guyana [giːˈɑːnə]. Guyana.
Guyanese [giːəˈniːz], *a.*, *s.* guyanés, *m.*
guzzle [gʌzl], *v.t.* beber mucho; engullir, tragar. — *v.i.* engullir.
guzzler [ˈgʌzlə], *s.* borrachín; pellejo.
gymnasium [dʒimˈneiziəm], *s.* gimnasio.
gymnast [ˈdʒimnæst], *s.* gimnasta, *m.f.*
gymnastic [dʒimˈnæstik], *a.* gimnástico.
gymnastics [dʒimˈnæstiks], *s.pl.* gimnástica.
gymnosophist [dʒimˈnɔsofist], *s.* gimnosofista, *m.f.*
gymnosperm [ˈdʒimnospəːm], *s.* (*bot.*) planta gimnosperma.
gymnospermous [dʒimnoˈspəːməs], *a.* (*bot.*) gimnospermo.
gynæceum [gainiˈsiəm], *s.* gineceo.
gynæcologist [gainiˈkɔlədʒist], *s.* ginecólogo.

gynæcology [gaini'kɔlədʒi], *s.* ginecología.
gynarchy ['gainɑːki], *s.* ginecocracia.
gyp [dʒip], *v.t.* (*fam.*) molestar mucho, jeringar; ***gyp s.o. out of sth.***, quitarle algo a alguien, pisarle algo a alguien.
gypseous ['dʒipsiəs], *a.* yesoso.
gypsum ['dʒipsəm], *s.* yeso; ***crude gypsum***, aljez; ***gypsum-pit***, yesal.
gypsy [GIPSY].
gyral ['dʒaiərəl], *a.* giratorio.
gyrate [dʒaiə'rəit], *v.i.* girar.
gyration [dʒaiə'reiʃən], *s.* giro, vuelta.
gyratory ['dʒaieərətəri], *a.* giratorio.
gyre [dʒaiə], *s.* giro, vuelta.
gyrfalcon [GERFALCON].
gyromancy ['dʒaiəromænsi], *s.* giromancia.
gyroscope ['dʒaiəroskoup], *s.* giroscopio.
gyrostatics [dʒaiəro'stætiks], *s.pl.* girostátcia.
gyve [dʒaiv], *v.t.* encadenar, engrillar.
gyves [dʒaivz], *s.pl.* (*ant.*) grillos, *m.pl.*

H

H, h [eitʃ], octava letra del alfabeto; ***H-bomb,*** bomba hache; ***to drop one's h's,*** pronunciar de una manera inculta.
ha! [hɑː], *interj.* ¡ah! ¡ja, ja, ja!
haberdasher [ˈhæbədæʃə], *s.* mercero.
haberdashery [ˈhæbədæʃəri], *s.* mercería.
habergeon [ˈhæbədʒən], *s.* coraza, cota de malla.
habiliment [həˈbilimənt], *s.* prenda de vestir.
habilitate [həˈbiliteit], *v.t.* habilitar.
habit [ˈhæbit], *s.* costumbre; hábito; ***habit of mind,*** costumbre mental; ***to be in the habit of,*** tener (la) costumbre de, acostumbrar, soler; ***to get into the habit of,*** coger la costumbre de, acostumbrarse a; ***to have got the habit,*** estar enviciado; (*equit.*) ***riding-habit,*** traje de montar, traje de amazona.
habitable [ˈhæbitəbl], *a.* habitable.
habitableness [ˈhæbitəblnis], *s.* habitabilidad.
habitat [ˈhæbitæt], *s.* habitación; medio.
habitation [hæbiˈteiʃən], *s.* habitación, vivienda.
habited [ˈhæbitid], *a.* vestido, ataviado.
habitual [həˈbitjuəl], *a.* habitual.
habituate [həˈbitjueit], *v.t.* habituar.
habitude [ˈhæbitjuːd], *s.* hábito, costumbre.
habitué [həˈbitjuei], *s.* asiduo; tertuliano; concurrente habitual.
hachure [hæˈʃuə], *s.* rayado. — *v.t.* sombrear con líneas, rayar.
hack (1) [hæk], *s.* azuela, hacha; pico, tajo; corte, cuchillada; ***hack-saw,*** sierra de armero. — *v.t.* machetear; cortar, picar, tajar; mellar; allanar *o* picar (*piedras*); dar un puntapié a; ***hack down,*** derribar a hachazos; ***hack to pieces,*** despedazar (a hachazos). — *v.i.* tajar, cortar; ***hacking cough,*** tos seca.
hack (2) [hæk], *a.* trillado, gastado; ***hack writer,*** escritorzuelo. — *s.* caballo de alquiler; rocín; (*fig.*) plumífero; (*pol.*) ***party hack,*** propagandista, *m.f.*
hackle [hækl], *s.* ***with one's hackles up,*** enfurecido, amoscado; ***to raise the hackles of,*** enfurecer, provocar, amoscar, amostazar.
hackman [ˈhækmən], *s.* (*pl.* **-men** [-men]) cochero de alquiler.
hackmatack [ˈhækmətæk], *s.* (*bot.*) alerce *o* lárice americano.
hackney [ˈhækni], *s.* caballo de silla; ***hackney-carriage,*** coche de alquiler. — *v.t.* gastar, trillar.
hackneyed [ˈhæknid], *a.* trillado, trivial.
haddock [ˈhædək], *s.* (*ict.*) pescadilla.
hade [heid], *s.* (*min.*) buzamiento, descenso escarpado.
Hades [ˈheidiːz], *s.* Hades, *m.inv.*; el infierno.
haemal [ˈhiːməl], *a.* perteneciente a la sangre.
haematite [ˈhiːmətait], *s.* hematita.
haematosis [hiːməˈtousis], *s.* hematosis, *f.inv.*
haemoglobin [hiːmoˈgloubin], *s.* hemoglobina.
haemophilia [hiːmoˈfiliə], *s.* hemofilia.
haemorrhage [ˈhemərid3], *s.* hemorragia.
haemorrhoids [ˈhemərɔidz], *s.pl.* hemorroides, *f.pl.*, almorranas, *f.pl.*
haft [hɑːft], *s.* mango, puño, empuñadura.
hag [hæg], *s.* bruja, tarasca; ***hag-ridden,*** dominado por una mujer.
haggard [ˈhægəd], *a.* desencajado.
haggis [ˈhægis], *s.* *plato escocés* (*picadillo hervido*).
haggish [ˈhægiʃ], *a.* de bruja, feo, horroroso.
haggle [hægl], *s.* regateo. — *v.t.* tajar, machetear. — *v.i.* regatear.
haggler [ˈhæglə], *s.* regatero, regatón.
hagiographer [hægiˈɔgrəfə], *s.* hagiógrafo.
hagiography [hægiˈɔgrəfi], *s.* hagiografía.
hagiolatry [hægiˈɔlətri], *s.* hagiolatría.
hagiology [hægiˈɔlədʒi], *s.* hagiología.
hah! [hɑː], *interj.* ¡ah! ¡ja, ja, ja!
ha-ha [ˈhɑː-hɑː], *s.* foso; zanja.
hail (1) [heil], *s.* granizo, pedrisco. — *v.i.* granizar.
hail (2) [heil], *s.* llamada; saludo; grito; ***within hail,*** al habla; ***to be hail-fellow-well-met with,*** ser campechano con. — *v.t.* llamar; saludar; aclamar. — *v.i.* — ***from,*** proceder se, ser (natural) de. — *interj.* ¡salve! ¡salud!
hailstone [ˈheilstoun], *s.* (piedra de) granizo.
hailstorm [ˈheilstɔːm], *s.* granizada.
hair [hɛə], *s.* pelo; cabello; cabellera; vello; ***hair-cloth,*** cilicio; tela de crin; (*fam.*) ***hair-do,*** peinado; ***hair-dresser,*** peluquero; peinador, peinadora; ***hair-dressing,*** peluquería; ***hair-raising,*** horripilante; ***hair shirt,*** cilicio; ***hair-sieve,*** tamiz de cerda; ***hair-splitting,*** bizantino; quisquilloso, chinche; sutilezas (*f.pl.*) *o* tiquismiquis (*m.pl.*) estériles; ***hair spring,*** muelle muy fino; ***head of hair,*** cabellera; ***to escape by a hair's breadth,*** librarse por un pelo [HAIRBREADTH]; (*fam.*) ***keep your hair on!*** ¡tranquilo! ¡tranquilícese! ¡cálmate!; ***to let one's hair down,*** echar una canita al aire, expansionarse; ***to split hairs,*** hilar excesivamente fino, andarse con tiquismiquis; ***to tear one's hair,*** mesarse los cabellos; ***not to turn a hair,*** no alterar ni un músculo de la cara, no alterarse en absoluto, quedarse tan fresco.
hairbreadth [ˈhɛəbredθ], *s.* (ancho de un) pelo; ***to have a hairbreadth escape,*** librarse de buena, escapar por un pelo.
hairiness [ˈhɛərinis], *s.* (lo) peludo.
hairless [ˈhɛəlis], *a.* pelón, calvo.
hairpin [ˈhɛəpin], *s.* horquilla; ***hairpin-bend,*** curva cerradísima.
hairy [ˈhɛəri], *a.* peludo, velloso, velludo, hirsuto.
Haiti [ˈheiti]. Haití, *m.*
Haitian [ˈheiʃən], *a.*, *s.* haitiano.
hake [heik], *s.* (*ict.*) merluza.
halberd [ˈhælbəd], *s.* alabarda.
halberdier [hælbəˈdiə], *s.* alabardero.
halcyon [ˈhælsiən], *a.* tranquilo, apacible, sereno; ***halcyon days,*** días tranquilos, *m.pl.* — *s.* (*orn.*) alción.
hale (1) [heil], *a.* sano, fuerte, robusto, vigoroso; entero, ileso; ***hale and hearty,*** sano y fuerte.
hale (2) [heil], *v.t.* tirar, halar, arrastrar.
half [hɑːf], *a.*, *adv.* medio; semi; a medias, mitad; ***half-asleep,*** medio dormido; (*fam.*) ***half-baked*** tonto, cretino; ***half-breed, half-caste,*** mestizo; ***half-dressed,*** a medio vestir; ***half-fare,*** medio billete; ***half-hearted,*** tibio, sin entusiasmo; ***at half-mast,*** a media asta; ***half measures,*** medias tintas, *f.pl.*; ***half-moon,*** media luna; ***half-price,*** (a) mitad de precio; ***half-seas-over,*** medio borracho; ***half-term,*** vacaciones de mitad de trimestre, *f.pl.*; ***half-timbered house,*** casa de marco de maderos; ***half-time,*** descanso; ***half-truth,*** verdad a medias; ***to meet s.o. half-way,*** transigir con alguien, llegar a una transacción con alguien; (*fam.*) ***half-wit,*** tonto, bobo. — *s.* (*pl.* **halves** [hɑːvz]) mitad; (*fam.*) ***better half,*** cara mitad, media naranja; ***better by half,*** mejor con mucho; ***by halves,*** a medias; ***to be too clever by half,*** pasarse de listo; ***to go halves,*** ir a medias, pagar a escote (*de dos*); ***half and half,*** mitad y mitad; ***an hour and a half,*** hora y media; ***in halves,*** en dos partes; (*fam.*) ***not half!*** ¡ya la creo!
halfpenny [ˈheipni], *s.* (*pl.* **halfpence, halfpennies** [ˈheipəns, -niz]) medio penique.
halfpennyworth [ˈheipəθ], *s.* valor de medio penique.
halibut [ˈhælibət], *s.* hipogloso, halibut.
hall [hɔːl], *s.* vestíbulo, hall, recibimiento; sala, salón; edificio, paraninfo; residencia.
hallelujah [hæliˈluːjə], *s.* (*igl.*) aleluya.

halliard [HALYARD].
hallo [HELLO].
halloo [hə'lu:], *s.* grita, vocería.— *v.t., v.i.* gritar, vocear; azuzar. — *interj.* ¡busca! ¡sus!
hallooing [hə'lu:iŋ], *s.* grita, vocería.
hallow ['hælou], *v.t.* consagrar, santificar; reverenciar.
Hallowe'en [hælou'i:n], *s.* víspera de Todos los Santos.
Hallowmas ['hæloumæs], *s.* fiesta de Todos los Santos; ***All-Hallows,*** día de Todos los Santos.
hallucinate [hə'l(j)u:sineit], *v.t.* alucinar. — *v.i.* alucinarse.
hallucination [həl(j)u:si'neiʃən], *s.* alucinación.
halo ['heilou], *s.* halo, nimbo, aureola.
halogen ['hælodʒən], *s.* halógeno.
halography [hə'lɔgrəfi], *s.* halografía.
haloid ['hælɔid], *a.* haloideo. — *s.* sal haloidea.
halt [hɔ:lt], *s.* alto, detención, parada. —*v.t.* detener, mandar hacer alto. — *v.i.* detenerse, hacer alto; cojear.
halter ['hɔ:ltə], *s.* cabestro, jáquima, ronzal; dogal, soga; (*ent.*) balancín. — *v.t.* poner el cabestro *o* ronzal a.
halting ['hɔ:ltiŋ], *a.* cojo; renqueante; vacilante.
halve [hɑ:v], *v.t.* partir en dos.
halves [hɑ:vz], *s.pl.* [HALF].
halyard ['hæljəd], *s.* (*mar.*) driza; ***throat halyards,*** drizas del foque mayor.
ham [hæm], *s.* jamón; (*fam.*) maleta, *m.*; ***ham-fisted, ham-handed,*** desmanotado, desmañado. — *v.t., v.i.* (*teat.*) machacar el papel.
hamadryad [hæmə'draiæd], *s.* amadríada.
hamartiology [hæmɑ:ti'ɔlədʒi], *s.* doctrina del pecado; tratado del pecado.
hamburger ['hæmbə:gə], *s.* hamburguesa.
hame [heim], *s.* horcate.
hamlet ['hæmlit], *s.* aldea, caserío, alquería.
hammer ['hæmə], *s.* martillo; macito, martinete; gatillo, percusor; pilón, maza; (*fig.*) martillo, verdugo; ***to bring under the hammer,*** vender en pública subasta. — *v.t.* martillar, golpear; clavar; machacar, martillear; ***hammer one's brains,*** devanarse los sesos; ***hammer out,*** sacar a martillazos; forjar a pulso. — *v.i.* martillear, dar golpes; ***hammer at,*** trabajar con ahinco en; ***hammer away,*** trabajar con ahinco; martillear.
hammerer ['hæmərə], *s.* martillador.
hammerhead ['hæməhed], *s.* (*ict.*) cornudilla, pez martillo.
hammering ['hæməriŋ], *s.* martilleo; martillazos, *m.pl.*
hammock ['hæmək], *s.* hamaca; coy.
hamper (1) ['hæmpə], *s.* canasta, cesto.
hamper (2) ['hæmpə], *v.t.* embarazar, estorbar, obstaculizar.
hamstring ['hæmstriŋ], *s.* tendón de la corva. — *v.t.* desjarretar; imposibilitar.
hand [hænd], *s.* mano, *f.*; maña, habilidad, destreza; manecilla, aguja (*de reloj*); peón, brazo, jornalero, operario; letra; firma, rúbrica; poder, influencia; ***all hands,*** toda la tripulación; todos; ***at hand,*** a mano; ***at first hand,*** de primera mano; ***at the hands of,*** a manos de; ***to have a free hand,*** tener carta blanca; ***to be a good hand at,*** tener buena mano para; ***hand-glass,*** espejo de mano; ***hand-mill,*** molinillo; ***hands off!*** ¡no tocar!; ***hand over fist,*** de miedo, de maravilla; ***hand to hand,*** cuerpo a cuerpo; ***hands up!*** ¡arriba las manos!; (*fig.*) ***old hand,*** perro viejo; ***on hand,*** a la mano; disponible; ***on one's hands,*** sin vender; a su cargo; ***to go on one's hands and knees,*** suplicar; ***on the one hand, on the other,*** por una parte, por otra; ***to be hand in glove with,*** estar confabulado con; ***to change hands,*** cambiar de dueño; ***to do by hand,*** hacer a mano; ***she's got him eating out of her hand,*** lo tiene metido en un puño; ***to fall into the hands of,*** caer en manos de; ***to get one's hand in,*** adquirir práctica; ***to get out of hand,*** desmandarse; ***to get the upper*** o ***whip hand,*** hacerse dueño de la situación; ***to have a hand in,*** tener que ver con, tomar parte en; ***to have in hand,*** estar ocupándose de; ***to lay hands on,*** echar mano a, coger, hacerse con; (*igl.*) imponer las manos a; ***to lend*** o ***give a hand,*** echar una mano, meter el hombro; ***to live from hand to mouth,*** vivir al día; ***to play into the hands of,*** seguir el juego a; ***to put one's hand to,*** emprender; ocuparse de; firmar; ***to put in hand,*** iniciar (los trámites de); ***to serve hand and foot,*** tratar a cuerpo de rey; ***to shoot out of hand,*** fusilar sin contemplaciones; ***to take a hand in,*** tomar parte en; ***to take in hand,*** ocuparse de, hacerse cargo de; ***to turn one's hand to,*** dedicarse a; ***to wash one's hands of,*** lavarse las manos de, desentenderse de. — *v.t.* dar; entregar; alargar; ***hand down,*** bajar; transmitir; ***hand in,*** entregar; ***hand out,*** repartir, distribuir; ***hand over,*** entregar; ***hand round,*** repartir; pasar de unos a otros.
handbag ['hændbæg], *s.* bolso.
handball ['hændbɔ:l], *s.* pelota; juego de pelota.
handbell ['hændbel], *s.* campanilla.
handbill ['hændbil], *s.* hoja volante, octavilla.
handbook ['hændbuk], *s.* manual, guía.
handbow ['hændbou], *s.* arco de mano.
handbreadth ['hændbredθ], *s.* palmo menor.
handcuff ['hændkʌf], *s.* manilla, esposas. — *v.t.* poner las esposas a, maniatar.
handful ['hændful], *s.* puñado, manojo; ***by handfuls,*** a manos llenas; ***this child is a handful,*** este niño es una buena pieza.
handicap ['hændikæp], *s.* desventaja; (*dep.*) handicap. — *v.t.* estorbar, entorpecer, poner trabas a.
handicraft ['hændikrɑ:ft], *s.* oficio, arte mecánica.
handicraftsman ['hændikrɑ:ftsmən], *s.* (*pl.* **-men** [-men]) artesano, artífice, mecánico.
handily ['hændili], *adv.* mañosamente, con destreza.
handiness ['hændinis], *s.* maña, destreza, habilidad.
handiwork ['hændiwə:k], *s.* obra, obraje.
handkerchief ['hæŋkətʃif], *s.* pañuelo.
handle [hændl], *s.* asa; astil; mango; manija; manubrio; puño; tirador; asidero, pretexto; tacto; (*fam.*) ***to fly off the handle,*** subirse por las paredes; ***handle-bar,*** manillar; ***handle-bar moustache,*** bigotazos, *m.pl.*; ***handle to one's name,*** título; tratamiento. —*v.t.* tocar, manosear; manejar, manipular; tratar; comerciar en; dirigir; poner mango a; ***to be hard to handle,*** ser difícil de manejar. — *v.i.* manejarse; usar las manos.
handler ['hændlə], *s.* el que maneja.
handless ['hændlis], *a.* manco, sin manos.
handling ['hændliŋ], *s.* toque, manoseo; manejo, manipulación.
handmaid(**en**) ['hændmeid(ən)], *s.* criada, doncella.
hand-me-down ['hænd-mi-daun], *s.* ***this is a hand-me-down from his brother,*** esto lo ha heredado de su hermano.
hand-out ['hænd-aut], *s.* reparto; hoja; nota.
hand-picked ['hænd-'pikt], *a.* escogido a mano.
handrail ['hændreil], *s.* pasamano.
handsel ['hænsəl], *s.* estrena, prenda, garantía.
handsome ['hænsəm], *a.* guapo; hermoso; generoso; ***a handsome sum of money,*** una bonita suma.
handsomeness ['hænsəmnis], *s.* (lo) guapo; elegancia, gracia; generosidad.
handspike ['hændspaik], *s.* (*mar.*) espeque.
handstaff ['hændstɑ:f], *s.* jabalina.
handwork ['hændwə:k], *s.* obra hecha a mano.
handwriting ['hændraitiŋ], *s.* letra; escritura.
handy ['hændi], *a.* diestro, mañoso, hábil; manual; manejable; cómodo, práctico, útil; a (la) mano;

to come in handy, venir bien, al pelo; ***handyman,*** hombre mañoso *o* habilidoso.

handywork [HANDIWORK].

hang [hæŋ], *s.* caída; ***hang-out,*** guarida, refugio, nido; ***hang-over,*** resaca; (*fam.*) ***hang-up,*** manía; ***I don't care a hang!*** ¡me importa un bledo!; ***to get the hang of,*** cogerle el manejo *o* tranquillo a. — *irr. v.t.* colgar; suspender; ahorcar; poner colgaduras en; pegar (*papel*); bajar (*la cabeza*); ***hang fire,*** estar en suspenso, interrumpido; ***hang it all!*** ¡por Dios! ¡demonios!; ***hang out,*** tender; desplegar; colgar; ***hang up,*** colgar; suspender; ***the meat was hung for two days,*** la carne estuvo colgada dos días; ***the prisoner was hanged,*** ahorcaron al preso. — *v.i.* colgar, pender, estar colgado *o* suspendido; caer (*prendas*); ser ahorcado; ***hang about,*** holgazanear; esperar, esperarse; rondar; ***hang back,*** resistirse a pasar adelante *o* a avanzar, vacilar; remolonear; ***hang in the balance,*** estar pendiente de un hilo; ***hang on,*** esperarse; colgar de; agarrarse (a); persistir; depender de; estar pendiente de; ***hang out,*** asomarse (por); (*fam.*) vivir, estar; ***hang over,*** cernerse sobre; ***to have hanging over one,*** tener encima; ***hang around,*** pegarse a; esperar; ***hang together,*** mantenerse unidos; tener sentido, ser convincente; ***hang upon,*** depender de; estar pendiente de.

hangdog [ˈhæŋdɔg], *a.* avergonzado; patibulario.

hanger [ˈhæŋə], *s.* colgadero; percha; campanillero; ***hanger-on,*** secuaz; simpatizante; parásito; pegote.

hanging [ˈhæŋiŋ], *a.* colgado, suspendido. — *s.* muerte en la horca, ejecución en el patíbulo; (*pl.*) colgaduras, *f.pl.*, cortinajes, *m.pl.*

hangman [ˈhæŋmən], *s.* (*pl.* **-men** [-men]) verdugo.

hangnail [ˈhæŋneil], *s.* padastro.

hank [hæŋk], *s.* madeja.

hanker [ˈhæŋkə], *v.i.* — ***after, for,*** anhelar, ansiar.

hankering [ˈhæŋkəriŋ], *s.* anhelo, ansia, deseo (***after, for,*** de).

hanky-panky [ˈhæŋki-ˈpæŋki], *s.* trapicheos, *m.pl.*, tapujos, *m.pl.*, líos, *m.pl.*

Hanseatic [hænsiˈætik], *a.* anseático.

hansom cab [ˈhænsəm ˈkæb], *s.* cabriolé.

hap [hæp], *s.* ***by hap,*** por casualidad.

ha'penny [HALFPENNY].

haphazard [hæpˈhæzəd], *a.* esporádico; poco sistemático, hecho a lo loco *o* sin orden ni concierto.

hapless [ˈhæplis], *a.* desventurado.

haply [ˈhæpli], *adv.* por casualidad.

ha'p'orth [HALFPENNYWORTH].

happen [ˈhæpən], *v.i.* pasar, ocurrir, suceder, acontecer; ***as it happens, it so happens that,*** da la casualidad (de) que; ***he happened to be out,*** por casualidad no estaba; ***happen upon,*** tropezar con, encontrarse con; ***whatever happens,*** pase lo que pase.

happening [ˈhæpəniŋ], *s.* acontecimiento, suceso, sucedido.

happiness [ˈhæpinis], *s.* felicidad, dicha.

happy [ˈhæpi], *a.* feliz, dichoso; afortunado; ***to be happy to,*** tener mucho gusto en.

harangue [həˈræŋ], *s.* arenga. — *v.t.* arengar.

haranguer [həˈræŋə], *s.* orador.

harass [ˈhærəs], *v.t.* acosar, hostigar, hostilizar.

harassment [ˈhærəsmənt], *s.* acoso, hostigamiento.

harbinger [ˈhɑːbindʒə], *s.* heraldo; precursor; anuncio, presagio. — *v.t.* presagiar, anunciar.

harbour [ˈhɑːbə], *s.* puerto; seguro; albergue, asilo, abrigo; ***harbour dues,*** derechos de puerto; ***harbour master,*** capitán de puerto. — *v.t.* abrigar, amparar, resguardar; hospedar, acoger, albergar. — *v.i.* refugiarse, ampararse.

harbourage [ˈhɑːbəridʒ], *s.* puerto; amparo, refugio.

habourer [ˈhɑːbərə], *s.* amparador, acogedor, albergador; encubridor.

harbourless [ˈhɑːbəlis], *a.* desamparado, desprovisto de asilo.

hard [hɑːd], *a.* duro; firme; endurecido; fuerte; arduo; difícil; severo, riguroso; sordo; ***hard and fast,*** rígido, inflexible; ***hard as nails,*** duro como la piedra; ***hard cash,*** dinero contante; ***hard drinker,*** gran bebedor; ***hard facts,*** hechos indiscutibles, *m.pl.*; ***hard-handed,*** trabajador; severo; ***hard-headed,*** duro, práctico; ***hard-hearted,*** empedernido, cruel, inhumano; ***hard-heartedness,*** dureza de corazón, insensibilidad; ***hard lines, hard luck,*** mala suerte; (*equit.*) ***hard-mouthed,*** boquiduro, de boca dura; ***hard of hearing,*** duro de oído; ***hard times,*** tiempos difíciles *o* duros, *m.pl.*; ***hard to please,*** difícil de agradar, exigente; ***hard to understand,*** difícil de entender; ***hard worker,*** persona muy trabajadora; ***to be hard on,*** ser duro para *o* con; ser destrozón con. — *adv.* duro, duramente, fuerte, fuertemente; difícilmente; con pesar; cerca; ***hard at it,*** al pie del cañón, dale que dale; ***hard-bitten,*** de carácter duro; ***hard-boiled egg,*** huevo pasado (por agua); ***hard-bound,*** estreñido; ***hard by,*** al lado, muy cerca; ***hard pressed,*** acosado, apremiado; ***hard pressed for time,*** falto de tiempo; ***hard put to it,*** en un aprieto; ***hard up,*** escaso de dinero; ***hard-wearing,*** resistente, duradero, sufrido; ***hard-working,*** trabajador, laborioso; ***to go hard with,*** ser duro para, costar caro a; ***to work hard,*** trabajar mucho *o* fuerte. — *s.* piso *o* suelo duro.

harden [hɑːdn], *v.t.* endurecer; curtir; encallecer; solidar; robustecer; hacer insensible. — *v.i.* endurecerse; empedernirse.

hardener [ˈhɑːdnə], *s.* el que *o* lo que endurece.

hardihood [ˈhɑːdihud], *s.* temeridad.

hardiness [ˈhɑːdinis], *s.* resistencia, robustez; intrepidez.

hardly [ˈhɑːdli], *adv.* apenas, casi no; difícilmente, mal; duramente; ***hardly ever,*** casi nunca.

hardness [ˈhɑːdnis], *s.* dureza; dificultad; crudeza (*del agua*).

hardship [ˈhɑːdʃip], *s.* privaciones, *f.pl.*, penalidades, *f.pl.*; apuros, *m.pl.*

hardtack [ˈhɑːdtæk], *s.* bizcocho duro.

hardware [ˈhɑːdwɛə], *s.* quincalla, ferretería; efectos materiales, *m.pl.*; (*Am.*) ***hardware dealer,*** armamento(s) [IRONMONGER].

hardwareman [ˈhɑːdwɛəmən], *s.* (*pl.* **-men** [-men]) quincallero, ferretero.

hardwood [ˈhɑːdwud], *s.* madera dura.

hardy [ˈhɑːdi], *a.* robusto; resistente; intrépido.

hare [hɛə], *s.* liebre, *f.*; ***hare-brained,*** descabellado, disparatado; casquivano, atolondrado; ***hare-lip,*** labio leporino; ***hare-lipped,*** labihendido; (*bot.*) ***hare's-ear,*** oreja de liebre; (*bot.*) ***hare's-foot,*** pie de liebre; (*bot.*) ***hare's lettuce,*** ajonjera; ***mad as a March hare,*** loco de atar; ***to run with the hare and hunt with the hounds,*** jugar a dos barajas. — *v.i.* (*fam.*) — ***off,*** salir disparado, largarse a escape.

harebell [ˈhɛəbel], *s.* (*bot.*) campánula.

harehound [ˈhɛəhaund], *s.* lebrel, galgo.

harem [hɑːˈriːm], *s.* harén, serrallo.

haremint [ˈhɛəmint], *s.* (*bot.*) yaro.

haricot [ˈhærikou], *s.* alubia, judía seca.

hark [hɑːk], *v.i.* oír, escuchar; atender; ***hark back to,*** volver a; recordar; remontarse a; ***always harking on about it!*** ¡siempre con la misma cantilena!

harlequin [ˈhɑːlikwin], arlequín.

harlequinade [hɑːlikwiˈneid], *s.* arlequinada.

harlot [ˈhɑːlət], *s.* ramera, prostituta, meretriz.

harlotry [ˈhɑːlətri], *s.* prostitución.

harm [hɑːm], *s.* daño; mal; perjuicio; ***out of harm's way,*** fuera de peligro, seguro, salvo; ***there's no harm in trying,*** no se pierde nada intentándolo. — *v.t.* dañar; hacer daño a; perjudicar.

harmful [ˈhɑ:mful], *a.* dañoso, dañino, nocivo, perjudicial.
harmfulness [ˈhɑ:mfulnis], *s.* (lo) dañoso *o* nocivo.
harmless [ˈhɑ:mlis], *a.* inofensivo, inocuo.
harmlessness [ˈhɑ:mlisnis], *s.* (lo) inofensivo *o* inocuo.
harmonic [hɑ:ˈmɔnik], *a.* armónico. — *s.* armónico; (*pl.*) armonía.
harmonica [hɑ:ˈmɔnikə], *s.* (*mús.*) armónica.
harmonicon [hɑ:ˈmɔnikən], *s.* (*mús.*) armónica, organillo.
harmonious [hɑ:ˈmouniəs], *a.* armónico; armonioso.
harmoniousness [hɑ:ˈmouniəsnis], *s.* armonía.
harmonist [ˈhɑ:mənist], *s.* armonista, *m.f.*
harmonium [hɑ:ˈmouniəm], *s.* (*mús.*) armonio.
harmonize [ˈhɑ:mənaiz], *v.t.* armonizar. — *v.i.* armonizarse.
harmonizer [ˈhɑ:mənaizə], *s.* armonizador.
harmony [ˈhɑ:məni], *s.* armonía.
harness [ˈhɑ:nis], *s.* arneses, *m.pl.*, arreos, *m.pl.*, guarniciones, *f.pl.*; (*mil.*) arnés; (*mec.*) equipo, aparejo; ***harness-maker,*** guarnicionero; ***harness-room,*** guardarnés; ***in harness,*** en activo; ***to die in harness,*** morir en la brecha *o* con las botas puestas. — *v.t.* poner las guarniciones a; enjaezar, atelajar; armar con arnés; represar (*las aguas de un río*); aprovechar.
harp [hɑ:p], *s.* (*mús., astron.*) arpa. — *v.i.* tocar *o* tañer el arpa. — *v.t., v.i.* ***harp on*** o ***upon,*** repetir, porfiar, machacar.
harping [ˈhɑ:piŋ], *s.* tañido del arpa; repetición enfadosa; (*pl., mar.*) cucharros, *m.pl.*; redondos de la proa, *m.pl.*
harpist [ˈhɑ:pist], *s.* arpista, *m.f.*
harpoon [hɑ:ˈpu:n], *s.* arpón. — *v.t.* arponear.
harpooner [hɑ:ˈpu:nə], *s.* arponero.
harpsichord [ˈhɑ:psikɔ:d], *s.* clavicordio.
harpy [ˈhɑ:pi], *s.* arpía; (*orn.*) arpella.
harquebus [ˈhɑ:kwibəs], *s.* arcabuz.
harquebusier [hɑ:kwibəˈsiə], *s.* arcabucero.
harridan [ˈhæridən], *s.* bruja, arpía.
harrier (1) [ˈhæriə], *s.* lebrel; (*dep.*) corredor (*a través del campo*).
harrier (2) [ˈhæriə], *s.* aguilucho; (*orn.*) ***harrier-eagle,*** atahorma.
harrow [ˈhærou], *s.* (*agric.*) grada de dientes, escarificador. — *v.t.* gradar, escarificar; torturar, atormentar.
harrowing [ˈhærouiŋ], *a.* desgarrador, acongojante, angustioso. — *s.* gradeo.
harry [ˈhæri], *v.t.* pillar, saquear, asolar; acosar.
harsh [hɑ:ʃ], *a.* áspero; duro, injusto; brusco, desabrido; agrio, acerbo; discordante, chillón.
harshness [ˈhɑ:ʃnis], *s.* aspereza; brusquedad; discordancia; dureza, rigor, severidad.
hart [hɑ:t], *s.* ciervo.
hartshorn [ˈhɑ:tshɔ:n], *s.* cuerno de ciervo.
hartstongue [ˈhɑ:tstʌŋ], *s.* (*bot.*) escolopendra.
harum-scarum [ˈhɛərəm-skɛərəm], *a.* tarambana, atolondrado.
haruspex [həˈrʌspeks], *s.* (*pl.* **haruspices** [həˈrʌspisi:z]) arúspice.
harvest [ˈhɑ:vist], *s.* cosecha, recolección; mies, *f.*; siega; ***grape harvest,*** vendimia. — *v.t.* cosechar; recoger.
harvester [ˈhɑ:vistə], *s.* (*máquina*) cosechadora; cosechero.
has [hæz], 3ª. *pers. sing. pres. ind.* [HAVE]. — *s.* (*fam.*) ***has-been,*** vejestorio, antigualla, vieja gloria.
hash [hæʃ], *s.* picadillo; lío, embrollo; chapucería; ***to make a hash of*** [HASH UP]. — *v.t.* picar; (*fam.*) ***hash up,*** hacer fatal, hacer una chapucería de.
hashish [ˈhæʃi:ʃ], *s.* hachís.
haslet [ˈheizlit], *s.* asadura de puerco.
hasp [hɑ:sp], *s.* aldaba de candado; broche. — *v.t.* cerrar con aldaba; abrochar.
hassock [ˈhæsək], *s.* cojín.
hastate [ˈhæsteit], *a.* (*bot.*) alabardado.
haste [heist], *s.* prisa, apresuramiento, premura; precipitación; ***to be in haste,*** estar de prisa, tener prisa; ***to make haste,*** darse prisa, apresurarse; ***more haste, less speed,*** vísteme despacio, que estoy *o* voy de prisa. — *v.t., v.i.* [HASTEN].
hasten [ˈheisən], *v.t.* acelerar, apresurar. — *v.i.* darse prisa, apresurarse.
hastiness [ˈheistinis], *s.* apresuramiento, precipitación; impaciencia.
hasty [ˈheisti], *a.* apresurado, precipitado; impaciente; inconsiderado.
hat [hæt], *s.* sombrero; ***cocked hat,*** tricornio, sombrero de tres picos; ***hat-band,*** cintillo (de sombrero); ***hat-box, hat-case,*** sombrerera; ***hat-maker,*** sombrerero; ***hat-pin,*** alfiler *o* pasador de sombrero; ***hat-trick,*** tres tantos; ***high hat,*** sombrero de copa; ***my hat!*** ¡por Dios!; ***Panama hat,*** sombrero de jipijapa; ***to pass the hat round,*** pasar el cepillo, hacer una colecta; ***to put on one's hat,*** ponerse el sombrero; ***to take off one's hat,*** quitarse el sombrero; (*fig.*) ***to take off one's hat to,*** descubrirse ante; ***to talk through one's hat,*** desbarrar, delirar; ***keep this under your hat,*** de esto no decir ni pío.
hatch (1) [hætʃ], *s.* (*orn.*) nidada, pollada. — *v.t.* empollar, incubar; (*fig.*) maquinar, tramar, urdir. — *v.i.* empollarse; salir del cascarón; madurarse; ***to count one's chickens before they are hatched,*** dar las cosas por supuestas.
hatch (2) [hætʃ], *s.* (*coc.*) torno; trampa; (*mar.*) escotilla.
hatch (3) [hætʃ], *v.t.* sombrear (*un grabado*).
hatchel [ˈhætʃəl], *s.* rastrillo. — *v.t.* rastrillar; (*fig.*) contrariar, fastidiar, impacientar.
hatcheller [ˈhætʃələ], *s.* rastrillador.
hatcher [ˈhætʃə], *s.* tramador, trazador.
hatchery [ˈhætʃəri], *s.* criadero.
hatchet [ˈhætʃit], *s.* destral, hacha pequeña, machado; ***to bury the hatchet,*** echar pelillos a la mar; ***to dig up*** (o ***take up***) ***the hatchet,*** hacer la guerra; ***hatchet-face,*** cara de cuchillo; ***hatchet-faced,*** de facciones enjutas.
hatching [ˈhætʃiŋ], *s.* incubación.
hatchment [ˈhætʃmənt], *s.* (*blas.*) escudo de armas.
hatchway [ˈhætʃwei], *s.* (*mar.*) escotilla.
hate [heit], *s.* odio, aversión. — *v.t.* odiar, aborrecer, detestar.
hateful [ˈheitful], *a.* aborrecible, detestable, odioso.
hatefulness [ˈheitfulnis], *s.* odiosidad.
hater [ˈheitə], *s.* aborrecedor.
hath [hæθ], (*ant.*) 3ª. *pers. sing. pres. ind.* [HAVE].
hating [ˈheitiŋ], *s.* aversión, aborrecimiento, (el) odiar *o* abominar.
hatred [ˈheitrid], *s.* odio, aversión, aborrecimiento.
hatted [ˈhætid], *a.* que lleva sombrero.
hatter [ˈhætə], *s.* sombrerero; ***as mad as a hatter,*** loco de remate.
hauberk [ˈhɔ:bə:k], *s.* (*mil.*) coraza, plaquín, camisote.
haughtiness [ˈhɔ:tinis], *s.* altanería, soberbia, altivez.
haughty [ˈhɔ:ti], *a.* soberbio, altivo, altanero.
haul [hɔ:l], *s.* tirón *o* estirón, halà; redada; (*fig.*) botín; ***a good haul,*** buena pesca. — *v.t.* tirar de, arrastrar; (*mar.*) ronzar, halar, aballestar, cazar; ***haul down the colours,*** arriar la bandera; ***haul home,*** cazar y atracar; ***haul aft the sheets,*** cazar las escotas; ***haul the wind,*** abarloar, ceñir el viento.
haulage [ˈhɔ:lidʒ], *s.* transporte(s); acarreo; ***haulage contractor,*** contratista de transportes, *m.*

hauling ['hɔ:liŋ], *s.* estirón, hala, (el) halar; ***hauling-line,*** guía.

haulm [hɔ:m], *s.* paja, rastrojo.

haunch [hɔ:ntʃ], *s.* anca, culata, grupa; (*arq.*) riñón de la bóveda; ***haunch of venison,*** pierna (*de venado*).

haunt [hɔ:nt], *s.* lugar que se frecuenta; querencia; guarida. — *v.t.* frecuentar, rondar; perseguir, obsesionar; aparecerse (a).

haunted ['hɔ:ntid], *a.* encantado, frecuentado por fantasmas.

hautboy ['oubɔi], *s.* (*mús.*) oboe.

have [hæv], *s.* (*pl.*) los ricos, privilegiados; ***the have-nots,*** los pobres, desposeídos, descamisados. — *irr. vt., v.i.* tener; ostentar; gozar de; contener; obtener; tomar; sentir, pasar; hablar; coger; vencer; dejar desconcertado *o* perplejo; (*fam.*) engañar, tomar el pelo a; tolerar, permitir; ***have (got) to do sth.,*** tener que hacer una cosa; ***have to do with,*** tener que ver con; ***he has his hair cut*** o ***a hair-cut,*** se corta el pelo; ***she had a dress made,*** se hizo un vestido; ***we are having him to stay,*** viene a pasar unos días con nosotros; ***I would have you know that,*** deseo comunicarle *o* hacerle saber que; ***he will have it that,*** se empeña en que + *indic.*; ***it's not to be had,*** no lo hay, no se puede conseguir; (*fam.*) ***you're having me on,*** me estás tomando el pelo; (*fam.*) ***we've had it,*** estamos listos, no hay nada que hacer; ***we can't have this,*** (esto) no se puede consentir *o* soportar; ***let him have it,*** dáselo; (*fam.*) pégale; (*fam.*) mátale, pégale un tiro; (*fam.*) díselo, suéltaselo; ***rumour has it that,*** se dice que, se rumorea que; ***have (sth.) on one,*** tener, llevar (algo) consigo; (*fam.*) ***have it in for,*** tenerla tomada con; (*fam.*) ***have it out,*** hablar claro, poner las cosas claras, resolver el asunto; ***I'll have you up for it,*** te llevaré a los tribunales. — *v. aux.* haber; ***have just,*** acabar de; ***had all the soldiers fought . . .,*** si hubiesen luchado todos los soldados . . .; ***you had better leave,*** conviene que *o* más vale que se vaya; ***I had rather die,*** preferiría morirme.

haven ['heivən], *s.* puerto; abrigo, asilo.

haver ['heivə], *v.i.* (*Esco.*) decir tonterías.

haversack ['hævəsæk], *s.* mochila, morral, macuto.

havoc ['hævək], *s.* estrago, destrucción; ***to play*** o ***wreak havoc,*** hacer (grandes) estragos.

haw (1) [hɔ:], *s.* (*bot.*) baya del espino blanco.

haw (2) [hɔ:], *v.i.* ***to hum and haw,*** no pronunciarse, no resolverse, vacilar.

Hawaii [hə'waii]. Hawai.

Hawaiian [hə'waijən], *a., s.* hawaiano.

hawk (1) [hɔ:k], *s.* halcón; ***hawk-eyed,*** de ojos de lince; (*ent.*) ***hawk-moth,*** esfinge; ***hawk-nosed,*** aguileño, de nariz aguileña; ***hawk-owl,*** surnia.

hawk (2) [hɔ:k], *v.t.* correr (*mercancías*).

hawk (3) [hɔ:k], *v.i.* gargajear.

hawker (1) ['hɔ:kə], *s.* halconero.

hawker (2) ['hɔ:kə], *s.* corredor, buhonero.

hawking (1) ['hɔ:kiŋ], *s.* cetrería.

hawking (2) ['hɔ:kiŋ], *s.* buhonería.

hawse [hɔ:z], *s.* (*mar.*) frente de los escobenes; ***hawse-hole,*** escobén; ***hawse-plugs,*** tacos de los escobenes, *m.pl.*

hawser ['hɔ:zə], *s.* (*mar.*) cable, estacha, guindaleza.

hawthorn ['hɔ:θɔ:n], *s.* (*bot.*) espino (blanco.)

hay [hei], *s.* heno; forraje; ***hay fever,*** fiebre del heno; ***hay-field,*** henar; ***hay-loft,*** henil; ***to make hay while the sun shines,*** al buen tiempo meterlo en casa, aprovechar las ocasiones.

haycock ['heikɔk], *s.* almiar, niara.

hayfork ['heifɔ:k], *s.* bieldo, horca.

haymaker ['heimeikə], *s.* segador (*de heno*).

haymaking ['heimeikiŋ], *s.* cosecha (*del heno*).

hayrick ['heirik], *s.* almiar, montón de heno.

hayseed ['heisi:d], *s.* patán, paleto; simiente de heno, *f.*

haystack ['heistæk], *s.* niara, almiar.

hazard ['hæzəd], *s.* azar; peligro, riesgo; ***road hazard,*** peligro *u* obstáculo en carretera; ***at all hazards,*** a toda costa, cueste lo que cueste. — ***v.t.*** arriesgar, exponer, aventurar, poner en riesgo. — *v.i.* arriesgarse, correr un albur, probar (la) suerte, aventurarse; correr riesgo.

hazardable ['hæzədəbl], *a.* que se puede aventurar; peligroso, osado, arriesgado.

hazarder ['hæzədə], *s.* jugador; el que arriesga.

hazardous ['hæzədəs], *a.* arriesgado, peligroso.

hazardousness ['hæzədəsnis], *s.* riesgo, peligro.

haze [heiz], *s.* neblina, calina, bruma. — *v.t.* (*mar.*) abrumar con trabajos pesados.

hazel ['heizəl], *a.* castaño, de color de avellana. — *s.* avellano; (*orn.*) ***hazel-grouse,*** ortega; ***hazel-nut,*** avellana.

haziness ['heizinis], *s.* calina, calígine; imprecisión.

hazing ['heiziŋ], *s.* tunda.

hazy ['heizi], *a.* brumoso, caliginoso; vago, confuso.

he [hi:], *pron. pers. masc.*, 3ª. *pers. sing.* él; ***he who, he that,*** el que, aquel que, quien; ***he-bear,*** oso; ***he-goat,*** macho cabrío.

head [hed], *s.* cabeza; cima; posición de jefe; extremo, punta; cara (*de una moneda*); título, encabezamiento; caudillo, jefe; res, cabeza de ganado; avance, adelantamiento, crisis, *f.inv.*; (*sing., ú. como pl.*) astas de ciervo *o* venado, *f.pl.*; (*mar.*) proa; nacimiento, fuente, *f.*, manantial; cofia; soltura (*del freno*); ***from head to foot,*** de pies a cabeza; ***head and shoulders above,*** mucho mejor que; ***head of a bed,*** cabecera; ***head of a cabbage,*** repollo de col; ***head of a cask,*** fondo de un barril; ***head of a sail,*** gratil; ***head-dress, head-gear,*** tocado, sombrero; ***head-first,*** de cabeza; ***head-hunter,*** cazador de cabezas; ***head-on,*** de frente; frontal; (*fig.*) ***head over heels,*** completamente; ***to be head over heels in debt,*** estar comido de deudas; ***head-piece,*** casco; ***head-sail,*** vela delantera; (*mar.*) ***head to sea,*** con la proa a la mar; ***two heads are better than one,*** más valen cuatro ojos que dos; ***to have a head for figures,*** tener cabeza para las cifras; ***to eat one's head off,*** comer como una lima; ***to give a horse his head,*** dar rienda suelta a un caballo; ***to go to one's head,*** subírsele a alguien a la cabeza; ***I can make neither head nor tail of it,*** no tiene pies ni cabeza; ***to make head against,*** hacer frente a; ***to play heads or tails,*** jugar a cara o cruz; ***to take it into one's head,*** metérsele a alguien en la cabeza; ***to win by a head,*** ganar por una cabeza; ***to hit the nail on the head,*** dar en el clavo; ***to give a figure out of one's head,*** inventarse una cifra; ***to do sth. over the head of s.o.,*** hacer algo sin consultar a alguien. — *v.t.* encabezar; dirigir; ponerse al frente de; poner título a; descabezar, desmochar; ***head off,*** atajar. — *v.i.* dirigirse; ***head for*** o ***towards,*** encaminarse a.

headache ['hedeik], *s.* dolor de cabeza; (*fig.*) quebradero de cabeza.

headboard ['hedbɔ:d], *s.* cabecera (de cama).

headed ['hedid], *a.* que tiene cabeza; titulado; ***headed for,*** con rumbo a, destinado a *o* para.

header ['hedə], *s.* caída de cabeza; cabezazo; ***to take a header,*** tirarse (al agua); pegarse un morrón *o* una morrada (en el suelo).

headily ['hedili], *adv.* locamente, impetuosamente.

headiness ['hedinis], *s.* locura, impetuosidad, fogosidad; embriaguez; fuerza embriagadora.

heading ['hediŋ], *s.* título, encabezamiento.

headland ['hedlənd], *s.* cabo, punta, promontorio.

headless ['hedlis], *a.* descabezado, degollado; acéfalo; inconsiderado.

headlight ['hedlait], *s.* (*mar.*) farol (*de tope*); faro (*de automóvil*).

headline ['hedlain], *s.* titular; ***to hit the headlines,*** salir en los periódicos, causar (una) sensación.

headlong ['hedlɔŋ], *a.* precipitado. — *adv.* de cabeza, precipitadamente.

headman [ˈhedmæn], *s.* jefe; cacique; capataz; encargado.
headmaster [hedˈmɑːstə], *s.* director (*de colegio*).
headmistress [hedˈmistris], *s.* directora.
headphone [ˈhedfoun], *s.* auricular.
headquarters [hedˈkwɔːtəz], *s.pl.* (*mil.*) cuartel general; casa central; sede.
headship [ˈhedʃip], *s.* jefatura, dirección.
headsman [ˈhedzmən], *s.* verdugo.
headstone [ˈhedstoun], *s.* lápida (sepulcral).
headstrong [ˈhedstrɔŋ], *a.* voluntarioso, testarudo.
headstrongness [ˈhedstrɔŋnis], *s.* (lo) voluntarioso, testarudez.
headway [ˈhedwei], *s.* progreso(s), adelanto(s); ***I can make no headway,*** no adelanto nada, no me cunde nada.
headwind [ˈhedwind], *s.* viento en contra, contrario.
heady [ˈhedi], *a.* impetuoso, fogoso; embriagador, espiritoso.
heal [hiːl], *v.t.* curar, sanar; remediar; purificar. — *v.i.* curar, curarse, sanar; cicatrizarse; remediarse; ***heal up,*** cicatrizarse.
healable [ˈhiːləbl], *a.* curable, sanable.
heald [hiːld], *s.* (*tej.*) lizo de un telar.
healer [ˈhiːlə], *s.* sanador, curador.
healing [ˈhiːliŋ], *a.* curativo, sanativo; cicatrizante. — *s.* cura, curación; cicatrización.
health [helθ], *s.* salud, *f.*, sanidad; ***bill of health,*** patente de sanidad; ***health-giving,*** saludable; ***health officer,*** inspector *o* visitador de sanidad; ***your health!*** ¡a su salud!
healthful [ˈhelθful], *a.* sano, saludable, salubre, salutífero.
healthfulness [ˈhelθfulnis], *s.* salud, salubridad, sanidad.
healthiness [ˈhelθinis], *s.* estado sano, sanidad, buena salud.
healthy [ˈhelθi], *a.* sano, fuerte; saludable.
heap [hiːp], *s.* montón, pila, cúmulo, rimero; (*pl., fam.*) muchísimos, muchísimas; ***in heaps,*** a montones. — *v.t.* amontonar, acumular, apilar.
heaper [ˈhiːpə], *s.* amontonador.
hear [hiə], *irr. v.t.* oír, escuchar; oír decir; ver (una causa); atender, hacer caso de; ***hear s.o. out,*** oír a alguien hasta el final; ***I heard that,*** oí decir que. — *v.i.* oír; ***hear about,*** oír hablar de; ***hear from,*** saber de; ***hear of,*** oír hablar de, tener noticias de; saber, enterarse de; ***I will not hear of it,*** no quiero ni hablar de ello; ***hear! hear!*** bravo!
hearer [ˈhiərə], s. oidor, oyente.
hearing [ˈhiəriŋ], *s.* oído; audición; (*for.*) vista (de una causa), examen de testigos; alcance del oído; ***hard of hearing,*** duro de oído; ***within hearing,*** al alcance del oído.
hearken [ˈhɑːkən], *v.i.* escuchar.
hearsay [ˈhiəsei], *s.* rumor, fama, voz común; ***by hearsay,*** de oídas.
hearse [həːs], *s.* coche *o* carroza fúnebre; ***hearse-cloth,*** palio, paño mortuorio; ***hearse-like,*** lúgubre, fúnebre. — *v.t.* poner en un coche fúnebre.
heart [hɑːt], *s.* corazón; alma; cogollo; copa(s) (*de la baraja*); ***he is a man after my own heart,*** es de los míos; ***at heart,*** en el fondo; ***to die of a broken heart,*** morir de pena, pesadumbre *o* tristeza; ***by heart,*** de memoria; ***cross my heart,*** palabra (de honor); ***to have one's heart in one's mouth,*** tener el alma entre los dientes; estar con el alma en un hilo; ***heart and soul,*** en cuerpo y alma; con toda el alma; ***heart-break,*** angustia, congoja, pena profunda; ***heart-breaking,*** desolador, desgarrador, que da muchísima pena, que le parte a uno el alma; ***heart-broken,*** desolado, tristísimo, que tiene el alma partida; ***heart disease,*** enfermedad del corazón; ***heart of the matter,*** quid del asunto; ***heart-rending,*** que parte el alma, desgarrador; (*bot.*) ***heart's ease,*** pensamiento, trinitaria; ***heart-sick,*** afligido, desconsolado; ***heart-strings,*** fibras del corazón, *f.pl.*; ***a heart-to-heart talk,*** una conversación íntima; ***heart transplant,*** trasplante de corazón; ***his heart is in the right place,*** tiene buen corazón; ***his heart sank,*** se le cayó el alma; ***to take the heart out of,*** desanimar; ***to take to heart,*** tomar muy en serio; apenarse por; ***to wear one's heart on one's sleeve,*** llevar el corazón en la mano.
heartache [ˈhɑːteik], *s.* dolor de corazón, aflicción.
heartburn [ˈhɑːtbəːn], *s.* acedía, ardor.
heartburning [ˈhɑːtbəːniŋ], *s.* descontento, envidia, rencor.
hearten [hɑːtn], *v.t.* animar, alentar.
heartfelt [ˈhɑːtfelt], *a.* sincero, cordial, de corazón, sentido hondamente.
hearth [hɑːθ], *s.* hogar; chimenea.
heartiness [ˈhɑːtinis], *s.* cordialidad; sinceridad; campechanía; vigor.
heartless [ˈhɑːtlis], *a.* sin corazón; cruel, inhumano, despiadado, sañudo.
heartlessness [ˈhɑːtlisnis], *s.* dureza de corazón, crueldad, saña.
hearty [ˈhɑːti], *a.* cordial; sincero; campechano; ***to be a hearty eater,*** tener buen diente.
heat [hiːt], *s.* calor; ardor; vehemencia; calefacción; celo; (*dep.*) eliminatoria; ***dead heat,*** empate; (*aer.*) ***heat-barrier,*** barrera térmica; ***heat-stroke,*** insolación; ***heat-wave,*** ola de calor; ***in heat,*** en celo; (*fig.*) ***to turn on the heat,*** apretar los tornillos. — *v.t.* calentar; acalorar. — *v.i.* calentarse; acalorarse; (*fig.*) ***to become*** o ***get heated,*** acalorarse.
heater [ˈhiːtə], *s.* calentador; estufa.
heath [hiːθ], *s.* (*bot.*) brezo; brezal; parque natural; (*orn.*) ***heath-cock,*** gallo silvestre.
heathen [ˈhiːðən], *a., s.* pagano; bárbaro.
heathenish [ˈhiːðəniʃ], *a.* pagano; bárbaro.
heathenism [ˈhiˈðənizəm], *s.* paganismo.
heathenize [ˈhiːðənaiz], *v.t.* hacer pagano.
heather [ˈheðə], *s.* brezo(s).
heathery [ˈheðəri], *a.* lleno *o* cubierto de brezos.
heathy [ˈhiːθi], *a.* matoso.
heating [ˈhiːtiŋ], *a.* calorífico. — *s.* calefacción; calentamiento.
heatless [ˈhiːtlis], *a.* frío, sin calor.
heave [hiːv], *s.* esfuerzo (*para solevar*); jadeo; náusea; (*geol.*) anchura (*de una falla*). — *irr. v.t.* levantar, solevar; lanzar, arrojar; exhalar; hinchar (*el pecho*); (*mar.*) halar; (*mar.*) ***heave the log,*** echar la corredera; (*mar.*) ***heave out,*** desaferrar (*una vela*); ***heave overboard,*** echar por la borda; ***heave round,*** virar (*un cabrestante*). — *v.i.* levantarse; subir y bajar; jadear; esforzarse; ***heave into sight,*** asomar en el horizonte; ***heave to,*** ponerse al pairo. — *interj.* ***heave ho!*** ¡iza!
heaven [ˈhevən], *s.* cielo; ***for heaven's sake!*** ¡por Dios!; ***good heavens!*** ¡válgame Dios!; ***heaven-born,*** celeste, angelical, divino; ***to move heaven and earth,*** mover cielo y tierra.
heavenliness [ˈhevənlinis], *s.* (lo) celestial.
heavenly [ˈhevənli], *a.* celestial, divino; delicioso.
heavenward [ˈhevənwəd], *a., adv.* hacia el cielo.
heaver [ˈhiːvə], *s.* (*mar.*) alzaprima; cargador.
heaves [hiːvz], *s. pl.* (*vet.*) huélfago.
heaviness [ˈhevinis], *s.* pesadez, pesantez; peso; pesadumbre; sopor.
heaving [ˈhiːviŋ], *s.* palpitación; (*mar.*) oleada, hinchazón de las olas, *f.*; ***heaving-line,*** estacha, calabrote.
heavy [ˈhevi], *a.* pesado, de peso; fuerte; denso, espeso; gravoso; cargado; soñoliento; ***to be heavy-handed,*** cargar la mano; ***heavy-duty,*** de servicio pesado; ***heavy-industry,*** industria pesada; ***heavy-weight,*** peso pesado; (*fig.*) de mucha categoría.
hebdomad [ˈhebdomæd], *s.* hebdómada.
hebdomadal, hebdomadary [hebˈdɔmədəl, -dəri], *a.* hebdomadario, semanal.

hebetation, hebetude [hebiˈteiʃən, ˈhebitju:d], *s.* estupidez, entorpecimiento, embotamiento.
Hebraic [hi:ˈbreiik], *a.* hebreo, hebraico.
Hebraism [ˈhi:breiizəm], *s.* hebraísmo.
Hebraist [ˈhi:breiist], *s.* hebraísta, hebraizante.
Hebraize [ˈhi:breiaiz], *v.t.* hebraizar, hacer hebreo, verter al hebreo. — *v.i.* volverse hebreo, adoptar costumbres hebreas.
Hebrew [ˈhi:bru:], *a.* hebraico, hebreo. — *s.* hebreo, judío, lengua hebrea.
hecatomb [ˈhekətu:m], *s.* hecatombe, *f.*
heck [hek], *s.* (*Am.*, *fam.*) ***what the heck!*** ¡qué diablos!
heckle [ˈhekl], *v.t.*, *v.i.* interrumpir, importunar con preguntas.
heckling [ˈhekliŋ], *s.* interrupciones, *f. pl.*
hectare [ˈhektεə], s. hectárea.
hectic [ˈhektik], *a.* agitado, ajetreado; febril.
hectogram [ˈhektogræm], *s.* hectogramo.
hectograph [ˈhektogræf], *s.* hectógrafo.
hectolitre [ˈhektoli:tə], *s.* hectolitro.
hectometre [ˈhektomi:tə], *s.* hectómetro.
hector [ˈhektə], *s.* matón, matasiete. — *v.t.* amenazar, intimidar con bravatas. — *v.i.* echar bravatas.
hedge [hedʒ], *s.* seto; vallado de zarzas; ***hedge-mustard,*** jaramago, erisimo; ***hedge-nettle,*** ortiga hedionda; (*orn.*) ***hedge-sparrow,*** acentor; ***quick-set hedge,*** seto vivo; ***stake hedge,*** cerca. — *v.t.* cercar con seto, vallar; ***hedge about*** o ***in,*** rodear, encerrar; poner obstáculos a; ***hedge a bet,*** hacer apuestas compensatorias; ***hedge off,*** separar con un seto. — *v.i.* contestar con evasivas, no querer comprometerse.
hedgehog [ˈhedʒhɔg], *s.* erizo.
hedgehop [ˈhedʒhɔp], *v.i.* volar rasando el suelo.
hedgerow [ˈhedʒrou], *s.* seto vivo.
hedging [ˈhedʒiŋ], *s.* cultivo y arreglo de setos; ***hedging-bill,*** podadera de setos.
hedonism [ˈhi:dənizəm], *s.* hedonismo.
hedonist [ˈhi:dənist], *s.* hedonista, *m.f.*
heed [hi:d], *s.* atención, caso; ***to give no heed to, take no heed of,*** no hacer caso de, echar en saco roto. — *v.t.* atender, prestar atención a, hacer caso de. — *v.i.* prestar atención, hacer caso.
heedful [ˈhi:dful], *a.* atento; cuidadoso; ***heedful of,*** atento a.
heedfulness [ˈhi:dfulnis], *s.* atención; cuidado.
heedless [ˈhi:dlis], *a,* desatento, negligente; distraído, descuidado, incauto, atolondrado.
heedlessness [ˈhi:dlisnis], *s.* falta de atención.
heel (I) [hi:l], *s.* (*anat.*) talón; tacón; parte inferior; (*fam.*) canalla; ***to be on the heels of,*** pisarle los talones a; ***to bring to heel,*** meter en cintura; ***to cool one's heels,*** hacer antesala; ***he was left cooling his heels,*** le dieron un plantón; ***down at heel,*** desaliñado, mal vestido; ***heel-maker,*** taconero; ***heel-piece,*** talón, tapa; ***to show a clean pair of heels, to take to one's heels,*** poner pies en polvorosa, darse a la fuga. — *v.t.*, *v.i.* (*dep.*) talonar.
heel (2) [hi:l], *v.i.* (*mar.*) escorar.
heeled [hi:ld], *a.* con tacones; (*fig.*) ***well-heeled,*** bien vestido.
heeler [ˈhi:lə], *s.* taconero.
heft [heft], *s.* peso, influencia. — *v.t.* sopesar, alzar en peso.
hefty [hefti], *a.* fornido, recio, corpulento; fuerte.
Hegelian [heiˈgi:liən], *a.*, *s.* hegeliano.
Hegelianism [heiˈgi:liənizəm], *s.* hegelianismo.
hegemonic [hegiˈmɔnik], *a.* hegemónico.
hegemony [hi(:)ˈgeməni], *s.* hegemonía.
hegira [ˈhedʒirə], *s.* hégira, égira.
heifer [ˈhefə], *s.* vaquilla, novilla; ***heifer calf,*** ternera.
heigh-ho! [ˈhei-ˈhou], *interj.* ¡bueno!
height [hait], *s.* altura, alto; altozano; estatura, talla, alzada; ***at its height,*** en su apogeo; ***the height of folly,*** el colmo de la locura.
heighten [haitn], *v.t.* realzar; levantar.
heightening [ˈhaitniŋ], *s.* adorno; realce.
heinous [ˈheinəs], *a.* atroz, nefando.
heinousness [ˈheinəsnis], *s.* (lo) atroz.
heir [εə], *s.* heredero; ***heir-apparent,*** heredero forzoso; ***heir at law,*** heredero legal; ***heir presumptive,*** heredero presunto; ***joint heir,*** coheredero.
heirdom [ˈεədəm], *s.* herencia, derecho de heredar; bienes heredados, *m. pl.*
heiress [ˈεəres], *s.* heredera.
heirless [ˈεəlis], *a.* sin heredero.
heirloom [ˈεəlu:m], *s.* (*for.*) bienes muebles vinculados, *m.pl.*; herencia; reliquia de familia.
heirship [ˈεəʃip], [HEIRDOM].
helcoid [ˈhelkɔid], *a.* parecido a una úlcera.
helcology [helˈkɔlədʒi], *s.* parte de la patología que trata de las úlceras.
heliacal [hi:ˈlaiəkəl], *a.* helíaco.
helical [ˈhelikəl], *a.* espiral; ***helical line,*** hélice, *f.*, espira.
helicoid [ˈhelikɔid], *a.* helicoidal. — *s.* (*geom.*) helicoide.
Helicon [ˈhelikən]. Helicón, Parnaso.
helicopter [ˈhelikɔptə], *s.* (*aer.*) helicóptero.
heliocentric(al) [hi:lioˈsentrik(əl)], *a.* heliocéntrico.
heliochrome [ˈhi:liokroum], *s.* (*foto.*) heliocromo.
heliograph [ˈhi:liogræf], *s.* heliógrafo. — *v.i.* hacer señales con el heliógrafo.
heliographic [hi:lioˈgræfik], *a.* heliográfico.
heliography [hi:liˈɔgrəfi], *s.* heliografía.
heliolatry [hi:liˈɔlətri], *s.* culto del sol.
heliometer [hi:liˈɔmitə], *s.* heliómetro.
helioscope [ˈhi:lioskoup], *s.* helioscopio.
heliostat [ˈhi:liostæt], *s.* helióstato.
heliotrope [ˈhi:liotroup], *s.* (*bot.*) heliotropo.
heliotype [ˈhi:liotaip], *s.* heliotipo; heliotipia. — *v.t.* reproducir por medio del heliotipo.
heliport [ˈhelipɔ:t], *s.* helipuerto.
helium [ˈhi:liəm], *s.* helio.
helix [ˈhi:liks], *s.* hélice; *f.*; voluta.
hell [hel], *s.* infierno; garito; (*impr.*) caja de letras inservibles; cajón de sastre; ***hell-bent,*** empeñado contra viento y marea (***on,*** en); ***hell-born,*** infernal; ***hell-cat,*** bruja; ***hell fire,*** tizonazos, *m.pl.*; ***hell-hound,*** perro del infierno, Cancerbero; demonio; verdugo; ***a hell of a racket,*** un ruidazo de mil demonios; ***like hell!*** ¡ni pensarlo!; ***oh, hell!*** ¡demonio(s)!; ***to give s.o. hell,*** echarle a alguien un broncazo de mil pares de demonios; ***to go hell for leather,*** ir flechado *o* disparado; ***go to hell!*** ¡vete al cuerno!; ***to raise hell,*** poner el grito en el cielo; ***what the hell?*** ¿qué demonios?
hellebore [ˈhelibɔ:], *s.* eléboro.
Hellenic [heˈli:nik], *a.* helénico.
Hellenism [ˈhelinizəm], *s.* helenismo.
Hellenist [ˈhelinist], *s.* helenista, *m.f.*
Hellenistic [heliˈnistik], *a.* helenístico.
hellenize [ˈhelinaiz], *v.t.* helenizar.
hellish [ˈheliʃ], *a.* infernal, diabólico.
hello! [heˈlou], *interj.* ¡hola!; vaya! (*sorpresa*); (*tele.*) diga, dígame.
hellwards [ˈhelwəd(z)], *adv.* hacia el infierno.
helm (I) [helm], *s.* (*mar.*) timón; caña *o* rueda del timón; gobernalle; dirección, gobierno, puesto de mando. — *v.t.* timonear, guiar.
helm (2) [helm], *s.* yelmo, capacete.
helmed [helmd], *a.* que lleva casco *o* yelmo.
helmet [ˈhelmit], *s.* casco; yelmo.
helmeted [ˈhelmitid], *a.* que lleva casco *o* yelmo.
helminth [ˈhelminθ], *s.* helminto.
helminthic [helˈminθik], *a.* helmíntico.
helminthology [helminˈθɔlədʒi], *s.* helmintología.

helmless [ˈhelmlis], *a.* sin timón.
helmport [ˈhelmpɔːt], *s.* (*mar.*) limera del timón.
helmsman [ˈhelmzmən], *s.* timonel, timonero.
helot [ˈhelət], *s.* ilota, *m.*
helotism, helotry [ˈhelətizem, -tri], *s.* ilotismo.
help [help], *s.* ayuda; auxilio, socorro; remedio; criada; ***to be a great help,*** ser una gran ayuda; ***home*** *o* ***house help,*** asistenta; ***mother's help,*** niñera; ***there's no help for it,*** no hay (más) remedio; ***to cry out for help,*** pedir socorro a gritos; ***with*** o ***by the help of,*** con ayuda de. — *v.t.* ayudar; auxiliar, socorrer; amparar; remediar, evitar; contribuir; servir; ***I cannot help it,*** no puedo remediarlo *o* evitarlo; ***I cannot help laughing,*** no puedo menos de reírme; ***it cannot be helped,*** no hay (más) remedio; ***God help us,*** Dios nos asista; ***help back,*** ayudar a regresar; ***help down,*** ayudar a bajar; (*fig.*) ***help forward,*** activar, promover; (*fig.*) ***help on,*** ayudar a progresar *o* medrar; ***help s.o. on with his coat,*** ayudar a alguien a ponerse el abrigo; ***help out,*** echar una mano a; ***help o.s. to,*** servirse; ***help up,*** ayudar a levantarse *o* subir; ***help yourself,*** sírvase usted; ***help out,*** prestar ayuda a, echar una mano a. — *v.i.* ayudar; servir; contribuir. — *interj.* ¡socorro!
helper [ˈhelpə], *s.* ayudador, ayudante; asistente; colaborador.
helpful [ˈhelpful], *a.* útil, provechoso; servicial.
helpfulness [ˈhelpfulnis], *s.* (lo) servicial.
helping [ˈhelpiŋ], *s.* ración; ***he had two helpings of meat,*** se sirvió carne dos veces.
helpless [ˈhelplis], *a.* impotente, incapaz; desamparado, indefenso.
helplessness [ˈhelplisnis], *s.* impotencia, incapacidad; desamparo, falta de defensa.
helpmate [ˈhelpmeit], *s.* compañero; esposo, esposa.
helter-skelter [ˈheltə-ˈskeltə], *adv.* atropelladamente.
helve [helv], *s.* mango, astil (*de hacha* o *destral*); ***to throw the helve after the hatchet,*** echar la soga tras el caldero. — *v.t.* poner mango o astil a.
Helvetian, Helvetic [helˈviːʃən, helˈvetik], *a., s.* helvético, helvecio.
hem (1) [hem], *s.* (*cost.*) dobladillo, bastilla, repulgo, orilla, borde; ribete — *v.t.* dobladillar, bastillar, repulgar; ***hem in,*** cercar.
hem (2) [hem], *v.i.* destoserse. — *interj.* ¡ejem!
hematite [HAEMATITE].
hematosis [HAEMATOSIS].
hemicrania [hemiˈkreiniə], *s.* hemicránea.
hemicycle [ˈhemisaikl], *s.* hemiciclo.
hemiplegia [hemiˈpliːdʒiə], *s.* hemiplejía.
hemiplegic [hemiˈpliːdʒik], *a.* hemipléjico.
hemipterous [heˈmiptərəs], *a.* hemíptero.
hemisphere [ˈhemisfiə], *s.* hemisferio.
hemispheric(al), [hemiˈsferik(əl)], *a.* hemisférico, semiesférico.
hemistich [ˈhemistik], *s.* (*poét.*) hemistiquio.
hemlock [ˈhemlɔk], *s.* (*bot.*) cicuta.
hemoglobin [HAEMOGLOBIN].
hemorrhage [HAEMORRHAGE].
hemorrhoids [HAEMORRHOIDS].
hemp [hemp], *s.* cáñamo; ***bastard-hemp,*** cañamón; ***hemp agrimony,*** eupatorio vulgar; ***hemp-beater,*** espadillador, espadador de cáñamo; ***hemp-brake,*** maza, espadilla; ***hemp-breaker,*** agramador; ***hemp-close,*** cañamar; ***hemp-comb,*** peine para el cáñamo; ***hemp-dresser,*** batidor; ***hemp-seed,*** cañamón; ***Indian hemp,*** hachís.
hempen [ˈhempən], *a.* cañameño.
hempy [ˈhempi], *a.* semejante al cáñamo.
hem-stitch [ˈhemstitʃ], *s.* vainica. — *v.t.* hacer vainica en.
hen [hen], *s.* gallina; hembra; ***brood-hen,*** gallina clueca; ***hen-coop, hen-house, hen-roost,*** gallinero; ***hen-party,*** reunión de mujeres.
henbane [ˈhenbein], *s.* (*bot.*) beleño.
hence [hens], *adv.* de aquí, desde aquí; fuera de aquí; por lo tanto, por esto; ***far hence,*** lejos de aquí; ***ten years hence,*** de aquí a diez años; (*ant.*) ***get thee hence!*** ¡largo de aquí!
henceforth, henceforward [hensˈfɔːθ, -ˈfɔːwəd], *adv.* de aquí en adelante.
henchman [ˈhentʃmən], *s.* secuaz; muñidor.
hendecagon [henˈdekəgən], *s.* endecágono.
hendecasyllable [hendekəˈsiləbəl], *s.* endecasílabo.
henna [ˈhenə], *s.* alheña.
hennery [ˈhenəri], *s.* gallinero.
henpeck [ˈhenpek], *v.t.* dominar, tener en un puño (*la mujer al marido*).
henpecked [ˈhenpekt], *a.* dominado por su mujer.
henry [ˈhenri], *s.* (*elec.*) henrio.
hepatic(al) [heˈpætik(əl)], *a.* hepático.
hepatica [heˈpætikə], *s.* hepática.
hepatite [ˈhepətait], *s.* hepatita.
hepatitis [hepəˈtaitis], *s.* hepatitis, *f.inv.*
heptachord [ˈheptəkɔːd], *s.* heptacordio.
heptad [ˈheptæd], *s.* setena.
heptagon [ˈheptəgən], *s.* heptágono.
heptagonal [hepˈtægənəl], *a.* heptagonal.
heptarchy [ˈheptɑːki], *s.* heptarquía.
Heptateuch [ˈheptətjuːk], *s.* Heptateuco.
her [həː], *pron.* (*caso acusativo* o *dativo de* **she**) la; le; ella; (*caso pos. de* **she**) su, sus, de ella.
herald [ˈherəld], *s.* heraldo; anunciador, precursor. — *v.t.* anunciar, presagiar, ser nuncio, premonición *o* precursor de.
heraldic [heˈrældik], *a.* heráldico.
heraldry [ˈherəldri], *s.* heráldica.
heraldship [ˈherəldʃip], *s.* heraldía.
herb [həːb], *s.* hierba; ***pot-herbs,*** hortalizas, *f.pl.*; ***sweet herbs,*** hierbas odoríferas.
herbaceous [həˈbeiʃəs], *a.* herbáceo.
herbage [ˈhəːbidʒ], *s.* herbaje; derecho de pastoreo.
herbaged [ˈhəːbidʒd], *a.* cubierto de hierba.
herbal [ˈhəːbəl], *a.* herbario.
herbalism [ˈhəːbəlizəm], *s.* conocimiento de las hierbas.
herbalist [ˈhəːbəlist], *s.* herbolario, herbario, botánico.
herbarium [həːˈbɛəriəm], *s.* herbario.
herbescent [həːˈbesənt], *a.* herbáceo.
herbivorous [həːˈbivərəs], *a.* herbívoro.
herbless [ˈhəːblis], *a.* sin hierbas.
herborization [həːbəraiˈzeiʃən], *s.* herborización.
herborize [ˈhəːbəraiz], *v.i.* herborizar.
herborizer [ˈhəːbəraizə], *s.* herborizante, herborizador.
herbous [ˈhəːbəs], *a.* herboso, herbáceo.
herbwoman [ˈhəːbwumən], *s.* herbolaria.
Herculean [həːkjuˈliən], *a.* hercúleo.
herd [həːd], *s.* manada; rebaño; piara; hato; muchedumbre; ***common herd,*** (el) vulgo; ***herd instinct,*** instinto gregario. — *v.t.* reunir, llevar en manadas. — *v.i.* — ***together,*** reunirse en manadas.
herdsman [ˈhəːdzmən], *s.* guarda de ganado, *m.*, manadero.
here [hiə], *adv.* aquí; acá; ***here and there,*** aquí y allá; ***here below,*** aquí abajo; ***here goes!*** ¡ahí va!; ***here it is,*** aquí lo tiene usted; aquí está; ***here's to you,*** a la salud de usted; ***that's neither here nor there,*** eso no viene *o* no hace al caso. — *interj.* ¡presente!
hereabouts [ˈhiərəbauts], *adv.* aquí alrededor, por aquí cerca.

hereafter [hiər'ɑ:ftə], *adv.* de aquí en adelante, en lo sucesivo. — *s.* (lo) futuro; vida futura.
hereat [hiər'æt], *adv.* a esto; en esto.
hereby ['hiə'bai], *adv.* por la presente, con esto.
hereditable [hi'reditəbl], *a.* heredable.
hereditament [heri'ditəmənt], *s.* (*for.*) bienes heredables, *m.pl.*
hereditary [hi'reditəri], *a.* hereditario.
herefrom [hiə'frɔm], *adv.* de aquí, desde aquí; a causa de esto.
herein [hiər'in], *adv.* aquí dentro; incluido.
hereinafter [hiərin'ɑ:ftə], *adv.* más abajo, más adelante; en lo sucesivo, a partir de ahora.
hereof [hiər'ɔv], *adv.* de esto; acerca de esto; de aquí.
hereon [hiər'ɔn], *adv.* sobre esto, sobre este punto.
heresiarch [he'ri:ziɑ:k], *s.* heresiarca, *m.f.*
heresy ['herisi], *s.* herejía.
heretic ['heritik], *s.* hereje.
heretical [he'retikəl], *a.* herético.
hereto [hiə'tu:], *adv.* a esto, a este fin.
heretofore [hiətu'fɔ:], *adv.* antes, hasta ahora. — *s.* tiempo pasado.
hereunder [hiər'ʌndə], *adv.* bajo esto; en virtud de esto.
hereunto [hiərʌn'tu:], *adv.* a esto, para esto.
hereupon [hiərə'pɔn], *adv.* sobre esto; en esto; en seguida.
herewith ['hiə'wið], *adv.* adjunto, con esto.
heritable ['heritəbl], *a.* que se puede heredar.
heritage ['heritidʒ], *s.* herencia; patrimonio.
hermaphrodite [hə:'mæfrodait], *a.*, *s.* hermafrodita, *m.f.*
hermaphroditic [hə:mæfro'ditik], *a.* hermafrodita.
hermaphroditism [hə:'mæfroditizəm], *s.* hermafroditismo.
hermeneutic(al) [hə:mi'nju:tik(əl)], *a.* hermenéutico.
hermeneutics [hə:mi'nju:tiks], *s.* hermenéutica.
hermetic [hə:'metik], *a.* hermético.
hermetically [hə:'metikəli], *adv.* herméticamente.
hermit ['hə:mit], *s.* ermitaño; ***hermit crab,*** ermitaño.
hermitage ['hə:mitidʒ], *s.* ermita.
hermitary ['hə:mitəri], *s.* celda de ermitaño (*aneja a un monasterio*).
hermitical [hə:'mitikəl], *a.* eremítico.
hernia ['hə:niə], *s.* hernia.
hernial ['hə:niəl], *a.* herniario.
hernshaw ['hə:nʃɔ:], *s.* garza.
hero ['hiərou], *s.* héroe; protagonista (*de un drama etc.*), *m.*; ***hero-worship,*** adoración; culto a los héroes.
heroic [hi'rouik], *a.* heroico. — *s.pl.*, exageraciones, *f.pl.*, expresiones extravagantes, *f.pl.*
heroically [hi'rouikəli], *adv.* heroicamente.
heroin ['heroin], *s.* heroína (*droga*).
heroine ['heroin], *s.* heroína.
heroism ['heroizəm], *s.* heroísmo; heroicidad.
heron ['herən], *s.* garza; airón; (*bot.*) pico de garza.
heronry ['herənri], *s.* lugar en que se crían (las) garzas.
herpes ['hə:pi:z], *s.* herpe, *m.f.*
herpetic [hə:'petik], *a.* herpético.
herpetism ['hə:pitizəm], *s.* herpetismo.
herpetology [hə:pi'tɔlədʒi], *s.* herpetología.
herring ['heriŋ], *s.* arenque; ***red herring,*** arenque ahumado; (*fig.*) pista falsa, cosa que despista.
herringbone ['heriŋboun], *s.* (*entarimados*) espinapez; (*tej.*) espiga.
hers [hə:z], *pron. pos. f.* suyo, suya, de ella; el suyo, la suya, los suyos, las suyas.
herself [hə'self], *pron. pers. f.* ella (misma); sí (misma); ***by herself,*** sola, por sí, por sí sola; ***she herself did it,*** ella (misma) lo hizo; ***she washes herself,*** se lava; ***she talks to herself,*** habla sola.
hersillon [hə:'silən], *s.* (*mil.*) caballo de Frisia.
hesitancy ['hezitənsi], *s.* vacilación, duda, indecisión.
hesitant ['hezitənt], *a.* vacilante, titubeante, irresoluto, indeciso.
hesitate ['heziteit], *v.i.* dudar, vacilar, titubear.
hesitation [hezi'teiʃən], *s.* irresolución, duda, titubeo, indecisión, vacilación.
Hesperus ['hespərəs], *s.* Héspero, Venus, estrella vespertina.
Hessian ['heʃən], *a.* perteneciente al ducado de Hesse; (*ent.*) ***Hessian fly,*** cecidomio.
hessian ['hesiən], *s.* arpillera.
hest [hest], *s.* (*ant.*) mandato, precepto, orden.
heteroclite ['hetəroklait], *a.*, *s.* heteróclito.
heterodox ['hetərodɔks], *a.* heterodoxo.
heterodoxy ['hetərodɔksi], *s.* heterodoxia.
heterogamous [hetə'rɔgəməs], *a.* (*bot.*) heterógamo.
heterogeneity, heterogeneousness [hetərodʒi'niiti, -'dʒi:niəsnis], *s.* heterogeneidad.
heterogeneous [hetəro'dʒi:niəs], *a.* heterogéneo.
hew [hju:], *irr. v.t.* tajar, cortar; labrar; desbastar; ***hew down,*** derribar a hachazos; ***hew in pieces,*** destrozar; ***hew out,*** modelar en bruto; ***hew one's way through,*** abrirse paso a hachazos por entre.
hewer [hju:ə], *s.* cortador de madera; cantero; desbastador; picapedrero.
hexachord ['heksəkɔ:d], *s.* hexacordo.
hexagon ['heksəgən], *s.* hexágono, seisavo.
hexagonal [hek'sægənəl], *a.* hexagonal, sexagonal, seisavado.
hexahedron [heksə'hi:drən], *s.* hexaedro.
hexameter [hek'sæmitə], *s.* hexámetro.
hexametric(al) [heksə'metrik(əl)], *a.* hexámetro, que se compone de hexámetros.
hexangular [hek'sæŋgulə], *a.* hexángulo, hexágono.
hexapod ['heksəpɔd], *s.* hexápodo.
hexastyle ['heksəstail], *s.* hexástilo.
hey! [hei], *interj.* ¡he! ¡eh!
heyday ['heidei], *s.* auge, apogeo. — *interj.* ¡hola!
hiatus [hai'eitəs], *s.* hiato; laguna, espacio, vacío; solución de continuidad.
hibernal [hai'bə:nəl], *a.* hibernal, hiemal, invernizo, invernal.
hibernate ['haibəneit], *v.i.* hibernar; invernar.
hibernation [haibə'neiʃən], *s.* hibernación; invernada.
Hibernian [hai'bə:niən], *a.*, *s.* hibernés, de Hibernia.
hibiscus [hi'biskəs], *s.* (*bot.*) hibisco.
hiccough [HICCUP].
hiccup ['hikʌp], *s.* hipo. — *v.i.* hipar, tener hipo.
hick [hik], *s.* (*fam.*) patán, paleto, palurdo.
hickory ['hikəri], *s.* nogal americano.
hidden [hidn], *a.* oculto; recóndito. — *p.p.* [HIDE].
hide (1) [haid], *s.* cuero; piel, *f.*; pellejo; ***to dress hides,*** curtir cueros; ***raw hide,*** cuero sin curtir; (*fam.*) ***I'll tan his hide for him,*** le voy a zurrar (la badana).
hide (2) [haid], *s.* paranza; ***hide-and-seek,*** escondite; ***to play hide-and-seek,*** jugar al escondite; ***hide-out,*** refugio. — *irr. v.t.* esconder; ocultar; encubrir; disimular. — *v.i.* esconderse; ocultarse.
hidebound ['haidbaund], *a.* rígido, intransigente; tradicionalista, chapado a la antigua.
hideous ['hidiəs], *a.* feísimo, horroroso, espantoso.
hideousness ['hidiəsnis], *s.* (lo) feísimo *etc.*
hiding (1) ['haidiŋ], *s.* (*fam.*) zurra, paliza.
hiding (2) ['haidiŋ], *s.* ocultación, (el) esconder(se); ***hiding-place,*** escondrijo; ***in hiding,*** escondido; ***to go into hiding,*** esconderse.

hidrotic [hi'drɔtik], *a.* (*med.*) hidrótico.
hie [hai], *v.t.* (*ant.*) apresurar. — *v.r.* darse prisa, apresurarse; ***hie thee home,*** apresúrate a volver a casa; ***hie thee,*** date prisa.
hierarch ['haiərɑ:k], *s.* jerarca, *m.*
hierarchic(al) [haiər'ɑ:kik(əl)], *a.* jerárquico.
hierarchism ['haiərɑ:kizəm], *s.* jerarquía.
hierarchy ['haiərɑ:ki], *s.* jerarquía.
hieratic(al) [haiə'rætik(əl)], *a.* hierático.
hieroglyph ['haiəroglif], *s.* jeroglífico. — *v.t.* escribir en jeroglíficos.
hieroglyphic [haiəro'glifik], *a.*, *s.* jeroglífico.
hierolatry [haiə'rɔlətri], *s.* hierolatría.
hierologic [haiəro'lɔdʒik], *s.* hierológico.
hierology [haiə'rɔlədʒi], *s.* hierología.
hieromancy ['hairomænsi], *s.* hieromancia.
hierophant ['hairofænt], *s.* hierofante.
hi-fi ['hai-'fai], *a.* (*fam.*, *rad.*) de alta fidelidad.
higgle [higl], *v.i.* regatear.
higgledy-piggledy ['higəldi-'pigəldi], *a.* (*fam.*) revuelto, desordenado. — *adv.* sin orden ni concierto, a lo loco.
high [hai], *a.* alto; elevado; (*altar, misa, calle*) mayor; (*color*) subido; altivo, altanero; (*carne*) pasado; (*caza*) manido; (*clero*) sumo; (*río*) crecido; (*velocidad*) gran(de); (*sonido*) agudo; (*viento*) fuerte; (*fam.*) bebido, borracho; drogado; ***high and dry,*** en seco, varado; ***high and mighty,*** altivo, altanero; ***high blood-pressure,*** hipertensión arterial; ***high-coloured,*** de color subido; ***high day,*** día solemne, *m.*, fiesta; ***high days and holidays,*** días de fiesta, *m.pl.*; ***high-handed,*** despótico; ***high-heeled,*** de tacones altos; ***to be on one's high-horse,*** estar en plan engreído; ***high-jump,*** salto de altura; ***to be in for the high-jump,*** estar listo, ir a ganársela; ***high-keyed,*** (*mus.*) agudo; impresionable; ***high life,*** alta sociedad; ***high living,*** vida regalada; ***high-minded,*** noble; ***high priest,*** sumo sacerdote; ***high road,*** carretera; camino real; ***high school,*** colegio de segunda enseñanza; ***high-spirited,*** fogoso, brioso, animoso; ***it was high time to do it,*** ya era hora de hacerlo; ***high-toned,*** de buen tono. — *adv.* arriba, alto; sumamente; altamente; fuertemente; ***high and low,*** por todas partes; ***high-born,*** noble, ilustre de nacimiento; ***high-powered,*** de mucho empuje; de mucha potencia; ***high-reaching,*** ambicioso, que pica alto; ***to aim high,*** picar alto; ***to hold one's head high,*** llevar la cabeza erguida; (*mar.*) ***to run high,*** estar (*la mar*) arbolada. — *s.* ***the Most High,*** el Altísmo; ***on high,*** en alto.
highball ['haibɔ:l], *s.* (*Am.*) güisqui con seltz.
highest ['haiist], *a.* *superl.* [HIGH]; (el) más alto; supremo, sumo, máximo, mayor.
highfalutin [haifə'lu:tin], *a.* (*fam.*) altisonante; versallesco; rebuscado, rimbombante.
highland ['hailənd], *a.* montañés. — *s.* país montañoso, montaña.
highlander ['hailəndə], *s.* montañés, serrano.
highly ['haili], *adv.* altamente; sumamente, en sumo grado, en gran manera, infinitamente; ***highly seasoned,*** que tiene mucho picante; ***highly strung,*** nervioso, de nervios delicados; ***to think highly of o.s.,*** tener gran concepto de sí mismo.
Highness ['hainis], *s.* Alteza (*título*).
highness ['hainis], *s.* altura, elevación.
hight [hait], *a.* (*ant.*) llamado, nombrado.
highty-tighty ['haiti-'taiti], [HOITY-TOITY].
highway ['haiwei], *s.* camino real; carretera.
highwayman ['haiweimən], *s.* bandolero, salteador (*de caminos*).
hijack ['haidʒæk], *v.t.* secuestrar (*aviones, camiones etc.*).
hijacker ['haidʒækə], *s.* secuestrador.
hike [haik], *s.* caminata, viaje a pie. — *v.i.* ir a pie.
hiker ['haikə], *s.* excursionista (a pie), *m.f.*

hilarious [hi'lɛəriəs], *a.* graciosísimo; muy alegre.
hilarity [hi'læriti], *s.* hilaridad; júbilo, alegría, regocijo.
hill [hil], *s.* monte, colina, collado, loma, otero, cerro; (*Am.*, *fam.*) ***hill-billy,*** zoquete, paleto.
hilliness ['hilinis], *s.* montuosidad.
hillock ['hilək], *s.* altillo, montecillo, montículo, altozano, cerrejón.
hillside ['hilsaid], *s.* ladera.
hilltop ['hiltɔp], *s.* cima, cumbre, (lo) alto.
hilly ['hili], *a.* montuoso.
hilt [hilt], *s.* puño, empuñadura; (*fig.*) ***(up) to the hilt,*** hasta las cachas; hasta los tuétanos; totalmente; de manera incondicional.
hilum ['hailəm], *s.* (*bot.*) hilo; (*anat.*) hilio.
him [him], *pron. pers. m.* (*acusativo*) lo, le; (*dativo*) le; (*disyuntivo*) él; ***give it to him,*** déselo Vd.
himself [him'self], *pron. pers. reflexivo.* (*nominativo*) él (mismo); (*acusativo y dativo*) se; (*disyuntivo*) sí (mismo); ***to say to o.s.,*** decir para sí; ***he will go himself,*** irá en persona; ***he will go by himself,*** irá solo.
hind (1) [haind], *a.* trasero, posterior; ***hind quarters,*** (cuarto) trasero; (*fam.*) ***to talk the hind-leg off a donkey,*** hablar por los codos.
hind (2) [haind], *s.* cierva.
hinder (1) ['hində], *v.t.* estorbar, obstaculizar; impedir; ***hinder from,*** impedir +*inf.* o que+ *subj.*
hinder (2) ['haində], *a.* [HIND (1)].
Hindi ['hindi], *s.* (*lengua*) indostaní, indostánico.
hindmost ['haindmoust], *a.* postrero, último.
hindrance ['hindrəns], *s.* impedimento, obstáculo, estorbo, embarazo.
Hindu [hin'du:], *a.*, *s.* hindú, indostánico.
Hindustani [hindu'stɑ:ni], *a.* indostánico, indostanés. — *s.* indostanés; (*lengua*) indostánico, indostaní.
hinge [hindʒ], *s.* gozne; bisagra; charnela; eje principal; (*anat.*) ***hinge-joint,*** coyuntura; ***hinge-post,*** quicial; ***to come off its hinges,*** desquiciarse. — *v.t.* engoznar, embisagrar, poner goznes o bisagras a. — *v.i.* (*fig.*) — ***on, upon,*** girar sobre; depender de.
hinny (1) ['hini], *s.* burdégano.
hinny (2) ['hini], *v.t.* relinchar.
hint [hint], *s.* indirecta, insinuación, indicación; (*pl.*) consejos, *m.pl.*, indicaciones, *f.pl.*; ***broad hint,*** indirecta bastante directa; ***to drop, let fall*** o ***throw out hints,*** tirar indirectas; ***to take the hint,*** darse por aludido. — *v.t.* insinuar, indicar, sugerir indirectamente. — *v.i.* echar una indirecta, echar indirectas; ***hint at,*** insinuar, dar a entender, hacer entrever.
hinterland ['hintəlænd], *s.* interior, hinterland.
hintingly ['hintiŋli], *adv.* con indirectas, con insinuaciones.
hip (1) [hip], *s.* (*anat.*) cadera; (*arq.*) caballete; ***hip bath,*** baño de asiento; ***hip-bone,*** cía; ***hip-pocket,*** bolsillo de cadera; (*arq.*) ***hip roof,*** techo a cuatro vertientes; ***hip-shot,*** renco; ***to smite hip and thigh,*** golpear despiadamente.
hip (2) [hip], *s.* (*bot.*) (fruta del) escaramujo; agavanzo.
hip! (3) [hip], *interj.* ***hip, hip, hurray!*** ¡hurra! ¡viva!
hippocampus [hipou'kæmpəs], *s.* hipocampo.
hippocras ['hipoukræs], *s.* hipocrás.
Hippocratism [hi'pɔkrətizəm], *s.* doctrina médica de Hipócrates.
hippodrome ['hipədroum], *s.* hipódromo; circo.
hippogriff ['hipougrif], *s.* hipogrifo.
hippophagy [hi'pɔfəgi], *s.* hipofagia.
hippopotamus [hipə'pɔtəməs], *s.* (*pl.* **hippopotamuses, hippopotami** ['hipə'pɔtəməsiz, -ai]), hipopótamo.
hipwort ['hipwə:t], *s.* escaramujo.

hircine [ˈhəːsain], *a.* cabrío, cabruno.
hire [haiə], *s.* alquiler, arriendo; jornal; ***for hire, on hire,*** para alquilar, de alquiler. — *v.t.* alquilar, arrendar; tomar en arriendo; contratar.
hireling [ˈhaiəliŋ], *a., s.* alquilón, mercenario.
hire purchase [ˈhaiə ˈpəːtʃis], *s.* compra a plazos.
hirer [ˈhaiərə], *s.* alquilador, arrendador.
hirsute [ˈhəːsjuːt], *a.* hirsuto; greñudo.
hirsuteness [ˈhəːsjuːtnis], *s.* (lo) hirsuto.
his [hiz], *a. pos.*, su, sus (de él); suyo, suya, suyos, suyas. — *pron.* (*pos.* o *genitivo de* **he**) *m.* el suyo, la suya, los suyos, las suyas (de él).
hispid [ˈhispid], *a.* híspido, cerdoso.
hiss [his], *s.* siseo; silbido. — *v.t., v.i.* sisear; silbar.
hissing [ˈhisiŋ], *s.* silbidos, silba; siseo.
hist! [hist], *interj.* ¡chito! ¡chitón! ¡silencio!
histologic(al) [histəˈlɔdʒik(əl)], *a.* histológico.
histologist [hisˈtɔlədʒist], *s.* histólogo.
histology [hisˈtɔlədʒi], *s.* histología.
historian [hisˈtɔːriən], *s.* historiador.
historic(al) [hisˈtɔrik(əl)], *a.* histórico.
historiographer [histɔriˈɔgrəfə], *s.* historiógrafo.
historiography [histɔriˈɔgrəfi], *s.* historiografía.
history [ˈhistəri], *s.* historia.
histrionic [histriˈɔnik], *a.* histriónico; teatral.
histrionics [histriˈɔniks], *s.pl.* histrionismo.
hit [hit], *s.* golpe; tiro certero; gran éxito; impacto; (*fam.*) ***to be a hit, to make a hit,*** ser un éxito; ***to make a hit with,*** caer en gracia a. — *v.t.* dar, pegar, golpear; asestar; herir, afectar; atinar, acertar; ***hit it off with,*** congeniar con; ***hit the mark,*** acertar, dar en el blanco; ***hit the nail on the head,*** dar en el clavo; ***hit the trail,*** ponerse en camino; ***it hits you in the eye,*** salta a la vista. — *v.i.* chocar, tocar; ***hit against,*** dar contra, chocar con; ***hit at,*** apuntar a; ***hit on, upon,*** encontrar; ocurrírsele (a uno); ***I hit on the idea,*** se me ocurrió la idea; ***hit or miss,*** a la buena de Dios; esporádico. — *pret., p.p.* [HIT].
hitch [hitʃ], *s.* (*fam.*) pega, dificultad; tirón; (*mar.*) vuelta de cabo; ***without a hitch,*** sin pega, sin problema. — *v.t.* atar; enganchar; (*mar.*) amarrar; mover a tirones; ***hitch up,*** subir(se), levantar.
hitch-hike [ˈhitʃ-haik], *v.i.* hacer autostop.
hitch-hiker [ˈhitʃ-haikə], *s.* autostopista, *m.f.*
hitch-hiking [ˈhitʃ-haikiŋ], *s.* autostop.
hither [ˈhiðə], *a.* citerior; ***on the hither side of,*** del lado de acá de. — *adv.* acá, hacia acá; ***come hither,*** ven acá; ***hither and thither,*** acá y acullá.
hithermost [ˈhiðəmoust], *a.* (el) más cercano.
hitherto [hiðəˈtuː], *adv.* hasta ahora.
hive [haiv], *s.* colmena; ***hive of activity,*** centro de actividad. — *v.t.* enjambrar; acopiar (*miel*); ***hive off,*** separar. — *v.i.* vivir aglomerados.
hiver [ˈhaivə], *s.* colmenero.
hives [haivz], *s.pl.* (*med.*) urticaria.
ho (a)! [hou], *interj.* ¡so!
hoar [hɔː], *a.* blanco, cano.
hoard [hɔːd], *s.* tesoro escondido; acumulación, acopio, acervo. — *v.t., v.i.* atesorar, guardar, acumular.
hoarder [ˈhɔːdə], s. persona muy dada a guardar cosas.
hoarding [ˈhɔːdiŋ], *s.* (el) acumular; valla provisional; cartelera.
hoar-frost [ˈhɔː-ˈfrɔst], *s.* escarcha.
hoariness [ˈhɔːrinis], *s.* (lo) canoso, canicie; vetustez.
hoarse [hɔːs], *a.* ronco.
hoarseness [ˈhɔːsnis], *s.* ronquera.
hoary [ˈhɔːri], *a.* cano, canoso; escarchado; venerable.
hoax [houks], *s.* engaño, engañifa, burla, bola, filfa. — *v.t.* engañar, burlar.
hob [hɔb], *s.* repisa interior del hogar.
hobble [hɔbl], *s.* cojera; traba; maniota. — *v.t.* poner trabas a, maniatar. — *v.i.* cojear.
hobbledehoy [ˈhɔbəldihɔi], *s.* mozalbete, gamberro.
hobby (1) [ˈhɔbi], *s.* pasatiempo, afición; ***hobby-horse,*** caballito (de niño); caballo mecedor; manía, tema obsesivo, obsesión.
hobby (2) [ˈhɔbi], *s.* (*orn.*) alcotán.
hobgoblin [hɔbˈgɔblin], *s.* duende, trasgo, cachidiablo.
hobnail [ˈhɔbneil], *s.* clavo (*de botas*). — *v.t.* clavetear (*botas*).
hob-nob [ˈhɔb-nɔb], *v.i.* codearse, alternar (***with,*** con).
hobo [ˈhoubou], *s.* (*Am.*) vagabundo.
hock (1) [hɔk], *s.* corva; (*animales*) corvejón, jarrete. — *v.t.* desjarretar.
hock (2) [hɔk], *s.* vino del Rin.
hock (3) [hɔk], *s.* (*Am., fam.*) empeño; ***hock-shop,*** casa de empeños. — *v.t.* empeñar.
hockey [ˈhɔki], *s.* hockey.
hockle [hɔkl], *v.t.* desjarretar.
hocus [ˈhoukəs], *v.t.* engañar, chasquear; atontar con drogas.
hocus-pocus [ˈhoukəs-ˈpoukəs], *s.* abracadabra; mistificación; treta.
hod [hɔd], *s.* cuezo; cubo para carbón; ***hod-carrier,*** peón de albañil.
hodge-podge [ˈhɔdʒ-pɔdʒ], *s.* (*fam.*) almodrote, bodrio; baturrillo, mezcolanza.
hodiernal [houdiˈəːnəl], *a.* de hoy, de hoy día.
hodman [ˈhɔdmən], *s.* peón de albañil.
hoe [hou], *s.* azada, azadón. — *v.t.* azadonar, sachar.
hoedown [ˈhoudaun], *s.* (*Am.*) bailoteo.
hoeing [ˈhouiŋ], *s.* sachadura.
hog [hɔg], *s.* cerdo, cochino, marrano, puerco; glotón; (*mar.*) escobón; ***to go the whole hog,*** llegar hasta el límite, echar el resto; ***hog-back,*** cerro escarpado; (*bot.*) ***hog-fennel,*** servato, ervato; ***hog-herd,*** porquero, porquerizo; ***hog-pen, hog-sty,*** pocilga, porqueriza; (*fam.*) ***hog-wash,*** músicas, *f.pl.*, gaitas, *f.pl.*; (*Am.*) [SWILL].
hoggish [ˈhɔgiʃ], *a.* cochino; glotón.
hoggishness [ˈhɔgiʃnis], *s.* porquería, cochinada, glotonería.
Hogmanay [hɔgməˈnei], *s.* (*Esco.*) Noche Vieja.
hogshead [ˈhɔgzhed], *s.* pipa, bocoy.
hoist [hɔist], *s.* cabria, malacate; montacargas, *m. inv.*, elevador; alzamiento. — *v.t.* alzar, izar, enarbolar.
hoisting-rope [ˈhɔistiŋ-roup], *s.* braga.
hoity-toity [ˈhɔiti-ˈtɔiti], *a.* petulante, presumido, fachendoso; displicente. — *interj.* ¡tate! ¡hombre!
hold [hould], *s.* agarro; agarradero, asidero; (*dep.*) presa; (*mar.*) cala, bodega; ***to catch, get*** o ***take hold of, to lay hold of*** u ***on,*** agarrar, coger, apoderarse de; ***to have a hold on*** u ***over,*** tener dominado, sujeto *o* cogido; tener mucha influencia sobre; ***to keep hold of,*** tener agarrado, no soltar. — *irr. v.t.* tener; retener, guardar; detener; detentar; sujetar; agarrar, coger; contener, tener cabida para; mantener; sostener; considerar; ocupar (*un puesto*); celebrar (*una reunión*); ***it won't hold any more,*** no cabe(n) más; ***hold back,*** retener, frenar, refrenar; ***hold down,*** sujetar; ***hold down a job,*** conservar un empleo, mostrarse adecuado para un empleo; ***hold the fort,*** defender el puesto; ***hold in,*** refrenar; (*tele.*) ***hold the line,*** no se retire; ***hold off,*** mantener a raya; ***hold out,*** (ex)tender; ***hold over,*** aplazar; ***hold one's own against,*** defenderse contra; ***hold to,*** obligar a cumplir; ***hold up,*** apoyar, sostener; levantar; detener; suspender; interrumpir; robar, saltear, atracar. — *v.i.* mantenerse firme, resistir, aguantar; detenerse; ser valedero; continuar; pegarse; ***hold back (from),*** no atreverse (a); ***hold forth,*** perorar; sentar cátedra; ***hold good*** o ***true,*** ser válido, valer; ***hold hard!*** ¡tente! ***hold on,*** agarrarse; aguantar; ***hold on!*** ¡espérate!; ***hold out,*** aguantar, resistir; ***hold out for,*** resistir

hasta conseguir; ***hold to,*** atenerse a; ***hold with,*** estar de acuerdo con; aprobar.

hold-all [ˈhould-ɔ:l], *s.* bolsa *o* saco de mano.

holdback [ˈhouldbæk], *s.* restricción, freno; (*carr.*) cejadero.

holder [ˈhouldə], *s.* tenedor, poseedor, posesor; titular; arrendatario, arrendador; agarrador, asidero, agarradero; mango, asa, puño; soporte; recipiente.

holdfast [ˈhouldfɑ:st], *s.* (*mec.*) grapa; apoyo, sostén.

holding [ˈhouldiŋ], *s.* tenencia, posesión; (*pl.*) terrenos, *m.pl.*; valores habidos, *m.pl.*

hold-up [ˈhould-ʌp], *s.* detención, interrupción; atraco.

hole [houl], *s.* agujero; cavidad; boquete; hoyo; rotura; (*calle*) bache; (*animales*) guarida; (*morada*) cuchitril; (*fig.*) ***in a hole,*** en un aprieto; (*fig.*) ***to make a hole in,*** dejar temblando; (*fig.*) ***to pick holes in,*** poner pegas *o* reparos a. — *v.t.* agujerear, perforar.

holiday [ˈhɔlidei], *a.* festivo, de fiesta, de vacaciones. — *s.* (día de) fiesta, día festivo; día de asueto; (*pl.*) vacaciones; ***holidays with pay,*** vacaciones retribuidas *o* pagadas; ***holiday camp,*** colonia veraniega. — *v.i.* pasar las vacaciones; veranear.

holiness [ˈhoulinis], *s.* santidad; ***His Holiness,*** Su Santidad.

Holland [ˈhɔlənd], Holanda.

holland [ˈhɔlənd], *s.* (*tej.*,) holanda; ***brown holland,*** holanda cruda; (*pl.*) ginebra.

hollo!, holl(o)a! [HELLO].

hollow [ˈhɔlou], *a.* hueco, ahuecado; (*ojos*) hundido; (*fig.*, *fam.*) vacío, falso; (*voz*) sepulcral, cavernoso; (*fam.*) ***to beat hollow,*** dar una paliza a, merendarse a. — *s.* hueco; cavidad; depresión, hondón; hondonada; ***hollow-root,*** moscatelina, palomilla. — *v.t.* — ***out,*** ahuecar; excavar; vaciar.

hollowness [ˈhɔlounis], *s.* oquedad, concavidad; (lo) vacío.

holly [ˈhɔli], *s.* acebo; agrifolio.

hollyhock [ˈhɔlihɔk], *s.* malvaloca, malvarrosa.

holm [houm], *s.* isleta (de río); rambla.

holm-oak [ˈhoum-ouk], *s.* (*bot.*) encina.

holocaust [ˈhɔləkɔ:st], *s.* holocausto.

holograph [ˈhɔlogrɑ:f], *s.* hológrafo.

holographic [hɔloˈgræfik], *s.* hológrafo.

holster [ˈhoulstə], *s.* pistolera, funda de pistola; ***holster-cap,*** tapafunda.

holt [hoult], *s.* bosque, monte.

holy [ˈhouli], *a.* santo, sagrado; ***Holy of Holies,*** sanctasanctórum, *m.inv.*; ***holy day,*** día de fiesta, *m.*, disanto; ***Holy Ghost, Holy Spirit,*** Espíritu Santo; ***Holy Land,*** Tierra Santa; ***Holy Office,*** Santo Oficio; ***holy oil,*** crisma, óleo; ***Holy Roman Empire,*** Sacro Imperio Romano; ***Holy See,*** (la) Santa Sede; ***Holy Thursday,*** jueves santo; día de la Ascensión; ***holy wars,*** cruzadas, *f.pl.*; ***holy water,*** agua bendita; ***holy-water sprinkler,*** hisopo; ***Holy Week,*** Semana Santa; ***holy writ,*** (la) Sagrada Escritura.

holystone [ˈhoulistoun], *s.* (*mar.*) piedra bendita. — *v.t.* (*mar.*) limpiar (la cubierta) con piedra bendita.

homage [ˈhɔmidʒ], *s.* homenaje; tributo; ***to do, pay*** *o* ***render homage to,*** rendir homenaje a.

home [houm], *a.* casero; doméstico, de casa; nacional; ***home life,*** vida de familia, hogareña; ***Home Office,*** Ministerio del Interior, de la Gobernación; ***home port,*** puerto de origen; ***home rule,*** autonomía; ***home straight,*** recta de llegada; ***home team,*** equipo de casa; ***hometown,*** ciudad *o* pueblo natal; ***to tell s.o. a few home-truths,*** decirle a alguien cuatro verdades. — *adv.* a casa; en casa; a fondo; ***home-born,*** doméstico, indígena; ***home-bred,*** casero; agreste, rudo; ***home-made,*** de fabricación casera, casero; ***to be home,*** estar de vuelta; ***to bring*** *o* ***drive home,*** hacer que convenza; remachar; ***to come home,*** volver a casa; ***to hit*** o ***strike home,*** herir en lo vivo; dar en el clavo *o* en el blanco; meter a fondo (*un clavo etc.*). — *s.* hogar, casa, domicilio; patria; asilo; (*dep.*) meta; ***at home,*** en casa; a gusto; ***make yourself at home,*** póngase cómodo; ***away from home,*** fuera de casa. — *v.i.* volver a casa.

homeless [ˈhoumlis], *a.* destituido; sin casa ni hogar; mostrenco.

homelike [ˈhoumlaik], *a.* semejante al hogar (doméstico); cómodo, agradable.

homeliness [ˈhoumlinis], *s.* sencillez; domesticidad; (*Am.*) fealdad.

homely [ˈhoumli], *a.* sencillo, llano; (*Am.*) feo, vulgar.

homeopathic [HOMŒOPATHIC].

homeopathy [HOMŒOPATHY].

Homeric [hoˈmerik], *a.* homérico.

homesick [ˈhoumsik], *a.* nostálgico, morriñoso; ***to be homesick (for),*** tener *o* sentir nostalgia *o* morriña (de).

homesickness [ˈhoumsiknis], *s.* nostalgia, morriña, añoranza.

homespun [ˈhoumspʌn], *a.* casero; basto; llanote. — *s.* tela de fabricación casera.

homestead [ˈhoumsted], *s.* granja; casa, caserío; heredad.

homeward(s) [ˈhoumwəd(z)], *a.* de regreso, de vuelta. — *adv.* hacia casa; hacia la patria; (*mar.*) ***homeward bound,*** con rumbo al puerto de origen.

homework [ˈhoumwə:k], *s.* tarea (escolar); (*fig.*) ***to do one's homework,*** documentarse.

homey [ˈhoumi], *a.* (*fam.*) acogedor, cómodo; vulgar.

homicidal [hɔmiˈsaidəl], *a.* homicida.

homicide [ˈhɔmisaid], *s.* homicidio; homicida, *m.f.*

homiletic(al) [hɔmiˈletik(əl)], *a.* homilético.

homiletics [hɔmiˈletiks], *s.pl.* homilética.

homilist [ˈhɔmilist], *s.* homilista, *m.f.*

homily [ˈhɔmili], *s.* homilía, sermoncillo.

homing [ˈhoumiŋ], *a.* (*mil.*) buscador del blanco; ***homing pigeon,*** paloma mensajera.

hominy [ˈhɔmini], *s.* maíz molido.

homœopathic [houmioˈpæθik], *a.* homeopático.

homœopathy [houmiˈɔpəθi], *s.* homeopatía.

homogeneity, homogeneousness [hɔmodʒəˈni:iti, -ˈdʒi:niəsnis], *s.* homogeneidad.

homogeneous [hɔmoˈdʒi:niəs], *a.* homogéneo.

homogenize [hɔˈmɔdʒənaiz], *v.t.* homogenizar, homogeneizar.

homograph [ˈhɔmogrɑ:f], *s.* homógrafo.

homographic [hɔmoˈgræfik], *a.* homógrafo.

homologation [hɔmɔloˈgeiʃən], *s.* homologación.

homologous [hɔˈmɔləgəs], *a.* homólogo.

homologue [ˈhɔmolɔg], *s.* cosa homóloga.

homonym [ˈhɔmonim], *s.* homónimo.

homonymous [hɔˈmɔniməs], *a.* homónimo.

homonymy [hɔˈmɔnimi], *s.* homonimia.

homophone [ˈhɔmofoun], *s.* palabra *o* letra homófona.

homophonous [hɔˈmɔfənəs], *a.* homófono.

homophony [hɔˈmɔfəni], *s.* homofonía.

homosexual [houmoˈseksjuəl], *a.*, *s.* homosexual.

homosexuality [houmoseksjuˈæliti], *s.* homosexualidad.

homunculus [hɔˈmʌŋkjuləs], *s.* homúnculo.

Honduran [hɔnˈdjuərən], *a.*, *s.* hondureño, *m.*, hondureña, *f.*

Honduras [hɔnˈdjuərəs]. Honduras, *f. sing.*

hone [houn], *s.* piedra de afilar. — *v.t.* afilar.

honest [ˈɔnist], *a.* honrado, probo; franco, sincero; (*mujer*) honesta.

honestly [ˈɔnistli], *adv.* honradamente; francamente, con franqueza.

honesty [ˈɔnisti], *s.* honradez.

honey [ˈhʌni], *s.* miel, *f.*; (*fam.*) cariño, vida mía; ***honey-ant,*** hormiga melífera; ***honey-bee,*** abeja de miel; ***honey-flower,*** ceriflor, *f.*; ***honey-mouthed, -tongued,*** melifluo, adulador; ***honey-sweet,*** dulce como la miel. — *v.t.* enmelar, cubrir con miel. — *v.i.* hablar con melosidad.

honeycomb [ˈhʌnikoum], *s.* panal.

honeycombed [ˈhʌnikoumd], *a.* apanalado; lleno (***with,*** de).

honeyed [ˈhʌnid], *a.* meloso, melifluo; enmelado, cubierto de miel.

honeyless [ˈhʌnilis], *a.* sin miel.

honeymoon [ˈhʌnimu:n], *s.* luna de miel, viaje de novios. — *v.i.* pasar la luna de miel.

honeymooner [ˈhʌnimu:nə], *s.* recién casado en viaje de novios.

honeysuckle [ˈhʌnisʌkl], *s.* madreselva.

Hong Kong [ˈhɔŋ ˈkɔŋ]. Hong Kong.

honk [hɔŋk], *s.* graznido (*de ganso*); bocinazo. — *v.t.* tocar (la bocina). — *v.i.* graznar; dar bocinazos.

honky-tonk [ˈhɔŋki-ˈtɔŋk], *s.* (*Am., fam.*) bar.

honorarium [ɔnəˈrɛəriəm], *s.* honorarios, *m.pl.*, emolumentos, *m.pl.*

honorary [ˈɔnərəri], *a.* honorario; ***honorary degree,*** título honorario.

honour [ˈɔnə], *s.* honor, honra; ***point of honour,*** pundonor, punto de honra; ***word of honour,*** palabra de honor; ***Your Honour,*** usía, su señoría; (***up***)***on my honour,*** a fe mía; ***to deem it an honour,*** honrarse, tener a honra; (*pl.*) distinción, sobresaliente; ***last honours,*** honras fúnebres; ***to do the honours of the house,*** hacer los honores de la casa. — *v.t.* honrar; (*com.*) hacer honor a; ***honour a cheque,*** aceptar y pagar un cheque.

honourable [ˈɔnərəbl], *a.* honorable, honrado, honroso.

honourableness [ˈɔnərəblnis], *s.* honorabilidad, honradez.

honourer [ˈɔnərə], *s.* honrador.

hooch [hu:tʃ], *s.* (*Am., fam.*) aguardiente.

hood [hud], *s.* capucha; capilla; capirote; caperuza; capota (*de coche*); muceta; gorrito (*de niño*); campana (*de hogar*); sombrerete (*de chimenea*); tapa (*de bomba*); (*mar.*) tambucho; caperuza (*de palo*). — *v.t.* encapuchar; tapar, ocultar.

hoodlum [ˈhu:dləm], *s.* (*Am., fam.*) matón, gorila.

hoodoo [ˈhu:du:], *s.* mal de ojo, aojo. — *v.t.* (*Am., fam.*) aojar.

hoodwink [ˈhudwiŋk], *v.t.* vendar los ojos a; embaucar.

hoof [hu:f], *s.* (*pl.* **hooves** [hu:vz]) casco, pezuña; ***hoof-bound,*** estrecho *o* corto de cascos; ***on the hoof,*** en pie, vivo. — *v.t.* hollar; (*fam.*) ***hoof it,*** ir a pie, hacer footing, ir pedibus andandibus.

hoofed [hu:ft], *a.* que tiene cascos, ungulado.

hook [huk], *s.* gancho; garfio: garra; anzuelo; corchete; colgadero; aliciente, atractivo; (*mús.*) rabo; ***by hook or by crook,*** a tuertas o a derechas; por las buenas o por las malas, como sea; ***hook-bill,*** pico encorvado; ***hook, line and sinker,*** totalmente; ***hook-nose,*** nariz aguileña; (*cost.*) ***hooks and eyes,*** corchetes y corchetas; ***hook-up,*** combinación; conexión; acoplamiento; ***radio hook-up,*** emisoras en combinación; (*fam.*) ***on one's own hook,*** por cuenta propia. — *v.t.* enganchar; coger (con gancho); garfear; encornar, dar una cornada a; pescar; encorvar; atraer, envolver; (*fam.*) robar; (*fam.*) ***hook it,*** largarse; (*fam.*) ***to get hooked on,*** hacerse adicto de; ***hook up,*** enganchar; abrochar. — *v.i.* — ***up*** o ***on,*** engancharse, acoplarse.

hookah [ˈhukə], *s.* narguile.

hooked [hukt], *a.* ganchudo; encorvado.

hooky [ˈhuki], *s.* (*fam.*) ***to play hooky,*** hacer novillos.

hooligan [ˈhu:ligən], *s.* gamberro.

hooliganism [ˈhu:ligənizəm], *s.* gamberrismo.

hoop [hu:p], *s.* aro; zuncho; ***hoop-skirt,*** miriñaque. — *v.t.* enarcar; enzunchar.

hooper [ˈhu:pə], *s.* tonelero.

hoopoe, hoopoo [ˈhu:pou, -pu:], *s.* abubilla.

hoot [hu:t], *s.* (*lechuza*) ululato; (*aut.*) bocinazo; toque (de sirena); risotada; grito; (*fam.*) ***he doesn't give two hoots,*** no se le da un ardite. — *v.t.* manifestar a gritos. — *v.i.* ulular; tocar la bocina; tocar la sirena; gritar; ***hoot at, off, out,*** abuchear, silbar.

hooter [ˈhu:tə], *s.* silbato, sirena (*de vapor*); (*aut.*) bocina.

hooting [ˈhu:tiŋ], *s.* ululatos, *m.pl.*; bocinazos, *m.pl. etc.* [HOOT].

hop (1) [hɔp], *s.* saltito, brinquito; vuelo; etapa; (*fam.*) baile, bailoteo. — *v.t.* atravesar (de un salto); (*fam.*) ***hop it!*** ¡lárgate! — *v.i.* saltar, brincar; saltar a la pata coja; ***hop off,*** bajarse (de); (*fam.*) largarse; ***hop on,*** subirse (a).

hop (2) [hɔp], *s.* (*bot.*) lúpulo; ***hop-picker,*** cosechador de lúpulos.

hope [houp], *s.* esperanza. — *v.t.* esperar. — *v.i.* esperar; confiar; ***hope against hope,*** esperar desesperando; ***hope for,*** esperar; ***hope for the best,*** tener fe; ***hope to,*** esperar.

hopeful [ˈhoupful], *a.* esperanzado; esperanzador; prometedor; ***to be hopeful that,*** tener esperanzas de que.

hopefully [ˈhoupfuli], *adv.* con esperanza(s).

hopeless [ˈhouplis], *a.* desesperado; desesperanzado; desahuciado; inútil.

hopelessly [ˈhouplisli], *adv.* sin esperanza(s), desesperadamente.

hopingly [ˈhoupiŋli], *adv.* con esperanza(s).

hoplite [ˈhɔplait], *s.* hoplita, *m.*

hopper [ˈhɔpə], *s.* el que salta a la pata coja; saltamontes, *m. inv.*; tolva.

hopple [hɔpl], [HOBBLE].

hopscotch [ˈhɔpskɔtʃ], *s.* la pata coja; el jugar a la pata coja; (*Am.*) rayuela.

horal, horary [ˈhɔ:rəl, ˈhɔrəri], *a.* horario; por horas.

Horatian [hɔˈreiʃən], *a.* horaciano.

horde [hɔ:d], *s.* horda; aduar.

horehound [ˈhɔ:haund], *s.* (*bot.*) marrubio.

horizon [həˈraizən], *s.* horizonte.

horizontal [hɔriˈzɔntl], *a.* horizontal.

horizontality [hɔrizɔnˈtæliti], *s.* horizontalidad.

hormone [ˈhɔ:moun], *s.* hormona.

horn [hɔ:n], *s.* cuerno, asta; trompa; bocina, claxon; (*pl.*) cuerna, cornamenta; ***horn-blower,*** trompetero; bocinero; ***horn of plenty,*** cornucopia, cuerno de la abundancia; ***on the horns of a dilemma,*** entre la espada y la pared. — *v.t.* poner cuernos a; acornear. — *v.i.* — ***in,*** entrometerse.

hornbeam [ˈhɔ:nbi:m], *s.* carpe, ojaranzo, carpinus.

hornbill [ˈhɔ:nbil], *s.* cálao.

hornblende [ˈhɔ:nblend], *s.* hornblenda.

hornbook [ˈhɔ:nbuk], *s.* cartilla.

horned [ˈhɔ:nd], *a.* cornudo; (*poét.*) cornígero; enastado; encornado; de cuerno.

hornet [ˈhɔ:nit], *s.* avispón; ***hornet-fly,*** avispón; ***to stir up a hornet's nest,*** armar un cisco, provocar fuerte oposición.

hornfish [ˈhɔ:nfiʃ], *s.* (*ict.*) aguja.

hornify [ˈhɔ:nifai], *v.t.* hacer semejante al cuerno.

horning [ˈhɔ:niŋ], *s.* media luna.

hornish [ˈhɔ:niʃ], *a.* duro; córneo.

hornless [ˈhɔ:nlis], *a.* que no tiene cuernos.

hornpipe [ˈhɔ:npaip], *s.* baile de marineros; chirimía.

hornsilver [ˈhɔ:nsilvə], *s,* (*min.*) plata córnea; cloruro de plata.

hornwork [ˈhɔ:nwə:k], *s.* (*fort.*) hornabeque.

horny [ˈhɔ:ni], *a.* hecho de cuerno; parecido al cuerno, córneo; calloso.

horography [hɔˈrɔgrəfi], *s.* gnomónica.

horologe [ˈhɔrəloudʒ], *s.* reloj.
horologic(al) [hɔrəˈlɔdʒik(əl)], *a.* que se refiere a la gnomónica.
horometry [hɔˈrɔmitri], *s.* horometría.
horoscope [ˈhɔrəskoup], *s.* horóscopo.
horrent [ˈhɔrənt], *a.* (*poét.*) erizado; horrendo.
horrible [ˈhɔribl], *a.* horrible, horroroso.
horribleness [ˈhɔriblnis], *s.* horribilidad.
horrid [ˈhɔrid], *a.* horrible, hórrido; desagradable, antipático.
horrific [hɔˈrifik], *a.* horrífico.
horrify [ˈhɔrifai], *v.t.* horrorizar.
horrifying [ˈhɔrifaiiŋ], *a.* horripilante, que da espanto.
horror [ˈhɔrə], *s.* horror; espanto; (*pl.*, *fam.*) melancolía; (espasmo de) horror; ***to have a horror of,*** tener horror a.
horse [hɔ:s], *s.* caballo; (*mil.*) caballería; caballete; potro. — *a.* caballar; hípico; ***clothes horse,*** tendal; ***dark horse,*** individuo desconocido, incógnita; (*fig.*) ***horse of a different colour,*** harina de otro costal; ***horse-bean,*** haba panosa *o* caballuna; ***horse-box,*** vagón para caballos; ***horse-breaker,*** domador de caballos; ***horse-chestnut,*** castaño de Indias; castaña de Indias; ***horse-collar,*** collera; ***horse-comb,*** almohaza; ***horse-dealer,*** chalán; ***horse-doctor,*** veterinario, albéitar; ***horse-dung,*** estiércol de caballos; ***horse-flesh,*** carne de caballo; (conjunto de) caballos; ***horse-fly,*** tábano; ***horse-guards,*** guardias de a caballo, *f.pl.*; ***horse-laugh,*** risotada; ***horse-leech,*** sanguijuela borriquera; ***horse-play,*** payasadas, *f.pl.*; ***horse-power,*** caballo de fuerza; ***horse-race,*** carrera de caballos; ***horse-radish,*** rábano picante; (*fam.*) ***horse-sense,*** sentido común; ***horse-show,*** concurso hípico; (*fig.*) ***horse trading,*** tejemaneje; (*fig.*) ***iron horse,*** locomotora; ***runaway horse,*** caballo desbocado; (*fig.*) ***white horses,*** borreguitos, *m.pl.*; (*fig.*) ***to back the wrong horse,*** apoyar al que pierde; (*fig.*) ***to change horses in mid-stream,*** cambiar de idea a mitad de camino; ***to eat like a horse,*** comer como una lima; ***to get on one's high horse,*** darse aires de suficiencia, ponerse en plan engreído *o* de superioridad; ***hold your horses!*** ¡pare (el carro)! ¡despacito! — *v.t.* proveer de caballo(s). — *v.i.* montar; (*fam.*) ***horse around*** *o* ***about,*** hacer payasadas.
horseback [ˈhɔ:sbæk], *s.* lomo de caballo; ***to ride on horseback,*** montar a caballo.
horsehair [ˈhɔ:shɛə], *s.* crin (de caballo).
horseman [ˈhɔ:smən], *s.* jinete; caballista, *m.*; (*mil.*) soldado de caballería.
horsemanship [ˈhɔ:smənʃip], *s.* equitación, manejo del caballo.
horsemint [ˈhɔ:smint], *s.* mastranzo.
horseshoe [ˈhɔ:sʃu:], *s.* herradura.
horsetail [ˈhɔ:steil], *s.* (*bot.*) cola de caballo.
horsewhip [ˈhɔ:swip], *s.* látigo. — *v.t.* azotar con látigo.
horsewoman [ˈhɔ:swumən], *s.* amazona.
horsy [ˈhɔ:si], *a.* caballar; hípico; caballuno; aficionado a los caballos; turfista, carrerista.
horticultural [hɔ:tiˈkʌltʃərəl], *a.* hortícola.
horticulture [ˈhɔ:tikʌltʃə], *s.* horticultura.
horticulturist [hɔ:tiˈkʌltʃərist], *s.* horticultor.
hosanna [houˈzænə], *s.* hosana. — *interj.* ¡hosana!
hose [houz], *s.* calzas, *f.pl.*, medias, *f.pl.*; calcetines, *m.pl.*; manga, manguera; ***hose-pipe,*** manguera, manga.
hosier [ˈhouziə], *s.* mediero, calcetero.
hosiery [ˈhouziəri], *s.* calcetería; calcetines, *m.pl.*, medias, *f.pl.*
hospice [ˈhɔspis], *s.* hospicio.
hospitable [ˈhɔspitəbl], *a.* hospitalario.
hospitableness [ˈhɔspitəblnis], *s.* hospitalidad.
hospital [ˈhɔspitl], *s.* hospital; hospicio; ***hospital ship,*** buque hospital; ***hospital wagon,*** carro de ambulancia; ***maternity hospital,*** hospital de maternidad.
hospitality [hɔspiˈtæliti], *s.* hospitalidad.
hospitalize [ˈhɔspitəlaiz], *v.t.* hospitalizar.
hospitaller [hɔsˈpitələ], *s.* hospitalario; hospitalero.
host (1) [houst], *s.* el que invita, anfitrión; huésped; hospedero, posadero; ***to reckon without one's host,*** hacer la cuenta sin la huéspeda.
host (2) [houst], *s.* hueste, sinnúmero.
host (3) [houst], *s.* (*relig.*) hostia.
hostage [ˈhɔstidʒ], *s.* rehén.
hostel [ˈhɔstəl], *s.* albergue, hostería; residencia (de estudiantes); ***youth hostel,*** albergue de la juventud.
hostelry [ˈhɔstəlri], *s.* posada, hostería, mesón, hospedería, hostal, parador.
hostess [ˈhoustes], *s.* anfitriona; posadera, mesonera; huéspeda; (*aer.*) azafata, aeromoza.
hostile [ˈhɔstail], *a.* hostil.
hostility [hɔsˈtiliti], *s.* hostilidad; ***to start hostilities,*** romper las hostilidades.
hostler [ˈɔslə], *s.* establero, palafrenero, mozo de paja y cebada.
hot [hɔt], *a.* caliente; cálido; caluroso; en caliente; ardiente; picante, fuerte; acalorado; vehemente; enérgico; apasionado; en celo; difícil, apurado (*situación*); (*fam.*) robado; ***hot air,*** palabrería; ***hot blast,*** bocanada de aire caliente; ***hot-blooded,*** fogoso; ***to go like hot cakes,*** venderse como pan bendito; ***hot-dog,*** perrito caliente; ***hot-foot,*** disparado, desalentado; ***hot-headed,*** exaltado; ***hot money,*** inversiones especulativas, *f.pl.*; ***hot mustard,*** mostaza muy picante; ***to be in hot water,*** estar metido en un lío; estar en un apuro; ***hot-water bottle,*** bolsa de agua caliente; ***to be burning hot,*** quemar; hacer mucho calor; ***to be hot on the heels of,*** pisarle los talones a; perseguir de cerca; (*fig.*) ***to get hot under the collar,*** sofocarse; ***to grow hot,*** calentarse; ***to make hot,*** calentar; ***piping hot,*** calentito.
hotbed [ˈhɔtbed], *s.* era, almajara; (*fig.*) foco, plantel, semillero.
hotchpot(ch) [ˈhɔtʃpɔt(ʃ)], *s.* olla podrida; batiburrillo, mezcolanza.
hotel [houˈtel], *s.* hotel.
hotelier [houˈteliə], *s.* hotelero.
hothouse [ˈhɔthaus], *s.* invernadero, invernáculo; ***hothouse atmosphere,*** ambiente ahogado *o* sofocante.
hotspur [ˈhɔtspə:], *s.* individuo temerario y fogoso.
Hottentot [ˈhɔtəntɔt], *s.* hotentote; cafre, salvaje.
hound [haund], *s.* perro; sabueso; podenco; (*fig.*) canalla; ***to ride to hounds,*** cazar con jauría. — *v.t.* perseguir, acosar.
hound's tongue [ˈhaundz ˈtʌŋ], *s.* (*bot.*) cinoglosa, viniebla.
hour [auə], *s.* hora; momento; ***after hours,*** fuera de horas; ***by the hour,*** por horas; ***hour-glass,*** reloj de arena; ***hour-hand,*** horario; ***hour-plate,*** esfera de reloj; ***to keep late hours,*** trasnochar; ***on the hour,*** a la hora en punto; ***small hours,*** altas horas de la noche; ***to strike the hour,*** dar la hora.
hourly [ˈauəli], *a.* de cada hora. — *adv.* a cada hora; frecuentemente.
house [haus], *a.* de (la) casa, domiciliario, doméstico. — *s.* casa; (*teat.*) sala, público, entrada; cámara; colegio; ***House of Commons,*** Cámara de los comunes; ***House of Lords,*** Cámara de los lores; (*Am.*) ***House of Representatives,*** Cámara de los representantes; ***house arrest,*** arresto domiciliario; ***house-boat,*** casa flotante; ***house-breaker,*** ladrón de casas; ***house-breaking,*** robo de casa, allanamiento de morada; ***house-coat,*** bata; ***house-dog,*** perro de casa *o* de guardia; ***house-fly,*** mosca doméstica; ***house-painter,*** pintor de brocha gorda; ***house-physician,*** médico residente; ***house-rent,*** alquiler de casa;

house-room, alojamiento; sitio en casa, cabida; ***house-trained,*** limpio, bien amaestrado; (*fam.*) ***to bring down the house,*** hacer venirse abajo el teatro (de aplausos); ***to carry out a house-to-house search,*** registrar *o* ir registrando de casa en casa; ***to keep house,*** llevar la casa; tener casa propia; ***to set one's house in order,*** poner orden en sus asuntos; ***it's on the house,*** invita la casa. — [hauz], *v.t.* alojar, hospedar, albergar, domiciliar; encajar; meter (en); estibar.

household [ˈhaushould], *a.* casero, doméstico; ***household furniture,*** menaje de una casa; ***household troops,*** guardia real; ***household word*** o ***name,*** nombre conocido de todo el mundo. — *s.* casa; familia.

householder [ˈhaushouldə], *s.* amo de casa; cabeza de familia; inquilino.

housekeeper [ˈhauski:pə], *s.* ama de llaves.

housekeeping [ˈhauski:piŋ], *a.* doméstico. — *s.* gobierno de la casa.

houseleek [ˈhausli:k], *s.* siempreviva, hierba puntera.

houseless [ˈhauslis], *a.* sin casa.

housemaid [ˈhausmeid], *s.* criada.

housetop [ˈhaustɔp], *s.* tejado; ***to shout from the housetops,*** pregonar a los cuatro vientos.

housewarming [ˈhauswɔ:miŋ], *s.* fiesta de estreno de una casa.

housewife [ˈhauswaif], *s.* ama de casa; madre de familia.

housewifely [ˈhauswaifli], *a.* de ama de casa; hacendoso.

housewifery [ˈhauswifri], *s.* gobierno de la casa; faenas domésticas, *f.pl.*

housing [ˈhauziŋ], *s.* alojamiento; vivienda, casas, *f.pl.*; almacenaje; (*mec.*) chumacera, caja, encaje; (*aut.*) cárter; (*arq.*) nicho; ***housing estate,*** urbanización; ***housing shortage,*** crisis de vivienda.

hovel [ˈhɔvəl], *s.* choza; casucha; cuchitril, tugurio.

hover [ˈhɔvə], *v.t.* cubrir con las alas. — *v.i.* cernerse; revolotear, aletear; ***hover around,*** rondar.

hovering [ˈhɔvəriŋ], *s.* revoloteo; (el) cernerse.

how [hau], *adv., conj.* cómo, de qué modo; cuánto; hasta qué punto; por qué; ***how do you do?*** mucho gusto; ***how far?*** ¿a qué distancia? ¿cuánto dista?; ***how few!*** ¡qué pocos!; ***how is it?*** ¿cómo está?; ***how little!*** ¡qué poco!; ***how long?*** ¿cuánto tiempo?; ***how many?*** ¿cuántos? ¿cuántas?; ***how much?*** ¿cuánto?; ***how so?*** ¿por qué? ¿cómo?; ***to know how to,*** saber (cómo); ***I know how difficult it is,*** sé lo difícil que es.

howbeit [hauˈbi:it], *adv.* sea como fuere.

however [hauˈevə], *adv.* como quiera que; por más que; por (muy) . . . que; ***however clever he is,*** por muy listo que sea; ***however much,*** por mucho que. — *conj.* sin embargo, no obstante, con todo.

howitzer [ˈhauitzə], *s.* (*artill.*) obús.

howl [haul], *s.* aullido, alarido; chillido; grito. — *v.t.* — ***down,*** hacer callar a gritos. — *v.i.* aullar, dar alaridos; chillar.

howler [ˈhaulə], *s.* (*fam.*) pifia; metedura de pata.

howlet [ˈhaulit], *s.* lechuza.

howling [ˈhauliŋ], *a.* aullante; ***a howling success,*** un éxito arrollador. — *s.* aullido(s).

howsoever [hausouˈevə], *adv.* como quiera que.

hoy [hɔi], *s.* (*mar.*) caraba.

hoyden [ˈhɔidən], *s.* tunantuela.

hub [hʌb], *s.* cubo; eje, centro; ***hub-cap,*** tapacubo(s).

hubbub [ˈhʌbʌb], *s.* barahunda, batahola, alboroto.

huckaback [ˈhʌkəbæk], *s.* (*tej.*) alemanisco.

huckleberry [ˈhʌklbəri], *s.* arándano.

hucklebone [ˈhʌklboun], *s.* taba.

huckster [ˈhʌkstə], *s.* buhonero, mercachifle. — *v.i.* revender, regatear.

hucksterage [ˈhʌkstəridʒ], *s.* regatonería; tráfico en géneros de poco valor.

hucksteress [ˈhʌkstris], *s.* regatona, revendedora.

huddle [hʌdl], *s.* pelotón, tropel; ***to go into a huddle,*** conferenciar en secreto. — *v.t.* apiñar, apelotonar. — *v.i.* apelotonarse; ***huddle up,*** acurrucarse.

hue [hju:], *s.* color; tinte; matiz; tono; ***hue and cry,*** alarma, clamor, griterío.

huff [hʌf], *s.* enojo, pique, ofendimiento; ***in a huff,*** enojado, ofendido. — *v.t.* (*damas*) soplar, comer(se). — *v.i.* — ***and puff,*** jadear.

huffish [ˈhʌfiʃ], *a.* enojadizo, susceptible.

huffishness [ˈhʌfiʃnis], *s.* mal humor, susceptibilidad.

huffy [ˈhʌfi], [HUFFISH].

hug [hʌg], *s.* abrazo apretado. — *v.t.* abrazar, apretar con los brazos, apretujar; ceñirse a; (*fig.*) acariciar; (*mar.*) navegar muy cerca de (*la costa*); ***to hug o.s. with glee,*** ponerse eufórico; congratularse.

huge [hju:dʒ], *a.* inmenso, enorme, ingente.

hugeness [ˈhju:dʒnis], *s.* inmensidad.

hugger-mugger [ˈhʌgə-mʌgə], *a.* confuso. — *adv.* a lo loco. — *s.* desorden, confusión.

Huguenot [ˈhju:gənou], *a., s.* hugonote.

hulk [hʌlk], *s.* (*mar.*) casco (arrumbado); carraca; armatoste.

hulking [ˈhʌlkiŋ], *a.* grande, pesado y desgarbado; ***hulking great fellow,*** hombretón; ***hulking great brute,*** animalote.

hull [hʌl], *s.* (*mar.*) casco; cáscara, vaina. — *v.t.* mondar, descascarar, desvainar; agujerear el casco de.

hullabaloo [hʌləbəˈlu:], *s.* alboroto, batahola, gritería, tumulto.

hullo! [hʌˈlou], [HELLO].

hum [hʌm], *s.* tarareo; zumbido(s); murmullo(s). — *v.t.* canturrear, tararear. — *v.i.* zumbar; canturrear; ***hum and haw,*** titubear, no resolverse; (*fam.*) ***to make things hum,*** activar las cosas.

human [ˈhju:mən], *a.* humano. — *s.* (ser) humano.

humane [hju:ˈmein], *a.* humano; humanitario; compasivo.

humanism [ˈhju:mənizəm], *s.* humanismo.

humanist [ˈhju:mənist], *s.* humanista, *m.f.*

humanitarian [hju:mæniˈtɛəriən], *a.* humanitario. — *s.* humanitario.

humanitarianism [hju:mæniˈtɛəriənizəm], *s.* humanitarismo.

humanity [hju:ˈmæniti], *s.* humanidad; (*pl.* **humanities** [-z]) humanidades.

humanize [ˈhju:mənaiz], *v.t.* humanizar.

humankind [ˈhju:mənˈkaind], *s.* humanidad, género humano.

humation [hju:ˈmeiʃən], *s.* entierro.

humble [hʌmbl], *a.* humilde; ***your humble servant,*** su (seguro) servidor; ***to eat humble-pie,*** retractarse y pedir perdón, achantarse. — *v.t.* humillar.

humble-bee [ˈhʌmbl-bi:], *s.* (*ent.*) abejorro.

humbleness [ˈhʌmblnis], *s.* humildad.

humbles [hʌmblz], *s.pl.* despojos (*m.pl.*) *o* casquería de venado.

humbling [ˈhʌmbliŋ], *s.* humillación.

humbug [ˈhʌmbʌg], *s.* hipocresía(s); farsa, engañifa; hipócrita, *m.f.*, farsante, *m.f.*; caramelo de menta. — *v.t.* embaucar.

humdrum [ˈhʌmdrʌm], *a.* ramplón, vulgarote, rutinario.

humeral [ˈhju:mərəl], *a.* humeral.

humerus [ˈhju:mərəs], *s.* (*anat.*) húmero.

humic [ˈhju:mik], *a.* perteneciente al suelo *o* tierra; ***humic acid,*** ácido húmico.

humid [ˈhju:mid], *a.* húmedo.

humidification [hju:midifiˈkeiʃən], *s.* humectación.

humidifier [hju:ˈmidifaiə], *s.* humectador.
humidify [hju:ˈmidifai], *v.t.* humedecer.
humidity [hju:ˈmiditi], *s.* humedad.
humiliate [hju:ˈmilieit], *v.t.* humillar.
humiliation [hju:miliˈeiʃən], *s.* humillación.
humility [hju:ˈmiliti], *s.* humildad.
humming [ˈhʌmiŋ], *a.* zumbador. — *s.* zumbido(s); ***humming-bird,*** colibrí, picaflor, pájaro mosca.
hummock [ˈhʌmək], *s.* montecillo, morón, mogote.
humor [HUMOUR].
humoral [ˈhju:mərəl], *a.* (*med.*) humoral.
humoralism [ˈhju:mərəlizəm], *s.* (*med.*) humorismo.
humorism [ˈhju:mərizəm], *s.* humorismo.
humorist [ˈhju:mərist], *s.* humorista, *m.f.*
humorous [ˈhju:mərəs], *a.* humorístico, chistoso, divertido.
humorousness [ˈhju:mərəsnis], *s.* jocosidad; gracejo; (lo) divertido.
humour [ˈhju:mə], *s.* humor; humorismo; humorada; capricho; ***broad humour,*** humor burdo *u* ordinario; ***to be in humour*** o ***in good humour,*** estar de buen humor *o* talante; ***to be out of humour*** o ***in ill humour,*** estar de mal humor; ***to be in the humour for,*** estar (de humor) para. — *v.t.* seguir el humor a, bailarle el agua a, darle gusto a.
humoursome [ˈhju:məsəm], *a.* caprichoso, antojadizo.
hump [hʌmp], *s.* giba, joroba; montículo; (*fam.*) ***it gives you the hump,*** te joroba; ***to have the hump,*** estar jorobado *o* harto. — *v.t.* (*fam.*) llevar a hombro.
humpback [ˈhʌmpbæk], *s.* giba, corcova, joroba; jorobado.
humpbacked [ˈhʌmpbækt], *a.* jorobado, giboso, corcovado; ***humpbacked bridge,*** puente de cambio de rasante.
humped [hʌmpt], *a.* jorobado, corcovado.
humpty-dumpty [ˈhʌmptiˈdʌmpti], *s.* persona rechoncha.
humpy [ˈhʌmpi], *a.* giboso.
humus [ˈhju:məs], *s.* humus, mantillo.
Hun [hʌn], *s.* huno.
hunch [hʌntʃ], *s.* (*fam.*) corazonada, sospecha; giba, corcova. — *v.t.* encorvar (*los hombros*).
hunchback [ˈhʌntʃbæk], *s.* joroba, corcova.
hunchbacked [ˈhʌntʃbækt], *a.* jorobado, giboso, corcovado.
hundred [ˈhʌndrəd], *a.* cien, ciento; ***a hundred times,*** cien veces. — *s.* cien, ciento; centenar; centena; ***in hundreds, by the hundred,*** a centenares.
hundredfold [ˈhʌndrədfould], *a.* céntuplo. — *adv.* cien veces; ***to increase a hundredfold,*** centuplicar.
hundredth [ˈhʌndrədθ], *a.* centésimo; ciento. — *s.* centésimo.
hundredweight [ˈhʌndrədweit], *s.* quintal.
Hungarian [hʌŋˈgɛəriən], *a., s.* húngaro.
Hungary [ˈhʌŋgəri]. Hungría.
hunger [ˈhʌŋgə], *s.* hambre, *f.*; ***hunger-strike,*** huelga de hambre; ***hunger is the best sauce,*** a buena hambre no hay pan duro; ***pang of hunger,*** raimiento de hambre. — *v.i.* hambrear; ***hunger after*** o ***for,*** ansiar.
hungry [ˈhʌŋgri], *a.* hambriento; pobre, estéril; ***to be hungry, feel hungry,*** tener hambre; ***to go hungry,*** pasar hambre.
hunk [hʌŋk], *s.* (*fam.*) (buen) pedazo; cacho, trozote.
hunt [hʌnt], *s.* caza; cacería; montería; partida de caza; jauría. — *v.t.* cazar; buscar; perseguir; recorrer, hacer la batida de; emplear en la caza; ***hunt down,*** buscar hasta cazar *o* hasta dar con; ***hunt out*** *o* ***up,*** buscar con ahinco *o* con afán. — *v.i.* cazar; buscar; ***hunt after*** o ***for,*** perseguir, buscar; ***to go hunting,*** ir de caza.
hunter [ˈhʌntə], *s.* cazador; montero; caballo de caza; podenco; saboneta.
hunting [ˈhʌntiŋ], *a.* de caza, cazador, cinegético; ***hunting-box,*** pabellón de caza; ***hunting-ground,*** cazadero; ***happy hunting ground,*** paraíso; ***hunting-horn,*** cuerno de caza; ***hunting-lodge,*** pabellón de caza. — *s.* caza; montería.
huntress [ˈhʌntris], *s.* cazadora.
huntsman [ˈhʌntsmən], *s.* montero; cazador.
hurdle [hə:dl], *s.* valla; (*fig.*) obstáculo. — *v.t.* saltar por encima de, salvar.
hurdy-gurdy [ˈhə:di-gə:di], *s.* (*mús.*) organillo.
hurl [hə:l], *s.* lanzamiento. — *v.t.* lanzar, arrojar.
hurling [ˈhə:liŋ], *s.* lanzamiento; hockey irlandés.
hurlyburly [ˈhə:libə:li], *s.* batahola, barullo, tumulto.
hurrah, hurray [hʌˈrɑ:, hʌˈrei], *v.i.* aclamar, aplaudir, vitorear. — *interj.* ¡viva! ¡hurra!
hurricane [ˈhʌrikən], *s.* huracán; ***hurricane-lamp,*** lámpara a prueba de viento; ***hurricane wind,*** viento huracanado.
hurried [ˈhʌrid], *a.* precipitado, apresurado.
hurry [ˈhʌri], *s.* prisa; ***hurry-scurry,*** confusamente, en tropel; ***in a hurry,*** de prisa; ***to be in a hurry,*** tener prisa; ***is there any hurry?*** ¿corre prisa?; ***what's the hurry?*** ¿qué prisa hay? — *v.t.* acelerar, dar prisa a, apresurar; ***hurry in,*** hacer entrar de prisa; ***hurry on*** o ***up,*** dar prisa a. — *v.i.* darse prisa, apresurarse; ***hurry after,*** correr detrás de, en pos de; ***hurry back,*** volver de prisa; ***hurry in,*** entrar de prisa; ***hurry off,*** salir de prisa; ***hurry over,*** pasar rápidamente; ***hurry over a thing,*** hacer una cosa con prisa; ***hurry up,*** darse prisa, apresurarse.
hurst [hə:st], *s.* bosquecillo, soto.
hurt [hə:t], *s.* herida, lesión; daño, perjuicio. — *irr. v.t.* lastimar, dañar; herir; perjudicar; ***to get hurt,*** herirse, lastimarse; sufrir; ***hurt s.o.'s feelings,*** herir los sentimientos de alguien, ofenderle. — *v.i.* doler; hacer daño; ***it hurts,*** duele; hace daño. — **hurt o.s.,** *v.r.* hacerse daño.
hurtful [ˈhə:tful], *a.* perjudicial.
hurtle [hə:tl], *v.i.* lanzarse, arrojarse con violencia; ***hurtle against,*** estrellarse contra.
husband [ˈhʌzbənd], *s.* marido, esposo. — *v.t.* administrar con prudencia, economizar.
husbandman [ˈhʌzbəndmən], *s.* agricultor, labrador, granjero.
husbandry [ˈhʌzbəndri], *s.* labranza, agricultura; economía; granjería; (buen) gobierno.
hush [hʌʃ], *a.* de silencio; secreto; ***very hush-hush,*** muy secreto, de mucho secreto. — *s.* silencio, quietud; ***hush-money,*** precio del silencio (de una persona). — *v.t.* apaciguar, callar, acallar; ***hush up,*** ocultar, mantener secreto, echar tierra a. — *v.i.* callar, estar(se) callado. — *interj.* ¡chitón! ¡silencio!
husk [hʌsk], *s.* cáscara; vaina; cascabillo. — *v.t.* descascarar, pelar, desvainar, mondar.
huskiness [ˈhʌskinis], *s.* ronquera; ronquedad, (lo) ronco.
husking [ˈhʌskiŋ], *s.* (el) descascarar.
husky (1) [ˈhʌski], *a.* (*voz*) cascada; ronco; (*fam.*) fornido, fortachón.
husky (2) [ˈhʌski], *s.* perro esquimal.
hussar [huˈzɑ:], *s.* (*mil.*) húsar.
hussy [ˈhʌsi], *s.* buena pieza, descarada, descocada.
husting [ˈhʌstiŋ], *s.* (*ant.*) asamblea; (*pl.*) reunión política, mitin.
hustle [hʌsl], *s.* prisa, actividad bulliciosa, bulla; empuje; ***hustle and bustle,*** ajetreo, bullicio. — *v.t.* dar prisa a, apresurar, meter prisa a; ***hustle out,*** echar a empujones. — *v.i.* darse prisa, moverse, menearse.
hustler [ˈhʌslə], *s.* (*fam.*) hombre de empuje, trafagón; matón.

hut [hʌt], *s.* cabaña, choza; cobertizo; (*de indígenas*) bohío.
hutch [hʌtʃ], *s.* conejera; jaula; arca; cabaña.
huzza [huˈzɑː], (*ant.*) *v.t.*, *v.i.* vitorear. — *interj.* ¡viva! ¡vítor!
hyacinth [ˈhaiəsinθ], *s.* (*bot.*) jacinto.
hyacinthine [haiəˈsinθain], *a.* jacintino.
hyæna [HYENA].
hyaline [ˈhaiəlin], *a.* hialino.
hybrid [ˈhaibrid], *a.*, *s.* híbrido.
hybridism [ˈhaibridizəm], *s.* hibridismo.
hybridize [ˈhaibridaiz], *v.t.*, *v.i.* hibridar.
hydatid [ˈhaideitid], *s.* hidátide, *f.*
hydra [ˈhaidrə], *s.* (*zool.*, *astron.*) hidra.
hydracid [haiˈdræsid], *s.* hidrácido.
hydragogue [ˈhaidrəgoug], *s.* hidragogo.
hydrangea [haiˈdreindʒə], *s.* (*bot.*) hortensia.
hydrant [ˈhaidrənt], *s.* boca de riego.
hydration [haiˈdreiʃən], *s.* hidratación.
hydrate [ˈhaidreit], *s.* hidrato. — *v.t.* hidratar.
hydraulic [haiˈdrɔːlik], *a.* hidráulico. — *s.* (*pl.*) hidráulica.
hydric [ˈhaidrik], *a.* hídrico.
hydriodic [haidriˈɔdik], *a.* iodo-hídrico.
hydrocarbon [haidroˈkɑːbən], *s.* hidrocarburo.
hydrocele [ˈhaidrosiːl], *s.* hidrocele, *f.*
hydrocephalus [haidroˈsefələs], *s.* hidrocéfalo.
hydrochlorate [haidroˈklɔːreit], *s.* hidroclorato, clorhidrato.
hydrochloric [haidroˈklɔrik], *a.* hidroclórico, clorhídrico.
hydrocyanic [haidrosaiˈænik], *a.* hidrociánico.
hydrodynamic [haidrodaiˈnæmik], *a.* hidrodinámico. — *s.* (*pl.*) hidrodinámica.
hydrofluoric [haidrofluˈɔrik], *a.* fluorhídrico.
hydrogen [ˈhaidrodʒən], *s.* hidrógeno; ***hydrogen bomb***, bomba de hidrógeno.
hydrogenate, hydrogenize [haiˈdrɔdʒəneit, -naiz], *v.t.* hidrogenar.
hydrogenous [haiˈdrɔdʒənəs], *a.* hidrogenado.
hydrographer [haiˈdrɔgrəfə], *s.* hidrógrafo.
hydrographic(al) [haidroˈgræfik(əl)], *a.* hidrográfico.
hydrography [haiˈdrɔgrəfi], *s.* hidrografía.
hydrokinetic [haidrokiˈnetik], *a.* hidromecánico.
hydrologic(al) [haidroˈlɔdʒik(əl)], *a.* hidrológico.
hydrology [haiˈdrɔlədʒi], *s.* hidrología.
hydrolysis [haiˈdrɔlisis], *s.* hidrólisis, *f. inv.*
hydromancy [ˈhaidromænsi], *s.* hidromancia.
hydromel [ˈhaidromel], *s.* hidromel, aguamiel, *f.*
hydrometallurgy [haidroˈmetələːdʒi], *s.* hidrometalurgia.
hydrometeor [haidroˈmiːtiɔː], *s.* hidrometeoro.
hydrometer [haiˈdrɔmitə], *s.* hidrómetro; pesalicores, *m. inv.*; fluviómetro.
hydrometric [haidroˈmetrik], *a.* hidrométrico; ***hydrometric pendulum***, péndulo hidrométrico.
hydrometry [haiˈdrɔmitri], *s.* hidrometría.
hydropathic [haidroˈpæθik], *a.* hidropático.
hydropathy [haiˈdrɔpəθi], *s.* hidropatía.
hydrophobia, hydrophoby [haidroˈfoubiə, haiˈdrɔfəbi], *s.* hidrofobia.
hydropic(al) [haiˈdrɔpik(əl)], *a.* hidrópico.
hydropsy [ˈhaidrɔpsi], *s.* hidropesía.
hydroscope [ˈhaidroskoup], *s.* hidroscopio.
hydrostat [ˈhaidrostæt], *s.* hidróstato.
hydrostatic(al) [haidroˈstætik(əl)], *a.* hidrostático.
hydrostatics [haidroˈstætiks], *s.pl.* hidrostática.
hydrosulphide [haidroˈsʌlfaid], *s.* hidrosulfuro, sulfhidrato.
hydrotherapeutic [haidroθerəˈpjuːtik], *a.*, *s.* hidroterápico; *s.pl.* [HYDROTHERAPY].
hydrotherapy [haidroˈθerəpi], *s.* hidroterapia, hidropatía.
hydrothermal [haidroˈθəːməl], *a.* hidrotermal.
hydrothorax [haidroˈθɔːræks], *s.* hidrotórax.
hydrous [ˈhaidrəs], *a.* hidratado.
hydrus [ˈhaidrəs], *s.* serpiente de agua, *f.*
hyena [haiˈiːnə], *s.* hiena.
hyetal [haiˈiːtl], *a.* pluvial.
hyetometer [haiiˈtɔmitə], *s.* pluvímetro.
hygiene [ˈhaidʒiːn], *s.* higiene, *f.*
hygienic [haiˈdʒiːnik], *a.* higiénico.
hygienist [ˈhaidʒinist], *s.* higienista, *m.f.*
hygrometer [haiˈgrɔmitə], *s.* higrómetro.
hygrometric(al) [haigroˈmetrik(əl)], *a.* higrométrico.
hygrometry [haiˈgrɔmitri], *s.* higrometría.
hygroscope [ˈhaigroskoup], *s.* higroscopio.
hygroscopic(al) [haigroˈskɔpik(əl)], *a.* higroscópico.
hyla [ˈhailə], *s.* rubeta.
hymen [ˈhaimən], *s.* himeneo; (*anat.*) himen.
hymeneal, hymenean [haimiˈniːəl, -ən], *a.* nupcial. — *s.* epitalamio.
Hymenoptera [haimənˈɔptərə], *s.pl.* (*ent.*) himenópteros, *m.pl.*
hymn [him], *s.* cántico; himno. — *v.t.* alabar con himnos. — *v.i.* cantar himnos.
hymnal [ˈhimnəl], *s.* libro de cánticos *o* de himnos, himnario.
hymnology [himˈnɔlədʒi], *s.* himnología.
hyoid [ˈhaiɔid], *a.*, *s.* hioides.
hyperæmia [haiperˈiːmiə], *s.* hiperemia.
hyperbola [haiˈpəːbələ], *s.* hipérbola.
hyperbole [haiˈpəːbəli], *s.* hipérbole, *f.*
hyperbolic(al) [haipəˈbɔlik(əl)], *a.* hiperbólico, ponderativo.
hyperbolize [haiˈpəːbəlaiz], *v.t.* expresar en lenguaje hiperbólico. — *v.i.* usar de hipérboles.
hyperborean [haipəbɔˈriːən], *a.*, *s.* hiperbóreo.
hypercritic [haipəˈkritik], *s.* hipercrítico.
hypercritical [haipəˈkritikəl], *a.* hipercrítico.
hyperdulia [haipəˈdjuːliə], *s.* hiperdulía.
hypericum [haiˈperikəm], *s.* (*bot.*) hipérico, hipericón.
hypermeter [haiˈpəːmitə], *s.* hipermetría.
hypertrophic [haipəˈtrɔfik], *a.* hipertrófico.
hypertrophied [haiˈpəːtrəfid], *a.* hipertrofiado.
hypertrophy [haiˈpəːtrəfi], *s.* hipertrofia. — *v.i.* hipertrofiarse.
hyphen [ˈhaifən], *s.* guión.
hyphenate [ˈhaifəneit], *v.t.* separar con guión; unir con guión; escribir con guión.
hyphenation [haifəˈneiʃən], *s.* empleo de guiones.
hypnosis [hipˈnousis], *s.* (*pl.* **hypnoses** [-iːz]) hipnosis, *f. inv.*
hypnotic [hipˈnɔtik], *a.* hipnótico.
hypnotism [ˈhipnətizəm], *s.* hipnotismo.
hypnotist [ˈhipnətist], *s.* hipnotizador.
hypnotize [ˈhipnətaiz], *v.t.* hipnotizar.
hypnotizer [ˈhipnətaizə], *s.* hipnotizador.
hypochondria [haipoˈkɔndriə], *s.* hipocondría.
hypochondriac [haipoˈkɔndriæk], *a.*, *s.* hipocondríaco.
hypocondrium [haipoˈkɔndriəm], *s.* (*anat.*) hipocondrio.
hypocrisy [hiˈpɔkrisi], *s.* hipocresía.
hypocrite [ˈhipokrit], *s.* hipócrita, *m.f.*
hypocritical [hipoˈkritikəl], *a.* hipócrita.
hypocycloid [haipoˈsaiklɔid], *s.* hipocicloide.
hypoderm [ˈhaipodəːm], *s.* hipodermis.
hypodermic [haipoˈdəːmik], *a.* subcutáneo, hipodérmico.
hypogastric [haipoˈgæstrik], *a.* hipogástrico.
hypogastrium [haipoˈgæstriəm], *s.* (*anat.*) hipogastro, bajovientre.
hypogeum [haipoˈdʒiːəm], *s.* hipogeo.
hypophosphite [haipoˈfɔsfait], *s.* hipofosfito.

hypostasis [hai'pɔstəsis], *s.* (*pl.* **hypostases** [-i:z]) hipóstasis, *f. inv.*
hypostatic(al) [haipo'stætik(əl)], *a.* hipostático.
hyposulphate [haipo'sʌlfeit], *s.* hiposulfato.
hyposulphite [haipo'sʌlfait], *s.* hiposulfito.
hypotenuse [hai'pɔtinju:z], *s.* hipotenusa.
hypothecate [hai'pɔθikeit], *v.t.* hipotecar, pignorar.
hypothecation [haipɔθi'keiʃən], *s.* pignoración.
hypothecator [hai'pɔθikeitə], *s.* el que pignora *o* da en hipoteca.
hypothesis [hai'pɔθisis], *s.* (*pl.* **hypotheses** [-i:z]) hipótesis, *f. inv.*
hypothetic(al) [haipo'θetik(əl)], *a.* hipotético.
hypsometer [hip'sɔmitə], *s.* hipsómetro.
hypsometric [hipso'metrik], *a.* hipsométrico.
hypsometry [hip'sɔmitri], *s.* hipsometría.
hyson ['haisən], *s.* cha.
hyssop ['hisəp], *s.* hisopo.
hysteria [his'tiəriə], *s.* (*med.*) histeria; (*fam.*) histerismo; exageraciones.
hysteric(al) [his'terik(əl)], *a.* histérico; exagerado.
hysterics [his'teriks], *s. pl.* histerismo, paroxismo histérico, ataque de nervios; ***to go into hysterics,*** ponerse histérico; (*fam.*) desternillarse de risa.
hysterotomy [histə'rɔtəmi], *s.* histerotomía.
hythe [haið], *s.* puerto pequeño.

I

I (1), **i** [ai], novena letra del alfabeto.
I (2) [ai], *pron. pers.* yo.
iambic [ai'æmbik], *a.* yámbico. — *s.* yambo; verso yámbico.
iambus [ai'æmbəs], *s.* (*pl.* **iambuses, iambi** [-iz, -bi:]) yambo.
Iberian [ai'biəriən], *a.* ibérico, ibero. — *s.* ibero.
ibex ['aibeks], *s.* (*zool.*) íbice, rebeco.
ibis ['aibis], *s.* (*orn.*) ibis, *f.*
Icarian [i'kɛəriən], *a.* icario.
ice [ais], *s.* hielo; helado; ***ice-age,*** edad del hielo; ***ice-bound,*** rodeado de hielos; aprisionado por los hielos; (*Am.*) ***ice-box*** [REFRIGERATOR]; ***ice-breaker,*** (barco) rompehielos, *m. inv.*; ***ice-cream,*** helado; ***ice-cream cone,*** cucurucho; ***ice-field,*** campo de hielo; ***ice-floe,*** hielo flotante; (*Am.*) ***ice-pack*** [PACK-ICE]; ***ice-rink,*** pista de hielo; ***ice-skating,*** patinaje sobre hielo; (*fig.*) ***to break the ice,*** romper el hielo; ***to cut no ice,*** no influir nada. — *v.t.* helar; escarchar, glasear. — *v.i.* — ***up*** o ***over,*** helarse.
iceberg ['aisbə:g], *s.* iceberg, témpano.
Iceland ['aislənd]. Islandia.
Icelander ['aisləndə], *s.* islandés, *m.f.*
Icelandic [ais'lændik], *a.* islandés. — *s.* islandés, *m.* (*idioma*).
iceman ['aismən], *s.* (*Am.*) vendedor de hielo.
ichneumon [ik'nju:mən], *s.* icneumon.
ichnographical [ikno'græfikəl], *a.* icnográfico.
ichnography [ik'nɔgrəfi], *s.* icnografía.
ichor ['aikɔ:], *s.* icor.
ichorous ['aikərəs], *a.* icoroso.
ichthyocolla [ikθio'kɔlə], *s.* colapez.
ichthyologic [ikθio'lɔdʒik], *a.* ictiológico.
ichthyologist [ikθi'ɔlədʒist], *s.* ictiólogo.
ichthyology [ikθi'ɔlədʒi], *s.* ictiología.
ichthyophagous [ikθi'ɔfəgəs], *a.* ictiófago.
ichthyophagy [ikθi'ɔfədʒi], *s.* ictiofagía.
ichthyosaurus [ikθio'sɔ:rəs], *s.* ictiosauro.
icicle ['aisikl], *s.* carámbano.
icily ['aisili], *adv.* fríamente, con gelidez, de manera glacial.
iciness ['aisinis], *s.* frigidez, frialdad, gelidez.
icing ['aisiŋ], *s.* formación de hielo; glaseado, capa de azúcar.
icon ['aikɔn], *s.* icono.
iconoclast [ai'kɔnoklæst], *s.* iconoclasta, *m.f.*
iconoclastic [aikɔno'klæstik], *a.* iconoclasta.
iconography [aikɔ'nɔgrəfi], *s.* iconografía.
icosahedron [aikɔsə'hi:drən], *s.* icosaedro.
icteric(al) [ik'terik(əl)], *a.* ictérico.
ictus ['iktəs], *s.* ictus, *m.*
icy ['aisi], *a.* helado; glacial; gélido.
I'd [aid], *contr. de* **I had, I should** *o* **I would.**
idea [ai'diə], *s.* idea; concepto; ***bright idea,*** idea luminosa; ***the very idea!*** ¡qué ocurrencia!; ***to get*** o ***form an idea of,*** darse *o* hacerse una idea de; ***to hit upon the idea of,*** ocurrírsele la idea de; ***what's the big idea?*** ¿qué se cree Vd. que está haciendo?
ideal [ai'diəl], *a.* ideal; perfecto. — *s.* ideal.
idealism [ai'diəlizəm], *s.* idealismo.
idealist [ai'diəlist], *s.* idealista, *m.f.*
idealistic [aidiə'listik], *a.* idealista.
ideality, idealness [aidi'æliti, ai'diəlnis], *s.* idealidad.
idealization [aidiəlai'zeiʃən], *s.* idealización.
idealize [ai'diəlaiz], *v.t., v.i.* idealizar.
identical [ai'dentikəl], *a.* idéntico.
identicalness [ai'dentikəlnis], *s.* (lo) idéntico.
identification [aidentifi'keiʃən], *s.* identificación.
identify [ai'dentifai], *v.t.* identificar. — *v.i.* — ***with,*** identificarse (con).
identity [ai'dentiti], *s.* identidad; ***identity card,*** carnet de identidad; ***to prove one's identity,*** demostrar la identidad de uno.
ideogram ['idiogræm], *s.* ideograma, *m.*
ideograph ['idiogrɑ:f], *s.* ideograma, *m.*
ideographic [idio'græfik], *a.* ideográfico.
ideography [idi'ɔgrəfi], *s.* ideografía.
ideologist [aidi'ɔlədʒist], *s.* ideólogo.
ideology [aidi'ɔlədʒi], *s.* ideología.
ides [aidz], *s.pl.* idus, *m. inv.*
idiocy ['idiəsi], *s.* idiotez, cretinez.
idiom ['idiəm], *s.* modismo; idiotismo; lenguaje, estilo.
idiomatic [idio'mætik], *a.* castizo, propio (*de una lengua*); idiomático.
idiopathic(al) [idio'pæθik(əl)], *a.* idiopático.
idiopathy [idi'ɔpəθi], *s.* idiopatía.
idiosyncrasy [idio'siŋkrəsi], *s.* idiosincrasia.
idiosyncratic [idiosiŋ'krætik], *a.* idiosincrásico.
idiot ['idiət], *s.* idiota, *m.f.*, imbécil, cretino; ***village idiot,*** tonto del pueblo.
idiotic [idi'ɔtik], *a.* idiota.
idiotize ['idiətaiz], *v.t.* embrutecer, volver tonto.
idle [aidl], *a.* ocioso; desocupado; parado, inactivo; holgazán, perezoso, vago; vano, inútil; fútil, vacío; (*elec.*) ***idle circuit,*** circuito muerto; ***idle fellow,*** vago; ***idle hours,*** ratos perdidos, *m.pl.*, horas de ocio, *f.pl.*; ***idle question,*** pregunta ociosa; ***idle rich,*** ricos ociosos, *m.pl.*; ***idle story,*** cuento de viejas; ***idle talk,*** charla frívola; ***idle thing,*** bagatela; ***idle wheel,*** rueda loca *o* intermedia; (*mec.*) ***to run idle,*** marchar en vacío *o* en mínima. — *v.t.* — ***away,*** perder *o* desperdiciar ociosamente. — *v.i.* vagar, haraganear; (*mec.*) marchar en vacío.
idleness ['aidlnis], *s.* ociosidad; desocupación; frivolidad; holgazanería.
idler ['aidlə], *s.* ocioso, vago.
idling ['aidliŋ], *s.* pereza, ociosidad; (*mec.*) marcha lenta.
idol [aidl], *s.* ídolo.
idolater [ai'dɔlətə], *s.* idólatra, *m.f.*
idolatress [ai'dɔlətris], *s.* mujer idólatra.
idolatrous [ai'dɔlətrəs], *a.* idólatra, idolátrico.
idolatrously [ai'dɔlətrəsli], *adv.* idolatradamente.
idolatry [ai'dɔlətri], *s.* idolatría.
idolize ['aidəlaiz], *v.t.* idolatrar.
idyll ['idil], *s.* idilio.
idyllic [ai'dilik], *a.* idílico, edénico.
if [if], *conj.* si; ***if only,*** ojalá + *subj.*; ***even if,*** aun cuando + *subj.* — *s.* duda; ***without ifs or buts*** o ***ifs and ands,*** sin si ni pero, *o* sin ambajes ni rodajes.
i'faith [i'feiθ], *adv.* (*ant.*) a fe mía.
igad! [i'gæd], *interj.* (*ant.*) por Dios.
igloo ['iglu:], *s.* iglú.
igneous ['igniəs], *a.* ígneo.
igniferous [ig'nifərəs], *a.* ignífero.
ignitable [ig'naitəbl], *a.* inflamable.
ignite [ig'nait], *v.t.* encender, inflamar. — *v.i.* encenderse, inflamarse.
ignition [ig'niʃən], *s.* ignición; (*mec.*) encendido; ***ignition key,*** llave de(l) contacto.
ignobility, ignobleness [igno'biliti, ig'noublnis], *s.* bajeza; vileza.
ignoble [ig'noubl], *a.* innoble, vil.
ignominious [igno'miniəs], *a.* ignominioso.
ignominy ['ignomini], *s.* ignominia.
ignoramus [ignə'reiməs], *s.* ignorante, necio.
ignorance ['ignərəns], *s.* ignorancia; desconocimiento.
ignorant ['ignərənt], *a.* ignorante; desconocedor; inculto; ***to be ignorant of,*** ignorar, desconocer.

ignore [igˈnɔː], *v.t.* no hacer caso de *o* a, hacer caso omiso de, desatender, desoír.
iguana [iˈgwɑːnə], *s.* iguana.
ileac [ILIAC].
ileum [ˈiliəm], *s.* (*anat.*) íleon.
ileus [ˈiliəs], *s.* ileo.
ilex [ˈaileks], *s.* (*pl.* **ilexes, ilices** [-iz, ˈailisiːz]) (*bot.*) encina.
iliac [ˈiliæk], *a.* ilíaco.
ilium [ˈiliəm], *s.* ilion.
ilk [ilk], *s.* jaez, especie, calaña.
I'll [ail], *contr. de* **I shall** *o* **I will.**
ill [il], *a.* malo, enfermo; ***ill-breeding,*** mala educación; ***to put an ill construction on,*** tomar a mal, interpretar en mal sentido; ***ill-feeling,*** rencor, hostilidad; ***ill-luck,*** desgracia; ***ill-nature,*** mal genio; ***ill-repute,*** mala fama; ***ill-temper,*** irritabilidad; ***ill-usage,*** malos tratos, *m.pl.*; ***ill-will,*** mala volundad, rencor; ***to bear ill will to,*** guardar rencor a; ***it's an ill wind (that blows no one any good),*** no hay mal que por bien no venga; ***to fall*** o ***be taken ill,*** caer *o* ponerse enfermo. — *adv.* mal; (*fig.*) ***ill-advised,*** inconsiderado, imprudente; ***ill at ease,*** mal a gusto; ***ill-bred,*** mal educado, mal criado; ***ill-considered,*** inconsiderado; ***ill-contrived,*** mal arreglado, mal organizado, mal ideado; ***ill-disposed,*** mal intencionado; mal dispuesto; ***ill-fated,*** mal hadado; aciago, funesto; ***ill-favoured,*** feo, mal parecido; ***ill-gotten,*** mal adquirido; ***ill-grounded,*** mal fundado; ***ill-humoured,*** malhumorado; ***ill-mannered,*** mal educado; ***ill-natured,*** malhumorado; ***ill-pleased,*** malcontento; ***ill-shaped,*** disforme, mal hecho; ***ill-starred,*** malhadado; ***ill-tempered,*** enojado; malhumorado, irritable; ***to take a thing ill,*** tomar una cosa a mal. — *s.* mal; ilación.
illation [iˈleiʃən], *s.* ilación.
illative [iˈleitiv], *a.* ilativo. — *s.* (conjunción) ilativa.
illegal [iˈliːgəl], *a.* ilegal.
illegality, illegalness [iliːˈgæliti, iˈliːgəlnis], *s.* ilegalidad.
illegibility [iledʒiˈbiliti], *s.* ilegibilidad.
illegible [iˈledʒibil], *a.* ilegible.
illegitimacy [iliˈdʒitiməsi], *s.* ilegitimidad.
illegitimate [iliˈdʒitimit], *a.* ilegítimo.
illiberal [iˈlibərəl], *a.* iliberal.
illiberality [ilibəˈræliti], *s.* falta de liberalidad, mezquindad.
illicit [iˈlisit], *a.* ilícito; ilegal.
illicitness [iˈlisitnis], *s.* ilicitud.
illimitable [iˈlimitəbl], *a.* ilimitable.
illiteracy, illiterateness [iˈlitərəsi, -itnis], *s.* analfabetismo.
illiterate [iˈlitərit], *a.* analfabeto.
illness [ˈilnis], *s.* enfermedad, mal, dolencia.
illogical [iˈlɔdʒikəl], *a.* ilógico, falto de lógica.
illogicality, illogicalness [ilɔdʒiˈkæliti, iˈlɔdʒiklnis], *s.* falta de lógica, contrasentido.
ill-treat [il-ˈtriːt], *v.t.* maltratar, tratar mal.
illume [iˈl(j)uːm], *v.t.* iluminar, aclarar; dorar.
illuminant [iˈl(j)uːminənt], *a.* iluminador, iluminante. — *s.* substancia iluminativa.
illuminate [iˈl(j)uːmineit], *v.t.* iluminar, alumbrar; (*b.a.*) miniar.
illuminati [il(j)uːmiˈnɑːtiː], *s.pl.* iluminados, *m.pl.*, alumbrados, *m.pl.*
illumination [il(j)uːmiˈneiʃən], *s.* iluminación; alumbrado.
illuminative [iˈl(j)uːminətiv], *a.* iluminativo.
illuminator [iˈl(j)uːmineitə], *s.* el que ilumina; iluminador, reflector (*lámpara, lente etc.*).
illumine [iˈl(j)uːmin], *v.t.* iluminar, alumbrar.
illusion [iˈl(j)uːʒən], *s.* ilusión, espejismo; ***to have no illusions,*** haber perdido todas las ilusiones; no engañarse; ***let us be under no illusion(s),*** no nos hagamos ilusiones, no nos engañemos; ***optical illusion,*** ilusión óptica, espejismo.
illusive [iˈl(j)uːsiv], *a.* ilusorio.
illusiveness [iˈl(j)uːsivnis], *s.* (lo) ilusorio.
illusory [iˈl(j)uːsəri], *a.* ilusorio.
illustrate [ˈiləstreit], *v.t.* ilustrar; ejemplificar.
illustration [iləsˈtreiʃən], *s.* ilustración; ejemplo.
illustrative [ˈiləstreitiv], *a.* illustrativo; ***to be illustrative of,*** ejemplificar.
illustrator [ˈiləstreitə], *s.* ilustrador.
illustrious [iˈlʌstriəs], *a.* ilustre, ínclito, preclaro.
illustriousness [iˈlʌstriəsnis], *s.* (lo) ilustre, (lo) esclarecido, (lo) preclaro.
I'm [aim], *contr. de* **I am.**
image [ˈimidʒ], *s.* imagen, *f.*; ***to be the very*** *o* ***spitting image of,*** ser (el) vivo retrato de *o* ser clavado a; ***to create*** o ***project an image of o.s.,*** crear un concepto de uno mismo; ***to live up to one's image,*** mantener el concepto que tiene la gente de uno. — *v.t.* representar, retratar; imaginar; reflejar.
imagery [ˈimidʒəri], *s.* (*b.a.*) imaginería; imágenes, *f.pl.*
imaginable [iˈmædʒinəbl], *a.* imaginable.
imaginary [iˈmædʒinəri], *a.* imaginario.
imagination [imædʒiˈneiʃən], *s.* imaginación; imaginativa.
imaginative [iˈmædʒinətiv], *a.* imaginativo.
imagine [iˈmædʒin], *v.t.* imaginar(se), figurar(se). — *v.i.* imaginarse, figurarse; ***just imagine!*** ¡imagínese!
imagining [iˈmædʒiniŋ], *s.* imaginación; imaginativa; (*pl.*) imaginaciones, *f.pl.*; figuraciones, *f.pl.*
imam [iˈmɑːm], *s.* imán.
imbecile [ˈimbisiːl], *a., s.* imbécil, cretino.
imbecility [imbiˈsiliti], *s.* imbecilidad, cretinez.
imbed, *v.t.* [EMBED].
imbibe [imˈbaib], *v.t.* beber(se); ***he imbibes whisky by the gallon,*** (se) bebe litros de whisky. — *v.i.* (*fam.*) empinar el codo.
imbiber [imˈbaibə], *s.* bebedor.
imbricated [ˈimbrikeitid], *a.* imbricado.
imbrication [imbriˈkeiʃən], *s.* imbricación.
imbroglio [imˈbrouliou], *s.* embrollo, enredo, lío.
imbue [imˈbjuː], *v.t.* imbuir, infundir, inculcar.
imitable [ˈimitəbl], *a.* imitable.
imitate [ˈimiteit], *v.t.* imitar; remedar.
imitation [imiˈteiʃən], *a.* de imitación, artificial. — *s.* imitación; remedo.
imitative [ˈimitətiv], *a.* imitativo; imitador.
imitator [ˈimiteitə], *s.* imitador.
immaculate [iˈmækjulit], *a.* inmaculado; impecable.
immaculateness [iˈmækjulitnis], *s.* (lo) inmaculado; (lo) impecable.
immalleable [iˈmæliəbl], *a.* no maleable.
immanence, immanency [ˈimənəns, -si], *s.* inmanencia.
immanent [ˈimənənt], *a.* inmanente.
Immanuel [iˈmænjuel]. Emanuel.
immaterial [iməˈtiəriəl], *a.* inmaterial, incorpóreo; sin importancia, indiferente; ***it is immaterial,*** no importa, da lo mismo.
immaterialism [iməˈtiəriəlizəm], *s.* idealismo.
immaterialist [iməˈtiəriəlist], *s.* idealista, *m.f.*
immateriality [imətiəriˈæliti], *s.* inmaterialidad, incorporeidad; (lo) indiferente, (lo) poco importante.
immaterialized [iməˈtiəriəlaizd], *a.* incorpóreo, espiritual.
immaterialness [iməˈtiəriəlnis], *s.* inmaterialidad.
immature [ˈimətʃɔː], *a.* inmaturo; verde.
immaturity, immatureness [iməˈtʃuəriti, -nis], *s.* inmadurez; falta de sazón.

immeasurability, immeasurableness [imeʒərə'biliti, i'meʒərəblnis], *s.* inconmensurabilidad.
immeasurable [i'meʒərəbl], *a.* inconmensurable.
immediacy [i'mi:djəsi], *s.* proximidad; (lo) inminente, (lo) urgente.
immediate [i'mi:djət], *a.* inmediato; instantáneo.
immediately [i'mi:djətli], *adv.* inmediatamente, en seguida, al instante, al momento; ***immediately opposite,*** justo enfrente.
immediateness [i'mi:djətnis], *s.* (lo) inmediato.
immedicable [i'medikəbl], *a.* inmedicable.
immemorial [imi'mɔ:riəl], *a.* inmemorial.
immemorially [imi'mɔ:riəli], *adv.* inmemorialmente, desde tiempo inmemorial.
immense [i'mens], *a.* inmenso, enorme.
immensity, immenseness [i'mensiti, -nis], *s.* inmensidad, vastedad.
immensurability [imenʃurə'biliti], *s.* inconmensurabilidad.
immensurable [i'menʃurəbl], *a.* inmensurable.
immerge [i'mə:dʒ], *v.t.* sumergir. — *v.i.* sumergirse.
immerse [i'mə:s], *v.t.* sumergir; ***immersed in thought,*** absorto.
immersion [i'mə:ʃən], *s.* inmersión, sumersión; ***baptism by immersion,*** bautismo por inmersión; ***immersion heater,*** termo.
immersionist [i'mə:ʃənist], *a., s.* inmersionista, *m.f.*
immethodical [imi'θɔdikəl], *a.* sin método.
immigrant ['imigrənt], *a., s.* inmigrante.
immigrate ['imigreit], *v.i.* inmigrar.
immigration [imi'greiʃən], *s.* inmigración.
imminence ['iminəns], *s.* inminencia.
imminent ['iminənt], *a.* inminente.
immiscibility [imisi'biliti], *s.* inmiscibilidad.
immiscible [i'misibl], *a.* inmiscible.
immitigable [i'mitigəbl], *a.* inmitigable.
immobile [i'moubail], *a.* inmóvil.
immobility [imo'biliti], *s.* inmovilidad.
immobilize [i'moubilaiz], *v.t.* inmovilizar.
immoderate [i'mɔdərit], *a.* inmoderado; intemperante; desorbitado.
immoderateness, immoderation [i'mɔdəritinis, imɔdə'reiʃən], *s.* inmoderación; intemperancia.
immodest [i'mɔdist], *a.* inmodesto, impúdico, deshonesto, indecente.
immodesty [i'mɔdisti], *s.* inmodestia, impudicia, indecencia.
immolate ['imoleit], *v.t.* inmolar.
immolation [imo'leiʃən], *s.* inmolación.
immolator ['imoleitə], *s.* inmolador.
immoral [i'mɔrəl], *a.* inmoral.
immorality [imɔ'ræliti], *s.* inmoralidad.
immortal [i'mɔ:təl], *a., s.* inmortal.
immortality [imɔ:'tæliti], *s.* inmortalidad.
immortalization [imɔ:təlai'zeiʃən], *s.* (el) inmortalizar.
immortalize [i'mɔ:təlaiz], *v.t.* inmortalizar.
immortelle [imɔ:'tel], *s.* (*bot.*) perpetua, siempreviva.
immovability [imu:və'biliti], *s.* inmovilidad; inamovilidad; inalterabilidad; inflexibilidad.
immovable [i'mu:vəbl], *a.* inmóvil; inamovible; fijo; inalterable; inflexible.
immune [i'mju:n], *a.* inmune; exento; ***he is immune to cold,*** no es friolero.
immunity [i'mju:niti], *s.* inmunidad; exención.
immunize ['imjunaiz], *v.t.* inmunizar.
immunologist [imju'nɔlədʒist], *s.* inmunólogo.
immunology [imju'nɔlədʒi], *s.* inmunología.
immure [i'mjuə:], *v.t.* emparedar.
immutability, immutableness [imju:tə'biliti, i'mju:təblnis], *s.* inmutabilidad.
immutable [i'mju:təbl], *a.* inmutable.

imp [imp], *s.* diablillo, trasgo, duende; (*fam.*) pillín, tunantuelo.
impact ['impækt], *s.* impacto; choque; efecto, impresión.
impaction [im'pækʃən], *s.* atasco; infarto.
impair [im'pɛə], *v.t.* perjudicar, debilitar, deteriorar, menoscabar, minar, disminuir.
impairment [im'pɛəmənt], *s.* deterioro, menoscabo, disminución.
impale [im'peil], *v.t.* empalar; empalizar.
impalpability [impælpə'biliti], *s.* impalpabilidad.
impalpable [im'pælpəbl], *a.* impalpable; intangible.
impanation [impə'neiʃən], *s.* impanación.
impanel [EMPANEL].
imparity [im'pæriti], *s.* disparidad.
impart [im'pɑ:t], *v.t.* comunicar, hacer saber; impartir.
impartial [im'pɑ:ʃəl], *a.* imparcial.
impartiality [impɑ:ʃi'æliti], *s.* imparcialidad.
impartible [im'pɑ:tibl], *a.* impartible.
impassability [impɑ:sə'biliti], *s.* (lo) intransitable; (lo) infranqueable; (lo) invadeable.
impassable [im'pɑ:səbl], *a.* intransitable; infranqueable; invadeable.
impasse [æm'pɑ:s], *s.* callejón sin salida; (*fig.*) obstáculo invencible; ***to reach an impasse,*** llegar a (un) punto muerto, estancarse.
impassibility, impassibleness [impæsi'biliti, im'pæsiblnis], *s.* impasibilidad; inalterabilidad.
impassible [im'pæsibl], *a.* impasible.
impassion [im'pæʃən], *v.t.* suscitar las pasiones de, enardecer.
impassionable [im'pæʃənəbl], *a.* conmovible.
impassionate [im'pæʃəneit], *v.t.* apasionar; enardecer.
impassioned [im'pæʃənd], *a.* apasionado, vehemente.
impassive [im'pæsiv], *a.* impasible, impávido.
impassiveness [im'pæsivnis], *s.* impasibilidad, impavidez.
impaste [im'peist], *v.t.* poner en forma de pasta; (*pint.*) empastar.
impatience [im'peiʃəns], *s.* impaciencia.
impatient [im'peiʃənt], *a.* impaciente; ***to become, get*** o ***grow impatient,*** impacientarse.
impeach [im'pi:tʃ], *v.t.* acusar, acriminar; procesar; censurar.
impeachable [im'pi:tʃəbl], *a.* procesable; censurable.
impeacher [im'pi:tʃə], *s.* acusador.
impeachment [im'pi:tʃmənt], *s.* procesamiento; imputación, acusación.
impeccability [impekə'biliti], *s.* impecabilidad.
impeccable [im'pekəbl], *a.* impecable.
impeccancy [im'pekənsi], *s.* incapacidad de pecar.
impeccant [im'pekənt], *a.* exento de pecar.
impecuniosity, impecuniousness [impikju:ni'ɔsiti, impi'kju:niəsnis], *s.* indigencia.
impecunious [impi'kju:niəs], *a.* indigente.
impede [im'pi:d], *v.t.* dificultar, estorbar; impedir.
impediment [im'pedimənt], *s.* impedimento, estorbo.
impedimenta [impedi'mentə], *s.pl.* (*mil.*) impedimenta, *f.sing.*; (*fam.*) equipaje, bártulos, *m.pl.*, trastos, *m.pl.*
impedimental [impedi'mentl], *a.* que impide, impeditivo.
impeditive [im'peditiv], *a.* impeditivo.
impel [im'pel], *v.t.* impeler; impulsar; obligar.
impellent [im'pelənt], *a.* impelente, impulsor. — *s.* móvil, motor; autor.
impeller [im'pelə], *s.* impulsor, motor.
impend [im'pend], *v.i.* ser inminente, cernerse, amagar.
impendence, impendency [im'pendəns, -i], *s.* inminencia, amago.

impendent [im'pendənt], *a.* inminente.
impending [im'pendiŋ], *a.* inminente.
impenetrability, impenetrableness [impenitrə'biliti, im'penitrəblnis], *s.* impenetrabilidad.
impenetrable [im'penitrəbl], *a.* impenetrable.
impenitence, impenitency [im'penitəns, -i], *s.* impenitencia.
impenitent [im'penitənt], *a.* impenitente.
impennate [im'peneit], *a.* impennado.
imperative [im'perətiv], *a.* imperativo, imperioso; fundamental. — *s.* mandato (perentorio); (*gram.*) imperativo.
imperceptibility, imperceptibleness [impəsepti'biliti, impə'septiblnis], *s.* imperceptibilidad, (lo) imperceptible.
imperceptible [impə'septibl], *a.* imperceptible, insensible.
imperception [impə'sepʃən], *s.* impercepción.
imperceptive, impercipient [impə'septiv, -'sipiənt], *a.* incapaz de percibir.
imperfect [im'pə:fikt], *a.* (*t. gram.*) imperfecto, defectuoso. — *s.* (*gram.*) imperfecto.
imperfection [impə'fekʃən], *s.* imperfección, defecto, desperfecto.
imperfectness [im'pə:fiktnis], *s.* imperfección, (lo) imperfecto.
imperforable [im'pə:fərəbl], *a.* imperforable.
imperforate(d) [im'pə:fəreit(id)], *a.* imperforado; sin dentar.
imperforation [impə:fə'reiʃən], *s.* imperforación.
imperial [im'piəriəl], *a.* imperial. — *s.* perilla; (*arq.*) cúpula morisca.
imperialism [im'piəriəlizəm], *s.* imperialismo.
imperialist [im'piəriəlist], *s.* imperialista, *m.f.*
imperialistic [impiəriə'listik], *a.* imperialista.
imperil [im'peril], *v.t.* poner en peligro.
imperious [im'piəriəs], *a.* imperioso; altanero.
imperiousness [im'piəriəsnis], *s.* (lo) imperioso; altanería.
imperishable [im'periʃəbl], *a.* imperecedero; inmarcesible.
impermanence, impermanency [im'pə:mənəns, -i], *s.* inestabilidad, (lo) provisional, (lo) transitorio.
impermanent [im'pə:mənənt], *a.* no permanente, fugaz.
impermeability [impə:miə'biliti], *s.* impermeabilidad.
impermeable [im'pə:miəbl], *a.* impermeable.
impersonal [im'pə:sənəl], *a.* impersonal.
impersonate [im'pə:səneit], *v.t.* hacerse pasar por; (*teat.*) representar.
impersonation [impə:sə'neiʃən], *s.* (*teat.*) representación; suplantación de personalidad.
impersonator [im'pə:səneitə], *s.* (*teat.*) representador; suplantador de personalidad.
impertinence, impertinency [im'pə:tinəns, -i], *s.* impertinencia, insolencia; ***the height of impertinence,*** el colmo de la insolencia.
impertinent [im'pə:tinənt], *a.* impertinente, insolente.
imperturbability [impətə:bə'biliti], *s.* imperturbabilidad, inalterabilidad.
imperturbable [impə'tə:bəbl], *a.* imperturbable, inalterable.
imperturbation [impə:tə'beiʃən], *s.* tranquilidad, serenidad, calma.
impervious [im'pə:viəs], *a.* impermeable; insensible.
imperviousness [im'pə:viəsnis], *s.* (lo) impermeable; (lo) insensible.
impetigo [impi'taigou], *s.* impétigo.
impetuosity, impetuousness [impetju'ɔsiti, im'petjuəsnis], *s.* impetuosidad.
impetuous [im'petjuəs], *a.* impetuoso.
impetus ['impitəs], *s.* ímpetu; impulsión; (*fig*). impulso.
impiety, impiousness [im'paiiti, 'impiəsnis], *s.* impiedad, irreligiosidad, irreverencia.
impinge [im'pindʒ], *v.i.* — ***upon*** o ***on,*** incidir en; chocar con; tocar en; invadir; hacerse sentir en.
impious ['impiəs], *a.* impío.
impish ['impiʃ], *a.* travieso, juguetón.
implacability, implacableness [implækə'biliti, im'plækəblnis], *s.* implacabilidad.
implacable [im'plækəbl], *a.* implacable, inexorable.
implacental [implæ'sentəl], *a.* que no tiene placenta. — *s.* mamífero que no tiene placenta.
implant [im'plɑ:nt], *v.t.* implantar; inculcar.
implantation [implɑ:n'teiʃən], *s.* implantación; (*fig.*) inculcación.
implausibility [implɔ:zi'biliti], *s.* inverosimilitud.
implausible [im'plɔ:zibl], *a.* inverosímil, poco creíble.
implead [im'pli:d], *v.t.* (*for.*) demandar, poner pleito a.
implement ['implimənt], *s.* herramienta, instrumento; (*pl.*) utensilios, *m.pl.*, aperos, *m.pl.*, útiles, *m.pl.*, enseres, *m.pl.* — [-ment], *v.t.* poner en práctica, cumplir.
implementation [implimen'teiʃən], *s.* puesta en práctica, ejecución, cumplimiento.
implicate ['implikeit], *v.t.* complicar; comprometer.
implication [impli'keiʃən], *s.* implicación; complicidad; ***the implication is that,*** esto implica *o* parece indicar que.
implicative [im'plikətiv], *a.* implicativo.
implicit [im'plisit], *a.* implícito; absoluto, total.
implicitness [im'plisitnis], *s.* (lo) implícito.
implied [im'plaid], *a.* implícito, sobreentendido.
implore [im'plɔ:], *v.t.* implorar, suplicar.
imploringly [im'plɔ:riŋli], *adv.* de (un) modo suplicante.
imply [im'plai], *v.t.* implicar, comportar, indicar; suponer, presuponer; querer decir, dar a entender, insinuar; ***to be implied,*** sobreentenderse.
impolite [impə'lait], *a.* descortés.
impoliteness [impə'laitnis], *s.* descortesía.
impolitic [im'pɔlitik], *a.* imprudente, indiscreto; poco político.
imponderability [impɔndərə'biliti], *s.* imponderabilidad; (lo) incalculable.
imponderable [im'pɔndərəbl], *a.* imponderable; incalculable.
imporous [im'pɔ:rəs], *a.* no poroso.
import ['impɔ:t], *s.* importación, artículo importado; significación; importancia; (*pl.*) (*com.*) importaciones, *f.pl.*; ***import duty,*** derechos de entrada, *m.pl.*; ***import licence,*** permiso de importación. — *v.t.* [im'pɔ:t], importar; significar. — *v.i.* importar.
importable [im'pɔ:təbl], *a.* importable.
importance [im'pɔ:təns], *s.* importancia, consideración.
important [im'pɔ:tənt], *a.* importante, de consideración.
importation [impɔ:'teiʃən], *s.* importación.
importer [im'pɔ:tə], *s.* importador.
importunacy, importunateness [im'pɔ:tjunəsi, -nitnis], *s.* importunidad.
importunate [im'pɔ:tjunit], *a.* importuno, insistente.
importune [im'pɔ:tju:n], *v.t.*, *v.i.* importunar, insistir.
importuner [impɔ:'tju:nə], *s.* importunador.
importunity [impɔ:'tju:niti], *s.* importunidad, insistencia.
imposable [im'pouzəbl], *a.* imponible.
impose [im'pouz], *v.t.* imponer; hacer aceptar. — *v.i.* — ***on, upon,*** abusar de.

imposing [im'pouziŋ], *a.* imponente, impresionante.
imposition [impə'ziʃən], *s.* imposición; carga; abuso.
impossibility [impɔsi'biliti], *s.* imposibilidad.
impossible [im'pɔsibl], *a.* imposible; ***to do the impossible,*** hacer lo imposible.
impost ['impoust], *s.* impuesto, tributo; (*arq.*) imposta.
impostor [im'pɔstə], *s.* impostor.
imposture [im'pɔstʃə], *s.* impostura.
impotence, impotency ['mpətəns, -i], *s.* impotencia.
impotent ['impətənt], *a.* impotente.
impound [im'paund], *v.t.* encerrar, acorralar; (*for.*) embargar, confiscar.
impoverish [im'pɔveriʃ], *v.t.* empobrecer, depauperar.
impoverishment [im'pɔvəriʃmənt], *s.* empobrecimiento.
impracticability, impracticableness [impræktikə'biliti, im'præktikəblnis], *s.* impracticabilidad, imposibilidad.
impracticable [im'præktikəbl], *a.* impracticable, infactible.
imprecate ['imprikeit], *v.t.* imprecar. — *v.i.* proferir imprecaciones.
imprecation [impri'keiʃən], *s.* imprecación.
imprecatory ['imprikeitəri], *a.* imprecatorio.
impregnable [im'pregnəbl], *a.* inexpugnable.
impregnate ['impregneit], *a.* preñado, fecundado. — *v.t.* impregnar; (em)preñar; imbuir; fecundar.
impregnation [impreg'neiʃən], *s.* impregnación; fecundación; fertilización.
impresario [impre'sɑ:riou], *s.* empresario.
imprescriptible [impri'skriptibl], *a.* imprescriptible.
impress ['impres], *s.* impresión; huella; sello, señal. — [im'pres], *v.t.* imprimir, estampar; impresionar; inculcar; hacer comprender; confiscar; reclutar (*a la fuerza*).
impressibility [impresi'biliti], *s.* (lo) impresionable.
impressible [im'presibl], *a.* impresionable.
impression [im'preʃən], *s.* impresión; huella; efecto; ***to make an impression,*** causar efecto; ***to make an impression on,*** impresionar; ***to have, get, be under the impression that,*** tener la impresión de que, dársele a uno la sensación de que.
impressionable [im'preʃənəbl], *a.* impresionable; susceptible.
impressionism [im'preʃənizəm], *s.* impresionismo.
impressionist [im'preʃənist], *s.* impresionista, *m.f.*
impressionistic [impreʃə'nistik], *a.* impresionista.
impressive [im'presiv], *a.* impresionante.
impressiveness [im'presivnis], *s.* (lo) impresionante; grandiosidad.
impressment [im'presmənt], *s.* expropiación; requisa; (*mil.*) leva, enganche.
imprest ['imprest], *s.* anticipo, pago adelantado.
imprint ['imprint], *s.* impresión; huella; (*impr.*) pie de imprenta. — [im'print], *v.t.* imprimir; estampar; grabar.
imprison [im'prizən], *v.t.* encarcelar.
imprisonment [im'prizənmənt], *s.* encarcelación; encarcelamiento; prisión; ***to serve a term of imprisonment,*** cumplir una condena.
improbability [imprɔbə'biliti], *s.* improbabilidad; inverosimilitud.
improbable [im'prɔbəbl], *a.* poco probable, improbable; inverosímil.
impromptu [im'prɔmptju:], *a.* improvisado; espontáneo. — *adv.* improvisadamente. — *s.* improvisación, actuación improvisada.
improper [im'prɔpə], *a.* impropio; indecoroso; incorrecto; ***improper fraction,*** fracción impropia.
impropriate [im'prouprieit], *v.t.* apropiarse; expropiar *o* secularizar (*bienes eclesiásticos*).
impropriation [improupri'eiʃən], *s.* secularización (*de bienes eclesiásticos*).
impropriety [impro'praiiti], *s.* impropiedad; inconveniencia; indecencia, indecoro.
improvable [im'pru:vəbl], *a.* mejorable.
improve [im'pru:v], *v.t.* mejorar; perfeccionar; aumentar; ***improve one's German,*** perfeccionarse el alemán. — *v.i.* mejorar(se); perfeccionarse; aumentar(se); hacer progresos; ***improve on*** o ***upon,*** mejorar; aventajar; enmendar la plana a.
improvement [im'pru:vmənt], *s.* mejora, mejoras, *f.pl.*; (*salud*) mejoría; mejoramiento; perfeccionamiento; (*agric.*) abono; enmienda, reforma; aprovechamiento; aumento, progreso, adelantamiento; ***to be an improvement on,*** representar un adelanto en comparación con.
improver [im'pru:və], *s.* adelantador, mejorador.
improvidence [im'prɔvidəns], *s.* imprevisión.
improvident [im'prɔvidənt], *a.* impróvido, imprevisor; pródigo, manirroto.
improvisate [im'prɔvizeit], *a.* improvisado, no premeditado.
improvisation [imprɔvai'zeiʃən], *s.* improvisación.
improvisatorial, improvisatory [imprəvaizə'tɔ:riəl, imprə'vaizətəri], *a.* improvisado.
improvise ['imprəvaiz], *v.t.* improvisar. — *v.i.* repentizar.
improviser, improvisator ['imprəvaizə, -eitə], *s.* improvisador; repentista, *m.f.*
imprudence [im'pru:dəns], *s.* imprudencia.
imprudent [im'pru:dənt], *a.* imprudente.
impuberal [im'pju:bərəl], *a.* impúber, impúbero.
impudence ['impjudəns], *s.* insolencia, desfachatez, descaro.
impudent ['impjudənt], *a.* insolente, descarado.
impudicity [impju'disiti], *s.* impudicicia.
impugn [im'pju:n], *v.t.* impugnar, poner en tela de juicio.
impugnable [im'pju:nəbl], *a.* impugnable.
impugner [im'pju:nə], *s.* impugnador.
impugnment [im'pju:nmənt], *s.* impugnación.
impulse ['impʌls], *s.* impulso; ímpetu; impulsión.
impulsion [im'pʌlʃən], *s.* impulsión.
impulsive [im'pʌlsiv], *a.* impulsivo.
impunity [im'pju:niti], *s.* impunidad; ***with impunity,*** impunemente.
impure [im'pjuə], *a.* impuro; adulterado.
impurity, impureness [im'pjuəriti, -nis], *s.* impureza; adulteración.
imputability, imputableness [impju:tə'biliti, im'pju:təblnis], *s.* imputabilidad.
imputable [im'pju:təbl], *a.* imputable.
imputation [impju'teiʃən], *s.* imputación.
impute [im'pju:t], *v.t.* imputar, atribuir.
imputer [im'pju:tə], *s.* imputador.
in [in], *adv.* dentro, adentro; ***day in, day out,*** día tras día; (*fam.*) ***in-crowd,*** el todo Madrid, *etc.*; ***to be the in-thing,*** estar de moda; ***to be in,*** estar, estar en casa, *etc.*; haber llegado; estar en el poder; ser (la) temporada (de); estar de moda, gozar de favor; ***to be in for,*** haber ido *o* venido para; haberse presentado a, haber solicitado; (*fam.*) ***you're in for it now,*** ya te la has jugado *o* liado, vas a cobrar, estás listo; ***what am I in for?*** ¿qué me esperará?; (*fam.*) ***to be in on it,*** estar en el ajo; ***to be (well) in with,*** estar (muy) metido con. — *prep.* en; dentro de; ***in the daytime,*** de día, durante el día; ***in better heart,*** de mejor ánimo; ***he hasn't got it in him to,*** no tiene agallas *o* capacidad para; ***there's not much in it,*** tiene poca sustancia; (*fam.*) por ahí se andan; ***one in ten,*** uno de cada diez; ***in that,*** en el sentido de que; ***in time (to),*** a tiempo (para); ***in (the fullness of) time,*** con el tiempo; ***in (good) time,*** con tiempo, con tiempo de

sobra; ***John is in town,*** ha llegado *o* ha venido Juan (a la ciudad); ***in a week, in a week's time,*** dentro de una semana, de aquí a ocho días; ***dressed in white,*** vestido de blanco; ***in a white dress,*** con un vestido blanco; ***all the money in the world,*** todo el dinero del mundo. — *s.pl.* ***ins and outs,*** recovecos, *m.pl.*; anfractuosidades, *f.pl.*; detalles, *m.pl.*; intríngulis, *m.inv.*

inability [inə'biliti], *s.* incapacidad; (el) no poder.

inaccessibility [inæksesi'biliti], *s.* inaccesibilidad.

inaccessible [inæk'sesibl], *a.* inaccesible.

inaccuracy [in'ækjurəsi], *s.* inexactitud.

inaccurate [in'ækjurit], *a.* inexacto.

inaction [in'ækʃən], *s.* inacción, falta de acción.

inactive [in'æktiv], *a.* inactivo, poco activo.

inactivity [inæk'tiviti], *s.* inactividad; inercia.

inadaptable [inə'dæptəbl], *a.* inadaptable.

inadequacy [in'ædikwəsi], *s.* insuficiencia; (lo) poco adecuado.

inadequate [in'ædikwit], *a.* inadecuado, poco adecuado; insuficiente.

inadequateness [in'ædikwitnis], *s.* insuficiencia.

inadmissible [inəd'misibl], *a.* inadmisible.

inadvertence, inadvertency [inəd'vəːtəns, -i], *s.* inadvertencia; falta de intencionalidad.

inadvertent [inəd'vəːtənt], *a.* inadvertido; no intencionado, hecho *o* dicho sin querer.

inadvisable [inəd'vaizəbl], *a.* poco aconsejable.

inalienable [in'eiliənəbl], *a.* inalienable.

inamorata [inæmɔ'rɑːtə], *s.* enamorada, amada.

inane [i'nein], *a.* estúpido, memo; vacío, hueco.

inanimate [in'ænimit], *a.* inanimado.

inanition [inə'niʃən], *s.* inanición.

inanity [i'næniti], *s.* estupidez, memez, sandez; (lo) vacío, (lo) hueco.

inappeasable [inə'piːzəbl], *a.* implacable.

inappellable [inə'peləbl], *a.* inapelable.

inappetence, inappetency [in'æpitəns, -i], *s.* inapetencia.

inapplicability [inæplikə'biliti], *s.* (lo) inaplicable; inadecuación.

inapplicable [in'æplikəbl], *a.* inaplicable; inadecuado.

inapplication [inæpli'keiʃən], *s.* inaplicación, desaplicación.

inapposite [in'æpəzit], *a.* no pertinente, fuera de propósito.

inappreciable [inə'priːʃəbl], *a.* insignificante.

inapprehensible [inæpri'hensibl], *a.* incomprensible, ininteligible.

inapproachable [inə'proutʃəbl], *a.* inaccesible, inabordable; inasequible.

inappropriate [inə'proupriit], *a.* poco apropiado; poco adecuado.

inappropriateness [inə'proupriitnis], *s.* impropiedad.

inapt [in'æpt], *a.* impropio.

inaptitude [in'æptitjuːd], *s.* ineptitud, insuficiencia.

inarch [in'ɑːtʃ], *v.t.* injertar por aproximación.

inarticulate [inɑː'tikjulit], *a.* inarticulado; incapaz de expresarse.

inarticulateness [inɑː'tikjulitnis], *s.* inarticulación; incapacidad de expresarse.

inartistic [inɑː'tistik], *a.* falto de gusto *o* talento artístico.

inasmuch [inəz'mʌtʃ], *adv.* ***inasmuch as,*** ya que, por cuanto que.

inattention [inə'tenʃən], *s.* desatención, distracción.

inattentive [inə'tentiv], *a.* desatento; distraído; descuidado.

inaudibility, inaudibleness [inɔːdi'biliti, in'ɔːdiblnis], *s.* dificultad *o* imposibilidad de oír(se).

inaudible [in'ɔːdibl], *a.* inaudible.

inaugural [in'ɔːgjurəl], *a.* inaugural.

inaugurate [in'ɔːgjureit], *v.t.* inaugurar.

inauguration [inɔːgju'reiʃən], *s.* inauguración; toma de posesión, instalación; apertura.

inauguratory [in'ɔːgjureitəri], *a.* inauguratorio.

inauspicious [inɔːs'piʃəs], *a.* poco propicio, desfavorable.

inauspiciousness [inɔːs'piʃəsnis], *s.* (lo) poco propicio, (lo) desfavorable.

inbeing ['inbiːiŋ], *s.* inherencia, inmanencia.

inboard ['inbɔːd], *a.* (*mar.*) interior, de dentro del casco. — *adv.* (*mec.*) hacia dentro, hacia el interior.

inborn ['inbɔːn], *a.* ingénito, innato.

inbred ['in'bred], *a.* innato, ingénito.

inbreed ['in'briːd], *v.t.* engendrar endogámicamente. — *v.i.* reproducirse endogámicamente.

inbreeding ['in'briːdiŋ], *s.* endogamia.

Inca ['iŋkə], *a.* incaico. — *s.* inca, *m.f.*

incalculable [in'kælkjuləbl], *a.* incalculable.

incandesce [inkæn'des], *v.i.* encandecer.

incandescence, incandescency [inkæn'desəns, -i], *s.* incandescencia.

incandescent [inkæn'desənt], *a.* incandescente.

incantation [inkæn'teiʃən], *s.* conjuro, ensalmo, sortilegio.

incapability, incapableness [inkeipə'biliti, in'keipəblnis], *s.* incapacidad, falta de capacidad.

incapable [in'keipəbl], *a.* incapaz; imposibilitado.

incapacious [inkə'peiʃəs], *a.* poco capaz, de poca capacidad.

incapacitate [inkə'pæsiteit], *v.t.* incapacitar, inhabilitar; imposibilitar (***from, for,*** para).

incapacitation [inkəpæsi'teiʃən], *s.* inhabilitación.

incapacity [inkə'pæsiti], *s.* incapacidad; insuficiencia.

incarcerate [in'kɑːsəreit], *v.t.* encarcelar.

incarceration [inkɑːsə'reiʃən], *s.* encarcelación, encarcelamiento.

incarnadine [in'kɑːnədin], *a.* encarnado. — *v.t.* volver encarnado.

incarnate [in'kɑːnit], *a.* encarnado. — [in'kɑːneit], *v.t.* encarnar.

incarnation [inkɑː'neiʃən], *s.* encarnación.

incautious [in'kɔːʃəs], *a.* incauto, imprudente.

incautiousness [in'kɔːʃəsnis], *s.* falta de cautela.

incendiarism [in'sendiərizəm], *s.* incendiarismo.

incendiary [in'sendiəri], *a., s.* incendiario.

incense (1) ['insens], *s.* incienso; ***incense burner,*** incensario. — *v.t.* incensar.

incense (2) [in'sens], *v.t.* exasperar, irritar, encolerizar.

incensement [in'sensmənt], *s.* exasperación, irritación.

incensive [in'sensiv], *a.* provocativo, incitativo.

incensor [in'sensə], *s.* incitador.

incensory [in'sensəri], *s.* incensario.

incentive [in'sentiv], *a.* incitativo. — *s.* incentivo, aliciente.

incept [in'sept], *v.t.* emprender; (*biol.*) recibir, tomar, asimilar, absorber.

inception [in'sepʃən], *s.* principio, comienzo.

inceptive [in'septiv], *a.* incipiente, incoativo.

incertitude [in'səːtitjuːd], *s.* incertidumbre.

incessable [in'sesəbl], *a.* incesable, incesante.

incessant [in'sesənt], *a.* incesante.

incest ['insest], *s.* incesto.

incestuous [in'sestjuəs], *a.* incestuoso.

inch [intʃ], *s.* pulgada; ***every inch an Englishman,*** inglés por los cuatro costados *o* hasta la médula; ***to know every inch of the area,*** conocer el terreno palmo a palmo; ***give him an inch and he'll take an ell,*** si le das la mano, se toma el brazo; ***inch by inch, by inches,*** palmo a palmo; ***within an inch,*** poco más o menos; ***within an inch of,*** a dos dedos de. — *v.i.* — ***forward,*** avanzar palmo a palmo.

inchoate [ˈinkoueit], *a.* incoado. — *v.t.* incoar, principiar. — *v.i.* empezar.
inchoately [ˈinkoueitli], *adv.* en el primer grado.
inchoation, [inkouˈeiʃən], *s.* principio.
inchoative [ˈinkoueitiv], *a.* incipiente, incoativo.
incidence [ˈinsidəns], *s.* incidencia; frecuencia; extensión.
incident [ˈinsidənt], *a.* incidente; propio (de). — *s.* incidente, episodio, lance, suceso.
incidental [insiˈdentəl], *a.* incidental, incidente; accesorio, casual; nimio; ***incidental expenses,*** gastos accesorios *o* secundarios, *m. pl.*
incidentally [insiˈdentəli], *adv.* a propósito, por cierto.
incinerate [inˈsinəreit], *v.t.* incinerar.
incineration [insinəˈreiʃən], *s.* incineración.
incipience, incipiency [inˈsipiəns, -i], *s.* principio.
incipient [inˈsipiənt], *a.* incipiente.
incise [inˈsaiz], *v.t.* tallar, grabar, hacer incisión en, cortar.
incised [inˈsaizd], *a.* inciso, cortado.
incision [inˈsiʒən], *s.* incisión.
incisive [inˈsaisiv], *a.* incisivo; mordaz.
incisiveness [inˈsaisivnis], *s.* (lo) incisivo.
incisor [inˈsaizə], *a.* incisivo. — *s.* diente incisivo.
incisory [inˈsaizəri], *a.* incisorio.
incitant [inˈsaitənt], *a.* incitante.
incitation [insaiˈteiʃən], *s.* incitación, instigación.
incite [inˈsait], *v.t.* incitar.
incitement [inˈsaitmənt], *s.* incitación; aliciente, incentivo.
inciter [inˈsaitə], *s.* incitador.
incitingly [inˈsaitiŋli], *adv.* incitantemente, de un modo incitante.
incivility [insiˈviliti], *s.* incivilidad, descortesía.
inclemency [inˈklemənsi], *s.* inclemencia; ***inclemency of weather,*** intemperie.
inclement [inˈklemənt], *a.* inclemente.
inclination [inkliˈneiʃən], *s.* inclinación; declive; tendencia; propensión; ***inclination for,*** afición a, predilección por; ***inclination to,*** deseo de.
inclinatory [inkliˈneitəri], *a.* inclinativo.
incline [ˈinklain], *s.* declive, pendiente. — [inˈklain], *v.t.* inclinar, ladear; ***to be*** o ***feel inclined to,*** inclinarse a, sentirse tentado de. — *v.i.* inclinarse, estar inclinado, ladearse, estar ladeado.
include [inˈklu:d], *v.t.* incluir; adjuntar; ***to be included in,*** figurar en.
including [inˈklu:diŋ], *prep.* incluido.
inclusion [inˈklu:ʒən], *s.* inclusión.
inclusive [inˈklu:siv], *a.* inclusivo; ***to be inclusive of,*** incluir; ***inclusive terms,*** precio global. — *adv.* inclusive.
inclusively [inˈklu:sivli], *adv.* inclusivamente, inclusive.
incognito [inˈkɔgnitou], *a.* incógnito. — *adv.* de incógnito. — *s.* incógnito.
incoherence, incoherency [inkouˈhiərəns, -i], *s.* incoherencia; incongruencia.
incoherent [inkouˈhiərənt], *a.* incoherente; incongruente.
incombustibility, incombustibleness [inkəmbʌstiˈbiliti,inkəmˈbʌstiblnis], *s.* incombustibilidad.
incombustible [inkəmˈbʌstibl], *a.* incombustible.
income [ˈinkʌm], *s.* ingreso(s), entrada(s); ***income-tax,*** impuesto sobre la renta; ***income-tax rebate,*** reembolso de impuestos; ***income-tax return,*** declaración de ingresos; ***private income,*** renta(s).
incomer [ˈinkʌmə], *s.* recién llegado.
incoming [ˈinkʌmiŋ], *a.* entrante; (*marea*) ascendente. — *s.* entrada; (*pl.*) ingresos, *m.pl.*
incommensurability [inkəmenʃərəˈbiliti], *s.* inconmensurabilidad.
incommensurable [inkəˈmenʃərəbl], *a.* inconmensurable.
incommensurate [inkəˈmenʃərit], *a.* desproporcionado.
incommode [inkəˈmoud], *v.t.* incomodar, molestar.
incommodious [inkəˈmoudiəs], *a.* incómodo, molesto.
incommodiousness, incommodity [inkəˈmoudiəsnis, inkəˈmɔditi], *s.* incomodidad, molestia.
incommunicability, incommunicableness [inkəmju:nikəˈbiliti, inkəˈmju:nikəblnis], *s.* incomunicabilidad.
incommunicable [inkəˈmju:nikəbl], *a.* incomunicable.
incommunicado [inkəmju:niˈkɑ:dou], *a.* incomunicado; ***to keep*** o ***hold s.o. incommunicado,*** mantener incomunicado a alguien.
incommunicative [inkəˈmju:nikətiv], *a.* poco comunicativo.
incommunicativeness [inkəˈmju:nikətivnis], *s.* carácter poco comunicativo.
incommutability [inkəmju:təˈbiliti], *s.* inconmutabilidad.
incommutable [inkəˈmju:təbl], *a.* inconmutable.
incomparability, incomparableness [inkɔmpərəˈbiliti, inˈkɔmpərəblnis], *s.* (lo) incomparable.
incomparable [inˈkɔmpərəbl], *a.* incomparable.
incompassionate [inkəmˈpæʃənit], *a.* incompasivo.
incompatibility [inkəmpætiˈbiliti], *s.* incompatibilidad.
incompatible [inkəmˈpætibl], *a.* incompatible.
incompetence, incompetency [inˈkɔmpitəns, -i], *s.* incompetencia, incapacidad.
incompetent [inˈkɔmpitənt], *a.* incompetente, incapaz.
incomplete [inkəmˈpli:t], *a.* incompleto.
incompleteness [inkəmˈpli:tnis], *s.* (lo) incompleto.
incompliance [inkəmˈplaiəns], *s.* indocilidad, desobediencia.
incomprehensibility, incomprehensibleness [inkɔmprihensiˈbiliti, inkɔmpriˈhensiblnis], *s.* incomprensibilidad.
incomprehensible [inkɔmpriˈhensibl], *a.* incomprensible.
incomprehension [inkɔmpriˈhenʃən], *s.* falta de comprensión.
incomprehensive [inkɔmpriˈhensiv], *a.* limitado, no exhaustivo.
incompressible [inkəmˈpresibl], *a.* incomprimible.
incomputable [inkəmˈpju:təbl], *a.* incalculable.
inconcealable [inkənˈsi:ləbl], *a.* que no se puede ocultar.
inconceivability, inconceivableness [inkənsi:vəˈbiliti, inkənˈsi:vəblnis], *s.* (lo) inconcebible.
inconceivable [inkənˈsi:vəbl], *a.* inconcebible.
inconclusive [inkənˈklu:siv], *a.* inconcluyente, poco convincente; indeterminado.
inconclusively [inkənˈklu:sivli], *adv.* de una manera no concluyente.
inconclusiveness [inkənˈklu:sivnis], *s.* (lo) inconcluyente; indeterminación.
incongruence, incongruity [inˈkɔŋgruəns, inkɔŋˈgru:iti], *s.* incongruencia.
incongruent [inˈkɔŋgruənt], *a.* incongruente.
incongruous [inˈkɔŋgruəs], *a.* incongruente.
incongruousness [inˈkɔŋgruəsnis], *s.* incongruencia.
inconsequence [inˈkɔnsikwəns], *s.* inconsecuencia.
inconsequent [inˈkɔnsikwənt], *a.* inconsecuente.
inconsequential [inkɔnsiˈkwenʃəl], *a.* inconsecuente; sin trascendencia, fútil.
inconsiderable [inkənˈsidərəbl], *a.* insignificante, de poca consideración.
inconsiderableness [inkənˈsidərəblnis], *s.* insignificancia, poca importancia.
inconsiderate [inkənˈsidərit], *a.* desconsiderado.
inconsiderateness [inkənˈsidəritnis], *s.* (lo) desconsiderado.

inconsistency [inkən'sistənsi], *s.* inconsecuencia, falta de consecuencia.
inconsistent [inkən'sistənt], *a.* inconsecuente, poco consecuente.
inconsolable [inkən'souləbl], *a.* inconsolable.
inconspicuous [inkən'spikjuəs], *a.* insignificante, anodino, que no llama la atención.
inconstancy [in'kɔnstənsi], *s.* inconstancia.
inconstant [in'kɔnstənt], *a.* inconstante, versátil.
incontestable [inkən'testəbl], *a.* incontestable, irrecusable.
incontinence, incontinency [in'kɔntinəns, -i], *s.* incontinencia.
incontinent [in'kɔntinənt], *a.* incontinente.
incontinently [in'kɔntinəntli], *adv.* incontinentemente; inmediatemente.
incontrovertible [inkɔntro'və:tibl], *a.* incontrovertible.
inconvenience [inkən'vi:niəns], *s.* incomodidad, molestia; inoportunidad. — *v.t.* incomodar, molestar.
inconvenient [inkən'vi:niənt], *a.* incómodo, molesto; inoportuno.
inconvertible [inkən'və:tibl], *a.* inconvertible.
inconvincible [inkən'vinsibl], *a.* inconvencible.
inco-ordinate [inkou-'ɔ:dinit], *a.* no coordinado, incoordinado.
incorporate [in'kɔ:pəreit], *v.t.* incorporar (***in, into,*** a); incluir, comprender; (*com.*) constituir en sociedad anónima.
incorporated [in'kɔ:pəreitid], *a.* incorporado; asociado; incorpóreo.
incorporation [inkɔ:pə'reiʃən], *s.* incorporación.
incorporeal [inkɔ:'pɔ:riəl], *a.* incorpóreo.
incorporeity [inkɔ:pə'ri:iti], *s.* incorporeidad.
incorrect [inkə'rekt], *a.* incorrecto, inexacto, erróneo.
incorrectness [inkə'rektnis], *s.* incorrección, inexactitud.
incorrigible [in'kɔridʒibl], *a.* incorregible; empecatado.
incorrigibility, incorrigibleness [inkɔridʒi'biliti, in'kɔridʒiblnis], *s.* incorregibilidad.
incorrodible [inkə'roudibl], *a.* que no puede corroerse.
incorrupt [inkə'rʌpt], *a.* incorrupto.
incorruptibility [inkərʌpti'biliti], *s.* incorruptibilidad.
incorruptible [inkə'rʌptibl], *a.* incorruptible.
incorruption [inkə'rʌpʃən], *s.* incorrupción.
incorruptive [inkə'rʌptiv], *a.* incorrupto.
incorruptness [inkə'rʌptnis], *s.* incorrupción.
incrassate [in'kræseit], *a.* encrasado. — *v.t.* espesar, encrasar. — *v.i.* espesarse.
incrassation [inkræ'seiʃən], *s.* engrasación, espesura.
incrassative [in'kræsətiv], *a.* incrasante, espesativo.
increasable [in'kri:səbl], *a.* aumentable.
increase ['inkri:s], *s.* aumento, incremento, crecimiento; alza; ganancia; ***to be on the increase,*** ir en aumento. — [in'kri:s], *v.t.* aumentar, incrementar, acrecentar; multiplicar. — *v.i.* aumentar, crecer; multiplicarse.
increasingly [in'kri:siŋli], *adv.* cada vez más.
increate ['inkrieit], *a.* (*poét.*) increado.
incredibility, incredibleness [inkredi'biliti, in'krediblnis], *a.* incredibilidad.
incredible [in'kredibl], *a.* increíble.
incredulity, incredulousness [inkri'dju:liti, in'kredjuləsnis], *s.* incredulidad.
incredulous [in'kredjuləs], *a.* incrédulo.
increment ['inkrimənt], *s.* incremento, aumento; añadidura; ***unearned increment,*** plusvalía.
incriminate [in'krimineit], *v.t.* inculpar, incriminar, acriminar.
incriminating [in'krimineitiŋ], *a.* incriminatorio, inculpatorio.
incrimination [inkrimi'neiʃən], *s.* criminación, acriminación, incriminación.
incriminatory [in'kriminətəri], *a.* acriminador, incriminador.
incrustation [inkrʌs'teiʃən], *s.* incrustación.
incubate ['inkjubeit], *v.t., v.i.* empollar, incubar; (*fig.*) madurar.
incubation [inkju'beiʃən], *s.* incubación, empolladura; ***incubation period,*** período de incubación.
incubator ['inkjubeitə], *s.* empollador; incubadora.
incubus ['inkjubəs], *s.* (*pl.* **incubuses, incubi** [-iz, -bai]) íncubo.
inculcate ['inkʌlkeit], *v.t.* inculcar.
inculcation [inkʌl'keiʃən], *s.* inculcación.
inculpable [in'kʌlpəbl], *s.* inculpable.
inculpableness [in'kʌlpəblnis], *s.* inculpabilidad.
inculpate ['inkʌlpeit], *v.t.* inculpar.
inculpation [inkʌl'peiʃən], *s.* inculpación.
inculpatory [in'kʌlpətəri], *a.* inculpador.
incumbency [in'kʌmbənsi], *s.* (*duración de un*) beneficio eclesiástico; incumbencia.
incumbent [in'kʌmbənt], *a.* que incumbe; obligatorio; ***to be incumbent on,*** incumbir a. — *s.* beneficiado; titular.
incur [in'kə:], *v.t.* incurrir en; contraer.
incurability, incurableness [inkjuərə'biliti, in'kjuərəblnis], *s.* incurabilidad, (lo) incurable.
incurable [in'kjuərəbl], *a., s.* incurable.
incurious [in'kjuəriəs], *a.* indiferente; poco curioso.
incursion [in'kə:ʃən], *s.* incursión, algara, irrupción.
incus ['iŋkəs], *s.* (*pl.* **incudes** ['iŋkjudi:z]) (*anat.*) yunque.
indebted [in'detid], *a.* adeudado; reconocido; obligado; ***to be indebted to,*** estar en deuda con.
indebtedness [in'detidnis], *s.* deuda(s); obligación; (el) estar en deuda (***to,*** con).
indecency [in'di:sənsi], *s.* indecencia, deshonestidad.
indecent [in'di:sənt], *a.* indecente, deshonesto; ***indecent assault,*** (intento de) violación; ***indecent exposure,*** (delito de) exhibicionismo impúdico.
indecipherable [indi'saifərəbl], *a.* indescifrable.
indecision [indi'siʒən], *s.* indecisión, irresolución.
indecisive [indi'saisiv], *a.* indeciso, irresoluto; dudoso; inconcluyente.
indecisiveness [indi'saisivnis], *s.* indecisión, irresolución; (lo) dudoso; (lo) inconcluyente.
indeclinable [indi'klainəbl], *a.* indeclinable.
indecorous [in'dekərəs], *a.* indecoroso.
indecorousness, indecorum [in'dekərəsnis, indi'kɔ:rəm], *s.* indecoro, falta de decoro, inconveniencia.
indeed [in'di:d], *adv.* en efecto; es más; verdaderamente, claro; ***yes, indeed!*** ¡sí, en efecto!; ***no, indeed!*** ¡no, por cierto!; ***indeed?*** ¿de veras?
indefatigability, indefatigableness [indifætigə'biliti, indi'fætigəblnis], *s.* (lo) infatigable.
indefatigable [indi'fætigəbl], *s.* infatigable.
indefeasibility [indifi:zi'biliti], *s.* irrevocabilidad.
indefeasible [indi'fi:zibl], *a.* (*for.*) irrevocable, inabrogable, inquebrantable.
indefectibility [indifekti'biliti], *s.* indefectibilidad.
indefectible [indi'fektibl], *a.* indefectible.
indefensible [indi'fensibl], *a.* indefendible, insostenible.
indefinable [indi'fainəbl], *a.* indefinible.
indefinite [in'definit], *a.* indefinido; indeterminado; incierto.
indefiniteness [in'definitnis], *s.* (lo) indeterminado.
indeliberate [indi'libərit], *a.* indeliberado, impremeditado.
indelibility [indeli'biliti], *s.* (lo) indeleble.
indelible [in'delibl], *a.* indeleble.
indelicacy [in'delikəsi], *s.* falta de delicadeza.

indelicate [in'delikit], *a.* poco delicado.
indemnification [indemnifi'keiʃən], *s.* indemnización, resarcimiento.
indemnify [in'demnifai], *v.t.* indemnizar, resarcir.
indemnity [in'demniti], *s.* indemnización, indemnidad, resarcimiento; ***indemnity bond,*** contrafianza.
indemonstrable [indi'mɔnstrəbl], *a.* indemostrable.
indent ['indent], *s.* mella, diente, cortadura dentada. — [in'dent], *v.t.* dentar, mellar, endentar; requisar; (*impr.*) sangrar. — *v.i.* ponerse dentado, mellarse; ***indent for,*** solicitar.
indentation [inden'teiʃən], *s.* mella, diente, muesca, piquete, corte, cortadura dentada.
indented [in'dentid], *a.* dentado; (*bot.*) dentellado.
indention [in'denʃən], *s.* abolladura, mella; (*impr.*) sangría.
indenture [in'dentʃə], *s.* (*for.*) escritura, contrato, instrumento, carta partida, documento; (*pl.*) contrato de aprendizaje. — *v.t.* obligar, ligar por contrato, escriturar.
independence [indi'pendəns], *s.* independencia; ***to gain*** o ***win one's independence,*** independizarse.
independent [indi'pendənt], *a.* independiente.
indescribable [indi'skraibəbl], *a.* indescriptible.
indestructibility [indistrʌkti'biliti], *s.* indestructibilidad.
indestructible [indis'trʌktibl], *a.* indestructible.
indeterminable [indi'tə:minəbl], *a.* indeterminable.
indeterminate [indi'tə:minit], *a.* indeterminado, indefinido.
indeterminateness, indetermination [indi'tə:minitnis, inditə:mi'neiʃən], *s.* indeterminación.
index ['indeks], *s.* (*pl.* **indexes, indices** ['indeksiz, 'indisi:z]) índice; ***index card,*** ficha; ***card index,*** fichero; ***cost of living index,*** índice del coste *o* costo de la vida; ***index gauge,*** compás de graduación, *m.*; ***index-plate,*** plataforma. — *v.t.* poner índice a; poner en el índice.
indexterity [indeks'teriti], *s.* falta de destreza.
India ['indiə]. India; ***India-paper,*** papel de China; ***India-rubber,*** caucho, goma.
Indiaman ['indiəmən], *s.* (*hist.*) barco que hace el comercio con la India.
Indian ['indiən], *a.* indio; índico; ***Indian corn,*** maíz; ***Indian cress,*** capuchina; ***Indian ink,*** tinta china; ***Indian meal,*** harina de maíz; ***Indian millet,*** alcandía; ***Indian Ocean,*** Océano Índico; ***Indian red,*** almagre; ***Indian summer,*** veranillo de San Martín; ***Red Indian,*** piel roja, *m.f.* — *s.* indio.
indicant ['indikənt], *a.* indicante.
indicate ['indikeit], *v.t.* indicar, señalar.
indication [indi'keiʃən], *s.* indicación, indicio, señal, *f.*
indicative [in'dikətiv], *a.*, *s.* indicativo; ***to be indicative of,*** indicar; delatar. — *s.* indicativo.
indicator ['indikeitə], *s.* indicador; (luz) intermitente, *f.*
indicatory [in'dikətəri], *a.* demostrativo, indicatorio.
indices ['indisi:z], *s.pl.* [INDEX].
indict [in'dait], *v.t.* acusar (*ante el juez*); procesar, encausar.
indictable [in'daitəbl], *a.* procesable, denunciable.
indictee [indai'ti:], *s.* acusado; procesado.
indicter [in'daitə], *s.* denunciante, acusador.
indiction [in'dikʃən], *s.* indicción.
indictment [in'daitmənt], *s.* acusación; sumaria.
Indies ['indiz], ***the,*** las Indias; (***the***) ***West Indies,*** (las) Antillas.
indifference [in'difərəns], *s.* indiferencia; desapego, desamor; (lo) mediocre.
indifferent [in'difərənt], *a.* indiferente; desapegado; mediano, mediocre.
indigence ['indidʒəns], *s.* indigencia.
indigenous [in'didʒinəs], *a.* indígena, nativo; innato; ***indigenous to,*** indígena de.
indigent ['indidʒənt], *a.* indigente.
indigestible [indi'dʒestibl], *a.* indigesto, indigerible.
indigestion [indi'dʒestʃən], *s.* indigestión; empacho.
indignant [in'dignənt], *a.* indignado; ***to make indignant,*** indignar; ***indignant at,*** indignado ante, contra.
indignantly [in'dignəntli], *adv.* con indignación.
indignation [indig'neiʃən], *s.* indignación; protesta.
indignity [in'digniti], *s.* indignidad; ultraje.
indigo ['indigou], *s.* añil, índigo; ***indigo-plant, indigo-tree,*** índigo, jiquilete.
indirect [indi'rekt], *a.* indirecto; ***indirect object,*** complemento indirecto; ***indirect taxation,*** contribución indirecta.
indirectness [indi'rektnis], *s.* (lo) indirecto.
indiscernible [indi'sə:nibl], *a.* indiscernible, imperceptible.
indisciplinable [in'disiplinəbl], *a.* indisciplinable.
indiscoverable [indis'kʌvərəbl], *a.* indescubrible.
indiscreet [indi'skri:t], *a.* indiscreto, imprudente; impolítico, inconsiderado.
indiscretion [indi'skreʃən], *s.* indiscreción, imprudencia.
indiscriminate [indis'kriminit], *a.* (hecho) sin distinción *o* a lo loco.
indiscriminating [indis'krimineitiŋ], *a.* indiscriminado, que obra sin distinguir *o* a lo loco.
indiscrimination [indiskrimi'neiʃən], *s.* falta de discernimiento.
indispensability, indispensableness [indispensə'biliti, indis'pensəblnis], *s.* (lo) indispensable.
indispensable [indis'pensəbl], *a.* indispensable, imprescindible.
indispose [indis'pouz], *v.t.* indisponer; ***to be indisposed,*** estar indispuesto.
indisposition, indisposedness [indispə'ziʃən, -'pouzidnis], *s.* indisposición; desavenencia.
indisputability, indisputableness [indispju:tə'biliti, indis'pju:təblnis], *s.* (lo) indiscutible.
indisputable [indis'pju:təbl], *a.* indiscutible.
indissolubility, indissolubleness [indisɔlju'biliti, indi'sɔljublnis], *s.* indisolubilidad.
indissoluble [indi'sɔljubl], *a.* indisoluble.
indistinct [indis'tiŋkt], *a.* indistinto, confuso, borroso, nebuloso.
indistinction [indis'tiŋkʃən], *s.* indistinción.
indistinctness [indis'tiŋktnis], *s.* (lo) confuso, (lo) borroso, (lo) nebuloso.
indistinguishable [indis'tiŋgwiʃəbl], *a.* indistinguible.
indite [in'dait], *v.t.* redactar, poner por escrito.
inditement [in'daitmənt], *s.* redacción.
inditer [in'daitə], *s.* redactor.
indium ['indiəm], *s.* indio (*metal.*).
individual [indi'vidjuəl], *a.* individual; personal; particular, determinado; uno por uno, por separado. — *s.* individuo, sujeto.
individualism [indi'vidjuəlizəm], *s.* individualismo.
individualist [indi'vidjuəlist], *s.* individualista, *m.f.*
individualistic [individjuə'listik], *a.* individualista.
individuality [individju'æliti], *s.* individualidad.
individualize [indi'vidjuəlaiz], *v.t.* individualizar, particularizar.
individuate [indi'vidjueit], *a.* individual. — *v.t.* individuar.
individuation [individju'eiʃən], *s.* individuación.
indivisibility, indivisibleness [indivizi'biliti, -'viziblnis], *s.* indivisibilidad.
indivisible [indi'vizibl], *a.* indivisible.

Indo-China [indou-ˈtʃainə]. Indochina.
Indo-Chinese [indou-tʃaiˈni:z], *a.*, *s.* indochino.
indocile [inˈdousail], *a.* indócil.
indocility [indouˈsiliti], *s.* indocilidad.
indoctrinate [inˈdɔktrineit], *v.t.* adoctrinar (***with***, en).
indoctrination [indɔktriˈneiʃən], *s.* adoctrinamiento.
Indo-European [indou-juərəˈpiən], *a.*, *s.* indoeuropeo.
Indo-Germanic [indou-dʒə:ˈmænik], *a.* indogermánico.
indolence [ˈindələns], *s.* indolencia.
indolent [ˈindələnt], *a.* indolente.
indomitable [inˈdɔmitəbl], *a.* indomable, indómito.
Indonesia [indouˈni:ziə]. Indonesia.
Indonesian [indouˈni:ziən], *a.*, *s.* indonesio.
indoor [ˈindɔ:], *a.* interior; de puertas adentro; de casa; de salón; ***indoor sports,*** deportes interiores, *m.pl.*; ***indoor swimming-pool,*** piscina cubierta.
indoors [inˈdɔ:z], *adv.* dentro; adentro; en casa; bajo techado.
indorse [ENDORSE].
indraught [ˈindrɑ:ft], *s.* aspiración, aire aspirado; corriente entrante; atracción hacia el interior.
indrawn [ˈindrɔ:n], *a.* sorbido, aspirado; llamado hacia el interior.
indubitable [inˈdju:bitəbl], *a.* indudable, indubitable.
indubitableness [inˈdju:bitəblnis], *s.* (lo) indudable.
induce [inˈdju:s], *v.t.* inducir; producir, provocar.
inducement [inˈdju:smənt], *s.* incentivo, aliciente, estímulo.
induct [inˈdʌkt], *v.t.* instalar; introducir; iniciar.
induction [inˈdʌkʃən], *s.* instalación; introducción; (*elec.*) inducción; ***induction coil,*** carrete de inducción; ***induction course,*** curso de introducción.
inductive [inˈdʌktiv], *a.* inductivo, inductor.
inductively [inˈdʌktivli], *adv.* por inducción, inductivamente.
inductivity [indʌkˈtiviti], *s.* inductividad.
inductometer [indʌkˈtɔmitə], *s.* inductómetro.
inductor [inˈdʌktə], *s.* instalador; (*elec.*) inductor.
indue [ENDUE].
indulge [inˈdʌldʒ], *v.t.* complacer; satisfacer; dar gusto a; consentir; (*com.*) prorrogar el plazo a. — *v.i.* — ***in,*** entregarse a, darse a.
indulgence [inˈdʌldʒəns], *s.* mimos, *m.pl.*, consentimiento, complacencia; satisfacción; (*com.*) prórroga; indulgencia.
indulgent [inˈdʌldʒənt], *a.* indulgente, complaciente.
indulger [inˈdʌldʒə], *s.* indulgente.
indult [inˈdʌlt], *s.* (*igl.*) indulto; dispensa.
indurate [ˈindjuəreit], *a.* duro, endurecido, obstinado, impenitente. — *v.t.* endurecer, hacer duro. — *v.i.* endurecerse, empedernirse.
induration [indjuəˈreiʃən], *s.* acción de endurecer, endurecimiento; dureza de corazón; (*med.*) dureza, induración.
industrial [inˈdʌstriəl], *a.* industrial, fabril.
industrialism [inˈdʌstriəlizəm], *s.* industrialismo.
industrialist [inˈdʌstriəlist], *s.* industrial.
industrialization [indʌstriəlaiˈzeiʃən], *s.* industrialización.
industrialize [inˈdʌstriəlaiz], *v.t.* industrializar.
industrious [inˈdʌstriəs], *a.* industrioso, laborioso, trabajador.
industry [ˈindəstri], *s.* industria; laboriosidad.
indwell [ˈinˈdwel], *v.t.* habitar. — *v.i.* residir, morar.
indweller [ˈindwelə], *s.* habitante.
indwelling [ˈinˈdweliŋ], *a.* morador, residente. — *s.* presencia, existencia interior.
inebriant [inˈi:briənt], *a.* embriagador, que embriaga. — *s.* lo que embriaga.
inebriate [inˈi:briit], *a.* ebrio. — *s.* borracho. — [-eit], *v.t.* embriagar.
inebriation [ini:briˈeiʃən], *s.* embriaguez, borrachera.
inedible [inˈedibl], *a.* no comestible, incomible.
inedited [inˈeditid], *a.* inédito.
ineffable [inˈefəbl], *a.* inefable.
ineffableness [inˈefəblnis], *s.* inefabilidad.
ineffaceable [iniˈfeisəbl], *a.* imborrable, indeleble.
ineffective [iniˈfektiv], *a.* ineficaz, inútil.
ineffectiveness [iniˈfektivnis], *s.* ineficacia.
ineffectual [iniˈfektjuəl], *a.* ineficaz, inútil.
ineffectualness [iniˈfektjuəlnis], *s.* ineficacia; (lo) inútil.
inefficacious [inefiˈkeiʃəs], *a.* ineficaz.
inefficacy, inefficaciousness, inefficiency, [inˈefikəsi, inefiˈkeiʃəsnis, iniˈfiʃənsi], *s.* ineficacia.
inefficient [iniˈfiʃənt], *a.* ineficaz.
inelastic [iniˈlæstik], *a.* poco flexible.
inelasticity [inilæsˈtisiti], *s.* falta de elasticidad *o* de flexibilidad.
inelegant [inˈeligənt], *a.* poco elegante.
inelegantly [inˈeligəntli], *adv.* sin elegancia.
ineligibility [inelidʒiˈbiliti], *s.* inelegibilidad.
ineligible [inˈelidʒibl], *a.* inelegible; que no tiene derecho (a).
ineluctable [iniˈlʌktəbl], *a.* ineluctable, inexorable.
inept [inˈept], *a.* inepto.
ineptitude, ineptness [inˈeptitju:d, -nis], *s.* ineptitud, incapacidad.
inequality [iniˈkwɔliti], *s.* desigualdad.
inequitable [inˈekwitəbl], *a.* poco equitativo.
inequity [inˈekwiti], *s.* injusticia.
ineradicable [iniˈrædikəbl], *a.* inextirpable.
inert [inˈə:t], *a.* inerte, inmóvil.
inertia [inˈə:ʃə], *s.* inercia.
inertness [inˈə:tnis], *s.* inmovilidad.
inescapable [inisˈkeipəbl], *a.* ineludible.
inessential [iniˈsenʃəl], *a.* no esencial, no fundamental.
inestimable [inˈestiməbl], *a.* inestimable, inapreciable.
inevitable [inˈevitəbl], *a.* inevitable.
inevitability, inevitableness [inevitəˈbiliti, inˈevitəblnis], *s.* (lo) inevitable.
inexact [inigˈzækt], *a.* inexacto.
inexcusable [iniksˈkju:zəbl], *a.* imperdonable, indisculpable.
inexcusableness [iniksˈkju:zəblnis], *s.* (lo) imperdonable.
inexhaustibility [inigˈzɔ:stibiliti], *s.* (lo) inagotable.
inexhaustible [inigˈzɔ:stibl], *a.* inagotable.
inexorability, inexorableness [ineksərəˈbiliti, inˈeksərəblnis], *s.* (lo) inexorable.
inexorable [inˈekzərəbl], *a.* inexorable.
inexpedience, inexpediency [inikˈspi:diəns, -i], *s.* inoportunidad; inconveniencia; imprudencia.
inexpedient [inikˈspi:diənt], *a.* inoportuno; inconveniente; imprudente.
inexpensive [inikˈspensiv], *a.* barato, económico.
inexperience [inikˈspiəriəns], *s.* inexperiencia; falta de experiencia; impericia.
inexperienced, inexpert [inikˈspiəriənst, inˈekspə:t], *a.* inexperto, novel.
inexpiable [inˈekspiəbl], *a.* inexpiable.
inexplicability, inexplicableness [ineksplikəˈbiliti, inˈeksplikəblnis], *s.* (lo) inexplicable.
inexplicable [inˈeksplikəbl], *a.* inexplicable.
inexplicit [inikˈsplisit], *a.* no explícito.
inexplorable [iniksˈplɔ:rəbl], *a.* inexplorable.
inexpressible [inikˈspresibl], *a.* inexpresable.
inexpressive [iniksˈpresiv], *a.* inexpresivo.

inextinguishability [inikstiŋgwiʃə'biliti], *s.* (lo) inextinguible.
inextinguishable [iniks'tiŋgwiʃəbl], *a.* inextinguible.
inextricability, inextricableness [inekstrikə'biliti, in'ekstrikəblnis], *s.* (lo) inextricable.
inextricable [in'ekstrikəbl], *a.* inextricable, intrincado.
infall ['infɔ:l], *s.* ataque, incursión; sitio por donde entra el agua en un estanque.
infallibility, infallibleness [infæli'biliti, in'fæliblnis], *s.* infalibilidad.
infallible [in'fælibl], *a.* infalible.
infamous ['infəməs], *a.* infame, ignominioso; infamante; tristemente famoso.
infamy, infamousness ['infəmi, -əsnis], *s.* infamia, ignominia.
infancy ['infənsi], *s.* infancia, niñez; (*for.*) minoría.
infant ['infənt], *a.* infantil; menor de edad; ***infant school,*** escuela de párvulos. — *s.* niño, niña, criatura; (*for.*) menor.
infanticidal [infænti'saidəl], *a.* infanticida.
infanticide [in'fæntisaid], *s.* infanticidio; infanticida, *m.f.*
infantile ['infəntail], *a.* infantil, pueril.
infantilism [in'fæntilizəm], *s.* infantilismo.
infantry ['infəntri], *s.* infantería.
infantryman ['infəntrimən], *s.* infante.
infarct [in'fɑ:kt], *s.* (*pat.*) infarto.
infatuate [in'fætjueit], *v.t.* atontar, enamoriscar; ***to get*** o ***become infatuated,*** enamoriscarse; encapricharse.
infatuation [infætju'eiʃən], *s.* enamoramiento; encaprichamiento.
infeasibility, infeasibleness [infi:zi'biliti, in'fi:ziblnis], *s.* impracticabilidad.
infeasible [in'fi:zibl], *a.* impracticable, no viable, no factible.
infect [in'fekt], *v.t.* infectar, inficionar, contagiar.
infection [in'fekʃən], *s.* infección, contagio.
infectious [in'fekʃəs], *a.* infeccioso, contagioso.
infectiously [in'fekʃəsli], *adv.* por infección.
infectiousness [in'fekʃəsnis], *s.* (lo) contagioso.
infective [in'fektiv], *a.* infeccioso, infectivo, contagioso.
infecund [in'fekʌnd], *a.* infecundo.
infecundity [infi'kʌnditi], *s.* infecundidad.
infelicitous [infi'lisitəs], *a.* poco feliz, desacertado.
infelicity [infi'lisiti], *s.* (lo) poco oportuno.
infer [in'fə:], *v.t.* inferir, deducir, colegir.
inferable [in'fə:rəbl], *a.* deducible.
inference ['infərəns], *s.* inferencia, deducción; ***to draw an inference,*** sacar una conclusión.
inferential [infə'renʃəl], *a.* ilativo.
inferentially [infə'renʃəli], *adv.* por inferencia.
inferior [in'fiəriə], *a.*, *s.* inferior.
inferiority [infiəri'ɔriti], *s.* inferioridad; ***inferiority complex,*** complejo de inferioridad.
infernal [in'fə:nəl], *a.* infernal.
inferno [in'fə:nou], *s.* infierno.
infertile [in'fə:tail], *a.* infecundo, estéril.
infertility [infə'tiliti], *s.* infecundidad, esterilidad.
infest [in'fest], *v.t.* infestar.
infestation [infes'teiʃən], *s.* infestación.
infidel ['infidəl], *a.*, *s.* infiel; pagano; descreído.
infidelity [infi'deliti], *s.* infidelidad; perfidia.
infighting ['infaitiŋ], *s.* lucha cuerpo a cuerpo (*en el boxeo*); luchas internas, *f.pl.*
infiltrate ['infiltreit], *v.t.* infiltrar. — *v.i.* infiltrarse.
infiltration [infil'treiʃən], *s.* infiltración.
infinite ['infinit], *a.*, *s.* infinito.
infiniteness ['infinitnis], *s.* (lo) infinito.
infinitesimal [infini'tesiməl], *a.* infinitesimal. — *s.* infinitésimo.
infinitive [in'finitiv], *a.* infinitivo. — *s.* (*gram.*) infinitivo.
infinitude [in'finitju:d], *s.* infinidad, infinitud; sinnúmero.
infinity [in'finiti], *s.* infinidad; sinnúmero; infinito.
infirm [in'fə:m], *a.* enfermizo; enclenque, débil; inestable, poco firme; ***infirm of purpose,*** irresoluto.
infirmary [in'fə:məri], *s.* enfermería; hospital.
infirmity [in'fə:miti], *s.* enfermedad, mal; debilidad, flaqueza; poca firmeza, inestabilidad.
infirmness [in'fə:mnis], *s.* debilidad; poca firmeza.
infix [in'fiks], *v.t.* fijar (en), encajar, clavar. — *s.* (*gram.*) infijo.
inflame [in'fleim], *v.t.* inflamar; azuzar, enardecer; ***to become inflamed,*** inflamarse.
inflammability, inflammableness [inflæmə'biliti, in'flæməblnis], *s.* (lo) inflamable.
inflammable [in'flæməbl], *a.* inflamable.
inflammation [inflə'meiʃən], *s.* inflamación.
inflammatory [in'flæmətəri], *a.* inflamatorio; incendiario.
inflate [in'fleit], *v.t.* inflar.
inflated [in'fleitid], *a.* inflado, hinchado.
inflation [in'fleiʃən], *s.* inflación.
inflationary [in'fleiʃənəri], *a.* inflacionista.
inflect [in'flekt], *v.t.* torcer, doblar, encorvar; modular; (*gram.*) declinar, conjugar.
inflection [in'flekʃən], *s.* inflexión.
inflectional [in'flekʃənəl], *a.* flexional.
inflexibility, inflexibleness [infleksi'biliti, in'fleksiblnis], *s.* inflexibilidad.
inflexible [in'fleksibl], *a.* inflexible.
inflexion [INFLECTION].
inflict [in'flikt], *v.t.* inferir, infligir; causar; descargar (*un golpe*).
infliction [in'flikʃən], *s.* imposición.
inflictive [in'fliktiv], *a.* que inflinge, punitivo.
inflorescence [inflɔ'resəns], *s.* inflorescencia; florescencia.
inflow ['inflou], *s.* flujo, afluencia. — [in'flou], *v.i.* afluir.
influence ['influəns], *s.* influencia, influjo; valimiento; (*elec.*) inducción; ***to have influence,*** ejercer influencia (***over,*** sobre); tener predicamento; tener influencia (***with,*** con); tener buenas aldabas. — *v.t.* influir en, influenciar.
influential [influ'enʃəl], *a.* influente; influyente, prestigioso.
influentially [influ'enʃəli], *adv.* por influencia.
influenza [influ'enzə], *s.* gripe, *f.*, trancazo.
influx ['inflʌks], *s.* influjo; afluencia.
influxion [in'flʌkʃən], *s.* infusión.
inform [in'fɔ:m], *v.t.* informar; comunicar, participar. — *v.i.* denunciar; dar parte.
informal [in'fɔ:məl], *a.* de confianza, sencillo, familiar, poco ceremonioso; sin etiquetas ni cumplidos; oficioso.
informality [infɔ:'mæliti], *s.* familiaridad, falta de ceremonia; sencillez; informalidad.
informant [in'fɔ:mənt], *s.* informador; denunciador.
information [infə'meiʃən], *s.* información; informes, *m.pl.*, datos, *m.pl.*; denuncia, delación; ***to gather information,*** tomar informes.
informative [in'fɔ:mətiv], *a.* informativo.
informed [in'fɔ:md], *a.* informado, al corriente; fidedigno.
informer [in'fɔ:mə], *s.* informador, informante; denunciante, delator; (*fam.*) soplón, chivato.
infraction [in'frækʃən], *s.* infracción.
infractor [in'fræktə], *s.* infractor.
infra dig ['infrə 'dig], *a.* que no se hace *o* que no se dice (por amor propio).
infrangibility, infrangibleness [infrændʒi'biliti, in'frændʒiblnis], *s.* (lo) infrangible.

infrangible [in'frændʒibl], *a.* infrangible, inquebrantable.
infra-red [infrə-'red], *a.* infrarrojo.
infrastructure ['infrəstrʌktʃə], *s.* infraestructura.
infrequence, infrequency [in'fri:kwəns, -i], *s.* infrecuencia, poca frecuencia.
infrequent [in'fri:kwənt], *a.* infrecuente, poco frecuente.
infringe [in'frindʒ], *v.t.* infringir; violar. — *v.i.* — ***on, upon,*** invadir.
infringement [in'frindʒmənt], *s.* infracción; transgresión, violación.
infringer [in'frindʒə], *s.* infractor.
infuriate [in'fjuərieit], *v.t.* enfurecer, poner furioso.
infuse [in'fju:z], *v.t.* infundir (***into,*** a).
infused [in'fju:zd], *a.* infundido, infuso.
infusibility, infusibleness [infju:zi'biliti, in'fju:ziblnis], *s.* infusibilidad.
infusible [in'fju:zibl], *a.* infusible, infundible.
infusion [in'fju:ʒən], *s.* infusión.
Infusoria [infju:'zɔ:riə], *s.pl.* infusorios, *m.pl.*
infusorial [infju:'zɔ:riəl], *a.* infusorio; ***infusorial earth,*** tierra de infusorios.
infusorian, infusory [infju:'zɔ:riən, in'fju:zəri], *a., s.* infusorio.
ingathering ['ingæðəriŋ], *s.* cosecha, recolección.
ingeminate [in'dʒemineit], *a.* repetido. — *v.t.* repetir.
ingenerable [in'dʒenərəbl], *a.* ingenerable.
ingenerate [in'dʒenərit], *a.* ingénito.
ingenious [in'dʒi:niəs], *a.* ingenioso; hábil.
ingeniousness [in'dʒi:niəsnis], *s.* ingeniosidad; habilidad.
ingenuity [indʒi'nju:iti], *s.* ingeniosidad; inventiva.
ingenuous [in'dʒenjuəs], *a.* ingenuo, cándido.
ingenuousness [in'dʒenjuəsnis], *s.* ingenuidad, candidez.
ingest [in'dʒest], *v.t.* ingerir.
ingesta [in'dʒestə], *s.pl.* alimento ingerido.
ingestion [in'dʒestʃən], *s.* ingestión.
ingle [iŋgl], *s.* fuego; ***ingle-nook,*** rincón del hogar.
inglorious [in'glɔ:riəs], *a.* ignominioso; sin fama; sanchopancesco.
ingloriousness [in'glɔ:riəsnis], *s.* ignominia; obscuridad.
ingoing ['ingouiŋ], *a.* entrante, que entra. — *s.* entrada, ingreso.
ingot ['iŋgət], *s.* lingote; ***ingot of copper,*** galápago de cobre; ***ingot of gold,*** tejo de oro; riel, barra de metal.
ingraft [ENGRAFT].
ingrain ['in'grein], *a.* teñido en rama; arraigado; ***ingrain carpet,*** alfombra teñida en rama. — *v.t.* teñir en rama; arraigar.
ingrained ['in'greind], *a.* teñido en rama; arraigado, innato.
ingrate ['ingreit], *a., s.* ingrato, desagradecido.
ingratiate [in'greiʃieit], *v.t.* captar *o* granjearse la simpatía de. — **ingratiate o.s.,** *v.r.* congraciarse (***with,*** con).
ingratiating [in'greiʃieitiŋ], *a.* obsequioso.
ingratitude [in'grætitju:d], *s.* ingratitud, desagradecimiento.
ingredient [in'gri:diənt], *s.* ingrediente.
ingress ['ingres], *s.* ingreso; acceso.
ingression [in'greʃən], *s.* ingreso.
ingrowing ['ingrouiŋ], *a.* que crece hacia dentro; ***ingrowing nail,*** uñero.
inguinal ['iŋgwinəl], *a.* inguinal.
ingulf [ENGULF].
ingurgitate [in'gə:dʒiteit], *v.i.* ingurgitar.
inhabit [in'hæbit], *v.t.* habitar, ocupar.
inhabitability [inhæbitə'biliti], *s.* habitabilidad.
inhabitable [in'hæbitəbl], *a.* habitable.
inhabitant [in'hæbitənt], *s.* habitante; vecino.
inhabited [in'hæbitid], *a.* habitado, poblado.
inhalant [in'heilənt], *s.* inhalador.
inhalation [inhə'leiʃən], *s.* inhalación.
inhale [in'heil], *v.t.* inhalar; tragar (el humo).
inharmonic [inhɑ:'mɔnik], *a.* dísono, inarmónico.
inharmonious [inhɑ:'mouniəs], *a.* discordante; inarmónico, poco armonioso, disonante.
inhere [in'hiə], *v.i.* ser inherente.
inherence, inherency [in'hiərəns, -i], *s.* inherencia.
inherent [in'hiərənt], *a.* inherente (***in,*** a).
inherit [in'herit], *v.t., v.i.* heredar.
inheritable [in'heritəbl], *a.* heredable; heredero.
inheritance [in'heritəns], *s.* herencia; patrimonio; (*Am.*) ***inheritance tax*** [DEATH-DUTIES].
inheritor [in'heritə], *s.* heredero.
inheritress [in'heritris], *s.* heredera.
inhibit [in'hibit], *v.t.* inhibir, cohibir; impedir; (*igl.*) prohibir.
inhibition [inhi'biʃən], *s.* inhibición.
inhibitory, inhibitive [in'hibitəri, -iv], *a.* inhibitorio.
inhospitable [in'hɔspitəbl], *a.* inhospitalario, inhóspito.
inhospitality [inhɔspi'tæliti], *s.* inhospitalidad.
inhuman [in'hju:mən], *a.* inhumano.
inhumanity [inhju:'mæniti], *s.* inhumanidad.
inhumation [inhju:'meiʃən], *s.* inhumación.
inhume [in'hju:m], *v.t.* inhumar.
inimical [in'imikəl], *a.* enemigo, hostil, contrario.
inimitability, inimitableness [inimitə'biliti, in'imitəblnis], *s.* (lo) inimitable.
inimitable [in'imitəbl], *a.* inimitable.
iniquitous [in'ikwitəs], *a.* inicuo.
iniquity [in'ikwiti], *s.* iniquidad.
initial [in'iʃəl], *a.* inicial. — *s.* (letra) inicial, *f.* — *v.t.* firmar *o* marcar con (las) iniciales.
initially [in'iʃəli], *adv.* inicialmente.
initiate [in'iʃiit], *a., s.* iniciado. — [-eit], *v.t.* iniciar, dar comienzo a.
initiating [in'iʃieitiŋ], *a.* iniciativo.
initiation [iniʃi'eiʃən], *s.* iniciación, comienzo.
initiative [in'iʃiətiv], *a.* iniciativo. — *s.* iniciativa; ***on one's own initiative,*** por propia iniciativa; ***to take the initiative,*** tomar la iniciativa.
initiator [in'iʃieitə], *s.* iniciador.
initiatory [in'iʃiətəri], *a.* iniciativo.
inject [in'dʒekt], *v.t.* inyectar; introducir.
injection [in'dʒekʃən], *s.* inyección.
injector [in'dʒektə], *s.* inyector.
injudicious [indʒu:'diʃəs], *a.* indiscreto, imprudente.
injudiciousness [indʒu:'diʃəsnis], *s.* indiscreción, imprudencia.
injunction [in'dʒʌŋkʃən], *s.* mandato, precepto; (*for.*) entredicho.
injure ['indʒə], *v.t.* herir, lastimar, lesionar, causar lesión a; dañar, causar daño a, perjudicar; ofender.
injurer ['indʒərə], *s.* agraviador, ofensor.
injurious [in'dʒuəriəs], *a.* dañoso, perjudicial, dañino, nocivo.
injuriousness [in'dʒuəriəsnis], *s.* (lo) nocivo, (lo) perjudicial.
injury ['indʒəri], *s.* herida, lesión; perjuicio, daño.
injustice [in'dʒʌstis], *s.* injusticia.
ink [iŋk], *s.* tinta; ***copying-ink,*** tinta de copiar; ***indelible*** o ***marking-ink,*** tinta indeleble, tinta de marcar; ***ink-ball,*** bala de entintar; ***ink-bottle,*** tintero, frasco de tinta; (*impr.*) ***ink duct,*** tintero de prensa; ***ink-eraser,*** raedor; (*impr.*) ***ink-roller,*** rulo, rodillo; ***invisible ink,*** tinta simpática. — *v.t.* entintar, dar tinta a, teñir con tinta, untar de tinta.
inkiness ['iŋkinis], *s.* entintamiento.

inkle [iŋkl], *s.* cinta.
inkling [ˈiŋkliŋ], *s.* atisbo; sospecha; barrunto; indicio.
inkmaker [ˈiŋkmeikə], *s.* fabricante de tinta.
inkstand, inkwell [ˈiŋkstænd, -wel], *s.* tintero.
inky [ˈiŋki], *a.* parecido a la tinta; manchado de tinta; cubierto de tinta.
inlaid [ˈinˈleid], *a.* ***inlaid work,*** taracea; ***inlaid floor,*** entarimado. — *pret., p.p.* [INLAY].
inland [ˈinlənd], *a.* interior; ***inland revenue,*** sección de impuestos de hacienda. — [inˈlænd], *adv.* tierra adentro. — [ˈinlənd], *s.* interior (del país).
inlander [ˈinləndə], *s.* habitante del interior.
in-law [ˈin-lɔ:], *s.* (*fam.*) político (*pariente*).
inlay [ˈinlei], *s.* taracea, embutido. — [inˈlei], *irr. v.t.* taracear; embutir, incrustar.
inlayer [ˈinˈleiə], *s.* incrustador, obrero que hace taracea, operario en taracea.
inlaying [ˈinˈleiiŋ], *s.* arte de taracear, embutir *o* incrustar.
inlet [ˈinlet], *s.* entrante, ensenada, cala, abra; boca de entrada; ***inlet valve,*** válvula de admisión.
inly [ˈinli], *adv.* interiormente.
inmate [ˈinmeit], *s.* residente; inquilino; asilado; preso; pupilo.
inmost [ˈinmoust], *a.* (más) interior; recóndito; íntimo.
inn [in], *s.* posada, mesón, fonda; venta; ***Inns of Court,*** colegios de abogados (*Londres*).
innards [ˈinədz], *s.pl.* tripas, *f.pl.*, intestinos, *m.pl.*
innate [iˈneit], *a.* innato, ingénito.
innately [iˈneitli], *adv.* de modo innato.
innateness [iˈneitnis], *s.* (lo) innato *o* ingénito.
innavigable [iˈnævigəbl], *a.* innavegable.
inner [ˈinə], *a.* interior; interno; secreto; íntimo; ***inner tube,*** cámara de aire.
innermost [ˈinəmoust], [INMOST].
innervation [inə:ˈveiʃən], *s.* inervación.
innings [ˈiniŋz], *s.* (*dep.*) turno, vez; (*fig.*) ***to have had a good innings,*** haber vivido *o* durado lo suyo.
innkeeper [ˈinki:pə], *s.* posadero, fondista, *m.f.*, mesonero; tabernero.
innocence [ˈinəsəns], *s.* inocencia.
innocent [ˈinəsənt], *a.* inocente. — *s.* inocente.
innocuous [iˈnɔkjuəs], *a.* innocuo.
innocuousness [iˈnɔkjuəsnis], *s.* innocuidad.
innominate [iˈnɔminit], *a.* innominado.
innovate [ˈinoveit], *v.t.* innovar. — *v.i.* hacer innovaciones.
innovation [inoˈveiʃən], *s.* innovación.
innovator [ˈinoveitə], *s.* innovador.
innoxious [iˈnɔkʃəs], *a.* innocuo, innocivo.
innoxiousness [iˈnɔkʃəsnis], *s.* innocuidad.
innuendo [injuˈendou], *s.* reticencia, insinuación.
innumerability, innumerableness [inju:mərəˈbiliti, iˈnju:mərəblnis], *s.* innumerabilidad.
innumerable [iˈnju:mərəbl], *a.* innumerable, innúmero.
inobservance [inəbˈzə:vəns], *s.* inobservancia.
inoculate [inˈɔkjuleit], *v.t., v.i.* inocular; vacunar.
inoculation [inɔkjuˈleiʃən], *s.* inoculación; vacuna.
inoculator [inˈɔkjuleitə], *s.* inoculador.
inodorous [inˈoudərəs], *a.* inodoro.
inoffensive [inəˈfensiv], *a.* inofensivo.
inoffensiveness [inəˈfensivnis], *s.* (lo) inofensivo.
inoperable [inˈɔpərəbl], *a.* inoperable.
inoperative [inˈɔpərətiv], *a.* inoperante.
inopportune [inˈɔpətju:n], *a.* inoportuno.
inopportuneness [inˈɔpətju:nnis], *s.* inoportunidad.
inordinate [inˈɔ:dinit], *a.* desmedido, desorbitado.
inordinateness [inˈɔ:dinitnis], *s.* (lo) desmedido.
inorganic [inɔ:ˈgænik], *a.* inorgánico.
inosculate [inˈɔskjuleit], *v.t.* unir por anastomosis. — *v.i.* anastomosarse.
inosculation [inɔskjuˈleiʃən], *s.* anastomosis, *f. inv.*
input [ˈinput], *s.* (potencia de) entrada; dinero invertido; consumo, gasto.
inquest [ˈinkwest], *s.* (*for.*) investigación *o* pesquisa judicial.
inquietude [inˈkwaiitju:d], *s.* inquietud, desasosiego.
inquire [inˈkwaiə], *v.t.* preguntar; ***inquire sth. of s.o.,*** preguntar algo a alguien. — *v.i.* preguntar; ***to inquire about,*** preguntar por; pedir informes sobre; ***to inquire after,*** preguntar por; ***inquire into,*** investigar, indagar.
inquirer [inˈkwaiərə], *s.* preguntador, preguntante; investigador; inquiridor.
inquiry [inˈkwaiəri], *s.* pregunta; encuesta; pesquisa, investigación; ***to hold a public inquiry,*** realizar una investigación oficial; ***to make inquiries,*** pedir informes.
inquisition [inkwiˈziʃən], *s.* inquisición; ***the Inquisition,*** la Inquisición.
inquisitional [inkwiˈziʃənəl], *a.* inquisitorial.
inquisitive [inˈkwizitiv], *a.* inquisitivo, curioso, preguntón.
inquisitiveness [inˈkwizitivnis], *s.* curiosidad.
inquisitor [inˈkwizitə], *s.* inquisidor; inquiridor, investigador.
inquisitorial [inkwiziˈtɔ:riəl], *a.* inquisitorial.
inroad [ˈinroud], *s.* incursión; ***to make inroads into,*** consumir una (gran) parte de.
inrush [ˈinrʌʃ], *s.* irrupción.
insalivate [inˈsæliveit], *v.t.* insalivar.
insalivation [insæliˈveiʃən], *s.* insalivación.
insalubrious [insəˈlju:briəs], *a.* insalubre.
insalubrity [insəˈlju:briti], *s.* insalubridad.
insane [inˈsein], *a.* demente.
insanitary [inˈsænitəri], *a.* antihigiénico, insano.
insanity [inˈsæniti], *s.* locura, demencia.
insatiable [inˈseiʃəbl], *a.* insaciable.
insatiableness, insatiateness [inˈseiʃəblnis, inˈseiʃiitnis], *s.* insaciabilidad.
insatiate [inˈseiʃiit], *a.* insaciable.
inscribe [inˈskraib], *v.t.* inscribir, dedicar.
inscriber [inˈskraibə], *s.* el que inscribe.
inscription [inˈskripʃən], *s.* inscripción; dedicatoria.
inscriptive [inˈskriptiv], *a.* inscrito.
inscrutability [inskru:təˈbiliti], *s.* inescrutabilidad.
inscrutable [inˈskru:təbl], *a.* inescrutable, inescudriñable.
inseam [ˈinsi:m], *s.* costura interior.
insect [ˈinsekt], *s.* insecto; bicho.
insecticide [inˈsektisaid], *s.* insecticida, *m.*
insection [inˈsekʃən], *s.* incisión.
insectivorous [insekˈtivərəs], *a.* insectívoro.
insecure [insiˈkjuə], *a.* inseguro, poco firme, poco seguro.
insecurity [insiˈkjuəriti], *s.* inseguridad.
inseminate [inˈsemineit], *v.t.* fecundar; sembrar.
insemination [inseminˈneiʃən], *s.* inseminación; fedundación.
insensate [inˈsenseit], *a.* insensato; insensible.
insensibility [insensiˈbiliti], *s.* insensibilidad; inconsciencia.
insensible [inˈsensibl], *a.* insensible; inconsciente.
insentient [inˈsenʃiənt], *a.* insensible.
inseparability, inseparableness [insepərəˈbiliti, inˈsepərəblnis], *s.* inseparabilidad.
inseparable [inˈsepərəbl], *a.* inseparable.
insert [inˈsə:t], *v.t.* insertar, intercalar; introducir.
insertion [inˈsə:ʃən], *s.* inserción, intercalación; (*cost.*) entredós, *m.*
inset [ˈinset], *s.* incrustación, cosa encajada; inserción. — [inˈset], *v.t.* incrustar, encajar; insertar.
inshore [ˈinˈʃɔ:], *a.* cercano a la orilla. — *adv.* hacia la orilla, cerca de la orilla.

inside [ˈinsaid], *a.* interior, interno; secreto, confidencial; (*fam.*) ***inside job,*** delito realizado con colaboración de los de dentro; (*dep.*) ***inside left*** (***right***), interior izquierdo (derecho). — [inˈsaid], *adv.* dentro, por dentro; adentro, hacia dentro. — [inˈsaid], *prep.* dentro de. — [inˈsaid, ˈinsaid], *s.* interior, parte de dentro; forro; contenido; (*pl.*, *fam.*) entrañas, *f.pl.*, tripas, *f.pl.*; ***on the inside,*** por dentro; (*fam.*) en el ajo; ***to know sth. inside out,*** saberse algo al dedillo; ***to turn inside out,*** volver del revés.
insidious [inˈsidiəs], *a.* insidioso.
insidiousness [inˈsidiəsnis], *s.* (lo) insidioso.
insight [ˈinsait], *s.* penetración (psicológica); perspicacia, intuición; ***to get an insight into,*** formarse una idea de.
insignia [inˈsigniə], *s. pl.* insignias, *f.pl.*
insignificance, insignificancy [insigˈnifikəns, -i], *s.* insignificancia.
insignificant [insigˈnifikənt], *a.* insignificante.
insincere [insinˈsiə], *a.* poco sincero, falso, hipócrita.
insincerity [insinˈseriti], *s.* falta de sinceridad, falsedad, hipocresía.
insinuate [inˈsinjueit], *v.t.* insinuar. — **insinuate o.s.,** *v.r.* insinuarse, introducirse.
insinuating [inˈsinjueitiŋ], *a.* insinuante, insinuador.
insinuation [insinjuˈeiʃən], *s.* insinuación.
insinuative [inˈsinjuətiv], *a.* insinuativo.
insinuator [inˈsinjueitə], *s.* insinuador.
insipid [inˈsipid], *a.* insípido, soso, insulso.
insipidity, insipidness [insiˈpiditi, inˈsipidnis], *s.* insipidez, sosería, insulsez.
insist [inˈsist], *v.i.* insistir; empeñarse; ***to insist on,*** insistir en, empeñarse en; ***to insist that,*** insistir en que, empeñarse en que.
insistence, insistency [inˈsistəns, -i], *s.* insistencia; empeño, ahinco.
insistent [inˈsistənt], *a.* insistente; porfiado.
insnare [ENSNARE].
insobriety [insoˈbraiiti], *s.* intemperancia.
insolate [ˈinsoleit], *v.t.* insolar.
insolation [insoˈleiʃən], *s.* insolación.
insole [ˈinsoul], *s.* plantilla.
insolence, insolency [ˈinsələns, -i], *s.* insolencia, descaro, desfachatez.
insolent [ˈinsələnt], *a.* insolente, descarado.
insolubility, insolubleness [insɔljuˈbiliti, inˈsɔljublnis], *s.* insolubilidad.
insoluble [inˈsɔljubl], *a.* insoluble.
insolvable [inˈsɔlvəbl], *a.* insoluble.
insolvency [inˈsɔlvənsi], *s.* insolvencia.
insolvent [inˈsɔlvənt], *a.* insolvente.
insomnia [inˈsɔmniə], *s.* insomnio.
insomnious [inˈsɔmniəs], *a.* insomne.
insomnolence [inˈsɔmnələns], *s.* falta de sueño.
insomuch [insouˈmʌtʃ], *adv.* de manera que, de suerte que; ***insomuch as,*** ya que, puesto que; por cuanto que; ***insomuch that,*** hasta el punto que.
inspect [inˈspekt], *v.t.* examinar, registrar, inspeccionar.
inspection [inˈspekʃən], *s.* inspección, registro, examen.
inspector [inˈspektə], *s.* inspector; revisor.
inspectorate [inˈspektərit], *s.* distrito, cargo *o* empleo de inspector.
insphere [inˈsfiə], *v.t.* colocar en una esfera.
inspirable [inˈspaiərəbl], *a.* inspirable.
inspiration [inspiˈreiʃən], *s.* inspiración; estro; ***to find inspiration in,*** inspirarse en.
inspiratory [inˈspaiərətəri], *a.* inspirador, inspirativo, inspiratorio.
inspire [inˈspaiə], *v.t.* inspirar; ***inspire sth. in s.o.,*** inspirar algo a alguien.
inspirer [inˈspaiərə], *s.* inspirador.
inspiring [inˈspaiəriŋ], *a.* inspirador, que inspira.
inspirit [inˈspirit], *v.t.* alentar, animar, estimular; infundir.
instability [instəˈbiliti], *s.* in(e)stabilidad; versatilidad.
install [inˈstɔːl], *v.t.* instalar; montar.
installation [instəˈleiʃən], *s.* instalación; montaje,
instalment [inˈstɔːlmənt], *s.* (*com.*) plazo; entrega; (*Am.*) ***instalment plan*** [HIRE PURCHASE].
instance [ˈinstəns], *s.* caso; ejemplo; vez, ocasión; ruego, instancia; ***at the instance of,*** a instancia de; ***for instance,*** por ejemplo; ***in the first instance,*** en primer lugar. — *v.t.* poner por caso, citar como ejemplo.
instancy [ˈinstənsi], *s.* insistencia, urgencia; instancia.
instant [ˈinstənt], *a.* inmediato, urgente; ***the fifth instant*** (o ***inst.***), el cinco del corriente (mes). — *s.* instante, momento; ***in an instant,*** en un instante; ***the instant that,*** así que, no bien, tan pronto como; ***this instant,*** al instante.
instantaneous [instənˈteiniəs], *a.* instantáneo.
instantly [ˈinstəntli], *adv.* al instante, instantáneamente, inmediatamente.
instate [inˈsteit], *v.t.* instalar.
instead [inˈsted], *adv.* en lugar de ello, en tu lugar *etc.*; ***instead of,*** en lugar de, en vez de.
instep [ˈinstep], *s.* empeine.
instigate [ˈinstigeit], *v.t.* instigar, instar.
instigation [instiˈgeiʃən], *s.* instigación; ***at the instigation of,*** a instigación de, a instancias de.
instigator [ˈinstigeitə], *s.* instigador.
instil(l) [inˈstil], *v.t.* instilar; (*fig.*) inculcar, infundir (***into,*** en, a).
instillation, instil(l)ment [instiˈleiʃən, inˈstilmənt], *s.* instilación; inculcación.
instinct [inˈstiŋkt], *a.* animado. — [ˈinstiŋkt], *s.* instinto.
instinctive [inˈstiŋktiv], *a.* instintivo.
institute [ˈinstitjuːt], *s.* instituto; (*pl.*) instituta. — *v.t.* instituir; incoar, iniciar.
institution [instiˈtjuːʃən], *s.* institución; fundación, establecimiento; iniciación; asilo; manicomio; (*fig.*) costumbre consagrada; persona muy conocida.
institutional, institutionary [instiˈtjuːʃənəl, -əri], *a.* institucional.
institutionalize [instiˈtjuːʃənəlaiz], *v.t.* reglamentar.
institutor [ˈinstitjuːtə], *s.* instituidor; fundador.
instruct [inˈstrʌkt], *v.t.* instruir; enseñar; dar instrucciones a, mandar.
instructer [INSTRUCTOR].
instructible [inˈstrʌktibl], *a.* instruible.
instruction [inˈstrʌkʃən], *s.* instrucción; ***on the instructions of,*** por orden de.
instructive [inˈstrʌktiv], *a.* instructivo.
instructiveness [inˈstrʌktivnis], *s.* (lo) instructivo.
instructor [inˈstrʌktə], *s.* instructor.
instructress [inˈstrʌktris], *s.* instructora.
instrument [ˈinstrumənt], *s.* instrumento; ***instrument panel,*** cuadro de mandos; ***negotiable instrument,*** cheque; (***set of***) ***instruments,*** instrumental; (*aer.*) ***to fly on instruments,*** volar por instrumentos. — *v.t.* (*mús.*) instrumentar.
instrumental [instruˈmentəl], *a.* instrumental; ***to be instrumental in,*** contribuir (materialmente) a, ayudar (de una manera fundamental) a.
instrumentalist [instruˈmentəlist], *s.* (*mús.*) instrumentista, *m.f.*
instrumentality [instrumenˈtæliti], *s.* agencia, mediación.
instrumentation [instrumenˈteiʃən], *s.* instrumentación.
insubordinate [insəˈbɔːdinit], *a.* insubordinado.
insubordination [insəbɔːdiˈneiʃən], *s.* insubordinación, indisciplina.

insubstantial [insəb'stænʃəl], *a.* insustancial; poco sólido; irreal.
insufferable [in'sʌfərəbl], *a.* insufrible, inaguantable.
insufficience, insufficiency [insə'fiʃəns, -i], *s.* insuficiencia.
insufficient [insə'fiʃənt], *a.* insuficiente; incapaz.
insufficiently [insə'fiʃəntli], *adv.* insuficientemente.
insufflate ['insəfleit], *v.t.* insuflar.
insufflation [insə'fleiʃən], *s.* soplo; (*med.*) insuflación.
insufflator ['insəfleitə], *s.* insuflador.
insular ['insjulə], *a.* insular; isleño; estrecho de miras, limitado.
insularity [insju'læriti], *s.* insularidad; estrechez de miras.
insulate ['insjuleit], *v.t.* aislar.
insulating ['insjuleitiŋ], *a.* aislador, aislante; ***insulating-tape,*** cinta aislante.
insulation [insju'leiʃən], *s.* aislamiento.
insulator ['insjuleitə], *s.* aislador.
insulin ['insjulin], *s.* insulina.
insult ['insʌlt], *s.* insulto; injuria; ***to add insult to injury,*** para mayor inri; ***to pocket an insult,*** encajar un insulto. — [in'sʌlt], *v.t.* insultar, injuriar.
insulter [in'sʌltə], *s.* insultador, denostador.
insulting [in'sʌltiŋ], *a.* insultante, injurioso.
insuperability, insuperableness [insju:pərə'biliti, in'sju:pərəblnis], *s.* (lo) insuperable.
insuperable [in'sju:pərəbl], *a.* insuperable.
insupportable [insə'pɔ:təbl], *a.* insoportable.
insupportableness [insə'pɔ:təblnis], *s.* (lo) insoportable.
insuppressible [insə'presibl], *a.* que no se puede suprimir.
insurable [in'ʃuərəbl], *a.* asegurable.
insurance [in'ʃuərəns], *s.* (*com.*) seguro; aseguramiento; seguros, *m.pl.*; ***accident insurance,*** seguro contra accidentes; ***endowment insurance,*** seguro dotal; ***fire insurance,*** seguro contra incendio; ***insurance agent,*** agente de seguros; ***insurance company,*** compañía de seguros; ***insurance policy,*** póliza de seguros; ***life insurance,*** seguro de vida.
insure [in'ʃuə], *v.t.* (*com.*) asegurar; afianzar, garantizar.
insurer [in'ʃuərə], *s.* asegurador.
insurgent [in'sə:dʒənt], *a., s.* insurrecto, sublevado.
insurmountable [insə'mauntəbl], *a.* insuperable, insalvable.
insurrection [insə'rekʃən], *s.* insurrección, rebelión, levantamiento.
insurrectional, insurrectionary [insə'rekʃənəl, -əri], *a.* insurreccional, rebelde.
insurrectionist [insə'rekʃənist], *s.* insurrecto.
insusceptible [insə'septibl], *a.* no susceptible, insensible.
intact [in'tækt], *a.* intacto; íntegro.
intactness [in'tæktnis], *s.* integridad.
intaglio [in'tɑ:ljou], *s.* entallo.
intake ['inteik], *s.* toma, entrada, admisión; cantidad admitida, número admitido.
intangibility, intangibleness [intændʒi'biliti, in'tændʒiblnis], *s.* (lo) intangible.
intangible [in'tændʒibl], *a.* intangible.
integer ['intidʒə], *s.* entero, número entero.
integral ['intigrəl], *a.* íntegro; integrante; integral; ***integral part,*** parte integrante. — *s.* (*mat.*) integral; ***integral calculus,*** cálculo integral.
integrate ['intigreit], *v.t.* integrar. — *v.i.* integrarse.
integration [inti'greiʃən], *s.* integración.
integrity [in'tegriti], *s.* integridad, rectitud, probidad.
integument [in'tegjumənt], *s.* integumento.
integumental, integumentary [integju'mentəl, -əri], *a.* integumentario.
intellect ['intilekt], *s.* intelecto.
intellection [inti'lekʃən], *s.* intelección.
intellective [inti'lektiv], *a.* intelectivo.
intellectual [inti'lektjuəl], *a., s.* intelectual.
intellectuality [intilektju'æliti], *s.* intelectualidad.
intelligence [in'telidʒəns], *s.* inteligencia; información, informes, *m.pl.*, noticias, *f.pl.*; ***intelligence quotient,*** cociente intelectual; ***intelligence test,*** prueba de inteligencia.
intelligent [in'telidʒənt], *a.* inteligente.
intelligentsia [inteli'dʒentsiə], *s.* intelectualidad.
intelligibility, intelligibleness [intelidʒi'biliti, in'telidʒiblnis], *s.* (lo) inteligible.
intelligible [in'telidʒibl], *a.* inteligible.
intemperance [in'tempərəns], *s.* intemperancia; inmoderación.
intemperate [in'tempərit], *a.* intemperante; inmoderado; severo.
intemperateness [in'tempəritnis], *s.* intemperancia; inmoderación; severidad.
intend [in'tend], *v.t.* pensar, proponerse; querer decir (***by***, con); destinar (***for***, para); ***intend to,*** pensar + *inf.*, tener (la) intención *o* (el) propósito de.
intendancy [in'tendənsi], *s.* intendencia.
intendant [in'tendənt], *s.* intendente.
intended [in'tendid], *s.* (*fam.*) prometido, prometida, novio, novia.
intendedly [in'tendidli], *adv.* intencionadamente.
intense [in'tens], *a.* intenso; fuerte; vivo; extremado; muy serio; vehemente; (*foto.*) duro (negativo).
intenseness [in'tensnis], *s.* intensidad; fuerza; suma seriedad; vehemencia.
intensifier [in'tensifaiə], *s.* intensificador; (*foto.*) baño para reforzar.
intensify [in'tensifai], *v.t.* intensificar; (*foto.*) reforzar (*un negativo*).
intension [in'tenʃən], *s.* intensión; (*lóg.*) contenido.
intensity [in'tensiti], *s.* intensidad, fuerza, vehemencia; (*foto.*) fuerza (*de un negativo*).
intensive [in'tensiv], *a.* intensivo; (*lóg.*) relativo al contenido; (*gram.*) enfático; ***intensive care,*** cuidados intensivos, *m.pl.*
intent [in'tent], *a.* absorto; resuelto, empeñado. — *s.* intento, propósito; ***to all intents and purposes,*** prácticamente, para todos los efectos; ***with intent to,*** con (el) propósito de.
intention [in'tenʃən], *s.* intención, propósito, finalidad; (*cir.*) ***healing by first intention,*** cura sin supuración; ***healing by second intention,*** cura por cicatrización.
intentional [in'tenʃənəl], *a.* intencionado.
intentness [in'tentnis], *s.* ahinco, porfía, empeño.
inter [in'tə:], *v.t.* sepultar.
interact ['intərækt], *s.* (*teat.*) entreacto; intermedio. — [intər'ækt], *v.i.* obrar recíprocamente.
interaction [intər'ækʃən], *s.* acción recíproca; influencia recíproca; interacción.
interarticular [intərɑ:'tikjulə], *a.* interarticular.
interbreed [intə'bri:d], *v.t.* cruzar, hibridar. — *v.i.* cruzarse, hibridar.
intercalary [in'tə:kələri], *a.* intercalar.
intercalate [in'tə:kəleit], *v.t.* intercalar, interpolar.
intercalation [intə:kə'leiʃən], *s.* intercalación, interpolación.
intercede [intə'si:d], *v.i.* interceder, mediar.
interceder [intə'si:də], *s.* intercesor.
interceding [intə'si:diŋ], *a.* intercesor.
intercept [intə'sept], *v.t.* interceptar.
interception [intə'sepʃən], *s.* interceptación.
interceptor [intə'septə], *s.* avión de caza.
intercession [intə'seʃən], *s.* intercesión, mediación.

intercessor [intə'sesə], *s.* intercesor, mediador; (*igl.*) obispo que administra una sede vacante.
intercessory [intə'sesəri], *a.*, *s.* intercesor.
interchain [intə'tʃein], *v.t.* encadenar (uno con otro).
interchange ['intətʃeindʒ], *s.* intercambio; (*prisioneros*) canje. — [intə'tʃeindʒ], *v.t.* intercambiar; alternar; (*prisioneros*) canjear. — *v.i.* intercambiarse; alternar.
interchangeability, interchangeableness ['intətʃeindʒə'biliti, intə'tʃeindʒəblnis], *s.* (lo) intercambiable.
interchangeable [intə'tʃeindʒəbl], *a.* intercambiable.
intercolumnar [intəkə'lʌmnə], *a.* intercolumnar.
intercolumniation [intəkəlʌmni'eiʃən], *s.* intercolumnio.
intercom ['intəkɔm], *s.* (*abrev. fam.*) sistema *o* aparato de intercomunicación.
intercommunicate [intəkə'mju:nikeit], *v.i.* comunicarse, intercomunicarse.
intercommunication [intəkəmju:ni'keiʃən], *s.* intercomunicación.
interconnect [intəkə'nekt], *v.t.* interconectar.
intercontinental [intəkɔnti'nentəl], *a.* intercontinental; ***intercontinental ballistic missile,*** proyectil balístico intercontinental.
intercostal [intə'kɔstəl], *a.* intercostal.
intercourse ['intəkɔ:s], *s.* comercio; trato; intercambio; ***sexual intercourse,*** trato sexual; ***social intercourse,*** trato social.
intercross [intə'krɔs], *v.t.* entrecruzar; hibridar, cruzar (castas). — *v.i.* entrecruzarse.
intercrossing [intə'krɔsiŋ], *s.* cruzamiento.
intercurrent [intə'kʌrənt], *a.* intercurrente.
intercutaneous [intekju:'teiniəs], *a.* intercutáneo.
interdenominational [intədinɔmi'neiʃənəl], *a.* interconfesional.
interdependence [intədi'pendəns], *s.* interdependencia.
interdependent [intədi'pendənt], *a.* interdependiente.
interdict ['intədikt], *s.* interdicto, entredicho; ***to place under an interdict,*** poner en entredicho. — [intə'dikt], *v.t.* interdecir, entredecir.
interdiction [intə'dikʃən], *s.* interdicción.
interdigital [intə'didʒitəl], *a.* interdigital.
interest ['intərest], *s.* interés; rédito; participación; ***to bear interest,*** devengar intereses; ***compound interest,*** interés compuesto; ***in the interest of,*** en interés de; ***to be of interest to,*** interesar, ser interesante para; ***to put out at interest,*** poner a interés *o* a rédito; ***rate of interest, interest rate,*** tipo de interés; ***to repay with interest,*** devolver con creces; ***simple interest,*** interés simple; ***to take an interest in,*** interesarse en *o* por. — *v.t.* interesar; ***to be interested in,*** interesarse en *o* por.
interesting ['intərestiŋ], *a.* interesante.
interfere [intə'fiə], *v.i.* — ***in,*** entrometerse, meterse, ingerirse, inmiscuirse, intervenir (en); ***interfere with,*** estorbar, obstaculizar; meterse con; interferir; (*fam.*) meter mano a.
interference [intə'fiərəns], *s.* entrometimiento, ingerencia(s), intervención; estorbo(s), obstáculo(s); interferencia(s); (*rad.*) parásitos.
interfering [intə'fiəriŋ], *a.* entremetido. — *s.* (el) entrometerse, *etc.*
interfuse [intə'fju:z], *v.t.* mezclar. — *v.i.* mezclarse.
interfusion [intə'fju:ʒən], *s.* mezcla, combinación.
interim ['intərim], *a.* interino, provisional. — *s.* intermedio, ínterin; ***in the interim,*** entre tanto, en el ínterin.
interior [in'tiəriə], *a.* interior, interno. — *s.* interior.
interjacent [intə'dʒeisənt], *a.* interyacente, interpuesto.
interject [intə'dʒekt], *v.t.* interponer, poner en medio, insertar. — *v.i.* interponerse, intervenir.
interjection [intə'dʒekʃən], *s.* (*gram.*) interjección; intervención, interposición; exclamación.
interjoin [intə'dʒɔin], *v.t.* unir mutuamente.
interlace [intə'leis], *v.t.*, *v.i.* entrelazar(se), entremezclar(se).
interlard [intə'lɑ:d], *v.t.* (*coc.*) mechar; entremezclar, entreverar.
interleave [intə'li:v], *v.t.* interfoliar, interpaginar, interpolar.
interline [intə'lain], *v.t.* interlinear, entrerrenglonar; (*cost.*) entretelar.
interlinear [intə'liniə], *a.* interlineal.
interlineation [intəlini'eiʃən], *s.* interlineación, entrerrenglonadura, corrección, interlineal.
interlining [intə'lainiŋ], *s.* (*cost.*) entretela.
interlink [intə'liŋk], *v.t.* eslabonar, encadenar.
interlock [intə'lɔk], *v.t.* trabar, engargantar, engranar. — *v.i.* entrelazarse, unirse.
interlocution [intəlo'kju:ʃən], *s.* interlocución, diálogo, plática.
interlocutor [intə'lɔkjutə], *s.* interlocutor.
interlocutory [intə'lɔkjutəri], *a.* dialogístico; interlocutorio.
interlope [intə'loup], *v.i.* entrometerse; ser intruso; traficar sin licencia.
interloper ['intəloupə], *s.* entrometido, intruso; (*com.*) intérlope.
interlude ['intəl(j)u:d], *s.* intermedio; descanso; entremés, *m.*; sainete; (*mús.*) interludio.
interlunar(y) [intə'lu:nə(ri)], *a.* interlunar.
intermarriage [intə'mæridʒ], *s.* matrimonio *o* casamiento de personas de distintas razas; matrimonio entre parientes.
intermarry [intə'mæri], *v.i.* casarse (*parientes* o *personas de distintas razas*).
intermeddle [intə'medl], *v.i.* entrometerse, inmiscuirse, ingerirse, mezclarse, meterse.
intermeddler [intə'medlə], *s.* entrometido.
intermediary [intə'mi:diəri], *a.*, *s.* intermediario; intermedio.
intermediate [intə'mi:diit], *a.* intermedio; medio. — [intə'mi:dieit], *v.i.* intervenir, mediar.
intermediately [intə'mi:diitli], *adv.* por intervención.
intermediation [intəmi:di'eiʃən], *s.* intervención, mediación.
intermedium [intə'mi:diəm], *s.* intermediario, intermedio; agente intermedio.
interment [in'tə:mənt], *s.* sepultura.
interminable [in'tə:minəbl], *a.* interminable, inacabable.
intermingle [intə'miŋgl], *v.t.* entremezclar. — *v.i.* entremezclarse.
intermission [intə'miʃən], *s.* intermisión; intermitencia; pausa, tregua; entreacto, descanso; (*Am., teat.*) [INTERVAL].
intermit [intə'mit], *v.t.* intermitir. — *v.i.* interrumpirse.
intermittent [intə'mitənt], *a.* intermitente.
intermittently [intə'mitəntli], *adv.* con intermisión, a intervalos.
intermix [intə'miks], *v.t.* entremezclar. — *v.i.* entremezclarse.
intermixture [intə'mikstʃə], *s.* entremezcladura, mezcla.
intermural [intə'mjuərəl], *a.* entremural.
intern ['intə:n], *s.* (*med.*) interno (*de hospital*). — [in'tə:n], *v.t.* recluir, internar.
internal [in'tə:nəl], *a.* interno; interior; ***internal combustion engine,*** motor de combustión interna *o* de explosión.
international [intə'næʃənəl], *a.* internacional; ***international date line,*** línea internacional de cambio de fecha; ***international law,*** derecho internacional *o* derecho de gentes. — *s.* Internacional, *f.*

internationalist [intəˈnæʃənəlist], *a.*, *s.* internacionalista, *m.f.*
internationalize [intəˈnæʃənəlaiz], *v.t.* internacionalizar.
internecine [intəˈni:sain], *a.* de exterminio mutuo.
internee [intə:ˈni:], *s.* internado, -da.
internment [inˈtə:nmənt], *s.* reclusión, internamiento.
internode [ˈintənoud], *s.* internodio.
internuncio [intəˈnʌnsiou], *s.* internuncio.
interosseous [intərˈɔsiəs], *a.* interóseo.
interpellate [inˈtə:peleit], *v.t.* interpelar.
interpellation [intə:peˈleiʃən], *s.* interpelación.
interpenetrate [intəˈpenitreit], *v.t.* penetrar completamente. — *v.i.* compenetrarse.
interplanetary [intəˈplænitəri], *a.* interplanetario.
interplay [ˈintəplei], *s.* interacción.
interpolate [inˈtə:poleit], *v.t.* interpolar.
interpolation [intə:poˈleiʃən], *s.* interpolación.
interpolator [inˈtə:poleitə], *s.* interpolador.
interpose [intəˈpouz], *v.t.* interponer. — *v.i.* interponerse, intervenir, mediar, intermediar.
interposition [intə:pəˈziʃən], *s.* interposición, mediación, intervención.
interpret [inˈtə:prit], *v.t.* interpretar.
interpretable [inˈtə:pritəbl], *a.* interpretable.
interpretation [intə:priˈteiʃən], *s.* interpretación.
interpretative [inˈtə:pritətiv], *a.* interpretativo.
interpreter [inˈtə:pritə], *s.* intérprete; interpretador.
interregnum [intəˈregnəm], *s.* interregno.
interrogate [inˈterogeit], *v.t.* interrogar. — *v.i.* hacer preguntas.
interrogation [interoˈgeiʃən], *s.* interrogatorio; interrogación; (*impr.*) ***mark*** o ***point of interrogation,*** interrogación, signo *o* punto de interrogación.
interrogative [intəˈrɔgətiv], *a.* interrogativo. — *s.* palabra interrogativa.
interrogator [inˈterogeitə], *s.* interrogador, preguntador.
interrogatory [intəˈrɔgətəri], *a.* interrogativo, interrogante.
interrupt [intəˈrʌpt], *v.t.* interrumpir.
interruptedly [intəˈrʌptidli], *adv.* interrumpidamente.
interrupter [intəˈrʌptə], *s.* interruptor; (*elec.*) interruptor.
interruption [intəˈrʌpʃən], *s.* interrupción.
interscapular [intəˈskæpjulə], *a.* interescapular.
intersecant [intəˈsi:kənt], *a.* cortante, separante.
intersect [intəˈsekt], *v.t.* cortar. — *v.i.* cruzarse, entrecortarse; intersecarse.
intersection [intəˈsekʃən], *s.* intersección; cruce.
interspace [ˈintəˈspeis], *s.* intervalo, espacio medio, intersticio.
intersperse [intəˈspə:s], *v.t.* esparcir, entremezclar; salpicar (***with,*** de).
interspersion [intəˈspə:ʃən], *s.* esparcimiento (*de una cosa entre otras*).
interspinal [intəˈspainəl], *a.* interespinal; interespinoso.
interstate [ˈintəsteit], *a.* interestatal.
interstellar [intəˈstelə], *a.* interestelar, intersideral.
interstice [inˈtə:stis], *s.* intersticio.
interstitial [intəˈstiʃəl], *a.* que tiene intersticios.
intertexture [intəˈtekstʃə], *s.* entretejido, entretejimiento, entretejedura.
intertropical [intəˈtrɔpikəl], *a.* intertropical.
intertwine, intertwist [intəˈtwain, -ˈtwist], *v.t.* entretejer, entrelazar; (*mar.*) acolchar.
interval [ˈintəvəl], *s.* intervalo; descanso; entreacto; pausa; ***at infrequent intervals,*** de tarde en tarde.
intervene [intəˈvi:n], *v.i.* mediar; interponerse; sobrevenir.
intervening [intəˈvi:niŋ], *a.* intermedio, que media.
intervention [intəˈvenʃən], *s.* intervención; ingerencia.
intervertebral [intəˈvə:tibrəl], *a.* intervertebral.
interview [ˈintəvju:], *s.* entrevista; interviú. — *v.t.* entrevistar, hacer una entrevista a; interviuar; ***to have an interview with,*** entrevistarse con.
interviewer [ˈintəvju:ə], *s.* el que entrevista *o* hace entrevistas; interviuador.
interweave [intəˈwi:v]. *irr. v.t.*, *v.i.* entretejer.
interweaving [intəˈwi:viŋ], *s.* entretejimiento.
interzonal [intəˈzounəl], *a.* interzonal.
intestacy [inˈtestəsi], *s.* falta de testamento.
intestate [inˈtestit], *a.* intestado.
intestinal [inˈtestinəl], *a.* intestinal.
intestine [inˈtestin], *a.* intestino. — *s.* intestino; (*pl.*) intestinos, *m.pl.*, tripas, *f.pl.*; ***large intestine,*** intestino grueso; ***small intestine,*** intestino delgado.
intimacy [ˈintiməsi], *s.* intimidad; trato sexual.
intimate [ˈintimit], *a.* íntimo; estrecho; profundo; ***to become intimate with,*** intimar con. — *s.* amigo íntimo *o* de confianza. — [ˈintimeit], *v.t.* insinuar, dar a entender; intimar, hacer saber.
intimation [intiˈmeiʃən], *s.* insinuación; intimación; indicio.
intimidate [inˈtimideit], *v.t.* intimidar, amedrentar.
intimidation [intimiˈdeiʃən], *s.* intimidación.
intimidating [inˈtimideitiŋ], *a.* intimidador, conminatorio, amenazador; ***intimidating prospect,*** perspectiva terrible, que da espanto.
into [ˈintu], *prep.* a, hacia (el interior de); en, dentro de.
intolerability, intolerableness [intɔlərəˈbiliti, inˈtɔlərəblnis], *s.* intolerabilidad, (lo) intolerable.
intolerable [inˈtɔlərəbl], *a.* intolerable, insoportable, insufrible, inaguantable.
intolerance [inˈtɔlərəns], *s.* intolerancia, intransigencia.
intolerant [inˈtɔlərənt], *a.* intolerante, falto de tolerancia, intransigente.
intolerantly [inˈtɔlərəntli], *adv.* con intolerancia.
intoleration [intɔləˈreiʃən], *s.* intolerantismo.
intomb [ENTOMB].
intonate [ˈintoneit], *v.i.* entonar.
intonation [intoˈneiʃən], *s.* entonación.
intone [inˈtoun], *v.t.*, *v.i.* entonar; salmodiar.
intoxicant [inˈtɔksikənt], *a.* embriagador. — *s.* bebida alcohólica.
intoxicate [inˈtɔksikeit], *v.t.* embriagar; (*med.*) intoxicar.
intoxication [intɔksiˈkeiʃən], *s.* embriaguez; (*med.*) intoxicación.
intractability, intractableness [intræktəˈbiliti, inˈtræktəblnis], *s.* indocilidad; (lo) insoluble.
intractable [inˈtræktəbl], *a.* indócil; insoluble.
intrados [inˈtreidɔs], *s.* intradós, *m.*
intramural [intrəˈmjuərəl], *a.* intramuros.
intransient [inˈtrɑ:nsiənt], *a.* inmutable, permanente.
intransigence [inˈtrænsidʒəns], *s.* intransigencia.
intransigent [inˈtrænsidʒənt], *a.* intransigente.
intransitive [inˈtrænsitiv], *a.* intransitivo.
intransmutability [intrænsmju:təˈbiliti], *s.* intransmutabilidad.
intransmutable [intrænsˈmju:təbl], *a.* intransmutable.
intravenous [intrəˈvi:nəs], *a.* intravenoso.
intrench [ENTRENCH].
intrepid [inˈtrepid], *a.* intrépido, denodado.
intrepidity [intriˈpiditi], *s.* intrepidez, denuedo.
intricacy, intricateness [ˈintrikəsi, -itnis], *s.* intrincación, (lo) intrincado, (lo) complejo, (lo) complicado.
intricate [ˈintrikit], *a.* intrincado, complicado.

intrigue [in'tri:g], *s.* intriga(s); embrollo; enredo (*de comedia*); galanteo, intriga amorosa. — *v.t.* intrigar. — *v.i.* intrigar; tener intrigas.
intriguer [in'tri:gə], *s.* intrigante; embrollador, entrometido.
intriguing [in'tri:giŋ], *a.* intrigante; enredador; (*fam.*) atrayente, fascinador.
intrinsic(al) [in'trinsik(əl)], *a.* intrínseco.
intrinsicalness [in'trinsikəlnis], *s.* valor *o* mérito intrínseco.
introduce [intro'dju:s], *v.t.* introducir, insertar, meter; presentar.
introducer [intro'dju:sə], *s.* introductor; presentador.
introduction [intro'dʌkʃən], *s.* introducción; presentación; ***letter of introduction,*** carta de presentación.
introductive [intro'dʌktiv], *a.* introductivo.
introductor [intro'dʌktə], *s.* introductor.
introductory [intro'dʌktəri], *a.* preliminar, introductivo, proemial.
introgression [intro'greʃən], *s.* ingreso.
introit ['introit], *s.* introito.
intromission [intro'miʃən], *s.* introducción, admisión, iniciación.
introspection [intro'spekʃən], *s.* introspección.
introspective [intro'spektiv], *a.* introspectivo; ***to be very introspective,*** ser muy llamado al interior.
introversion [intro'və:ʃən], *s.* introversión.
introvert ['introvə:t], *a.*, *s.* introvertido.
introverted [intro'və:tid], *a.* introvertido.
intrude [in'tru:d], *v.t.* introducir; imponer. — *v.i.* meterse (indebidamente), intrusarse; pegarse (***upon,*** a); estorbar, molestar; ***am I intruding?*** ¿estorbo? ¿molesto?
intruder [in'tru:də], *s.* intruso.
intrusion [in'tru:ʒən], *s.* intrusión.
intrusive [in'tru:siv], *a.* intruso.
intrusiveness [in'tru:sivnis], *s.* (lo) intruso.
intrust [ENTRUST].
intuition [intju'iʃən], *s.* intuición.
intuitive [in'tju:itiv], *a.* intuitivo.
intumesce [intju'mes], *v.i.* entumecerse.
intumescence, intumescency [intju'mesəns, -i], *s.* entumecimiento, intumescencia.
intumescent [intju'mesənt], *a.* intumescente.
inula ['injulə], *s.* (*bot.*) énula campana.
inulin ['injulin], *s.* inulina.
inundate ['inʌndeit], *v.t.* inundar; abrumar.
inundation [inʌn'deiʃən], *s.* inundación; (*fig.*) avalancha.
inure [i'njuə], *v.t.* avezar, habituar, acostumbrar.
inured [i'njuəd], *a.* avezado, hecho (***to,*** a).
inurement [i'njuəmənt], *s.* costumbre, (el) estar avezado.
inutility [inju'tiliti], *s.* inutilidad.
invade [in'veid], *v.t.* invadir; usurpar.
invader [in'veidə], *s.* invasor; usurpador.
invading [in'veidiŋ], *a.* invasor.
invaginate [in'vædʒineit], *v.t.* invaginar.
invagination [invædʒi'neiʃən], *s.* invaginación.
invalid [in'vælid], *a.* inválido, nulo. — ['invəlid], *s.* enfermo, inválido; ***invalid chair,*** sillón para inválido(s). — ['invəli:d], *v.t.* matricular en el registro de inválidos; ***invalid out of the army,*** licenciar por invalidez.
invalidate [in'vælideit], *v.t.* invalidar.
invalidation [invæli'deiʃən], *s.* invalidación.
invalidism ['invəli:dizəm], *s.* invalidez crónica.
invalidity, invalidness [invə'liditi, in'vælidnis], *s.* invalidez; (*for.*) nulidad, inhabilitación.
invaluable [in'væljuəbl], *a.* inestimable, inapreciable.
invariability, invariableness [invɛəriə'biliti, in'vɛəriəblnis], *a.* invariabilidad.
invariable [in'vɛəriəbl], *a.* invariable.
invasion [in'veiʒən], *s.* invasión; violación.
invasive [in'veisiv], *a.* invasor.
invective [in'vektiv], *a.* ofensivo, injurioso. — *s.* invectiva(s), improperio(s).
inveigh [in'vei], *v.i.* — ***against,*** invectivar, pronunciarse vehementemente contra.
inveigher [in'veiə], *s.* declamador, ultrajador.
inveigle [in'vi:gl], *v.t.* engatusar; ***inveigle into,*** engatusar para que, inducir a.
inveiglement [in'vi:glmənt], *s.* embaimiento.
inveigler [in'vi:glə], *s.* engatusador.
invent [in'vent], *v.t.* inventar; idear; inventarse.
invention [in'venʃən], *s.* invención; invento.
inventive [in'ventiv], *a.* inventivo, ingenioso.
inventiveness [in'ventivnis], *s.* inventiva.
inventor [in'ventə], *s.* inventor.
inventorial [invən'tɔ:riəl], *a.* perteneciente al inventario.
inventory ['invəntəri], *s.* inventario. — *v.t.* inventariar.
inventress [in'ventris], *s.* inventora.
Inverness [invə'nes], *s.* macferlán.
inverse ['in'və:s], *a.* inverso, invertido.
inversion [in'və:ʃən], *s.* inversión.
invert ['invə:t], *s.* invertido. — [in'və:t], *v.t.* invertir.
invertebrate [in'və:tibrit], *a.*, *s.* invertebrado.
inverted [in'və:tid], *a.* invertido; ***in inverted commas,*** entre comillas.
invest [in'vest], *v.t.* (*com.*) invertir; investir, dar, conferir; (*mil.*) sitiar, cercar.
investigable [in'vestigəbl], *a.* investigable.
investigate [in'vestigeit], *v.t.* investigar, indagar.
investigation [investi'geiʃən], *s.* investigación, indagación.
investigative [in'vestigeitiv], *a.* investigador.
investigator [in'vestigeitə], *s.* investigador, indagador.
investiture [in'vestitʃə], *s.* investidura; instalación.
investment [in'vestmənt], *s.* (*com.*) inversión; investidura, instalación; (*mil.*) sitio, cerco; (*pl.*, *com.*) inversiones, *f.pl.*, valores en cartera, *m.pl.*; ***investment trust,*** compañía inversionista.
investor [in'vestə], *s.* inversionista, *m.f.*
inveteracy, inveterateness [in'vetərəsi, -ritnis], *s.* (lo) inveterado.
inveterate [in'vetərit], *a.* inveterado; habitual; empedernido.
invidious [in'vidiəs], *a.* aborrecible, detestable, odioso; injusto, imparcial.
invidiousness [in'vidiəsnis], *s.* (lo) odioso; (lo) injusto.
invigilate [in'vidʒileit], *v.i.* vigilar (*durante un examen*).
invigorate [in'vigəreit], *v.t.* vigorizar, fortificar, tonificar.
invigorating [in'vigəreitiŋ], *a.* vigorizador, tonificante, reconfortante.
invigoration [invigə'reiʃən], *s.* vigorización, tonificación.
invincibility, invincibleness [invinsi'biliti, in'vinsiblnis], *s.* (lo) invencible.
invincible [in'vinsibl], *a.* invencible.
inviolability, inviolableness [invaiələ'biliti, in'vaiələblnis], *s.* inviolabilidad.
inviolable [in'vaiələbl], *a.* inviolable.
inviolate [in'vaiəlit], *a.* inviolado; inviolable.
invisibility, invisibleness [invizi'biliti, in'viziblnis], *s.* invisibilidad.
invisible [in'vizibl], *a.* invisible; ***invisible ink,*** tinta simpática.
invitation [invi'teiʃən], *s.* invitación; convite.
invitatory [in'vaitətəri], *a.* invitador.
invite [in'vait], *v.t.* invitar; convidar.

inviter [in'vaitə], *s.* invitador; convidador.
inviting [in'vaitiŋ], *a.* seductor, atrayente; incitante, provocativo; apetitoso.
invitingness [in'vaitiŋnis], *s.* (lo) seductor.
invocation [invo'keiʃən], *s.* invocación; evocación.
invoice ['invɔis], *s.* factura. — *v.t.* facturar.
invoke [in'vouk], *v.t.* invocar; evocar.
involucral [invə'l(j)u:krəl], *a.* involucral.
involucrate [invə'l(j)u:krit], *a.* involucrado.
involucre, involucrum [invə'l(j)u:kə, -rəm], *s.* (*bot.*) involucro.
involuntariness [in'vɔləntərinis], *s.* (lo) involuntario.
involuntary [in'vɔləntəri], *a.* involuntario.
involute ['invəl(j)u:t], *a.* intrincado; enrollado en espiral; vuelto hacia dentro. — *s.* involuta.
involution [invə'l(j)u:ʃən], *s.* intrincación; involución; elevación a potencias.
involve [in'vɔlv], *v.t.* enredar, enmarañar; complicar, comprometer; implicar, comportar, suponer; ***to get involved in,*** meterse en, verse embrollado, metido *o* envuelto en; ***to get involved with s.o.,*** liarse con alguien.
involved [in'vɔlvd], *a.* intrincado, complicado, complejo.
involvement [in'vɔlvmənt], *s.* envolvimiento; apuro; enredo; complicación.
invulnerability, invulnerableness [invʌlnərə'biliti, in'vʌlnərəblnis], *s.* invulnerabilidad.
invulnerable [in'vʌlnərəbl], *a.* invulnerable.
inward ['inwəd], *a.* interior, interno. — *adv.* [INWARDS].
inwardly ['inwədli], *adv.* para sí; [INWARDS].
inwardness ['inwədnis], *s.* (lo) poco comunicativo.
inwards ['inwədz], *adv.* hacia dentro, para dentro; interiormente.
inweave ['in'wi:v], *v.t.* entretejer, enlazar.
inwrought ['in'rɔ:t], *a.* labrado, incrustado, embutido.
iodic [ai'ɔdik], *a.* yodado.
iodide ['aiodaid], *s.* yoduro.
iodine ['aiodi:n], *s.* yodo.
iodism ['aiodizəm], *s.* yodismo.
iodize ['aiodaiz], *v.t.* yodurar.
iodoform [ai'oudofɔ:m], *s.* yodoformo.
ion ['aiən], *s.* ion.
Ionic [ai'ɔnik], *a.* jónico.
iota [ai'outə], *s.* iota; ápice, pizca.
ipecac, ipecacuanha ['ipikæk, ipikækju'ɑ:nə], *s.* ipecacuana.
ipomœa [ipo'mi:ə], *s.* ipomea.
Iran [i'rɑ:n]. (el) Irán.
Iranian [i'reiniən], *a., s.* iranio, iraní.
Iraq [i'rɑ:k]. (el) Irak.
Iraqi [i'rɑ:ki], *a., s.* iraquí.
irascibility, irascibleness [iræsi'biliti, i'ræsiblnis], *s.* irascibilidad.
irascible [i'ræsibl], *a.* irascible.
irate [ai'reit], *a.* encolerizado, airado.
ire [aiə], *s.* ira, iracundia.
ireful ['aiəful], *a.* iracundo.
Ireland ['aiələnd]. Irlanda.
iridaceous [iri'deiʃəs], *a.* irideo.
iridesce [iri'des], *v.i.* irisar.
iridescence [iri'desəns], *s.* irisación, tornasol.
iridescent [iri'desənt], *a.* iridescente, irisado, tornasolado.
iridium [i'ridiəm], *s.* iridio.
iris ['aiəris], *s.* (*anat., ópt.*) iris, *m.*; (*bot.*) flor de lis, *f.*
Irish ['aiəriʃ], *a.* irlandés. — *s.* irlandés (*idioma*); ***the Irish,*** los irlandeses *o* el pueblo irlandés.
Irishism [aiəriʃizəm], *s.* locución irlandesa.
Irishman ['aiəriʃmən], *s.* irlandés.
Irishwoman ['aiəriʃwumən], *s.* irlandesa.
iritis [aiə'raitis], *s.* iritis, *f. inv.*

irk [ə:k], *v.t. impers.* fastidiar, encocorar.
irksome ['ə:ksəm], *a.* fastidioso, molesto, cargante.
irksomeness ['ə:ksəmnis], *s.* molestia, fastidio.
iron ['aiən], *a.* de hierro, férreo; ***iron age,*** edad del hierro; ***to have an iron constitution,*** tener (una) complexión de hierro; ***iron-curtain,*** telón de acero; ***iron-foundry,*** fundición de hierro; ***iron-hearted,*** duro, inflexible; rígido; ***iron lung,*** pulmón de acero; ***iron-mould,*** mancha de orín, de hierro; ***iron-ore,*** mineral de hierro; ***iron rations,*** ración mínima *o* superbásica; ***iron-worker,*** herrero. — *s.* hierro; plancha; (*pl.*) hierros, *m.pl.*, grilletes, *m.pl.*; ***bar iron,*** hierro en barras; ***cast iron,*** hierro colado; ***iron-bound,*** zunchado con hierro; férreo, inflexible; ***sheet iron,*** hierro en planchas; ***smoothing iron,*** plancha; ***to have too many irons in the fire,*** tener demasiados asuntos entre manos; ***to put*** o ***throw into irons,*** echar grillos a; ***to strike while the iron is hot,*** a hierro candente, batir de repente. — *v.t.* planchar; aherrojar; herrar; ***iron out,*** allanar; (*fig.*) solucionar. — *v.i.* planchar.
ironclad ['aiənklæd], *a., s.* acorazado.
ironer ['aiənə], *s.* planchadora.
ironic(al) [ai'rɔnik(əl)], *a.* irónico.
ironing ['aiəniŋ], *s.* planchado; ***ironing board,*** tabla de planchar.
ironmonger ['aiənmʌŋgə], *s.* ferretero; quincallero; ***ironmonger's shop,*** ferretería.
ironmongery ['aiənmʌŋgəri], *s.* ferretería, quincallería.
ironside ['aiənsaid], *s.* acorazado.
ironware ['aiənwɛə], *s.* (*artículos de*) ferretería.
ironwood ['aiənwud], *s.* madera de hierro; palo de hierro.
ironwork ['aiənwə:k], *s.* herraje(s); (*pl.*) herrería.
ironwort ['aiənwə:t], *s.* siderita.
irony ['aiərəni], *s.* ironía.
Iroquois ['irəkwɔi], *s.* (*pl.* **Iroquois** [-kwɔiz]) iroqués.
irradiance, irradiancy [i'reidiəns, -i], *s.* irradiación; luminosidad.
irradiate [i'reidieit], *v.t.* irradiar; iluminar; derramar. — *v.i.* lucir, brillar.
irradiation [ireidi'eiʃən], *s.* irradiación; esplendor, brillo.
irrational [i'ræʃənəl], *a.* irracional.
irrationality [iræʃə'næliti], *s.* irracionalidad.
irreclaimable [iri'kleiməbl], *a.* irrecuperable; irredimible, incorregible.
irreconcilable [irəkon'sailəbl], *a.* irreconciliable; intransigente.
irreconcilableness [irekən'sailəblnis], *s.* (lo) irreconciliable.
irrecoverable [iri'kʌvərəbl], *a.* irrecuperable; incobrable.
irrecuperable [iri'kju:pərəbl], *a.* irrecuperable.
irredeemable [iri'di:məbl], *a.* irredimible; no reembolsable.
irreducible [iri'dju:sibl], *a.* irreducible.
irrefragable [i'refrəgəbl], *a.* irrefragable.
irrefutable [i'refjutəbl], *a.* irrefutable, irrecusable.
irregular [i'regjulə], *a.* irregular; no previsto por el reglamento, que no se conforma con los cánones, que no se ajusta a las normas. — *s.* (*mil.*) irregular, guerrillero.
irregularity [iregju'læriti], *s.* irregularidad; anomalía; chanchullo.
irrelative [i'relətiv], *a.* inconexo.
irrelevance [i'relevəns], *s.* inconexión; impertinencia; inaplicabilidad.
irrelevant [i'reləvənt], *a.* inaplicable, no pertinente, fuera de propósito; ***to be irrelevant to,*** no hacer al caso de, no tener nada que ver con.
irrelevantly [i'reləvəntli], *adv.* fuera de propósito.
irrelievable [iri'li:vəbl], *a.* irremediable, irreparable.
irreligious [iri'lidʒəs], *a.* irreligioso, impío.

irremediable [iri'mi:diəbl], *a.* irremediable, irreparable.
irremediableness [iri'mi:diəblnis], *s.* (lo) irremediable.
irremissible [iri'misibl], *a.* irremisible.
irremissibleness [iri'misiblnis], *s.* (lo) irremisible.
irremovable [iri'mu:vəbl], *a.* inamovible; inmutable.
irreparability [irepərə'biliti], *s.* (lo) irreparable.
irreparable [i'repərəbl], *a.* irreparable.
irrepealable [iri'pi:ləbl], *a.* inabrogable, irrevocable.
irreplaceable [iri'pleisəbl], *a.* irreemplazable, insustituible.
irreprehensible [irepri'hensibl], *a.* irreprensible.
irrepressible [iri'presibl], *a.* irreprimible, incontenible, irrefrenable; indomable.
irreproachable [iri'proutʃəbl], *a.* intachable, irreprochable.
irreprovable [iri'pru:vəbl], *a.* irreprensible, irreprochable.
irresistance [iri'zistəns], *s.* pasividad, paciencia.
irresistibility, irresistibleness [irizisti'biliti, iri'zistiblnis], *s.* fuerza *o* poder irresistible.
irresistible [iri'zistibl], *a.* irresistible.
irresoluble [i'rezəljubl], *a.* irresoluble.
irresolubleness [i'rezəljublnis], *s.* calidad de irresoluble.
irresolute [i'rezəl(j)u:t], *a.* irresoluto, indeciso.
irresoluteness [i'rezəl(j)u:tnis], *s.* irresolución.
irresolution [irezə'l(j)u:ʃən], *s.* irresolución, indecisión.
irresolvable [iri'zɔlvəbl], *a.* insoluble.
irrespective [iri'spektiv], *a.* ***irrespective of,*** prescindiendo de, independiente(mente) de.
irresponsibility [irispɔnsi'biliti], *s.* irresponsabilidad.
irresponsible [iri'spɔnsibl], *a.* irresponsable.
irresponsive [iri'spɔnsiv], *a.* que no responde.
irretentive [iri'tentiv], *a.* que no retiene.
irretraceable [iri'treisəbl], *a.* que no se puede desandar.
irretrievable [iri'tri:vəbl], *a.* irrecuperable.
irreverence [i'revərəns], *s.* irreverencia.
irreverent [i'revərənt], *a.* irreverente.
irreversibility, irreversibleness [irivə:si'biliti, iri'və:siblnis], *s.* irreversibilidad, irrevocabilidad.
irreversible [iri'və:sibl], *a.* irreversible, irrevocable.
irrevocability, irrevocableness [irevəkə'biliti, i'revəkəblnis], *s.* irrevocabilidad.
irrevocable [i'revəkəbl], *a.* irrevocable, inabrogable.
irrigable ['irigəbl], *a.* regadizo.
irrigate ['irigeit], *v.t.* regar; (*med.*) irrigar.
irrigation [iri'geiʃən], *s.* riego; (*med.*) irrigación; ***irrigation channel,*** acequia, canal de riego.
irrigator ['irigeitə], *s.* carro de riego; (*med.*) irrigador.
irritability, irritableness [iritə'biliti, 'iritəblnis], *s.* irritabilidad; mal humor.
irritable ['iritəbl], *a.* irritable; que tiene mal humor.
irritant ['iritənt], *a.*. *s.* irritante.
irritate ['iriteit], *v.t.* poner de mal humor; fastidiar, molestar; (*fam.*) picar.
irritating ['iriteitiŋ], *a.* irritador, irritante; que pone de mal humor, exasperante; fastidioso, molesto.
irritation [iri'teiʃən], *s.* irritación; mal humor; fastidio; (*fam.*) comezón, picazón, cosa que pica.
irritative, irritatory ['iriteitiv, -əri], *a.* irritador, irritante.
irruption [i'rʌpʃən], *s.* irrupción.
irruptive [i'rʌptiv], *a.* irruptor.
ischiatic [iski'ætik], *a.* isquiático.
ischium ['iskiəm], *s.* isquión.
Ishmaelite ['iʃmeiəlait], *s.* ismaelita, *m.f.*
isinglass ['aiziŋglɑ:s], *s.* colapez, cola de pescado.
Islam ['izlɑ:m], *s.* islam, islamismo.
Islamic [iz'læmik], *a.* islámico.
Islamism ['izləmizəm] [ISLAM].
island ['ailənd], *a.* isleño. — *s.* isla; (*circulación*) refugio.
islander ['ailəndə], *s.* isleño.
isle [ail], *s.* isla.
Isle of Man [ail əv mæn]. Isla de Man.
islet ['ailit], *s.* isleta; (*despec.*) islote.
ism ['izəm], *s.* ismo.
isobar ['aisoubɑ:], *s.* isobaro; isobara.
isobaric [aisou'bærik], *a.* isobárico.
isochromatic [aisoukro'mætik], *a.* isocromático.
isochronal, isochronous [ai'sɔkrənəl, -əs], *a.* isócrono.
isolate ['aisoleit], *v.t.* aislar; separar.
isolated ['aisoleitid], *a.* aislado; solitario, retirado; esporádico.
isolation [aiso'leiʃən], *s.* aislamiento; separación; apartamiento; ***isolation hospital,*** hospital de aislamiento.
isolationism [aiso'leiʃənizəm], *s.* aislacionismo.
isolationist [aiso'leiʃənist], *a.*, *s.* aislacionista, *m.f.*
isomeric [aisou'merik], *a.* isomérico.
isomerism [ai'sɔmərizəm], *s.* isomerismo.
isometric(al) [aisou'metrik(əl)], *a.* isométrico.
isomorphism [aisou'mɔ:fizəm], *s.* isomorfismo.
isomorphous [aisou'mɔ:fəs], *a.* isomorfo.
isosceles [ai'sɔsili:z], *a.* isósceles.
isotherm ['aisoθə:m], *s.* línea isoterma.
isothermal [aiso'θə:məl], *a.* isotermo.
isotope ['aisotoup], *s.* isotope, isotopo.
Israel ['izreil]. Israel.
Israeli [iz'reili], *a.*, *s.* israelí.
Israelite ['izrəlait], *s.* israelita, *m.f.*
issuable ['iʃuəbl, 'isjuəbl], *a.* emisible.
issue ['iʃu:, 'isju:], *s.* salida, egreso; distribución; emisión; edición, impresión, tirada; número, entrega; cuestión, problema, punto en disputa; resultado, consecuencia; sucesión, prole; (*med.*) flujo; ***at issue,*** en disputa; ***to evade the issue,*** esquivar la cuestión; ***to face the issue,*** afrontar la situación; ***to force the issue,*** forzar una decisión; ***issue of blood,*** pérdida de sangre; ***to join*** o ***take issue with,*** discutir con, oponerse a; ***point at issue,*** punto que se discute, punto en cuestión; ***without issue,*** sin sucesión. — *v.t.* distribuir; emitir, poner en circulación; publicar, promulgar; ***issue an arrest-warrant,*** dar una orden de arresto *o* de detención. — *v.i.* salir, manar, fluir; provenir.
issued ['iʃu:d, 'isju:d], *a.* expedido; emitido.
issueless ['iʃu:lis, 'isju:lis], *a.* sin sucesión.
issuing ['iʃu:iŋ, 'isju:iŋ], *s.* salida.
Isthmian ['isθmiən], *a.* ístmico.
isthmus ['is(θ)məs], *s.* istmo.
it [it], *pron. neut.* (*pl.* **they** [ðei]) él, ella, ello; lo, la; le; ***far from it,*** ni mucho menos; ***to be (hard) at it,*** estar dale que dale; ***how goes it?*** ¿qué tal?; ***it is I,*** soy yo; (*fam.*) ***it's me,*** soy yo; ***it is two o'clock,*** son las dos; ***it's raining,*** llueve; ***it's warm,*** hace calor; ***that's it,*** eso es; se acabó; (*fam.*) ***he thinks he's it,*** se cree muy importante; ***this is it,*** llegó la hora; (*fam.*) ***to be with it,*** estar a la última; ***the worst of it . . .,*** lo malo *o* peor (es que) . . . ; ***you're it,*** tú te quedas.
Italian [i'tæljən], *a.*, *s.* italiano.
italianize [i'tæljənaiz], *v.t.* italianizar.
italic [i'tælik], *a.* itálico; (*impr.*) bastardillo. — *s.* (letra) bastardilla.
italicize [i'tælisaiz], *v.t.* poner en letra bastardilla; subrayar.
Italy ['itəli]. Italia.

itch [itʃ], *s.* sarna, picor, picazón, *f.*, comezón, *f.*, prurito. — *v.i.* picar; sentir comezón *o* picazón, sentir prurito; ***itch to,*** estar deseando, rabiar por.

itching [ˈitʃiŋ], *a.* que pica. — *s.* escozor, picazón, *f.*, picor, comezón, *f.*, prurito.

itchy [ˈitʃi], *a.* que pica.

item [ˈaitəm], *adv.* ítem; otrosí, además. — *s.* partida; artículo; número; noticia, suelto; detalle; punto, tema.

itemize [ˈaitəmaiz], *v.t.* detallar, especificar, pormenorizar.

iterant [ˈitərənt], *a.* iterativo.

iterate [ˈitəreit], *v.t.* iterar, reiterar, repetir.

iteration [itəˈreiʃən], *s.* iteración.

iterative [ˈitərətiv], *a.* iterativo; (*gram.*) frecuentativo.

itinerant [aiˈtinərənt], *a.* ambulante; errante.

itinerary [aiˈtinərəri], *s.* itinerario, ruta; guía de viajeros.

itinerate [aiˈtinəreit], *v.i.* viajar, seguir un itinerario.

its [its], *a.* su(s). — *pron.* (el) suyo, (la) suya *etc.*

it's [its], *abrev. de* **it is.** es; está.

itself [itˈself], *pron.* (*nominativo*) él mismo, ella misma, ello mismo; (*acusativo, dativo*) se; (*disyuntivo*) sí (mismo, -ma).

I've [aiv], *abrev. de* **I have.** (yo) he; (yo) tengo.

ivied [ˈaivid], *a.* cubierto de hiedra.

ivory [ˈaivəri], *a.* de marfil, ebúrneo. — *s.* marfil; (*pl.* **ivories** [-iz]) teclas, *f.pl.*; cosas de marfil, *f.pl.*; bolas de billar, *f.pl.*; (*fam.*) dientes, *m.pl.*

Ivory Coast [ˈaivəri ˈkoust], **the.** la Costa de Marfil.

ivy [ˈaivi], *s.* hiedra.

J

J, j [dʒei], décima letra del alfabeto.
jab [dʒæb], *s.* (*fam., inyección*) pinchazo; jeringazo; hurgonazo; codazo; (*dep.*) golpe inverso. — *v.t.* pinchar; jeringar; hurgonear; dar un codazo a.
jabber [ˈdʒæbə], *s.* algarabía, guirigay. — *v.t.* farfullar, chapurrear. — *v.i.* parlotear, hablar por los codos.
jabberer [ˈdʒæbərə], *s.* farfullador; parlanchín.
jaborandi [dʒæbəˈrændi], *s.* jaborandi, pilocarpo.
jacaranda [dʒækəˈrændə], *s.* (*bot.*) jacaranda, abey.
jacinth [ˈdʒæsinθ], *s.* (*min.*) circón.
Jack [dʒæk], *a.* Juanito; ***Jack Frost,*** el Invierno; ***Jack Ketch,*** el verdugo; ***Jack of all trades (and master of none),*** aprendiz de todo (maestro de nada).
jack (1) [dʒæk], *s.* (*mec.*) gato; marinero; mozo; macho (*de varios animales*); sacabotas, *m. inv.*; torno de asador; boliche; sota (*de la baraja*); (*ict.*) lucio; ***jack-boot,*** bota militar fuerte; bota de montar; ***jack-in-office,*** (funcionario) engreído, mequetrefe; ***jack-in-the-box,*** caja sorpresa; (*fig.*) culo de mal asiento; ***jack-knife,*** navaja; ***jack-o'-lantern,*** fuego fatuo. — *v.t.* — ***up,*** alzar con gato; aumentar.
jack (2) [dʒæk], *s.* (*mar.*) bandera de proa.
jackal [ˈdʒækɔːl], *s.* chacal.
jackanapes [ˈdʒækəneips], *s. inv.* mequetrefe.
jackass [ˈdʒækæs], *s.* burro, asno.
jackdaw [ˈdʒækdɔː], *s.* (*orn.*) grajilla, corneja, chova.
jacket [ˈdʒækit], *s.* chaqueta, americana; (sobre)-cubierta; camisa.
jackpot [ˈdʒækpɔt], *s.* (*juego*) bote; premio gordo; ***he hit the jackpot,*** le tocó el premio gordo *o* la suerte; se puso las botas.
jackscrew [ˈdʒækskruː], *s.* gato cornaquí.
jackstaff [ˈdʒækstɑːf], *s.* asta de bandera.
jackstone [ˈdʒækstoun], *s.* taba.
jackstraw [ˈdʒækstrɔː], *s.* (*fig.*) mequetrefe; (*pl.*) juego de las pajitas.
Jacob [ˈdʒeikəb]. Jacob; ***Jacob's ladder,*** (*bot.*) polemonio azul; (*mar.*) escala de jarcias; ***Jacob's staff,*** bordón de peregrino; báculo de Jacob; astrolabio.
Jacobin [ˈdʒækobin], *s.* (*pol.*) jacobino; (*igl.*) dominico; pichón capuchino.
Jacobinic(al) [dʒækoˈbinik(əl)], *a.* jacobínico.
Jacobinism [ˈdʒækobinizəm], *s.* jacobinismo.
jacobinize [ˈdʒækobinaiz], *v.t.* infundir los principios de los jacobinos a.
Jacobite [ˈdʒækobait], *a., s.* jacobita, *m.f.*
jaconet [ˈdʒækonet], *s.* chaconá, chaconada.
jade (1) [dʒeid], *s.* (*min.*) jade.
jade (2) [dʒeid], *s.* rocín, jamelgo; mujerzuela. — *v.t.* cansar, rendir; estragar.
jaded [ˈdʒeidid], *a.* amargado; ***to have a jaded palate,*** tener el paladar *o* gusto estragado; ***jaded outlook,*** enfoque amargado.
jag (1) [dʒæg], *s.* diente, púa, mella; roto, siete. — *v.t.* dentar, mellar, rasgar; engancharse; ***jag one's shirt on a nail,*** engancharse la camisa en un clavo.
jag (2) [dʒæg], *s.* (*fam.*) turca, pítima.
jagged, jaggy [ˈdʒægid, ˈdʒægi], *a.* dentado, serrado; desigual, mellado.
jaggedness [ˈdʒægidnis], *s.* melladura, estado de dentellado.
jaguar [ˈdʒægjuə], *s.* jaguar.
jail [dʒeil], *s.* cárcel, *f.* — *v.t.* encarcelar.
jailbird [ˈdʒeilbəːd], *s.* presidiario; malhechor.
jailer [ˈdʒeilə], *s.* carcelero; alcaide.
jalap [ˈdʒæləp], *s.* jalapa.
jalousie [ˈdʒæluːziː], *s.* celosía.
jam (1) [dʒæm], *s.* mermelada; ***money for jam,*** pan comido.
jam (2) [dʒæm], *s.* apretura, apiñamiento; aprieto, lío; ***jam session,*** sesión de jazz improvisado; ***to get into a jam,*** meterse en un lío. — *v.t.* apiñar, apretar; atascar; interferir; encasquetar. — *v.i.* agolparse, apiñarse; atascarse.
Jamaica [dʒəˈmeikə]. Jamaica; (*bot.*) ***Jamaica pepper,*** pimienta; ***Jamaica rum,*** ron de Jamaica; ***Jamaica wood,*** brasilete; palo campeche; caoba fina.
Jamaican [dʒəˈmeikən], *a., s.* jamaiquino, jamaicano.
jamb [dʒæm], *s.* jamba, quicial, montante.
jamboree [dʒæmbəˈriː], *s.* reunión de niños exploradores; (*fam.*) francachela.
jangle [dʒæŋgl], *s.* sonido discordante; disputa, altercado, querella, riña. — *v.t.* hacer sonar discordemente. — *v.i.* sonar discordemente.
jangler [ˈdʒæŋglə], *s.* parlanchín, disputador.
jangling [ˈdʒæŋgliŋ], *s.* sonido discordante; charla; riña, pendencia.
janitor [ˈdʒænitə], *s.* conserje, portero; (*Am.*) [CARETAKER; PORTER].
janizary [ˈdʒænizəri], *s.* genízaro.
Jansenism [ˈdʒænsənizəm], *s.* jansenismo.
January [ˈdʒænjuəri], *s.* enero.
Japan [dʒəˈpæn]. el Japón.
japan [dʒəˈpæn], *s.* laca negra japonesa; obra japonesa charolada. — *v.t.* charolar con laca japonesa.
Japanese [dʒæpəˈniːz], *a., s.* japonés, *m.*
jape [dʒeip], *s.* broma, burla.
Japhetic [dʒəˈfetik], *a.* jafético.
japonica [dʒəˈpɔnikə], *s.* rosal japonés.
jar (1) [dʒɑː], *s.* choque; sacudida; escopetazo, sorpresa desagradable; discordia. — *v.t.* chocar; sacudir; (hacer) vibrar. — *v.i.* chocar, ser discorde; (*colores*) no hacer juego; ***jar on*** o ***upon,*** enervar, poner los nervios de punta a.
jar (2) [dʒɑː], *s.* tarro; frasco; bote; (*agua*) botija, jarra; (*de gran tamaño*) tinaja.
jar (3) [dʒɑː], *s.* (*fam.*) ***on the jar,*** entreabierta (*puerta*).
jardinière [ʒɑːdiniˈɛə], *s.* jardinera; florero.
jargon [ˈdʒɑːgən], *s.* jerga; jerigonza(s), algarabía(s).
jarring [ˈdʒɑːriŋ], *a.* chocante; discordante; enervante. — *s.* sacudidas, *f.pl.*; discordias, *f.pl.*
jasmine [ˈdʒæzmin], *s.* (*bot.*) jazmín.
jasper [ˈdʒæspə], *s.* jaspe.
jaundice [ˈdʒɔːndis], *s.* ictericia; (*fig.*) envidia. — *v.t.* dar ictericia a; dar envidia a; amargar.
jaundiced [ˈdʒɔːndist], *a.* itérico, ictericiado; cetrino; (*fig.*) envidioso; amargado, desengañado.
jaunt [dʒɔːnt], *s.* paseo (tranquilo); excursión. — *v.i.* ir con calma, pasear despacio.
jauntiness [ˈdʒɔːntinis], *s.* viveza, garbo.
jaunty [ˈdʒɔːnti], *a.* garboso, gallardo; vivaracho; pizpireta, *f.*
Javanese [dʒɑːvəˈniːz], *a., s.* javanés.
javelin [ˈdʒævlin], *s.* jabalina.
jaw [dʒɔː], *s.* mandíbula; quijada; (*fam.*) cháchara(s), palique; (*pl.*) (*fig.*) boca, fauces, *f.pl.*; ***jaw-bone,*** quijada, mandíbula; (*fam.*) ***jaw-breaker,*** trabalenguas, *m. inv.*; palabra kilométrica; (*fam.*) ***jaw-jaw,*** charloteo, palabrería. — *v.i.* (*fam.*) charlotear, hablar por los codos, darle a la sinhueso.
jay [dʒei], *s.* (*orn.*) arrendajo; ***jay-walker,*** peatón descuidado *o* inconsciente.
jazz [dʒæz], *s.* jazz; (*fam.*) monsergas, *m.pl.* — *v.t.* sincopar; (*fam.*) ***jazz (up),*** animar, echar ajilimójili a.
jazzy [ˈdʒæzi], *a.* chillón, llamativo, aparatoso.
jealous [ˈdʒeləs], *a.* celoso; vigilante; ***to be jealous of,*** tener celos de.
jealousy, jealousness [ˈdʒeləsi, -nis], *s.* celo(s); celo, vigilancia.

jeer [dʒiə], *s.* mofa, befa, escarnio. — *v.t.* mofarse de, burlarse de, befar, escarnecer. — *v.i.* — ***at,*** mofarse de, burlarse de.

jeerer [ˈdʒiərə], *s.* mofador, escarnecedor.

jeering [ˈdʒiəriŋ], *a.* mofador. — *s.* mofa, befa, escarnio.

jeeringly [ˈdʒiəriŋli], *adv.* con escarnio.

Jehovah [dʒiˈhouvə]. Jehová, *m.*

jejune [dʒiˈdʒu:n], *a.* insípido; estéril, seco.

jejunum [dʒiˈdʒu:nəm], *s.* (*anat.*) yeyuno.

jellied [ˈdʒelid], *a.* en gelatina.

jelly [ˈdʒeli], *s.* jalea; gelatina; ***jelly-fish,*** medusa; aguamar; ***jelly-roll,*** (*Am.*) [SWISS ROLL]. — *v.t.* convertir en jalea *o* gelatina.

jemmy [ˈdʒemi], *s.* palanqueta, pie de cabra.

jennet [ˈdʒenit], *s.* burra, jumenta; jaca española.

jenny [ˈdʒeni], *s.* torno, máquina para hilar; jumenta, burra, asna, borrica; ***jenny-wren,*** reyezuelo.

jeopardize [ˈdʒepədaiz], *v.t.* arriesgar, comprometer, exponer, poner en peligro; minar.

jeopardy [ˈdʒepədi], *s.* peligro, riesgo.

jerboa [dʒə:ˈbouə], *s.* (*zool.*) gerbo.

jeremiad [dʒeriˈmaiæd], *s.* jeremiada.

jerk (1) [dʒə:k], *s.* tirón, sacudida, sacudimiento; brinco, salto, respingo; (*equit.*) sobarbada; (*mar.*) socollada, gualdrapazo. — *v.t.* sacudir, mover a tirones; arrojar. — *v.i.* moverse a sacudidas, avanzar a tirones.

jerk (2) [dʒə:k], *v.t.* atasajar (*carne*).

jerker [ˈdʒə:kə], *s.* tirador, sacudidor.

jerkin [ˈdʒə:kin], *s.* justillo; jubón.

jerky [ˈdʒə:ki], *a.* espasmódico, desigual, nervioso.

jerry-builder [ˈdʒeri-bildə], *s.* mal constructor.

jerry-built [ˈdʒeri-bilt], *a.* mal construido, de pacotilla.

jersey [ˈdʒə:zi], *s.* jersey.

Jerusalem [dʒəˈru:sələm]. Jerusalén; ***Jerusalem artichoke,*** cotufa, pataca, aguaturma.

jess [dʒes], *s.* pihuela.

jessamine [ˈdʒesəmin] [JASMINE].

jest [dʒest], *s.* chanza, broma; ***in jest,*** en broma, de guasa. — *v.i.* bromear, chancear(se).

jester [ˈdʒestə], *s.* bufón.

jesting [ˈdʒestiŋ], *a.* bromista, chancero. — *s.* bromas, *f.pl.*, chanzas, *f.pl.*

jestingly [ˈdʒestiŋli], *adv.* en broma.

Jesuit [ˈdʒezjuit], *a.*, *s.* jesuita, *m.*

Jesuitic(al) [dʒezjuˈitik(əl)], *a.* jesuítico.

Jesuitism [ˈdʒezjuitizəm], *s.* jesuitismo.

Jesus [ˈdʒi:zəs]. Jesús, *m.*

jet (1) [dʒet], *s.* chorro; surtidor; mechero; ***jet-(aero)plane,*** avión de reacción; ***jet-engine,*** motor de reacción a chorro; ***jet-propelled,*** de impulsión a chorro. — *v.i.* salir en chorro, chorrear.

jet (2) [dʒet], *s.* (*min.*) azabache; ***jet-black,*** negro (como el) azabache.

jetsam [ˈdʒetsəm], *s.* (*mar.*) echazón, *f.*; (*for.*) pecio.

jettison [ˈdʒetisən], *s.* (*mar.*) echazón, *f.*; (*for.*) pecio. — *v.t.* (*mar.*) echar, arrojar al mar; tirar por la borda; despedir.

jetty [ˈdʒeti], *s.* malecón, muelle, (des)embarcadero.

Jew [dʒu:], *s.* judío.

jewel [ˈdʒu:əl], *s.* joya; alhaja; (*reloj*) rubí; ***jewel-box, jewel-case,*** joyero. — *v.t.* adornar con piedras preciosas.

jeweller [ˈdʒu:ələ], *s.* joyero.

jewellery [ˈdʒu:əlri], *s.* joyas, *f.pl.*, pedrería, joyería; ***cheap jewellery,*** bisutería.

Jewess [ˈdʒu:es], *s.* judía.

jewfish [ˈdʒu:fiʃ], *s.* guasa.

Jewish [ˈdʒu:iʃ], *a.* judío, judaico.

Jewry [ˈdʒuəri], *s.* judería.

Jew's harp [dʒu:z hɑ:p], *s.* birimbao.

Jezebel [ˈdʒezəbel], *s.* mujer cruel y viciosa.

jib (1) [dʒib], *s.* aguilón, pescante (de una grúa); (*mar.*) foque; ***jib-boom,*** botalón de foque; ***cut of one's jib,*** cara, expresión, aspecto, pergeño.

jib (2) [dʒib], *v.i.* plantarse; (*fig.*) resistirse (***at,*** a).

jibe [GIBE].

jiffy [ˈdʒifi], *s.* (*fam.*) instante, momento, periquete; ***in a jiffy,*** en un santiamén.

jig [dʒig], *s.* jiga; plantilla; anzuelo emplomado; (*min.*) criba. — *v.i.* bailar una jiga; bailotear; ***jig about,*** moverse a saltitos.

jigger (1) [ˈdʒigə], *s.* criba; (*ing.*) aparejo hidráulico; (*min.*) enganche; aparato con movimiento de vaivén; (*mar.*) aparejuelo; (*mar.*) cangreja de mesana. — *v.t.* (*fam.*) — ***up,*** jeringar, amolar; estropear; (*fam.*) ***I'm jiggered if I will!*** ¡ni hablar!

jigger (2) [ˈdʒigə], *s.* (*ent.*) nigua, pulga.

jiggery-pokery [ˈdʒigəri-ˈpoukəri], *s.* (*fam.*) tejemaneje(s), chanchullos, *m.pl.*

jig-saw [ˈdʒig-sɔ:], *s.* sierra de vaivén; ***jig-saw puzzle,*** rompecabezas, *m.inv.*

jilt [dʒilt], *v.t.* (*fam.*) dar calabazas a.

jim-jams [ˈdʒim-dʒæmz], *s. pl.* (*fam.*) grima.

jimmy, (*Am.*) [JEMMY].

jingle [dʒiŋgl], *s.* cascabeleo, retintín; rima infantil; (*propaganda*) musiquilla. — *v.t.* hacer sonar. — *v.i.* cascabelear, tintinear.

jingo [ˈdʒiŋgou], *s.* (*fam.*) patriotero; ***by jingo!*** ¡caramba!

jingoism [ˈdʒiŋgouizəm], *s.* patriotería.

jingoist [ˈdʒiŋgouist], *s.* patriotero.

jingoistic [dʒingouˈistik], *a.* patriotero, chauvinista.

jinks [dʒiŋks], *s.pl.* (*fam.*) ***high jinks,*** jolgorio, juerga.

jinn [dʒin], *s.* genio, espíritu, duende.

jinx [dʒiŋks], *s.* (*fam.*) gafe; ***to put a*** o ***the jinx on,*** gafar.

jitters [ˈdʒitəz], *s.pl.* nervios, *m.pl.*, nerviosismo; ***to give the jitters,*** poner nervioso; ***to have the jitters,*** estar nervioso; no poder estarse quieto.

job [dʒɔb], *s.* trabajo, tarea; empleo, puesto; (*fam.*) asunto, cosa; (*fam.*) robo; ***a bad job,*** cosa mal hecha; mala cosa; ***by the job,*** a destajo; (*fam.*) ***it's a good job that,*** menos mal que; ***to do a good job, make a good job of it,*** hacerlo bien; ***job lot,*** lote suelto de chismes *o* cachivaches; (*fam., pol.*) ***jobs for the boys,*** enchufes, *m. pl.*, enchufismo; (*fam.*) ***just the job,*** perfecto; justo lo que hace falta; ***odd job,*** tarea suelta, trabajo casual; ***odd-job man,*** hombre que hace de todo; (*fam.*) ***it's quite a job to get there,*** cuesta trabajo llegar hasta allí; ***to be on the job,*** estar trabajando; estar al pie del cañón; ***to lie down on the job,*** cruzarse de brazos; ***to be out of a job,*** estar sin trabajo. — *v.t.* alquilar; ceder por contrato; comprar y vender como corredor. — *v.i.* especular; trabajar a destajo.

jobber [ˈdʒɔbə], *s.* destajista, *m.*; agiotista, *m.*, corredor, intermediario; chanchullero.

jobbery [ˈdʒɔbəri], *s.* chanchullos, *m.pl.*; agiotaje.

jobbing [ˈdʒɔbiŋ], *s.* comercio de intermediario; trabajo a destajo.

jockey [ˈdʒɔki], *s.* jockey. — *v.t.* — ***into,*** embaucar para que. — *v.i.* — ***for position,*** maniobrar para conseguir un sitio bueno.

jocose [dʒoˈkous], *a.* jocoso, festivo.

jocoseness, jocosity [dʒoˈkousnis, -ˈkɔsiti], *s.* jocosidad.

jocular [ˈdʒɔkjulə], *a.* jocoso, divertido.

jocularity [dʒɔkjuˈlæriti], *s.* jocosidad, festividad.

jocund [ˈdʒɔkʌnd], *a.* jocundo.

jocundity, jocundness [dʒoˈkʌnditi, ˈdʒɔkʌndnis], *s.* jocundidad.

jodhpurs [ˈdʒɔdpə:z], *s.pl.* pantalones de montar, *m. pl.*

jog [dʒɔg], *s.* empujoncito, sacudida ligera; trote, paso corto; estímulo. — *v.t.* empujar *o* sacudir levemente; estimular; ***jog the memory,*** refrescar

la memoria. — *v.i.* — ***along,*** andar despacio *o* al trote corto.
jogging [ˈdʒɔgiŋ], *s.* traqueteo, sacudimiento.
joggle [dʒɔgl], *v.t.* mover, sacudir levemente.
John [dʒɔn]. Juan; muchacho; tipo nacional; ***John Bull,*** símbolo del inglés; ***John Dory,*** fabro, dorado.
join [dʒɔin], *v.t.* juntar, unir; ensamblar, acoplar; empalmar; unirse a, reunirse con; ingresar en, hacerse socio de; alistarse en; (*com.*) asociarse con; ***join battle,*** trabar batalla; ***join forces,*** unirse, hacer causa común; ***join hands,*** darse las manos; ***join up,*** juntar, unir. — *v.i.* juntarse, unirse; ***join in,*** tomar parte, participar en; ***join up,*** alistarse; ***join up with,*** asociarse con, unirse a.
joiner [ˈdʒɔinə], *s.* ebanista, *m.*, carpintero de obra prima, ensamblador.
joinery [ˈdʒɔinəri], *s.* carpintería, ebanistería.
joining [ˈdʒɔiniŋ], *s.* unión, *f.*, juntura; coyuntura; bisagra; (*carp.*) ***joining press,*** cepo.
joint [dʒɔint], *a.* mutuo, (en) común, colectivo; conjunto, combinado; ***joint account,*** cuenta indistinta, en participación; ***joint chiefs of staff,*** estado mayor conjunto; ***joint committee,*** comisión mixta; ***joint heir,*** coheredero; ***joint owner,*** copropietario; ***joint property,*** propiedad indivisa; ***joint responsibility,*** responsabilidad solidaria; ***joint stock company,*** sociedad anónima. — *s.* junta, juntura; coyuntura, articulación; nudo; empalme; ensambladura; bisagra; redondo (*de carne*); (*fam.*) sitio; tugurio, tabernucho; ***out of joint,*** descoyuntado; ***to put s.o.'s nose out of joint,*** alterar humillando a alguien. — *v.t.* juntar, unir; articular; ensamblar.
jointed [ˈdʒɔintid], *a.* nudoso; articulado.
jointer [ˈdʒɔintə], *s.* (*carp.*) juntera.
jointly [ˈdʒɔintli], *adv.* conjuntamente.
jointure [ˈdʒɔintʃə], *s.* (*for.*) viudedad.
joist [dʒɔist], *s.* viga, vigueta.
joke [dʒouk], *s.* broma; chiste; cosa de risa; ***bad joke,*** broma pesada; chiste malo; ***no joke,*** cosa seria; ***practical joke,*** bromazo; ***to crack a joke,*** decir un chiste; ***to play a joke on,*** gastar una broma a; ***he can take a joke,*** tiene aguante, sabe encajar las bromas; ***to tell a joke,*** contar un chiste; ***to treat as a joke,*** tomar a broma, a chunga, a guasa. — *v.t.* ***joke one's way into,*** conseguir burla burlando. — *v.i.* bromear, hablar en broma, guasear; (*fam.*) ***you're joking*** (***of course***)***!*** ¡no hablas en serio, claro!
joker [ˈdʒoukə], *s.* bromista, *m.f.*; guasón; comodín (*naipe*).
joking [ˈdʒoukiŋ], *a.* de broma, de guasa. — *s.* (el) bromear, (el) guasear; ***no joking,*** en serio.
jokingly [ˈdʒoukiŋli], *adv.* con tono de broma *o* de chunga.
jollification [dʒɔlifiˈkeiʃən], *s.* jolgorio, juerga.
jollity [ˈdʒɔliti], *s.* alegría, regocijo; jolgorio.
jolly [ˈdʒɔli], *a.* alegre, regocijado; jovial; divertido; (*fam.*) alegrete; ***Jolly Roger,*** bandera negra de los piratas. — *adv.* muy; ***jolly good,*** muy bueno, estupendo; muy bien, estupendamente; ***he'll jolly well have to,*** no va a tener más remedio (que). — *v.t.* — (***along***), animar con bromas.
jolly-boat [ˈdʒɔli-bout], *s.* (*mar.*) esquife.
jolt [dʒoult], *s.* sacudida; salto, tumbo. — *v.t.* dar una sacudida *o* un empujon a. — *v.i.* dar saltos *o* tumbos, bambolearse.
jolting [ˈdʒoultiŋ], *s.* sacudidas; bamboleo; traqueteo.
jongleur [ʒɔŋˈgləː], *s.* juglar.
jonquil [ˈdʒɔnkwil], *s.* junquillo.
Jordan [dʒɔːdn]. Jordán (*río*); Jordania (*país*).
Jordanian [dʒɔːˈdeiniən], *a.*, *s.* jordano.
joss [dʒɔs], *s.* ídolo *o* dios chino; ***joss-stick,*** pebete.
jostle [dʒɔsl], *v.t.* empujar, dar empujones, empellones *o* codazos a.
jot [dʒɔt], *s.* jota, pizca; ***I don't care a jot,*** me importa un bledo. — *v.t.* — ***down,*** apuntar.
jotter [ˈdʒɔtə], *s.* taco de notas, bloc de cartas.
jotting [ˈdʒɔtiŋ], *s.* (el) apuntar.
joule [dʒuːl], *s.* julio.
journal [ˈdʒəːnəl], *s.* diario; periódico; revista; (*mec.*) mangueta, gorrón; ***journal-bearing,*** cojinete; ***journal-box,*** caja de grasa.
journalese [dʒəːnəˈliːz], *s.* (*despec.*) estilo periodístico.
journalism [ˈdʒəːnəlizəm], *s.* periodismo.
journalist [ˈdʒəːnəlist], *s.* periodista, *m.f.*
journalistic [dʒəːnəˈlistik], *a.* periodístico.
journey [ˈdʒəːni], *s.* viaje. — *v.i.* viajar.
journeyman [ˈdʒəːnimən], *s.* jornalero; oficial (*de un oficio*).
joust [dʒaust], *s.* justa, torneo. — *v.i.* justar, lidiar.
jovial [ˈdʒouviəl], *a.* jovial, alegre, festivo.
joviality [dʒouviˈæliti], *s.* jovialidad, buen humor, regocijo.
jowl [dʒaul], *s.* carrillo, quijada; (*fig.*) ***cheek by jowl,*** (muy) juntos.
joy [dʒɔi], *a.* de gozo, de diversión; ***joy ride,*** paseo *o* excursión en coche *etc.*; (*mec.*) ***joy stick,*** palanca de gobierno. — *s.* alegría, júbilo, regocijo; ***a joy to the eye,*** un gozo para la retina; ***I wish you joy,*** le doy la enhorabuena; ***to jump with*** o ***for joy,*** brincar de gozo.
joyful [ˈdʒɔiful], *a.* alegre, gozoso, regocijado, jubiloso.
joyfulness [ˈdʒɔifulnis], *s.* gozo, júbilo, alegría.
joyless [ˈdʒɔilis], *a.* triste, sin gozo, sin alegría, lúgubre.
joylessness [ˈdʒɔilisnis], *s.* tristeza, melancolía.
joyous [ˈdʒɔiəs], *a.* alegre, gozoso, festivo.
joyousness [ˈdʒɔiəsnis], *s.* regocijo.
jubilant [ˈdʒuːbilənt], *a.* alborozado, jubiloso, eufórico.
jubilate [ˈdʒuːbileit], *v.i.* alegrarse, regocijarse, jubilar.
jubilation [dʒuːbiˈleiʃən], *s.* júbilo, regocijo, euforia.
jubilee [ˈdʒuːbiliː], *s.* jubileo; quincuagésimo aniversario.
Judaic(al) [dʒuːˈdeiik(əl)], *a.* judaico.
Judaism [ˈdʒuːdeiizəm], *s.* judaísmo.
judaize [ˈdʒuːdeiaiz], *v.i.* judaizar.
judaizer [ˈdʒuːdeiaizə], *s.* judaizante.
Judas-tree [ˈdʒuːdəs-triː], *s.* árbol de Judas.
judge [dʒʌdʒ], *s.* juez, *m.*; magistrado; conocedor, perito; ***to be no judge of,*** no entender de. — ***v.t.*** juzgar, estimar; considerar. — *v.i.* juzgar; ***judging from,*** a juzgar por.
judgeship [ˈdʒʌdʒʃip], *s.* judicatura, magistratura.
judg(e)ment [ˈdʒʌdʒmənt], *s.* juicio; sentencia, fallo; entendimiento, discernimiento; opinión; ***against my better judgment,*** con muchas reservas; ***in my judgment,*** a mi juicio; ***judgment-seat,*** tribunal; ***last judgment,*** juicio final; ***to the best of my judgment,*** según mi leal saber y entender; ***to sit in judgment on,*** juzgar, enjuiciar.
judicable [ˈdʒuːdikəbl], *a.* que puede ser juzgado.
judicative [ˈdʒuːdikətiv], *a.* judicativo.
judicatory [ˈdʒuːdikətəri], *a.* judicial; jurídico. — *s.* tribunal de justicia, justicia, judicatura.
judicature [ˈdʒuːdikətʃə], *s.* judicatura, magistratura; juzgado.
judicial [dʒuːˈdiʃəl], *a.* judicial.
judiciary [dʒuːˈdiʃəri], *a.* judiciario; judicial. — *s.* administración de justicia; magistratura.
judicious [dʒuːˈdiʃəs], *a.* juicioso, prudente, sensato.
judiciousness [dʒuːˈdiʃəsnis], *s.* buen juicio, sensatez.
jug [dʒʌg], *s.* jarro, cántaro; (*fam.*) chirona. — ***v.t.*** (*fam.*) meter en chirona; estofar; ***jugged hare,*** liebre estofada.
juggernaut [ˈdʒʌgənɔːt], *s.* armatoste.

juggle [dʒʌgl], *s.* juego de manos. — *v.t.* — ***s.o. out of sth.,*** pisarle algo a alguien, chafarle algo a alguien. — *v.i.* hacer juegos de manos *o* malabares; hacer trampas; ***juggle with figures,*** barajar las cifras.
juggler [ˈdʒʌglə], *s.* malabarista, *m.f.*; (*ant.*) juglar.
jugglery, juggling [ˈdʒʌgləri, -liŋ], *s.* juegos malabares, *m.pl.*, malabarismo; chanchullo(s).
jugular [ˈdʒʌgjulə], *a.* yugular. — *s.* vena yugular.
juice [dʒu:s], *s.* zumo, jugo; (*fam.*) electricidad; (*fam.*) gasolina; ***digestive juices,*** jugos digestivos; (*aut., fam.*) ***to step on the juice,*** pisar a fondo.
juiciness [ˈdʒu:sinis], *s.* jugosidad; suculencia.
juicy [ˈdʒu:si], *a.* jugoso, zumoso; suculento; sabroso, picante.
jujube [ˈdʒu:dʒu:b], *s.* azufaifa; pastilla (de azufaifa); ***jujube-tree,*** azufaifo.
juke-box [ˈdʒu:k-bɔks], *s.* tocadiscos tragaperras, *m. inv.*
julep [ˈdʒu:lep], *s.* julepe.
julienne [ʒu:liˈen], *s.* sopa juliana.
July [dʒu:ˈlai], *s.* julio.
jumble [dʒʌmbl], *s.* revoltijo, masa confusa, confusión, mezcolanza, embrollo; ***jumble sale,*** venta *o* saldo de objetos usados *o* de segunda mano. — *v.t.* mezclar, revolver confusamente, confundir, embrollar.
jumbo [ˈdʒʌmbou], *a.* enorme, gigantesco. — *s.* (*fam.*) elefante.
jump [dʒʌmp], *s.* salto, brinco; lanzamiento (en paracaídas); (*equit.*) barrera; ***to give a jump,*** dar un salto; ***to have the jump on,*** llevar la ventaja a; ***jump in prices,*** alza de precios; (*fam.*) ***take a running jump!*** ¡vete a freír espárragos! — *v.t.* saltar (por encima de); hacer saltar; ***jump the gun,*** adelantarse, anticiparse; ***jump the queue,*** colarse; ***jump the rails,*** salirse de la vía; ***jump ship,*** desertar del barco. — *v.i.* saltar, dar saltos, brincar; lanzarse (en paracaídas); ***jump at,*** lanzarse sobre; apresurarse a aprovechar, faltarle a uno tiempo para aceptar; ***jump down,*** bajar(se) de un salto; ***jump in the lake!*** ¡vete a freír espárragos!; ***jump on,*** saltar a; (*fig.*) echar una bronca a; ***jump over,*** saltar por (encima de); ***jump to conclusions,*** hacer juicios temerarios.
jumper (1) [ˈdʒʌmpə], *s.* saltador; barrena de percusión; hilo de cierre.
jumper (2) [ˈdʒʌmpə], *s.* jersey.
jumpiness [ˈdʒʌmpinis], *s.* nerviosismo.
jumping [ˈdʒʌmpiŋ], *a.* saltador. — *s.* salto(s); ***jumping-board,*** trampolín; ***jumping-off point,*** trampolín; (*mil.*) base avanzada.
jumpy [ˈdʒʌmpi], *a.* nervioso, asustadizo.
junction [ˈdʒʌŋkʃən], *s.* juntura, unión; cruce (*de caminos*); confluencia (*de ríos*); (estación de) empalme; ***junction box,*** caja de empalmes.
juncture [ˈdʒʌŋktʃə], *s.* juntura; coyuntura; trance.
June [dʒu:n], *s.* junio.
jungle [dʒʌŋgl], *s.* selva; jungla; manigua; (*fig.*) maraña; ***jungle-fever,*** fiebre palúdica.
junior [ˈdʒu:niə], *a., s.* menor; (más) joven; más nuevo; subalterno; hijo; ***junior partner,*** socio menos antiguo; (*Am.*) ***John Smith Junior*** (***Jr.***), John Smith, hijo; ***she is three years my junior,*** le llevo tres años.
juniper [ˈdʒu:nipə], *s.* (*bot.*) enebro, junípero; ***juniper-berry,*** nebrina.
junk (1) [dʒʌŋk], *s.* (*mar.*) junco.
junk (2) [dʒʌŋk], *s.* trastos viejos, *m.pl.*; chatarra; baratijas, *f.pl.*; (*fig.*) paparruchas, *f.pl.*
junkie [ˈdʒʌŋki], *s.* (*fam.*) drogadicto.
junket [ˈdʒʌŋkit], *s.* dulce de leche cuajada; juerga. — *v.i.* juerguearse.
junketing [ˈdʒʌŋkitiŋ], *s.* festín, tiberio.
junta [ˈdʒʌntə], *s.* (*pol.*) junta.
junto [ˈdʒʌntou], *s.* camarilla.
jural [ˈdʒuərəl], *a.* forénsico.
Jurassic [dʒuˈræsik], *a.* jurásico.
jurat [ˈdʒuəræt], *s.* jurado, magistrado.
juratory [ˈdʒuərətəri], *a.* juratorio.
juridic(al) [dzu:ˈridik(əl], *a.* jurídico.
jurisconsult [dʒuərisˈkɔnsʌlt], *s.* jurisconsulto.
jurisdiction [dʒuərisˈdikʃən], *s.* jurisdicción; potestad.
jurisdictional [dʒuərisˈdikʃənəl], *a.* jurisdiccional.
jurisdictive [dʒuərisˈdiktiv], *a.* que tiene jurisdicción.
jurisprudence [dʒuərisˈpru:dəns], *s.* jurisprudencia.
jurisprudent [dʒuərisˈpru:dənt], *a., s.* jurisperito, jurisprudente.
jurist [ˈdʒuərist], *s.* jurista, *m.*, legista, *m.*, jurisperito, jurisconsulto.
juror [ˈdʒuərə], *s.* (*for.*) jurado (*miembro de un jurado*).
jury [ˈdʒuəri], *s.* (*for.*) jurado (*cuerpo* e *institución*); ***grand jury,*** gran jurado de acusación; ***jury-box,*** tribuna del jurado; ***petty jury,*** jurado de juicio.
juryman [ˈdʒuərimən], *s.* jurado (*individuo*).
jurymast [ˈdʒuərimɑ:st], *s.* (*mar.*) bandola.
jussive [ˈdʒʌsiv], *a.* (*gram.*) imperativo, de mandato.
just [dʒʌst], *a.* justo; recto; exacto. — *adv.* justamente, exactamente, ni más ni menos; precisamente; sólo, no más; apenas; recién, recientemente; en el instante; completamante, precisamente; ***just about,*** poco más o menos; ***just arrived,*** recién llegado; ***I have just arrived,*** acabo de llegar; ***just as,*** en el momento en que; lo mismo que; ***just as you please,*** como usted guste; ***just beyond,*** una pizca más allá (de); ***just by,*** justo al lado (de); ***he is just a child,*** no es más que un niño; ***to have but just time,*** tener el tiempo justo; ***I was just going,*** estaba a punto de irme; ***just imagine!*** ¡imagínese!; ***just let me see,*** vamos a ver; ***just now,*** ahora mismo; hace un momento; ***just so,*** exactamente, eso mismo.
justice [ˈdʒʌstis], *s.* justicia; juez; ***court of justice,*** tribunal de justicia; ***justice of the peace,*** juez de paz; ***to do justice to,*** hacer justicia a; hacer honor a; ***to do o.s. justice,*** quedar bien; estar bien *o* muy bien; ***poetic justice,*** castigo de Dios.
justiceship [ˈdʒʌstisʃip], *s.* justiciazgo, judicatura.
justiciary [dʒʌsˈtiʃəri], *a.* judicial. — *s.* juez, magistrado.
justifiable [ˈdʒʌstifaiəbl], *a.* justificable.
justifiableness [ˈdʒʌstifaiəblnis], *s.* posibilidad de ser justificado.
justifiably [ˈdʒʌstifaiəbli], *adv.* justificadamente.
justification [dʒʌstifiˈkeiʃən], *s.* justificación; descargo, defensa.
justificative, justificatory [ˈdʒʌstifikeitiv, -əri], *a.* justificativo, defensivo.
justificator [ˈdʒʌstifikeitə], *s.* justificador, defensor.
justifier [ˈdʒʌstifaiə], *s.* justificador.
justify [ˈdʒʌstifai], *v.t.* justificar; ***to be justified in,*** tener motivo para.
justle [dʒʌsl], *v.t.* [JOSTLE].
justly [dʒʌstli], *adv.* con justicia.
justness [ˈdʒʌstnis], *s.* justicia; equidad.
jut [dʒʌt], *s.* saliente. — *v.i.* sobresalir, resaltar.
jute [dʒu:t], *s.* yute.
juvenescence [dʒu:vəˈnesəns], *s.* rejuvenecimiento.
juvenescent [dʒu:vəˈnesənt], *a.* rejuveneciente.
juvenile [ˈdʒu:vənail], *a.* juvenil; de *o* para menores; ***juvenile delinquent,*** delincuente menor; ***juvenile delinquency,*** delincuencia de menores. — *s.* (niño) menor de edad; (*teat.*) ***juvenile lead,*** galán joven.
juxtapose [dʒʌkstəˈpouz], *v.t.* yuxtaponer.
juxtaposition [dʒʌkstəpəˈziʃən], *s.* yuxtaposición.

K

K, k [kei], undécima letra del alfabeto.
kale [keil], *s.* (*bot.*) col rizada.
kaleidoscope [kəˈlaidəskoup], *s.* caleidoscopio.
kaleidoscopic [kəlaidəˈskɔpik], *a.* caleidoscópico.
kalmia [ˈkælmiə], *s.* calmia.
Kalmuck [ˈkælmʌk], *s.* calmuco.
Kanaka [kəˈnækə], *a.*, *s.* hawaiano.
kangaroo [kæŋgəˈruː], *s.* canguro; ***kangaroo court,*** tribunal sin autoridad.
Kantian [ˈkæntiən], *a.*, *s.* kantiano.
Kantianism [ˈkæntiənizəm], *s.* kantismo.
kaolin [ˈkeiəlin], *s.* caolín.
kapok [ˈkeipɔk], *s.* miraguano.
karat [ˈkærət], *s.* quilate.
katabolism [kəˈtæbolizəm], *s.* catabolismo.
kauri [ˈkauri], *s.* (*bot.*) kauri.
kayak [ˈkaijæk], *s.* kayak.
kedge [kedʒ], *s.* anclote.
kedgeree [ˈkedʒəriː], *s.* guiso de sobras de pescado.
keel [kiːl], *s.* quilla; (*mar.*) ***on an even keel,*** en iguales calados; (*fig.*) en equilibrio, derecho, firme. — *v.i.* — ***over,*** (*mar.*) dar de quilla; volcar(se); (*fam.*, *fig.*) caerse, desplomarse.
keelage [ˈkiːlidʒ], *s.* (*mar.*) derechos de quilla, *m.pl.*
keelhaul [ˈkiːlhɔːl], *v.t.* (*mar.*) pasar por debajo de la quilla (*castigo*).
keen [kiːn], *a.* agudo; afilado; penetrante, sutil; mordaz; perspicaz; vivo, ardiente; entusiasta; ***to be keen on,*** ser aficionado a; ser (muy) partidario de; ***I'm not very keen on him,*** no me gusta demasiado, no es santo de mi devoción; ***to be keen to,*** tener vivo deseo de, tener mucho interés en *o* por.
keenness [ˈkiːnnis], *s.* agudeza; viveza; perspicacia; sutileza; interés, deseo; entusiasmo, aplicación.
keep [kiːp], *s.* mantenimiento; manutención; custodia; guardia; torreón; (*fam.*) ***for keeps,*** para siempre; ***to earn one's keep,*** trabajar por la comida. — *irr. v.t.* tener, mantener, retener, conservar, guardar, custodiar, cuidar, defender; reservar; impedir, detener, entretener; dirigir, atender a (*una tienda*); llevar (*los libros de comercio*); sostener, proveer, mantener; proseguir, continuar, seguir; celebrar, solemnizar; guardar, cumplir, observar; poner por escrito; ***keep (s.o.) awake,*** no dejar dormir a (alguien); ***keep away,*** tener alejado; ***keep back,*** retener, guardar; tener a raya, rechazar; ***keep one's bed,*** guardar cama; (*com.*) ***keep books,*** llevar (los) libros; ***keep by,*** guardar; tener guardado *o* en reserva; tener a mano; ***keep company with,*** acompañarse de, estar con; ***keep down,*** sujetar; tener dominado *o* sometido; ***keep one's eye on,*** no perder de vista; tener vigilado; (*de peligro*) ***keep from,*** defender, guardar; ***keep s.o. from,*** impedir a alguien que + *subj.*; ***keep sth. from s.o.,*** ocultar algo a alguien; ***keep in,*** refrenar, reprimir, contener, tener en sujeción; (re)tener en casa; ***keep in awe,*** tener asombrado *o* pasmado; ***keep sth. in mind,*** tener presente una cosa; (*mar.*) ***keep the land aboard,*** mantenerse inmediato a la tierra; ***keep late hours,*** trasnochar; ***keep off,*** tener alejado; ***keep on,*** seguir con, tener; ***keep out,*** impedir que entre, no permitir entrar; (*mar.*) ***keep the sea,*** mantenerse mar afuera; ***keep strict silence,*** guardar riguroso silencio; ***keep one's temper,*** contenerse, no enfadarse; ***keep sth. to o.s.,*** no soltar prenda de algo; ***keep under,*** sujetar, tener en sujeción; tener sojuzgado; ***keep up,*** conservar; mantener; ***keep s.o. waiting,*** hacer esperar a alguien. — *v.i.* mantenerse, sostenerse; continuar; perseverar; permanecer, quedar; residir, vivir; conservarse fresco *o* bien; ***keep aloof,*** apartarse, alejarse, mantenerse aparte; no entremeterse; vivir ajeno; (*fam.*) ***keep at it,*** persistir, perseverar; ***keep away,*** no (ven)ir, no acercarse; ***keep back,*** mantenerse apartado; no atreverse a figurar *o* hacer *o* decir mucho; ***keep in,*** quedarse en casa; ***keep in with,*** mantener buenas relaciones con; ***keep off,*** no acercarse; mantenerse distante, no arrimarse; (*fam.*) ***if the rain keeps off,*** si sigue sin llover; ***keep on,*** insistir (en), empeñarse (en); decir una y otra vez; ***keep out,*** no entrar, mantenerse alejado; ***keep still,*** estarse quieto; ***keep to one's bed,*** guardar cama; ***keep strictly to the text,*** atenerse a la letra; ***keep up with,*** ir al paso de; mantenerse a la altura de; mantenerse al día *o* al tanto de.
keeper [ˈkiːpə], *s.* guarda, *m.f.*; custodio; guardián, carcelero; tenedor; guardabosque; (*fam.*) portero, guardameta, *m.*; ***Lord Keeper of the Great Seal,*** Guardasellos del Rey, *m.inv.*, Gran Canciller.
keepership [ˈkiːpəʃip], *s.* guardería, alcaidía.
keeping [ˈkiːpiŋ], *s.* mantenimiento; cargo; custodia; cuidado; defensa; posesión; ***to be in keeping with,*** ir a tono con, estar en consonancia con, estar de acuerdo con.
keepsake [ˈkiːpseik], *s.* recuerdo.
keg [keg], *s.* cuñete, barrilete.
kelp [kelp], *s.* quelpo.
kelpie [ˈkelpi], *s.* (*Esco.*) duende del agua.
Kelt [CELT].
Keltic [CELTIC].
ken [ken], *s.* (*fam.*) alcance de la vista; conocimiento, saber; comprensión; ***beyond our ken,*** inasequible para nuestra inteligencia. — *v.t.* (*Esco.*) saber; conocer; reconocer.
kennel [ˈkenəl], *s.* perrera; jauría. — *v.t.* tener en perrera; meter en perrera.
kentledge [ˈkentlidʒ], *s.* (*mar.*) enjunque.
Kenya [ˈkenjə, ˈkiːnjə]. Kenia.
Kenyan [ˈkenjən, ˈkiːnjən], *a.*, *s.* keniano.
kepi [ˈkepi], *s.* quepis, *m. inv.*
keratitis [kerəˈtaitis], *s.* queratitis, *f. inv.*
kerb [kəːb], *s.* bordillo, encintado (de la acera); ***kerb-stone,*** bordillo.
kerchief [ˈkəːtʃif], *s.* pañuelo, pañoleta.
kermes [ˈkəːmiːz], *s.* quermes, *m. inv.*, grana; (*bot.*) coscojo; coscoja.
kermis [ˈkəːmis], *s.* quermese, *f.*
kern [kəːn], *s.* (*impr.*) hombro (*de una letra*).
kernel [ˈkəːnəl], *s.* almendra; grano; (*fig.*) meollo, médula, núcleo; ***there's not a kernel of truth in it,*** no tiene el más mínimo fundamento.
kernelled [ˈkəːnəld], *a.* que tiene almendra.
kernelly [ˈkəːnəli], *a.* almendrado, lleno de almendras.
kernelwort [ˈkəːnəlwəːt], *s.* escrofularia.
kerosene, kerosine [kerosiːn], *s.* keroseno.
kersey [ˈkəːzi], *s.* buriel.
kestrel [ˈkestrəl], *s.* (*orn.*) cernícalo.
ketch [ketʃ], *s.* queche.
ketchup [ˈketʃəp], *s.* salsa de tomate.
ketone [ˈkiːtoun], *s.* (*quím.*) ketona.
kettle [ketl], *s.* cafetera; ***tea-kettle,*** tetera; ***here's a (pretty) kettle of fish!*** ¡vaya un lío!
kettledrum [ˈketldrʌm], *s.* timbal.
kettledrummer [ˈketldrʌmə], *s.* timbalero, atabalero.
key (1) [kiː], *s.* llave; clave; cuña, chaveta; (*arq.*) dovela; (*artill.*) sotrozo; (*enc.*) clavija; (*elec.*) llave, *f.*, conmutador; tecla (*de piano etc.*); tono; ***in a high key,*** en tono alto; ***in key,*** en armonía, de acuerdo; (*mús.*) ***key action,*** teclado; ***pass*** o ***skeleton key,*** llave maestra; ***to be under lock and key,*** estar bajo siete llaves. — *v.t.* enchavetar, acuñar; templar, afinar; ***key up,*** elevar el nivel de; excitar.
key (2) [kiː], *s.* (*mar.*) cayo, isleta.
keyboard [ˈkiːbɔːd], *s.* teclado.
keyed [kiːd], *a.* que tiene llaves *o* teclas; templado, afinado; ***to be all keyed up,*** estar sobreexcitado.

keyhole [ˈki:houl], *s.* ojo (*de la cerradura*).
keystone [ˈki:stoun], *s.* (*arq.*) piedra clave.
khaki [ˈkɑ:ki], *a., s.* caqui.
khan [kɑ:n], *s.* kan, khan.
Khartoum [kɑ:ˈtu:m]. Jartum.
khedive [keˈdi:v], *s.* jedive, kedive.
Khmer [kmɛə]. Kmer.
kibble [kibl], *s.* (*min.*) cubo de hierro.
kibe [kaib], *s.* grieta (*en la piel*); sabañón ulcerado.
kibosh [ˈkaibɔʃ], *s.* (*fam.*) ***to put the kibosh on,*** acabar *o* dar al traste con.
kick [kik], *s.* puntapié; patada, coz; (*armas*) culatazo, retroceso; fuerza (*de una bebida*); protesta, queja; (*fam.*) gozada; (*fam.*) ***what is the kick-back?*** ¿qué pagan?; ***kick-off,*** saque inicial; ***I get a kick out of it,*** me emociona, me encanta, me entusiasma; (*fam.*) ***to do sth. for kicks,*** hacer algo de sport *o* por la gozada. — *v.t.* patear, tirar coces a; (*fam.*) ***kick the bucket,*** estirar la pata, diñarla; (*fam.*) ***I felt like kicking myself,*** me entró mucha furia conmigo mismo, me puse furioso conmigo mismo. — *v.i.* patear, dar patadas, dar puntapiés, dar coces; (*fam.*) oponerse; sublevarse; quejarse; ***kick against the pricks,*** dar coces contra el aguijón; ***kick off,*** (*dep.*) sacar; (*fam.*) empezar; ***kick out,*** echar a puntapiés *o* a patadas; (*fam.*) ***kick up a shindy,*** armar un escándalo *o* un follón.
kicker [ˈkikə], *s.* pateador, coceador; (*fam.*) quejumbroso.
kicking [ˈkikiŋ], *s.* coces, *f.pl.*, pataleo; quejas, *f.pl.*
kid [kid], *s.* cabrito; cabritilla; carne de cabrito; (*mar.*) gamella; (*fam.*) niño, crío, chiquillo; ***to treat with kid-gloves,*** dar trato(s) de guante blanco a. — *v.t.* (*fam.*) tomar el pelo a. — *v.i.* parir cabritos.
kiddle [kidl], *s.* presa *o* represa en un río con redes *o* trampas para pescar.
kidnap [ˈkidnæp], *v.t.* secuestrar.
kidnapper [ˈkidnæpə], *s.* secuestrador.
kidnapping [ˈkidnæpiŋ], *s.* secuestro.
kidney [ˈkidni], *s.* riñón; ***kidney-bean,*** judía, habichuela; ***kidney-shaped,*** reniforme; ***kidney-vetch,*** vulneraria; (*bot.*) ***kidney-wort,*** ombligo; ***of the same kidney,*** del mismo jaez.
kilderkin [ˈkildəkin], *s.* medio barril (*de* 18 *galones*).
kill [kil], *s.* matanza; (*fig.*) ***to be in at the kill,*** presenciar el final; (*fig.*) ***to go in for the kill,*** proponerse acabar con; ***kill-joy,*** aguafiestas, *m.f. inv.* — *v.t.* matar; apagar; acabar con, suprimir; ahogar; derrotar; ***kill o.s. with work,*** matarse trabajando; ***kill two birds with one stone,*** matar dos pájaros de un tiro. — *v.i.* matar; hacer una impresión irresistible.
killdee, killdeer [ˈkildi:, -diə], *s.* (*orn.*) egialites, *m.*, frailecillo norteamericano.
killer [ˈkilə], *s.* matador; asesino; ***to be a real killer,*** ser mortífero.
killing [ˈkiliŋ], *a.* que mata; destructivo; abrumador; (*fam.*) de carcajada, graciosísimo. — *s.* matanza; (*fig.*) golpe acertado, gran acierto, gran éxito.
kiln [kiln], *s.* horno.
kiln-dry [ˈkiln-ˈdrai], *v.t.* secar en horno.
kilo [ˈki:lou], *pref., abrev.* [KILOGRAM(ME)].
kilocycle [ˈkilosaikl], *s.* kilociclo.
kilogram(me) [ˈkilogræm], *s.* kilo(gramo).
kilogrammetre [kiloˈgræmitə], *s.* kilográmetro.
kilolitre [ˈkiloli:tə], *s.* kilolitro.
kilometre [ˈkilomi:tə], *s.* kilómetro.
kilometric [kiloˈmetrik], *a.* kilométrico.
kilowatt [ˈkilowɔt], *s.* kilovatio.
kilt [kilt], *s.* falda escocesa.
kimono [kiˈmounou], *s.* quimono.
kin [kin], *a.* allegado. — *s.* familia, parientes, *m.pl.*, parentela; deudos, *m.pl.*; parentesco; ***next of kin,*** pariente(s) más cercano(s); (*despec.*) ***they are of a kin,*** son de la misma ralea *o* calaña.
kind [kaind], *a.* bueno; benigno; amable; ***kind-hearted,*** bondadoso, de buen corazón; ***to be kind to,*** ser bueno con, ser amable con; ***to be so kind as to,*** tener la amabilidad *o* la bondad de. — *adv.* (*fam.*) ***kind of,*** en cierto sentido, hasta cierto punto, por lo menos. — *s.* clase, género, tipo, especie, suerte; ***a kind of,*** una especie de, un a modo de; ***human kind,*** género humano; ***nothing of the kind!*** ¡nada de eso! ¡en absoluto!; ***of a kind,*** de una misma clase; (*despec.*) de la misma calaña, del mismo jaez; ***of all kinds,*** de todas clases; ***of the (same) kind,*** del mismo estilo, por el estilo; ***to pay in kind,*** pagar en especie.
kindergarten [ˈkindəgɑ:tn], *s.* jardín de infancia.
kind-heartedness [kaind-ˈhɑ:tidnis], *s.* bondad, benevolencia.
kindle [kindl], *v.t.* encender; inflamar. — *v.i.* encenderse; inflamarse.
kindliness [ˈkaindlinis], *s.* bondad, benevolencia.
kindly [ˈkaindli], *a.* bondadoso, benévolo, benigno. — *adv.* ***kindly wait here,*** haga el favor de esperar aquí; ***to take kindly to,*** aceptar de buen grado; ***we'd take it kindly if,*** agradeceríamos que.
kindness [ˈkaindnis], *s.* bondad; benevolencia; cariño, afecto; amabilidad, favor.
kindred [ˈkindrid], *a.* allegado, afín. — *s.* parentesco; parentela; afinidad.
kine [kain], *s.pl.* (*ant.*) vacas, *f.pl.*
kinematics [kiniˈmætiks], *s. pl.* (*fís.*) cinemática.
kinetic [kaiˈnetik], *a.* cinético.
kinetics [kaiˈnetiks], *s. pl.* cinética.
king [kiŋ], *s.* rey; (*ajedrez, cartas*) rey; ***king-bird,*** tirano, muscícapa; ***king-bolt,*** perno pinzote, perno real; ***king-crab,*** límulo; (*bot.*) ***king-cup,*** botón de oro; ***king-pin,*** perno real; (*arq.*) ***king-post,*** pendolón, colgante; ***king-size,*** tamaño extra; ***King's English,*** inglés correcto; ***king's evil,*** escrófula.
kingcraft [ˈkiŋkrɑ:ft], *s.* arte de reinar.
kingdom [ˈkiŋdəm], *s.* reino.
kingfisher [ˈkiŋfiʃə], *s.* (*orn.*) martín pescador.
kinghood [ˈkiŋhud], *s.* soberanía, dignidad de rey.
kinglet [ˈkiŋlit], *s.* reyezuelo; régulo.
kingly, kinglike [ˈkiŋli, -laik], *a.* real, regio.
kingship [ˈkiŋʃip], *s.* majestad, dignidad real.
kingspear [ˈkiŋspiə], *s.* gamón.
kink [kiŋk], *s.* anilla, rizo, coca; (*fam.*) rareza, chifladura; ***he's got a kink,*** es un tío raro. — *v.i.* formar cocas, rizos etc.
kinky [ˈkiŋki], *a.* ensortijado; crespo, encarrujado; (*fam.*) raro, chiflado.
kino [ˈki:nou], *s.* quino.
kinsfolk [ˈkinzfouk], *s.* parientes, parentela, *m.pl.*
kinship [ˈkinʃip], *s.* parentesco.
kinsman [ˈkinzmən], *s.* pariente, deudo.
kinswoman [ˈkinzwumən], *s.* parienta.
kiosk [ˈkiɔsk], *s.* quiosco.
kip (1) [kip], *s.* (*ten.*) piel de res pequeña; ***kip-leather, kip-skin,*** becerro.
kip (2) [kip], *s.* (*fam.*) sueño, sueñecito.
kipper [ˈkipə], *s.* arenque ahumado; tío, individuo. — *v.t.* curar (pescado) al humo.
kirk [kə:k], *s.* (*Esco.*) iglesia.
kirtle [kə:tl], *s.* capa, manto; chupa larga.
kirtled [kə:tld], *a.* vestido con manto *o* capa.
kismet [ˈkizmet], *s.* hado, destino.
kiss [kis], *s.* beso, ósculo; roce; merengue; ***kiss-curl,*** aladar. — *v.t.* besar; ***kiss the rod,*** bajar la cerviz; ***kiss good-bye,*** dar un beso de despedida. — *v.i.* besar(se); rozar(se); tocarse levemente.
kisser [ˈkisə], *s.* (*fam.*) hocico.
kist [kist], *s.* (*Esco.*) arca, cofre; ataúd de piedra prehistórico.

kit [kit], *s.* avíos, *m.pl.*, equipo; herramental; instrumental; estuche; equipaje; juego; botiquín; ***kit-bag,*** mochila.

kitchen [ˈkitʃin], *s.* cocina; (*ant.*) ***kitchen-boy, kitchen-knave,*** pinche, marmitón; ***kitchen garden,*** huerto; (*ant.*) ***kitchen maid, kitchen wench,*** fregona; ***kitchen-range,*** cocina económica, fogón; ***kitchen utensils,*** batería de cocina.

kite [kait], *s.* (*orn.*) milano; cometa; (*com.*) crédito ficticio; (*mar.*) sobrejuanete; foque volante; (*fam.*) fullero; ***to fly a kite,*** remontar una cometa; (*fam.*) echar un globo sonda.

kith [kiθ], *s.* ***kith and kin,*** parientes y amigos, *m.pl.*

kitten [kitn], *s.* gatito. — *v.i.* parir (la gata).

kittenish [ˈkitəniʃ], *a.* de gatito; juguetón; coquetón.

kittiwake [ˈkitiweik], *s.* (*orn.*) risa (*especie de gaviota*).

kitty (1) [ˈkiti], *s.* gatito, minino.

kitty (2) [ˈkiti], *s.* (*juego*) bote; puesta; ***to have sth. in the kitty,*** tener algo guardado.

kleptomania [kleptoˈmeiniə], *s.* cleptomanía.

kleptomaniac [kleptoˈmeiniæk], *a.*, *s.* cleptómano.

knack [næk], *s.* tranquillo, manejo, truco; maña, tino.

knacker [ˈnækə], *s.* matarife de caballos.

knapsack [ˈnæpsæk], *s.* mochila.

knapweed [ˈnæpwi:d], *s.* cabezuela; centáurea.

knave [neiv], *s.* bribón, bellaco, truhán; sota (*de naipes*).

knavery, knavishness [ˈneivəri, -iʃnis], *s.* bribonería, bellaquería, truhanería.

knavish [ˈneiviʃ], *a.* pícaro, ruin.

knead [ni:d], *v.t.* amasar, heñir.

kneader [ˈni:də], *s.* amasador.

kneading [ˈni:diŋ], *s.* amasadura, (el) amasar; ***kneading trough,*** amasadera, artesa, masera.

knee [ni:], *s.* rodilla; (*mec.*) codillo, ángulo; ***knee breeches,*** calzón corto; ***knee-cap,*** rodillera, rótula; ***knee deep,*** metido hasta las rodillas; ***knee high,*** hasta la rodilla; ***knee-joint,*** articulación de la rodilla; ***knee-pan,*** rótula, choquezuela; ***to bring (s.o.) to his knees,*** humillar, obligar (a alguien) a bajar la cerviz; ***to fall on one's (bended) knees,*** caer de rodillas; ***to go down on one's knees to,*** suplicar de rodillas. — *v.t.* dar un rodillazo *o* rodillazos a; (*pantalones*) hacer rodilleras en.

kneel [ni:l], *v.i.* arrodillarse, ponerse de rodillas; estar de rodillas.

knell [nel], *s.* doble, toque de difuntos; (*fig.*) anuncio fatídico; ***to toll the knell of,*** anunciar la muerte *o* el fin de. — *v.t.* anunciar a toque de campana. — *v.i.* doblar, tocar a muerto.

knickerbockers [ˈnikəbɔkəz], *s.pl.* calzón corto, pantalón corto.

knickers [ˈnikəz], *s.pl.* bragas, *f.pl.*

knick-knack [ˈniknæk], *s.* (*fam.*) chuchería, bujería, baratija.

knife [naif], *s.* (*pl.* **knives** [naivz]) cuchillo; navaja; cuchilla; navajilla; ***he has got his knife into me,*** la tiene tomada conmigo. — *v.t.* acuchillar, dar una cuchillada *o* cuchilladas a.

knight [nait], *s.* caballero; caballo (*del ajedrez*); ***knight-errant,*** caballero andante; ***knight-errantry,*** caballería andante. — *v.t.* armar caballero.

knighthead [ˈnaithed], *s.* (*mar.*) tragante exterior del bauprés; ***knighthead of the windlass,*** cepos (*m. pl.*) *o* bitas (*f.pl.*) del molinete; ***knightheads of the gears,*** guindastes, *m. pl.*

knighthood [ˈnaithud], *s.* caballería, dignidad de caballero.

knightliness [ˈnaitlinis], *s.* caballerosidad.

knightly [ˈnaitli], *a.* caballeresco.

knit [nit], *irr. v.t.* hacer, tejer (a punto de aguja); ***to knit together,*** enlazar, unir; ***knit one's brow,*** fruncir el entrecejo; ***knit up,*** enmallar; concluir. — *v.i.* hacer punto *o* malla; soldarse, trabarse; ***knit together,*** enlazarse, unirse.

knittable [ˈnitəbl], *a.* capaz de ser tejido *o* unido.

knitter [ˈnitə], *s.* calcetero, mediero.

knitting [ˈnitiŋ], *s.* trabajo de punto; (el) hacer calceta; unión, *f.*; ***knitting machine,*** máquina de hacer punto; ***knitting needle,*** aguja de hacer punto; ***knitting work,*** trabajo de punto.

knittle [nitl], *s.* (*mar.*) sardineta, cordoncillo de bolsa.

knob [nɔb], *s.* protuberancia; bulto; nudo; perilla; botón; puño (*de bastón*); ***door-knob,*** tirador de puerta.

knobbed, knobby [nɔbd, ˈnɔbi], *a.* nudoso; terco, obstinado, difícil.

knobbiness [ˈnɔbinis], *s.* (lo) nudoso.

knock [nɔk], *s.* golpe; porrazo, topetazo; llamada, toque, aldabonazo; (*dep.*) peloteo; juego preliminar; ***to be able to take the knocks,*** aguantar *o* encajar los golpes. — *v.t.* dar, pegar, golpear; (*fam.*) poner verde; ***knock down,*** echar por tierra de un golpe, derribar; rebajar; adjudicar; ***knock down to the highest bidder,*** rematar al mejor postor; ***knock in,*** hundir a golpes; hacer entrar por medio de golpes; (*fam.*) ***knock off,*** birlar; despachar, espabilarse (*una cosa*); ***knock on the head,*** dar en la cabeza a; dar al traste con; ***knock out,*** sacar, quitar a golpes; dejar fuera de combate, noquear; privar del conocimiento; ***knock over,*** tirar; ***knock together,*** apañar, hacer chapuceramente; ***knock up,*** rendir, agotar; despertar; apañar; (*Am., fam.*) dejar embarazada. — *v.i.* llamar a la puerta; golpear, dar golpes; ***knock about,*** andar por ahí; ***knock off,*** dar de mano.

knock-about [ˈnɔk-əbaut], *a.* de payasada(s) (*farsas*); de batalla; ***knock-about suit,*** traje de batalla.

knock-down [ˈnɔk-daun], *a.* derribador; ***knock-down price,*** reserva, precio mínimo.

knocker [ˈnɔkə], *s.* golpeador; aldaba, llamador.

knocking [ˈnɔkiŋ], *s.* aldabazo, aldabonazo, llamada a la puerta; golpes, *m.pl.*, golpeteo.

knock-kneed [ˈnɔk-ˈni:d], *a.* zambo, patizambo.

knoll (1) [noul], *s.* loma, otero.

knoll (2) [noul], [KNELL].

knot (1) [nɔt], *s.* nudo; lazo; grupo, corrillo; (*mar.*) nudo; ***to get a knot in one's throat,*** hacérsele un nudo en la garganta a uno; ***hard knot,*** nudo apretado; ***loose knot,*** nudo flojo; ***running knot*** o ***slip-knot,*** nudo corredizo; (*fig.*) ***tied up in knots,*** hecho un lío. — *v.t.* anudar, atar con nudos. — *v.i.* formar nudos, hacer nudos; enmarañarse.

knot (2) [nɔt], *s.* (*orn.*) canuto.

knotgrass [ˈnɔtgrɑ:s], *s.* (*bot.*) centinodia.

knotted [ˈnɔtid], *a.* nudoso; anudado.

knottiness [ˈnɔtinis], *s.* (lo) nudoso; (lo) difícil *o* complicado.

knotty [ˈnɔti], *a.* nudoso; difícil, complicado, espinoso.

knout [naut], *s.* knut.

know [nou], *s.* conocimiento; ***know-all, know-it-all,*** sabelotodo, sabihondo, marisabidilla, *f.*; ***know-how,*** conocimiento técnico; experiencia, pericia; ***to be in the know,*** estar enterado, estar en el ajo. — *irr. v.t., v.i.* saber; conocer; ***know about,*** (llegar a) saber, (llegar a) enterarse de; ***know best,*** saber lo que más conviene; ***you ought to know better!*** ¡vergüenza debiera darte!; ***know how to,*** saber (cómo) + *inf.*; ***know of,*** saber de, tener noticia de; ***I know what I'm doing,*** yo sé lo que me hago; ***know what's what,*** saber cuántas son cinco; ***he has never been known to laugh,*** no se recuerda que haya reído nunca; ***to get*** o ***come to know,*** (llegar a) conocer, (llegar a) enterarse de.

knowable [ˈnouəbl], *a.* conocible.

knowing [ˈnouiŋ], *a.* sabio; malicioso; ***knowing look,*** mirada de inteligencia.

knowingly [ˈnouiŋli], *adv.* a sabiendas; con (cierta) malicia.

knowledge [ˈnɔlidʒ], *s.* conocimiento(s); saber; ciencia; ***to be common knowledge,*** ser del dominio público; ***to the best of my knowledge,*** según mi leal saber y entender; ***not to my knowledge,*** que yo sepa, no; ***without my knowledge,*** sin saberlo yo.

knowledgeable [ˈnɔlidʒəbl], *a.* sabio, erudito.

known [noun], *a.* reconocido; ***well-known person,*** persona conocida; ***to make known,*** hacer saber, participar, publicar; ***as is well known,*** como es sabido, como se sabe; ***the known facts,*** los datos que constan. — *p.p.* [KNOW].

knuckle [nʌkl], *s.* nudillo; jarrete; (*mec.*) junta de charnela; ***knuckle-duster,*** puño de hierro. — *v.i.* — ***down*** (***to***), ponerse con ahinco (a); ponerse de codos; ***knuckle under,*** someterse, achantarse.

knur(**l**) [nəː(l)], *s.* (*madera*) nudo.

knurled, knurry [nəːld, ˈnəːri], *a.* lleno de nudos, nudoso.

kobold [ˈkɔbould], *s.* gnomo.

koniscope [ˈkɔniskoup], *s.* coniscopio.

kopeck [ˈkoupek], *s.* copec.

kopje [ˈkɔpi], *s.* colina, montecillo.

Koran [kɔˈrɑːn], *s.* Alcorán, Corán.

Korea [kəˈriə]. Corea, *f.*

Korean [kəˈriən], *a.*, *s.* coreano.

kosher [ˈkouʃə], *a.* (*coc.*) preparado según la ley judía.

kow-tow [ˈkau-ˈtau], *v.i.* inclinarse; ***kow-tow to,*** acceder servilmente a, hacer la pelotilla a.

kow-towing [ˈkau-ˈtauiŋ], *a.* servil, adulón. — *s.* pelotilleo, adulonería, servilismo.

kraal [krɑːl], *s.* poblado de hotentotes; corral, redil.

kraft [krɑːft], *s.* (*Am.*) [BROWN PAPER].

kudos [ˈkjuːdɔs], *s. pl.* renombre, prestigio.

Kuwait [k(j)uːˈweit]. Kuwait.

Kuwaiti [k(j)uːˈweiti], *a.*, *s.* kuwaití.

kymograph [ˈkaimogrɑːf], *s.* cimógrafo.

L

L, l [el]. duodécima letra del alfabeto.
la [lɑ:], *s.* (*mús.*) la, *m.*
laager [ˈlɑ:gə], *s.* (*Sud Africa*) campamento.
labarum [ˈlæbərəm], *s.* lábaro.
labdanum [ˈlæbdənəm], *s.* [LADANUM].
label [leibl], *s.* etiqueta; rótulo, marbete; tejuelo; apodo. — *v.t.* poner etiqueta a; rotular; apodar; clasificar como.
labellum [ləˈbeləm], *s.* (*bot.*) labelo; (*ent.*) apéndice del labro *o* lóbulo de la trompa.
labial [ˈleibiəl], *a.* labial. — *s.* letra labial.
labiate, labiated [ˈleibiət, leibieitid], *a.*, *s.* (*bot.*) labiado.
labiodental [ˈleibioˈdentəl], *a.*, *s.* labiodental, *f.*
labionasal [ˈleibioˈneizəl], *a.*, *s.* labionasal, *f.*
labium [ˈleibiəm], *s.* (*pl.* **labia** [ˈleibiə]) labio.
laboratory [ləˈbɔrətri], *s.* laboratorio.
laborious, laboursome [ləˈbɔ:riəs, ˈleibəsəm], *a.* trabajoso, penoso; lento, pesado.
laboriousness [ləˈbɔ:riəsnis], *s.* (lo) trabajoso; (lo) lento.
labour [ˈleibə], *a.* de trabajo, laboral, obrero; (*pol.*) laborista; ***labour camp,*** campo *o* campamento de trabajo; ***labour dispute,*** conflicto laboral; ***Labour Exchange,*** bolsa de trabajo; ***labour turnover,*** rotación de la mano de obra. — *s.* trabajo; labor, faena; esfuerzo; pena; mano de obra; clase obrera; (dolores del) parto; ***hard labour,*** trabajos forzados, *m.pl.*; ***to be in labour,*** estar de parto; ***labour of love,*** trabajo hecho por amor *o* afición; ***labour-saving,*** que ahorra trabajo; ***skilled labour,*** obreros especializados, *m.pl.* — *v.t.* insistir machaconamente en, machacar. — *v.i.* hacer (*algo*) trabajosamente; afanarse; hacer mucho esfuerzo; (*mar.*) cabecear, balancearse; moverse difícilmente, avanzar con dificultad; ***labour under,*** sufrir; ***labour under a delusion,*** padecer un error.
labourer [leibərə], *s.* obrero; jornalero, bracero, peón; (*agricultura*) labriego.
labouring [ˈleibəriŋ], *a.* de trabajo; trabajador. — *s.* trabajo(s).
labradorite [ˈlæbrədɔ:rait], *s.* labradorita.
labrum [ˈlæbrəm], *s.* labro.
laburnum [ləˈbə:nəm], *s.* (*bot.*) laburno, codeso.
labyrinth [ˈlæbirinθ], *s.* laberinto, dédalo.
labyrinthine [læbiˈrinθain], *a.* laberíntico.
lac [læk], *s.* laca.
lace [leis], *s.* encaje; puntilla; blonda; galón; cordón; lazo; ***lace-frame,*** telar para encajes; ***lace-maker,*** encajero; ***lace-work,*** encaje. — *v.t.* atar con lazos *o* cordones; adornar con encajes; enlazar; (*bebidas*) echar licor a. — *v.i.* (*fam.*) ***lace into,*** dar una paliza a.
Lacedæmonian [læsidiˈmouniən], *a.*, *s.* lacedemón, lacedemonio.
lacerate [ˈlæsəreit], *v.t.* lacerar; (*fig.*) herir.
laceration [læsəˈreiʃən], *s.* laceración.
lacewing [ˈleiswiŋ], *s.* crisopo.
laches [ˈleitʃiz], *s.* (*for.*) negligencia culpable; negligencia, dejadez.
lachrymal [ˈlækriməl], *a.* lagrimal.
lachrymatory [ˈlækrimətəri], *a.* lacrimatorio.
lachrymose [ˈlækrimous], *a.* lacrimoso, lloroso.
lacing [ˈleisiŋ], *s.* (el) atar con cordones; (el) adornar con encajes; adorno de encaje(s).
lacinia [ləˈsiniə], *s.* lacinia.
laciniate(d) [ləˈsinieit(id)], *a.* laciniado.
lack [læk], *s.* falta, carencia; necesidad; ***for lack of,*** por falta de. — *v.t.* carecer de, necesitar; ***he lacks enthusiasm,*** carece de entusiasmo, le falta entusiasmo.
lackadaisical [lækəˈdeizikəl], *a.* despreocupado, indiferente, distraído.
lackaday! [ˈlækədei], *interj.* (*ant.*) ¡ay de mí!
lackey [ˈlæki], *s.* lacayo; secuaz servil.
lacking [ˈlækiŋ], *a.* carente, falto; (*fam.*) ***he's completely lacking,*** es una nulidad integral; ***he's lacking in courage,*** le falta valor.
lacklustre [ˈlæklʌstə], *a.* deslustrado, falto de brillo.
laconic(al) [ləˈkɔnik(əl)], *a.* lacónico.
laconism [ˈlækɔnizəm], *s.* laconismo.
lacquer [ˈlækə], *s.* laca; ***lacquer-work,*** objetos de laca, *m.pl.* — *v.t.* laquear.
lacquering [ˈlækəriŋ], *s.* laqueado.
lacrimal [LACHRYMAL].
lacrosse [ləˈkrɔs], *s.* lacrosse.
lactary [ˈlæktəri], *a.* lácteo, lactario.
lactate [ˈlækteit], *s.* lactato.
lactation [lækˈteiʃən], *s.* lactancia; lactación.
lacteal [ˈlæktiəl], *a.* lácteo, quilífero.
lacteous [ˈlæktiəs], *a.* lácteo, lactario.
lactescence [lækˈtesəns], *s.* lactescencia.
lactescent [lækˈtesənt], *a.* lácteo, lactario.
lactic [ˈlæktik], *a.* láctico.
lactiferous [lækˈtifərəs], *a.* lactífero.
lactometer [lækˈtɔmitə], *s.* lactómetro, galactómetro.
lactumen [ˈlæktjumən], *s.* lactumen.
lacuna [ləˈkju:nə], *s.* laguna, claro, blanco.
lacunar [ləˈkju:nə], *s.* lagunar.
lacustral, lacustrine [ləˈkʌstrəl, -trin], *a.* lacustre.
lad [læd], *s.* mozo, muchacho, joven, mozalbete, rapaz; (*fam.*) ***he's quite a lad!*** ¡qué tío!
ladanum [ˈlædənəm], *s.* ládano.
ladder [ˈlædə], *s.* escalera (*de mano*); escala; carrera (*en la media*); (*mar.*) ***accommodation ladder,*** escala real; ***extension ladder,*** escalera doble, escalera de extensión; ***ladder ropes,*** brandales, *m.pl.*; (*mar.*) ***quarter*** o ***poop ladder,*** escala de popa *o* de toldilla; ***quarter-deck ladder,*** escala del alcázar; ***rope ladder,*** escala (de cuerda).
laddie [ˈlædi], *s.* (*fam.*) [LAD].
lade [leid], *irr. v.t.* cargar, poner (sobre); vaciar; sacar (agua); echar (en), verter. — *v.i.* (*mar.*) hacer agua, abrir agua.
la-di-da [lɑ:-di-ˈdɑ], *a.* de muchas campanillas; muy afectado; de postín.
lading [ˈleidiŋ], *s.* carga, cargamento, cargazón, *f.*, flete; (*com.*) ***bill of lading,*** conocimiento *o* póliza de embarque.
Ladino [lɑ:ˈdi:nou], *a.*, *s.* ladino.
ladle [leidl], *s.* cucharón, cuchara grande; vertidor; (*artill.*) cuchara; (*hidr.*) álabe, paleta (*de rueda hidráulica*). — *v.t.* servir, verter *o* sacar con cucharón; achicar (*el agua*); poner paletas a (*una rueda hidráulica*).
ladleful [ˈleidlful], *s.* cucharonada.
lady [ˈleidi], *s.* señora; dama; ***ladies and gentlemen,*** (señoras y) señores; ***Lady Day,*** Día de la Anunciación, *m.*; ***lady-fern,*** aspidio; ***lady-in-waiting,*** dama de honor; ***lady-killer,*** conquistador, tenorio; ***lady-like,*** fino; elegante; distinguido; ***lady-love,*** amada, novia; ***lady's maid,*** doncella; ***lady's man*** o ***ladies' man,*** periquito entre ellas; (*bot.*) ***lady's mantle,*** alquimila, pie de león; (*bot.*) ***lady's-slipper,*** zueco; (*bot.*) ***lady's smock,*** cardamina; ***young lady,*** señorita.
ladybird [ˈleidibə:d], *s.* (*ent.*) mariquita, vaca de San Antón.
ladyship [ˈleidiʃip], *s.* señoría; ***Your Ladyship,*** Su Señoría.
lag (1) [læg], *s.* retraso, demora. — *v.i.* — ***behind,*** rezagarse, quedarse atrás; retrasarse.
lag (2) [læg], *v.t.* revestir, forrar (*cañerías*).
lag (3) [læg], *s.* (*fam.*) ***old lag,*** presidiario.
lager [ˈlɑ:gə], *s.* cerveza tipo Pilsen.
laggard, lagger [ˈlægəd, ˈlægə], *s.* rezagado; perezoso, remolón.

lagging [ˈlægiŋ], *s.* forro(s) (*de cañería*).
lagoon [ləˈguːn], *s.* laguna.
laic [ˈleiik], *a.* [LAY (3)]. — *s.* [LAYMAN].
laical [ˈleiikəl], *a.* [LAY (3)].
laicize [ˈleiisaiz], *v.t.* laicizar.
lair [lɛə], *s.* cubil, guarida, madriguera, cueva.
laird [lɛəd], *s.* (*Esco.*) hacendado; señor, amo.
laity [ˈleiiti], *s.* legos, *m.pl.*, laicado.
lake [leik], *s.* lago; (*pint.*) laca; ***lake dwelling,*** vivienda *o* habitación lacustre; ***Lake poets,*** lakistas, *m.pl.*
lam [læm], *v.t.*, *v.i.* — ***into,*** dar una paliza a.
lama [ˈlɑːmə], *s.* lama, *m.*
lamaism [ˈlɑːməizəm], *s.* lamaísmo.
lamb [læm], *s.* cordero; borrego; carne de cordero; ***lamb-chop,*** chuleta de cordero; ***lamb-fry,*** criadilla; ***lamb-like,*** (manso) como un cordero; ***lamb's wool,*** lana de cordero; (*fig.*) ***mutton dressed as lamb,*** la mona aunque se vista de seda . . . (mona se queda). — *v.i.* parir (*corderos*).
lambaste [læmˈbeist], *v.t.* dar una paliza a; poner como un trapo.
lambent [ˈlæmbənt], *a.* vacilante; centelleante.
lambkin [ˈlæmkin], *s.* corderito.
lambrequin [ˈlæmbrikin], *s.* lambrequín; guardamalleta.
lambskin [ˈlæmskin], *s.* corderina, piel de cordero.
lame [leim], *a.* cojo; lisiado; (*fig.*) flojo; ***to be lame,*** cojear; (*fam.*) ***lame duck,*** herido; incapacitado; rezagado; ***to make lame,*** dejar cojo. — *v.t.* lisiar, encojar.
lamella [ləˈmelə], *s.* (*pl.* **lamellæ** [ləˈmeliː]) laminilla.
lamellar [ləˈmelə], *a.* laminar.
lamellate(d) [ˈlæmeleit(id)], *a.* laminado, hojaldrado.
lamelliform [læˈmelifɔːm], *a.* lameliforme.
lameness [ˈleimnis], *s.* cojera; incapacidad; flojera.
lament [ləˈment], *s.* lamento, llanto. — *v.t.* llorar a, lamentar. — *v.i.* lamentarse, llorar.
lamentable [ˈlæmentəbl], *a.* lamentable, deplorable; lastimero.
lamentation [læmenˈteiʃən], *s.* lamento.
lamenting [ləˈmentiŋ], *s.* lamentación.
lamina [ˈlæminə], *s.* (*pl.* **laminæ** [ˈlæminiː]) lámina.
laminable [ˈlæminəbl], *a.* laminable.
laminar [ˈlæminə], *a.* laminar.
laminate [ˈlæmineit], *a.* laminado. — *v.t.* batir *o* laminar en hojas *o* láminas delgadas.
laminated [ˈlæmineitid], *a.* laminado.
Lammas [ˈlæməs]. (*igl.*) fiesta del día primero de agosto.
lammergeyer [ˈlæməˈgaiə], *s.* (*orn.*) quebrantahuesos, *m.inv.*
lamp [læmp], *s.* lámpara, farol; quinqué, velón, candil; faro; bombilla.
lampblack [ˈlæmpblæk], *s.* negro de humo; ***lamp-burner,*** mechero, piquera; ***lamp-chimney,*** tubo de lámpara; ***lamp-holder,*** portalámparas, *m.inv.*; ***lamp-post,*** pie de farol; ***lamp-shade,*** pantalla de lámpara.
lamplight [ˈlæmplait], *s.* luz de lámpara; luz artificial.
lamplighter [ˈlæmplaitə], *s.* farolero, lamparero; cerillero, encendedor de lámparas.
lampoon [læmˈpuːn], *s.* pasquín, libelo, panfleto. — *v.t.* pasquinar; satirizar.
lampooner [læmˈpuːnə], *s.* escritor de pasquines.
lamprey [ˈlæmpri], *s.* lamprea.
lanary [ˈlænəri], *s.* almacén para lana.
lanate [ˈlæneit], *a.* lanoso; (*bot.*) lanudo.
Lancastrian [lænˈkæstriən], *a.*, *s.* lancastriano.
lance [lɑːns], *s.* lanza; ***to break a lance for s.o.,*** romper una lanza por alguien, dar la cara por alguien; (*mil.*) ***lance-corporal,*** soldado de primera. — *v.t.* (a)lancear, dar una lanzada a; abrir con lanceta.
lanceolate [ˈlɑːnsioleit], *a.* lanceolado.
lancer [ˈlɑːnsə], *s.* lancero; (*pl.*) lanceros (*danza*).
lancet [ˈlɑːnsit], *s.* (*cir.*) lanceta, sangradera; (*arq.*) arco puntiagudo; (*ent.*) trompetilla.
lancewood [ˈlɑːnswud], *s.* palo de lanza.
lancinate [ˈlɑːnsineit], *v.t.* lancinar.
land [lænd], *s.* tierra; terreno; país; ***dry land,*** tierra firme; ***land agent,*** corredor de fincas; ***land forces,*** fuerzas terrestres *o* de tierra; ***landlubber,*** marinero de agua dulce; ***land reform,*** reforma(s) agraria(s); ***land-tax,*** impuesto sobre tierras; ***native land,*** patria; ***promised land,*** tierra de promisión; (*mar.*) ***to make land,*** llegar a tierra *o* arribar; ***to see how the land lies,*** tantear el terreno. — *v.t.* desembarcar; descargar; poner en tierra; conseguir (*un empleo etc.*); asestar (*un golpe*); ***I have been landed with this job,*** me han encajado *o* endosado este trabajo. — *v.i.* desembarcar; (*aer.*) aterrizar; (*aer.*, *en el mar*) amerizar, amarar; (*luna*) alunizar; ***land on one's feet,*** caer de pie; ***land up at*** o ***in,*** ir a parar a.
landau [ˈlændɔː], *s.* landó.
landed [ˈlændid], *a.* hacendado, que tiene fincas; ***landed gentry,*** pequeña aristocracia; ***landed property,*** bienes raíces, *m.pl.* — *p.p.* [LAND].
landfall [ˈlændfɔːl], *s.* (*mar.*) arribada, aterrada.
landgrave [ˈlændgreiv], *s.* langrave.
landgraviate [lændˈgreiviit], *s.* langraviato.
landholder [ˈlændhouldə], *s.* terrateniente; hacendado.
landing [ˈlændiŋ], *s.* desembarco (*de gente*); desembarque (de cargamentos); (*aer.*) aterrizaje; descansillo, rellano (de escalera); ***landing-craft,*** lanchón de desembarco; (*mar.*) ***landing-place*** o ***-stage,*** desembarcadero; ***landing-run,*** recorrido de aterrizaje; ***landing-strip,*** pista de aterrizaje.
landlady [ˈlandleidi], *s.* dueña; patrona (*de pensión*).
landless [ˈlændlis], *a.* sin tierras; desheredado.
landlocked [ˈlændlɔkt], *a.* cercado de tierra, mediterráneo.
landlord [ˈlændlɔːd], *s.* dueño; patrón; posadero.
landmark [ˈlændmɑːk], *s.* mojón; guía; punto destacado; (*fig.*) jalón; (*pl.*, *mar.*) marcas, *f.pl.*
landowner [ˈlændounə], *s.* terrateniente; hacendado.
landscape [ˈlændskeip], *s.* paisaje; ***landscape gardener,*** arquitecto de jardines; ***landscape painter,*** paisajista, *m.f.*
landslide [ˈlændslaid], *s.* desprendimiento de tierra *o* de tierras; (*fig.*, *elección*) triunfo arrollador.
landslip [ˈlændslip], [LANDSLIDE].
landsman [ˈlændzmən], *s.* hombre de (la) tierra.
landward [ˈlændwəd], *adv.* hacia la tierra.
lane [lein], *s.* camino; (*ciudad*) callejón; (*autopista*) carril; (*mar.*) ruta, derrotero.
language [ˈlæŋgwidʒ], *s.* idioma, *m.*, lengua; lenguaje; ***bad language,*** palabrotas, *f.pl.*, tacos, *m.pl.*; ***to use bad language,*** ser mal hablado; ***modern languages,*** lenguas vivas; ***strong language,*** palabras mayores, *f.pl.*
languid [ˈlæŋgwid], *a.* lánguido.
languidness [ˈlæŋgwidnis], *s.* languidez.
languish [ˈlæŋgwiʃ], *v.i.* languidecer, consumirse; ***languish for,*** suspirar por.
languishing [ˈlæŋgwiʃiŋ], *a.* lánguido, decaído; sentimental. — *s.* languidez, (el) languidecer.
languishment [ˈlæŋgwiʃmənt], *s.* languidez, languidecimiento.
languor [ˈlæŋgə], *s.* languidez; desfallecimiento.
languorous [ˈlæŋgərəs], *a.* lánguido.
laniard [LANYARD].
laniferous, lanigerous [læˈnifərəs, læˈnidʒərəs], *a.* lanudo, lanoso, lanífero, lanuginoso, velludo.
lank [læŋk], *a.* alto y flaco; lacio (*pelo*).
lank(i)ness [ˈlæŋk(i)nis], *s.* flacura; (lo) lacio.

lanky [ˈlæŋki], *a.* (*fam.*) larguirucho.
lanner [ˈlænə], *s.* (*orn.*) alcotán.
lanolin [ˈlænolin], *s.* lanolina.
lansquenet [ˈlænskənet], *s.* lansquenete; sacanete.
lantern [ˈlæntən], *s.* farol, fanal; linterna; ***lantern-jack,*** fuego fatuo; ***lantern-jawed,*** carienjuto; ***lantern jaws,*** carilargo; ***lantern-maker,*** linternero; ***magic lantern,*** linterna mágica.
lanyard [ˈlænjəd], *s.* (*mar.*) acollador; (*artill.*) correa tirafrictor.
Lao [lau], *s.* lengua oficial de Laos.
Laodicean [leiodiˈsi:ən], *a.* laodicense; (*fig.*) indiferente, tibio, irreligioso.
Laos [laus]. Laos.
Laotian [ˈlauʃən], *a.*, *s.* laosiano.
lap (1) [læp], *s.* falda; regazo; seno; traslapo, solapo; (*dep.*) vuelta; etapa; ***lap-dog,*** perrillo faldero; ***lap-joint,*** junta *o* ensambladura solapada; (*cost.*) ***lap-seam,*** costura rebatida; ***to live in the lap of luxury,*** vivir con mucho regalo. — *v.t.* (*cost.*) traslapar, solapar; (*dep.*) aventajar (en una vuelta entera). — *v.i.* traslaparse.
lap (2) [læp], *s.* lamedura. — *v.t.* lamer, bañar; ***lap up,*** beber a lenguetadas; (*fam.*) ***they'll lap it up,*** les va a encantar; se lo tragan seguro. — *v.i.* lamer.
laparotomy [læpəˈrɔtəmi], *s.* laparotomía.
lapel [ləˈpel], *s.* solapa.
lapful [ˈlæpful], *s.* lo que puede caber en el regazo.
lapidary [ˈlæpidəri], *a.*, *s.* lapidario.
lapidate [ˈlæpideit], *v.t.* lapidar.
lapidation [læpiˈdeiʃən], *s.* lapidación.
lapidific [læpiˈdifik], *a.* lapidífico.
lapidification [læpidifiˈkeiʃən], *s.* lapidificación.
lapidist [ˈlæpidist], *s.* lapidario.
lapis lazuli [ˈlæpis ˈlæzjulai], *s.* lapislázuli.
Lapland [ˈlæplænd]. Laponia.
Laplander [ˈlæplændə], *s.* lapón, *m.* (*habitante*).
Lapp [læp], *s.* lapón, *m.* (*habitante, idioma*).
lapse [læps], *s.* lapso, decurso, transcurso; lapsus, *m. inv.*, descuido, incuria; recaída; (*for.*) caducidad, prescripción; ***with the lapse of time,*** con el transcurso del tiempo. — *v.i.* transcurrir; incurrir (***into,*** en); recaer (***into,*** en); (*for.*) caducar, prescribir.
lapsed [læpst], *a.* ***lapsed Catholic,*** católico no practicante. — *p.p.* [LAPSE].
lapwing [ˈlæpwiŋ], *s.* (*orn.*) avefría.
larboard [ˈlɑ:bəd], *s.* babor.
larcener, larcenist [ˈlɑ:sənə, -ist], *s.* ladrón.
larceny [ˈlɑ:səni], *s.* (*for.*) latrocinio; ***grand larceny,*** robo mayor; ***petty larceny,*** robo menor.
larch [lɑ:tʃ], *s.* (*bot.*) alerce.
lard [lɑ:d], *s.* manteca de cerdo. — *v.t.* (*coc.*) mechar; (*fig.*) adornar (***with,*** con), salpicar (***with,*** de).
larder [ˈlɑ:də], *s.* despensa.
lardy [ˈlɑ:di], *a.* mantecoso.
large [lɑ:dʒ], *a.* grande; amplio; cuantioso; ***as large as life,*** de tamaño natural; en persona; ***large-scale,*** de *o* en gran escala; ***large-sized,*** de gran tamaño. — *adv.* ***by and large,*** en general, en términos generales. — *s.* ***at large,*** en libertad, suelto; en general.
largely [ˈlɑ:dʒli], *adv.* en gran parte.
largeness [ˈlɑ:dʒnis], *s.* grandor, (lo) grande.
larger, largest [ˈlɑ:dʒə, -ist], *compar.*, *superl.* [LARGE]; (el) más grande, (el) mayor.
largess(e) [lɑ:ˈdʒes], *s.* largueza; dádiva.
lariat [ˈlæriət], *s.* lazo.
lark (1) [lɑ:k], *s.* (*orn.*) alondra; ***to rise with the lark,*** levantarse con el gallo.
lark (2) [lɑ:k], *s.* (*fam.*) calaverada, travesura, broma; (*fam.*) cachondeo; ***to go on a lark,*** organizar un poco de juerga *o* de cachondeo. — *v.i.* — ***about,*** tontear; enredar; dedicarse al cachondeo.
larkspur [ˈlɑ:kspə:], *s.* (*bot.*) delfinio, espuela de caballero.
larrup [ˈlærəp], *v.t.* (*fam.*) zurrar, zurriagar, tundir.
larva [ˈlɑ:və], *s.* larva.
larval [ˈlɑ:vəl], *a.* larval.
larvate, larvated [ˈlɑ:veit, lɑ:ˈveitid], *a.* larvado.
laryngeal [ləˈrindʒiəl], *a.* laríngeo.
laryngitis [lærinˈdʒaitis], *s.* laringitis, *f. inv.*
laryngoscope [læˈriŋgoskoup], *s.* laringoscopio.
laryngoscopy [læriŋˈgɔskəpi], *s.* laringoscopia.
laryngotomy [læriŋˈgɔtəmi], *s.* laringotomía.
larynx [ˈlæriŋks], *s.* laringe, *f.*
Lascar [ˈlæskɑ:], *s.* láscar.
lascivious [ləˈsiviəs], *a.* lascivo.
lasciviousness [ləˈsiviəsnis], *s.* lascivia.
lash [læʃ], *s.* látigo, tralla, azote; (*anat.*) pestaña; (*golpe*) latigazo; (*fig.*) (el) fustigar. — *v.t.* azotar; atar, sujetar; fustigar; trincar; vituperar; excitar. — *v.i.* chasquear; ***lash out,*** gastarse mucho dinero; ser espléndido; ***lash out at,*** pegar un puñetazo a; (*fig.*) soltar una andanada a.
lashing [ˈlæʃiŋ], *s.* ligadura, atadura; cabo de cuerda, lazo; (*mar.*) amarra, amarradura; (castigo de) azotes; (el) fustigar; (*mar.*) ***lashing rings,*** argollas de amura, *f.pl.*; ***lashing rope,*** braga.
lasket [ˈlæskit], *s.* (*mar.*) badaza de boneta.
lass [læs], *s.* chica, zagala, moza.
lassie [ˈlæsi], *s.* muchachita, niña, mozuela.
lassitude [ˈlæsitju:d], *s.* lasitud.
lasso [læˈsu:], *s.* lazo, guasco, mangana. — *v.t.* lazar, manganear.
lassoer [læˈsu:ə], *s.* lazador.
last (1) [lɑ:st], *a.* último, postrero; pasado; final, extremo; ***last but not least,*** por último pero no el último; ***last but one,*** penúltimo; ***last but two,*** antepenúltimo; ***to be on one's last legs,*** estar en las últimas; ***last night,*** anoche; ***the last thing I want,*** lo último que quiero; lo que menos pretendo; ***last week,*** la semana pasada; ***to have the last word,*** hablar el último. — *adv.* la última vez, por última vez. — *s.* término, fin, conclusión; (el) último; (lo) último; ***at last,*** por fin, al fin; finalmente; ***we shall never hear the last of this,*** esto no nos lo dejarán olvidar; ***to see the last of,*** perder de vista; ***to the last,*** hasta el fin, hasta lo último.
last (2) [lɑ:st], *v.i.* durar; resistir; continuar; ***last out,*** (per)durar.
last (3) [lɑ:st], *s.* (*zap.*) horma; ***last-maker,*** hormero. — *v.t.* ahormar.
lastage [ˈlɑ:stidʒ], *s.* (*mar.*) espacio para el cargamento; (*ant.*) lastre.
laster [ˈlɑ:stə], *s.* (*zap.*) ahormador.
lasting [ˈlɑ:stiŋ], *a.* duradero, perdurable. — *s.* (*tej.*) sempiterna.
lastingness [ˈlɑ:stiŋnis], *s.* durabilidad.
lastly [ˈlɑ:stli], *adv.* finalmente, por último.
latch [lætʃ], *s.* picaporte; ***latch-key,*** llavín; ***latch-string,*** cordón de aldaba; ***on the latch,*** cerrado con picaporte.
latchet [ˈlætʃit], *s.* cordón de zapato.
late [leit], *a.* tardío; (hora) avanzada; reciente, de hace poco; difunto; antiguo, ex; ***as late as,*** todavía en; ***late-comer,*** recién llegado; rezagado, (el) que llega tarde; ***to keep late hours,*** trasnochar; ***late lamented,*** difunto . . . que en paz descanse; ***late nineteenth century,*** (de) finales del siglo diecinueve; ***of late years,*** de *o* en estos últimos años; ***it is late,*** es tarde; ***it's getting late,*** se hace tarde; ***you're late,*** llegas tarde; ***the train is late,*** el tren lleva retraso; ***it was five minutes late,*** llegó con cinco minutos de retraso; ***he was late (in) applying,*** presentó tarde la solicitud, tardó en presentar la solicitud. — *adv.* tarde; ***better late than never,*** más vale tarde que nunca; ***late in the afternoon,*** a última hora de la tarde; ***late in life,*** (cuando era) ya mayor;

late in the year, (cuando iba) ya avanzado el año; ***to stay up late,*** trasnochar. — *s.* ***of late,*** últimamente.

lateen [lə'ti:n], *a.* latino; (*mar.*) ***lateen-sail,*** vela latina.

lateener [lə'ti:nə], *s.* falucho.

lately ['leitli], *adv.* recientemente, últimamente; hace poco.

latency ['leitənsi], *s.* estado latente, (lo) latente.

lateness ['leitnis], *s.* retraso; (lo) tardío; (lo) avanzado.

latent ['leitənt], *a.* latente.

later ['leitə], *a.* posterior, más reciente. — *adv.* más tarde, luego, después; ***later on,*** más tarde, luego; ***sooner or later,*** tarde *o* temprano.

lateral ['lætərəl], *a.* lateral.

Lateran ['lætərən], *a.* lateranense.

latest ['leitist], *a.* (el) más reciente; (lo) más tarde. — *s.* ***at the latest,*** a más tardar.

latex ['leiteks], *s.* látex.

lath [lɑ:θ], *s.* listón.

lathe [leið], *s.* torno; ***lathe-bed,*** banco de torno.

lather ['lɑ:ðə], *s.* jabonadura(s), espuma (de jabón), espumas, *f.pl.* — *v.t.* enjabonar. — *v.i.* espumar, hacer espuma.

lathery ['lɑ:ðəri], *a.* espumoso.

lathing ['leiðiŋ], *s.* enlistonado.

Latin ['lætin], *a.* latino; (*fam.*) latino, meridional. — *s.* latín; (*fam.*) latino, meridional.

Latin-American ['lætin-ə'merikən], *a., s.* latinoamericano, hispanoamericano.

Latinism ['lætinizəm], *s.* latinismo.

Latinist ['lætinist], *s.* latinista, *m.f.*

Latinity [læ'tiniti], *s.* latinidad.

latinize ['lætinaiz], *v.t.* latinizar. — *v.i.* emplear latinismos.

latish ['leitiʃ], *a.* algo tardío. — *adv.* algo tarde, tardecillo.

latitude ['lætitju:d], *s.* latitud; amplitud; libertad.

latitudinal [læti'tju:dinəl], *a.* latitudinal.

latitudinarian [lætitju:di'nɛəriən], *a., s.* latitudinario.

latitudinarianism [lætitju:di'nɛəriənizəm], *s.* latitudinarismo.

latria [lə'traiə], *s.* latría.

latrine [lə'tri:n], *s.* letrina.

latter ['lætə], *a.* posterior, moderno, más reciente; éste, el último; ***latter-day,*** de nuestros días; ***Latter-day Saints,*** (el) pueblo mormón.

lattice ['lætis], *s.* celosía, rastel, enrejado de listoncillos. — *v.t.* enrejar, poner celosías a; hacer un enrejado para.

Latvia ['lætvia]. Letonia, Latvia.

Latvian ['lætviən], *a., s.* letón, *m.*, latvio; (*idioma*) letón, *m.*

laud [lɔ:d], *s.* elogio, alabanza; (*pl.*) (*igl.*) laudes, *f.pl.* — *v.t.* alabar, celebrar, elogiar, loar; ***laud to the skies,*** poner sobre las estrellas.

laudability, laudableness [lɔ:də'biliti, 'lɔ:dəblnis], *s.* (lo) laudable.

laudable ['lɔ:dəbl], *a.* laudable, loable.

laudanum ['lɔdnəm], *s.* láudano.

laudative, laudatory ['lɔ:dətiv, -təri], *a.* laudatorio. — *s.* panegírico.

laugh [lɑ:f], *s.* risa; risotada; ***to have the last laugh,*** reírse el último. — *v.t.* — ***down,*** ridiculizar, hacer callar a carcajadas; — ***off,*** tomar a risa. — *v.i.* reírse; ***laugh at,*** reírse de; ***laugh in s.o.'s face,*** reírsele a alguien en las barbas; ***he who laughs last laughs longest,*** el que se ríe el último se ríe el mejor; ***laugh up one's sleeve,*** reírse para su sayo.

laughable ['lɑ:fəbl], *a.* risible, irrisorio.

laugher ['lɑ:fə], *s.* reidor.

laughing ['lɑ:fiŋ], *a.* risueño, reidor; ***laughing eyes,*** ojos alegres, *m.pl.* — *s.* risa(s); ***laughing-gas,*** gas hilarante; ***laughing matter,*** cosa de risa; ***laughing stock,*** hazmerreír.

laughingly ['lɑ:fiŋli], *adv.* alegremente, entre risas.

laughter ['lɑ:ftə], *s.* risas, *f.pl.*

launch [lɔ:ntʃ], *s.* (*mar.*) botadura (de un buque); lanzamiento; (*mar.*) lancha. — *v.t.* botar (al agua); iniciar, dar principio a, lanzar. — *v.i.* lanzarse.

launching ['lɔ:ntʃiŋ], *s.* botadura; lanzamiento; ***launching pad,*** plataforma de lanzamiento.

launder ['lɔ:ndə], *v.t.* lavar.

launderer ['lɔ:ndərə], *s.* lavandero.

launderette [lɔ:ndə'ret], *s.* lavandería automática.

laundress ['lɔ:ndris], *s.* lavandera.

laundry ['lɔ:ndri], *s.* lavandería; lavadero; (*fam.*) ropa lavada, colada.

laureate ['lɔ:riit], *a.* laureado. — *s.* (poeta) laureado.

laureateship ['lɔ:riitʃip], *s.* dignidad de poeta laureado.

laurel ['lɔrəl], *s.* laurel; lauro, corona de laurel; ***to crown with laurel,*** laurear.

laurelled ['lɔrəld], *a.* laureado, coronado con laurel.

Laurentian [lɔ'renʃən], *a.* lorenziano.

laurustine, laurustinus ['lɔrəstain, lɔrəs'tainəs], *s.* durillo, viburno.

lava ['lɑ:və], *s.* lava(s).

lavatory ['lævətəri], *s.* váter, retrete; lavatorio; ***public lavatory,*** urinarios públicos, *m.pl.*

lave [leiv], *v.t.* lavar, bañar.

lavender ['lævində], *s.* espliego; lavanda; ***lavender water,*** agua de lavanda.

laver ['leivə], *s.* aguamanil, jofaina.

lavish ['læviʃ], *a.* pródigo, espléndido; suntuoso, opíparo; profuso. — *v.t.* prodigar; ***lavish care upon,*** prodigar atenciones a, colmar de atenciones.

lavishness ['læviʃnis], *s.* prodigalidad; profusión.

law [lɔ:], *s.* ley, *f.*; derecho; regla; ***by law,*** según la ley; ***civil law,*** derecho civil; ***common law,*** derecho consuetudinario; ***in law,*** según (el) derecho; ***law and order,*** (el) orden (público); ***law-abiding,*** observante de la ley; formal; ***law-breaker,*** transgresor de la ley; ***to go to law,*** recurrir a los tribunales; ***to have the law on,*** llevar a los tribunales; ***to lay down the law (on),*** sentar cátedra (de); ***to practise (law),*** ejercer (de abogado); ***to take the law into one's own hands,*** tomarse la justicia por su mano.

law(ks)! [lɔ:(ks)], *interj.* (*ant.*) ¡Dios mío!

lawful ['lɔ:ful], *a.* legal, legítimo, lícito.

lawfulness ['lɔ:fulnis], *s.* legalidad, legitimidad, (lo) lícito.

lawgiver ['lɔ:givə], *s.* legislador.

lawgiving ['lɔ:giviŋ], *a.* legislativo.

lawless ['lɔ:lis], *a.* ilegal; desenfrenado; que obra con desacato.

lawlessness ['lɔ:lisnis], *s.* ilegalidad; desenfreno; desacato.

lawmaker ['lɔ:meikə], *s.* legislador.

lawn (1) [lɔ:n], *s.* césped; ***lawn-mower,*** cortacéspedes, *m.inv.*

lawn (2) [lɔ:n], *s.* (*tej.*) linón.

lawsuit ['lɔ:s(j)u:t], *s.* pleito, litigio, proceso.

lawyer ['lɔ:jə], *s.* abogado; jurisconsulto.

lax [læks], *a.* laxo; descuidado, negligente, falto de disciplina *o* de rigor.

laxation [læk'seiʃən], *s.* laxación.

laxative ['læksətiv], *a.* laxativo, laxante. — *s.* laxante.

laxity, laxness ['læksiti, -nis], *s.* laxitud; relajación, relajamiento; negligencia, incuria.

lay (1) [lei], *pret.* [LIE (2)].

lay (2) [lei], *s.* disposición; situación; caída, sesgo; (*fam.*) negocio. — *irr. v.t.* poner, colocar, dejar; tender, extender; acostar; derribar, acabar con; apuntar (*un cañón*); hacer (*apuestas*); echar (*culpas,* *cimientos*); presentar (*reclamación*); matar (*polvo*); poner (*mesa, huevos*); aquietar; preparar; conjurar; apostar (*dinero*); formar (*planes*); tender (*vías, caminos*); ***lay aside, away,*** guardar; poner a un lado; ***lay bare,*** poner *o* dejar al descubierto; ***lay by,*** guardar; ***lay claim to,*** reclamar; ***lay down,*** deponer (*las armas*); establecer; trazar; ***lay the dust,*** (a)sentar el polvo; ***lay eyes on,*** echar la vista encima a; ***lay fears,*** calmar, ahuyentar (los) temores; ***lay hands on,*** poner la mano encima a; ***lay hold of,*** agarrar; ***lay one's hopes on,*** cifrar las esperanzas en; ***lay in,*** almacenar; ***lay low,*** derribar; ***lay off,*** despedir (*a un obrero*); ***lay on,*** instalar; asestar, descargar (*golpes*); ***lay it on thick,*** cargar la mano; ***lay open,*** exponer; poner al descubierto; ***lay out,*** disponer; trazar; desembolsar; ***lay stress on,*** hacer hincapié en; (*mar.*) ***lay to,*** poner al pairo; ***lay up,*** guardar; obligar a guardar cama; ***to be laid up,*** estar fuera de servicio *o* guardado *o* encamado; ***lay waste,*** asolar. — *v.i.* poner; apostar; ***lay about one,*** dar palos a un lado y a otro; ***lay into s.o.,*** dar una paliza a alguien; (*mar.*) ***lay to,*** ponerse al pairo.

lay (3) [lei], *a.* laico; lego; profano; ***lay-clerk,*** sochantre.

lay (4) [lei], *s.* balada, lay.

layer [leiə], *s.* capa; lecho; (*alb.*) hilada; (*geol.*) estrato; (*agric.*) acodo; (gallina) ponedora. — *v.t.* (*agric.*) acodar.

layering [ˈleiəriŋ], *s.* (*agric.*) acodadura.

layette [leiˈet], *s.* canastilla.

lay-figure [ˈlei-ˈfigə], *s.* maniquí.

laying [ˈleiiŋ], *a.* situado, colocado; (*mar.*) anclado; ***laying hen,*** gallina ponedora. — *s.* colocación; tendido; postura (*del huevo*); ***laying-on of hands,*** imposición de manos.

layman [ˈleimən], *s.* lego, seglar; profano.

layout [ˈleiaut], *s.* plan; disposición, trazado.

laystall [ˈleistɔ:l], *s.* establo.

lazar [ˈlæzə], *s.* lázaro, lazarino, leproso.

lazaret, lazaretto [læzəˈret, -ou], **lazar-house** [ˈlæzə-haus], *s.* lazareto.

lazar-like, lazarly [ˈlæzə-laik, ˈlazəli], *a.* lazarino.

lazarwort [ˈlæzəwə:t], *s.* laserpicio.

laze [leiz], *v.t.* — ***away,*** malgastar por pereza, perder en el ocio *o* con el ocio. — *v.i.* holgazanear.

laziness [ˈleizinis], *s.* pereza, indolencia, holgazanería.

lazuli [ˈlæzjulai], *s.* lapislázuli.

lazy [ˈleizi], *a.* perezoso; holgazán; ***lazy-bones,*** vago, gandul.

lea [li:], *s.* prado, pradera.

leach [li:tʃ], *s.* cenizas de lejía, *f.pl.*; colada; lixiviación. — *v.t.* lixiviar; colar (*la ropa*).

leachy [ˈli:tʃi], *a.* penetrable, permeable, poroso.

lead (1) [led], *s.* (*min.*) plomo; (*impr.*) interlínea, regleta; (*mar.*) sonda, escandallo; (*lápiz*) mina; ***black-lead,*** lápiz-plomo, plombagina, grafito; ***deep-sea lead,*** escandallo mayor; ***hand-lead, lead-line,*** sondaleza; ***lead-pencil,*** lápiz; ***red lead,*** almagra, almagre; ***sugar of lead,*** azúcar de plomo, acetato de plomo; ***white lead,*** albayalde; ***yellow lead,*** albayalde calcinado; (*mar.*) ***to heave the lead,*** echar la sonda. — *v.t.* emplomar, forrar *o* guarnecer con plomo; (*impr.*) interlinear, espaciar, regletear.

lead (2) [li:d], *s.* delantera, cabeza; primacía, hegemonía, dirección, mando; iniciativa; ejemplo; guía; indicación; (*dep.*) liderato; (*juego*) mano; (*teat.*) papel principal; (*perros*) traílla, correa; (*elec.*) conductor; ***to be in the lead,*** ir en cabeza; ***to take the lead*** (***over***), tomar la delantera (a); tomar la iniciativa. — *v.t.* llevar; conducir, guiar; encabezar; dirigir, mandar; mover, incitar (***to,*** a); ***lead astray,*** llevar por mal camino; ***lead on,*** animar, incitar (***to,*** a); (*fig.*) ***lead s.o. up the garden path,*** tomarle el pelo a alguien; ***lead the way,*** enseñar el camino; ser el primero. — *v.i.* llevar la delantera; tener el mando; ser el primero; conducir (***to,*** a); (*juego*) salir, ser mano; ***lead off,*** empezar; abrir el juego; ***lead up to,*** conducir a, preparar el terreno para.

leaden [ˈledən], *a.* de plomo; plomizo; plúmbeo; apesadumbrado; ***leaden-footed,*** lento, con paso lento; ***leaden-hearted,*** insensible; apesadumbrado.

leader [ˈli:də], *s.* jefe; caudillo; (*pol.*) dirigente, líder; guía, *m.f.*; conductor; cuadrillero; cabecilla (*de guerrilleros, rebeldes, etc.*); caballo delantero; (*orquesta*) primer violín, (*Am.*) director; (*periódico*) artículo de fondo; (*min.*) filón; (*mec.*) rueda motriz.

leadership [ˈli:dəʃip], *s.* dirección, liderato; jefatura; mando; iniciativa; ***powers of leadership,*** dotes de mando, *f.pl.*

leading (1) [ˈli:diŋ], *a.* principal; primero; capital; ***leading article,*** artículo de fondo, editorial; ***leading man, lady,*** primer galán, primera actriz; ***leading question,*** pregunta capciosa. — *s.* conducción; dirección; ***leading-strings,*** andadores, *m.pl.*

leading (2) [ˈlediŋ], *s.* emplomadura; (*impr.*) interlineación.

leadsman [ˈledzmən], *s.* (*mar.*) sondeador.

leadwort [ˈledwə:t], *s.* velesa.

leaf [li:f], *s.* (*pl.* **leaves** [li:vz]) (*bot.*) hoja; ***to shake like a leaf,*** temblar como un azogado; ***to take a leaf from s.o.'s book,*** seguir el ejemplo de alguien; ***to turn over a new leaf,*** enmendarse. —*v.t.* — ***through,*** hojear. — *v.i.* echar hojas *o* las hojas.

leafage [ˈli:fidʒ], *s.* follaje.

leafed, leafy [li:ft, ˈli:fi], *a.* frondoso; hojoso.

leafiness [ˈli:finis], *s.* (lo) frondoso.

leafless [ˈli:flis], *a.* áfilo, deshojado, sin follaje.

leaflet [ˈli:flit], *s.* hoja volante, octavilla; folleto.

leaf-stalk [ˈli:f-stɔ:k], *s.* (*bot.*) pecíolo.

league [li:g], *s.* liga; legua; ***League of Nations,*** Sociedad de (las) Naciones; ***in league with,*** aliado con; conchabado con. — *v.t.* ligar. — *v.i.* coligarse, conchabarse.

leagued [li:gd], *a.* confederado, aliado.

leak [li:k], *s.* vía de agua, gotera; salida, escape, fuga; rendija; filtración; (*pol.*) revelación; ***to spring a leak,*** (empezar a) hacer agua; ***to stop a leak,*** cegar una vía de agua. — *v.t.* (*pol.*) divulgar. — *v.i.* hacer agua; salirse; gotear; ***leak in,*** infiltrarse; ***leak out,*** filtrarse; (*fig.*) trascender (un secreto).

leakage [ˈli:kidʒ], *s.* goteo; filtración; (*com.*) avería; pérdida, merma.

leaky [ˈli:ki], *a.* llovedizo; que hace agua; que (se) rezuma.

leal [li:əl], *a.* (*Esco.*) leal, sincero, fiel; ***the land of the leal,*** la morada de los bienaventurados, la Gloria.

lean (1) [li:n], *a.* magro, escaso; delgado. — *s.* carne magra *o* mollar.

lean (2) [li:n], *v.t.* apoyar, recostar. — *v.i.* ladearse; inclinarse; apoyarse; ***lean against,*** apoyarse en; ***lean upon,*** acodarse en.

leaning [ˈli:niŋ], *s.* inclinación, propensión, tendencia.

leanly [ˈli:nli], *adv.* pobremente.

leanness [ˈli:nnis], *s.* delgadez; magrez; carestía.

lean-to [ˈli:n-tu:], *s.* (*arq.*) colgadizo.

leap [li:p], *s.* salto, brinco; ***leap-frog,*** fil derecho, pídola; ***leap in the dark,*** salto en el vacío; ***leap-year,*** año bisiesto; ***by leaps and bounds,*** a pasos agigantados. — *v.t.* salvar de un salto. — *v.i.* saltar, brincar; ***leap over,*** saltar por encima (de).

leaper [ˈli:pə], *s.* saltador, brincador.

leapingly [ˈli:piŋli], *adv.* a brincos, a saltos.

learn [lə:n], *irr. v.t.* aprender; saber, enterarse de. — *v.i.* aprender, enterarse; ***live and learn,*** vivir para ver.

learnable [ˈlə:nəbl], *a.* que puede aprenderse.
learned [ˈlə:nid], *a.* docto, erudito, sabio.
learner [ˈlə:nə], *s.* principiante; aprendiz; estudiante.
learning [ˈlə:niŋ], *s.* ciencia; saber; erudición; estudio, (el) aprender.
lease [li:s], *s.* (*for.*) arriendo; arrendamiento; (*Am.*) contrato de alquiler; ***to let out on lease,*** dar en arriendo; ***to take on a new lease of life,*** recobrar su vigor; renovarse. — *v.t.* arrendar; dar en arriendo; tomar en arriendo; (*Am.*) [LET].
leasehold [ˈli:should], *a.* arrendado. — *s.* arrendamiento; bienes raíces arrendados, *m.pl.*
leaseholder [ˈli:shouldə], *s.* arrendador.
leaser [ˈli:sə], *s.* arrendatario.
leash [li:ʃ], *s.* traílla, correa; ***to strain at the leash,*** estar impaciente; (*fig.*) tascar el freno. — *v.t.* atraillar, atar con correa.
least [li:st], *a.* menor; más pequeño; mínimo; menos importante. — *adv.* menos. — *s.* ***at least,*** al menos, a lo menos, por lo menos; ***at the*** (***very***) ***least,*** lo menos, como poco; ***not in the least,*** en absoluto; ***to say the least,*** que digamos.
leat [li:t], *s.* cauce, caz.
leather [ˈleðə], *a.* de cuero; ***leather belt,*** correa; ***leather belting,*** correaje; ***leather dresser,*** curtidor. — *s.* cuero; piel (curtida); ***patent leather,*** charol. — *v.t.* guarnecer con cuero; zurrar.
leatherette [leðəˈret], *s.* cuero artificial.
leatherhead [ˈleðəhed], *s.* (*orn.*) frailecico; (*fig.*) tonto, lerdo.
leathern [ˈleðən], *a.* de cuero.
leathery [ˈleðəri], *a.* correoso; curtido (*piel etc.*).
leave [li:v], *s.* permiso; licencia; ***by your leave,*** con permiso de usted; ***leave of absence,*** licencia; ***leave-taking,*** despedida; ***on leave,*** de licencia, de permiso, de vacaciones; ***to take one's leave of,*** despedirse de; ***to take French leave,*** despedirse a la francesa; ***without so much as a 'by your leave',*** sin decir oxte ni moxte. — *irr. v.t.* dejar, abandonar; salir de, marcharse de; legar; ceder; entregar; ***leave it at that,*** déjalo estar; vale, basta; ***leave it to me,*** déjalo de mi cuenta, yo me encargo de eso; ***it leaves much to be desired,*** deja mucho que desear; ***four from eight leaves four,*** ocho menos cuatro son cuatro; ***leave alone,*** dejar en paz, no meterse con; no tocar, dejar; ***leave behind,*** dejar atrás; ***leave off,*** no ponerse, quitarse; ***leave out,*** omitir, prescindir de. — *v.i.* salir, irse, marcharse; ***leave off smoking,*** dejar de fumar.
leaved [li:vd], *a.* de hojas.
leaven [ˈlevən], *s.* levadura. — *v.t.* leudar; penetrar e influir; (*fig.*) ***leaven the mixture,*** echar un poco de ajilimójili a la cosa; ***leavened bread,*** pan de levadura.
leavening [ˈlevəniŋ], *s.* levadura; mezcla; influencia; elemento.
leaves [li:vz], *s.pl.* [LEAF].
leaving [ˈli:viŋ], *s.* partida, marcha; (*pl.*) sobras, *f.pl.*, residuos, *m.pl.*, restos, *m.pl.*
Lebanese [lebəˈni:z], *a.*, *s.* libanés, *m.*
Lebanon [ˈlebənən]. el Líbano.
lecher [ˈletʃə], *s.* hombre lujurioso.
lecherous [ˈletʃərəs], *a.* lujurioso, libidinoso.
lechery, lecherousness [ˈletʃəri, -rəsnis], *s.* lujuria, libidinosidad.
lecithin [ˈlesiθin], *s.* lecitina.
lectern [ˈlektə:n], *s.* facistol.
lection [ˈlekʃən], *s.* lección.
lectionary [ˈlekʃənəri], *s.* leccionario.
lector [ˈlektə], *s.* lector.
lecture [ˈlektʃə], *s.* conferencia; explicación; (*fam.*) sermón; ***curtain lecture,*** reconvención entre esposos; ***lecture hall*** o ***room,*** sala de conferencias, aula. — *v.t.* dar lecciones a; (*fam.*) sermonear. — *v.i.* dar conferencias; explicar.
lecturer [ˈlektʃərə], *s.* conferenciante; profesor (adjunto).
lectureship [ˈlektʃəʃip], *s.* cargo de profesor.
led [led], *a.* ***led horse,*** caballo de mano. — *pret.*, *p.p.* [LEAD (2)].
ledge [ledʒ], *s.* repisa, (re)borde; antepecho; anaquel; retallo; (*pl.*) (*mar.*) barrotes, *m.pl.*, latas de los baos, *f.pl.*
ledger [ˈledʒə], *s.* (*com.*) libro mayor; traviesa de andamio; solera de emparrillado.
lee [li:], *a.* (*mar.*) sotaventado; (*mar.*) ***lee shore,*** costa de sotavento; ***lee side,*** banda de sotavento; ***lee tide,*** marea de donde viene el viento; ***to have lee room,*** disponer de sitio suficiente (*para maniobrar*). — *s.* (*mar.*) sotavento; socaire; ***under the lee,*** a sotavento.
leech (1) [li:tʃ], *s.* sanguijuela; ***artificial leech,*** ventosa.
leech (2) [li:tʃ], *s.* (*mar.*) caídas, *m.pl.*; ***leech lines,*** apagapenoles, *m.pl.*; ***leech-rope,*** relinga de las caídas.
leek [li:k], *s.* (*bot.*) puerro.
leer [liə], *s.* mirada insistente, mirada lasciva. — *v.i.* mirar con lascivia.
leeringly [ˈliəriŋli], *adv.* lujuriosamente.
lees [li:z], *s.pl.* heces, *f.pl.*, posos, *m.pl.*, sedimento, zurrapa, lías, *f.pl.*
leeward [ˈlu:əd], *a.* (*mar.*) a *o* de sotavento, sotaventeado, roncero; ***leeward-tide,*** marea en la dirección del viento. — *adv.* a *o* hacia sotavento. — *s.* sotavento; ***to leeward,*** a sotavento; ***to fall to leeward,*** sotaventarse; ***to stand to leeward,*** virar de bordo en redondo.
leeway [ˈli:wei], *s.* (*mar.*) deriva; atraso; ***to have a lot of leeway to make up,*** tener mucho que recuperar; ***not to leave much leeway for,*** dejar poco margen para.
left (1) [left], *a.*, *s.* izquierdo; ***left-wing,*** de izquierdas, izquierdista.
left (2) [left] *a.* ***left-luggage*** (***office***), consigna; ***left-overs,*** sobras, *f.pl.* — *pret.*, *p.p.* [LEAVE].
left-hand [ˈleft-hænd], *a.* (*aut.*) (conducción) por la izquierda; (*lado*) (mano) izquierda; ***on the left-hand side,*** a mano izquierda.
left-handed [ˈleft-ˈhændid], *a.* zurdo; (*fig.*) desmañado, torpe; malicioso, de segunda intención; morganático.
leftist [ˈleftist], *a.*, *s.* izquierdista, *m.f.*
left-winger [ˈleft-ˈwiŋə], *s.* izquierdista, *m.f.*
leg [leg], *s.* pierna; (*animales*) pata; pie *o* pata (*de un mueble*); caña (*de media* o *de bota*); (*geom.*) lado (*de un triángulo*); pernil (*de carne de cerdo*); muslo (*de pollo*); (*fig.*) etapa; ***to be on one's legs again,*** haberse repuesto; ***to be on one's last legs,*** estar en las últimas *o* dando las boqueadas; ***to get*** (***up***) ***on one's hind legs,*** ponerse gallo *o* chulo; ***to get one's sea legs,*** acostumbrarse a la vida de a bordo; ***to give a leg up,*** ayudar a subir; ***not to have a leg to stand on,*** no tener razón de ninguna clase, no poder decir nada para justificarse; (*fam.*) ***to pull s.o.'s leg,*** tomarle el pelo a alguien; ***stretch one's legs,*** estirar las piernas.
legacy [ˈlegəsi], *s.* legado, herencia; ***legacy duty,*** derechos de herencia, *m.pl.*; ***legacy hunter,*** (el) que anda a caza de herencias.
legal [ˈli:gəl], *a.* legal; jurídico; ***legal adviser,*** asesor jurídico.
legality [liˈgæliti], *s.* legalidad; legitimidad.
legalization [li:gəlaiˈzeiʃən], *s.* legalización.
legalize [ˈli:gəlaiz], *v.t.* legalizar.
legate [ˈlegit], *s.* legado.
legatee [legəˈti:], *s.* legatorio.
legateship [ˈlegitʃip], *s.* legacía.
legation [liˈgeiʃən], *s.* legación.
legato [liˈgɑ:tou], *adv.* (*mús.*) ligado.
legator [liˈgeitə], *s.* testador, el que haciendo testamento deja legados.
legend [ˈledʒənd], *s.* leyenda; letrero, inscripción.

legendary ['ledʒəndəri], *a.* legendario.
leger ['ledʒə], *a.* (*ant.*) ligero, delicado; (*mús.*) ***leger-lines,*** líneas adicionales al pentagrama; ***leger-space,*** espacio comprendido por estas líneas.
legerdemain [ledʒədi'mein], *s.* juego de manos, prestidigitación; trapacería.
legged ['legid], *a.* de piernas, que tiene piernas; ***three-legged,*** de tres pies.
legging ['legiŋ], *s.* polaina.
Leghorn [le'gɔ:n], *s.* sombrero de paja; gallina.
legibility [ledʒi'biliti], *s.* legibilidad.
legible ['ledʒibl], *a.* legible.
legion ['li:dʒən], *s.* legión, *f.*; gran número; ***their numbers are legion,*** son innumerables.
legionary ['li:dʒənəri], *a., s.* legionario.
legislate ['ledʒisleit], *v.i.* legislar.
legislation [ledʒis'leiʃən], *s.* legislación.
legislative ['ledʒislətiv], *a.* legislativo.
legislator ['ledʒisleitə], *s.* legislador.
legislatorial [ledʒislə'tɔ:riəl], *a.* perteneciente *o* relativo a la legislación *o* a una legislatura.
legislatorship ['ledʒisleitəʃip], *s.* oficio de legislador.
legislatress ['ledʒisleitris], *s.* legisladora.
legislature ['ledʒislətʃə], *s.* legislatura.
legist ['li:dʒist], *s.* legista, *m.f.*, jurisconsulto.
legitimacy, legitimateness [li'dʒitiməsi, -mitnis], *s.* legitimidad.
legitimate [li'dʒitimit], *a.* legítimo; admisible; genuino, auténtico. — [li'dʒitimeit], *v.t.* legitimar.
legitimation [lidʒiti'meiʃən], *s.* legitimación.
legitimist [li'dʒitimist], *s.* legitimista, *m.f.*
legitimize [li'dʒitimaiz], *v.t.* legitimar.
legume, legumen ['legju:m, le'gju:mən], *s.* legumbre.
leguminous [le'gju:minəs], *a.* leguminoso.
leisure ['leʒə], *s.* ocio, tiempo libre; desocupación; ***at leisure,*** sin ocupación; sin obligaciones; sin prisas, con tiempo; ***at one's leisure,*** a conveniencia de uno; ***to be at leisure,*** estar desocupado; ***leisure hours,*** horas libres, *f.pl.*, horas de ocio, *f.pl.*
leisured ['leʒəd], *a.* acomodado; desocupado.
leisureliness ['leʒəlinis], *s.* (lo) tranquilo (de).
leisurely ['leʒəli], *a.* pausado, lento, parsimonioso. — *adv.* despacio, con calma.
leitmotiv ['laitmouti:f], *s.* tema constante, *m.*, leitmotiv.
lemma (1) ['lemə], *s.* (*log., mat.*) lema.
lemma (2) ['lemə], *s.* (*bot.*) lemnáceo, lentícula.
lemon ['lemən], *a.* hecho *o* sazonado con limón; de color de limón; ***lemon coloured,*** cetrino; ***lemon drop,*** pastilla de limón; ***lemon grove,*** limonar; ***lemon squash,*** limonada; ***lemon tree,*** limonero. — *s.* limón; ***candied lemon,*** acitrón.
lemonade [lemə'neid], *s.* limonada; gaseosa de limón.
lemur ['li:mə], *s.* lémur.
lend [lend], *v.t.* prestar; ***lend one's aid,*** prestar ayuda; ***lend an ear,*** prestar atención, prestar oído; ***lend a hand,*** echar una mano, ayudar.
lendable ['lendəbl], *a.* prestable, prestadizo.
lender ['lendə], *s.* prestador, prestamista, *m.f.*
lending ['lendiŋ], *a.* ***lending library,*** biblioteca circulante. — *s.* préstamo, empréstito.
lene [li:n], *a.* suave, no aspirado. — *s.* consonante no aspirada.
length [leŋθ], *s.* longitud, largo, largura, largor; extensión, duración; eslora; alcance; tramo; corte (*de tela*); punto, extremo; ***at length,*** al fin, finalmente; extensamente; (*b.a.*) ***full length,*** de cuerpo entero; ***to go to great lengths*** (*to*), desvivirse (por); ***to write at great length,*** escribir largo y tendido, escribir largamente.
lengthen ['leŋθən], *v.t.* alargar, prolongar. — *v.i.* alargarse, prolongarse.
lengthening ['leŋθəniŋ], *s.* alargamiento, prolongación.
lengthwise ['leŋθwaiz], *adv.* longitudinalmente; a lo largo.
lengthy ['leŋθi], *a.* bastante largo, demasiado largo; prolijo.
leniency ['li:niənsi], *s.* benevolencia, indulgencia.
lenient ['li:niənt], *a.* benévolo, indulgente, lenitivo.
lenify ['lenifai], *v.t.* lenificar.
lenitive ['lenitiv], *a.* lenitivo.
lenity ['leniti], *s.* lenidad.
lens [lenz], *s.* (*pl.* **lenses** ['lenziz]) (*ópt.*) lente, *f.*; (*anat.*) cristalino.
Lent [lent]. (la) Cuaresma.
Lenten ['lentən], *a.* cuaresmal; pobre, escaso.
lenticular, lentiform [len'tikjulə, 'lentifɔ:m], *a.* lenticular.
lentiginous [len'tidʒinəs], *a.* (*bot., zool.*) pecoso; casposo.
lentil ['lentil], *s.* (*bot.*) lenteja.
lentisk ['lentisk], *s.* lentisco.
Leo ['li:ou], *s.* (*astron., astrol.*) León.
leonine ['li:onain], *a.* leonino.
leopard ['lepəd], *s.* leopardo.
leopard's-bane ['lepədz-bein], *s.* dorónico.
lepadide ['lepədaid], *s.* lápade, *f.*
leper ['lepə], *s.* leproso.
Lepidoptera [lepi'dɔptərə], *s.pl.* lepidópteros, *m.pl.*
lepidopterous [lepi'dɔptərəs], *a.* lepidóptero.
leporine ['lepərain], *a.* lebruno; leporino.
leprose ['leprous], *a.* (*bot.*) casposo; escamoso.
leprosity [lə'prɔsiti], *s.* calidad de escamoso *o* casposo.
leprosy ['leprəsi], *s.* lepra.
leprous ['leprəs], *a.* leproso.
leprousness ['leprəsnis], *s.* leprosidad.
Lepus ['li:pəs], *s.* (*astron.*) Liebre, *f.*
Lesbian ['lezbiən], *a., s.* lesbiana.
lese-majesty ['li:z-mædʒisti], *s.* lesa majestad.
lesion ['li:ʒən], *s.* lesión.
Lesotho [lə'soutou]. Lesotho.
less [les], *a.* menor, inferior; menos. — *adv.* menos; ***to grow less,*** disminuir(se); ***less and less,*** cada vez menos; ***to make less,*** disminuir, aminorar; ***more or less,*** más o menos; ***no less than,*** nada menos que; ***no less a person than,*** no otro que, nada menos que.
lessee [le'si:], *s.* arrendatario.
lessen ['lesən], *v.t.* aminorar, disminuir, reducir. — *v.i.* disminuir(se), mermar, menguar.
lesser ['lesə], *a.* menor, más pequeño; inferior.
lesson ['lesən], *s.* lección; clase; escarmiento; ***to give English lessons,*** dar clases de inglés; (*fig.*) ***to learn one's lesson,*** escarmentar.
lessor ['lesə], *s.* arrendador.
lest [lest], *conj.* para que no, a fin de que no, por miedo de que.
let (1) [let], *s.* alquiler. — *v.t.* dejar, permitir; alquilar, arrendar; ***he won't let me,*** no me deja, no me lo permite; ***let him come!*** ¡que venga!; ***let us go!*** ¡vamos! ¡vámonos!; ***let alone,*** no tocar; dejar en paz; ***let alone,*** sin pensar en, ni mucho menos; ***let well alone,*** dejar las cosas estar; más valer no meneallo; ***let be,*** dejar en paz; ***let by,*** dejar pasar; ***let down,*** bajar; deshinchar; ***don't let me down!*** ¡no me falles!; ***let down lightly,*** no ponerse en plan demasiado duro con; ***let o.s. down by,*** descolgarse con; fallar al + *inf.*; ***let fly at,*** disparar contra; soltar contra; ***let go,*** soltar; vender; dejar (pasar); ***let o.s. go,*** expansionarse; dejarse, descuidarse; desahogarse; ***let in,*** dejar entrar, abrir (la puerta) a; hacer pasar; ***let o.s. in for,*** meterse en, exponerse a; ***let into a secret,*** revelar un secreto a; ***let know,***

hacer saber a, avisar a, comunicar a; ***let loose,*** soltar; ***let off,*** disparar; perdonar, dejar libre; ***let out,*** dejar salir, abrir (la puerta) a; poner en libertad; soltar; divulgar; alquilar; dejar apagarse; (*cost.*) echar de largo, dar de ancho; ***let through,*** dejar pasar (por). — *v.i.* alquilarse (***at, for,*** en); (*fam.*) ***let on,*** irse de la lengua; (*fam.*) ***let up,*** cejar. — *pret., p.p.* [LET].

let (2) [let], *s.* (*ant.*) ***without let or hindrance,*** sin estorbo ni obstáculo.

lethal [ˈliːθəl], *a.* letal, mortal.

lethargic(al) [leˈθɑːdʒik(əl)], *a.* letárgico.

lethargy [ˈleθədʒi], *s.* letargo, aletargamiento; ***to fall into (a) lethargy,*** aletargarse.

Lethe [ˈliːθi]. Leteo.

Lethean [ˈliːθiən], *a.* leteo.

lethiferous [leˈθifərəs], *a.* mortífero.

Lett [let], *s.* letón.

letter [ˈletə], *s.* carta; letra; (*pl.*) letras; ***letter-book,*** libro copiador; ***letter-box,*** buzón; ***letter-carrier,*** cartero; ***letter-case,*** cartera; ***letter-file,*** guardacartas, *m.inv.*; ***letter of exchange,*** letra de cambio; ***letter of licence,*** moratoria; (*for.*) ***letter rogatory,*** suplicatoria; ***letters of safe-conduct,*** salvoconducto. — *v.t.* estampar con letras; rotular.

lettered [ˈletəd], *a.* letrado, instruido.

lettering [ˈletəriŋ], *s.* letrero, rótulo, inscripción.

letterpress [ˈletəpres], *a.* impreso. — *s.* impresión, obra impresa; texto.

lettuce [ˈletis], *s.* (*bot.*) lechuga.

leucine [ˈljuːsin], *s.* leucina.

leucocyte [ˈljuːkosait], *s.* leucocito.

leucoma [ljuːˈkoumə], *s.* albugo.

leucorrhœa [ljuːkəˈriə], *s.* leucorrea, flores blancas, *f.pl.*

Levant [leˈvænt], *s.* oriente medio.

Levanter [leˈvæntə], *s.* viento de levante.

Levantine [leˈvæntain], *a.* de oriente medio.

levantines [leˈvæntainz], *s.pl.* (*tej.*) levantín.

levator [liˈveitə], *s.* músculo elevador; (*cir.*) levantador.

levee [ˈlevi], *s.* corte, *f.*, besamanos, *m.inv.*, recepción; dique, ribero.

level [ˈlevəl], *a.* llano, plano, raso; nivelado, igual; equilibrado, juicioso; ***dead level,*** completamente llano *o* nivelado; ***to do one's level best,*** hacer todo lo que se puede; ***level-crossing,*** paso a nivel; ***to keep a level head,*** no perder la cabeza; ***level-headed,*** juicioso, sensato; ***level with,*** al nivel de; ***to make level,*** nivelar. — *adv.* a nivel, ras con ras. — *s.* nivel; ras; plano, llano; ***on a level with,*** al mismo nivel que; a ras con; a flor de; a la altura de. — *v.t.* nivelar; enrasar; aplanar, allanar; desmontar; ***level an accusation at,*** acusar, denunciar; ***level down,*** rebajar; ***level off,*** aplanar, nivelar; ***level to the ground,*** arrasar; ***level up,*** igualar. — *v.i.* — ***at,*** apuntar (*un arma*) a; ***level off,*** nivelarse; enderezarse (*un avión para aterrizar*); estabilizarse (*precios*).

leveller [ˈlevələ], *s.* nivelador; (*pol.*) igualitario.

levelling [ˈlevəliŋ], *s.* nivelación; aplanamiento; allanamiento; arrasamiento; igualación; (*alb.*) enrasado.

levelness [ˈlevəlnis], *s.* igualdad, (lo) plano; (lo) nivelado; (lo) uniforme.

lever [ˈliːvə], *s.* palanca. — *v.t., v.i.* apalancar.

leverage [ˈliːvəridʒ], *s.* apalancamiento; palancadas, *f.pl.*; (*fig.*) buenas aldabas, *f.pl.*, enchufe, influencia(s).

leveret [ˈlevəret], *s.* (*zool.*) lebrato, lebratillo.

leviable [ˈleviəbl], *a.* exigible.

leviathan [liˈvaiəθən], *s.* leviatán.

levigate [ˈlevigeit], *v.t.* levigar; pulverizar.

levigation [leviˈgeiʃən], *s.* levigación; pulverización.

levitate [ˈleviteit], *v.i.* elevarse en el aire, despegar; levitar.

levitation [leviˈteiʃən], *s.* elevación en el aire, despegue; levitación.

Levite [ˈliːvait], *s.* levita, *m.*

Levitic(al) [leˈvitik(əl)], *a.* levítico.

levity [ˈleviti], *s.* levedad, ligereza; frivolidad.

levulose [ˈlevjulous], *s.* levulosa.

levy [ˈlevi], *s.* leva, recluta, enganche; (*for.*) embargo; exacción, recaudación; impuesto. — *v.t.* reclutar, enganchar; (*for.*) embargar; exigir, recaudar.

lewd [l(j)uːd], *a.* lascivo, impúdico; deshonesto, obsceno.

lewdness [ˈl(j)uːdnis], *s.* lascivia, impudicicia; deshonestidad, obscenidad.

lexical [ˈleksikəl], *a.* léxico.

lexicographer [leksiˈkɔgrəfə], *s.* lexicógrafo.

lexicographic [leksikoˈgræfik], *a.* lexicográfico.

lexicography [leksiˈkɔgrəfi], *s.* lexicografía.

lexicological [leksikoˈlɔdʒikəl], *a.* lexicológico.

lexicologist [leksiˈkɔlədʒist], *s.* lexicólogo.

lexicology [leksiˈkɔlədʒi], *s.* lexicología.

lexicon [ˈleksikən], *s.* léxico, lexicón.

liability [laiəˈbiliti], *s.* riesgo, exposición; responsabilidad; obligación; compromiso, carga; deuda; (*pl.* **liabilities** [-tiz]) (*com.*) pasivo, deudas pasivas, *f.pl.*

liable [ˈlaiəbl], *a.* expuesto (***to,*** a); propenso (***to,*** a); responsable (***for,*** de); obligado; ***liable to duty,*** sujeto a derechos (de aduana).

liaise [liːˈeiz], *v.i.* — ***between,*** hacer el enlace entre.

liaison [liːˈeizən], *s.* enlace; lío, relaciones amorosas, *f.pl.*; ***liaison officer,*** oficial de enlace.

liana [liˈɑːnə], *s.* liana.

liar [ˈlaiə], *s.* mentiroso, embustero.

lias [ˈlaiəs], *s.* (*geol.*) liásico.

libation [laiˈbeiʃən], *s.* libación.

libel [ˈlaibəl], *s.* calumnia, difamación. — *v.t., v.i.* calumniar, difamar.

libeller [ˈlaibələ], *s.* calumniador, difamador.

libelling [ˈlaibəliŋ], *s.* difamación.

libellous [ˈlaibələs], *a.* difamatorio, calumnioso.

liberal [ˈlibərəl], *a.* liberal; generoso; tolerante; abundante; ***liberal arts,*** artes liberales, *f.pl.*; ***liberal-minded,*** tolerante; ***liberal profession,*** carrera liberal. — *s.* liberal.

liberalism [ˈlibərəlizəm], *s.* liberalismo.

liberality [libəˈræliti], *s.* liberalidad, largueza.

liberalize [ˈlibərəlaiz], *v.t.* liberalizar, hacer liberal.

liberate [ˈlibəreit], *v.t.* liberar; libertar; librar.

liberation [libəˈreiʃən], *s.* liberación.

liberator [ˈlibəreitə], *s.* libertador.

Liberia [laiˈbiəriə]. Liberia.

Liberian [laiˈbiəriən], *a., s.* liberiano.

libertarian [libəˈtɛəriən], *a., s.* libertario.

libertinage, libertinism [ˈlibətinidʒ, -izəm], *s.* libertinaje; desenfreno.

libertine [ˈlibətain], *a., s.* libertino, disoluto.

liberty [ˈlibəti], *s.* libertad; ***at liberty,*** en libertad, libre; ***to be at liberty to,*** ser libre de; tener permiso para; ***to take liberties,*** tomarse (muchas) confianzas.

libidinous [liˈbidinəs], *a.* libidinoso.

libidinousness [liˈbidinəsnis], *s.* libidinosidad.

libido [liˈbidou], *s.* libido, *f.*

Libra [ˈlaibrə], *s.* (*astron., astrol.*) Libra.

librarian [laiˈbrɛəriən], *s.* bibliotecario.

librarianship [laiˈbrɛəriənʃip], *s.* empleo *u* oficio de bibliotecario; bibliotecnia.

library [ˈlaibrəri], *s.* biblioteca.

libration [laiˈbreiʃən], *s.* libración.

librettist [liˈbretist], *s.* autor de libretos.

libretto [liˈbretou], *s.* libreto.

Libya [ˈlibiə]. Libia.

Libyan [ˈlibiən], *a., s.* libio.

lice [lais], *s.pl.* [LOUSE].
licebane [ˈlaisbein], *s.* (*bot.*) albarraz, hierba piojera.
licence [ˈlaisəns], *s.* licencia; permiso; autorización, título, cédula; ***driving licence,*** carnet de conducir.
licensable [ˈlaisənsəbl], *a.* permisible.
license [ˈlaisəns], *s.* (*Am.*) [LICENCE]. — *v.t.* licenciar, dar licencia a; autorizar, conceder permiso para.
licensee [laisənˈsi:], *s.* concesionario, titular de una autorización.
license-plate [ˈlaisəns-pleit], *s.* (*Am., aut.*) [NUMBER-PLATE].
licenser [ˈlaisənsə], *s.* persona que da licencia.
licentiate [laiˈsenʃiit], *s.* licenciado.
licentious [laiˈsenʃəs], *a.* licencioso, disoluto.
licentiousness [laiˈsenʃesnis], *s.* licencia, libertinaje.
lichen [ˈlaikən], *s.* liquen.
lich-gate [ˈlitʃ-geit], *s.* puerta de cementerio.
licit [ˈlisit], *a.* lícito.
licitness [ˈlisitnis], *s.* licitud.
lick [lik], *s.* lametón, lengüetada; (*fam.*) ***at a hell of a lick,*** disparado, como una flecha. — *v.t.* lamer; (*fam.*) dar una paliza a, zurrar; (*fam.*) vencer; ***lick the boots of,*** hacer la pelotilla a; ***lick clean,*** limpiar a lametones; ***lick into shape,*** dar forma a; meter en cintura; ***lick one's lips*** o ***chops,*** relamerse.
licker [ˈlikə], *s.* lamedor; (*mec.*) lubricador (*automático*).
licking [ˈlikiŋ], *s.* lametones, *m.pl.*; (*fam., fig.*) paliza.
lickspittle [ˈlikspitl], *s.* lameculos, *m.f. inv.*
licorice, liquorice [ˈlikəris], *s.* regaliz.
lictor [ˈliktə], *s.* lictor.
lid [lid], *s.* tapa, tapadera; (*bot.*) opérculo; guardapolvo (*de reloj*); ***eye-lid,*** párpado; (*fam.*) ***that's put the lid on it!*** ¡estamos listos *o* aviados!
lie (1) [lai], *s.* mentira, embuste; ***white lie,*** mentirilla; ***to give the lie to,*** dar el mentís (a), desmentir. — *v.i.* mentir.
lie (2) [lai], *s.* disposición; ***lie of the land,*** configuración del terreno; situación. — *v.i.* acostarse, estar acostado, echarse, estar echado, tumbarse, estar tumbado, tenderse, estar tendido; estar (situado), encontrarse; yacer; (*nieve*) cuajar; extenderse; (*for.*) ser admisible; ***let sleeping dogs lie,*** más vale no menearlo; ***lie about,*** estar desperdigados; holgazanear; ***lie back,*** recostarse, echarse (para) atrás; ***lie down,*** acostarse, echarse, tumbarse, tenderse; (*fam.*) ***lie down under it, take it lying down,*** tragarlo, aguantarlo sin chistar; ***lie in,*** consistir en; ***lie in state,*** estar de cuerpo presente; ***lie in wait for,*** acechar, estar al acecho de; ***lie low,*** estar escondido; estar agazapado; (*mar.*) ***lie to,*** estar *o* ponerse al pairo; ***lie up,*** descansar, guardar cama; (*bíb.*) ***lie with,*** acostarse, yacer con; (*responsabilidad*) corresponder a, tocar; ***it does not lie with me,*** no me corresponde a mí.
Liechtenstein [ˈliktənstɑin]. Liechtenstein.
lief [li:f], *adv.* de buena gana.
liege [li:dʒ], *a.* ligio; feudatorio. — *s.* vasallo; señor de vasallos.
liegeman [ˈli:dʒmən], *s.* vasallo.
lien [ˈliən], *s.* (*for.*) derecho de retención, embargo preventivo; gravamen, obligación.
lienteric [liənˈterik], *a.* lientérico.
lientery [ˈlaiəntəri], *s.* lientería.
lieu [lju:], *s.* ***in lieu of,*** en lugar de, en vez de.
lieutenancy [lefˈtenənsi], *s.* tenencia; lugartenencia; tenientazgo.
lieutenant [lefˈtenənt], *s.* teniente; lugarteniente; (*mil.*) teniente.
lieutenantship [lefˈtenəntʃip], *s.* tenencia, tenientazgo, oficio de lugarteniente.

life [laif], *a.* vitalicio, de por vida; ***life-annuity,*** fondo vitalicio; ***life-belt,*** (cinturón) salvavidas, *m.inv.*; ***life-blood,*** sangre vital, *f.*; (*fig.*) vida; ***life-buoy,*** boya salvavidas; ***life-insurance,*** seguro de vida; ***life-line,*** cable de salvamento; ***life-sentence,*** condena a cadena perpetua. — *s.* vida, vivir; existencia; vivacidad, animación; vigencia, validez; ***to be the life and soul of the party,*** ser el alma de la fiesta; ***for life,*** para toda la vida; ***for the life of me,*** así me maten; ***from life,*** del natural; ***never in my life,*** en mi vida; ***not on your life!*** ¡ni hablar!; ***this is the life***; ¡esto sí que es vida!; ¡esto es jauja!; ***to the life,*** a lo vivo.
lifeboat [ˈlaifbout], *s.* lancha salvavidas.
life-giving [ˈlaif-giviŋ], *a.* vivificante.
lifeguard [ˈlaifgɑ:d], *s.* guardia de corps.
lifeless [ˈlaiflis], *a.* muerto, sin vida, exánime.
lifelessly [ˈlaiflisli], *adv.* sin espíritu, sin vigor.
lifelike [ˈlaiflaik], *a.* que parece vivo, natural.
lifelong [ˈlaiflɔŋ], *a.* de toda la vida.
lifesized [ˈlaifsaizd], *a.* de tamaño natural.
lifetime [ˈlaiftaim], *s.* curso de la vida.
lift [lift], *s.* alzamiento; esfuerzo para levantar; empuje, ayuda; ascensor, elevador; montacargas, *m.inv.*; (*pl., mar.*) amantillos, *m.pl.*; ***at one lift,*** de un golpe; ***to give s.o. a lift,*** ayudar a alguien a levantarse; llevar en coche. — *v.t.* alzar, levantar, elevar; transportar; suprimir, quitar; plagiar; robar; ***not to be prepared to lift a finger to help,*** no estar dispuesto a molestarse en absoluto; ***lift one's hat,*** quitarse el sombrero; ***lift up,*** levantar, alzar. — *v.i.* levantarse, disiparse.
lifter [ˈliftə], *s.* alzador, elevador; calzo; (*fam.*) ratero, ladrón.
lifting [ˈliftiŋ], *s.* (el) levantar; levantamiento; ***lifting-jack,*** gato, cric.
ligament [ˈligəmənt], *s.* (*anat.*) ligamento; ligazón, *f.*; ligadura, traba.
ligamental, ligamentous [ligəˈmentəl, -təs], *a.* ligamentoso.
ligate [laiˈgeit], *v.t.* (*cir.*) atar con ligadura.
ligation [laiˈgeiʃən], *s.* ligación.
ligature [ˈligətʃə], *s.* (*cir., mec., mús.*) ligadura; (*impr.*) letras ligadas, *f.pl.*
light (1) [lait], *a.* claro; blanco. — *s.* luz, *f.*; lumbre; fuego; faro; aspecto, punto de vista; (*pl.*) luces, entendimiento; ***against the light,*** a contraluz; ***at first light,*** al rayar el día; ***in the light of,*** a la luz de; ***light-bulb,*** bombilla; ***light-keeper,*** torrero; ***light-wave,*** onda luminosa; ***light-year,*** año luz; ***to bring*** (***come***) ***to light,*** sacar (salir) a la luz; (*fam.*) ***to give a light to,*** dar fuego a; ***to put a light to,*** encender; ***to see the light,*** darse cuenta; ver la luz; ***to throw light on,*** arrojar luz sobre. — *v.t.* encender; alumbrar, iluminar. — *v.i.* brillar; ***light up,*** encenderse, iluminarse, alumbrarse; (*fam.*) encender un pitillo.
light (2) [lait], *a.* ligero, leve; alegre, ameno; (*mar.*) en lastre; (*f.c.*) vacío; ***light-armed,*** armado ligeramente; ***light-fingered,*** largo de uñas; ***light-footed,*** ligero de pies; ***light-headed,*** casquivano; mareado, aturdido; delirante; ***light-hearted,*** alegre, festivo; ***light-horse,*** caballería ligera; ***light literature,*** literatura ligera *o* amena; (*dep.*) ***light-weight,*** peso ligero; (*fam.*) de poca importancia; ***to make light of,*** no dar importancia a; ***to travel light,*** viajar ligero.
light (3) [lait], *v.i.* — ***upon,*** dar con, tropezar con, encontrarse con; posarse en.
lighten (1) [laitn], *v.t.* iluminar, alumbrar; hacer más claro. — *v.i.* iluminarse; clarear, hacerse más claro; relampaguear.
lighten (2) [laitn], *v.t.* aligerar; aliviar; alegrar, regocijar. — *v.i.* aligerarse; alegrarse.
lightening [ˈlaitəniŋ], *s.* aligeramiento, (el) aliviar *etc.*
lighter (1) [ˈlaitə], *a.* más claro.

lighter (2) ['laitə], *a.* más ligero.
lighter (3) ['laitə], *s.* (*mar.*) lanchón, gabarra.
lighter (4) ['laitə], *s.* alumbrador, encendedor; ***cigarette lighter,*** encendedor, mechero.
lighterage ['laitəridʒ], *s.* gabarraje.
lighterman ['laitəmən], *s.* lanchonero, gabarrero.
lighthouse ['laithaus], *s.* faro.
lighting ['laitiŋ], *s.* iluminación; alumbrado; ***lighting engineering,*** luminotecnia; ***lighting point,*** toma de corriente; ***lighting-up time,*** hora de encender los faros.
lightless ['laitlis], *a.* obscuro, sin luz, falto de luz.
lightly ['laitli], *adv.* ligeramente, a la ligera.
lightness ['laitnis], *s.* ligereza; agilidad; claridad, luminosidad.
lightning ['laitniŋ], *a.* de relámpago(s), relampagueante. — *s.* relámpago(s), rayo(s), relampagueo; ***lightning conductor,*** pararrayos, *m.inv.*; ***lightning-proof,*** a prueba de rayos; (*fam.*) ***as quick as lightning,*** como una pólvora, cual centella.
lights ['laits], *s.pl.* bofes, *m.pl.*
lightship ['laitʃip], *s.* buque-faro.
lightsome ['laitsəm], *a.* alegre, festivo, juguetón; (*poét.*) luminoso.
ligneous ['ligniəs], *a.* leñoso.
lignite ['lignait], *s.* lignito.
lignum-vitæ ['lignəm-'vaiti:], *s.* guayaco, guayacán, palo santo.
ligulate ['ligjuleit], *a.* (flor) acintillada, semiflosculosa *o* ligulada.
ligure ['ligjuə], *s.* ligurio.
like [laik], *a.* igual; parecido, semejante; lo mismo que, como; propio, característico; ***like father, like son,*** de tal palo, tal astilla; ***in a like manner,*** de igual modo; ***to be like,*** parecerse, ser parecido (a); ***to be as like as two peas,*** parecerse como dos gotas de agua, ser clavados. — *prep.* como, del mismo modo que, igual que; ***like anything,*** hasta más no poder; ***like (a) fury,*** hecho una furia; ***like this*** o ***that,*** así, de este modo; ***sth. like,*** algo así como; ***to look like,*** parecer (que), tener trazas (de); ***what is he like?*** ¿cómo es (él)?; ***that's (just) like him,*** eso es muy de él; ***I feel like taking a walk,*** me apetece dar un paseo. — *s.* igual; cosa parecida; ***he has not his like,*** no tiene igual; (*fam.*) ***the like,*** cosas por el estilo, cosas así; ***to give like for like,*** pagar en la misma moneda; ***likes and dislikes,*** gustos *o* aficiones y antipatías. — *v.t.* gustar, gustarle a uno; querer; ***I like tea,*** me gusta el té; ***how do you like it?*** ¿qué le parece?; ¿le gusta?; ***to like better*** o ***best,*** preferir, gustarle a uno más. — *v.i.* ***as you like,*** como (usted) quiera; ***if you like,*** si usted quiere; ***I should like to,*** me gustaría, quisiera.
likelihood, likeliness ['laiklihud, -nis], *s.* probabilidad; verosimilitud.
likely ['laikli], *a.* probable; verosímil; a propósito; (*ironía*) ***a likely story,*** con que sí ¿eh?; ***it is likely enough,*** es bastante probable. — *adv.* probablemente.
liken ['laikən], *v.t.* comparar; asemejar.
likeness ['laiknis], *s.* semejanza, parecido; igualdad; aire; retrato; ***a speaking likeness,*** un retrato fiel.
likewise ['laikwaiz], *adv.* también, asimismo, igualmente; además.
liking ['laikiŋ], *s.* inclinación, gusto, afición; preferencia.
lilac ['lailək], *a.* de color de lila. — *s.* lila, lilas.
liliaceous [lili'eiʃəs], *a.* liliáceo.
lilied ['lilid], *a.* adornado con lirios.
Lilliputian [lili'pju:ʃən], *a., s.* liliputiense.
lilt [lilt], *s.* canción; ritmo. — *v.t., v.i.* bailar *o* cantar alegremente.
lily ['lili], *s.* lirio; azucena; flor de lis, *f.*; ***day lily,*** hemerocálide; ***lily of the valley,*** muguete, lirio de los valles; (*fam.*) ***lily-livered,*** gallina, cobarde.
lilywort ['liliwə:t], *s.* liliácea.
Lima ['li:mə]. ***Lima wood,*** brasilete; ***Lima beans,*** habas de Lima, *f.pl.*
limaceous [li'meiʃəs], *a.* limáceo.
limb [lim], *s.* miembro (*del cuerpo*); rama (*de árbol*); (*astron.*) limbo; ***to be out on a limb,*** estar en situación expuesta, estar en un aprieto.
limber ['limbə], *a.* ágil, flexible. — *s.* (*artill.*) armón, avantrén; (*mar.*) imbornal de varenga. — *v.t.* hacer flexible; enganchar el armón a. — *v.i.* — ***up,*** enganchar el armón; agilitarse, flexibilizarse.
limberness ['limbənis], *s.* flexibilidad, agilidad.
limbless ['limlis], *a.* desmembrado.
limbo ['limbou], *s.* limbo.
lime (1) [laim], *s.* cal, *f.*; ***lime-burner,*** calero; ***lime-kiln,*** calera; ***lime-light,*** luz de calcio; (*fig.*) (luz de) candilejas; ***to get in the lime-light,*** singularizarse, significarse, señalarse; ***lime water,*** agua de cal. — *v.t.* encalar; untar *o* coger con liga; (*agric.*) abonar con cal; (*alb.*) unir con argamasa *o* mezcla.
lime (2) [laim], *s.* (*bot.*) lima; ***lime-juice,*** zumo de lima; ***lime-tree,*** limero.
lime (3) [laim], *s.* (*bot.*) tilo, tila.
limerick ['limərik], *s.* copla humorística, especie de aleluya.
limestone ['laimstoun], *s.* piedra de cal, piedra caliza.
limit ['limit], *s.* límite; término; confín; ***to go (to) the limit,*** seguir hasta el final; echar el resto; ***to know no limit,*** no tener límite(s) *o* fin; ***that's the limit!*** ¡es el colmo! — *v.t.* limitar; restringir.
limitary ['limitəri], *a.* limitáneo, limítrofe.
limitation [limi'teiʃən], *s.* limitación; restricción; (*for.*) prescripción.
limited ['limitid], *a.* limitado, restringido; ***limited company,*** sociedad limitada; ***limited partnership,*** sociedad en comandita.
limiter ['limitə], *s.* limitador.
limitless ['limitlis], *a.* ilimitado.
limn [lim], *v.t.* pintar.
limner ['limnə], *s.* pintor.
limning ['limiŋ], *s.* pintura.
limous ['laiməs], *a.* fangoso.
limp (1) [limp], *a.* lacio; flojo; flexible.
limp (2) [limp], *s.* cojera. — *v.i.* cojear; (*fig.*) renquear.
limper ['limpə], *s.* cojo.
limpet ['limpit], *s.* lapa.
limpid ['limpid], *a.* límpido, cristalino, diáfano.
limpidity, limpidness [lim'piditi, 'limpidnis], *s.* limpidez, diafanidad, claridad.
limping ['limpiŋ], *a.* cojo; renqueante.
limpingly ['limpiŋli], *adv.* con cojera; renqueante.
limy ['laimi], *a.* calizo; viscoso, pegajoso.
Linaceae [li'neisii], *s.pl.* lináceas, *f.pl.*
linaceous [li'neiʃəs], *a.* lináceo.
linch-pin ['lintʃ-pin], *s.* sotrozo; pezonera.
linden (-tree) ['lindən (-tri:)], *s.* (*bot.*) tilo.
line [lain], *s.* línea; renglón; cuerda; cordel; (*pesca*) sedal; (*com.*) ramo, género; (*f.c.*) vía; (*poesía*) verso; hilera, fila; (*cara*) arruga; (*fam.*) especialidad, fuerte; (*fam.*) profesión, trabajo; (*fam.*) plan, norma(s), principios, *m.pl.*; (*f.c.*) ***branch line,*** ramal; (*fam.*) ***hard lines,*** mala suerte; ***junction line,*** línea de empalme; ***line engraving,*** grabado de líneas; (*f.c.*) ***line-keeper,*** guardavía, *m.*; ***line-reel,*** carretel de la caña de pescar; (*fam.*) ***to shoot a line,*** darse bombo; (*fam.*) ***to toe the line,*** conformarse, someterse; ***to write a few lines,*** escribir cuatro líneas *o* renglones. — *v.t.* linear, rayar, reglar; arrugar; alinear; medir con cordel; forrar, revestir; ***line one's pockets,*** ponerse las botas, forrarse; ***line the streets,*** ocupar las aceras; ***line up,*** alinear, poner en fila. — *v.i.* — ***up,*** alinearse, ponerse en fila; hacer, formar cola.

lineage [ˈliniidʒ], *s.* linaje, prosapia, abolengo.
lineal [ˈliniəl], *a.* lineal; en línea recta.
lineally [ˈliniəli], *adv.* en línea recta.
lineament [ˈliniəmənt], *s.* lineamento, facción.
linear [ˈliniə], *a.* lineal; longitudinal; ***linear measure,*** medida de longitud.
lineate(d) [ˈlinieit(id)], *a.* señalado con líneas.
lineation [liniˈeiʃən],*s.* delineación, dibujo de líneas.
lined [laind], *a.* rayado; forrado; arrugado.
lineman [ˈlainmən], *s.* tendedor de hilos telegráficos.
linen [ˈlinin], *s.* lino; lienzo; hilo; ropa blanca; ***bleached linen,*** lienzo blanqueado; ***change of linen,*** muda de ropa; ***linen cambric,*** olán batista, cambray; ***linen damask,*** damasco de hilo, alemanisco; ***linen draper,*** lencero; ***linen goods, linen trade,*** lencería; ***table linen,*** mantelería.
liner [ˈlainə], *s.* (*mar.*) vapor de línea; transatlántico.
line-up [ˈlain-ʌp], *s.* alineación, formación.
ling (1) [liŋ], *s.* (*bot.*) brezo ; (*bot.*) ***ling-aloe,*** lináloe.
ling (2) [liŋ], *s.* (*ict.*) abadejo.
linger [ˈliŋgə], *v.i.* demorarse, dilatarse, entretenerse.
lingerer [ˈliŋgərə], *s.* el que tarda *o* dilata.
lingerie [ˈlɛ̃:ʒəri:], *s.* ropa interior, lencería.
lingering [ˈliŋgəriŋ], *a.* lento, tardo, prolongado, moroso. — *s.* tardanza, dilación.
lingo [ˈliŋgou], *s.* (*fam.*) jerga, galimatías, *m.inv.*
lingual [ˈliŋgwəl], *a.* lingual.
linguist [ˈliŋgwist], *s.* lingüista, *m.f.*
linguistic [liŋˈgwistik], *a.* lingüístico.
linguistics [liŋˈgwistiks], *s.* lingüística.
liniment [ˈlinimənt], *s.* linimento.
lining [ˈlainiŋ], *s.* forro; (*mec.*) revestimiento; guarnición (*de freno*).
link [liŋk], *s.* eslabón; (*mec.*) varilla (*de conexión*); hacha de viento; enlace; (*mec.*) ***link motion,*** cuadrante de la corredera. — *v.t.* eslabonar; enlazar; ligar; unir. — *v.i.* — ***up,*** eslabonarse; enlazarse; ligarse; unirse.
links [liŋks], *s.pl.* campo de golf.
linkage [ˈliŋkidʒ], *s.* eslabonamiento, enlace; (*mec.*) varillaje.
linkboy [ˈliŋkbɔi], *s.* paje de hacha.
linnet [ˈlinit], *s.* (*orn.*) pardillo.
lino [ˈlainou], *s. abrev. de* [LINOLEUM].
linoleum [liˈnouliəm], *s.* linóleo.
linotype [ˈlainotaip], *s.* linotipia.
linseed [ˈlinsi:d], *s.* linaza; ***linseed-oil,*** aceite de linaza.
linstock [ˈlinstɔk], *s.* botafuego.
lint [lint], *s.* hilas, *f.pl.*
lintel [lintl], *s.* (*arq.*) dintel.
lion [ˈlaiən], *s.* léon; (*fig.*) celebridad; (*astron., astrol.*) León; ***lion-like,*** aleonado; (*bot.*) ***lion's foot,*** pie de león; ***lion's share,*** parte del león; (*bot.*) ***lion's tail,*** leonura; (*fig.*) ***literary lion,*** gerifalte de la literatura; ***to put one's head in(to) the lion's mouth,*** meterse en la boca del lobo.
lioness [ˈlaiənes], *s.* leona.
lionize [ˈlaiənaiz], *v.t.* agasajar con mucho fausto, recibir como una celebridad *o* un héroe.
lip [lip], *s.* labio; borde; pico (*de jarro*); (*fam.*) insolencia(s); ***lip-reading,*** interpretación del movimiento de los labios; ***lip-salve,*** pomada para los labios; ***lip service,*** cosa dicha de boquilla, jarabe de pico; ***to pay lip-service to,*** acatar sólo en apariencia, fingir respeto por; ***lip-stick,*** barra de labios, lápiz labial, *m.*; ***to hang on the lips of,*** estar pendiente de las palabras de; ***to keep a stiff upper lip,*** no inmutarse, no alterarse, no afectarse; ***to smack one's lips,*** relamerse.
lipothymy [liˈpɔθimi], *s.* lipotimia.
lipped [lipt], *a.* labiado, que tiene labios.
lipper [ˈlipə], *s.* (*mar.*) mar picada.
liquable [ˈlikwəbl], *a.* licuable.
liquate [ˈlikweit], *v.t.* licuar. — *v.i.* licuarse.
liquation, liquefaction [liˈkweiʃən, likwiˈfækʃən], *s.* licuación, licuefacción.
liquefiable [ˈlikwifaiəbl], *a.* licuable, liquidable.
liquefy [ˈlikwifai], *v.t.* licuar, liquidar. — *v.i.* licuarse, liquidarse.
liquescence [liˈkwesəns], *s.* licuescencia.
liquescent [liˈkwesənt], *a.* licuescente.
liqueur [liˈkjuə], *s.* licor.
liquid [ˈlikwid], *a.* líquido; límpido; (*com.*) ***liquid assets,*** activo líquido; (*com.*) ***liquid securities,*** valores realizables, *m.pl.* — *s.* líquido; (*fon.*) líquida.
liquidambar [likwiˈdæmbə], *s.* liquidámbar; ***liquidambar-tree,*** ocozol, estoraque.
liquidate [ˈlikwideit], *v.t.* liquidar.
liquidation [likwiˈdeiʃən], *s.* liquidación.
liquidator [ˈlikwideitə], *s.* liquidador.
liquidity, liquidness [liˈkwiditi, ˈlikwidnis], *s.* liquidez; fluidez.
liquor [ˈlikə], *s.* licor, bebida alcohólica.
liquorice [LICORICE].
lisle thread [ˈlail ˈθred], *s.* hilo de escocia.
lisp [lisp], *s.* ceceo; balbucencia. — *v.t., v.i.* cecear; balbucir.
lisper [ˈlispə], *s.* el que cecea; el que balbucea.
lisping [ˈlispiŋ], *a.* ceceoso; balbuciente.
lissom [ˈlisəm], *a.* flexible, ágil.
list (1) [list], *s.* lista; catálogo; nómina; matrícula; rol; ***Army List,*** nómina del ejército; ***black list,*** lista negra; ***Navy List,*** nómina de la marina. — *v.t.* registrar, matricular; poner en una lista, hacer una lista de; enumerar; (*com.*) cotizar, facturar.
list (2) [list], *s.* (*tej.*) orilla, borde (*del paño*), lista, cenefa, tira; (*carp.*) tabloncillo; (*arq.*) filete, listón, orla, barandal. — *v.t.* guarnecer con cenefas *o* listones.
list (3) [list], *s.* (*mar.*) inclinación, escora. — *v.i.* dar a la banda, inclinarse a la banda, escorar.
lists (4) [lists], *s.* liza (*para torneos*); (*fig.*) ***enter the lists,*** salir a la palestra.
listed [ˈlistid], *a.* en la lista; (*com.*) cotizado.
listel [ˈlistəl], *s.* listel, filete.
listen [ˈlisən], *v.i.* escuchar, oír, atender; ***listen to reason,*** atender a razones; ***listen in,*** escuchar por radio; escuchar a hurtadillas.
listener [ˈlisnə], *s.* oyente, radioyente; escucha, *m.f.*; ***listeners hear no good of themselves,*** quien escucha, su mal oye.
listerine [ˈlistərin], *s.* (*farm., marca de fábrica*) listerina.
Listerism [ˈlistərizəm], *s.* listerismo.
listing [ˈlistiŋ], *s.* orilla (*de paño*), cenefa, tira.
listless [ˈlistlis], *a.* lánguido, apático, indiferente, que no tiene interés por nada.
listlessness [ˈlistlisnis], *s.* languidez, apatía, indiferencia.
litany [ˈlitəni], *s.* letanía.
literal [ˈlitərəl], *a.* literal.
literalist [ˈlitərəlist], *a.* escrupulosamente exacto. — *s.* el que se adhiere a la letra; positivista, *m.f.*
literally [ˈlitərəli], *adv.* literalmente, al pie de la letra.
literalness [ˈlitərəlnis], *s.* sentido literal, (lo) literal.
literary [ˈlitərəri], *a.* literario.
literate [ˈlitərit], *a., s.* literato.
literati [litəˈrɑ:ti], *s.pl.* literatos, *m.pl.*
literatim [litəˈreitim], *adv.* letra por letra, a la letra; literalmente.
literature [ˈlitrəʃə], *s.* literatura; (*fig.*) literatura de propaganda; (*fig.*) todos los datos (referentes a un asunto).
litharge [ˈliθɑ:dʒ], *s.* litarge, litargirio, almártaga.
lithate [ˈliθeit], *s.* urato.
lithe [laið], *a.* ágil y esbelto; ligero; flexible.

litheness [ˈlaiðnis], *s.* agilidad y esbeltez; agilidad; flexibilidad.
lithesome [ˈlaiðsəm], *a.* ágil, flexible.
lithia [ˈliθiə], *s.* litina.
lithiasis [liˈθaiəsis], *s.* litiasis, *f. inv.*
lithic [ˈliθik], *a.* lítico.
lithium [ˈliθiəm], *s.* litio.
lithogenesy [liθoˈdʒenisi], *s.* litogenesia.
lithograph [ˈliθograːf], *s.* litografía. — *v.t., v.i.* litografiar.
lithographer [liˈθɔgrəfə], *s.* litógrafo.
lithographic [liθoˈgræfik], *a.* litográfico.
lithography [liˈθɔgrəfi], *s.* litografía.
lithoid, lithoidal [ˈliθɔid, liˈθɔidəl], *a.* litoideo.
lithologic(al) [liθəˈlɔdʒik(əl)], *a.* litológico.
lithologist [liˈθɔlədʒist], *s.* litólogo.
lithology [liˈθɔlədʒi], *s.* litología.
lithophyte [ˈliθofait], *s.* litófito.
lithotomist [liˈθɔtəmist], *s.* litotomista, *m.f.*
lithotomy [liˈθɔtəmi], *s.* litotomía.
lithotrite [ˈliθotrait], *s.* litotrictor.
lithotrity [liˈθɔtriti], *s.* litotricia.
Lithuania [liθjuˈeiniə]. Lituania.
Lithuanian [liθjuˈeiniən], *a., s.* lituano.
litigant [ˈlitigənt], *a., s.* litigante; pleiteante.
litigate [ˈlitigeit], *v.t., v.i.* litigar; pleitear.
litigation [litiˈgeiʃən], *s.* litigio, litigación; pleito.
litigator [ˈlitigeitə], *s.* litigante, pleiteador.
litigious [liˈtidʒəs], *a.* litigioso.
litigiousness [liˈtidʒəsnis], *s.* propensión a pleitear.
litmus [ˈlitməs], *s.* tornasol.
litotes [laiˈtoutiːz], *s.* lítote, *f.*
litre [ˈliːtə], *s.* litro.
litter [ˈlitə], *s.* litera, parihuela, andas, *f.pl.*; (*animales*) camada, lechigada, ventregada; cama de paja; desorden, revoltijo; basura, desperdicios, *m.pl.* — *v.t.* hacer un lecho de paja para; parir; sembrar *o* llenar (de); ***littered with,*** sembrado de; ***littered with mistakes,*** plagado de faltas. — *v.i.* (*animales*) parir.
littérateur [litəræˈtəː], *s.* literato.
little [litl], *a.* poco; pequeño; menudo; reducido; chico; ***little money,*** poco dinero; ***a little money,*** un poco de dinero; ***a little house,*** una casa pequeña, una casita; ***the little ones,*** los pequeños, los chiquillos, la gente menuda; ***his little ways,*** sus cosas *o* cositas; ***the little people,*** los duendes, las hadas. — *adv.* poco; ***little does he know that,*** no tiene (ni) la menor sospecha de que; ***not a little displeased,*** harto disgustado. — *s.* poco; ***for a little,*** durante un poco *o* un rato; por muy poco (*dinero*); ***little by little,*** poco a poco; ***to make little of,*** sacar poco en claro de; ***not a little,*** no poco.
littleness [ˈlitlnis], *s.* pequeñez; poquedad; mezquindad.
littoral [ˈlitərəl], *a., s.* litoral.
liturgic(al) [liˈtəːdʒik(əl)], *a.* litúrgico.
liturgy [ˈlitədʒi], *s.* liturgia.
live [laiv], *a.* vivo; ardiente; (*impr.*) útil; (*elec.*) con corriente; cargado (*proyectiles*); ***live-box,*** porta-animálculos (*para el microscopio*), *m. inv.*; ***live coal,*** brasa; (*bot.*) ***live oak,*** encina americana; ***live-stock,*** ganado; ***to be a live wire,*** ser una pólvora. — [liv], *v.t.* pasar, llevar (*una vida*); ***live down,*** lograr borrar; ***live out,*** vivir hasta el fin (de). — *v.i.* vivir, tener vida, existir; subsistir, mantenerse; (*mar.*) estar *o* quedar a flote, salvarse; ***live and learn,*** vivir para ver; ***live at No. 2 Smith St.,*** vivir en el dos de la calle Smith; ***live from hand to mouth,*** vivir al día; ***live in,*** dormir en (la) casa; ***live in a dream,*** vivir soñando; ***live in sin,*** estar liado con; ***live up to,*** vivir en conformidad con; ***live up to one's promise,*** cumplir lo prometido; ***live within one's means,*** vivir con arreglo a los ingresos.
liveable [ˈlivəbl], *a.* digno de vida.
livelihood [ˈlaivlihud], *s.* vida, mantenimiento, sustento; subsistencia.
liveliness [ˈlaivlinis], *s.* vida, viveza, vivacidad, animación.
livelong [ˈlivlɔŋ, ˈlaivlɔŋ], *a.* todo, entero; ***all the livelong day,*** todo el (santo) día.
lively [ˈlaivli], *a.* vivo, vivaz, animado, alegre. — *adv.* vigorosamente, enérgicamente; vivamente, a lo vivo; aprisa.
liver (1) [ˈlivə], *s.* hígado; ***liver complaint,*** dolencia hepática.
liver (2) [ˈlivə], *s.* ***fast liver,*** vividor, calavera.
livered [ˈlivəd], *a.* de hígado, que tiene hígado.
liveried [ˈlivərid], *a.* que lleva librea.
Liverpudlian [livəˈpʌdliən], *a., s.* de *o* natural de Liverpool.
liverwort [ˈlivəwəːt], *s.* hepática.
livery [ˈlivəri], *s.* librea; cochería de alquiler; ***livery coach,*** carruaje de alquiler; ***livery horse,*** caballo de alquiler; ***livery stable,*** pensión de caballos; cochería de alquiler.
liveryman [ˈlivərimən], *s.* dueño de cochería de alquiler; ciudadano de honor de Londres; (*pl.* **liverymen**) criados de librea, *m.pl.*
lives [laivz], *s.pl.* [LIFE]; [livz] 3*a pers. sing. pres. indic.* [LIVE].
livestock [ˈlaivstɔk], *s.* ganado.
livid [ˈlivid], *a.* lívido, cárdeno, amoratado; (*fam.*) ***to be livid,*** estar furioso.
lividity, lividness [liˈviditi, ˈlividnis], *s.* lividez; furia.
living [ˈliviŋ], *a.* vivo, viviente. — *s.* vida; sustento; modo de vivir; ***to be fond of good living,*** gustarle a alguien vivir bien; ***to earn one's living,*** ganarse la vida; ***the living,*** los vivos; ***living-room,*** cuarto de estar.
lixivial [likˈsiviəl], *a.* lixiviado, lejivial.
lixiviate [likˈsivieit], *a.* convertido en lejía, lixiviado. — *v.t.* lixiviar; hacer lejía de.
lizard [ˈlizəd], *s.* (*zool.*) lagarto.
llama [ˈlɑːmə], *s.* (*zool.*) llama.
lo! [lou], *interj.* ***lo and behold!,*** ¡he aquí! ¡ved aquí! ¡mirad!
loach [loutʃ], *s.* (*ict.*) locha.
load [loud], *s.* carga; peso; ***load-line, load-water-line,*** línea de flotación; (*fam.*) ***loads of,*** montones (*m.pl.*) de; ***loads of money, food,*** *etc.*, montones de dinero, dinero a espuertas, comida a manta *etc.* — *v.t.* cargar (***with,*** con, de); ***load down with,*** agobiar con, de; ***load with honours,*** colmar de honores; ***loaded question,*** pregunta capciosa, malintencionada. — *v.i.* — ***up,*** cargar.
loader [ˈloudə], *s.* cargador.
loading [ˈloudiŋ], *a.* de carga; cargador. — *s.* carga, (el) cargar.
loadstar [LODESTAR].
loadstone [LODESTONE].
loaf (1) [louf], *s.* (*pl.* **loaves** [louvz]) hogaza de pan, pan; ***loaf of sugar,*** pilón de azúcar; ***loaf sugar,*** azúcar de pilón; (*fam.*) ***use your loaf!*** ¡no seas negado!
loaf (2) [louf], *v.i.* haraganear, holgazanear, gandulear.
loafer [ˈloufə], *s.* haragán, holgazán, gandul; azotacalles, *m.inv.*
loam [loum], *s.* marga. — *v.t.* echar marga a.
loamy [ˈloumi], *a.* margoso.
loan [loun], *s.* préstamo; (*com.*) empréstito; ***to ask for the loan of, ask for on loan,*** pedir prestado; ***loan-word,*** préstamo lingüístico. — *v.t.* prestar.
loath [louθ], *a.* poco dispuesto; ***to be loath to,*** no querer, sentir desgana *o* repugnancia ante la idea de; ***nothing loath,*** animosamente, con presteza.
loathe [louð], *v.t.* detestar, aborrecer, sentir asco de.

loathing [ˈlouðiŋ], *s.* repugnancia, asco.
loathingly [ˈlouðiŋli], *adv.* con repugnancia, con asco; de mala gana.
loathness [ˈlouθnis], *s.* desgana, repugnancia.
loathsome [ˈlouðsəm], *a.* repugnante, nauseabundo, asqueroso.
loathsomeness [ˈlouðsəmnis], *s.* (lo) repugnante *o* asqueroso.
loaves [louvz], *s.pl.* [LOAF].
lob [lɔb], *s.* voleo alto (*en tenis*). — *v.t.* volear por alto; (*fam.*) lanzar, echar.
lobate(d) [ˈloubeit(id)], *a.* lobulado.
lobby [ˈlɔbi], *s.* vestíbulo; pasillo; antecámara; (*pol.*) camarilla de cabilderos. — *v.t.*, *v.i.* (*pol.*) cabildear.
lobbying [ˈlɔbiiŋ], *s.* (*pol.*) cabildeo.
lobbyist [ˈlɔbiist], *s.* (*pol.*) cabildero.
lobe [loub], *s.* lóbulo.
lobed [loubd], *a.* lobado, lobulado.
lobelia [loˈbi:liə], *s.* (*bot.*) lobelia.
loblolly [ˈlɔblɔli], *s.* polenta.
lobster [ˈlɔbstə], *s.* langosta; bogavante; ***lobster-pot,*** langostera.
lobulate [ˈlɔbjulit], *a.* lobulado.
lobule [ˈlɔbju:l], *s.* lobulillo.
local [ˈloukəl], *a.* local, vecinal, de la localidad; ***local anaesthetic,*** anestésico local; (*tele.*) ***local call,*** llamada urbana; ***local colour,*** colorido local, costumbres de la comarca, *f.pl.*; ***local government,*** administración local; ***local remedy,*** remedio externo; ***local train,*** tren de cercanías. — *s.* (*fam.*) (la) taberna; (*fam.*) ***the locals,*** el vecindario.
locale [louˈkɑ:l], *s.* ambiente; lugar, escenario (de acontecimientos).
localism [ˈloukəlizəm], *s.* localismo; costumbre local.
locality [loˈkæliti], *s.* localidad; posición, situación.
localization [loukəlaiˈzeiʃən], *s.* localización.
localize [ˈloukəlaiz], *v.t.* localizar.
locate [loˈkeit], *v.t.* colocar; situar; localizar, encontrar.
location [loˈkeiʃən], *s.* colocación, ubicación; sitio, localidad; situación, posición; (*f.c.*) trazado de la línea; (*cine.*) rodaje de exteriores.
loch [lɔx, lɔk], *s.* (*Esco.*) lago; ría.
lochia [ˈloukiə], *s.pl.* loquios, *m.pl.*
lock (1) [lɔk], *s.* cerradura; traba, retén; llave (*de arma de fuego*); presa (*lucha libre*); (*canales*) esclusa, compuerta; (*med.*) ***lock-jaw,*** trismo, tétano; ***lock-keeper,*** esclusero; ***lock-nut,*** contratuerca; ***lock-out,*** lockout, cierre, paro (de patronos); ***lock, stock and barrel,*** con todos los bártulos; ***under lock and key,*** bajo siete llaves. — *v.t.* enclavar, trabar; cerrar con llave, echar la llave a; hacer pasar por una esclusa; ***to be locked in combat,*** estar con la lucha trabada; ***lock in,*** encerrar; ***lock out,*** cerrar la puerta a, dejar en la calle; excluir; ***lock up,*** encerrar, recluir; trabar, inmovilizar. — *v.i.* cerrarse (con llave); trabarse; ***lock up,*** cerrar con llave, echar la llave.
lock (2) [lɔk], *s.* guedeja.
lockage [ˈlɔkidʒ], *s.* materiales de una esclusa, *m.pl.*; diferencia de nivel en un canal de esclusas; portazgo *o* derechos (*m.pl.*) de esclusa.
locker [ˈlɔkə], *s.* alacena *o* cajón (*que se cierra con llave*); taquilla; consigna automática.
locket [ˈlɔkit], *s.* guardapelo, medallón.
lockram [ˈlɔkrəm], *s.* lienzo basto, estopa.
locksmith [ˈlɔksmiθ], *s.* cerrajero.
lock-up [ˈlɔk-ʌp], *s.* (*fam.*) encierro; cárcel.
locomobile [ˈloukomobi:l], *a.*, *s.* locomóvil.
locomotion [loukoˈmouʃən], *s.* locomoción.
locomotive [loukoˈmoutiv], *a.* locomotor, locomotriz, locomóvil. — *s.* (*f.c.*) locomotora.
locomotor [loukoˈmoutə], *a.* locomotor, locomotriz; ***locomotor ataxia,*** ataxia locomotriz.
locular [ˈlɔkjulə], *a.* locular, loculado.
locum-tenens [loukəm-ˈti:nenz], *s.* (*pl.* **-tenentes** [tiˈnenti:z]) interino.
locust [ˈloukəst], *s.* langosta; (*bot.*) ***locust-tree,*** algarrobo.
locution [loˈkju:ʃən], *s.* locución.
lode [loud], *s.* (*min.*) filón, veta.
lodestar [ˈloudstɑ:], *s.* estrella polar; (*fig.*) norte.
lodestone [ˈloudstoun], *s.* piedra imán.
lodge [lɔdʒ], *s.* casita; casa de campo; casa de guarda; portería; (*masonería*) logia; pabellón (de caza). — *v.t.* alojar, hospedar; colocar, depositar; introducir; incrustar; ***lodge a complaint,*** formular una protesta. — *v.i.* alojarse, hospedarse; ir a parar; fijarse, incrustarse.
lodger [ˈlɔdʒə], *s.* huésped.
lodging [ˈlɔdʒiŋ], *s.* alojamiento, hospedaje; habitación, aposento, cuarto; (*pl.*) pensión; habitaciones, *f.pl.*; ***lodging house,*** pensión, casa de huéspedes; ***board and lodging,*** pensión completa.
lodgment [ˈlɔdʒmənt], *s.* alojamiento; (*mil.*) posición ganada; depósito.
loft [lɔft], *s.* desván; pajar.
loftiness [ˈlɔftinis], *s.* elevación; encumbramiento; excelsitud, sublimidad; altivez, altanería, soberbia.
lofty [ˈlɔfti], *a.* elevado; encumbrado; excelso; sublime; altivo, altanero, soberbio.
log (1) [lɔg], *s.* leño, toza, tronco; ***log-cabin,*** cabaña (hecha) de troncos; (*pol.*) ***log-rolling,*** cabildeo de politicastros; ***to be as easy as falling off a log,*** ser tirado; ***to sleep like a log,*** dormir como un tronco *o* un lirón.
log (2) [lɔg], *s.* (*mar.*) corredera; ***log-book,*** cuaderno de bitácora; diario de a bordo; libro de vuelo(s).
loganberry [ˈlougənbəri], *s.* (*fam.*) mora; (*bot.*) frambuesa negra norteamericana; ***loganberry bush,*** moral.
logarithm [ˈlɔgəriðəm], *s.* logaritmo.
logarithmic(al) [lɔgəˈriðmik(əl)], *a.* logarítmico.
loggerhead [ˈlɔgəhed], *s.* (*ant.*) zote, necio; ***to be at loggerheads,*** estar a matar, en pleno desacuerdo *o* en plena desavenencia; ***to come to loggerheads,*** chocar.
logging [ˈlɔgiŋ], *s.* explotación forestal; transporte de leños.
logic [ˈlɔdʒik], *s.* lógica.
logical [ˈlɔdʒikəl], *a.* lógico.
logician [loˈdʒiʃən], *s.* lógico.
logistic [loˈdʒistik], *a.* logístico.
logistics [loˈdʒistiks], *s.pl.* logística.
logman [ˈlɔgmən], *s.* leñero.
logogram [ˈlɔgogræm], *s.* abreviatura *o* signo que indica una palabra; logogrifo.
logograph [ˈlɔgogrɑ:f], *s.* palabra escrita.
logogriph [ˈlɔgogrif], *s.* logogrifo, enigma en verso.
logomachy [lɔˈgoməki], *s.* logomaquia; juego de formar anagramas.
log-roll [ˈlɔg-roul], *v.i.* (*Am.*) hacer rodar tozas; (*pol.*) cabildear.
logwood [ˈlɔgwud], *s.* palo de Campeche, palo de tinte.
loin [lɔin], *s.* ijada, ijar; lomo; (*bíb.*) ***to gird up one's loins,*** aprestarse (a), apercibirse para la acción; ***loin-cloth,*** taparrabo.
Loire [lwɑ:]. Loira.
loiter [ˈlɔitə], *v.i.* detenerse, estar detenido, pararse, estar parado; callejear.
loiterer [ˈlɔitərə], *s.* callejero; el que se para *o* detiene en la calle.
loitering [ˈlɔitəriŋ], *s.* (el) pararse *o* detenerse en la calle.
lolium [ˈlouliəm], *s.* (*bot.*) joyo, cizaña.
loll [lɔl], *v.i.* colgar, estar colgando (hacia fuera); estar tirado desmadejadamente; ***the dog's tongue was lolling out,*** el perro iba con la

lengua (colgando) fuera; ***loll about,*** estar repantigado.

Lollard [ˈlɔlɑːd], *s.* lolardo.

lollipop [ˈlɔlipɔp], *s.* pirulí.

Lombardy [ˈlɔmbədi]. Lombardía.

loment [ˈloument], *s.* (*bot.*) lomento.

London [ˈlʌndən], *a.* londinense; (*bot.*) ***London pride,*** saxífraga irlandesa. — *s.* Londres.

Londoner [ˈlʌndənə], *s.* londinense.

lone [loun], *a.* solitario, solo; señero; ***lone wolf,*** solitario.

loneliness [ˈlounlinis], *s.* soledad.

lonely [ˈlounli], *a.* solitario, solo.

loneness [ˈlounnis], *s.* soledad.

loner [ˈlounə], *s.* individualista, *m.f.*

lonesome [ˈlounsəm], *a.* solitario, solo, triste.

lonesomeness [ˈlounsəmnis], *s.* soledad, abandono; sensación de soledad.

long (1) [lɔŋ], *a.* largo, extenso, prolongado; (*com.*) bien provisto; ***long-bow,*** arco; ***at long date,*** a largo plazo; ***long-distance,*** de gran distancia; (corredor) de fondo; (*tele.*) interurbano; ***long-jump,*** salto de longitud; ***long-legged,*** zanquilargo; ***long measure,*** medida de longitud; ***a long mile,*** una milla larga; ***long-range,*** de gran alcance; de gran autonomía; ***in the long run,*** a la larga; ***long-sighted,*** présbita; (*fig.*) sagaz, previsor; ***long-term,*** a largo plazo; ***long wave,*** onda larga; ***long-winded,*** prolijo; ***two feet long,*** de dos pies de largo. — *adv.* mucho, mucho tiempo, largo tiempo; ***as long as*** o ***so long as,*** mientras; siempre que, con tal que; ***as long as I live,*** mientras (yo) viva; ***to be long in,*** tardar en; ***all (the) day long,*** todo el santo día; ***for long,*** (por) mucho tiempo; ***how long is it since?*** ¿cuánto tiempo hace que?; ***long after,*** mucho después; ***long ago*** o ***long since,*** hace mucho tiempo; ***long before,*** mucho antes; ***long drawn out,*** prolongado, dilatado; ***long live!*** ¡viva!; ***long-lived,*** de vida larga, longevo; ***long-playing,*** de larga duración; ***long-standing,*** existente desde hace *o* hacía mucho tiempo; ***long-suffering,*** pacienzudo, sufrido; ***so long!*** ¡hasta luego! — *s.* largo, longitud; sílaba larga; (*mús.*) longa; ***before long,*** dentro de poco, en breve; antes de mucho; ***it takes long to do it,*** lleva mucho (tiempo) hacerlo; ***the long and the short of it,*** en resumidas cuentas.

long (2) [lɔŋ], *v.i.* — ***for, after, to,*** ansiar, anhelar, añorar; suspirar por.

longanimity [lɔŋgəˈnimiti], *s.* longanimidad.

longboat [ˈlɔŋbout], *s.* lancha, chalupa.

longer [ˈlɔŋgə], *a.* más largo. — *adv.* más tiempo; ***how much longer?*** ¿cuánto más tiempo?; ***no longer,*** ya no.

longeval, longevous [lɔnˈdʒiːvəl, -vəs], *a.* longevo.

longevity [lɔnˈdʒeviti], *s.* longevidad.

longhand [ˈlɔŋhænd], *s.* escritura *o* letra normal.

longing [ˈlɔŋiŋ], *s.* anhelo, ansia, ansiedad.

longingly [ˈlɔŋiŋli], *adv.* con ansiedad.

longish [ˈlɔŋ(g)iʃ], *a.* algo largo.

longitude [ˈlɔndʒitjuːd], *s.* longitud.

longitudinal [lɔndʒiˈtjuːdinəl], *a.* longitudinal.

longness [ˈlɔŋnis], *s.* largura.

longshoreman [ˈlɔŋʃɔːmən], *s.* (*Am.*) [DOCKER].

longspun [ˈlɔŋspʌn], *a.* dilatado, prolijo.

longways [ˈlɔŋweiz], *adv.* longitudinalmente, a lo largo.

loo [luː], *s.* (*fam.*) váter.

look [luk], *s.* mirada; aspecto; ***by the look of things,*** según parece; a juzgar por las apariencias; ***good looks,*** buen parecer; ***look-out,*** vigilancia, observación; vigía; ***look-out tower,*** atalaya; ***to be on the look-out for,*** estar al acecho de; ***that's his look-out,*** allá él, eso es cosa suya; ***to get*** o ***have a look in,*** poder participar; tener posibilidad de ganar; ***to have*** o ***take a look at,*** echar un vistazo *o* una ojeada a; ***to have a look for,*** buscar; ***I don't like the look of it,*** me da mala espina, no me tiene buen cariz. — *v.t.* expresar con la mirada; (*edad*) representar; ***look (s.o.) in the face,*** mirar cara a cara; ***look out,*** buscar, sacar, elegir; ***look over,*** echar un vistazo a; ***he looks the part,*** tiene aspecto de lo que es; ***look up,*** buscar, consultar; (*fam.*) hacer una visita a; ***look (s.o.) up and down,*** mirar de hito en hito *o* de arriba abajo. — *v.i.* mirar; parecer; tener aire de; (*joven, viejo*) resultar, estar; buscar; ***look about,*** mirar alrededor *o* en torno; ***look about for,*** andar buscando; ***look after,*** cuidar de; ocuparse de; ***look at,*** mirar; ***it's not much to look at,*** resulta muy poquita cosa; ***look away,*** desviar *o* apartar la vista; ***look back,*** mirar hacia atrás; ***look back on,*** recordar, evocar; ***look before you leap,*** antes que te cases, mira lo que haces; ***look down on,*** dominar; (*fig.*) mirar por encima del hombro; ***look for,*** buscar; esperar; ***look forward to,*** tener ilusión por, esperar con ilusión; ***look here!*** ¡oiga! ¡un momento!; (*fam.*) ***look in,*** pasar(se) por (la) casa (***on,*** de); ver la televisión; ***look into,*** investigar, indagar; ***look like,*** parecerse a; tener aspecto de; ***it looks like rain,*** parece que va a llover; ***look on,*** estar de espectador, mirar (sin más); ***look on to,*** dar a; ***look out!*** ¡cuidado! ¡ojo!; ***look out for,*** buscar; estar a la expectativa de; tener cuidado con; ***look out of,*** mirar por; ***look out on,*** dar a; ***look round,*** volver la cabeza; ***look through,*** mirar por; hojear; buscar entre; ***look to,*** ocuparse de; acudir a, tener puestas las esperanzas en; ***look to s.o. to do sth.,*** contar con alguien para que haga algo; ***look up,*** levantar los ojos; mejorar; ***look up to,*** respetar, admirar; ***look well,*** tener buen aspecto *o* buena cara; ***it looks well on you,*** te sienta bien.

looker [ˈlukə], *s.* observador, espectador; mirón.

looking [ˈlukiŋ], *a.* ***good*** o ***fine looking,*** guapo, bien parecido. — *s.* mirada; expectación; ***looking-glass,*** espejo.

loom (1) [luːm], *s.* telar; (*mar.*) guión del remo.

loom (2) [luːm], *s.* amago, aparición. — *v.i.* presentarse, amagar, asomar.

looming [ˈluːmiŋ], *s.* (*ópt.*) espejismo.

loon (1) [luːn], *s.* bobo, necio.

loon (2) [luːn], *s.* (*orn.*) somorgujo.

loop [luːp], *s.* lazo, gaza, nudo; ojal, presilla, alamar; anillo; recodo, comba, curva, vuelta; (*fort.*) aspillera; (*mec.*) abrazadera, anilla; (*aer.*) rizo; ***loop-maker,*** ojaladero, presillero. — *v.t.* enlazar; asegurar con una presilla; hacer gazas, formar festones *o* curvas en; ***loop the loop,*** rizar el rizo. — *v.i.* serpentear; formar lazos.

looped [luːpt], *a.* ojalado, lleno de ojales.

looper [ˈluːpə], *s.* engazador.

loophole [ˈluːphoul], *s.* aspillera, tronera; (*fig.*) escapatoria.

loopholed [ˈluːphould], *a.* que tiene troneras *o* aspilleras.

loose [luːs], *a.* suelto, desatado; flojo; holgado; (*rueda*) loco; (*cable*) desconectado; poco exacto *o* concreto, mal construido; incoherente; (*moralidad*) relajado; (*mujer*) fácil; (*med.*) ***loose in the bowels,*** suelto de vientre; ***loose change,*** suelto; ***loose end,*** cabo suelto; ***to be at a loose end,*** no tener nada que hacer; ***to break loose,*** desatarse; escaparse; desencadenarse; ***to cast*** o ***let loose,*** soltar; ***to come, get*** o ***work loose,*** aflojarse, desatarse; ***to play fast and loose with,*** andarse con un juego de tira y afloja con. — *s.* libertad; soltura; ***to be on the loose,*** estar en libertad; estar de juerga. — *v.t.* soltar; desatar; aflojar; ***loose one's hold on,*** soltar, dejar irse. — *v.i.* — ***off,*** dispararse.

loosely [ˈluːsli], *adv.* sueltamente, flojamente; con desenvoltura; negligentemente; holgadamente; sin cohesión.

loosen [luːsn], *v.t.* desatar, aflojar, soltar. — *v.i.* desatarse, aflojarse, soltarse; ***loosen up,*** desentumecerse.

looseness [ˈlu:snis], *s.* soltura, flojedad, holgura; (*moralidad*) relajación; (*med.*) diarrea.
loosening [ˈlu:səniŋ], *a.* laxante. — *s.* laxación; (el) aflojar, (el) soltar.
loosestrife [ˈlu:sstraif], *s.* (*bot.*) lasimaquia.
loot [lu:t], *s.* botín. — *v.t.* saquear, pillar.
looter [ˈlu:tə], *s.* saqueador.
looting [ˈlu:tiŋ], *s.* saqueo, pillaje.
lop [lɔp], *v.t.* — ***off,*** desmochar, descabezar, cercenar; cortar de un hachazo.
lope [loup], *s.* paso largo y rápido. — *v.i.* ir a medio galope, correr a paso largo.
lopsided [lɔpˈsaidid], *a.* más pesado de un lado que de otro, ladeado; (*fig.*) desequilibrado.
loquacious [loˈkweiʃəs], *a.* locuaz.
loquaciousness, loquacity [loˈkweiʃəsnis, loˈkwæsiti], *s.* locuacidad.
loquat [ˈloukwɔt], *s.* níspero (del Japón).
lord [lɔ:d], *s.* señor; lord; ***House of Lords,*** Cámara de los Lores; ***Lord Chamberlain,*** Camarero Mayor; ***Lord Chief Justice,*** Presidente del tribunal supremo (*de Inglaterra*); ***Lord Mayor,*** alcalde; ***Lord's Day,*** día del Señor; ***Lord's Prayer,*** padrenuestro; ***Lord's Supper,*** Sacramento de la Eucaristía. — *v.t.* (*fam.*) ***lord it,*** hacer el señor; mandar despóticamente; ***lord it over,*** señorear, dominar, tener metido en un puño; tener avasallado.
lordliness [ˈlɔ:dlinis], *s.* señorío; dignidad; altivez.
lordling [ˈlɔ:dliŋ], *s.* señoritingo.
lordly [ˈlɔ:dli], *a.* señorial; señoril.
lordship [ˈlɔ:dʃip], *s.* señoría; dominio, señorío; ***Your Lordship,*** Su Señoría.
lore [lɔ:], *s.* saber (popular); ciencia.
lorgnette [lɔ:ˈnjet], *s.* impertinentes, *m.pl.*
loriot [ˈlɔriət], *s.* (*orn.*) oropéndola.
loris [ˈlɔris], *s.* (*zool.*) loris, *m.*
Lorraine [lɔˈrein]. Lorena.
lorry [ˈlɔri], *s.* camión.
Los Angeles [lɔs ˈændʒili:z]. Los Angeles.
lose [lu:z], *irr. v.t.* perder; hacer perder; ***lose face,*** desprestigiarse; ***lose ground,*** perder terreno; ***lose one's heart to,*** prendarse de; ***lose one's mind,*** perder el juicio; ***lose patience,*** perder la paciencia; ***lose sight of,*** perder de vista; ***lose one's temper,*** enfadarse, perder los estribos; ***lose sth. to,*** perder algo en favor de; ***lose one's way,*** perderse, extraviarse; ***to be lost,*** estar perdido; ***to get lost,*** perderse; ***get lost!*** ¡desaparece! ¡lárgate!; ***he has just lost his father,*** acaba de perder a su padre, acaba de morírsele su padre; ***that lost him his job,*** eso le hizo perder el empleo. — *v.i.* perder; atrasar (*reloj*); ***lose out,*** perderse algo.
loser [ˈlu:zə], *s.* perdedor, perdidoso; ***to be a good*** o ***bad loser,*** tener buen *o* mal perder; ***to come off the loser,*** salir perdiendo.
losing [ˈlu:ziŋ], *a.* perdedor; vencido. — *s.* pérdida, diminución, merma.
loss [lɔs], *s.* pérdida; ***loss of face,*** desprestigio; ***to be at a loss,*** estar perplejo, no saber qué hacer; ***to be at a loss for,*** no encontrar, no dar con; ***to be at a loss to,*** no saber cómo (*hacer algo*); ***to be a dead loss,*** ser una nulidad; ***to sell at a loss,*** vender con pérdida; ***it's your loss,*** usted se lo pierde.
lost [lɔst], *a.* perdido; ***lost-property office,*** (*Am.*) ***lost and found,*** oficina de objetos perdidos; ***lost in thought,*** absorto, ensimismado; ***the remark was not lost on him,*** no dejó de advertir esta observación; ***lost to,*** insensible a. — *pret.*, *p.p.* [LOSE].
lot [lɔt], *adv.* ***a lot, lots,*** mucho; ***a lot*** o ***lots better,*** mucho mejor. — *s.* lote; porción; suerte; solar (de construcción); gran cantidad; tipo, sujeto; colección, partida; ***a lot of, lots of,*** muchísimo, la mar de; ***a lot of people,*** mucha gente; ***a bad lot,*** un mal sujeto; ***to draw lots,*** echar suertes; ***it fell to his lot,*** le cupo en suerte; ***the lot,*** todo; ***to throw in one's lot with,*** unirse a la suerte de.
loth [louθ] [LOATH].
lothario [loˈθɑ:riou], *s.* libertino, tunante.
lotion [ˈlouʃən], *s.* loción.
lottery [ˈlɔtəri], *s.* lotería, rifa; ***lottery office,*** lotería, expendeduría de billetes de lotería.
lotto [ˈlɔtou], *s.* lotería (*juego casero*).
lotus [ˈloutəs], *s.* (*bot.*) loto, ninfea, nenúfar, almez, azufaifo; ***lotus-eater,*** lotófago, ocioso; ***lotus-tree,*** loto, almez.
loud [laud], *a.* alto, recio, fuerte; (*colores*) llamativo, chillón, charro; (*mal gusto*) chabacano, ordinario.
loudly [ˈlaudli], *adv.* ruidosamente; fuerte, recio; a gritos; en voz alta.
loudness [ˈlaudnis], *s.* ruido, sonoridad; (*fam.*) (lo) llamativo, mal gusto.
loudspeaker [laudˈspi:kə], *s.* altavoz, *m.*
lough [lɔx, lɔk], *s.* lago, laguna.
Louis [ˈlu:i]. Luis.
louis [ˈlu:i], *s.* luis de oro.
Louisa, Louise [luˈi:zə, luˈi:z]. Luisa.
Louisiana [lui:ziˈænə]. Luisiana.
lounge [laundʒ], *s.* salón; sala (de estar); (*mueble*) sofá, *m.*, canapé; holganza; ***lounge suit,*** traje de calle. — *v.i.* arrellanarse; holgazanear, gandulear; pasearse lentamente.
lounger [ˈlaundʒə], *s.* haragán, holgazán, ocioso, gandul, azotacalles, *m.inv.*
lour [LOWER (2)].
louse [laus], s. (*pl.* **lice** [lais]) piojo; pulgón. — *v.t.* despiojar.
lousewort [ˈlauswə:t], *s.* (*bot.*) albarraz; hierba piojera.
lousiness [ˈlauzinis], *s.* (lo) piojoso; (lo) pésimo.
lousy [ˈlauzi], *a.* piojoso; (*fam.*, *fig.*) infame, fatal, pésimo; (*obsc.*) mierdento; ***lousy trick,*** judiada, cabronada.
lout [laut], *s.* patán, zafio; gamberro.
loutish [ˈlautiʃ], *a.* grosero.
Louvain [lu:ˈvein]. Lovaina.
louver [ˈlu:və], *s.* (*arq.*) lumbrera, lucerna; ***louver-boards,*** tejadillos, *m.pl.*
lovable [ˈlʌvəbl], *a.* que inspira amor, que se hace querer.
love [lʌv], *a.* de amor; amoroso. — *s.* amor (***of, for,*** de, a); cariño; querer; (*pers.*) amante, amado, amada, querido, querida; (*fam.*) preciosidad, amor; (*tenis*) cero; ***for love,*** por amor; (*fam.*) gratis; ***for the love of,*** por (el) amor de; (*fam.*) ***not for love nor money,*** por nada del mundo; a ningún precio; ***to be (madly) in love with,*** estar (locamente) enamorado de; ***to fall in love with,*** enamorarse de; ***to give*** o ***send one's love,*** mandar cariñosos saludos a; ***to make love to,*** hacer el amor a; cortejar; ***love at first sight,*** flechazo; ***love-affair,*** amores, *m.pl.*, amorío(s), lío amoroso; (*orn.*) ***love-bird,*** periquito; (*fig.*) tortolito; ***love-feast,*** ágape; (*bot.*) ***love-in-a-mist,*** neguilla; pasionaria; (*bot.*) ***love-lies-bleeding,*** amaranto; ***love-lorn,*** abandonado del amante, suspirando de amor; ***love-making,*** trato sexual; galanteo(s); ***love-match,*** matrimonio de amor. — *v.t.* querer; amar; ser muy aficionado a; ***he loves figs,*** le encantan *o* le chiflan los higos; ***I should love to,*** me encantaría + *inf.*
lovelace [ˈlʌvleis], *s.* seductor, libertino.
loveless [ˈlʌvlis], *a.* falto de amor, sin amor.
loveliness [ˈlʌvlinis], *s.* belleza, hermosura; encanto; exquisitez.
lovely [ˈlʌvli], *a.* hermoso, encantador; exquisito; precioso.
lover [ˈlʌvə], *s.* amante; amador; enamorado; amigo (***of,*** de), aficionado (***of,*** a); (*pl.*) amantes; novios, *m.pl.*; ***lover of nature,*** enamorado de la naturaleza.
lovesick [ˈlʌvsik], *a.* enfermo de mal de amores.
lovesome [ˈlʌvsəm], *a.* amable.

loving [ˈlʌviŋ], *a.* amoroso; tierno, cariñoso; ***loving-kindness,*** cariño; misericordia. — *s.* afecto; ***loving-cup,*** copa que pasa de mano en mano entre amigos.
lovingness [ˈlʌviŋnis], *s.* cariño, ternura, afecto.
low (1) [lou], *a.* bajo, poco elevado, pequeño; económico, barato, módico; profundo, hondo; (*fig.*) abatido, decaído, desanimado; ***low-born,*** de humilde cuna; (*fam.*) ***low brow,*** poco culto; ***low-church,*** evangélico, opuesto al ritualismo; ***low churchman,*** partidario del evangelismo, enemigo del ritualismo, *m.f.*; ***low comedy,*** comedia burlesca; ***Low Countries,*** Países Bajos, *m.pl.*; ***low fever,*** calentura lenta; ***low latitude,*** latitud cercana al ecuador; ***Low Mass,*** misa privada *o* rezada; ***low-minded,*** ruin, vil; ***low neck,*** escote; ***low-necked,*** escotado; ***to have a low opinion of,*** tener un concepto poco favorable de; ***low-pitched,*** grave (de tono); ***in low spirits*** o ***low-spirited,*** abatido, desanimado; ***Low Sunday,*** domingo de cuasimodo; ***low tide*** o ***water,*** marea baja, aguas de menguante, *f.pl.*, reflujo, bajamar (*del mar*), *f.*, estiaje (*del río*); ***low trick,*** mala jugada *o* partida; ***in a low voice,*** en voz baja; ***to be low on,*** andar mal *o* escaso de. — *adv.* bajo.
low (2) [lou], *s.* mugido, berrido. — *v.i.* mugir, dar mugidos, berrear.
lowbell [ˈloubel], *s.* cencerro; esquila.
lower (1) [louə], *a.* más bajo; bajo, inferior; (*impr.*) ***lower case,*** caja baja; ***Lower Empire,*** Bajo Imperio. — *v.t.* bajar, poner más bajo *o* en lugar inferior, descender; abajar, agachar, humillar, abatir; rebajar, disminuir, minorar; (*mar.*) ***lower the sails,*** arriar las velas. — *v.i.* bajar, disminuirse, minorarse, menguar; (*mar.*) ***lower away,*** arriar. — **lower o.s.,** *v.r.* — ***to,*** rebajarse a.
lower (2) [lauə], *v.i.* encapotarse (*el cielo*); ponerse ceñudo.
lowering [ˈlauəriŋ], *a.* sombrío, encapotado (*cielo*).
lowermost, lowest [ˈlouəmoust, ˈlouist], *a.* (el) más bajo; bajísimo, ínfimo.
lowing [ˈlouiŋ], *s.* mugidos, *m.pl.*, bramidos, *m.pl.*
lowland [ˈlouland], *s.* tierra baja; (*pl.* **Lowlands**) tierras bajas de Escocia, *f.pl.*
lowlander [ˈlouləndə], *s.* abajeño, llanero.
lowliness [ˈloulinis], *s.* humildad.
lowly [ˈlouli], *a.* humilde; vil, ruin, despreciable; bajo, rastrero. — *adv.* humildemente, modestamente; vilmente.
lowness [ˈlounis], *s.* (lo) bajo; (lo) vil; humildad; postración.
loxodrome [ˈlɔkzodroum], *s.* loxodromia.
loxodromic [lɔksoˈdrɔmik], *a.* loxodrómico; ***loxodromic line,*** línea loxodrómica.
loyal [ˈlɔiəl], *a.* leal, fiel.
loyalist [ˈlɔiəlist], *s.* realista, *m.f.*; legitimista, *m.f.*; gubernamental; republicano.
loyalty [ˈlɔiəlti], *s.* lealtad, fidelidad.
lozenge [ˈlɔzindʒ], *s.* (*farm.*) pastilla; (*geom.*) rombo; (*blas.*) losanje.
lozenged [ˈlɔzindʒd], *a.* rombal, que tiene forma de rombo *o* losanje.
lubber [ˈlʌbə], *s.* bobalicón.
lubberly [ˈlʌbəli], *a.* bobo, torpe.
lubricant [ˈl(j)u:brikənt], *a.*, *s.* lubricante, lubrificante.
lubricate [ˈl(j)u:brikeit], *v.t.* lubricar, lubrificar, engrasar.
lubricating [ˈl(j)u:brikeitiŋ], *a.* lubricante.
lubrication [l(j)u:briˈkeiʃən], *s.* lubricación, lubrificación, engrase.
lubricator [ˈl(j)u:brikeitə], *s.* lubricador, engrasador.
lubricity [l(j)u:ˈbrisiti], *s.* lubricidad.
lubricous [ˈl(j)u:brikəs], *a.* lúbrico.
Lucan [ˈl(j)u:kən], *a.* Lucano.
luce [l(j)u:s], *s.* (*ict.*) lucio.
lucent [ˈl(j)u:sənt], *a.* luciente.
lucerne [l(j)u:ˈsə:n], *s.* (*bot.*) alfalfa; ***lucerne-field,*** alfalfal.
lucid [ˈl(j)u:sid], *a.* lúcido.
lucidity, lucidness [l(j)u:ˈsiditi, ˈl(j)u:sidnis], *s.* lucidez.
Lucifer [ˈl(j)u:sifə]. Lucifer.
Luciferian [l(j)u:siˈfiəriən], *a.* luciferino.
luck [lʌk], *s.* suerte, *f.*, ventura, fortuna; azar; ***bad, hard*** o ***ill luck,*** mala suerte; ***better luck tomorrow!*** mañana será otro día; ***for luck,*** para traer (la) (buena) suerte; ***good luck,*** (buena) suerte, fortuna; ***run of luck,*** racha de suerte; ***to be in luck,*** estar de suerte; ***to be down on one's luck*** o ***out of luck,*** no estar de suerte, tener la negra; ***no such luck!*** ¡no caerá esa breva!; ***to try one's luck,*** probar fortuna; ***with any luck,*** si Dios quiere, malo será (que no + *subj.*).
luckily [ˈlʌkili], *adv.* por fortuna, afortunadamente, felizmente.
luckiness [ˈlʌkinis], *s.* (buena) fortuna, (buena) suerte; felicidad.
luckless [ˈlʌklis], *a.* desafortunado, desdichado, desventurado; desgraciado, infeliz.
lucky [ˈlʌki], *a.* afortunado, venturoso; propicio, bienhadado, favorable; ***to be born under a lucky star,*** nacer en buena hora; ***to be lucky,*** tener (buena) suerte; ***lucky dip,*** tómbola; ***lucky hit, break,*** (una) suerte.
lucrative [ˈl(j)u:krətiv], *a.* lucrativo, provechoso.
lucre [ˈl(j)u:kə], *s.* lucro.
Lucretia [l(j)u:ˈkri:ʃjə]. Lucrecia.
Lucretius [l(j)u:ˈkri:ʃəs]. Lucrecio.
lucubrate [ˈl(j)u:kjubreit], *v.i.* lucubrar.
lucubration [l(j)u:kjuˈbreiʃən], *s.* lucubración.
lucubratory [ˈl(j)u:kjubrətəri], *a.* que se lucubra.
luculent [ˈl(j)u:kjulənt], *a.* luciente, claro; evidente, diáfano.
Lucullus [l(j)u:ˈkʌləs]. Luculo.
Lucy [ˈlu:si]. Lucía.
ludicrous [ˈl(j)u:dikrəs], *a.* irrisorio, ridículo.
ludicrousness [ˈl(j)u:dikrəsnis], *s.* ridiculez, (lo) irrisorio.
luff [lʌf], *s.* (*mar.*) gratil, cachete de proa; orzada; ***to keep one's luff,*** orzar; (*mar.*) ***luff-tackle,*** aparejo de bolinear; ***to spring the luff,*** partir el puño. — *v.t.* ***luff up,*** tomar por avante. — *v.i.* orzar.
lug [lʌg], *s.* (*fam.*) oreja; asa, agarradera; (*fam.*) tirón, estirón; (*mar.*) ***lug sail,*** vela al tercio. — *v.t.* tirar (de); (*mar.*) halar; ***lug away*** o ***off,*** arrastrar, llevarse arrastrando; (*fig.*) ***lug in,*** traer a colación.
luggage [ˈlʌgidʒ], *s.* equipaje; (*f.c.*) ***luggage van,*** furgón de equipajes.
lugger [ˈlʌgə], *s.* (*mar.*) lugre.
lugubrious [l(j)u:ˈg(j)u:briəs], *a.* lúgubre.
lugworm [ˈlʌgwə:m], *s.* (*zool.*) arenícola.
Luke [l(j)u:k]. Lucas, *m.*
lukewarm [ˈl(j)u:kwɔ:m], *a.* tibio.
lukewarmness [ˈl(j)u:kwɔ:mnis], *s.* tibieza.
lull [lʌl], *s.* calma, recalmón; tregua, respiro. — *v.t.* calmar, sosegar; arrullar, adormecer.
lullaby [ˈlʌləbai], *s.* canción de cuna, nana.
Lulu [ˈlu:lu:]. *dim. de* [LOUISA, LOUISE].
lumbago [lʌmˈbeigou], *s.* lumbago.
lumbar [ˈlʌmbə], *a.* lumbar.
lumber (1) [ˈlʌmbə], *s.* madera(s); trastos viejos, *m.pl.*; balumba; (*Am.*) árboles, *m.pl.*; (*Am.*) ***lumber-jack,*** leñador, hachero; ***lumber-mill,*** aserradero; ***lumber-room,*** trastero, camaranchón; ***lumber-yard,*** almacén de maderas. — *v.t.* cortar, aserrar (*árboles* o *troncos*); amontonar, atestar.
lumber (2) [ˈlʌmbə], *v.i.* andar *o* moverse pesadamente.
lumbering [ˈlʌmbəriŋ], *a.* pesado (*en el andar*), torpe.

lumberman [ˈlʌmbəmən], *s.* hachero.
luminary [ˈl(j)uːminəri], *s.* lumbrera, luminar, astro.
luminescence [l(j)uːmiˈnesəns], *s.* luminescencia.
luminescent [l(j)uːmiˈnesənt], *a.* luminescente.
luminiferous [l(j)uːmiˈnifərəs], *a.* luminífero.
luminous [ˈl(j)uːminəs], *a.* luminoso, luciente; lúcido.
luminousness, luminosity [ˈl(j)uːminəsnis, l(j)uːmiˈnɔsiti], *s.* luminosidad.
lump [lʌmp], *s.* trozo, pedazo; terrón (de azúcar); (*anat.*) bulto, hinchazón, *f.*; protuberancia; pella; masa; ***to have a lump in one's throat,*** tener un nudo en la garganta, hacérsele a uno un nudo en la garganta; ***lump of dough*** o ***stodge,*** mazacote, ladrillazo; (*pers.*) zoquete; ***lump sum,*** suma global. — *v.t.* — ***together,*** juntar, englobar; (*fam.*) ***lump it,*** aguantarse.
lumping [ˈlʌmpiŋ], *a.* (*fam.*) ***lumping great brute,*** animalazo.
lumpish [ˈlʌmpiʃ], *a.* amazacotado, apelmazado; grumoso.
lumpishness [ˈlʌmpiʃnis], *s.* (lo) amazacotado, (lo) apelmazado; (lo) grumoso.
lumpy [ˈlʌmpi], *a.* [LUMPISH]; (*mar.*) picado.
lunacy [ˈl(j)uːnəsi], *s.* locura, demencia.
lunar [ˈl(j)uːnə], *a.* lunar, lunario.
lunarian [l(j)uːˈnɛəriən], *a., s.* lunario.
lunate(d) [ˈl(j)uːneit(id)], *a.* lunado, luniforme.
lunatic [ˈl(j)uːnətik], *a., s.* lunático; demente; ***lunatic fringe,*** extremistas chalados, *m.pl.*
lunation [l(j)uːˈneiʃən], *s.* lunación.
lunch, luncheon [lʌntʃ, ˈlʌntʃən], *s.* comida, almuerzo; ***to have meat for lunch,*** comer *o* almorzar carne. — *v.i.* comer, almorzar.
lunette [l(j)uːˈnet], *s.* (*arq., fort.*) luneta.
lung [lʌŋ], *s.* pulmón; ***iron lung,*** pulmón de acero.
lunge [lʌndʒ], *s.* estocada; arremetida. — *v.i.* (*esgr.*) dar una estocada; arremeter (***at,*** contra).
lungwort [ˈlʌŋwəːt], *s.* (*bot.*) pulmonaria.
luniform [ˈl(j)uːnifɔːm], *a.* luniforme, lunado.
lunisolar [ˈl(j)uːnisoulə], *a.* lunisolar.
lunt [lʌnt], *s.* mecha (*de cañón*); bocanada (*de humo*); llamarada.
lunular [ˈl(j)uːnjulə], *a.* lunado.
lunulate(d) [ˈl(j)uːnjuleit(id)], *a.* (*bot.*) lunado.
lupin(e) [ˈl(j)uːpin], *s.* (*bot.*) altramuz.
lurch (1) [ləːtʃ], *s.* sacudida, tumbo, tambaleo; (*mar.*) guiñada. — *v.i.* dar *o* pegar sacudidas *o* tumbos, tambalearse; (*mar.*) guiñar, cabecear; ***lurch along,*** ir dando tumbos.
lurch (2) [ləːtʃ], *s.* ***to leave in the lurch,*** dejar en la estacada, en el atolladero, dejar plantado.
lure [l(j)uə], *s.* señuelo, reclamo; aliciente. — *v.t.* atraer (con señuelo *o* reclamo), tentar, seducir, encandilar.
lurid [ˈl(j)uərid], *a.* lívido, cárdeno; (*colores*) chillón, llamativo; (*periodismo*) sensacionalista, escandaloso; espeluznante, tremebundo.
lurk [ləːk], *v.i.* estar agazapado, emboscado *o* en acecho.
lurker [ˈləːkə], *s.* acechador.
lurking [ˈləːkiŋ], *a.* escondido, en acecho; ***lurking doubt,*** dudilla; ***lurking suspicion,*** sospechilla, recelillo. — *s.* acecho; ***lurking-place,*** emboscada; escondrijo, guarida.
luscious [ˈlʌʃəs], *a.* delicioso, exquisito, sabroso; hermoso.
lusciousness [ˈlʌʃəsnis], *s.* melosidad, dulzura; lo sabroso *o* exquisito; hermosura.
lush (1) [lʌʃ], *a.* jugoso, suculento, lozano.
lush (2) [lʌʃ], *s.* licor. — *v.t.* emborrachar. — *v.i.* beber.
lust, lustfulness [lʌst, ˈlʌstfulnis], *s.* lascivia, lujuria; avidez, codicia. — *v.i.* — ***after,*** codiciar, ansiar.
lustful [ˈlʌstful], *a.* lujurioso, lascivo.
lustfulness [LUST].
lustily [ˈlʌstili], *adv.* fuertemente, vigorosamente, robustamente, con fuerza.
lustiness [ˈlʌstinis], *s.* vigor, lozanía, robustez.
lustral [ˈlʌstrəl], *a.* lustral, lústrico.
lustration [lʌsˈtreiʃən], *s.* lustración.
lustre [ˈlʌstə], *s.* lustre, brillo; viso; araña (*de cristal*); lustro.
lustreless [ˈlʌstəlis], *a.* deslustrado, sin brillo.
lustring [ˈlʌstriŋ], *s.* lustrina.
lustrous [ˈlʌstrəs], *a.* lustroso, brillante.
lustrum [ˈlʌstrəm], *s.* lustro.
lustwort [ˈlʌstwəːt], *s.* (*bot.*) rocío del sol.
lusty [ˈlʌsti], *a.* robusto, forzudo, vigoroso, fornido.
lute (1) [l(j)uːt], *s.* (*mús.*) laúd.
lute (2) [l(j)uːt], *s.* raspador de ladrillares; lutén *o* lodo y cemento para junturas. — *v.t.* enlodar, tapar con lodo; enrasar (un ladrillar).
luteolin [ˈl(j)uːtiəlin], *s.* luteína.
lutestring [ˈl(j)uːtstriŋ], *s.* cuerda de laúd.
Luther [ˈl(j)uːθə]. Lutero.
Lutheran [ˈl(j)uːθərən], *a., s.* luterano.
Lutheranism [ˈl(j)uːθərənizəm], *s.* luteranismo.
lutist [ˈl(j)uːtist], *s.* tañedor de laúd.
lutose [ˈl(j)uːtouz], *a.* lodoso, cenagoso.
luxate [ˈlʌkseit], *v.t.* luxar.
luxation [lʌkˈseiʃən], *s.* luxación.
Luxemb(o)urg [ˈlʌksəmbəːg]. Luxemburgo.
luxuriance [lʌkˈzjuriəns], *s.* lozanía, frondosidad, exuberancia.
luxuriant [lʌkˈzjuəriənt], *a.* lozano, frondoso, lujuriante, exuberante.
luxuriate [lʌkˈzjuərieit], *v.i.* crecer con exuberancia, lozanear; (*fig.*) deleitarse, regodearse; (*fig.*) vivir con lujo.
luxurious [lʌkˈzjuəriəs], *a.* lujoso, suntuoso.
luxuriousness [lʌkˈzjuəriəsnis], *s.* suntuosidad, lujo.
luxury [ˈlʌkʃəri], *s.* lujo.
lycanthropy [laiˈkænθrəpi], *s.* licantropía.
lyceum [laiˈsiəm], *s.* liceo.
lycopodium [laikoˈpoudiəm], *s.* licopodio.
lyddite [ˈlidait], *s.* lidita.
Lydia [ˈlidiə]. Lidia.
Lydian [ˈlidiən], *a., s.* lidio.
lye (1) [lai], *s.* lejía.
lye (2) [lai], *s.* (*f.c.*) desviadero.
lying (1) [ˈlaiiŋ], *a.* falso, mentiroso. — *s.* mentiras, falsedades.
lying (2) [ˈlaiiŋ], *a.* echado, yacente; sito, situado; ***lying down,*** acostado; (*mar.*) ***lying-to,*** al pairo. — *s.* ***lying-in,*** parto; ***lying-in hospital,*** casa de maternidad.
lymph [limf], *s.* linfa.
lymphate, lymphated [ˈlimfeit, limˈfeitid], *a.* linfático.
lymphatic [limˈfætik], *a.* linfático. — *s.* vaso linfático.
lynch [lintʃ], *v.t.* linchar; ***lynch-law,*** ley del linchamiento.
lynching [ˈlintʃiŋ], *s.* linchamiento.
lynx [liŋks], *s.* lince; ***lynx-eyed,*** de ojos de lince.
Lyons [ˈliɔ̃]. Lyón, Lyons, León de Francia.
lyrate [ˈlaiəreit], *a.* de forma de lira.
lyre [ˈlaiə], *s.* (*mús.*) lira; (*orn.*) ***lyre-bird,*** pájaro lira.
lyric [ˈlirik], *a.* lírico. — *s.* (poesía) lírica; letra (de una canción); (*pl.*) letra.
lyrical [ˈlirikəl], *a.* [LYRIC].
lyricism [ˈlirisizəm], *s.* lirismo.
lyrist [ˈlaiərist, ˈlirist], *s.* (*mús.*) lirista, *m.f*; (*poeta*) lírico.
lysis [ˈlaisis], *s.* lisis, *f.*

M

M, m [em], decimotercera letra del alfabeto.
ma [ˈmɑː], *s.* (*fam.*) mamá, *f.*
ma'am [mæm, mɑːm], *s.* señora.
mac [mæk], *s.* (*fam.*) [MACKINTOSH].
macabre [məˈkɑːbr], *a.* macabro.
macadam [məˈkædəm], *s.* macadán.
macadamize [məˈkædəmaiz], *v.t.* macadamizar.
macaque [məˈkɑːk], *s.* (*zool.*) macaco.
macaroni [mækəˈrouni], *s.* macarrones, *m.pl.*
macaronic [mækəˈrɔnik], *a.* macarrónico.
macaronics [mækəˈrɔniks], *s.pl.* poesía macarrónica.
macaroon [mækəˈruːn], *s.* macarrón (de almendras).
macassar [məˈkæsə], *s.* aceite macasar.
macaw [məˈkɔː], *s.* (*orn.*) guacamayo.
Macbeth [mækˈbeθ]. Macbet.
Maccabean [mækəˈbiən], *a.* de los macabeos.
mace [meis], *s.* maza; macis, *f.inv.*
mace-bearer, macer [ˈmeis-bεərə, ˈmeisə], *s.* macero.
macerate [ˈmæsəreit], *v.t.* macerar.
maceration [mæsəˈreiʃən], *s.* maceración.
Mach [mæk], *s.* (*aer.*) número Mach.
Machiavelli [mækiəˈveli]. Maquiavelo.
Machiavellian [mækiəˈveliən], *a.* maquiavélico. — *s.* maquiavelista, *m.f.*
Machiavell(ian)ism [mækiəˈvel(iən)izəm], *s.* maquiavelismo.
machicolation [mætʃikəˈleiʃən], *s.* (*arq.*) matacán.
machinate [ˈmækineit], *v.t.*, *v.i.* maquinar.
machination [mækiˈneiʃən], *s.* maquinación.
machinator [ˈmækineitə], *s.* maquinador.
machine [məˈʃiːn], *s.* máquina, aparato; (*pol.*) camarilla; ***machine-gunner,*** ametrallador; ***machine-made,*** hecho a máquina; ***machine-tool,*** máquina herramienta. — *v.t.* trabajar a máquina.
machine-gun [məˈʃiːn-gʌn], *s.* ametralladora. — *v.t.* ametrallar.
machinery [məˈʃiːnəri], *s.* maquinaria, mecanismo.
machinist [məˈʃiːnist], *s.* maquinista, *m.f.*, mecánico; operario (*de una máquina*).
mackerel [ˈmækərəl], *s.* escombro, caballa; ***mackerel sky,*** cielo aborregado.
mackintosh [ˈmækintɔʃ], *s.* impermeable.
mackle [mækl], *s.* maculatura. — *v.t.* macular, repintar.
macrobian [məˈkroubiən], *s.* macrobiano.
macrocephalous [mækroˈsefələs], *a.* macrocéfalo.
macrocosm [ˈmækroukɔzəm], *s.* macrocosmo.
macula [ˈmækjulə], *s.* mácula.
maculate [ˈmækjulit], *a.* maculado. — [ˈmækjuleit], *v.t.* macular.
maculation [mækjuˈleiʃən], *s.* mácula, mancilla.
mad [mæd], *a.* loco, demente; furioso, rabioso; disparatado; ***as mad as a hatter,*** loco como una cabra; ***to be mad about,*** estar loco por; (*Am.*) estar furioso con *o* por; ***to drive mad,*** volver loco; (*Am.*) ***to get mad,*** ponerse furioso; ***to go mad,*** volverse loco; ***like mad,*** como un loco.
Madagascar [mædəˈgæskə]. Madagascar.
madam [ˈmædəm], *s.* señora, madama.
madcap [ˈmædkæp], *a.*, *s.* botarate, cabeza loca; casquivano.
madden [mædn], *v.t.* enloquecer; enfurecer.
maddening [ˈmædniŋ], *a.* exasperante; ***it's maddening,*** es para exasperar a cualquiera.
madder [ˈmædə], *s.* (*bot.*) rubia. — *v.t.* teñir con rubia.
madefaction [mædiˈfækʃən], *s.* humedecimiento.
Madeira [məˈdiərə], *s.* Madera; vino de Madera; ***Madeira Islands,*** islas de Madera.
madhouse [ˈmædhaus], *s.* manicomio, casa de locos.
madman [ˈmædmən], *s.* loco, orate.
madness [ˈmædnis], *s.* locura; insensatez; furia, rabia.
madonna [məˈdɔnə], *s.* Madona, Señora.
Madras [məˈdrɑːs]. Madrás.
madrepore [ˈmædripɔː], *s.* madrépora.
Madrid [məˈdrid]. Madrid.
madrigal [ˈmædrigəl], *s.* madrigal.
Madrilenian [mædriˈliːniən], *a.*, *s.* madrileño, matritense.
madwort [ˈmædwəːt], *s.* (*bot.*) aliso, marrubio.
Mæcenas [mi(ː)ˈsiːnæs]. Mecenas.
maelstrom [ˈmeilstrɔm], *s.* vorágine.
mænad [ˈmiːnæd], *s.* ménade.
magazine [mægəˈziːn], *s.* revista (ilustrada); (*mil.*) almacén; polvorín; (*mar.*) pañol de pólvora, santabárbara; recámara, cargador (*de un fusil*).
Magdalen, Magdalene [ˈmægdəlin, mægdəliːn]. Magdalena.
Magellan [məˈgelən]. Magallanes, *m.*
magenta [məˈdʒentə], *s.* magenta.
maggot [ˈmægət], *s.* gusano; cresa.
maggoty [ˈmægəti], *a.* lleno de gusanos, agusanado, gusaniento.
magi [ˈmeidʒai], *s.pl.* magos, *m.pl.*; (los) Reyes Magos.
magian [ˈmeidʒiən], *a.* de los magos; de los Reyes Magos.
magic [ˈmædʒik], *a.* mágico; ***magic lantern,*** linterna mágica; ***magic wand,*** varita mágica *o* de las virtudes. — *s.* magia; ***as if by magic,*** como por ensalmo.
magical [ˈmædʒikəl], *a.* mágico.
magically [ˈmædʒikəli], *adv.* mágicamente, milagrosamente.
magician [məˈdʒiʃən], *s.* mago; prestidigitador.
magisterial [mædʒisˈtiəriəl], *a.* magisterial.
magistery [ˈmædʒistəri], *s.* magisterio.
magistracy [ˈmædʒistrəsi], *s.* magistratura.
magistrate [ˈmædʒistreit], *s.* magistrado; juez.
Magna Carta [ˈmægnə ˈkɑːtə]. (la) Carta Magna.
magnanimity [mægnəˈnimiti], *s.* magnanimidad, generosidad.
magnanimous [mægˈnænimәs], *a.* magnánimo, generoso.
magnate [ˈmægneit], *s.* magnate.
magnesia [mægˈniːʒə], *s.* magnesia.
magnesian [mægˈniːʒən], *a.* magnesiano, magnésico.
magnesium [mægˈniːziəm], *s.* magnesio.
magnet [ˈmægnit], *s.* imán; ***horseshoe magnet,*** imán de herradura.
magnetic(al) [mægˈnetik(əl)], *a.* magnético; ***magnetic field,*** campo magnético; ***magnetic tape,*** cinta magnética.
magnetics [mægˈnetiks], *s.pl.* magnética.
magnetism [ˈmægnitizəm], *s.* magnetismo.
magnetizable [ˈmægnitaizəbl], *a.* magnetizable.
magnetization [mægnitaiˈzeiʃən], *s.* magnetización.
magnetize [ˈmægnitaiz], *v.t.* magnetizar; imantar.
magnetizer [ˈmægnitaizə], *s.* magnetizador.
magneto [mægˈniːtou], *s.* magneto.
magnifiable [ˈmægnifaiəbl], *a.* capaz de ser aumentado.
magnification [mægnifiˈkeiʃən], *s.* aumento, amplificación.
magnificence [mægˈnifisəns], *s.* magnificencia; esplendor, grandiosidad.
magnificent [mægˈnifisənt], *a.* magnífico; grandioso.

magnifier [ˈmægnifaiə], *s.* lente de aumento, *f.*
magnify [ˈmægnifai], *v.t.* aumentar, amplificar; exagerar.
magnifying [ˈmægnifaiiŋ], *a.* de aumento, que aumenta, amplificante, que amplifica; ***magnifying glass,*** lente de aumento, *f.*
magniloquence [mægˈnilokwəns], *s.* altilocuencia.
magniloquent [mægˈnilokwənt], *a.* grandílocuo.
magnitude [ˈmægnitju:d], *s.* magnitud.
magnolia [mægˈnouliə], *s.* magnolia.
magnum [ˈmægnəm], *s.* botella de dos litros.
magpie [ˈmægpai], *s.* (*orn.*) urraca, picaza, marica.
Magyar [ˈmægjɑ:], *a., s.* magiar.
maharaja [mɑ:həˈrɑ:dʒə], *s.* maharajá, *m.*
mahlstick [ˈmɑ:lstik], *s.* tiento de pintor.
mahogany [məˈhɔgəni], *s.* caoba.
Mahomet [məˈhɔmit], [MOHAMMED].
maid [meid], *s.* doncella; criada; soltera; ***lady's maid,*** doncella; ***maid of honour,*** dama de honor; ***nursery maid,*** niñera; (*fam.*) ***old maid,*** solterona.
maiden [ˈmeidən], *a.* de virgen, de joven, virgíneo, virginal; ***maiden name,*** apellido de soltera; (*pol.*) ***maiden speech,*** primer discurso; (*mar.*) ***maiden voyage,*** viaje inaugural. — *s.* doncella; virgen; soltera.
maidenhair [ˈmeidənhɛə], *s.* (*bot.*) culantrillo; (*ant.*) brenca.
maidenhead, maidenhood, maidhood [ˈmeidənhed, -hud, ˈmeidhud], *s.* virginidad, doncellez.
maidenlike [ˈmeidənlaik], *a.* virginal, virgíneo, doncellil.
maidenliness [ˈmeidənlinis], *s.* pudor, recato, modestia.
maidenly [ˈmeidənli], *a.* virginal, virgíneo, pudoroso.
mail (1) [meil], *s.* (cota de) malla.
mail (2) [meil], *s.* correo, correspondencia; ***mailbag,*** valija, mala; (*Am.*) ***mail-box,*** buzón; ***mailcoach,*** correo; diligencia; ***mail-steamer,*** vapor correo; ***mail-train,*** correo; tren correo; ***royal mail,*** mala real. — *v.t.* echar al correo; enviar por correo.
mailman [ˈmeilmæn] (*Am.*) [POSTMAN].
maim [meim], *v.t.* mutilar, lisiar, mancar, tullir.
maimed [meimd], *a.* mutilado, manco, tullido.
main (1) [mein], *a.* grande; mayor; principal; más importante; (*mar.*) ***main-brace,*** brazo mayor; ***main road,*** carretera; (*mar.*) ***main-sheet,*** escota mayor; (*Am.*) ***Main Street America,*** el hombre de la calle (norteamericano); (*mar.*) ***maintopmast,*** mastelero mayor; (*mar.*) ***maintopsail,*** vela de gavia; (*mar.*) ***main-topyard,*** verga de gavia; ***main wall,*** pared maestra; (*mar.*) ***main-yard,*** verga mayor. — *s.* alta mar; (*pl.*) cloaca colectora; cañería maestra; cable eléctrico de alimentación; ***in the main,*** principalmente; ***Spanish Main,*** (el) mar de las Antillas.
main (2) [mein], *s.* ***with might and main,*** con todas sus fuerzas.
Maine [mein]. Maine.
mainland [ˈmeinlænd], *s.* continente, tierra firme.
mainly [ˈmeinli], *adv.* principalmente, mayormente.
mainmast [ˈmeinmɑ:st], *s.* (*mar.*) palo mayor.
mainsail [ˈmeinsəl], *s.* (*mar.*) vela mayor.
maintain [meinˈtein], *v.t.* mantener; sostener.
maintainable [meinˈteinəbl], *a.* sostenible.
maintenance [ˈmeintənəns], *s.* mantenimiento; sostenimiento; manutención; conservación.
maisonette [meizəˈnet], *s.* casita, hotelito.
maize [meiz], *s.* maíz.
majestic [məˈdʒestik], *a.* majestuoso.
majesty [ˈmædʒisti], *s.* majestad; majestuosidad.
majolica [məˈdʒɔlikə], *s.* (*cerá.*) mayólica.
major [ˈmeidʒə], *a.* mayor; principal; importante, trascendental. — *s.* (*mil.*) comandante; (*for.*) mayor de edad; (proposición) mayor; ***majordomo,*** mayordomo; ***major-general,*** general de división. — *v.i.* (*Am.*) — ***in,*** especializarse en.
Majorca [məˈjɔ:kə]. Mallorca.
majority [məˈdʒɔriti], *s.* mayoría, mayor parte, mayor número; mayoría de edad.
majuscule [ˈmædʒəskjul], *s.* mayúscula.
make [meik], *s.* hechura; confección; fabricación; marca; ***make-up,*** composición; invención; maquillaje; (*fam.*) ***to be on the make,*** barrer para dentro. — *irr. v.t.* hacer; crear; constituir; ganar (*dinero*); dar, producir (*dinero*); pronunciar (*un discurso*); cometer (*una falta*); hacerse (*una reputación*); llegar a, alcanzar; poner (*nervioso*); calcular; (*fam.*) ***make the best of it,*** sacarle a una cosa el mejor partido posible; (*fam.*) ***you'll have to make the best of a bad job,*** no tienes más remedio que aguantarte; ***it's made for him,*** le viene pintado; ***make good,*** reparar; compensar; completar; cumplir; ***make the grade,*** dar la talla; ***make into,*** convertir *o* transformar en; (*fam.*) ***make it,*** llegar; ***make of,*** deducir de; ***I can't make anything of it,*** no le veo sentido, no lo entiendo en absoluto; ***make out,*** (*cheque*) extender; distinguir, divisar; descifrar; entender; (*fingir*) hacer ver; ***make over,*** ceder, traspasar; ***make rich,*** enriquecer; (*fam., fig.*) ***it makes you sick,*** es indignante; ***make up,*** hacer; preparar; inventar(se); completar; (*impr.*) compaginar; (*ropa*) confeccionar; pintar, maquillar; (*lumbre*) echar más carbón *o* leña a; subsanar, compensar; (*tiempo*) recuperar; ***make it up,*** hacer las paces; ***to be made up of,*** componerse de; ***she'll make him a good wife,*** será buena esposa para él; ***make s.o.,*** ser causa del éxito de alguien; ***I made him go,*** le hice ir, le obligué a ir; ***that makes ten,*** con éste son *o* van diez; ***we've got it made,*** ya está, ya lo tenemos; ***make or break, make or mar,*** hacer la fortuna (felicidad) o ser la ruina (desgracia) de. — *v.i.* ***make after,*** salir en persecución de; ***make as if*** o ***as though to,*** hacer como si; ***make away with,*** suprimir; eliminar; llevarse; ***make away with o.s.,*** suicidarse; ***make believe,*** fingir(se); ***make for,*** dirigirse a; contribuir a, fomentar, favorecer; (*fam.*) ***make good,*** llegar; ***make off,*** largarse, darse a la fuga; ***make off with,*** llevarse, alzarse con; ***make out,*** arreglárselas, defenderse (bien); ***how did you make out?*** ¿ qué tal te fue ?; ***make to,*** ir a, hacer ademán de; ***make towards,*** dirigirse a; ***make up,*** maquillarse; hacer las paces; ***make up for,*** compensar; recuperar (el tiempo perdido); ***make up to,*** hacer la pelotilla a.
makebelieve [ˈmeikbili:v], *a.* simulado, inventado. — *s.* simulación, invención.
maker [ˈmeikə], *s.* hacedor, creador, autor; artífice, fabricante.
makeshift [ˈmeikʃift], *a.* improvisado; provisional. — *s.* improvisación, recurso, cosa provisional *o* improvisada.
makeweight [ˈmeikweit], *s.* complemento del peso.
making [ˈmeikiŋ], *s.* formación; hechura; elementos necesarios, *m.pl.*; ***he's got the makings of a good lawyer,*** tiene madera de (buen) abogado; ***in the making,*** haciéndose, en vías de formación; ***it was his making,*** él fue la causa; ***it was the making of him,*** fue lo que le llevó al éxito *o* a triunfar *o* a encontrar su camino en la vida.
Malabar [ˈmæləbɑ:]. Malabar.
Malacca [məˈlækə]. Malaca.
malachite [ˈmæləkait], *s.* malaquita.
malacology [mæləˈkɔlədʒi], *s.* malacología.
maladjustment [mæləˈdʒʌstmənt], *s.* ajuste defectuoso; inadaptación (*psicológica*).
maladministration [mælədminisˈtreiʃən], *s.* mala administración, mal gobierno, desgobierno.
maladroit [mæləˈdrɔit], *a.* desmañado, torpe; falto de tacto.
malady [ˈmælədi], *s.* enfermedad, dolencia, mal.
Malaga [ˈmæləgə]. Málaga.
malaga [ˈmæləgə], *s.* vino de Málaga.

Malagasy Republic [ˈmæləˈgæsi]. República Malgache.
malaise [mæˈleiz], *s.* malestar; desazón, desasosiego.
malapropism [ˈmæləprɔpizəm], *s.* disparate lingüístico.
malaria [məˈlɛəriə], *s.* (*med.*) paludismo, malaria.
malarial, malarious [məˈlɛəriəl, -riəs], *a.* palúdico.
Malawi [məˈlɑːwi]. Malawi.
Malawian [məˈlɑːwian], *a.*, *s.* malawiano.
Malay [məˈlei], *a.*, *s.* malayo, *m.*
Malaya [məˈleiə]. Malaya.
Malayan [məˈleiən], *a.*, *s.* malayo, *m.*
Malaysia [məˈleizjə]. Malasia.
Malaysian [məˈleizjən], *a.*, *s.* malasio.
malcontent [ˈmælkəntent], *a.*, *s.* malcontento, descontento.
malcontentedness [mælkənˈtentidnis], *s.* descontento, disgusto.
male [meil], *a.* macho; masculino; varón; ***male child,*** hijo varón; ***male fern,*** helecho macho; ***male nurse,*** enfermero; ***male screw,*** tornillo (macho). — *s.* varón; macho.
malediction [mæliˈdikʃən], *s.* maldición.
Maldives [ˈmɔːldivz]. Maldivas.
Maldivian [mɔːlˈdiviən], *a.*, *s.* maldivo.
malefactor [ˈmælifæktə], *s.* malhechor.
malefic [məˈlefik], *a.* maléfico.
maleficent [məˈlefisənt], *a.* maléfico.
malevolence [məˈlevələns], *s.* malevolencia, malignidad.
malevolent [məˈlevələnt], *a.* malévolo, maligno.
malfeasance [mælˈfiːzəns], *s.* conducta ilícita; fechoría.
malformation [mælfɔːˈmeiʃən], *s.* deformación, deformidad.
malformed [mælˈfɔːmd], *a.* mal formado, contrahecho, deformado.
Mali [ˈmɑːli]. Malí.
Malian [ˈmɑːliən], *a.*, *s.* maliense.
malic [ˈmeilik], *a.* málico.
malice [ˈmælis], *s.* rencor, mala intención; encono.
malicious [məˈliʃəs], *a.* rencoroso, malintencionado; enconado.
maliciousness [məˈliʃəsnis], [MALICE].
malign [məˈlain], *a.* maligno. — *v.t.* calumniar, difamar, baldonar.
malignancy [məˈlignənsi], *s.* malignidad; malevolencia.
malignant [məˈlignənt], *a.* maligno.
malignity [məˈligniti], *s.* malignidad.
malinger [məˈliŋgə], *v.i.* fingirse enfermo.
malingerer [məˈliŋgərə], *s.* enfermo fingido.
malingering [məˈliŋgəriŋ], *a.* que se finge enfermo. — *s.* enfermedad fingida.
malkin [ˈmɔːkin], *s.* (*ant.*) gato.
mall [mɔːl, mæl], *s.* paseo, alameda.
mallard [ˈmæləd], *s.* (*orn.*) ánade *o* pato real.
malleability [mæliəˈbiliti], *s.* maleabilidad.
malleable [ˈmæliəbl], *a.* maleable.
malleableness [ˈmæliəblnis], *s.* maleabilidad.
malleate [ˈmælieit], *v.t.* martillar, martillear.
malleation [mæliˈeiʃən], *s.* maleación.
malleolar [ˈmælioulə], *a.* maleolar.
malleolus [mæˈliələs], *s.* maléolo.
mallet [ˈmælit], *s.* mazo.
mallow [ˈmælou], *s.* (*bot.*) malva; ***marsh mallow,*** malvavisco, bombón (de merengue blando).
malmsey [ˈmɑːmzi], *s.* malvasía.
malnutrition [mælnjuːˈtriʃən], *s.* desnutrición, inanición.
malodorous [mælˈoudərəs], *a.* maloliente.
malpractice [mælˈpræktis], *s.* procedimiento(s) ilícito(s).
malt [mɔːlt], *s.* malta; ***malt-liquor,*** cerveza.
Malta [ˈmɔːltə]. Malta.
Maltese [mɔːlˈtiːz], *a.*, *s.* maltés, *m.*
Malthusian [mælˈθjuːziən], *a.*, *s.* maltusiano.
malting [ˈmɔːltiŋ], *s.* maltaje.
maltster [ˈmɔːltstə], *s.* cervecero, preparador de malta.
maltreat [mælˈtriːt], *v.t.* maltratar.
maltreatment [mælˈtriːtmənt], *s.* malos tratos, *m.pl.*
malvaceous [mælˈveiʃəs], *a.* malváceo.
malversation [mælvəːˈseiʃən], *s.* malversación.
mam(m)a [məˈmɑː], *s.* mamá; (*ant.*) mama, teta.
mameluke [ˈmæmiluːk], *s.* mameluco.
mammal [ˈmæməl], *s.* mamífero.
Mammalia [mæˈmeiliə], *s.pl.* mamíferos, *m.pl.*
mammalian [mæˈmeiliən], *a.* mamífero.
mammary [ˈmæməri], *a.* mamario.
mammee [mæˈmiː], *s.* mamey.
mammifer [ˈmæmifə], *s.* mamífero.
mammiferous [mæˈmifərəs], *a.* mamífero.
mammiform [ˈmæmifɔːm], *a.* mamiforme; atetado.
mammilla [mæˈmilə], *s.* mamila, mamella.
mammillary [ˈmæmiləri], *a.* mamilar.
mammillated [ˈmæmileitid], *a.* mamellado, apezonado.
mammock [ˈmæmək], *s.* pedazo, fragmento. — *v.t.* hacer pedazos, despedazar.
mammon [ˈmæmən], *s.* becerro de oro.
mammoth [ˈmæməθ], *a.* mastodonte, gigantesco. — *s.* mamut.
man [mæn], *s.* (*pl.* **men** [men]) hombre; varón; el género humano; criado, servidor; soldado; peón (*ajedrez*); pieza (*damas*); ***good man,*** (*moralmente*) hombre de pro, hombre de bien; hombre que vale; ***head man,*** jefe; ***man-about-town,*** señorito; hombre de mundo; ***man-eater,*** caníbal; ***man-eating,*** antropófago; ***man-hater,*** misántropo; mujer que aborrece a los hombres; ***man-hole,*** registro, pozo; ***man-hour,*** hora-hombre; ***man-hunt,*** persecución (de un criminal); ***man-in-the-street,*** hombre de la calle, hombre medio; ***man-killer,*** homicida, *m.f.*; ***man of means,*** hombre de posibles; ***man of parts,*** hombre de buenas prendas; ***man-of-war,*** buque de guerra; ***man of his word,*** hombre de palabra; ***man of the world,*** hombre de mundo; ***man overboard!*** ¡hombre al agua!; ***man-power,*** mano de obra; potencial humano; ***man to man,*** de hombre a hombre; ***officers and men,*** oficiales y soldados; ***per man,*** por barba *o* por cabeza; ***to a man,*** como un solo hombre *o* unánimamente. — *v.t.* tripular, dotar, amarinar; guarnecer; proveer de gente armada; servir.
manacle [ˈmænəkl], *s.* manilla; (*pl.*) esposas, *f.pl.* — *v.t.* maniatar, esposar, poner esposas a.
manage [ˈmænidʒ], *v.t.* manejar, manipular; dirigir, regir, regentar, gobernar, administrar; conseguir (hacer); poder con; ***can you manage two more?*** ¿puedes llevarte dos más ?; ***can you manage tomorrow?*** ¿puedes venir *o* hacerlo *etc.* mañana? — *v.i.* arreglárselas, ingeniárselas (para lograr); ir tirando; ***manage without,*** pasarse sin.
manageable [ˈmænidʒəbl], *a.* manejable; tratable; dócil; flexible.
manageableness [ˈmænidʒəblnis], *s.* flexibilidad; docilidad.
management [ˈmænidʒmənt], *s.* manejo; gobierno; negociación, gestión, *f.*, administración; (*com.*) gerencia, dirección; empresa.
manager [ˈmænidʒə], *s.* director, gerente, jefe; administrador, apoderado; empresario.
managerial [mæniˈdʒiəriəl], *a.* directivo, administrativo, empresarial.
managing [ˈmænidʒiŋ], *a.* directivo; ***managing director,*** director gerente.
Managua [məˈnægjuə]. Managua.

manatee [mænə'ti:], *s.* (*zool.*) manatí, vaca marina.
manciple ['mænsipl], *s.* mayordomo.
mandarin ['mændərin], *s.* mandarín; (naranja) mandarina.
mandarine ['mændəri:n], *s.* (*bot.*) mandarina.
mandate ['mændeit], *s.* mandato.
mandated ['mændeitid], *a.* bajo mandato.
mandatory ['mændətəri], *a.* obligatorio. — *s.* mandatario.
mandible ['mændibl], *s.* mandíbula.
mandibular [mæn'dibjulə], *a.* mandibular.
mandibulate [mæn'dibjulit], *a.* mandibulado.
mandolin, mandoline ['mændəlin, -li:n], *s.* (*mús.*) mandolina.
mandragora, mandrake [mæn'drægərə, 'mændreik], *s.* (*bot.*) mandrágora.
mandrel ['mændril], *s.* mandril.
mane [mein], *s.* crin, *f.*, crines, *f.pl.*; melena (*de león*).
maned [meind], *a.* crinado.
manes ['meini:z], *s.pl.* manes, *m.pl.*
manful ['mænful], *a.* viril; valiente, denodado, esforzado; estoico, impasible.
manfulness ['mænfulnis], *s.* virilidad; valentía; estoicismo.
manganate ['mæŋgənit], *s.* manganato.
manganese [mæŋgə'ni:z], *s.* manganeso.
manganic [maŋ'gænik], *a.* mangánico.
manganous ['mæŋgənəs], *a.* manganoso.
mange [meindʒ], *s.* (*vet.*) sarna, roña.
mangel-wurzel ['mæŋgəl-'wə:zəl], *s.* (*bot.*) remolacha forrajera.
manger ['meindʒə], *s.* pesebre; ***dog in the manger,*** perro del hortelano.
manginess ['meindʒinis], *s.* (lo) sarnoso.
mangle [mæŋgl], *s.* exprimidor (de la ropa). — *v.t.* lacerar, desgarrar, mutilar; destrozar, estropear.
mangler ['mæŋglə], *s.* destrozador.
mangling ['mæŋgliŋ], *s.* (el) destrozar.
mango ['mæŋgou], *s.* (*bot.*) mango.
mangrove ['mæŋgrouv], *s.* (*bot.*) manglar; ***mangrove swamp,*** manglar, pantano de manglares.
mangy ['meindʒi], *a.* sarnoso.
manhandle ['mænhændl], *v.t.* mover a brazo; (*fig.*) maltratar.
manhole ['mænhoul], *s.* registro, pozo de visita; agujero de hombre.
manhood ['mænhud], *s.* virilidad; masculinidad, hombradía; naturaleza humana.
mania ['meiniə], *s.* manía; ***to have a mania for,*** ser maniático de, sentir auténtica locura por.
maniac ['meiniæk], *a.* maníaco, maniático. — *s.* maniático, demente.
maniacal [mə'naiəkəl], *a.* maníaco.
manic ['mænik], *a.* maníaco; ***manic depression,*** psicosis maníacodepresiva; ***manic depressive,*** maníacodepresivo.
Manichæism [mæni'kiizəm], *s.* maniqueísmo.
Manichæan [mæni'kiən], *a.*, *s.* maniqueo.
manichord ['mænikɔ:d], *s.* manicordio.
manicure ['mænikjuə], *s.* manicura. — *v.t.* hacer (la) manicura a.
manicurist ['mænikjuərist], *s.* manicuro, manicura.
manifest ['mænifest], *a.* manifiesto. — *s.* (*mar.*) manifiesto, conocimiento, hoja de ruta. — *v.t.* manifestar.
manifestation [mænifes'teiʃən], *s.* manifestación.
manifestness ['mænifestnis], *s.* evidencia palpable.
manifesto [mæni'festou], *s.* (*pol.*) manifiesto, proclama.
manifold ['mænifould], *a.* multíplice, múltiple, numeroso, diverso, vario. — *s.* (*mec.*) tubo múltiple. — *v.t.* sacar muchas copias de.
manikin ['mænikin], *s.* maniquí; hombrecillo.
Manil(l)a [mə'nilə]. Manila.
manil(l)a [mə'nilə], *s.* cigarro filipino; abacá, *m.*, cáñamo de Manila.
manioc ['mæniɔk], *s.* (*bot.*) cazabe, mandioca.
maniple ['mænipl], *s.* manípulo.
manipular [mə'nipjulə], *a.* manipular.
manipulate [mə'nipjuleit], *v.t.* manipular, manejar.
manipulation [mənipju'leiʃən], *s.* manipulación, manejo.
manipulative [mə'nipjulətiv], *a.* manipulante.
manipulator [mə'nipjuleitə], *s.* manipulador.
mankind [mænkaind], *s.* la humanidad, el género humano, los hombres.
manlike ['mænlaik], *a.* varonil, masculino.
manliness ['mænlinis], *s.* virilidad, masculinidad, hombr(ad)ía.
manly ['mænli], *a.* varonil, viril; valeroso, valiente.
manna ['mænə], *s.* maná; (*bot.*) ládano, mangla.
mannequin ['mænikin], *s.* modelo, *f.*; maniquí.
manner ['mænə], *s.* manera, modo; aire, porte; ademán; forma; (*pl.*) modales, *m.pl.*; maneras, costumbres, *f.pl.*; ***after the manner of,*** a la manera de, a la, a lo; ***all manner of,*** toda clase de; ***by all manner of means,*** no faltaba más, por supuesto; ***by no manner of means,*** de ningún modo; ***in a manner of speaking,*** por decirlo así; en cierto sentido; ***in his own manner,*** a su manera; ***in such a manner as,*** de tal suerte que; ***in the manner of,*** a la manera de, a guisa de; ***in this manner,*** así, de este modo; ***to the manner born,*** avezado desde la cuna.
mannered ['mænəd], *a.* amanerado.
mannerism ['mænərizəm], *s.* amaneramiento; manierismo; movimiento característico.
mannerist ['mænərist], *s.* manierista *m.f.*; amanerado.
mannerliness ['mænəlinis], *s.* buena educación, urbanidad.
mannerly ['mænəli], *a.* cortés, urbano.
mannikin [MANNEQUIN].
mannish ['mæniʃ], *a.* hombruno.
manœuvrable [mə'nu:vrəbl], *a.* maniobrable.
manœuvre [mə'nu:və], *s.* maniobra. — *v.t.* hacer maniobrar; ***he manœuvred us into an impossible position,*** nos metió con artilugios en una situación insostenible. — *v.i.* maniobrar; tramar, intrigar.
manœuvrer [mə'nu:vrə], *s.* maniobrista, *m.f.*
manœuvring [mə'nu:vriŋ], *s.* maniobras, *f.pl.*
manometer [mæ'nɔmitə], *s.* manómetro.
manometrical [mænə'metrikəl], *a.* manométrico.
manor-(house) ['mænə-(haus)], *s.* finca solariega; casa solariega, casa señorial, palacio.
manorial [mə'nɔ:riəl], *a.* señorial; solariego.
manse [mæns], *s.* (*Esco.*) casa del párroco.
manservant ['mænsə:vənt], *s.* criado.
mansion ['mænʃən], *s.* casa grande, palacio, residencia señorial; (*pl.*) edificio de pisos.
manslaughter ['mænslɔ:tə], *s.* homicidio (no premeditado).
mantelet, mantlet ['mæntlit], *s.* capotillo; (*mil.*) mantelete.
mantelpiece ['mæntlpi:s], *s.* chimenea.
mantilla [mæn'tilə], *s.* mantilla.
mantis ['mæntis], *s.* (*ent.*) mantis, *f.*; ***praying mantis,*** mantis religiosa.
mantissa [mæn'tisə], *s.* (*mat.*) mantisa.
mantle [mæntl], *s.* manto; manteo; manguito incandescente. — *v.t.* velar, cubrir, tapar, ocultar.
manual ['mænjuəl], *a.* manual, a mano. — *s.* manual; (*mús.*) teclado (de órgano).
manually ['mænjuəli], *adv.* a mano.
manufactory [mænju'fæktəri], *s.* fábrica.
manufacture [mænju'fæktʃə], *s.* fabricación; manufactura. — *v.t.* fabricar; manufacturar, elaborar.
manufacturer [mænju'fæktʃərə], *s.* fabricante, manufacturero.

manufacturing [mænju'fæktʃəriŋ], *a.* fabril, manufacturero. — *s.* fabricación.
manumission [mænju'miʃən], *s.* manumisión.
manumit [mænju'mit], *v.t.* manumitir.
manure [mə'njuə], *s.* estiércol, abono. — *v.t.* estercolar, abonar.
manuscript ['mænjuskript], *a.*, *s.* manuscrito.
Manx [mæŋks], *a.* de la isla de Man. — *s.* lengua de la isla de Man.
Manxman ['mæŋksmən], *s.* (*pl.* **-men** [-men]) habitante de la isla de Man.
many ['meni], *a.* muchos; ***as many as,*** tantos como; ***how many?*** ¿cuántos?; ***many-coloured,*** multicolor, policromo, abigarrado; ***many-flowered,*** de muchas flores, multifloro; ***many-hued,*** matizado; ***many people,*** muchas personas, *f.pl.*, mucha gente; ***many-sided,*** multilátero; polifacético; ***many times, many a time,*** muchas veces; ***so many,*** tantos; ***he told me in so many words to clear out,*** lo que vino a decirme fue que me largara; ***too many,*** demasiados; ***one too many,*** uno de más. — *s.* muchos; ***as many more, as many again,*** otros tantos; ***a good many, a great many,*** un buen número (de), muchísimos; ***the many,*** la mayoría, la(s) masa(s).
manyplies ['meniplaiz], *s.* omaso, libro (*de los rumiantes*).
map [mæp], *s.* mapa, *m.*, carta geográfica; plano; ***map-maker,*** cartógrafo; ***map-making,*** cartografía; ***off the map,*** apartado, remoto, lejano; ***to put a place on the map,*** hacer que sea conocido *o* que se conozca un sitio. — *v.t.* hacer *o* trazar el mapa de; ***map out,*** proyectar, planear, trazar.
maple [meipl], *s.* (*bot.*) arce, plátano falso, meple; ***maple sugar,*** azúcar de arce; ***maple syrup,*** almíbar de arce; ***maple wood,*** arce.
mar [mɑ:], *v.t.* estropear, echar a perder; desfigurar; (*placer*) aguar.
marabout ['mærəbu:t], *s.* morabito.
marasmus [mə'ræzməs], *s.* marasmo.
maraud [mə'rɔ:d], *v.t.*, *v.i.* merodear.
marauder [mə'rɔ:də], *s.* merodeador.
marauding [mə'rɔ:diŋ], *a.* merodeante. — *s.* merodeo.
maravedi [mærə'veidi], *s.* maravedí.
marble [mɑ:bl], *a.* de mármol, marmóreo. — *s.* mármol; canica (*bolita de juego*); (*impr.*) piedra de imponer; (*pl.*) juego de canicas; ***marble-mason, marble-polisher,*** marmolista, *m.*; ***marble-works,*** marmolería.
marbled [mɑ:bld], *a.* marmóreo; marmoleño; jaspeado.
marbling ['mɑ:bliŋ], *s.* marmoración; jaspeadura.
marbly ['mɑ:bli], *a.* marmóreo.
marc [mɑ:k], *s.* hollejo.
marcasite ['mɑ:kəzait], *s.* marcasita, marquesita, pirita blanca.
March [mɑ:tʃ]. marzo; ***ides of March,*** idus de marzo, *m.pl.*
march (1) [mɑ:tʃ], *s.* marcha; ***to steal a march on,*** ganar por la mano; ***slow march,*** paso lento; ***march-past,*** desfile. — *v.t.* hacer marchar, ***march out,*** hacer salir. — *v.i.* marchar; ***march on,*** seguir caminando; ***march out,*** irse, salir; ***march past,*** desfilar; ***march up,*** adelantar, avanzar. — *interj.* ***quick march!*** ¡de frente, marchen!
march (2) [mɑ:tʃ], *s.* marca (frontera).
marching ['mɑ:tʃiŋ], *a.* en marcha. — *s.* marcha; ***to give s.o. their marching orders,*** echar con cajas destempladas a alguien.
marchioness ['mɑ:ʃənes], *s.* marquesa.
marchpane ['mɑ:tʃpein], *s.* mazapán.
marcid ['mɑ:sid], *a.* demacrado.
marconigram [mɑ:'kounigræm], *s.* marconigrama, *m.*
mare [mɛə], *s.* yegua; (*fig.*) ***mare's nest,*** cuento, camelo; (*bot.*) ***mare's tail,*** cola de caballo.
Margaret ['mɑ:g(ə)rit]. Margarita.
margaric [mɑ:'gærik], *a.* margárico.
margarine [mɑ:dʒə'ri:n], *s.* margarina.
margarite ['mɑ:gərait], *s.* (*min.*) margarita, perla mica.
margin ['mɑ:dʒin], *s.* margen, *m.*; margen, *f.* (de río); reserva; sobrante; ***in the margin,*** en el margen, al margen; ***margin of error,*** margen de error; ***margin of safety,*** margen de seguridad.
marginal ['mɑ:dʒinəl], *a.* marginal; tangencial; ***marginal note,*** acotación.
marginate ['mɑ:dʒineit], *a.* marginado.
margrave ['mɑ:greiv], *s.* margrave.
margraviate [mɑ:'greivieit], *s.* margraviato.
marguerite [mɑ:gə'ri:t], *s.* (*bot.*) margarita.
Maria [mə'raiə]. María; (*fam.*) ***Black Maria,*** coche celular.
Marian (1) [MARION (2)].
Marian (2) ['mɛəriən], *a.* mariano.
Marie Antoinette [mæ'ri: æntwæ'net]. María Antonieta.
marigold ['mærigould], *s.* (*bot.*) caléndula, maravilla.
marinade [mæri'neid], *s.* escabeche. — ['mærineid], *v.t.* (*also* **marinate** [-neit]) marear; rociar (***with,*** con); rehogar.
marine [mə'ri:n], *a.* marino, marítimo. — *s.* marina; soldado de infantería de marina; (*pl.*) infantería de marina; ***tell that to the marines,*** a otro perro con ese hueso.
mariner ['mærinə], *s.* marino, marinero.
Mariolatry [mɛəri'ɔlətri], *s.* mariolatría.
Marion (1) ['mæriən 'mɛəriən], *m.* Mariano.
Marion (2) ['mæriən, 'mɛəriən], *f.* Mariana.
marionette [mæriə'net], *s.* marioneta.
marital ['mæritəl], *a.* marital; ***marital status,*** estado civil.
maritime ['mæritaim], *a.* marítimo.
marjoram ['mɑ:dʒərəm], *s.* (*bot.*) mejorana; orégano.
Mark [mɑ:k]. Marcos.
mark (1) [mɑ:k], *s.* señal; (que distingue) marca; impresión; huella; indicio; mancha; (*examen*) calificación, nota; (*dep.*) raya; meta; ***high, low water mark,*** nivel de marea alta, baja; ***to hit the mark,*** dar en el blanco, acertar; ***to leave one's mark,*** hacer *o* dejar huella *o* mella; ***to make one's mark,*** firmar con una cruz; (*fig.*) señalarse, significarse; ***man of mark,*** hombre de mucha talla, distinción *o* categoría; ***to miss the mark,*** errar *o* marrar el golpe; ***up to the mark,*** satisfactorio, que vale; que da la talla, que está a la altura de las circunstancias; ***wide of the mark,*** totalmente desacertado *o* errado. — *v.t.* señalar; marcar; indicar (*el precio de*); manchar; (*examen*) calificar, poner nota a; distinguir; notar, fijarse en, reparar en; ***mark down,*** rebajar (*el precio de*); apuntar; señalar; ***mark off,*** señalar; separar; delimitar; ***mark out,*** trazar; indicar; jalonar; ***mark time,*** marcar el paso; ***mark up,*** poner, indicar.
mark (2) [mɑ:k], *s.* (*numis.*) marco.
marked [mɑ:kt], *a.* marcado, señalado; notable, acusado; ***marked man,*** hombre condenado *o* señalado con el dedo.
marker ['mɑ:kə], *s.* marcador; ficha.
market ['mɑ:kit], *s.* mercado; venta; bolsa; plaza; ***black market,*** mercado negro, estraperlo; ***in the market for,*** interesado en la compra de; ***market-garden,*** huerto; huerta; ***market-gardener,*** hortelano; ***market-place,*** mercado; plaza; ***market price,*** precio de mercado *o* corriente; ***market research,*** análisis de mercados; ***on the market,*** de venta; en (la) bolsa; ***to play the market,*** jugar a la bolsa; ***ready market,*** fácil salida. — *v.t.* vender, poner a la venta. — *v.i.* venderse, tener salida.
marketable ['mɑ:kitəbl], *a.* comerciable, vendible.

marketing [ˈmɑːkitiŋ], *s.* venta, comercialización.
marking [ˈmɑːkiŋ], *s.* marcación; ***marking ink,*** tinta de marcar.
marksman [ˈmɑːksmən], *s.* tirador.
marksmanship [ˈmɑːksmənʃip], *s.* buena puntería.
marl (1) [mɑːl], *s.* marga, greda. — *v.t.* margar, abonar con marga.
marl (2) [mɑːl], *v.t.* (*mar.*) coser con merlín, empalomar, trincafiar.
marlaceous [mɑːˈleiʃəs], *a.* margoso.
marline [ˈmɑːlin], *s.* (*mar.*) merlín; ***marline-spike,*** pasador. — *v.t.* [MARL (2)].
marmalade [ˈmɑːməleid], *s.* mermelada de naranjas (*o* de otros agrios).
marmoreal [mɑːˈmɔːriəl], *a.* marmóreo.
marmose [ˈmɑːmous], *s.* marmoso.
marmot [ˈmɑːmət], *s.* (*zool.*) marmota, monote.
maroon (1) [məːˈruːn], *a.* castaño. — *s.* cimarrón, color castaño.
maroon (2) [məˈruːn], *s.* (pirotécnica) morterete.
maroon (3) [məˈruːn], *v.t.* abandonar en una costa desierta; dejar abandonado *o* aislado; ***to be marooned,*** verse abandonado *o* aislado.
marquee [mɑːˈkiː], *s.* marquesina; gran tienda.
marquess [ˈmɑːkwis], *s.* marqués.
marquetry [ˈmɑːkitri], *s.* marquetería, ataracea.
marquis [ˈmɑːkwis], *s.* marqués.
marquisate [ˈmɑːkwizit], *s.* marquesado.
marquise [mɑːˈkiːz], *s.* marquesa.
marriage [ˈmæridʒ], *s.* matrimonio; boda, casamiento; ***by marriage,*** por afinidad, político; ***marriage-contract,*** contrato de matrimonio; ***marriage-licence,*** permiso para casarse; ***marriage-lines,*** partida de matrimonio; ***marriage of convenience,*** boda de conveniencia; ***marriage-portion,*** dote.
marriageable [ˈmæridʒəbl], *a.* casadero.
married [ˈmærid], *a.* casado; matrimonial; ***married couple,*** matrimonio; ***to get married,*** casarse (***to,*** con).
marrow [ˈmærou], *s.* médula, tuétano; meollo; ***marrow-bone,*** caña *o* hueso medular; (***vegetable***) ***marrow,*** calabacín.
marrowish [ˈmærouiʃ], *a.* meduloso.
marrowless [ˈmæroulis], *a.* sin médula.
marrowy [ˈmæroui], *a.* meduloso, medular.
marry [ˈmæri], *v.t.* casar. — *v.i.* casarse; ***marry into,*** emparentar con.
Mars [mɑːz]. Marte.
Marsellaise [mɑːsəˈleiz]. Marsellesa.
Marseilles [mɑːˈseilz]. Marsella.
marsh [mɑːʃ], *s.* pantano, ciénaga, marisma, marjal; ***marsh land,*** lugar pantanoso; (*bot.*) ***marsh-mallow,*** malvavisco; (*bot.*) ***marsh-marigold,*** calta; ***salt marsh,*** saladar.
marshal [ˈmɑːʃəl], *s.* (*mil.*) mariscal; maestro de ceremonias; (*Am.*) jefe de policía; oficial del tribunal de justicia. — *v.t.* ordenar, organizar, poner en orden, formar (las tropas). — *v.i.* formar, ponerse en orden.
marshaller [ˈmɑːʃələ], *s.* ordenador, arreglador.
marshalship [ˈmɑːʃəlʃip], *s.* mariscalía, mariscalato.
marshy [ˈmɑːʃi], *a.* pantanoso.
marsupial [mɑːˈsjuːpiəl], *a.*, *s.* marsupial.
mart [mɑːt], *s.* emporio; mercado; (*sala de*) ventas.
Martello tower [mɑːˈtelou ˈtauə], *s.* atalaya.
marten [ˈmɑːtin], *s.* (*zool.*) marta; garduña; piel de marta.
Martial [ˈmɑːʃəl]. Marcial.
martial [ˈmɑːʃəl], *a.* marcial; ***court martial,*** consejo de guerra; ***martial law,*** (la) ley marcial, estado de sitio.
Martian [ˈmɑːʃən], *a.*, *s.* marciano.
Martin [ˈmɑːtin]. Martín.
martin [ˈmɑːtin], *s.* (*orn.*) avión.
martinet [mɑːtiˈnet], *s.* ordenancista, *m.f.*
martingale [ˈmɑːtiŋgeil], *s.* martingala.
Martinique [mɑːtiˈniːk]. Martinica.
Martinmas [ˈmɑːtinməs]. fiesta de San Martín (11 *de noviembre*).
martyr [ˈmɑːtə], *s.* mártir. — *v.t.* martirizar.
martyrdom [ˈmɑːtədəm], *s.* martirio.
martyrize [ˈmɑːtiraiz], *v.t.* martirizar.
martyrologist [mɑːtiˈrɔlədʒist], *s.* martirologista, *m.f.*
martyrology [mɑːtiˈrɔlədʒi], *s.* martirologio.
marvel [ˈmɑːvəl], *s.* maravilla; prodigio; ***to do*** o ***work marvels,*** hacer *u* obrar milagros *o* maravillas. — *v.i.* maravillarse (***at,*** de).
marvellous [ˈmɑːvələs], *a.* maravilloso.
Marxism [ˈmɑːksizəm], *s.* marxismo.
Marxist [ˈmɑːksist], *a.*, *s.* marxista, *m.f.*
Mary [ˈmɛəri]. María.
marzipan [ˈmɑːzipæn], *s.* mazapán.
Masai [ˈmɑːsai], *a.*, *s.* masai.
mascara [mæsˈkɑːrə], *s.* (*marca registrada*) rimmel.
mascot [ˈmæskɔt], *s.* mascota.
masculine [ˈmæskjulin], *a.* masculino; varonil; ***masculine woman,*** mujer hombruna.
masculinity [mæskjuˈliniti], *s.* masculinidad.
mash [mæʃ], *s.* mezcla; amasijo; baturrillo; (*fabricación de cerveza*) malta remojada; (*agric.*) afrecho remojado; (*coc.*) puré. — *v.t.* majar, machacar, aplastar; mezclar; ***mashed potato,*** puré de patata(s).
mashy [ˈmæʃi], *a.* machacado, aplastado.
mask [mɑːsk], *s.* máscara; careta; antifaz; mascarilla; ***death mask,*** mascarilla; ***gas mask,*** careta antigás; ***oxygen mask,*** mascarilla de oxígeno; ***to take off one's mask,*** quitarse la careta. — *v.t.* enmascarar; ocultar; ***masked ball,*** baile de máscaras.
masker [ˈmɑːskə], *s.* máscara, mascarón.
maslin [ˈmæslin], *s.* mezcla de granos, especialmente de trigo y centeno.
masochism [ˈmæsokizəm], *s.* masoquismo.
masochist [ˈmæsokist], *s.* masoquista, *m.f.*
mason [ˈmeisən], *s.* albañil; masón; ***mason-bird,*** trepatroncos, *m.inv.*
masonic [məˈsɔnik], *a.* masónico; ***masonic lodge,*** logia de francmasones.
masonry [ˈmeisənri], *s.* albañilería; mampostería; (franc)masonería.
masque [mɑːsk], *s.* mascarada, mojiganga.
masquerade [mɑːskəˈreid], *s.* mascarada, (baile de) máscaras; (*fig.*) farsa. — *v.i.* enmascararse; ***masquerade as,*** ir disfrazado de; hacer el papel de.
masquerader [mɑːskəˈreidə], *s.* máscara, mascarón, *m.f.*
mass (1) [mæs], *s.* masa; montón; mole; ***in the mass,*** en conjunto; ***mass production,*** fabricación en serie; ***the masses,*** las masas. — *v.t.* reunir en masa, juntar. — *v.i.* juntarse.
mass (2) [mæs, mɑːs], *s.* (*relig.*) misa; ***High Mass,*** misa mayor; ***Low Mass,*** misa rezada.
massacre [ˈmæsəkə], *s.* carnicería, matanza, mortandad. — *v.t.* hacer una matanza de; (*fig.*) hacer una chapucería de; (*lenguas*) chapurrear, hablar pésimamente.
massage [ˈmæsɑːʒ], *s.* masaje. — *v.t.* dar masaje a.
masseur [mæˈsəː], *s.m.*, **masseuse** [mæˈsəːz], *s.f.* masajista, *m.f.*
massive [ˈmæsiv], *a.* masivo, en masa; ingente.
massiveness [ˈmæsivnis], *s.* solidez; (lo) masivo.
mast (1) [mɑːst], *s.* (*mar.*) mástil; palo; asta; (*pl.*, *mar.*) arboladura; (*mar.*) ***main mast,*** palo mayor; (*mar.*) ***mizen mast,*** palo de mesana; ***to sail before the mast,*** ser *o* servir de marinero. — *v.t.* (*mar.*) arbolar.
mast (2) [mɑːst], *s.* (*bot.*) bellota; fabuco (*del haya etc.*).

master [ˈmɑːstə], *a.* maestro; magistral; ***master builder,*** maestro de obras; ***master key,*** llave maestra; ***master mind,*** inteligencia superior, ingenio; ***master stroke,*** golpe maestro. — *s.* maestro (*de escuela*); profesor (de segunda enseñanza) (*de colegio*); maestre (*de una orden*); señor; amo, dueño (*de perro, casa etc.*); jefe; señorito; (*mar.*) patrón; ***like master, like man,*** cual es el amo, tal es el criado; ***Master of Arts,*** licenciado en filosofía y letras; ***Master of the Rolls,*** archivero general; ***to be master of the situation,*** dominar *o* ser dueño de la situación; ***past master,*** maestro consumado. — *v.t.* dominar; llegar a dominar; domar; ser maestro en; sobreponerse a.

masterdom [ˈmɑːstədəm], *s.* mando, dominio.

masterful [ˈmɑːstəful], *a.* dominante.

masterless [ˈmɑːstəlis], *a.* libre, independiente; rebelde; indómito.

masterliness [ˈmɑːstəlinis], *s.* maestría.

masterly [ˈmɑːstəli], *a.* magistral; maestro; perfecto. — *adv.* de mano maestra.

masterpiece [ˈmɑːstəpiːs], *s.* obra maestra.

mastery [ˈmɑːstəri], *s.* maestría; dominio; superioridad.

masthead [ˈmɑːsthed], *s.* tope (del mástil).

mastic [ˈmæstik], *s.* mástique, almáciga.

masticate [ˈmæstikeit], *v.t.* masticar.

mastication [mæstiˈkeiʃən], *s.* masticación.

masticator [ˈmæstikeitə], *s.* masticador.

masticatory [ˈmæstikeitəri], *a., s.* masticatorio.

mastiff [ˈmæstif], *s.* mastín.

mastless [ˈmɑːstlis], *a.* desarbolado.

mastodon [ˈmæstədɔn], *s.* mastodonte.

mastoid [ˈmæstɔid], *a.* mastoides. — *s.* mastoides, *m.inv.*

masturbate [ˈmæstəbeit], *v.i.* masturbarse.

masturbation [mæstəˈbeiʃən], *s.* masturbación.

mat [mæt], *s.* estera; esterilla; (*puerta*) felpudo; (*mesa*) salvamanteles, *m.inv.*; (*encaje*) tapetito; (*pelo*) mata. — *v.t.* esterar. — *v.i.* enmarañarse, enredarse.

matador [ˈmætədɔː], *s.* matador, espada, *m.*, diestro.

match (1) [mætʃ], *s.* cerilla, fósforo; (*artill.*) mecha; ***match-box,*** cajita de cerillas, fosforera.

match (2) [mætʃ], *s.* igual; compañero; pareja; matrimonio; (*dep.*) partido; concurso, certamen; ***good match,*** buena pareja; (*para matrimonio*) buen partido; ***to be a match for,*** hacer juego con; (*fig.*) poder con; ***to meet one's match,*** encontrarse con la horma de su zapato; ***match-maker,*** casamentero. — *v.t.* emparejar; parear; igualar; competir con; hacer juego con; ***match (s.o.) against,*** hacer que (alguien) compita con. — *v.i.* hacer juego, casar.

matchet [ˈmætʃit], *s.* machete.

matching [ˈmætʃiŋ], *a.* que hace juego (***with,*** con).

matchless [ˈmætʃlis], *a.* incomparable, sin igual, sin par.

matchlessness [ˈmætʃlisnis], *s.* (lo) incomparable.

matchwood [ˈmætʃwud], *s.* madera de fósforos; ***to make matchwood of sth.,*** hacer algo astillas, trizas *o* añicos.

mate (1) [meit], *s.* cónyuge, consorte, *m.f.*, pareja; (*fam.*) compadre; camarada, *m.f.*, compañero; (*mar.*) segundo de a bordo; (*orn., zool.*) macho, hembra. — *v.t.* casar; parear. — *v.i.* casarse; parearse.

mate (2) [meit], *s.* (*ajedrez*) mate.

mater [ˈmeitə], *s.* (*anat.*) máter; (*fam.*) madre, mamá.

material [məˈtiəriəl], *a.* material; esencial, importante; considerable. — *s.* material; tejido, tela; ***raw material,*** materia prima, primera materia; ***writing materials,*** recado de escribir, artículos de escritorio, *m.pl.*

materialism [məˈtiəriəlizəm], *s.* materialismo.

materialist [məˈtiəriəlist], *s.* materialista, *m.f.*

materialistic [mətiəriəˈlistik], *a.* materialista.

materiality [mətiəriˈæliti], *s.* materialidad; corporeidad.

materialization [mətiəriəlaiˈzeiʃən], *s.* materialización; realización.

materialize [məˈtieriəlaiz], *v.t.* materializar. — *v.i.* materializarse; realizarse; cuajar; presentarse, aparecer.

materially [məˈtiəriəli], *adv.* materialmente; esencialmente.

materialness [məˈtiəriəlnis], *s.* materialidad; importancia.

maternal [məˈtəːnəl], *a.* maternal; materno.

maternally [məˈtəːnəli], *adv.* maternalmente.

maternity [məˈtəːniti], *s.* maternidad.

math [mæθ], *s.* cosecha del heno.

mathematical [mæθiˈmætikəl], *a.* matemático.

mathematician [mæθiməˈtiʃən], *s.* matemático.

mathematics [mæθiˈmætiks], *s.pl.* matemática(s).

Mat(h)ilda [məˈtildə]. Matilde.

matinal [ˈmætinəl], *a.* matinal, matutino.

matinée [ˈmætinei], *s.* (*teat.*) función de (la) tarde.

matins [ˈmætinz], *s.pl.* maitines, *m.pl.*

matrice [ˈmeitris], [MATRIX].

matricidal [ˈmeitrisaidl], *a.* relativo al matricidio.

matricide [ˈmeitrisaid], *s.* matricidio (*acción*); matricida, *m.f.*

matricula [məˈtrikjulə], *s.* matrícula.

matriculate [məˈtrikjuleit], *v.t.* matricular. — *v.i.* matricularse.

matriculation [mətrikjuˈleiʃən], *s.* matriculación; requisitos *o* examen de ingreso.

matrimonial [mætriˈmouniəl], *a.* matrimonial, marital, conyugal.

matrimony [ˈmætriməni], *s.* matrimonio, casamiento; ***to be joined in (holy) matrimony,*** unirse en matrimonio.

matrix [ˈmeitriks], *s.* matriz, *f.*; (*impr.*) matriz, *f.*, molde; (*geol.*) quijo.

matron [ˈmeitrən], *s.f.* matrona; ama de llaves; (*med.*) enfermera jefa.

matte [mæt], *a.* mate de cobre.

matter [ˈmætə], *s.* (*med.*) materia; asunto, cuestión; tema; cosa; motivo; ***a matter of,*** cosa de; ***as a matter of course,*** por rutina, automáticamente; ***it is a matter of course,*** es automático; ***matter of fact,*** hecho positivo; prosaico, práctico; ***as a matter of fact,*** en realidad, el caso es que; ***matter of form,*** (puro) formulismo; ***matter in hand,*** asunto de que se trata; ***to make matters worse,*** para colmo de desgracias; ***no matter,*** no importa; ***no matter how,*** de cualquier modo; ***printed matter,*** impresos, *m.pl.*; ***for that matter,*** tampoco; la verdad es que; ***what's the matter?*** ¿qué pasa?; ***what's the matter with that?*** ¿qué tiene eso de malo?; ***what's the matter with you?*** ¿qué te pasa? — *v.i.* importar; ***it does not matter,*** no importa, no le hace.

Matthew [ˈmæθjuː]. Mateo.

matting [ˈmætiŋ], *s.* esteras, *f.pl.*, esterado; (*mar.*) empalletado.

mattins [MATINS].

mattock [ˈmætək], *s.* azadón.

mattress [ˈmætrəs], *s.* colchón; ***spring mattress,*** colchón de muelles.

maturate [ˈmætjureit], *v.t.* madurar; (*med.*) hacer supurar. — *v.i.* madurar; (*med.*) supurar.

maturation [mætjuˈreiʃən], *s.* maduración; (*med.*) supuración.

maturative [məˈtjuərətiv], *a.* madurativo.

mature [məˈtjuə], *a.* maduro; (*com.*) pagadero, vencido. — *v.t.* (hacer) madurar. — *v.i.* madurar; (*com.*) vencer.

matureness, maturity [məˈtjuənis, məˈtjuəriti], *s.* madurez; (*com.*) vencimiento.

matutinal [məˈtjuːtinəl], *a.* matutino.

maudlin [ˈmɔːdlin], *a.* sensiblero, sentimentalón.

maul [mɔ:l], *s.* (*mar.*) mandarria. — *v.t.* herir, destrozar; causar destrozos en; (*fam.*) manosear, sobar.
Maundy [ˈmɔ:ndi], *s.* ***Maundy Thursday,*** jueves santo.
Mauritania [ˈmɔriˈteiniə]. Mauritania.
Mauritanian [ˈmɔriˈteiniən], *a., s.* mauritano.
Mauritian [məˈriʃən], *a., s.* mauriciano.
Mauritius [məˈriʃəs]. Mauricio.
mausoleum [mɔ:səˈliəm], *s.* mausoleo, panteón.
mauve [mouv], *a., s.* morado.
maverick [ˈmævərik], *s.* (*Am.*) cimarrón; disidente.
maw [mɔ:], *s.* (*rumiantes*) cuajar; (*orn.*) molleja; estómago; (*fam.*) buche; (*fig.*) ***maws of death,*** fauces de la muerte, *f.pl.*
mawkish [ˈmɔ:kiʃ], *a.* sensiblero; empalagoso, dulzón.
mawkishness [ˈmɔ:kiʃnis], *s.* sensiblería; empalagosería.
maxilla [mækˈsilə], *s.* (*anat.*) hueso maxilar.
maxillary [mækˈsiləri], *a.* maxilar.
maxim [ˈmæksim], *s.* máxima, apotegma, *m.*, aforismo.
maximum [ˈmæksiməm], *a.* máximo. — *s.* máximum, máximo.
May (1) [mei]. mayo; (*bot.*) ***May-apple,*** mandrágora; (*bot.*) ***may-blossom,*** espina blanca, maya; ***May day,*** (fiesta del) primero de mayo; (*bot.*) ***may-flower,*** maya, flor de mayo; ***may-fly,*** mosca de mayo; (*bot.*) ***may-lily,*** lirio de los valles; ***May queen,*** maya; (*bot.*) ***may-weed,*** manzanilla loca. — *v.i.* ***to go maying,*** participar en la(s) fiesta(s) de mayo.
may (2) [mei], *irr. v. aux.* poder; ser posible; tener permiso (para); ***I may go,*** es posible que *o* puede que vaya; ***may I?*** ¿se puede?; ¿me permite (usted)?; ***it may be that,*** puede (ser) que; ***may you be happy!*** ¡(le deseo) que sea feliz!
maybe, mayhap [meiˈbi:, -ˈhæp], *adv.* quizá(s), tal vez, acaso.
mayhem [ˈmeihem], *s.* (*for.*) mutilación criminal; (*fam.*) bullicio, alboroto.
mayonnaise [meiəˈneiz], *s.* (salsa) mayonesa.
mayor [mɛə], *s.* alcalde.
mayoralty [ˈmɛərəlti], *s.* alcaldía, funciones de alcalde, *f.pl.*
mayoress [ˈmɛəres], *s.* alcaldesa, corregidora; mujer *o* hija del alcalde.
maypole [ˈmeipoul], *s.* mayo, árbol de mayo.
mazard [ˈmæzɑ:d], *s.* (*bot.*) guinda.
mazarine [ˈmæzərin], *a., s.* color azul subido.
maze [meiz], *s.* laberinto, dédalo; (*fig.*) enredo; perplejidad; ***to be in a maze,*** estar confuso, perplejo. — *v.t.* enredar; dejar perplejo.
mazurka [məˈzə:kə], *s.* mazurca.
mazy [ˈmeizi], *a.* laberíntico, intrincado, embrollado.
me [mi:], *pron. pers.* me, a mí; ***with me,*** conmigo.
mead (1) [mi:d], *s.* aguamiel, hidromiel, meloja.
mead (2) [mi:d], *s.* (*poét.*) prado.
meadow [ˈmedou], *s.* prado, pradera; ***meadow land,*** pastos, *m.pl.*; (*bot.*) ***meadow-sweet,*** ulmaria, barba de cabra.
meadowy [ˈmedoui], *a.* de pradera; lleno de prados.
meagre [ˈmi:gə], *a.* escaso, exiguo; ***meagre pittance,*** miseria.
meagreness [ˈmi:gənis], *s.* escasez, exigüidad.
meal (1) [mi:l], *s.* comida; ***meal-time,*** hora de comer.
meal (2) [mi:l], *s.* harina gruesa; ***meal-man,*** harinero; ***meal-tub,*** artesa para harina; ***meal-worm,*** gusanillo de harina.
mealiness [ˈmi:linis], *s.* melosidad; calidad harinosa.
mealy [ˈmi:li], *a.* harinoso, farináceo; meloso; ***mealy-mouthed,*** hipócrita; mojigato.
mean (1) [mi:n], *a.* mezquino; humilde, pobre; tacaño.
mean (2) [mi:n], *a.* medio. — *s.* medio; promedio, término medio; media; (*pl.*) medios, *m.pl*; ***by all means,*** no faltaba más; ***by any means,*** sea como sea, por cualquier medio; ***by fair means or foul,*** por medios lícitos o ilícitos; ***by means of,*** por medio de; ***by no means, not by any means,*** de ninguna manera, de ningún modo; ***by some means or other,*** de una manera u otra; ***by this*** *o* ***that means,*** de este modo, por ese medio; ***to be a man of means,*** ser (un) hombre de medios; ***ways and means,*** medios y arbitrios, *m.pl.*
mean (3) [mi:n], *v.t. irr.* querer decir (***by,*** con); significar (***to,*** para); destinar (***for,*** a); pensar, proponerse; ***I didn't mean to do it,*** lo hice sin querer; ***he means business,*** lo dice en serio; ***he means it,*** va en serio. — *v.i.* — ***well*** *o* ***ill,*** tener buenas *o* malas intenciones.
meander [miˈændə], *s.* meandro; serpenteo. — *v.i.* serpentear; divagar.
meandering [miˈændəriŋ], *a.* que serpentea; que divaga (mucho). — *s.* meandros, *m.pl.*; rodeos, *m.pl.*, divagaciones, *f.pl.*
meaning [ˈmi:niŋ], *s.* significado, significación, sentido; acepción; ***double meaning,*** sentido doble, equívoco; ***what is the meaning of this?*** ¿(puede saberse) qué significa esto?
meaningful [ˈmi:niŋful], *a.* significante.
meaningless [ˈmi:niŋlis], *a.* sin sentido.
meanness [ˈmi:nnis], *s.* mezquindad; tacañería.
meantime, meanwhile [ˈmi:nˈtaim, -ˈwail], *adv.* mientras tanto, entretanto. — *s.* ínterin.
measled [mi:zld], *a.* enfermo de sarampión.
measles [mi:zlz], *s.pl.* sarampión; ***German measles,*** rubéola.
measly [ˈmi:zli], *a.* pobre, mezquino, miserable, despreciable.
measurable [ˈmeʒərəbl], *a.* mensurable; apreciable.
measurableness [ˈmeʒərəblnis], *s.* mensurabilidad.
measure [ˈmeʒə], *s.* medida; regla; (*mús.*) compás, *m.*; ***beyond measure,*** en exceso; ***dry measure,*** medida para áridos; ***for good measure,*** para mayor abundancia; ***in great measure,*** en gran parte; ***in some measure,*** hasta cierto punto; en cierto sentido; ***made to measure,*** hecho a medida; ***to take measures,*** tomar medidas. — *v.t.* medir; (*fig.*) ***measure one's length,*** medir el suelo. — *v.i.* medir; ***measure up to,*** mostrarse adecuado para, a la altura de.
measured [ˈmeʒəd], *a.* medido, acompasado; moderado, pausado; deliberado; ***to speak in measured tones,*** hablar con comedimiento.
measureless [ˈmeʒəlis], *a.* sin medida, inconmensurable.
measurement [ˈmeʒəmənt], *s.* medida; medición, mensuración.
measurer [ˈmeʒərə], *s.* medidor; (*terrenos*) agrimensor.
measuring [ˈmeʒəriŋ], *s.* medición.
meat [mi:t], *s.* carne, *f.*; (*ant.*) comida, alimento; (*fig.*) sustancia, enjundia; ***chopped*** o ***minced meat,*** carne picada; ***cold meat,*** fiambre; ***meat-ball,*** albóndiga; ***meat-hook,*** escarpia; ***meat-pie,*** empanada; ***meat-safe,*** fresquera; ***one man's meat is another man's poison,*** lo que a uno cura a otro mata.
meatus [mi:ˈeitəs], *s.* meato.
meaty [ˈmi:ti], *a.* carnoso; (*fig.*) sustancioso, de (mucha) enjundia.
mechanic [miˈkænik], *s.* mecánico.
mechanical [miˈkænikəl], *a.* mecánico; maquinal.
mechanics [miˈkæniks], *s. pl.* mecánica; técnica.
mechanism [ˈmekənizəm], *s.* mecanismo.
mechanist [ˈmekənist], *s.* mecánico, maquinista, *m.f.*
mechanize [ˈmekənaiz], *v.t.* mecanizar; motorizar.
meconate [ˈmekəneit], *s.* (*quím.*) meconato.
meconic [miˈkɔnik], *a.* mecónico.

meconium [mi'kouniəm], *s.* (*quím.*) meconio, alhorre.
medal [medl], *s.* medalla.
medallion [mi'dæljən], *s.* medallón.
medallist ['medəlist], *s.* medallista, *m.f.*; persona condecorada con una medalla; ***gold medallist***, medallista de oro.
meddle [medl], *v.i.* meterse, entremeterse, entrometerse, ingerirse; ***don't meddle in what doesn't concern you***, no te metas en lo que no te importa.
meddler ['medlə], *s.* entremetido, entrometido.
meddlesome ['medlsəm], *a.* entremetido.
meddlesomeness ['medlsəmnis], *s.* entremetimiento, entrometimiento.
meddling ['medliŋ], *a.* entremetido, oficioso, intrigante. — *s.* entremetimiento, entrometimiento, intromisión; tercerías, *f.pl.*
media (1) ['mi:diə], *s.pl.* [MEDIUM].
media (2) ['mi:diə], *s.* (*anat.*) túnica media de un vaso.
mediæval [MEDIEVAL].
medial ['mi:diəl], *a.* medio, del medio, del centro.
median ['mi:diən], *a.* mediano; del medio.
mediant ['mi:diənt], *s.* (*mús.*) tercera.
mediate ['mi:diit], *a.* mediato. — ['mi:dieit], *v.i.* mediar, intervenir.
mediation [mi:di'eiʃən], *s.* mediación; intervención; interposición; intercesión; tercería.
mediatize ['mi:diətaiz], *v.t.* mediatizar.
mediator ['mi:dieitə], *s.* mediador, medianero.
medic ['medik], *s.* (*fam.*) estudiante de medicina; médico.
medical ['medikəl], *a.* médico; de medicina. — *s.* (*fam.*) chequeo (médico).
medicament ['medikəmənt], *s.* medicamento, remedio.
medicaster ['medikæstə], *s.* medicastro.
medicate ['medikeit], *v.t.* medicinar, hacer medicinal.
medication [medi'keiʃən], *s.* medicación.
medicative ['medikətiv], *a.* medicinal.
medicinal [me'disinəl], *a.* medicinal, médico, de médico.
medicine [medsn], *s.* medicina, medicamento; ***to give s.o. a taste of his own medicine***, pagar a alguien con la misma moneda; ***medicine chest***, botiquín; ***medicine man***, curandero.
medieval [medi'i:vəl], *a.* medieval.
medievalism [medi'i:vəlizəm], *s.* medievalismo.
medievalist [medi'i:vəlist], *s.* medievalista, *m.f.*
mediocre [mi:di'oukə], *a.* mediocre, mediano.
mediocrity [mi:di'ɔkriti], *s.* mediocridad, medianía.
meditate ['mediteit], *v.i.* meditar, reflexionar.
meditation [medi'teiʃən], *s.* meditación, reflexión.
meditative ['meditətiv], *a.* meditativo, meditabundo, pensativo.
Mediterranean [meditə'reiniən], *a.* mediterráneo. — *s.* Mediterráneo.
medium [mi:diəm], *a.* mediano, (inter)medio, regular; ***medium-sized***, de tamaño mediano *o* medio. — *s.* (*pl.* **media** ['mi:diə]) medio; (*pers.*, *pl.* **mediums**) médium, *m.f.*; ***to strike a happy medium***, encontrar el justo medio *o* el término medio; ***through the medium of***, por medio de; ***the media***, los medios de información *o* comunicación.
medlar ['medlə], *s.* (*bot.*) níspero (*arbol y fruto*).
medley ['medli], *s.* mezcla, mezcolanza; miscelánea, fárrago; (*mús.*) popurrí, *m.*
medulla [me'dʌlə], *s.* (*anat.*) médula, medula.
medullar(y) [me'dʌlə(ri)], *a.* medular.
medusa [mi'dju:zə], *s.* medusa.
meek [mi:k], *a.* manso, sumiso, dócil.
meekness ['mi:knis], *s.* mansedumbre, sumisión, docilidad.

meerschaum ['miəʃəm], *s.* espuma de mar.
meet (1) [mi:t], *a.* (*bíb.*) conveniente, propio, adecuado, apropiado.
meet (2) [mi:t], *s.* reunión *o* concurso (*de cazadores*). — *irr. v.t.* encontrar; hallar; encontrarse con; recibir, esperar; conocer; enfrentarse con; hacer frente a; (*obligaciones*) satisfacer; pagar; (*deberes*) cumplir (con); (*lo estipulado*) conformarse a; unirse con; ***meet one's death***, encontrar la muerte; ***meet one's expenses***, cubrir los gastos; ***meet half-way***, partir la diferencia con; llegar a una transacción con; ***meet one's maker***, rendir cuentas a Dios; ***meet one's Waterloo***, encontrarse con la horma de su zapato; ***to go to meet***, ir a recibir, ir al encuentro de; ***I met him in Paris***, le conocí en París. — *v.i.* encontrarse; reunirse; conocerse; verse; enfrentarse; unirse; ***meet with***, encontrarse con; sufrir; ***till we meet again***, hasta la vista, hasta más ver; ***where shall we meet?*** ¿dónde quedamos (para reunirnos)?
meeting ['mi:tiŋ], *s.* reunión; sesión; encuentro; cita; concurso; confluencia (de ríos); ***meeting-place***, lugar de reunión, sitio de (la) cita.
meetness ['mi:tnis], *s.* conveniencia, (lo) propio, (lo) adecuado, (lo) apropiado.
megalith ['megəliθ], *s.* megalito.
megalithic [megə'liθik], *a.* megalítico.
megalomania [megəlo'meiniə], *s.* megalomanía.
megalomaniac [megəlo'meiniæk], *a.*, *s.* megalómano.
megaphone ['megəfoun], *s.* megáfono, portavoz, *m.*
megrim ['mi:grim], *s.* jaqueca.
melancholia [melən'kouliə], *s.* melancolía.
melancholic [melən'kɔlik], *a.* melancólico.
melancholy ['melənkəli], *a.* melancólico. — *s.* melancolía, hipocondria.
Melanesia [melə'ni:ʃə]. Melanesia.
mélange [mei'lɑ̃:(n)ʒ], *s.* mezcla.
melanosis [melə'nousis], *s.* (*med.*) melanosis, *f.inv.*
Melbourne ['melbən]. Melburne.
Melchior ['melkiɔ:]. Melchor.
Melchizedek, Melchisedec [mel'kizədek]. Melquisedec.
mêlée, melee ['melei], *s.* refriega, reyerta.
melic ['melik], *a.* mélico, lírico.
melilot ['melilɔt], *s.* mililoto, trébol dulce.
melinite ['melinait], *s.* melinita.
meliorate ['mi:liəreit], *v.t.* mejorar. — *v.i.* mejorarse.
melioration [mi:liə'reiʃən], *s.* mejora, mejoramiento.
melissa [me'lisə], *s.* melisa.
melliferous [me'lifərəs], *a.* melífero.
mellifluence [me'lifluəns], *s.* melifluidad.
mellifluent, mellifluous [me'lifluənt, -fluəs], *a.* melifluo, melificado.
mellow ['melou], *a.* maduro; sazonado; (*fig.*) dulce, suave; meloso; (*vino*) añejo.— *v.t.* madurar, sazonar; suavizar. — *v.i.* madurar(se).
mellowness ['melounis], *s.* madurez; sazón; dulzura, suavidad; melosidad.
mellowy ['meloui], *a.* dulce, suave.
melodic [mi'lɔdik], *a.* melódico.
melodious [mi'loudiəs], *a.* melodioso.
melodiousness [mi'loudiəsnis], *s.* (lo) melodioso.
melodist ['melodist], *s.* melodista, *m.f.*
melodize ['melodaiz], *v.t.* hacer melodioso. — *v.i.* hacer melodía.
melodrama ['melodrɑ:mə], *s.* melodrama, *m.*
melodramatic [melodrə'mætik], *a.* melodramático.
melodramatist [melo'dræmətist], *s.* autor de melodramas.
melody ['melədi], *s.* melodía.
melon ['melən], *s.* melón.

melt [melt], *irr. v.t.* (*metal.*) fundir; derretir; disolver; (*fig.*) ablandar; ***melt a heart of stone,*** ablandar las piedras; ***melt down,*** fundir. — *v.i.* (*metal.*) fundirse; derretirse; disolverse; ablandarse; ***melt away,*** disiparse, desvanecerse; ***melt into tears,*** deshacerse *o* derretirse en lágrimas.

melter [ˈmeltə], *s.* fundidor; crisol.

melting [ˈmeltiŋ], *a.* fundente. — *s.* fusión, derretimiento; ***melting-pan,*** cazo; ***melting-point,*** punto de fusión; (*lit., fig.*) ***melting-pot,*** crisol.

melton [ˈmeltən], *s.* melton.

member [ˈmembə], *s.* miembro; socio; individuo; (*parlamento*) diputado.

membered [ˈmembəd], *a.* (*blas.*) membrado.

membership [ˈmembəʃip], *s.* calidad de miembro *o* socio; asociación, sociedad; número de miembros *o* socios; ***membership fee,*** cuota de socio.

membranaceous, membraneous, membranous, membraniform [membrəˈneiʃəs, memˈbreiniəs, ˈmembrənəs, memˈbreinifɔ:m], *a.* membranáceo; membranoso; membraniforme.

membrane [ˈmembrein], *s.* (*anat.*) membrana; trozo de pergamino.

memento [miˈmentou], *s.* recuerdo.

memo [ˈmemou], *s. abrev. de* [MEMORANDUM].

memoir [ˈmemwɑ:], *s.* memoria; (*pl.*) memorias, *f.pl.*

memorable [ˈmemərəbl], *a.* memorable.

memorandum [meməˈrændəm], *s.* (*pl.* **memoranda** [-də]) memoria, nota; (*pol.*) memorándum.

memorial [miˈmɔ:riəl], *a.* conmemorativo. — *s.* memorial; monumento (*conmemorativo*).

memorialist [miˈmɔ:riəlist], *s.* memorialista, *m.f.*; suplicante.

memorialize [miˈmɔ:riəlaiz], *v.t.* conmemorar; dirigir un memorial a.

memorize [ˈmeməraiz], *v.t.* aprender de memoria.

memory [ˈmeməri], *s.* memoria, retentiva; recuerdo; ***from memory,*** de memoria; ***in memory of,*** en memoria *o* recuerdo de.

men [men], *s.pl.* [MAN].

menace [ˈmenəs], *s.* amenaza; (*fam.*) peligro para la humanidad; pelmazo de marca. — *v.t., v.i.* amenazar.

menacer [ˈmenəsə], *s.* amenazador.

menacing [ˈmenəsiŋ], *a.* amenazante, amenazador.

menacingly [ˈmenəsiŋli], *adv.* de una manera amenazadora.

ménage [meˈnɑ:ʒ], *s.* casa; familia.

menagerie [miˈnædʒəri], *s.* colección *o* casa de fieras.

mend [mend], *s.* remiendo; (*cost.*) zurcido; ***to be on the mend,*** ir mejor *o* mejorando. — *v.t.* reparar, componer, arreglar; remendar; enmendar, mejorar; (*cost.*) zurcir; ***mend one's ways,*** enmendarse. — *v.i.* mejorar(se).

mendable [ˈmendəbl], *a.* reparable.

mendacious [menˈdeiʃəs], *a.* mendaz.

mendaciousness, mendacity [menˈdeiʃesnis, -ˈdæsiti], *s.* mendacidad.

mendicancy [ˈmendikənsi], *s.* mendicidad.

mendicant [ˈmendikənt], *a., s.* mendicante.

mendicity [menˈdisiti], *s.* mendicidad.

mending [ˈmendiŋ], *s.* reparación, compostura, (el) arreglar; (*cost.*) zurcidura; ropa de repaso; ***invisible mending,*** remiendo(s) invisible(s).

menfolk [ˈmenfouk], *s.* hombres (de la familia), *m.pl.*

menhir [ˈmenhiə], *s.* menhir.

menial [ˈmi:niəl], *a.* doméstico; servil; bajo. — *s.* criado; lacayo.

meninges [meˈnindʒi:z], *s.pl.* [MENINX].

meningitis [meninˈdʒaitis], *s.* meningitis, *f.inv.*

meninx [ˈmeniŋks], *s.* (*pl.* **meninges** [meˈnindʒi:z]) meninge, *f.*

meniscus [meˈniskəs], *s.* menisco.

menology [meˈnɔlədʒi], *s.* menologio.

menopause [ˈmenopɔ:z], *s.* menopausia.

menorrhagia [menoˈreidʒiə], *s.* menorragia.

menses [ˈmensi:z], *s.pl.* menstruo.

menstrual [ˈmenstruəl], *a.* menstrual.

menstruate [ˈmenstrueit], *v.i.* menstruar.

menstruation [menstruˈeiʃən], *s.* menstruación.

menstruous [ˈmenstruəs], *a.* menstruoso.

menstruum [ˈmenstruəm], *s.* (*quím.*) menstruo.

mensurability [menʃərəˈbiliti], *s.* mensurabilidad.

mensurable [ˈmenʃərəbl], *a.* mensurable.

mensural [ˈmenʃərəl], *a.* mensural.

mensuration [mensjuəˈreiʃən], *s.* mensura, medición, medida.

mental [mentl], *a.* mental; espiritual, anímico, psíquico; ***mental arithmetic,*** cálculo mental; ***mental deficiency,*** deficiencia mental; ***mental defective,*** deficiente mental; ***mental home*** *o* ***hospital,*** manicomio; ***mental reservation,*** reserva mental.

mentha [ˈmenθə], *s.* menta.

menthol [ˈmenθɔl], *s.* mentol.

mention [ˈmenʃən], *s.* mención, alusión. — *v.t.* mencionar, hacer mención de, hablar de, decir; ***don't mention it!*** ¡no hay de que! ¡de nada!; ***not to mention,*** sin contar.

mentionable [ˈmenʃənəbl], *a.* mencionable.

mentor [ˈmentə], *s.* mentor.

menu [ˈmenju:], *s.* lista de platos, minuta; ***set menu,*** menú.

Mephistopheles [mefisˈtofili:z]. Mefistófeles.

mephitic(al) [meˈfitik(əl)], *a.* mefítico.

mephitis [meˈfaitis], *s.* mefitis, *f.inv.*

mercantile [ˈmə:kəntail], *a.* mercantil; mercante; comercial.

mercantilism [ˈmə:kəntailizəm], *s.* mercantilismo.

mercenariness [ˈmə:sinərinis], *s.* venalidad.

mercenary [ˈmə:sinəri], *a., s.* mercenario.

mercer [ˈmə:sə], *s.* mercero, sedero.

mercerize [ˈmə:səraiz], *v.t.* (*tint.*) mercerizar.

mercership [ˈmə:səʃip], *s.* mercería.

mercery [ˈmə:səri], *s.* mercería, sedería.

merchandise [ˈmə:tʃəndaiz], *s.* mercancía, mercadería, géneros, *m.pl.* — *v.t., v.i.* comerciar, negociar, traficar.

merchant [ˈmə:tʃənt], *a.* mercantil; mercante; comercial; ***merchant iron,*** hierro en barras; ***merchant navy,*** marina mercante; ***merchant seaman,*** marinero mercante; ***merchant ship*** o ***vessel,*** buque mercante. — *s.* comerciante, negociante, traficante; (*ant.*) mercader.

merchantman [ˈmə:tʃəntmən], *s.* barco, buque mercante.

merciful [ˈmə:siful], *a.* misericordioso, compasivo.

mercifulness [ˈmə:sifulnis], *s.* misericordia, piedad, compasión, clemencia.

merciless [ˈmə:silis], *a.* despiadado, desalmado.

mercilessly [ˈmə:silisli], *adv.* sin misericordia, sin piedad, cruelmente.

mercilessness [ˈmə:silisnis], *s.* falta de misericordia, falta de compasión.

mercurial [mə:ˈkjuəriəl], *a.* mercurial, mercúrico, de mercurio; (*fig.*) activo, vivo. — *s.* (*med.*) preparado mercurial.

mercurialize [mə:ˈkjuəriəlaiz], *v.t.* someter a un tratamiento mercurial; (*foto.*) tratar con mercurio.

Mercury [ˈmə:kjuri], *s.* (*astron., mit.*) Mercurio.

mercury [ˈmə:kjuri], *s.* mercurio; (*bot.*) mercurial, *f.*

mercy [ˈmə:si], *s.* misericordia, clemencia, compasión, piedad; favor, merced; gracia; ***at the mercy of,*** a merced de; ***to cry for mercy,*** pedir compasión; ***to show mercy,*** usar de misericordia; ***one must be thankful for small mercies,*** menos da una piedra; ***mercy killing,*** eutanasia.

mere (I) [miə], *a.* mero, simple, puro, nada más que; ***mere words,*** pura palabrería.

mere (2) [miə], *s.* lago.
merely [ˈmiəli], *adv.* meramente, simplemente, puramente, sólo, solamente, nada más que.
meretricious [meriˈtriʃəs], *a.* de oropel; chabacano.
meretriciousness [meriˈtriʃəsnis], *s.* chabacanería.
merganser [mə:ˈgænsə], *s.* mergo, mergánsar.
merge [mə:dʒ], *v.t.* fundir, unir; fusionar. — *v.i.* fundirse; fusionarse; ***merge into,*** fundirse con, convertirse en, ir fundiéndose con *o* convirtiéndose en.
merger [ˈmə:dʒə], *s.* fusión.
meridian [məˈridiən], *a.* meridiano. — *s.* (*astron.*, *geog.*) meridiano; mediodía.
meridional [məˈridiənəl], *a.* meridional.
meringue [məˈræŋ], *s.* merengue.
merino [məˈri:nou], *a.* merino. — *s.* paño merino; carnero merino.
merit [ˈmerit], *s.* mérito. — *v.t.* merecer, ser digno de.
meritorious [meriˈtɔ:riəs], *a.* meritorio; benemérito.
meritoriousness [meriˈtɔ:riəsnis], *s.* (lo) meritorio.
merlin [ˈmə:lin], *s.* (*orn.*) merlín, esmerejón.
merlon [ˈmə:lən], *s.* merlón.
mermaid [ˈmə:meid], *s.* sirena.
merman [ˈmə:mən], *s.* tritón.
Merovingian [meroˈvindʒiən], *a.*, *s.* merovingio.
merriment, merriness [ˈmerimənt, -nis], *s.* alegría, regocijo, alborozo; hilaridad.
merry [ˈmeri], *a.* alegre, regocijado, alborozado; (*borracho*) alegre, alegrillo; ***to make merry,*** divertirse, juerguearse; ***merry-andrew,*** bufón, chocarrero; ***Merry Christmas!*** ¡Felices Pascuas!; ***merry-go-round,*** tiovivo, caballitos, *m.pl.*; ***merry-making,*** juerga, holgorio, júbilo.
mesenteric [mesənˈterik], *a.* mesentérico.
mesentery [ˈmesəntəri], *s.* mesenterio.
mesh [meʃ], *s.* malla; red, trampa; (*mec.*) engranaje; (*pl.* **meshes** [-iz]) red, trampa; (*mec.*) ***to be in mesh,*** estar engranado. — *v.t.* enredar. — *v.i.* engranar (***with,*** con).
meshy [ˈmeʃi], *a.* hecho de malla; reticular.
mesmeric [mezˈmerik], *a.* mesmérico.
mesmerism [ˈmezmərizəm], *s.* mesmerismo, hipnotismo.
mesmerist [ˈmezmərist], *s.* magnetizador.
mesmerization [mezməraiˈzeiʃən], *s.* mesmerización.
mesmerize [ˈmezməraiz], *v.t.* hipnotizar, magnetizar; fascinar, hechizar.
mesmerizer [ˈmezməraizə], *s.* persona que hipnotiza.
mesocarp [ˈmesokɑ:p], *s.* mesocarpio.
mess (1) [mes], *s.* revoltijo, lío, desorden; porquería, bazofia; ***to be in a mess,*** estar revuelto; estar en un lío; estar hecho una porquería; ***to make a mess of,*** ensuciar, poner perdido; destrozar; hacer mal; hacer una chapuza de. — *v.t.* ***mess about,*** causar trastorno a; dar la marcha a; ***mess up,*** estropear, desarreglar; ensuciar. — *v.i.* ***mess about,*** entretenerse; hurgar *o* andar (en); ***mess about with,*** manosear; hurgar *o* andar en.
mess (2) [mes], *s.* (*mar.*, *mil.*) mesa de oficiales; rancho. — *v.i.* comer juntos, arrancharse.
message [ˈmesidʒ], *s.* mensaje; recado; encargo.
messenger [ˈmesindʒə], *s.* mensajero; recadero, mandadero; ***messenger boy,*** botones, *m. inv.*; (*mar.*) virador.
Messiah [miˈsaiə] (**the**). (el) Mesías.
messmate [ˈmesmeit], *s.* compañero de rancho, comensal.
Messrs. [ˈmesəz], *s.pl.* (*abrev. de* **Messieurs**) Señores, *m.pl.*
messuage [ˈmeswidʒ], *s.* (*for.*) heredad.
messy [ˈmesi], *a.* revuelto; sucio.
metabolic [metəˈbɔlik], *a.* metabólico.
metabolism [meˈtæbəlizəm], *s.* metabolismo.
metacarpal [metəˈkɑ:pl], *a.* metacarpiano, del metacarpo.
metacarpus [metəˈkɑ:pəs], *s.* (*anat.*) metacarpo.
metacentre [metəˈsentə], *s.* metacentro.
metachromatism [metəˈkroumətizəm], *s.* cambio de color.
metage [ˈmi:tidʒ], *s.* medición de carbón.
metal [metl], *a.* metálico, de metal. — *s.* metal; grava (*de carretera*); (*f.c.*) balasto; (*fig.*) temple, ánimo; ***metal polish,*** limpiametales; ***metal work,*** metalistería. — *v.t.* guarnecer con metal; balastar (*una vía férrea*); (*carreteras*) macadamizar.
metalepsis [metəˈlepsis], *s.* metalepsis, *f.inv.*
metaleptic [metəˈleptik], *a.* metaléptico.
metallic [miˈtælik], *a.* metálico.
metalliferous [metəˈlifərəs], *a.* metalífero.
metalline [ˈmetəlain], *a.* metálico.
metallist [ˈmetəlist], *s.* metalario.
metallization [metəlaiˈzeiʃən], *s.* metalización.
metallize [ˈmetəlaiz], *v.t.* metalizar.
metallographer [metəˈlɔgrəfə], *s.* metalógrafo.
metallography [metəˈlɔgrəfi], *s.* metalografía.
metalloid [ˈmetəlɔid], *a.*, *s.* metaloide.
metalloidal [metəˈlɔidəl], *a.* metaloide.
metallurgic(al) [metəˈlə:dʒik(əl)], *a.* metalúrgico.
metallurgist [meˈtælədʒist], *s.* metalúrgico, metalario, metalista, *m.f.*
metallurgy [meˈtælədʒi], *s.* metalurgia.
metameric [metəˈmerik], *a.* metamérico.
metamorphic [metəˈmɔ:fik], *a.* metamórfico.
metamorphism [metəˈmɔ:fizəm], *s.* metamorfismo.
metamorphose [metəˈmɔ:fouz], *v.t.* metamorfosear.
metamorphosis [metəˈmɔ:fəsis], *s.* (*pl.* **metamorphoses** [-i:z]) metamorfosis, *f.inv.*
metaphor [ˈmetəfə], *s.* metáfora.
metaphoric(al) [metəˈfɔrik(əl)], *a.* metafórico.
metaphrastic [metəˈfræstik], *a.* metafrástico.
metaphysic(al) [metəˈfizik(əl)], *a.* metafísico.
metaphysician [metəfiˈziʃən], *s.* metafísico.
metaphysics [metəˈfiziks], *s.* metafísica.
metaplasm [ˈmetəplæzəm], *s.* metaplasmo.
metastasis [meˈtæstəsis], *s.* metástasis, *f.inv.*
metathesis [meˈtæθisis], *s.* metátesis, *f.inv.*
mete [mi:t], *v.t.* — ***out,*** distribuir, repartir; (*fam.*) dar, imponer.
metempsychosis [metempsiˈkousis], *s.* (*pl.* **metempsychoses** [-i:z]) metempsícosis, *f.inv.*
meteor [ˈmi:tiə], *s.* meteoro.
meteoric [mi:tiˈɔrik], *a.* meteórico.
meteorism [mi:tiərizəm], *s.* meteorismo.
meteorite [ˈmi:tiərait], *s.* meteorito.
meteoritic [mi:tiəˈritik], *a.* meteórico.
meteorolite [ˈmi:tiərəlait], *s.* meteorolito.
meteorologic(al) [mi:tiərəˈlɔdʒik(əl)], *a.* meteorológico.
meteorologist [mi:tiəˈrɔlədʒist], *s.* meteorólogo.
meteorology [mi:tiəˈrɔlədʒi], *s.* meteorología.
meteoroscope [ˈmi:tiərəskoup], *s.* meteoroscopio.
meter [ˈmi:tə], *s.* contador.
methane [ˈmi:θein], *s.* metano.
metheglin [meˈθeglin], *s.* aguamiel, hidromiel, *f.*
methinks [miˈθiŋks], *v. impers.* (*ant.*) tengo para mí, paréceme.
method [ˈmeθəd], *s.* método; sistema, *m.*, procedimiento.
methodical [miˈθɔdikəl], *a.* metódico, sistemático.
Methodism [ˈmeθədizəm], *s.* (*relig.*) metodismo.
Methodist [ˈmeθədist], *s.* metodista, *m.f.*
methodize [ˈmeθədaiz], *v.t.* metodizar, sistematizar.
methodology [meθəˈdɔlədʒi], *s.* metodología.
methyl [ˈmeθil], *s.* metilo.

methylated spirit [ˈmeθileitid ˈspirit], *s.* alcohol metílico.
methylene [ˈmeθili:n], *s.* metileno.
methylic [meˈθilik], *a.* metílico.
metonymical [metəˈnimikəl], *a.* metonímico.
metonymy [meˈtɔnimi], *s.* metonimia.
metope [ˈmetoup], *s.* métopa.
metoposcopy [metəˈpɔskəpi], *s.* metoposcopia.
metre [ˈmi:tə], *s.* metro.
metric(al) [ˈmetrik(əl)], *a.* métrico.
metrician, metrist [meˈtriʃən, ˈmetrist], *s.* metrista, *m.f.*, versificador.
metrological [metrəˈlɔdʒikəl], *a.* metrológico.
metrology [meˈtrɔlədʒi], *s.* metrología.
metronome [ˈmetrənoum], *s.* metrónomo.
metropolis [miˈtrɔpəlis], *s.* metrópoli, *f.*
metropolitan [metrəˈpɔlitən], *a.*, *s.* metropolitano.
metrorrhagia [metrəˈreidʒiə], *s.* metrorragia.
mettle [metl], *s.* temple, brío, ánimo; ***to put s.o. on his mettle,*** picarle el amor propio a alguien.
mettled [metld], *a.* (*f.c.*) terraplenado; cubierto de grava.
mettlesome [ˈmetlsəm], *a.* fogoso, brioso, animoso.
mettlesomeness [ˈmetlsəmnis], *s.* vivacidad, brío, fuego, ardor.
Meuse [mə:z] (**River**). Mosa.
mew (1) [mju:], *s.* (*orn.*) gaviota.
mew (2) [mju:], *s.* maullido. — *v.i.* maullar.
mew (3) [mju:], *s.* muda (*de las aves de caza*). — *v.t.* poner en la muda; enjaular, encerrar. — *v.i.* mudar las plumas (*las aves*).
mewing (1) [ˈmju:iŋ], *s.* maullido(s).
mewing (2) [ˈmju:iŋ], *a.* que muda. — *s.* muda (*de las aves de caza*).
mewl [mju:l], *s.* lloriqueo; maullido. — *v.i.* lloriquear; maullar.
mews [mju:z], *s.* caballeriza; cochera.
Mexican [ˈmeksikən], *a.*, *s.* mejicano.
Mexico [ˈmeksikou]. México.
mezzanine [ˈmetsəni:n], *s.* entresuelo.
mezzotint [ˈmedzoutint], *s.* media tinta; grabado mezzotinto.
mi [mi:], *s.* (*mús.*) mi, la nota E.
Miami [maiˈæmi]. Miami.
miaow [miˈau], *s.* miau. — *v.i.* maullar.
miasma [miˈæzmə], *s.* (*pl.* **miasmata** [miˈæzmətə]) miasma, *m.*
miasmal, miasmatic [miˈæzməl, miæzˈmætik], *a.* miasmático.
mica [ˈmaikə], *s.* mica.
micaceous [maiˈkeiʃəs], *a.* micáceo.
mice [mais], *s.pl.* [MOUSE].
Michael [ˈmaikəl]. Miguel.
Michaelmas [ˈmiklməs], *s.* día de San Miguel; sanmiguelada.
Michelangelo [maikəlˈændʒilou]. Miguel Angel.
Michigan [ˈmiʃigən]. Michigan.
mickey [ˈmiki], *s.* (*fam.*) ***to take the mickey out of,*** tomarle el pelo a.
microbe [ˈmaikroub], *s.* microbio.
microbial, microbic [maiˈkroubiəl, -bik], *a.* microbiano.
microbicide [maiˈkroubisaid], *s.* microbicida, *m.*
microbiology [maikroubaiˈɔlədʒi], *s.* microbiología.
microcephaly [maikrouˈsefəli], *s.* microcefalia.
microcephalic, microcephalous [ˈmaikrouseˈfælik, ˈmaikrouˈsefələs], *a.* microcéfalo.
micrococcal [maikrouˈkɔkəl], *a.* micrococal.
micrococcus [maikrouˈkɔkəs], *s.* micrococo.
microcosm [ˈmaikrokɔzəm], *s.* microcosmo.
microcosmical [maikroˈkɔzmikəl], *a.* microcósmico.
micrography [maiˈkrɔgrəfi], *s.* micrografía.
micrometer [maiˈkrɔmitə], *s.* micrómetro.
micrometric(al) [maikroˈmetrik(əl)], *a.* micrométrico.
micrometry [maiˈkrɔmitri], *s.* micrometría.
Micronesia [maikroˈni:ʃə]. Micronesia.
microphone [ˈmaikrəfoun], *s.* micrófono.
microphyte [ˈmaikrəfait], *s.* micrófito.
microscope [ˈmaikrəskoup], *s.* microscopio.
microscopic(al) [maikrəˈskɔpik(əl)], *a.* microscópico.
microscopist [maiˈkrɔskəpist], *s.* microscopista, *m.f.*
microscopy [maiˈkrɔskəpi], *s.* microscopia.
micturition [miktjuəˈriʃən], *s.* micción.
micturate [ˈmiktjuəreit], *v.i.* orinar.
mid [mid], *a.* medio; ***in mid-air,*** en medio del aire; en pleno vuelo; ***in mid-course,*** a media carrera; ***mid-day,*** (las) doce; mediodía; del mediodía; ***in mid-season,*** en mitad de temporada; ***mid-week,*** en medio de la semana.
midden [midn], *s.* muladar.
middle [midl], *a.* medio; intermedio; de en medio; central; mediano; ***middle-age,*** mediana edad; ***middle-aged,*** de mediana edad, de edad madura; ***Middle Ages,*** edad media; ***middle class(es),*** clase media; ***middle distance,*** segundo término; (*mar.*) ***middle-jig,*** segundo foque; ***middle-sized,*** de tamaño mediano, de mediana estatura; (*dep.*) ***middle-weight,*** peso medio. — *s.* centro, medio, mitad; cintura, estómago; ***about the middle of May,*** a mediados de mayo; ***in the middle of,*** en medio de; en pleno; ***in the middle of the afternoon,*** al mediodía; a media tarde.
middleman [ˈmidlmæn], *s.* intermediario; corredor.
middlemost [ˈmidlmoust], *a.* más del centro.
middling [ˈmidliŋ], *a.* mediano; regular, mediocre.
middy [ˈmidi], *s. abrev. de* [MIDSHIPMAN].
midge [midʒ], *s.* mosquito, cínife.
midget [ˈmidʒit], *s.* enano; ***midget submarine,*** submarino de bolsillo.
midi-skirt [ˈmidi-skə:t], *s.* midifalda.
midland [ˈmidlənd], *a.* del centro, del interior.
Midlands [ˈmidləndz], **the.** condados del centro de Inglaterra, *m.pl.*
midnight [ˈmidnait], *a.*, *s.* (de) (las) doce de la noche; (de) media noche; ***to burn the midnight oil,*** quemarse las cejas.
midriff [ˈmidrif], *s.* diafragma, *m.*
midshipman [ˈmidʃipmən], *s.* guardiamarina, *m.*
midships [ˈmidʃips], *adv.* en medio del buque.
midst [midst], *prep.* (*poét.*) entre. — *s.* centro, medio; ***in the midst of,*** en medio de.
midsummer [ˈmidsʌmə], *s.* medio del verano; pleno verano; solsticio estival; fiesta de San Juan.
midway [ˈmidˈwei], *adv.* a mitad de(l) camino.
midwife [ˈmidwaif], *s.* (*pl.* **midwives** [-waivz]) partera, comadrona.
midwifery [ˈmidwifri], *s.* partería.
midwinter [midˈwintə], *s.* pleno invierno; ***in midwinter,*** en pleno invierno.
mien [mi:n], *s.* aire, semblante; porte.
miffed [mift], *a.* (*fam.*) disgustado, fastidiado.
might (1) [mait], *s.* fuerza, poder; poderío; ***with might and main,*** con todas sus fuerzas.
might (2) [mait], *pret. condicional* [MAY]; podría; es posible; ***they might come,*** podrían venir; es posible que vengan.
mightiness [ˈmaitinis], *s.* poder, poderío; fuerza; grandeza.
mighty [ˈmaiti], *a.* poderoso; fuerte; enorme, grande. — *adv.* muy, enormemente.
mignonette [minjəˈnet], *s.* (*bot.*) reseda.
migraine [ˈmi:grein], *s.* jaqueca.
migrant [ˈmaigrənt], *a.* migratorio; de paso (*ave*). — *s.* inmigrante; peregrino, nómada, *m.f.* (*ave*).

migrate [mai'greit], *v.i.* emigrar.
migrating [mai'greitiŋ], *a.* migratorio.
migration ['mai'greiʃən], *s.* migración.
migratory ['maigrətəri], *a.* migratorio; nómada; ***migratory bird,*** ave de paso.
Mike [maik]. (*fam.*) Miguel; (*fam.*) ***for the love of Mike,*** por (el amor de) Dios.
mike [maik], *s.* (*fam.*) micro.
Milan [mi'læn]. Milán.
Milanese [milə'ni:z], *a.*, *s.* milanés, *m.*, milanesa, *f.*
milch [miltʃ], *a.* lechero; ***milch cow,*** vaca lechera.
mild [maild], *a.* suave; manso, blando; apacible; dulce; (*meteorol.*) templado; (*pat.*) benigno; leve, ligero; ***mild steel,*** acero dulce.
mildew ['mildju:], *s.* mildiu; añublo; moho. — *v.t.* enmohecer; añublar. — *v.i.* enmohecerse; añublarse.
mildly ['maildli], *adv.* ***to put it mildly,*** por no decir más, que digamos.
mildness ['maildnis], *s.* suavidad; levedad; templanza.
mile [mail], *s.* milla (1.609 metros); ***nautical mile,*** (1.852 metros), milla náutica *o* marina.
mileage ['mailidʒ], *s.* número de millas, distancia en millas, kilometraje; ***mileage book,*** (billete) kilométrico.
milepost, milestone ['mailpoust, -stoun], *s.* piedra miliar(ia); mojón; (*fig.*) ***to be a milestone,*** hacer época, ser hito *o* jalón.
milfoil ['milfɔil], *s.* (*bot.*) cientoenrama, milenrama, milhojas, *f.inv.*
miliaria [mili'ɛəriə], *s.* fiebre miliar.
miliary ['miliəri], *a.* miliar.
milieu ['mi:ljə:], *s.* (medio) ambiente.
militancy ['militənsi], *s.* belicosidad.
militant ['militənt], *a.* militante, belicoso, agresivo. — *s.* militante.
militarily ['militərili], *adv.* militarmente.
militarism ['militərizəm], *s.* militarismo.
militarize ['militəraiz], *v.t.* militarizar.
military ['militəri], *a.* militar, de guerra. — *s.* ***the military,*** los militares.
militate ['militeit], *v.i.* militar; ***militate against,*** militar contra; ***militate in favour of,*** militar a favor de.
militia [mi'liʃə], *s.* milicia, guardia nacional.
militiaman [mi'liʃəmən], *s.* miliciano.
milk [milk], *s.* leche; ***milk-and-water,*** débil, flojo; ***milk can,*** lechera, cántara; ***milk diet,*** régimen lácteo; ***milk-fever,*** fiebre láctea; ***milk of human kindness,*** compasión, humanidad; ***milk of lime,*** lechada de cal; ***milk of magnesia,*** leche de magnesia; ***milk-pail,*** ordeñadero, colodra; (*bot.*) ***milk-thistle,*** titimalo; ***milk tooth,*** diente de leche; ***powdered milk,*** leche en polvo; ***skim(med) milk,*** leche desnatada; ***whole milk,*** leche sin desnatar; ***it's no use crying over spilt milk,*** a lo hecho pecho. — *v.t.* ordeñar; (*fig.*) chupar. — *v.i.* dar leche.
milker ['milkə], *s.* ordeñador; vaca lechera.
milkiness ['milkinis], *s.* lactescencia, (lo) lechoso.
milkmaid ['milkmeid], *s.* lechera.
milkman ['milkmən], *s.* lechero.
milkpan ['milkpæn], *s.* lechera, ordeñadero.
milksop ['milksɔp], *s.* sopa de leche; (*fig.*) marica, *m.*
milkwoman ['milkwumən], *s.* lechera.
milkwort ['milkwə:t], *s.* enforbio, polígala.
milky ['milki], *a.* lechoso; ***Milky Way,*** vía láctea.
mill [mil], *s.* molino; fábrica; taller; tejeduría, hilandería, fábrica de tejidos *o* de hilados; caz; ***mill-board,*** cartón doble, cartón de encuadernar; ***mill-dam,*** esclusa, represa; ***mill-hand,*** obrero de molino; ***mill-hopper,*** tolva de molino; ***mill-pond,*** alberca, represa de molino; ***mill-wheel,*** rueda de molino; ***it's all grist to his mill,*** todo ello le sirve para su objeto; ***to go through the mill,*** sufrir mucho *o* muchas penalidades, pasarlo muy mal, pasar las de Caín, pasarlas moradas; ***to put through the mill,*** someter a un régimen muy duro, hacer pasar muchos sufrimientos. — *v.t.* moler; (*mec.*) fresar; (*numis.*) acordonar; (*tej.*) abatanar; (*chocolate*) batir. — *v.i.* — ***about, around,*** pulular, hormiguear.
millenarian [mili'nɛəriən], *a.*, *s.* milenario.
millenary [mi'lenəri], *a.*, *s.* milenario.
millennial [mi'leniəl], *a.* milenario.
millennium [mi'leniəm], *s.* milenario, milenio.
milleped, millepede ['miliped, -pi:d], *s.* miriápodo.
millepore ['milipɔ:], *s.* miléporo.
miller ['milə], *s.* molinero.
millesimal [mi'lesiməl], *a.* milésimo.
millet ['milit], *s.* mijo.
milliard ['miliɑ:d], *s.* mil millones.
milliary ['miliəri], *a.* miliario. — *s.* piedra miliar.
millibar ['milibɑ:], *s.* (*meteorol.*) milibar.
milligram(me) ['miligræm], *s.* miligramo.
millilitre ['milili:tə], *s.* mililitro.
millimetre ['milimi:tə], *s.* milímetro.
milliner ['milinə], *s.* modista, *m.f.*, sombrerera.
millinery ['milinəri], *s.* modistería; sombrerería.
milling ['miliŋ], *s.* molienda; (*monedas*) acordonamiento, cordoncillo; ***milling-machine,*** fresadora.
million ['miljən], *s.* millón.
millionaire [miljə'nɛə], *s.* millonario.
millionth ['miljənθ], *a.* millonésimo. — *s.* millonésima.
milliped, millipede [MILLEPED, MILLEPEDE].
millpond ['milpɔnd], *s.* represa de molino; (*fig.*) balsa de aceite.
millstone ['milstoun], *s.* muela, piedra molar; ***to have a millstone about one's neck,*** tener una soga al cuello, llevar encima una losa.
millwright ['milrait], *s.* constructor de molinos.
milt [milt], *s.* bazo; lechecillas, *f.pl.* — *v.t.* (*ict.*) fecundar, aovar.
milter ['miltə], *s.* pez macho.
mime [maim], *s.* mimo; mímica, pantomima. — *v.t.* remedar, hacer en pantomima. — *v.i.* representar una pantomima.
mimeograph ['mimiəgrɑ:f], *s.* mimeógrafo.
mimer ['maimə], *s.* mimo.
mimesis [mi'mi:sis], *s.* mimesis, *f.inv.*
mimetic [mi'metik], *a.* mímico, imitativo.
mimic ['mimik], *a.* mímico. — *s.* imitador; remedador. — *v.t.* imitar; remedar.
mimicry ['mimikri], *s.* mímica, imitación, remedo.
mimosa [mi'mouzə], *s.* (*bot.*) mimosa.
mimosis [mi'mousis], *s.* (*med.*) semejanza.
minaret ['minəret], *s.* minarete, alminar.
minatory ['minətəri], *a.* conminatorio.
mince [mins], *s.* carne picada. — *v.t.* picar; desmenuzar; ***not to mince matters*** o ***words,*** no tener pelos en la lengua. — *v.i.* andar con pasos menuditos; hablar remilgadamente.
mincemeat ['minsmi:t], *s.* picadillo; carne picada; conserva de fruta picada; ***to make mincemeat of,*** hacer picadillo de; (*fig.*) merendarse (a).
mincepie ['mins'pai], *s.* pastel de pasas y especias.
mincing ['minsiŋ], *a.* afectado, remilgado.
mincingly ['minsiŋli], *adv.* remilgadamente; a pasitos cortos.
mind [maind], *s.* mente; espíritu; ánimo; opinión, parecer; juicio; inteligencia, entendimiento; ***to bear*** o ***keep in mind,*** tener presente, en cuenta; ***to call to mind,*** traer a la memoria; ***to change one's mind,*** cambiar de opinión, mudar de parecer; ***to give one's mind to,*** aplicarse a; ***to give s.o. a piece of one's mind,*** decir a alguien cuatro verdades; ***I have a good mind to go,*** (casi) estoy por ir, de buena gana iría; ***to have in mind,*** pensar en, tener pensado; ***to know***

one's own mind, saber lo que uno quiere; ***to make up one's mind (to),*** decidirse, resolverse (a); tomar partido; ***of one mind,*** unánimes; ***out of one's mind,*** no en su juicio; (como) loco; ***out of sight, out of mind,*** ojos que no ven, corazón que no siente; ***time out of mind,*** tiempo inmemorial; ***to put s.o. in mind of,*** recordarle a alguien; ***to be in one's right mind,*** estar en sus cabales; ***to set one's mind on,*** resolverse a; ***it slipped my mind,*** se me escapó de la memoria; se me fue de la cabeza; ***to speak one's mind,*** hablar con franqueza; ***with one mind,*** unánimemente. — *v.t.* notar, mirar, fijarse en; hacer caso de; cuidar; importar; ***mind your own business,*** métase en lo que le importa; ***mind the step,*** ¡cuidado con el escalón!, ¡ojo con el escalón! — *v.i.* tener inconveniente; importar; tener cuidado; ***mind!*** ¡ojo! ¡cuidado!; ***mind you,*** le advierto que, ahora bien; conste que; ***never mind,*** no importa, no le hace; ***I don't mind,*** no me importa, da igual; (*fam.*) ***I don't mind if I do,*** acepto muy gustoso; ***do you mind if I smoke?*** ¿le importa que fume?

minded [ˈmaindid], *a.* inclinado, propenso, dispuesto.

mindedness [ˈmaindidnis], *s.* inclinación, disposición.

mindful [ˈmaindful], *a.* atento, diligente; cuidadoso, vigilante; ***mindful of,*** que tiene en cuenta, atento a.

mindfulness [ˈmaindfulnis], *s.* cuidado, atención, prudencia.

mindless [ˈmaindlis], *a.* irreflexivo; estúpido.

mine (1) [main], *pron.* mío, míos, *m.pl.*, mía, mías, *f.pl.*; el mío, lo mío etc.; ***a friend of mine,*** un amigo mío.

mine (2) [main], *s.* mina; ***mine-detector,*** detector de minas; ***mine-field,*** campo de minas; (*mar.*) ***mine-layer,*** buque minador; (*mar.*) ***mine-sweeper,*** dragaminas, *m.inv.* — *v.t.* minar; extraer; explotar; (*mil.*) sembrar minas en. — *v.i.* minar; explotar una mina; dedicarse a la minería.

miner [ˈmainə], *s.* minero.

mineral [ˈminərəl], *a., s.* mineral; ***mineral oil,*** petróleo; ***mineral water,*** agua mineral; gaseosa.

mineralization [minərəlaiˈzeiʃən], *s.* mineralización.

mineralize [ˈminərəlaiz], *v.t.* mineralizar.

mineralizer [ˈminərəlaizə], *s.* mineralizador.

mineralogic(al) [minərəˈlɔdʒik(əl)], *a.* mineralógico.

mineralogist [minəˈrælədʒist], *s.* mineralogista, *m.f.*

mineralogy [minəˈrælədʒi], *s.* mineralogía.

minever [MINIVER].

mingle [miŋgl], *v.t.* mezclar; confundir. — *v.i.* mezclarse; confundirse; alternar (***with,*** con).

mingling [ˈmiŋgliŋ], *s.* (el) mezclar; (el) alternar.

mingy [ˈmindʒi], *a.* (*fam.*) tacaño, roñoso.

miniate [ˈminieit], *v.t.* miniar.

miniature [ˈminjətʃə], *a.* en miniatura; diminuto, de bolsillo. — *s.* miniatura.

miniaturist [ˈminjətʃərist], *s.* miniaturista, *m.f.*

minikin [ˈminikin], *s.* cosa baladí; alfilerito.

minim [ˈminim], *s.* mínimo; (*mús.*) mínima, blanca.

minimal [ˈminiməl], *a.* mínimo.

minimize [ˈminimaiz], *v.t.* reducir al mínimo, minimizar; atenuar, quitar importancia a.

minimum [ˈminiməm], *a.* mínimo. — *s.* mínimo, mínimum.

mining [ˈmainiŋ], *a.* minero. — *s.* minería; explotación de minas; extracción; ***mining engineer,*** ingeniero de minas.

minion [ˈminjən], *s.* favorito, valido, paniaguado; secuaz; (*impr.*) miñona.

mini-skirt [ˈmini-skəːt], *s.* minifalda.

minister [ˈministə], *s.* ministro; pastor; ***Prime Minister,*** primer ministro. — *v.t., v.i.* ministrar; (*igl.*) oficiar; atender (***to,*** a).

ministerial [minisˈtiəriəl], *a.* ministerial; de ministro.

ministerialism [minisˈtiəriəlizəm], *s.* ministerialismo.

ministering [ˈministəriŋ], *a.* ministrador, ministrante. — *s.* (el) atender (***to,*** a).

ministrant [ˈministrənt], *a., s.* ministrante; oficiante.

ministration [minisˈtreiʃən], *s.* servicio, agencia; (*igl.*) ministerio, oficio eclesiástico.

ministry [ˈministri], *s.* ministerio; (*igl.*) sacerdocio.

minium [ˈminiəm], *s.* minio, azarcón.

miniver [ˈminivə], *s.* (*zool.*) marta.

mink [miŋk], *s.* visón, piel de visón.

minnow [ˈminou], *s.* pececillo, alevín.

minor [ˈmainə], *a.* menor; menor de edad; secundario, subalterno; sin importancia; (*mús.*) ***minor key,*** tono menor; (*med.*) ***minor operation,*** operación secundaria. — *s.* menor (de edad).

Minorca [miˈnɔːkə]. Menorca.

minorite [ˈmainərait], *a.* franciscano. — *s.* minorita, *m.*

minority [maiˈnɔriti], *a.* de minoría, minoritario. — *s.* minoría; minoridad, menor edad.

Minos [ˈmainɔs]. Minos, *m.*

minotaur [ˈmainətɔː], *s.* minotauro.

minster [ˈminstə], *s.* catedral, *f.*, iglesia abacial.

minstrel [ˈminstrəl], *s.* juglar, trovador; cómico (disfrazado de negro).

minstrelsy [ˈminstrəlsi], *s.* arte del trovador; gaya ciencia.

mint (1) [mint], *a.* de menta. — *s.* (*bot.*) hierbabuena, menta.

mint (2) [mint], *a.* nuevo, sin usar. — *s.* casa de moneda; ***mint of money,*** (un) dineral. — *v.t.* acuñar; (*fig.*) inventar.

mintage [ˈmintidʒ], *s.* moneda acuñada; braceaje; derecho de cuño.

minter [ˈmintə], *s.* acuñador; forjador, inventor.

minuend [ˈminjuend], *s.* minuendo.

minuet [minjuˈet], *s.* minueto, minué.

minus [ˈmainəs], *a.* negativo. — *prep.* menos, sin. — *s.* (*signo*) menos, *m.*

minuscule [ˈminəskjuːl], *a.* minúsculo. — *s.* minúscula.

minute (1) [ˈminit], *s.* minuto; momento, instante; minuta, nota; (*pl.*) actas, *f.pl.*; ***minute-book,*** libro de actas; ***minute-hand,*** minutero; ***this very minute,*** en este instante; ahora mismo. — *v.t.* minutar, levantar acta de.

minute (2) [maiˈnjuːt], *a.* menudo, diminuto; minucioso.

minutely [maiˈnjuːtli], *adv.* exactamente; circunstanciadamente; minuciosamente; con minuciosidad; detalladamente.

minuteness [maiˈnjuːtnis], *s.* menudencia, minucia; minuciosidad; (lo) diminuto.

minutia [ˈmainjuːʃə], *s.* (*ú. más en pl.* **minutiæ** [maiˈnjuːʃii]) detalle(s) minucioso(s).

minx [miŋks], *s.* (*zool.*) marta; (*fig.*) bribona; moza descarada.

miracle [ˈmirəkəl], *s.* milagro; ***miracle play,*** auto (*drama religioso*).

miraculous [miˈrækjuləs], *a.* milagroso.

miraculously [miˈrækjuləsli], *adv.* milagrosamente, de milagro.

miraculousness [miˈrækjuləsnis], *s.* (lo) milagroso.

mirage [miˈrɑːʒ], *s.* espejismo.

mire [maiə], *s.* fango; lodo, cieno. — *v.t.* enlodar, encenagar.

miriness [ˈmaiərinis], *s.* (lo) fangoso.

mirky [MURKY].

mirror [ˈmirə], *s.* espejo; (*aut.*) retrovisor. — *v.t.* reflejar.

mirth, mirthfulness [mə:θ, ˈmə:θfulnis], *s.* alegría, regocijo; hilaridad, risas, *f.pl.*
mirthful [ˈmə:θful], *a.* alegre, regocijado; dado a la hilaridad *o* a la risa.
mirthless [ˈmə:θlis], *a.* sin alegría, triste.
miry [ˈmaiəri], *a.* fangoso, cenagoso.
misadventure [misədˈventʃə], *s.* desgracia, desventura; accidente.
misalliance [misəˈlaiəns], *s.* mal casamiento, casamiento desigual.
misallied [misəˈlaid], *a.* mal casado.
misanthrope, misanthropist [ˈmisənθroup, miˈsænθrəpist], *s.* misántropo.
misanthropic(al) [misənˈθrɔpik(əl)], *a.* misantrópico.
misanthropy [miˈsænθrəpi], *s.* misantropía.
misapplication [misæpliˈkeiʃən], *s.* aplicación equivocada, mala aplicación; abuso.
misapply [misəˈplai], *v.t.* aplicar mal; hacer mal uso de.
misapprehend [misæpriˈhend], *v.t.* entender mal.
misapprehension [misæpriˈhenʃən], *s.* mala inteligencia; error, concepción equivocada; ***to labour under a misapprehension,*** padecer un error.
misappropriate [misəˈprouprieit], *v.t.* malversar.
misappropriation [misəproupriˈeiʃən], *s.* malversación.
misbecome [misbiˈkʌm], *v.t.* no favorecer; no decir nada bueno de.
misbegotten [misbiˈgɔtn], *a.* bastardo, ilegítimo.
misbehave [misbiˈheiv], *v.i.* portarse mal; (*niño*) ser malo.
misbehaved [misbiˈheivd], *a.* mal educado, que se porta mal.
misbehaviour [misbiˈheivjə], *s.* mala conducta, mal comportamiento.
misbelief [misbiˈli:f], *s.* falsa creencia, error; incredulidad.
misbelieve [misbiˈli:v], *v.t.* no creer, no dar crédito a.
misbeliever [misbiˈli:və], *s.* incrédulo, infiel.
misbelieving [misbiˈli:viŋ], *a.* incrédulo, infiel, heterodoxo.
miscalculate [misˈkælkjuleit], *v.t.* calcular mal.
miscalculation [miskælkjuˈleiʃən], *s.* mal cálculo, cálculo equivocado *o* desacertado; desacierto.
miscall [misˈkɔ:l], *v.t.* equivocar el nombre de.
miscarriage [misˈkæridʒ], *s.* malparto, aborto; malogro; extravío; fracaso; ***miscarriage of justice,*** error judicial.
miscarry [misˈkæri], *v.i.* malparir, abortar; malograrse; extraviarse.
miscast [misˈkɑ:st], *v.t.* (*teat.*) repartir mal los papeles de *o* entre.
miscegenation [misidʒiˈneiʃən], *s.* entrecruzamiento de razas.
miscellanea [misiˈleiniə], *s.* miscelánea.
miscellaneous [misiˈleiniəs], *a.* misceláneo, mezclado, diverso, mixto.
miscellany [miˈseləni], *s.* miscelánea.
mischance [misˈtʃɑ:ns], *s.* mala suerte, infortunio, accidente.
mischarge [misˈtʃɑ:dʒ], *v.t.* cargar en cuenta indebidamente.
mischief [ˈmistʃif], *s.* travesura, diablura; daño, mal; malicia; ***to get into mischief,*** meterse en un lío; (*niños*) travesear; (*fam.*) ***little mischief,*** diablillo; ***to make mischief,*** meter cizaña; enredar; ***mischief-maker,*** enredador, chismoso, cizañero; ***mischief-making,*** enredador, chismoso, cizañero; (el) enredar *o* meter cizaña.
mischievous [ˈmistʃivəs], *a.* dañoso, perjudicial; malo; malicioso; travieso, revoltoso.
mischievousness [ˈmistʃivəsnis], *s.* malicia; malignidad, maldad; (*niño*) picardía, travesura.
miscibility [misiˈbiliti], *s.* cualidad miscible, (lo) miscible.
miscible [ˈmisibl], *a.* miscible, mezclable.
miscitation [missaiˈteiʃən], *s.* cita falsa *o* equivocada.
miscite [misˈsait], *v.t.* citar falsamente *o* equivocadamente.
misclaim [misˈkleim], *s.* pretensión mal fundada.
misconceive [miskənˈsi:v], *v.t.* interpretar mal; formar un concepto erróneo de.
misconception [miskənˈsepʃən], *s.* concepto erróneo; mala interpretación.
misconduct [misˈkɔndəkt], *s.* mala conducta; adulterio. — [miskənˈdʌkt], *v.t.* dirigir *o* administrar mal. — **misconduct o.s.,** *v.r.* portarse mal.
misconjecture [miskənˈdʒektʃə], *s.* conjetura falsa *o* equivocada. — *v.t., v.i.* hacer conjeturas falsas (de).
misconstruction [miskənˈstrʌkʃən], *s.* mala interpretación.
misconstrue [miskənˈstru:], *v.t.* interpretar mal torcer el sentido de.
miscount [ˈmisˈkaunt], *s.* error de cuenta. — *v.t.* contar mal. — *v.i.* descontarse.
miscreant [ˈmiskriənt], *a., s.* malandrín.
misdate [misˈdeit], *v.t.* fechar falsamente.
misdeal [misˈdi:l], *v.t.* dar mal (*las cartas*).
misdeed [misˈdi:d], *s.* delito; fechoría.
misdemean [misdiˈmi:n] **o.s.,** *v.r.* conducirse mal, portarse mal.
misdemeanour [misdiˈmi:nə], *s.* mala conducta; delito; fechoría.
misdirect [misdiˈrekt], *v.t.* dirigir mal; orientar equivocadamente.
misdirection [misdiˈrekʃən], *s.* mala dirección; orientación equivocada; instrucciones erróneas, *f.pl.*
misdoer [misˈdu:ə], *s.* malhechor.
misdoubt [misˈdaut], *v.t., v.i.* dudar (de), recelar.
misemploy [misimˈplɔi], *v.t.* hacer mal uso de, emplear mal.
misentry [misˈentri], *s.* nota equivocada, inserción errónea.
miser [ˈmaizə], *s.* avaro.
miserable [ˈmizərəbl], *a.* melancólico, triste; desgraciado, lastimoso, infeliz, cuitado; mezquino; (*tiempo*) tristón.
miserableness [ˈmizərəblnis], *s.* melancolía, tristeza; (lo) mezquino.
miserere [mizəˈriəri], *s.* (*igl.*) miserere.
miserly [ˈmaizəli], *a.* avariento, tacaño.
misery [ˈmizəri], *s.* (honda) tristeza, aflicción, desgracia; miseria; ***to put an animal out of its misery,*** matar un animal para que deje de sufrir.
misestimate [misˈestimeit], *v.t.* calcular mal.
misfashion [misˈfæʃən], *v.t.* formar mal, hacer mal.
misfeasance [misˈfi:zəns], *s.* (*for.*) ejecución ilícita.
misfire [misˈfaiə], *s.* falla de tiro. — *v.i.* fallar (*un arma de fuego*); (*fig.*) salir el tiro por la culata.
misfit [ˈmisfit], *s.* cosa mal ajustada; traje que no cae bien; (*pers.*) inadaptado.
misform [misˈfɔ:m], *v.t.* formar mal, deformar.
misfortune [misˈfɔ:tʃən], *s.* desgracia; infortunio; desventura; ***misfortunes never come singly,*** las desgracias nunca vienen solas.
misgiving [misˈgiviŋ], *s.* recelo, duda; ***to have misgivings,*** tener recelos *o* dudas, no tenerlas todas consigo.
misgotten [misˈgɔtn], *a.* mal adquirido, mal ganado.
misgovern [misˈgʌvən], *v.t.* desgobernar, gobernar mal.
misgovernment [misˈgʌvənmənt], *s.* desgobierno, mala administración, desbarajuste.
misguidance [misˈgaidəns], *s.* dirección falsa *o* errada; extravío.
misguide [misˈgaid], *v.t.* dirigir mal; aconsejar mal; descarriar, extraviar.

misguided [mis'gaidid], *a.* equivocado, poco conveniente.
mishandle [mis'hændl], *v.t.* manejar mal; maltratar.
mishap ['mishæp], *s.* contratiempo, accidente, percance.
mishmash ['miʃmæʃ], *s.* (*fam.*) mezcolanza.
misinform [misin'fɔ:m], *v.t.* informar mal, dar informes erróneos a.
misinformation [misinfə'meiʃən], *s.* informes erróneos *o* falsos, *m.pl.*
misinstruct [misin'strʌkt], *v.t.* informar mal, instruir mal.
misintelligence [misin'telidʒəns], *s.* informes erróneos, *m.pl.*; desacuerdo.
misinterpret [misin'tə:prit], *v.t.* interpretar mal, entender mal.
misinterpretation [misintə:pri'teiʃən], *s.* mala interpretación; tergiversación.
misjoin [mis'dʒɔin], *v.t.* unir, ajustar, acomodar *o* adecuar mal.
misjudge [mis'dʒʌdʒ], *v.t.* juzgar mal, formar conceptos erróneos de. — *v.i.* engañarse, equivocarse, errar.
misjudg(e)ment [mis'dʒʌdʒmənt], *s.* juicio falso, erróneo *o* injusto; idea falsa.
mislay [mis'lei], *v.t.* extraviar, traspapelar.
mislead [mis'li:d], *v.t.* extraviar, descaminar, descarriar, despistar; engañar.
misleading [mis'li:diŋ], *a.* falso, engañoso.
misled [mis'led], *a.* extraviado, perdido.
mismanage [mis'mænidʒ], *v.t.* administrar mal, dirigir mal.
mismanagement [mis'mænidʒmənt], *s.* desgobierno, desbarajuste, mala administración, mala dirección.
misname [mis'neim], *v.t.* trasnombrar, dar un nombre falso a.
misnomer [mis'noumə], *s.* nombre impropio.
misogamist [mi'sɔgəmist], *s.* misógamo.
misogamy [mi'sɔgəmi], *s.* misogamia.
misogynist [mi'sɔdʒinist], *s.* misógino.
misogyny [mi'sɔdʒini], *s.* misoginia.
misplace [mis'pleis], *v.t.* colocar mal, poner fuera de lugar.
misprint ['misprint], *s.* errata, error de imprenta. — [mis'print], *v.t.* imprimir mal, hacer erratas en.
misprision [mis'priʒən], *s.* (*for.*) ocultación de delito, negligencia culpable.
mispronounce [misprə'nauns], *v.t.* pronunciar mal *o* incorrectamente.
mispronunciation [misprənʌnsi'eiʃən], *s.* pronunciación incorrecta.
misquotation [miskwou'teiʃən], *s.* cita falsa *o* equivocada.
misquote [mis'kwout], *v.t.* citar mal *o* equivocadamente.
misrate [mis'reit], *v.t.* valuar mal.
misread [mis'ri:d], *v.t.* leer mal; interpretar mal.
misreckon [mis'rekən], *v.t.* calcular mal.
misreckoning [mis'rekəniŋ], *s.* cálculo erróneo.
misrelate [misri'leit], *v.t.* relacionar equivocadamente.
misreport [misri'pɔ:t], *v.t.* dar cuenta equivocada de; tergiversar, falsificar; citar inexactamente.
misrepresent [misrepri'zent], *v.t.* falsificar, tergiversar.
misrepresentation [misreprizen'teiʃən], *s.* falsificación, tergiversación.
misrule [mis'ru:l], *s.* desgobierno. — *v.t.* desgobernar.
Miss [mis]. Señorita.
miss (1) [mis], *s.* traviesa; coqueta.
miss (2) [mis], *s.* tiro errado; desacierto; malogro, fracaso; ***to give sth. a miss,*** omitir, suprimir, dejar algo. — *v.t.* errar, no acertar; perder; no encontrar; no entender, no cazar, no captar; echar de menos, echar en falta; ***he missed his footing,*** se le fue el pie; ***it just missed him,*** faltó poquísimo para que le diese; ***miss an opportunity,*** desaprovechar una ocasión; ***miss out,*** omitir; prescindir de; pasar por alto; ***you've missed the point,*** no has captado la idea; ***he misses nothing,*** ve crecer la hierba. — *v.i.* errar el blanco; fallar; (*aut.*) ratear; (*fam.*) ***miss by miles,*** marrar totalmente el golpe.
missal ['misəl], *s.* misal.
missel-thrush ['misəl-θrʌʃ], *s.* tordo.
misshape [mis'ʃeip], *v.t.* deformar.
misshapen [mis'ʃeipən], *a.* deforme, disforme, contrahecho.
missile ['misail], *s.* proyectil; misil; arma arrojadiza.
missing ['misiŋ], *a.* perdido; extraviado; (*mil.*) desaparecido; ausente; ***to be missing,*** faltar.
mission ['miʃən], *s.* misión.
missionary ['miʃənəri], *a.*, *s.* misionero.
missis ['misiz], *s.* (*fam.*) (***the*** —), (la) parienta.
Mississippi [misi'sipi]. Misisipí, *m.*
missive ['misiv], *a.* misivo. — *s.* misiva.
misspeak [mis'spi:k], *v.t.* pronunciar mal.
misspell [mis'spel], *v.t.* deletrear mal, escribir con mala ortografía.
misspelling [mis'speliŋ], *s.* ortografía incorrecta, error de ortografía.
misspend [mis'spend], *v.t.* malgastar.
misstate [mis'steit], *v.t.* exponer mal, expresar mal.
misstatement [mis'steitmənt], *s.* relación inexacta.
missus [MISSIS].
missy ['misi], *s.* (*festivo*) señorita.
mist [mist], *s.* neblina; ***Scotch mist,*** llovizna; ***sea-mist,*** bruma. — *v.t.* — ***over,*** empañar. — *v.i.* empañarse.
mistakable [mis'teikəbl], *a.* confundible.
mistake [mis'teik], *s.* equivocación; error; falta; ***by mistake,*** por equivocación; sin querer; ***and no mistake!*** de verdad, de remate; sin solución; con ganas; ***to make a mistake,*** cometer una falta, equivocarse. — *irr. v.t.* entender mal; confundir, equivocar; ***mistake for,*** tomar por, equivocar con; ***to be mistaken,*** equivocarse, engañarse.
mistaken [mis'teikən], *a.* incorrecto, erróneo, equivocado. — *p.p.* [MISTAKE].
mistakenly [mis'teikənli], *adv.* equivocadamente.
misteach [mis'ti:tʃ], *irr. v.t.* instruir mal, enseñar mal.
Mister ['mistə]. (*abrev.* **Mr.**) Señor.
misterm [mis'tə:m], *v.t.* dar un nombre equivocado a.
mistime [mis'taim], *v.t.* hacer a deshora; cronometrar mal.
mistimed [mis'taimd], *a.* inoportuno; mal calculado (*tiempo*).
mistiness ['mistinis], *s.* brumosidad; borrosidad.
mistletoe ['misəltou], *s.* (*bot.*) muérdago.
mistranslate [mistrɑ:ns'leit], *v.t.* traducir inexactamente, traducir mal.
mistranslation [mistrɑ:ns'leiʃən], *s.* traducción inexacta *o* infiel.
Mistress ['mistris]. (*abrev.* **Mrs.** ['misiz]) Señora.
mistress ['mistris], *s.* ama de casa; (*ant.*) dueña; (*escuela*) maestra, profesora; amante, querida; señora.
mistrial [mis'traiəl], *s.* (*for.*) causa *o* pleito viciado de nulidad, por error, empate *o* desacuerdo del jurado.
mistrust [mis'trʌst], *s.* recelo, desconfianza. — *v.t.* dudar de, recelar de, desconfiar de.
mistrustful [mis'trʌstful], *a.* desconfiado, receloso suspicaz.
mistrustfulness [mis'trʌstfulnis], *s.* desconfianza, suspicacia, recelo.
mistune [mis'tju:n], *v.t.* desafinar, desentonar.

mistutor [mis'tju:tə], *v.t.* instruir mal.
misty ['misti], *a.* nebuloso, brumoso; caliginoso; empañado; vago, vaporoso.
misunderstand [misʌndə'stænd], *v.t.* entender mal, comprender mal, trasoír.
misunderstanding [misʌndə'stændiŋ], *s.* equivocación, concepto erróneo; desavenencia; malentendido, mala inteligencia.
misuse [mis'ju:s], *s.* abuso, mal uso; maltratamiento. — [mis'ju:z], *v.t.* emplear mal; abusar de; maltratar.
mite (1) [mait], *s.* (*lit.*, *fig.*) ardite; (*peso*) óbolo, grano de arena; (*fig.*) pizca; (*infantil*) niñito.
mite (2) [mait], *s.* (*zool.*) ácaro.
mitigable ['mitigəbl], *a.* mitigable.
mitigant ['mitigənt], *a.* mitigante, lenitivo.
mitigate ['mitigeit], *v.t.* mitigar.
mitigation [miti'geiʃən], *s.* mitigación.
mitigatory ['mitigeitəri], *a.* mitigador, mitigativo; (*med.*) sedativo, lenitivo, calmante.
mitral ['maitrəl], *a.* mitral.
mitre (1) ['maitə], *s.* (*igl.*) mitra. — *v.t.* conferir mitra a.
mitre (2) ['maitə], *s.* (*carp.*) inglete. — *v.t.* ingletear.
mitred (1) ['maitəd], *a.* mitrado.
mitred (2) ['maitəd], *a.* (*carp.*) ingleteado.
mitt [mit], *s.* (*fam.*) mitón; guante de béisbol; (*fam.*) ***to give the frozen mitt to,*** recibir fríamente.
mitten [mitn], *s.* mitón.
mix [miks], *s.* mezcla; ***mix-up,*** confusión, lío, enredo. — *v.t.* mezclar; (*harina, argamasa etc.*) amasar; (*bebidas*) preparar; (*ensalada*) aderezar; confundir; ***to get (all) mixed up,*** confundirse, armarse un lío; ***to get mixed up in,*** meterse en, comprometerse en, complicarse en; ***mix up,*** confundir, trabucar. — *v.i.* mezclarse; asociarse (***with,*** con); frecuentar la compañía (***with,*** de); ***mix in (high) society,*** alternar en sociedad.
mixed [mikst], *a.* mixto; mezclado; (*galletas etc.*) variado, surtido; ***to have mixed feelings about,*** tener una postura ambivalente *o* poco resuelta ante; no estar muy seguro de.
mixer ['miksə], *s.* mezclador; (*pers.*) ***good mixer,*** persona sociable, persona que tiene (el) don de gentes.
mixture ['mikstʃə], *s.* mezcla.
miz(z)en ['mizən], *s.* (*mar.*) mesana; ***mizen-mast,*** palo de mesana; ***mizen-shrouds,*** jarcia de mesana.
mizzle [mizl], *s.* (*prov.*) mollizna. — *v.i.* (*prov.*) molliznar.
mnemonic(al) [ne'mɔnik(əl)], *a.* (m)nemotécnico.
mnemonics [ne'mɔniks], *s.pl.* (m)nemónica, (m)nemotecnia.
moan [moun], *s.* gemido, quejido; queja. — *v.i.* gemir; quejarse.
moanful ['mounful], *a.* quejumbroso.
moat [mout], *s.* foso. — *v.t.* rodear con foso.
mob [mɔb], *s.* muchedumbre; turba, populacho; pandilla; ***mob-rule,*** dominación de la turba. — *v.t.* atropellar, atacar en masa; festejar tumultuosamente.
mobile ['moubail], *a.* móvil.
mobility [mo'biliti], *s.* movilidad.
mobilization [moubilai'zeiʃən], *s.* movilización.
mobilize ['moubilaiz], *v.t.* movilizar. — *v.i.* movilizarse.
moccasin ['mɔkəsin], *s.* mocasín.
mock [mɔk], *a.* fingido, simulado; burlesco; ***mock battle,*** simulacro de batalla. — *s.* burla; ***to make mock of,*** burlarse de. — *v.t.* burlarse de, mofarse de; (*fig.*) defraudar. — *v.i.* burlarse, mofarse.
mocker ['mɔkə], *s.* burlador, mofador.
mockery ['mɔkəri], *s.* burla, mofa, befa.
mocking ['mɔkiŋ], *a.* burlón; (*orn.*) ***mocking-bird,*** sinsonte; (*orn.*) ***mocking-thrush,*** mirlo burlón. — *s.* burlas, *f.pl.*, befas, *f.pl.*, escarnio.
mockingly ['mɔkiŋli], *adv.* con mofa, con burla, irónicamente.
modal [moudl], *a.* modal.
modality [mo'dæliti], *s.* modalidad.
mode [moud], *s.* modo; manera; moda.
model [mɔdl], *a.* modelo; ***model prison,*** cárcel modelo. — *s.* modelo; (*norma*) patrón; (*arq.*) maqueta; (*pers.*) modelo, *m.f.*; maniquí; horma, molde. — *v.t.* modelar, moldear; trazar el diseño de. — *v.i.* servir de modelo.
modeller ['mɔdlə], *s.* modelador, diseñador, trazador.
modelling ['mɔdliŋ], *a.* modelador. — *s.* modelado.
moderate ['mɔdərit], *a.* moderado; mediano; (*precio*) módico. — *s.* moderado. — ['mɔdəreit], *v.t.* moderar, templar; (*igl.*) presidir (*reunión*). — *v.i.* moderarse; amainar; (*igl.*) presidir (*reunión*).
moderation [mɔdə'reiʃən], *s.* moderación; ***in moderation,*** con moderación.
moderator ['mɔdəreitə], *s.* moderador; árbitro; (*mec.*) regulador; concordador; presidente.
moderatorship ['mɔdəreitəʃip], *s.* funciones de moderador, *f.pl.*
moderatrix ['mɔdəreitriks], *s.* moderadora.
modern ['mɔdən], *a.*, *s.* moderno.
modernism ['mɔdənizəm], *s.* modernismo.
modernist ['mɔdənist], *s.* modernista, *m.f.*
modernize ['mɔdənaiz], *v.t.* modernizar. — *v.i.* modernizarse.
modernness ['mɔdənnis], *s.* novedad; (lo) moderno.
modest ['mɔdist], *a.* modesto; moderado; púdico.
modesty ['mɔdisti], *s.* modestia; moderación; pudor.
modicum ['mɔdikəm], *s.* mínimo, poquito.
modifiable ['mɔdifaiəbl], *a.* modificable.
modification [mɔdifi'keiʃən], *s.* modificación.
modifier ['mɔdifaiə], *s.* modificador.
modify ['mɔdifai], *v.t.* modificar. — *v.i.* modificarse.
modillion [mɔ'diljən], *s.* modillón, cartela.
modish ['moudiʃ], *a.* a la moda, de moda, en boga.
modishly ['moudiʃli], *adv.* a la moda, según la moda.
modishness ['moudiʃnis], *s.* afición a la moda; elegancia.
modular ['mɔdjulə], *a.* modular.
modulate ['mɔdjuleit], *v.t.* modular.
modulation [mɔdju'leiʃən], *s.* (*mús.*) modulación; (*arq.*) módulo.
module ['mɔdju:l], *s.* módulo.
modulus ['mɔdjuləs], *s.* módulo.
modus ['moudəs], *s.* modo.
mofette [mou'fet], *s.* mofeta.
mogul ['mougʌl], *s.* mogol; (*fig.*) magnate.
mohair ['mouhɛə], *s.* moer.
Mohammed [mo'hæmid]. Mahoma, *m.*
Mohammedan [mo'hæmidən], *a.*, *s.* mahometano.
Mohammedanism [mo'hæmidənizəm], *s.* mahometismo.
Mohawk ['mouhɔ:k], *a.*, *s.* mohock.
moiety ['mɔiiti], *s.* mitad; parte (pequeña), elemento (pequeño), mínimo.
moire, moiré [mwɑ:, 'mwɑ:rei], *s.* moaré, muaré.
moist [mɔist], *a.* húmedo; jugoso.
moisten ['mɔisən], *v.t.* humedecer, mojar levemente.
moistener ['mɔisənə], *s.* humedecedor.
moisture, moistness ['mɔistʃə, 'mɔistnis], *s.* humedad; jugosidad.
moke [mouk], *s.* burro.
molar ['moulə], *a.* molar. — *s.* (diente) molar, muela.
molasses [mo'læsiz], *s.* melaza; (*Am.*) [TREACLE].
Moldavian [mɔl'deiviən], *a.*, *s.* moldavo.

mole (1) [moul], *s.* (*zool.*) topo; (*ent.*) ***mole-cricket,*** topogrillo, grillotalpa; (*fam.*) ***mole-eyed,*** cegato.
mole (2) [moul], *s.* (*anat.*) lunar.
mole (3) [moul], *s.* (*mar.*) muelle; espolón, malecón.
molecular [mo'lekjulə], *a.* molecular.
molecule ['mɔlikju:l], *s.* molécula.
molehill ['moulhil], *s.* topera; ***to make a mountain out of a molehill,*** hacer una montaña de un grano de arena, sacar las cosas de quicio.
moleskin ['moulskin], *s.* piel de topo.
molest [mo'lest], *v.t.* importunar, fastidiar; meterse con.
molestation [moules'teiʃən], *s.* importunidad, vejación; (el) meterse (con alguien).
moll [mɔl], *s.* (*fam.*) amiga, querindanga, querindola.
mollient ['mɔliənt], *a.* emoliente, molitivo.
mollifier ['mɔlifaiə], *s.* emoliente; mitigador; (*fig.*) pacificador.
mollify ['mɔlifai], *v.t.* molificar; calmar, mitigar, suavizar.
mollusc ['mɔlʌsk], *s.* molusco.
mollycoddle ['mɔlikɔdl], *s.* (*fam.*) alfeñique, niño mimado. — *v.t.* mimar.
molten ['moultən], *a.* fundido; líquido. — *p.p.* [MELT].
molybdate [mə'libdeit], *s.* (*quím.*) molibdato.
molybdenum [mə'libdənəm], *s.* molibdeno.
moment ['moumənt], *s.* momento; instante; importancia, trascendencia; (***at***) ***any moment*** (***now***), de un momento a otro; ***at*** o ***for the moment,*** de momento, por ahora; ***in a moment,*** en un momento; (*futuro*) dentro de un momento.
momentarily ['mouməntərili], *adv.* momentáneamente.
momentary ['mouməntəri], *a.* momentáneo.
momentous [mo'mentəs], *a.* importantísimo, trascendental.
momentously [mo'mentəsli], *adv.* de (una) manera trascendental.
momentousness [mo'mentəsnis], *s.* gravedad, importancia, trascendencia.
momentum [mo'mentəm], *s.* momento; ímpetu; ***to gather momentum,*** cobrar impulso; acelerarse.
monachal ['mɔnəkəl], *a.* monacal, monástico.
monachism ['mɔnəkizəm], *s.* monaquismo, monacato.
Monaco ['mɔnəkou]. Mónaco.
monad ['mɔnæd], *s.* mónada.
monadic(al) [mɔ'nædik(əl)], *a.* de mónada.
monarch ['mɔnək], *s.* monarca, *m.*
monarchal, monarchic(al) [mɔ'nɑ:kəl, mɔ'nɑ:kik(əl)], *a.* monárquico.
monarchically [mɔ'nɑ:kikli], *adv.* monárquicamente.
monarchism ['mɔnəkizəm], *s.* monarquismo.
monarchist ['mɔnəkist], *s.* monárquico.
monarchy ['mɔnəki], *s.* monarquía.
monastery ['mɔnəstəri], *s.* monasterio.
monastic(al) [mə'næstik(əl)], *a.* monástico; monasterial; monacal.
monastically [mə'næstikli], *adv.* monásticamente.
monasticism [mə'næstisizəm], *s.* monasticidad.
Monday ['mʌndi], *s.* lunes.
Monegasque [mɔnə'gæsk], *a.*, *s.* monegasco.
monetary ['mʌnitəri], *a.* monetario, pecuniario.
monetization [mʌnitai'zeiʃən], *s.* monetización.
monetize ['mʌnitaiz], *v.t.* monetizar.
money ['mʌni], *s.* dinero; plata; moneda; ***bad money,*** moneda falsa; ***even money,*** cuenta redonda; ***money-bag,*** bolso, talega; (*fig., sing.*) ***money-bags,*** ricachón; ***money-box,*** hucha; caja; ***money-broker,*** corredor de cambios; ***money-changer,*** cambista, *m.f.*; ***money-changing,*** cambio de divisas; ***money-grubbing,*** tacaño, roñoso; tacañería; ***money-lender,*** prestamista, *m.f.*; ***money-market,*** lonja, bolsa, mercado monetario; ***money-order,*** giro postal, libranza postal; ***paper money,*** papel moneda; ***ready money,*** dinero contante; ***to make money,*** ganar dinero; ***to be made of money, to be rolling in money, to have pots of money,*** tener dinero a espuertas; (*com.*) ***to put out money,*** poner dinero a interés.
moneyed ['mʌnid], *a.* adinerado.
moneyer ['mʌniə], *s.* monedero.
moneywort ['mʌniwə:t], *s.* (*bot.*) lisimaquia, mimularia.
monger ['mʌŋgə], *s.* comerciante, tratante; propalador de. . . .
Mongolia [mɔŋ'gouliə]. Mongolia.
Mongolian [mɔŋ'gouliən], *a.*, *s.* mongol, *m.*
mongoose ['mɔŋgu:s], *s.* (*pl.* **mongooses** [-iz]) mangosta.
mongrel ['mʌŋgrəl], *a.* mestizo, cruzado. — *s.* perro callejero.
monism ['mɔnizəm], *s.* monismo.
monition [mo'niʃən], *s.* amonestación.
monitive ['mɔnitiv], *a.* monitorio.
monitor ['mɔnitə], *s.* (*escuelas*) monitor; (*rad.*) radiorreceptor de contrastación; escucha. — *v.t.* vigilar; regular; contrastar; (*rad.*) radiocaptar.
monitorial [mɔni'tɔ:riəl], *a.* monitorio.
monitory ['mɔnitəri], *a.* monitorio, instructivo. — *s.* amonestación.
monitress ['mɔnitris], *s.* admonitora.
monk [mʌŋk], *s.* monje; fraile; (*bot.*) ***monk's hood,*** acónito, acónito napelo.
monkery ['mʌŋkəri], *s.* monasterio; vida monástica.
monkey ['mʌŋki], *s.* mono; mico; diablillo; (*mec.*) maza; ***monkey business,*** trampas, *f.pl.*; tapujos, *m.pl.*; ***monkey-nut,*** cacahuete; (*bot.*) ***monkey-puzzle,*** arancaria; (*fam.*) ***monkey-suit,*** smoking, esmoquin; ***monkey-tricks,*** travesuras, *f.pl.*; ***monkey-wrench,*** llave inglesa; ***to make a monkey of,*** tomar el pelo a; ***to play the monkey,*** hacer monerías. — *v.i.* — ***about,*** hacer payasadas.
monkish ['mʌŋkiʃ], *a.* frailuno, de monje.
monochord ['mɔnokɔ:d], *a.* monocorde. — *s.* monocordio.
monochromatic [mɔnokro'mætik], *a.* monocromático.
monochrome ['mɔnokroum], *a.*, *s.* monocromo.
monocle ['mɔnəkl], *s.* monóculo.
monocotyledon [mɔnokɔti'li:dən], *s.* monocotiledón.
monocotyledonous [mɔnokɔti'li:dənəs], *a.* monocotiledóneo.
monocular, monoculous [mɔ'nɔkjulə, -ləs], *a.* monóculo.
monody ['mɔnədi], *s.* monodia.
monogamist [mɔ'nɔgəmist], *s.* monógamo.
monogamous [mɔ'nɔgəməs], *a.* monógamo.
monogamy [mɔ'nɔgəmi], *s.* monogamia.
monogram ['mɔnəgræm], *s.* monograma, *m.*
monograph ['mɔnəgrɑ:f], *s.* monografía.
monographic(al) [mɔnə'græfik(əl)], *a.* monográfico.
monography [mɔ'nɔgrəfi], *s.* monografía.
monolith ['mɔnoliθ], *s.* monolito.
monolithic [mɔno'liθik], *a.* monolítico.
monologist [mɔ'nɔlədʒist], *s.* monologista, *m.f.*
monologue ['mɔnəlɔg], *s.* monólogo.
monomane ['mɔnomein], *s.* monómano.
monomania [mɔno'meiniə], *s.* monomanía.
monomaniac [mɔno'meiniæk], *a.* monomaníaco, monomaniático. — *s.* monómano.
monopetalous [mɔno'petələs], *a.* monopétalo.
monoplane ['mɔnoplein], *s.* monoplano.

monopolist [mɔ'nɔpəlist], *s.* monopolista, *m.f.*
monopolization [mɔnɔpəlai'zeiʃən], *s.* monopolización; acaparamiento.
monopolize [mɔ'nɔpəlaiz], *v.t.* monopolizar; acaparar.
monopolizer [mɔ'nɔpəlaizə], *s.* acaparador.
monopoly [mɔ'nɔpəli], *s.* monopolio; ***state monopoly,*** monopolio estatal.
monorail ['mɔnoreil], *s.* monocarril.
monosyllabic [mɔnosi'læbik], *a.* monosilábico.
monosyllable ['mɔnosiləbl], *s.* monosílabo.
monotheism ['mɔnoθiizm], *s.* monoteísmo.
monotheist ['mɔnoθiist], *s.* monoteísta, *m.f.*
monotheistic [mɔnoθi'istik], *a.* monoteístico, monoteísta.
monotone ['mɔnotoun], *s.* monotonía.
monotonous [mə'nɔtənəs], *a.* monótono.
monotonously [mə'nɔtənəsli], *adv.* de un modo monótono.
monotony [mə'nɔtəni], *s.* monotonía; solo tono.
Monotype ['mɔnotaip], *s.* (*impr., marca registrada*) monotipia.
monoxide [mɔn'ɔksaid], *s.* monóxido.
monsoon [mɔn'su:n], *s.* monzón, *m.*
monster ['mɔnstə], *a.* monstruoso; enorme. — *s.* monstruo.
monstrance ['mɔnstrəns], *s.* (*igl.*) custodia.
monstrosity [mɔns'trɔsiti], *s.* monstruosidad.
monstrous ['mɔnstrəs], *a.* monstruoso.
monstrousness ['mɔnstrəsnis], *s.* monstruosidad, enormidad.
Montenegro [mɔnti'ni:grou]. Montenegro.
Montevideo [mɔntivi'deiou]. Montevideo.
month [mʌnθ], *s.* mes; ***he won't do it in a month of Sundays,*** no lo conseguirá aunque le den un siglo para hacerlo.
monthly ['mʌnθli], *a.* mensual. — *adv.* mensualmente. — *s.* publicación mensual.
monticle ['mɔntikl], *s.* montecillo, montículo.
Montreal [mɔntri'ɔ:l]. Montreal.
monument ['mɔnjumənt], *s.* monumento.
monumental [mɔnju'mentəl], *a.* monumental; notable; (*fam.*) garrafal.
moo [mu:], *s.* mugido. — *v.i.* mugir, hacer mu.
mooch [mu:tʃ], *v.i.* — ***about,*** andar perdido, dar valsones; ***mooch along,*** andar arrastrando los pies.
mood (1) [mu:d], *s.* estado anímico; ***to be in a good*** (***bad***) ***mood,*** estar de buen (mal) humor; ***to be in the mood*** (***for***)***,*** estar (de vena) (para).
mood (2) [mu:d], *s.* (*gram.*) modo.
moodily ['mu:dili], *adv.* caprichosamente; con mal humor.
moodiness ['mu:dinis], *s.* mal humor; melancolía; caprichosidad.
moody ['mu:di], *a.* de mal humor; tristón, melancólico; caprichoso, versátil.
moon [mu:n], *s.* luna; (*poét.*) mes, *m.*; ***once in a blue moon,*** de higos a brevas. — *v.i.* — ***about,*** mirar a las musarañas; andar distraído.
moonbeam ['mu:nbi:m], *s.* rayo de luna.
moon-calf ['mu:n-kɑ:f], *s.* bobo, tonto.
moon-daisy ['mu:n-deizi], *s.* (*bot.*) margarita mayor, crisantemo, floriblanco.
moon-eyed ['mu:n-aid], *a.* de ojos lunáticos.
moon-fern ['mu:n-fə:n], *s.* (*bot.*) botriquio, helecho común.
moonflower ['mu:nflauə], *s.* (*bot.*) ipomea nocturna.
moonish ['mu:niʃ], *a.* lunático.
moonless ['mu:nlis], *a.* sin luna, sin claridad de luna.
moonlight ['mu:nlait], *s.* claro de luna, luz de la luna; ***moonlight flit,*** mudanza a la chita callando.
moonlit ['mu:nlit], *a.* iluminado por la luna; de luna.
moonseed ['mu:nsi:d], *s.* cualquier planta del género *Menispermo.*
moonshine ['mu:nʃain], *s.* claridad de la luna; (*fig.*) pamplinas, *f.pl.*; sandeces, *f.pl.*; música celestial; (*Am.*) licor destilado clandestinamente.
moonshiner ['mu:nʃainə], *s.* (*Am.*) fabricante de licor ilegal.
moonstone ['mu:nstoun], *s.* adularia.
moonstruck ['mu:nstrʌk], *a.* lunático.
moonwort ['mu:nwə:t], *s.* lunaria.
moony ['mu:ni], *a.* tristón, melancólico; absorto, alelado.
Moor [muə], *s.* moro.
moor (1) [muə], *s.* páramo, brezal; (*orn.*) ***moor-buzzard,*** circo.
moor (2) [muə], *v.t.* (*mar.*) amarrar. — *v.i.* (*mar.*) echar las amarras.
moorcock ['muəkɔk], *s.* (*orn.*) macho de la cerceta; lagópedo de Escocia.
moorhen ['muəhen], *s.* cerceta.
mooring ['muəriŋ], *s.* (*mar.*) amarra; ***mooring-ground,*** amarradero.
Moorish ['muəriʃ], *a.* moro, morisco, moruno.
moorland ['muələnd], *s.* paramera, brezal.
moose [mu:s], *s.* (*zool.*) alce, anta.
moot [mu:t], *a.* discutible. — *s.* asamblea, reunión. — *v.t.* proponer (para ser discutido).
mop [mɔp], *s.* fregasuelos, *m.inv.*, trapo del suelo; mata, greña (de pelo). — *v.t.* fregar *o* limpiar con trapo; ***mop up,*** limpiar (secando); (*fam.*) beberse, zamparse; (*fam.*) acabar con; (*mil.*) ***mopping-up operations,*** operaciones de limpieza, *f.pl.*
mope [moup], *s.* (*ú. más en pl.* **mopes**) murrias, *f.pl.*, depresión; (*fam.*) ***to have the mopes,*** andar *o* estar triste, tristón *o* deprimido. — *v.i.* estar triste, tristón, deprimido *o* abatido.
mopish ['moupiʃ], *a.* triste, tristón, deprimido, alicaído, melancólico.
mopishness ['moupiʃnis], *s.* abatimiento, melancolía.
moquette [mɔ'ket], *s.* moqueta.
moraine [mɔ'rein], *s.* (*geol.*) morena.
moral ['mɔrəl], *a.* moral, ético; virtuoso, honesto; ***moral victory,*** victoria moral. — *s.* moraleja; (*pl.*) moral, *f.*; moralidad; costumbres, *f.pl.*
morale [mɔ'rɑ:l], *s.* moral, *f.*
moralist ['mɔrəlist], *s.* moralista, *m.f.*
morality [mɔ'ræliti], *s.* moralidad, moral, *f.*
moralization [mɔrəlai'zeiʃən], *s.* moralización.
moralize ['mɔrəlaiz], *v.t., v.i.* moralizar.
moralizer ['mɔrəlaizə], *s.* moralizador.
moralizing ['mɔrəlaiziŋ], *a.* moralizador. — *s.* (el) moralizar, moralización.
morally ['mɔrəli], *adv.* moralmente; (*fam.*) prácticamente, casi.
morass [mə'ræs], *s.* cenagal, lodazal.
moratorium [mɔrə'tɔ:riəm], *s.* moratoria.
Moravian [mɔ'reiviən], *a., s.* moravo.
morbid ['mɔ:bid], *a.* morboso, malsano.
morbidity, morbidness [mɔ:'biditi, 'mɔ:bidnis], *s.* morbosidad, (lo) malsano.
mordacious [mɔ:'deiʃəs], *a.* mordaz.
mordacity [mɔ:'dæsiti], *s.* mordacidad.
mordant ['mɔ:dənt], *a.* mordaz.
mordent ['mɔ:dənt], *s.* (*mús.*) mordente.
more [mɔ:], *a.* más; ***more haste, less speed,*** cuanto más se corre, menos se anda. — *adv.* más; ***more and more,*** cada vez más; ***more or less,*** más o menos; ***the more the merrier,*** cuantos más, mejor; ***the more one has, the more one wants,*** cuanto más se tiene, más se quiere; ***neither more nor less,*** ni más ni menos; ***to be no more,*** no existir ya, haber dejado de existir; ***once more,*** una vez más; ***so much the more,*** tanto más.
morel [mɔ'rel], *s.* crespilla, colmenilla múrgura; hierba mora, solano.

moreover [mɔːr'ouvə], *adv.* además, por otra parte.
mores [mou'riːz], *s.pl.* costumbres, *f.pl.*
Moresque [mɔ'resk], *a.* morisco.
morganatic [mɔːgə'nætik], *a.* morganático.
morgue [mɔːg], *s.* (*Am.*) depósito de cadáveres.
moribund ['mɔribʌnd], *a.* moribundo.
morion ['mɔriən], *s.* morrión.
morisco [mɔ'riskou], *a.* morisco. — *s.* morisco; danza morisca; arabesco.
morling ['mɔːliŋ], *s.* lana muerta.
Mormon ['mɔːmən], *a.* mormónico. — *s.* mormón.
Mormonism ['mɔːmənizəm], *s.* mormonismo.
morn [mɔːn], *s.* (*poét.*) mañana, aurora, alborada.
morning ['mɔːniŋ], *a.* de mañana, matutino, matinal; ***morning coat,*** chaqué; ***morning gown,*** salto de cama; ***morning star,*** lucero del alba. — *s.* mañana; ***early in the morning,*** muy de mañana, por la mañana temprano; ***first thing tomorrow morning,*** mañana a primera hora; ***good morning,*** buenos días; ***tomorrow morning,*** mañana por la mañana.
Moroccan [mə'rɔkən], *a., s.* marroquí.
Morocco [mə'rɔkou]. Marruecos, *m.*
morocco [mo'rɔkou], *s.* (*cuero*) marroquí, tafilete.
morose [mə'rous], *a.* malhumorado, hosco, mohino, sombrío.
moroseness [mə'rousnis], *s.* mal humor, hosquedad.
Morpheus ['mɔːfiəs]. Morfeo.
morphia, morphine ['mɔːfiə, -fiːn], *s.* morfina.
morphinism ['mɔːfinizəm], *s.* morfinismo.
morphinomania [mɔːfiːnou'meiniə], *s.* morfinomanía.
morphological [mɔːfə'lɔdʒikəl], *a.* morfológico.
morphology [mɔː'fɔlədʒi], *s.* morfología.
morphosis [mɔː'fousis], *s.* morfosis, *f.inv.*
morris ['mɔris], *s.* danza morisca, mojiganga.
morrow ['mɔrou], *s.* (*poét.*) mañana; día siguiente; ***on the morrow,*** al día siguiente.
Morse [mɔːs], *s.* ***Morse code,*** alfabeto Morse.
morsel [mɔːsl], *s.* pedacito; bocado.
mort [mɔːt], *s.* muerte, *f.*
mortal [mɔːtl], *a., s.* mortal.
mortality [mɔː'tæliti], *s.* mortalidad.
mortally ['mɔːtəli], *adv.* mortalmente, a muerte; (*fam.*) extremadamente.
mortar ['mɔːtə], (*mil.*) *s.* mortero; argamasa; almirez; ***mortar-board,*** esparavel; tocado profesorial; (*mil.*) ***mortar-bomb,*** proyectil de mortero.
mortgage ['mɔːgidʒ], *s.* hipoteca. — *v.t.* hipotecar.
mortgageable ['mɔːgidʒəbl], *a.* hipotecable.
mortgagee [mɔːgə'dʒiː], *s.* acreedor hipotecario.
mortgager ['mɔːgidʒə], *s.* deudor hipotecario.
mortician [mɔː'tiʃən], (*Am.*) [UNDERTAKER].
mortiferous [mɔː'tifərəs], *a.* mortífero, mortal.
mortification [mɔːtifi'keiʃən], *s.* mortificación; humillación; ***mortification of the flesh,*** mortificación de la carne.
mortify ['mɔːtifai], *v.t.* mortificar; (*fig.*) humillar, abochornar. — *v.i.* mortificarse, gangrenarse.
mortifying ['mɔːtifaiiŋ], *a.* mortificante; humillante.
mortise ['mɔːtis], *s.* mortaja, muesca. — *v.t.* hacer una mortaja en.
mortmain ['mɔːtmein], *s.* (*der.*) manos muertas, *f.pl.*
mortuary ['mɔːtjuəri], *a.* mortuorio. — *s.* depósito de cadáveres.
mosaic [mo'zeiik], *s.* mosaico.
mosaic(al) [mo'zeiik(əl)], *a.* mosaico.
Moscow ['mɔskou]. Moscú.
Moselle [mou'zel]. Mosela, *m.*
Moses ['mouziz]. Moisés, *m.*
Moslem ['mʌzləm], *a., s.* musulmán.
mosque [mɔsk], *s.* mezquita.
mosquito [mɔs'kiːtou], *s.* mosquito; ***mosquito net,*** mosquitero.
moss [mɔs], *s.* musgo; pantano; ***moss-grown,*** musgoso; ***moss-rose,*** rosa musgosa; ***moss-trooper,*** bandido, bandolero.
mossiness ['mɔsinis], *s.* (lo) musgoso.
mossy ['mɔsi], *a.* musgoso.
most [moust], *a.* la mayor parte de, la mayoría de; ***for the most part,*** en su mayor parte; ***most people,*** la mayor parte de las personas. — *adv.* sumamente; en extremo, en sumo grado; ***most of all,*** sobre todo, máxime. — *s.* el mayor número, la mayor parte, los más; ***at (the) most,*** a lo sumo, cuando más; ***to make the most of,*** sacar el mejor partido posible de.
mostly ['moustli], *adv.* principalmente; en su mayor parte.
mote [mout], *s.* mota.
motet [mou'tet], *s.* motete.
moth [mɔθ], *s.* polilla; mariposa (nocturna); ***moth-eaten,*** apolillado; (*fig.*) carcomido, maltrecho.
moth-ball ['mɔθ-bɔːl], *s.* bola de naftalina; (*fig.*) ***moth-ball fleet,*** flota de reserva; ***to put into moth-balls,*** retirar del servicio activo.
mother ['mʌðə], *a.* (de) madre, materno; maternal; ***Mother Church,*** (la) santa madre iglesia; iglesia metropolitana; ***mother country,*** (madre) patria; ***mother love,*** amor materno; ***mother tongue,*** lengua materna; ***mother wit,*** ingenio, inteligencia. — *s.* madre; ***mother-in-law,*** suegra, madre política; ***mother of pearl,*** nacarino; nácar, madreperla. — *v.t.* servir de madre a; ahijar; mimar.
motherhood ['mʌðəhud], *s.* maternidad.
motherland ['mʌðəlænd], *s.* (madre) patria.
motherless ['mʌðəlis], *a.* sin madre, huérfano de madre.
motherliness ['mʌðəlinis], *s.* cariño maternal, (lo) maternal.
motherly ['mʌðəli], *a.* maternal.
motherwort ['mʌðəwəːt], *s.* (*bot.*) agripalma.
mothy ['mɔθi], *a.* apolillado.
motif [mou'tiːf], *s.* motivo; tema, *m.*
motion ['mouʃən], *s.* movimiento; (*mec.*) marcha, operación; mecanismo, juego; (*pol.*) moción; ademán; señal; (*med.*) evacuación; (*for.*) pedimento; ***motion picture,*** película cinematográfica; ***to carry a motion,*** (hacer) adoptar una moción; ***to propose a motion,*** presentar una moción; ***to set in motion,*** poner en marcha; ***(in) slow motion,*** (a) cámara lenta; ***he goes through the motions of suffering grief,*** hace ver que está muy condolido. — *v.i.* hacer señas.
motionless ['mouʃənlis], *a.* inmóvil.
motivate ['moutiveit], *v.t.* motivar.
motivation [mouti'veiʃən], *s.* motivación.
motive ['moutiv], *a.* motor, motriz; ***motive power,*** fuerza motriz. — *s.* motivo; móvil.
motley ['mɔtli], *a.* abigarrado, multicolor, vestido de colorines; variado, mezclado; ***motley crew,*** grupo (de gente) muy dispar. — *s.* traje abigarrado; mezcla de colores; payaso, gracioso con traje de colores.
motor ['moutə], *a.* motor, motriz; ***motor-boat,*** motora; ***motor-car,*** coche automóvil; ***motor-cycle,*** motocicleta. — *s.* motor; (*fam.*) automóvil. — *v.i.* ir *o* viajar en automóvil.
motorcade ['moutəkeid], *s.* desfile de coches.
motoring ['moutəriŋ], *s.* automovilismo.
motorist ['moutərist], *s.* automovilista, *m.f.*
motorman ['moutəmæn], *s.* conductor de tren *o* tranvía eléctrico.
motorway ['moutəwei], *s.* autopista.
Motswana [mɔt'swɑːnə], *s.* (*sing.*) botswanés, *m.*
mottle [mɔtl], *s.* mancha. — *v.t.* jaspear, motear; abigarrar.
mottled [mɔtld], *a.* jaspeado, moteado; abigarrado,

pintarrajado, pintojo; ***mottled soap,*** jabón de Marsella.

motto [ˈmɔtou], *s.* divisa; lema, *m.*

moufflon [ˈmu:flɔn], *s.* musmón.

mould (1) [mould], *s.* moho; mantillo. — *v.i.* enmohecerse.

mould (2) [mould], *s.* matriz, molde; modelo, patrón; (*mar.*) grúa de tablas; (*arq.*) moldura. — *v.t.* amoldar; moldear; modelar; moldurar; galibar; vaciar. — *v.i.* tomar hechura *o* forma.

mouldable [ˈmouldəbl], *a.* amoldable; moldeable.

moulder (1) [ˈmouldə], *s.* moldeador; vaciador.

moulder (2) [ˈmouldə], *v.t.* desmoronar, consumir; reducir a polvo. — *v.i.* desmoronarse, consumirse; reducirse a polvo.

mouldering [ˈmouldəriŋ], *a.* que (se) reduce a polvo; que (se) consume.

mouldiness [ˈmouldinis], *s.* moho, enmohecimiento.

moulding [ˈmouldiŋ], *s.* (*arq.*) moldura, lengüeta; amoldamiento; vaciamiento.

mouldy [ˈmouldi], *a.* mohoso, enmohecido.

moulinet [mu:liˈnet], *s.* molinete.

moult [moult], *s.* (*zool.*) muda. — *v.i.* mudar (*el pelo, la pluma etc.*).

moulting [ˈmoultiŋ], *s.* muda (*de pluma*).

mound [maund], *s.* montículo; terrero; terraplén; (*blas.*) mundo, esfera. — *v.t.* amontonar; terraplenar.

mount [maunt], *s.* (*top.*) monte; (*equit.*) cabalgadura, montura; (*joy.*) engaste; base, soporte. — *v.t.* montar; subir; subir a *o* en; proveer de caballo(s); engastar; ***to mount guard,*** montar guardia; ***to mount the throne,*** subir al trono *o* solio. — *v.i.* montar; montarse; ascender; aumentar.

mountain [ˈmauntin], *a.* de montaña, serrano, montañés. — *s.* montaña; monte; (*pl.*) (la) sierra; (*bot.*) ***mountain ash,*** serbal; ***mountain chain,*** cordillera; ***mountain climber,*** montañero, alpinista, *m.f.*; ***mountain climbing,*** montañismo, alpinismo; (*zool.*) ***mountain lion,*** puma; ***mountain-railway,*** ferrocarril funicular; ***mountain range,*** sierra; ***mountain sickness,*** mal de las montañas; (*Hisp. Am.*) soroche; ***mountainside,*** falda *o* ladera (de montaña); ***seas mountains high,*** olas como montañas; ***to make a mountain out of a molehill,*** hacer una montaña de un grano de arena, sacar las cosas de quicio.

mountaineer [mauntiˈniə], *s.* montañero, alpinista, *m.f.* — *v.i.* dedicarse *o* ser aficionado al alpinismo.

mountaineering [mauntiˈniəriŋ], *s.* montañismo, alpinismo.

mountainous [ˈmauntinəs], *a.* montañoso; (*fig.*) enorme.

mountainousness [ˈmauntinəsnis], *s.* (lo) montañoso.

mountebank [ˈmauntibæŋk], *s.* saltimbanqui; charlatán.

mounting [ˈmauntiŋ], *a.* creciente. — *s.* montadura; montaje; engaste; soporte.

mourn [mɔ:n], *v.t.* llorar, lamentar; llevar luto por. — *v.i.* lamentarse, dolerse; estar de luto.

mourner [ˈmɔ:nə], *s.* enlutado; doliente; plañidera.

mournful [ˈmɔ:nful], *a.* lúgubre, triste; lastimero.

mournfulness [ˈmɔ:nfulnis], *s.* (lo) lúgubre; (lo) lastimero.

mourning [ˈmɔ:niŋ], *s.* luto; duelo; lamentación; ***to be in mourning,*** estar de luto; ***to be in mourning for,*** llevar luto por; ***to come out of mourning,*** dejar el luto; ***deep mourning,*** luto riguroso; ***to go into mourning,*** tomar el luto; ***half mourning,*** medio luto.

mouse [maus], *s.* (*pl.* **mice** [mais]) ratón; (*mar.*) barrilete; ***mouse-coloured,*** pardusco; (*bot.*) ***mouse-ear,*** velosillo, pelosilla; ***mouse-hole,*** agujero de ratón; (*bot.*) ***mouse-tail,*** miosuro; ***mouse-trap,*** ratonera. — *v.i.* cazar ratones.

mouser [ˈmausə], *s.* cazador de ratones.

mousing [ˈmausiŋ], *s.* caza de ratones.

moustache [məsˈtɑ:ʃ], *s.* bigote, mostacho.

mouth [mauθ], *s.* boca; (des)embocadura; boquilla; ***down in the mouth,*** alicaído, deprimido; ***to keep one's mouth shut,*** callar(se); ***it makes one's mouth water,*** se le hace a uno la boca agua; ***mouth-organ,*** armónica; ***mouth-piece,*** boquilla; (*tele.*) micrófono; (*fig.*) portavoz; ***not to open one's mouth,*** no decir esta boca es mía; ***to shut s.o.'s mouth,*** (hacer) callar a alguien. — [mauð], *v.t.* proferir (*insultos*). — *v.i.* hablar con voz hueca.

mouthful [ˈmauθful], *s.* bocado.

mouthing [ˈmauðiŋ], *s.* pronunciación afectada.

mouthless [ˈmauθlis], *a.* desbocado.

movable [ˈmu:vəbl], *a.* movible. — *s.* (*pl.*) bienes muebles, *m.pl.*

movableness [ˈmu:vəblnis], *s.* movilidad.

move [mu:v], *s.* movimiento; paso, acción; maniobra; jugada; ***get a move on!*** ¡date prisa! ¡espabílate!; ***make a move,*** dar un paso; hacer una jugada; ***on the move,*** en movimiento; en marcha; de viaje; ***whose move is it?*** ¿a quién le toca (mover)?; ***to miss one's move,*** perder una jugada. — *v.t.* mover; trasladar, mudar; inducir, persuadir; menear; (*sentimientos*) conmover, enternecer; excitar, incitar; proponer; hacer mover, exonerar (*el vientre*); ***to be moved,*** conmoverse; ***move away,*** apartar, quitar; ***move a motion,*** proponer una moción; ***move on,*** hacer circular; adelantar; ***move to laughter,*** mover a risa; ***move up,*** ascender, subir. — *v.i.* moverse; mudarse, trasladarse; andar, marchar, funcionar; menearse; hacer una jugada; exonerarse (*el vientre*); ***move about*** o ***around,*** cambiar de sitio, ir y venir; ***move along,*** circular; ***move away,*** alejarse, retirarse, apartarse; ***move down,*** bajar, descender; ***move forward,*** avanzar, adelantarse; ***move in,*** instalarse (en), entrar (en); ***move out,*** salir; marcharse; mudarse (de casa); ***move off,*** alejarse; ***move round,*** dar vueltas, girar; ***move that,*** proponer que; ***move up,*** subir, ascender.

movement [ˈmu:vmənt], *s.* movimiento; (*com.*) actividad; circulación (*de dinero*); (*mús.*) tiempo; (*mec.*) mecanismo; (*med.*) defecación.

mover [ˈmu:və], *s.* movedor; móvil; autor; (*Am.*) [REMOVER]; ***prime mover,*** promotor, primer motor; máquina motriz.

movie [ˈmu:vi], *s.* película.

moving [ˈmu:viŋ], *a.* motor, motriz; movedor; movedizo; conmovedor, patético; emocionante; ***moving staircase,*** escalera mecánica. — *s.* (el) mover(se); (el) mudar de casa, mudanza(s).

mow [mou], *irr. v.t.* segar; ***mow down,*** derribar, barrer.

mower [mouə], *s.* segador; segadora mecánica.

mowing [ˈmouiŋ], *s.* siega; ***mowing machine,*** segadora mecánica.

Mozarab [mɔˈzærəb], *s.* mozárabe.

Mozarabic [mɔˈzærəbik], *a.* mozárabe.

much [mʌtʃ], *a.* mucho; ***much ado about nothing,*** mucho ruido y pocas nueces. — *adv.* mucho; muy; grandemente; con mucho; ***as much again,*** otro tanto; ***as*** o ***so much as,*** tanto como; ***as much more,*** otro tanto; ***how much?*** ¿cuánto?; ***however much,*** por mucho que; ***so much,*** tanto; ***so much the better,*** tanto mejor; ***too much*** o ***over much,*** demasiado; ***I thought as much,*** ya me lo figuraba; ***much as I should like,*** por más que yo quisiera; ***much obliged,*** muy *o* sumamente agradecido, agradecidísimo; ***much the same,*** más o menos lo mismo; ***not so much as*** (*a*), ni siquiera. — *s.* mucho; ***not much of a job,*** un empleíllo (de mala muerte); ***to make much of,*** dar (mucha) importancia a; ***(not) to think much of,*** estimar en mucho (en poco).

muchness [ˈmʌtʃnis], *s.* (*fam.*) ***much of a muchness,*** lo mismo poco más o menos, por el estilo;

they're much of a muchness, por ahí se andan, son por el estilo.
mucilage [ˈmjuːsilidʒ], *s.* mucílago.
mucilaginous [mjuːsiˈlædʒinəs], *a.* mucilaginoso.
muck [mʌk], *s.* estiércol; (*fig.*) mierda, porquería; ***muck-heap, muck-hill,*** estercolero, muladar; (*fam.*) ***muck-up,*** lío, follón. — *v.t.* estercolar, abonar; (*fam.*) ***to muck up,*** estropear, jeringar; hacer una chapucería de. — *v.i.* — ***about,*** perder el tiempo; hacer el tonto; ***muck about with,*** andar en; sobar; tontear con; ***muck in (with),*** echar una mano.
muck-rake [ˈmʌk-reik], *v.i.* escarbar cosas escabrosas; murmurar.
mucky [ˈmʌki], *a.* (*fam.*) sucio, puerco, guarro; asqueroso.
mucosity [mjuːˈkɔsiti], *s.* mucosidad.
mucous [ˈmjuːkəs], *a.* mucoso; mocoso.
mucus [ˈmjuːkəs], *s.* mucosidad; moco.
mud [mʌd], *s.* barro, lodo, fango; ***to get stuck in the mud,*** atollarse; ***mud-bath,*** lodos, *m.pl.*; ***mud-wall,*** tapia de adobe; (*fig.*) ***to sling mud at,*** llenar de fango, vilipendiar.
muddiness [ˈmʌdinis], *s.* (lo) barroso; (lo) turbio.
muddle [mʌdl], *s.* barullo, confusión; lío, embrollo; ***to get into a muddle,*** embrollarse; armarse un lío; ***to make a muddle,*** armar un lío.— *v.t.* confundir, aturdir; ***muddle up,*** embrollar. — *v.i.* ***muddle along*** o ***through,*** salir del paso a lo loco.
muddled, muddle-headed [mʌdld, ˈmʌdl-ˈhedid], *a.* atontado; aturullado, atolondrado.
muddy [ˈmʌdi], *a.* barroso; turbio. — *v.t.* enlodar; enturbiar.
mudguard [ˈmʌdgɑːd], *s.* (*aut.*) guardabarros, *m.inv.*
mudlark [ˈmʌdlɑːk], *s.* (*fam.*) galopín.
mudwort [ˈmʌdwəːt], *s.* limosela.
muezzin [muːˈezin], *s.* muecín, almuecín, almuédano.
muff (1) [mʌf], *s.* manguito.
muff (2) [mʌf], *v.t.* fallar, marrar; ***muff it,*** marrar, fallar el golpe.
muffin [ˈmʌfin], *s.* mollete; bodigo.
muffle (1) [mʌfl], *s.* (*mec.*) mufla. — *v.t.* amortiguar; embozar, arrebujar; enfundar (*un tambor*). — *v.i.* — ***up,*** arrebujarse, embozarse.
muffle (2) [mʌfl], *s.* (*anat., zool.*) hocico, morro.
muffled [mʌfld], *a.* sordo.
muffler [ˈmʌflə], *s.* embozo, bufanda, tapaboca, *m.*; guante de púgil; sordina; silenciador; (*Am.*) [SILENCER].
mufti [ˈmʌfti], *s.* muftí; (*mil.*) traje de paisano.
mug (1) [mʌg], *s.* taza, tazón; jarra, jícara; (*fam.*) hocico, jeta.
mug (2) [mʌg], *s.* (*fam.*) besugo; (*fam.*) ***it's a mug's game,*** es negocio de tontos.
mug (3) [mʌg], *v.t.* — ***up,*** empollarse, embotellarse.
mugging [ˈmʌgiŋ], *s.* vapuleo, asalto.
muggy, muggish [ˈmʌgi, ˈmʌgiʃ], *a.* bochornoso.
mugwort [ˈmʌgwəːt], *s.* (*bot.*) artemisa vulgar.
mugwump [ˈmʌgwʌmp], *s.* (*Am., pol.*) votante independiente; tonto.
mulatress [mjuːˈlætris], *s.* mulata.
mulatto [mjuːˈlætou], *s.* mulato.
mulberry [ˈmʌlbəri], *s.* (*bot.*) mora; ***mulberry-tree,*** morera.
mulch [mʌltʃ], *s.* estiércol. — *v.t.* estercolar.
mulct [mʌlkt], *s.* multa. — *v.t.* multar; ***mulct of,*** quitar.
mule (1) [mjuːl], *s.* mulo; (*fam.*) terco; (*mec.*) máquina de hilar intermitente; planta híbrida; ***mule-chair,*** jamuga; ***mule-driver*** [MULETEER]; (*mec.*) ***mule-jenny,*** hilandera; ***mule track,*** camino de herradura.
mule (2) [mjuːl], *s.* babucha.
muleteer [mjuːliˈtiə], *s.* muletero, mulero, acemilero, arriero.
mulish [ˈmjuːliʃ], *a.* mular; híbrido; (*fig.*) terco.
mulishness [ˈmjuːliʃnis], *s.* terquedad.
mull (1) [mʌl], *v.t.* calentar (vino, cerveza *etc.*) con especias.
mull (2) [mʌl], *v.t.* — ***over,*** meditar, reflexionar en.
mullein [ˈmʌlin], *s.* (*bot.*) verbasco.
mullet [ˈmʌlit], *s.* (*ict.*) (***red***) salmonete; (***grey***) mújol.
mulligatawny [mʌligəˈtɔːni], *s.* sopa india.
mullion [ˈmʌljən], *s.* parteluz, *m.*
multangular [mʌlˈtæŋgjulə], *a.* multangular.
multicapsular [mʌltiˈkæpsjulə], *a.* multicapsular.
multicoloured [ˈmʌltikʌləd], *a.* multicolor; abigarrado.
multidentate [mʌltiˈdenteit], *a.* multidentado.
multifarious [mʌltiˈfɛəriəs], *a.* múltiple, vario, diverso.
multifariousness [mʌltiˈfɛəriəsnis], *s.* multiplicidad, variedad, diversidad.
multiflorous [mʌltiˈflɔːrəs], *a.* multifloro.
multiform [ˈmʌltifɔːm], *a.* multiforme.
multiformity [mʌltiˈfɔːmiti], *s.* multiformidad.
multilateral [mʌltiˈlætərəl], *a.* multilátero.
multiloquent [mʌlˈtiləkwənt], *a.* moltilocuo.
multimillionaire [mʌltimiljəˈnɛə], *a., s.* multimillonario.
multiparous [mʌlˈtipərəs], *a.* multípara.
multipartite [mʌltiˈpɑːtait], *a.* multipartido.
multiped [ˈmʌltiped], *a., s.* multípedo.
multiple [ˈmʌltipl], *a.* múltiple; ***multiple firm,*** casa de muchas sucursales; ***multiple stores,*** cadena de (grandes) almacenes. — *s.* múltiplo.
multiplex [ˈmʌltipleks], *a.* multíplice.
multipliable, multiplicable [ˈmʌltiplaiəbl, mʌltiˈplikəbl], *a.* multiplicable.
multiplicand [mʌltipliˈkænd], *s.* multiplicando.
multiplication [mʌltipliˈkeiʃən], *s.* multiplicación; ***multiplication table,*** tabla de multiplicar.
multiplicative [mʌltiˈplikətiv], *a.* multiplicador, multiplicativo.
multiplicator [ˈmʌltiplikeitə], *s.* multiplicador.
multiplicity [mʌltiˈplisiti], *s.* multiplicidad.
multiplier [ˈmʌltiplaiə], *s.* multiplicador.
multiply [ˈmʌltiplai], *v.t.* multiplicar. — *v.i.* multiplicarse.
multipolar [mʌltiˈpoulə], *a.* multipolar.
multitude [ˈmʌltitjuːd], *s.* multitud; muchedumbre.
multitudinous [mʌltiˈtjuːdinəs], *a.* multitudinario, muy numeroso.
multitudinousness [mʌltiˈtjuːdinəsnis], *s.* (lo) multitudinario, (lo) numerosísimo.
multivalve [ˈmʌltivælv], *a., s.* multivalvo.
multure [ˈmʌltʃə], *s.* maquila.
mum (1) [mʌm], *a.* (*fam.*) callado; ***to keep mum,*** callar(se), guardar silencio; ***mum's the word!*** ¡chitón!
mum (2) [mʌm], *s.* (*fam.*) mamá.
mumble [mʌmbl], *v.t.* mascullar. — *v.i.* hablar entre dientes.
mumbler [ˈmʌmblə], *s.* mascullador.
mumblingly [ˈmʌmbliŋli], *adv.* entre dientes.
mumbo-jumbo [ˈmʌmbou-ˈdʒʌmbou], *s.* (*fam.*) fetiche; conjuro; mistificaciones, *f.pl.*; mistiquerías, *f.pl.*
mummer [ˈmʌmə], *s.* máscara, *m.f.*; momero.
mummery [ˈmʌməri], *s.* mascarada; momería, mojiganga; ceremoniosidades, *f.pl.*
mummification [mʌmifiˈkeiʃən], *s.* momificación.
mummiform [ˈmʌmifɔːm], *a.* en forma de momia.
mummify [ˈmʌmifai], *v.t.* momificar. — *v.i.* momificarse.

mumming [ˈmʌmiŋ], *s.* mascarada, mojiganga, momería.
mummy (1) [ˈmʌmi], *s.* momia.
mummy (2) [ˈmʌmi], *s.* (*fam.*) mamá, mamaíta.
mump [mʌmp], *v.i.* (*fam.*) quejarse, protestar.
mumpish [ˈmʌmpiʃ], *a.* protestón, gruñón.
mumps [mʌmps], *s. inv.* parótidas, *f.pl.*, paperas.
munch [mʌntʃ], *v.t.* rumiar, ronzar. — *v.i.* ronchar.
mundane [ˈmʌndein], *a.* mundano.
municipal [mjuːˈnisipl], *a.* municipal.
municipality [mjuːnisiˈpæliti], *s.* municipalidad, municipio.
munificence [mjuːˈnifisəns], *s.* munificencia.
munificent [mjuːˈnifisənt], *a.* munífico.
muniment [ˈmjuːnimənt], *s.* (*ant.*) medio de defensa; (*pl. for.*) escritura de propiedad.
munition [mjuːˈniʃən], *s.* (*ú. más en pl.*) municiones, *f.pl.*; ***munitions dump,*** depósito de municiones. — *v.t.* municionar.
mural [ˈmjuərəl], *a.* mural; vertical, escarpado. — *s.* pintura mural; mural.
murder [ˈməːdə], *s.* asesinato; homicidio; ***murder will out,*** un crimen no puede ocultarse; ***to get away with murder,*** matarlas callando; ***to shout*** o ***cry*** (***blue***) ***murder,*** poner el grito en el cielo. — *v.t.* asesinar; (*fig.*) destrozar, estropear; (*teat. etc.*) degollar.
murderer [ˈməːdərə], *s.* asesino, homicida, *m.f.*
murderess [ˈməːdəris], *s.* asesina.
murderous [ˈməːdərəs], *a.* asesino, homicida; sanguinario.
murex [ˈmjuəreks], *s.* (*zool.*) múrice.
muriate [ˈmjuəriit], *s.* (*quím.*) muriato, clorhidrato.
muriatic [mjuəriˈætik], *a.* muriático, clorhídrico.
murk [məːk], *s.* oscuridad, lobreguez.
murky [ˈməːki], *a.* oscuro, lóbrego, tenebroso.
murkiness [ˈməːkinis], *s.* lobreguez, tinieblas, *f.pl.*
murmur [ˈməːmə], *s.* murmullo; queja; susurro, rumor; (*med.*) ***cardiac murmur,*** rumor cardíaco. — *v.t., v.i.* murmurar; susurrar; murmullar.
murmurer [ˈməːmərə], *s.* murmurador, descontento.
murmuring [ˈməːməriŋ], *a.* susurrante; murmurante. — *s.* murmullo(s).
murrain [ˈmʌrin], *s.* morrina.
murrey [ˈmʌri], *a.* morado, rojo oscuro.
muscat, muscatel [ˈmʌskət, mʌskəˈtel], *s.* moscatel.
muscardine [ˈmʌskədain], *s.* muscardina.
muscle [mʌsl], *s.* músculo; (*fig.*) fuerza muscular. — *v.i.* — ***in*** (***on***), entrarse (en), intrusarse (en), meterse (por la fuerza) (en).
muscoid [ˈmʌskɔid], *a.* musgoso.
Muscovite [ˈmʌskovait], *a., s.* moscovita, *m.f.*
Muscovy [ˈmʌskəvi]. Moscovia; ***Muscovy duck,*** pato almizclado.
muscular [ˈmʌskjulə], *a.* muscular; musculoso, membrudo, fornido.
muscularity [mʌskjuˈlæriti], *s.* musculosidad.
muse (1) [mjuːz], *s.* musa; numen, estro.
muse (2) [mjuːz], *v.i.* meditar, reflexionar; estar distraído.
muser [ˈmjuːzə], *s.* soñador.
museum [mjuːˈziəm], *s.* museo.
mush [mʌʃ], *s.* gachas, *f.pl.*; (*fig., fam.*) sensiblerías, *f.pl.*, sentimentalismos, *m.pl.*; blandenguerías, *f.pl.*; sandeces, *f.pl.*
mushroom [ˈmʌʃrum], *s.* hongo; (*comestible*) seta, champiñón; ***mushroom cloud,*** hongo atómico. — *v.i.* aparecer de la noche a la mañana; crecer extraordinariamente.
mushy [ˈmʌʃi], *a.* (*fam.*) pulposo, mollar; (*fig.*) sensiblero, sentimentaloide.
music [ˈmjuːzik], *s.* música; ***music-hall,*** (teatro de) variedades; ***music-master,*** profesor de música; ***music-stand,*** atril, facistol; ***music-stool,*** banqueta o taburete de piano; ***to face the music,*** enfrentarse con las consecuencias; pagar el pato, cargar con el muerto; ***to set to music,*** musicar, poner música a.
musical [ˈmjuːzikəl], *a.* musical, músico; armonioso; armónico; aficionado a la música; ***musical box,*** caja de música; ***musical comedy,*** zarzuela, comedia musical. — *s.* musical.
musician [mjuːˈziʃən], *s.* músico.
musicianship [mjuːˈziʃənʃip], *s.* maestría musical.
musicology [mjuːziˈkɔlədʒi], *s.* musicología.
musing, museful [ˈmjuːziŋ, -ful], *a.* meditabundo.
musk [mʌsk], *s.* almizcle, olor de almizcle; (*bot.*) almizcleña; (*bot.*) ***musk-apple,*** manzana camuesa; ***musk-beetle,*** calicromo; (*bot.*) ***musk-cherry,*** cereza almizcleña; ***musk-deer,*** ciervo almizclero; (*bot.*) ***musk-grape,*** moscatel; (*bot.*) ***musk-melon,*** melón almizclero; ***musk-ox,*** buey almizclero; (*bot.*) ***musk-pear,*** mosqueruela, pera almizcleña; ***musk-rat,*** rata almizclera; (*bot.*) ***musk-rose,*** rosa almizcleña.
musked [mʌskt], *a.* almizclado.
musket [ˈmʌskit], *s.* mosquete; ***musket-shot,*** mosquetazo, fusilazo.
musketeer [mʌskiˈtiə], *s.* mosquetero.
musketry [ˈmʌskitri], *s.* mosquetería; fusilería.
muskiness [ˈmʌskinis], *s.* olor de almizcle.
musky [ˈmʌski], *a.* almizclado, almizclero, almizcleño.
Muslim [ˈmʌzlim] [MOSLEM].
muslin [ˈmʌzlin], *s.* muselina; ***cambric muslin,*** batista.
musquash [ˈmʌskwɔʃ], *s.* (piel de) rata almizclera.
muss [mʌs], *v.t.* — ***about,*** sobar, manosear.
mussel [mʌsl], *s.* mejillón.
Mussulman [ˈmʌslmən], *s.* [MOSLEM].
must (1) [mʌst], *s.* (*fam.*) ***it's a must,*** es obligado. — *v. aux.* deber; deber de; ser necesario *o* preciso; ***he must go now,*** tiene que ir(se) ahora; ***he must keep his word,*** debe cumplir lo prometido; ***it must be here,*** debe de estar aquí; ***there must be a solution,*** debe de haber una solución; tiene que haber una solución; ***it must be*** (***about***) ***four o'clock,*** serán las cuatro.
must (2) [mʌst], *s.* (*vino*) mosto.
must (3) [mʌst], *s.* moho.
mustang [ˈmʌstæŋ], *s.* potro mesteño.
mustard [ˈmʌstəd], *s.* mostaza; ***mustard-gas,*** gas mostaza; ***mustard-paper, mustard-poultice,*** sinapismo; ***mustard-pot,*** mostacera.
musteline [ˈmʌstəliːn], *a.* mustelino.
muster [ˈmʌstə], *s.* asamblea; (*mil.*) revista; lista, matrícula; rol; ***muster-book,*** libro de revistas; ***muster-master,*** comisario de revista; ***muster-roll,*** matrícula de revista; (*mar.*) rol de la tripulación; ***to pass muster,*** pasar revista; colar. — *v.t.* reunir, juntar; cobrar (*ánimo etc.*); revistar, pasar revista a. — *v.i.* reunirse, juntarse.
mustiness [ˈmʌstinis], *s.* moho; ranciedad; olor a humedad.
musty [ˈmʌsti], *a.* mohoso, enmohecido; rancio; que huele a humedad.
mutability [mjuːtəˈbiliti], *s.* mutabilidad.
mutable [ˈmjuːtəbl], *a.* mudable, inestable.
mutableness [ˈmjuːtəblnis], *s.* mutabilidad.
mutation [mjuːˈteiʃən], *s.* mutación, mudanza.
mute [mjuːt], *a.* mudo. — *s.* mudo; sordina; letra muda. — *v.t.* apagar, poner sordina a.
mutely [ˈmjuːtli], *adv.* en silencio, calladamente.
muteness [ˈmjuːtnis], *s.* mudez, mutismo.
mutilate [ˈmjuːtileit], *v.t.* mutilar.
mutilation [mjuːtiˈleiʃən], *s.* mutilación.
mutineer [mjuːtiˈniə], *s.* amotinador, amotinado, sedicioso.
mutinous [ˈmjuːtinəs], *a.* amotinado, sedicioso.
mutinousness [ˈmjuːtinəsnis], *s.* amotinamiento, sedición.

mutiny ['mju:tini], *s.* amotinamiento, motín. — *v.i.* amotinarse, sublevarse.
mutism ['mju:tizəm], *s.* mutismo.
mutter ['mʌtə], *s.* murmullo; rumor. — *v.t.* murmurar; mascullar. — *v.i.* murmurar.
mutterer ['mʌtərə], *s.* gruñón, rezongador.
muttering ['mʌtəriŋ], *a.* mascullante. — *s.* refunfuño.
mutton [mʌtn], *s.* carne de carnero; ***leg of mutton,*** pierna de cordero; ***mutton chop,*** chuleta de cordero; ***mutton-fist,*** manaza; ***mutton-ham,*** pierna de carnero salada y curada.
mutual ['mju:tʃuəl], *a.* mutuo, común, recíproco; ***mutual consent,*** común acuerdo.
mutuality [mju:tʃu'æliti], *s.* mutualidad; reciprocidad.
mutually ['mju:tʃuəli], *adv.* mutuamente, recíprocamente.
mutuary ['mju:tjuəri], *s.* mutuatario.
muzzle [mʌzl], *s.* (*anat.*) hocico, morro; bozal; mordaza; boca (*de arma de fuego*); ***muzzle-loader,*** arma que se carga por la boca; ***muzzle-velocity,*** velocidad inicial. — *v.t.* abozalar; amordazar.
muzzy ['mʌzi], *a.* confuso, borroso, nebuloso.
my [mai], *a.* mi, mis. — *interj.* (***oh***) ***my!*** ¡Dios mío!
mycology [mai'kɔlədʒi], *s.* micología.
myocardium [maio'kɑ:diəm], *s.* miocardio.
myography [mai'ɔgrəfi], *s.* miografía.
myope ['maioup], *s.* miope, *m.f.*
myopia [mai'oupiə], *s.* miopía.
myopic [mai'ɔpik], *a.* miope.
myosis [mai'ousis], *s.* miosis, *f.inv.*
myosotis [maio'soutis], *s.* (*bot.*) miosota.
myriad ['miriəd], *s.* miríada.
myriagram ['miriəgræm], *s.* miriagramo.
myrialitre ['miriəli:tə], *s.* mirialitro.
myriametre ['miriəmi:tə], *s.* miriametro.
myriapod ['miriəpɔd], *s.* miriápodo.
Myriapoda [miri'æpədə], *s.pl.* miriápodos, *m.pl.*, miriópodos, *m.pl.*
myrmidon ['mə:midən], *s.* secuaz; esbirro.
myrrh [mə:], *s.* mirra.
myrrhic ['mə:rik], *a.* mirrado, mirrino.
myrtiform ['mə:tifɔ:m], *a.* mirtiforme.
myrtle [mə:tl], *s.* mirto, arrayán.
myself [mai'self], *pron. pers.* yo mismo, yo; me, a mí, a mí mismo.
mysterious [mis'tiəriəs], *a.* misterioso.
mysteriousness [mis'tiəriəsnis], *s.* (lo) misterioso.
mystery ['mistəri], *s.* misterio; arcano; (*ant.*) profesión, oficio; (*teat.*) auto sacramental, misterio; ***mystery novel,*** novela policíaca.
mystic ['mistik], *s.* místico.
mystic(al) ['mistik(əl)], *a.* místico.
mysticism ['mistisizəm], *s.* misticismo; mística.
mystification [mistifi'keiʃən], *s.* mistificación; superchería; perplejidad, desconcierto.
mystify ['mistifai], *v.t.* mistificar; desconcertar, dejar perplejo.
myth [miθ], *s.* mito.
mythic(al) ['miθik(əl)], *a.* mítico; fabuloso.
mythologic(al) [miθə'lɔdʒik(əl)], *a.* mitológico.
mythologist [mi'θɔlədʒist], *s.* mitologista, *m.f.*, mitólogo.
mythologize [mi'θɔlədʒaiz], *v.t.* convertir en mito; interpretar mitológicamente.
mythology [mi'θɔlədʒi], *s.* mitología.

N

N, n [en], décimocuarta letra del alfabeto.
nab [næb], *v.t.* (*fam.*) coger; birlar.
nabob [ˈneibɔb], *s.* nabab; potentado.
nacelle [nɑːˈsel], *s.* (*aer.*) barquilla; góndola.
nacre [ˈneikə], *s.* nácar.
nacreous [ˈneikriəs], *a.* nacarado, nacarino.
nadir [ˈneidiə], *s.* nadir.
nag [næg], *s.* (*despec.*) jaco, rocín, jamelgo; (*pers.*) regañona. — *v.t.* importunar, dar la lata a. — *v.i.* — ***at,*** regañar.
naiad [ˈnaiæd], *s.* náyade, *f.*
nail [neil], *s.* uña; clavo; ***nail-brush,*** cepillo para las uñas; ***nail-cleaner,*** limpiauñas, *m.inv.*; ***nail-clippers,*** cortauñas, *m.inv.*; ***nail-maker,*** clavero; ***on the nail,*** a toca teja; ***to bite one's nails,*** comerse *o* morderse las uñas; ***to hit the nail on the head,*** dar en el clavo. — *v.t.* clavar; clavetear; enclavar; ***nail down,*** sujetar con clavos; (*fig.*) ***nail a lie,*** descubrir una mentira; ***nail up,*** cerrar con clavos *o* clavado.
nailer [ˈneilə], *s.* fabricante de clavos.
nailery [ˈneiləri], *s.* fábrica de clavos.
nainsook [ˈneinsuk], *s.* nansú.
naissant [ˈneisənt], *a.* (*blas.*) naciente.
naïve [nɑːˈiːv], *a.* ingenuo, cándido.
naïveté [nɑːˈiːvtei], *s.* ingenuidad, candidez.
naked [ˈneikid], *a.* desnudo; al descubierto; ***stark naked,*** en cueros vivos; ***with the naked eye,*** a simple vista; ***the naked truth,*** la pura verdad.
nakedness [ˈneikidnis], *s.* desnudez.
namby-pamby [ˈnæmbi-ˈpæmbi], *a.* (*fam.*) soso; ñoño. — *s.* (*fam.*) mirliflor; marica; pamplina.
name [neim], *s.* nombre; (*familia*) apellido; reputación, fama; título; linaje; ***by the name of,*** bajo el nombre de; ***to call names,*** poner motes a, decir injurias a; ***Christian name,*** nombre de pila; ***in name,*** de nombre; ***in God's name,*** por el amor de Dios; ***in the name of,*** en nombre de, de parte de; ***to make a name for o.s.,*** significarse, singularizarse, particularizarse; ***name-day,*** fiesta onomástica, día del santo, *m.*, santo; ***what is his name?*** ¿cómo se llama? — *v.t.* nombrar; apellidar, llamar, poner nombre a; mentar; elegir; mencionar; (*precio, dato etc.*) señalar, fijar, especificar, designar; citar; proferir; ***to be named,*** llamarse.
named [neimd], *a.* nombrado; ***above named,*** arriba citado.
nameless [ˈneimlis], *a.* anónimo, innominado.
namely [ˈneimli], *adv.* a saber.
namesake [ˈneimseik], *s.* homónimo; tocayo.
nankeen [nænˈkiːn], *s.* nanquín.
nanny [ˈnæni], *s.* niñera; ***nanny-goat,*** cabra.
nap (1) [næp], *s.* sueñecito, siesta; ***to have*** o ***take a nap,*** descabezar un sueño, dormir *o* echar la siesta. — *v.i.* dormitar; ***to catch napping,*** coger desprevenido.
nap (2) [næp], *s.* lanilla, flojel.
nap (3) [næp], *s.* juego de cartas; (*fam.*) ***to go nap,*** jugarse el todo.
napalm [ˈneipɑːm], *s.* (*mil.*) gelatina de gasolina, napalm.
nape [neip], *s.* nuca, cogote.
napery [ˈneipəri], *s.* ropa blanca; artículos de lienzo; mantelería.
naphtha [ˈnæfθə], *s.* nafta.
naphthalene, naphthaline [ˈnæfθəliːn], *s.* naftalina.
naphthol [ˈnæfθɔl], *s.* naftol.
napkin [ˈnæpkin], *s.* servilleta; ***napkin-ring,*** servilletero.
Naples [neiplz]. Nápoles, *m.*
napless [ˈnæplis], *a.* sin pelusa, raído.
Napoleon [nəˈpouliən]. Napoleón.
napoleon [nəˈpouliən], *s.* napoleón.
napper [ˈnæpə], *s.* (*vulg.*) cabeza, crisma, cholla.
nappy [ˈnæpi], *s.* (*fam., abrev. de* **napkin**) pañal.
Narbonne [nɑːˈbɔn]. Narbona.
narcissus [nɑːˈsisəs], *s.* (*pl.* **narcissuses, narcissi** [-əsiz, -ai] (*bot.*) narciso.
narcolepsy [ˈnɑːkəlepsi], *s.* narcolepsia.
narcosis [nɑːˈkousis], *s.* (*pl.* **narcoses** [-iːz]) narcosis, *f. inv.*
narcotic [nɑːˈkɔtik], *a., s.* narcótico.
narcotine [ˈnɑːkətiːn], *s.* narcotina.
narcotism [ˈnɑːkətizəm], *s.* narcotismo.
narcotize [ˈnɑːkətaiz], *v.t.* narcotizar.
nard [nɑːd], *s.* nardo.
nark [nɑːk], *s.* (*fam.*) soplón. — *v.t.* (*fam.*) fastidiar, poner negro; ***nark it!*** ¡déjate de eso!; ¡bobadas!
narrate [nəˈreit], *v.t.* narrar, relatar.
narration [nəˈreiʃən], *s.* narración, relato.
narrative [ˈnærətiv], *a.* narrativo. — *s.* narrativa; relato.
narrator [nəˈreitə], *s.* narrador.
narratory [nəˈreitəri], *a.* narrativo.
narrow [ˈnærou], *a.* estrecho, angosto; estrecho de miras; ***narrow circumstances,*** estrechez, estrecheces, *f.pl.*; ***to have a narrow escape,*** librarse por los pelos, librarse de buena; ***narrow-gauge,*** (de) vía estrecha; ***narrow majority,*** mayoría escasa; ***narrow-minded,*** estrecho de miras. — *s.* (*pl.*) estrecho. — *v.t.* estrechar. — *v.i.* estrecharse.
narrowing [ˈnærouiŋ], *s.* estrechamiento; (el) estrechar(se).
narrowly [ˈnærouli], *adv.* estrechamente; apenas, por los pelos.
narrowness [ˈnærounis], *s.* estrechez, angostura; (*pers.*) estrechez de miras.
narwhal [ˈnɑːwəl], *s.* (*zool.*) narval.
nasal [neizl], *a.* nasal; gangoso; ***nasal twang,*** gangueo. — *s.* letra nasal; hueso nasal.
nasality [neiˈzæliti], *s.* nasalidad.
nasally [ˈneizəli], *adv.* nasalmente, con sonido nasal; ***to speak nasally,*** ganguear.
nascent [ˈneisənt], *a.* naciente.
naseberry [ˈneizbəri], *s.* (*bot.*) níspero.
nastiness [ˈnɑːstinis], *s.* antipatía; mala intención; (lo) feo; (lo) sucio; (lo) difícil.
nasturtium [nəˈstəːʃəm], *s.* (*bot.*) capuchina, nasturcia.
nasty [ˈnɑːsti], *a.* antipático, desagradable; mal intencionado; feo; sucio, asqueroso; difícil; (*fam.*) ***he's a nasty piece of work,*** es muy mala persona; ***it's beginning to look nasty,*** la cosa empieza a ponerse fea.
natal [neitl], *a.* natal.
natality [nəˈtæliti], *s.* natalidad.
natatorial [neitəˈtɔːriəl], *a.* natatorio.
natatory [ˈneitətəri], *a.* natatorio.
Nathaniel [nəˈθænjəl]. Nataniel.
nation [ˈneiʃən], *s.* nación; ***nation-wide,*** por toda la nación.
national [ˈnæʃənəl], *a.* nacional; ***national debt,*** deuda pública. — *s.* nacional, *m.f.*
nationalism [ˈnæʃənəlizəm], *s.* nacionalismo.
nationalist [ˈnæʃənəlist], *a., s.* nacionalista, *m.f.*
nationalistic [næʃənəˈlistik], *a.* nacionalista.
nationality [næʃəˈnæliti], *s.* nacionalidad.
nationalize [ˈnæʃənəlaiz], *v.t.* nacionalizar.
native [ˈneitiv], *a.* nativo; natal; originario; natural; oriundo; patrio; ***native land,*** patria, tierra; ***native place,*** lugar *o* suelo natal; ***native soil,*** terruño, tierra natal; ***native tongue*** o ***native language,*** lengua materna.— *s.* nacional; natural; indígena; nativo.

nativeness [ˈneitivnis], *s.* (lo) nativo; (lo) originario; (lo) natural.
nativity [nəˈtiviti], *s.* natividad.
Nato [ˈneitou], *s.* (*pol.*) Otan, *f.*
natron [ˈneitrən], *s.* natrón.
natter [ˈnætə], *s.* (*fam.*) palique; ***to have a natter,*** tener un rato de palique; echar un párrafo. — *v.i.* paliquear.
nattiness [ˈnætinis], *s.* garbo, (*fam.*) elegancia.
natty [ˈnæti], *a.* garboso, (*fam.*) elegante, fino; apuesto; majo.
natural [ˈnætʃərəl], *a.* natural. — *s.* (*fam.*) cosa *o* persona de éxito seguro; (*mús.*) becuadro.
naturalism [ˈnætʃərəlizəm], *s.* naturalismo.
naturalist [ˈnætʃərəlist], *s.* naturalista, *m.f.*
naturalistic [nætʃərəˈlistik], *a.* naturalista.
naturalization [nætʃərəlaiˈzeiʃən], *s.* naturalización; ***naturalization papers,*** carta de naturaleza.
naturalize [ˈnætʃərəlaiz], *v.t.* naturalizar.
naturalness [ˈnætʃərəlnis], *s.* naturalidad.
nature [ˈneitʃə], *s.* naturaleza; (*pers.*) índole, *f.*; natural; ***from nature,*** del natural; al natural; ***good nature,*** buen natural; ***ill nature,*** mal carácter; ***in the nature of things,*** siendo las cosas como son, siendo la vida como es.
naught [nɔːt], *s.* nada, cero; ***to bring to naught, set at naught,*** reducir a la nada; dar al traste con, hacer fracasar; quitar toda importancia a, no dar (ninguna) importancia a; ***to come to naught,*** reducirse a la nada; fracasar, no cuajar, quedarse en nada *o* en agua de cerrajas *o* borrajas.
naughtiness [ˈnɔːtinis], *s.* travesura, picardía, maldad.
naughty [ˈnɔːti], *a.* travieso, pícaro, malo.
Nauru [nɔːˈruː]. Nauru.
Nauruan [nɔːˈruːən], *a.*, *s.* nauruano.
nausea [ˈnɔːsiə], *s.* náusea(s), basca(s).
nauseate [ˈnɔːsieit], *v.t.*, *v.i.* causar náusea(s), dar asco (a).
nauseating [ˈnɔːsieitiŋ], *a.* nauseabundo; asqueroso.
nauseous [ˈnɔːsiəs], *a.* nauseabundo; asqueroso.
nauseousness [ˈnɔːsiəsnis], *s.* náuseas, *f.pl.*; asquerosidad.
nautical [ˈnɔːtikəl], *a.* náutico.
naval [ˈneivəl], *a.* naval; ***naval dockyard,*** arsenal; ***naval officer,*** marino (de la armada).
Navarre [nəˈvɑː]. Navarra.
nave [neiv], *s.* (*arq.*) nave.
navel [ˈneivəl], *s.* ombligo; ***navel cord,*** cordón umbilical; ***navel-gall,*** matadura; ***navel-shaped,*** umbilicado.
navelwort [ˈneivəlwəːt], *s.* (*bot.*) oreja de monje.
navigability, navigableness [nævigəˈbiliti, ˈnævigəblnis], *s.* navegabilidad.
navigable [ˈnævigəbl], *a.* navegable; gobernable, dirigible.
navigate [ˈnævigeit], *v.t.*, *v.i.* navegar; marear, dirigir (un buque).
navigation [næviˈgeiʃən], *s.* navegación, náutica; mareaje.
navigator [ˈnævigeitə], *s.* navegador, navegante; mareante, piloto.
navvy [ˈnævi], *s.* bracero, peón (caminero).
navy [ˈneivi], *s.* marina, armada; ***merchant navy,*** marina mercante; ***navy blue,*** azul marino.
nawab [nəˈwɑːb], *s.* nabab; potentado.
nay [nei], *adv.* (*ant.*) no; más aun, es más; mejor dicho. — *s.* negativa.
Nazarene [næzəˈriːn], *a.*, *s.* nazareno.
Nazareth [ˈnæzərəθ]. Nazaret.
naze [neiz], *s.* cabo, promontorio.
neap [niːp], *a.* — ***tide,*** marea muerta.
Neapolitan [niəˈpɔlitən], *a.*, *s.* napolitano.
near [niə], *a.* cercano, próximo, inmediato, vecino; (*relación*) estrecho, íntimo; fiel; ***near-by,*** cercano, próximo; (*fam.*) ***near the knuckle,*** verdecillo; ***near seal,*** imitación de piel de foca; (*aut.*, *países donde se circula por la izquierda*) ***near side,*** lado izquierdo, (*aut.*, *otros países*) lado derecho; ***near-sighted,*** miope, corto de vista; ***near-sightedness,*** miopía; ***it was a near thing,*** escapé por un pelo. — *adv.* cerca; ***near at hand,*** a la mano; ***near by,*** cerca, al lado; ***to draw, come*** o ***go near,*** acercarse. — *prep.* cerca de, junto a. — *v.t.*, *v.i.* acercarse (a).
nearly [ˈniəli], *adv.* casi; cerca (de); por poco; ***I nearly lost it,*** por poco lo pierdo; (*fam.*) ***we nearly bought it,*** faltó poco para que lo comprásemos.
nearness [ˈniənis], *s.* proximidad, cercanía; intimidad.
neat [niːt], *a.* pulcro; primoroso; ordenado; (*bebidas alcohólicas*) puro, sin mezcla; bien proporcionado.
neatness [ˈniːtnis], *s.* pulcritud; primor; orden, limpieza; pureza.
Nebuchadnezzar [nebjukədˈnəzə]. Nabucodonosor.
nebula [ˈnebjulə], *s.* (*pl.* **nebulae** [-li]) nebulosa.
nebular [ˈnebjulə], *a.* relativo a las nebulosas; nebuloso.
nebulous [ˈnebjuləs], *a.* nebuloso.
nebulosity, nebulousness [nebjuˈlɔsiti, ˈnebjuləsnis], *s.* nebulosidad; (lo) nebuloso.
necessarily [ˈnesisərili], *adv.* necesariamente, forzosamente.
necessariness [ˈnesisərinis], *s.* necesidad.
necessary [ˈnesisəri], *a.* necesario, forzoso, preciso; ***to be necessary,*** ser necesario *o* preciso; hacer falta; ***to do more than is necessary,*** hacer más de lo necesario. — *s.* (lo) necesario.
necessitate [niˈsesiteit], *v.t.* exigir, requerir.
necessitous [niˈsesitəs], *a.* necesitado, indigente.
necessity [niˈsesiti], *s.* necesidad, precisión; exigencia; ***necessity knows no law,*** la necesidad carece de ley; ***of necessity,*** de *o* por necesidad, forzosamente.
neck [nek], *s.* cuello; (*animales*) pescuezo; (*botellas*) gollete; garganta; (*violín, guitarra etc.*) clavijero; (*arq.*) collarino; (*geog.*) istmo; (*cost.*) ***low neck,*** escote; ***neck and crop,*** totalmente; (*carreras*) ***neck and neck,*** parejos; ***neck-line,*** escote; ***neck or nothing,*** todo o nada; ***stiff neck,*** tortícolis, *f. inv.*; ***to break one's neck,*** desnucarse; (*fam.*) ***to get it in the neck,*** cobrar, cargársela; (*fam.*) ***to have a lot of neck,*** ser un descarado, tener mucha cara; (*fam.*) ***he is a pain in the neck,*** es un pelmazo *o* tostón; (*fam.*) ***to stick one's neck out,*** exponerse, arriesgarse; ***to wring the neck*** (***of***), torcer el pescuezo (a). — *v.i.* (*fam.*) besuquearse, sobarse.
neckerchief [ˈnekətʃiːf], *s.* corbata, pañuelo de cuello.
necking [ˈnekiŋ], *s.* (*fam.*) sobo, manoseo.
necklace [ˈnekləs], *s.* collar.
necktie [ˈnektai], *s.* corbata.
necrological [nekrəˈlɔdʒikəl], *a.* necrológico.
necrologist [neˈkrɔlədʒist], *s.* necrologista, *m.f.*
necrology [neˈkrɔlədʒi], *s.* necrología.
necromancer [ˈnekromænsə], *s.* nigromante.
necromancy [ˈnekromænsi], *s.* nigromancia.
necromantic [nekroˈmæntik], *a.* nigromántico.
necropolis [neˈkrɔpəlis], *s.* necrópolis, *f. inv.*
necrosis [neˈkrousis], *s.* necrosis, *f. inv.*
necrotomy [neˈkrɔtəmi], *s.* necrotomía.
nectar [ˈnektə], *s.* néctar.
nectarean, nectareous [nekˈtɛəriən, -iəs], *a.* nectáreo.
nectarine [ˈnektərin], *a.* nectarino. — *s.* melocotón nectarino.
nectary [ˈnektəri], *s.* nectario.
née [nei], *a.* nacida; ***Carmen Jones, née García,*** Carmen Jones, nacida García.

need [niːd], *s.* necesidad; requisito; indigencia; urgencia; ***need for patience,*** necesidad de paciencia; ***to have need of,*** be o ***stand in need of,*** tener necesidad de, necesitar; ***in case of need,*** en caso de necesidad; ***if need be,*** de ser necesario *o* preciso, si fuese menester; ***in need,*** necesitado. — *v.t.* necesitar (de), precisar; requerir, exigir; ***he needs it,*** lo necesita, le hace falta; ***he needs to see him,*** necesita verle; ***he needs watching,*** hay que vigilarle; ***it need not be done,*** no es preciso que se haga; ***time is needed,*** hace falta tiempo.
needful [ˈniːdful], *a.* necesario, preciso.
needfulness [ˈniːdfulnis], *s.* necesidad.
neediness [ˈniːdinis], *s.* necesidad, estrechez.
needle [niːdl], *s.* aguja; ***magnetic needle,*** aguja de marear; ***needle-case,*** alfiletero; (*ict.*) ***needle-fish,*** aguja; ***needle-holder,*** portaagujas, *m.inv.*; ***needle-shaped,*** acicular. — *v.t.* (*fam.*) chinchar, decir pullas a.
needless [ˈniːdlis], *a.* innecesario, superfluo, inútil; ***needless to say,*** huelga *o* sobra decir (que), ni que decir tiene (que).
needlessly [ˈniːdlisli], *adv.* sin necesidad.
needlessness [ˈniːdlisnis], *s.* (lo) innecesario.
needlewoman [ˈniːdlwumən], *s.* costurera.
needlework [ˈniːdlwəːk], *s.* costura; bordado.
needs [niːdz], *adv.* necesariamente; ***I must needs go,*** es menester *o* fuerza es que vaya; ***it must needs be,*** es menester; ***needs must when the Devil drives,*** a la fuerza ahorcan. — *s.* (*pl.*) [NEED].
needy [ˈniːdi], *a.* necesitado, menesteroso.
ne'er [nɛə], *contr.* (*poét.*) [NEVER].
nefarious [niˈfɛəriəs], *a.* ilícito, vituperable, inicio.
nefariousness [niˈfɛəriəsnis], *s.* (lo) ilícito, (lo) vil, iniquidad.
negate [niˈgeit], *v.t.* negar, anular, invalidar.
negation [niˈgeiʃən], *s.* negación.
negative [ˈnegətiv], *a.* negativo. — *s.* negativa, denegación; (*foto.*) negativo. — *v.t.* denegar, poner veto a, votar en contra de.
negativeness [ˈnegətivnis], *s.* (lo) negativo.
neglect [niˈglekt], *s.* descuido, abandono; negligencia; dejadez; incuria; ***to fall into neglect,*** caer en desuso. — *v.t.* descuidar, desatender; abandonar; (*deber*) faltar a; dejar (tener) abandonado; ***neglect to do sth.,*** dejar de, olvidarse de hacer algo.
neglectful [niˈglektful], *a.* negligente, dejado.
neglectfulness [niˈglektfulnis], [NEGLIGENCE].
negligee [ˈnegliʒei], *s.* salto de cama.
negligence [ˈneglidʒəns], *s.* negligencia, descuido, incuria, dejadez.
negligent [ˈneglidʒənt], *a.* negligente, dejado.
negligible [ˈneglidʒibl], *a.* insignificante, despreciable.
negotiability [nigouʃiəˈbiliti], *s.* negociabilidad.
negotiable [niˈgouʃiəbl], *a.* negociable; (*camino etc.*) transitable.
negotiate [niˈgouʃieit], *v.t.* negociar; gestionar; agenciar; (*obstáculo*) salvar; abrirse camino por; (*curva*) tomar; (*estrecho*) abocar. — *v.i.* negociar.
negotiation [nigouʃiˈeiʃən], *s.* negociación; gestión; ***to enter into negotiation,*** iniciar negociaciones, empezar a negociar; ***under negotiation,*** bajo negociaciones.
negotiator [niˈgouʃieitə], *s.* negociador; gestor.
Negress [ˈniːgres], *s.* (*a veces pey.*) negra.
Negro [ˈniːgrou], *s.* (*pl.* **Negroes** [-z]) (*a veces pey.*) negro.
Negroid [ˈniːgrɔid], *a.*, *s.* negroide.
negrophile [ˈniːgrofail], *a.*, *s.* negrófilo.
Negus [ˈniːgəs]. Negus, *m.*
Nehemiah [niiˈmaiə]. Neemías, *m.*
neigh [nei], *s.* relincho. — *v.i.* relinchar.
neighbour [ˈneibə], *s.* vecino; prójimo. — *v.t.* ser vecino de; estar contiguo a, estar cerca de.
neighbourhood [ˈneibəhud], *s.* vecindad, vecindario; ***in the neighbourhood of,*** en las inmediaciones de, alrededor de.
neighbouring [ˈneibəriŋ], *a.* vecino, cercano.
neighbourliness [ˈneibəlinis], *s.* buena vecindad.
neighbourly [ˈneibəli], *a.* de buen vecino, amistoso.
neighing [ˈneiiŋ], *s.* relincho(s).
neither [ˈnaiðə], *a.* ninguno (de los dos); ni uno ni otro. — *adv.* ni; ***neither . . . nor,*** ni . . . ni. — *conj.* ni; tampoco; ni . . . tampoco.
Nemesis [ˈnemisis], *s.* (*mit.*) Némesis, *f.*
nemesis [ˈnemisis], *s.* justicia.
nenuphar [ˈnenjufɑː], *s.* nenúfar.
neologic(al) [niəˈlɔdʒik(əl)], *a.* neológico.
neologism [niˈɔlədʒizəm], *s.* neologismo.
neologist [niˈɔlədʒist], *s.* neólogo.
neology [niˈɔlədʒi], *s.* neología.
neomenia [niouˈmiːniə], *s.* neomenia.
neon [ˈniːɔn], *s.* (*quím.*) neón; ***neon light,*** lámpara de neón; ***neon lighting,*** alumbrado de neón.
neophobia [niouˈfoubiə], *s.* neofobia.
neophyte [ˈnioufait], *s.* neófito.
neoplasm [ˈniouplæzəm], *s.* neoplasma, *m.*
neoplatonism [niouˈpleitənizəm], *s.* neoplatonismo.
neoteric(al) [niouˈterik(əl)], *a.* neotérico.
Nepal [nəˈpɔːl]. Nepal.
Nepalese [nepəˈliːz], *a.*, *s.* nepalés, *m.*
nepenthe [neˈpenθi], *s.* nepente.
nephew [ˈnevjuː], *s.* sobrino.
nephrite [ˈnefrait], *s.* nefrita.
nephritic [neˈfritik], *a.* nefrítico. — *s.* remedio nefrítico.
nephritis [neˈfraitis], *s.* nefritis, *f. inv.*
nepotism [ˈnepətizəm], *s.* nepotismo.
Neptune [ˈneptjuːn]. Neptuno.
nereid [ˈniəriid], *s.* nereida.
Nero [ˈniərou]. Nerón.
nerve [nəːv], *s.* nervio; (*bot.*) nervadura; (*fam.*) descaro, frescura; (*pl.*) nervios, *m.pl.*, nerviosidad, nerviosismo; ***nerve-cell,*** neurona; célula nerviosa; ***nerve-centre,*** centro nervioso; (*fig.*) punto neurálgico; ***nerve-racking,*** que agota *o* crispa los nervios; ***it gets on my nerves,*** me crispa los nervios, me saca de quicio; ***to lose one's nerve,*** perder la cabeza. — **nerve o.s.,** *v.r.* — ***to,*** acorazarse para.
nerved [nəːvd], *a.* nervudo.
nerveless [ˈnəːvlis], *a.* sin nervio.
nerviness, nervousness [ˈnəːvinis, -vəsnis], *s.* nerviosidad, nerviosismo.
nervous [ˈnəːvəs], *a.* nervioso; miedoso; ***nervous breakdown,*** crisis nerviosa; ***nervous exhaustion,*** agotamiento nervioso.
nervure [ˈnəːvjuə], *s.* nervadura.
nervy [ˈnəːvi], *a.* nervioso.
nescience [ˈnesiəns], *s.* nesciencia.
ness [nes], *s.* cabo, promontorio.
nest [nest], *s.* nido; nidada; juego (de cajones); ***nest-egg,*** nidal; (*fig.*) ahorros, *m.pl.*; ***nest of thieves,*** cueva de ladrones. — *v.i.* anidar, nidificar; buscar nido.
nestle [nesl], *v.i.* apretarse, acurrucarse, arrimarse; ***nestle up to,*** arrimarse a, apretarse contra.
nestling [ˈnes(t)liŋ], *s.* pajarito (en el nido).
net (1) [net], *a.* neto, líquido; ***net income,*** renta neta; ***net price,*** precio neto. — *v.t.* producir en neto.
net (2) [net], *s.* red, *f.*; redecilla; tul; ***net-maker,*** redero. — *v.t.* coger, pescar *o* cazar con red; conseguir, apropiarse.
nether [ˈneðə], *a.* más bajo, inferior; ***nether regions,*** infierno.

Netherlands [ˈneðələndz], **the.** los Países Bajos. — *a.* neerlandés.
nethermost [ˈnəðəmoust], *a.* más bajo, inferior.
nett [net], *a.* [NET (I)].
netting [ˈnetiŋ], *s.* obra de malla; redes, *f.pl.*
nettle [netl], *s.* (*bot.*) ortiga; ***nettle-rash,*** urticaria. — *v.t.* picar, provocar, irritar.
network [ˈnetwəːk], *s.* malla; red.
neuralgia [njuəˈrældʒə], *s.* neuralgia.
neuralgic [njuəˈrældʒik], *a.* neurálgico.
neurasthenia [njuərəsˈθiːniə], *s.* neurastenia.
neurasthenic [njuərəsˈθenik], *a., s.* neurasténico.
neurologist [njuəˈrɔlədʒist], *s.* neurólogo.
neurology [njuəˈrɔlədʒi], *s.* neurología.
neuropter [njuəˈrɔptə], *s.* neuróptero.
neurosis [njuəˈrousis], *s.* (*pl.* **neuroses** [-siːz]) neurosis, *f. inv.*
neurotic [njuəˈrɔtik], *a., s.* neurótico.
neurotomy [njuəˈrɔtəmi], *s.* neurotomía.
neuter [ˈnjuːtə], *a.* neutro.
neutral [ˈnjuːtrəl], *a.* neutral; neutro. — *s.* neutral; (*aut.*) ***in neutral,*** en punto muerto.
neutrality [njuːˈtræliti], *s.* neutralidad.
neutralization [njuːtrəlaiˈzeiʃən], *s.* neutralización.
neutralize [ˈnjutːrəlaiz], *v.t.* neutralizar.
neutron [ˈnjuːtrɔn], *s.* neutrón.
Nevada [niˈvɑːdə]. Nevada.
never [ˈnevə], *adv.* nunca, jamás; de ningún modo; por más (que); ***never a one,*** ni uno; ***never a word,*** ni una palabra; ***never again,*** nunca más; ***never-ceasing,*** incesante; ***never-ending,*** perpetuo, continuo, de nunca acabar; ***never-failing,*** infalible, inagotable; ***never mind,*** no importa; (*fam.*) ***to buy sth. on the never-never,*** comprar algo a plazos; ***be it never so great,*** por mucho que sea; ***be it never so little,*** por poco que sea.
nevermore [nevəˈmɔː], *adv.* nunca jamás.
nevertheless [nevəðəˈles], *adv.* sin embargo, no obstante, con todo.
new [njuː], *a.* nuevo; fresco; tierno; ***new bread,*** pan fresco, pan tierno; ***New Britain,*** Nueva Bretaña; ***New England,*** Nueva Inglaterra; ***New Guinea,*** Nueva Guinea; ***New Mexico,*** Nuevo Méjico; ***new moon,*** luna nueva, novilunio; ***New Orleans,*** Nueva Orleáns; ***new rich,*** nuevo rico; ***New Testament,*** Nuevo Testamento; ***New World,*** (el) Nuevo Mundo; ***New Year,*** año nuevo; ***to see the New Year in,*** celebrar el año nuevo; ***New York,*** Nueva York; ***New Yorker,*** neoyorquino; ***New Zealand,*** Nueva Zeland(i)a; ***New Zealander,*** neozelandés, *m.* — *adv.* recientemente; modernamente; nuevamente, de nuevo; ***new-born,*** recién nacido; ***new-fangled,*** recién inventado, moderno; ***new-laid egg,*** huevo fresco.
newcomer [ˈnjuːkʌmə], *s.* recién llegado.
newel [ˈnjuːəl], *s.* (*arq.*) nabo, bolo (de escalera); poste, pilar.
Newfoundland [ˈnjuːfaundˈlænd], *s.* Terranova; perro de Terranova.
newish [ˈnjuːiʃ], *a.* bastante nuevo.
newly [ˈnjuːli], *adv.* recientemente, recién; ***newly wed,*** recién casado.
newness [ˈnjuːnis], *s.* novedad; inexperiencia.
news [njuːz], *s.* noticias, *f.pl.*; nuevas, *f.pl.*; novedades, *f.pl.*; aviso; gacetilla; actualidades, *f.pl.*; ***news agency,*** agencia de noticias; ***news-bulletin,*** (boletín de) noticias; ***news-items,*** noticias, *f.pl.*, actualidades, *f.pl.*; ***news-reel,*** noticiario, actualidades (*cinematográficas*); ***news-stand,*** quiosco de periódicos; ***no news is good news,*** falta de noticias, buena señal; ***this was news to me,*** me cogió de nuevas; ***what is the news?*** ¿qué hay de nuevo? ¿qué noticias hay?
newsagent [ˈnjuːzeidʒənt], *s.* vendedor de periódicos; agente de prensa.
newsboy [ˈnjuːzbɔi], *s.* mozo vendedor de periódicos.
newsmonger [ˈnjuːzmʌŋgə], *s.* gacetista, *m.f.*
newspaper [ˈnjuːspeipə], *s.* periódico, diario.
newspaperman [ˈnjuːspeipəmæn], *s.* (*pl.* **-men** [-men]) periodista, *m.*
newsreader [ˈnjuːzriːdə], *s.* (*rad.*) locutor.
newsroom [ˈnjuːzruːm], *s.* redacción; sala de lectura.
newsvendor [ˈnjuːzvendə], *s.* vendedor de periódicos.
newswriter [ˈnjuːzraitə], *s.* gacetero, gacetillero, noticiero.
newsy [ˈnjuːzi], *a.* (*fam.*) que tiene muchas noticias, informativo.
newt [njuːt], *s.* tritón.
next [nekst], *a.* próximo, siguiente; vecino, inmediato, de al lado; ***the next best thing,*** lo mejor después de eso; ***next but one,*** el siguiente no, el otro; (***on***) ***the next day,*** al día siguiente; ***the next of kin,*** los parientes más cercanos, deudos más próximos, *m.pl.*; ***next time,*** la próxima vez; ***next to,*** junto a, al lado de; ***next to impossible,*** casi imposible, que raya en lo imposible; ***next to nothing,*** casi nada; ***in next to no time,*** en menos de nada; ***next week,*** la semana que viene; ***next year,*** el año que viene. — *adv.* luego, después; ahora; ***what next?*** y luego ¿qué? y ahora ¿qué?
nexus [ˈneksəs], *s.* nexo.
Niagara [naiˈægərə]. Niágara.
nib [nib], *s.* plumín.
nibble [nibl], *s.* mordisco. — *v.t.* mordiscar, mordisquear, picar.
nibs [nibz], *s.* (*fam.*) ***his nibs,*** su señoría, el jefe.
Nicaragua [nikəˈrægjuə]. Nicaragua.
Nicaraguan [nikəˈrægjuən], *a., s.* nicaragüense, *m.f.*
Nice [niːs]. Niza.
nice [nais], *a.* simpático; agradable; bonito; primoroso, meticuloso; sutil, delicado; ***nice and hot,*** calentito; ***it's nice and warm,*** hace un calorcito muy agradable; ***nice point,*** punto sutil, sutileza; ***nice-looking,*** guapo; (*fam.*) ***not nice,*** feo.
nicely [ˈnaisli], *adv.* muy bien, estupendamente.
niceness [ˈnaisnis], *s.* simpatía, (lo) simpático; delicadeza, sutileza.
nicety [ˈnaisiti], *s.* delicadeza, sutileza; exactitud; refinamiento; ***to a nicety,*** con la mayor precisión; (*pl.*) minucias, *f.pl.*
niche [nitʃ], *s.* nicho.
Nicholas [ˈnikələs]. Nicolás, *m.*
Nick [nik], (*dim.*) [NICHOLAS]; ***Old Nick,*** Patillas.
nick (I) [nik], *s.* muesca; mella; ***in the*** (***very***) ***nick of time,*** (justo) a tiempo. — *v.t.* mellar; (*fam.*) birlar.
nick (2) [nik], *s.* (*fam.*) chirona, cárcel. — *v.t.* (*fam.*) trincar; enchiquerar.
nickel [ˈnikəl], *s.* níquel; ***nickel-plated,*** niquelado; ***nickel-plater,*** niquelador; ***nickel-silver,*** metal blanco.
nickering [ˈnikəriŋ], *s.* (el) birlar.
nick-nack [KNICK-KNACK].
nickname [ˈnikneim], *s.* apodo, mote. — *v.t.* apodar, motejar.
nicotine [ˈnikətiːn], *s.* nicotina.
nidification [nidifiˈkeiʃən], *s.* nidificación.
niece [niːs], *s.* sobrina.
Niger [ˈnaidʒə], **the.** el Níger (*país*).
Nigeria [naiˈdʒiəriə]. Nigeria.
Nigerian [naiˈdʒierian], *a., s.* nigeriano.
niggard [ˈnigəd], *a., s.* tacaño, cicatero, avaro.
niggardliness [ˈnigədlinis], *s.* tacañería, cicatería, avaricia.
niggardly [ˈnigədli], *a.* tacaño, cicatero, avaro.

niggle [nigl], *v.i.* inquietarse por pequeñeces; ***niggle at,*** inquietar.
niggling [ˈnigliŋ], *a.* nimio, minucioso, insignificante; inquietante.
nigh [nai], *a.* (*ant.*) cercano — *adv.* cerca. — *prep.* cerca de; ***to draw nigh,*** avecinarse; ***nigh at hand,*** a la mano, al lado.
night [nait], *s.* noche, *f.*; ***at*** o ***by night,*** de noche; ***good night,*** buenas noches; ***last night,*** anoche; ***night-club,*** cabaret nocturno, club nocturno, boite; ***night-light,*** lamparilla de noche, mariposa; ***night-school,*** instituto nocturno; ***night-shift,*** turno *o* tanda de noche; (*Am.*) ***night-stick*** [TRUNCHEON]; ***night-walk,*** paseo de noche; ***night-walker,*** somnámbulo; ***night-walking,*** somnambulismo; ***night-watch,*** ronda de noche; ***night-watchman,*** sereno; vigilante; ***to have a night out on the town,*** andar *o* ir de picos pardos; ***to spend the night,*** hacer noche, pasar la noche, pernoctar, dormir; ***the maid's night out,*** la noche que libra la muchacha.
nightbird [ˈnaitbəːd], *s.* pájaro nocturno; (*fig.*, *fam.*) trasnochador.
nightcap [ˈnaitkæp], *s.* gorro de dormir; (*fig.*) (la) última copa antes de acostarse.
nightdress [ˈnaitdres], *s.* camisa de dormir; camisón.
nightfall [ˈnaitfɔːl], *s.* anochecer.
nightfire [ˈnaitfaiə], *s.* fuego de Santelmo; fuego fatuo.
nightgown [ˈnaitgaun], [NIGHTDRESS].
nightie [ˈnaiti], (*fam.*) [NIGHTDRESS].
nightingale [ˈnaitiŋgeil], *s.* (*orn.*) ruiseñor.
nightjar [ˈnaitdʒaː], *s.* (*orn.*) chotacabras, *m. inv.*
nightless [ˈnaitlis], *a.* que no tiene noche(s).
nightly [ˈnaitli], *a.* nocturno. — *adv.* de noche, por la(s) noche(s).
nightmare [ˈnaitmɛə], *s.* pesadilla.
nightshade [ˈnaitʃeid], *s.* (*bot.*) hierbamora, belladona, beleño.
nigrescent [naiˈgresənt], *a.* negruzco, ennegrecido.
nihilism [ˈnaiilizəm], *s.* nihilismo.
nihilist [ˈnaiilist], *s.* nihilista, *m.f.*
nil [nil], *s.* nada; cero.
Nile [ˈnail]. Nilo.
nimble [nimbl], *a.* ágil, ligero, activo; ***nimble-footed,*** ligero de pies; ***nimble-witted,*** listo, despejado, de mucha rapidez mental.
nimbleness [ˈnimblnis], *s.* agilidad, ligereza.
nimbus [ˈnimbəs], *s.* (*pl.* **nimbuses, nimbi** [-əsiz, -ai]) nimbo.
nincompoop [ˈniŋkəmpuːp], *s.* necio, mastuerzo, cantamañanas, *m.inv.*
nine [nain], *a.*, *s.* nueve; (*fam.*) ***dressed up to the nines,*** hecho un brazo de mar.
ninefold [ˈnainfould], *adv.* nueve veces.
ninepins [ˈnainpinz], *s.* bolos, *m.pl.*, juego de bolos; ***to go down like ninepins,*** morir como chinches.
nineteen [nainˈtiːn], *a.*, *s.* diecinueve, diez y nueve; ***to talk nineteen to the dozen,*** hablar por los codos.
nineteenth [nainˈtiːnθ], *a.* décimonoveno, décimonono; diecinueve (*títulos*). — *s.* décimonovena parte; diecinueve (*fechas*).
ninetieth [ˈnaintiəθ], *a.*, *s.* nonagésimo, noventavo.
ninety [ˈnainti], *a.*, *s.* noventa.
ninny [ˈnini], *s.* (*despec.*) bobo, simplón; marica.
ninth [nainθ], *a.* novena (*t. títulos*); nono (*sólo títulos de papas*). — *s.* novena parte; nueve (*fechas*).
niobium [naiˈoubiəm], *s.* niobio.
nip (1) [nip], *s.* pellizco; mordisco; (*fig.*) frío, fresquete; ***there's a nip in the air,*** hace fresquete. — *v.t.* pellizcar, tirar un pellizco a; cortar (el frío); ***nip in the bud,*** cortar en ciernes.
nip (2) [nip], *v.i.* (*fam.*) — ***along,*** ir corriendo; ir en un momento; ***nip in,*** entrar de prisa *o* en un momento; ***nip off,*** largarse.
nip (3) [nip], *s.* (*fam.*) trago, sorbo.
nipper [ˈnipə], *s.* (*fam.*) chiquillo, chaval, rapaz.
nippers [ˈnipəz], *s.pl.* pinzas, *f.pl.*, tenazas, *f.pl.*; alicates, *m.pl.*
nipple [nipl], *s.* pezón; (*biberón*, *anat. masculina*) tetilla; (*mec.*) boquilla.
nipplewort [ˈniplwəːt], *s.* (*bot.*) lapsana.
nippy [ˈnipi], *a.* (*fam.*) frío, fresquillo; ***it's nippy,*** hace fresquillo *o* fresquete, hace un biruje *o* un gris.
nit [nit], *s.* liendre, *f.*; (*fam.*) [NITWIT].
nitrate [ˈnaitreit], *s.* nitrato.
nitre [ˈnaitə], *s.* nitro.
nitric [ˈnaitrik], *a.* nítrico.
nitrogen [ˈnaitrədʒen], *s.* nitrógeno.
nitro-glycerine [naitrou-ˈglisərin], *s.* nitroglicerina.
nitrous [ˈnaitrəs], *a.* nitroso.
nitty [ˈniti], *a.* lendroso.
nitwit [ˈnitwit], *s.* (*fam.*) cretino.
nival [ˈnaivəl], *a.* nevoso.
niveous [ˈniviəs], *a.* níveo.
no [nou], *a.* ninguno; ***no man*** o ***no one,*** nadie; ***no man's land,*** tierra de nadie; ***no matter,*** no importa; ***no more of this,*** basta de eso; ***to no purpose,*** en vano, inútilmente; ***with no,*** sin. — *adv.* no. — *s.* no, voto negativo.
Noah [ˈnouə]. Noé, *m.*
nob (1) [nɔb], *s.* (*fam.*) señor(ón).
nob (2) [nɔb], *s.* (*fam.*) cabeza.
nobble [nɔbl], *v.t.* (*caballo*) narcotizar; (*cosa*) birlar; (*pers.*) sobornar.
nobiliary [nouˈbiliəri], *a.* nobiliario.
nobilitate [nouˈbiliteit], *v.t.* ennoblecer, hacer noble.
nobilitation [noubiliˈteiʃən], *s.* ennoblecimiento.
nobility, nobleness, noblesse [nouˈbiliti, ˈnoublnis, nouˈbles], *s.* nobleza.
noble [noubl], *a.* noble. — *s.* noble.
nobleman [ˈnoublmən], *s.* noble.
noblewoman [ˈnoublwumən], *s.* mujer noble.
nobody [ˈnoubɔdi], *pron.* nadie, ninguno. — *s.* nulidad; ***to be a nobody,*** no ser nada.
noctambulism [nɔkˈtæmbjulizəm], *s.* noctambulismo.
noctambulist [nɔkˈtæmbjulist], *s.* noctámbulo.
nocturnal [nɔkˈtəːnəl], *a.* nocturno.
nocturne [ˈnɔktəːn], *s.* (*mús.*) nocturno.
nod [nɔd], *s.* cabezada; señal hecha con la cabeza; reverencia, inclinación de la cabeza; (*fam.*) ***Land of Nod,*** sueño, mu, *f.* — *v.i.* asentir con la cabeza; dar cabezadas, cabecear; ***nod off,*** dormirse.
nodal [ˈnoudəl], *a.* nodal.
noddle [nɔdl], *s.* (*fam.*) cholla, mollera.
noddy [ˈnɔdi], *s.* bobo.
node [noud], *s.* nodo; nodo.
nodose [ˈnoudous], *a.* nudoso.
nodosity [nouˈdɔsiti], *s.* nudosidad.
nodular [ˈnɔdjulə], *a.* nodular.
nodule [ˈnɔdjuːl], *s.* nódulo.
nog [nɔg], *s.* bote; (*mar.*) cabilla para escotas; clavija; perno; cerveza fuerte.
noggin [ˈnɔgin], *s.* vaso (pequeño).
nogging [ˈnɔgiŋ], *s.* tabique.
noise [nɔiz], *s.* ruido; (*fam.*) ***big noise,*** pez gordo. — *v.t.* — ***abroad,*** divulgar.
noiseless [ˈnɔizlis], *a.* sin ruido, silencioso.
noiselessness [ˈnɔizlisnis], *s.* silencio.
noisiness [ˈnɔizinis], *s.* ruido, bullicio.
noisome [ˈnɔisəm], *a.* apestoso, maloliente, fétido.
noisomeness [ˈnɔisəmnis], *s.* mal olor, fetidez.
noisy [ˈnɔizi], *a.* ruidoso, bullicioso.

noli-me-tangere [noulai-mi:-ˈtændʒəri], *s.* (*med.*) noli me tángere, *m.*; (*fam.*) no me toques, *m.*
nomad [ˈnoumæd], *a.*, *s.* nómada, *m.f.*
nomadic [nouˈmædik], *a.* nómada.
nom-de-plume [nɔm-də-ˈplu:m], *s.* seudónimo.
nomenclator [ˈnoumenkleitɔ:], *s.* nomenclator.
nomenclature [nouˈmenklətʃə], *s.* nomenclatura.
nominal [ˈnɔminəl], *a.* nominal.
nominalism [ˈnɔminəlizəm], *s.* nominalismo.
nominalist [ˈnɔminəlist], *a.*, *s.* nominalista, *m.f.*
nominally [ˈnɔminəli], *adv.* nominalmente, de nombre.
nominate [ˈnɔmineit], *v.t.* nombrar; proponer.
nomination [nɔmiˈneiʃən], *s.* nombramiento; propuesta.
nominative [ˈnɔminətiv], *a.* nominativo. — *s.* nominativo.
nominator [ˈnɔmineitə], *s.* nominador.
nominee [nɔmiˈni:], *s.* persona nombrada *o* propuesta.
non-acceptance [nɔn-ækˈseptəns], *s.* no aceptación, inaceptación.
nonage [ˈnounidʒ], *s.* minoridad.
nonagenarian [nounədʒiˈnɛəriən], *a.*, *s.* nonagenario.
nonagesimal [nɔnəˈdʒesiməl], *a.* nonagésimo.
non-aggression [nɔn-əˈgreʃən], *s.* no agresión.
nonagon [ˈnɔnəgən], *s.* nonágono.
non-alcoholic [nɔn-ælkəˈhɔlik], *a.* no alcohólico.
non-appearance [nɔn-əˈpiərəns], *s.* (el) no aparecer, (el) no asomar; ausencia; (*for.*) no comparencia.
non-attendance [nɔn-əˈtendəns], *s.* (el) no asistir.
nonce [nɔns], *s.* ***for the nonce,*** de momento, por ahora.
nonchalance [ˈnɔnʃələns], *s.* desembarazo, desenfado; desparpajo; indiferencia.
nonchalant [ˈnɔnʃələnt], *a.* desembarazado, desenfadado; que tiene desparpajo; indiferente.
non-combatant [nɔn-ˈkɔmbətənt], *a.* no combatiente.
non-commissioned [nɔn-kəˈmiʃənd], *a.* (*mil.*) — ***officer,*** cabo, sargento *o* suboficial.
non-committal [nɔn-kəˈmitəl], *a.* circunspecto, que no quiere comprometerse.
non-condensing [nɔn-kənˈdensiŋ], *a.* sin condensador.
non-conductor [nɔn-kənˈdʌktə], *s.* (*fís.*) mal conductor, aislante.
nonconformist [nɔnkənˈfɔ:mist], *a.*, *s.* disidente, *m.f.*, no conformista, *m.f.*, inconformista.
nonconformity [nɔnkənˈfɔ:miti], *s.* disidencia, no conformismo, inconformismo.
non-delivery [nɔn-diˈlivəri], *s.* falta de envío *o* de entrega.
nondescript [ˈnɔndiskript], *a.* indefinible; mediocre; mostrenco.
none [nʌn], *adv.* no; de ningún modo; nada; ***none the less,*** no obstante; ***he was none the better (the worse) for it,*** no por ello salió mejor (peor) librado. — *pron. indef.* nadie, ninguno, ninguna; nada; ***none of that,*** nada de eso; ***he has none,*** no tiene.
nonentity [nɔnˈentiti], *s.* nulidad, cero a la izquierda.
nones [nounz], *s.pl.* nonas, *f.pl.*; (*igl.*) nona.
nonesuch [ˈnʌnsʌtʃ], *s.* sin par.
non-execution [nɔn-eksiˈkju:ʃən], *s.* falta de ejecución.
non-intervention [nɔn-intəˈvenʃən], *s.* ***non-intervention policy,*** política de no intervención.
non-iron [ˈnɔn-ˈaiən], *a.* que no necesita plancha.
nonpareil [nɔnpəˈrel], *s.* sin igual; (*impr.*) nonparel.
non-payment [nɔn-ˈpeimənt], *s.* falta de pago.
nonplus [nɔnˈplʌs], *v.t.* dejar turulato *o* estupefacto.
non-resident [nɔn-ˈrezidənt], *a.* no residente, no fijo.
nonsense [ˈnɔnsəns], *s.* desatino, disparate, insensatez; ***to make a nonsense of sth.,*** hacer que algo resulte ridículo; ***no nonsense!*** ¡formalidad!; ***piece of nonsense,*** tontería.
nonsensical [nɔnˈsensikəl], *a.* desatinado, disparatado.
nonsensicalness [nɔnˈsensikəlnis], *s.* disparate; (lo) disparatado.
non-shrink [ˈnɔn-ˈʃriŋk], *a.* sanforizado.
nonsolvency [nɔnˈsɔlvənsi], *s.* insolvencia.
nonsolvent [nɔnˈsɔlvənt], *a.* insolvente.
nonsuit [nɔnˈs(j)u:t], *s.* (*der.*) desistimiento. — *v.t.* absolver de la instancia.
non-voter [nɔn-ˈvoutə], *s.* abstencionista, *m.f.*
noodle [nu:dl], *s.* (*fam.*) bobo; (*fam.*) cabeza; (*coc.*) tallarín, fideo.
nook [nuk], *s.* rincón, escondrijo; ***to search every nook and cranny,*** buscar exhaustivamente.
noon, noonday, noontide [nu:n, ˈnu:ndei, ˈnu:ntaid], *s.* mediodía, *m.*; punto culminante, apogeo.
noose [nu:s], *s.* lazo, nudo corredizo; gaza; (*ahorcar*) dogal. — *v.t.* lazar, coger con lazo.
nopal [noupl], *s.* nopal.
nor [nɔ:], *conj.* ni, no; tampoco; ***nor was this all,*** y esto no era todo.
norm [nɔ:m], *s.* norma; pauta, modelo.
normal [ˈnɔ:məl], *a.* normal; (*geom.*) perpendicular.
Norman [ˈnɔ:mən], *a.*, *s.* normando.
norman [ˈnɔ:mən], *s.* (*mar.*) burel del molinete.
Normandy [ˈnɔ:məndi]. Normandía.
Norse [nɔ:s], *a.* escandinavo, noruego. — *s.* (*ant. idioma*) nórdico.
north [nɔ:θ], *a.* del norte, septentrional; ***North Africa,*** Africa del Norte; ***North America,*** Norteamérica; ***North Carolina,*** Carolina del Norte; ***north-east,*** nordeste; ***North Sea,*** Mar del Norte; ***north-west,*** noroeste. — *s.* norte, septentrión.
northerly [ˈnɔ:ðəli], *a.* del norte, septentrional.
northern [ˈnɔ:ðən], *a.* del norte, septentrional; ***Northern Ireland,*** Irlanda del Norte.
northernmost [ˈnɔ:ðənmoust], *a.* (el) más septentrional.
northward [ˈnɔ:θwəd], *a.*, *adv.* hacia el norte. — *s.* norte.
northwards [ˈnɔ:θwədz], *adv.* hacia el norte.
Norway [ˈnɔ:wei]. Noruega.
Norwegian [nɔ:ˈwi:dʒən], *a.*, *s.* noruego.
nose [nouz], *s.* nariz; (*animal*) hocico; (*vehículo*) morro; olfato; (*mar.*) proa; ***nose-bag,*** cebadera, morral; ***nose-band,*** muserola; ***nose-dive,*** picado vertical; ***Roman nose,*** nariz aguileña; ***snub nose,*** nariz chata; ***turned-up nose,*** nariz respingada; ***to blow one's nose,*** sonarse; ***to follow one's nose,*** ir todo seguido; dejarse llevar por el instinto; ***to have a good nose for,*** tener buen olfato para; (*fig.*) ***to lead by the nose,*** tener en un puño; ***to look down one's nose at,*** mirar por encima del hombro; ***to pay through the nose,*** pagar un ojo de la cara; ***to poke one's nose into everything,*** querer mangonearlo todo; ***to turn up one's nose at,*** hacer feos a; ***under the very nose of,*** en las barbas de. — *v.t.* husmear, olfatear; restregar la nariz contra; ***nose out,*** descubrir husmeando; ***nose one's way,*** avanzar con precaución. — *v.i.* — ***about,*** curiosear.
nosebleed [ˈnouzbli:d], *s.* hemorragia nasal.
nosed [nouzd], *a.* con nariz.
nosegay [ˈnouzgei], *s.* ramillete.
noseless [ˈnouzlis], *a.* desnarigado.
nosography [nɔˈsɔgrəfi], *s.* nosografía.
nosology [nɔˈsɔlədʒi], *s.* nosología.
nostalgia [nɔsˈtældʒiə], *s.* nostalgia.

nostril [ˈnɔstril], *s.* ventana de la nariz, *f.*
nostrum [ˈnɔstrəm], *s.* remedio secreto, panacea.
nosy [ˈnouzi], *a.* (*fam.*) curiosón, fisgón; ***nosy parker,*** fisgón.
not [nɔt], *adv.* no; ***not half!*** ¡ya lo creo!; ***not likely!*** ¡ni hablar! ¡ni soñarlo!; ***he had not so much as heard,*** ni siquiera había oído; ***not thinking that,*** sin pensar que; ***not to say,*** por no decir; ***I think not,*** creo que no; ***why not?*** ¿cómo no? ¿porqué no?
notability [noutəˈbiliti], *s.* notabilidad.
notable [ˈnoutəbl], *a.* notable, señalado. — *s.* persona notable, notabilidad.
notableness [ˈnoutəblnis], *s.* notabilidad.
notary [ˈnoutəri], *s.* notario.
notation [nouˈteiʃən], *s.* notación.
notch [nɔtʃ], *s.* mella, muesca. — *v.t.* mellar, hacer muescas en.
note [nout], *s.* nota; apunte; billete (de banco); (*com.*) vale; pagaré; ***note-book,*** cuaderno; libro de apuntes; ***of note,*** notable; ***to make a note of,*** apuntar; ***to take note of,*** tomar nota de; ***to take notes,*** tomar notas, tomar *o* sacar apuntes. — *v.t.* notar, observar, advertir; anotar, apuntar.
noted [ˈnoutid], *a.* conocido, famoso, célebre.
noteworthy [ˈnoutwəːði], *a.* notable, digno de notarse.
nothing [ˈnʌθiŋ], *adv.* en nada; de ninguna manera; ***nothing daunted,*** sin arredrarse. — *s.* nada; nadería; friolera; (*mat.*) cero; ***for nothing,*** gratuitamente, de balde; ***to be good for nothing,*** no servir para nada, ser inútil; ***to be nothing to,*** no importar a; ***to come to nothing,*** quedarse en nada; ***to have nothing to do with,*** no tener nada que ver con; ***to make nothing of,*** no sacar nada de, no comprender; ***nothing to speak of,*** poca cosa; ***nothing ventured, nothing gained,*** quien no se arriesga no cruza la mar; ***there's nothing for it, but...,*** no hay más remedio que....
nothingness [ˈnʌθiŋnis], *s.* (la) nada; insignificancia.
notice [ˈnoutis], *s.* aviso; informe; observación, nota, reparo; cuidado, atención; conocimiento; cartel, anuncio; plazo; ***notice-board,*** tablón *o* tablero de anuncios; ***until further notice,*** hasta nuevo aviso; ***short notice,*** poca anticipación; ***worthy of notice,*** digno de atención; ***to attract notice,*** atraer la atención; ***to give notice,*** avisar, hacer saber; ***to give notice of,*** notificar, hacer saber; (*patrón*) ***to give notice to s.o.,*** despedir; (*empleado*) despedirse; ***to give short notice,*** dar corto plazo, conceder un breve plazo; ***to take notice of,*** observar, notar, advertir; hacer caso de; ***to be under notice,*** estar despedido, llevar dimisorias. — *v.t.* advertir, reparar en, fijarse en, notar, hacer caso de.
noticeable [ˈnoutisəbl], *a.* evidente, perceptible; notable.
notification [noutifiˈkeiʃən], *s.* notificación.
notify [ˈnoutifai], *v.t.* notificar, comunicar, hacer saber; avisar.
notion [ˈnouʃən], *s.* noción, idea; capricho; inclinación; (*pl. Am.*) [HABERDASHERY].
notional [ˈnouʃənəl], *a.* nocional; especulativo.
notoriety [noutəˈraiiti], *s.* mala fama; escándalo; notoriedad.
notorious [noˈtɔːriəs], *a.* (tristemente) famoso; notorio.
notoriousness [noˈtɔːriəsnis], *s.* mala fama; notoriedad.
notwithstanding [nɔtwiðˈstændiŋ], *adv.* no obstante, empero. — *conj.* aun cuando; ***notwithstanding (that),*** pese a que, a pesar de que. — *prep.* a pesar de, no obstante.
nought [NAUGHT].
noun [naun], *s.* sustantivo, nombre.
nourish [ˈnʌriʃ], *v.t.* nutrir, alimentar; sustentar, mantener; (*fig.*) fomentar, alentar.
nourishable [ˈnʌriʃəbl], *a.* nutritivo, nutricio.
nourisher [ˈnʌriʃə], *s.* nutridor, alimentador.
nourishing [ˈnʌriʃiŋ], *a.* alimenticio, nutritivo.
nourishment [ˈnʌriʃmənt], *s.* alimento, nutrimento, sustento; nutrición.
nouveau riche [ˈnuːvou ˈriːʃ], *s.* nuevo rico.
Nova Scotia [ˈnouvə ˈskouʃə]. Nueva Escocia.
novation [nouˈveiʃən], *s.* novación.
novel [ˈnɔvəl], *a.* nuevo, novedoso, original, insólito. — *s.* novela.
novelette [nɔvəˈlet], *s.* novela corta.
novelettish [nɔvəˈletiʃ], *a.* folletinesco.
novelist [ˈnɔvəlist], *s.* novelista, *m.f.*
novelty [ˈnɔvəlti], *s.* novedad, innovación.
November [noˈvembə], *s.* noviembre.
novice [ˈnɔvis], *s.* novato, principiante, *m.f.*; (*igl.*) novicio.
novitiate [nouˈviʃiit], *s.* noviciado.
now [nau], *adv.* ahora; ya; ahora bien; ***he should be there by now,*** ya debe de haber llegado; ***from now on,*** (de ahora) en adelante; ***how now?*** ¿qué tal ahora? ¿ahora qué?; ***just now,*** ahora mismo; hace un momento; ***now... now...,*** ora... ora...; ya... ya...; ***now and again*** o ***now and then,*** de vez en cuando, de cuando en cuando; ***right now,*** ahora mismo; ***it was now two o'clock,*** eran ya las dos. — *conj.* ahora bien, pues; ***now that,*** ya que. — *s.* (el) ahora.
nowadays [ˈnauədeiz], *adv.* hoy en día.
nowhere [ˈnouwɛə], *adv.* en ninguna parte, en ningún sitio.
nowise [ˈnouwaiz], *adv.* de ningún modo, de ninguna manera.
noxious [ˈnɔkʃəs], *a.* novico; (*fam.*) apestoso.
nozzle [nɔzl], *s.* tobera, inyector; boquerel (*de manguera*).
nub [nʌb], *s.* (*fam.*) ***the nub of the matter,*** el quid del asunto.
Nubian [ˈnjuːbiən], *a., s.* nubio.
nubile [ˈnjuːbail], *a.* núbil.
nuclear [ˈnjuːkliə], *a.* nuclear; ***nuclear-powered,*** de impulsión nuclear.
nucleus [ˈnjuːkliəs], *s.* (*pl.* **nuclei** [-kliai]) núcleo.
nude [njuːd], *a.* desnudo. — *s.* (*b.a.*) desnudo.
nudge [nʌdʒ], *s.* codazo leve, codacito. — *v.t.* dar un codacito a, tocar levemente con el codo.
nudism [ˈnjuːdizəm], *s.* desnudismo.
nudist [ˈnjuːdist], *a., s.* desnudista, *m.f.*
nudity [ˈnjuːditi], *s.* desnudez.
nugatory [ˈnjuːgətəri], *a.* fútil.
nugget [ˈnʌgit], *s.* pepita (*de oro*).
nuggety [ˈnʌgiti], *a.* abundante en pepitas.
nuisance [ˈnjuːsəns], *s.* molestia, fastidio, lata; ***to be a nuisance, make a nuisance of o.s.,*** ser una lata *o* un tostón, dar la lata *o* el tostón; ***what a nuisance!*** ¡qué lata!
null [nʌl], *a.* nulo; ineficaz, inútil; inválido.
nullify [ˈnʌlifai], *v.t.* anular, invalidar.
nullity [ˈnʌliti], *s.* nulidad.
Numantia [njuːˈmænʃə]. Numancia.
numb [nʌm], *a.* entumecido; insensible; ***numb with cold,*** aterido de frío; ***numb with fear,*** paralizado de miedo. — *v.t.* entumecer; insensibilizar; entorpecer.
number [ˈnʌmbə], *s.* número; cifra; (*pl., poét.*) versos, *m.pl.*; ***a number of,*** algunos, varios; ***back number,*** número atrasado; (*fig.*) ***number one,*** uno mismo, sí mismo; ***to look after number one,*** cuidarse, cuidar de uno mismo; (*fig.*) ***quite a number!*** ¡menuda papeleta!; ***round numbers,*** números redondos; (*fig.*) ***I've got your number,*** ya me lo conozco a usted, le tengo calado. — *v.t.* numerar; contar; poner número a; ascender a; ***to be numbered among,*** figurar entre; ***his days are numbered,*** tiene los días contados.
numberer [ˈnʌmbərə], *s.* contador, numerador.

numbering [ˈnʌmbəriŋ], *s.* numeración.
numberless [ˈnʌmbəlis], *a.* innumerable, sin número.
number-plate [ˈnʌmbə-pleit], *s.* (*aut.*) (placa de) matrícula.
numb-fish [ˈnʌm-fiʃ], *s.* (*ict.*) torpedo.
numbles [nʌmblz], *s.pl.* entrañas de venado, *m.pl.*
numbness [ˈnʌmnis], *s.* entumecimiento; aterimiento; insensibilidad.
numerable [ˈnju:mərəbl], *a.* numerable.
numeracy [ˈnju:mərəsi], *s.* talento numérico.
numeral [ˈnju:mərəl], *a.* numeral. — *s.* número, cifra, guarismo.
numerally [ˈnju:mərəli], *adv.* numéricamente; individualmente.
numerary [ˈnju:mərəri], *a.* numerario.
numerate [ˈnju:mərit], *a.* poseyendo talento numérico. — [-eit], *v.t.* numerar, contar.
numeration [nju:məˈreiʃən], *s.* numeración.
numerator [ˈnju:məreitə], *s.* contador; (*arit.*) numerador.
numeric(al) [nju:ˈmerik(əl)], *a.* numérico.
numerically [nju:ˈmerikəli], *adv.* numéricamente; individualmente.
numerous [ˈnju:mərəs], *a.* numeroso; muchos.
numerousness [ˈnju:mərəsnis], *s.* numerosidad.
Numidia [nju:ˈmidiə]. Numidia.
Numidian [nju:ˈmidiən], *a.*, *s.* númida, *m.f.*
numismatic [nju:mizˈmætik], *a.* numismático.
numismatics [nju:mizˈmætiks], *s.pl.* numismática.
numismatographer [nju:mizməˈtɔgrəfə], *s.* numismatógrafo.
numismatography [nju:mizməˈtɔgrəfi], *s.* numismatografía.
numismatologist [nju:mizməˈtɔlədʒist], *s.* numismático.
numismatology [nju:mizməˈtɔlədʒi], *s.* numismática.
numskull [ˈnʌmskʌl], *s.* zote, lerdo.
nun [nʌn], *s.* monja; (*orn.*) paro.
nun-buoy [ˈnʌn-boi], *s.* (*mar.*) boya de barrilete.
nuncio [ˈnʌnʃiou], *s.* nuncio (*apostólico*).
nuncupative [ˈnʌŋkjupeitiv], *a.* nuncupativo.
nunnery [ˈnʌnəri], *s.* convento de monjas.
nuphar [ˈnju:fɑ:], *s.* nenúfar amarillo.
nuptial [ˈnʌpʃəl], *a.* nupcial; ***nuptial ode,*** epitalamio.
nuptials [ˈnʌpʃəlz], *s.pl.* nupcias, *f.pl.*, bodas, *f.pl.*
Nuremberg [ˈnjuərəmbə:g]. Nuremberga.
nurse [nə:s], *s.* enfermera; nodriza, ama de cría; niñera; ***dry nurse,*** ama seca; ***male nurse,*** enfermero; ***to put to nurse,*** poner ama a; ***wet nurse,*** ama de leche. — *v.t.* cuidar; criar, amamantar; (*fig.*) alimentar, abrigar, acariciar; fomentar; curar, tratar (*una enfermedad*); ***nurse a grievance,*** estar resentido. — *v.i.* ser enfermera.
nursemaid [ˈnə:smeid], *s.* niñera.
nursery [ˈnə:səri], *s.* cuarto de (los) niños; (*bot.*) criadero, vivero, semillero; (*fig.*) plantel; ***nursery rhymes,*** canciones infantiles, *f.pl.*; ***nursery school,*** jardín de infancia.
nursing [ˈnə:siŋ], *a.* de lactancia; ***nursing mother,*** mujer parturienta. — *s.* lactancia; crianza; asistencia; profesión de enfermera; ***nursing home,*** sanatorio, clínica.
nursling [ˈnə:sliŋ], *s.* criatura, niño de pecho.
nurture [ˈnə:tʃə], *s.* nutrición; (*fig.*) educación. — *v.t.* nutrir; criar, educar.
nut [nʌt], *s.* (*nogal*) nuez; (*avellano*) avellana; (*mec.*) tuerca; (*fam.*) cabeza; (*fam.*) chalado; (*pl.*) frutos secos, *m.pl.*; (*fam.*) ***nut-case,*** chalado; ***nut-crackers,*** cascanueces, *m.inv.*; ***nut-gall,*** agalla de monte; ***nut-oil,*** aceite de cacahuetes; ***nut-tree,*** avellano; (*fam.*) ***to be nuts about, on,*** estar chalado por *o* con; ***to drive nuts,*** volver loco *o* mochales; (*fig.*) ***to be a hard nut to crack,*** ser hueso duro de roer, ser duro de pelar.
nutation [nju:ˈteiʃən], *s.* nutación.
nut-brown [ˈnʌt-braun], *a.* avellanado.
nuthatch [ˈnʌthætʃ], *s.* (*orn.*) trepatroncos, *m.inv.*
nutmeg [ˈnʌtmeg], *s.* nuez moscada.
nutria [ˈnju:triə], *s.* (*zool.*) nutria.
nutrient [ˈnju:triənt], *a.* nutritivo. — *s.* alimento.
nutriment [ˈnju:trimənt], *s.* nutrimento, alimento.
nutrition [nju:ˈtriʃən], *s.* nutrición, alimentación.
nutritional [nju:ˈtriʃənəl], *a.* nutritivo.
nutritious [nju:ˈtriʃəs], *a.* nutritivo, alimenticio.
nutritive [ˈnju:tritiv], *a.* nutritivo.
nutshell [ˈnʌtʃel], *s.* cáscara de nuez; (*fig.*) ***in a nutshell,*** en resumidas cuentas, en resumen.
nutty [ˈnʌti], *a.* de nuez *o* de avellana; (*fam.*) chalado, chiflado.
nux vomica [ˈnʌks ˈvɔmikə], *s.* (*bot.*) nuez vómica.
nuzzle [nʌzl], *v.t.* hocicar; acariciar con el hocico. — *v.i.* — ***up to,*** arrimarse cariñosamente *o* mimosamente a.
nymph [nimf], *s.* ninfa.
nympha [ˈnimfə], *s.* (*zool.*) ninfa.
nymphæa [nimˈfi:ə], *s.* (*bot.*) ninfea.
nymphlike [ˈnimflaik], *a.* ninfal.
nymphomania [nimfoˈmeiniə], *s.* ninfomanía, furor uterino.
nymphomaniac [nimfoˈmeiniæk], *s.* ninfómana.

O

O (1), **o** [ou], décimoquinta letra del alfabeto.
O! (2) [OH!].
oaf [ouf], *s.* (*fam.*) zoquete, patán, palurdo; zafio.
oafish ['oufiʃ], *a.* zoquete, patán; zafio.
oafishness ['oufiʃnis], *s.* zoquetería; zafiedad.
oak [ouk], *s.* (*bot.*) roble; ***cork oak,*** alcornoque, roble de corcho; ***evergeen oak,*** encina; ***oak-apple,*** agalla; ***oak bark,*** corteza de roble; ***oak gall,*** bugalla; ***oak grove,*** robledo, robledal; ***scarlet oak,*** coscoja.
oaken ['oukən], *a.* roblizo, de roble.
oakum ['oukəm], *s.* (*mar.*) estopa (*para calafatear*).
oaky ['ouki], *a.* de roble; fuerte, duro.
oar [ɔ:], *s.* remo; remero; ***oar-maker,*** remero; ***to put one's oar in,*** meter baza; (*fig.*) ***to rest on one's oars,*** dormirse en los laureles; ***to ship*** (***unship***) ***oars,*** armar (desarmar) los remos. — *v.t.* mover a remo. — *v.i.* remar, bogar.
oared [ɔ:d], *a.* provisto de remos.
oarlock ['ɔ:lɔk], (*Am.*) [ROWLOCK].
oarsman ['ɔ:zmən], *s.* (*pl.* **oarsmen** [-men]) remador, remero.
oasis [ou'eisis], *s.* (*pl.* **oases** [-si:z]) oasis, *m.inv.*
oast [oust], *s.* horno para lúpulo.
oat [out], *s.* (*bot.*) avena; ***oat-field,*** avenal; (*fig.*) ***to sow one's wild oats,*** pasar las mocedades, correrla.
oaten ['outən], *a.* de avena, aveníceo.
oath [ouθ], *s.* juramento; jura; reniego; blasfemia; ***on oath,*** bajo juramento; ***to put*** (***s.o.***) ***on oath,*** hacer prestar juramento; ***to take an*** o ***the oath,*** prestar juramento.
oatmeal ['outmi:l], *s.* harina de avena, gachas, *f.pl.*, puches, *m.pl.*
obbligato [ɔbli'gɑ:tou], *s.* (*mús.*) obligado.
obduracy, obdurateness ['ɔbdjurəsi, -ritnis], *s.* obstinación, terquedad.
obdurate ['ɔbdjurit], *a.* obstinado, terco; empedernido.
obedience [o'bi:diəns], *s.* obediencia.
obedient [o'bi:diənt], *a.* obediente; dócil, sumiso.
obeisance [o'beisəns], *s.* reverencia; acato, acatamiento; ***to pay obeisance to,*** tributar homenaje a.
obelisk ['ɔbilisk], *s.* obelisco; (*impr.*) obelo, cruz, *f.*
obese [o'bi:s], *a.* obeso, gordo.
obesity, obeseness [o'bi:siti, -nis], *s.* obesidad.
obey [o'bei], *v.t.* obedecer; acatar. — *v.i.* obedecer, ser obediente.
obfuscate ['ɔbfʌskeit], *v.t.* ofuscar.
obfuscation [ɔbfʌs'keiʃən], *s.* ofuscación.
obit ['oubit], *s.* (*ant.*) óbito.
obitual [o'bitjuəl], *a.* obituario.
obituary [o'bitjuəri], *a.* obituario, necrológico. — *s.* obituario, nota necrológica.
object ['ɔbdʒikt], *a.* de objeto *o* cosa; (*ópt.*) ***object glass*** o ***lens,*** objetivo; ***object lesson,*** lección prática. — *s.* objeto; cosa; artículo; (*despec.*) facha, mamarracho; (*gram.*) objeto; ***money no object,*** no importa el dinero. — [əb'dʒekt], *v.t.* objetar. — *v.i.* objetar; poner objeción, poner reparos; ***if you don't object,*** si no tiene inconveniente.
objectify [əb'dʒektifai], [OBJECTIVIZE].
objection [əb'dʒekʃən], *s.* objeción, reparo; dificultad, inconveniente; ***to make*** o ***raise objections,*** objetar, poner reparos; ***I have no objection,*** no tengo, no hay inconveniente.
objectionable [əb'dʒekʃənəbl], *a.* objetable; (*pers.*) ofensivo, molesto, desagradable.
objective [əb'dʒektiv], *a.*, *s.* objetivo.
objectivity [ɔbdʒek'tiviti], *s.* objetividad.
objectivize [əb'dʒektivaiz], *v.t.* objetivar.
objectless ['ɔbdʒiktlis], *a.* sin objeto.
objector [əb'dʒektə], *s.* objetante.
objurgate ['ɔbdʒəgeit], *v.t.* reprender, reconvenir.
objurgation [ɔbdʒə'geiʃən], *s.* reprensión, reconvención.
objurgatory [əb'dʒə:gətəri], *a.* reprobatorio.
oblate (1) ['ɔbleit], *a.* aplastado en los polos.
oblate (2) ['ɔbleit], *s.* oblata.
oblateness [ɔ'bleitnis], *s.* aplastamiento.
oblation [o'bleiʃən], *s.* oblación.
obligate ['ɔbligeit], *v.t.* (*fam.*) obligar.
obligation [ɔbli'geiʃən], *s.* obligación; compromiso; (*igl.*) ***day of obligation,*** fiesta de precepto; ***to be under an obligation to,*** estar en deuda con (*una persona*); ***to be under*** (***an***) ***obligation to*** (+*inf.*), tener obligación de (+*inf.*), verse obligado a (+*inf.*); ***without obligation,*** sin compromiso.
obligatory [o'bligətəri], *a.* obligatorio.
oblige [o'blaidʒ], *v.t.* obligar; complacer, dar gusto a, hacer un favor a; ***I am much obliged (for),*** estoy muy agradecido *o* reconocido (por *o* de); ***I should be much obliged if,*** le agradecería mucho que; ***oblige with,*** hacer el favor de. — *v.i.* ser complaciente.
obliging [o'blaidʒiŋ], *a.* complaciente, servicial, atento.
oblique [o'bli:k], *a.* oblicuo, sesgado; indirecto, evasivo.
obliquely [o'bli:kli], *adv.* oblicuamente, al sesgo; indirectamente.
obliqueness, obliquity [o'bli:knis, o'blikwiti], *s.* oblicuidad, sesgo.
obliterate [o'blitəreit], *v.t.* borrar; destruir, arrasar, aniquilar; (*med.*) obliterar.
obliteration [oblitə'reiʃən], *s.* (el) borrar; destrucción, arrasamiento, aniquilación; (*med.*) obliteración.
oblivion [o'bliviən], *s.* olvido; ***to sink into oblivion,*** caer en el olvido; ir perdiendo el conocimiento, ir hundiéndose en la inconsciencia.
oblivious [o'bliviəs], *a.* olvidado, inconsciente.
obliviousness [o'bliviəsnis], *s.* olvido.
oblong ['ɔblɔŋ], *a.* alargado, apaisado; (*geom.*) oblongo. — *s.* cuadrilongo.
obloquy ['ɔbləkwi], *s.* infamia, baldón, vilipendio.
obnoxious [ɔb'nɔkʃəs], *a.* detestable, ofensivo, odioso.
obnoxiousness [əb'nɔkʃəsnis], *s.* odiosidad, (lo) odioso.
oboe ['oubou], *s.* oboe.
oboist ['oubouist], *s.* oboe (*músico*).
obol, obolus ['ɔbɔl, 'ɔbələs], *s.* óbolo.
obovate [ɔb'ouveit], *a.* (*bot.*) trasovado.
obreption [ɔb'repʃən], *s.* obrepción.
obreptitious [ɔbrep'tiʃəs], *a.* obrepticio.
obscene [ɔb'si:n], *a.* obsceno; indecente; repugnante.
obsceneness, obscenity [ɔb'si:nnis, -'seniti], *s.* obscenidad; indecencia; repugnancia.
obscurantism [ɔbskju'ræntizəm], *s.* obscurantismo.
obscurantist [ɔbskjuə'ræntist], *a.*, *s.* obscurantista, *m.f.*
obscuration [ɔbskjuə'reiʃən], *s.* obscurecimiento.
obscure [əb'skjuə], *a.* oscuro; abstruso, recóndito. — *v.t.* obscurecer; ocultar.
obscurely [əb'skjuəli], *adv.* obscuramente; ocultamente; confusamente; opacamente.
obscurity, obscureness [əb'skjuəriti, -nis], *s.* obscuridad; (lo) abstruso.
obsequies ['ɔbsikwiz], *s.pl.* exequias, *f.pl.*
obsequious [əb'si:kwiəs], *a.* servil, adulón.
obsequiousness [əb'si:kwiəsnis], *s.* servilismo.

observable [əb'zə:vəbl], *a.* observable; notable.
observance [əb'zə:vəns], *s.* observancia, cumplimiento, acatamiento; uso, práctica, costumbre.
observant [əb'zə:vənt], *a.* observador; atento, observante. — *s.* observante.
observation [ɔbzə'veiʃən], *s.* observación; experiencia; ***under observation,*** vigilado.
observatory [əb'zə:vətəri], *s.* observatorio.
observe [əb'zə:v], *v.t.* observar. — *v.i.* advertir, comentar.
observer [əb'zə:və], *s.* observador.
observing [əb'zə:viŋ], *a.* observador; observante.
obsess [əb'ses], *v.t.* obsesionar, causar obsesión a.
obsession [əb'seʃən], *s.* obsesión.
obsolescence [ɔbsə'lesəns], *s.* caída en desuso.
obsolescent [ɔbsə'lesənt], *a.* que cae en desuso; que envejece.
obsolete ['ɔbsəli:t], *a.* anticuado, en desuso; obsoleto; (*biol.*) atrofiado.
obsoleteness ['ɔbsəli:tnis], *s.* desuso; (*biol.*) atrofia.
obstacle ['ɔbstəkəl], *s.* obstáculo; impedimento; inconveniente; ***obstacle race,*** carrera de obstáculos.
obstetric(al) [ɔb'stetrik(əl)], *a.* obstétrico.
obstetrician [ɔbsti'triʃən], *s.* obstétrico.
obstetrics [əb'stetriks], *s.* obstetricia.
obstinacy, obstinateness ['ɔbstinəsi, -nitnis], *s.* obstinación, terquedad; porfía.
obstinate ['ɔbstinit], *a.* obstinado, terco; porfiado.
obstreperous [əb'strepərəs], *a.* rebelde, desmandado, díscolo, chulo.
obstreperousness [əb'strepərəsnis], *s.* rebeldía, indocilidad, chulería.
obstruct [əb'strʌkt], *v.t.* obstruir, cegar; estorbar, dificultar, obstaculizar.
obstruction [əb'strʌkʃən], *s.* obstrucción; estorbo.
obstructionism [əb'strʌkʃənizəm], *s.* obstruccionismo.
obstructionist [əb'strʌkʃənist], *a.*, *s.* obstruccionista, *m.f.*
obstructive [əb'strʌktiv], *a.* obstructivo.
obstruent ['ɔbstruənt], *a.* (*med.*) opilativo. — *s.* (*med.*) obstrucción.
obtain [əb'tein], *v.t.* obtener, adquirir; conseguir, lograr. — *v.i.* existir, imperar.
obtainable [əb'teinəbl], *a.* asequible, que se puede conseguir.
obtrude [əb'tru:d], *v.t.* imponer. — *v.i.* ser importuno; entrometerse.
obtrusion [əb'tru:ʒən], *s.* imposición; entrometimiento.
obtrusive [əb'tru:siv], *a.* importuno, indiscreto; entrometido.
obturate ['ɔbtjuəreit], *v.t.* obturar.
obturation [ɔbtjuə'reiʃən], *s.* obturación.
obturator ['ɔbtjuəreitə], *s.* obturador.
obtuse [əb'tju:s], *a.* obtuso; (*fig.*) obtuso, embotado, lerdo; ***obtuse-angled,*** obtusángulo.
obtuseness [əb'tju:snis], *s.* estupidez, embotamiento; (lo) obtuso.
obtusion [əb'tju:ʒən], *s.* embotamiento, estado de obtuso.
obverse ['ɔbvə:s], *a.* del anverso. — *s.* anverso.
obviate ['ɔbvieit], *v.t.* obviar, evitar, precaver.
obvious ['ɔbviəs], *a.* evidente, palmario, obvio.
obviously ['ɔbviəsli], *adv.* evidentemente.
obviousness ['ɔbviəsnis], *s.* evidencia, claridad; (*fig.*) trasparencia.
ocarina [ɔkə'ri:nə], *s.* ocarina.
occasion [ə'keiʒən], *s.* ocasión; vez; motivo; ***as occasion requires,*** de acuerdo con las circunstancias; ***if you have occasion to go to,*** si (por casualidad) va Vd. alguna vez a; ***on occasion,*** de vez en cuando; ***on the first occasion,*** la primera vez; ***on the occasion of,*** con ocasión de, con motivo de; ***to rise to the occasion,*** estar a la altura de las circunstancias. — *v.t.* ocasionar, originar.
occasionable [ə'keiʒənəbl], *a.* que puede ser ocasionado.
occasional [ə'keiʒənəl], *a.* poco frecuente; uno que otro; ***an*** o ***the occasional visit,*** alguna que otra visita.
occasionally [ə'keiʒənəli], *adv.* de vez en cuando.
occasioner [ə'keiʒənə], *s.* causante.
occident ['ɔksidənt], *s.* occidente; ocaso, poniente.
occidental [ɔksi'dentl], *a.* occidental.
occipital [ɔk'sipitl], *a.* (*anat.*) occipital.
occiput ['ɔksipət], *s.* (*anat.*) occipucio.
occlude [ə'klu:d], *v.t.* ocluir, obliterar.
occlusion [ə'klu:ʒən], *s.* (*med.*) oclusión.
occult [ɔ'kʌlt], *a.* oculto; misterioso, sobrenatural, mágico.
occultation [ɔkʌl'teiʃən], *s.* (*astron.*, *astrol.*) ocultación, desaparición.
occultism [ɔ'kʌltizəm], *s.* ocultismo.
occultist [ɔ'kʌltist], *s.* ocultista, *m.f.*
occultly [ɔ'kʌltli], *adv.* ocultamente.
occultness [ɔ'kʌltnis], *s.* carácter oculto.
occupancy ['ɔkjupənsi], *s.* ocupación, tenencia, posesión.
occupant ['ɔkjupənt], *s.* ocupante; inquilino.
occupation [ɔkju'peiʃən], *s.* ocupación; toma de posesión; tenencia; inquilinato.
occupational [ɔkju'peiʃənəl], *a.* de oficio; ***occupational hazards,*** gajes del oficio, *m.pl.*; ***occupational therapy,*** terapia laboral.
occupier ['ɔkjupaiə], *s.* ocupante, inquilino.
occupy ['ɔkjupai], *v.t.* ocupar; habitar; emplear, pasar. — **occupy o.s.,** *v.r.* — ***in*** o ***with,*** ocuparse de, en *o* con.
occur [ə'kə:], *v.i.* ocurrir, acontecer; darse, aparecer; ocurrirse; ***it occurred to me that,*** se me ocurrió que.
occurrence [ə'kʌrəns], *s.* acontecimiento, suceso, acaecimiento; ***to be of frequent occurrence,*** suceder a menudo.
ocean ['ouʃən], *s.* océano; (*fig.*) ***oceans of,*** la mar de.
oceanic [ouʃi'ænik], *a.* oceánico.
ocellate(d) ['ɔseleit(id)], *a.* ojoso.
ocelot ['ousilɔt], *s.* (*zool.*) ocelote.
ochre ['oukə], *s.* ocre.
ochreous ['oukriəs], *a.* ocroso.
o'clock [ə'klɔk], *partícula.* ***what o'clock is it?*** ¿qué hora es?; ***it is four o'clock,*** son las cuatro.
octagon ['ɔktəgən], *s.* octágono.
octagonal [ɔk'tægənəl], *a.* octagonal.
octahedral [ɔktə'hi:drəl], *a.* octaédrico.
octahedron [ɔktə'hi:drən], *s.* octaedro.
octane ['ɔktein], *s.* octano; ***high octane fuel,*** gasolina de alto octanaje.
octangular [ɔk'tæŋgjulə], *a.* octangular.
octave ['ɔktiv], *s.* octava.
Octavian [ɔk'teiviən]. Octavio.
octavo [ɔk'teivou], *a.* en octavo.
octennial [ɔk'teniəl], *a.* de ocho años.
octet [ɔk'tet], *s.* octeto.
octillion [ɔk'tiliən], *s.* octillón.
October [ɔk'toubə], *s.* octubre.
octogenarian [ɔktoudʒi'nɛəriən], *a.*, *s.* octogenario.
octopetalous [ɔktou'petələs], *a.* (*bot.*) octopétalo.
octopus ['ɔktəpəs], *s.* (*ict.*) pulpo.
octosyllabic [ɔktousi'læbik], *a.* octosílabo, octosilábico.
octosyllable ['ɔktousiləbl], *s.* octosílabo.
octroi ['ɔktrwɑ:], *s.* fielato.
octuple [ɔk'tjupl], *a.* óctuplo.
ocular ['ɔkjulə], *a.* ocular.
oculist ['ɔkjulist], *s.* oculista, *m.f.*

odalisque [ˈoudəlisk], *s.* odalisca.
odd [ɔd], *a.* impar; desigual; suelto, desparejado; sobrante; raro, extraño; tal cual, algún, alguna; ***fifty odd,*** cincuenta y pico, cincuenta y tantos; ***odd jobs,*** trabajos dispares, *m.pl.*; ***to be odd man out,*** estar de non, sobrar, estar de más; singularizarse, significarse, señalarse; ***odd moments,*** ratos perdidos, *m.pl.*; ***on the odd occasion,*** alguna vez; ***at odd times,*** a horas intempestivas, a deshora; de vez en cuando; ***the odd tree,*** algún árbol (que otro).
oddity [ˈɔditi], *s.* rareza, excentricidad; persona *o* cosa singular.
oddly [ˈɔdli], *adv.* extrañamente, de una manera rara *o* curiosa; ***oddly enough,*** es curioso, pero....
oddment [ˈɔdmənt], *s.* retazo; retal; artículo suelto.
oddness [ˈɔdnis], *s.* disparidad, desigualdad; rareza, extravagancia, singularidad.
odds [ɔdz], *s.pl.* ventaja, superioridad; probabilidades, *f.pl.*; puntos de ventaja, *m.pl.*; ***against odds,*** contra una fuerza superior; ***to be at odds,*** estar reñido(s) *o* de punta (***with,*** con); ***to give odds,*** dar ventaja; (*fam.*) ***it makes no odds,*** da igual; ***odds and ends,*** chismes, *m.pl.*, trastos, *m.pl.*, cachivaches, *m.pl.*; ***the odds are that,*** lo más probable *o* seguro es que; ***to set at odds,*** enemistar; (*fam.*) ***what's the odds?*** ¿qué más da?
ode [oud], *s.* oda.
Odessa [oˈdesə]. Odesa.
odious [ˈoudiəs], *a.* odioso, aborrecible, detestable.
odiousness [ˈoudiəsnis], *s.* odiosidad.
odium [ˈoudiəm], *s.* odio; oprobio.
odometer [ouˈdɔmitə], *s.* cuenta kilómetros.
odontalgia [ɔdɔnˈtældʒə], *s.* odontalgia.
odontalgic [ɔdɔnˈtældʒik], *a.* odontálgico.
odontograph [oˈdɔntogrɑ:f], *s.* odontógrafo.
odontoid [oˈdɔntɔid], *a.* odontoide, odontóideo.
odontology [ɔdɔnˈtɔlədʒi], *s.* odontología.
odorant [ˈoudərənt], *a.* odorífero.
odoriferous [oudəˈriferəs], *a.* odorífero.
odoriferousness [oudəˈrifərəsnis], *s.* perfume, fragancia.
odorous [ˈoudərəs], *a.* oloroso, oliente.
odorousness [ˈoudərəsnis], *s.* olor, aroma, fragancia.
odour [ˈoudə], *s.* olor; tufillo; (*fig.*) ***to be in bad odour with,*** no ser santo de la devoción de.
odourless [ˈoudəlis], *a.* inodoro.
odyssey [ˈɔdisi], *s.* odisea.
œcumenic(al) [ECUMENIC(AL)].
œdema [i:ˈdi:mə], *s.* edema, *m.*
œdematous [i:ˈdemətəs], *a.* edematoso.
Oedipus [i:ˈdipəs]. Edipo.
œsophagus [i:ˈsɔfəgəs], *a.* esófago.
œstrum [ˈi:strəm], *s.* brama; (*poét.*) estro.
œstrus [ˈi:strəs], *s.* tábano.
of [ɔv *acentuado,* əv *sin acentuación*], *prep.* de; ***of course,*** por supuesto; ***of late,*** últimamente; ***a friend of mine,*** un amigo mío; ***of old,*** antaño; ***of all things,*** precisamente; ***how kind of you (to...)!*** ¡qué amable ha sido usted (al...)!; ***to dream of,*** soñar con; ***I was robbed of my money,*** me robaron el dinero; ***it smells of roses,*** huele a rosas; ***to think of,*** pensar en.
off [ɔf], *a.* apartado, alejado; lateral; libre; suspendido; abandonado; quitado; (*elec., agua etc.*) desconectado, cortado, apagado; (*comida*) pasado; (*leche*) cortado; ***on the off chance,*** por si acaso; ***to have an off day,*** estar sin inspiración; estar flojo; ***off season,*** estación muerta; (*aut.*) ***off-side,*** (*paises donde se circula por la izquierda*) lado derecho; (*otros paises*) lado izquierdo; ***off street,*** calle lateral, traversía. — *adv.* lejos, a distancia; fuera; ***day off,*** dia libre; ***hands off!*** ¡las manos quietas!; ***hats off!*** ¡hay que descubrirse!; ***there is nothing off,*** no hay descuento; ***on and off*** o ***off and on,*** esporádicamente, a intervalos, intermitentemente; ***to have one's shoes off,*** estar descalzo; ***a little way off,*** a poca distancia; ***the wedding is off,*** se ha deshecho la boda; ***to be off,*** marcharse; ***to be badly off,*** estar mal de dinero; ***to be well off,*** tener una posición acomodada, estar bien de dinero; ***to see s.o. off,*** (ir a) despedir a alguien. — *prep.* lejos de, fuera de; separado de; de, desde; (*mar.*) a la altura de; frente a; al lado de; ***off-beat,*** poco ortodoxo, excéntrico; ***off-colour,*** malucho; ***to speak off the cuff,*** hablar improvisadamente; ***off one's head*** o ***rocker,*** chalado; ***off-key,*** fuera de tono; ***off the mark,*** despistado; ***off-shore,*** costanero; (*dep.*) ***off-side,*** fuera de juego; ***off-stage,*** entre bastidores; ***off the beaten track,*** apartado. — *interj.* ¡fuera!; ***off with you!*** ¡fuera de aquí!
offal [ˈɔfəl], *s.* despojos, *m.pl.*, casquería.
offence [əˈfens], *s.* ofensa, agravio, afrenta; delito; (*mil.*) ofensiva; ***to give offence,*** ofender; ***no offence meant,*** sin ánimo de ofender; ***to take offence,*** ofenderse, molestarse.
offend [əˈfend], *v.t.* ofender; ***to be offended,*** ofenderse, tomar la cosa a mal. — *v.i.* — ***against,*** pecar contra; violar.
offender [əˈfendə], *s.* ofensor; delincuente; culpable; ***first offender,*** delincuente sin antecedentes penales.
offense [OFFENCE].
offensive [əˈfensiv], *a.* ofensivo, injurioso; repugnante, asqueroso. — *s.* ofensiva.
offensiveness [əˈfensivnis], *s.* (lo) ofensivo.
offer [ˈɔfə], *s.* ofrecimiento; oferta. — *v.t.* ofrecer; brindar, deparar, presentar; ***offer resistance,*** oponer resistencia. — *v.i.* — ***to*** + *inf.*, ofrecer, ofrecerse a.
offerer [ˈɔfərə], *s.* ofrecedor, oferente.
offering [ˈɔfəriŋ], *s.* ofrecimiento; ofrenda; ***burnt offering,*** holocausto; ***votive offering,*** exvoto.
offertory [ˈɔfətəri], *s.* ofrenda; ofertorio; ***offertory box,*** cepillo (de la limosna).
offhand [ˈɔfˈhænd], *a.* brusco, descortés. — *adv.* sin pensarlo, sin consultarlo; así, de repente.
office [ˈɔfis], *s.* oficina; despacho; (*abogado*) bufete; (*med., Am.*) consultorio; oficio; cargo; ***to be in office,*** estar en el poder; estar en *o* desempeñar el cargo; estar en funciones; ***Foreign Office,*** Ministerio de Asuntos Exteriores; ***Home Office,*** Ministerio de Gobernación, del Interior; ***office-worker,*** oficinista, *m.f.*; ***to take office,*** tomar el poder; ***good offices,*** buenos oficios.
officer [ˈɔfisə], *s.* oficial; funcionario; agente (de policía); ***customs officer,*** aduanero; ***staff officer,*** oficial de estado mayor. — *v.t.* mandar; proveer de oficiales; ***to be well officered,*** tener buena oficialidad.
official [əˈfiʃəl], *a.* oficial; autorizado. — *s.* oficial; burocracia.
officialdom [əˈfiʃəldəm], *s.* círculos oficiales, *m.pl.*; funcionariado.
officialism [əˈfiʃəlizəm], *s.* burocracia.
officiality [əfiʃiˈæliti], *s.* oficialidad, cosa oficial.
officially [əˈfiʃəli], *adv.* oficialmente.
officiate [əˈfiʃieit], *v.i.* oficiar; ***officiate as,*** oficiar de.
officiating [əˈfiʃieitiŋ], *a.* oficiante.
officinal [ɔˈfisinəl], *a.* oficinal; (*farm.*) (*droga*) oficinal.
officious [əˈfiʃəs], *a.* oficioso, entrometido.
officiousness [əˈfiʃəsnis], *s.* oficiosidad.
offing [ˈɔfiŋ], *s.* ***in the offing,*** cerca (de la costa); en perspectiva.
offish [ˈɔfiʃ], *a.* arisco, huraño, esquivo.
offprint [ˈɔfprint], *s.* tirada aparte, separata.
offset [ˈɔfset], *s.* compensación; (*agric.*) acodo; (*arq.*) retallo; (*impr.*) offset; (*mec.*) recodo. — *v.t.* [ɔfˈset], compensar; acodar; retallar.
offshoot [ˈɔfʃu:t], *s.* vástago; ramal.

offspring [ˈɔ:fspriŋ], *s.* vástago; prole, descendencia; resultado.
offward [ˈɔfwəd], *adv.* (*mar.*) hacia el largo de la costa.
oft [ɔft], (*poét.*) [OFTEN].
often [ˈɔ(:)fən], *adv.* a menudo, muchas veces, con frecuencia; ***as often as,*** siempre que, tantas veces como; ***as often as not, more often than not,*** casi siempre; ***every so often,*** cada cierto tiempo; ***how often?*** ¿cuántas veces?; ***not often,*** pocas veces; ***so often,*** tantas veces; ***too often,*** demasiado a menudo.
ogee [oˈdʒi:], *s.* cimacio, gola.
ogival [oˈdʒaivəl], *a.* ogival.
ogive [ˈoudʒaiv], *s.* ojiva; nervadura.
ogle [ougl], *s.* mirada insinuante, de amor. — *v.t.*, *v.i.* echar miradas amorosas *o* incitantes (a); comerse con los ojos.
ogre [ˈougə], *s.* ogro.
oh! [ou], *interj.* ¡oh! ¡ay!
ohm [oum], *s.* (*elec.*) ohmio.
ohmic [ˈoumik], *a.* óhmico.
oho! [ouˈhou], *interj.* ¡aja!
oil [ɔil], *s.* aceite; (*geol.*) petróleo; (*pint.*) óleo; ***oil-beetle,*** carraleja; ***oil-can,*** aceitera; ***oil-field,*** campo petrolífero; ***oil industry,*** industria petrolera; ***oil lamp,*** velón, candil, quinqué; ***oil-painting,*** pintura al óleo; (*Am.*, *aut.*) ***oil-pan*** [SUMP]; ***oil-press,*** almazara; ***oil-shop,*** aceitería; ***oil-stove,*** estufa de aceite; ***oil-tanker,*** barco petrolero; camión petrolero; ***palm oil,*** aceite de palma; ***to burn the midnight oil,*** quemarse las cejas; (*fig.*) ***to pour oil on troubled waters,*** calmar los ánimos; (*fig.*) ***to strike oil,*** enriquecerse de pronto. — *v.t.* engrasar, aceitar, lubri(fi)car.
oilcake [ˈɔilkeik], *s.* torta de linaza, torta de borujo.
oilcloth [ˈɔilklɔθ], *s.* hule.
oiler [ˈɔilə], *s.* aceitador; buque aceitero.
oiliness [ˈɔilinis], *s.* (lo) aceitoso, (lo) oleaginoso.
oilman [ˈɔilmæn], *s.* (*pl.* **-men** [-men]) petrolero.
oilskin [ˈɔilskin], *s.* hule; impermeable.
oily [ˈɔili], *a.* aceitoso; oleaginoso; (*fig.*) zalamero; empalagoso, suavón.
ointment [ˈɔintmənt], *s.* pomada, ungüento.
O.K. [ˈouˈkei], *a.* bueno, conforme; ***that's O.K.,*** vale, está bien. — *s.* visto bueno. — *v.t.* dar el visto bueno a. — *interj.* ¡muy bien! ¡vale! ¡de acuerdo!
old [ould], *a.* viejo; anciano; antiguo; añejo; de edad (de); ***to be old enough,*** tener bastante edad; ***to be twenty years old,*** tener veinte años; ***to grow old,*** envejecer; ***how old are you?*** ¿cuántos años tiene Vd.?; ***of old,*** antiguamente; ***in days of old,*** en tiempos de Maricastaña; ***old age,*** vejez, senectud; ***old age pension,*** subsidio de vejez; ***at the ripe old age of seventy,*** ya con sus buenos setenta años; ***old bachelor,*** solterón; ***old boy,*** antiguo alumno; viejo; vejete; ***he's well in with the old boy network,*** tiene muy buen enchufe; ***old chap*** *o* ***fellow,*** viejo; vejete; ***old-fashioned,*** anticuado, pasado de moda; ***old maid,*** solterona; ***old-maidish,*** de solterona; remilgado; ***old man,*** viejo, anciano; (*fam.*) (el) pariente; ***Old Spanish,*** castellano antiguo; ***old wine,*** vino añejo; ***old woman,*** vieja, anciana; (*fam.*) (la) parienta.
olden [ˈouldən], *a.* antiguo, viejo; ***in olden days*** o ***times,*** antiguamente.
oldish [ˈouldiʃ], *a.* algo viejo, tirando a viejo, que va para viejo.
oldness [ˈouldnis], *s.* vejez; antigüedad.
oleaceous [ouliˈeiʃəs], *a.* oleáceo.
oleaginous [ouliˈædʒinəs], *a.* oleaginoso.
oleander [ouliˈændə], *s.* (*bot.*) adelfa, baladre.
oleaster [ouliˈæstə], *s.* (*bot.*) oleastro.
oleate [ˈoulieit], *s.* oleato.
oleic [oˈli:ik], *a.* oleico.
olein [ˈouliin], *s.* oleína.
oleometer [ouliˈɔmitə], *s.* oleómetro.
olfactory [ɔlˈfæktəri], *a.* olfativo, olfatorio.
olibanum [ɔˈlibənəm], *s.* olíbano.
oligarch [ˈɔligɑ:k], *s.* oligarca, *m.*
oligarchic(al) [ɔliˈgɑ:kik(əl)], *a.* oligárquico.
oligarchy [ˈɔligɑ:ki], *s.* oligarquía.
olivaceous [ɔliˈveiʃəs], *a.* oliváceo.
olivary [ˈɔlivəri], *a.* oliviforme, olivario.
olive [ɔliv], *a.* aceitunado. — *s.* olivo; oliva; aceituna; ***olive-bearing,*** olivífero; ***olive-green,*** aceitunado; ***olive grove,*** olivar; ***olive oil,*** aceite de oliva; ***olive-tree,*** olivo, aceituno; ***wild olive,*** acebuchina; ***wild olive tree,*** acebuche.
Oliver [ˈɔlivə]. Oliverio.
Olympiad [oˈlimpiæd], *s.* olimpíada.
Olympian [oˈlimpiən], *a.* olímpico. — *s.* (ser) olímpico.
Olympic [oˈlimpik], *a.* olímpico; ***the Olympic Games,*** los juegos olímpicos.
Olympus [oˈlimpəs], *s.* (el) Olimpo.
Oman [ouˈmɑ:n]. (el) Omán.
ombre [ˈɔmbə], *s.* tresillo (*juego de naipes*).
omega [ˈoumigə], *s.* omega.
omelet(te) [ˈɔmlit], *s.* tortilla.
omen [ˈoumen], *s.* presagio; ***of ill omen,*** de mal agüero; ***good omen,*** buena señal.
omentum [oˈmentəm], *s.* omento.
ominous [ˈɔminəs], *a.* nefasto; siniestro; ominoso; de mal agüero, que no augura nada bueno; amenazador, torvo, ceñudo.
ominousness [ˈɔminəsnis], *s.* (lo) siniestro.
omissible [oˈmisibl], *a.* que se puede omitir.
omission [oˈmiʃən], *s.* omisión; olvido, supresión.
omissive [oˈmisiv], *a.* que omite, que olvida.
omit [oˈmit], *v.t.* omitir; suprimir; ***omit to*** + *inf.*, dejar de + *inf.*
omnibus [ˈɔmnibəs], *a.* general, para todo. — *s.* autobús, *m.*; ómnibus, *m.inv.*
omnifarious [ɔmniˈfɛəriəs], *a.* omnímodo, de todos los géneros.
omniparous [ɔmˈnipərəs], *a.* omníparo.
omnipotence, omnipotency [ɔmˈnipətəns, -i], *s.* omnipotencia.
omnipotent [ɔmˈnipətənt], *a.* omnipotente, todopoderoso.
omnipresence [ɔmniˈprezəns], *s.* omnipresencia, ubicuidad.
omnipresent [ɔmniˈprezənt], *a.* omnipresente, ubicuo.
omniscience [ɔmˈnisiəns], *s.* omnisciencia.
omniscient [ɔmˈnisiənt], *a.* omnisciente, omnisapiente.
omnium [ˈɔmniəm], *s.* (*bolsa*) el agregado valor de las diferentes acciones, obligaciones *etc.* en que un empréstito está fundado; (*fam.*) mezcla, confusión, barullo.
omnivorous [ɔmˈnivərəs], *a.* omnívoro.
omoplate [ˈoumopleit], *s.* omóplato.
omphalic [ɔmˈfælik], *a.* umbilical.
on [ɔn], *adv.* ***the brakes are on,*** el freno está puesto; ***it's not on,*** no vale, no puede ser, no hay posibilidad; no cuela; ***the lights are on,*** las luces están encendidas; ***what's on at the cinema?*** ¿qué ponen en el cine?; ***to go on*** (***doing sth.***), seguir (haciendo algo); ***to live on,*** seguir viviendo. — *prep.* en, sobre; acerca de, sobre, de; ***on account of,*** a causa de; ***on no account,*** de ninguna manera; bajo ningún concepto; ***on arriving,*** al llegar; ***on his arrival*** o ***arriving,*** a su llegada; ***on an average,*** por término medio; ***on board,*** a bordo (de); ***on the cheap,*** a base de gastar poco; ***on condition that,*** con tal que; ***on the contrary,*** al contrario; ***on foot,*** a pie; ***to be on one's guard,*** estar en guardia; ***on horseback,*** a caballo; ***on the left,*** a la (mano) izquierda; ***on my part,*** por mi parte; ***on the***

point of, a punto de; ***on purpose,*** a propósito, adrede; ***on the right,*** a la (mano) derecha; ***on the side,*** como plan secundario; ***on every side,*** por todos lados; ***to have on tap,*** tener a mano; ***on second thoughts,*** pensándolo bien; ***on the wing,*** volando; ***the drinks are on me,*** invito yo; ***to live on,*** vivir de.

onager [ˈɔnəgə], *s.* (*zool.*) onagro.

onanism [ˈounənizəm], *s.* onanismo.

once [wʌns], *adv.* una vez; antiguamente, en otro tiempo; ***at once,*** en seguida, inmediatamente; ***all at once,*** de repente; (todo) de una vez; todos juntos; (***just***) ***for once,*** una vez siquiera; ***once*** (***and***) ***for all,*** una vez para siempre; ***once in a while,*** de vez en cuando, de tarde en tarde; ***once more,*** una vez más, otra vez; ***once upon a time,*** érase que se era; ***once bit, twice shy,*** gato escaldado del agua fría huye.

one [wʌn], *a.* un, uno, una; único, solo; un tal, cierto; ***it's all one to me,*** a mí me da exactamente igual; ***one by one,*** uno a uno; ***he is one of the family,*** es de la familia; ***one or two,*** unos cuantos, algunos; ***his one concern,*** su única preocupación; ***one-eyed,*** tuerto; ***one-handed,*** manco; (*fam.*) ***one-horse,*** de mala muerte; (*despec.*) ***one-horse town,*** pueblo *o* ciudad de mala muerte; ***one-sided,*** unilateral; desigual; desequilibrado; parcial; ***one-time,*** antiguo; ***one-track mind,*** que tiene monobsesión; ***one-way,*** de dirección única. — *pron.* uno, una; alguno; (la) una; se, uno; ***each and every one,*** todos y cada uno; ***one Harry,*** un tal Enrique; ***the little ones,*** los pequeños; la gente menuda; ***the red ones,*** los colorados; ***one another,*** uno(s) a otro(s); ***one does not know,*** no se sabe; ***one must work,*** hay que trabajar; ***that one,*** ése, aquél *etc.*; ***the one who,*** el que; ***the one...the other,*** el uno ...el otro. — *s.* ***at one,*** unidos, reconciliados.

oneness [ˈwʌnnis], *s.* unidad; unión; unicidad.

onerous [ˈɔnərəs], *a.* oneroso, pesado, gravoso.

one's [wʌnz], *pron. pos.* [ONE]; su, sus, de uno.

oneself [wʌnˈself], *pron. reflexivo.* uno mismo; se; sí (mismo); ***by oneself,*** solo; por sí mismo; ***to come to oneself,*** volver en sí.

one-upmanship [ˈwʌn-ˈʌpmənʃip], *s.* arte de aventajar al adversario.

onion [ˈʌnjən], *s.* cebolla; ***onion-bed,*** cebollar.

onlooker [ˈɔnlukə], *s.* espectador.

only [ˈounli], *a.* solo, único. — *adv.* sólo, solamente, tan sólo, no . . . sino, no más que, únicamente; ***if only,*** ojalá . . ., quién . . .; ***only just,*** por los pelos, raspandillo. — *conj.* sólo que.

onomatopœia [ɔnəmætəˈpiə], *s.* onomatopeya.

onrush [ˈɔnrʌʃ], *s.* arremetida, embestida; ímpetu.

onset [ˈɔnset], *s.* asalto, ataque; acceso; comienzo.

onslaught [ˈɔnslɔːt], *s.* embestida (furiosa).

ontological [ɔntoˈlɔdʒikəl], *a.* ontológico.

ontologist [ɔnˈtɔlədʒist], *s.* ontólogo.

ontology [ɔnˈtɔlədʒi], *s.* ontología.

onus [ˈounəs], *s.* carga, responsabilidad.

onward [ˈɔnwəd], *adj.* progresivo. — (*t.* **onwards** [ˈɔnwədz]), *adv.* (hacia) adelante.

onyx [ˈɔniks], *s.* ónice.

oolite [ˈouəlait], *s.* oolito.

oolitic [ouəˈlitik], *a.* oolítico.

oological [ouəˈlɔdʒikəl], *a.* oológico.

oology [ouˈɔlədʒi], *s.* oología.

ooze [uːz], *s.* lama, cieno. — *v.t.* rezumar. — *v.i.* rezumar(se).

oozing [ˈuːziŋ], *a.* rezumante. — *s.* rezumo.

oozy [ˈuːzi], *a.* legamoso, limoso, cenagoso.

opacity [oˈpæsiti], *s.* opacidad.

opal [ˈoupəl], *s.* ópalo.

opalescence [oupəˈlesəns], *s.* opalescencia.

opalescent [oupəˈlesənt], *a.* opalino, iridiscente, opalescente.

opaline [ˈoupəlain], *a.* opalino.

opaque [oˈpeik], *a.* opaco; (*vidrio*) esmerilado.

opaqueness [oˈpeiknis], *s.* opacidad.

open [ˈoupən], *a.* abierto; descubierto; desplegado; destapado; desembarazado; (*pers.*) llano, franco; libre; extendido; (*mente*) receptivo; (*com.*) pendiente; ***in the open air,*** al aire libre; al raso, a la intemperie; ***open-cast mining,*** minería a cielo abierto; ***open country,*** terreno abierto; ***in open court,*** en pleno tribunal; ***open-eyed,*** vigilante, alerta; ***open fields,*** campo raso; ***open-handed,*** espléndido, dadivoso; ***open-hearted,*** abierto, franco; ***to keep an open mind,*** estar dispuesto a admitir nuevas ideas; ***an open question,*** una cuestión pendiente; ***an open secret,*** un secreto a voces; ***open shame,*** vergüenza pública; ***in the open street,*** en medio de la calle, en plena calle; ***to be open to question,*** ser dudoso, discutible; ***to draw open,*** abrir (de par en par); ***to lay open,*** descubrir; ***to lie open,*** exponerse; ***slightly open,*** entreabierto. — *v.t.* abrir; descubrir; destapar; desplegar; extender; inaugurar, iniciar; explorar; ***open up,*** abrir; explorar; franquear. — *v.i.* abrirse; comenzar; extenderse; estrenarse; ***open into,*** comunicar con; desembocar en; ***open on*** (***to***), dar a, mirar a; ***open up,*** romper el fuego; (*fam.*) franquearse; ***open with,*** empezar con.

opener [ˈoupənə], *s.* abridor.

opening [ˈoupəniŋ], *s.* abertura; apertura; estreno; oportunidad, ocasión; brecha; claro; salida.

openly [ˈoupənli], *adv.* abiertamente; francamente; públicamente; al descubierto.

openness [ˈoupənnis], *s.* espaciosidad; (lo) abierto; (*fig.*) franqueza.

openwork [ˈoupənwəːk], *s.* (*cost.*) calado, deshilado.

opera (1) [ˈɔpərə], *s.* ópera; ***comic*** o ***light opera,*** zarzuela; ***opera-glass***(***es***), gemelos de teatro, *m.pl.*; (*fam.*) ***opera-goer,*** aficionado a la ópera; ***opera-hat,*** clac; ***opera-singer,*** cantante de ópera, operista, *m.f.*

opera (2) [ˈɔpərə], *s.pl.* [OPUS].

operameter [ɔpəˈræmitə], *s.* operámetro.

operate [ˈɔpəreit], *v.t.* hacer funcionar, accionar; actuar; impulsar; manejar, dirigir. — *v.i.* funcionar; operar; (*med.*) ***operate for,*** operar de; ***operate on,*** producir efecto en; (*med.*) operar.

operatic [ɔpəˈrætik], *a.* de ópera, operístico.

operating [ˈɔpəreitiŋ], *a.* operante. — *s.* (el) operar *etc.*; ***operating expenses,*** gastos de explotación, *m.pl.*; (*med.*) ***operating table,*** mesa de operaciones; (*med.*) ***operating theatre,*** quirófano.

operation [ɔpəˈreiʃən], *s.* operación; intervención (quirúrgica); funcionamiento; explotación; manejo; ***in operation,*** en funcionamiento; en vigor; ***to come into operation,*** empezar a funcionar; entrar en vigor; ***to put into operation,*** hacer funcionar; poner por obra.

operational [ɔpəˈreiʃənəl], *a.* de operaciones; en condiciones de servicio.

operative [ˈɔpərətiv], *a.* operativo, operador; (*cir.*) operatorio; en vigor; ***operative word,*** palabra clave *o* fundamental. — *s.* operario.

operator [ˈɔpəreitə], *s.* operario; (*cir.*) operador; agente; (*fam.*) ***smart*** o ***smooth operator,*** vivales, *m.inv.*; (***telephone***) ***operator,*** telefonista, *m.f.*

operculum [ɔˈpəːkjuləm], *s.* (*pl.* **opercula** [-kjulə]) opérculo.

operetta [ɔpəˈretə], *s.* opereta; zarzuela.

ophidian [ɔˈfidiən], *a.*, *s.* ofidio.

ophite [ˈɔfait], *s.* ofita.

ophthalmia [ɔfˈθælmiə], *s.* oftalmía.

ophthalmic [ɔfˈθælmik], *a.* oftálmico.

ophthalmologist [ɔfθælˈmɔlədʒist], *s.* oftalmólogo.

ophthalmology [ɔfθælˈmɔlədʒi], *s.* oftalmología.

ophthalmoscope [ɔfˈθælməskoup], *s.* oftalmoscopio.

ophthalmy [ɔfˈθælmi], *s.* oftalmía.

opiate [ˈoupiit], *a.* opiático. — *s.* opiata, narcótico.

opine [ɔˈpain], *v.t.*, *v.i.* opinar.

opiniative [ə'pinjətiv], [OPINIONATED].
opinion [ə'pinjən], *s.* opinión, *f.*, parecer, juicio, concepto; ***to have a high opinion of,*** tener buen concepto de; ***in my opinion,*** en mi opinión, a mi parecer *o* juicio; ***to be of the opinion that,*** ser de parecer que; ***public opinion,*** la opinión (pública); ***public opinion poll,*** sondaje de opinión pública.
opinionated [ə'pinjəneitid], *a.* dogmático; intransigente.
opium ['oupiəm], *s.* opio; ***opium-addict,*** opiómano; ***opium den,*** fumadero de opio.
opopanax [ə'pɔpənæks], *s.* opopónaco.
opossum [ə'pɔsəm], *s.* (*zool.*) zarigüeya.
oppilation [ɔpi'leiʃən], *s.* opilación.
opponent [ə'pounənt], *a.* contrario, antagónico. — *s.* adversario, contrario; competidor, contrincante.
opportune ['ɔpətju:n], *a.* oportuno.
opportuneness ['ɔpətju:nnis], *s.* (lo) oportuno.
opportunism ['ɔpətju:nizəm], *s.* oportunismo.
opportunist ['ɔpətju:nist], *s.* oportunista, *m.f.*
opportunity [ɔpə'tju:niti], *s.* oportunidad, ocasión; ***opportunity makes the thief,*** la ocasión hace el ladrón.
opposable [ə'pouzəbl], *a.* oponible.
oppose [ə'pouz], *v.t.* oponerse a; oponer; resistarse a; resistir; combatir.
opposed [ə'pouzd], *a.* contrario, opuesto; encontrado; ***as opposed to,*** en contraste con; ***to be opposed to,*** oponerse a.
opposer [ə'pouzə], *s.* antagonista, *m.f.*, adversario; opugnador; rival.
opposite ['ɔpəzit], *a.* opuesto, contrario; de enfrente; encontrado; ***opposite number,*** equivalente, igual, colega. —*s.* (lo) contrario, (lo) opuesto. — *prep.* frente a, enfrente de.
oppositely ['ɔpəzitli], *adv.* opuestamente.
oppositeness ['ɔpəzitnis], *s.* contraste; situación opuesta.
opposition [ɔpə'ziʃən], *s.* oposición; resistencia; competencia; ***to set up*** (***shop***) ***in opposition to,*** establecerse en competencia con.
oppress [ə'pres], *v.t.* oprimir; agobiar.
oppression [ə'preʃən], *s.* opresión; agobio.
oppressive [ə'presiv], *a.* opresivo; agobiante; (*ambiente, tiempo*) sofocante, bochornoso.
oppressiveness [ə'presivnis], *s.* opresión, carácter opresivo; (lo) bochornoso.
oppressor [ə'presə], *s.* opresor.
opprobrious [ə'proubriəs], *a.* oprobioso, infamante.
opprobriousness [ə'proubriəsnis], *s.* oprobio.
opprobrium [ə'proubriəm], *s.* oprobio.
oppugn [ə'pju:n], *v.t.* opugnar, combatir.
opt [ɔpt], *v.i.* optar; ***opt for,*** optar por; ***opt out,*** quedarse fuera, retirarse, rajarse.
optative ['ɔptətiv], *a.*, *s.* optativo; (*gram.*) modo optativo.
optic(**al**) ['ɔptik(əl)], *a.* óptico.
optician [ɔp'tiʃən], *s.* óptico.
optics ['ɔptiks], *s.* óptica.
optimism ['ɔptimizəm], *s.* optimismo.
optimist ['ɔptimist], *s.* optimista, *m.f.*
optimistic [ɔpti'mistik], *a.* optimista.
option ['ɔpʃən], *s.* opción.
optional ['ɔpʃənəl], *a.* facultativo, potestativo, discrecional.
optometer [ɔp'tɔmitə], *s.* optómetro.
opulence ['ɔpjuləns], *s.* opulencia.
opulent ['ɔpjulənt], *a.* opulento.
opus ['oupəs], *s.* (*pl.* **opera** ['ɔpərə]) opus, *m.*
opuscule [o'pʌskju:l], *s.* opúsculo.
or [ɔ:], *conj.* o, u; ***either . . . or,*** o . . . o, o . . . o bien.
oracle ['ɔrəkl], *s.* oráculo.
oracular [ɔ'rækjulə], *a.* de oráculo; (*fig.*) doctoral; misterioso.
oral ['ɔ:rəl], *a.* oral.
orange ['ɔrindʒ], *a.* anaranjado, de naranja; ***orange-coloured,*** anaranjado. — *s.* (*bot.*) naranja; ***orange blossom,*** azahar; ***orange-tree,*** naranjo.
orangeade [ɔrin'dʒeid], *s.* naranjada.
orangery ['ɔrindʒəri], *s.* invernadero para naranjos.
orang-outang [ɔ'ræŋ-u'tæŋ], *s.* (*zool.*) orangután.
oration [ɔ'reiʃən], *s.* oración, discurso.
orator ['ɔrətə], *s.* orador.
oratorical [ɔrə'tɔrikəl], *a.* oratorio.
oratorio [ɔrə'tɔ:riou], *s.* oratorio.
oratory ['ɔrətəri], *s.* oratoria; oratorio.
orb [ɔ:b], *s.* orbe. — *v.t.* rodear, cercar.
orbed [ɔ:bd], *a.* circular, esférico, redondo.
orbicular [ɔ:'bikjulə], *a.* orbicular.
orbiculate(**d**) [ɔ:'bikjuleit(id)], *a.* orbicular.
orbit ['ɔ:bit], *s.* órbita; ***to go into orbit,*** entrar en órbita. — *v.i.* girar.
orbital ['ɔ:bitəl], *a.* orbital.
orca ['ɔ:kə], *s.* orca, orco.
orchard ['ɔ:tʃəd], *s.* huerta, huerto; pomar.
orchestra ['ɔ:kistrə], *s.* orquesta; ***orchestra seat,*** butaca.
orchestral [ɔ:'kestrəl], *a.* orquestal.
orchestrate ['ɔ:kistreit], *v.t.* orquestar, instrumentar.
orchestration [ɔ:kis'treiʃən], *s.* orquestación, instrumentación.
orchid ['ɔ:kid], *s.* orquídea.
orchidaceous [ɔ:ki'deiʃəs], *a.* orquidáceo.
ordain [ɔ:'dein], *v.t.* ordenar; decretar; mandar; (*igl.*) ***to ordain as*** (***a***) ***priest,*** ordenar de sacerdote.
ordainer [ɔ:'deinə], *s.* ordenador.
ordeal [ɔ:'di:(ə)l], *s.* ordalía; prueba dura, experiencia dura, sufrimiento.
order ['ɔ:də], *s.* (*método*) orden, *m.*; (*mandato*) orden, *f.*; (*com.*) encargo, pedido; (*com.*) libranza; (*pl.*, *igl.*) órdenes sagradas, *f.pl.*; (*com.*) ***by order and on account of,*** por orden y por cuenta de; ***in order,*** en regla, en orden; ***in order to,*** para, con el fin de; ***to keep in order,*** tener en buen estado; ***to put*** o ***set in order,*** ordenar, arreglar; ***law and order,*** orden, *m.*; ***made to order,*** hecho de encargo; ***old order,*** antiguo régimen; (*com.*) ***order-book,*** libro de pedidos; (*mec.*) ***out of order,*** averiado; no funciona; (*igl.*) ***to take orders,*** ordenarse; ***till further orders,*** hasta nueva orden. — *v.t.* mandar, ordenar; disponer; (*com.*) pedir, encargar; (*igl.*) ordenar, conferir las órdenes sagradas a; ***order away*** o ***off,*** despedir, mandar salir; ***order in,*** mandar entrar, mandar traer; ***order out,*** mandar salir; ***order up,*** mandar subir. — *interj.* (*mil.*) ***order arms!*** ¡descansen!
orderless ['ɔ:dəlis], *a.* sin orden, desordenado, irregular.
orderliness ['ɔ:dəlinis], *s.* método, orden, *m.*
orderly ['ɔ:dəli], *a.* ordenado; sistemático; en orden; ***orderly officer,*** oficial del día. — *s.* ordenanza, *m.*
ordinal ['ɔ:dinəl], *a.* ordinal. — *s.* número ordinal; (*igl.*) ritual.
ordinance ['ɔ:dinəns], *s.* ordenanza; decreto.
ordinary ['ɔ:dinəri], *a.* corriente, vulgar; ordinario; normal. — *s.* ordinario (de la misa); ***out of the ordinary,*** extraordinario.
ordinate ['ɔ:dinit], *a.* regular, ordenado, metódico. — *s.* (*geom.*) ordenada.
ordinately ['ɔ:dinitli], *adv.* de una manera regular.
ordination [ɔ:di'neiʃən], *s.* (*igl.*) ordenación; disposición, buen orden, arreglo.
ordnance ['ɔ:dnəns], *s.* artillería; pertrechos, *m.pl.*, intendencia; ***ordnance map,*** mapa del estado mayor, *m.*

ordure [ˈɔ:djuə], *s.* excremento; inmundicia.
ore [ɔ:], *s.* mineral; mena.
organ [ˈɔ:gən], *s.* (*fisiol.*, *mús.*) órgano; ***organ-blower,*** entonador; ***organ-grinder,*** organillero; (*mús.*) ***organ stop,*** registro (de órgano).
organdie [ˈɔ:gəndi], *s.* organdí.
organic [ɔ:ˈgænik], *a.* orgánico.
organism [ˈɔ:gənizəm], *s.* organismo.
organist [ˈɔ:gənist], *s.* organista, *m.f.*
organization [ɔ:gənaiˈzeiʃən], *s.* organización; organismo.
organize [ˈɔ:gənaiz], *v.t.* organizar; (*fam.*) conseguir, proporcionar. — *v.i.* organizarse.
organizer [ˈɔ:gənaizə], *s.* organizador.
organographic(al) [ɔ:gənoˈgræfik(əl)], *a.* organográfico.
organography [ɔ:gəˈnɔgrəfi], *s.* organografía.
organology [ɔ:gəˈnɔlədʒi], *s.* organología.
orgasm [ˈɔ:gæzəm], *s.* orgasmo.
orgeat [ˈɔ:dʒiæt], *s.* horchata.
orgiastic [ɔ:dʒiˈæstik], *a.* orgiástico.
orgy [ˈɔ:dʒi], *s.* orgía.
oriel [ˈɔ:riəl], *s.* mirador.
orient [ˈɔ:riənt], *a.* oriental. — *s.* oriente. — [ˈɔ:rient], *v.t.* orientar.
oriental [ɔ:riˈentl], *a.* oriental, del oriente, de oriente; exótico. — *s.* oriental.
orientalism [ɔ:riˈentəlizəm], *s.* orientalismo.
orientalist [ɔ:riˈentəlist], *s.* orientalista, *m.f.*
orientalize [ɔ:riˈentəlaiz], *v.t.* orientalizar.
orientate [ˈɔ:rienteit], *v.t.* orientar.
orientation [ɔ:rienˈteiʃən], *s.* orientación.
orifice [ˈɔrifis], *s.* orificio.
oriflamme [ˈɔriflæm], *s.* oriflama.
origan, origanum [ˈɔrigən, ɔˈrigənəm], *s.* (*bot.*) orégano.
origin [ˈɔridʒin], *s.* origen, procedencia.
original [əˈridʒinəl], *a.* original; originario; primitivo; ***original sin,*** pecado original. — *s.* original; prototipo.
originality [əridʒiˈnæliti], *s.* originalidad.
originalness [əˈridʒinəlnis], *s.* originalidad.
originate [əˈridʒineit], *v.t.* originar, crear. — *v.i.* originarse, tener su origen, surgir en primer lugar *o* primitivamente.
origination [əridʒiˈneiʃən], *s.* creación.
originator [əˈridʒineitə], *s.* creador.
oriole [ˈɔ:rioul], *s.* (*orn.*) oropéndola.
orison [ˈɔrizən], *s.* (*ant.*) oración, plegaria.
Orkney Islands [ˈɔ:kni ˈailəndz]. (Las) Orcadas.
orle [ɔ:l], *s.* orla.
orlop [ˈɔ:lɔp], *s.* (*mar.*) sollado.
ormolu [ˈɔ:məlu:], *s.* bronce dorado.
ornament [ˈɔ:nəmənt], *s.* adorno, ornamento, ornato. — [ˈɔ:nəment], *v.t.* adornar, ornamentar.
ornamental [ɔ:nəˈmentl], *a.* de adorno, ornamental.
ornamentation [ɔ:nəmenˈteiʃən], *s.* ornamentación; ornamento.
ornate [ɔ:ˈneit], *a.* recargado, exagerado.
ornateness [ɔ:ˈneitnis], *s.* (lo) recargado, exageración.
ornithological [ɔ:niθəˈlɔdʒikəl], *a.* ornitológico.
ornithologist [ɔ:niˈθɔlədʒist], *s.* ornitólogo.
ornithology [ɔ:niˈθɔlədʒi], *s.* ornitología.
ornithomancy [ˈɔ:ˈniθomænsi], *s.* ornitomancia.
orographic [ɔroˈgræfik], *a.* orográfico.
orography [ɔˈrɔgrəfi], *s.* orografía.
orological [ɔrəˈlɔdʒikəl], *a.* orológico.
orology [ɔˈrɔlədʒi], *s.* orología.
orotund [ˈɔ:rotʌnd], *a.* rotundo.
orphan [ˈɔ:fən], *a.*, *s.* huérfano; (*Am.*) ***orphan asylum,*** orfanato. — *v.t.* dejar huérfano.
orphanage [ˈɔ:fənidʒ], *s.* orfandad; orfanato; (los) huérfanos.
orphanhood [ˈɔ:fənhud], *s.* orfandad; (los) huérfanos.
Orphean, Orphic [ɔ:ˈfi:ən, ˈɔ:fik], *a.* órfico.
Orpheus [ˈɔ:fiəs]. Orfeo.
orrery [ˈɔrəri], *s.* planetario.
orris [ˈɔris], *s.* galón, trencilla; (*bot.*) lirio; ***orris-root,*** raíz de iris florentina.
orthochromatic [ɔ:θoukroˈmætik], *a.* ortocromático.
orthodox [ˈɔ:θədɔks], *a.* ortodoxo; formal, convencional, correcto.
orthodoxy [ˈɔ:θədɔksi], *s.* ortodoxia.
orthoepical [ɔ:θouˈepikəl], *a.* ortológico.
orthoepist [ˈɔ:θouepist], *s.* ortólogo.
orthoepy [ˈɔ:θouepi], *s.* ortología.
orthogon [ˈɔ:θəgɔn], *s.* ortogonio.
orthogonal [ɔ:ˈθɔgənəl], *a.* ortogonal.
orthographer, orthographist [ɔ:ˈθɔgrəfə, -ist], *s.* ortógrafo.
orthographic [ɔ:θəˈgræfik], *a.* ortográfico.
orthography [ɔ:ˈθɔgrəfi], *s.* ortografía.
orthopædic [ɔ:θəˈpi:dik], *a.* ortopédico.
orthopædics, orthopædy [ɔ:θəˈpi:diks, ˈɔ:θəpi:di], *s.* ortopedia.
Orthoptera [ɔ:ˈθɔptərə], *s.pl.* (*ent.*) ortópteros, *m.pl.*
ortolan [ˈɔ:tələn], *s.* (*orn.*) hortelano; verderol.
oryx [ˈɔriks], *s.* (*zool.*) orix.
oscillate [ˈɔsileit], *v.i.* oscilar, fluctuar.
oscillating, oscillatory [ˈɔsileitiŋ, -əri], *a.* oscilante, oscilatorio.
oscillation [ɔsiˈleiʃən], *s.* oscilación.
oscillator [ˈɔsileitə], *s.* oscilador.
oscillograph [ɔˈsiləgræf], *s.* oscilógrafo.
oscitation [ɔsiˈteiʃən], *s.* oscitancia.
osculation [ɔskjuˈleiʃən], *s.* osculación.
osculatory [ˈɔskjulətəri], *a.* osculatorio.
osier [ˈouziə], *s.* mimbre; mimbrera.
osmic [ˈɔzmik], *a.* ósmico.
osmium [ˈɔzmiəm], *s.* osmio.
osmosis [ɔzˈmousis], *s.* osmosis, *f.*
osmotic [ɔzˈmɔtik], *a.* osmótico.
osprey [ˈɔsprei], *s.* (*orn.*) quebrantahuesos, *m.inv.*
ossarium [ɔˈsɛəriəm], *s.* osario.
osseous [ˈɔsiəs], *a.* óseo.
ossicle [ˈɔsikəl], *s.* osículo.
ossification [ɔsifiˈkeiʃən], *s.* osificación.
ossify [ˈɔsifai], *v.t.* osificar. — *v.i.* osificarse.
ossifrage [ˈɔsifridʒ], *s.* osífraga.
ossuary [ˈɔsjuəri], *s.* osario.
osteitis [ɔstiˈaitis], *s.* osteítis, *f. inv.*
Ostend [ɔsˈtend]. Ostende.
ostensible [ɔsˈtensibl], *a.* supuesto, pretendido, aparente.
ostentation [ɔstenˈteiʃən], *s.* fausto, boato, pompa, aparato; ostentación.
ostentatious [ɔstenˈteiʃəs], *a.* ostentoso, fastuoso, pomposo, aparatoso.
ostentatiousness [ɔstenˈteiʃəsnis], *s.* (lo) ostentoso, (lo) pomposo, fastuosidad.
osteogeny [ɔstiˈɔdʒini], *s.* osteogenía.
osteography [ɔstiˈɔgrəfi], *s.* osteografía.
osteologist [ɔstiˈɔlədʒist], *s.* osteólogo.
osteology [ɔstiˈɔlədʒi], *s.* osteología.
osteoma [ɔstiˈoumə], *s.* osteoma, *m.*
osteotomy [ɔstiˈɔtəmi], *s.* osteotomía.
ostiary [ˈɔstiəri], *s.* ostiario.
ostler [ˈɔslə], *s.* mozo de cuadra.
ostlery [ˈɔsləri], *s.* hostería.
ostosis [ɔsˈtousis], *s.* osificación.
ostracean [ɔsˈtreisiən], *a.* ostráceo.
ostracism [ˈɔstrəsizəm], *s.* ostracismo.

ostracize [ˈɔstrəsaiz], *v.t.* condenar al ostracismo.
ostreiculture [ˈɔstriikʌltʃə], *s.* ostricultura.
ostrich [ˈɔstritʃ], *s.* avestruz, *f.*
Ostrogoth [ˈɔstrogɔθ], *s.* ostrogodo.
otalgia [oˈtældʒə], *s.* otalgia.
Othello [ɔˈθelou]. Otelo.
other [ˈʌðə], *a.* otro; ***the other day,*** el otro día; ***every other day,*** un día sí y otro no; (*fam.*) ***if he doesn't like it, he can do the other thing,*** si no le gusta, que se aguante. — *adv.* — ***than,*** otra cosa que (no sea); ***other than this,*** como no sea esto, como no sea así. — *pron.* (el) otro *etc.*; ***the others, other ones,*** los otros, los demás; ***somebody or other,*** alguien, no sé quién.
otherwise [ˈʌðəwaiz], *adv.* de otro modo; si no, de lo contrario, de no ser así, como no sea así.
otherworldly [ˈʌðəˈwəːldli], *a.* ultramundano; místico, no de este mundo.
otic [ˈoutik], *a.* ótico.
otiose [ˈouʃious], *a.* ocioso.
otitis [oˈtaitis], *s.* otitis, *f. inv.*
otolith [ˈoutoliθ], *s.* otolito.
otologist [oˈtɔlədʒist], *s.* otólogo.
otology [oˈtɔlədʒi], *s.* otología.
otoscope [ˈoutoskoup], *s.* otoscopio.
otoscopy [oˈtɔskəpi], *s.* otoscopia.
ototomy [oˈtɔtəmi], *s.* ototomía.
otter [ˈɔtə], *a.* ***otter-coloured,*** alutrado. — *s.* nutria; ***otter skin,*** piel de nutria; ***sea otter,*** nutria de mar.
Ottoman [ˈɔtəmən], *a., s.* otomano.
ottoman [ˈɔtəmən], *s.* (*mueble*) otomana; (*tej.*) otomán.
ouch! [autʃ], (*interj.*) ¡uy! ¡ay!
ought [ɔːt], *v. aux.* debe, debería, debiera; ***you ought to be ashamed,*** vergüenza debiera darte.
ounce [auns], *s.* onza.
our [auə], *a.* nuestro, nuestra, nuestros, nuestras; ***the Our Father,*** el Padrenuestro.
ourang [ɔˈræng], [ORANG-OUTANG].
ours [auəz], *pron.* el nuestro, la nuestra, los nuestros, las nuestras.
ourself [auəˈself], *pron.* (*pl.* **ourselves** [-ˈselvz]) nosotros (mismos), nosotras (mismas); ***between ourselves,*** entre nosotros, entre tú y yo.
ousel [ˈuːzəl], *s.* (*orn.*) mirlo.
oust [aust], *v.t.* desposeer; desalojar; desahuciar.
ousting [ˈaustiŋ], *s.* (*for.*) evicción, desahucio, despojo.
out [aut], *a.* externo; distante, remoto, lejano. — *adv.* fuera, afuera, hacia fuera; ***to be out,*** no estar (en casa); no estar de moda; quedar cesante; (*fuego etc.*) estar extinguido, apagado; salir a luz; estar fuera de juego; ***to be out for the count,*** estar k.o.; (*libro*) ***just out,*** que acaba de publicarse; ***out at heels,*** con los tacones rotos; ***out and out,*** completamente; consumado; (***it is***) ***out of stock,*** no hay más, agotado; (*fam.*) ***the best thing out,*** lo mejor que existe; ***to come out on strike,*** declararse en huelga; ***to fall out with,*** reñir con; ***to hear s.o. out,*** escuchar a alguien hasta el final; ***to set out,*** ponerse en camino, partir; ***to speak out,*** hablar sin rodeos; ***way out,*** salida. — *prep.* ***out of,*** fuera de; de; entre; de entre; por; sin; ***out of breath,*** sin aliento; ***out of character,*** impropio; fuera de propósito; ***out of humour,*** de mal humor; ***out of idleness,*** por pereza; ***out of kindness,*** por amistad; (*fig.*) ***out of line with,*** en desacuerdo con; ***out of measure,*** desmesurado; ***out of one's mind,*** fuera de sí; ***time out of mind,*** tiempo inmemorial; ***out of order,*** descompuesto, averiado; desordenado; ***I am out of paper,*** se me acabó el papel, ya no me queda papel; ***to get out of patience,*** perder la paciencia; ***to be out of a place*** o ***job,*** estar sin colocación; ***out of print,*** agotado; ***it is out of the question,*** no puede ser; ***out of sight,*** fuera del alcance de la vista; ***out of sight, out of mind,*** ojos que no ven, corazón que no siente; ***out of sorts,*** indispuesto; (*lit.*) ***out of step,*** que no lleva el (mismo) paso; (*fig.*) en desacuerdo; ***out of time,*** discordante; ***out of tune,*** desentonado; ***out of the way,*** lejano, inaccesible, desviado. — *v.t.* (*fam.*) expulsar, expeler, despojar. — *interj.* ¡fuera! ¡fuera de aquí!; ***out with it!*** ¡hable Vd. sin rodeos!
outact [autˈækt], *v.t.* superar.
outargue [autˈɑːgjuː], *v.t.* hacer callar, reducir al silencio (con argumentos).
outback [ˈautbæk], *s.* (*Australia*) interior.
outbid [autˈbid], *v.t.* sobrepujar, pujar *o* licitar más que; ofrecer más que.
outboard [ˈautbɔːd], *a.* (de) fuera de borda.
outbound [ˈautbaund], *a.* de ida, de salida.
outbrave [autˈbreiv], *v.t.* aventajar en valor.
outbrazen [autˈbreizən], *v.t.* ganar en descaro.
outbreak [ˈautbreik], *s.* erupción, brote; ramalazo; estallido.
outbuild [autˈbild], *v.t.* construir mejor *o* más que.
outbuilding [ˈautbildiŋ], *s.* dependencia; anexo.
outburst [ˈautbəːst], *s.* explosión; ramalazo; estallido.
outcast [ˈautkɑːst], *s.* paria, *m.f.*; proscrito; desechado de *o* por la sociedad.
outclass [autˈklɑːs], *v.t.* ser superior a, aventajar (con mucho).
outcome [ˈautkʌm], *s.* resultado, consecuencia.
outcrop [ˈautkrɔp], *s.* afloramiento.
outcry [ˈautkrai], *s.* clamor, protesta (ruidosa); vocerío, griterío.
outdare [autˈdɛə], *v.t.* osar, atreverse más que.
outdated [autˈdeitid], *a.* anticuado, trasnochado.
outdistance [autˈdistəns], *v.t.* dejar atrás.
outdo [autˈduː], *v.t.* sobrepujar, superar, exceder; ***not to be outdone,*** para no ser menos.
outdoor [ˈautdɔː], *a.* al aire libre.
outdoors [autˈdɔːz], *adv.* al aire libre, fuera de casa.
outdrink [autˈdriŋk], *v.t.* beber más que.
outer [ˈautə], *a.* exterior, externo; ***outer cover,*** cubierta (de neumático); ***outer space,*** espacio exterior.
outermost [ˈautəmoust], *a.* extremo; (el) más exterior.
outface [autˈfeis], *v.t.* desafiar, arrostrar.
outfall [ˈautfɔːl], *s.* desembocadura.
outfit [ˈautfit], *s.* equipo; ajuar; traje; instrumental; (*fam.*) unidad (militar); (*fam.*) organización. — *v.t.* equipar.
outfitter [ˈautfitə], *s.* abastecedor; armador; ***outfitter's*** (***shop***), camisería.
outflank [autˈflæŋk], *v.t.* (*mil.*) flanquear.
outflow [ˈautflou], *s.* salida; efusión; desagüe.
outgeneral [autˈdʒenərəl], *v.t.* (*mil.*) vencer en táctica.
outgoing [ˈautgouiŋ], *a.* saliente.
outgoings [ˈautgouiŋz], *s.pl.* gastos, *m.pl.*, egresos, *m.pl.*
outgrow [autˈgrou], *v.t.* crecer más que; ser ya mayor para.
outgrowth [ˈautgrouθ], *s.* excrecencia; consecuencia.
outhouse [ˈauthaus], *s.* dependencia, anejo (*de un edificio*).
outing [ˈautiŋ], *s.* excursión, paseo.
outlandish [autˈlændiʃ], *a.* estrafalario, estrambótico.
outlast [autˈlɑːst], *v.t.* sobrevivir a, durar más que.
outlaw [ˈautlɔː], *s.* proscrito, forajido. — *v.t.* proscribir, declarar fuera de la ley.
outlawed [ˈautlɔːd], *a.* proscrito.
outlawry [ˈautlɔːri], *s.* proscripción, rebeldía.
outlay [ˈautlei], *s.* gastos, *m.pl.*, desembolso; ***initial outlay,*** gastos iniciales.
outlet [ˈautlit], *s.* salida; desagüe; toma de corriente.

outline [ˈautlain], *s.* (*dib.*, *pint.*) contorno, perfil; trazado; bosquejo; ***in outline,*** a grandes rasgos. — *v.t.* perfilar; trazar, bosquejar; prefigurar; ***to be outlined against,*** destacarse contra.

outlive [autˈliv], *v.t.* sobrevivir a, durar más tiempo que.

outlook [ˈautluk], *s.* opinión, punto de vista; perspectiva.

outlying [ˈautlaiiŋ], *a.* periférico.

outmanœuvre [autməˈnu:və], *v.t.* superar en la táctica.

outmarch [autˈmɑ:tʃ], *v.t.* dejar atrás.

outmeasure [autˈmeʒə], *v.t.* exceder en medida.

outmost [ˈautmoust], *a.* más exterior.

outnumber [autˈnʌmbə], *v.t.* exceder en número.

outpace [autˈpeis], *v.t.* dejar atrás.

outpatient [ˈautpeiʃənt], *s.* enfermo externo (del hospital).

outpost [ˈautpoust], *s.* avanzadilla.

outpouring [ˈautpɔ:riŋ], *s.* efusión; chorro.

output [ˈautput], *s.* producción; producto; rendimiento; (*elec.*) potencia de salida; ***output valve,*** válvula de salida.

outrage [ˈautreidʒ], *s.* atrocidad; ultraje; atropello; escándalo. — *v.t.* escandalizar; atropellar, violar.

outrageous [autˈreidʒəs], *a.* atroz; escandaloso; monstruoso.

outrageousness [autˈreidʒəsnis], *s.* atrocidad; (lo) escandaloso.

outreach [autˈri:tʃ], *v.t.* pasar más allá de; alcanzar más que; — ***o.s.,*** excederse, extralimitarse.

outreason [autˈri:zən], *v.t.* vencer en argumento.

outride [autˈraid], *v.t.* ganar la delantera a. — *v.i.* andar a caballo junto al estribo de un carruaje.

outrider [ˈautraidə], *s.* batidor; motociclista de escolta, *m.*

outrigger [ˈautrigə], *s.* (*mar.*) botalón; bote con portarremos exterior; balancín.

outright [ˈautrait], *a.* completo, total; cabal; franco. [autˈrait], *adv.* de una vez.

outrun [autˈrʌn], *v.t.* correr más que; vencer (*en una carrera*).

outsail [autˈseil], *v.t.* navegar más y mejor que.

outsell [autˈsel], *v.t.* vender más que.

outset [ˈautset], *s.* principio, comienzo; ***from the outset,*** desde el *o* un principio.

outshine [autˈʃain], *v.t.* brillar más que; (*fig.*) eclipsar.

outside [ˈautˈsaid], *a.* exterior, externo; superficial; ajeno; extremo. — *adv.* (a) fuera. — *prep.* fuera de; más allá de. — *s.* exterior; superficie; apariencia; ***at the outside,*** a lo sumo, cuando más; a más tardar; ***on the outside,*** por fuera.

outsider [autˈsaidə], *s.* forastero, extraño; intruso; (*carreras de caballos etc.*) outsider.

outsize [ˈautsaiz], *a.* de tamaño excepcional *o* extraordinario.

outskirts [ˈautskə:ts], *s.pl.* alrededores, *m.pl.*; afueras, *f.pl.*; cercanías, *f.pl.*

outsmart [autˈsmɑ:t], *v.t.* (*fam.*) [OUTWIT].

outspeak [autˈspi:k], *v.t.* hablar más que, exceder en locuacidad.

outspoken [autˈspoukən], *a.* franco, que no tiene pelos en la lengua.

outspread [autˈspred], *a.* extendido; desplegado; abierto.

outstanding [autˈstændiŋ], *a.* sobresaliente, destacado, descollante, relevante; pendiente, no pagado.

outstare [autˈstɛə], *v.t.* aguantar la mirada a.

outstay [autˈstei], *v.t.* quedarse más tiempo que; ***outstay one's welcome,*** quedarse demasiado tiempo, quedarse más de la cuenta, abusar.

outstretch [autˈstretʃ], *v.t.* extender, alargar.

outstrip [autˈstrip], *v.t.* aventajar; dejar atrás.

outtalk [autˈtɔ:k], *v.t.* hablar más que.

outvote [autˈvout], *v.t.* vencer en las urnas; rechazar por votación; ***to be outvoted,*** verse derrotado en las elecciones, en las urnas *o* en la votación.

outwalk [autˈwɔ:k], *v.t.* andar más que, dejar atrás.

outward [ˈautwəd], *a.* exterior, externo; superficial; aparente; ***outward journey,*** viaje de ida. — *adv.* (*t.* **outwards**) hacia fuera; ***outward bound,*** con rumbo a un puerto extranjero.

outwardly [ˈautwədli], *adv.* exteriormente; aparentemente, en apariencia.

outwardness [ˈautwədnis], *s.* exterioridad; extroversión.

outwards [ˈautwədz], *adv.* [OUTWARD (*adv.*)].

outwear [autˈwɛə], *v.t.* durar más tiempo que.

outweigh [autˈwei], *v.t.* exceder en peso, pesar más que.

outwit [autˈwit], *v.t.* ser más listo que, burlar.

outwork [ˈautwə:k], *s.* (*fort.*) obra exterior, obra avanzada.

outworn [ˈautˈwɔ:n], *a.* (*fig.*) anticuado, trasnochado.

ouzel [ˈu:zəl], *s.* (*orn.*) mirlo.

ova [ˈouvə], *s.pl.* [OVUM].

oval [ˈouvəl], *a.* oval(ado). — *s.* óvalo.

ovarian [ouˈvɛəriən], *a.* ovárico.

ovarious [ovˈvɛəriəs], *a.* de huevos.

ovaritis [ouvəˈraitis], *s.* ovaritis, *f.inv.*

ovary [ˈouvəri], *s.* (*anat.*) ovario; (*orn.*) overa, huevera.

ovate(d) [ˈouveit(id)], *a.* ovado.

ovation [ouˈveiʃən], *s.* ovación.

oven [ˈʌvən], *s.* horno; hornillo.

over [ˈouvə], *a.* adicional; de más; acabado, terminado; ***it's all over,*** se acabó. — *adv.* (por) encima; al otro lado; de un lado a otro; al revés, trastocado; enfrente; al dorso; ***all over,*** por todas partes; ***all the world over,*** por todo el mundo; ***children of fourteen and over,*** niños de catorce años o más; ***he is muddy all over,*** está todo lleno de barro; ***all over again,*** otra vez, vuelta a empezar; ***over against,*** enfrente de; por contraste a; ***over and over again,*** una y otra vez; ***over-anxious,*** demasiado inquieto; ***over-busy,*** demasiado ocupado; ***over here,*** acá; por aquí; ***over-modest,*** demasiado modesto; ***over-nice,*** remilgado; ***over there,*** allá; ***ten times over,*** diez veces seguidas. — *prep.* sobre, (por) encima de; al otro lado de; por, a través de; más allá de; más de; acerca de; por causa de; superior a; ***all over the city,*** por toda la ciudad; ***to be over forty,*** tener más de cuarenta años; ***how long will you be over it?*** ¿cuánto tiempo le llevará (hacerlo)?; ***over and above,*** además de; en exceso de; ***over the way,*** enfrente, al otro lado.

overact [ˈouvərˈækt], *v.t.*, *v.i.* exagerar (un papel).

overall [ˈouvərɔ:l], *a.* total, global.

overalls [ˈouvərɔ:lz], *s.pl.* guardapolvo, mono.

overarch [ˈouvəˈɑ:tʃ], *v.t.* abovedar.

overawe [ˈouvərˈɔ:], *v.t.* intimidar; impresionar (fuertemente).

overbalance [ˈouvəˈbæləns], *s.* exceso de peso; falta de equilibrio. — *v.t.*, *v.i.* (hacer) perder el equilibrio.

overbear [ˈouvəˈbɛə], *irr. v.t.* agobiar, abrumar; dominar, imponerse a. — *v.i.* dar demasiado fruto.

overbearing [ˈouvəˈbɛəriŋ], *a.* despótico, dominante.

overbid [ˈouvəˈbid], *v.t.* pujar, ofrecer más que. — *v.i.* ofrecer demasiado.

overblow [ˈouvəˈblou], *v.t.* disipar, esparcir (soplando). — *v.i.* soplar demasiado fuerte.

overblown [ˈouvəˈbloun], *a.* marchito; pasado.

overboard [ˈouvəbɔ:d], *adv.* (*mar.*) al mar, al agua; por la borda; ***man overboard!*** ¡hombre al agua!; ***to throw overboard,*** echar por la borda.

overboil [ˈouvəˈbɔil], *v.t., v.i.* hervir *o* cocer demasiado.
overbold [ˈouvəˈbould], *a.* descarado; temerario.
overburden [ˈouvəˈbə:dn], *v.t.* sobrecargar, agobiar.
overbuy [ˈouvəˈbai], *v.t.* comprar muy caro; comprar demasiado.
overcareful [ˈouvəˈkɛəfʌl], *a.* demasiado cuidadoso.
overcast [ouvəˈkɑ:st], *a.* encapotado, nublado, cerrado. — *v.t.* anublar, oscurecer; sobrehilar; cicatrizar. — *v.i.* nublarse.
overcautious [ˈouvəˈkɔ:ʃəs], *a.* demasiado cauto, precavido, cauteloso.
overcharge [ˈouvətʃɑ:dʒ], *s.* sobrecarga; recargo. — [ouvəˈtʃɑ:dʒ], *v.t.* sobrecargar; recargar; cobrar más de lo justo, cobrar de más.
overcloud [ˈouvəˈklaud], *v.t.* cubrir de nubes, nublar.
overcoat [ˈouvəkout], *s.* abrigo, gabán.
overcome [ˈouvəˈkʌm], *v.t.* vencer; superar; rendir; sobrecoger (***with,*** de).
overconfidence [ˈouvəˈkɔnfidəns], *s.* confianza excesiva.
overconfident [ˈouvəˈkɔnfidənt], *a.* demasiado confiado, muy confiado.
overcrowd [ˈouvəˈkraud], *v.t.* atestar; congestionar; superpoblar.
overcrowding [ˈouvəˈkraudiŋ], *s.* congestionamiento; superpoblación.
overdo [ˈouvəˈdu:], *irr. v.t.* exagerar, hacer excesivamente, excederse en; guisar excesivamente; ***overdo it,*** pasarse, excederse; recargar las tintas negras; sacar las cosas de quicio.
overdone [ˈouvəˈdʌn], *a.* exagerado; demasiado guisado *o* pasado. — *p.p.* [OVERDO].
overdose [ˈouvədous], *s.* dosis excesiva, *inv.*
overdraft [ˈouvədrɑ:ft], *s.* (*com.*) giro en descubierto; ***to have an overdraft,*** tener la cuenta en descubierto.
overdraw [ˈouvəˈdrɔ:], *irr. v.t.* (*com.*) girar en descubierto.
overdress [ˈouvəˈdres], *v.t., v.i.* vestir exageradamente.
overdrink [ˈouvəˈdriŋk], *v.i.* beber con exceso.
overdrive [ˈouvədraiv], *s.* (*aut.*) superdirecta. — [ouvəˈdraiv], *v.t.* agobiar.
overdue [ˈouvəˈdju:], *a.* atrasado; (*com.*) vencido y no pagado.
overeat [ˈouvərˈi:t], *v.i.* comer demasiado.
overeating [ˈouvərˈi:tiŋ], *s.* (el) comer con exceso.
overemployment [ˈouvərimˈplɔimənt], *s.* superempleo.
overestimate [ˈouvərˈestimit], *s.* presupuesto excesivo. — [ˈouvərˈestimeit], *v.t.* supervalorar, dar un valor excesivo a.
overexcite [ˈouvərikˈsait], *v.t.* sobreexcitar.
overexcitement [ˈouvərikˈsaitmənt], *s.* sobreexcitación.
overexpose [ˈouvəriksˈpouz], *v.t.* (*foto.*) sobrerevelar.
overexposure [ˈouvəriksˈpouʒə], *s.* (*foto.*) sobrerevelado.
overfeed [ˈouvəˈfi:d], *v.t.* sobrealimentar. — *v.i.* comer con exceso.
overfeeding [ˈouvəˈfi:diŋ], *s.* sobrealimentación.
overflow [ˈouvəflou], *s.* desbordamiento; (cañería de) desagüe. — [ouvəˈflou], *v.i.* salirse, derramarse, desbordarse; rebosar; ***overflow with,*** rebosar de; ***the river overflowed its banks,*** el río se desbordó.
overflowing [ˈouvəˈflouiŋ], *a.* (*fig.*) rebosante (***with,*** de); ***full to overflowing,*** lleno a rebosar.
overfree [ˈouvəˈfri:], *a.* demasiado libre; pródigo.
overfull [ˈouvəˈful], *a.* demasiado lleno.
overgrow [ˈouvəˈgrou], *irr. v.t.* revestir; entapizar; cubrir con plantas; crecer más que. — *v.i.* crecer *o* desarrollarse demasiado.
overgrown [ˈouvəˈgroun], *a.* entapizado, revestido, cubierto; demasiado grande, muy espigado. — *p.p.* [OVERGROW].
overgrowth [ˈouvəgrouθ], *s.* maleza, vegetación exuberante.
overhang [ˈouvəhæŋ], *s.* alero; proyección. — [ouvəˈhæŋ], *v.t., v.i.* sobresalir (por encima de); estar pendiente (sobre); (*fig.*) amenazar.
overhanging [ouvəˈhæŋiŋ], *a.* suspendido, colgado sobre.
overhaste, overhastiness [ˈouvəˈheist, -inis], *s.* precipitación.
overhasty [ˈouvəˈheisti], *a.* precipitado, demasiado apresurado.
overhaul [ˈouvəhɔ:l], *s.* (*mec.*) repaso, revisión. — [ouvəˈhɔ:l], *v.t.* repasar, revisar; alcanzar.
overhead [ˈouvəhed], *a.* de arriba; aéreo; elevado. — [ˈouvəˈhed], *adv.* por lo alto, por encima de la cabeza, arriba. — [ˈouvəhedz], *s.pl.* (*com.*) gastos generales, *m.pl.*
overhear [ˈouvəˈhiə], *v.t.* oír (por casualidad), acertar a oír; sorprender.
overheat [ˈouvəˈhi:t], *v.t.* recalentar.
overindulge [ˈouvərinˈdʌldʒ], *v.t.* mimar demasiado. — *v.i.* — ***in,*** entregarse con exceso a; tomar demasiado.
overjoyed [ouvəˈdʒɔid], *a.* loco de alegría; ***to be overjoyed at,*** no caber de contento con.
overkind [ˈouvəˈkaind], *a.* excesivamente benévolo.
overkindness [ˈouvəˈkaindnis], *s.* bondad excesiva.
overlade [ˈouvəˈleid], *v.t.* sobrecargar.
overland [ˈouvəlænd], *a.* [ouvəˈlænd], *adv.* por tierra, por vía terrestre.
overlap [ˈouvəlæp], *s.* solapo, traslapo; coincidencia. — [ouvəˈlæp], *v.t.* traslapar, solapar, cruzar sobre, cubrir. — *v.i.* coincidir en parte; traslaparse.
overlay [ˈouvəlei], *s.* capa, cubierta. — [ouvəˈlei], *v.t.* cubrir; dar una capa a.
overleaf [ouvəˈli:f], *adv.* al dorso, a la vuelta.
overlie [ˈouvəˈlai], *v.t.* descansar, estar tendido sobre.
overload [ˈouvəloud], *s.* sobrecarga, carga excesiva. — [ouvəˈloud], *v.t.* sobrecargar.
overlook [ˈouvəˈluk], *v.t.* dominar con la vista; dar a, caer a; vigilar; pasar por alto; no fijarse en; omitir; perdonar; hacer la vista gorda ante.
overlord [ˈouvəlɔ:d], *s.* jefe supremo.
overmatch [ˈouvəmætʃ], *s.* fuerza superior; persona con fuerza *o* destreza superior. — [ˈouvəˈmætʃ], *v.t.* vencer, superar, sobrepujar.
overmeasure [ˈouvəˈmeʒə], *s.* medida excesiva, porción excesiva, colmo. — *v.t.* dar demasiada estimación, importancia a.
overmuch [ˈouvəˈmʌtʃ], *a., adv.* demasiado.
over-nice [ˈouvə-ˈnais], *a.* demasiado escrupuloso; remilgado.
overnight [ˈouvənait], *a.* de la noche, nocturno, de noche; ***overnight train,*** tren nocturno. — [ouvəˈnait], *adv.* de la noche a la mañana; ***to become famous overnight,*** hacerse célebre de la noche a la manaña; ***to stay overnight,*** pasar la noche, pernoctar; quedarse hasta el día siguiente.
overpass [ˈouvəpɑ:s], *s.* paso elevado. — [ouvəˈpɑ:s], *v.t.* pasar, salvar; transgredir; pasar por alto.
overpay [ˈouvəˈpei], *v.t.* pagar demasiado.
overpayment [ˈouvəˈpeimənt], *s.* pago excesivo.
overpeople [ˈouvəˈpi:pl], *v.t.* superpoblar.
overplus [ˈouvəˈplʌs], *s.* sobrante.
overpower [ˈouvəˈpauə], *v.t.* subyugar, dominar, vencer; embargar, embriagar.
overpowering [ˈouvəˈpauəriŋ], *a.* abrumador, aplastante; embargante, embriagador.
overproduction [ˈouvəprəˈdʌkʃən], *s.* superproducción.
overrate [ouvəˈreit], *v.t.* supervalorar.

overreach [ˈouvəˈriːtʃ], *v.t.* extenderse más allá de. — **overreach o.s.,** *v.r.* extralimitarse, excederse, pasarse.
override [ouvəˈraid], *irr. v.t.* pasar por encima de; fatigar, reventar (un caballo); prescindir de, hacer caso omiso de.
overriding [ˈouvəˈraidiŋ], *a.* predominante.
overripe [ˈouvəˈraip], *a.* demasiado maduro, pocho.
overrule [ouvəˈruːl], *v.t.* anular, invalidar; (*for.*) denegar.
overrun [ouvəˈrʌn], *v.t.* ocupar rápidamente *o* precipitadamente; invadir, infestar; (*tiempo*) exceder de, pasar de.
overscrupulous [ˈouvəˈskruːpjuləs], *a.* demasiado escrupuloso.
oversea(s) [ˈouvəˈsiː(z)], *a.* de ultramar. — **overseas** [ˈouvəˈsiːz], *adv.* en ultramar; en el extranjero; al extranjero.
oversee [ˈouvəˈsiː], *irr. v.t.* vigilar, superentender; fiscalizar.
overseer [ˈouvəsiə], *s.* capataz; superintendente; sobrestante.
oversell [ˈouvəˈsel], *v.t.* vender demasiado.
overset [ˈouvəˈset], *v.t.* volcar, hacer volcar.
overshadow [ˈouvəˈʃædou], *v.t.* sombrear, dar sombra a; eclipsar.
overshoe [ˈouvəʃuː], *s.* chanclo.
overshoot [ˈouvəˈʃuːt], *irr. v.t.* tirar más allá de; sobrepasar; ***overshoot the mark,*** pasar de la raya, excederse; ***overshoot the runway,*** ir a aterrizar más allá de la pista, pasarse.
oversight [ˈouvəsait], *s.* descuido; inadvertencia; equivocación; vigilancia.
oversimplification [ˈouvəsimplifiˈkeiʃən], *s.* supersimplificación.
oversimplify [ouvəˈsimplifai], *v.t.* simplificar demasiado *o* excesivamente.
overskirt [ˈouvəskəːt], *s.* sobrefalda.
oversleep [ˈouvəˈsliːp], *v.i.* dormir demasiado; ***I overslept,*** se me pegaron las sábanas, me dormí.
oversleeves [ˈouvəsliːvz], *s.pl.* mangotes, *m.pl.*
overspend [ˈouvəˈspend], *v.t.* gastar más de (*la suma asignada*). — *v.i.* gastar demasiado.
overspent [ˈouvəˈspent], *a.* apurado, agotado, extenuado.
overspread [ˈouvəˈspred], *v.t.* desparramar, esparcir; extenderse sobre, cubrir.
overspill [ˈouvəspil], *s.* desbordamiento (de población).
overstate [ˈouvəˈsteit], *v.t.* exagerar.
overstep [ˈouvəˈstep], *v.t.* exceder; ***overstep the mark,*** propasarse; ***overstep the bounds,*** extralimitarse.
overstock [ˈouvəˈstɔk], *s.* surtido excesivo. — [ouvəˈstɔk], *v.t.* abarrotar; ***to be overstocked with,*** tener surtido excesivo de.
overstore [ˈouvəˈstɔː], *v.t.* aprovisionar con exceso.
overstrain [ˈouvəˈstrein], *s.* fatiga *o* tensión excesiva. — *v.t.* fatigar excesivamente.
overstretch [ˈouvəˈstretʃ], *v.t.* estirar demasiado.
overstrung [ˈouvəˈstrʌŋ], *a.* sobreexcitado, nervioso; [ˈouvəstrʌŋ], cruzado (*piano*).
overt [ˈouvəːt], *a.* abierto, manifiesto.
overtake [ˈouvəˈteik], *v.t.* alcanzar, pasar, dejar atrás; adelantar(se) a; (*fig.*) coger, sorprender.
overtask [ˈouvəˈtɑːsk], *v.t.* atarear demasiado.
overtax [ˈouvəˈtæks], *v.t.* agobiar con impuestos; (*fig.*) agobiar, oprimir. — **overtax o.s.,** *v.r.* esforzarse demasiado, cansarse.
overthrow [ˈouvəθrou], *s.* derribo, vuelco; derrocamiento. — [ouvəˈθrou], *v.t.* echar abajo; volcar; derrocar, derribar.
overtime [ˈouvətami], *s.* horas extraordinarias, *f.pl.*
overtire [ˈouvəˈtaiə], *v.t.* fatigar con exceso.
overtone [ˈouvətoun], *s.* (*mús.*) armónico; (*fig.*) sugestión, resonancia; nota, tono.
overtop [ˈouvəˈtɔp], *v.t.* descollar sobre.
overture [ˈouvətjuə], *s.* (*mús.*) obertura; proposición; sondeo.
overturn [ˈouvətəːn], *s.* vuelco, volteo; derrocamiento; trastorno; (*com.*) movimiento de mercancías. — [ouvəˈtəːn], *v.t.* volcar, voltear; trastornar; derrocar. — *v.i.* volcarse; zozobrar.
overvalue [ˈouvəˈvæljuː], *v.t.* sobrevalorar, estimar demasiado, ponderar.
overwatch [ˈouvəˈwɔtʃ], *v.t.* cansar con vigilias.
overweary [ˈouvəˈwiəri], *v.t.* cansar de más.
overween [ˈouvəˈwiːn], *v.i.* presumir.
overweening [ˈouvəˈwiːniŋ], *a.* presuntuoso, altanero, orgulloso; ***overweening pride,*** soberbia, orgullo desorbitado.
overweight [ˈouvəˈweit], *a.* excesivamente pesado; ***to be overweight,*** pesar demasiado *o* de más; ***this parcel is two kilos overweight,*** este paquete excede en dos kilos al peso permitido. — *s.* peso excesivo, sobrepeso.
overwhelm [ouvəˈwelm], *v.t.* abrumar; anonadar; inundar; ***to overwhelm with favours,*** colmar de favores.
overwhelming [ouvəˈwelmiŋ], *a.* abrumador, arrollador, aplastante.
overwork [ˈouvəˈwəːk], *s.* exceso de trabajo, trabajo excesivo. — *v.t.* hacer trabajar con exceso. — *v.i.* trabajar demasiado.
overwrought [ˈouvəˈrɔːt], *a.* sobreexcitado, excitadísimo, muy nervioso, con los nervios de punta.
ovicular [ouˈvikjulə], *a.* ovicular.
Ovid [ˈɔvid]. Ovidio.
oviduct [ˈouvidʌkt], *s.* oviducto.
oviferous [ouˈvifərəs], *a.* ovífero.
oviform [ˈouvifɔːm], *a.* oviforme.
ovine [ˈouvain], *a.* ovino.
oviparous [ouˈvipərəs], *a.* ovíparo.
ovoid [ˈouvɔid], *a.* ovoide.
ovolo [ˈouvoulou], *s.* óvolo.
ovoviviparous [ouvouviˈvipərəs], *a.* ovovivíparo.
ovule [ˈouvjuːl], *s.* óvulo.
ovum [ˈouvəm], *s.* (*pl.* **ova** [ˈouvə]) (*biol.*) huevo.
owe [ou], *v.t.* deber; ***to owe a grudge,*** guardar rencor a. — *v.i.* tener deudas.
owing [ˈouiŋ], *a.* debido; ***to be owing to,*** deberse a, obedecer a. — *prep.* ***owing to,*** debido a, a causa de, por.
owl [aul], *s.* (*orn.*) lechuza (común); ***little owl,*** mochuelo; ***barn-owl,*** lechuza; ***long-eared owl,*** búho; ***screech owl,*** estrige.
owlet [ˈaulit], *s.* lechuza pequeña, mochuelo.
owlish [ˈauliʃ], *a.* de lechuza, de búho, semejante a la lechuza; estólido.
own (1) [oun], *a.* propio, suyo, particular; ***of one's own accord,*** espontáneamente; ***off one's own bat,*** por cuenta propia, por su cuenta; ***it's his own fault,*** tiene la culpa él; ***in one's own hand, with one's own hand,*** de su puño y letra; ***my own self,*** yo mismo. — *pron.* (lo) mío; ***a home of one's own,*** una casa propia; ***on one's own,*** por su cuenta; solo; ***to come into one's own,*** entrar en posesión de lo suyo; conseguir el espaldarazo (oficial); ***to get one's own back,*** tomar la revancha; vengarse; ***to hold one's own,*** defenderse (bien). — *v.t.* poseer, ser dueño de.
own (2) [oun], *v.i.* — ***to*** o ***up to,*** reconocer, confesar.
owner [ˈounə], *s.* proprietario; dueño, amo.
ownerless [ˈounəlis], *a.* sin dueño; mostrenco.
ownership [ˈounəʃip], *s.* propiedad; posesión.
ox [ɔks], *s.* (*pl.* **oxen** [ˈɔksən]) buey; ***ox-bow lake,*** recodo de un río; ***ox-driver,*** boyero; (*bot.*) ***ox-eye,*** ojo de buey; ***ox-fly,*** tábano; ***ox-goad,*** aguijada; ***ox-herd,*** boyero; ***ox-stall,*** boyera, boyeriza; ***ox-tongue,*** lengua de buey; (*bot.*) buglosa.
oxalate [ˈɔksəleit], *s.* oxalato.
oxalic [ɔkˈsælik], *a.* oxálico.

oxen [ˈɔksən], *s.pl.* [OX].
oxidant [ˈɔksidənt], *s.* oxidante.
oxidate [ˈɔksideit], *v.t.* oxidar.
oxidation [ɔksiˈdeiʃən], *s.* oxidación.
oxide [ˈɔksaid], *s.* óxido.
oxidize [ˈɔksidaiz], *v.t.*, *v.i.* oxidar(se).
oxlip [ˈɔkslip], *s.* prímula.
Oxonian [ɔkˈsouniən], *a.*, *s.* oxoniense.
oxtail [ˈɔksteil], *s.* rabo de toro; ***oxtail soup,*** sopa de rabo de toro.
oxyacetylene [ɔksiəˈsetili:n], *a.* oxiacetilénico; ***oxyacetylene burner,*** soplete oxiacetilénico.
oxygen [ˈɔksidʒən], *s.* oxígeno.
oxygenate [ˈɔksidʒineit], *v.t.* oxigenar.
oxygenation [ɔksidʒiˈneiʃən], *s.* oxigenación.
oxygenic [ɔksiˈdʒenik], *a.* oxigenado.
oxygenizable [ˈɔksidʒinaizəbl], *a.* oxigenable.
oxygenize [ˈɔksidʒinaiz], *v.t.* oxigenar.
oxygenous [ɔkˈsidʒənəs], *a.* de oxígeno.
oxyhydrogen [ɔksiˈhaidrədʒən], *s.* gas oxhídrico.
oxysalt [ˈɔksisɔ:lt], *s.* oxisal, *f.*
oxytone [ˈɔksitoun], *a.*, *s.* (*gram.*) oxítono, agudo.
oyer [ˈɔiə], *s.* (*for.*) audición, vista, audiencia.
oyez! [ouˈjes], *interj.* ¡oíd!
oyster [ˈɔistə], *s.* ostra; ostión, ostrón; ***oyster-bed, oyster-farm,*** criadero de ostras; (*orn.*) ***oyster-catcher,*** ostrero; ***oyster-culture,*** ostricultura; ***oyster-dredger,*** pescador de ostras; ***oyster-woman,*** vendedora de ostras.
ozone [ˈouzoun], *s.* ozono.
ozonic, ozonous [ouˈzounik, ˈouzənəs], *a.* que contiene ozono.
ozonize [ˈouzounaiz], *v.t.* ozonizar, ozonificar.
ozonometer [ouzouˈnɔmitə], *s.* ozonómetro.

P

P, p [pi:], décimosexta letra del alfabeto; ***to mind one's P's and Q's,*** andarse con tiento.
pa [pɑ:], *s.* (*fam.*) papá, *m.*
pabulum [ˈpæbjuləm], *s.* pábulo.
paca [ˈpækə], *s.* (*zool.*) paca.
pace [peis], *s.* paso; marcha; velocidad; ***to keep pace with,*** llevar el mismo paso de, ajustar el paso a, (*fig.*) mantenerse al día de; ***to put s.o. through his paces,*** poner a alguien a la prueba; hacer que alguien demuestre su valer; ***to quicken one's pace,*** apretar, acelerar el paso; ***to set the pace,*** dar la pauta. — *v.t.* medir a pasos; (*dep.*) marcar el paso para (alguien). — *v.i.* ***about,*** pasearse (por); ***pace up and down,*** pasearse de arriba (para) abajo.
pacemaker [ˈpeismeikə], *s.* (*med.*) marcapaso; (*dep.*) el que abre carrera; el que da la pauta.
pacer [ˈpeisə], *s.* amblador; el que lleva el paso.
pacha [PASHA].
pachyderm [ˈpækidə:m], *s.* paquidermo.
pachydermatous [pækiˈdə:mətəs], *a.* paquidermo.
pacific [pəˈsifik], *a.* pacífico.
pacificate [pəˈsifikeit], *v.t.* pacificar, apaciguar.
pacification [pæsifiˈkeiʃən], *s.* pacificación, apaciguamiento.
pacificator [pəˈsifikeitə], *s.* pacificador, apaciguador.
pacificatory [ˈpæsifikeitəri], *a.* pacificador.
pacifier [ˈpæsifaiə], *s.* pacificador; (*Am.*) [DUMMY].
pacifism [ˈpæsifizəm], *s.* pacifismo.
pacifist [ˈpæsifist], *a.*, *s.* pacifista, *m.f.*
pacify [ˈpæsifai], *v.t.* pacificar, apaciguar, calmar.
pack [pæk], *s.* bulto, fardo; paquete; carga; cajetilla (de pitillos); jauría (de perros); manada (de lobos); baraja (de cartas); sarta (de mentiras); ***pack animal,*** acémila; ***pack-cloth,*** arpillera; ***pack-horse,*** caballo de carga; ***pack-ice,*** témpanos flotantes, *m.pl.*; ***pack-saddle,*** albarda, basto; ***pack-thread,*** bramante; ***pack-train,*** reata. — *v.t.* hacer (la maleta); meter (en); empaquetar; embalar; envasar; (*fig.*) atestar, llenar hasta los topes (***with,*** de); (***in***) apretar, meter apretadamente; ***to be packed,*** estar atestado, hasta los topes, de bote en bote, repleto; ***to send packing,*** despedir con cajas destempladas; (*fam.*) ***pack it in*** o ***up,*** dejarlo; desistir; renunciar; dar de mano; ***pack off,*** mandar, despachar. — *v.i.* hacer la(s) maleta(s); ***pack up,*** hacer el equipaje; (*fam.*) liar el petate; dar de mano.
package [ˈpækidʒ], *s.* paquete; envase; bulto; ***package deal,*** contrato global; ***package tour,*** viaje turístico con todo incluido. — *v.t.* empaquetar; envasar.
packer [ˈpækə], *s.* embalador.
packet [ˈpækit], *s.* paquete; (*mar.*) paquebote; (*pitillos*) cajetilla; (*fam.*) ***to make a packet,*** hacerse de oro.
packing [ˈpækiŋ], *s.* embalaje; envase; empaquetadura; ***packing-case,*** cajón de embalaje.
packman [ˈpækmən], *s.* (*pl.* **-men** [-men]) buhonero.
pact [pækt], *s.* pacto; ***to make a pact,*** firmar un pacto.
pad (1) [pæd], *s.* almohadilla; cojinete; (*fam.*) cuchitril, cubil. — *v.t.* rellenar, forrar; acolchar; meter paja *o* ripio en (*un escrito*).
pad (2) [pæd], *v.i.* — ***about,*** andar, pisar ligero.
padding [ˈpædiŋ], *s.* relleno; (*fig.*) paja, ripio.
paddle [pædl], *s.* canalete, zagual; paleta; ***paddle-board,*** paleta (de rueda); ***paddle-box,*** tambor; ***paddle-door,*** paradera; ***paddle-steamer,*** vapor de paletas; ***paddle-wheel,*** rueda de paletas. — *v.t.* impulsar con canalete. — *v.i.* remar con canalete; chapotear, meter los pies en el agua.
paddling-pool [ˈpædliŋ-pu:l], *s.* piscina infantil.
paddock [ˈpædək], *s.* prado; corral, cercado; potrero.
Paddy [ˈpædi], *s.* forma cariñosa de [PATRICK]; (*fam.*) irlandés.
padlock [ˈpædlɔk], *s.* candado. — *v.t.* cerrar con candado, echar el candado a.
padre [ˈpɑ:drei], *s.* (*mil.*, *mar.*) cura castrense, capellán.
pæan [ˈpi:ən], *s.* himno de triunfo.
pagan [ˈpeigən], *a.*, *s.* pagano.
paganish [ˈpeigəniʃ], *a.* pagano.
paganism [ˈpeigənizəm], *s.* paganismo.
paganize [ˈpeigənaiz], *v.t.* paganizar. — *v.i.* paganizarse.
page (1) [peidʒ], *s.* paje; botones, *m.inv.* — *v.t.* buscar llamando, hacer llamar por el botones.
page (2) [peidʒ], *s.* página; plana; ***front page,*** portada; primera plana; ***full-page,*** a toda página. — *v.t.* paginar, foliar; ***page*** (***up***), compaginar.
pageant [ˈpædʒənt], *a.* espectacular, ostentoso, fastuoso. — *s.* fausto, pompa; espectáculo brillante; procesión, desfile.
pageantry [ˈpædʒəntri], *s.* fausto, pompa, fasto, aparato.
paginate [ˈpædʒineit], *v.t.* paginar, foliar.
pagination, paging [pædʒiˈneiʃən, ˈpeidʒiŋ], *s.* paginación, foliación.
pagoda [pəˈgoudə], *s.* pagoda.
paid [peid], *a.* ***paid-up,*** pagado, al día; ***paid-up capital,*** capital desembolsado; ***paid-up share,*** acción liberada. — *pret.*, *p.p.* [PAY].
pail [peil], *s.* cubo, pozal; balde.
pailful [ˈpeilful], *s.* (lo que cabe en un) cubo.
paillasse [pælˈjæs], *s.* jergón.
pain [pein], *s.* dolor; ***labour pains,*** dolores del parto; ***on pain of death,*** so pena de muerte; ***pain-killer,*** droga mitigadora; ***shooting pains,*** dolores punzantes, *m.pl.*; ***to be in pain,*** estar con dolor(es); ***to take pains with*** o ***to,*** esmerarse en; ***I have a pain in my side,*** me duel e el costado. — *v.t.* doler, dar lástima.
painful [ˈpeinful], *a.* doloroso; penoso; nada grato.
painfulness [ˈpeinfulnis], *s.* (lo) doloroso; (lo) penoso.
painless [ˈpeinlis], *a.* sin dolor, indoloro.
painlessness [ˈpeinlisnis], *s.* ausencia de dolor.
painstaker [ˈpeinzteikə], *s.* el que se esmera.
painstaking [ˈpeinzteikiŋ], *a.* esmerado, (muy) cuidadoso, meticuloso.
paint [peint], *s.* pintura; colorete, afeites, *m.pl.*; ***coat of paint,*** capa de pintura; ***paint-box,*** caja de colores; ***paint-brush,*** pincel; brocha. — *v.t.* pintar. — *v.i.* pintarse.
painter (1) [ˈpeintə], *s.* pintor, *m.*, pintora, *f.*
painter (2) [ˈpeintə], *s.* (*mar.*) amarra (de un bote).
painting [ˈpeintiŋ], *s.* pintura, arte pictórico; cuadro, pintura; coloración.
pair [pɛə], *s.* pareja; par; unos, unas; yunta (*de bueyes*); ***pair of scissors, of spectacles,*** (par de) tijeras, (de) anteojos. — *v.t.* parear, aparear; igualar; hermanar, casar. — *v.i.* hacer pareja; parearse, aparearse; igualarse; hermanarse.
pairing [ˈpɛəriŋ], *s.* pareamiento, pareo.
pajamas [pəˈdzɑ:məz], *s.pl.* (*Am.*) [PYJAMAS].
Pakistan [pɑ:kisˈtɑ:n]. el Paquistán.
Pakistani [pɑ:kisˈtɑ:ni], *a.*, *s.* paquistanés, paquistaní.
pal [pæl], *s.* (*fam.*) camarada, *m.f.*, compinche, *m.f.*, compadre.
palace [ˈpælis], *s.* palacio.
paladin [ˈpælədin], *s.* paladín.
palæographer [pæliˈɔgrəfə], *s.* paleógrafo.

palæographic(al) [pælio'græfik(əl)], *a.* paleográfico.
palæography [pæli'ɔgrəfi], *s.* paleografía.
palæologist [pæli'ɔlədʒist], *s.* paleólogo.
palæontological [pæliɔntə'lɔdʒikəl], *a.* paleontológico.
palæontologist [pæliɔn'tɔlədʒist], *s.* paleontólogo.
palæontology [pæliɔn'tɔlədʒi], *s.* paleontología.
palæstra [pæ'lestrə], *s.* palestra.
palanquin [pælən'ki:n], *s.* palanquín.
palatable ['pælətəbl], *a.* sabroso, apetitoso; aceptable.
palatal ['pælətəl], *a., s.* palatal.
palatalize ['pælətəlaiz], *v.t.* palatalizar.
palate ['pælit], *s.* paladar.
palatial [pə'leiʃəl], *a.* (*fig.*) señorial, suntuoso.
palatinate [pə'lætinit], *s.* palatinado.
palatine ['pælətain], *a., s.* palatino.
palaver [pə'lɑ:və], *s.* parlamento; (*fam.*) monserga; (*fam.*) jaleo, pesadez.
pale (1) [peil], *a.* pálido; descolorido; claro; tenue, pobre; ***pale-face,*** rostropálido; ***pale-faced,*** de rostro pálido; ***to grow pale,*** palidecer. — *v.i.* palidecer, ponerse pálido; (*fig.*) ***pale before,*** resultar insignificante en comparación con.
pale (2) [peil], *s.* empalizada; ***to be beyond the pale,*** ser insoportable, ser el colmo; pasar de la raya.
paleness ['peilnis], *s.* palidez.
paleographer [PALÆOGRAPHER].
Palestine ['pælistain]. Palestina.
Palestinian [pælis'tinjən], *a., s.* palestino.
palette ['pælit], *s.* (*pint.*) paleta; ***palette-knife,*** espátula.
palfrey ['pɔ:lfri], *s.* palafrén.
palimpsest ['pælimpsest], *s.* palimpsesto.
palindrome ['pælindroum], *s.* palíndromo.
paling ['peiliŋ], *s.* palizada, estacada, valla.
palinode ['pælinoud], *s.* palinodia.
palisade [pæli'seid], *s.* empalizada, estacada. — *v.t.* empalizar.
palish ['peiliʃ], *a.* algo pálido, paliducho.
pall (1) [pɔ:l], *s.* (*igl.*) palio; palia; paño mortuorio; ***pall-bearer,*** portaféretro; ***pall of smoke,*** capa *o* nube de humo, humareda.
pall (2) [pɔ:l], *v.i.* perder el sabor *o* el interés, dejar de interesar, empezar a hartar; ***it palls on one,*** acaba hartando.
palladium [pə'leidiəm], *s.* (*fig.*) paladión; (*min.*) paladio.
pallet (1) ['pælit], *s.* jergón.
pallet (2) ['pælit], *s.* (*mec.*) uña; paleta; ***pallet-knife,*** espátula.
palliate ['pælieit], *v.t.* paliar, mitigar.
palliation [pæli'eiʃən], *s.* paliación, mitigación.
palliative ['pæliətiv], *a., s.* paliativo, lenitivo.
pallid ['pælid], *a.* pálido.
pallor, pallidness ['pælə, -idnis], *s.* palidez.
palm (1) [pɑ:m], *s.* (*bot.*) palma; ***to carry off the palm,*** llevarse la palma; (*orn.*) ***palm-bird,*** tejedor; ***palm-grove,*** palmar; ***Palm Sunday,*** domingo de Ramos.
palm (2) [pɑ:m], *s.* palma; (*medida*) palmo; (*mar.*) rempujo; ***to grease s.o.'s palm,*** untar la mano a alguien. — *v.t.* escamotear; ***palm off on,*** endosar, encajar a.
Palma-Christi ['pælmə-'kristi], *s.* (*bot.*) palmacristi, higuera infernal.
palmar ['pælmə], *a.* palmar.
palmary ['pælməri], *a.* digno de premio.
palmate(d) ['pælmeit(id)], *a.* palmar, palmeado, palmípedo.
palmer ['pɑ:mə], *s.* palmero, peregrino, romero; palmeta; tahur.
palmetto [pæl'metou], *s.* (*bot.*) palmera enana, palmito.
palmiferous [pæl'mifərəs], *a.* palmífero.
palmiped ['pælmiped], *a.* palmípedo, palmeado. — *s.* palmeado.
palmistry ['pɑ:mistri], *s.* quiromancia.
palmy ['pɑ:mi], *a.* palmeado; palmar; glorioso, espléndido, floreciente, próspero, triunfal.
palp [pælp], *s.* (*pl.* **palpi** [-ai]) palpo.
palpability [pælpə'biliti], *s.* palpabilidad.
palpable ['pælpəbl], *a.* palpable.
palpation [pæl'peiʃən], *s.* palpación, palpamiento, palpadura.
palpitate ['pælpiteit], *v.i.* palpitar, latir.
palpitation [pælpi'teiʃən], *s.* palpitación, latido.
palpus ['pælpəs], [PALP].
palsied ['pɔ:lzid], *a.* paralizado, paralítico, perlático.
palsy ['pɔ:lzi], *s.* parálisis, *f. inv.*, perlesía. — *v.t.* paralizar.
palter ['pɔ:ltə], *v.i.* usar de rodeos; petardear; regatear.
palterer ['pɔ:ltərə], *s.* petardista, *m.f.*
paltriness ['pɔ:ltrinis], *s.* (lo) fútil, (lo) baladí, (lo) insignificante; (lo) miserable.
paltry ['pɔ:ltri], *a.* fútil, insignificante.
paludal [pə'lju:dəl], *a.* palúdico, palustre.
paly ['peili], *a.* (*blas.*) barrado, palado.
pampas ['pæmpəs], *s.pl.* pampas, *f.pl.*
pamper ['pæmpe], *v.t.* mimar, consentir.
pampered ['pæmpəd], *a.* mimado, consentido.
pamperer ['pæmpərə], *s.* mimador.
pamphlet ['pæmflit], *s.* folleto; hoja.
pamphleteer [pæmfli'tiə], *s.* folletista, *m.f.*
pan [pæn], *s.* cazuela, cacerola; (*masa*) artesa; (*carp.*) quicio; (*min.*) gamella; (*fusil*) cazoleta; (*fam.*) tazón; (***brain-)pan,*** sesera; ***it is just a flash in the pan,*** es una cosa que ha salido por chiripa, sonó la flauta por casualidad. — *v.t.* (*oro*) separar en la gamella; (*fam.*) poner verde a. — *v.i.* (*fam.*) ***pan out,*** resultar; salir bien.
panacea [pænə'siə], *s.* panacea.
panache [pæ'næʃ], *s.* penacho.
Panama [pænə'mɑ:]. Panamá, *m.*
Panamanian [pænə'meiniən], *a., s.* panameño.
pancake ['pænkeik], *s.* filloa; ***pancake landing,*** aterrizaje en desplome *o* de vientre.
pancratic [pæn'krætik], *a.* pancrático.
pancreas ['pæŋkriəs], *s.* páncreas, *m.inv.*
pancreatic [pæŋkri'ætik], *a.* pancreático.
pandect ['pændekt], *s.* digesto, recopilación; (*pl.*) pandectas, *f.pl.*
pandemonium [pændi'mouniəm], *s.* ruidazo, estruendo, pandemonio.
pander ['pændə], *s.* alcahuete. — *v.t.* mimar, consentir. — *v.i.* alcahuetear; ***pander to,*** dar gusto a (siempre), consentir.
panderess ['pændəris], *s.* alcahueta.
pane [pein], *s.* cristal; (hoja de) vidrio.
panegyric [pæni'dʒirik], *s.* panegírico.
panegyric(al) [pæni'dʒirik(əl)], *a.* panegírico.
panegyrist [pæni'dʒirist], *a., s.* panegirista, *m.f.*
panegyrize ['pænidʒiraiz], *v.t.* panegirizar, hacer el panegírico de.
panel ['pænəl], *s.* panel; (*puerta*) entrepaño; (*techo*) artesón; (*cost.*) paño; (*instrumentos*) tablero, cuadro, salpicadero; (*discusión televisada etc.*) panel, cuadro; (*pint.*) tabla.
panelled ['pænəld], *a.* con paneles; artesonado; de tableros.
panelling ['pænəliŋ], *s.* paneles, *m.pl.*; entrepaños, *m.pl.*; artesonado.
pang [pæŋ], *s.* punzada (*de dolor*), dolor agudo; ***pangs of conscience,*** remordimiento(s), pena; ***pangs of hunger,*** vacío en el estómago, sensación de vacío.

panic ['pænik], *a.* pánico. — *s.* (terror) pánico; (*bot.*) ***panic-grass,*** mijo común; ***panic-stricken,*** presa del pánico. — *v.i.* llenarse de pánico, ser presa del pánico.
panicky ['pæniki], *a.* asustadizo.
panicle ['pænikl], *s.* panícula, panoja, panocha.
paniculated [pə'nikjuleitid], *a.* apanojado.
panification [pænifi'keiʃən], *s.* panificación.
pannier ['pæniə], *s.* canasto; cuévano; serón; ***pannier-bags,*** alforjas, *f.pl.*; carteras, *f.pl.*
pannikin ['pænikin], *s.* cazo, cacillo.
panoply ['pænəpli], *s.* panoplia.
panorama [pænə'rɑ:mə], *s.* panorama, *m.*
panoramic [pænə'ræmik], *a.* panorámico.
pansy ['pænzi], *s.* (*bot.*) pensamiento; (*fam.*) marica, *m.*
pant [pænt], *v.i.* jadear, resollar; ***pant after, for,*** anhelar, suspirar por.
pantaloon [pæntə'lu:n], *s.* pantalón; gracioso, bufón; (*pl.*) pantalones, *m.pl.*, calzones, *m.pl.*
pantechnicon [pæn'teknikən], *s.* camión de mudanzas.
pantheism ['pænθiizəm], *s.* panteísmo.
pantheist ['pænθiist], *s.* panteísta, *m.f.*
pantheistic(al) [pænθi'istik(əl)], *a.* panteístico.
pantheologist [pænθi'ɔlədʒist], *s.* panteólogo.
pantheology [pænθi'ɔlədʒi], *s.* panteología.
pantheon ['pænθiən], *s.* panteón.
panther ['pænθə], *s.* pantera.
panties ['pæntiz], *s.pl.* bragas, *f.pl.*, braguitas, *f.pl.*
pantile ['pæntail], *s.* baldosa; teja.
panting ['pæntiŋ], *a.* jadeante. — *s.* jadeo, resuello; palpitación.
pantograph ['pæntogrɑ:f], *s.* pantógrafo.
pantographic [pænto'græfik], *a.* pantográfico.
pantography [pæn'tɔgrəfi], *s.* pantografía.
pantomime ['pæntəmaim], *s.* pantomima; espectáculo cómico navideño.
pantomimic [pænto'mimik], *a.* pantomímico.
pantomimist [pæntə'maimist], *s.* pantomimo.
pantry ['pæntri], *s.* despensa.
pants [pænts], *s.pl.* calzoncillos, *m.pl.*; (*Am.*) pantalones, *m.pl.*; (*fam.*, *fig.*) ***to catch s.o. with his pants down,*** coger desprevenido a alguien.
pap [pæp], *s.* papilla; gachas, *f.pl.*
papa [pə'pɑ:], *s.* papá.
papacy ['peipəsi], *s.* papado, pontificado.
papal ['peipəl], *a.* papal, pontifical.
papaverous [pə'peivərəs], *a.* papaveráceo, amapolado.
papaw [pə'pɔ:], *s.* (*bot.*) (*árbol*) papayo; (*fruto*) papaya.
paper ['peipə], *s.* papel; periódico; (*académico*) ponencia, comunicación; artículo; documento; (*pl.*) papeles, documentos, documentación; examen; ***brown paper,*** papel de embalar, de estraza; ***cream-laid paper,*** papel acantillado; ***emery paper,*** papel esmeril; ***laid paper,*** papel acantillado; ***large paper,*** papel marquilla; ***litmus-paper,*** papel de tornasol; ***mathematics paper,*** ejercicio de matemática, (los) temas de matemática; ***monthly paper,*** revista mensual; ***on paper,*** sobre el papel; ***on paper the team is good,*** en teoría, es bueno el equipo; ***paper-clip,*** sujetapapeles, *m.inv.*, abrazadera; ***paper-cutter,*** cortapapeles, *m.inv.*; ***paper-folder,*** plegadera; ***paper-hanger,*** empapelador; ***paper-hanging,*** empapelado; ***paper-knife,*** plegadera; ***paper-weight,*** pisapapeles, *m.inv.*; ***quarterly paper,*** revista trimestral; ***quire of paper,*** mano de papel, *f.*; ***ream of paper,*** resma de papel; ***sand-paper,*** papel de lija; ***waste paper,*** papeles usados; ***weekly paper,*** revista semanal; ***wrapping-paper,*** papel de envolver. — *v.t.* empapelar.
papescent [pə'pesənt], *a.* pulposo, carnoso.
papier-mâché ['pæpjei-'mæʃei], *s.* cartón piedra.
papilionaceous [pəpiliə'neiʃəs], *a.* papilionáceo, amariposado.
papillary, papillous [pə'piləri, -əs], *a.* papilar.
papist ['peipist], *s.* papista, *m.f.*
papistic(al) [pə'pistik(əl)], *a.* papístico, papal.
papistry ['peipistri], *s.* papismo.
pappose, pappous ['pæpous, -pəs], *a.* velloso, velludo.
pappus ['pæpəs], *s.* (*bot.*) vilano.
pappy ['pæpi], *a.* jugoso, mollar.
papula, papule ['pæpjulə, -pju:l], *s.* pápula.
papular, papulous ['pæpjulə, -ləs], *a.* lleno de pápulas.
papyrography [pæpi'rɔgrəfi], *s.* papirografía.
papyrus [pə'paiərəs], *s.* (*pl.* **papyri** [-rai]) papiro.
par [pɑ:], *s.* (*com.*) par; paridad; nivel; ***above par,*** a premio; ***at par,*** a la par; ***below par,*** a descuento; (*fig.*) malucho; (*fig.*) de calidad inferior a la normal; (*fig.*) ***to be on a par with,*** estar al nivel de, ser igual a, correr parejas con; ***par value,*** valor nominal.
parable ['pærəbl], *s.* parábola.
parabola [pə'ræbələ], *s.* (*geom.*) parábola.
parabolic(al) [pærə'bɔlik(əl)], *a.* parabólico.
paraboloid [pə'ræbəlɔid], *s.* paraboloide.
parachronism [pə'rækrənizəm], *s.* paracronismo.
parachute ['pærəʃu:t], *s.* paracaídas, *m. inv.* — *v.i.* lanzarse en paracaídas.
parachutist ['pærəʃu:tist], *s.* paracaidista, *m.f.*
paraclete ['pærəkli:t], *s.* paráclito, paracleto.
parade [pə'reid], *s.* (*mil.*) parada, desfile; paseo; alarde; ***parade ground,*** plaza de armas. — *v.t.* formar en parada; desfilar (por); pasear (por); hacer gala *o* alarde de. — *v.i.* desfilar, formar en parada.
paradigm ['pærədaim], *s.* paradigma, *m.*
paradisaic(al), paradisiac(al) [pærədi'seiik(əl), -di'siæk(əl)], *a.* paradisíaco.
paradise ['pærədais], *s.* paraíso.
paradox ['pærədɔks], *s.* paradoja.
paradoxical [pærə'dɔksikəl], *a.* paradójico.
paraffin ['pærəfin], *s.* petróleo (de alumbrado); ***paraffin wax,*** parafina.
paragoge [pærə'goudʒi], *s.* (*gram.*) paragoge.
paragogic(al) [pærə'gɔdʒik(əl)], *a.* paragógico.
paragon ['pærəgən], *s.* dechado; ***paragon of virtue,*** dechado de virtudes; (*impr.*) parangona.
paragraph ['pærəgrɑ:f], *s.* párrafo; suelto; ***new*** o ***fresh paragraph,*** punto y aparte.
Paraguay ['pærəgwai]. el Paraguay.
Paraguayan [pærə'gwaiən], *a.*, *s.* paraguayo.
parakeet ['pærəki:t], *s.* (*orn.*) perico, periquito.
paralipsis [pærə'lipsis], *s.* (*ret.*) paralipsis, *f. inv.*
parallactic(al) [pærə'læktik(əl)], *a.* paraláctico.
parallax ['pærəlæks], *s.* paralaje, *f.*
parallel ['pærəlel], *a.* paralelo, en paralelo; ***to run parellel to,*** ir paralelo *o* paralela a. — *s.* (*geom.*, *fort.*) paralela; (*geog.*, *fig.*) paralelo; (*pl.*, *impr.*) doble raya vertical; ***to have no parallel,*** no poder compararse con nada; ***without parallel,*** nunca visto. — *v.t.* ir paralelo a; correr parejas con; ***to be paralleled by,*** tener su paralelo en.
parallelism ['pærəlelizəm], *s.* paralelismo.
parallelogram [pærə'leləgræm], *s.* paralelogramo.
paralogism [pə'rælədʒizəm], *s.* paralogismo.
paralogize [pə'rælədʒaiz], *v.i.* paralogizar.
paralysation [pærəlai'zeiʃən], *s.* paralización.
paralyse ['pærəlaiz], *v.t.* paralizar.
paralysis [pə'rælisis], *s.* parálisis, *f.*
paralytic [pærə'litik], *a.* paralítico; (*fam.*) completamente trompa, *m. f.* — *s.* paralítico.
paralyze [PARALYSE].
parameter [pə'ræmitə], *s.* parámetro.
paramorphism [pærə'mɔ:fizəm], *s.* paramorfismo.

paramount [ˈpærəmaunt], *a.* supremo, capital.
paramour [ˈpærəmuə], *s.* cortejo, amante, querido, querida.
paranymph [ˈpærənimf], *s.* paraninfo; padrino; intercesor.
paranoia [pærəˈnɔiə], *s.* paranoia.
parapet [ˈpærəpit], *s.* parapeto.
paraphernalia [pærəfəˈneiliə], *s.pl.* bienes parafernales, *m.pl.*; avios, *m.pl.*; atavíos, *m.pl.*, galas, *f.pl.*; trámites, *m.pl.*
paraphrase [ˈpærəfreiz], *s.* paráfrasis, *f.inv.* — *v.t.* parafrasear.
paraphraser [ˈpærəfreizə], *s.* parafraseador.
paraphrast [pˈærəfræst], *s.* parafraste.
paraphrastic(al) [pærəˈfræstik(əl)], *a.* parafrástico.
parasite [ˈpærəsait], *s.* parásito.
parasitic(al) [pærəˈsitik(əl)], *a.* parásito, parasítico.
parasitism [ˈpærəsitizəm], *s.* parasitismo.
parasol [pærəˈsɔl, ˈpærəsɔl], *s.* parasol, sombrilla, quitasol.
paratrooper [ˈpærətru:pə], *s.* paracaidista, *m.*
parboil [ˈpɑ:bɔil], *v.t.* sancochar.
parbuckle [ˈpɑ:bʌkl], *s.* tiravira.
parcel [ˈpɑ:səl], *s.* paquete; lío; parcela; ***parcel of ground,*** solar, lote, parcela de terreno; ***parcel post,*** servicio de paquetes postales. — *v.t.* dividir, partir; repartir, distribuir; ***parcel out,*** parcelar; repartir; ***parcel up,*** empaquetar, embalar.
parcener [ˈpɑ:sinə], *s.* coheredero.
parch [pɑ:tʃ], *v.t.* (re)secar, quemar, agostar.
parched [pɑ:tʃt], *a.* reseco; muerto de sed.
parching [ˈpɑ:tʃiŋ], *a.* abrasador, ardiente.
parchment [ˈpɑ:tʃmənt], *s.* pergamino, vitela.
pard [pɑ:d], *s.* leopardo.
pardon [pɑ:dn], *s.* perdón; indulto; remisión; ***general pardon,*** amnistía (general); ***I beg your pardon,*** le pido perdón, perdone; ***I beg your pardon?*** ¿cómo (dice)? — *v.t.* perdonar, dispensar; (*der.*) indultar; ***pardon me,*** dispense Vd.
pardonable [ˈpɑ:dnəbl], *a.* perdonable, excusable, disculpable.
pardonableness [ˈpɑ:dnəblnis], *s.* disculpabilidad.
pardoner [ˈpɑ:dnə], *s.* perdonador.
pardoning [ˈpɑ:dniŋ], *s.* (el) perdonar.
pare [pɛə], *v.t.* adelgazar; mondar; cortar; ***pare down,*** reducir, ir reduciendo.
paregoric [pæriˈgɔrik], *a.*, *s.* paregórico.
parent [ˈpɛərənt], *a.* madre, matriz; ***parent house,*** casa madre. — *s.* padre (*m.*) *o* madre (*f.*); (*pl.*) padres, *m.pl.*
parentage [ˈpɛərəntidʒ], *s.* familia, linaje, alcurnia; nacimiento.
parental [pəˈrentl], *a.* de los padres, paternal.
parentalism [pəˈrentəlizəm], *s.* paternalismo.
parenthesis [pəˈrenθisis], *s.* (*pl.* **-theses** [-θisi:z]) paréntesis, *m.inv.*; ***in parentheses,*** entre paréntesis.
parenthetic(al) [pærənˈθetik(əl)], *a.* parentético; explicativo.
parenthetically [pærənˈθetikəli], *adv.* entre paréntesis.
parenthood [ˈpɛərənthud], *s.* paternidad *o* maternidad, (el) ser padre(s), (el) tener hijo(s).
parenticide [pəˈrentisaid], *s.* parricida, *m.f.*; (*acto*) parricidio.
parentless [ˈpɛərəntlis], *a.* sin padres, huérfano.
paresis [ˈpærisis], *s.* (*pat.*) paresia.
parget [ˈpɑ:dʒit], *s.* yeso; enlucido. — *v.t.* enyesar; enlucir.
parhelion [pɑ:ˈhi:liən], *s.* parhelio.
pariah [ˈpæriə], *s.* paria, *m.f.*
Parian [ˈpɛəriən], *a.*, *s.* pario.
parietal [pəˈraiitl], *a.* parietal.
paring [ˈpɛəriŋ], *s.* raedura, peladura, raspadura; ***paring-knife,*** tranchete, trinchete, cuchilleja.

Paris [ˈpæris]. París, *m.*
parish [ˈpæriʃ], *a.* parroquial; ***parish church,*** parroquia, iglesia parroquial; ***parish council,*** concejo parroquial; ***parish priest,*** párroco. — *s.* parroquia.
parishioner [pəˈriʃənə], *s.* feligrés, *m.f. inv.*
Parisian [pəˈriziən], *a.*, *s.* parisiense, parisién, parisino.
parisyllabic [pærisiˈlæbik], *a.* parisilábico.
parity [ˈpæriti], *s.* paridad.
park [pɑ:k], *s.* parque; ***artillery-park,*** parque de artillería; ***car park,*** aparcamiento. — *v.t.* estacionar, aparcar; (*fam.*) poner, dejar. — *v.i.* estacionarse, aparcar.
parking [ˈpɑ:kiŋ], *s.* estacionamiento, aparcamiento; ***no parking,*** prohibido estacionarse; ***parking lights,*** luces de situación, *f.pl.*; (*Am.*) ***parking lot,*** aparcamiento; ***parking meter,*** parquímetro.
parkway [ˈpɑ:kwei], [MOTORWAY].
parlance [ˈpɑ:ləns], *s.* lenguaje.
parley [ˈpɑ:li], *s.* parlamento; ***to come to a parley,*** parlamentar. — *v.i.* parlamentar.
parliament [ˈpɑ:ləmənt], *s.* parlamento; cortes, *f.pl.*; ***Houses of Parliament,*** el Parlamento; ***Member of Parliament,*** diputado.
parliamentarian [pɑ:limənˈtɛəriən], *a.*, *s.* parlamentario.
parliamentarism [pɑ:liˈmentərizəm], *s.* parlamentarismo.
parliamentary [pɑ:liˈmentəri], *a.* parlamentario.
parlour [ˈpɑ:lə], *s.* salón, saloncito, sala, salita; locutorio; ***parlour game,*** juego de salón; ***parlour-maid,*** camarera.
Parmesan [pɑ:məˈzæn], *a.*, *s.* parmesano; ***Parmesan cheese,*** queso de Parma.
Parnassus [pɑ:ˈnæsəs]. (el) Parnaso.
parochial [pəˈroukiəl], *a.* parroquial; (*fig.*) estrecho, de miras estrechas, provinciano.
parochiality [pərouki'æliti], *s.* parroquialidad.
parodic [pəˈrɔdik], *a.* paródico.
parodist [ˈpærədist], *s.* parodista, *m.f.*
parody [ˈpærədi], *s.* parodia. — *v.t.* parodiar.
parole [pəˈroul], *s.* palabra de honor; (*mil.*) santo y seña; ***on parole,*** bajo palabra; ***to put on parole,*** poner en libertad bajo palabra.
paronomasia [pærənəˈmeisiə], *s.* paronomasia.
paronym [ˈpærənim], *s.* voz parónima.
paronymous [pəˈrɔniməs], *a.* paronímico, parónimo.
paronymy [pəˈrɔnimi], *s.* paronimia.
parotid [pəˈrɔtid], *a.* parotídeo. — *s.* parótida.
paroxysm [ˈpærəksizəm], *s.* paroxismo, acceso, arrebato.
paroxysmal [pærəkˈsizməl], *a.* paroxismal.
parquet, parquetry [ˈpɑ:ki, ˈpɑ:kitri], *s.* parquet; entarimado; piso de taracea *o* mosaico de madera.
parr [pɑ:], *s.* murgón, esguín.
parricidal [pæriˈsaidl], *a.* parricida.
parricide [ˈpærisaid], *s.* parricida, *m.f.*; (*acto*) parricidio.
parrot [ˈpærət], *s.* papagayo, loro; ***parrot fashion,*** como un loro, como un papagayo; (*ict.*) ***parrot-fish,*** escaro.
parry [ˈpæri], *v.t.*, *v.i.* parar; quitar; desviar; esquivar.
parry(ing) [ˈpæri(iŋ)], *s.* parada; reparo; quite.
parse [pɑ:z], *v.t.* (*gram.*) analizar.
Parsee [pɑ:ˈsi:], *a.*, *s.* parsi.
parsimonious [pɑ:siˈmouniəs], *a.* frugal, parco; mezquino.
parsimoniously [pɑ:siˈmouniəsli], *adv.* frugalmente, parcamente; mezquinamente.
parsimoniousness, parsimony [pɑ:siˈmouniəsnis, ˈpɑ:siməni], *s.* frugalidad, parquedad; mezquindad.

parsing ['pɑ:ziŋ], *s.* (*gram.*) análisis, *m. inv.*
parsley ['pɑ:sli], *s.* (*bot.*) perejil.
parsnip ['pɑ:snip], *s.* (*bot.*) chirivía.
parson ['pɑ:sən], *s.* cura, *m.*, clérigo, párroco; pastor.
parsonage ['pɑ:sənidʒ], *s.* curato, rectoría, casa del cura *o* del pastor.
part [pɑ:t], *s.* parte; porción; (*mec.*) pieza; (*teat.*) papel; lugar, comarca; deber; (*pl.*) prendas, *f.pl.*; región, lugares, *m.pl.*; ***for my part,*** por mi parte, por lo que a mí toca; ***foreign parts,*** países extranjeros, *m.pl.*, el extranjero; ***in part,*** en parte; ***in parts,*** en parte; ***man of parts,*** hombre de buenas prendas; ***that is part and parcel of the same problem,*** forma parte integrante del mismo problema; ***part owner,*** condueño; ***private parts,*** partes pudendas, *f.pl.*, vergüenzas, *f.pl.*; ***to play a part,*** hacer, representar *o* desempeñar un papel; ***to take in good part,*** tomar a buena parte; ***to take part in,*** tomar parte en, participar en. — *v.t.* separar, partir, dividir; ***part one's hair,*** hacerse la raya. — *v.i.* separarse; ***part from,*** despedirse de; separarse de; ***part with,*** desprenderse de.
partake [pɑ:'teik], *irr. v.t.*, *v.i.* — ***of,*** tomar, comer, beber (de); ***partake in,*** participar en.
partaker [pɑ:'teikə], *s.* partícipe, participante, *m.f.*; cómplice, *m.f.*
partaking [pɑ:'teikiŋ], *s.* participación; complicidad.
parterre [pɑ:'tɛə], *s.* parterre, arriate.
parthenogenesis [pɑ:θinou'dʒenisis], *s.* partenogénesis, *f.inv.*
partial ['pɑ:ʃəl], *a.* parcial; ***to be partial to,*** ser aficionado a.
partiality [pɑ:ʃi'æliti], *s.* parcialidad, preferencia; afición (***for,*** a).
partially ['pɑ:ʃəli], *adv.* parcialmente, en parte.
participant [pɑ:'tisipənt], *a.*, *s.* partícipe, participante; combatiente.
participate [pɑ:'tisipeit], *v.i.* participar, tomar parte (***in,*** en); (*beneficiarse de*) participar (***in,*** de).
participation [pɑ:tisi'peiʃən], *s.* participación.
participator [pɑ:'tisipeitə], *s.* participante.
participial [pɑ:ti'sipiəl], *a.* participial.
participle ['pɑ:tisipl], *s.* (*gram.*) participio.
particle ['pɑ:tikl], *s.* partícula.
parti-coloured ['pɑ:ti-kʌləd], *a.* abigarrado.
particular [pə'tikjulə], *a.* particular; concreto, específico; escrupuloso, minucioso; exigente; ***that particular one,*** concretamente ése; ***to be very particular about,*** ser muy exigente en relación con. — *s.* particular, particularidad; pormenor, detalle; ***in particular,*** en particular, particularmente, especialmente; ***to go into particulars,*** entrar en detalles, concretar.
particularity [pətikju'læriti], *s.* particularidad.
particularize [pə'tikjuləraiz], *v.t.* particularizar, especificar, detallar. — *v.i.* entrar en detalles.
particularly [pə'tikjuləli], *adv.* en particular, particularmente, especialmente.
parting ['pɑ:tiŋ], *s.* despedida; separación; bifurcación; raya (*del pelo*); ***parting of the ways,*** momento de la separación; bifurcación de los caminos.
partisan ['pɑ:tizæn], *a.* partidista; ***partisan spirit,*** partidismo. — *s.* guerrillero, partisano.
partition [pɑ:'tiʃən], *s.* partición, división, separación; tabique. — *v.t.* partir, dividir, separar.
partitive ['pɑ:titiv], *a.*, *s.* partitivo.
partly ['pɑ:tli], *adv.* en parte.
partner ['pɑ:tnə], *s.* socio; compañero, camarada, *m.f.*; cónyuge; pareja; (*com.*) ***sleeping partner,*** socio comanditario. — *v.t.* acompañar, ser pareja de; ***to be partnered,*** ir acompañado de, tener como *o* de pareja.
partnership ['pɑ:tnəʃip], *s.* asociación; sociedad; vida en común; ***to enter into partnership with,*** asociarse con, hacerse socio de.
partridge ['pɑ:tridʒ], *s.* (*orn.*) perdiz, *f.*
parturient [pɑ:'tjuəriənt], *a.* parturienta.
parturition [pɑ:tjuə'riʃən], *s.* parto, parturición.
party ['pɑ:ti], *s.* partido; grupo; facción; partida; pelotón; reunión; tertulia; fiesta, guateque; parte; individuo; interesado; ***to be party to,*** estar interesado en; ser parte (*o* complice) en; ***party line,*** línea *o* política de partido; ***party politics,*** politiqueo, partidismo; ***party ticket,*** candidatura (*apoyada por un partido*); (*constr.*) ***party wall,*** (pared) medianera.
parvenu ['pɑ:vənju:], *a.*, *s.* advenedizo, arribista, *m.f.*
parvis ['pɑ:vis], *s.* (*arq.*) atrio.
Paschal ['pɑ:skəl], *a.* pascual.
pasha ['pæʃə], *s.* bajá, *m.*
pasque-flower ['pɑ:sk-flauə], *s.* pulsatila.
pasquinade [pæskwi'neid], *s.* pasquín, pasquinada.
pass [pɑ:s], *s.* (*geog.*) puerto, paso, desfiladero; (*mil.*) pase; salvoconducto; (*teat.*) pase, entrada de favor; (*examen*) aprobado; ***pass-mark,*** aprobado; ***things have come to a pretty pass,*** hemos llegado a una situación lamentable; ***to make a pass,*** intentar ligar, echar un piropo. — *v.t.* pasar; pasar por delante de; adelantar, dejar atrás a; cruzarse con; aprobar; expresar; pronunciar, dictar; (*Am.*) [OVERTAKE]; ***pass by,*** pasar por alto; ***pass off,*** (hacer) pasar; ***pass o.s. off as,*** hacerse pasar por; ***pass over,*** excluir; ***pass round,*** pasar de mano en mano; ***pass up,*** subir; (*fig.*) renunciar a; ***will you pass me the bread?*** ¿me hace el favor de pasar el pan? — *v.i.* pasar; aprobar; ***in passing,*** de paso, de pasada; ***to come to pass,*** acontecer, suceder; ***pass away,*** fallecer; ***pass by,*** pasar de largo; pasar delante de; ***pass out,*** desmayarse; ***pass through,*** pasar por.
passable ['pɑ:səbl], *a.* transitable; pasable, discreto.
passably ['pɑ:səbli], *adv.* tolerablemente, medianamente, discretamente.
passage ['pæsidʒ], *s.* paso; (*mar.*, *mús.*) pasaje; (*arq.*) passillo; galería; callejón; pasadizo; (*escrito*) trozo; (*pol.*) trámites (*de una ley*); ***bird of passage,*** ave de paso; ***passage of arms,*** paso de armas; ***passage of time,*** paso, transcurso del tiempo; ***in the passage of time,*** andando el tiempo; ***rough passage,*** travesía movida.
passant ['pæsənt], *a.* (*blas.*) pasante.
passenger ['pæsindʒə], *s.* pasajero, viajero.
passer, passer-by ['pɑ:sə, -'bai], *s.* transeúnte, paseante.
passing ['pɑ:siŋ], *a.* pasajero, fugaz; ***passing fancy,*** capricho del momento. — *adv.* muy, excepcionalmente. — *s.* paso; tránsito; ***passing bell,*** toque de difuntos.
passion ['pæʃən], *s.* pasión; (acceso de) cólera; ***to fly into a passion,*** encolerizarse, montar en cólera; ***to have a passion for,*** tener (auténtica) locura por; (*bot.*) ***passion-flower,*** pasionaria.
passionate ['pæʃənit], *a.* apasionado; colérico; ardiente, vivo, intenso, vehemente.
passionateness ['pæʃənitnis], *s.* vehemencia.
passionless ['pæʃənlis], *a.* frío, sin pasiones.
passive ['pæsiv], *a.* pasivo; inactivo, inerte. — *s.* (*gram.*) voz pasiva, *f.*
passiveness, passivity ['pæsivnis, pæ'siviti], *s.* pasividad, (lo) pasivo.
Passover ['pɑ:souvə], *s.* pascua de los hebreos.
passport ['pɑ:spɔ:t], *s.* pasaporte.
password ['pɑ:swə:d], *s.* santo y seña, *m.*
past [pɑ:st], *a.* pasado, transcurrido; ***for some time past,*** (desde) hace ya (algún) tiempo; ***past master,*** maestro consumado (***at,*** en); ***that's past,*** ha pasado, pasó. — *adv.* por delante; ***to rush past,*** pasar precipitadamente. — *prep.* más allá de; por delante de; más de; después de; ***it's past nine,*** son las nueve pasadas; (*fam.*) ***I***

wouldn't put it past him, es capaz de todo, no me chocaría nada; ***past belief,*** increíble; ***past comprehension,*** incomprensible; ***past doubt,*** fuera de duda; ***past hope,*** sin esperanza; desahuciado. — *s.* pasado; antecedentes, *m.pl.*; ***woman with a past,*** mujer que tiene historia.

paste [peist], *s.* pasta; engrudo; ***paste diamonds,*** bisutería. — *v.t.* empastar; engrudar; (*fam.*) pegar.

pasteboard [ˈpeistbɔ:d], *s.* cartón.

pastel [ˈpæstəl], *a.*, *s.* pastel.

pastern [ˈpæstə:n], *s.* cuartilla (*del caballo*).

pasteurize [ˈpæstəraiz], *v.t.* pasteurizar.

pastille [ˈpæsti:l], *s.* pastilla.

pastime [ˈpɑ:staim], *s.* pasatiempo, afición.

pastor [ˈpɑ:stə], *s.* (*igl.*) pastor.

pastoral [ˈpɑ:stərəl], *a.* pastoral; (*lit.*) pastoril. — *s.* (*igl.*) pastoral, *f.*; pastorela.

pastorate, pastorship [ˈpɑ:stərit, -ʃip], *s.* curato.

pastry [ˈpeistri], *s.* pasta; pastas, *f.pl.*; pasteles, *m.pl.*; pastelería; ***flaky pastry,*** hojaldre; ***pastry-cook,*** pastelero.

pasturage [ˈpɑ:stjuridʒ], *s.* [PASTURE].

pasture [ˈpɑ:stʃə], *s.* pasto, pastura; dehesa. — *v.t.* pastar, apacentar, pastorear. — *v.i.* pastar, pacer.

pasty (1) [ˈpeisti], *a.* pálido.

pasty (2) [ˈpæsti], *s.* empanadilla.

Pat [pæt], forma cariñosa de [PATRICIA; PATRICK].

pat [pæt], *a.* oportuno, pintiparado. — *adv.* ***to have sth. off pat,*** saberse algo al dedillo; [PATLY]. — *s.* palmadita, palmada; golpecito; caricia. — *v.t.* dar palmaditas a; dar una palmada en; acariciar con la mano; (*fig.*) ***pat on the back,*** felicitar. — *v.i.* andar con un trotecito ligero.

Patagonia [pætəˈgouniə]. Patagonia.

patch [pætʃ], *s.* remiendo; parche; lunar postizo; mancha; parcela pequeña, cuadro; (*fam.*) ***it's not a patch on,*** no se puede ni comparar con. — *v.t.* remendar; apañar; ***patch up,*** remendar *o* reparar provisionalmente; (*fam.*) ***patch it up,*** hacer las paces.

patcher [ˈpætʃə], *s.* remendón, chafallón.

patchouli [ˈpætʃuli], *s.* planta *o* perfume pachulí.

patchwork [ˈpætʃwə:k], *s.* remiendo; centón, obra de retazos; confusión, masa confusa.

patchy [ˈpætʃi], *a.* desigual, poco uniforme.

pate [peit], *s.* (*fam.*) cabeza, testa; coronilla.

pated [ˈpeitid], *a.* que tiene cabeza.

patella [pəˈtelə], *s.* (*anat.*) rótula.

paten [pætn], *s.* plato; placa; (*igl.*) patena.

patent [ˈpeitənt], *a.* patente, palmario; de patente, patentado; ***letters patent,*** patente de privilegio; ***patent leather,*** charol; ***patent medicine,*** específico. — *s.* patente, *f.*; privilegio; ***patent office,*** oficina de patentes. — *v.t.* patentar.

patentee [peitənˈti:], *s.* dueño de una patente.

patentor [ˈpeitəntə], *s.* el que expide una patente.

pater [ˈpeitə], *s.* (*fam.*) padre, papá, *m.*

paterfamilias [peitəfæˈmiljəs], *s.* padre de familia.

paternalism [pəˈtə:nəˈlism], *s.* gobierno paternal.

paternal [pəˈtə:nəl], *a.* paternal; paterno.

paternity [pəˈtə:niti], *s.* paternidad; origen, linaje.

paternoster [ˈpætəˈnɔstə], *s.* paternóster, padrenuestro, rosario; (*arq.*) contera.

path [pɑ:θ], *s.* camino, senda, vereda, sendero; (*fig.*) curso, trayectoria; órbita; (*tempestad*) marcha; ***bridle path,*** camino de herradura; ***cinder path,*** pista de ceniza.

pathetic [pəˈθetik], *a.* patético; lastimoso, de pena.

pathless [ˈpɑ:θlis], *a.* sin camino, sin senda.

pathologic(al) [pæθəˈlɔdʒik(əl)], *a.* patológico.

pathologist [pəˈθɔlədʒist], *s.* patólogo.

pathology [pəˈθɔlədʒi], *s.* patología.

pathos [ˈpeiθɔs], *s.* patetismo, (lo) patético.

pathway [ˈpɑ:θwei], *s.* senda, sendero, vereda.

patience [ˈpeiʃəns], *s.* paciencia; (*bot.*) romaza; solitario (*juego de naipes*); ***to lose patience,*** perder la paciencia, impacientarse; montar en cólera; ***to try s.o.'s patience,*** probar la paciencia a alguien, tentar de *o* la paciencia a alguien.

patient [ˈpeiʃənt], *a.* paciente, sufrido. — *s.* paciente, enfermo.

patly [ˈpætli], *adv.* a propósito, en punto, oportunamente, convenientemente.

patness [ˈpætnis], *s.* (lo) oportuno, oportunidad, conveniencia.

patois [ˈpætwɑ:], *s.* dialecto, jerga.

patriarch [ˈpeitriɑ:k], *s.* patriarca, *m.*

patriarchal, patriarchic [peitriˈɑ:kəl, -ik], *a.* patriarcal.

patriarchate, patriarchship [ˈpeitriɑ:kit, -ʃip], *s.* patriarcado.

Patricia [pəˈtriʃə]. Patricia.

patrician [pəˈtriʃən], *a.*, *s.* patricio.

patricide [ˈpætrisaid], *s.* (*pers.*) parricida, *m.f.*; (*acto*) parricidio.

Patrick [ˈpætrik]. Patricio.

patrimonial [pætriˈmouniəl], *a.* patrimonial.

patrimony [ˈpætriməni], *s.* patrimonio.

patriot [ˈpeitriət], *s.* patriota, *m.f.*

patriotic [pætriˈɔtik], *a.* patriótico; (*pers.*) patriota; ***he's very patriotic,*** es muy patriota.

patriotism [ˈpætriətizəm], *s.* patriotismo.

patrol [pəˈtroul], *s.* patrulla; ronda; (*Am.*) ***patrolman,*** guardia muncipal, *m.*, (*Hisp. Am.*) patrullero; (*Am.*) ***patrol wagon*** [BLACK MARIA]. — *v.t.* patrullar (por); rondar (por). — *v.i.* patrullar; rondar, hacer la ronda.

patron [ˈpeitrən], *s.* cliente, parroquiano; (*igl.*) patrono; patrocinador (*de una empresa*); ***patron (of the arts),*** mecenas, *m.inv.*; protector.

patronage [ˈpætrənidʒ], *s.* patronato; patrocinio; mecenazgo; ***under the patronage of,*** patrocinado por.

patronal [pəˈtrounəl], *a.* patronal.

patroness [ˈpeitrənes], *s.* cliente, *f.*; protectora; patrona; patrocinadora.

patronize [ˈpætrənaiz], *v.t.* ser cliente de; patrocinar; (*fig.*) tratar con aire protector.

patronizing [ˈpætrənaiziŋ], *a.* (*fig.*) protector.

patronymic [pætroˈnimik], *a.*, *s.* patronímico.

patten [ˈpætən], *s.* chanclo, zueco.

patter [ˈpætə], *s.* jerga *o* labia (publicitaria); parloteo; (ruido de) pasitos ligeros; tamborileo; golpeteo. — *v.i.* — ***about,*** andar con pasitos ligeros; tamborilear.

pattern [ˈpætən], *s.* modelo; patrón; dibujo; mosaico; paradigma, *m.*; ***to follow the pattern set by,*** seguir la pauta de. — *v.t.* modelar (***on,*** sobre).

patty [ˈpæti], *s.* empanadilla.

paucity [ˈpɔ:siti], *s.* exigüidad, orfandad, escasez.

Paul [pɔ:l]. Pablo.

Pauline (1) [ˈpɔ:li:n]. Paulina.

Pauline (2) [ˈpɔ:lain], *a.* paulino.

paunch [pɔ:ntʃ], *s.* panza, barriga.

paunchy [ˈpɔ:ntʃi], *a.* panzudo, barrigón.

pauper [ˈpɔ:pə], *s.* pobre, indigente.

pauperism [ˈpɔ:pərizəm], *s.* pauperismo.

pauperize [ˈpɔ:pəraiz], *v.t.* depauperar, empobrecer, reducir a la pobreza.

pause [pɔ:z], *s.* pausa; ***to give pause to,*** dar que pensar a. — *v.i.* hacer una pausa, detenerse (brevemente).

pausingly [ˈpɔ:ziŋli], *adv.* con (muchas) pausas.

pave [peiv], *v.t.* pavimentar, enlosar; ***pave the way for,*** preparar el terreno a, abrir el camino a.

pavement [ˈpeivmənt], *s.* acera; pavimento.

paver, paviour [ˈpeivə, ˈpeivie], *s.* empedrador, solador.

pavilion [pəˈviljən], *s.* pabellón; (*dep.*) vestuario, caseta.

paving [ˈpeiviŋ], *s.* pavimento, pavimentación; ***paving-stone,*** losa, baldosa; ***paving-tile,*** baldosa loseta.

paviour [PAVER].

paw [pɔ:], *s.* pata; garra, zarpa. — *v.t.* dar zarpazos a; (*fam.*) manosear, sobar; ***paw the ground,*** piafar.

pawl [pɔ:l], *s.* (*mar.*) linguete, trinquete; (*mec.*) retén, seguro; diente (de encaje); paleta (de reloj); (*mar.*) ***supporter of the pawl,*** descanso del linguete; (*mar.*) ***hanging pawls,*** linguetes de por alto.

pawn (1) [pɔ:n], *s.* peón (*de ajedrez*).

pawn (2) [pɔ:n], *s.* empeño; ***in pawn,*** en prenda; ***pawn ticket,*** papeleta de empeño. — *v.t.* empeñar, dejar en prenda, pignorar; ***he has pawned his boots,*** está empeñado hasta las cejas.

pawnbroker [ˈpɔ:nbroukə], *s.* prestamista, *m.f.*, prendero; (*for.*) comodatario.

pawnee [pɔ:ˈni:], *s.* prestamista, *m.f.*, prestador.

pawner [ˈpɔ:nə], *s.* prendador.

pawnshop [ˈpɔ:nʃɔp], *s.* casa de empeños, prendería; monte de piedad.

pay [pei], *s.* paga, sueldo, salario; pago; ***in the pay of,*** a sueldo de, al servicio de; ***on half-pay,*** a medio sueldo; ***pay-clerk,*** pagador, habilitado; ***pay-day,*** día de (la) paga; ***pay-list,*** nómina; ***pay-load,*** carga útil; ***pay-office,*** pagaduría; ***pay-packet,*** sobre de la paga; ***pay-roll,*** nómina. —*irr. v.t.* pagar; costear; liquidar; ***pay attention,*** prestar atención; ***pay back,*** devolver, restituir; reembolsar; pagar en *o* con la misma moneda; ***pay a call*** o ***visit,*** hacer una visita; ***pay cash down,*** pagar al contado; hacer un pago inicial; ***pay in,*** ingresar; ***pay in full,*** pagar del todo, saldar; ***pay off,*** saldar; pagar y despedir; ajustar (*una cuenta*); ***pay out,*** desembolsar; (*mar.*) soltar, largar; (*fig.*, *fam.*) ajustarle a alguien las cuentas; ***he who pays the piper calls the tune,*** el que paga, manda. — *v.i.* pagar; rendir, ser rentable *o* provechoso; compensar; ***pay up,*** pagar (de mala gana); ***pay with interest,*** pagar con creces; ***you'll pay for it,*** ya me la(s) pagarás; ***pay through the nose,*** costarle a uno un ojo de la cara; ***it doesn't pay to do it,*** vale más no hacerlo, no compensa hacerlo.

payable [ˈpeiəbl], *a.* pagadero.

payee [peiˈi:], *s.* (*com.*) portador.

payer [ˈpeiə], *s.* pagador.

paymaster [ˈpeimɑ:stə], *s.* oficial pagador, habilitado; ***Paymaster-General,*** ordenador de pagos.

payment [ˈpeimənt], *s.* pago; ***full payment,*** saldo finiquito; ***in payment for,*** en pago de; ***monthly payment,*** mensualidad; ***on payment of,*** mediante pago de; ***to present for payment,*** presentar al cobro; ***to suspend payment,*** hacer suspensión de pagos.

pea [pi:], *s.* (*pl.* **peas, pease** [-z]) guisante; chícharo; ***as like as two peas in a pod,*** clavados; ***pea-gun, pea-shooter,*** cerbatana; (*ent.*) ***pea-weevil,*** gorgojo.

peace [pi:s], *s.* paz, *f.*; ***at peace,*** en paz; ***peace-loving,*** amante de la paz; ***peace-maker,*** pacificador, conciliador; ***peace-offering,*** sacrificio propiciatorio; ***peace-officer,*** agente del orden público; ***to hold one's peace,*** callarse, guardar silencio; ***to keep the peace,*** mantener la paz *o* el orden (público); ***to make peace,*** hacer las paces; ***to sue for peace,*** negociar con miras a la paz.

peaceable [ˈpi:səbəl], *a.* pacífico; sosegado.

peaceableness [ˈpi:səblnis], *s.* tranquilidad, sosiego.

peaceful [ˈpi:sful], *a.* tranquilo, pacífico.

peacefulness [ˈpi:sfulnis], *s.* tranquilidad, calma.

peach [pi:tʃ], *s.* melocotón; ***peach-tree,*** melocotonero; (*fig.*) preciosidad, monada.

peachy [ˈpi:tʃi], *a.* (*fam.*) estupendo, de rechupete.

peacock [ˈpi:kɔk], *s.* (*orn.*) pavo real, pavón.

peahen [ˈpi:hen], *s.* (*orn.*) pava real.

peak [pi:k], *s.* pico, cumbre, *f.*, cima, cúspide, *f.*; (*fig.*) auge, apogeo; punta; (*gorra*) visera; ***peak hours,*** horas punta, *f.pl.*; ***peak traffic,*** movimiento máximo.

peaked [pi:kt], *a.* de visera.

peaky [ˈpi:ki], *a.* (*fam.*) pálido, enfermucho, que tiene mala cara.

peal [pi:l], *s.* repique; repiqueteo; juego de campanas; ***peal of laughter,*** risotada, carcajada; ***peal of thunder,*** trueno. — *v.t.* tocar a vuelo. — *v.i.* repicar; tronar.

peanut [ˈpi:nʌt], *s.* cacahuete; ***to earn peanuts,*** ganar una miseria; ***peanut-butter,*** manteca de cachuete.

pear [pɛə], *s.* (*bot.*) pera; ***pear-tree,*** peral.

pearl [pə:l], *s.* perla; aljófar; ***mother of pearl,*** madreperla, nácar; (*bot.*) ***pearl-barley,*** cebada perlada. — *v.t.* perlar; adornar con perlas.

pearled [pə:ld], *a.* perlado, aljofarado.

pearly [ˈpə:li], *a.* perlino, de perla(s).

peasant [ˈpezənt], *a.*, *s.* campesino, labrador.

peasantry [ˈpezəntri], *s.* campesinos, *m.pl.*, gente del campo, campesinado.

peascod [ˈpi:zkɔd], *s.* vaina de guisantes.

pease [pi:z], *s.pl.* [PEA].

peat [pi:t], *s.* turba; ***peat-bog,*** turbera; ***peat-moss,*** musgo de pantano.

peaty [ˈpi:ti], *a.* turboso.

pebble [pebl], *s.* guijarro, guija, china; ***he thinks he's the only pebble on the beach,*** se cree que no hay más que él. — *v.t.*, *v.i.* granular.

pebbly [ˈpebli], *a.* guijarroso, guijoso.

peccability [pekəˈbiliti], *s.* fragilidad, debilidad (moral).

peccable [ˈpekəbl], *a.* pecable.

peccadillo [pekəˈdilou], *s.* pecadillo, falta leve, *f.*

peccancy [ˈpekənsi], *s.* defecto, vicio, disposición al pecado.

peccant [ˈpekənt], *a.* pecador, pecante; vicioso, defectuoso.

peck (1) [pek], *s.* medida de áridos (9.087 *litros*).

peck (2) [pek], *s.* picotada, picotazo. — *v.t.* picar, picotear. — *v.i.* comiscar; ***peck at one's food,*** comer con remilgos *o* como un pajarito.

pecker [ˈpekə], *s.* picoteador; (zapa)pico; (*orn.*) picoverde; (*fam.*) ***to keep one's pecker up,*** no dejarse desanimar.

peckish [ˈpekiʃ], *a.* (*fam.*) ***to feel peckish,*** tener hambrecilla.

pectin [ˈpektin], *s.* pectina.

pectinal [ˈpektinəl], *a.* pectíneo.

pectinate(d) [ˈpektineit(id)], *a.* pectiniforme.

pectoral [ˈpektərəl], *a.* pectoral. — *s.* (*mil.*) peto; (*igl.*) pectoral.

peculate [ˈpekjuleit], *v.t.* (*ant.*) desfalcar, malversar.

peculation [pekjuˈleiʃən], *s.* peculado, desfalco, malversación.

peculator [ˈpekjuleitə], *s.* peculador, malversador, desfalcador.

peculiar [piˈkju:liə], *a.* peculiar; singular; particular; ***peculiar to,*** privativo de; propio de; (*fam.*) ***she's a bit peculiar,*** es un poco rara.

peculiarity [pikju:liˈæriti], *s.* particularidad, peculiaridad, rasgo característico.

pecuniary [piˈkju:niəri], *a.* pecuniario.

pecunious [piˈkju:niəs], *a.* adinerado.

pedagogic [pedəˈgɔdʒik], *a.* pedagógico.

pedagogics [pedəˈgɔdʒiks], *s.* pedagogía.

pedagogue [ˈpedəgɔg], *s.* pedagogo; pedante.

pedagogy, pedagogism [ˈpedəgɔdʒi, -gɔdʒizəm], *s.* pedagogía; pedantismo.

pedal [pedl], *s.* pedal; ***pedal brake,*** freno de pie *o* de pedal. — *v.t.* mover pedaleando. — *v.i.* pedalear.

pedant [ˈpedənt], *s.* pedante.

pedantic [pi'dæntik], *a.* pedante, pedantesco.
pedantry ['pedəntri], *s.* pedantería.
peddle [pedl], *v.t.* vender por las calles *o* de casa en casa, andar vendiendo. — *v.i.* andar vendiendo cosas, ser buhonero.
peddler, (*Am.*) [PEDLAR].
peddling ['pedliŋ], *s.* buhonería; comercio, venta, tráfico.
pedestal ['pedistəl], *s.* pedestal, peana.
pedestrian [pi'destriən], *a.* de peatón, para peatones; (*fig.*) pedestre, ramplón. — *s.* peatón.
pediatric [pi:di'ætrik], *a.* pediátrico.
pediatrician [pi:diə'triʃən], *s.* pedíatra, *m.f.*
pediatrics [pi:di'ætriks], *s.* pediatría.
pedicle ['pedikl], *s.* pedículo.
pedicular, pediculous [pi'dikjulə, -ləs], *a.* pedicular.
pedigree ['pedigri:], *a.* de casta, de raza. — *s.* árbol genealógico; genealogía, ascendencia; pedigrí.
pediment ['pedimənt], *s.* (*arq.*) frontón.
pedlar ['pedlə], *s.* buhonero; revendedor.
pedometer [pi'dɔmitə], *s.* pedómetro.
peduncle [pi'dʌŋkl], *s.* pedúnculo.
peduncular [pi'dʌŋkjulə], *a.* peduncular.
pee [pi:], *s.* (*obsc.*) ***to have a pee,*** hacer pis. — *v.i.* (*obsc.*) hacer pis.
peek [pi:k], *s.* mirada furtiva. — *v.i.* irse a las vistillas; ***peek at,*** mirar a hurtadillas.
peel [pi:l], *s.* piel, mondadura(s), peladura(s). — *v.t.* mondar, pelar; quitar; ***peel off,*** quitar(se). — *v.i.* — ***off,*** pelarse; desconcharse; (*fam.*) desnudarse.
peeler ['pi:lə], *s.* mondador, pelador.
peeling(s) ['pi:liŋ(z)], *s.* (*pl.*) mondadura(s), peladura(s).
peep (I) [pi:p] [PEEK]; ***peep-hole,*** mirilla; ***peep-show,*** mundonuevo; (*fam.*) escenas pornográficas, *f.pl.* — *v.i.* asomar, empezar a aparecer, despuntar.
peep (2) [pi:p], *s.* pío. — *v.i.* piar; (*fam.*) ***let's have no peep out of you,*** tú, a callar.
peeper ['pi:pə], *s.* (*fam.*) ojo.
Peeping Tom ['pi:piŋ 'tɔm], *s.* mirón.
peer (I) [piə], *s.* par; igual; noble.
peer (2) [piə], *v.i.* — ***at, into,*** mirar de cerca, mirar con ojos de miope.
peerage ['piəridʒ], *s.* paría, nobleza.
peeress ['piəres], *s.* paresa.
peerless ['piəlis], *a.* sin par, incomparable, sin igual.
peerlessly ['piəlisli], *adv.* incomparablemente.
peerlessness ['piəlisnis], *s.* superioridad incomparable.
peeved [pi:vd], *a.* (*fam.*) de mal humor; ofendido.
peevish ['pi:viʃ], *a.* desabrido, malhumorado.
peevishness ['pi:viʃnis], *s.* desabrimiento, mal humor.
peewit [PEWIT].
peg [peg], *s.* clavija; estaca; pinza (*de la ropa*); colgadero, gancho; (*fig.*) pretexto; punto de apoyo; ***peg-leg,*** pata de palo; ***to be a square peg in a round hole,*** ser un inadaptado; ***to take down a peg,*** bajar los humos a. — *v.t.* enclavijar; (*precios*) fijar, estabilizar; ***peg down,*** estaquillar; ***peg out,*** señalar con estacas; tender con pinzas. — *v.i.* — ***away,*** machacar (***at,*** en); tener tesón; (*fam.*) ***peg out,*** estirar la pata.
Pegasus ['pegəsəs]. Pegaso.
pegging ['pegiŋ], *s.* pernería.
Peggy ['pegi]. forma cariñosa de **Margaret.**
pegmatite ['pegmətait], *s.* pegmatita.
pejorative [pi'dʒɔrətiv], *a.* despectivo, peyorativo.
Peke [pi:k], *s.* (*fam.*) (perro) pequinés.
Pekin(g) [pi:'kin, -iŋ]. Pequín, Pekín.
Pekinese, Pekingese [pi:ki'ni:z, pi:kiŋ'i:z], *a., s.* pequinés; ***Pekinese (dog),*** (perro) pequinés.
pekoe ['pekou], *s.* te negro superior.
pelagic [pi'lædʒik], *a.* pelágico, oceánico.
pelargonium [pelɑ:'gouniəm], *s.* pelargonio.
pelerine ['pelərin], *s.* pelerina, manteleta.
pelican ['pelikən], *s.* (*orn.*) pelícano.
pelisse [pe'li:s], *s.* pelliza.
pell [pel], *s.* (*ant.*) piel, *f.*, pellejo, cuero; pergamino.
pellet ['pelit], *s.* bolita; bodoque; perdigón.
pellicle ['pelikl], *s.* película, cutícula, telilla.
pellitory ['pelitəri], *s.* (*bot.*) cañarroya; ***pellitory of Spain,*** pelitre, manzanilla pelitre.
pell-mell ['pel-'mel], *adv.* a trochemoche, al (buen) tuntún, sin orden ni concierto.
pellucid [pe'lju:sid], *a.* translúcido, diáfano, cristalino.
pellucidity, pellucidness [pelju:'siditi, pe'lju:sidnis], *s.* diafanidad; (*fís.*) pelucidad.
pelt (I) [pelt], *s.* pellejo; piel.
pelt (2) [pelt], *s.* (*fam.*) ***(at) full pelt,*** a todo correr. — *v.t.* tirar, lanzar; apedrear; ***pelt with questions,*** acribillar (a preguntas). — *v.i.* azotar, batir (*la lluvia*); ir a todo gas.
pelting ['peltiŋ], *a.* furioso, que cae con fuerza (*lluvia etc.*). — *s.* golpeo; lluvia (*de piedras etc.*).
peltry ['peltri], *s.* peletería, corambre, pieles, *f.pl.*, pellejos, *m.pl.*
pelvic ['pelvik], *a.* pélvico.
pelvimeter [pel'vimitə], *s.* pelvímetro.
pelvis ['pelvis], *s.* (*pl.* **pelves** [-i:z]) pelvis, *f.inv.*
pemmican ['pemikən], *s.* carne seca, cecina, mojama.
pen (I) [pen], *s.* corral; redil. — *v.t.* — ***in, up,*** encerrar, accorralar.
pen (2) [pen], *s.* pluma; ***fountain pen,*** estilográfica; ***pen-drawing, pen-sketch,*** dibujo a pluma; ***pen-name,*** seudónimo; (*Am.*) ***pen point*** [NIB]; ***pen-stroke,*** plumazo; ***slip of the pen,*** error de pluma, lapsus. — *v.t.* escribir, redactar.
penal ['pi:nəl], *a.* penal; gravoso; ***penal servitude,*** presidio, trabajos forzados, *m.pl.*
penalize ['pi:nəlaiz], *v.t.* castigar, sancionar; penar; perjudicar.
penalty ['penəlti], *s.* castigo, pena, sanción; (*dep.*) penalti; ***penalty-kick,*** golpe de castigo.
penance ['penəns], *s.* penitencia.
penates [pe'neiti:z], *s.pl.* penates, *m.pl.*
pence [pens], *s.pl.* [PENNY].
penchant ['pɔ:nʃɔ̃:], *s.* tendencia, inclinación, predilección, afición.
pencil ['pensəl], *s.* lápiz; pincel; (*ópt.*) hacecillo (*de luz*); ***pencil-case,*** lapicero; ***pencil-sharpener,*** sacapuntas, *m.inv.* — *v.t.* dibujar, escribir con lápiz.
pendant ['pendənt], *s.* pendiente, medallón; arete; araña (*de lámpara*); (*mar.*) amante, gallardete; apéndice; (*arq.*) adorno que cuelga.
pendency ['pendənsi], *s.* suspensión; dilación, demora.
pendent ['pendənt], *a., s.* pendiente.
pendentive [pen'dentiv], *s.* (*arq.*) pechina.
pending ['pendiŋ], *a.* pendiente. — *prep.* hasta.
pendulous ['pendjuləs], *a.* colgante.
pendulum ['pendjuləm], *s.* péndulo.
penetrability, penetrableness [penitrə'biliti, 'penitrəblnis], *s.* penetrabilidad.
penetrable ['penitrəbl], *a.* penetrable.
penetrant ['penitrənt], *a.* penetrante.
penetrate ['penitreit], *v.t., v.i.* penetrar (en).
penetrating ['penitreitiŋ], *a.* penetrante.
penetration [peni'treiʃən], *s.* penetración.
penetrative ['penitrətiv], *a.* penetrante, penetrativo.
penguin ['pengwin], *s.* (*orn.*) pingüino, pájaro bobo.
penholder ['penhouldə], *s.* portaplumas, *m.inv.*
penicillin [peni'silin], *s.* penicilina.
peninsula [pe'ninsjulə], *s.* península.
peninsular [pe'ninsjulə], *a.* peninsular.
penis ['pi:nis], *s.* (*pl.* **penes** [-i:z]) (*anat.*) pene.

penitence [ˈpenitəns], *s.* penitencia; contrición, arrepentimiento.
penitent [ˈpenitənt], *a.* penitente; contrito, arrepentido. — *s.* penitente.
penitential [peniˈtenʃəl], *a.* penitencial.
penitentiary [peniˈtenʃəri], *a.* penitenciario. — *s.* presidio.
penitently [ˈpenitəntli], *adv.* con penitencia; arrepentidamente.
penknife [ˈpennaif], *s.* navajilla, cortaplumas, *m.inv.*
penmanship [ˈpenmənʃip], *s.* caligrafía.
penna [ˈpenə], *s.* (*orn.*) pena.
pennant [ˈpenənt], *s.* gallardete; banderola, estandarte.
pennate(**d**) [ˈpeneit(id)], *a.* pennado.
penniless [ˈpenilis], *a.* sin dinero, sin blanca, indigente.
pennilessness [ˈpenilisnis], *s.* pobreza.
pennon [ˈpenən], *s.* pendón.
penny [ˈpeni], *s.* (*pl.* **pennies, pence** [ˈpeniz, pens]) penique; ***in for a penny, in for a pound,*** de perdidos, al río; ***penny-a-liner,*** gacetillero; ***penny dreadful,*** folletín; ***penny-in-the-slot machine,*** tragaperras, *m.inv.*; ***penny wise pound foolish,*** mezquino en lo pequeño, derrochador en lo grande; (*fam.*) ***now the penny's dropped,*** ya caigo; ***to cost a pretty penny,*** costar un dineral *o* bastante dinerete; ***to turn an honest penny,*** ganar honradamente (algo de) dinero; ***to be without a penny,*** estar a la cuarta pregunta.
pennyroyal [peniˈrɔiəl], *s.* (*bot.*) poleo.
pennyweight [ˈpeniweit], *s.* peso de 1,555 gramos.
pennyworth [ˈpenəθ, ˈpeniwəːθ], *s.* valor de un penique; pizca.
penology [piːˈnɔlədʒi], *s.* penología.
pensile [ˈpensail], *a.* pensil.
pension [ˈpenʃən], *s.* pensión; jubilación; retiro; ***old-age pension,*** subsidio de vejez. — *v.t.* pensionar; ***pension off,*** jubilar.
pensionable [ˈpenʃənəbl], *a.* ***pensionable age,*** edad de la jubilación.
pensionary [ˈpenʃənəri], *a.* pensionado. — *s.* pensionista, *m.f.*, pensionado.
pensioner [ˈpenʃənə], *s.* pensionista, *m.f.*, pensionado; (*mil., mar.*) inválido.
pensive [ˈpensiv], *a.* pensativo, meditabundo.
pensiveness [ˈpensivnis], *s.* estado pensativo *o* meditabundo.
penstock [ˈpenstɔk], *s.* paradera (del caz).
pent [pent], *a.* — ***up,*** reprimido, contenido.
pentachord [ˈpentəkɔːd], *s.* pentacordio.
pentad [ˈpentæd], *s.* grupo de cinco cosas.
pentagon [ˈpentəgən], *s.* pentágono.
pentagonal [penˈtægənəl], *a.* pentágono, pentagonal.
pentameter [penˈtæmitə], *a.* pentamétrico. — *s.* pentámetro.
pentarchy [ˈpentɑːki], *s.* pentarquía.
Pentateuch [ˈpentətjuːk], *s.* Pentateuco.
Pentecost [ˈpentikɔst], *s.* Pentecostés, *m.*
penthouse [ˈpenthaus], *s.* cobertizo, colgadizo; casa de azotea, ático.
penult [piˈnʌlt], *s.* penúltima (sílaba).
penultimate [piˈnʌltimit], *a.* penúltimo.
penumbra [piˈnʌmbrə], *s.* penumbra.
penurious [piˈnjuəriəs], *a.* indigente, miserable, pobrísimo.
penuriousness [piˈnjuəriəsnis], *s.* indigencia.
penury [ˈpenjuri], *s.* penuria; indigencia, estrechez.
penwiper [ˈpenwaipə], *s.* limpiaplumas, *m.inv.*
peon [ˈpiːən], *s.* peón; criado.
peony [ˈpiəni], *s.* (*bot.*) peonía.
people [piːpl], *s.* pueblo; nación; gente; personas; habitantes; padres, familia; ***common people,*** vulgo, plebe; ***old people,*** (los) viejos; ***people say,*** se dice. — *v.t.* poblar.
pep [pep], *s.* (*fam.*) vigor, energía, arrestos, *m.pl.*; ***pep-talk,*** palabras para infundir aliento, *f.pl.* — *v.t.* — ***up,*** animar, estimular; echarle ajilimójili a.
pepper [ˈpepə], *s.* pimienta; pimiento. — *v.t.* sazonar con pimienta; acribillar.
peppercorn [ˈpepəkɔːn], *s.* semilla *o* grano de pimienta; (*fig.*) bagatela, minucia.
peppergrass, pepperwort [ˈpepəgrɑːs, -wəːt], *s.* (*bot.*) lepidio.
peppermint [ˈpepəmint], *s.* (*bot.*) menta, piperita; pastilla de menta.
peppery [ˈpepəri], *a.* picante; (*fig.*) de malas pulgas.
pepsine [ˈpepsin], *s.* pepsina.
peptone [ˈpeptoun], *s.* peptona.
per [pəː], *prep.* por; ***per annum,*** al año; ***per cent,*** por ciento; ***per diem,*** diario, al día; ***per se,*** por sí mismo, de por sí.
peradventure [pərədˈventʃə], *adv.* (*ant.*) por ventura, acaso.
perambulate [pəˈræmbjuleit], *v.t.* recorrer, transitar por. — *v.i.* deambular.
perambulation [pəræmbjuˈleiʃən], *s.* recorrido, visita de inspección.
perambulator [pəˈræmbjuleitə], *s.* cochecito de niño.
percale [pəːˈkeil], *s.* (*tej.*) percal.
perceivable [pəˈsiːvəbl], *a.* perceptible.
perceive [pəˈsiːv], *v.t.* darse cuenta de, comprender; percibir, advertir.
percentage [pəˈsentidʒ], *a.* porcentual. — *s.* porcentaje, tanto por ciento; proporción.
perceptibility [pəˈseptiˈbiliti], *s.* perceptibilidad.
perceptible [pəˈseptibl], *a.* perceptible.
perception [pəˈsepʃən], *s.* percepción; penetración, perspicacia; comprensión.
perceptive [pəˈseptiv], *a.* penetrante, perspicaz, observador.
perceptivity [pəːsepˈtiviti], *s.* penetración, perspicacia.
perch (1) [pəːtʃ], *s.* (*ict.*) perca.
perch (2) [pəːtʃ], *s.* medida de longitud (5,299 metros); percha, alcándara; posición elevada *o* en alto. — *v.t.* colocar (en alto *o* en tenguerengue). — *v.i.* posarse; encaramarse; colocarse (en alto *o* en tenguerengue).
perchance [pəˈtʃɑːns], *adv.* tal vez, acaso, por ventura.
perchloride [pəˈklɔːraid], *s.* percloruro.
percipient [pəˈsipiənt], *a.* perceptor.
percolate [ˈpəːkəleit], *v.t.*, *v.i.* (in)filtrar(se).
percolation [pəːkəˈleiʃən], *s.* (in)filtración.
percolator [ˈpəːkəleitə], *s.* filtro; cafetera filtradora.
percuss [pəˈkʌs], *v.t.* percutir.
percussion [pəˈkʌʃən], *s.* percusión; ***percussion-cap,*** cápsula fulminante; ***percussion hammer,*** martillo neumático.
perdition [pəːˈdiʃən], *s.* perdición.
peregrinate [ˈperigrineit], *v.i.* peregrinar.
peregrination [perigriˈneiʃən], *s.* peregrinación.
peregrine [ˈperigrin], *a.* peregrino; ***peregrine falcon,*** halcón peregrino.
peremptoriness [pəˈremptərinis], *s.* carácter perentorio, (lo) perentorio.
peremptory [pəˈremptəri], *a.* perentorio; imperioso.
perennial [pəˈreniəl], *a.* perenne. — *s.* planta vivaz.
perfect [ˈpəːfikt], *a.* perfecto; ***he's a perfect stranger to me,*** me es totalmente desconocido. — *s.* (*gram.*) (tiempo) perfecto. — [pəˈfekt], *v.t.* perfeccionar.
perfectibility [pəfektiˈbiliti], *s.* perfectibilidad.
perfectible [pəˈfektibl], *a.* perfectible.
perfection [pəˈfekʃən], *s.* perfección; ***to perfection,*** a la perfección.

perfectionist [pə'fekʃənist], *s.* perfeccionista, *m.f.*
perfective [pə'fektiv], *a.* perfectivo.
perfectly ['pə:fiktli], *adv.* perfectamente; ***perfectly well,*** perfectamente.
perfervid [pə'fə:vid], *a.* fervidísimo.
perfidious [pə'fidiəs], *a.* pérfido.
perfidiousness, perfidy [pə'fidiəsnis, 'pə:fidi], *s.* perfidia.
perfoliate [pə:'foulieit], *a.* (*bot.*) perfoliado.
perforate ['pə:fəreit], *v.t.* perforar, horadar; dentar (sellos).
perforation [pə:fə'reiʃən], *s.* perforación, horadación; (*sellos*) dentado.
perforator ['pə:fəreitə], *s.* perforador(a), taladrador(a).
perforce [pə'fɔ:s], *adv.* por fuerza, necesariamente.
perform [pə'fɔ:m], *v.t.* hacer; ejecutar; interpretar; desempeñar; representar; poner; cumplir; realizar. — *v.i.* tocar (*un instrumento*); representar; actuar; funcionar.
performance [pə'fɔ:məns], *s.* ejecución; interpretación; desempeño; realización; actuación; rendimiento; (*mec.*) functionamiento; ***to put up a good performance,*** hacer un buen papel, estar muy bien.
performer [pə'fɔ:mə], *s.* artista, *m.f.*; ejecutante.
perfume ['pə:fju:m], *s.* perfume. — [pə'fju:m], *v.t.* perfumar.
perfumer [pə'fju:mə], *s.* perfumador, perfumista, *m.f.*
perfumery [pə'fju:məri], *s.* perfumería, perfumes, *m.pl.*
perfuming [pə'fju:miŋ], *a.* que perfuma. — *s.* (el) perfumar.
perfunctoriness [pə'fʌŋktərinis], *s.* manera superficial *o* somera (de hacer algo).
perfunctory [pə'fʌŋktəri], *a.* superficial, somero, a la ligera, por encima.
pergola ['pə:gələ], *s.* pérgola, glorieta, cenador.
perhaps [pə'hæps], *adv.* quizá(s), tal vez, acaso, puede (que).
peri ['piəri], *s.* peri, *f.*, hada.
perianth ['periænθ], *s.* (*bot.*) periantio.
pericardial [peri'kɑ:diəl], *a.* pericardino.
pericardium [peri'kɑ:diəm], *s.* (*anat.*) pericardio.
pericarp ['perikɑ:p], *s.* (*bot.*) pericarpo.
pericranium [peri'kreiniəm], *s.* (*anat.*) pericráneo.
perigee ['peridʒi:], *s.* (*astron.*) perigeo.
perigonium [peri'gouniəm], *s.* perigonio.
perihelion [peri'hi:liən], *s.* perihelio.
peril ['peril], *s.* peligro, riesgo, trance; ***to stand in*** o ***to be in peril,*** peligrar, estar en peligro.
perilous ['periləs], *a.* peligroso, arriesgado, aventurado, expuesto.
perilousness ['periləsnis], *s.* peligro, situación peligrosa.
perimeter [pə'rimitə], *s.* perímetro.
period ['piəriəd], *s.* período; época; término; (*Am. gram.*) [FULL STOP]; clase, hora; (*med.*) regla; ***period furniture,*** muebles de época, *m.pl.*
periodic(al) [piəri'ɔdik(əl)], *a.* periódico; esporádico. — *s.* publicación periódica, revista (periódica).
periodicity, periodicalness [piəriə'disiti, piəri'ɔdikəlnis], *s.* periodicidad; (lo) esporádico.
periosteum [peri'ɔstiəm], *s.* (*anat.*) periostio.
periostitis [periɔs'taitis], *s.* periostitis, *f. inv.*
peripatetic [peripə'tetik], *a.*, *s.* peripatético.
peripheral [pə'rifərəl], *a.* periférico.
periphery [pə'rifəri], *s.* periferia.
periphrasis [pə'rifrəsis], *s.* (*pl.* **periphrases** [-si:z]) perífrasis, *f.inv.*
periphrase ['perifreiz], *v.t.* designar indirectamente. — *v.i.* perifrasear.
periphrastic [peri'fræstik], *a.* perifrástico.
periscope ['periskoup], *s.* periscopio.
periscopic [peri'skɔpik], *a.* periscópico.
perish ['periʃ], *v.t.* deteriorar, echar a perder; ***to be perished with cold,*** estar aterido. — *v.i.* perecer; deteriorarse; ***perish the thought!*** ¡ni por pensamiento! ¡no lo quiera Dios!
perishable ['periʃəbl], *a.* perecedero; corruptible, que no se conserva bien.
perishableness, perishability ['periʃəblnis, periʃə'biliti], *s.* carácter perecedero; carácter corruptible.
perisher ['periʃə], *s.* (*fam.*) tío, tipo; ***little perisher,*** granujilla, pillete; pobrecillo
perishing ['periʃiŋ], *a.* (*fam.*) ***it's perishing (cold),*** hace un frío que pela; ***perishing idiot,*** idiota de tomo y lomo, *m.f.*
perisperm ['perispə:m], *s.* perispermo.
peristaltic [perə'stæltik], *a.* peristáltico.
peristyle ['peristail], *s.* peristilo.
peritoneum [peri'touniəm], *s.* (*anat.*) peritoneo.
peritonitis [perito'naitis], *s.* peritonitis, *f.inv.*
periwig ['periwig], *s.* peluca; peluquín.
periwinkle (1) ['periwiŋkl], *s.* litorina, caracol marino.
periwinkle (2) ['periwiŋkl], *s.* (*bot.*) pervinca.
perjure ['pə:dʒə], *v.r.* ***perjure o.s.,*** perjurar(se).
perjurer ['pə:dʒərə], *s.* perjuro.
perjury ['pə:dʒəri], *s.* perjurio; ***to commit perjury,*** jurar en falso, perjurar.
perk (1) [pə:k], *v.i.* (*fam.*) — ***up,*** cobrar ánimo, animarse, reanimarse.
perk (2) [pə:k], *abrev. de* [PERQUISITE].
perky ['pə:ki], *a.* (*fam.*) animado, alegre.
perm [pə:m], *s.* (*fam.*) permanente, *f.*; ***to have a perm,*** hacerse la permanente.
permanence, permanency ['pə:mənəns, -i], *s.* permanencia, estabilidad.
permanent ['pə:mənənt], *a.* permanente, estable; ***permanent wave,*** ondulación, permanente; ***permanent way,*** vía férrea, ferrocarril.
permanganate [pə'mæŋgənit], *s.* permanganato.
permeability [pə:miə'biliti], *s.* permeabilidad.
permeable ['pə:miəbl], *a.* permeable.
permeate ['pə:mieit], *v.t.* penetrar, calar.
permeation [pə:mi'eiʃən], *s.* penetración, infiltración.
permeative ['pə:mieitiv], *a.* permeativo, penetrativo.
permissible [pə'misibl], *a.* permisible, admisible.
permission [pə'miʃən], *s.* permiso.
permissive [pə'misiv], *a.* permisivo.
permit ['pə:mit], *s.* permiso; licencia. — [pə'mit], *v.t.* permitir; ***permit of,*** permitir, admitir; ***weather permitting,*** si lo permite el tiempo.
permutable [pə'mju:təbl], *a.* permutable.
permutation [pə:mju'teiʃən], *s.* permutación.
permute [pə'mju:t], *v.t.* permutar.
pernicious [pə'niʃəs], *a.* pernicioso.
perniciousness [pə'niʃəsnis], *s.* perniciosidad.
pernickety [pə'nikiti], *a.* (*fam.*) exigente, difícil, maniático.
perorate ['perəreit], *v.i.* perorar.
peroration [perə'reiʃən], *s.* peroración.
peroxide [pə'rɔksaid], *s.* peróxido.
peroxidize [pə'rɔksidaiz], *v.t.*, *v.i.* peroxidar.
perpendicular [pə:pən'dikjulə], *a.*, *s.* perpendicular.
perpendicularity [pə:pəndikju'læriti], *s.* perpendicularidad.
perpetrate ['pə:pitreit], *v.t.* perpetrar.
perpetration [pə:pi'treiʃən], *s.* perpetración.
perpetrator ['pə:pitreitə], *s.* perpetrador.
perpetual [pə'petʃuəl], *a.* perpetuo, perenne; ***perpetual motion,*** movimiento perpetuo.
perpetuate [pə'petjueit], *v.t.* perpetuar.

perpetuation [pəːpetju'eiʃən], *s.* perpetuación.
perpetuity [pəːpi'tjuːiti], *s.* perpetuidad.
Perpignan [perpi'njã]. Perpiñán.
perplex [pə'pleks], *v.t.* confundir, dejar perplejo.
perplexed [pə'plekst], *a.* perplejo, confuso.
perplexing [pə'pleksiŋ], *a.* desconcertante, que causa perplejidad.
perplexity, perplexedness [pə'pleksiti, -idnis], *s.* perplejidad.
perquisite ['pəːkwizit], *s.* gaje.
perquisition [pəːkwi'ziʃən], *s.* pesquisa.
perron ['perɔn], *s.* (*arq.*) escalinata.
perroquet ['peroukei], *s.* cotorra.
perry ['peri], *s.* sidra de peras.
persecute ['pəːsikjuːt], *v.t.* perseguir; acosar.
persecution [pəːsi'kjuːʃən], *s.* persecución; ***persecution mania,*** manía persecutoria.
persecutor ['pəːsikjuːtə], *s.* perseguidor; acosador.
perseverance [pəːsi'viərəns], *s.* perseverancia; persistencia.
persevere [pəːsi'viə], *v.i.* perseverar; persistir, empeñarse.
persevering [pəːsi'viəriŋ], *a.* perseverante; persistente, porfiado.
Persia ['pəːʃə]. Persia.
Persian ['pəːʃən], *a.*, *s.* persa, *m.f.*; ***Persian cat,*** gato de Angora; ***the Persian Gulf,*** el Golfo Pérsico; ***Persian lamb,*** caracul.
Persic ['pəːsik], *a.* pérsico.
persimmon [pə'simən], *s.* fruto del dióspiro.
persist [pə'sist], *v.i.* persistir, porfiar, empeñarse, insistir.
persistence, persistency [pə'sistəns, -i], *s.* persistencia, insistencia, porfía, pertinacia.
persistent, persisting [pə'sistənt, -iŋ], *a.* persistente, porfiado, pertinaz.
persistently, persistingly [pə'sistəntli, -iŋli], *adv.* con persistencia, con insistencia, con porfía.
person ['pəːsən], *s.* persona, *f.*; ***displaced person,*** refugiado; ***in person,*** en persona, personalmente.
personable ['pəːsənəbl], *a.* de buena presencia, bien parecido.
personage ['pəːsənidz], *s.* personaje.
personal ['pəːsənəl], *a.* personal; privado; corporal; ***to become*** o ***get personal,*** empezar a hacer alusiones de tipo personal; ***to make a personal appearance,*** aparecer en persona; ***personal estate,*** bienes muebles, *m.pl.*
personality [pərsə'næliti], *s.* personalidad.
personalize ['pəːsənəlaiz], *v.t.* personalizar.
personalty ['pəːsənəlti], *s.* bienes muebles, *m.pl.*
personate ['pəːsəneit], *v.t.* representar, hacer el papel de; hacerse pasar por, fingir ser.
personation [pəːsə'neiʃən], *s.* personificación; usurpación del nombre de otro.
personator ['pəːsəneitə], *s.* el que hace el papel de otro *o* se hace pasar por otro.
personification [pəsɔnifi'keiʃən], *s.* personificación.
personify [pə'sɔnifai], *v.t.* personificar.
personnel [pəːsə'nel], *s.* personal; ***personnel manager,*** jefe de(l) personal.
perspective [pə'spektiv], *s.* perspectiva; ***in perspective,*** en perspectiva; bien enfocado.
perspicacious [pəːspi'keiʃəs], *a.* perspicaz.
perspicaciousness, perspicacity [pəːspi'keiʃəsnis, pəːspi'kæsiti], *s.* perspicacia.
perspicuity [pəːspi'kjuːiti], *s.* perspicuidad.
perspicuous [pə'spikjuəs], *a.* perspicuo.
perspiration [pəːspi'reiʃən], *s.* transpiración, sudor; ***to be bathed in perspiration,*** estar empapado de transpiración *o* de sudor.
perspiratory [pə'spaiərətəri], *a.* sudorífico.
perspire [pə'spaiə], *v.i.* transpirar, sudar.
persuade [pə'sweid], *v.t.* persuadir; convencer (***of,*** de); ***he persuaded him to go,*** le convenció de que *o* para que fuese.
persuader [pə'sweidə], *s.* persuador, persuadidor.
persuasible [pə'sweisibl], *a.* persuasible.
persuasion [pə'sweiʒən], *s.* persuasión; creencia; secta; ***power(s) of persuasion,*** persuasiva.
persuasive [pə'sweisiv], *a.* persuasivo.
persuasiveness [pə'sweisivnis], *s.* persuasiva.
persulphate [pə'sʌlfeit], *s.* persulfato.
pert [pəːt], *a.* impertinente, insolente, descarado, respondón.
pertain [pə'tein], *v.i.* pertenecer, referirse (***to,*** a), tener que ver, relacionarse (***to,*** con).
pertaining [pə'teiniŋ], *a.* perteneciente, relativo (***to,*** a).
pertinacious [pəːti'neiʃəs], *a.* pertinaz.
pertinacity [pəːti'næsiti], *s.* pertinacia; porfía.
pertinence, pertinency, pertinentness ['pəːtinəns, -i, -nəntnis], *s.* pertinencia; oportunidad.
pertinent ['pəːtinənt], *a.* pertinente; oportuno, atinado.
pertness ['pəːtnis], *s.* impertinencia, descaro, frescura.
perturb [pə'təːb], *v.t.* perturbar, inquietar, agitar.
perturbable [pə'təːbəbl], *a.* perturbable.
perturbation [pəːtəː'beiʃən], *s.* perturbación, agitación.
perturbator, perturber ['pəːtəːbeitə, pə'təːbə], *s.* perturbador, agitador.
Peru [pə'ruː]. el Perú.
Perugia [pə'ruːdʒiə]. Perusa.
peruke [pə'ruːk], *s.* peluca, peluquín; ***perukemaker,*** peluquero.
perusal [pə'ruːzəl], *s.* lectura atenta.
peruse [pə'ruːz], *v.t.* leer con atención, examinar.
Peruvian [pə'ruːviən], *a.*, *s.* peruano; ***Peruvian bark,*** quina.
pervade [pəː'veid], *v.t.* penetrar, impregnar; difundirse por.
pervasion [pəː'veiʒən], *s.* penetración, impregnación; difusión.
pervasive [pəː'veisiv], *a.* penetrante, que lo impregna todo.
perverse [pə'vəːs], *a.* perverso, avieso, depravado.
perverseness, perversity [pə'vəːsnis, -iti], *s.* perversidad; contumacia.
perversion [pə'vəːʃən], *s.* perversión; pervertimiento.
perversive [pə'vəːsiv], *a.* perversivo.
pervert ['pəːvəːt], *s.* pervertido; apóstata, *m.f.*, renegado. — [pəː'vəːt], *v.t.* pervertir; malear; estragar; hacer mal uso de. — *v.i.* caer en el error.
perverter [pə'vəːtə], *s.* pervertidor.
pervertible [pə'vəːtibl], *a.* pervertible.
pervious ['pəːviəs], *a.* penetrable, permeable; ***pervious to light,*** diáfano.
perviousness ['pəːviəsnis], *s.* penetrabilidad, permeabilidad.
pesky ['peski], *a.* (*Am. fam.*,) molesto, cargante.
pessary ['pəsəri], *s.* pesario.
pessimism ['pesimizəm], *s.* pesimismo.
pessimist ['pesimist], *s.* pesimista, *m.f.*
pessimistic [pesi'mistik], *a.* pesimista.
pest [pest], *s.* plaga; animal, insecto *o* bicho dañino; (*fam.*) pelma, *m.*; tostón, lata.
pester ['pestə], *v.t.* molestar, importunar, cargar, amolar.
pestiferous [pes'tifərəs], *a.* pestífero.
pestilence ['pestiləns], *s.* pestilencia.
pestilent ['pestilənt], *a.* pestilente.
pestilential [pesti'lenʃəl], *a.* pestilencial.
pestle ['pesl], *s.* pistadero, majadero de mortero, mano de almirez, *f.* — *v.t.* majar, moler en un mortero. — *v.i.* emplear un pistadero.
pet (I) [pet], *a.* doméstico, domesticado, de casa; favorito, predilecto; ***pet hate,*** pesadilla, cosa especialmente antipática; ***pet name,*** apodo *o*

mote cariñoso; ***he's on to his pet subject again,*** ya está con la cantilena de siempre. — *s.* animal doméstico *o* de casa; favorito, persona especialmente mimada; (*fam.*) querido, rico; (*fam.*) ***he's a real pet!*** ¡qué simpaticón es! — *v.t.* mimar, consentir; sobar, manosear. — *v.i.* sobarse, pegarse un lote.

pet (2) [pet], *s.* ***to fly into a pet,*** coger un berrinche *o* una rabieta.

petal [petl], *s.* pétalo.

petal(l)ed, petalous [petld, ˈpetələs], *a.* que tiene pétalos.

petard [peˈtɑ:d], *s.* petardo; ***to be hoist with one's own petard,*** salirle a uno el tiro por la culata.

Peter [ˈpi:tə]. Pedro; ***to rob Peter to pay Paul,*** desnudar a un santo para vestir a otro.

peter [ˈpi:tə], *v.i.* — ***out,*** ir acabándose *o* agotándose poco a poco; quedarse en agua de borrajas *o* de cerrajas.

petiolate [ˈpetioleit], *a.* peciolado.

petiole [ˈpetioul], *s.* pecíolo.

petition [piˈtiʃən], *s.* petición; memorial, súplica, instancia. — *v.t.* suplicar, rogar, dirigir un memorial *o* una instancia a.

petitionary [piˈtiʃənəri], *a.* petitorio, suplicante.

petitioner [piˈtiʃənə], *s.* peticionario, memorialista, *m.*, suplicante.

Petrarch [ˈpetrɑ:k]. Petrarca, *m.*

petrel [ˈpetrəl], *s.* (*orn.*) petrel; (*fig.*) ***stormy petrel,*** enfant terrible.

petrifaction, petrification [petriˈfækʃən, petrifiˈkeiʃən], *s.* petrificación.

petrify [ˈpetrifai], *v.t.* petrificar. — *v.i.* petrificarse.

petrifying [ˈpetrifaiiŋ], *a.* petrificante.

petrography [peˈtrɔgrəfi], *s.* petrografía.

petrol [ˈpetrəl], *s.* gasolina; ***petrol-pump,*** surtidor de gasolina; ***petrol tank,*** depósito de (la) gasolina; (*mar.*) ***petrol tanker,*** petrolero, (*aut.*) camióntanque, *m.*

petroleum [piˈtrouliəm], *s.* petróleo.

petroliferous [petroˈlifərəs], *a.* petrolífero.

petrology [peˈtrɔlədʒi], *s.* petrología.

petrous [ˈpi:trəs], *a.* pétreo, petroso.

petticoat [ˈpetikout], *a.* (propio) de (las) mujeres, de mujer. — *s.* enagua(s), *f.*(*pl.*); combinación; falda can-can.

pettifogger [ˈpetifɔgə], *s.* picapleitos, *m.inv.*, leguleyo, sofista, *m.*

pettifoggery [ˈpetifɔgəri], *s.* nimiedad(es), sofistería(s).

pettifogging [ˈpetifɔgiŋ], *a.* insignificante, nimio; lleno de sofisterías.

pettiness [ˈpetinis], *s.* pequeñez, insignificancia; (lo) mezquino.

pettish [ˈpetiʃ], *a.* quisquilloso, susceptible, malhumorado, enojadizo.

pettishness [ˈpetiʃnis], *s.* mal humor, quisquillosidad, susceptibilidad.

petty [ˈpeti], *a.* pequeño, insignificante; frívolo; mezquino; ***petty cash,*** cantidades pequeñas, *f.pl.*; ***petty expenses,*** gastos menores, *m.pl.*; ***petty king,*** reyezuelo; (*der.*) ***petty larceny,*** hurto menor; (*mar.*) ***petty officer,*** suboficial; (*der.*) ***petty thief,*** ladronzuelo.

petulance, petulancy [ˈpetjuləns, -i], *s.* mal humor, mal genio.

petulant [ˈpetjulənt], *a.* enojadizo, malhumorado.

petunia [piˈtju:niə], *s.* (*bot.*) petunia.

pew [pju:], *s.* banco de iglesia; (*fam.*) asiento; ***take a pew!*** ¡toma asiento!

pewit [ˈpi:wit], *s.* (*orn.*) avefría, frailecillo.

pewter [ˈpju:tə], *s.* peltre.

pewterer [ˈpju:tərə], *s.* peltrero.

phaeton [ˈfeitən], *s.* faetón.

phalanx [ˈfælænks], *s.* (*pl.*, *mil. griega* **phalanxes** [ˈfælæŋksiz]; *anat.*, *zool.* **phalanges** [fəˈlændʒi:z]) falange, *f.*

phallic [ˈfælik], *a.* fálico.

phantasm [ˈfæntæzəm], *s.* fantasma, *m.*

phantasmagoria [fæntæzməˈgɔ:riə], *s.* fantasmagoría.

phantasmagoric [fæntæzməˈgɔrik], *a.* fantasmagórico.

phantom [ˈfæntəm], *a.* fantasmal, espectral. — *s.* fantasma, *m.*, espectro.

pharisaic(al) [færiˈseiik(əl)], *a.* farisaico.

pharisaism [ˈfæriseiizəm], *s.* farisaísmo.

Pharisee [ˈfærisi:], *s.* fariseo.

pharmaceutic(al) [fɑ:məˈsju:tik(əl)], *a.* farmacéutico.

pharmaceutics [fɑ:məˈsju:tiks], *s.pl.* farmacéutica.

pharmacologist [fɑ:məˈkɔlədʒist], *s.* farmacólogo.

pharmacology [fɑ:məˈkɔlədʒi], *s.* farmacología.

pharmacopœia [fɑ:məkoˈpiə], *s.* farmacopea.

pharmacy [ˈfɑ:məsi], *s.* farmacia.

pharyngoscope [fæˈriŋgoskoup], *s.* faringoscopio.

pharynx [ˈfæriŋks], *s.* faringe, *f.*

phase [feiz], *s.* fase, *f.*

pheasant [ˈfezənt], *s.* (*orn.*) faisán.

phenacetin [fiˈnæsitin], *s.* fenacetina.

phenol [ˈfi:nɔl], *s.* fenol, ácido fénico.

phenomenal [fiˈnɔminəl], *a.* fenomenal.

phenomenon [fiˈnɔminən], *s.* (*pl.* **phenomena** [-minə]) fenómeno.

phenyl [ˈfi:nil], *s.* (*quím.*) fenilo.

phew! [fju:], *interj.* ¡uf!

phial [faiəl], *s.* redoma, frasco.

Philadelphia [filəˈdelfiə]. Filadelfia.

Philadelphian [filəˈdelfiən], *a.* (*geog.*) de Filadelfia, filadelfiano; de Ptolomeo Filadelfo. — *s.* filadelfiano.

philander [fiˈlændə], *v.i.* flirtear, mariposear.

philanderer [fiˈlændərə], *s.* tenorio, galanteador.

philanthropic(al) [filənˈθrɔpik(əl)], *a.* filantrópico.

philanthropy [fiˈlænθrəpi], *s.* filantropía; humanidad.

philanthropist [fiˈlænθrəpist], *s.* filántropo.

philatelic [filəˈtelik], *a.* filatélico.

philatelist [fiˈlætəlist], *s.* filatelista, *m.f.*

philately [fiˈlætəli], *s.* filatelia.

philharmonic [filhɑ:ˈmɔnik], *a.* filarmónico.

philhellene, philhellenist [filˈheli:n, filheˈli:nist], *s.* filheleno.

Philip [ˈfilip]. Felipe; ***Philip the Fair,*** Felipe el hermoso.

philippic [fiˈlipik], *s.* filípica.

Philippine [ˈfilipi:n], *a.* filipino. — *a. s.*, ***the Philippines*** o ***Philippine Islands,*** (las islas) Filipinas.

Philistine [ˈfilistain], *a.*, *s.* filisteo; (*fig.*) inculto, ignorante, bárbaro.

philological [filəˈlɔdʒikəl], *a.* filológico.

philologist [fiˈlɔlədʒist], *s.* filólogo.

philology [fiˈlɔlədʒi], *s.* filología.

philomel [ˈfilomel], *s.* (*poét.*) filomela.

philosopher [fiˈlɔsəfə], *s.* filósofo; ***philosopher's stone,*** piedra filosofal.

philosophic(al) [filoˈsɔfik(əl)], *a.* filosófico.

philosophize [fiˈlɔsəfaiz], *v.i.* filosofar.

philosophy [fiˈlɔsəfi], *s.* filosofía; ***philosophy of life,*** filosofía de la vida.

philotechnic [filoˈteknik], *a.* filotécnico.

philter, philtre [ˈfiltə], *s.* filtro.

phimosis [faiˈmousis], *s.* fimosis, *f.inv.*

phiz [fiz], *s.* (*fam.*) jeta.

phlebitis [fliˈbaitis], *s.* flebitis, *f.inv.*

phlebotomist [fliˈbɔtəmist], *s.* flebótomo, flebotomiano.

phlebotomy [fliˈbɔtəmi], *s.* flebotomía.

phlegm [flem], *s.* flema; (*fig.*) flema, pachorra, cachaza.

phlegmasia [fleg'meiziə], *s.* flegmasia.
phlegmatic [fleg'mætik], *a.* flemático, cachazudo.
phlegmon ['flegmɔn], *s.* flemón.
phlogistic [flo'dʒistik], *a.* flogístico.
phlogiston [flo'dʒistɔn], *s.* flogisto.
phlox [flɔks], *s.* flox, *f.*
phobia ['foubiə], *s.* fobia.
Phoebe ['fi:bi]. Febe.
phoebe bird ['fi:bi bə:d], *s.* aguador.
Phoebus ['fi:bəs]. Febo.
Phœnician [fi'ni:ʃən], *a.*, *s.* fenicio.
phœnix ['fi:niks], *s.* fénix, *m.*
phone (1) [foun], *s.* (*abrev.*, *fam.* [TELEPHONE]); ***he is on the phone,*** está hablando por teléfono; (*Am.*) ***phone-booth*** [CALL-BOX, KIOSK]. — *v.t.* ***phone*** (***up***), dar un telefonazo a. — *v.i.* ***phone for,*** llamar *o* pedir por teléfono; ***phone up,*** dar un telefonazo.
phone (2) [foun], [PHONEME].
phoneme ['founi:m], *s.* fonema, *m.*
phonemic [fo'ni:mik], *a.* fonémico.
phonemics [fo'ni:miks], *s.pl.* fonémica.
phonetic [fo'netik], *a.* fonético.
phonetician [founi'tiʃən], *s.* fonetista, *m.f.*
phonetics [fo'netiks], *s.pl.* fonética.
phonetist ['founitíst], *s.* fonetista, *m.f.*
phonic ['founik], *a.* fónico.
phonograph ['founogræf], *s.* fonógrafo; (*Am.*) [GRAMOPHONE].
phonography [fo'nɔgrəfi], *s.* fonografía.
phonology [fo'nɔlədʒi], *s.* fonología.
phonometer [fo'nɔmitə], *s.* fonómetro.
phonometric [founo'metrik], *a.* fonométrico.
phonometry [fo'nɔmitri], *s.* fonometría.
phon(e)y ['founi], *a.* (*fam.*) falso, fingido, simulado, simulacro de. — *s.* (*pers.*) farsantón, fantasmón; cosa falsificada, camelo.
phosphate ['fɔsfeit], *s.* fosfato.
phosphatic [fɔs'fætik], *a.* fosfático.
phosphor ['fɔsfə], *s.* fósforo.
phosphorate ['fɔsfəreit], *v.t.* fosforar.
phosphoresce [fɔsfə'res], *v.i.* fosforescer.
phosphorescence [fɔsfə'resəns], *s.* fosforescencia.
phosphorescent [fɔsfə'resənt], *a.* fosforescente.
phosphoric [fɔs'fɔrik], *a.* fosfórico.
phosphorite ['fɔsfərait], *s.* fosforita.
phosphorescence [fɔsfə'resəns], *s.* forsforescencia.
phosphorize ['fɔsfəraiz], *v.t.* fosforar.
phosphorus ['fɔsfərəs], *s.* fósforo.
phosphuret ['fɔsfjuret], *s.* fosfuro.
photo ['foutou], *s.* (*fam.*) foto, *f.*; ***photo-electric cell,*** célula fotoeléctrica; ***photo-finish,*** resultado (comprobado por) fotocontrol.
photocopy ['foutoukɔpi], *s.* fotocopia.
photogenic [fouto'dʒenik], *a.* fotogénico.
photograph ['foutəgræf], *s.* fotografía. — *v.t.* fotografiar, retratar.
photographer [fə'tɔgrəfə], *s.* fotógrafo.
photographic [fouto'græfik], *a.* fotográfico.
photography [fə'tɔgrəfi], *s.* fotografía.
photogravure [foutogrə'vjuə], *s.* fotograbado.
photolithograph [fouto'liθəgræf], *v.t.* fotolitografiar.
photolithographic [foutoliθo'græfik], *a.* fotolitográfico.
photolithography [foutoli'θɔgrəfi], *s.* fotolitografía.
photometer [fou'tɔmitə], *s.* fotómetro.
photometric [fouto'metrik], *a.* fotométrico.
photometry [fou'tɔmitri], *s.* fotometría.
photophone ['foutofoun], *s.* fotófono.
photosphere ['foutosfiə], *s.* fotosfera.
phototypography [foutotai'pɔgrəfi], *s.* fototipografía.
phototypy ['foutotaipi], *s.* fototipia.
phrase [freiz], *s.* frase, *f.*, locución, expresión; ***to have a good turn of phrase,*** expresarse con elegancia; ***phrase-book,*** libro de frases. — *v.t.* expresar; (*mús.*) frasear.
phraseologist [freizi'ɔlədʒist], *s.* fraseologista, *m.f.*
phraseology [freizi'ɔlədʒi], *s.* fraseología.
phrenetic [fri'netik], *a.* frenético, espasmódico.
phrenitis [fri'naitis], *s.* frenitis, *f.inv.*, fiebre cerebral.
phrenologic(al) [frenə'lɔdʒik(əl)], *a.* frenológico.
phrenologist [fre'nɔlədʒist], *s.* frenólogo.
phrenology [fre'nɔlədʒi], *s.* frenología.
phrenopathy [fre'nɔpəθi], *s.* frenopatía.
Phrygian ['fridʒən], *a.*, *s.* frigio.
phthisical ['θaisikəl], *a.* tísico.
phthisis ['θaisis], *s.* tisis, *f.inv.*
phylactery [fi'læktəri], *s.* filacteria.
phyllite ['filait], *s.* filita.
phyllome ['filoum], *s.* (*bot.*) hoja.
phyllotaxis [filo'tæksis], *s.* filotaxia.
phylloxera [fi'lɔksərə], *s.* filoxera.
phylogeny [fai'lɔdʒəni], *s.* filogenia.
physic ['fizik], *s.* (*ant.*) medicina; purga. — *v.t.* medicinar; purgar.
physical ['fizikəl], *a.* físico; material.
physician [fi'ziʃən], *s.* médico; (*ant.*) físico.
physicist ['fizisist], *s.* físico.
physics ['fiziks], *s.* física.
physiognomic(al) [fiziɔ'nɔmik(əl)], *a.* fisonómico.
physiognomist [fizi'ɔnəmist], *s.* fisónomo, fisonomista, *m.f.*
physiognomy [fizi'ɔnəmi], *s.* fisonomía; estudio de la fisionomía; fisionomía.
physiologic(al) [fiziə'lɔdʒik(əl)], *a.* fisiológico.
physiologist [fizi'ɔlədʒist], *s.* fisiólogo.
physiology [fizi'ɔlədʒi], *s.* fisiología.
physiotherapy [fizio'θerəpi], *s.* fisioterapia.
physique [fi'zi:k], *s.* físico, complexión.
phytologist [fai'tɔlədʒist], *s.* fitólogo.
phytology [fai'tɔlədʒi], *s.* fitología.
pia mater ['paiə 'meitə], *s.* (*anat.*) piamáter, *f.*
pianissimo [pi:ə'nisimou], *a.*, *adv.* (*mús.*) pianísimo.
pianist ['pi:ənist], *s.* pianista, *m.f.*
piano [pi'ænou], *a.*, *adv.* piano. — *s.* (*mús.*) piano; ***grand piano,*** piano de cola; ***baby grand piano,*** piano de media cola; ***upright piano,*** piano vertical; ***piano tuner,*** afinador de pianos; ***to play the piano,*** tocar el piano.
pianoforte [piænou'fɔ:ti], *s.* (*mús.*) pianoforte.
piastre [pi'æstə], *s.* piastra.
piazza [pi'ætsə], *s.* plaza; pórtico, galería.
pibroch ['pi:brɔk], *s.* música marcial tocada con la gaita; gaita.
pica (1) ['paikə], *s.* (*med.*) pica.
pica (2) ['paikə], *s.* (*impr.*) cícero.
Picardy ['pikədi]. la Picardía.
picaroon [pikə'ru:n], *s.* pirata, *m.*; pícaro.
pick [pik], *s.* pico, piqueta; ganzúa; (derecho de) elección; (lo) más escogido; ***it's your pick,*** ahora eliges tú; ***pick-up,*** recogida; (*elec.*) fonocaptor. — *v.t.* escoger, elegir, seleccionar; (*flores*) coger; (*fruta*) recoger; (*huesos*) roer; (*cerradura*) forzar (con ganzúa); hurgarse (*en la nariz*); mondarse (*los dientes*); ***to have a bone to pick with,*** tener un asunto que ventilar con; ***pick off,*** matar de un tiro *o* con tiros sucesivos; ***pick out,*** elegir, seleccionar; identificar; divisar; ***pick over,*** mirar *o* examinar revolviendo; ***pick s.o.'s pocket,*** robar la cartera a; ***pick a quarrel,*** buscar camorra; ***pick to pieces,*** criticar acerbamente, poner de vuelta y media; ***pick up,*** recoger; recuperar; encontrar por casualidad; saber, aprender por casualidad *o* a lo loco, ir aprendiendo poco a poco *o* sobre la marcha *o* sin sistema *o* sin esfuerzo; (*rad.*) captar; cazar; (*arrestar*) pillar,

pescar; (*fig.*) ***pick up the pieces,*** volver a organizarse, rehacerse la vida; ***pick one's way through,*** andar con mucho tiento por entre. — *v.i.* — ***and choose,*** eligir con muchas exigencias; ***pick on s.o.,*** meterse con alguien; (*fam.*) ***pick up,*** ir mejor, restablecerse.

pickaback [ˈpikəbæk], *adv.* sobre los hombros.

pickaxe [ˈpikæks], *s.* pico, piqueta, zapapico.

picked [pikt], *a.* selecto, escogido.

picker [ˈpikə], *s.* el que recoge.

pickerel [ˈpikərəl], *s.* (*ict.*) sollo.

picket [ˈpikit], *s.* estaca; piquete. — *v.t.* cercar con piquete(s). — *v.i.* poner piquete(s); estar de guardia (*los piquetes*).

pickings [ˈpikiŋz], *s.pl.* recolección; ganancias, *f.pl.*; lo que se saca (*de un robo etc.*); sobras, *f.pl.*

pickle [pikl], *s.* escabeche, salmuera, adobo; encurtido; (*fam.*) diablillo, picaruelo; ***a fine*** (***old***) ***pickle,*** un buen lío; ***mixed pickles,*** variantes en vinagre, *f.pl.* — *v.t.* escabechar, adobar; conservar en vinagre; encurtir.

picklock [ˈpiklɔk], *s.* ganzúa.

pickpocket [ˈpikpɔkit], *s.* ratero, carterista, *m.f.*

Pickwickian [pikˈwikiən], *a.* optimista; no literal.

picnic [ˈpiknik], *s.* comida *o* merienda en el campo; (*fam.*) pan comido, cosa tirada. — *v.i.* comer *o* merendar en el campo.

pictotee [pikoˈti:], *s.* (*bot.*) clavel moteado.

picrate [ˈpikreit], *s.* (*geol.*) picrato.

picric [ˈpikrik], *a.* pícrico.

Pict [pikt], *s.* picto.

pictograph [ˈpiktogræf], *s.* pictografía.

pictorial [pikˈtɔ:riəl], *a.* pictórico; gráfico, ilustrado.

picture [ˈpiktʃə], *s.* cuadro; pintura; retrato; fotografía estampa; descripción; imagen; (*pl.*) ***the pictures,*** el cine; ***to be in the picture,*** estar al corriente; ***to be the picture of health,*** ser la salud en persona, estar vendiendo salud; ***to put in the picture,*** poner al tanto; ***the other side of the picture,*** el reverso de la medalla. — *v.t.* pintar, retratar, describir.

picturesque [piktʃəˈresk], *a.* pintoresco.

picturesqueness [piktʃəˈresknis], *s.* (lo) pintoresco.

piddle [pidl], *v.i.* (*fam.*) mear; hacer(se) pis.

piddler [ˈpidlə], *s.* (*fam.*) meón.

piddling [ˈpidliŋ], *a.* (*fam.*) insignificante.

pidgin [ˈpidʒin], *s.* ***it's not my pidgin,*** no es cosa mía, allá películas; ***pidgin English,*** inglés chapurrado, *m.*

pie (1) [pai], *s.* pastel, empanada; (*Am.*) tarta, tarteleta; ***to have a finger in every pie,*** estar metido en todo.

pie (2) [pai], *s.* mezcla confusa de tipos de imprenta.

piebald [ˈpaibɔ:ld], *a.*, *s.* (animal) pío, (animal) manchado, (animal) abigarrado.

piece [pi:s], *s.* pieza; pedazo, trozo; retazo; ***all in one piece,*** intacto; sano y salvo, ileso, incólume; ***bits and pieces,*** cachivaches, *m.pl.*; chismes; *m.pl.*; bártulos, *m.pl.*; ***by the piece,*** por pieza; ***fowling piece,*** escopeta; ***in pieces,*** destrozado, hecho pedazos; ***to be of a piece with,*** ir en consonancia con; ***piece of advice,*** consejo; ***piece of folly,*** locura; ***piece of furniture,*** mueble; ***piece of ground,*** solar, terreno; (*fam.*) ***to give a piece of one's mind to,*** decir cuatro verdades a; ***piece of news,*** noticia; ***piece of work,*** trabajo; ***piece-work,*** trabajo a destajo; ***ten-penny piece,*** moneda de diez peniques; ***to break to pieces,*** hacer pedazos; ***to come to pieces,*** deshacerse; ***to cut*** o ***hack to pieces,*** destrozar, despedazar; (*fig.*) poner verde; (*fig.*) ***to go to pieces,*** desfondarse; ***to take to pieces,*** desarmar, desmontar. — *v.t.* — ***together,*** juntar; atar (los) cabos (de).

piecemeal [ˈpi:smi:l], *a.* esporádico, fragmentario. — *adv.* esporádicamente, fragmentariamente, a retazos.

pied [paid], *a.* manchado, pío, de varios colores, abigarrado.

Piedmont [ˈpi:dmɔnt]. Piamonte.

Piedmontese [pi:dmɔnˈti:z], *a.*, *s.* piamontés.

pier [piə], *s.* (*mar.*) embarcadero, desembarcadero, muelle, malecón; (*arq.*) pila; pilar, columna; estribo (*de puente*); (*arq.*) entrepaño; ***pier-glass,*** espejo de cuerpo entero; ***pier-table,*** consola.

pierce [piəs], *v.t.* penetrar; taladrar, perforar, horadar; pinchar; agujerear; traspasar, atravesar; ***pierced with sorrow,*** traspasado *o* transido de dolor. — *v.i.* penetrar.

piercing [ˈpiəsiŋ], *a.* penetrante; agudo.

piercingness [ˈpiəsiŋnis], *s.* (lo) penetrante.

pierrot [ˈpiərou], *s.* payaso, bufón, cómico.

pietism [ˈpaitizəm], *s.* pietismo.

pietist [ˈpaiitist], *s.* pietista, *m.f.*

piety [ˈpaiiti], *s.* piedad, devoción, santidad.

piffle [pifl], *s.* disparates, *m.pl.*, sandeces, *f.pl.*

piffling [ˈpifliŋ], *a.* fútil, baladí, insignificante.

pig [pig], *s.* cerdo; (*fig.*) puerco, cochino, marrano; ***guinea pig,*** conejillo de Indias; ***to buy a pig in a poke,*** comprar a ciegas; hacer un mal negocio; (*fam.*) ***to make a pig of o.s.,*** pegarse un atracón, darse un hartazgo; ***pig-headed,*** cabezota, tozudo; ***pig-iron,*** hierro en barras; ***sucking pig,*** lechoncillo. — *v.t.* (*fam.*) ***pig it,*** vivir a lo puerco.

pigeon [ˈpidʒən], *s.* paloma; ***carrier-pigeon,*** paloma mensajera; ***wild pigeon,*** paloma torcaz; ***pigeon-hearted,*** cobarde; ***pigeon-house,*** palomar; ***pigeon-shooting,*** tiro a pichón.

pigeon-hole [ˈpidʒən-houl], *s.* casilla. — *v.t.* encasillar; archivar.

pigeonry [ˈpidʒənri], *s.* palomar.

piggery [ˈpigəri], *s.* pocilga, zahurda.

piggish [ˈpigiʃ], *a.* (de) cochino; glotón.

piggy [ˈpigi], *s.* (*infantil*) [PIGLET]; ***piggy-bank,*** hucha (en forma de cerdito).

piglet [ˈpiglit], *s.* cerdito, cochinillo, lechón.

pigmean [pigˈmiən], *a.* (de) pigmeo.

pigment [ˈpigmənt], *s.* pigmento.

pigmy [ˈpigmi], *a.*, *s.* pigmeo.

pigskin [ˈpigskin], *s.* piel de cerdo.

pigsty [ˈpigstai], *s.* pocilga.

pigtail [ˈpigteil], *s.* coleta; trenza.

pike (1) [paik], *s.* pica; (*ict.*) lucio.

pike (2) [paik], *s.* (*Am.*, *aut.*) [MOTORWAY].

piked [paikt], *a.* puntiagudo.

pikeman [ˈpaikmən], *s.* piquero.

pikestaff [ˈpaikstɑ:f], *s.* asta de pica; ***it's as plain as a pikestaff,*** salta a la vista; es de cajón.

pilar [ˈpailə], *a.* piloso.

pilaster [piˈlæstə], *s.* pilastra.

Pilate [ˈpailət]. Pilatos, *m.*

pilchard [ˈpiltʃəd], *s.* sardina arenque.

pile (1) [pail], *s.* pila, montón, rimero; (*arq.*) mole; (*fam.*) caudal, fortuna; cúmulo; ***atomic pile,*** pila atómica; ***to make one's pile,*** hacer su agosto; ***pile-up,*** accidente múltiple. — *v.t.* apilar, amontonar; colmar; ***pile on,*** dar cada vez más; prodigar; ***pile it on,*** recargar las tintas negras; ***pile up,*** amontonar, acumular. — *v.i.* — ***up,*** amontonarse, acumularse.

pile (2) [pail], *s.* pilote; ***pile-driver,*** martinete.

pile (3) [pail], *s.* (*tej.*) pelillo; (*alfombra*) pelo.

piles [pailz], *s.pl.* (*med.*) almorranas, *f.pl.*, hemorroides, *f.pl.*

pilework [ˈpailwə:k], *s.* pilotaje, estructura de pilotes.

pilfer [ˈpilfə], *v.t.* ratear, sisar. — *v.i.* andar de robo.

pilferer [ˈpilfərə], *s.* ratero, sisón.

pilfering [ˈpilfəriŋ], *s.* ratería, sisa.

pilgrim [ˈpilgrim], *s.* peregrino, romero. — *v.i.* peregrinar, ir de romería.

pilgrimage [ˈpilgrimidʒ], *s.* peregrinación, romería; ***to make a pilgrimage,*** ir en peregrinación.

pill [pil], *s.* píldora, pastilla; ***a bitter pill,*** un trago (amargo).

pillage [ˈpilidʒ], *s.* pillaje, saqueo. — *v.t.* pillar, saquear.

pillager [ˈpilədʒə], *s.* saqueador.

pillar [ˈpilə], *s.* pilar, columna; (*fig.*) puntal, sostén; ***to go from pillar to post,*** ir de (la) Ceca a (la) Meca.

pillarbox [ˈpiləbɔks], *s.* buzón.

pillared [ˈpiləd], *a.* sostenido con columnas.

pillbox [ˈpilbɔks], *s.* fortín, nido de ametralladoras.

pillion [ˈpiljən], *s.* grupa; ***pillion seat,*** asiento de atrás; ***to ride pillion,*** ir de paquete.

pillory [ˈpiləri], *s.* picota. — *v.t.* poner en la picota.

pillow [ˈpilou], *s.* almohada, cabezal; (*mec.*) cojín, cojinete; (*mar.*) ***pillow of the bowsprit,*** tragante del bauprés; ***pillow-case,*** funda de almohada. — *v.t.* poner sobre la almohada; servir de almohada.

pilose, pilous [ˈpailous, -ləs], *a.* piloso, velloso.

pilosity [piˈlɔsiti], *s.* vellosidad.

pilot [ˈpailət], *s.* piloto; práctico; ***pilot-boat,*** bote del práctico; ***pilot-balloon,*** globo de ensayo; (*orn.*) ***pilot-bird,*** pájaropiloto; (*ict.*) ***pilot-fish,*** piloto; (*aut.*) ***pilot-light,*** luz de situación. — *v.t.* dirigir, guiar, gobernar; pilotar, pilotear.

pilotage, piloting [ˈpailətidʒ, -iŋ], *s.* pilotaje, practicaje.

pimento [piˈmentou], *s.* pimiento.

pimp [pimp], *s.* chulo, alcahuete. — *v.i.* chulear, alcahuetar.

pimpernel [ˈpimpənel], *s.* pimpinela.

pimping [ˈpimpiŋ], *a.* (*fam.*) enclenque.

pimple [pimpl], *s.* grano.

pimpled [pimpld], *a.* granujiento.

pimply [ˈpimpli], *a.* granujoso, que tiene granos.

pin [pin], *s.* alfiler; clavija; perno; (*pl., fam.*) (los) remos, (las) piernas; ***I don't care two pins,*** no se me da un bledo; ***pin-case,*** alfiletero; ***pin-head,*** cabeza de alfiler; (*fig.*) ***pin money,*** dinerillo (para los gastos pequeños); ***pin-point,*** punta de alfiler; ***pin-prick,*** alfilerazo; pullita; ***pin-stripe trousers,*** pantalón a rayas; ***pin-up,*** foto de chica guapa, pin-up; ***pins and needles,*** hormiguillo. — *v.t.* prender *o* asegurar con alfileres; sujetar (con perno); ***pin down,*** inmovilizar; obligar a concretar, conseguir que se concrete; ***pin-point,*** concretar, punctualizar, localizar *o* identificar con exactitud; ***pin sth. on s.o.,*** encajarle a alguien la culpa de algo; ***pin up,*** sujetar con alfileres, horquillas *etc.*

pinafore [ˈpinəfɔ:], *s.* delantal.

pince-nez [pɑ:ns-ˈnei], *s.* quevedos, *m.pl.*

pincers [ˈpinsəz], *s.pl.* tenazas, *f.pl.*, pinzas, *f.pl.*

pinch [pintʃ], *s.* pellizco; ***at a pinch,*** en caso de apuro; apretando mucho; ***pinch of salt,*** pizca de sal; ***pinch of snuff,*** polvo de rapé; (*fam.*) aprieto, apuro; ***to feel the pinch,*** sentirse apurado, pasar apuros. — *v.t.* pellizcar, tirar un pellizco *o* pellizcos a; (*fam.*) birlar; (*fam.*) coger, prender; ***he pinched his finger,*** se cogió un dedo. — *v.i.* apretar (*zapatos etc.*); (*fig.*) ***pinch and scrape,*** hacer muchas economías, gastar lo menos posible.

pinchbeck [ˈpintʃbek], *a.* de similor; falsificado. — *s.* similor.

pinchfist [ˈpintʃfist], *s.* avaro.

pincushion [ˈpinkuʃən], *s.* acerico.

Pindar [ˈpində]. Píndaro.

Pindaric [pinˈdærik], *a.* pindárico.

pine (1) [pain], *s.* pino; ***pine-cone,*** piña; ***pine-kernel,*** piñón; ***pine-marten,*** marta; ***pine-needle,*** pinocha; ***pine-wood,*** pinar.

pine (2) [pain], *v.i.* languidecer, consumirse; ***pine after*** o ***for,*** penar por, suspirar por; ***pine away,*** languidecer, morirse de pena.

pineapple [ˈpainæpl], *s.* piña.

pinfold [ˈpinfould], *s.* redil.

ping [piŋ], *s.* silbido (*de una bala*), zas.

ping-pong [ˈpiŋ-pɔŋ], *s.* ping-pong, *m.*

pining [ˈpainiŋ], *a.* lánguido.

pinion [ˈpinjən], *s.* ala (de ave); (*mec.*) piñón. — *v.t.* cortar las alas de; sujetar (los brazos de).

pink (1) [piŋk], *a.* (de) rosa, rosado; (*pol.*) rojillo. — *s.* clavellina; (*fam.*) ***in the pink (of health),*** vendiendo salud, rozagante.

pink (2) [piŋk], *v.t., v.i.* picar.

pinker [ˈpiŋkə], *s.* recortador; picador.

pinkeye [ˈpiŋkai], *s.* conjuntivitis (catarral), *f.inv.*

pinking [ˈpiŋkiŋ], *s.* recortadura; picadura; (*aut.*) (el) picar.

pinkish, pinky [ˈpiŋkiʃ, ˈpiŋki], *a.* rosado.

pinna [ˈpinə], *s.* (*zool.*) ala, aleta; (*anat.*) pabellón externo del oído.

pinnace [ˈpinis], *s.* (*mar.*) pinaza.

pinnacle [ˈpinəkl], *s.* cumbre; pináculo, chapitel.

pinnate(d) [ˈpineit(id)], *a.* (*bot.*) pinado, alado.

pinnatifid [piˈnætifid], *a.* pinatifido.

pinnigrade [ˈpinigreid], *a.* (*zool.*) pinípedo.

pinnock [ˈpinək], *s.* (*orn.*) paro.

pinnule [ˈpinju:l], *s.* (*bot.*) pínula, hojuela; (*zool.*) aleta pequeña.

pint [paint], *s.* pinta; ***you can't get a pint into a half-pint pot,*** no se pueden pedir peras al olmo.

pintle [pintl], *s.* clavija; macho de timón.

pinwheel [ˈpinwi:l], *s.* molinete de juegos artificiales; rueda de engranaje con clavijas.

pinworm [ˈpinwə:m], *s.* gusano pequeño.

piolet [piˈoulei], *s.* pico de trepador de hielo.

pioneer [paiəˈniə], *s.* explorador; zapador; colonizador; iniciador, pionero; promotor; ***to be a pioneer in,*** ser de los primeros en. — *v.t.* iniciar, promover, preparar el terreno para. — *v.i.* explorar.

pious [paiəs], *a.* piadoso, pío, devoto.

pip (1) [pip], *s.* (*fruto*) pepita.

pip (2) [pip], *s.* (*aves*) pepita; moquillo; (*fam.*) ***to give s.o. the pip,*** sacar de quicio a alguien; (*fam.*) ***to have the pip,*** estar fastidiado; estar mustio.

pip (3) [pip], *s.* (*juego*) punto; (*uniforme*) estrella.

pip (4) [pip], *v.t.* derrotar; herir (con bala); ***to be pipped at the post,*** verse vencido *o* superado en el último momento.

pipe [paip], *s.* tubo, caño, conducto, cañería, tubería; cañón; caramillo, flauta; silbato, chiflo; pito; manga; pipa; (*pl.*) gaita; tubería(s); ***pipe-cleaner,*** limpiapipas, *m.inv.*; ***pipe-dream,*** castillo en el aire, espejismo; ***pipe-laying*** instalación de cañerías; (*mil.*) ***pipe-major,*** gaitero mayor; ***pipe-stock,*** terraja; ***pipe-tobacco,*** tabaco de pipa; ***pipe-wrench,*** llave de caños; (*fam.*) ***put that in your pipe and smoke it!*** ¡chúpate ésa! — *v.t.* (*flauta*) tocar; decir (*con voz atiplada*); conducir (*por cañerías etc.*); llamar (*con silbato*). — *v.i.* tocar el caramillo *etc.*; (*fam.*) ***pipe down,*** callarse; (*fam.*) ***pipe up,*** arrancar a hablar, meter baza de pronto.

pipeline [ˈpaiplain], *s.* oleoducto; conducción. — *v.t.* llevar por oleoducto.

piper [ˈpaipə], *s.* flautista, *m.f.*; gaitero.

pipette [pɪˈpet], *s.* pipeta.

piping [ˈpaipiŋ], *adv.* — ***hot,*** muy caliente. — *s.* cordoncillo; gemidos; tuberías, cañerías; (*mar.*) raya de cuerda; (*cost.*) cordoncillo, vivo.

pipet [ˈpipit], *s.* (*orn.*) alondra.

pipkin [ˈpipkin], *s.* pucherito, ollita.

pippin [ˈpipin], *s.* (*bot.*) esperiega, camuesa.

pip-squeak [ˈpip-skwi:k], *s.* mequetrefe.

piquancy [ˈpi:kənsi], *s.* (lo) picante.

piquant [ˈpi:kənt], *a.* sabroso, picante.

pique [pi:k], *s.* pique; resentimiento; ***to be in a***

pique, estar resentido. — *v.t.* picar, herir. — **pique o.s.,** *v.r.* — ***(up)on,*** picarse de.
piquet [pi'ket], *s.* séptimo, juego de los ciento.
piracy ['paiərəsi], *s.* piratería.
Piraeus [pai'riəs]. el Pireo.
pirate ['paiərit], *s.* pirata, *m.*; (*fig.*) plagiario; ***pirate radio,*** emisora ilícita. — *v.t.* pillar; robar; publicar fraudulentamente; ***pirated edition,*** edición clandestina *o* fraudulenta.
piratical [pai'rætikəl], *a.* pirático.
piroque [pi'roug], *s.* piragua.
pirouette [piru'et], *s.* pirueta. — *v.i.* hacer piruetas.
piscatorial, piscatory [piskə'tɔ:riəl, 'piskətəri], *a.* piscatorio.
pisciculture ['pisikʌltʃə], *s.* piscicultura.
piscina [pi'si:nə], *s.* piscina.
piscivorous [pi'sivərəs], *a.* piscívoro, ictiófago.
pish! [piʃ], *interj.* ¡quita allá!
pismire ['pismaiə], *s.* hormiga.
piss [pis], *s.* (*obsc.*) orina. — *v.i.* orinar, mear.
pissasphalt ['pisəsfælt], *s.* pisasfalto.
pistachio [pis'tɑ:ʃou], *s.* (*bot.*) pistacho; alfóncigo.
pistil ['pistil], *s.* pistilo.
pistol ['pistəl], *s.* pistola, revólver.
pistole [pis'toul], *s.* pistola.
piston ['pistən], *s.* émbolo, pistón; (*mús.*) llave, *f.*, pistón; (*mec.*) ***piston boss,*** cubo de émbolo; ***piston pin,*** pasador de pistón; ***piston ring,*** aro de pistón; ***piston rod,*** vástago de émbolo; ***piston stroke,*** carrera del émbolo.
pit [pit], *s.* hoyo, hoya; pozo; mina; abismo; (*teat.*) platea; boca (del estómago); (*Am., de frutas*) [STONE]; ***coal pit,*** mina de carbón; ***pit-head,*** boca de pozo (*de mina*). — *v.t.* marcar con hoyos; picar; ***pit one's brains against,*** medir la inteligencia con; competir intelectualmente con.
pitapat ['pitəpæt], *s.* palpitación acelerada; pasos ligeros, *m.pl.*; tamborileo. — *adv.* de una manera palpitante. — *v.i.* tamborilear.
Pitcairn [pit'kɛən]. La isla de Pitcairn.
pitch (1) [pitʃ], *s.* pez, *f.*, brea; ***as dark as pitch,*** oscuro como boca de lobo; ***pitch-black,*** negro como el azabache.
pitch (2) [pitʃ], *s.* pendiente, *f.*, declive; lanzamiento, echada; (grado de) inclinación; (*mús.*) diapasón, tono; (*mar.*) cabezada; (*dep.*) terreno, campo; (*com.*) puesto; (*fig.*) extremo, punto; ***pitch-farthing,*** (juego de) hoyuelo; (*mús.*) ***pitch-pipe,*** tono, diapasón; ***to queer s.o.'s pitch,*** chafarle a alguien el plan. — *v.t.* arrojar, lanzar; poner, plantar; graduar el tono de; entonar; contar (un cuento); ***pitched battle,*** batalla campal. — *v.i.* caerse (***into,*** en); (*mar.*) ***pitch and toss,*** cabecear; ***pitch forward,*** caer(se) de bruces *o* de cabeza; ***pitch in,*** ponerse (en serio) con ello, poner manos a la obra; ***pitch into,*** arremeter contra; emprenderla con.
pitcher (1) ['pitʃə], *s.* cántaro, jarro.
pitcher (2) ['pitʃə], *s.* (*béisbol*) botador.
pitchfork ['pitʃfɔ:k], *s.* horca, bieldo; (*mús.*) diapasón; ***to rain pitchforks,*** llover chuzos, a cántaros. — *v.t.* ***pitchfork s.o. into sth.,*** meter violentamente a alguien en algo.
pitchiness ['pitʃinis], *s.* obscuridad, negrura.
pitching ['pitʃiŋ], *a.* en declive. — *s.* (*mar.*) cabeceo.
pitchy ['pitʃi], *a.* embreado, piceo, peceño.
piteous ['pitiəs], *a.* lastimero, patético, conmovedor.
piteousness ['pitiəsnis], *s.* (lo) lastimero, patético *o* conmovedor.
pitfall ['pitfɔ:l], *s.* escollo; trampa.
pith [piθ], *s.* tegumento; médula (espinal); (*fig.*) enjundia, sustancia.
pithiness ['piθinis], *s.* (*fig.*) expresividad.
pithy ['piθi], *a.* (*fig.*) expresivo.
pitiable ['pitiəbl], *a.* lastimoso; enternecedor.
pitiful ['pitiful], *a.* lastimoso; enternecedor.
pitifulness ['pitifulnis], *s.* (lo) lastimoso; (lo enternecedor.
pitiless ['pitilis], *a.* cruel, despiadado.
pitilessness ['pitilisnis], *s.* crueldad, (lo) cruel.
pitman ['pitmən], *s.* (*pl.* **-men** [-men]) aserrador de foso, pocero.
piton ['pitɔ], *s.* (*alpinismo*) barra, estaca (para fijar una cuerda en los precipicios).
pittance ['pitəns], *s.* miseria.
pitted ['pitid], *a.* picado, cacarañado.
pituita [pi'tju:itə], *s.* pituita.
pituitary [pi'tju:itəri], *a.* (*anat.*) pituitario; ***pituitary gland,*** glándula pituitaria.
pituitous [pi'tju:itəs], *a.* pituitoso.
pity ['piti], *s.* misericordia, compasión; lástima; piedad; ***for pity's sake,*** ¡por piedad!; ***it's a pity that,*** es lástima que; ***to take pity on,*** compadecerse de; ***what a pity!*** ¡qué pena! — *v.t.* tener lástima de, compadecerse de.
Pius ['paiəs]. Pío.
pivot ['pivət], *s.* pivote; quicio; espiga, espigón, gorrón; (*fig.*) eje, polo, punto central. — *v.t.* colocar sobre un eje; proveer de pivote. — *v.i.* girar sobre un eje.
pixy, pixie ['piksi], *s.* (*pl.* **pixies** [-siz]) duende(cito).
pizzle [pizl], *s.* vergajo (*de buey*).
placard ['plækɑ:d], *s.* cartel, pancarta. — *v.t.* poner carteles en, llenar de carteles.
placate [plə'keit], *v.t.* aplacar, apaciguar; contentar.
place [pleis], *s.* sitio, lugar; local; paraje; puesto; plaza; (*a la mesa*) cubierto; (*fam.*) ***at his place,*** en su casa; ***in the first place,*** en primer lugar; ***in his place,*** en su lugar; ***to put s.o. in his place,*** bajarle a alguien los humos; ***in no place,*** en ninguna parte; ***in place,*** en su sitio; oportuno; ***in place of,*** en lugar de; ***it is not his place to,*** no le corresponde a él + *inf.*; ***out of place,*** fuera de su sitio; fuera de lugar; ***place of worship,*** templo; ***there's no place like home,*** como la casa de uno no hay; ***to be in the right place at the right time,*** estar en el sitio oportuno en el momento oportuno; ***to give place to,*** ceder el paso a; ***to know one's place,*** ser respetuoso; (*libro*) ***to lose one's place,*** perder el sitio, la página, la línea; ***to take place,*** tener lugar, verificarse; ***to take the place of,*** sustituir. — *v.t.* colocar, situar; identificar; ***to be placed,*** colocarse; ***place a bet,*** apostar.
placenta [plə'sentə], *s.* placenta.
placer ['pleisə], *s.* (*geol.*) placer; (*min.*) lavadero de oro.
placid ['plæsid], *a.* plácido, tranquilo, apacible, sosegado.
placidity [plə'siditi], *s.* placidez, serenidad.
plagiarism ['pleidʒjərizəm], *s.* plagio.
plagiarist ['pleidʒjərist], *s.* plagiario.
plagiarize ['pleidʒjəraiz], *v.t.* plagiar. — *v.i.* cometer plagios.
plagiary ['pleidʒjəri], *s.* plagio.
plague [pleig], *s.* plaga; peste, *f.*; ***a plague on him!*** ¡Dios le confunda! — *v.t.* plagar, infestar; (*fig.*) importunar; atormentar.
plaguy ['pleigi], *a.* (*fam.*) fastidioso.
plaice [pleis], *s.* (*ict.*) platija.
plaid [plæd], *s.* manta escosesa; tartán.
plain [plein], *a.* llano, sencillo; sin adorno(s); liso, sin dibujo(s); natural, puro; claro, evidente; vulgar, sin gracia; ***in plain clothes,*** con traje de calle; ***plain-clothes policeman,*** policía no uniformado; ***plain cooking,*** cocina sencilla; ***plain-dealing,*** sincero, de buena fe; ***in plain English,*** hablandò en plata; ***plain-spoken,*** franco; ***the plain truth,*** la verdad monda y lironda *o* lisa y llana; ***it is plain that,*** es evidente que; ***I'll be plain with you,*** le voy a hablar claro. — *adv.* llanamente, claro. — *s.* llanura, llano.
plainly ['pleinli], *adv.* llanamente; claramente, evidentemente.

plainness [ˈpleinnis], *s.* evidencia; sencillez, (lo) sencillo; llaneza, franqueza; fealdad.
plainsong [ˈpleinsɔŋ], *s.* (*igl.*) canto llano.
plaint [pleint], *s.* querella, demanda; (*poét.*) queja.
plaintiff [ˈpleintif], *s.* (*for.*) demandante.
plaintive [ˈpleintiv], *a.* lastimero, plañidero.
plaintiveness [ˈpleintivnis], *s.* tono lastimero, (lo) lastimero.
plait [plæt], *s.* (*cost.*) pliegue, plegado; trenza (*de cabellos*). — *v.t.* trenzar; plegar.
plaiting [ˈplætiŋ], *s.* trenza, trenzado.
plan [plæn], *s.* proyecto, plan; plano; esquema, *m.*; programa, *m.*; ***five-year plan,*** plan quinquenal; ***to draw a plan,*** levantar un plano. — *v.t.* planear, planificar; proyectar; idear. — *v.i.* hacer planes; ***plan to,*** proponerse, pensar.
planchet [ˈplɑːntʃit], *s.* cospel.
planchette [plɑːnˈʃet], *s.* plancheta, tabla de escritura mesmérica.
plane [plein], *a.* plano, llano. — *s.* plano; nivel; esfera; (*fam.*) avión; ala; cepillo, garlopa. — *v.t.* (a)cepillar; ***plane down,*** alisar; ***plane off,*** desbastar. — *v.i.* volar; planear.
plane-tree [ˈplein-triː], *s.* (*bot.*) plátano.
planer [ˈpleinə], *s.* acepillador; (*impr.*) tamborilete.
planet [ˈplænit], *s.* planeta, *m.*
planetarium [plæniˈtɛəriəm], *s.* planetario.
planetary [ˈplænitəri], *a.* planetario.
planimeter [plæˈnimitə], *s.* planímetro.
planimetric(al) [plæniˈmetrik(əl)], *a.* planimétrico.
planimetry [plæˈnimitri], *s.* planimetría.
planing [ˈpleiniŋ], *s.* acepilladura.
planish [ˈplæniʃ], *v.t.* allanar, aplanar, alisar, pulir.
planisher [ˈplæniʃə], *s.* planador, aplanador, alisador.
planisphere [ˈplænisfiə], *s.* planisferio.
plank [plæŋk], *s.* tabla (gruesa), tablón; (*pl.*) tablas, *f.pl.*; (*fig.*) ***the main plank in his policy,*** el punto fundamental de su política. — *v.t.* entarimar, entablar, enmaderar; (*min.*) encofrar.
planking [ˈplæŋkiŋ], *s.* tablazón, *f.*; tablaje; maderamen (de cubierta).
plankton [ˈplæŋktən], *s.* plancton.
planned [plænd], *a.* planificado; ***planned economy,*** economía dirigida.
planner [ˈplænə], *s.* proyectista, *m.f.*, calculista, *m.f.*; ***town planner,*** urbanista, *m.f.*
planning [ˈplæniŋ], *s.* planificación; ***family planning,*** control de la natalidad; ***planning board,*** comisión planificadora.
plant [plɑːnt], *s.* (*bot.*) planta; (*tec.*) fábrica; instalación; equipo; ***plant-life,*** vida vegetal. — *v.t.* plantar, sembrar; colocar, instalar.
plantain [ˈplæntin], *s.* (*bot.*) llantén; plátano.
plantation [plɑːnˈteiʃən], *s.* plantación; hacienda.
planter [ˈplɑːntə], *s.* plantador; colono.
plantigrade [ˈplæntigreid], *a.*, *s.* plantígrado.
planting [ˈplɑːntiŋ], *s.* (el) plantar.
plaque [plɑːk], *s.* placa.
plash [plæʃ], *s.* chapoteo, chapaleteo. — *v.i.* chapotear, chapalear.
plasm, plasma [ˈplæzəm, ˈplæzmə], *s.* plasma, *m.*
plasmic [ˈplæzmik], *a.* plasmático.
plaster [ˈplɑːstə], *s.* yeso; argamasa; enlucido; emplasto; ***court plaster,*** tafetán inglés; ***mustard plaster,*** sinapismo; ***plaster cast,*** vaciado; tablilla de yeso; ***plaster of Paris,*** escayola; ***plaster work,*** enyesado; enlucido; ***sticking plaster,*** esparadrapo. — *v.t.* enyesar; enlucir; emplastar; revocar; (*fig.*) embadurnar, llenar *o* cubrir (***with,*** de); (*fam.*) ***to be plastered,*** tener una pítima.
plasterer [ˈplɑːstərə], *s.* yesero; enlucidor; revocador.
plastering [ˈplɑːstəriŋ], *s.* enyesado; enlucido.
plastic [ˈplæstik], *a.* (de) plástico; ***plastic art,*** plástica; ***plastic surgery,*** cirugía plástica *o* estética. — *s.* plástico.
plasticine [ˈplæstisiːn], *s.* plasticina.
plasticity [plæsˈtisiti], *s.* plasticidad.
plastics [ˈplæstiks], *s.pl.* plástica.
plastron [ˈplæstrɔn], *s.* plastrón; pechera; peto.
plat [plæt], *s.* trenza. — *v.t.* trenzar.
plate [pleit], *s.* plato; plancha; lámina; chapa; vajilla; (*foto.*) placa; (placa de la) dentadura postiza; ***gold plate,*** vajilla de oro; ***hot plate,*** plancha caliente; ***plate-glass,*** vidrio *o* cristal cilindrado; (*foto.*) ***plate-holder,*** portaplacas, *m.inv.*; (*f.c.*) ***plate layer,*** peón; ***plate-rack,*** escurreplatos, *m.inv.*; ***silver plate,*** vajilla de plata; ***soup plate,*** sopero; ***to hand s.o. sth. on a plate,*** servirle algo a alguien en bandeja; ***to have a lot on one's plate,*** tener mucho trabajo, no dar abasto. — *v.t.* planchear; platear; dorar; niquelar.
plateau [ˈplætou], *s.* meseta, altiplanicie, *f.*
plateful [ˈpleitful], *s.* plato (lleno).
platform [ˈplætfɔːm], *s.* plataforma; tablado; estrado; tarima; tribuna; (*f.c.*) andén.
plating [ˈpleitiŋ], *s.* enchapado; capa metálica; niquelado; blindaje.
platinum [ˈplætinəm], *s.* platino; ***platinum blonde,*** rubia platino.
platitude [ˈplætitjuːd], *s.* perogrullada, trivialidad.
Plato [ˈpleitou]. Platón, *m.*
platonic [pləˈtɔnik], *a.* platónico.
Platonism [ˈpleitənizəm], *s.* platonismo.
Platonist [ˈpleitənist], *s.* platónico.
platoon [pləˈtuːn], *s.* (*mil.*) pelotón.
platter [ˈplætə], *s.* fuente; plato grande; (*Am.*) [DISH].
platting [ˈplætiŋ], *s.* trenza; (el) trenzar.
plaudit [ˈplɔːdit], *s.* aplauso, aprobación.
plausibility, plausibleness [plɔːziˈbiliti, ˈplɔːziblnis], *s.* especiosidad; apariencia.
plausible [ˈplɔːzibl], *a.* especioso; aparente.
play [plei], *s.* juego; recreo; obra, pieza dramática; ***fair (foul) play,*** juego limpio (sucio); ***to make great play with,*** recalcar, insistir en, darle (mucha) importancia a; ***in play,*** en juego; ***to come into play,*** entrar en juego; ***out of play,*** fuera de juego; ***play on words,*** juego de palabras; ***play-pen,*** corralito (de niño); ***play-time,*** hora de recreo. — *v.t.* jugar, jugar a, jugar contra; tocar, tañer; hacer jugar; hacer el papel de, desempeñar; hacer uso de, valerse de; ***play back,*** repetir (lo grabado); ***play down,*** quitar importancia a; ***play second fiddle,*** hacer un papel secundario; ***play the fool,*** hacer(se) el tonto; ***play the game,*** jugar limpio; ***play a joke,*** hacer una broma; ***play off,*** desempatar; ***be played out,*** estar rendido *o* agotado; ***play a trick on,*** hacer una mala pasada a; ***play truant,*** hacer novillos, *m.pl.*; ***play (s.o.) up,*** dar guerra a (alguien); ***play up,*** hacer resaltar. — *v.i.* jugar; divertirse; tocar; representar; (*agua*) correr; (*luz*) reverberar; ***play fast and loose with,*** dar la marcha a; ***play for time,*** tratar de ganar tiempo; ***play into the hands of,*** ponerse a merced de; hacerle el juego a; ***play upon,*** valerse de, aprovecharse de; ***play up to,*** hacer la pelotilla a.
playbill [ˈpleibil], *s.* cartel de teatro.
playboy [ˈpleibɔi], *s.* (*fam.*) señorito juerguista, *m.*, joven vividor.
player [ˈpleiə], *s.* jugador; actor; músico.
playfellow [ˈpleifelou], *s.* compañero de juego.
playful [ˈpleiful], *a.* juguetón.
playgoer [ˈpleigouə], *s.* aficionado al teatro.
playground [ˈpleigraund], *s.* patio de recreo.
playhouse [ˈpleihaus], *s.* teatro.
playing-card [ˈpleiiŋ-kɑːd], *s.* naipe.
plaything [ˈpleiθiŋ], *s.* juguete.
playwright [ˈpleirait], *s.* autor dramático, dramaturgo.

plea [pli:], *s.* disculpa, pretexto; alegato; contestación a la demanda; petición, ruego, instancia; ***to put in a plea for,*** hablar por, en favor de.
plead [pli:d], *v.t.* defender; alegar; ***plead (not) guilty,*** declararse (no) culpable; ***plead ignorance,*** pretextar ignorancia. — *v.i.* rogar, suplicar; declararse, confesarse; (*der.*) abogar; ***plead with s.o. for sth.,*** rogar *o* suplicar a alguien que haga *o* conceda algo.
pleadable [ˈpli:dəbl], *a.* defendible; alegable.
pleader [ˈpli:də], *s.* defensor, abogado.
pleading [ˈpli:diŋ], *s.* súplicas, *f.pl.*; alegatos, *m.pl.*
pleasant [ˈplezənt], *a.* agradable, grato; ameno; simpático.
pleasantness [ˈplezəntnis], *s.* (lo) agradable.
pleasantry [ˈplezəntri], *s.* dicho gracioso, chiste, chocarrería, humorada.
please [pli:z], *v.t.* agradar, dar gusto a, complacer, contentar; ***to be pleased (with),*** estar contento (con), estar satisfecho (de); ***to be pleased to,*** complacerse en, serle a uno grato + *inf.*; ***I am pleased to meet you,*** tengo mucho gusto en conocerle; ***to be hard to please,*** ser muy exigente, no conformarse fácilmente. — *v.i.* gustar; ***if you please,*** si Vd. no tiene inconveniente; (*ironía*) ¡imagínese!; ***please go in,*** tenga Vd. la bondad de entrar, haga Vd. el favor de entrar, entre Vd. por favor, sírvase Vd. entrar. — **please o.s.,** *v.r.* hacer lo que a uno le da la gana; ***please yourself,*** como Vd. quiera.
pleased [pli:zd], *a.* contento, satisfecho.
pleasing [ˈpli:ziŋ], *a.* agradable, grato.
pleasurable [ˈpleʒərəbl], *a.* agradable, que da mucho gusto.
pleasure [ˈpleʒə], *s.* placer; gusto; ***it is a pleasure,*** se lo hago con mucho gusto; ***at pleasure,*** a voluntad; ***pleasure-boat,*** barca *o* barco de recreo; ***pleasure-ground,*** parque *o* jardín de recreo; ***pleasure-trip,*** viaje de recreo, excursión turística; ***to take pleasure in,*** complacerse en, disfrutar + *p.a.*; ***what is your pleasure?*** ¿qué desea Vd.?
pleat [pli:t], *s.* pliegue; (*pl.*) plisado. — *v.t.* plegar, plisar.
plebeian [pliˈbiən], *a.*, *s.* plebeyo.
plebeianism [pliˈbiənizəm], *s.* plebeyez.
plebiscite [ˈplebisit], *s.* plebiscito.
plebs [plebz], *s.* (*fam.*) plebe, *f.*
plectrum [ˈplektrəm], *s.* (*pl.* **plectra** [-trə]) plectro.
pledge [pledʒ], *s.* prenda; promesa, voto; ***as a pledge of,*** en prenda de, en señal de; ***to put in pledge,*** empeñar. — *v.t.* empeñar, dar en prenda; prometer; dar (*la palabra*); brindar por. — **pledge o.s.,** *v.r.* — ***to,*** prometer, comprometerse a.
Pleiads, Pleiades [ˈplaiədz, -ədi:z], (*astron.*) las Pléyades, *f.pl.*
plenary [ˈpli:nəri], *a.* plenario; ***plenary session,*** sesión plenaria.
plenipotentiary [plenipoˈtenʃəri], *a.*, *s.* plenipotenciario.
plenitude [ˈplenitju:d], *s.* plenitud.
plenteous [ˈplentiəs], *a.* abundante, copioso.
plenteousness [ˈplentiəsnis], *s.* abundancia, copia; fertilidad.
plentiful [ˈplentiful], *a.* abundante, copioso.
plenty [ˈplenti], *s.* abundancia, profusión; ***horn of plenty,*** cuerno de la abundancia; ***plenty of,*** bastante, de sobra; ***I have plenty of...,*** tengo bastante..., mucho..., una buena cantidad de....
plenum [ˈpli:nəm], *s.* pleno.
pleonasm [ˈpli:onæzəm], *s.* pleonasmo.
pleonastic(al) [pli:oˈnæstik(əl)], *a.* pleonástico.
plethora [ˈpleθərə], *s.* plétora.
plethoric [pleˈθɔ:rik], *a.* pletórico.
pleura [ˈpluərə], *s.* (*anat.*) pleura.
pleurisy [ˈpluərisi], *s.* (*pat.*) pleuresía, pleuritis, *f.inv.*
pleuritic(al) [pluəˈritik(əl)], *a.* pleurítico.
plexiform [ˈpleksifɔ:m], *a.* reticular, complicado.
plexus [ˈpleksəs], *s.* (*anat.*) plexo; trabazón, *f.*, red, *f.*
pliability, pliableness [plaiəˈbiliti, ˈplaiəblnis], *s.* docilidad; flexibilidad.
pliable [ˈplaiəbl], *a.* dócil; blando; flexible; doblegable.
pliancy [ˈplaiənsi], *s.* flexibilidad; docilidad; blandura; elasticidad.
pliant [ˈplaiənt], *a.* flexible; dócil; plegable; manejable.
pliantness [ˈplaiəntnis], *s.* flexibilidad; docilidad.
pliers [ˈplaiəz], *s.pl.* alicates, *m.pl.*; ***flat-pointed pliers,*** alicates de boca; ***sharp-pointed pliers,*** alicates de punta.
plight (1) [plait], *s.* apuro, aprieto; situación apurada.
plight (2) [plait], *v.t.* empeñar.
Plimsoll line [ˈplimsəl ˈlain], *s.* línea Plimsoll, línea de carga máxima.
plimsolls [ˈplimsəlz], *s.pl.* zapatillas de goma, *f.pl.*, bambas, *f.pl.*
plinth [plinθ], *s.* plinto.
Pliny [ˈplini]. Plinio.
Pliocene [ˈplaiosi:n], *s.* (*geol.*) plioceno.
plod [plɔd], *v.i.* afanarse, trabajar penosamente; andar fatigosamente; ***plod on,*** caminar trabajosamente.
plodder [ˈplɔdə], *s.* trafagón, hombre trabajador; estudiantón.
plodding [ˈplɔdiŋ], *a.* laborioso; perseverante.
plop [plɔp], *s.* plaf. — *v.t.* dejar caer haciendo plaf. — *v.i.* caer haciendo plaf.
plot [plɔt], *s.* parcela, terreno; solar; cuadro, bancal; complot, conspiración; argumento, trama, intriga. — *v.t.* trazar; tramar; maquinar. — *v.i.* conspirar, intrigar.
plotter [ˈplɔtə], *s.* conjurado, conspirador; maquinador, tramador.
plotting [ˈplɔtiŋ], *s.* intrigas, *f.pl.*, conspiraciones, *f.pl.*
plough [plau], *s.* arado; ***snow-plough,*** (máquina) quitanieves, *f.inv.* — *v.t.* arar; surcar (*los mares*); quitar (*la nieve*); (*fam.*) (*suspender*) catear, cargarse; (*com.*) ***plough back (in),*** reinvertir; ***plough up,*** arrancar *o* levantar con (el) arado. — *v.i.* arar; ***plough through,*** abrirse (trabajosamente) paso por; arrollar; leerse.
ploughboy [ˈplaubɔi], *s.* yuguero, mozo de arado.
ploughing [ˈplauiŋ], *s.* (el) arar.
ploughman [ˈplaumən], *s.* (*pl.* **-men** [-men]) arador, yuguero.
ploughshare [ˈplauʃɛə], *s.* reja de arado.
ploughtail [ˈplauteil], *s.* mancera.
plover [ˈplʌvə], *s.* (*orn.*) chorlito.
plow (*Am.*) [PLOUGH].
pluck (1) [plʌk], *s.* (*fam.*) valor, denuedo, agallas, *f.pl.*
pluck(2) [plʌk], *v.t.* arrancar; coger; pelar, desplumar; (*mús.*) puntear; ***pluck up courage,*** hacer de tripas corazón, sacar fuerzas de flaqueza. — *v.i.* — ***at,*** tirar de, dar tirones a.
plucky [ˈplʌki], *a.* (*fam.*) valiente, animoso, denodado, esforzado.
plug [plʌg], *s.* tapón; taco; (*elec.*) enchufe; (*aut.*) bujía; (*fam.*) propaganda machacona (comercial); ***plug-hole,*** sumidero. — *v.t.* tapar, obturar; (*dientes*) empastar; (*fam.*) pegar un tiro a; dedicar (una) propaganda machacona a; ***plug in,*** enchufar. — *v.i.* (*fam.*) ***plug away,*** seguir erre que erre, seguir dándole a la cosa; dedicarse con ahinco (***at,*** a).
plum [plʌm], *s.* (*bot.*) ciruela; ***plum-cake,*** plum-cake; (*fam.*) cosa estupenda; (*fam.*) ***plum job,***

enchufazo, destino *o* puesto estupendo; ***plum tree,*** ciruelo.

plumage [ˈplu:midʒ], *s.* plumaje, plumazón.

plumb [plʌm], *a.* a plomo, vertical; recto. — *adv.* a plomo, verticalmente; totalmente. — *s.* plomada. — *v.t.* sondar, sondear.

plumbago [plʌmˈbeigou], *s.* plombagina.

plumbean, plumbeous [ˈplʌmbiən, -biəs], *a.* plúmbeo, plúmbico.

plumber [ˈplʌmə], *s.* fontanero.

plumbiferous [plʌmˈbifərəs], *a.* plumbífero.

plumbing [ˈplʌmiŋ], *s.* fontanería.

plume [plu:m], *s.* pluma; penacho. — *v.t.* emplumar. — **plume o.s.,** *v.r.* componerse (las plumas); jactarse, vanagloriarse.

plumeless [ˈplu:mlis], *a.* implume.

plumiferous [plu:ˈmifərəs], *a.* plumífero.

plumiped [ˈplu:miped], *a.* plumípedo, calzado. — *s.* ave calzada.

plummet [ˈplʌmit], *s.* plomada. — *v.i.* caer a plomo.

plumose, plumous [ˈplu:mous, -məs], *a.* plúmeo, plumoso.

plump [plʌmp], *a.* regordete, rechoncho, rollizo; ***plump-faced,*** carilleno. — *adv.* de lleno, de golpe. — *v.t.* — ***down,*** soltar, dejar caer de golpe. — *v.i.* — ***for,*** optar por.

plumpness [ˈplʌmpnis], *s.* gordura.

plumula, plumule [ˈplu:mjulə, -ju:l], *s.* (*bot.*) plúmula.

plumy [ˈplu:mi], *a.* plumado, plumoso, empenachado.

plunder [ˈplʌndə], *s.* pillaje, saqueo, rapiña; botín, despojo. — *v.t.* pillar, saquear.

plunderer [ˈplʌndərə], *s.* pillador, saqueador.

plunge [plʌndʒ], *s.* zambullida, chapuzón; salto. — *v.t.* zambullir, chapuzar; arrojar, precipitar; hundir. — *v.i.* zambullirse, sumergirse; arrojarse; (*caballo*) corcovear; (*buque*) cabecear.

plungeon [ˈplʌndʒən], *s.* (*orn.*) somorgujo, mergo.

plunger [ˈplʌndʒə], *s.* buzo; (*mec.*) chupón, émbolo.

pluperfect [ˈplu:ˈpə:fikt], *a., s.* pluscuamperfecto.

plural [ˈpluərəl], *a., s.* plural.

pluralism [ˈpluərəlizəm], *s.* pluralidad; pluralismo.

plurality [pluəˈræliti], *s.* pluralidad.

pluralize [ˈpluərəlaiz], *v.t.* pluralizar.

plurally [ˈpluərəli], *adv.* en plural.

plus [plʌs], *a., adv.* más; (*mat., elec.*) positivo; ***plus-fours,*** pantalones de golf, bombachos, *m.pl.*

plush [plʌʃ], *a.* afelpado; (*fam.*) lujoso. — *s.* tripe, felpa.

Plutarch [ˈplu:tɑ:k]. Plutarco.

plutarchy [ˈplu:tɑ:ki], *s.* plutocracia.

Pluto [ˈplu:tou]. Plutón.

plutocracy [plu:ˈtɔkrəsi], *s.* plutocracia.

plutocrat [ˈplu:tokræt], *s.* plutócrata, *m.f.*

plutocratic [plu:toˈkrætik], *a,* plutocrático.

pluvial [ˈplu:viəl], *a.* pluvial. — *s.* (*igl.*) capa pluvial.

pluviograph [ˈplu:viogrɑ:f], *s.* pluviógrafo.

pluviometer [plu:viˈɔmitə], *s.* pluviómetro.

pluvious [ˈplu:viəs], *a.* lluvioso.

ply (1) [plai], *s.* pliegue, doblez; capa; cabo; ***three-ply,*** de tres capas *o* cabos.

ply (2) [plai], *v.t.* manejar, usar (vigorosamente); ejercer, practicar; importunar, acosar; ***ply s.o. with drink,*** hacer beber a alguien; ***ply with questions,*** acosar con preguntas. — *v.i.* — ***between,*** hacer el servicio entre; ***ply for hire,*** buscar cliente(s).

pneumatic [nju:ˈmætik], *a.* neumático; ***pneumatic drill,*** perforadora (de aire comprimido); ***pneumatic tyre,*** neumático.

pneumatics [nju:ˈmætiks], *s.pl.* neumática.

pneumatology [nju:məˈtɔlədʒi], *s.* neumatología.

pneumonia [nju:ˈmouniə], *s.* (*pat.*) pulmonía; ***to get pneumonia,*** coger una pulmonía.

pneumonic [nju:ˈmɔnik], *a.* neumónico.

poa [ˈpouə], *s.* (*bot.*) poa.

poach (1) [poutʃ], *v.t.* (*huevos*) escalfar.

poach (2) [poutʃ], *v.t.* cazar *o* pescar furtivamente (*en terreno vedado*); (*fig.*) invadir. — *v.i.* cazar *o* pescar furtivamente; ***poach on s.o. else's territory,*** meterse en el terreno de otro.

poacher [ˈpoutʃə], *s.* cazador *o* pescador furtivo.

poaching [ˈpoutʃiŋ], *s.* caza *o* pesca furtiva.

pock [pɔk], *s.* hoyuelo de viruela; ***pock-marked,*** picado de viruelas.

pocket [ˈpɔkit], *s.* bolsillo; (*fig.*) bolsa; cavidad; ***pocket-battleship,*** acorazado de bolsillo; (*Am.*) ***pocket-book,*** [PURSE]; ***pocket-handkerchief,*** pañuelo (de bolsillo); ***pocket-knife,*** navaja, cortaplumas, *m.inv.*; ***pocket-money,*** paga, dinerillo, propina; ***to be in pocket, out of pocket,*** salir ganando, perdiendo; ***to line one's pockets,*** forrarse, lucrarse; ***to pick s.o.'s pocket,*** quitarle a alguien la cartera. — *v.t.* embolsar, meterse en el bolsillo; apropiarse; ***pocket an insult,*** tragarse un insulto; ***pocket one's pride,*** aguantarse, achantarse, tragarse el orgullo.

pocketful [ˈpɔkitful], *s.* bolsillo, lo que cabe en un bolsillo.

pocky [ˈpɔki], *a.* picado de viruelas.

pod [pɔd], *s.* (*bot.*) vaina. — *v.i.* criar vainas; hincharse.

podagra [pɔˈdægrə], *s.* podagra.

podge [pɔdʒ], *s.* (*fam.*) persona gordinflona, fondón.

podgy [ˈpɔdʒi], *a.* gordinflón, rechoncho, regordete, fondón.

podium [ˈpoudiəm], *s.* podio.

poem [ˈpouim], *s.* poema, *m.*, poesía.

poesy [ˈpouizi], *s.* (*ant.*) poesía.

poet [ˈpouit], *s.* poeta, *m.*

poetaster [pouiˈtæstə], *s.* poetastro.

poetess [ˈpouites], *s.* poetisa.

poetic(al) [pouˈetik(əl)], *a.* poético; ***it's poetic justice,*** le está bien empleado; castigo de Dios.

poetics [pouˈetiks], *s.pl.* poética, arte poética.

poetize [ˈpouitaiz], *v.i.* poetizar, versificar.

poetry [ˈpouitri], *s.* poesía.

pogrom [ˈpougrɔm], *s.* pogrom.

poignancy [ˈpɔinjənsi], *s.* patetismo.

poignant [ˈpɔinjənt], *a.* conmovedor, patético.

point [pɔint], *s.* punta; punto; (*geog.*) cabo, promontorio; aguja, agujeta; (*f.c.*) aguja; cola, rabo; sal, *f.*; intención; chiste, agudeza; cuestión; pormenor, detalle; objeto, punto, fin; momento, instante; puntería; grado (*de una escala*); rasgo, característica; (*mar.*) rumbo; (*com.*) entero; (*gram.*) signo de puntuación, punto final; (*impr.*) punto tipográfico; puntura; (*pl., f.c.*) cambiavía, *m.inv.*, agujas, *f.pl.*; ***at the point of death,*** en artículo de muerte; ***to be beside the point,*** no venir al caso; ***in point,*** a propósito, al caso; ***in point of fact,*** en realidad; ***on all points,*** en todos los aspectos; ***on the points,*** de puntillas; ***to be on the point of,*** estar a punto de; ***point-blank,*** directo; a quemarropa; a bocajarro; categóricamente, tajantemente; ***point-duty,*** control de la circulación; ***point of no return,*** decisión irrevocable; momento decisivo; ***point of order,*** cuestión de procedimiento; ***point of view,*** punto de vista; ***points to be remembered,*** cosas que han de tenerse en cuenta; ***point-to-point,*** carrera de caballos a campo traviesa; ***to come to the point,*** ir al grano, concretar; ***to keep, stick to the point,*** ceñirse al tema, no salirse del tema; ***to speak to the point,*** ir al grano; ***to carry one's point,*** salirse con la suya; ***to make the point that,*** señalar que; ***to score a point,*** ganar un tanto; ***to stretch a point,*** hacer una excepción; ser benévolo. — *v.t.* apuntar; aguzar, afilar; dirigir, asestar; (*gram.*) puntuar; ***point out,*** indicar, señalar; (*alb.*) unir con mortero, rellenar. — *v.i.* señalar; (*perro*) parar, mostrar la caza;

point at, señalar con el dedo; ***point to,*** señalar, indicar.
pointed [ˈpɔintid], *a.* puntiagudo; agudo, aguzado, afilado de punta; (*arq.*) ojival; (*fig.*) directo; satírico; intencionado, lleno de intención.
pointedly [ˈpɔintidli], *adv.* con intención.
pointedness [ˈpɔintidnis], *s.* (lo) directo, (lo) inequívoco; intención.
pointer [ˈpɔintə], *s.* indicador; índice; apuntador puntero; aguja; buril, punta; perro perdiguero; manecilla de reloj; (*f.c.*) palanca de aguja; (*pl.*, *astron.*) ***the Pointers,*** las dos estrellas de la Osa Mayor, en cuya dirección se halla la estrella polar.
pointing [ˈpɔintiŋ], *s.* puntuación; indicación, señalamiento; puntería; aguzadura, afiladura; (*mar.*) rabo de rata; (*com.*) marca; (*alb.*) mamposteado, relleno de juntas.
pointless [ˈpɔintlis], *a.* inútil, sin objeto.
pointsman [ˈpɔintsmən], *s.* (*pl.* **-men** [-men]) (*f.c.*) guardagujas, *m.inv.*.
poise [pɔiz], *s.* contrapeso, pesa; equilibrio; aplomo, serenidad; aire, porte. — *v.t.* equilibrar; balancear; contrapesar; ***to be poised,*** estar suspendido, cernerse; ***to be poised to,*** estar aprestado para. — *v.i.* ***to poise to,*** aprestarse a, ponerse en facha de.
poison [ˈpɔizən], *a.* venenoso; (*bot.*) ***poison-elder,*** zumaque; ***poison-gas,*** gas tóxico; ***poison-ivy,*** zumaque; ***poison-nut,*** nuez vómica; ***poison-pen letter,*** anónimo. — *s.* veneno, ponzaña. — *v.t.* envenenar, emponzoñar.
poisoner [ˈpɔizənə], *s.* envenenador.
poisoning [ˈpɔizəniŋ], *s.* envenenamiento.
poisonous [ˈpɔizənəs], *a.* venenoso, ponzoñoso, tóxico.
poisonousness [ˈpɔizənəsnis], *s.* venenosidad, (lo) venenoso.
poke [pouk], *s.* empujón; codazo; hurgonazo. — *v.t.* empujar; dar un codazo a; hurgar, atizar; meter (***into,*** en); ***poke fun at,*** meterse con, tomar el pelo a, burlarse de; (*fam.*) ***poke one's nose into,*** (entro)meterse en. — *v.i.* — ***about, around,*** andar hurgando *o* husmeando.
poker (1) [ˈpoukə], *s.* hurgón.
poker (2) [ˈpoukə], *s.* (*juego*) póker; ***poker face,*** cara de estaca.
pokeweed [ˈpoukwi:d], *s.* (*bot.*) hierba carmín.
poky [ˈpouki], *a.* (*fam.*) pequeñujo, pequeñajo, angustioso, apretado; ***poky little cinema,*** cinucho; ***poky little place,*** cuchitril.
Poland [ˈpoulənd]. Polonia.
Polar [ˈpoulə], *a.* (*mar.*) polar.
polariscope [pouˈlæriskoup], *s.* polariscopio.
polarity [pouˈlæriti], *s.* polaridad.
polarization [poulәraiˈzeiʃən], *s.* polarización.
polarize [ˈpouləraiz], *v.t.* polarizar.
Pole [poul], *s.* polaco, polaca.
pole (1) [poul], *s.* (*geog.*, *elec.*) polo.
pole (2) [poul], *s.* palo; asta (*de bandera*); (*dep.*) pértiga; (*telégrafos*) poste, palo; (*fam.*) ***up the pole,*** chiflado, mochales.
poleaxe [ˈpoulæks], *s.* hachuela de mano. — *v.t.* desnucar; (*fig.*) dar al traste con.
polecat [ˈpoulkæt], *s.* (*zool.*) veso, turón; mofeta.
polemic(al) [pɔˈlemik(əl)], *a.* polémico.
polemic [pɔˈlemik], *s.* polémica.
polemics [pɔˈlemiks], *s.pl.* polémica.
police [pəˈli:s], *s.* policía; ***police constable*** o ***police officer,*** agente de policía; ***police force,*** cuerpo de policía; ***police state,*** estado policía; ***police station,*** comisaría; cuartelillo. — *v.t.* vigilar, patrullar; mantener servicio de policía en.
policeman [pəˈli:smən], *s.* policía, *m.*, guardia, *m.*
policewoman [pəˈli:swumən], *s.* agente femenino de policía, mujer policía.
policy [ˈpɔlisi], *s.* política; programa político; norma(s); póliza (de seguros).
poliomyelitis [poulioumaiiˈlaitis], *s.* (*pat.*) poliomielitis, *f.inv.*
Polish [ˈpouliʃ], *a.*, *s.* polaco.
polish [ˈpɔliʃ], *s.* pulimento; lustre, brillo, bruñido; (*zapatos*) betún, crema; cera; (*fig.*) finura, perfección. — *v.t.* sacar brillo a; pulir; encerar; pulimentar; (*fam.*) ***polish off,*** acabar con; zamparse; (*fam.*) ***polish up one's German,*** perfeccionar su alemán, dar *o* pegar un repaso a su alemán.
polished [ˈpɔliʃt], *a.* fino; cuidado; esmerado, elegante.
polisher [ˈpɔliʃə], *s.* pulidor; enceradora.
polishing [ˈpɔliʃiŋ], *s.* pulimento.
polite [pəˈlait], *a.* cortés; ***polite society,*** sociedad fina, (la) buena sociedad.
politeness [pəˈlaitnis], *s.* cortesía.
politic [ˈpɔlitik], *a.* político; conveniente.
political [pəˈlitikəl], *a.* político; ***political science,*** ciencias políticas.
politician [pɔliˈtiʃən], *s.* político.
politics [ˈpɔlitiks], *s.pl.* política; ***what are his politics?*** ¿cómo respira políticamente?; ***to go into politics,*** dedicarse a la política.
polity [ˈpɔliti], *s.* gobierno; estado.
polka [ˈpɔlkə], *s.* polca.
poll [poul], *s.* votación, elección, votos, *m.pl.*; lista electoral; urnas; sondeo; encuesta; ***poll-tax,*** capitación; ***to go to the poll(s),*** acudir a las urnas; ***to take a poll,*** hacer una encuesta. — *v.t.* recibir (votos); descabezar; descornar. — *v.i.* votar.
pollack [ˈpɔlək], *s.* abadejo, pescadilla.
pollard [ˈpɔləd], *s.* árbol desmochado; (*ict.*) esperinque; animal mocho. — *v.t.* desmochar.
pollen [ˈpɔlən], *s.* (*bot.*) polen.
poller [ˈpoulə], *s.* desmochador; votante.
polling [ˈpouliŋ], *s.* votación; escrutinio; ***polling-booth,*** cabina *o* caseta de votar; colegio electoral.
polliwog [ˈpɔliwɔg], *s.* renacuajo.
pollute [pəˈl(j)u:t], *v.t.* contaminar; ensuciar; corromper.
pollutedness [pəˈl(j)u:tidnis], *s.* contaminación; corrupción.
polluter [pəˈl(j)u:tə], *s.* contaminador; corruptor.
pollution [pəˈl(j)u:ʃən], *s.* contaminación; corrupción.
polo [ˈpoulou], *s.* (*dep.*) polo.
polonaise [pɔləˈneiz], *s.* (*mús.*) polonesa; (*sast.*) polaca.
poltroon [pɔlˈtru:n], *s.* cobarde, gallina.
poltroonery [pɔlˈtru:nəri], *s.* cobardía.
poltroonish [pɔlˈtru:niʃ], *a.* pusilánime.
poly [ˈpouli], *s.* zamarrilla.
polyandry [pɔliˈændri], *s.* poliandria.
polyanthus [pɔliˈænθəs], *s.* (*bot.*) primavera.
polyarchy [ˈpɔliɑ:ki], *s.* poliarquía.
polychromatic [pɔlikrouˈmætik], *a.* policromático.
polychrome [ˈpɔlikroum], *s.* policromo.
polygamist [pɔˈligəmist], *s.* polígamo.
polygamous [pɔˈligəməs], *a.* polígamo.
polygamy [pɔˈligəmi], *s.* poligamia.
polygastric [pɔliˈgæstrik], *a.* poligástrico.
polygenesis [pɔliˈdʒenisis], *s.* poligénesis, *f.inv.*
polyglot [ˈpɔliglɔt], *a.*, *s.* políglota, poliglota.
polygon [ˈpɔligən], *s.* polígono.
polygonal [pɔˈligənəl], *a.* poligonal, polígono.
polygraphy [pɔˈligrəfi], *s.* poligrafía.
polygraphic(al) [pɔliˈgræfik(əl)], *a.* poligráfico.
polyhedral [pɔliˈhi:drəl], *a.* poliédrico.
polyhedron [pɔliˈhi:drən], *s.* poliedro.
Polynesia [pɔliˈni:ziə]. Polinesia.
Polynesian [pɔliˈni:ziən], *a.*, *s.* polinesio.
polynome [ˈpɔlinoum], *s.* polinomio.
polyp [ˈpɔlip], *s.* (*zool.*) pólipo.

polypetalous [pɔli'petələs], *a.* polipétalo.
polyphase ['pɔlifeiz], *a.* (*elec.*) polifásico.
polypody ['pɔlipədi], *s.* (*bot.*) polipodio.
polypus ['pɔlipəs], *s.* (*pl.* **polypi** [-pai]) pólipo.
polyscope ['pɔliskoup], *s.* poliscopio.
polysepalous [pɔli'sepələs], *a.* polisépalo.
polysyllabic [pɔlisi'læbik], *a.* polisílabo, polisilábico.
polysyllable [pɔli'siləbl], *s.* polisílabo.
polytechnic [pɔli'teknik], *a.* politécnico. — *s.* escuela politécnica.
polytheism ['pɔliθi:izəm], *s.* politeísmo.
polytheist ['pɔliθi:ist], *s.* politeísta, *m.f.*
polytheistic(al) [pɔliθi:'istik(əl)], *a.* politeísta.
polythene ['pɔliθi:n], *s.* politene.
pomace ['pʌmis], *s.* desecho de manzanas.
pomaceous [pɔ'meiʃəs], *a.* pomáceo.
pomade, pomatum [pɔ'mɑ:d, pɔ'meitəm], *s.* pomada. — *v.t.* untar con pomada.
pome [poum], *s.* pomo.
pomegranate ['pɔməgrænit], *s.* (*bot.*)g ranada; ***pomegranate tree,*** granado.
pommel ['pʌməl], *s.* pomo; perilla. — *v.t.* apalear, aporrear, dar puñetazos a.
pommelling ['pʌməliŋ], *s.* paliza, puñetazos, *m.pl.*
pommie, pommy ['pɔmi], *s.* (*Australia, fam.*) inmigrante inglés.
pomp [pɔmp], *s.* pompa, fausto.
Pompeii [pɔm'pei]. Pompeya.
Pompey ['pɔmpi]. Pompeyo.
pom-pom ['pɔm-pɔm], *s.* cañón automático antiaéreo.
pomposity, pompousness [pɔm'pɔsiti, 'pɔmpəsnis], *s.* pomposidad; rimbombancia; fatuidad.
pompous ['pɔmpəs], *a.* pomposo; rimbombante; fatuo.
pond [pɔnd], *s.* estanque (*artificial*); charca (*natural*); ***pond life,*** seres acuáticos, *m.pl.*
ponder ['pɔndə], *v.t., v.i.* meditar (en), reflexionar (sobre).
ponderer ['pɔndərə], *s.* meditador.
ponderous ['pɔndərəs], *a.* pesadísimo; trabajoso.
ponderousness ['pɔndərəsnis], *s.* (lo) pesadísimo; (lo) trabajoso.
pong [pɔŋ], *s.* (*fam.*) tufo.
poniard ['pɔnjɑ:d], *s.* puñal. — *v.t.* herir con puñal, dar de puñaladas a.
pontiff ['pɔntif], *s.* pontífice.
pontifical [pɔn'tifikəl], *a.* pontifical, pontificio.
pontificals [pɔn'tifikəlz], *s.pl.* pontificales, *m.pl.*
pontificate [pɔn'tifikit], *s.* pontificado. — [-keit], *v.i.* pontificar.
Pontius Pilate ['pɔnʃəs 'pailət]. Poncio Pilato(s).
pontlevis [pɔnt'levis], *s.* puente levadizo; (*equit.*) (el) constante encabritarse del caballo.
pontoon [pɔn'tu:n], *s.* pontón; ***pontoon bridge,*** puente de pontones.
pony ['pouni], *s.* (*pl.* **ponies** [-iz]) jaca, caballito, pony; (*Am., fam.*) chuleta.
poodle [pu:dl], *s.* perro de lanas, caniche.
pooh! [pu:], *interj.* ¡bah!
pooh-pooh ['pu:-pu:], *v.t.* acoger con desdén; negar importancia a.
pool [pu:l], *s.* charca; estanque; charco; poza; (*Am., juego*) billar; polla; fusión de intereses; fondo común; ***football pools,*** quinielas, *f.pl.*; ***swimming pool,*** piscina; ***typing pool,*** sala de mecanógrafas. — *v.t.* juntar, mancomunar, fundir.
poop [pu:p], *s.* popa; toldilla. — *v.t.* empopar, abordar por la popa.
poor [puə], *a.* pobre; malo, de mala calidad; flojo, bajo; ***as poor as a church mouse,*** más pobre que una rata; ***poor-box,*** cepillo de los pobres; ***to have poor health,*** tener mala salud; ***poor-house,*** casa de caridad; ***poor-rate,*** contribución que se pagaba para socorrer a los necesitados; ***poor-spirited,*** pusilánime, apocado. — *s.pl.* ***the poor,*** los pobres.
poorly ['puəli], *a.* malito. — *adv.* pobremente; mal.
poorness ['puənis], *s.* pobreza.
pop (1) [pɔp], *s.* (ligera) detonación; (*corcho*) taponazo; pum; (*fam.*) gaseosa; ***pop-eyed,*** de ojos saltones; ***pop-gun,*** taco, tirabala. — *v.t.* (*fam.*) hacer saltar; meter de sopetón; espetar, disparar; ***pop the question,*** declararse. — *v.i.* (*fam.*) estallar, reventar; ***pop in,*** asomarse un momento; entrar de sopetón; ***pop off,*** diñarla; largarse; ***pop out,*** salir un momento; salir de sopetón; ***pop up,*** asomar, aparecer (de sopetón).
pop (2) [pɔp], *s.* (*Am., fam.*) papá, *m.*
pop (3) [pɔp], *s.* (*fam.*) música ye-yé; ***pop-concert,*** concierto de música ye-yé; ***pop-singer,*** cantante ye-yé; ***pop-song,*** canción ye-yé.
popcorn ['pɔpkɔ:n], *s.* rosetas, *f.pl.*, palomitas, *f.pl.*
pope [poup], *s.* papa, *m.*; ***pope's head,*** escobillón para limpiar techos.
popedom ['poupdəm], *s.* papado, papazgo.
popery ['poupəri], *s.* (*despec.*) papismo.
popinjay ['pɔpindʒei], *s.* (*ant., orn.*) papagayo, loro; picamaderos, *m.inv.*; (*fig.*) pisaverde.
popish ['poupiʃ], *a.* papista.
poplar ['pɔplə], *s.* (*bot.*) álamo; ***black poplar,*** chopo.
poplin ['pɔplin], *s.* (*tej.*) popelina.
poppy ['pɔpi], *s.* (*bot.*) amapola; adormidera; ***poppy-head,*** cabeza de adormidera.
poppycock ['pɔpikɔk], *s.* (*fam.*) majaderías, *f.pl.*
populace ['pɔpjulis], *s.* pueblo, población; plebe, populacho.
popular ['pɔpjulə], *a.* popular; ***to be popular,*** ser popular, tener aceptación, tener (muchas) simpatías.
popularity [pɔpju'læriti], *s.* popularidad; aceptación.
popularization [pɔpjulərai'zeiʃən], *s.* divulgación.
popularize ['pɔpjuləraiz], *v.t.* popularizar, divulgar, vulgarizar.
populate ['pɔpjuleit], *v.t.* poblar.
population [pɔpju'leiʃən], *s.* población, habitantes, *m.f.pl.*
populous ['pɔpjuləs], *a.* populoso.
populousness ['pɔpjuləsnis], *s.* (lo) populoso.
porbeagle ['pɔ:bi:gl], *s.* tiburón.
porcelain ['pɔ:slin], *s.* porcelana.
porch [pɔ:tʃ], *s.* pórtico; vestíbulo; entrada.
porcine ['pɔ:sain], *a.* porcino.
porcupine ['pɔ:kjupain], *s.* (*zool.*) puerco espín.
pore (1) [pɔ:], *s.* poro.
pore (2) [pɔ:], *v.i.* — ***over,*** estudiar detenidamente, estar absorto en.
porgy ['pɔ:dʒi], *s.* pargo, pagro.
pork [pɔ:k], *s.* (carne de) cerdo; ***pork-butcher,*** carnicero de cerdo; ***pork chop,*** chuleta de cerdo; ***pork-pie,*** empanada de (carne de) cerdo.
porker ['pɔ:kə], *s.* (*fam.*) cerdo.
porky ['pɔ:ki], *a.* (*fam.*) gordoncho.
pornographic [pɔ:nə'græfik], *a.* pornográfico.
pornography [pɔ:'nɔgrəfi], *s.* pornografía.
porosity, porousness [pɔ:'rɔsiti, 'pɔ:rəsnis], *s.* porosidad.
porous ['pɔ:rəs], *a.* poroso.
porphyritic [pɔ:fi'ritik], *a.* porfídico.
porphyry ['pɔ:firi], *s.* pórfido.
porpoise ['pɔ:pəs], *s.* (*zool.*) marsopa, puerco marino.
porridge ['pɔridʒ], *s.* gachas de avena, *f.pl.*
porringer ['pɔrindʒə], *s.* escudilla.
port (1) [pɔ:t], *a.* portuario. — *s.* puerto; ***free port,*** puerto franco; ***port of call,*** puerto de escala, escala; ***to put into port,*** entrar a puerto *o* en puerto.

port (2) [pɔ:t], *s.* (*mar.*) porta, portilla; (*cañón*) tronera; (*mec.*) lumbrera.
port (3) [pɔ:t], *s.* (*mar.*) babor. — *v.t.* — ***the helm,*** poner el timón a babor.
port (4) [pɔ:t], *s.* vino de Oporto, oporto.
portable [ˈpɔ:təbl], *a.* portátil.
portage [ˈpɔ:tidʒ], *s.* porteo; transporte.
portal [pɔ:tl], *s.* portal; puerta grande, portón.
portcullis [pɔ:tˈkʌlis], *s.* rastrillo.
portend [pɔ:ˈtend], *v.t.* presagiar, augurar.
portent [ˈpɔ:tent], *s.* portento; presagio, augurio.
portentous [pɔ:ˈtentəs], *a.* portentoso.
porter [ˈpɔ:tə], *s.* mozo; portero; porteador; cerveza negra.
porterage [ˈpɔ:təridʒ], *s.* porte.
portfire [ˈpɔ:tfaiə], *s.* lanzafuegos, *m.inv.*, botafuego.
portfolio [pɔ:tˈfouliou], *s.* carpeta; cartera; ***Minister without Portfolio,*** ministro sin cartera.
porthole [ˈpɔ:thoul], *s.* (*mar.*) ojo de buey, portilla.
portico [ˈpɔ:tikou], *s.* pórtico.
portion [ˈpɔ:ʃən], *s.* porción, parte; dote; ración. — *v.t.* — ***out,*** repartir, dividir.
portioner [ˈpɔ:ʃənə], *s.* repartidor.
portionless [ˈpɔ:ʃənlis], *a.* indotado, sin dote.
portliness [ˈpɔ:tlinis], *s.* gordura.
portly [ˈpɔ:tli], *a.* grueso, gordo; barrigón.
portmanteau [pɔ:tˈmæntou], *s.* baúl de viaje; ***portmanteau word,*** palabra híbrida.
Porto Rico [pɔ:tou ˈri:kou]. Puerto Rico.
portrait [ˈpɔ:trit], *s.* retrato; ***full-length portrait,*** retrato de cuerpo entero; ***half-length portrait,*** retrato de medio cuerpo; ***portrait-painter,*** retratista, *m.f.*
portraiture [ˈpɔ:tritjə], *s.* arte de retratar; retratos, *m.pl.*
portray [pɔ:ˈtrei], *v.t.* retratar, describir.
portrayal [pɔ:ˈtreiəl], *s.* representación gráfica.
Portugal [ˈpɔ:tʃugəl]. Portugal.
Portuguese [pɔ:tʃuˈgi:z], *a., s.* portugués, *m.*
pose [pouz], *s.* postura; pose, *f.*, afectación. — *v.t.* plantear (*un problema*); hacer, formular (*una pregunta*). — *v.i.* posar; darse tono; ***pose as,*** dárselas de.
poser [ˈpouzə], *s.* (*fam.*) pregunta *o* problema (*m.*) difícil, problemón.
posh [pɔʃ], *a.* (*fam.*) pera; de postín; elegantón.
posit [ˈpɔzit], *v.t.* (*lóg.*) proponer, postular.
position [pəˈziʃən], *s.* posición; situación; colocación; emplazamiento; postura, opinión; cargo, puesto; ***to be in a position to,*** estar en condiciones *o* situación de. — *v.t.* colocar, disponer.
positive [ˈpɔzitiv], *a.* positivo; afirmativo; categórico; ***I am positive,*** estoy seguro. — *s.* (*foto., gram.*) positivo.
positiveness [ˈpɔzitivnis], *s.* (lo) positivo *o* categórico.
positivism [ˈpɔzitivizəm], *s.* positivismo.
positivist [ˈpɔzitivist], *s.* positivista, *m.f.*
posology [pɔˈsɔlədʒi], *s.* (*med.*) posología.
posse [ˈpɔsi], *s.* (*Am.*) grupo de gente armada; partida, pelotón; ***in posse,*** en potencia.
possess [pəˈzes], *v.t.* poseer; tener, gozar de. — **possess o.s.,** *v.r.* — ***of,*** apoderarse de.
possessed [pəˈzest], *a.* poseído, poseso; ***one possessed,*** energúmeno.
possession [pəˈzeʃən], *s.* posesión; ***to take possession of,*** apoderarse de; entrar en posesión de, tomar posesión de.
possessive [pəˈzesiv], *a.* posesivo; absorbente; dominante. — *s.* (*gram.*) posesivo.
possessor [pəˈzesə], *s.* poseedor, posesor; (*com.*) portador.
possessory [pəˈzesəri], *a.* posesorio.
possibility [pɔsiˈbiliti], *s.* posibilidad; eventualidad.
possible [ˈpɔsibl], *a.* posible; eventual; ***as much as possible,*** todo lo posible, cuanto sea posible; ***as often as possible,*** lo más frecuentemente posible; ***as soon as possible,*** cuanto antes; ***it is possible that,*** puede (ser) que, es posible que.
possibly [ˈpɔsibli], *adv.* posiblemente; ***I cannot possibly,*** me es totalmente imposible; ***if I possibly can,*** de no serme totalmente imposible.
possum [ˈpɔsəm], *s.* (*fam.*) zarigüeya [OPOSSUM]; ***to play possum,*** hacerse el muerto *o* el dormido.
post (1) [poust], *s.* correo; ***by post,*** por correo; ***by return of post,*** a vuelta de correo; ***to go to the post,*** ir a correos *o* a echar una carta; ***post-bag,*** saco de correspondencia; saca de correos; ***post-box,*** buzón; ***post-card,*** (tarjeta) postal, *f.*; ***post-chaise,*** silla de posta; ***post free,*** franco de porte; ***post-haste,*** a toda prisa, quemando etapas; ***post-office,*** (oficina de) correos; ***post-office box,*** apartado (de correos); ***post-paid,*** (con) franqueo pagado. — *v.t.* echar al correo, mandar por correo; ***to keep posted about*** o ***on,*** tener al corriente de.
post (2) [poust], *s.* poste; ***as deaf as a post,*** sordo como una tapia; ***to go from pillar to post,*** ir de la ceca a la meca. — *v.t.* fijar, pegar.
post (3) [poust], *s.* puesto, cargo; destino. — *v.t.* (*mil.*) destinar.
postage [ˈpoustidʒ], *s.* franqueo, porte; ***postage stamp,*** sello de correo.
postal [ˈpoustəl], *a.* postal; ***postal order,*** giro postal, orden postal de pago.
post-date [poust-ˈdeit], *v.t.* posfechar.
poster [ˈpoustə], *s.* cartel; anuncio; póster.
poste restante [poust resˈtɑ:nt], *s.* lista de correos.
posterior [pɔsˈtiəriə], *a.* posterior. — *s.* trasero.
posteriority [pɔstiəriˈɔriti], *s.* posterioridad.
posterity [pɔsˈteriti], *s.* posteridad.
postern [ˈpɔstən], *s.* puerta trasera; (*fort.*) poterna.
postfix [ˈpoustfiks], *s.* (*gram.*) posfijo.
postgraduate [poustˈgrædjuit], *a., s.* posgraduado.
posthumous [ˈpɔstjuməs], *a.* póstumo.
postilion [pɔsˈtiliən], *s.* postillón.
postliminy [poustˈlimini], *s.* (*der.*) postliminio.
postman [ˈpoustmən], *s.* cartero.
postmark [ˈpoustmɑ:k], *s.* matasellos, *m.inv.* — *v.t.* matar (el sello de).
postmaster [ˈpoustmɑ:stə], *s.* administrador de correos.
postmeridian [poustməˈridiən], *a.* postmeridiano.
post-mortem [poust-ˈmɔ:təm], *s.* autopsia.
post-obit [poust-ˈoubit], *a.* (*for.*) válido después de la muerte.
postpone [pousˈpoun], *v.t.* aplazar.
postponement [pousˈpounmənt], *s.* aplazamiento.
postscript [ˈpousskript], *s.* posdata.
postulant [ˈpɔstjulənt], *s.* postulante, postulanta.
postulate [ˈpɔstjulit], *s.* postulado. — [-eit], *v.t.* postular.
postulation [pɔstjuˈleiʃən], *s.* postulación.
postulatory [ˈpɔstjuleitəri], *a.* postulatorio, supuesto.
posture [ˈpɔstʃə], *s.* postura, actitud. — *v.i.* adoptar una pose.
post-war [ˈpoust-ˈwɔ:], *a.* de la posguerra. — *s.* posguerra.
posy [ˈpouzi], *s.* ramillete de flores.
pot (1) [pɔt], *s.* olla, marmita, puchero; maceta; tarro, pote; ***chamber pot,*** orinal; ***flower-pot,*** tiesto; ***pot-belly,*** barriga; ***pot-bellied,*** barrigón, barrigudo, panzudo; ***pot-boiler,*** obra hecha de prisa para ganarse la vida; ***pot-cheese,*** requesón; ***pot-herb,*** hortaliza; ***pot-hole,*** bache; (*geol.*) marmita; ***pot-holer,*** espeleólogo; ***pot-holing,*** espeleología; ***pot-house,*** tabernucho; ***pot-lead,*** grafito; ***to take pot-luck,*** hacer penitencia; comer lo que haya; ***to take a pot-shot at,*** pegar, disparar un tiro a lo loco a; ***it is like the pot***

calling the kettle black, dijo la sartén a la caldera, ¡quítate allá culinegra!; (*fam.*) ***to go to pot,*** echarse a perder; ***to have pots of money,*** tener montones de dinero; ***to keep the pot boiling,*** ganar bastante para vivir; hacer que la cosa siga adelante. — *v.t.* conservar (en pote); poner (en tiesto); cocer, estofar; (*fam.*) matar a tiros.

pot (2) [pɔt], *s.* (*fam.*) grifa, marihuana.

potable [ˈpoutəbl], *a.* potable.

potage [pɔˈtɑːʒ], *s.* potaje.

potash [ˈpɔtæʃ], *s.* potasa.

potassium [pɔˈtæsiəm], *s.* potasio.

potation [pouˈteiʃən], *s.* potación; (*pl.*) libaciones, *f.pl.*

potato [pəˈteitou], *s.* (*bot.*) patata; papa, *f.*; ***new potatoes,*** patatas nuevas; ***potato-chips,*** (*Am.*) [CRISPS]; ***potato starch,*** almidón; ***sweet potato,*** batata; boniato; (*Hisp. Am.*) camote.

poteen [pouˈtiːn], *s.* aguardiente (irlandés).

potency, potentness [ˈpoutənsi, -təntnis], *s.* potencia, fuerza; (lo) contundente; eficacia.

potent [ˈpoutənt], *a.* potente; contundente; fuerte.

potentate [ˈpoutənteit], *s.* potentado, magnate.

potential [poˈtenʃəl], *a.*, *s.* potencial.

potentiality [potenʃiˈæliti], *s.* potencialidad.

potentilla [poutənˈtilə], *s.* (*bot.*) cincoenrama.

potentiometer [potenʃiˈɔmitə], *s.* potenciómetro.

pother [ˈpɔðə], *s.* cisco, alboroto.

pothook [ˈpɔthuk], *s.* garabato.

potion [ˈpouʃən], *s.* poción.

pot-pourri [pou-puːˈriː], *s.* (*coc.*) mezcolanza, batiburrillo; (*mús.*) popurrí.

potsherd [ˈpɔtʃəːd], *s.* casco, tiesto.

pottage [ˈpɔtidʒ], *s.* potaje.

pottager [ˈpɔtidʒə], *s.* escudilla.

potter (1) [ˈpɔtə], *s.* alfarero; ***potter's field,*** cementerio de (los) pobres; ***potter's wheel,*** torno de alfarero.

potter (2) [ˈpɔtə], *v.i.* — ***about,*** trajinar (sin provecho).

pottery [ˈpɔtəri], *s.* alfarería; cerámica.

potty [ˈpɔti], *a.* (*fam.*) chalado.

pouch [pautʃ], *s.* bolsa; morral, zurrón (*de caza*); petaca (*de tabaco*); cartuchera.

poulterer [ˈpoultərə], *s.* pollero.

poultice [ˈpoultis], *s.* bizma, emplasto, cataplasma. — *v.t.* bizmar.

poultry [ˈpoultri], *s.* aves de corral, *f.pl.*; ***poultry farm,*** granja avícola; ***poultry farmer*** o ***keeper,*** avicultor.

pounce [pauns], *s.* salto repentino; ataque repentino. — *v.i.* — ***on, upon,*** saltar sobre, abalanzarse *a o* sobre, precipitarse sobre.

pouncet-box [ˈpaunsit-bɔks], *s.* cajita agujereada para polvos.

pound (1) [paund], *s.* (*numis., peso*) libra.

pound (2) [paund], *s.* corral de concejo.

pound (3) [paund], *v.t.* golpear, aporrear; machacar; moler, pulverizar; bombardear insistentemente; (*olas*) estrellarse contra, batir. — *v.i.* golpear, aporrear; ***pound along,*** correr pesadamente.

poundage [ˈpaundidʒ], *s.* impuesto sobre cada libra.

pounder [ˈpaundə], *s.* ***six-pounder,*** uno de seis libras.

pour [pɔː], *v.t.* echar, verter; arrojar; derramar; escanciar (*vino*); ***pour away, out,*** vaciar. — *v.i.* correr, fluir (abundantemente); ***pour in, out,*** entrar, salir a raudales; ***pour with rain,*** diluviar, llover a cántaros; ***it never rains but it pours,*** las desgracias nunca vienen solas.

pourer [ˈpɔːrə], *s.* escanciador.

pouring [ˈpɔːriŋ], *a.* ***pouring rain,*** diluvio.

pout [paut], *s.* pucherito. — *v.i.* hacer pucheritos; poner mal gesto.

pouter [ˈpautə], *s.* (*orn.*) paloma buchona.

poverty [ˈpɔvəti], *s.* pobreza, miseria.

powder [ˈpaudə], *s.* polvo; polvos (*de la cara*); pólvora; ***powder-box, powder-compact,*** polvera; ***powder-flask, powder-horn,*** polvorín, cebador; cuerno de pólvora; ***powder-magazine,*** polvorín, santabárbara; ***powder-puff,*** borla de empolvar; ***powder-room,*** (cuarto) tocador. — *v.t.* pulverizar; polvorear (***with,*** de); ***powder one's face,*** echarse polvos, ponerse polvos; ***powdered milk,*** leche en polvo; (*Am.*) ***powdered sugar*** [CASTOR SUGAR].

powdery [ˈpaudəri], *a.* polvoriento; empolvado; en polvo; pulverizado.

power [pauə], *s.* poder; potencia; poderío; atribución, autoridad; fuerza, energía; facultad; ***to be in power,*** estar en el poder; ***power-cut,*** apagón, corte de luz; (*pl.*) restricciones, *f.pl.*; ***power-loom,*** telar mecánico; ***power of attorney,*** procuración, poder; ***power-shovel,*** excavadora mecánica; ***power-station,*** central eléctrica; ***the powers that be,*** las autoridades constituidas; ***the Western Powers,*** las potencias occidentales.

powerful [ˈpauəful], *a.* poderoso; potente; fuerte; intenso; contundente.

powerfulness [ˈpauəfulnis], *s.* poderío; fuerza, energía.

powerless [ˈpauəlis], *a.* sin poder, impotente.

powerlessness [ˈpauəlisnis], *s.* impotencia; incapacidad.

pow-wow [ˈpau-wau], *s.* junta india; conferencia, parlamento.

pox [pɔks], *s.* viruelas, *f.pl.*; (*fam.*) sífilis, *f.inv.*

practicability [præktikəˈbiliti], *s.* factibilidad, viabilidad.

practicable [ˈpræktikəbl], *a.* practicable, factible, hacedero, viable.

practical [ˈpræktikəl], *a.* práctico; ***practical joke,*** bromazo.

practically [ˈpræktikəli], *adv.* prácticamente; casi.

practicalness [ˈpræktikəlnis], *s.* carácter práctico.

practice [ˈpræktis], *s.* práctica; uso, costumbre; ejercicio; (*de abogado* o *médico*) clientela; prácticas; normas, *f.pl.*; ***in practice,*** en la práctica; (*dep.*) en forma, entrenado; ***to put into practice,*** llevar a la práctica, poner en práctica; ***to make a practice of,*** tener por costumbre; ***to be out of practice,*** haber perdido la costumbre; estar desentrenado; ***practice makes perfect,*** la práctica hace maestro(s).

practician [prækˈtiʃən], *s.* práctico.

practise [ˈpræktis], *v.t.* practicar; ejercitar, ejercer; hacer prácticas de, hacer ejercicios de, entrenarse en; ensayarse a. — *v.i.* ensayarse; ejercer; practicar (la medicina).

practised [ˈpræktist], *a.* experto, experimentado.

practiser [ˈpræktisə], *s.* practicante, el que practica, el que ejerce (una profesión).

practising [ˈpræktisiŋ], *a.* practicante; en ejercicio, que ejerce.

practitioner [prækˈtiʃənə], *s.* facultativo, práctico; ***general practitioner,*** médico de medicina general.

prætor [ˈpriːtɔː], *s.* pretor.

prætorial [priːˈtɔːriəl], *a.* pretorial.

prætorium [priˈtɔːriəm], *s.* pretorio.

pragmatic(al) [prægˈmætik(əl)], *a.* pragmático.

pragmatism [ˈprægmətizəm], *s.* (*filos.*) pragmatismo.

pragmatist [ˈprægmətist], *s.* pragmatista, *m.f.*

Prague [prɑːg]. Praga.

prairie [ˈprɛəri], *s.* pradera; sabana; pampa; (*orn.*) ***prairie chicken,*** chocha; (*zool.*) ***prairie dog,*** aranata.

praise [preiz], *s.* alabanza, elogio, encomio. — *v.t.* alabar, elogiar, encomiar; ***praise to the skies,*** poner por las nubes *o* sobre las estrellas.

praiseworthiness [ˈpreizwəːðinis], *s.* (lo) loable.

praiseworthy [ˈpreizwəːði], *a.* loable, digno de alabanza.
praline [ˈpræliːn], *s.* (*bot.*) almendra garapiñada.
pram [præm], *s.* (*abrev.*) [PERAMBULATOR]; (*fam.*) cochecito (de niño).
prance [prɑːns], *s.* cabriola. — *v.i.* cabriolar, encabritarse; ***prance about,*** dar valsones.
prancing [ˈprɑːnsiŋ], *s.* cabriolas, *f.pl.*
prang [præŋ], *v.t.* (*fam.*) estrellarse.
prank [præŋk], *s.* travesura, broma, bromazo; ***to get up to one's pranks,*** hacer de las suyas.
prankish [ˈpræŋkiʃ], *a.* travieso.
prate [preit], *v.i.* charlar, parlotear.
prater [ˈpreitə], *s.* charlatán.
prating [ˈpreitiŋ], *s.* cháchara(s), parloteo.
pratique [prəˈtiːk], *s.* (*mar.*) libre plática.
prattle [prætl], *s.* garrulería, parloteo, cháchara; balbuceo. — *v.i.* parlotear; balbucear.
prattler [ˈprætlə], *s.* parlanchín, charlatán.
prawn [prɔːn], *s.* gamba; ***Dublin Bay prawn, king prawn, Chinese prawn,*** langostino.
praxis [ˈpræksis], *s.* praxis, *f.*
pray [prei], *v.t.* rogar, suplicar, implorar. — *v.i.* rezar, orar; ***pray be silent,*** le(s) ruego (que) guarde(n) silencio; ***pray for,*** rogar, pedir (algo; por alguien).
prayer [prɛə], *s.* oración, rezo, plegaria; ruego, súplica; ***Lord's prayer,*** padrenuestro; ***prayer-book,*** devocionario, misal; ***to say one's prayers,*** rezar.
prayerfulness [ˈprɛəfulnis], *s.* devoción; inclinación a rezar.
praying [ˈpreiiŋ], *s.* rezos, *m.pl.*
preach [priːtʃ], *v.t.* predicar; (*fig.*) aconsejar, fomentar; ***practise what one preaches,*** predicar con el ejemplo. — *v.i.* predicar; ***preach at s.o.,*** sermonear a alguien, echar un sermón a alguien; ***preach to deaf ears,*** predicar en (el) desierto.
preacher [ˈpriːtʃə], *s.* predicador.
preaching [ˈpriːtʃiŋ], *s.* predicación; sermoneo.
preacquaint [priːəˈkweint], *v.t.* comunicar *o* advertir de antemano.
preadmonish [priːədˈmɔniʃ], *v.t.* advertir de antemano.
preamble [priːˈæmbl], *s.* preámbulo.
prearrange [priːəˈreindʒ], *v.t.* arreglar *o* fijar de antemano.
prebend [ˈprebənd], *s.* prebenda; prebendado.
prebendary [ˈprebəndəri], *s.* prebendado, racionero.
precarious [priˈkɛəriəs], *a.* precario; poco seguro.
precariousness [priˈkɛəriəsnis], *s.* (lo) precario; incertidumbre.
precast [ˈpriːˈkɑːst], *a.* (*constr.*) prefabricado.
precaution [priˈkɔːʃən], *s.* precaución.
precautionary [priˈkɔːʃənri], *a.* preventivo, de precaución.
precede [priˈsiːd], *v.t.* preceder (a), anteceder (a). — *v.i.* preceder.
precedence [priˈsiːdəns], *s.* precedencia, preferencia; ***to take precedence over,*** primar sobre.
precedent [priˈsiːdənt], *a.* precedente, antecedente. — [ˈpresidənt], *s.* precedente, antecedente.
preceding [priˈsiːdiŋ], *a.* precedente.
precentor [priˈsentə], *s.* chantre, capiscol.
precept [ˈpriːsept], *s.* precepto; (*for.*) mandato.
preceptive [priˈseptiv], *a.* preceptivo.
preceptor [priˈseptə], *s.* preceptor.
preceptorial [priːsepˈtɔːriəl], *a.* preceptoral.
preceptory [priˈseptəri], *a.* preceptoral. — *s.* preceptoría.
preceptress [priˈseptris], *s.* preceptora.
precession [priˈseʃən], *s.* precedencia; (*astron.*) precesión.
precinct [ˈpriːsiŋkt], *s.* recinto, ámbito; (*Am.*) zona, distrito.
precious [ˈpreʃəs], *a.* valioso; precioso; ***precious style,*** estilo preciosista.
preciousness [ˈpreʃəsnis], *s.* preciosidad; preciosismo.
precipice [ˈpresipis], *s.* precipicio, despeñadero.
precipitance, precipitancy [priˈsipitəns, -i], *s.* precipitación.
precipitant [priˈsipitənt], *a.* precipitado. — *s.* (*quím.*) precipitante.
precipitate [priˈsipitit], *a.*, *s.* precipitado. — [priˈsipiteit], *v.t.* precipitar. — *v.i.* precipitarse.
precipitation [prisipiˈteiʃən], *s.* precipitación, apresuramiento; (*quím.*) precipitado.
precipitous [priˈsipitəs], *a.* escarpado.
precipitousness [priˈsipitəsnis], *s.* (lo) escarpado.
précis [ˈpreisiː], *s.* resumen.
precise [priˈsais], *a.* preciso, exacto; meticuloso.
precisely [priˈsaisli], *adv.* exactamente; en punto.
precision, preciseness [priˈsiʒən, -ˈsaisnis], *s.* precisión, exactitud.
preclude [priˈkluːd], *v.t.* excluir; imposibilitar.
preclusion [priˈkluːʒən], *s.* exclusión.
precocious [priˈkouʃəs], *a.* precoz.
precociousness, precocity [priˈkouʃəsnis, -ˈkɔsiti], *s.* precocidad.
precognition [priːkəgˈniʃən], *s.* precognición.
precompose [priːkəmˈpouz], *v.t.* componer de antemano.
preconceive [priːkənˈsiːv], *v.t.* preconcebir.
preconceived [priːkənˈsiːvd], *a.* preconcebido.
preconception [priːkənˈsepʃən], *s.* preconcepción.
preconcert [priːkənˈsəːt], *v.t.* concertar *o* acordar de antemano.
precursor [priːˈkəːsə], *s.* precursor.
predator [ˈpredətə], *s.* predator; animal de rapiña.
predatory [ˈpredətəri], *a.* rapaz, de presa, de rapiña, de predator.
predecease [priːdiˈsiːs], *v.t.* morir antes que.
predecessor [ˈpriːdisesə], *s.* predecesor; antecesor.
predestinate [priːˈdestineit], *v.t.* predestinar.
predestination [priːdestiˈneiʃən], *s.* predestinación.
predestine [priːˈdestin], *v.t.* predestinar.
predeterminate [priːdiˈtəːminit], *a.* predeterminado.
predetermination [priːditəːmiˈneiʃən], *s.* predeterminación.
predetermine [priːdiˈtəːmin], *v.t.* predeterminar.
predial [ˈpriːdiəl], *a.* predial.
predicable [ˈpredikəbl], *a.*, *s.* predicable.
predicament [priˈdikəmənt], *s.* apuro, aprieto, trance apurado, situación difícil; (*filos.*) predicamento.
predicate [ˈpredikit], *s.* predicado. — [ˈpredikeit], *v.t.* (*lóg.*) predicar.
predication [prediˈkeiʃən], *s.* (*lóg.*) predicación, aseveración.
predict [priˈdikt], *v.t.* predecir, pronosticar.
predictable [priˈdiktəbl], *a.* pronosticable, previsible.
prediction [priˈdikʃən], *s.* predicción, pronóstico, vaticinio.
predictive [priˈdiktiv], *a.* que predice, profético.
predictor [priˈdiktə], *s.* vaticinador.
predigestion [priːdiˈdʒestʃən], *s.* peptonización del alimento, digestión artificial.
predilection [priːdiˈlekʃən], *s.* predilección.
predisponent [priːdisˈpounənt], *a.* predisponente.
predispose [priːdisˈpouz], *v.t.* predisponer.
predisposition [priːdispəˈziʃən], *s.* predisposición.
predominance, predominancy [priˈdɔminəns, -i], *s.* predominio.
predominant [priˈdɔminənt], *a.* predominante.
predominate [priˈdɔmineit], *v.i.* predominar, prevalecer.

pre-elect [pri:-i'lekt], *v.t.* nombrar *o* elegir de antemano.
pre-election [pri:-i'lekʃən], *s.* elección anterior.
pre-eminence [pri:-'eminəns], *s.* preeminencia, supremacía, primacía.
pre-eminent [pri:-'eminənt], *a.* preeminente, relevante.
pre-empt [pri:-'empt], *v.t.* adelantarse a, anticiparse a; ***pre-empt the situation,*** anticiparse a los acontecimientos.
pre-emption [pri:-'empʃən], *s.* anticipación.
pre-emptive [pri:-'emptiv], *a.* anticipado; ***pre-emptive attack,*** ataque anticipado.
preen [pr:n], *v.t.* limpiar y arreglar (sus plumas) (*las aves*). — **preen o.s.,** *v.r.* pavonearse; acicalarse.
pre-engage [pri:-in'geidʒ], *v.t.* apalabrar, contratar de antemano.
pre-engagement [pri:-in'geidʒmənt], *s.* compromiso anterior.
pre-establish [pri:-is'tæbliʃ], *v.t.* preestablecer, establecer de antemano.
pre-exist [pri:-ig'zist], *v.i.* preexistir.
pre-existence [pri:-ig'zistəns], *s.* preexistencia.
pre-existent [pri:-ig'zistənt], *a.* preexistente.
prefab ['pri:fæb], *s.* (*fam.*) casa prefabricada.
prefabricate [pri:'fæbrikeit], *v.t.* prefabricar.
preface ['prefis], *s.* prefacio, prólogo. — *v.t.* prologar; comenzar; decir a modo de prólogo a.
prefatory ['prefətəri], *a.* preliminar.
prefect ['pri:fekt], *s.* prefecto; monitor.
prefecture ['pri:fektʃə], *s.* prefectura.
prefer [pri'fə:], *v.t.* preferir.
preferable ['prefərəbl], *a.* preferible.
preference ['prefərəns], *s.* preferencia; predilección; prelación; ***preference shares,*** acciones preferentes, *f.pl.*
preferential [prefə'renʃəl], *a.* preferente, de preferencia.
preferment [pri'fə:mənt], *s.* primacía; ascenso; preferencia; puesto eminente.
prefiguration [pri:figjuə'reiʃən], *s.* prefiguración.
prefigurative [pri:'figjuərətiv], *a.* que prefigura.
prefigure [pri:'figə], *v.t.* prefigurar.
prefix ['pri:fiks], *s.* prefijo. — [pri:'fiks], *v.t.* prefijar.
preform [pri:'fɔ:m], *v.t.* formar de antemano.
preformation [pri:fɔ:'meiʃən], *s.* preformación.
pregnancy ['pregnənsi], *s.* embarazo.
pregnant ['pregnənt], *a.* embarazada, encinta, en estado (interesante); (*fig.*) ***pregnant pause,*** pausa preñada *o* cargada de tensiones, emociones *etc.*
preheat ['pri:'hi:t], *v.t.* precalentar.
prehensile [pri'hensail], *a.* prensil.
prehension [pri'henʃən], *s.* prensión.
prehistoric(al) [pri:his'tɔrik(əl)], *a.* prehistórico.
prejudge ['pri:'dʒʌdʒ], *v.t.* prejuzgar.
prejudgment ['pri:'dʒʌdʒmənt], *s.* prejuicio.
prejudice ['predʒudis], *s.* prejuicio, prevención; (*for.*) perjuicio; ***without prejudice to,*** sin perjuicio de. — *v.t.* perjudicar; predisponer (***against,*** contra).
prejudiced ['predʒudist], *a.* parcial, interesado; que tiene prevención (***against,*** contra); que tiene prejuicios; ***to be prejudiced against,*** tener prevención contra.
prejudicial [predʒu'diʃəl], *a.* perjudicial.
prelacy ['preləsi], *s.* prelacía.
prelate ['prelit], *s.* prelado.
prelateship ['prelitʃip], *s.* prelatura, prelacía.
preliminary [pri'liminəri], *a.* preliminar. — *s.* (*pl.*) preliminares, *m.pl.*
prelude ['prelju:d], *s.* preludio. — [pri'lju:d], *v.t.* preludiar; presagiar.

premarital [pri:'mæritəl], *a.* premarital.
premature ['pri:mətʃuə], *a.* prematuro.
prematureness ['pri:mətʃuənis], *s.* (lo) prematuro.
premeditate [pri:'mediteit], *v.t.* premeditar.
premeditated [pri:'mediteitid], *a.* premeditado.
premeditation [pri:medi'teiʃən], *s.* premeditación.
premier ['premiə], *a.* primero, principal. — *s.* primer ministro.
première ['premiɛə], *s.* estreno.
premiership ['premiəʃip], *s.* cargo de primer ministro.
premise ['premis], *s.* (*lóg.*) premisa.
premises ['premisiz], *s.pl.* local.
premium ['pri:miəm], *s.* premio; (*com., mar.*) prima; ***to be at a premium,*** estar sobre la par; (*fig.*) tener demanda, estar (muy) solicitado.
premonish [pri:'mɔniʃ], *v.t.* prevenir, advertir.
premonition [pri:mə'niʃən], *s.* presentimiento; premonición.
premonitory [pri'mɔnitəri], *a.* premonitorio.
prenatal ['pri:'neitəl], *a.* prenatal.
prenominate [pri:'nɔmineit], *v.t.* nombrar primero.
prenomination [pri:nɔmi'neiʃən], *s.* acción de nombrar primero.
prentice ['prentis], *s.* aprendiz.
preoccupancy [pri:'ɔkjupənsi], *s.* ocupación previa.
preoccupation [pri:ɔkju'peiʃən], *s.* preocupación; ocupación previa.
preoccupied [pri:'ɔkjupaid], *a.* preocupado.
preoccupy [pri:'ɔkjupai], *v.t.* preocupar.
preordain ['pri:ɔ:'dein], *v.t.* preordenar; (*teo.*) predestinar, preordinar.
preordinance, preordination [pri:'ɔ:dinəns, pri:ɔ:di'neiʃən], *s.* preordinación.
prep [prep], *s.* (*fam.*) (la) tarea.
prepacked ['pri:'pækt], *a.* (que viene ya) empaquetado.
prepaid ['pri:'peid], *a.* (con) porte pagado.
preparation [prepə'reiʃən], *s.* preparación; preparativo(s); preparado.
preparative [pri'pærətiv], *a.* preparativo.
preparatory [pri'pærətəri], *a.* preparatorio, previo, preliminar; ***prep(aratory) school,*** (*Am.*) [PUBLIC SCHOOL]. — *adv.* — ***to,*** antes de, con miras a.
prepare [pri'pɛə], *v.t.* preparar; disponer; prevenir. — *v.i.* prepararse; disponerse; prevenirse. — **prepare o.s.,** *v.r.* — ***for the worst,*** prepararse para lo peor.
prepared [pri'pɛəd], *a.* preparado, dispuesto; ***to be prepared to,*** estar dispuesto a.
preparedly [pri'pɛəridli], *adv.* preventivamente.
preparedness [pri'pɛəridnis], *s.* estado de preparación (*mil. etc.*).
preparer [pri'pɛərə], *s.* preparador.
prepay ['pri:'pei], *v.t.* pagar por adelantado.
prepayment ['pri:'peimənt], *s.* pago adelantado.
prepense [pri:'pens], *a.* premeditado.
preperception [pri:pə'sepʃən], *s.* percepción previa.
preponderance, preponderancy [pri'pɔndərəns, -i], *s.* preponderancia.
preponderant [pri'pɔndərənt], *a.* preponderante.
preponderate [pri'pɔndəreit], *v.t.* predominar. — *v.i.* preponderar, prevalecer.
preponderating [pri'pɔndəreitiŋ], *a.* preponderante.
preponderation [pripɔndə'reiʃən], *s.* preponderancia.
preposition [prepə'ziʃən], *s.* preposición.
prepositional [prepə'ziʃənəl], *a.* preposicional, prepositivo.
prepositive [pri'pɔzitiv], *a.* prefijo, antepuesto. — *s.* partícula, prepositiva.
prepossess [pri:pə'zes], *v.t.* predisponer (favorablemente).

prepossessing [pri:pəˈzesiŋ], *a.* atractivo, que atrae, que apetece.
prepossession [pri:pəˈzeʃən], *s.* predisposición (favorable).
preposterous [priˈpɔstərəs], *a.* absurdo, ridículo, disparatado.
preposterousness [priˈpɔstərəsnis], *s.* (lo) disparatado.
prepotent [pri:ˈpoutənt], *a.* prepotente.
prepuce [ˈpri:pju:s], *s.* (*anat.*) prepucio.
pre-Raphaelite [pri:-ˈræfəlait], *a.*, *s.* (*b.a.*) prerrafaelista, *m.f.*
prerequisite [pri:ˈrekwizit], *s.* requisito (previo).
preresolve [pri:riˈzɔlv], *v.t.* resolver anticipadamente.
prerogative [priˈrɔgətiv], *s.* prerrogativa.
presage [ˈpresidʒ], *s.* presagio. — [preˈseidʒ], *v.t.* presagiar.
presageful [ˈpresidʒful], *a.* lleno de presagios.
presbyopia [prezbiˈoupiə], *s.* (*ópt.*) presbicia.
presbyter [ˈprezbitə], *s.* presbítero.
Presbyterian [prezbiˈtiəriən], *a.*, *s.* (*relig.*) presbiteriano.
Presbyterianism [prezbiˈtiəriənizəm], *s.* (*relig.*) presbiterianismo.
presbytery [ˈprezbitəri], *s.* presbiterio.
prescience [ˈpresiəns], *s.* presciencia.
prescient [ˈpresiənt], *a.* presciente.
prescribe [priˈskraib], *v.t.*, *v.i.* prescribir; (*med.*) recetar.
prescript [ˈpri:skript], *s.* regla, norma; (*filos.*) prescrito.
prescriptible [priˈskriptibl], *a.* prescriptible.
prescription [priˈskripʃən], *s.* prescripción; (*med.*) receta.
prescriptive [priˈskriptiv], *a.* de prescripción; autorizado por la costumbre; (*for.*) adquirido por prescripción.
presence [ˈprezəns], *s.* presencia; asistencia; ***in the presence of,*** en presencia de; ***presence-chamber,*** salón de recepción; ***presence of mind,*** presencia de ánimo.
present (1) [ˈprezənt], *a.* actual, presente; ***to be present at,*** asistir a; ***present company excepted,*** mejorando lo presente; ***present-day,*** actual, contemporáneo; ***those present,*** los asistentes. — *s.* presente; (*gram.*) tiempo presente; ***at present,*** actualmente; de momento; ***for the present,*** por ahora.
present (2) [ˈprezənt], *s.* regalo, obsequio; ***to make a present of,*** regalar. — [priˈzent], *v.t.* presentar; representar; ofrecer; deparar; exponer; ***present arms!*** ¡presenten armas!; ***present with,*** presentar; obsequiar con.
presentability [prizentəˈbiliti], *s.* calidad de presentable, (lo) presentable.
presentable [priˈzentəbl], *a.* presentable.
presentation [prezənˈteiʃən], *s.* presentación; obsequio; (*com.*) ***on presentation of,*** a presentación de; ***presentation copy,*** ejemplar de regalo.
presentee [prezənˈti:], *s.* (*igl.*) presentado (*a un beneficio*).
presenter [priˈzentə], *s.* presentador; obsequiador.
presentiment [priˈzentimənt], *s.* presentimiento.
presently [ˈprezəntli], *adv.* luego, después; (*Am.*) actualmente.
presentment [priˈzentmənt], *s.* presentación; retrato, representación, semejanza; (*for.*) denuncia, acusación.
preservable [priˈzə:vəbl], *a.* preservable; conservable.
preservation [prezəˈveiʃən], *s.* preservación; conservación.
preservative [priˈzə:vətiv], *a.* preservativo; conservativo. — *s.* preservativo.
preserve [priˈzə:v], *s.* conserva, confitura, compota; (*caz.*) coto, vedado. — *v.t.* conservar; preservar; ***preserve from,*** guardar de.
preserved [priˈzə:vd], *a.* en conserva.
preserver [priˈzə:və], *s.* preservador; conservador; conservero.
preside [priˈzaid], *v.i.* presidir; ***preside over,*** presidir, ocupar la presidencia de.
presidency [ˈprezidənsi], *s.* presidencia.
president [ˈprezidənt], *s.* presidente, presidenta, *f.*
presidential [preziˈdenʃəl], *a.* presidencial.
presidentship [ˈprezidəntʃip], *s.* presidencia.
presider [priˈzaidə], *s.* presidente.
presiding [priˈzaidiŋ], *a.* presidente, que preside.
presidium [priˈsidiəm], *s.* (*pol.*) presidium (*soviético*).
press [pres], *a.* de prensa; de imprenta; (*mil.*) de enganche; ***press-agency,*** agencia de información; ***press agent,*** agente de publicidad; ***press-box,*** tribuna de la prensa; ***press-clipping*** o ***cutting,*** recorte de prensa; ***press-conference,*** conferencia *o* rueda de prensa; ***press-gallery,*** tribuna de la prensa; ***press-gang,*** patrulla de enganche, levadores, *m.pl.*; ***press-release,*** comunicado; ***press-room,*** taller de imprenta; ***press-stud,*** botón automático; ***press-work,*** impresión, tirada. — *s.* (*mec.*, *periodismo*) prensa; imprenta; (*gente*) tropel, apiñamiento; presión, empuje; apremio, prisa, urgencia; (*mil.*) leva, enganche; ***to have a good*** (***bad***) ***press,*** tener buena (mala) prensa; ***in press,*** en prensa; ***to go to press,*** entrar en prensa. — *v.t.* apretar, comprimir, estrujar; oprimir; apremiar; enganchar, hacer levas de; planchar; prensar; pulsar; insistir (a); ***to be pressed for time, money,*** estar apurado de tiempo, dinero; ***press one's point,*** insistir en su idea *o* punto de vista, porfiar. — *v.i.* urgir, apremiar; apiñarse; ***press on*** o ***forward,*** seguir adelante; ***time presses,*** el tiempo apremia.
pressing [ˈpresiŋ], *a.* urgente, apremiante, acuciante. — *s.* (el) planchar.
pressman [ˈpresmən], *s.* (*pl.* **-men** [-men]) periodista, *m.*
pressure [ˈpreʃə], *s.* presión; apremio, premura, urgencia; impulso; tensión; ***to bring pressure to bear on s.o.,*** presionar a alguien; ***high blood pressure,*** tensión alta; ***low blood pressure,*** tensión baja; ***pressure-cooker,*** olla de *o* a presión; ***pressure-gauge,*** manómetro; ***pressure-group,*** grupo de presión; ***to work under pressure,*** trabajar con premura.
pressurize [ˈpreʃəraiz], *v.t.* presionar; ***they pressurized him into doing it,*** le presionaron de tal forma que se vio obligado a hacerlo.
pressurized [ˈpreʃəraizd], *a.* de *o* a presión.
prestidigitation [prestididʒiˈteiʃən], *s.* prestidigitación.
prestige [presˈti:ʒ], *s.* prestigio; ***to lose prestige,*** desprestigiarse.
prestressed [ˈpri:ˈstrest], *a.* (*constr.*) pretensado.
presumable [priˈz(j)u:məbl], *a.* presumible.
presumably [priˈz(j)u:məbli], *adv.* según cabe presumir, es de suponer (que).
presume [priˈz(j)u:m], *v.t.* presumir, suponer, dar por supuesto; ***presume to,*** tomarse la libertad de, atreverse a. — *v.i.* suponer; ***presume on*** o ***upon,*** abusar de.
presumption [priˈzʌmpʃən], *s.* suposición; presunción; ***the presumption is that,*** se presume que, se da por supuesto que.
presumptive [priˈzʌmptiv], *a.* presunto; presuntivo.
presumptuous [priˈzʌmptjuəs], *a.* presuntuoso, presumido.
presumptuousness [priˈzʌmptjuəsnis], *s.* presunción, presuntuosidad.
presuppose [pri:səˈpouz], *v.t.* presuponer.
pretence [priˈtens], *s.* pretexto; fingimiento; apariencia; pretensión; ***to make a pretence of,*** fingir, simular; ***on false pretences,*** con fraude, con engaño; ***on*** o ***under pretence of,*** so pretexto de.

pretend [pri'tend], *v.t.* fingir, simular, aparentar; ***pretend to be deaf,*** fingir *o* hacer ver que se es sordo, fingir ser sordo, hacerse el sordo. — *v.i.* — ***to,*** pretender; ***he pretends to courage,*** pretende ser valiente.
pretended [pri'tendid], *a.* pretendido.
pretender [pri'tendə], *s.* pretendiente; fingidor.
pretension [pri'tenʃən], *s.* pretensión.
pretentious [pri'tenʃəs], *a.* pretencioso; presuntuoso; cursi.
pretentiousness [pri'tenʃəsnis], *s.* (lo) pretencioso; presuntuosidad; cursilería, (lo) crusi.
preterite ['pretərit], *a.*, *s.* pretérito.
preterition [pretə'riʃən], *s.* preterición.
pretermission [pri:tə'miʃən], *s.* pretermisión.
pretermit [pri:tə'mit], *v.t.* pretermitir.
preternatural [pri:tə'nætʃərəl], *a.* preternatural.
pretext ['pri:tekst], *s.* pretexto; ***on pretext of,*** so pretexto *o* capa de.
pretor [PRÆTOR].
prettiness ['pritinis], *s.* (lo) bonito, lindeza.
pretty ['priti], *a.* bonito, lindo, (*fam.*) guapo, (*fam.*) mono; ***a pretty mess you made of it!*** ¡bonito *o* valiente lío ha armado Vd.!; ***a pretty penny,*** dinerillo, un buen pico; ***pretty-pretty,*** remilgado, delicadísimo, de mírame y no me toques. — *adv.* bastante, muy; ***pretty nearly,*** por poco; ***pretty well,*** bastante bien; ***he is sitting pretty,*** está como quiere.
prevail [pri'veil], *v.i.* prevalecer; predominar, preponderar; reinar, imperar; ***to be prevailed upon to,*** dejarse convencer para; ***prevail over,*** prevalecer sobre; ***prevail upon,*** presuadir, convencer.
prevailing [pri'veiliŋ], *a.* predominante; prevaleciente; reinante, imperante; general; ***prevailing winds,*** vientos dominantes, *m.pl.*
prevalence, prevalency ['prevələns, -i], *s.* predominio; uso frecuente, costumbre.
prevalent ['prevələnt], *a.* prevaleciente; predominante; reinante; general, común.
prevaricate [pri'værikeit], *v.i.* andarse con evasivas, tergiversar.
prevarication [priværi'keiʃən], *s.* evasivas, sofismas, tergiversación.
prevaricator [pri'værikeitə], *s.* sofista, tergiversador.
prevenient [pri'vi:niənt], *a.* preveniente, preventivo.
prevent [pri'vent], *v.t.* impedir; evitar; estorbar.
preventable [pri'ventəbl], *a.* evitable.
preventative [pri'ventətiv], [PREVENTIVE].
preventer [pri'ventə], *s.* estorbador, persona que impide; (*mar.*) berlinga, soga, perno auxiliar.
prevention [pri'venʃən], *s.* prevención; el impedir, el evitar.
preventive [pri'ventiv], *a.* preventivo, impeditivo; preservativo, profiláctico. — *s.* preservativo.
preview ['pri:vju:], *s.* vista anticipada; (*teat.*) preestreno; (*cine*) avance. — *v.t.* ver de antemano.
previous ['pri:viəs], *a.* previo, anterior; (*fam.*) prematuro. — *prep.* — ***to,*** antes de.
previously ['pri:viəsli], *adv.* previamente, anteriormente, antes.
prevision [pri:'viʒən], *s.* previsión.
pre-war ['pri:-'wɔ:], *a.* de antes de la guerra.
prey [prei], *s.* presa; víctima, *f.*; ***bird of prey,*** ave de rapiña; ***to be*** o ***fall a prey to,*** ser presa de, ser víctima de. — *v.i.* — ***on*** o ***upon,*** vivir de, alimentarse de; (*fig.*) ***prey on*** o ***on the mind of,*** atormentar, angustiar.
price [prais], *s.* precio; ***at any price,*** a toda costa, cueste lo que cueste; ***not at any price,*** de ninguna manera, bajo ningún concepto, ni hablar, por nada del mundo; ***cost price,*** precio de coste; ***price control,*** control de (los) precios; ***price cutting,*** reducción de precios, rabajas, *f.pl.*; ***price fixing,*** fijación *o* estabilización de precios; ***price list,*** lista de precios; ***to set a price (up)on s.o.'s head,*** poner a precio la cabeza de alguien. — *v.t.* tasar, fijar el precio de.
priceless ['praislis], *a.* sin precio; inapreciable, que no tiene precio; (*fam.*) divertidísimo, graciosísimo.
prick [prik], *s.* pinchazo; punzada; alfilerazo; ***to kick against the pricks,*** tirar coces contra el aguijón. — *v.t.* pinchar; punzar; agujerear; remorder (*la conciencia*); ***prick up one's ears,*** aguzar las orejas. — *v.i.* — ***up,*** prestar atención; animarse.
pricket ['prikit], *s.* cervato *o* gamo de un año.
pricking ['prikiŋ], *s.* picazón, *f.*, picor, escozor.
prickle [prikl], *s.* espina, pincho, púa; picazón, *f.*, picor, escozor.
prickly ['prikli], *a.* espinoso, lleno de púas; quisquilloso; ***prickly heat,*** sarpullido de calor; (*bot.*) ***prickly pear,*** higo chumbo; chumbera; ***prickly person,*** cascarrabias, *m.inv.*
pride [praid], *s.* orgullo; ***overweening pride,*** soberbia; ***to take pride in,*** tener a gala, enorgullecerse de; ***to take pride of place,*** ocupar el puesto de honor. — **pride o.s.,** *v.r.* — ***on,*** preciarse de.
prideful ['praidful], *a.* soberbio, orgulloso.
prier [praiə], *s.* fisgón.
priest [pri:st], *s.* cura, *m.*, sacerdote; ***priest-ridden*** dominado por el clero.
priestcraft ['pri:stkrɑ:ft], *s.* intriga eclesiástica.
priestess [pri:s'tes], *s.* sacerdotisa.
priesthood ['pri:sthud], *s.* sacerdocio; clero.
priestly ['pri:stli], *a.* sacerdotal.
prig [prig], *s.* presumido, engreído, persona pagada de sí (misma); pedante; gazmoño.
priggish ['prigiʃ], *a.* presumido, engreído, pagado de sí (mismo); pedante; gazmoño.
priggishness ['prigiʃnis], *s.* presunción, engreimiento; pedantería.
prim [prim], *a.* ñoño, remilgado, monjil; ***prim and proper,*** melindroso, muy recatado.
primacy ['praiməsi], *s.* primacía.
primage ['praimidʒ], *s.* (*mar.*) capa.
primal ['praiməl], *a.* primal.
primarily ['praimərili], *adv.* principalmente, ante todo.
primariness ['praimərinis], *s.* primacía.
primary ['praiməri], *a.* primario; ***primary school,*** escuela (primaria). — *s.* (lo) principal; elección preliminar; (*orn.*) pluma primaria; (*elec.*) circuito primario.
primate ['praimit], *s.* (*igl.*) primado; (*zool.*) primate.
primateship ['praimitʃip], *s.* (*igl.*) primacía.
primatial [prai'meiʃəl], *a.* primacial.
prime (1) [praim], *a.* primero; básico; primo; selecto, superior, de primera calidad; ***prime beef,*** carne de primera calidad; ***prime minister,*** primer ministro. — *s.* flor, (lo) mejor; ***prime of life,*** flor de la edad.
prime (2) [praim], *v.t.* cebar (*una arma*); imprimar; instruir, informar de antemano; preparar; (*fam.*) hacer achisparse (a alguien).
primeness ['praimnis], *s.* excelencia, buena calidad.
primer (1) ['praimə], *s.* cartilla; (*impr.*) ***great primer,*** letra de dieciocho puntos; ***long primer,*** letra de diez puntos.
primer (2) ['praimə], *s.* (*artill.*) pistón, fulminante, cebador.
primeval [prai'mi:vəl], *a.* original, primitivo, prístino.
priming ['praimiŋ], *s.* cebo (*de las armas*); preparación; (*pint.*) primera capa.
primiparous [prai'mipərəs], *a.* primípara.
primitive ['primitiv], *a.* primitivo; rudimentario. — *s.* primitivo.
primitiveness ['primitivnis], *s.* (lo) primitivo; (lo) rudimentario.

primness [ˈprimnis], *s.* (lo) remilgado, (lo) ñoño, (lo) monjil.
primogenital [praimoˈdʒenitəl], *a.* primogénito.
primogenitor [praimoˈdʒenitə], *s.* progenitor.
primogeniture [praimoˈdʒenitʃə], *s.* primogenitura.
primordial [praiˈmɔːdiəl], *a.* primordial.
primrose [ˈprimrouz], *s.* (*bot.*) primavera; ***primrose path,*** caminito de rosas.
prince [prins], *s.* príncipe; infante; ***Prince of Darkness,*** Príncipe de las tinieblas; ***Prince of Peace,*** Príncipe de la Paz.
princedom [ˈprinsdəm], *s.* principado.
princelike [ˈprinslaik], *a.* de príncipe.
princeliness [ˈprinslinis], *s.* magnificencia.
princeling [ˈprinsliŋ], *s.* principillo.
princely [ˈprinsli], *a.* principesco, magnífico.
princess [prinˈses], *s.* princesa.
principal [ˈprinsipəl], *a.* principal. — *s.* director; (*arq.*) jamba de fuerza; (*for.*) principal.
principality [prinsiˈpæliti], *s.* principado.
principle [ˈprinsipl], *s.* principio; ***in principle,*** en principio; ***on principle,*** por principio, por cuestión de principios; (*fam.*) porque sí, porque no.
print [print], *s.* impresión; letra; estampa, grabado; (*foto.*) impresión, positiva; (*tej.*) estampado; ***in print,*** impreso; en letra(s) de molde; disponible; ***out of print,*** agotado. — *v.t.* imprimir; estampar; grabar; escribir con letra de molde *o* con mayúsculas.
printed [ˈprintid], *a.* impreso; ***printed fabric,*** tejido estampado; ***printed matter,*** impresos, *m.pl.*
printer [ˈprintə], *s.* impresor.
printing [ˈprintiŋ], *s.* tipografía; impresión; tirada; ***printing-house, printing office,*** imprenta; ***printing-ink,*** tinta de imprenta; ***printing press,*** prensa tipográfica, imprenta.
prior [praiə], *a.* anterior, previo. — *adv.* — ***to,*** antes de. — *s.* prior.
priorate [ˈpriaərit], *s.* priorato.
prioress [ˈpraiəres], *s.* priora.
priority [praiˈɔriti], *s.* prioridad; preferencia; precedencia; prelación; ***in order of priority,*** por orden de preferencia *o* prelación; ***to get one's priorities right,*** hacer las cosas por orden de importancia, organizarse bien.
priorship [ˈpraiəʃip], *s.* priorato, priorazgo.
priory [ˈpraiəri], *s.* priorato.
prise [PRIZE (2)].
prism [ˈprizəm], *s.* prisma, *m.*
prismatic(al) [prizˈmætik(əl)], *a.* prismático.
prismoid [ˈprizmɔid], *a.* prismoide, en forma de prisma.
prison [prizn], *s.* cárcel, *f.*, prisión; ***prison camp,*** campo de concentración; ***prison-house,*** cárcel, *f.*; ***prison-van,*** coche celular; ***to put in prison,*** encarcelar, meter en la cárcel.
prisoner [ˈpriznə], *s.* prisionero; preso; reo, acusado; ***prisoner's base,*** rescate (*juego de muchachos*); ***prisoner of war,*** prisionero de guerra; ***to take prisoner,*** hacer prisionero.
prissy [ˈprisi], *a.* (*fam.*) [PRIM].
pristine [ˈpristain], *a.* prístino; impecable, inmaculado.
prithee [ˈpriði], *interj.* (*ant.*, *contr. de* **I pray thee**) te ruego.
prittle-prattle [ˈpritl-prætl], *s.* cháchara, *f.pl.*
privacy [ˈpraivəsi, ˈprivəsi], *s.* independencia; intimidad; secreto, reserva.
private [ˈpraivit], *a.* privado; particular; reservado; íntimo; ***to be private,*** estar solo; ser privado; ***in private,*** en privado; ***private (and confidential),*** confidencial; ***private enterprise,*** iniciativa(s) privada(s); ***private hearing,*** vista a puerta cerrada; ***private income,*** renta(s) personal(es), ingresos personales, *m.pl.*; ***in private life,*** en la intimidad; ***private parts,*** partes pudendas, *f.pl.*; ***private secretary,*** secretario particular; ***private view,*** inauguración privada; ***strictly private,*** muy reservado. — *s.* soldado raso.
privateer [praivəˈtiə], *s.* corsario. — *v.i.* navegar en corso.
privateering [praivəˈtiəriŋ], *s.* corso.
privately [ˈpraivitli], *adv.* secretamente, en privado; ***to sell privately,*** vender a un particular.
privateness [ˈpraivitnis], *s.* (lo) privado *o* reservado.
privation [praiˈveiʃən], *s.* privaciones, *f.pl.*, estrecheces, *f.pl.*
privative [ˈprivətiv], *a.* privativo. — *s.* carácter privativo; (*gram.*) prefijo negativo.
privet [ˈprivit], *s.* (*bot.*) aligustre.
privilege [ˈprivilidʒ], *s.* privilegio; prerrogativa; ***Parliamentary privilege,*** inmunidad parlamentaria. — *v.t.* privilegiar; ***I was privileged to,*** me cupo el privilegio de.
privily [ˈprivili], *adv.* privadamente; reservadamente.
privy [ˈprivi], *a.* privado; ***to be privy to,*** tener conocimiento secreto de; ser cómplice en; ***privy parts,*** partes pudendas, *f.pl.*; ***privy purse,*** gastos personales del rey, *m.pl.* — *s.* retrete.
prize (1) [praiz], *s.* premio; presa; ***first prize,*** primer premio; premio mayor; premio gordo; ***to be a lawful prize,*** ser de buena presa; ***prize-fight,*** pugilato, contienda de boxeo; ***prize-fighter,*** púgil, boxeador profesional; ***prize-fighting,*** pugilato, boxeo; ***prize fool,*** tonto de campeonato; ***prize-giving,*** distribución de premios; ***prize money,*** parte de presa; ***prize-winner,*** premiado; ***to draw a prize,*** sacar un premio. — *v.t.* apreciar, estimar.
prize (2), **prise** [praiz], *v.t.* — ***open,*** alzaprimar; abrir con palanca.
prizeman [ˈpraizmən], *s.* (*pl.* **-men** [-men]) laureado.
pro (1) [prou], *prep.* en pro de; (*fam.*) ***pro tem,*** provisional(mente). — *s.* (*pl.*) ***pros and cons,*** el pro y el contra.
pro (2) [prou], *s.* (*fam.*) professional.
probability [prɔbəˈbiliti], *s.* probabilidad.
probable [ˈprɔbəbl], *a.* probable.
probang [ˈproubæŋ], *s.* (*cir.*) sonda esofágica.
probate [ˈproubeit], *a.* (*for.*) testamentario. — *s.* comprobación (*de un testamento*), copia auténtica (*de un testamento*).
probation [proˈbeiʃən], *s.* probación; (*for.*) libertad condicional; ***on probation,*** bajo libertad condicional; a prueba.
probational, probationary [proˈbeiʃənəl, -əri], *a.* de libertad condicional; de prueba.
probationer [proˈbeiʃənə], *s.* persona en régimen de libertad condicional; novicio; aprendiz.
probative [ˈproubətiv], *a.* probatorio.
probe [proub], *s.* sonda; cohete de sonda; (*fig.*) investigación (***into,*** de); (*fam.*) globo sonda, *m.* — *v.t.* sondar, tentar; investigar, indagar.
probity [ˈproubiti], *s.* probidad.
problem [ˈprɔbləm], *s.* problema, *m.*; ***problem child,*** niño problema.
problematic(al) [prɔbləˈmætik(əl)], *a.* problemático.
proboscis [proˈbɔsis], *s.* (*pl.* **proboscides, proboscises** [-sidiːz, -siːz]) probóscide; (*irónico*) narizota.
procedural [proˈsiːdʒərəl], *a.* de procedimiento, procesal.
procedure [proˈsiːdʒə], *s.* procedimiento; proceder; tramitación, trámites, *m.pl.*
proceed [proˈsiːd], *v.i.* proceder; continuar, proseguir; ***proceed against,*** proceder contra, procesar; ***proceed from,*** proceder de, provenir de; ***proceed on one's way,*** (pro)seguir su camino; ***proceed to,*** proceder a; ir a; ponerse a;

proceed to say, decir a continuación; ***proceed with,*** seguir haciendo.
proceeding [pro'si:diŋ], *s.* proceder; procedimiento; (*pl.*) actas, *f.pl.*; proceso; ***to take proceedings (against),*** formular demanda (a), instruir causa (contra).
proceeds ['prousi:dz], *s.pl.* producto, ganancia.
process ['prouses], *s.* proceso; procedimiento; tratamiento; ***in the process of,*** en vías de; ***in the process of time,*** andando el tiempo, con el transcurso del tiempo. — *v.t.* elaborar, someter a un procedimiento *o* a un tratamiento.
procession [pro'seʃən], *s.* desfile; (*relig.*) procesión; ***funeral procession,*** cortejo fúnebre.
processional [pro'seʃənəl], *a.* procesional. — *s.* (libro) procesional.
proclaim [pro'kleim], *v.t.* proclamar.
proclaimer [pro'kleimə], *s.* proclamador.
proclamation [prɔklə'meiʃən], *s.* proclama; proclamación.
proclitic [pro'klitik], *a.* proclítico.
proclivity [pro'kliviti], *s.* proclividad.
proconsul [prou'kɔnsəl], *s.* procónsul.
proconsular [prou'kɔnsjulə], *a.* proconsular.
proconsulate, proconsulship [prou'kɔnsjulit, -səlʃip], *s.* proconsulado.
procrastinate [pro'kræstineit], *v.i.* andarse con dilaciones.
procrastination [prokræsti'neiʃən], *s.* dilaciones, *f.pl.*, dilatorias, *f.pl.*; morosidad.
procrastinator [pro'kræstineitə], *s.* moroso.
procreant ['proukriənt], *a.* procreante.
procreate ['proukrieit], *v.t.* procrear.
procreative ['proukrieitiv], *a.* procreador, generativo.
procreativeness [proukri'eitivnis], *s.* facultad de procrear.
procreator ['proukrieitə], *s.* procreador.
proctor ['prɔktə], *s.* (*for.*) procurador; censor (*de una universidad*).
proctorage ['prɔktəridʒ], *s.* procuración.
proctorship ['prɔktəʃip], *s.* cargo de procurador.
procumbent [prou'kʌmbənt], *a.* postrado, yacente.
procurable [pro'kjuərəbl], *a.* asequible, proporcionable.
procuration [prɔkju'reiʃən], *s.* (*for.*) procuración; gestión; alcahuetería.
procurator ['prɔkjureitə], *s.* procurador; apoderado.
procuratorship ['prɔkjureitəʃip], *s.* cargo de procurador.
procure [pro'kjuə], *v.t.* conseguir; procurar; proporcionar. — *v.i.* alcahuetear.
procurement [pro'kjuəmənt], *s.* alcahuetería; obtención, logro; procuración.
procurer [pro'kjuərə], *s.* tercero, alcahuete, (*fam.*) gancho.
procuress ['prɔkjuəris], *s.* alcahueta, tercera.
prod [prɔd], *s.* empujón (con el dedo); pinchazo. — *v.t.* empujar (con el dedo); pinchar.
prodigal ['prɔdigəl], *a.*, *s.* pródigo; ***prodigal son,*** hijo pródigo.
prodigality [prɔdi'gæliti], *s.* prodigalidad.
prodigious [prə'didʒəs], *a.* prodigioso, portentoso.
prodigiousness [prə'didʒəsnis], *s.* (lo) prodigioso, (lo) portentoso.
prodigy ['prɔdidʒi], *s.* prodigio; ***infant prodigy,*** niño prodigio.
prodomic [pro'dɔmik], *a.* prodómico.
produce ['prɔdju:s], *s.* producto(s). — [prə'dju:s], *v.t.* producir; (*geom.*) prolongar; presentar, sacar, mostrar; (*teat.*) poner en escena, dirigir. — *v.i.* producir, dar fruto.
producer [prə'dju:sə], *s.* (*teat.*) director de escena; productor; realizador.
producible [prə'dju:sibl], *a.* producible.
product ['prɔdʌkt], *s.* producto; ***gross national product,*** producto nacional bruto.
production [prə'dʌkʃən], *s.* producción; (*teat.*) realización; representación.
productive [prə'dʌktiv], *a.* productivo; fecundo; ***productive of,*** que produce, que fomenta, que causa; abundante *o* prolífico en.
productiveness, productivity [prə'dʌktivnis, prɔdʌk'tiviti], *s.* productividad; fecundidad; ***productivity agreement,*** convenio relativo a la productividad.
proem ['prouem], *s.* proemio.
proemial [pro'i:miəl], *a.* proemial.
profanation [prɔfə'neiʃən], *s.* profanación.
profane [prə'fein], *a.* profano; obsceno, soez. — *v.t.* profanar.
profaneness [prə'feinnis], *s.* profanidad, (lo) profano.
profaner [prə'feinə], *s.* profanador.
profanity [prə'fæniti], *s.* profanidad; blasfemia; obscenidad.
profess [prə'fes], *v.t.* profesar; declarar, confesar; manifestar; ***profess to be,*** pretender *o* querer ser. — *v.i.* profesar. — **profess o.s.,** *v.r.* — ***unable to etc.,*** declararse incapaz de *etc.*
professed [prə'fest], *a.* declarado; pretendido; profeso.
profession [prə'feʃən], *s.* profesión.
professional [prə'feʃənəl], *a.* profesional; de profesión; ***professional classes,*** clase profesional. — *s.* profesional; ***to turn professional,*** hacerse profesional.
professor [prə'fesə], *s.* catedrático; ***Professor Walsh,*** el profesor Walsh.
professorial [prɔfi'sɔ:riəl], *a.* de catedrático; numerario; profesoral.
professorship [prə'fesəʃip], *s.* cátedra.
proffer ['prɔfə], *v.t.* brindar, ofrecer.
proficiency [prə'fiʃənsi], *s.* capacidad, aptitud.
proficient [prə'fiʃənt], *a.* capacitado, apto; ***proficient in,*** con buenos conocimientos de.
profile ['proufail], *s.* perfil; ***in profile,*** de perfil. — *v.t.* perfilar.
profit ['prɔfit], *s.* provecho; beneficio, ganancia; ***gross profit,*** ganancia total *o* en bruto; ***net profit,*** beneficio neto, ganancia neta; ***profit and loss,*** ganancias y pérdidas, *f.pl.* — *v.t.* servir a, aprovechar a, ser útil a. — *v.i.* — ***by, from,*** aprovechar, sacar provecho *o* partido de.
profitability, profitableness [prɔfitə'biliti, 'prɔfitəblnis], *s.* (lo) provechoso; rentabilidad.
profitable ['prɔfitəbl], *a.* provechoso, lucrativo; rentable.
profiteer [prɔfi'tiə], *s.* logrero, logrón; explotador. — *v.i.* logrear, ser logrón; explotar.
profitless ['prɔfitlis], *a.* infructuoso.
profligacy ['prɔfligəsi], *s.* libertinaje.
profligate ['prɔfligit], *a.*, *s.* libertino, disoluto.
profound [prə'faund], *a.* profundo, hondo.
profundity [prə'fʌnditi], *s.* profundidad, hondura.
profuse [prə'fju:s], *a.* profuso; exuberante.
profuseness, profusion [prə'fju:snis, prə'fju:ʒən], *s.* profusión; exuberancia.
progenitor [pro'dʒenitə], *s.* progenitor.
progeniture [pro'dʒenitʃə], *s.* progenitura.
progeny ['prɔdʒini], *s.* progenie, *f.*, prole, *f.*, progenitura.
prognathism ['prɔgnəθizəm], *s.* prognatismo.
prognathous [prɔg'neiθəs], *a.* prognato.
prognosis [prɔg'nousis], *s.* (*pl.* **prognoses** [-si:z]) prognosis, *f.inv.*; vaticinio, pronóstico.
prognostic [prɔg'nɔstik], *a.* pronosticador. — *s.* pronóstico.
prognosticable [prɔg'nɔstikəbl], *a.* pronosticable.
prognosticate [prɔg'nɔstikeit], *v.t.* pronosticar.

prognostication [prɔgnɔsti'keiʃən], *s.* pronosticación; pronóstico.
prognosticator [prɔg'nɔstikeitə], *s.* pronosticador, vaticinador.
programme ['prougræm], *s.* programa, *m.* — *v.t.* programar (*máquinas calculadoras*).
programmer ['prougræmə], *s.* programador (*de máquinas calculadoras*).
progress ['prougres], *s.* progreso(s), adelanto(s); marcha, curso; ***in progress,*** en vía(s) de realizarse; ***to make progress,*** adelantar, hacer progresos; ***progress report,*** informe sobre el progreso *o* sobre los progresos. — [pro'gres], *v.i.* progresar, hacer progresos; avanzar, marchar; cundir.
progression [pro'greʃən], *s.* progresión.
progressional [pro'greʃənəl], *a.* de progresión.
progressist [prou'gresist], *a.*, *s.* progresista, *m.f.*
progressive [pro'gresiv], *a.*, *s.* progresivo.
progressiveness [pro'gresivnis], *s.* (lo) progresivo.
prohibit [prou'hibit], *v.t.* prohibir; vedar.
prohibition [prouhi'biʃən], *s.* prohibición; veda; ***prohibition law,*** ley seca.
prohibitionism [prouhi'biʃənizəm], *a.* prohibicionismo.
prohibitionist [prouhi'biʃənist], *s.* prohibicionista (*de bebidas alcohólicas*), *m.f.*
prohibitive, prohibitory [prou'hibitiv, prou'hibitəri], *a.* prohibitivo.
project ['prɔdʒekt], *s.* proyecto; plan. — [pro'dʒekt], *v.t.* proyectar. — *v.i.* sobresalir.
projectile [pro'dʒektail], *a.* proyectante; arrojadizo. — *s.* proyectil.
projecting [pro'dʒektiŋ], *a.* saledizo, saliente.
projection [prə'dʒekʃən], *s.* proyección; saliente, resalte.
projector [prə'dʒektə], *s.* proyector.
prolapse ['proulæps], *s.* prolapso.
prolate ['prouleit], *a.* (*geom.*) prolongado hacia los polos.
prolegomenon [proule'gɔminən], *s.* (*u. más en pl.* **prolegomena** [-ə]) prolegómeno.
prolepsis [prou'lepsis], *s.* (*pl.* **prolepses** [-si:z]) prolepsis, *f.inv.*
proletarian [prouli'tɛəriən], *a.*, *s.* proletario.
proletariat(e) [prouli'tɛəriət], *s.* proletariado.
proliferate [pro'lifəreit], *v.i.* proliferar.
proliferation [prolifə'reiʃən], *s.* proliferación.
prolific [prə'lifik], *a.* prolífico, fecundo.
prolificness [prə'lifiknis], *s.* fecundidad.
prolix ['prouliks], *a.* prolijo.
prolixity [prou'liksiti], *s.* prolijidad.
prolocutor [prou'lɔkjutə], *s.* presidente (*de una asamblea*); portavoz, *m.*
prologue ['proulɔg], *s.* prólogo. — *v.t.* prologar.
prolong [pro'lɔŋ], *v.t.* prolongar; alargar.
prolongation [proulɔŋ'geiʃən], *s.* prolongación.
prom [prɔm], *s.* (*fam.*, *abrev.*) [PROMENADE] paseo marítimo.
promenade [prɔmi'nɑ:d], *s.* paseo; paseo marítimo; ***promenade concert,*** concierto durante el cual se pasea el público; (*mar.*) ***promenade-deck,*** cubierta de paseo. — *v.i.* pasear(se).
promenader [prɔmi'nɑ:də], *s.* paseante.
Prometheus [pro'mi:θiəs]. Prometeo.
prominence ['prɔminəns], *s.* prominencia; eminencia; (lo) destacado.
prominent ['prɔminənt], *a.* prominente; saltón, protuberante; eminente, sobresaliente, destacado, relevante.
promiscuity, promiscuousness [prɔmis'kju:iti, prə'miskjuəsnis], *s.* promiscuidad.
promiscuous [prə'miskjuəs], *a.* promiscuo.
promise ['prɔmis], *s.* promesa; ***to be of*** o ***have*** (***great***) ***promise,*** prometer (mucho); ***to break one's promise,*** faltar a su palabra; ***to keep one's promise,*** cumplir su palabra *o* promesa; ***under promise of,*** bajo (su) palabra de. — *v.t.* prometer; augurar. — *v.i.* prometer; ***promised land,*** tierra de promisión.
promising ['prɔmisiŋ], *a.* prometedor, que promete.
promissory ['prɔmisəri], *a.* promisorio; ***promissory note,*** pagaré, *m.*
promontory ['prɔməntəri], *s.* promontorio.
promote [prə'mout], *v.t.* promover; fomentar; (*rango*) ascender; apoyar; (*com.*) fundar, financiar; gestionar; promocionar.
promoter [prə'moutə], *s.* promotor, promovedor; fundador; (*dep.*) empresario.
promotion [prə'mouʃən], *s.* promoción; fomento; ascenso.
promotive [prə'moutiv], *a.* promovedor, que protege.
prompt [prɔmpt], *a.* puntual; pronto, inmediato; en punto; ***prompt payment,*** pronto pago. — *s.* (*teat.*) apunte; (*teat.*) ***prompt-book,*** libro del apuntador *o* traspunte; ***prompt-box,*** concha del apuntador. — *v.t.* mover, incitar, provocar; inspirar; (*teat.*) apuntar; (*fam.*) soplar.
prompter ['prɔmptə], *s.* incitador, instigador; (*teat.*) apuntador.
promptitude, promptness ['prɔmptitju:d, 'prɔmptnis], *s.* puntualidad; prontitud, presteza, diligencia.
promptly ['prɔmptli], *adv.* puntualmente; sin dilación; con rapidez.
promulgate ['prɔmʌlgeit], *v.t.* promulgar; proclamar, publicar.
promulgation [prɔmʌl'geiʃən], *s.* promulgación; publicación, declaración oficial.
promulgator ['prɔmʌlgeitə], *s.* promulgador; publicador.
prone [proun], *a.* postrado; prono; ***prone to,*** propenso a.
proneness ['prounnis], *s.* postración; propensión.
prong [prɔŋ], *s.* punta; púa, pincho; diente.
prongbuck, pronghorn ['prɔŋbʌk, -hɔ:n], *s.* (*zool.*) antílope norteamericano.
pronged [prɔŋd], *a.* dentado, provisto de púas.
pronominal [prou'nɔminəl], *a.* pronominal.
pronoun ['prounaun], *s.* pronombre.
pronounce [prə'nauns], *v.t.* pronunciar. — *v.i.* pronunciarse.
pronounceable [prə'naunsəbl], *a.* pronunciable.
pronounced [prə'naunst], *a.* pronunciado, marcado, fuerte.
pronouncement [prə'naunsmənt], *s.* declaración; juicio, opinión.
pronouncing [prə'naunsiŋ], *a.* de pronunciación.
pronunciation [prənʌnsi'eiʃən], *s.* pronunciación.
proof [pru:f], *a.* normal en graduación (*de alcohol*); ***proof against,*** insensible a; a prueba de. — *s.* prueba; ***cast-iron proof,*** prueba irrefutable *o* incontrovertible; ***the proof of the pudding is in the eating,*** la calidad se demuestra con el uso; ***proof-reader,*** corrector de pruebas; ***proof-reading,*** corrección de pruebas; ***proof-sheet,*** prueba; ***to bring*** *o* ***put to the proof,*** poner a prueba; ***to stand the proof of time,*** demostrar a lo largo de los años su valer. — *v.t.* impermeabilizar.
prop [prɔp], *s.* apoyo, sostén; puntal; (*agric.*) rodrigón; (*min.*) entibo. — *v.t.* apoyar, sostener; apuntalar; entibar.
propagable ['prɔpəgəbl], *a.* propagable.
propaganda [prɔpə'gændə], *a.* propagandístico. — *s.* propaganda (política).
propagandist [prɔpə'gændist], *s.* propagandista, *m.f.*
propagate ['prɔpəgeit], *v.t.* propagar. — *v.i.* propagarse.
propagation [prɔpə'geiʃən], *s.* propagación.
propagative ['prɔpəgeitiv], *a.* propagativo.

propagator [ˈprɔpəgeitə], *s.* propagador.
propel [prəˈpel], *v.t.* impulsar; propulsar; impeler.
propellent [prəˈpelənt], *a., s.* propulsor.
propeller [prəˈpelə], *s.* hélice, *f.*
propensity [prəˈpensiti], *s.* propensión, tendencia.
proper [ˈprɔpə], *a.* propio; conveniente, apropiado, adecuado; decoroso, decente; exacto, justo, correcto; (*gram.*) propio; hecho y derecho; consumado; ***China proper,*** la China propiamente dicha; (*gram.*) ***proper noun*** o ***name,*** nombre propio; (*fam.*) ***a proper rascal,*** un sinvergüenza de tomo y lomo; ***in the proper sense,*** en el sentido exacto (de la palabra); ***what is proper,*** (lo) propio; (lo) adecuado.
properly [ˈprɔpəli], *adv.* bien, debidamente, como es debido, como Dios manda, en condiciones; correctamente; (*fam.*) totalmente.
property [ˈprɔpəti], *s.* propiedad; bienes, *m.pl.*; hacienda; (*pl., teat.*) accesorios, *m.pl.*; ***man of property,*** hacendado; ***personal property,*** bienes muebles.
prophecy [ˈprɔfisi], *s.* profecía, vaticinio.
prophesy [ˈprɔfisai], *v.t., v.i.* profetizar, vaticinar.
prophet [ˈprɔfit], *s.* profeta, *m.*
prophetess [ˈprɔfites], *s.* profetisa.
prophetic [proˈfetik], *a.* profético.
prophylactic [prɔfiˈlæktik], *a., s.* (*med.*) profiláctico.
prophylaxis [prɔfiˈlæksis], *s.* profilaxis, *f.inv.*
propinquity [proˈpiŋkwiti], *s.* propincuidad.
propitiate [prəˈpiʃirit], *v.t.* propiciar; conciliar.
propitiation [prəpiʃiˈeiʃən], *s.* propiciación; expiación.
propitiator [prəˈpiʃieitə], *s.* propiciador.
propitiatory [prəˈpiʃieitəri], *a., s.* propiciatorio.
propitious [prəˈpiʃəs], *a.* propicio.
propitiousness [prəˈpiʃəsnis], *s.* (lo) propicio.
proponent [prəˈpounənt], *s.* proponedor, proponente.
proportion [prəˈpɔːʃən], *s.* proporción; ***in proportion,*** en proporción; ***in proportion as,*** a medida que; ***in proportion to,*** en proporción con; a medida de; ***out of proportion,*** desproporcionado; ***to be out of proportion,*** no guardar proporción; ***to lose all sense of proportion,*** perder completamente el sentido de la proporción. — *v.t.* proporcionar.
proportionable [prəˈpɔːʃənəbl], *a.* proporcionable.
proportionableness [prəˈpɔːʃənəblnis], *s.* proporcionalidad.
proportionably [prəˈpɔːʃənəbli], *adv.* proporcionadamente, proporcionablemente.
proportional [prəˈpɔːʃənəl], *a.* proporcional, en proporción; (*pol.*) ***proportional representation,*** representación proporcional. — *s.* (*mat.*) proporcional.
proportionate [prəˈpɔːʃənit], *a.* proporcionado. — [-eit], *v.t.* proporcionar, ajustar.
proportionless [prəˈpɔːʃənlis], *a.* desproporcionado, sin proporción.
proposal [prəˈpouzl], *s.* propuesta; proposición; oferta; ***proposal of marriage,*** declaración de matrimonio.
propose [prəˈpouz], *v.t.* proponer. — *v.i.* declararse; ***propose to,*** tener idea de, pensar; ***propose (to s.o.),*** declararse (a alguien).
proposer [prəˈpouzə], *s.* proponedor, proponente.
proposition [prɔpəˈziʃən], *s.* proposición; oferta; empresa, cosa, asunto, problema, *m.*; ***it's not a paying proposition,*** no es rentable.
propound [prəˈpaund], *v.t.* proponer.
propounder [prəˈpaundə], *s.* proponedor, proponente.
proprietary [prəˈpraiətəri], *a.* (de) propietario; ***proprietary brand,*** marca registrada. — *s.* propietaro, dueño; pertenencia, propiedad.
proprietor [prəˈpraiətə], *s.* propietario, dueño.
proprietorship [prəˈpraiətəʃip], *s.* propiedad; dominio.
proprietress [prəˈpraiətris], *s.* propietaria, dueña.
propriety [prəˈpraiiti], *s.* corrección, decoro.
props [prɔps], *s.pl.* (*fam., teat.*) guardarropía.
propulsion [prəˈpʌlʃən], *s.* propulsión; impulso.
propulsive [prəˈpʌlsiv], *a.* propulsor, impelente.
pro rata [prou ˈrɑːtə], *frase adv.* prorrata.
prorogation [prourouˈgeiʃən], *s.* prorrogación; prórroga.
prorogue [proˈroug], *v.t.* prorrogar; (*pol.*) suspender (las sesiones del Parlamento).
prosaic [proˈzeiik], *a.* prosaico.
prosaism [ˈprouzeiizəm], *s.* proaísmo.
proscenium [proˈsiːniəm], *s.* proscenio.
proscribe [proˈskraib], *v.t.* proscribir.
proscriber [proˈskraibə], *s.* proscriptor.
proscript [ˈprouskript], *s.* proscrito.
proscription [proˈskripʃən], *s.* proscripción.
proscriptive [proˈskriptiv], *a.* proscriptivo.
prose [prouz], *a.* de prosa, en prosa. — *s.* prosa; traducción inversa; ***prose-writer,*** prosista, *m.f.*
prosecute [ˈprɔsikjuːt], *v.t.* proseguir, continuar; (*for.*) procesar, demandar.
prosecution [prɔsiˈkjuːʃən], *s.* prosecución; cumplimiento; (*for.*) procesamiento; (*for.*) parte actora, demandante; fiscal.
prosecutor [ˈprɔsikjuːtə], *s.* (*for.*) demandante, acusador; ***public prosecutor,*** fiscal.
prosecutrix [ˈprɔsikjuːtriks], *s.* (*pl.* **prosecutrices** [-trisiz]) (*for.*) acusadora, demandante.
proselyte [ˈprɔsilait], *s.* prosélito.
proselytism [ˈprɔsilitizəm], *s.* proselitismo.
proselytize [ˈprɔsilitaiz], *v.t.* hacer prosélito(s) de. — *v.i.* hacer prosélitos.
prosily [ˈprouzili], *adv.* con mucha verbosidad.
prosody [ˈprɔsədi], *s.* métrica.
prosopopœia [prɔsopoˈpiə], *s.* (*ret.*) prosopopeya.
prospect [ˈprɔspekt], *s.* perspectiva; panorama, *m.*; probabilidad, posiblidad; ***to have in prospect,*** tener en perspectiva; ***to have no prospects,*** no tener porvenir; ***to hold out the prospect of,*** dar *u* ofrecer esperanzas de. — [prɔsˈpekt], *v.t.* explorar, hacer prospecciones en. — *v.i.* realizar prospecciones (***for,*** en busca de).
prospective [prəsˈpektiv], *a.* presunto; esperado, probable; futuro.
prospector [prəsˈpektə], *s.* (*min.*) prospector.
prospectus [prəsˈpektəs], *s.* prospecto.
prosper [ˈprɔspə], *v.t.* favorecer, hacer medrar. — *v.i.* prosperar, florecer, medrar.
prosperity, prosperousness [prɔsˈperiti, ˈprɔspərəsnis], *s.* prosperidad.
prosperous [ˈprɔspərəs], *a.* próspero; floreciente; acomodado.
prostate [ˈprɔsteit], *s.* (*anat.*) próstata.
prostatic [prɔsˈtætik], *a.* prostático.
prosthesis [ˈprɔsθisis], *s.* prótesis, *f.*
prostitute [ˈprɔstitjuːt], *s.* prostituta. — *v.t.* prostituir.
prostitution [prɔstiˈtjuːʃən], *s.* prostitución.
prostrate [ˈprɔstreit], *a.* postrado, prosternado; abatido; (*biol.*) tendido. — *v.t.* postrar; abatir. — **prostrate o.s.,** *v.r.* postrarse.
prostration [prɔsˈtreiʃən], *s.* postración; abatimiento; (*med.*) agotamiento, adinamia.
prosy [ˈprouzi], *a.* prolijo, largo y pesado; prosaico.
protagonist [proˈtægənist], *s.* protagonista, *m.f.*
protasis [ˈprɔtəsis], *s.* prótasis, *f.inv.*
protatic [proˈtætik], *a.* protático.
protean [ˈproutiən], *a.* proteico.
protect [proˈtekt], *v.t.* proteger.
protection [proˈtekʃən], *s.* protección; salvoconducto; (*pol.*) proteccionismo.
protectionism [proˈtekʃənizəm], *s.* proteccionismo.

protectionist [pro'tekʃənist], *a., s.* proteccionista, *m.f.*
protective [pro'tektiv], *a.* protector; proteccionista. — *s.* amparo, resguardo.
protector [pro'tektə], *s.* protector.
protectoral, protectorial [pro'tektərəl, proutek'tɔ:riəl], *a.* (de) protector.
protectorate [pro'tektərit], *s.* protectorado; protectoría.
protectorship [pro'tektəʃip], *s.* protectorado.
protectress [pro'tektris], *s.* protectriz, protectora.
protectrix [pro'tektriks], (*pl.* **protectrices** [-risiz]) [PROTECTRESS].
protein ['prouti:n], *s.* proteína.
protend [pro'tend], *v.t.* tender, alargar.
protest ['proutest], *s.* protesta; protestación; (*com.*) protesto; ***under protest,*** contra la voluntad de uno, mal que le pese a uno. — [pro'test], *v.t.* protestar; ***protest one's innocence,*** declarar enérgicamente su inocencia. — *v.i.* protestar (***at,*** de; ***against,*** contra).
Protestant ['prɔtistənt], *a., s.* protestante.
Protestantism ['prɔtistəntizəm], *s.* protestantismo.
protestation [prɔtes'teiʃən], *s.* protesta; protestación; declaración.
protester [pro'testə], *s.* persona que protesta.
protocol ['proutəkɔl], *s.* protocolo. — *v.t.* protocolizar, protocolar.
protomartyr ['proutomɑ:tə], *s.* protomártir.
protoplasm ['proutoplæzəm], *s.* protoplasma, *m.*
prototype ['proutotaip], *s.* prototipo.
prototypical [prouto'tipikəl], *a.* prototípico.
protoxide [pro'tɔksaid], *s.* protóxido.
protoxidize [pro'tɔksidaiz], *v.t.* protoxidar.
protract [pro'trækt], *v.t.* alargar, prolongar, dilatar; (*geom.*) levantar (*un plano*) con el transportador.
protracted [pro'træktid], *a.* largo, prolongado.
protraction [pro'trækʃən], *s.* prolongación.
protractor [pro'træktə], *s.* (*geom.*) transportador; (*anat.*) músculo extensor.
protrude [pro'tru:d], *v.t.* hacer salir, sacar. — *v.i.* (sobre)salir, salir fuera.
protruding [pro'tru:diŋ], *a.* saliente, que sobresale; ***protruding eyes,*** ojos saltones, *m.pl.*
protrusion [pro'tru:ʒən], *s.* (el) salir *o* avanzar hacia fuera.
protrusive [pro'tru:siv], *a.* saliente, protuberante.
protuberance [pro'tju:bərəns], *s.* protuberancia.
protuberant [pro'tju:bərənt], *a.* protuberante.
proud [praud], *a.* orgulloso; soberbio; espléndido, magnífico; ***to be proud of,*** estar orgulloso de, enorgullecerse de; ***proud flesh,*** carnosidad, bezo. — *adv.* ***to do o.s. proud,*** darse buena vida, pegarse una vidorra; ***to do s.o. proud,*** tratar a alguien a cuerpo de rey.
prove [pru:v], *v.t.* probar; demostrar; confirmar. — *v.i.* resultar, ser; ***it proved difficult,*** fue difícil; ***it proved otherwise,*** no fue así.
proven ['prouvən], *a.* probado, demostrado. — *p.p. irr.* [PROVE].
provenance ['prɔvinəns], *s.* procedencia.
Provençal [prɔvən'sɑ:l], *a., s.* provenzal.
Provence [prɔ'vɔns]. Provenza.
provender ['prɔvində], *s.* forraje; (*fam.*) pitanza.
proverb ['prɔvə:b], *s.* refrán.
proverbial [prə'və:biəl], *a.* proverbial.
provide [prə'vaid], *v.t.* proveer (***with,*** de); proporcionar. — *v.i.* — ***against,*** precaverse de; ***provide for,*** prevenir; proporcionar lo necesario para; asegurar el porvenir de; ***provide that,*** estipular que; ***to be well provided for,*** tener todo lo necesario, no faltarle a uno nada; ***the Lord will provide,*** Dios proveerá.
provided [prə'vaidid], *conj.* (***that***) siempre que, con tal (de) que.
providence ['prɔvidəns], *s.* providencia; previsión; ***Providence,*** la Providencia.
provident ['prɔvidənt], *a.* previsor.
providential [prɔvi'denʃəl], *a.* providencial.
provider [prə'vaidə], *s.* proveedor.
province ['prɔvins], *s.* provincia; (*fig.*) incumbencia; competencia; ***it's not my province,*** no es de mi incumbencia *o* competencia.
provincial [prə'vinʃəl], *a.* provincial, de provincia; (*despec.*) provinciano. — *s.* provinciano.
provincialism [prə'vinʃəlizəm], *s.* provincialismo.
provision [prə'viʒən], *s.* provisión; disposición; previsión; (*pl.*) provisiones, *f.pl.*, víveres, *m.pl.*; ***to make provision for,*** prevenir; asegurar el porvenir de. — *v.t.* aprovisionar, abastecer.
provisional [prə'viʒənəl], *a.* provisional, interino.
proviso [prə'vaizou], *s.* estipulación; salvedad.
provisor [prə'vaizə], *s.* proveedor.
provisorily [prə'vaizərili], *adv.* condicionalmente.
provisory [prə'vaizəri], *a.* provisorio; condicional.
provocation [prɔvə'keiʃən], *s.* provocación.
provocative [prə'vɔkətiv], *a.* provocativo, provocador.
provoke [prə'vouk], *v.t.* provocar; incitar; causar, motivar; indignar, irritar.
provoker [prə'voukə], *s.* provocador.
provoking [prə'voukiŋ], *a.* provocativo.
provost ['prɔvəst], *s.* preboste; provisor; (*Esco.*) alcalde; (*Ingl.*) director de colegio; (*mil.*) ***provost marshal,*** capitán preboste.
provostship ['prɔvəstʃip], *s.* prebostazgo.
prow [prau], *s.* proa, tajamar.
prowess ['praues], *s.* destreza; (gran) capacidad.
prowl [praul], *s.* ronda; ***to be on the prowl,*** rondar. — *v.i.* rondar, merodear.
prowler ['praulə], *s.* rondador, merodeador.
proximate ['prɔksimit], *a.* inmediato, próximo.
proximately ['prɔksimitli], *adv.* inmediatamente, próximamente.
proximity [prɔk'simiti], *s.* proximidad, cercanía.
proxy ['prɔksi], *s.* procuración, poder; poderhabiente; ***to marry by proxy,*** casarse por poderes.
prude [pru:d], *s.* mojigato, gazmoño.
prudence ['pru:dəns], *s.* prudencia.
prudent, prudential ['pru:dənt, pru:'denʃəl], *a.* prudente; prudencial.
prudery ['pru:dəri], *s.* mojigatería, gazmoñería.
prudish ['pru:diʃ], *a.* mojigato, gazmoño.
prune (1) [pru:n], *s.* ciruela pasa.
prune (2) [pru:n], *v.t.* podar, escamondar.
pruner ['pru:nə], *s.* podador.
pruniferous [pru:'nifərəs], *a.* que produce ciruelas.
pruning ['pru:niŋ], *s.* poda, escamonda; ***pruning-hook, pruning-knife,*** podadera.
prurience, pruriency ['pruriəns, -i], *s.* lujuria, lascivia; prurito.
prurient ['pruəriənt], *a.* lujurioso, lascivo.
prurigo [pru'raigou], *s.* prurigo.
Prussia ['prʌʃə]. Prusia.
Prussian ['prʌʃən], *a., s.* prusiano; ***Prussian blue,*** azul de Prusia.
prussiate ['prʌsiit], *s.* prusiato.
prussic ['prʌsik], *a.* prúsico; ***prussic acid,*** ácido prúsico.
pry [prai], *v.t.* alzaprimar, levantar con palanca; ***pry out a secret,*** arrancar un secreto, sonsacar a alguien, meterle los dedos a alguien. — *v.i.* fisgar, fisgonear; curiosear; ***pry into other people's business,*** (entro)meterse en asuntos ajenos.
prying ['praiiŋ], *a.* fisgón, curioso, entrometido.
psalm [sɑ:m], *s.* salmo; cántico.
psalmist ['sɑ:mist], *s.* salmista, *m.*
psalmody ['sælmədi], *s.* salmodia.
psalter ['sɔltə], *s.* salterio.

psaltery [ˈsɔltəri], *s.* (*mús.*) salterio.
pseudo [ˈsjuːdou], *a.* seudo; falso, pretendido.
pseudomorphous [sjuːdouˈmɔːfəs], *a.* seudomorfo.
pseudonym [ˈsjuːdonim], *s.* seudónimo.
pseudonymous [sjuːˈdɔniməs], *a.* seudónimo.
pseudoscope [ˈsjuːdoskoup], *s.* seudoscopio.
pshaw! [pʃɔː], *interj.* ¡bah!
psoriasis [soˈraiəsis], *s.* (*med.*) soriasis, *f.inv.*
Psyche [ˈsaiki]. Psique.
psyche [ˈsaiki], *s.* psique, *f.*
psychiatrist [saiˈkaiətrist], *s.* psiquiatra, *m.f.*
psychiatry [saiˈkaiətri], *s.* psiquiatría.
psychic [ˈsaikik], *a.* psíquico; (*fam.*) clarividente.
psychoanalyse [saikoˈænəlaiz], *v.t.* psicoanalizar.
psychoanalysis [saikouəˈnælisis], *s.* psicoanálisis, *m.inv.*
psychoanalyst [saikoˈænəlist], *s.* psicoanalista, *m.f.*
psychological [saikoˈlɔdʒikəl], *a.* psicológico.
psychologist [saiˈkɔlədʒist], *s.* psicólogo.
psychology [saiˈkɔlədʒi], *s.* psicología.
psychopath [ˈsaikopæθ], *s.* psicópata, *m.f.*
psychopathic [saikoˈpæθik], *a.* psicopático.
psychosis [saiˈkousis], *s.* psicosis, *f.inv.*
psychrometer [saiˈkrɔmitə], *s.* psicómetro.
ptarmigan [ˈtɑːmigən], *s.* (*orn.*) perdiz blanca.
ptisan [ˈtizən], *s.* tisana.
Ptolemy [ˈtɔləmi]. Tolomeo.
ptomaine [ˈtoumein], *s.* ptomaína.
ptyalin [ˈtaiəlin], *s.* ptialina.
ptyalism [ˈtaiəlizəm], *s.* tialismo.
pub [pʌb], *s.* (*fam.*, *abrev.*) [PUBLIC HOUSE]; taberna; ***pub-crawl,*** chateo (de tasca en tasca); ***to go on a pub-crawl,*** ir de chateo, ir a copear, ir de copeo.
puberty [ˈpjuːbəti], *s.* pubertad.
pubes [ˈpjuːbiːz], *s.* pubis, *m.inv.*
pubescence [pjuːˈbesəns], *s.* pubescencia.
pubescent [pjuːˈbesənt], *a.* pubescente.
pubic [ˈpjuːbik], *a.* púbico.
public [ˈpʌblik], *a.* público; ***public address system,*** sistema acústico amplificador; ***public enemy,*** enemigo público; ***public house,*** taberna; ***public school,*** colegio interno (privado); (*Am.*) escuela (pública), instituto; ***public spirit,*** civismo, espíritu cívico. — *s.* público; ***in public,*** en público.
publican [ˈpʌblikən], *s.* tabernero; publicano.
publication [pʌbliˈkeiʃən], *s.* publicación.
publicist [ˈpʌblisist], *s.* publicista, *m.f.*
publicity [pʌbˈlisiti], *s.* publicidad; propaganda comercial.
publicize [ˈpʌblisaiz], *v.t.* publicar, dar publicidad a, anunciar.
publish [ˈpʌbliʃ], *v.t.* publicar, editar.
publisher [ˈpʌbliʃə], *s.* editor.
publishing [ˈpʌbliʃiŋ], *s.* publicación (*de libros*); ***publishing house,*** editorial, casa editorial.
puccoon [pəˈkuːn], *s.* (*bot.*) orcaneta, onoquiles, *f.inv.*
puce [pjuːs], *a.*, *s.* (de) color castaño rojizo.
puck [pʌk], *s.* duende.
pucker [ˈpʌkə], *s.* fruncido. — *v.t.* fruncir, arrugar (*entrecejo*); arrugar (*labios*).
puckish [ˈpʌkiʃ], *a.* travieso; ***puckish humour,*** espíritu juguetón, humor travieso.
pudding [ˈpudiŋ], *s.* postre dulce; ***black pudding,*** morcilla; ***rice pudding,*** arroz con leche.
puddle [pʌdl], *s.* charco. — *v.t.* pudelar.
puddler [ˈpʌdlə], *s.* (*fund.*) pudelador.
puddling [ˈpʌdliŋ], *s.* (*fund.*) pudelación; ***puddling furnace,*** horno de pudelar.
puddly [ˈpʌdli], *a.* lleno de charcos.
pudency [ˈpjuːdənsi], *s.* pudor, recato.
pudge [pʌdʒ], *s.* (*fam.*) gordiflón, gordinflón, regordete.
pudgy [ˈpʌdʒi], *a.* (*fam.*) gordiflón, gordinflón, regordete.
puerile [ˈpjuərail], *a.* pueril.
puerility [pjuəˈriliti], *s.* puerilidad.
puerperal [pjuːˈəːpərəl], *a.* puerperal; ***puerperal fever,*** fiebre puerperal, *f.*
puet [ˈpjuːit], *s.* gallineta.
puff [pʌf], *s.* soplo, soplido; resuello; (*viento*) racha; bocanada; humareda; (*coc.*) pastelillo de crema; (*publicidad*) bombo; (*bot.*) ***puff-ball,*** bejín; (*coc.*) ***puff-pastry,*** hojaldre. — *v.t.* soplar; ***puff out,*** echar, arrojar (*humo*); ***puff up,*** hinchar, inflar. — *v.i.* soplar; ***puff and blow,*** jadear; resollar, resoplar; ***puff at,*** chupar; ***puff like a grampus,*** resoplar como una locomotora; ***puff out,*** salir echando humo.
puffed [pʌft], *a.* hinchado; ***to be puffed,*** estar sin aliento; ***to be puffed up,*** estar engreído.
puffer [ˈpʌfə], *s.* soplador; (*infantil*) trenecito.
puffin [ˈpʌfin], *s.* (*orn.*) frailecillo.
puffiness [ˈpʌfinis], *s.* (lo) esponjoso; abotargamiento.
puffy [ˈpʌfi], *a.* esponjoso; abotargado.
pug [pʌg], *s.* perro dogo pequeño, doguillo; ***pug-dog,*** perro dogo pequeño; ***pug-nosed,*** de nariz respingona *o* chata.
pugilism [ˈpjuːdʒilizəm], *s.* pugilato, pugilismo.
pugilist [ˈpjuːdʒilist], *s.* púgil.
pugilistic [pjuːdʒiˈlistik], *a.* de pugilato.
pugnacious [pʌgˈneiʃəs], *a.* pugnaz, belicoso; chulo.
pugnacity [pʌgˈnæsiti], *s.* pugnacidad, belicosidad; chulería.
puissance [ˈpwiːsəns], *s.* pujanza.
puissant [ˈpwiːsənt], *a.* pujante.
puke [pjuːk], *v.t.*, *v.i.* vomitar.
pukka [ˈpʌkə], *a.* (*fam.*) fetén.
pulchritude [ˈpʌlkritjuːd], *s.* belleza.
pule [pjuːl], *v.i.* lloriquear, gemir.
puling [ˈpjuːliŋ], *a.* que lloriquea. — *s.* lloriqueo.
pull [pul], *s.* tirón; chupada; (*fam.*) trago; tirador (*de campanilla*); (*impr.*) prueba, (primeras) pruebas; (*influencia*) enchufe, buenas aldabas, *f.pl.*; (*fam.*) ***it's a long pull,*** es un buen trecho, es una buena caminata; es una buena subida; (*fam.*) ***to have*** o ***take a pull,*** echar un trago. — *v.t.* tirar de; arrastrar; (*músculo*) torcerse; ***pull about,*** manosear; estropear; ***pull along,*** arrastrar; ***pull back,*** tirar hacia atrás de; ***pull down,*** tirar hacia abajo de; derribar; rebajar; ***pull faces,*** hacer muecas, visajes; ***pull a fast one on s.o.,*** dársela a alguien, dar gato por liebre a alguien; ***pull in,*** tirar hacia dentro de; (*cuerda*) cobrar; detener (*a un delincuente*); ***pull off,*** arrancar (de un tirón); (*fam.*) ***pull it off,*** conseguirlo; ***pull on,*** tirar de; ***pull out,*** sacar; arrancar; estirar; ***pull no punches*** [PUNCH (I)]; ***pull through,*** sacar (de), ayudar a vencer; ***pull to pieces,*** deshacer, destrozar; (*una hipótesis etc.*) dar al traste con; (*pers.*) poner de vuelta y media; ***pull the trigger,*** apretar el gatillo; ***pull up,*** arrancar; parar; (*pers.*) llamar la atención a. — *v.i.* tirar, dar un tirón; ***pull at,*** tirar de; chupar; ***pull in,*** llegar al andén (*el tren*); parar junto a la acera; ***pull out,*** salir de la estación, arrancar; (*mil.*) retirarse; ***pull through,*** salir de una enfermedad *o* de un apuro; ***pull up,*** pararse, detenerse; mejorar. — **pull o.s.,** *v.r.* — ***together,*** sobreponerse.
pullet [ˈpulit], *s.* polla, pollita.
pulley [ˈpuli], *s.* polea; (*mar.*) garrucha.
pullover [ˈpulouvə], *s.* jersey.
Pullman car [ˈpulmən ˈkɑː], *s.* vagón pullman.
pullulate [ˈpʌljuleit], *v.i.* pulular.
pulmonary [ˈpʌlmənəri], *a.* pulmonar. — *s.* (*bot.*) pulmonaria.
pulmonic [pʌlˈmɔnik], *a.* pulmonar, pulmoníaco. — *s.* pectoral; tísico.

pulp [pʌlp], *s.* pulpa; pasta (*de papel*). — *v.t.* hacer pulpa.
pulpiness, pulpousness [ˈpʌlpinis, -əsnis], *s.* (lo) pulposo.
pulpous [ˈpʌlpəs], *a.* pulposo; mollar.
pulpit [ˈpulpit], *s.* púlpito.
pulpwood [ˈpʌlpwud], *s.* pulpa de madera, pasta de madera, celulosa.
pulsate [pʌlˈseit], *v.i.* latir; vibrar.
pulsatile [ˈpʌlsətail], *a.* pulsátil, pulsativo, latiente; de percusión.
pulsation [pʌlˈseiʃən], *s.* latido; vibración; pulsación.
pulsative [ˈpʌlsətiv], *a.* pulsativo.
pulsator [pʌlˈseitə], *s.* pulsómetro.
pulsatory [ˈpʌlsətəri], *a.* pulsátil, pulsativo, latiente.
pulse [pʌls], *s.* pulso; ***to feel s.o.'s pulse,*** tomarle el pulso a alguien. — *v.i.* latir; vibrar.
pulseless [ˈpʌlslis], *a.* sin pulso.
pulsimeter [pʌlˈsimitə], *s.* pulsímetro.
pulverizable [ˈpʌlvəraizəbl], *a.* pulverizable.
pulverization [pʌlvəraiˈzeiʃən], *s.* pulverización.
pulverize [ˈpʌlvəraiz], *v.t.* pulverizar.
pulverizer [ˈpʌlvəraizə], *s.* pulverizador.
puma [ˈpju:mə], *s.* puma.
pumice [ˈpʌmis], *s.* piedra pómez.
pummel [ˈpʌməl], *v.t.* apuñear, aporrear.
pump [pʌmp], *s.* bomba; zapatilla; (*mar.*) ***pump-box,*** mortero de bomba; (*mar.*) ***pump-brake,*** guimbalete; freno *o* amortiguador hidráulico; (*mar.*) ***to man the pump,*** armar la bomba. — *v.t.* bombear; (*fam.*) ***pump s.o.*** (***for information***), meterle a alguien los dedos, sonsacar a alguien; ***pump s.o.'s hand,*** estrecharle violentamente a alguien la mano; ***pump in,*** inyectar; ***pump out,*** achicar; (*neumático*) ***pump up,*** inflar.
pumper [ˈpʌmpə], *s.* bombero; (*fam.*) sonsacador.
pumpkin [ˈpʌmpkin], *s.* (*bot.*) calabaza.
pun [pʌn], *s.* equívoco, retruécano; juego de palabras. — *v.i.* hacer retruécanos.
Punch [pʌntʃ]. Polichinela, *m.*; ***Punch and Judy show,*** guiñol, cristobillas, *f.pl.*
punch (1) [pʌntʃ], *s.* puñetazo; ***punch-drunk,*** groggy, grogui; ***to pull no punches,*** no tener pelos en la lengua, no andarse con chiquitas. — *v.t.* picar; golpear, dar puñetazos a.
punch (2) [pʌntʃ], *s.* (*mec.*) punzón. — *v.t.* punzar, taladrar.
punch (3) [pʌntʃ], *s.* (*bebida*) ponche; ***punch-bowl,*** ponchera.
puncheon [ˈpʌntʃən], *s.* punzón; (*carp.*) montante, pie derecho; tonel.
puncher [ˈpʌntʃə], *s.* punzón.
punchinello [pʌntʃiˈnelou], *s.* polichinela, *m.*
punctilio [pʌŋkˈtiliou], *s.* puntillo; pundonor; etiqueta.
punctilious [pʌŋkˈtiliəs], *a.* puntilloso; pundonoroso; etiquetero.
punctiliously [pʌŋkˈtiliəsli], *adv.* con (extrema) exactitud *o* puntualidad, con una exactitud *o* puntualidad exagerada.
punctiliousness [pʌŋkˈtiliəsnis], *s.* exactitud *o* puntualidad extrema *o* exagerada.
punctual [ˈpʌŋktjuəl], *a.* puntual.
punctuality [pʌŋktjuˈæliti], *s.* puntualidad.
punctually [ˈpʌŋktjuəli], *adv.* puntualmente; (hora) en punto.
punctuate [ˈpʌŋktjueit], *v.t.* puntuar; (*fig.*) interrumpir (***with,*** con).
punctuation [pʌŋktjuˈeiʃən], *s.* puntuación.
puncture [ˈpʌŋktʃə], *s.* pinchazo; perforación; punción; ***to get a puncture,*** tener un pinchazo, pinchar. — *v.t.* pinchar; perforar; punzar.
pundit [ˈpʌndit], *s.* entendido, técnico.
pungency [ˈpʌndʒənsi], *s.* picante; mordacidad; (lo) acre.
pungent [ˈpʌndʒənt], *a.* picante; acre; mordaz.
Punic [ˈpju:nik], *a.* púnico.
puniness [ˈpju:ninis], *s.* (lo) escuchimizado, (lo) encanijado, (lo) enclenque; (lo) insignificante.
punish [ˈpʌniʃ], *v.t.* castigar; (*fig.*) fustigar; tratar con dureza.
punishable [ˈpʌniʃəbl], *a.* punible.
punishing [ˈpʌniʃiŋ], *a.* durísimo, fuertísimo, exigentísimo.
punishment [ˈpʌniʃmənt], *s.* castigo; trato(s) duro(s); ***to take one's punishment like a man,*** aguantar estoicamente el *o* un castigo.
punitive, punitory [ˈpju:nitiv, -təri], *a.* punitivo.
punk [pʌŋk], *a.* (*fam.*) malo, flojo. — *s.* yesca, *f.*
punnet [ˈpʌnit], *s.* cestito.
punster [ˈpʌnstə], *s.* equivoquista, *m.f.*
punt (1) [pʌnt], *s.* batea. — *v.i.* ir en batea.
punt (2) [pʌnt], *v.i.* jugar, hacer apuestas.
punt (3) [pʌnt], *s.* puntapié (*a la pelota*). — *v.t.* dar un puntapié a (*la pelota*).
punter [ˈpʌntə], *s.* jugador.
puny [ˈpju:ni], *a.* canijo, enclenque, escuchimizado; insignificante, despreciable.
pup [pʌp], *s.* cachorro. — *v.i.* (*perra*) parir.
pupa [ˈpju:pə], *s.* (*pl.* **pupæ** [-pi:]) crisálida, ninfa.
pupil [ˈpju:pəl], *s.* pupila (*del ojo*); alumno; (*for.*) pupilo.
pupilage [ˈpju:pilidʒ], *s.* alumnado; (*for.*) pupilaje.
pupil(l)ary [ˈpju:piləri], *a.* pupilar.
puppet [ˈpʌpit], *s.* títere, marioneta; muñeco, monigote; ***puppet-play, puppet-show,*** (función de) títeres.
puppy [ˈpʌpi], *s.* perrillo, cachorro; (*fig.*) mequetrefe.
puppyish [ˈpʌpiiʃ], *a.* de perrito; de mequetrefe.
purblind [ˈpə:blaind], *a.* cegato.
purchasable [ˈpə:tʃisəbl], *a.* comprable.
purchase [ˈpə:tʃis], *s.* compra, adquisición; agarre firme; apalancamiento; ***to get purchase,*** encontrar dónde agarrarse; ***to have purchase,*** tener dónde agarrarse; ***purchase tax,*** impuesto de venta. — *v.t.* comprar, adquirir.
purchaser [ˈpə:tʃisə], *s.* comprador.
purchasing [ˈpə:tʃəsiŋ], *a.* de compra; ***purchasing power,*** poder adquisitivo. — *s.* compra, adquisición.
pure [pjuə], *a.* puro.
purée [ˈpjuərei], *s.* (*coc.*) puré.
pureness [ˈpjuənis], *s.* (lo) puro.
purfle [pə:fl], *s.* orla. — *v.t.* orlar.
purgation [pə:ˈgeiʃən], *s.* purgación, purgamiento.
purgative [ˈpə:gətiv], *a.* purgativo, purgante, purgador. — *s.* purgante, purga.
purgatorial [pə:gəˈtɔ:riəl], *a.* purgatorio; expiatorio; del purgatorio.
purgatory [ˈpə:gətəri], *s.* purgatorio.
purge [pə:dʒ], *s.* purga, purgante; depuración. — *v.t.* purgar; purificar, depurar.
purger [ˈpə:dʒə], *s.* purgador.
purging [ˈpə:dʒiŋ], *a.* purgativo, purgante. — *s.* purgación.
purification [pjuərifiˈkeiʃən], *s.* purificación, depuración.
purificator, purifier [ˈpjuərifikeitə, -faiə], *s.* purificador.
puriform [ˈpjuərifɔ:m], *a.* puriforme.
purify [ˈpjuərifai], *v.t.* purificar, depurar; acrisolar.
purifying [ˈpjuərifaiiŋ], *a.* purificante, depurador. — *s.* purificación.
purin [ˈpjuərin], *s.* purina.
purism [ˈpjuərizəm], *s.* purismo.
purist [ˈpjuərist], *s.* purista, *m.f.*
Puritan [ˈpjuəritən], *a.*, *s.* puritano.
puritanic(al) [pjuəriˈtænik(əl)], *a.* puritano.
Puritanism [ˈpjuəritənizəm], *s.* puritanismo.

purity [ˈpjuəriti], *s.* pureza.
purl (1) [pəːl], *s.* murmullo. — *v.i.* murmurar.
purl (2) [pəːl], *s.* punto de media invertido. — *v.i.* hacer un punto de media invertido.
purlieu [ˈpəːljuː], *s.* linde; (*pl.*) alrededores, *m.pl.*
purling [ˈpəːliŋ], *a.* murmurante, que murmura. — *s.* murmullo.
purloin [pəːˈlɔin], *v.t.* robar, hurtar, sustraer.
purloiner [pəːˈlɔinə], *s.* ladrón.
purloining [pəːˈlɔiniŋ], *s.* robo, hurto.
purple [pəːpl], *a.* purpúreo, morado; ***purple patch*** o ***passage,*** trozo *o* pasaje de estilo elocuente *o* altisonante. — *s.* púrpura, morado. — *v.t.* purpurar. — *v.i.* purpurear; ruborizarse.
purplish, purply [ˈpəːpliʃ, -pli], *a.* algo purpúreo.
purport [ˈpəːpɔːt], *s.* sentido, significado; tenor, idea fundamental; intención. — [pəːˈpɔːt], *v.t.* significar, indicar; ***purport to*** + *inf.*, pretender.
purpose [ˈpəːpəs], *s.* propósito, objeto, finalidad; intención; resolución, decisión; ***novel with a purpose,*** novela de tesis; ***strength of purpose,*** resolución, decisión; ***for the purpose of,*** con el propósito *o* la finalidad de; ***on purpose,*** adrede, aposta, de própósito, intencionadamente; ***to good purpose,*** con efecto, con buenos resultados; ***to no purpose,*** inútilmente, sin efecto; ***to serve the purpose,*** servir para el caso. — *v.t.* proponer(se), proyectar.
purposeful [ˈpəːpəsful], *a.* decidido, resuelto.
purposeless [ˈpəːpəslis], *a.* sin objeto.
purposely [ˈpəːpəsli], *adv.* adrede, de propósito.
purr [pəː], *s.* ronroneo. — *v.t.* decir suavemente. — *v.i.* ronronear.
purring [ˈpəːriŋ], *s.* ronroneo.
purse [pəːs], *s.* bolsa; portamonedas, *m.inv.*; premio; colecta; ***to hold the purse-strings,*** administrar el dinero; ***well-lined purse,*** bolsa llena; ***you cannot make a silk purse out of a sow's ear,*** de ruin paño nunca buen sayo. — *v.t.* embolsar; fruncir (los labios).
purseful [ˈpəːsful], *s.* bolsa (llena).
purser [ˈpəːsə], *s.* (*mar.*) contador; sobrecargo.
purslane [ˈpəːslin], *s.* (*bot.*) verdolaga.
pursuable [pəˈsjuːəbl], *a.* proseguible.
pursuance [pəˈsjuːəns], *s.* ***in pursuance of,*** con arreglo a, en cumplimiento de.
pursuant [pəˈsjuːənt], *a.* ***pursuant to,*** de conformidad con.
pursue [pəˈsjuː], *v.t.* seguir, perseguir, dar caza a. — *v.i.* proseguir.
pursuer [pəˈsjuːə], *s.* perseguidor; (*for.*) demandante.
pursuit [pəˈsjuːt], *s.* persecución; caza; busca; ocupación; pasatiempo; ***in pursuit of,*** en pos de; en perseguimiento de; en busca de; ***pursuit plane,*** avión de caza.
pursuivant [ˈpəːsivənt], *s.* (*mil.*, *blas.*) persevante.
pursy [ˈpəːsi], *a.* asmático; engreído por el dinero.
purulence, purulency [ˈpjuəruləns, -i], *s.* purulencia.
purulent [ˈpjuərulənt], *a.* purulento.
purvey [pəːˈvei], *v.t.* proveer, suministrar, surtir, abastecer. — *v.i.* proveer, surtir.
purveyance [pəːˈveiəns], *s.* abastecimiento, suministro, abasto.
purveyor [pəːˈveiə], *s.* abastecedor, proveedor, suministrador.
purview [ˈpəːvjuː], *s.* alcance, esfera, ámbito.
pus [pʌs], *s.* (*med.*) pus.
push [puʃ], *s.* empujón; empuje; ***at a push,*** apurando mucho; ***to get the push,*** ser despedido; ***push-bike,*** bici; ***push-button,*** pulsador, botón eléctrico; ***push-chair,*** silla de ruedas; (*fam.*) ***push-over,*** pan comido, cosa tirada. — *v.t.* empujar; impeler; apretar; avanzar; promover, impulsar; apremiar; apurar; ***push away,*** apartar de un empujón; ***push back,*** empujar hacia atrás; ***push forward,*** empujar hacia adelante; ***push in,*** meter a empujones; ***push off,*** desatracar; ***push one's luck,*** fiarse *o* confiarse demasiado; ***push out,*** expulsar; ***push through,*** hacer aceptar a la fuerza; ***to be pushed for,*** andar muy escaso de. — *v.i.* empujar, dar un empujón; ***push forward,*** seguir adelante, avanzar; ***push off,*** desatracarse; largarse; ***push one's way in*** o ***through,*** abrirse paso a empujones. — *interj.* ¡empujar!; ***push on!*** ¡adelante!
pushing [ˈpuʃiŋ], *a.* emprendedor; agresivo.
pushpin [ˈpuʃpin], *s.* juego de alfileres, juego de pajitas.
pusillanimity [pjuːsiləˈnimiti], *s.* pusilanimidad.
pusillanimous [pjuːsiˈlæniməs], *a.* pusilánime, apocado.
puss [pus], *s.* minino, michito; (*fig.*) chavala, niña; jeta.
pussy [ˈpusi], *s.* minino, michito; (*fig.*) chavala.
pussy-cat [ˈpusi-kæt], *s.* gatito, misito.
pussy-willow [ˈpusi-wilou], *s.* sauce de hoja sedosa.
pustular [ˈpʌstjulə], *a.* (*bot.*) pustuloso.
pustulate [ˈpʌstjuleit], *v.i.* llenarse de pústulas.
pustule [ˈpʌstjuːl], *s.* pústula.
pustulous [ˈpʌstjuləs], *a.* pustuloso.
put [put], *v.t.* poner; colocar; meter; lanzar (*un peso*); formular, hacer (*una pregunta*); proponer, someter a votación; presentar, expresar, interpretar; calcular (***at,*** en); verter, traducir (***into,*** a); ***be hard put to it to,*** verse negro para, verse apurado para; ***put it about that,*** propagar, propalar la idea de que; ***put across,*** comunicar, expresar; conseguir que se acepte (*una cosa*); (*fam.*) ***put one across s.o.,*** tomarle el pelo a alguien, dársela a alguien; ***put aside,*** poner a un lado; prescindir de; ***put away,*** guardar; (*fam.*) zamparse (*comida*); (*fam.*) meter en la cárcel *o* en un manicomio; ***put back,*** devolver a su sitio; retrasar, atrasar; aplazar; ***put by,*** poner a un lado; guardar; ***put down,*** sofocar, acabar con; soltar, dejar; apuntar, anotar; deponer (*las armas*); ***put sth. down to,*** achacar algo a; ***put forth,*** sacar, publicar; echar; producir; ***put forward,*** presentar, proponer; adelantar; ***put o.s. forward,*** ofrecerse; ***put in,*** meter, introducir; presentar; interponer; dedicar (*tiempo*); ***put off,*** aplazar; desanimar, disuadir, quitar las ganas a; despistar, desorientar, desconcertar; dar largas a; contestar con evasivas; ***put on,*** ponerse; (*fam.*) ***put it on,*** exagerar; darse tono, ser cursi; ***put out,*** extender; asomar; sacar; echar (*hojas etc.*); apagar; molestar, incomodar; desconcertar; ***put over,*** comunicar, expresar; conseguir que se acepte (*una idea*); ***put o.s. over,*** causar (muy) buena impresión; ***put right,*** arreglar; corregir, rectificar; poner en hora; ***put sth. to s.o.,*** proponerle algo a alguien; ***put through,*** llevar a cabo; conseguir que se apruebe (*una cosa*); ***put through to,*** poner con; ***put together,*** juntar; montar; ***put up,*** montar, construir; envainar (*la espada*); abrir (*el paraguas*); subir, aumentar; ofrecer (*un premio*); poner, contribuir con, aportar (*dinero*); levantar (*la caza*); nombrar; alojar; ***put up to,*** incitar, animar a. — *v.i.* (*mar.*) ***put about,*** cambiar de rumbo; (*mar.*) ***put in,*** entrar en *o* a puerto; (*mar.*) ***put in at,*** hacer escala en; ***put in for,*** pedir, solicitar; (*mar.*) ***put out,*** hacerse a la mar; ***put up at,*** alojarse en; ***put up with,*** aguantar, soportar; ***put upon,*** abusar de.
putative [ˈpjuːtətiv], *a.* putativo.
puteal [ˈpjuːtiəl], *s.* brocal de pozo.
putlog [ˈputlɔg], *s.* (*arq.*) almojaya.
put-off [ˈput-ɔf], *s.* pretexto; evasiva.
putrefaction [pjuːtriˈfækʃən], *s.* putrefacción.
putrefactive [ˈpjuːtrifæktiv], *a.* putrefactivo.
putrefiable [ˈpjuːtrifaiəbl], *a.* que puede pudrirse.
putrefy [ˈpjuːtrifai], *v.t.*, *v.i.* pudrir(se), podrecer(se).
putrescence [pjuːˈtresəns], *s.* putrescencia.
putrescent [pjuːˈtresənt], *a.* putrescente.

putrid [ˈpjuːtrid], *a.* pútrido, putrefacto.
putridity [pjuːˈtriditi], *s.* putridez.
putt [pʌt], *s.* golpe corto (*golf*). — *v.t.* golpear (*la pelota de golf*) suavemente.
puttee [ˈpʌti], *s.* polaina, banda arrollada a la pierna.
putter (1) [ˈpʌtə], *s.* uno de los palos del juego de golf, putter.
putter (2) [ˈputə], *s.* ponedor, persona que pone; ***putter-on,*** instigador, incitador; fingidor; cursi.
putting (1) [ˈpʌtiŋ], *s.* golpeadura suave (*golf*); ***putting-green,*** espacio en el campo de golf donde se halla el hoyo.
putting (2) [ˈputiŋ], *s.* (el) poner; (el) lanzar.
puttock [ˈpʌtək], *s.* milano.
putty [ˈpʌti], *s.* masilla. — *v.t.* enmasillar.
put-up [ˈput-ʌp], *a.* apañado; ***put-up job,*** cosa apañada de antemano.
puzzle [pʌzl], *s.* enigma, *m.*; misterio; acertijo; ***jigsaw puzzle,*** rompecabezas, *m.inv.* — *v.t.* desconcertar, dejar, perplejo; ***puzzle out,*** descifrar, resolver. — *v.i.* — ***over,*** devanarse los sesos (para descifrar).
puzzled [pʌzld], *a.* perplejo; ***a puzzled look,*** una mirada perpleja *o* de perplejidad.
puzzler [ˈpʌzlə], *s.* enigma, *m.*, problema difícil, *m.*, problemón, papeleta.
puzzling [ˈpʌzliŋ], *a.* enigmático, misterioso; desconcertante.
pycnite [ˈpiknait], *s.* variedad de topacio.
pye [PIE (2)].
pygmean [pigˈmiːən], *a.* de pigmeo.
pygmy [ˈpigmi], *a.* de pigmeo. — *s.* pigmeo, enano.
pyjamas [piˈdʒɑːməz], *s.pl.* pijama, *m.inv.*
pylon [ˈpailən], *s.* pilón; torre (de conducción eléctrica).
pyloric [paiˈlɔrik], *a.* (*anat.*) pilórico.
pylorus [paiˈlɔːrəs], *s.* (*anat.*) píloro.
pyorrhoea [paiəˈriə], *s.* piorrea.
pyracanth [ˈpairəkænθ], *s.* piracanto.
pyramid [ˈpirəmid], *s.* pirámide, *f.*
pyramidal [piˈræmidəl], *a.* piramidal.
pyre [paiə], *s.* pira; hoguera.
Pyrenean [piriˈniːən], *a.* pirenaico, de los Pirineos.
Pyrenees [piriˈniːz], **the.** los Pirineos.
pyretic [paiˈretik], *a.* pirético.
pyretology [pairiˈtɔlədʒi], *s.* piretología.
pyrexia [paiˈreksiə], *s.* pirexia.
pyrites [paiˈraitiːz], *s.* pirita.
pyritic [paiˈritik], *a.* piritoso.
pyrogallic [pairoˈgælik], *a.* pirogálico.
pyrogenous [paiˈrɔdʒinəs], *a.* priógeno.
pyrography [paiˈrɔgrəfi], *s.* pirografía.
pyrolign(e)ous [pairoˈlign(i)əs], *a.* pirolignoso.
pyrology [paiˈrɔlədʒi], *s.* pirología.
pyrometer [paiˈrɔmitə], *s.* pirómetro.
pyrometry [paiˈrɔmitri], *s.* pirometría.
pyrophorous [paiˈrɔfərəs], *a.* piroforoso.
pyrophorus [paiˈrɔfərəs], *s.* piróforo.
pyrophotometer [pairoˈfoutɔmitə], *s.* pirofotómetro.
pyroscope [ˈpairoskoup], *s.* piroscopio.
pyrotechnic(al) [pairoˈteknik(əl)], *a.* pirotécnico.
pyrotechnics, pyrotechny [pairoˈtekniks, ˈpairotekni], *s.* pirotecnia.
pyroxene [paiˈrɔksiːn], *s.* piroxena.
Pyrrhic [ˈpirik], *a.* pírrico; ***Pyrrhic victory,*** victoria pírrica, triunfo pírrico.
Pythagoras [paiˈθægərəs]. Pitágoras, *m.*
Pythagorean [paiθægəˈriːən], *a.* pitagórico.
Pythagorism [paiˈθægərizəm], *s.* pitagorismo.
python [ˈpaiθən], *s.* pitón.
pythoness [ˈpaiθənes], *s.* pitonisa.
pythonic [paiˈθɔnik], *a.* pitónico.
pyx [piks], *s.* copón, píxide, *f.*

Q

Q, q [kju:], decimoséptima letra del alfabeto; ***to mind one's p's and q's,*** andarse con (mucho) cuidado *o* con (mucho) tiento.
Qatar [ˈkɑ:tɑ:]. Katar, Qatar.
quack (1) [kwæk], *s.* graznido (*de pato*). — *v.i.* parpar, graznar (el pato).
quack (2) [kwæk], *a.* de curandero; mixtificado. — *s.* curandero, medicastro, charlatán de feria.
quackery [ˈkwækəri], *s.* charlatanismo, curandería, curanderismo.
quackish [ˈkwækiʃ], *a.* curanderil.
quad [kwɔd], *s.* patio (cuadrangular); (*fam.*) chirona; (*pl., fam.*) cuatrillizos, *m.pl.*
quadragenarian [kwɔdrədʒiˈnɛəriən], *a., s.* cuadragenario.
quadragesima [kwɔdrəˈdʒesimə], *s.* cuadragésima.
quadragesimal [kwɔdrəˈdʒesiməl], *a.* cuadragesimal.
quadrangle [ˈkwɔdræŋgl], *s.* (*geom.*) cuadrángulo; (*arq.*) patio.
quadrangular [kwɔˈdræŋgjulə], *a.* cuadrangular.
quadrant [ˈkwɔdrənt], *s.* cuadrante.
quadrantal [kwɔˈdræntəl], *a.* cuadrantal.
quadrat [ˈkwɔdrit], *s.* (*impr.*) cuadrado, cuadratín.
quadrate [ˈkwɔdrit], *a.* cuadrado. — *s.* (*anat.*) hueso cuadrado; (*astrol.*) aspecto cuadrado; (*mús.*) becuadro. — [kwɔˈdreit, ˈkwɔdreit], *v.t., v.i.* cuadrar.
quadratic [kwɔˈdrætik], *a.* cuadrado; (*mat.*) de segundo grado; (*cristal.*) cuadrático. — *s.* cuadrática, ecuación de segundo grado.
quadrature [ˈkwɔdrətʃə], *s.* cuadratura, cuadrado; (*mec.*) escuadreo.
quadrel [ˈkwɔdrəl], *s.* (*arq.*) piedra cuadrada.
quadrennial [kwɔˈdreniəl], *a.* cuadrenial.
quadrennially [kwɔˈdreniəli], *adv.* cada cuatro años.
quadricycle [ˈkwɔdrisaikl], *s.* cuadriciclo.
quadriga [kwɔˈdraigə], *s.* cuadriga.
quadrilateral [kwɔdriˈlætərəl], *a., s.* cuadrilátero.
quadrille [kwɔˈdril], *s.* contradanza; cuatrillo; cuadrilla.
quadrillion [kwɔˈdriljən], *s.* cuatrillón.
quadrinomial [kwɔdriˈnoumiəl], *a.* cuadrínomo. — *s.* cuadrinomio.
quadripartite [kwɔdriˈpɑ:tait], *a., s.* cuadripartido.
quadrisyllable [kwɔdriˈsiləbl], *s.* cuadrisílabo.
quadrivium [kwɔˈdriviəm], *s.* cuadrivio.
quadroon [kwɔˈdru:n], *s.* cuarterón.
quadrumane [ˈkwɔdrumein], *s.* cuadrumano.
quadrumanous [kwɔˈdru:mənəs], *a.* cuadrumano.
quadruped [ˈkwɔdruped], *a., s.* cuadrúpedo.
quadrupedal [kwɔˈdru:pidəl], *a.* cuadrupedal.
quadruple [ˈkwɔdrupl], *a.* cuádruple. — *s.* cuádruplo. — *v.t.* (*v.i.*) cuadruplicar(se).
quadruplet [ˈkwɔdruplit], *s.* cuatrillizo.
quadruplex [ˈkwɔdrupleks], *a.* cuádruple.
quadruplicate [kwɔˈdru:plikit], *a.* cuadruplicado. — [-keit], *v.t.* cuadruplicar.
quadruplication [kwɔdru:pliˈkeiʃən], *s.* cuadruplicación.
quadruply [ˈkwɔdrupli], *adv.* al cuádruplo, cuatro veces.
quaff [kwɔf], *v.t., v.i.* libar.
quagga [ˈkwægə], *s.* cuaga.
quaggy [ˈkwægi], *a.* pantanoso.
quagmire [ˈkwægmaiə], *s.* cenagal, tremedal.
quail (1) [kweil], *s.* (*orn.*) codorniz.
quail (2) [kweil], *v.i.* temblar de miedo, estar atemorizado.
quailing [ˈkweiliŋ], *a.* que tiembla de miedo, tembloroso. — *s.* tiemblo.
quaint [kweint], *a.* curioso, original; pintoresco; típico; excéntrico, extravagante.
quaintness [ˈkweintnis], *s.* (lo) curioso; (lo) pintoresco *etc.*
quake [kweik], *s.* estremecimiento, temblor; (*abrev. fam. de* EARTHQUAKE]), terremoto. — *v.i.* estremecerse, temblar.
Quaker [ˈkweikə], *a., s.* cuáquero.
Quakerish [ˈkweikəriʃ], *a.* de cuáquero.
Quakerism [ˈkweikərizəm], *s.* cuaquerismo.
quaking [ˈkweikiŋ], *a.* que tiembla, tembloroso. — *s.* estremecimientos, *m.pl.*, temblores, *m.pl.*
qualification [kwɔlifiˈkeiʃən], *s.* calificación; requisito, condición; mérito, título; capacidad; limitación, restricción, reserva; ***without qualification,*** sin reservas.
qualified [ˈkwɔlifaid], *a.* capacitado, con capacidad, competente, con títulos *o* méritos (***to, for,*** para); limitado, con reservas.
qualifier [ˈkwɔlifaiə], *s.* (*gram.*) calificativo.
qualify [ˈkwɔlifai], *v.t.* calificar; capacitar, hacer competente; dar título a; autorizar; habilitar (***to, for,*** para); modificar, limitar; decir *o* expresar con reservas. — *v.i.* capacitarse, hacerse *o* ser competente (***to,*** para); hacerse *o* ser merecedor (***for,*** de) *o* acreedor (***for,*** a).
qualifying [ˈkwɔlifaiiŋ], *a.* (examen) eliminatorio.
qualitative [ˈkwɔlitətiv], *a.* cualitativo.
quality [ˈkwɔliti], *s.* calidad; (*pers.*) cualidad; ***good quality,*** (de) buena calidad; ***good qualities,*** buenas cualidades; (*ant.*) ***the quality,*** la aristocracia.
qualm [kwɑ:m], *s.* escrúpulo; reparo; ***to have no qualms about,*** no tener empacho en.
quandary [ˈkwɔndəri], *s.* incertidumbre, *f.*, perplejidad, duda, dilema, *m.*; ***to be in a quandary,*** verse en un dilema.
quantify [ˈkwɔntifai], *v.t.* cuantificar.
quantitative, quantitive [ˈkwɔntitətiv, -tiv], *a.* cuantitativo.
quantity [ˈkwɔntiti], *s.* cantidad; ***unknown quantity,*** incógnita; ***quantity surveyor,*** aparejador.
quantum [ˈkwɔntəm], *a.* cuántico. — *s.* (*fís.*) cuanto; unidad cuántica; cantidad.
quarantine [ˈkwɔrənti:n], *s.* cuarentena. — *v.t.* poner en cuarentena.
quarrel [ˈkwɔrəl], *s.* riña, disputa, pendencia; desavenencia; ***to pick a quarrel with,*** buscarle camorra a. — *v.i.* reñir, disputar, pelear.
quarreller [ˈkwɔrələ], *s.* pendenciero, camorrista, *m.f.*
quarrelling [ˈkwɔrəliŋ], *a.* disputador. — *s.* riñas, *f.pl.*, disputas, *f.pl.*, pendencias, *f.pl.* desacuerdo.
quarrelsome [ˈkwɔrəlsəm], *a.* pendenciero, peleón.
quarrelsomeness [ˈkwɔrəlsəmnis], *s.* temperamento pendenciero; chulería.
quarrier [ˈkwɔriə], *s.* cantero.
quarry (1) [ˈkwɔri], *s.* cantera, pedrera. — *v.t.* sacar, extraer (piedra) de una cantera.
quarry (2) [ˈkwɔri], *s.* pieza (de caza), caza, presa.
quarryman [ˈkwɔrimən], *s.* cantero, cavador de cantera; picapedrero.
quart [kwɔ:t], *s.* cuarto de galón (*aprox.* 1,13 *litros*); cuarta.
quartan [ˈkwɔ:tən], *a.* cuartanal. — *s.* (*med.*) cuartana.
quarter [ˈkwɔ:tə], *a.* cuarto. — *s.* cuarto, cuarta parte; cuartel; trimestre; barrio; (*mar.*) cuarta, cuadra de popa; cantón; fuente, procedencia; ***to give no quarter,*** no dar cuartel; (*pl.*) alojamiento; cuartel; ***from all quarters,*** de todos lados; ***at close quarters,*** muy de cerca, casi a las manos; ***to take up quarters,*** alojarse. — *v.t.* cuartear; descuartizar; cuartelar; alojar; acuartelar, acantonar. — *v.i.* alojarse.

quarterage [ˈkwɔ:təridʒ], *s.* sueldo trimestral; acuartelamiento.
quarter-day [ˈkwɔ:tə-dei], *s.* día en que se pagan los alquileres.
quarter-deck [ˈkwɔ:tə-dek], *s.* (*mar.*) alcázar.
quarter-final [ˈkwɔ:tə-ˈfainəl], *s.* cuarto de final; (*pl.*) cuartos de final, *m.pl.*
quartering [ˈkwɔ:təriŋ], *s.* acción de alojar, acuartelamiento; descuartizamiento.
quarterly [ˈkwɔ:təli], *a.* trimestral. — *adv.* trimestralmente; por cuartos. — *s.* revista *o* publicación trimestral.
quartermaster [ˈkwɔ:təmɑ:stə], *s.* (*mil.*) intendente; furriel, comisario; (*mar.*) cabo de mar.
quartern [ˈkwɔ:tən], *a.* de cuatro. — *s.* cuarta.
quartet [kwɔ:ˈtet], *s.* cuarteto.
quarto [ˈkwɔ:tou], *a.* en cuarto. — *s.* papel en cuarto; libro en cuarto.
quartz [kwɔ:tz], *s.* (*min.*) cuarzo.
quartzite [ˈkwɔ:tzait], *s.* (*geol.*) cuarcita.
quartzose, quartzy [ˈkwɔ:tsouz, ˈkwɔ:tsi], *a.* cuarzoso.
quash [kwɔʃ], *v.t.* anular, invalidar.
quasi [ˈkweizai], *adv.* cuasi-, -oide; ***quasi-divine,*** divinoide.
quasimodo [kwæsiˈmoudou], *s.* domingo de cuasimodo.
quassia [ˈkwɔʃə, ˈkwæʃiə], *s.* (*bot.*) cuasia.
quatercentenary [kwætəsenˈti:nəri], *s.* cuarto centenario.
quaternary [kwɔˈtə:nəri], *a.* cuaternario.
quatrain [ˈkwɔtrein], *s.* estrofa de cuatro versos.
quatrefoil [ˈkæt(r)əfɔil], *s.* hoja *o* flor cuadrifoliada.
quaver [ˈkweivə], *s.* trino; temblor; trémolo; (*mús.*) corchea. — *v.i.* gorjear, trinar; temblar.
quavering [ˈkweivəriŋ], *a.* tembloroso, trémulo. — *s.* trinos, *m.pl.*; temblores, *m.pl.*
quay [ki:], *s.* muelle, desembarcadero.
quean [kwi:n], *s.* mujer de mala vida; moza.
queasiness [ˈkwi:zinis], *s.* náuseas, *f.pl.*; propensión a la náusea; malestar.
queasy [ˈkwi:zi], *a.* que tiene *o* siente náuseas; delicado, muy escrupuloso; ***to have a queasy stomach,*** sentir náuseas.
queen [kwi:n], *s.* reina; dama; ***queen bee,*** abeja reina; ***queen dowager,*** reina viuda; ***queen-like,*** de reina; ***queen mother,*** reina madre. — *v.t.* hacer reina; ***queen it,*** hacerse la reina, darse tono.
queenliness [ˈkwi:nlinis], *s.* dignidad de reina.
queenly [ˈkwi:nli], *a.* de reina.
queer [kwiə], *a.* raro, extraño; excéntrico; misterioso; malucho; ***there's sth. queer about this,*** aquí hay gato encerrado; (*fam.*) ***in Queer Street,*** mal de fondos, a la cuarta pregunta. — *s.* (*fam.*) maricón. — *v.t.* — ***the pitch for,*** chafarle (algo) a.
queerish [ˈkwiəriʃ], *a.* rarillo.
queerly [ˈkwiəli], *adv.* de (un) modo raro; (*fam.*) ***to feel queerly,*** sentirse raro.
queerness [ˈkwiənis], *s.* (lo) raro, (lo) extraño.
quell [kwel], *v.t.* reprimir; sofocar; calmar.
queller [ˈkwelə], *s.* sojuzgador; mitigador.
quench [kwentʃ], *v.t.* apagar, extinguir; saciar; enfriar (*hierro*).
quenchable [ˈkwentʃəbl], *a.* apagable, extinguible.
quencher [ˈkwentʃə], *s.* trago.
quenchless [ˈkwentʃlis], *a.* inextinguible; inapagable.
quercitron [ˈkwə:sitrən], *s.* roble negro norteamericano y su cáscara.
quern [kwə:n], *s.* molinillo para especias.
querulous [ˈkweruləs], *a.* quejumbroso, quejicoso.
querulousness [ˈkweruləsnis], *s.* tendencia a quejarse.
query [ˈkwiəri], *s.* pregunta; duda. — *v.t.* preguntar sobre, indagar; poner en duda. — *v.i.* preguntar, hacer preguntas.
quest [kwest], *s.* búsqueda; pesquisa; ***in quest of,*** en busca de. — *v.i.* — ***for,*** ir en busca de.
question [ˈkwestʃən], *s.* pregunta; interrogación; cuestión; problema, *m.*; asunto; ***beyond all question,*** fuera de (toda) duda; ***the matter in question,*** el asunto del que se trata; ***the question is,*** se trata de; ***question mark,*** punto de interrogación; interrogante; ***that is the question,*** ahí está el quid; ***that's beside the question,*** eso no tiene nada que ver; ***that is out of the question,*** eso es imposible; ***there is no question about it,*** no cabe duda; ***there is no question of,*** no hay la menor posibilidad de; ***to ask a question,*** hacer una pregunta; ***to beg the question,*** ser una petición de principio; ***to call in question,*** poner en duda. — *v.t.* preguntar; interrogar; poner en duda, dudar de; recusar, objetar a. — *v.i.* hacer preguntas, preguntar; indagar.
questionable [ˈkwestʃənəbl], *a.* discutible, argüible; problemático; dudoso.
questionableness [ˈkwestʃənəblnis], *s.* (lo) discutible; (lo) dudoso.
questionary [ˈkwestʃənəri], *s.* cuestionario.
questioner [ˈkwestʃənə], *s.* preguntador, inquiridor.
questioning [ˈkwestʃəniŋ], *s.* (el) preguntar; (el) indagar.
questionnaire [kwestʃəˈnɛə], *s.* cuestionario.
queue [kju:], *s.* cola. — *v.i.* ***queue (up),*** hacer cola.
quibble [kwibl], *s.* sutileza; retruécano; sofistería, sofisma, *m.* — *v.i.* sutilizar; usar de sofisterías; usar de evasivas.
quibbler [ˈkwiblə], *s.* sofista, *m.f.*, equivoquista, *m.f.*
quick [kwik], *a.* rápido; pronto; vivo; fino; agudo; ***quick-change actor,*** transformista, *m.f.*; ***quick-freeze,*** de congelación rápida; ***quick-sighted,*** de vista aguda; ***quick-tempered,*** de genio vivo; ***quick-witted,*** listo, despierto; ***to be quick,*** darse prisa; ser rápido; ***to be quick to catch on,*** cogerlas al vuelo. — *adv.* [*t.* QUICKLY] rápido, con rápidez, de prisa; ***quick, march!*** ¡de frente, marchen! — *s.* carne viva; ***the quick and the dead,*** los vivos y los muertos; ***to cut*** o ***sting to the quick,*** herir en lo vivo.
quicken [ˈkwikən], *v.t.* acelerar; avivar; ***quicken the appetite,*** aguzar el apetito; ***quicken one's step,*** avivar el paso. — *v.i.* acelerarse; avivarse.
quickfiring [ˈkwikˈfaiəriŋ], *a.* de tiro rápido.
quickie [ˈkwiki], *s.* (*fam.*) pregunta rápida.
quicklime [ˈkwiklaim], *s.* cal viva.
quickly [ˈkwikli], *adv.* [QUICK]; de prisa, aprisa; pronto, en seguida.
quickness [ˈkwiknis], *s.* rapidez; prontitud; presteza; viveza; agudeza; penetración.
quicksand [ˈkwiksænd], *s.* arena movediza.
quickset [ˈkwikset], *a.* ***quickset hedge,*** seto vivo. — *s.* planta viva.
quicksilver [ˈkwiksilvə], *s.* azogue. — *v.t.* azogar.
quicksilvered [ˈkwiksilvəd], *a.* cubierto de azogue.
quickstep [ˈkwikstep], *s.* (*mús.*) pasacalle, *m.*
quid (1) [kwid], *s.* mascada (*de tabaco*).
quid (2) [kwid], *s.* (*fam.*) libra (esterlina).
quiescence [kwaiˈesəns], *s.* quietud, reposo.
quiescent [kwaiˈesənt], *a.* tranquilo; quieto; latente.
quiet [ˈkwaiət], *a.* callado, silencioso; tranquilo; quedo; discreto, no llamativo (*color*); encalmado (*comercio*); ***to be quiet,*** callarse; estar tranquilo; ***to keep quiet,*** estarse callado. — *s.* silencio; tranquilidad; sosiego; ***on the quiet,*** a la chita callando. — *v.t.* aquietar. — *v.i.* — ***down,*** aquietarse, sosegarse. — *interj.* (***be***) ***quiet!*** ¡cállate!
quieten [ˈkwaiətn], *v.t.*, *v.i.* [QUIET].
quietism [ˈkwaiətizəm], *s.* quietismo.
quietist [ˈkwaiətist], *s.* quietista, *m.f.*
quietness [ˈkwaiətnis], *s.* tranquilidad, calma.

quietude ['kwaiətju:d], *s.* quietud, tranquilidad, reposo, sosiego.
quietus [kwai'i:təs], *s.* quitanza, finiquito, carta de pago; golpe de gracia.
quill [kwil], *s.* pluma (*de ave*); cañón (*de pluma*); púa (*de puerco espín*); devanador; estría; ***men of the quill,*** los escritores, *m.pl.*, profesión de las letras. — *v.t.* plegar, encañonar; desplumar, arrancar plumas de; (*cost.*) rizar, hacer un encarrujado en.
quillon ['ki:jɔŋ], *s.* gavilán (*de espada*).
quilt [kwilt], *s.* colcha, cobertor. — *v.t.* acolchar; estofar; acojinar.
quilter ['kwiltə], *s.* colchero, acolchador.
quilting ['kwiltiŋ], *s.* acción de acolchar, colchadura; (*mar.*) cajera; (*tej.*) piqué.
quina ['kwainə], *s.* quina.
quinary ['kwainəri], *a.*, *s.* quinario.
quince [kwins], *s.* membrillo; ***quince cheese,*** carne de membrillo; ***quince jelly,*** jalea de membrillo; ***quince tree,*** membrillero, membrillo.
quincentenary [kwinsen'ti:nəri], *s.* quinto centenario.
quincuncial [kwin'kʌnʃəl], *a.* dispuesto al tresbolillo.
quincunx ['kwinkʌŋks], *s.* quincuence, tresbolillo.
quindecagon [kwin'dekəgən], *s.* (*geom.*) quindecágono.
quinia ['kwiniə], *s.* quinina.
quinine [kwi'ni:n], *s.* quinina.
quinol ['kwinəl], *s.* hidroquinona.
quinquagenarian [kwiŋkwədʒə'nɛəriən], *a.*, *s.* quincuagenario.
quinquagesima [kwiŋkwə'dʒesimə], *s.* quincuagésima.
quinquennial [kwin'kweniəl], *a.* quinquenal.
quinquina [kin'ki:nə, kwin'kwainə], *s.* (*bot.*) quina.
quinsy ['kwinzi], *s.* angina.
quint [kwint], *s.* quinta; conjunto de cinco; (*mús.*) quinta.
quintain ['kwintin], *s.* estafermo.
quintal ['kwintəl], *s.* quintal.
quintessence [kwin'tesəns], *s.* quintaesencia.
quintessential [kwinti'senʃəl], *a.* quintaesenciado, depuradísimo.
quintet(**te**) [kwin'tet], *s.* quinteto.
quintile ['kwintil], *s.* quintil.
quintillion [kwin'tiljən], *s.* quintillón (*en Ing. y Francia* = 1 seguido de 30 ceros, *en los EE. UU.* = 1 seguido de 18 ceros).
quintuple ['kwintjupl], *a.* quíntuplo. — *v.t.*, *v.i.* quintuplicar(se).
quintuplet ['kwintjuplit], *s.* quintillizo.
quip [kwip], *s.* chiste, broma, zumba; agudeza. — *v.i.* bromear.
quire [kwaiə], *s.* mano (*de papel*).
quirk [kwə:k], *s.* rareza; peculiaridad; agudeza.
quirky ['kwə:ki], *a.* raro, excéntrico, caprichoso.
quirt [kwə:t], *s.* rebenque.
quisling ['kwizliŋ], *s.* quisling, *m.*, colaboracionista, *m.f.*
quit [kwit], *a.* libre; absuelto; ***to be quit of,*** estar *o* verse libre de; ***to get quit of,*** deshacerse de; zafarse de. — *v.t.* dejar, abandonar; renunciar a, desistir de. — *v.i.* despedirse (de), marcharse (de); rajarse; ***to give notice to quit,*** dar aviso para que se marche.
quitch-grass ['kwitʃ-grɑ:s], *s.* (*bot.*) grama.
quitclaim ['kwitkleim], *s.* (*for.*) renuncia.
quite [kwait], *adv.* completamente; perfectamente; bastante; ***I quite understand,*** comprendo perfectamente; ***I don't quite understand,*** no lo entiendo del todo, no lo acabo de entender; ***it's quite good,*** no está mal; ***quite a dozen,*** doce por lo menos; ***quite seriously,*** completamente en serio; ***quite so,*** en efecto; ***quite somebody,*** ¡una auténtica personalidad!
quits [kwits], *a.* (*fam.*) en paz; ***to cry quits,*** darse por vencido.
quittance ['kwitəns], *s.* quitanza; remuneración, recompensa.
quitter ['kwitə], *s.* el que se da fácilmente por vencido.
quiver (1) ['kwivə], *s.* carcaj, aljaba.
quiver (2) ['kwivə], *s.* temblor. — *v.i.* estremecerse, temblar.
quivering ['kwivəriŋ], *a.* temblón, tembloroso. — *s.* temblor, estremecimiento.
quixotic [kwik'sɔtik], *a.* quijotesco.
quixotism ['kwiksətizəm], *s.* quijotismo; quijotería.
quiz [kwiz], *s.* encuesta; acertijo; concurso a base de preguntas. — *v.t.* interrogar; interrogar con la mirada.
quizzical ['kwizikəl], *a.* burlón, irónico, de sorna.
quod [kwɔd], *s.* (*fam.*) chirona [QUAD].
quodlibet ['kwɔdlibet], *s.* equívoco, cuodlibeto; (*mús.*) miscelánea burlesca.
quoin [kwɔin], *s.* rincón, ángulo, esquina; (*impr.*, *mec.*) cuña; (*arq.*) diente, adaraja, clave (*f.*) de arco, piedra angular.
quoit [k(w)ɔit], *s.* herrón, tejo; (*pl.*) juego de tejos.
quondam ['kwɔndæm], *a.* antiguo, de antaño.
quorum ['kwɔ:rəm], *s.* quórum.
quota ['kwoutə], *s.* cupo; cuota; contingente.
quotable ['kwoutəbl], *a.* citable.
quotation [kwou'teiʃən], *s.* cita; citación; (*com.*) cotización; (*impr.*) ***quotation marks,*** comillas, *f.pl.*
quote [kwout], *s.* (*fam.*) cita. — *pl.* (*impr.*, *fam.*) comillas, *f.pl.* [QUOTATION MARKS]. — *v.t.* citar; (*com.*) cotizar.
quoter ['kwoutə], *s.* citador; cotizador.
quoth [kwouθ], *v. defec. pret.* (*ant.*); ***quoth I,*** dije yo; ***quoth he,*** dijo él.
quotidian [kwo'tidiən], *a.* cotidiano, diario. — *s.* cosa diaria; (*med.*) calentura cotidiana.
quotient ['kwouʃənt], *s.* cociente.

R

R, r [ɑ:]. decimoctava letra del alfabeto; (*fam.*) ***the three R's,*** lectura, escritura, y aritmética (**reading, 'riting, 'rithmetic**).
rabbet [ˈræbit], *s.* rebajo; ensambladura; ***rabbet plane,*** guillame; (*mar.*) alefriz. — *v.t.* embarbillar; ensamblar (a rebajo).
rabbi, rabbin [ˈræbai, ˈræbin], *s.* rabí, rabino.
rabbinic [rəˈbinik], *a.* rabínico. — *s.* habla rabínica.
rabbinical [rəˈbinikəl], *a.* rabínico.
rabbinism [ˈræbinizəm], *s.* rabinismo.
rabbinist [ˈræbinist], *s.* rabinista, *m.f.*
rabbit [ˈræbit], *s.* conejo; ***doe rabbit,*** coneja; ***Welsh rabbit,*** rebanada de pan con queso tostado; ***young rabbit,*** gazapo, gazapillo; ***rabbit-hole, rabbit-warren,*** conejera; ***rabbit-hutch,*** conejera. — *v.i.* cazar conejos; apiñarse.
rabble [ræbl], *s.* gentuza, chusma, turba, populacho, canalla; barra de pudelar.
rabid [ˈræbid], *a.* rabioso; fanático.
rabies [ˈreibi:z], *s.* rabia, hidrofobia.
race (1) [reis], *s.* raza; casta, estirpe; pueblo, nación; sabor (*vino*); ***human race,*** género humano.
race (2) [reis], *s.* carrera; ***mill race,*** caz, saetín; ***boat race,*** regata; ***race meeting,*** carreras (de caballo), *f.pl.* — *v.t.* hacer correr; competir con. — *v.i.* correr, embalarse; competir; ir de prisa.
race (3) [reis], *s.* raíz, *f.*; ***race-ginger,*** raíz de gengibre sin moler.
racecourse [ˈreiskɔ:s], *s,* estadio; hipódromo.
racehorse [ˈreishɔ:s], *s.* caballo de carreras.
raceme [rəˈsi:m], *s.* (*bot.*) racimo.
racemose, racemous [ˈræsiməs], *a.* racimoso.
racer [ˈreisə], *s.* caballo de carrera; coche de carrera; corredor.
racetrack [ˈreistræk], (*Am.*) [RACECOURSE].
rachis [ˈrækis], *s.* (*pl.* **rachides** [ˈrækidi:z]) (*bot.*) raquis, *m.inv.*; cañón de pluma.
rachitic [rəˈkitik], *a.* (*med.*) raquítico.
rachitis [rəˈkaitis], *s.* (*med.*) raquitis, *f.inv.*
racial [ˈreiʃəl], *a.* racial.
racialism, racism [ˈreiʃəlizəm, ˈreisizəm], *s.* racismo.
racialist, racist [ˈreiʃəlist, ˈreisist], *a.*, *s.* racista, *m.f.*
raciness [ˈreisinis], *s.* vivacidad, gracia picante; casticismo.
racing [ˈreisiŋ], *a.* de carrera(s); ***racing-car,*** coche de carreras, bólido; ***racing-circuit,*** pista de carreras; autódromo; ***racing driver,*** corredor (automovilista). — *s.* carreras, *f.pl.*
rack (1) [ræk], *s.* estante; percha; redecilla (*del equipaje*); astillero; armero; rambla; potro (*de tormento*); suplicio; cremallera; jirones de nubes; ***bottle rack,*** botellero; ***rack and pinion,*** (de) cremallera y piñón; ***rack railway,*** ferrocarril de cremallera. — *v.t.* atormentar, torturar; trasegar, embotellar; ***rack one's brains,*** devanarse los sesos.
rack (2) [ræk], *s.* ***to go to rack and ruin,*** caer en estado de ruina, hundirse, echarse a perder, ir de cabeza.
racket (1) [ˈrækit], *s.* estrépito, barahúnda, ruidazo, jaleo; traqueteo; (*fam.*) trampa; estafa, timo; estraperlo.
racket (2) [ˈrækit], *s.* raqueta (*de tenis*).
racketeer [rækiˈtiə], *s.* estafador; (*mercado negro*) estraperlista, *m.f.*
racketeering [rækiˈtiəriŋ], *s.* estafas, *f.pl.*; estraperlo.
rackety [ˈrækiti], *a.* bullicioso, ruidoso.
racking [ˈrækiŋ], *a.* (*dolor*) terrible, atroz.
racoon [rəˈku:n], *s.* mapache.
racy [ˈreisi], *a.* vivo, gracioso y picante, que tiene gracia y sal; castizo.
radar [ˈreidɑ:], *s.* radar; ***radar screen,*** pantalla de radar; ***radar station,*** estación de radar; ***radar technology,*** técnica(s) radárica(s).
raddle [rædl], *s.* almagre. — *v.t.* pintar de almagre.
radial [ˈreidiəl], *a.* radial.
radian [ˈreidiən], *s.* (*geom.*) radián.
radiance, radiancy [ˈreidiəns, -i], *s.* resplandor; brillo.
radiant [ˈreidiənt], *a.* radiante; brillante; resplendeciente.
radiate [ˈreidiit], *a.* radiado. — [ˈreidieit], *v.t.* radiar, irradiar; difundir. — *v.i.* (ir)radiarse.
radiation [reidiˈeiʃən], *s.* radiación; irradiación.
radiator [ˈreidieitə], *s.* radiador.
radical [ˈrædikəl], *a.*, *s.* radical.
radicalism [ˈrædikəlizəm], *s.* radicalismo.
radicalness [ˈrædikəlnis], *s.* naturaleza radical.
radication [rædiˈkeiʃən], *s.* radicación.
radicle [ˈrædikl], *s.* raicilla, radícula.
radio [ˈreidiou], *s.* radio, *f.*; ***over the radio,*** por radio; ***radio announcer,*** locutor; ***radio broadcast,*** emisión; ***radio listener,*** radioyente; ***radio play,*** comedia radiofónica; ***radio station,*** emisora. — *v.t.* radiar; transmitir por radio.
radioactive [reidiouˈæktiv], *a.* radioactivo.
radioactivity [reidiouækˈtiviti], *s.* radioactividad.
radioamplifier [reidiouˈæmplifaiə], *s.* radioamplificador.
radiodetector [reidioudiˈtektə], *s.* detector de ondas eléctricas.
radiogram [ˈreidiougræm], *s.* radiograma, *m.*; radiogramola.
radiograph [ˈreidiougræf], *s.* radiografía. — *v.t.* radiografiar.
radiographer [reidiˈɔgrəfə], *s.* radiografista, *m.f.*
radiography [reidiˈɔgrəfi], *s.* radiografía.
radiologist [reidiˈɔlədʒist], *s.* radiólogo.
radiology [reidiˈɔlədʒi], *s.* radiología.
radiometer [reidiˈɔmitə], *s.* radiómetro.
radiophare [ˈreidioufɛə], *s.* estación baliza, radio faro.
radiotelegraphy [reidioutiˈlegrəfi], *s.* radiotelegrafía.
radiotherapy [reidiouˈθerəpi], *s.* radioterapia.
radish [ˈrædiʃ], *s.* rábano.
radium [ˈreidiəm], *s.* radio.
radius [ˈreidiəs], *s.* (*pl.* **radii** [-ai]) radio.
radix [ˈreidiks], *s.* (*pl.* **radices** [-isi:z]) raíz, *f.*; (*mat.*) base, *f.*; (*gram.*) radical.
raffia [ˈræfiə], *s.* rafia.
raffish [ˈræfiʃ], *a.* disoluto, encanallado.
raffle [ræfl], *s.* rifa, sorteo. — *v.t.* rifar, sortear.
raft [rɑ:ft], *s.* balsa, almadía. — *v.t.* transportar en balsa.
rafter [ˈrɑ:ftə], *s.* viga, cabrio, traviesa, costanera. — *v.t.* construir con vigas.
raftsman [ˈrɑ:ftsmən], *s.* (*pl.* **-men** [-men]) almadiero.
rag (1) [ræg], *s.* trapo, andrajo, harapo, trapajo; periodicucho; ***in rags,*** harapiento; ***rag dealer, rag picker,*** trapero; ***rag, tag and bobtail,*** morralla, gentucilla, chusma; (*fam*) ***rag trade,*** industria del vestido *o* industria de los trapos (de moda); ***to feel like a rag,*** estar hecho papilla; ***to put on one's glad rags,*** endomingarse.
rag (2) [ræg], *s.* broma pesada; novatada; ***Rag Week,*** semana festiva estudiantil. — *v.t.* hacer una broma pesada a; dar una novatada a.
ragamuffin [ˈrægəmʌfin], *s.* golfo; zarrapastroso.
rage [reidʒ], *s.* rabia, furor, furia; ***to be all the rage,*** hacer furor. — *v.i.* rabiar; bramar.
ragged [ˈrægid], *a.* andrajoso, haraposo, harapiento; desigual, mellado.
raggedness [ˈrægidnis], *s.* (lo) haraposo, andrajoso *o* harapiento; (lo) desigual.

raging [ˈreidʒiŋ], *a.* rabioso; furioso; bramador.
raglan [ˈræglən], *s.* raglán.
ragman [ˈrægmæn], *s.* (*pl.* **-men** [-men]) trapero.
ragoût [rəˈgu:], *s.* estofado, guisado.
ragpicker [ˈrægpikə], *s.* trapero.
ragtag [ˈrægtæg], *s.* (***and bobtail***) [RAG].
ragtime [ˈrægtaim], *s.* (*mús.*) tiempo sincopado.
ragwort [ˈrægwə:t], *s.* hierba de Santiago.
raid [reid], *s.* incursión, correría, algara; entrada *o* irrupción repentina; ***air-raid,*** ataque aéreo, bombardeo aéreo. — *v.t.* hacer incursiones *o* algaras en; entrar *o* irrumpir repentinamente en; atacar; bombardear.
rail (1) [reil], *s.* barandilla, baranda, pasamano; (*mar.*) batayola, cairel; carril, riel, raíl; (*orn.*) rascón; ***by rail,*** por ferrocarril, en tren; ***to go*** *o* ***run off the rails,*** descarrilar, salirse de la vía; (*fig.*) despistarse; salirse de madre. — *v.t.* poner barandilla a; ***rail in,*** cercar con barandilla; ***rail off,*** separar con barandilla *o* con (una) cuerda.
rail (2) [reil], *v.i.* — ***at*** o ***against,*** despotricar de; desatarse en improperios contra.
railhead [ˈreilhed], *s.* final *o* término de la vía; (*mil.*) estación de ferrocarril para víveres y municiones.
railing [ˈreiliŋ], *s.* barandilla, pasamano, antepecho; verja.
raillery [ˈreiləri], *s.* burlas, *f.pl.*
railroad [ˈreilroud], *s.* (*Am.*) [RAILWAY]. — *v.t.* meter precipitadamente (en), empujar *o* lanzar (a).
railway [ˈreilwei], *a.* ferroviario. — *s.* ferrocarril; vía férrea; ***narrow-gauge railway,*** ferrocarril de vía estrecha; ***railway-carriage,*** vagón; ***railway-compartment,*** departamento; ***railway-engine,*** locomotora; ***railway-guard,*** jefe de(l) tren; ***railway-platform,*** andén; ***railway-porter,*** mozo (de estación); ***railway station,*** estación (de ferrocarril).
railwayman [ˈreilweimən], *s.* (*pl.* **-men** [-men]) ferroviario.
raiment [ˈreimənt], *s.* vestido, vestimenta.
rain [rein], *s.* lluvia; ***pouring rain,*** diluvio; ***rain gauge,*** pluviómetro; ***to pour with rain,*** llover a cántaros, diluviar. — *v.i.* llover; ***to rain cats and dogs, rain pitchforks,*** llover a cántaros, llover chuzos de punta; ***rain or shine,*** con lluvia o con sol.
rainbow [ˈreinbou], *s.* arco iris.
raincoat [ˈreinkout], *s.* impermeable.
raindrop [ˈreindrɔp], *s.* gota de lluvia.
rainfall [ˈreinfɔ:l], *s.* (cantidad de) lluvia; precipitación.
raininess [ˈreininis], *s.* (lo) lluvioso.
rainproof [ˈreinpru:f], *a.* impermeable.
rainstorm [ˈreinstɔ:m], *s.* aguacero, temporal de lluvia(s) *o* de agua(s).
rainwater [ˈreinwɔ:tə], *s.* agua (de lluvia).
rainy [ˈreini], *a.* lluvioso, de lluvia, de (mucha) agua.
raise [reiz], *s.* (*Am.*) [RISE]. — *v.t.* levantar, alzar, elevar; subir; erigir, erguir; ascender (*de categoría*); sacar a flote (*un barco*); reclutar (*un ejército*); cultivar (*un cultivo*); resucitar (*a los muertos*); suscitar, fomentar (*las dudas, las esperanzas*); izar, enarbolar (*una bandera*); criar (*animales*); reunir (*dinero*); poner (*pegas, objeciones*); plantear, suscitar (*problemas*); levantar (*un sitio, la voz*); ***raise one's hat,*** descubrirse; ***raise Cain,*** poner el grito en el cielo.
raiser [ˈreizə], *s.* fundador; cultivador; productor; educador; ***cattle raiser,*** ganadero; ***fire raiser,*** incendiario.
raisin [ˈreizin], *s.* pasa (*de uva*).
raising [ˈreiziŋ], *s.* elevación, levantamiento; cría (*de ganado*).
raj [rɑ:dʒ], *s.* soberanía, señorío, dominio.
raja, rajah [ˈrɑ:dʒə], *s.* rajá.
rake (1) [reik], *s.* (*agric.*) rastro; rastrillo; mielga. — *v.t.* rastrillar; (*fig.*) ***rake together,*** reunir a duras penas; (*fig.*) ***rake up,*** sacar a relucir *o* colación; (*fig.*) ***rake over the coals,*** volver sobr lo antiguo.
rake (2) [reik], *s.* libertino, tuno, calavera, *m.*
rake (3) [reik], *s.* (*mar.*) lanzamiento. — *v.i.* inclinarse.
rakehell [ˈreikhel], *s.* disoluto, libertino, perdido.
raki [ˈrɑ:ki], *s.* coñac turco.
raking [ˈreikiŋ], *a.*, *s.* rastrilleo, rastrillada, roza; terreno arrastrado.
rakish (1) [ˈreikiʃ], *a.* corrompido, libertino, perdido, licencioso.
rakish (2) [ˈreikiʃ], *a.* (*mar.*) de mástiles muy inclinados.
rakishness (1) [ˈreikiʃnis], *s.* libertinaje, disolución.
rakishness (2) [ˈreikiʃnis], *s.* (*mar.*) caída, inclinación de los palos.
rally (1) [ˈræli], *s.* reunión; rally. — *v.i.* reunirse; (*mil.*) rehacerse; recuperarse.
rally (2) [ˈræli], *v.t.* ridiculizar, embromar. — *v.i.* bromear.
rallying point [ˈræliiŋ pɔint], *s.* punto de reunión.
Ralph [rælf, reif]. Rodolfo.
ram [ræm], *s.* carnero, morueco; (*astron., astrol.*) ***the Ram,*** Aries, *m.*; ariete, espolón; pisón. — *v.t.* embestir; arremeter contra; abordar.
ramble [ræmbl], *s.* excursión (por el campo). — *v.i.* vagar; divagar.
rambler [ˈræmblə], *s.* excursionista, *m.f.*; divagador; ***rambler rose,*** rosal trepador.
rambling [ˈræmbliŋ], *a.* errante; divagador; destartalado. — *s.* excursionismo; divagación.
ramé [ræˈmei], *a.* (*blas.*) adornado.
ramekin [ˈræmikin], *s.* (*coc.*) plato compuesto de queso, huevos y migas de pan, etc.
ramose, ramous, rameous [ˈreimous, -məs, -miəs], *a.* ramoso.
ramification [ræmifiˈkeiʃən], *s.* ramificación.
ramify [ˈræmifai], *v.i.* ramificarse.
rammer [ˈræmə], *s.* pisón; baqueta (de fusil).
ramp [ræmp], *s.* rampa; estafa.
rampage [ræmˈpeidʒ], *s.* alboroto; motín; ***to go on the*** o ***a rampage,*** desmandarse, desbocarse, volverse loco, perder los estribos, entregarse al desenfreno.
rampancy [ˈræmpənsi], *s.* exuberancia; desenfreno.
rampant [ˈræmpənt], *a.* exuberante, desbordante; de locura; desenfrenado; (*blas.*) rampante.
rampart [ˈræmpɑ:t], *s.* (*fort.*) terraplén; muralla, baluarte.
rampion [ˈræmpiən], *s.* rapónchigo.
ramrod [ˈræmrɔd], *s.* baqueta, atacador.
ramshackle [ˈræmʃækl], *a.* desvencijado, destartalado.
ranch [rɑ:ntʃ], *s.* rancho; hacienda.
rancher, ranchman (*pl.* **-men**) [ˈrɑ:ntʃə, -mən (*pl.* -men)], *s.* hacendado; ganadero; ranchero.
rancid [ˈrænsid], *a.* rancio, rancioso.
rancidity [rænˈsiditi], *s.* rancidez.
rancorous [ˈræŋkərəs], *a.* rencoroso.
rancour [ˈræŋkə], *s.* rencor, encono.
randan [ˈrændæn], *s.* ***to go on the randan,*** irse de juerga *o* de picos pardos.
random [ˈrændəm], *a.* hecho *o* dicho al azar; casual, aleatorio; ***random sample,*** muestra cogida al azar; ***random shot,*** tiro disparado al azar *o* a lo loco. — *s.* ***at random,*** al azar; ***to speak at random,*** hablar a lo loco, sin orden ni concierto.
randy [ˈrændi], *a.* cachondo, calentón.
ranee [ˈrɑ:ni:], *s.* esposa de rajá.
range [reindʒ], *s.* alcance; autonomía, radio de acción; gama; escala; serie; surtido; extensión; ***cattle range,*** dehesa; ***firing range,*** campo de tiro; ***kitchen range,*** fogón; ***mountain range,*** sierra, cordillera; ***within range,*** a tiro; ***within range of,*** al alcance de; ***to take the range,*** cal-

cular la distancia. — *v.t.* ordenar, colocar, alinear. — *v.i.* — ***between,*** oscilar, fluctuar, variar, extenderse entre; ***range over,*** recorrer.
range-finder [ˈreindʒ-faində], *s.* telémetro.
ranger [ˈreindʒə], *s.* guardabosque(s).
ranging [ˈreindʒiŋ], *s.* (el) ordenar, (el) colocar.
rank (1) [ræŋk], *s.* categoría; rango; grado; graduación; fila, hilera; ***the ranks, the rank and file,*** la tropa; la masa; ***officer risen from the ranks,*** oficial patatero; ***to join the ranks,*** alistarse. — *v.t.* clasificar, ordenar; conceptuar. — *v.i.* clasificarse, figurar; ***rank above,*** ser superior a; ***rank among,*** figurar entre; ***rank as,*** equivaler a; ***rank with,*** equipararse con; ***rank high,*** ser tenido en gran estima.
rank (2) [ræŋk], *a.* lozano, exuberante; rancio; (*fam.*) redomado.
rankle [ræŋkl], *v.t.* irritar, escocer; ***it rankles (me) still,*** todavía (me) escuece. — *v.i.* irritarse.
rankling [ˈræŋkliŋ], *a.* que irrita *o* escuece. — *s.* irritación.
rankness [ˈræŋknis], *s.* (lo) lujuriante; rancidez.
ransack [ˈrænsæk], *v.t.* desvalijar; saquear; registrar de arriba abajo.
ransom [ˈrænsəm], *s.* rescate; redención. — *v.t.* rescatar; redimir.
rant [rænt], *v.i.* desvariar, desbarrar (a gritos); vociferar.
ranter [ˈræntə], *s.* declamador, vociferador.
ranting [ˈræntiŋ], *a.* vociferante. — *s.* (el) desbarrar.
ranula [ˈrænjulə], *s.* ránula.
ranunculus [rəˈnʌŋkjuləs], *s.* ranúnculo.
rap [ræp], *s.* golpe seco, golpecito; ***I don't care a rap,*** (no) me importa un bledo; ***to take the rap,*** pagar el pato. — *v.t.* golpear; ***rap out,*** espetar; ***rap s.o. over the knuckles,*** (*lit.*) darle a alguien en los nudillos; (*fig.*) echar una bronca *o* un rapapolvo a alguien. — *v.i.* golpear; ***rap at the door,*** llamar a la puerta.
rapacious [rəˈpeiʃəs], *a.* rapaz.
rapaciousness, rapacity [rəˈpeiʃəsnis, rəˈpæsiti], *s.* rapacidad.
rape (1) [reip], *s.* violación, estrupro; destrucción. — *v.t.* violar, forzar, estuprar.
rape (2) [reip], *s.* (*bot.*) colza.
Raphael [ˈræfeil]. Rafael.
rapid [ˈræpid], *a.* rápido, veloz. — *s.* (*pl.*) rápidos, *m.pl.*, rabión.
rapidity, rapidness [rəˈpiditi, ˈræpidnis], *s.* rapidez, celeridad.
rapier [ˈreipiə], *s.* estoque.
rapine [ˈræpin], *s.* rapiña.
rapprochement [ræˈprɔʃmɔŋ], *s.* acercamiento.
rapscallion [ræpˈskæljən], *s.* tunante, granuja, bribón.
rapt [ræpt], *a.* embelesado, extasiado; ***to listen with rapt attention,*** escuchar absorto.
rapture [ˈræptʃə], *s.* éxtasis, *m.inv.*, arrebatamiento, arrobamiento, embelesamiento.
rapturous [ˈræptʃərəs], *a.* delirante, extático.
rapturously [ˈræptʃərəsli], *adv.* con éxtasis.
rare (1) [rɛə], *a.* raro; muy poco frecuente; muy poco usado.
rare (2) [rɛə], *a.* (*coc.*) poco pasado.
rarebit [ˈrɛəbit], *s.* ***Welsh rarebit,*** *v.* [RABBIT].
rarefaction [rɛəriˈfækʃən], *s.* rarefacción, enrarecimiento.
rarefy [ˈrɛərifai], *v.t.* enrarecer. — *v.i.* enrarecerse.
rarely [ˈrɛəli], *adv.* rara vez, pocas veces.
rareness, rarity [ˈrɛənis, ˈrɛəriti], *s.* rareza, (lo) raro; (lo) poco frecuente; (lo) poco usado.
rascal [ˈrɑːskəl], *s.* bribón, pícaro, bellaco, tunante, truhán, pillo, granuja.
rascality [rɑːsˈkæliti], *s.* bribonería, bellaquería, truhanería.
rascallion [rɑːsˈkæljən], [RAPSCALLION].
rascally [ˈrɑːskəli], *a.* de pícaro, de pillo, truhanesco.
rase [RAZE].
rash (1) [ræʃ], *a.* temerario, precipitado, inconsiderado.
rash (2) [ræʃ], *s.* erupción, sarpullido.
rasher [ˈræʃə], *s.* loncha (de jamón).
rashness [ˈræʃnis], *s.* temeridad, precipitación.
rasp [rɑːsp], *s.* raspador, escofina; tono áspero. — *v.t.* raspar, escofinar; decir con tono áspero. — *v.i.* rechinar.
raspberry [ˈrɑːzbəri], *s.* frambuesa; ***raspberry bush,*** frambueso.
rasper [ˈrɑːspə], *s.* raspador.
rasping [ˈrɑːspiŋ], *a.* áspero, bronco. — *s.* raspaduras, *f.pl.*
rat [ræt], *s.* rata; (*fig.*) canalla, *m.*; desertor; chivato; ***to smell a rat,*** verle las orejas al lobo; olerse algo. — *v.i.* cazar ratas; rajarse; desertar; chivarse, ir con el soplo; ***rat on,*** delatar, traicionar. — *interj.* ***rats!*** (*fam.*) ¡narices!
ratable [ˈreitəbl], *a.* imponible, sujeto a contribución; tasable.
ratafia [rætəˈfiə], *s.* ratafia.
rat catcher [ˈræt kætʃə], *s.* cazarratas, *m.inv.*
ratch [rætʃ], *s.* trinquete.
ratchet [ˈrætʃit], *s.* trinquete.
rate [reit], *s.* relación; proporción; tanto (por ciento); razón; velocidad, paso; tasa, precio; tipo; tarifa; ***at a cheap rate,*** a un precio reducido; ***at the rate of,*** a razón de; ***at any rate,*** de todas formas; ***at that rate,*** de ese modo; ***first rate,*** de primera clase; (*pl.*) contribución (municipal). — *v.t.* tasar, valorar, valuar; clasificar; apreciar; imponer contribución a; reñir, regañar; ***rate s.o. highly,*** tener muy buen concepto de alguien. — *v.i.* valer.
ratepayer [ˈreitpeiə], *s.* contribuyente.
rather [ˈrɑːðə], *adv.* más bien; mejor; primero, antes; algo, bastante; ***or rather,*** mejor dicho; ***I had*** (o ***would***) ***rather,*** preferiría, me gustaría más; ***I rather expected it,*** la verdad es que no me choca, la verdad es que me lo esperaba. — *interj.* ¡ya lo creo!
ratification [rætifiˈkeiʃən], *s.* ratificación.
ratifier [ˈrætifaiə], *s.* ratificador.
ratify [ˈrætifai], *v.t.* ratificar.
rating [ˈreitiŋ], *s.* clasificación; tasación; contribución; (*mar.*) clase; marinero.
ratio [ˈreiʃiou], *s.* razón, *f.*, relación, proporción.
ratiocinant [ræʃiˈɔsinənt], *a.* raciocinador, razonador.
ratiocination [ræʃiɔsiˈneiʃən], *s.* raciocinación.
ration [ˈræʃən], *s.* ración; ***ration book,*** cartilla de racionamiento; ***off the ration,*** no racionado. — *v.t.* racionar.
rational [ˈræʃənəl], *a.* racional, razonable.
rationale [ræʃəˈnɑːl], *s.* razón fundamental, *f.*
rationalism [ˈræʃənəlizəm], *s.* racionalismo.
rationalist [ˈræʃənəlist], *a., s.* racionalista, *m.f.*
rationality, rationalness [ræʃəˈnæliti, ˈræʃənəlnis], *s.* racionalidad.
rationalization [ræʃənəlaiˈzeiʃən], *s.* racionalización.
rationalize [ˈræʃənəlaiz], *v.t.* racionalizar.
rationing [ˈræʃəniŋ], *s.* racionamiento.
Ratisbon [ˈrætisbɔn]. Ratisbona.
ratite [ˈrætait], *s.* (*orn.*) corredora.
ratline, ratling [ˈrætlin, ˈrætliŋ], *s.* (*mar.*) flechaste.
ratoon [rəˈtuːn], *s.* serpollo; retoño de caña de azúcar.
rat-tail [ˈræt-teil], *s.* (*carp.*) lima de cola de rata.
rattan [rəˈtæn], *s.* roten *o* rota; junquillo, bejuco.
ratteen [rəˈtiːn], *s.* ratina.
ratter [ˈrætə], *s.* gato *o* perro ratonero.
ratting [ˈrætiŋ], *s.* (*fam.*) chivatazo, soplo.

rattle [rætl], *s.* tableteo; matraqueo; golpeteo; matraca, carraca; sonajero; charla, parloteo; cascabel; ***death rattle,*** estertor; ***rattle-brained, rattle-headed,*** casquivano. — *v.t.* hacer sonar como una matraca; sacudir; (*fam., fig.*) aturrullar, desconcertar, meter miedo a; (*fam.*) ***rattle off,*** enumerar rápidamente. — *v.i.* sonar; crujir; castañetear; tabletear; repiquetear; (*fam.*) ***rattle on,*** parlotear.

rattler (1) [ˈrætlə], *s.* parlanchín, tarabilla.

rattler (2) [ˈrætlə], *s.* crótalo.

rattlesnake [ˈrætlsneik], *s.* serpiente de cascabel, crótalo; ***rattlesnake-root,*** lechera.

rattling [ˈrætliŋ], *a.* que traquetea; (*fam.*) ***at a rattling pace,*** a mucha velocidad. — *adv.* (*fam.*) ***rattling good,*** estupendo.

rat-trap [ˈræt-træp], *s.* ratonera.

ratty [ˈræti], *a.* (*fam.*) cabreado.

raucous [ˈrɔːkəs], *a.* ronco; estridente.

ravage [ˈrævidʒ], *s.* estrago, destrucción, destrozo. — *v.t.* asolar, destruir; saquear; ajar (*la piel*).

rave [reiv], *v.i.* delirar, desvariar; ***rave about,*** hacerse lenguas de; pirrarse por; ***rave at,*** injuriar como un demente.

ravellings [ˈrævəliŋz], *s.pl.* hilachas, *f.pl.*

raven [ˈreivən], *s.* cuervo, grajo.

ravening, ravenous [ˈrævəniŋ, -əs], *a.* hambriento, famélico.

ravenously [ˈrævənəsli], *adv.* ***to be ravenously hungry,*** tener un hambre canina.

ravine [rəˈviːn], *s.* barranco, desfiladero.

raving [ˈreiviŋ], *a.* delirante, loco (perdido). — *adv.* ***raving mad,*** loco de atar. — *s.* delirio, desvarío.

ravish [ˈræviʃ], *v.t.* violar, forzar, estuprar; raptar; embelesar.

ravisher [ˈræviʃə], *s.* violador, forzador.

ravishing [ˈræviʃiŋ], *a.* arrebatador, embelesador, embriagador.

ravishment [ˈræviʃmənt], *s.* violación; rapto; éxtasis, *m.inv.*, arrobamiento.

raw [rɔː], *a.* crudo; en bruto; novato; ***raw-boned,*** descarnado, huesudo; ***raw cotton,*** algodón en rama; ***raw deal,*** trato injusto, injusticia; ***raw flesh,*** carne viva; ***raw hand,*** novato; ***raw hide,*** cuero crudo; ***raw material,*** materia prima; materia bruta; ***raw meat,*** carne cruda; ***raw recruit,*** soldado bisoño; ***raw silk,*** seda en rama; ***raw spirits,*** alcohol puro; ***raw sugar,*** azúcar crudo. — *s.* ***to get on the raw,*** herir en lo vivo.

rawness [ˈrɔːnis], *s.* crudeza; (lo) crudo; falta de experiencia.

ray (1) [rei], *s.* rayo; (*bot.*) bráctea. — *v.t.* radiar. — *v.i.* emitir rayos.

ray (2) [rei], *s.* (*ict.*) raya.

ray-grass [ˈrei-grɑːs], *s.* vallico.

Raymond [ˈreimənd]. Ramón, Raimundo.

rayon [ˈreiɔn], *s.* (*tej.*) rayón.

raze [reiz], *v.t.* arrasar, asolar.

razee [ræˈziː], *s.* (*mar.*) buque rebajado.

razor [ˈreizə], *s.* navaja de afeitar; colmillo de jabalí; ***electric razor,*** maquinilla eléctrica; (*orn.*) ***razor-bill,*** alca; ***razor blade,*** hoja *o* cuchilla de afeitar; ***razor case,*** navajero; ***razor shell,*** navaja (marisco); ***razor strop,*** suavizador; ***safety razor,*** maquinilla de afeitar.

re (1) [rei], *s.* (*mús.*) re.

re (2) [riː], *prep.* (*for., com.*) acerca de, ref.

reabsorb [ˈriːəbˈsɔːb], *v.t.* reabsorber.

reabsorption [ˈriːəbˈsɔːpʃən], *s.* reabsorción.

reaccess [ˈriːækses], *s.* (*med.*) recidiva.

reach [riːtʃ], *s.* alcance; distancia; extensión; capacidad; tramo, sección; (*mar.*) bordada; ***beyond reach, out of reach,*** fuera de alcance; ***within (easy) reach,*** al alcance. — *v.t.* alcanzar, llegar a; lograr; ***reach out one's hand,*** alargar la mano. — *v.i.* extenderse; ***reach after*** o ***for,*** hacer esfuerzos para alcanzar; requerir; ***reach out to,*** alargar la mano *o* el brazo para (coger).

react [riːˈækt], *v.i.* reaccionar.

reacting [riːˈæktiŋ], *a.* reactivo. — *s.* reacción.

reaction [riːˈækʃən], *s.* reacción; resistencia.

reactionary, reactionist [riːˈækʃənəri, -ist], *a., s.* reaccionario.

reactive [riːˈæktiv], *a.* reactivo.

reactivity [riːækˈtiviti], *s.* reactividad.

reactor [riːˈæktə], *s.* reactor; (*quím.*) reactivo.

read [riːd], *v.t.* (*pret., p.p.* **read** [red]) leer; estudiar; interpretar; ***read the future,*** leer (en) el futuro; ***read out,*** anunciar; ***read over,*** repasar; ***read s.o.'s palm,*** decirle la buenaventura a alguien; ***read proofs,*** corregir pruebas; ***read too much into sth.,*** buscarle tres pies al gato. — *v.i.* leer; decir, rezar; indicar, marcar (*termómetro*); ***read about,*** enterarse de; leer; ***I've read about it,*** lo he leído; ***read aloud,*** leer en voz alta; ***read between the lines,*** leer entre líneas; ***read on,*** seguir leyendo; ***read through,*** leerse de cabo a rabo.

readability, readableness [riːdəˈbiliti, ˈriːdəblnis], *s.* calidad de legible; amenidad.

readable [ˈriːdəbl], *a.* leíble; ameno.

reader [ˈriːdə], *s.* lector; libro de lectura; (*impr.*) corrector; (*universidad*) profesor adjunto.

readership [ˈriːdəʃip], *s.* (número de) lectores (*de un periódico*); (*universidad*) adjuntía.

readily [ˈredili], *adv.* fácilmente; con presteza.

readiness [ˈredinis], *s.* prontitud; buena disposición; buena voluntad; preparación; ***in readiness,*** preparado.

reading [ˈriːdiŋ], *s.* lectura; estudio; interpretación; lección; ***reading book,*** libro de lectura; ***reading room,*** sala de lectura.

readjust [ˈriːəˈdʒʌst], *v.t.* reajustar; reacomodar; volver a orientar (de nuevo).

readjustment [ˈriːəˈdʒʌstment], *s.* reajuste; reacomodo; nueva orientación.

readmission [ˈriːədˈmiʃən], *s.* readmisión.

readmit [ˈriːədˈmit], *v.t.* readmitir, volver a admitir.

readmittance [ˈriːədˈmitəns], *s.* readmisión.

ready [ˈredi], *a.* listo, preparado (***for, to,*** para); pronto; dispuesto; ***ready answer,*** respuesta fácil; respuesta para todo; ***ready for action,*** dispuesto para el combate, lanza en ristre; ***ready for anything,*** dispuesto a todo; ***ready for use, to use,*** listo para usar(se); ***ready money,*** dinero efectivo, dinero contante y sonante; ***ready wit,*** ingenio despierto; ***to get*** o ***make ready,*** preparar(se) (***for, to,*** para), disponer(se) (***for, to,*** a). — *adv.* ***ready-made,*** hecho; ***ready-made suit,*** traje hecho. — *s.* ***at the ready,*** listo; apercibido; en ristre.

reaffirm [ˈriːəˈfəːm], *v.t.* afirmar de nuevo, reiterar.

reafforest [ˈriːəˈfɔrist], *v.t.* repoblar de árboles.

reafforestation [ˈriːəfɔriˈsteiʃən], *s.* repoblación forestal.

reagent [riːˈeidʒənt], *s.* reactivo.

real [riəl], *a.* real; verdadero; auténtico, legítimo; efectivo; ***real estate,*** bienes raíces, *m.pl.*

realgar [riːˈælgɑː], *s.* rejalgar.

realism [ˈriəlizəm], *s.* realismo.

realist [ˈriəlist], *s.* realista, *m.f.*

realistic [riəˈlistik], *a.* realista.

reality [riːˈæliti], *s.* realidad; ***in reality,*** en la realidad.

realizable [ˈriəlaizəbl], *a.* realizable.

realization [riəlaiˈzeiʃən], *s.* realización; comprensión, (el) comprender *o* darse cuenta (de).

realize [ˈriəlaiz], *v.t.* realizar; darse cuenta de, comprender.

really [ˈriəli], *adv.* en realidad; realmente; verdaderamente; ***really?*** ¿ de veras ?

realm [relm], *s.* reino; (*fig.*) esfera, campo.

realtor [ˈriəltə], *s.* (*Am.*) agente de fincas.

realty [ˈriəlti], *s.* (*der.*) bienes raíces, *m.pl.*; (*Am.*) [REAL ESTATE].

ream [riːm], *s.* resma (de papel); (*pl., fig.*) montones, *m.pl.*, muchísimo.
reamer [ˈriːmə], *s.* escariador.
reanimate [ˈriːˈænimeit], *v.t.* reanimar; resucitar.
reap [riːp], *v.t.*, *v.i.* segar; cosechar; (*fig.*) ***reap a fine*** o ***rich harvest,*** hacer su agosto.
reaper [ˈriːpə], *s.* segador; segadora (mecánica).
reaping [ˈriːpiŋ], *s.* siega; ***reaping-machine,*** segadora.
reappear [ˈriːəˈpiə], *v.i.* reaparecer, volver a aparecer.
reappearance [ˈriːəˈpiərəns], *s.* reaparición.
reapply [ˈriːəˈplai], *v.t.* aplicar de nuevo. — *v.i.* presentarse de nuevo; presentar una nueva solicitud.
reappoint [ˈriːəˈpɔint], *v.t.* nombrar de nuevo.
reappointment [ˈriːəˈpɔintmənt], *s.* nuevo nombramiento.
rear (1) [riə], *a.* posterior; trasero; zaguero; de cola; ***rear admiral,*** contraalmirante; ***rear lamp,*** piloto *o* luz de cola. — *s.* trasera; espalda; raga; parte posterior; fondo; cola; retaguardia; ***in the rear,*** a retaguardia; ***to bring up the rear,*** cerrar la marcha.
rear (2) (riə], *v.t.* criar; erigir, alzar. — *v.i.* encabritarse, empinarse.
rearguard [ˈriəgɑːd], *s.* retaguardia.
rearm [ˈriːˈɑːm], *v.t.*, *v.i.* rearmar(se).
rearmament [ˈriːˈɑːməmənt], *s.* rearme.
rearmost [ˈriəmoust], *a.* último, postrero.
rearrange [ˈriːəˈreindʒ], *v.t.* arreglar *u* ordenar de nuevo.
rearrangement [ˈriːəˈreindʒmənt], *s.* nuevo arreglo.
rearward [ˈriəwəd], *a.* posterior, último. — *adv.* (*t.* **rearwards** [-wədz]) hacia atrás. — *s.* retaguardia.
reascend [ˈriːəˈsend], *v.i.* volver a subir, subir de nuevo.
reascension [ˈriːəˈsenʃən], *s.* nueva ascensión.
reascent [ˈriːəˈsent], *s.* nueva subida.
reason [ˈriːzən], *s.* razón; motivo, causa; ***by reason of,*** a causa de; ***within reason,*** dentro de lo razonable; ***it stands to reason,*** es lógico, es evidente; ***to listen to*** o ***see reason,*** atender a razones, entrar en razón. — *v.t.*, *v.i.* razonar, discurrir.
reasonable [ˈriːzənəbl], *a.* razonable; justo, equitativo; sensato; módico, asequible; prudencial; justificado, motivado; discreto.
reasonableness [ˈriːzənəblnis], *s.* razón, *f.*, racionalidad; (lo) razonable *etc.*
reasoner [ˈriːzənə], *s.* razonador, dialéctico.
reasoning [ˈriːzəniŋ], *s.* raciocinio, razonamiento; argumento; discurso.
reasonless [ˈriːzənlis], *a.* desrazonable, sin razón.
reassemble [ˈriːəˈsembl], *v.t.* reunir, juntar de nuevo. — *v.i.* reunirse de nuevo.
reassert [ˈriːəˈsəːt], *v.t.* reafirmar, reiterar.
reassume [ˈriːəˈsjuːm], *v.t.* reasumir.
reassumption [ˈriːəˈsʌmpʃən], *s.* reasunción.
reassurance [ˈriːəˈʃuərəns], *s.* seguridades, *f.pl.*, garantías, *f.pl.*; reaseguro.
reassure [ˈriːəˈʃuə], *v.t.* asegurar de nuevo; tranquilizar.
reassuring [ˈriːəˈʃuəriŋ], *a.* tranquilizador, que tranquiliza; alentador.
reattempt [ˈriːəˈtempt], *v.t.* ensayar de nuevo.
rebaptize [ˈriːbæpˈtaiz], *v.t.* rebautizar.
rebate (1) [ˈriːbeit], *s.* (*com.*) descuento, rebaja. — [riːˈbeit], *v.t.* rebajar, descontar.
rebate (2) [riːˈbeit], *s.* (*carp.*) encaje; ranura; cepillo; majadero; asperón. — *v.t.* practicar una ranura en.
rebec [ˈriːbek], *s.* rabel.
rebel [ˈrebəl], *a.*, *s.* rebelde. — [riˈbel], *v.i.* rebelarse, sublevarse.
rebellion [riˈbeljən], *s.* rebelión, sublevación.
rebellious [riˈbeljəs], *a.* rebelde, insubordinado.
rebelliousness [riˈbeljəsnis], *s.* insubordinación, rebeldía.
reblossom [ˈriːˈblɔsəm], *v.i.* florecer de nuevo.
rebore [ˈriːˈbɔː], *s.* (*mec.*) rectificado. — *v.t.* rectificar.
rebound (1) [ˈriːbaund], *s.* rebote; retroceso; ***on the rebound,*** de rechazo. — [riːˈbaund], *v.i.* rebotar.
rebound (2) [ˈriːˈbaund], *a.* (*libro*) reencuadernado.
rebuff [riˈbʌf], *s.* desaire, rechazo. — *v.t.* desairar, rechazar.
rebuild [ˈriːˈbild], *v.t.* (*pret.*, *p.p.* **rebuilt** [-ˈbilt]) reedificar, reconstruir.
rebuke [riˈbjuːk], *s.* reprimenda, reprensión. — *v.t.* dar una reprimenda a, reprender.
rebuker [riˈbjuːkə], *s.* reprensor.
rebus [ˈriːbəs], *s.* jeroglífico.
rebut [riˈbʌt], *v.t.* refutar, rebatir.
rebuttal [riˈbʌtl], *s.* refutación.
recalcitrant [riˈkælsitrənt], *a.* recalcitrante, reacio.
recalescence [ˈriːkəˈlesəns], *s.* recalescencia.
recall [riˈkɔːl], *s.* llamada (*para que alguien vuelva*); retirada; llamada a escena; (***gone***) ***beyond recall,*** irremisiblemente olvidado. — *v.t.* llamar, hacer volver; retirar; recordar, traer a la memoria.
recant [riˈkænt], *v.t.* retractar. — *v.i.* retractarse, desdecirse, cantar la palinodia.
recantation [riːˈkænˈteiʃən], *s.* retractación, palinodia.
recanter [riˈkæntə], *s.* persona que se retracta.
recapitulate [riːkəˈpitjuleit], *v.t.* recapitular, resumir.
recapitulation [riːkəpitjuˈleiʃən], *s.* recapitulación, resumen.
recapitulatory [riːkəˈpitjulətəri], *a.* recapitulatorio.
recapture [ˈriːˈkæptʃə], *s.* represa; recobro, recuperación. — *v.t.* represar; recobrar, recuperar; volver a coger *o* a capturar *o* a prender.
recast [ˈriːˈkɑːst], *v.t.* (*pret.*, *p.p.* **recast**) refundir.
recede [riˈsiːd], *v.i.* retroceder, retirarse; alejarse; bajar.
receipt [riˈsiːt], *s.* recepción; cobranza; recibo; (*pl.*) ingresos, *m.pl.*, entradas, *f.pl.*; ***receipt book,*** libro de ingresos; ***on receipt of,*** al recibir; ***to acknowledge receipt of,*** acusar recibo de; ***I am in receipt of your letter,*** obra en mi poder su carta. — *v.t.* poner el recibí a.
receipted [riˈsiːtid], *a.* que lleva el recibí.
receivable [riˈsiːvəbl], *a.* admisible; por cobrar.
receive [riˈsiːv], *v.t.* recibir; admitir; cobrar, percibir; acoger; ***receive warmly,*** acoger calurosamente *o* cariñosamente.
receiver [riˈsiːvə], *s.* recibidor; (*rad.*) receptor; (*tele.*) auricular; (*der.*) síndico (*de quiebra*).
receivership [riˈsiːvəʃip], *s.* receptoría; sindicatura.
receiving [riˈsiːviŋ], *a.* receptor, que recibe; ***receiving set,*** (aparato) receptor. — *s.* recepción; cobranza.
recension [riˈsenʃən], *s.* recensión; revisión crítica.
recent [ˈriːsənt], *a.* reciente; ***in recent years,*** en los últimos años.
recently [ˈriːsəntli], *adv.* recientemente, últimamente; hace poco.
recentness [ˈriːsəntnis], *s.* origen reciente, novedad.
receptacle [riˈseptəkl], *s.* receptáculo, recipiente.
receptibility [riseptiˈbiliti], *s.* receptividad.
reception [riˈsepʃən], *s.* recepción; recibimiento; acogida; admisión, ingreso; ***reception room,*** sala de recibo.
receptionist [riˈsepʃənist], *s.* recepcionista, *f.*
receptive [riˈseptiv], *a.* receptivo.
recess [riˈses], *s.* hueco, nicho; vacaciones, *f.pl.*; suspensión; intermedio; ***in the farthest recesses of,*** en lo más recóndito de.
recession [riˈseʃən], *s.* retroceso; (*com.*) recesión.
rechange [ˈriːˈtʃeindʒ], *v.t.* volver a cambiar.

recharge [ˈriːˈtʃɑːdʒ], *v.t.* volver a cargar; acusar de nuevo.
recherché [riˈʃɛəʃei], *a.* rebuscado.
recidivism [riˈsidivizəm], *s.* reincidencia.
recidivist [riˈsidivist], *s.* reincidente.
recipe [ˈresipi], *s.* receta.
recipient [riˈsipiənt], *s.* recibidor; receptor; el que recibe *o* reciba.
reciprocal [riˈsiprəkəl], *a.* recíproco, mutuo. — *s.* recíproca.
reciprocality, reciprocalness [risiprəˈkæliti, riˈsiprəkəlnis], *s.* reciprocidad.
reciprocate [riˈsiprəkeit], *v.t.* corresponder a, devolver; reciprocar; (*mec.*) dar movimiento de vaivén a. — *v.i.* corresponder; (*mec.*) oscilar, alternar.
reciprocating [riˈsiprəkeitiŋ], *a.* (*mec.*) alternativo, de vaivén.
reciprocation [risiprəˈkeiʃən], *s.* reciprocación
reciprocity [resiˈprɔsiti], *s.* reciprocidad.
recision [riˈsiʒən], *s.* rescisión.
recital [riˈsaitl], *s.* relación; enumeración; recital.
recitation [resiˈteiʃən], *s.* recitación; recitado.
recitative [resitəˈtiːv], *a.* recitativo. — *s.* recitado.
recite [riˈsait], *v.t.* recitar; relatar, referir, narrar, contar; citar. — *v.i.* recitar; declamar.
reciter [riˈsaitə], *s.* recitador; declamador.
reck [rek], *v.t.* tener en cuenta. — *v.i.* preocuparse; (*poét.*) importar.
reckless [ˈreklis], *a.* temerario, irreflexivo; (*acto*) imprudente.
recklessness [ˈreklisnis], *s.* temeridad, irreflexión, imprudencia.
reckon [ˈrekən], *v.t.* calcular; ***reckon as,*** considerar como; ***reckon up,*** calcular, echar la cuenta de. — *v.i.* calcular; ***reckon on, upon,*** contar con; ***reckon with,*** tener en cuenta.
reckoner [ˈrekənə], *s.* calculador; ***ready reckoner,*** libro de cálculos hechos.
reckoning [ˈrekəniŋ], *s.* cálculo, cómputo; cuenta; ajuste de cuentas; (*mar.*) ***dead reckoning,*** estima; ***day of reckoning,*** día de ajustar las cuentas; ***out in one's reckoning,*** equivocado en el cálculo.
reclaim [ˈriːˈkleim], *v.t.* reclamar; recuperar; ganar; hacer utilizable; reformar.
reclaimable [ˈriːˈkleiməbl], *a.* reclamable; utilizable.
reclamation [rekləˈmeiʃən], *s.* reclamación; recuperación; utilización; ***land reclamation,*** rescate de terrenos.
recline [riˈklain], *v.t.* reclinar, recostar. — *v.i.* reclinarse, recostarse.
reclining [riˈklainiŋ], *a.* reclinado, recostado; reclinable.
reclose [ˈriːˈklouz], *v.t.* volver a cerrar.
recluse [riˈkluːs], *a., s.* recluso; solitario.
reclusion [riˈkluːʒən], *s.* reclusión; recogimiento, soledad, aislamiento.
recognition [rekəgˈniʃən], *s.* reconocimiento.
recognizable [ˈrekəgnaizəbl], *a.* reconocible.
recognizance [riˈkɔ(g)nizəns], *s.* reconocimiento; (*der.*) obligación.
recognize [ˈrekəgnaːz], *v.t.* reconocer.
recoil [riˈkɔil], *s.* retroceso; reculada; culatazo. — *v.i.* retroceder, recular.
recoin [ˈriːˈkɔin], *v.t.* acuñar de nuevo.
recoinage [ˈriːˈkɔinidʒ], *s.* nueva acuñación.
recollect [rekəˈlekt], *v.t.* recordar, acordarse de.
recollection [rekəˈlekʃən], *s.* recuerdo.
recollective [rekəˈlektiv], *a.* recordativo.
recombine [ˈriːkəmˈbain], *v.t.* combinar de nuevo.
recommence [ˈriːkəˈmens], *v.t., v.i.* volver a comenzar, comenzar de nuevo.
recommend [rekəˈmend], *v.t.* recomendar; ***recommend warmly,*** encarecer.
recommendable [rekəˈmendəbl], *a.* recomendable.
recommendation [rekəmenˈdeiʃən], *s.* recomendación; ***warm recommendation,*** encarecimiento.
recommendatory [rekəˈmendətəri], *a.* recomendatario.
recommender [rekəˈmendə], *s.* recomendante.
recommit [ˈriːkəˈmit], *v.t.* confiar de nuevo; trasladar de nuevo; volver a prender *o* encarcelar; cometer de nuevo.
recommitment, recommittal [ˈriːkəˈmitmənt, -ˈmitl], *s.* acto de volver a confiar, trasladar *o* encarcelar.
recompense [ˈrekəmpens], *s.* recompensa, remuneración, retribución. — *v.t.* recompensar, retribuir, remunerar.
recompose [ˈriːkəmˈpouz], *v.t.* volver a calmar, tranquilizar; recomponer, volver a componer; volver a ajustar; rehacer.
recomposition [ˈriːkɔmpəˈziʃən], *s.* recomposición.
reconcilable [rekənˈsailəbl], *a.* reconciliable.
reconcile [ˈrekənsail], *v.t.* reconciliar. — *v.r.* ***reconcile o.s. to,*** resignarse (*to*, a).
reconcilement [ˈrekənsailmənt], *s.* reconciliación.
reconciler [ˈrekənsailə], *s.* reconciliador, conciliador.
reconciliation [rekənsiliˈeiʃən], *s.* conciliación, reconciliación.
reconciliatory [rekənˈsiliətəri], *a.* reconciliador.
recondense [ˈriːkənˈdens], *v.t.* volver a condensar.
recondite [ˈrekəndait], *a.* recóndito.
recondition [ˈriːkənˈdiʃən], *v.t.* (*mec.*) reacondicionar; rectificar.
reconfirm [ˈriːkənˈfəːm], *v.t.* reconfirmar.
reconnaissance [riˈkɔnisəns], *s.* (*mil.*) reconocimiento; exploración.
reconnoitre [rekəˈnɔitə], *v.t.* (*mil.*) reconocer; explorar. — *v.i.* hacer un reconocimiento, batir el campo.
reconquer [ˈriːˈkɔŋkə], *v.t.* reconquistar.
reconquest [ˈriːˈkɔŋkwest], *s.* reconquista.
reconsecrate [ˈriːˈkɔnsikreit], *v.t.* volver a consagrar.
reconsecration [ˈriːkɔnsiˈkreiʃən], *s.* nueva consagración.
reconsider [ˈriːkənˈsidə], *v.t.* volver a considerar volver a pensar.
reconsideration [ˈriːkənsidəˈreiʃən], *s.* nueva consideración, nueva reflexión.
reconstruct [ˈriːkənˈstrʌkt], *v.t.* reconstruir, reedificar.
reconstruction [ˈriːkənˈstrʌkʃən], *s.* reconstrucción, reedificación.
reconvene [ˈriːkənˈviːn], *v.t.* reunir de nuevo, convocar de nuevo.
reconvention [ˈriːkənˈvenʃən], *s.* reconvención.
reconversion [ˈriːkənˈvəːʃən], *s.* reconversión.
reconvert [ˈriːkənˈvəːt], *v.t.* volver a convertir.
record [ˈrekɔːd], *s.* registro; partida; expediente; acta, documento, relación; antecedentes, *m.pl.*, historial, carrera; disco (gramofónico); récord, marca; (*pl.*) archivo(s); inform(es); anales, *m.pl.*, memorias, *f.pl.*; ***off the record,*** no oficial, confidencial; entre nosotros; ***on record,*** registrado; que consta; que se conoce; ***record breaker,*** el que supera la marca; ***record changer,*** cambiadiscos, *m.inv.*; ***record crop,*** cosecha sin precedentes; ***record library,*** discoteca; ***record office,*** archivo, registro; ***record time,*** tiempo récord; ***to beat*** o ***break the record,*** batir la marca *o* el récord; ***to be*** o ***go on record,*** constar; ***to keep to the record,*** ceñirse al asunto; ***to place on record,*** dejar constancia de; ***to set up a record,*** establecer una marca *o* un récord. — [riˈkɔːd], *v.t.* registrar; inscribir; anotar; consignar; hacer constar; grabar (*un disco etc.*).
recorder (I) [riˈkɔːdə], *s.* registrador, archivero; juez municipal; (*mec.*) indicador; ***recorder of deeds,*** registrador de la propiedad.

recorder (2) [ri'kɔ:də], *s.* (*mús.*) caramillo; flauta dulce.
recording [ri'kɔ:diŋ], *a.* registrador; magnetofónico. — *s.* registro; grabación.
recount (1) [ri'kaunt], *v.t.* referir, relatar.
recount (2) ['ri:kaunt], *s.* recuento. — ['ri:'kaunt], *v.t.* recontar.
recoup [ri:'ku:p], *v.t.* recuperar; resarcirse de.
recourse [ri'kɔ:s], *s.* recurso; ***to have recourse to,*** recurrir a, echar mano de.
recover (1) [ri'kʌvə], *v.t.* recobrar, recuperar; rescatar; (volver a) ganar; reembolsar(se). — *v.i.* reponerse, restablecerse; volver en sí; (*for.*) ganar un pleito.
recover (2) ['ri:'kʌvə], *v.t.* volver a cubrir *o* tapar.
recoverable [ri'kʌvərəbl], *a.* recuperable.
recovery [ri'kʌvəri], *s.* recobro, recuperación; restablecimiento; mejoría; rescate; (*for.*) reivindicación; ***past all recovery,*** irremisiblemente perdido.
recreant ['rekriənt], *a.*, *s.* cobarde; traidor.
recreate (1) ['rekrieit], *v.t.* recrear, divertir. — *v.i.* recrearse, divertirse.
recreate (2) ['ri:kri'eit], *v.t.* recrear.
recreation (1) [rekri'eiʃən], *s.* recreo; pasatiempo, diversión; ***recreation ground,*** campo de deportes.
recreation (2) ['ri:kri'eiʃən], *s.* recreación.
recreative ['rekrieitiv], *a.* recreativo.
recriminate [ri'krimineit], *v.t.* recriminar; reconvenir. — *v.i.* recriminar.
recrimination [rikrimi'neiʃən], *s.* recriminación; reconvención.
recross ['ri:'krɔs], *v.t.* volver a atravesar; volver a pasar; volver a cruzar. — *v.i.* volver a cruzarse.
recrudesce [ri:kru:'des], *v.i.* recrudecer(se).
recrudescence [ri:kru:'desəns], *s.* recrudescencia, recrudecimiento.
recruit [ri'kru:t], *s.* (*mil.*) recluta, *m.* — *v.t.* (*mil.*) reclutar, alistar; restablecer. — *v.i.* restablecerse.
recruiter [ri'kru:tə], *s.* reclutador.
recruiting, recruitment [ri'kru:tiŋ, -mənt], *s.* reclutamiento.
rectal ['rektəl], *a.* rectal.
rectangle ['rektæŋgl], *s.* rectángulo.
rectangular [rek'tæŋgjulə], *a.* rectangular.
rectifiable ['rektifaiəbl], *a.* rectificable.
rectification [rektifi'keiʃən], *s.* rectificación.
rectifier ['rektifaiə], *s.* rectificador.
rectify ['rektifai], *v.t.* rectificar.
rectigrade ['rektigreid], *a.* rectígrado.
rectilineal, rectilinear [rekti'liniəl, -'liniə], *a.* rectilíneo.
rectitude ['rektitju:d], *s.* rectitud, probidad.
recto ['rektou], *s.* recto.
rector ['rektə], *s.* rector.
rectoral, rectorial ['rektərəl, rek'tɔ:riəl], *a.* rectoral.
rectorate, rectorship ['rektərit, -ʃip], *s.* rectorado, rectoría.
rectory ['rektəri], *s.* rectoría, casa rectoral.
rectrix ['rektriks], *s.* (*pl.* **rectrices** [-trisi:z]) pluma timonera.
rectum ['rektəm], *s.* (*anat.*) recto.
recumbence, recumbency [ri'kʌmbəns, -i], *s.* reclinación; reposo.
recumbent [ri'kʌmbənt], *a.* reclinado, recostado, yacente.
recuperate [ri'kju:pəreit], *v.t.* recobrar, recuperar. — *v.i.* restablecerse, reponerse.
recuperation [rikju:pə'reiʃən], *s.* recuperación; restablecimiento, convalecencia.
recuperative [ri'kju:pərətiv], *a.* recuperativo.
recur [ri'kə:], *v.i.* repetirse, volver a darse, volver a pasar.
recurrence, recurrency [ri'kʌrəns, -i], *s.* repetición; reaparición; periodicidad.
recurrent [ri'kʌrənt], *a.* repetido; periódico; (*anat.*) recurrente.
recurvation ['ri:kə:'veiʃən], *s.* encorvadura; flexión hacia atrás.
recurve ['ri:'kə:v], *v.t.* recorvar. — *v.i.* recorvarse.
recurved, recurvous ['ri:'kə:vd, -'kə:vəs], *a.* (*bot.*, *zool.*) recorvado.
recusancy ['rekjuzənsi], *s.* recusación, disidencia.
recusant ['rekjuzənt], *a.*, *s.* recusante, disidente.
recusation [rekju'zeiʃən], *s.* (*der.*) recusación.
red [red], *a.* rojo; colorado; encarnado; tinto; encendido; ***red-cap,*** cardelina; policía militar, *m.*; ***red-haired,*** pelirrojo; ***red-handed,*** en flagrante, con las manos en la masa; ***red-hot,*** candente, al rojo; entusiasmadísimo; de última hora; ***red herring,*** pista falsa, ardid para despistar; ***red letter day,*** día señalado *o* memorable; ***Red Riding Hood,*** Caperucita Roja; ***Red Sea,*** Mar Rojo; ***red tape,*** papeleo; ***to paint the town red,*** andar de picos pardos. — *s.* rojo, encarnado, colorado; ***to be in the red,*** estar en deuda, tener la cuenta en descubierto.
redan [ri'dæn], *s.* (*fort.*) estrella.
redbird ['redbə:d], *s.* (*orn.*) cardenal.
redbreast ['redbrest], *s.* petirrojo.
redbud ['redbʌd], *s.* ciclamor.
redbug ['redbʌg], *s.* nigua.
redcoat ['redkout], *s.* (*fam.*) soldado.
redden [redn], *v.t.* enrojecer, teñir de rojo. — *v.i.* enrojecer, ruborizarse.
reddish ['rediʃ], *a.* rojizo.
reddle [redl], *s.* almagre, almazarrón.
redeem [ri'di:m], *v.t.* redimir; rescatar; desempeñar; amortizar; cumplir (*una promesa*); expiar.
redeemable [ri'di:məbl], *a.* redimible; rescatable; amortizable.
redeemer [ri'di:mə], *s.* redentor; rescatador; ***the Redeemer,*** el Redentor.
redeeming [ri'di:miŋ], *a.* que redime; ***redeeming virtue,*** virtud que salva; (*for.*) ***redeeming feature,*** circunstancia atenuante.
redeliberate ['ri:di'libəreit], *v.i.* redeliberar.
redeliver ['ri:di'livə], *v.t.* entregar de nuevo.
redemption [ri'dempʃən], *s.* redención; rescate; desempeño; amortización.
redemptive [ri'demptiv], *a.* redentor.
redevelop ['ri:di'veləp], *v.t.* desarrollar de nuevo.
redevelopment ['ri:di'veləpmənt], *s.* nuevo desarrollo.
redhead ['redhed], *s.* pelirrojo.
redingote ['rediŋgout], *s.* redingote.
redirect ['ri:di'rekt], *v.t.* reexpedir.
rediscover ['ri:dis'kʌvə], *v.t.* descubrir de nuevo.
redistribute ['ri:dis'tribju:t], *v.t.* volver a distribuir.
redistribution ['ri:distri'bju:ʃən], *s.* nueva distribución.
redness ['rednis], *s.* rojez, (lo) rojo.
redo ['ri:'du:], *v.t.* rehacer.
redolence, redolency ['redoləns, -i], *s.* perfume, fragancia.
redolent ['redolənt], *a.* perfumado, fragante; ***to be redolent of,*** hacer pensar en.
redouble ['ri:'dʌbl], *v.t.*, *v.i.* redoblar(se).
redoubt [ri'daut], *s.* reducto.
redoubtable [ri'dautəbl], *a.* temible.
redound [ri'daund], *v.i.* redundar (**to,** en *o* en beneficio de).
redraft ['ri:'drɑ:ft], *s.* nuevo dibujo *o* diseño; nuevo borrador. — *v.t.* dibujar *o* diseñar *o* trazar de nuevo; hacer un nuevo borrador de.
redraw ['ri:'drɔ:], *v.t.* dibujar de nuevo; trazar de nuevo.
redress (1) [ri'dres], *s.* reparación; compensación; resarcimiento; derecho a satisfacción. — *v.t.*

reparar; compensar; resarcir; corregir; ***redress the balance,*** restablecer el equilibrio; ***redress a wrong,*** deshacer un entuerto.
redress (2) [ˈriːˈdres], *v.t.* vestir de nuevo. — *v.i.* vestirse de nuevo.
redressive [riˈdresiv], *a.* correctivo.
redshank [ˈredʃæŋk], *s.* (*orn.*) totano, archibebe.
redskin [ˈredskin], *s.* piel roja, *m.*
redstart [ˈredstɑːt], *s.* (*orn.*) colirrojo.
reduce [riˈdjuːs], *v.t.* reducir; disminuir; rebajar; (*mil.*) degradar; abreviar. — *v.i.* adelgazar, perder peso.
reducible [riˈdjuːsibl], *a.* reductible, reducible.
reduction [riˈdʌkʃən], *s.* reducción; disminución; rebaja.
reductive [riˈdʌktiv], *a.* reductivo.
redundance, redundancy [riˈdʌndəns, -i], *s.* redundancia; (el) estar de más, (el) sobrar.
redundant [riˈdʌndənt], *a.* redundante; que sobra; ***to be redundant,*** estar de más, sobrar.
reduplicate [ˈriːˈdjuːplikit], *a.* reduplicado. — [-keit], *v.t.* reduplicar; repetir.
reduplication [ˈriːdjuːpliˈkeiʃən], *s.* reduplicación; repetición.
redwing [ˈredwiŋ], *s.* (*orn.*) malvís, *m.*
redwood [ˈredwud], *s.* (*bot.*) secuoya.
redye [ˈriːˈdai], *v.t.* teñir de nuevo, volver a teñir.
re-echo [ˈriː-ˈekou], *v.t.* repetir. — *v.i.* resonar, repetirse, repercutir.
reed [riːd], *s.* (*bot.*) caña, carrizo, junquillo; (*mús.*) lengüeta, caramillo; (*poét.*) saeta, flecha; peine de tejedor; (*arq.*) baqueta; ***reed organ,*** armonio.
reed-bunting [ˈriːd-bʌntiŋ], *s.* (*orn.*) verderón.
reeded [ˈriːdid], *a.* cubierto de cañas.
re-edify [ˈriː-ˈedifai], *v.t.* reedificar.
reedy [ˈriːdi], *a.* cañado, cañoso, lleno de cañas; (*mús.*) de tono agudo y delgado.
reef (1) [riːf], *s.* (*mar.*) rizo. — *v.t.* (*mar.*) tomar rizos de, arrizar.
reef (2) [riːf], *s.* arrecife, escollo; (*min.*) filón.
reefer (1) [ˈriːfə], *s.* (*mar.*) arrizador; chaquetón.
reefer (2) [ˈriːfə], *s.* (*fam.*) pitillo de marihuana (*o* grifa).
reefy [ˈriːfi], *a.* lleno de arrecifes.
reek [riːk], *s.* vaho; hedor. — *v.i.* vahear, humear; ***reek of,*** heder a, oler fuertemente a.
reeky [ˈriːki], *a.* humeante; ahumado.
reel (1) [riːl], *s.* devanadera, broca; carrete; carretel; rollo, cinta, película; ***off the reel,*** seguido. — *v.t.* devanar, aspar; ***reel off,*** recitar de carrerilla.
reel (2) [riːl], *v.i.* hacer eses, tambalearse; ***my head reels,*** me da vueltas la cabeza.
reel (3) [riːl], *s.* baile escocés.
re-elect [ˈriː-iˈlekt], *v.t.* reelegir.
re-election [ˈriː-iˈlekʃən], *s.* reelección.
re-eligibility [ˈriː-elidʒiˈbiliti], *s.* estado reelegible.
re-eligible [ˈriː-ˈelidʒibl], *a.* reelegible.
re-embark [ˈriː-imˈbɑːk], *v.t., v.i.* (*mar.*) reembarcar(se).
re-embarkation, re-embarcation [ˈriː-embɑː-ˈkeiʃən], *s.* reembarque.
re-embody [ˈriː-imˈbɔdi], *v.t.* reincorporar.
re-enact [ˈriː-iˈnækt], *v.t.* revalidar, promulgar de nuevo (*una ley*); reconstruir.
re-enactment [ˈriː-iˈnæktmənt], *s.* restablecimiento (*de una ley*).
re-engage [ˈriː-inˈgeidʒ], *v.t.* contratar de nuevo.
re-engagement [ˈriː-inˈgeidʒmənt], *s.* nuevo ataque; nuevo contrato; reenganche.
re-enlist [ˈriː-inˈlist], *v.t.* reenganchar. — *v.i.* reengancharse.
re-enlistment [ˈriː-inˈlistmənt], *s.* reenganche.
re-enter [ˈriː-ˈentə], *v.t., v.i.* volver a entrar (en).
re-entrance, re-entry [ˈriː-ˈentrəns, ˈriː-ˈentri], *s.* nueva entrada.
re-establish [ˈriː-isˈtæbliʃ], *v.t.* restablecer, restaurar.
re-establishment [ˈriː-isˈtæbliʃmənt], *s.* restablecimiento, restauración.
reeve [riːv], *v.t.* (*mar.*) laborear.
re-examination [ˈriː-igzæmiˈneiʃən], *s.* nuevo examen.
re-examine [ˈriː-igˈzæmin], *v.t.* reexaminar, volver a examinar.
re-export [ˈriː-ˈekspɔːt], *s.* reexportación. — [ˈriː-iksˈpɔːt], *v.t.* reexportar, volver a exportar.
re-exportation [ˈriː-ekspɔːˈteiʃən], *s.* reexportación.
refection [riˈfekʃən], *s.* refección.
refectory [riˈfektəri], *s.* refectorio.
refer [riˈfəː], *v.t.* referir; remitir. — *v.i.* referirse, hacer alusión (***to,*** a).
referable [riˈfəːrəbl], *a.* referible.
referee [refəˈriː], *s.* árbitro.
reference [ˈrefərəns], *s.* referencia; alusión; recomendación, informes, *m.pl.*; (*impr.*) llamada; ***reference number,*** número de referencia; ***reference work*** o ***work of reference,*** libro *u* obra de consulta; ***terms of reference,*** enunciado; ***to have*** o ***bear no reference to,*** no tener nada que ver con; ***to make reference to,*** hacer referencia *o* alusión a; ***with*** o ***in reference to,*** (con) respecto a, en cuanto a, con referencia a.
referendary [refəˈrendəri], *a.* referendario.
referendum [refəˈrendəm], *s.* referéndum.
refill [ˈriːfil], *s.* recambio. — [ˈriːˈfil], *v.t.* llenar de nuevo.
refine [riˈfain], *v.t.* refinar; purificar, acrisolar. — *v.i.* — ***on, upon,*** mejorar, superar.
refined [riˈfaind], *a.* fino; refinado, afectado.
refinedness, refinement [riˈfaindnis, -mənt], *s.* finura, urbanidad; refinamiento, afectación.
refiner [riˈfainə], *s.* refinador.
refinery [riˈfainəri], *s.* refinería.
refining [riˈfainiŋ], *s.* refinación.
refit [ˈriːˈfit], *s.* reparación, compostura. — [riːˈfit], *v.t., v.i.* reparar(se), componer(se).
reflect [riˈflekt], *v.t.* reflejar. — *v.i.* reflexionar; ***reflect on*** o ***upon,*** reflexionar sobre; no decir bien de, mostrar *o* revelar bajo una luz poco favorable.
reflection, reflexion [riˈflekʃən], *s.* reflejo; reflexión; ***to cast reflections on,*** hacer reflejos en; (*fig.*) comentar desfavorablemente.
reflective [riˈflektiv], *a.* reflexivo.
reflector [riˈflektə], *s.* reflector; reverbero.
reflex [ˈriːfleks], *a.* reflejo. — *s.* reflejo; (*anat.*) acción refleja.
reflexibility [rifleksiˈbiliti], *s.* reflexibilidad.
reflexible [riˈfleksibl], *a.* reflexible.
reflexive [riˈfleksiv], *a.* reflexivo; (*fís.*) reflector.
refloat [ˈriːˈflout], *v.t.* sacar a flote. — *v.i.* volver a flotar.
reflorescence [ˈriːflɔːˈresəns], *s.* acción de reflorecer.
reflourish [ˈriːˈflʌriʃ], *v.i.* reflorecer.
reflow [ˈriːˈflou], *v.i.* refluir.
refluence, refluency [ˈrefluəns, -i], *s.* reflujo.
refluent [ˈrefluənt], *a.* refluente.
reflux [ˈriːflʌks], *s.* reflujo.
reforest [ˈriːˈfɔrist], [REAFFOREST].
reforestation [ˈriːfɔrisˈteiʃən], [REAFFORESTATION].
reform (1) [riˈfɔːm], *s.* reforma. — *v.t.* reformar, rehacer, formar de nuevo. — *v.i.* rehacerse.
reform (2) [ˈriːˈfɔːm], *v.t.* reformar, rehacer, formar de nuevo. — *v.i.* rehacerse.
reformation (1) [refəˈmeiʃən], *s.* reformación; reforma; ***the Reformation,*** la Reforma.
reformation (2) [ˈriːfɔːˈmeiʃən], *s.* reformación; nueva formación.
reformative [riˈfɔːmətiv], *a.* reformador, reformatorio.
reformatory [riˈfɔːmətəri], *a., s.* reformatorio.

reformer [ri'fɔːmə], *s.* reformador, reformista, *m.f.*
reforming [ri'fɔːmiŋ], *a.* reformador.
reformist [ri'fɔːmist], *a.* reformador. — *s.* reformista, *m.f.*
refound ['riː'faund], *v.t.* refundar.
refract [ri'frækt], *v.t.* refractar, refringir.
refracting [ri'fræktiŋ], *a.* refringente.
refraction [ri'frækʃən], *s.* refracción.
refractive [ri'fræktiv], *a.* refractor, refringente.
refractometer [riːfræk'təmitə], *s.* refractómetro.
refractor [ri'fræktə], *s.* refractor; telescopio de refracción.
refractoriness [ri'fræktərinis], *s.* (lo) refractario, (lo) reacio.
refractory [ri'fræktəri], *a.* refractario, reacio.
refrain (1) [ri'frein], *s.* estribillo; cantilena.
refrain (2) [ri'frein], *v.i.* contenerse; ***refrain from,*** abstenerse de.
reframe ['riː'freim], *v.t.* rehacer; volver a enmarcar.
refrangibility [rifrændʒi'biliti], *s.* refrangibilidad.
refrangible [ri'frændʒibl], *a.* refrangible, capaz de refracción.
refresh [ri'freʃ], *v.t.* refrescar; reavivar, reanimar; ***try to refresh your memory,*** haga memoria.
refresher [ri'freʃə], *s.* refresco; ***refresher course,*** curso de repaso.
refreshing [ri'freʃiŋ], *a.* refrescante; alentador.
refreshment [ri'freʃmənt], *s.* refresco; descanso; refrigerio; ***refreshment stall,*** quiosco de refrescos; ***to take some refreshment,*** tomar (comer, beber) algo.
refrigerant [ri'fridʒərənt], *a.*, *s.* refrigerante, refrigerativo.
refrigerate [ri'fridʒəreit], *v.t.* refrigerar.
refrigerating [ri'fridʒəreitiŋ], *a.* refrigerante; ***refrigerating plant*** o ***machine,*** máquina de hacer hielo.
refrigeration [rifridʒə'reiʃən], *s.* refrigeración.
refrigerative [ri'fridʒərətiv], *a.* refrigerante, refrigerativo.
refrigerator [ri'fridʒəreitə], *s.* nevera; refrigerador; frigorífico; ***refrigerator car,*** vagón frigorífico; ***refrigerator ship,*** buque frigorífico.
refuel ['riː'fjuːəl], *v.t.*, *v.i.* reaprovisionar(se) de combustible.
refuge ['refjuːdʒ], *s.* refugio, asilo; ***to take refuge,*** refugiarse; guarecerse, resguardarse.
refugee [refju'dʒiː], *s.* refugiado; ***refugee camp,*** campo de refugiados.
refulgence, refulgency [ri'fʌldʒəns, -i], *s.* refulgencia, resplandor.
refulgent [ri'fʌldʒənt], *a.* refulgente, resplandeciente.
refund ['riːfʌnd], *s.* reembolso. — [riː'fʌnd], *v.t.* devolver, reintegrar, reembolsar; (*com.*) consolidar.
refundable [riː'fʌndəbl], *a.* reembolsable.
refurbish ['riː'fəːbiʃ], *v.t.* restaurar, remozar.
refusal [ri'fjuːzəl], *s.* negativa; denegación; opción (exclusiva).
refuse (1) ['refjuːs], *s.* basura; deshechos, *m.pl.*, desperdicios, *m.pl.*; ***refuse dump,*** basurero, basural, vertedero (de basura); ***refuse lorry,*** camión de (la) basura.
refuse (2) [ri'fjuːz], *v.t.* rehusar; denegar; rechazar; ***refuse o.s. sth.,*** privarse de algo. — *v.i.* decir que no, negarse, no querer; ***he refused to speak,*** se negó a hablar, no quiso hablar.
refutable ['refjutəbl], *a.* refutable, rebatible.
refutation [refju'teiʃən], *s.* refutación.
refutatory ['refjuteitəri], *a.* refutatorio.
refute [ri'fjuːt], *v.t.* refutar, rebatir.
regain ['riː'gein], *v.t.* recobrar, recuperar; volver a tomar, volver a ganar.
regal ['riːgəl], *a.* regio; majestuoso.
regale [ri'geil], *v.t.* regalar, festejar, agasajar. — ***regale o.s.,*** *v.r.* regalarse.
regalement [ri'geilmənt], *s.* regalo, regalamiento.
regalia [rigeiliə], *s.pl.* insignias reales, *f.pl.*, insignias de la corona.
regality [riː'gæliti], *s.* soberanía; realeza.
regard [ri'gɑːd], *s.* respeto, consideración, miramiento, deferencia; mirada; (*pl.*) recuerdos, *m.pl.*; ***to have a high regard for,*** tener mucho respeto por; tener muy buen concepto de; ***having regard to, regard being had to,*** considerando, en vista de; ***in*** o ***with regard to,*** (con) respecto a, en cuanto a; ***out of regard for,*** por respeto a; ***without regard to,*** sin tener en cuenta; (***with***) ***kind regards,*** (con) muchos recuerdos. — ***v.t.*** considerar (***as,*** como); observar, mirar; respetar (***highly,*** mucho); ***as regards,*** por lo que se refiere a *o* respecta a.
regardful [ri'gɑːdful], *a.* atento (***of,*** a).
regarding [ri'gɑːdiŋ], *prep.* (con) respecto a, en cuanto a.
regardless [ri'gɑːdlis], *a.* ***regardless of consequences,*** sin reparar en las consecuencias. — *adv.* sin miramientos, sin tener en cuenta nada, sin hacer caso de nada; (*fam.*) ***to go*** o ***bash ahead regardless,*** tirar por la calle de en medio.
regatta [ri'gætə], *s.* regata.
regency ['riːdʒənsi], *s.* regencia.
regeneracy [ri'dʒenərəsi], *s.* regeneración.
regenerate [ri'dʒenərit], *a.* regenerado. — ['riː-'dʒenəreit], *v.t.* regenerar.
regenerating, regenerative, regeneratory ['riː-'dʒenəreitiŋ, -rətiv, -rətəri], *a.* regenerador, regenerativo.
regeneration ['riːdʒenə'reiʃən], *s.* regeneración.
regent ['riːdʒənt], *a.*, *s.* regente.
regentship ['riːdʒəntʃip], *s.* regencia.
regerminate ['riː'dʒəːmineit], *v.i.* retoñar.
regicide ['redʒisaid], *s.* regicidio (*crimen*); regicida, *m.f.* (*persona*).
régime [rei'ʒiːm], *s.* régimen.
regimen ['redʒimən], *s.* (*med.*, *gram.*) régimen.
regiment ['redʒimənt], *s.* regimiento. — [-ment], *v.t.* organizar rígidamente.
regimental [redʒi'mentl], *a.* regimentario, de(l) regimiento.
regimentals [redʒi'mentlz], *s.pl.* uniforme (regimentario).
regimentation [redʒimen'teiʃən], *s.* organización rígida.
Reginald ['redʒinəld]. Reinaldo.
region ['riːdʒən], *s.* región; ***in the region of,*** del orden de.
regional ['riːdʒənəl], *a.* regional.
regionalism ['riːdʒənəlizəm], *s.* regionalismo.
regionalist ['riːdʒənəlist], *a.* regionalista. — *s.* regionalista, *m.f.*
register ['redʒistə], *s.* registro; archivo; lista; padrón; matrícula; (*mec.*) indicador, registrador; ***cash register,*** caja registradora; (***parish***) ***register,*** registro parroquial; ***register office,*** juzgado municipal; ***register ton,*** tonelada de registro. — *v.t.* registrar; inscribir; matricular; indicar, manifestar; certificar; facturar. — *v.i.* registrarse; inscribirse; matricularse; (*impr.*) estar en registro.
registrar ['redʒistrɑː], *s.* registrador; secretario (de universidad).
registrarship ['redʒistrɑːʃip], *s.* funciones de registrador *etc.*
registration [redʒis'treiʃən], *s.* registro; inscripción; matrícula; facturación; asiento, partida; ***registration fee,*** derechos de matrícula, *m.pl.*; ***registration number,*** matrícula.
registry ['redʒistri], *s.* registro, archivo; secretaría; ***registry office,*** juzgado municipal; registro civil; ***to marry at a registry office,*** casarse por lo civil; ***servants' registry,*** agencia de colocaciones.
regius ['riːdʒiəs], *a.* (de fundación) real.

reglet [ˈreglit], *s.* (*arq.*) filete; (*impr.*) regleta, corondel.
regnant [ˈregnənt], *a.* reinante.
regraft [ˈri:ˈgrɑ:ft], *v.t.* volver a injertar.
regress [ˈri:gres], *s.* retroceso; retrogradación. — [riˈgres], *v.i.* retroceder; retrogradar.
regression [riˈgreʃən], *s.* regresión.
regressive [riˈgresiv], *a.* regresivo, retrógrado.
regret [riˈgret], *s.* pesar, sentimiento; remordimiento; (*pl.*) excusas, *f.pl.*; ***to my regret,*** con pesar mío, a mi pesar. — *v.t.* sentir; lamentar; arrepentirse de.
regretful [riˈgretful], *a.* pesaroso, arrepentido.
regretfully [riˈgretfuli], *adv.* con pesar.
regrettable [riˈgretəbl], *a.* lamentable, deplorable.
regular [ˈregjulə], *a.* regular; ordenado, metódico; normal; uniforme; periódico; asiduo, habitual; (*fam.*) verdadero, de verdad; ***as regular as clockwork,*** como un reloj; ***regular officer,*** militar de carrera. — *s.* (*igl.*) regular; militar de carrera; cliente asiduo *o* habitual.
regularity [regjuˈlæriti], *s.* regularidad; método; uniformidad.
regularly [ˈregjuləli], *adv.* periódicamente.
regulate [ˈregjuleit], *v.t.* regular; graduar; ajustar.
regulation [regjuˈleiʃən], *a.* reglamentario. — *s.* regulación; reglamento, regla; (*pl.*) reglamento; (*mil.*) ordenanzas, *f.pl.*
regulator [ˈregjuleitə], *s.* regulador.
regurgitate [ˈri:gə:dʒiteit], *v.t.* volver a arrojar. — *v.i.* regurgitar.
regurgitation [ˈri:gə:dʒiˈteiʃən], *s.* regurgitación.
rehabilitate [ˈri:həˈbiliteit], *v.t.* rehabilitar.
rehabilitation [ˈri:həbiliˈteiʃən], *s.* rehabilitación.
rehash [ˈri:ˈhæʃ], *s.* (*fam.*) refrito. — *v.t.* hacer un refrito de.
rehearing [ˈri:ˈhiəriŋ], *s.* (*der.*) nueva vista.
rehearsal [riˈhə:səl], *s.* ensayo.
rehearse [riˈhə:s], *v.t.* ensayar.
reheat [ˈri:ˈhi:t], *v.t.* recalentar.
rehouse [ˈri:ˈhauz], *v.t.* dar nueva vivienda a.
reign [rein], *s.* reinado; dominio; ***in the reign of,*** bajo el reinado de; ***reign of terror,*** reinado del terror. — *v.i.* reinar; imperar.
reigning [ˈreiniŋ], *a.* reinante; imperante.
reimburse [ˈri:imˈbə:s], *v.t.* reembolsar; indemnizar.
reimbursement [ˈri:imˈbə:smənt], *s.* reembolso; indemnización.
reimpress [ˈri:imˈpres], *v.t.* reimprimir.
reimpression [ˈri:imˈpreʃən], *s.* reimpresión.
reimprison [ˈri:imˈprizən], *v.t.* volver a encarcelar.
reimprisonment [ˈri:imˈprizənmənt], *s.* nuevo encarcelamiento.
rein [rein], *s.* rienda; ***to give rein to,*** dar rienda suelta a; ***to keep a tight rein on s.o.,*** atar (muy) corto a alguien. — *v.t.* — ***in, back,*** (re)frenar. — *v.i.* — ***in,*** (re)frenarse.
reincarnation [ˈri:inkɑ:ˈneiʃən], *s.* reencarnación.
reincorporate [ˈri:inˈkɔ:pəreit], *v.t.* reincorporar.
reindeer [ˈreindiə], *s.* reno.
reinforce [ˈri:inˈfɔ:s], *v.t.* reforzar; ***reinforced concrete,*** hormigón armado.
reinforcement [ˈri:inˈfɔ:smənt], *s.* refuerzo; (*ing.*) armadura (*del hormigón armado*).
reinless [ˈreinlis], *a.* sin riendas; desenfrenado.
reinsert [ˈri:inˈsə:t], *v.t.* insertar de nuevo.
reinsertion [ˈri:inˈsə:ʃən], *s.* reinserción.
reinstall [ˈri:inˈstɔ:l], *v.t.* reinstalar, restablecer.
reinstallation, reinstalment [ˈri:instəˈleiʃən, ˈri:inˈstɔ:lmənt], *s.* reinstalación, restablecimiento, rehabilitación.
reinstate [ˈri:inˈsteit], *v.t.* reinstalar, reintegrar, restablecer, rehabilitar.
reinstatement [ˈri:inˈsteitmənt], *s.* reintegración, restablecimiento.
reinsurance [ˈri:inˈʃuərəns], *s.* reaseguro.
reinsure [ˈri:inˈʃuə], *v.t.* reasegurar.
reintegrate [ˈri:ˈintigreit], *v.t.* reintegrar.
reintegration [ˈri:intiˈgreiʃən], *s.* reintegración.
reintroduce [ˈri:intrəˈdju:s], *v.t.* volver a introducir.
reintroduction [ˈri:intrəˈdʌkʃən], *s.* reintroducción.
reinvest [ˈri:inˈvest], *v.t.* reinvertir.
reinvestment [ˈri:inˈvestmənt], *s.* reinversión.
reinvestigate [ˈri:inˈvestigeit], *v.t.* investigar de nuevo.
reinvestigation [ˈri:investiˈgeiʃən], *s.* nueva investigación.
reinvigorate [ˈri:inˈvigəreit], *v.t.* volver a dar vigor a; vigorizar.
reissue [ˈri:ˈiʃu:], *s.* reimpresión. — *v.t.* reimprimir; reexpedir; reemitir; reestrenar.
reiterate [ˈri:ˈitəreit], *v.t.* reiterar.
reiteration [ˈri:itəˈreiʃən], *s.* reiteración.
reject [ˈri:dʒekt], *s.* cosa defectuosa. — [riˈdʒekt], *v.t.* rechazar; denegar; rehusar; desechar.
rejectable [riˈdʒektəbl], *a.* rechazable; desechable.
rejection [riˈdʒekʃən], *s.* rechazamiento; denegación; negativa.
rejoice [riˈdʒɔis], *v.t.*, *v.i.* alegrar(se), regocijar(se).
rejoicing [riˈdʒɔisiŋ], *a.* alegre, gozoso. — *s.* alegría, regocijo.
rejoin [ˈri:ˈdʒɔin], *v.t.* volver a juntarse con, reunirse con; reincorporarse a. — [riˈdʒɔin], *v.i.* (*for.*) replicar.
rejoinder [riˈdʒɔində], *s.* réplica, contrarréplica.
rejoint [ˈri:ˈdʒɔint], *v.t.* (*alb.*) rejuntar.
rejudge [ˈri:ˈdʒʌdʒ], *v.t.* juzgar de nuevo.
rejuvenate [riˈdʒu:vəneit], *v.t.* rejuvenecer, remozar.
rejuvenation, rejuvenescence [ridʒu:vəˈneiʃən, -ˈnesəns], *s.* rejuvenecimiento, remozamiento.
rekindle [ˈri:ˈkindl], *v.t.* reencender, reavivar.
reland [ˈri:ˈlænd], *v.t.*, *v.i.* desembarcar de nuevo; (*aer.*) aterrizar de nuevo.
relapse [riˈlæps], *s.* recaída; reincidencia; (*med.*) recidiva. — *v.i.* recaer; reincidir.
relate [riˈleit], *v.t.* relatar, referir; relacionar; emparentar. — *v.i.* relacionarse (*con*).
related [riˈleitid], *a.* afín, conexo, emparentado; ***he is related to me,*** es pariente mío.
relating to [riˈleitiŋ tu], *frase prep.* que concierne, que se refiere a.
relation [riˈleiʃən], *s.* relato; relación; parentesco; pariente, deudo; ***in relation to,*** respecto a, en relación con.
relationship [riˈleiʃənʃip], *s.* parentesco; afinidad.
relative [ˈrelətiv], *a.* relativo. — *s.* pariente; (*gram.*) pronombre relativo.
relatively [ˈrelətivli], *adv.* relativamente; ***there are relatively few,*** hay relativamente pocos.
relativeness [ˈrelətivnis], *s.* (lo) relativo.
relativism [ˈrelətivizəm], *s.* relativismo.
relativity [reləˈtiviti], *s.* relatividad.
relax [riˈlæks], *v.t.* relajar, aflojar; mitigar. — *v.i.* esparcirse, distraerse; descansar; (*fam.*) tranquilizarse, tomar las cosas con calma.
relaxation [ˈri:lækˈseiʃən], *s.* relajación, relajamiento, aflojamiento; esparcimiento, distracción, recreo; descanso; distensión.
relaxing [riˈlæksiŋ], *a.* que descansa. — *s.* relajación; distensión.
relay (1) [ˈri:lei], *s.* parada; posta; relevo; (*elec.*) relé; (*rad.*) retransmisión; ***relay-race,*** carrera de relevos. — [riˈlei], *v.t.* (*rad.*) retransmitir.
relay (2) [ˈri:ˈlei], *v.t.* volver a poner.
release [riˈli:s], *s.* liberación; (el) soltar; descargo; estreno general; (*der.*) cesión; (*foto.*) disparador. — *v.t.* libertar; soltar; descargar; aflojar; estrenar; (*der.*) ceder.
relegate [ˈreligeit], *v.t.* relegar.
relegation [reliˈgeiʃən], *s.* relegación.

relent [ri'lent], *v.i.* ceder; ablandarse; desenojarse; enternecerse.
relentless [ri'lentlis], *a.* inexorable, implacable.
relet ['ri:'let], *v.t.* volver a alquilar.
relevance, relevancy ['reləvəns, -i], *s.* pertinencia.
relevant ['reləvənt], *a.* pertinente, que hace al caso, que tiene que ver.
reliability [rilaiə'biliti], *s.* seguridad; formalidad.
reliable [ri'laiəbl], *a.* seguro, de confianza, de fiar; formal; de fuente fidedigna.
reliance [ri'laiəns], *s.* confianza (***on,*** en); dependencia (***on,*** de).
reliant [ri'laiənt], *a.* ***to be reliant upon,*** depender de.
relic ['relik], *s.* reliquia; vestigio.
relict ['relikt], *s.* viuda.
relief [ri'li:f], *s.* alivio; desahogo; consuelo; socorro, auxilio; (*mil.*) relevo; (*b.a.*) relieve; (*fam.*) ***that's a relief!*** ¡menos mal!; ***relief map,*** mapa en relieve; ***relief train,*** tren suplementario; ***relief work,*** trabajos de socorro, *m.pl.*; ***to throw into relief,*** poner de relieve, hacer resaltar.
relieve [ri'li:v], *v.t.* aliviar; desahogar; consolar; tranquilizar; socorrer, auxiliar; relevar; ***relieve nature,*** hacer del cuerpo; ***relieve one's feelings,*** desahogarse.
relight ['ri:'lait], *v.t.* volver a encender.
religion [ri'lidʒən], *s.* religión.
religiosity [rilidʒi'ɔsiti], *s.* religiosidad.
religious [ri'lidʒəs], *a.* religioso; concienzudo. — *s.* religioso, *m.*, religiosa, *f.*
religiously [ri'lidʒəsli], *adv.* sin falta, puntualmente, religiosamente.
religiousness [ri'lidʒəsnis], *s.* religiosidad.
reline ['ri:'lain], *v.t.* reforrar.
relinquish [ri'liŋkwiʃ], *v.t.* abandonar, renunciar a.
relinquishment [ri'liŋkwiʃmənt], *s.* abandono, renuncia.
reliquary ['relikwəri], *s.* relicario.
relish ['reliʃ], *s.* sabor; fruición. — *v.t.* saborear; gozar, disfrutar de; ***I don't relish it,*** no me apetece *o* seduce nada.
relishable ['reliʃəbl], *a.* gustoso, sabroso, apetitoso.
relive ['ri:'liv], *v.t.* volver a vivir, vivir de nuevo, revivir.
reload ['ri:'loud], *v.t.* volver a cargar.
relucent [ri'lu:sənt], *a.* reluciente.
reluctance [ri'lʌktəns], *s.* resistencia; repugnancia; desgana; (*elec.*) reluctancia.
reluctant [ri'lʌktənt], *a.* maldispuesto; reacio; ***to be reluctant to,*** resistirse a.
reluctantly [ri'lʌktəntli], *adv.* de mala gana.
rely [ri'lai], *v.i.* — ***on,*** contar con, confiar en, fiarse de; depender de.
remain [ri'mein], *v.i.* quedarse, permanecer; ***remain unchanged*** o ***the same,*** seguir siendo igual; ***it remains to be done,*** está *o* queda por hacer; ***it remains to be seen,*** está por ver.
remainder [ri'meində], *s.* residuo; resto; remanente; (*der.*) reversibilidad; (*arit.*) residuo.
remains [ri'meinz], *s.pl.* restos, *m.pl.*; residuos, *m.pl.*; ruinas, *f.pl.*
remake ['ri:'meik], *v.t.* rehacer, hacer de nuevo.
remand [ri'ma:nd], *s.* reencarcelamiento; ***to be on remand,*** estar detenido. — *v.t.* reencarcelar.
remark [ri'ma:k], *s.* observación; nota; comentario. — *v.t.* observar, notar. — *v.i.* hacer una observación *o* un comentario.
remarkable [ri'ma:kəbl], *a.* notable, extraordinario.
remarkableness [ri'ma:kəblnis], *s.* (lo) notable, (lo) extraordinario.
remarriage ['ri:'mæridʒ], *s.* segundas nupcias, *f.pl.*
remarry ['ri:'mæri], *v.t.*, *v.i.* volver a casar(se).
remediable [ri'mi:diəbl], *a.* remediable, reparable.
remedial [ri'mi:diəl], *a.* remediador; curativo, terapéutico.
remediless ['remədilis], *a.* sin remedio, irremediable, incurable.
remedy ['remədi], *s.* remedio; ***it is past remedy,*** no tiene remedio; ***there is no remedy but,*** no hay más remedio que. — *v.t.* remediar.
remelt ['ri:'melt], *v.t.* refundir.
remember [ri'membə], *v.t.* acordarse de, recordar; tener presente; ***remember me to him!*** ¡dele Vd. recuerdos míos! — *v.i.* recordar, acordarse.
remembrance [ri'membrəns], *s.* recuerdo; memoria; recordación.
remembrancer [ri'membrənsə], *s.* recordador; recordatorio.
remind [ri'maind], *v.t.* recordar; ***remind s.o. of sth.,*** recordarle algo a alguien.
reminder [ri'maində], *s.* advertencia; ***give him a gentle reminder,*** recuérdaselo dulcemente *o* de cierta manera.
reminisce [remi'nis], *v.i.* recordar el pasado, complacerse en los recuerdos.
reminiscence [remi'nisəns], *s.* reminiscencia.
reminiscent [remi'nisənt], *a.* recordativo; evocador.
remiss [ri'mis], *a.* descuidado, negligente, remiso.
remissible [ri'misibl], *a.* remisible.
remission [ri'miʃən], *s.* remisión.
remissness [ri'misnis], *s.* descuido, negligencia, incuria.
remissory [ri'misəri], *a.* remisorio.
remit [ri'mit], *v.t.*, *v.i.* remitir.
remittance [ri'mitəns], *s.* remesa; giro.
remittent [ri'mitənt], *a.* remitente.
remitter [ri'mitə], *s.* remitente.
remnant ['remnənt], *s.* resto; residuo; remanente; retal; (*pl.*) restos, *m.pl.*
remodel ['ri:'mɔdl], *v.t.* volver a modelar; rehacer.
remonstrance [ri'mɔnstrəns], *s.* protesta; reconvención.
remonstrant [ri'mɔnstrənt], *a.* protestatario.
remonstrate ['remənstreit], *v.i.* protestar; ***remonstrate with,*** reconvenir a.
remora ['remɔ:ra], *s.* (*ict.*) rémora.
remorse [ri'mɔ:s], *s.* remordimientos, *m.pl.*
remorseful [ri'mɔ:sful], *a.* lleno de remordimientos, arrepentido.
remorseless [ri'mɔ:slis], *a.* inexorable, implacable.
remorselessness [ri'mɔ:slisnis], *s.* (lo) inexorable, (lo) implacable.
remote [ri'mout], *a.* remoto, lejano; distante; ***remote control,*** mando a distancia.
remoteness [ri'moutnis], *s.* alejamiento, apartamiento, (lo) remoto.
remould ['ri:'mould], *v.t.* moldear de nuevo, dar nueva forma a.
remount ['ri:'maunt], *s.* (*mil.*) remonta. — *v.t.* remontar. — *v.i.* volver a subir.
removable [ri'mu:vəbl], *a.* que se puede quitar, separable.
removal [ri'mu:vəl], *s.* (el) quitar *o* separar; mudanza, traslado; eliminación, supresión; ***removal van,*** camión de mudanzas, capitoné.
remove [ri'mu:v], *v.t.* quitar; sacar; suprimir, eliminar; trasladar; separar; ***remove from office,*** destituir. — *v.i.* mudarse, trasladarse.
removed [ri'mu:vd], *a.* apartado, distante; ***cousin once removed,*** primo segundo.
remover [ri'mu:və], *s.* agente de mudanzas; (***pl.***) mudanzas, *f.pl.*
remunerable [ri'mju:nərəbl], *a.* remunerable, retribuible.
remunerate [ri'mju:nəreit], *v.t.* remunerar, retribuir.
remuneration [rimju:nə'reiʃən], *s.* remuneración, retribución.

remunerative [ri'mju:nərətiv], *a.* remunerador.
remunerator [ri'mju:nəreitə], *s.* remunerador.
renaissance [ri'neisəns], *s.* renacimiento.
renal ['ri:nəl], *a.* renal.
rename ['ri:'neim], *v.t.* dar nuevo nombre a.
renard ['renɑ:d], *s.* (*ant.*) vulpeja.
renascence ['ri:'næsəns], *s.* renacimiento.
renascent [ri:'næsənt], *a.* renaciente.
rend [rend], *v.t.* desgarrar; lacerar; ***rend asunder,*** hender, escindir.
render ['rendə], *v.t.* hacer; volver; dar; verter; interpretar; derretir; ***render accounts,*** dar cuenta; ***render into,*** verter al; ***render a service,*** prestar un servicio; ***render thanks,*** dar gracias.
rendering ['rendəriŋ], *s.* traducción, versión; realización; interpretación.
rendezvous ['rɔndeivu:], *s.* (lugar de una) cita. — *v.i.* darse cita, encontrarse.
rendition [ren'diʃən], *s.* ejecución; versión.
renegade, renegado ['renigeid, reni'geidou], *s.* renegado, apóstata, *m.f.*
renew [ri'nju:], *v.t.* renovar; reanudar.
renewable [ri'nju:əbl], *a.* renovable.
renewal [ri'nju:əl], *s.* renovación; reanudación.
renewed [ri'nju:d], *a.* renovado; nuevo; ***with renewed vigour,*** con nuevo (*o* redoblado) vigor.
reniform ['renifɔ:m], *a.* reniforme.
rennet ['renit], *s.* cuajo.
renominate ['ri:'nɔmineit], *v.t.* nombrar de nuevo.
renounce [ri'nauns], *v.t.*, *v.i.* renunciar (a).
renouncement [ri'naunsmənt], *s.* renuncia.
renouncer [ri'naunsə], *s.* renunciador.
renovate ['renoveit], *v.t.* renovar; reformar.
renovation [reno'veiʃən], *s.* renovación; reforma(s).
renovator ['renoveitə], *s.* renovador.
renown [ri'naun], *s.* renombre, fama, nombradía.
renowned [ri'naund], *a.* renombrado, célebre, afamado.
rent (1) [rent], *s.* alquiler; arriendo, arrendamiento; ***rent-free,*** sin pagar alquiler. — *v.t.* alquilar; arrendar; dar en arrendamiento; tomar en arrendamiento; (***house***) ***to rent,*** se alquila (esta casa).
rent (2) [rent], *s.* rasgón, desgarrón; cisma.
rentable ['rentəbl], *a.* arrendable.
rental [rentl], *s.* alquiler; arriendo.
renunciation [rinʌnsi'eiʃən], *s.* renunciación, renunciamiento, renuncia.
reobtain ['ri:əb'tein], *v.t.* obtener de nuevo.
reoccupy ['ri:'ɔkjupai], *v.t.* reocupar.
reopen ['ri:'oupən], *v.t.* volver a abrir, reabrir.
reopening ['ri:'oupəniŋ], *s.* reapertura.
reordain ['ri:ɔ:'dein], *v.t.* volver a ordenar.
reorganization [ri:ɔ:gənai'zeiʃən], *s.* reorganización.
reorganize ['ri:'ɔ:gənaiz], *v.t.* reorganizar.
rep [rep], *s.* (*tej.*) reps, *m.inv.*
repack ['ri:'pæk], *v.t.* reempaquetar; volver a hacer (*una maleta*).
repair (1) [ri'pɛə], *s* reparación; remiendo; compostura, arreglo; ***to keep in repair,*** conservar en buen estado; ***out of repair,*** descompuesto, en mal estado; ***repair shop,*** taller de reparaciones. — *v.t.* reparar; remendar; componer.
repair (2) [ri'pɛə], *v.i.* — ***to,*** retirarse a, recogerse a; ir a.
repairable [ri'pɛərəbl], *a.* reparable.
repairer [ri'pɛərə], *s.* reparador, restaurador.
repairing [ri'pɛəriŋ], *s.* (el) reparar, componer *etc.*
repaper ['ri:'peipə], *v.t.* empapelar de nuevo.
reparable ['repərəbl], *a.* reparable.
reparation [repə'reiʃən], *s.* reparación; satisfacción; (*pl.*) indemnizaciones, *f.pl.*; ***to make reparations,*** dar satisfacción; ***to make reparations for,*** compensar de, indemnizar por.
reparative [ri'pærətiv], *a.* reparatorio, reparativo.
repartee [repɑ:'ti:], *s.* respuesta aguda; discreteo. — *v.i.* dar respuestas agudas.
repartition [repɑ:'tiʃən], *s.* reparto, repartición.
repass ['ri:'pɑ:s], *v.t.*, *v.i.* repasar, volver a pasar.
repast [ri'pɑ:st], *s.* colación.
repasture ['ri:'pɑ:stʃə], *s.* alimento, sustento.
repatriate ['ri:'pætrieit], *v.t.* repatriar.
repay ['ri:'pri], (*pret.*, *p.p.* **repaid**), *v.t.* pagar; restituir, devolver; corresponder a; ***repay a visit,*** devolver *o* pagar una visita.
repayable ['ri:'peiəbl], *a.* reembolsable, pagadero.
repayment ['ri:'peimənt], *s.* reembolso, pago; devolución.
repeal [ri'pi:l], *s.* revocación, abrogación. — *v.t.* revocar, abrogar.
repealable [ri'pi:ləbl], *a.* revocable, abrogable.
repealer [ri'pi:lə], *s.* revocador.
repeat [ri'pi:t], *s.* (*mús.*) repetición; (*rad.*) retransmisión. — *v.t.* repetir, reiterar; recitar. — *v.i.* repetirse.
repeatedly [ri'pi:tidli], *adv.* repetidas veces, reiteradamente.
repeater [ri'pi:tə], *s.* rifle de repetición; (*elec.*) repetidor.
repeating [ri'pi:tiŋ], *a.* que repite, de repetición, repetidor.
repel [ri'pel], *v.t.* rechazar, repeler. — *v.i.* ser repulsivo.
repellency [ri'pelənsi], *s.* repulsión, fuerza repulsiva.
repellent [ri'pelənt], *a.* repulsivo, repugnante; que ahuyenta.
repent [ri'pent], *v.i.* arrepentirse.
repentance [ri'pentəns], *s.* arrepentimiento, contrición.
repentant [ri'pentənt], *a.* arrepentido, contrito.
repeople ['ri:'pi:pl], *v.t.* repoblar.
repercuss ['ri:pə'kʌs], *v.t.* repercutir.
repercussion ['ri:pə'kʌʃən], *s.* repercusión, resonancia.
repercussive ['ri:pə'kʌsiv], *a.* repercusivo.
repertoire ['repətwɑ:], *s.* repertorio.
repertory ['repətəri], *s.* repertorio; ***repertory company*** o ***theatre,*** teatro de repertorio.
repetition [repi'tiʃən], *s.* repetición, reiteración.
repine [ri'pain], *v.i.* quejarse; afligirse.
repining [ri'painiŋ], *s.* (el) afligirse.
replace ['ri:'pleis], *v.t.* reponer, devolver a su sitio, colocar de nuevo; sustituir, reemplazar.
replaceable ['ri:'pleisəbl], *a.* sustituible, reemplazable.
replacement ['ri:'pleismənt], *s.* repuesto; (***pers.***) sustituto; reposición; reemplazo.
replant ['ri:'plɑ:nt], *v.t.* replantar.
replenish [ri'pleniʃ], *v.t.* reponer; reaprovisionar.
replenishment [ri'pleniʃmənt], *s.* reposición; reaprovisionamiento.
replete [ri'pli:t], *a.* repleto.
repleteness, repletion [ri'pli:tnis, ri'pli:ʃən], *s.* repleción, plenitud; hartazgo.
replevin [ri'plevin], *s.* (*der.*) auto de desembargo.
replica ['replikə], *s.* copia exacta, reproducción exacta.
reply [ri'plai], *s.* respuesta, contestación. — *v.t.*, *v.i.* responder, contestar.
repolish ['ri:'pɔliʃ], *v.t.* repulir.
report [ri'pɔ:t], *s.* informe; parte, *m.*; información, reportaje, crónica (*de periódico*); (*ruido*) estampido, detonación; memoria (anual); ***report has it that,*** corre la voz de que. — *v.t.* informar acerca de; dar parte de; denunciar (*un delito*); ***report that,*** informar *o* comunicar que. — *v.i.* hacer un informe (***on,*** de); presentarse, personarse.
reporter [ri'pɔ:tə], *s.* reportero; periodista, *m.f.*; ***reporters' gallery,*** tribuna de periodistas.

reporting [ri'pɔ:tiŋ], *s.* reportaje(s); periodismo.
repose [ri'pouz], *s.* reposo, descanso. — *v.t.* — ***hope in,*** cifrar las esperanzas en; ***repose trust in,*** poner confianza en, tener fe en. — *v.i.* reposar, descansar.
repository [ri'pɔzitəri], *s.* repositorio; depósito, almacén, guardamuebles, *m.inv.*; depositario.
repossess ['ri:po'zes], *v.t.* recobrar, recuperar.
repossession ['ri:po'zeʃən], *s.* recuperación.
repoussé [ri'pu:sei], *a.* repujado.
reprehend [repri'hend], *v.t.* reprender.
reprehensibility, reprehensibleness [reprihensi'biliti, -'hensiblnis], *s.* (lo) reprobable.
reprehensible [repri'hensibl], *a.* reprensible, reprobable, censurable.
reprehension [repri'henʃən], *s.* reprensión.
reprehensive [repri'hensiv], *a.* de reprensión.
represent [repri'zent], *v.t.* representar.
representable [repri'zentəbl], *a.* representable.
representation [reprizen'teiʃən], *s.* representación.
representative [repri'zentətiv], *a.* representativo, representante. — *s.* representante.
representativeness [repri'zentətivnis], *s.* carácter representativo.
repress [ri'pres], *v.t.* reprimir, sofocar.
repression [ri'preʃən], *s.* represión.
repressive [ri'presiv], *a.* represivo.
reprieve [ri'pri:v], *s.* respiro; suspensión; indulto. — *v.t.* indultar, suspender la pena de muerte de.
reprimand ['reprimɑ:nd], *s.* reprimenda. — [*t.* repri'mɑ:nd], *v.t.* reprender, reconvenir.
reprint ['ri:print], *s.* reimpresión. — ['ri:'print], *v.t.* reimprimir.
reprisal [ri'praizəl], *s.* represalia.
reprise [ri'pri:z], *s.* represa; (*mús.*) repetición; estribillo.
reproach [ri'proutʃ], *s.* reproche; oprobio, baldón. — *v.t.* reprochar; ***reproach s.o. for sth.,*** reprochar algo a alguien.
reproachable [ri'proutʃəbl], *a.* reprochable, censurable, reprensible.
reproachful [ri'proutʃful], *a.* acusador, reprensor.
reprobate ['reprobeit], *a.*, *s.* réprobo; (*fam.*) granuja, sinvergüenza.
reprobation [repro'beiʃən], *s.* reprobación, desaprobación, condenación.
reprobative, reprobatory ['reprobeitiv, 'reprobeitəri], *a.* reprobatorio, reprobador.
reproduce [ri:pro'dju:s], *v.t.* reproducir.
reproducer [ri:pro'dju:sə], *s.* reproductor.
reproducible [ri:pro'dju:sibl], *a.* reproductible.
reproduction [ri:pro'dʌkʃən], *s.* reproducción; trasunto.
reproductive, reproductory [ri:pro'dʌktiv, -'dʌktəri], *a.* reproductor, reproductivo.
reproof [ri'pru:f], *s.* reconvención, reproche.
reprovable [ri'pru:vəbl], *a.* reprensible, censurable.
reprove [ri'pru:v], *v.t.* reprobar, reprender.
reprover [ri'pru:və], *s.* reprensor, reprobador.
reprovingly [ri'pru:viŋli], *adv.* en tono de reprobación.
reprovision ['ri:pro'viʒən], *v.t.* reaprovisionar.
reptant ['reptənt], *a.* (*hist. nat.*) reptante; rastrero.
reptile ['reptail], *a.*, *s.* reptil.
reptilian [rep'tiliən], *a.*, *s.* reptil.
republic [ri'pʌblik], *s.* república.
republican [ri'pʌblikən], *a.*, *s.* republicano.
republicanism [ri'pʌblikənizəm], *s.* republicanismo.
republicanize [ri'pʌblikənaiz], *v.t.* republicanizar.
republication ['ri:pʌbli'keiʃən], *s.* reedición.
republish ['ri:'pʌbliʃ], *v.t.* reeditar.
repudiate [ri'pju:dieit], *v.t.* repudiar; rechazar, negar, negarse a reconocer.
repudiation [ripju:di'eiʃən], *s.* repudiación; repudio.
repugnance [ri'pʌgnəns], *s.* repugnancia, aversión, sensación de asco.
repugnant [ri'pʌgnənt], *a.* repugnante; repulsivo; ***to be repugnant to,*** repugnar.
repulse [ri'pʌls], *s.* repulsa; rechazo. — *v.t.* repulsar; rechazar.
repulsion [ri'pʌlʃən], *s.* repulsión; aversión, repugnancia.
repulsive [ri'pʌlsiv], *a.* repulsivo, repelente, repugnante.
repulsiveness [ri'pʌlsivnis], *s.* (lo) repulsivo, (lo) repugnante.
reputability, reputableness [repjutə'biliti, 'repjutəblnis], *s.* (lo) respetable, (lo) honroso.
reputable ['repjutəbl], *a.* acreditado; de buena fama *o* reputación.
reputation [repju'teiʃən], *s.* reputación, fama.
repute [ri'pju:t], *s.* reputación, fama; ***by repute,*** según dice la fama; ***of repute,*** de (mucha) fama, (muy) acreditado; ***a house of ill repute,*** una casa de mala fama. — *v.t.* reputar; ***to be reputed to be,*** tener fama de, ser tenido por.
reputed [ri'pju:tid], *a.* supuesto, pretendido.
request [ri'kwest], *s.* ruego, petición, solicitud; instancia; demanda; ***at the request of,*** a petición de, a solicitud de; a instancia(s) de; ***on request,*** a petición; ***request programme,*** programa de peticiones, *m.*; ***request stop,*** parada discrecional. — *v.t.* rogar, pedir, solicitar.
requiem ['rekwiəm], *s.* réquiem.
require [ri'kwaiə], *v.t.* requerir, exigir.
requirement [ri'kwaiəmənt], *s.* requisito; necesidad; requerimiento.
requisite ['rekwizit], *a.* necesario, preciso, indispensable. — *s.* requisito; ***toilet requisites,*** artículos de aseo, *m.pl.*
requisition [rekwi'ziʃən], *s.* (*mil.*) requisa; demanda; pedido. — *v.t.* (*mil.*) requisar.
requital [ri'kwaitəl], *s.* compensación; desquite.
requite [ri'kwait], *v.t.* (re)compensar; desquitar; corresponder a.
rerail ['ri:'reil], *v.t.* volver a encarrilar.
reredos ['riədɔs], *s.* retablo.
resail ['ri:'seil], *v.i.* reembarcarse.
resale ['ri:'seil], *s.* reventa.
resalute ['ri:sə'l(j)u:t], *v.t.* volver a saludar.
rescind [ri'sind], *v.t.* rescindir.
rescindable [ri'sindəbl], *a.* rescindible.
rescission [ri'siʒən], *s.* rescisión.
rescissory [ri'sisəri], *a.* rescisorio.
rescript ['ri:'skript], *s.* rescripto.
rescue ['reskju:], *s.* salvamento; rescate; ***to go to the rescue of,*** acudir en socorro de. — *v.t.* salvar; rescatar; librar.
rescuer ['reskjuə], *s.* salvador, rescatador; libertador.
research [ri'sə:tʃ], *s.* investigación, investigaciones, *f.pl.* — *v.t.*, *v.i.* investigar, hacer investigaciones (en).
researcher [ri'sə:tʃə], *s.* investigador.
reseat ['ri:'si:t], *v.t.* poner asiento nuevo a; (*mec.*) reasentar.
resect ['ri:'sekt], *v.t.* (*cir.*) resecar.
resection ['ri:'sekʃən], *s.* resección.
reseda [ri'si:də], *s.* (*bot.*) reseda; color grisverde muy pálido.
reseize ['ri:'si:z], *v.t.* volver a coger.
resell ['ri:'sel], *v.t.* revender, volver a vender.
resemblance [ri'zembləns], *s.* parecido; semejanza; ***to bear no resemblance to,*** no parecerse (en) nada a.
resemble [ri'zembl], *v.t.* parecerse a, asemejarse a; ***he resembles his father,*** tiene parecido con su padre, se parece a su padre.
resent [ri'zent], *v.t.* tomar a mal; ofenderse por; estar resentido por.
resentful [ri'zentful], *a.* resentido; ofendido.

resentfulness [ri'zentfulnis], *s.* resentimiento.
resentment [ri'zentmənt], *s.* resentimiento.
reservation [rezə'veiʃən], *s.* reserva; salvedad; plaza reservada.
reserve [ri'zə:v], *s.* reserva; suplente; ***in reserve,*** de reserva; ***reserve price,*** precio mínimo. — *v.t.* reservar.
reserved [ri'zə:vd], *a.* reservado, reservón, poco comunicativo.
reservedness [ri'zə:vidnis], *s.* reserva, cautela, circunspección.
reservist [ri'zə:vist], *s.* reservista, *m.f.*
reservoir ['rezəvwɑ:], *s.* depósito (*de agua*); embalse, pantano; aljibe; (*com.*) fondo de reserva.
reset ['ri:'set], *v.t.* reajustar; reengastar; recomponer; regraduar.
resetting ['ri:'setiŋ], *s.* (*impr.*) recomposición.
resettle ['ri:'setl], *v.t.* restablecer; reasentar; repoblar.
resettlement ['ri:'setlmənt], *s.* restablecimiento; reinstalación.
reshape ['ri:'ʃeip], *v.t.* reformar, dar nueva forma a.
reship ['ri:'ʃip], *v.t.* reembarcar; reexpedir.
reshipment ['ri:'ʃipmənt], *s.* reembarco; reembarque; reexpedición.
reshuffle ['ri:'ʃʌfl], *s.* (*fig.*) reajuste, reorganización. — *v.t.* reajustar, reorganizar.
reside [ri'zaid], *v.i.* residir, morar.
residence ['rezidəns], *s.* residencia; domicilio, morada; permanencia, estancia.
resident ['rezidənt], *a.* residente. — *s.* residente; vecino.
residential [rezi'denʃəl], *a.* residencial.
residual, residuary [ri'zidjuəl, ri'zidjuəri], *a.* residual; ***residuary legatee,*** heredero universal; (*elec.*) ***residual magnetism,*** magnetismo remanente.
residue ['rezidju:], *s.* residuo, resto.
residuum [ri'zidjuəm], *s.* (*pl.* **residua** [-juə]) residuo.
resign [ri'zain], *v.t.* renunciar a; ceder. — *v.i.* dimitir, renunciar. — **resign o.s.,** *v.r.* — resignarse (***to,*** a).
resignation [rezig'neiʃən], *s.* resignación; dimisión, renuncia; ***to give in one's resignation,*** presentar la dimisión.
resigned [ri'zaind], *a.* resignado.
resilience, resiliency [ri'ziliəns, -i], *s.* elasticidad; resistencia; poder de recuperación.
resilient [ri'ziliənt], *a.* elástico; resistente.
resin ['rezin], *s.* resina.
resiniferous [rezi'nifərəs], *a.* resinífero.
resinous ['rezinəs], *a.* resinoso.
resist [ri'zist], *v.t.* resistir, resistir a; oponerse a. — *v.i.* resistir.
resistance [ri'zistəns], *s.* resistencia; oposición; (*elec.*) ***resistance box,*** caja de resistencias; ***resistance coil,*** bobina de resistencia; ***to offer resistance,*** oponer resistencia.
resistant, resistent [ri'zistənt], *a.* resistente.
resistible [ri'zistibl], *a.* resistible.
resisting [ri'zistiŋ], *a.* resistente.
resistless [ri'zistlis], *a.* irresistible.
resistlessness [ri'zistlisnis], *s.* (lo) irresistible.
resole ['ri:'soul], *v.t.* (*zap.*) sobresolar.
resolute ['rezol(j)u:t], *a.* resuelto, decidido.
resoluteness ['rezol(j)u:tnis], *s.* resolución, decisión.
resolution [rezo'l(j)u:ʃən], *s.* resolución; decisión; acuerdo (de una junta *o* asamblea); ***good resolutions,*** buenos propósitos, *m.pl.*; ***to pass a resolution,*** tomar un acuerdo.
resolvable [ri'zɔlvəbl], *a.* soluble.
resolve [ri'zɔlv], *s.* resolución, decisión. — *v.t.* resolver. — *v.i.* resolverse (***into,*** en); ***resolve to,*** resolver + *inf.*, resolverse a, acordar + *inf.*
resolvedly [ri'zɔlvidli], *adv.* resueltamente, decididamente.
resolvedness [ri'zɔlvidnis], *s.* resolución.
resolvent [ri'zɔlvənt], *a.* disolvente, resolvente. — *s.* disolvente, solutivo.
resolver [ri'zɔlvə], *s.* el que resuelve.
resolving [ri'zɔlviŋ], *s.* resolución.
resonance ['rezənəns], *s.* resonancia.
resonant ['rezənənt], *a.* resonante, sonoro.
resonator ['rezəneitə], *s.* resonador.
resorb [ri'sɔ:b], *v.t.* reabsorber.
resorcin [ri'zɔ:sin], *s.* resorcina.
resorption [ri'sɔ:pʃən], *s.* reabsorción, resorción.
resort [ri'zɔ:t], *s.* recurso; ***health resort,*** balneario; ***as a last resort, in the last resort,*** como último recurso, en último caso; ***seaside resort,*** playa; ***summer resort,*** lugar de veraneo; ***to have resort to,*** recurrir a. — *v.i.* — ***to,*** recurrir a, acudir a, echar mano de.
resound [ri'zaund], *v.i.* resonar, retumbar.
resounding [ri'zaundiŋ], *a.* resonante; clamoroso.
resource [ri'sɔ:s], *s.* recurso; arbitrio; medio; expediente; inventiva.
resourceful [ri'sɔ:sful], *a.* fértil en recursos, ingenioso, inventivo.
resourcefulness [ri'sɔ:sfulnis], *s.* inventiva, ingenio.
resourceless [ri'sɔ:slis], *a.* sin recursos, desprovisto de medios.
resow ['ri:'sou], *v.t.* volver a sembrar.
respect [ri'spekt], *s.* respeto, consideración; respecto; (*pl.*) respetos, *m.pl.*, saludos, *m.pl.*; ***in all respects, in every respect,*** por todos conceptos; ***in other respects,*** por lo demás, por otra parte; ***in respect of,*** respecto a; por concepto de; ***in some respect(s),*** en cierto sentido, desde algunos puntos de vista; ***in this respect,*** a este respecto; ***out of respect to,*** por consideración a; ***to pay one's respects,*** cumplimentar; ***with respect to,*** (con) respecto a. — *v.t.* respetar; acatar, atenerse a.
respectability, respectableness [rispektə'biliti, ri'spektəblnis], *s.* respetabilidad; decencia.
respectable [ri'spektəbl], *a.* respetable, estimable; decente.
respecter [ri'spektə], *s.* respetador; ***to be no respecter of persons,*** no respetar a nadie.
respectful [ri'spektful], *a.* respetuoso.
respectfully [ri'spektfuli], *adv.* respetuosamente; ***yours respectfully,*** le saluda respetuosamente.
respectfulness [ri'spektfulnis], *s.* (lo) respetuoso; respetuosidad.
respecting [ri'spektiŋ], *prep.* con respecto a, tocante a, en cuanto a.
respective [ri'spektiv], *a.* respectivo.
respiration [respi'reiʃən], *s.* respiración.
respirator ['respireitə], *s.* respirador; careta antigás.
respiratory [re'spirətəri], *a.* respiratorio.
respire [ri'spaiə], *v.t.*, *v.i.* respirar.
respite ['resp(a)it], *s.* respiro, tregua; suspensión; prórroga: ***without respite,*** sin tregua, sin respirar; ***to give no respite to,*** no dejar respirar, no dejar descansar.
resplendence, resplendency [ri'splendəns, -i], *s.* resplandor, fulgor.
resplendent [ri'splendent], *a.* resplandeciente, brillante.
respond [ri'spɔnd], *v.i.* responder; ***respond to,*** reaccionar a *o* ante.
respondent [ri'spɔndənt], *s.* demandado.
response [ri'spɔns], *s.* respuesta; reacción.
responsibility [rispɔnsi'biliti], *s.* responsabilidad (***for,*** de).
responsible [ri'spɔnsibl], *a.* responsable (***for,*** de); de responsabilidad.
responsive [ri'spɔnsiv], *a.* sensible.
responsiveness [ri'spɔnsivnis], *s.* sensibilidad.
responsory [ri'spɔnsəri], *s.* responsorio.
rest (I) [rest], *s.* descanso, reposo; paz, *f.*; apoyo;

(*mús.*) pausa, silencio; ***at rest,*** en paz; inmóvil; ***rest cure,*** cura de reposo; ***rest home,*** casa de reposo; residencia *o* asilo de ancianos; ***to get a good night's rest,*** dormir bien; ***to take a rest,*** descansar. — *v.t.* descansar, apoyar (***on,*** en, sobre). — *v.i.* descansar, reposar; posarse (***on,*** en); apoyarse (***on,*** en); (*fig.*) estribar (***upon,*** en); ***rest assured that,*** tenga la seguridad *o* la certeza de que; ***rest with,*** depender de, ser asunto de; ***there the matter rested,*** ahí quedó la cosa.

rest (2) [rest], *s.* resto; ***the rest,*** (*sing.*) lo demás, (*pl.*) los demás; ***for the rest,*** por lo demás.

restart [ˈriːˈstɑːt], *v.t.* empezar de nuevo, volver a empezar; (*motor*) volver a arrancar, volver a poner en marcha.

restatement [ˈriːˈsteitmənt], *s.* nueva exposición.

restaurant [ˈrestərɔːnt], *s.* restaurante, restaurán, restorán.

restful [ˈrestful], *a.* tranquilo; que descansa.

rest-harrow [ˈrest-hærou], *s.* (*bot.*) detienebuey.

resting [ˈrestiŋ], *s.* reposo; descanso; ***resting-place,*** lugar de descanso; ***last resting-place,*** última morada.

restitution [restiˈtjuːʃən], *s.* restitución; indemnización; ***to make restitution for,*** indemnizar de.

restive [ˈrestiv], *a.* inquieto; indócil, ingobernable.

restiveness [ˈrestivnis], *s.* inquietud; indocilidad.

restless [ˈrestlis], *a.* desasosegado, inquieto; desvelado.

restlessness [ˈrestlisnis], *s.* desasosiego, inquietud; desvelo.

restock [ˈriːˈstɔk], *v.t.* reaprovisionar, reponer; repoblar (de árboles).

restorable [riˈstɔːrəbl], *a.* restituible.

restoration [restɔːˈreiʃən], *s.* restauración; restitución.

restorative [risˈtɔːrətiv], *a., s.* reconstituyente.

restore [riˈstɔː], *v.t.* restaurar; restituir, devolver; ***restore to life,*** devolver la vida a.

restorer [riˈstɔːrə], *s.* restaurador; restituidor; reparador; ***hair restorer,*** loción capilar.

restrain [riˈstrein], *v.t.* contener, refrenar; reprimir; ***restrain s.o. from doing sth.,*** impedir a alguien que haga algo, disuadir a alguien de hacer algo.

restraint [riˈstreint], *s.* moderación, comedimiento; restricción.

restrict [riˈstrikt], *v.t.* restringir, limitar.

restriction [riˈstrikʃən], *s.* restricción, limitación.

restrictive [riˈstriktiv], *a.* restrictivo.

restringency [riˈstrindʒənsi], *s.* restringencia.

restringent [riˈstrindʒənt], *a.* restringente, restriñente.

restroom [ˈrestruːm], (*Am.*) [TOILET].

result [riˈzʌlt], *s.* resultado; ***as a result,*** por consiguiente; ***as a result of,*** a consecuencia de, de resultas de. — *v.i.* producirse como consecuencia; ***nothing resulted from it,*** no dio resultado; ***result in,*** dar por resultado, conducir a, tener como consecuencia.

resultant [riˈzʌltənt], *a., s.* resultante.

resulting [riˈzʌltiŋ], *a.* resultante; (*for.*) ***resulting use,*** usufructo resultante.

resumable [riˈzjuːməbl], *a.* que se puede reasumir.

resume [riˈzjuːm], *v.t.* reanudar; ***resume one's seat,*** volver a ocupar su asiento. — *v.i.* reanudarse.

résumé [ˈrezjuːmei], *s.* resumen.

resumption [riˈzʌmpʃən], *s.* reasunción; reanudación.

resupinate [riˈs(j)uːpineit], *a.* (*bot.*) boca arriba, supino.

resupination [ris(j)uːpiˈneiʃən], *s.* posición supina.

resurge [ˈriːsəːdʒ], *v.i.* resurgir, renacer, reaparecer.

resurgence [riˈsəːdʒəns], *s.* resurgimiento.

resurgent [riˈsəːdʒənt], *a.* resurrecto.

resurrect [rezəˈrekt], *v.t.* resucitar; (*fam.*) desenterrar.

resurrection [rezəˈrekʃən], *s.* resurrección.

resurvey [ˈriːˈsəːvei], *s.* revisión. — [ˈriːsəːˈvei], *v.t.* volver a ver, rever.

resuscitate [riˈsʌsiteit], *v.t.* resucitar.

resuscitation [risʌsiˈteiʃən], *s.* resucitación.

resuscitator [riˈsʌsiteitə], *s.* resucitador.

ret [ret], *v.t.* enriar (*cáñamo* o *lino*).

retable [riˈteibl], *s.* retablo.

retail [ˈriːteil], *a., adv.* al por menor. — *s.* venta al por menor; ***by retail,*** al por menor. — [riːˈteil], *v.t.* vender al por menor; contar, repetir. — *v.i.* venderse al por menor.

retailer [ˈriːteilə], *s.* vendedor al por menor.

retain [riˈtein], *v.t.* retener; guardar, quedarse con, conservar; contratar; (*der.*) ajustar (*a un abogado*).

retainer [riˈteinə], *s.* criado; adherente.

retaining [riˈteiniŋ], *a.* que retiene; que conserva; ***retaining fee,*** ajuste, anticipo; ***retaining wall,*** muro de contención.

retake [ˈriːˈteik], *s.* repetición, parte filmada más de una vez. — *v.t.* volver a tomar; reconquistar; volver a filmar.

retaliate [riˈtælieit], *v.i.* vengarse, tomar represalias.

retaliation [ritæliˈeiʃən], *s.* venganza, represalias, *f.pl.*

retaliative, retaliatory [riˈtæliətiv, -təri], *a.* de venganza, de represalia.

retard [riˈtɑːd], *v.t.* retardar, retrasar, demorar.

retardation, retardment [ritɑːˈdeiʃən, riˈtɑːdmənt], *s.* retardo, retardación, retraso.

retardative, retardatory [riˈtɑːdətiv, -təri], *a.* retardador; retardatario.

retch [retʃ, riːtʃ], *v.i.* tener bascas *o* arcadas.

retell [ˈriːˈtel], *v.t.* repetir, volver a contar.

retention [riˈtenʃən], *s.* retención; conservación.

retentive [riˈtentiv], *a.* retentivo.

retentiveness [riˈtentivnis], *s.* retentiva.

reticence [ˈretisəns], *s.* reserva; retraimiento.

reticent [ˈretisənt], *a.* reservado, retraído.

reticle [ˈretikl], [RETICULE].

reticular [riˈtikjulə], *a.* reticular.

reticulate, reticulated [riˈtikjulit, -leitid], *a.* reticular.

reticulation [ritikjuˈleiʃən], *s.* disposición reticular.

reticule [ˈretikjuːl], *s.* retículo.

reticulum [riˈtikjuləm], *s.* retículo; (*zool.*) redecilla.

retiform [ˈretifɔːm], *a.* retiforme.

retina [ˈretinə], *s.* retina.

retinue [ˈretinjuː], *s.* comitiva, séquito.

retire [riˈtaiə], *v.t.* jubilar; retirar. — *v.i.* jubilarse; retirarse (*esp. mil.*); recogerse (*a dormir*).

retired [riˈtaiəd], *a.* jubilado; retirado; ***to put on the retired list,*** jubilar.

retirement [riˈtaiəmənt], *s.* jubilación; retiro; retirada; retraimiento; ***retirement pension,*** jubilación, (pensión de) retiro; ***to live in retirement,*** vivir en el retiro.

retiring [riˈtaiəriŋ], *a.* retraído, reservado; modesto; referente a la jubilación; ***retiring member,*** miembro saliente.

retort (1) [riˈtɔːt], *s.* réplica (mordaz). — *v.t.* redargüir. — *v.i.* replicar.

retort (2) [riˈtɔːt], *s.* retorta.

retorter [riˈtɔːtə], *s.* el que replica.

retortion [riˈtɔːʃən], *s.* retorcedura, retorsión; represalia.

retouch [ˈriːˈtʌtʃ], *s.* retoque. — *v.t.* retocar.

retoucher [ˈriːˈtʌtʃə], *s.* (*foto.*) retocador.

retrace [ˈriːˈtreis], *v.t.* volver a trazar; repasar; ***retrace one's steps,*** desandar lo andado, volver sobre sus pasos.

retract [riˈtrækt], *v.t.* retractar; retraer, encoger; replegar. — *v.i.* retractarse; encogerse.

retractable, retractible [riˈtræktəbl], *a.* retractable, retráctil; replegable.

retractation, retraction [riːtræk'teiʃən, ri'trækʃən], *s.* retractación, retracción.
retractile [ri'træktail], *a.* retráctil.
retractive [ri'træktiv], *a.* que tiende a retractar.
retractor [ri'træktə], *s.* el que *o* lo que retracta; (*anat.*) músculo contractor; (*cir.*) retractor; (*armas de fuego*) expulsor.
retread ['riː'tred], *v.t.* recauchutar (*neumáticos*).
retreat [ri'triːt], *s.* retiro, refugio; retirada; retreta; ***to beat a retreat,*** batirse en retirada. — *v.i.* retirarse; retroceder.
retrench [ri'trentʃ], *v.t.* cercenar. — *v.i.* economizar.
retrenchment [ri'trentʃmənt], *s.* cercenamiento; economías, *f.pl.*
retrial ['riː'traiəl], *s.* (*for.*) nuevo proceso; revisión.
retribute [ri'tribjuːt], *v.t.* retribuir, dar en pago.
retribution [retri'bjuːʃən], *s.* justo castigo; desquite.
retributive, retributory [ri'tribjutiv, -təri], *a.* de castigo.
retrievability, retrievableness [ritriːvə'biliti, ri'triːvəblnis], *s.* (lo) recuperable; (lo) reparable.
retrievable [ri'triːvəbl], *a.* recuperable; reparable.
retrieval [ri'triːvl], *s.* cobranza; recobro; recuperación; reparación.
retrieve [ri'triːv], *v.t.* cobrar; recobrar; recuperar; reparar; resarcirse de.
retriever [ri'triːvə], *s.* perro cobrador *o* perdiguero.
retroactive [retrou'æktiv], *a.* retroactivo.
retrocede [retro'siːd], *v.t.* (*for.*) hacer retrocesión de. — *v.i.* retroceder.
retrocession [retro'seʃən], *s.* (*for.*) retrocesión; retroceso.
retroflex ['retrofleks], *a.* doblado hacia atrás.
retroflexion [retro'flekʃən], *s.* retroflexión.
retrogradation [retrogrei'deiʃən], *s.* retrogradación.
retrograde ['retrogreid], *a.* retrógrado. — *v.i.* retrogradar; retroceder.
retrogression [retro'greʃən], *s.* retrogradación; retrogresión; retroceso.
retrogressive [retro'gresiv], *a.* retrógrado.
retrospect ['retrospekt], *s.* retrospección; ***in retrospect,*** retrospectivamente.
retrospection [retro'spekʃən], *s.* retrospección.
retrospective [retro'spektiv], *a.* retrospectivo; ***retrospective to,*** con efecto retrospectivo *o* retroactivo a partir de.
retroussé [ri'truːsei], *a.* respingado.
retroversion [retro'vəːʃən], *s.* retroversión.
retry ['riː'trai], *v.t.* (*for.*) rever; procesar de nuevo.
return [ri'təːn], *s.* vuelta, regreso, retorno; devolución, restitución; reaparición; respuesta; recompensa; informe, relación; (*arq.*) marco; ganancia, rédito; ingresos, *m.pl.*; (*impuestos*) declaración (*de ingresos*); (*pl.*) estadísticas, *f.pl.*, cifras, *f.pl.*; resultados, *m.pl.*; ***by return (of post),*** a vuelta de correo; ***many happy returns!*** ¡muchas felicidades!; ***in return (for),*** a cambio (de), en recompensa (de); ***return match,*** (partido de) desquite, revancha; ***return ticket,*** billete de ida y vuelta. — *v.t.* devolver; producir; elegir; ***return an answer,*** dar respuesta; ***return a favour,*** corresponder a un favor; ***return good for evil,*** devolver bien por mal; ***return thanks,*** dar gracias; ***return a verdict,*** dar *o* pronunciar un dictamen *o* fallo; ***return a visit,*** pagar una visita. — *v.i.* volver, regresar, retornar; responder, reponer (*pret.*), replicar; reaparecer; (*for.*) revertir; ***return to one's parents,*** volver con sus padres; ***return to a subject,*** volver a un tema.
returnable [ri'təːnəbl], *a.* restituible; (*for.*) devolutivo — *s.* casco, envase vacío.
returning officer [ri'təːniŋ ɔfisə], *s.* escudriñador.
reunion ['riː'juːniən], *s.* reunión, *f.*; reconciliación; ***to celebrate a reunion,*** volver a reunirse.
reunite ['riːjuː'nait], *v.t.* reunir, volver a reunir; reconciliar. — *v.i.* reunirse, volver a reunirse; reconciliarse.
rev [rev], *s.* (*fam.*) acelerón. — *v.t.* — ***(up) an engine,*** acelerar, dar *o* pegar acelerones a un motor.
reveal [ri'viːl], *v.t.* revelar, descubrir.
revealing [ri'viːliŋ], *a.* revelador, significativo.
reveille [ri'væli], *s.* (*mil.*) diana.
revel ['revəl], *s.* jarana, juerga; ***to hold high revel,*** andar de jarana. — *v.i.* jaranear, estar *o* ir de juerga; ***revel in,*** deleitarse en, regodearse con.
revelation [revə'leiʃən], *s.* revelación.
reveller ['revələ], *s.* jaranero, juerguista, *m.f.*
revelry ['revəlri], *s.* jolgorio, jarana, juerga.
revendication [riːvendi'keiʃən], *s.* reivindicación.
revenge [ri'vendʒ], *s.* venganza; ***to take revenge for,*** vengarse de. — *v.t.* vengar; ***to be revenged on,*** vengarse de.
revengeful [ri'vendʒful], *a.* vengativo.
revengefulness [ri'vendʒfulnis], *s.* (lo) vengativo; sed *o* ansia de venganza.
revenger [ri'vendʒə], *s.* vengador.
revengingly [ri'vendʒiŋli], *adv.* con venganza.
revenue ['revinjuː], *s.* rentas públicas, *f.pl.*; (*com.*) rédito; ingreso(s); ***Inland Revenue,*** delegación de contribuciones; (*mar.*) ***revenue cutter,*** guardacostas, *m.inv.*, escampavía, *f.*; ***revenue officer,*** aduanero, empleado de aduana.
reverberant [ri'vəːbərənt], *a.* repercusivo; resonante, retumbante.
reverberate [ri'vəːbəreit], *v.i.* resonar, retumbar; (*t. luz*) reverberar.
reverberation [rivəːbə'reiʃən], *s.* retumbo, eco; reverberación.
reverberator [ri'vəːbəreitə], *s.* reverberador, reverbero.
reverberatory [ri'vəːbərətəri], *a.* de reverbero, que reverbera. — *s.* horno de reverbero.
revere [ri'viə], *v.t.* reverenciar, venerar; acatar.
reverence ['revərəns], *s.* reverencia, veneración; acatamiento; ***to do (o pay) reverence,*** rendir homenaje; (*fam.*) ***saving your reverence,*** salvo vuestro respeto. — *v.t.* reverenciar, venerar; acatar.
reverencer ['revərənsə], *s.* reverenciador.
reverend ['revərənd], *a.* reverendo, venerable; (*título, abrev.* **Rev.**) Reverendo; ***Most Reverend, Right Reverend,*** Reverendísimo.
reverent ['revərənt], *a.* reverente; respetuoso.
reverential [revə'renʃəl], *a.* reverencial; respetuoso.
reverer [ri'viərə], *s.* venerador.
reverie ['revəri], *s.* ensueño(s), ensoñación; (*mús.*) fantasía.
revers [ri'viə], *s.* (*pl.* **revers** [-'viəz]) solapa(s).
reversal [ri'vəːsəl], *s.* inversión; cambio total; (*for.*) revocación.
reverse [ri'vəːs], *a.* inverso, invertido; contrario; (*mec.*) de marcha atrás. — *s.* (lo) contrario; revés, *m.*, contratiempo; reverso (*de una moneda*); revés (*de una tela*); marcha atrás; ***quite the reverse,*** todo lo contrario; ***reverse operation,*** operación inversa; ***reverse turn,*** cambio de dirección; ***to suffer a reverse,*** sufrir un revés. — *v.t.* invertir; cambiar totalmente de; volver al revés; poner en marcha atrás; (*for.*) revocar. — *v.i.* dar marcha atrás.
reversedly, reversely [ri'vəːsidli, ri'vəːsli], *adv.* al revés.
reversible [ri'vəːsibl], *a.* reversible; (*for.*) revocable.
reversing [ri'vəːsiŋ], *a.* de marcha atrás. — *s.* (el) dar marcha atrás (a).
reversion [ri'vəːʃən], *s.* reversión; salto atrás.
reversionary [ri'vəːʃənəri], *a.* (*for.*) reversible.
revert [ri'vəːt], *v.i.* volver; (*for.*) revertir; (*biol.*) saltar atrás.

revertible [ri'vɘ:tibl], *a.* reversible.
revet [ri'vet], *v.t.* revestir.
revetment [ri'vetmɘnt], *s.* revestimiento.
revictual ['ri:'vitl], *v.t.* reavituallar. — *v.i.* repostar.
review [ri'vju:], *s.* revista; repaso; (*for.*) revisión; reseña, recensión (*de un libro*). — *v.t.* pasar revista a, revistar; repasar; (*for.*) rever; reseñar (*un libro*).
reviewer [ri'vju:ɘ], *s.* crítico.
revile [ri'vail], *v.t.* vituperar, ultrajar, injuriar, vilipendiar.
revilement [ri'vailmɘnt], *s.* vituperio(s), ultraje(s), vilipendio(s).
reviler [ri'vailɘ], *s.* injuriador, vilipendiador.
revindicate ['ri:'vindikeit], *v.t.* reivindicar.
revisal [ri'vaizɘl], *s.* revisión.
revise [ri'vaiz], *s.* (*impr.*) segunda prueba; ***second revise,*** tercera prueba. — *v.t.* revisar; repasar, releer; corregir.
reviser, revisor [ri'vaizɘ], *s.* revisor; (*impr.*) corrector de pruebas.
revision [ri'viʒɘn], *s.* repaso; revisión; (*impr.*) corrección.
revisit ['ri:'vizit], *v.t.* volver a visitar, visitar de nuevo.
revisory [ri'vaizɘri], *a.* revisor.
revitalize ['ri:'vaitɘlaiz], *v.t.* revivificar, vivificar de nuevo.
revival [ri'vaivɘl], *s.* renacimiento; renovación; reanimación; (*teat.*) reposición; despertar religioso.
revivalist [ri'vaivɘlist], *s.* predicador protestante que recorre un país para despertar la fe.
revive [ri'vaiv], *v.t.* reanimar; restablecer; avivar; despertar; reponer. — *v.i.* reanimarse; renacer; renovarse.
reviver [ri'vaivɘ], *s.* vivificador.
revivification ['ri:vivifi'keiʃɘn], *s.* revivificación.
revivify ['ri:'vivifai], *v.t.* revivificar; (*quím.*) reactivar.
revocability, revocableness [revokɘ'biliti, 'revokɘblnis], *s.* revocabilidad.
revocable ['revokɘbl], *a.* revocable.
revocation [revo'keiʃɘn], *s.* revocación; derogación.
revoke [ri'vouk], *v.t.* revocar; derogar. — *v.i.* renunciar (*naipes*).
revolt [ri'voult], *s.* rebelión, sublevación. — *v.t.* dar asco a. — *v.i.* rebelarse, sublevarse.
revolter [ri'voultɘ], *s.* rebelde, sublevado.
revolting [ri'voultiŋ], *a.* asqueroso, repugnante, repulsivo.
revolute ['revol(j)u:t], *a.* (*bot.*) enrollado hacia atrás.
revolution [revo'l(j)u:ʃɘn], *s.* revolución; ciclo; rotación.
revolutionary, revolutionist [revo'l(j)u:ʃɘnɘri, -nist], *a.*, *s.* revolucionario.
revolutionize [revo'l(j)u:ʃɘnaiz], *v.t.* revolucionar.
revolve [ri'vɔlv], *v.i.* girar, dar vueltas; (*astron.*) revolverse; (*fig.*) ***revolve round,*** depender de.
revolver [ri'vɔlvɘ], *s.* revólver.
revolving, revolvable [ri'vɔlviŋ, -ɘbl], *a.* giratorio.
revue [ri'vju:], *s.* revista.
revulsion [ri'vʌlʃɘn], *s.* repulsión, repugnancia; (*med.*) revulsión.
revulsive [ri'vʌlsiv], *a.* (*med.*) revulsivo.
reward [ri'wɔ:d], *s.* premio, recompensa, galardón. — *v.t.* premiar, recompensar, galardonar.
rewarding [ri'wɔ:diŋ], *a.* remunerador; que proporciona muchas satisfacciones.
reweigh ['ri:'wei], *v.t.* repesar.
reword ['ri:'wɘ:d], *v.t.* volver a formular con otras palabras.
rewrite ['ri:'rait], *v.t.* refundir; escribir de nuevo.
reynard ['reinɑ:d], *s.* zorro.
rhapontic [rei'pɔntik], *s.* rapóntico.
rhapsodist ['ræpsɘdist], *s.* rapsodista, *m.f.*
rhapsodize ['ræpsɘdaiz], *v.i.* extasiarse (***over,*** ante), entusiasmarse (***over,*** con).
rhapsody ['ræpsɘdi], *s.* rapsodia; éxtasis, *m.inv.*
rhea ['ri:ɘ], *s.* ñandú.
Rhenish ['reniʃ], *a.* del Rin. — *s.* vino del Rin.
rheometer [ri:'ɔmitɘ], *s.* reómetro.
rheophore ['ri:ofɔ:], *s.* reóforo.
rheostat ['ri:ostæt], *s.* reóstato.
rhesus ['ri:sɘs], *s.* macaco de la India.
rhetoric ['retɘrik], *s.* retórica.
rhetorical [ri'tɔrikɘl], *a.* retórico.
rhetorician [retɘ'riʃɘn], *s.* retórico.
rheum [ru:m], *s.* reuma; catarro.
rheumatic [ru:'mætik], *a.* reumático.
rheumatism ['ru:mɘtizɘm], *s.* reuma, *m.*
rheumy ['ru:mi], *a.* catarroso; (*fig.*) húmedo y frío.
Rhine [rain]. Rin, *m.*
Rhineland ['rainlænd]. Renania.
rhinitis [rai'naitis], *s.* rinitis, *f.inv.*
rhinoceri(c)al, rhinocerotic [raino'seri(k)ɘl, rainose'rɔtik], *a.* rinoceróntico.
rhinoceros [rai'nɔsɘrɘs], *s.* rinoceronte; ***female rhinoceros,*** abada.
rhinoplastic [raino'plæstik], *a.* rinoplástico.
rhinoplasty ['rainoplæsti], *s.* rinoplastia.
rhizome, rhizoma ['raizoum, rai'zoumɘ], *s.* rizoma.
rhizopod ['raizopɔd], *s.* animal rizópodo.
Rhodes [roudz]. Rodas, *f.*
Rhodesia [ro'di:ʃɘ]. Rodesia.
Rhodesian [ro'di:ʃɘn], *a.*, *s.* rodesiano.
rhodium ['roudiɘm], *s.* rodio.
rhododendron [roudo'dendrɘn], *s.* rododendro.
rhomb, rhombus [rɔmb, 'rɔmbɘs], *s.* rombo; (*blas.*) losange.
rhombic ['rɔmbik], *a.* rombal.
rhombohedron [rɔmbo'hi:drɘn], *s.* romboedro.
rhomboid ['rɔmbɔid], *s.* romboide.
rhomboidal [rɔm'bɔidɘl], *a.* romboidal.
Rhone [roun]. Ródano.
rhubarb ['ru:bɑ:b], *s.* ruibarbo.
rhumb [rʌm(b)], *s.* (*mar.*) rumbo.
rhyme [raim], *s.* rima; poesía; ***without rhyme or reason,*** sin ton ni son, sin qué ni por qué. — *v.t.*, *v.i.* rimar.
rhymer, rhymester ['raimɘ, -stɘ], *s.* versificador, rimador.
rhythm ['riðɘm], *s.* ritmo, cadencia; (*med.*) periodicidad.
rhythmic(al) ['riðmik(ɘl)], *a.* rítmico, cadencioso, acompasado.
rib [rib], *s.* costilla; (*mec.*) pestaña, reborde; (*bot.*) nervadura (de la hojas); (*mar.*) cuaderna; (*mar.*) ligazón, *f.*; (*arq.*) faja, listón, nervadura, nervio; viga (de tejado); cabrio; varilla (*de paraguas*); tirante, varenga de hierro; (*pl.*) (*mar.*) costillaje. — *v.t.* encarrujar; afianzar con rebordes *o* pestañas; marcar con rayas, listones *o* filetes; (*fam.*) tomar el pelo a, meterse con.
ribald ['ribɘld], *a.* obsceno, indecente; irreverente y regocijado.
ribaldry ['ribɘldri], *s.* obscenidad, indecencia; irreverencia regocijada.
riband ['ribɘnd], *s.* cinta.
ribbed [ribd], *a.* encarrujado, guarnecido de costillas.
ribbon ['ribɘn], *s.* cinta; galón; (*pl.*) (*fam.*) perifollos, *m.pl.*; ***ribbon grass,*** alpiste; ***slashed to ribbons,*** corticheado, lleno de tijeretazos. — *v.t.* encintar. — *v.i.* serpear, serpentear.
ribwort ['ribwɘ:t], *s.* llantén.
rice [rais], *s.* arroz; ***rice field,*** arrozal; ***rice paper,*** papel de paja de arroz; papel de China; ***rice-pudding,*** arroz con leche.
rich [ritʃ], *a.* rico; feraz; (*pey.*) dulzón, empalagoso,

empachoso; denso (*color*); sonoro (*voz*); generoso (*vino*); ***rich pickings,*** pingües ganancias, *f.pl.*; (*fam.*) ***that's rich!*** ¡vaya gracia! ¡esa sí que es buena!; ***to be rich in,*** ser fértil en.

Richard [ˈritʃəd]. Ricardo.

riches [ˈritʃiz], *s.pl.* riqueza, caudales, *m.pl.*

richness [ˈritʃnis], *s.* riqueza; fertilidad; (lo) dulzón *o* empalagoso; (lo) sonoro; (lo) denso; (lo) generoso.

rick (1) [rik], *s.* niara, almiar. — *v.t.* hacinar.

rick (2) [rik], *s.* torcedura. — *v.t.* torcer.

rickets [ˈrikits], *s.* raquitismo.

rickety [ˈrikiti], *a.* desvencijado, tambaleante; (*med.*) raquítico.

rickshaw [ˈrikʃɔ:], *s.* carricoche (chino, japonés).

ricochet [ˈrikoʃei], *s.* rebote. — *v.i.* rebotar.

rictus [ˈriktəs], *s.* rictus.

rid [rid], *irr. v.t.* librar, desembarazar, quitar de encima; ***to be rid of,*** verse libre de; ***get rid of,*** deshacerse de, librarse de; ***you're well rid of him,*** estás mejor sin él.

riddance [ˈridəns], *s.* libramiento; ***good riddance (to bad rubbish),*** menos mal que se ha ido, (a) enemigo que huye, puente de plata.

riddle (1) [ridl], *s.* acertijo, adivinanza; enigma, *m.*

riddle (2) [ridl], *s.* criba. — *v.t.* cribar; acribillar; ***riddled with bullets,*** acribillado a balazos.

ride [raid], *s.* paseo (*a caballo, en coche etc.*); viaje; cabalgata; camino de herradura; ***to take for a ride,*** dar un paseo a; (*fig., fam.*) tomar el pelo a, dársela a. — *irr. v.t.* montar *o* ir montado en *o* sobre; recorrer (a caballo, en coche *etc.*) (*una distancia*); surcar (*los mares*); ***ride down,*** atropellar, hollar; ***ride out the storm,*** capear al temporal. — *irr. v.i.* montar a caballo, cabalgar; ir *o* dar un paseo (*a caballo, en coche etc.*); (*mar.*) ***ride at anchor,*** estar fondeado *o* surto; ***ride roughshod over everything and everybody,*** pasar por encima de todo y de todos, no respetar a nada ni a nadie, no pararse en barras.

rider [ˈraidə], *s.* jinete, caballero; ciclista, *m.f.*; (*mar.*) sobreplán, *f.*; corolario.

ridge [ridʒ], *s.* espinazo; cadena de montes, sierra; cresta; (*agric.*) caballón; (*arq.*) caballete (del tejado); ***ridge-pole,*** parhilera. — *v.t.* (*agric.*) encaballar.

ridgy [ˈridʒi], *a.* rugoso; lleno de surcos, carriles *o* carrileras; accidentado.

ridicule [ˈridikju:l], *s.* ridículo, burla, irrisión; ***to subject to ridicule,*** poner en ridículo. — *v.t.* ridiculizar, hacer burla *o* mofa de.

ridiculous [riˈdikjuləs], *a.* ridículo.

ridiculousness [riˈdikjuləsnis], *s.* (lo) ridículo.

riding [ˈraidiŋ], *a.* cabalgante; ***riding at anchor,*** fondeado, surto. — *s.* equitación; ***riding-boots,*** botas de montar, *f.pl.*; ***riding-habit,*** traje de montar; ***riding-school,*** escuela de equitación; ***riding-whip,*** fusta.

rife [raif], *a.* que reina, que pulula, que se multiplica, que se encuentra en todas partes; ***rumour is rife,*** cunden los rumores.

riff-raff [ˈrif-ræf], *s.* gentucilla, gente de medio pelo, chusma.

rifle (1) [raifl], *s.* fusil; (*caz., dep.*) rifle; ***rifle butt,*** culata (de fusil); ***rifle range,*** campo de tiro; ***rifle shot,*** tiro de fusil, fusilazo.

rifle (2) [raifl], *v.t.* robar; saquear; revolver y robar.

rifleman [ˈraiflmən], *s.* (*pl.* **-men** [-men]) riflero; fusilero.

rifler [ˈraiflə], *s.* saqueador.

rift [rift], *s.* hendidura, rendija, grieta; (*fig.*) escisión, cisma. — *v.t.* hender. — *v.i.* henderse.

rig (1) [rig], *s.* (*mar.*) aparejo; atuendo; avíos, *m.pl.* — *v.t.* (*mar.*) aparejar, enjarciar; ***rig out,*** ataviar; ***rig up,*** improvisar.

rig (2) [rig], *s.* timo. — *v.t.* apañar; ***rig an election,*** dar pucherazo; ***rig the market,*** manipular la bolsa.

rigadoon [rigəˈdu:n], *s.* rigodón.

rigescent [riˈdʒesənt], *a.* que se envara *o* pone rígido.

rigger [ˈrigə], *s.* (*mar.*) aparejador.

rigging [ˈrigiŋ], *s.* (*mar.*) aparejo, jarcia, cordaje.

riggish [ˈrigiʃ], *a.* rijoso.

right [rait], *a.* recto; derecho; correcto, exacto; verdadero; justo; indicado, apropiado, conveniente, debido; cuerdo; favorable; ***all right!*** ¡bueno! ¡de acuerdo! ¡conforme! ¡está bien! ¡vale!; ***to be all right,*** estar bien; ***I'm all right, Jack!*** ¡a mí, plin! ¡a los demás que los zurzan!; ***as right as rain,*** perfectamente; tan fresco, tan campante; ***to be right,*** tener razón; ***to be right to,*** hacer bien en; ***right angle,*** ángulo recto; ***right-angled,*** de ángulo recto; ***right-handed,*** que se sirve de la mano derecha; ***right-handed screw,*** tornillo de rosca a la derecha; ***right-hand man,*** brazo derecho; (*fam.*) ***a right idiot,*** un imbécil integral; ***he's the right man,*** es el hombre pintiparado, que hace falta; ***to be in one's right mind,*** estar en sus cabales; ***right-minded,*** honrado, recto; prudente; ***right wing,*** (*dep.*) ala derecha; (*pol.*) derecha; [RIGHT-WING, RIGHT-WINGER]; ***to put*** o ***set right,*** arreglar, poner remedio a; ***that's right,*** exacto, justo. — *adv.* directamente; a derechas; bien; completamente, del todo; exactamente, correctamente; a la derecha; muy; ***right about!*** ¡derecha!; ***right and left,*** a diestro y siniestro; ***right away,*** en el acto, en seguida; ***right here,*** aquí mismo; ***right now,*** ahora mismo; ***right or wrong,*** con razón o sin ella, a tuertas o a derechas; ***Right Reverend,*** Reverendísimo. — *s.* derecho; título, privilegio; derecha; (*boxeo*) derechazo; ***by right(s),*** en justicia; ***by right of,*** por razón de; ***to be in the right,*** tener razón; ***in his own right,*** por derecho propio; (*pol.*) ***he is of the right,*** es de derechas; ***to*** o ***on the right,*** a la derecha; ***right of way,*** derecho de paso; preferencia, prioridad; (*Am.*) [PERMANENT WAY]. — *v.t.* poner remedio a; enderezar; corregir, rectificar; ***right a wrong,*** deshacer un entuerto.

righteous [ˈraitʃəs], *a.* justo, honrado, probo.

righteousness [ˈraitʃəsnis], *s.* rectitud, honradez, probidad.

righter [ˈraitə], *s.* ***righter of wrongs,*** enderezador de agravios, deshacedor de entuertos.

rightful [ˈraitful], *a.* legítimo; justo, equitativo.

rightfulness [ˈraitfulnis], *s.* derechura; equidad; rectitud, justicia.

rightness [ˈraitnis], *s.* rectitud, justicia; derechura.

right-wing [ˈrait-wiŋ], *a.* (*pol.*) derechista.

right-winger [ˈrait-ˈwiŋə], *s.* (*dep.*) extremo derecha; (*pol.*) derechista, *m.f.*

rigid [ˈridʒid], *a.* rígido; inflexible.

rigidity, rigidness [riˈdʒiditi, ˈridʒidnis], *s.* rigidez; inflexibilidad.

rigmarole [ˈrigmərəul], *s.* galimatías, *m.inv.*, monserga.

rigor [ˈrigə], *s.* (*Am.*) [RIGOUR]; ***rigor mortis,*** rigor de la muerte, rigidez cadavérica.

rigorism [ˈrigərizəm], *s.* rigorismo.

rigorist [ˈrigərist], *s.* rigorista, *m.f.*

rigorous [ˈrigərəs], *a.* riguroso; severo; inflexible.

rigour, rigorousness [ˈrigə, ˈrigərəsnis], *s.* rigurosidad, rigor; severidad.

rile [rail], *v.t.* (*fam.*) irritar, sacar de quicio.

rill [ril], *s.* arroyuelo.

rillet [ˈrilit], *s.* arroyuelo.

rim [rim], *s.* borde; reborde; canto (*de moneda*); brocal (*de pozo* o *de escudo*); llanta (*de rueda*).

rime (1) [raim], *s.* [RHYME].

rime (2) [raim], *s.* escarcha. — *v.t.* cubrir de escarcha.

rimy [ˈraimi], *a.* lleno de escarcha.

rind [raind], *s.* corteza; piel, *f.*; cáscara.

ring (1) [riŋ], *s.* anillo, sortija; círculo; anilla (*de cortina*); argolla (*de hierro*); cuadrilátero (*de boxeo*);

plaza, redondel (*de toros*); corro *o* corrillo (*de gente*); pandilla (*de delincuentes*); ***ring-a-ring-o'-roses,*** juego del corro; (***dark***) ***rings round*** o ***under the eyes,*** ojeras, *f.pl.*; ***ring-shaped,*** circular, en forma de anillo; (*fam.*) ***to run rings round,*** dar ciento y raya a. — *v.t.* cercar, rodear (***by, with,*** de); formar (un) corro alrededor de; poner un anillo a.

ring (2) [riŋ], *s.* campanada, tañido; toque; llamada (*a la puerta*); telefonazo; sonido (metálico); ***I'll give you a ring,*** te pegaré un telefonazo; ***to have the ring of truth,*** sonar a verdad. — *irr. v.t.* tocar, tañer; (hacer) sonar; ***ring out,*** anunciar a toque de campana; ***ring up,*** llamar (por teléfono). — *irr. v.i.* sonar; resonar (***with,*** con); repicar; llamar (*a la puerta*); zumbar (*los oídos*); ***ring off,*** colgar (*el teléfono*); ***ring true,*** sonar a verdad.

ringdove [ˈriŋdʌv], *s.* paloma torcaz.

ringed [riŋd], *a.* anillado.

ringer [ˈriŋə], *s.* campanero.

ringing [ˈriŋiŋ], *a.* resonante; retumbante. — *s.* anillamiento; campaneo, repique; zumbido(s).

ringleader [ˈriŋli:də], *s.* cabecilla, *m.*

ringlet [ˈriŋlit], *s.* rizo, bucle, tirabuzón.

ringmaster [ˈriŋmɑ:stə], *s.* director de pista, director de circo.

ringworm [ˈriŋwə:m], *s.* tiña; culebrilla; cardador.

rink [riŋk], *s.* pista; ***skating-rink,*** pista de patinar.

rinse [rins], *s.* aclarado; enjuague. — *v.t.* aclarar; enjuagar.

rinsing [ˈrinsiŋ], *s.* aclarado; enjuague.

riot [ˈraiət], *s.* revuelta, motín, alboroto; ***to run riot,*** desmandarse. — *v.i.* alborotarse, amotinarse.

rioter [ˈraiətə], *s.* alborotador, amotinado(r).

riotous [ˈraiətəs], *a.* alborotado; desenfrenado; bullicioso.

riotousness [ˈraiətəsnis], *s.* desorden, alboroto; bullicio; desenfreno.

rip (1) [rip], *s.* rasgón, rasgadura; ***rip-cord,*** cuerda para abrir el paracaídas; ***rip panel,*** faja de rasgadura; ***rip-saw,*** sierra de hender. — *v.t.* rasgar; romper, abrir; destripar; descoser; ***rip open*** o ***up,*** hender, lacerar, rasgar, romper, rajar, partir; (*cost.*) descoser; ***rip out*** o ***away,*** cortar, destripar, arrancar, destrozar; descoser, soltar; ***rip off,*** arrancar, quitar con violencia; ***rip up,*** destrozar, desgarrar; ***rip out an oath,*** jurar con violencia. — *v.i.* henderse, rasgarse, romperse; ***let it rip!*** ¡más rápido!

rip (2) [rip], *s.* ***young rip,*** pillo.

riparian [raiˈpɛəriən], *a.* ribereño.

riparious [raiˈpɛəriəs], *a.* ribereño.

ripe [raip], *a.* maduro; sazonado, en sazón; acabado, consumado; colorado, rosado; ***to be ripe for,*** estar (listo) para.

ripen [ˈraipən], *v.t., v.i.* madurar; sazonar(se).

ripeness [ˈraipnis], *s.* madurez; sazón, *f.*

riposte [riˈpɔst], *s.* estocada; respuesta aguda, réplica. — *v.i.* replicar con viveza.

ripper [ˈripə], *s.* rasgador; destripador; (*fam.*) persona *o* cosa estupenda; ***Jack the Ripper,*** Jack, el destripador.

ripping [ˈripiŋ], *a.* (*fam.*) estupendo. — *s.* rasgadura; descosedura, deshiladura; laceración; (*mar.*) ***ripping-iron,*** descalcador; (*aer.*) ***ripping-line,*** cabo de desgarre (con que se maneja la faja de desgarre); (*aer.*) ***ripping-panel,*** faja de desgarre.

ripple [ripl], *s.* ondulación; rizo, onda; murmullo (del agua). — *v.t.* rizar, hacer ondear; desgargolar (*el cáñamo*). — *v.i.* rizarse, ondear; murmurar.

rippling [ˈripliŋ], *a.* que se riza, murmura *etc.* — *s.* escarceo, ondulación.

riprap [ˈripræp], *s.* (*alb.*) cascajo, broma, ripio; cimiento hecho de cascajo. — *v.t.* (*Am., alb.*) reforzar con broma.

rip-roaring [ˈrip-ˈrɔ:riŋ], *a.* ruidosísimo; animadísimo; alegrísimo; violento; tremendo.

rise [raiz], *s.* subida; alza; elevación; ascenso; crecida; cuesta; nacimiento; origen; ***to give rise to,*** dar origen a, dar lugar a. — *irr. v.i.* subir; alzarse, levantarse; salir (*el sol*); ascender; nacer, brotar; hincharse; sublevarse; suspenderse (*la sesión*); ***rise to,*** mostrarse capaz de; ***rise to one's feet,*** levantarse, ponerse en pie; ***rise to the occasion,*** ponerse a la altura de las circunstancias.

riser [ˈraizə], *s.* el que se levanta; (*carp.*) contrahuella; (*elec. etc.*) conductor *o* tubo ascendente; ***early riser,*** madrugador; ***late riser,*** el que se levanta tarde.

risibility [riziˈbiliti], *s.* risibilidad; ***to tickle s.o.'s risibility,*** hacerle gracia a alguien, hacer reír a alguien.

risible [ˈrizibl], *a.* risible.

rising [ˈraiziŋ], *a.* naciente; ascendiente; (*astron., astrol.*) saliente, que sale; (*terreno*) en cuesta, que sube; ***rising generation,*** nueva generación. — *s.* sublevación, levantamiento; salida, orto; término *o* clausura (*de sesión*).

risk [risk], *s.* riesgo, peligro; ***at the risk of,*** con riesgo *o* peligro de; ***at the risk of boring you,*** aunque peque de pesado; ***to run a*** o ***the risk of,*** correr riesgo *o* peligro de. — *v.t.* arriesgar, poner en riesgo *o* en peligro, exponer; aventurar; ***risk failure*** o ***failing,*** exponerse a un fracaso *o* a fracasar.

risky [ˈriski], *a.* expuesto, arriesgado; aventurado.

risqué [ˈriskei], *a.* escabroso, indecente, verde.

rissole [ˈrisoul], *s.* (*aprox.*) croqueta.

rite [rait], *s.* rito; ***funeral rites,*** exequias, *f.pl.*

ritual [ˈritjuəl], *a., s.* ritual; sacral.

ritualism [ˈritjuəlizəm], *s.* ritualismo.

ritualist [ˈritjuəlist], *a., s.* ritualista, *m.f.*

ritualistic [ritjuəˈlistik], *a.* ritualista.

ritually [ˈritjuəli], *adv.* según el ritual, conforme al ritual *o* a los ritos.

rival [ˈraivəl], *a.* rival, competidor. — *s.* rival, competidor, contrincante. — *v.t.* rivalizar con, competir con.

rivalry [ˈraivəlri], *s.* rivalidad, emulación, competencia.

riven [ˈrivən], *a.* hendido.

river [ˈrivə], *a.* fluvial. — *s.* río; ***down river,*** río abajo; ***river basin,*** cuenca de río; ***river bed,*** lecho de río; ***up river,*** río arriba.

riverside [ˈrivəsaid], *a.* ribereño, de la orilla (de un río). — *s.* ribera, orilla, margen, *f.* (de un río).

rivet [ˈrivit], *s.* remache, roblón. — *v.t.* remachar; clavar; ***to have one's eyes riveted*** (***on sth.***), tener la mirada clavada (en algo).

riveting [ˈrivitiŋ], *a.* cautivador, encantador. — *s.* robladura, remache.

Riviera [riviˈɛərə], *s.* costa azul, Riviera.

rivulet [ˈrivjulit], *s.* riachuelo, arroyo.

roach (1) [routʃ], *s.* (*ict.*) escarcho.

roach (2) [routʃ], *s.* (*mar.*) alunamiento.

roach (3) [routʃ], (*Am.*) [COCKROACH].

road [roud], *s.* carretera; camino; calle; (*pl.*) (*mar.*) rada; ***across the road,*** al otro lado de la calle, enfrente; ***high road, main road,*** camino real, carretera; ***to be on the road,*** estar en carretera; estar de viaje; ***to be on the road to success,*** estar camino del triunfo, en vías de triunfar; ***road accident,*** accidente de tráfico *o* de carretera; ***road block,*** obstáculo *o* barrera de carretera; ***road hog,*** volantista de cuidado, *m.f.*, asesino de carretera; ***road-making,*** construcción de carreteras; ***road map,*** mapa de carreteras; ***road sense,*** instinto automovilístico; ***road sweeper,*** barrendero; ***road traffic,*** tráfico rodado; ***road transport,*** transporte vial *o* por carretera; ***road vehicle,*** vehículo de carretera; ***side road,*** camino secundario; ***turnpike road,*** camino de peaje.

roadman [ˈroudmæn], *s.* (*pl.* **-men** [-men]) peón caminero.

roadside [ˈroudsaid], *s.* borde de la carretera.

roadstead [ˈroudsted], *s.* rada, fondeadero; ensenada.
roadster [ˈroudstə], *s.* automóvil de turismo; (*Am.*) [TWO-SEATER]; bicicleta de carreras; caballo de aguante; (*mar.*) barco capaz de fondear en una rada.
roadway [ˈroudwei], *s.* calzada.
roam [roum], *v.t.* rodar, vagar por. — *v.i.* vagar, callejear.
roamer [ˈroumə], *s.* vagabundo, hombre errante.
roan [roun], *a.* ruano, roano, sabino, rosillo. — *s.* caballo ruano; badana de color ruano; color ruano.
roar [rɔː], *s.* rugido, bramido; estruendo; griterío; ***roar of laughter,*** risotada. — *v.i.* rugir, bramar.
roarer [ˈrɔːrə], *s.* bramador.
roaring [ˈrɔːriŋ], *a.* rugiente, bramador; (*fig.*) tremendo, enorme, de aúpa; floreciente. — *s.* (*vet.*) ronquido.
roast [roust], *a.* asado; tostado; ***roast beef,*** rosbif; ***roast meat,*** asado, carne asada. — *s.* asado, carne asada; carne para asar; tueste, tostadura; ***roast of beef,*** carne de vaca (buena) para asar; (*Am.*) cuarto. — *v.t.* asar; tostar (*café*); calcinar; (*metal.*) calcinar. — *v.i.* asarse; tostarse.
roaster [ˈroustə], *s.* asador; tostador; cocinero que asa; pollo *o* lechón propio para ser asado.
roasting [ˈroustiŋ], *s.* acción de asar; tostadura; torrefacción; calcinación; (*fam.*) censura; rechifla, burla; ***roasting-jack*** o ***roasting-spit,*** asador, espetón, pincho.
rob [rɔb], *v.t.* robar, hurtar; ***rob s.o. of sth.,*** robar algo a alguien; ***rob Peter to pay Paul,*** desnudar a un santo para vestir a otro.
robber [ˈrɔbə], *s.* ladrón; ***highway robber,*** salteador, bandolero.
robbery [ˈrɔbəri], *s.* robo, hurto, latrocinio; ***to commit highway robbery,*** saltear.
robe [roub], *s.* túnica, manto; toga, traje talar; hábito sotana; ***bath robe,*** albornoz; ***christening robe(s),*** traje de cristianar *o* de acristianar; ***counsellor's robe,*** ropaje; ***master of the robes,*** jefe del guardarropa. — *v.t.* vestir, ataviar, vestir de gala *o* de ceremonia. — *v.i.* vestirse.
Robert [ˈrɔbət]. Roberto.
robin [ˈrɔbin], *s.* (*orn.*) pechicolorado, petirrojo.
roborant [ˈroubərənt], *a.* roborante, roborativo.
robot [ˈroubɔt], *s.* robot; autómata, *m.*
robust [roˈbʌst], *a.* robusto, vigoroso.
robustness [roˈbʌstnis], *s.* robustez, vigor.
roc [rɔk], *s.* rocho, ruc.
Rochelle (La) [rɔˈʃel (lɑː)]. La Rochela.
rochet (1) [ˈrɔtʃit], *s.* (*igl.*) roquete.
rochet (2) [ˈrɔtʃit], *s.* (*ict.*) trigla roja.
rock (1) [rɔk], *s.* roca; peña; peñasco; (*mar.*) escollo; (*fam.*) diamante; ***rock-bottom,*** más bajo, mínimo; ***to get down to rock bottom,*** llegar al fondo; ***rock-bound,*** rodeado de peñascos; ***rock candy,*** azúcar cande; ***rock crystal,*** cristal de roca; ***rock rose,*** heliantemo; ***rock salt,*** sal gema; ***the Rock,*** el Peñón; ***on the rocks,*** (bebida) con hielo; sin cinco, tronado; ***his marriage is on the rocks,*** su matrimonio ha fracasado.
rock (2) [rɔk], *v.t.* mecer, balancear; sacudir. — *v.i.* mecerse, balancearse; sacudirse; ***rock with laughter,*** desternillarse de risa.
rocker [ˈrɔkə], *s.* balancín; mecedora; (*fam.*) ***off one's rocker,*** chalado.
rockery [ˈrɔkəri], *s.* jardín rocoso, cuadro alpino.
rocket [ˈrɔkit], *s.* cohete; (*bot.*) oruga; (*fam.*) reprimenda; bronca; (*fam.*) ***to give s.o. a rocket,*** echarle a alguien una bronca. — *v.i.* subir como un cohete.
rockiness [ˈrɔkinis], *s.* (lo) rocoso, (lo) peñascoso.
rocking [ˈrɔkiŋ], *a.* mecedor; ***rocking-chair,*** mecedora; ***rocking-horse,*** caballo mecedor, caballo de balancín, caballito.
rocky (1) [ˈrɔki], *a.* rocoso, peñascoso; duro, despiadado; ***Rocky Mountains,*** Montañas Rocosas, *f.pl.*
rocky (2) [ˈrɔki], *a.* (*fam.*) inestable.
rococo [roˈkoukou], *a.*, *s.* rococó.
rod [rɔd], *s.* vara; varilla; caña (*de pescar*); barra (*de cortina*); pértica (*medida*); (*mec.*) vástago; (*mec.*) ***connecting-rod,*** biela; ***to give the rod,*** dar azotes, azotar; ***to rule with a rod of iron,*** gobernar con mano de hierro; ***to spare the rod,*** excusar la vara.
rodent [ˈroudənt], *a.*, *s.* roedor.
Roderick [ˈrɔdərik]. Rodrigo.
rodomontade [rɔdomɔnˈteid], *s.* fanfarronada. — *v.i.* fanfarronear.
roe [rou], *s.* hueva; ***soft roe,*** lechas, *f.pl.*
roebuck, roe-deer [ˈroubʌk, ˈrou-diə], *s.* corzo, corza.
rogation [roˈgeiʃən], *s.* (*igl.*) rogativa; rogación.
rogatory [roˈgeitəri], *a.* rogatorio.
rogue [roug], *s.* bribón, tunante, pícaro, pillo, bellaco, granuja; ***rogue elephant,*** elefante bravo que vive por su cuenta; ***rogues' gallery,*** fichero de delincuentes.
roguery [ˈrougəri], *s.* picardía, bellaquería.
roguish [ˈrougiʃ], *a.* pícaro, picaresco; travieso.
roguishness [ˈrougiʃnis], *s.* picardía.
roil [rɔil], *v.t.* enturbiar.
roister [ˈrɔistə], *s.* jaranero. — *v.i.* jaranear.
rôle [roul], *s.* papel; ***to play a rôle,*** hacer un papel.
roll [roul], *s.* rollo; rodillo; pergamino; lista, rol, nómina; bollo; (*cir.*) mecha; (*arq.*) voluta; retumbo; tronar (*del cañón*); redoble (*del tambor*); trino; balanceo (*del barco*); movimiento; rodar; fajo (*de billetes*); ***to call the roll,*** pasar lista; ***french roll,*** panecillo; ***roll call,*** lista (acto de pasar lista); ***roll-film,*** película en rollo; ***roll of the waves,*** oleaje; ***roll-top desk,*** buró de tapa rodadera. — *v.t.* hacer rodar; allanar (*con rodillo*); liar (*cigarrillo*); vibrar (*la lengua*); enrollar, abarquillar; vibrar (*la voz*); laminar (*metales*); ***roll the drum,*** redoblar el tambor; ***roll the eyes,*** poner los ojos en blanco; ***roll one's own,*** liarse sus cigarrillos; (*fig.*) bandeárselas por su cuenta; ***roll up,*** arrollar, enrollar; arremangar(se) (*las mangas*). — *v.i.* rodar; revolcarse; ondular (*el terreno*); retumbar; bambolearse; balancearse; ***roll about,*** rodar, andar de acá para allá; ***roll down,*** bajar rodando; ***roll*** o ***be rolling in money,*** nadar en la abundancia; ***roll up,*** llegar (en coche); aparecer, presentarse.
roller [ˈroulə], *s.* rodillo; tambor; apisonadora; rulo; (*cir.*) venda enrollada; ola larga, tumbo; roldana; ***roller bearing,*** cojinete de rodillos; ***roller coaster,*** montaña rusa; ***roller skates,*** patines de ruedas, *m.pl.*; ***roller skating,*** patinaje sobre ruedas; ***roller towel,*** toalla continua; ***steam roller,*** apisonadora.
rollick [ˈrɔlik], *v.i.* juguetear.
rollicking [ˈrɔlikiŋ], *a.* jovial; retozón, juguetón; travieso.
rolling [ˈrouliŋ], *a.* rodadero; rodadizo, rodador, rodante; ondulado (*terreno*); (*metal.*) ***rolling-mill,*** taller para laminar; laminador; ***rolling-pin,*** rodillo de pastelero; ***rolling-stock,*** material rodante; ***rolling stone,*** (*geol.*) galga, canto rodado; (*fig.*) culo de mal asiento; ***a rolling stone gathers no moss,*** piedra movediza, nunca moho la cobija; (*mar.*) ***rolling tackle,*** aparejo de rolin. — *s.* acto de rodar, rodadura; balanceo; cuneo; revuelco; fajamiento; enrollamiento; (*aer.*) escora lateral.
roll-on [ˈroul-ɔn], *s.* tubular.
roly-poly [ˈrouli-ˈpouli], *a.* rechoncho, gordiflón. — *s.* pudín en forma de rollo; (*fam.*) persona gordiflona.
Romaic [roˈmeiik], *a.* romaico.
Roman [ˈroumən], *a.* romano; romanesco; papal, católico romano; ***Roman candle,*** candela romana; ***Roman nose,*** nariz aguileña. — *s.* romano; romanesco; católico romano.

roman [ˈroumən], *a.* (*impr.*) ***roman letter, roman type,*** letra romana, tipo romano. — *s.* (*mar.*) romano.

Romance [roˈmæns], *a.* romance; neolatino.

romance [roˈmæns], *s.* romance; cuento, novela, ficción; idilio amoroso, amores, *m.pl.*; (*mús.*) romanza. — *v.i.* contar novelas; soñar; exagerar.

romancer [roˈmænsə], *s.* romancero; visionario; embustero.

Romanesque [roumәˈnesk], *a.* (*arq.*) románico.

Romania [rouˈmeiniә]. Rumania.

Romanian [rouˈmeiniәn], *a., s.* rumano.

Romanic [roˈmænik], [ROMANCE].

Romanism [ˈroumənizəm], *s.* romanismo.

Romanist [ˈroumənist], *a., s.* romanista, *m.f.*

Romanize [ˈroumənaiz], *v.t.* romanizar; convertir al catolicismo.

romantic [roˈmæntik], *a.* romántico; sentimental. — *s.* romántico.

romanticism [roˈmæntisizəm], *s.* romanticismo.

romanticist [roˈmæntisist], *s.* (escritor) romántico.

romanticize [roˈmæntisaiz], *v.t.* hacer romántico.

Romany [ˈroumәni], *a., s.* gitano; caló.

Rome [roum]. Roma; ***when in Rome do as the Romans do,*** adonde fueres, haz como vieres.

Romish [ˈroumiʃ], *a.* (católico) romano.

romp [rɔmp], *s.* retozo, trisca; ***to have a romp,*** retozar. — *v.i.* retozar, triscar, juguetear; ***romp home,*** ganar *o* triunfar fácilmente, ser el primero con mucho.

rompish [ˈrɔmpiʃ], *a.* retozón.

Romulus [ˈrɔmjuləs]. Rómulo.

rondeau [ˈrɔndou], *s.* rondó.

rondelle [ˈrɔndel], *s.* rondel.

rondo [ˈrɔndou], *s.* rondó.

rood [ru:d], *s.* cruz, *f.*, crucifijo.

roof [ru:f], *s.* tejado; ***coach*** o ***carriage roof,*** imperial; ***flat roof,*** azotea; ***inside roof,*** techo; ***roof of the mouth,*** cielo de la boca; ***roof-tile,*** teja; ***roof-tree,*** cumbrera; ***thatched roof,*** techumbre (de paja); (*fam.*) ***to raise the roof,*** poner el grito en el cielo; ***with a roof*** (***over one's head***), bajo tejado; ***without a roof over one's head,*** sin casa, sin hogar. — *v.t.* poner tejado a, techar.

roofing [ˈru:fiŋ], *s.* (*arq.*) techado; tejado(s), techo(s); material para tejados *o* para techos; ***roofing-slate,*** pizarra de techar.

rook (1) [ruk], *s.* (*orn.*) grajo, graja. — *v.t.* (*fam.*) estafar, timar.

rook (2) [ruk], *s.* (*ajedrez*) torre.

rookery [ˈrukəri], *s.* colonia de grajos.

rookie [ˈruki], *s.* novato.

rooky [ˈruki], *a.* habitado por cornejas.

room [ru:m], *s.* habitación, cuarto; sitio, cabida; (*pl.*) alojamiento; ***back room,*** cuarto de detrás; cuarto interior; ***dining-room,*** comedor; ***double room,*** habitación de matrimonio; ***drawing-room,*** salón; ***front room,*** cuarto de delante; ***lecture room,*** aula; ***living-room,*** cuarto de estar; ***room and board,*** pensión completa; ***room divider,*** tabique; ***room-mate,*** compañero de cuarto; ***room service,*** servicio (de las habitaciones); ***single room,*** habitación individual; ***sitting-room,*** salón; ***to make room for,*** hacer sitio *o* lugar a; abrir paso a; ***there's no room for them,*** no caben.

roomer [ˈru:mə], [LODGER].

roomful [ˈru:mful], *s.* lo que cabe en una habitación.

roominess [ˈru:minis], *s.* espaciosidad, amplitud, holgura.

roomy [ˈru:mi], *a.* espacioso, holgado, amplio.

roost [ru:st], *s.* percha; gallinero; sueño, reposo (*de las aves domésticas*); (*fam.*) lugar de descanso; ***to rule the roost,*** dominar, mandar, tener vara alta, gobernar el cotarro. — *v.i.* dormir, descansar (*las aves*) en una percha; (*fam.*) alojarse, acostarse; (*fig.*) ***the chickens have come home to roost,*** ha llegado la hora de pagar.

rooster [ˈru:stə], *s.* gallo.

root [ru:t], *s.* raíz, *f.*; tronco; (*mús.*) base, *f.*, nota fundamental; (*mat.*) ***cube root,*** raíz cúbica; ***root and branch,*** del todo, por completo; ***the root of all evil,*** la fuente *o* el origen de todo mal *o* de todos los males; ***square root,*** raíz cuadrada; ***to lie at the root of sth.,*** ser la fuente, la causa *o* el origen de algo; ***to put down one's roots,*** echar raíces, afincarse; ***to take*** o ***strike root,*** echar raíces, arraigarse. — *v.t.* hozar; sacar hozando; ***root out*** o ***up,*** desarraigar, arrancar, extirpar, sacar de raíz; ***to be rooted to the spot,*** quedar(se) clavado en el sitio; ***to have sth. rooted in one's mind,*** tener *o* llevar una cosa metida en la cabeza. — *v.i.* hozar; arraigar(se); (*Am.*) ***root for,*** hacer propaganda por.

rooted [ˈru:tid], *a.* arraigado.

rootlet [ˈru:tlit], *s.* raicilla.

rootstock [ˈru:tstɔk], *s.* (*bot.*) rizoma; (*fig.*) origen.

rooty [ˈru:ti], *a.* lleno de raíces; radicoso.

rope [roup], *s.* cuerda; soga, maroma; ***bolt rope,*** relinga; ***buoy rope,*** orinque; ***entering rope,*** guardamancebo del portalón; (*mar.*) ***rope-bands,*** envergues, *m.pl.*; ***rope-dancer,*** volatín, bailarín de cuerda; ***rope-ladder,*** escala de cuerdas; ***rope trick,*** truco de las cuerdas; ***rope-walk,*** cordelería; ***rope-walker,*** volatinero, maromero; ***rope work,*** trabajo hecho de cuerdas; ***rope yard,*** cordelería; ***rope yarn,*** filástica; (*mar.*) ***ropes of a ship,*** jarcias, *f.pl.*, cordaje; ***to be at the end of one's rope,*** estar sin recursos; estar en las últimas; ***to give s.o. the rope's end,*** castigar a uno golpeándole con un cabo de cuerda; ***to give s.o. more rope,*** darle a alguien más facilidades, más confianza *etc.*; (*fig.*) ***to know the ropes,*** conocer el paño. — *v.t.* atar, amarrar con una cuerda; ***rope in,*** entruchar, persuadir; ***rope off,*** rodear *o* cercar con cuerdas; ***to be roped together,*** ir atados (juntos). — *v.i.* hacer hebra (*un licor*).

ropery [ˈroupəri], *s.* cordelería; (*fam.*) tunantería.

ropiness [ˈroupinis], *s.* viscosidad; (lo) malejo.

ropish, ropy [ˈroupiʃ, ˈroupi], *a.* viscoso, pegajoso, glutinoso; (**ropy,** *fig., fam.*) malejo, flojo.

Roquefort [ˈrɔkfɔ:], *s.* queso de Roquefort.

roquet [ˈroukei], *s.* choque de dos bolas (*croquet*). — *v.t.* dar con la bola propia a la de otro.

rorqual [ˈrɔ:kwəl], *s.* (*ict.*) rorcual, balenóptero.

rosaceous [roˈzeiʃəs], *a.* (*bot.*) rosáceo.

rosaniline [rozˈænilain], *s.* rosanilina.

rosary [ˈrouzəri], *s.* (*igl.*) rosario; guirnalda *o* corona de rosas; macizo *o* jardín de rosales, rosaleda; (*fig.*) crestomatía; ***to say one's rosary,*** rezar el rosario.

rose (1) [rouz], *pret.* [RISE].

rose (2) [rouz], *a.* de color de rosa, rosado. — *s.* rosa; color de rosa; roseta (*de regadera*); (*arq.*) rosetón; ***rose-bay,*** adelfa, baladre; ***rose-bud,*** capullo de rosa; ***rose-bush,*** rosal; ***rose-tree,*** rosal; (*arq.*) ***rose-window,*** rosetón; (*prov.*) ***no rose without its thorn,*** no hay rosa sin espina.

roseate [ˈrouziit], *a.* rosado, róseo.

rosemary [ˈrouzməri], *s.* romero.

roseola [roˈzi:olə], *s.* roséola.

rosette [roˈzet], *s.* escarapela; (*arq.*) rosetón.

rosewater [ˈrouzwɔ:tə], *s.* agua de rosas.

rosewood [ˈrouzwud], *s.* palisandro; palo de rosa.

Rosicrucian [rouziˈkru:ʃən], *a., s.* rosacruz.

rosin [ˈrɔzin], *s.* colofonia. — *v.t.* dar con colofonia a.

roster [ˈrɔstə], *s.* lista; registro.

rostral [ˈrɔstrəl], *a.* rostral.

rostrate [ˈrɔstrit], *a.* (*zool.*) rostrado.

rostrum [ˈrɔstrəm], *s.* tribuna; estrado; (*mar., zool.*) rostro.

rosy [ˈrouzi], *a.* de rosa, rosado; sonrosado; (*fig.*)

prometedor, halagüeño, muy favorable; ***with rosy cheeks,*** de mejillas sonrosadas; ***rosy-hued,*** rosado, de color de rosa; ***rosy prospects, rosy future,*** porvenir halagüeño, *m.*

rot [rɔt], *s.* putrefacción, podredumbre; (*fam.*) tonterías, *f.pl.*; sandeces, *f.pl.*; ***to stop the rot setting in,*** impedir que empiecen a degenerar las cosas. — *v.t., v.i.* pudrir(se); corromper(se).

rota [ˈroutə], *s.* lista; orden, *m.*

rotary [ˈroutəri], *a.* rotatorio, rotativo; (*impr.*) ***rotary press,*** prensa rotativa.

rotate [roˈteit], *v.t.* hacer girar; alternar. — *v.i.* girar, dar vueltas; alternar.

rotation [roˈteiʃən], *s.* rotación, turno, alternación; ***in rotation*** o ***by rotation,*** por turno, alternativamente; ***rotation of crops,*** rotación de cultivos.

rotative, rotatory [ˈroutətiv, -təri], *a.* rotante, rotatorio, rotativo; turnante; ***rotative press,*** (prensa) rotativa.

rotator [roˈteitə], *s.* lo que hace rodar, lo que causa rotación; (*anat.*) músculo rotador; hélice (de la corredera); (*elec.*) rotor.

rote [rout], *s.* repetición rutinaria; estudio de memoria mecánica; ***by rote,*** de coro, maquinalmente.

Rotifera [roˈtifərə], *s.pl.* rotíferos, *m.pl.*, infusorios rodadores, *m.pl.*

rotiform [ˈroutifɔ:m], *a.* rotiforme, en forma de rueda *o* estrella.

rotor [ˈroutə], *s.* pieza giratoria; (*hidr.*) rotor, rueda móvil de una turbina; (*elec.*) pequeño motor; (*aut.*) rotor.

rotten [rɔtn], *a.* podrido, putrefacto; corrompido; carcomido; (*fam.*) infame, pésimo; ***rotten egg,*** huevo podrido; ***rotten trick,*** mala faena; (*fam.*) ***to feel rotten,*** estar malísimo, encontrarse fatal.

rottenness [ˈrɔtnnis], *s.* podredumbre, putrefacción; mala calidad *o* estado.

rottenstone [ˈrɔtnstoun], *s.* trípol *o* trípoli.

rotter [ˈrɔtə], *s.* (*fam.*) persona indeseable; canalla.

rotund [roˈtʌnd], *a.* rotundo; orondo.

rotunda [roˈtʌndə], *s.* rotonda.

rotundity [roˈtʌnditi], *s.* rotundidad, redondez.

rouble [ru:bl], *s.* rublo.

roué [ˈru:ei], *s.* libertino.

Rouen [ˈru:ɔ̃]. Ruán.

rouge [ru:ʒ], *s.* arrebol, afeite, colorete. — *v.t., v.i.* pintar(se), arrebolar(se), dar(se) colorete.

rough [rʌf], *a.* áspero; tosco; quebrado, escabroso, fragoso; duro; encrespado; bruto, rudo, bronco; borrascoso, tempestuoso; movido; aproximado; desgreñado; ***rough diamond,*** diamante en bruto; ***rough draft,*** boceto, bosquejo; ***to make a rough draft,*** hacer un boceto *o* borrador, bosquejar; ***at a rough guess,*** a ojo de buen cubero; ***rough rider,*** jinete arrojado; domador de caballos; ***rough sea,*** mar alborotado; (*alb.*) ***rough setter,*** mampostero; ***rough sketch,*** boceto, bosquejo; ***rough weather,*** tiempo borrascoso; ***to be rough and ready,*** ser elemental *o* basto, hacer las cosas en plan elemental; ***to get rough with s.o.,*** ponerse en plan duro con alguien. — *adv.* aproximadamente; ***to rough-hew,*** desbastar; ***rough-shod,*** herrado con ramplones; ***to ride roughshod over everybody,*** ponerse el mundo por montera; ***rough-spoken,*** brusco *o* basto de palabra. — *s.* terreno escabroso; matón; ***in the rough,*** en bruto; ***rough and tumble,*** lucha, forcejeo; ***to take the rough with the smooth,*** estar a las duras y a las maduras. — *v.t.* hacer *o* poner áspero; ***rough it,*** vivir duro; ***rough out,*** bosquejar, abocetar; ***rough up,*** dar una paliza a.

roughcast [ˈrʌfkɑ:st], *s.* modelo tosco; (*alb.*) mortero grueso; mezcla gruesa. — [rʌfˈkɑ:st], *v.t.* bosquejar.

roughen [rʌfn], *v.t., v.i.* poner(se) áspero.

roughly [ˈrʌfli], *adv.* ásperamente *etc.*; aproximadamente.

roughness [ˈrʌfnis], *s.* aspereza; tosquedad; (lo) aproximado; (lo) bruto *etc.*

roulette [ru:ˈlet], *s.* ruleta.

round [raund], *a.* redondo; (*fig.*) rotundo, categórico; ***round-faced,*** carirredondo; ***round sum,*** cifra redonda; ***round table,*** mesa redonda; ***round trip,*** viaje de ida y vuelta; ***to make round,*** hacer redondo, redondear. — *adv.* alrededor; ***all round,*** por todos lados; ***all (the) year round,*** durante todo el año; ***for 3 miles round,*** en 5 kilómetros a la redonda; ***3 feet round,*** un metro en redondo; ***there's not enough to go round,*** no hay (bastante) para todos; ***my head is going round,*** me da vueltas la cabeza. — *prep.* alrededor de; ***round (about) 3 o'clock,*** a eso de las tres; ***round the corner,*** a la vuelta de la esquina; ***round the house,*** por la casa; ***to get round s.o.,*** persuadir *o* convencer a alguien engatusándole, embaucar con adulaciones. — *s.* círculo, esfera; rutina; recorrido (*del lechero etc.*); rodaja (*de carne etc.*); ronda (*de bebidas, copas*); (*deporte*) vuelta, circuito; (*boxeo*) asalto; (*mil.*) cartucho, tiro, disparo; ronda; ***round-up,*** rodeo, recogida (*del ganado*); redada; ***to go the rounds,*** ir de ronda; hacer el recorrido de siempre; ir de boca en boca. — *v.t.* redondear; ***round off,*** redondear; ***round up,*** recoger (*el ganado*); juntar; hacer una redada de. — *v.i.* — ***on,*** volverse contra.

roundabout [ˈraundəbaut], *a.* indirecto, tortuoso. — *s.* (*tráfico*) rotonda; tío vivo.

roundel, roundelay [ˈraundəl, ˈraundilei], *s.* baile en círculo; melodía que se canta en rueda.

roundhand [ˈraundhænd], *s.* letra redonda.

roundhouse [ˈraundhaus], *s.* (*mar.*) toldilla; (*f.c.*) casa de máquinas.

rounding [ˈraundiŋ], *s.* redondeamiento; (*mar.*) aforro de un cabo.

roundish [ˈraundiʃ], *a.* casi redondo, redondillo.

roundly [ˈraundli], *adv.* rotundamente; categóricamente.

roundness [ˈraundnis], *s.* redondez; rotundidad.

roundsman [ˈraundzmən], *s.* (*pl.* **-men** [-men]) repartidor; proveedor casero; (*Am.*) policía que hace rondas, *m.*

rouse [rauz], *v.t.* despertar; excitar, provocar; levantar (*la caza*); (*mar.*) halar, arronzar; ***rouse s.o. to fury,*** provocar la furia de, enfurecer, poner furioso. — *v.i.* despertar(se).

rouser [ˈrauzə], *s.* despertador, excitador.

rousing [ˈrauziŋ], *a.* (*canción, discurso*) apasionante que apasiona.

Roussillon [ru:si:ˈjɔn]. Rosellón.

roust [raust], *v.t.* (*fam.*) despertar, sacudir; ***roust out,*** obligar a levantarse *o* a salir. — *v.i.* moverse enérgicamente.

roustabout [ˈraustəbaut], *s.* (*Am.*) peón portuario (*de río*); haragán.

rout (1) [raut], *s.* desbandada, derrota total; fuga desordenada; ***to put to rout,*** derrotar completamente. — *v.t.* derrotar completamente, arrollar, poner en fuga.

rout (2) [raut], *v.t.* — ***out,*** arrancar hozando; (*carp.*) rebajar.

route [ru:t], *s.* ruta, itinerario, camino; ***route map,*** (mapa del) itinerario; ***route march,*** marcha (de entrenamiento). — *v.t.* encaminar, encauzar, dirigir.

router [ˈrautə], *s.* (*carp.*) cepillo de machihembrar, moldear *etc.* — *v.t.* hacer molduras en.

routine [ru:ˈti:n], *a.* rutinario. — *s.* rutina, hábito, costumbre; práctica diaria *o* regular.

rove (1) [rouv], *s.* vagabundeo, correría. — *v.t.* recorrer vagando. — *v.i.* vagar, errar; ***rove the seas,*** piratear.

rove (2) [rouv], *s.* mecha, mecha estirada. — *v.t.* pasar por un ojete; cardar (*la lana*); estirar y torcer (*la mecha*).

rove (3) [rouv], *s.* arandela de remache.

rover [ˈrouvə], *s.* vagabundo; pirata, *m.*
roving (1) [ˈrouviŋ], *a.* errante, vagabundo; ambulante; andariego; ***roving eye,*** mirada errante y pecadora.
roving (2) [ˈrouviŋ], *s.* ***roving frame,*** mechera en fino.
row (1) [rou], *s.* hilera, fila; ringlera; andana; ***in a row,*** en fila; seguidos.
row (2) [rou], *s.* remadura; paseo en bote. — *v.t.* mover a remo; llevar remando; ***row s.o. across the river,*** pasar a alguien en barca (al otro lado del río); ***row a race,*** hacer una carrera (de remo). — *v.i.* remar, bogar; ***row for the shore,*** dirigirse (a remo) a tierra; ***row hard,*** remar fuerte.
row (3) [rau], *s.* ruido; jaleo, alboroto, escándalo, follón; bronca, pelea, camorra; tremolina, trifulca, zapatiesta; ***there was a devil of a row,*** se armó una discusión de mil pares de demonios; ***to kick up a row,*** armar un follón, poner el grito en el cielo. — *v.t.* echar una bronca a, reñir. — *v.i.* pelearse, reñir; armar camorra, alborotar.
rowan [ˈrauən, ˈrouən], *s.* (*bot.*) serbal.
rowboat [ˈroubout], *s.* (*mar.*) bote, barca *o* lancha (de remos).
rowdy [ˈraudi], *a., s.* gamberro, pendenciero, alborotador, camorrista, *m.f.*, bravucón, bergante.
rowdyism [ˈraudiizəm], *s.* gamberrismo, pendencias, alboroto.
rowel [ˈrauəl], *s.* rodaja de espuela; (*equit.*) sedal. — *v.t.* poner sedal a.
rower [ˈrouə], *s.* remero, bogador.
rowlock [ˈrʌlək], *s.* chumacera.
royal [ˈrɔiəl], *a.* real, regio; ***to have a right royal time,*** divertirse en grande. — *s.* (*fam.*) personaje real; (*mar.*) juanete, sobrejuanete; punta superior del asta (del ciervo).
royalism [ˈrɔiəlizəm], *s.* realismo, monarquismo.
royalist [ˈrɔiəlist], *a., s.* realista, *m.f.*, monárquico.
royalty [ˈrɔiəlti], *s.* realeza; personajes reales, *m.pl.*; (*pl.*) derechos de autor, *m.pl.*
rub [rʌb], *s.* frotamiento; roce, rozadura; ***there's the rub,*** ahí está la cosa *o* el quid. — *v.t.* frotar; ***rub away,*** quitar *o* borrar frotando; erosionar; ***rub hard,*** frotar fuerte, restregar; ***rub in,*** hacer penetrar frotando; (*fam.*) ***don't rub it in!*** ¡no me lo restriegues!; ***rub off,*** borrar, quitar frotando; ***rub out,*** borrar; (*fam.*) cargarse, eliminar; ***rub shoulders with,*** codearse con; ***rub up,*** sacar brillo a; ***rub up the wrong way,*** frotar a contrapelo; (*fam., fig.*) ofender; caer gordo a. — *v.i.* — ***along,*** ir tirando, vivir de mala manera; (*ideas etc.*) ***rub off,*** quedarse, pegarse; ***rub on*** o ***against,*** rozar.
rub-a-dub [ˈrʌb-ə-ˈdʌb], *s.* rataplán.
rubber [ˈrʌbə], *a.* de caucho, de goma. — *s.* caucho; goma; goma (de borrar); (*bridge*) juego; (*pl.*) (*calzado*) chanclos, *m.pl.*; ***rubber band,*** goma, gomilla; ***rubber-neck,*** turista desaforado; ***rubber plantation,*** cauchal, *m.*; ***rubber solution,*** disolución de goma; ***rubber stamp,*** sello *o* estampilla de goma; ***rubber tree,*** árbol del caucho.
rubberize [ˈrʌbəraiz], *v.t.* engomar, cubrir de goma *o* de caucho.
rubbing [ˈrʌbiŋ], *s.* frotamiento(s), roce(s), fricción; ***rubbing alcohol,*** (*Am.*) [SURGICAL SPIRIT].
rubbish [ˈrʌbiʃ], *s.* basura; desperdicio(s), deshecho(s); (*fig.*) tonterías, *f.pl.*, sandeces, *f.pl.*, disparates, *m.pl.*; ***rubbish bin,*** cubo de la basura; ***rubbish dump,*** basural, basurero, vertedero (de basuras).
rubbishy [ˈrʌbiʃi], *a.* de pacotilla, de mala muerte, desprovisto de valor.
rubble [rʌbl], *s.* escombros, *m.pl.*, cascote(s); cascajos, *m.pl.*; ***rubble-work,*** mampostería.
rubescence, rubicundicity [ru:ˈbesəns, ru:biˈkʌnditi], *s.* rubescencia; rubicundez.
rubescent, rubicund [ru:ˈbesənt, ˈru:bikənd], *a.* rubescente; rubicundo.
rubiaceous [ru:biˈeiʃəs], *a.* rubiáceo.
Rubicon [ˈru:bikən]. Rubicón, *m.*
rubied [ˈru:bid], *a.* adornado con rubíes.
rubigo [ru:ˈbaigou], *s.* añublo, tizón.
rubric [ˈru:brik], *s.* rúbrica.
rubrical [ˈru:brikəl], *a.* de rúbrica.
rubricate [ˈru:brikeit], *v.t.* rubricar.
ruby [ˈru:bi], *a.* color de rubí. — *s.* rubí; color de rubí.
ruche [ru:ʃ], *s.* (*cost.*) golilla, lechuguilla.
ruck (1) [rʌk], *s.* arruga. — *v.t.* arrugar, ajar. — *v.i.* arrugarse.
ruck (2) [rʌk], *s.* ***the ruck,*** el montón, vulgo; (*dep.*) el grueso del pelotón (*en una carrera*).
rucksack [ˈruksæk], *s.* mochila, morral.
rudder [ˈrʌdə], *s.* (*mar.*) timón; gobernalle; (*mar.*) ***rudder-chain,*** varón del timón; ***rudder-hole,*** limera del timón; (*mar.*) ***rudder-pintles,*** machos del timón, *m.pl.*; ***rudder-post,*** (*mar.*) codaste; (*aer.*) eje del timón; ***rudder-stock,*** cabeza del timón.
ruddiness [ˈrʌdinis], *s.* rubicundez.
ruddle [rʌdl], *s.* almagre. — *v.t.* marcar con almagre.
ruddy [ˈrʌdi], *a.* coloradote, rubicundo; (*fam.*) maldito, puñetero; ***ruddy complexion,*** tez sanguínea.
rude [ru:d], *a.* grosero, descortés, mal educado; inculto; rudo, tosco; (*canción, chiste etc.*) verde; ***don't be rude!*** ¡no seas grosero!; ***how rude!*** ¡qué grosero!; ***a rude awakening,*** una sorpresa desagradable; ***to be in rude health,*** estar vendiendo salud, gozar de una salud insultante.
rudeness [ˈru:dnis], *s.* grosería, descortesía; rudeza, tosquedad.
rudiment [ˈru:dimənt], *s.* rudimento.
rudimental [ru:diˈmentəl], *a.* rudimental.
rudimentarily [ru:diˈmentərili], *adv.* de un modo rudimentario.
rudimentary [ru:diˈmentəri], *a.* rudimentario.
rue (1) [ru:], *s.* (*bot.*) ruda.
rue (2) [ru:], *s.* pesar, arrepentimiento. — *v.t.* arrepentirse de, lamentar; ***you'll rue it,*** te pesará. — *v.i.* arrepentirse.
rueful [ˈru:ful], *a.* contrito; vergonzoso.
ruefulness [ˈru:fulnis], *s.* tristeza, pesar, pena, aflicción.
ruff (1) [rʌf], *s.* (*cost.*) lechuguilla.
ruff (2) [rʌf], *s.* fallada. — *v.t.* fallar.
ruffian [ˈrʌfiən], *a.* brutal, violento. — *s.* rufián, canalla, *m.*; ***ruffian-like,*** arrufianado.
ruffianly [ˈrʌfiənli], *a.* arrufianado.
ruffle (1) [rʌfl], *s.* (*cost.*) volante; redoble (*de tambor*); rizo, escarceo. — *v.t.* fruncir; descomponer; perturbar, incomodar; agitar, rizar. — *v.i.* arrugarse; descomponerse; rizarse (*el agua*).
ruffle (2) [rʌfl], *s.* redoble (*de tambor*). — *v.i.* redoblar (*el tambor*).
rufous [ˈru:fəs], *a.* rufo, rojizo.
rug [rʌg], *s.* alfombrilla; manta (de viaje).
rugby [ˈrʌgbi], *s.* rugby.
rugged [ˈrʌgid], *a.* áspero, escabroso, fragoso; recio, vigoroso, robusto; rudo, bronco.
ruggedness [ˈrʌgidnis], *s.* (lo) áspero; (lo) recio *etc.*
rugose [ˈru:gous], *a.* rugoso.
rugosity [ru:ˈgɔsiti], *s.* rugosidad.
ruin [ˈru:in], *s.* ruina; arruinamiento; perdición; (*pl.*) ruinas, *f.pl.*; ***to be the ruin of,*** perder (a); ***to lay in ruins,*** asolar. — *v.t.* arruinar; perder, hundir; echar a perder, estropear; estragar.
ruination [ru:iˈneiʃən], *s.* arruinamiento, ruina, perdición.
ruinous [ˈru:inəs], *a.* ruinoso; funesto, desastroso.
rulable [ˈru:ləbl], *a.* gobernable.
rule [ru:l], *s.* regla; norma; mando, dominio, gobierno; (*mec.*) metro; ***as a rule,*** por regla

general; ***rule of the road,*** reglamento del tráfico; ***rule of three,*** regla de tres; ***rule of thumb,*** regla práctica, sistema práctico y sencillo; ***rules (and regulations),*** reglamento; ***standing rule,*** estatuto, norma fija; ***to be the rule,*** ser la norma; ser de precepto; ***to make it a rule to,*** tener por norma *o* por sistema + *inf.* — *v.t.* mandar, gobernar; regir; trazar, tirar (*una línea*); trazar rayas en (*el papel*); ***be ruled by,*** estar dominado por; guiarse por; ***rule out,*** excluir, descartar. — *v.i.* mandar, gobernar; reinar, imperar; ***rule over,*** mandar en, gobernar (a); ***rule that,*** decretar que; estipular que.

ruler [ˈruːlə], *s.* regla; gobernante, dirigente.

ruling [ˈruːliŋ], *a.* reinante, imperante. — *s.* (*for.*) decisión, fallo; rayado; ***ruling-pen,*** tiralíneas, *m.inv.*

rullion [ˈrʌljən], *s.* zapato de cuero sin adobar.

rum (1) [rʌm], *s.* ron.

rum (2) [rʌm], *a.* (*fam.*, *Ingl.*) extraño, singular, raro.

Rumania [ruːˈmeiniə], [ROMANIA].

Rumanian [ruːˈmeiniən], [ROMANIAN].

rumba [ˈrʌmbə], *s.* rumba.

rumble (1) [rʌmbl], *s.* retumbo; ruido sordo; ***rumble seat,*** ahitepudras, *m.inv.* — *v.i.* retumbar; sonar (*el estómago*).

rumble (2) [rʌmbl], *v.t.* (*fam.*) calar (*algo* o *a alguien*).

rumbler [ˈrʌmblə], *s.* lo que hace un ruido sordo y continuo.

rumbustious [rʌmˈbʌstʃəs], *a.* bullicioso, alborotador.

rumen [ˈruːmen], *s.* (*zool.*) omaso, panza.

ruminant [ˈruːminənt], *a.* (*zool.*) rumiante; (*fig.*) rumiador, meditativo. — *s.* (*zool.*) rumiante.

ruminate [ˈruːmineit], *v.t.* rumiar, masticar; (*fig.*) reflexionar, considerar. — *v.i.* reflexionar, pensar con reflexión *o* con madurez, rumiar.

rumination [ruːmiˈneiʃən], *s.* rumia, rumiadura; (*fig.*) meditación.

ruminative [ˈruːminətiv], *a.* reflexivo, meditabundo, dado a la meditación.

rummage [ˈrʌmidʒ], *s.* búsqueda; ***rummage sale,*** venta de prendas usadas. — *v.i.* — ***for,*** buscar revolviéndolo todo; ***rummage about in,*** hurgar *o* remover en, trastear en.

rummager [ˈrʌmidʒə], *s.* buscador, revolvedor.

rummy (1) [ˈrʌmi], *s.* (*naipes*) rummy.

rummy (2) [ˈrʌmi], *a.* (*fam.*) raro.

rumour [ˈruːmə], *s.* rumor, runrún; ***false rumour,*** bulo. — *v.t.* rumorear, propalar; ***it is rumoured,*** se rumorea (que).

rump [rʌmp], *s.* rabadilla *u* obispillo de ave; ancas, *f.pl.*, grupa; solomo de vaca; (*despec.*) trasero, nalgas, *f.pl.*

rumple [rʌmpl], *s.* pliegue, arruga; ajamiento. — *v.t.* arrugar, chafar.

rumpus [ˈrʌmpəs], *s.* bulla, batahola; ***to kick up a rumpus,*** armar un cisco.

rumpy [ˈrʌmpi], *s.* gato sin cola originario de la isla de Man.

run [rʌn], *a.* ***badly run,*** mal dirigido; ***well run,*** bien dirigido; ***run down,*** agotado; (*elec.*) descargado. — *s.* carrera; corrida; paseo en coche; trayecto, recorrido; jornada; (*mar.*) singladura; duración, vida; (*teat.*) serie de representaciones; (*mús.*) glisado, fermata; (*agric.*) terreno de pasto; (*com.*) demanda (**on,** de); (*com.*) tendencia; progreso, marcha, desarrollo, curso; ***the common run,*** el común de las gentes; ***to have a good*** o ***bad run of luck,*** tener una racha de buena *o* mala suerte; ***in the long run,*** a la larga; ***to be on the run,*** ir *o* andar huido; (*aut.*) ***run-in,*** rodaje; ***run of the mill,*** corriente y moliente; ***run on the bank,*** asedio del banco; ***run-through,*** ensayo, prueba; ***to give s.o. a run for his money,*** hacerle a alguien sudar (una cosa); ***to have the run of,*** disponer (libremente) de. — *irr. v.t.* correr; dirigir, organizar (*un negocio*); manejar (*una máquina*); gobernar (*la casa etc.*); burlar, forzar (*un bloqueo*); pasar (*contrabando*); hacer (*un recado*); trazar (*una línea*); tener (*fiebre, coche*); ***run down,*** atropellar; acorralar, cazar; (*fig.*) criticar, poner verde, meterse con; ***be run down,*** padecer (un) agotamiento; ***run in,*** tener en rodaje (*un coche*); (*fam.*) meter en la cárcel; ***it is being run in,*** está en rodaje; ***run into,*** hacer chocar con; ***he ran the car into the wall,*** embistió la pared con el coche; ***run off,*** vaciar; tirar, imprimir; ***run over,*** atropellar; ***run your eye over it,*** échele un vistazo; ***run one's hand over,*** pasar la mano por, recorrer con la mano; ***run through,*** atravesar, espetar (*con la espada*); ***run up,*** izar (*la bandera*); ***run up debts,*** entramparse; incurrir en deudas; ***run up a house,*** construir de prisa una casa. — *irr. v.i.* correr; seguir; ir, extenderse; circular; derretirse, deshacerse; correrse (*un color, la pintura*); competir (*en una carrera*); presentarse (*como aspirante* o *candidato*); mantenerse en cartelera (*una obra*); (*mec.*) andar, marchar, funcionar; (*med.*) supurar, echar pus; ***run across,*** topar(se) con, encontrarse con; ***run away,*** huir, escaparse, fugarse; desbocarse (*un caballo* o *una persona*); ***run away with,*** irse con, fugarse con, largarse con; ganar sin trabajo (ninguno); ***run down,*** acabarse la cuerda (*al reloj*); descargarse (*una batería*); ***run dry,*** quedarse seco *o* sin agua; ***run for,*** presentarse a, para; ***run high,*** crecerse (*el río*); (*fig.*) ***feeling ran high,*** se exaltaron los ánimos; ***run in,*** entrar corriendo; ***it runs in the family,*** es (una) cosa (habitual) de esta familia, es (una) cosa que se da en esta familia; ***run into,*** chocar con; encontrarse con, topar(se) con; ascender a; ***run on,*** seguir; (*fam.*) ***he does run on!*** ¡habla por los codos!; ***his thoughts were running on a holiday,*** le daba vueltas en la cabeza (a) la idea de unas vacaciones; ***run out,*** salir corriendo; acabarse; ***we've run out of sugar,*** se nos ha acabado el azúcar; nos hemos quedado sin azúcar; ***run over,*** salirse, desbordarse; ***run short of,*** quedarse casi sin, encontrarse con poco; ***run through,*** gastarse (*el dinero, una fortuna etc.*); leerse de prisa; hojear; ***run to,*** llegar a; ascender a; (*fam.*) ***I can't run to that,*** no puedo gastarme tanto; ***run up,*** acudir corriendo; ***run up against,*** encontrarse con; ***run upon,*** concentrarse en; ***be running with,*** tener montones de, estar lleno de; chorrear (*sudor*).

runabout [ˈrʌnəbaut], *s.* (*aut.*) coche ligero.

runaway [ˈrʌnəwei], *a.* fugitivo; desbocado (*caballo*); ***runaway marriage,*** matrimonio que sigue a la fuga de los novios de casa de sus padres; ***runaway victory,*** triunfo fácil. — *s.* fugitivo.

runcinate [ˈrʌnsinit], *a.* (*bot.*) dentado hacia atrás.

rundlet [ˈrʌndlit], *s.* barrilejo.

rune [ruːn], *s.* runa.

rung (1) [rʌŋ], *pret.*, *p.p.* [RING].

rung (2) [rʌŋ], *s.* peldaño, escalón; travesaño; (*mar.*) varenga; (*mar.*) ***rung-heads,*** escoas, *f.pl.*, puntas de escoa, *f.pl.*

runic [ˈruːnik], *a.* rúnico, runo. — *s.* (*impr.*) tipo rúnico

runlet, runnel [ˈrʌnlit, ˈrʌnəl], *s.* arroyuelo.

runner [ˈrʌnə], *s.* corredor; mensajero; contrabandista, *m.f.*; ordenanza; vástago; agente, factor; maquinista, *m.*; fugitivo; corredera, muela, volandera; alguacil, corchete; anillo movible; (*bot.*) serpa, jerpa; (*hidr.*) rueda móvil (*de turbina*); pasador corredizo; ***gun runner,*** traficante de armas; ***long-distance runner,*** corredor de fondo; (*mar.*) ***runner of a crowfoot,*** perigallo de araña; (*mar.*) ***runner of a tackle,*** amante de aparejo; ***runner-up,*** subcampeón, segundo ganador.

running [ˈrʌniŋ], *a.* corriente; corredizo; cursivo; continuo; (*med.*) supurante; ***running hand,*** letra corrida; (*impr.*) ***running head(line)*** o ***title,*** título de página; (*mar.*) ***running rigging,*** cabos de labor, *m.pl.*; ***running start,*** salida lanzada; ***run-***

ning water, agua corriente; agua via. — *adv.* seguido, en sucesión; ***twice running,*** dos veces seguidas. — *s.* carrera, corrida; curso; marcha, funcionamiento; dirección, gestión; ***to be in the running,*** estar entre los posibles; ***running-board,*** estribo.
runnion [ˈrʌnjən], *s.* pelafustán, pandorgo.
runny [ˈrʌni], *a.* muy líquido, demasiado líquido.
runt [rʌnt], *s.* redrojo; enano, retaco.
runway [ˈrʌnwei], *s.* (*Am.*) lecho, cauce, madre, *f.*; senda; (*f.c.*) vía; (*aer.*) pista de aterrizaje.
rupee [ru:ˈpi:], *s.* rupia.
rupture [ˈrʌptʃə], *s.* rompimiento, rotura; (*med.*) quebradura, hernia; ruptura. — *v.t.* romper, quebrar. — *v.i.* abrirse, romperse, quebrarse.
rupturewort [ˈrʌptʃəwə:t], *s.* milengrana, herniaria.
rural [ˈruərəl], *a.* rural, campestre, campesino, rústico.
rurality, ruralness [ruəˈræliti, ˈruərəlnis], *s.* calidad de rural.
ruralize ˈruərəlaiz], *v.t.* dar forma campestre a.
ruse [ru:z], *s.* ardid, artimaña.
rush (1) [rʌʃ], *s.* (*bot.*) junco; ***rush-bottomed,*** con asiento de junco; ***rush rope,*** aderra.
rush (2) [rʌʃ], *s.* ímpetu; acometida, embestida; torrente, tropel; prisa; carrera precipitada, precipitación; (*Am.*) lucha violenta; demanda (***on,*** de); bocanada (*de aire*); ***rush hour,*** hora punta; ***rush order,*** pedido urgente; ***it is not worth a rush,*** no vale un ardite. — *v.t.* dar prisa a, precipitar; despachar *o* ejecutar de prisa; asaltar; (*fam.*) hacer pagar; ***rush through,*** aprobar de prisa. — *v.i.* arrojarse, precipitarse, abalanzarse; agolparse; embestir, acometer; ***rush in,*** entrar de rondón; ***rush forward,*** arrojarse con ímpetu; ***rush in upon,*** entrar sin avisar, sorprender; ***rush out,*** salir precipitadamente.
rushy [ˈrʌʃi], *a.* juncoso, cubierto de juncos.
rusk [rʌsk], *s.* galleta dura; tostada (*para niño*).
russet [ˈrʌsit], *a.* bermejo, rojizo. — *s.* color bermejo; (*bot.*) manzana asperiega.
Russia [ˈrʌʃə]. Rusia; ***Russia leather,*** cuero *o* piel de Rusia.
Russian [ˈrʌʃən], *a.*, *s.* ruso.
rust [rʌst], *s.* óxido, herrumbre, orín; (*bot.*) roya; ***rust-proof, rust-resistant,*** inoxidable. — *v.t.*, *v.i.* oxidar(se), aherrumbrar(se).
rustic [ˈrʌstik], *a.* rústico, aldeano; palurdo. — *s.* patán, palurdo, paleto.
rusticate [ˈrʌstikeit], *v.t.* (*univ.*) suspender temporal *o* provisionalmente. — *v.i.* rusticar.
rustication [rʌstiˈkeiʃən], *s.* (*univ.*) suspensión temporal *o* provisional; rusticación.
rusticity [rʌsˈtisiti], *s.* rusticidad.
rustiness [ˈrʌstinis], *s.* (lo) oxidado, (lo) herrumbroso.
rustle [rʌsl], *s.* susurro(s); crujido(s). — *v.t.* (hacer) susurrar; (hacer) crujir; robar (*ganado*). — *v.i.* susurrar; crujir.
rustler [ˈrʌslə], *s.* ladrón de ganado.
rusty [ˈrʌsti], *a.* oxidado, herrumbroso; ***my Spanish is very rusty,*** tengo muy oxidado el español, se me ha oxidado mucho el español.
rut (1) [rʌt], *s.* rodera, rodada, carril, carrilera; rutina; (*fig.*) ***to be in a rut,*** estar metido en una rutina, llevar una vida rutinaria. — *v.t.* hacer rodades *o* carrileras en.
rut (2) [rʌt], *s.* celo; ***to be in rut,*** estar en celo; ***season of rut,*** época del celo.
rutabaga [ru:təˈbeigə], (*Am.*) [SWEDE].
rutaceous [ru:ˈteiʃəs], *a.* rutáceo.
Ruth [ru:θ]. Rut.
ruth [ru:θ], *s.* (*ant.*) compasión, conmiseración.
Ruthenia [ru:ˈθi:niə]. Rutenia.
ruthenium [ru:ˈθi:niəm], *s.* rutenio.
ruthless [ˈru:θlis], *a.* despiadado, implacable; sañudo.
ruthlessness [ˈru:θlisnis], *s.* crueldad, implacabilidad.
rutted [ˈrʌtid], *a.* lleno de baches.
rutting [ˈrʌtiŋ], *a.* en celo. — *s.* celo; ***rutting season,*** época del celo.
ruttish [ˈrʌtiʃ], *a.* cachondo, salido; que hace carriles *o* rodadas.
rutty [ˈrʌti], *a.* lleno de surcos.
Rwanda [ruˈændə]. Ruanda.
Rwandese [ruænˈdi:z], *a.*, *s.* ruandés, *m.*
rye [rai], *s.* centeno; (*Am.*, *fam.*) whisky destilado de centeno; ***rye bread,*** pan de centeno; ***rye grass,*** ballico, grama de centeno; ***rye straw,*** paja centenaza.
ryot [ˈraiət], *s.* (*en la India*) labrador, labriego, villano.

S

S, s [es], *s.* décimonona letra del alfabeto.
Saar [sɑ:]. Sarre.
sabal [ˈseibəl], *s.* sabal.
sabbatarian [sæbəˈtɛəriən], *a.*, *s.* sabatario.
sabbatarianism, sabbatism [sæbəˈtɛəriənizəm, ˈsæbətizəm], *s.* observancia rígida del sábado.
sabbath [ˈsæbəθ], *s.* sábado (judío); domingo (cristiano).
sabbatic(al) [səˈbætik(əl)], *a.* sabático; ***sabbatical year,*** año sabático.
Sabian [ˈseibiən], *a.*, *s.* sabeo, (persona) que adora el sol.
Sabianism [ˈseibiənizəm], *s.* sabeísmo.
Sabine [ˈsæbain], *a.*, *s.* sabino.
sabine [ˈsæbain], *s.* (*bot.*) sabina.
sable [seibl], *a.* (*blas.*) sable, negro; (*poét.*) negro. — *s.* (*zool.*) marta, marta cebellina.
sabot [ˈsæbou], *s.* zueco, almadreña; (*artill.*) salero de granada.
sabotage [ˈsæbətɑ:ʒ], *s.* sabotaje(s); ***to commit an act of sabotage,*** hacer un sabotaje. — *v.t.* sabotear.
saboteur [sæbəˈtə:], *s.* saboteador.
sabre [ˈseibə], *s.* sable. — *v.t.* herir con sable.
sabre-rattling [ˈseibə-ˈrætliŋ], *s.* patriotería; bravuconería; amenazas belicosas.
sac [sæk], *s.* (*biol.*) saco.
saccate [ˈsækeit], *a.* en forma de bolsa *o* saco.
sacchariferous [sækəˈrifərəs], *a.* sacarífero.
saccharine [ˈsækərin], *a.* sacarino, azucarado. — (**saccharin(e)**), *s.* sacarina.
saccharoid [ˈsækərɔid], *a.* sacaroideo.
saccharose [ˈsækərous], *s.* sacarosa.
saccharous [ˈsækərəs], *a.* sacarino, azucarado.
sacerdotal [sæsəˈdoutəl], *a.* sacerdotal.
sacerdotalism [sæsəˈdoutəlizəm], *s.* carácter y métodos sacerdotales; clericalismo.
sachem [ˈseitʃəm], *s.* (*Am.*) cacique indio.
sachet [ˈsæʃei], *s.* sobrecito, paquetito, saquito.
sack (1) [sæk], *s.* saco; costal; (*postal*) saca; (*sast.*) saco; (*fam.*) despido; (*fam.*) ***to give the sack,*** echar, despedir; (*fam.*) ***he got the sack,*** le echaron (del trabajo). — *v.t.* ensacar; (*fam.*) despedir.
sack (2) [sæk], *s.* (*mil.*) saqueo; ***to put to sack,*** saquear, entregar al saqueo. — *v.t.* saquear.
sackbut [ˈsækbʌt], *s.* sacabuche.
sackcloth [ˈsækklɔθ], *s.* arpillera; cilicio; ***in sackcloth and ashes,*** con hábito de penitencia; en plan de pedir perdón.
sacker [ˈsækə], *s.* saqueador.
sackful [ˈsækful], *s.* saco lleno.
sacking [ˈsækiŋ], *s.* arpillera.
sacque [sæk], *s.* (*cost.*) saco.
sacrament [ˈsækrəmənt], *s.* sacramento; ***to receive the sacrament,*** comulgar; ***to receive the last sacraments,*** recibir los últimos sacramentos *o* la extremaunción *o* el viático.
sacramental [sækrəˈmentəl], *a.* sacramental.
sacramentarian, sacramentary [sækrəmenˈtɛəriən, -ˈmentəri], *a.*, *s.* sacramentario.
sacrarium [sæˈkrɛəriəm], *s.* (*igl.*) sagrario.
sacred [ˈseikrid], *a.* sagrado; sacro; ***sacred music,*** música sacra; ***is nothing sacred?*** ¿no hay nada sagrado? ¿no se respeta nada?
sacredness [ˈseikridnis], *s.* (lo) sagrado.
sacrifice [ˈsækrifais], *s.* sacrificio; inmolación; víctima. — *v.t.* sacrificar; inmolar. — *v.i.* sacrificar, ofrecer sacrificios.
sacrificer [ˈsækrifaisə], *s.* sacrificador.
sacrificial [sækriˈfiʃəl], *a.* sacrificatorio, de sacrificio.
sacrilege [ˈsækrilidʒ], *s.* sacrilegio.
sacrilegious [sækriˈlidʒəs], *a.* sacrílego.
sacristan [ˈsækristən], *s.* sacristán.
sacristy [ˈsækristi], *s.* sacristía.
sacrosanct [ˈsækrosæŋkt], *a.* sacrosanto.
sacrum [ˈseikrəm], *s.* sacro.
sad [sæd], *a.* triste; ***he left a sadder and a wiser man,*** partió habiendo aprendido una dura lección; ***it's a sad business,*** es una cosa que da pena; ***a sad mistake,*** una equivocación que da pena; ***to grow sad,*** entristecerse; ***to make sad,*** entristecer, poner triste.
sadden [sædn], *v.t.* entristecer. — *v.i.* entristecerse.
saddle [sædl], *s.* silla; (*bicicleta*) sillín; collado (*de montaña*); cuarto trasero (*de una res*); (*fig.*) ***in the saddle,*** en el mando, en el poder; ***pack-saddle,*** albarda; ***saddle-bag,*** alforja; ***saddle-bow,*** arzón; ***saddle-cloth,*** sudadero; ***saddle-galled,*** lastimado por la silla; ***saddle-tree,*** fuste de silla. — *v.t.* ensillar; ***saddle up,*** ensillar; ***saddle s.o. with sth.,*** cargar *o* encajar algo a alguien. — **saddle o.s.,** *v.r.* — ***with,*** cargar con.
saddlebacked [ˈsædlbækd], *a.* ensillado.
saddler [ˈsædlə], *s.* sillero; talabartero, guarnicionero.
saddlery [ˈsædləri], *s.* talabartería, guarnicionería; guarniciones, *f.pl.*, arneses, *m.pl.*
Sadducee [ˈsædjusi:], *s.* saduceo.
Sadduceeism [ˈsædjusi:izəm], *s.* saduceísmo.
sadism [ˈseidizəm], *s.* sadismo.
sadist [ˈseidist], *s.* sádico.
sadistic [səˈdistik], *a.* sádico.
sadness [ˈsædnis], *s.* tristeza, melancolía.
safe [seif], *a.* seguro; salvo, ileso; prudente; confiable; ***it is safe to say,*** se puede decir con toda seguridad; ***safe and sound,*** sano y salvo; ***safe conduct,*** salvoconducto; ***safe load,*** carga máxima; ***to be in safe keeping,*** estar en buenas manos; ***to be on the safe side,*** para mayor seguridad; ***to be safe from,*** estar a salvo de, al abrigo de; ***to play safe,*** jugar sobre seguro. — *s.* caja de caudales; fresquera; ***safe-blower,*** ladrón de cajas de caudales.
safeguard [ˈseifgɑ:d], *s.* salvaguardia, protección. — *v.t.* salvaguardar, proteger.
safely [ˈseifli], *adv.* sano y salvo; con toda seguridad (*o* confianza).
safeness [ˈseifnis], *s.* seguridad, (lo) seguro.
safety [ˈseifti], *s.* seguridad; ***safety belt,*** cinturón de seguridad; ***safety catch,*** seguro, fiador; ***safety curtain,*** telón de seguridad; ***safety first,*** (***campaign***), (campaña de) prudencia en (la) carretera; (*min.*) ***safety lamp,*** lámpara de seguridad; ***safety measure,*** medida de seguridad *o* de precaución; ***to take safety measures,*** tomar medidas de seguridad *o* de precaución; ***safety net,*** red de seguridad; ***safety pin,*** imperdible; ***safety razor,*** maquinilla de afeitar; ***safety valve,*** válvula de seguridad; (*fig.*) aliviadero.
saffian [ˈsæfiən], *s.* cuero de cabra *o* carnero curtido con zumaque y teñido de amarillo *o* rojo.
safflower [ˈsæflauə], *s.* alazor, cártamo, azafrán bastardo.
saffron [ˈsæfrən], *a.* azafranado, de color de azafrán. — *s.* azafrán.
sag [sæg], *s.* comba, combadura; pandeo, hundimiento; flecha (*de un cable*); baja (*de precios*). — *v.i.* combarse; flechar; ceder; bajar; flaquear, disminuir; (*mar.*) sotaventarse.
saga [ˈsɑ:gə], *s.* saga.
sagacious [səˈgeiʃəs], *a.* sagaz.
sagaciousness, sagacity [səˈgeiʃəsnis, səˈgæsiti], *s.* sagacidad.
sagamore [ˈsægəmɔ:], *s.* (*Am.*) cacique indio.
sagapenum [sægəˈpi:nəm], *s.* sagapeno.

sage (1) [seidʒ], *s.* (*bot.*) salvia; ***sage brush,*** artemisa.
sage (2) [seidʒ], *a.*, *s.* sabio.
sageness [ˈseidʒnis], *s.* sapiencia.
saggar [ˈsægɑː], *s.* caja refractaria para cocer porcelana fina.
sagittal [ˈsædʒitəl], *a.* sagital.
Sagittarius [sædʒiˈtɛəriəs]. Sagitario.
sago [ˈseigou], *s.* sagú.
saguaro [sæˈgwɑːrou], *s.* pitahaya.
Sahara [səˈhɑːrə]. Sahara, *m.*
Saharan [səˈhɑːrən], *a.* sahárico.
sahib [ˈsɑːib], *s.* señor (*tratamiento indio*).
said [sed], *a.* citado, (ante)dicho. — *p.p.* [SAY].
sail [seil], *s.* (*mar.*) vela; excursión *o* paseo en barco; aspa (*de molino*); ***fleet of seventeen sail of the line,*** escuadra de diecisiete navíos de línea; ***fore-sail,*** trinquete; ***fore-stay-sail,*** trinquetilla; ***fore-top-gallant-sail,*** juanete de proa; ***in, under*** o ***with full sail,*** a todo trapo; ***main-sail,*** vela mayor; ***main-top-gallant-sail,*** juanete mayor; ***mizzen-sail,*** mesana; ***mizzen-top-gallant-sail,*** juanete de mesana; ***mizzen-top-sail,*** sobremesana; ***sail-loft,*** almacén de velas; ***sail-maker,*** fabricante de velas; ***stay-sail,*** vela de estay; ***to make sail, to set sail,*** hacerse a la vela; ***to strike sail,*** arriar una vela. — *v.t.* gobernar (*una embarcación*); navegar por (*el mar, un río etc.*). — *v.i.* navegar; ir en barco; darse a la vela; zarpar, partir; flotar, deslizarse; ***sail along,*** deslizarse suavemente; ***sail along the coast,*** costear; ***sail back,*** volver a puerto; ***sail before the wind,*** navegar viento en popa; ***sail close to the wind,*** ceñir el viento; (*fig.*) atravesar *o* pasar por una coyuntura precaria *o* un momento precario; (*fam.*) ***sail into,*** atacar, embestir; echar una resplandina a.
sailable [ˈseiləbl], *a.* navegable.
sailcloth [ˈseilklɔθ], *s.* lona.
sailer [ˈseilə], *s.* velero; ***good sailer, fine sailer,*** barco marinero.
sailing [ˈseiliŋ], *a.* de vela; ***sail(ing)-boat,*** barca de vela; velero; ***sailing-ship,*** barco *o* buque de vela, velero. — *s.* navegación, (el) navegar; salida, zarpa, (el) zarpar; ***sailing orders,*** últimas instrucciones, *f.pl.*; (*fam.*) ***that's*** o ***it's plain sailing,*** es cosa de coser y cantar.
sailor [ˈseilə], *s.* marinero; (*oficial*) marino; ***to be a bad*** o ***poor sailor,*** marearse fácilmente; ***sailor suit,*** traje de marinero.
sailyard [ˈseiljɑːd], *s.* verga.
sainfoin [ˈseinfɔin], *s.* pipirigallo.
saint [seint; *antes de nombre* sint, sənt], *a.*, *s.* santo, santa; San, Santo, Santa; ***patron saint,*** patrón; ***St. Bernard (dog),*** perro de San Bernardo; ***St. James,*** Santiago; ***Court of St. James,*** corte de San Jaime; ***St. Valentine's Day,*** día de San Valentín, *m.*; (*med.*) ***St. Vitus' dance,*** baile de San Vito. — *v.t.* canonizar.
sainted [ˈseintid], *a.* santo; (*fam.*) ***my sainted aunt!*** ¡por Dios (y por todos los santos)!
sainthood [ˈseinthud], *s.* santidad.
saintlike, saintly [ˈseintlaik, ˈseintli], *a.* (propio de) santo.
saintliness [ˈseintlinis], *s.* santidad.
sake [seik], *s.* motivo, mor; ***art for art's sake,*** el arte por el arte; ***for brevity's sake,*** en obsequio a la brevedad; ***for God's sake, for goodness' sake,*** por (el amor de) Dios; ***for my sake,*** por mí; ***do it for my sake,*** hágalo por mí; ***for the sake of,*** por; en atención a; ***let's say for the sake of argument,*** vamos a suponer que, admitamos que; ***for your sake,*** por Vd., por su bien; ***to talk for its own sake,*** hablar por hablar.
saker [ˈseikə], *s.* (*artill.*, *orn.*) sacre.
sal [sæl], *s.* (*farm.*, *quím.*) sal, *f.*; ***sal ammoniac,*** sa amoníaca; ***sal soda,*** sosa, carbonato de sodio; ***sal volatile,*** sal volátil.
sala(a)m [səˈlɑːm], *s.* zalema. — *v.t.*, *v.i.* hacer zalemas (a).
salability, salableness [seiləˈbiliti, ˈseiləblnis], *s.* (lo) vendible; facilidad de venta, salida.
salable [ˈseiləbl], *a.* vendible, de fácil venta.
salacious [səˈleiʃəs], *a.* salaz.
salaciousness, salacity [səˈleiʃəsnis, səˈlæsiti], *s.* salacidad.
salad [ˈsæləd], *s.* ensalada; ***fruit salad,*** ensalada *o* macedonia de frutas; ***salad dressing,*** aliño; ***salad oil,*** aceite para ensaladas; ***salad bowl, salad dish,*** ensaladera.
salal [ˈsæləl], *s.* arbusto perenne de California (*Gaultheria shallon*).
Salamanca [sæləˈmæŋkə]. Salamanca.
salamander [ˈsæləmændə], *s.* salamandra; salamanquesa; (*min.*) ***salamander's hair*** o ***wool,*** asbesto, amianto.
salamandrine [sæləˈmændrain], *a.* salamandrino.
salami [səˈlɑːmi], *s.* salchichón.
salaried [ˈsælərid], *a.* asalariado.
salary [ˈsæləri], *s.* sueldo.
sale [seil], *s.* venta; saldo, liquidación; ***for*** o ***on sale,*** de venta, en venta, se vende; (*com.*) ***on sale or return,*** contrato de retroventa; (***public***) ***sale,*** (pública) subasta; ***sale by auction,*** subasta, almoneda; ***sale price,*** precio de venta; ***sales tax,*** impuesto sobre las ventas; ***sale value,*** valor en el mercado.
saleable, saleableness *etc.* [SALABLE, SALABLENESS *etc.*].
salep [ˈsæləp], *s.* salep.
saleratus [sæləˈreitəs], *s.* (*coc.*) bicarbonato de sosa *o* potasa para usos culinarios.
saleroom [ˈseilruːm], *s.* sala de subastas.
salesgirl [ˈseilzgəːl], *s.f.* vendedora; dependienta de tienda.
salesman [ˈseilzmən], *s.* (*pl.* **-men** [-men]) vendedor; dependiente de tienda; ***travelling salesman,*** viajante (de comercio).
salesmanship [ˈseilzmənʃip], *s.* arte de vender, mercadotecnia.
saleswoman [ˈseilzwumən], *s.* (*pl.* **-women** [-wimin]) vendedora; dependienta de tienda.
Salian [ˈseiliən], *a.*, *s.* salio.
Salic [ˈseilik], *a.* sálico; ***Salic law,*** ley sálica.
salicaceous [sæliˈkeiʃəs], *a.* salicíneo.
salicetum [sæliˈsiːtəm], *s.* salceda.
salicin(e) [ˈsælisin], *s.* salicina.
salicylate [sæˈlisileit], *s.* salicilato.
salicylic [sæliˈsilik], *a.* salicílico.
salience [ˈseiliəns], *s.* (lo) saliente; relieve; ***to give salience to,*** poner de relieve.
salient [ˈseiliənt], *a.* sobresaliente, descollante. — *s.* (*mil.*) saliente.
saliferous [sæˈlifərəs], *a.* salífero.
salifiable [ˈsælifaiəbl], *a.* salificable.
salify [ˈsælifai], *v.t.* salificar.
saline [ˈseilain], *a.* salino. — *s.* saladar; salina.
salineness [ˈseilainnis], *s.* calidad de salino.
salinometer [sæliˈnɔmitə], *s.* pesasales, *m.inv.*
salinous [səˈlainəs], *a.* salino.
saliva [səˈlaivə], *s.* saliva.
salival, salivary [səˈlaivəl, səˈlaivəri], *a.* salival; salivoso.
salivant [ˈsælivənt], *a.*, *s.* sialogogo.
salivate [ˈsæliveit], *v.i.* salivar.
salivation [sæliˈveiʃən], *s.* salivación.
sallow (1) [ˈsælou], *a.* cetrino, amarillento.
sallow (2) [ˈsælou], *s.* sauce.
sallowness [ˈsælounis], *s.* (lo) cetrino.
sally [ˈsæli], *s.* salida; incursión, algara; (*arq.*) saledizo, vuelo; ***sallies of wit,*** ocurrencias chistosas, *f.pl.* — *v.i.* salir, hacer una salida; ***sally forth,*** salir (resueltamente).
sallyport [ˈsælipɔːt], *s.* (*fort.*) surtida.

salmagundi [sælmə'gʌndi], *s.* salpicón; (*fig.*) mescolanza.
salmon ['sæmən], *a.*, *s.* salmón; color (de) salmón; ***salmon trout,*** trucha asalmonada.
salol ['seilɔl], *s.* salol.
Salome [sæ'loumi]. Salomé.
Salomonic [sælo'mɔnik], *a.* salomónico.
salon ['sælɔŋ], *s.* salón.
saloon [sə'lu:n], *s.* salón; (*f.c.*) coche salón; cámara (*de un barco*); (*aut.*) turismo; taberna; ***saloon keeper,*** tabernero.
salsify ['sælsifi], *s.* salsifí.
salt [sɔ:lt], *a.* salado; (*agua*) salobre; ***salt meat,*** carne salada, cecina; ***salt spring,*** fuente de agua salada. — *s.* sal, *f.*; (*pl.*) sales medicinales; (*mar.*) ***old salt,*** lobo de mar; ***rock salt,*** sal gema; ***salt cellar,*** salero; ***salt-maker,*** salinero; ***salt mines,*** minas de sal, *f.pl.*; ***salt pit,*** saladar; ***the salt of the earth,*** lo mejor del mundo; ***he's not worth his salt,*** no vale el pan que come. — *v.t.* salar; (*fig.*) ***salt away,*** guardar (para el futuro).
saltant ['sæltənt], *a.* saltante.
salter ['sɔ:ltə], *s.* salador; salinero.
saltiness ['sɔ:ltinis], *s.* (lo) salado.
salting ['sɔ:ltiŋ], *s.* (el) salar; ***salting-tub,*** saladero.
saltish ['sɔ:ltiʃ], *a.* algo salado.
saltmarsh ['sɔ:ltmɑ:ʃ], *s.* saladar.
saltness ['sɔ:ltnis], *s.* salinidad.
saltpeter, saltpetre ['sɔ:ltpi:tə], *s.* nitro, salitre; ***saltpetre-maker,*** nitrero, salitrero; ***saltpetre works,*** nitrería, salitrería.
saltwater ['sɔ:ltwɔ:tə], *a.* (*pescado*) de mar, de agua salada.
saltworks ['sɔ:ltwə:ks], *s.* salinas, *f.pl.*
saltwort ['sɔ:ltwə:t], *s.* barrilla, sosa.
salty ['sɔ:lti], *a.* salado; salobre.
salubrious [sə'l(j)u:briəs], *a.* salubre, saludable, salutífero.
salubriousness, salubrity [sə'l(j)u:briəsnis, sə'l(j)u:briti], *s.* salubridad.
salutariness ['sæl(j)utərinis], *s.* (lo) conveniente.
salutary ['sæl(j)utəri], *a.* saludable, salubre; salutífero, curativo; que escarmienta, conveniente.
salutation [sæl(j)u'teiʃən], *s.* salutación; bienvenida, parabién.
salutatory [sæ'l(j)u:tətəri], *a.* de salutación. — *s.* discurso de bienvenida; (*gram.*) vocativo.
salute [sə'l(j)u:t], *s.* saludo (*con la mano*); (*mil. y mar.*) salva. — *v.t.*, *v.i.* saludar (*con la mano*), saludar militarmente.
salvability, salvableness [sælvə'biliti, 'sælvəblnis], *s.* posibilidad de ser redimido *o* de salvarse.
salvable ['sælvəbl], *a.* que puede salvarse.
Salvador (El) [(el) 'sælvədɔ:]. El Salvador.
Salvador(e)an [sælvə'dɔ:r(i)ən], *a.*, *s.* salvadoreño.
salvage ['sælvidʒ], *s.* salvamento; objetos salvados, *m.pl.* — *v.t.* salvar.
salvarsan ['sælvəsən], *s.* salvarsán.
salvation [sæl'veiʃən], *s.* salvación; ***Salvation Army,*** Ejército de Salvación.
salve (1) [sælv], *s.* ungüento. — *v.t.* curar con ungüento; aliviar.
salve (2) [sælv], *v.t.* (*mar.*) salvar.
salver ['sælvə], *s.* salvilla, bandeja.
salvia ['sælviə], *s.* salvia.
salvo (1) ['sælvou], *s.* salvedad, reserva.
salvo (2) ['sælvou], *s.* (*mil.*) salva.
Sam [sæm]. (*abrev.*) [SAMUEL].
Samaritan [sə'mæritən], *a.*, *s.* samaritano; ***good Samaritan,*** buen samaritano.
same [seim], *a.* mismo, igual; ***the same,*** el mismo, lo mismo, la misma, los mismos, las mismas; todo uno; otro tanto; ***all the same,*** a pesar de todo; ***exactly the same,*** idéntico; ***if it is (all) the same to you,*** si a Vd. le es igual; ***it is all the same (to me),*** lo mismo (me) da; (para mí) es todo uno; ***the same . . . as,*** lo mismo . . . que; ***much the same as,*** más o menos como; ***the same to you,*** igualmente.
sameness ['seimnis], *s.* igualdad, identidad; monotonía.
samlet ['sæmlit], *s.* salmón joven.
sammy ['sæmi], *v.t.* humedecer (*cueros*).
Samoa [sə'mouə]. Samoa.
Samoan [sə'mouən], *a.*, *s.* samoano.
Samothrace ['sæmoθreis]. Samotracia.
samovar ['sæmovɑ:], *s.* samovar.
samp [sæmp], *s.* (*Am.*) maíz molido grueso.
samphire ['sæmfaiə], *s.* hinojo marino.
sample [sɑ:mpl], *s.* muestra; ***sample book,*** muestrario; ***sample copy,*** ejemplar de muestra; ***sample room,*** cuarto de muestras. — *v.t.* probar, catar; sacar una muestra de; muestrear.
sampler ['sɑ:mplə], *s.* probador, catador; (*cost.*) dechado; ***bottom samplers,*** catadores de fondo; (*ing.*) ***soil sampler,*** cuchara de sondeo.
sampling ['sɑ:mpliŋ], *s.* muestreo.
Samuel ['sæmjuəl]. Samuel.
Samson ['sæmsən]. Sansón.
sanative ['sænətiv], *a.* curativo, sanativo.
sanativeness ['sænətivnis], *s.* calidad de sanativo.
sanatorium [sænə'tɔ:riəm], *s.* sanatorio, casa de salud.
sanatory ['sænətəri], *a.* sanativo.
sanctification [sæŋktifi'keiʃən], *s.* santificación.
sanctifier ['sæŋktifaiə], *s.* santificador.
sanctify ['sæŋktifai], *v.t.* santificar.
sanctimonious [sæŋkti'mouniəs], *a.* beato, santurrón.
sanctimoniously [sæŋkti'mouniəsli], *adv.* con beatería *o* santurronería, con tono (de) beato *o* (de) santurrón.
sanctimoniousness, sanctimony [sæŋkti'mouniəsnis, 'sæŋktiməni], *s.* santurronería.
sanction ['sæŋkʃən], *s.* sanción; autorización. — *v.t.* sancionar; autorizar.
sanctity ['sæŋktiti], *s.* santidad; inviolabilidad.
sanctuary ['sæŋktjuəri], *s.* santuario; refugio (sagrado); ***to take sanctuary,*** acogerse a sagrado; refugiarse.
sanctum ['sæŋktəm], *s.* lugar sagrado; refugio; ***inner sanctum,*** sanctasanctórum.
sand [sænd], *s.* arena; (*pl.*) arenal, playa; ***fine sand,*** arenilla(s); ***sand bag,*** saco de arena; saco terrero; ***sand bank,*** banco de arena; ***sand bar,*** barra de arena; ***sand-blast(ing),*** chorro de arena; ***sand box,*** salvadera, arenillero; (*f.c.*) depósito de arena, caja de enarenar; ***sand-castle,*** castillo de arena; ***sand dune,*** duna; (*ent.*) ***sand fly,*** jijene; ***sand glass,*** reloj de arena; ***sand hill,*** duna; ***sand shoes,*** (zapatillas) playeras, *f.pl.* — *v.t.* enarenar.
sandal [sændl], *s.* sandalia; abarca; ***hempen sandal,*** alpargata.
sandalwood ['sændlwud], *s.* sándalo.
sandarac(h) ['sændəræk], *s.* sandáraca; tuya.
sanderling ['sændəliŋ], *s.* (*orn.*) churrilla.
sandiness ['sændinis], *s.* (lo) arenoso.
sandpaper ['sændpeipə], *s.* (papel de) lija. — *v.t.* lijar.
sandpiper ['sændpaipə], *s.* (*orn.*) andarríos, *m.inv.*, lavandera.
sandpit ['sændpit], *s.* arenal.
sandstone ['sændstoun], *s.* (piedra) arenisca.
sandstorm ['sændstɔ:m], *s.* tempestad de arena.
sandwich ['sændwidʒ], *s.* sándwich, emparedado; ***sandwich board,*** cartelón; ***sandwich man,*** hombre-anuncio. — *v.t.* colocar entre dos capas *o* entre dos cosas; intercalar, insertar; apretujar.
sandy ['sændi], *a.* arenoso; (*persona*) ***sandy (-haired),*** pelirrojo.
sane [sein], *a.* cuerdo; sensato.
saneness ['seinnis], *s.* cordura; sensatez.
sangaree [sæŋgə'ri:], *s.* sangría (*bebida*).

Sangrail [sæŋ'greil], *s.* grial.
sanguiferous [sæŋ'gwifərəs], *a.* sanguífero, sanguificativo.
sanguification [sæŋgwifi'keiʃən], *s.* sanguificación.
sanguifier ['sæŋgwifaiə], *s.* cosa sanguificable.
sanguify ['sæŋgwifai], *v.t.* sanguificar. — *v.i.* criar sangre.
sanguinariness ['sæŋgwinərinis], *s.* (lo) sanguinario; lo sangriento.
sanguinary ['sæŋgwinəri], *a.* sanguinario; sangriento; con efusión de sangre.
sanguine ['sæŋgwin], *a.* optimista; confiado; ***don't be too sanguine,*** no se confíe Vd. demasiado. — *s.* color (de) sangre.
sanguineness ['sæŋgwinnis], *s.* (exceso de) optimismo.
sanguineous [sæŋ'gwiniəs], *a.* sanguino, sanguíneo, sanguinoso; encarnado.
Sanhedrin, Sanhedrim ['sænidrin, -drim], *s.* sanedrín.
sanicle ['sænikl], *s.* sanícula.
sanies ['seinii:z], *s.* sanie(s), *f.*, icor.
sanious ['seiniəs], *a.* sanioso, icoroso.
sanitarian [sæni'tɛəriən], *a.*, *s.* sanitario.
sanitarium [sæni'tɛəriəm], (*Am.*) [SANATORIUM].
sanitary ['sænitəri], *a.* sanitario; ***sanitary cordon,*** cordón sanitario; ***sanitary corps,*** cuerpo de sanidad; ***sanitary towel,*** paño higiénico, compresa higiénica.
sanitation [sæni'teiʃən], *s.* sanidad; instalación sanitaria; servicios, *m.pl.*; higiene; saneamiento.
sanity ['sæniti], *s.* cordura; sensatez.
San José [sæn hou'zei]. San José.
San Juan [sæn 'hwɑ:n]. San Juan.
San Marino [sæn mə'ri:nou]. San Marino.
San Salvador [sæn sælvə'dɔ:]. San Salvador.
Sanskrit, Sanscrit ['sænskrit], *a.*, *s.* sánscrito.
Santa Claus ['sæntə 'klɔ:z]. Papá Noel, *m.*
Santiago [sænti'ɑ:gou]. Santiago.
Santo Domingo ['sæntou dɔ'miŋgou]. Santo Domingo.
santonica [sæn'tɔnikə], *s.* santónico.
santonin(e) ['sæntonin], *s.* santonina.
sap (1) [sæp], *s.* savia; jugo. — *v.t.* extraer la savia de.
sap (2) [sæp], *s.* zapa. — *v.t.* zapar; minar. — *v.i.* hacer labor de zapa.
sap (3) [sæp], *s.* (*fam.*) panoli.
sapajou ['sæpədʒu:], *s.* sapajú, zamba.
sapan-wood ['sæpən-wud], *s.* sapán.
sapful ['sæpful], *a.* lleno de savia.
sapid ['sæpid], *a.* sápido, sabroso, gustoso.
sapience ['seipiəns], *s.* sabiduría; sapiencia.
sapient ['seipiənt], *a.* sapiente.
sapiential [seipi'enʃəl], *a.* sapiencial.
sapless ['sæplis], *a.* seco, sin jugo.
sapling ['sæpliŋ], *s.* árbol joven; pimpollo; (*fam.*) jovenzuelo.
sapodilla [sæpo'dilə], *s.* zapotillo, chicozapote.
saponaceous [sæpo'neiʃəs], *a.* saponáceo.
saponifiable [sə'pɔnifaiəbl] *a.* saponificable.
saponification [səpɔnifi'keiʃən], *s.* saponificación.
saponify [sə'pɔnifai], *v.t.* saponificar.
saporific sæpə'rifik], *a.* saporífero.
sapper ['sæpə], *s.* (*mil.*) zapador.
Sapphic ['sæfik], *a.*, *s.* sáfico.
sapphire ['sæfaiə], *a.* zafirino. — *s.* zafiro.
Sappho ['sæfou]. Safo, *f.*
sappiness ['sæpinis], *s.* (lo) lleno de savia, (lo) jugoso; (lo) enérgico.
sappy ['sæpi], *a.* lleno de savia, jugoso; enérgico.
saraband ['særəbænd], *s.* zarabanda.
Saracen ['særəsən], *a.*, *s.* sarraceno.
Saracenic [særə'senik], *a.* sarracénico.
Saragossa [særə'gɔsə]. Zaragoza.
Sarah ['sɛərə]. Sara.
sarcasm ['sɑ:kæzəm], *s.* sarcasmo.
sarcastic [sɑ:'kæstik], *a.* sarcástico.
sarcastically [sɑ:'kæstikəli], *adv.* sarcásticamente.
sarcenet ['sɑ:snit], [SARSENET].
sarcocarp ['sɑ:kokɑ:p], *s.* sarcocarpio.
sarcocele ['sɑ:kosi:l], *s.* sarcocele.
sarcocolla [sɑ:ko'kɔlə], *s.* sarcocola.
sarcologic(al) [sɑ:ko'lɔdʒik(əl)], *a.* sarcológico.
sarcology [sɑ:'kɔlədʒi], *s.* sarcología.
sarcoma [sɑ:'koumə], *s.* sarcoma.
sarcomatous [sɑ:'kɔmətəs], *a.* sarcomatoso.
sarcophagus [sɑ:'kɔfəgəs], *s.* (*pl.* **sarcophaguses, sarcophagi** [sɑ:'kɔfəgəsiz, -gai], sarcófago.
sard [sɑ:d], *s.* sardio.
sardine (1) [sɑ:'di:n], *s.* (*ict.*) sardina; ***packed like sardines,*** como sardinas en banasta.
sardine (2) ['sɑ:din], *s.* (*joy.*) sardio.
Sardinia [sɑ:'diniə]. Cerdeña.
Sardinian [sɑ:'diniən], *a.*, *s.* sardo.
sardius ['sɑ:diəs], *s.* sardio.
sardonic [sɑ:'dɔnik], *a.* sardónico, burlón.
sardonically [sɑ:'dɔnikəli], *adv.* irónicamente, con sarcasmo.
sardonyx ['sɑ:doniks], *s.* sardónice, *f.*
Sargasso Sea [sɑ:'gæsou 'si:]. mar de los Sargazos.
sargasso [sɑ:'gæsou], *s.* sargazo.
sari ['sɑ:ri], *s.* sari, *m.*
sark [sɑ:k], *s.* (*Esco.*) camisa.
sarsaparilla [sɑ:səpə'rilə], *s.* zarzaparrilla.
sarsenet ['sɑ:sinit], *s.* tafetán de Florencia.
sartorial [sɑ:'tɔ:riəl], *a.* indumentario; (*anat.*) sartorio.
sash (1) [sæʃ], *s.* faja; (*mil.*) fajín.
sash (2) [sæʃ], *s.* marco (*de ventena*); ***sash cord,*** cuerda (para contrapesos de ventana); ***sash window,*** ventana de guillotina.
sassafras ['sæsəfræs], *s.* sasafrás, *m.*
Satan ['seitən]. Satanás, *m.*
satanic(al) [sə'tænik(əl)], *a.* satánico, diabólico.
satchel ['sætʃəl], *s.* cartera, cabás.
sate [seit], *v.t.* saciar, hartar.
sateen [sə'ti:n], *s.* satén.
satellite ['sætəlait], *a.*, *s.* satélite.
satiate ['seiʃiit], *a.* harto, ahito. — ['seiʃieit], *v.t.* saciar, hartar.
satiation [seiʃi'eiʃən], *s.* saciedad, hartura.
satiety [sə'taiiti], *s.* saciedad, hartazgo.
satin ['sætin], *s.* (*tej.*) raso; ***satin damask,*** raso adamascado; ***satin flower,*** lunaria.
satinet [sæti'net], *s.* satinete; rasete.
satinwood ['sætinwud], *s.* palo aguita, palo áloe, doradillo.
satiny ['sætini], *a.* arrasado.
satire ['sætaiə], *s.* sátira.
satiric(al) [sə'tirik(əl)], *a.* satírico.
satirist ['sætirist], *s.* (escritor) satírico.
satirize ['sætiraiz], *v.t.* satirizar.
satisfaction [sætis'fækʃən], *s.* satisfacción; compensación, pago.
satisfactoriness [sætis'fæktərinis], *s.* (lo) satisfactorio.
satisfactory [sætis'fæktəri], *a.* satisfactorio; ***to be satisfactory,*** dar buen resultado, valer.
satisfied ['sætisfaid], *a.* satisfecho, contento; pagado. — *p.p.* [SATISFY]; ***I'm not satisfied,*** no me convence; ***to be easily satisfied,*** pasarse con poco, conformarse con poco.
satisfy ['sætisfai], *v.t.* satisfacer; contentar; convencer. — *v.i.* satisfacer.
satrap ['sætrəp], *s.* sátrapa, *m.*

satrapy ['sætrəpi], *s.* satrapía.
saturable ['sætʃərəbl], *a.* saturable.
saturant ['sætʃərənt], *a.*, *s.* saturante.
saturate ['sætʃəreit], *v.t.* saturar; embeber, empapar, impregnar.
saturation [sætʃə'reiʃən], *s.* saturación.
Saturday ['sætədei], *s.* sábado.
Saturn ['sætə:n]. Saturno.
Saturnalia [sætə'neiliə], *s.* saturnales, *f.pl.*
Saturnalian [sætə'neiliən], *a.* de las saturnales; saturnal, licencioso.
Saturnian [sə'tə:niən], *a.* saturnal; feliz, dichoso.
saturnine ['sætənain], *a.* saturnino; ***saturnine poisoning,*** saturnismo.
saturnite ['sætənait], *s.* saturnita.
satyr ['sætə], *s.* sátiro.
satyriasis [sæti'raiəsis], *s.* satiriasis, *f.inv.*
satyric [sə'tirik], *a.* satírico.
sauce [sɔ:s], *s.* salsa; (*fam.*) desfachatez, frescura; ***apple sauce,*** salsa de manzana; ***sauce boat, sauce dish,*** salsera; ***to give a little sauce to,*** echarle un poco de ajilimójili a. — *v.t.* condimentar, echar salsa a.
saucebox ['sɔ:sbɔks], *s.* (muchacho) descarado.
saucepan ['sɔ:spæn], *s.* cacerola, cazo.
saucer ['sɔ:sə], *s.* platillo; ***flying saucer,*** platillo volante; ***saucer eyes,*** ojos como platos, *m.pl.*
sauciness ['sɔ:sinis], *s.* descaro, descoco, frescura.
saucy ['sɔ:si], *a.* descarado; respondón.
Saudi Arabia ['saudi ə'reibiə]. Arabia Saudita.
Saudi Arabian. ['saudi ə'reibiən], *a.*, *s.* árabe saudita.
sauerkraut ['sauəkraut], *s.* chucruta.
Saul [sɔ:l]. Saúl; (*San Pablo*) Saulo.
sauna ['sɔ:nə], *s.* sauna.
saunter ['sɔ:ntə], *s.* paseo (lento y tranquilo). — *v.i.* pasear(se) (despacio y con tranquilidad).
saurian ['sɔ:riən], *a.*, *s.* saurio.
sausage ['sɔsidʒ], *s.* salchicha; ***garlic sausage,*** chorizo; ***sausages (of all kinds),*** embutidos, *m.pl.*; ***sausage meat,*** relleno para salchichas; ***sausage roll,*** empanadilla de salchicha.
sauté ['soutei], *a.* (*coc.*) ***sauté potatoes,*** patatas salteadas, *f.pl.*
savage ['sævidʒ], *a.* salvaje; bárbaro; feroz, sañudo. — *s.* salvaje. — *v.t.* atacar con ferocidad, desgarrar.
savageness, savagery ['sævidʒnis, 'sævədʒəri], *s.* salvajismo, salvajería; barbarie, *f.*; ferocidad, saña.
savanna(h) [sæ'vænə], *s.* sabana.
savant ['sævɔŋ], *s.* erudito, sabio.
save (1) [seiv], *conj.* ***save that,*** salvo que, excepto que, a menos que. — *prep.* salvo, excepto, menos.
save (2) [seiv], *v.t.* salvar; librar; ahorrar, economizar; guardar, conservar; ***save face,*** salvar las apariencias; ***save o.s. trouble,*** ahorrarse *o* evitarse molestias *o* latas; ***God save the Queen!*** ¡Dios guarde a la Reina! — *v.i.* ahorrar.
saveloy ['sævəlɔi], *s.* embutido seco.
saver ['seivə], *s.* ahorrador.
savin ['sævin], *s.* sabina.
saving ['seiviŋ], *a.* ahorrativo; económico; que economiza; ***saving clause,*** cláusula que contiene una salvedad; ***saving grace,*** mérito que compensa *o* redime. — *prep.* salvo, excepto; ***saving those present,*** mejorando lo presente. — *s.* ahorro, economía; (*pl.*) ahorros, *m.pl.*; ***savings account,*** cuenta de ahorros; ***savings bank,*** caja de ahorros.
saviour ['seivjə], *s.* salvador; ***the Saviour,*** el Salvador.
savoir-faire [sævwɑ:-'fɛə], *s.* habilidad, maña.
savory ['seivəri], *s.* (*bot.*) ajedrea; tomillo salsero.
savour ['seivə], *s.* sabor, gustillo, gusto. — *v.t.* saborear. — *v.i.* — ***of,*** saber (a), oler (a), tener sabor, gusto *u* olor (de).
savouriness ['seivərinis], *s.* (lo) salado; sabor.
savourless ['seivəlis], *a.* insípido, insulso.
savoursome ['seivəsəm], *a.* sabroso.
savoury ['seivəri], *a.* salado; sabroso. — *s.* cosa salada; ***savouries and sweetmeats,*** lo salado y lo dulce.
Savoy [sə'vɔi]. Saboya.
savoy [sə'vɔi], *s.* (*bot.*) col de Saboya.
Savoyard [sə'vɔiɑ:d], *a.*, *s.* saboyano.
savvy ['sævi], *s.* (*fam.*) experiencia. — *v.i.* (*fam.*) ***savvy?*** ¿ comprende ? ¿ entiende ?
saw (1) [sɔ:], *s.* sierra; ***fret-saw,*** sierra de calar *o* de punto; ***hand-saw,*** sierra *o* serrucho de mano. — *irr. v.t.* serrar, aserrar. — *irr. v.i.* serrar; serrarse.
saw (2) [sɔ:], *pret.* [SEE].
saw (3) [sɔ:], *s.* refrán, dicho, proverbio.
sawbones ['sɔ:bounz], *s.* (*fam.*) sacapotras, *m.inv.*
sawbuck ['sɔ:bʌk], *s.* cabrilla de aserrar.
sawdust ['sɔ:dʌst], *s.* aserraduras, *f.pl.*, serrín.
sawhorse ['sɔ:hɔ:s], *s.* caballete, cabrilla.
sawmill ['sɔ:mil], *s.* aserradero.
sawn [sɔ:n], *a.* aserrado; *p.p. irreg.* [SAW].
sawpit ['sɔ:pit], *s.* aserradero.
sawwort ['sɔ:wə:t], *s.* serrátula.
sawyer ['sɔ:jə], *s.* aserrador, serrador, chiquichaque.
sax (1) [sæks], *s.* hachuela *o* martillo de pizarrero.
sax (2) [sæks], *s.* (*fam.*) sax, saxofón.
saxatile, saxicolous ['sæksətail, sæks'ikələs], *a.* saxátil.
saxe [sæks], *s.* (*foto.*) papel de Sajonia, papel albuminado; ***saxe-blue,*** azul de Sajonia.
saxhorn ['sækshɔ:n], *s.* bombardino; bombardón.
saxifrage ['sæksifridʒ], *s.* saxífraga.
Saxon ['sæksən], *a.*, *s.* sajón.
Saxony ['sæksəni]. Sajonia.
saxophone ['sæksəfoun], *s.* saxofón.
say [sei], *s.* decir, dicho; voz (*uso de la palabra*); ***let him have his say,*** que hable él; ***to have no say,*** no tener voz ni voto. — *irr. v.t.* decir; afirmar; rezar; ***it is said, people say,*** se dice; ***that is to say,*** es decir, o sea; ***say grace,*** bendecir la mesa; ***to say the least,*** por lo menos, que digamos; ***say mass,*** decir misa; ***to say nothing of,*** sin contar, por no hablar de; ***I should say so!*** ¡ya lo creo!; ***you don't say so!*** ¡no me diga!; ***say what you like*** (o ***will***), diga lo que quiera, diga lo que diga; ***easier said than done,*** se dice muy pronto; ***no sooner said than done,*** dicho y hecho; ***there is a lot to be said for that,*** (es una cosa que) tiene muchas ventajas; ***he did not have much to say for himself,*** apenas si abrió la boca; ***that doesn't say much for his intelligence,*** eso dice poco *o* no dice mucho de su inteligencia; ***my watch says . . .,*** yo tengo las . . .; ***shall we say 3 o'clock?*** ¿ quedamos para las tres ? — *irr. v.i.* decir, hablar; ***say,*** digamos, por ejemplo; ***I say!*** ¡oiga!; ***say on,*** seguir hablando; ***it goes without saying,*** ni que decir tiene; ***needless to say,*** ni que decir tiene, huelga decir.
saying ['seiiŋ], *s.* dicho, proverbio, adagio, sentencia; ***as the saying goes,*** come suele decirse.
scab [skæb], *s.* costra, postilla; roña; escabro; esquirol. — *v.i.* boicotear una huelga.
scabbard ['skæbəd], *s.* vaina (*de espada*).
scabbed, scabby [skæbd, 'skæbi], *a.* postilloso, costroso; ruin, vil.
scabbiness ['skæbinis], *s.* (lo) costroso *o* roñoso.
scabies ['skeibi:z], *s.* sarna.
scabrous ['skæbrəs], *a.* escabroso; áspero, rugoso.
scabious (2) ['skeibiəs], *s.* escabiosa.
scabrous ['skæbrəs], *a.* escabroso, áspero, rugoso.
scabrousness ['skæbrəsnis], *s.* escabrosidad; aspereza.
scabwort ['skæbwə:t], *s.* énula campana.
scad [skæd], *s.* (*ict.*) escombro; sábalo, alosa.

scaffold [ˈskæfəld], *s.* patíbulo, cadalso. — *v.t.* poner andamios a, en.
scaffolding [ˈskæfəldiŋ], *s.* andamio(s), andamiaje.
scaglia [ˈskɑːljə], *s.* piedra caliza italiana.
scagliola [skɑːˈljoulə], *s.* estuco, escayola.
scalliwag [ˈskæliwæg], *s.* (*fam.*) bribón, tunante.
scald [skɔːld], *s.* escaldadura. — *v.t.* escaldar; limpiar con agua muy caliente.
scale (1) [skeil], *s.* platillo de balanza; (***pair of***) ***scales,*** balanza; ***to tip the scales,*** inclinar la balanza; ***to turn the scales,*** ser decisivo, hacer que cambien las tornas.
scale (2) [skeil], *s.* (*zool., bot.*) escama. — *v.t.* escamar, quitar las escamas a; descostrar, quitar la costra a; raspar; quitar el sarro a (*los dientes*). — *v.i.* — (***off***), descamarse; descostrarse; (*pintura, yeso etc.*) desconcharse; ***scale over,*** llenarse de escamas.
scale (3) [skeil], *s.* (*mús., mat.*) escala; ***on a large scale,*** en gran escala; ***on a small scale,*** en pequeña escala; ***to scale,*** según escala. — *v.t.* (*montañas*) escalar, trepar a; ***scale down,*** reducir según escala; ir reduciendo.
scalene [ˈskeiliːn], *a.* escaleno. — *s.* (*geom.*) (triángulo) escaleno.
scaliness [ˈskeilinis], *s.* escamosidad.
scaling (1) [ˈskeiliŋ], *s.* (el) escamar.
scaling (2) [ˈskeiliŋ], *s.* (el) escalar; (*mil.*) escalamiento; ***scaling-ladder,*** escala de sitio, escala de asalto.
scallion [ˈskæljən], *s.* chalote; cebolleta, (*Am.*) [SPRING-ONION].
scallop [ˈskæləp, ˈskɔləp], *s.* (*ict.*) vieira; venera, pechina, concha (*de peregrino*); (*cost.*) festón; ***scallop shell,*** venera, concha de vieira. — *v.t.* festonear.
scalp [skælp], *s.* cuero cabelludo. — *v.t.* quitar el cuero cabelludo a; (*Am., fam.*) comprar y revender.
scalpel [ˈskælpəl], *s.* escalpelo, bisturí.
scalper [ˈskælpə], *s.* (*Am., fam.*) revendedor de billetes; escalpelo.
scalping [ˈskælpiŋ], *s.* (el) quitar el cuero cabelludo (a).
scaly [ˈskeili], *a.* escamoso.
scammony [ˈskæməni], *s.* escamonea.
scamp (1) [skæmp], *s.* bribón, granuja.
scamp (2) [skæmp], *v.t.* frangollar.
scamper [ˈskæmpə], *s.* carrera precipitada. — *v.i.* — ***away,*** salir de estampía.
scan [skæn], *v.t.* escudriñar; examinar, explorar; otear; (*poét.*) escandir. — *v.i.* (*poét.*) estar bien medido.
scandal [ˈskændəl], *s.* escándalo; difamación; ***scandal bearer,*** correveidile; ***scandal monger,*** murmurador; ***what a scandal! it's a scandal!*** ¡qué vergüenza!
scandalize [ˈskændəlaiz], *v.t.* escandalizar; difamar. — *v.i.* murmurar.
scandalous [ˈskændələs], *a.* escandaloso; vergonzoso; difamatorio, calumnioso.
scandalousness [ˈskændələsnis], *s.* (lo) escandaloso.
scandent [ˈskændənt], *a.* trepador.
Scandinavia [skændiˈneiviə]. Escandinavia.
Scandinavian [skændiˈneiviən], *a., s.* escandinavo.
scanner [ˈskænə], *s.* antena direccional giratoria; dispositivo explorador.
scanning [ˈskæniŋ], *s.* escrutinio; (*poét.*) escansión.
scansion [ˈskænʃən], *s.* escansión.
scansorial, scansorious [skænˈsɔːriəl, -ˈsɔːriəs], *a.* trepador.
scant [skænt], *a.* escaso, parvo, exiguo; ***to pay scant attention to,*** prestar *o* dedicar poca atención a. — *v.t.* escatimar. — *v.i.* (*mar.*) caer (*el viento*).
scant(i)ness [ˈskænt(i)nis], *s.* (lo) escaso, exigüidad.
scantling [ˈskæntliŋ], *s.* cuartón, madero, barrote; escantillón; colección de cuartones; (*pl.*) (*mar.*) grúas de tablas, *f.pl.*
scanty [ˈskænti], *a.* escaso, parvo, exiguo; insuficiente; ***to be scantily dressed,*** estar, ir *o* andar escaso de ropa.
scape [skeip], *s.* (*bot.*) escapo, bohordo; (*ent.*) cuerno, antena; (*orn.*) cañón de una pluma; (*arq.*) fuste de una columna.
scapegoat [ˈskeipgout], *s.* cabeza de turco, víctima propiciatoria; ***to be a scapegoat for,*** pagar las culpas de.
scapegrace [ˈskeipgreis], *s.* bribón, pillo.
scapement [ˈskeipmənt], *s.* escape (*de reloj*).
scaphander [skəˈfændə], *s.* escafandra.
scaphoid [ˈskæfɔid], *a.* navicular, en forma de nave; escafoideo. — *s.* (*anat.*) escafoides, *m.*
scapula [ˈskæpjulə], *s.* escápula, omóplato, espaldilla, hueso de la espaldilla.
scapular(y) [ˈskæpjulə(ri)], *a.* escapular. — *s.* (*igl.*) escapulario; (*cir.*) vendaje para el omóplato.
scar (1) [skɑː], *s.* cicatriz, *f.*; chirlo, costurón. — *v.t.* marcar con una cicatriz.
scar (2) [skɑː], *s.* peñasco, farallón, roca pelada.
scar (3) [skɑː], *s.* (*ict.*) escaro.
scarab [ˈskærəb], *s.* ateuco, escarabajo sagrado.
scaramouch [ˈskærəmuːʃ], *s.* fanfarrón; truhán.
scarce [skɛəs], *a.* escaso; ***to be scarce,*** escasear; ***to make o.s. scarce,*** desaparecer, quitarse de en medio, largarse.
scarcely [ˈskɛəsli], *adv.* apenas, no bien; difícilmente; ***scarcely anybody,*** casi nadie; ***scarcely ever,*** casi nunca.
scarceness, scarcity [ˈskɛəsnis, -iti], *s.* escasez.
scare [skɛə], *s.* susto, sobresalto. — *v.t.* asustar, espantar; ***scare away*** o ***off,*** espantar, ahuyentar; ***to be scared stiff,*** estar muerto de miedo.
scarecrow [ˈskɛəkrou], *s.* espantapájaros, *m.inv.*; (*fig.*) espantajo; esperpento, adefesio.
scaremonger [ˈskɛəmʌŋgə], *s.* alarmista, *m.f.*
scarf (1) [skɑːf], *s.* (*pl.* **scarfs, scarves** [skɑːfs, skɑːvz]) bufanda; pañuelo (de la cabeza); ***scarf pin,*** alfiler de corbata.
scarf (2) [skɑːf], *s.* ensambladura francesa. — *v.t.* unir con ensambladura francesa.
scarfing [ˈskɑːfiŋ], *s.* ensambladura francesa.
scarfskin [ˈskɑːfskin], *s.* epidermis, *f.inv.*
scarification [skærifiˈkeiʃən], *s.* escarificación.
scarificator [ˈskærifikeitə], *s.* escarificador.
scarifier [ˈskærifaiə], *s.* escarificador.
scarify [ˈskærifai], *v.t.* escarificar; (*fig.*) criticar severamente.
scarious, scariose [ˈskɛəriəs, ˈskɛərious], *a.* (*bot.*) escarioso.
scarlatina [skɑːləˈtiːnə], *s.* escarlatina.
scarlet [ˈskɑːlit], *a.* de color escarlata, de grana; ***scarlet fever,*** escarlatina; ***scarlet oak,*** coscoja; ***scarlet runner,*** judía (inglesa).— *s.* escarlata, grana.
scarp [skɑːp], *s.* escarpa; declive. — *v.t.* escarpar. — *v.i.* hacer escarpa.
scarry [ˈskɑːri], *a.* lleno de cicatrices.
scary [ˈskɛəri], *a.* (*fam.*) medroso, asustadizo; que da miedo.
scat! [skæt], *interj.* ¡zape!
scathe [skeið], *v.t.* fustigar.
scatheless [ˈskeiðlis], *a.* ileso, indemne.
scathing [ˈskeiðiŋ], *a.* mordaz, cáustico, acerbo.
scatological [skætoˈlɔdʒikəl], *a.* (*pat.*) escatológico.
scatology [skæˈtɔlədʒi], *s.* (*pat.*) escatología.
scatter [ˈskætə], *s.* desparramamiento; dispersión. — *v.t.* esparcir, desparramar, desperdigar; dispersar. — *v.i.* desparramarse; dispersarse.
scatterbrain [ˈskætəbrein], *s.* casquivano, cabeza de chorlito.
scatterbrained [ˈskætəbreind], *a.* casquivano, atolondrado.

scattered [ˈskætəd], *a.* disipado; disperso; desparramado, esparcido; irregular, esporádico; a lo loco.
scavenge [ˈskævindʒ], *v.i.* recoger basuras (de las calles); andar buscando comida (por las calles).
scavenger [ˈskævindʒə], *s.* basurero; animal que se alimenta de carroña; ***scavenger beetle,*** escarabajo, clavicornio.
scenario [siˈnɑːriou], *s.* guión; argumento.
scend [send], *s.* arfada. — *v.i.* (*mar.*) arfar, cabecear (un buque).
scene [siːn], *s.* escena; panorama, *m.*; teatro; ***behind the scenes,*** entre bastidores; ***the scene of the crime,*** el escenario *o* teatro del crimen; ***scene-painter,*** pintor escenógrafo; ***scene-shifter,*** tramoyista, *m.f.*; ***change of scene,*** cambio de aire(s); ***to come on the scene,*** llegar (al sitio), asomar *o* presentarse (en el sitio); ***to make a scene,*** armar un escándalo, armarla; ***to set the scene,*** crear el ambiente.
sceneful [ˈsiːnful], *a.* abundante en escenas *o* imágenes.
scenery [ˈsiːnəri], *s.* paisaje; (*teat.*) decorado(s).
scenic [ˈsiːnik], *a.* escénico, pintoresco.
scenographer [siːˈnɔgrəfə], *s.* escenógrafo.
scenographical [siːnoˈgræfikəl], *a.* escenográfico.
scenography [siːˈnɔgrəfi], *s.* escenografía.
scent [sent], *s.* perfume, aroma, *m.*; olor; olfato; pista, rastro. — *v.t.* perfumar; olfatear; olerse; ***scent out,*** husmear. — *v.i.* — ***of,*** oler a.
scentless [ˈsentlis], *a.* inodoro, sin olor.
sceptic [ˈskeptik], *s.* escéptico.
sceptical [ˈskeptikəl], *a.* escéptico.
scepticism [ˈskeptisizəm], *s.* escepticismo.
sceptre [ˈseptə], *s.* cetro.
schedule [ˈʃedjuːl], *s.* lista, catálogo, inventario; apéndice; cuestionario; programa, *m.*; horario; plan; calendario; ***to be behind schedule,*** ir *o* andar atrasado *o* retrasado; ***on schedule,*** puntual, a la hora, en la fecha prevista, de acuerdo con el plan previsto; ***a tight schedule,*** un programa apretado *o* de muy poco margen. — *v.t.* inventariar, catalogar; incluir en un horario, programa *etc.*; proyectar, programar; ***scheduled for demolition,*** se prevé su demolición.
Scheldt [ʃelt]. Escalda, *m.*
schema [ˈskiːmə], *s.* cuadro, sinopsis, *f.inv.*; diagrama, *m.*; esquema, *m.*
schematic [skiːˈmætik], *a.* esquemático.
scheme [skiːm], *s.* plan, proyecto, designio; diseño, bosquejo, diagrama, *m.*, traza; modelo, esquema, *m.*, planta; sistema, *m.*, disposición, arreglo; ardid, treta, artificio; ***colour scheme,*** combinación de colores; ***rhyme scheme,*** combinación de rimas; (*arq.*) ***scheme arch,*** arco rebajado. — *v.t.* idear, proyectar; urdir, tramar. — *v.i.* formar un plan, hacer proyectos; intrigar.
schemer [ˈskiːmə], *s.* intrigante, maquinador.
schiller [ˈʃilə], *s.* (*min.*) brillo bronceado peculiar de ciertos minerales.
schism [ˈsizəm], *s.* cisma, *m.*
schismatic(al) [sizˈmætik(əl)], *a.* cismático. — (**schismatic**), *s.* cismático.
schismatize [ˈsizmətaiz], *v.t.* inducir al cisma. — *v.i.* tomar parte en un cisma.
schist [ʃist], *s.* esquisto.
schistose, schistous, schistic [ˈʃistous, -təs, -tik], *a.* esquistoso.
schnaps [ʃnæps], *s.* ginebra de Holanda.
scholar [ˈskɔlə], *s.* escolar, colegial; erudito, sabio; becario; ***classical scholar,*** clasicista, *m.f.*; ***day scholar,*** alumno externo; ***fellow scholar,*** compañero de estudios.
scholarly [ˈskɔləli], *a.* (de) erudito.
scholarship [ˈskɔləʃip], *s.* erudición; beca.
scholastic(al) [skɔˈlæstik(əl)], *a.* escolástico; ***scholastic prowess,*** capacidad para los estudios.
scholasticism [skɔˈlæstisizəm], *s.* escolasticismo.
scholiast [ˈskouliæst], *s.* escoliador.
scholium [ˈskouliəm], *s.* escolio.
school (1) [skuːl], *a.* escolar, de escuela, de colegio *etc.* — *s.* escuela; ***at school,*** en el colegio *etc.*; ***primary*** o ***elementary school,*** (*estatal*) escuela (de primera enseñanza); (*particular*) colegio; ***public school,*** colegio interno particular; ***secondary, high*** o ***grammar school,*** (*estatal*) instituto (de segunda enseñanza); (*particular*) colegio; ***university school,*** escuela, facultad; ***to go to school,*** ir al colegio *etc.* — *v.t.* instruir, enseñar; disciplinar; amaestrar.
school (2) [skuːl], *s.* banco (*de peces*), cardumen.
schoolboy [ˈskuːlbɔi], *s.* colegial.
schoolfellow [ˈskuːlfelou], *s.* compañero de colegio.
schoolgirl [ˈskuːlgəːl], *s.* colegiala.
schoolhouse [ˈskuːlhaus], *s.* escuela; colegio.
schooling [ˈskuːliŋ], *s.* instrucción; enseñanza.
schoolman [ˈskuːlmən], *s.* (*filos.*) escolástico.
schoolmaster [ˈskuːlmɑːstə], *s.* maestro de escuela; profesor de colegio.
schoolmate [ˈskuːlmeit], *s.* compañero de colegio.
schoolmistress [ˈskuːlmistris], *s.* maestra de escuela; profesora de colegio.
schoolroom [ˈskuːlruːm], *s.* (sala de) clase.
schoolteacher [ˈskuːltiːtʃə], *s.* maestro *o* maestra de escuela; profesor *o* profesora de colegio.
schooner (1) [ˈskuːnə], *s.* (*mar.*) goleta.
schooner (2) [ˈskuːnə], *s.* (*fam.*) vaso alto para cerveza.
sciatica [saiˈætikə], *s.* ciática.
sciatic(al) [saiˈætik(əl)], *a.* ciático.
science [ˈsaiəns], *s.* ciencias (exactas), *f.pl.*; física y química; ciencia; ***science fiction,*** ciencia ficción.
scientific [saiənˈtifik], *a.* científico.
scientifically [ˈsaiənˈtifikəli], *adv.* científicamente.
scientist [ˈsaiəntist], *s.* hombre de ciencia, científico.
scimitar [ˈsimitɑː], *s.* cimitarra.
scintilla [sinˈtilə], *s.* centella, chispa; partícula.
scintillate [ˈsintileit], *v.i.* chispear, centellear, destellar.
scintillation [sintiˈleiʃən], *s.* centelleo, destello.
sciolist [ˈsaiolist], *s.* semisabio, erudito a la violeta.
scion [ˈsaiən], *s.* (*agric.*) esqueje, plantón; vástago.
scioptic [saiˈɔptik], *a.* escióptico.
Scipio [ˈskipiou]. Escipión.
scirrhosity [siˈrɔsiti], *s.* calidad de escirroso.
scirrhous [ˈsirəs], *a.* (*med.*) cirroso, escirroso, endurecido.
scirrhus [ˈsirəs], *s.* (*med.*) cirro, escirro; tumor endurecido.
scissel [ˈsisəl], *s.* desperdicios (*m.pl.*), desechos (*m.pl.*) *o* recortes (*m.pl.*) de metal; escoria.
scission [ˈsiʃən], *s.* corte, división, partición, separación.
scissor [ˈsizə], *v.t., v.i.* cortar(se) con tijeras.
scissors [ˈsizəz], *s.pl.* tijeras, *f.pl.*
scissure [ˈsiʃjə], *s.* cisura, cortadura, hendidura; cisma, *m.*, escisión.
sceroma [skliˈroumə], *s.* escleroma, *m.*
sclerosis [skliˈrousis], *s.* esclerosis, *f.inv.*
sclerotic [skliˈrɔtik], *a.* escleroso, esclerótico. — *s.* esclerótica.
sclerotica [skliˈrɔtikə], *s.* esclerótica.
sclerotitis [skleroˈtaitis], *s.* esclerotitis, *f.inv.*
scoff [skɔf], *s.* mofa, befa. — *v.i.* mofarse, burlarse; ***scoff at,*** mofarse de, hacer befa de.
scoffer [ˈskɔfə], *s.* burlón, mofador.
scoffingly [ˈskɔfiŋli], *adv.* con mofa y escarnio.
scold [skould], *s.* regañona. — *v.t., v.i.* regañar.
scolding [ˈskouldiŋ], *s.* regaño, trepe, reprensión; ***scolding match,*** pelotera.
scoliosis [skouliˈousis], *s.* escoliosis, *f.inv.*
scollop [ˈskɔləp], [SCALLOP].

scolopendra [skɔlo'pendrə], *s.* escolopendra, ciempiés, *m.inv.*
scomber ['skɔmbə], *s.* (*ict.*) escombro.
sconce (1) [skɔns], *s.* cobertizo, saledizo; (*fort.*) defensa, baluarte, fortín. — *v.t.* fortificar con baluarte.
sconce (2) [skɔns], *s.* farolillo, linterna, linterna sorda; candelabro de pared; (*fam.*) sentido, juicio, seso; (*fam.*) cabeza.
sconce (3) [skɔns], *s.* (*univ.*) multa por ligera travesura; anaquel fijo. — *v.t.* multar.
scone [skɔn, skoun], *s.* bollo escocés.
scoop [sku:p], *s.* pala; paleta; achicador; cuchara; reportaje sensacional que publica un periódico antes que los demás. — *v.t.* sacar con pala *o* cuchara; adelantarse (a alguien) en la publicación de una noticia; ***scoop out,*** excavar; achicar; ***scoop up,*** recoger rápidamente *o* de un golpe (*naipes etc.*).
scooper ['sku:pə], *s.* achicador, vaciador; cavador.
scoot [sku:t], *v.i.* (*fam.*) largarse.
scooter ['sku:tə], *s.* patín; patineta; vespa.
scope [skoup], *s.* alcance, magnitud, envergadura; ***free*** o ***full scope,*** ancho campo, rienda suelta; ***to have free scope,*** tener carta blanca; ***to give scope to,*** ofrecer posibilidades a; ***there is scope for,*** hay campo para; ***it is within his scope,*** está dentro de su alcance *o* de sus posibilidades; tiene capacidad para ello.
scorbutic [skɔ:'bju:tik], *a.* escorbútico.
scorch [skɔ:tʃ], *v.t.* chamuscar; quemar, abrasar, agostar; curtir mucho. — *v.i.* quemarse, agostarse, abrasarse (*las plantas*); (*fam.*) ***scorch along,*** ir como un relámpago.
scorcher ['skɔ:tʃə], *s.* (*fam.*) día de calorazo, *m.*
scorching ['skɔ:tʃiŋ], *a.* abrasador, achicharrante; (*fig.*) acerbo, mordaz.
score [skɔ:], *s.* muesca, incisión; entalladura; raya; (*dep.*) tanteo; (*mús.*) partitura; (*número*) veinte, veintena; ***by the score,*** a montones; ***to keep*** (***the***) ***score,*** (*dep.*) tantear; (*fig.*) llevar la cuenta; ***on that score,*** a ese respecto; ***on the score of,*** en cuanto a; con motivo de; ***to pay off*** o ***settle old scores,*** ajustar *o* saldar cuentas viejas; ***scoreboard,*** marcador; ***what's the score?*** ¿cómo están? ¿cómo estamos? — *v.t.* hacer muescas en; rayar; (*dep.*) marcar (*un tanto* o *un gol*); (*dep.*) ganar (*puntos*); (*dep.*) apuntar; (*mús.*) orquestar, instrumentar. — *v.i.* — (***heavily***), ganarse (muchos) puntos, apuntarse (muchos) tantos; sacar (muy) buena(s) nota(s); ***score off s.o.,*** llevar la ventaja a alguien.
scorer ['skɔ:rə], *s.* marcador; tanteador, goleador.
scoria ['skɔ:riə], *s.* escoria.
scoriaceous [skɔri'eiʃəs], *a.* escoriáceo.
scorification [skɔrifi'keiʃən], *s.* escorificación.
scoriform ['skɔrifɔ:m], *a.* escoriforme.
scorify ['skɔrifai], *v.t.* escorificar.
scoring ['skɔ:riŋ], *s.* rayado; orquestación.
scorn [skɔ:n], *s.* desdén, desprecio. — *v.t.* desdeñar, despreciar; ***scorn to,*** negarse orgullosamente a, no dignarse + *inf.*
scorner ['skɔ:nə], *s.* desdeñador, despreciador.
scornful ['skɔ:nful], *a.* desdeñoso, despreciativo.
scornfulness ['skɔ:nfulnis], *s.* desdén, desprecio; (lo) desdeñoso.
Scorpio ['skɔ:piou]. Escorpión.
scorpion ['skɔ:piən], *s.* escorpión, alacrán; (*bib.*) escorpión; ***scorpion grass,*** alacranera.
Scot [skɔt], *s.* escocés, *m.*, escocesa, *f.*
scot [skɔt], *s.* escote; ***to go scot-free,*** no pagar nada; librarse totalmente, salir impune.
Scotch [skɔtʃ], *a.* (*whisky*) escocés; ***Scotch thistle,*** cardo borriquero. — *s.* whisky escocés.
scotch (1) [skɔtʃ], *s.* calza, cuña. — *v.t.* calzar.
scotch (2) [skɔtʃ], *v.t.* (*fig.*) dar al traste con.
Scotchman ['skɔtʃmən], [SCOTSMAN].
scoter ['skoutə], *s.* (*orn.*) ánade negro.
scotia ['skouʃə], *a.* (*arq.*) escocia, nacela.
Scotism ['skoutizəm], *s.* escotismo.
Scotist ['skoutist], *s.* escotista, *m.f.*
Scotland ['skɔtlənd]. Escocia; ***Scotland Yard,*** cuartel central de la policía metropolitana de Londres.
scotoma [sko'toumə], *s.* (*med.*) escotoma, *m.*
scotomy ['skɔtəmi], *s.* (*med.*) escotomía.
Scotsman ['skɔtsmən], *s.* (*pl.* **-men** [-men]) escocés, *m.*
Scotswoman ['skɔtswumən], *s.* (*pl.* **-women** [-wimin]) escocesa, *f.*
scottie ['skɔti], *s.* terrier escocés.
Scottish ['skɔtiʃ], *a.* escocés. — *s.* escocés (*lengua*), *m.*
scoundrel ['skaundrəl], *s.* bribón; pícaro, granuja; sinvergüenza, pillo.
scoundrelly ['skaundrəli], *a.* pícaro.
scour (1) [skauə], *v.t.* refregar, restregar.
scour (2) [skauə], *v.t.* — ***the country,*** recorrer, explorar el terreno, batir el monte; ***scour for,*** recorrer en busca de. — *v.i.* — ***about in search of,*** buscar por todas partes.
scourer ['skauərə], *s.* estropajo.
scourge [skə:dʒ], *s.* azote, flagelo; disciplina; plaga; ***the Scourge of God,*** el azote de Dios (Atila). — *v.t.* azotar, flagelar; asolar.
scourger ['skə:dʒə], *s.* disciplinante, flagelante.
scouring ['skauəriŋ], *s.* (el) refregar *etc.*
scout (1) [skaut], *s.* (*mil.*) explorador, escucha, batidor; ***boy scout,*** explorador. — *v.i.* (*mil.*) explorar, reconocer.
scout (2) [skaut], *v.t.* rechazar con desdén; reírse de, burlarse de, escarnecer.
scoutmaster ['skautma:stə], *s.* jefe de exploradores.
scow [skau], *s.* lanchón, gabarra.
scowl [skaul], *s.* mirada torva *o* ceñuda. — *v.i.* mirar ceñuda *o* torvamente.
scowling ['skauliŋ], *s.* ceño.
scowlingly ['skauliŋli], *adv.* con ceño.
scrabble [skræbl], *s.* garabato(s). — *v.t.* garabatear. — *v.i.* garabatear; ***scrabble for,*** porfiar por coger.
scrag [skræg], *s.* pescuezo. — *v.t.* torcer el pescuezo a.
scragginess ['skræginis], *s.* escualidez; (lo) flacucho.
scraggy, scragged ['skrægi, 'skrægid], *a.* áspero, escabroso, desigual; descarnado, flacucho.
scramble [skræmbl], *s.* arrebatiña, lucha precipitada; ***scramble up,*** subida precipitada. — *v.t.* revolver; ***scrambled eggs,*** huevos revueltos, *m.pl.* — *v.i.* (*aer.*) prepararse inmediatamente para despegar; ***scramble over,*** pasar precipitadamente por encima de; ***scramble over*** o ***for,*** disputarse precipitadamente; ***scramble up,*** trepar precipitadamente a; subir gateando a.
scrap (1) [skræp], *s.* pizca, fragmento; (*pl.*) sobras, *f.pl.*, desperdicios, *m.pl.*; ***not a scrap,*** ni pizca; ***scrap book,*** álbum de recortes; ***scrap heap,*** montón de deshechos; ***to throw on to the scrap heap,*** desechar, tirar; ***scrap iron,*** hierro viejo, chatarra; (*fig.*) ***scrap of paper,*** papel mojado. — *v.t.* suprimir, desechar; desguazar (*un barco*).
scrap (2) [skræp], *s.* (*fam.*) pelea, zipizape. — *v.i.* (*fam.*) pelearse, reñir.
scrape [skreip], *s.* raspadura, raedura; ruido de raspar; aprieto, apuro, lío. — *v.t.* raspar, raer; restregar (*los pies*); rascar (*un instrumento*); (ar)rebañar (*un plato*); ***scrape acquaintance with,*** conseguir (a duras penas) conocer; ***scrape off,*** quitar raspando; ***scrape together*** o ***up,*** reunir con mucho trabajo, conseguir a duras penas reunir. — *v.i.* — ***against,*** rozar; ***scrape along,*** ir tirando (de mala manera); ***scrape through,*** aprobar por los pelos *o* de mala manera (*un examen*).

scraper [ˈskreipə], *s.* raspador, raedera; ***shoe-scraper,*** limpiabarros, *m.inv.*; (*fam.*) ***violin-scraper,*** rascatripas, *m.f.inv.*

scraping [ˈskreipiŋ], *s.* (el) raspar *etc.*; (*pl.*) raspaduras, *f.pl.*

scrappy [ˈskræpi], *a.* deslavazado, hecho a retazos.

scratch (1) [skrætʃ], *a.* improvisado; reunido precipitadamente.

scratch (2) [skrætʃ], *s.* rasguño, arañazo; raya; (*dep.*) línea de partida; ***to start from scratch,*** empezar desde el principio *o* desde la nada, empezar sin nada; (***not***) ***to be*** o (***not***) ***to come up to scratch,*** (no) estar en condiciones; (no) estar a la altura de las circunstancias; (no) dar la talla. — *v.t.* rasguñar, arañar; rascar; rayar (*un cristal etc.*); escarbar (*la tierra*); (*fam.*) suprimir, borrar; ***scratch out,*** tachar; ***scratch s.o.'s eyes out,*** sacarle a alguien los ojos (con las uñas). — *v.i.* (*pluma*) raspear; (*gallina*) escarbar. — **scratch o.s.,** *v.r.* (*sin querer*) arañarse; (*adrede*) rascarse.

scratchingly [ˈskrætʃiŋli], *adv.* rascando, arañando.

scrawl [skrɔ:l], *s.* garabatos, *m.pl.* — *v.t.*, *v.i.* escribajear, garabatear.

scrawler [ˈskrɔ:lə], *s.* garabateador.

scrawniness [ˈskrɔ:ninis], *s.* escualidez.

scrawny [ˈskrɔ:ni], *a.* escuálido, flacucho.

scream [skri:m], *s.* grito, chillido; (*fam.*) ***he's a scream,*** es graciosísimo. — *v.t.* gritar, vociferar. — *v.i.* gritar, chillar, vociferar.

screaming [ˈskri:miŋ], *s.* gritos, *m.pl.*, griterío, chillidos, *m.pl.*

scree [skri:], *s.* (*geol.*) ladera cubierta de piedra movediza.

screech [skri:tʃ], *s.* chillido; ***screech hawk,*** chotacabras, *f.inv.*; ***screech owl,*** autillo, estrige. — *v.i.* chillar, dar chillidos; ***the car screeched to a halt,*** el coche paró con gran estrépito de frenos.

screechy [ˈskri:tʃi], *a.* chillón, agudo, estridente.

screed [skri:d], *s.* tirada larga y tendida; cartapacio.

screen [skri:n], *s.* pantalla; biombo; mampara; tamiz; cortina; (*foto.*) retícula; ***safety screen,*** pantalla de seguridad; ***screen test,*** prueba cinematográfica *o* para el cine. — *v.t.* ocultar, encubrir, tapar; proteger, abrigar; tamizar; proyectar; investigar.

screenings [ˈskri:niŋz], *s.pl.* desperdicios, *m.pl.*, granzas, *f.pl.*

screw [skru:], *s.* tornillo; rosca; tuerca; espiral, *f.*; hélice, *f.*; (*fam.*) sueldo; ***he has a screw loose,*** le falta un tornillo; ***to put the screw(s) on,*** apretar a alguien los tornillos (las clavijas); ***screw bolt,*** perno roscado; ***screw-eyes,*** armellas, *f.pl.*; ***screw head,*** cabeza de tornillo; ***screw jack,*** gato, cric; ***screw plate, screw stock,*** terraja; ***screw wrench,*** llave inglesa, desvolvedor. — *v.t.* atornillar; ***screw down,*** fijar con tornillos; ***screw in,*** hacer entrar atornillando; ***screw out,*** desatornillar; ***screw up,*** tensar; ***screw up one's courage,*** hacer de tripas corazón.

screwdriver [ˈskru:draivə], *s.* destornillador.

screwy [ˈskru:i], *a.* (*fam.*) chiflado, chalado.

scribble [skribl], *s.* garabato. — *v.t.*, *v.i.* garabatear, escribajear.

scribbler [ˈskriblə], *s.* mal escritor, escritor de poca fama.

scribbling pad [ˈskribliŋ pæd], *s.* bloc (de escribir).

scribe [skraib], *s.* amanuense, escriba, *m.* — *v.t.* rayar, marcar, puntear; (*carp.*) juntar, ajustar, ensamblar, corrocar, esgarabotar.

scrim [skrim], *s.* tejido muy fuerte de algodón *o* lino usado en la tapicería de muebles.

scrimmage [ˈskrimidʒ], *s.* arrebatiña, zipizape.

scrimp [skrimp], *v.t.* escatimar. — *v.i.* — ***and scrape,*** cicatear; ***we've got to scrimp and scrape,*** tenemos que hacer muchas economías.

scrimping [ˈskrimpiŋ], *a.* mezquino, escatimoso.

scrimpy [ˈskrimpi], *a.* (*fam.*) muy pequeño, muy estrecho.

scrimshaw [ˈskrimʃɔ:], *v.t.*, *v.i.* decorar (marfil, conchas etc.) con tallados, dibujos de color *etc.*

scrip [skrip], *s.* cédula; (*com.*) vale, pagaré.

script [skript], *s.* letra (cursiva); (*for.*) escritura; manuscrito; guión (*de cine etc.*); ***script-writer,*** guionista, *m.f.*

scriptural [ˈskriptʃərəl], *a.* bíblico; (*for.*) escrituario.

scripture [ˈskriptʃə], *s.* Sagrada Escritura; (*clase de*) Historia Sagrada.

scrivener [ˈskrivənə], *s.* (*ant.*) escribano; escribiente.

scrofula [ˈskrɔfjulə], *s.* escrófula.

scrofulism [ˈskrɔfjulizəm], *s.* escrofulismo.

scrofulous [ˈskrɔfjuləs], *a.* escrofuloso.

scroll [skroul], *s.* rollo (de papel *o* de pergamino); (*arq.*) voluta; ***scroll-saw,*** sierra de contornear.

scrotal [ˈskroutəl], *a.* escrotal.

scrotocele [ˈskroutosi:l], *s.* escrotocele, *f.*

scrotum [ˈskroutəm], *s.* escroto.

scrounge [skraundʒ], *s.* (*fam.*) ***to be on the scrounge,*** andar de gorra, andar sableando, andar pegando sablazos. — *v.t.* sacar a base de gorronería *o* de sablazos; birlar. — *v.i.* vivir de gorra, gorronear, sablear.

scrub (1) [skrʌb], *s.* fregado. — *v.t.* fregar, restregar; (*fam.*) suprimir.

scrub (2) [skrʌb], *s.* maleza, matas *f.pl.*, monte bajo.

scrubbing [ˈskrʌbiŋ], *s.* fregado; ***scrubbing-brush,*** cepillo para *o* de fregar.

scrubby [ˈskrʌbi], *a.* (*terreno*) cubierto de maleza.

scruff [skrʌf], *s.* pellejo (***of the neck,*** del cerviguillo).

scruffy [ˈskrʌfi], *a.* desaliñado, desaseado, desastrado.

scrum, scrummage [skrʌm, ˈskrʌmidʒ], *s.* (*rugby*) mêlée, *f.*

scrumptious [ˈskrʌmpʃəs], *a.* (*fam.*) exquisito, delicioso.

scruple [skru:pl], *s.* escrúpulo; ***to have no scruples about,*** no tener escrúpulos acerca de; no tener reparo(s) en. — *v.i.* tener escrúpulos, reparos *o* dudas; ***scruple to,*** dudar (por cuestión de escrúpulos) en.

scrupulous [ˈskru:pjuləs], *a.* escrupuloso; meticuloso.

scrupulousness, scrupulosity [ˈskru:pjuləsnis, skru:pjuˈlɔsiti], *s.* escrupulosidad; meticulosidad.

scrutineer [skru:tiˈniə], *s.* escudriñador; escrutador.

scrutinize [ˈskru:tinaiz], *v.t.* escudriñar; escrutar; examinar.

scrutinous [ˈskru:tinəs], *a.* penetrante.

scrutiny [ˈskru:tini], *s.* escrutinio; examen.

scud [skʌd], *s.* carrera rápida; nubes impulsadas por el viento, *f.pl.*; espuma (del mar). — *v.i.* correr (ante el viento), deslizarse rápidamente; (*mar.*) ***scud before the wind,*** correr viento en popa.

scuff [skʌf], *v.t.* hacer una rozadura a.

scuffle [skʌfl], *s.* zipizape, refriega. — *v.i.* armar zipizapes.

scull [skʌl], *s.* espadilla; remo ligero; bote pequeño. — *v.t.* cinglar. — *v.i.* remar con espadilla.

scullboat [ˈskʌlbout], *s.* barquillo, botecito; (*mar.*) serení.

sculler [ˈskʌlə], *s.* bote de espadilla; remero de bote; cinglador.

scullery [ˈskʌləri], *s.* (cuarto del) fregadero; trascocina.

scullion [ˈskʌljən], *s.* marmitón, galopín de cocina, pinche; sollastre; ***scullion wench,*** fregona.

sculper [ˈskʌlpə], *s.* buril, cincel.

sculpin [ˈskʌlpin], *s.* (*ict.*) coto espinoso.

sculptor [ˈskʌlptə], *s.* escultor.

sculptress [ˈskʌlptris], *s.* escultora.

sculptural [ˈskʌlptʃərəl], *a.* escultórico.

sculpture [ˈskʌlptʃə], *s.* escultura. — *v.t.* esculpir.

sculpturesque [skʌlptʃəˈresk], *a.* escultural.
scum [skʌm], *s.* hez, *f.*; espuma; natorra; chusma, canalla; ***the scum of the earth,*** la hez. — *v.t.* despumar; desnatar.
scumble [skʌmbl], *s.* unión de colores, glacis, *m.inv.* — *v.t.* (*pint.*) dar glacis a.
scummy [ˈskʌmi], *a.* espumoso; cubierto de escoria; (*fam.*) ***scummy people,*** gente de medio pelo.
scupper [ˈskʌpə], *s.* (*mar.*) imbornal, embornal; ***scupper-hole,*** imbornal, embornal; ***scupper-nails,*** estoperoles, *m.pl.* — *v.t.* hundir (*un barco*).
scurf [skəːf], *s.* caspa; costra.
scurfiness [ˈskəːfinis], *s.* (lo) casposo; (lo) costroso.
scurfy [ˈskəːfi], *a.* casposo; costroso.
scurrility, scurrilousness [skʌˈriliti, ˈskʌriləsnis], *s.* procacidad, obscenidad, (lo) procaz *u* obsceno.
scurrilous [ˈskʌriləs], *a.* procaz, obsceno.
scurry [ˈskʌri], *s.* carrera precipitada. — *v.i.* correr (con pasitos menudos); ***scurry away,*** escabullirse.
scurvied [ˈskəːvid], *a.* escorbútico.
scurviness [ˈskəːvinis], *s.* ruindad, vileza.
scurvy [ˈskəːvi], *a.* vil, ruin. — *s.* escorbuto; ***scurvy grass,*** coclearia.
scutate [ˈskjuːteit], *a.* (*zool.*) escutiforme; (*bot.*) escuteliforme.
scutch [skʌtʃ], *s.* estopa; ***scutch blade,*** agramadera. — *v.t.* agramar, tascar, espadar, espadillar (*lino etc.*).
scutcheon [ˈskʌtʃən], *s.* escudo de armas; ***a blot on one's scutcheon,*** baldón.
scutellate [ˈskjuːteleit], *a.* escutelado.
scutiform [ˈskjuːtifɔːm], *a.* escutiforme.
scuttle (1) [skʌtl], *s.* cubo (de *o* del carbón).
scuttle (2) [skʌtl], *s.* carrera, fuga precipitada. — *v.i.* (echar a) correr; ***scuttle away,*** escabullirse.
scuttle (3) [skʌtl], *s.* (*naut.*) escotilla. — *v.t.* (*naut.*) barrenar, dar barreno a; agujerear el fondo de.
scythe [saið], *s.* guadaña. — *v.t.* guadañar.
scythed [saiðd], *a.* armado de guadaña.
Scythian [ˈsiðiən], *a., s.* escita, *m.f.*
sea [siː], *s.* mar, *m.f.*; (*fig.*) ***all at sea,*** desorientado, despistado, desconcertado; ***at sea,*** en el mar, embarcado; ***beyond the sea,*** allende los mares; ***by sea,*** por mar, en barco; ***choppy sea,*** mar picada; ***to go to sea,*** hacerse marinero; (*fam.*) ***to be half seas over,*** estar trompa, *inv.*; ***heavy sea,*** mar gruesa; ***on the high seas,*** en alta mar; ***high (-running) sea,*** mar arbolada; ***to put to sea,*** hacerse a la mar; ***sea bass,*** serrano; ***sea bird,*** ave marina; ***sea biscuit,*** bizcocho (duro); ***sea-borne,*** transportado por mar; ***sea bream,*** besugo; ***sea breeze,*** brisa de mar; ***sea brief,*** carta marítima; ***sea calf,*** becerro marino; ***sea captain,*** capitán de mar; ***sea cow,*** vaca marina, manatí; ***sea dog,*** lobo de mar; ***sea eagle,*** águila pescadora; ***sea fight,*** combate naval; ***sea fowl,*** ave marina; ***sea front,*** paseo marítimo; ***sea-girt,*** rodeado *o* cercado por el mar; ***sea green,*** verdemar; ***sea hog,*** puerco marino; ***sea horse,*** hipocampo; ***sea kale,*** berza marina; ***to get one's sea legs,*** acostumbrarse a la vida de barco *o* de a bordo; ***sea level,*** nivel del mar; ***sea maid, sea maiden,*** sirena; ***sea mew,*** gaviota; ***sea mist,*** bruma (marítima); ***sea nettle,*** ortiga de mar; ***sea ooze,*** cieno de mar; ***sea otter,*** nutria marina; (*pint.*) ***sea piece,*** marina; ***sea pool,*** laguna de agua salada, albufera; ***sea power,*** potencia naval; ***sea raven,*** cormorán; ***sea room,*** sitio para maniobrar; ***sea rover,*** corsario, pirata, *m.*; ***sea serpent,*** serpiente de mar, *f.*; ***sea shanty,*** canción marinera; ***sea shark,*** tiburón; ***sea-tossed,*** batido por el mar; ***sea urchin,*** erizo de mar; ***sea wall,*** dique (marítimo); ***sea water,*** agua de(l) mar; ***sea wolf,*** lobo marino.
seaboard [ˈsiːbɔːd], *a.* costanero, costero. — *s.* costa, litoral.
seafarer [ˈsiːfɛərə], *s.* navegante; marinero.
seafaring [ˈsiːfɛəriŋ], *a.* marinero. — *s.* vida marinera.
seafood [ˈsiːfuːd], *s.* pescado; (*Am.*) [FISH]; mariscos, *m.pl.*
seagoing [ˈsiːgouiŋ], *a.* de alta mar.
seagull [ˈsiːgʌl], *s.* gaviota.
seal (1) [siːl], *s.* (*zool.*) foca. — *v.i.* cazar focas.
seal (2) [siːl], *s.* sello; precinto; ***great seal,*** sello real; ***to set one's seal on,*** poner su sello a. — *v.t.* sellar; cerrar; precintar; lacrar; (*fig.*) decidir; ***seal off,*** separar (herméticamente); ***seal up,*** cerrar (herméticamente).
sealer (1) [ˈsiːlə], *s.* cazador de focas.
sealer (2) [ˈsiːlə], *s.* sellador.
sealing wax [ˈsiːliŋ wæks], *s.* lacre.
sealskin [ˈsiːlskin], *s.* piel de foca.
seam [siːm], *s.* costura; junta, juntura; arruga; (*cir.*) sutura; filón, veta; ***to burst at the seams,*** descoserse; (*fig.*) ***to be bursting at the seams,*** estar estallando; (*mar.*) ***to pay the seams,*** embrear las costuras. — *v.t.* coser; juntar; arrugar (*la cara*).
seaman [ˈsiːmən], *s.* marinero; ***able-bodied seaman,*** marinero de primera.
seamanlike [ˈsiːmənlaik], *a.* marinero, de buen marinero.
seamanly [ˈsiːmənli], *a.* marino, marinesco.
seamanship [ˈsiːmənʃip], *s.* marinería, (pericia) náutica.
seamless [ˈsiːmlis], *a.* sin costura; ***seamless stockings,*** medias sin costura, *f.pl.*
seamstress [ˈsemstris], *s.* costurera.
seamy [ˈsiːmi], *a.* miserable, vil; (*fig.*) ***the seamy side,*** el revés de la medalla.
sean [SEINE].
séance [ˈseiɔns], *s.* sesión de espiritismo.
seaplane [ˈsiːplein], *s.* hidroavión.
seaport [ˈsiːpɔːt], *s.* puerto de mar.
sear (1) [siə], *a.* seco, ajado, agostado, marchito (*hojas, flores, plantas*). — *v.t.* abrasar; agostar; secar, marchitar; chamuscar; ***searing pain,*** dolor punzante.
sear (2) [siə], *s.* (*arma.*) fiador que mantiene el gatillo en seguro; ***sear spring,*** muelle real.
search [səːtʃ], *s.* busca, búsqueda; registro; reconocimiento; ***in search of,*** en busca de; ***to make a search,*** practicar un registro; ***right of search,*** derecho de visita; ***search party,*** equipo de búsqueda; ***search warrant,*** mandamiento judicial de registro, auto *u* orden de registro. — *v.t.* buscar; registrar; explorar, examinar. — *v.i.* buscar; (*cir.*) tentar, sondar; ***search after*** o ***for,*** buscar; ***search for weapons,*** registrar en busca de armas; ***search into,*** investigar.
searcher [ˈsəːtʃə], *s.* buscador; registrador; (*artill.*) gato de registro; (*cir.*) explorador, sonda, tienta; (*ópt.*) buscador.
searching [ˈsəːtʃiŋ], *a.* penetrante, escrutador; agudo; que exige mucho, exigente; hecho a fondo, exhaustivo. — *s.* busca.
searchlight [ˈsəːtʃlait], *s.* reflector; foco.
seascape [ˈsiːskeip], *s.* marina.
seashell [ˈsiːʃel], *s.* concha (marina).
seashore [ˈsiːʃɔː], *s.* playa, orilla del mar.
seasick [ˈsiːsik], *a.* mareado; ***to be seasick,*** estar mareado; marearse.
seasickness [ˈsiːsiknis], *s.* mareo.
seaside [ˈsiːsaid], *s.* playa; orilla del mar; ***seaside resort,*** sitio de veraneo en la costa, playa; ***to go to the seaside,*** ir (a veranear) a una playa.
season [ˈsiːzən], *s.* estación (del año); tiempo; época; temporada; ***the season,*** (*vida social, teatro, deportes*) la temporada; ***at this season of the year,*** en esta época (del año); ***close season,*** veda; (*fig.*) ***in due season,*** en su momento; ***the four seasons,*** las cuatro estaciones; ***it's not in season, it's out of season,*** (ahora) no es temporada; ***fruit in season,*** fruta del tiempo; ***with***

the compliments of the Season, deseándole felices Pascuas *o* Navidades; ***at the height of the season,*** en plena temporada; (*fig.*) ***out of season,*** fuera de sazón; ***open season,*** tiempo de caza; (*com.*) ***slack season,*** temporada floja; ***season ticket,*** (billete de) abono. — *v.t.* sazonar, condimentar; curar (*madera etc.*); acostumbrar; templar. — *v.i.* curarse.

seasonable [ˈsi:zənəbl], *a.* propio de la estación; oportuno.

seasonal [ˈsi:zənəl], *a.* de acuerdo con la estación *o* con la época del año.

seasoned [ˈsi:zənd], *a.* (*tropas*) aguerridas.

seasoning [ˈsi:zəniŋ], *s.* aderezo, condimento; cura (*de la madera*); (*fig.*) ajilimójili.

seat [si:t], *s.* asiento; silla; (*teat.*) localidad; (*en el Parlamento*) escaño; residencia; sede (*del gobierno*); fondillos (*del pantalón*), *m.pl.*; (*fig.*) ***to take a back seat,*** hacer un papel secundario, pintar poco; ***country seat,*** casa solariega; ***seat back,*** respaldo; ***seat belt,*** cinturón de seguridad; ***seat of learning,*** centro de erudición, universidad; ***to have a seat in Parliament,*** ser diputado. — *v.t.* sentar; asentar; poner asiento a; tener asientos *o* cabida para; ***be seated,*** sentarse; estar sentado.

seater [ˈsi:tə], *a.*, *s.* ***two-seater (car),*** (coche de) dos plazas; ***two-seater (plane),*** (avión) biplaza.

seating [ˈsi:tiŋ], *s.* asientos, *m.pl.*; ***seating capacity,*** cabida (de personas sentadas).

seaward [ˈsi:wəd], *a.* del lado del mar; dirigido hacia el mar.

seawards [ˈsi:wədz], *adv.* hacia el mar.

seaway [ˈsi:wei], *s.* (*mar.*) ruta marítima.

seaweed [ˈsi:wi:d], *s.* alga(s).

seaworthiness [ˈsi:wə:ðinis], *s.* buen estado (de una embarcación).

seaworthy [ˈsi:wə:ði], *a.* marinero, en buen estado para hacerse a la mar.

sebaceous [siˈbeiʃəs], *a.* sebáceo, seboso.

sebacic [siˈbæsik], *a.* sebácico; ***sebacic acid,*** ácido sebácico.

sebate [ˈsi:beit], *s.* sebato.

secant [ˈsi:kənt, ˈsekənt], *a.*, *s.* secante.

secede [siˈsi:d], *v.i.* separarse.

seceder [siˈsi:də], *s.* separatista, *m.f.*

secession [siˈseʃən], *s.* secesión, separación.

secessionism [siˈseʃənizəm], *s.* separatismo.

secessionist [siˈseʃənist], *a.*, *s.* secesionista, *m.f.*, separatista, *m.f.*

seclude [siˈklu:d], *v.t.* aislar. — **seclude o.s.,** *v.r.* aislarse.

secluded [siˈklu:did], *a.* aislado, apartado, retirado, solitario. — *p.p.* [SECLUDE].

seclusion [siˈklu:ʒən], *s.* apartamiento, aislamiento, retiro.

second (1) [ˈsekənd], *a.* segundo; otro; ***second best,*** segundo; de *o* en segundo lugar; ***to come off second best,*** salir perdiendo; ***second class,*** segunda clase; ***second cousin,*** primo segundo; ***to play second fiddle,*** hacer un papel secundario; ***second-hand,*** de segunda mano, de lance; ***second-hand bookseller,*** librero de viejo; ***second-hand bookshop,*** librería de viejo; ***second-hand clothes,*** ropa de segunda mano; ***second-hand information,*** informes de segunda mano, *m.pl.*; ***to be second in command,*** ser el segundo de a bordo; ***second lieutenant,*** alférez; ***to be second nature,*** ser innato; ***second-rate,*** de segunda (clase *o* categoría); ***second sight,*** doble vista, intuición, clarividencia; ***second son,*** segundón; ***he's had second thoughts,*** (se) lo ha pensado mejor; ***on second thoughts,*** pensándolo mejor; ***to be second to none,*** no tener que envidiarle nada a nadie, ser como el mejor; ***the second largest town,*** la mayor ciudad después de la primera. — *adv.* en segundo lugar; ***to travel second,*** viajar en segunda. — *s.* segundo; (*mús.*) segundo; (*dep.*) segundo, padrino; (*pl.*, *com.*) artículos de segunda calidad *o* con algún desperfecto, *m.pl.*; ***to come in second,*** llegar el segundo; ***to come a poor second,*** llegar el segundo a gran distancia del primero. — *v.t.* secundar, apoyar.

second (2) [ˈsekənd], *s.* (*tiempo*) segundo; (*reloj.*) ***second hand,*** segundero; ***just a second!*** ¡un momentito nada más!

second (3) [siˈkɔnd], *v.t.* trasladar temporalmente.

secondariness [ˈsekəndərinis], *s.* propiedad de ser secundario; (lo) secundario.

secondary [ˈsekəndəri], *a.* secundario; subalterno, subordinado; (*elec.*, *fís. etc.*) secundario; (*elec.*) ***secondary battery,*** acumulador; ***secondary school,*** colegio (de segunda enseñanza); instituto. — *s.* lugarteniente, diputado, delegado, subalterno; (*astron.*) círculo secundario; (*orn.*) pluma grande de la segunda articulación; planeta secundario, satélite; (*ent.*) ala posterior.

seconder [ˈsekəndə], *s.* el que apoya *o* secunda una proposición.

secondly [ˈsekəndli], *adv.* en segundo lugar.

secrecy [ˈsi:krisi], *s.* secreto; reserva, discreción; ***in (strict) secrecy,*** en (el mayor) secreto; ***to swear s.o. to secrecy,*** exigirle a alguien promesa de guardar el secreto; ***to be sworn to secrecy,*** haber dado su palabra de guardar el secreto.

secret [ˈsi:krit], *a.* secreto; clandestino; oculto; ***top secret,*** de sumo secreto. — *s.* secreto; ***in secret,*** en secreto; ***to be in the secret,*** estar en el secreto *o* en el ajo; ***to keep a secret,*** guardar un secreto; ***an open secret,*** un secreto a voces.

secretarial [sekriˈtɛəriəl], *a.* de *o* para secretario(s), secretaria(s).

secretariat [sekriˈtɛəriət], *s.* secretaría; secretariado.

secretary [ˈsekrətəri], *s.* secretario; secretaria; ***private secretary,*** secretario *o* secretaria particular; (*orn.*) ***secretary bird,*** secretario, serpentario; ***Secretary-General,*** Secretario General; ***Secretary of State,*** Ministro de Estado; (*Am.*) Ministro de Asuntos Exteriores; ***Secretary of State for the Home Department*** o ***Home Secretary,*** Ministro del Interior.

secretaryship [ˈsekrətəriʃip], *s.* secretaría, cargo de secretario.

secrete [siˈkri:t], *v.t.* esconder, ocultar; (*med.*) segregar, secretar.

secretion [siˈkri:ʃən], *s.* (*med.*) secreción.

secretive [ˈsi:kritiv], *a.* reservado, reservón, poco comunicativo; sigiloso; ***to be secretive about,*** no soltar prenda de.

secretiveness [ˈsi:kritivnis], *s.* (lo) reservado *etc.*

secretly [ˈsi:kritli], *adv.* en secreto, con mucho secreto; ***he was secretly pleased about it,*** en el fondo se alegraba (de ello).

secretness [ˈsi:kritnis], *s.* secreto.

secretory [siˈkri:təri], *a.* secretorio.

sect [sekt], *s.* secta.

sectant [ˈsektənt], *s.* (*mat.*) sectante.

sectarian [sekˈtɛəriən], *a.*, *s.* sectario.

sectarianism [sekˈtɛəriənizəm], *s.* sectarismo.

sectary [ˈsektəri], *a.*, *s.* sectario.

sectile [ˈsektail], *a.* sectil.

section [ˈsekʃən], *s.* sección; sector; zona; tramo (*de una vía, de una carretera*). — *v.t.* tajar, cortar.

sectional [ˈsekʃənəl], *a.* seccional; fabricado en secciones; regional, local.

sectionalism [ˈsekʃənəlizəm], *s.* regionalismo.

sector [ˈsektə], *s.* sector.

secular [ˈsekjulə], *a.* secular; seglar. — *s.* seglar.

secularity [sekjuˈlæriti], *s.* secularidad.

secularization [sekjuləraiˈzeiʃən], *s.* secularización.

secularize [ˈsekjuləraiz], *v.t.* secularizar.

secure [siˈkjuə], *a.* seguro; firme; ***secure against*** o ***from,*** a salvo de; ***to be secure in the knowledge that,*** tener la seguridad *o* tranquilidad de saber que. — *v.t.* asegurar; afianzar; conseguir, obtener, recabar.

secureness [si'kjuənis], *s.* seguridad, (lo) seguro; falta de cuidado.
security [si'kjuəriti], *a.* ***top security,*** de sumo secreto. — *s.* seguridad; protección; fianza, prenda; fiador; (*pl.*) títulos, *m.pl.*, valores, *m.pl.*, obligaciones, *f.pl.*; ***social security,*** seguro social; ***to lend money on security,*** prestar dinero sobre fianza; ***to stand security for,*** salir fiador de.
sedan [si'dæn], *s.* silla de manos; (*Am.*, *aut.*) [SALOON].
sedate [si'deit], *a.* tranquilo, sosegado; serio.
sedateness [si'deitnis], *s.* serenidad; seriedad.
sedative ['sedətiv], *a.*, *s.* sedante, calmante.
sedentariness ['sedəntərinis], *s.* (lo) sedentario.
sedentary ['sedəntəri], *a.* sedentario.
sedge [sedʒ], *s.* juncia.
sedgy ['sedʒi], *a.* abundante en juncias.
sediment ['sedimənt], *s.* sedimento(s), poso(s).
sedimental, sedimentary [sedi'mentəl, -təri], *a.* sedimentario, sedimental.
sedimentation [sedimen'teiʃən], *s.* sedimentación.
sedition [si'diʃən], *s.* sedición.
seditious [si'diʃəs], *a.* sedicioso.
seditiousness [si'diʃəsnis], *s.* (lo) sedicioso.
seduce [si'dju:s], *v.t.* seducir; desviar, tentar.
seducer [si'dju:sə], *s.* seductor.
seduction, seducement [si'dʌkʃən, si'dju:smənt], *s.* seducción.
seductive [si'dʌktiv], *a.* seductor.
seductress [si'dʌktris], *s.* seductora.
sedulous ['sedjuləs], *a.* asiduo, diligente.
sedulousness, sedulity ['sedjuləsnis, si'dju:liti], *s.* asiduidad, diligencia.
see (I) [si:], *irr. v.t.* ***to have seen life,*** tener experiencia de la vida; ***he's not fit to be seen in public,*** no puede salir a la calle de esa guisa; ***see the back of,*** perder de vista; ***see company,*** recibir visitas; ***see daylight,*** ver el cielo abierto; ***see fit,*** tener por conveniente; tener a bien; ***see out,*** ver, quedarse *etc.* hasta el fin; ***see page 5,*** véase la página 5; ***see the point,*** comprender, ver el sentido de; ***see s.o. home,*** acompañar a alguien a casa; ***see s.o. off,*** ir a despedir a alguien; ***see s.o. through,*** ayudar a alguien hasta el fin; ***see sth. through,*** ver realizada una cosa; ***see a thing done,*** ver hacer una cosa. — *irr. v.i.* ***as far as the eye can see,*** hasta donde alcanza la vista; ***I don't know what he sees in her,*** ¿qué le verá (a semejante mujer)?; ***I see,*** ya veo; ya comprendo; ***let me see,*** déjeme pensar; ***let's see,*** veamos, vamos a ver; ***see after,*** cuidar de; ***see into,*** examinar a fondo; ***see through,*** calar, penetrar; [SEE-THROUGH]; ***see to,*** atender, servir; ***see (to it) that,*** procurar que, cuidar de que. — **see one another,** *v.r.* verse, visitarse. — *interj.* ***see!*** ¡mira!
see (2) [si:], *s.* sede, *f.*; ***Holy See,*** Santa Sede.
seed [si:d], *s.* semilla; simiente, *f.*; semen; germen; casta, progenie, *f.*; ***seed (of a fruit),*** pepita, cuesco; ***seed bed,*** semillero; ***seed cake,*** torta de semillas aromáticas; ***seed plot,*** semillero; ***seed potato,*** patata de siembra; ***seed time,*** siembra; ***to go*** o ***run to seed,*** espigarse; echarse a perder; ***to sow seeds of doubt in s.o.'s mind,*** sembrarle a alguien la duda. — *v.t.* sembrar; (*dep.*) seleccionar. — *v.i.* echar las semillas.
seeder ['si:də], *s.* sembradora.
seediness ['si:dinis], *s.* desaseo; sordidez.
seedling ['si:dliŋ], *s.* planta de semillero.
seedsman ['si:dzmən], *s.* vendedor de semillas.
seedy ['si:di], *a.* lleno de semillas; (*fig.*) sórdido, de mala muerte; raído, de capa caída; malucho, pachucho.
seeing ['si:iŋ], *conj.* ***seeing*** o ***seeing that,*** visto que. — *s.* vista, visión; (el) ver; ***seeing is believing,*** ver es creer.
seek [si:k], *irr. v.t.* buscar; pretender; ambicionar; ***seek advice from s.o.,*** pedirle consejo(s) a alguien, asesorarse con alguien; ***seek out,*** buscar con afán; (buscar y) dar con; ***seek to,*** pretender, intentar + *inf.* — *irr. v.i.* buscar; ***seek after*** o ***for,*** buscar, ir *o* andar en busca de.
seeker ['si:kə], *s.* buscador.
seem [si:m], *v.i.* parecer; aparentar; ***I seem to know him,*** me parece que le conozco; ***he's older than he seems,*** tiene más años de los que aparenta; ***what seems to be the trouble?*** ¿qué pasa? ¿pasa algo? ¿occurre algo? ¿qué pasa aquí?
seeming ['si:miŋ], *a.* aparente, teórico, fingido.
seemingly ['si:miŋli], *adv.* al parecer, aparentemente.
seemliness ['si:mlinis], *s.* decoro, decencia.
seemly ['si:mli], *a.* decoroso, decente.
seep [si:p], *v.i.* rezumarse, filtrarse.
seepage ['si:pidʒ], *s.* filtración.
seer [siə], *s.* adivino, vidente.
seersucker ['siəsʌkə], *s.* sirsaca.
seesaw ['si:sɔ:], *a.* de vaivén, oscilante. — *s.* balancín; columpio de tabla; (*fig.*) vaivén. — *v.i.* balancearse, columpiarse; moverse con vaivén.
seethe [si:ð], *v.i.* hervir, bullir; pulular, hormiguear; ***he's seething,*** está negro; está que trina; ***seethe with,*** hervir de.
seether ['si:ðə], *s.* caldera, marmita.
see-through ['si:-thru:], *a.* transparente; ***see-through dress,*** vestido transparente.
segment ['segmənt], *s.* segmento; gajo. — [seg'ment], *v.t.* segmentar.
segmental [seg'mentəl], *a.* segmentario; (*arq.*) escarzano (*arco*).
segmentary ['segməntəri], *a.* segmentario; segmentado.
segmentation [segmen'teiʃən], *s.* segmentación.
segregate ['segrigit], *a.* segregado, separado. — ['segrigeit], *v.t.* segregar, separar.
segregation [segri'geiʃən], *s.* segregación, separación; segregación (racial).
segregationist [segri'geiʃənist], *a.*, *s.* segregacionista, *m.f.*
seigneur [sein'jə:], *s.* (*der.*) señor.
seigneury ['seinjəri], *s.* señoría, señorío.
seignorage ['seinjəridʒ], *s.* señoreaje; derecho de braceaje.
seignorial [sein'jɔ:riəl], *a.* señorial.
Seine [sein]. Sena.
seine [sein], *s.* jábega. — *v.t.*, *v.i.* pescar con jábega.
seisin [SEIZIN].
seismic(al) ['saizmik(əl)], *a.* sísmico.
seismograph, seismometer ['saizmogrɑ:f, saiz'mɔmitə], *s.* sismógrafo, sismómetro.
seismology [saiz'mɔlədʒi], *s.* sismología.
seizable ['si:zəbl], *a.* embargable.
seize [si:z], *v.t.* asir, agarrar; tomar, coger violentamente; apoderarse de; embargar, decomisar; prender, apresar; captar; ***to be seized with,*** ser presa de. — *v.i.* — ***(up)on,*** agarrarse a; (*mec.*) ***seize up,*** agarrotarse.
seizer ['si:zə], *s.* agarrador; secuestrador.
seizin ['si:zin], *s.* (*for.*) posesión, acto de poseer; cosa poseída; toma de posesión.
seizing ['si:ziŋ], *s.* toma de posesión; (*mar.*) trinca, traba; aferramiento, ligadura.
seizure ['si:ʒə], *s.* (el) asir, captar *etc.*; prendimiento, captura; ataque, acceso; agarrotamiento; embargo, comiso.
sejant, sejeant ['si:dʒənt], *a.* (*blas.*) sentado.
selachian [si'leikiən], *a.*, *s.* selacio.
seldom ['seldəm], *adv.* raramente, rara vez, pocas veces.
select [si'lekt], *a.* selecto, escogido. — *v.t.* elegir, escoger; seleccionar.
selection [si'lekʃən], *s.* selección; elección; tría.

selective [si'lektiv], *a.* selectivo; ***selective tuning,*** sintonización selectiva.
selectness [si'lektnis], *s.* (lo) selecto.
selector [si'lektə], *s.* (*dep.*) seleccionador; (*elec.*) selector.
selenite ['selinait], *s.* selenita, *m.f.*
selenium [si'li:niəm], *s.* selenio.
selenography [seli'nɔgrəfi], *s.* selenografía.
self [self], *a.* mismo; (*color*) unicolor. — *pron.* se; sí (mismo) *etc.* — *s.* (*pl.* **selves** [selvz]) uno (mismo); (el) yo; (all) ***by o.s.,*** (completamente) solo, *m.*, sola, *f.*; ***he's not his old self,*** ya no es el que fue.
self-abasement ['self-ə'beismənt], *s.* humillación de sí mismo.
self-acting ['self-'æktiŋ], *a.* automático.
self-addressed ['self-ə'drest], *a.* ***self-addressed envelope,*** sobre con la dirección de uno mismo.
self-advertisment ['self-əd'və:tismənt], *s.* autobombo.
self-appointed ['self-ə'pɔintid], *a.* autonombrado, designado por uno mismo.
self-assurance ['self-ə'ʃuərəns], *s.* aplomo, seguridad en sí mismo.
self-centred ['self-'sentəd], *a.* egocéntrico.
self-complacency ['self-kəm'pleisənsi], *s.* (auto)-suficiencia.
self-composed ['self-kəm'pouzd], *a.* imperturbable, que no se altera fácilmente.
self-conceit ['self-kən'si:t], *s.* presunción, fatuidad.
self-conceited ['self-kən'si:tid], *a.* presuntuoso, fatuo.
self-confidence ['self-'kɔnfidəns], *s.* confianza en sí mismo.
self-conscious ['self-'kɔnʃəs], *a.* tímido, cohibido, corto.
self-consciousness ['self-'kɔnʃəsnis], *s.* timidez, cohibición, cortedad.
self-contained ['self-kən'teind], *a.* independiente; completo en sí mismo.
self-control ['self-kən'troul], *s.* dominio de sí mismo, autodominio.
self-convicted ['self-kən'viktid], *a.* convicto por confesión propia.
self-criticism ['self-'kritisizəm], *s.* autocrítica.
self-defeating ['self-di'fi:tiŋ], *a.* contraproducente.
self-defence ['self-di'fens], *s.* defensa propia, autodefensa.
self-delusion ['self-di'l(j)u:ʒən], *s.* engaño de sí mismo, autoengaño.
self-denial ['self-di'naiəl], *s.* abnegación.
self-denying ['self-di'naiiŋ], *a.* abnegado.
self-determination ['self-ditə:mi'neiʃən], *s.* autodeterminación.
self-discipline ['self-'disiplin], *s.* autodisciplina.
self-educated ['self-'edukjeitid], *a.* autodidacta.
self-effacing ['self-i'feisiŋ], *a.* modesto.
self-employed ['self-im'plɔid], *a.* ***to be self-employed,*** trabajar para uno mismo *o* por cuenta propia.
self-esteem ['self-is'ti:m], *s.* buen concepto de sí mismo, amor propio.
self-evident ['self-'evidənt], *a.* patente, evidente por sí mismo; ***self-evident proposition,*** verdad de Perogrullo.
self-explanatory ['self-iks'plænətəri], *a.* que se explica solo.
self-expression ['self-iks'preʃən], *s.* expresión de la propia personalidad.
self-fulfilment ['self-ful'filmənt], *s.* realización de la propia personalidad.
self-government ['self-'gʌvənmənt], *s.* autogobierno, autonomía.
self-heal ['self-'hi:l], *s.* (*bot.*) sanícula.
self-importance ['self-im'pɔ:təns], *s.* engreimiento.
self-imposed ['self-im'pouzd], *a.* autoimpuesto, impuesto por uno mismo.
self-incriminating ['self-in'krimineitiŋ], *a.* autoacusador.
self-induction ['self-in'dʌkʃən], *s.* autoinducción.
self-indulgence ['self-in'dʌldʒəns], *s.* intemperancia; comodonería.
self-indulgent ['self-in'dʌldʒənt], *a.* intemperante; comodón.
self-inflicted ['self-in'fliktid], *a.* (herida) autoinfligida.
self-interest ['self-'intərəst], *s.* interés, *m.*, egoísmo.
self-knowledge ['self-'nɔlidʒ], *s.* conocimiento de uno mismo.
self-love ['self-'lʌv], *s.* amor propio.
self-made ['self-'meid], *a.* ***self-made man,*** hijo de sus propias obras.
self-moving ['self-'mu:viŋ], *a.* automotor.
self-opinionated ['self-o'pinjəneitid], *a.* terco, testarudo.
self-pity ['self-'piti], *s.* autocompasión.
self-portrait ['self-'pɔ:trit], *s.* autorretrato.
self-possessed ['self-pə'zest], *a.* seguro de sí mismo, dueño de sí mismo.
self-preservation ['self-prezə'veiʃən], *s.* autoconservación.
self-propelled ['self-pro'peld], *a.* autopropulsado.
self-regulating ['self-'regjuleitiŋ], *a.* que se regula solo, autoregulador.
self-reliant ['self-ri'laiənt], *a.* que sabe valerse solo.
self-reproach ['self-ri'proutʃ], *s.* remordimiento(s).
self-respect ['self-ri'spekt], *s.* amor propio, dignidad.
self-respecting ['self-ri'spektiŋ], *a.* que se precia; ***no self-respecting person,*** nadie que se precie.
self-righteous ['self-'raitʃəs], *a.* farisaico, santurrón.
self-sacrifice ['self-'sækrifais], *s.* sacrificio; abnegación.
self-sacrificing ['self-'sækrifaisiŋ], *a.* abnegado.
self-satisfaction ['self-'sætis'fækʃən], *s.* suficiencia, satisfacción de sí mismo.
self-satisfied ['self-'sætisfaid], *a.* satisfecho, pagado de sí mismo, suficiente.
self-seeking ['self-'si:kiŋ], *a.* egoísta. — *s.* egoísmo.
self-service ['self-'sə:vis], *s.* autoservicio.
self-starter ['self-'stɑ:tə], *s.* (*aut.*) arranque automático.
self-styled ['self-'staild], *a.* autollamado, supuesto, sedicente.
self-sufficiency ['self-sə'fiʃənsi], *s.* independencia, autosuficiencia; confianza en sí mismo.
self-sufficient ['self-sə'fiʃənt], *a.* independiente, autosuficiente; seguro de sí mismo.
self-supporting ['self-sə'pɔ:tiŋ], *a.* con recursos propios, que vive de su propio trabajo.
self-taught ['self-'tɔ:t], *a.* autodidacta.
self-will ['self-'wil], *s.* voluntariosidad.
self-willed ['self-'wild], *a.* voluntarioso.
self-winding ['self-'waindiŋ], *a.* de cuerda automática.
selfish ['selfiʃ], *a.* egoísta, interesado.
selfishness ['selfiʃnis], *s.* egoísmo.
selfless ['selflis], *a.* desinteresado, abnegado.
selfsame ['selfseim], *a.* mismo, mismísimo.
sell [sel], *irr. v.t.* vender; hacer aceptar; traicionar; ***house to sell, to be sold,*** se vende casa; ***you've been sold!*** ¡te han tomado el pelo!; ***sell at auction,*** vender en almoneda *o* en pública subasta; ***sell at retail,*** vender a destajo *o* al por menor; ***sell back,*** revender; ***sell for ready money,*** vender al contado; (*com.*) ***sell long stock,*** vender acciones que uno posee en abundancia; ***sell off*** o ***out,*** vender (todas las existencias de), saldar, liquidar; ***sell on credit,*** vender al fiado (*o* a plazos); ***I'm not sold on the idea,*** no me acaba

de convencer la idea; ***sell under the counter,*** vendor bajo mano; ***sell wholesale,*** vender al por mayor. — *irr. v.i.* venderse, estar en venta; ***sell out*** o ***up,*** venderlo todo, realizar; ***it sells well,*** se vende bien, tiene buena venta.

seller [ˈselə], *s.* vendedor.

selling [ˈseliŋ], *a.* de venta; vendible. — *s.* venta; ***selling price,*** precio de venta.

seltzer [ˈseltzə], *s.* agua de Seltz.

selvage [ˈselvidʒ], *s.* (*tej.*) hirma, orilla de paño; orilla, borde, orla; lista; (*min.*) salbanda; (*pl.*) (*mar.*) estrobos, *m.pl.*

selves [selvz], *s.pl.* [SELF].

semantic [siˈmæntik], *a.* semántico.

semantics [siˈmæntiks], *s.* semántica.

semaphore [ˈseməfɔ:], *s.* semáforo; disco; telégrafo de señales.

semaphoric(al) [seməˈfɔrik(əl)], *a.* semafórico.

semasiology [semeisiˈɔlədʒi], *s.* semasiología, semántica.

semblance [ˈsembləns], *s.* apariencia; aspecto; visos, *m.pl.*, trazas, *f.pl.*; señal.

semeiology [si:maiˈɔlədʒi], *s.* semiología.

semen [ˈsi:men], *s.* semen; (*bot.*) simiente, *f.*

semester [siˈmestə], *s.* semestre.

semi- [ˈsemi], *prefijo.* semi, medio; ***semi-darkness,*** penumbra; ***semi-detached,*** (casa) semiindependiente; ***semi-official,*** semioficial, paraoficial; (*joy.*) ***semi-precious,*** semiprecioso; ***semi-skilled,*** semiespecializado.

semiannual [semiˈænjuəl], *a.* semianual, semestral.

semiannular [semiˈænjulə], *a.* semianular.

semibreve [ˈsemibri:v], *s.* (*mús.*) semibreve, *f.*, redonda; ***semibreve rest,*** aspiración de semibreve.

semicircle [ˈsemisə:kl], *s.* semicírculo, medio círculo, hemiciclo.

semicircular, semicircled [semiˈsə:kjulə, ˈsemisə:kld], *a.* semicircular.

semicircumference [semisəˈkʌmfərəns], *s.* semicircunferencia.

semicolon [ˈsemikoulən], *s.* punto y coma.

semidiameter [semidaiˈæmitə], *s.* semidiámetro.

semidiaphanous [semidaiˈæfənəs], *a.* semidiáfano.

semidouble [semiˈdʌbl], *a.* (*bot.*) semidoble. — *s.* (*igl.*) semidoble.

semifinal [semiˈfainəl], *a.*, *s.* semifinal, *f.*

semifinalist [semiˈfainəlist], *s.* semifinalista, *m.f.*

semifloret [semiˈflɔ:ret], *s.* semiflósculo.

semifluid [semiˈflu:id], *a.* semiflúido.

semilunar [semiˈlu:nə], *a.* semilunar.

semimonthly [semiˈmʌnθli], *a.* quincenal. — *s.* publicación quincenal.

seminal [ˈseminəl], *a.* seminal; primigenio, embrionario.

seminar [ˈseminɑ:], *s.* seminario.

seminarist [ˈseminərist], *s.* seminarista, *m.f.*

seminary [ˈseminəri], *s.* seminario.

semination [semiˈneiʃən], *s.* sembradura; propagación, diseminación.

semiordinate [semiˈɔ:dinit], *s.* semiordenada.

semi-precious [semi-ˈpreʃəs], *a.* (*joy.*) semiprecioso.

semiquaver [ˈsemikweivə], *s.* semicorchea.

semispherical [semiˈsferikəl], *a.* semiesférico.

Semite [ˈsemait, ˈsi:mait], *s.* semita, *m.f.*

Semitic [siˈmitik], *a.* semítico. — *s.* lengua semítica.

semitone [ˈsemitoun], *s.* semitono.

semivocal [semiˈvoukəl], *a.* semivocal.

semivowel [ˈsemivauəl], *s.* semivocal, *f.*

semiweekly [semiˈwi:kli], *a.* bisemanal. — *s.* publicación bisemanal.

semolina [semoˈli:nə], *s.* sémola.

sempiternal [sempiˈtə:nəl], *a.* sempiterno.

sempstress [ˈsempstris], *s.* costurera.

senate [ˈsenit], *s.* senado; ***senate house,*** senado; claustro (de la Universidad).

senator [ˈsenətə], *s.* senador.

senatorial [senəˈtɔ:riəl], *a.* senatorial.

senatorship [ˈsenətəʃip], *s.* senaduría.

send [send], *irr. v.t.* enviar, mandar; despachar; remitir; expedir; lanzar; poner (*un telegrama*); volver (*loco etc.*); ***send away,*** despedir; enviar lejos; ***send back,*** devolver; mandar volver; ***send down,*** expulsar (de la Universidad); ***send for,*** enviar a buscar, enviar a llamar, enviar por; ***send in,*** hacer entrar *o* pasar; presentar; ***send off,*** mandar; despedir; ***send on,*** reexpedir, hacer seguir; mandar delante; ***send out,*** arrojar, despedir; emitir; ***send s.o. packing*** o ***about his business,*** mandar a alguien a paseo; ***send up,*** mandar subir; (*fam.*) remedar, parodiar; ***send word,*** mandar aviso *o* recado.

sender [ˈsendə], *s.* remitente; (*elec.*) transmisor.

send-off [ˈsend-ɔf], *s.* (*fam.*) despedida.

Seneca [ˈsenikə]. Séneca, *m.*

Senegal [seniˈgɔ:l]. Senegal.

Senegalese [senigɔ:ˈli:z], *a.*, *s.* senegalés, *m.*

senescent [siˈnesənt], *a.* que envejece.

seneschal [ˈseniʃəl], *s.* senescal.

senile [ˈsi:nail], *a.* senil; ***to be senile,*** estar chocho.

senility [siˈniliti], *s.* senilidad; debilidad senil.

senior [ˈsi:niə], *a.* mayor, más viejo; más antiguo; de rango superior; ***he's senior to me,*** es mayor que yo; tiene categoría superior a la mía. — *s.* mayor; miembro más antiguo; ***he's 2 years my senior,*** me lleva dos años.

seniority [si:niˈɔriti], *s.* antigüedad.

senna [ˈsenə], *s.* sena.

sensation [senˈseiʃən], *s.* sensación; ***to be, cause*** o ***create a sensation,*** causar sensación; ***it's a sensation!*** ¡es formidable!

sensational [senˈseiʃənəl], *a.* sensacional.

sensationalism [senˈseiʃənəlizəm], *s.* sensacionalismo.

sense [sens], *s.* sentido; juicio; buen sentido; inteligencia; sensación; opinión, parecer; significado, acepción, significación; ***common sense,*** sentido común; ***in a sense,*** en cierto sentido; ***in the best sense,*** en el buen sentido de la palabra; ***in the broad sense,*** en el sentido más amplio; ***sense of hearing, sight*** *etc.*, oído, vista *etc.*; ***sense of humour,*** sentido del humor; ***a sense of pleasure,*** una sensación de placer; ***to bring s.o. to his senses,*** hacer a alguien entrar en razón, hacer reaccionar a alguien; ***it doesn't make sense,*** no tiene sentido; ***to be out of one's senses,*** haber perdido el juicio; ***to take leave of one's senses,*** perder el juicio; ***to talk sense,*** hablar con cordura; no decir tonterías. — *v.t.* sentir, percibir; ***sense the danger,*** darse cuenta del peligro.

senseless [ˈsenslis], *a.* insensible, inerte, sin conocimiento, sin sentido; disparatado, insensato.

senselessness [ˈsenslisnis], *s.* insensatez.

sensibility [sensiˈbiliti], *s.* sensibilidad; finura, precisión (*de instrumentos*).

sensible [ˈsensibl], *a.* sensato, juicioso; razonable, acertado; ***that's a sensible thing to do,*** eso me parece razonable; ***to be sensible of,*** ser consciente de.

sensibleness [ˈsensiblnis], *s.* sensatez, juicio; lo razonable.

sensitive [ˈsensitiv], *a.* sensible; susceptible; impresionable; (*foto.*) sensibilizado; sensitivo (*instrumentos*); (*bot.*) ***sensitive plant,*** sensitiva.

sensitiveness, sensitivity [ˈsensitivnis, sensiˈtiviti], *s.* sensibilidad; lo impresionable; susceptibilidad; delicadeza.

sensitize [ˈsensitaiz], *v.t.* hacer sensible; (*foto.*) sensibilizar.

sensorial [senˈsɔ:riəl], *a.* sensorio, sensorial.

sensorium [senˈsɔ:riəm], *s.* sensorio.

sensory [ˈsensəri], *a.*, *s.* sensorio.

sensual [ˈsensjuəl], *a.* sensual; lujurioso, lascivo, voluptuoso.
sensualism [ˈsensjuəlizəm], *s.* sensualismo, sensualidad.
sensualist [ˈsensjuəlist], *s.* persona sensual; (*filos.*) sensualista, *m.f.*
sensuality [sensjuˈæliti], *s.* sensualidad, voluptuosidad.
sensualize [ˈsensjuəlaiz], *v.t.* hacer sensual, lascivo *o* voluptuoso.
sensuous [ˈsensjuəs], *a.* sensual; mórbido.
sensuousness [ˈsensjuəsnis], *s.* sensualidad.
sentence [ˈsentəns], *s.* (*gram.*) frase, oración; (*for.*) sentencia, fallo; condena; ***death sentence,*** sentencia a pena de muerte; ***life sentence,*** condena a reclusión perpetua; ***to pass sentence,*** pronunciar sentencia, fallar; ***to serve one's sentence,*** cumplir (la) condena. — *v.t.* condenar, sentenciar.
sentential [senˈtenʃəl], *a.* (*gram.*) oracional.
sententious [senˈtenʃəs], *a.* sentencioso.
sententiousness [senˈtenʃəsnis], *s.* estilo sentencioso.
sentience [ˈsenʃəns], *s.* sensibilidad, sensitividad.
sentient [ˈsenʃənt], *a.* sensible, sensitivo.
sentiment [ˈsentimənt], *s.* sentimiento; opinión, *f.*, parecer; ***excess of sentiment,*** mucho sentimentalismo; ***to wallow in sentiment,*** regodearse con los sentimentalismos, entregarse a la sensiblería.
sentimental [sentiˈmentəl], *a.* sentimental; sensiblero, sentimentalón; romántico.
sentimentalism, sentimentality [sentiˈmentəlizəm, sentimenˈtæliti], *s.* sentimentalismo, sensiblería.
sentimentalist [sentiˈmentəlist], *s.* persona sensiblera; romántico.
sentimentalize [sentiˈmentəlaiz], *v.t.* tratar *o* enfocar de una manera sentimental *o* sensiblera. — *v.i.* entregarse al sentimentalismo *o* a la sensiblería.
sentinel, sentry [ˈsentinəl, ˈsentri], *s.* centinela, *m.*; ***sentry box,*** garita de centinela; ***sentry go,*** turno de centinela; ***to stand sentry,*** estar de centinela; hacer centinela.
sepal [ˈsepəl], *s.* sépalo.
separability [sepərəˈbiliti], *s.* separabilidad.
separable [ˈsepərəbl], *a.* separable.
separate [ˈsepərit], *a.* separado; suelto. — [ˈsepəreit], *v.t.* separar; desprender; apartar. — *v.i.* separarse; desprenderse; apartarse.
separately [ˈsepəritli], *adv.* por separado, individualmente.
separation [sepəˈreiʃən], *s.* separación.
separatist [ˈsepərətist], *s.* separatista, *m.f.*
separative [ˈsepərətiv], *a.* separativo.
separator [ˈsepəreitə], *s.* separador.
sepia [ˈsi:piə], *a.* de color sepia. — *s.* (*pint.*) sepia; (*ict.*) jibia.
sepoy [ˈsi:pɔi], *s.* cipayo.
sepsis [ˈsepsis], *s.* sepsis, *f.*
septal [ˈseptəl], *a.* septal.
September [sepˈtembə], *s.* septiembre.
septenary [sepˈti:nəri], *a.* septenario. — *s.* septena; septenio.
septennial [sepˈteniəl], *a.* sieteñal.
septentrional [sepˈtentriounəl], a septentrional.
septet [sepˈtet], *s.* septena; (*mús.*) septeto.
septic [ˈseptik], *a.* séptico; ***septic tank,*** pozo séptico.
septicæmia [septiˈsi:miə], *s.* septicemia.
septillion [sepˈtiljən], *s.* septillón.
septuagenary [septjuəˈdʒi:nəri], *a.* septuagenario.
Septuagesima [septjuəˈdʒesimə], *s.* septuagésima.
septuagesimal [septjuəˈdʒesiməl], *a.* septuagésimo.
septum [ˈseptəm], *s.* (*pl.* **septa** [-tə]) septo.
septuple [ˈseptjupl], *a.* séptuplo. — *v.t.*, *v.i.* septuplicar, septuplicarse.
sepulchral [siˈpʌlkrəl], *a.* sepulcral.
sepulchre [ˈsepəlkə], *s.* sepulcro, sepultura. — *v.t.* sepultar.
sepulture [ˈsepəltʃə], *s.* sepultura, sepelio.
sequacious [siˈkweiʃəs], *a.* servil; consecuente.
sequaciousness, sequacity [siˈkweiʃəsnis, siˈkwæsiti], *s.* servilismo.
sequel [ˈsi:kwəl], *s.* consecuencia, resultado; secuela; ***in the sequel,*** posteriormente.
sequela [siˈkwi:lə], *s.* secuela.
sequence [ˈsi:kwəns], *s.* sucesión, orden, serie; secuencia.
sequent [ˈsi:kwənt], *a.* siguiente, subsiguiente.
sequester [siˈkwestə], *v.t.* separar, retirar, apartar; (*for.*) secuestrar.
sequestered [siˈkwestəd], *a.* aislado, remoto.
sequestrable [siˈkwestrəbl], *a.* que se puede secuestrar.
sequestrate [ˈsi:kwistreit], *v.t.* (*for.*) secuestrar; confiscar.
sequestration [si:kwisˈtreiʃən], *s.* (*for.*) secuestro; separación, reclusión, retiro.
sequestrator [ˈsi:kwistreitə], *s.* secuestrador.
sequestrum [siˈkwestrəm], *s.* (*pl.* **sequestra** [-trə]) (*cir.*) secuestro.
sequin [ˈsi:kwin], *s.* lentejuela; (*moneda*) cequí.
sequoia [siˈkwɔiə], *s.* secoya.
seraglio [seˈrɑ:ljou], *s.* serrallo.
seraph [ˈserəf], *s.* (*pl.* **seraphim** [ˈserəfim]) serafín.
seraphic(al) [seˈræfik(əl)], *a.* seráfico.
seraphina, seraphine [serəˈfi:nə, ˈserəfi:n], *s.* serafina, organillo de salón, órgano portátil.
Serb, Serbian [sə:b, ˈsə:biən], *a.*, *s.* servio.
Serbia [ˈsə:biə]. Servia.
Serbo-Croat [ˈsə:bou-ˈkrouæt], *s.* (*idioma*) servocroata, *m.*
Serbo-Croatian [ˈsə:bou-krouˈeiʃən], *a.*, *s.* servocroata, *m.f.*
sere [SEAR (1), (2)].
serein [səˈræn], *s.* sereno.
serenade [sereˈneid], *s.* serenata. — *v.t.* dar serenata a.
serene [siˈri:n], *a.* sereno, sosegado; ***Most Serene,*** serenísimo.
serenity, sereneness [siˈreniti, siˈri:nnis], *s.* serenidad.
serf [sə:f], *s.* siervo (de la gleba).
serfdom [ˈsə:fdəm], *s.* servidumbre.
serge [sə:dʒ], *s.* estameña; sarga.
sergeant [ˈsɑ:dʒənt], *s.* (*mil.*) sargento; ***sergeant-at-arms,*** macero; ***sergeant-major,*** sargento instructor.
sergeantship [ˈsɑ:dʒəntʃip], *s.* sargentía.
serial [ˈsiəriəl], *a.* en serie, consecutivo; de serie; por entregas. — *s.* serial, novela por entregas; ***radio serial,*** serial radiofónico.
serialize [ˈsiəriəlaiz], *v.t.* publicar como serial *o* por entregas.
serially [ˈsiəriəli], *adv.* en serie; por serie; por entregas.
sericate [ˈserikit], *a.* sedoso; velludo.
sericeous [siˈriʃiəs], *a.* sérico, sedoso, lustroso como la seda.
sericultural [seriˈkʌltʃərəl], *a.* sericícola.
sericulture [ˈserikʌltʃə], *s.* sericicultura.
series [ˈsiəri:z], *s.* serie, *f.*
serin [ˈserin], *s.* (*orn.*) verdecillo.
seringa [siˈriŋgə], *s.* (*bot.*) siringa.
serio-comic(al) [ˈsiəriou-ˈkɔmik(əl)], *a.* jocoserio, seriocómico.
serious [ˈsiəriəs], *a.* serio; grave; ***to be serious,*** tomar la(s) cosa(s) en serio, dejarse de bromas, de chistes *o* de gracias; ***he's serious*** (***about it***), la

cosa va en serio; ***you can't be serious!*** ¡no me lo digas! ¿me lo dices en serio?

seriously [ˈsiəriəsli], *adv.* seriamente; gravemente; ***seriously wounded,*** herido de gravedad; ***to take seriously,*** tomar en serio.

seriousness [ˈsiəriəsnis], *s.* seriedad; gravedad.

serjeant [SERGEANT].

sermon [ˈsəːmən], *s.* sermón; ***collection of sermons,*** sermonario; ***funeral sermon,*** oración fúnebre.

sermonize [ˈsəːmənaiz], *v.t.* sermonear; echar un sermón *o* sermones a. — *v.i.* sermonear.

seron, seroon [ˈsiərɔn, siˈruːn], *s.* churla.

serosity [siˈrɔsiti], *s.* serosidad.

serotherapy [siəroˈθerəpi], *s.* seroterapia.

serotinous [siˈrɔtinəs], *a.* serondo, serótino.

serous [ˈsiərəs], *a.* seroso.

serpent [ˈsəːpənt], *s.* serpiente, *f.*, sierpe, *f.*; (*mús.*) serpentón; (*piro.*) buscapiés, *m.inv.*; (*astron.*) Serpiente.

serpentine [ˈsəːpəntain], *a.* serpentino. — *s.* (*min.*) serpentina. — *v.i.* serpentear.

serpiginous [səˈpidʒinəs], *a.* serpiginoso.

serpigo [səˈpaigou], *s.* serpigo.

serrate, serrated [ˈsereit, siˈreitid], *a.* dentellado; (*bot.*) serrado.

serration [siˈreiʃən], *s.* endentadura.

serried [ˈserid], *a.* apretado, apiñado.

serum [ˈsiərəm], *s.* (*pl.* **sera, serums** [ˈsiərə, -rəmz]) suero.

servable [ˈsəːvəbl], *a.* servible.

servant [ˈsəːvənt], *s.* criado, sirviente; servidor; ***your obedient servant,*** su seguro servidor; ***servant girl, servant maid, woman servant,*** criada; ***servant man,*** criado.

serve [səːv], *s.* (*tenis*) saque. — *v.t.* servir; estar al servicio de; ser útil a; manejar, hacer funcionar; abastecer; (*for.*) entregar (*una citación*); cumplir (*una condena*); cubrir (*el macho a la hembra*); (*tenis*) sacar; ***it serves you right,*** te está bien empleado; ***it served its turn,*** sirvió para el caso, fue útil en aquella ocasión, bastó en aquel momento. — *v.i.* servir (***as, for,*** de, para); ***serve at table,*** servir a la mesa.

server [ˈsəːvə], *s.* servidor; criado de mesa; (*igl.*) acólito; bandeja; (*dep.*) saque.

service [ˈsəːvis], *s.* servicio; (*igl.*) oficio; (*dep.*) saque; vajilla; (*mar.*) forro de cable; (*aut.*) revisión; ***on active service,*** en activo; en acto de servicio; ***at your service,*** a la disposición de Vd.; ***coffee service,*** juego de café; ***diplomatic service,*** cuerpo diplomático; ***to do s.o. a service,*** hacer *o* prestar un servicio a alguien; ***it is of no service,*** no sirve para nada; ***to be of service to,*** ser útil a, servir a; ***out of service,*** no funciona; ***to see service,*** prestar servicio, servir; ***service lift,*** montacargas, *m.inv.*; ***service station,*** gasolinera, estación de servicio; ***service (-tree),*** serbal. — *v.t.* (*aut.*) revisar, mantener.

serviceable [ˈsəːvisəbl], *a.* servible, útil; aprovechable.

serviceableness [ˈsəːvisəblnis], *s.* utilidad; (lo) aprovechable.

servient [ˈsəːviənt], *a.* (*for.*) subordinado.

serviette [səːviˈet], *s.* servilleta; ***serviette ring,*** servilletero.

servile [ˈsəːvail], *a.* servil.

servility [səːˈviliti], *s.* servilismo.

serving [ˈsəːviŋ], *a.* sirviente; en activo; en funciones; ***serving maid,*** criada, sirvienta; ***serving man,*** criado, sirviente. — *s.* (el) servir; (*mar.*) ***serving mallet,*** maceta de forrar; ***serving of (the) summons,*** entrega de citación.

servitor [ˈsəːvitə], *s.* (*Esco.*) bedel.

servitude [ˈsəːvitjuːd], *s.* servidumbre; ***penal servitude,*** trabajos forzados, *m.pl.*

sesame [ˈsesəmi], *s.* sésamo; ***open, sesame!*** ¡ábrete, sésamo!

sesamoid [ˈsesəmɔid], *a.*, *s.* (*anat.*) sesamoideo.

sesquioxide [seskwiˈɔksaid], *s.* sesquióxido.

sesquipedal, sesquipedalian [ˈseskwipedəl, seskwipiˈdeiliən], *a.* sesquipedal.

sesquitertian [seskwiˈtəːʃən], *a.* sesquitercio.

sessile [ˈsesail], *a.* sésil.

session [ˈseʃən], *s.* sesión; curso (*académico*); ***petty sessions,*** tribunal de primera instancia; ***to be in session,*** celebrar sesión, sesionar.

sessional [ˈseʃənəl], *a.* de sesión; de fin de curso.

sesterce [ˈsestəːs], *s.* sestercio.

set [set], *a.* rígido, inflexible; yerto; permanente; forzado; listo; fijo; decidido (de antemano); prescrito, establecido; señalado; resuelto, decidido, empeñado; formal, regular; arreglado, ajustado, puesto; ***set books,*** textos del programa, *m.pl.*; ***set fight,*** batalla campal; ***set menu,*** menú; ***(are we) all set?*** ¿estamos (listos)?; ***to be all set for,*** estar (completamente) listo para; ***at the set time,*** a la hora señalada; ***he gave a set speech,*** pronunció un discurso preparado; ***to be quite set in one's purpose,*** estar totalmente resuelto; ***to be set on sth.,*** estar empeñado en algo; ***to be set on doing sth.,*** estar empeñado en hacer algo; ***to be dead set against,*** oponerse tajantemente a, ser totalmente contrario a. — *s.* juego, serie, conjunto; grupo, colección; batería; equipo; tren; cubierto; (*tenis*) set; pollazón; clase; banda, cuadrilla; triscamiento (*de una sierra*); caída (*de una prenda*); corte, ajuste; dirección, curso; posición; sesgo, tendencia; esqueje, planta de trasplante; decorado(s), montaje; ***set of chairs,*** juego de sillas; ***set of diamonds,*** aderezo de diamantes; ***set of dishes,*** vajilla; ***set of horses,*** tiro *o* tronco de caballos; ***coffee set,*** juego de café; ***toilet set,*** juego de tocador; ***wireless set,*** (aparato) de radio, (radio-) receptor; ***battery set,*** radio de pilas, *f.*; ***generating set,*** grupo electrógeno; ***the smart set,*** la gente bien, el mundo elegante; ***a set of thieves,*** una banda de ladrones; ***this makes up the set,*** esto completa el juego; ***to make a dead set at s.o.,*** tomarla abiertamente con alguien; ***to make a dead set at a man,*** ponerle los puntos a un hombre; ***to have a shampoo and set,*** hacerse lavar y marcar el pelo; ***to be on the set,*** estar en plató. — *v.t.* poner, colocar; situar; engastar, montar; arreglar, ajustar, graduar, regular; componer; marcar, fijar; desplegar; triscar; armar, tender; endurecer, cuajar, fraguar; apretar; señalar; imponer, establecer; dar; asignar; plantear; ***set the table,*** poner la mesa; ***set to music,*** poner música a; ***set out a plan,*** exponer un plan; ***set s.o. in front of s.o. (else),*** anteponer una persona a otra; ***set the value of sth. at,*** valorar algo en; ***the story is set in Madrid,*** la acción tiene lugar *o* se desarrolla en Madrid; ***set the alarm-clock for eight,*** poner el despertador para las ocho; ***set the time,*** fijar la hora; ***set the fashion,*** imponer la moda; ***set the trend,*** dar la pauta; ***set the record,*** establecer el récord *o* la marca; ***set course for,*** poner rumbo a; ***set an example,*** dar ejemplo; ***set an exam,*** poner un examen; ***set sth. going,*** poner algo en marcha; ***set s.o. laughing,*** hacer reír a alguien; ***that set me thinking,*** eso me hizo pensar; ***set sth. against sth. (else),*** contraponer una cosa a otra; ***set aside,*** poner a un lado, poner aparte; dedicar, asignar; desechar; desestimar; anular; ***set back,*** detener; retrasar; ***set down,*** depositar; poner por escrito, consignar; ***set down to,*** atribuir, achacar a; ***set forth,*** exponer, explicar; ***set off,*** hacer estallar; realzar, acentuar; ***set (on),*** azuzar; (*fam.*) ***set s.o. off,*** provocar a alguien, hacer que una persona se dispare; ***set out,*** exponer, explicar; ***set up,*** erigir, levantar; crear, fundar, instituir; constituir; componer; armar, montar; poner; establecer; sentar; ***be well set up for,*** estar bien provisto de; ***set one person against another,*** indisponer a una persona con otra; ***set at liberty,*** poner en libertad; ***set at naught,*** dar al traste con; ***set at rest,*** tranquilizar; ***set fire to,*** pegar fuego a; ***set the Thames on fire,*** descubrir la pólvora; ***set the teeth on edge,*** dar dentera; ***set one's hand to,*** poner manos a; firmar; ***set one's house in order,*** arreglar sus asuntos; ***set one's heart on,*** empeñarse en, tener muchísima ilusión por; ***set right*** o ***to rights,*** enderezar, poner remedio a; ***set sail,*** hacerse a la vela; ***set great store by,*** dar mucha importancia a; ***set a task,*** imponer una tarea; ***set up house,*** poner casa. — *v.i.* ponerse (*el sol*); cuajarse, coagularse, fraguar, endurecerse, solidificarse; fijarse (*un color*); caer, sentar bien (*una prenda*); estar de muestra (*un perro*); ***the tide is set in his favour,*** tiene las circunstancias a su favor, lleva el viento de popa; ***set about a task,*** emprender una tarea; ***set about doing sth.,*** ponerse a hacer algo; ***set about s.o.,*** atacar a, emprenderla con alguien; ***set about each other,*** venir *o* llegar a las manos; ***set down,*** aterrizar; ***set forth,*** ponerse en camino; ***set in,*** comenzar; declararse; afianzarse; cerrar; fluir (*la marea*); ***the rain has set in for the day,*** el día se ha metido en agua; ***set off*** o ***set out,*** ponerse en camino; salir, ***set out to,*** ponerse a; proponerse; ***set to,*** ponerse a la obra; ***set to work,*** ponerse a trabajar, poner manos a la obra; ***set up,*** establecerse; ***set up for o.s.,*** (empezar a) trabajar por su cuenta *o* independientemente; ***set up in business,*** poner un negocio; ***set upon,*** acometer, asaltar. — **set o.s.,** *v.r.* — ***to work,*** ponerse a trabajar; ***set o.s. up as judge,*** erigirse en juez.

setaceous [si'teiʃəs], *a.* cerdoso.

setback ['setbæk], *s.* revés, *m.*, contratiempo, contrariedad.

setbolt ['setboult], *s.* prisionero, botador, perno.

set-down ['set-daun], *s.* reprimenda; (*fam.*) peluca.

set-off ['set-ɔf], *s.* relieve, realce; (*arq.*) saliente; (*impr.*) tiznadura.

seton ['si:tən], *s.* (*cir.*, *vet.*) sedal.

setose, setous ['si:tous, -təs], *a.* cerdoso.

set-square ['set-skwɛə], *s.* cartabón.

Se-Tswana [sə-'swɑ:nə], *s.* (*lengua*) setswana.

settee [se'ti:], *s.* canapé, sofá, *m.*

setter ['setə], *s.* persona que monta, coloca *etc.*; perdiguero, sétter; ***diamond setter,*** joyero; (*impr.*) ***typesetter,*** cajista, *m.f.*

setting ['setiŋ], *s.* puesta, colocación; engaste, montadura, montura; escena, escenario, marco; ajuste; (*mús.*) arreglo, versión; ***setting lotion,*** fijador; ***setting-up,*** erección; fundación, creación, establecimiento; (*impr.*) composición.

settle [setl], *s.* escaño, arquibanco. — *v.t.* colocar; asentar; fijar, asegurar; establecer; colonizar, poblar; calmar, sosegar; ajustar, liquidar, saldar, pagar; resolver, dirimir; ***it's all settled,*** está todo resuelto; ***settle one's affairs,*** arreglar sus asuntos; ***that settles it!*** ¡no hay más que decir! — *v.i.* instalarse; establecerse; posarse; asentarse; clarificarse; sedimentarse; calmarse; normalizarse; ***the snow is settling,*** está cuajando la nieve; ***the weather is settling,*** el tiempo se está normalizando; ***settle down,*** asentar la cabeza; ***he can't settle down anywhere,*** es un culo de mal asiento; ***he's settling down at his new job,*** se está acostumbrando a su nuevo trabajo; ***settle down for the night,*** arreglarse para pasar la noche; ***settle down to work,*** aplicarse al trabajo; ***I will not settle for less than £100,*** no me conformo con menos de £100; ***things are settling into shape,*** las cosas empiezan a cobrar forma; ***settle on sth.,*** decidir algo; ***settle on a date,*** convenir en una fecha; ***settle up,*** ajustar cuentas.

settled [setld], *a.* fijo; arreglado; establecido; asentado; saldado; seguro; poblado.

settlement ['setlmənt], *s.* establecimiento; ajuste, pago, saldo, liquidación; acuerdo, arreglo, solución; ***to reach a settlement,*** llegar a un acuerdo *o* a un acomodo; colonización, (el) poblar; colonia, caserío, poblado, núcleo de población; (*for.*) asignación; (*for.*) dote.

settler ['setlə], *s.* colonizador, poblador; colono.

settling ['setliŋ], *s.* ajuste; arreglo.

set-to ['set-'tu:], *s.* zipizape, pelea; disputa.

set-up ['set-ʌp], *s.* tinglado; sistema, *m.*; organización.

seven ['sevən], *a.*, *s.* siete.

sevenfold ['sevənfould], *a.* séptuplo. — *adv.* siete veces.

seventeen [sevən'ti:n], *a.*, *s.* diez y siete, diecisiete.

seventeenth [sevən'ti:nθ], *a.* décimo séptimo, diez y siete.

seventh ['sevənθ], *a.* séptimo; siete. — *s.* séptimo, séptima parte; (*mús.*) séptima.

seventieth ['sevəntiiθ], *a.* septuagésimo, setenta. — *s.* septuagésimo; setentavo.

seventy ['sevənti], *a.*, *s.* setenta; ***the seventies,*** los años setenta.

sever ['sevə], *v.t.* separar; cortar; cercenar; romper (*relaciones*).

several ['sevərəl], *a.* varios, *m.pl.*; respectivos, *m.pl.*; distintos, *m.pl.*

severally ['sevərəli], *adv.* separadamente, individualmente; respectivamente; ***jointly and severally,*** solidariamente.

severalty ['sevərəlti], *s.* (*for.*) posesión privativa de un terreno.

severance ['sevərəns], *s.* separación; cercenamiento; ruptura.

severe [si'viə], *a.* severo; riguroso; grave; intenso; violento; austero, adusto.

severity, severeness [si'veriti, si'viənis], *s.* severidad; rigor; gravedad; intensidad; violencia; adustez.

Seville [se'vil]. Sevilla.

Sevillian [se'viliən], *a.*, *s.* sevillano, hispalense.

sew [sou], *irr. v.t.*, *v.i.* coser; ***sew up,*** coser.

sewage ['sj:uidʒ], *s.* aguas de albañal, *f.pl.*; aguas residuales, *f.pl.*; ***sewage disposal,*** eliminación de aguas residuales; ***sewage farm,*** instalación depuradora de aguas residuales.

sewer (1) ['souə], *s.* persona que cose.

sewer (2) ['sju:ə], *s.* albañal, cloaca, alcantarilla; ***sewer gas,*** emanaciones de las cloacas, *f.pl.*

sewerage ['sju:əridʒ], *s.* alcantarillado; sistema de cloacas, *m.*

sewing ['souiŋ], *s.* (labor de) costura; ***sewing-machine,*** máquina de coser; ***sewing-needle,*** aguja de coser; ***sewing-thread,*** hilo de coser.

sex [seks], *s.* sexo; (*acto*) acto sexual, coito; sexualidad; ***the fair sex,*** el bello sexo; ***sex appeal,*** atractivo sexual; atracción sexual; ***sex education,*** educación sexual; ***sex maniac,*** maníaco sexual.

sexagenarian [seksədʒi'nɛəriən], *a.*, *s.* sesentón.

sexagenary [seksə'dʒi:nəri], *a.* sexagenario.

Sexagesima [seksə'dʒesimə], *s.* sexagésima.

sexagesimal [seksə'dʒesiməl], *a.* sexagesimal.

sexangular [seks'æŋgjulə], *a.* sexángulo, hexágono, sexangular.

sexennial [seks'eniəl], *a.* que dura seis años, que acontece cada seis años.

sexless ['sekslis], *a.* sin sexo; asexuado.

sexologist [seks'ɔlədʒist], *s.* sexólogo.

sextain ['sekstin], *s.* sextilla.

sextant ['sekstənt], *s.* sextante.

sextet [seks'tet], *s.* sexteto.

sextile ['sekstail], *s.* sextil.

sextillion [seks'tiljən], *s.* sextillón.

sexton ['sekstən], *s.* (*igl.*) sacristán.

sextuple ['sekstjupl], *a.* séxtuplo.

sexual ['seksjuəl], *a.* sexual.

sexuality [seksju'æliti], *s.* sexualidad.

sexy ['seksi], *a.* de gran atractivo sexual; verde, escabroso; provocativo; cachondo.

sgraffito [zgræ'fi:tou], *s.* esgrafiado.

shabbiness ['ʃæbinis], *s.* (lo) raído, zarrapastroso, usado, costroso.

shabby [ˈʃæbi], *a.* raído, zarrapastroso, usado, costroso; ***shabby treatment,*** trato(s) mezquino(s).

shack [ʃæk], *s.* cabaña, casucha, chabola. — *v.i.* (*fam.*) ***shack up with s.o.,*** (irse *o* largarse a) vivir con alguien.

shackle [ʃækl], *s.* grillo, grillete; (*pl.*) hierros, *m.pl.*; trabas, *f.pl.*; ***the shackles of convention,*** las trabas del convencionalismo. — *v.t.* poner grillos a; poner trabas a.

shad [ʃæd], *s.* sábalo.

shade [ʃeid], *s.* sombra, umbría; matiz, tonalidad; pantalla (*de lámpara*); visera (*de gorra*); (*color*) tono, tonalidad; (*sentido, opinión etc.*) matiz; ***in the shade of,*** a la sombra de; ***to put s.o. in the shade,*** hacer sombra a alguien; ***a shade more,*** un poquito *o* una pizca más; ***a shade of,*** una pizca de; ***the shades of night,*** las sombras de la noche *o* nocturnas; ***sun shade,*** quitasol, parasol; ***window shade,*** visillo; (*pl.*, *Am.*) [BLINDS, VENETIAN]. — *v.t.* dar sombra a; sombrear; ***shade down,*** difuminar. — *v.i.* — ***away*** (***off***) ***into,*** ir transformándose poco a poco en.

shadeless [ˈʃeidlis], *a.* que carece de sombra.

shader [ˈʃeidə], *s.* persona *o* cosa que obscurece.

shadily [ˈʃeidili], *adv.* sospechosamente, de una manera sospechosa.

shadiness ˈʃeidinis], *s.* sombra; (lo) umbroso.

shading [ˈʃeidiŋ], *s.* (*b.a.*) degradación; sombreado.

shadow [ˈʃædou], *s.* sombra; (*pl.*, *relig.*) las tinieblas; ***shadow boxing,*** (el) hacer sombra; (*pol.*) ***shadow cabinet,*** equipo ministerial de la oposición; ***the shadow of death,*** la sombra de la muerte; ***without a shadow of doubt,*** sin asomo de duda, sin la menor duda; ***he is but a shadow of his former self,*** no es ni sombra de lo que fue. — *v.t.* oscurecer; sombrear; seguir y vigilar; ***I have been shadowed,*** me han seguido; ***shadow forth,*** presagiar.

shadowy [ˈʃædoui], *a.* tenebroso; borroso; ***a shadowy form,*** una figura borrosa *o* nebulosa.

shady [ˈʃeidi], *a.* sombreado, umbrío, umbroso; (*fam.*) sospechoso, turbio.

shaft [ʃɑ:ft], *s.* flecha, dardo, saeta; mango (de un arma *o* de una herramienta); (*mec.*) eje, árbol; (*arq.*) caña, fuste (*de columna*); (*carr.*) vara; humero, cañón (*de chimenea*); cañón (*de pluma*); (*min.*) pozo (*de mina*); pozo (*de ascensor*); ***camshaft,*** árbol de levas; ***driving shaft,*** árbol motor; ***shaft of irony*** o ***sarcasm,*** pulla, puyazo; ***shaft of light,*** rayo de luz; ***ventilating shaft,*** respiradero.

shag [ʃæg], *s.* pelo áspero y lanudo; (*tej.*) felpa; tabaco picado.

shagginess [ˈʃæginis], *s.* (lo) lanudo *etc.*

shaggy [ˈʃægi], *a.* lanudo, velludo, peludo, hirsuto; afelpado.

shagreen [ʃæˈgri:n], *s.* (piel de) zapa; chagrén.

shah [ʃɑ:], *s.* cha, *m.*

shake [ʃeik], *s.* sacudida; estremecimiento; meneo; movimiento (*de la cabeza*); (*mús.*) trino; (*fam.*) instante; ***milk shake,*** batido; (*fam.*) ***no great shakes,*** ninguna maravilla; ***in a brace of shakes,*** en un santiamén; ***shake up,*** meneón; convulsión; conmoción; reorganización. — *irr. v.t.* sacudir; estremecer; agitar; menear; mover (con violencia); hacer (re)temblar; hacer tambalearse; perturbar; (*fam.*) sorprender; estrechar (*la mano*); ***shake down,*** bajar *o* hacer bajar sacudiendo *o* a sacudidas; ***shake hands,*** estrecharse la mano; ***shake one's head,*** mover la cabeza; ***shake off,*** sacudirse (a); librarse de; despistar; ***shake out,*** hacer salir sacudiendo *o* a sacudidas; ***shake to bits,*** deshacer a sacudidas; ***shake up,*** sacudir, menear, pegar un meneón a; alterar, inquietar. — *irr. v.i.* estremecerse; agitarse; (re)temblar (***at, with,*** de); trepidar; (*mús.*) trinar, hacer gorgoritos; ***shake with laughter,*** desternillarse de risa. — *interj.* (*fam.*) ***shake*** (***on it***)***!*** ¡chócala!

shakedown [ˈʃeikdaun], *s.* cama improvisada.

shaker [ˈʃeikə], *s.* (***cocktail***) ***shaker,*** coctelera.

Shakespearean, Shakespearian [ʃeiksˈpiəriən], *a.* shakespeariano.

shaking [ˈʃeikiŋ], *s.* sacudidas, *f.pl.*; meneo; traqueteo; estremecimiento, temblores, *m.pl.*

sha(c)ko [ˈʃækou], *s.* chacó.

shaky [ˈʃeiki], *a.* trémulo, tembloroso; precario, tambaleante.

shale [ʃeil], *s.* esquisto; ***shale oil,*** aceite de esquistos.

shall [ʃæl], *irr. v. aux. defec.* (*expresa el futuro*) ***I shall do it,*** lo haré; ***shall we come tomorrow?*** ¿venimos mañana?; (*expresa deber u obligación en la 2a y 3a persona*) ***he shall do it,*** tiene que hacerlo.

shalloon [ʃæˈlu:n], *s.* chalón.

shallop [ˈʃæləp], *s.* chalupa; bote abierto.

shallot [ʃəˈlɔt], *s.* chalote, ascalonia, cebolleta.

shallow [ˈʃælou], *a.* poco profundo; bajo; llano; somero, superficial; (*mar.*) ***shallow-bodied,*** de poco calado; ***shallow-brained, shallow-pated,*** ligero de cascos, aturdido. — *s.* (*pl.*, *mar.*) bajos, *m.pl.*, bajío. — *v.i.* hacerse menos profundo.

shallowness [ˈʃælounis], *s.* poca profundidad; (*fig.*) frivolidad; superficialidad.

sham [ʃæm], *a.* falso, simulado, fingido; ***sham fight,*** simulacro de combate. — *s.* fraude, impostura, engaño; simulacro; impostor, farsante; ***it's all a sham,*** es todo engaño; ***he's just a big sham,*** es un farsante de aúpa. — *v.t.* fingir, simular. — *v.i.* fingirse.

shamble [ʃæmbl], *v.i.* andar arrastrando los pies; moverse renqueando.

shambles [ʃæmblz], *s.pl.* matadero, degolladero; carnicería; (*como sing.*) confusión, caos, *m.*; ***the whole thing was a shambles,*** todo ello fue una catástrofe; aquello fue un (auténtico) caos.

shambling [ˈʃæmbliŋ], *a.* pesado, lento.

shame [ʃeim], *s.* vergüenza; deshonra; pena, lástima; ***for shame! shame on you! the shame of it!*** ¡qué vergüenza!; ***what a shame!*** ¡qué lástima! ¡qué pena! — *v.t.* avergonzar, abochornar; ***shame s.o. into doing sth.,*** avergonzar a alguien para que tenga que hacer algo. — *interj.* ¡que vergüenza!

shamefaced [ˈʃeimfeist], *a.* vergonzoso.

shamefacedness [ˈʃeimfeistnis], *s.* vergüenza; pudor.

shameful [ˈʃeimful], *a.* vergonzoso, ignominioso; escandaloso; deshonroso.

shamefully [ˈʃeimfuli], *adv.* vergonzosamente; (*fig.*) ***shamefully ignorant,*** de una ignorancia vergonzosa *o* que da vergüenza.

shameless [ˈʃeimlis], *a.* desvergonzado, sin vergüenza.

shamelessness [ˈʃeimlisnis], *s.* desvergüenza.

shammy [ˈʃæmi], *s.* gamuza [CHAMOIS]; ***shammy leather,*** piel de gamuza.

shampoo [ʃæmˈpu:], *s.* champú; ***shampoo and set,*** lavado y marcado. — *v.t.* lavar con champú.

shamrock [ˈʃæmrɔk], *s.* trébol.

shandy [ˈʃændi], *s.* cerveza con gaseosa.

shanghai [ʃæŋˈhai], *v.t.* (*mar.*) embarcar a base de engaños y emborrachamiento; llevarse con engaños.

Shangri-la [ˈʃæŋri-ˈlɑ:]. (*aprox.*) Jauja.

shank [ʃæŋk], *s.* zanca; caña; (*impr.*) cuerpo (*del tipo*); (*mec.*) mango; (*zap.*) enfranque (de la suela); (*bot.*) pedicelo, pedúnculo; (*mar.*) ***shank of an anchor,*** asta de ancla; ***spindle shank,*** pierna de huso; ***to ride Shanks's mare*** o ***pony,*** ir en el coche de San Fernando.

shanked [ʃæŋkt], *a.* ***long-shanked*** o ***spindle-shanked,*** zancudo, de zancas largas.

shan't [ʃɑ:nt], (*fam.*) *abrev. de* **shall not** [SHALL].

shanty (1) [ˈʃænti], *s.* (*pl.* **shanties** [-iz]) cabaña, choza, chabola.

shanty (2) [ˈʃænti], *s.* (*pl.* **shanties** [-iz]) ***sea-***

shanty, canción marinera, saloma.

shantytown [ˈʃæntiˈtaun], *s.* barrio de chabolas.

shape [ʃeip], *s.* forma; figura; configuración; contorno; ***not in any shape or form,*** bajo ningún concepto; ***in good shape,*** en buenas condiciones, en buen estado; sano y fuerte, en forma; ***in poor shape,*** en malas condiciones, en mal estado; enfermo, débil; ***to get into shape,*** poner(se) en condiciones; preparar(se); ***to knock*** o ***put into shape,*** dar forma a; dar una estructura a; organizar; ***to get out of shape,*** perder la forma, deformarse; desentrenarse; ***the shape of things to come,*** el cariz del porvenir; ***to take shape,*** tomar forma *o* cuerpo, plasmarse; irse perfilando. — *v.t.* formar, dar forma *o* perfil a; modelar; (*fig.*) determinar, condicionar; dirigir.

shapeless [ˈʃeiplis], *a.* informe; sin forma.

shapelessness [ˈʃeiplisnis], *s.* (lo) informe; inconcreción.

shapeliness [ˈʃeiplinis], *s.* forma hermosa, forma atractiva; buen talle; morbidez.

shapely [ˈʃeipli], *a.* bien formado; proporcionado; de buen talle; mórbido.

shard [ʃɑ:d], *s.* tiesto, casco; élitro (*de un coleóptero*).

share [ʃɛə], *s.* parte, *f.*, porción; participación; (*com.*) acción; ***equal shares,*** partes iguales; ***fair share,*** parte *o* porción equitativa; ***to go shares, pay each his own share,*** pagar a escote; ***to have a share in,*** tomar parte, participar en; ***share-cropper,*** aparcero; [SHARE-OUT]. — *v.t.* compartir; ***share out,*** repartir, distribuir. — *v.i.* (*aportar*) participar, tomar parte (***in,*** en); (*sacar*) participar (***in,*** de); ***share and share alike,*** repartirse las cosas a partes iguales.

shareholder [ˈʃɛəhouldə], *s.* (*com.*) accionista, *m.f.*

share-out [ˈʃɛər-aut], *s.* reparto.

shark [ʃɑ:k], *s.* (*ict.*) tiburón; (*fam.*) estafador; ***shark skin,*** piel de tiburón.

sharp [ʃɑ:p], *a.* afilado, cortante; nítido, marcado; brusco, repentino; listo, vivo; agudo; fino; astuto; cáustico, acerbo, acre; ***sharp bend,*** curva cerrada; ***sharp customer,*** vivales, *m.inv.*; ***sharp-edged,*** afilado, de filo cortante; ***sharp-eyed, sharp-sighted,*** de vista penetrante, que tiene vista de lince; ***sharp-faced, sharp-featured,*** cariaguileño; ***sharp-pointed,*** de punta aguda, puntiagudo; ***sharp-witted,*** agudo de ingenio. — *adv.* ***at 3 o'clock sharp,*** a las 3 en punto; ***and be sharp about it!*** ¡y date prisa!; ***look sharp!*** ¡muévete!; ***to turn sharp left,*** coger la primera a la izquierda. — *s.* (*mús.*) sostenido.

sharpen [ˈʃɑ:pən], *v.t.* afilar, sacar punta a; aguzar; agudizar, hacer más intenso. — *v.i.* agudizarse, hacerse más intenso.

sharpener [ˈʃɑ:pənə], *s.* afilador; amolador; aguzador; ***knife sharpener,*** afilacuchillos, *m.inv.*, chaira; ***pencil sharpener,*** sacapuntas, *m.inv.*

sharper [ˈʃɑ:pə], *a. compar. de* [SHARP]. — *s.* estafador; fullero.

sharpness [ˈʃɑ:pnis], *s.* (lo) afilado, cortante *etc.*; brusquedad; nitidez; viveza, agudeza; finura; aspereza, mordacidad.

sharpshooter [ˈʃɑ:pʃu:tə], *s.* francotirador.

shatter [ˈʃætə], *v.t.* destrozar, hacer añicos *o* pedazos, estrellar, desbaratar. — *v.i.* romperse, hacerse añicos.

shattered [ˈʃætəd], *a.* destrozado; ***she felt completely shattered,*** se sintió totalmente anonadada, se quedó totalmente desfondada.

shattering [ˈʃætəriŋ], *a.* que destroza, demoledor; fulgurante; contundente.

shattery [ˈʃætəri], *a.* desmenuzable, quebradizo.

shave [ʃeiv], *s.* afeitado, rasurado; ***to have a shave,*** afeitarse; ***to have a close*** o ***narrow shave,*** escaparse por un pelo; ***that was a close shave!*** ¡nos hemos librado por un pelo *o* por los pelos! ¡ha faltado poquísimo para que nos diéramos un trompazo! — *v.t.* afeitar, rasurar; acepillar; rozar, pasar rozando. — *v.i.* afeitarse, hacerse la barba.

shaveling [ˈʃeivliŋ], *s.* (*despec.*) hombre rapado; monje, fraile.

shaven [ˈʃeivən], *a.* ***clean-shaven,*** (bien) afeitado.

shaver [ˈʃeivə], *s.* ***electric shaver,*** afeitadora eléctrica; ***young shaver,*** rapaz, chaval.

shaving [ˈʃeiviŋ], *s.* afeitada; raedura, rasura; acepilladura, raspadura; (*pl.*) acepilladuras, *f.pl.*, alisaduras, *f.pl.*, virutas, *f.pl.*, raeduras, *f.pl.*; ***shaving blade,*** navaja de afeitar; ***shaving brush,*** brocha de afeitar; ***shaving cloth,*** paño de afeitar; ***shaving cream,*** crema de afeitar; ***shaving dish,*** bacía; ***shaving lotion,*** loción para después del afeitado; ***shaving soap,*** jabón para afeitarse; ***shaving stick,*** jabón de afeitar.

shaw [ʃɔ:], *s.* soto, bosquecillo.

shawl [ʃɔ:l], *s.* chal; mantón.

she [ʃi:], *a.* ***she-devil,*** diabla; ***she-goat,*** cabra; ***she-ass,*** burra, borrica. — *pron. fem.* ella; hembra; ***she who,*** la que.

sheaf [ʃi:f], *s.* (*pl.* **sheaves** [ʃi:vz]) (*agric.*) gavilla; haz, *m.*; fajo. — *v.t.* (*agric.*) agavillar.

shear [ʃiə], *irr. v.t.* esquilar, trasquilar; ***shear off,*** cortar, cercenar; ***shear through,*** cortar, hender; (*fig.*) hender, surcar.

shearer [ˈʃiərə], *s.* esquilador, trasquilador.

shearing [ˈʃiəriŋ], *s.* esquileo; (*pl.*) lana esquilada; ***shearing-machine,*** esquiladora mecánica; ***shearing-time,*** esquileo.

shears [ʃiəz], *s.pl.* tijeras (grandes), *f.pl.*; (*mec.*) cizalla.

shearwater [ˈʃiəwɔ:tə], *s.* (*orn.*) pico-tijera.

sheat-fish [ˈʃi:t-fiʃ], *s.* siluro.

sheath [ʃi:θ], *s.* vaina; funda; estuche; ***sheath knife,*** navaja (que tiene vaina *o* funda).

sheathe [ʃi:ð], *v.t.* envainar, enfundar; (*mec.*) revestir.

sheathing [ˈʃi:ðiŋ], *s.* forro, revestimiento.

sheave [ʃi:v], *v.t.* (*agric.*) agavillar.

Sheba [ˈʃi:bə]. Sabá.

shebang [ʃiˈbæŋ], *s.* (*fam.*) ***the whole shebang,*** todo el asunto, toda la pesca.

shed (1) [ʃed], *irr. v.t.* verter (*lágrimas, luz*); derramar (*sangre*); despojarse de (*la ropa, las hojas*); mudar (*la piel*); (*fig.*) ***shed light on,*** arrojar luz sobre. — *irr. v.i.* mudar.

shed (2) [ʃed], *s.* cobertizo.

shedder [ˈʃedə], *s.* derramador; animal que muda.

shedding [ˈʃediŋ], *s.* derramamiento; vertimiento; muda (*de plumas, piel etc.*).

sheen [ʃi:n], *s.* brillo, lustre.

sheeny [ˈʃi:ni], *a.* brillante, lustroso.

sheep [ʃi:p], *s. inv.* oveja; carnero; (*pl.*) ganado ovino *o* lanar; (*fig.*) persona *o* gente gregaria; grey, *f.*; ***black sheep,*** garbanzo negro, oveja negra; ***sheep-cote*** [SHEEPFOLD]; ***sheep-dip,*** baño desinfectante para ovejas; ***sheep-dog,*** perro pastor; ***sheep-farmer,*** ganadero de ganado lanar; ***sheep-farming,*** ganadería de ganado lanar; ***sheep-hook,*** cayado; (*fig.*) ***sheep-like,*** borreguil, gregario; ***sheep-shearing,*** esquileo; ***sheep-tick,*** garrapata; ***sheep-walk,*** carneril, dehesa; ***to make sheep's eyes at,*** mirar con ojos de carnero a medio degollar.

sheepfold [ˈʃi:pfould], *s.* redil, majada, aprisco.

sheepish [ˈʃi:piʃ], *a.* vergonzoso.

sheepishness [ˈʃi:piʃnis], *s.* (lo) vergonzoso.

sheepshead [ˈʃi:pshed], *s.* (*ict.*) sargo.

sheepskin [ˈʃi:pskin], *s.* badana, piel de carnero; ***sheepskin jacket,*** zamarra.

sheer (1) [ʃiə], *a.* puro, completo; cabal, consumado; escarpado; diáfano; fino; ***sheer nonsense!*** ¡pura tontería!; ***this is sheer robbery,*** es un robo con todas las de la ley. — *adv.* de golpe; a pico.

sheer (2) [ʃiə], *v.i.* — ***off,*** (*mar.*) desviarse; (*fam.*) largarse.

sheer-hulk [ˈʃiə-hʌlk], *s.* chata de arbolar.

sheer-legs [ˈʃiə-legz], *s.pl.* cabria de arbolar.
sheers [ʃiəz], *s.pl.* cabria de arbolar; machina, grúa de tijeras.
sheet [ʃi:t], *s.* hoja, lámina, plancha (*de cualquier materia*); sábana; cuartilla, hoja (*de papel*); extensión (*de agua*); (*mar.*) escota; (*poét.*) vela; (*fig.*) ***sheet anchor,*** áncora de salvación; ***sheet cable,*** cable mayor; ***sheet glass,*** vidrio plano, luna; ***sheet hole,*** escotera; ***sheet lightning,*** fucilazo(s); ***sheet piling,*** pilotaje; (*mar.*) ***topsail sheets,*** escotines, *m.pl.*; ***winding sheet,*** mortaja; ***to haul aft the sheets,*** cazar las escotas; ***to sail with flowing sheets,*** navegar a escota larga. — *v.t.* ensabanar, envolver en sábanas, poner sábanas en, proveer de sábanas; amortajar; extender en láminas *u* hojas.
sheeting [ˈʃi:tiŋ], *s.* tela para sábanas; (*metal.*) laminado; (*hidr.*, *min.*) encofrado.
sheikh [ʃi:k, ʃeik], *s.* jeque.
shekel [ˈʃekəl], *s.* siclo; (*pl.*, *fam.*) dinero.
shelf [ʃelf], *s.* (*pl.* **shelves** [ʃelvz]) estante; anaquel; (*mar.*) bajío, banco de arena; (*geol.*) escalón (*de roca*); ***continental shelf,*** plataforma submarina; ***to get left on the shelf,*** quedarse para vestir santos.
shell [ʃel], *s.* casco; cáscara (*de nuez, de huevo etc.*); (*bot.*) silicua; vaina, vainilla (*de legumbres*); concha; caparazón (*de cangrejo etc.*); (*fund.*) camisa *o* revestimiento de horno; (*artill.*) proyectil, obús, *m.*, granada; (*mar.*) casco *o* caja de motón; ***shell fire,*** cañoneo, bombardeo, fuego de artillería; ***shell gold,*** oro de concha, oro molido; ***shell-proof,*** a prueba de bomba; ***shell shock,*** shock producido por los bombardeos; ***shell silver,*** plata de concha; ***shell work,*** obra de concha; ***tortoise shell,*** carey, concha de tortuga; ***to come out of one's shell,*** salir de su concha; ***to retire into one's shell,*** meterse en su concha. — *v.t.* pelar, desvainar, descascarar; (*mil.*) bombardear. — *v.i.* (*fam.*) ***shell out,*** desembolsar dinero.
shellac [ˈʃelæk], *s.* goma laca en hojuelas. — *v.t.* barnizar con laca.
shellbark [ˈʃelbɑ:k], *s.* caria.
sheller [ˈʃelə], *s.* desgranador, descascarador.
shellfish [ˈʃelfiʃ], *s. inv.* crustáceo; (*pl.*) mariscos, *m.pl.*
shelling [ˈʃeliŋ], *s.* descascaramiento, desgranamiento, desgrane; bombardeo.
shelly [ˈʃeli], *a.* conchado, conchudo, cubierto de conchas.
shelter [ˈʃeltə], *s.* abrigo, refugio; albergue; protección, amparo; ***to seek shelter,*** buscar cobijo; ***under shelter,*** al abrigo. — *v.t.* abrigar; amparar; proteger. — *v.i.* abrigarse, ponerse al abrigo, refugiarse, cobijarse; ***shelter from the rain,*** ponerse al abrigo de la lluvia.
sheltered [ˈʃeltəd], *a.* abrigado; resguardado del viento; protegido de lo desagradable.
shelterless [ˈʃeltəlis], *a.* desamparado; desabrigado.
shelve (1) [ʃelv], *v.t.* (*fig.*) dar carpetazo a.
shelve (2) [ʃelv], *v.i.* estar en declive.
shelves [ʃelvz], *s.pl.* [SHELF].
shelving (1) [ˈʃelviŋ], *s.* estantería; anaquelería.
shelving (2) [ˈʃelviŋ], *a.* en declive.
shemozzle [ʃiˈmɔzl], *s.* (*fam.*) barahúnda, revuelo, alboroto; ***make a shemozzle,*** armar un cisco.
shenanigans [ʃiˈnænigənz], *s.pl.* (*fam.*) chanchullos, *m.pl.*, tejemaneje(s).
shepherd [ˈʃepəd], *s.* pastor; ***shepherd dog,*** perro pastor; ***shepherd's crook,*** cayado; (*bot.*) ***shepherd's pouch,*** bolsa de pastor.— *v.t.* guiar.
shepherdess [ˈʃepədes], *s.* pastora, zagala.
sherbet [ˈʃə:bət], *s.* sorbete.
sherd [ʃə:d], *s.* tiesto, casco.
sherif [ʃeˈri:f], s. jerife.
sheriff [ˈʃerif], *s.* sheriff.
sheriffdom [ˈʃerifdəm], *s.* jurisdicción del sheriff.
sherry [ˈʃeri], *s.* (vino de) Jerez, jerez.
Shetland Islands [ˈʃetlənd ailəndz], **the.** Las Islas Shetland.
shew [ʃou], *irr. v.t.*, *v.i.* [SHOW].
shibboleth [ˈʃiboleθ], *s.* formulismo.
shie [SHY].
shield [ʃi:ld], *s.* escudo; broquel, rodela; (*mec.*) blindaje; (*blas.*) escudo de armas; ***shield-bearer,*** escudero. — *v.t.* escudar; amparar, defender; resguardar, proteger.
shift [ʃift], *s.* cambio; cambio de sitio; movimiento; tanda, turno; truco, estratagema, *f.*, recurso; vestido (*de mujer*) en estilo de camisa; ***to make shift for o.s.,*** defenderse solo, apañárselas solo; ***to make shift to,*** ingeniárselas para; ***to make shift with,*** arreglárselas con; ***to make shift without,*** arreglárselas sin. — *v.t.* cambiar (de sitio), trasladar, mover. — *v.i.* cambiar (de sitio); cambiar de casa; moverse; menearse; (*fam.*) ir como el viento; ***shift for o.s.,*** defenderse solo, apañárselas solo.
shiftless [ˈʃiftlis], *a.* inútil, incapaz; perezoso e inquieto.
shifty [ˈʃifti], *a.* taimado; huidizo, escurridizo, furtivo.
shillalah, shillela(g)h [ʃiˈleilə], *s.* cachiporra.
shilling [ˈʃiliŋ], *s.* chelín.
shilly-shally [ˈʃili-ʃæli], *s.* vacilaciones, *f.pl.*, titubeos, *m.pl.* — *v.i.* vacilar, titubear.
shim [ʃim], *s.* cuña, chaveta, plancha *etc.* que sirve de relleno. — *v.t.* tapar, rellenar, cuñar.
shimmer [ˈʃimə], *s.* luz trémula, débil resplandor. — *v.i.* rielar, relucir.
shimmering, shimmery [ˈʃiməriŋ, -ri], *a.* reluciente; trémulo.
shimmy (1) [ˈʃimi], *s.* (*fam.*) camisa (*de mujer*).
shimmy (2) [ˈʃimi], *s.* baile de movimientos temblorosos; (*aut.*) abaniqueo de las ruedas delanteras. — *v.i.* bailar el shimmy; (*aut.*) oscilar las ruedas delanteras.
shin [ʃin], *s.* espinilla; jarrete; ***shin pad,*** guardaespinilla, *m.inv.*, guardatibia, *m.inv.* — *v.i.* — ***up,*** trepar.
shindy [ˈʃindi], *s.* alboroto, zapatiesta; ***to kick up a shindy,*** armar una zapatiesta.
shine [ʃain], *s.* brillo, lustre; buen tiempo; ***to give a shine to,*** dar lustre, sacar brillo a; (*fam.*) ***to take a shine to,*** cogerle simpatía a; ***rain or shine,*** llueva o haga sol; (*fig.*) pase lo que pase. — (*irr.*) *v.t.* sacar brillo a, limpiar; pulir. — *v.i.* brillar, relucir, resplandecer; (*fig.*) brillar, lucirse.
shiner [ˈʃainə], *s.* persona *o* cosa que brilla; (*fam.*) moneda de oro; pez plateado; (ojo) morado, ojo a la virulé.
shingle (1) [ʃiŋgl], *s.* (*arq.*) ripia; corte a lo garçon. — *v.t.* cortar el pelo a lo garçon; techar con ripia.
shingle (2) [ʃiŋgl], *s.* guijos, *m.pl.*, guijarral.
shingle (3) [ʃiŋgl], *v.t.* (*metal.*) cinglar.
shingles [ʃiŋglz], *s.* (*med.*) herpes, *m.f.*, *pl.*
shingly [ˈʃiŋgli], *a.* guijarroso, guijarreño.
shining [ˈʃainiŋ], *a.* brillante, radiante, luciente, resplandeciente, luminoso, lustroso. — *s.* lucimiento.
Shintoism [ˈʃintouizəm], *s.* sintoísmo.
shiny [ˈʃaini], *a.* lustroso, brillante, luciente, resplandeciente.
ship [ʃip], *s.* barco, buque, navío; ***to abandon ship,*** abandonar el barco; ***to clear a ship for action,*** alistar un buque para el combate; ***merchant ship,*** buque mercante; ***on board ship,*** a bordo; ***ship breaker,*** desguazador de barcos; ***ship canal,*** canal de navegación; ***ship chandlery,*** cabuyería; tienda de efectos navales; ***ship fever,*** tifus, *m.inv.*; ***ship of the line,*** navío de alto bordo, navío de línea; ***ship of war,*** buque de guerra; ***ship owner,*** naviero, armador; ***ship's biscuit,*** galleta de munición, galleta muy dura; ***ship's boy,*** paje de escoba, grumete; ***ship's carpenter,*** carpintero de ribera; ***ship's company,*** tripulación; ***ship's doctor,*** médico de a bordo; ***ship's***

papers, documentación del buque; ***ship's stores,*** matalotaje; ***store ship,*** navío almacén. — *v.t.* embarcar; izar; armar; enviar, expedir; ***ship a sea,*** embarcar agua (*una ola*). — *v.i.* embarcarse.

shipboard [ˈʃipbɔ:d], *s.* (*mar.*) bordo; ***a-shipboard, on shipboard,*** a bordo.

shipbuilder [ˈʃipbildə], *s.* ingeniero naval, constructor de barcos.

shipbuilding [ˈʃipbildiŋ], *s.* construcción naval.

shipload [ˈʃiploud], *s.* cargazón, *f.*, cargamento.

shipmaster [ˈʃipmɑ:stə], *s.* patrón, capitán de buque.

shipmate [ˈʃipmeit], *s.* camarada de a bordo, *m.*

shipment [ˈʃipmənt], *s.* embarque; expedición; cargamento; envío, remesa.

shipper [ˈʃipə], *s.* remitente; exportador.

shipping [ˈʃipiŋ], *a.* naval; marítimo; de la marina mercante; de embarque. — *s.* barcos, *m.pl.*, buques, *m.pl.*; marina; (*com.*) embarque, expedición; ***shipping agent,*** consignatario de buques; ***shipping articles,*** contrata de marinero; ***shipping bill,*** factura de embarque; ***shipping charges,*** gastos de embarque, *m.pl.*; ***shipping clerk,*** dependiente de muelle; ***shipping master,*** persona que contrata marineros.

shipshape [ˈʃipʃeip], *a.*, *adv.* en buen orden.

shipworm [ˈʃipwə:m], *s.* tiñuela.

shipwreck [ˈʃiprek], *s.* naufragio. — *v.t.* hacer naufragar; ***to be shipwrecked,*** naufragar.

shipwrecked [ˈʃiprekt], *a.* náufrago.

shipwright [ˈʃiprait], *s.* carpintero de ribera.

shipyard [ˈʃipjɑ:d], *s.* astillero.

shire [ʃaiə], *s.* condado; ***shire horse,*** percherón.

shirk [ʃə:k], *s.* [SHIRKER]. — *v.t.* eludir, evitar, esquivar; faltar a; desentenderse de; ***shirk one's duty,*** faltar al deber. — *v.i.* remolonear, hacerse el remolón, escurrir el bulto.

shirker [ˈʃə:kə], *s.* persona que falta a su deber; remolón, el que escurre el bulto.

shirr [ʃə:], *s.* (*cost.*) frunce, fruncimiento, acordonamiento; hilo de goma tejido en una tela para hacerla elástica. — *v.t.* (*cost.*) fruncir, gandujar, acordonar.

shirred [ʃə:d], *p.p.* [SHIRR]. — *a.* (*cost.*) acordonado, fruncido; (*tej.*) elástico.

shirt [ʃə:t], *s.* camisa; ***shirt-collar,*** cuello de camisa; ***shirt-front,*** pechera de camisa; ***shirt-sleeve,*** manga de camisa; ***to be in one's shirt-sleeves,*** estar en mangas de camisa; ***shirt-tail,*** faldón de camisa; (*fam.*) ***keep your shirt on!*** ¡tranquilícese! ¡no se sulfure!

shirting [ˈʃə:tiŋ], *s.* tela para camisas.

shirt-waist [ˈʃə:t-weist], (*Am.*) [BLOUSE].

shirty [ˈʃə:ti], *a.* (*fam.*) malhumorado; ***to get shirty,*** amoscarse, mosquearse.

shist [ʃist], *s.* esquisto; [SCHIST].

shiver (1) [ˈʃivə], *s.* temblor; escalofrío, tiritón; estremecimiento; (*fam.*) ***it gives me the shivers,*** me da grima *o* dentera. — *v.i.* temblar; tiritar; estremecerse.

shiver (2) [ˈʃivə], *s.* fragmento; astilla. — *v.i.* — ***to pieces,*** hacerse añicos.

shivering [ˈʃivəriŋ], *a.* temblante *etc.* — *s.* (el) temblar *etc.*

shivery [ˈʃivəri], *a.* estremecido; tembloroso; friolero; ***to feel shivery,*** tener escalofríos.

shoal (1) [ʃoul], *s.* banco (*de peces*), cardumen; muchedumbre. — *v.i.* reunirse en gran número.

shoal (2) [ʃoul], *s.* bajío, banco de arena. — *v.i.* disminuir en profundidad.

shoaly [ˈʃouli], *a.* lleno de bajíos.

shock (1) [ʃɔk], *s.* choque; shock; sacudida; encuentro violento, encontronazo; temblor (*de tierra*); sorpresa (desagradable); escándalo; (*med.*) shock; (*elec.*) calambre; ***it was a great shock to him,*** le causó una impresión muy fuerte; ***shock absorber,*** amortiguador; ***shock tactics,*** táctica de sorpresa; ***shock therapy,*** terapia de shock; ***shock treatment,*** tratamiento de shock; ***shock troops,*** tropas de asalto, *f.pl.* — *v.t.* sorprender (desagradablemente); impresionar (fuertemente); escandalizar; ***to be shocked,*** escandalizarse.

shock (2) [ʃɔk], *s.* (*agric.*) tresnal.

shock (3) [ʃɔk], *s.* ***shock of hair,*** mechón, greña.

shocker [ˈʃɔkə], *s.* porquería, birria; ***he's a shocker,*** es tremendo.

shocking [ˈʃɔkiŋ], *a.* espantoso; escandaloso, ofensivo; ***it's shocking,*** es una vergüenza; ***he has shocking taste,*** tiene un gusto pésimo.

shockingly [ˈʃɔkiŋli], *adv.* horriblemente, terriblemente; ***it's a shockingly bad book,*** es un libro infame.

shockproof [ˈʃɔkpru:f], *a.* a prueba de golpes; (*persona*) imperturbable.

shod [ʃɔd], *pret.*, *p.p.* [SHOE]; ***shod with,*** calzado de.

shoddy [ˈʃɔdi], *a.* inferior; de pacotilla. — *s.* lana regenerada; (*fig.*) pacotilla.

shoe [ʃu:], *s.* zapato; herradura; zapata; ***horse-shoe,*** herradura; ***shoe black,*** limpiabotas, *m.inv.*; ***shoe blacking,*** betún para zapatos; ***shoe brush,*** cepillo de *o* para zapatos; ***shoe lace,*** cordón de zapato; ***shoe polish,*** betún, crema; ***shoe shop,*** zapatería; ***on a shoe string,*** con muy poco dinero, a lo barato; ***to cast a shoe,*** desherrarse (*un animal*); (*fam.*) ***to be in s.o.'s shoes,*** hallarse en el pellejo de alguien; ***to step into s.o. else's shoes,*** ocupar el puesto de otro; ***wooden shoes,*** zuecos, *m.pl.* — *irr. v.t.* calzar; herrar (*un caballo*); (*mar.*) ***shoe the anchor,*** calzar el ancla.

shoehorn [ˈʃu:hɔ:n], *s.* calzador.

shoeing [ˈʃu:iŋ], *s.* (el) herrar.

shoemaker [ˈʃu:meikə], *s.* zapatero.

shoemaking [ˈʃu:meikiŋ], *s.* zapatería, fabricación de calzado.

shoer [ˈʃu:ə], *s.* herrador (de caballerías).

shoestring [ˈʃu:striŋ], (*Am.*) [SHOE LACE].

shole [ʃoul], *s.* (*mar.*) solero, tornapunta.

shoo [ʃu:], *v.t.* ahuyentar (*gallinas etc.*). — *interj.* ¡so! ¡fuera!

shoot [ʃu:t], *s.* renuevo, retoño, vástago; partida de caza; rabión; resbaladero; empuje (*de un arco*). — *irr. v.t.* disparar, tirar, descargar; matar *o* herir con arma de fuego; fusilar; rodar, filmar; (*dep.*) marcar, meter; saltar sobre; salvar, atravesar; echar (*red, dados, rayos*); verter, vaciar; ***shoot dead,*** matar a tiros; ***shoot down,*** derribar, abatir; rebatir; ***shoot out,*** arrojar; ***shoot a question,*** espetar una pregunta; ***shoot through,*** atravesar de un tiro; ***shoot up,*** asaltar a tiros. — *irr. v.i.* tirar; disparar; (*dep.*) chutar, tirar; punzar, dar punzadas; brotar; lanzarse, salir disparado; ***shoot back,*** devolver el tiro; ***shoot in,*** entrar como un disparo; ***shoot off*** o ***out,*** salir como una bala; ***shoot past,*** pasar embalado; ***shoot to,*** precipitarse a; ***shoot to kill,*** tirar a matar; ***shoot up,*** crecer, espigar; ***the price has shot up,*** el precio ha subido vertiginosamente; ***the temperature shot up,*** se desbocó el termómetro.

shooter [ˈʃu:tə], *s.* tirador.

shooting [ˈʃu:tiŋ], *a.* creciente; punzante etc.; ***shooting pain,*** dolor punzante; ***shooting star,*** estrella fugaz. — *s.* caza con escopeta; tiro; tiroteo; latido doloroso, punzada; coto de caza; derecho de cazar; ***shooting brake,*** furgoneta, rubia; ***shooting gallery,*** galería de tiro (al blanco); ***shooting jacket,*** cazadora; ***shooting match,*** concurso de tiro; ***shooting range,*** campo de tiro; ***shooting stick,*** (*dep.*) bastón asiento; (*impr.*) acuñador, desacuñador; atacador.

shop [ʃɔp], *s.* tienda; (*pl.*) tiendas, comercio; (*fábrica*) taller; ***baker's shop,*** panadería; ***bookseller's shop,*** librería; ***chemist's shop,*** farmacia; ***jeweller's shop,*** joyería; ***silversmith's shop,*** platería; ***stationer's shop,*** papelería; ***watchmaker's shop,*** relojería; ***shop assistant,*** dependiente, dependienta; ***shop girl,***

muchacha de tienda; (*fábrica*) ***shop steward,*** enlace sindical; ***shop window,*** escaparate; ***to set up shop,*** abrir una tienda; ***to shut up shop,*** cerrar la tienda; (*fig.*) dar de mano; ***to talk shop,*** hablar del trabajo, del oficio. — *v.i.* ir de compras; ***to go shopping,*** ir de compras.

shopkeeper [ˈʃɔpki:pə], *s.* tendero.

shoplifter [ˈʃɔpliftə], *s.* ladrón de tiendas; (mujer) mechera.

shoplifting [ˈʃɔpliftiŋ], *s.* robo en las tiendas.

shopper [ˈʃɔpə], *s.* comprador.

shopping [ˈʃɔpiŋ], *s.* compras, *f.pl.*; ***shopping centre,*** zona comercial.

shop-soiled [ˈʃɔp-sɔild], *a.* estropeado, deteriorado.

shopwalker [ˈʃɔpwɔ:kə], *s.* vigilante (de almacén).

shop-worn [ˈʃɔp-wɔ:n], (*Am.*) [SHOP-SOILED].

shore (1) [ˈʃɔ:], *s.* playa; ribera; orilla; ***on shore,*** en tierra.

shore (2) [ʃɔ:], *s.* puntal. — *v.t.* — (***up***), apuntalar.

shorn [ʃɔ:n], *p.p.* [SHEAR]; (*fig.*) ***shorn of,*** despojado de.

short [ʃɔ:t], *a.* corto; breve; (*pers.*) bajo; escaso, falto; (*fig.*) seco, brusco; quebradizo; ***it's short for,*** es forma abreviada de, es abreviatura de; ***short-bodied,*** pequeño de cuerpo; ***short change,*** vuelta de menos; [SHORT-CHANGE]; ***short circuit,*** cortocircuito; [SHORT-CIRCUIT]; ***short cut,*** atajo; ***short-haired,*** de pelo corto; ***short-handed,*** falto de mano de obra; ***short list,*** lista de aspirantes posibles; [SHORT-LIST]; ***short-lived,*** efímero, pasajero, de breve vida; ***short memory,*** poca memoria, memoria corta; ***short-necked,*** cuellicorto; ***short-range,*** de corto *o* poco alcance; ***short-sighted,*** miope, corto de vista; (*fig.*) falto de previsión; ***short-sightedness,*** miopía, cortedad de vista; (*fig.*) falta de previsión; ***short-tempered,*** de mal genio, de poca paciencia; ***short-term,*** de corto plazo, a corto plazo; ***to work short time,*** trabajar (en) jornadas reducidas; ***short-waisted,*** corto de talle; ***short wave,*** onda corta; ***a short while,*** un rato, un ratito; ***in a short while,*** dentro de un ratito *o* de poco tiempo; ***short-winded,*** corto de respiración; ***to be short, cut a long story short,*** para abreviar, en resumidas cuentas; ***to be short of,*** estar falto de, andar escaso de. — *adv.* ***nothing short of,*** nada menos que; ***short of stealing,*** como no sea a base de robar; ***to come*** o ***fall short of,*** no llegar a, no responder a, defraudar algo; ***to cut short,*** terminar prematuramente; interrumpir; ***to run short of,*** acabársele a uno; ***we are running short of petrol,*** se nos acaba la gasolina; ***to stop short,*** detenerse de repente; ***to stop short of,*** detenerse antes de llegar a. — *s.* (*fam.*) película corta; (*fam.*) cortocircuito; (*pl.*) pantalón corto; (*Am.*) [PANTS; BRIEFS]; ***for short,*** para abreviar; ***in short,*** en suma, en resumen; ***the long and the short of it,*** en resumidas cuentas, en resumen.

shortage [ˈʃɔ:tidʒ], *s.* falta, escasez.

shortbread, shortcake [ˈʃɔ:tbred, ˈʃɔ:tkeik], *s.* mantecada, torta escocesa.

short-change [ˈʃɔ:t-ˈtʃeindʒ], *v.t.* devolver de menos.

short-circuit [ˈʃɔ:t-ˈsə:kit], *v.t., v.i.* cortocircuitar(se).

shortcoming [ˈʃɔ:tkʌmiŋ], *s.* defecto, imperfección, deficiencia.

shorten [ʃɔ:tn], *v.t.* acortar, abreviar, reducir. — *v.i.* acortarse, abreviarse, reducirse.

shortening [ˈʃɔ:tniŋ], *s.* acortamiento; abreviación; reducción; manteca de hojaldre.

shortfall [ˈʃɔ:tfɔ:l], *s.* déficit.

shorthand [ˈʃɔ:thænd], *s.* taquigrafía, estenografía; ***to take shorthand,*** escribir al dictado; ***to take sth. down in shorthand,*** apuntar algo taquigráficamente; ***shorthand-typist,*** taquimeca (-nógrafa); ***shorthand writer,*** taquígrafo.

shortish [ˈʃɔ:tiʃ], *a.* cortillo; (*pers.*) bajillo.

short-list [ˈʃɔ:t-ˈlist], *v.t.* poner a alguien en la lista de los posibles.

shortly [ˈʃɔ:tli], *adv.* en breve, dentro de poco, próximamente; secamente, bruscamente; ***shortly after,*** poco después.

shortness [ˈʃɔ:tnis], *s.* (lo) corto; (lo) breve, brevedad; (lo) brusco; flaqueza (*de memoria*); ***shortness of breath,*** respiración dificultosa.

shot [ʃɔt], *pret., p.p.* [SHOOT]. — *a.* (*tej.*) batido, tornasolado; ***shot silk,*** seda tornasolada, muaré. — *s.* bala, proyectil; tiro, disparo; balazo; (*fam.*) foto, *f.*; perdigones, *m.pl.*; (*dep.*) peso; (*dep.*) golpe, tirada, tiro; inyección, dosis, *f.inv.*; (el) probar; (el) adivinar; ***big shot,*** pez gordo; ***bird shot,*** perdigones, *m.pl.*; ***buck shot,*** perdigones, *m.pl.*; ***cannon shot,*** cañonazo; ***crack shot,*** tirador experto; ***deer shot,*** munición de balines; ***fowling shot,*** munición menuda; ***good shot,*** buena escopeta, buen tirador; ***good shot!*** ¡muy bien!; ***grape shot,*** metralla; ***like a shot,*** como una bala; ***not by a long shot,*** ni con mucho, ni mucho menos; ***moon shot,*** lanzamiento de un cohete a la luna; ***shot between wind and water,*** balazo a flor del agua; ***shot gauge,*** vitola para calibrar proyectiles; ***a shot in the arm,*** un estímulo *o* acicate; ***a shot of whisky,*** un trago *o* traguete de whisky; ***shot plug,*** tapabalazo; ***shot pouch,*** perdigonera; ***shot tower,*** torre para hacer municiones; ***to exchange shots,*** tirotearse; (*fig.*) ***to have a shot at,*** probar suerte de; ***to take a shot at,*** tirar a.

shotgun [ˈʃɔtgʌn], *s.* escopeta; ***shotgun wedding,*** casamiento forzoso, boda de penalty.

should [ʃud], *pret.* [SHALL]; (*aux. de modo condicional*) ***I should like to go,*** me gustaría ir; (*indica deber*) ***you should go,*** deberías ir.

shoulder [ˈʃouldə], *s.* hombro; espalda(s); lomo; andén, arcén; ***shoulder blade, bone,*** paletilla, omóplato; (*mil.*) ***shoulder knot,*** charretera mocha, capona; ***shoulder of pork,*** pernil; ***shoulder pad,*** hombrera; ***shoulder strap,*** correón; tirante; ***to give s.o. the cold shoulder,*** volver la espalda *o* hacer el vacío a alguien; ***to put one's shoulder to the wheel,*** arrimar el hombro; ***to rub shoulders with,*** codearse con; ***to stand shoulder to shoulder,*** estar hombro con hombro. — *v.t.* llevar al hombro; echarse a las espaldas, cargar con; ***shoulder arms!*** ¡armas al hombro!; ***shoulder one's way through,*** abrirse paso empujando con el hombro.

shout [ʃaut], *s.* grito, voz. — *v.t., v.i.* gritar, dar voces (de); ***shout down,*** hacer callar a gritos, acallar a gritos, hundir a gritos.

shouting [ˈʃautiŋ], *s.* gritería; vocerío.

shove [ʃʌv], *s.* empujón, empellón. — *v.t.* empujar, dar un empujón *o* empujones a; ***shove out,*** empujar hacia fuera, hacer salir a empujones. — *v.i.* empujar, pegar empujones; (*mar.*) ***shove off,*** alejarse; (*fam.*) largarse.

shovel [ˈʃʌvəl], *s.* pala; ***fire shovel,*** badila; (*juego*) ***shovel board,*** (el) tejo; ***shovel hat,*** sombrero de teja. — *v.t.* traspalar; quitar con pala; ***shovel food into one's mouth,*** meterse comida en la boca sin parar, comer sin respirar.

shovelful [ˈʃʌvəlful], *s.* palada.

shoveller [ˈʃʌvələ], *s.* palero.

shovelling [ˈʃʌvəliŋ], *s.* traspaleo.

show, shew [ʃou], *s.* exhibición; exposición; pompa, aparato, boato; manifestación; demostración; apariencia, fachada, fingimiento; (*teat.*) función, espectáculo; (*ganado*) feria; ***dumb show,*** pantomima; ***on show,*** expuesto; ***in open show,*** públicamente, delante de todo el mundo; ***show boat,*** barco teatro; ***show business,*** vida de teatro, de cine y de televisión, farándula; ***show case,*** vitrina; ***show girl,*** vicetiple, *f.*; corista, girl, *f.*; ***show ground,*** campo de feria; ***show jumping,*** hipismo; ***show of hands,*** votación a mano alzada; ***show piece,*** pieza más lucida; pieza muy lucida; ***show window,*** escaparate; (*fam.*) ***to give the show away,*** echarlo todo a rodar, descubrir el pastel, delatarse; ***to make a show of,*** fingir, simular; hacer alarde *o* gala de; ***to make*** o ***put up a good show,*** estar bien, hacer un buen papel; (*fam.*) ***the whole show,*** todo el asunto *o* negocio, toda la pesca; (*fam.*) ***to run the whole show,*** mangonearlo todo. — *irr. v.t.* enseñar; mostrar; probar, demostrar; manifestar, exteriorizar; indicar, señalar; exhibir; (*películas*) proyectar, poner; (*pérdida etc.*) arrojar; ***show in,*** hacer pasar; ***show off,*** lucir, hacer alarde *o* gala de; ***show out,*** acompañar a la puerta; ***show one's teeth,*** enseñar los dientes; ***show up,*** hacer subir; descubrir, revelar, poner de relieve *o* de manifiesto; revelar bajo un aspecto desfavorable. — *irr. v.i.* verse, notarse, aparecer; transparentarse; ***show off,*** lucirse; chulear(se); ***show up,*** aparecer, presentarse, asomar.

showbread, shewbread [ˈʃoubred], *s.* panes de proposición, *m.pl.*

show-down [ˈʃou-daun], *s.* (*fam.*) hora de la verdad, ajuste de cuentas, enfrentamiento.

shower [ˈʃauə], *s.* chubasco, chaparrón; ducha; (*fig.*) lluvia, rociada; ***heavy shower,*** aguacero; ***shower bath,*** ducha. — *v.t.* regar, derramar con abundancia; ***shower with,*** colmar de. — *v.i.* llover, caer un chubasco *o* chubascos; (*fig.*) llover.

showery [ˈʃauəri], *a.* chubascoso, de chubascos.

showiness [ˈʃouinis], *s.* aparatosidad, (lo) vistoso *etc.*

showman [ˈʃoumən], *s.* empresario; (*fig.*) fantasmón, farsantón.

showmanship [ˈʃoumənʃip], *s.* teatralidad; capacidad para presentar espectáculos.

show-off [ˈʃou-ɔf], *s.* persona que le gusta mucho lucirse. [SHOW OFF].

showroom [ˈʃouru:m], *s.* sala de exposición.

showy [ˈʃoui], *a.* vistoso, aparatoso, ostentoso, llamativo.

shrapnel [ˈʃræpnəl], *s.* metralla.

shred [ʃred], *s.* triza, jirón, tira; fragmento; ***to be in shreds,*** estar hecho trizas; ***to tear an argument to shreds,*** hacer pedazos un argumento; ***without a shred of evidence,*** sin la más ligera prueba. — *v.t.* hacer trizas *o* tiras; desmenuzar; deshilar (*carne*).

shredded [ˈʃredid], *a.* trojezado, desmenuzado, hecho trizas.

shrew [ʃru:], *s.* (*zool.*) musaraña; arpía, tarasca; ***The Taming of the Shrew,*** *La doma de la bravía* o *La fierecilla domada.*

shrewd [ʃru:d], *a.* listo, perspicaz, sagaz; astuto.

shrewdness [ˈʃru:dnis], *s.* perspicacia, sagacidad; astucia.

shrewish [ˈʃru:iʃ], *a.* regañona.

shrewishly [ˈʃru:iʃli], *adv.* de muy mal humor, regañando.

shrewishness [ˈʃru:iʃnis], *s.* mal genio.

shrewmouse [ˈʃru:maus], *s.* (*zool.*) musgaño, musaraña.

shriek [ʃri:k], *s.* chillido, grito agudo; ***with shrieks of laughter,*** con grandes risotadas. — *v.i.* chillar, gritar; ***shriek with laughter,*** reírse a grandes carcajadas; ***shriek with pain,*** chillar de dolor.

shrieking [ˈʃri:kiŋ], *a.* chillón. — *s.* chillidos, *m.pl.*, gritos, *m.pl.*

shrift [ʃrift], *s.* (*igl.*) confesión; penitencia; ***to give short shrift to,*** echar con cajas destempladas.

shrike [ʃraik], *s.* alcaudón.

shrill [ʃril], *a.* chillón, agudo, estridente. — *v.i.* chillar.

shrillness [ˈʃrilnis], *s.* (lo) estridente *o* chillón.

shrimp [ʃrimp], *s.* camarón, quisquilla; (*fig.*) retaco, renacuajo. — *v.i.* pescar camarones.

shrine [ʃrain], *s.* santuario, lugar sagrado; sepulcro de santo; relicario.

shrink [ʃriŋk], *irr. v.t.* contraer; reducir; mermar; (*mec.*) ***shrink on,*** montar (*una pieza*) en caliente. — *irr. v.i.* encogerse, contraerse; reducirse; mermar, disminuir; ***shrink away*** o ***back*** (***from*** o ***at***), acobardarse, amilanarse (ante).

shrinkage [ˈʃriŋkidʒ], *s.* encogimiento, contracción; reducción; (*com.*) merma, pérdida.

shrinking [ˈʃriŋkiŋ], *a.* apocado, tímido. — *s.* contracción; reducción; (*com.*) merma, pérdida; (*pers.*, *fig.*) acobardamiento, amilanamiento.

shrive [ʃraiv], *irr. v.t.*, *v.i.* (*igl.*) confesar; confesarse.

shrivel [ˈʃrivəl], *v.t.* secar, marchitar; arrugar. — *v.i.* — ***up,*** apergaminarse, avellanarse; arrugarse, encogerse.

shrivelled-up [ˈʃrivəld-ʌp], *a.* apergaminado, avellanado, sarmentoso.

shroud [ʃraud], *s.* mortaja, sudario; (*fig.*) velo; (*pl.*, *mar.*) obenques, *m.pl.*; (*fig.*) ***a shroud of mystery,*** un velo de misterio. — *v.t.* amortajar; (*fig.*) velar, ocultar; ***to be shrouded in,*** estar envuelto en.

Shrove Tuesday [ˈʃrouv ˈtju:zd(e)i]. martes de carnestolendas, *m.inv.*, martes de carnaval, *m.inv.*

Shrovetide [ˈʃrouvtaid]. carnaval.

shrub [ʃrʌb], *s.* arbusto.

shrubbery [ˈʃrʌbəri], *s.* arbustos, *m.pl.*; maleza(s), matorral(es).

shrubby [ˈʃrʌbi], *a.* lleno de arbustos.

shrug [ʃrʌg], *s.* encogimiento de hombros. — *v.t.* — ***one's shoulders,*** encogerse de hombros; ***shrug sth. off,*** tratar con indiferencia una cosa, sacudirse una cosa. — *v.i.* encogerse de hombros.

shrunken [ˈʃrʌŋkən], *a.* encogido; (*fig.*) disminuido. — *p.p.* [SHRINK].

shuck [ʃʌk], *s.* cáscara, vaina; (*Am.*) concha (*de marisco*). — *v.t.* descascarar, descortezar, pelar; quitar la concha a (*una ostra*).

shudder [ˈʃʌdə], *s.* temblor, estremecimiento; vibración, trepidación; ***a shudder ran through him,*** le recorrió el cuerpo un estremecimiento; ***he realized with a shudder that,*** se estremeció al darse cuenta de que. — *v.i.* temblar (violentamente), estremecerse; vibrar (violentamente), trepidar.

shuffle [ʃʌfl], *s.* (el) barajar, turno de barajar; (el) arrastrar los pies; ***he walks with a shuffle,*** anda arrastrando los pies. — *v.t.* barajar; revolver; ***shuffle one's feet,*** arrastrar los pies; ***shuffle off,*** sacudirse. — *v.i.* barajar; arrastrar los pies; ***shuffle along,*** ir arrastrando los pies.

shun [ʃʌn], *v.t.* rehuir, evitar; retraerse de, apartarse de, recatarse de; ***shun the world,*** vivir en el apartamiento.

shunt [ʃʌnt], *s.* desviación; (*elec.*) derivador de corriente, shunt. — *v.t.* desviar; (*f.c.*) apartar; (*elec.*) derivar, shuntar. — *v.i.* (*f.c.*) hacer maniobras.

shunter [ˈʃʌntə], *s.* (*f.c.*) guardagujas, *m.inv.*

shunting [ˈʃʌntiŋ], *s.* (*f.c.*) maniobras, *f.pl.*

shush! [ʃʌʃ], *interj.* (*fam.*) ¡chit!

shut [ʃʌt], *irr. v.t.* cerrar; ***shut the door in s.o.'s face,*** cerrarle a alguien la puerta en las narices; ***shut down,*** cerrar; parar; [SHUT-DOWN]; ***shut in,*** encerrar; rodear; cercar; ***shut off,*** cortar (*el agua etc.*); aislar (***from,*** de); ***shut out,*** excluir; negar la entrada a; ***shut up,*** (en)cerrar; obturar; acallar, hacer callar. — *irr. v.i.* cerrar(se); ***shut up,*** callarse.

shut-down [ˈʃʌt-daun], *s.* cierre.

shut-eye [ˈʃʌt-ai], *s.* (*fam.*) ***to get some shut-eye,*** (ir a) dormir (un poco).

shutter [ˈʃʌtə], *s.* postigo, contraventana; (*foto.*) obturador; ***to put up the shutters,*** cerrar el negocio.

shuttle [ʃʌtl], *s.* (*tej.*) lanzadera; ***shuttle-service,*** servicio de transporte rápido (*entre dos sitios poco distantes entre sí*). — *v.t.* transportar rápidamente (*entre dos sitios*). — *v.i.* ir y venir (*entre dos sitios*).

shuttlecock [ˈʃʌtlkɔk], *s.* volante.

shy (I) [ʃai], *a.* tímido, corto, vergonzoso; ***to be*** o ***fight shy of,*** rehuir, esquivar. — *v.i.* espantarse; ***shy away from,*** espantarse ante, zafarse de.

shy (2) [ʃai], *s.* tiro, echada; ***coconut shy,*** tiro al coco; ***have a shy at,*** probar, intentar. — *v.t.* lanzar, arrojar.
shyness [ˈʃainis], *s.* timidez; vergüenza; recato.
shyster [ˈʃaistə], *s.* (*Am., fam.*) tramposo.
si [si:], *s.* (*mús.*) si.
Siam [saiˈæm]. Siam.
Siamese [saiəˈmi:z], *a., s.* siamés.
Siberia [saiˈbiəriə]. Siberia.
Siberian [saiˈbiəriən], *a., s.* siberiano.
sibilant [ˈsibilənt], *a.* sibilante.
sibilation [sibiˈleiʃən], *s.* (lo) silbante.
sibyl [ˈsibil], *s.* sibila, profetisa.
sibylline [ˈsibilain], *a.* sibilino.
sicamore [SYCAMORE].
siccate [ˈsikeit], *v.t.* desecar.
siccation [siˈkeiʃən], *s.* desecación.
siccative [ˈsikətiv], *a., s.* (*pint.*) secante, secativo, desecativo.
siccity [ˈsiksiti], *s.* sequedad, aridez.
Sicilian [siˈsiliən], *a., s.* siciliano.
Sicily [ˈsisili]. Sicilia.
sick (1) [sik], *a.* malo, enfermo; mareado; harto; ***sick headache,*** jaqueca con náuseas; ***to be sick at heart,*** llevar la muerte en el alma; ***to be sick of,*** estar harto de; ***to get sick of,*** coger asco a; ***to report sick,*** darse de baja (por enfermedad); ***to take sick,*** caer enfermo, enfermar; (*fig.*) ***you make me sick!*** ¡me sacas de quicio! — *s.* ***sick-bay,*** enfermería; ***sick-bed,*** lecho de enfermo; ***sick benefit,*** subsidio de enfermedad; ***sick-flag,*** bandera amarilla; ***sick-leave,*** permiso por enfermedad; ***sick nurse,*** enfermera; ***sick pay,*** [SICK BENEFIT]; ***sick room,*** cuarto del enfermo; (*pl.*) ***the sick,*** los enfermos, *m.pl.*
sick (2) [sik], *v.t.* azuzar.
sicken [ˈsikən], *v.t.* poner enfermo; dar asco a. — *v.i.* enfermar; ***sicken at,*** sentir náuseas por (ante); ***sicken for,*** añorar; mostrar síntomas de.
sickening [ˈsikəniŋ], *a.* nauseabundo, asqueroso, repugnante.
sickeningly [ˈsikəniŋli], *adv.* (*fam.*) ***sickeningly punctual,*** de una puntualidad que da asco.
sickish [ˈsikiʃ], *a.* malucho.
sickle [sikl], *s.* hoz, *f.*
sickliness [ˈsiklinis], *s.* achacosidad, estado enfermizo; insalubridad.
sickly [ˈsikli], *a.* enfermizo, achacoso; lánguido, endeble; malsano; nauseabundo; empalagoso; ***to grow sickly*** (o ***become sickly***), perder la salud.
sickness [ˈsiknis], *s.* enfermedad, falta de salud; náusea(s).
side [said], *a.* lateral; de lado; secundario; indirecto; (*mil.*) ***side arms,*** armas de cinto, *f.pl.*, armas blancas, *f.pl.*; ***side door,*** puerta lateral; ***side glance,*** mirada de soslayo *o* de refilón; ***side issue,*** cuestión secundaria; ***side light,*** luz lateral; [SIDELIGHT]; ***side road,*** carretera secundaria; (*aer.*) ***side slip,*** deslizamiento lateral; ***side street,*** calle lateral; ***side stroke,*** natación de costado; ***side whiskers,*** patillas, *f.pl.* — *s.* lado, costado; margen, orilla; ladera, falda; bando, facción, partido; parte, *f.*; (*mar.*) bordo, banda, costado; cara, faz, *f.*; lazo de parentesco; (*dep.*) equipo; ijada (*de animal*); (*pl.*) aspectos, *m.pl.*, facetas, *f.pl.* (*de una cuestión*); ***by the side of,*** al lado de; ***on all sides,*** por todas partes; ***on that side,*** de *o* por aquel lado; (*fam.*) ***on the side,*** bajo cuerda; ***to be on the side of,*** estar de parte de; ***to look on the bright side,*** ser optimista; ***on the far side,*** en el lado de allá; ***to be on the large side,*** ser algo grande, ser grandecito, pecar de grande; ***on the maternal side,*** por parte de madre; ***on the other side,*** del *o* al otro lado; ***to get on the right*** o ***good side of s.o.,*** congraciarse con alguien; ponerse a bien con alguien; ***to be on the safe side,*** para mayor seguridad, para estar más seguro, para tener margen de seguridad; ***on this side,*** a, de *o* por este lado; ***whose side are you on?*** ¿de parte de quién estás?; ***our side,*** nuestro equipo, los nuestros; ***right side,*** cara (*de una tela*); ***side by side,*** lado a lado; ***side of bacon,*** falda *o* flanco de bacon *o* de jamón; ***to split one's sides,*** reventarse de risa; ***to take sides,*** tomar partido; ***wrong side,*** revés (*de una tela*), *m.* — *v.t.* cubrir (*las tapas de un libro*). — *v.i.* — ***with,*** ponerse de parte de.
sideboard [ˈsaidbɔ:d], *s.* aparador.
sideboards, sideburns [ˈsaidbɔ:dz, -bə:nz], *s.pl.* (*fam.*) patillas, *f.pl.*
sidecar [ˈsaidkɑ:], *s.* sáicar.
sided [ˈsaidid], *sufijo.* de lados; ***eight-sided,*** ochavado.
sideface [ˈsaidfeis], *s.* perfil.
sidelight [ˈsaidlait], *s.* (*fig.*) detalle accesorio.
sideline [ˈsaidlain], *s.* ocupación accesoria, empleo accesorio; afición accesoria.
sidelong [ˈsaidlɔŋ], *a.* lateral, de lado. — *adv.* lateralmente, de lado; de soslayo.
sideral, sidereal [ˈsaidərəl, saiˈdiəriəl], *a.* sidéreo, sideral.
siderography [sidəˈrɔgrəfi], *s.* siderografía.
siderurgy [ˈsidəˈrə:dʒi], *s.* siderurgia.
side-saddle [ˈsaid-sædl], *adv.* a mujeriegas. — *s.* silla de mujer.
sideshow [ˈsaidʃou], *s.* caseta (*de feria*); (*fig.*) cosa *o* función secundaria.
sidestep [ˈsaidstep], *s.* esquivada lateral. — *v.t.* (*fam.*) evitar, soslayar.
sidetrack [ˈsaidtræk], *s.* apartadero. — *v.t.* desviar, apartar.
sidewalk [ˈsaidwɔ:k], *s.* (*Am.*) [PAVEMENT].
sideward(s) [ˈsaidwəd(z)], *a.* oblicuo, de soslayo. — *adv.* de lado, de costado.
sideways [ˈsaidweiz], *adv.* de lado, oblicuamente, al través.
siding [ˈsaidiŋ], *s.* (*f.c.*) apartadero.
sidle [saidl], *v.i.* — ***up to,*** acercarse furtiva *o* servilmente a.
siege [si:dʒ], *s.* sitio, asedio, cerco; ***to lay siege to,*** poner sitio a; ***to raise a siege,*** levantar un sitio.
Sienese [si:əˈni:z], *a., s.* sienés, *m.*
sienite [ˈsaiənait], *s.* sienita.
sienna [siˈenə], *s.* (tierra de) siena; ***burnt sienna,*** (tierra de) siena tostada.
Sierra Leone [siˈɛərə liˈoun]. Sierra Leona.
Sierra Leonean [siˈɛərə liˈouniən], *a., s.* sierraleonés, *m.*
sieve [siv], *s.* tamiz, cedazo, criba; coladera. — *v.t.* tamizar, cerner, cribar.
sievemaker [ˈsivmeikə], *s.* cedacero.
sift [sift], *v.t.* cerner, tamizar, cribar; examinar; separar, entresacar.
sifter [ˈsiftə], *s.* cribador; criba, cedazo, tamiz.
sigh [sai], *s.* suspiro; ***to breathe a sigh of relief,*** respirar. — *v.t.* decir suspirando; ***sigh away the time,*** consumir el tiempo en suspiros. — *v.i.* suspirar (***after, for,*** por).
sighingly [ˈsaiiŋli], *adv.* con suspiros, suspirando.
sight [sait], *s.* vista; visión; espectáculo, escena; cosa digna de verse; (*fam.*) facha, espantajo, mamarracho; mira (*de fusil*); (*pl.*) cosas de interés turístico, *f.pl.*; ***at sight, on sight,*** a simple vista; ***at first sight,*** a primera vista; ***by sight,*** de vista; ***to know by sight,*** conocer de vista; ***in sight,*** a la vista; ***to come in*** o ***into sight,*** (empezar a) aparecer, asomar; ***out of sight,*** invisible; [SIGHT-READ]; ***to catch sight of,*** divisar, columbrar, alcanzar a ver; ***to have second sight,*** ser clarividente; ***to have one's sights set on sth.,*** tener la vista puesta en; ***to lose sight of,*** perder de vista; ***to set one's sights too high,*** picar demasiado alto; ***what a sight he is!*** ¡qué facha, qué pinta (tiene)!; (***with***)***in sight of,*** a la vista de. — *v.t.* avistar; divisar; apuntar (*un arma*).
sighted [ˈsaitid], *a.* vidente.

sightless [ˈsaitlis], *a.* ciego; invisible.
sightliness [ˈsaitlinis], *s.* hermosura, belleza; vistosidad.
sightly [ˈsaitli], *a.* hermoso; agradable a la vista; vistoso.
sight-read [ˈsait-ˈri:d], *v.t.*, *v.i.* ejecutar a la primera lectura; leer sin preparación.
sightseeing [ˈsaitsi:iŋ], *s.* turismo, visita de sitios de interés. — *v.i.* ***to go sightseeing,*** visitar los monumentos, hacer turismo.
sightseer [ˈsaitsiə], *s.* turista, *m.f.*
sigmoid [ˈsigmɔid], *a.* sigmoideo.
sign [sain], *s.* señal, *f.*; indicio; signo; huella, vestigio, traza; letrero, rótulo; ***by signs,*** por señas; ***in sign of,*** en señal de; ***there was no sign of it,*** no se veía ni rastro *o* ni el menor indicio de ello; ***to show signs of,*** dar muestras de; tener *o* llevar trazas de; ***sign language,*** lenguaje de señas; ***sign painter,*** pintor de letreros; ***sign writer,*** rotulista, *m.* — *v.t.* firmar; signar; ***signed and sealed,*** firmado y lacrado; ***sign away,*** ceder; ***sign sth. over to s.o.,*** cederle algo a alguien (por escrito); ***sign up,*** contratar; fichar. — *v.i.* firmar; ***sign off,*** terminar; ***sign up,*** fichar.
signal [ˈsignəl], *a.* señalado, notable. — *s.* seña, señal, *f.*, aviso; (*f.c.*) señal, *f.*; indicio; signo; (*pl.*) (cuerpo de) transmisiones; ***sailing signals,*** señales de hacerse a la vela, *f.pl.*; ***signal box,*** garita de señales; (*mar.*) ***signal code,*** código *o* sistema de señales; ***signal flag,*** bandera de señales; ***signal light,*** fanal. — *v.t.*, *v.i.* señalar, indicar; hacer señales *o* señas; enviar señales; comunicar por señales.
signalize [ˈsignəlaiz], *v.t.* señalar, distinguir; singularizar.
signally [ˈsignəli], *adv.* insignemente, grandemente; señaladamente.
signalman [ˈsignəlmən], *s.* guardavía, *m.*
signatory [ˈsignətəri], *a.*, *s.* firmante, signatario.
signature [ˈsignətʃə], *s.* firma; rúbrica; (*impr.*, *mús.*) signatura; marca, sello; ***signature tune,*** sintonía.
signboard [ˈsainbɔ:d], *s.* letrero.
signer [ˈsainə], *s.* firmante.
signet [ˈsignit], *s.* sello; signáculo; timbre; ***signet ring,*** sortija de sello.
significance, significancy [sigˈnifikəns, -i], *s.* significación; significado; importancia.
significant [sigˈnifikənt], *a.* significativo; importante; expresivo.
signification [signifiˈkeiʃən], *s.* significación; significado, sentido.
significative [sigˈnifikətiv], *a.* significativo; indicativo.
signify [ˈsignifai], *v.t.* significar; manifestar; dar a entender; denotar, representar. — *v.i.* importar, ser de importancia *o* consecuencia; ***it doesn't signify,*** no importa.
signiory [ˈsi:njɔ:ri], *s.* señorío, dominio.
signpost [ˈsainpoust], *s.* indicador de dirección.
Sikh [si:k], *s.* sik.
Sikkim [ˈsikim]. Sikkim.
silage [ˈsailidʒ], *s.* forraje conservado en silo.
silence [ˈsailəns], *s.* silencio; ***in dead silence,*** con un silencio absoluto *o* total; ***to put to silence,*** reducir al silencio, hacer callar; ***silence gives consent,*** quien calla otorga. — *v.t.* imponer silencio a; mandar (*o* hacer) callar; cerrar la boca a; acallar; silenciar; amortiguar; (*mil.*) apagar el fuego (*del enemigo*). — *interj.* ¡silencio!
silencer [ˈsailənsə], *s.* (*aut.*) silenciador.
silent [ˈsailənt], *a.* silencioso; callado; ***to be silent, keep, remain silent,*** callar(se), guardar silencio, permanecer en silencio; ***to fall silent,*** callar, enmudecer; ***silent film,*** película muda; (*Am.*, *com.*) ***silent partner*** [SLEEPING PARTNER].
silentiary [ˈsaiˈlenʃəri], *s.* silenciario.
silentness [ˈsailəntnis], *s.* silencio.
silex [ˈsaileks], *s.* sílice, *f.*
silhouette [silu:ˈet], *s.* silueta; ***in silhouette,*** en silueta. — *v.t.* hacer destacarse *o* resaltar (*en silueta*); ***to be silhouetted against,*** destacarse sobre *o* contra.
silica [ˈsilikə], *s.* sílice, *f.*
silicate [ˈsilikit], *s.* silicato.
silicic [siˈlisik], *a.* silícico.
silicious [siˈliʃəs], *a.* silíceo, silícico.
silicle [ˈsilikəl], *s.* silícula.
silicon [ˈsilikən], *s.* silicio.
silicone [ˈsilikoun], *s.* silicona.
silicosis [siliˈkousis], *s.* silicosis, *f.inv.*
siliqua [ˈsilikwə], *s.* silicua.
siliquous, siliquose [ˈsilikwəs, -kwous], *a.* silicuoso.
silk [silk], *a.* de seda; ***silk hat,*** sombrero de copa. — *s.* seda; (*pl.*) sedería; ***figured silk,*** seda labrada; ***raw silk,*** seda en rama; ***shot silk,*** seda tornasolada; ***silk cotton,*** seda vegetal; ***silk growing,*** sericultura; ***silk mercer,*** sedero; ***watered silk,*** muaré.
silken [ˈsilkən], *a.* de seda, sedoso.
silkiness [ˈsilkinis], *s.* (lo) sedoso.
silkworm [ˈsilkwə:m], *s.* gusano de seda.
silky [ˈsilki], *a.* sedoso.
sill [sil], *s.* alféizar; antepecho; repisa; umbral (*de puerta*).
silliness [ˈsilinis], *s.* tontería, bobería.
silly [ˈsili], *a.* tonto, bobo; ***to make s.o. look silly,*** poner a alguien en ridículo.
silo [ˈsailou], *s.* silo.
silt [silt], *s.* aluvión, sedimento(s). — *v.t.*, *v.i.* — (***up***), rellenar(se) *u* obstruir(se) con sedimentos.
Silurian [saiˈlju:riən], *a.*, *s.* siluriano.
silvan [ˈsilvən], *a.* de los bosques, selvático.
silver [ˈsilvə], *a.* de plata, plateado; ***silver birch,*** abedul blanco; ***silver fir,*** abeto blanco; ***silver foil,*** hoja de plata; ***silver paper,*** papel de plata; ***silver wedding,*** bodas de plata, *f.pl.*; ***every cloud has a silver lining,*** no hay mal que por bien no venga. — *s.* plata; cubiertos (*m.pl.*) *o* vajilla de plata; ***silver-plated,*** plateado; [SILVER-PLATE]. — *v.t.* platear.
silverfish [ˈsilvəfiʃ], *s.* (*zool.*) lepisma.
silvering [ˈsilvəriŋ], *s.* capa *o* baño de plata; plateado, plateadura; azogado (*espejo*).
silver-plate [ˈsilvə-ˈpleit], *v.t.* platear; azogar.
silversmith [ˈsilvəsmiθ], *s.* platero; orfebre.
silverware [ˈsilvəwɛə], *s.* plata labrada; efectos de plata, *m.pl.*; vajilla de plata.
silverweed [ˈsilvəwi:d], *s.* agrimonia.
silvery [ˈsilvəri], *a.* plateado; argentino.
Silvester [silˈvestə]. Silvestre.
Simeon [ˈsimiən]. Simeón.
simian [ˈsimiən], *a.* simiesco. — *s.* simio.
similar [ˈsimilə], *a.* similar, semejante, parecido.
similarity [simiˈlæriti], *s.* semejanza, parecido.
simile [ˈsimili], *s.* símil.
similitude [siˈmilitju:d], *s.* similitud, semejanza; comparación; parecido.
simioid, simious [ˈsimiɔid, ˈsimiəs], *a.* simiesco.
simmer [ˈsimə], *v.t.* hacer hervir a fuego lento. — *v.i.* hervir a fuego lento; (*fam.*) estar a punto de estallar.
Simon [ˈsaimən]. Simón; ***Simon Pure,*** genuino, puro, verdadero.
simoniac, simoniacal [siˈmouniæk, simoˈnaiəkəl], *a.* simoníaco.
simony [ˈsaimoni], *s.* simonía.
simoom, simoon [siˈmu:m, siˈmu:n], *s.* simún.
simper [ˈsimpə], *s.* sonrisa afectada *o* boba. — *v.i.* sonreírse bobamente.
simpering [ˈsimpəriŋ], *a.* bobo y melindroso.
simperingly [ˈsimpəriŋli], *adv.* sonriendo tontamente *o* afectadamente.

simple [simpl], *a.* sencillo; simple; puro; llano; fácil; ingenuo, cándido, inocente; mero; bobo, necio, mentecato; ***simple-hearted,*** sencillo, franco, sincero; ***simple-minded,*** simple, mentecato; ***simple-mindedness,*** simpleza, mentecatez. — *s.* (*med.*) simple.

simpleton ['simpltən], *s.* simplón, *m.*, gaznápiro, bobalicón.

simplicity, simpleness [sim'plisiti, 'simplnis], *s.* sencillez; llaneza; ingenuidad, candor; simplicidad; simpleza, sandez.

simplification [simplifi'keiʃən], *s.* simplificación.

simplify ['simplifai], *v.t.* simplificar.

simply ['simpli], *adv.* sencillamente, simplemente; ***it is simply beautiful!*** ¡es una auténtica preciosidad!; ***simply impossible,*** totalmente imposible; ***you simply must!*** ¡no tienes más remedio!

simulacrum [simju'leikrəm], *s.* (*pl.* **simulacra** [-krə]) simulacro.

simulant ['simjulənt], *a.* que simula, imita *o* finge; de forma (de).

simulate ['simjuleit], *v.t.* simular, fingir.

simulation [simju'leiʃən], *s.* simulación, fingimiento.

simultaneity, simultaneousness [siməltə'ni:iti, siməl'teiniəsnis], *s.* simultaneidad.

simultaneous [siməl'teiniəs], *a.* simultáneo.

sin [sin], *s.* pecado; ***sin offering,*** sacrificio propiciatorio; ***the seven deadly sins,*** los siete pecados capitales; ***to fall into sin,*** caer en pecado; ***to live in sin,*** vivir amancebado(s). — *v.i.* pecar.

Sinai ['sainiai]. Sinaí.

sinapism ['sinəpizəm], *s.* sinapismo.

Sinbad ['sinbæd]. Simbad.

since [sins], *adv.* desde entonces, después; ***ever since,*** a partir de entonces, desde entonces; ***long since,*** (desde) hace mucho (tiempo); ***not long since,*** (desde) hace poco. — *conj.* puesto que, ya que. — *prep.* desde, después de, a partir de.

sincere [sin'siə], *a.* sincero; sentido; franco; ***yours sincerely,*** le saluda cordialmente.

sincerity [sin'seriti], *s.* sinceridad; franqueza.

sine [sain], *s.* (*mat.*) seno.

sinecure ['s(a)inikjuə], *s.* sinecura; (*fam.*) enchufe.

sinew ['sinju:], *s.* tendón; nervio, fibra.

sinewy ['sinjui], *a.* nervudo, vigoroso; (*carne*) que tiene mucho nervio.

sinful ['sinful], *a.* pecaminoso; (*pers.*) pecador.

sinfulness ['sinfulnis], *s.* pecaminosidad; maldad.

sing [siŋ], *irr. v.t.* cantar; ***sing out,*** gritar, vocear; ***sing to sleep,*** dormir cantando, arrullar; (*fig.*) ***sing a different song,*** cambiar de tono, recoger velas. — *v.i.* (*pájaros*) cantar, trinar; (*oídos*) zumbar; ***sing small,*** achantarse.

Singapore [siŋ(g)ə'pɔ:]. Singapur.

Singaporean [siŋ(g)ə'pɔ:riən], *a., s.* singapurense, *m.f.*

singe [sindʒ], *v.t.* chamuscar; quemar las puntas de.

singer ['siŋə], *s.* cantante; cantor.

Singhalese [siŋgə'li:z], *a., s.* cingalés, *m.*

singing ['siŋiŋ], *a.* cantante; ***singing bird,*** pájaro cantor. — *s.* canto; zumbido (*de los oídos*); ***singing master,*** maestro de canto.

single [siŋgl], *a.* único; solo; simple; (*cuarto*) individual; (*billete*) sencillo; (*sin casar*) soltero; (*combate*) singular; ***single-breasted,*** sin cruzar; ***single-chamber,*** unicameral; ***single-engined,*** monomotor; ***single file,*** fila india; ***single-handed,*** solo, sin ayuda; ***single-minded,*** firme, resuelto; [SINGLE-SEATER]; (*esgr.*) ***single-stick,*** bastón; ***single-track,*** de vía única; ***not a single word,*** ni una sola palabra. — *s.pl.* (*tenis*) juego de simples *o* de individuales. — *v.t.* — ***out,*** escoger, elegir; distinguir, señalar.

singleness ['siŋglnis], *s.* (***of purpose***) firmeza, resolución.

single-seater ['siŋgl-'si:tə], *a.* monoplaza. — *s.* monoplaza, *m.*

singlet ['siŋglit], *s.* camiseta.

singly ['siŋgli], *adv.* individuamente; uno a uno.

singsong ['siŋsɔŋ], *a.* monótono, de cadencia uniforme; ***to talk in a singsong voice,*** hablar con tono cantarín. — *s.* concierto espontáneo.

singular ['siŋgjulə], *a.* singular.

singularity [siŋgju'læriti], *s.* particularidad, singularidad.

singularize ['siŋgjuləraiz], *v.t.* singularizar, individualizar, particularizar.

Sinic ['sinik], *a.* chinesco, chino.

sinical ['sinikəl], *a.* (*geom.*) relativo al seno (de un arco).

sinister ['sinistə], *a.* siniestro; avieso, torvo; aciago.

sinistrous ['sinistrəs], *a.* siniestro; avieso; aciago.

sink [siŋk], *s.* fregadero, pila; sumidero; sentina. — *irr. v.t.* hundir, sumir, sumergir; abrir, cavar; perforar (*un pozo*); invertir (*dinero*); hincar (*los dientes*); olvidar, suprimir (*diferencias*). — *v.i.* hundirse; menguar, declinar; ponerse (*el sol*); dejarse caer; ***my heart sank,*** se me cayó el alma a los pies; ***sink in,*** penetrar, calar; tener efecto, hacer mella; ***sink on one's knees,*** caer de rodillas; ***sink under,*** hundirse bajo.

sinkable ['siŋkəbl], *a.* hundible, sumergible.

sinker ['siŋkə], *s.* hundidor; plomada; ***die sinker, punch sinker,*** tallador, abridor *o* grabador en hueco.

sinking ['siŋkiŋ], *a.* que se hunde *etc.* — *s.* hundimiento; sumergimiento; cavadura; abatimiento (*de ánimo*); abertura (*de un pozo etc.*); (*com.*) ***sinking fund,*** fondo de amortización.

sinless ['sinlis], *a.* sin pecado.

sinlessness ['sinlisnis], *s.* impecabilidad.

sinner ['sinə], *s.* pecador, pecadora.

sinologist [si'nɔlədʒist], *s.* sinólogo.

sinology [si'nɔlədʒi], *s.* sinología.

sinople ['sinopl], *s.* (*blas.*) sinople.

sinter ['sintə], *s.* toba, incrustación.

sinuate ['sinjuit], *a.* sinuoso, tortuoso; (*bot.*) festoneado. — ['sinjueit], *v.i.* formar meandros, serpentear.

sinuation [sinju'eiʃən], *s.* corvadura, tortuosidad.

sinuosity [sinju'ɔsiti], *s.* sinuosidad, tortuosidad.

sinuous ['sinjuəs], *a.* sinuoso, tortuoso.

sinus ['sainəs], *s.* (*med. etc.*) seno; cavidad, concavidad; ***sinus trouble,*** sinusitis, *f.*

sinusitis [sainə'saitis], *s.* sinusitis, *f.inv.*

sip [sip], *s.* sorbo; ***little sip,*** sorbito. — *v.t.* beber a sorbos; saborear; chupar. — *v.i.* beber a sorbos.

siphon ['saifən], *s.* sifón. — *v.t.* sacar con sifón.

sipper ['sipə], *s.* sorbedor.

sippet ['sipit], *s.* sopita, sopilla, sopa, pan empapado en agua *u* otra bebida.

Sir [sə:]. (*título inglés*) sir.

sir [sə:], *s.* señor; caballero; ***Dear Sir,*** muy señor mío.

sire [saiə], *s.* padre, progenitor; (*caballo*) semental; (*tratamiento*) señor. — *v.t.* engendrar.

siren ['saiərən], *s.* sirena.

Sirius ['siriəs]. (*astron.*) Sirio.

sirloin ['sə:lɔin], *s.* solomillo.

sirocco [si'rɔkou], *s.* siroco.

sirrah ['sira:], *s.* buen hombre.

sirup [SYRUP].

sirupy [SYRUPY].

sisal ['saisəl], *s.* sisal, henequén; cáñamo sisal.

siskin ['siskin], *s.* (*orn.*) verderón.

sissy ['sisi], *s.* marica, *m.*, mariquita, *m.*

sister ['sistə], *s.* hermana; (*igl.*) (*tratamiento*) Sor; ***foster sister,*** hermana de leche; ***sister ship,*** barco gemelo; ***sister-in-law,*** cuñada, hermana política; ***Sister of Mercy,*** Hermana de la Caridad; ***step-sister,*** hermanastra.

sisterhood [ˈsistəhud], *s.* hermandad; cofradía de mujeres.
sisterly [ˈsistəli], *a.* de hermana, como hermana.
sistrum [ˈsistrəm], *s.* (*pl.* **sistrums, sistra** [-z, -trə]) sistro.
sit [sit], *irr. v.t.* sentar; montar, ir montado en (*un caballo*); ***sit an examination,*** examinarse; ***sit sth. out,*** aguantar una cosa hasta el final; ***sit out a dance,*** no bailar. — *v.i.* sentarse; estar sentado; reunirse (*en junta*), celebrar junta *o* sesión; empollar (*las aves*); sentar (***well, badly,*** bien, mal) (*la ropa*); (*como modelo*) posar; ***sit back*** (***and do nothing***), estarse mano sobre mano; ***sit down,*** sentarse; (*fam.*) ***sit down under abuse,*** aguantar sin chistar los improperios; ***sit for,*** posar para, servir de modelo a; ***sit for one's picture,*** hacerse retratar; ***sit on a committee,*** ser (miembro) de una junta; ***the house sits on a rise,*** la casa está asentada *o* situada en un altozano; (*fam.*) ***sit on s.o.,*** hacer callar a alguien; (*fam.*) ***sit on sth.,*** dar al traste con algo; ***sit still!*** ¡estate quieto!; ***sit up,*** incorporarse; ponerse derecho; (*por la noche*) trasnochar; velar; ***sit up and take notice,*** poner el oído, aguzar las orejas, prestar (mucha) atención; ***this will make him sit up,*** esto no se lo espera, esto le dará en qué pensar.
sit-down [ˈsit-daun], *a.* ***sit-down strike,*** huelga de brazos caídos.
site [sait], *s.* solar; emplazamiento, sitio. — *v.t.* situar.
sit-in [ˈsit-in], *s.* ocupación protestataria.
sit(i)ology [sit(i)ˈɔlədʒi], *s.* sitología.
sitter [ˈsitə], *s.* persona sentada; modelo (*de pintor*); ave *o* gallina clueca; (*fam.*) cosa tirada (*de fácil*).
sitting [ˈsitiŋ], *a.* sentado; (*fam.*) ***sitting duck,*** blanco fácil; cosa tirada. — *s.* sentada; nidada; sesión; reunión, *f.*; ***sitting room,*** cuarto de estar; ***at a*** o ***one sitting,*** de una sentada.
situate [ˈsitjueit], *a.* sito.
situation [sitjuˈeiʃən], *s.* situación; emplazamiento; colocación, empleo.
six [siks], *a., s.* seis, *m.*; ***at sixes and sevens,*** en estado de desorden; en confusión; desorganizado(s); patas arriba; ***it's six of one and half-a-dozen of the other,*** viene a ser lo mismo; ***six-footer,*** hombre de un metro ochenta; ***six-shooter,*** revólver de seis tiros.
sixfold [ˈsiksfould], *a.* séxtuplo. — *adv.* seis veces.
sixpence [ˈsikspəns], *s.* seis peniques.
sixpenny [ˈsikspəni], *a.* de seis peniques; (*fig.*) mezquino, miserable, ruin.
sixscore [ˈsikskɔː], *a.* ciento veinte.
sixteen [siksˈtiːn], *a., s.* diez y seis, dieciséis, *m.*
sixteenth [siksˈtiːnθ], *a.* décimosexto. — *s.* dieciseisavo.
sixth [ˈsiksθ], *a.* sexto; (*fecho*) seis. — *s.* sexto, sexta parte; (*mús.*) sexta.
sixtieth [ˈsikstiəè], *a.* sexagésimo, sesenta. — *s.* (una) sexagésima parte, sesentavo.
sixty [ˈsiksti], *a., s.* sesenta; ***the sixties,*** los años sesenta; ***to be in one's sixties,*** estar en los sesenta.
sizable, [ˈsaizəbl], *a.* de tamaño considerable; bastante grande.
sizar [ˈsaizə], *s.* becario.
size (1) [saiz], *s.* tamaño; talla; dimensión; número (*de zapatos*); medida; volumen; diámetro; magnitud, cuantía; ***cut s.o. down to size,*** bajarle a alguien los humos. — *v.t.* clasificar por tamaños; apreciar, evaluar; ***size up,*** calar, averiguar de qué pie cojea (una persona).
size (2) [saiz], *s.* cola; apresto. — *v.t.* encolar; aprestar.
sizeable [SIZABLE].
sized (1) [saizd], *a.* sisado; calibrado; de (tal) tamaño.
sized (2) [saizd], *a.* encolado.
siziness [ˈsaizinis], *s.* viscosidad.
sizing (1) [ˈsaiziŋ], *s.* calibradura.
sizing (2) [ˈsaiziŋ], *s.* encoladura, encolado.
sizy [ˈsaizi], *a.* viscoso, pegajoso.
sizzle [sizl], *s.* sonido chirriante; chisporroteo. — *v.i.* chisporrotear, churruscar; crepitar (*al freírse*).
skate (1) [skeit], *s.* patín; ***roller skate,*** patín de ruedas. — *v.i.* patinar.
skate (2) [skeit], *s.* (*ict.*) raya.
skater [ˈskeitə], *s.* patinador.
skating [ˈskeitiŋ], *s.* patinaje; ***skating-rink,*** pista de patinaje.
skedaddle [skiˈdædl], *v.i.* (*fam.*) tomar las de Villadiego, largarse, poner pies en polvorosa.
skeet [skiːt], *s.* (*mar.*) bañadera.
skein [skein], *s.* madeja.
skeletal [ˈskelitəl], *a.* de (del) esqueleto; esquelético.
skeleton [ˈskelitən], *a.* reducido; esquemático; en esqueleto, en armazón; ***skeleton key,*** llave maestra. — *s.* esqueleto; osamenta; esquema; armadura; ***to be reduced to a skeleton,*** estar en los huesos; ***skeleton in the cupboard,*** deshonra familiar.
skeptic, skeptical, skepticism [SCEPTIC *etc.*].
sketch [sketʃ], *s.* esbozo, croquis, *m.inv.*; bosquejo, boceto; (*teat.*) pieza corta; ***sketch-book,*** libro de dibujos. — *v.t.* esbozar, bosquejar, dibujar. — *v.i.* hacer bosquejos.
sketchily [ˈsketʃili], *adv.* de un modo abocetado, a manera de bosquejo; superficialmente.
sketchiness [ˈsketʃinis], *s.* modo abocetado; estado incompleto; hechura ligera; superficialidad.
sketchy [ˈsketʃi], *a.* bosquejado, abocetado, esquiciado; incompleto; ligero; superficial.
skew [skjuː], *a.* oblicuo, sesgado, atravesado, torcido, al sesgo, de través; (*fam.*) ***skew-whiff,*** torcido. — *s.* oblicuidad, sesgo; mirada de soslayo. — *v.t.* sesgar. — *v.i.* sesgarse; mirar de soslayo.
skewer [ˈskjuːə], *s.* (*coc.*) brocheta; espetón. — *v.t.* espetar.
ski [skiː], *s.* esquí; ***ski-boot,*** bota de *o* para esquiar; ***ski-jump,*** salto de esquí; ***ski-lift,*** telesquí, telesilla, *m.*; ***ski-pants,*** pantalón de *o* para esquiar; ***ski-slope,*** pista de *o* para esquiar. — *v.i.* esquiar.
skid [skid], *s.* patinazo; resbalón; (*mar.*) varadera; (*aer.*) patín; ***skid mark,*** señal de patinazo. — *v.i.* patinar; resbalar(se).
skidaddle, skiddoo [skiˈdædl, skiˈduː], [SKEDADDLE].
skidding [ˈskidiŋ], *s.* (el) patinar.
skier [ˈskiːə], *s.* esquiador.
skiff [skif], *s.* esquife.
skiing [ˈskiːiŋ], *s.* (el) esquiar; esquí; ***to go skiing,*** hacer esquí.
skilful [ˈskilful], *a.* diestro; hábil; mañoso; primoroso; experto, perito.
skill, skilfulness [skil, ˈskilfulnis], *s.* destreza; habilidad; maña; pericia.
skilled [skild], *a.* diestro; hábil; experto; especializado.
skillet [ˈskilit], *s.* cacerola.
skim [skim], *v.t.* quitar la nata a, desnatar; quitar la espuma a, espumar; rozar, pasar rasando *o* raspando. — *v.i.* — ***along,*** deslizarse, ir veloz(mente); ***skim over,*** pasar rasando *o* raspando; ***skim over*** o ***through,*** tratar *o* examinar a la ligera *o* con superficialidad; hojear rápidamente.
skimmer [ˈskimə], *s.* espumadera.
skim-milk [ˈskim-milk], *s.* leche desnatada.
skimp [skimp], *v.t.* escatimar; hacer de una manera superficial. — *v.i.* economizar.
skimpy [ˈskimpi], *a.* escaso, (muy) corto.
skin [skin], *s.* piel, *f.*; epidermis, *f.inv.*; cutis, *m.inv.* (*de la cara*); pellejo; (*ten.*) cuero; corteza, pellejo (*de la fruta*); nata (*de la leche*); odre, pellejo, cuero (*del vino*); (*fam.*) ***by the skin of one's teeth,*** por los pelos; ***skin-deep,*** superficial, epidérmico; ***skin disease,*** enfermedad de la piel; ***skin diving,*** natación submarina, buceo; ***skin graft***(***ing***), injerto de piel; ***soaked to the skin,*** calado hasta

los huesos; ***to be (nothing but) skin and bone,*** estar en los huesos, ser escuálido; ***to have a thick skin,*** tener mucha cara; ser insensible; ***to save one's skin,*** salvar el pellejo *o* la pelleja. — *v.t.* desollar; despellejar; pelar, mondar; (*fam.*) ***skin alive,*** desollar vivo. — *v.i.* — ***over,*** cicatrizarse.

skinflint [ˈskinflint], *s.* avaro, tacaño.

skinned [skind], *a.*, *sufijo.* de piel . . .; ***dark-skinned,*** de piel oscura.

skinner [ˈskinə], *s.* desollador; peletero.

skinniness [ˈskininis], *s.* escualidez; (lo) flacucho.

skinny [ˈskini], *a.* flaco, descarnado.

skint [skint], *a.* (*fam.*) ***to be skint,*** no tener ni un céntimo, no tener ni cinco.

skip (1) [skip], *s.* brinco, salto. — *v.t.* — ***it!*** ¡déjalo! ¡olvídalo!; ***skip (over),*** omitir, saltar(se). — *v.i.* saltar (a la comba); saltar (*de un tema a otro*); escabullirse.

skip (2) [skip], *s.* (*min.*) jaula.

skipper [ˈskipə], *s.* saltador, brincador; (*mar.*) patrón; (*dep.*) capitán.

skipping [ˈskipiŋ], *s.* (el) saltar (a la comba); comba (*juego*); ***skipping-rope,*** comba.

skippingly [ˈskipiŋli], *adv.* a saltos, a brincos.

skirmish [ˈskəːmiʃ], *s.* escaramuza. — *v.i.* escaramuzar.

skirmisher [ˈskəːmiʃə], *s.* escaramuzador.

skirret [ˈskirit], *s.* chirivía.

skirt [skəːt], *s.* falda; saya; sayuela, enagua; (*sast.*) faldón; faldones (de la silla de montar); orilla, borde, margen; (*fam.*) muchacha, mujer; ***divided skirt,*** saya en forma de pantalones muy anchos; ***skirts of a city,*** contornos, alrededores de una ciudad, *m.pl.*; ***skirts of a country,*** confines de un país, *m.pl.* — *v.t.* ladear, bordear, orillar; poner cenefa a.

skirting [ˈskəːtiŋ], *s.* ***skirting-board,*** zócalo, rodapié.

skit [skit], *s.* sátira; burla; parodia, caricatura.

skittish [ˈskitiʃ], *a.* nervioso, asustadizo, espantadizo (*caballo etc.*); caprichoso, liviano; juguetón.

skittishness [ˈskitiʃnis], *s.* lo nervioso *etc.*

skittle [skitl], *s.* bolo; (*pl.*) juego de bolos; ***skittle alley,*** bolera.

skive (1) [skaiv], *v.t.* (*ten.*) raspar, adelgazar.

skive (2) [skaiv], *v.i.* (*fam.*) gandulear, remolonear.

skiver (1) [ˈskaivə], *s.* cuero hendido con cuchillo; cuero para pastas; cuchillo *o* máquina de adelgazar.

skiver (2) [ˈskaivə], *s.* (*fam.*) gandul, remolón.

skulduggery [skʌlˈdʌgəri], *s.* tejemaneje(s).

skulk [skʌlk], *v.i.* acechar, ocultarse; rondar; remolonear.

skulker [ˈskʌlkə], *s.* acechador; remolón.

skull [skʌl], *s.* cráneo; calavera; ***skull-cap,*** casquete, gorro.

skunk [skʌŋk], *s.* mofeta; (*Arg.*, *Guat.*, *Hond.*) zorrillo, mapurite; (*fam.*) sinvergüenza, *m.f.*; (*bot.*) ***skunk-cabbage,*** hierba fétida (de la familia del yaro).

sky [skai], *s.* cielo; ***sky blue, sky-coloured,*** azul celeste, cerúleo; (*poét.*) ***sky-born,*** nacido en el cielo; ***sky-high,*** por las nubes; ***to blow sky-high,*** volar en mil pedazos; ***sky writing,*** escritura aérea; ***to praise s.o. to the skies,*** poner a alguien por las nubes.

skyey [ˈskaii], *a.* etéreo.

skyish [ˈskaiiʃ], *a.* azulado.

skylark [ˈskailaːk], *s.* (*orn.*) alondra, calandria. — *v.i.* (*fam.*) jaranear.

skylarking [ˈskailaːkiŋ], *s.* jarana.

skylight [ˈskailait], *s.* claraboya, tragaluz, *m.*

skyline [ˈskailain], *s.* línea del horizonte, perfil, silueta.

sky-rocket [ˈskai-rɔkit], *s.* cohete, volador. — *v.i.* subir como un cohete; ponerse por las nubes (*los precios*).

skysail [ˈskaisəl], *s.* (*mar.*) periquito.

skyscraper [ˈskaiskreipə], *s.* rascacielos, *m.inv.*

skyward(s) [ˈskaiwəd(z)], *adv.* hacia el cielo.

slab [slæb], *s.* losa; plancha; tabla; laja; tajada gruesa (*de carne*); bloque; tableta.

slack (1) [slæk], *a.* flojo; perezoso; descuidado; (*com.*) encalmado; ***business is slack,*** se vende poco; hay poco movimiento; ***slack period,*** período *o* momento de poco movimiento *o* de poca actividad; ***slack water,*** repunte de la marea. — *s.* (lo) flojo; (*pl.*) pantalones (flojos), *m.pl.* — *v.i.* (*fam.*) trabajar poco, remolonear; ***slack off,*** disminuir, decaer; reducirse; amainar; cejar.

slack (2) [slæk], *s.* (*min.*) cisco.

slacken [ˈslækən], *v.t.* aflojar; disminuir, reducir. — *v.i.* aflojarse; ceder, cejar; amainar (*el viento*).

slacker [ˈslækə], *s.* remolón, gandul.

slackness [ˈslæknis], *s.* flojedad; descuido; pereza.

slag [slæg], *s.* escoria; ***slag heap,*** escorial.

slake [sleik], *v.t.* apagar.

slam (1) [slæm], *s.* portazo; golpazo. — *v.t.* cerrar de un portazo, cerrar dando *o* pegando un portazo; (*fig.*) fustigar; ***slam down,*** soltar dando un golpazo; ***slam shut,*** cerrar de golpe *o* dando un portazo. — *v.i.* — (***shut***), cerrarse de un golpazo *o* de un portazo.

slam (2) [slæm], *s.* (*cartas*) capote.

slamming [ˈslæmiŋ], *s.* (*fig.*) ***to give s.o. a slamming,*** fustigar, vapulear a alguien; echarle a alguien un broncazo.

slander [ˈslaːndə], *s.* calumnia(s), difamación. — *v.t.* calumniar, difamar.

slanderer [ˈslaːndərə], *s.* calumniador.

slanderous [ˈslaːndərəs], *a.* calumnioso.

slang [slæŋ], *s.* argot; germanía (de ladrones *o* delincuentes). — *v.t.* poner como un trapo, poner verde.

slangy [ˈslæŋi], *a.* de argot; ***slangy term,*** vulgarismo.

slant [slaːnt], *s.* inclinación, sesgo; enfoque, punto de vista. — *v.t.* inclinar, sesgar; enfocar. — *v.i.* inclinarse, sesgarse.

slant-eyed [ˈslaːnt-aid], *a.* de ojos sesgados.

slanting [ˈslaːntiŋ], *a.* inclinado, sesgado, oblicuo.

slantingly, slantwise [ˈslaːntiŋli, -waiz], *adv.* sesgadamente, oblicuamente, de través.

slap [slæp], *adv.* justo, de lleno, totalmente; ***slap (bang) in the middle,*** justo en medio *o* en la mitad; ***he ran slap into a tree,*** embistió de lleno un árbol. — *s.* manotada, palmada; bofetada, bofetón, sopapo; (*fig.*) ***slap in the face,*** desaire; golpe rudo; ***slap on the back,*** palmada en la espalda; ***it needs an extra slap of paint,*** necesita *o* le hace falta otra manita de pintura. — *v.t.* dar *o* pegar una bofetada a; ***slap down,*** soltar de un golpazo; (*fig.*) aplastar, dejar aniquilado.

slapdash [ˈslæpdæʃ], *a.* descuidado, chapucero, hecho a lo loco; que hace las cosas a lo loco *o* de prisa y corriendo.

slap-happy [ˈslæp-ˈhæpi], *a.* (*fig.*) inconsciente, despreocupado.

slapstick [ˈslæpstik], *a.* chaplinesco. — *s.* payasadas, *f.pl.*

slap-up [ˈslæp-ʌp], *a.* por todo lo alto, en toda la regla; ***slap-up do,*** fiesta por todo lo alto; ***slap-up meal,*** comilona.

slash [slæʃ], *s.* cuchillada; jabeque, chirlo; corte (*feroz*), tajo.— *v.t.* achuchillar, cortar (*ferozmente*), dar *o* pegar un tajo *o* tajos a; rebajar muchísimo. — *v.i.* — (***about***), dar tajos a un lado y a otro.

slat [slæt], *s.* tablilla; ***blind-slat,*** tablilla de persiana.

slatch [slætʃ], *s.* (*mar.*) socaire; seno de un cabo; intervalo de buen tiempo.

slate (1) [sleit], *s.* pizarra; esquisto; (*Am.*, *pol.*) lista de candidatos, programa de partido, *m.*; ***slate blue,*** azul pizarra; ***slate-coloured,*** de color de pizarra, apizarrado, pizarreño; ***slate pencil,*** pizarrín; ***slate quarry,*** pizarral, cantera de pizarra; ***slate roof,*** tejado de pizarra; ***to wipe the slate clean,*** hacer tabla rasa; ***to wipe clean off the slate,*** borrar completamente. — *v.t.* cubrir con pizarra, empizarrar.

slate (2) [sleit], *v.t.* (*fam.*) criticar severamente, censurar severamente, fustigar.

slater [ˈsleitə], *s.* pizarrero.

slattern [ˈslætən], *s.* mujer desaliñada, pazpuerca.

slatternliness [ˈslætənlinis], *s.* desaseo, desaliño.

slatternly [ˈslætənli], *a.* puerco, desaliñado. — *adv.* desaliñadamente.

slaty [ˈsleiti], *a.* pizarreño.

slaughter [ˈslɔːtə], *s.* matanza; carnicería; sacrificio (*de reses*); ***like a lamb to the slaughter,*** sumiso como un cordero. — *v.t.* hacer una carnicería de; matar; sacrificar.

slaughterer, slaughterman [ˈslɔːtərə, -mən], *s.* matarife, jifero; asesino.

slaughterhouse [ˈslɔːtəhaus], *s.* matadero.

Slav [slɑːv, slæv], *a., s.* eslavo.

slave [sleiv], *s.* esclavo, esclava; siervo; ***slave-born,*** nacido en la esclavitud; ***slave-driver,*** negrero; ***slave-holder,*** proprietario de esclavos; ***slave labour,*** trabajadores forzados, *m.pl.*; ***slave labour camp,*** campamento de trabajadores forzados; ***slave trade, slave traffic,*** trata de esclavos; ***white slave traffic,*** trata de blancas; ***to be a slave to duty,*** ser esclavo del deber. — *v.i.* trabajar como un esclavo, sudar tinta.

slaver (1) [ˈsleivə], *s.* negrero; buque negrero.

slaver (2) [slævə], *s.* baba. — *v.i.* babosear.

slaverer [ˈslævərə], *s.* baboso.

slavery [ˈsleivəri], *s.* esclavitud; servidumbre.

Slavic [ˈslævik], [SLAVONIC].

slavish [ˈsleiviʃ], *a.* servil.

slavishness [ˈsleiviʃnis], *s.* servilismo.

Slavism [ˈslɑːvizəm], *s.* eslavismo.

Slavonic, Slavic, Slavonian [sləˈvɔnik, ˈslævik, sləˈvouniən], *a., s.* eslavo; esclavón.

slaw [slɔː], *s.* ensalada de col.

slay (1) [slei], *irr. v.t.* matar, asesinar; (*fam. fig.*) ***this will really slay you!*** con esto te vas a partir de risa.

slay (1), **sley** [slei], *s.* (*tej.*) peine, carda.

slayer [ˈsleiə], *s.* matador, asesino; ***man-slayer,*** homicida, *m.*

sleave [sliːv], *s.* (*ant.*) seda en rama, hilo destorcido. — *v.t.* desenredar, destorcer.

sleaziness [ˈsliːzinis], *s.* (lo) sucio *etc.*

sleazy, sleezy [ˈsliːzi], *a.* sucio; desvencijado; de medio pelo.

sledge, sled [sledʒ, sled], *s.* trineo, rastra, narria. — *v.t., v.i.* transportar *o* viajar en trineo, rastra, narria.

sledge-hammer [ˈsledʒ-hæmə], *s.* acotillo, macho.

sleek [sliːk], *a.* liso; lustroso; pulcro; meloso, zalamero. — *v.t.* alisar, pulir; suavizar.

sleekness [ˈsliːknis], *s.* lisura; lustre.

sleeky [ˈsliːki], *a.* liso; taimado, zalamero.

sleep [sliːp], *s.* sueño; ***sleep-walker,*** sonámbulo; ***sleep-walking,*** sonambulismo; ***to go to sleep,*** dormirse, quedarse dormido; ***my leg has gone to sleep,*** se me ha dormido la pierna; ***to put*** o ***send to sleep,*** dormir, adormecer; matar. — *irr. v.t.* — ***away,*** pasar durmiendo; ***sleep it off,*** dormir la mona. — *v.i.* dormir; ***sleep away*** o ***on!*** ¡siga durmiendo!; ***sleep like a log*** o ***top,*** dormir como un tronco *o* como un lirón; ***sleep on it!*** ¡consúltelo con la almohada!; ***sleep soundly,*** dormir profundamente *o* a pierna suelta; ***sleep through (sth.),*** seguir durmiendo durante, no despertarse durante.

sleeper [ˈsliːpə], *s.* durmiente; (*f.c.*) coche-cama, *m.*; (*f.c.*) traviesa; ***to be a light*** o ***heavy sleeper,*** tener el sueño ligero *o* profundo.

sleepiness [ˈsliːpinis], *s.* somnolencia, sueño.

sleeping [ˈsliːpiŋ], *a.* durmiente; ***Sleeping Beauty,*** Bella Durmiente; (*com.*) ***sleeping partner,*** socio comanditario. — *s.* ***sleeping-bag,*** saco de *o* para dormir; (*f.c.*) ***sleeping-car, sleeping-coach,*** coche-cama, *m.*; ***sleeping-draught, sleeping-potion,*** soporífero; ***sleeping sickness,*** enfermedad del sueño; ***sleeping-tablet*** o ***sleeping-pill,*** comprimido *o* pastilla para dormir.

sleepless [ˈsliːplis], *a.* desvelado, insomne.

sleeplessness [ˈsliːplisnis], *s.* desvelo, insomnio.

sleepy [ˈsliːpi], *a.* soñoliento; adormecido, amodorrado; soporífero; ***sleepy-head,*** dormilón.

sleet [sliːt], *s.* aguanieve, *f.* — *v.i.* caer aguanieve.

sleety [ˈsliːti], *a.* de aguanieve; como aguanieve.

sleeve [sliːv], *s.* manga; (*mec.*) manguito; ***sleeve-band,*** vuelta de manga; ***sleeve-buttons,*** botones de manga, *m.pl.*; (*mec.*) ***sleeve coupling,*** junta de manguito; (*mec.*) ***sleeve nut,*** manguito de tuerca; ***to laugh in one's sleeve,*** reírse con disimulo *o* para sí; ***to wear one's heart on one's sleeve,*** llevar el corazón en la mano; ***to have sth. up one's sleeve,*** estar urdiendo *o* tramando algo, tener algo en reserva.

sleeved [sliːvd], *a.* que tiene manga(s).

sleeveless [ˈsliːvlis], *a.* sin manga(s), que no tiene manga(s).

sleigh [slei], *s.* trineo; ***sleigh bell,*** cascabel; ***sleigh ride,*** paseo en trineo. — *v.i.* ir en trineo.

sleighing [ˈsleiiŋ], *s.* paseo(s) en trineo.

sleight [slait], *s.* ***sleight of hand,*** escamoteo, prestidigitación.

slender [ˈslendə], *a.* esbelto, delgado, fino; corto, escaso, limitado; tenue, remoto; ***slender hope,*** esperanza tenue.

slenderness [ˈslendənis], *s.* esbeltez; (lo) corto, (lo) escaso; (lo) tenue.

sleuth [sluːθ], *s.* sabueso; detective; ***sleuth-hound,*** sabueso; detective.

slew (1) [sluː], *v.t.* — ***(round),*** torcer. — *v.i.* — ***(round),*** torcerse.

slew (2) [sluː], *pret.* [SLAY].

slice [slais], *s.* tajada, lonja, loncha; raja; rebanada; rodaja; estrelladera; ***a slice of life,*** una estampa de la vida; ***a large slice of the population,*** una apreciable proporción de los habitantes. — *v.t.* partir en lonchas *etc.*; rebanar; tajar, cortar; ***slice off,*** rebanar.

slicer [ˈslaisə], *s.* rebanador; (*joy.*) aparato de hender, sierra circular.

slick [slik], *a.* liso, lustroso; aceitoso; astuto, mañoso, listo, hábil; (*fam.*) puro, mero. — *adv.* directamente. — *s.* mancha de petróleo.

slicker [ˈslikə], *s.* embaucador; impermeable.

slide [slaid], *s.* tapa corrediza; (*foto.*) diapositiva; (*foto.*) portaplacas, *m.inv.*; resbalón, resbaladura; portaobjetos (*para el microscopio*), *m.inv.*; declive; encaje (*de un bastidor*); muesca; resbaladero; (*geol.*) falla, dislocación de una veta; desprendimiento (*de rocas*); (*mús.*) ligado, portamento; (*mec.*) guía; pasador (*para el pelo*); ***slide-projector,*** proyector de *o* para diapositivas. — *irr. v.t.* hacer colar. — *v.i.* resbalar(se); deslizarse; ***slide in,*** colarse; ***slide into,*** introducirse suavemente; ***slide over,*** pasar por alto; ***to let things slide,*** dejar rodar la bola.

slide-bolt [ˈslaid-boult], *s.* pestillo corredizo, cerrojo de seguridad.

slide-box [ˈslaid-bɔks], *s.* caja de válvulas de distribución.

slide-rail [ˈslaid-reil], *s.* (*f.c.*) aguja, contracarril.

slide-rest [ˈslaid-rest], *s.* (*mec.*) soporte de corredera.

slide-rule [ˈslaid-ruːl], *s.* regla de cálculo; medida *o* escala de corredera.

slider [ˈslaidə], *s.* resbalador; cursor.

sliding [ˈslaidiŋ], *a.* corredizo; resbaladizo, escurridizo; ***sliding door,*** puerta de corredera; ***sliding knot,*** nudo corredizo; ***sliding scale,*** escala graduada; ***sliding seat,*** banca corrediza (*de bote*). — *s.* deslizamiento; ***sliding-place,*** deslizadero, resbaladero.

slight [slait], *a.* leve; ligero; escaso; tenue; delgado; pequeño; ***not in the slightest,*** ni en lo más mínimo. — *s.* desaire, feo. — *v.t.* desairar; desatender; menospreciar.

slighting [ˈslaitiŋ], *a.* despreciativo. — *s.* menosprecio.

slightness [ˈslaitnis], *s.* insignificancia; pequeñez; delgadez.

slim [slim], *a.* delgado, esbelto; escaso; hábil, artero. — *v.i.* adelgazar.

slime [slaim], *s.* limo, légamo, fango, cieno; babaza; (*fig.*) lodo, cieno. — *v.t.*, *v.i.* enfangar(se), enlodar(se), ensuciar(se) con limo, légamo, babaza *etc.*

sliminess [ˈslaiminis], *s.* limosidad; viscosidad, mucosidad; (*fig.*) servilismo.

slimming [ˈslimiŋ], *a.* que adelgaza, adelgazador; (*vestido*) que hace delgado. — *s.* (el) adelgazar; adelgazamiento.

slimy [ˈslaimi], *a.* viscoso; limoso; pegajoso; legamoso; mucoso; (*fig.*) servil; vil, repulsivo.

sling (1) [sliŋ], *s.* honda; (*cir.*) cabestrillo; vendaje; barbiquejo; (*mil.*) charpa, portafusil; (*mar.*) eslinga, balso; (*mar.*) ***slings of the buoy,*** guarnición de la boya; ***slings of the yard,*** cruz de la verga. — *v.t.* lanzar, tirar, arrojar; tirar con honda; embragar, eslingar, izar; poner en cabestrillo.

sling (2) [sliŋ], *s.* (*Am.*) bebida de ginebra con azúcar y nuez moscada.

slinger [ˈsliŋə], *s.* hondero, pedrero.

slingshot [ˈsliŋʃɔt], *s.* honda, tirachinos, *m.inv.*

slink [sliŋk], *irr. v.i.* andar furtivamente; ***slink along,*** andar sinuosamente; ***slink away,*** escabullirse, escurrirse.

slip (1) [slip], *s.* (*agric.*) esqueje; lengua (*de tierra*); (*impr.*) galerada; tira, lista (*de papel*); ***slip of a girl,*** muchachilla, jovenzuela.

slip (2) [slip], *s.* resbalón; desliz; falta, equivocación, lapso; (*geol.*) falla, dislocación; (*mar.*) grada; combinación (*de mujer*); funda (*de almohada*); ***slip of the pen,*** lapsus (calami); ***slip of the tongue,*** lapsus (linguae); ***slip-up,*** metedura de pata; ***to give the slip,*** dar esquinazo a, sacudirse (a); (*prov.*) ***there's many a slip 'twixt cup and lip,*** de la mano a la boca desaparece la sopa. — *v.t.* deslizar; introducir; dislocarse (*un disco*); escapar a, librarse de; ***slip a cable,*** soltar un cable; ***slip in,*** meter deslizando, insinuar; ***slip into,*** introducir en; ***it has slipped my mind, it slips my mind,*** se me ha ido el santo al cielo; ***slip off,*** quitarse (en un momento); ***slip on,*** ponerse (en un momento). — *v.i.* deslizarse, resbalar(se); dislocarse; (*fam.*) empezar a ir para abajo, pegar un bajón; ***his foot slipped,*** se le fue el pie; ***slip away, off,*** o ***out,*** escabullirse, salir, *o* irse desapercibido; ***slip back,*** volver con sigilo *o* desapercibido; ***slip by,*** pasar inadvertido; pasar sin sentir; ***slip down,*** bajarse (*las medias etc.*); ***slip through,*** colarse, infiltrarse; ***slip up,*** resbalar(se); (*fam.*) meter la pata; ***let slip a chance,*** desaprovechar una ocasión; ***he let the secret slip out,*** se le fue la lengua, se fue de la lengua.

slip-board [ˈslip-bɔːd], *s.* (*mar.*) corredera.

slip-cover [ˈslip-kʌvə], *s.* funda de mueble.

slip-knot [ˈslip-nɔt], *s.* nudo corredizo.

slipper [ˈslipə], *s.* zapatilla; babucha.

slippered [ˈslipəd], *a.* con zapatillas.

slipperiness [ˈslipərinis], *s.* (lo) resbaladizo.

slippery [ˈslipəri], *a.* resbaladizo, resbaloso escurridizo; viscoso; (*fig.*) escurridizo.

slipshod [ˈslipʃɔd], *a.* (*fig.*) descuidado, *f.*; chapucero.

slipslop [ˈslipslɔp], *s.* aguachirle, *f.*

slipstream [ˈslipstriːm], *s.* (*aer.*) viento de la hélice.

slipway [ˈslipwei], *s.* grada.

slit [slit], *s.* raja, hendidura, corte; abertura. — *irr. v.t.* rajar, hender, cortar; ***slit s.o.'s throat,*** degollar a alguien, cortarle a alguien el pescuezo.

sliver [ˈslivə], *s.* raja; tira; torzal. — *v.t.* cortar en rajas *o* tiras.

slob [slɔb], *s.* mastuerzo.

slobber [ˈslɔbə], *s.* baba; sensiblería. — *v.i.* babear, babosear; ***slobber over,*** besuquear; entusiasmarse estúpidamente por.

sloe [slou], *s.* endrino; endrina.

slog [slɔg], *s.* trabajo pesado; caminata. — *v.t.* golpear (desmañadamente). — *v.i.* sudar tinta, afanarse; patear, caminar trabajosamente.

slogan [ˈslougən], *s.* grito de combate; lema, *m.*, eslógan.

sloop [sluːp], *s.* (*mar.*) balandra, chalupa; (*mar.*) ***sloop of war,*** corbeta.

slop (1) [slɔp], *s.* (*pl.*) agua sucia, lavazas, *f.pl.*; aguachirle, *f.*; (*despec.*) atole, gachas, *f.pl.*; (*mar.*, *fam.*) ropa barata y mal hecha; ***slop-shop,*** tienda de ropa barata; ***slop-work,*** chapucería; ***slop-basin, slop-bucket,*** barreño; ***slop-bowl, slop-pail,*** cubo *o* tina para aguas sucias. — *v.i.* — ***over,*** derramarse, desbordarse.

slop (2) [slɔp], *s.* (*fam.*) policía, *m.*

slope [sloup], *s.* (*geol.*, *min.*) inclinación, sesgo, escotadura; (*f.c.*) talud; declive, descenso; loma, falda, bajada, repecho, recuesto; ladera, vertiente; (*fort.*) rampa, escarpa; (*mil.*) ***at the slope,*** al hombro. — *v.t.* sesgar, partir *o* cortar en sesgo; formar en declive; (*cost.*) escotar; ***slope arms!*** ¡armas al hombro! — *v.i.* inclinarse, declinar, estar en declive; ir oblicuamente, moverse en plano inclinado.

sloping [ˈsloupiŋ], *a.* al sesgo, inclinado, en declive.

sloppiness [ˈslɔpinis], *s.* (lo) desaliñado; (lo) sentimentalón; (lo) sensiblero.

sloppy [ˈslɔpi], *a.* aguoso; lleno de charcos; mojado; cenagoso; descuidado, desaliñado; sentimentalón, sensiblero.

slosh [slɔʃ], *s.* lodo blando, aguachirle, *f.* — *v.t.* (*fam.*) echar; pegar. — *v.i.* — ***about,*** chapotear.

slot [slɔt], *s.* (*mec.*) ranura; muesca; rastro, pista, huella; ***slot-machine,*** tragaperras, *f.inv.* — *v.t.* hacer una ranura *o* muesca en.

sloth [slouθ], *s.* pereza, dejadez, indolencia, acidia; (*zool.*) perezoso.

slothful [ˈslouθful], *a.* perezoso, indolente, holgazán.

slothfulness [ˈslouθfulnis], *s.* pereza, indolencia.

slouch [slautʃ], *s.* postura desgarbada; ***slouch hat,*** sombrero gacho. — *v.t.* poner gacho, bajar el ala de. — *v.i.* andar con aire desgalichado; ***sit slouched in a chair,*** estar sentado desgarbadamente en una silla.

slough (1) [slau], *s.* lodazal, fangal, cenagal; (*fig.*) abismo.

slough (2) [slʌf], *s.* camisa (*de serpiente*); (*med.*) escara, tejido muerto. — *v.t.* echar (fuera) (*una costra*); (*zool.*) mudar (la piel). — *v.i.* desprenderse, caerse.

sloughy [ˈslaui], *a.* fangoso, pantanoso, lodoso.

Slovak [ˈslouvæk], *a.*, *s.* eslovaco.

sloven [ˈslʌvən], *s.* persona desaseada *o* desaliñada.

Slovene [ˈslouviːn], *a.*, *s.* esloveno.

Slovenian [slouˈviːniən], *a.*, *s.* esloveno.

slovenliness [ˈslʌvənlinis], *s.* desaliño; desaseo; dejadez.

slovenly [ˈslʌvənli], *a.* desaliñado; desaseado; descuidado; dejado.

slow [slou], *a.* lento; tardo; ***slow and deliberate,*** pausado; ***slow-motion,*** (hecho *o* realizado) a cámara lenta; ***slow-witted,*** torpe, tardo, lento; ***to be slow,*** ser lento; (*reloj.*) atrasar, retrasar; ***to be slow to,*** tardar en; ***to be slow to anger,*** no enfadarse fácilmente, tener mucho aguante. — *adv.* lento, despacio. — *v.t.* — ***down*** o ***up,*** retardar; reducir la velocidad *o* la marcha de;

reducir el ritmo de. — *v.i.* — ***down*** o ***up,*** ir más despacio, amainar.

slowcoach [ˈsloukoutʃ], *s.* (*fam.*) tardón, lentote.

slowly [ˈslouli], *adv.* despacio; (***terribly***) ***slowly,*** lentamente, con mucha lentitud; ***slowly but surely,*** lenta pero seguramente.

slowness [ˈslounis], *s.* lentitud; tardanza.

slow-worm [ˈslou-wəːm], *s.* lución, *m.*

sludge [slʌdʒ], *s.* sedimento(s).

slue [sluː], [SLEW (I)].

slug (I) [slʌg], *s.* babosa.

slug (2) [slʌg], *s.* (*artill.*) posta; (*impr.*) lingote.

slug (3) [slʌg], *v.t.* (*fam.*) pegar, pegar un puñetazo a.

sluggard [ˈslʌgəd], *s.* dormilón; perezosón; pachorrudo.

sluggish [ˈslʌgiʃ], *a.* perezoso; lento; pachorrudo.

sluggishness [ˈslʌgiʃnis], *s.* pereza; lentitud; pachorra.

sluice [sluːs], *s.* esclusa; canal; ***sluice-gate,*** compuerta; ***sluice-way,*** saetín, caz. — *v.t.* regar; lavar; echar.

slum [slʌm], *s.* barrio bajo, suburbio, barriada pobre. — *v.i.* visitar los barrios bajos; ***go slumming,*** ir(se) de juerga por los barrios bajos.

slumber [ˈslʌmbə], *s.* sueño (tranquilo); inactividad, estancamiento. — *v.i.* dormir (tranquilo); dormitar; estarse sin hacer nada.

slumberous [ˈslʌmbərəs], *a.* soñoliento; tranquilo.

slummock [ˈslʌmək], *v.i.* moverse con pereza y desgarbadamente; arrellanarse, repantigarse.

slump [slʌmp], *s.* baja; bajón; crac, crisis económica, *f.* — *v.i.* bajar; hundirse; dejarse caer pesadamente, desplomarse.

slur [sləː], *s.* baldón; borrón; (*mús.*) ligado; ***to cast a slur upon,*** baldonar, echar un baldón a *o* en; poner en duda. — *v.t.* pronunciar de manera borrosa, confusa *o* poco clara; ***slur over a letter,*** comerse una letra.

slush [slʌʃ], *s.* nieve sucia y deshecha, barro de nieve; (*fig.*) sentimentalismos, *m.pl.*, cursilerías, *f.pl.*

slushy [ˈslʌʃi], *a.* fangoso; sensiblero.

slut [slʌt], *s.* mujerzuela; perra.

sluttish [ˈslʌtiʃ], *a.* puerco, desaliñado.

sly [slai], *a.* astuto, taimado; socarrón; disimulado; ***on the sly,*** a hurtadillas.

slyboots [ˈslaibuːts], *s.* camastrón, mosquita muerta.

slyness [ˈslainis], *s.* astucia; socarronería; disimulo.

smack (I) [smæk], *s.* (*mar.*) cúter, queche.

smack (2) [smæk], *adv.* ¡zas!; ***smack on the nose,*** en las mismísimas narices. — *s.* manotada, golpe; rechupete; beso sonoro. — *v.t.* dar una manotada a; pegar, golpear; relamerse; besar sonoramente; ***smack one's lips,*** chuparse los labios, relamerse. — *v.i.* dar manotadas; besarse sonoramente.

smack (3) [smæk], *s.* dejo; sabor(cillo). — *v.i.* — ***of,*** saber a, tener un dejo *o* gustillo de.

smacker [ˈsmækə], *s.* (*fam.*) beso sonoro; bofetón; (*Am.*) dólar.

small [smɔːl], *a.* pequeño; chico; menudo; diminuto; insignificante; menor; bajo (*de estatura*); escaso, exiguo; flojo, diluido; fino, delgado; ***small arms,*** armas cortas (*de fuego*), *f.pl.*; (*fig.*) ***small beer,*** cosa(s) de poca monta; ***small capital,*** versalita; ***small change,*** suelto, dinero menudo; ***small coal,*** cisco, carbón menudo; ***small craft,*** embarcaciones menores, *f.pl.*; ***to be a small eater,*** comer poco, comer como un pajarito; ***small fry,*** morralla; gente menuda; ***small game,*** caza menor; ***small-holding,*** parcela, minifundio; ***small hours,*** altas horas, *f.pl.*; ***small intestine,*** intestino delgado; ***small letter,*** minúscula; ***small matters,*** menudencias, *f.pl.*; ***small-minded,*** estrecho de miras; ***small print,*** tipo pequeño; ***to small purpose,*** con poco fruto; ***small rate,*** precio bajo; ***small-scale,*** de *o* en pequeña escala; ***small talk,*** charla intrascendente; ***small-time,*** de poca importancia, de poca monta; ***small voice,*** voz delgada, vocecita; ***small wares,*** mercería; ***in a small way,*** en pequeña escala; ***to feel small,*** sentirse humillado; ***to make small,*** achicar. — *adv.* en tono bajo *o* suave; ***to cut small,*** desmenuzar; ***to think small of,*** tener en poco. — *s.* parte estrecha de una cosa; cosa pequeña; (lo) pequeño; (*pl.*) paños menores, *m.pl.*; ***in small,*** en pequeño; ***small of the back,*** (la) parte más estrecha de la espalda.

smallage [ˈsmɔːlidʒ], *s.* apio silvestre.

smaller [ˈsmɔːlə], *a. compar.*, **smallest** [ˈsmɔːlist], *a. superl.* [SMALL]; menor.

smallish [ˈsmɔːliʃ], *a.* pequeñito, algo pequeño, menudo.

smallness [ˈsmɔːlnis], *s.* pequeñez, (lo) pequeño; insignificancia; exigüidad.

smallpox [ˈsmɔːlpɔks], *s.* viruelas, *f.pl.*

smalt [smɔːlt], *s.* esmalte; (*pint.*) esmaltín.

smarmy [ˈsmɑːmi], *a.* (*fam.*) gachón, empalagoso.

smart (I) [smɑːt], *a.* listo, vivo; hábil; despierto; ladino, astuto; elegante; pulcro; aseado; ***smart set,*** gente de buen tono.

smart (2) [smɑːt], *s.* escozor; picor. — *v.i.* escocer; picar; ***it makes my tongue smart,*** me escuece en la lengua; ***you shall smart for it,*** me la pagarás; ***smart under*** o ***with,*** resentirse de.

smarten [smɑːtn], *v.t.* hermosear, embellecer.

smartness [ˈsmɑːtnis], *s.* agudeza, viveza, despejo, vivacidad; elegancia.

smarty [ˈsmɑːti], *s.* (*fam.*) listillo, cuco.

smash [smæʃ], *s.* choque, encontronazo; golpe violento, golpazo; (*com.*) quiebra; ***smash-and-grab*** (***raid***), robo relámpago; ***smash hit,*** exitazo; (*fam.*) ***smash-up,*** choque, encontronazo. — *v.t.* romper (con violencia), destrozar, hacer pedazos *o* trizas; lanzar con violencia (***against,*** contra), aplastar (***against,*** contra). — *v.i.* romperse, deshacerse; (*com.*) quebrar, arruinarse; ***it smashed to bits,*** se hizo añicos.

smasher [ˈsmæʃə], *s.* (*fam.*) bombón, *m.*

smashing [ˈsmæʃiŋ], *a.* (*fam.*) estupendo, bárbaro.

smattering [ˈsmætəriŋ], *s.* ***to have a smattering of,*** tener alguna ideílla *o* nocioncilla de; tener un barnicillo de.

smear [smiə], *s.* embadurnamiento, mancha; ***smear campaign,*** campaña de calumnias. — *v.t.* embadurnar, manchar, untar.

smeary [ˈsmiəri], *a.* embadurnado.

smell [smel], *s.* olor; (*sentido del*) olfato; ***bad smell,*** mal olor. — *irr. v.t.* oler; olfatear; ***smell out,*** descubrir husmeando; ***smell a rat,*** olerse algo, escamarse. — *v.i.* oler (**of,** a).

smelling [ˈsmeliŋ], *a.* ***foul-smelling,*** hediondo, que huele mal; ***sweet-smelling,*** oloroso, odorífero. — *s.* (el) oler; ***smelling-bottle,*** frasco de sales; ***smelling-salts,*** sales (aromáticas), *f.pl.*

smelt (I) [smelt], *pret.*, *p.p.* [SMELL].

smelt (2) [smelt], *s.* (*ict.*) esperlán.

smelt (3) [smelt], *v.t.* (*fund.*) fundir.

smelter [ˈsmeltə], *s.* fundidor.

smeltery [ˈsmeltəri], *s.* fundición.

smelting [ˈsmeltiŋ], *s.* fundición; ***smelting furnace,*** horno de fundición; ***smelting house,*** fundición; ***smelting pot,*** cubilote; ***smelting works,*** fundición.

smilax [ˈsmailæks], *s.* esmílax, esmiláceo.

smile [smail], *s.* sonrisa; ***to raise a smile,*** forzar una sonrisa; provocar una sonrisa. — *v.t.* expresar con una sonrisa. — *v.i.* sonreír(se); ***smile at, on*** o ***upon,*** sonreír a.

smiling [ˈsmailiŋ], *a.* sonriente, risueño.

smilingly [ˈsmailiŋli], *adv.* con cara risueña, sonriendo, con sonrisa.

smirch [sməːtʃ], *v.t.* tiznar; mancillar, desdorar.

smirk [sməːk], *s.* sonrisa boba *o* afectada. — *v.i.* sonreírse afectadamente.

smirking [ˈsməːkiŋ], *a.* satisfecho; afectado.

smite [smait], *s.* golpe, porrazo. — *irr. v.t.* herir, golpear; afligir; castigar; encantar, ganar *o* robar (el corazón); llegar al alma a, conmover, enternecer; doler, apenar, pesar; ***smite off,*** cortar, partir *o* romper de un golpe. — *v.i.* chocar; venir con fuerza repentina.

smiter [ˈsmaitə], *s.* golpeador; persona *o* animal que hiere, que aflige, que castiga, *etc.*

smith [smiθ], *s.* herrero; (*en composición*) artífice; ***smith and farrier,*** herrador; ***smith's hammer,*** destajador.

smithereens [smiðəˈriːnz], *s.pl.* añicos, *m.pl.*; ***to smash to smithereens,*** hacer añicos.

smithery [ˈsmiθəri], *s.* herrería, taller *u* oficio del herrero.

smithy [ˈsmiði], *s.* fragua, forja.

smock [smɔk], *s.* (*ant.*) camisa (*de mujer*); blusa (*de labrador*); ***smock-frock,*** blusa de labrador.

smoke [smouk], *s.* humo; ***smoke-black,*** negro humo; ***smoke-bomb,*** bomba fumígena; ***smoke-burner, smoke-consumer,*** aparato fumívoro; ***smoke-consuming,*** fumívoro; ***smoke-jack,*** torno de asador movido por el humo; (*mar.*) ***smoke-sail,*** guardahumo; ***smoke-screen,*** cortina de humo; ***smoke-signal,*** señal de humo; ***smoke-stack,*** chimenea; ***smoke-tight,*** impenetrable al humo; (*fig.*) ***to end in smoke,*** volverse humo, quedarse en agua de borrajas; ***to have a smoke,*** fumar un pitillo; ***there's no smoke without fire,*** cuando el río suena, agua lleva. — *v.t.* fumar; curar al humo, poner al humo, ahumar; sahumar; ennegrecer; ***smoke out,*** ahumar, ahogar con humo; hacer salir por medio del humo. — *v.i.* humear, echar humo; fumar; ***please do not smoke,*** se ruega no fumar.

smoked [smoukt], *a.* ahumado.

smoke-dry [ˈsmouk-drai], *v.t.* ahumar, curar, secar al humo.

smokeless [ˈsmouklis], *a.* sin humo; desahumado; ***smokeless zone,*** zona libre de humo.

smoker [ˈsmoukə], *s.* fumador; sahumador; caja de ahumar abejas; (*fam.*) coche para fumadores.

smokiness [ˈsmoukinis], *s.* fumosidad.

smoking [ˈsmoukiŋ], *a.* humeante, fumante.—*s.* (el) fumar; (el) ahumar; ***no smoking (allowed),*** se prohibe fumar; (*Ingl.*) ***smoking compartment,*** (*Am.*) ***smoking car,*** vagón para fumadores; ***smoking-jacket,*** chaqueta batín; ***smoking-room,*** fumadero, cuarto de fumar.

smoky [ˈsmouki], *a.* humeante; humoso; ahumado.

smolt [smoult], *s.* (*ict.*) murgón, esguín.

smolder [SMOULDER].

smooch [smuːtʃ], *v.i.* (*fam.*) besuquearse.

smooth [smuːð], *a.* liso; terso; suave: llano, igual, uniforme; tranquilo; (*despec.*) meloso, suavón; ***smooth-shaven,*** (bien) afeitado; ***smooth-sliding,*** que se desliza suavemente; ***smooth-spoken, smooth-tongued,*** meloso, suavón, zalamero. — *v.t.* alisar; suavizar; allanar; ***smooth away,*** eliminar suavemente; ***smooth down,*** calmar, tranquilizar; ***smooth over,*** resolver suavemente; ***smooth the way for,*** allanar el camino de *o* para.

smoothing-iron [ˈsmuːðiŋ-aiən], *s.* plancha.

smoothly [ˈsmuːðli], *adv.* con suavidad; ***go smoothly,*** ir sobre ruedas.

smoothness [ˈsmuːðnis], *s.* lisura; tersura; suavidad.

smother [ˈsmʌðə], *v.t.* ahogar, sofocar; apagar; contener; suprimir; ***smother in*** o ***with attention,*** colmar de atenciones.

smoulder [ˈsmouldə], *v.i.* arder lentamente; arder sin llama; arder en rescoldo; (*fig.*) estar latente.

smouldering [ˈsmouldəriŋ], *a.* que arde lentamente; latente, oculto; ***smouldering hatred,*** odio sordo *o* contenido; ***smouldering look,*** mirada de furia contenida.

smudge [smʌdʒ], *s.* mancha (borrosa), borrón; tiznón. — *v.t.* manchar (borrosamente), echar un borrón *o* borrones en; tiznar (***with,*** de).

smudgy [ˈsmʌdʒi], *a.* manchado, borroso, lleno de borrones *o* de tiznones.

smug [smʌg], *a.* satisfecho, pagado de sí (mismo), que tiene buen concepto de sí (mismo).

smuggle [smʌgl], *v.t.* pasar de contrabando; ***smuggle in*** o ***out,*** entrar *o* sacar de contrabando *o* de matute *o* clandestinamente. — *v.i.* hacer contrabando, matutear.

smuggled [smʌgld], *a.* de contrabando.

smuggler [ˈsmʌglə], *s.* contrabandista, *m.f.*, matutero.

smuggling [ˈsmʌgliŋ], *s.* contrabando, matute.

smugness [ˈsmʌgnis], *s.* satisfacción de sí mismo; presunción.

smut [smʌt], *s.* tiznón; mancha; (*fig.*) indecencia, verdulez; (*bot.*) tizón, tizoncillo. — *v.t.* tiznar, manchar.

smuttiness [ˈsmʌtinis], *s.* (*fig.*) indecencia, verdulez.

smutty [ˈsmʌti], *a.* tiznado, manchado con tizne; (*bot.*) atizonado; (*fig.*) indecente, verde.

Smyrna [ˈsməːnə]. Esmirna.

snack [snæk], *s.* tentempié, piscolabis, *m.inv.*, bocadillo; ***snack-bar,*** cafetería.

snaffle [snæfl], *s.* bridón. — *v.t.* enfrenar; (*fam.*) birlar.

snag [snæg], *s.* nudo (*de la madera*); protuberancia; tocón; raigón; pitón; tropiezo, pero, pega; ***to strike*** o ***hit a snag,*** tropezar *o* chocar con una pega; ***that's the snag,*** ésa es la pega, ahí está la cosa; ***there's a snag,*** hay una pega; ***what's the snag?*** ¿qué pega hay? ¿en qué consiste la pega?

snagged [snægd], *a.* lleno de raigones; nudoso.

snaggy [ˈsnægi], *a.* lleno de troncos (*o* tocones); (*carp.*) nudoso; parecido a un tócon.

snail [sneil], *s.* caracol (de tierra); ***snail-clover,*** mielga; ***at a snail's pace,*** a paso de tortuga.

snake [sneik], *s.* culebra, serpiente; ***snake-bite,*** mordedura *o* picadura de serpiente; ***snake charmer,*** encantador de serpientes; (*fig., pers.*) ***snake in the grass,*** peligro oculto; enemigo oculto, traidor; ***snake-weed,*** bistorta, dragontea. — *v.t.* arrastrar, mover sinuosamente. — *v.i.* culebrear, serpear, serpentear.

snaky [ˈsneiki], *a.* de culebra; culebrino, serpentino; tortuoso; que serpentea; solapado; traidor; (*Am.*) lleno de culebras.

snap [snæp], *a.* repentino, imprevisto, de sorpresa; ***snap election,*** elección por sorpresa; ***snap judgment,*** decisión precipitada; ***snap shot,*** disparo rápido sin apuntar [SNAPSHOT]. — *s.* chasquido; castañetazo; cierre de resorte; bocado, mordisco; vigor; (*foto., fam.*) instantánea; ***soft snap,*** ganga; ***snap bolt,*** pestillo de golpe; ***snap fastener,*** corchete de presión; ***snap switch,*** interruptor de resorte. — *v.t.* romper; hacer saltar; chasquear; castañetear; (*foto., fam.*) sacar una instantánea de; ***he snaps his fingers at it,*** le trae al fresco; ***snap shut,*** cerrar de golpe; ***snap up,*** tirarse sobre. — *v.i.* romperse, saltar; chasquear; ***snap at,*** tirar un bocado a; responder brúscamente a; aceptar (algo) sin pensar; ***snap off,*** soltarse, saltar, partirse; ***snap out of it,*** reaccionar; ***snap shut,*** cerrarse de golpe.

snapdragon [ˈsnæpdrægən], *s.* hierba becerra, antirrino.

snapper [ˈsnæpə], *s.* ratero; punta del látigo; triquitraque, buscapiés, *m.inv.*; (*pl.*) castañuelas, *f.pl.*

snapping [ˈsnæpiŋ], *a.* saltadizo; ***snapping turtle,*** gran tortuga voraz. — *s.* acción de estallar, chasquear *etc.* [SNAP].

snappish [ˈsnæpiʃ], *a.* irritable, arisco.

snappishness [ˈsnæpiʃnis], *s.* irritabilidad.

snappy [ˈsnæpi], *a.* vivo, rápido; ***make it snappy!*** ¡rápido!

snapshot [ˈsnæpʃɔt], *s.* (foto) instantánea. — *v.t., v.i.* hacer una instantánea (a).

snare [snɛə], *s.* trampa, lazo; celada, red, asechanza. — *v.t.* atrapar, hacer caer en una trampa; enredar, tender celadas *o* lazos a.

snarl [snɑːl], *s.* gruñido; regaño. — *v.i.* gruñir, enseñar los dientes; regañar.

snarler [ˈsnɑːlə], *s.* gruñón; regañón.

snarly [ˈsnɑːli], *a.* gruñón; regañón; enredado.

snatch [snætʃ], *s.* arrebatamiento; (*fam.*) robo; ***in snatches,*** a ratitos, en los ratitos perdidos; poquito a poco; a retazos, fragmentariamente; ***snatch of music,*** trocito de música. — *v.t.* arrebatar, coger violenta y groseramente; ***don't snatch!*** ¡no lo cojas así!; ***snatch a moment's rest,*** aprovechar para descansar un momento; ***they've all been snatched up,*** se han acabado *o* agotado todos en nada de tiempo.

snath, snathe, snead [snæθ, sneiθ, sniːd], *s.* mango de guadaña.

snazzy [ˈsnæzi], *a.* (*fam.*) elegantón.

sneak [sniːk], *s.* soplón, acusica. — *v.i.* ir con el soplo, chivarse; ***sneak in,*** colarse, entrar a hurtadillas; ***sneak off, out,*** o ***away,*** salir a hurtadillas *o* furtivamente, escabullirse, escurrirse; ***sneak on s.o.,*** chivarse.

sneakers [ˈsniːkəz], *s.pl.* (*Am.*) zapatos de playa, *m.pl.*

sneaking [ˈsniːkiŋ], *a.* furtivo, oculto; ***to have a sneaking admiration for s.o.,*** a pesar de todo *o* en el fondo sentir cierta admiración por alguien; ***sneaking doubt, qualm,*** dudilla, escrupulillo, reparillo. — *s.* (el) chivarse.

sneer [sniə], *s.* expresión de burla y de displicencia. — *v.i.* hablar de una manera burlona y displicente; ***sneer at,*** burlarse con displicencia de.

sneering [ˈsniəriŋ], *a.* burlón y displicente.

sneeze [sniːz], *s.* estornudo. — *v.i.* estornudar; ***it's not to be sneezed at,*** no es moco de pavo; ahí es nada.

sneezing [ˈsniːziŋ], *s.* estornudos, *m.pl.*

snick [snik], *s.* corte pequeño, tijeretada. — *v.t.* cortar (con tijeras).

sniff [snif], *s.* husmeo; venteo; sorbo por la nariz. — *v.t.* oler, olfatear, husmear; ***sniff up,*** sorber por la nariz. — *v.i.* sorber por la nariz; ***sniff at,*** husmear; despreciar, hacer feos a.

snigger [ˈsnigə], *s.* risilla, risita. — *v.i.* reírse tontamente.

snip [snip], *s.* tijeretada; recorte; pedacito; (*fam.*) ganga; cosa tirada; ***snip of a girl,*** muchachilla. — *v.t.* cortar de un tijeretazo, recortar, cercenar.

snipe [snaip], *s.* agachadiza, becardón. — *v.i.* tirar desde un escondrijo, paquear; ***snipe at,*** tirotear.

sniper [ˈsnaipə], *s.* paco.

snippet [ˈsnipit], *s.* recorte; trocillo.

snip-snap [ˈsnip-ˈsnæp], *s.* diálogo picante.

snivel [snivl], *s.* moquita; gimoteo, pucheros, *m.pl.* — *v.i.* lloriquear, hacer pucheros.

sniveller [ˈsnivlə], *s.* llorón, lloraduelos, *m.inv.*, jeremías, *m.f.inv.*

snivelling [ˈsnivəliŋ], *a.* llorón, que hace pucheros; mocoso. — *s.* pucheros, *m.pl.*

snob [snɔb], *s.* esnob, cursi.

snobbery, snobbishness [ˈsnɔbəri, -iʃnis], *s.* (e)snobismo, cursilería.

snobbish [ˈsnɔbiʃ], *a.* esnob, cursi.

snood [snuːd], *s.* redecilla; cendal (*de pesca*).

snook (1) [snuːk], *s.* pez tropical parecido al lucio.

snook (2) [snuːk], *s.* ***to cock a snook at,*** sacarle la lengua a; ***to cock a snook at society,*** ponerse el mundo por montera.

snooker [ˈsnuːkə], *s.* snooker.

snoop [snuːp], *s.* fisgón, entremetido. — *v.i.* fisgonear, curiosear.

snooper [ˈsnuːpə], *s.* husmeador; espía, *m.*

snooty [ˈsnuːti], *a.* (*fam.*) creído, altivo.

snooze [snuːz], *s.* siestecita, sueñecillo. — *v.i.* dormitar, descabezar un sueño.

snore [snɔː], *s.* ronquido. — *v.i.* roncar.

snorer [ˈsnɔːrə], *s.* roncador.

snoring [ˈsnɔːriŋ], *s.* ronquido(s).

snort [snɔːt], *s.* resoplido, bufido. — *v.i.* resoplar, bufar.

snot [snɔt], *s.* moco.

snotty (1) [ˈsnɔti], *a.* mocoso.

snotty (2) [ˈsnɔti], *s.* (*mar., fam.*) guardiamarina, *m.*

snout [snaut], *s.* hocico, morro; ***snout-beetle,*** gorgojo; ***snout-ring,*** narigón para puercos.

snouted [ˈsnautid], *a.* hocicudo.

snow [snou], *s.* nieve; (*fam.*) cocaína; ***snow-bird,*** pinzón de las nieves; ***snow-blind,*** cegado por la nieve; ***snow-blindness,*** ceguera causada por el reflejo de la nieve; ***snow-bound,*** aislado por la nieve; ***snow-bunting,*** verderón de las nieves; ***snow-capped,*** coronado de nieve; ***snow-plough,*** (máquina) quitanieves, *m.inv.*; ***snow-shoe,*** raqueta de nieve; ***snow-slip,*** alud; ***Snow White,*** Blancanieves, *f.*; ***snow-white,*** nevado; blanco como la nieve; (*poet.*) de nieve, níveo. — *v.t.* — ***in, under,*** o ***up,*** cubrir, obstruir, detener *o* aprisionar con nieve; ***to be snowed up,*** estar aislado por la nieve; (*fig.*) ***snow under,*** abrumar. — *v.i.* nevar.

snowball [ˈsnoubɔːl], *s.* bola de nieve. — *v.t., v.i.* lanzar bolas de nieve (a). — *v.i.* aumentar como una bola de nieve.

snowdrift [ˈsnoudrift], *s.* acumulación de nieve, ventisquero.

snowdrop [ˈsnoudrɔp], *s.* campanilla blanca.

snowfall [ˈsnoufɔːl], *s.* nevada, nevasca.

snowflake [ˈsnoufleik], *s.* copo de nieve; (*orn.*) verderón de las nieves; (*bot.*) campanilla.

snowman [ˈsnoumæn], *s.* figura de nieve; ***the abominable snowman,*** el abominable hombre de las nieves.

snowstorm [ˈsnoustɔːm], *s.* nevasca, borrasca de nieve.

snowy [ˈsnoui], *a.* nevoso, de nieves; (*poét.*) níveo.

snub [snʌb], *a.* ***snub-nosed,*** chato. — *s.* desaire; sofión. — *v.t.* dar un sofión a; desairar; repulsar.

snuff [snʌf], *s.* rapé; ***snuff-box,*** tabaquera. — *v.t.* despabilar; ***snuff out,*** apagar, extinguir; ***snuff up,*** aspirar, sorber por la nariz.

snuffers [ˈsnʌfəz], *s.pl.* despabiladeras, *f.pl.*

snuffle [snʌfl], *s.* mocos, *m.pl.*; ***to have the snuffles,*** tener mocos. — *v.i.* tener mocos, sorberse los mocos.

snug [snʌg], *a.* a gustito, abrigadito, calentito.

snuggery [ˈsnʌgəri], *s.* (*fam.*) sitio cómodo *o* abrigadito.

snuggle [snʌgl], *v.i.* arrimarse; apretarse; ***snuggle up to,*** arrimarse a, apretarse contra.

so [sou], *adv.* así; de igual manera; por tanto, por lo tanto; tan, tanto; ***and so,*** conque; ***and so on*** o ***forth,*** y así sucesivamente; ***I hope so,*** así lo espero; ***if so,*** de ser así; ***just so, exactly so,*** exactamente, precisamente, justo; ***it is not so,*** no es así, no es cierto; ***only more so,*** sólo que más aún; ***some six or so,*** unos seis o así; ***so am I,*** yo también; ***So-and-So,*** fulano (de tal); (*despec.*) ***he's a real so-and-so,*** ¡es un auténtico tal!; ***so as to,*** de manera que; ***so be it,*** así sea; ***so-called,*** llamado; ***so far,*** hasta aquí, hasta ahora; ***so far so good,*** hasta ahora *o* hasta aquí bien *o* vale; ***so far this year,*** en lo que va de año; ***so good,*** tan bueno; ***it so happens that,*** da la casualidad de que; ***so it does! so it is!*** pues sí, es cierto; ***so many,*** tantos; ***so much*** (***as***), tanto (como); ***ever so much, little,*** muchísimo, poquísimo; ***so much so that,*** tan es así que; ***so-so,*** mediano, regular, pasadero, mediocre; así así, medianamente, regularmente; ***so that,*** de manera que; para que, a fin de que (+ *subj.*); ***so to say, so to speak,*** por decirlo así, como si dijéramos; ***so what?*** ¿y qué?; ***I think so,*** creo que sí; ***I don't think so,*** no lo creo; ***I thought so!*** ¡ya me lo imaginaba *o* figuraba!; ***I'm so sorry!—I should think so too!*** ¡lo siento muchísimo!—¡ya puede usted sentirlo!; ***I told you so,*** ya te lo decía *o* dije; ***why so? how so?*** ¿por qué? ¿cómo es eso? — *conj.* conque; así que.

soak [souk], *s.* remojo; (*fam.*) borrachín; ***to give a good soak to,*** mojar mucho *o* a fondo; ***to have a good soak,*** bañarse mucho *o* a fondo. — *v.t.* empapar, mojar, remojar, poner en remojo; (*fam.*) desplumar, clavar, ordeñar; ***to get soaked to the skin,*** calarse hasta los huesos; ***soak up,*** absorber(se). — *v.i.* estar en remojo; ***soak in*** o ***through,*** penetrar (en); (*fig.*) ***it hasn't soaked in,*** no se ha dado cuenta.

soaking [ˈsoukiŋ], *a.* ***to be soaking wet,*** estar hecho una sopa; estar pingando. — *s.* remojo; ***to get a soaking,*** ponerse pingando.

soaky [ˈsouki], *a.* empapado, calado, mojado.

soap [soup], *s.* jabón; ***soap-ball,*** bola de jabón; ***soap-boiler,*** caldera para jabón; jabonero; ***soap-bubble,*** pompa de jabón; ***soap-dish,*** jabonera; ***soap factory,*** jabonería; ***soap-maker,*** jabonero; ***soap opera,*** folletín radiofónico; (*bot.*) ***soap-plant,*** amole; ***soap powder,*** jabón en polvo; (*fam.*) ***soft soap,*** coba. — *v.t.* (en)jabonar; dar coba, dar jabón.

soapberry-tree [ˈsoupberi-triː], *s.* sapindo, jaboncillo.

soapflake [ˈsoupfleik], *s.* (*ú. más en pl.*) copos de jabón, *m.pl.*

soapstone [ˈsoupstoun], *s.* esteatita, galaxía; jaboncillo, jabón de sastre.

soapsuds [ˈsoupsʌdz], *s.pl.* jabonaduras, *f.pl.*

soapwort [ˈsoupwəːt], *s.* saponaria, jabonera.

soapy [ˈsoupi], *a.* jabonoso, saponáceo.

soar [sɔː], *s.* vuelo, remonte. — *v.i.* remontarse; encumbrarse; cernerse; volar a gran altura.

soaring [ˈsɔːriŋ], *a.* que se remonta; (*fig.*) sublime, elevado.

sob [sɔb], *a.* (*fam.*) sentimental, cursi. — *s.* sollozo. — *v.i.* sollozar.

sober [ˈsoubə], *a.* sobrio; serio; moderado; sereno; ***as sober as a judge,*** serenísimo; ***sober-minded,*** serio; ***to get sober,*** serenarse; ***in sober earnest,*** muy en serio; ***to be stone-cold sober,*** estar serenísimo. — *v.t.* volver sobrio; ***sober down*** o ***up,*** serenar. — *v.i.* — ***down*** o ***up,*** serenarse.

soberness, sobriety [ˈsoubənis, soˈbraiiti], *s.* sobriedad; templanza; moderación; seriedad; calma; serenidad.

sobriquet [ˈsoubrikei], *s.* apodo.

soccer [ˈsɔkə], *s.* fútbol.

sociability [souʃəˈbiliti], *s.* sociabilidad.

sociable [ˈsouʃəbl], *a.* sociable.

social [ˈsouʃəl], *a.* social; ***social outcast,*** paria social; ***social worker,*** asistente social. — *s.* reunión, *f.*, velada.

socialism [ˈsouʃəlizəm], *s.* socialismo.

socialist [ˈsouʃəlist], *a.*, *s.* socialista, *m.f.*

socialistic [souʃəˈlistik], *a.* socialista.

socialize [ˈsouʃəlaiz], *v.t.* socializar. — *v.i.* cultivar el trato social, alternar en sociedad.

society [soˈsaiiti], *s.* sociedad; mundo elegante, alta sociedad; ***fashionable society,*** (la) alta sociedad; ***society news,*** noticias de sociedad, *f.pl.*; ***to go into society,*** entrar en sociedad.

Socinian [soˈsiniən], *a.* sociniano.

Socinianism [soˈsiniənizəm], *s.* socinianismo.

sociological [souʃiəˈlɔdʒikəl], *a.* sociológico.

sociologist [souʃiˈɔlədʒist], *s.* sociólogo.

sociology [souʃiˈɔlədʒi], *s.* sociología.

sock (1) [sɔk], *s.* calcetín; (*fig.*) comedia.

sock (2) [sɔk], *s.* reja de arado.

sock (3) [sɔk], *s.* golpe, puñetazo. — *v.t.* (*fam.*) pegar, dar, golpear.

socket [ˈsɔkit], *s.* encaje; casquillo; cubo; portalámparas, *m.inv.*; enchufe; cuenca (*del ojo*); alvéolo (*del diente*).

socle [soukl], *s.* (*arq.*) zócalo.

Socrates [ˈsɔkrətiːz]. Sócrates, *m.*

Socratic [soˈkrætik], *a.* socrático.

sod (1) [sɔd], *s.* césped; terrón; ***under the sod,*** bajo la tierra.

sod (2) [sɔd], *s.* (*obsc.*) cabrón.

soda [ˈsoudə], *s.* sosa, soda; ***soda-fountain,*** sifón; ***soda-water,*** agua de soda; agua de seltz; gaseosa; sifón.

sodality [soˈdæliti], *s.* cofradía, hermandad.

sodden [sɔdn], *a.* empapado; saturado; embrutecido por el alcohol. — *v.t.* empapar, calar.

sodium [ˈsoudiəm], *s.* sodio.

sodomite [ˈsɔdəmait], *s.* sodomita, *m.*

sodomy [ˈsɔdəmi], *s.* sodomía.

sofa [ˈsoufə], *s.* sofá, *m.*

soffit [ˈsɔfit], *s.* (*arq.*) sofito.

soft [sɔft], *a.* blando; muelle; fofo; suave, dulce; (*sombrero*) flexible; (*pan*) tierno; (*empleo*) fácil, facilón; (*bebida*) no alcohólica; ***as soft as silk,*** suave como la seda *o* como una seda; (*fam.*) ***soft in the head,*** tonto (de la cabeza); ***soft-headed,*** memo, lelo; ***soft-hearted,*** blando (de corazón).

soften [sɔfn], *v.t.* ablandar; reblandecer; volver blando; enternecer; suavizar; templar. — *v.i.* ablandarse; reblandecerse *etc.*

softening [ˈsɔfniŋ], *a.* suavizador; emoliente. — *s.* ablandamiento; reblandecimiento; enternecimiento; ***softening of the brain,*** reblandecimiento cerebral.

softish [ˈsɔftiʃ], *a.* blandillo; blanducho.

softly [ˈsɔftli], *adv.* blandamente; suavemente; ***to speak softly,*** hablar quedo *o* bajito.

softness [ˈsɔftnis], *s.* blandura, fofez; suavidad, dulzura; (*metal.*) ductilidad.

soggy [ˈsɔgi], *a.* blanducho.

soil (1) [sɔil], *s.* tierra; suelo; ***native soil,*** suelo natal.

soil (2) [sɔil], *s.* estiércol; ***soil-pipe,*** tubo de desagüe sanitario. — *v.t.* ensuciar, manchar. — *v.i.* ensuciarse, mancharse.

soil (3) [sɔil], *v.t.* dar alcacel (*al ganado*).

soiling (1) [ˈsɔiliŋ], *s.* ensuciamiento.

soiling (2) [ˈsɔiliŋ], *s.* alcacel.

soirée [ˈswɑːrei], *s.* velada, sarao.

sojourn [ˈsɔdʒən], *s.* estancia, permanencia. — *v.i.* estar, permanecer, residir (durante una temporada).

sojourner [ˈsɔdʒənə], *s.* transeúnte, residente temporal.

sol (1) [sɔl], *s.* sueldo (*moneda*); sol (*moneda*).

sol (2) [sɔl], *s.* (*mús.*) sol.

sol (3) [sɔl], *s.* (*fam.*) ***Old Sol,*** Febo, el sol.

solace [ˈsɔlis], *s.* consuelo, alivio; solaz. — *v.t.* consolar, aliviar; solazar.

solan [ˈsoulən], *s.* bubia.

solanaceous [souləˈneiʃəs], *a.* solanáceo.

solar [ˈsoulə], *a.* solar; ***solar plexus,*** plexo solar; (*foto.*) ***solar print,*** impresión heliográfica; ***solar spot,*** mancha solar; ***solar system,*** sistema solar.

solarium [soˈlɛəriəm], *s.* (*pl.* **solaria** [-riə]) solarium.

solatium [soˈleiʃəm], *s.* (*pl.* **solatia** [-ʃiə]) indemnización por daños *o* sufrimiento.

solder [ˈsɔldə], *s.* soldadura. — *v.t.*, *v.i.* soldar(se).

solderer [ˈsɔldərə], *s.* soldador.

soldering [ˈsɔldəriŋ], *s.* soldadura; ***soldering-iron,*** soldador.

soldier [ˈsouldʒə], *s.* soldado; militar; ***old soldier,*** veterano; ***soldier-like*** [SOLDIERLY]; ***tin soldier,*** soldado de plomo. — *v.i.* militar, ser soldado.

soldiering [ˈsouldʒəriŋ], *s.* (el) militar; carrera de militar.

soldierly [ˈsouldʒəli], *a.* soldadesco; militar, marcial.

soldiery [ˈsouldʒəri], *s.* soldadesca; tropa; servicio militar.

sole (1) [soul], *s.* planta del pie; suela del zapato; fondo, suelo. — *v.t.* solar, echar suelas a.

sole (2) [soul], *s.* (*ict.*) lenguado.
sole (3) [soul], *a.* solo, único; único, exclusivo; ***sole right,*** exclusiva.
solecism [ˈsɔlisizəm], *s.* solecismo.
solecistic [sɔliˈsistik], *a.* incorrecto.
solecize [ˈsɔlisaiz], *v.i.* (*ant.*) cometer solecismos.
solemn [ˈsɔləm], *a.* solemne, grave.
solemnness [ˈsɔləmnis], *s.* solemnidad, gravedad.
solemnity [sɔˈlemniti], *s.* solemnidad.
solemnization [sɔləmnaiˈzeiʃən], *s.* solemnización, celebración.
solemnize [ˈsɔləmnaiz], *v.t.* solemnizar, celebrar, celebrar solemnemente.
solen [ˈsoulən], *s.* navaja (*marisco*).
solenoid [ˈsoulənɔid], *s.* solenoide.
soleus [soˈli:əs], *s.* sóleo.
sol-fa [sɔl-ˈfɑ:], *s.* (*mús.*) solfa; solfeo. — *v.t.*, *v.i.* solfear.
solfeggio [sɔlˈfedʒiou], *s.* (*mús.*) solfeo.
solicit [səˈlisit], *v.t.* solicitar; importunar; intentar seducir; gestionar, procurar. — *v.i.* ofrecerse (como prostituta).
solicitation [səlisiˈteiʃən], *s.* solicitación; incitación.
solicitor [səˈlisitə], *s.* abogado; notario; ***Solicitor-General,*** subfiscal de la Corona.
solicitous [səˈlisitəs], *a.* solícito; muy atento.
solicitude [səˈlisitju:d], *s.* solicitud; extrema atención.
solid [ˈsɔlid], *a.* sólido; macizo; unánime; denso; ***solid citizen,*** persona de fundamento; ***solid gold, tyre,*** oro, neumático macizo; ***we waited three solid hours,*** estuvimos esperando nuestras tres buenas horas. — *s.* sólido.
solidarity [sɔliˈdæriti], *s.* solidaridad.
solidification [sɔlidifiˈkeiʃən], *s.* solidificación.
solidify [sɔˈlidifai], *v.t.* solidificar. — *v.i.* solidificarse.
solidity, solidness [sɔˈliditi, ˈsɔlidnis], *s.* solidez; (lo) sólido; macicez, (lo) macizo *etc.*
soliloquize [səˈliləkwaiz], *v.i.* soliloquiar, hacer un soliloquio.
soliloquy [səˈliləkwi], *s.* soliloquio.
soliped [ˈsɔliped], *s.* solípedo.
solipsism [ˈsɔlipsizəm], *s.* solipsismo.
solitaire [sɔliˈtɛə], *s.* solitario; (*Am.*, *naipes*) [PATIENCE].
solitariness [ˈsɔlitərinis], *s.* soledad, (lo) solitario.
solitary [ˈsɔlitəri], *a.* solitario; solo, único; ***in solitary confinement,*** incomunicado; ***not a solitary one,*** ni uno (solo). — *s.* solitario.
solitude [ˈsɔlitju:d], *s.* soledad.
solmization [sɔlmaiˈzeiʃən], *s.* (*mús.*) solfa.
solo [ˈsoulou], *s.* solo; ***solo flight,*** vuelo a solas.
soloist [ˈsoulouist], *s.* solista, *m.f.*
Solomon [ˈsɔləmən]. Salomón; (*bot.*) ***Solomon's seal,*** sello de Salomón.
solstice [ˈsɔlstis], *s.* solsticio.
solstitial [sɔlˈstiʃəl], *a.* solsticial.
solubility [sɔljuˈbiliti], *s.* solubilidad.
soluble [ˈsɔljubl], *a.* soluble.
solution [səˈl(j)u:ʃən], *s.* solución.
solvable [ˈsɔlvəbl], *a.* soluble.
solve [sɔlv], *v.t.* resolver, solucionar; adivinar, acertar.
solvency [ˈsɔlvənsi], *s.* solvencia.
solvent [ˈsɔlvənt], *a.*, *s.* solvente.
Somali [soˈmɑ:li] *a.*, *s.* somalí, *m.f.*
Somalia [soˈmɑ:liə]. Somalia.
somatic [soˈmætik], *a.* somático.
somatology [souməˈtɔlədʒi], *s.* somatología.
sombre [ˈsɔmbə], *a.* sombrío; tétrico; lúgubre.
sombrous [ˈsɔmbrəs], *a.* (*poét.*) sombrío.
some [sʌm], *a.* alguno, algún; unos, *m.pl.*, unos cuantos, *m.pl.*; un poco de, algo de; ***some days ago,*** hace algunos días; ***have you some money?*** ¿tienes algún dinero?; ***here's some money for you,*** aquí tienes un poco de dinero; ***some people,*** algunas personas, *f.pl.*; ***after some time,*** después de algún tiempo; ***some other time,*** otra vez, otro día; ***some actor fellow or other,*** un tío que es *o* era actor; ***that's some car!*** ¡vaya (un) coche! — *adv.* unos, unas, aproximadamente, alrededor de; ***some 15 people,*** unas 15 personas; ***some £80,*** alrededor de £80. — *pron.* algunos, *m.pl.*; algo, un poco; ***some say yes and some say no,*** algunos dicen que sí y otros que no; ***some of what you said,*** una parte de lo que dijo usted.
somebody [ˈsʌmbɔdi], *pron.* alguien; ***somebody else,*** algún otro, otra persona; ***to be somebody,*** ser un personaje; ***he thinks he's somebody,*** se cree alguien.
somehow [ˈsʌmhau], *adv.* de algún modo, de alguna manera.
somersault [ˈsʌməsɔ:lt], *s.* salto mortal. — *v.i.* dar un salto mortal.
something [ˈsʌmθiŋ], *adv.* algo, algún tanto; (*fam.*) ***this is something like it,*** esto sí que me gusta. — *s.* alguna cosa, algo; ***something else,*** otra cosa; ***to have something to do,*** tener que hacer.
sometime [ˈsʌmtaim], *adv.* algún día; antiguamente; en algún tiempo; en otro tiempo; ***sometime last week,*** durante la semana pasada; ***sometime very soon,*** dentro de muy poco (tiempo).
sometimes [ˈsʌmtaimz], *adv.* algunas veces, de vez en cuando, a veces.
somewhat [ˈsʌmwɔt], *adv.* algo, algún tanto; un poco; ***somewhat busy,*** algo ocupado. — *s.* algo; un poco.
somewhere [ˈsʌmwɛə], *adv.* en alguna parte; ***somewhere else,*** en alguna otra parte.
somite [ˈsoumait], *s.* segmento teórico del cuerpo de un articulado.
somnambulism [sɔmˈnæmbjulizəm], *s.* somnambulismo.
somnambulist [sɔmˈnæmbjulist], *s.* somnámbulo.
somniferous [sɔmˈnifərəs], *a.* somnífero, soporífero.
somnific [sɔmˈnifik], *a.* narcótico, soporífero.
somniloquism, somniloquy [sɔmˈniləkwizəm, somˈniləkwi], *s.* somnilocuencia.
somniloquist [sɔmˈniləkwist], *s.* somnilocuo.
somnolence, somnolency [ˈsɔmnələns, -i], *s.* somnolencia.
somnolent [ˈsɔmnələnt], *a.* soñoliento; soporífero, adormecedor.
son [sʌn], *s.* hijo; ***son-in-law,*** yerno, hijo político; (*obsc.*) ***son of a bitch,*** hijo de puta; (*fam.*) ***son of a gun,*** tuno, pillastre.
sonant [ˈsounənt], *a.* (*gram.*) sonante; sonoro.
sonata [soˈnɑ:tə], *s.* sonata.
song [sɔŋ], *s.* canción; canto; cantar; copla; ***drinking song,*** canción de taberna; ***an old song,*** una vieja cantilena; ***song-bird,*** ave cantora; ***song-book,*** cancionero; ***the Song of Songs,*** el Cantar de los Cantares; ***song-writer,*** compositor de canciones; ***to burst into (a) song,*** romper a cantar; ***there's no need to make a song and dance,*** no es para tanto; ***to sell for a (mere) song,*** vender tirado; (*fig.*) ***to sing another song,*** bajar el tono; recoger velas; ***to sing the same song,*** cantar la misma cantinela.
songful [ˈsɔŋful], *a.* melodioso.
songless [ˈsɔŋlis], *a.* sin canto; que no canta.
songster [ˈsɔŋstə], *s.* cantor; poeta, *m.*; pájaro cantor.
songstress [ˈsɔŋstris], *s.* cantora; cantante; cantatriz.
sonifer [ˈsɔnifə], *s.* sonífero.
soniferous, sonorific [sɔˈnifərəs, sɔnəˈrifik], *a.* sonante, sonoro.
sonnet [ˈsɔnit], *s.* soneto. — *v.i.* celebrar con soneto(s); sonetear.
sonneteer [sɔnəˈtiə], *s.* sonetista, *m.f.*

sonny [ˈsʌni], *s.* (*fam.*) hijito.
sonometer [sɔˈnɔmitə], *s.* sonómetro.
sonority, sonorousness [sɔˈnɔriti, ˈsɔnərəsnis], *s.* sonoridad, (lo) sonoro.
sonorous [ˈsɔnərəs], *a.* sonoro; cadencioso.
sonship [ˈsʌnʃip], *s.* filiación.
soon [su:n], *adv.* pronto; dentro de poco; al poco rato; ***soon after,*** poco después; ***as soon as,*** en cuanto, tan pronto como; ***as soon as possible,*** lo antes posible, cuanto antes; ***how soon?*** ¿cuándo *o* a qué hora será?; ***I would just as soon stay,*** me da lo mismo quedarme.
sooner [ˈsu:nə], *adv. compar.* [SOON]; más pronto; antes; ***the sooner the better,*** cuanto antes mejor; ***sooner or later,*** tarde o temprano; ***no sooner had he come than . . .,*** apenas había llegado, cuando . . .; ***no sooner said than done,*** dicho y hecho; ***the sooner we start the sooner we finish,*** cuanto antes empecemos, antes terminaremos; ***I would sooner die,*** antes la muerte; ***I would sooner go,*** preferiría ir.
soonest [ˈsu:nist], *adv. superl.* [SOON]; (lo) más pronto; (***at***) ***the soonest,*** lo más pronto, lo antes posible.
soot [sut], *s.* hollín. — *v.t.* manchar, ensuciar *o* cubrir de hollín.
sooth [su:θ], *s.* (*ant.*) verdad; ***in sooth,*** en verdad.
soothe [su:ð], *v.t.* calmar; aliviar, mitigar; suavizar.
soothing [ˈsu:ðiŋ], *a.* calmante, tranquilizador; suavizante.
soothingly [ˈsu:ðiŋli], *adv.* con dulzura, con suavidad; con tono tranquilizador.
soothsayer [ˈsu:θseiə], *s.* adivino, adivina.
sootiness [ˈsutinis], *s.* fuliginosidad.
sooty [ˈsuti], *a.* lleno de hollín, fuliginoso.
sop [sɔp], *s.* sopa; cosa ideada para calmar *o* para granjearse simpatías. — *v.t.* — (***up***), empapar, absorber.
sophism [ˈsɔfizəm], *s.* sofisma, *m.*
sophist [ˈsɔfist], *s.* sofista, *m.f.*
sophistic(al) [soˈfistik(əl)], *a.* sofístico.
sophisticate [soˈfistikit], *s.* persona mundana *o* sofisticada, hombre de mundo. — [-eit], *v.t.* sofisticar.
sophisticated [soˈfistikeitid], *a.* mundano; sofisticado; avanzado, complejo.
sophistication [sofistiˈkeiʃən], *s.* mundanería; sofisticación; (lo) avanzado, (lo) complejo.
sophistry [ˈsɔfistri], *s.* sofistería.
Sophoclean [sɔfəˈkli:ən], *a.* sofocleo.
Sophocles [ˈsɔfəkli:z]. Sófocles, *m.*
sophomore [ˈsɔfəmɔ:], *s.* (*Am.*) estudiante de segundo año.
soporiferous [sɔpəˈrifərəs], *a.* soporífero.
soporiferousness [sɔpəˈrifərəsnis], *s.* (lo) soporífero.
soporific [sɔpəˈrifik], *a., s.* soporífero.
sopping [ˈsɔpiŋ], *a.* empapadísimo, mojadísimo, pingando.
soppy [ˈsɔpi], *a.* bobo, tonto de la mano, lelo, zonzo.
soprano [səˈprɑ:nou], *s.* soprano, tiple.
sorb [sɔ:b], *s.* serba; serbal; ***sorb-apple,*** serba.
sorbet [ˈsɔ:bit], *s.* sorbete.
sorcerer [ˈsɔ:sərə], *s.* hechicero, brujo, encantador.
sorceress [ˈsɔ:səris], *s.* hechicera, bruja.
sorcery [ˈsɔ:səri], *s.* hechizo(s), hechicería, brujería.
sordid [ˈsɔ:did], *a.* sórdido; bajo, vil; despreciable.
sordidness [ˈsɔ:didnis], *s.* sordidez; bajeza, vileza.
sordine [ˈsɔ:di:n], *s.* sordina.
sore [sɔ:], *a.* dolorido; doloroso; vehemente, violento; extremo; enojado; ***sore ears,*** dolor de oídos; ***sore eyes,*** dolor de ojos; (*ant.*) ***sore sight,*** espectáculo doloroso; ***sore throat,*** dolor de garganta. — *adv.* (*poét*) penosamente, con gran pena. — *s.* llaga; úlcera; matadura (*del ganado*); memoria dolorosa.
soreness [ˈsɔ:nis], *s.* dolor; inflamación; (lo) dolorido.
sorghum [ˈsɔ:gəm], *s.* sorgo, zahina; (*Am.*) melaza de sorgo.
sorites [sɔˈraiti:z], *s.* sorites, *m.inv.*
sorority [sɔˈrɔriti], *s.* (*Am.*) club *o* hermandad de mujeres.
sorrel (1) [ˈsɔrəl], *a.* alazán (rojo). — *s.* color alazán *o* roano; alazán (*de un animal*).
sorrel (2) [ˈsɔrəl], *s.* (*bot.*) acedera, acetosa, romaza; ***field-sorrel*** o ***meadow-sorrel,*** acedera pequeña; ***wood-sorrel,*** acederilla.
sorrow [ˈsɔrou], *s.* pesar, dolor, pesadumbre, sentimiento, pena, aflicción, tristeza; amargura; desgracia, infortunio; duelo, luto; ***to my great sorrow,*** con gran sentimiento mío. — *v.i.* apenarse, afligirse.
sorrowful [ˈsɔroful], *a.* pesaroso, afligido, doliente, desconsolado; doloroso, lastimoso, triste.
sorrowfulness [ˈsɔrofulnis], *s.* tristeza, aflicción, pesar.
sorrowing [ˈsɔrouiŋ], *a.* afligido, desconsolado. — *s.* aflicción, lamentación, tristeza.
sorry [ˈsɔri], *a.* afligido, pesaroso; apenado; arrepentido; penoso, lastimoso; triste; pobre, ruin; ***I am sorry*** (***about it***), lo siento; ***I am sorry for him,*** le compadezco; ***you'll be sorry for it,*** se arrepentirá, le pesará; ***looking very sorry for himself,*** cabizbajo, con aire triste; ***I am so sorry,*** lo siento mucho; ***sorry sight,*** espectáculo doloroso; ***to be sorry that,*** sentir que.
sort [sɔ:t], *s.* clase, *f.*; especie, *f.*; suerte, *f.*; ***a sort of,*** una especie de; ***after a*** o ***in a sort,*** en cierto sentido; ***all sorts of people,*** toda clase de gentes; ***of all sorts,*** de toda(s) clase(s); ***it takes all sorts,*** de todo hay; ***a good sort,*** un buen chico, una buena persona; ***in like sort,*** de la misma suerte; ***nothing of the sort,*** nada de eso; ***out of sorts,*** indispuesto; malhumorado; ***sth. of the sort,*** algo por el estilo; ***sort of,*** algo. — *v.t.* separar; distribuir en grupos; dividir en clases; clasificar; escoger; colocar, arreglar, ordenar; ***sort out,*** escoger y arreglar (*u* ordenar); (*fam.*) ***sort s.o. out,*** ajustarle a alguien las cuentas; ***sort over,*** clasificar. — *v.i.* acomodarse, ajustarse, convenir; unirse, hermanarse.
sortable [ˈsɔ:təbl], *a.* separable; clasificable.
sorter [ˈsɔ:tə], *s.* (*correos*) triador de cartas.
sortie [ˈsɔ:ti], *s.* salida.
sortilege [ˈsɔ:tilidʒ], *s.* sortilegio.
so-so [ˈsou-ˈsou], *a.* mediano, regular, pasadero, mediocre. — *adv.* así así, medianamente, regularmente.
sot [sɔt], *s.* borrachín.
sottish [ˈsɔtiʃ], *a.* embrutecido por la bebida.
sottishness [ˈsɔtiʃnis], *s.* embrutecimiento, emborrachamiento.
sou [su:], *s.* (*aprox.*) blanca, real; ***without a sou,*** sin blanca.
soubrette [su:ˈbret], *s.* (*teat.*) cómica.
soubriquet [SOBRIQUET].
sough [sʌf], *s.* susurro. — *v.i.* susurrar.
sought [sɔ:t], *a.* (***much***) ***sought-after,*** (muy) solicitado. — *pret., p.p.* [SEEK].
soul [soul], *s.* alma; ***All Souls' Day,*** Día de los Difuntos, *m.*; ***he cannot call his soul his own,*** no tiene ni un momento para sí; ***the life and soul of the party,*** el alma de la fiesta; ***upon my soul!*** ¡por vida mía!
soulful [ˈsoulful], *a.* sentimental, lacrimoso, patético.
soulfulness [ˈsoulfulnis], *s.* sentimentalismo.
soulless [ˈsoullis], *a.* desalmado.
sound (1) [saund], *a.* sano; firme, sólido; formal, de confianza; sensato, de fundamento; acertado, razonable; bueno, ortodoxo; profundo; solvente; ***safe and sound,*** sano y salvo; ***sound in wind***

and limb, de cuerpo sano; ***of sound mind,*** de mente sana; en su juicio cabal.
sound (2) [saund], *a.* sonoro, de(l) sonido. — *s.* sonido; ruido; ***sound barrier,*** barrera del sonido; ***sound effects,*** efectos sonoros, *m.pl.*; ***sound-proof,*** insonorizado; ***sound recording,*** grabación; ***sound track,*** banda sonora; ***sound wave,*** onda sonora; ***I don't care for the sound of it,*** no me apetece *o* no me seduce la idea. — *v.t.* (hacer) sonar; tocar; entonar; ***sound the alarm,*** dar la voz de alarma; ***sound the charge,*** tocar el zafarrancho de combate. — *v.i.* sonar, resonar; parecer, resultar.
sound (3) [saund], *s.* (*mar.*) estrecho, brazo de mar.
sound (4) [saund], *s.* sonda. — *v.t.* sondar; (*fig.*) sondear; (*med.*) auscultar.
sounder [ˈsaundə], *s.* (*elec.*) resonador; (*mar.*) sondeador.
sounding (2) [ˈsaundiŋ], *s.* (*mar.*) sondeo; (*pl.*) sondas, *f.pl.*; (*mar.*) ***sounding-lead,*** escandallo; ***board,*** caja de resonancia; secreto.
sounding (2) [ˈsaundiŋ], *s.* (*mar.*) sondeo; (*pl.*) sondas, *f.pl.*; (*mar.*) ***sounding-lead,*** escandallo; ***sounding-line,*** sondaleza.
soundless [ˈsaundlis], *a.* silencioso.
soundly [ˈsaundli], *adv.* bien; a fondo.
soundness [ˈsaundnis], *s.* (lo) sano *etc.*
soup [su:p], *s.* (*coc.*) sopa; caldo; ***clear soup,*** consomé; (*fam.*) ***in the soup,*** en apuros; ***milk soup,*** sopas de leche, *f.pl.*; ***mock-turtle soup,*** sopa de tortuga imitada; ***pea soup,*** sopa de guisantes; ***soup-ladle,*** cucharón; ***soup-plate,*** (plato) sopero; ***soup-tureen,*** sopera; ***thick soup,*** puré.
soupçon [ˈsu:psɔ̃], *s.* pizca, poquito.
sour [sauə], *a.* agrio, ácido, acedo, avinagrado; huraño, desabrido; ***sour apple,*** manzana agria; manzana verde; ***sour dock,*** acedera; ***sour grapes!*** ¡están verdes!; ***sour grass,*** acedera pequeña; ***to taste sour,*** tener un gusto agrio; ***to turn sour,*** volverse agrio. — *v.t.* agriar; avinagrar; hacer fermentar (*la cal*); malear; (*fig.*) amargar. — *v.i.* agriarse; avinagrarse; malearse; cortarse; fermentar.
source [sɔ:s], *s.* fuente, *f.*; nacimiento; procedencia, origen; ***to have from a good source,*** saber de buena tinta.
sourish [ˈsauəriʃ], *a.* agrillo, agrete.
sourness [ˈsauənis], *s.* acedía, acidez, (lo) agrio; desabrimiento, aspereza.
sourpuss [ˈsauəpus], *s.* (*fam.*) cara de vinagre, cascarrabias, *m.f.inv.*
souse (1) [saus], *s.* escabeche, adobo, salmuera; zambullida, chapuz; cabeza, patas *u* orejas de cerdo adobadas. — *v.t.* escabechar; zambullir; mojar. — *v.i.* zambullirse; (*Am.*) emborracharse.
souse (2) [saus], *adv.* zas, de cabeza, con violencia. — *s.* ataque repentino (*del halcón*). — *v.i.* arrojarse con violencia.
souse (3) [saus], *v.t.* golpear violentamente.
south [sauθ], *a.* meridional, del mediodía, del sur; ***South Africa,*** Sudáfrica; ***South African,*** sudafricano; ***South America,*** Sudamérica; ***South American,*** sudamericano; ***South Carolina,*** Carolina del Sur; ***south-east,*** sudeste, del sudeste; sudeste; ***south-easter,*** temporal *o* viento del sudeste; ***south-easterly,*** al sudeste, hacia el sudeste; del sudeste; ***south-eastern,*** del sudeste; ***South Pole,*** Polo Sur; ***South Seas,*** mares del Sur, *m.* o *f.pl.*; ***South Vietnam,*** Vietnam del sur; ***South Vietnamese,*** survietnamita, *m.f.*; ***south-west,*** sudoeste, del sudoeste; sudoeste; ***south-wester,*** vendaval del sudoeste; (prenda) sueste; ***south-westerly,*** del sudoeste; hacia el sudoeste; del sudoeste; ***south-western, south-westward,*** hacia el sudoeste; ***south wind,*** viento del sur. — *adv.* hacia el sur; del sur (*viento*). — *s.* mediodía, *m.*; sur.
souther [ˈsauθə], *s.* viento *o* borrasca del sur.
southerly [ˈsʌðəli], *a.* meridional, hacia el sur. — *adv.* del sur.
southern [ˈsʌðən], *a.* meridional; del sur; situado en el *o* al sur; ***Southern Cross,*** Cruz del Sur; ***Southern Yemen,*** el Yemen Meridional; ***Southern Yemenite,*** sudyemenita, *m.f.*
southernmost [ˈsʌðənmoust], *a. superl.* [SOUTHERN]; (el) más meridional. — *adv.* lo más al sur.
southernwood [ˈsʌðənwud], *s.* abrótano, lombriguera.
southing [ˈsauθiŋ], *a.* que camina hacia el sur. — *s.* diferencia de latitud medida hacia el sur.
southmost [ˈsauθmoust], [SOUTHERNMOST].
southpaw [ˈsauθpɔ:], *a.*, *s.* (*dep.*) zurdo.
southron [ˈsʌðrən], *s.* habitante del sur, meridional.
southward [ˈsauθwəd], *a.* situado hacia el sur. — *adv.* hacia el mediodía; ***southward of the line,*** al sur del ecuador.
souvenir [ˈsu:vəniə], *s.* recuerdo.
sovereign [ˈsɔvrin], *a.* soberano, soberana. — *s.* soberano, soberana; ***golden sovereign,*** libra esterlina de oro.
sovereignty [ˈsɔvrinti], *s.* soberanía.
soviet [ˈsouvjit, sɔvjit], *a.* soviético. — *s.* soviet.
sow (1) [sau], *s.* cerda; (*fund.*) galápago; ***sow-bread,*** pamporcino; ***sow-bug,*** cochinilla de tierra; ***sow-thistle,*** cerraja, cardo ajonjero.
sow (2) [sou], *irr. v.t.* sembrar; ***sow discord,*** sembrar cizaña; ***sow doubt in s.o.'s mind,*** sembrarle a alguien la duda; (*fig., fam.*) ***sow one's wild oats,*** correr sus mocedades, correrla. — *v.i.* sembrar; ***as a man sows, so must he reap,*** tal siembras, tal recogerás.
sowing [ˈsouiŋ], *s.* siembra; (el) sembrar; ***sowing machine,*** sembradora; ***sowing time,*** sementera.
soya [ˈsɔiə], *s.* soja; ***soya-bean,*** (semilla de) soja.
sozzled [sɔzld], *a.* (*fam.*) trompa, *inv.*
spa [spɑ:], *s.* balneario.
space [speis], *a.* espacial, del espacio, interplanetario; ***space age,*** era del espacio; ***space bar,*** barra espaciadora (*máquina de escribir*); ***space-capsule,*** cápsula espacial; ***space-craft, space-ship,*** nave espacial, astronave; ***space-man,*** hombre del espacio, astronauta, *m.*; ***space-probe,*** sondeo *o* sondaje del espacio; ***space-station,*** estación espacial; ***space-suit,*** traje espacial. — *s.* espacio; sitio; hueco; ***in the space of,*** por espacio de; ***outer space,*** espacio exterior; ***short space of time,*** breve período de tiempo. — *v.t.* espaciar; (*impr.*) regletear.
spacial [SPATIAL].
spacing [ˈspeisiŋ], *s.* espaciamiento.
spacious [ˈspeiʃəs], *a.* espacioso; amplio; anchuroso; extenso; capaz.
spaciousness [ˈspeiʃəsnis], *s.* espaciosidad; amplitud.
spade [speid], *s.* (*agric.*) pala; (*pl.*) (*cartas*) espadas, *f.pl.*; picos, *m.pl.*; ***to call a spade a spade,*** llamar al pan pan (y al vino vino); ***spade-work,*** trabajo preliminar.
spadeful [ˈspeidful], *s.* palada.
spadille [spəˈdil], *s.* espadilla.
spadix [ˈspeidiks], *s.* (*pl.* **spadices** [speiˈdaisi:z]) espádice.
spado [ˈspeidou], *s.* eunuco.
spaghetti [spəˈgeti], *s.* espaguetis, *m.pl.*
Spain [spein]. España.
spall [spɔ:l], *s.* astilla.
spalt [spɔ:lt], *s.* (*fund.*) espalto.
span (1) [spæn], *s.* palmo; extensión, alcance; espacio, lapso; duración; tronco (*de caballos*); yunta (*de bueyes*); envergadura (*de ala*); ojo, luz (*de puente*); tramo, trecho; arcada, entramado; vano; ***a span of,*** una extensión de; ***the average span of life,*** la duración media de la vida; ***for a brief span,*** durante un corto espacio (de tiempo); ***the whole span of problems,*** toda la gama de problemas. — *v.t.* medir (*a palmos*); extenderse

sobre, tender un puente sobre; abarcar, abrazar; emparejar (*caballos*).
span (2) [spæn], *pret. ant.* [SPIN].
spandrel [ˈspændrəl], *s.* (*arq.*) tímpano; enjuta, embecadura.
spangle [spæŋgl], *s.* lentejuela. — *v.t.* adornar con lentejuelas.
spangled [spæŋgld], *a.* estrellado (*cielo*); ***spangled with,*** tachonado de.
Spaniard [ˈspænjəd], *s.* español.
spaniel [ˈspænjəl], *s.* perro de aguas.
Spanish [ˈspæniʃ], *a.*, *s.* español; hispano; castellano (*idioma*); ***Spanish-American,*** hispanoamericano; (*bot.*) ***Spanish bayonet,*** yuca; ***Spanish black,*** negro de España; corcho quemado; ***Spanish broom,*** retama (de olor); ***Spanish chalk,*** esteatita, jaboncillo; ***Spanish fly,*** cantárida; ***Spanish leather,*** cordobán; ***Spanish mackerel,*** escombro; ***Spanish Main,*** (las) Antillas; ***Spanish moss,*** musgo negro; ***Spanish soap,*** jabón de Castilla; ***Spanish-speaking,*** hispanohablante, de habla española.
Spanishness [ˈspæniʃnis], *s.* españolidad, españolismo.
spank (1) [spæŋk], *s.* azote (en las nalgas). — *v.t.* zurrar, manotear.
spank (2) [spæŋk], *v.i.* — ***along,*** correr, ir volando.
spanker (1) [ˈspæŋkə], *s.* persona *o* cosa que da azotes (en las nalgas).
spanker (2) [ˈspæŋkə], *s.* (*mar.*) cangreja de mesana.
spanking (1) [ˈspæŋkiŋ], *s.* zurra, azotaina.
spanking (2) [ˈspæŋkiŋ], *a.* rápido (*paso*); fuerte (*viento*); ***he had a spanking time,*** lo pasó en grande.
spanless [ˈspænlis], *a.* que no se puede abarcar *o* medir.
spanner [ˈspænə], *s.* (*mec.*) llave de tuercas, *f.*; llave inglesa; ***to throw a spanner in the works,*** meter un palo en la rueda, torpedear la cosa.
spar (1) [spɑː], *s.* (*min.*) espato.
spar (2) [spɑː], *s.* (*mar.*) berlinga, percha, borón; palo, mástil, verga; asna, cabrial, cabrio (de grúa *o* cabria); tranca, cerreta, barra; (*pl.*) arboladuras, *f.pl.*; ***spar-buoy,*** baliza; ***spar-deck,*** cubierta de guindaste.
spar (3) [spɑː], *s.* boxeo; riña, altercado; pelea de gallos con espolones cubiertos. — *v.i.* (*boxeo*) fintar; entrenarse.
sparable [ˈspærəbl], *s.* (*zap.*) puntilla, tachuela.
spare [spɛə], *a.* de reserva, de repuesto, de recambio; de sobra, sobrante; libre, desocupado; disponible; enjuto; ***have you any spare cigarettes?*** ¿tienes algún cigarrillo que darme?; ***spare rib,*** costilla de cerdo con poca carne; ***in my spare time,*** en mis ratos libres *o* de ocio. — *s.* (pieza de) repuesto, recambio. — *v.t.* ahorrar, escatimar, economizar; evitar; privarse de, prescindir de, pasarse sin; perdonar, hacer gracia de; ***spare the life,*** perdonar la vida; ***spare the rod and spoil the child,*** la letra con sangre entra; ***to have sth. to spare,*** tener algo de sobra; ***I have no time to spare for that,*** no puedo dedicarle tiempo a eso. — **spare o.s.,** *v.r.* cuidarse, ahorrarse molestias.
spareness [ˈspɛənis], *s.* enjutez, (lo) enjuto.
sparing [ˈspɛəriŋ], *a.* parco (***of, in,*** en).
sparingness [ˈspɛəriŋnis], *s.* parquedad, (lo) parco.
spark [spɑːk], *s.* chispa; centella; (*fig.*) chispazo; (*fam.*) ***bright spark,*** tipo listo; tipo animado; ***not a spark of life,*** ni un átomo de vida; (*Am.*) ***spark-plug*** [SPARKING-PLUG]; (*pl.*, *fam.*) telegrafista, *m.* — *v.t.* — ***off,*** ser el chispazo que origina *u* originó, originar. — *v.i.* chispear, centellear, echar chispas.
sparking-plug [ˈspɑːkiŋ-plʌg], *s.* bujía (de encendido).
sparkle [spɑːkl], *s.* centelleo; destello; brillo; (*fig.*) viveza. — *v.i.* centellear, destellar, brillar; ser *o* estar alegrísimo; ser espumoso (*de ciertos vinos*).
sparkler [ˈspɑːklə], *s.* (*fam.*) bengala; (*fam.*) diamante.
sparkling [ˈspɑːkliŋ], *a.* centelleante, brillante; alegrísimo; (*ingenio*) chispeante; ***sparkling wine,*** vino espumoso.
sparring [ˈspɑːriŋ], *s.* (el) boxeo; ***a sparring partner,*** un sparring.
sparrow [ˈspærou], *s.* gorrión; ***sparrow-hawk,*** gavilán.
sparse [spɑːs], *a.* escaso, poco denso; (*pelo*) ralo; disperso.
sparsely [ˈspɑːsli], *adv.* con poca densidad; con grandes huecos; ***sparsely furnished,*** con muy pocos muebles; ***sparsely populated,*** (muy) poco poblado.
sparseness [ˈspɑːsnis], *s.* (lo) escaso, (lo) poco denso *etc.*
Sparta [ˈspɑːtə]. Esparta.
Spartan [ˈspɑːtən], *a.*, *s.* espartano.
spasm [ˈspæzəm], *s.* espasmo; calambre; arranque, ramalazo; ***to work in spasms,*** trabajar por impulsos *o* esporádicamente.
spasmodic [spæzˈmɔdik], *a.* espasmódico.
spastic [ˈspæstik], *a.*, *s.* espástico.
spat (1) [spæt], *pret.*, *p.p.* [SPIT (3)].
spat (2) [spæt], *s.* freza; masa de ostras jóvenes.
spat (3) [spæt], *s.* (*ú. más en pl.*) botines, *m.pl.*
spate [speit], *s.* crecida; avenida; (*fig.*) torrente; ***in spate,*** crecido.
spathe [speið], *s.* espata.
spathic [ˈspæθik], *a.* espático.
spatial [ˈspeiʃəl], *a.* espacial, del espacio.
spatter [ˈspætə], *v.t.* salpicar; rociar (***with,*** de).
spatula [ˈspætjulə], *s.* espátula.
spatulate [ˈspætjulit], *a.* espatulado, en forma de espátula.
spavin [ˈspævin], *s.* (*vet.*) esparaván.
spawn [spɔːn], *s.* (*ict.*) freza, huevas, *f.pl.*; (*fam.*) prole. — *v.t.* (*fam.*) procrear. — *v.i.* desovar, frezar.
spawner [ˈspɔːnə], *s.* pez hembra.
spawning [ˈspɔːniŋ], *s.* freza, desove; ***spawning time,*** desove.
spay [spei], *v.t.* castrar (*las hembras de los animales*).
speak [spiːk], *irr. v.t.* hablar; decir; ***speak one's mind,*** decir lo que se piensa; ***speak sense,*** hablar con sentido; ***speak the truth,*** decir la verdad. — *v.i.* hablar; ***speak about,*** hablar de; ***speak for,*** hablar por; ***speak for itself,*** hablar por sí mismo, ser evidente; ***speak well for,*** decir mucho en favor de; ***speak out,*** hablar claro; atreverse a hablar; ***speak thick,*** hablar gordo, con lengua de trapo; ***speak through the nose,*** hablar gangoso; ***speak to,*** (*lit.*) hablar con; (*fig.*) hablar a; ***speak to the point,*** hablar sin rodeos, ir al grano; ***speak up,*** hablar más fuerte; ***so to speak,*** por así decirlo; como si dijéramos; (*teléfono*) ***speaking!*** ¡al habla! soy yo.
speakable [ˈspiːkəbl], *a.* decible.
speak-easy [ˈspiːk-ˈiːzi], *s.* (*Am.*) taberna clandestina.
speaker [ˈspiːkə], *s.* el que habla; orador; (*Am.*) libro de declamación; presidente de un cuerpo cualquiera; ***Speaker of the House of Commons,*** Presidente de la Cámara de los Comunes.
speakership [ˈspiːkəʃip], *s.* presidencia de una asamblea legislativa.
speaking [ˈspiːkiŋ], *a.* parlante, hablante, que habla; para hablar; ***English-speaking,*** de habla inglesa; ***speaking likeness,*** retrato viviente; ***they are not on speaking terms,*** no se hablan. — *s.* habla; discurso; declamación; ***speaking-trumpet,*** megáfono; ***speaking-tube,*** tubo acústico.
spear [spiə], *s.* lanza; venablo; azagaya; (*poét.*) lancero; arpón de pesca; (*bot.*) brizna; ***spear-grass,*** hierba de los prados; ***spear-head,*** punta de lanza. — *v.t.* alancear; atravesar con arpón. — *v.i.* brotar.

spearmint [ˈspiəmint], *s.* hierbabuena puntiaguda, menta verde.
spearwood [ˈspiəwud], *s.* eucalipto; acacia.
spearwort [ˈspiəwəːt], *s.* ranúnculo.
special [ˈspeʃəl], *a.* especial; extraordinario.
specialist [ˈspeʃəlist], *s.* especialista, *m.f.*
speciality [speʃiˈæliti], *s.* especialidad; ***speciality of the house,*** especialidad de la casa.
specialize [ˈspeʃəlaiz], *v.t.* especializar. — *v.i.* especializarse.
specially [ˈspeʃəli], *adv.* especialmente, sobre todo.
specialness [ˈspeʃəlnis], *s.* (lo) especial.
specialty [ˈspeʃəlti], *s.* especialidad; (*for.*) obligación firmada formalmente.
specie [ˈspiːʃiː], *s.* dinero contante, efectivo, moneda, metálico, numerario.
species [ˈspiːʃiz], *s. inv.* especie, *f.*
specific [spiˈsifik], *a.* específico; concreto; expreso; ***specific gravity,*** peso específico; ***specific heat,*** calor específico. — *s.* (*med.*) específico.
specification [spesifiˈkeiʃən], *s.* especificación; plan (detallado).
specificness [spiˈsifiknis], *s.* (lo) específico.
specify [ˈspesifai], *v.t.* especificar, concretar, detallar, particularizar.
specimen [ˈspesimən], *s.* espécimen; ejemplar; muestra; ***fine specimen,*** ejemplarón; ***specimen signature,*** firma espécimen; (*fam.*) ***what a specimen!*** ¡vaya tipejo! ¡qué tío!
specious [ˈspiːʃəs], *a.* especioso.
speciousness [ˈspiːʃəsnis], *s.* (lo) especioso.
speck [spek], *s.* manchita; motita; pizca, partícula; (*coc.*) tocino.
speckle [spekl], *s.* motita. — *v.t.* motear (***with,*** de), llenar de manchitas.
spectacle [ˈspektəkl], *s.* espectáculo; escena; (*pl.*) lentes, *m.pl.*, anteojos, *m.pl*, gafas, *f.pl*; ***to see everything through rose-coloured spectacles,*** verlo todo color de rosa; ***spectacle-case,*** estuche de gafas.
spectacled [ˈspektəkəld], *a.* que lleva lentes *o* gafas.
spectacular [spekˈtækjulə], *a.* espectacular; aparatoso.
spectator [spekˈteitə], *s.* espectador.
spectral [ˈspektrəl], *a.* espectral.
spectre [ˈspektə], *s.* espectro, fantasma, *m.*; aparecido.
spectrology [spekˈtrɔlədʒi], *s.* espectrología.
spectroscope [ˈspektroskoup], *s.* espectroscopio.
spectroscopic [spektroˈskɔpik], *a.* espectroscópico.
spectrum [ˈspektrəm], *s.* (*pl.* **spectra** [-trə]) espectro; prisma, *m.*
specular [ˈspekjulə], *a.* especular.
speculate [ˈspekjuleit], *v.i.* especular; conjeturar.
speculation [spekjuˈleiʃən], *s.* especulación; conjetura(s).
speculative [ˈspekjulətiv], *a.* especulativo; conjetural.
speculativeness [ˈspekjulətivnis], *s.* (lo) especulativo.
speculator [ˈspekjuleitə], *s.* especulador; (*teat.*) revendedor de billetes.
speculum [ˈspekjuləm], *s.* (*pl.* **specula** [-lə]) (*cir.*) espéculum; (*ópt.*) espejo.
speech [spiːtʃ], *s.* habla; lenguaje; idioma, *m.*; discurso; (*teat.*) parlamento; ***direct speech,*** discurso *o* estilo directo; ***free speech,*** libertad de palabra; (*gram.*) ***indirect speech, reported speech,*** discurso *o* estilo indirecto; ***Speech Day,*** día de distribución de premios, *m.*; ***speech-maker,*** orador; ***speech therapy,*** terapia lingüística; ***to make*** o ***deliver a speech,*** hacer *o* pronunciar un discurso.
speechify [ˈspiːtʃifai], *v.i.* (*fam.*) discursear.
speechless [ˈspiːtʃlis], *a.* mudo; estupefacto, turulato.
speechlessness [ˈspiːtʃlisnis], *s.* mudez; estupefacción.
speed [spiːd], *a.* de velocidad *o* marcha; ***speed counter,*** contador de velocidades; ***speed gauge, indicator*** o ***recorder,*** cuentarrevoluciones, *m.inv.*, velocímetro; ***speed limit,*** velocidad máxima, límite de velocidad. — *s.* velocidad, rapidez; prisa, presteza; marcha; ***with all speed,*** a toda prisa; ***at full speed,*** a toda velocidad, a todo correr; ***full speed ahead!*** ¡todo avante! ¡a toda máquina!; ***God speed!*** ¡vaya con Dios!; ***good speed!*** ¡buen viaje!; ***to make speed,*** apresurarse. — *irr. v.t.* ayudar, favorecer; despedir; ***speed up,*** acelerar; activar; dar prisa a. — *v.i.* prosperar, medrar; apresurarse, darse prisa; exceder la velocidad permitida; ***speed along,*** ir volando; ***speed past,*** pasar como un rayo.
speedboat [ˈspiːdbout], *s.* (canoa) motora.
speediness [ˈspiːdinis], *s.* celeridad, rapidez, velocidad; diligencia, prontitud, prisa.
speedometer [spiːˈdɔmitə], *s.* cuentakilómetros, *m.inv.*, velocímetro.
speedwell [ˈspiːdwel], *s.* verónica.
speedy [ˈspiːdi], *a.* ligero, rápido, veloz; presuroso; diligente, pronto.
speleology [spiːliˈɔlədʒi], *s.* espeleología.
spell (1) [spel], *s.* hechizo, encanto, ensalmo. — *v.t.* encantar, hechizar.
spell (2) [spel], *s.* tanda, turno; rato, temporada, período; racha; ***bad spell,*** mala racha; ***by spells,*** por turnos, a ratos. — *v.t.* revezar, reemplazar, relevar.
spell (3) [spel], *irr. v.t.* deletrear; descifrar; significar; ***how do you spell...?*** ¿cómo se escribe ...?; ***spell out,*** deletrear poco a poco; ***spell sth. out for s.o.,*** explicarle algo a alguién de un modo muy sencillo *o* elemental. — *v.i.* (saber) deletrear, escribir con buena ortografía.
spellbind [ˈspelbaind], *v.t.* encantar, fascinar.
spellbound [ˈspelbaund], *a.* hechizado, embelesado, encantado.
speller [ˈspelə], *s.* deletreador, persona que deletrea; ***to be a bad speller,*** no saber ortografía.
spelling [ˈspeliŋ], *s.* acción de deletrear, deletreo, manera de deletrear; ortografía; ***spelling bee,*** concurso de ortografía; ***spelling-book,*** cartilla.
spelter [ˈspeltə], *s.* (*com.*) cinc; peltre.
spelt-wheat [ˈspelt-wiːt], *s.* escanda, espelta.
spend [spend], *irr. v.t.* gastar; consumir; disipar, malgastar, echar a perder; ocupar, pasar, emplear; (*mar.*) ***spend a mast,*** perder un palo; ***spend time,*** pasar tiempo. — *v.i.* gastar dinero, hacer gastos; gastarse, consumirse.
spender [ˈspendə], *s.* gastador.
spending [ˈspendiŋ], *s.* gasto; ***spending-money,*** dinero para gastos personales.
spendthrift [ˈspendθrift], *s.* pródigo, manirroto, malgastador, derrochador.
sperm [spəːm], *s.* esperma, semen; esperma de ballena; ***sperm oil,*** aceite de esperma; ***sperm whale,*** cachalote.
spermaceti [spəːməˈseti], *s.* esperma de ballena; ***spermaceti oil,*** aceite de esperma.
spermatic [spəːˈmætik], *a.* espermático.
spermatize [ˈspəːmətaiz], *v.i.* arrojar esperma.
spermatology [spəːməˈtɔlədʒi], *s.* espermatología.
spermatorrhœa [spəːmətoˈriə], *s.* espermatorrea.
spermatozoon [spəːmətoˈzouɔn], *s.* (*pl.* **spermatozoa** [-zouə]) espermatozoo.
spew [spjuː], *s.* vómito(s). — *v.t., v.i.* vomitar.
sphacelate [ˈsfæsileit], *v.i.* esfacelar(se).
sphacelus [ˈsfæsiləs], *s.* esfacelo.
sphenoid [ˈsfiːnɔid], *a.* esfenoidal. — *s.* (*anat.*) esfenoides, *m.inv.*
sphere [sfiə], *s.* esfera; ***that is outside his sphere,*** eso no cae dentro de su cometido; ***sphere of activity,*** esfera *o* campo de actividad; ***sphere of***

influence, zona de influencia; ***sphere of music,*** esfera *o* mundillo de la música.
spherical [ˈsferikəl], *a.* esférico.
sphericity [sfeˈrisiti], *s.* esfericidad.
spheroid [ˈsfiərɔid], *s.* esferoide.
spheroidal [sfiəˈrɔidəl], *a.* esferoidal.
spherule [ˈsferjuːl], *s.* esférula.
sphincter [ˈsfiŋktə], *s.* esfínter.
sphinx [sfiŋks], *s.* esfinge, *f.*; ***sphinx-like,*** de esfinge, esfingido.
sphygmic [ˈsfigmik], *a.* esfígmico.
spice [spais], *s.* especia; (*fig.*) ajilimójili. — *v.t.* (*coc.*) especiar, echar especias a; echar ajilimójili a.
spicery [ˈspaisəri], *s.* especiería.
spiciness [ˈspaisinis], *s.* (lo) picante.
spick-and-span [ˈspik-ənd-ˈspæn], *a.* más limpio que una patena; pulcro; flamante.
spicular [ˈspaikjulə], *a.* espicular.
spicule [ˈspaikjuːl], *s.* espícula; aguja (*del hielo*).
spicy [ˈspaisi], *a.* especiado, picante; (*fig.*) sabroso, picante.
spider [ˈspaidə], *s.* araña; ***spider-crab,*** centollo, centolla; ***spider's web,*** telaraña; ***spider-wort,*** pasajera.
spidery [ˈspaidəri], *a.* muy delgado, delgadillo, finillo; de patas de araña.
spigot [ˈspigət], *s.* espiche, espita; (*mec.*) espiga.
spike [spaik], *s.* pincho, púa; escarpia, alcayata; espigón; clavo (*de zapato*); (*bot.*) espliego; (*bot.*) espiga; (*Am., zap.*) ***spike heel*** [STILETTO HEEL]. — *v.t.* sujetar con clavos, pinchos, escarpias *etc.*; clavetear; enclavijar; clavar (*un cañon*); inutilizar, dar al traste con.
spikelet [ˈspaiklit], *s.* espiguilla.
spikenard [ˈspaiknɑːd], *s.* espicanardo; nardo.
spiky [ˈspaiki], *a.* erizado; armado de púas; claveteado.
spile [spail], *s.* tarugo, espiche; estaca. — *v.t.* abrir (*un barril*) y ponerle espita *o* tapón; clavar estacas *o* pilotes a.
spill (1) [spil], *s.* alegrador, pajuela.
spill (2) [spil], *s.* derramamiento; caída, vuelco; ***spill-way,*** aliviadero, vertedero. — *irr. v.t.* derramar, verter; tirar; desarzonar; quitar viento (*a una vela*); (*fam.*) ***spill the beans,*** tirar de la manta. — *v.i.* derramarse, verterse; (*fam.*) cantar.
spiller [spilə], *s.* sedal (*de caña de pescar*).
spilling lines [ˈspiliŋ lainz], *s.pl.* (*mar.*) trapas de las velas, *f.pl.*
spin [spin], *s.* giro, vuelta; barrena; paseo (*en coche etc.*). — *irr. v.t.* hilar; retorcer; hacer girar; ***spin out,*** alargar, prolongar; (*fig.*) contar sin acabar; ***spin out a speech,*** hacer un discurso muy largo; ***spin a yarn,*** contar un cuento. — *v.i.* hilar; correr hilo a hilo; girar; (*aer.*) entrar *o* caer en barrena; ***my head is spinning,*** me da vueltas la cabeza.
spinach [ˈspinidʒ], *s.* espinaca(s).
spinal [ˈspainəl], *a.* espinal; ***spinal column,*** columna vertebral, espinazo; ***spinal cord*** o ***marrow,*** médula espinal.
spindle [spindl], *s.* huso; broca; (*mec.*) eje, gorrón, carretel, torno, astil, aguja, peón, árbol; (*mar.*) pínola, fierro, maza; ***spindle-legged, spindle-shanked,*** zanquivano; ***spindle-shaped,*** ahusado, fusiforme; ***spindle-tree,*** bonetero. — *v.i.* (*bot.*) espigarse.
spin-drier [ˈspin-ˈdraiə], *s.* secador centrífugo.
spindrift [ˈspindrift], *s.* rocío del mar.
spine [spain], *s.* espinazo, espina dorsal; (*bot.*) espina, púa delgada; lomo (*de un libro*).
spinel [spiˈnel], *s.* espinela.
spineless [ˈspainlis], *a.* invertebrado; flojo, falto de voluntad.
spinet [spiˈnet], *s.* espineta.
spiniferous [spaiˈnifərəs], *a.* espinoso, espinífero.
spinnaker [ˈspinəkə] *s.* ala *o* arrastradera grande, balón.
spinner [ˈspinə], *s.* hilandero, hilandera; máquina de hilar; araña de jardín.
spinneret [ˈspinəret], *s.* (*zool.*) fileras, *f.pl.*, órgano hilandero (*de las arañas y gusanos de seda*).
spinney [ˈspini], *s.* bosquecillo, soto.
spinning [ˈspiniŋ], *a.* girante; ***spinning top,*** peonza, trompo. — *s.* hilado, hilatura, (el) hilar; ***spinning-jenny, spinning-mule,*** máquina de hilar; ***spinning tackle,*** curricán; ***spinning-wheel,*** rueca.
spinose [ˈspainous], *a.* espinoso.
spinosity [spaiˈnɔsiti], *s.* dificultad, enredo, cosa espinosa.
Spinozism [spiˈnouzizəm], *s.* espinosismo.
spinster [ˈspinstə], *s.* soltera; (*despec.*) ***old spinster,*** solterona.
spiny [ˈspaini], *a.* espinoso.
spiracle [ˈspairəkl], *s.* espiráculo.
Spiræa [spaiˈriə], *s.* espírea.
spiral [ˈspaiərəl], *a.* espiral; ***spiral staircase,*** escalera de caracol. — *s.* espiral, *f.* — *v.i.* dar vueltas en espiral; bajar en espiral; (*fig.*) ***spiral down*** (***into***), ir hundiéndose (en).
spirant [ˈspaiərənt], *a., s.* espirante.
spire [spaiə], *s.* (*arq.*) aguja, chapitel; torre. — *v.i.* elevarse (en torre).
spirit [ˈspirit], *s.* espíritu; ánimo; brío, denuedo; humor; temple; alcohol; (*pl.*) alcohol; (*pl.*) ánimo; ***animal spirits,*** ruda vitalidad, brío; ***community spirit,*** espíritu de comunidad, espíritu cívico, civismo; ***evil spirit,*** espíritu maligno; ***fighting spirit,*** espíritu combativo, combatividad, acometividad; ***to be in high spirits,*** estar animadísimo, eufórico; ***the Holy Spirit,*** el Espíritu Santo; ***to be in low spirits,*** estar (muy) desanimado, abatido; ***raw spirits,*** alcohol puro; ***spirit lamp,*** lámpara de alcohol; ***spirit-level,*** nivel de aire; ***spirits of wine,*** espíritu de vino; ***spirit stove,*** estufa de parafina; ***to keep up one's spirits,*** no desanimarse, no abatirse; ***to raise s.o.'s spirits,*** animar a alguien; ***to show spirit,*** mostrarse animoso. — *v.t.* — ***away*** o ***off,*** hacer desaparecer sigilosamente, escamotear, llevarse misteriosamente.
spirited [ˈspiritid], *a.* animoso; fogoso, brioso; ***high-spirited,*** animoso; enérgico; de mucha vitalidad; ***low-spirited,*** apocado; ***mean-spirited,*** mezquino, de alma mezquina.
spiritedness [ˈspiritidnis], *s.* (lo) animoso, (lo) enérgico *etc.*
spiritism [ˈspiritizəm], *s.* espiritismo.
spiritless [ˈspiritlis], *a.* apocado, que tiene poco ánimo.
spiritous [ˈspiritəs], *a.* espiritoso.
spiritual [ˈspiritjuəl], *a.* espiritual.
spiritualism [ˈspiritjuəlizəm], *s.* espiritismo.
spiritualist [ˈspiritjuəlist], *s.* espiritista, *m.f.*
spiritualistic [spiritjuəˈlistik], *a.* espiritista.
spirituality [spiritjuˈæliti], *s.* espiritualidad.
spiritualization [spiritjuəlaiˈzeiʃən], *s.* espiritualización.
spiritualize [ˈspiritjuəlaiz], *v.t.* espiritualizar.
spirituous [ˈspiritjuəs], *a.* espiritoso, espirituoso.
spirituousness [ˈspiritjuəsnis], *s.* (lo) espirituoso.
spirt [SPURT].
spissated [ˈspiseitid], *a.* espesado.
spit (1) [spit], *s.* azadada.
spit (2) [spit], *s.* espetón, asador; lengua de tierra. — *v.t.* espetar, ensartar.
spit (3) [spit], *s.* saliva, salivazo, escupitajo. — *irr. v.t.* escupir; esputar; arrojar. — *v.i.* escupir; chisporrotear; bufar; ***spit with rain,*** chispear.
spitch-cock [ˈspitʃ-kɔk], *s.* anguila tajada y asada. — *v.t.* tajar y asar (*anguilas*).

spite [spait], *s.* rencor, despecho, ojeriza, odio, mala voluntad, malevolencia; (*in*) ***spite of,*** a pesar de, a despecho de. — *v.t.* mortificar, causar pena a.

spiteful [ˈspaitful], *a.* rencoroso, malévolo, maligno.

spitefulness [ˈspaitfulnis], *s.* rencor, despecho, malevolencia, malignidad, encono.

spitfire [ˈspitfaiə], *s.* fierabrás, *m.inv.*

spitter [ˈspitə], *s.* el que éspeta; escupidor; gamezno.

spittle [spitl], *s.* saliva, salivazo.

spittoon [spiˈtu:n], *s.* escupidera.

spitz [spits], *s.* perro de Pomerania.

spiv [spiv], *s.* (*fam.*) vivales, *m.inv.*; estraperlista, *m.f.*

splanchnic [ˈsplæŋknik], *a.* esplácnico.

splanchnology [splæŋkˈnɔlədʒi], *s.* esplacnología.

splash [splæʃ], *s.* salpicadura, rociada; (*ruido*) chapoteo; mancha (*de color*); ***splash-board,*** alero, guardabarros, *m.inv.*; ***to make a splash,*** dar el golpe, gastar la tira. — *v.t.* salpicar, rociar. — *v.i.* chapotear; ***splash out,*** gastar la tira.

splashdown [ˈsplæʃdaun], *s.* amerizaje.

splashy [ˈsplæʃi], *a.* líquido; lodoso.

splatter [ˈsplætə], *v.t.*, *v.i.* chapotear, guachapear, chapalear; salpicar, rociar.

splay [splei], *a.* esparcido; pesado; ***splay-foot***(***ed***), zancajoso; ***splay-mouth,*** boquiancho. — *s.* bisel, chaflán; alféizar; derrame. — *v.t.* biselar; despald(ill)ar (*un caballo*); extender (sin gracia).

spleen [spli:n], *s.* (*anat.*) bazo; rencor; esplín, melancolía, hipocondria; ***to vent one's spleen,*** descargar la bilis (***on,*** contra).

spleenful [ˈspli:nful], *a.* bilioso; colérico, regañón; melancólico.

spleenwort [ˈspli:nwə:t], *s.* escolopendra, doradillo, culantrillo.

spleeny [ˈspli:ni], *a.* bilioso; melancólico; irritable, enfadadizo.

splendent [ˈsplendənt], *a.* esplendente; resplandeciente.

splendid [ˈsplendid], *a.* espléndido, magnífico. — *interj.* ¡estupendo!

splendour [ˈsplendə], *s.* esplendor; brillantez; magnificencia.

splenetic [spliˈnetik], *a.* bilioso, atrabiliario.

splenic [ˈsplenik], *a.* esplénico.

splice [splais], *s.* empalme; junta. — *v.t.* empalmar; juntar; (*fam.*) casar, unir en matrimonio; (*mar.*) ***splice the main-brace,*** servir una ración de ron; beber; (*fam.*) ***to get spliced,*** casarse, echarse la soga al cuello.

splicing [ˈsplaisiŋ], *s.* empalme; junta.

splint [splint], *s.* tablilla; (*vet.*) sobrehueso. — *v.t.* entablillar.

splinter [ˈsplintə], *s.* astilla. — *v.t.* astillar. — *v.i.* astillarse.

split [split], *a.* partido, hendido, rajado; resquebrajado; cuarteado; ***split loyalties,*** lealtades divididas, *f.pl.*; ***split party,*** partido dividido *o* en cisma; ***split personality,*** personalidad desdoblada. — *s.* hendidura, raja; resquebrajadura; cuarteadura; división, cisma, *m.*; (*fam.*) ***to do the splits,*** despatarrarse. — *irr. v.t.* partir, hender, rajar; resquebrajar; cuartear; dividir, causar cisma en; ***split the difference,*** partir la diferencia; ***split hairs,*** hilar demasiado fino *o* delgado, sutilizar mucho *o* demasiado, andarse con muchos *o* demasiados tiquismiquis; ***split one's sides laughing,*** desternillarse de risa. — *v.i.* partirse, henderse, rajarse; resquebrajarse; cuartearse; dividirse; bifurcarse; desdoblarse; (*fam.*) ***split*** (***on s.o.***), soplar, ir con el soplo, chivarse (contra alguien), delatar (a alguien); ***split up,*** separarse, irse cada uno por su camino *o* por su lado.

splodge, splotch [splɔdʒ, splɔtʃ], *s.* borrón, manchón, embadurnamiento.

splurge [splə:dʒ], *s.* fachenda. — *v.i.* fachendear.

splutter [ˈsplʌtə], *s.* farfulla; chisporroteo. — *v.i.* farfullar; chisporrotear.

spoil [spɔil], *s.* (*sing. o pl.*) botín, despojo. — *v.t.* estropear, echar a perder; mimar, consentir (*niños*). — *v.i.* estropearse, echarse, a perder, deteriorarse; ***to be spoiling for an argument,*** estar deseando discutir; ***to be spoiling for a fight,*** estar deseando pelear(se).

spoilsport [ˈspɔilspɔ:t], *s.* aguafiestas, *m.f.inv.*

spoke (1) [spouk], *s.* rayo; (*fig.*) ***to put a spoke in s.o.'s wheel,*** chafar a alguien, estropearle a alguien el plan.

spoke (2), **spoken** [ˈspouk(ən)], *pret.*, *p.p.* [SPEAK].

spokesman [ˈspouksmən], *s.* portavoz; ***act as spokesman for,*** hacer de *o* ser portavoz de.

spoliation [spouliˈeiʃən], *s.* despojo; (*for.*) expoliación.

spoliator [ˈspoulieitə], *s.* expoliador.

spondaic [spɔnˈdeiik], *a.* espondaico.

spondee [ˈspɔndi:], *s.* espondeo.

spondyl [ˈspɔndil], *s.* espóndilo.

spondylitis [spɔndiˈlaitis], *s.* espondilosis, *f.inv.*

sponge [spʌndʒ], *s.* esponja; (*artill.*) lanada, escobillón; ***sponge-bag,*** esponjera; ***sponge-cake,*** bizcocho; ***sponge-tree,*** cuje; ***to throw up the sponge,*** darse por vencido. — *v.t.* mojar *o* lavar con esponja; borrar; embeber; ***sponge up,*** absorber. — *v.i.* esponjarse; ***sponge on,*** vivir a costa de, dar sablazos a.

spongelet [ˈspʌndʒlit], *s.* esponja pequeña, esponjita; (*bot.*) espongiola.

sponger [ˈspʌndʒə], *s.* sablista, *m.f.*, gorrón.

sponginess [ˈspʌndʒinis], *s.* esponjosidad.

sponging [ˈspʌndʒiŋ], *s.* (el) limpiar con esponja; (*fig.*) gorronería.

spongiole [ˈspʌndʒioul], *s.* espongiola.

spongy, spongeous, spongious [ˈspʌndʒi, -iəs], *a.* esponjoso; embebido, empapado.

sponsion [ˈspɔnʃən], *s.* fianza, acto de salir fiador por otro.

sponson [ˈspɔnsən], *s.* barbeta.

sponsor [ˈspɔnsə], *s.* fiador; padrino *o* madrina; patrocinador. — *v.t.* patrocinar; promover, fomentar; apadrinar.

sponsorship [ˈspɔnsəʃip], *s.* patrocinio; ***under the sponsorship of,*** patrocinado por.

spontaneity, spontaneousness [spɔntəˈni:iti, spɔnˈteiniəsnis], *s.* espontaneidad.

spontaneous [spɔnˈteiniəs], *a.* espontáneo.

spontoon [spɔnˈtu:n], *s.* espontón.

spoof [spu:f], *s.* (*fam.*) engaño, broma. — *v.t.* engañar, hacer una broma a.

spook [spu:k], *s.* (*fam.*) fantasma, *m.*, aparición, aparecido.

spooky [ˈspu:ki], *a.* espectral, horripilante.

spool [spu:l], *s.* carrete; canilla; carretel. — *v.t.* ovillar, encanillar, devanar, encañar.

spoom [spu:m], *v.i.* navegar a toda vela; ir *o* correr de prisa.

spoon [spu:n], *s.* cuchara; ***dessert-spoon,*** cucharilla de postre; ***spoon-bait, spoon-hook,*** anzuelo de cuchara; ***table-spoon,*** cuchara grande; ***teaspoon,*** cucharilla; ***to be born with a silver spoon in one's mouth,*** nacer en la abundancia. — *v.t.* sacar *o* alzar con cuchara. — *v.i.* pescar con anzuelo de cuchara; ponerse amartelado; besuquearse.

spoonbill [ˈspu:nbil], *s.* (*orn.*) espátula, ave de cuchara.

Spoonerism [ˈspu:nərizəm], *s.* trastrueque de sílabas.

spoonful [ˈspu:nful], *s.* cucharada.

spoonwort [ˈspu:nwə:t], *s.* coclearia.

spoony [ˈspu:ni], *a.* (*fam.*) amartelado; sobón; ***to be spoony on,*** estar amartelado con.

spoor [spu:ə], *s.* rastro, pista, huella de animal salvaje. — *v.i.* seguir el rastro *o* la pista.

sporadic [spɔˈrædik], *a.* esporádico.

spore [spɔ:], *s.* (*bot, biol.*) espora.

sport [spɔ:t], *s.* deporte; juego, diversión; broma, burla; objeto de broma *o* de burla; juguete; (*bot.*) mutación; (*pl.*) deportes, *m.pl.*, juegos, *m.pl.*; (*fam.*) ***good sport,*** buen perdedor; buen chico; ***in sport,*** en broma; ***to make sport of,*** mofarse de; ***sports car,*** coche de sport; ***sports commentator,*** comentarista de deportes *o* deportivo, *m.f.*; ***sports ground,*** campo de deportes; ***sports jacket,*** chaqueta de sport; ***sports page,*** página de deportes *o* deportiva. — *v.t.* gastar, ostentar, lucir. — *v.i.* divertirse, holgar, retozar.

sportful [ˈspɔ:tful], *a.* retozón.

sporting [ˈspɔ:tiŋ], *a.* deportivo; de caza; ***to have a sporting chance,*** tener ciertas posibilidades de escaparse, de librarse *o* de conseguir algo.

sportive [ˈspɔ:tiv], *a.* juguetón, retozón; festivo.

sportsman [ˈspɔ:tsmən], *s.* deportista, *m.f.*; cazador; (*fam.*) caballero (cumplido).

sportsmanlike [ˈspɔ:tsmənlaik], *a.* deportivo; caballeroso.

sportsmanship [ˈspɔ:tsmənʃip], *s.* deportividad.

sportswoman [ˈspɔ:tswumən], *s.* deportista.

sporty [ˈspɔ:ti], *a.* deportivo.

sporule [ˈspɔ:rju:l], *s.* espórula.

spot [spɔt], *a.* inmediato, en el mismísimo momento, en el mismísimo sitio; ***spot cash,*** dinero contante (y sonante); ***to pay spot cash,*** pagar a toca teja; ***spot check,*** inspección *o* comprobación repentina. — *s.* sitio, lugar, paraje; punto; mancha; (*cara*) grano; (*rad.*) espacio; (*fam.*) ***a spot of,*** un poco de; ***a spot of trouble,*** un poco de lío, cisco, jaleo *etc.*; ***beauty spot,*** lunar (*cutáneo*); sitio de gran belleza natural; ***on the spot,*** en el mismísimo sitio; sobre el terreno; en el acto; (*fam.*) ***to put on the spot,*** poner en un aprieto *o* apuro, poner en un brete; ***to have a soft spot for s.o.,*** sentir debilidad por alguien; ***to be in a tight spot,*** estar en un aprieto; ***to know s.o.'s weak spots,*** saber de qué pie cojea uno, conocerle a alguien los puntos flacos; ***he broke out*** o ***came out in spots,*** le salió un sarpullido; ***to knock spots off s.o.,*** dar ciento y raya a alguien. — *v.t.* manchar; salpicar; darse cuenta de, fijarse en, detectar; divisar. — *v.i.* — ***with rain,*** chispear.

spotless [ˈspɔtlis], *a.* inmaculado, limpísimo.

spotlessness [ˈspɔtlisnis], *s.* (lo) inmaculado.

spotlight [ˈspɔtlait], *s.* proyector; faro giratorio; foco de luz.

spotted [ˈspɔtid], *a.* manchado, moteado; ***spotted fever,*** tabardillo pintado. — *p.p.* [SPOT].

spotter [ˈspɔtə], *s.* vigilante; observador; coleccionista (*de matrículas etc.*), *m.f.*

spotty [ˈspɔti], *a.* lleno de manchas; lleno de granos.

spousal [ˈspauzəl], *a.* nupcial, conyugal. — *s.pl.* nupcias, *f.pl.*

spouse [spauz], *s.* esposo, esposa, cónyuge.

spout [spaut], *s.* caño; pitón, pitorro; surtidor; canilla de tonel, espita; canalón, gárgola; pico (*de cafetera, de tetera*); chorro; ***rain-spout,*** chaparrón, turbión; (*fam.*) ***up the spout,*** empeñado, en prenda; acabado; ***water-spout,*** surtidor; tromba *o* manga de agua. — *v.t.* echar, arrojar; (*fig.*) declamar; (*fam.*) empeñar. — *v.i.* chorrear; brotar; (*fig.*) perorar.

sprain [sprein], *s.* torcedura, esguince. — *v.t.* torcer, distender; ***sprain one's ankle,*** torcerse el tobillo.

sprat [spræt], *s.* sardineta; arenque pequeño.

sprawl [sprɔ:l], *s.* desparramamiento. — *v.i.* arrellanarse; tumbarse; extenderse; desparramarse; ***he was sprawled in his chair,*** estaba repantigado en el sillón.

spray (1) [sprei], *s.* rociada; agua pulverizada; espuma; atomizador; rocío, riego por aspersión. — *v.t.* rociar; regar; pulverizar. — *v.i.* pulverizarse.

spray (2) [sprei], *s.* ramita.

sprayer [ˈspreiə], *s.* rociador, pulverizador.

spread [spred], *a.* extendido, esparcido; cubierto, untado; puesta (*la mesa*); (*joy.*) de poco brillo. — *s.* extensión; propagación; despliegue; diferencia; envergadura (*de alas*); cobertor, cubrecama; (*fam.*) comilona, festín; ***middle-aged spread,*** barriga de la edad madura. — *irr. v.t.* extender; desplegar; esparcir, desparramar; poner (*la mesa*); untar; ***spread abroad,*** propagar, divulgar. — *v.i.* extenderse; esparcirse; propagarse, difundirse; ***spread out,*** abrirse, separarse, desplegarse. — **spread o.s.,** *v.r.* (*fig.*) explayarse; gastar a base de bien.

spreadeagle [ˈspredi:gl], *v.t.* espanzurrar; (*fig.*) desparramar.

spreader [ˈspredə], *s.* esparcidor; divulgador; propagador; separador.

spreading [ˈspredinŋ], *a.* dilatado, extenso; (*bot.*) divergente; frondoso (*de un árbol*).

spree [spri:], *s.* juerga, parranda; ***to go on the spree,*** irse de juerga; ***spending spree,*** locura de gastar, orgía de compras. — *v.i.* irse de juerga.

sprig [sprig], *s.* ramita; pimpollo, renuevo; puntilla; espiga. — *v.t.* adornar con ramitas.

sprigged [sprigd], *a.* (*tej.*) estampado de ramas.

sprightliness [ˈspraitlinis], *s.* viveza, vivacidad; desenvoltura.

sprightly [ˈspraitli], *a.* despierto, vivaracho, vivo.

spring [spriŋ], *a.* primaveral, de primavera; de muelle(s); ***spring-board,*** trampolín; ***spring clean***(***ing***), limpieza de primavera; ***spring-latch,*** picaporte; ***spring lock,*** cerradura de golpe; ***spring-mattress,*** somier, colchón de muelles; ***spring onion,*** cebolleta; ***spring tide,*** marea viva. — *s.* primavera; muelle, resorte; elasticidad; salto, brinco; fuente, *f.*, manantial, hontanar; (*fig.*) móvil, causa; ***hot springs,*** termas, *f.pl.*, caldas, *f.pl.* — *irr. v.t.* hacer saltar; volar; abrir de repente, soltar; (*fam.*) ***he sprang it on us all of a sudden,*** nos lo espetó de repente *o* de buenas a primeras, nos soltó el escopetazo; ***the ship sprang a leak,*** al barco se le abrió una vía de agua. — *v.i.* saltar, brincar; brotar, nacer; surgir, provenir, dimanar (***from,*** de); (*mec.*) combarse, torcerse; ***spring at*** o ***upon,*** abalanzarse a *o* sobre; ***spring back,*** saltar hacia atrás; ***spring forth,*** brotar; ***spring forward,*** lanzarse *o* abalanzarse hacia adelante; ***spring up,*** brotar; levantarse de pronto *o* de un salto; ***where did he spring from?*** ¿de dónde salió ése?

springbok [ˈspriŋbɔk], *s.* gacela (del sur de África).

springe [sprindʒ], *s.* (*caza*) lazo, trampa.

springer [ˈspriŋə], *s.* saltador, brincador.

springiness [ˈspriŋinis], *s.* elasticidad, fuerza elástica.

springtime [ˈspriŋtaim], *s.* (época de) primavera.

springy [ˈspriŋi], *a.* elástico; (*hierba*) muelle.

sprinkle [spriŋkl], *s.* [SPRINKLING]. — *v.t.* asperjar (*de agua bendita*); rociar, salpicar (***with,*** de); espolvorear (*de azúcar*). — *v.i.* (*impers.*) caer unas gotas.

sprinkler [ˈspriŋklə], *s.* rociador; regadera; (*igl.*) hisopo.

sprinkling [ˈspriŋkliŋ], *s.* rociada, rociadura; aspersión; poco, pizca; ***a sprinkling of knowledge,*** un barniz de cultura; ***a sprinkling of rain,*** (unas) gotas de lluvia.

sprint [sprint], *s.* esprint; carrera. — *v.i.* (*dep.*) esprintar; correr.

sprinter [ˈsprintə], *s.* esprínter.

sprit [sprit], *s.* (*mar.*) botavara.

sprite [sprait], *s.* duende, trasgo, hada.

spritsail [ˈspritsəl], *s.* (*mar.*) cebadera.

sprocket [ˈsprɔkit], *s.* diente de rueda de cadena; ***sprocket-gear,*** engranaje de rueda de cadena; ***sprocket-wheel,*** rueda de cadena.

sprout [spraut], *s.* brote; retoño; ***Brussels sprouts,*** coles de Bruselas, *f.pl.* — *v.t.* echar. — *v.i.* brotar, retoñar, germinar; surgir.

spruce [spru:s], *a.* apuesto, pulcro, atildado, peripuesto. — *s.* (*bot.*) picea, abeto falso *o* rojo; ***spruce fir,*** pinabete. — *v.t.* (*fam.*) ***spruce up,***

poner elegante, poner decente, asear. — **spruce o.s.,** *v.r.* — ***up,*** acicalarse.
spruceness [ˈspru:snis], *s.* atildamiento.
sprung [sprʌŋ], *a.* provisto de muelles *o* resortes. — *p.p.* [SPRING].
spry [sprai], *a.* ágil, activo.
spryness [ˈsprainis], *s.* agilidad; presteza.
spud [spʌd], *s.* (*agric.*) escarda; laya; (*cir.*) limpiaojos, *m.inv.*; (*fam.*) patata, papa.
spue [spju:], *v.t., v.i.* [SPEW].
spume [spju:m], *s.* espuma; espumarajo. — *v.i.* espumar, echar *o* hacer espuma.
spumescent [spju:ˈmesənt], *a.* espumante.
spumous, spumy [ˈspju:məs, -i], *a.* espumoso, espumajoso, espumante.
spun [spʌn], *a.* ***spun glass,*** hilacha de vidrio; ***spun gold*** o ***silver,*** hilo de oro *o* plata; ***spun silk,*** (borra de) seda hilada; ***spun yarn,*** meollar. — *pret., p.p.* [SPIN].
spunk [spʌŋk], *s.* yesca; (*fam.*) coraje, ánimo, denuedo.
spunky [ˈspʌŋki], *a.* (*fam.*) que tiene agollas; enfadadizo, enojadizo.
spur [spə:], *s.* espuela; espolón; estribo; aguijón; estímulo, acicate; uña puntiaguda; pincho; (*mar.*) escora; (*arq.*) riostra; ***spur-gear, spur-wheel,*** rueda dentada; ***spur-gearing,*** engranaje de ruedas dentadas; ***on the spur of the moment,*** impulsivamente, sin reflexionar; ***win one's spurs,*** alcanzar distinción, hacerse un nombre. — *v.t.* espolear, aguijonear, picar; ***spur on,*** estimular, incitar, animar. — *v.i.* picar espuelas.
spurge [spə:dʒ], *s.* lechetrezna, titímalo, euforbio, tártago; ***spurge-laurel,*** lauréola, mecereón.
spurious [ˈspjuəriəs], *a.* espurio; falso; (*bot.*) aparente.
spuriousness [ˈspjuəriəsnis], *s.* falsedad, (lo) falso; adulteración.
spurn [spə:n], *s.* desdén; coz, *f.*, puntapié. — *v.t.* desdeñar, rechazar.
spurning [ˈspə:niŋ], *s.* menosprecio, desdén.
spurred [spə:d], *a.* con espuelas; con espolones; (*biol.*) atizonado.
spurrier [ˈspʌriə], *s.* el que hace espuelas.
spurry [ˈspʌri], *s.* (*bot.*) espérgula.
spurt [spə:t], *s.* chorretada, borbotón; esfuerzo supremo; ramalazo, estallido (*de una pasión*). — *v.t.* arrojar en chorro, espurriar. — *v.i.* salir en chorro, borbotar; hacer un esfuerzo supremo.
sputnik [ˈsputnik], *s.* sputnik.
sputter [ˈspʌtə], *s.* chisporroteo; farfulla. — *v.i.* echar saliva (al hablar); chisporrotear; farfullar.
sputtering [ˈspʌtəriŋ], *a.* que chisporrotea. — *s.* chisporroteo.
sputum [ˈspju:təm], *s.* esputo.
spy [spai], *s.* espía, *m.f.*; ***spy ring,*** banda de espías. — *v.t.* divisar, columbrar; ***spy out,*** explorar, reconocer. — *v.i.* espiar, ser espía; ***spy on,*** espiar (a).
spy-glass [ˈspai-glɑ:s], *s.* catalejo.
spy-hole [ˈspai-houl], *s.* mirilla.
squab [skwɔb], *a.* implume, acabado de salir de la cáscara; regordete, rechoncho. — *s.* (*orn.*) pichón, pichoncillo; cojín; canapé.
squabble [skwɔbl], *s.* riña, disputa, pelea, desavenencia. — *v.i.* reñir, disputar, pelearse.
squabbler [ˈskwɔblə], *s.* pendenciero.
squad [skwɔd], *s.* escuadra; pelotón; ***squad car,*** coche patrulla.
squadron [ˈskwɔdrən], *s.* (*mar.*) escuadra; (*mil.*) escuadrón; (*aer.*) escuadrilla; ***squadron-leader,*** comandante.
squalid [ˈskwɔlid], *a.* sórdido; mezquino.
squalidness [ˈskwɔlidnis], *s.* sordidez, (lo) sórdido; mezquindad, (lo) mezquino.
squall [skwɔ:l], *s.* chillido, berrido; borrasca; ***rain squall,*** chubasco. — *v.i.* chillar, berrear.
squaller [ˈskwɔ:lə], *s.* berreón.
squally [ˈskwɔ:li], *a.* borrascoso; chubascoso.
squalor [ˈskwɔlə], *s.* sordidez; miseria.
squama [ˈskweimə], *s.* escama.
squamose, squamous [ˈskweimous, -məs], *a.* escamoso.
squander [ˈskwɔndə], *v.t.* despilfarrar, derrochar, malgastar; disipar.
squanderer [ˈskwɔndərə], *s.* derrochador, derrochón.
square [skwɛə], *a.* cuadrado; en ángulo recto, en cuadro, a escuadra; claro y directo; rotundo; justo, equitativo; honrado; abundante; en regla; (*fam.*) carca; ***2 foot square,*** 2 pies en cuadro; ***square brackets,*** corchetes, *m.pl.*; ***square dance,*** cuadrilla, danza de figuras; ***square dealing,*** honradez, buena fe; ***2 square feet,*** 2 pies cuadrados; ***square meal,*** comida en regla; ***square rig,*** aparejo de cruzamen; ***square-rigged,*** de aparejo de cruzamen; ***square sail,*** vela en cruz *o* redonda; ***to be square,*** estar en paz; estar igualados *o* empatados; ***to get square with,*** desquitarse con. — *adv.* de cara, directamente. — *s.* cuadro, cuadrado; escuadra; plaza; casilla; (*fam.*) carca, *m.f.*; ***square of the circle,*** cuadratura del círculo. — *v.t.* cuadrar; escuadrar; cuadricular; elevar al cuadrado; ajustar, saldar; (*fam.*) sobornar; ***square one's shoulders,*** cuadrarse; ***square up,*** enderezar; ***square the yards,*** poner las vergas en cruz. — *v.i.* cuadrar, concordar; ***square up,*** saldar cuentas, pagar; ***square up to s.o.,*** cuadrarse con alguien, enfrentarse resueltamente con alguien. — **square o.s.,** *v.r.* justificarse, sincerarse.
squarely [ˈskwɛəli], *adv.* (*fig.*) resueltamente, sin titubeos; ***fairly and squarely,*** resueltamente.
squareness [ˈskwɛənis], *s.* cuadratura; honradez.
squaring [ˈskwɛəriŋ], *s.* cuadratura; escuadreo; cuadriculación; escuadrición; ***squaring shears,*** cizallas de escuadrar, *f.pl.*
squarrose, squarrous [ˈskwɔ:rous, -rəs], *a.* (*biol.*) áspero, escamoso.
squash (1) [skwɔʃ], *s.* aplastamiento; cosa blanda; agolpamiento, apiñamiento (*de personas*); limonada, naranjada; pulpa; maceración; despachurramiento; (*dep.*) juego de pelota; ***squash-beetle,*** coleóptero crisomélido; ***squash-vine,*** cidracayote, cucúrbita; ***summer squash,*** cidracayote de verano. — *v.t.* aplastar; apretar, apiñar; estrujar; despachurrar; apabullar; confutar. — *v.i.* aplastarse; despachurrarse; agolparse, apiñarse.
squash (2) [skwɔʃ], *s.* (*bot.*) calabaza.; (*Am.*) [MARROW].
squashy [ˈskwɔʃi], *a.* blanducho; zumoso.
squat [skwɔt], *a.* rechoncho; achaparrado. — *s.* postura en cuclillas. — *v.i.* agacharse; sentarse en cuclillas; establecerse en un sitio sin título para ello.
squatter [ˈskwɔtə], *s.* colono *o* residente intruso.
squaw [skwɔ:], *s.* (*Am.*) mujer *o* esposa india.
squawk [skwɔ:k], *s.* graznido; (*fam.*) chillido. — *v.i.* graznar; (*fam.*) chillar.
squeak [skwi:k], *s.* chirrido, chillido; ***to have a narrow squeak,*** escaparse por un pelo. — *v.i.* chirriar; chillar; cantar, soplar.
squeaker [ˈskwi:kə], *s.* soplón.
squeal [skwi:l], *s.* chillido, grito agudo. — *v.i.* chillar; (*fam.*) soplar, dar el soplo.
squealer [ˈskwi:lə], *s.* soplón, chivato.
squeamish [ˈskwi:miʃ], *a.* remilgado; delicado.
squeamishness [ˈskwi:miʃnis], *s.* remilgo, escrúpulo; delicadeza; sensación de asco.
squeegee [ˈskwi:dʒi:], *s.* rodillo *o* escobilla de goma para restregar superficies mojadas. — *v.t.* restregar con rodillo de goma.
squeeze [skwi:z], *s.* apretón, estrujón, apretujón; apretura; apiñamiento; presión; restricción (*de crédito etc.*); ***to put the squeeze on,*** apretar los tornillos a; ***to be in a tight squeeze,*** estar en un

aprieto, en un brete. — *v.t.* apretar; estrujar; oprimir; sacar el jugo a; ***squeeze in,*** hacer entrar apretando; ***squeeze out,*** hacer salir apretando; exprimir; excluir, eliminar; ***squeeze through,*** hacer pasar apretando; ***squeeze one's way,*** abrirse paso entre apreturas. — *v.i.* introducirse, deslizarse, pasar entre apreturas.

squeezer [ˈskwi:zə], *s.* exprimidor; ***lemon-squeezer,*** exprimidor de limones.

squelch [skweltʃ], *v.t.* despachurrar. — *v.i.* despachurrarse; andar chapoteando.

squib [skwib], *s.* (*piro.*) buscapiés, *m.inv.*; (*fig.*) pasquín; (*fig.*) ***damp squib,*** petardo.

squid [skwid], *s.* calamar, chipirón.

squill [skwil], *s.* (*bot.*) escila, albarrana; (*zool.*) esquila.

squint [skwint], *a.* (***squint-eyed***) bizco, bisojo. — *s.* estrabismo; mirada bizca; (*fam.*) vistazo; ***to have a squint,*** bizquear; ***to have*** o ***take a squint at,*** echar un vistazo *o* una ojeada a. — *v.i.* bizquear; ***squint at,*** mirar bizco (a).

squinting [ˈskwintiŋ], *a.* bizco. — *s.* estrabismo.

squire [ˈskwaiə], *s.* escudero; hacendado. — *v.t.* acompañar.

squirm [skwə:m], *v.i.* retorcerse; sufrir; serpentear; ***squirm out of,*** librarse vilmente *o* arteramente de, zufarse de.

squirrel [ˈskwirəl], *s.* ardilla.

squirt [skwə:t], *s.* surtidor; chorro; jeringazo; (*fam.*) mequetrefe, chisgarabís, *m.inv.* — *v.t.* lanzar en surtidor, expulsar a chorro; jeringar. — *v.i.* — ***out,*** salir en surtidor *o* a chorro(s).

squirt-gun [ˈskwə:t-gʌn], *s.* jeringa.

Sri Lanka [sri: ˈlʌŋkə]. Sri-Lanka.

stab [stæb], *s.* puñalada; (*fam.*) ***have*** o ***take a stab at it,*** probar a hacerlo, intentarlo. — *v.t.* apuñalar, dar una puñalada a.

stability, stableness [stəˈbiliti, ˈsteiblnis], *s.* estabilidad; fijeza, firmeza.

stabilize [ˈsteibilaiz], *v.t.* estabilizar, normalizar. — *v.i.* estabilizarse, normalizarse.

stable (1) [steibl], *a.* estable; fijo, firme.

stable (2) [steibl], *s.* cuadra, caballeriza; ***riding stables,*** escuela hípica; ***stable-boy, stableman,*** mozo de cuadra. — *v.t.* poner en (la) cuadra.

stack [stæk], *s.* niara, almiar (*de heno*); rimero, pila, hacina, montón; (*mil.*) pabellón (*de fusiles*); cañón (*de chimenea*). — *v.t.* hacinar, amontonar; poner (*las armas*) en pabellón; ***the cards were stacked against us,*** teníamos las circunstancias en contra.

stadia (1) [ˈsteidiə], *s.* estadia.

stadium [ˈsteidiəm], *s.* (*pl.* **stadia** (2) [ˈsteidiə]) estadio.

staff [stɑ:f], *s.* palo; pértiga; vara, bastón (*de mando*); báculo; sostén; asta; báculo pastoral; regla de medir; jalón, mira; (*cir.*) guía, *f.*, sonda acanalada; estado mayor, plana mayor; personal (técnico *o* administrativo), cuadro; profesorado; servidumbre; (*arq.*) cartón piedra; (*mús.*) pentagrama, *m.*; ***medical staff,*** personal médico; cuerpo de sanidad militar; ***staff of a newspaper,*** redacción de un periódico; ***staff officer,*** oficial de estado mayor; ***staff room,*** sala de profesores; ***teaching staff,*** cuadro de profesores, personal docente. — *v.t.* dotar de personal.

stag [stæg], *s.* ciervo, venado; (*fam.*) varón; toro castrado; (*Bolsa*) especulador, alcista a corto plazo, *m.f.*; ***stag-beetle,*** ciervo volante; ***stag-party,*** reunión de hombres solos, *f.*

stage [steidʒ], *s.* (*teat.*) escena; escenario, tablado, tablas, *f.pl.*; teatro; entarimado, estrado, plataforma; parada; jornada, etapa; estado, grado; piso, escalón; portaobjeto; ***at this stage,*** a estas alturas; ***by short stages,*** a cortas jornadas; en pequeñas etapas; ***stage coach,*** diligencia; ***stage direction,*** acotación; ***stage door,*** entrada de artistas; ***stage driver,*** mayoral, cochero de diligencia; ***stage fright,*** miedo al público; ***stage hand,*** metesillas, *m.inv.*, tramoyista, *m.*; ***stage manager,*** director de escena; ***stage name,*** nombre artístico; ***stage-struck,*** loco por el teatro; ***stage whisper,*** aparte; ***to go off the stage,*** abandonar la escena; ***to quit the stage,*** retirarse del teatro; ***to go on the stage,*** adoptar la carrera del teatro; ***to produce*** o ***put on the stage,*** poner en escena. — *v.t.* (*teat.*) poner en escena; representar; organizar, montar.

stager [ˈsteidʒə], *s.* caballo de diligencia; ***old stager,*** veterano.

stagger [ˈstægə], *s.* tambaleo; vacilación; (*aer.*) decalaje; (*pl.*) (*vet.*) vértigo, vahido. — *v.t.* asombrar; hacer tambalear; escalonar; ***staggered hours,*** horas escalonadas, *f.pl.* — *v.i.* tambalearse, hacer eses; titubear, flaquear.

staggering [ˈstægəriŋ], *a.* tambaleante; asombroso. — *s.* tambaleo, titubeo.

staghound [ˈstæghaund], *s.* sabueso, perro para cazar ciervos.

staging [ˈsteidʒiŋ], *s.* andamiaje; tráfico en diligencias; puesta en escena.

stagnant [ˈstægnənt], *a.* estancado, detenido, estantío; paralizado; (*com.*) inactivo.

stagnate [stægˈneit], *v.i.* estancarse, detenerse; estar estancado; paralizarse.

stagnation, stagnancy [stægˈneiʃən, ˈstægnənsi], *s.* estancamiento; paralización.

staid [steid], *a.* serio, formal; tieso.

staidness [ˈsteidnis], *s.* seriedad, formalidad; (lo) tieso.

stain [stein], *s.* mancha; tinte, tintura; mácula. — *v.t.* manchar; teñir, colorar; mancillar; ***stained glass,*** vidrio de color; ***stained-glass window,*** vidriera (de colores). — *v.i.* mancharse.

stainless [ˈsteinlis], *a.* inmaculado; ***stainless steel,*** acero inoxidable.

stair [stɛə], *s.* escalón, peldaño; escalera; (*pl.*) escalera(s); ***flight of stairs,*** (tramo de) escalera; ***spiral*** o ***winding stairs,*** escalera de caracol; ***stair-carpet,*** alfombra de escalera; ***stair-rod,*** varilla para alfombra de escalera.

staircase [ˈstɛəkeis], *s.* escalera.

stairway [ˈstɛəwei], *s.* escalera.

stake [steik], *s.* estaca, poste; hoguera; (*agric.*) rodrigón; (*carr.*) telero; bigorneta; (*com.*) interés, *m.*, premio; apuesta (*en los juegos*); ***at stake,*** en juego; en peligro; ***I have a great deal at stake,*** me va mucho en este juego *o* en este asunto; ***to die at the stake,*** morir en la hoguera. — *v.t.* estacar; apostar, jugar, aventurar; ***stake all,*** jugárselo todo, jugarse el todo por el todo.

stalactic, stalactitic [stəˈlæktik, stæləkˈtitik], *a.* estalactítico.

stalactite [ˈstæləktait], *s.* estalactita.

stalagmite [ˈstæləgmait], *s.* estalagmita.

stalagmitic [stæləgˈmitik], *a.* estalagmítico.

stale [steil], *a.* rancio; viejo; añejo; pasado, trasnochado; ***stale air,*** aire viciado; ***stale bread,*** pan duro; ***stale news,*** noticia(s) vieja(s); ***to be*** o ***feel stale,*** estar, sentirse cansado *o* sin entusiasmo.

stalemate [ˈsteilmeit], *s.* tablas, *f.pl.* (*ajedrez*); (*fig.*) ***to reach stalemate,*** llegar a (un) punto muerto.

staleness [ˈsteilnis], *s.* (lo) rancio; (lo) viejo *etc.*

stalk (1) [stɔ:k], *s.* (*bot.*) tallo; pedúnculo; troncho (*de ciertas hortalizas*); raspa (*de uva*).

stalk (2) [stɔ:k], *v.t.*, *v.i.* acechar (*para cazar*). — *v.i.* andar con paso enérgico y aire de impaciencia; ***stalk about,*** andar de un lado para otro con paso airado.

stall (1) [stɔ:l], *s.* pesebre; cuadra; establo; puesto; caseta; tenderete; (*teat.*) butaca; (*igl.*) sitial de coro. — *v.t.* encerrar *o* meter en cuadra *o* establo. — *v.i.* calarse (*un motor*).

stall (2) [stɔ:l], *v.t.* — ***off,*** mantener a raya con evasivas; dar largas a. — *v.i.* andarse con evasivas, dar largas a la cosa; ***quit stalling,*** ¡déjate de evasivas!

stallion [ˈstæljən], *s.* caballo padre.

stalwart [ˈstɔːlwət], *a.* fornido, forzudo, membrudo; fiel, constante, leal, acérrimo. — *s.* persona forzuda; partidario acérrimo.

stamen [ˈsteimən], *s.* estambre.

stamina [ˈstæminə], *s.* resistencia, aguante, fibra, vigor.

staminal [ˈstæminəl], *a.* (*bot.*) estaminal; vital, vigoroso.

staminate [ˈstæminit], *a.* estaminífero.

stamineous [stəˈminiəs], *a.* estamíneo, estaminoso.

stammer [ˈstæmə], *s.* tartamudeo, balbuceo. — *v.t.*, *v.i.* tartamudear, balbucear.

stammerer [ˈstæmərə], *s.* tartamudo; farfalloso.

stamp [stæmp], *s.* sello; timbre, póliza; marca, impresión; estampilla; estampa; cuño, troquel; calaña; patada; ***postage stamp,*** sello de correos; ***Stamp Act,*** ley del timbre; ***stamp album,*** álbum (para sellos); ***stamp collecting,*** filatelia; ***stamp dealer,*** comerciante de sellos (postales); ***stamp duty,*** impuesto del timbre; ***stamp machine,*** máquina (expendedora) de sellos; ***to bear the stamp of,*** llevar el sello de. — *v.t.* sellar; estampar, imprimir; estampillar; marcar, señalar; bocartear; ***stamp one's foot,*** dar patadas en el suelo; ***stamp out,*** apagar pisoteando; extirpar. — *v.i.* patear; patalear; piafar; ***stamp on,*** hollar, pisotear.

stampede [stæmˈpiːd], *s.* estampida, fuga precipitada, huida en tropel. — *v.t.*, *v.i.* (hacer) huir en tropel, en desorden.

stamper [ˈstæmpə], *s.* estampador; impresor; bocarte, pilón, punzón de forja, martinete de fragua; triturador de pólvora; mano de almirez; pisón.

stamping [ˈstæmpiŋ], *s.* selladura; timbre, timbrado; estampado (*de telas*); pateo, pataleo; ***stamping-mill,*** bocarte.

stance [stɑːns], *s.* postura; ***to take up a stance,*** adoptar una postura.

stanch [stɑːntʃ], *a.* [STAUNCH]. — *v.t.*, *v.i.* restañar(se).

stanchion [ˈstænʃən], *s.* puntal; pie derecho; candelero; montante.

stanchness [ˈstɑːntʃnis], [STAUNCHNESS].

stand [stænd], *s.* posición, postura; resistencia; puesto; quiosco; stand (*de una exposición*); (*dep.*) tribuna; tarima, plataforma, estrado; estante; soporte, sostén; parada, punto (*de taxis*); atril (*de música*); ***one-night stand,*** actuación de una (sola) noche; ***to make a stand (against),*** oponerse (a), oponer resistencia (a); cuadrarse (ante); ***to take a firm stand,*** adoptar una actitud firme, cuadrarse; ***to take one's stand on,*** basarse en, tomar como punto fundamental; ***to take the stand,*** comparecer. — *v.t.* poner, colocar (derecho *o* de pie); aguantar, soportar, sufrir, resistir; resistir a (*un escrutinio etc.*); ***I can't stand him,*** no lo aguanto, no lo soporto, no lo puedo sufrir, no lo puedo ver; ***he doesn't stand a chance,*** no existe ni la menor posibilidad de que lo consiga; ***I'll stand the drinks,*** invito yo, convido yo; ***he stood his ground,*** no vaciló, no cejó, se mantuvo firme; no dio su brazo a torcer; ***stand (s.o.) in good stead,*** ser útil a, servir; ***it stands the test,*** da (muy) buen resultado, resulta (muy) bien; ***he doesn't stand the test,*** no da la talla; (*fig.*) ***he stood me up for an hour,*** me dio un plantón de una hora. — *v.i.* estar *o* estarse (de pie), tenerse (de pie); hallarse; levantarse; quedarse; tener vigencia *o* validez, regir, valer; (per)durar; estar parado; pararse; medir; ***stand about doing nothing,*** estarse sin hacer nada, estarse mano sobre mano; ***stand aside,*** apartarse, hacerse a un lado; ***stand at ease!*** ¡en su lugar, descansen!; ***stand back,*** retroceder, echarse hacia atrás; ***stand by,*** estar preparado; estar cerca; atenerse a, cumplir; dar apoyo a; no abandonar; ***stand down,*** retirarse; ***stand fast*** o ***firm,*** mantenerse firme; ***stand for,*** significar; representar; presentarse (*como aspirante* o *candidato*) para; ***I won't stand for it,*** no (se) lo aguanto, no (se) lo consiento; ***stand in,*** suplir, sustituir, reemplazar (***for,*** a); (*mar.*) acercarse (***to,*** a); ***you're standing in the light,*** me quitas la luz; ***stand in need of,*** necesitar, estar necesitado de; ***you're standing in the way,*** me estorbas; ***stand off,*** apartarse; ***stand out,*** destacarse, perfilarse (***against,*** contra); (*fig.*) descollar, sobresalir; (*fig.*) ***stand out against,*** insistir en oponerse a; (*fig.*) ***stand out for,*** aguantar para conseguir; ***stand still,*** estarse quieto; ***stand to reason,*** ser lógico; ***stand to win (lose),*** llevar las de ganar (de perder); ***stand up,*** levantarse, ponerse de pie; (*fig.*) ***stand up for,*** defender, dar *o* sacar la cara por; volver por; (*fig.*) ***stand up to,*** resistir a, hacer frente a; ***stand (up)on ceremony,*** andarse con cumplidos; ***how do we stand?*** ¿cómo estamos? ¿cómo está la cosa?; ***we don't know where we stand,*** no sabemos a qué atenernos.

standard [ˈstændəd], *a.* normal; corriente; uniforme, estereotipado; reglamentario, legal, de ley; aceptado, reconocido; ***standard English,*** inglés correcto, *m.*; ***standard measure,*** medida tipo; ***standard model,*** modelo corriente; ***standard work,*** obra fundamental; obra clásica. — *s.* norma; tipo; patrón; modelo; pauta; nivel; criterio; estandarte, bandera; poste, pie; ***gold standard,*** patrón oro; ***standard-bearer,*** portaestandarte, abanderado; ***standard lamp,*** lámpara de pie; ***standard of living,*** nivel de vida.

standardization [stændədaiˈzeiʃen], *s.* (el) uniformar.

standardize [ˈstændədaiz], *v.t.* hacer uniforme, uniformar.

stand-by [ˈstænd-bai], *s.* recurso seguro; persona de confianza.

stand-in [ˈstænd-in], *s.* sustituto.

standing [ˈstændiŋ], *a.* derecho, de pie, en pie, erecto; permanente, estable; constante; vigente; parado; estancado; ***standing army,*** ejército permanente; ***standing committee,*** comisión permanente; ***standing crop,*** cosecha sin cortar; ***standing order,*** pedido regular; orden de pago; ***standing orders,*** reglamento; ***standing rigging,*** jarcia muerta. — *s.* posición; situación; sitio; reputación; importancia, categoría; duración, antigüedad; ***of good (high) standing,*** de buena reputación; ***of old (long) standing,*** de toda la vida; ***standing room,*** sitio para estar de pie.

stand-offish [ˈstænd-ˈɔfiʃ], *a.* reservón, esquivo; endiosado, que tiene aire de superioridad.

standpoint [ˈstændpɔint], *s.* punto de vista.

standstill [ˈstændstil], *s.* alto, parada; ***be at a standstill,*** estar en punto muerto.

stanhope [ˈstænəp], *s.* cabriolé ligero.

stannic [ˈstænik], *a.* estannífero.

stannite [ˈstænait], *s.* (*min.*) estannita; (*quím.*) estannito.

stanza [ˈstænzə], *s.* estancia, estrofa.

stapes [ˈsteipiːz], *s.* (*anat.*) estribo.

staphyle [ˈstæfili], *s.* úvula.

staphylitis [stæfiˈlaitis], *s.* inflamación de la úvula.

staphylococcus [stæfiloˈkɔkəs], *s.* (*pl.* **staphylococci** [-kai]) estafilococo.

staple (1) [steipl], *a.* principal; corriente. — *s.* producto principal.

staple (2) [steipl], *s.* fibra (*textil*). — *v.t.* clasificar (*hebras*).

staple (3) [steipl], *s.* grapa, armella. — *v.t.* grapar.

stapled [steipld], *a.* de fibra, de hebra; ***long-stapled,*** de hebra larga; ***short-stapled,*** de hebra corta.

stapler (1) [ˈsteiplə], *s.* clasificador de lanas.

stapler (2) [ˈsteiplə], *s.* grapadora.

star [stɑː], *a.* estelar; ***star player,*** superjugador; ***star role,*** papel de protagonista. — *s.* estrella; astro; (*impr.*) asterisco; ***to be born under a lucky star,*** nacer con suerte; ***to thank one's***

lucky stars, darle gracias a Dios; ***North Star*** o ***Pole Star,*** estrella polar; (*bot.*) ***star of Bethlehem,*** leche de gallina; ***Stars and Stripes,*** barras y estrellas, *f.pl.* — *v.t.* estrellar, sembrar de estrellas; (*teat.*) presentar como estrella; señalar con asterisco. — *v.i.* ser estrella.

starboard [ˈstɑːbəd], *a.* de estribor. — *s.* estribor.

starch [stɑːtʃ], *s.* almidón; fécula; (*fig.*) tiesura; ***starch-maker,*** almidonero. — *v.t.* almidonar.

starched [stɑːtʃt], *a.* almidonado; tieso.

starcher [ˈstɑːtʃə], *s.* almidonador.

starch(i)ness [ˈstɑːtʃ(i)nis], *s.* almidonamiento; tiesura.

starchy [ˈstɑːtʃi], *a.* almidonado; de almidón; (*med.*) feculoso; (*fig.*) tieso, entonado.

stardom [ˈstɑːdəm], *s.* estrellato.

stare [stɛə], *s.* mirada fija. — *v.t.* — (***s.o.***) ***in the face,*** saltar a la vista. — *v.i.* — (***at***), mirar fijamente (a), clavar la vista en.

starer [ˈstɛərə], *s.* persona que mira fijamente.

starfish [ˈstɑːfiʃ], *s.* estrella de mar.

star-gazer [ˈstɑː-geizə], *s.* astrónomo; astrólogo; (*fam.*) iluso.

staring [ˈstɛəriŋ], *a.* que mira fijamente; llamativo, chillón; (ojo) saltón.

stark [stɑːk], *a.* tieso, rígido; completo, total, puro; adusto, severo; desnudo, pelado; ***stark nonsense,*** pura tontería. — *adv.* completamente, totalmente; ***stark mad,*** rematadamente loco; ***stark naked,*** completamente desnudo, en cueros vivos.

starless [ˈstɑːlis], *a.* sin estrellas.

starlet [ˈstɑːlit], *s.* aspirante a estrella, estrella novicia.

starlight [ˈstɑːlait], *a.* estrellado. — *s.* luz de las estrellas.

starlike [ˈstɑːlaik], *a.* estrellado; brillante, como una estrella.

starling [ˈstɑːliŋ], *s.* (*orn.*) estornino.

starlit [ˈstɑːlit], *a.* iluminado por las estrellas.

starred [stɑːd], *a.* estrellado; señalado con asterisco; ***ill-starred,*** malhadado.

starry [ˈstɑːri], *a.* estrellado; sembrado de estrellas; ***starry-eyed,*** ilusionado, lleno de ilusión.

star-shaped [ˈstɑː-ʃeipt], *a.* de forma de estrella.

star-shell [ˈstɑː-ʃel], *s.* granada *o* bomba luminosa.

star-spangled [ˈstɑː-spæŋgld], *a.* estrellado.

start [stɑːt], *s.* principio, comienzo; salida; arranque; ventaja; sobresalto, respingo, repullo; ***by fits and starts,*** esporádicamente; ***false start,*** comienzo falso; ***for a start,*** para empezar; ***to get a start on,*** coger la delantera a; ***to get off to a flying start,*** salir viento en popa; empezar estupendamente; ***to give a start,*** pegar un respingo, sobresaltarse; ***to give*** (***s.o., sth.***) ***a start,*** dar (una) ventaja (a); dar un susto (a), sobresaltar; ***to have a good start in life,*** nacer de pie; ***to make a good start in life,*** empezar con éxito la vida de trabajo; ***to make an early start,*** empezar pronto *o* temprano, madrugar. — *v.t.* empezar, comenzar, iniciar, dar comienzo *o* principio a; causar, dar origen a; (*aut. etc.*) poner en marcha, (hacer) arrancar; (*caza*) levantar, ojear; (*carrera*) dar la señal de salida a. — *v.i.* empezar, comenzar; iniciarse; salir, ponerse en camino; arrancar, ponerse en marcha; sobresaltarse, dar *o* pegar un respingo; ***start after,*** salir en persecución de; ***start back,*** emprender el viaje de regreso; ***start*** (***out***) ***for,*** salir para, ponerse en camino hacia; ***start from nothing, start from scratch,*** empezar sin nada *o* de la nada, empezar a cero; empezar desde el principio; ***start off*** o ***out,*** salir, ponerse en camino; ***start on,*** emprender; ***start to,*** empezar a, comenzar a, ponerse a; ***start up,*** arrancar, ponerse en marcha.

starter [ˈstɑːtə], *s.* stárter, juez de salida; (*aut.*) (motor de) arranque.

starting [ˈstɑːtiŋ], *a.* de salida, de partida; de arranque; (*carrera*) ***starting gate,*** barrera de salida; ***starting handle,*** manivela (de arranque); ***starting point,*** punto de partida; ***starting price,*** precio inicial; ***starting switch,*** botón de arranque.

startle [stɑːtl], *v.t.* asustar, sobrecoger; alarmar.

startling [ˈstɑːtliŋ], *a.* alarmante; asombroso, sorprendente; (*color*) chillón; (*vestido*) llamativo.

starvation [stɑːˈveiʃən], *s.* hambre, *f.*; inanición; ***starvation diet,*** régimen de hambre; ***starvation wage,*** salario misérrimo.

starve [stɑːv], *v.t.* matar de hambre; ***starve out,*** rendir por hambre. — *v.i.* morir(se) de hambre; pasar hambre; ***starve to death,*** morir(se) de hambre; ***I'm starving!*** ¡estoy muerto de hambre! — **starve o.s.,** *v.r.* comer poquísimo.

starveling [ˈstɑːvliŋ], *a.* hambriento, muerto de hambre, famélico. — *s.* animal extenuado por el hambre.

starving [ˈstɑːviŋ], *a.* hambriento, famélico.

stash [stæʃ], *v.t.* — ***away,*** esconder, guardar clandestinamente.

state [steit], *a.* del estado, de estado, estatal; de gala. — *s.* estado, condición; fausto, pompa, dignidad; ***in a state of*** (o ***to***), en estado de; ***in state,*** con gran pompa, de gran ceremonia; ***state affairs,*** negocios públicos, *m.pl.*, asuntos de estado, *m.pl.*; ***state control,*** dirección *o* control estatal; ***state education,*** enseñanza pública; ***state of emergency,*** estado de urgencia *o* de excepción; ***state room,*** salón de ceremonias; (*Am.*) ***Secretary of State,*** Ministro de Asuntos Exteriores; (*Am.*) ***State Department,*** Ministerio de Asuntos Exteriores; ***the States,*** (los) Estados Unidos; ***to be in a terrible state,*** estar totalmente deshecho, estar fatal; ***to get into a state,*** ponerse nervioso, exaltarse, perder los estribos; ***to lie in state,*** estar de cuerpo presente; ***what a state of affairs!*** ¡bonito estado de cosas! — *v.t.* afirmar, declarar; decir, manifestar, consignar, hacer constar; exponer, enunciar, aseverar; ***as stated above,*** según consta arriba; ***state a case,*** exponer su opinión *o* criterio; (*documento*) ***state your name and address,*** ponga *o* diga su nombre y dirección.

state-controlled [ˈsteit-kənˈtrould], *a.* regido por el estado.

statecraft [ˈsteitkrɑːft], *s.* política, arte de gobernar.

stated [ˈsteitid], *a.* indicado; establecido, regular, fijo. — *p.p.* [STATE].

statehood [ˈsteithud], *s.* categoría de estado.

stateless [ˈsteitlis], *a.* apátrida.

stateliness [ˈsteitlinis], *s.* grandeza, majestad, pompa, dignidad.

stately [ˈsteitli], *a.* majestuoso, imponente; ***stately home,*** casa solariega.

statement [ˈsteitmənt], *s.* afirmación; declaración; manifestación; relación; informe; (*com.*) estado de cuenta; ***to make a statement,*** prestar declaración, declarar.

stateroom [ˈsteitrum], *s.* (*mar.*) camarote de lujo.

statesman [ˈsteitsmən], *s.* estadista, *m.*, hombre de estado.

statesmanlike [ˈsteitsmənlaik], *a.* (propio) de estadista.

statesmanship [ˈsteitsmənʃip], *s.* arte de gobernar.

static(al) [ˈstætik(əl)], *a.* estático.

statics [ˈstætiks], *s.pl.* estática; (*rad.*) ruidos parásitos *o* atmosféricos, *m.pl.*

station [ˈsteiʃən], *s.* puesto; sitio; condición *o* posición social; ***marry beneath one's station,*** hacer una boda poco lucida; (*f.c.*) estación; (*rad.*) emisora; (*mar.*) apostadero; (*mil.*) puesto militar; punto de marca (en agrimensura); (*igl.*) estación; (*f.c.*) ***station manager,*** (*ant.*), ***station master,*** jefe de estación; ***Stations of the Cross,*** (estaciones de la) Vía Crucis; ***to make the Stations of the Cross,*** hacer la Vía Crucis. — *v.t.* colocar, situar; estacionar; apostar; destinar.

stationary [ˈsteiʃənəri], *a.* estacionario, inmóvil, parado; estantío; (*astron.*) estacional.

stationer [ˈsteiʃənə], *s.* papelero.

stationery [ˈsteiʃənəri], *s.* papelería, efectos de escritorio, *m.pl.*

statistic [stəˈtistik], *s.* estadística, dato; (*pl.*) estadística; estadísticas, *f.pl.*, datos, *m.pl.*

statistical [stəˈtistikəl], *a.* estadístico.

statistician, statist [stætisˈtiʃən, ˈsteitist], *s.* estadístico, experto en estadísticas.

statuary [ˈstætjuəri], *a.* estatuario. — *s.* estatuario; estatuaria, estatuas, *f.pl.*

statue [ˈstætju:], *s.* estatua.

statuesque [stætju:ˈesk], *a.* escultural.

statuette [stætju:ˈet], *s.* figurilla, estatuilla.

stature [ˈstætʃə], *s.* estatura, talla; (*fig.*) ***not to have sufficient stature,*** no dar la talla.

status [ˈsteitəs], *s.* estado; condición; categoría; ***status quo,*** estatu quo; ***status symbol,*** símbolo de prestigio social.

statute [ˈstætju:t], *s.* estatuto, ley, *f.*; ***statute book,*** código de leyes; ***statute law,*** derecho escrito.

statutory [ˈstætjutəri], *a.* reglamentario, estatutario.

staunch [stɔ:ntʃ], *a.* leal, fiel; firme, constante. — *v.t.*, *v.i.* [STANCH].

staunchness [ˈstɔ:ntʃnis], *s.* firmeza, constancia; lealtad.

stave [steiv], *s.* duela (de tonel); palo; (*mús.*) pentagrama, *m.* — *v.t.* — ***in,*** desfondar, hundir; ***stave off,*** evitar, tener a raya; aplazar.

staves [steivz], *s.pl. reg.* [STAVE]. — *pl. irr.* [STAFF].

stay (1) [stei], *s.* estancia, permanencia; visita; suspensión, prórroga. — *v.t.* detener, contener, poner freno a; (*for.*) suspender, aplazar; engañar *o* entretener (*el hambre*); ***stay one's hand,*** contenerse. — *v.i.* quedar(se), permanecer; hospedarse, estar; ***stay for lunch,*** quédese a comer; ***they stayed for the races,*** se quedaron a ver las carreras; ***stay away,*** no ir, no venir, no asomar; no presentarse; ***stay behind,*** quedarse; ***stay in,*** quedarse en casa, no salir; ***stay on,*** seguir, continuar; ***stay out,*** quedarse fuera, no entrar; no participar (***of,*** en); ***stay put,*** seguir en su sitio, no moverse; (*fig.*) seguir erre que erre; ***stay up,*** velar, trasnochar, no acostarse; ***where are you staying?*** ¿dónde estás?

stay (2) [stei], *s.* sostén, soporte, puntal; ballena (*de corsé*); (*pl.*) corsé. — *v.t.* sostener, apuntalar.

stay (3) [stei], *s.* (*mar.*) estay; ***stay-sail,*** vela de estay.

stay-at-home [ˈstei-ət-houm], *a.*, *s.* (hombre) casero *o* que sale poco.

stayer [ˈsteiə], *s.* persona *o* animal de resistencia *o* de aguante.

staying-power [ˈsteiiŋ-pauə], *s.* resistencia, aguante.

stead [sted], *s.* lugar, sitio; ***in his stead,*** en su lugar; ***stand in good stead,*** servir *o* ser útil a.

steadfast [ˈstedfɑ:st], *a.* constante; firme; resuelto.

steadfastness [ˈstedfɑ:stnis], *s.* constancia; firmeza; resolución; fijeza.

steadily [ˈstedili], *adv.* firmemente, fijamente; regularmente; sin parar; sin pestañear; ***steadily better,*** cada vez mejor.

steadiness [ˈstedinis], *s.* firmeza, fijeza; estabilidad; constancia, uniformidad; regularidad; seriedad, formalidad; sensatez; serenidad, sangre fría.

steady [ˈstedi], *a.* firme, fijo; estable; regular, constante, uniforme; ininterrumpido, continuo; serio, formal; sensato; diligente; sereno, tranquilo; ***steady job,*** empleo seguro; ***steady pace,*** paso regular; ***to make steady going,*** hacer constantes progresos. — *adv.* (*fam.*) ***to go steady with s.o.,*** estar en relaciones formales con uno. — *s.* (*fam.*) novio *o* novia (formal). — *v.t.* afianzar, asegurar; estabilizar; calmar, tranquilizar. — *v.i.* afianzarse, estabilizarse; calmarse, tranquilizarse; sentar la cabeza. — **steady o.s.,** *v.r.* (hacer lo posible por) serenarse; ***steady o.s. against sth.,*** apoyarse contra algo, agarrarse a algo. — *interj.* ***steady!*** ¡calma!, ¡tranquilo!, ¡con tiento!, ¡despacio!; ***steady*** (***on***)***!*** ¡calma!, ¡cuidado!

steak [steik], *s.* filete (de carne); ***beef-steak,*** biftec; ***steak and kidney pie,*** empanada de carne con riñones; ***steak house,*** tasca, restaurante (especializado en carne de vaca).

steal [sti:l], *irr. v.t.* robar, hurtar; ***steal a glance*** (***at s.o.***), mirar a hurtadillas; irse a las vistillas; ***steal a march on,*** sorprender; ganar por la mano; ***steal the show,*** llevarse la palma. — *v.i.* — ***along,*** deslizarse sin ruido; ***steal away*** o ***off,*** escabullirse, marcharse a hurtadillas; ***steal down, up, forth, out, in*** o ***into,*** bajar, subir, salir, entrar, meterse a hurtadillas; ***steal up on s.o.,*** acercarse a uno sin hacer ruido.

stealing [ˈsti:liŋ], *s.* robo, hurto.

stealth [stelθ], *s.* sigilo; cautela; ***by stealth,*** a hurtadillas, a escondidas.

stealthily [ˈstelθili], *adv.* a hurtadillas.

stealthiness [ˈstelainis], *s.* sigilo; cautela; (lo) furtivo.

stealthy [ˈstelθi], *a.* furtivo; clandestino, secreto; sigiloso; cauteloso.

steam [sti:m], *s.* vapor, vaho; ***full steam ahead,*** todo avante, a toda máquina; ***high-pressure steam,*** vapor a alta presión; ***steam-chest,*** cámara de vapor; ***steam-dome,*** cámara de distribución; ***steam-engine,*** máquina de vapor; ***steam-gauge,*** manómetro; ***steam-hammer,*** maza de fragua; ***steam-plough,*** arado de vapor; ***steam-whistle,*** silbato, sirena, pito; ***the steam is on,*** hay presión; ***to let off steam,*** (*fig.*) desahogarse; (*lit.*) descargar (el) vapor; ***superheated*** (o ***supercharged***) ***steam,*** vapor recalentado; ***with all steam on,*** a todo vapor. — *v.t.* saturar con vapor; (*coc.*) cocer al vapor; poner en vapor; empañar (*ventanas etc.*). — *v.i.* generar vapor; echar vapor; empañarse; evaporarse.

steamboat [ˈsti:mbout], *s.* vapor, buque de vapor; vapor de río.

steamroller [ˈsti:mroulə], *s.* apisonadora. — *v.t.* ***he steamrollered his way through,*** se abrió paso violentamente; ***they steamrollered the bill through Parliament,*** hicieron aprobar a la fuerza el proyecto de ley, impusieron por la fuerza la aprobación del proyecto de ley.

steamship [ˈsti:mʃip], *s.* vapor, embarcación *o* buque de vapor; ***steamship company,*** compañía naviera.

steamy [ˈsti:mi], *a.* vaporoso; ***atmosphere of steamy heat,*** ambiente de calor húmedo; ***to be steamy,*** hacer un calor húmedo.

stearic [stiˈærik], *a.* esteárico.

stearin [ˈsti:ərin], *s.* estearina.

steatite [ˈsti:ətait], *s.* esteatita.

steed [sti:d], *s.* corcel.

steel [sti:l], *a.* acerado; de acero. — *s.* acero; afilón; eslabón; ***alloy steel,*** acero de aleación; ***cast steel,*** acero colado *o* fundido; ***cold steel,*** arma blanca; ***steel engraving,*** grabado en acero; ***steel industry,*** industria siderúrgica; ***steel mill*** o ***works,*** acería, fábrica de acero; ***steel wool,*** estropajo de aluminio; ***tool steel,*** acero superior para herramientas cortantes. — *v.t.* acerar, revestir de acero; (*fig.*) fortalecer. — **steel o.s.,** *v.r.* (*fig.*) fortalecerse, acorazarse.

steel-clad [ˈsti:l-klæd], *a.* revestido de acero, acorazado.

steeliness [ˈsti:linis], *s.* (lo) acerado; (lo) inflexible, (lo) duro.

steely [ˈsti:li], *a.* acerado, de acero; (*fig.*) inflexible, duro.

steelyard [ˈsti:ljɑ:d], *s.* romana.

steep (1) [sti:p], *a.* escarpado, empinado, abrupto; (*fam.*) fuerte.

steep (2) [sti:p], *v.t.* empapar, impregnar; remojar. — *v.i.* estar en remojo.

steeping [ˈsti:piŋ], *s.* remojo; (el) remojar.

steeple [sti:pl], *s.* campanario, aguja.
steeplechase [ˈsti:pltʃeis], *s.* carrera de obstáculos; carrera de vallas.
steeplejack [ˈsti:pldʒæk], *s.* reparador de campanarios, *etc.*
steeply [ˈsti:pli], *adv.* ***to rise steeply,*** subir fuertemente (*precios*).
steepness [ˈsti:pnis], *s.* (lo) escarpado.
steer (1) [stiə], *s.* novillo; buey (joven).
steer (2) [stiə], *v.t.* dirigir, guiar; conducir (*un coche*); gobernar (*una embarcación*). — *v.i.* conducir; gobernar; ***steer for,*** dirigirse a; ***steer clear of,*** evitar, rehuir.
steerage [ˈstiəridʒ], *s.* entrepuente; tercera clase; gobierno, dirección; ***steerage passenger,*** pasajero de tercera clase; (*mar.*) ***steerage way,*** velocidad mínima; ***to have steerage way,*** tener salida para navegar.
steering [ˈstiəriŋ], *s.* (*mar.*) gobierno; (*aut.*) dirección; ***steering committee,*** junta de iniciativas; (*mar.*) ***steering-wheel,*** rueda del timón; (*aut.*) volante.
steersman [ˈstiəzmən], *s.* (*mar.*) timonel, timonero.
stellar [ˈstelə], *a.* estelar.
stellate [ˈsteleit], *a.* estrellado.
stem [stem], *s.* (*bot.*) tallo; pie (*de copa*); cañón (*de pipa*); (*mec.*) vástago; (*gram.*) tema, *m.*; espiga (*de llave*); (*naut.*) roda, tajamar; ***from stem to stern,*** de proa a popa; (*fig.*) de cabo a rabo. — *v.t.* represar (*agua*); desgranar (*uvas etc.*); contener, detener; ***stem the tide*** o ***torrent,*** contener *o* detener la marea, el torrente. — *v.i.* — ***from,*** provenir de, proceder de, tener su origen en.
stempel, stemple [stempl], *s.* estemple.
stench [stentʃ], *s.* hedor, hediondez, fetidez.
stencil [ˈstensəl], *s.* patrón picado; estarcido. — *v.t.* estarcir.
stenograph [ˈstenogræf], *s.* escrito taquigráfico; máquina estenográfica; (*Am.*) [SHORTHAND].
stenographer [steˈnɔgrəfə], *s.* taquígrafo, estenógrafo.
stenographic [stenoˈgræfik], *a.* estenográfico.
stenography [steˈnɔgrəfi], *s.* taquigrafía, estenografía.
stentor [ˈstentə], *s.* estentor.
stentorian [stenˈtɔ:riən], *a.* estentóreo.
step [step], *s.* paso; pisada; huella; escalón, peldaño, grada; estribo; grado; (*mar.*) carlinga; (*mús.*) intervalo; (*mec.*) rangua; medida, paso, gestión; (*mec.*) ***step-box,*** rangua; ***step-ladder,*** escalera de tijera; ***step by step,*** paso a paso; ***it's a good step,*** es un buen trecho; ***to be in step with,*** llevar el paso con; estar conforme con; ***to be out of step,*** no ir al paso; estar en desacuerdo; estar desfasado; ***to retrace one's steps,*** volver sobre sus pasos, desandar lo andado; ***to take a step,*** dar un paso; ***to take steps to,*** tomar medidas para; ***watch your step!,*** ¡vaya con cuidado!; (*pl.*) escalera; escalinata; ***folding steps,*** escalera de tijera. — *v.t.* escalonar; ***step up,*** aumentar, acelerar. — *v.i.* dar un paso; andar, caminar; pisar; ***step this way,*** pase por aquí; ***step aside,*** apartarse, hacerse a un lado; ***step back,*** dar un paso atrás, retroceder; ***step down,*** bajar; retirarse, renunciar; (*elec.*) ***step-down transformer,*** transformador para reducir voltajes; ***step in,*** entrar; (*fig.*) intervenir; ***step on,*** pisar, hollar; ***step on it,*** darse prisa; (*aut.*) acelerar; ***step out,*** salir; apearse; apretar el paso; ***step over,*** pasar sobre; evitar pisar; ***step up,*** subir.
stepbrother [ˈstepbrʌðə], *s.* hermanastro.
stepchild [ˈsteptʃaild], (*pl.* **stepchildren** [-tʃildrən]) *s.* hijastro, alnado.
stepdaughter [ˈstepdɔ:tə], *s.* hijastra.
stepfather [ˈstepfɑ:ðə], *s.* padrastro.
stephanite [ˈstefənait], *s.* (*min.*) negrillo.
Stephen [ˈsti:vən]. Esteban.
stepmother [ˈstepmʌðə], *s.* madrastra.
stepney [ˈstepni], *s.* (*ant.*) rueda de recambio.
steppe [step], *s.* estepa.
stepping-stone [ˈstepiŋ-stoun], *s.* estriberón; pasadera; (*fig.*) escalón.
stepsister [ˈstepsistə], *s.* media hermana, hermanastra.
stepson [ˈstepsʌn], *s.* hijastro.
stercoraceous [stə:koˈreiʃəs], *a.* estercolizo, estercoráceo.
stere [stiə], *s.* estéreo, metro cúbico.
stereographic [ˈsteriogræfik], *a.* estereográfico.
stereography [steriˈɔgrəfi], *s.* estereografía.
stereometer [steriˈɔmitə], *s.* estereómetro.
stereometry [steriˈɔmitri], *s.* estereometría.
stereophonic [sterioˈfɔnik], *a.* estereofónico.
stereophony [steriˈɔfəni], *s.* estereofonía.
stereoscope [ˈsterioskoup], *s.* estereoscopio.
stereoscopic [sterioˈskɔpik], *a.* estereoscópico.
stereotomy [steriˈɔtəmi], *s.* estereotomía.
stereotype [ˈsteriotaip], *s.* estereotipo, clisé. — *v.t.* estereotipar, clisar.
stereotyper [ˈsteriotaipə], *s.* estereotipador.
stereotyping [ˈsteriotaipiŋ], *s.* estereotipia, clisado.
stereotypography [steriotaiˈpɔgrəfi], *s.* estereotipia.
sterile [ˈsterail], *a.* estéril.
sterility [steˈriliti], *s.* esterilidad.
sterilization [sterilaiˈzeiʃən], *s.* esterilización.
sterilize [ˈsterilaiz], *v.t.* esterilizar.
sterilizer [ˈsterilaizə], *s.* esterilizador.
sterling [ˈstə:liŋ], *a.* de ley, auténtico; de toda confianza; ***pound sterling,*** libra esterlina; ***sterling silver,*** plata de ley. — *s.* libra(s) esterlina(s); ***sterling area,*** area de la libra esterlina.
stern (1) [stə:n], *a.* severo, adusto.
stern (2) [stə:n], *s.* (*mar.*) popa; ***stern-fast,*** codera; ***stern-frame,*** cuaderna; ***stern-post,*** codaste.
sternmost [ˈstə:nmoust], *a.* popel.
sternness [ˈstə:nnis], *s.* severidad, adustez.
sternum [ˈstə:nəm], *s.* esternón.
sternway [ˈstə:nwei], *s.* cía.
stertorous [ˈstə:tərəs], *a.* estertoroso.
stethoscope [ˈsteθəscoup], *s.* estetoscopio.
stethoscopic [steθəˈskɔpik], *a.* estetoscópico.
stethoscopy [steˈθɔskəpi], *s.* estetoscopía.
stetson [ˈstetsən], *s.* sombrero vaquero.
stevedore [ˈsti:vədɔ:], *s.* estibador.
stew [stju:], *s.* (*coc.*) estofado; guisado, guiso; (*fam.*) apuro; atufamiento; ***stew-pan,*** cazuela, cacerola; ***stew-pot,*** olla; (*fam.*) ***to get into a stew,*** apurarse; atufarse. — *v.t.* estofar; guisar; ***stewed fruit,*** compota.
steward [ˈstju:əd], *s.* administrador; mayordomo; camarero.
stewardess [ˈstju:ədes], *s.* (*mar.*) camarera; (*aer.*) azafata, aeromoza.
stewardship [ˈstju:ədʃip], *s.* mayordomía.
sthenic [ˈsθenik], *a.* esténico.
stibium [ˈstibiəm], *s.* estibio.
stick [stik], *s.* palo; bastón; garrote; (*mus., fam.*) batuta; pastilla (*de jabón*); barra (*de lacre*); tallo (*de espárrago etc.*); (*fam.*) ***old stick,*** vejete; ***stick of furniture,*** mueble; (*pl.*) leña, astillas, *f.pl.*; (*mar.*) arboladura. — *irr. v.t.* — (***up, down, together***) pegar, encolar; clavar, hincar; picar, pinchar; (*fam.*) meter, poner; ***stick in,*** meter; ***stick out,*** sacar, asomar; (*fam.*) ***stick it*** (***out***), aguantar(lo) hasta el final; (*fig.*) ***stick one's neck out,*** exponerse, arriesgarse; (*fam.*) ***stick up,*** atracar, asaltar (*para robar*); ***stick 'em up!*** ¡manos arriba!; ***to be stuck for an answer,*** no saber en absoluto qué contestar; ***to get stuck,*** meterse y no poder salir; ***we're stuck with him now,*** ya no podemos quitárnosle de encima. —

v.i. pegarse: adherirse (*to,* a); atascarse; estar cogido, estar enganchado; pararse; estar parado; quedarse; (*fam.*) ***stick around!*** ¡quédate!, espérate por aquí!; ***stick at sth.,*** perseverar con algo; resistirse a hacer algo; ***stick at it!*** ¡persevera!; ***stick at nothing,*** no pararse en barras; ***stick by,*** no abandonar, permanecer fiel a, no fallar; ***stick fast,*** no moverse; ***stick out,*** sobresalir; ***it sticks out a mile,*** salta a la vista, es evidente de toda evidencia; ***stick out for,*** aguantar hasta conseguir; ***stick out like a sore thumb,*** saltar a la vista; ***stick to (s.o.),*** permanecer fiel a; pegarse a; ***stick to (sth.),*** aferrarse a (algo), atenerse a (algo); ***stick to one's guns,*** no dar su brazo a torcer; ***stick together,*** seguir juntos, mantenerse unidos; ***stick up,*** sobresalir, asomar (por encima); ponerse de punta (*los pelos*); ***stick up for,*** defender, sacar la cara por.

sticker [ˈstikə], *s.* persona tenaz y perseverante *o* de tesón; etiqueta engomada; (*Am.*) [LABEL; TAG (I)].

stickiness [ˈstikinis], *s.* pegajosidad; viscosidad; (*fig.*) (lo) difícil.

sticking-plaster [ˈstikiŋ-plɑːstə], *s.* esparadrapo.

stick-in-the-mud [ˈstik-in-ðə-mʌd], *a., s.* retrógrado, carca; rutinario.

stickle [stikl], *v.i.* porfiar por menudencias.

stickleback [ˈstiklbæk], *s.* (*ict.*) espino.

stickler [ˈstiklə], *s.* rigorista, *m.f.*; exigente.

stick-up [ˈstik-ʌp], *s.* (*fam.*) atraco a mano armada.

sticky [ˈstiki], *a.* pegajoso, viscoso; engomado; (*fig.*) bochornoso; difícil; ***to come to a sticky end,*** acabar mal.

stiff [stif], *a.* rígido, tieso; firme; duro; almidonado; espeso; tenso, tirante; entumecido; envarado; exorbitante; fuerte, recio; difícil; frío, etiquetero, estirado; ***stiff breeze,*** brisa fuerte, brisote; ***stiff gale,*** galerna fuerte; ***stiff neck,*** tortícolis, *f.inv.*; ***stiff-necked,*** estirado; testarudo, terco; ***to grow stiff,*** atiesarse; endurecerse; ***to be stiff in the legs,*** tener entumecidas las piernas; ***to be stiff with cold,*** estar aterido; ***to feel stiff,*** tener agujetas; ***stiff upper lip,*** impasibilidad, inmutabilidad. — *s.* persona tiesa, estirada; (*fam.*) cadáver, fiambre; (*fam.*) caballo lento.

stiffen [ˈstifən], *v.t.* poner tieso, atiesar; endurecer; reforzar, fortalecer; espesar; envarar; aterir *o* arrecir de frío. — *v.i.* atiesarse, ponerse tieso; endurecerse; fortalecerse, robustecerse; obstinarse; espesarse; enderezarse; envararse; aterirse *o* arrecirse.

stiffener [ˈstifnə], *s.* contrafuerte; ballena, tensor.

stiffly [ˈstifli], *adv.* fríamente; tiesamente; tercamente.

stiffness [ˈstifnis], *s.* rigidez; tiesura; inflexibilidad; dureza; espesura; entumecimiento; (lo) fuerte; (lo) difícil; (lo) frío *o* estirado.

stifle [staifl], *v.t.* ahogar, sofocar; suprimir. — *v.i.* ahogarse.

stifling [ˈstaifliŋ], *a.* sofocante, ahogador; bochornoso.

stigma [ˈstigmə], *s.* estigma, *m.*; tacha, baldón; desdoro.

stigmatic [stigˈmætik], *a.* (*bot.*) estigmático; de estigma.

stigmatize [ˈstigmətaiz], *v.t.* estigmatizar.

stile (I) [stail], *s.* portillo con escalones.

stile (2) [stail], *s.* (*carp.*) larguero.

stiletto [stiˈletou], *s.* estilete; (*cost.*) ojeteador, punzón; (*zap.*) ***stiletto heel,*** tacón de aguja.

still (I) [stil], *a.* quieto, quedo, inmóvil; ***keep still!*** ¡estate quieto!, ¡no te muevas!; ***stand still,*** estarse quieto, no moverse; ***still life,*** naturaleza muerta, bodegón; (*ant.*) ***still voice,*** voz queda; ***still water,*** agua mansa; ***still waters run deep,*** no te fíes del agua mansa; ***still wine,*** vino no espumoso. — *adv.* todavía, aún; ***he's still there,*** sigue ahí; ***people are still coming in,*** la gente sigue entrando; ***still more,*** aún más, más aún. — *conj.* con todo, a pesar de todo, sin embargo. — *s.* silencio; quietud; (*cine.*) vista fija. — *v.t., v.i.* calmar(se), tranquilizar(se), aquietar(se).

still (2) [stil], *s.* alambique.

stillbirth [ˈstilbəːθ], *s.* parto malogrado.

stillborn [ˈstilbɔːn], *a.* nacido muerto; (*fig.*) frustrado, (*proyecto*) malogrado; (*fig.*) ***to be stillborn,*** no cuajar; ***his plans were stillborn,*** sus proyectos no cuajaron *o* se quedaron en agua de borrajas *o* cerrajas.

stillness [ˈstilnis], *s.* inmovilidad; quietud; tranquilidad.

stilly [ˈstili], *a.* (*poét.*) [STILL (I)].

stilt [stilt], *s.* zanco.

stilted [ˈstiltid], *a.* afectado, altisonante.

stimulant [ˈstimjulənt], *a., s.* estimulante.

stimie [STYMIE].

stimied [STYMIED].

stimulant [ˈstimjulənt], *a., s.* estimulante.

stimulate [ˈstimjuleit], *v.t.* estimular; fomentar, favorecer.

stimulation [stimjuˈleiʃən], *s.* estímulo; fomento.

stimulating [ˈstimjuleitiŋ], *a.* estimulante; sugestivo, sugeridor.

stimulative [ˈstimjulətiv], *a.* estimulante, estimulador. — *s.* estímulo.

stimulus [ˈstimjuləs], *s.* (*pl.* **stimuli** [-lai]) estímulo; incentivo, aliciente.

sting [stiŋ], *s.* aguijón; picadura; escozor, picazón; (*remordimiento*) punzada. — *irr. v.t.* picar; pinchar; escocer; remorder (*la conciencia*); (*fam.*) clavar. — *v.i.* picar, escocer.

stinginess [ˈstindʒinis], *s.* tacañería.

stinging-nettle [ˈstiŋiŋ-netl], *s.* ortiga.

stingy [ˈstindʒi], *a.* tacaño, miserable.

stink [stiŋk], *s.* hedor, mal olor; ***stink-bomb,*** bomba fétida; (*despec.*) ***stink-pot,*** persona maloliente; (*fam.*) ***to raise a stink,*** poner el grito en el cielo, armarla. — *irr. v.t.* — **out,** hacer oler muy mal, hacer que apeste. — *v.i.* heder, apestar, oler muy mal.

stinker [ˈstiŋkə], *s.* (*fam.*) canalla, *m.*

stinking [ˈstiŋkiŋ], *a.* hediondo, apestoso. — *adv.* ***to be stinking rich,*** ser (un) ricachón, estar podrido de dinero.

stint [stint], *s.* sesión *o* turno (*de trabajo*); ***to do a good stint,*** hacer una buena sesión. — *v.t.* escatimar. — *v.i.* escatimar, ser mezquino *o* miserable. — **stint o.s.,** *v.r.* estrecharse, apretarse el cinturón.

stipe [staip], *s.* estipe.

stipend [ˈstaipend], *s.* estipendio.

stipendiary [staiˈpendiəri], *a., s.* estipendiario.

stipple [stipl], *s.* punteado. — *v.t., v.i.* puntear.

stippling [ˈstipliŋ], *s.* graneo, punteado.

stipulate [ˈstipjuleit], *v.t.* estipular, especificar, particularizar.

stipulation [stipjuˈleiʃən], *s.* estipulación, requisito.

stipule [ˈstipjuːl], *s.* estípula.

stir [stəː], *s.* revuelo; conmoción; agitación; sensación; ***to cause a stir,*** causar sensación. — *v.t.* remover; agitar; menear; revolver; mover; hurgar; despertar, conmover; ***stir up,*** excitar; ***stir before use,*** agítese antes de usarse; ***stir the fire,*** atizar, avivar la lumbre. — *v.i.* moverse, menearse; ponerse en movimiento, levantarse (de la cama).

stirrer [ˈstəːrə], *s.* agitador; excitador; mecedor (*de líquidos*); ***early stirrer,*** madrugador.

stirring [ˈstəːriŋ], *a.* apasionante, emocionante; inspirador.

stirrup [ˈstirəp], *s.* estribo; (*zap.*) tirapié; (*mar.*) estribo; ***stirrup-leather,*** ación.

stitch [stitʃ], *s.* punto, puntada; (*cir.*) punto (de sutura); (*dolor*) punzada, calambre; (*agric.*) caballón; ***a stitch in time saves nine,*** una puntada a tiempo . . .; ***not a stitch on,*** en cueros vivos; (*fam.*) ***he is in stitches,*** se desternilla de risa. — *v.t.* coser; (*cir.*) suturar; ***stitch up,*** remendar.

stitcher [ˈstitʃə], *s.* cosedor, cosedora; ribeteadora.

stitching [ˈstitʃiŋ], *s.* puntos, *m.pl.*, puntadas, *f.pl.*; costura; pespunte, punto atrás.

stoat [stout], *s.* armiño.

stock [stɔk], *a.* de surtido; (*fig.*) ***stock answer,*** respuesta consagrada. — *s.* (*finanzas y comercio*) provisión, surtido, existencia; inventario; capital, caudal; título, bono, acción, valores, *m.pl.*; enseres, *m.pl.*, muebles, *m.pl.*; [LIVESTOCK]; patrón (*de injerto*); estirpe, linaje, raza, tronco; cepa; (*de fusil*) caja, culata; (*bot.*) alhelí; (*coc.*) caldo; (*f.c.*) ***rolling stock,*** material rodante; (*mec.*) terraja; cepo (*del ancla, del yunque*); corbatín, alzacuello; (*teat.*) repertorio; (*pl.*) cepo (*castigo*); (*mar.*) grada de construcción, astillero; (*finanzas*) valores públicos, *m.pl.*; ***stock company,*** (*com.*) sociedad de valores, (*teat.*) compañía de repertorio; ***Stock Exchange,*** Bolsa de valores; ***stock jobber,*** agiotista, *m.*; ***stock jobbing,*** agiotaje; ***stock taking,*** inventario, balance; ***stock turnover,*** movimiento de existencias; ***in stock,*** hay existencias; ***it's his stock in trade,*** es lo suyo, es su oficio; ***out of stock,*** vendido, agotado; ***to take stock,*** hacer inventario; (*fig.*) ***to take stock of,*** evaluar, hacer apreciación de; ***to be in the stocks,*** estar en la picota; (*fig.*) ***to be on the stocks,*** estar preparándose; (*fig.*) ***to have on the stocks,*** estar preparando. — *v.t.* abastecer, proveer, surtir; tener existencias de; poblar, sembrar de; almacenar; tener en almacén; vender, trabajar.

stockade [stɔˈkeid], *s.* estacada, empalizada. — *v.t.* empalizar, rodear de empalizadas.

stock-breeder [ˈstɔk-bri:də], *s.* ganadero.

stock-breeding [ˈstɔk-bri:diŋ], *s.* ganadería.

stockbroker [ˈstɔkbroukə], *s.* corredor de valores; bolsista, *m.*

stock-dove [ˈstɔk-dʌv], *s.* paloma torcaz.

stockfish [ˈstɔkfiʃ], *s.* bacalao seco, pejepalo.

stockholder [ˈstɔkhouldə], *s.* accionista, *m.f.*

Stockholm [ˈstɔkhoum]. Estocolmo.

stockinet [stɔkiˈnet], *s.* tejido de punto.

stocking [ˈstɔkiŋ], *s.* media.

stockist [ˈstɔkist], *s.* distribuidor.

stockmarket [ˈstɔkmɑ:kit], *s.* bolsa, mercado de valores.

stock-pile [ˈstɔk-pail], *s.* reserva, acopio, acumulación. — *v.t.* hacer acopio de, acumular.

stockroom [ˈstɔkrum], *s.* almacén.

stock-still [ˈstɔk-ˈstil], *a.* totalmente inmóvil.

stocky [ˈstɔki], *a.* rechoncho, achaparrado.

stodgy [ˈstɔdʒi], *a.* pesado, apelmazado, amazacotado; ***stodgy lump of stuff,*** ladrillazo.

Stoic [ˈstouik], *s.* estoico.

stoic(al) [ˈstouik(əl)], *a.* estoico.

stoicism [ˈstouisizəm], *s.* estoicismo.

stoke [stouk], *v.t.* alimentar, cebar; atizar, avivar.

stokehold [ˈstoukhould], *s.* (*mar.*) sala de calderas.

stoker [ˈstoukə], *s.* fogonero.

stole (1) [stoul], *s.* estola.

stole (2) [stoul], **stolen** [ˈstoulən], *pret.*, *p.p.* [STEAL].

stolid [ˈstɔlid], *a.* cachazudo, flemático; impasible.

stolidity [stɔˈliditi], *s.* cachaza, flema; impasibilidad.

stolon [ˈstoulɔn], *s.* estolón.

stoma [ˈstoumə], *s.* (*pl.* **stomata** [-tə]) estoma, *m.*

stomach [ˈstʌmək], *s.* estómago; ***it turns my stomach,*** me revuelve el estómago *o* las tripas; ***stomach upset,*** trastorno de tripa; ***to have a stomach upset,*** tener mal el estómago. — *v.t.* tragar, aguantar.

stomachal [ˈstʌməkəl], *a.* estomacal.

stomacher [ˈstʌməkə], *s.* peto, estomaguero.

stomachic [stoˈmækik], *a.*, *s.* estomocal.

stomatitis [stouməˈtaitis], *s.* estomatitis, *f.*

stomp [stɔmp], *v.i.* — ***about,*** andar pegando patadas.

stone [stoun], *a.* de piedra. — *s.* piedra; lápida, piedra sepulcral; (*joya*) piedra preciosa; (*med.*) piedra, cálculo; (*de las frutas*) hueso; (*Ingl.*) (peso de) 14 libras; ***flint stone,*** pedernal; ***stone-breaker*** o ***stone-crusher,*** picapedrero; trituradora de piedra; ***stone-chat,*** collalba; ***stone-crop,*** chubarba, fabacrasa, ombligo de Venus; ***stone-cutter,*** picapedrero, cantero; ***stone-fruit,*** fruta de hueso; ***stone-mason,*** albañil; cantero; ***stone-pit*** *o* ***stone-quarry,*** cantera; ***to leave no stone unturned,*** remover Roma con Santiago; ***within a stone's throw,*** muy cerca, al lado. — *v.t.* apedrear, lapidar; deshuesar (*la fruta*).

stone-blind [ˈstoun-ˈblaind], *a.* completamente ciego.

stone-cold [ˈstoun-ˈkould], *a.* frío como la piedra.

stone-dead [ˈstoun-ˈded], *a.* muerto como una piedra.

stone-deaf [ˈstoun-ˈdef], *a.* sordo como una tapia.

stone-dumb [ˈstoun-ˈdʌm], *a.* completamente mudo.

stoneware [ˈstounwɛə], *s.* gres, *m.*

stonework [ˈstounwə:k], *s.* obra de sillería.

stoniness [ˈstouninis], *s.* carácter pedregoso *o* pétreo; dureza, inflexibilidad, insensibilidad.

stony [ˈstouni], *a.* pétreo; pedregoso; como la *o* una piedra; (*fig.*) empedernido; (*fig.*) frío, glacial; (*fam.*) ***to be stony broke,*** estar tronado, sin blanca; ***stony-hearted,*** duro de corazón.

stooge [stu:dʒ], *s.* hombre de paja; paniaguado; fantoche, pelele.

stook [stuk], *s.* tresnal. — *v.t.* apilar en tresnales.

stool [stu:l], *s.* taburete, escabel; sillico; (*bot.*) planta madre; cimbel, señuelo; (*med.*) cámaras, defecaciones, *f.pl.*; ***to go to stool,*** hacer del cuerpo; (*fam.*) ***stool pigeon,*** gancho; (*fam.*) soplón, espía, *m.f.* — *v.i.* (*med.*) hacer del cuerpo; (*bot.*) echar renuevos.

stoop (1) [stu:p], *s.* inclinación, cargazón de espaldas; rebajamiento; ***to walk with a stoop,*** andar encorvado. — *v.t.* inclinar, bajar, abatir. — *v.i.* inclinarse, encorvarse; andar encorvado; ser cargado de espaldas; ***stoop to,*** rebajarse a.

stoop (2) [stu:p], *s.* (*Am.*) escalinata de entrada.

stooping [ˈstu:piŋ], *a.* inclinado; encorvado; doblado; cargado (de espaldas). — *s.* inclinación.

stop [stɔp], *s.* parada; alto; pausa; paro; detención; estancia; escala; apeadero; registro (*órgano*); llave (*instrumento de viento*); traste (*guitarra*); punto; tapón; tarugo; (*consonante*) oclusiva; estorbo, impedimento; coto; (*mec.*) tope, retén, fiador; (*ópt.*) diafragma, *m.*; ***full stop,*** punto final; ***dead stop,*** parada en seco; ***request stop,*** parada discrecional; ***without a stop,*** sin parar; ***to come to a stop,*** pararse, venir a parar; ***to put a stop to,*** atajar, poner fin a; (*fig.*) ***to pull out all the stops,*** echar el resto, poner toda la carne en el asador; ***stop press,*** noticias de última hora, *f.pl.*; al cerrar (*la edición*); ***stop sign(al),*** señal de alto *o* parada; ***stop valve,*** válvula de cierre *o* de regulación; ***stop watch,*** cronómetro. — *v.t.* parar, detener; contener; estorbar; evitar, impedir; terminar, poner fin a; suspender, cancelar, cortar, interrumpir; dejar de; tapar, cerrar, cegar; empastar (*una muela*); ***stop up,*** obstruir, bloquear; atascar, represar; ***stop thief!*** ¡al ladrón!; ***stop it!*** ¡déjate de eso!, ¡basta!, ¡basta ya!; ***stop that noise!*** ¡suprimir ese ruido!, ¡basta ya de ruido!, ¡ya está bien de ruido!; ***stop a gap,*** tapar un hueco; ***stop s.o.'s mouth,*** taparle la boca a alguien; ***stop one's ears,*** taparse los oídos; ***there is nothing to stop me,*** no hay nada que me lo impida; ***stop s.o. (from) doing sth.,*** impedir a uno hacer *o* que haga algo; ***he stopped himself stealing with a great deal of effort,*** haciendo un gran esfuerzo, se abstuvo de robar; ***he was going to blurt it out but stopped***

himself in time, se le iba la lengua, pero reaccionó a tiempo; ***I have stopped smoking,*** he dejado de fumar; ***she never stops talking,*** no para de hablar, habla sin parar; ***stop sth. happening,*** evitar que ocurra algo; ***stop (payment on) a cheque,*** (dar orden de) suspender el pago de un cheque; ***stop the electricity supply,*** cortar el suministro de electricidad; ***stop all leave,*** cancelar todos los permisos. — *v.i.* parar(se), detenerse; hacer alto; cesar; acabarse, terminarse; cortarse; interrumpirse; quedarse, alojarse; ***I'm stopping with my brother,*** me hospedo, estoy *o* paro en casa de mi hermano: ***stop at nothing,*** no pararse en barras; ***stop away,*** ausentarse, no asistir; ***stop by,*** pasarse (por), pasar brevemente; ***stop dead*** o ***short,*** pararse en seco; ***stop in,*** quedarse en casa; ***stop over,*** pasar la noche; hacer parada *o* escala; ***stop up,*** seguir levantado, no acostarse. — **stop o.s.,** *v.r.* ***I stopped myself in time,*** me detuve a tiempo. — *interj.* ¡pare!, ¡alto!

stopcock [ˈstɔpkɔk], *s.* llave *o* espita de paso *o* cierre.

stop-gap [ˈstɔp-gæp], *s.* recurso temporal sustituto; (*fam.*) tapaagujeros, *m.inv.*

stopover [ˈstɔpouvə], *s.* parada intermedia.

stoppage [ˈstɔpidʒ], *s.* paro; suspensión; cesación; detención; huelga; (*med.*) oclusión.

stopper [ˈstɔpə], *s.* tapón; taco, tarugo; obturador, tapador; (*mar.*) boza. — *v.t.* (en)taponar, tapar.

stopping [ˈstɔpiŋ], *s.* empaste (de un diente); ***stopping-place,*** escala.

stopple [stɔpl], *s.* tapón. — *v.t.* entaponar, cerrar con tapón.

storage [ˈstɔːridʒ], *s.* almacenaje.

storax [ˈstɔːræks], *s.* estoraque; ***storax-tree,*** estoraque.

store [ˈstɔː], *s.* acopio, provisión; almacén, depósito; tienda, almacén; (*pl.*) víveres, *m.pl.*, provisiones, *f.pl.*; bastimentos, *m.pl.*, municiones, *f.pl.*; ***army stores,*** pertrechos de guerra, *m.pl.*; ***what is in store for me?*** ¿qué me espera?, ¿qué me tienen reservado?; ***what do you have in store for him?*** ¿qué le tenéis reservado?; ***to put*** o ***set great store by,*** dar *o* conceder mucha importancia a. — *v.t.* almacenar; tener guardado; ***store away,*** guardar; archivar; ***store up,*** acumular.

storehouse [ˈstɔːhaus], *s.* almacén, depósito; (*fig.*) mina, acervo.

storekeeper [ˈstɔːkiːpə], *s.* almacenista, *m.f.*, almacenero, guardalmacén; tendero, comerciante; (*mar.*) pañolero.

storeroom [ˈstɔːruːm], *s.* despensa; (*mar.*) pañol de víveres.

store-ship [ˈstɔː-ʃip], *s.* buque nodriza.

storey [ˈstɔːri], *s.* piso, planta; ***four-storey house,*** casa de cuatro pisos.

storied [ˈstɔːrid], *a.* que tiene pisos, de (tantos) pisos; ***three-storied,*** de tres pisos.

stork [stɔːk], *s.* cigüeña.

stork's-bill [ˈstɔːks-bil], *s.* (*bot.*) geranio.

storm [stɔːm], *s.* tormenta, temporal; ***rain storm,*** temporal de lluvia(s); ***snow storm,*** temporal de nieve(s); ***wind storm,*** tempestad; ***storm cloud,*** nubarrón; ***storm of laughter,*** explosión de risas; ***storm of protest,*** lluvia de protestas; ***storm troops,*** tropas de asalto, *f.pl.*; (*fig.*) ***to raise a storm,*** provocar *u* originar mucho revuelo; (*mil.*) ***to take by storm,*** tomar por asalto; (*fam.*) ***storm in a tea-cup,*** tormenta *o* tempestad en un vaso de agua. — *v.t.* (*mil.*) asaltar, tomar por asalto. — *v.i.* rabiar, despotricar, tronar (***at,*** contra).

storminess [ˈstɔːminis], *s.* (lo) tempestuoso *etc.*

stormy [ˈstɔːmi], *a.* tempestuoso, borrascoso; turbulento, violento.

story (1) [ˈstɔːri], *s.* historia; cuento; anécdota; trama, argumento; (*fam.*) bola, embuste; ***fairy story,*** cuento de hadas; ***true story,*** historia verdadera *o* verídica; ***funny story,*** chiste; ***that's quite another story,*** ésa es harina de otro costal; ***as the story goes,*** según cuenta la historia; ***story-teller,*** cuentista, *m.f.*

story (2) [STOREY].

stoup [stuːp], *s.* pila (de agua bendita).

stout [staut], *a.* fuerte, recio; macizo; gordo; fornido; valiente, animoso; resuelto; firme; ***stout-hearted,*** valiente, resuelto. — *s.* cerveza negra fuerte.

stoutness [ˈstautnis], *s.* gordura, (lo) gordo; valor; solidez.

stove (1) [stouv], *pret., p.p.* [STAVE].

stove (2) [stouv], *s.* estufa; hornilla, cocina.

stow [stou], *v.t.* meter, poner, colocar; hacinar; (*mar.*) estibar, arrumar; ***stow away,*** esconder, guardar. — *v.i.* — ***away,*** viajar de polizón.

stowage [ˈstouidʒ], *s.* estiba, arrumaje; bodega; almacenaje.

stowaway [ˈstouəwei], *s.* polizón, llovido.

stower [ˈstouə], *s.* estibador.

strabismus [strəˈbizməs], *s.* estrabismo.

Strabo [ˈstreibou]. Estrabón.

straddle [ˈstrædl], *s.* actitud equívoca; (*com.*) operación de bolsa con opción de compra y venta. — *v.t.* montar a horcajadas sobre; estar a caballo sobre; llenar por todas partes; (*artill.*) horquillar (*el blanco*).

Stradivarius [strædiˈvɛəriəs]. Estradivario.

strafe [strɑːf], *v.t.* bombardear intensamente; ametrallar en vuelo bajo.

straggle [strægl], *v.i.* extraviarse; dispersarse; rezagarse; desparramarse; estar disperso *o* esparcido; ***straggling branches,*** ramas dispersas, *f.pl.*; ***straggling soldier,*** soldado rezagado.

straggler [ˈstræglə], *s.* rezagado; extraviado; rama extendida; objeto aislado.

straggling, straggly [ˈstrægliŋ, -li], *a.* rezagado; disperso; esparcido.

straight [streit], *a.* recto; derecho; erguido; lacio (*pelo*); honrado; franco; sencillo; serio; puro (*bebida*); en orden, en regla; ***as straight as a die,*** más derecho que una vela; ***let me be straight with you,*** te voy a ser franco; ***let's get things straight,*** vamos a concretar *o* a puntualizar, vamos a poner los puntos sobre las íes, vamos a ver si nos entendemos, entendámonos; ***straight answer,*** respuesta directa; ***straight face,*** cara seria; ***straight fight,*** lucha limpia; ***straight whisky,*** whisky a secas; ***to put things straight,*** poner en orden *o* arreglar *u* ordenar las cosas. — *adv.* directo, directamente; inmediatamente; francamente; puro, sin mezcla; ***straight ahead*** o ***on,*** todo recto, todo seguido; ***straight away*** o ***off,*** en seguida, inmediatamente; ***to come straight to the point,*** ir directamente al grano; ***to go straight,*** enmendarse; vivir dentro de la ley; ir en línea recta; ***to go straight home,*** irse derecho a casa; ***to look s.o. straight in the eye,*** mirarle a alguien a la cara. — *s.* (*póker*) escalera; ***the straight,*** la recta; ***the straight and narrow,*** el buen camino.

straighten [streitn], *v.t.* enderezar, poner derecho; poner en orden; ***straighten out,*** resolver, desenmarañar. — *v.i.* — ***up,*** enderezarse; erguirse.

straightforward [streitˈfɔːwəd], *a.* sencillo, sin complicaciones; abierto, sin recámara; franco.

straightforwardness [streitˈfɔːwədnis], *s.* sencillez.

straightness [ˈstreitnis], *s.* rectitud, derechura; honradez.

straightway [ˈstreitwei], *adv.* en seguida, inmediatamente.

strain (1) [strein], *s.* estirpe, linaje; elemento; ***strain of madness,*** vena de locura.

strain (2) [strein], *s.* tensión, tirantez; esfuerzo (excesivo); fatiga; torcedura; torsión, deformación; carga; presión; tenor, estilo; (*pl., mús.*) son, acordes, *m.pl.*; ***mental strain,*** agotamiento nervioso; ***in the same strain,*** del mismo tenor; ***to be a strain on one's credulity,*** ser sumamente inverosímil; ***to put a strain on sth.,*** pedir *o* exigir mucho a, cargar mucho a; ***to take the strain of sth.,*** llevar el peso de algo. — *v.t.* estirar, tensar, poner tirante; deformar; torcerse (*músculo, ligamento etc.*); cansar (*la vista*); abusar de; forzar, hacer violencia a; hacer tirante, crear tirantez en; aguzar (*el oído*); filtrar, colar; ***strain one's eyes to see,*** forzar la vista para ver; esforzarse por ver; ***strain courtesy,*** extremar la cortesía; ***strain a point,*** hacer una excepción *o* concesión; ***strain the law to help s.o.,*** hacer violencia a la ley para ayudar a alguien. — *v.i.* esforzarse; padecer; colar; ***strain to,*** hacer grandes esfuerzos para; (*fig.*) ***strain at the leash (to),*** tener una impaciencia loca (por).

strained [streind], *a.* tirante, de mucha tirantez; ***strained atmosphere,*** ambiente tirante *o* en que se nota mucha tirantez; ***strained muscle,*** músculo forzado; ***strained relations,*** relaciones tirantes, *f.pl.*; ***strained smile,*** sonrisa forzada.

strainer [ˈstreinə], *s.* colador.

strait [streit], *a.* ***strait-jacket,*** camisa de fuerza; ***strait-laced,*** estricto, severo; gazmoño. — *s.* (*geog.*) estrecho; (*pl.*) (*geog.*) estrecho; apuro, aprieto; ***to be in dire straits,*** verse sumamente apurado; encontrarse en una situación sumamente comprometida.

straiten [streitn], *v.t.* estrechar.

straitened [streitnd], *a.* ***to live in straitened circumstances,*** vivir con estrechez *o* con estrecheces.

strake [streik], *s.* traca.

stramonium [strəˈmouniəm], *s.* estramonio.

strand (1) [strænd], *s.* arenal, playa. — *v.t.* varar; ***to be stranded,*** quedarse desamparado *o* colgado *o* sin medio de transporte; ***to leave stranded,*** dejar colgado *o* en la estacada. — *v.i.* encallar; varar(se).

strand (2) [strænd], *s.* hebra, filamento; cabo, ramal.

strange [streindʒ], *a.* extraño, raro, peregrino; nuevo, desconocido; ***he's strange to this sort of thing,*** esto es nuevo para él.

strangely [ˈstreindʒli], *adv.* de una manera rara.

strangeness [ˈstreindʒnis], *s.* rareza, (lo) raro, (lo) extraño; novedad.

stranger [ˈstreindʒə], *s.* desconocido; forastero; extraño; ***he's a stranger to me,*** para mí es desconocido, no lo conozco; ***he's no stranger to hunger,*** ha pasado muchas hambres.

strangle [stræŋgl], *v.t.* estrangular; ahogar.

stranglehold [ˈstræŋglhould], *s.* (*dep.*) collar de fuerza; (*fig.*) dominio total; ***to have a stranglehold on,*** tener asido por la garganta; (*fig.*) tener totalmente dominado.

strangler [ˈstræŋglə], *s.* estrangulador.

strangulated [ˈstræŋgjuleitid], *a.* (*med.*) estrangulado.

strangulation [stræŋgjuˈleiʃən], *s.* estrangulación; ahogamiento.

strap [stræp], *s.* correa; tira, banda; trabilla; (*fam.*) ***strap-hanger,*** persona que viaja de pie en un tren *etc.* (y que se agarra a las correas que cuelgan del techo); ***shoulder-strap,*** tirante; (*mil.*) capona. — *v.t.* atar con correa.

strapless [ˈstræplis], *a.* sin trabillas.

strapping [ˈstræpiŋ], *a.* (*fam.*) robusto; fuertote, fornido; ***strapping fellow,*** muchacho grandullón, chicarrón.

Strasbourg [ˈstræzbəːg]. Estrasburgo.

strata [ˈstrɑːtə, ˈstreitə], *s.pl.* [STRATUM].

stratagem [ˈstrætədʒəm], *s.* estratagema, *f.*

strategic [strəˈtiːdʒik], *a.* estratégico.

strategist [ˈstrætidʒist], *s.* estratega, *m.*, estratégico.

strategy [ˈstrætidʒi], *s.* estrategia.

strath [stræθ], *s.* (*Esco.*) valle extenso.

stratification [strætifiˈkeiʃən], *s.* estratificación.

stratiform [ˈstrætifɔːm], *a.* estratiforme.

stratify [ˈstrætifai], *v.t.* estratificar.

stratigraphic(al) [strætiˈgræfik(əl)], *a.* estratigráfico.

stratigraphy [strəˈtigrəfi], *s.* estratigrafía.

stratocracy [strəˈtɔkrəsi], *s.* dictadura militar.

stratocruiser [ˈstrætokruːzə], *s.* avión estratosférico.

stratosphere [ˈstrætosfiə], *s.* estratosfera.

stratum [ˈstrɑːtəm, ˈstreitəm], *s.* (*pl.* **strata** [ˈstrɑːtə, ˈstreitə]) estrato; capa; ***social strata,*** estratos (*m.pl.*) *o* categorías (*f.pl.*) *o* niveles (*m.pl.*) sociales.

stratus [ˈstreitəs], *s.* estrato.

straw [strɔː], *a.* de paja; pajizo; falso, simulado; ***straw bed,*** jergón de paja; ***straw hat,*** sombrero de paja. — *s.* paja; pajita; ***a straw in the wind,*** un indicio de cómo van las cosas; ***I don't care a straw,*** me importa un comino; ***it's not worth a straw,*** no vale un higo; ***it's the last straw!*** ¡es el colmo!; ***straw-coloured,*** pajizo, de color paja; ***straw-loft,*** pajar, pajera, almiar; ***straw-worm,*** gorgojo; ***to clutch at a straw,*** agarrarse a un clavo ardiendo; ***to drink through a straw,*** sorber con una pajita; ***the last straw breaks the camel's back,*** la bestia cargada, el sobornal la mata.

strawberry [ˈstrɔːbəri], *s.* fresa; fresón; ***strawberry-tree,*** madroño.

strawy [ˈstrɔːi], *a.* pajizo, hecho de paja.

stray [strei], *a.* extraviado, descarriado; perdido; aislado, inconexo; ***a few stray instances,*** unos cuantos casos aislados; ***stray bullet,*** bala perdida. — *s.* animal extraviado; niño desamparado; (*pl.*) (*rad.*) parásitos, *m.pl.* — *v.i.* descarriarse, extraviarse; perderse; vagar, errar.

streak [striːk], *s.* raya; lista; faja; línea; veta, vena; racha; (*min.*) raspadura (*mar.*) hilada; ***streak of lightning,*** relámpago; ***streak of madness,*** vena de locura; ***to have a yellow streak,*** tener una veta de cobardía. — *v.t.* rayar, listar, gayar. — *v.i.* ir como un rayo; ***streak past,*** pasar como un rayo.

streaky [ˈstriːki], *a.* rayado, listado; entreverado.

stream [striːm], *s.* corriente; arroyo, riachuelo; río; torrente, raudal; flujo, chorro; riada; rayo; curso; grupo (*colegio*); ***against the stream,*** contra la corriente; ***down stream,*** río abajo; ***in a continuous stream,*** ininterrumpidamente; ***in streams,*** en tropel; ***stream anchor,*** anclote; ***stream tin,*** casiterita de aluvión; ***up stream,*** río arriba. — *v.t.* verter, derramar; clasificar en grupos. — *v.i.* correr, fluir, manar; flamear, tremolar; ***her hair was streaming in the wind,*** el pelo le flotaba en el aire; ***eyes streaming with tears,*** ojos arrasados de lágrimas; ***stream out,*** salir a chorros *o* en tropel.

streamer [ˈstriːmə], *s.* flámula, gallardete, banderola; serpentina.

streamlet [ˈstriːmlit], *s.* arroyuelo, hilo de agua.

streamline [ˈstriːmlain], *v.t.* aerodinamizar; (*fig.*) perfilar; perfeccionar, hacer más eficaz.

streamlined [ˈstrːimlaind], *a.* aerodinámico, fuselado.

streamy [ˈstriːmi], *a.* surcado de arroyos.

street [striːt], *s.* calle; ***at street level,*** a nivel de la calle; a ras de la calle; ***cross street,*** travesía; (*fig.*) ***he's streets ahead of him,*** le da ciento y raya; ***high street, main street,*** calle mayor, calle real; (*fig.*) ***it's right up my street,*** de eso entiendo mucho; esto es lo mío; esto es justo lo que a mí me gusta; ***one-way street,*** calle de dirección única; ***side-street,*** calle lateral; bocacalle; ***street accident,*** accidente de circulación; ***street door,*** puerta de la calle; ***street lamp,*** farol; ***street lighting,*** alumbrado público; ***street musician,*** músico callejero; ***street railway,*** tranvía, *m.*, ferrocarril urbano; ***streetwalker,*** buscona, puta callejera; ***the man in the street,*** el hombre de la calle; (*fam.*) ***to be on***

Queer Street, estar tronado; (*fig.*) ***to be streets ahead of s.o.,*** aventajar con mucho a alguien.
streetcar [ˈstriːtkɑː], (*Am.*) [TRAM-CAR].
strength [streŋθ], *s.* fuerza, vigor; robustez, consistencia, solidez; potencia; resistencia; intensidad; número (*de tropas etc.*); ***give me strength!*** ¡Dios me dé paciencia!; ***he is working at full strength,*** está trabajando a todo trabajar *o* a todo tren; ***my strength is exhausted,*** se me acabaron las fuerzas; ***on the strength of this . . .,*** basándose en esto; ***strength of character,*** firmeza de carácter; ***strength of mind,*** fortaleza espiritual; (*finanzas*) ***strength of the pound,*** valor *o* pujanza de la libra; (*mec. etc.*) ***to be (working) at full strength,*** funcionar a máxima potencia; ***to come in strength,*** venir en número nutrido; ***to save one's strength,*** conservar las fuerzas.
strengthen [ˈstreŋθən], *v.t.* fortalecer, vigorizar, robustecer; reforzar; fortificar; confirmar.
strenuous [ˈstrenjuəs], *a.* arduo, de mucho esfuerzo, que exige mucho esfuerzo; enérgico.
strenuousness [ˈstrenjuəsnis], *s.* (lo) arduo.
streptococcus [streptoˈkɔkəs], *s.* (*pl.* **streptococci** [-kai]) estreptococo.
streptomycin [streptoˈmaisin], *s.* estreptomicina.
stress [stres], *s.* tensión; presión; esfuerzo; (*gram.*) acento; ***to lay stress upon,*** hacer hincapié en, dar (mucha) importancia a, poner de relieve. — *v.t.* subrayar, recalcar, insistir en; (*gram.*) acentuar; (*mec.*) tensar.
stretch [stretʃ], *s.* estirón; elasticidad; esfuerzo (*de la imaginación*); extensión, trecho, tramo (*de carretera etc.*); período, lapso (*de tiempo*); ***at a stretch,*** de un tirón; ***by no stretch of the imagination,*** ni remotamente; ***for hours at a stretch,*** hora tras hora, durante horas (sin interrupción); ***for three days at a stretch,*** durante tres dias sin interrupcion; ***to work at full stretch,*** trabajar a todo tren *o* a velocidad máxima. — *v.t.* estirar; ensanchar; alargar, tender, extender; (*fig.*) forzar, violentar; ***let's stretch a point in this case,*** vamos a ser flexibles *o* hacer una excepción en este caso; ***stretch out one's hand,*** tender la mano. — *v.i.* estirarse; dar de sí; desperezarse; extenderse; ***stretch out,*** (*pers.*) tenderse; (*paisaje etc.*) extenderse.
stretcher [ˈstretʃə], *s.* estirador; camilla; (*alb.*) soga; ***glove-stretcher,*** ensanchador de guantes; ***stretcher-bearer,*** camillero.
stretching [ˈstretʃiŋ], *s.* estiramiento, (el) estirar *etc.*
strew [struː], *irr. v.t.* esparcir, desparramar; sembrar (***with,*** de).
stria [ˈstraiə], *s.* (*arq.*) estría.
striate [ˈstraieit], *a.* estriado. — *v.t.* estriar.
striated [straiˈeitid], *a.* estriado.
striation [straiˈeiʃən], *s.* estriación.
stricken [ˈstrikən], *a.* herido; afligido; ***stricken in years,*** decrépito, de edad provecta; ***to be stricken with grief,*** estar apesadumbrado por el dolor; ***to be stricken with guilt,*** estar agobiado por un remordimiento, estar agobiado por la *o* una sensación de culpabilidad. — *p.p.* [STRIKE].
strict [strikt], *a.* estricto; riguroso; severo; ***in the strict sense of the word,*** en el sentido exacto de la palabra; ***in the strictest confidence,*** con el más absoluto secreto; ***to have strict orders to,*** tener la consigna tajante de.
strictly [ˈstriktli], *adv.* estrictamente; rigurosamente; severamente; ***strictly forbidden,*** terminantemente prohibido; ***strictly speaking,*** en rigor, estrictamente hablando, hablando con propiedad; ***that's not strictly true,*** eso no es absolutamente cierto, eso es verdad sólo hasta cierto punto.
strictness [ˈstriktnis], *s.* exactitud, puntualidad; rigor; rigidez; severidad; (lo) terminante.
stricture [ˈstriktʃə], *s.* crítica *o* censura acerba; (*med.*) estrechez, constricción; ***to pass strictures on,*** criticar acerbamente.
stride [straid], *s.* tranco, zancada, paso largo; ***to make great strides,*** hacer grandes progresos; ***he took it in his stride,*** lo hizo sin esfuerzo *o* sin dificultad; no se aterró por ello; ***to get into one's stride,*** entrar en faena. — *irr. v.t.* montar a horcajadas; salvar, cruzar de una zancada. — *v.i.* andar a pasos largos, dar zancadas; ***stride up to s.o.,*** acercarse resueltamente a alguien.
stridency [ˈstraidənsi], *s.* estridencia; (lo) chillón; (lo) estrepitoso.
strident [ˈstraidənt], *a.* estridente; chillón; estrepitoso; llamativo.
stridor [ˈstraidɔː], *s.* estridor.
stridulation [stridjuˈleiʃən], *s.* estridor, chirrido.
strife [straif], *s.* disputa, contienda, lucha, disensión; refriega; porfía; ***party strife,*** lucha de partidos, banderías, *f.pl.*; ***internal strife,*** luchas internas, *f.pl.*
strike [straik], *s.* huelga; hallazgo, descubrimiento (*de un filón*); golpe; ataque; ganga, golpe de suerte; rasero; ***general strike,*** huelga general; ***sympathy strike,*** huelga por solidaridad; ***to be on strike,*** estar en huelga; ***hunger strike,*** huelga de hambre; ***strike pay,*** subsidio de huelga; ***strike-breaker,*** esquirol; ***come out*** o ***go on strike,*** ponerse, declararse en huelga; ***air strike,*** ataque aéreo. — *irr. v.t.* pegar, dar un golpe a; golpear; herir; percutir; alcanzar; atacar; asestar, dar; tocar, pulsar (*una cuerda*); acuñar, troquelar; frotar, encender (*una cerilla*); dar, chocar con; estrellarse, chocar contra; encontrar, descubrir, topar con; tomar, adoptar (*actitud, postura*); rasar, nivelar; ***he struck the table with his fist,*** descargó un puñetazo en la mesa; ***he was struck by a bullet,*** le alcanzó una bala; ***the tree was struck by lightning,*** cayó un rayo en el árbol; ***strike sparks (fire) from,*** sacar chispas (fuego) de; ***strike root,*** echar raíces, arraigar; ***strike s.o. blind (deaf, dumb),*** cegar (ensordecer, enmudecer) a alguien; ***strike s.o. with horror,*** dejar horrorizado a alguien; ***my head struck the wall,*** me di con la cabeza en la pared; ***it strikes me that . . .,*** se me ocurre que . . .; ***what strikes me is . . .,*** lo que me extraña (sorprende) es que . . .; ***has it ever struck you that . . .?*** ¿se te ha ocurrido alguna vez que . . .?; ***it strikes me as being very unlikely,*** me parece muy improbable; ***that's how it strikes me,*** eso es lo que pienso yo; ***how does he strike you?*** ¿qué te parece (él)?; ***I was very much struck by his efficiency,*** me impresionó mucho su eficacia; ***strike a lead,*** encontrar un filón; ***strike oil,*** encontrar petróleo; ***strike it rich,*** descubrir un buen filón; ***strike camp,*** levantar el camp(ament)o; ***strike the flag,*** arriar la bandera; ***strike home,*** dar en lo vivo; ***strike an average,*** calcular el promedio; ***strike a balance,*** hallar un equilibrio; ***strike a bargain,*** cerrar un trato; ***strike a hard bargain,*** hacer un trato con máximo provecho; ***he strikes a hard bargain,*** es un hombre duro de pelar; (*fig.*) ***strike a chord,*** resultar simpático; tener eco; ***this one strikes my fancy,*** éste me agrada *o* me convence mucho; (*fam.*) ***strike s.o. for money,*** dar un sablazo a alguien; (*fam.*) ***strike all of a heap,*** dejar turulato, atónito; ***strike back,*** devolver el golpe; ***strike down,*** tumbar, derribar; ***strike off,*** cortar, cercenar; borrar, tachar; tirar, imprimir; rebajar; ***strike out,*** borrar, tachar; ***strike through,*** tachar; penetrar; ***strike up,*** iniciar, (empezar a) tocar; entablar; ***strike up a friendship,*** trabar amistad. — *v.i.* golpear; sonar, dar la hora; atacar; declarar la huelga; encenderse (*fuego, cerilla*); arraigar, echar raíces; (*mar.*) arriar el pabellón; (*mar.*) encallar, embarrancar; ***strike against,*** dar, chocar contra; ***strike at,*** asestar un golpe a, acometer; ***strike across country,*** ir a campo traviesa; ***strike into,*** adentrarse *o* penetrar en; ***strike off,*** desviarse; ***strike on an idea,*** dar con *u* ocurrírsele a uno una idea; ***strike out,***

(empezar a) repartir golpes; ***strike out wildly,*** repartir golpes a diestro y siniestro; ***strike out for o.s.,*** empezar a bandeárselas solo *o* a apañárselas por su cuenta; ***strike through,*** atravesar, pasar por; ***strike up,*** comenzar a tocar (*la música*); ***when one's hour strikes,*** cuando le llega a uno la hora.

striker [ˈstraikə], *s.* huelgista, *m.f.*; (*mec.*) percutor.

striking [ˈstraikiŋ], *a.* que llama la atención, impresionante, asombroso; ***the resemblance between them is striking,*** se parecen asombrosamente; ***striking figure,*** figura arrogante, bizarra *o* valiente.

string [striŋ], *s.* cuerda; cordel, guita; fila, hilera; sarta (*de perlas, de mentiras*); retahila (*de tacos etc.*); ristra (*de cebollas, de ajos*); (*bot.*) fibra; (*pl., mús.*) instrumentos de cuerda, *m.pl.*; ***string beans,*** judías verdes, *f.pl.*; (*fam.*) ***to have several strings to one's bow,*** tener varios recursos; ***to (be able to) pull strings,*** tener enchufe(s), estar enchufado, tener buenas aldabas, (poder) ejercer influencia. — *v.t.* ensartar; (*mús.*) encordar; quitar las fibras a (*las judías*); ***string out,*** extender en fila; ***string together,*** compaginar; (*fam.*) ***string up,*** ahorcar, colgar, linchar. — *v.i.* — ***out,*** extenderse en fila.

stringed [striŋd], *a.* — ***instrument,*** instrumento de cuerda.

stringency [ˈstrindʒənsi], *s.* severidad, rigor; (*com.*) tirantez.

stringent [ˈstrindʒənt], *a.* estricto, riguroso, severo; (*com.*) tirante.

stringy [ˈstriŋi], *a.* fibroso.

strip [strip], *s.* tira; lámina (*de metal*); faja, franja (*de tierra*); lista, listón (*de madera*); jirón (*de nube*); ***strip cartoon,*** historieta. — *v.t.* desnudar, desvestir; (*mec.*) estropear; (*mec.*) desmontar; ***strip bare,*** desnudar totalmente; dejar totalmente pelado; ***strip of,*** despojar de; ***strip off,*** quitar. — *v.i.* desnudarse.

stripe [straip], *s.* raya, lista; azote, azotazo; cardenal; (*mil.*) galón. — *v.t.* rayar, listar.

stripling [ˈstripliŋ], *s.* mozalbete, mozuelo.

stripper [ˈstripə], *s.* estriptisista.

striptease [ˈstripˈti:z], *a., s.* striptease.

strive [straiv], *irr. v.i.* esforzarse (***to,*** por), afanarse (***after, for,*** por lograr); luchar (***against,*** contra).

stroke (1) [strouk], *s.* golpe; choque; jugada; tacada; remada, bogada; brazada; campanada; (*mec.*) carrera, vaivén, tiempo; (*med.*) ataque, apoplejía; trazo, rasgo; plumada; raya, tilde; (*impr.*) barra; pincelada, brochazo; primer remero; desgracia, infortunio; esfuerzo, hazaña; ***at a (one) stroke,*** de un golpe; ***with one fell stroke,*** de un (solo) golpe fatal; ***type of stroke,*** estilo (*de brazada*); ***good stroke!*** ¡muy bien!; ***he doesn't do a stroke (of work),*** no da golpe; ***stroke of diplomacy,*** éxito diplomático; ***stroke of genius,*** rasgo de genio, genialidad; ***stroke of wit,*** rasgo de ingenio, agudeza; ***stroke of luck,*** (golpe de) suerte; ***stroke of fortune,*** golpe de fortuna; ***by a stroke of luck,*** por suerte; ***a good stroke of business,*** un buen negocio; ***great*** o ***master stroke,*** golpe maestro; ***on the stroke of 10,*** al (acabar de) dar las 10; ***two-stroke engine,*** motor de dos tiempos; ***stroke of a piston,*** embolada; ***stroke of lightning,*** rayo; (*med.*) ***to have a stroke,*** tener un infarto; ***at*** o ***with one stroke of the pen,*** de un plumazo; ***to row stroke,*** remar en el primer puesto, ser el primer remero. — *v.t.* remar en el primer puesto de.

stroke (2) [strouk], *s.* caricia; ***stroke of the hand,*** caricia con la mano. — *v.t.* acariciar; frotar suavemente; pasar la mano sobre *o* por.

stroll [stroul], *s.* paseo, vuelta; ***to take a stroll,*** dar un paseo. — *v.i.* pasear(se), dar un paseo, deambular, callejear.

stroller [ˈstroulə], *s.* paseante.

strolling [ˈstrouliŋ], *a.* ambulante.

stroma [ˈstroumə], *s.* (*pl.* **stromata** [-tə]) (*anat.*) estroma.

strong [strɔŋ], *a.* fuerte; recio; robusto; resistente; profundo, intenso; (*partidario*) acérrimo; (*café, té*) cargado; (*protesta etc.*) enérgico; (*verbo*) irregular; (*com.*) pujante; ***a thousand strong,*** de (número de) mil; ***strong-arm, strong-handed,*** de mano dura; ***strong-armed,*** de brazos fuertes; ***strong-bodied,*** corpulento, de mucho cuerpo, membrudo, fornido; ***strong-box,*** caja fuerte *o* de caudales; ***strong-minded,*** decidido, resuelto; de firmes creencias; ***strong words*** o ***language,*** palabras mayores *o* duras, *f.pl.*; ***to be strong in sth.,*** estar fuerte en algo. — *adv.* con vigor; ***to be going strong,*** ir estupendamente *o* viento en popa.

stronghold [ˈstrɔŋhould], *s.* fortaleza, plaza fuerte; reducto, baluarte.

strongly [ˈstrɔŋli], *adv.* fuertemente, vigorosamente; firmemente; ***to feel strongly about,*** tener opiniones *o* ideas muy vehementes acerca de; (*carta etc.*) ***strongly worded,*** enérgicamente expresado, expresado con energía.

strontia [ˈstrɔnʃə], *s.* estronciana.

strontium [ˈstrɔnʃəm], *s.* estroncio.

strop [strɔp], *s.* suavizador (*de navajas*); (*mar.*) estrobo. — *v.t.* suavizar.

strophe [ˈstroufi], *s.* (*poét.*) estrofa.

stroppy [ˈstrɔpi], *a.* (*fam.*) irascible.

structural [ˈstrʌktʃərəl], *a.* estructural.

structure [ˈstrʌkʃə], *s.* estructura; fábrica; construcción, edificio.

struggle [strʌgl], *s.* lucha; contienda; esfuerzo; porfía; pugna; pelea; disputa. — *v.i.* luchar; bregar; esforzarse; porfiar; pugnar; forcejear.

strum [strʌm], *v.t.* rasguear (*la guitarra*).

struma [ˈstru:mə], *s.* (*pl.* **strumæ** (-mi:]) estruma.

strumming [ˈstrʌmiŋ], *s.* guitarreo, rasgueo, punteo.

strumpet [ˈstrʌmpit], *s.* ramera, meretriz.

strut (1) [strʌt], *s.* pavonada. — *v.i.* pavonearse, contonearse.

strut (2) [strʌt], *s.* (*carp.*) jabalcón, tornapunta; (*aer.*) montante; (*min.*) adema.

strutting [ˈstrʌtiŋ], *s.* pavoneo, contoneo.

strychnine [ˈstrikni:n], *s.* estricnina.

Stuart [ˈstju:ət]. Estuardo.

stub [stʌb], *s.* (*agric.*) tocón; colilla (*de cigarrillo*); cabo (*de lápiz*); talón (*de cheque*); ***stub-book,*** libro talonario. — *v.t.* (*agric.*) limpiar; arrancar; ***stub out,*** apagar aplastando; ***stub a toe,*** lastimarse un dedo (del pie) tropezando.

stubbiness [ˈstʌbinis], *s.* (lo) achaparrado.

stubble [stʌbl], *s.* (*agric.*) rastrojo; barba.

stubborn [ˈstʌbən], *a.* terco, testarudo, tozudo, porfiado, contumaz; tenaz, tesonudo; inflexible.

stubbornness [ˈstʌbənnis], *s.* terquedad, testarudez; tenacidad.

stubby [ˈstʌbi], *a.* achaparrado.

stucco [ˈstʌkou], *s.* estuco; ***stucco-work,*** estuco, estucaco. — *v.t., v.i.* estucar.

stuck-up [ˈstʌk-ʌp], *a.* engreído; altivo.

stud (1) [stʌd], *s.* tachón, taco (*de bota*); botón (*de camisa*). — *v.t.* tachonar; sembrar (***with,*** de); ***star-studded,*** estrellado.

stud (2) [stʌd], *s.* yeguada, caballada; caballeriza; ***stud book,*** registro genealógico de caballos; ***stud farm,*** acaballadero, potrero; ***stud horse,*** caballo padre.

studding-sails [ˈstʌdiŋ-seilz], *s.pl.* (*mar.*) alas, *f.pl.*

student [ˈstju:dənt], *s.* estudiante; (*erudito*) estudioso; ***student body,*** estudiantado.

studentship [ˈstju:dəntʃip], *s.* beca.

studied [ˈstʌdid], *a.* estudiado; premeditado, intencionado. — *p.p.* [STUDY].

studio [ˈstju:diou], *s.* estudio; taller; (*rad., cine. etc.*) estudio.

studious [ˈstju:diəs], *a.* estudioso, aplicado; muy atento, solícito.

studiousness [ˈstju:diəsnis], *s.* estudiosidad, aplicación.

study [ˈstʌdi], *s.* estudio; taller; despacho; cuarto de trabajo; ***study group,*** grupo de estudio; ***to be in a brown study,*** estar en Babia. — *v.t.*, *v.i.* estudiar; ***study under s.o.,*** estudiar con alguien, estudiar dirigido por alguien.

stuff [stʌf], *s.* material, materia prima; sustancia; paño, tela; chismes, *m.pl.* trastos, *m.pl.*, cosas, *f.pl.*; bobadas, *f.pl.*, tonterías, *f.pl.*; (*mar.*) ***thick stuff,*** tablones, *m.pl.*; ***poor stuff,*** cosa floja; (*fig.*, *fam.*) ***hot stuff,*** cosa *o* persona estupenda; (*fam.*) ***take all your stuff with you,*** llévate todas tus cosas; ***there's good stuff in it,*** tiene cosas buenas; ***stuff and nonsense!*** ¡sandeces!, ¡necedades! — *v.t.* atestar, atiborrar; atascar, tapar; rellenar, embutir; disecar; ***stuff away,*** engullir, zampar(se); ***her head is stuffed with stories,*** tiene la cabeza llena de cuentos. — *v.i.* atracarse, ponerse morado (*de comer*). — **stuff o.s.,** *v.r.* — ***with food,*** atiborrarse (de comida).

stuffiness [ˈstʌfinis], *s.* mala ventilación; bochorno.

stuffing [ˈstʌfiŋ], *s.* (*coc.*) relleno.

stuffy [ˈstʌfi], *a.* mal ventilado, ahogado, cargado; de bochorno; (*fig.*) estirado; pesado, aburrido; ***it's stuffy in here,*** aquí huele a encerrado.

stultification [stʌltifiˈkeiʃən], *s.* embotamiento.

stultify [ˈstʌltifai], *v.t.* entontecer; entorpecer, embotar.

stum [stʌm], *s.* mosto, vino remostado. — *v.t.* remostar, azufrar (*el vino*).

stumble [stʌmbl], *s.* tropiezo, tropezón, traspié. — *v.i.* tropezar, dar un traspié; ***stumble on, across*** o ***upon,*** dar *o* tropezar con, encontrarse con; (*fig.*) ***stumble through,*** hacer a trompicones; leer de mala manera.

stumbler [ˈstʌmblə], *s.* tropezador.

stumbling-block [ˈstʌmbliŋ-blɔk], *s.* escollo, tropiezo, obstáculo.

stump (1) [stʌmp], *s.* tocón, cepa; muñón; raigón (*de muela*); cabo; colilla; poste (*críquet*); (*fam.*) pierna; (*fam.*) ***to stir one's stumps,*** moverse, menearse; ***to be up a stump,*** estar en un brete; ***stump speaker,*** propagandista electoral, *m.f.* — *v.t.* desconcertar, dejar perplejo; ***stump the country,*** recorrer el país pronunciando discursos; ***stump up the cash,*** aflojar la pasta de mala gana. — *v.i.* — ***along*** o ***about,*** andar pesadamente; ***stump up,*** pagar de mala gana.

stump (2) [stʌmp], *s.* (*dib.*) esfumino. — *v.t.* (*dib.*) esfuminar.

stumpy [ˈstʌmpi], *a.* achaparrado; ***stumpy individual,*** retaco.

stun [stʌn], *v.t.* aturdir, atontar; pasmar, asombrar.

stunner [ˈstʌnə], *s.* (*fam.*) chica de bandera.

stunning [ˈstʌniŋ], *a.* (*fam.*) asombroso, imponente, bárbaro.

stunt (1) [stʌnt], *s.* treta, truco; maniobra (publicitaria *o* sensacionalista); (*aer.*) vuelo acrobático. — *v.i.* (*aer.*) hacer acrobacias (aéreas).

stunt (2) [stʌnt], *v.t.* impedir el crecimiento *o* desarrollo de, atrofiar.

stunted [ˈstʌntid], *a.* atrofiado; achaparrado.

stunting [ˈstʌntiŋ], *s.* (*aer.*) acrobacias (aéreas), *f.pl.*

stupe [stju:p], *s.* (*med.*) fomento, compresa.

stupefacient [stju:piˈfeiʃənt], *a.*, *s.* estupefaciente.

stupefaction [stju:piˈfækʃən], *s.* estupefacción, estupor, pasmo.

stupefy [ˈstju:pifai], *v.t.* abobar, atontar, entontecer; embrutecer; dejar estupefacto.

stupendous [stju:ˈpendəs], *a.* asombroso, pasmoso; imponente.

stupendousness [stju:ˈpendəsnis], *s.* (lo) asombroso *etc.*

stupid [ˈstju:pid], *a.* estúpido, tonto, mentecato, necio.

stupidity [stju:ˈpiditi], *s.* estupidez, tontería, necedad, sandez.

stupor [ˈstju:pə], *s.* atontamiento; embrutecimiento; estupor.

sturdiness [ˈstə:dinis], *s.* robustez, fuerza; (lo) duro, (lo) resistente.

sturdy [ˈstə:di], *a.* robusto, fuerte; duro, resistente; firme.

sturgeon [ˈstə:dʒən], *s.* esturión.

stutter [ˈstʌtə], *s.* tartamudez; ***to have a stutter,*** ser tartamudo. — *v.t.* balbucir, balbucear. — *v.i.* tartamudear, balbucear.

stutterer [ˈstʌtərə], *s.* tartamudo.

sty (1) [stai], *s.* (*pl.* **sties** [-z]) zahurda, cochinera; (*fig.*) ***pig-sty,*** pocilga.

sty (2), **stye** [stai], *s.* (*pl.* **styes** [-z]) (*med.*) orzuelo (del ojo).

Stygian [ˈstidʒiən], *a.* estigio.

style [stail], *s.* estilo; moda; elegancia; tratamiento; título; (*cir.*) estilete; (*ant.*) buril; ***to be in style,*** estar de moda; ***to travel in style,*** viajar por todo lo alto. — *v.t.* cortar a la moda, estilizar; nombrar, intitular. — **style o.s.,** *v.r.* darse el título de, intitularse.

stylet [ˈstailit], *s.* estilete; punzón; (*zool.*) púa.

stylish [ˈstailiʃ], *a.* elegante, de buen estilo, a la moda.

stylist [ˈstailist], *s.* estilista, *m.f.*

stylize [ˈstailaiz], *v.t.* estilizar.

stylograph [ˈstailogræf], *s.* estilógrafo.

styloid [ˈstailɔid], *a.* estiloideo.

stylus [ˈstailəs], *s.* estilo; punzón; (*gramófono*) aguja.

stymie [ˈstaimi], *v.t.* (*dep.*, *esp. golf*) obstruir.

stymied [ˈstaimid], *a.* (*fam.*) aviado; ***now we're stymied!*** ¡menudo problemón (nos plantea esto)!

styptic [ˈstiptik], *a.*, *s.* estíptico; astrictivo.

stypticity [stipˈtisiti], *s.* estipticidad.

styrax [ˈstaiəræks], *s.* estoraque.

Styx [stiks], *s.* (*mit.*) (*río* o *laguna*) Estigia.

suable [ˈsju:əbl], *a.* que puede ser perseguido en justicia.

suasion [ˈsweiʒən], *s.* persuasión.

suasive (*ant.*), **suasory** [ˈsweiziv, -zəri], *a.* persuasivo, suasorio.

suave [swɑ:v], *a.* afable; empalagoso, zalamero.

suavity [ˈswɑ:viti], *s.* afabilidad; empalagosidad, zalamería.

subacid [ˈsʌbˈæsid], *a.* agrillo; (*quím.*) subácido.

subacrid [ˈsʌbˈækrid], *a.* asperillo.

subaerial [ˈsʌbˈɛəriəl], *a.* subaéreo.

sub-agent [ˈsʌb-eidʒənt], *s.* subagente, subejecutor.

sub-almoner [ˈsʌb-ˈɑ:mənə], *s.* teniente de limosnero.

subalpine [sʌbˈælpain], *a.* subalpino.

subaltern [ˈsʌbəltən], *a.* subalterno, subordinado; (*lóg.*) (proposición) particular. — *s.* oficial subalterno; alférez.

subalternate [sʌbɔ:lˈtə:nit], *a.* sucesivo; subalterno, subordinado. — *s.* (*lóg.*) proposición particular.

subaqueous [ˈsʌbˈeikwiəs], *a.* subacuático.

subarctic [sʌbˈɑ:ktik], *a.* subártico.

sub-base [ˈsʌb-ˈbeis], *s.* (*arq.*) miembro más bajo de una base.

sub-bass [ˈsʌb-ˈbeis], *s.* (*mús.*) registro grave (*de un órgano*).

subcarbonate [ˈsʌbˈkɑ:bənit], *s.* subcarbonato.

subchanter [ˈsʌbˈtʃɑ:ntə], *s.* sochantre.

subcommittee [ˈsʌbkəmiti], *s.* subcomisión.

subconscious [ˈsʌbˈkɔnʃəs], *a.* subconsciente. — *s.* ***the subconscious,*** el subconsciente, la subconsciencia.

subcontract [ˈsʌbˈkɔntrækt], *s.* subcontrato. — [sʌbkənˈtrækt], *v.t.* subcontratar.

subcontractor [ˈsʌbkəntræktə], *s.* subcontratista, *m.f.*
subcontrary [ˈsʌbˈkɔntrəri], *a.* (*lóg.*) (proposición) subcontraria.
subcutaneous [ˈsʌbkjuːˈteiniəs], *a.* subcutáneo.
subdeacon [ˈsʌbˈdiːkən], *s.* subdiácono.
subdeaconship [ˈsʌbˈdiːkənʃip], *s.* subdiaconato.
subdean [ˈsʌbˈdiːn], *s.* subdecano.
subdelegate [ˈsʌbˈdeligit], *s.* subdelegado. — [-geit], *v.t.* subdelegar.
subdelegation [ˈsʌbdeliˈgeiʃən], *s.* subdelegación.
subdivide [ˈsʌbdiˈvaid], *v.t.*, *v.i.* subdividir(se).
subdivision [ˈsʌbdiviʒən], *s.* subdivisión.
subdominant [ˈsʌbˈdɔminənt], *s.* (*mús.*) subdominante, *f.*
subdue [səbˈdjuː], *v.t.* sojuzgar, subyugar, someter, dominar, domeñar; domar; amansar, suavizar.
subdued [səbˈdjuːd], *a.* suave; tenue; discreto; apagado; poco animado; poco fuerte.
sub-edit [ˈsʌb-ˈedit], *v.t.* corregir.
sub-editor [ˈsʌb-ˈeditə], *s.* subredactor.
subfamily [ˈsʌbfæmili], *s.* (*biol.*) subfamilia.
subgenus [ˈsʌbdʒiːnəs], *s.* (*biol.*) subgénero.
sub-heading [ˈsʌb-hediŋ], *s.* subtítulo.
subjacent [sʌbˈdʒeisənt], *a.* subyacente.
subject [ˈsʌbdʒikt], *a.* sujeto; (*pueblo*) sojuzgado; ***subject to,*** sujeto a; expuesto a; propenso a; ***subject to correction,*** bajo corrección. — *s.* tema, *m.*; asunto; materia; (*univ.*) asignatura, materia; (*gram.*) sujeto; (*pol.*) súbdito; (*med.*) individuo, caso. — [səbˈdʒekt], *v.t.* someter.
subjection [səbˈdʒekʃən], *s.* sujeción; sometimiento.
subjective [səbˈdʒektiv], *a.* subjetivo.
subjectivism [səbˈdʒektivizəm], *s.* subjetivismo.
subjectivity [sʌbdʒekˈtiviti], *s.* subjetividad.
subjoin [ˈsʌbˈdʒɔin], *v.t.* adjuntar.
subjugate [ˈsʌbdʒjugeit], *v.t.* subyugar, sojuzgar, someter.
subjugation [sʌbdʒuˈgeiʃən], *s.* subyugación, sojuzgamiento, sometimiento.
subjunctive [səbˈdʒʌŋktiv], *a.*, *s.* (*gram.*) subjuntivo.
sub-kingdom [ˈsʌb-kiŋdəm], *s.* subreino.
sublease [ˈsʌbˈliːs], *s.* subarriendo. — *v.t.* subarrendar.
sub-lessee [ˈsʌb-leˈsiː], *s.* subarrendatario.
sub-lessor [ˈsʌb-leˈsɔː], *s.* subarrendador.
sublet [ˈsʌbˈlet], *v.t.* realquilar.
sublimate [ˈsʌblimit], *s.* (*quím.*) sublimado. — [-meit], *v.t.* sublimar.
sublimation [sʌbliˈmeiʃən], *s.* sublimación.
sublimatory [ˈsʌblimeitəri], *a.* sublimatorio.
sublime [səˈblaim], *a.* sublime. — *s.* (lo) sublime. — *v.t.* sublimar.
sublimity [səˈblimiti], *s.* sublimidad.
sublingual [sʌbˈliŋgwəl], *a.* sublingual.
sublunar, sublunary [sʌbˈluːnə, sʌbˈluːnəri], *a.* sublunar.
submarine [sʌbməˈriːn], *a.*, *s.* submarino.
submaxillary [ˈsʌbmækˈsiləri], *a.* submaxilar.
submediant [ˈsʌbˈmiːdiənt], *s.* (*mús.*) superdominante, *f.*
submerge [səbˈməːdʒ], *v.t.* sumergir; inundar, anegar. — *v i.* sumergirse.
submergence, submersion [səbˈməːdʒəns, -ˈməːʃən], *s.* sumersión.
submersible [səbˈməːsibl], *a.*, *s.* sumergible.
submission [səbˈmiʃən], *s.* sumisión; sometimiento; rendición; presentación.
submissive [səbˈmisiv], *a.* sumiso; rendido.
submissiveness [səbˈmisivnis], *s.* sumisión; rendimiento.
submit [səbˈmit], *v.t.* someter; presentar, aducir; rendir; ***I submit that . . .,*** me permito decir *o* sugerir que. — *v.i.* someterse, rendirse; ***submit to,*** aceptar resignadamente; conformarse con.
submultiple [ˈsʌbˈmʌltipl], *s.* submúltiplo.
subnormal [ˈsʌbˈnɔːməl], *a.* subnormal; (*temperatura*) bajo la normal. — *s.* (*mat.*) subnormal.
suboctave [ˈsʌbˈɔktiv], *a.* subóctuplo.
suborder [ˈsʌbɔːdə], *s.* (*bot.*, *zool.*) suborden; (*arq.*) orden subordinado.
subordinacy [səˈbɔːdinəsi], *s.* subordinación, sujeción.
subordinate [səˈbɔːdinit], *a.* subordinado; secundario, menos importante. — *s.* subordinado. — [səˈbɔːdineit], *v.t.* subordinar.
subordination [səbɔːdiˈneiʃən], *s.* subordinación.
suborn [sʌˈbɔːn], *v.t.* sobornar, cohechar.
subornation [sʌbɔːˈneiʃən], *s.* soborno, cohecho.
suborner [sʌˈbɔːnə], *s.* sobornador, cohechador.
subpœna [sʌbˈpiːnə], *s.* (*for.*) citación, comparendo. — *v.t.* (*for.*) citar, emplazar.
subpolar [ˈsʌbˈpoulə], *a.* subpolar.
subrector [ˈsʌbˈrektə], *s.* subrector.
subreption [sʌbˈrepʃən], *s.* subrepción.
subrogation [sʌbroˈgeiʃən], *s.* subrogación.
sub rosa [ˈsʌb ˈrouzə], *a.* secreto. — *adv.* sub rosa, en secreto, en confianza.
subscribe [səbˈskraib], *v.t.* suscribir; contribuir; firmar, rubricar. — *v.i.* suscribir; ***subscribe to a paper,*** abonarse a un periódico; ***subscribe to an idea,*** suscribir *o* abonar una idea.
subscriber [səbˈskraibə], *s.* suscriptor, abonado; infrascrito, firmante.
subscript [ˈsʌbskript], *a.*, *s.* cosa escrita debajo de otra.
subscription [səbˈskripʃən], *s.* suscripción; abono; cuota.
subsection [ˈsʌbsekʃən], *s.* subdivisión.
subsecutive [səbˈsekjutiv], *a.* subsiguiente, subsecuente.
subsequence [ˈsʌbsikwəns], *s.* subsecuencia.
subsequent [ˈsʌbsikwənt], *a.* subsiguiente; posterior, ulterior. — *adv.* — ***to this,*** a raíz de esto, posteriormente a esto.
subsequently [ˈsʌbsikwəntli], *adv.* posteriormente, con posterioridad, luego, más tarde.
subserve [səbˈsəːv], *v.t.* servir, ayudar, estar subordinado a. — *v.i.* servir como subordinado.
subservience, subserviency [səbˈsəːviəns, -i], *s.* subordinación; servilismo.
subservient [səbˈsəːviənt], *a.* subordinado; servil.
subside [səbˈsaid], *v.i.* (*agua*) bajar; (*viento*) amainar; (*emoción*) calmarse; desplomarse; dejarse caer; (*tierra*) hundirse.
subsidence [ˈsʌbsidəns], *s.* socavón, hundimiento; (*agua*) bajada.
subsidiary [səbˈsidiəri], *a.* subsidiario; secundario; (*com.*) afiliado. — *s.* filial, *f.*
subsidize [ˈsʌbsidaiz], *v.t.* subvencionar.
subsidy [ˈsʌbsidi], *s.* subvención.
subsist [səbˈsist], *v.i.* subsistir; sustentarse; ***subsist on,*** sustentarse con.
subsistence [səbˈsistəns], *s.* subsistencia; manutención; ***subsistence allowance,*** dietas, *f.pl.*
subsistent [səbˈsistənt], *a.* subsistente.
subsoil [ˈsʌbsɔil], *s.* subsuelo.
substance [ˈsʌbstəns], *s.* sustancia; enjundia; ***man of substance,*** hombre de posibles.
substandard [ˈsʌbˈstændəd], *a.* inferior, deficiente.
substantial [səbˈstænʃəl], *a.* sustancial; sustancioso, enjundioso; (*suma, cantidad*) importante, considerable; sólido, consistente, fuerte; acomodado, de posición acomodada.
substantiality [səbstænʃiˈæliti], *s.* sustancialidad.
substantially [səbˈstænʃəli], *adv.* en esencia, fundamentalmente.
substantiate [səbˈstænʃieit], *v.t.* demostrar *o* hacer constar (la validez de); justificar; comprobar.

substantiation [səbstænʃiˈeiʃən], *s.* demostración; justificación; comprobación.
substantival [sʌbstənˈtaivəl], *a.* (*gram.*) sustantivo.
substantive [ˈsʌbstəntiv], *a.*, *s.* (*gram.*) sustantivo.
substitute [ˈsʌbstitju:t], *a.* sustituto, suplente. — *s.* (*pers.*) sustituto, suplente; (*mil.*) reemplazo; (*cosa*) sucedáneo. — *v.t.* sustituir; ***substitute Z for X,*** sustituir X por Z, sustituir X con Z.
substitution [sʌbstiˈtju:ʃən], *s.* sustitución.
substratum [ˈsʌbˈstrɑ:təm, -streitəm], *s.* (*pl.* **substrata** [-ˈstrɑ:tə, -ˈstreitə]) sustrato.
substructure [ˈsʌbˈstrʌktʃə], *s.* subestructura.
subtangent [ˈsʌbˈtændʒənt], *s.* (*geom.*) subtangente.
subtenant [ˈsʌbˈtenənt], *s.* realquilado.
subtend [sʌbˈtend], *v.t.* (*geom.*) subtender.
subtense [sʌbˈtens], *s.* (*geom.*) subtensa.
subterfuge [ˈsʌbtəfju:dʒ], *s.* subterfugio, treta.
subterranean, subterraneous [sʌbtəˈreiniən, sʌbtəˈreiniəs], *a.* subterráneo.
subtile [sʌtl], *a.* sutil.
subtility [sʌbˈtiliti], *s.* sutileza, sutilidad.
subtilize [ˈsʌtilaiz], *v.t.*, *v.i.* sutilizar.
subtle [sʌtl], *a.* sutil; fino, delicado; tenue; artero, astuto.
subtlety [ˈsʌtlti], *s.* sutileza; finura, delicadeza; agudeza; astucia.
subtly [ˈsʌtli], *adv.* sutilmente; finamente, delicadamente; astutamente.
subtract [səbˈtrækt], *v.t.*, *v.i.* (*arit.*) restar.
subtraction [səbˈtrækʃən], *s.* sustracción; (*arit.*) resta.
subtrahend [ˈsʌbtrəhend], *s.* substraendo, sustraendo.
subtreasurer [ˈsʌbˈtreʒərə], *s.* subtesorero.
subtropic(al) [ˈsʌbˈtrɔpik(əl)], *a.* subtropical.
suburb [ˈsʌbə:b], *s.* barrio *o* barriada de las afueras; (*pl.*) afueras, *f.pl.*
suburban [səˈbə:bən], *a.* de las afueras; ***suburban train,*** tren de cercanías.
suburbanite [səˈbə:bənait], *s.* habitante de las afueras *o* de los barrios exteriores.
subvention [səbˈvenʃən], *s.* subvención, subsidio.
subversion [səbˈvə:ʃən], *s.* subversión.
subversive [səbˈvə:siv], *a.* subversivo.
subvert [səbˈvə:t], *v.t.* subvertir, trastornar.
subverter [səbˈvə:tə], *s.* subversor, trastornador.
subvertible [səbˈvə:tibl], *a.* subvertible, trastornable.
subway [ˈsʌbwei], *s.* paso subterráneo, paso inferior; (*Am.*, *f.c.*) [TUBE; UNDERGROUND].
succedaneous [sʌksiˈdeiniəs], *a.* sucedáneo.
succedaneum [sʌksiˈdeiniəm], *s.* (*pl.* **succedanea, succedaneums** [-niə, -niəmz]) sucedáneo, sustituto; (*med.*) sucedáneo.
succeed [səkˈsi:d], *v.i.* tener éxito, triunfar, salir bien; suceder, seguir; heredar; ***nothing succeeds like success,*** lo que más éxito tiene es el éxito mismo; ***succeed in life,*** triunfar en la vida; ***succeed in doing sth.,*** lograr hacer algo.
succeeding [səkˈsi:diŋ], *a.* sucesivo; subsiguiente; futuro, venidero.
success [səkˈses], *s.* (buen) éxito, acierto, triunfo; logro, cosa lograda; ***he was a great success,*** tuvo mucho éxito; ***to meet with success,*** tener éxito, prosperar, medrar.
successful [səkˈsesful], *a.* afortunado, feliz, que tiene éxito; logrado; próspero; acertado; ***to be successful,*** tener éxito, salir bien; ***to be successful in doing sth.,*** lograr, conseguir hacer algo.
successfully [səkˈsesfuli], *adv.* felizmente, con (buen) éxito.
successfulness [səkˈsesfulnis], *s.* éxito, acierto.
succession [səkˈseʃən], *s.* sucesión; serie; ***in succession,*** sucesivamente; ***three times in succession,*** tres veces seguidas.
successive [səkˈsesiv], *a.* sucesivo; consecutivo.
successively [səkˈsesivli], *adv.* sucesivamente; ***and so on successively,*** y así sucesivamente.
successor [səkˈsesə], *s.* sucesor; heredero.
succinate [ˈsʌksineit], *s.* (*quím.*) succinato.
succinct [səkˈsiŋkt], *a.* sucinto, conciso.
succinctness [səkˈsiŋktnis], *s.* (lo) sucinto, concisión.
succinic [sʌkˈsinik], *a.* succínico.
succotash [ˈsʌkotæʃ], *s.* (*Am.*) potaje de maíz y habas.
succour [ˈsʌkə], *s.* socorro, auxilio; sustento. — *v.t.* socorrer, auxiliar.
succuba, succubus [ˈsʌkjubə, -bəs], *s.* (*pl.* **succubæ, succubi** [ˈsʌkjubi, -bai]) súcubo.
succulence, succulency [ˈsʌkjuləns, -i], *s.* suculencia, (lo) suculento.
succulent [ˈsʌkjulənt], *a.* suculento.
succumb [səˈkʌm], *v.i.* sucumbir; ***succumb to,*** sucumbir ante.
succussion [səˈkʌʃən], *s.* sucusión.
such [sʌtʃ], *a.* tal; semejante; ***such a problem,*** un problema de este tipo; ***there's no such thing,*** no hay tal (cosa); ***such cheek!*** ¡semejante descaro!; ***such as,*** tal como; ***as such,*** como tal; ***such and such a,*** tal o cual; ***such as to,*** (tal) como para; ***such is the position,*** ésta es la situación, así es la cosa; ***such a small amount,*** una cantidad tan pequeña. — *pron.* — ***as,*** quienes, los que.
suchlike [ˈsʌtʃlaik], *a.* tal, semejante. — *pron.* ***and suchlike,*** y demás, y otras cosas por el estilo.
suck [sʌk], *s.* chupada; ***to give suck to,*** amamantar, dar de mamar a. — *v.t.* chupar; mamar; libar; ***suck in,*** sorber(se); aspirar (*aire*); ***suck out,*** extraer *o* sacar chupando *o* con bomba; ***suck up,*** absorber(se). — *v.i.* chupar; mamar; libar; (*fam.*) ***suck up to,*** hacer la pelotilla a; ***to teach one's grandmother to suck eggs,*** predicar a los conversos *o* a los convertidos.
sucker [ˈsʌkə], *s.* chupador; mamón, chupón; (*mec.*) émbolo; sopapo de bomba; (*bot.*) pimpollo, serpollo; (*zool. etc.*) ventosa; (*fam.*) primo, tonto, bobo, iluso.
sucking-fish [ˈsʌkiŋ-fiʃ], *s.* rémora.
sucking-pig [ˈsʌkiŋ-pig], *s.* lechón, lechoncillo.
suckle [sʌkl], *v.t.* amamantar, dar de mamar a; criar. — *v.i.* lactar.
suckling [ˈsʌkliŋ], *s.* mamón.
sucrose [ˈsju:krous], *s.* sucrosa.
suction [ˈsʌkʃən], *s.* succión; ***suction-pump,*** bomba aspirante.
Sudan [su(:)ˈdɑ:n], **the.** el Sudán.
Sudanese [su:dəˈni:z], *a.*, *s.* sudanés, *m.*
sudatory [ˈsju:dətəri], *a.* sudatorio.
sudden [ˈsʌdən], *a.* repentino; súbito; ***all of a sudden,*** de repente; ***on a sudden,*** súbitamente.
suddenly [ˈsʌdənli], *adv.* de repente, de pronto.
suddenness [ˈsʌdənnis], *s.* (lo) repentino; (lo) imprevisto; brusquedad.
sudoriferous [sju:dəˈrifərəs], *a.* sudorífero.
sudorific [sju:dəˈrifik], *a.*, *s.* sudorífico.
suds [sʌdz], *s.pl.* jabonaduras, *f.pl.*
sue [sju:], *v.t.*, *v.i.* demandar, poner pleito (a), entablar juicio; ***sue for,*** rogar, pedir, suplicar; (*for.*) ***sue for damages,*** demandar por daños y perjuicios.
suède [sweid], *s.* ante.
suet [ˈs(j)u:it], *s.* sebo, saín.
suety [ˈs(j)u:iti], *a.* seboso.
Suez Canal [ˈs(j)u:iz kəˈnæl], **the.** el Canal de Suez.
suffer [ˈsʌfə], *v.t.* sufrir; padecer; aguantar; experimentar; tolerar; ***he suffered the same fate,*** le cupo la misma suerte. — *v.i.* sufrir, padecer; ***how I suffered!*** ¡lo que sufrí!; ***you will suffer for it,*** (me) lo pagarás, te pesará; ***suffer from,*** padecer (de); adolecer de; estar aquejado de; ***suffer from the effects of,*** resentirse de.
sufferable [ˈsʌfərəbl], *a.* sufrible, sufridero, pasadero, tolerable, soportable.

sufferably [ˈsʌfərəbli], *adv.* de un modo soportable.
sufferance [ˈsʌfərəns], *s.* tolerancia; ***on sufferance,*** por tolerancia; ***it is beyond sufferance,*** es más de lo que puede aguantarse.
sufferer [ˈsʌfərə], *s.* sufridor; paciente; víctima, *f.*; ***fellow-sufferer,*** compañero de infortunio(s).
suffering [ˈsʌfəriŋ], *a.* que sufre, doliente; enfermo. — *s.* sufrimiento; padecimiento; dolor.
suffice [səˈfais], *v.t.* satisfacer, ser suficiente para, bastar a. — *v.i.* bastar, ser suficiente, alcanzar.
sufficiency [səˈfiʃənsi], *s.* (lo) suficiente, (lo) bastante; ***to have a sufficiency,*** tener un (buen) pasar.
sufficient [səˈfiʃənt], *a.* suficiente, bastante; ***to be sufficient,*** bastar, ser suficiente.
sufficiently [səˈfiʃəntli], *adv.* suficientemente, bastante.
suffix [ˈsʌfiks], *s.* sufijo. — *v.t.* añadir sufijo a.
suffocate [ˈsʌfəkeit], *v.t., v.i.* ahogar(se), asfixiar(se).
suffocating [ˈsʌfəkeitiŋ], *a.* sofocante, sofocador, asfixiante.
suffocation [sʌfəˈkeiʃən], *s.* sofocación, asfixia, ahogo.
suffragan [ˈsʌfrəgən], *a., s.* (*igl.*) sufragáneo.
suffrage [ˈsʌfridʒ], *s.* sufragio; voto; aprobación; ***universal suffrage,*** sufragio universal; ***to get the suffrage,*** obtener el derecho de votar.
suffragette [sʌfrəˈdʒet], *s.* sufragista.
suffragist [ˈsʌfrədʒist], *s.* votante; sufragista, *m.f.*
suffuse [səˈfju:z], *v.t.* bañar, cubrir; difundir.
suffusion [səˈfju:ʒən], *s.* difusión; (*med.*) sufusión.
sufi [ˈsu:fi], *s.* sufí, sofí.
sugar [ˈʃugə], *s.* azúcar; ***brown sugar,*** azúcar negro *o* moreno; ***grape sugar,*** glucosa; ***maple sugar,*** azúcar de arce; ***loaf sugar, sugar-loaf,*** azúcar de pilón, pan de azúcar; ***sugar-beet,*** remolacha azucarera; ***sugar-bowl,*** azucarero; ***sugar candy,*** azúcar cande; ***sugar-cane,*** caña de azúcar; (*Am.*) ***sugar-daddy,*** viejo rico que mantiene con lujo a una mujer joven; ***sugar-loaf*** [LOAF SUGAR]; ***sugar-mill,*** trapiche, ingenio; ***sugar of lead,*** acetato de plomo; ***sugar-plantation,*** cañaveral (azucarero); ***sugar-plum,*** dulce, confite, golosina; ***sugar syrup,*** melado; ***sugar-tongs,*** tenacillas, *f.pl.*; ***white sugar,*** azúcar blanco. — *v.t.* azucarar, endulzar, confitar; ***sugar the pill,*** dorar la píldora. — *v.i.* granularse, cristalizarse.
sugar-coated [ˈʃugə-ˈkoutid], *a.* confitado, garapiñado.
sugary [ˈʃugəri], *a.* azucarado; (*fig.*) meloso, almibarado.
suggest [səˈdʒest], *v.t.* sugerir, indicar; proponer; (*hipnosis*) sugestionar; ***I suggest trying this,*** propongo que se intente esto.
suggestion [səˈdʒestʃən], *s.* sugerencia, indicación; propuesta; (*hipnosis*) sugestión.
suggestive [səˈdʒestiv], *a.* incitante, provocativo, sicalíptico; ***suggestive of,*** sugeridor de.
suicidal [sju:iˈsaidl], *a.* suicida.
suicide [ˈsju:isaid], *s.* suicidio; (*pers.*) suicida, *m.f.*; ***to commit suicide,*** suicidarse.
suint [swint], *s.* grasa natural de la lana.
suit [s(j)u:t], *s.* traje (*para hombres*); traje de chaqueta (*para mujeres*); (*amor*) cortejo; (*naipes*) palo; petición, súplica; (*for.*) pleito; ***suit of armour,*** armadura; ***to bring a suit,*** armar un pleito (***against,*** a); ***to follow suit,*** servir del palo; (*fig.*) hacer igual, lo mismo *u* otro tanto. — *v.t.* adaptar, acomodar, adecuar; (*ropa*) sentar bien a, favorecer; ***that skirt suits you,*** esa falda le va, esa falde le cae bien; (*comida*) sentar bien a, caer bien a; (*hora etc.*) convenir, venir bien a; ***they are well suited*** (***to each other***), van bien juntos; hacen juego; hacen buena pareja. — **suit o.s.,** *v.r.* hacer lo que le de la gana a uno; ***suit yourself,*** como usted quiera.
suitability [s(j)u:təˈbiliti], *s.* (lo) adecuado, (lo) apropiado, idoneidad; conveniencia.
suitable [ˈs(j)u:təbl], *a.* adecuado, apropiado, idóneo; conveniente; ***very suitable for,*** muy indicado para.
suitcase [ˈs(j)u:tkeis], *s.* maleta.
suite [swi:t], *s.* suite, *f.*; juego; séquito, comitiva, acompañamiento; ***suite of apartments,*** suite de habitaciones; ***bedroom suite,*** juego de dormitorio.
suitor [ˈs(j)u:tə], *s.* pretendiente, galán; (*for.* demandante.
sulk [sʌlk], *s.* enfurruñamiento, disgusto; ***to go into a sulk,*** ponerse mohino; (*pl.*) mohina, mal humor; ***to have the sulks,*** estar mohino; ***to get the sulks,*** amohinarse. — *v.i.* enfurruñarse, disgustarse.
sulkiness [ˈsʌlkinis], *s.* mohina, mal humor, enfurruñamiento.
sulky [ˈsʌlki], *a.* mohino, malhumorado, resentido, enfurruñado.
sullen [ˈsʌlən], *a.* (*pers.*) hosco, ceñudo; malhumorado; resentido; (*cosas*) plomizo, ceñudo.
sullenly [ˈsʌlənli], *adv.* hoscamente, con ceño.
sullenness [ˈsʌlənnis], *s.* hosquedad; malhumor; resentimiento.
sully [ˈsʌli], *s.* mancha, mancilla. — *v.t., v.i.* manchar(se), mancillar(se); empañar(se).
sulphate [ˈsʌlfeit], *s.* sulfato. — *v.t.* sulfatar.
sulphide [ˈsʌlfaid], *s.* sulfuro.
sulphite [ˈsʌlfait], *s.* sulfito.
sulphonamide [sʌlˈfounəmaid], *s.* sulfamida.
sulphur [ˈsʌlfə], *s.* azufre; ***sulphur drugs,*** sulfamidas. — *v.t.* azufrar.
sulphurate [ˈsʌlfjurit], *a.* sulfurado, sulfúreo. — [-eit], *v.t.* sulfurar, azufrar.
sulphuration [sʌlfjuˈreiʃən], *s.* sulfatación, sulfatado.
sulphureousness [sʌlˈfjuəriəsnis], *s.* calidad de sulfúreo.
sulphureous, sulphurous, sulphury [sʌlˈfjuəriəs, ˈsʌlfərəs, ˈsʌlfəri], *a.* sulfúreo, azufrado, azufroso.
sulphuric [sʌlˈfjuərik], *a.* sulfúrico.
sulphurwort [ˈsʌlfəwə:t], *s.* servato.
sulphydric [sʌlˈfaidrik], *a.* sulfhídrico.
sultan [ˈsʌltən], *s.* sultán.
sultana [sulˈtɑ:nə], *s.* sultana; (*fruta*) pasa de Corinto.
sultanate [ˈsʌltənit], *s.* sultanato.
sultriness [ˈsʌltrinis], *s.* bochorno.
sultry [ˈsʌltri], *a.* bochornoso, sofocante.
sum [sʌm], *s.* suma; total; cantidad, importe; ***in sum,*** en suma, en resumen; ***good round sum,*** una buena cantidad; ***sum agreed upon,*** cantidad alzada; ***lump sum,*** suma global. — *v.t.* — ***up,*** resumir; recapitular; evaluar rápidamente. — *v.i.* — ***up,*** resumir; recapitular; ***sum up . . .,*** en resumen. . . .
sumac [ˈsju:mæk, ˈʃu:mæk], *s.* zumaque.
Sumatra [sju:ˈmɑ:trə]. Sumatra.
summarily [ˈsʌmərili], *adv.* sumariamente; resumidamente, en resumen.
summarize [ˈsʌməraiz], *v.t.* resumir, compendiar.
summary [ˈsʌməri], *a.* sumario; compendioso, sucinto, resumido; (*for.*) ***summary justice,*** justicia sumaria. — *s.* resumen, sumario, compendio.
summation [sʌˈmeiʃən], *s.* adición; recapitulación, resumen; suma total.
summer [ˈsʌmə], *a.* de verano, veraniego, estival; ***summer resort,*** lugar de veraneo; ***summer time,*** hora de verano; ***summer school,*** escuela de verano. — *s.* verano, estío; ***Indian summer,*** veranillo de San Martín; ***a summer's day,*** un día de verano; ***to spend the summer,*** veranear, pasar el verano. — *v.i.* (*esp. Am.*) veranear.
summer-boarder [ˈsʌmə-ˈbɔ:də], *s.* veraneante.
summer-fallow [ˈsʌmə-ˈfælou], *v.t.* barbechar en verano.

summer-house [ˈsʌmə-haus], *s.* cenador, glorieta.
summertree [ˈsʌmətri:], *s.* viga maestra, solera.
summery [ˈsʌməri], *a.* veraniego, estival.
summit [ˈsʌmit], *s.* cima, cumbre, *f.*; ápice; cúspide, *f.*; ***summit conference,*** conferencia (en la) cumbre.
summon [ˈsʌmən], *v.t.* llamar, convocar; (*for.*) citar, emplazar; ***summon up,*** evocar (*un recuerdo*); ***summon up courage,*** cobrar ánimo, sacar fuerzas de flaqueza; ***summon away,*** llamar aparte; mandar ir; ***summon back,*** mandar volver.
summoner [ˈsʌmənə], *s.* emplazador.
summons [ˈsʌmənz], *s.* (*for.*) citación; requerimiento. — *v.t.* (*for.*) citar; mandar acudir.
sump [sʌmp], *s.* (*min.*) sumidero; (*aut.*) sumidero del cárter.
sumptuary [ˈsʌmptjuəri], *a.* suntuario.
sumptuous [ˈsʌmptjuəs], *a.* suntuoso; opíparo.
sumptuously [ˈsʌmptjuəsli], *adv.* suntuosamente, con mucho fausto.
sumptuousness, sumptuosity [ˈsʌmptjuəsnis, sʌmptjuˈɔsiti], *s.* suntuosidad.
sun [sʌn], *a.* solar. — *s.* sol; ***in the sun,*** al sol, bajo el sol; ***sun-bathing,*** baño(s) de sol; ***sun-bird,*** suimanga; ***sun-blind,*** store; ***sun-bonnet,*** papalina; ***sun-dial,*** reloj de sol; ***sun glasses,*** gafas de sol, *f.pl.*; ***sun-lamp,*** lámpara de cuarzo; ***to have a place in the sun,*** tener un lugar *o* un sitio suyo; ***under the sun,*** de *o* en este mundo. — *v.t.* asolear. — **sun o.s.,** *v.r.* tomar el sol.
sunbathe [ˈsʌnbeið], *v.i.* tomar el sol *o* un baño de sol *o* baños de sol.
sunbeam [ˈsʌnbi:m], *s.* rayo de sol.
sunburn [ˈsʌnbə:n], *s.* quemadura del sol, solanera; bronceado. — *v.i.* quemarse al sol; tostarse al sol.
sunburnt [ˈsʌnbə:nt], *a.* tostado (por el sol), bronceado.
sundae [ˈsʌndei], *s.* copa (de helado) ilustrada.
Sunday [ˈsʌndi, ˈsʌndei], *a.* dominical; dominguero; (*fam.*) ***Sunday best,*** trapos de (a)cristianar, *m.pl.*; (***dressed up***) ***in one's Sunday best,*** endomingado; ***Sunday school,*** escuela dominical. — *s.* domingo; ***Easter Sunday,*** domingo de Resurrección; ***Palm Sunday,*** domingo de Ramos.
sunder [ˈsʌndə], *v.t.* hender.
sundew [ˈsʌndju:], *s.* (*bot.*) rocío del sol.
sundown [ˈsʌndaun], *s.* puesta del sol; ***at sundown,*** al anochecer.
sundry [ˈsʌndri], *a.* diversos; ***all and sundry,*** todo el mundo.
sundries [ˈsʌndriz], *s.pl.* (*com.*) géneros diversos, *m.pl.*
sunflower [ˈsʌnflauə], *s.* girasol.
sunken [ˈsʌŋkən], *a.* hundido; ***sunken eyes,*** ojos hundidos, *m.pl.*
sunless [ˈsʌnlis], *a.* sin sol; nublado.
sunlight [ˈsʌnlait], *s.* (luz del) sol; luz solar.
sunlike [ˈsʌnlaik], *a.* parecido al sol; resplandeciente.
Sunna [ˈsʌnə], *s.* Suna.
sunny [ˈsʌni], *a.* soleado, lleno de sol; ***sunny day,*** día de sol, *m.*; (*fig.*) ***sunny side,*** lado bueno *o* risueño; ***it is sunny,*** hace sol.
sun-proof [ˈsʌn-pru:f], *a.* a prueba de sol.
sunrise [ˈsʌnraiz], *s.* salida del sol, orto; ***from sunrise to sunset,*** de sol a sol.
sunset [ˈsʌnset], *s.* puesta del sol, ocaso.
sunshade [ˈsʌnʃeid], *s.* quitasol, parasol, sombrilla.
sunshine [ˈsʌnʃain], *s.* luz *o* claridad del sol, sol; ***in the sunshine,*** al sol.
sunshiny [ˈsʌnʃaini], *a.* lleno de sol; resplandeciente; claro como el sol; (*fig.*) risueño.
sunspot [ˈsʌnspɔt], *s.* mancha solar.
sunstroke [ˈsʌnstrouk], *s.* insolación.
sunup [ˈsʌnʌp], *s.* (*Am.*) [DAWN; SUNRISE].
sunward [ˈsʌnwəd], *adv.* hacia el sol.
sunwise [ˈsʌnwaiz], *adv.* con el sol.
sup [sʌp], *s.* (*fam.*) sorbo. — *v.t., v.i.* beber a sorbos. — *v.i.* cenar.
super [ˈs(j)u:pə], *a.* (*fam.*) estupendo, bárbaro; (*fam.*) ***how super!*** ¡qué bien!; ***to have a super time,*** pasarlo bárbaro.
superable [ˈs(j)u:pərəbl], *a.* superable.
superableness [ˈs(j)u:pərəblnis], *s.* cualidad (*o* estado) de superable.
superabound [s(j)u:pərəˈbaund], *v.i.* sobreabundar.
superabundance [s(j)u:pərəˈbʌndəns], *s.* superabundancia.
superabundant [s(j)u:pərəˈbʌndənt], *a.* superabundante.
superadd [s(j)u:pərˈæd], *v.t.* sobreañadir.
superaddition [s(j)u:pərəˈdiʃən], *s.* sobreañadidura.
superannuate [s(j)u:pərˈænjueit], *v.t.* jubilar; dar retiro a.
superannuated [s(j)u:pərˈænjueitid], *a.* jubilado; anticuado. — *p.p.* [SUPERANNUATE].
superannuation [s(j)u:pərænjuˈeiʃən], *s.* jubilación; ***superannuation contribution,*** cuota de jubilación *o* retiro.
superb [s(j)u:ˈpə:b], *a.* soberbio, espléndido, magnífico.
supercargo [ˈs(j)u:pəkɑ:gou], *s.* sobrecargo.
super-charged [ˈs(j)u:pə-ˈtʃɑ:dʒd], *a.* superpotenciado.
superciliary [s(j)u:pəˈsiliəri], *a.* superciliar.
supercilious [s(j)u:pəˈsiliəs], *a.* displicente; desdeñoso; suficiente.
superciliousness [s(j)u:pəˈsiliəsnis], *s.* displicencia, desdén; suficiencia.
supereminence, (*ant.*) **supereminency** [s(j)u:pərˈeminens, -i], *s.* supereminencia.
supereminent [s(j)u:pərˈeminənt], *a.* supereminente, eminentísimo.
supererogation [s(j)u:pəreroˈgeiʃən], *s.* supererogación.
supererogatory [s(j)u:pəreˈrɔgətəri], *a.* supererogatorio.
superessential [s(j)u:pəriˈsenʃəl], *a.* sobreesencial.
superexcellence [s(j):upərˈeksiləns], *s.* sobreexcelencia.
superficial [s(j)u:pəˈfiʃəl], *a.* superficial.
superficiality [s(j)u:pəfiʃiˈæliti], *s.* superficialidad.
superficially [s(j)u:pəˈfiʃəli], *adv.* superficialmente; someramente; por encima.
superficies [s(j)u:pəˈfiʃii:z], *s. inv.* superficie, *f.*
superfine [ˈs(j)u:pəˈfain], *a.* superfino.
superfluity [s(j)u:pəˈflu:iti], *s.* superfluidad, superabundancia.
superfluous [s(j)u:ˈpə:fluəs], *a.* superfluo, que sobra.
superheterodyne [s(j)u:pəˈhetərodain], *a.* (*radio*) superheterodínico. — *s.* superheterodino.
superhuman [s(j)u:pəˈhju:mən], *a.* sobrehumano.
superimpose [s(j)u:pərimˈpouz], *v.t.* sobreponer.
superincumbent [s(j)u:pərinˈkʌmbənt], *a.* superyacente.
superinduce [s(j)u:pərinˈdju:s], *v.t.* sobreañadir.
superintend [s(j)u:pərinˈtend], *v.t.* dirigir; vigilar supervisar.
superintendence, superintendency [s(j)u:pərinˈtendəns, -i], *s.* superintendencia; inspección vigilación.
superintendent [s(j)u:pərinˈtendənt], *a.* que supervisa. — *s.* superintendente; inspector, supervisor comisario (de policía).
superior [s(j)u:ˈpiəriə], *a.* superior; (*despec.*) displicente, altivo; protector; ***mother superior*** superiora. — *s.* superior.
superiority [s(j)u:piəriˈɔriti], *s.* superioridad primacía.

superlative [s(j)uː'pəːlətiv], *a., s.* superlativo; ***to talk in superlatives,*** ser muy exagerado hablando.
superlatively [s(j)uː'pəːlətivli], *adv.* superlativamente; a la perfección, de (un) modo inmejorable.
superlativeness [s(j)uː'pəːlətivnis], *s.* excelencia.
superman ['s(j)uːpəmæn], *s.* superhombre.
supermarket ['s(j)uːpəmɑːkit], *s.* supermercado.
supernal [s(j)uː'pəːnəl], *a.* superno.
supernatural [s(j)uːpə'nætʃərəl], *a.* sobrenatural. — *s.* (lo) sobrenatural.
supernaturalism [s(j)uːpə'nætʃərəlizəm], *s.* sobrenaturalismo.
supernumerary [s(j)uːpə'njuːmərəri], *a., s.* supernumerario. — *s.* (*teat.*) comparsa, *m.f.*
superpose [s(j)uːpə'pouz], *v.t.* sobreponer, superponer.
superposition [s(j)uːpəpə'ziʃən], *s.* superposición.
superpower ['s(j)uːpəpauə], *s.* superpotencia.
superscribe [s(j)uːpə'skraib], *v.t.* sobrescribir.
superscription [s(j)uːpə'skripʃən], *s.* sobrescrito.
supersede [s(j)uːpə'siːd], *v.t.* sustituir, reemplazar; superar.
supersedeas [s(j)uːpə'siːdiəs], *s.* (*for.*) auto de sobreseimiento.
supersedure [s(j)uːpə'siːdʒə], (*Am.*) [SUPERSESSION].
supersession [s(j)uːpə'seʃən], *s.* (*for.*) sobreseimiento.
supersonic [s(j)uːpə'sɔnik], *a.* supersónico.
superstition [s(j)uːpə'stiʃən], *s.* superstición.
superstitious [s(j)uːpə'stiʃəs], *a.* supersticioso.
superstructure ['s(j)uːpəstrʌktʃə], *s.* superestructura; (*mar.*) obra muerta.
supertanker ['s(j)uːpətæŋkə], *s.* superpetrolero.
supertax ['s(j)uːpətæks], *s.* impuesto adicional; impuesto suplementario.
supervene [s(j)uːpə'viːn], *v.i.* sobrevenir, supervenir; seguir.
supervenient [s(j)uːpə'viːniənt], *a.* superveniente.
supervention [s(j)uːpə'venʃən], *s.* supervención, superveniencia, sobrevenida.
supervise ['s(j)uːpəvaiz], *v.t.* dirigir; vigilar; supervisar.
supervision [s(j)uːpə'viʒən], *s.* superintendencia; vigilación; (el) dirigir.
supervisor ['s(j)uːpəvaizə], *s.* supervisor; revisor; interventor; director.
supervisory ['s(j)uːpəvaizəri], *a.* de supervisión; ***in a supervisory capacity,*** en calidad de supervisor *o* de director.
supination [s(j)uːpi'neiʃən] *s.* supinación, posición supina.
supine ['s(j)uːpain], *a.* supino; pasivo, inactivo, indolente. — *s.* (*gram.*) supino.
supineness ['s(j)uːpainnis], *s.* pasividad, inactividad, indolencia.
supper ['sʌpə], *s.* cena; ***supper-time***, hora de cenar; ***The Lord's Supper,*** la (santísima) comunión; ***The Last Supper***, la (Ultima) Cena; ***to have supper,*** cenar, tomar la cena.
supperless ['sʌpəlis], *a.* sin cenar.
supplant [sə'plɑːnt], *v.t.* suplantar; desbancar.
supplanter [sə'plɑːntə], *s.* suplantador.
supplanting [sə'plɑːntiŋ], *s.* suplantación.
supple [sʌpl], *a.* flexible; elástico. — *v.t., v.i.* flexibilizar(se), hacer(se) flexible.
supplement ['sʌplimənt], *s.* suplemento; apéndice. — [-ment], *v.t.* complementar, suplir; completar.
supplemental, supplementary [sʌpli'mentəl, -əri], *a.* suplemental; suplementario; supletorio; adicional; secundario.
suppleness ['sʌplnis], *s.* flexibilidad; elasticidad.
suppletory ['sʌplitəri], *a.* (*for.*) supletorio.
suppliance ['sʌpliəns], *s.* ruego, súplica.
suppliant ['sʌpliənt], *a., s.* suplicante.
supplicant ['sʌplikənt], *a., s.* suplicante.
supplicate ['sʌplikeit], *v.t.* suplicar, rogar, impetrar.
supplication [sʌpli'keiʃən], *s.* súplica; (*igl.*) preces, *f.pl.*, plegaria.
supplicatory ['sʌplikeitəri], *a.* suplicatorio.
supplier [sə'plaiə], *s.* suministrador, proveedor, abastecedor.
supply [sə'plai], *s.* suministro abastecimiento, provisión; surtido, existencias, *f.pl.*; ***supply and demand,*** oferta y demanda; ***supply line,*** vía de abastecimiento; ***supply ship,*** buque nodriza; (*pl.* **supplies**) provisiones, *f.pl.*, víveres, *m.pl.*, pertechos, *m.pl.* — *v.t.* proveer, suministrar, surtir; (*mil. etc.*) abastecer, aprovisionar; (*general, fig.*) facilitar, proporcionar, brindar.
support [sə'pɔːt], *s.* apoyo; sostén; soporte, pilar; respaldo; ***in support of,*** en apoyo de. — *v.t.* apoyar; sostener; apuntalar; respaldar; mantener; (*tolerar*) soportar; ***this supports his statement,*** esto confirma su declaración. — **support o.s.,** *v.r.* mantenerse, ganarse la vida.
supportable [sə'pɔːtəbl], *a.* soportable; sostenible.
supporter [sə'pɔːtə], *s.* partidario; (*dep.*) aficionado, hincha, *m.f.*, forofo; (*mec.*) soporte, sostén; (*blas.*) tenante; ***supporters' club,*** pena deportiva.
supporting [sə'pɔːtiŋ], *a.* de apoyo; (*cine., teat.*) secundario.
suppose [sə'pouz], *v.t.* suponer; ***let us suppose (that),*** supongamos (que), pongamos por caso; ***supposing that,*** suponiendo que, en el supuesto de que; ***suppose we try it like this?*** ¿y si lo intentamos así? ***he's ready I suppose,*** estará listo, ¿verdad?; ***he is supposed to know,*** en teoría, lo debía saber; ***it's supposed to be very good,*** dicen que es muy bueno; ***I suppose so,*** supongo (que sí); ***oh, I suppose so,*** si te empeñas, si no hay más remedio.
supposed [sə'pouzd], *a.* supuesto; pretendido.
supposedly [sə'pouzidli], *adv.* según se supone; en teoría.
supposition [sʌpo'ziʃən], *s.* suposición; supesto; conjetura.
suppositional [sʌpə'ziʃənəl], *a.* supositivo, hipotético, conjetural.
supposititious [səpɔsi'tiʃəs], *a.* supositicio.
suppository [sə'pɔzitəri], *s.* supositorio.
suppress [sə'pres], *v.t.* suprimir; sofocar.
suppression [sə'preʃən], *s.* supresión.
suppressive [sə'presiv], *a.* supreviso.
suppressor [sə'presə], *s.* supresor.
suppurate ['sʌpjureit], *v.i.* supurar.
suppuration [sʌpju'reiʃən], *s.* supuración.
suppurative ['sʌpjurətiv], *a., s.* supurativo.
supranational [s(j)uːprə'næʃənəl], *a.* supranacional.
suprarenal [s(j)uːprə'riːnəl], *a.* suprarrenal.
supremacy [s(j)uː'preməsi], *s.* supremacia.
supreme [s(j)uː'priːm], *a.* supremo; ***Supreme Court,*** el tribunal supremo.
supremely [s(j)uːpriːmli], *adv.* sumamente, en sumo grado.
sural ['sjuərəl], *a.* sural.
surcharge ['səːtʃɑːdʒ], *s.* recargo; sobrecarga. — [səː'tʃɑːdʒ], *v.t.* recargar; sobrecargar.
surcingle ['səːsiŋgl], *s.* sobrecincha.
surcoat ['səːkout], *s.* sobretodo, gabán; sobrevesta.
surculose ['səːkjulous], *a.* lleno de vástagos.
surd [səːd], *a.* (*fonét.*) sordo; (*mat.*) orracional. — *s.* sonido sordo; número irracional.
surdity ['səːditi], *s.* sordera.
sure [ʃɔː, ʃuə], *a.* seguro, cierto; firme; ***as sure as fate,*** con toda seguridad; como un clavo; ***to be sure!*** ¡claro!; ***are you quite sure?*** ¿está seguró del todo?; ***I'm sure about that,*** estoy seguro de ello; ***I'm not so sure about that,*** no diría yo tanto; ***to be sure that...,*** estar seguro de que...; ***he is sure to come,*** es seguro que vendrá; ***be sure to do it,*** no dejes de hacerlo; ***I don't know for sure,*** no lo sé con seguridad; ***that's for sure,***

eso es seguro; ***to make sure***, asegurarse, cerciorase. — *adv.* ***sure!*** si, ¡claro!, ¡ya lo creo!; ***sure enough***, efectivamente; a buen seguro.
sure-footed [ˈʃɔ-ˈfutid], *a.* de pie firme, con pie firme.
surely [ˈʃɔːli], *adv.* seguramente, ciertamente; por supuesto; ***surely!*** con mucho gusto; ***surely he hasn't said that***, ¿será posible que haya dicho eso?; ***surely not!*** ¡no me digas!; ¿será posible?; ***you'll come, surely?*** vendrás, ¿verdad?
sureness [ˈʃɔːnis], *s.* seguridad, certeza; firmeza; (lo) certero.
surety [ˈʃuəriti], *s.* garantía, fianza; fiador, garante; ***to stand surety for***, salir garante por, ser fiador de.
suretyship [ˈʃuəritiʃip], *s.* seguridad, fianza.
surf [səːf], *s.* oleaje; rompiente(s).
surface [ˈsəːfis], *s.* superficie; cara; exterior; ***temporary surface***, firme provisional; ***on the surface***, a primera vista; ***surface (mail)***, por vía terrestra *o* marítima; (*fís.*) ***surface tension***, tensión superficial. — *v.t.* poner superficie a; alisar; recubrir, revestir. — *v.i.* salir a la superficie, emerger (*un submarino*); asomar.
surfacer [ˈsəːfisə], *s.* cepillo mecánico, máquina de alisar *o* cepillar madera.
surface-air missile [ˈsəːfis-ɛə ˈmisail], *s.* proyectil tierra-aire.
surfboard [ˈsːəfbɔːd], *s.* acuaplano.
surfeit [ˈsəˈfit], *s.* hartura, saciedad; empacho, atracón; exceso. — *v.t.* hartar, saciar. — **surfeit o.s.,** *v.r.* — (***with***), hartarse (de), saciarse (de).
surge [səːdʒ], *s.* oleaje, oleada; (*fig.*) ola, oleada. — *v.i.* hervir, bullir, agitarse; embravecerse (*el mar*).
surgeon [ˈsəːdʒən], *s.* cirujano; (*mil.*, *mar.*) médico, físico; ***veterinary surgeon***, veterinario; (*Am.*) ***surgeon-general***, médico mayor, jefe de sanidad (militar *o* naval).
surgery [ˈsəːdʒəri], *s.* cirugía; (*sala*) consultorio; ***surgery hours***, horas de consulta, *f.pl.*; ***plastic surgery***, cirugía estética.
surgical [ˈsəːdʒikəl], *a.* quirúrgico; ***surgical spirit***, alcohol.
surliness [ˈsəːlinis], *s.* hosquedad, aspereza, desabrimiento.
surly [ˈsəːli], *a.* hosco, áspero, desabrido.
surmise [səˈmaiz], *s.* conjetura, suposición. — *v.t.* conjeturar, suponer. — *v.i.* hacer conjeturas.
surmount [səˈmaunt], *v.t.* vencer, superar.
surmountable [səˈmauntəbl], *a* vencible, superable.
surname [ˈsəːneim], *s.* apellido. — *v.t.* apellidar.
surpass [səˈpɑːs], *v.t.* superar, sobrepujar, sobrepasar, aventajar.
surpassing [səˈpɑːsiŋ], *a.* sobresaliente, incomparable, excepcional, extraordinario.
surplice [ˈsəːplis], *s.* (*igl.*) sobrepelliz, *f.*
surplus [ˈsəːpləs]. *a.* sobrante, de sobra. — *s.* excedente; sobrante; (*com.*) superávit; ***Government Surplus***, excedentes oficiales, *m.pl.*
surprise [səˈpraiz], *a.* de sorpresa, inesperado. — *s.* sorpresa; extrañeza; ***to my surprise***, con sorpresa mía; ***to take by surprise***, tomar por sorpresa, coger desprevenido. — *v.t.* sorprender; extrañar, chocar; coger desprevenido; ***to be surprised at*** o ***by***, sorprenderse de, extrañarse de.
surprising [səˈpraiziŋ], *a.* soprendente, chocante.
surrealism [səˈriəlizəm], *s.* surrealismo.
surrealist [səˈriəlist], *a.*, *s.* surrealista, *m.f.*
surrender [səˈrendə], *s.* rendición; entrega; renuncia; abandono. — *v.t.* rendir; entregar; renunciar a. — *v.i.* rendirse; entregarse.
surrepetitious [sʌrəpˈtiʃəs], *a.* subrepticio, furtivo.
surrey [ˈsʌri], *s.* (*Am.*) birlocho.
surrogate [ˈsʌrogeit], *s.* sustituto; (*igl.*) vicario.
surround [səˈraund], *s.* marco; borde. — *v.t.* cercar, rodear, circundar.
surrounding [səˈraundiŋ], *a.* de alrededor, circundante, circunvecino. — *s.* (*pl.*) alrededores, *m.pl.*, contornos, *m.pl.*; ambiente, medio; medio ambiente.
surtax [ˈsəːtæks], *s.* impuesto adicional.
surveillance [səˈveiləns], *s.* vigilancia.
survey [ˈsəːvei], *s.* medición; inspección; reconocimiento; examen; estudio; encuesta; visión; informe (*económico*). — [səˈvei], *v.t.* inspeccionar; reconocer; examinar; estudiar; dar una visión de.
surveying [səˈveiiŋ], *s.* agrimensura.
surveyor [səˈveiə], *s.* agrimensor, topógrafo; inspector; ***surveyor of the custom-house***, vista de aduana, *m.*
surveyorship [səˈveiəʃip], *s.* profesión *o* empleo de agrimensor.
survival [səˈvaivəl], *s.* supervivencia.
survive, [səˈvaiv], *v.t.* sobrevivir (a). — *v.i.* sobrevivir; (*fig.*) perdurar, subsistir.
survivor [səˈvaivə], *s.* superviviente.
Susan [ˈsuːzən]. Susana.
susceptibility [səseptiˈbiliti], *s.* susceptibilidad; sensibilidad.
susceptible [səˈseptibl], *a.* susceptible; sensible; enamoradizo; ***to be susceptible of***, admitir; ***it is susceptible of improvement***, cabe mejorarlo.
susceptibly [səˈseptibli], *adv.* de una manera susceptible.
suspect [ˈsʌspekt], *a.*, *s.* sospechoso. — [səsˈpekt], *v.t.* sospechar (de); recelar *o* recelarse de; ***he is suspected of murder***, es sospechoso de haber cometido un asesinato.
suspend [səsˈpend], *v.t.* suspender; ***he was suspended for 1 year***, le retiraron el permiso, la licencia *etc.* por 1 año; ***suspend payment***, hacer suspensión de pagos.
suspended [səsˈpendid], *a.* suspendido; ***suspended animation***, muerte aparente, *f.*
suspender [səsˈpendə], suspendedor; (*pl.*) ligas, *f.pl.*, tirantes (de las medias *o* los calcetines), *m.pl.*; (*Am.*) [BRACES].
suspense [səsˈpens], *s.* incertidumbre, duda, zozobra; suspensión; suspense; tensión; ***to be in suspense***, estar en vilo.
suspension [səsˈpenʃən], *s.* suspensión; ***suspension bridge***, puente colgante; (*mil.*) ***suspension of hostilities***, suspensión de hostilidades.
suspensive [səsˈpensiv], *a.* suspensivo.
suspensory [səsˈpensəri], *a.*, *s.* suspensorio.
suspicion [səsˈpiʃən], *s.* sospecha; desconfianza, recelo, suspicacia; (*fam.*) pizca.
suspicious [səsˈpiʃəs], *a.* suspicaz, desconfiado, receloso; sospechoso; ***to be suspicious about sth.***, redelarse *o* sospechar (de) algo; ***it looks very suspicious***, resulta muy sospechoso.
suspiciously [səsˈpiʃəsli], *adv.* con recelo, desconfiadamante; de modo sospechoso.
suspiciousness [səsˈpiʃəsnis], *s.* recelo; (lo) sospechoso.
sustain [səsˈtein], *v.t.* sostener, mantener; apoyar; ***sustain a loss***, sufrir una pérdida; ***sustain injuries***, sufrir *o* recibir heridas.
sustainable [səsˈteinəbl], *a.* sostenible; sustentable.
sustainer [səsˈteinə], *s.* sostenedor; sustentador; (*fig.*) protector.
sustenance [ˈsʌstənəns], *s.* sustento.
susurration [sʌsjuˈreiʃən], *s.* susurro.
sutler [ˈsʌtlə], *s.* vivandero.
suture [ˈsjuːtʃə], *s.* (*cir.*) sutura. — *v.t.* suturar, coser.
suzerain [ˈsuːzərin], *s.* soberano.
suzerainty [ˈsuːzrənti], *s.* soberanía.
svelte [svelt], *a.* esbelto.
swab [swɔb], *s.* estropajo; trapo; (*mar.*) lampazo; (*artill.*) escobillón; (*med.*) algodón, torunda. — *v.t.* limpiar con estropajo *etc.*; (*mar.*) lampacear; fregar; enjugar.

swaddle [swɔdl], *v.t.* envolver en pañales.
swaddling clothes [ˈswɔdliŋ klouðz], *s.pl.* pañales, *m.pl.*
swag [swæg], *s.* (*fam.*) botín.
swage [sweidʒ], *v.t.* (*metal.*) estampar.
swagger [ˈswægə], *a.* (*fam.*) de mucho estilo. — *s.* pavoneo, contoneo. — *v.i.* pavonearse, contonearse.
swaggering [ˈswægəriŋ], *a.* con pavoneo *o* contoneo; ***swaggering gait,*** andares chulescos, *m.pl.* — *s.* pavoneo, contoneo; ademanes chulescos, *m.pl.*
Swahili [swɑːˈhiːli], *a., s.* swahili, *m.f.*
swain [swein], *s.* zagal; enamorado.
swallow (1) [ˈswɔlou], *s.* (*orn.*) golondrina; (*natación*) ***swallow-dive,*** salto del ángel; (*carp.*) ***swallow-tail,*** cola de milano; ***swallow-tailed coat,*** frac.
swallow (2) [ˈswɔlou], *s.* trago. — *v.t.* tragar; engullir, deglutir; (*fig.*) tragarse (*un insulto etc.*); creerse (*una mentira etc.*); ***swallow up,*** tragar(se); ***swallow one's words,*** tragarse las palabras, desdecirse, retractarse. — *v.i.* tragar.
swallow-wort [ˈswɔlou-wəːt], *s.* celidonia.
swamp [swɔmp], *s.* pantano; marisma; (*bot.*) ***swamp-oak,*** roble de los pantanos. — *v.t.* inundar; desbordar; (*fig.*) abrumar, apabullar.
swampy [ˈswɔmpi], *a.* pantanoso.
swan [swɔn], *s.* (*orn.*) cisne; ***swan-song,*** canto del cisne; (*Am.*) ***swan-dive*** [SWALLOW-DIVE]. — *v.i.* (*fig., fam.*) ***swan*** (***about***), dar valsones.
swank [swæŋk], *s.* (*fam.*) fachenda, chulería. — *v.i.* (*fam.*) fachendear, chulear(se), darse tono; dárselas de elegante.
swanky [ˈswæŋki], *a.* (*fam.*) fachendoso, chulo; elegantón.
swansdown [ˈswɔnzdaun], *s.* plumón de cisne; (*tej.*) moletón, paño de vicuña.
swanskin [ˈswɔnskin], *s.* piel de cisne, *f.*; lanilla.
swap, swop [swɔp], *s.* (*fam.*) (inter)cambio, cambalache, trueque. — *v.t.* (*fam.*) (inter)cambiar, cambalachear, trocar. — *v.i.* (*fam.*) hacer cambalaches *o* trueques.
sward [swɔːd], *s.* césped.
swarm [swɔːm], *s.* enjambre; muchedumbre. — *v.i.* enjambrar; (*fig.*) pulular, bullir, hormiguear (***with,*** de).
swart [swɔːt], *a.* (*ant.*) prieto.
swarthiness [ˈswɔːðinis], *s.* morenez, (lo) moreno, (lo) morenote.
swarthy [ˈswɔːði], *a.* atezado, moreno.
swash [swɔʃ], *s.* chapoteo. — *v.i.* chapotear, chapalear; fanfarronear.
swashbuckler [ˈswɔʃbʌklə], *s.* matasiete, espadachín, fanfarrón.
swashbuckling [ˈswɔʃbʌkliŋ], *a.* valentón, fanfarrón, baladrón. — *s.* fanfarria, valentonadas, *f.pl.*, baladronadas, *f.pl.*
swashy [ˈswɔʃi], *a.* pastoso, aguanoso, lodoso.
swastika [ˈswɔstikə], *s.* esvástica, cruz gamada.
swat [swɔt], *v.t.* matar (*moscas*).
swath [swɔːθ], *s.* ringla *o* ringlera de mies segada.
swathe [sweið], *s.* venda; faja. — *v.t.* fajar; envolver; vendar.
sway [swei], *s.* balanceo; oscilación; vaivén; cimbreo; imperio, dominio; ascendiente, influencia; ***to hold sway over,*** tener dominio sobre. — *v.t.* balancear, mecer; inclinar; mover, influir en; (*mar.*) ***sway up,*** guindar, izar. — *v.i.* balancearse; oscilar; tambalearse; bambolearse; mecerse.
Swazi [ˈswɑːzi], *a., s.* swazi, *m.f.*
Swaziland [ˈswɑːzilænd]. Swazilandia.
sweal [swiːl], *v.t., v.i.* quemar(se), chamuscar(se); (*fig.*) derretir(se).
swear [swɛə], *irr. v.t.* jurar; ***swear in,*** tomar juramento a, hacer prestar juramento a; ***to be sworn in,*** prestar juramento. — *v.i.* jurar; soltar tacos, decir palabrotas, blasfemar; ***swear black and blue,*** echar sapos y culebras; ***swear roundly,*** jurar y perjurar; ***swear like a trooper,*** jurar como un carretero; ***swear at,*** maldecir; decir *o* echar pestes de; ***swear by,*** jurar por; creer ciegamente en; ***I would swear to it,*** juraría que fue así.
swearer [ˈswὲərə], *s.* jurador.
swearword [ˈswɛəwəːd], *s.* taco, palabrota.
sweat [swet], *s.* sudor; ***by the sweat of one's brow,*** con el sudor de la frente; ***to be in a sweat,*** estar sudando; (*fig.*) estar apurado; ***cold sweat,*** escalofríos, *m.pl.*; (*fam.*) ***old sweat,*** veterano; ***running with sweat,*** chorreando sudor; ***sweat gland,*** glándula sudorípara; ***sweat shop,*** taller en que se explota al obrero; ***what a sweat!*** ¡qué trabajo! — *v.t.* sudar; explotar (*a los obreros*); ***sweat blood,*** sudar la gota gorda, sudar tinta. — *v.i.* sudar.
sweatband [ˈswetbænd], *s.* badana (*del sombrero*).
sweater [ˈswetə], *s.* suéter.
sweating [ˈswetiŋ], *a.* sudoroso. — *s.* (el) sudar; explotación (*de obreros*); ***sweating room,*** sudadero.
sweaty [ˈsweti], *a.* sudoroso; sudado, sudoso.
Swede [swiːd], *s.* (*pers.*) sueco, sueca.
swede [swiːd], *s.* nabo sueco.
Sweden [swiːdn]. Suecia.
Swedish [ˈswiːdiʃ], *a., s.* sueco.
sweep [swiːp], *s.* barrido; (*paisaje etc.*) extensión; (*movimiento de máquina etc.*) recorrido; (*vista etc.*) alcance; (*de conocimientos etc.*) envergadura; (*traje etc.*) vuelo; (*carretera etc.*) curva, vuelta, giro; redada (*de la policía*); (*pers.*) barrendero; ***chimney-sweep,*** deshollinador, limpiachimeneas, *m.inv.*; remo (*largo y pesado*); aspa (*de molino*); cigoñal (*de pozo*); ***to make a clean sweep of,*** hacer tabla rasa de, cambiar totalmente. — *irr. v.t.* barrer; limpiar barriendo; (*chimenea*) deshollinar; ((*minas*) rastrear, dragar; ***sweep along,*** arrastrar; ***sweep aside,*** apartar *o* rechazar bruscamente *o* con impaciencia; ***sweep away,*** barrer totalmente, arrastrar; borrar totalmente; (*fig.*) ***sweep under the carpet,*** darle carpetazo a; ***sweep up,*** barrer, limpiar barriendo; (*fig.*) ***sweep s.o. off his*** o ***her feet,*** arrebatar a alguien; (*fig.*) ***sweep the board,*** llevárselo todo, copar. — *irr. v.i.* barrer; ***sweep by, past,*** o ***through,*** pasar rápidamente, majestuosamente *o* altivamente; ***sweep down on,*** descender rápidamente sobre, abalanzarse sobre.
sweeper [ˈswiːpə], *s.* barrendero; (máquina) barredera; ***chimney-sweeper,*** deshollinador, limpiachimeneas, *m.inv.*; ***carpet-sweeper,*** barredera de alfombra; (*mar.*) ***mine-sweeper,*** (buque) dragaminas, *m.*
sweeping [ˈswiːpiŋ], *a.* excesivamente amplio, categórico *o* tajante. — *s.* barrido; (*pl.*) barreduras, *f.pl.*
sweepstake(s) [ˈswiːpsteik(z)], *s.* lotería (*esp. de carreras de caballos*); carrera de caballos.
sweet [swiːt], *a.* dulce; azucarado; oloroso, fragante; fresco; melodioso, suave; encantador, amable, bonito; (*tierra*) fértil; (*bot.*) ***sweet-basil,*** alba haca; (*bot.*) ***sweet-cicely,*** perifollo; ***sweet-corn,*** maíz; (*bot.*) ***sweet-flag, sweet-rush,*** cálamo aromático; ***sweet-oil,*** aceite de oliva; ***sweet-gum,*** ocozol; ***sweet-potato,*** batata; (*bot.*) ***sweet-pea,*** guisante de olor; ***sweet-tongued*** o ***sweet-spoken,*** melifluo; ***sweet-smelling,*** odorífero, fragante; ***sweet-tempered,*** de carácter dulce; ***sweet-scented,*** perfumado; ***sweet-toothed,*** goloso; (*bot.*) ***sweet-willow, sweet-gale,*** mirto holandés; (*bot.*) ***sweet-william,*** minutisa; ***how sweet!*** ¡qué mono!, ¡qué coquetón!, ¡qué tierno! — *s.* caramelo; dulce; postre; (*pl.*) caramelos, *m.pl.*; dulces, *m.pl.*
sweetbreads [ˈswiːtbredz], *s. pl.* lechecillas, *f.pl.*, mollejas, *f.pl.*
sweetbrier, sweetbriar [ˈswiːtˈbraiə], *s.* eglantina.
sweeten [swiːtn], *v.t.* endulzar, azucarar; dulcificar; (*farm.*) edulcorar.

sweetener [ˈswi:tnə], *s.* edulcorante; dulcificador.
sweetening [ˈswi:tniŋ], *a.*, *s.* (lo) dulcificante.
sweetheart [ˈswi:thɑ:t], *s.* novio; novia.
sweetie [ˈswi:ti], *s.* (*fam.*) cariño.
sweeting [ˈswi:tiŋ], *s.* (*bot.*) camuesa; (*ant.*) cariño.
sweetish [ˈswi:tiʃ], *a.* algo dulce, dulcecillo.
sweetmeat [ˈswi:tmi:t], *s.* golosina, confitura.
sweetness [ˈswi:tnis], *s.* dulzor; dulzura, ternura; fragrancia; (*fam.*) ***he was all sweetness and light,*** estaba *o* estuvo encantador *o* desconocido.
swell [swel], *a.* (*fam.*) elegantísimo; (*fam.*) estupendo, bárbaro; (*fam.*) ***we had a swell time,*** lo pasamos de órdago. — *s.* mar de fondo, marejada; (*mús.*) pedal de expresión; (*fam.*) personaje, pez gordo; (*fam.*) ***the swells,*** la gente de buen tono. — *irr. v.t.* hinchar, inflar; abultar; engrosar; aumentar; acrecentar. — *v.i.* hincharse, inflarse; abultarse; crecer, aumentar(se); ***my hand swelled up,*** se me hinchó la mano; ***swell to a great amount,*** elevarse a una fuerte suma; ***swell out,*** hincharse; ampollarse.
swelling [ˈsweliŋ], *a.* que (se) hincha, (se) infla *etc.*; tumescente; ***swelling sea,*** mar embravecido. — *s.* hinchazón, *f.*; (*med.*) tumefacción; chichón, bulto; protuberancia.
swelter [ˈsweltə], *v.t.* sofocar, achicharrar, abrumar de calor. — *v.i.* abrasarse, achicharrarse, ahogarse, sudar la gota gorda.
swerve [swə:v], *s.* desvío *o* viraje repentino; esguince, regate. — *v.t.* desviar, torcer; dar efecto a (*una pelota*). — *v.i.* desviarse; torcer(se); virar.
swift [swift], *a.* veloz, raudo; ***swift of foot,*** de pies ligeros. — *s.* (*orn.*) vencejo; (*mec.*) devanadera.
swift-footed [ˈswift-ˈfutid], *a.* veloz, de pies ligeros.
swifter (1) [ˈswiftə], *s.* (*mar.*) tortor, andaribel; falso obenque.
swifter (2) [ˈswiftə], *a.* (*compar. de* [SWIFT]).
swiftly [ˈswiftli], *adv.* velozmente, rápidamente, ligeramente.
swiftness [ˈswiftnis], *s.* velocidad, ligereza, celeridad; prontitud.
swig [swig], *s.* trago. — *v.t.*, *v.i.* beber (a grandes tragos).
swill [swil], *s.* (*para cerdos etc.*) bazofia; aguachirle; tragantada. — *v.t.* lavar, limpiar con agua; beber (a grandes tragos); tragar(se). — *v.i.* emborracharse, beber mucho.
swiller [ˈswilə], *s.* borrachín.
swim [swim], *s.* (el) nadar, nadada, nado; ***swim-bladder,*** vejiga natatoria (*de los peces*); ***to go for a swim, to have a swim,*** bañarse, ir a nadar; ***to be in the swim,*** estar metido (*en sociedad etc.*). — *irr. v.t.* pasar, cruzar a nado. — *v.i.* nadar; ***to swim with the tide,*** seguir la corriente; ***my head is swimming,*** me da vueltas la cabeza.
swimmer [ˈswimə], *s.* nadador.
swimming [ˈswimiŋ], *a.* natatorio; de natación. — *s.* natación; ***swimming-costume,*** bañador, traje de baño; ***swimming-place,*** nadadero; ***swimming-bath*** o ***-pool,*** piscina.
swimmingly [ˈswimiŋli], *adv.* (*fam.*) viento en popa, a las mil maravillas.
swimsuit [ˈswims(j)u:t], *s.* traje de baño.
swindle [swindl], *s.* estafa, timo. — *v.t.* estafar, timar.
swindler [ˈswindlə], *s.* estafador, timador.
swine [swain], *s. inv.* marrano, puerco, cerdo; (*fig.*) canalla, *m.f.*; (*ict.*) ***sea-swine,*** marsopa; ***swine-fever,*** peste de los puercos, *f.*; ***swine-herd,*** porquero, porquerizo; (*bot.*) ***swine-thistle,*** cerraja, cardo ajonjero.
swing [swiŋ], *s.* columpio; vaivén, oscilación; balanceo, movimiento; viraje; (*mús.*) swing; (*mús.*) ritmo; (*boxeo*) golpe lateral; ***swing-bridge,*** puente giratorio; ***swing-door,*** puerta giratoria; ***in full swing,*** en plena marcha, en pleno funcionamiento; ***to go with a swing,*** ir viento en popa. — *irr. v.t.* columpiar; balancear; hacer oscilar; menear; hacer girar; hacer bascular; (*fam.*) ***swing the lead,*** contar una mentira (para zafarse de algo). — *v.i.* columpiarse; balancearse; oscilar; menearse; girar; bascular; (*fam.*) ***you'll swing for it,*** te ahorcarán, te lincharán.
swingeing [ˈswindʒiŋ], *a.* (*fam.*) durísimo, feroz; morrocotudo.
swinging [ˈswiŋiŋ], *a.* oscilante; (*mús.*) rítmico; (*fig.*, *fam.*) novedoso, torremolinesco.
swingle [swiŋgl], *s.* espadilla. — *v.t.* espadillar.
swinish [ˈswainiʃ], *a.* porcuno; (*fig.*) canallesco.
swinishness [ˈswainiʃnis], *s.* (lo) canallesco.
swipe [swaip], *s.* (*fam.*) tortazo. — *v.t.* dar un tortazo a; birlar.
swirl [swə:l], *s.* torbellino; remolino. — *v.i.* arremolinarse, girar.
swish [swiʃ], *s.* silbido (*del látigo*); crujido, frufrú. — *v.t.* agitar, blandir, menear. — *v.i.* silbar, sonar; crujir.
Swiss [swis], *a.*, *s.* suizo; ***Swiss chard,*** acelga; ***Swiss Guards,*** guardia suiza; ***Swiss roll,*** brazo de gitano.
switch [switʃ], *s.* vara, varilla; trenza postiza, postizo; (*Am.*, *f.c.*) aguja; desviación; (*elec.*) interruptor, conmutador; cambio; ***switch lever,*** palanca de aguja; (*Am.*) ***switch-man,*** guardaagujas, *m.inv.*; ***to do a switch,*** pegar el cambiazo; ***to make a switch,*** hacer un cambio. — *v.t.* cambiar; (*f.c.*) desviar, cambiar de vía; (*elec.*) derivar; ***switch round,*** intercambiar (de sitio); ***switch on,*** encender; conectar, poner; ***switch off,*** apagar; desconectar, quitar; parar (*el motor*). — *v.i.* cambiar; ***switch over to,*** cambiar a; ***switch round,*** intercambiar los sitios; ***switch on,*** encender; enchufar, poner; ***switch off,*** apagar; desconectar.
switchback [ˈswitʃbæk], *s.* (*dep.*) montaña rusa.
switchboard [ˈswitʃbɔ:d], *s.* (*elec.*) cuadro de distribución; centralita (*de teléfono*).
Switzerland [ˈswitsələnd]. Suiza.
swivel [ˈswivəl], *s.* torniquete; eslabón giratorio; lanzadera (*de un telar de cintas*); (*artill.*) ***swivel-gun,*** colisa, pedrero; ***swivel-chair,*** silla giratoria; ***swivel-door,*** puerta giratoria; ***swivel-joint,*** junta articulada, rótula. — *v.t.*, *v.i.* — ***round,*** (hacer) girar.
swollen [ˈswoulən], *a.* hinchado; henchido; crecido; ***swollen with pride,*** henchido de orgullo. — *p.p.* [SWELL].
swoon [swu:n], *s.* desmayo, desvanecimiento; ***to fall in a swoon,*** caerse desmayado. — *v.i.* desmayarse, desvanecerse, perder el sentido.
swoop [swu:p], *s.* calada, descenso súbito; arremetida; redada; ***in one (fell) swoop,*** de un (solo) golpe. — *v.i.* abatirse, calarse, lanzarse; abalanzarse.
swop [SWAP].
sword [sɔ:d], *s.* espada; ***to put to the sword,*** pasar a cuchillo; ***sword-arm,*** brazo derecho; ***sword-belt,*** talabarte, cinturón; ***sword-guard, sword-hilt,*** empuñadura; ***sword-knot,*** borla de espada; ***sword-law,*** ley del más fuerte; ***sword-play,*** esgrima; manejo de la espada; ***with fire and sword,*** a sangre y fuego.
swordfish [ˈsɔ:dfiʃ], *s.* (*ict.*) pez espada, *m.*
sword-shaped [ˈsɔ:d-ʃeipt], *a.* ensiforme.
swordsman [ˈsɔ:dzmən], *s.* (*pl.* **swordsmen** [-men]) esgrimidor; espadachín.
sworn [swɔ:n], *a.* ***sworn enemy,*** enemigo jurado; ***sworn statement,*** declaración jurada. — *p.p.* [SWEAR].
swot [swɔt], *s.* (*fam.*) empollón. — *v.t.*, *v.i.* (*fam.*) empollar.
sybarite [ˈsibərait], *s.* sibarita, *m.f.*
sybaritic [sibəˈritik], *a.* sibarítico.
sycamore [ˈsikəmɔ:], *s.* (*bot.*) socomoro.
sycophancy [ˈsikəfənsi], *s.* servilismo, adulación.
sycophant [ˈsikəfænt], *s.* sicofante; adulador, cobista, *m.f.*

sycophantic [sikəˈfæntik], *a.* adulatorio; servil.
syenite [ˈsaiənait], *s.* sienita.
syenitic [saiəˈnitik], *a.* sienítico.
syllabary [ˈsiləbəri], *s.* silabario.
syllabic [siˈlæbik], *a.* silábico.
syllabicate [siˈlæbikeit], *v.t.* silabear.
syllabication [silæbiˈkeiʃən], *s.* silabeo.
syllable [ˈsiləbl], *s.* sílaba.
syllabus [ˈsiləbəs], *s.* (*pl.* **syllabuses, syllabi** [-iz, ˈsiləbai]) programa, *m.*
syllepsis [siˈlepsis], *s.* (*pl.* **syllepses** [-si:z]) silepsis, *f. inv.*
syllogism [ˈsilodʒizəm], *s.* silogismo.
syllogistic [siloˈdʒistik], *a.* silogístico.
syllogize [ˈsilodʒaiz], *v.i.* silogizar.
sylph [silf], *s.* sílfide, *f.*
sylvan [SILVAN].
symbol [ˈsimbəl], *s.* símbolo.
symbolic(al) [simˈbɔlik(əl)], *a.* simbólico.
symbolism [ˈsimbəlizəm], *s.* simbolismo.
symbolist [ˈsimbəlist], *s.* simbolista, *m.f.*
symbolization [simbəlaiˈzeiʃən], *s.* simbolización.
symbolize [ˈsimbəlaiz], *v.t.* simbolizar.
symmetric(al) [siˈmetrik(əl)], *a.* simétrico.
symmetrize [ˈsimitraiz], *v.t.* dar simetría a.
symmetry [ˈsimitri], *s.* simetría.
sympathetic [simpəˈθetik], *a.* compasivo; comprensivo; simpatizante, solidario; simpático; ***to be sympathetic to,*** simpatizar con.
sympathize [ˈsimpəθaiz], *v.i.* compadecerse (***with,*** de); simpatizar (***with,*** con).
sympathizer [ˈsimpəθaizə], *s.* simpatizante (***with,*** de), solidario (***with,*** de).
sympathy [ˈsimpəθi], *s.* compasión, conmiseración; comprensión; simpatía, solidaridad; ***to be in sympathy with,*** simpatizar con; ***to be out of sympathy with,*** no simpatizar con; ***to express one's sympathy*** (***on the occasion of bereavement***), acompañar en el sentimiento (***with,*** a); ***to extend one's sympathy to,*** dar el pésame a; ***to strike in sympathy with,*** declararse en huelga por solidaridad con.
symphonic [simˈfɔnik], *a.* sinfónico.
symphonious [simˈfouniəs], *a.* armonioso.
symphonist [ˈsimfənist], *s.* sinfonista, *m.f.*
symphony [ˈsimfəni], *s.* sinfonía.
symphysis [ˈsimfisis], *s.* sínfisis, *f.inv.*
symposium [simˈpouziəm], *s.* (*pl.* **symposia, symposiums** [simˈpouziə, -iəmz]) simposio, coloquio.
symptom [ˈsimptəm], *s.* síntoma, *m.*
symptomatic [simptəˈmætik], *a.* sintomático.
symptomatology [simptəməˈtɔlədʒi], *s.* sintomatología.
synæresis [siˈniərisis], *s.* sinéresis, *f.inv.*
synæsthesia [sinisˈθi:ziə], *s.* sinestesia.
synagogue [ˈsinəgɔg], *s.* sinagoga.
synalepha [sinəˈli:fə], *s.* sinalefa.
synarthrosis [sinɑ:ˈθrousis], *s.* sinartrosis, *f.inv.*
synchromesh [ˈsiŋkromeʃ], *s.* (*aut.*) cambio sincronizado.
synchronism [ˈsiŋkrənizəm], *s.* sincronismo.
synchronization [siŋkrənaiˈzeiʃən], *s.* sincronización.
synchronize [ˈsiŋkrənaiz], *v.t.* sincronizar. — *v.i.* sincronizarse, ser sincrónico.
synchronous [ˈsiŋkrənəs], *a.* sincrónico, síncrono.
synclinal [sinˈklainəl], *a.* (*geol.*) sinclinal.
syncopate [ˈsiŋkəpeit], *v.t.* sincopar.
syncopation [siŋkəˈpeiʃən], *s.* (*mús.*) síncopa.
syncope [ˈsiŋkəpi], *s.* (*med., lenguaje*) síncope; (*mús.*) síncopa.
syncretism [ˈsiŋkritizəm], *s.* sincretismo.
syndic [ˈsindik], *s.* síndico.
syndicalism [ˈsindikəlizəm], *s.* sindicalismo.
syndicalist [ˈsindikəlist], *a., s.* sindicalista, *m.f.*
syndicate [ˈsindikit], *s.* sindicato; sindicatura; síndico; trust. — [-keit], *v.t., v.i.* sindicar(se).
syndrome [ˈsindroum], *s.* síndrome.
syne [sain], *adv.* (*Esco.*) tiempo atrás, hace tiempo.
synecdoche [siˈnekdoki], *s.* (*ret.*) sinécdoque, *f.*
synergy [ˈsinədʒi], *s.* (*fisiol.*) sinergia.
synod [ˈsinəd], *s.* sínodo.
synodal, synodic(al) [ˈsinədəl, siˈnɔdik(əl)], *a.* sinódico, sinodal.
synonym [ˈsinənim], *s.* sinónimo.
synonymize [siˈnɔnimaiz], *v.t.* hacer uso de sinónimos.
synonymous [siˈnɔniməs], *a.* sinónimo.
synonymy [siˈnɔnimi], *s.* sinonimia.
synopsis [siˈnɔpsis], *s.* (*pl.* **synopses** [-si:z]) sinopsis, *f.inv.*
synoptic [siˈnɔptik], *a.* sinóptico.
synovia [siˈnouviə], *s.* sinovia.
syntactic [sinˈtæktik], *a.* sintáctico.
syntax [ˈsintæks], *s.* sintaxis, *f. inv.*
synthesis [ˈsinθisis], *s.* (*pl.* **syntheses** [-si:z]) síntesis, *f. inv.*
synthesize, synthetize [ˈsinθisaiz, -taiz], *v.t.* sintetizar.
synthetic(al) [sinˈθetik(əl)], *a.* sintético.
syntonic [sinˈtɔnik], *a.* sintónico, sintonizado.
syntonization [sintənaiˈzeiʃən], *s.* sintonización.
syntonize [ˈsintənaiz], *v.t.* sintonizar.
syphilis [ˈsifilis], *s.* (*med.*) sífilis, *f. inv.*
syphilitic [sifiˈlitik], *a., s.* sifilítico.
syphon [ˈsaifən], *s.* sifón.
Syracuse [ˈsaiərəkju:z]. Siracusa.
syren [SIREN].
Syria [ˈsiriə]. Siria.
Syriac [ˈsiriæk], *a., s.* siriaco, siríaco.
Syrian [ˈsiriən], *a., s.* sirio.
syringa [siˈriŋgə], *s.* (*bot.*) jeringuilla.
syringe [ˈsirindʒ], *s.* jeringa. — *v.t.* jeringar.
syrup [ˈsirəp], *s.* almíbar; (*Am.*) [TREACLE]; (*med.*) jarabe.
syrupy [ˈsirəpi], *a.* parecido a jarabe, espeso como el almíbar.
system [ˈsistəm], *s.* sistema, *m.*; método, régimen; (*fisiol., bot.*) sistema; (*geol.*) formación; ***railway-system,*** red de ferrocarriles, *f.*
systematic(al) [sistəˈmætik(əl)], *a.* sistemático, metódico.
systematization [sistimətaiˈzeiʃən], *s.* sistematización.
systematize [ˈsistəmətaiz], *v.t.* sistematizar, metodizar.
systemic [sisˈtemik], *a.* sistemático.
systole [ˈsistəli], *s.* (*fisiol.*) sístole, *f.*
systolic [sisˈtɔlik], *a.* sistólico.
syzygy [ˈsizidʒi], *s.* (*astron.*) sicigia.

T

T, t [ti:], vigésima letra del alfabeto; ***to a T,*** a la perfección.

tab [tæb], *s.* oreja; etiqueta; (*fam.*) ***to keep tabs on,*** controlar, tener controlado.

tabard [ˈtæbəd], *s.* tabardo.

tabby [ˈtæbi], *a.* atigrado. — *s.* gato romano, gato atigrado.

tabernacle [ˈtæbənækl], *s.* tabernáculo.

table [teibl], *s.* mesa; (*mat.*) tabla; (*estadística*) cuadro; (*arq.*) tablero; (*hist.*) ***Round Table,*** Tabla Redonda; ***table-cloth,*** mantel; ***table-cover,*** cubremesa, *m.*; ***table-land,*** meseta; ***table-linen,*** mantelería; ***table-mat,*** salvamanteles, *m.inv.*; ***table-napkin,*** servilleta; ***table of contents,*** tabla *o* índice de materias; ***table-service, table-ware,*** vajilla; ***table-talk,*** conversación de sobremesa; ***table-tennis,*** tenis de mesa, *m.*, ping-pong; (*fam.*) ***under the table,*** borracho perdido; ***to lay*** o ***set the table,*** poner la mesa; ***to clear the table,*** levantar *o* despejar la mesa; (*fam.*) ***to turn the tables*** (***on s.o.***), coger la ventaja (a alguien), volver las tornas (contra alguien); ***the tables are turned,*** se ha vuelto la tortilla, se cambiaron las tornas. — *v.t.* poner sobre el tapete, presentar; plantear, proponer.

tableau [ˈtæblou], *s.* (*pl.* **tableaux** [ˈtæblou(z)]) cuadro vivo.

tablespoon [ˈteiblspu:n], *s.* cuchara grande.

tablespoonful [ˈteiblspu:nful], *s.* cucharada.

tablet [ˈtæblit], *s.* tableta; pastilla; lápida (*sepulcral etc.*); bloc (*de papel*); (*med.*) pastilla, comprimido.

taboo [təˈbu:], *a.* (de) tabú; prohibido. — *s.* tabú; prohibición. — *v.t.* declarar tabú; (*fig.*) prohibir, vedar.

tabor [ˈteibɔ:], *s.* tamboril.

tabouret [ˈtæbərit], *s.* tamborilete; taburete; bastidor de bordar.

tabular [ˈtæbjulə], *a.* tabular.

tabulate [ˈtæbjuleit], *v.t.* tabular.

tabulation [tæbjuˈleiʃən], *s.* tabulación.

tabulator [ˈtæbjuleitə], *s.* tabulador.

tacamahac [ˈtækəməhæk], *s.* tacamaca.

tachometer [təˈkɔmitə], *s.* tacómetro.

tachygraph [ˈtækigrɑ:f], *s.* taquígrafo.

tachygraphic [tækiˈgræfik], *a.* taquigráfico.

tachygraphy [təˈkigrəfi], *s.* taquigrafía.

tachymeter [təˈkimitə], *s.* taquímetro.

tachymetry [təˈkimitri], *s.* taquimetría.

tacit [ˈtæsit], *a.* tácito.

taciturn [ˈtæsitə:n], *a.* taciturno.

taciturnity [tæsiˈtə:niti], *s.* taciturnidad.

Tacitus [ˈtæsitəs]. Tácito.

tack [tæk], *s.* tachuela; hilván; (*mar.*) bordada, virada; amura; rumbo; línea de política, conducta; ***to get down to brass tacks,*** concretar, ir al grano; ***to try another tack,*** probar otro enfoque *u* otra táctica. — *v.t.* clavar con tachuelas; hilvanar; ***tack sth. down,*** sujetar *o* afianzar algo con tachuelas; ***tack on,*** añadir, agregar. — *v.i.* virar, cambiar de bordada; ***— on,*** (*fam.*) caer.

tack-claw [ˈtæk-klɔ:], *s.* sacatachuelas, *m.inv.*, sacabrocas, *m.inv.*

tackle [tækl], *s.* (*mar.*) aparejo, maniobra, motonería, jarcia, cuadernal; equipo, avíos, *m.pl.*, enseres, *m.pl.*; (*fútbol*) carga; ***stay-tackle,*** candelón, candeletón, estrinque; ***fore-tackle,*** aparejo del trinquete; ***main-tackle,*** aparejo real; ***tack-tackle,*** aparejo de amurar; ***tackle-hooks,*** ganchos de aparejos, *m.pl.*; ***tackle-fall,*** tira de aparejo; ***tackle-block,*** motón de aparejo, polea. — *v.t.* agarrar, coger, asir; atacar; (*dep.*) atajar, blocar; (*tema etc.*) abordar, acometer; (*problema etc.*) enfrentarse con, atreverse con.

tackling [ˈtækliŋ], *s.* (*dep.*) (el) atajar, (el) blocar; (el) abordar, *etc.*

tact [tækt], *s.* tacto; discreción, diplomacia; tino.

tactful [ˈtæktful], *a.* con tacto, diplomático, discreto.

tactfulness [ˈtæktfulnis], *s.* tacto, diplomacia, discreción.

tactic [ˈtæktik], *a.* táctico. — *s.* táctica; (*pl.*) táctica.

tactical [ˈtæktikəl], *a.* táctico.

tactician [tækˈtiʃən], *s.* táctico.

tactile [ˈtæktail], *a.* táctil.

tactility [tækˈtiliti], *s.* calidad de táctil.

tactless [ˈtæktlis], *a.* falto de tacto *o* tino, indiscreto.

tadpole [ˈtædpoul], *s.* renacuajo.

tænia [ˈti:niə], *s.* banda, cinta, faja; tenia, solitaria.

taffeta, taffety [ˈtæfitə, ˈtæfiti], *s.* (*tej.*) tafetán.

taffrail [ˈtæfreil], *s.* (*mar.*) coronamiento.

Taffy [ˈtæfi], *s.* (*fam.*) galés, *m.*

taffy [ˈtæfi], *s.* caramelo, melcocha; (*fam.*) coba, halago.

tag (1) [tæg], *s.* etiqueta; rótulo; extremo (*del rabo*); tirador (*de una bota*); pingajo, arrapiezo; muletilla, estribillo. — *v.t.* clavetear, herretear; atar, marcar con marbete *o* rótulo. — *v.i.* ***— along, behind,*** ir rezagado, ir a la zaga; ***tag on to s.o.,*** pegarse a alguien.

tag (2) [tæg], *s.* (*juego*) marro; ***to play tag,*** jugar al marro.

Tagalog [tɑ:ˈgɑ:lɔg], *s.* tagalo.

tail [teil], *s.* cola; rabo; (*astron.*) cola (*de un cometa*); (*mús.*) rabito (*de una nota*); (*sast.*) faldón; (*alb.*) cola *o* entrega (*de un sillar*); ***bobbed tail*** o ***bob-tail,*** cola cortada; (*mar.*) ***tail-block,*** motón (*de rabiza*); ***tail-coat,*** chaqué, frac; ***tail-end,*** zaga, rabera; cola; extremo; (*fam.*) restos, *m.pl.*, lo que queda *o* sobra; ***tail-light,*** luz piloto *o* trasera; ***tail-piece,*** apéndice; florón; (*aer.*) ***tail-spin,*** barrena de cola; ***tail-unit,*** conjunto de cola; (*pl.*) (*ropa*) frac; ***heads or tails?*** ¿cara o cruz? — *v.t.* seguir (de cerca). — *v.i.* formar cola; ***tail off,*** ir disminuyendo *o* en disminución; ***tail after s.o.,*** seguir a alguien a disgusto.

tailed [teild], *a.* que tiene rabo *o* cola.

tailing [ˈteiliŋ], *s.* (*alb.*) entrega; (*pl.*) restos, *m.pl.*, desechos, *m.pl.*

tailless [ˈteillis], *a.* rabón, sin rabo.

tailor [ˈteilə], *s.* sastre. — *v.t.* entallar (*un traje*).

tailoring [ˈteiləriŋ], *s.* sastrería.

taint [teint], *s.* mancha; infección; corrupción; olor; contaminación. — *v.t.* manchar; (*fama etc.*) mancillar; (*carne etc.*) corromper; (*aire etc.*) viciar, contaminar.

Taiwan [taiˈwæn]. Taiwán; *v.* [CHINA].

take [teik], *s.* toma; (*com.*, *fam.*) entradas, *f.pl.*, ingresos, *m.pl.*; (*cine.*) toma. — *irr. v.t.* tomar; coger; llevar; aceptar; aguantar; (*ajedrez etc.*) comer; (*consejos*) seguir; (*barrera*) saltar; (*periódico etc.*) abonarse a, estar abonado a; (*juramento*) prestar; (*ocasión*) aprovechar, coger; (*foto, billete*) sacar; (*paso, paseo*) dar; (*excursión, viaje*) hacer; ***I take it that you know,*** presumo *o* supongo que (lo) sabrás; ***it takes 3 days to get there,*** se tarda tres días en llegar; ***it takes 3 people to do it,*** hacen falta tres personas para hacerlo; (*fam.*) ***he can take it,*** sabe aguantarlo todo, todo (se) lo aguanta; ***the devil take it!*** ¡maldita sea!; ***take aback,*** desconcertar, dejar perplejo; ***take amiss,*** tomar a mal; ***take apart,*** deshacer, desmontar; ***take away,*** llevarse; quitar; (*mat.*) restar; ***take back,*** aceptar *o* recibir (*de nuevo*); (volver) a quitar (***from,*** a); devolver; retractar, desdecirse de; ***take by storm,*** tomar por asalto; ***take down,*** bajar; descolgar; tomar nota de, poner por escrito; (*mec.*) desmontar; (*fam.*) ***take s.o. down a peg or two,*** bajarle a alguien los humos; ***take for,*** tomar por, confundir con; (*fam.*) ***we've been taken for a ride,*** nos han tomado el pelo; ***take for a walk,*** llevar de paseo; ***take for granted,*** dar por supuesto; ***take from,*** quitar a; privar de; (*mat.*) restar de; ***take in,*** comprender; asimilar(se);

incluir, abarcar; (*ropa*) remeter; admitir, recibir, acoger, recoger; aceptar; reducir, disminuir; (*vela*) desmontar; (*huéspedes*) tomar; (*fam.*) embaucar, tomar el pelo a; ***take in hand,*** ocuparse (seriamente) de; ***take off,*** quitarse (*ropa*); quitar, rebajar; (*fam.*) imitar; ***take on,*** tomar (sobre sí), asumir; emprender; desafiar, enfrentarse con; coger, contratar; coger, aceptar; ***take out,*** sacar; quitar; (*fam.*) ***it takes it out of you,*** te cansa, te agota; (*fam.*) ***he took it out on me,*** se desahogó metiéndose conmigo, como desquite se ensañó conmigo, se vengó en mí; ***take over,*** tomar posesión de, apoderarse de; encargarse de; (*econ.*) absorber(se); ***take to bits*** *o* ***to pieces,*** desmontar, desarmar, deshacer; ***take to task,*** reprender; ***take up,*** subir; (re)coger; (*alfombra*) quitar; (*cargo*) tomar posesión de; ***take up residence,*** sentar sus reales, afincarse; empezar a vivir (en); ***take up room,*** ocupar sitio, abultar; ***take up time,*** ocupar tiempo; quitar tiempo; ***take up a story,*** continuar un relato; ***take up a study,*** empezar a estudiar una cosa; ***take s.o. up on sth.,*** disputar con alguien sobre algo; tomarle a alguien la palabra; ***I shall take this matter up in the appropriate quarter,*** pienso hacer una denuncia oficial, voy a formular una protesta oficial; ***I may well take you up on that,*** a lo mejor te tomo la palabra; ***take upon o.s.,*** tomar sobre sí, asumir; ***take it upon o.s. to,*** atreverse a, tomar la iniciativa de, tener a bien *con infin.*; ***I am very taken with it,*** me gusta mucho, lo encuentro muy apetecible. — *v.i.* coger (bien); pegar (bien); resultar (bien); arraigar; cuajar; (*vacuna*) prender; ***take after,*** salir a; (*aer.*) ***take off,*** despegar; (*fam.*) largarse; (*fam.*) ***take on,*** ponerse histérico; hacer aspavientos; ***don't take on so!*** ¡no seas (tan) exagerado!; ***take over,*** tomar el relevo; tomar posesión; ***take to s.o.,*** cogerle simpatía *o* cariño a alguien; ***I took to him at once,*** me gustó de entrada *o* desde el primer momento; ***we took to each other at once,*** simpatizamos en seguida; ***take to sth.,*** cogerle afición a algo, aficionarse a algo; ***take to drink,*** darse a la bebida; ***he took to going for long walks,*** le dio por dar grandes paseos; (*fam.*) ***take up with,*** trabar amistad con; ligar con.

take-off [ˈteik-ɔf], *s.* (*aer.*) despegue; imitación, parodia, remedo.

takeover [ˈteikouvə], *s.* toma de posesión; absorción; ***takeover bid,*** oferta para comprar una empresa.

taker [ˈteikə], *s.* tomador.

taking [ˈteikiŋ], *a.* atractivo, encantador. — *s.* toma, conquista; (*pl.*) recaudación, taquilla.

talaria [təˈlεəriə], *s.pl.* talares, *m.pl.*

talc [tælk], *s.* talco; [TALCUM POWDER].

talcoid, talcose, talcous [ˈtælkɔid, ˈtælkous, ˈtælkəs], *a.* talcoso.

talc-schist [ˈtælk-ʃist], *s.* talquita.

talcum powder [ˈtælkəm paudə], *s.* polvo de talco.

tale [teil], *s.* cuento, narración, relato; fábula, conseja; (*fam.*) ***to tell tales,*** contar secretos, ir con el soplo; ***old wives' tales,*** chismes de comadre, *m.pl.*; ***tale-bearer, tale-teller,*** acusica, *m.f.*, soplón; correveidile.

tale-bearing [ˈteil-bεəriŋ], *a.* acusica, soplón. — *s.* (el) ir con el soplo, (el) acusar.

talent [ˈtælənt], *s.* talento; (*ant.*) talento (*peso* o *moneda*).

talented [ˈtæləntid], *a.* talentoso, talentudo.

talesman [ˈteilzmən], *s.* (*pl.* **talesmen** [-men]) jurado suplente.

talion [ˈtæljən], *s.* talión.

talipot [ˈtælipɔt], *s.* palmera de las Indias.

talisman [ˈtælizmən], *s.* talismán.

talk [tɔ:k], *s.* conversación; charla; plática; (*despec.*) cháchara(s), palabrería; ***small talk,*** charla, palique; ***talk of the town,*** comidilla de la ciudad; ***there is talk of,*** se habla de. — *v.t.* hablar; decir; ***talk down,*** hacer callar a base de hablar más fuerte; (*aer.*) dirigir *o* guiar el aterrizaje de; ***talk into,*** convencer para que; ***talk out of,*** convencer para que no, disuadir de; ***talk over,*** hablar (de); comentar; convencer; ***I'll talk it over with him,*** lo voy a hablar con él; ***talk round,*** convencer; ***talk sense!*** ¡no diga usted dislates! — *v.i.* hablar; charlar; ***talk to,*** hablar con; ***talk down to,*** hablar a, hablar con tono displicente *o* protector a.

talkative [ˈtɔ:kətiv], *a.* hablador, locuaz, charlatán.

talkativeness [ˈtɔ:kətivnis], *s.* locuacidad.

talker [ˈtɔ:kə], *s.* persona que habla (mucho); ***good talker,*** persona que habla bien.

talking [ˈtɔ:kiŋ], *a.* parlante; ***talking doll,*** muñeca parlante. — *s.* — ***point,*** tema (a discutir), *m.*

talking-to [ˈtɔ:kiŋ-tu:], *s.* (*fam.*) reprimenda, bronca, rapapolvo; ***to give s.o. a good talking-to,*** echarle a alguien un buen rapapolvo.

tall [tɔ:l], *a.* alto; grande; ***he's only five feet tall,*** tiene sólo cinco pies de alto; (*fam.*) ***that's a tall order!*** ¡menuda tarea!, ¡menuda papeleta!, ¡ahí es nada!, ¡pues no es nada lo que piden!; (*fam.*) ***that's a tall story!*** ¡menudo cuento!, ¡cualquiera se traga semejante cuento!

tallboy [ˈtɔ:lbɔi], *s.* cómoda alta.

tallness [ˈtɔ:lnis], *s.* altura, (lo) alto.

tallow [ˈtælou], *s.* sebo; ***tallow-candle,*** vela de sebo; ***tallow-chandler,*** velero; ***tallow-chandler's (shop),*** velería; (*bot.*) ***tallow-tree,*** árbol del sebo.

tallow-faced [ˈtælou-feist], *a.* pálido como la cera.

tallowy [ˈtæloui], *a.* seboso, sebáceo.

tally [ˈtæli], *s.* tarja, tara; cuenta, número; ***tally-stick,*** tarja; ***to keep tally,*** llevar la cuenta. — *v.t.* tarjar; acomodar, ajustar. — *v.i.* cuadrar, concordar, compaginar, coincidir, corresponder.

tally-ho [ˈtæli-ˈhou], *s.* coche de cuatro caballos. — *interj.* grito del cazador de zorros.

tallyman [ˈtælimæn], *s.* tendero que vende a tarja, tarjador, tarjero.

Talmud [ˈtælmud], *s.* talmud.

Talmudical [tælˈmudikəl], *a.* talmúdico.

Talmudist [ˈtælmudist], *s.* talmudista, *m.*

talon [ˈtælən], *s.* garra, uña; monte (de la baraja); talón de hoja de espada.

talus [ˈteiləs], *s.* (*pl.* **tali** [ˈteilai]) (*anat.*) astrágalo, tobillo; (*geol.*) talud, inclinación, pendiente, *f.*

tamable [ˈteiməbl], *a.* domable, domesticable.

tamarack [ˈtæməræk], *s.* alerce.

tamarind [ˈtæmərind], *s.* tamarindo.

tamarisk [ˈtæmərisk], *s.* taray.

tambour [ˈtæmbə], *s.* (*mús.*, *arq.*) tambor; ***tambour frame,*** bastidor. — *v.t.* bordar en bastidor.

tambourine [tæmbəˈri:n], *s.* pandereta, pandero.

tame [teim], *a.* domesticado, domado; manso, dócil; soso, insulso; aburrido. — *v.t.* domar, domesticar; amansar; reprimir.

tameness [ˈteimnis], *s.* mansedumbre, *f.*; sumisión; sosería, insulsez.

tamer [ˈteimə], *s.* domador.

Tamerlane [ˈtæməlein]. Tamerlán.

Tamil [ˈtæməl], *a.*, *s.* tamil.

taming [ˈteimiŋ], *s.* doma, domadura; amansamiento; ***'The Taming of the Shrew',*** 'La fierecilla domada'.

tam-o'-shanter [tæm-o-ˈʃæntə], (*fam.*) **tammy-(shanter)** [ˈtæmi(-ʃæntə)], *s.* boina escocesa.

tamp [tæmp], *v.t.* — ***down,*** apisonar; ***tamp in,*** atacar, tupir; apelmazar.

tamper [ˈtæmpə], *v.i.* — ***with,*** andar *o* hurgar en, meter mano en.

tampion [ˈtæmpiən], *s.* (*artill.*) tapabocas, *m.inv.*

tampon [ˈtæmpən], *s.* (*cir.*) tapón. — *v.t.* taponar.

tan [tæn], *a.* tostado; de color canela; (de color) marrón (*zapatos*). — *s.* bronceado, tostado; casca; color canela *o* café con leche; ***tan-bark,*** casca; ***tan-yard,*** tenería. — *v.t.* broncear, tostar; curtir, adobar; atezar; ***tan s.o.'s hide,*** zurrarle a alguien la badana. — *v.i.* tostarse, broncearse.

tanager [ˈtænədʒə], *s.* (*orn.*) tánagra.
tandem [ˈtændəm], *adv.* uno delante de otro, en tándem. — *s.* tándem.
tang [tæŋ], *s.* saborcillo, regustillo; olorcillo; tañido.
Tanganyika [ˈtæŋgəˈnjiːkə]. Tangañica.
tangency [ˈtændʒənsi], *s.* tangencia.
tangent [ˈtændʒənt], *a.*, *s.* (*geom.*) tangente; ***to go*** o ***fly off at a tangent,*** salirse por la tangente.
tangential [tænˈdʒenʃəl], *a.* tangencial.
tangerine [tændʒəˈriːn], *s.* mandarina.
tangibility [tændʒiˈbiliti], *s.* tangibilidad.
tangible [ˈtændʒibl], *a.* tangible; palpable; concreto.
Tangier(s) [tænˈdʒiə(z)]. Tánger.
tangle [tæŋgl], *s.* enredo, maraña; embrollo, confusión, barullo; (*bot.*) laminaria; ***to be in a tangle,*** estar enmarañado; estar hecho un lío; ***to get into a tangle,*** hacerse un lío. — *v.t.* enredar, enmarañar; embrollar, embarullar. — *v.i.* enredarse; embrollarse.
tank [tæŋk], *s.* tanque; cisterna; depósito; (*mil.*) tanque, carro de combate; ***petrol tank,*** depósito de (la) gasolina; (*f.c.*) ***tank-engine,*** locomotora ténder; ***tank lorry,*** camión cisterna; ***water tank,*** depósito de agua, aljibe.
tankage [ˈtæŋkidʒ], *s.* cabida *o* capacidad de un tanque.
tankard [ˈtæŋkəd], *s.* jarro, bock, pichel.
tanker [ˈtæŋkə], *s.* (*mar.*) petrolero; buque cisterna; camión cisterna; (*aer.*) avión nodriza.
tannate [ˈtænit], *s.* tanato.
tanned [tænd], *a.* curtido; tostado (del sol), bronceado. — *p.p.* [TAN].
tanner [ˈtænə], *s.* curtidor; (*fam.*, *ant.*) (moneda de) seis peniques.
tannery [ˈtænəri], *s.* tenería, curtiduría.
tannic [ˈtænik], *a.* tánico; ***tannic acid,*** ácido tánico.
tannin [ˈtænin], *s.* tanino.
tanning [ˈtæniŋ], *s.* curtido, curtimiento; (*fam.*) paliza, zurra.
tansy [ˈtænzi], *s.* tanaceto.
tantalize [ˈtæntəlaiz], *v.t.* atormentar; encandilar, provocar; exasperar; tener en vilo.
tantalizing [ˈtæntəlaiziŋ], *a.* que atormenta, que exaspera *etc.*; ***it's tantalizing,*** se me ponen los dientes largos; es desesperante.
tantalum [ˈtæntələm], *s.* (*quím.*) tantalio.
tantamount [ˈtæntəmaunt], *a.* equivalente; ***to be tantamount to,*** equivaler a, venir a ser.
tantivy [tænˈtivi], *adv.* (*ant.*) a galope, a rienda suelta.
tantrum [ˈtæntrəm], *s.* berrinche, pataleta, rabieta.
Tanzania [tænzəˈniə]. Tanzania.
Tanzanian [tænzəˈniən], *a.*, *s.* tanzaniano.
tap [tæp], *s.* (*agua*) grifo; (*gas*) llave; espita (*de barril*); (*elec.*) toma; (*mec.*) macho (*de terraja*); ***on tap,*** del barril, al grifo; (*fig.*) a mano; ***to give a tap on the shoulder,*** dar un golpecito *o* una palmadita en el hombro. — *v.t.* espitar, poner espita a (*un barril*); sangrar (*un árbol*); explotar (*recursos*, *yacimientos*); (*elec.*) hacer una derivación en; intervenir (*una línea telefónica*); (*mec.*) aterrajar; dar golpecitos *o* palmaditas a *o* en.
tap-dance [ˈtæp-ˈdɑːns], *s.* zapateado. — *v.i.* zapatear.
tape [teip], *s.* cinta; ***sticky tape,*** cinta adhesiva; ***red tape,*** balduque; (*fig.*) papeleo, expedienteo; ***tape-measure,*** cinta métrica. — *v.t.* grabar en cinta (magnetofónica); (*fam.*) ***I've got him taped,*** le tengo calado.
taper [ˈteipə], *a.* cónico; ahusado. — *s.* cirio; candela, bujía; disminución gradual. — *v.t.* afilar, ahusar, adelgazar. — *v.i.* ahusarse; ***taper away*** o ***off,*** ir adelgazándose; ir en disminución.
tape-recorder [ˈteip-rikɔːdə], *s.* magnetófono, magnetofón.
tape-recording [ˈteip-rikɔːdiŋ], *s.* grabación en cinta.
tapestry [ˈtæpistri], *s.* tapiz; tapicería. — *v.t.* tapizar.
tapeworm [ˈteipwəːm], *s.* tenia, (lombriz) solitaria.
tapioca [tæpiˈoukə], *s.* tapioca.
tapir [ˈteipə], *s.* (*zool.*) tapir.
tappet [ˈtæpit], *s.* (*mec.*) alzaválvulas, *m.inv.*, levantaválvulas, *m.inv.*
tapping [ˈtæpiŋ], *s.* golpecitos, *m.pl.*, golpeteo; (*cir.*) paracentesis, *f. inv.*
tapster [ˈtæpstə], *s.* mozo de taberna.
tar (1) [tɑː], *s.* alquitrán, brea, pez (líquida); ***coal-tar,*** alquitrán de hulla; ***mineral-tar,*** alquitrán mineral; (*mar.*) ***tar-brush,*** escopero; ***tar-water,*** agua de alquitrán. — *v.t.* alquitranar, embrear, dar brea a; ***tar and feather,*** embrear y emplumar; ***tarred with the same brush,*** otro que tal, ídem de lienzo, que cojea del mismo pie.
tar (2) [tɑː], *s.* (*fam.*) marinero.
tarantella [tærənˈtelə], *s.* tarantela.
tarantula [təˈræntjulə], *s.* tarántula.
tardigrade [ˈtɑːdigreid], *a.*, *s.* (*zool.*) tardígrado.
tardily [ˈtɑːdili], *adv.* morosamente, tardíamente.
tardiness [ˈtɑːdinis], *s.* tardanza; lentitud, morosidad, parsimonia.
tardy [ˈtɑːdi], *a.* tardío; lento, moroso, parsimonioso.
tare (1) [tɛə], *s.* (*bot.*) arveja; (*en la Biblia*) cizaña.
tare (2) [tɛə], *s.* (*com.*) tara. — *v.t.* destarar.
target [ˈtɑːgit], *s.* blanco; objetivo; ***sitting target,*** blanco tirado *o* facilísimo; ***to be on target,*** ir hacia el blanco; ***target practice*** o ***shooting,*** tiro al blanco.
Targum [ˈtɑːgəm], *s.* targum.
tariff [ˈtærif], *s.* tarifa, arancel; derecho de aduana; ***tariff protection,*** protección arancelaria. — *v.t.* tarifar.
tarlatan [ˈtɑːlətən], *s.* tarlatana.
tarmac [ˈtɑːmæk], *s.* alquitranado; pista.
tarn [tɑːn], *s.* lago pequeño entre montañas.
tarnish [ˈtɑːniʃ], *s.* deslustre, empañadura, mancha. — *v.t.* deslustrar, deslucir, empañar. — *v.i.* deslustrarse, empañarse; perder el brillo.
tarot [ˈtɑːro], *s.* naipe de dibujos alegóricos.
tarpaulin [tɑːˈpɔːlin], *s.* lona (embreada).
tarragon [ˈtærəgən], *s.* (*bot.*) tarragón, estragón.
tarring [ˈtɑːriŋ], *s.* embreadura.
tarry (1) [ˈtɑːri], *a.* alquitranado, embreado.
tarry (2) [ˈtæri], *v.i.* demorarse, entretenerse; tardar.
tarsal [ˈtɑːsəl], *a.* del tarso.
tarsus [ˈtɑːsəs], *s.* (*pl.* **tarsi** [-sai]) tarso.
tart (1) [tɑːt], *a.* acre; ácido; agrio; (*fig.*) áspero, brusco.
tart (2) [tɑːt], *s.* tarta, tarteleta.
tart (3) [tɑːt], *s.* (*fam.*) fulanilla, mujercilla, putilla. — *v.r.* (*fam.*) ***tart o.s. up,*** acicalarse, ponerse de tiros largos.
tartan [ˈtɑːtən], *s.* (*tej.*) tartán.
Tartar [ˈtɑːtə], *s.* tártaro; ***to catch a Tartar,*** hallar la horma de su zapato; (*fam.*) ***she's a real Tartar,*** es una auténtica tarasca.
tartar [ˈtɑːtə], *s.* tártaro; (*odont.*) sarro; ***cream of tartar,*** crémor tártaro.
Tartarean [tɑːˈtɛəriən], *a.* tartáreo.
tartareous [tɑːˈtɛəriəs], *a.* tartáreo.
tartaric [tɑːˈtærik], *a.* tartárico.
tartarize [ˈtɑːtəraiz], *v.t.* tartarizar.
Tartarus [ˈtɑːtərəs]. (el) Tártaro.
Tartary [ˈtɑːtəri]. Tartaria.
tartness [ˈtɑːtnis], *s.* acidez; aspereza.
tartrate [ˈtɑːtreit], *s.* tartrato.
task [tɑːsk], *s.* tarea; faena; empresa, misión; ***to take to task,*** llamar la atención a (***for,*** por), echar una reprimenda a (***for,*** por).

task-force [ˈtɑːsk-fɔːs], *s.* agrupación de fuerzas; fuerza especial.
taskmaster [ˈtɑːskmɑːstə], *s.* capataz; amo.
Tasmania [tæzˈmeiniə]. Tasmania.
Tasmanian [tæzˈmeiniən], *a.*, *s.* tasmanio, *m.*
tassel [tæsl], *s.* borla; (*bot.*) penacho. — *v.t.* adornar con borlas.
tasselled [tæsld], *a.* adornado con borlas.
taste [teist], *s.* gusto; sabor (***of,*** a); sorbo; pizca (*para probar*); buen gusto; afición; ***just a taste,*** una pizca nada más; ***in good*** o ***bad taste,*** de buen *o* mal gusto; ***to taste,*** al gusto, a discreción; ***to acquire a taste for,*** cogerle *o* tomarle gusto a; ***to have a taste for,*** tener afición a; ***he has a taste for it,*** le tiene afición, le gusta; ***it is not to my taste,*** no es de mi agrado; ***taste-bud,*** papila del gusto. — *v.t.* gustar; notar un sabor de; probar, catar. — *v.i.* saber, tener sabor; ***taste of,*** saber a, tener sabor a; ***it tastes good,*** está bueno.
tasteful [ˈteistful], *a.* de buen gusto; hecho con gusto.
tastefully [ˈteistfuli], *adv.* con buen gusto.
tastefulness [ˈteistfulnis], *s.* buen gusto.
tasteless [ˈteistlis], *a.* insípido, insulso, soso; (*fig.*) de mal gusto; ***tasteless joke,*** chiste de mal gusto.
tastelessness [ˈteistlisnis], *s.* insipidez, insulsez; falta de (buen) gusto, mal gusto.
taster [ˈteistə], *s.* catador.
tasty [ˈteisti], *a.* sabroso, apetitoso.
ta-ta! [tæ-ˈtɑː], *interj.* (*fam.*) adiosito.
Tatar [TARTAR].
tatter [ˈtætə], *s.* andrajo, harapo, pingajo, guiñapo, jirón; ***to be in tatters,*** estar hecho un andrajo. — *v.t.* hacer harapos *o* andrajos.
tatterdemalion [tætədiˈmeiliən], *s.* zarrapastrón, andrajoso.
tattered [ˈtætəd], *a.* andrajoso, harapiento. — *p.p.* [TATTER].
tatting [ˈtætiŋ], *s.* encaje de frivolité.
tattle [tætl], *s.* cháchara, parloteo, picoteo. — *v.i.* charlar, parlotear, chismear.
tattler [ˈtætlə], *s.* charlatán; chismoso; (*orn.*) chorlito.
tattoo (1) [təˈtuː], *s.* tatuaje. — *v.t.* tatuar(se).
tattoo (2) [təˈtuː], *s.* (*mil.*) retreta; parada militar. — *v.i.* tamborilear.
tattooing (1) [təˈtuːiŋ], *s.* tatuaje.
tattooing (2) [təˈtuːiŋ], *s.* tamborileo.
taunt [tɔːnt], *s.* mofa, sarcasmo, escarnio. — *v.t.* mofarse de; ***taunt s.o. with sth.,*** reprocharle algo a alguien *o* echarle algo en cara a alguien.
taunter [ˈtɔːntə], *s.* mofador, zumbón.
tauntingly [ˈtɔːntiŋli], *adv.* con mofa, en son de burla; con tono de reproche.
tauriform [ˈtɔːrifɔːm], *a.* de forma de toro; (*astron.*) referente a Tauro.
taurine [ˈtɔːrain], *a.* taurino; (*astron.*) relativo a Tauro.
tauromachy [tɔːˈrɔməki], *s.* tauromaquia.
Taurus [ˈtɔːrəs]. (*astron.*, *astrol.*) Tauro.
taut [tɔːt], *a.* tenso, tirante; (*mar.*) ***to haul*** o ***make taut,*** tesar, tensar.
tauten [ˈtɔːtən], *v.t.* tesar, tensar.
tautness [ˈtɔːtnis], *s.* tensión, tirantez.
tautological [tɔːtəˈlɔdʒikəl], *a.* tautológico.
tautologist [tɔːˈtɔlədʒist], *s.* tautológico.
tautologize [tɔːˈtɔlədʒaiz], *v.i.* usar de tautologías.
tautology [tɔːˈtɔlədʒi], *s.* tautología.
tavern [ˈtævən], *s.* taberna, figón.
tavern-keeper [ˈtævən-ˈkiːpə], *s.* tabernero.
taw (1) [tɔː], *s.* canica (de vidrio).
taw (2) [tɔː], *v.t.* curtir (*pieles*) en blanco.
tawdriness [ˈtɔːdrinis], *s.* charrería, (lo) oropelesco, (lo) charro.
tawdry [ˈtɔːdri], *a.* charro, oropelesco.
tawny [ˈtɔːni], *a.* leonado.
tax [tæks], *s.* contribución, impuesto, tributo; carga, exacción; ***tax-collector*** o ***-gatherer,*** recaudador de contribuciones; ***tax-list,*** cédula *o* lista de contribuyentes; (*Biblia*) censo de contribuyentes; ***tax-payer,*** contribuyente; ***tax-rate,*** cupo. — *v.t.* gravar, imponer impuestos *o* tributos a; tasar; (*fig.*) cargar, abrumar; acusar, censurar; ***this taxes one's strength,*** esto le agota a uno las fuerzas.
taxable [ˈtæksəbl], *a.* imponible.
taxation [tækˈseiʃən], *s.* tributación; impuestos, *m.pl.*; contribuciones, *f.pl.*; sistema tributario.
tax-free [ˈtæks-ˈfriː], *a.* exento de impuestos.
taxi [ˈtæksi], *s.* taxi; ***taxi-driver,*** taxista, *m.*; ***taxi-meter,*** taxímetro; ***taxi-rank,*** ***taxi-stand,*** parada de taxis. — *v.i.* ir en taxi; (*aer.*) correr por tierra, carretear.
taxidermist [ˈtæksidəːmist], *s.* taxidermista, *m.f.*
taxidermy [ˈtæksidəːmi], *s.* taxidermia.
taxonomy [tækˈsɔnəmi], *s.* taxonomía.
tea [tiː], *s.* té; merienda; ***high tea,*** merienda-cena; ***tea-caddy,*** bote para (el) té; ***tea-cosy,*** cubretetera, *m.*; ***tea-cup,*** taza para té; ***tea-pot,*** tetera; (*pl.*) ***tea-leaves,*** hojas de té, *f.pl.*
teach [tiːtʃ], *v.t.* enseñar; (*fig.*) ***teach s.o. a lesson,*** escarmentar a alguien. — *v.i.* enseñar, dar clases.
teachable [ˈtiːtʃəbl], *a.* que se le puede enseñar.
teacher [ˈtiːtʃə], *s.* maestro, maestra (*de escuela*); profesor, profesora (*de colegio, de instituto* o *universitario*); ***teacher training,*** formación pedagógica; ***teacher training college,*** escuela normal.
teaching [ˈtiːtʃiŋ], *a.* docente; pedagógico; ***teaching staff,*** personal docente, profesorado. — *s.* enseñanza; instrucción; pedagogía; magisterio.
teak(wood) [ˈtiːk(wud)], *s.* teca.
teal [tiːl], *s.* cerceta, trullo.
team [tiːm], *s.* equipo; tiro (*de caballos*); yunta (*de bueyes*); ***team spirit,*** espíritu de equipo. — *v.i.* — ***up,*** formar un equipo, asociarse; ***team up, with,*** asociarse con, unirse con.
teamster [ˈtiːmstə], *s.* tronquista, *m.f.*
tear (1) [tɛə], *s.* rasgón, desgarrón; ***wear and tear,*** desgaste, uso. — *irr. v.t.* rasgar, desgarrar; romper (*el papel*); ***tear apart,*** deshacer, despedazar; ***tear away,*** arrancar, arrebatar; ***tear down,*** arrancar; derribar, echar abajo; ***tear off,*** arrancar; ***tear up,*** romper (*el papel*); arrancar de cuajo. — *irr. v.i.* rasgarse; romperse; ***tear along,*** ir flechado; ***tear by*** o ***past,*** pasar como un rayo; ***tear down the road,*** ir flechado por la calle. — *v.r.* ***tear o.s. away,*** desasirse, desprenderse.
tear (2) [tiə], *s.* lágrima; ***tear gas,*** gas lacrimógeno, *m.*; (*pl.*) lágrimas, llanto.
tear-away [ˈtɛər-əˈwei], *a.*, *s.* impetuoso.
tearful [ˈtiəful], *a.* lloroso, llorón.
tearless [ˈtiəlis], *a.* sin lágrimas.
tease [tiːz], *s.* guasón, embromador; guasa, pitorreo; burla, toreo. — *v.t.* hacer rabiar; tomar el pelo a; cardar (*el paño*).
teasel [ˈtiːzəl], *s.* (*bot.*) cardencha; carda.
teaseler [ˈtiːzlə], *s.* pelaire; carda.
teaser [ˈtiːzə], *s.* (*fam.*) guasón; (*elec.*) excitador de una dínamo; (*fam.*) rompecabezas, *m.inv.*, acertijo.
teaspoon [ˈtiːspuːn], *s.* cucharita, cucharilla.
teaspoonful [ˈtiːspuːnful], *s.* cucharadita.
teat [tiːt], *s.* pezón; teta; boquilla, tetilla.
technical [ˈteknikəl], *a.* técnico; ***technical school,*** escuela laboral; ***technical term,*** tecnicismo; ***technical offence,*** cuasidelito.
technicality [tekniˈkæliti], *s.* cosa técnica; detalle técnico; tecnicismo; ***a mere technicality,*** una cosa puramente técnica *o* mecánica.
technician [tekˈniʃən], *s.* técnico.
technics [tekniks], *s.pl.* técnica; tecnicismo.
technique [tekˈniːk], *s.* técnica.
technological [teknəˈlɔdʒikəl], *a.* tecnológico.

technologist [tek'nɔlədʒist], *s.* tecnólogo.
technology [tek'nɔlədʒi], *s.* tecnología.
tectonic [tek'tɔnik], *a.* tectónico. — *s.* (*pl.*) tectónica.
Ted, Teddy ['ted(i)]. Eduardito.
ted [ted], *v.t.* henear, rastrillar, esparcir el heno.
tedder ['tedə], *s.* heneador.
tedding ['tediŋ], *s.* henaje.
teddy-bear ['tedi-'bεə], *s.* osito (de trapo).
Te Deum ['ti: 'di:əm], *s.* tedéum.
tedious ['ti:diəs], *a.* latoso, pesado, aburrido; tedioso.
tediousness, tedium ['ti:diəsnis, 'ti:diəm], *s.* pesadez, tedio, aburrimiento.
tee [ti:], *s.* nombre de la letra T *o* cualquier objeto en forma de T; (*dep.*) meta; (*juego de golf*) montoncillo donde se coloca la pelota antes de lanzarla, tee. — *v.t.* colocar (*la pelota*) en el tee.
teem [ti:m], *v.i.* pulular, abundar; ***teem with***, pulular de; abundar en; estar plagado de.
teeming ['ti:miŋ], *a.* pululante; abundante, numerosísimo.
teenage ['ti:neidʒ], *a.* adolescente (de 13 a 19 años). — *s.* adolescencia (de 13 a 19 años).
teenager ['ti:neidʒə], *s.* adolescente, joven de 13 a 19 años.
teens [ti:nz], *s.pl.* edad de 13 a 19 años; ***to be still in one's teens***, no haber cumplido aún los 20.
teeny (weeny) ['ti:ni ('wi:ni)], *a.* (*infantil*) chiquitín, pequeñito.
teetee ['ti:ti:], *s.* (*zool.*) tití.
teeter ['ti:tə], *s.* balance, vaivén. — *v.i.* balancearse; (*fig.*) tambalearse, vacilar.
teeth [ti:θ], *s.pl.* [TOOTH].
teethe [ti:ð], *v.i.* echar los dientes, dentar.
teething ['ti:*y*iŋ], *s.* dentición, (el) echar los dientes; ***teething-ring***, chupador.
teetotal [ti:'toutəl], *a.* abstemio.
teetotal(l)er [ti:'toutələ], *s.* abstemio.
teetotalism [ti:'toutəlizəm], *s.* abstinencia completa de bebidas alcohólicas.
teetotum [ti:'toutəm], *s.* perinola.
tegmen ['tegmən], *s.* (*pl.* **tegmina** [-ə]) tegmen.
tegument ['tegjumənt], *s.* tegumento.
tegumentary [tegju'mentəri], *a.* tegumentario.
tehee ['ti:'hi:], *s.* risita.
telamon ['teləmən], *s.* telamón.
telautograph [tel'ɔ:togrɑ:f], *s.* telautógrafo.
telegram ['teligræm], *s.* telegrama, *m.*; ***to send a telegram***, poner un telegrama.
telegraph ['teligrɑ:f], *a.* telegráfico; ***telegraph line***, línea telegráfica; ***telegraph pole***, poste telegráfico. — *s.* telégrafo. — *v.t.*, *v.i.* telegrafiar.
telegraphic [teli'græfik], *a.* telegráfico.
telegraphist [ti'legrəfist], *s.* telegrafista, *m.f.*
telegraphy [ti'legrəfi], *s.* telegrafía; ***wireless telegraphy***, telegrafía sin hilos.
telemeter [ti'lemitə], *s.* telémetro.
telemetry [ti'lemitri], *s.* telemetría.
teleologic(al) [teliə'lɔdʒik(əl)], *a.* teleológico.
teleology [teli'ɔlədʒi], *s.* teleología.
telepathic [teli'pæθik], *a.* telepático.
telepathy [ti'lepəθi], *s.* telepatía.
telephone ['telifoun], *s.* teléfono; ***telephone box*** o ***kiosk***, cabina de teléfono, locutorio; ***telephone call***, llamada telefónica; ***long-distance telephone call***, conferencia; ***telephone directory*** o ***book***, guía telefónica; ***telephone exchange***, central telefónica; ***telephone number***, número de teléfono; ***telephone operator***, telefonista, *m.f.*; ***to be on the telephone***, estar hablando por teléfono; ***to come to the telephone***, ponerse al teléfono. — *v.t.*, *v.i.* telefonear, llamar por teléfono.
telephonic [teli'fɔnik], *a.* telefónico.
telephonist [ti'lefənist], *s.* telefonista, *m.f.*
telephony [ti'lefəni], *s.* telefonía.

teleprinter ['teliprintə], *s.* teleimpresor.
telescope ['teliskoup], *s.* telescopio; catalejo (*anteojo de larga vista*). — *v.t.* telescopar; enchufar; acortar. — *v.i.* telescoparse; enchufarse; acortarse.
telescopic [telis'kɔpik], *a.* telescópico; de enchufe.
teletype ['telitaip], *s.* teletipo.
teleview ['telivju:], *v.t.*, *v.i.* ver por televisión.
televiewer ['telivju:ə], *s.* televidente, telespectador.
televise ['telivaiz], *v.t.* transmitir por televisión, televisar.
television [teli'viʒən], *s.* televisión; ***television set***, aparato de televisión, televisor.
Telex ['teleks], *s.* (*marca de fábrica*) télex.
tell [tel], *irr. v.t.* decir; contar (*un cuento*); notar; determinar; ***I told him to leave***, le dije que se fuera; ***he was told that***, le dijeron que; ***you can always tell***, se nota siempre; ***you can never tell***, nunca se sabe; ***it's not easy to tell whether***, no es fácil saber *o* determinar si; (*fam.*) ***you're telling me!*** ¡no hace falta que me lo diga!; (*fam.*) ***tell off***, echar una resplandina a, echar una reprimenda a; ***who told you (about it)?*** ¿quién te lo dijo? — *v.i.* decir; hacer mella, dejar huella; hacerse sentir *o* notar; surtir efecto; (*fam.*) soplar, ir con el soplo, chivarse, chivatear (***on***, contra).
teller ['telə], *s.* relator, narrador; escrutador (*de votos etc.*); (*Am.*) [CASHIER]; ***paying teller***, pagador; ***receiving teller***, cobrador; ***entering teller***, contador.
telling ['teliŋ], *a.* contundente, convincente; revelador; eficaz. — *s.* narración; ***there is no telling***, no hay manera de saberlo, ¡quién sabe!
tell-tale ['tel-teil], *a.* revelador, indicador. — *s.* soplón, acusón, acusica, correveidile; (*mar.*) axiómetro.
telluric [te'ljuərik], *a.* telúrico.
tellurion [tel'juəriən], *s.* planetario.
telly ['teli], *s.* (*fam.*) tele, *f.*
telpherage ['telfəridʒ], *s.* transporte automático (*por medio de teleférico*).
Telugu ['teləgu:], *a.*, *s.* telugu.
temerity [ti'meriti], *s.* temeridad.
temper ['tempə], *s.* temple; (mal) humor, (mal) genio; temperamento; ***bad, hot, quick temper***, mal genio, genio vivo; ***good temper***, buen humor; ***to have a foul temper***, tener muy malas pulgas; ***to keep one's temper***, contenerse; ***to lose one's temper***, perder la paciencia. — *v.t.* templar, temperar; moderar, mitigar.
tempera ['tempərə], *s.* (*pint.*) pintura al temple.
temperament ['temprəmənt], *s.* temperamento; genio cambiante; (*mús.*) temple.
temperamental [temprə'mentəl], *a.* temperamental; de impulsos repentinos, caprichoso.
temperance ['tempərəns], *s.* templanza, moderación; ***temperance hospital*** u ***hotel***, sitio en el que no se venden bebidas alcohólicas.
temperate ['tempərit], *a.* templado; sobrio, abstemio, moderado.
temperateness ['tempəritnis], *s.* templanza, moderación.
temperature ['tempərətʃə], *s.* temperatura; (*med.*) fiebre, *f.*
tempered ['tempəd], *a.* templado; ***good-tempered***, de genio benigno, de buen humor; ***ill-tempered***, geniudo, de mal humor; ***even-tempered***, de humor igual; ***hot-tempered***, irascible.
tempest ['tempist], *s.* tempestad, tormenta.
tempestuous [tem'pestjuəs], *a.* tempestuoso, proceloso, borrascoso.
tempestuousness [tem'pestjuəsnis], *s.* (lo) tempestuoso.
Templar ['templə], *s.* templario.
template, templet ['templit], *s.* patrón; gálibo; solera.

temple (1) [templ], *s.* templo.
temple (2) [templ], *s.* (*anat.*) sien, *f.*
tempo [ˈtempou], *s.* (*mús.*) tiempo; (*fig.*) ritmo.
temporal (1) [ˈtempərəl], *a.* temporal.
temporal (2) [ˈtempərəl], *s.* (*anat.*) (hueso) temporal.
temporality [tempəˈræliti], *s.* temporalidad.
temporarily [ˈtempərərili], *adv.* temporalmente, provisionalmente.
temporariness [ˈtempərərinis], *s.* (lo) temporal, (lo) provisional.
temporary [ˈtempərəri], *a.* temporal, provisional, interino.
temporize [ˈtempəraiz], *v.i.* contemporizar.
tempt [tempt], *v.t.* tentar (***to***, a); seducir; ***tempt Providence,*** tentar a Dios *o* al Cielo; ***to be tempted to,*** sentirse tentado de.
temptation [tempˈteiʃən], *s.* tentación; aliciente.
tempter [ˈtemptə], *s.* tentador.
tempting [ˈtemptiŋ], *a.* tentador, seductor; apetitoso.
temptingly [ˈtemptiŋli], *adv.* de (una) manera tentadora.
temptress [ˈtemptris], *s.* tentadora.
ten [ten], *a.*, *s.* diez.
tenable [ˈtenəbl], *a.* sostenible.
tenacious [tiˈneiʃəs], *a.* tenaz.
tenaciously [tiˈneiʃəsli], *adv.* tenazmente, con tenacidad.
tenacity, tenaciousness [tiˈnæsiti, tiˈneiʃəsnis], *s.* tenacidad; tesón.
tenaculum [tiˈnækjuləm], *s.* (*pl.* **tenacula** [-lə]) tenáculo.
tenail, tenaille [teˈneil], *s.* (*fort.*) tenaza.
tenancy [ˈtenənsi], *s.* arriendo, inquilinato.
tenant [ˈtenənt], *s.* arrendatario, inquilino; residente. — *v.t.* alquilar; ocupar.
tenantless [ˈtenəntlis], *a.* desarrendado, sin inquilinos.
tenantry [ˈtenəntri], *s.* inquilinos, *m.pl.*
tench [tentʃ], *s.* (*ict.*) tenca.
tend (1) [tend], *v.t.* cuidar, tener cuidado de, vigilar; servir, manejar.
tend (2) [tend], *v.i.* tender, tener tendencia, propender, tener propensión (***to***, a).
tendency [ˈtendənsi], *s.* tendencia, propensión, proclividad; inclinación.
tendentious [tenˈdenʃəs], *a.* tendencioso.
tender (1) [ˈtendə], *a.* tierno; (*fig.*) delicado; (*fig.*) sensible; (*herida etc.*) dolorido; ***tender age,*** tierna edad; ***tender-hearted,*** tierno de corazón, compasivo. — *v.t.* (*ant.*) enternecer.
tender (2) [ˈtendə], *s.* (*com.*) oferta; proposición; licitatión; ***legal tender,*** moneda corriente; ***it is legal tender,*** es de curso legal. — *v.t.* (*com.*) presentar; dar; ofrecer en pago. — *v.i.* ofertar, hacer una oferta; licitar.
tender (3) [ˈtendə], *s.* (*f.c.*) ténder; (*mar.*) gabarra.
tenderfoot [ˈtendəfut], *s.* recién llegado; novato, principiante.
tenderling [ˈtendəliŋ], *s.* pitón de asta de venado.
tenderloin [ˈtendəlɔin], *s.* (*Am.*) filete.
tenderly [ˈtendəli], *adv.* tiernamente, con ternura.
tenderness [ˈtendənis], *s.* ternura; delicadeza; sensibilidad.
tendinous [ˈtendinəs], *a.* tendinoso.
tendon [ˈtendən], *s.* (*anat.*) tendón.
tendril [ˈtendril], *s.* (*bot.*) zarcillo, tijereta (de las vides), *f.pl.*
tenebrous [ˈtenibrəs], *a.* (*poét.*) tenebroso.
tenement [ˈtenimənt], *s.* habitación; vivienda, morada; (*for.*) heredamiento; ***tenement*** (***house***), casa de vecindad.
tenementary [teniˈmentəri], *a.* (*for.*) arrendable.
tenesmus [teˈnezməs], *s.* (*med.*) tenesmo, pujo.
tenet [ˈtenit, ˈtiːnit], *s.* dogma, *m.*, principio, credo.
tenfold [ˈtenfould], *a.* décuplo. — *adv.* diez veces, de modo décuplo.
tennis [ˈtenis], *s.* tenis, *m.*; ***tennis ball,*** pelota de tenis; ***tennis court,*** pista *o* cancha de tenis; ***tennis player,*** tenista, *m.f.*; ***tennis racket,*** raqueta de tenis.
tenon [ˈtenən], *s.* (*carp.*) espiga, almilla; ***tenon saw,*** serrucho. — *v.t.* espigar, despatillar; juntar a espiga y mortaja.
tenor [ˈtenə], *a.* (*mús.*) de tenor. — *s.* tenor; ***the even tenor of one's way,*** el curso regular de su vida.
tenotomy [teˈnɔtəmi], *s.* tenotomía.
tenpenny [ˈtenpəni], *a.* de diez peniques, que vale diez peniques.
tenpins [ˈtenpinz], *s.* bolos, *m.pl.*; ***tenpin bowling,*** juego de los bolos.
tense (1) [tens], *a.* tenso; tirante, estirado. — *v.t.* tensar, tesar; estirar. — *v.i.* — ***up,*** tensar.
tense (2) [tens], *s.* (*gram.*) tiempo.
tenseness [ˈtensnis], *s.* tirantez; tensión.
tensile [ˈtensail], *a.* tensor; de tensión; dúctil.
tension [ˈtenʃən], *s.* tensión; tirantez; ***nervous tension,*** tensión nerviosa; ***political tension,*** tirantez política.
tensor [ˈtensɔː], *s.* tensor.
tent [tent], *s.* tienda (de campaña); (*cir.*) lechino, tapón; ***tent-peg,*** estaca de tienda; ***tent-pole,*** mástil de tienda; ***to pitch tents,*** armar (las) tiendas; ***to strike tents,*** desarmar *o* plegar (las) tiendas, levantar el campo. — *v.i.* acampar bajo tiendas.
tentacle [ˈtentəkl], *s.* tentáculo.
tentacular [tenˈtækjulə], *a.* tentacular.
tentative [ˈtentətiv], *a.* tentativo; de tanteo, de ensayo; provisional.
tenter [ˈtentə], *s.* (*tej.*) tendedor; (*tej.*) ***tenter-hooks,*** escarpias, *f.pl.*, alcayatas, *f.pl.*; (*fig.*) ***to be on tenter-hooks,*** estar sobre ascuas *o* en vilo. — *v.t.* (*tej.*) estirar.
tenth [tenθ], *a.* décimo, diez; (*título*) diez; (*fecha*) diez. — *s.* décimo; décima parte.
tenthly [ˈtenθli], *adv.* en décimo lugar.
tenuity [teˈnjuːiti], *s.* tenuidad; raridad.
tenuous [ˈtenjuəs], *a.* tenue.
tenure [ˈtenjuə], *s.* tenencia; posesión.
tepid [ˈtepid], *a.* templaducho; calentucho; (*fig.*) tibio.
tepidity [teˈpiditi], *s.* (lo) templaducho; (lo) calentucho; (*fig.*) tibieza.
teratology [terəˈtɔlədʒi], *s.* teratología.
tercentenary [təːsenˈtiːnəri], *a.* tricentésimo. — *s.* tricentenario.
tercet [ˈtəːsit], *s.* terceto.
terebinth [ˈteribinθ], *s.* terebinto.
teredo [teˈriːdou], *s.* teredo.
Terence [ˈterəns]. Terencio.
tergiversate [ˈtəːdʒivəseit], *v.i.* tergiversar.
tergiversation [təːdʒivəˈseiʃən], *s.* evasiva; subterfugio.
term [təːm], *s.* término; plazo, período; trimestre (escolar); duración; mandato; ***during his term of office,*** durante su posesión del puesto; ***in the long term,*** a largo plazo; (*pl.*) condiciones, *f.pl.*; tarifa, precio; relaciones, *f.pl.*; ***in plain terms,*** en términos sencillos; ***in set terms,*** en términos establecidos *o* concretos; ***terms of reference,*** enunciado, puntos de consulta, *m.pl.*; ***not on any terms,*** bajo ningun concepto; ***what are your terms?*** ¿cúales son sus condiciones?; ***to come to terms,*** llegar a un acuerdo; ***he can't come to terms with the idea,*** no se resigna a aceptar la idea; ***to offer easy terms,*** ofrecer facilidades de pago; ***to be on good terms with,*** estar en buenas relaciones con; ***not to be on speaking terms,*** no hablarse. — *v.t.* denominar, llamar; nombrar; calificar de.

termagant [ˈtəːməgənt], *s.* arpía, tarasca.
terminable [ˈtəːminəbl], *a.* limitable.
terminal [ˈtəːminəl], *a.* terminal, final; trimestral; ***terminal disease,*** enfermedad mortal. — *s.* terminal, *m.f.*; (*elec.*) borne; ***air terminal,*** terminal (aérea), *f.*
terminate [ˈtəːmineit], *v.t., v.i.* terminar(se).
termination [təːmiːˈneiʃən], *s.* terminación.
terminative [ˈtəːminətiv], *a.* terminativo.
terminer [ˈtəːminə], *s.* (*for.*) vista.
terminology [təːmiˈnɔlədʒi], *s.* terminología.
terminus [ˈtəːminəs], *s.* (*pl.* **termini** [-ai]) término; (*f.c.*) estación terminal.
termite [ˈtəːmait], *s.* termita, *m.*, hormiga blanca.
tern (1) [təːn], *a.* ternario. — *s.* terna, terno.
tern (2) [təːn], *s.* (*orn.*) golondrina de mar.
ternary [ˈtəːnəri], *a.* ternario, trino. — *s.* terna, terno, ternario.
ternate [ˈtəːneit], *a.* ternario.
terne-plate [ˈtəːn-pleit], *s.* hojalata (*con baño de aleación de estaño-plomo*).
Terpsichorean [təːpsiˈkɔːriən], *a.* de Terpsícore.
terrace [ˈteris], *s.* terraza; terraplén; (*tejado*) azotea; gradas, *f.pl.*; hilera de casas; ***terrace house,*** casa en hilera. — *v.t.* terraplenar; formar terrazas en.
terracotta [ˈterəˈkɔtə], *s.* terracota.
terrain [teˈrein], *s.* terreno.
terrapin [ˈterəpin], *s.* tortuga de agua dulce.
terraqueous [teˈreikwiəs], *a.* terráqueo.
terreplein [ˈtɛəplein], *s.* (*fort.*) terraplén.
terrestrial [tiˈrestriəl], *a.* terrestre.
terret [ˈterit], *s.* portarriendas, *m.inv.*
terrible [ˈteribl], *a.* terrible, pavoroso, horroroso, espantoso; (*fam.*) infame, malísimo, pésimo.
terribleness [ˈteriblnis], *s.* (lo) terrible.
terribly [ˈteribli], *adv.* terriblemente; (*fam.*) tremendamente; ***terribly difficult,*** dificilísimo; ***terribly selfish,*** tremendamente egoísta.
terrier [ˈteriə], *s.* terrier; ***fox-terrier,*** perro zorrero.
terrific [təˈrifik], *a.* tremendo; inmenso, ingente; (*fam.*) soberbio, imponente.
terrify [ˈterifai], *v.t.* aterrorizar.
territorial [teriˈtɔːriəl], *a.* territorial; ***Territorial Army,*** reserva (del ejército); ***territorial waters,*** aguas jurisdiccionales, *f.pl.* — *s.* reservista, *m.*
territory [ˈteritəri], *s.* territorio.
terror [ˈterə], *s.* terror, espanto, pavor; (*fam.*) ***to be a real terror,*** ser de cuidado *o* de armas tomar.
terrorism [ˈterərizəm], *s.* terrorismo.
terrorist [ˈterərist], *s.* terrorista, *m.f.*
terrorize [ˈterəraiz], *v.t.* aterrorizar; someter al terrorismo.
Terry [ˈteri]. *abrev. de* [TERENCE].
terse [təːs], *a.* conciso; brusco.
terseness [ˈtəːsnis], *s.* concisión; brusquedad.
tertian [ˈtəːʃən], *a.* terciano. — *s.* (*med.*) terciana.
tertiary [ˈtəːʃəri], *a., s.* terciario.
tessellate [ˈtesəleit], *v.t.* formar con teselas.
tessellated [ˈtesəleitid], *a.* teselado, de mosaico.
tessellation [tesəˈleiʃən], *s.* teselado, mosaico.
tessera [ˈtesərə], *s.* (*pl.* **tesserae** [-iː, -ai]) tesela; tésera.
tessitura [tesiˈtuərə], *s.* (*mús.*) tesitura.
test [test], *s.* prueba; ensayo; examen; piedra de toque; (*educ., psic.*) test; (*fig.*) ***acid test,*** prueba de fuego; ***test flight,*** vuelo de ensayo; ***test match,*** partido internacional de cricket *o* de rugby; ***test-pilot,*** piloto de pruebas; ***test-tube,*** tubo de ensayo, probeta; ***to put to the test,*** poner a prueba; ***to stand the test,*** soportar la prueba; (*fig.*) demostrar su validez; (*pers.*) dar la talla. — *v.t.* probar, ensayar; examinar; graduar (*la vista*).
testacean [tesˈteiʃən], *a., s.* testáceo.
testaceous [tesˈteiʃəs], *a.* testáceo.
testament [ˈtestəmənt], *s.* testamento; ***Old Testament,*** Antiguo *o* Viejo Testamento; ***New Testament,*** Nuevo Testamento.
testamentary [testəˈmentəri], *a.* testamentario.
testate [ˈtestit], *a.* testado.
testator [tesˈteitə], *s.* testador.
testatrix [tesˈteitriks], *s.* (*pl.* **testatrixes, testatrices** [-ksiz, -siːz]) testadora.
tester [ˈtestə], *s.* ensayador; (*quím.*) reactivo; (*arq.*) baldaquino.
testicle [ˈtestikl], *s.* testículo.
testicular [tesˈtikjulə], *a.* testicular.
testiculate [tesˈtikjulit], *a.* en forma de testículo; que tiene testículos.
testification [testifiˈkeiʃən], *s.* testificación.
testifier [ˈtestifaiə], *s.* testigo, testificador.
testify [ˈtestifai], *v.t.* (*for.*) testificar, atestiguar, testimoniar, atestar. — *v.i.* dar testimonio; servir de testigo.
testimonial [testiˈmouniəl], *s.* recomendación; certificado.
testimony [ˈtestiməni], *s.* testimonio; testimonios, *m.pl.*; ***in testimony whereof,*** en fe *o* en testimonio de lo cual.
testiness [ˈtestinis], *s.* irascibilidad.
testis [ˈtestis], *s.* (*pl.* **testes** [ˈtestiːz]) testículo, teste.
testudo [tesˈtjuːdou], *s.* testudo; (*zool.*) tortuga.
testy [ˈtesti], *a.* irascible; ***testy old blighter,*** viejo cascarrabias, *m.inv.*
tetanic [teˈtænik], *a.* tetánico.
tetanoid [ˈtetənɔid], *a.* parecido al tétano.
tetanus [ˈtetənəs], *s.* tétano(s).
tetchy [ˈtetʃi], *a.* irascible.
tête-à-tête [ˈteit-ɑː-ˈteit], *adv.* cara a cara, a solas. — *s.* entrevista a solas; (*mueble*) confidente.
tether [ˈteðə], *s.* traba, maniota, atadura; ***I am at the end of my tether,*** no puedo *o* no aguanto más; se me acabó la paciencia. — *v.t.* atar con cuerda, atar, trabar.
tetrachord [ˈtetrəkɔːd], *s.* tetracordio.
tetragon [ˈtetrəgən], *s.* tetrágono, cuadrilátero.
tetragonal [teˈtrægənəl], *a.* tetrágono, cuadrangular.
tetrahedron [tetrəˈhiːdrən], *s.* tetraedro.
tetralogy [teˈtrælədʒi], *s.* tetralogía.
tetrameter [teˈtræmitə], *s.* (*poét.*) tetrámetro.
tetrarch [ˈtetrɑːk], *s.* tetrarca, *m.*
tetrarchy [ˈtetrɑːki], *s.* tetrarquía.
tetter [ˈtetə], *s.* herpes, *m.f.pl.*
Teuton [ˈtjuːtən], *s.* teutón, tudesco.
Teutonic [tjuːˈtɔnik], *a.* teutónico, tudesco. — *s.* teutón, tudesco.
Texan [ˈteksən], *a., s.* tejano.
Texas [ˈteksəs]. Tejas, *m.*
text [tekst], *s.* texto; (*impr.*) ***text hand,*** letra cursiva grande.
textbook [ˈtekstbuk], *s.* libro de texto.
textile [ˈtekstail], *a.* textil. — *s.* textil, tejido.
textual [ˈtekstjuəl], *a.* textual.
textualist [ˈtekstjuəlist], *s.* textualista, *m.f.*
texture [ˈtekstʃə], *s.* textura; tejido.
Thai [tai], *a., s.* tailandés, *m.*
Thailand [ˈtailænd]. Tailandia.
thallium [ˈθæliəm], *s.* talio.
Thames [temz], *s.* Támesis, *m.*; ***not to set the Thames on fire,*** no haber inventado la pólvora; no ser nada del otro jueves.
than [ðæn], *conj.* que; ***you have more money than I,*** Vd. tiene más dinero que yo; ***fewer than ten,*** menos de diez; ***more time than I have,*** más tiempo del que tengo; ***earlier than expected,*** más pronto de lo que se creía.
thane [θein], *s.* (*ant.*) caballero; señor.
thank [θæŋk], *s.* (*sólo en plural*) gracias, *f.pl.*;

agradecimiento; ***thanks to,*** gracias a. — *v.t.* dar las gracias a, agradecer; ***I thanked him,*** le di las gracias; ***I thank you for it,*** se lo agradezco; ***you have only yourself to thank,*** no le puedes echar la culpa a nadie más que a ti mismo; ***I'll thank you to keep a civil tongue in your head!*** ¡tenga usted la bondad de comedirse! — *interj.* (*sólo en plural*) ¡gracias!

thankful [ˈθæŋkful], *a.* agradecido, reconocido; ***I'm thankful I didn't go,*** me alegro de no haber ido.

thankfully [ˈθæŋkfuli], *adv.* con gratitud.

thankfulness [ˈθæŋkfulnis], *s.* agradecimiento, reconocimiento, gratitud.

thankless [ˈθæŋklis], *a.* ingrato.

thanklessness [ˈθæŋklisnis], *s.* desagradecimiento, ingratitud.

thanksgiving [ˈθæŋksgiviŋ], *s.* acción de gracias; ***Thanksgiving (Day),*** fiesta nacional de los Estados Unidos.

that [ðæt], *a.* (*pl.* **those** [ðouz]) ese, esa; aquel, aquella; ***that way,*** por ahí, por allí, por ese lado. — *adv.* tan; ***that far,*** tan lejos; ***that much,*** tanto. — *conj.* que; (***so***) ***that,*** para que, a fin de que; de modo que, de forma que, de manera que, de suerte que; ***in that,*** en que, por cuanto. — *pron.* ése, ésa, eso; aquél, aquélla, aquello; que, quien, el cual, la cual, lo cual; el, la lo; ***that which,*** lo que; ***what of that?*** ¿y qué?, ¿qué importa eso?; ***that is,*** es decir, a saber; ***that may be,*** puede ser, es posible; ***so that's that!*** ¡se acabó; ***at that,*** al oír *o* saber esto; ***it's not very good, at that,*** tampoco es ninguna maravilla, que digamos; ***like that,*** de esa manera; (***just***) ***like that,*** en el acto, sin más.

thatch [θætʃ], *s.* barda; paja. — *v.t.* bardar; techar con paja; ***thatched roof,*** techumbre de paja.

thatcher [ˈθætʃə], *s.* techador; bardador.

thaumaturgical [θɔːməˈtəːdʒikəl], *a.* taumatúrgico.

thaumaturgist [ˈθɔːmətəːdʒist], *s.* taumaturgo.

thaumaturgy [ˈθɔːmətəːdʒi], *s.* taumaturgia.

thaw [θɔː], *s.* deshielo. — *v.t., v.i.* deshelar(se); derretir(se); ablandar(se).

the [ðə, *delante de vocal* ði, *con énfasis* ðiː], *art.* el, la, los, las; ***the clear and the abstruse,*** lo evidente y lo recóndito; ***Charles the Fifth,*** Carlos Quinto; ***the Smiths,*** los Smith; ***the pity of it!*** ¡qué pena!; ***he is the man,*** es el hombre pintiparado. — *adv.* ***the more . . . the more . . .,*** cuanto más . . . más; ***the sooner the better,*** cuanto antes mejor.

theatre [ˈθiətə], *s.* teatro; ***theatre-goer,*** aficionado al teatro.

theatre-going [ˈθiətə-gouiŋ], *a.* teatrero.

theatrical [θiˈætrikəl], *a.* teatral; de teatro; exagerado.

theatricals [θiˈætrikəlz], *s.pl.* funciones teatrales, *f.pl.*; ***amateur theatricals,*** funciones de aficionados, *f.pl.*

thee [ðiː], *pron.* (*ant., poét.*) te, ti; ***with thee,*** contigo.

theft [θeft], *s.* hurto, robo.

their [ðɛə], *pron. pos.* su, sus; suyo, suya, suyos, suyas; de ellos, de ellas.

theism [ˈθiːizəm], *s.* teísmo.

theistic(al) [θiːˈistik(əl)], *a.* teísta.

them [ðem], *pron.* los, las; les; ellos, ellas; ***them and us,*** ellos y nosotros.

thematic [θiˈmætik], *a.* temático.

theme [θiːm], *s.* tema, *m.*; (*cine.*) ***theme music,*** música sintónica.

themselves [ðemˈselvz], *pron.* ellos (mismos), ellas (mismas); sí (mismos, mismas).

then [ðen], *adv.* entonces; en aquel tiempo, a la sazón; luego, después; ***now and then,*** de vez en cuando; ***by then,*** para entonces; ***from then on,*** a partir de entonces; ***what then?*** y entonces, ¿qué?; ¿qué pasó luego?; ***and then again,*** y adémas; y por otra parte; ***the then Prime Minister,*** el primer ministro del momento. — *conj.* pues; por tanto; en ese caso, entonces; ***now . . . then . . .,*** bien . . . bien, ora . . . ora . . .; ***now then,*** ahora bien; ***well then,*** pues bien.

thence [ðens], *adv.* (*de lugar*) de allí, desde allí; (*fig.*) de ahí, por eso, por esa razón, por ese motivo.

thenceforth, thenceforward [ðensˈfɔːθ, ðensˈfɔːwəd], *adv.* desde entonces, a partir de entonces, de allí en adelante.

theocracy [θiˈɔkrəsi], *s.* teocracia.

theocratic(al) [θioˈkrætik(əl)], *a.* teocrático.

theodicy [θiˈɔdisi], *s.* teodicea.

theodolite [θiˈɔdəlait], *s.* teodolito.

theogony [θiˈɔgəni], *s.* teogonía.

theologian [θioˈloudʒən], *s.* teólogo.

theological [θioˈlɔdʒikəl], *a.* teológico; teologal.

theologize [θiˈɔlədʒaiz], *v.i.* teologizar.

theologue [ˈθioloug], *s.* (*Am.*) estudiante de teología.

theology [θiˈɔlədʒi], *s.* teología.

theorem [ˈθiərəm], *s.* teorema, *m.*

theoretic(al) [θiəˈretik(əl)], *a.* teórico.

theorist [ˈθiərist], *s.* teórico; (*despec.*) teorizante.

theorize [ˈθiəraiz], *v.i.* teorizar.

theory [ˈθiəri], *s.* teoría; ***in theory,*** en teoría.

theosophic(al) [θiəˈsɔfik(əl)], *a.* teosófico.

theosophist [θiˈɔsəfist], *s.* teósofo.

theosophy [θiˈɔsəfi], *s.* teosofía.

therapeutic(al) [θerəˈpjuːtik(əl)], *a.* terapéutico

therapeutics [θerəˈpjuːtiks], *s.* terapéutica.

therapeutist [θerəˈpjuːtist], *s.* terapeuta, *m.f.*

therapy [ˈθerəpi], *s.* terapia; terapéutica.

there [ðɛə], *adv.* ahí; allí, allá; ***there they are,*** allí están; helos ahí; (*impers.*) ***there is*** o ***there are,*** hay; ***here and there,*** aquí y allá; ***who goes there?*** ¿quién vive?; ***who's there?*** ¿quién es?, ¿quién llama?; ***there was once,*** había una vez; ***over there,*** por allí, por allá, allí; ***out there,*** (por) ahí fuera; (por) allí fuera; allá; ***there and back,*** ida y vuelta; ***there and then,*** en el acto; (*fam.*) ***he's all there,*** no tiene (ni) un pelo de tonto; (*fam.*) ***he's not all there,*** le falta un tornillo, está un poco chalado. — *interj.* ¡toma!, ¡vaya!, ¡ya ves!; ***there! there!*** ¡cálmate!, ¡vamos!

thereabout(s) [ˈðɛərəbaut(s)], *adv.* por ahí.

thereafter [ðɛərˈɑːftə], *adv.* después de eso, a partir de entonces.

thereat [ðɛərˈæt], *adv.* al oír *o* saber esto.

thereby [ðɛəˈbai], *adv.* con eso, de ese modo, así.

therefore [ˈðɛəfɔː], *adv.* por esto, por eso, por tanto, por lo tanto, por consiguiente.

therefrom [ðɛəˈfrɔm], *adv.* de allí.

therein [ðɛərˈin], *adv.* allí dentro; en eso.

thereinafter [ðɛərinˈɑːftə], *adv.* posteriormente.

thereof [ðɛərˈɔv], *adv.* de ello; ***the meaning thereof,*** su sentido, su significación.

thereon [ðɛərˈɔn], *adv.* sobre eso.

Theresa [təˈriːzə, təˈreizə]. Teresa.

thereto [ðɛəˈtuː], *adv.* a ello.

thereunder [ðɛərˈʌndə], *adv.* bajo ese título; debajo de eso.

thereupon [ðɛərəˈpɔn], [THEREAT].

therewith [ðɛəˈwið], *adv.* con eso; acto seguido.

theriac [ˈθiəriæk], *a.* teriacal, triacal.

therm [θəːm], *s.* (*fís.*) unidad térmica.

thermal [ˈθəːməl], *a.* (*fís.*) térmico; termal.

thermic [ˈθəːmik], *a.* térmico.

thermionic [θəːmaiˈɔnik], *a.* termoiónico; ***thermionic valve,*** lámpara termoiónica.

thermodynamics [θəːmoudaiˈnæmiks], *s.* termodinámica.

thermoelectric [θəːmouiˈlektrik], *a.* termoeléctrico.

thermoelectricity [θəːmouelekˈtrisiti], *s.* termoelectricidad.

thermometer [θə'mɔmitə], *s.* termómetro.
thermometric [θə:mo'metrik], *a.* termométrico.
thermometry [θə'mɔmitri], *s.* termometría.
thermonuclear ['θə:mou'nju:kliə], *a.* termonuclear.
Thermopylae [θə:'mɔpili:]. (las) Termópilas.
Thermos ['θə:mɔs], *s.* (*marca de fábrica*) ***Thermos flask,*** termo.
thermoscope ['θə:moskoup], *s.* termoscopio.
thermostat ['θə:mostæt], *s.* termostato.
thesaurus [θi'sɔ:rəs], *s.* tesoro (léxico).
these [ði:z], *dem. a.pl.* [THIS], estos, estas. — *dem. pron. pl.* [THIS], éstos, éstas.
thesis ['θi:sis], *s.* (*pl.* **theses** [-i:z]) tesis, *f. inv.*
Thespian ['θespiən], *a.* de Tespis; trágico, dramático. — *s.* comediante.
theurgy ['θiədji], *s.* teurgia.
thew [θju:], *s.* tendón, músculo; (*pl.*) fuerza muscular, energía, vigor.
they [ðei], *pron. pl.* [HE, SHE *o* IT], ellos, ellas.
thick [θik], *a.* grueso; espeso; denso; tupido; poblado; turbio; viscoso; lerdo, zote; ***thick air,*** aire viciado; ***thick accent,*** acento cerrado; (*fam.*) ***thick with,*** lleno de; ***it is 2 inches thick,*** tiene 2 pulgadas de espesor; (*fam.*) ***they're very thick,*** son íntimos; (*fam.*) ***as thick as thieves,*** uña y carne; (*fam.*) ***it's a bit thick!*** ¡no hay derecho!; ***thick of hearing,*** duro de oído. — *adv.* ***to speak thick,*** tener lengua de trapo; ***to put the paint on thick,*** echar mucha pintura; (*fig.*) ***to lay it on thick,*** exagerar la nota; recargar las tintas negras. — *s.* grueso, espesor; ***in the thick of the fight,*** en lo más reñido de la pelea; ***in the thick of the crowd,*** en lo más apretado del gentío; ***through thick and thin,*** en la dicha y en la desdicha; ***to be in the thick of it,*** estar metido de hoz y de coz.
thicken ['θikən], *v.t., v.i.* espesar(se); ***the plot thickens,*** se complica la trama.
thickener ['θikənə], *s.* espesador.
thickening ['θikəniŋ], *a.* espesativo. — *s.* espesamiento; espesador.
thicket ['θikit], *s.* matorral.
thick-headed, thick-skulled ['θik-'hedid, 'θik-'skʌld], *a.* lerdo, estúpido.
thickish ['θikiʃ], *a.* espesillo.
thick-lipped ['θik-'lipt], *a.* bezudo.
thickly ['θikli], *adv.* espesamente; ***thickly settled,*** (*sitio*) muy poblado.
thickness ['θiknis], *s.* espesor; grosor, grueso; densidad.
thickset ['θikset], *a.* achaparrado, rechoncho, grueso; muy espeso, denso.
thick-skinned ['θik-'skind], *a.* (*fig.*) insensible, de cara dura.
thief [θi:f], *s.* (*pl.* **thieves** [θi:vz]) ladrón.
thieve [θi:v], *v.t., v.i.* hurtar, robar.
thievery ['θi:vəri], *s.* hurto, latrocinio; ***piece of thievery,*** robo.
thievish ['θi:viʃ], *a.* ladrón, rapaz.
thievishness ['θi:viʃnis], *s.* propensión al latrocinio.
thigh [θai], *s.* muslo; ***thigh-bone,*** fémur.
thill [θil], *s.* limonera, lanza, vara (de carruaje).
thimble [θimbl], *s.* (*cost.*) dedal; (*mec.*) manguito; (*mar.*) guardacabo; ***thimble-berry,*** frambuesa negra.
thin [θin], *a.* delgado; flaco; ligero; (*aire*) tenue, sutil; (*sopa, sangre*) pobre; (*papel*) fino; (*pelo*) ralo; (*cosecha etc.*) escaso; ***to be thin on the ground,*** escasear, ser pocos, haber pocos; ***to grow thin*** o ***thinner,*** adelgazar, enflaquecer. — *v.t.* — ***out,*** aclarar. — *v.i.* adelgazar; aclararse; reducirse, disminuir.
thine [ðain], *a.* (*ant., poét.*) tu, tus. — *pron.* (*ant., poét.*) el tuyo, la tuya *etc.*
thing [θiŋ], *s.* cosa; ***above all things,*** sobre todo; ***as things stand,*** tal y como están las cosas; ***for one thing,*** para empezar; ***he doesn't know the first thing about it,*** no tiene la más mínima idea del asunto; (*fam.*) ***it's not the done thing,*** (eso) no se hace; ***no such thing!*** ¡nada de eso!; ***poor*** (***little***) ***thing!*** ¡pobre!, ¡pobrecito!; ***take your things and go!*** ¡coge tus cosas *o* tus bártulos y vete!; (***that***) ***of all things!*** ¡precisamente eso!; ***the best thing,*** lo mejor; ***the only thing,*** lo único; ***the thing is,*** lo importante es; el caso es que; ***the thing of the moment,*** lo que está de moda, lo que se estila; (*fam.*) ***to have a thing*** (***about***), tener manía con, estar obsesionado; (*fam.*) ***to know a thing or two,*** saber cuántas son cinco; ***to make a good thing out of it,*** beneficiarse, forrarse; ***things are looking up,*** las cosas empiezan a ir mejor.
thingummy, thingumabob ['θiŋəmi, θiŋəməbɔb], *s.* chisme.
think [θiŋk], *irr. v.t., v.i.* pensar; ***as you think fit,*** como usted quiera, como mejor le parezca; ***he thought it proper*** o ***right to,*** creyó conveniente *con. inf.*, le pareció conveniente *u* oportuno *con inf.*, tuvo a bien *con inf.* — *v.i.* pensar, creer; ***think about, of,*** pensar en; ***think of,*** (*tener un concepto de*) pensar de, opinar de; ***think about, of*** (*con ger.*), pensar en la posibilidad de; ***I think so,*** creo que sí; ***I don't think so,*** creo que no, no creo, no lo creo; ***I thought so!*** ¡ya me lo figuraba!, ¡ya me parecía a mí!; ***I should think so!*** ¡ya lo creo!; ***I can't think properly,*** no puedo discurrir bien.
thinker ['θiŋkə], *s.* pensador.
thinking ['θiŋkiŋ], *a.* pensante; racional. — *s.* pensamiento(s); ***wishful thinking,*** ilusiones, *f.pl.*, espejismos, *m.pl.*, utopías, *f.pl.*; ***that's*** (***just***) ***wishful thinking,*** eso es lo que usted quisiera; ***way of thinking,*** modo de pensar; ***to my way of thinking,*** a mi modo de ver.
think-tank ['θiŋk-tæŋk], *s.* (*fam.*) equipo de deliberadores.
thinly ['θinli], *adv.* ligeramente; ***thinly populated,*** de baja densidad de población, poco poblado.
thinness ['θinnis], *s.* delgadez; (*fig.*) tenuidad; (*pelo, vegetación*) raleza.
thin-skinned ['θin-'skind], *a.* de piel fina; (*fig.*) sensible.
third [θə:d], *a.* tercer(o); ***third-class, third-rate,*** de baja categoría, de tercera clase, de tercer orden; (*títulos*) tercero; ***third-party insurance,*** seguro contra tercera persona. — *adv.* ***to travel third*** (***class***), viajar en tercera (clase). — *s.* tercio, tercera parte; (*fechas*) tres; (*mús.*) tercera.
thirdly ['θə:dli], *adv.* en tercer lugar.
thirst [θə:st], *s.* sed; ansia, afán; ***to quench one's thirst,*** apagar la sed. — *v.i.* ***to thirst for*** o ***after,*** tener sed de, ansiar vivamente.
thirstiness ['θə:stinis], *s.* sed, *f.*
thirsty ['θə:sti], *a.* sediento; ***to be thirsty,*** tener sed; ***how thirsty I am!*** !qué sed tengo!; ***to make thirsty,*** dar sed.
thirteen [θə:'ti:n], *a., s.* trece.
thirteenth [θə:'ti:nθ], *a.* decimotercio, decimotercero, trece; (*títulos*) trece. — *s.* decimotercio, trezavo; (*fechas*) trece.
thirtieth ['θə:tiəθ], *a.* trigésimo, treinta. — *s.* trigésimo, treintavo; (*fechas*) treinta.
thirty ['θə:ti], *a., s.* treinta.
this [ðis], *a.* (*pl.* **these** [ði:z]) este, esta. — *pron.* éste, ésta, esto.
thistle ['θisəl], *s.* (*bot.*) cardo; (*mil.*) abrojo; ***carline thistle,*** carlina, ajonjera; ***fuller's thistle,*** cardón, cardencha, cardo de batanero; ***milk-thistle,*** cardo lechoso; ***prickly thistle,*** acanto; ***Scotch thistle,*** cardo escocés; ***Order of the Thistle,*** orden del Cardo, *f.*
thistledown ['θisəldaun], *s.* papo *o* vilano (de cardo).
thistle-finch ['θisəl-fintʃ], *s.* jilguero.
thistly ['θisli], *a.* lleno de cardos; espinoso; erizado.
thither [ðiðə], *adv.* allá; ***hither and thither,*** acá y allá.
tho' [ðou], *conj., contr.* [THOUGH].

thole [θoul], *s.* (*mar.*) tolete.
thole-pin [ˈθoul-pin], *s.* tolete.
tholus [ˈθouləs], *s.* (*pl.* **tholi** [-lai]) (*arq.*) cúpula.
Thomas [ˈtɔməs]. Tomás, *m.*
Thomist [ˈtoumist], *s.* tomista, *m.f.*
thong [θɔŋ], *s.* correa.
thoracic [θɔ:ˈræsik], *a.* torácico.
thorax [ˈθɔ:ræks], *s.* (*pl.* **thoraces** [ˈθɔ:rəsi:z]) (*anat.*) tórax.
thorium [ˈθɔ:riəm], *s.* torio.
thorn [θɔ:n], *s.* (*rosa, fig.*) espina; (*cactos*) púa, pincho; ***thorn-bush,*** espino, abrojo. — *v.t.* pinchar (con una espina); ***to be upon thorns,*** estar en ascuas.
thorn-apple [ˈθɔ:n-æpl], *s.* (*bot.*) estramonio.
thornback [ˈθɔ:nbæk], *s.* (*ict.*) raya espinosa.
thorny [ˈθɔ:ni], *a.* espinoso.
thorough [ˈθʌrə], *a.* completo, exhaustivo, hecho a fondo; (*pers.*) concienzudo, minucioso.
thoroughbred [ˈθʌrəbred], *a.* de casta, de pura sangre. — *s.* (*caballo*) pura sangre, *m.f.*
thoroughfare [ˈθʌrəfɛə], *s.* vía pública; calle; carretera; ***no thoroughfare,*** prohibido el paso.
thoroughgoing [ˈθʌrəgouiŋ], *a.* completo, consumado; de cuerpo entero.
thoroughly [ˈθʌrəli], *adv.* completamente, por completo, totalmente; a fondo; ***thoroughly fed-up,*** harto hasta más no poder.
thoroughness [ˈθʌrənis], *s.* (lo) completo, (lo) exhaustivo *etc.*
thoroughwort [ˈθʌrəwə:t], *s.* eupatorio.
thorp [θɔ:p], *s.* pueblo, aldea, lugar, caserío.
those [ðouz], *a. pl.* [THAT]; esos; esas; aquellos, aquellas. — *pron. pl.* [THAT]; ésos, ésas; aquéllos, aquéllas; ***those who,*** los que, las que, quienes; ***those of,*** los de, las de.
thou [ðau], *pron. pers.* (*ant., poét.*) tú. — *v.t.* tutear; ***to thee-and-thou,*** tutear, dar trato demasiado familiar a.
though [ðou], *adv.* sin embargo. — *conj.* aunque, bien que, aun cuando; si bien; ***as though,*** como si.
thought [θɔ:t], *s.* pensamiento; consideración, reflexión; idea, intención, propósito; ***it's a nice thought, but . . .,*** la idea es bonita, pero . . ., sería un detalle bonito, pero . . .; ***he gives no thought to others,*** no piensa para nada en los demás; ***on second thoughts,*** pensándolo bien, bien pensado; ahora que caigo; ***thought-processes,*** procesos cogitativos, *m.pl.*
thoughtful [ˈθɔ:tful], *a.* pensativo, meditabundo; considerado; atento; ***how thoughtful!*** ¡qué detallista!; ***he's always very thoughtful,*** hace las cosas con mucho interés; siempre tiene detalles.
thoughtfulness [ˈθɔ:tfulnis], *s.* atención, solicitud, interés, *m.*
thoughtless [ˈθɔ:tlis], *a.* irreflexivo, incauto; desconsiderado, que no piensa en los demás.
thoughtlessness [ˈθɔ:tlisnis], *s.* irreflexión; desconsideración.
thousand [ˈθauzənd], *a., s.* mil.
thousandth [ˈθauzəndθ], *a., s.* milésimo.
thraldom [ˈθrɔ:ldəm], *s.* servidumbre, *f.*, esclavitud.
thrall [θrɔ:l], *s.* siervo, esclavo; servidumbre, *f.*, esclavitud.
thrash [θræʃ], *v.t.* zurrar; sacudir, cascar; ***thrash out a matter,*** ventilar un asunto. — *v.i.* — ***about,*** revolcarse; debatirse; [THRESH].
thrasher [ˈθræʃə], *s.* (*orn.*) malvís, *m.*; (*ict.*) ***thrasher (shark),*** zorra de mar.
thrashing [ˈθræʃiŋ], *s.* zurra, vapuleo, paliza; ***to give s.o. a thrashing,*** dar una tunda a alguien; [THRESHING].
thread [θred], *s.* hilo, hebra; (*mec.*) rosca, filete; ***to hang by a thread,*** colgar *o* pender de un hilo; ***to lose the thread,*** perder el hilo; ***to pick up the thread again,*** coger *o* reanudar el hilo. — *v.t.* enhebrar; ensartar; roscar, aterrajar; ***thread one's way through,*** abrirse paso por, colarse a través de.
threadbare [ˈθredbɛə], *a.* raído, gastado; (*fig.*) manido, trillado.
thread-like [ˈθred-laik], *a.* filiforme.
threadworm [ˈθredwə:m], *s.* ascáride, *f.*, lombriz intestinal.
thready [ˈθredi], *a.* filamentoso.
threat [θret], *s.* amenaza; amago.
threaten [θretn], *v.t.* amenazar; amagar; ***threaten with death,*** amenazar de muerte. — *v.i.* amenazar.
threatener [ˈθretnə], *s.* amenazador.
threatening [ˈθretniŋ], *a.* amenazador, amenazante, conminatorio. — *s.* amenazas, *f.pl.*
threateningly [ˈθretniŋli], *adv.* con amenaza(s), de una manera amenazante.
three [θri:], *a., s.* tres, *m.*; (*bot.*) ***three-cleft,*** trífido; ***three-cornered,*** triangular; ***three-cornered hat,*** tricornio, sombrero de tres picos; ***three-decker,*** navío de tres puentes; ***three deep,*** de tres en fondo; ***three-dimensional,*** tridimensional; ***three-forked,*** de tres dientes; ***three-legged,*** de tres piernas *o* patas; ***three-masted,*** de tres mástiles; (*elec.*) ***three-phase,*** trifásico; ***three-piece suit,*** terno; ***three-piece suite,*** tresillo; ***three-ply,*** triple, de tres capas; madera contrachapada de tres capas; ***three-quarter,*** de tres cuartos; ***three-quarter coat,*** abrigo tres cuartos; ***three-stringed,*** de tres cuerdas; ***three-valve(d),*** trivalvado, trivalvo, trivalvular; ***three-way,*** de tres pasos, vías *o* direcciones; ***three-way valve,*** válvula de paso triple; ***three-wheeler,*** coche triciclo.
threefold [ˈθri:fould], *a.* triple.
threepence [ˈθrepəns], *s.* tres peniques, *m.pl.*
threepenny [ˈθrepəni], *a.* de tres peniques; (*ant.*) ***threepenny bit,*** moneda de tres peniques.
threescore [ˈθri:skɔ:], *a., s.* sesenta.
threnody [ˈθrenədi], *s.* treno.
thresh [θreʃ], *v.t.* trillar; desgranar.
threshing [ˈθreʃiŋ], *a.* de (la) trilla. — *s.* trilla; ***threshing floor,*** era; ***threshing machine,*** trilladora.
threshold [ˈθreʃould], *s.* umbral.
thrice [θrais], *adv.* tres veces.
thrift [θrift], *s.* economía, ahorro; frugalidad.
thriftiness [ˈθriftinis], *s.* economía, ahorro; frugalidad; (lo) parco.
thriftless [ˈθriftlis], *a.* malgastador, pródigo, manirroto.
thrifty [ˈθrifti], *a.* económico, parco, que gasta poco.
thrill [θril], *s.* emoción (fuerte); gozada, gustazo; calambrín de gusto; estremecimiento (*de miedo etc.*) — *v.t.* emocionar; alucinar; dar (un) gustazo a; estremecer (*de miedo etc.*). — *v.i.* emocionarse; darse (un) gustazo; estremecerse.
thrilling [ˈθriliŋ], *a.* emocionante; alucinante; que da mucho gustirrín *o* gustazo; estremecedor.
thrive [θraiv], *irr. v.i.* medrar; prosperar; florecer.
thriving [ˈθraiviŋ], *a.* próspero, floreciente, pujante.
throat [θrout], *s.* garganta; cuello; ***he has a sore throat,*** le duele la garganta; ***sore throat,*** dolor de garganta; (*fig.*) ***he sticks in my throat,*** se me ha atravesado; ***it stuck in my throat,*** se me atragantó; ***throat-band,*** ahogadero; ***to clear one's throat,*** carraspear; ***to cut the throat of,*** degollar, cortarle el cuello a; ***to jump down the throat of,*** enfadarse muchísimo con.
throatwort [ˈθroutwə:t], *s.* (*bot.*) hermosilla.
throaty [ˈθrouti], *a.* ronco.
throb [θrɔb], *s.* latido, palpitación, pulsación; trepidación. — *v.i.* latir, palpitar; trepidar.
throbbing [ˈθrɔbiŋ], *a.* palpitante. — *s.* latido(s), *etc.*
throes [θrouz], *s. pl.* ***throes of childbirth,*** dolores del parto, *m.pl.*; ***throes of death,*** agonía (de la

muerte); ***they are in the throes of working out a solution,*** están luchando *o* debatiéndose por encontrar *o* idear una solución.

thrombosis [θrɔm'bousis], *s.* (*med.*) trombosis, *f. inv.*

throne [θroun], *s.* trono.

throng [θrɔŋ], *s.* muchedumbre, *f.*, multitud, tropel, gentío. — *v.t.* llenar de bote en bote, atestar, pulular por. — *v.i.* pulular; acudir en tropel(es); apiñarse.

throttle [θrɔtl], *s.* (*mec.*) regulador, válvula reguladora; (*aut.*) acelerador. — *v.t.* ahogar, estrangular. — *v.i.* — ***down*** o ***back,*** cerrar el regulador, decelerar.

through [θru:], *a.* continuo; ***through traffic,*** tráfico de tránsito, tráfico interurbano; ***through train,*** tren directo. — *adv.* de parte a parte; (desde el principio) hasta el final; (*Am.*) inclusive; ***to be wet through,*** estar calado hasta los huesos; ***to be English through and through,*** ser inglés por los cuatro costados; ***to carry through,*** llevar a cabo *o* a término; (*fam.*) ***to see it through,*** llegar hasta el final, aguantar hasta el final. — *prep.* a través de; por entre; por; por medio de; gracias a, por mediación de.

throughout [θru:'aut], *adv.* en todo, por todas partes; todo el tiempo, desde el principio hasta el fin. — *prep.* por todo, en todo; a lo largo de todo, de un extremo a otro de; durante todo.

throw [θrou], *s.* tiro, tirada, echada, lanzamiento; jugada; (*dados*) lance; (*lucha libre*) derribo; (*mec.*) golpe, carrera, recorrido; ***within a stone's throw,*** a tiro de piedra *o* ballesta. — *irr. v.t.* echar, tirar, lanzar, arrojar; (*luz etc.*) proyectar; desmontar, desarzonar; despedir; derribar; mudar (*la piel*); quitarse, soltar; (*mec.*) impeler, empujar; (*fig., fam.*) confundir, desconcertar; echar al suelo; (*alfarería*) formar, dar forma a; (*seda, hilo*) torcer; descartarse de (*un naipe*); ***throw about,*** esparcir, arrojar de un lado a otro; (*fig., fam.*) ***throw one's weight about,*** chulear(se); ***throw money about,*** tirar el dinero; ***throw a bridge across*** o ***over a river,*** tender un puente sobre un río; ***throw aside,*** echar a un lado; ***throw away,*** tirar; ***throw back,*** devolver; rechazar (con desprecio); ***throw down,*** echar por tierra, derribar; ***throw down the gauntlet,*** arrojar el guante; (*dep.*) ***throw in,*** sacar; añadir; ***with travel expenses thrown in,*** con (los) gastos de viaje incluidos; ***throw in one's lot with,*** unirse a, hacer causa común con; (*aut.*) ***throw in the clutch,*** embragar; ***throw off,*** sacudirse; quitarse de encima; (*mec.*) desconectar, desembragar; ***throw pursuers off (the trail),*** despistar a los perseguidores; ***throw open,*** abrir de golpe *o* de par en par; ***throw out,*** echar fuera; despedir; poner de patitas en la calle; ***throw out a hint,*** echar una indirecta; ***throw out of gear,*** desengranar, desembragar; (*fig.*) desarticular; ***throw over,*** dejar, abandonar; romper con; ***throw overboard,*** echar *o* tirar por la borda; ***throw together,*** unir (casualmente); ***throw up,*** lanzar al aire; (*fig.*) renunciar a; (*fam.*) vomitar, devolver; construir de prisa; (*fig.*) ***throw up*** o ***in the sponge,*** darse por vencido, arrojar la toalla. — *v.i.* (*fam.*) ***throw up,*** devolver; (*fam.*) ***it makes me throw up,*** me asquea, me da asco.

throwaway ['θrouəwei], *a.* ***throwaway remark,*** cosa dicha al desgaire.

throwback ['θroubæk], *s.* salto atrás; (*biol.*) reversión.

thrower ['θrouə], *s.* lanzador, tirador; torcedor (de seda).

throw-in ['θrou-in], *s.* (*dep.*) saque (de banda).

throwing ['θrouiŋ], *s.* tiro.

throw-out ['θrou-aut], *s.* cosa desechada *o* inútil.

throwster ['θroustə], *s.* torcedor (de seda).

thrum (1) [θrʌm], *s.* (*naut.*) cabos, *m.pl.*; (*tej.*) borla; hilo basto.

thrum (2) [θrʌm], *s.* (*mús.*) tecleo, rasgueo. — *v.t., v.i.* teclear (en), rasguear.

thrush (1) [θrʌʃ], *s.* (*orn.*) tordo.

thrush (2) [θrʌʃ], *s.* (*med.*) afta; (*vet.*) higo.

thrust [θrʌst], *s.* empuje; acometida, arremetida; empellón; estocada; lanzada; puñalada; cornada; aguijonada; (*min.*) derrumbe; (*mec.*) ***thrust-bearing,*** cojinete axial *o* de empuje. — *irr. v.t., v.i.* empujar; impulsar, impeler; meter, introducir; clavar, hincar; ***thrust aside,*** apartar de un empujón *o* rechazar bruscamente; ***thrust away,*** rechazar; ***thrust back,*** empujar hacia atrás; arrollar, hacer retroceder; ***thrust forward,*** empujar hacia adelante; ***thrust in,*** meter a la fuerza; ***thrust out,*** sacar, echar fuera; ***thrust through,*** atravesar, pasar de parte a parte; ***thrust upon,*** imponer, obligar a aceptar. — *v.i.* empujar; ***thrust at,*** intentar asestar una estocada a; ***he thrust at me with a knife,*** intentó asestarme una cuchillada; ***thrust forward*** o ***on,*** seguir adelante, seguir avanzando; ***thrust through,*** abrirse camino a viva fuerza. — *v.r.* ***thrust o.s. in,*** meterse; ***thrust o.s. upon,*** forzar su compañía a.

thud [θʌd], *s.* ruido *o* golpe sordo; porrazo; baque. — *v.i.* hacer *o* caer *o* moverse con (un) ruido sordo.

thug [θʌg], *s.* bestia, bruto; asesino.

thumb [θʌm], *s.* pulgar; ***he's under her thumb,*** lo tiene metido en un puño; ***thumb index,*** (índice de) uñero; ***thumb-stall,*** dedil; (*Am.*) ***thumb-tack*** [DRAWING-PIN]; ***to be all thumbs,*** ser *o* estar torpísimo, no hacer nada a derechas; (*fig.*) ***to twiddle one's thumbs,*** estar mirando (a) las musarañas; ***thumbs up (down),*** signo de aprobación (desaprobación). — *v.t.* manosear; ***thumb a lift,*** conseguirse un viaje haciendo autostop; ***thumb through,*** hojear.

thumbnail ['θʌmneil], *s.* uña del pulgar.

thumbprint ['θʌmprint], *s.* impresión del pulgar.

thumbscrew(s) ['θʌmskru:(z)], *s.* empulgueras, *f.pl.*; tuerca de cabeza prismática.

thump [θʌmp], *s.* golpazo, porrazo; baque, ruido sordo; trastazo. — *v.t.* golpear, aporrear. — *v.i.* latir pesadamente; funcionar *o* vibrar con ruido sordo.

thumping ['θʌmpiŋ], *adv.* (*fam.*) extraordinariamente; ***thumping good book,*** libro estupendo; ***thumping great fellow,*** gigantón. — *s.* golpeteo; golpazos, *m.pl.*, porrazos, *m.pl.*

thunder ['θʌndə], *s.* trueno(s); (*fig.*) estruendo; ***thunder-cloud,*** nubarrón (de tormenta); ***thunder-storm,*** tormenta de truenos; ***to steal s.o.'s thunder,*** chafarle algo a alguien (haciéndolo *o* diciéndolo primero). — *v.i.* tronar; (*fig.*) ***thunder against,*** tronar contra; ***thunder along,*** ir *o* pasar con estruendo.

thunderbolt ['θʌndəboult], *s.* rayo; (*fig.*) escopetazo.

thunderclap ['θʌndəklæp], *s.* trueno, tronido.

thunderer ['θʌndərə], *s.* (*Júpiter*) tonante *o* tronante.

thundering ['θʌndəriŋ], *adv.* (*fam.*) extraordinariamente; ***thundering good,*** estupendo, fenomenal.

thunderous ['θʌndərəs], *a.* atronador.

thunderstruck ['θʌndəstrʌk], *a.* atónito, estupefacto.

thurible ['θju:ribl], *s.* (*igl.*) turíbulo.

thurifer ['θju:rifə], *s.* turiferario.

thuriferous [θju:'rifərəs], *a.* turífero.

thurification [θju:rifi'keiʃən], *s.* turificación.

Thursday ['θə:zd(e)i], *s.* jueves, *m. inv.*; ***Maundy Thursday,*** jueves santo.

thus [ðʌs], *adv.* así; ***thus far,*** hasta aquí.

thuya ['θu:jə], *s.* (*bot.*) tuya.

thwack [θwæk], [WHACK].

thwart [θwɔ:t], *s.* (*mar.*) banco (de remeros). — *v.t.* frustrar; impedir; contrariar.

thy [ðai], *a. pos.* (*ant., poét.*) tu, tus.

thyme [taim], *s.* tomillo.

thymol ['θaimɔl], *s.* timol.

thymus [ˈθaiməs], *s.* (*pl.* **thymi** [-mai]) (*anat.*) timo.
thyroid [ˈθairɔid], *a.* tiroideo; ***thyroid gland,*** tiroides, *m.inv.*
thyrsus [ˈθəːsəs], *s.* (*pl.* **thyrsi** [-sai]) (*bot.*) tirso.
thyself [ðaiˈself], *pron. refl.* (*ant.*, *poét.*) tú mismo; te; ti (mismo).
tiara [tiˈɑːrə], *s.* tiara; diadema.
Tiber [ˈtaibə]. Tíber.
Tiberius [taiˈbiəriəs]. Tiberio.
Tibet [tiˈbet]. (el) Tibet.
Tibetan [tiˈbetən], *a.*, *s.* tibetano.
tibia [ˈtibiə], *s.* tibia.
tibial [ˈtibiəl], *a.* tibial.
tic [tik], *s.* (*med.*) tic (nervioso).
tick (1) [tik], *s.* tictac (del reloj); señal, *f.*; ***in two ticks,*** en un santiamén, en un pispás. — *v.t.* poner una señal (de aprobación) a; (*fam.*) ***tick s.o. off,*** echar un rapapolvo *o* una reprimenda a, cantar las cuarenta a. — *v.i.* hacer tictac (*el reloj*); (*aut.*) ***tick over,*** marchar en vacío; (*fam.*) ***what makes him tick?*** ¿por dónde respira?
tick (2) [tik], *s.* (*zool.*) garrapata.
tick (3) [tik], *s.* (*fam.*) ***on tick,*** al fiado.
ticker tape [ˈtikə teip], *s.* cinta de teleimpresor.
ticket [ˈtikit], *s.* billete; (*teat.*, *cine. etc.*) entrada; localidad; etiqueta, rótulo; talón; (*Am.*, *pol.*) candidatura; (*Am.*, *fam.*) multa; (*fam.*) ***that's the ticket!*** ¡justo lo que hace falta! — *v.t.* poner etiqueta a, rotular.
ticking (1) [ˈtikiŋ], *s.* tictac; ***ticking-off,*** bronca, resplandina; ***to give s.o. a ticking-off,*** echar una bronca *o* una resplandina a alguien.
ticking (2) [ˈtikiŋ], *s.* (*tej.*) terliz, cutí.
tickle [tikl], *s.* cosquilla(s). — *v.t.* cosquillear, hacer cosquillas a; divertir, hacer gracia a; (*fam.*) ***he was tickled pink by it,*** le gustó la mar; ***to be tickled to death,*** morirse de risa. — *v.i.* sentir cosquillas; ***it tickles,*** me hace cosquillas.
tickler [ˈtiklə], *s.* el que hace cosquillas; (*fam.*) rompecabezas, *m.inv.*, problema difícil, *m.*
tickling [ˈtikliŋ], *s.* cosquillas, *f.pl.*; cosquilleo.
ticklish [ˈtikliʃ], *a.* cosquilloso; peliagudo, espinoso; ***to be ticklish,*** ser cosquilloso, tener cosquillas; ***it's a ticklish business,*** es asunto peliagudo *o* engorroso.
ticklishness [ˈtikliʃnis], *s.* (lo) cosquilloso; (lo) peliagudo *o* engorroso; susceptibilidad.
tick-tock [ˈtik-tɔk], *s.* tictac.
tidal [taidl], *a.* de marea; ***tidal wave,*** maremoto; ola de marea.
tid-bit [ˈtid-bit], [TIT-BIT].
tide [taid], *s.* marea; corriente, *f.*; flujo, curso, marcha; tendencia; ***ebb tide,*** bajamar, *f.*; reflujo del mar; ***flood tide,*** creciente, *f.*; ***high tide,*** pleamar, *f.*; marea alta; cumbre, apogeo; ***low tide,*** bajamar, *f.*, menguante, marea baja; ***neap tide,*** agua muerta; ***spring tide,*** agua viva; ***to go against the tide,*** ir contra la corriente; ***to go with the tide,*** seguir la corriente; ***to turn the tide,*** cambiar el curso *o* la suerte. — *v.t.* — ***s.o. over,*** ayudar a alguien a salir del paso. — *v.i.* — ***on,*** seguir, continuar.
tide-gate [ˈtaid-geit], *s.* compuerta de marea.
tideless [ˈtaidlis], *a.* sin marea.
tidesman [ˈtaidzmən], *s.* aduanero de puerto.
tide-way [ˈtaid-wei], *s.* canal de marea.
tidiness [ˈtaidinis], *s.* pulcritud; buen orden.
tidings [ˈtaidiŋz], *s.pl.* nuevas, *f.pl.*, noticias, *f.pl.*; (*ant.*) albricias, *f.pl.*
tidy [ˈtaidi], *a.* ordenado, en orden; (bien) arreglado; (*pers.*) pulcro; metódico; (*fig.*, *fam.*) bastante, considerable; ***to get the house tidy,*** arreglar la casa; ***to have a tidy mind,*** tener una inteligencia metódica; (*fig.*, *fam.*) ***a tidy bit,*** una suma considerable. — *v.t.*, *v.i.* — (***up***), arreglar *u* ordenar (las cosas), poner (las cosas) en orden.
tie [tai], *s.* lazo; vínculo; atadura, ligazón; (*mús.*) ligadura; (*prenda*) corbata; (*arq.*) tirante; (*f.c.*) traviesa; (*dep.*) empate; (*dep.*) ***cup-tie,*** partido eliminatorio; ***to end in a tie,*** terminar en empate, terminar empatados. — *v.t.* atar; ligar; unir, enlazar; vincular; (*mús.*) ligar; ***tie down,*** sujetar; afianzar; ***tie s.o. down,*** obligar a alguien; ***tie up,*** atar; invertir (*dinero*); (*mar.*) atracar; ***to be tied up*** (***with***), estar ocupado (con); estar liado (con); ***my money is tied up with,*** tengo el dinero metido en. — *v.i.* empatar; (*mar.*) ***tie up,*** atracar. — **tie o.s.,** *v.r.* ***he doesn't want to tie himself down,*** no quiere comprometerse.
tier [tiə], *s.* grada; fila, hilera, ringlera; (*mar.*) andana.
tierce [tiəs], *s.* (*mús.*) tercera; (*igl.*) tercia; tercerola; tercera (en el juego de los cientos); (*esgr.*) tercera posición.
tiercet [ˈtəːsit], *s.* (*poét.*) [TERCET].
tiff [tif], *s.* riña, discusión; ***to have a tiff,*** reñir, discutir.
tiffin [ˈtifin], *s.* almuerzo.
tiger [ˈtaigə], *s.* tigre; (*bot.*) ***tiger lily,*** tigridia; (*piedra*) ***tiger's eye,*** ojo de gato.
tigerish [ˈtaigəriʃ], *a.* atigrado; feroz.
tight [tait], *a.* apretado; estrecho; ajustado; tirante; duro; (*curva*) cerrada; (*situación*) apurada, comprometida; (*fig.*, *dinero*) escaso; (*fig.*, *pers.*) agarrado, tacaño; (*fam.*) que tiene una curda *o* una trompa; ***it's a tight fit,*** entra muy justo; está muy duro; ***to be in a tight corner, spot*** o ***squeeze,*** verse en un aprieto *o* apuro; ***tight-rope,*** cuerda tirante; ***tight-rope walker,*** volatinero, equilibrista, *m.f.*, funámbulo. — *adv.* bien, fuertemente; (*fig.*, *fam.*) ***tight-fisted,*** agarrado, tacaño; ***tight-fitting,*** ajustado; ***to hold tight,*** agarrarse bien; ***to sit tight,*** estarse quieto, no moverse. — *s.* (*pl.*) traje de malla.
tighten [taitn], *v.t.* apretar; (*cuerda etc.*) atiesar.
tightness [ˈtaitnis], *s.* (lo) apretado *etc.*
tightwad [ˈtaitwɔd], (*Am.*) [MISER].
tigress [ˈtaigris], *s.* tigresa.
tile [tail], *s.* teja; baldosa; azulejo; (*fig.*, *fam.*) ***to have a tile loose,*** faltarle a uno un tornillo; (*fig.*, *fam.*) ***to go on the tiles,*** andar de picos pardos. — *v.t.* poner ladrillos *o* azulejos a.
till (1) [til], *conj.* hasta que. — *prep.* hasta.
till (2) [til], *s.* caja (registradora).
till (3) [til], *v.t.* cultivar, labrar.
tillable [ˈtiləbl], *a.* laborable.
tillage [ˈtilidʒ], *s.* labranza, cultivo.
tiller [ˈtilə], *s.* labrador; (*mar.*) caña del timón.
tilt [tilt], *s.* inclinación, ladeo; justa, torneo; ***to give a tilt to,*** inclinar, ladear; ***on the tilt,*** inclinado; ***at full tilt,*** a toda velocidad. — *v.t.* inclinar, ladear. — *v.i.* inclinarse, ladearse; justar; ***tilt at,*** arremeter contra.
tilter [ˈtiltə], *s.* justador.
tilth [tilθ], *s.* cultivo, labranza.
tilting [ˈtiltiŋ], *a.* inclinado, ladeado. — *s.* justas, *f.pl.*, torneos, *m.pl.*
Tim [tim]. *dim. de* [TIMOTHY].
timbal [ˈtimbəl], *s.* timbal.
timber [ˈtimbə], *s.* madera (de construcción); maderamen, maderaje; árboles de monte, *m.pl.*; (*mar.*) cuaderna; viga, madero; ***standing timber,*** árboles en pie, *m.pl.*; ***timber work,*** madera, maderamen; ***timber land,*** tierras maderables, *f.pl.*; ***timber merchant,*** maderero; ***timber yard,*** almacén de madera. — *v.t.* enmaderar.
timbered [ˈtimbəd], *a.* enmaderado; arbolado, cubierto de bosques.
timbering [ˈtimbəriŋ], *s.* maderamen; (*min.*) entibación.
timbre [ˈtimbə], *s.* timbre.
timbrel [ˈtimbrəl], *s.* pandero, pandereta.
time [taim], *s.* tiempo; hora; período; plazo; rato; momento; vez; horas (de trabajo), *f.pl.*, jornada;

época, tiempos, *m.pl.*; temporada, estación; (*mús.*) compás, *m.*, paso;

(*tiempo en general*) ***at this moment in time,*** en este momento de la historia; ***in the course of time,*** con el transcurso del tiempo; ***in time, as time passes,*** con el tiempo, andando el tiempo; ***race against time,*** carrera contra reloj; ***spare time,*** ratos libres, *m.pl.*; ***time-honoured,*** consagrado, clásico, sacramental, secular; ***time and tide,*** tiempo y sazón; ***time and tide wait for no man,*** tiempo ni hora no se ata con la soga; ***to be pressed for time,*** estar apurado de tiempo; ***time presses,*** el tiempo apremia; ***to gain time,*** ganar tiempo; ***to have plenty of time,*** tener tiempo de sobra; ***I have no time for that sort of thing,*** no tengo paciencia con esas cosas, no puedo con esas cosas, esas cosas me impacientan *o* me ponen nervioso; ***to have a good*** (***bad***) ***time,*** pasarlo bien (mal); ***to have a rough time,*** pasarlas canutas; ***to kill time,*** hacer tiempo, pasar el rato; ***he lost no time in doing it,*** no tardó en hacerlo; ***to make up for lost time,*** recuperar el tiempo perdido; (*fig.*) ***to mark time,*** estancarse; ***to play for time,*** tratar de *o* querer ganar tiempo; ***take your time!*** ¡hazlo con calma!; ***time will tell,*** el tiempo dirá;

(*período de tiempo*) ***a long time,*** mucho tiempo; ***a short time,*** poco tiempo, un rato; ***a long*** (***short***) ***time ago,*** hace mucho (tiempo), hace poco (tiempo); ***a short time after,*** poco después; ***all in good time,*** todo se andará, ya llegaremos a eso; ***I'll do it in my own good time,*** ya lo haré cuando me parezca bien; (*dep.*) ***extra time,*** prórroga; ***for a time,*** durante un (cierto) tiempo; ***for some time past,*** de algún tiempo a esta parte; ***for the time being,*** de momento, por el momento, por ahora; ***in a short time,*** en breve; ***in five days' time,*** de aquí a cinco días, dentro de cinco días; ***in no time at all,*** en nada de tiempo; ***it takes time to do it,*** lleva tiempo hacerlo; (*foto.*) ***time-exposure,*** exposición; (*fam.*) ***to do time,*** cumplir una condena; ***within the agreed time,*** dentro del plazo convenido;

(*hora*) ***closing*** (***opening***) ***time,*** hora de cerrar (abrir); ***standard time,*** hora normal; ***summer time,*** hora de verano; ***time!*** ¡es la hora!; ***time keeper,*** reloj cronómetro; cronometador, apuntador del tiempo; ***time lag,*** intervalo, lapso de tiempo; ***time-table,*** horario; programa, *m.*; ***time-signal,*** señal horaria; ***to arrive ahead of*** (***behind***) ***time,*** llegar adelantado (atrasado); ***to arrive on time,*** llegar a la hora; ***he arrived bang on time,*** llegó puntual como un clavo; ***what's the time?*** ¿qué hora es?; ***what time do you make it?*** ¿qué hora tienes?

(*momento*) ***and about time too!*** ¡ya era hora!; ***any time,*** en cualquier momento; ***any time now,*** de un momento a otro; ***to arrive*** (***just***) ***in time*** (***to***), llegar (justo) a tiempo (para); ***to arrive in good time,*** llegar con tiempo (de sobra); ***at a given time,*** en un momento dado; ***at one time,*** en un momento determinado; ***at no time,*** nunca, en ningún momento; ***at that time,*** (por *o* en aquel) entonces, a la sazón; ***at all times,*** en todo momento; ***at the same time,*** al mismo tiempo, al par, a la vez; ***at this particular time,*** en este preciso momento; ***at the time of the Suez crisis*** o ***Suez affair,*** cuando la crisis de Suez *o* cuando lo de Suez; ***by that time,*** para entonces; ***by the time he comes . . .,*** para cuando llegue . . .; ***from this*** (***that***) ***time on,*** de ahora (entonces) en adelante; ***it's high time that,*** ya es hora de que; ***now is the time to . . .,*** ha llegado la hora de . . ., ha llegado el momento de . . .; ***this is no time for*** (***playing***) ***games,*** no es éste momento de jugar *o* de juegos; ***when the time comes,*** cuando llegue la hora *o* el momento;

(*ocasión, vez*) ***at times,*** a veces; ***at various times,*** en diversas ocasiones; ***each time, every time,*** cada vez; todas las veces; ***for the first*** (***last***) ***time,*** por primera (última) vez; ***many times, many a time,*** muchas veces; ***several times,*** varias veces; ***time after time, time and again,*** una y otra vez; ***three times,*** tres veces; ***third time lucky,*** a la tercera va la vencida; ***this, last, next time,*** esta, la última, la próxima vez; ***three at a time,*** tres a la vez, de tres en tres;

(*época*) ***at one time,*** en tiempos; ***at the present time,*** en la actualidad; ***in my time,*** en mis tiempos; ***in our time,*** en nuestra época; ***in times to come,*** en (los) tiempos (años) venideros; ***I remember the time when . . .,*** me acuerdo de cuando . . .; ***the good old times,*** los buenos tiempos de antes; ***to be behind the times,*** haberse quedado en su tiempo *o* atrasado; ***to keep abreast of*** o ***up with the times,*** mantenerse al día *o* a la altura de los tiempos;

(*mús.*) ***to beat time,*** llevar el compás; ***to get out of time,*** perder el ritmo *o* el compás; ***to mark time,*** marcar el paso.

timeful [ˈtaimful], *a.* oportuno.

timeless [ˈtaimlis], *a.* eterno, intemporal.

timeliness [ˈtaimlinis], *s.* (lo) oportuno.

timely [ˈtaimli], *a.* oportuno.

time-serving [ˈtaim-sə:viŋ], *a.* contemporizador. — *s.* contemporización.

timeworn [ˈtaimwɔ:n], *a.* gastado por el tiempo; (*fig.*) llevado y traído, consabido.

timid [ˈtimid], *a.* tímido, corto.

timidity, timidness [tiˈmiditi, ˈtimidnis], *s.* timidez, cortedad.

timing [ˈtaimiŋ], *s.* medida del tiempo; regulación del tiempo; (*dep.*) cronometraje; ***right timing,*** selección del momento oportuno.

timocracy [tiˈmɔkrəsi], *s.* timocracia.

timorous [ˈtimərəs], *a.* tímido; timorato, medroso.

timorously [ˈtimərəsli], *adv.* tímidamente; medrosamente.

timorousness [ˈtimərəsnis], *s.* timidez; medrosidad, (lo) medroso.

Timothy [ˈtiməθi]. Timoteo.

timothy [ˈtiməθi], *s.* (*bot.*) fleo.

tin [tin], *a.* de estaño; de hojalata; (*fam.*) de pacotilla; ***tin can,*** lata; ***tin soldier,*** soldado de plomo. — *s.* estaño; lata; hojalata; (*fam.*) pasta, parné; ***tin-smith,*** hojalatero. — *v.t.* estañar; conservar en lata.

tincal [ˈtiŋkəl], *s.* atíncar.

tincture [ˈtiŋktʃə], *s.* (*farm.*) tintura; (*fig.*) barnicillo. — *v.t.* tinturar; teñir, colorear.

tinder [ˈtində], *s.* yesca; ***tinder-box,*** yescas, *f.pl.*

tine [tain], *s.* diente (*de tenedor*); púa (*de rastrillo etc.*).

tinea [ˈtiniə], *s.* (*med.*) tiña.

tinfoil [ˈtinfɔil], *s.* hoja de estaño.

ting [tiŋ], [TINKLE].

tinge [tindʒ], *s.* tinte; matiz. — *v.t.* teñir (***with,*** de); matizar (***with,*** de).

tingle [tiŋgl], *v.i.* doler (de frío); (*fig.*) ***tingle with excitement,*** estremecerse de emoción.

tingling [ˈtiŋgliŋ], *s.* dolor (de frío); estremecimiento.

tinker [ˈtiŋkə], *s.* calderero, remendón. — *v.i.* — ***with,*** andar en, hurgar en; ***tinker about,*** trajinar.

tinkle [tiŋkl], *s.* retintín; campanilleo. — *v.t.* hacer retiñir; hacer campanillear. — *v.i.* retiñir; campanillear.

tinkling [ˈtiŋkliŋ], *s.* retintín; campanilleo.

tinned [tind], *a.* en lata.

tinner [ˈtinə], *s.* estañero; minero de estaño.

tinny [ˈtini], *a.* de hojalatilla, que parece de lata, que suena a lata; (*fig.*) de pacotilla, de mala muerte.

tinsel [ˈtinsəl], *a.* de oropel; (*fig.*) de relumbrón, de oropel. — *s.* oropel; (*fig.*) relumbrón, oropel. — *v.t.* adornar con oropel.

tint [tint], *s.* tinte, matiz. — *v.t.* teñir, matizar.

tinware [ˈtinwɛə], *s.* objetos de hojalata, *m.pl.*

tiny [ˈtaini], *a.* diminuto, muy menudo, muy pequeñito.

tip (1) [tip], *s.* punta; cabo, extremo; contera, regatón; virola; casquillo; yema (*del dedo*); puntera (*del zapato*); boquilla, filtro (*de cigarrillo*); ***at the tip of one's fingers,*** al dedillo; ***from tip to toe,*** de pies a cabeza; ***I have it on the tip of my tongue,*** lo tengo en la punta de la lengua. — *v.t.* poner contera *etc.* a; guarnecer la punta de.
tip (2) [tip], *s.* golpecito. — *v.t.* golpear, tocar *o* chocar ligeramente.
tip (3) [tip], *s.* propina. — *v.t.* dar (una) propina a.
tip (4) [tip], *s.* (*fam.*) soplo; confidencia; consejo; pronóstico; ***tip-off,*** soplo, aviso confidencial; ***to be a hot tip,*** ser un ganador seguro; ***to give a tip,*** dar un consejo; dar el soplo *o* advertir (*a la policía*). — *v.t.* ***I tip him to win,*** pronostico que ganará él; ***tip off,*** avisar, soplar; ***tip the wink,*** avisar.
tip (5) [tip], *s.* vertedero, escombrera. — *v.t.* inclinar, ladear; voltear, verter, volcar; abatir, levantar (*un asiento*); ***tip away,*** verter, echar; ***tip one's hat,*** tocarse el sombrero; ***tip over,*** tirar, volcar; (*fig.*) ***tip the scales,*** inclinar la balanza, ser decisivo; ***tip up,*** inclinar, ladear; volcar; hacer caer. — *v.i.* inclinarse, ladearse; tambalearse; perder el equilibrio, caer; volcarse; abatirse, levantarse; bascular.
tippet [ˈtipit], *s.* palatina, esclavina.
tipple [tipl], *s.* bebida. — *v.i.* empinar el codo.
tippler [ˈtiplə], *s.* bebedor.
tippling [ˈtipliŋ], *s.* (el) beber.
tipsily [ˈtipsili], *adv.* como borracho.
tipstaff [ˈtipstɑːf], *s.* palo herrado; vara (de alguacil); alguacil, ministril.
tipsy [ˈtipsi], *a.* achispado, alegrete.
tiptoe [ˈtiptou], *s.* punta del pie; ***to walk on tiptoe,*** andar de puntillas. — *v.i.* andar de puntillas.
tiptop [ˈtipˈtɔp], *a.* (*fam.*) de órdago, espléndido, de primera, soberbio.
tip-up [ˈtip-ʌp], *a.* basculante; abatible.
tirade [taiˈreid], *s.* diatriba, invectiva.
tire (1) [taiə], *v.t.* cansar, fatigar; aburrir; ***tire out,*** extenuar. — *v.i.* cansarse, fatigarse; aburrirse; ***tire of,*** cansarse de, aburrirse con.
tire (2) [taiə], *s.* (*Am.*) [TYRE].
tired [ˈtaiəd], *a.* cansado, fatigado; aburrido; ***tired out,*** agotado, molido; ***to be tired of sth.,*** estar harto de algo.
tiredness [ˈtaiədnis], *s.* cansancio, fatiga.
tireless [ˈtaiəlis], *a.* incansable, infatigable.
tiresome [ˈtaiəsəm], *a.* molesto, fastidioso, pesado, aburrido.
tiresomeness [ˈtaiəsəmnis], *s.* molestia, fastidio, pesadez, aburrimiento.
tiring [ˈtaiəriŋ], *a.* cansado, que cansa.
'tis [tiz], *abrev. de* **it is,** es; está.
tissue [ˈtiʃ(j)uː, ˈtisjuː], *s.* (*biol.*) tejido; tisú, gasa; (*fig.*) sarta; enredijo; ***tissue paper,*** papel de seda; ***paper tissue,*** (*marca de fábrica*) kleenex.
tit (1) [tit], *s.* (*orn.*) paro.
tit (2) [tit], *s.* (*despec.*) teta; pezón.
tit (3) [tit], *s.* (*sólo en la frase*) ***tit for tat,*** donde las dan las toman.
titanic [taiˈtænik], *a.* titánico, gigantesco; ***titanic task,*** obra de romanos.
titanium [taiˈteiniəm], *s.* titanio.
tit-bit [ˈtit-bit], *s.* golosina; bocado apetitoso.
tithable [ˈtaiðəbl], *a.* diezmable, sujeto al diezmo.
tithe [taið], *s.* diezmo; décimo, décima parte; pizca. — *v.t.* diezmar. — *v.i.* pagar el diezmo.
tithe-collector, tither [ˈtaið-kəlektə, ˈtaiðə], *s.* diezmero.
tithing [ˈtaiðiŋ], *s.* diezmo.
titillate [ˈtitileit], *v.t.* estimular, excitar, encandilar.
titillation [titiˈleiʃən], *s.* (el) excitar.
titivate [ˈtitiveit], *v.t., v.i.* emperejilar(se), emperifollar(se).
titlark [ˈtitlɑːk], *s.* pipí de matorral.
title [taitl], *s.* título; ***title-page,*** frontispicio, portada; (*teat.*) ***title-rôle,*** papel principal; ***title to property,*** derecho *o* título de propiedad.
titled [taitld], *a.* de título, que tiene título.
titleless [ˈtaitllis], *a.* sin título.
titmouse [ˈtitmaus], *s.* (*pl.* **titmice** [ˈtitmais]) paro.
titrate [ˈtaitreit], *v.t.* (*quím.*) valorar.
titter [ˈtitə], *s.* risita, risilla. — *v.i.* reírse tonta y nerviosamente.
tittering [ˈtitəriŋ], *s.* risitas, *f.pl.*, risillas, *f.pl.*
tittle [titl], *s.* ápice; ***not one jot or tittle,*** ni un ápice.
tittle-tattle [ˈtitl-tætl], *s.* chismes, *m.pl.*, chismorreo. — *v.i.* chismorrear.
titular [ˈtitjulə], *a.* titular; nominal.
titulary [ˈtitjuləri], *a.* titular.
to [tu(ː)], *con inf.* ***I have things to do,*** tengo cosas que hacer; ***there are things still to be done,*** quedan *o* faltan (todavía) cosas por hacer; ***it makes me sad just to recall it,*** sólo con recordarlo me entristezco. — [tuː], *adv.* ***to and fro,*** de un lado para otro; ***to bring to,*** hacer volver en sí; ***to come to,*** volver en sí; (*mar.*) ***to lay to,*** ponerse al pairo. — [tu(ː)], *prep.* a; hacia; para; ***he's going to Seville,*** va a Sevilla; ***the road to Seville,*** la carretera de Sevilla; ***from house to house,*** de casa en casa; ***he was kind to me,*** fue bueno *o* amable conmigo; ***here's to you!*** ¡por usted!; ***secretary to,*** secretario de; ***to my mind,*** para mi punto de vista, según mi modo de ver.
toad [toud], *s.* sapo.
toad-eater [ˈtoud-iːtə], *s.* [TOADY].
toadflax [ˈtoudflæks], *s.* linaria.
toadstone [ˈtoudstoun], *s.* estelón, estelión.
toadstool [ˈtoudstuːl], *s.* hongo (venenoso).
toady [ˈtoudi], *s.* (*despec.*) pelotillero, lameculos, *m.inv.* — *v.i.* hacer la pelotilla (***to,*** a).
toast [toust], *s.* pan tostado; (rebanada de pan) tostada; brindis, *m.inv.*; ***piece of toast,*** tostada. — *v.t.* tostar; brindar por.
toaster [ˈtoustə], *s.* tostadora.
tobacco [təˈbækou], *a.* tabacalero, de tabaco. — *s.* tabaco; ***tobacco-pouch,*** petaca.
tobacconist [təˈbækənist], *s.* tabaquero, estanquero; ***tobacconist's (shop),*** tabaquería, estanco.
toboggan [təˈbɔgən], *s.* trineo. — *v.i.* deslizarse (sobre la nieve) en trineo.
toccata [təˈkɑːtə], *s.* (*mús.*) tocata.
tocsin [ˈtɔksin], *s.* campanada de alarma; campana de alarma.
today [tuˈdei], *adv.* hoy, hoy día, actualmente. — *s.* día de hoy, actualidad.
toddle [tɔdl], *s.* pasitos inseguros, *m.pl.*; (*fam.*) ***to go for a toddle,*** ir a dar un paseo. — *v.i.* hacer pinitos; (*fam.*) ***toddle off,*** irse, largarse.
toddler [ˈtɔdlə], *s.* niño que hace pinitos; niño, pequeño.
toddy [ˈtɔdi], *s.* ponche.
to-do [tu-ˈduː], *s.* lío, jaleo, cisco, tiberio.
toe [tou], *s.* dedo (del pie); punta (*del pie, de calzado, media etc.*); puntera (*de calzado, media etc.*); ***big toe,*** dedo gordo; ***from top to toe,*** de pies a cabeza; ***to be on one's toes,*** estar alerta; estar con los cinco sentidos puestos en el asunto; ***to tread on the toes of,*** pisar; (*fig.*) ofender, molestar. — *v.t.* — ***the line,*** conformarse, acatar (las) órdenes, bajar la cerviz.
toff [tɔf], *s.* (*fam.*) señor, señorón.
toffee [ˈtɔfi], *s.* tofe, caramelo de melaza; ***toffee-apple,*** manzana garrapiñada; ***toffee-nosed,*** pera, que tiene aire de suficiencia.
tog [tɔg], *s.* (*pl.*) (*fam.*) trapos, *m.pl.* — *v.t.* ataviar; ***to get togged up,*** ataviarse. — *v.r.* ***tog o.s. up,*** ataviarse.
toga [ˈtougə], *s.* toga.
together [tuˈgeðə], *adv.* junto, juntos, juntamente; a la vez, a un tiempo; seguido; ***to be together in,***

estar juntos en; ir a medias en; ***together with,*** junto con; ***to pull o.s. together,*** recobrarse; reaccionar; sobreponerse.

togetherness [tu'geðənis], *s.* unión, compañerismo, solidaridad.

toggle ['tɔgl], *s.* (*mar.*) cazonete de aparejo; (*mec.*) palanca acodada; ***toggle-joint,*** junta de codillo.

Togo ['tougou]. el Togo.

Togolese [tougo'li:z], *a., s.* togolés, *m.*, togolesa.

toil [tɔil], *s.* trabajo duro, fatiga, esfuerzo. — *v.i.* afanarse, fatigarse; ***toil along,*** avanzar penosamente; ***toil up the hill,*** subir trabajosamente la cuesta.

toilet ['tɔilit], *s.* tocado; lavabo, retrete, wáter; ***toilet facilities,*** servicios, *m.pl.*; ***toilet paper,*** papel higiénico; ***toilet requisites,*** avíos de tocador, *m.pl.*; ***toilet set,*** juego de tocador; ***toilet soap,*** jabón de tocador; ***toilet water,*** agua de tocador.

toilful, toilsome ['tɔilful, -səm], *a.* penoso, trabajoso, fatigoso.

toils [tɔilz], *s. pl.* red, lazo.

toilsomeness ['tɔilsəmnis], *s.* (lo) penoso *etc.*

toilworn ['tɔilwɔ:n], *a.* agotado, rendido.

token ['toukən], *s.* señal, indicio; prenda; ficha, disco; cupón, bono; ***as a token of,*** en señal de; ***token payment,*** pago nominal; ***token resistance,*** resistencia simbólica.

Tokyo, Tokio ['toukiou]. Tokio.

tolerable ['tɔlərəbl], *a.* tolerable, soportable; (*fig.*) regular, pasable.

tolerableness ['tɔlərəblnis], *s.* (lo) tolerable.

tolerably ['tɔlərəbli], *adv.* tolerablemente; mediana mente.

tolerance ['tɔlərəns], *s.* tolerancia.

tolerant ['tɔlərənt], *a.* tolerante.

tolerate ['tɔləreit], *v.t.* tolerar.

toleration [tɔlə'reiʃən], *s.* tolerancia (*esp. religiosa*).

toll (I) [toul], *s.* peaje, pontazgo, portazgo; balance, número de víctimas, bajas *etc.*; ***toll-bar, toll-gate,*** barrera de peaje; ***toll-call,*** conferencia interurbana; ***toll-gatherer,*** peajero; ***toll-house,*** oficina de portazgo; ***to take (a) heavy toll (of),*** hacer grandes estragos (entre).

toll (2) [toul], *s.* tañido de campanas. — *v.t.* tañer, doblar, tocar. — *v.i.* doblar (*las campanas*).

tolling ['touliŋ], *s.* tañido, (el) doblar.

tolu [to'lu:], *s.* (*farm.*) tolú; (*bot.*) árbol de tolú.

Tom [tɔm]. *abrev. de* [THOMAS]; Tomasín, Tomasito; ***every Tom, Dick and Harry,*** cada quisque, todo hijo de vecino; ***Tom Thumb,*** Pulgarcito; ***peeping Tom,*** mirón clandestino.

tomahawk ['tɔməhɔ:k], *s.* tomahawk, hacha de guerra de los pieles rojas.

tomato [tə'mɑ:tou], *s.* tomate; ***tomato plant,*** tomatera.

tomb [tu:m], *s.* tumba, sepulcro.

tombac ['tɔmbæk], *s.* tombac.

tomboy ['tɔmbɔi], *s.* chicote, *m.*

tombstone ['tu:mstoun], *s.* lápida sepulcral.

tom(-cat) ['tɔm(-kæt)], *s.* (gato) macho.

tom-cod ['tɔm-kɔd], *s.* microgado.

tome [toum], *s.* tomo, volumen; (*fam.*) librote.

tomentous [to'mentəs], *a.* (*bot.*) tomentoso.

tomfool [tɔm'fu:l], *s.* botarate.

tomfoolery [tɔm'fu:ləri], *s.* botaratadas, *f.pl.*

Tommy ['tɔmi]. *dim. de* [THOMAS]; Tomasito.

tommy ['tɔmi], *s.* (*fam.*) soldado inglés; ***tommy-gun,*** (pistola) ametralladora (*de la marca* Thompson); (*fam.*) ***tommy-rot,*** sandeces, *f.pl.*

tomorrow [tə'mɔrou], *adv.* mañana; ***day after tomorrow,*** pasado mañana. — *s.* mañana, *m.*

tomtit ['tɔmtit], *s.* paro.

tomtom ['tɔmtɔm], *s.* tantán.

ton [tʌn], *s.* tonelada; (*fam.*) ***tons of,*** la mar de, montones de.

tonal ['tounəl], *a.* (*mús.*) tonal.

tonality [to'næliti], *s.* tonalidad.

tone [toun], *s.* tono; tonalidad; ***to change one's tone,*** cambiar de tono; ***to lower one's tone,*** bajar el tono; ***to lower the tone,*** dar (un) tono ordinario a, quitar categoría a. — *v.t.* entonar; ***tone down,*** suavizar; bajar un poco; modificar; ***tone up,*** entonar, tonificar, vigorizar; subir un poco. — *v.i.* — ***in with,*** armonizar con, hacer juego con, ir bien con.

Tonga ['tɔŋə]. Tonga.

tongs [tɔŋz], *s.pl.* tenazas, *f.pl.*, tenacillas, *f.pl.*

tongue [tʌŋ], *s.* lengua; (*zapato, mec.*) lengüeta; ***to give tongue,*** (ponerse a) ladrar; ***to hold one's tongue,*** callarse; (***to speak***) ***with tongue in cheek,*** (hablar) con sorna; ***tongue-twister,*** trabalenguas, *m.inv.*

tongued [tʌŋd], *a.* que tiene lengua; ***soft-tongued*** o ***smooth-tongued,*** de palabra suave *o* melosa.

tongue-tied ['tʌŋ-taid], *a.* que tiene poca facilidad de palabra, que se hace un lío al hablar; tímido, corto.

tonic ['tɔnik], *a.* tónico. — *s.* (*med.*) tónico; (*mús.*) tónica; ***tonic*** (***water***), (agua) tónica.

tonicity [to'nisiti], *s.* tonicidad.

tonight [tu'nait], *adv., s.* esta noche.

tonnage ['tʌnidʒ], *s.* tonelaje.

tonsil ['tɔnsil], *s.* amígdala.

tonsillar ['tɔnsilə], *a.* tonsilar.

tonsillitis [tɔnsi'laitis], *s.* amigdalitis, *f.inv.*, anginas, *f.pl.*

tonsorial [tɔn'sɔ:riəl], *a.* barberil.

tonsure ['tɔnʃə], *s.* tonsura.

tontine ['tɔnti:n], *s.* tontina.

Tony ['touni]. *dim. de* [ANTHONY]; Antoñito, Toño.

too [tu:], *adv.* demasiado; muy; también, además; ***too much,*** demasiado; ***too many,*** demasiados; ***I did it too,*** también yo lo hice; ***and it's expensive too,*** y (además) es caro.

tool [tu:l], *s.* herramienta; utensilio; instrumento; (*pl.*) útiles, *m.pl.*, herramental; ***edge tools,*** instrumentos cortantes, *m.pl.*; ***tool bag,*** bolsa de herramientas; ***tool box*** o ***chest,*** caja, estuche de herramientas; ***tool kit,*** juego de herramientas; ***tool shed,*** cobertizo para herramientas. — *v.t.* labrar con herramienta; estampar en seco, filetear.

tooling ['tu:liŋ], *s.* estampación en seco, fileteado.

toot [tu:t], *s.* toquecito (de claxon, bocina, trompa). — *v.t.* sonar, tocar. — *v.i.* tocar la bocina, dar un bocinazo.

tooth [tu:θ], *s.* (*pl.* **teeth** [ti:θ]) diente, muela; (*mec.*) diente; (*peine*) púa; ***false teeth,*** dentadura postiza; ***in the teeth of,*** contra viento y marea de; ***set of teeth,*** dentadura; ***to cut one's teeth,*** echar los dientes; (*fig.*) ***to cut one's teeth on,*** estrenarse con; ***to gnash one's teeth,*** crujir los dientes; ***to have a sweet tooth,*** ser goloso; ***tooth and nail,*** como gato panza arriba, con todas sus fuerzas, hasta con los dientes; ***to pick one's teeth,*** hurgarse (en) los dientes con un palillo; (*fig.*) ***to show one's teeth,*** enseñar *o* mostrar los dientes. — *v.t.* dentar, endentar; (*mec.*) engranar.

toothache ['tu:θeik], *s.* dolor de muelas.

toothbrush ['tu:θbrʌʃ], *s.* cepillo de dientes.

toothed [tu:θt], *a.* dentado, de *o* con dientes, serrado; ***big-toothed,*** dentón.

toothless ['tu:θlis], *a.* desdentado.

toothpaste ['tu:θpeist], *s.* pasta dentífrica, pasta de dientes.

toothpick ['tu:θpik], *s.* palillo, mondadientes, *m.inv.*

toothsome ['tu:θsəm], *a.* sabroso, apetitoso.

toothwort ['tu:θwə:t], *s.* (*bot.*) dentaria.

toothy ['tu:θi], *a.* dentón, dentudo.

tootle [tu:tl], *s.* flauteado; serie de notas breves. — *v.i.* tocar (*la flauta etc.*).

too-too ['tu:-'tu:], *adv.* exageradamente.

top (I) [tɔp], *a.* (el) más alto; cimero, superior; (*piso*) último, alto; primero, máximo, sumo;

principal; de arriba; ***at top speed,*** a máxima velocidad; (*fam.*) ***top dog,*** mandamás, *m.inv.*, el que manda; (*fam.*) ***the top dogs,*** los de arriba; ***top hat,*** chistera, sombrero de copa; (*mar.*) ***top-mast,*** mastelero; (*fam.*) ***top-notch,*** de primera (categoría); (*fam.*) ***top-notcher,*** persona *o* cosa de primera (categoría); (*mar.*) ***top-sail,*** gavia; (*mar.*) ***top-timber,*** barraganete. — *adv.* ***to come top,*** ser ganador, clasificarse en primer lugar; ***top secret,*** de sumo secreto. — *s.* cima; copa (*de árbol*); cumbre, *f.*; cúspide, *f.*, ápice; remate; coronilla (*de cabeza*); (lo) más alto; superficie, *f.*; jefe; cabeza (*de página*); (*fig.*) auge, cima, cumbre, *f.*; (*de vehículo*) capota; ***at the top,*** en lo alto; (*fig.*) a la cabeza; ***from top to bottom,*** de arriba abajo; ***from top to toe,*** de pies a cabeza. — *v.t.* desmochar, descabezar; coronar, rematar; exceder, descollar por encima de; aventajar; alcanzar la cumbre de; encabezar (*lista, clasificación etc.*); (*fam.*) apiolar, cargarse a; ***top off,*** acabar, rematar; ***to top it all,*** para colmo de desdichas; ***top up,*** llenar del todo; acabar de llenar.

top (2) [tɔp], *s.* (*juguete*) peonza, trompo; ***to sleep like a top,*** dormir como un tronco; ***whipping top,*** peonza.

topaz [ˈtoupæz], *s.* topacio.

topcoat [ˈtɔpkout] (*Am.*) [OVERCOAT].

tope [toup], *v.i.* beber, emborracharse.

toper (1) [ˈtoupə], *s.* bebedor.

toper (2) [ˈtoupə], *s.* (*orn.*) paro.

topgallant [tɔpgælənt, təˈgælənt], *s.* (*mar.*) juanete.

tophus [ˈtoufəs], *s.* (*med.*) tofo; (*min.*) toba.

topic [ˈtɔpik], *s.* tema, asunto, materia.

topical [ˈtɔpikəl], *a.* de interés actual, de actualidad.

topicality [tɔpiˈkæliti], *s.* actualidad, interés actual.

topknot [ˈtɔpnɔt], *s.* moño, copete; (*fam.*) cholla.

topmost [ˈtɔpmoust], *a.* (el) más alto.

topographer [təˈpɔgrəfə], *s.* topógrafo.

topographical [tɔpoˈgræfikəl], *a.* topográfico.

topography [təˈpɔgrəfi], *s.* topografía.

toponym [ˈtɔpənim], *s.* topónimo.

toponymic [tɔpəˈnimik], *a.* toponímico.

toponymics, toponymy [tɔpəˈnimiks, təˈpɔnimi], *s.* toponimia.

topper [ˈtɔpə], *s.* (*fam.*) sombrero de copa.

topping [ˈtɔpiŋ], *a.* (*fam.*) estupendo, soberbio. — *s.* (*coc.*) lo que va encima, crema de adorno.

topple [tɔpl], *v.t.* derribar, hacer caer, hacer venirse abajo. — *v.i.* tambalearse; venirse abajo; ***topple down,*** venirse abajo, desplomarse; ***topple over,*** caerse, volcarse.

topsy-turvy [ˈtɔpsi-ˈtəːvi], *a.* desordenado, hecho un lío, hecho un barullo. — *adv.* patas arriba, en desorden.

toque [touk], *s.* toca.

tor [tɔː], *s.* tolmo, tormo.

torch [tɔːtʃ], *s.* antorcha, tea; linterna (*eléctrica*); (*fam.*) ***to carry a torch for,*** sentir un amor no correspondido por; ***torch-bearer,*** portahachón, hachero.

torchlight [ˈtɔːtʃlait], *s.* luz de antorcha; ***torchlight procession,*** desfile de portahachones.

torment [ˈtɔːment], *s.* tormento, suplicio. — [tɔːˈment], *v.t.* atormentar, torturar.

tormentor [tɔːˈmentə], *s.* atormentador.

tornado [tɔːˈneidou], *s.* tornado, huracán.

torpedo [tɔːˈpiːdou], *s.* torpedo; ***torpedo boat,*** torpedero. — *v.t.* torpedear.

torpid [ˈtɔːpid], *a.* aletargado, amodorrado, embotado; lentísimo.

torpidity, torpidness [tɔːˈpiditi, ˈtɔːpidnis], *s.* amodorramiento, embotamiento; lentitud.

torpor [ˈtɔːpə], *s.* letargo, modorra, sopor.

torque [tɔːk], *s.* par de torsión.

torrefaction [tɔriˈfækʃən], *s.* torrefacción.

torrent [ˈtɔrənt], *s.* torrente, raudal.

torrential [təˈrenʃəl], *a.* torrencial.

torrid [ˈtɔrid], *a.* tórrido.

torridity [təˈriditi], *s.* (lo) tórrido.

torsion [ˈtɔːʃən], *s.* torsión.

torso [ˈtɔːsou], *s.* torso.

tort [tɔːt], *s.* (*for.*) tuerto, agravio.

tortoise [ˈtɔːtəs], *s.* (*zool.*) tortuga (terrestre); ***tortoise-shell,*** carey.

tortuosity [tɔːtjuˈɔsiti], *s.* tortuosidad.

tortuous [ˈtɔːtjuəs], *a.* tortuoso.

torture [ˈtɔːtʃə], *s.* suplicio, tortura, tormento, martirio; ***torture-chamber,*** cámara de suplicio. — *v.t.* torturar, atormentar, dar tormento a, martirizar; ***torture the truth,*** tergiversar, violentar la verdad.

torturer [ˈtɔːtʃərə], *s.* atormentador, verdugo.

torus [ˈtɔːrəs] *s.* (*pl.* **tori** [rai]) (*arq.*) toro.

Tory [ˈtɔːri], *a., s.* (*pol.*) conservador.

tosh! [tɔʃ], *interj.* ¡memeces!, *f.pl.*

toss [tɔs], *s.* echada, tirada; caída; ***it's a toss up,*** cualquier cosa puede pasar; está en el aire. — *v.t.* sacudir, menear; zarandear; echar, tirar; lanzar al aire; ***toss in a blanket,*** mantear; ***toss aside,*** echar a un lado; ***toss off,*** beberse de un trago. — *v.i.* agitarse; cabecear, balancearse; mecerse; ***toss and turn,*** revolverse, dar vueltas (en la cama); ***toss (up),*** sortear, echar a cara o cruz.

tossing [ˈtɔsiŋ], *s.* sacudimiento; meneo; manteamiento; cornada.

tot (1) [tɔt], *s.* traguito, copita; nene, crío.

tot (2) [tɔt], *v.t., v.i.* (*solo en la frase*) ***tot up,*** echar la cuenta (de).

total [toutl], *a.* total; completo, absoluto. — *s.* total, suma. — *v.t.* sumar. — *v.i.* sumar, ascender a.

totalitarian [toutæliˈtɛəriən], *a.* totalitario.

totalitarianism [toutæliˈtɛəriənizəm], *s.* totalitarismo.

totality [touˈtæliti], *s.* totalidad.

totalizator [ˈtoutəlaizeitə], *s.* (*apuestas*) totalizador.

totalize [ˈtoutəlaiz], *v.t.* totalizar.

totally [ˈtoutəli], *adv.* totalmente.

tote (1) [tout], *abrev. de* [TOTALIZATOR].

tote (2) [tout], *v.t.* (*Am., fam.*) llevar (con esfuerzo).

totem [ˈtoutəm], *s.* tótem; ***totem pole,*** poste totémico.

totter [ˈtɔtə], *v.i.* bambolearse, tambalearse.

tottering [ˈtɔtəriŋ], *a.* vacilante; tambaleante.

totteringly [ˈtɔtəriŋli], *adv.* de un modo tambaleante.

toucan [ˈtuːkən], *s.* tucán.

touch [tʌtʃ], *s.* tacto; roce; (*fig.*) contacto; (*pint.*) pincelada; (*gesto*) rasgo; mano; pizca, poquito; (*fam.*) sablazo; ***to put the finishing touch to (sth.),*** dar el último toque *o* la última mano a; ***it has the touch of Picasso,*** se ve la mano de Picasso; ***to be in touch (with),*** estar en contacto (con); estar al tanto; (*dep.*) ***into touch,*** fuera de juego; ***to be out of touch (with),*** haber perdido el contacto (con); haberse quedado atrás *o* anticuado; ***to get in touch with,*** ponerse en contacto con; ***to keep in touch (with),*** mantener el contacto (con); mantenerse al corriente (de); ***a touch of humour,*** un dejo de humor; ***to have a touch of flu,*** tener un poco de gripe. — *v.t.* tocar; palpar, tentar; rozar; tomar, probar; conmover, enternecer; afectar; ***don't touch!*** ¡no tocar!; ***he is deeply touched,*** está profundamente conmovido *o* emocionado; ***I never touch wine,*** el vino, no lo pruebo; ***no one can touch him,*** nadie puede compararsele; ***this problem touches me personally,*** este problema me afecta a mí (personalmente); (*dep.*) ***touch down,*** poner (*el balón*) en tierra; ***touch off,*** desencadenar, provocar; (*fam.*) ***touch s.o. for money,*** dar un sablazo a alguien; ***touch up,*** retocar; ***touch wood!*** ¡toca madera! — *v.i.* tocarse; rozarse; lindar; ***touch down,*** aterrizar; amerizar; alunizar; posarse; ***touch (in) at,*** tocar en, hacer

escala en; ***touch on*** o ***upon,*** tocar, aludir brevemente a.
touchable [ˈtʌtʃəbl], *a.* tangible, palpable.
touch-and-go [ˈtʌtʃ-ənd-ˈgou], *a.* dudoso, precario; ***it's touch-and-go whether we get there on time*** (***or not***), estamos en vilo por si no llegamos a la hora.
touchdown [ˈtʌtʃdaun], *s.* aterrizaje; amerizaje.
touched [ˈtʌtʃt], *a.* (*fam.*) tocado, chiflado, sonado.
touchiness [ˈtʌtʃinis], *s.* susceptibilidad; irascibilidad.
touching [ˈtʌtʃiŋ], *a.* conmovedor, emocionante, patético. — *prep.* tocante a, en cuanto a.
touchingly [ˈtʌtʃiŋli], *adv.* tiernamente, de modo conmovedor.
touchline [ˈtʌtʃlain], *s.* (*dep.*) línea de banda, de toque, lateral.
touchstone [ˈtʌtʃstoun], *s.* piedra de toque.
touch-typing [ˈtʌtʃ-ˈtaipiŋ], *s.* mecanografía al tacto.
touchwood [ˈtʌtʃwud], *s.* yesca.
touchy [ˈtʌtʃi], *a.* susceptible, quisquilloso.
tough [tʌf], *a.* (*comida etc.*) correoso, estropajoso; duro; fuerte; (*en el uso*) resistente; (*Am.*) ***tough guy,*** duro; ***tough luck,*** mala suerte, mala pata; ***tough trip,*** viaje duro. — *s.* (*fam.*) matón.
toughen [ˈtʌfən], *v.t.* endurecer, hacer duro. — *v.i.* endurecer(se).
toughish [ˈtʌfiʃ], *a.* algo duro, durillo.
toughness [ˈtʌfnis], *s.* (lo) correoso; dureza; (lo) fuerte *etc.*
Toulon [tu:ˈlɔ̃]. Tolón.
Toulouse [tu:ˈlu:z]. Tolosa (de Francia).
tour [tuə], *s.* viaje; jira; excursión; (*dep.*) vuelta; ***circular tour,*** viaje redondo; (***guided***) ***tour,*** visita (con guía); ***on tour,*** de viaje; (*teat. etc.*) de jira; ***to make a tour of,*** hacer un viaje por, recorrer. — *v.t.* hacer un viaje por, recorrer. — *v.i.* viajar en plan de turismo, hacer turismo; ***to go touring,*** hacer (un viaje de) turismo.
Touraine [tu:ˈrein]. (la) Turena.
touring [ˈtuəriŋ], *a.* turístico, de turismo. — *s.* turismo.
tourist [ˈtuərist], *a.* turístico; ***tourist class,*** clase turística. — *s.* turista, *m.f.*
tourmaline [ˈtuəməli:n], *s.* turmalina.
tournament [ˈtuənəmənt], *s.* torneo; concurso.
tourney [ˈtuəni], *s.* torneo. — *v.i.* tornear.
tourniquet [ˈtuənikei], *s.* (*cir.*) torniquete.
Tours [ˈtuə]. Turs.
tousle, towsle [tauzl], *v.t.* desmelenar, despeinar, enmarañar.
tout [taut], *s.* gancho; revendedor (*de entradas etc.*); pronosticador (*de carreras*). — *v.i.* — (***for***), solicitar.
tow (1) [tou], *s.* remolque; ***on*** o ***in tow,*** a remolque; ***to take in tow,*** coger *o* tomar *o* llevar a remolque; ***tow-line, tow-rope,*** cable de remolque; (*mar.*) cable de sirga. — *v.t.* remolcar, llevar a remolque.
tow (2) [tou], *s.* estopa.
towage [ˈtouidʒ], *s.* remolque.
towboat [ˈtoubout], *s.* remolcador.
toward(s) [tuˈwɔ:d(z)], *prep.* hacia, con dirección a; ***attitude towards sth.*** o ***s.o.,*** postura ante algo *o* alguien.
towel [ˈtauəl], *s.* toalla; ***towel-rail,*** toallero. — *v.t.* — (***down***), secar con toalla.
tower [ˈtauə], *s.* torre, *f.*; campanario (*de iglesia*); ***Tower of London,*** torre de Londres. — *v.i.* elevarse, encumbrarse, alzarse; ***tower above*** o ***over,*** dominar por completo; (*fig.*) no admitir la menor comparación con, descollar de forma absoluta entre.
towered [ˈtauəd], *a.* torreado, flanqueado *o* guarnecido de torres.
towering [ˈtauəriŋ], *a.* altísimo, elevadísimo; escarpadísimo; (*furia*) incontenible, violentísimo.
towing [ˈtouiŋ], *s.* remolque.
town [taun], *s.* ciudad; población; pueblo; municipio; ***new town,*** poblado de absorción; (*fig.*) ***to go to town*** (***on***), emplearse a fondo (en); echar el resto (con); (*fig., fam.*) ***to paint the town red,*** ir de jarana, ir de picos pardos; ***town clerk,*** secretario del ayuntamiento; ***town council,*** ayuntamiento, concejo municipal; ***town councillor,*** concejal; ***town hall,*** ayuntamiento, casa consistorial; ***town planning,*** urbanismo.
township [ˈtaunʃip] *s.* municipio.
townsman [ˈtaunzmən], *s.* ciudadano.
towsle [TOUSLE].
toxic [ˈtɔksik], *a.* tóxico.
toxicology [tɔksiˈkɔlədʒi], *s.* toxicología.
toxin [ˈtɔksin], *s.* toxina.
toy [tɔi], *s.* juguete; ***toy car, train*** *etc.*, coche, tren *etc.* de juguete; ***toy maker,*** juguetero, fabricante de juguetes; ***toy soldier,*** soldadito (de plomo *etc.*). — *v.i.* — ***with,*** jugar con; divertirse con; ***toy with an idea,*** acariciar una idea, darle vueltas a una idea.
toyshop [ˈtɔiʃɔp], *s.* juguetería, tienda de juguetes.
trace (1) [treis], *s.* huella, traza, rastro, indicio, vestigio; pizca; dejo; ***without a trace of,*** sin rastro *o* asomo de. — *v.t.* trazar; calcar; rastrear, seguir la huella de; delinear; encontrar, averiguar; ***trace back,*** (hacer) remontar a.
trace (2) [treis], *s.* tirante; correa, ronzal; ***to kick over the traces,*** sacar los pies del plato; darle la patada a todo.
traceable [ˈtreisəbl], *a.* que es posible trazar, rastrear, encontrar, *o* averiguar.
tracer [ˈtreisə], *s.* trazador; calcador; tiralíneas, *m.inv.*; persona encargada de buscar; ***tracer bullet,*** bala trazante; (*fís.*) ***tracer element,*** elemento trazador.
tracery [ˈtreisəri], *s.* (*arq.*) tracería.
trachea [trəˈki:ə], *s.* (*pl.* **tracheas, tracheae** [-z, trəˈki:i:]) tráquea.
tracheal [trəˈki:əl], *a.* traqueal.
tracheotomy [trækiˈɔtəmi], *s.* traqueotomía.
trachoma [trəˈkoumə], *s.* tracoma.
trachyte [ˈtrækait], *s.* (*min.*) traquita.
tracing [ˈtreisiŋ], *s.* calco; descubrimiento; rastreo; ***tracing paper,*** papel de calco.
track [træk], *s.* huella, rastro; senda, camino; (*dep.*) pista; (*de rueda*) rodada; marcha, trayectoria; (*f.c.*) vía; (*Am., f.c.*) [PLATFORM]; ***forest track,*** camino forestal; ***mule track,*** camino de herradura; ***off the track,*** descarrilado; (*fig.*) extraviado; ***side track,*** vía muerta; ***single, double track,*** vía única, doble; ***to be on s.o.'s track,*** estar sobre la pista de alguien; ***to be on the right*** (***wrong***) ***track,*** ir por buen (mal) camino; ***to follow in s.o.'s track,*** seguir en pos de alguien; ***to get off the beaten track,*** apartarse del camino trillado; ***to have a one-track mind,*** tener monobsesión; ***to keep track of,*** seguir la pista de; mantenerse al corriente de; ***to lose track of s.o.,*** perderle la pista a alguien; ***to throw s.o. off the track,*** despistar a alguien, poner a alguien sobre una pista falsa; (*f.c.*) ***track maintenance,*** conservación de la vía (férrea); (*Am.*) ***track racing,*** carreras (*f.pl.*) *o* ciclismo en pista; (*Am.*) ***track sports,*** deportes de pista, *m.pl.* — *v.t.* rastrear; seguir la pista de; seguir la trayectoria de; (*mar.*) sirgar; ***track down,*** seguir hasta dar con; averiguar el paradero de.
trackage [ˈtrækidʒ], *s.* remolque, sirgadura; (*Am.*) sistema de vías, *m.*
tracker [ˈtrækə], *s.* (*mar.*) sirguero; seguidor, rastreador; ***tracker dog,*** perro rastreador.
tracking [ˈtrækiŋ], *s.* rastreo; ***tracking station,*** estación *o* centro de rastreo.
trackless [ˈtræklis], *a.* sin rastro *o* huellas; sin caminos, impenetrable.
trackway [ˈtrækwei], *s.* vía (de ferrocarril).

tract (1) [trækt], *s.* extensión, trecho; ***digestive tract,*** canal digestivo; ***respiratory tract,*** vías respiratorias, *f.pl.*
tract (2) [trækt], *s.* folleto; (*relig.*) tracto.
tractability [træktə'biliti], *s.* docilidad.
tractable ['træktəbl], *a.* dócil, manejable.
tractate ['trækteit], *s.* tratado.
tractility [træk'tiliti], *s.* ductilidad.
traction ['trækʃən], *s.* tracción; ***traction-engine,*** locomóvil, máquina de tracción; ***traction-wheel,*** rueda de tracción.
tractive ['træktiv], *a.* (*mec.*) de tracción, tractor, tractivo.
tractor ['træktə], *s.* tractor; ***tractor-drawn,*** arrastrado por tractor; ***tractor-driver,*** tractorista, *m.f.*
trade [treid], *s.* comercio; negocio; tráfico; profesión, oficio; (*fam.*) ***the trade,*** el ramo, los del ramo; ***a carpenter by trade,*** de oficio carpintero; ***Department of Trade (and Industry),*** Ministerio de Comercio; ***foreign trade,*** comercio exterior; ***free trade,*** libre cambio; ***trade discount,*** descuento comercial; ***trade mark,*** marca de fábrica, marca (registrada); ***trade name,*** razón social; nombre de fábrica; ***trade price,*** precio para el comerciante; ***trade school,*** escuela de artes y oficios; ***trade winds,*** vientos alisios, *m.pl.* — *v.t.* comerciar; vender; cambiar; ***trade in,*** dar como parte del pago; ***trade off,*** deshacerse (*de algo*). — *v.i.* comerciar, traficar, negociar; ***trade in,*** tratar en; ***trade on,*** aprovecharse de, explotar.
trader ['treidə], *s.* comerciante; traficante; (buque) carguero; ***Free Trader,*** librecambista, *m.f.*
tradesman ['treidzmən], *s.* comerciante, tendero; artesano; ***tradesmen's entrance,*** puerta de servicio.
trade(s)-union ['treid(z)-'ju:niən], *a.* sindical, sindicalista. — *s.* sindicato.
trade(s)-unionism ['treid(z)-'ju:niənizəm], *s.* sindicalismo.
trade(s)-unionist ['treid(z)-'ju:niənist], *s.* sindicalista, *m.f.*
trading ['treidiŋ], *a.* comercial, mercantil. — *s.* compraventa; comercio; ***trading post,*** factoría; ***trading stamp,*** cupón (comercial).
tradition [trə'diʃən], *s.* tradición.
traditional [trə'diʃənəl], *a.* tradicional.
traditionalism [trə'diʃənəlizəm], *s.* tradicionalismo.
traditionary [trə'diʃənəri], *a.* tradicional.
traduce [trə'dju:s], *v.t.* calumniar; vituperar.
traducer [trə'dju:sə], *s.* calumniador; vituperador.
traffic ['træfik], *s.* tráfico; (*aut.*) tráfico (rodado), circulación; (*Am.*) ***traffic circle*** [ROUNDABOUT]; ***traffic jam,*** atasco, embotellamiento; ***traffic lights,*** señales luminosas, *f.pl.*, semáforo, disco; ***white slave traffic,*** trata (*de blancas*). — *v.i.* traficar, comerciar (***in,*** en).
trafficator ['træfikeitə], *s.* (*aut.*) indicador de luz intermitente, intermitente, *f.*
trafficker ['træfikə], *s.* traficante.
tragacanth ['trægəkænθ], *s.* tragacanto.
tragedian [trə'dʒi:diən], *s.* trágico.
tragedienne [trədʒi:di'en], *s.* trágica.
tragedy ['trædʒidi], *s.* tragedia.
tragic ['trædzik], *a.* trágico.
tragically ['trædʒikəli], *adv.* trágicamente.
tragi-comedy [trædʒi-'kɔmədi], *s.* tragicomedia.
tragi-comic(al) [trædʒi-'kɔmik(əl)], *a.* tragicómico.
trail [treil], *s.* pista, rastro, huella; camino, senda, sendero; estela; cola (*de vestido*); ***Wyoming trail,*** ruta de Wyoming. — *v.t.* seguir la pista de (*alguien*); rastrear (*algo*); arrastrar; seguir (*un coche*); bajar (*las armas*). — *v.i.* arrastrarse; ***trail behind,*** rezagarse, ir a la zaga; ***trail away*** o ***off,*** ir desapareciendo, ir desvaneciéndose, ir debilitándose.
trailer ['treilə], *s.* (*aut.*) remolque; (*Am.*) [CARAVAN]; (*cine.*) avance, tráiler; (*bot.*) tallo rastrero.
trailing ['treiliŋ], *a.* que va rezagado.
train [trein], *s.* tren; séquito; recua (*de mulas*); cola (*de vestido*); reguero (*de pólvora*); hilo (*del pensamiento*); ***by train,*** en tren, por ferrocarril; ***down train,*** tren descendente; ***express train,*** tren expreso, exprés, *m.*; ***fast train,*** (tren) rápido; ***goods train,*** tren de mercancías; ***in train,*** en (vías de) preparación; ***slow train,*** tren correo, tren ómnibus; ***through train,*** tren directo; ***train-bearer,*** caudatorio; ***up train,*** tren ascendente. — *v.t.* formar, preparar; adiestrar; enseñar; educar; (*dep.*) entrenar; apuntar (*un arma*); guiar (*una planta*). — *v.i.* formarse; adiestrarse; entrenarse.
trained [treind], *a.* formado; diplomado; preparado; capacitado; adiestrado; amaestrado; enseñado, educado; disciplinado.
trainee [trei'ni:], *s.* aprendiz.
trainer ['treinə], *s.* instructor; entrenador; preparador (físico); domador.
training ['treiniŋ], *s.* formación; preparación; instrucción; (*de animales etc.*) adiestramiento; ejercicios, *m.pl.*; (*dep.*) entrenamiento; capacitación; ***training camp,*** campo de instrucción; ***training centre,*** centro de formación laboral; ***training college,*** escuela normal; ***training-ship,*** buque-escuela; (*dep.*) ***to be out of training,*** estar desentrenado.
train-oil ['trein-ɔil], *s.* aceite de ballena.
traipse [TRAPES].
trait [trei(t)], *s.* rasgo, característica.
traitor ['treitə], *s.* traidor.
traitorous ['treitərəs], *a.* traidor; traicionero.
traitorousness ['treitərəsnis], *s.* traición, perfidia.
traitress ['treitris], *s.* traidora.
Trajan ['treidʒən]. Trajano.
traject ['trædʒekt], *s.* trayecto; travesía. — [trə'dʒekt], *v.t.* (hacer) pasar a través de.
trajectory [trə'dʒektəri], *s.* trayectoria.
tram [træm], *s.* tranvía, *m.*
tram-car ['træm-kɑ:], *s.* tranvía, *m.*
tramline ['træmlain], *s.* vía, carril de tranvía.
trammel ['træməl], *s.* (*pl.*) trabas, *f.pl.*, impedimentos, *m.pl.* — *v.t.* trabar, impedir, estorbar.
tramontane [træ'mɔntein], *a.* tramontano. — *s.* extranjero.
tramp [træmp], *s.* vagabundo; (*despec.*) puta; fulana; caminata; ruido (de pasos pesados); ***tramp (steamer),*** (vapor) volandero. — *v.t.* patear(se); pisar con fuerza. — *v.i.* marchar pesadamente; ir a pie; pisar fuerte; ***tramp on,*** pisotear, hollar.
trample [træmpl], *s.* pisoteo. — *v.t.* pisar, pisotear, hollar; ***trample underfoot,*** pisotear, hollar. — *v.i.* pisar fuerte; ***trample on,*** pisotear; (*fig.*) tratar sin miramientos.
trance [trɑ:ns], *s.* trance, rapto, éxtasis, *m.inv.*, arrobamiento; (*med.*) catalepsia; ***to go into a trance,*** caer en trance.
tranquil ['træŋkwil], *a.* tranquilo, apacible, sosegado.
tranquillity [træŋ'kwiliti], *s.* tranquilidad, calma, sosiego.
tranquillize ['træŋkwilaiz], *v.t.* tranquilizar, sosegar, aquietar.
tranquillizer ['træŋkwilaizə], *s.* (*med.*) tranquilizante.
transact [træn'zækt], *v.t.* despachar, tramitar, gestionar.
transaction [træn'zækʃən], *s.* negocio, transacción, operación (comercial); tramitación; (*pl.*) actas, *f.pl.*, memorias, *f.pl.*
transactor [træn'zæktə], *s.* negociador, gestor.
transalpine [trænz'ælpain], *a.* transalpino.
transatlantic [trænzət'læntik], *a.* tra(n)satlántico. — *s.* americano; ***transatlantic (steamer),*** tra(n)satlántico.

transcend [træn'send], *v.t.* sobrepujar, exceder de, rebasar.
transcendence, transcendency [træn'sendəns, -i], *s.* trascendencia.
transcendent [træn'sendənt], *a.* trascendente, trascendental.
transcendental [trænsen'dentəl], *a.* (*filos.*) trascendental.
transcendentalism [trænsen'dentəlizəm], *s.* transcendentalismo.
transcribe [træn'skraib], *v.t.* transcribir; (*mús.*) transcribir.
transcriber [træn'skraibə], *s.* copista, *m.f.*
transcript, transcription ['trænskript, træn'skripʃən], *s.* transcripción; (*mús.*) transcripción.
transept ['trænsept], *s.* (*arq.*) crucero.
transfer ['trænsfə:], *s.* traslado; (*dinero*) transferencia; (*f.c. etc.*) transbordo; (*dep.*) traspaso; (*cromo*) calcomanía. — [træns'fə:], *v.t.* trasladar; (*dinero*) transferir; (*f.c. etc.*) transbordar; (*dep.*) traspasar. — *v.i.* trasladarse; (*f.c. etc.*) transbordar.
transferable ['træns'fə:rəbl], *a.* transferible.
transference ['trænsfərəns], *s.* transferencia.
transferor [træns'fə:rə], *s.* cesionista, *m.f.*
transfiguration [trænsfigju'reiʃən], *s.* transfiguración.
transfigure [træns'figə], *v.t.* transfigurar.
transfix [træns'fiks], *v.t.* traspasar; dejar atónito *o* estupefacto; dejar transido (*de dolor*).
transfixion [træns'fikʃən], *s.* transfixión.
transform [træns'fɔ:m], *v.t.* transformar.
transformable [træns'fɔ:məbl], *a.* transformable.
transformation [trænsfɔ:'meiʃən], *s.* transformación.
transformative [træns'fɔ:mətiv], *a.* transformativo.
transformer [træns'fɔ:mə], *s.* transformador; (*elec.*) transformador.
transfuse [træns'fju:z], *v.t.* transfundir.
transfusion [træns'fju:ʒən], *s.* transfusión; ***to give a transfusion to,*** hacer una transfusión a.
transgress [trænz'gres], *v.t.* transgredir, traspasar, contravenir, infringir, violar. — *v.i.* cometer (una) transgresión; pecar.
transgression [trænz'greʃən], *s.* transgresión; pecado.
transgressor [trænz'gresə], *s.* transgresor; pecador.
tranship [træn'ʃip], *v.t.* (*mar.*) transbordar.
transhipment [træn'ʃipmənt], *s.* transbordo.
transience, transientness ['trænziəns, 'trænziəntnis], *s.* (lo) transitorio, (lo) pasajero.
transient ['trænziənt], *a.* transitorio, pasajero, efímero.
transistor [træn'zistə], *s.* transistor; ***transistor (radio),*** radio de transistores, transistor.
transit ['trænsit], *s.* tránsito; ***in transit,*** de *o* en tránsito.
transition [træn'ziʃən], *s.* tránsito, paso, transición.
transitional, transitionary [træn'ziʃənəl, -əri], *a.* de transición.
transitive ['trænzitiv], *a.* (*gram.*) transitivo.
transitoriness ['trænzitərinis], *s.* (lo) transitorio, (lo) pasajero.
transitory ['trænzitəri], *a.* transitorio, pasajero.
translatable [trænz'leitəbl], *a.* traducible.
translate [trænz'leit], *v.t.* traducir, verter; trasladar.
translation [trænz'leiʃən], *s.* traducción, versión; traslado.
translator [trænz'leitə], *s.* traductor.
transliterate [trænz'litəreit], *v.t.* transcribir.
translocation [trænzlo'keiʃən], *s.* cambio de sitio.
translucence, translucency [trænz'l(j)u:səns, -i], *s.* translucidez.
translucent, translucid [trænz'l(j)u:sənt, -sid], *a.* translúcido.
transmigrant [trænz'maigrənt], *a., s.* transmigrante.
transmigrate ['trænzmai'greit], *v.i.* transmigrar.
transmigration [trænzmai'greiʃən], *s.* transmigración.
transmigratory [trænz'maigrətri], *a.* transmigratorio.
transmissible [trænz'misibl], *a.* transmisible.
transmission [trænz'miʃən], *s.* transmisión; (*Am.*) [GEAR-BOX].
transmissive [trænz'misiv], *a.* transmitido, transmisor.
transmit [trænz'mit], *v.t.* transmitir.
transmittal [trænz'mitl], *s.* transmisión.
transmitter [trænz'mitə], *s.* transmisor.
transmitting station [trænz'mitiŋ 'steiʃən], *s.* estación transmisora, emisora.
transmogrification [trænzmɔgrifi'keiʃən], *s.* metamorfosis, *f.inv.*
transmogrify [trænz'mɔgrifai], *v.t.* transformar; metamorfosear; cambiar (*como por ensalmo*).
transmutability [trænzmju:tə'biliti], *s.* transmutabilidad.
transmutable [trænz'mju:təbl], *a.* transmutable.
transmutation [trænzmju:'teiʃən], *s.* transmutación.
transmute [trænz'mju:t], *v.t.* transmutar, metamorfosear.
transom ['trænsəm], *s.* (*arq.*) travesaño, montante; (*artill.*) telera.
transparency [træns'pærənsi], *s.* transparencia; (*foto. etc.*) diapositiva.
transparent [træns'pærənt], *a.* trasparente, diáfano; (*fig.*) clarísimo.
transpierce [træns'piəs], *v.t.* traspasar, penetrar.
transpiration [trænspi'reiʃən], *s.* transpiración.
transpire [træns'paiə], *v.i.* (*fig.*) revelarse; (*fam.*) resultar (***that,*** que).
transplant ['trænsplɑ:nt], *s.* trasplante. — [træns'plɑ:nt], *v.t.* trasplantar.
transplantable [træns'plɑ:ntəbl], *a.* trasplantable.
transplantation, transplanting [trænsplɑ:n'teiʃən, -'plɑ:ntiŋ], *s.* trasplantación; trasplante.
transplanter [træns'plɑ:ntə], *s.* trasplantador.
transport ['trænspɔ:t], *s.* transporte; ***Ministry of Transport,*** Ministerio de Transportes. — [træns'pɔ:t], *v.t.* transportar; deportar.
transportable [træns'pɔ:təbl], *a.* transportable.
transportation [trænspɔ:'teiʃən], *s.* transportación; transporte; acarreo; deportación.
transporter [træns'pɔ:tə], *s.* transportador.
transposal, transposing [træns'pouzəl, -iŋ], *s.* transposición.
transpose [træns'pouz], *v.t.* transponer; (*mús.*) transportar.
transposer [træns'pouzə], *s.* (*mús.*) transpositor.
transposition [trænspo'ziʃən], *s.* transposición; (*mús.*) transporte.
transubstantiate [trænsəb'stænʃieit], *v.t.* transubstanciar.
transubstantiation [trænsəbstænʃi'eiʃən], *s.* transubstanciación.
Transvaal ['trɑ:nz'vɑ:l], **the.** Transval.
Transvaaler ['trɑ:nz'vɑ:lə], *s.* (*pers.*) habitante del Transval.
transversal [trænz'və:səl], *a.* transversal. — *s.* (línea) transversal, *f.*
transverse ['trænzvə:s], *a.* transversal. — *s.* (lo) transverso.
trap [træp], *s.* trampa; cepo; lazo; tartana, coche de dos ruedas; (*mec.*) sifón; (*fam.*) boca; (*pl.*) (*fam.*) bártulos, *m.pl.*; ***mouse-trap,*** ratonera; ***to get caught in the trap, to fall into the trap,*** caer en la trampa *o* en el lazo; (*fam.*) ***shut your trap!*** ¡cállate la boca! — *v.t.* entrampar; atrapar; coger con (la *o* una) trampa, coger con lazo; ***trap out,*** enjaezar; (*fam.*) adornar, emperejilar.
trapdoor ['træp'dɔ:], *s.* trampa; (*teat.*) escotillón.

trapes [treips], *v.i.* andar (con fatiga) de un lado para otro; ***they trapesed all over the town,*** se patearon la ciudad entera.
trapeze [trəˈpi:z], *s.* trapecio; ***trapeze artist,*** trapecista, *m.f.*
trapezium [trəˈpi:ziəm], *s.* (*pl.* **trapezia, trapeziums** [-ziə, -ziəmz]) (*geom.*) trapecio.
trapezoid [trəˈpi:zɔid], *s.* trapezoide.
trapper [ˈtræpə], *s.* cazador (con trampas).
trappings [ˈtræpiŋz], *s.pl.* jaeces (*de caballo*), *m.pl.*; (*cost.*) arreos, *m.pl.*, adornos, *m.pl.*, atavíos, *m.pl.*
trash [træʃ], *s.* basura, desperdicios, *m.pl.*; (*fig.*) cosa(s) de pacotilla, birria(s), porquería(s); (*pers.*) gentucilla; (*fam.*, *despec.*) ***white trash,*** gentuza blanca.
trashy [ˈtræʃi], *a.* de pacotilla, malejo.
trauma [ˈtrɔ:mə], *s.* (*cir.*) trauma, *m.*; traumatismo.
traumatic [trɔ:ˈmætik], *a.* traumático.
traumatism [ˈtrɔ:mətizəm], *s.* traumatismo.
travail [ˈtræveil], *s.* parto, dolores del parto, *m.pl.*; (*fig.*) fatiga, labor penosa. — *v.i.* estar de parto, tener dolores de parto; afanarse, trabajar penosamente.
travel [ˈtrævəl], *s.* viaje(s); (el) viajar; (*mec.*) recorrido; ***travel sickness,*** mareo; ***travel-soiled*** o ***-stained,*** sucio *o* manchado del viaje *o* de viajar; ***travel-worn,*** rendido de viajar. — *v.t.* viajar por, recorrer. — *v.i.* viajar; ***this wine doesn't travel well,*** este vino viaja mal; (*fam.*) ***he's certainly travelling!*** ¡cómo va el tío!; ¡qué bestia!; ¡qué velocidad lleva!
travelled [ˈtrævəld], *a.* que ha viajado, que ha visto mundo.
traveller [ˈtrævələ], *s.* viajero; pasajero, ***commercial traveller,*** viajante; ***fellow traveller,*** compañero de viaje; ***traveller's cheque,*** cheque de viajero; (*bot.*) ***traveller's joy,*** clemátide, *f.*; ***traveller's tales,*** cuentos de viajero, *m.pl.*
travelling [ˈtrævəliŋ], *a.* ambulante; ***travelling crane,*** grúa puente *o* móvil. — *s.* (el) viajar, viajes, *m.pl.*; ***travelling bag,*** bolsa de viaje; ***travelling clock,*** reloj de viaje; ***travelling expenses,*** gastos de viaje, *m.pl.*
travelogue [ˈtrævəlɔg], *s.* documental de viaje(s).
traversable [trəˈvə:səbl], *a.* atravesable; (*for.*) negable, contestable.
traverse [ˈtrævə:s, trəˈvə:s], *a.* transversal, oblicuo; ***traverse course,*** rumbo compuesto. — *s.* travesaño; (*fort.*) través, *m.*; (*geom.*) línea transversal; (*mar.*) bordada en dirección oblicua. — *v.t.* atravesar, cruzar; recorrer, pasar por; (*for.*) oponerse a. — *v.i.* (*alpinismo*) subir oblicuamente.
travestied [ˈtrævəstid], *a.* parodiado.
travesty [ˈtrævəsti], *s.* parodia. — *v.t.* parodiar; disfrazar.
trawl [trɔ:l], *s.* red barredera, jábega; ***trawl line,*** palangre. — *v.t.* rastrear, pescar con jábega *o* palangre. — *v.i.* hacer la pesca con jábega.
trawler [ˈtrɔ:lə], *s.* barco para la pesca con jábega, palangrero, jabeguero.
trawling [ˈtrɔ:liŋ], *s.* pesca con jábega *o* al rastreo.
tray [trei], *s.* bandeja; batea; cubeta; platillo.
treacherous [ˈtretʃərəs], *a.* traidor, traicionero; falso, engañoso; movedizo.
treachery [ˈtretʃəri], *s.* traición, perfidia.
treacle [tri:kl], *s.* melaza.
treacly [ˈtri:kli], *a.* almibarado, meloso.
tread [tred], *s.* paso; pisada; huella; (modo de) andar *o* pisar; pisa (de uva); suela; (*neumático*) (banda de) rodamiento; (*mar.*) longitud de quilla. — *v.t.* pisar; gallear; ***tread the boards,*** pisar las tablas; ***tread down,*** hollar; ***tread underfoot,*** pisotear, hollar. — *v.i.* pisar; andar; ***tread carefully*** o ***warily,*** andar(se) con pies de plomo; ***tread in the footsteps of,*** seguir los pasos de; ***tread on*** o ***upon,*** pisotear; ***tread on air,*** estar eufórico *o* como unas pascuas; ***tread on s.o.'s corns*** o ***toes,*** herir *o* molestar a alguien; ***tread on s.o.'s heels,*** pisar los talones a alguien; ***tread softly,*** andar despacito.
treadle [tredl], *s.* pedal, cárcola.
treadmill [ˈtredmil], *s.* molino de rueda de escalones, molino de disciplina; (*fig.*) noria, tajo.
treason [ˈtri:zən], *s.* traición; ***high treason,*** alta traición.
treasonable [ˈtri:zənəbl], *a.* traidor, traicionero, desleal, pérfido.
treasonableness [ˈtri:zənəblnis], *s.* traición.
treasonably [ˈtri:zənəbli], *adv.* traidoramente.
treasure [ˈtreʒə], *s.* tesoro; joya; preciosidad; ***she is a treasure,*** es una alhaja; ***treasure-chest,*** arca *o* cofre de(l) tesoro; ***treasure-trove,*** hallazgo inesperado de un tesoro. — *v.t.* atesorar; apreciar muchísimo, guardar como oro en paño.
treasurer [ˈtreʒərə], *s.* tesorero.
treasureship [ˈtreʒərəʃip], *s.* tesorería.
treasury [ˈtreʒəri], *s.* tesorería, tesoro; ***Treasury,*** hacienda, ministerio de hacienda.
treat [tri:t], *s.* regalo; gustazo, gozada, cosa estupenda; (convite) extraordinario; excursión; ***it's my treat,*** invito yo; ***to stand treat,*** invitar, convidar; (*fam.*) ***it works a treat,*** funciona de maravilla. — *v.t.* tratar; invitar, convidar; ***treat royally,*** tratar a cuerpo de rey. — *v.i.* — ***of,*** tratar de, versar sobre; ***treat with,*** tratar *o* negociar con.
treatise [ˈtri:tiz], *s.* tratado.
treatment [ˈtri:tmənt], *s.* trato(s); tratamiento; (*med.*) tratamiento; ***inhuman treatment,*** tratos inhumanos, *m.pl.*
treaty [ˈtri:ti], *s.* tratado.
treble [trebl], *a.* triple; (*mús.*) sobreagudo; atiplado; de tiple; ***treble clef,*** clave de sol. — *s.* triple; (*mús.*) tiple. — *v.t.* triplicar. — *v.i.* triplicarse.
tree [tri:], *s.* árbol; horma (*de zapato*); arzón (*de silla de montar*); ***family tree,*** árbol genealógico; ***fruit tree,*** (árbol) frutal; ***tree-line,*** altitud que alcanzan los árboles; ***tree of knowledge*** (***of good and evil***), árbol de la ciencia (del bien y del mal); ***tree of life,*** árbol de la vida; ***tree-surgeon,*** cirujano de árboles; (*fig.*, *fam.*) ***up a tree,*** en un apuro, entre la espada y la pared; (*fig.*, *fam.*) ***bark up the wrong tree,*** andar descaminado *o* despistado, equivocarse, estar equivocado.
treeless [ˈtri:lis], *a.* sin árboles, pelado.
treenail [ˈtri:neil], *s.* (*mar.*) clavija.
treetop [ˈtri:tɔp], *s.* copa de árbol.
trefoil [ˈtri:fɔil], *s.* trébol.
trek [trek], *s.* caminata; ***pony-trek,*** excursión a caballo. — *v.i.* caminar trabajosamente; viajar (en carromato).
trellis [ˈtrelis], *s.* enrejado.
trellised [ˈtrelist], *a.* enrejado.
tremble [trembl], *s.* temblor; estremecimiento. — *v.i.* temblar (***with,*** de; ***at,*** ante); estremecerse (***with,*** de; ***at,*** ante).
trembling [ˈtrembliŋ], *a.* trémulo, tembloroso. — *s.* temblor(es); estremecimiento(s).
tremendous [triˈmendəs], *a.* tremendo.
tremolo [ˈtreməlou], *s.* (*mús.*) trémolo.
tremor [ˈtremə], *s.* temblor; estremecimiento; vibración; ***earth tremor,*** temblor de tierra.
tremulous [ˈtremjuləs], *a.* trémulo.
tremulousness [ˈtremjuləsnis], *s.* temblor(es).
trench [trentʃ], *s.* trinchera; zanja; ***trench warfare,*** guerra de trincheras. — *v.t.* atrincherar; hacer zanjas en.
trenchant [ˈtrentʃənt], *a.* cortante; mordaz, incisivo.
trencher [ˈtrentʃə], *s.* trinchador; trinchero; tajadero.
trencherman [ˈtrentʃəmən], *s.* comilón; ***to be a good trencherman,*** tener buen diente *o* saque.
trend [trend], *s.* tendencia; boga, moda. — *v.i.* tender.

trendy [ˈtrendi], *a.* (*fam.*) modernísimo, novedoso, a la última (moda).

Trent [trent]. Trento; ***Council of Trent,*** Concilio de Trento.

trepan [triˈpæn], *s.* trépano. — *v.t.* trepanar.

trepanation [trepəˈneiʃən], *s.* (*cir.*) trepanación.

trephine [triˈfi:n], *s.* trefino. — *v.t.* trepanar.

trepidation [trepiˈdeiʃən], *s.* agitación, azoramiento, turbación.

trespass [ˈtrespəs], *s.* intrusión; entrada ilegal; transgresión; pecado, culpa; ***forgive us our trespasses,*** perdónanos nuestras deudas. — *v.i.* entrar ilegalmente (en finca ajena); ***trespass against,*** infringir, violar; pecar contra; (*fig.*) ***trespass upon another's preserve,*** meterse en el terreno de otro.

trespasser [ˈtrespəsə], *s.* intruso; transgresor; pecador.

tress [tres], *s.* trenza.

tressed [trest], *a.* trenzado.

trestle [tresl], *s.* bastidor (*de mesa*), armadura; caballete; tijera; ***trestle-table,*** mesa de tijera.

trews [tru:z], *s.pl.* (*Esco.*) pantalones hechos de tela tartán, *m.pl.*

trey [trei], *s.* (el) tres (*de los naipes* o *dados*).

triad (ˈtraiəd], *a.* (*quím.*) trivalente. — *s.* tríada; (*mús.*) acorde ternario.

triadic [traiˈædik], *a.* trino; trivalente.

trial [ˈtraiəl], *s.* prueba, ensayo; tentativa; concurso; (*for.*) proceso, juico, vista (de una causa); aflicción, adversidad; ***by trial and error,*** a base de probar diversas posibilidades; ***to be on trial,*** estar en juicio; estar a prueba; ***to bring to trial,*** enjuiciar, procesar; ***to stand trial,*** comparecer, ser procesado; ***trial by jury,*** juicio con jurado; ***trial run*** o ***trip,*** viaje de ensayo.

triangle [ˈtraiæŋgl], *s.* triángulo.

triangular [traiˈæŋgjulə], *a.* triangular.

triangulate [traiˈæŋgjuleit], *v.t.* triangular.

triangulation [traiæŋgjuˈleiʃən], *s.* triangulación.

tribal [ˈtraibəl], *a.* tribal.

tribalism [ˈtraibəlizəm], *s.* tribalismo, organización tribal.

tribe [traib], *s.* tribu; (*fig.*) ralea; (*fam.*) ***tribe of kids,*** turba de niños.

tribesman [ˈtraibzmən], *s.* miembro de una tribu.

tribrach [ˈtribræk], *s.* tribraquio.

tribulation [tribjuˈleiʃən], *s.* tribulación, congoja.

tribunal [traiˈbju:nəl], *s.* tribunal.

tribunate [ˈtribjunit], *s.* tribunado.

tribune [ˈtribju:n], *s.* tribuna; tribuno.

tributary [ˈtribjutəri], *a.* tributario. — *s.* tributario; afluente.

tribute [ˈtribju:t], *s.* tributo; homenaje.

trice [trais], *s.* instante; ***in a trice,*** en un santiamén. — *v.t.* (*mar.*) izar, trincar.

tricennial [traiˈseniəl], *a.* tricenal.

triceps [ˈtraiseps], *s.* tríceps, *m.inv.*

trichina [triˈki:nə], *s.* (*med.*) triquina.

trichinosis [trikiˈnousis], *s.* triquinosis, *f.inv.*

trick [trik], *s.* truco; burla; engaño; trampa; maña; travesura; ardid; espejismo; juego de manos; (*cartas*) baza; peculiaridad (*de estilo etc.*); (*fam.*) ***dirty trick,*** mala pasada, faena; ***trick photography,*** trucaje; ***trick question,*** pregunta de pega *o* de mala idea; ***to get up to one's old tricks,*** volver a las andadas; ***to play a trick on,*** engañar, burlar. — *v.t.* engañar; embaucar; burlar; ***trick s.o. into doing sth.,*** conseguir con treta(s) que alguien haga *o* hiciese algo; ***trick s.o. out of sth.,*** quitarle algo a alguien con engaño, pisarle *o* chafarle algo a alguien con engaño; ***trick out,*** ataviar, adornar.

trickery [ˈtrikəri], *s.* engaños, *m.pl.*, trampas, *f.pl.*, tretas, *f.pl.*, astucias, *f.pl.*,

trickiness [ˈtrikinis], *s.* (lo) difícil, (lo) delicado; (lo) engorroso.

trickle [trikl], *s.* hilillo, chorrillo. — *v.i.* gotear, salir en hilillo.

trickster [ˈtrikstə], *s.* tramposo; estafador, timador.

tricksy [ˈtriksi], *a.* engañoso.

tricky [ˈtriki], *a.* difícil, delicado, sutil; engorroso; (*pers.*) artero, taimado.

tricolour [ˈtrikələ], *a.* tricolor. — *s.* bandera tricolor.

tricycle [ˈtraisikl], *s.* triciclo.

trident [ˈtraidənt], *s.* tridente.

tridentate [traiˈdenteit], *a.*, *s.* tridente.

tried [traid], *a.* probado; leal, fiel. — *p.p.* [TRY].

triennial [traiˈeniəl], *a.* trienal.

trier [ˈtraiə], *s.* (*fam.*) persona de tesón, persona que no se da fácilmente por vencido.

trifid [ˈtraifid], *a.* trífido.

trifle [traifl], *s.* bagatela, friolera, fruslería; (*coc.*) dulce de bizcocho borracho y natillas. — *adv.* algo, una pizca, un poquito; ***a trifle annoyed,*** una pizca molesto. — *v.t.* — ***away,*** perder *o* desperdiciar frívolamente. — *v.i.* tontear; ***trifle with,*** jugar con.

trifler [ˈtraiflə], *s.* hombre frívolo, mujer frívola.

trifling [ˈtraifliŋ], *a.* insignificante; frívolo.

triflingly [ˈtraifliŋli], *adv.* de una manera frívola.

triflingness [ˈtraifliŋnis], *s.* (lo) insignificante; (lo) frívolo.

trifoliate [traiˈfouliit], *a.* trifoliado.

triform [ˈtraifɔ:m], *a.* triforme.

trigger [ˈtrigə], *s.* gatillo; disparador; ***to pull the trigger,*** apretar el gatillo. — *v.t.* — ***off,*** dar origen a, ocasionar; provocar, hacer estallar.

trigger-happy [ˈtrigə-ˈhæpi], *a.* de gatillo fácil.

triglyph [ˈtraiglif], *s.* (*arq.*) tríglifo.

trigonal [ˈtrigonəl], *a.* trigonal.

trigonometric(al) [trigənoˈmetrik(əl)], *a.* trigonométrico.

trigonometry [trigəˈnɔmitri], *s.* trigonometría.

trihedral [traiˈhi:drəl], *a.* triedro.

trihedron [traiˈhi:drən], *s.* triedro.

trilateral [traiˈlætərəl], *a.* trilateral.

trilby [ˈtrilbi], *s.* sombrero de terciopelo flojo.

trilingual [traiˈliŋgwəl], *a.* trilingüe.

triliteral [traiˈlitərəl], *a.* trilítero.

trill [tril], *s.* trino, gorjeo; (*mús.*, *fonét.*) quiebro; vibración; trinado. — *v.t.* pronunciar con vibración. — *v.i.* trinar, gorjear.

trillion [ˈtriljən], *s.* (*en Inglaterra, Francia, y España*) trillón; (*Am.*) billón.

trilobate [traiˈloubeit], *a.* (*bot.*) trilobado.

trilogy [ˈtrilədʒi], *s.* trilogía.

trim [trim], *a.* acicalado; arreglado; en buen orden *o* estado; ***a trim figure,*** un buen tipo. — *s.* orden, estado, condición, disposición; recorte; (*mar.*) asiento; adorno, ribete, guarnición; ***trim of the hold,*** nivelación de la estiba; ***trim of the sails,*** orientación del velamen; ***in good trim,*** en orden, en regla; ***to get things into trim,*** arreglar *o* poner en orden las cosas; ***to have a trim,*** arreglarse *o* (re)cortarse el pelo. — *v.t.* arreglar, ajustar, disponer; (re)cortar, podar; atusar; despabilar; alisar, pulir; adornar, ribetear, guarnecer; (*mar.*) equilibrar; ***trim the hold,*** nivelar la estiba; ***trim the sails,*** orientar el velamen; ***trim off,*** cortar lo que sobra; ***trim up,*** arreglar, componer.

trimester [triˈmestə], *s.* (*Am.*) trimestre.

trimeter [ˈtrimitə], *s.* trimetro.

trimly [ˈtrimli], *adv.* bien, en buen orden, en regla, elegantemente.

trimmer [ˈtrimə], *s.* guarnecedor; (*carp.*) solera; recortadora, desbastadora; (*cost.*) ribeteador.

trimming [ˈtrimiŋ], *s.* guarnición (*de vestido*), galón, orla, franja; arreglo, ajuste; poda; (*mar.*) estiba (de la cala); orientación (*de las velas*); (*carp.*) desbaste; (*pl.*) accesorios, *m.pl.*

trimness [ˈtrimnis], *s.* buen orden; elegancia, esbeltez.
trinal [ˈtrainəl], *a.* trino.
trine [train], *s.* juego de tres; (*teo.*) (la) Trinidad; (*astron.*) (el) aspecto de los planetas cuando distan entre sí 120°.
Trinidad and Tobago [ˈtrinidæd ænd toˈbeigou]. Trinidad-Tobago.
Trinidadian [triniˈdædiən], *a.*, *s.* trinitario.
Trinitarian [triniˈtɛəriən], *a.*, *s.* trinitario.
trinitrotoluene [trainaitroˈtɔluiːn], *s.* (*abrev.* **T.N.T.**) trinitrotolueno.
trinity [ˈtriniti], *s.* trinidad; ***Holy Trinity,*** Santísima Trinidad.
trinket [ˈtriŋkit], *s.* dije, chuchería.
trinomial [traiˈnoumiəl], *a.* (*biol.*) de tres nombres; (*mat.*) de tres términos. — *s.* (*alg.*) trinomio.
trio [ˈtriːou], *s.* trío.
triolet [ˈtriːolit], *s.* trioleto.
Triones [traiˈouniːz], *s.pl.* (*astron.*) Triones, *m.pl.*
trip [trip], *s.* viaje (corto), excursión; tropiezo, traspié; zancadilla; desliz; (*mec.*) trinquete, disparo; (*mar.*) bordada; ***business trip,*** viaje de negocios; (*Am.*) ***round trip,*** viaje de ida y vuelta; ***to take a trip,*** hacer un viaje. — *v.t.* — ***up,*** echar *o* poner la zancadilla a. — *v.i.* — ***along,*** ir con paso ligero; ***trip up,*** tropezar.
tripartite [traiˈpɑːrtait], *a.* tripartito.
tripe [traip], *s.* callos, *m.pl.*; (*fig.*, *fam.*) sandeces, *f.pl.*, estupideces, *f.pl.*, gaitas, *f.pl.*
tripetalous [traiˈpetələs], *a.* tripétalo.
triphthong [ˈtrifθɔŋ], *s.* triptongo.
triple [tripl], *a.*, *s.* triple. — *v.t.* triplicar.
triplet [ˈtriplit], *s.* trillizo; (*mús.*, *poét.*) terceto.
triplex [ˈtripleks], *a.*, *s.* tríplice.
triplicate [ˈtriplikit], *a.* triplicado; ***in triplicate,*** por triplicado. — [ˈtriplikeit], *v.t.* triplicar.
triplication [tripliˈkeiʃən], *s.* triplicación.
triplicity [triˈplisiti], *s.* triplicidad.
tripod [ˈtraipɔd], *s.* trípode.
tripper [ˈtripə], *s.* excursionista, *m.f.*
tripping [ˈtripiŋ], *a.* ligero, ágil.
triptych [ˈtriptik], *s.* tríptico.
trireme [ˈtrairiːm], *s.* trirreme.
trisagion [triˈsægiən], *s.* trisagio.
trisect [traiˈsekt], *v.t.* trisecar.
trisection [traiˈsekʃən], *s.* trisección.
Tristram [ˈtristrəm]. Tristán.
trisyllabic [traisiˈlæbik], *a.* trisilábico.
trisyllable [traiˈsiləbl], *s.* trisílabo.
trite [trait], *a.* trillado, trivial, vulgar.
triteness [ˈtraitnis], *s.* trivialidad, vulgaridad.
triton [ˈtraitən], *s.* tritón.
tritone [ˈtraitoun], *s.* trítono.
triturate [ˈtritjureit], *v.t.* triturar.
trituration [tritjuˈreiʃən], *s.* trituración.
triumph [ˈtraiʌmf], *s.* triunfo. — *v.i.* triunfar, salir airoso; ***triumph over,*** triunfar de.
triumphal [traiˈʌmfəl], *a.* triunfal; ***triumphal arch,*** arco de triunfo.
triumphant [traiˈʌmfənt], *a.* triunfante, airoso.
triumvir [traiˈʌmvə], *s.* triunviro.
triumvirate [traiˈʌmvirit], *s.* triunvirato.
triune [ˈtraijuːn], *a.* trino y uno.
trivet [ˈtrivit], *s.* trébedes, *f.pl.*
trivial [ˈtriviəl], *a.* fútil, baladí, insignificante.
triviality [triviˈæliti], *s.* futilidad, (lo) baladí, insignificancia.
trivium [ˈtriviəm], *s.* trivio.
tri-weekly [traiˈwiːkli], *a.* trisemanal.
trochaic [troˈkeiik], *a.* trocaico.
troche [trouk, trouʃ], *s.* trocisco.
trochee [ˈtroukiː], *s.* troqueo.
trochlea [ˈtrɔkliə], *s.* tróclea.
trochoid [ˈtrɔkɔid], *a.* trocoideo. — *s.* trocoide.
troglodyte [ˈtrɔglədait], *s.* troglodita, *m.f.*
trogon [ˈtrougən], *s.* (*orn.*) trogón.
troika [ˈtrɔikə], *s.* troica.
Trojan [ˈtroudʒən], *a.*, *s.* troyano.
troll (1) [troul], *s.* gnomo, duende.
troll (2) [troul], *v.i.* andorrear, corretear.
trolley [ˈtrɔli], *s.* mesita de ruedas, carrito; carretilla; trole; ***trolley bus,*** trolebús, *m.*; (*Am.*) ***trolley car,*** tranvía; ***trolley pole,*** trole.
trollop [ˈtrɔləp], *s.* pindonga, pécora.
trombone [ˈtrɔmˈboun], *s.* trombón.
troop [truːp], *s.* tropa; cuadrilla, banda; tropel; (*mar.*) ***troop carrier,*** transporte (de tropas); ***troop train,*** tren militar. — *v.t.* atropar, agrupar; ***troop the colour,*** presentar la bandera. — *v.i.* agruparse; ***troop away*** o ***off,*** salir *o* alejarse en tropel; ***troop up*** o ***together,*** atroparse, formar grupo.
trooper [ˈtruːpə], *s.* soldado de caballería; ***to swear like a trooper,*** jurar como un carretero.
troopial [ˈtruːpiəl], *s.* (*orn.*) turpial, turicha.
troopship [ˈtruːpʃip], *s.* transporte (de tropas).
trope [troup], *s.* tropo.
trophy [ˈtroufi], *s.* trofeo.
tropic [ˈtrɔpik], *s.* trópico.
tropical [ˈtrɔpikəl], *a.* tropical.
tropological [trɔpəˈlɔdʒikəl], *a.* tropológico.
tropology [trɔˈpɔlədʒi], *s.* tropología.
trot [trɔt], *s.* trote; ***at a trot,*** al trote; ***fox trot,*** fox; ***to be always on the trot,*** no parar, llevar una vida ajetreada; ***to keep s.o. on the trot,*** no dejar descansar a alguien; ***slow*** o ***easy trot,*** trote corto. — *v.t.* hacer trotar; ***trot out,*** probar (*un caballo*) al trote; (*fig.*) sacar a relucir *o* a colación. — *v.i.* trotar, ir al trote.
troth [trouθ], *s.* palabra, fe, fidelidad; ***to plight*** o ***pledge one's troth,*** empeñar su palabra; prometerse, desposarse.
trotter [ˈtrɔtə], *s.* trotón; manita *o* pie (*de cerdo, carnero etc.*).
trotting [ˈtrɔtiŋ], *a.* trotador, trotón. — *s.* trote.
troubadour [ˈtruːbədɔː], *s.* trovador.
trouble [trʌbl], *s.* pena, molestia; apuro, aprieto; lío; dificultad, pega, inconveniente; trabajo, esfuerzo; engorro; mal, enfermedad; avería, fallo; conflicto, disturbio, agitación; (*pl.*) disturbios, *m.pl.*; ***engine trouble,*** avería(s) de(l) motor, *f.pl.*; ***heart trouble,*** enfermedad cardíaca; ***money troubles,*** problemas de dinero, *m.pl.*; ***stomach trouble,*** molestias de estómago, *f.pl.*; ***to ask for trouble,*** buscarse un lío; ***to drown one's troubles,*** beber para olvidar; ***to give s.o. trouble,*** causarle molestia a alguien; ***he had some trouble (in) getting it,*** tuvo (algunas) dificultades para conseguirlo, le costó (cierto) trabajo conseguirlo; ***to be in trouble,*** estar en un apuro; tener dificultades; ***to get into trouble,*** meterse en un lío; ***to get s.o. into trouble,*** comprometer a alguien, meter en un lío a alguien; ***to look for trouble where there is none,*** buscarle tres pies al gato; ***to make trouble for s.o.,*** amargarle la vida a alguien; ***it's no trouble,*** no es molestia; ***it's no trouble to do it,*** no cuesta trabajo *o* nada hacerlo; (***always***) ***providing it's no trouble,*** siempre que Vd. buenamente pueda *o* que no le cause extorsión; ***to get out of trouble,*** salir de apuros; ***to get s.o. out of trouble,*** sacar de apuros a alguien; ***to save o.s. the trouble,*** ahorrarse el trabajo; ***to stir up trouble,*** sembrar cizaña; ***to go to the trouble of,*** tomarse la molestia de; ***it's too much trouble,*** es mucha *o* demasiada molestia; ***what's the trouble?, what seems to be the trouble?*** ¿qué pasa?, ¿pasa algo?; ***it's not worth the trouble,*** no vale la pena; ***trouble-free,*** libre de dificultades *o* de problemas; ***trouble-maker,*** alborotador; agitador; ***trouble-shooter,*** uno que soluciona problemas. — *v.t.* afligir; inquietar, preocupar;

agitar; turbar, perturbar; molestar, importunar, incomodar; ***I'm sorry to trouble you,*** siento (tener que) molestarle *o* causarle un trastorno. — *v.i.* (*fam.*) preocuparse; molestarse; tomarse molestias; (*fam.*) (***please***) ***don't trouble,*** (le ruego) no se moleste.

troubled [trʌbld], *a.* turbado; preocupado; turbulento, agitado; (*fig.*) ***to fish in troubled waters,*** pescar a río revuelto.

troublesome [ˈtrʌblsəm], *a.* molesto, pesado, fastidioso; difícil, dificultoso; importuno.

troublesomeness [ˈtrʌblsəmnis], *s.* (lo) molesto *etc.*

troublous [ˈtrʌbləs], *a.* agitado, turbulento, inquieto.

trough [trɔf], *s.* artesa; canal; seno (*de ola*); (*meteorol.*) mínimo de presión; ***drinking-trough,*** abrevadero; ***feeding-trough,*** comedero; ***kneading-trough,*** artesa.

trounce [trauns], *v.t.* (*fam.*) zurrar, dar una paliza a.

troupe [tru:p], *s.* compañía (*de teatro etc.*)

trousering [ˈtrauzəriŋ], *s.* paño (para pantalones).

trousers [ˈtrauzəz], *s.pl.* pantalones, *m.pl.*; (*fig.*) ***to wear the trousers,*** llevar los pantalones.

trousseau [ˈtru:sou], *s.* ajuar (de novia).

trout [traut], *s.* (*ict.*) trucha.

trowel [ˈtrauəl], *s.* paleta, llana; (*hort.*) desplantador.

Troy [trɔi]. Troya.

troy [trɔi], *s.* (peso) troy.

truancy [ˈtru:ənsi], *s.* (el) hacer novillos.

truant [ˈtru:ənt], *s.* novillero; ***to play truant,*** hacer novillos, hacer rabona.

truce [tru:s], *s.* tregua.

truck (1) [trʌk], *s.* camión; carretilla (*de mano*); vagón (*de mercancías*); (*Am.*) [LORRY].

truck (2) [trʌk], *s.* trueque, cambio; pago en especie; cachivaches, *m.pl.*; ***to have no truck with,*** no tratar con, no (querer) tener nada que ver con.

truckage [ˈtrʌkidʒ], *s.* (*Am.*) camionaje; acarreo, carreteo.

truckle [trʌkl], *v.i.* someterse con servilismo (***to,*** a).

truckle-bed [ˈtrʌkl-bed], *s.* carriola.

truckman [ˈtrʌkmən], *s.* carretero; camionero.

truculence [ˈtrʌkjuləns], *s.* agresividad, chulería.

truculent [ˈtrʌkjulənt], *a.* agresivo, chulo.

trudge [trʌdʒ], *v.i.* caminar trabajosamente, andar penosamente.

true [tru:], *a.* verdadero; verídico; fiel, leal; uniforme, a nivel; ***to come true,*** realizarse, cumplirse; ***true-hearted,*** de corazón, sincero, leal, fiel; ***true to life,*** conforme con la realidad; ***that's true,*** es verdad, es cierto; ***it's only too true,*** ¡por desgracia, es totalmente cierto!

true-blue [ˈtru:-ˈblu:], *a.*, *s.* conservador hasta los tuétanos.

true-born [ˈtru:-bɔ:n], *a.* legítimo, de casta.

true-bred [ˈtru:-bred], *a.* de pura sangre, de casta legítima.

trueness [ˈtru:nis], *s.* veracidad; sinceridad, fidelidad.

truffle [trʌfl], *s.* trufa, criadilla de tierra.

truffled [trʌfld], *a.* trufado, guarnecido con trufas.

truism [ˈtru:izəm], *s.* perogrullada, tópico.

trull [trʌl], *s.* ramera.

truly [ˈtru:li], *adv.* verdaderamente, realmente; ***yours truly,*** le saluda atentamente.

trump [trʌmp], *s.* triunfo (*naipes*); (*fig.*) ***to play one's trump card,*** jugar la baza de triunfos. — *v.t.* ganar; ***trump up,*** inventar(se), forjar. — *v.i.* triunfar.

trumped-up [ˈtrʌmpt-ʌp], *a.* inventado, forjado, falso.

trumpery [ˈtrʌmpəri], *a.* frívolo; de relumbrón. — *s.* oropel.

trumpet [ˈtrʌmpit], *a.* de trompeta. — *s.* trompeta; trompetilla; bocina; clarín; ***ear-trumpet,*** trompetilla acústica; ***to blow one's own trumpet,*** darse bombo; (*bot.*) ***trumpet-creeper,*** jazmín trompeta; ***trumpet-fish,*** centrisco. — *v.t.*, *v.i.* pregonar a son de trompeta; trompetear, tocar la trompeta; (*fig.*) divulgar.

trumpeter [ˈtrʌmpitə], *s.* trompeta, *m.*, trompetero; (*orn.*) agamí.

trumpeting [ˈtrʌmpitiŋ], *s.* trompeteo; berrido(s) (del elefante); (*fig.*) berrido(s).

trumpet-tongued [ˈtrʌmpit-ˈtʌŋd], *a.* vocinglero.

truncate [ˈtrʌŋkeit], *a.* truncado, trunco. — [trʌŋˈkeit], *v.t.* truncar.

truncated [trʌŋˈkeitid], *a.* truncado, trunco.

truncation [trʌŋˈkeiʃən], *s.* truncamiento.

truncheon [ˈtrʌntʃən], *s.* (cachi)porra. — *v.t.* aporrear.

trundle [trʌndl], *s.* ruedecilla; carriola; ***trundle-bed,*** carriola. — *v.t.* hacer rodar. — *v.i.* rodar pesadamente; ir sobre ruedas.

trunk [trʌŋk], *s.* tronco; baúl; trompa (de elefante); (*Am.*, *aut.*) [BOOT (1)]; ***swimming trunks,*** traje de baño, bañador; ***trunk call,*** conferencia (interurbana); ***trunk hose,*** calzas, *f.pl.*, trusas, *f.pl.*; ***trunk line,*** línea principal de transporte; ***trunk-maker,*** cofrero; ***trunk road,*** carretera nacional.

trunnion [ˈtrʌnjən], *s.* muñón.

truss [trʌs], *s.* lío, fardo; armazón; (*arq.*) entramado; (*med.*) braguero. — *v.t.* atar, liar; espetar; apuntalar; (*mar.*) aferrar.

trust [trʌst], *s.* confianza; responsabilidad, deber; obligación; cargo; fideicomiso; (*com.*) trust; monopolio, cartel; ***to hold in trust,*** guardar en depósito; ***to sell on trust,*** vender a crédito *o* al fiado; ***National Trust,*** sociedad de conservación de monumentos de interés nacional; ***position of trust,*** puesto *o* cargo de confianza; ***trust company,*** compañía fideicomisaria; ***trust deed of sale,*** escritura de venta condicionada. — *v.t.* confiar en, fiarse de; (*com.*) dar al fiado; esperar; ***he is not to be trusted,*** no es de fiar; ***trust him!*** ¡fíate de él!; (*ironía*) eso es muy de él. — *v.i.* confiar; esperar; ***I trust not,*** espero que no; ***trust to luck,*** confiar en la suerte.

trustee [trʌsˈti:], *s.* depositario; fideicomisario; administrador; síndico.

trusteeship [trʌsˈti:ʃip], *s.* cargo de fideicomisario *etc.*

trustful [ˈtrʌstful], *a.* confiado.

trustfulness [ˈtrʌstfulnis], *s.* confianza.

trustiness [ˈtrʌstinis], *s.* fidelidad, lealtad.

trusting [ˈtrʌstiŋ], *a.* confiado.

trustingly [ˈtrʌstiŋli], *adv.* con confianza.

trustworthiness [ˈtrʌstwə:ðinis], *s.* (lo) digno de confianza, formalidad, seriedad; (lo) seguro, (lo) fidedigno.

trustworthy [ˈtrʌstwə:ði], *a.* digno de confianza, formal, serio; seguro, fidedigno.

trusty [ˈtrʌsti], *a.* fiel, leal; seguro.

truth [tru:θ], *s.* verdad; exactitud; ***the plain truth,*** la pura verdad; ***in truth,*** en verdad.

truthful [ˈtru:θful], *a.* veraz; verídico; exacto.

truthfulness [ˈtru:θfulnis], *s.* veracidad.

truthless [ˈtru:θlis], *a.* falso.

try [trai], *s.* intento, tentativa; ensayo; (*rugby*) prueba. — *v.t.* intentar; probar; ensayar; (*for.*) procesar, juzgar; ver (*una causa*); (*metal.*) refinar; (*fam.*) desesperar, exasperar; ***try one's luck,*** probar fortuna *o* suerte; ***try on,*** probarse (*una prenda*); (*fam.*) ***try it on,*** intentar dar el pego, intentar dársela a alguien; ***try out,*** probar, someter a prueba. — *v.i.* probar, intentarlo, hacer la prueba; esforzarse, hacer esfuerzos; ***try and do it,*** prueba a hacerlo; ***try for,*** intentar conseguir *o* alcanzar; ***try hard,*** hacer muchos esfuerzos, hacer esfuerzos denodados; ***try to,*** *con inf.*, tratar de, intentar, procurar, pretender.

trying [ˈtraiiŋ], *a.* molesto, fastidioso, desesperante.

try-on [ˈtrai-ɔn], *s.* (*fam.*) intento de engaño *o* de timo.

try-out [ˈtrai-aut], *s.* prueba, ensayo.

tryst [traist], *s.* cita; lugar de cita. — *v.i.* darse cita.
tsetse [ˈsetsi], *s.* tsetsé, *f.*
tub [tʌb], *s.* tina; cuba; artesón; (*baño*) bañera; (*barco*) carcamán. — *v.t.* entinar, encubar.
tuba [ˈtju:bə], *s.* (*mús.*) tuba.
tube [tju:b], *s.* tubo; cámara (*de neumático*); (*f.c.*) metro; (*Am., rad.*) [VALVE].
tubeless [ˈtju:blis], *a.* (*neumático*) sin cámara.
tuber [ˈtju:bə], *s.* tubérculo.
tubercle [ˈtju:bəkl], *s.* tubérculo.
tubercular [tjuˈbə:kjulə], *a.* tubercular; (*med.*) tuberculoso.
tuberculosis [tjubə:kjuˈlousis], *s.* tuberculosis, *f.inv.*; ***s.o. suffering from pulmonary tuberculosis,*** tísico.
tuberculous [tjuˈbə:kjuləs], *a.* tuberculoso; tísico.
tuberose [ˈtju:bərous], *s.* tuberosa.
tuberosity [tju:bəˈrɔsiti], *s.* tuberosidad.
tuberous [ˈtju:bərəs], *a.* tuberoso.
tubing [ˈtju:biŋ], *s.* tubería; tubos, *m.pl.*, tuberías, *f.pl.*, cañerías, *f.pl.*
tubular [ˈtju:bjulə], *a.* tubular.
tubule [ˈtju:bju:l], *s.* túbulo, tubito.
tuck [tʌk], *s.* pliegue, alforza; golosinas, *f.pl.*; (*fam.*) pitanza. — *v.t.* plegar, alforzar; ***tuck away,*** guardar con mucho cuidado; (*fam.*) engullirse, zamparse; ***tuck in,*** remeter (*la ropa de la cama*); ***tuck up,*** arremangar(se); arropar. — *v.i.* (*fam.*) ***tuck in,*** engullir, zampar.
tucker [ˈtʌkə], *s.* canesú; alforzador. — *v.t.* (*Am., fam.*) ***tucker out,*** fatigar, moler.
tuck-in [ˈtʌk-in], *s.* (*fam.*) comilona.
Tuesday [ˈtju:zdi], *s.* martes, *m.inv.*; ***Shrove Tuesday,*** martes de carnaval.
tufa, tuff [ˈtju:fə, tʌf], *s.* toba, tufo.
tufaceous [tju:ˈfeiʃəs], *a.* tobáceo, toboso.
tuft [tʌft], *s.* penacho; copete; cresta; mechón, tupé; pera, perilla; manojo; macizo (*de plantas*). — *v.t.* empenachar; adornar con crestas *etc.*; bardear (*un colchón*).
tufted, tufty [ˈtʌftid, ˈtʌfti], *a.* copetudo; penachudo.
tug [tʌg], *s.* tirón, estirón; forcejeo; (*mar.*) remolcador. — *v.t.* tirar de, halar; remolcar. — *v.i.* tirar; forcejear.
tugboat [ˈtʌgbout], *s.* remolcador.
tug-of-war [ˈtʌg-əv-ˈwɔ:], *s.* lucha de la cuerda; (*fig.*) forcejeo, tira y afloja.
tuition [tju:ˈiʃən], *s.* enseñanza, instrucción; ***private tuition,*** clases particulares, *f.pl.*
tulip [ˈtju:lip], *s.* tulipán; ***tulip tree,*** tulipero.
tulle [tju:l], *s.* tul.
tumble [tʌmbl], *s.* caída, vuelco, tumbo, voltereta; desorden; ***to take a tumble,*** caerse, darse un batacazo. — *v.t.* derribar, tumbar; ***tumble (sth.) over,*** volcar; ***tumble (sth.) out,*** echar en desorden. — *v.i.* caerse; dar tumbos; ***tumble down,*** desplomarse, venirse abajo; ***tumble into (out of) bed,*** caer(se) en (de) la cama; ***tumble out,*** salir en desorden; ***to go tumbling over and over,*** ir rodando, ir dando tumbos; ***tumble to,*** caer en, caer en la cuenta de.
tumble-down [ˈtʌmbl-daun], *a.* ruinoso, desvencijado.
tumbler [ˈtʌmblə], *s.* vaso; cubilete; volatinero; tambor giratorio; rodete (*de cerradura*); piñón (*de escopeta*); (*orn.*) pichón volteador.
tumbrel, tumbril [ˈtʌmbrəl], *s.* carreta, chirrión; (*artill.*) furgón, carro de artillería.
tumefaction [tju:miˈfækʃən], *s.* tumefacción.
tumefy [ˈtju:mifai], *v.t.* entumecer. — *v.i.* entumecerse.
tumid [ˈtju:mid], *a.* túmido; (*med.*) hinchado.
tummy [ˈtʌmi], *s.* (*fam.*) estómago.
tumour [ˈtju:mə], *s.* tumor.
tumular [ˈtju:mjulə], *a.* tumulario.
tumult [ˈtju:mʌlt], *s.* tumulto, alboroto.
tumultuary [tjuˈmʌltjuəri], *a.* tumultuario.
tumultuous [tjuˈmʌltjuəs], *a.* tumultuoso.
tumultuousness [tjuˈmʌltjuəsnis], *s.* (lo) tumultuoso, (lo) alborotado, turbulencia.
tumulus [ˈtju:mjuləs], *s.* (*pl.* **tumuli** [ˈtju:mjuli:]) túmulo.
tun [tʌn], *s.* tonel; tonelada.
tuna [ˈtju:nə], *s.* atún.
tune [tju:n], *s.* música, musiquilla; melodía; tonada, tonadilla, aire; armonía; ***in tune,*** afinado, templado; afinadamente; (*fig.*) ***in tune with,*** a tono con, en consonancia con, de acuerdo con; ***out of tune,*** desafinado, destemplado; desafinadamente; (*fig.*) ***out of tune with,*** que desentona con; ***to the tune of,*** en la cantidad de; por valor de; (*fam.*) ***to change one's tune,*** cambiar de tono, recoger velas. — *v.t.* (*mús.*) afinar, templar; (*rad.*) centrar; (*rad.*) ***tune in,*** sintonizar; (*aut.*) ***tune (up),*** poner a punto. — *v.i.* (*rad.*) ***tune in (to a station),*** coger (una emisora); ***the orchestra is tuning (up),*** la orquesta está afinando (*los instrumentos*).
tuneful [ˈtju:nful], *a.* armonioso, melodioso.
tuneless [ˈtju:nlis], *a.* sin armonía, disonante.
tuner [ˈtju:nə], *s.* afinador; (sistema) sintonizador.
tungstate [ˈtʌŋsteit], *s.* tungestato.
tungsten [ˈtʌŋstən], *s.* tungsteno.
tungstic [ˈtʌŋstik], *a.* túngstico.
tunic [ˈtju:nik], *s.* túnica; guerrera.
tunicate [ˈtju:nikeit], *a.* tunicado.
tunicle [ˈtju:nikl], *s.* (*igl.*) tunicela.
tuning [ˈtju:niŋ], *a.* sintonizador. — *s.* afinación; sintonización (de radio); (*mús.*) (el) afinar.
tuning-fork [ˈtju:niŋ-fɔ:k], *s.* diapasón.
tuning-hammer, tuning-key [ˈtju:niŋ-hæmə, -ki:], *s.* templador, llave de afinador.
Tunis [ˈtju:nis]. Túnez (*ciudad*).
Tunisia [tjuˈniziə]. Túnez (*país*).
Tunisian [tjuˈniziən], *a., s.* tunecino.
tunnage [ˈtʌnidʒ], *s.* derecho de tonelaje.
tunnel [tʌnəl], *s.* túnel; galería. — *v.t.* abrir un túnel a través de; horadar. — *v.i.* construir un túnel; excavar.
tunnelling [ˈtʌnəliŋ], *s.* construcción de túneles; horadación.
tunny [ˈtʌni], *s.* atún.
tup [tʌp], *s.* (*zool.*) morueco; cabeza (*del martinete*).
tupelo [ˈtju:pilou], *s.* (*bot.*) nisa.
turban [ˈtə:bən], *s.* turbante.
turbaned [ˈtə:bənd], *a.* cubierto con turbante.
turbary [ˈtə:bəri], *s.* turbera.
turbid [ˈtə:bid], *a.* turbio.
turbidity [tə:ˈbiditi], *s.* turbiedad.
turbinal, turbinate [ˈtə:binəl, ˈtə:bineit], *a.* de forma de peonza.
turbine [ˈtə:bain], *s.* turbina.
turbojet [ˈtə:bodʒet], *a., s.* (de) turborreactor.
turboprop [ˈtə:boprɔp], *a., s.* (de) turbohélice.
turbot [ˈtə:bət], *s.* (*ict.*) rodaballo.
turbulence, turbulency [ˈtə:bjuləns, -i], *s.* turbulencia.
turbulent [ˈtə:bjulənt], *a.* turbulento, levantisco.
Turcoman [ˈtə:komæn], *a., s.* turcomano.
turd [tə:d], *s.* zurullo, mierda.
Turdus [ˈtə:dəs], *s.* (*orn.*) tordo.
tureen [tju:ˈri:n], *s.* sopera; ***soup-tureen,*** sópera.
turf [tə:f], *s.* césped; tapín; ***the Turf,*** las carreras, el hipódromo; ***turf accountant,*** corredor de apuestas. — *v.t.* encespedar, cubrir con césped *o* con tapines.
turfiness [ˈtə:finis], *s.* (lo) esponjoso.
turfy [ˈtə:fi], *a.* esponjoso.
turgid [ˈtə:dʒid], *a.* turgente; hinchado, ampuloso.
turgidity, turgidness [tə:ˈdʒiditi, ˈtə:dʒidnis], *s.* turgencia; hinchazón, *f.*, ampulosidad.

Turk [tə:k], *s.* turco; (*bot.*) ***turk's cap,*** martagón.

Turkey [ˈtə:ki]. Turquía.

turkey [ˈtə:ki], *s.* pavo; ***turkey-buzzard,*** aura; ***turkey-cock,*** gallipavo; ***turkey-hen,*** pava.

Turkish [ˈtə:kiʃ], *a.* turco; ***Turkish bath,*** baño turco. — *s.* (*idioma*) turco.

turmeric [ˈtə:mərik], *s.* cúrcuma.

turmoil [ˈtə:mɔil], *s.* tumulto, baraúnda, alboroto, disturbio.

turn [tə:n], *s.* vuelta; giro; revolución; curva, recodo (*de la carretera*); paseo (*en barco, coche*); cambio; turno, vez; disposición (*de ánimo*); (*fam.*) susto; (*fam.*) desmayo; (*teat.*) número;
(*turno, vez*) ***by turns,*** por turnos, alternativamente; ***in turn,*** por turno; a su vez; ***in his turn,*** a su vez; ***out of turn,*** fuera de turno *o* de orden; ***it's your turn,*** le toca a usted; ***to take a turn at,*** echar una mano en; ***to take one's turn,*** esperar su turno *o* la vez; ***I'll take a turn at the wheel now,*** ahora conduzco yo; ***to take turns,*** turnarse;
(*movimiento, cambio de dirección etc.*) (*fig.*) ***at every turn,*** a cada paso, a cada momento; ***to take a turn,*** dar una vuelta;
(*cambio etc.*) ***at the turn of the century,*** al iniciarse el nuevo siglo; ***to take a turn for the better,*** cambiar para mejor, empezar a mejorar algo; ***to take a turn for the worse,*** cambiar para peor, empezar a empeorar algo;
(*calidad*) ***turn of phrase,*** giro (lingüístico), estilo; ***to show a sudden turn of speed,*** apresurar repentinamente el paso;
(*rotación etc.*) (***done***) ***to a turn,*** en su punto; a la perfección;
(*actividad para con otro*) ***bad turn,*** flaco servicio, mala pasada; ***good turn,*** favor, (buen) servicio; ***one good turn deserves another,*** bien con bien se paga; hoy por ti, mañana por mí. —
v.t. volver; girar, dar vueltas a; (*llave*) dar vuelta a; echar; (*esquina*) doblar; (*estómago*) revolver; (*leche*) cortar, agriar; (*mec.*) tornear;
(*dirigir etc., lit., fig.*) ***turn against,*** predisponer en contra de; ***turn aside,*** desviar; ***turn away,*** apartar; despedir; ***turn back,*** hacer retroceder; doblar (*una página*); ***turn a blind eye,*** hacer la vista gorda; ***turn down,*** doblar (hacia abajo); rechazar; no aceptar; ***turn one's hand to,*** dedicarse a, ponerse a trabajar en; ***turn in,*** doblar hacia dentro; entregar (*a la policía etc.*); ***turn out,*** echar, expulsar; ***turn out of town,*** echar *o* expulsar de la ciudad; ***to be well turned out,*** ir bien vestido; ***turn over*** (***to***), entregar (a); ***turn tail,*** volver grupas; ***turn up,*** volver hacia arriba; levantar; descubrir; subir (*una manga*);
(*cambiar*) ***he has turned forty,*** ha cumplido los cuarenta (años); ***turn down,*** bajar (*el gas etc.*); ***turn into,*** convertir en; (*traducir*) verter a; ***turn off,*** apagar (*la luz, la radio*); cerrar (*el grifo*); cortar (*el gas, el agua, la corriente*); ***turn on,*** encender, dar (*la luz*); poner (*la radio*); abrir (*el grifo*); abrir la llave de; (*fig., fam.*) ***it turns me on,*** me anima, me excita, me pone en vena; ***turn out,*** apagar (*la luz*); vaciar (*un bolsillo*); producir, fabricar; (*fig.*) ***turn over a new leaf,*** enmendarse, hacer vida nueva, cambiar de vida; ***turn up,*** subir (*el gas, la radio*);
(*dar vueltas a*) ***turn over,*** volver; volcar; pasar (*la página*); dar vueltas a (*en la cabeza*). —
v.i. volver(se); girar, dar vueltas; (*coche, avión*) virar; torcer; hacerse, ponerse, volverse; (*leche*) cortarse, agriarse; (*tiempo*) cambiar; (*marea*) repuntar;
(*dirigirse etc., lit., fig.*) ***turn about,*** dar la vuelta; dar vueltas; (*mil.*) ***about turn!*** media vuelta—¡ar!; ***turn against,*** cobrar aversión a; rebelarse contra; ***turn around,*** dar la vuelta; ***turn aside*** o ***away,*** apartarse, desviarse, alejarse; volver la espalda; ***turn back,*** volver (atrás); (*fig.*) volverse atrás; ***turn from,*** apartarse de; ***turn in,*** doblarse hacia dentro; (*fam.*) acostarse; ***turn to,*** recurrir a, acudir a; ***they all turned to and cleaned the house,*** pusieron todos manos a la obra y limpiaron la casa; ***turn up,*** doblarse hacia arriba;
(*cambiar etc.*) ***turn into,*** convertirse en; ***turn out,*** resultar; ***turn out to be,*** resultar (ser); ***turn out well,*** resultar bien, salir bien; ***turn to,*** convertirse en; ***turn up,*** aparecer, presentarse, asistir; ***turn white,*** ponerse blanco *o* pálido.
(*darse vueltas etc.*) ***turn over,*** volcar; (*en la cama*) volverse; ***turn round,*** volverse; girar.

turnbuckle [ˈtə:nbʌkl], *s.* tarabilla, torniquete, tensor de tornillo.

turncoat [ˈtə:nkout], *s.* chaquetero, renegado; ***to become a turncoat,*** volver la chaqueta.

turned-up [ˈtə:nd-ʌp], *a.* respingón (*nariz*).

turner [ˈtə:nə], *s.* tornero.

turnery [ˈtə:nəri], *s.* tornería.

turning [ˈtə:niŋ], *s.* vuelta, revuelta, recodo; ángulo; bocacalle, *f.*; (*aut.*) ***turning circle,*** diámetro de giro; ***turning lathe,*** torno; (*fig.*) ***turning of the tide,*** momento decisivo, momento de cambiar la suerte; ***turning-point,*** punto decisivo.

turnip [ˈtə:nip], *s.* nabo.

turnkey [ˈtə:nki:], *s.* carcelero, llavero (*de una cárcel*).

turnout [ˈtə:naut], *s.* concurrencia, asistencia; (*com.*) producto neto; (*fam.*) atuendo.

turnover [ˈtə:nouvə], *s.* (*com.*) volumen de negocios *o* de ventas; transacciones, *f.pl.*; rotación de existencias; empanadilla; vuelco, voltereta.

turnpike [ˈtə:npaik], *s.* camino de portazgo, barrera de portazgo; ***turnpike keeper,*** guardabarrera, *m.f.*; ***turnpike road,*** autopista de peaje.

turnsole [ˈtə:nsoul], *s.* (*bot.*) heliotropo, tornasol, girasol.

turnspit [ˈtə:nspit], *s.* rueda de asador; galopín (*que hace girar el asador*).

turnstile [ˈtə:nstail], *s.* torniquete.

turnstone [ˈtə:nstoun], *s.* (*orn.*) revuelvepiedras, *m.inv.*

turntable [ˈtə:nteibl], *s.* (*f.c.*) placa giratoria; (*gramófono*) plato giratorio.

turn-up [ˈtə:n-ʌp], *s.* vuelta (*de los pantalones*); (*fam.*) trifulca; ***that's a turn-up for the books!*** ¡eso sí que es algo nuevo! ¡eso sí que no me lo esperaba!

turpentine [ˈtə:pəntain], *s.* trementina, aguarrás, *m.*; (*bot.*) ***turpentine-tree,*** terebinto.

turpitude [ˈtə:pitju:d], *s.* vileza, infamia.

turquoise [ˈtə:kwʌz], *s.* turquesa; ***turquoise-blue,*** de azul turquesa, turquesado.

turret [ˈtʌrit], *s.* torreón; torrecilla; (*submarino, tanque*) torreta.

turreted [ˈtʌritid], *a.* que tiene torres, torreado.

turtle [tə:tl], *s.* (*zool.*) tortuga (de mar); ***to turn turtle,*** volverse quilla arriba *o* patas arriba; ***turtle-dove,*** tórtola; ***turtle-necked sweater,*** jersey de cuello de cisne; ***turtle-shell,*** carey.

Tuscan [ˈtʌskən], *a., s.* toscano.

Tuscany [ˈtʌskəni]. (la) Toscana.

tush! [tʌʃ], *interj.* ¡bah!

tusk [tʌsk], *s.* colmillo.

tusked, tusky [tʌskt, ˈtʌski], *a.* colmilludo.

tussle [tʌsl], *s.* forcejeo; agarrada. — *v.i.* forcejear.

tussock [ˈtʌsək], *s.* montecillo de hierbas, mata.

tussore [tʌˈsɔ:], *s.* gusano de seda de la India; seda tusá.

tut! [tʌt], *interj.* ¡bah! ¡vaya!

tutelage [ˈtju:tilidʒ], *s.* tutela.

tutelar, tutelary [ˈtju:tilə, ˈtju:tiləri], *a.* tutelar.

tutor [ˈtju:tə], *s.* profesor (particular); preceptor; (*for.*) tutor. — *v.t.* dar clase(s) a; instruir.

tutorial [tju:ˈtɔ:riəl], *a.* de instrucción. — *s.* seminario; clase particular, *f.*

tutoring [ˈtju:təriŋ], *s.* clases particulares, *f.pl.*

tutorship [ˈtju:təʃip], *s.* (*for.*) tutela.

tutsan [ˈtʌtsən], *s.* (*bot.*) todabuena.

tutty [ˈtʌti], *s.* atutía, tutía.

tuxedo [tʌkˈsi:dou], (*Am.*) [DINNER-JACKET].

tuwhit tuwhoo [tu:ˈwit tu:ˈwu:], *s.* grito de la lechuza.
twaddle [twɔdl], *s.* disparates, *m.pl.*, tonterías, *f.pl.* — *v.i.* parlotear.
twain [twein], *a.*, *s.* (*ant.*) dos.
twang [twæŋ], *s.* (*mús.*) punteado, rasgueo; (*fonética*) gangueo, timbre nasal. — *v.t.* puntear, rasguear. — *v.i.* ganguear, vibrar.
'twas [twɔz], *contr. de* **it was.**
tweak [twi:k], *s.* pellizco retorcido. — *v.t.* pellizcar retorciendo.
tweed [twi:d], *s.* mezclilla, chéviot.
tweedy [ˈtwi:di], *a.* que lleva traje de mezclilla; (*fig.*) prosaico.
tweet [twi:t], *s.* piada, gorjeo. — *v.i.* piar, gorjear.
tweeter [ˈtwi:tə], *s.* (*elec.*) altavoz para superfrecuencias.
tweezers [ˈtwi:zəz], *s.pl.* pinzas, *f.pl.*
twelfth [twelfθ], *a.* duodécimo; (*títulos*) doce; ***Twelfth Night,*** día *o* noche de Reyes. — *s.* duodécima parte; (*mús.*) duodécima; (*fechas*) doce.
twelve [twelv], *a.*, *s.* doce; ***twelve-bore,*** del calibre doce; ***twelve good men and true,*** (los) doce jurados; ***twelve o'clock,*** las doce; ***to be twelve,*** tener doce años.
twelvemonth [ˈtwelvmʌnθ], *s.* año, doce meses.
twentieth [ˈtwentiəθ], *a.* vigésimo; (*títulos*) veinte. — *s.* vigésima parte; (*fechas*) veinte.
twenty [ˈtwenti], *a.*, *s.* veinte; ***to be twenty,*** tener veinte años.
'twere [twɔ:], (*ant.*) *contr. de* **it were.**
twice [twais], *adv.* dos veces; el doble; ***twice as much, twice as many,*** el doble; ***to do sth. twice over,*** volver a hacer algo (por segunda vez).
twice-told [ˈtwais-tould], *a.* repetido.
twiddle [twidl], *s.* vuelta, giro. — *v.t.* hacer girar; juguetear con; ***twiddle one's thumbs,*** voltear los pulgares; (*fig.*) mirar (a) las muscarañas, mirarse el ombligo.
twig (I) [twig], *s.* ramita; (*anat.*) ramal pequeña.
twig (2) [twig], *v.t.*, *v.i.* (*fam.*) captar, cazar.
twilight [ˈtwailait], *a.* crepuscular. — *s.* crepúsculo; ***at twilight,*** al anochecer; ***in the twilight of his years,*** en el crepúsculo de su vida.
'twill [twil], *contr. de* **it will.**
twill [twil], *s.* tela cruzada *o* asargada. — *v.t.* cruzar, asargar.
twin [twin], *a.* gemelo, mellizo; ***twin beds,*** camas gemelas, *f.pl.*; ***twin-cylinder,*** de dos cilindros; ***twin-engined,*** bimotor; ***twin-jet,*** birreactor; (*aer.*, *mar.*) ***twin-screw,*** bihélice; ***twin town,*** ciudad gemela. — *s.* gemelo, gemela. — *v.t.* hacer gemelas (*ciudades*).
twine [twain], *s.* guita, bramante, torzal. — *v.t.* tejer; torcer, retorcer; abrazar, ceñir; enrollar. — *v.i.* enroscarse; entrelazarse; entretejerse.
twinge [twindʒ], *s.* punzada, dolor agudo; ***twinge of conscience,*** remordimiento.
twinkle [twinkl], *s.* parpadeo; centelleo; ***in a twinkle,*** en un periquete. — *v.i.* parpadear, pestañear; centellear, titilar.
twinkling [ˈtwiŋkliŋ], *a.* titilante, centelleante; risueño. — *s.* centelleo; parpadeo; ***in the twinkling of an eye,*** en un abrir y cerrar de ojos.
twirl [twɔ:l], *s.* giro; molinete; pirueta; rasgo (*de la pluma*). — *v.t.*, *v.i.* (hacer) girar rápidamente; ensortijar(se), enroscar(se).
twist [twist], *s.* torsión; tirón; torcimiento, torcedura; rasgo; efecto (*de la pelota*); quiebro, sesgo; vuelta, recodo; rosca; torzal; mecha, trenza; rollo (*de tabaco*); (*mús.*) twist; (*fam.*) trampa; ***twists and turns,*** vueltas y revueltas, *f.pl.*; ***an unexpected twist,*** un giro imprevisto; ***it's a twist,*** ¡aquí hay trampa! — *v.t.* torcer; retorcer; enroscar; enrollar; trenzar, entrelazar; dar efecto a (*la pelota*); (*fam.*) estafar; ***twist s.o.'s arm,*** presionar a alguien. — *v.i.* torcerse, retorcerse; enroscarse, ensortijarse; serpentear; bailar el twist.
twisted [ˈtwistid], *a.* (*fam.*) retorcido; ***twisted sense of humour,*** humor negro.
twister [ˈtwistə], *s.* torcedor, soguero; torcedero; (*fam.*) tramposo.
twisting [ˈtwistiŋ], *a.* sinuoso, serpentino; que retuerce. — *s.* torsión; torcedura; entretejido; serpenteo.
twit [twit], *s.* (*fam.*) imbécil, tonto. — *v.t.* guasearse de.
twitch [twitʃ], *s.* tirón, sacudida; contracción, crispamiento. — *v.t.* dar un tirón a. — *v.i.* crisparse; moverse nerviosamente.
twitch-grass [ˈtwitʃ-grɑ:s], *s.* (*bot.*) cantinodia, sanguinaria.
twitter [ˈtwitə], *s.* gorjeo, piada; (*fam.*) agitación; revuelo. — *v.i.* gorjear, piar; (*fam.*) agitarse.
'twixt [twikst], *contr. de* [BETWIXT].
two [tu:], *a.*, *s.* dos, *m.inv.*; ***to be two,*** tener dos años; ***in two,*** en dos (partes); ***in twos, two by two,*** de dos en dos; ***to put two and two together,*** atar cabos; ***two-edged,*** de doble filo; ***two-faced,*** disimulado; (*fig.*) ***to be two-faced,*** tener dos caras; ***two-handed,*** de dos manos; para dos manos; ***two-headed,*** de dos cabezas; bicéfalo; ***two-legged,*** bípedo; ***two-ply,*** de dos tramas; de dos hilos; de dos láminas; ***two-seater,*** (*coche etc.*) de dos plazas; (*aer.*) biplaza, *m.*; ***two-sided,*** bilateral; ***two-step,*** paso doble; ***two-storey,*** de dos pisos; ***two-stroke engine,*** motor de dos tiempos; ***two-tone,*** bicolor; ***two-way switch,*** conmutador bidireccional.
twofold [ˈtu:fould], *a.* duplicado, doble. — *adv.* doblemente.
twopence [ˈtʌpəns], *s.* dos peniques.
twopenny [ˈtʌpəni], *a.* (del valor) de dos peniques; (*fig.*) de tres al cuarto; (*fig.*, *ant.*) ***twopenny ha'penny,*** de tres al cuarto, de mala muerte.
tycoon [taiˈku:n], *s.* taicón (*japonés*); (*fam.*) magnate.
tyke [taik], *s.* perrucho; tipejo, tiete.
tympan [ˈtimpən], *s.* tímpano.
tympanitis [timpəˈnaitis], *s.* timpanitis, *f.inv.*
tympanum [ˈtimpənəm], *s.* (*pl.* **tympana** [-nə]) tímpano.
type [taip], *s.* tipo; (*impr.*) tipo, letra de imprenta; tipos, *m.pl.*; ***type-case,*** caja de imprenta; ***type-founder,*** fundidor de letra de imprenta; ***type-foundry,*** fundición de tipos; ***type-metal,*** metal de imprenta; ***type-setting,*** tipografía; ***type-setter,*** cajista, *m.f.*; ***type-script,*** mecanografiado. — *v.t.* [TYPEWRITE]; clasificar, asignar a un grupo. — *v.i.* escribir a máquina.
typewrite [ˈtaiprait], *v.t.* escribir a máquina, pasar a máquina, mecanografiar.
typewriter [ˈtaipraitə], *s.* máquina de escribir; ***typewriter ribbon,*** cinta de máquina de escribir.
typewriting [ˈtaipraitiŋ], *s.* mecanografía, dactilografía.
typhoid [ˈtaifɔid], *a.* tifoideo. — *s.* fiebre tifoidea.
typhoon [taiˈfu:n], *s.* tifón.
typhus [ˈtaifəs], *s.* tifo, tifus, *m.inv.*
typical [ˈtipikəl], *a.* típico; propio; ***that's typical of him,*** eso es muy de él.
typify [ˈtipifai], *v.t.* tipificar, simbolizar, representar.
typing [ˈtaipiŋ], *s.* mecanografía.
typist [ˈtaipist], *s.* mecanógrafa, mecanógrafo.
typographer [taiˈpɔgrəfə], *s.* tipógrafo.
typographic(al) [taipoˈgræfik(əl)], *a.* tipográfico.
typography [taiˈpɔgrəfi], *s.* tipografía.
tyrannic(al) [tiˈrænik(əl)], *a.* tiránico.
tyrannicide [tiˈrænisaid], *s.* tiranicidio; (*pers.*) tiranicida, *m.f.*
tyrannize [ˈtirənaiz], *v.t.*, *v.i.* tiranizar.
tyrannous [ˈtirənəs], *a.* tiránico.
tyranny [ˈtirəni], *s.* tiranía, tiranización.
tyrant [ˈtairənt], *s.* tirano.
Tyre [taiə]. Tiro.

tyre [taiə], *s.* neumático; cubierta; ***tyre-burst,*** reventón; ***tyre puncture,*** pinchazo; ***flat tyre,*** neumático desinflado; ***non-skid tyre,*** neumático antideslizante; ***spare tyre,*** neumático de recambio.

Tyrian [ˈtiriən], *a., s.* tirio.

tyro [ˈtaiərou], *s.* novicio, principiante.

Tyrol [tiˈroul], (**the**). (el) Tirol.

Tyrolean, Tyrolese [tirɔˈliən, -ˈli:z], *a., s.* tirolés, *m.*

tzar [zɑ:], *s.* zar.

tzarina [zɑ:ˈri:nə], *s.* zarina.

U

U, u [ju:], *s.* vigésima primera letra del alfabeto.
Ubiquitarian [ju:bikwi'tɛəriən], *a.*, *s.* ubiquitario.
ubiquitary [ju:'bikwitəri], *a.* ubicuo, omnipresente. — *s.* ubiquitario.
ubiquitous [ju:'bikwitəs], *a.* omnipresente, ubicuo.
ubiquity [ju:'bikwiti], *s.* omnipresencia, ubicuidad.
U-boat ['ju:-bout], *s.* submarino alemán.
udder ['ʌdə], *s.* ubre, *f.*
Uganda [ju:'gændə]. Uganda.
Ugandan [ju:'gændən], *a.*, *s.* ugandés, *m.*
ugh! [ʌ], *interj.* ¡puf!
uglify ['ʌglifai], *v.t.* afear.
ugliness ['ʌglinis], *s.* fealdad, (lo) feo.
ugly ['ʌgli], *a.* feo; (*fam.*) ***things are beginning to look ugly,*** la cosa se está poniendo fea, la cosa empieza a tomar mal cariz; (*fam.*) ***he's in an ugly mood,*** está de malas; ***to be as ugly as sin,*** ser más feo que Picio.
uhlan ['u:lən], *s.* (*mil.*) ulano.
ukase ['ju:keis], *s.* ucase.
Ukraine [ju'krein]. (**the**). Ucrania.
Ukrainian [ju'kreiniən], *a.*, *s.* ucranio; ***the Ukrainian Soviet Socialist Republic,*** la República Socialista Soviética de Ucrania.
ulcer ['ʌlsə], *s.* úlcera.
ulcerate ['ʌlsəreit], *v.t.* ulcerar. — *v.i.* ulcerarse.
ulceration [ʌlsə'reiʃən], *s.* ulceración.
ulcered ['ʌlsəd], *a.* ulcerado.
ulcerous ['ʌlsərəs], *a.* ulceroso.
uliginous [ju:'lidʒinəs], *a.* uliginoso.
ulmaceous [ʌl'meiʃəs], *a.* ulmáceo.
ulna ['ʌlnə], *s.* (*anat.*) cúbito.
ulnar ['ʌlnə], *a.* cubital.
Ulster ['ʌlstə]. Úlster.
ulster ['ʌlstə], *s.* úlster.
Ulsterman ['ʌlstəmən], *s.* habitante de(l) Úlster.
ulterior [ʌl'tiəriə], *a.* ulterior, posterior; ***ulterior motive*** o ***design,*** móvil oculto.
ultimate ['ʌltimit], *a.* último, final; esencial, fundamental; extremo, sumo. — ['ʌltimeit], *v.t.* terminar, finalizar. — *v.i.* resultar (***in,*** en).
ultimately ['ʌltimitli], *adv.* últimamente; por fin, a la larga.
ultimatum [ʌlti'meitəm], *s.* (*pl.* **ultimata** [ʌlti'meitə]) ultimátum.
ultimo ['ʌltimou], *adv.* (*contr.* **ult.**) del mes pasado.
ultra- ['ʌltrə], *prefijo* ultra; ***to be ultra-fashionable,*** ir a la ultimísima.
ultra ['ʌltrə], *a.* extremo, exagerado. — *s.* extremista, ultra, *m.f.*
ultramarine [ʌltrəmə'ri:n], *a.* (*color*) ultramarino. — *s.* azul ultramarino.
ultra-modern [ʌltrə-'mɔdən], *a.* ultramoderno.
ultramontane [ʌltrə'mɔntein], *a.* ultramontano.
ultramundane [ʌltrə'mʌndein], *a.* ultramundano.
ultra-violet [ʌltrə-'vaiəlit], *a.* ultravioleta.
ululate ['ju:ljuleit], *v.i.* ulular.
ululation [ju:lju'leiʃən], *s.* ululatos, *m.pl.*
umbel ['ʌmbəl], *s.* (*bot.*) umbela.
umbellate, umbelliferous ['ʌmbəleit, ʌmbə'lifərəs], *a.* umbelado, umbelífero.
umber ['ʌmbə], *s.* (*pint.*) sombra.
umbilic(al) [ʌm'bilik(əl)], *a.* umbilical; ***umbilical cord,*** cordón umbilical.
umbilicus [ʌmbi'laikəs], *s.* (*pl.* **umbilici** [-'laisi]) ombligo.
umbles ['ʌmbəlz], [NUMBLES].
umbo ['ʌmbou], *s.* umbo; umbón (*de escudo*).
umbra ['ʌmbrə], *s.* (*astron.*) sombra.
umbrage ['ʌmbridʒ], *s.* resentimiento, pique; ***to take umbrage,*** ofenderse, picarse.
umbrageous [ʌm'breidʒəs], *a.* umbroso.
umbrageousness [ʌm'breidʒəsnis], *s.* umbrosidad.
umbrella [ʌm'brelə], *s.* paraguas, *m.inv.*; (*mil.*) cortina de fuego; ***umbrella-stand,*** paragüero.
Umbria ['ʌmbriə]. (la) Umbría.
umlaut ['umlaut], *s.* metafonía.
umpire ['ʌmpaiə], *s.* árbitro. — *v.t.*, *v.i.* arbitrar.
umpteen ['ʌmp'ti:n], *a.*, *s.* muchísimos, innumerables.
umpteenth ['ʌmp'ti:nθ], *a.* enésimo.
unabashed [ʌnə'bæʃt], *a.* sin avergonzarse, sin ruborizarse.
unabated [ʌnə'beitid], *a.* sin disminución, sin amainar.
unabbreviated [ʌnə'bri:vieitid], *a.* no abreviado, sin abreviar; íntegro.
unable [ʌn'eibl], *a.* incapaz; imposibilitado; ***to be unable to do sth.,*** no poder hacer una cosa.
unabridged [ʌnə'bridʒd], *a.* no abreviado, sin abreviar; íntegro.
unabsolved [ʌnəb'zɔlvd], *a.* no absuelto.
unaccented [ʌnək'sentid], *a.* átono, no acentuado.
unacceptable [ʌnək'septəbl], *a.* inaceptable.
unacceptability, unacceptableness [ʌnəkseptə'biliti, ʌnək'septəblnis], *s.* (lo) inaceptable.
unaccepted [ʌnək'septid], *a.* inaceptado, no aceptado.
unaccommodating [ʌnə'kɔmədeitiŋ], *a.* poco servicial, poco complaciente.
unaccompanied [ʌnə'kʌmpənid], *a.* no acompañado; (*mús.*) sin acompañamiento.
unaccomplished [ʌnə'kʌmpliʃt], *a.* inacabado; de pocas dotes.
unaccountable [ʌnə'kauntəbl], *a.* inexplicable; (*pers.*) no responsable.
unaccountableness [ʌnə'kauntəblnis], *s.* (lo) inexplicable.
unaccountably [ʌnə'kauntəbli], *adv.* de una manera inexplicable.
unaccounted for [ʌnə'kauntid fɔ:], *a.* sin noticias; sin explicación; desaparecido; ***three are still unaccounted for,*** sigue sin haber noticias de tres de ellos.
unaccustomed [ʌnə'kʌstəmd], *a.* insólito; ***to be unaccustomed to doing sth.,*** no tener (la) costumbre de hacer algo.
unacknowledged [ʌnək'nɔlidʒd], *a.* no reconocido; (*carta etc.*) sin contestación, por contestar.
unacquainted [ʌnə'kweintid], *a.* ignorante; ***to be unacquainted with,*** no conocer, ignorar.
unacquired [ʌnə'kwaiəd], *a.* no adquirido.
unacquitted [ʌnə'kwitid], *a.* no absuelto.
unadaptable [ʌnə'dæptəbl], *a.* inadaptable.
unaddressed [ʌnə'drest], *a.* sin dirección.
unadjusted [ʌnə'dʒʌstid], *a.* inadaptado.
unadopted [ʌnə'dɔptid], *a.* no adoptado.
unadorned [ʌnə'dɔ:nd], *a.* sin adorno(s), sencillo.
unadulterated [ʌnə'dʌltəreitid], *a.* sin mezcla, puro; sin adulterar.
unadventurous, unadventuresome [ʌnəd'ventʃərəs, ʌnəd'ventʃəsəm], *a.* poco emprendedor, poco lanzado.
unadvisable [ʌnəd'vaizəbl], *a.* poco aconsejable.
unadvised [ʌnəd'vaizd], *a.* no aconsejado.
unadvisedly [ʌnəd'vaizidli], *adv.* imprudentemente.
unaesthetic [ʌni:s'θetik], *a.* antiestético.
unaffected [ʌnə'fektid], *a.* sin afectación, natural, sencillo; no afectado.
unaffectedly [ʌnə'fektidli], *adv.* sin afectación, de una manera natural.
unaffectedness [ʌnə'fektidnis], *s.* ausencia de afectación, naturalidad, sencillez.

unaffectionate [ʌnəˈfekʃənit], *a.* poco cariñoso.
unafflicted [ʌnəˈfliktid], *a.* no afligido, no apenado.
unafraid [ʌnəˈfreid], *a.* sin temor, sin miedo.
unaided [ʌnˈeidid], *a.* sin auxilio, sin ayuda.
unaired [ʌnˈɛəd], *a.* no ventilado.
unalienated [ʌnˈeiliəneitid], *a.* no enajenado.
unalleviated [ʌnəˈli:vieitid], *a.* sin alivio; sin tregua, interminable.
unallied [ʌnəˈlaid], *a.* no aliado; no relacionado.
unallowable [ʌnəˈlauəbl], *a.* inadmisible.
unallowed [ʌnəˈlaud], *a.* no permitido.
unalloyed [ʌnəˈlɔid], *a.* sin mezcla, puro.
unalterable [ʌnˈɔ:ltərəbl], *a.* que no (se) puede cambiar, invariable, inmutable.
unaltered [ʌnˈɔ:ltəd], *a.* que no ha cambiado; ***it remains quite unaltered,*** no ha cambiado nada.
unambiguous [ʌnæmˈbigjuəs], *a.* sin ambigüedad(es), inequívoco.
unambitious [ʌnæmˈbiʃəs], *a.* que no tiene ambiciones.
un-American [ʌn-əˈmerikən], *a.* anti(norte)-americano.
unamiable [ʌnˈeimiəbl], *a.* poco amable.
unamiableness [ʌnˈeimiəblnis], *s.* falta de amabilidad.
unanimity [ju:nəˈnimiti], *s.* unanimidad.
unanimous [ju:ˈnæniməs], *a.* unánime.
unanimousness [ju:ˈnæniməsnis], *s.* unanimidad.
unannounced [ʌnəˈnaunst], *a.* sin ser anunciado; sin anunciar.
unanswerable [ʌnˈɑ:nsərəbl], *a.* incontestable, irrebatible.
unanswered [ʌnˈɑ:nsəd], *a.* no contestado, incontestado, por contestar, sin contestar.
unappealable [ʌnəˈpi:ləbl], *a.* inapelable.
unappeasable [ʌnəˈpi:zəbl], *a.* implacable.
unappetizing [ʌnˈæpitaiziŋ], *a.* poco apetitoso; poco apetecible; (*fam., pers.*) poco atractivo.
unappreciated [ʌnəˈpri:ʃieitid], *a.* que no se aprecia.
unappreciative [ʌnəˈpri:ʃətiv], *a.* poco agradecido; poco entusiasta.
unapprehended [ʌnæpriˈhendid], *a.* sin detener.
unapprehensive [ʌnæpriˈhensiv], *a.* sin temer nada; inconsciente.
unapproachable [ʌnəˈproutʃəbl], *a.* inaccesible; inabordable, intratable.
unapproachableness [ʌnəˈproutʃəblnis], *a.* inaccesibilidad; intratabilidad.
unapproved [ʌnəˈpru:vd], *a.* no aprobado, sin aprobar.
unapt [ʌnˈæpt], *a.* poco adecuado, poco conveniente.
unarmed [ʌnˈɑ:md], *a.* inerme, indefenso.
unarranged [ʌnəˈreindʒd], *a.* sin concertar; imprevisto.
unartistic [ʌnɑ:ˈtistik], *a.* nada artístico, poco artístico.
unashamed [ʌnəˈʃeimd], *a.* descarado, desvergonzado.
unasked [ʌnˈɑ:skt], *a.* no solicitado, no pedido; no invitado, sin ser llamado *o* invitado.
unaspirated [ʌnˈæspireitid], *a.* (*letra*) no aspirada.
unassailable [ʌnəˈseiləbl], *a.* inatacable; inexpugnable; irrebatible.
unassimilated [ʌnəˈsimileitid], *a.* no asimilado.
unassisted [ʌnəˈsistid], *a.* sin ayuda, por sí solo.
unassuming [ʌnəˈsju:miŋ], *a.* modesto, sencillo, sin pretensiones.
unassured [ʌnəˈʃjuəd], *a.* poco seguro.
unattached [ʌnəˈtætʃt], *a.* suelto; no prometido, soltero; (*mil.*) de reemplazo; (*for.*) no embargado.
unattackable [ʌnəˈtækəbl], *a.* inatacable.
unattainable [ʌnəˈteinəbl], *a.* inasequible, inalcanzable.
unattained [ʌnəˈteind], *a.* no alcanzado.
unattempted [ʌnəˈtemptid], *a.* no intentado.
unattended [ʌnəˈtendid], *a.* sin guardia; sin servicio; sin personal.
unattested [ʌnəˈtestid], *a.* inatestiguado.
unattractive [ʌnəˈtræktiv], *a.* poco atractivo.
unattractiveness [ʌnəˈtræktivnis], *s.* falta de atractivo.
unauthenticated [ʌnɔ:ˈθentikeitid], *a.* no legalizado.
unauthorized [ʌnˈɔ:θəraizd], *a.* no autorizado.
unavailable [ʌnəˈveiləbl], *a.* indisponible; inasequible; (*libro*) agotado.
unavailing [ʌnəˈveiliŋ], *a.* infructuoso, inútil, vano.
unavoidable [ʌnəˈvɔidəbl], *a.* inevitable, ineludible.
unavoidableness [ʌnəˈvɔidəblnis], *s.* inevitabilidad.
unaware [ʌnəˈwɛə], *a.* inconsciente; desprevenido; ***to be unaware that,*** ignorar que; ***I am not unaware that,*** no ignoro que, no se me oculta que.
unawares [ʌnəˈwɛəz], *adv.* de improviso, inopinadamente; ***to catch s.o. unawares,*** coger desprevenido a alguien.
unawed [ʌnˈɔ:d], *a.* sin pavor, sin temor.
unbacked [ʌnˈbækt], *a.* sin respaldo; (*fig.*) sin apoyo, sin respaldo.
unbaked [ʌnˈbeikt], *a.* no cocido.
unbalance [ʌnˈbæləns], *s.* desequilibrio. — *v.t.* desequilibrar, trastornar.
unbalanced [ʌnˈbælənst], *a.* desequilibrado; trastornado; (*com.*) no saldado.
unbaptized [ʌnbæpˈtaizd], *a.* no bautizado, sin bautizar.
unbar [ʌnˈbɑ:], *v.t.* desatrancar, quitar la barra de.
unbearable [ʌnˈbɛərəbl], *a.* insoportable, insufrible, inaguantable.
unbeatable [ʌnˈbi:təbl], *a.* inmejorable; imbatible.
unbeaten [ʌnˈbi:tn], *a.* imbatido; no mejorado; invicto.
unbecoming [ʌnbiˈkʌmiŋ], *a.* impropio (***for, in, to,*** de); indecoroso; poco airoso, poco elegante.
unbefitting [ʌnbiˈfitiŋ], *a.* impropio.
unbefriended [ʌnbiˈfrendid], *a.* sin amigos, sin (el) apoyo de amigos.
unbeknown [ʌnbiˈnoun], *a.* no sabido. — *adv.* ***unbeknown to me,*** sin saberlo yo.
unbelief [ʌnbiˈli:f], *s.* incredulidad; descreimiento.
unbelievable [ʌnbiˈli:vəbl], *a.* increíble.
unbeliever [ʌnbiˈli:və], *s.* no creyente, incrédulo, descreído.
unbelieving [ʌnbiˈli:viŋ], *a.* incrédulo; descreído.
unbend [ʌnˈbend], *v.t.* desencorvar, enderezar. — *v.i.* enderezarse; flexibilizarse; distenderse; (*fig.*) expansionarse.
unbending [ʌnˈbendiŋ], *a.* inflexible; tieso, rígido.
unbias(s)ed [ʌnˈbaiəst], *a.* imparcial.
unbidden [ʌnˈbidn], *a.* sin que nadie se lo diga (dijese), sin que nadie se lo mande (mandase).
unbind [ʌnˈbaind], *v.t.* desatar.
unbleached [ʌnˈbli:tʃt], *a.* sin blanquear.
unblemished [ʌnˈblemiʃt], *a.* sin mácula, inmaculado.
unblenching [ʌnˈblentʃiŋ], *a.* impertérrito.
unblended [ʌnˈblendid], *a.* sin mezcla.
unblest [ʌnˈblest], *a.* no bendito, sin bendecir.
unblushing [ʌnˈblʌʃiŋ], *a.* que no se ruboriza, sin ruborizarse.
unbolt [ʌnˈboult], *v.t.* descorrer el cerrojo de, abrir.
unborn [ʌnˈbɔ:n], *a.* que no ha nacido todavía.
unbosom [ʌnˈbuzəm], *v.t.* descubrir, revelar. — **unbosom o.s.,** *v.r.* desahogarse, sincerarse (***to,*** con).
unbound [ʌnˈbaund], *a.* (libro) no encuadernado, sin encuadernar.
unbounded [ʌnˈbaundid], *a.* sin límites, ilimitado; desenfrenado.

unbowed [ʌnˈbaud], *a.* sin bajar la cerviz, sin domar, invicto.
unbraid [ʌnˈbreid], *v.t.* destrenzar.
unbribable [ʌnˈbraibəbl], *a.* insobornable.
unbridle [ʌnˈbraidl], *v.t.* desembridar.
unbridled [ʌnˈbraidld], *a.* desembridado; desenfrenado.
unbroken [ʌnˈbroukən], *a.* intacto, entero; ininterrumpido, continuo, sin solución de continuidad; imbatido; no domado; indómito.
unbrotherly [ʌnˈbrʌðəli], *a.* poco fraternal.
unbuckle [ʌnˈbʌkl], *v.t.* deshebillar.
unburden [ʌnˈbəːdn], *v.t.* descargar; aliviar. — **unburden o.s.,** *v.r.* desahogarse.
unburied [ʌnˈberid], *a.* insepulto.
unbusinesslike [ʌnˈbiznislaik], *a.* poco práctico; sin instinto comercial.
unbutton [ʌnˈbʌtn], *v.t.* desabotonar, desabrochar.
uncage [ʌnˈkeidʒ], *v.t.* desenjaular.
uncalled-for [ʌnˈkɔːld-fɔː], *a.* innecesario; inmerecido.
uncancelled [ʌnˈkænsəld], *a.* no anulado, sin cancelar.
uncanny [ʌnˈkæni], *a.* misterioso, extraño; (*fam.*) especial.
uncap [ʌnˈkæp], *v.t.* destapar, descubrir.
uncared-for [ʌnˈkɛəd-fɔː], *a.* descuidado, desamparado, abandonado.
uncase [ʌnˈkeis], *v.t.* sacar de una caja *o* de un estuche.
unceasing [ʌnˈsiːsiŋ], *a.* incesante, sin cesar.
unceasingly [ʌnˈsiːsiŋli], *adv.* incesantemente, sin cesar.
uncensored [ʌnˈsensəd], *a.* no censurado, sin censurar.
unceremonious [ʌnseriˈmouniəs], *a.* descortés, brusco; poco formulista; sin ceremonias.
unceremoniously [ʌnseriˈmouniəsli], *adv.* sin miramientos; lisa y llanamente.
unceremoniousness [ʌnseriˈmouniəsnis], *s.* falta de ceremonia; brusquedad.
uncertain [ʌnˈsəːtən], *a.* incierto, dudoso; indeciso, vacilante; variable.
uncertainty [ʌnˈsəːtənti], *s.* incertidumbre, duda; irresolución, indecisión.
uncertificated [ʌnsəːˈtifikitid], *a.* sin título.
uncertified [ʌnˈsəːtifaid], *a.* no certificado.
unchain [ʌnˈtʃein], *v.t.* desencadenar; libertar.
unchallengeable [ʌnˈtʃælindʒəbl], *a.* incuestionable, incontrovertible, incontestable.
unchallenged [ʌnˈtʃælindʒd], *a.* incontestado.
unchangeable [ʌnˈtʃeindʒəbl], *a.* invariable, inmutable, inalterable.
unchangeableness [ʌnˈtʃeindʒəblnis], *s.* invariabilidad, inmutabilidad.
unchanged [ʌnˈtʃeindʒd], *a.* que no ha cambiado, que sigue sin cambio.
unchanging [ʌnˈtʃeindʒiŋ], *a.* que no cambia; monótono.
uncharitable [ʌnˈtʃæritəbl], *a.* poco caritativo, poco benévolo.
uncharitableness [ʌnˈtʃæritəblnis], *s.* (lo) poco caritativo, (lo) poco benévolo.
unchaste [ʌnˈtʃeist], *a.* impúdico, deshonesto.
unchastised [ʌntʃæsˈtaizd], *a.* sin castigo, sin castigar.
unchecked [ʌnˈtʃekt], *a.* desenfrenado; no comprobado. — *adv.* sin refrenar; sin comprobar.
unchristened [ʌnˈkrisənd], *a.* no bautizado, sin bautizar.
unchristian [ʌnˈkristʃən], *a.* anticristiano; poco cristiano.
uncial [ˈʌnsiəl], *a.* uncial. — *s.* (letra) uncial.
unciform [ˈʌnsifɔːm], *a.* unciforme.
uncinate [ˈʌnsineit], *a.* uncinado.
uncircumcised [ʌnˈsəːkəmsaizd], *a.* incircunciso.
uncircumscribed [ʌnˈsəːkəmskraibd], *a.* incircunscrito.
uncivil [ʌnˈsivəl], *a.* incivil, descortés.
uncivilized [ʌnˈsivilaizd], *a.* no civilizado, sin civilizar; bárbaro, salvaje.
unclad [ʌnˈklæd], *a.* desnudo, sin vestir.
unclaimed [ʌnˈkleimd], *a.* no reclamado, sin reclamar.
unclasp [ʌnˈklɑːsp], *v.t.* desabrochar; desengarzar; desatar, abrir.
unclassifiable [ʌnˈklæsifaiəbl], *a.* inclasificable.
uncle [ʌŋkl], *s.* tío; (*fam.*) prestamista, *m.f.*; (*fam.*) ***Uncle Sam,*** tío Sam (*símbolo de los Estados Unidos*).
unclean [ʌnˈkliːn], *a.* sucio, desaseado; inmundo, impuro.
uncleanliness, uncleanness [ʌnˈklenlinis, ʌnˈkliːnnis], *s.* suciedad; impureza.
uncleansed [ʌnˈklenzd], *a.* sin limpiar.
unclench [ʌnˈklentʃ], *v.t.* abrir, desapretar.
uncloak [ʌnˈklouk], *v.t.* (*fig.*) revelar, descubrir.
unclog [ʌnˈklɔg], *v.t.* desatrancar.
unclothed [ʌnˈklouðd], *a.* desnudo, sin vestir.
unclouded [ʌnˈklaudid], *a.* sin nubes; (*fig.*) sin amenazas, despejado.
unco [ˈʌnkou], *adv.* (*Esco.*) extraordinariamente; en extremo, demasiado.
uncock [ʌnˈkɔk], *v.t.* desmontar.
uncoil [ʌnˈkɔil], *v.t.* desenrollar. — *v.i.* desenrollarse; desovillarse; desanillarse, desenroscarse.
uncoined [ʌnˈkɔind], *a.* no acuñado.
uncollected [ʌnkəˈlektid], *a.* disperso; no recogido; (*pago etc.*) no cobrado, sin cobrar.
uncoloured [ʌnˈkʌləd], *a.* sin color; descolorado; en blanco; objetivo, imparcial.
uncombed [ʌnˈkoumd], *a.* despeinado, sin peinar.
uncomeliness [ʌnˈkʌmlinis], *s.* desgarbo.
uncomely [ʌnˈkʌmli], *a.* desgarbado.
uncomfortable [ʌnˈkʌmfətəbl], *a.* incómodo; molesto; penoso, desagradable; ***to be uncomfortable,*** estar incómodo; estar inquieto; ***to feel uncomfortable about sth.,*** estar inquieto por algo; ***to make life uncomfortable for s.o.,*** amargarle la vida a alguien.
uncomfortableness [ʌnˈkʌmfətəblnis], *s.* incomodidad; malestar.
uncommitted [ʌnkəˈmitid], *a.* no comprometido; no alineado.
uncommon [ʌnˈkɔmən], *a.* poco común, poco *o* nada frecuente; insólito; especial.
uncommonly [ʌnˈkɔmənli], *adv.* raramente, rara vez; extraordinariamente; ***not uncommonly,*** con cierta frecuencia, no pocas veces.
uncommonness [ʌnˈkɔmənnis], *s.* infrecuencia; (lo) poco frecuente.
uncommunicative [ʌnkəˈmjuːnikətiv], *a.* poco comunicativo; poco expresivo; reservado.
uncommunicativeness [ʌnkəˈmjuːnikətivnis], *s.* reserva.
uncompassionate [ʌnkəmˈpæʃənit], *a.* poco compasivo.
uncompensated [ʌnˈkɔmpenseitid], *a.* sin compensación.
uncomplaining [ʌnkəmˈpleiniŋ], *a.* resignado, sumiso; que no se queja.
uncompleted [ʌnkəmˈpliːtid], *a.* inacabado, inconcluso, sin terminar.
uncomplimentary [ʌnkɔmpliˈmentəri], *a.* poco halagüeño, nada lisonjero, desfavorable.
uncomplying [ʌnkəmˈplaiiŋ], *a.* poco complaciente.
uncompounded [ʌnkəmˈpaundid], *a.* no compuesto, sencillo.
uncompressed [ʌnkəmˈprest], *a.* no comprimido.
uncompromising [ʌnˈkɔmprəmaiziŋ], *a.* intransigente, inflexible.

unconcealed [ʌnkənˈsiːld], *a.* no escondido, patente.
unconcern [ʌnkənˈsəːn], *s.* sangre fría, frialdad; calma, tranquilidad; indiferencia.
unconcerned [ʌnkənˈsəːnd], *a.* indiferente; tranquilo; despreocupado.
unconcernedly [ʌnkənˈsəːnidli], *adv.* con sangre fría; indiferentemente.
uncondensed [ʌnkənˈdenst], *a.* no compendiado, sin compendiar.
unconditional [ʌnkənˈdiʃənəl], *a.* incondicional, sin condiciones, *f.pl.*
unconditioned [ʌnkənˈdiʃənd], *a.* no condicionado.
unconfessed [ʌnkɔnˈfest], *a.* inconfeso.
unconfined [ʌnkənˈfaind], *a.* sin límites, sin trabas, sin estorbos.
uncongealed [ʌnkənˈdʒiːld], *a.* no cuajado, sin cuajar.
uncongenial [ʌnkənˈdʒiːniəl], *a.* poco simpático; incompatible; ***uncongenial job,*** trabajo *o* empleo que a uno no le va.
uncongeniality, uncongenialness [ʌnkəndʒiːniˈæliti, ʌnkənˈdʒiːniəlnis], *s.* poca simpatía; incompatibilidad.
unconnected [ʌnkəˈnektid], *a.* inconexo; no relacionado, sin relación.
unconquerable [ʌnˈkɔŋkərəbl], *a.* inconquistable, invencible.
unconquered [ʌnˈkɔŋkəd], *a.* invicto, sin vencer.
unconscientious [ʌnkɔnʃiˈenʃəs], *a.* poco concienzudo, poco meticuloso.
unconscionable [ʌnˈkɔnʃənəbl], *a.* desmedido, enorme.
unconscious [ʌnˈkɔnʃəs], *a.* inconsciente; sin conocimiento, que ha perdido el conocimiento; no intencionado, dicho *o* hecho sin querer.
unconsciously [ʌnˈkɔnʃəsli], *adv.* inconscientemente; involuntariamente, sin querer.
unconsciousness [ʌnˈkɔnʃəsnis], *s.* inconsciencia; pérdida de conocimiento.
unconsecrated [ʌnˈkɔnsikreitid], *a.* no consagrado, sin consagrar.
unconstitutional [ʌnkɔnstiˈtjuːʃənəl], *a.* anticonstitucional, inconstitucional.
unconstrained [ʌnkənˈstreind], *a.* espontáneo, libre, voluntario, sin constreñimientos.
unconsumed [ʌnkənˈsjuːmd], *a.* no consumido.
uncontaminated [ʌnkənˈtæmineitid], *a.* incontaminado, sin contaminaciones.
uncontested [ʌnkənˈtestid], *a.* incontestado, indiscutido.
uncontrollable [ʌnkənˈtrouləbl], *a.* ingobernable, irrefrenable, irresistible; incontrolable.
uncontrolled [ʌnkənˈtrould], *a.* libre, sin trabas, sin control.
unconventional [ʌnkənˈvenʃənəl], *a.* poco convencional, poco ortodoxo.
unconventionality [ʌnkənvenʃəˈnæliti], *s.* (lo) poco convencional, (lo) poco ortodoxo, extravagancia.
unconverted [ʌnkənˈvəːtid], *a.* no convertido, sin convertir.
unconvicted [ʌnkənˈviktid], *a.* no declarado culpable.
unconvinced [ʌnkənˈvinst], *a.* no convencido.
unconvincing [ʌnkənˈvinsiŋ], *a.* poco convincente.
uncooked [ʌnˈkukt], *a.* sin guisar, crudo.
uncork [ʌnˈkɔːk], *v.t.* descorchar, destapar.
uncorrected [ʌnkəˈrektid], *a.* sin corregir.
uncorrupted [ʌnkəˈrʌptid], *a.* incorrupto.
uncouple [ʌnˈkʌpl], *v.t.* desacoplar; soltar, zafar.
uncouth [ʌnˈkuːθ], *a.* grosero, zafio; rudo, que tiene el pelo de la dehesa, cerril.
uncouthness [ʌnˈkuːθnis], *s.* grosería; cerrilismo.
uncover [ʌnˈkʌvə], *v.t.* descubrir, destapar; revelar; dejar al descubierto. — *v.i.* descubrirse.
uncovered [ʌnˈkʌvəd], *a.* descubierto, sin cubierta.
uncreated [ʌnkriˈeitid], *a.* increado.
uncritical [ʌnˈkritikəl], *a.* sin sentido crítico; poco exigente.
uncropped [ʌnˈkrɔpt], *a.* no segado; no cortado.
uncross [ʌnˈkrɔs], *v.t.* descruzar.
uncrossed [ʌnˈkrɔst], *a.* (*cheque*) sin cruzar.
uncrown [ʌnˈkraun], *v.t.* descoronar.
uncrowned [ʌnˈkraund], *a.* no coronado; sin corona; destronado.
unction [ˈʌŋkʃən], *s.* unción, ungimiento; ungüento, untura; celo, fervor; efusión; ***extreme unction,*** extremaunción.
unctuous [ˈʌŋktjuəs], *a.* untuoso; zalamero, meloso.
unctuousness [ˈʌŋktjuəsnis], *s.* untuosidad; celo fingido *o* afectado; zalamería.
uncultivable [ʌnˈkʌltivəbl], *a.* incultivable.
uncultivated [ʌnˈkʌltiveitid], *a.* sin cultivar.
uncultured [ʌnˈkʌltʃəd], *a.* inculto, iletrado.
uncurbable [ʌnˈkəːbəbl], *a.* indomable.
uncurbed [ʌnˈkəːbd], *a.* indómito.
uncurl [ʌnˈkəːl], *v.t., v.i.* desrizar(se), desenroscar(se).
uncurtailed [ʌnkəːˈteild], *a.* no abreviado; sin reducción.
uncustomary [ʌnˈkʌstəməri], *a.* insólito.
uncut [ʌnˈkʌt], *a.* sin cortar; sin labrar, en bruto, sin tallar; intonso.
undamaged [ʌnˈdæmidʒd], *a.* indemne; intacto.
undated [ʌnˈdeitid], *a.* sin fecha.
undaunted [ʌnˈdɔːntid], *a.* impávido, impertérrito; intrépido, denodado; sin arredrarse.
undecayed [ʌndiˈkeid], *a.* intacto, sin deterioro(s).
undeceive [ʌndiˈsiːv], *v.t.* desengañar, desilusionar; sacar de engaño a.
undecided [ʌndiˈsaidid], *a.* no decidido *o* resuelto; pendiente; (*pers.*) indeciso.
undecipherable [ʌndiˈsaifərəbl], *a.* indescifrable.
undecisive [ʌndiˈsaisiv], *a.* no decisivo; vacilante, irresoluto.
undeclinable [ʌndiˈklainəbl], *a.* (*gram.*) indeclinable.
undefeated [ʌndiˈfiːtid], *a.* imbatido, invicto.
undefended [ʌndiˈfendid], *a.* sin defensa, indefenso.
undefiled [ʌndiˈfaild], *a.* inmaculado, impoluto.
undefinable [ʌndiˈfainəbl], *a.* indefinible.
undefined [ʌndiˈfaind], *a.* no definido, indefinido.
undelayed [ʌndiˈleid], *a.* sin demora(s).
undelivered [ʌndiˈlivəd], *a.* no entregado, sin entregar.
undemonstrative [ʌndiˈmɔnstrətiv], *a.* poco efusivo, poco expresivo.
undeniable [ʌndiˈnaiəbl], *a.* innegable.
undenominational [ʌndinɔmiˈneiʃənəl], *a.* no sectario.
undependable [ʌndiˈpendəbl], *a.* informal, que no es de fiar.
under [ˈʌndə], *a.* inferior. — *adv.* debajo; ***to bring under,*** someter; ***to go under,*** hundirse; ***to keep under,*** tener en sujeción; (*fam.*) tener metido en un puño. — *prep.* debajo de, por debajo de; (*fig.*) bajo; ***under age,*** menor de edad; ***under 21,*** de menos de 21 años; ***under arms,*** bajo las armas; ***under lock and key,*** bajo llave; ***under oath,*** bajo juramento; ***under pressure (from),*** bajo presión (de), presionado (por); ***under sail,*** a la vela; ***under sentence of death,*** reo de muerte; ***under the hand of,*** firmado por; (*fam.*) ***under the influence,*** bebido, borracho; ***under the necessity of,*** en la necesidad de; (*fam.*) ***under the nose of,*** en las barbas de; ***under (the) threat of,*** bajo (la) amenaza de; (*fam.*) ***to feel*** o ***to be under the weather,*** estar alicaído; encontrarse malucho; ***under way,*** en camino; ***we're under way,*** (*mar.*) ya zarpamos; (*f.c.*) ya arrancamos.
underbelly [ˈʌndəbeli], *s.* (*aer. etc.*) panza.

underbid [ʌndəˈbid], *v.t.* ofrecer menos que.
underbrush [ˈʌndəbrʌʃ], *s.* maleza.
undercarriage [ˈʌndəkæridʒ], *s.* (*aer.*) tren de aterrizaje.
undercharge [ʌndəˈtʃɑːdʒ], *v.t.* cobrar de menos *o* menos del precio justo.
underclothes [ˈʌndəklouðz], *s.pl.* ropa interior, paños menores, *m.pl.*
underclothing [ˈʌndəklouðiŋ], *s.* [UNDERCLOTHES].
undercoat [ˈʌndəkout], *s.* (*pint.*) primera capa.
undercurrent [ˈʌndəkʌrənt], *s.* corriente submarina, resaca; (*fig.*) tendencia oculta, ambiente sordo.
undercut [ˈʌndəkʌt], *s.* solomillo, filete (*de carne*). — [ʌndəˈkʌt], *v.t.* vender más barato que.
underdeveloped [ʌndədiˈveləpt], *a.* subdesarrollado; (*foto.*) revelado insuficientemente.
underdog [ˈʌndədɔg], *s.* (*fig.*) desvalido, desheredado, descamisado.
underdone [ʌndəˈdʌn], *a.* (*coc.*) poco pasado.
underestimate [ʌndərˈestimit], *s.* estimación (demasiado) baja; presupuesto (demasiado) bajo. — [-meit], *v.t.* subestimar, apreciar (demasiado) poco; presupuestar (demasiado) bajo.
underexpose [ʌndəriksˈpouz], *v.t.* (*foto.*) relevar de menos.
underfeed [ʌndəˈfiːd], *v.t.* subalimentar.
underfoot [ʌndəˈfut], *adv.* debajo de los pies.
undergo [ʌndəˈgou], *v.t.* sufrir, experimentar; (*med.*) ***undergo an operation,*** operarse.
undergraduate [ʌndəˈgrædjuit], *s.* estudiante (universitario) no licenciado.
underground [ˈʌndəgraund], *a.* subterráneo; (*fig.*) clandestino. — [ʌndəˈgraund], *adv.* bajo tierra, subterráneamente; (*fig.*) clandestinamente. — [ˈʌndəgraund], *s.* (*f.c.*) metro; (*mil.*) resistencia; movimiento clandestino.
undergrowth [ˈʌndəgrouθ], *s.* matorrales, *m.pl.*, maleza.
underhand, underhanded [ˈʌndəˈhænd, -id], *a.* clandestino, hecho bajo cuerda, solapado, poco directo, poco limpio.
underlay [ˈʌndəlei], *s.* (*impr.*) calzo, realce. — [ʌndəˈlei], *v.t.* (*impr.*) calzar; reforzar.
underlie [ʌndəˈlai], *v.t.* estar debajo de; ser la razón fundamental de, ser la causa de.
underline [ʌndəˈlain], *v.t.* subrayar.
underling [ˈʌndəliŋ], *s.* inferior, subordinado; secuaz, paniagudo, hechura.
underlining [ʌndəˈlainiŋ], *s.* subrayada.
underlying [ʌndəˈlaiiŋ], *a.* (*geol.*) subyacente; fundamental, básico.
undermine [ʌndəˈmain], *v.t.* (*min.*) zapar, socavar; (*fig.*) minar.
underminer [ʌndəˈmainə], *s.* zapador; minador.
undermost [ˈʌndəmoust], *a.* (el) más bajo, ínfimo. — *adv.* debajo del todo.
underneath [ʌndəˈniːθ], *adv.* debajo, por debajo. — *prep.* debajo de.
undernourished [ʌndəˈnʌriʃt], *a.* desnutrido.
undernourishment [ʌndəˈnʌriʃmənt], *s.* desnutrición.
underpaid [ʌndəˈpeid], *a.* mal pagado, mal retribuido.
underpants [ˈʌndəpænts], (*Am.*) [PANTS].
underpass [ˈʌndəpɑːs], *s.* paso inferior.
underpin [ʌndəˈpin], *v.t.* socalzar, apuntalar.
underpinning [ʌndəˈpiniŋ], *s.* apuntalamiento.
underplay [ˈʌndəˈplei], *v.t.*, *v.i.* (*teat.*) hacer (*un papel*) sin alardes.
underplot [ˈʌndəplɔt], *s.* intriga accesoria, trama secreta; (*teat.*) acción secundaria.
underpopulated [ʌndəˈpɔpjuleitid], *a.* poco poblado.
underpraise [ʌndəˈpreiz], *v.t.* no elogiar suficientemente.
underprice [ʌndəˈprais], *v.t.* valorar muy bajo.
underprize [ʌndəˈpraiz], *v.t.* apreciar en menos de su valor.
underproduction [ʌndəprəˈdʌkʃən], *s.* producción insuficiente.
underprop [ʌndəˈprɔp], *v.t.* sostener, apuntalar, poner puntales a.
underrate [ʌndəˈreit], *v.t.* apreciar en demasiado poco; subestimar; no hacer justicia a.
underripe [ʌndəˈraip], *a.* poco maduro.
underscore [ʌndəˈskɔː], *v.t.* subrayar.
undersea [ʌndəˈsiː], (*Am.*) [UNDERWATER].
under-secretary [ˈʌndə-ˈsekrətri], *s.* subsecretario.
undersell [ʌndəˈsel], *v.t.* vender (*las cosas*) a un precio más bajo que.
undershirt [ˈʌndəʃəːt], *s.* (*Am.*) camiseta.
underside [ˈʌndəsaid], *s.* cara inferior, revés, *m.*, envés, *m.*
undersign [ʌndəˈsain], *v.t.* (*ant.*) firmar.
undersigned [ˈʌndəˈsaind], *a.*, *s.* ***the undersigned,*** (el) infrascrito, ***we the undersigned,*** (nosotros) los infrascritos.
undersized [ˈʌndəsaizd], *a.* de tamaño exiguo *o* insuficiente.
underskirt [ˈʌndəskəːt], *s.* enagua, refajo.
understaffed [ʌndəˈstɑːft], *a.* falto de personal.
understand [ʌndəˈstænd], (*irr.*) *v.t.*, *v.i.* entender, comprender; tener entendido; sobretender; ***to give to understand,*** dar a entender (que); ***they understand each other,*** se entienden.
understandable [ʌndəˈstændəbl], *a.* comprensible.
understanding [ʌndəˈstændiŋ], *a.* comprensivo. — *s.* entendimiento; inteligencia; comprensión; acuerdo, arreglo, avenencia; simpatía, comprensión mutua; ***good understanding,*** buena armonía; ***on the understanding that...,*** con tal que, bien entendido que...; ***to come to an understanding,*** llegar a un acuerdo.
understate [ʌndəˈsteit], *v.t.* declarar incompletamente; decir sin el debido énfasis *o* con (demasiada) modestia.
understatement [ˈʌndəsteitmənt], *s.* declaración modesta *o* incompleta; (*gram.*) atenuación; ***that's the understatement of the year!*** ¡y usted que lo diga! ¡y que lo digas!
understood [ʌndəˈstud], *a.* sobrentendido. — *p.p.* [UNDERSTAND]; ***be it understood,*** que conste (que); ***that is understood,*** se da por supuesto.
understudy [ˈʌndəstʌdi], *s.* (*teat.*) suplente. — *v.t.* doblar, suplir; aprender un papel para suplir.
undertake [ʌndəˈteik], *irr. v.t.* emprender, acometer; tomar a cargo; comprometerse a hacer; encargarse de.
undertaker [ˈʌndəteikə], *s.* director de pompas fúnebres.
undertaking [ʌndəˈteikiŋ], *s.* empresa; compromiso, promesa; (*for.*) garantía.
undertone [ˈʌndətoun], *s.* voz baja; (*fig.*) fondo; ***in an undertone,*** en voz baja.
undertow [ˈʌndətou], *s.* (*mar.*) resaca.
undervaluation [ʌndəvæljuˈeiʃən], *s.* valorización demasiado baja; subestimación.
undervalue [ʌndəˈvæljuː], *v.t.* valorar *o* valorizar demasiado bajo; subestimar.
underwater [ˈʌndəwɔːtə], *a.* submarino.
underwear [ˈʌndəwɛə], *s.* [UNDERCLOTHES].
underweight [ʌndəˈweit], *a.* de poco peso, de peso insuficiente.
underwood [ˈʌndəwud], *s.* matorrales, *m.pl.*, monte bajo.
underworld [ˈʌndəwəːld], *s.* averno, infierno; (*criminal*) hampa, inframundo, submundo, bajos fondos, *m.pl.*
underwrite [ˈʌndərait], *v.t. irr.* subscribir; asegurar, reasegurar.

underwriter [ˈʌndəraitə], *s.* suscriptor de valores; asegurador; (*pl.*) compañía aseguradora.
undescribable [ʌndiˈskraibəbl], *a.* indescriptible.
undeserved [ʌndiˈzə:vd], *a.* inmerecido, injusto, inmérito.
undeserving [ʌndiˈzə:viŋ], *a.* indigno; que no merece.
undesignedly [ʌndiˈzainidli], *adv.* sin designio premeditado.
undesigning [ʌndiˈzainiŋ], *a.* desinteresado.
undesirable [ʌndiˈzaiərəbl], *a.* poco deseable, indeseable. — *s.* (*fam.*, *pers.*) indeseable.
undesired [ʌndiˈzaiəd], *a.* que no se desea, no deseado.
undetected [ʌndiˈtektid], *a.* no descubierto, sin descubrir.
undetermined [ʌndiˈtə:mind], *a.* sin especificar.
undeterred [ʌndiˈtə:d], *a.* impertérrito, sin arredrarse.
undeveloped [ʌndiˈveləpt], *a.* sin desarrollar; (terrenos) sin explotar; (*foto.*) sin revelar; inmaturo.
undeviating [ʌnˈdi:vieitiŋ], *a.* constante, sin vacilaciones; inexorable.
undigested [ʌndiˈdʒestid], *a.* no digerido, sin digerir.
undignified [ʌnˈdignifaid], *a.* poco decoroso; poco serio.
undiluted [ʌndaiˈl(j)u:tid], *a.* sin diluir, puro.
undiminished [ʌndiˈminiʃt], *a.* no disminuido; sin merma.
undimmed [ʌnˈdimd], *a.* sin merma (de luz).
undiplomatic [ʌndipləˈmætik], *a.* poco diplomático.
undiscerned [ʌndiˈsə:nd], *a.* desapercibido.
undiscernible [ʌndiˈsə:nibl], *a.* imperceptible, invisible.
undiscerning [ʌndiˈsə:niŋ], *a.* sin discernimiento.
undischarged [ʌndisˈtʃɑ:dʒd], *a.* (*com.*) no pagado, sin pagar; (*mil.*) sin licenciar.
undisciplinable [ʌnˈdisiplinəbl], *a.* indisciplinable.
undisciplined [ʌnˈdisiplind], *a.* indisciplinado.
undisclosed [ʌndisˈklouzd], *a.* no descubierto, no revelado.
undiscovered [ʌndisˈkʌvəd], *a.* no descubierto, por descubrir.
undiscriminating [ʌndisˈkrimineitiŋ], *a.* sin discernimiento; poco exigente.
undisguised [ʌndisˈgaizd], *a.* sin disfraz; abierto, franco.
undismayed [ʌndisˈmeid], *a.* impávido; no desanimado; sin arredrarse.
undisputed [ʌndisˈpju:tid], *a.* indiscutido.
undissolvable [ʌndiˈzɔlvəbl], *a.* indisoluble.
undissolved [ʌndiˈzɔlvd], *a.* no disuelto.
undistinguishable [ʌndisˈtiŋgwiʃəbl], *a.* indistinguible.
undistinguished [ʌndisˈtiŋgwiʃt], *a.* sin distinción, sin pena ni gloria.
undistorted [ʌndisˈtɔ:tid], *a.* no deformado; (*fig.*) sin desnaturalizar, no falseado, no tergiversado.
undisturbed [ʌndisˈtə:bd], *a.* tranquilo; ***to leave things undisturbed,*** dejar las cosas como están; ***to leave s.o. undisturbed,*** no molestar a alguien, dejar a alguien en paz.
undivided [ʌndiˈvaidid], *a.* indiviso, íntegro, entero; ***I want your undivided attention,*** quiero que me presten toda su atención.
undo [ʌnˈdu:], *v.t. irr.* deshacer; desatar; desabrochar; abrir; ***undo a door,*** abrir una puerta; ***undo one's hair,*** soltarse el pelo; (*fig.*) ***to be undone,*** estar perdido *o* arruinado; ***come undone,*** desatarse, deshacerse; ***leave undone,*** dejar sin hacer; ***remain undone,*** quedar por hacer.
undock [ʌnˈdɔk], *v.t.* sacar (*un buque*) de un dique *o* dársena. — *v.i.* salir del dique *o* del puerto.
undoer [ʌnˈdu:ə], *s.* el que deshace; el que arruina.
undoing [ʌnˈdu:iŋ], *s.* ruina, perdición; ***this was his undoing,*** esto fue su perdición, esto le perdió.
undoubted [ʌnˈdautid], *a.* indudable, indiscutible.
undoubtedly [ʌnˈdautidli], *adv.* sin duda, indudablemente.
undoubting [ʌnˈdautiŋ], *a.* que no duda.
undreamed-of, undreamt-of [ʌnˈdri:md-ɔv, ʌnˈdremt-ɔv], *a.* no soñado, inimaginable.
undress [ˈʌnˈdres], *s.* traje de casa; ***undress*** (***uniform***)***,*** uniforme de diario, de cuartel; ***to be in undress,*** estar de trapillo. — *v.t.* desnudar; desvendar (*una herida*). — *v.i.* desnudarse, desvestirse.
undressed [ʌnˈdrest], *a.* desnudo, sin vestir; (*com.*) en bruto; en rama; sin curtir; no cepillado (*madera*); (*coc.*) sin aliño.
undrinkable [ʌnˈdriŋkəbl], *a.* imbebible, que no hay quien lo beba.
undue [ʌnˈdju:], *a.* indebido; excesivo, desmedido.
undulate [ˈʌndjuleit], *v.i.* ondular.
undulated [ˈʌndjuleitid], *a.* ondulado.
undulating [ˈʌndjuleitiŋ], *a.* ondulante; ondulado.
undulation [ʌndjuˈleiʃən], *s.* ondulación.
undulatory [ˈʌndjulətri], *a.* ondulatorio.
unduly [ʌnˈdju:li], *adv.* indebidamente; excesivamente.
undutiful [ʌnˈdju:tiful], *a.* poco cumplidor; irrespetuoso, insumiso.
undutifulness [ʌnˈdju:tifulnis], *s.* (lo) poco cumplidor; irrespetuosidad.
undyed [ʌnˈdaid], *a.* sin teñir.
undying [ʌnˈdaiiŋ], *a.* inmortal, imperecedero; ***undying love,*** amor eterno.
unearned [ʌnˈə:nd], *a.* inmerecido; no ganado; ***unearned income,*** renta de inversiones.
unearth [ʌnˈə:θ], *v.t.* desenterrar; (*fig.*) descubrir.
unearthing [ʌnˈə:θiŋ], *s.* desenterramiento; (*fig.*) descubrimiento.
unearthly [ʌnˈə:θli], *a.* sobrenatural, espectral, fantasmagórico; (*fam.*) (*hora*) intempestiva.
uneasily [ʌnˈi:zili], *adv.* con inquietud, de una manera inquieta.
uneasiness [ʌnˈi:zinis], *s.* inquietud, intranquilidad, desasosiego.
uneasy [ʌnˈi:zi], *a.* inquieto, intranquilo, desasosegado; ***to become uneasy,*** inquietarse, intranquilizarse, desasosegarse; ***I am uneasy about it,*** (esto) me inquieta *o* me tiene inquieto.
uneatable [ʌnˈi:təbl], *a.* incomible, que no hay quien lo coma.
uneconomic [ʌni:kəˈnɔmik], *a.* antieconómico.
unedifying [ʌnˈedifaiiŋ], *a.* poco edificante.
uneducated [ʌnˈedjukeitid], *a.* inculto.
unemotional [ʌniˈmouʃənəl], *a.* poco sentimental; impasible; objetivo.
unemployable [ʌnimˈplɔiəbl], *a.* inútil, que no sirve para el trabajo.
unemployed [ʌnimˈplɔid], *a.* parado, sin trabajo, sin empleo; cesante; (*com.*) sin invertir. — *s.* (*pl.*) ***the unemployed,*** los parados.
unemployment [ʌnimˈplɔimənt], *s.* paro (forzoso), desempleo; ***unemployment benefit,*** subsidio de paro.
unencumbered [ʌninˈkʌmbəd], *a.* desembarazado.
unending [ʌnˈendiŋ], *a.* inacabable, interminable.
unendowed [ʌninˈdaud], *a.* sin dote(s).
unendurable [ʌninˈdjuərəbl], *a.* intolerable, insoportable, insufrible.
unenduring [ʌninˈdjuəriŋ], *a.* no duradero, de poca duración.
unengaged [ʌninˈgeidʒd], *a.* no comprometido; libre; desocupado.
unengaging [ʌninˈgeidʒiŋ], *a.* poco atractivo.
unenlightened [ʌninˈlaitnd], *a.* poco inteligente, poco inspirado.

unenterprising [ʌn'entəpraiziŋ], *a.* poco emprendedor, sin iniciativa, de poca(s) iniciativa(s).
unentertaining [ʌnentə'teiniŋ], *a.* de poco interés, poco divertido.
unenviable [ʌn'enviəbl], *a.* poco envidiable.
unenvied [ʌn'envid], *a.* poco envidiado.
unequal [ʌn'i:kwəl], *a.* desigual; ***unequal to,*** insuficiente para, sin capacidad para, sin fuerzas para.
unequalled [ʌn'i:kwəld], *a.* inigualado, sin igual, sin par.
unequivocal [ʌni'kwivəkəl], *a.* inequívoco.
unerring [ʌn'ə:riŋ], *a.* infalible, certero.
unessential [ʌni'senʃəl], *a.* no esencial.
uneven [ʌn'i:vən], *a.* desigual; irregular; desnivelado; impar.
unevenness [ʌn'i:vənnis], *s.* desigualdad; irregularidad; desnivelación, desnivel.
uneventful [ʌni'ventful], *a.* sin accidentes *o* acontecimientos; tranquilo.
unexampled [ʌnig'zɑ:mpld], *a.* sin igual.
unexceptionable [ʌnik'sepʃənəbl], *a.* intachable, impecable.
unexceptional [ʌnik'sepʃənəl], *a.* corriente, vulgar.
unexciting [ʌnik'saitiŋ], *a.* poco interesante *o* emocionante, anodino.
unexhausted [ʌnig'zɔ:stid], *a.* sin agotar.
unexpected [ʌniks'pektid], *a.* inesperado, imprevisto, inopinado.
unexpended [ʌniks'pendid], *a.* sin gastar, no gastado.
unexpensive [ʌniks'pensiv], *a.* barato, económico.
unexperienced [ʌniks'piəriənst], *a.* inexperto; no experimentado.
unexpired [ʌniks'paiəd], *a.* no vencido, no caducado.
unexplainable [ʌniks'pleinəbl], *a.* inexplicable.
unexplained [ʌniks'pleind], *a.* inexplicado.
unexplored [ʌniks'plɔ:d], *a.* sin explorar.
unexposed [ʌniks'pouzd], *a.* no expuesto; inexpuesto.
unexpressed [ʌniks'prest], *a.* tácito, sobrentendido; no expresado, sin expresar.
unexpressive [ʌniks'presiv], *a.* poco expresivo.
unexpurgated [ʌn'ekspəgeitid], *a.* sin expurgar, íntegro; ***unexpurgated version,*** texto íntegro.
unfaded [ʌn'feidid], *a.* no marchitado, sin ajar.
unfading [ʌn'feidiŋ], *a.* inmarcesible.
unfailing [ʌn'feiliŋ], *a.* inagotable; indefectible; infalible.
unfair [ʌn'fɛə], *a.* injusto; sin equidad; (*juego*) sucio; abusivo; ***how unfair!*** ¡no hay derecho!
unfairness [ʌn'fɛənis], *s.* injusticia; suciedad.
unfaithful [ʌn'feiθful], *a.* infiel.
unfaithfulness [ʌn'feiθfulnis], *s.* infidelidad.
unfaltering [ʌn'fɔ:ltəriŋ], *a.* resuelto, firme, sin fallar.
unfalteringly [ʌn'fɔ:ltəriŋli], *adv.* sin vacilar.
unfamiliar [ʌnfə'miliə], *a.* nuevo, desconocido; ***to be unfamiliar with,*** no conocer, desconocer; ***I am unfamiliar with it,*** no me es familiar.
unfashionable [ʌn'fæʃənəbl], *a.* pasado de moda, fuera de moda; que no está de moda; poco actual.
unfashionableness [ʌn'fæʃənəblnis], *s.* (lo) fuera de moda.
unfasten [ʌn'fɑ:sən], *v.t.* desatar; desabrochar; soltar; ***to come unfastened,*** soltarse.
unfatherly [ʌn'fɑ:ðəli], *a.* falto de comprensión paternal.
unfathomable [ʌn'fæðəməbl], *a.* insondable.
unfavourable [ʌn'feivərəbl], *a.* desfavorable; adverso, poco propicio.
unfeasible [ʌn'fi:zibl], *a.* impracticable, no factible.
unfed [ʌn'fed], *a.* sin alimento, sin alimentar.
unfeeling [ʌn'fi:liŋ], *a.* insensible; sin sentimientos.
unfeigned [ʌn'feind], *a.* no fingido; verdadero, sincero, auténtico.
unfenced [ʌn'fenst], *a.* sin cerca, sin valla.
unfermented [ʌnfə'mentid], *a.* no fermentado, sin fermentar.
unfertile [ʌn'fə:tail], *a.* infecundo.
unfetter [ʌn'fetə], *v.t.* desencadenar; quitar los grillos a.
unfettered [ʌn'fetəd], *a.* sin trabas.
unfilial [ʌn'filiəl], *a.* indigno *o* impropio de un hijo.
unfinished [ʌn'finiʃt] *a.* inacabado, no terminado, sin acabar, sin terminar; incompleto.
unfit [ʌn'fit], *a.* incapaz (***to,*** de); no apto, poco adecuado (***for,*** para); (*dep.*) lesionado.
unfitted [ʌn'fitid], *a.* que no está preparado (***for,*** para); que no tiene capacidad (***for,*** para).
unfitting [ʌn'fitiŋ], *a.* impropio, poco adecuado.
unfix [ʌn'fiks], *v.t.* desatar, desprender, soltar.
unflagging [ʌn'flægiŋ], *a.* infatigable, incansable.
unfledged [ʌn'fledʒd], *a.* implume; (*fig.*) inmaturo.
unflinching [ʌn'flintʃiŋ], *a.* impávido.
unfold [ʌn'fould], *v.t.* desplegar, desdoblar; (*fig.*) descubrir, revelar; exponer. — *v.i.* desplegarse *etc.*
unforced [ʌn'fɔ:st], *a.* natural; dicho *o* hecho con naturalidad.
unfordable [ʌn'fɔ:dəbl], *a.* invadeable.
unforeseeable [ʌnfɔ:'si:əbl], *a.* imprevisible.
unforeseen [ʌnfɔ:'si:n], *a.* imprevisto, inopinado.
unforgettable [ʌnfə'getəbl], *a.* inolvidable.
unforgivable [ʌnfə'givəbl], *a.* imperdonable, que no tiene perdón.
unforgiving [ʌnfə'giviŋ], *a.* implacable, que no perdona; rencoroso.
unforgotten [ʌnfə'gɔtn], *a.* no olvidado, que no se olvida, que no se ha olvidado.
unformed [ʌn'fɔ:md], *a.* sin formar; en embrión; rudimentario.
unfortified [ʌn'fɔ:tifaid], *a.* no fortificado, sin fortificar.
unfortunate [ʌn'fɔ:tʃənit], *a.* desgraciado, desventurado, desafortunado. — *s.* desgraciado, desventurado.
unfortunately [ʌn'fɔ:tʃənitli], *adv.* desgraciadamente, por desgracia, desafortunadamente.
unfortunateness [ʌn'fɔ:tʃənitnis], *s.* infortunio, desgracia.
unfounded [ʌn'faundid], *a.* infundado, sin fundamento.
unframed [ʌn'freimd], *a.* sin marco, no enmarcado.
unfrequented [ʌnfri'kwentid], *a.* poco frecuentado, solitario.
unfrequently [ʌn'fri:kwəntli], *adv.* rara vez, raramente, pocas veces.
unfriendliness [ʌn'frendlinis], *s.* hostilidad; antipatía.
unfriendly [ʌn'frendli], *a.* hostil; antipático; poco amistoso.
unfrock [ʌn'frɔk], *v.t.* (*igl.*) exclaustrar.
unfruitful [ʌn'fru:tful], *a.* infructuoso.
unfruitfulness [ʌn'fru:tfulnis], *s.* infructuosidad.
unfulfilled [ʌnful'fild], *a.* incumplido.
unfurl [ʌn'fə:l], *v.t.* desplegar.
unfurnished [ʌn'fə:niʃt], *a.* desamueblado.
unfurrowed [ʌn'fʌroud], *a.* (*entrecejo*) sin fruncir.
ungainliness [ʌn'geinlinis], *s.* desgarbo, falta de gracia.
ungainly [ʌn'geinli], *a.* desgarbado.
ungallant [ʌn'gælənt], *a.* poco galante, descortés.
ungarnished [ʌn'gɑ:niʃt], *a.* no guarnecido; sin adornos.
ungarrisoned [ʌn'gærisənd], *a.* sin guarnición.
ungartered [ʌn'gɑ:təd], *a.* sin liga(s).
ungathered [ʌn'gæðəd], *a.* no recogido; (*cost.*) no encogido.

ungauged [ʌn'geidʒd], *a.* no medido.
ungenerous [ʌn'dʒenərəs], *a.* poco generoso.
ungenial [ʌn'dʒi:niəl], *a.* poco simpático.
ungenteel [ʌndʒen'ti:l], *a.* poco urbano, poco fino.
ungentle [ʌn'dʒentl], *a.* poco suave.
ungentlemanliness [ʌn'dʒentlmənlinis], *s.* falta de caballerosidad.
ungentlemanly, ungentlemanlike [ʌn'dʒentlmənli, -laik], *a.* poco caballeroso, indigno de un caballero.
ungird [ʌn'gə:d], *v.t.* desceñir.
unglazed [ʌn'gleizd], *a.* sin vidriar, no vidriado; deslustrado; (*papel, tela*) sin satinar.
ungloved [ʌn'glʌvd], *a.* sin guantes.
ungodliness [ʌn'gɔdlinis], *s.* impiedad, irreligión.
ungodly [ʌn'gɔdli], *a.* impío, irreligioso; (*fam.*) atroz, espantoso; intempestivo.
ungovernable [ʌn'gʌvənəbl], *a.* ingobernable, indisciplinable.
ungraceful [ʌn'greisful], *a.* poco airoso, desgarbado; poco delicado.
ungracious [ʌn'greiʃəs], *a.* poco delicado; poco gentil.
ungraciousness [ʌn'greiʃəsnis], *s.* (lo) poco delicado; (lo) poco gentil.
ungrammatical [ʌngrə'mætikəl], *a.* antigramatical.
ungrateful [ʌn'greitful], *a.* desagradecido, ingrato.
ungratefully [ʌn'greitfuli], *adv.* con ingratitud, desagradecidamente.
ungratefulness [ʌn'greitfulnis], *s.* ingratitud, desagradecimiento.
ungratified [ʌn'grætifaid], *a.* no satisfecho, sin satisfacer.
ungrounded [ʌn'graundid], *a.* sin fundamento, infundado, inmotivado.
ungrudging [ʌn'grʌdʒiŋ], *a.* generoso.
ungrudgingly [ʌn'grudʒiŋli], *adv.* de buena gana, sin escatimar.
ungual ['ʌŋgwəl], *a.* ungular.
unguarded [ʌn'gɑ:did], *a.* indefenso, sin defensa; imprudente; descuidado; ***in an unguarded moment,*** en un momento de descuido.
unguardedly [ʌn'gɑ:didli], *adv.* incautamente.
unguent ['ʌŋgwənt], *s.* ungüento.
unguided [ʌn'gaidid], *a.* sin guía, sin orientación.
ungulate ['ʌŋgjulit], *a., s.* ungulado.
ungum [ʌn'gʌm], *v.t.* despegar.
unhallowed [ʌn'hæloud], *a.* sin consagrar, sin santificar.
unhampered [ʌn'hæmpəd], *a.* desembarazado, sin estorbos.
unhand [ʌn'hænd], *v.t.* quitar las manos a, soltar.
unhandy [ʌn'hændi], *a.* poco hábil, desmañado; poco manejable, incómodo.
unhappily [ʌn'hæpili], *adv.* desgraciadamente, por desgracia; infelizmente, desdichadamente.
unhappiness [ʌn'hæpinis], *s.* desgracia, infelicidad, desdicha.
unhappy [ʌn'hæpi], *a.* desgraciado, infeliz, desdichado; infausto.
unharmed [ʌn'hɑ:md], *a.* indemne, ileso, incólume.
unharmonious [ʌnhɑ:'mouniəs], *a.* inarmónico.
unharness [ʌn'hɑ:nis], *v.t.* (*caballos etc.*) desenjaezar.
unhatched [ʌn'hætʃt], *a.* no incubado.
unhealthiness [ʌn'helθinis], *s.* insalubridad; mala salud.
unhealthy [ʌn'helθi], *a.* enfermizo, achacoso; insalubre, insano; malsano.
unheard [ʌn'hə:d], *a.* sin ser oído; ***unheard-of,*** inaudito.
unheeded [ʌn'hi:did], *a.* desapercibido, inadvertido.
unheedful, unheeding [ʌn'hi:dful, -iŋ], *a.* sin hacer caso, que no hace caso.
unhelpful [ʌn'helpful], *a.* poco servicial; inútil.
unhesitating [ʌn'heziteitiŋ], *a.* que no vacila, que no titubea; ***he gave me an unhesitating reply,*** me contestó sin vacilar *o* sin titubear.
unhesitatingly [ʌn'heziteitiŋli], *adv.* sin vacilar, con presteza.
unhewn [ʌn'hju:n], *a.* bruto, en bruto; sin labrar.
unhinge [ʌn'hindʒ], *v.t.* desgoznar; desquiciar.
unhitch [ʌn'hitʃ], *v.t.* desatar; desenganchar.
unholiness [ʌn'houlinis], *s.* impiedad.
unholy [ʌn'houli], *a.* impío; (*fam.*) de miedo.
unhonoured [ʌn'ɔnəd], *a.* sin honor; despreciado.
unhook [ʌn'huk], *v.t., v.i.* descolgar(se); desenganchar(se); desabrochar(se); desaferrar(se).
unhoop [ʌn'hu:p], *v.t.* quitar los cercos de.
unhoped-for [ʌn'houpt-fɔ:], *a.* inesperado, fortuito.
unhopeful [ʌn'houpful], *a.* que tiene pocas esperanzas.
unhorse [ʌn'hɔ:s], *v.t.* desarzonar.
unhoused [ʌn'hauzd], *a.* sin casa.
unhurried [ʌn'hʌrid], *a.* parsimonioso, pausado.
unhurriedly [ʌn'hʌridli], *adv.* con mucha parsimonia.
unhurt [ʌn'hə:t], *a.* ileso, incólume, indemne.
unhygienic [ʌnhai'dʒi:nik], *a.* antihigiénico.
unicorn ['ju:nikɔ:n], *s.* unicornio.
unidentified [ʌnai'dentifaid], *a.* no identificado, sin identificar.
unification [ju:nifi'keiʃən], *s.* unificación.
uniflorous [ju:ni'flɔ:rəs], *a.* unifloro.
uniform ['ju:nifɔ:m], *a., s.* uniforme.
uniformity [ju:ni'fɔ:miti], *s.* uniformidad.
uniformly ['ju:nifɔ:mli], *adv.* uniformemente.
unify ['ju:nifai], *v.t.* unificar, unir.
unilateral [ju:ni'lætərəl], *a.* unilateral.
unimaginable [ʌni'mædʒinəbl], *a.* inimaginable.
unimpaired [ʌnim'pɛəd], *a.* intacto; sin disminuir, sin merma; sin deterioro(s).
unimpeachable [ʌnim'pi:tʃəbl], *a.* irrecusable; irreprochable, intachable.
unimpeded [ʌnim'pi:did], *a.* sin obstáculo(s), sin estorbo(s).
unimportance [ʌnim'pɔ:təns], *s.* poca importancia.
unimportant [ʌnim'pɔ:tənt], *a.* poco importante, sin importancia.
unimposing [ʌnim'pouziŋ], *a.* poco impresionante, que no hace impacto, que resulta muy poca cosa.
unimpressive [ʌnim'presiv], *a.* poco impresionante, poco convincente.
unimproved [ʌnim'pru:vd], *a.* sin mejorar, sin mejora(s).
uninfectious [ʌnin'fekʃəs], *a.* no contagioso.
uninflammable [ʌnin'flæməbl], *a.* incombustible.
uninfluential [ʌninflu'enʃəl], *a.* poco influyente.
uninformed [ʌnin'fɔ:md], *a.* poco instruido, ignorante; poco enterado.
uninhabitable [ʌnin'hæbitəbl], *a.* inhabitable.
uninhabited [ʌnin'hæbitid], *a.* inhabitado, sin habitantes.
uninitiated [ʌni'niʃieitid], *a.* no iniciado.
uninjured [ʌn'indʒəd], *a.* incólume, ileso, indemne.
uninspired [ʌnin'spaiəd], *a.* falto de inspiración; mediocre, ramplón.
uninspiring [ʌnin'spaiəriŋ], *a.* poco apasionante; ramplón, vulgar, aburrido.
uninstructed [ʌnin'strʌktid], *a.* sin instrucción, ignorante.
uninstructive [ʌnin'strʌktiv], *a.* poco instructivo.
uninsulated [ʌn'insjuleitid], *a.* (*elec.*) descubierto, sin aislar.
uninsured [ʌnin'ʃuəd], *a.* no asegurado, sin seguro.
unintelligent [ʌnin'telidʒənt], *a.* poco inteligente.
unintelligibility, unintelligibleness [ʌntelidʒi'biliti, ʌnin'telidʒiblnis], *s.* ininteligibilidad.

unintelligible [ʌnin'telidʒibl], *a.* ininteligible.
unintelligibly [ʌnin'telidʒibli], *adv.* de una manera ininteligible.
unintended, unintentional [ʌnin'tendid, ʌnin'tenʃənəl], *a.* no intencionado, involuntario, dicho *o* hecho sin querer.
unintentionally [ʌnin'tenʃənəli], *adv.* involuntariamente, sin querer.
uninterested [ʌn'intrəstid], *a.* que no tiene interés, que no demuestra interés.
uninteresting [ʌn'intrəstiŋ], *a.* poco interesante, falto de interés; aburrido.
uninterrupted [ʌnintə'rʌptid], *a.* ininterrumpido, sin interrupción.
uninterruptedly [ʌnintə'rʌptidli], *adv.* ininterrumpidamente, sin interrupción.
uninvested [ʌnin'vestid], *a.* sin invertir.
uninvestigated [ʌnin'vestigeitid], *a.* no investigado.
uninvited [ʌnin'vaitid], *a.* no invitado; (*fig.*) gratuito.
union ['ju:niən], *s.* unión, *f.*; enlace; (*mec.*) (manguito de) unión; ***customs union,*** unión aduanera; ***trade union,*** sindicato, gremio obrero; (*fam.*) ***Union Jack,*** bandera del Reino Unido.
unionism ['ju:niənizəm], *s.* sindicalismo; ***Unionism*** (*G.B. esp. Irlanda del Norte, Escocia*) partido conservador.
unionist ['ju:niənist], *a.*, *s.* unionista, *m.f.*; sindicalista, *m.f.*; (*pol.*) ***Unionist*** (*G.B. esp. Irlanda del Norte, Escocia*) conservador.
Union of Soviet Socialist Republics ['ju:niən əv 'souviət 'souʃəlist ri'pʌbliks], **the.** la Unión de Repúblicas Socialistas Soviéticas.
uniparous [ju:'nipərəs], *a.* unípara.
unipersonal [ju:ni'pə:sənəl], *a.* (*gram.*) unipersonal.
unique [ju:'ni:k], *a.* único.
uniquely [ju:'ni:kli], *adv.* de una manera única.
uniqueness [ju:'ni:knis], *s.* (lo) único; (lo) excepcional.
unisexual [ju:ni'seksjuəl], *a.* unisexual.
unison ['ju:nisən], *s.* (*mús.*) unísono; ***in unison,*** al unísono.
unisonal, unisonous [ju:'nisənəl, -əs], *a.* unísono.
unit ['ju:nit], *s.* unidad; (*mec.*) grupo, dispositivo.
Unitarian [ju:ni'tɛəriən], *a.*, *s.* unitario.
unitary ['ju:nitəri], *a.* unitario.
unite [ju:'nait], *v.t.* unir, juntar; unificar; casar. — *v.i.* unirse, juntarse.
united [ju:'naitid], *a.* unido.
United Arab Republic [ju:'naitid 'ærəb ri'pʌblik], **the.** la República Arabe Unida.
United Kingdom (of Great Britain and Northern Ireland) [ju:'naitid 'kiŋdəm (əv greit 'brit(ə)n ənd 'nɔ:ðən 'aiələnd)], **the.** el Reino Unido (de Gran Bretaña e Irlanda del Norte).
unitedly [ju:'naitidli], *adv.* unidamente, juntamente; de acuerdo.
United Nations [ju:'naitid 'neiʃənz], **the.** las Naciones Unidas.
United States (of America) [ju:'naitid steits (əv ə'merikə)], **the.** (los) Estados Unidos (de América).
uniter [ju:'naitə], *s.* unificador.
unity ['ju:niti], *s.* unidad; unión, *f.*, armonía.
univalve ['ju:nivælv], *a.*, *s.* univalvo.
univalved, univalvular ['ju:nivælvd, ju:ni'vælvjulə], *a.* univalvo.
universal [ju:ni'və:səl], *a.* universal; general; ***universal coupling, universal joint,*** junta universal *o* cardánica.
universality [ju:nivə:'sæliti], *s.* universalidad.
universalize [ju:ni'və:səlaiz], *v.t.* universalizar.
universally [ju:ni'və:səli], *adv.* universalmente.
universe ['ju:nivə:s], *s.* universo.
university [ju:ni'və:siti], *a.* universitario. — *s.* universidad.
univocal ['ju:'nivoukəl], *a.* unívoco.
unjust [ʌn'dʒʌst], *a.* injusto.
unjustifiable [ʌndʒʌsti'faiəbl], *a.* injustificable.
unjustifiably [ʌndʒʌsti'faiəbli], *adv.* injustificadamente.
unjustified [ʌn'dʒʌstifaid], *a.* injustificado.
unkempt [ʌn'kempt], *a.* despeinado, desgreñado; desaseado.
unkind [ʌn'kaind], *a.* poco benévolo, poco caritativo; duro, cruel, malo; malintencionado.
unkindly [ʌn'kaindli], *a.* poco benévolo, poco caritativo.
unkindness [ʌn'kaindnis], *s.* falta de cariño, desamor; dureza, crueldad; (lo) poco caritativo *etc.*
unkingly [ʌn'kiŋli], *a.* indigno *o* impropio de un rey.
unknit [ʌn'nit], *v.t.* deshacer; (*entrecejo*) desfruncir.
unknot [ʌn'nɔt], *v.t.* deshacer el nudo *o* los nudos de, desatar.
unknowing [ʌn'nouiŋ], *a.* inconsciente, ignorante.
unknowingly [ʌn'nouiŋli], *adv.* sin darse cuenta, sin saberlo; involuntariamente, sin querer.
unknown [ʌn'noun], *a.* desconocido, ignoto; incógnito; ***unknown quantity,*** incógnita; ***unknown warrior*** o ***soldier,*** soldado desconocido. — *adv.* ***unknown to him,*** sin saberlo él, sin que él lo supiese. — *s.* (lo) desconocido.
unlaboured [ʌn'leibəd], *a.* natural, no forzado.
unlace [ʌn'leis], *v.t.* desatar; desenlazar.
unlade [ʌn'leid], *v.t.* descargar.
unlading [ʌn'leidiŋ], *s.* descarga.
unladylike [ʌn'leidilaik], *a.* impropio de una señora, de mal tono.
unlamented [ʌnlə'mentid], *a.* no llorado, no sentido.
unlatch [ʌn'lætʃ], *v.t.* abrir (levantando el picaporte).
unlawful [ʌn'lɔ:ful], *a.* ilegítimo, ilícito, ilegal.
unlawfulness [ʌn'lɔ:fulnis], *s.* ilegalidad, ilegitimidad.
unlearn [ʌn'lə:n], *v.t.* desaprender.
unlearned [ʌn'lə:nid], *a.* indocto, ignorante.
unleash [ʌn'li:ʃ], *v.t.* destraillar; soltar; descencadenar.
unleavened [ʌn'levənd], *a.* sin levadura, ázimo; ***unleavened bread,*** (pan) ázimo.
unless [ʌn'les], *conj.* a menos que, a no ser que, si no.
unlettered [ʌn'letəd], *a.* iletrado.
unlicensed [ʌn'laisənst], *a.* no autorizado; sin licencia, sin permiso.
unlighted [ʌn'laitid], *a.* no iluminado, sin alumbrar.
unlike [ʌn'laik], *a.* poco parecido; (*elec.*) de signo contrario. — *adv.* a diferencia de, en contraste con.
unlikelihood, unlikeliness [ʌn'laiklihud, -nis], *s.* improbabilidad.
unlikely [ʌn'laikli], *a.* inverosímil; poco probable, improbable, difícil.
unlikeness [ʌn'laiknis], *s.* poco parecido.
unlimber [ʌn'limbə], *v.t.* (*mil.*) quitar el armón *o* el avantrén a (*un cañón*).
unlimited [ʌn'limitid], *a.* ilimitado, sin límite(s).
unlined (1) [ʌn'laind], *a.* sin arrugas; sin rayas.
unlined (2) [ʌn'laind], *a.* sin forrar.
unlink [ʌn'liŋk], *v.t.* deslabonar.
unliquidated [ʌn'likwideitid], *a.* no liquidado, pendiente de pago.
unlit [ʌn'lit], *a.* sin alumbrado.
unload [ʌn'loud], *v.t.* descargar.
unloading [ʌn'loudiŋ], *s.* descarga.
unlock [ʌn'lɔk], *v.t.* abrir (*con llave*); resolver (*enigma etc.*).
unlooked-for [ʌn'lukt-fɔ:], *a.* inopinado, inesperado.
unloose [ʌn'lu:s], *v.t.* soltar, desatar.

unlovable [ʌn'lʌvəbl], *a.* antipático.
unloved [ʌn'lʌvd], *a.* que no es amado.
unlovely [ʌn'lʌvli], *a.* feo, sin gracia, desgarbado.
unloving [ʌn'lʌviŋ], *a.* nada cariñoso.
unluckily [ʌn'lʌkili], *adv.* por desgracia, desgraciadamente; infaustamente.
unluckiness [ʌn'lʌkinis], *s.* mala suerte.
unlucky [ʌn'lʌki], *a.* desgraciado, desdichado, infortunado, desafortunado; aciago, nefasto; ***to be unlucky,*** tener mala suerte; ***it's unlucky,*** trae mala suerte.
unmade [ʌn'meid], *a.* (*cama*) sin hacer.
unmaidenly [ʌn'meidənli], *a.* impropio de una doncella.
unmake [ʌn'meik], *v.t.* deshacer.
unman [ʌn'mæn], *v.t.* acobardar; afeminar; emascular, castrar; (*mil.*) desguarnecer.
unmanageable [ʌn'mænidʒəbl], *a.* inmanejable; ingobernable, indócil.
unmanly [ʌn'mænli], *a.* poco varonil, de poca hombría.
unmannered [ʌn'mænəd], *a.* mal educado, mal criado.
unmannerliness [ʌn'mænəlinis], *s.* mala educación; malos modales, *m.pl.*
unmannerly [ʌn'mænəli], *a.* mal educado, mal criado; descortés.
unmarked [ʌn'mɑ:kt], *a.* sin marcar; ileso; (*dep.*) desmarcado.
unmarketable [ʌn'mɑ:kitəbl], *a.* invendible, incomerciable.
unmarriageable [ʌn'mæridʒəbl], *a.* incasable.
unmarried [ʌn'mærid], *a.* soltero, célibe.
unmask [ʌn'mɑ:sk], *v.t.* desenmascarar, quitar la careta a. — *v.i.* quitarse la máscara.
unmast [ʌn'mɑ:st], *v.t.* (*mar.*) desarbolar.
unmastered [ʌn'mɑ:stəd], *a.* sin domar; sin dominar.
unmatchable [ʌn'mætʃəbl], *a.* incomparable.
unmatched [ʌn'mætʃt], *a.* incomparable, sin igual, sin par.
unmeaning [ʌn'mi:niŋ], *a.* sin significación, sin sentido.
unmeant [ʌn'ment], *a.* involuntario, dicho *o* hecho sin querer.
unmeasurable [ʌn'meʒərəbl], *a.* inmensurable; incalculable.
unmeasured [ʌn'meʒəd], *a.* sin límites, sin medida; sin medir.
unmeet [ʌn'mi:t], *a.* impropio; poco conveniente; poco apropiado (***for,*** para).
unmelodious [ʌnmi'loudiəs], *a.* poco melodioso.
unmentionable [ʌn'menʃənəbl], *a.* nefando inconfesable.
unmentioned [ʌn'menʃənd], *a.* no mencionado.
unmerciful [ʌn'mə:siful], *a.* despiadado, sin piedad.
unmercifully [ʌn'mə:sifuli], *adv.* despiadadamente, sin piedad.
unmerited [ʌn'meritid], *a.* inmerecido.
unmindful [ʌn'maindful], *a.* olvidado (***of,*** de); ***to be unmindful of,*** no pensar en.
unmistakable [ʌnmis'teikəbl], *a.* inconfundible; inequívoco.
unmitigated [ʌn'mitigeitid], *a.* no mitigado; total; (*fam.*) ***unmitigated rubbish,*** soberana tontería; (*ant., fam.*) ***unmitigated rogue,*** bribón redomado.
unmixed [ʌn'mikst], *a.* sin mezcla, puro.
unmodified [ʌn'mɔdifaid], *a.* sin modificación.
unmolested [ʌnmɔ'lestid], *a.* tranquilo. — *adv.* sin que nadie se meta con uno.
unmoor [ʌn'muə], *v.t.* (*mar.*) desamarrar; desaferrar. — *v.i.* soltar amarras.
unmortgaged [ʌn'mɔ:gidʒd], *a.* no hipotecado, libre de hipoteca.
unmotherly [ʌn'mʌðəli], *a.* de (una) madre desnaturalizada.
unmounted [ʌn'mauntid], *a.* desmontado; (*piedra*) sin engastar; (*foto etc.*) sin encuadrar.
unmourned [ʌn'mɔ:nd], *a.* no llorado.
unmoved [ʌn'mu:vd], *a.* impasible, sin conmoverse.
unmusical [ʌn'mju:zikəl], *a.* poco aficionado a la música; poco armónico.
unmutilated [ʌn'mju:tileitid], *a.* no mutilado, sin mutilar; intacto.
unmuzzle [ʌn'mʌzl], *v.t.* quitar el bozal a.
unnamed [ʌn'neimd], *a.* innominado; sin nombre, anónimo.
unnatural [ʌn'nætʃərəl], *a.* antinatural; (*padre, madre*) desnaturalizado; poco natural, afectado.
unnavigable [ʌn'nævigəbl], *a.* innavegable.
unnavigated [ʌn'nævigeitid], *a.* que no ha sido navegado.
unnecessarily [ʌn'nesəserili], *adv.* sin necesidad, innecesariamente.
unnecessariness [ʌn'nesəserinis], *s.* (lo) innecesario.
unnecessary [ʌn'nesəseri], *a.* innecesario; ***it is unnecessary to say that . . .,*** excusado decir que. . . .
unneeded [ʌn'ni:did], *a.* innecesario.
unneighbourly [ʌn'neibəli], *a.* impropio de un buen vecino; poco amistoso *o* poco atento *o* poco servicial con los vecinos.
unnerve [ʌn'nə:v], *v.t.* amilanar, acobardar.
unnoticed [ʌn'noutist], *a.* desapercibido, inadvertido; ***to go unnoticed,*** pasar desapercibido.
unnumbered [ʌn'nʌmbəd], *a.* innumerable, sin número; no numerado.
unobjectionable [ʌnəb'dʒekʃənəbl], *a.* intachable; que no se le pueden poder reparos.
unobservant [ʌnəb'zə:vənt], *a.* poco observador.
unobserved [ʌnəb'zə:vd], *a.* desapercibido.
unobstructed [ʌnəb'strʌktid], *a.* libre, sin obstáculos; expedito.
unobtainable [ʌnəb'teinəbl], *a.* que no se puede conseguir.
unobtrusive [ʌnəb'tru:siv], *a.* discreto; sencillo.
unoccupied [ʌn'ɔkjupaid], *a.* desocupado; (*habitación*) vacío; (*empleo*) vacante; (*zona*) despoblado.
unofficial [ʌnə'fiʃəl], *a.* no oficial; extraoficial; oficioso.
unopened [ʌn'oupənd], *a.* sin abrir.
unopposed [ʌnə'pouzd], *a.* sin resistencia *u* oposición.
unordered [ʌn'ɔ:dəd], *a.* sin ordenar; no encargado.
unorganized [ʌn'ɔ:gənaizd], *a.* no organizado, sin organizar.
unoriginal [ʌnə'ridʒinəl], *a.* poco original.
unorthodox [ʌn'ɔ:θədɔks], *a.* nada convencional; poco ortodoxo; heterodoxo.
unostentatious [ʌnɔsten'teiʃəs], *a.* modesto, sencillo, no ostentoso.
unostentatiously [ʌnɔsten'teiʃəsli], *adv.* sin ostentación.
unowned [ʌn'ound], *a.* sin dueño; no reconocido.
unpacified [ʌn'pæsifaid], *a.* sin pacificar.
unpack [ʌn'pæk], *v.t.* deshacer (*las maletas*); desempaquetar, desembalar.
unpaid [ʌn'peid], *a.* sin pagar, por pagar; (*com.*) pendiente (*de pago*); ***unpaid work,*** trabajo sin retribuir.
unpainted [ʌn'peintid], *a.* sin pintar.
unpaired [ʌn'pɛəd], *a.* desapareado.
unpalatable [ʌn'pælətəbl], *a.* de mal sabor, incomible; (*fig.*) desagradable.
unparalleled [ʌn'pærəleld], *a.* sin paralelo; sin igual, sin par, incomparable; sin precedentes.
unpardonable [ʌn'pɑ:dənəbl], *a.* imperdonable, inexcusable, que no tiene perdón.

unpardoned [ʌnˈpɑːdənd], *a.* no perdonado.
unparliamentary [ʌnpɑːliˈmentəri], *a.* antiparlamentario; contrario a los usos parlamentarios.
unpatriotic [ʌnpætriˈɔtik], *a.* antipatriótico.
unpatronized [ʌnˈpætrənaizd], *a.* sin protección; que no tiene clientela; sin mecenazgo.
unpaved [ʌnˈpeivd], *a.* sin pavimentar; sin adoquinar.
unpeg [ʌnˈpeg], *v.t.* desclavijar.
unpensioned [ʌnˈpenʃənd], *a.* sin pensión.
unpeople [ʌnˈpiːpl], *v.t.* despoblar.
unperceived [ʌnpəˈsiːvd], *a.* desapercibido, inadvertido.
unperceptive [ʌnpəˈseptiv], *a.* poco observador; (*fig.*) poco penetrante.
unperformed [ʌnpəˈfɔːmd], *a.* (*teat.*) sin representar.
unperturbed [ʌnpəˈtəːbd], *a.* impertérrito, sin alterarse.
unpick [ʌnˈ pik], *v.t.* descoser.
unpin [ʌnˈpin], *v.t.* desprender; desclavijar.
unpitying [ʌnˈpitiiŋ], *a.* despiadado, sin piedad.
unplaced [ʌnˈpleist], *a.* (*dep.*) no colocado.
unpleasant [ʌnˈplezənt], *a.* desagradable; poco grato; antipático, desabrido.
unpleasantness [ʌnˈplezəntnis], *s.* (lo) desagradable; disgusto.
unpleasing [ʌnˈpliːziŋ], *a.* desagradable, poco grato.
unplumbed [ʌnˈplʌmd], *a.* no sondado, sin sondar.
unpolished [ʌnˈpɔliʃt], *a.* sin pulir; (*joy.*) en bruto; (*fig.*) tosco.
unpoetic [ʌnpouˈetik], *a.* poco poético; prosaico.
unpolluted [ʌnpɔˈl(j)uːtid], *a.* sin contaminar.
unpopular [ʌnˈpɔpjulə], *a.* impopular, poco popular, que tiene poca aceptación.
unpopularity [ʌnpɔpjuˈlæriti], *s.* impopularidad, poca popularidad, poca aceptación.
unpractical [ʌnˈpræktikəl], *a.* poco práctico.
unpractised [ʌnˈpræktist], *a.* inexperto, imperito.
unprecedented [ʌnˈpresidentid], *a.* sin precedentes, inaudito.
unpredictable [ʌnpriˈdiktəbl], *a.* imposible de predecir; de reacciones imprevisibles, que nunca se sabe lo que va a hacer.
unprejudiced [ʌnˈpredʒudist], *a.* sin prejuicios; imparcial.
unpremeditated [ʌnpriːˈmediteitid], *a.* no premeditado.
unprepared [ʌnpriˈpɛəd], *a.* no preparado, sin preparar; desprevenido.
unpreparedness [ʌnpriˈpɛəridnis], *s.* falta de preparación; desprevención.
unprepossessing [ʌnpriːpəˈzesiŋ], *a.* poco atractivo, poco atrayente.
unpresentable [ʌnpriˈzentəbl], *a.* mal apersonado, poco presentable.
unpressed [ʌnˈprest], *a.* sin planchar.
unpretending [ʌnpriˈtendiŋ], *a.* sin fingimiento(s), sincero.
unpretentious [ʌnpriˈtenʃəs], *a.* sin pretensiones; sencillo.
unprevailing [ʌnpriˈveiliŋ], *a.* infructuoso, inútil.
unprincipled [ʌnˈprinsipld], *a.* falto de principios, sin conciencia *o* escrúpulos, cínico.
unprinted [ʌnˈprintid], *a.* sin imprimir; (*tej.*) sin estampar.
unprivileged [ʌnˈprivilidʒd], *a.* sin privilegios.
unproductive [ʌnprəˈdʌktiv], *a.* improductivo; infructuoso.
unprofessional [ʌnprəˈfeʃənəl], *a.* poco profesional; indigno de *o* contrario a la ética profesional; profano.
unprofitable [ʌnˈprɔfitəbl], *a.* improductivo, infructuoso; nada lucrativo.
unprofitableness [ʌnˈprɔfitəblnis], *s.* inutilidad, infructuosidad.
unprofitably [ʌnˈprɔfitəbli], *adv.* inútilmente, sin provecho.
unpromising [ʌnˈprɔmisiŋ], *a.* poco prometedor, poco halagüeño.
unpronounceable [ʌnprəˈnaunsəbl], *a.* impronunciable.
unpropitious [ʌnprəˈpiʃəs], *a.* poco propicio, adverso.
unprotected [ʌnprəˈtektid], *a.* desvalido, indefenso, sin protección.
unproved [ʌnˈpruːvd], *a.* no probado.
unprovided [ʌnprəˈvaidid], *a.* desprovisto; ***unprovided for,*** desvalido; imprevisto, inesperado.
unprovocative [ʌnprəˈvɔkətiv], *a.* que no provoca, inofensivo.
unprovoked [ʌnprəˈvoukt], *a.* no provocado, sin provocación.
unpublished [ʌnˈpʌbliʃt], *a.* inédito; no publicado.
unpunctual [ʌnˈpʌŋktʃuəl], *a.* poco puntual.
unpunished [ʌnˈpʌniʃt], *a.* impune, sin castigo.
unqualified [ʌnˈkwɔlifaid], *a.* incompetente; sin título; no capacitado; categórico; sin reservas; ***unqualified success,*** éxito rotundo.
unqueenly [ʌnˈkwiːnli], *a.* indigno *o* impropio de una reina.
unquenchable [ʌnˈkwentʃəbl], *a.* inextinguible; insaciable.
unquenched [ʌnˈkwentʃt], *a.* no apagado; sin saciar.
unquestionable [ʌnˈkwestʃənəbl], *a.* indiscutible, incuestionable.
unquestioned [ʌnˈkwestʃənd], *a.* indiscutido.
unquestioning [ʌnˈkwestʃəniŋ], *a.* (*obediencia etc.*) ciego; que lo acepta todo sin objeciones.
unquiet [ʌnˈkwaiət], *a.* inquieto, desasosegado. — *s.* inquietud, desasosiego.
unquietness [ʌnˈkwaiətnis], *s.* inquietud, desasosiego.
unquotable [ʌnˈkwoutəbl], *a.* imposible de citar (por lo obsceno).
unquote [ˈʌnkwout], 'fin de la cita'.
unravel [ʌnˈrævəl], *v.t.* desenmarañar, desenredar; desembrollar; descifrar. — *v.i.* deshacerse; (*relato*) desarrollarse.
unread [ʌnˈred], *a.* no leído, sin leer; indocto, inculto.
unreadable [ʌnˈriːdəbl], *a.* (*letra*) ilegible; (*fig.*) insoportable, pesadísimo.
unreadiness [ʌnˈredinis], *s.* falta de preparación; desprevención.
unready [ʌnˈredi], *a.* no preparado, sin preparar; desprevenido, desapercibido.
unreal [ʌnˈriəl], *a.* irreal, no real; ilusorio, quimérico, fantasmagórico.
unrealistic [ʌnriəˈlistik], *a.* poco realista; poco práctico; imposible (de realizar); impracticable; disparatado, absurdo.
unreality [ʌnriˈæliti], *s.* irrealidad, (lo) ilusorio *etc.*
unrealizable [ʌnˈriəlaizəbl], *a.* irrealizable.
unreason [ʌnˈriːzən], *s.* sinrazón, *f.*
unreasonable [ʌnˈriːznəbl], *a.* irrazonable; excesivo, exorbitante.
unreasonableness [ʌnˈriːznəblnis], *s.* (lo) irrazonable; (lo) excesivo.
unreasoning [ʌnˈriːzniŋ], *a.* irracional.
unrecognizable [ʌnˈrekəgnaizəbl], *a.* irreconocible.
unreconciled [ʌnˈrekənsaild], *a.* no reconciliado, irreconciliado.
unrecorded [ʌnriˈkɔːdid], *a.* (*cifra etc.*) no registrado, sin registrar; (*palabras etc.*) no consignado, sin consignar; (*disco*) no grabado, sin grabar.
unrecoverable [ʌnriˈkʌvrəbl], *a.* irrecuperable.
unredeemed [ʌnriˈdiːmd], *a.* (*promesas etc.*) sin cumplir; (*cosas en prenda*) sin desempeñar; (*errores*) sin compensar, no compensado, sin mitigar, no mitigado.

unredressed [ʌnri'drest], *a.* sin enmendar, sin remediar.
unreduced [ʌnri'dju:st], *a.* no reducido; no rebajado; sin amainar, sin disminuir.
unrefined [ʌnri'faind], *a.* no refinado; sin refinar; no fino.
unreflecting [ʌnri'flektiŋ], *a.* irreflexivo.
unreformable [ʌnri'fɔ:məbl], *a.* irreformable; incorregible.
unreformed [ʌnri'fɔ:md], *a.* no reformado; sin corregir.
unregarded [ʌnri'gɑ:did], *a.* desatendido.
unregenerate [ʌnri'dʒenərit], *a.* sin regenerar.
unregistered [ʌn'redʒistəd], *a.* no registrado, no inscrito; (*carta*) sin certificar.
unregretted [ʌnri'gretid], *a.* no sentido, no lamentado, no llorado.
unregulated [ʌn'regjuleitid], *a.* sin regular.
unrehearsed [ʌnri'hə:st], *a.* improvisado; sin ensayar.
unrelated [ʌnri'leitid], *a.* inconexo; sin relación; ***unrelated to,*** que no tiene relación con.
unrelenting [ʌnri'lentiŋ], *a.* implacable; inflexible.
unreliable [ʌnri'laiəbl], *a.* (*pers.*) informal, poco serio; (*servicio etc.*) poco seguro, inseguro.
unrelieved [ʌnri'li:vd], *a.* monótono; continuo.
unrelished [ʌn'reliʃt], *a.* que no apetece.
unremarkable [ʌnri'mɑ:kəbl], *a.* poco notable.
unremarked [ʌnri'mɑ:kt], *a.* desapercibido.
unremedied [ʌn'remidid], *a.* sin remediar.
unremembered [ʌnri'membəd], *a.* no recordado.
unremitting [ʌnri'mitiŋ], *a.* incesante, constante.
unremittingly [ʌnri'mitiŋli], *adv.* incesantemente, sin cejar.
unremunerated [ʌnri'mju:nəreitid], *a.* sin remunerar.
unremunerative [ʌnri'mju:nərətiv], *a.* no remunerador; (*fam.*) poco remunerador.
unrepaired [ʌnri'pɛəd], *a.* no reparado, sin reparar.
unrepealable [ʌnri'pi:ləbl], *a.* irrevocable.
unrepealed [ʌnri'pi:ld], *a.* no revocado.
unrepeatable [ʌnri'pi:təbl], *a.* que no puede repetirse; imposible de citar (por lo obsceno).
unrepentant [ʌnri'pentənt], *a.* impenitente.
unrepresentative [ʌnrepri'zentətiv], *a.* poco representativo, poco típico.
unrepresented [ʌnrepri'zentid], *a.* sin representación.
unreprieved [ʌnri'pri:vd], *a.* sin indultar.
unrequested [ʌnri'kwestid], *a.* no solicitado.
unrequired [ʌnri'kwaiəd], *a.* innecesario.
unrequited [ʌnri'kwaitid], *a.* no correspondido.
unreserved [ʌnre'zə:vd], *a.* incondicional, sin reservas; no reservado; franco, directo.
unreservedly [ʌnri'zə:vidli], *adv.* incondicionalmente, sin reservas.
unresisted [ʌnri'zistid], *a.* que no encuentra resistencia *u* oposición.
unresisting [ʌnri'zistiŋ], *a.* que no resiste, que no ofrece resistencia.
unresolved [ʌnri'zɔlvd], *a.* irresoluto; sin resolver.
unresponsive [ʌnris'pɔnsiv], *a.* insensible; poco expresivo; poco entusiasta.
unrest [ʌn'rest], *s.* inquietud, desasosiego, desazón; (*política etc.*) agitación, disturbios, *m.pl.*, desórdenes, *m.pl.*
unrestrained [ʌnri'streind], *a.* desenfrenado, sin refrenar.
unrestricted [ʌnri'striktid], *a.* sin restricción, sin restricciones; libre.
unrewarded [ʌnri'wɔ:did], *a.* no recompensado, sin recompensa.
unrewarding [ʌnri'wɔ:diŋ], *a.* que proporciona pocas satisfacciones; infructuoso.
unriddle [ʌn'ridl], *v.t.* descifrar.
unrig [ʌn'rig], *v.t.* (*mar.*) desaparejar.
unrighteous [ʌn'raitʃəs], *a.* injusto; inicuo.
unrighteousness [ʌn'raitʃəsnis], *s.* injusticia; inicuidad.
unripe [ʌn'raip], *a.* no maduro, verde; (*fig.*) inmaduro.
unripeness [ʌn'raipnis], *s.* falta de madurez, poca madurez.
unrivalled [ʌn'raivəld], *a.* sin rival, sin igual, sin par, incomparable.
unrivet [ʌn'rivit], *v.t.* quitar los remaches de.
unrobe [ʌn'roub], *v.t.* quitar el vestido a, desnudar. — *v.i.* quitarse el vestido, desnudarse.
unroll [ʌn'roul], *v.t.* desenrollar; (*fig.*) desplegar. — *v.i.* desenrollarse; (*fig.*) desenvolverse.
unromantic [ʌnrou'mæntik], *a.* poco romántico; prosaico.
unroof [ʌn'ru:f], *v.t.* levantar el tejado de, destechar.
unroot [ʌn'ru:t], *v.t.* desarraigar, desenraizar.
unrope [ʌn'roup], *v.t.* desatar.
unruffled [ʌn'rʌfld], *a.* impertérrito, sin inmutarse.
unruled [ʌn'ru:ld], *a.* (*papel*) sin rayar.
unruliness [ʌn'ru:linis], *s.* indocilidad, indisciplina.
unruly [ʌn'ru:li], *a.* indócil, ingobernable, indisciplinable, revoltoso.
unsaddle [ʌn'sædl], *v.t.* (*jinete*) desarzonar; (*caballo*) desensillar.
unsafe [ʌn'seif], *a.* inseguro; (*situación etc.*) expuesto.
unsaid [ʌn'sed], *a.* sin decir; ***he left this unsaid,*** lo calló.
unsaleable [ʌn'seiləbl], *a.* invendible.
unsalted [ʌn'sɔ:ltid], *a.* sin sal; sin salar.
unsanctioned [ʌn'sæŋkʃənd], *a.* sin sancionar.
unsated [ʌn'seitid], *a.* sin saciar.
unsatisfactorily [ʌnsætis'fæktərili], *adv.* de una manera poco satisfactoria.
unsatisfactory [ʌnsætis'fæktəri], *a.* poco satisfactorio; que no satisface.
unsatisfied [ʌn'sætisfaid], *a.* insatisfecho, no satisfecho; no convencido.
unsatisfying [ʌn'sætisfaiiŋ], *a.* que no satisface; insuficiente, poco convincente; que proporciona pocas satisfacciones.
unsavoury [ʌn'seivəri], *a.* desagradable, repugnante; ***unsavoury reputation,*** mala fama.
unsay [ʌn'sei], *v.t.* desdecirse de.
unscarred [ʌn'skɑ:d], *a.* sin cicatrices.
unscathed [ʌn'skeiðd], *a.* ileso, incólume, indemne.
unscholarly [ʌn'skɔləli], *a.* impropio de un erudito; poco riguroso.
unschooled [ʌn'sku:ld], *a.* sin instrucción, no instruido.
unscientific [ʌnsaiən'tifik], *a.* poco científico.
unscorched [ʌn'skɔ:tʃt], *a.* sin chamuscar.
unscramble [ʌn'skræmbl], *v.t.* descifrar.
unscratched [ʌn'skrætʃt], *a.* sin arañar; intacto, como nuevo.
unscreened [ʌn'skri:nd], *a.* no abrigado; (*elec.*) descubierto.
unscrew [ʌn'skru:], *v.t.* destornillar, desatornillar.
unscrupulous [ʌn'skru:pjuləs], *a.* poco escrupuloso, sin escrúpulos, desaprensivo, cínico.
unscrupulousness [ʌn'skru:pjuləsnis], *s.* falta de escrúpulos, desaprensión.
unscrupulously [ʌn'skru:pjuləsli], *adv.* sin escrúpulos, desaprensivamente.
unseal [ʌn'si:l], *v.t.* desellar, abrir.
unsearchable [ʌn'sə:tʃəbl], *a.* insondable.
unseasonable [ʌn'si:znəbl], *a.* intempestivo, inoportuno; inconveniente; impropio; fuera de tiempo *o* sazón; prematuro, tardío.
unseasoned [ʌn'si:zənd], *a.* no sazonado, sin sazonar; inmaduro; (*madera*) verde; (*tropas*) no aguerrido; sin experiencia.

unseat [ʌn'si:t], *v.t.* quitar el asiento a; desarzonar; (*gobierno*) derribar, derrocar.
unseaworthy [ʌn'si:wə:ði], *a.* que no está en condiciones de navegar, poco marinero.
unseconded [ʌn'sekəndid], *a.* no secundado, sin apoyo.
unsecured [ʌnsi'kjuəd], *a.* inseguro, sin afianzar.
unseeing [ʌn'si:iŋ], *a.* que no ve, ciego.
unseemliness [ʌn'si:mlinis], *s.* (lo) impropio, (lo) indecoroso, (lo) inconveniente.
unseemly [ʌn'si:mli], *a.* impropio, indecoroso, inconveniente.
unseen [ʌn'si:n], *a.* invisible; oculto; desapercibido; (*traducción*) que no se ha visto antes. — *s.* materia para traducción que no se ha visto antes.
unselfish [ʌn'selfiʃ], *a.* desinteresado, abnegado, altruista, desprendido.
unselfishness [ʌn'selfiʃnis], *s.* desinterés, *m.*, abnegación, altruismo, desprendimiento.
unsensitized [ʌn'sensitaizd], *a.* (*foto.*) no sensibilizado.
unserviceable [ʌn'sə:visəbl], *a.* inútil, inservible.
unserviceableness [ʌn'sə:visəblnis], *s.* inutilidad.
unsettle [ʌn'setl], *v.t.* trastornar, perturbar; inquietar, intranquilizar.
unsettled [ʌn'setld], *a.* (*pers.*) inquieto, intranquilo; (*tiempo, situación etc.*) inestable, variable, poco seguro; (*fecha*) no fijo; (*cuestión*) pendiente, sin resolver; (*deuda*) sin pagar; (*tierra*) sin colonizar, sin poblar.
unsettledness [ʌn'setldnis], *s.* inquietud; incertidumbre; inestabilidad.
unsew [ʌn'sou], *v.t.* decoser.
unsex [ʌn'seks], *v.t.* privar de la sexualidad.
unshackle [ʌn'ʃækl], *v.t.* desencadenar, quitar las trabas a.
unshaded [ʌn'ʃeidid], *a.* sin sombra; no sombreado.
unshakable [ʌn'ʃeikəbl], *a.* firme; inquebrantable; imperturbable.
unshaken [ʌn'ʃeikən], *a.* firme; impertérrito.
unshapely [ʌn'ʃeipli], *a.* de forma fea, disforme, desproporcionado.
unshaven [ʌn'ʃeivən], *a.* no afeitado, sin afeitar.
unsheathe [ʌn'ʃi:ð], *v.t.* desenvainar.
unsheltered [ʌn'ʃeltəd], *a.* desabrigado, sin protección.
unship [ʌn'ʃip], *v.t.* (*mar.*) desembarcar, descargar; desmontar (*el timón*); desarmar (*un remo*).
unshod [ʌn'ʃɔd], *a.* descalzo; (*caballo*) desherrado.
unshorn [ʌn'ʃɔ:n], *a.* sin esquilar.
unshrinkable [ʌn'ʃriŋkəbl], *a.* inencogible.
unshrinking [ʌn'ʃriŋkiŋ], *a.* impávido, intrépido, sin vacilar.
unshriven [ʌn'ʃrivən], *a.* sin confesión.
unsighted [ʌn'saitid], *a.* invidente.
unsightliness [ʌn'saitlinis], *s.* fealdad.
unsightly [ʌn'saitli], *a.* feo, que hiere (a) la vista.
unsigned [ʌn'saind], *a.* sin firmar.
unsinkable [ʌn'siŋkəbl], *a.* imposible de hundir.
unsisterly [ʌn'sistəli], *a.* indigno *o* impropio de una hermana.
unsized [ʌn'saizd], *a.* (*tejido*) sin apresto; (*papel*) sin cola.
unskilful [ʌn'skilful], *a.* poco hábil, desmañado, torpe.
unskilfulness [ʌn'skilfulnis], *s.* inhabilidad, torpeza, impericia, desmaña.
unskilled [ʌn'skild], *a.* no capacitado; (*obrero*) no especializado; (*trabajo*) que no requiere habilidad.
unslaked [ʌn'sleikt], *a.* (*sed*) sin apagar.
unsling [ʌn'sliŋ], *v.t.* (*mar.*) quitar las relingas de, deslingar.
unsmoked [ʌn'smoukt], *a.* no ahumado, sin ahumar.
unsociable [ʌn'souʃəbl], *a.* insociable, poco sociable.
unsociableness, unsociability [ʌn'souʃəblnis, ʌnʃouʃə'biliti], *s.* insociabilidad.
unsocial [ʌn'souʃəl], *a.* insocial.
unsoiled [ʌn'sɔild], *a.* sin manchar.
unsold [ʌn'sould], *a.* no vendido, sin vender.
unsoldierlike, unsoldierly [ʌn'souldʒəlaik, -li], *a.* poco militar; impropio de un militar.
unsolicited [ʌnsə'lisitid], *a.* no solicitado.
unsolvable [ʌn'sɔlvəbl], *a.* irresoluble, insoluble.
unsolved [ʌn'sɔlvd], *a.* (*cuestión, problema*) sin resolver, no resuelto, por resolver; (*misterio*) sin explicar, sin aclarar.
unsophisticated [ʌnsə'fistikeitid], *a.* sencillo; natural; ingenuo; elemental.
unsorted [ʌn'sɔ:tid], *a.* (*correo*) sin triar.
unsought [ʌn'sɔ:t], *a.* no buscado, no solicitado.
unsound [ʌn'saund], *a.* poco firme, poco sólido; defectuoso; erróneo, falso; perturbado.
unsoundness [ʌn'saundnis], *s.* falta de solidez; (lo) defectuoso; (lo) erróneo, falsedad; perturbación (*mental*).
unsown [ʌn'soun], *a.* no sembrado.
unsparing [ʌn'spɛəriŋ], *a.* pródigo, generoso; incansable; que no regatea (*esfuerzos*).
unsparingly [ʌn'spɛəriŋli], *adv.* generosamente, pródigamente, profusamente; sin regatear (*esfuerzos*).
unspeakable [ʌn'spi:kəbl], *a.* abominable, execrable, nefando.
unspeakably [ʌn'spi:kəbli], *adv.* de una manera execrable.
unspecified [ʌn'spesifaid], *a.* no especificado, no detallado; sin precisar.
unspent [ʌn'spent], *a.* no gastado, sin gastar.
unspoilt, unspoiled [ʌn'spɔilt, -d], *a.* no estropeado, sin estropear; intacto; (*niños etc.*) no mimado, sin mimar; (*ecología etc.*) en su estado natural.
unspotted [ʌn'spɔtid], *a.* sin mancha(s); puro, inmaculado.
unsprung [ʌn'sprʌŋ], *a.* sin muelles.
unstable [ʌn'steibl], *a.* inestable, poco firme.
unstableness [ʌn'steiblnis], *s.* inestabilidad.
unstaid [ʌn'steid], *a.* nada ceremonioso.
unstaidness [ʌn'steidnis], *s.* poca ceremoniosidad.
unstained [ʌn'steind], *a.* sin manchar.
unstamped [ʌn'stæmpt], *a.* sin franquear, sin sello.
unstanched [ʌn'stɑ:ntʃt], *a.* sin restañar.
unstatesmanlike [ʌn'steitsmənlaik], *a.* indigno *o* impropio de un hombre de estado.
unsteadiness [ʌn'stedinis], *s.* inestabilidad, poca seguridad, falta de firmeza; (*equilibrio*) tambaleo; (*conducta*) poca constancia, inconstancia.
unsteady [ʌn'stedi], *a.* inestable, inseguro, poco firme; (*equilibrio*) tambaleante; (*conducta*) poco constante, inconstante.
unstinted, unstinting [ʌn'stintid, -iŋ], *a.* generoso; ***with unstinted effort,*** sin escatimar esfuerzos.
unstirred [ʌn'stə:d], *a.* impasible.
unstop [ʌn'stɔp], *v.t.* destaponar.
unstrained [ʌn'streind], *a.* fácil, sin tensiones; (*arroz etc.*) sin colar.
unstressed [ʌn'strest], *a.* inacentuado, átono.
unstring [ʌn'striŋ], *v.t. irr.* desencordar; (*perlas*) desensartar.
unstudied [ʌn'stʌdid], *a.* hecho *o* dicho con naturalidad *o* sin afectación.
unstudious [ʌn'stju:diəs], *a.* poco estudioso.
unsubdued [ʌnsəb'dju:d], *a.* no disminuido; indómito.
unsubmissive [ʌnsəb'misiv], *a.* insumiso.
unsubstantial [ʌnsəb'stænʃəl], *a.* insustancial; poco sólido.
unsuccessful [ʌnsək'sesful], *a.* que no tiene éxito, que no acierta, que fracasa; inútil, infructuoso; ***to be unsuccessful,*** fracasar; fallar; malograrse;

to be unsuccessful in doing sth., no lograr hacer algo, no conseguir hacer algo.
unsuccessfully [ʌnsək'sesfuli], *adv.* sin éxito, en vano.
unsuccessfulness [ʌnsək'sesfulnis], *s.* falta de éxito, fracaso, desacierto.
unsuitable [ʌn's(j)u:təbl], *a.* no apto, no adecuado, poco apropiado, poco idóneo.
unsuitability, unsuitableness [ʌns(j)u:tə'biliti, ʌn's(j)u:təblnis], *s.* poca idoneidad.
unsuited [ʌn's(j)u:tid], *a.* no apto, poco adecuado (***to, for,*** para).
unsullied [ʌn'sʌlid], *a.* inmaculado, impoluto.
unsung [ʌn'sʌŋ], *a.* no cantado; no elogiado, no celebrado; ***unsung hero,*** héroe sin reconocer.
unsupplied [ʌnsə'plaid], *a.* sin suministrar.
unsupported [ʌnsə'pɔ:tid], *a.* sin apoyo, no respaldado; (*testimonio etc.*) no corroborado.
unsuppressed [ʌnsə'prest], *a.* no suprimido.
unsure [ʌn'ʃuə], *a.* inseguro, poco seguro; ***to be unsure of o.s.***, tener poca confianza en sí (mismo), tener poca seguridad (en sí mismo).
unsurmountable [ʌnsə'mauntəbl], *a.* insuperable.
unsurpassed [ʌnsə'pɑ:st], *a.* insuperado, inmejorado.
unsusceptible [ʌnsə'septibl], *a.* no susceptible.
unsuspected [ʌnsəs'pektid], *a.* insospechado.
unsuspecting [ʌnsəs'pektiŋ], *a.* confiado; desprevenido; sin recelos, sin sospechas.
unsuspicious [ʌnsəs'piʃəs], *a.* confiado, bien pensado.
unswathe [ʌn'sweið], *v.t.* desfajar.
unsweetened [ʌn'swi:tnd], *a.* sin endulzar, no azucarado.
unswerving [ʌn'swə:viŋ], *a.* (*fig.*) inquebrantable, firme, inconmovible.
unsworn [ʌn'swɔ:n], *a.* no juramentado.
unsymmetrical [ʌnsi'metrikəl], *a.* asimétrico; desproporcionado.
unsympathetic [ʌnsimpə'θetik], *a.* poco compasivo; poco comprensivo; frío, insensible; que simpatiza poco (***to,*** con).
unsynchronized [ʌn'siŋkrənaizd], *a.* sin sincronizar.
unsystematic [ʌnsisti'mætik], *a.* poco sistemático.
untack [ʌn'tæk], *v.t.* quitar las tachuelas a.
untainted [ʌn'teintid], *a.* impoluto; no corrompido.
untamable [ʌn'teiməbl], *a.* indomable, indómito.
untamed [ʌn'teimd], *a.* sin domar, no domado.
untangle [ʌn'tæŋgl], *v.t.* desenmarañar.
untapped [ʌn'tæpt], *a.* sin explotar.
untarnished [ʌn'tɑ:niʃt], *a.* (*fig.*) no empañado, sin mancilla.
untasted [ʌn'teistid], *a.* sin probar.
untaught [ʌn'tɔ:t], *a.* no enseñado.
untaxed [ʌn'tækst], *a.* libre de impuestos.
unteachable [ʌn'ti:tʃəbl], *a.* incapaz de aprender; imposible de enseñar.
untenable [ʌn'tenəbl], *a.* insostenible.
untenanted [ʌn'tenəntid], *a.* que no tiene inquilinos.
untended [ʌn'tendid], *a.* sin atender, abandonado.
untested [ʌn'testid], *a.* no probado; no puesto a prueba; sin probar.
unthanked [ʌn'θæŋkt], *a.* sin recibir gracias.
unthankful [ʌn'θæŋkful], *a.* ingrato, desagradecido.
unthankfully [ʌn'θæŋkfuli], *adv.* con ingratitud, desagradecidamente.
unthankfulness [ʌn'θæŋkfulnis], *s.* ingratitud, desagradecimiento.
unthinkable [ʌn'θiŋkəbl], *a.* impensable, inconcebible.
unthinking [ʌn'θiŋkiŋ], *a.* irreflexivo.
unthinkingly [ʌn'θiŋkiŋli], *adv.* irreflexivamente, sin pensar.
unthought-of [ʌn'θɔ:t-ɔv], *a.* inaudito.
unthread [ʌn'θred], *v.t.* (*tela*) deshebrar; (*aguja*) desenhebrar; (*perlas*) desensartar.
untidily [ʌn'taidili], *adv.* sin orden, desordenadamente.
untidiness [ʌn'taidinis], *s.* desorden; desaliño.
untidy [ʌn'taidi], *a.* desordenado; desaliñado.
untie [ʌn'tai], *v.t.* desatar; soltar.
until [ʌn'til], *conj.* hasta que, mientras no. — *prep.* hasta; ***until now,*** hasta ahora.
untilled [ʌn'tild], *a.* no labrado, sin labrar, baldío.
untimeliness [ʌn'taimlinis], *s.* inoportunidad, (lo) intempestivo; (lo) prematuro.
untimely [ʌn'taimli], *a.* inoportuno, intempestivo; prematuro. — *adv.* antes de tiempo.
untiring [ʌn'taiəriŋ], *a.* infatigable, incansable.
untitled [ʌn'taitld], *a.* sin título.
unto ['ʌntu(:)], *prep.* a.
untold [ʌn'tould], *a.* nunca contado; incalculable, incontable. — *frase adv.* ***to leave untold,*** callar, dejar en el tintero.
untomb [ʌn'tu:m], *v.t.* exhumar.
untouchable [ʌn'tʌtʃəbl], *a., s.* intocable.
untouched [ʌn'tʌtʃt], *a.* sin tocar; intacto; incólume; (*comida*) sin probar; insensible (***by,*** a).
untoward [ʌntə'wɔ:d], *a.* adverso, aciago, nefasto; inconveniente; ***sth. untoward,*** un *o* algún contratiempo.
untraceable [ʌn'treisəbl], *a.* imposible de encontrar.
untrained [ʌn'treind], *a.* sin formar, sin formación; (*dep.*) sin entrenar; (*animales*) sin amaestrar.
untrammelled [ʌn'træməld], *a.* sin trabas, libre, desembarazado.
untransferable [ʌntrænz'fə:rəbl], *a.* intransferible.
untranslatable [ʌntrænz'leitəbl], *a.* intraducible.
untravelled [ʌn'trævəld], *a.* que no ha viajado; inexplorado.
untried [ʌn'traid], *a.* no probado, sin probar; (*der., pers.*) sin procesar; (*der., causa*) sin ver.
untrimmed [ʌn'trimd], *a.* sin cortar; (*carp.*) sin alisar, sin desbastar.
untrod(den) [ʌn'trɔd(n)], *a.* no hollado, no pisado; (*nieve etc.*) virgen.
untroubled [ʌn'trʌbld], *a.* tranquilo; no perturbado (***by,*** por).
untrue [ʌn'tru:], *a.* falso; ficticio; (*pers.*) desleal; ***to be untrue to one's promise,*** incumplir su promesa; claudicar.
untruss [ʌn'trʌs], *v.t.* desatar.
untrustworthy [ʌn'trʌstwə:ði], *a.* indigno de confianza, informal, poco serio; no fidedigno; pérfido; poco seguro; ***he's thoroughly untrustworthy,*** no se puede uno fiar de él en absoluto.
untruth [ʌn'tru:θ], *s.* mentira, falsedad.
untruthful [ʌn'tru:θful], *a.* mentiroso, falso.
unturned [ʌn'tə:nd], *a.* (*en la frase*) ***to leave no stone unturned,*** remover Roma con Santiago; agotar todas las posibilidades.
untutored [ʌn'tju:təd], *a.* poco instruido, indocto; sin educar.
untwine, untwist [ʌn'twain, ʌn'twist], *v.t.* destorcer; desenlazar; desenroscar.
unused [ʌn'ju:zd], *a.* nuevo, sin usar; sin estrenar; [ʌn'ju:st] no acostumbrado (***to,*** a).
unusual [ʌn'ju:ʒuəl], *a.* excepcional; poco frecuente, insólito; raro.
unutterable [ʌn'ʌtərəbl], *a.* indecible; impronunciable; ***unutterable idiot,*** imbécil mayúsculo.
unvalued [ʌn'vælju:d], *a.* no valorado; menospreciado.
unvanquished [ʌn'væŋkwiʃt], *a.* invicto.
unvaried [ʌn'vɛərid], *a.* uniforme, invariable, monótono.
unvarnished [ʌn'vɑ:niʃt], *a.* no barnizado, sin barnizar; (*fig.*) escueto; ***the plain, unvarnished truth,*** la verdad monda y lironda.
unvarying [ʌn'vɛəriiŋ], *a.* invariable; constante.

unveil [ʌn'veil], *v.t.* quitar el velo a; descubrir.
unventilated [ʌn'ventileitid], *a.* sin ventilar, sin aire, sin ventilación.
unverifiable [ʌn'verifaiəbl], *a.* no comprobable.
unverified [ʌn'verifaid], *a.* sin comprobar.
unversed [ʌn'və:st], *a.* poco versado, poco ducho.
unviolated [ʌn'vaiəleitid], *a.* inviolado.
unvoiced [ʌn'vɔist], *a.* no expresado; (*gram.*) sordo.
unvouched-for [ʌn'vautʃt-fɔ:], *a.* no garantizado.
unwalled [ʌn'wɔ:ld], *a.* desamurallado; sin tapiar, sin tapia.
unwanted [ʌn'wɔntid], *a.* no querido, no deseado; superfluo.
unwarily [ʌn'wɛərili], *adv.* incautamente.
unwariness [ʌn'wɛərinis], *s.* imprudencia.
unwarlike [ʌn'wɔ:laik], *a.* poco belicoso, pacífico.
unwarrantable [ʌn'wɔrəntəbl], *a.* injustificable, indisculpable.
unwarranted [ʌn'wɔrəntid], *a.* injustificado; no autorizado; sin garantía.
unwary [ʌn'wɛəri], *a.* incauto, imprudente.
unwashed [ʌn'wɔʃt], *a.* no lavado, sin lavar; (*fig.*) ***the great unwashed,*** el populacho, el vulgo.
unwavering [ʌn'weivəriŋ], *a.* (*pers.*) que no vacila, sin titubeos; (*pers., voluntad*) firme, (*voluntad*) inquebrantable.
unweaned [ʌn'wi:nd], *a.* no destetado, sin destetar.
unwearied [ʌn'wiərid], *a.* infatigable.
unwearying [ʌn'wiəriiŋ], *a.* incansable, infatigable.
unweave [ʌn'wi:v], *v.t.* destejer.
unwed(ded) [ʌn'wed(id)], *a.* no casado, soltero.
unwelcome [ʌn'welkəm], *a.* que viene mal; inoportuno; molesto.
unwell [ʌn'wel], *a.* indispuesto, malo.
unwept [ʌn'wept], *a.* no llorado, no lamentado.
unwholesome [ʌn'houlsəm], *a.* poco saludable; malsano; que desazona.
unwholesomeness [ʌn'houlsəmnis], *s.* (lo) poco saludable; (lo) malsano.
unwieldiness [ʌn'wi:ldinis], *s.* (lo) pesado y difícil de manejar.
unwieldy [ʌn'wi:ldi], *a.* pesado y difícil de manejar.
unwilling [ʌn'wiliŋ], *a.* que no quiere, que se resiste, reacio, recalcitrante; ***he is unwilling to go,*** se resiste a ir.
unwillingly [ʌn'wiliŋli], *adv.* de mala gana, a regañadientes.
unwillingness [ʌn'wiliŋnis], *s.* mala gana, desgana, resistencia, renuencia.
unwind [ʌn'waind], *irr. v.t.* desliar, deshacer. — *v.i.* desliarse; distenderse; (*fig., fam.*) descansar, distenderse, expansionarse.
unwisdom [ʌn'wizdəm], *s.* imprudencia.
unwise [ʌn'waiz], *a.* poco prudente, imprudente, inconsiderado.
unwitnessed [ʌn'witnist], *a.* sin testigo(s).
unwitting [ʌn'witiŋ], *a.* inconsciente.
unwittingly [ʌn'witiŋli], *adv.* sin saberlo, inconscientemente.
unwomanly [ʌn'wumənli], *a.* indigno *o* impropio de una mujer; poco femenino.
unwonted [ʌn'wountid], *a.* inusitado, insólito.
unwontedness [ʌn'wountidnis], *s.* (lo) insólito.
unwooded [ʌn'wudid], *a.* sin árboles, sin bosques.
unworkable [ʌn'wə:kəbl], *a.* impracticable; (*mina*) inexplotable.
unworkmanlike [ʌn'wə:kmənlaik], *a.* chapucero.
unworldliness [ʌn'wə:ldlinis], *s.* falta de mundo *o* de mundanería.
unworldly [ʌn'wə:ldli], *a.* poco mundano.
unworn [ʌn'wɔ:n], *a.* nuevo, sin estrenar; sin (des)gastar.
unworthiness [ʌn'wə:ðinis], *s.* indignidad, falta de mérito.
unworthy [ʌn'wə:ði], *a.* indigno, sin mérito.
unwounded [ʌn'wu:ndid], *a.* ileso.
unwrap [ʌn'ræp], *v.t.* desenvolver, deshacer.
unwritten [ʌn'ritn], *a.* no escrito; en blanco; ***unwritten law,*** ley no escrita.
unwrought [ʌn'rɔ:t], *a.* sin forjar, no trabajado; ***unwrought wax,*** cera virgen.
unyielding [ʌn'ji:ldiŋ], *a.* inflexible, que no cede, que no ceja.
unyoke [ʌn'jouk], *v.t.* desuncir.
unzip [ʌn'zip], *v.t.* desabrochar, abrir la cremallera de.
up [ʌp], *a.* ascendente; de arriba; ***up train,*** tren ascendente. — *adv.* arriba; hacia arriba, para arriba; en lo alto; ***up and down,*** de acá para allá; ***to be up,*** estar levantado; ***to be up all night,*** no acostarse en toda la noche; ***to be up against it,*** estar en un aprieto; ***to be up against s.o.,*** habérselas con alguien; ***we are up against the unions now,*** hemos topado con los sindicatos; ***to be up in arms,*** estar sublevado(s); ***to be up for sale,*** estar de *o* en venta; ***to be up with the leaders,*** estar a la altura de los primeros; ***it's all up,*** ya no hay nada que hacer, se acabó; ***Chelsea is two goals up,*** el Chelsea lleva dos goles de ventaja; ***he's well up in maths.,*** está muy fuerte en matemáticas; ***the sun is up,*** ha salido el sol; ***the tide is up,*** ha subido la marea; ***time is up,*** es la hora; ***what's up?*** ¿qué pasa?; ***what's up with you?*** ¿qué te pasa?; ***there is sth. up,*** algo pasa, algo se trama; ***he is up to sth.,*** está tramando algo; ***it is up to you,*** allá usted, usted verá; de usted depende; ***it is up to me to tell him,*** me toca a mí decírselo; ***to bring up to date,*** actualizar; ***to come*** o ***crop up,*** plantearse, surgir, terciarse; ***to get worked up about sth.,*** excitarse por algo, exaltarse por algo; ***to stand up,*** ponerse de pie, levantarse; ***to store up,*** almacenar, guardar; (*fig.*) guardar. — *prep.* en lo alto de, encima de; subido a; ***up against,*** contra; ***up till*** o ***to,*** hasta; ***up a tree,*** subido a un árbol; ***up the river,*** río arriba; ***up the road,*** calle arriba. — *s.* (*pl.*) ***ups and downs,*** altibajos, *m.pl.* — *v.t.* — ***anchor,*** levar anclas. — *v.i.* — ***and go,*** coger e irse. — *interj.* ***up*** (***with***)***...!*** ¡arriba...!; ***ups-a-daisy!*** ¡upa!, ¡aúpa!
up-and-coming ['ʌp-ənd-'kʌmiŋ], *a.* (*fam.*) prometedor, que viene empujando.
upas ['ju:pəs], *s.* (*bot.*) antiaro.
upbraid [ʌp'breid], *v.t.* reprender.
upbraiding [ʌp'breidiŋ], *s.* reprimenda, reconvención.
upbringing ['ʌpbriŋiŋ], *s.* educación, crianza.
up-country ['ʌp-'kʌntri], *a.* del interior. — [ʌp-'kʌntri], *adv.* en el interior; al interior. — *s.* ['ʌp-'kʌntri], interior.
update [ʌp'deit], *v.t.* poner al día.
upend [ʌp'end], *v.t.* poner vertical.
upgrade ['ʌpgreid], *s.* cuesta en subida; (*fig.*) ***on the upgrade,*** mejorando, prosperando. — [ʌp'greid], *v.t.* subir *o* ascender de categoría.
upgrowth ['ʌpgrouθ], *s.* (*Am.*) crecimiento, aumento.
upheaval [ʌp'hi:vəl], *s.* solevantamiento; convulsión.
upheave [ʌp'hi:v], *v.t.* solevantar. — *v.i.* solevantarse.
uphill ['ʌphil], *a.* ascendente; (*fig.*) arduo, penoso. — [ʌp'hil], *adv.* cuesta arriba.
uphold [ʌp'hould], *v.t. irr.* defender; apoyar.
upholder [ʌp'houldə], *s.* defensor.
upholster [ʌp'houlstə], *v.t.* tapizar.
upholsterer [ʌp'houlstərə], *s.* tapicero.
upholstery [ʌp'houlstəri], *s.* tapicería; tapizado.
upkeep ['ʌpki:p], *s.* manutención; conservación; (*máquinas etc.*) sostenimiento.
upland ['ʌplənd], *a.* elevado, alto. — *s.* terreno elevado, tierras altas, *f.pl.*
uplift ['ʌplift], *s.* elevación; edificación, inspiración. — [ʌp'lift], *v.t.* elevar; edificar, inspirar.

upmost [ˈʌpmoust], *a. superl.* [UP].
upon [əˈpɔn], *prep.* [ON]; ***upon my word!*** ¡santos cielos!; ***upon my honour!*** ¡a fe mía!
upper [ˈʌpə], *a. compar.* [UP]; superior; más elevado; de arriba; ***upper class(es),*** clase superior; (*autobús*) ***upper deck,*** piso de arriba; ***to have the upper hand,*** tener la ventaja; tener vara alta. — *s.* (*pl.*) pala (*del calzado*); (*fam.*) ***to be on one's uppers,*** andar de capa caída.
upper-case [ˈʌpə-keis], *a.* (*impr.*) caja alta.
uppercut [ˈʌpəkʌt], *s.* (*boxeo*) puñetazo de abajo arriba.
uppermost [ˈʌpəmoust], *a.* (el) más alto; predominante; *superl.* [UP].
Upper Volta [ˈʌpə ˈvɔltə]. (el) Alto Volta.
uppish [ˈʌpiʃ], *a.* (*fam.*) engreído, petulante, chulo.
uppishness [ˈʌpiʃnis], *s.* (*fam.*) engreimiento, petulancia, chulería.
upraise [ʌpˈreiz], *v.t.* elevar, levantar.
upright [ˈʌprait], *a.* vertical; derecho; (*fig.*) recto, íntegro, probo. — *adv.* derecho, vertical(mente); (*fam.*) ***bolt upright,*** derecho como un huso. — *s.* montante.
uprightness [ˈʌpraitnis], *s.* honradez, rectitud.
uprise [ʌpˈraiz], *v.i.* levantarse.
uprising [ʌpˈraiziŋ], *s.* levantamiento, sublevación, insurrección, alzamiento; (*sol*) salida.
uproar [ˈʌprɔ:], *s.* alboroto, gritería, batahola, escándalo.
uproarious [ʌpˈrɔ:riəs], *a.* tumultuoso, clamoroso; (*fam.*) de carcajada.
uproariously [ʌpˈrɔ:riəsli], *adv.* tumultuosamente; a carcajadas.
uproot [ʌpˈru:t], *v.t.* desarraigar, extirpar, arrancar; (*agric.*) descuajar.
ups-a-daisy! [ˈʌps-ə-ˈdeizi], *interj.* [UP].
upset [ˈʌpset], *a.* (re)volcado; (*Am.*) ***upset price,*** primera oferta; precio mínimo; ***to have an upset stomach,*** tener el estómago fastidiado. — *s.* disgusto; trastorno; revés, *m.*, contratiempo; vuelco. — [ʌpˈset], *v.t.* disgustar; trastornar; contrariar; perturbar, alterar, desconcertar; volcar, derribar; ***he is very upset about it,*** está muy disgustado. — **upset o.s.,** *v.r.* disgustarse; apurarse.
upsetting [ʌpˈsetiŋ], *a.* inquietante, perturbador.
upshot [ˈʌpʃɔt], *s.* resultado, consecuencia.
upside [ˈʌpsaid], *s.* parte *o* lado superior; ***upside down,*** al revés, patas arriba; ***to turn everything upside down,*** revolverlo todo, ponerlo todo patas arriba.
upstairs [ʌpˈstɛəz], *a.* de arriba. — *adv.* arriba, en el piso superior *o* de arriba. — *s.* el piso *o* la parte de arriba.
upstanding [ʌpˈstændiŋ], *a.* recto, honrado.
upstart [ˈʌpstɑ:t], *a.*, *s.* arribista, *m.f.*, advenedizo.
upstream [ˈʌpˈstri:m], *adv.* aguas arriba, río arriba; ***to swim upstream,*** nadar contra la corriente.
upstroke [ˈʌpstrouk], *s.* (*de la pluma*) trazo hacia arriba; (*mec.*) carrera ascendente.
upsurge [ˈʌpsə:dʒ], *s.* brote; aumento; recrudecimiento.
uptake [ˈʌpteik], *s.* (*sólo en la frase*) ***to be quick on the uptake,*** cazarlas al vuelo.
upthrust [ˈʌpθrʌst], *s.* (*geol.*) solevantamiento.
up-to-date [ˈʌp-tə-ˈdeit], *a.* actual, del día, del momento.
upturn [ˈʌptə:n], *s.* (*Am.*) mejora; alza, aumento. — [ʌpˈtə:n], *v.t.* volver hacia arriba; volcar.
upward [ˈʌpwəd], *a.* ascendente, ascensional; al alza; pendiente.
upwards [ˈʌpwədz], *adv.* hacia arriba; ***to look upward(s),*** mirar hacia arriba. — *frase adv.* ***upwards of an hour,*** más de una hora.
Urals [ˈjuərəlz], **the.** *s.pl.* los Urales.
uranite [ˈjuərənait], *s.* uranita.
uranium [juˈreiniəm], *s.* uranio; ***uranium-reactor,*** reactor nuclear de uranio.
uranoelectricity [jureinouelikˈtrisiti], *s.* uranoelectricidad.
uranographic [jureinoˈgræfik], *a.* uranográfico.
uranography [juərəˈnɔgrəfi], *s.* uranografía.
uranometry [juərəˈnɔmitri], *s.* uranometría.
Uranus [ˈjuərənəs]. (*astron.*, *astrol.*) Urano.
urate [ˈjuəreit], *s.* urato.
urban [ˈə:bən], *a.* urbano; ***urban guerrilla,*** guerrillero urbano, tupamaro; ***urban renewal,*** renovación urbana.
urbane [ə:ˈbein], *a.* urbano, cortés.
urbanism [ˈə:bənizəm], *s.* urbanismo.
urbanity [ə:ˈbæniti], *s.* urbanidad, cortesía.
urbanization [ə:bənaiˈzeiʃən], *s.* urbanización.
urbanize [ˈə:bənaiz], *v.t.* urbanizar.
urchin [ˈə:tʃin], *s.* pillete, pilluelo, golfillo; (*zool.*) ***sea urchin,*** erizo de mar.
Urdu [ˈuədu:], *s.* urdu, *m.*
ureter [ju:ˈri:tə], *s.* uréter.
urethra [ju:ˈri:θrə], *s.* uretra.
urethral [ju:ˈri:θrəl], *a.* uretral.
urethritis [ju:ri:ˈθraitis], *s.* uretritis, *f.inv.*
urge [ə:dʒ], *s.* impulso, instinto, pujo; ansia. — *v.t.* impulsar, instar, incitar (**to,** a); exhortar (**to,** a); ***urge on,*** animar, aguijonear. — *v.i.* — ***that,*** pedir *o* recomendar con insistencia que.
urgency [ˈə:dʒənsi], *s.* urgencia; insistencia.
urgent [ˈə:dʒənt], *a.* urgente; apremiante; insistente; ***it is urgent,*** es urgente, urge.
urgently [ˈə:dʒəntli], *adv.* urgentemente, con urgencia; con insistencia; ***I need it urgently,*** me urge.
uric [ˈjuərik], *a.* (*quím.*) úrico.
urinal [ˈjuərinəl], *s.* orinal; urinario.
urinary [ˈjuərinəri], *a.* urinario.
urination [juəriˈneiʃən], *s.* urinación, micción.
urinate [ˈjuərineit], *v.t.* orinar. — *v.i.* orinar, mear.
urine [ˈjuərin], *s.* orina, orines, *m.pl.*
urn [ə:n], *s.* urna; tetera.
urologist [juəˈrɔlədʒist], *s.* urólogo.
urology [juəˈrɔlədʒi], *s.* urología.
uroscopy [juəˈrɔskəpi], *s.* uroscopia.
Ursa [ˈə:sə]. (*astron.*) Osa (***Major,*** Mayor; ***Minor,*** Menor).
ursine [ˈə:sain], *a.* ursino.
urticaceous [ə:tiˈkeiʃəs], *a.* urticáceo.
urticaria [ə:tiˈkɛəriə], *s.* urticaria.
Uruguay [ˈjuərəgwai]. (el) Uruguay.
Uruguayan [juərəˈgwaiən], *a.*, *s.* uruguayo.
us [ʌs], *pron. pers. pl.* nos; nosotros.
usable [ˈju:zəbl], *a.* servible, utilizáble.
usage [ˈju:sidʒ], *s.* uso; ***ill usage,*** malos tratos, *m.pl.*
usance [ˈju:zəns], *s.* (*com.*) plazo; (*com.*) interés, *m.*, renta.
use [ju:s], *s.* uso, empleo; utilidad; (*for.*) usufructo; ***to be of use,*** ser útil, servir; ***can I be of (any) use?*** ¿puedo hacer algo? ¿puedo ayudar?; ***it's (of) no use,*** es inútil; ***to be in use,*** estar en uso, estar usándose; ***to have no use for,*** no necesitar; (*fam.*) no apreciar; tener un concepto desfavorable de; ***to make use of,*** servirse de; ***to make good use of, to put to good use,*** aprovechar, sacar partido de; ***what's the use of it?*** ¿de qué sirve?; (*fam.*) ***what's the use?*** ¿para qué? — [ju:z], *v.t.* usar (de), emplear, utilizar, servirse de; (*for.*) usufructuar; ***use up,*** consumir, agotar; ***use ill,*** tratar mal. — [ju:st], *v. aux.* ***I used to go,*** solía ir, acostumbraba ir, iba; ***to be used to,*** estar acostumbrado a; ***to get used to,*** acostumbrarse a, habituarse a.
useful [ˈju:sful], *a.* útil.
usefully [ˈju:sfuli], *adv.* útilmente; ventajosamente, provechosamente, con provecho.

usefulness [ˈju:sfulnis], *s.* utilidad.
useless [ˈju:slis], *a.* inútil; inservible.
uselessly [ˈju:slisli], *adv.* inútilmente, en vano.
uselessness [ˈju:slisnis], *s.* inutilidad, (lo) inútil.
user [ˈju:zə], *s.* usuario.
usher [ˈʌʃə], *s.* portero, ujier; acomodador; anunciador. — *v.t.* — ***in,*** introducir, anunciar; hacer pasar (con mucha ceremonia); ***usher out,*** acompañar a la puerta (con mucha ceremonia).
usherette [ʌʃəˈret], *s.* (*teat.*, *cinema*) acomodadora.
usual [ˈju:ʒuəl], *a.* normal, corriente; usual, acostumbrado, habitual; ***as usual,*** como de costumbre, como siempre.
usually [ˈju:ʒuəli], *adv.* normalmente, generalmente, por regla general.
usucapt [ˈju:zjukæpt], *v.t.* (*for.*) usucapir.
usufruct [ˈju:zjufrʌkt], *s.* (*for.*) usufructo.
usufructuary [ju:zjuˈfrʌktjuəri], *s.* usufructuario.
userer [ˈju:ʒərə], *s.* usurero.
usurious [ju:ˈʒuəriəs], *a.* usurario.
usurp [ju:ˈzə:p], *v.t.* usurpar.
usurpation [ju:zə:ˈpeiʃən], *s.* usurpación.
usurper [ju:ˈzə:pə], *s.* usurpador.
usurping [ju:ˈzə:piŋ], *a.* usurpador. — *s.* usurpación.
usury [ˈju:ʒuəri], *s.* usura; ***to practise usury,*** usurear.
ut [ʌt], *s.* (*mús.*) ut, do.
utensil [ju:ˈtensil], *s.* utensilio, herramienta, útil.
uterine [ˈju:tərain], *a.* uterino.
uterus [ˈju:tərəs], *s.* (*pl.* **uteri** [-rai]) útero, matriz.
utilitarian [ju:tiliˈtɛəriən], *a.* utilitario, funcional. — *s.* utilitarista, *m.f.*
utilitarianism [ju:tiliˈtɛəriənizəm], *s.* utilitarismo.
utility [ju:ˈtiliti], *s.* utilidad; conveniencia; (*pl.* **utilities** [-z]) servicios, *m.pl.*
utilizable [ˈju:tilaizəbl], *a.* utilizable, aprovechable.
utilize [ˈju:tilaiz], *v.t.* utilizar, servirse de, hacer uso de.
utmost, uttermost [ˈʌtmoust, ˈʌtəmoust], *a.* extremo, sumo, último. — *s.* todo (lo) posible, (lo) máximo, (lo) sumo; ***at the utmost,*** a lo más; ***to do one's utmost,*** hacer todo lo posible, hacer cuanto pueda uno.
Utopia [ju:ˈtoupiə]. Utopía.
Utopian [ju:ˈtoupiən], *a.* utópico. — *s.* utopista, *m.f.*
utricle [ˈju:trikl], *s.* utrículo.
utricular [ju:ˈtrikjulə], *a.* utricular.
utter (1) [ˈʌtə], *a.* completo, absoluto, total; extremo; puro.
utter (2) [ˈʌtə], *v.t.* pronunciar, proferir; emitir; publicar; poner en circulación.
utterable [ˈʌtərəbl], *a.* pronunciable; proferible.
utterance [ˈʌtərəns], *s.* pronunciación; palabras, *pl.*; (*cheques etc.*) emisión; manifestación, declaración; ***to give utterance to,*** manifestar, declarar.
utterer [ˈʌtərə], *s.* el que pronuncia *o* profiere; emisor, divulgador.
utterly [ˈʌtəli], *adv.* absolutamente, totalmente.
uttermost [ʌtəˈmoust], [UTMOST].
uvea [ˈju:viə], *s.* úvea.
uvula [ˈju:vjulə], *s.* úvula; galillo, campanilla.
uvular [ˈju:vjulə], *a.* uvular.
uxorious [ʌksˈɔ:riəs], *a.* gurrumino.
uxoriousness [ʌkˈsɔ:riəsnis], *s.* gurrumina.

V

V, v [vi:], *s.* vigésima segunda letra del alfabeto; ***V-shaped,*** en V.

vacancy [ˈveikənsi], *s.* (lo) vacío, vacuidad, vaciedad; habitación vacante; (*puesto*) vacante, *f.*; ***to fill a vacancy,*** proveer una vacante.

vacant [ˈveikənt], *a.* vacío; vacante; libre, desocupado; vago, distraído.

vacate [vəˈkeit], *v.t.* desocupar (*una casa*); dejar vacante (*un puesto*); dejar libre (*un asiento*).

vacation [vəˈkeiʃən], *s.* vacación, vacaciones, *f.pl.*

vaccinate [ˈvæksineit], *v.t.* vacunar.

vaccination [væksiˈneiʃən], *s.* vacunación; vacuna.

vaccine [ˈvæksi:n], *s.* vacuna.

vacillate [ˈvæsileit], *v.i.* vacilar, titubear.

vacillating [ˈvæsileitiŋ], *a.* vacilante, titubeante.

vacillation [væsiˈleiʃən], *s.* vacilación, titubeo.

vacuity [vəˈkju:iti], *s.* vacuidad.

vacuous [ˈvækjuəs], *a.* vacío; necio, casquivano; (*fís.*) vacuo.

vacuum [ˈvækjuəm], *s.* (*fís.*) vacío; ***vacuum-brake,*** freno de vacío; ***vacuum-cleaner,*** aspiradora; ***vacuum-flask,*** termo.

vade-mecum [ˈveidi-ˈmi:kəm], *s.* vademécum.

vagabond [ˈvægəbɔnd], *a.*, *s.* vagabundo; ***to be a vagabond,*** ser vagabundo, vagabundear.

vagabondage, vagabondism [ˈvægəbɔndidʒ, -izəm], *s.* vagabundeo.

vagabondize [ˈvægəbɔndaiz], *v.i.* vagabundear.

vagary [ˈveigəri], *s.* capricho, extravagancia.

vagina [vəˈdʒainə], *s.* vagina.

vaginal [vəˈdʒainəl], *a.* vaginal.

vagrancy [ˈveigrənsi], *s.* vagancia, vagabundeo.

vagrant [ˈveigrənt], *a.* vagabundo; errante, errático. — *s.* vagabundo.

vague [veig], *a.* (*recuerdo etc.*) vago, borroso; indefinido, indistinto, impreciso; (*temperamento*) poco concreto; nebuloso; distraído.

vagueness [ˈveignis], *s.* vaguedad; (lo) vago, borroso, impreciso *etc.*

vain [vein], *a.* vano, inútil; vanidoso, presumido; ***in vain,*** en vano, en balde.

vainglorious [veinˈglɔ:riəs], *a.* vanaglorioso, jactancioso.

vaingloriously [veinˈglɔ:riəsli], *adv.* vanagloriosamente, con jactancia.

vaingloriousness, vainglory [veinˈglɔ:riəsnis, veinˈglɔ:ri], *s.* vanagloria, jactancia.

vainly [ˈveinli], *adv.* inútilmente, en vano; vanidosamente.

vainness [ˈveinnis], *s.* vanidad, (lo) vanidoso, envanecimiento.

vair [vɛə], *s.* (*blas.*) vero.

valance [ˈvæləns], *s.* cenefa, doselera.

vale (1) [veil], *s.* valle; ***vale of tears,*** valle de lágrimas.

vale! (2) [ˈveili], *interj.* vale, adiós.

valediction [væliˈdikʃən], *s.* despedida, adiós, *m.inv.*, vale.

valedictory [væliˈdiktəri], *a.* de despedida. — *s.* discurso de despedida.

valence, valency [ˈveiləns, -i], *s.* (*quím.*) valencia.

Valencia [vəˈlenʃə]. Valencia.

Valencian [vəˈlenʃən], *a.*, *s.* valenciano.

Valentine [ˈvæləntain]. Valentín.

valentine [ˈvæləntain], *s.* felicitación amorosa *o* jocosa del día de San Valentín; novio *o* novia escogido en este día.

valerian [vəˈliəriən], *s.* (*bot.*) valeriana.

valerianate, valerate [vəˈliəriənit, ˈvælərit], *s.* (*quím.*) valerianato.

valet [ˈvælit], *s.* ayuda de cámara.

valetudinarian, valetudinary [vælitju:diˈnɛəriən, væliˈtju:dinəri], *a.*, *s.* valetudinario.

valiant [ˈvæljənt], *a.* valeroso, denodado.

valid [ˈvælid], *a.* válido, valedero; vigente, en vigor.

validate [ˈvælideit], *v.t.* validar.

validity [vəˈliditi], *s.* validez.

valise [vəˈli:z], *s.* maleta.

valkyrie [ˈvælkiri], *s.* valquiria.

Valladolid [vælədɔˈlid], *a.* vallisoletano.

valley [ˈvæli], *s.* valle.

valorous [ˈvælərəs], *a.* bizarro, esforzado, denodado.

valour [ˈvælə], *s.* valentía, bizarría.

valuable [ˈvæljuəbl], *a.* valioso; estimable. — *s.* (*pl.*) objetos de valor, *m.pl.*

valuableness [ˈvæljuəblnis], *s.* valor; precio.

valuation [væljuˈeiʃən], *s.* valuación; tasación.

valuator [ˈvæljueitə], *s.* tasador.

value [ˈvælju:], *s.* valor; valía; ***to set a value on,*** poner un precio a; (*fam.*) ***wonderful value,*** una auténtica ganga; de precio muy interesante. — *v.t.* valorar, tasar (***at,*** en); apreciar, estimar.

valueless [ˈvæljulis], *a.* sin valor.

valuer [ˈvæljuə], *s.* tasador.

valvate [ˈvælvit], *a.* valvular.

valve [vælv], *s.* válvula; (*bot.*, *zool.*) valva.

valvular [ˈvælvjulə], *a.* valvular.

vamoose [vəˈmu:s], *v.i.* (*fam.*) largarse.

vamp (1) [væmp], *s.* empella; remiendo. — *v.t.* poner empella a; remendar; (*mús.*) improvisar.

vamp (2) [væmp], *s.* vampiresa, vampi, *f.* — *v.t.* encandilar.

vampire [ˈvæmpaiə], *s.* vampiro; (*fig.*) vampiresa.

vampirism [ˈvæmpaiərizəm], *s.* vampirismo.

van (1) [væn], *s.* (*mil.*) vanguardia; ***to be in the van,*** ir a vanguardia.

van (2) [væn], *s.* camioneta; (*f.c.*) furgón.

vanadium [vəˈneidiəm], *s.* vanadio.

vandal [ˈvændəl], *s.* vándalo; (*fig.*) gamberro.

vandalic [vænˈdælik], *a.* vandálico.

vandalism [ˈvændəlizəm], *s.* vandalismo; (*fig.*) gamberrismo.

vane [vein], *s.* paleta (*de hélice*); aspa (*de molino*); barba (*de pluma*); ***weather vane,*** veleta.

vang [væŋ], *s.* (*mar.*) osta.

vanguard [ˈvæŋgɑ:d], *s.* vanguardia; ***to be in the vanguard,*** ir en vanguardia.

vanilla [vəˈnilə], *s.* vainilla.

vanish [ˈvæniʃ], *v.i.* desaparecer, desvanecerse.

vanishing [ˈvæniʃiŋ], *a.* que desaparece; ***vanishing cream,*** crema facial. — *s.* desaparición; desvanecimiento; fuga; ***vanishing point,*** punto de fuga.

vanity [ˈvæniti], *s.* vanidad; ***vanity case,*** neceser (de belleza).

vanquish [ˈvæŋkwiʃ], *v.t.* vencer.

vanquishable [ˈvæŋkwiʃəbl], *a.* vencible.

vanquisher [ˈvæŋkwiʃə], *s.* vencedor.

vantage [ˈvɑ:ntidʒ], *s.* (*tenis*) ventaja; ***vantage ground,*** posición ventajosa; ***vantage point,*** atalaya, mirador; sitio panorámico.

vapid [ˈvæpid], *a.* insípido, insulso.

vapidity, vapidness [vəˈpiditi, ˈvæpidnis], *s.* insipidez, insulsez.

vaporization [veipəraiˈzeiʃən], *s.* vaporización.

vaporize [ˈveipəraiz], *v.t.* vaporizar, vaporear. — *v.i.* vaporizarse, vaporearse.

vaporous [ˈveipərəs], *a.* vaporoso; (*fig.*) nebuloso.

vapour [ˈveipə], *s.* vapor; vaho, exhalación. — *v.i.* evaporarse, vahear.

variability, variableness [vɛəriəˈbiliti, ˈvɛəriəblnis], *s.* variabilidad, (lo) variable.

variable [ˈvɛəriəbl], *a.*, *s.* variable.

variance [ˈvɛəriəns], *s.* disidencia, desacuerdo, desavenencia, disensión; ***to be at variance (with),*** estar en desacuerdo con, estar de punta con.
variant [ˈvɛəriənt], *a., s.* variante, *f.*
variation [vɛəriˈeiʃən], *s.* variación; cambio.
varicella [væriˈselə], *s.* varicela.
varicocele [ˈværikosi:l], *s.* varicocele.
varicoloured [ˈvɛərikʌləd], *a.* variopinto.
varicose [ˈværikous], *a.* varicoso; ***varicose veins,*** varices, *f.pl.*
varied [ˈvɛərid], *a.* vario, variado.
variegate [ˈvɛərigeit], *v.t.* (entre)mezclar.
variegated [ˈvɛərigeitid], *a.* abigarrado.
variegation [vɛəriˈgeiʃən], *s.* abigarramiento; jaspeado.
variety [vəˈraiəti], *s.* variedad, diversidad; (*teat.*) teatro de variedades.
variola [vəˈraiələ], *s.* (*med.*) viruela(s).
varioloid [vəˈraiəlɔid], *s.* varioloide, *f.*
variolous [vəˈraiələs], *a.* varioloso, virolento.
various [ˈvɛəriəs], *a.* diverso(s).
variously [ˈvɛəriəsli], *adv.* diversamente, de diversos modos.
varix [ˈvɛəriks], *s.* (*pl.* **varices** [ˈværisi:z]) (*cir.*) variz, *f.*, varice, *f.*, várice, *f.*
varnish [ˈvɑ:niʃ], *s.* barniz; esmalte; ***nail varnish,*** esmalte de uñas. — *v.t.* barnizar; laquear, esmaltar; (*fig.*) paliar, disimular.
varnisher [ˈvɑ:niʃə], *s.* barnizador; esmaltador.
varnishing [ˈvɑ:niʃiŋ], *s.* barnizado; esmaltado.
varsity [ˈvɑ:siti], *s.* (*fam.*) universidad.
vary [ˈvɛəri], *v.t., v.i.* variar; cambiar.
varying [ˈvɛəriiŋ], *a.* variable; diverso.
vascular [ˈvæskjulə], *a.* vascular.
vascularity [væskjuˈlæriti], *s.* vascularidad.
vasculose [ˈvæskjulous], *a.* vasculoso.
vase [vɑ:z], *s.* jarrón; florero.
Vaseline [ˈvæsili:n], *s.* (*marca de fábrica*) vaselina.
vasomotor [ˈveizoˈmoutə], *a.* (*anat.*) vasomotor.
vassal [ˈvæsəl], *s.* vasallo.
vassalage [ˈvæsəlidʒ], *s.* vasallaje.
vast [vɑ:st], *a.* vasto, inmenso, enorme.
vastly [ˈvɑ:stli], *adv.* en sumo grado; ***vastly different,*** totalmente distinto; ***vastly superior,*** sin punto de comparación.
vastness [ˈvɑ:stnis], *s.* vastedad, inmensidad, enormidad.
vasty [ˈvɑ:sti], *a.* (*poét.*) vasto, inmenso.
vat [væt], *s.* tina, tinaja.
Vatican [ˈvætikən], *a.* vaticano; ***Vatican City,*** ciudad vaticana; ***Vatican Council,*** concilio vaticano. — *s.* ***the Vatican,*** (el) Vaticano.
vaticinate [væˈtisineit], *v.t.* vaticinar. — *v.i.* hacer pronosticaciones.
vaticination [vætisiˈneiʃən], *s.* vaticinio(s).
vaudeville [ˈvɔ:dəvil], *s.* (teatro de) variedades.
vault (1) [vɔ:lt], *s.* bóveda; bodega; sepultura, tumba; ***vault of heaven,*** bóveda celeste. — *v.t.* (*arq.*) abovedar.
vault (2) [vɔ:lt], *s.* salto, voltereta. — *v.i.* saltar, voltear.
vaulted [ˈvɔ:ltid], *a.* abovedado.
vaulting [ˈvɔ:ltiŋ], *s.* abovedado; saltos, *m.pl.*; ***vaulting horse,*** potro de madera.
vaunt [vɔ:nt], *v.t.* alardear de, jactarse de. — *v.i.* vanagloriarse, jactarse.
vaunted [ˈvɔ:ntid], *a.* cacareado; ***the much vaunted,*** el tan cacareado.
vaunting [ˈvɔ:ntiŋ], *a.* jactancioso. — *s.* jactancias, *f.pl.*
vauntingly [ˈvɔ:ntiŋli], *adv.* con jactancias.
veal [ˈvi:l], *s.* ternera, carne de ternera; ***veal-chop,*** chuleta de ternera; ***veal-cutlet,*** filete de ternera.
vector [ˈvektə], *s.* vector.
vectorial [vekˈtɔ:riəl], *a.* vectorial.
vedette [viˈdet], *s.* (*mil.*) centinela de avanzada; ***vedette boat,*** buque escucha, *m.*
veer [viə], *v.i.* virar, cambiar de dirección.
veering [ˈviəriŋ], *s.* (*mar.*) virada(s).
veery [ˈviəri], *s.* (*orn.*) tordo canoro.
vegetable [ˈvedʒitəbl], *a., s.* vegetal; ***vegetable garden,*** huerto; ***vegetable kingdom,*** reino vegetal; ***vegetable marrow,*** calabacín. — *s.* (*pl.*) verduras, *f.pl.*, hortalizas, *f.pl.*; (*secas*) legumbres, *f.pl.*
vegetal [ˈvedʒitəl], *a.* vegetal.
vegetarian [vedʒiˈtɛəriən], *a., s.* vegetariano.
vegetarianism [vedʒiˈtɛəriənizəm], *s.* vegetarianismo.
vegetate [ˈvedʒiteit], *v.i.* vegetar.
vegetation [vedʒiˈteiʃən], *s.* vegetación.
vegetative [ˈvedʒitətiv], *a.* vegetativo.
vehemence, vehemency [ˈvi:əməns, -i], *s.* vehemencia; violencia.
vehement [ˈvi:əmənt], *a.* vehemente; violento.
vehicle [ˈvi:ikl], *s.* vehículo.
vehicular [viˈhikjulə], *a.* de (los) vehículos, para vehículos; ***vehicular traffic,*** tráfico rodado.
veil [veil], *s.* velo; ***to draw a veil over,*** correr un velo sobre; ***to take the veil,*** profesar, tomar el velo. — *v.t.* velar.
veiling [ˈveiliŋ], *s.* (*foto.*) velo; material para velos.
veilless [ˈveillis], *a.* sin velo.
vein [vein], *s.* (*anat.*) vena; (*min.*) veta, filón; (*fig.*) veta; (*bot.*) nervio.
veined [veind], *a.* venoso; veteado; avetado.
veining [ˈveiniŋ], *s.* veteado.
veinstone [ˈveinstoun], *s.* (*min.*) ganga.
veiny [ˈveini], [VEINED].
velar [ˈvi:lə], *a.* velar.
velleity [veˈli:iti], *s.* veleidad.
vellicate [ˈvelikeit], *v.t.* (*med.*) velicar.
vellication [veliˈkeiʃən], *s.* (*med.*) velicación.
vellum [ˈveləm], *s.* vitela.
velocipede [viˈlɔsipi:d], *s.* velocípedo.
velocity [viˈlɔsiti], *s.* velocidad; celeridad.
velours [vəˈluə], *s.* tela *o* felpa aterciopelada.
velum [ˈvi:ləm], *s.* (*pl.* **vela** [ˈvi:lə]) velo del paladar.
velvet [ˈvelvit], *a.* de terciopelo, aterciopelado. — *s.* terciopelo; ***to be on velvet,*** vivir en plan sibarita.
velveteen [velviˈti:n], *s.* velludillo, pana.
velveting [ˈvelvitiŋ], *s.* (tela de) terciopelo.
velvety [ˈvelviti], *a.* aterciopelado.
venal [ˈvi:nəl], *a.* venal.
venality [vi:ˈnæliti], *s.* venalidad.
venation [vi:ˈneiʃən], *s.* nervadura.
vend [vend], *v.t.* vender.
vendee [venˈdi:], *s.* (*for.*) adquiridor, comprador.
vendetta [venˈdetə], *s.* enemistad.
vendibleness [ˈvendiblnis], *s.* (lo) vendible.
vendible [ˈvendibl], *a.* vendible.
vending [ˈvendiŋ], *s.* venta, distribución; ***vending machine,*** máquina expendedora.
vendor [ˈvendə], *s.* vendedor; vendedor ambulante, buhonero.
veneer [viˈniə], *s.* chapa, enchapado; (*fig.*) barniz, apariencia. — *v.t.* chapear, plaquear; (*fig.*) encubrir.
veneering [viˈniəriŋ], *s.* enchapado, chapeado.
venerable [ˈvenərəbl], *a.* venerable; (*título*) (el) venerable.
venerableness [ˈvenərəblnis], *s.* (lo) venerable, respetabilidad.
venerate [ˈvenəreit], *v.t.* venerar, reverenciar.
veneration [venəˈreiʃən], *s.* veneración, reverencia.
venerator [ˈvenəreitə], *s.* venerador.

venereal [vi'niəriəl], *a.* venéreo; ***venereal disease,*** enfermedad venérea.
venery ['venəri], *s.* acto venéreo, venus, *f.inv.*
Venetian [vi'ni:ʃən], *a., s.* veneciano; ***Venetian blinds,*** persianas, *f.pl.*
Venezuela [veni'zweilə]. Venezuela.
Venezuelan [veni'zweilən], *a., s.* venezolano.
vengeance ['vendʒəns], *s.* venganza; (*fam.*) ***with a vengeance,*** con gana(s).
vengeful ['vendʒful], *a.* vengativo.
venial ['vi:niəl], *a.* venial.
Venice ['venis]. Venecia.
venison ['venzən], *s.* carne de venado.
venom ['venəm], *s.* veneno; (*fig.*) virulencia.
venomous ['venəməs], *a.* venenoso; (*fig.*) virulento; (*lengua*) viperina.
venomousness ['venəməsnis], *s.* venenosidad; virulencia.
venous ['vi:nəs], *a.* venoso.
vent (1) [vent], *s.* agujero, orificio; respiradero, salida (*de aire*); (*artill.*) fogón; (*fund.*) bravera; (*mec.*) lumbrera, válvula de purga; ***to give vent to,*** dar salida *o* expresión *o* rienda suelta a; ***to give vent to one's feelings,*** desahogarse. — *v.t.* proveer de abertura(s); purgar; (*fig.*) desahogar, descargar, expresar; ***vent one's spleen,*** descargar la bilis; ***vent one's cruelty*** o ***savagery on,*** ensañarse con.
vent (2) [vent], *s.* abertura (*de prenda de vestir*).
venthole ['venthoul], *s.* respiradero.
ventilate ['ventileit], *v.t.* ventilar; (*fig.*) ***ventilate one's grievances,*** ventilar sus quejas.
ventilation [venti'leiʃən], *s.* ventilación.
ventilator ['ventileitə], *s.* ventilador.
ventral ['ventrəl], *a.* ventral.
ventricle ['ventrikl], *s.* ventrículo.
ventricular [ven'trikjulə], *a.* ventricular.
ventriloquism, ventriloquy [ven'triləkwizəm, -kwi], *s.* ventriloquia.
ventriloquist [ven'triləkwist], *s.* ventrílocuo.
venture ['ventʃə], *s.* empresa (arriesgada), aventura; especulación. — *v.t.* aventurar; arriesgar. — *v.i.* aventurarse; arriesgarse; atreverse (***to,*** a); ***venture abroad*** o ***out,*** atreverse a salir; ***venture on,*** embarcarse en, arriesgarse en; ***nothing venture, nothing win*** o ***gain,*** quien no se aventura, no ha ventura.
venturesome, venturous ['ventʃəsem, -rəs], *a.* (*pers.*) aventurero, osado, intrépido, emprendedor; (*empresa etc.*) aventurado, azaroso.
venturesomeness, venturousness ['ventʃəsəmnis, -rəsnis], *s.* arrojo, intrepidez.
venue ['venju:], *s.* lugar *o* sitio de reunión; escenario; (*for.*) lugar de los hechos; (*esgr.*) pase.
Venus ['vi:nəs]. (*astron., astrol.*) Venus, *m.*; (*mit.*) Venus, *f.*
veracious [və'reiʃəs], *a.* verídico, veraz.
veracity [və'ræsiti], *s.* veracidad.
veranda(h) [və'rændə], *s.* terraza, galería.
verb [və:b], *s.* verbo.
verbal ['və:bəl], *a.* verbal; oral, de palabra.
verbalism ['və:bəlizəm], *s.* palabrería, verbalismo.
verbalize ['və:bəlaiz], *v.t., v.i.* expresar(se) con palabras.
verbally ['və:bəli], *adv.* de palabra, verbalmente.
verbatim [və'beitim], *a.* textual. — *adv.* palabra por palabra.
verbena [və:'bi:nə], *s.* (*bot.*) verbena.
verberation [və:bə'reiʃən], *s.* verberación.
verbiage ['və:biidʒ], *s.* verbosidad, palabrería.
verbose [və:'bous], *a.* verboso, prolijo.
verbosely [və:'bousli], *adv.* con verbosidad, prolijamente.
verboseness, verbosity [və:'bousnis, və:'bɔsiti], *s.* verbosidad, palabrería.
verdancy ['və:dənsi], *s.* verdor.
verdant ['və:dənt], *a.* verde.
verdict ['və:dikt], *s.* (*for.*) veredicto, fallo; dictamen.
verdigris ['və:digris], *s.* (*quím.*) cardenillo, verdete.
verditer ['və:ditə], *s.* verde de tierra.
verdure ['və:dʒə], *s.* verdor; frondosidad, lozanía.
verdured, verdurous ['və:dʒəd, -rəs], *a.* verdoso, lozano.
verge (1) [və:dʒ], *s.* borde, margen; orilla; ***on the verge of,*** al borde de; ***to be on the verge of,*** estar a punto de. — *v.i.* — ***on,*** estar al borde de, rayar en.
verge (2) [və:dʒ], *s.* fuste; eje (*de reloj*).
verger ['və:dʒə], *s.* alguacil de vara; sacristán.
veridical [və'ridikəl], *a.* verídico.
verification [verifi'keiʃən], *s.* comprobación.
verify ['verifai], *v.t.* comprobar; acreditar.
verily ['verili], *adv.* (*ant.*) en verdad.
verisimilar [veri'similə], *a.* verosímil.
verisimilitude [verisi'militju:d], *s.* verosimilitud.
veritable ['veritəbl], *a.* verdadero.
verity ['veriti], *s.* verdad, veracidad.
verjuice ['və:dʒu:s], *s.* agrazada; (*fig.*) aspereza.
vermeil ['və:meil], *s.* plata dorada; (*poét.*) bermellón.
vermicelli [və:mi'seli], *s.* fideos, *m.pl.*
vermicide ['və:misaid], *s.* vermicida, *m.*
vermicular [və'mikjulə], *a.* vermicular.
vermiform ['və:mifɔ:m], *a.* vermiforme.
vermifuge ['və:mifju:dʒ], *a., s.* vermífugo.
vermil(l)ion [və'miljən], *a.* bermejo. — *s.* bermellón.
vermin ['və:min], *s.* (*bichos pequeños*) sabandijas, *f.pl.*; (*bichos grandes*) alimañas, *f.pl.*; (*fig.*) sabandija, insecto, parásito; (*fig.*) gentuza, chusma.
verminous ['və:minəs], *a.* lleno de sabandijas; infestado de ratones; lleno de piojos, piojoso.
vermivorous [və:'mivərəs], *a.* vermívoro.
vermouth ['və:məθ], *s.* vermut.
vernacular [və'nækjulə], *a.* vernáculo. — *s.* lengua vernácula; (*fam.*) lenguaje corriente.
vernal ['və:nəl], *a.* vernal.
vernier ['və:niə], *s.* (*mat. etc.*) vernier.
Verona [və'rounə]. Verona.
Veronese [vero'ni:z], *a., s.* veronés, *m.*
veronica [və'rɔnikə], *s.* (*bot.*) verónica.
Versailles [vɛə'sai]. Versalles.
versatile ['və:sətail], *a.* adaptable; polifacético; polivalente.
versatility [və:sə'tiliti], *s.* (lo) adaptable; (lo) polifacético; (lo) polivalente.
verse [və:s], *s.* estrofa; poesías, *f.pl.*; poesía, verso; versículo (*de la Biblia*); ***in verse,*** en verso.
versed [və:st], *a.* versado (***in,*** en).
versicle ['və:sikl], *s.* versículo.
versification [və:sifi'keiʃən], *s.* versificación.
versifier ['və:sifaiə], *s.* versificador.
versify ['və:sifai], *v.t., v.i.* versificar.
version ['və:ʃən], *s.* versión.
verso ['və:sou], *s.* reverso.
verst [və:st], *s.* versta.
versus ['və:səs], *prep.* contra.
vertebra ['və:tibrə], *s.* (*pl.* **vertebræ** ['və:tibri:]) vértebra.
vertebral ['və:tibrəl], *a.* vertebral.
vertebrate ['və:tibrit], *a., s.* (*zool.*) vertebrado.
vertex ['və:teks], *s.* (*pl.* **vertices** ['və:tisi:z]) vértice; (*astron.*) cenit; ápice.
vertical ['və:tikəl], *a., s.* vertical.
verticalness ['və:tikəlnis], *s.* verticalidad.
vertiginous [və:'tidʒinəs], *a.* vertiginoso.
vertiginousness [və:'tidʒinəsnis], *s.* (lo) vertiginoso.

vertigo [ˈvəːtigou], *s.* (*pl.* **vertigines** [vəːˈtidʒiniːz]) vértigo.
vervain [ˈvəːvein], *s.* (*bot.*) verbena.
verve [vəːv], *s.* energía, brío.
very [ˈveri], *a.* mismo; ***at that very moment,*** en aquel mismo instante; ***it's the very thing,*** es justo lo que queremos; ***the very idea!*** ¡a quién se le ocurre!; ***the very truth,*** la pura verdad. — *adv.* muy; ***very good,*** muy bueno, buenísimo; muy bien; ***very well,*** muy bien; ***very well, then,*** si usted se empeña, si eso es lo que usted quiere; ***very much,*** mucho, muchísimo; ***very much better*** (***worse***), muchísimo mejor (peor); ***that's very kind of you,*** es usted muy amable; ***the very best,*** el, la, lo mejor que hay; ***to do one's very best,*** hacer todo lo posible; ***at the very most,*** todo lo más, a lo sumo; ***are you busy? very,*** ¿estás ocupado? mucho.
vesania [viˈseiniə], *s.* vesania.
vesicate [ˈvesikeit], *v.t.* avejigar.
vesicatory [ˈvesikeitəri], *a.*, *s.* vejigatorio.
vesicle [ˈvesikl], *s.* vejiguilla, vesícula.
vesicular [viˈsikjulə], *a.* vesicular.
vesiculate [viˈsikjulit], *a.* vesiculoso.
Vesper [ˈvespə], *s.* Véspero, estrella vespertina.
vespers [ˈvespəz], *s.pl.* (*igl.*) vísperas, *f.pl.*
vessel [ˈvesəl], *s.* vaso; vasija, recipiente; nave, buque; ***blood vessel,*** vaso sanguíneo.
vest (1) [vest], *s.* camiseta; (*Am.*) chaleco.
vest (2) [vest], *v.t.* investir; conferir, conceder; hacer titular de.
vestal [ˈvestəl], *a.*, *s.* vestal.
vested [ˈvestid], *a.* (*for.*) inalienable, establecido; ***vested interests,*** intereses creados, *m.pl.*
vestibule [ˈvestibjuːl], *s.* vestíbulo.
vestige [ˈvestidʒ], *s.* vestigio, rastro.
vestigial [vesˈtidʒiəl], *a.* vestigial.
vestment [ˈvestmənt], *s.* vestidura.
vestry [ˈvestri], *s.* sacristía.
vesture [ˈvestʃə], *s.* vestidura; (*for.*) toda vegetación menos los árboles.
Vesuvius [viˈsuːviəs]. (el) Vesubio.
vet [vet], *s.* (*abrev. de* [VETERINARIAN]) veterinario. — *v.t.* (*fam.*) repasar, revisar; investigar.
vetch [vetʃ], *s.* arveja.
veteran [ˈvetərən], *a.* veterano. — *s.* veterano, excombatiente.
veterinarian [vetəriˈnɛəriən], *s.* veterinario.
veterinary [ˈvetərinəri], *a.* veterinario; ***veterinary science,*** veterinaria; ***veterinary surgeon,*** veterinario.
veto [ˈviːtou], *s.* veto. — *v.t.* poner veto a, vetar.
vex [veks], *v.t.* molestar, fastidiar, contrariar, disgustar.
vexation [vekˈseiʃən], *s.* molestia, fastidio, contrariedad, disgusto.
vexatious [vekˈseiʃəs], *a.* molesto, fastidioso, que contraría, que disgusta.
vexatiousness [vekˈseiʃəsnis], *s.* (lo) molesto, (lo) fastidioso.
vexed [vekst], *a.* molesto, de fastidio; discutido, llevado y traído; ***vexed question,*** cuestión batallona.
vexing [ˈveksiŋ], [VEXATIOUS].
via [ˈvaiə], *prep.* por.
viability [vaiəˈbiliti], *s.* viabilidad.
viable [ˈvaiəbl], *a.* viable.
viaduct [ˈvaiədʌkt], *s.* viaducto.
vial [ˈvaiəl], *s.* frasco pequeño, frasquete.
viand [ˈvaiənd], *s.* vianda; (*pl.*) manjares, *m.pl.*
viaticum [vaiˈætikəm], *s.* (*pl.* **viatica** [-kə]) viático.
vibrant [ˈvaibrənt], *a.* vibrante (***with,*** de).
vibrate [vaiˈbreit], *v.t.* hacer vibrar. — *v.i.* vibrar; trepidar.
vibratile [ˈvaibrətail], *a.* vibrátil.
vibrating [vaiˈbreitiŋ], *a.* vibrante; trepidante.
vibration [vaiˈbreiʃən], *s.* vibración; trepidación.
vibratory [ˈvaibrətəri], *a.* vibratorio.
Viburnum [vaiˈbəːnəm], *s.* (*bot.*) viburno, mundillo.
vicar [ˈvikə], *s.* vicario; pastor (protestante), párroco.
vicarage [ˈvikəridʒ], *s.* casa del párroco.
vicarial [viˈkɛəriəl], *a.* vicario.
vicarious [viˈkɛəriəs], *a.* vicario; experimentado a través de otro.
vicariously [viˈkɛəriəsli], *adv.* a través de otro.
vicarship [ˈvikəʃip], *s.* vicariato, vicaría.
vice (1) [vais], *s.* vicio; resabio (*de caballo*); ***vice squad,*** brigada contra el vicio.
vice (2) [vais], *s.* (*mec.*) tornillo de banco.
vice (3) [vais], *prep.* (*prefijo*) en lugar de, en vez de; ***vice-admiral,*** vicealmirante; ***vice-admiralty,*** vicealmirantazgo; ***vice-chairman,*** vicepresidente; ***vice-chancellor,*** vicecanciller; (*univ.*) rector; ***vice-consul,*** vicecónsul; ***vice-consulate,*** viceconsulado; ***vice-presidency,*** vicepresidencia; ***vice-president,*** vicepresidente.
vicegerency [ˈvaisˈdʒerənsi], *s.* vicegerencia.
vicegerent [ˈvaisˈdʒerənt], *a.*, *s.* vicegerente.
viceregal [ˈvaisˈriːgəl], *a.* virreinal.
vicereine [ˈvaisrein], *s.* virreina.
viceroy [ˈvaisrɔi], *s.* virrey.
viceroyalty, viceroyship [vaisˈrɔiəlti, ˈvaisrɔiʃip], *s.* virreinato.
vice versa [ˈvaisi ˈvəːsə], *adv.* viceversa, a la inversa.
vicinage [ˈvisinidʒ], [VICINITY].
vicinal [ˈvisinəl], *a.* vecinal, vecino.
vicinity [viˈsiniti], *s.* vecindad, proximidad; contornos, *m.pl.*, alrededores, *m.pl.*
vicious [ˈviʃəs], *a.* cruel, rencoroso, sañudo; resabiado; perverso; (*ant.*) vicioso; ***vicious circle,*** círculo vicioso; ***with vicious intent,*** con malas intenciones.
viciousness [ˈviʃəsnis], *s.* vicio, depravación; rencor, saña; malas intenciones, *f.pl.*
vicissitude [viˈsisitjuːd], *s.* (*úsase más en pl.*) vicisitud, peripecia.
vicissitudinous [visisiˈtjuːdinəs], *a.* azaroso, accidentado.
victim [ˈviktim], *s.* víctima, *f.*; ***to fall a victim to,*** ser víctima de; ***victim of circumstance,*** víctima de las circunstancias.
victimization [viktimaiˈzeiʃən], *s.* persecución; represalias, *f.pl.*
victimize [ˈviktimaiz], *v.t.* meterse (injustamente) con, tomarla con.
Victor [ˈviktə]. Víctor.
victor [ˈviktə], *s.* vencedor, triunfador.
Victoria [vikˈtɔːriə]. Victoria.
Victorian [vikˈtɔːriən], *a.* victoriano; decimonónico. — *s.* victoriano.
victorious [vikˈtɔːriəs], *a.* victorioso, triunfante, vencedor.
victoriousness [vikˈtɔːriəsnis], *s.* (lo) victorioso.
victory [ˈviktəri], *s.* victoria, triunfo.
victual [vitl], *s.* (*pl.*) vituallas, *f.pl.*, víveres, *m.pl.* — *v.t.* abastecer, avituallar.
victualler [ˈvitlə], *s.* proveedor, abastecedor; hostalero.
victualling [ˈvitliŋ], *s.* abastecimiento; víveres, *m.pl.*, vituallas, *f.pl.*
vicuna [viˈkjuːnə], *s.* vicuña.
vide [ˈvaidi], *v. imper.* vide, véase.
videlicet [viˈdiːliset], *adv.* a saber.
video [ˈvidiou], *a.* de vídeo. — *s.* vídeo.
viduage [ˈvidjuidʒ], *s.* viudez.
vie [vai], *v.i.* rivalizar, porfiar.
Vienna [viˈenə]. Viena.
Viennese [viəˈniːz], *a.*, *s.* vienés, *m.*
Vietnam [vjetˈnæm]. (el) Vietnam.

Vietnamese [vjetnæ'mi:z], *a.* vietnamita. — *s.* vietnamita, *m.f.*; (*idioma*) vietnamés, *m.*
view [vju:], *s.* vista; panorama, perspectiva; visión; mirada, ojeada; parecer, opinión; criterio; ***at first view,*** a primera vista; ***in my view,*** en mi opinión; ***in view of,*** en vista de; ***on view,*** expuesto a la vista; ***point of view,*** punto de vista; opinión; ***to have s.o. in view,*** tener alguien en perspectiva; ***to take a closer view of,*** examinar más de cerca; ***what's your view?*** ¿qué opina usted? ¿cuál es su parecer?; ***with a view to,*** con miras a. — *v.t.* ver, mirar, contemplar; examinar; considerar.
viewer ['vju:ə], *s.* espectador; (*de televisión*) telespectador, televidente.
viewfinder ['vju:faində], *s.* (*foto.*) visor.
viewless ['vju:lis], *a.* sin vista(s).
viewpoint ['vju:pɔint], *s.* punto de vista; mirador.
vigesimal [vi'dʒezimәl], *a.* vigésimo.
vigil ['vidʒil], *s.* vigilia; vela; ***to keep vigil,*** velar.
vigilance ['vidʒiləns], *s.* vigilancia.
vigilant ['vidʒilənt], *a.* vigilante, alerta, atento.
vigilante [vidʒi'lænti], *s.* vigilante.
vignette [vi'njet], *s.* viñeta.
vigorous ['vigərəs], *a.* vigoroso; (*fig.*) enérgico.
vigorously ['vigərəsli], *adv.* vigorosamente; con energía.
vigour, vigorousness ['vigə, -rəsnis], *s.* vigor; energía.
Viking ['vaikiŋ], *a., s.* vikingo.
vile [vail], *a.* vil, odioso, detestable, infame; asqueroso, repugnante; (*fam.*) pésimo.
vileness ['vailnis], *s.* vileza; (lo) odioso; (lo) infame *etc.*
vilification [vilifi'keiʃən], *s.* difamación, vilipendio.
vilifier ['vilifaiə], *s.* difamador.
vilify ['vilifai], *v.t.* difamar, vilipendiar.
villa ['vilə], *s.* chalet, hotelito; casa de campo, quinta.
village ['vilidʒ], *a.* de pueblo, aldeano. — *s.* pueblo, pueblecito, aldea, lugar.
villager ['vilidʒə], *s.* aldeano; ***the villagers,*** los del pueblo.
villain ['vilən], *s.* villano; (*teat., novela etc.*) malo, traidor; ***the villain of the piece,*** el malo.
villainous ['vilənəs], *a.* vil, infame; (*fam.*) pésimo; ***villainous-looking,*** de aspecto patibulario; de aspecto infame.
villainy, villainousness ['viləni, -əsnis], *s.* maldad, infamia.
villein ['vilin], *s.* (*ant.*) villano.
villeinage ['vilinidʒ], *s.* (*ant.*) villanaje.
villosity [vi'lɔsiti], *s.* vellosidad.
villous, villose ['viləs, 'vilous], *a.* velloso.
vim [vim], *s.* (*fam.*) energía, brío.
vinaigrette [vinei'gret], *s.* vinagrera; (*salsa*) vinagreta.
Vincent ['vinsənt]. Vicente.
vincible ['vinsibl], *a.* vencible.
vinculum ['viŋkjuləm], *s.* (*pl.* **vincula** ['viŋkjulə]) (*mat.*) vínculo.
vindicate ['vindikeit], *v.t.* vindicar; justificar. — **vindicate o.s.,** *v.r.* justificarse.
vindication [vindi'keiʃən], *s.* vindicación; justificación.
vindicator ['vindikeitə], *s.* vindicador.
vindicatory ['vindikeitəri], *a.* vindicatorio; justificativo.
vindictive [vin'diktiv], *a.* vengativo, rencoroso.
vindictiveness [vin'diktivnis], *s.* (lo) vengativo, (lo) rencoroso, rencor.
vine [vain], *s.* vid, *f.*; (*enredadera*) parra; ***vine-dresser,*** viñador; ***vine-knife,*** podadera; ***vine-shoot,*** sarmiento; ***vine-stock,*** cepa.
vine-clad ['vain-klæd], *a.* cubierto de viñas.
vinegar ['vinigə], *s.* vinagre.
vinegary, vinegarish ['vinigəri, -gəriʃ], *a.* avinagrado, vinagroso.
vinery ['vainəri], *s.* invernadero; emparrado.
vineyard ['vinjɑ:d], *s.* viña, viñedo.
vinosity [vai'nɔsiti], *s.* vinosidad.
vinous, vinose ['vainəs, -ous], *a.* vinoso.
vintage ['vintidʒ], *a.* ***vintage car,*** coche veterano *o* de época; ***vintage wine,*** vino añejo *o* de calidad; ***vintage year,*** buen año. — *s.* vendimia; cosecha.
vintager ['vintidʒə], *s.* vendimiador.
vintner ['vintnə], *s.* vinatero.
vinyl ['vainil], *s.* vinilo.
viol ['viəl], *s.* (*mús., ant.*) viola, violón; (*mus., ant.*) ***double bass viol,*** contrabajo.
Viola ['vaiələ]. Viola.
viola (1) [vi'oulə], *s.* (*mús.*) viola.
viola (2) [vai'oulə], *s.* (*bot.*) viola.
violaceous [vaiəlei'ʃəs], *a.* violáceo.
violate ['vaiəleit], *v.t.* violar; infringir, quebrantar.
violation [vaiə'leiʃən], *s.* violación.
violator ['vaiəleitə], *s.* violador.
violence ['vaiələns], *s.* violencia; ***to do violence to,*** violentar.
violent ['vaiələnt], *a.* violento; intenso.
violently ['vaiələntli], *adv.* con violencia, violentamente.
violet ['vaiəlit], *a.* violado. — *s.* violeta.
violin [vaiə'lin], *s.* (*mús.*) violín; ***first violin,*** primer violín.
violinist [vaiə'linist], *s.* violinista, *m.f.*
violoncellist [vaiələn'tʃelist], *s.* violoncelista, *m.f.*
violoncello [vaiələn'tʃelou], *s.* violoncelo.
viper ['vaipə], *s.* víbora; (*bot.*) ***viper-grass,*** escorzonera.
viperine, viperish, viperous ['vaipərain, -iʃ, -əs], *a.* viperino.
virago [vi'rɑ:gou], *s.* fiera, tarasca; virago.
vireo ['viriou], *s.* (*orn.*) víreo.
virescent [vi'resənt], *a.* (*bot.*) verdoso.
Virgil ['və:dʒil]. Virgilio.
Virgilian [və:'dʒiliən], *a.* virgiliano.
virgin ['və:dʒin], *a., s.* virgen; (*bot.*) ***virgin's bower,*** clemátide, *f.*
virginal ['və:dʒinəl], *a.* virginal. — *s.* (*mús.*) espineta, virginal.
Virginia [və'dʒiniə]. Virginia; ***Virginia tobacco,*** (tabaco de) Virginia, *m.*
virginity [və'dʒiniti], *s.* virginidad.
viridescent [viri'desənt], *a.* verdoso.
viridity [vi'riditi], *s.* verdor.
virile ['virail], *a.* viril.
virility [vi'riliti], *s.* virilidad.
virtual ['və:tʃuəl], *a.* virtual; ***it's a virtual certainty,*** es casi seguro.
virtuality [və:tʃu'æliti], *s.* virtualidad.
virtually ['və:tʃuəli], *adv.* prácticamente.
virtue ['və:tʃu:], *s.* virtud; ***by*** *o* ***in virtue of,*** en virtud de; ***to make a virtue of necessity,*** poner a mal tiempo buena cara; ***a woman of easy virtue,*** una mujer de vida alegre.
virtueless ['və:tʃu:lis], *a.* sin virtud.
virtuosity [və:tju'ɔsiti], *s.* virtuosismo.
virtuoso [və:tju'ouzou], *a.* de virtuoso. — *s.* virtuoso.
virtuous ['və:tʃuəs], *a.* virtuoso.
virtuousness ['və:tʃuəsnis], *s.* virtud, (lo) virtuoso.
virulence, virulency ['vir(j)uləns, -i], *s.* virulencia.
virulent ['vir(j)ulənt], *a.* virulento.
virulently ['vir(j)uləntli], *adv.* con virulencia.
virus ['vaiərəs], *s.* virus; ***virus disease,*** enfermedad de virus.
visa ['vi:zə], *s.* visado.
visage ['vizidʒ], *s.* rostro, semblante, faz, *f.*; (*fig.*) cariz.

vis-à-vis [ˈviːz-ɑː-viː], *prep.* frente a. — *s.* interlocutor.
viscera [ˈvisərə], *s.pl.* vísceras, *f.pl.*
visceral [ˈvisərəl], *a.* visceral.
viscid, viscous [visid, ˈviskəs], *a.* viscoso.
viscosity, viscidity [visˈkɔsiti, viˈsiditi], *s.* viscosidad.
viscount [ˈvaikaunt], *s.* vizconde.
viscountess [ˈvaikauntes], *s.* vizcondesa.
viscountship, viscountcy [ˈvaikauntʃip, -si], *s.* vizcondado.
viscous [ˈviskəs], [VISCID].
vise [vais], *s.* (*Am.*) [VICE (2)].
visé [ˈviːˈzei], [VISA].
visibility [viziˈbiliti], *s.* visibilidad.
visible [ˈvizibl], *a.* visible.
Visigoth [ˈvizigɔθ], *s.* visigodo.
Visigothic [viziˈgɔθik], *a.* visigodo, visigótico.
vision [ˈviʒən], *s.* visión.
visionary [ˈviʒənəri], *a.*, *s.* visionario.
visit [ˈvizit], *s.* visita; ***to pay a visit on*** o ***to,*** hacer una visita a; ***to repay*** o ***return a visit,*** pagar una visita. — *v.t.* visitar; ***to visit sth. on s.o.,*** castigar a alguien con algo, mandar algo (malo) a alguien. — *v.i.* hacer visitas; ***to go visiting,*** ir de visita; (*despec.*) ir de visiteo.
visitant [ˈvizitənt], *a.*, *s.* visitante.
visitation [viziˈteiʃən], *s.* visitación; (*fam.*) visitón.
visiting [ˈvizitiŋ], *a.* visitante; de visita; ***visiting professor,*** catedrático visitante *o* en visita. — *s.* (el) visitar; ***visiting card,*** tarjeta de visita.
visitor [ˈvizitə], *s.* visitante; turista, *m.f.*; ***we have visitors,*** tenemos visita; ***visitor's book,*** libro de visitas.
visor [ˈvaizə], *s.* visera.
visored [ˈvaizəd], *a.* con visera.
vista [ˈvistə], *s.* vista, panorama, *m.*
visual [ˈviʒjuəl], *a.* visual.
visualize [ˈviʒjuəlaiz], *v.t.* representarse mentalmente, imaginarse; prever; ***I can't visualize it*** (***happening***), no lo veo probable, no me parece probable.
vital [vaitl], *a.* (*fig.*) vital; enérgico, dinámico; (*fam.*) ***vital statistics,*** medidas vitales, *f.pl.* — *s.pl.* partes vitales, *f.pl.*, vísceras, *f.pl.*
vitalism [ˈvaitəlizəm], *s.* vitalismo.
vitalist [ˈvaitəlist], *s.* vitalista, *m.f.*
vitality [vaiˈtæliti], *s.* vitalidad.
vitalize [ˈvaitəlaiz], *v.t.* vitalizar, vivificar.
vitally [ˈvaitəli], *adv.* vitalmente; ***it's vitally important,*** es de capital importancia, es fundamental.
vitamin [ˈvitəmin], *s.* vitamina; ***vitamin deficiency,*** avitaminosis, *f.*
vitaminize [ˈvitəminaiz], *v.t.* vitaminar.
vitellin [viˈtelin], *s.* (*quím.*) vitelina.
vitiate [ˈviʃieit], *v.t.* viciar, corromper; invalidar.
vitiation [viʃiˈeiʃən], *s.* corrupción; invalidación.
viticultural [vitiˈkʌltʃərəl], *a.* vitícola.
viticulture [ˈvitikʌltʃə], *s.* viticultura.
viticulturist [vitiˈkʌltʃərist], *s.* vitícola, *m.f.*, viticultor.
vitreous [ˈvitriəs], *a.* vítreo; ***vitreous enamel,*** esmalte vítreo.
vitreousness [ˈvitriəsnis], *s.* vitreosidad, vidriosidad.
vitrescence [viˈtresəns], *s.* vitrificación.
vitrescent, vitrescible [viˈtresənt, -ibl], *a.* vitrificable.
vitrifaction [vitriˈfækʃən], *s.* vitrificación.
vitrifiable [ˈvitrifaiəbl], *a.* vitrificable.
vitrification [vitrifiˈkeiʃən], *s.* vitrificación.
vitriform [ˈvitrifɔːm], *a.* vitriforme.
vitrify [ˈvitrifai], *v.t.* vitrificar. — *v.i.* vitrificarse.
vitriol [ˈvitriəl], *s.* vitriolo; (*fig.*) acerbidad, saña, acíbar.
vitriolated [ˈvitriəleitid], *a.* vitriolado.
vitriolic [vitriˈɔlik], *a.* vitriólico; (*fig.*) feroz, acerbo, atroz, sañudo.
vitriolize [ˈvitriəlaiz], *v.t.* convertir en vitriolo.
vituline [ˈvitjulain], *a.* becerril, de ternero.
vituperate [viˈtjuːpəreit], *v.t.* vituperar, denostar. — *v.i.* proferir vituperios *o* injurias.
vituperation [vitjuːpəˈreiʃən], *s.* vituperio, denuesto(s).
vivacious [viˈveiʃəs], *a.* animado, vivo, lleno de vitalidad.
vivaciousness, vivacity [viˈveiʃəsnis, viˈvæsiti], *s.* vivacidad, viveza, animación.
vivarium [vaiˈvɛəriəm], *s.* (*pl.* **vivaria, vivariums** [-riə, -riəmz]) vivero.
vivary [ˈvaivəri], [VIVARIUM].
viva voce [ˈvaivə ˈvousi], *adv.* de viva voz, de palabra.
vivid [ˈvivid], *a.* vivo; intenso; gráfico.
vividness [ˈvividnis], *s.* viveza; intensidad; (lo) gráfico.
vivification [vivifiˈkeiʃən], *s.* vivificación.
vivify [ˈvivifai], *v.t.* vivificar.
viviparous [viˈvipərəs], *a.* vivíparo.
vivisect [viviˈsekt], *v.t.* hacer la vivisección de. — *v.i.* realizar vivisecciones.
vivisection [viviˈsekʃən], *s.* vivisección.
vixen [ˈviksən], *s.* zorra, raposa; (*fig.*) fiera.
viz. [viz], *adv. contr.* [VIDELICET].
vizier [ˈviziə], *s.* visir.
vizierate, viziership [viˈziərit, viˈziəʃip], *s.* dignidad de visir.
vocable [ˈvoukəbl], *s.* vocablo, voz, *f.*
vocabulary [voˈkæbjuləri], *s.* vocabulario.
vocal [ˈvoukəl], *a.* vocal; (*fam.*) ruidoso, que se hace sentir; vociferante; ***vocal chords,*** cuerdas vocales, *f.pl.*
vocalist [ˈvoukəlist], *s.* cantante, *m.f.*
vocalization [voukəlaiˈzeiʃən], *s.* vocalización.
vocalize [ˈvoukəlaiz], *v.t.* cantar. — *v.i.* vocalizar(se).
vocation [voˈkeiʃən], *s.* vocación.
vocational [voˈkeiʃənəl], *a.* vocacional.
vocative [ˈvɔkətiv], *a.*, *s.* vocativo.
vociferate [voˈsifəreit], *v.t.*, *v.i.* vociferar.
vociferation [vosifəˈreiʃən], *s.* vociferación.
vociferous [voˈsifərəs], *a.* vociferante, vocinglero, clamoroso.
vociferously [voˈsifərəsli], *adv.* clamorosamente, a voz en grito.
vodka [ˈvɔdkə], *s.* vodka, *m.*
vogue [voug], *s.* moda; boga; ***in vogue,*** de moda, en boga.
voice [vɔis], *s.* voz, *f.*; ***voice-box,*** laringe, *f.*; ***to be in*** (***good***) ***voice,*** estar en voz; ***to give voice to,*** dar expresión a, expresar; ***to have no voice in,*** no tener ni voz ni voto en, no tener arte ni parte en, no pintar nada en; ***to raise one's voice,*** levantar la voz; ***in a loud voice,*** con voz fuerte; ***in a low voice,*** con voz queda; ***with one voice,*** a una (voz). — *v.t.* expresar; hacerse eco de; (*fonét.*) sonorizar. — *v.i.* (*fonét.*) sonorizarse.
voiced [vɔist], *a.* (*fonét.*) sonoro.
voiceless [ˈvɔislis], *a.* mudo; afónico; (*fonét.*) sordo.
void [vɔid], *a.* vacío; (*for.*) nulo, inválido; ***void of,*** desprovisto de. — *s.* vacío; hueco. — *v.t.* vaciar; anular.
voidable [ˈvɔidəbl], *a.* anulable.
voidance [ˈvɔidəns], *s.* invalidación.
voidness [ˈvɔidnis], *s.* (lo) vacío; invalidez.
volant [ˈvoulənt], *a.* volante; ligero.
volatile [ˈvɔlətail], *a.* volátil; (*fig.*) voluble.
volatility [vɔləˈtiliti], *s.* volatilidad; volubilidad.
volatilization [vɔlətilaiˈzeiʃən], *s.* volatilización.
volatilize [vɔˈlætilaiz], *v.t.* volatilizar. — *v.i.* volatilizarse.

volcanic [vɔl'kænik], *a.* volcánico.
volcano [vɔl'keinou], *s.* volcán; ***active volcano,*** volcán (en) activo; ***erupting volcano,*** volcán en erupción; ***extinct volcano,*** volcán apagado *o* extinto.
vole [voul], *s.* (*zool.*) campañol.
volition [vo'liʃən], *s.* voluntad; volición; ***of one's own volition,*** por voluntad propia, espontáneamente.
volitive ['vɔlitiv], *a.* volitivo.
volley ['vɔli], *s.* descarga; salva; (*dep.*) voleo (de la pelota). — *v.t.* enviar *o* hacer una descarga de; (*dep.*) volear.
volleyball ['vɔlibɔ:l], *s.* balonvolea, *m.*, voleibol.
volt [voult], *s.* (*elec.*) voltio.
voltage ['voultidʒ], *s.* (*elec.*) voltaje.
voltameter [vɔl'tæmitə], *s.* voltámetro.
voltmeter ['vɔltmi:tə], *s.* voltímetro.
volubility [vɔlju'biliti], *s.* locuacidad.
voluble ['vɔljubl], *a.* locuaz.
volubly ['vɔljubli], *adv.* con locuacidad.
volume ['vɔlju:m], *s.* (*libro*) tomo, volumen; (*agua etc.*) caudal; cantidad; ***work in three volumes,*** obra en tres tomos.
volumetric [vɔlju'metrik], *a.* volumétrico.
voluminous [vɔ'l(j)u:minəs], *a.* voluminoso, abultado.
voluminousness [vɔ'l(j)u:minəsnis], *s.* (lo) voluminoso.
voluntarily ['vɔləntərili], *adv.* voluntariamente; espontáneamente.
voluntariness ['vɔləntərinis], *s.* (lo) voluntario.
voluntary ['vɔləntəri], *a.* voluntario; espontáneo. — *s.* (*mús.*) solo.
volunteer [vɔlən'tiə], *a.*, *s.* voluntario. — *v.t.* ofrecer voluntariamente. — *v.i.* ofrecerse voluntariamente; (*mil.*) alistarse como voluntario.
voluptuary [və'lʌptjuəri], *s.* hombre voluptuoso, sibarita, *m.f.*
voluptuous [və'lʌptjuəs], *a.* voluptuoso; sibarita.
voluptuousness [və'lʌptjuəsnis], *s.* voluptuosidad.
volute [vɔ'l(j)u:t], *a.* de espiral. — *s.* voluta.
voluted [vɔ'l(j)u:tid], *a.* de volutas.
volution [vɔ'l(j)u:ʃən], *s.* espiral, *f.*
volvulus ['vɔlvjuləs], *s.* (*med.*) miserere.
vomit ['vɔmit], *s.* vómito(s). — *v.t.* vomitar, arrojar. — *v.i.* tener vómitos.
vomiting ['vɔmitiŋ], *s.* vómito(s).
vomitory (1) ['vɔmitəri], *a.* vomitivo, emético.
vomitory (2) ['vɔmitəri], *s.* vomitorio.
voodoo ['vu:du:], *s.* vudú.
voracious [vɔ'reiʃəs], *a.* voraz.
voracity [vɔ'ræsiti], *s.* voracidad.
vortex ['vɔ:teks], *s.* (*pl.* **vortexes, vortices** [-teksiz, -tisi:z]) vórtice; (*fig.*) vorágine, *f.*
vortical, vortiginous ['vɔ:tikəl, vɔ:'tidʒinəs], *a.* vortiginoso.
votary ['voutəri], *s.* (*relig.*) devoto; partidario, sectario.
vote [vout], *s.* voto; sufragio; votación; ***by a majority vote,*** por mayoría de votos; ***casting vote,*** voto decisivo; ***the miners' vote,*** los votos de los mineros; ***to cast a vote,*** dar un voto; ***to put to the vote*** o ***to take a vote on,*** someter a votación; ***vote of confidence,*** voto de confianza; ***vote of thanks,*** voto de gracias. — *v.t.* votar; ***vote in,*** elegir por votación; ***vote down,*** derrotar *o* desechar por votación. — *v.i.* votar (***for,*** por); ***vote that,*** resolver por voto que; (*fig.*, *fam.*) proponer que.
voter ['voutə], *s.* votante.
voting ['voutiŋ], *s.* votación.
votive ['voutiv], *a.* votivo.
vouch [vautʃ], *v.t.* afirmar, garantizar, atestiguar. — *v.i.* — ***for,*** responder de (*una cosa*); confirmar (*un hecho*); responder por (*una persona*).
voucher ['vautʃə], *s.* bono, vale; (documento) comprobante; (certificado) justificante.
vouchsafe [vautʃ'seif], *v.t.* otorgar, conceder; dignarse dar *o* hacer.
voussoir ['vu:swɑ:], *s.* (*arq.*) dovela.
vow [vau], *s.* voto, promesa solemne; ***to take*** (***the***) ***vows,*** profesar. — *v.t.* hacer voto de, prometer solemnemente, jurar. — *v.i.* hacer voto (***to,*** de).
vowel ['vauəl], *s.* vocal, *f.*; ***vowel sound,*** sonido vocálico.
voyage ['vɔiidʒ], *s.* viaje (por mar). — *v.t.* navegar. — *v.i.* viajar por mar, navegar.
voyager ['vɔiidʒə], *s.* viajero; viandante.
Vulcan ['vʌlkən]. Vulcano.
vulcanite ['vʌlkənait], *s.* vulcanita.
vulcanization [vʌlkənai'zeiʃən], *s.* vulcanización.
vulcanize ['vʌlkənaiz], *v.t.* vulcanizar.
vulgar ['vʌlgə], *a.* ordinario, chabacano; cursi; (*chiste*) verde, indecente; (*latín*) vulgar. — *s.* (*pl.*) ***the vulgar,*** (el) vulgo.
vulgarism ['vʌlgərizəm], *s.* vulgarismo.
vulgarity, vulgarness [vʌl'gæriti, 'vʌlgənis], *s.* ordinariez, chabacanería; cursilería; indecencia.
vulgarization [vʌlgərai'zeiʃən], *s.* vulgarización.
vulgarize ['vʌlgəraiz], *v.t.* vulgarizar.
Vulgate ['vʌlgeit], *s.* (*igl.*) vulgata.
vulnerability [vʌlnərə'biliti], *s.* vulnerabilidad; sensibilidad.
vulnerable ['vʌlnərəbl], *a.* vulnerable; sensible.
vulnerary ['vʌlnərəri], *a.* vulnerario. — *s.* (medicamento) vulnerario.
vulpine ['vʌlpain], *a.* vulpino, raposino, zorruno.
vulture ['vʌltʃə], *s.* buitre.
vulturine, vulturish, vulturous ['vʌltʃərain, -iʃ, -əs], *a.* buitrero, de buitre.
vulva ['vʌlvə], *s.* vulva.

W

W, w [ˈdʌblju:], vigésima tercera letra del alfabeto.

wad (1) [wɔd], *s.* fajo (*de billetes*); rollo, lío (*de papeles*); guata; borra (*para rellenar, acolchar etc.*). — *v.t.* rellenar, forrar; acolchar.

wad (2) [wɔd], *s.* quijo de manganeso y cobalto.

wadding [ˈwɔdiŋ], *s.* guata; borra; algodón en rama; taco; entretela, entreforro; relleno.

waddle [wɔdl], *s.* anadeo. — *v.i.* anadear.

wade [weid], *v.t.* vadear. — *v.i.* caminar por el agua (*o* por el lodo *etc.*); (*fig.*) ***wade into s.o.,*** emprenderla con alguien, arremeter contra alguien; (*fig.*) ***wade through,*** leerse (trabajosamente).

wader [ˈweidə], *s.* (*orn.*) ave zancuda; (*pl.*) botas (altas) de goma, *f.pl.*

wafer [ˈweifə], *s.* (*comestible*) barquillo; (*de lacre etc.*) oblea; (*igl.*) hostia. — *v.t.* cerrar *o* pegar con oblea.

wafery [ˈweifəri], *a.* delgado y ligero, como una oblea.

waffle [wɔfl], *s.* tortita; (*fig.*) palabrería; paja.

waft [wɔft], *s.* soplo (*de aire* o *de olor*); (*mar.*) bandera de señales. — *v.t.* llevar por el aire. — *v.i.* ***waft away,*** irse por los aires.

wag [wæg], *s.* meneo, movimiento; (*pers.*) guasón, bromista, *m.f.*; ***to play the wag,*** estar de chunga. — *v.t.* menear, mover, agitar; ***the dog wags its tail,*** el perro menea el rabo *o* la cola. — *v.i.* moverse, menearse.

wage [weidʒ], *s.* salario, jornal, paga; pago, premio; (*pl.*) salario, paga, jornal; ***wage-earner,*** asalariado, jornalero; ***wage-freeze,*** congelación de (los) salarios. — *v.t.* (*batalla*) dar, librar; ***wage war,*** hacer la guerra; ***wage a campaign,*** hacer una campaña.

wager [ˈweidʒə], *s.* apuesta; ***to lay a wager,*** apostar, hacer una apuesta. — *v.t.* apostar. — *v.i.* apostar (***that,*** a que).

waggery [ˈwægəri], *s.* zumba, guasa.

waggish [ˈwægiʃ], *a.* zumbón, guasón, chacotero.

waggishness [ˈwægiʃnis], *s.* jocosidad, (lo) zumbón.

waggle [wægl], *s.* meneo. — *v.t.* menear. — *v.i.* menearse.

wag(g)on [ˈwægən], *s.* carro; carreta; (*f.c.*) vagón; (*mil.*) furgón; ***wagon maker,*** carretero; ***wagon load,*** carretada; (*fam.*) ***to be on the wagon,*** no beber (alcohol).

wag(g)onage [ˈwægənidʒ], *s.* (*Am.*) carretaje.

wag(g)oner [ˈwægənə], *s.* carretero.

wag(g)onette [wægəˈnet], *s.* carricoche, birlocho.

Wagnerian [vɑ:gˈniəriən], *a.*, *s.* wagneriano.

wagtail [ˈwægteil], *s.* nevatilla, aguzanieves, *m.inv.*

waif [weif], *s.* (niño) expósito, niño abandonado *o* desamparado.

wail [weil], *s.* lamento, gemido; (*de niño*) vagido. — *v.i.* lamentarse, gemir; gimotear.

wailing [ˈweiliŋ], *s.* lamentos, *m.pl.*, gemidos, *m.pl.*; ***Wailing Wall,*** muro de las lamentaciones.

wain [wein], *s.* carro; ***the Wain,*** el Carro.

wainscot [ˈweinskət], *s.* zócalo. — *v.t.* poner zócalo a.

wainscoting [ˈweinskətiŋ], *s.* zócalo(s).

waist [weist], *s.* cintura; talle; (*mar.*) combés, *m.*; (*fig.*) cuello.

waistband [ˈweistbænd], *s.* pretina.

waistcloth [ˈweistklɔθ], *s.* taparrabo, taparrabos, *m.inv.*

waistcoat [ˈweiskout], *s.* chaleco.

waist-deep [ˈweist-di:p], *adv.* hasta la cintura.

wait [weit], *s.* espera; ***to have a long wait,*** (tener que) esperar mucho tiempo; ***to lie in wait for,*** acechar, estar al acecho de. — *v.i.* esperar, aguardar; ***wait at table,*** servir a la mesa; ***wait on*** o ***upon,*** servir como criado; presentar sus respetos a; (*decisión*) depender de; ***wait for,*** esperar, aguardar; ***keep*** (***s.o.***) ***waiting,*** hacer esperar (*a alguien*); ***wait and see,*** espera y verás; (*fam.*) ***wait about,*** estar esperando.

waiter [ˈweitə], *s.* camarero, mozo; ***dumb-waiter,*** montaplatos, *m.inv.*

waiting [ˈweitiŋ], *a.* que sirve; ***waiting-maid,*** doncella. — *s.* espera; servicio; ***gentleman-in-waiting,*** gentilhombre de cámara; ***lady-in-waiting,*** dama de honor; ***waiting-list,*** lista de solicitantes *o* de interesados; ***waiting-room,*** sala de espera; antesala.

waitress [ˈweitris], *s.* camarera.

waive [weiv], *v.t.* prescindir de, no exigir.

waiver [ˈweivə], *s.* dispensa.

wake (1) [weik], *s.* velatorio; velorio. — *v.t. irr.* despertar; ***wake up,*** despertar, llamar. — *v.i.* — (***up***), despertar, despertarse. — *interj.* ***wake up!*** ¡despiértate!

wake (2) [weik], (*mar.*) estela; ***in the wake of,*** en pos de; a raíz de.

wakeful [ˈweikful], *a.* despierto, desvelado; vigilante, alerta.

wakefulness [ˈweikfulnis], *s.* desvelo, insomnio; vigilancia.

waken [ˈweikən], *v.t.* despertar. — *v.i.* despertar(se).

waker [ˈweikə], *s.* ***to be an early waker,*** ser madrugador.

wake-robin [ˈweik-ˈrɔbin], *s.* (*bot.*) aro, yaro.

waking [ˈweikiŋ], *a.* despierto; ***in one's waking hours,*** en las horas en que se está despierto.

wale [weil], *s.* (*mar.*) cinta; relieve (*de tejidos*).

Wales [weilz]. Gales, *f.*

walk [wɔ:k], *s.* paseo; paso, (modo de) andar; recorrido, ronda; paseo, alameda; ***walk of life,*** profesión; condición social; ***it's only a five-minute walk from here,*** desde aquí no se tarda más de cinco minutos andando *o* a pie; ***to go for*** o ***have*** o ***take a walk,*** dar un paseo *o* una vuelta. — *v.t.* pasear, llevar de paseo; andar, recorrer; (*fig.*, *fam.*) ***walk off a headache,*** darse un paseo para quitarse un dolor de cabeza; (*fig.*, *fam.*) ***walk one's lunch off,*** dar un paseo para bajar la comida; ***walk one's round,*** hacer su recorrido *o* ronda; ***walk a horse,*** llevar un caballo al paso; (*fig.*, *fam.*) ***walk s.o. off his legs,*** obligar a alguien a andar una barbaridad; ***walk the streets,*** callejear, andar por *o* azotar las calles; ***walk the wards,*** hacer prácticas de medicina. — *v.i.* andar, ir a pie; pasear(se); (*fantasma*) aparecerse; ***walk about,*** pasear(se); ***walk away,*** irse, alejarse; ***walk back,*** volver(se), regresar a pie; ***walk down,*** bajar andando; ***walk in,*** entrar; ***please walk in,*** entre(n) sin llamar; ***walk into s.o.,*** tropezar con alguien; ***walk off,*** irse, marcharse; ***walk off with everything,*** llevárselo todo, alzarse con el santo y la limosna; ***walk on,*** pisar; ***to be walking on air,*** estar muy ufano *o* eufórico; ***walk out,*** salir(se); declararse en huelga; ***walk out on s.o.,*** dejar (plantado) a alguien; ***walk*** (***all***) ***over s.o.,*** tratar a alguien a patadas; ***walk up,*** subir andando; ***walk up to s.o.,*** llegarse a alguien; ***walk up and down,*** ir de un lado para otro; ***we walked ten miles,*** recorrimos diez millas (andando).

walker [ˈwɔ:kə], *s.* (el) que anda; ***to be a great walker,*** ser gran andarín.

walkie-talkie [ˈwɔ:ki-ˈtɔ:ki], *s.* emisor-receptor portátil.

walking [ˈwɔ:kiŋ], *a.* ambulante; (*fig.*, *fam.*) ***walking encyclopedia,*** enciclopedia ambulante. — *s.* (el) andar, (el) pasear; ***walking-pace,*** paso de andadura; ***walking-stick,*** bastón; ***walking-tour,*** excursión a pie, caminata.

walk-on [ˈwɔ:k-ɔn], *a.* (*teat.*) de figurante.

walkout [ˈwɔ:kaut], *s.* salida; huelga; ***there was a walkout,*** se salió todo el mundo.

wall [wɔ:l], *s.* pared; muro; (*de jardín, de campo*) tapia; (*de ciudad, de fortaleza*) muralla; ***partition wall,*** tabique; (*fig.*) ***to go to the wall,*** sucumbir, hundirse; (*fig.*) ***to have one's back to the wall,***

estar entre la espada y la pared; (*fig.*) ***walls have ears,*** las paredes oyen; (*elec.*) ***wall-plug, wall-socket,*** enchufe de pared. — *v.t.* murar; amurallar; ***wall in*** o ***up,*** emparedar, tapiar.

wallaby [ˈwɔləbi], *s.* ualabi.

Wallachian [wɔˈleikiən], *a., s.* valaco.

wallet [ˈwɔlit], *s.* cartera.

wall-eye [ˈwɔ:l-ai], *s.* (*med.*) ojo desviado.

wall-eyed [ˈwɔ:l-aid], *a.* que tiene los ojos desviados.

wallflower [ˈwɔ:lflauə], *s.* (*bot.*) alhelí; (*fam.*) mujer sin pareja (en un baile); ***to be a wallflower,*** comer pavo.

Walloon [wɔˈlu:n], *a., s.* valón.

wallop [ˈwɔləp], *s.* (*fam.*) golpazo, trompazo; (*fam.*) cerveza. — *v.t.* zurrar.

wallow [ˈwɔlou], *v.i.* revolcarse; (*fig.*) regodearse; (*fig.*) nadar; ***wallow in riches,*** nadar en la opulencia; ***wallow in sentiment,*** regodearse con el sentimentalismo, entregarse a la sensiblería.

wallowing [ˈwɔlouiŋ], *s.* revolcamiento; (*fig.*) regodeo; ***wallowing place,*** revolcadero.

wallpaper [ˈwɔ:lpeipə], *s.* papel pintado.

wallwort [ˈwɔ:lwə:t], *s.* (*bot.*) cañarroya.

walnut [ˈwɔ:lnʌt], *s.* (*bot.*) nuez; (*color*) (de) nogalina; (madera de) nogal; ***walnut-tree,*** nogal.

walrus [ˈwɔ:lrəs], *s.* (*zool.*) morsa.

Walter [ˈwɔ:ltə]. Gualterio.

waltz [wɔ:lts], *s.* vals, *m.* — *v.i.* valsar, bailar el vals; (*fig.*) ***he waltzed across the room,*** atravesó la habitación dando valsones.

waltzer [ˈwɔ:ltsə], *s.* valsador.

wan [wɔn], *a.* macilento.

wand [wɔnd], *s.* (*insignia de autoridad*) vara; varita (*de virtudes* o *mágica*).

wander [ˈwɔndə], *v.i.* vagar, andar vagando, andar perdido; deambular (*por las calles*); (*pensamiento*) divagar; ***wander off the subject,*** salirse del tema, divagar; ***he wandered about the world,*** anduvo viajando por el mundo.

wanderer [ˈwɔndərə], *s.* vagamundo, nómada, *m.f.*

wandering [ˈwɔndəriŋ], *a.* errabundo, errante; distraído. — *s.* (el) vagar, (el) andar viajando *etc.*; (*pl.*) andanzas, *f.pl.*, viajes, *m.pl.*; (*med.*) delirios, *m.pl.*

wanderlust [ˈwɔndəlʌst], *s.* ansia de viajar *o* de ver mundo.

wane [wein], *s.* (*luna, fig.*) mengua, menguante; (*fig.*) disminución, declinación; ***to be on the wane,*** menguar; ir disminuyendo. — *v.i.* menguar; disminuir.

wangle [wæŋgl], *s.* (*fam.*) chanchullo, trampa. — *v.t.* (*fam.*) conseguir con trampas.

waning [ˈweiniŋ], *a.* (*luna*) menguante; (*fig.*) decadente. — *s.* (*luna*) menguante, mengua; (*fig.*) disminución, decadencia.

wanness [ˈwɔnnis], *s.* palidez, (lo) macilento.

want [wɔnt], *s.* falta, carencia; miseria, pobreza; necesidad; ***for want of,*** por falta de; ***to be in want,*** estar necesitado; ***to die of want,*** morir de miseria; ***for want of anything better,*** a falta de algo mejor. — *v.t.* querer, desear; necesitar; exigir, requerir; ***he wants £500 for the car,*** pide 500 libras por el coche; ***you're wanted on the phone,*** le llaman por teléfono; ***all I want is money,*** lo único que necesito es dinero; (*fam.*) ***you want to be careful,*** debes andarte con cuidado; (*fam.*) ***it wants painting,*** necesita una mano de pintura. — *v.i.* — ***for,*** carecer de; ***they want for nothing,*** no les falta (de) nada.

wanted [ˈwɔntid], *a.* ***the wanted man,*** el hombre buscado (*por la policía*); ***'wanted',*** 'se busca'.

wanting [ˈwɔntiŋ], *a.* deficiente; ***he is wanting in determination,*** le falta decisión.

wanton [ˈwɔntən], *a.* lascivo, impúdico; caprichoso; injustificado, inmotivado, gratuito. — *s.* descocado, descocada. — *v.t.* — ***away,*** disipar, malgastar. — *v.i.* holgar, retozar.

wantonly [ˈwɔntənli], *adv.* lascivamente, de manera impúdica; injustificadamente, sin motivo.

wantonness [ˈwɔntənnis], *s.* lascivia; (lo) caprichoso; (lo) gratuito, falta de motivo.

war [wɔ:], *s.* guerra; ***articles of war,*** código militar *o* naval; ***cold war,*** guerra fría; ***engine of war,*** ingenio bélico; ***hot*** o ***shooting war,*** guerra de tiros; ***man-of-war,*** buque de guerra; ***to be at war,*** estar en guerra; (*fig.*) ***to have been in the wars,*** estar maltrecho; ***to declare war on,*** declarar la guerra a; ***to go to war,*** hacer *o* emprender la guerra; (*fig.*) ***we shall not go to war over this,*** no vamos a reñir por esto; ***to make*** o ***wage war (on),*** hacer la guerra (a); ***war-bride,*** novia de guerra; ***war-cry,*** grito de guerra; ***war-dance,*** danza de guerra; ***war-dog,*** veterano; ***to put on a war footing,*** poner en pie de guerra; ***war-loan,*** préstamo *o* empréstito de guerra; ***war material,*** material bélico; ***war memorial,*** monumento a los caídos; ***war of nerves,*** guerra de nervios; ***war of words,*** lucha *o* forcejeo verbal; (*ant.*) ***War Office,*** Ministerio de la Guerra; ***war to the death*** o ***to the knife,*** guerra a muerte. — *v.i.* (*fig.*) batallar.

warble [wɔ:bl], *s.* trino, gorjeo. — *v.t., v.i.* trinar, gorjear.

warbler [ˈwɔ:blə], *s.* gorjeador; ave canora; curruca.

warbling [ˈwɔ:bliŋ], *a.* canoro, gorjeador. — *s.* gorjeo, cantos, *m.pl.*, trinos, *m.pl.*

ward [wɔ:d], *s.* (*for.*) tutela, custodia; (*for., pers.*) pupilo; (*pol.*) distrito electoral; (*de hospital, asilo etc.*) sala, crujía; (*de cárcel*) ala, pabellón; (*de llave*) guarda; ***in ward,*** bajo tutela; ***ward of court,*** persona bajo custodia del tribunal; ***to walk the wards,*** hacer prácticas de medicina. — *v.t.* guardar, proteger, defender; ***ward off,*** parar, evitar; rechazar.

warden [ˈwɔ:dən], *s.* guardián; (*de colegio universitario*) director; alcaide; (*Am.*, [PRISON GOVERNOR]).

wardenship [ˈwɔ:dənʃip], *s.* oficio *o* dignidad de un guardián, de un director *etc.*

warder [ˈwɔ:də], *s.* carcelero.

wardrobe [ˈwɔ:droub], *s.* guardarropa, *m.*; vestidos, *m.pl.*; (*teat.*) vestuario, guardarropía.

wardroom [ˈwɔ:dru(:)m], *s.* (*mar.*) cámara de oficiales; (*mil.*) cuarto de guardia.

wardship [ˈwɔ:dʃip], *s.* tutela.

ware [wɛə], *s.* loza; ***table-ware,*** vajilla de mesa; (*pl.*) mercancías, *f.pl.*, géneros, *m.pl.*

warehouse [ˈwɛəhaus], *s.* almacén, depósito; ***warehouse-keeper,*** guardaalmacén; ***warehouse rent,*** almacenaje. — [ˈwɛəhauz], *v.t.* almacenar.

warehouseman [ˈwɛəhausmən], *s.* almacenero, almacenista, *m.*

warehousing [ˈwɛəhauziŋ], *s.* almacenaje.

warfare [ˈwɔ:fɛə], *s.* guerra; ***germ warfare,*** guerra bacteriológica; ***nuclear warfare,*** guerra nuclear.

warhead [ˈwɔ:hed], *s.* cabeza de guerra.

warily [ˈwɛərili], *adv.* cautelosamente; ***to go warily,*** andarse con cuidado *o* con precaución *o* con precauciones.

wariness [ˈwɛərinis], *s.* cautela, precaución.

warlike [ˈwɔ:laik], *a.* guerrero, belicoso, marcial.

warlock [ˈwɔ:lɔk], *s.* (*Esco.*) hechichero, brujo.

warlord [ˈwɔ:lɔ:d], *s.* adalid.

warm [wɔ:m], *a.* caliente; (*día, acogida*) caluroso; (*clima*) cálido; (*discusión*) acalorado; cariñoso; ***warm-blooded,*** de sangre caliente; (*fig., fam.*) ardiente, apasionado; (*fig.*) ***warm-hearted,*** afectuoso, cariñoso; ***to be warm,*** (*cosa*) estar caliente; (*pers.*) tener calor; (*tiempo*) hacer calor; (*fig., en juegos infantiles*) quemarse; ***to get warm,*** calentarse; entrar en calor; ***to keep sth. warm,*** conservar caliente; ***to keep s.o. warm,*** conservar el calor a alguien; ***to keep o.s. warm,*** mantenerse caliente; ***to make warm,*** calentar, poner caliente. — *s.* (*fam.*) ***British warm,*** abrigo militar. — *v.t.* calentar; (*habitación*) caldear; (*fig.*) alegrar, regocijar; ***warm up,*** calentar (*un motor* *etc.*), recalentar (*la comida*). — *v.i.* — (***up***), calentarse; caldearse; (*discusión*) acalorarse; (*dep.*) hacer ejercicio(s) para entrar en calor; ***warm to,*** ir cobrando afición *o* gusto a.

warming-pan [ˈwɔːmiŋ-pæn], *s.* calentador.

warmness, warmth [ˈwɔːmnis, ˈwɔːmθ], *s.* calor; (*de emoción*) ardor; (*de amistad*) cordialidad; entusiasmo.

warmonger [ˈwɔːmʌŋgə], *s.* belicista, *m.f.*

warn [wɔːn], *v.t.* advertir, avisar; amonestar; ***warn s.o. of sth.,*** advertirle algo a alguien; ***warn against,*** prevenir contra; ***warn off,*** advertir que no *o* indicar que no *con subj.*; ***warn off sth.,*** prevenir contra.

warning [ˈwɔːniŋ], *a.* de aviso, de advertencia. — *s.* advertencia, aviso; ***to be a warning to,*** servir de advertencia *o* de escarmiento a.

warp [wɔːp], *s.* urdimbre; comba, alabeo; torcedura; deformación; (*fig.*) sesgo, prejuicio; ***warp-beam,*** plegador de urdimbre, enjullo; ***warp-thread, warp-wire,*** lizo. — *v.t.* urdir; torcer; combar, alabear; deformar. — *v.i.* alabearse, combarse; torcerse; deformarse.

warpath [ˈwɔːpɑːθ], *s.* (*fig., fam.*) ***to be on the warpath,*** andar buscando camorra.

warped [wɔːpt], *a.* deformado; torcido; combado; (*fam.*) retorcido.

warper [ˈwɔːpə], *s.* urdidor.

warping [ˈwɔːpiŋ], *s.* deformación; alabeo, combadura.

warplane [ˈwɔːplein], *s.* (*Am.*) avión militar.

warrant [ˈwɔrənt], *s.* (*for.*) auto; autorización, poder; (*papel*) cédula, certificado; (*mil.*) orden, mandato; ***warrant of arrest,*** orden de prisión; ***warrant officer,*** suboficial; contramaestre. — *v.t.* autorizar; justificar; asegurar, garantizar.

warrantable [ˈwɔrəntəbl], *a.* garantizable; justificable.

warranted [ˈwɔrəntid], *a.* garantizado, con garantía.

warrantee [wɔrənˈtiː], *s.* (*for.*) afianzado.

warrantor, warranter [ˈwɔrəntə], *s.* garante.

warranty [ˈwɔrənti], *s.* (*for.*) garantía.

warren [ˈwɔrən], *s.* conejera; vivar, madriguera; (*fig.*) laberinto; ***this place is a warren,*** esto es un laberinto.

warrior [ˈwɔriə], *s.* guerrero, soldado.

Warsaw [ˈwɔːsɔː]. Varsovia.

warship [ˈwɔːʃip], *s.* buque *o* barco de guerra.

wart [wɔːt], *s.* verruga; ***wart-hog,*** facóquero.

wartime [ˈwɔːtaim], *a.* de tiempos de guerra. — *s.* tiempo de guerra.

wartwort [ˈwɔːtwəːt], *s.* (*bot.*) verrucaria.

warty [ˈwɔːti], *a.* verrugoso.

war-worn [ˈwɔː-wɔːn], *a.* gastado *o* devastado por la guerra.

wary [ˈwɛəri], *a.* cauto, cauteloso, precavido.

wash [wɔʃ], *s.* lavado; baño; ropa sucia, ropa para lavar; ***weekly wash,*** colada; (*mar.*) estela, remolinos, *m.pl.*; enjuague; lavazas, *f.pl.*; (*pint.*) aguada; ***wash-board,*** tabla de lavar; (*carp.*) rodapié; (*mar.*) falca; ***hog-wash,*** bazofia; (*fig.*) memeces, *f.pl.*; ***wash-bowl,*** jofaina, palangana; ***wash-(hand) basin,*** palangana, lavabo, jofaina; ***wash-(hand) stand,*** palanganero, aguamanil; ***wash-house,*** lavadero; ***wash-leather,*** gamuza; ***wash-tub,*** tina de lavar. — *v.t.* lavar; bañar; ***wash away,*** llevarse, arrastrar; quitar (*lo sucio*) lavando; ***wash down,*** regar (*la comida*) con vino *etc.*; ***wash-out,*** suprimir; (*fig.*) abandonar; ***wash (up) the dishes,*** fregar los platos. — *v.i.* lavar; lavarse; ***wash up,*** fregar; ***it washes well,*** (se) lava bien; (*fig., fam.*) ***it won't wash,*** no cuela, es inaceptable.

washable [ˈwɔʃəbl], *a.* lavable.

wash-and-wear [ˈwɔʃ-ənd-ˈwɛə], *a.* de lava y pon.

washed-out [ˈwɔʃt-ˈaut], *a.* (*fam.*) pálido, desteñido, descolorido.

washed-up [ˈwɔʃt-ˈʌp], *a.* (*fam.*) fracasado.

washer [ˈwɔʃə], *s.* (*mec.*) arandela; zapatilla, cuero (*de grifo*).

washerwoman [ˈwɔʃəwumən], *s.* lavandera.

washing [ˈwɔʃiŋ], *s.* lavado; ropa para lavar; ***washing-machine,*** lavadora; ***washing powder,*** jabón en polvo; ***washing-up,*** platos para lavar, *m.pl.*; fregado.

wash-out [ˈwɔʃ-aut], *s.* (*fam.*) fracaso, desastre.

washrag [ˈwɔʃræg], (*Am.*) [FACE-CLOTH].

washy [ˈwɔʃi], *a.* acuoso, clarucho.

wasp [wɔsp], *s.* avispa; ***wasp's nest,*** avispero.

waspish [ˈwɔspiʃ], *a.* mordaz, áspero, irascible.

waspishness [ˈwɔspiʃnis], *s.* mordacidad, aspereza, irascibilidad.

wassail [ˈwɔsəl], *s.* francachela, borrachera, orgía; cerveza aderezada con azúcar y especias.

wastage [ˈweistidʒ], *s.* desperdicio, pérdida(s).

waste [weist], *a.* de desperdicio; inútil, que no interesa, que sobra; (*terreno*) baldío, yermo; ***to lay waste,*** asolar, devastar; ***waste-paper,*** papeles viejos *o* usados, *m.pl.*; ***waste products,*** desperdicios, *m.pl.*; ***waste(-paper) basket,*** papelera. — *s.* desperdicio(s); pérdida(s); derroche, despilfarro; desecho(s), basura; desierto, yermo; ***to go*** o ***run to waste,*** desperdiciarse, perderse; ***waste-pipe,*** (tubo de) desagüe; ***it's a waste of time,*** es tiempo perdido. — *v.t.* desperdiciar; desaprovechar; echar a perder; malgastar; derrochar; ***waste time,*** perder el tiempo. — *v.i.* desperdiciarse; ***waste away,*** irse consumiendo; ir mermando.

wasteful [ˈweistful], *a.* pródigo, malgastador, manirroto; que desperdicia; antieconómico.

wastefully [ˈweistfuli], *adv.* con (mucho) derroche *o* desperdicio; de una manera antieconómica.

wastefulness [ˈweistfulnis], *s.* despilfarro; (lo) antieconómico.

waster, wastrel [ˈweistə, ˈweistrəl], *s.* haragán, zángano.

wasting [ˈweistiŋ], *s.* consunción; (el) desperdiciar *etc.*

watch [wɔtʃ], *s.* vigilancia; vigilia, vela; guardia; ronda; centinela, vigía, *m.*; reloj de bolsillo *o* de pulsera; ***on the watch,*** alerta, sobre aviso, ojo avizor, a la espera; ***to keep watch,*** velar, vigilar; estar de guardia; ***to keep a close watch on s.o.,*** vigilar de cerca a alguien; ***to keep watch over,*** velar (por); ***to set a watch,*** poner un reloj; ***to set a watch on s.o.,*** mandar que se vigile a alguien; ***watch box,*** garita; ***watch-case,*** relojera; ***watch chain,*** leontina; ***watch committee,*** junta de vigilancia; ***watch fire,*** hoguera de vigilancia; ***watch glass,*** cristal de reloj; ***watch-house,*** portería; (*mil.*) cuarto de guardia; ***watch tower,*** atalaya. — *v.t.* guardar; vigilar; observar, mirar, ver, contemplar; acechar, espiar; (*fam.*) ser cuidadoso con, prestar atención a; ***did you watch the television last night?*** ¿viste la televisión anoche?; (*fam.*) ***you'd better watch it!*** ¡cuidado con lo que haces!; (*fam.*) ***watch your step!*** ¡ándate con tiento! ¡ten cuidado!; ***he's watching (for) his chance (to),*** está al acecho de una ocasión (de). — *v.i.* ver, mirar; observar; vigilar; velar; (*Am.*) ***watch for,*** esperar, estar a la espera de; ***watch out,*** estar al tanto; tener cuidado; ***watch out for,*** estar a la mira de; guardarse de, tener cuidado con; ***watch over,*** vigilar, velar, velar por.— *interj.* ***watch it!*** ¡ojo! ¡cuidado!; ***watch out!*** ¡cuidado! ¡ojo!

watchdog [ˈwɔtʃdɔg], *s.* perro de guardia; (*fig.*) cancerbero.

watcher [ˈwɔtʃə], *s.* observador; vigilante, persona que vela (*a un enfermo*).

watchful [ˈwɔtʃful], *a.* vigilante, observador, atento, despierto.

watchfulness [ˈwɔtʃfulnis], *s.* vigilancia, atención, cuidado.

watching [ˈwɔtʃiŋ], *s.* vigilancia, atención.

watchkey [ˈwɔtʃkiː], *s.* llave de reloj.

watchmaker [ˈwɔtʃmeikə], *s.* relojero; ***watchmaker's (shop)***, relojería.

watchmaking [ˈwɔtʃmeikiŋ], *s.* relojería.

watchman [ˈwɔtʃmən], *s.* sereno; guarda, *m.*; vigilante.

watchword [ˈwɔtʃwəːd], *s.* (*ant.*, *mil.*) santo y seña, consigna; lema, *m.*

water [ˈwɔːtə], *s.* agua; orina, orines, *m.pl.*; (*tej.*) viso;

(*en general*) ***holy water,*** agua bendita; ***rainwater,*** agua de lluvia; ***spring water,*** agua de manantial; (*astron.*, *astrol.*) ***Water-bearer,*** Acuario; (*pint.*) ***water-colour,*** acuarela; (*pint.*) ***water-colour painting,*** acuarela; ***water-diviner,*** zahorí, alumbrador de aguas; ***water-nymph,*** náyade, *f.*;

(*océano, río etc.*; *mar.*) ***high water,*** marea alta; ***home waters,*** aguas nacionales, *f.pl.*; ***low water,*** marea baja, bajamar; ***slack water,*** repunte de la marea; ***still*** o ***stagnant water,*** agua estancada; ***territorial waters,*** aguas territoriales *o* jurisdiccionales, *f.pl.*; ***by*** o ***on land and water,*** por tierra y (por) mar; ***to back water,*** ciar; ***to take on water,*** tomar agua; ***water-line,*** línea de flotación;

(*uso doméstico etc.*) ***boiling water,*** agua hirviendo; ***cold water,*** agua fría; ***hard water,*** agua dura; ***hot water,*** agua caliente; ***lavender water,*** (agua de) lavanda; ***mineral water,*** agua mineral; ***orange-flower water,*** agua de azahar; ***rose-water,*** agua de rosas; ***runnng water,*** agua corriente; ***soft water,*** agua blanda; ***table water,*** agua de mesa *o* mineral; ***toilet-water,*** agua de tocador; ***water-bottle,*** cantimplora; ***water carrier*** o ***bearer,*** aguador; ***water-cart,*** carro de riego; camión de riego; ***water-closet,*** (*abrev.* ***W.C.***) retrete, váter, inodoro; ***water-ice,*** polo; sorbete; ***water-jug,*** jarro de(l) agua *o* para agua; ***water-pistol,*** pistola de agua; ***water-rate,*** contribución de consumo de agua; ***water-supply,*** abastecimiento de aguas; ***water-tank,*** depósito de agua, cisterna; ***water-tap,*** grifo; ***water-trough,*** abrevadero; ***to put (s.o.) on bread and water,*** poner a dieta; ***to turn on the water,*** dejar correr el agua; abrir el grifo; *v. también bajo* '*mec.*';

(*natación*) ***water-skiing,*** esquí aquático; ***water-sports,*** deportes acuáticos, *m.pl.*; ***water-wings,*** nadaderas, *f.pl.*;

(*med.*) ***water on the brain,*** hidrocefalía; ***water on the knee,*** derrame sinovial; ***to take the waters,*** tomar las aguas;

(*fisiol.*) ***to make water,*** mear, orinar, hacer aguas;

(*bot.*, *zool.*) ***water-bird, water-fowl,*** ave acuática, *f.*; ***water-flower,*** flor acuática; ***water-hemlock,*** cicuta acuática; ***water-hen,*** polla de agua; ***water-lily,*** nenúfar; ***water-melon,*** sandía; ***water-mint,*** hierbabuena acuática; ***water-mite,*** cresa de agua; ***water-plant,*** planta acuática; ***water-plantain,*** alisma; ***water-rat,*** rata de agua; ***water-spider,*** esquila;

(*quím.*) ***distilled water,*** agua destilada; ***fresh water,*** agua dulce; ***heavy water,*** agua pesada; ***salt water,*** agua salada;

(*mec.*) ***water-ballast,*** lastre de agua; ***water-butt,*** tonel de agua; ***water-gauge,*** indicador de nivel del agua; ***water-level,*** nivel del agua; ***water-meter,*** hidrómetro; ***water-mill,*** molino de agua, aceña; ***water-parting*** [WATERSHED]; ***water-pipe,*** tubería *o* cañería (de agua); ***water-power,*** energía *o* fuerza hidráulica; ***water-softener,*** ablandador de agua; ***water-tower,*** arca *o* torre de aguas; ***water-wheel,*** rueda hidráulica; noria; (*v. también bajo* '*uso doméstico*');

(*fig.*) ***he spends money like water,*** gasta el dinero como agua *o* abundantemente *o* a espuertas; ***much water has flowed under the bridge (since then),*** ya ha llovido desde entonces; ***of the first water,*** de primera, de lo mejor; ***still waters run deep,*** líbrate del agua mansa; ***to fish in troubled waters,*** pescar a río revuelto; ***to get into deep water(s),*** meterse en un lío; ***to hold water,*** estar bien fundado, tener fundamento; ***that won't hold water,*** carece de fundamento, (eso) no cuela; ***to throw*** o ***pour cold water on,*** echar un jarro de agua fría a.

— *v.t.* regar; bañar; aguar, diluir; (*com.*) ***water capital,*** emitir un número excesivo de acciones. — *v.i.* abrevar; lagrimear; llorar; (*mar.*) hacer aguada; ***my eyes water,*** me lloran los ojos; ***my mouth is watering,*** se me hace la boca agua.

water-borne [ˈwɔːtə-bɔːn], *a.* transportado en barco.

water-cooled [ˈwɔːtə-kuːld], *a.* refrigerado por agua.

watercourse [ˈwɔːtəkɔːs], *s.* corriente de agua, arroyo; lecho de río, cauce.

watercress [ˈwɔːtəkres], *s.* berro(s).

waterfall [ˈwɔːtəfɔːl], *s.* cascada, catarata.

waterfront [ˈwɔːtəfrʌnt], *s.* muelle(s).

wateriness [ˈwɔːtərinis], *s.* acuosidad.

watering [ˈwɔːtəriŋ], *s.* riego; (el) dar de beber (*a los animales*); lagrimeo; (*mar.*) aguada; ***watering-boat,*** barco aguador; ***watering-can, watering-pot,*** regadera; ***watering-cart,*** carro de regar; ***watering-place,*** abrevadero; balneario.

waterless [ˈwɔːtəlis], *a.* sin agua, seco.

waterlogged [ˈwɔːtəlɔgd], *a.* anegado; empapado.

waterman [ˈwɔːtəmən], *s.* barquero.

watermark [ˈwɔːtəmɑːk], *s.* (*de papel*) filigrana.

waterproof [ˈwɔːtəpruːf], *a.*, *s.* impermeable. — *v.t.* impermeabilizar.

watershed [ˈwɔːtəʃed], *s.* divisoria de aguas; vertiente, cuenca.

waterside [ˈwɔːtəsaid], *s.* orilla del agua, ribera.

water-ski [ˈwɔːtə-ˈskiː], *v.i.* practicar el esquí acuático.

waterspout [ˈwɔːtəspaut], *s.* manga, tromba marina.

waterspring [ˈwɔːtəspriŋ], *s.* fuente, *f.*, manantial, ojo de agua.

watertight [ˈwɔːtətait], *a.* estanco, hermético; (*fig.*) incontrovertible; ***watertight compartment,*** compartimiento estanco.

waterway [ˈwɔːtəwei], *s.* canal *o* río navegable.

waterworks [ˈwɔːtəwəːks], *s.* obras hidráulicas, *f.pl.*; central depuradora, *f.*

watery [ˈwɔːtəri], *a.* acuoso; (*ojos*) húmedo, lloroso; (*sopa etc.*) clarucho, flojo; ***to go to a watery grave,*** morir ahogado.

watt [wɔt], *s.* (*elec.*) vatio.

wattle (1) [wɔtl], *s.* barba.

wattle (2) [wɔtl], *s.* zarzo. — *v.t.* enzarzar, entrelazar *o* entretejer con mimbres.

wave [weiv], *s.* (*mar.*) ola; (*radio etc.*) onda; (*fig.*) ondulación; (*fig.*, *de pers.*) oleada; señal (*f.*) *o* ademán (de la mano), saludo (con la mano); ***heat wave,*** ola de calor; ***long wave,*** onda larga; ***medium wave,*** onda media; ***short wave,*** onda corta; ***very short wave,*** hiperfrecuencia, onda alta; ***sound wave,*** onda sonora; ***to come in waves,*** llegar en oleadas; (*rad.*) ***wave-band,*** banda de frecuencias, banda de ondas; ***wave-length,*** frecuencia, longitud de onda; ***wave of strikes,*** oleada de huelgas; ***with a wave of his hand,*** saludando con la mano, haciendo una señal con la mano. — *v.t.* agitar; blandir; hacer tremolar; ondear; ondular; ***wave aside,*** apartar *o* rechazar con un ademán de la mano; ***wave goodbye,*** decir adiós con la mano; ***wave s.o. on,*** hacer señas a alguien para que siga. — *v.i.* saludar, hacer señas con la mano; ondear, flotar.

waved [weivd], *a.* ondulado; ondeado.

waveless [ˈweivlis], *a.* sin olas, tranquilo.

wavelet [ˈweivlit], *s.* olita, cabrilla.

waver [ˈweivə], *v.i.* titubear, vacilar; flaquear.

waverer [ˈweivərə], *s.* irresoluto, indeciso.

wavering [ˈweivəriŋ], *a.* indeciso, irresoluto, vacilante. — *s.* indecisión, irresolución, titubeo, vacilación.

waveringly [ˈweivəriŋli], *adv.* con titubeos, con vacilación.

waving [ˈweiviŋ], *a.* ondulante; que se agita. — *s.* ondulación; agitación; ademanes, *m.pl.* (*de despedida, de bienvenida etc.*).

wavy [ˈweivi], *a.* (*pelo etc.*) ondulado; ondulante, ondeado.

wax (1) [wæks], *s.* cera; ***ear wax,*** cera de los oídos, cerumen; ***cobbler's wax,*** cerote; ***sealing-wax,*** lacre; (*bot.*) ***wax-flower,*** ceriflor; ***wax taper,*** blandón, cirio. — *v.t.* encerar.

wax (2) [wæks], *v.i.* (*luna*) crecer; (*ant., poét.*) ponerse, hacerse, volverse.

waxen [ˈwæksən], *a.* de cera.

waxwork [ˈwækswəːk], *s.* figura *u* obra de cera; (*pl.*) museo de figuras de cera.

waxy [ˈwæksi], *a.* ceroso.

way [wei], *s.* camino (***to,*** de); vía; dirección, sentido; trecho, distancia; paso; costumbre; modo, forma, manera; método, sistema, *m.*; (*mar.*) marcha, andar, velocidad;

(*camino, dirección etc.*) ***across the way,*** enfrente; ***all the way,*** durante todo el camino *o* el viaje; ***by the way,*** al lado del camino; ***by way of,*** por (vía de); ***on the way,*** en el camino, durante el viaje; ***on the way to,*** camino de; ***to feel one's way,*** andar a tientas; ***to find one's way,*** encontrar el camino; ***to go one's own way,*** seguir su camino; ***to go out of one's way,*** desviarse de su camino, hacer un rodeo; ***to know one's way around,*** conocer el terreno; ***to lead the way,*** llevar la delantera, ir (el) primero; ***to lose one's way,*** perderse; ***to make one's way,*** abrir camino (***through,*** por); dirigirse (***to,*** a); ***to make way*** (***for***), abrir paso (a), despejar el camino (para); ***this way,*** por aquí; ***that way,*** por allí; ***way in,*** entrada; ***way out,*** salida; ***on the way in,*** al entrar, entrando; ***on the way out,*** al salir, saliendo; ***way through,*** paso; ***under way,*** en marcha;

(*fig., dirección etc.*) ***by the way,*** a propósito, por cierto; ***once in a way,*** de vez en cuando; ***on the way out,*** (que va) desapareciendo, a punto de desaparecer; ***to be on the way out,*** estar en decadencia, empezar a caer en desuso; ***out of the way,*** apartado, alejado; ***to be in the way,*** estorbar; ***to feel one's way,*** tantear el camino, proceder con tiento; ***there are no two ways about it,*** no tiene vuelta de hoja; ***to get out of the way,*** quitar(se) de en medio; ***out of harm's way,*** fuera de peligro; ***to give way,*** ceder (el paso); entregarse (a las emociones); ***to go a long way towards,*** contribuir mucho *o* grandemente a; ***to go out of one's way to,*** molestarse mucho con tal de, desvivirse por; ***to keep out of the way,*** quitar(se) de en medio; mantener(se) apartado *o* a un lado; ***not to know which way to turn,*** no saber qué hacer; ***to make one's way,*** abrirse camino, hacer carrera; ***he's on the way up,*** va triunfando; ***to see one's way to,*** ver la forma de, encontrar (una) manera de; ***to work one's way through,*** ir haciendo poco a poco, ir leyendo *o* estudiando poco a poco;

(*manera de estar, hacer, pensar etc.*) ***by way of,*** a modo de, a título de; ***in a way,*** en cierto modo, en cierto sentido; ***in a bad way,*** en mal estado, en malas condiciones; maltrecho; malamente; ***in a big way,*** en gran escala; por todo lo alto; ***in a small way,*** en pequeña escala; en plan modesto; ***in every way,*** en todos los sentidos; (***in***) ***my*** (***own***) ***way,*** a mi manera; ***in no way,*** de ninguna manera, en absoluto; (*fam.*) ***in the family way,*** embarazada; ***in the way of,*** como, en plan de; (***in***) ***this*** o ***that way,*** de este *o* ese modo, así; ***I feel the same way,*** yo opino lo mismo, soy del mismo parecer; ***to have*** o ***get one's way,*** salirse con la suya; ***he always wants his own way,*** quiere salirse siempre con la suya; ***to get into the way of doing sth.,*** irse habituando a hacer algo; ***to go one's own way,*** ser muy suyo; ***to have a way with,*** saber manejar; ***to have a way with people,*** tener (el) don de gentes; ***to know one's way around,*** bandeárselas; saber defenderse; ***to mend one's ways,*** enmendarse, cambiar de vida; ***way of thinking,*** modo *o* manera de pensar; ***way of life,*** modo *o* manera de vivir, estilo de vida; ***there's a right way and a wrong way to do it,*** se puede hacer bien y se puede hacer mal; ***where there's a will there's a way,*** querer es poder; ***there are ways and means*** (***of doing sth.***), existen métodos (de hacer algo);

(*distancia*) ***a good way,*** un buen trecho; ***a long way off,*** muy lejos, a mucha distancia; ***a short way off,*** no muy lejos, a poca distancia.

way-bill [ˈwei-bil], *s.* hoja de ruta.

wayfarer [ˈweifɛərə], *s.* viandante, caminante.

wayfaring [ˈweifɛəriŋ], *a.* (*ant.*) que viaja, que va de viaje *o* de camino.

wayfaring-tree [ˈweifɛəriŋ-triː], *s.* viburno.

waylay [weiˈlei], *v.t.* acechar; detener en el camino.

waymark [ˈweimɑːk], *s.* hito, poste indicador.

wayside [ˈweisaid], *a.* del borde del camino; ***wayside inn,*** posada de camino. — *s.* orilla *o* borde del camino; ***by the wayside,*** al borde de la carretera.

wayward [ˈweiwəd], *a.* voluntarioso, caprichoso, díscolo, rebelde.

waywardness [ˈweiwədnis], *s.* voluntariedad, indocilidad.

we [wiː], *pron. pers. pl.* nosotros, nosotras.

weak [wiːk], *a.* débil; flaco; flojo; tenue; claro, poco cargado; ***to grow weak,*** debilitarse; ***to have weak eyes,*** tener la vista cansada; ***weak side*** o ***point,*** lado *o* punto débil *o* flaco; ***weak-headed,*** de cabeza débil; (*fig., fam.*) ***weak-kneed,*** poco enérgico, flojo; ***weak-minded,*** vacilante, débil de voluntad; (*med.*) imbécil.

weaken [ˈwiːkən], *v.t.* debilitar; atenuar; disminuir, reducir. — *v.i.* debilitarse, flaquear; atenuarse; disminuir, desfallecer.

weakening [ˈwiːkniŋ], *a.* debilitante. — *s.* debilitación, enflaquecimiento.

weakling [ˈwiːkliŋ], *s.* enclenque, canijo.

weakly [ˈwiːkli], *a.* enclenque, enfermizo, achacoso. — *adv.* débilmente; tenuemente; flojamente.

weakness [ˈwiːknis], *s.* debilidad, flaqueza, flojedad; endeblez; lado débil *o* flaco; tenuidad; falta de carácter.

weal (1) [wiːl], *s.* verdugón, cardenal.

weal (2) [wiːl], *s.* (*ant.*) bienestar; ***common*** o ***public weal,*** bien público.

weald [wiːld], *s.* (*ant.*) bosque.

wealth [welθ], *s.* riqueza(s); (*fig.*) abundancia, gran caudal, acopio.

wealthily [ˈwelθili], *adv.* ricamente, opulentamente.

wealthy [ˈwelθi], *a.* rico, adinerado, acaudalado, pudiente. — *s.* (*pl.*) ***the wealthy,*** los ricos.

wean [wiːn], *v.t.* destetar; (*fig.*) ***wean s.o. from sth.,*** ir apartando a alguien de algo.

weaning [ˈwiːniŋ], *s.* destete.

weanling [ˈwiːnliŋ], *a.* recién destetado. — *s.* niño *o* animal recién destetado.

weapon [ˈwepən], *s.* arma.

weaponed [ˈwepənd], *a.* armado.

weaponless [ˈwepənlis], *a.* desarmado, sin armas.

weaponry [ˈwepənri], *s.* armas, *f.pl.*, armamento.

wear [wɛə], *s.* uso; degaste; ropa, prenda(s); duración, resistencia; ***for everyday wear,*** de uso diario, para todo trote; ***for hard wear,*** duradero, resistente; ***wear and tear,*** desgaste (normal); ***winter*** (***summer***) ***wear,*** ropa de invierno (de verano); ***light wear,*** ropa ligera, prendas ligeras, *f.pl.*; ***the worse for wear,*** gastado por el uso; ***to look the worse for wear, to show signs of wear,*** dar indicios *o* señales de deterioro; (*fig.*) estar maltrecho. — (*irr.*) *v.t.* llevar, usar, gastar;

traer *o* llevar puesto; calzar; tener, mostrar, exhibir; ponerse; desgastar; (*fig.*, *fam.*) admitir; consentir, aguantar; ***I have nothing to wear,*** no tengo nada que ponerme; (*fig.*, *fam.*) ***I won't wear that,*** no lo consentiré, no lo consiento; (*fig.*) ***wear the trousers*** o ***breeches,*** llevar los pantalones; (*fig.*) ***wear one's heart on one's sleeve,*** llevar el corazón en la mano; ***wear away,*** gastar, desgastar; raer; consumir; ***wear down,*** desgastar; (*fig.*) agotar, ir acabando con; ***wear out,*** desgastar; romper con el uso; agotar, rendir. — *v.i.* durar; ***it wears well,*** dura mucho, es duradero; ***wear away,*** desgastarse, gastarse, consumirse; ***wear off,*** pasar(se), desaparecer; (*pint.*) borrarse; (*tiempo etc.*) ***wear on,*** transcurrir, ir pasando; ***wear out,*** usarse, romperse con el uso, consumirse.

wearer [ˈwɛərə], *s.* el que lleva (*una prenda etc.*).

wearily [ˈwiərili], *adv.* con fatiga y hastío.

weariness [ˈwiərinis], *s.* fatiga, hastío.

wearing [ˈwɛəriŋ], *a.* cansado, agotador. — *s.* (el) llevar; ***wearing apparel,*** prendas de vestir, *f.pl.*

wearisome [ˈwiərisəm], *a.* cansado, pesado, fastidioso, aburrido.

wearisomeness [ˈwiərisəmnis], *s.* (lo) cansado *etc.*

weary [ˈwiəri], *a.* fatigado, cansado; hastiado; aburrido. — *v.t.* fatigar, cansar; hastiar, aburrir. — *v.i.* — (***of***), hartarse (de), cansarse (de), aburrirse (de).

weasand [ˈwi:zənd], *s.* tráquea; gaznate.

weasel [ˈwi:zl], *s.* (*zool.*) comadreja.

weather [ˈweðə], *s.* tiempo; intemperie, *f.*; ***bad weather,*** mal tiempo; ***cloudy weather,*** tiempo cubierto; ***fine weather,*** buen tiempo; ***wet*** o ***rainy weather,*** tiempo lluvioso; ***weather permitting,*** si el tiempo lo permite; ***the weather is bad,*** hace mal tiempo; ***to be out in the weather,*** estar a la intemperie; (*fig.*) ***to be under the weather,*** estar deprimido, estar poco animado; (*fig.*) ***to keep a weather-eye open,*** estar ojo avizor, estar alerta; (*fig.*) ***to make heavy weather of,*** encontrar difícil; ***weather-board,*** tabla de chilla; ***weather-bureau,*** servicio meteorológico; ***weather-chart, weather-map,*** mapa meteorológico, *m.*; ***weather-forecast,*** parte *o* boletín meteorológico, pronóstico del tiempo; (*mar.*) ***weather-gauge, -gage,*** barlovento; ***weather-glass,*** barómetro. — *v.t.* desgastar (*la piedra etc.*); curtir (*la madera*); (*mar.*) doblar (*un cabo*); (*fig.*) superar; ***weather the storm,*** capear el temporal. — *v.i.* curtirse; desgastarse.

weather-beaten [ˈweðə-bi:tn], *a.* curtido por la intemperie; azotado por los elementos.

weather-bound [ˈweðə-baund], *a.* parado *o* aislado por el mal tiempo.

weathercock [ˈweðəkɔk], *s.* veleta.

weathered [ˈweðəd], *a.* gastado por el tiempo; (*tez etc.*) curtido por el tiempo.

weathering [ˈwəðəriŋ], *s.* (*geol.*) desgaste (por la acción atmosférica); exposición a la intemperie.

weatherly [ˈweðəli], *a.* (*mar.*) de barlovento, de bolina.

weatherman [ˈweðəmæn], *s.* hombre del tiempo.

weatherproof [ˈweðəpru:f], *a.* a prueba de mal tiempo, resistente a la intemperie.

weave (1) [wi:v], *s.* tejido; (*tec.*) textura. — *v.t. irr.* tejer; trenzar; entretejer, entrelazar; urdir, tramar; (*fig.*) ***weave one's way,*** abrirse camino serpeando. — *v.i.* tejer.

weave (2) [wi:v], *v.i.* serpentear.

weaver [ˈwi:və], *s.* tejedor; (*zool.*) araña tejedora; (*orn.*) ***weaver-bird,*** tejedor.

weaving [ˈwi:viŋ], *s.* tejeduría; ***weaving machine,*** telar; ***weaving mill,*** tejeduría.

web [web], *s.* tejido; (*de araña*) telaraña; (*fig.*) red; (*de pato etc.*) membrana (interdigital); ***web-foot,*** pie palmado.

webbed [webd], *a.* palmado, palmípedo; unido por una membrana.

webbing [ˈwebiŋ], *s.* cinta para cinchas, cincha, petral.

webby [ˈwebi], *a.* membranoso.

web-footed [ˈweb-futid], *a.* palmado, palmípedo.

wed [wed], *v.t.* casarse con; casar, unir en matrimonio; ***to be wedded to one's opinions,*** estar aferrado a sus opiniones. — *v.i.* casarse, matrimoniar.

wedded [ˈwedid], *a.* casado; conyugal; ***wedded bliss,*** dicha conyugal.

wedding [ˈwediŋ], *s.* boda, casamiento, nupcias, *f.pl.*, bodas, *f.pl.*, enlace, unión, *f.*; ***golden wedding,*** bodas de oro; ***silver wedding,*** bodas de plata; ***wedding breakfast,*** banquete de boda, lunch; ***wedding-day,*** día de bodas, *m.*; ***wedding-cake,*** tarta *o* pastel de boda; ***wedding-dress,*** traje de boda; ***wedding-march,*** marcha nupcial; ***wedding-ring,*** anillo *o* sortija de boda.

wedge [wedʒ], *s.* cuña; calza; alzaprima; (*geom.*) prisma triangular; ***it's the thin end of the wedge,*** así se empieza, la cosa irá a — más. *v.t* acuñar, meter cuña(s) a, sujetar con cuña(s), calzar.

wedlock [ˈwedlɔk], *s.* matrimonio.

Wednesday [ˈwenzdi], *s.* miércoles, *m.inv.*; ***Ash Wednesday,*** miércoles de ceniza.

wee [wi:], *a.* (*Esco.*) chiquitito, pequeñín. — *frase adv.* ***a wee bit,*** un poquito, un poquitín.

weed (1) [wi:d], *s.* mala hierba, hierbajo; cizaña; (*fam.*) (***the***) ***weed,*** tobaco; (*fig.*, *fam.*) flacucho, enclenque; ***weed-killer,*** herbicida, *m.* — *v.t.* escardar, desyerbar, sachar; ***weed out,*** arrancar; (*fig.*) extirpar.

weed (2) [wi:d], *s.* (*ant.*) vestido; ***widow's weeds,*** luto de viuda.

weeder [ˈwi:də], *s.* escardador, desyerbador.

weedhook [ˈwi:dhuk], *s.* escarda, sacha.

weeding [ˈwi:diŋ], *s.* escardadura, escarda.

weedless [ˈwi:dlis], *a.* sin malas hierbas, limpio de hierbajos.

weedy [ˈwi:di], *a.* lleno de malas hierbas *o* de hierbajos; (*fig.*) flacucho, enclenque, desmirriado.

week [wi:k], *s.* semana; ***week-day,*** día de trabajo, *m.*, día laborable, *m.*; ***on week-days, on a week-day,*** entre semana; ***this day week, today week,*** de hoy en ocho días.

weekend [ˈwi:kˈend], *s.* fin de semana.

weekly [ˈwi:kli], *a.* semanal. — *adv.* semanalmente, todas las semanas. — *s.* periódico semanal, semanario.

ween [wi:n], *v.t.* (*ant.*, *poét.*) pensar, creer, imaginar.

weep [wi:p], (*irr.*) *v.t.* llorar, lamentar; derramar (*lágrimas*). — *v.i.* llorar; ***she wept all night long,*** pasó la noche llorando; ***she wept over the death of her father,*** lloró la muerte de su padre.

weeper [ˈwi:pə], *s.* plañidera.

weeping [ˈwi:piŋ], *a.* llorón, que llora; ***weeping willow,*** sauce llorón. — *s.* llanto, lloro.

weepy [ˈwi:pi], *a.* lloroso.

weever [ˈwi:və], *s.* (*ict.*) traquino, dragón marino.

weevil [ˈwi:vil], *s.* (*ent.*) gorgojo.

weft [weft], *s.* trama (*de tejidos*).

weigh [wei], *v.t.* pesar; (*fig.*) ***weigh*** (***up***), sopesar; (*fig.*, *fam.*) ***weigh up,*** calar (*a una persona*); ***I soon weighed him up,*** pronto le calé; ***weigh sth. against sth. else,*** sopesar una cosa frente a otra; ***weigh down,*** sobrecargar; (*fig.*) agobiar (***with,*** de); ***weigh anchor,*** levar anclas. — *v.i.* pesar; ***it weighs three kilos,*** pesa tres kilos; (*fam.*) ***weigh in with,*** aportar, meter baza diciendo, salir con; (*fig.*) ***it weighs little with him,*** influye poco en él.

weigh-bridge [ˈwei-bridʒ], *s.* báscula-puente.

weighing [ˈweiiŋ], *s.* (el) pesar; ***weighing machine,*** báscula.

weight [weit], *s.* peso; pesa (*de plomo, hierro etc.*); ***weights and measures,*** pesos (*m.pl.*) y medidas (*f.pl.*); ***set of weights,*** pesas, *f.pl.*; ***by weight,*** al peso; ***gross weight,*** peso bruto; ***net weight,*** peso neto; ***standard weight,*** peso legal *o* normal; (*fig.*) ***to be worth one's weight in gold,*** valer su peso en oro; ***to make up the weight,*** completar el peso; ***to lose weight,*** adelgazar; ***to put on weight,*** engordar; ***to be over-weight,*** estar gordo; (*fig.*) ***to pull one's weight,*** trabajar lo suyo; (*fam.*) ***to throw one's weight about,*** chulearse; (*fig.*) ***to carry great weight*** (***with***), tener mucho predicamento (con), influir poderosamente (en); (*dep.*) ***putting the weight,*** lanzamiento de pesos; (*dep.*) ***weight-lifting,*** levantamiento de pesos; (*dep.*) ***weight-training,*** ejercicios realizados con pesas, *m.pl.* — *v.t.* cargar; sobrecargar; sujetar con un peso.

weightiness [ˈweitinis], *s.* peso; (*fig.*) peso, importancia; gravedad.

weightless [ˈweitlis], *a.* sin peso, ingrávido.

weighty [ˈweiti], *a.* pesado; (*fig.*) de peso, importante; grave.

weir [wiə], *s.* azud; cañal; presa.

weird [wiəd], *a.* extraño, raro; fantasmagórico, espectral; (*Shakespeare*) ***the Weird Sisters,*** las brujas.

welcome [ˈwelkəm], *a.* bienvenido; grato, agradable; ***a good cigar is always welcome,*** un buen puro siempre viene bien; (*Am.*) ***you're welcome!*** ¡de nada! ¡no hay de qué!; ***you're welcome to it,*** está a su disposición; ***you are welcome to try it,*** es usted muy dueño de intentarlo. — *s.* bienvenida, (buena) acogida *o* recepción. — *v.t.* dar la bienvenida a; acoger, recibir; aceptar, aprobar. — *interj.* ¡bien venido!

welcomer [ˈwelkəmə], *s.* persona que acoge *o* que da la bienvenida.

welcoming [ˈwelkəmiŋ], *a.* acogedor; de bienvenida.

weld [weld], *s.* soldadura. — *v.t., v.i.* soldar(se).

welder [ˈweldə], *s.* soldador.

welding [ˈweldiŋ], *s.* soldadura; ***welding torch,*** soplete soldador.

welfare [ˈwelfɛə], *s.* bienestar, bien, prosperidad; asistencia social; ***welfare state,*** estado asistencial; ***welfare work,*** trabajos de asistencia social, *m.pl.*; ***welfare worker,*** asistente social.

welkin [ˈwelkin], *s.* (*poét.*) bóveda celeste, firmamento; ***to make the welkin ring,*** atronar el espacio.

well (1) [wel], *s.* pozo; fuente, *f.*, manantial; copa (*de tintero*); caja *o* hueco (*de escalera*); ***well-borer,*** pocero; ***well-curb,*** brocal de pozo; ***well-drain,*** desagüe; ***well-hole,*** boca de pozo; ***well-spring,*** fuente, *f.*, manantial; ***well-water,*** agua de pozo. — *v.i.* manar, fluir, brotar.

well (2) [wel], *a.* bueno; ***are you well?*** ¿qué tal está?; ***to get well,*** reponerse; ***well and good,*** de acuerdo; ***to be well-off*** o ***well-to-do,*** tener el riñón bien cubierto *o* vida acomodada. — *adv.* bien; ***as well as,*** así como; ***well enough,*** bastante bien; ***well-aimed,*** certero; ***well-appointed,*** bien equipado; bien amueblado; ***well-attended,*** muy concurrido; ***well-balanced,*** (bien) equilibrado; ***well-behaved,*** (bien) educado; formal; manso; ***well-beloved,*** bienquisto; ***well-born,*** bien nacido; ***well-bred,*** bien criado; culto; de buena raza; ***well-built,*** sólido, bien construido; (*pers.*) fornido; ***well-chosen,*** elegido cuidadosamente; (*palabras*) acertado; ***well-deserved,*** merecido; ***well-disposed,*** favorable, bien dispuesto; ***well-favoured,*** bien parecido, agraciado; ***well-fed,*** bien nutrido; ***well-founded,*** (bien) fundado; ***well-groomed,*** bien vestido y aseado; ***well-informed,*** instruido; enterado, impuesto (***about,*** de); (*fuente*) bien informada; ***well-intentioned,*** bien intencionado; ***well-kept,*** (muy) cuidado; ***well-known,*** (muy) conocido; ***well-meaning,*** bien intencionado; ***well-nigh,*** casi, punto menos que; ***well-read,*** muy leído; ***well-spent,*** bien gastado, bien empleado; ***well-stocked,*** bien provisto; ***well-thought-out,*** bien razonado, bien ideado; ***well-turned,*** bien hecho; bien expresado; ***well-worded,*** bien expresado, bien dicho; ***well-worn,*** usado, gastado; trillado. — *interj.* ¡bien! ¡bueno! ¡ah! ¡vaya!; ***well, then,*** pues bien; ***all's well!*** ¡sereno!

well-being [ˈwel-ˈbi:iŋ], *s.* bienestar.

well-doing [ˈwel-ˈdu:iŋ], *a.* benéfico. — *s.* beneficencia.

wellington (**boot**) [ˈweliŋtən (bu:t)], *s.* bota de goma.

well-wisher [ˈwel-wiʃə], *s.* amigo, persona que quiere bien a otra.

Welsh [welʃ], *a.* galés; ***Welsh rabbit,*** tostada con queso. — *s.* (*idioma*) galés, *m.*; (*pl.*) ***the Welsh,*** los galeses.

Welshman [ˈwelʃmən], *s.* galés, *m.*

welt [welt], *s.* ribete; (*de zapato*) vira; costurón, verdugón. — *v.t.* poner vira a.

welter [ˈweltə], *s.* confusión, tumulto; mar (***of,*** de); oleaje. — *v.i.* revolcarse; (*poét.*) hincharse (las olas).

wen [wen], *s.* (*med.*) lobanillo.

wench [wentʃ], *s.* moza, mozuela. — *v.i.* (*ant.*) putañear.

wend [wend], *v.t.* ***wend one's way,*** dirigirse, seguir su camino; ***wend one's way through,*** abrirse camino por, atravesar.

were [wə:], *pl. del. pret., subj. pasado* [BE]; ***as it were,*** como si dijéramos; ***as if it were,*** como si fuese.

werwolf, werewolf [ˈwə:wulf, ˈwiəwulf], *s.* (*folklore*) hombre-lobo, licántropo.

Wesleyan [ˈwezliən], *a., s.* wesleyano.

west [west], *a.* del oeste, occidental; ***the West Country,*** los condados del suroeste (británico). — *adv.* al oeste, hacia el oeste; (*fam.*) ***to go west,*** fracasar, fallar, finiquitar. — *s.* oeste, occidente.

westerly [ˈwestəli], *a.* del oeste. — *s.pl.* (**Westerlies**) vientos del oeste, *m.pl.*

western [ˈwestən], *a.* occidental, de occidente. — *s.* novela *o* película de vaqueros y de tiros.

westerner [ˈwestənə], *s.* hombre del oeste.

westernmost [ˈwestənmoust], *a.* (el) más occidental.

West Indian [west ˈindiən], *a., s.* antillano.

West Indies [west ˈindiz]. Antillas, *f.pl.*

westward [ˈwestwəd], *a.* occidental, del oeste. — (*t.* **westwards** [ˈwestwədz]) *adv.* hacia (el) oeste, al oeste.

wet [wet], *a.* mojado; húmedo; (*adrede*) humedecido; (*pint.*) fresco; (*día, clima etc.*) lluvioso; (*Am.*) no prohibicionista; (*fam.*) soso, bobo; (*fam.*) ***wet blanket,*** aguafiestas, *m.f.inv.*; (*elec.*) ***wet cell,*** pila húmeda; ***wet day,*** día de lluvia, *m.*; ***wet nurse,*** ama de cría, nodriza; (*foto.*) ***wet plate,*** placa de colodión; (*quím.*) ***wet process,*** vía húmeda; ***wet season,*** estación de las lluvias; ***wet weather,*** tiempo lluvioso; ***to be wet through,*** estar calado *o* mojado hasta los huesos; ***to get wet,*** mojarse; (*fam.*) ***don't be so wet!*** ¡no seas bobo! — *s.* humedad; tiempo húmedo; lluvia, agua. — *v.t.* mojar, humedecer; ***wet one's bed,*** orinarse en la cama.

wether [ˈweðə], *s.* carnero castrado.

wetness [ˈwetnis], *s.* humedad; (lo) lluvioso.

wetting [ˈwetiŋ], *s.* mojada, mojadura, remojo; ***to get a wetting,*** mojarse.

wettish [ˈwetiʃ], *a.* algo mojado, algo húmedo.

whack [wæk], *s.* (*fam.*) trastazo, porrazo; tentativa; lote, porción; ***to do one's whack,*** hacer su parte; ***to have a whack at it,*** intentarlo. — *v.t.* vapulear, golpear; ***they whacked the other team,*** se merendaron al equipo contrario.

whacker [ˈwækə], *s.* (*fam.*) vapuleador; (*fam.*) ejemplar inmenso.

whacking [ˈwækiŋ], *a.* (*fam.*) enorme; ***a whacking great car,*** un cochazo enorme. — *s.* (*fam.*) paliza, tunda.

whale [weil], *s.* ballena; ***sperm whale,*** cachalote; ***whale-boat, whale-ship,*** (barco) ballenero; (*fig., fam.*) ***a whale of a difference,*** una diferencia enorme. — *v.i.* ir a la pesca de la ballena.
whalebone [ˈweilboun], *s.* (barba de) ballena.
whaler [ˈweilə], *s.* (barco) ballenero.
whaling [ˈweiliŋ], *s.* pesca de ballenas; ***whaling station,*** estación ballenera.
wharf [wɔ:f], *s.* (*pl.* **wharfs, wharves** [wɔ:fs, wɔ:vz]) muelle, embarcadero, desembarcadero.
wharfage [ˈwɔ:fidʒ], *s.* muellaje.
wharfinger [ˈwɔ:findʒə], *s.* propietario de muelle.
what [wɔt], *a.* qué; el, la, los, las . . . que; ***buy what hat you like,*** compra el sombrero que quieras; ***what a man!*** ¡qué hombre! — *adv.* (en) parte, entre; ***what with one thing and another,*** entre unas cosas y otras. — *conj.* que; (*ant.*) ***but what,*** que no; ***there is not a day but what it rains,*** no hay día que no llueva. — *pron.* (*interr.*) qué, cuál; ***what else?*** ¿qué más?; ***what for?*** ¿para qué?; ***so what?*** ¿y qué?; ***what if...?*** ¿y si . . .?, ¿qué pasaría si . . .?; ***what of it?, what of that?*** y eso ¿qué importa?; (*rel.*) lo que; ***say what you like,*** diga lo que quiera; ***come what may,*** venga lo que venga; ***and what not,*** y qué sé yo más; ***to know what's what,*** saber cuántas son cinco. — *interj.* ¡qué! ¡cómo! ¡eh!
what-d'ye-call-him [ˈwɔt-djə-kɔ:l-(h)im], *pron.* fulano, ése.
what-d'ye-call-it [ˈwɔt-djə-kɔ:l-it], *s.* cosa, chisme.
whatever, whatsoever [wɔtˈevə, wɔtsouˈevə], *a.* cualquier; ***whatever the price,*** al precio que sea; ***nothing whatever,*** nada en absoluto. — *pron.* lo que, todo lo que; ***whatever you like,*** lo que quiera; ***whatever you say,*** diga usted lo que diga; ***or whatever,*** o lo que sea; ***whatever do you want?*** pero ¿qué diablos quiere usted?
whatnot [ˈwɔtnɔt], *pron.* ***and whatnot,*** y qué sé yo. — *s.* juguetero.
what's-his-name [ˈwɔts-iz-neim], *pron.* (*fam.*) fulano (de tal).
whatsoever [WHATEVER].
wheal [wi:l], *s.* roncha, cardenal.
wheat [wi:t], *s.* trigo.
wheaten [wi:tn], *a.* de trigo.
wheatfield [ˈwi:tfi:ld], *s.* trigal.
wheedle [wi:dl], *v.t.* ***wheedle s.o. into,*** engatusar a alguien para que + *subj.*; ***wheedle sth. out of s.o.,*** (son)sacarle algo a alguien.
wheel [wi:l], *s.* rueda; (*aut.*) (***steering-***)***wheel,*** volante; (*mar.*) timón; (*mil.*) conversión; ***cog-wheel,*** rueda dentada; ***driving-wheel,*** rueda motriz; ***fly-wheel,*** volante (de máquinas); ***front-wheel,*** rueda delantera; ***rear-wheel,*** rueda trasera; (*aut.*) ***to take the wheel,*** llevar el volante, conducir; ***to torture on the wheel,*** enrodar; ***wheel-base,*** distancia entre ejes, batalla; ***wheel-chair,*** silla *o* sillón de ruedas; ***wheel of fortune,*** rueda de la fortuna. — *v.t.* hacer rodar *o* girar; (*bicicleta*) empujar; (*cochecito de niño*) empujar, pasear. — *v.i.* rodar; girar; (*pájaros*) revolotear; (*mil.*) cambiar de frente; ***wheel round,*** volverse de repente, girar sobre los talones.
wheelbarrow [ˈwi:lbærou], *s.* carretilla.
wheeled [wi:ld], *a.* rodado; de ruedas.
wheeler [ˈwi:lə], *s.* caballo de vara(s); biciclista, *m.f.*; rodador, girador; vapor de ruedas; ***three-wheeler,*** triciclo.
wheelhouse [ˈwi:lhaus], *s.* (*mar.*) caseta del timón, timonera.
wheelwright [ˈwi:lrait], *s.* carretero, ruedero.
wheeze [wi:z], *s.* resuello asmático; (*fam.*) idea, broma, truco. — *v.i.* resollar asmáticamente.
wheezing, wheezy [ˈwi:ziŋ, ˈwi:zi], *a.* asmático.
whelk (1) [welk], *s.* buccino.
whelk (2) [welk], *s.* grano, pústula.
whelp [welp], *s.* cachorro; (*mar.*) diente (de engranaje). — *v.i.* parir.
when [wen], *adv., conj.* cuando. — *pron.* (*rel.*) en que; (*interr.*) ¿cuándo?; ***the moment when,*** el momento en que; ***since when,*** y desde entonces.
whence [wens], *adv.* (*rel.*) por lo que; por consiguiente; (*interr.*) ¿de dónde?
when(so)ever [wen(sou)ˈevə], *conj.* cuandoquiera que; siempre que.
where [wɛə], *conj.* donde. — *adv.* (*rel.*) en que; (*interr.*) ¿dónde?; ¿adónde?
whereabouts [wɛərəˈbauts], *adv.* (*interr.*) dónde, de qué lado, hacia dónde, hacia qué sitio; ***whereabouts is it?*** ¿dónde está exactamente? — [ˈwɛərəbauts], *s.pl.* paradero.
whereas [wɛərˈæz], *conj.* mientras que; (*for.*) visto que, por cuanto, considerando que.
whereat [wɛərˈæt], *adv.* a lo cual, ante lo cual.
whereby [wɛəˈbai], *adv.* por lo cual, por medio de lo cual.
wherefore [ˈwɛəfɔ:], *adv.* por qué; por lo cual, por lo tanto. — *s.* porqué, motivo, razón; ***the why and the wherefore,*** el porqué.
wherein [wɛərˈin], *adv.* (en) donde, en que; en lo que.
whereof [wɛərˈɔv], *adv.* de lo cual, del cual, de que; cuyo.
whereon [wɛərˈɔn], *adv.* en que, sobre que, sobre lo cual.
wheresoever [wɛəsouˈevə], [WHEREVER].
whereto [wɛəˈtu:], *adv.* a que, a lo que.
whereupon [wɛərəˈpɔn], *adv.* en esto, al oír *o* ver esto, con lo cual, después de lo cual, acto seguido.
wherever [wɛərˈevə], *adv.* dondequiera que; por dondequiera que; ***sit wherever you like,*** siéntate donde quieras; (*interr.*) ¿dónde?; (*fam.*) ***wherever did you buy that?*** ¿dónde diablos compraste eso?
wherewith [wɛəˈwið], *adv.* con que, con lo cual.
wherewithal [ˈwɛəwiðɔ:l], *adv.* [WHEREWITH]. — *s.* (el) con qué, (el) cónquibus.
wherry [ˈweri], *s.* chalana.
wherryman [ˈwerimæn], *s.* barquero.
whet [wet], *s.* (*fig.*) afiladura, aguzadura. — *v.t.* (*fig.*) afilar, amolar; aguzar; excitar, estimular, despertar; ***whet the appetite,*** abrir el apetito.
whether [ˈweðə], *conj.* si, que; ***I don't know whether he is at home,*** no sé si estará *o* está en casa; ***whether . . . or . . .,*** tanto si . . . como (si); ***whether they come or not,*** vengan o no (vengan); ***I doubt whether he'll come,*** dudo que venga.
whetstone [ˈwetstoun], *s.* piedra de afilar, amoladera.
whew! [hju:], *interj.* ¡uf!
whey [wei], *s.* suero (de la leche).
wheyey, wheyish [ˈweii, ˈweiiʃ], *a.* seroso.
which [witʃ], *a.* (*interr.*) ¿qué?; ***which way?*** ¿por dónde? — *pron.* (*rel.*) que; lo cual; el cual, la cual, los cuales, las cuales; ***all of which,*** todo lo cual, todo esto; ***both of which,*** los dos, ambos; (*interr.*) ¿cuál? ¿qué?
whichever [witʃˈevə], *a.* cualquier. — *pron.* cualquiera, el que, la que.
whiff [wif], *s.* soplo; vaharada, bocanada, fumarada; fumada, chupada; tufo, olorcillo; ***to get a whiff of,*** oler; coger un poco de (*aire etc.*). — *v.t., v.i.* oler.
whiffle [wifl], *v.i.* variar, cambiar; vacilar.
Whig [wig], *a., s.* (*pol.*) liberal.
Whiggery, Whiggism [ˈwigəri, ˈwigizəm], *s.* doctrina política de los Whigs.
while [wail], *conj.* (*t.* **whilst** [wailst]) mientras (que). — *s.* rato; ***a good while,*** un buen rato; ***a long while,*** un rato largo; ***all the while,*** y a todo esto; ***just a short*** o ***little while*** (***ago***), (hace) un ratito *o* ratillo nada más; ***for a while,*** durante un rato; durante algún tiempo; ***between whiles,*** mientras tanto, en medio; ***once in a while,*** de vez en cuando; (*fam.*) ***to be worth while,*** valer *o* merecer la pena. — ***v.t. while***

away, (*tiempo etc.*) pasar (ociosamente), entretener, matar.

whim [wim], *s.* capricho, antojo; (*min.*) malacate.

whimper [ˈwimpə], *s.* quejido. — *v.i.* gimotear, lloriquear.

whimpering [ˈwimpəriŋ], *s.* gimoteo, lloriqueo.

whims(e)y [ˈwimzi], *s.* capricho; fantasía.

whimsical [ˈwimzikəl], *a.* (*pers. etc.*) caprichoso; (*noción etc.*) fantástico; (*sonrisa etc.*) entre burlón y distraído.

whimsicality [wimziˈkæliti], *s.* fantasía, extravagancia.

whin [win], *s.* (*bot.*) aulaga, aliaga, tojo.

whine [wain], *s.* gemido, quejido. — *v.i.* gemir, gimotear, quejarse; (*bala*) silbar.

whining [ˈwainiŋ], *a.* quejumbroso. — *s.* quejumbrosidad, gimoteo; silbido.

whinny [ˈwini], *s.* relincho suave. — *v.i.* relinchar suavemente.

whip [wip], *s.* látigo; azote; (***riding-***)***whip,*** fusta; (***bull-***)***whip,*** rebenque; (*pol.*) oficial disciplinario de partido; ***lash of the whip,*** latigazo; ***to have*** o ***hold the whip-hand,*** tener el mando, tener la ventaja, tener la sartén por el mango. — *v.t.* azotar; (*nata*) batir; (*fig., fam.*) dar una paliza a, vencer; ***whip away,*** arrebatar (***from,*** a); (*pol.*) ***whip in,*** llamar (*para que vote*); ***whip off, on,*** quitarse, ponerse (*una prenda*) en un momento; ***whip out,*** sacar de repente; ***whip up,*** provocar, fomentar, suscitar. — *v.i.* ***whip round*** o ***through,*** (*el viento*) azotar; ***whip round,*** volverse de repente; (*fam.*) hacer una colecta.

whipcord [ˈwipkɔ:d], *s.* tralla (del látigo); tela fuerte de estambre.

whiplash [ˈwiplæʃ], *s.* trallazo, latigazo. — *v.t.* azotar.

whipper [ˈwipə], *s.* azotador.

whipper-snapper [ˈwipəsnæpə], *s.* (*fam.*) mequetrefe.

whippet [ˈwipit], *s.* (perro) lebrel.

whipping [ˈwipiŋ], *s.* azotaina; vapuleo; paliza; ***whipping top,*** peonza.

whippletree [ˈwipltri:], *s.* (*carr.*) balancín, volea.

whipsaw [ˈwipsɔ:], *s.* serrucho.

whipstaff [ˈwipstɑ:f], *s.* piño del látigo.

whirl [wə:l], *s.* giro, volteo; (*agua etc.*) remolino; (*humo etc.*) espiral, *f.* — *v.t.* hacer girar, voltear. — *v.i.* girar, dar vueltas; arremolinarse; ***my head is whirling,*** me da vueltas la cabeza.

whirligig [ˈwə:ligig], *s.* (*juguete*) perinola, molinete; tiovivo; (*ent.*) girino; (*fig.*) torbellino.

whirlpool [ˈwə:lpu:l], *s.* remolino; torbellino; (*fig.*) vorágine, *f.*

whirlwind [ˈwə:lwind], *s.* torbellino, manga de viento.

whirr [wə:], *s.* zumbido; aleteo. — *v.i.* zumbar, runrunear; batir.

whirring [ˈwə:riŋ], *s.* zumbido(s).

whisk [wisk], *s.* (*coc.*) batidor; (*bot.*) escobilla; ***in a whisk,*** en un periquete; ***with a whisk of the broom,*** de un escobazo. — *v.t.* batir; ***whisk away*** o ***off,*** quitar *o* llevarse rápidamente; arrebatar. — *v.i.* ***whisk round,*** girar rápidamente.

whisker [ˈwiskə], *s.* patilla; pelo (de la barba); (*pl.*) bigotes, *m.pl.*; ***side whiskers,*** patillas.

whiskered [ˈwiskəd], *a.* patilludo; bigotudo.

whisk(e)y [ˈwiski], *s.* whisky, güisqui.

whisper [ˈwispə], *s.* cuchicheo; susurro; murmullo; ***in a whisper,*** en voz baja. — *v.t.* decir al oído *o* en voz baja. — *v.i.* cuchichear; susurrar; murmurar.

whisperer [ˈwispərə], *s.* cuchicheador.

whispering [ˈwispəriŋ], *a.* que cuchichea, susurra *o* murmulla. — *s.* cuchicheo; susurros, *m.pl.*; murmullos, *m.pl.*

whist [wist], *s.* (*naipes*) whist.

whistle [wisl], *s.* pito, silbato; pitido, silbido, silbo; (*fam.*) ***to wet one's whistle,*** humedecerse el gaznate. — *v.t.* silbar; ***whistle up,*** llamar con un silbido *o* silbando; (*fig., fam.*) reunir apresuradamente. — *v.i.* silbar.

whistler [ˈwislə], *s.* silbador.

whistling [ˈwisliŋ], *a.* silbante. — *s.* silbidos, *m.pl.*

whit [wit], *s.* pizca; ***not a whit,*** ni pizca, en absoluto; ***not a whit the wiser,*** sin enterarse en absoluto, sin saber en absoluto más que antes.

white [wait], *a.* blanco; pálido; (*pelo*) cano; ***white coffee,*** café con leche; (*fig.*) ***white elephant,*** objeto costoso e inútil; (*fig.*) ***white horses,*** borreguitos blancos, *m.pl.*; ***white hot,*** candente; (*Am.*) ***White House,*** Casa Blanca; ***white lead,*** albayalde; ***white lie,*** mentirilla; ***White Russian,*** ruso blanco; ***white slave trade,*** trata de blancas; ***to grow*** o ***go*** o ***turn white,*** ponerse pálido *o* lívido, palidecer; (*fig.*) ***to show the white feather,*** mostrarse gallina; ***he sees everything in black and white,*** no sabe matizar; no se anda con medias tintas; ***white-collar,*** profesional; de oficina, oficinesco; ***white-livered,*** cobarde. — *s.* blanco; (*del ojo*) blanco; (*de huevo*) clara; (*de la nieve*) ampo; (*pl.*) flores blancas, *f.pl.*; ropa blanca; flor de harina; ***to turn up the whites of one's eyes,*** poner los ojos en blanco.

whitebait [ˈwaitbeit], *s.* (*ict.*) boquerones, *m.pl.* chanquetes, *m.pl.*

whitecaps [ˈwaitkæps], *s.pl.* (*mar.*) borreguitos, *m.pl.*

whited sepulchre [ˈwaitid ˈseplkə], *s.* sepulcro blanqueado.

whitefish [ˈwaitfiʃ], *s.* (*ict.*) albur.

whiten [waitn], *v.t.* blanquear. — *v.i.* ponerse blanco *o* lívido.

whiteness [ˈwaitnis], *s.* blancura; palidez; lividez.

whitening [ˈwaitniŋ], *s.* blanqueo; enjalbegadura.

whitesmith [ˈwaitsmiθ], *s.* hojalatero.

whitethorn [ˈwaitθɔ:n], *s.* (*bot.*) espino blanco.

whitewash [ˈwaitwɔʃ], *s.* (*alb.*) (lechada de) cal, jalbegue. — *v.t.* blanquear, encalar, enjalbegar; (*fig.*) encubrir *o* paliar las faltas *o* los defectos de, quitar importancia a los delitos de.

whitewasher [ˈwaitwɔʃə], *s.* blanqueador, enjalbegador.

whitewashing [ˈwaitwɔʃiŋ], *s.* blanqueo, enjalbegadura; (*fig.*) (el) encubrir las faltas de *etc.*

whither [ˈwiðə], *adv.* (*lit.*) adonde; (*interr.*) ¿adónde?

whithersoever [wiðəsouˈevə], *adv.* adondequiera que.

whiting [ˈwaitiŋ], *s.* (*ict.*) pescadilla; tiza, blanco de España.

whitish [ˈwaitiʃ], *a.* blanquecino, blancuzco.

whitishness [ˈwaitiʃnis], *s.* color blanquecino.

whitleather [ˈwitleðə], *s.* cuero baldés.

whitlow [ˈwitlou], *s.* (*med.*) panadizo; ***whitlow-wort,*** nevadilla.

Whit Monday [ˈwit ˈmʌndi], *s.* lunes de Pentecostés, *m.inv.*

Whitsun [ˈwitsən], *a.* de Pentecostés. — *s.* Pentecostés, *m.*

Whit Sunday, Whitsunday [ˈwitˈsʌndi], *s.* domingo de Pentecostés.

Whitsuntide [ˈwitsəntaid], *s.* pascua de Pentecostés.

whittle [witl], *v.t.* ***whittle*** (***away*** o ***down***), tallar *o* cercenar poco a poco; (*fig.*) ir reduciendo *o* rebajando (muy) poco a poco.

whity [ˈwaiti], *a.* blanquecino.

whiz(z) [wiz], *s.* silbido, zumbido; (*fam.*) ***whiz-kid,*** lumbrera (joven), fenómeno. — *v.i.* silbar; zumbar; (*fig.*) zamparse; despacharse; ***he whizzed through the book,*** se zampó el libro (sin respirar); ***he whizzed through the job,*** se despachó en un santiamén el trabajo.

whizzing [ˈwiziŋ], *a.* silbante. — *s.* silbidos, *m.pl.*, zumbidos, *m.pl.*

who [hu:], *pron.* (*interr.*) ¿quién?, ¿quiénes?; (*fam.*) ***who is he looking for?*** ¿a quién busca?;

(*rel.*) que, quien, quienes, el (la, los, las) que; ***he who,*** el que; ***those who,*** los que.
whoa! [wouə], *interj.* ¡so!
whodunit [huːˈdʌnit], *s.* (*fam.*) novela policíaca.
whoever, whosoever [huːˈevə, huːsouˈevə], *pron.* (*indef.*) quienquiera que; ***whoever says that is a liar,*** el que lo diga miente; (*interr.*) ¿quién?; ***whoever said that?*** ¿quién diablos dijo eso?
whole [houl], *a.* todo, entero, completo, total; íntegro, intacto; ileso, sano; ***the whole book,*** todo el libro; ***nothing was left whole,*** no quedó nada intacto, no quedó títere con cabeza; ***whole number,*** número entero; ***whole-wheat,*** de trigo integral; ***whole-wheat bread,*** pan integral. — *s.* todo, total, totalidad, conjunto; ***the whole of Spain,*** toda España; ***as a whole,*** en conjunto; ***on the whole,*** por lo general, en general.
wholehearted [houlˈhɑːtid], *a.* incondicional, de todo corazón, sin reservas.
wholeheartedly [houlˈhɑːtidli], *adv.* de todo corazón, sin reservas.
wholemeal [ˈhoulmiːl], *a.* íntegro, de harina integral. — *s.* harina integral.
wholeness [ˈhoulnis], *s.* integridad.
wholesale [ˈhoulseil], *a.* al por mayor; (*fig.*) general, en masa; ***wholesale dealer,*** comerciante al por mayor, mayorista, *m.*; ***wholesale price,*** precio al por mayor; (*fig.*) ***wholesale slaughter,*** matanza general. — *adv.* al por mayor; (*fig.*) en masa, sin distinción. — *s.* venta al por mayor.
wholesaler [ˈhoulseilə], *s.* comerciante al por mayor, mayorista, *m.*
wholesome [ˈhoulsəm], *a.* sano, saludable.
wholesomeness [ˈhoulsəmnis], *s.* (lo) sano, (lo) saludable.
wholly [ˈhoulli], *adv.* completamente, totalmente, enteramente; del todo.
whom [huːm], *pron.* (*interr.*) ¿a quién?; ***of whom?*** ¿de quién?; ***with whom?*** ¿con quién? *etc.*; (*rel.*) que, a quien; ***all of whom,*** todos los cuales, todos ellos.
whom(so)ever [huːm(sou)ˈevə], *pron.* (*indef.*) a quienquiera que, a quienesquiera que.
whoop [huːp], *s.* grito, alarido; (*med.*) estertor, gallo. — *v.t.* (*fam.*) ***whoop it up,*** alborotar, echar una cana al aire. — *v.i.* dar alaridos, gritar, vocear.
whooping-cough [ˈhuːpiŋ-kɔf], *s.* tos ferina, *f.*
whop [wɔp], *v.t.* (*fam.*) zurrar, pegar.
whopper [ˈwɔpə], *s.* (*fam.*) cosa enorme, ejemplar inmenso; trola colosal.
whopping [ˈwɔpiŋ], *a.* (*fam.*) enorme, colosal; ***whopping great brute,*** animalazo, pedazo de animal.
whore [hɔː], *s.* puta, ramera. — *v.i.* putañear.
whoredom [ˈhɔːdəm], *s.* puterío.
whoremonger [ˈhɔːmʌŋgə], *s.* putañero.
whorl [wəːl], *s.* espiral, *f.*; (*bot.*) verticilo.
whortleberry [ˈwəːtlbəri], *s.* arándano.
whose [huːz], *pron.* (*poss.*) [WHO, WHICH]; (*rel.*) cuyo; de quien, de quienes; (*interr.*) ¿de quién?, ¿de quiénes?
whosoever [WHOEVER].
why [wai], *adv.* (*interr.*) ¿por qué?, ¿para qué?; ***why so much argument?*** ¿a qué tanto discutir?; (*rel.*) ***the reason why,*** la razón por la cual. — *s.* ***the why*** (***and the wherefore***), el porqué. — *interj.* ¡pero! ¡pero si!; ¡hombre!; ***why, I didn't mean that!*** ¡pero si no quería decir eso!
wick [wik], *s.* mecha, pabilo.
wicked [ˈwikid], *a.* malo, perverso, malvado, impío, inicuo; (*fam.*) infame.
wickedly [ˈwikidli], *adv.* malvadamente, inicuamente; (*fam.*) terriblemente.
wickedness [ˈwikidnis], *s.* maldad, iniquidad, perversidad.
wicker [ˈwikə], *s.* mimbre; ***wicker basket,*** cesto de mimbre.
wickerwork [ˈwikəwəːk], *s.* cestería; rejilla.
wicket [ˈwikit], *s.* postigo, portillo; (*cricket*) palos, *m.pl.*; terreno; (*fig., fam.*) ***sticky wicket,*** aprieto; situación comprometida.
wide [waid], *a.* ancho; amplio; dilatado; extenso; ***wide-angle lens,*** objetivo de ángulo ancho; ***wide difference,*** diferencia grande; ***ten feet wide,*** de diez pies de ancho; ***wide-eyed,*** con los ojos (inocentones) muy abiertos; ***wide of the mark,*** totalmente equivocado, que tiene poco o nada que ver; ***wide-mouthed,*** boquiancho. — *adv.* lejos; ***far and wide,*** por todos lados, en todas partes; a lo largo y a lo ancho del país; ***wide awake,*** bien despierto; ***wide open,*** abierto de par en par.
widen [waidn], *v.t.* ensanchar; (*fig.*) ampliar. — *v.i.* ensancharse.
wideness [ˈwaidnis], *s.* anchura.
widespread [ˈwaidspred], *a.* muy difundido, muy corriente.
widgeon [ˈwidʒən], *s.* (*orn.*) ánade silbador.
widow [ˈwidou], *s.* viuda; ***to become a widow,*** enviudar. — *v.t.* dejar viuda.
widowed [ˈwidoud], *a.* viudo, viuda.
widower [ˈwidouə], *s.* viudo.
widowhood [ˈwidouhud], *s.* viudez.
width [witθ], *s.* ancho; anchura.
wield [wiːld], *v.t.* manejar, empuñar; (*poder, autoridad*) ejercer, poseer.
wieldy [ˈwiːldi], *a.* manejable.
wife [waif], *s.* (*pl.* **wives** [waivz]) mujer, *f.*, esposa; señora; (*fam.*) ***the wife,*** la parienta; (*Shakespeare*) ***'The Merry Wives of Windsor',*** 'Las alegres comadres de Windsor'; ***old wives' tale,*** cuento de viejas.
wifehood [ˈwaifhud], *s.* estado de mujer casada.
wifeless [ˈwaiflis], *a.* sin mujer, sin esposa.
wifelike, wifely [ˈwaiflaik, ˈwaifli], *a.* de esposa.
wig [wig], *s.* peluca, peluquín; ***wig-maker,*** peluquero.
wigan [ˈwigən], *s.* (*tej.*) forro basto que se usa para refuerzo.
wigged [wigd], *a.* con peluca.
wigging [ˈwigiŋ], *s.* (*fam.*) peluca, resplandina.
wiggle [wigl], *s.* meneo; culebreo. — *v.t.* menear de prisa. — *v.i.* menearse *o* moverse mucho.
wigwam [ˈwigwæm], *s.* tienda de indios.
wild [waild], *a.* (*animal, pers.*) salvaje; (*planta*) silvestre; (*lugar*) campestre, agreste; (*gato, cabra*) montés; (*indócil*) montaraz, cerril; (*animal doméstico huido*) cimarrón; (*animal, pers.*) bravo, bravío, indómito, fiero; (*reunión, época etc.*) turbulento, alborotado; (*vida etc.*) desarreglado, desordenado; (*en general*) violento, furioso, impetuoso, desmandado; loco, alocado, insensato; disparatado, descabellado, desatinado; estrafalario; ***wild ass,*** onagro; ***wild beast,*** fiera; ***wild boar,*** jabalí; ***wild duck,*** pato salvaje; ***wild goat,*** cabra montés; ***wild goose,*** ánsar *o* ganso bravo; (*fig.*) ***we're on a wild goose chase,*** esto no conduce a nada; ***wild oats,*** avena loca; (*fig.*) ***to sow one's wild oats,*** correr las mocedades; ***wild olive tree,*** acebuche; ***wild-eyed,*** de mirada extraviada; (*fam.*) ***to be wild about sth.,*** estar loco por algo; ***to be wild with s.o.,*** estar furioso con alguien; (*fam.*) ***to get wild,*** ponerse furioso; ***to go*** o ***run wild,*** desmandarse; volver al estado salvaje; ***to grow wild,*** crecer libre; ***to have a wild youth,*** tener una juventud desordenada; ***to make a wild guess,*** conjeturar a lo loco; ***it drives*** o ***makes me wild,*** me saca de quicio; ***those were wild years,*** aquellos años fueron turbulentos. — *s.* yermo; tierra virgen; soledad(es).
wildcat [ˈwaildkæt], *s.* gato montés; (*fig.*) ***wildcat scheme,*** proyecto descabellado; ***wildcat strike,*** huelga sorpresa (no autorizada por el sindicato).
wilderness [ˈwildənis], *s.* desierto, yermo; soledad(es).

wildfire ['waildfaiə], *s.* fuego fatuo *o* griego; ***to spread like wildfire,*** propagarse como el fuego, extenderse como un reguero de pólvora.
wildfowl ['waildfaul], *s.* ánades, *m.f.pl.,* aves salvajes, *f.pl.*
wilding ['waildiŋ], *a.* (*poét.*) inculto, silvestre. — *s.* manzana silvestre.
wildlife ['waildlaif], *s.* fauna.
wildly ['waildli], *adv.* furiosamente; desordenadamente; locamente, insensatamente; frenéticamente; ***to shoot wildly,*** disparar a lo loco; ***to hit out wildly,*** dar golpes al (buen) tuntún; ***to dash about wildly,*** correr de un lado para otro como un loco.
wildness ['waildnis], *s.* estado salvaje; carácter salvaje; violencia, brutalidad, ferocidad; impetuosidad; rudeza, selvatiquez; tumulto; travesura, desvarío, extravío; irregularidad; extravagancia; frenesí.
wile [wail], *s.* (*pl.*) ardides, *m.pl.,* tretas, *f.pl.* — *v.t.* ***wile away,*** pasar, entretener (*el tiempo*).
wilful ['wilful], *a.* (*pers.*) voluntarioso, testarudo; (*acción*) premeditado, intencionado, deliberado.
wilfulness ['wilfulnis], *s.* voluntariosidad, (lo) voluntarioso.
wiliness ['wailinis], *s.* astucia, artería.
Will [wil]. *abrev. de* [WILLIAM].
will [wil], *s.* voluntad; testamento; ***good, ill will,*** buena, mala voluntad; ***free will,*** libre albedrío; ***against one's will,*** contra su voluntad; ***at will,*** a voluntad, a discreción; ***with a will,*** muy gustosamente, resueltamente; ***where there's a will there's a way,*** querer es poder. — *v.t.* querer; (*der.*) legar. — *v.aux.irr. defect.* ***he will go,*** irá; ***I will get it,*** estoy resuelto a conseguirlo; ***do as you will,*** haz lo que quieras; ***will you come?*** ¿quiere venir? ¿vendrás?
willed [wild], *p.p.* [WILL]. — *a.* ***ill-willed,*** que tiene mala voluntad; ***self-willed,*** voluntarioso, testarudo.
William ['wiljəm]. Guillermo.
willing ['wiliŋ], *a.* que quiere, que está dispuesto, que se presta gustosamente (***to,*** a); ***God willing,*** Dios mediante, si Dios quiere.
willingly ['wiliŋli], *adv.* de buena gana, con gusto, gustosamente.
willingness ['wiliŋnis], *s.* (el) querer, (el) estar dispuesto (***to,*** a).
will-o'-the-wisp ['wil-o-ðə-wisp], *s.* fuego fatuo.
willow ['wilou], *s.* (*bot.*) sauce; ***weeping willow,*** sauce llorón.
willowy ['wiloui], *a.* (*fig.*) cimbreño, juncal.
willy-nilly ['wili-'nili], *adv.* de buen o mal grado, de grado o por fuerza, queriendo o sin querer, quiera o no.
wilt (1) [wilt], *v.t.* marchitar. — *v.i.* marchitarse, agostarse; (*fig.*) aplanarse.
wilt (2) [wilt], (*ant.*) 2ª *pers. sing. pres. indic.* [WILL].
wily ['waili], *a.* astuto, taimado.
wimple [wimpl], *s.* griñón.
win [win], *s.* triunfo; (*en concursos*) acierto. — *v.t.* ganar; lograr, conseguir; (*fig.*) ***win*** (***over*** o ***round***), captar(se), granjear(se). — *v.i.* ganar, triunfar; (*en concursos*) acertar; ***win through to,*** alcanzar; ***he won on the pools,*** le tocaron las quinielas.
wince [wins], *v.i.* acusar visiblemente el golpe, el dolor, *etc.,* dar muestras de dolor *etc.*
winch [wintʃ], *s.* malacate. — *v.t.* ***winch*** (***up***), guindar.
wind (1) [wind], *s.* viento, aire; resuello, aliento; (*mús.*) instrumentos de viento, *m.pl.*; ventosidad, flato; ***gust of wind,*** ráfaga *o* racha de viento; (*dep.*) ***second wind,*** fuerzas renovadas, *f.pl.*; (*fig.*) ***there's a revolution in the wind,*** se masca la revolución, hay ambiente de revolución; (*mar.*) ***to run before the wind,*** correr con el viento; ***to break wind,*** ventosear; (*fig.*) ***to get wind of,*** oler(se); (*fig.*) ***to sail close to the wind,*** exponerse al entredicho; ponerse en situación precaria; (*fig.*) ***to take the wind out of s.o.'s sails,*** quitarle a alguien los bríos, cortarle a alguien las alas; ***to throw caution to the winds,*** dejarse de precauciones, tirar por la calle de en medio; (*fam.*) ***to put the wind up s.o.,*** meterle a alguien el resuello para dentro; (*fam.*) ***wind-bag,*** charlatán; ***wind-break,*** mampara contra el viento; ***wind-gauge,*** anemómetro; ***wind-jammer,*** (*prenda*) anorak; (*barco*) velero.
wind (2) [waind], *v.t. irr.* enrollar, enroscar; devanar, ovillar; torcer, retorcer; ***wind off,*** desenrollar, devanar; ***wind round,*** ceñir, rodear; dar vueltas a, girar; ***wind up,*** ovillar; dar cuerda a; atirantar; izar (*con una máquina*); terminar, concluir; (*com.*) liquidar; (*fig.*) ***to be (all) wound up,*** estar con mucha tensión; estar muy excitado; ***wind its way,*** serpentear, pasar haciendo rodeos. — *v.i.* serpentear, culebrear; enroscarse; ***wind up,*** terminar, acabar; (*com.*) liquidar.
windage ['windidʒ], *s.* (*artill.*) viento (de un cañón).
winded ['windid], *a.* jadeante, sin aliento *o* resuello; ***short-winded,*** corto de resuello; ***long-winded,*** de buenos pulmones; (*fig.*) interminable, prolijo.
winder ['waində], *s.* devanador; (máquina) devanadera; llave para dar cuerda; (*mar.*) carretel.
windfall ['windfɔ:l], *s.* fruta caída del árbol; (*fig.*) ganancia inesperada, cosa llovida del cielo.
windflower ['windflauə], *s.* (*bot.*) anémone, *f.*
windgall ['windgɔ:l], *s.* (*vet.*) aventadura.
windhover ['windhɔvə], *s.* (*orn.*) cernícalo.
windiness ['windinis], *s.* (lo) ventoso; (*fam.*) (el) tener canguelo.
winding ['waindiŋ], *a.* tortuoso, sinuoso, serpentino; ***winding staircase,*** escalera de caracol. — *s.* (el) dar cuerda; tortuosidad; vueltas, *f.pl.,* recodos, *m.pl.*; (*elec.*) bobinado, devanado; ***winding frame,*** devanadera; ***winding sheet,*** mortaja, sudario.
winding-up ['waindiŋ-'ʌp], *s.* conclusión; (*com.*) liquidación.
windlass ['windləs], *s.* torno; malacate; (*mar.*) molinete.
windless ['windlis], *a.* sin viento; sin resuello.
windmill ['windmil], *s.* molino de viento.
window ['windou], *s.* ventana; ventanilla; escaparate; ***shop window, show window,*** escaparate; ***bay window,*** cierro (de cristales); mirador; ***French window,*** puerta ventana; ***rose window,*** rosetón; ***window blind,*** estore; celosía; ***window-cleaner,*** limpiacristales, *m.inv.*; ***window-frame,*** marco de ventana; ***window-ledge,*** alféizar; ***window-pane,*** cristal; ***window-seat,*** asiento junto a una ventana *o* ventanilla; ***window-shutter,*** postigo, contraventana; ***window sash,*** bastidor de ventana de guillotina; ***window shade,*** visillo; ***window-sill,*** antepecho, repisa de ventana; ***window dresser,*** escaparatista, *m.f.*; ***window dressing,*** decoración de escaparates; (*fig.*) fachada, camuflaje, apariencias, *f.pl.*
windowed ['windoud], *a.* fenestrado.
window-shop ['windou-ʃɔp], *v.i.* mirar escaparates (sin intención de comprar).
windpipe ['windpaip], *s.* tráquea; gaznate.
windsails ['windseilz], *s.pl.* (*mar.*) mangueras de viento, *f.pl.*
windscreen ['windskri:n], *s.* (*aut.*) parabrisas, *m.inv.*; ***windscreen-wiper,*** limpiaparabrisas, *m.inv.*
windshield ['windʃi:ld], (*Am.*) [WINDSCREEN].
windward ['windwəd], *a.* al viento, del viento, de barlovento. — *adv.* al viento, a barlovento. — *s.* barlovento; ***to lie to windward,*** barloventear.
windy ['windi], *a.* ventoso, expuesto al viento, de viento; ***it is windy,*** hace viento; (*fam.*) ***to be windy,*** tener canguelo.
wine [wain], *s.* vino; ***red wine,*** vino tinto; ***white wine,*** vino blanco; ***wine-cellar, wine-vault,*** bodega; ***wine-cooler,*** enfriadera; ***wine-glass,***

vaso para vino, copa; ***wine-grower,*** viticultor, viñador; ***wine-merchant,*** vinatero; ***wine-skin,*** odre; bota de vino; ***wine-taster,*** catavinos, *m.inv.*

winebibber [ˈwainbibə], *s.* borrachín.

winepress [ˈwainpres], *s.* lagar.

winery [ˈwainəri], *s.* candiotera.

wing [wiŋ], *s.* ala; (*aut.*) aleta; (*teat.*) bastidor; (*fam.*) brazo; ***to be on the wing,*** estar volando; ***to be under the wing of,*** estar bajo la protección de; ***to take wing,*** levantar *o* alzar el vuelo; ***wing-case, wing-sheath,*** élitro; ***wing-chair,*** sillón de orejas; ***wing-span, wing-spread,*** envergadura (de las alas). — *v.t.* herir en el ala *o* en el brazo; ***wing one's way*** (***to***), volar *o* ir volando (a). — *v.i.* volar.

winged [wiŋd], *a.* alado.

wingless [ˈwiŋlis], *a.* sin alas; (*ent.*) áptero.

wink [wiŋk], *s.* guiño; ***to have forty winks,*** descabezar un sueñecito; ***not to get a wink of sleep,*** no pegar ojo; (*fam.*) ***to tip the wink,*** chivarse, ir con el soplo. — *v.t.* guiñar. — *v.i.* guiñar (el ojo); parpadear; pestañear; (*luz*) titilar; ***wink at,*** guiñar el ojo a; (*fig.*) hacer la vista gorda ante.

winking [ˈwiŋkiŋ], *a.* que guiña; que pestañea; que centellea. — *s.* guiños, *m.pl.*; pestañeo; (*fig.*) centelleo.

winkle [wiŋkl], *s.* bígaro. — *v.t.* — ***out,*** hacer salir; sacar con dificuldad *o* hurgando; sonsacar.

winner [ˈwinə], *s.* ganador, vencedor; acertante.

winning [ˈwiniŋ], *a.* que gana, que vence; que toca; al que le toca; victorioso, triunfante; persuasivo, encantador, atractivo; ganancioso; premiado; ***winning smile,*** sonrisa atrayente *o* seductora. — *s.* (el) ganar; ***winning-post,*** poste de llegada; (*pl.*) ganancias, *f.pl.*

winnow [ˈwinou], *v.t.*, *v.i.* aventar, ahechar.

winnower [ˈwinouə], *s.* aventador.

winnowing [ˈwiŋouiŋ], *s.* (*pl.*) aventamiento; ahechadura; ***winnowing-fork,*** bieldo.

winsome [ˈwinsəm], *a.* atrayente, retrechero.

winter [ˈwintə], *a.* invernal, de invierno. — *s.* invierno; ***winter-cherry,*** alquebenje; ***winter season,*** invernada. — *v.i.* invernar, pasar el invierno.

wintergreen [ˈwintəgri:n], *s.* (*bot.*) pirola.

wintriness [ˈwintrinis], *s.* (lo) invernal.

wintry [ˈwintri], *a.* de invierno, invernal, invernizo; (*fig.*) glacial.

winy [ˈwaini], *a.* vinoso.

winze [winz], *s.* (*min.*) pozo de comunicación, pozo ciego.

wipe [waip], *s.* limpión. — *v.t.* limpiar, secar, enjugar; ***wipe one's eyes,*** enjugarse las lágrimas; ***wipe away*** o ***off,*** quitar con un trapo; ***wipe out,*** borrar; suprimir; liquidar; destruir del todo, aniquilar; (*fig.*, *fam.*) ***wipe the floor with s.o.,*** merendarse a alguien, darle ciento y raya a alguien.

wiper [ˈwaipə], *s.* paño, trapo; toalla; (*coche etc.*) frotador; (*mec.*) excéntrica, álabe, leva.

wiping [ˈwaipiŋ], *s.* limpieza, (el) limpiar, enjugar *etc.*

wire [waiə], *s.* alambre; (*elec.*) hilo, cable; telegrama, *m.*; ***wire cutters,*** cortaalambres, *m.inv.*; ***wire fence,*** alambrado; ***wire gauge,*** calibrador para alambres; ***wire netting,*** tela metálica; ***to pull wires,*** mover (los) hilos; (*Am.*, *fam.*) tener enchufes *o* agarraderas. — *v.t.* alambrar; instalar la red eléctrica de. — *v.t.*, *v.i.* telegrafiar.

wiredrawer [ˈwaiədrɔ:ə], *s.* estirador (de metales).

wiredrawing [ˈwaiədrɔ:iŋ], *s.* estiramiento, tirado.

wireless [ˈwaiəlis], *a.* inalámbrico, sin hilos. — *s.* radio, *f.*; ***wireless(-telegraphy),*** radiotelegrafía; ***wireless(-telephony),*** radiotelefonía; ***wireless operator*** o ***engineer,*** radiotelegrafista, *m.f.*; ***wireless set,*** receptor de radio; ***wireless-station,*** emisora; ***wireless-transmission,*** emisión. — *v.t.*, *v.i.* comunicar *o* transmitir por radiotelegrafía *o* radiotelefonía.

wirepuller [ˈwaiəpulə], *s.* (*fam.*) enchufista, *m.f.*

wirepulling [ˈwaiəpuliŋ], *s.* (*fam.*) enchufismo.

wirework [ˈwaiəwə:k], *s.* enrejado; (*pl.*) fábrica de tirado, trefilería.

wiring [ˈwaiəriŋ], *s.* alambrado; instalación *o* colocación de alambres (eléctricos); cablería.

wiry [ˈwaiəri], *a.* de alambre, de hilo metálico; nervudo; (*med.*) (*pulso*) débil.

wisdom [ˈwizdəm], *s.* sabiduría; saber; cordura, prudencia; ***wisdom tooth,*** muela del juicio.

wise (1) [waiz], *a.* sabio; prudente, juicioso, sensato; acertado; enterado (***to,*** de), noticioso (***to,*** de); ***a wise man,*** un sabio; ***the Wise Men,*** los Reyes Magos, *m.pl.*; (*Am.*, *fam.*, *irón.*) ***wise guy,*** chistoso, gracioso; ***it is not wise to do it,*** no es aconsejable hacerlo; (*fam.*) ***to get wise to,*** enterarse de, percatarse de; ***to put s.o. wise,*** explicarle a alguien el caso *o* la situación, poner al corriente a alguien; ***a word to the wise is enough,*** al buen entendedor pocas palabras (bastan). — *v.i.* (*fam.*) ***wise*** (***up***), espabilarse.

wise (2) [waiz], *s.* (*ant.*) guisa, modo; ***in this wise,*** de esta guisa; ***in no wise,*** de ningún modo.

wiseacre [ˈwaizeikə], *s.* sabihondo, sábelotodo.

wisecrack [ˈwaizkræk], *s.* (*fam.*) chiste, cuchufleta.

wish [wiʃ], *s.* deseo (***for,*** de); ***best wishes!*** ¡muchas felicidades!; (*carta*) ***with best wishes,*** saludos, *m.pl.*; ***make a wish,*** pide algo *o* alguna cosa. — *v.t.* desear; ***wish good day,*** dar los buenos días a. — *v.i.* desear, querer; ***wish for,*** desear; ***as you wish,*** como quieras; ***I wish I knew!*** ¡quién (lo) supiera!; ***I wish you well,*** le deseo buena suerte.

wishbone [ˈwiʃboun], *s.* espoleta, hueso de la suerte.

wishful [ˈwiʃful], *a.* deseoso (***for, to,*** de); ***wishful thinking,*** sueños dorados, *m.pl.*, espejismos, *m.pl.*, utopías, *f.pl.*; ***to indulge in wishful thinking,*** hacerse ilusiones.

wishy-washy [ˈwiʃi-ˈwɔʃi], *a.* (*fam.*) (*fig.*, *cosa*) flojete, de poca sustancia; (*fig.*, *pers.*) tambaleante, falto de firmeza.

wisp [wisp], *s.* manojillo (*de hierba*); mechón (*de pelo*); jirón (*de nube*).

wistful [ˈwistful], *a.* pensativo y tristón, melancólicamente meditabundo; místico.

wistfulness [ˈwistfulnis], *s.* (lo) místico.

wit [wit], *s.* ingenio; agudeza; sal, *f.*; (*hombre*) chistoso, chusco; (*pl.*) juicio; inteligencia; ***half-wit,*** mentecato; ***to be at one's wit's end,*** haber agotado todos los recursos, no saber ya qué hacer *o* decir; ***to have*** *o* ***keep one's wits about one,*** estar ojo avizor; ***to have lost one's wits, to be out of one's wits,*** haber perdido el juicio; ***to have the wit to,*** tener la presencia de ánimo de; ***to live by one's wits,*** vivir del aire, vivir de gorra; ***to use one's wits,*** valerse de su ingenio, utilizar el cacumen.

witch [witʃ], *s.* bruja, hechicera; ***witch-doctor,*** hechicero, curandero; ***witch-hunt,*** persecución (*política*).

witchcraft, witchery [ˈwitʃkrɑ:ft, -əri], *s.* brujería, hechicería.

witch-hazel [ˈwitʃ-heizl], *s.* [WYCH-HAZEL].

with [wið], *prep.* con; en compañía de; ***with all speed,*** a toda prisa; ***away with you!*** ¡fuera de aquí!; ***with that . . .,*** dicho esto . . .; ***to shiver with cold,*** tiritar de frío; ***covered with,*** cubierto de, lleno de; ***the girl with the blue hat,*** la chica del sombrero azul; ***it varies with the time of year,*** varía según la época; ***with no snags at all,*** sin pega ninguna.

withal [wiðˈɔ:l], *adv.* además, a más de esto; pese a todo.

withdraw [wiðˈdrɔ:], *v.t. irr.* retirar; retractar. — *v.i.* retirarse; recogerse; (*dep.*) abandonar.

withdrawal [wiðˈdrɔ:əl], *s.* (*mil.*) retirada; (*fondos*) (el) retirar; (*palabras*) retractación; (*espiritual*) recogimiento, retiro; ***withdrawal symptoms,***

síntomas resultantes de la abstinencia, *m.pl.*, síndrome de abstinencia.
withdrawing [wiðˈdrɔ:iŋ], *a.* que se retira. — *s.* retirada.
withdrawn [wiðˈdrɔ:n], *a.* (*pers.*) reservado, retraído, introvertido.
withe [waið], *s.* mimbre, junco; vencejo; (*mec.*) mango flexible.
wither [ˈwiðə], *v.t.* marchitar, secar, ajar; (*fam.*) fulminar. — *v.i.* marchitarse, secarse, ajarse; (*pers.*) ***wither away,*** irse marchitando; (*fig.*) irse atrofiando *o* extinguiendo *o* desvaneciendo.
withered [ˈwiðəd], *a.* seco, marchito.
witheredness [ˈwiðədnis], *s.* sequedad, marchitez.
withering [ˈwiðəriŋ], *a.* abrasador; (*fam., mirada etc.*) fulminante.
withers [ˈwiðəz], *s.pl.* crucero, cruz (*del caballo etc.*), *f.*
withhold [wiðˈhould], *v.t. irr.* retener; (*permiso, autorización*) denegar, negar, rehusar.
within [wiðˈin], *adv.* dentro; por dentro; ***from within,*** desde dentro. — *prep.* dentro de; al alcance de; ***within hearing,*** al alcance del oído; ***within a short distance,*** a poca distancia; ***within a short time,*** dentro de poco (tiempo); ***within an ace of,*** a pique de; ***within an inch of,*** a dos dedos de; ***within an hour,*** antes de *o* en el espacio de una hora; ***within my power,*** en mi poder; ***to live within one's income,*** vivir con arreglo a sus ingresos.
without [wiðˈaut], *adv.* fuera, por fuera; ***from without,*** desde fuera. — *prep.* sin; falto de; fuera de; ***it goes without saying,*** ni que decir tiene, huelga decir (***that,*** que).
withstand [wiðˈstænd], *v.t. irr.* oponerse a, resistir (a), hacer resistencia a; aguantar.
witless [ˈwitlis], *a.* tonto, necio.
witlessness [ˈwitlisnis], *s.* necedad.
witness [ˈwitnis], *s.* testigo; espectador; testimonio, prueba, atestación; ***in witness of,*** en fe de; ***in witness thereof,*** en fe de lo cual; ***to bear witness to,*** atestiguar, dar fe de; ***witness for the defence,*** testigo de descargo; ***witness for the prosecution,*** testigo de cargo; ***eye witness,*** testigo de vista, testigo ocular; ***to call to witness,*** tomar por testigo. — *v.t.* ser testigo de, asistir a, presenciar, ver; atestar, atestiguar; dar fe de; ***witness my hand,*** en fe de lo cual firmo. — *v.i.* dar testimonio.
witted [ˈwitid], *a.* ***quick-witted,*** vivo de ingenio; ***slow-witted, half-witted,*** mentecato, estúpido.
witticism [ˈwitisizəm], *s.* agudeza, ocurrencia, rasgo de ingenio.
wittily [ˈwitili], *adv.* con gracia, con sal, con donaire, ingeniosamente, agudamente.
wittiness [ˈwitinis], *s.* gracia, sal, donaire, ingenio, agudeza.
wittingly [ˈwitiŋli], *adv.* a sabiendas, sabiéndolo.
witty [ˈwiti], *a.* gracioso, salado, ingenioso, chistoso, agudo.
wives [waivz], *s.pl.* [WIFE].
wizard [ˈwizəd], *a.* (*fam.*) estupendo, soberbio. — *s.* mago, brujo, hechicero.
wizen [wizn], *v.i.* arrugarse, apergaminarse.
wizened [wiznd], *a.* arrugado, apergaminado, acartonado, avellanado, sarmentoso.
woad [woud], *s.* (*bot.*) glasto, hierba pastel.
wobble [wɔbl], *v.i.* bailar, bambolear, tambalearse; oscilar; (*fig.*) vacilar.
woe [wou], *s.* pena, dolor, aflicción, pesar, pesadumbre; calamidad, desgracia, infortunio. — *interj.* ***woe is me!*** ¡ay de mí!; ***woe to the vanquished!*** ¡ay de los vencidos!
woebegone [ˈwoubigɔn], *a.* desconsolado, afligido, apesadumbrado, triste.
woeful [ˈwouful], *a.* desconsolado, triste, afligido; deplorable, lamentable.
woefulness [ˈwoufulnis], *s.* aflicción, tristeza.
wold [would], *s.* campiña.
wolf [wulf], *s.* (*pl.* **wolves** [wulvz]) lobo; (*fig., fam.*) don juan, tenorio; ***to cry wolf,*** gritar 'al lobo'; ***to keep the wolf from the door,*** mantener a raya al *o* el hambre; ***wolf-dog, wolf-hound,*** perro-lobo; ***wolf-fish,*** lobo marioni; ***wolf's bane,*** acónito. — *v.t.* zampar(se), engullir(se) (*la comida*).
wolfish [ˈwulfiʃ], *a.* lobuno; (*fig.*) rapaz.
wolfishly [ˈwulfiʃli], *adv.* como un lobo, con rapacidad.
wolfram [ˈwulfrəm], *s.* volframio.
woman [ˈwumən], *s.* (*pl.* **women** [ˈwimin]) mujer, *f.*; ***daily woman,*** asistenta; ***old woman,*** vieja, anciana; ***young woman,*** joven, *f.*; ***woman doctor,*** mujer médico, médica; ***woman-hater,*** misógino; ***women's lib.,*** movimiento de liberación femenina.
womanhood [ˈwumənhud], *s.* femineidad; sexo femenino, (las) mujeres, *f.pl.*; edad adulta.
womanish [ˈwuməniʃ], *a.* mujeril, femenil; (más) propio de mujer (que de hombre); afeminado.
womanishness [ˈwuməniʃnis], *s.* afeminamiento.
womanize [ˈwumənaiz], *v.i.* andar de mujeres.
womanizer [ˈwumənaizə], *s.* mujeriego.
womankind [ˈwumənkaind], *s.* sexo femenino, (las) mujeres, *f.pl.*
womanliness [ˈwumənlinis], *s.* femineidad, feminidad.
womanly [ˈwumənli], *a.* femenino, mujeril, de mujer.
womb [wu:m], *s.* matriz, *f.*; útero; (*fig.*) seno.
women [ˈwimin], *s.pl.* [WOMAN].
wonder [ˈwʌndə], *s.* admiración, asombro, pasmo; maravilla, portento, prodigio, milagro; ***the Seven Wonders of the World,*** las siete maravillas del mundo; ***no wonder!*** ¡no es de extrañar!; ***for a wonder,*** cosa extraña *o* rara; ***it is no*** o ***little*** o ***small wonder that . . .,*** no es extraño que; ***to work wonders,*** hacer maravillas *o* milagros; ***wonder-worker,*** milagrero, taumaturgo. — *v.t., v.i.* preguntarse; extrañarse, sorprenderse, maravillarse; ***I wonder!*** ¡quizá!, ¡quién sabe!; ***I wonder why,*** ¿por qué será?, me gustaría saber por qué; ***I wonder what he wants?*** ¿qué querrá?; ***I wonder if it's true,*** pienso si será verdad; ***I shouldn't wonder,*** no me chocaría nada; ***wonder at,*** extrañarse de, sorprenderse de, maravillarse de.
wonderful [ˈwʌndəful], *a.* asombroso, maravilloso, admirable, portentoso, pasmoso, prodigioso.
wonderfulness [ˈwʌndəfulnis], *s.* (lo) maravilloso; (lo) pasmoso.
wonderland [ˈwʌndəlænd], *s.* país de las maravillas.
wonderment [ˈwʌndəmənt], *s.* admiración, asombro.
wondrous [ˈwʌndrəs], *a.* maravilloso, portentoso, pasmoso.
wonky [ˈwɔŋki], *a.* (*fam.*) defectuoso, que no anda bien; torcido; (*ideas*) equivocado, erróneo.
wont [wount], *a.* ***to be wont to,*** soler, acostumbrar. — *s.* costumbre, hábito; ***it is his wont to,*** suele, acostumbra, tiene por costumbre.
won't [wount], (*fam., abrev.*) **will not.**
wonted [ˈwountid], *a.* (*Am.* o *ant.*) acostumbrado, habitual.
woo [wu:], *v.t.* cortejar; (*fig.*) solicitar; (*fig.*) buscar el apoyo *o* el favor de; ***woo sleep,*** conciliar el sueño. — *v.i.* cortejar, hacer la corte.
wood [wud], *s.* madera; bosque; monte; ***fire-wood,*** leña; ***drift-wood,*** madera de flotación, madera de deriva; ***small wood,*** leña menuda *o* brusca; ***wood alcohol, wood spirit,*** alcohol de madera; ***wood-ant,*** hormiga leonada; ***wood-carving,*** grabado en madera; ***wood-pigeon,*** paloma torcaz; ***wood-pile,*** montón de leña; ***wood-pulp,*** pulpa de madera, celulosa; ***wood-rasp,*** escofina; ***wood-shavings,*** virutas, *f.pl.*; (*bot.*) ***wood-sorrel,*** aleluya; ***wood-thrush,*** tordo pardo;

(*zool.*) ***wood-tick,*** carcoma; ***touch wood!*** ¡toca madera!; ***he can't see the wood for the trees,*** los árboles no le dejan ver el bosque; ***to take to the woods,*** echarse al monte. — *v.t.* proveer de leña; cubrir con bosques.

woodbine [ˈwudbain], *s.* madreselva.

woodchuck [ˈwudtʃʌk], *s.* (*orn.*) marmota grande de América.

woodcock [ˈwudkɔk], *s.* chochaperdiz, *f.*

woodcraft [ˈwudkrɑ:ft], *s.* conocimiento del bosque; pericia en montería; arte de trabajar la madera.

woodcut [ˈwudkʌt], *s.* viñeta, grabado en madera.

woodcutter [ˈwudkʌtə], *s.* leñador; grabador en madera.

wooded [ˈwudid], *a.* arbolado, cubierto *o* poblado de bosques.

wooden [wudn], *a.* de madera, de palo; (*fig.*) inexpresivo, sin gracia.

woodland [ˈwudlənd], *s.* bosque, monte, arbolado.

woodlark [ˈwudlɑ:k], *s.* totovía.

woodless [ˈwudlis], *a.* sin bosques.

woodlouse [ˈwudlaus], *s.* cochinilla.

woodman [ˈwudmən], *s.* leñador; guardabosque, *m.*

woodnymph [ˈwudnimf], *s.* napea, orea, oréade, oréada.

woodpecker [ˈwudpekə], *s.* pájaro carpintero.

woodruff [ˈwudrəf], *s.* (*bot.*) aspérula.

woodshed [ˈwudʃed], *s.* leñera.

woodwind [ˈwudwind], *s.* (*mús.*) instrumentos de viento de madera, *m.pl.*

woodwork [ˈwudwə:k], *s.* (obra de) carpintería; ebanistería; maderaje.

woodworm [ˈwudwə:m], *s.* carcoma.

woody [ˈwudi], *a.* arbolado; leñoso.

wooer [ˈwu:ə], *s.* galanteador, pretendiente, cortejador.

woof [wu:f], *s.* trama.

wooing [ˈwu:iŋ], *s.* galanteo.

wool [wul], *s.* lana; ***all wool,*** (de) pura lana; (*fig.*) ***dyed in the wool,*** acérrimo, empedernido; ***fleece wool,*** lana de vellón; (*fig.*) ***to pull the wool over s.o.'s eyes,*** embaucar a alguien; ***wire-wool,*** estropajo de aluminio; ***wool-comber,*** cardador; ***wool-combing,*** cardadura; (*fig.*) ***wool-gatherer,*** distraído; (*fig.*) ***wool-gathering,*** ensimismamiento, absorción; (*fig.*) ***to go wool-gathering,*** estar en Babia.

wool-bearing [ˈwul-bɛəriŋ], *a.* lanar.

woollen [ˈwulən], *a.* de lana, en lana. — *s.* tela de lana.

woolliness [ˈwulinis], *s.* (*fig.*) (lo) vago, confuso *etc.*

woolly [ˈwuli], *a.* lanudo, lanoso; (*fig.*) vago, confuso, inconcreto, impreciso; borroso. — *s.pl.* (**woollies** [ˈwuliz]) ropa de lana, jerseys de lana, *m.pl.*

woolpack [ˈwulpæk], *s.* fardo de lana; (*nube*) cúmulo.

Woolsack [ˈwulsæk], *s.* saco de lana (*asiento del Gran Canciller de la Cámara de los Lores*).

word [wə:d], *s.* palabra; vocablo, voz, *f.*; noticia; recado, mensaje; (*mil.*) santo y seña; ***the Word,*** el Verbo; (*pl.*) (*mús.*) letra; ***by word of mouth,*** verbalmente; ***he never said a word,*** no dijo palabra, calló; ***he said in so many words that,*** vino a decirme que; ***this means in so many words,*** esto viene a decir que; ***in a word,*** no hay que darle vueltas; (***just***) ***say the word,*** basta con una palabra tuya; ***man of his word,*** hombre de palabra, hombre que tiene palabra; ***mark my word(s),*** si no . . . al tiempo, fíjese bien en lo que le digo; ***take my word for it,*** se lo aseguro; ***to be as good as one's word,*** cumplir su palabra *o* lo prometido; ***not to breathe a word,*** no decir (ni) palabra; ***to eat one's words,*** desdecirse; ***to give one's word,*** dar su palabra; ***to have a word with,*** hablar con; ***to have words,*** discutir; ***to keep one's word,*** cumplir su palabra; ***to leave word,*** dejar recado; ***to put in a word for s.o.,*** decir una palabrita a favor de alguien; ***to send word,*** mandar recado; ***to take s.o. at his word,*** cogerle a alguien la palabra; ***upon my word!*** ¡a fe mía!; ***without a word,*** sin decir palabra, sin chistar; ***word came that,*** llegó la noticia de que; ***words fail me!*** ¡me deja de una pieza!; ***word for word,*** textualmente; ***word of honour,*** palabra (de honor). — *v.t.* ***how shall I word it?*** ¿cómo lo pongo?, ¿cómo lo expreso?

wordiness [ˈwə:dinis], *s.* verbosidad, prolijidad, palabrería.

wording [ˈwə:diŋ], *s.* redacción, términos, *m.pl.*; fraseología, estilo.

wordless [ˈwə:dlis], *a.* sin palabras.

wordy [ˈwə:di], *a.* verboso, prolijo.

work [wə:k], *s.* trabajo; empleo, ocupación; labor, tarea, faena; obra;

(*trabajo*) ***domestic work,*** trabajo de casa, labor casera; ***good works,*** buenas obras; ***piece of work,*** trabajo; obra; ***piece-work,*** trabajo a destajo; ***social work,*** asistencia social; ***to be hard at work,*** estar muy atareado; ***to do one's work,*** hacer su trabajo; ***to have one's work cut out,*** tener trabajo para rato *o* mucho que hacer; ***you'll have your work cut out!*** ¡trabajo te mando!; ***to make short work of sth.,*** despachar algo rápidamente; ***to set to work,*** ponerse a trabajar, poner manos a la obra; ***to set s.o. to work,*** poner a trabajar a alguien; ***work-bag,*** saco de labor; ***work-box,*** caja de labor; ***work-bench,*** banco de trabajo; ***work-mate,*** compañero de trabajo;

(*empleo*) ***day's work,*** jornada; ***to be at work,*** estar trabajando; ***to be in work,*** tener trabajo; ***to be out of work,*** estar sin trabajo, estar parado; ***to put s.o. out of work,*** dejar a alguien sin trabajo;

(*de arte, literatura etc.*) ***complete works,*** obras completas; ***standard work,*** obra clásica; ***the works of Byron,*** las obras de Byron; ***work of art,*** obra de arte; ***work of reference,*** libro de consulta;

(*pl.*) (*mec. etc.*) (*de una máquina*) mecanismo; (*sitio de trabajo*) fábrica, taller(es); ***public works,*** obras públicas *o* estatales; ***road works,*** obras; ***works foreman,*** capataz; (*fam.*) ***to give sth. the works,*** emplearse a fondo en algo; echar el resto en algo; tratar algo a bombo y platillo(s).

— *v.t.* hacer funcionar, operar; hacer trabajar; accionar; mover; producir, motivar; manufacturar; hacer, efectuar; bordar; tallar; trabajar; explotar; cultivar, labrar; maniobrar; hacer fermentar; (*impr.*) tirar;

(*esfuerzo físico*) ***work*** (***sth.***) ***in,*** introducir (algo) poco a poco; ***work into,*** meter, introducir (con maña); ***work one's passage,*** pagarse el pasaje a base de trabajo; ***work one's way,*** abrirse camino; ***work out*** (***a mine***), agotar (una mina);

(*esfuerzo mental etc.*) (*fam.*) ***work it,*** lograrlo; agenciárselas, arreglárselas; ***work off,*** eliminar gradualmente; ***work off one's feelings,*** desahogarse; ***work out*** (***a problem***), resolver (un problema); ***work out*** (***a sum***), calcular (una cantidad); ***work out*** (***an idea***), desarrollar (una idea); ***work out*** (***a plan***), idear (un plan); ***work up,*** excitar, exaltar, emocionar; ***to get worked up,*** sofocarse, exaltarse, excitarse; (*ant.*) he ***wrought great wonders,*** realizó grandes maravillas.

— *v.i.* trabajar; funcionar, marchar; ser eficaz, surtir efecto, obrar; dar resultado; fermentar; (*fam.*) ***it works a treat,*** funciona a las mil maravillas; ***to get sth. working,*** hacer funcionar algo; ***the scheme won't work,*** el plan no es práctico; ***work hard,*** trabajar mucho, trabajar de firme *o* con ahínco; ***work in*** o ***into,*** penetrar poco a poco, colarse; ***work loose,*** soltarse, aflojarse; ***work off,*** separarse, soltarse; ***work on,*** trabajar en; reparar; investigar; atenerse a, basarse en; ***work on*** o ***upon,*** influir; ***work out,*** resultar *o* salir bien *o* mal; resolverse; costar, venir a salir por; ***it works out at £10,*** viene a ser unas diez

libras; ***work round,*** volverse lentamente; ***work through,*** penetrar; hacer con esfuerzo; ***work up,*** subir lentamente.
— *v.r.* ***work o.s. to death,*** matarse a trabajar *o* trabajando; ***work o.s. up to*** o ***into a higher position,*** conseguir a pulso un puesto superior.

workable [ˈwəːkəbl], *a.* práctico, factible; explotable, laborable.

workaday [ˈwəːkədei], *a.* rutinario, de cada día; prosaico.

workday [ˈwəːkdei], *s.* día de trabajo, *m.*, día laborable, *m.*

worker [ˈwəːkə], *s.* trabajador, obrero; operario; ***research worker,*** investigador; ***skilled worker,*** obrero especializado; ***worker-priest,*** cura obrero, *m.*

workhouse [ˈwəːkhaus], *s.* hospicio, asilo (de los pobres), casa de misericordia; (*Am.*) casa de corrección.

working [ˈwəːkiŋ], *a.* de trabajo; que funciona; de explotación; ***working-class,*** clase obrera; ***working party,*** grupo de trabajo; ***working majority,*** mayoría suficiente; ***working man,*** trabajador, obrero; ***working partner,*** socio activo. — *s.* trabajo; (el) trabajar; manejo; operación, funcionamiento; laboreo; fermentación; labores, *m.pl.*; ***working day,*** dia laborable, *m.*, jornada.

workman [ˈwəːkmən], *s.* obrero; trabajador; operario.

workmanlike [ˈwəːkmənlaik], *a.* bien hecho, bien ejecutado, hecho a conciencia; competente.

workmanship [ˈwəːkmənʃip], *s.* trabajo (habilidoso *o* esmerado); ejecución; hechura, confección; ***the workmanship is very good,*** está muy bien hecho.

workmate [ˈwəːkmeit], *s.* compañero de trabajo.

work-out [ˈwəːk-aut], *s.* (sesión de) entrenamiento; prueba, ensayo.

workroom, workshop [ˈwəːkrum, -ʃɔp], *s.* taller; obrador.

work-shy [ˈwəːk-ʃai], *a.* vago, remolón.

workwoman [ˈwəːkwumən], *s.* obrera.

world [wəːld], *a.* mundial; ***world power,*** potencia mundial. — *s.* mundo; ***a world of (a) difference,*** toda la diferencia del mundo; ***for all the world as if...,*** exactamente como si...; ***half the world,*** medio mundo; (*igl.*) ***in the world,*** en el siglo; ***man of the world,*** hombre de mundo; ***not for all the world,*** por nada del mundo; ***since the world began,*** desde que el mundo es mundo; ***the world of fashion,*** el mundillo de la moda; ***this world and the next,*** este mundo y el otro; ***to bring into the world,*** traer al mundo; ***to come into the world,*** venir al mundo; ***to come down in the world,*** venir a menos; ***to feel on top of the world,*** estar eufórico, estar como unas pascuas; ***to see the world,*** ver mundo. — *frase adv.* (*fig.*) ***to think the world of,*** tener un concepto altísimo de; ***world without end,*** por los siglos de los siglos.

worldliness [ˈwəːldlinis], *s.* mundanería.

worldling [ˈwəːldliŋ], *s.* mundano, persona mundana.

worldly [ˈwəːldli], *a.* mundano; ***to be worldly-wise,*** tener (mucho) mundo.

world-wide [ˈwəːld-waid], *a.* mundial.

worm [wəːm], *s.* gusano; (*mec.*) tornillo sin fin; ***earth-worm,*** lombriz, *f.*; ***glow-worm,*** luciérnaga, gusano de luz; ***silk-worm,*** gusano de seda. — *v.t.* ***worm sth. out of s.o.,*** sonsacarle algo a alguien. — *v.i.*, *v.r.* ***worm (o.s.) into,*** insinuarse en; ***worm (o.s.) through,*** atravesar *o* pasar serpenteando.

worm-eaten [ˈwəːm-iːtn], *a.* comido de los gusanos, carcomido; (*fig.*) apolillado.

wormwood [ˈwəːmwud], *s.* ajenjo.

wormy [ˈwəːmi], *a.* lleno de gusanos *o* de carcoma.

worn [wɔːn], *p.p.* [WEAR]; llevado, gastado etc.; ***worn out,*** usado, gastado; ***to be worn out,*** estar rendido; estar quemado.

worrier [ˈwʌriə], *s.* persona que se preocupa por todo.

worry [ˈwʌri], *s.* preocupación, inquietud. — *v.t.* preocupar, inquietar; (*perro*) molestar, acosar, intentar morder. — *v.i.* preocuparse, inquietarse; ***don't worry!*** ¡no se preocupe!, ¡pierda usted cuidado!, ¡descuide!

worrying [ˈwʌriiŋ], *a.* inquietante, que causa preocupación.

worse [wəːs], *a.*, *adv. compar.* [BAD (I)], peor; ***he is none the worse for it,*** no le ha hecho daño ninguno, ne le ha venido mal en absoluto; ***so much the worse,*** tanto peor; ***the worse for wear,*** deteriorado, estropeado, maltrecho; ***to grow worse,*** empeorar; ***to make worse,*** empeorar; ***worse and worse,*** cada vez peor; ***worse luck!*** ¡por desgracia!; ***worse than ever,*** peor que nunca.

worsen [wəːsn], *v.t.* agravar; empeorar. — *v.i.* empeorar(se).

worship [ˈwəːʃip], *s.* culto; adoración; veneración; ***Your Worship,*** vuestra merced, su señoría, usía. — *v.t.* adorar, venerar; rendir culto a.

worshipful [ˈwəːʃipful], *a.* honorable.

worshipper [ˈwəːʃipə], *s.* adorador, devoto.

worshipping [ˈwəːʃipiŋ], *a.* adorador, adorante. — *s.* culto; adoración.

worst [wəːst], *a. superl.* [BAD (I)], (el) peor. — *adv. superl.* [BADLY, ILL], peor. — *s.* lo peor; ***at (the) worst!*** en el peor de los casos; ***do your worst,*** ¡haga todo lo que quiera!; ***I can only think the worst,*** no me queda más remedio que interpretarlo de la manera más desfavorable; ***if the worst comes to the worst,*** si sucede lo peor; ***to make the worst of,*** enfocar de la manera más pesimista; ***the worst (of it) is,*** lo malo es, lo peor es; ***the worst is yet to come,*** (aún) falta lo peor; ***to get the worst over,*** salvar el bache, vencer la cuesta; ***to get the worst of it,*** salir perdiendo, llevar la peor parte. — *v.t.* derrotar, vencer.

worsted [ˈwustid], *a.* de estambre. — *s.* estambre.

worth [wəːθ], *a.* que vale, por valor de, equivalente a; digno de, que merece; ***to be worth,*** valer; merecer; ***to be worth while,*** valer la pena; ***for what it's worth,*** si es que interesa; ***it's not worth it, it's not worth the trouble,*** no vale la pena; ***the book is not worth reading,*** no merece la pena leer ese libro. — *s.* valor; valía, mérito; ***£2 worth of records,*** discos por valor de dos libras; ***50 pesetas worth of cigarettes,*** 50 ptas. de cigarrillos.

worthily [ˈwəːðili], *adv.* dignamente.

worthiness [ˈwəːðinis], *s.* mérito.

worthless [ˈwəːθlis], *a.* que no vale nada.

worthlessness [ˈwəːθlisnis], *s.* indignidad; falta de mérito.

worthy [ˈwəːði], *a.* digno (*of*, de), merecedor (*of*, de); valioso, estimable, apreciable; notable. — *s.* personaje, notable.

would [wud], *pret. y subj.* [WILL]; ***would to God,*** ¡pluguiera a Dios!, ¡ojalá!

would-be [ˈwud-biː], *a.* supuesto, pretendido; seudo, titulado; ***a would-be painter,*** un aspirante a pintor, uno que presume de pintor.

wound (I) [wuːnd], *s.* herida; lesión, daño; (*fig.*) ***to lick one's wounds,*** lamer *o* restañar sus heridas. — *v.t.* herir; dañar, lastimar; ***wound to the quick,*** herir en lo vivo.

wound (2) [waund], *pret.*, *p.p.* [WIND (2)].

wounded [ˈwuːndid], *p.p.* [WOUND (I)], *a.* herido. — *s. pl.* ***the wounded,*** los heridos.

wounding [ˈwuːndiŋ], *a.* hiriente, mordaz, ofensivo. — *s.* heridas, *f.pl.*

wrack [ræk], *s.* (*bot.*) fuco; ***sea-wrack,*** algas (*arrojadas por el mar*), *f.pl.*; ***cloud-wrack,*** celajes, *m.pl.*; jirones de nubes, *m.pl.*; ruina; ***to***

go to wrack and ruin, arruinarse, echarse a perder.
wraith [reiθ], *s.* fantasma, *m.*, espectro, aparecido.
wrangle [ræŋgl], *s.* riña, pelotera, disputa; regateo. — *v.t.* (*Am.*, *caballos*) encargarse de. — *v.i.* reñir, disputar; regatear.
wrangler [ˈræŋglə], *s.* disputador, pendenciero; (*Am.*) el que se encarga de *o* se ocupa de caballos.
wrangling [ˈræŋgliŋ], *s.* (el) reñir, riñas, *f.pl. etc.*
wrap [ræp], *s.* bata; abrigo; manto. — *v.t.* ***wrap (up),*** envolver; abrigar, arropar, arrebujar; (*fig.*) ***to be wrapped up in,*** estar absorto en, estar sumido en, estar entregado a; no pensar más que en. — *v.i.* abrigarse, arroparse, arrebujarse.
wrapper [ˈræpə], *s.* envoltura, envoltorio; faja (*de periódico*).
wrapping [ˈræpiŋ], *a.* de envolver. — *s.* envoltorio(s).
wrath [rɔ(:)θ], *s.* ira.
wrathful [ˈrɔ(:)θful], *a.* airado.
wreak [ri:k], *v.t.* infligir; ***wreak havoc,*** hacer estragos; ***wreak vengeance on,*** vengarse en; ***wreak one's wrath on,*** descargar la ira en.
wreath [ri:θ], *s.* (*fúnebre*) corona; (*festivo*) guirnalda; espiral, *f.*, penacho (*de humo*).
wreathe [ri:ð], *v.t.* enguirnaldar; ceñir; tejer; ***to be wreathed in smiles,*** estar muy risueño. — *v.i.* enroscarse, formar espirales.
wreck [rek], *s.* naufragio; barco naufragado; destrucción, ruina; (*fam.*) ***to be a wreck,*** estar hecho un desastre. — *v.t.* hacer naufragar; (*f.c.*) hacer descarrilar; (*fig.*) dar al traste con, echar a perder *o* a rodar; (*mar.*) ***to be wrecked,*** naufragar.
wreckage [ˈrekidʒ], *s.* restos de naufragio, *m.pl.*, pecios, *m.pl.*; escombros, *m.pl.*; ruina.
wrecker [ˈrekə], *s.* demoledor; (*mar.*) raquero, ladrón de barcos, ladrón de naufragios; ***train wrecker,*** descarrilador.
wren [ren], *s.* troglodito, reyezuelo.
wrench [rentʃ], *s.* arranque violento, sacudida violenta; torcedura, esguince; (*mec.*) llave inglesa; (*fig.*) momento doloroso *o* angustioso (*de separación etc.*). — *v.t.* arrancar, arrebatar (***from s.o.,*** a alguien); torcer; ***wrench open,*** abrir violentamente, forzar; ***wrench out,*** sacar violentamente; ***he wrenched his foot,*** se torció un pie.
wrest [rest], *s.* tirón; (*ant.*, *mús.*) templador. — *v.t.* ***wrest sth. from s.o.,*** arrancar *o* arrebatar algo a alguien. — *v.r.* ***wrest o.s. free,*** desprenderse *o* zafarse violentamente.
wrestle [resl], *s.* lucha (a brazo partido). — *v.i.* luchar a brazo partido; forcejear; (*fig.*) contender, disputar, luchar.
wrestler [ˈreslə], *s.* luchador (de lucha libre).
wrestling [ˈresliŋ], *s.* lucha libre.
wretch [retʃ], *s.* desgraciado, infeliz, pobre diablo; ***little wretch,*** diablillo; ***you wretch!*** ¡canalla!
wretched [ˈretʃid], *a.* (*pers.*) desgraciado, desdichado; (*pers.*, *despec.*) vil, miserable, despreciable; (*cosas*) horrible, malísimo; (*fig.*, *esp. exclamativo*) condenado, maldito.
wretchedness [ˈretʃidnis], *s.* (lo) desgraciado *etc.*; abatimiento, tristeza.
wriggle [rigl], *s.* movimiento, meneo; serpenteo. — *v.t.* menear, mover; retorcer; ***wriggle one's way into,*** deslizarse en; ***wriggle one's way through,*** deslizarse con movimientos de gusano por. — *v.i.* menearse; retorcerse; serpentear, culebrear; ***wriggle along,*** culebrear, moverse culebreando; ***wriggle away,*** escabullirse *o* escaparse *o* alejarse culebreando; ***wriggle into,*** deslizarse en; ***wriggle out of,*** escaparse retorciéndose; (*fig.*) zafarse de.
wring [riŋ], *s.* torcedura, torsión; ***to give clothes a wring,*** retorcer la ropa. — *v.t. irr.* torcer, retorcer; exprimir, escurrir; acongojar, apenar; ***wring the neck of,*** retorcerle el pescuezo a; ***wring out,*** arrancar (por la fuerza); ***wring money from,*** sacar *o* arrancar dinero a.
wringer [ˈriŋə], *s.* escurridor; máquina de exprimir.
wrinkle [riŋkl], *s.* arruga, pliegue. — *v.t.* arrugar, fruncir. — *v.i.* arrugarse, hacer arrugas.
wrinkly [ˈriŋkli], *a.* arrugado.
wrist [rist], *s.* muñeca; ***wrist-watch,*** reloj de pulsera.
wristlet [ˈristlit], *s.* pulsera; ***wristlet-watch,*** reloj de pulsera.
writ [rit], *s.* escritura; escrito; (*for.*) orden, auto, mandato, mandamiento; decreto judicial; (*fig.*) autoridad; ***Holy Writ,*** Sagrada Escritura; ***to issue a writ against s.o.,*** demandar a alguien en juicio.
write [rait], *v.t. irr.* escribir; ***write a good hand,*** tener buena letra; ***write down,*** apuntar, anotar; poner por escrito; hacer constar; (*com.*) rebajar *o* reducir el precio de, reducir el valor nominal de; ***write sth. down as useless,*** resolver que algo es inútil; ***write in,*** escribir, insertar; inscribir *o* añadir (*en la lista de candidatos*); ***write music,*** hacer música; ***write off,*** escribir de prisa *o* de corrido; (*com.*) borrar (por incobrable); quitar; (*fig.*) anular, cancelar; ***write sth. off as a dead loss,*** dar algo por totalmente perdido; ***write out,*** copiar, transcribir; escribir por entero; redactar; extender (*un cheque*); ***write songs,*** hacer canciones; ***write up,*** escribir una crónica *o* una reseña *o* un reportaje sobre *o* de; poner al día; dar bombo a; (*fig.*) ***his guilt is written all over him,*** lleva escrita la culpa en el rostro. — *v.i.* escribir; ***he wrote of his good fortune,*** describió su suerte; ***write back,*** contestar; ***write for, write in for*** o ***write off for*** (***sth.***), escribir pidiendo (algo); ***we write to each other,*** nos escribimos, nos carteamos; ***write for a living,*** ganarse la vida escribiendo; ***write as a hobby,*** escribir de *o* por afición.
write-off [ˈrait-ɔf], *s.* (*fam.*) pérdida total.
writer [ˈraitə], *s.* escritor, autor; ***the (present) writer,*** el que esto escribe.
write-up [ˈrait-ʌp], *s.* (*fam.*) crónica; ***to give a big write-up,*** dar mucho bombo a.
writhe [raið], *v.i.* retorcerse.
writing [ˈraitiŋ], *s.* (el) escribir; escritura; profesión de escritor; (***hand-***)***writing,*** letra; ***his writings,*** sus escritos, *m.pl.*; ***in writing,*** por escrito; ***in one's own writing,*** de su puño y letra; ***writing-case,*** recado de escribir; ***writing-desk,*** escritorio; ***writing-pad,*** bloc; ***writing-paper,*** papel de escribir.
wrong [rɔŋ], *a.* equivocado, erróneo, incorrecto, desacertado; malo; injusto; inoportuno; ***a wrong decision,*** una decisión equivocada *o* desacertada; ***to come at the wrong moment,*** llegar en mal momento; ***to be wrong,*** estar equivocado, equivocarse; engañarse; no tener razón; ***to be the wrong way round,*** estar del revés; ***to be the wrong side of fifty,*** pasar ya de los cincuenta, tener ya más de (los) cincuenta años; ***to get out of the wrong side of bed,*** levantarse por los pies de la cama; ***don't take the wrong one,*** no cojas el que no es; ***he took the wrong one,*** cogió el que no era *o* uno que no era; ***there's sth. wrong with him,*** algo le pasa; ***what's wrong with you?*** ¿qué te pasa?; ***what's wrong with dancing?*** (el) bailar ¿qué tiene de malo?; (*fam.*) ***wrong in the head,*** chiflado. — *adv.* mal; ***to go wrong,*** (empezar a) funcionar mal, estropearse; (empezar a) ir por mal camino, andar en malos pasos. — *s.* mal; injusticia; perjuicio; entuerto; ***to be in the wrong,*** no tener razón; ***to put s.o. in the wrong,*** hacer que alguien quede mal; ***to do wrong,*** hacer mal; ***to do s.o. wrong, to do wrong to*** o ***by s.o.,*** hacerle mal a alguien; ***wrong-doer,*** malhechor; ***wrong-doing,*** maldad, fechorías, *f.pl.* — *v.t.* agraviar, ofender; cometer una injusticia con.
wrongful [ˈrɔŋful], *a.* equivocado; injusto; ilícito.
wrongheaded [rɔŋˈhedid], *a.* tercamente equivocado, equivocado y testarudo.

wrongheadedness [rɔŋ'hedidnis], *s.* (lo) terco y equivocado.
wrongly ['rɔŋli], *adv.* equivocadamente; injustamente; sin razón.
wrongness ['rɔŋnis], *s.* (lo) equivocado; (lo) injusto *etc.*
wroth [rouθ], *a.* airado.
wrought [rɔ:t], *a.* forjado; ***wrought iron,*** hierro forjado. — (*ant.*) *p.p. irr.* [WORK].
wry [rai], *a.* torcido; irónico, sarcástico; dicho con sorna; ***wry face,*** mueca.
wryneck ['rainek], *s.* (*orn.*) torcecuello; (*med.*) tortícolis, *f.inv.*
wryness ['rainis], *s.* ironía, sarcasmo.
wych-elm ['witʃ-elm], *s.* olmo escocés.
wych-hazel ['witʃ-heizl], *s.* (*bot.*) Hamamelis de Virginia.

X

X, x [eks], vigésima cuarta letra del alfabeto.
xanthic [ˈzænθik], *a.* xántico.
xanthine [ˈzænθain], *s.* xantina, jantina.
Xantippe [zænˈtipi]. Jantipa. — *s.* (*fig.*) esposa regañona.
Xavier [ˈzæviə]. Javier, Xavier.
xebec [ˈziːbek], *s.* (*mar.*) jabeque.
xenon [ˈzenɔn], *s.* xeno, xenón.
xenophobe [ˈzenəfoub], *a.*, *s.* xenófobo.
xenophobia [zenəˈfoubiə], *s.* xenofobia.
Xenophon [ˈzenəfən]. Jenofonte.
xerophagy [zeˈrɔfədʒi], *s.* jerofagia.
xerophthalmy [zerɔfˈθælmi], *s.* jeroftalmía.
xerosis [zeˈrousis], *s.* xerodermia.
xiphoid [ˈzifɔid], *a.* xifoideo. — *s.* xifoides, *m.inv.*
Xmas [ˈkrisməs], *s.* *abrev. de* [CHRISTMAS].
X-ray [ˈeks-rei], *s.* rayo X; radiografía. — *v.t.* radiografiar, sacar una radiografía de; mirar por rayos.
xylogen [ˈzailodʒən], *s.* xilógeno.
xylographical [zailoˈgræfikəl], *a.* xilográfico.
xylography [zaiˈlɔgrəfi], *s.* xilografía.
xylol [ˈzailəl], *s.* xileno.
xylonite [ˈzailənait], *s.* xilonita, *m.*
xylophone [ˈzailəfoun], *s.* xilófono.

Y

Y, y [wai], vigésima quinta letra del alfabeto.

yacht [jɔt], *s.* balandro; (motor) yate; ***yacht club,*** club náutico; ***yacht race,*** regata de balandros *o* de yates. — *v.i.* navegar en balandro; viajar en yate.

yachting [ˈjɔtiŋ], *s.* (deporte de) (la) vela.

yachtsman [ˈjɔtsmən], *s.* balandrista; dueño de un yate.

yah! [jɑː], *interj.* ¡bah!

yahoo [jəˈhuː], *s.* patán, bruto.

yak [jæk], *s.* (*zool.*) yak.

Yale lock [ˈjeil ˈlɔk], *s.* (*marca registrada*) cerradura Yale.

yam [jæm], *s.* (*bot.*) ñame.

Yank [jæŋk], *s. abrev. despec. de* [YANKEE].

yank [jæŋk], *s.* (*fam.*) tirón. — *v.t.* (*fam.*) dar un tirón de; sacar de un tirón.

Yankee [ˈjæŋki], *a., s.* (*fam.*) yanqui, *m.f.*

yap [jæp], *s.* gañido; parloteo. — *v.i.* ladrar (con ladrido corto); parlotear.

yard (1) [jɑːd], *s.* yarda, vara; (*mar.*) verga; ***main yard,*** verga mayor.

yard (2) [jɑːd], *s.* patio; corral; ***back yard,*** patio (trasero), corral; ***dock yard,*** astillero; ***junk yard,*** depósito de chatarra; chamarilería; ***timber yard,*** almacén de maderas; ***navy yard,*** arsenal; ***Scotland Yard*** o ***the Yard,*** jefatura de la policía de Londres. — *v.t.* acorralar, apriscar; almacenar.

yardarm [ˈjɑːdɑːm], *s.* (*mar.*) penol.

yardstick [ˈjɑːdstik], *s.* vara de medir; (*fig.*) rasero.

yarn [jɑːn], *s.* hilo, hilado, hilaza; (*fig.*) ***to spin a yarn,*** contar un cuento chino.

yarrow [ˈjærou], *s.* (*bot.*) milenrama, milhojas, *f.inv.*

yataghan [ˈjætəgən], *s.* yatagán.

yaw [jɔː], *s.* (*mar.*) guiñada; (*aer.*) derrape. — *v.i.* (*mar.*) guiñar, dar guiñadas; (*aer.*) derrapar.

yawl [jɔːl], *s.* (*mar.*) yola.

yawn [jɔːn], *s.* bostezo. — *v.i.* bostezar; (*fig.*) ***yawn open,*** abrirse de par en par.

yawner [ˈjɔːnə], *s.* bostezador.

yawning [ˈjɔːniŋ], *a.* bostezante, que bosteza. — *s.* (el) bostezar, bostezos, *m.pl.*

yclad [iˈklæd], *a.* (*ant.*) vestido.

ycleped, yclept [iˈklept], *a.* (*ant.*) llamado.

ye [jiː], *pron. pl.* (*ant.*) [THOU]; vosotros, vos.

yea [jei], *adv.* (*ant.*) sí; en verdad, verdaderamente, ciertamente; ***yea or nay,*** sí o no. — *s.* sí; voto afirmativo; ***the yeas and nays,*** los votos en pro y en contra.

year [jəː], *s.* año; (*pl.*) años, edad; ***by the year,*** al año; ***every other year,*** cada dos años; ***last year,*** el año pasado; ***leap year,*** año bisiesto; ***once a year,*** una vez al año; ***so far this year,*** en lo que va de año; ***these last few years,*** (en) estos últimos años; ***to grow in years,*** envejecer; ***year in, year out,*** año tras año; ***year of grace,*** año de gracia; ***year-book,*** anuario.

yearling [ˈjəːliŋ], *s.* añojo, primal.

yearly [ˈjəːli], *a.* anual. — *adv.* anualmente.

yearn [jəːn], *v.i.* anhelar; ***yearn after*** o ***for sth.,*** anhelar, ansiar *o* añorar algo, suspirar por algo; ***yearn to do sth.,*** anhelar, ansiar *o* añorar hacer algo, suspirar por hacer algo.

yearning [ˈjəːniŋ], *s.* anhelo, ansia, añoranza.

yeast [jiːst], *s.* levadura.

yeasty [ˈjiːsti], *a.* espumoso; (*fig.*) frívolo.

yelk [jelk], [YOLK].

yell [jel], *s.* grito, alarido; chillido. — *v.t.* gritar, decir a gritos. — *v.i.* gritar, dar alaridos; chillar.

yelling [ˈjeliŋ], *a.* que grita *etc.* — *s.* gritos, *m.pl.*, alaridos, *m.pl.*

yellow [ˈjelou], *a.* amarillo; (*fam.*) gallina; ***to go yellow,*** ponerse amarillo; ***to show up yellow,*** amarillear; ***yellow fever,*** fiebre amarilla. — *s.* amarillo.

yellow-bird [ˈjelou-bəːd], *s.* jilguero.

yellow-hammer [ˈjelou-hæmə], *s.* ave tonta, *f.*

yellowish [ˈjelouiʃ], *a.* amarillento.

yellowishness [ˈjelouiʃnis], *s.* (lo) amarillento.

yellowness [ˈjelounis], *s.* amarillez, color amarillo.

yelp [jelp], *s.* gañido. — *v.i.* gañir.

yelping [ˈjelpiŋ], *s.* gañido(s).

Yemen [ˈyemən]. (el) Yemen.

Yemeni [ˈyeməni], *a., s.* yemenita, *m.f.*

yen (1) [jen], *s.* (*fam.*) deseo, gana.

yen (2) [jen], *s.* yen.

yeoman [ˈjoumən], *s.* (*pl.* **yeomen** [ˈjoumen]) hacendado; ***Yeoman of the Guard,*** alabardero de la Casa Real.

yeomanry [ˈjoumənri], *s.* hacendados, *m.pl.*; cuerpo voluntario de caballería.

yes [jes], *adv., s.* sí; ***yes man,*** cobista, *m.f.*, pelotillero.

yesterday [ˈjestədei], *adv., s.* ayer.

yesteryear [ˈjestəjəː], *adv.* (*poét.*) antaño.

yesternight [ˈjestənait], *s., adv.* (*poét.*) anoche.

yet [jet], *adv.* todavía, aún; ***as yet,*** todavía, hasta ahora, hasta aquí; ***not yet,*** todavía no, aún no; ***yet again,*** otra vez más; ***yet more,*** todavía más, más aún. — *conj.* con todo, pese a todo; ***and yet,*** y sin embargo, pero con todo.

yew [juː], *s.* (*bot.*) tejo.

Yiddish [ˈjidiʃ], *s.* idioma fundado en un dialecto alemán medieval usado por los judíos de la Europa Oriental.

yield [jiːld], *s.* rendimiento; producto; (*agric.*) cosecha. — *v.t.* producir, dar, rendir; ***yield up,*** entregar. — *v.i.* rendirse, someterse; ceder; ***yield to temptation,*** ceder ante *o* caer en la tentación.

yielding [ˈjiːldiŋ], *a.* que cede; flexible.

yippee! [jiˈpiː], *interj.* (*fam.*) ¡estupendo!, ¡bárbaro!

yod [jɔd], *s.* yod, *f.*

yodel [joudl], *s.* canción tirolesa. — *v.i.* cantar a la tirolesa.

yoga [ˈjougə], *s.* yoga, *m.*

yogi [ˈjougi], *s.* yogui.

yogurt, yogh(o)urt [ˈjɔgət], *s.* yogur.

yoke [jouk], *s.* yugo; yunta (*de bueyes etc.*); (*mec.*) horquilla; culata; (*arq.*) traviesa, tirante; balancín; percha; (*cost.*) canesú; ***to throw off the yoke,*** sacudir(se) el yugo. — *v.t.* uncir; acoplar; (*fig.*) sojuzgar.

yokel [ˈjoukəl], *s.* palurdo, patán, gañán.

yolk [jouk], *s.* yema (de huevo).

yon, yonder [jɔn, ˈjɔndə], *a.* aquel. — *adv.* allá, a lo lejos.

yore [jɔː], *s.* (*poét., usado en la frase adv.*) ***of yore,*** de antaño.

you [juː], *pron.* tú, usted, vosotros, ustedes; te, os; ti; ***for you,*** para ti, para usted *etc.*; ***with you,*** contigo, con usted *etc.*; ***you can't do that here,*** eso no se puede hacer aquí; ***you artists,*** ustedes *o* vosotros los artistas; ***away with you!*** ¡largo de aquí!; (*fam.*) ***get away with you!*** ¡no digas tonterías, hombre!; ***if I were you,*** yo en su *o* tu lugar, yo que tú *o* usted; ***between you and me,*** entre tú y yo; ***now there's a car for you!*** ¡vaya coche!, ése sí que es un coche!

young [jʌŋ], *a.* joven; pequeño; nuevo; mozo, juvenil; tierno, verde; ***young child,*** niño; ***a young man (woman),*** un (una) joven; ***a young lady,*** una señorita; ***the young people,*** los jóvenes, *m.pl.*, la gente joven; ***the night is young,*** la noche es joven; ***to look young,*** tener aire joven. — *s.* ***with young,*** preñada, encinta; (*sentido pl.*) cría; ***the young,*** los jóvenes, la gente joven.

younger [ˈjʌŋgə], *a. compar.* [YOUNG]; más joven; menor; ***Pliny the Younger,*** Plinio el Joven; ***Herrera the Younger,*** Herrera el Mozo.

youngest [ˈjʌŋgist], *a. superl.* [YOUNG]; (el) más joven, (el) menor.

youngish [ˈjʌŋiʃ], *a.* bastante joven, más bien joven.

youngster [ˈjʌŋstə], *s.* muchacho, muchacha, joven, *m.f.*

your [jɔː], *a.* (*pos.*) tu, tus; vuestro, vuestros, vuestra, vuestras; su, sus.

yours [jɔːz], *pron.* (*pos.*) el tuyo; el vuestro; el suyo *etc.*; ***yours truly,*** su seguro servidor (S.S.S.); ***it's all yours,*** ahí queda eso.

yourself [jɔːˈself], *pron.* (*refl.*) (*pl.* **yourselves** [jɔːˈselvz]) tú (mismo), usted (mismo) *etc.*

youth [juːθ], *s.* juventud; (los) jóvenes, *m.pl.*; (*pers.*) joven; ***youth hostel,*** albergue para jóvenes.

youthful [ˈjuːθful], *a.* juvenil, joven.

youthfulness [ˈjuːθfulnis], *s.* juventud; vigor *o* espíritu juvenil.

yttrium [ˈitriəm], *s.* itrio.

yucca [ˈjʌkə], *s.* (*bot.*) yuca.

Yugoslav [juːgoˈslɑːv], *a.*, *s.* yugo(e)slavo.

Yugoslavia [juːgoˈslɑːviə]. Yugo(e)slavia.

Yule [juːl], *s.* Navidad; ***Yule-log,*** leño navideño; ***Yule-tide,*** (pascua de) Navidad, Navidades.